TALMUD BAVLI
תלמוד בבלי
D1778346

Scriptural Index

Urim VeTumim – a parchment bearing the Ineffable Name of God that was inserted into the breastplate worn by the **Kohen Gadol.** When a request for Divine instruction was put to it, the letters engraved on the breastplate's precious stones would glow, spelling out the Divine message. The *Urim VeTumim* disappeared during the destruction of the First Temple.

variable [chatas] offering – a special type of **chatas** offering whose quality varies in accordance with the sinner's financial resources. He is liable to a regular *chatas* offering of a female lamb or kid only if he is a person of means. Should he be poor, he is required to bring only two turtledoves or two young pigeons, one as a *chatas* and the other as an **olah.** If he is very poor, he brings a tenth of an **ephah** of fine flour for a **minchah**.

v'lad hatumah – derivate **tumah;** see **tumah**.

v'lad v'lad hatumah – See **tumah**.

Women's Courtyard – the Courtyard of the **Temple** that faced the eastern wall of the main Courtyard.

yavam – See **yibum**.

yetzer hara – Evil Inclination.

ye'ush – abandonment. This refers to an owner's despairing of recovering his lost or stolen property.

yevamah – See **yibum**.

yibum – levirate marriage. When a man dies childless, the **Torah** provides for one of his brothers to marry the widow. This marriage is called *yibum*. Pending this, the widow is forbidden to marry anyone else. The surviving brother, upon whom the obligation to perform the **mitzvah** of *yibum* falls, is called the *yavam*. The widow is called the *yevamah*. *Yibum* is effected only through cohabitation. If the brother should refuse to perform *yibum*, he must release her from her *yibum*-bond by performing the alternate rite of *chalitzah,* in which she removes his shoe before the court and spits before him and declares: *So should be done to the man who will not build his brother's house* (*Deuteronomy* 25:5-10).

Yisrael [pl. **Yisraelim**] – (a) Jew; (b) Israelite (in contradistinction to **Kohen** or **Levi**).

Yom Kippur – Day of Atonement; a day of prayer, penitence, fasting and abstention from **melachah**.

Yom Tov [pl. **Yamim Tovim**] – holiday; the festival days on which the Torah prohibits **melachah**. Specifically, it refers to the first and last days of **Pesach,** the first day of **Succos, Shemini Atzeres, Shavuos, Yom Kippur** and the two days of **Rosh Hashanah**. Outside of **Eretz Yisrael,** an additional day of **Yom Tov** is added to each of these festivals, except **Yom Kippur** and **Rosh Hashanah**.

Yovel – fiftieth year [Jubilee]; the year following the conclusion of a set of seven **shemittah** cycles. On **Yom Kippur** of that year, the **shofar** is sounded to proclaim freedom for the Jewish servants, and to signal the return to the original owner of fields sold in **Eretz Yisrael** during the previous forty-nine years.

zakein mamrei – a sage who refuses to accept a ruling of the Great Sanhedrin, and who continues to rule contrary to their decision.

zav [pl. **zavim**] – a man who has become **tamei** because of a specific type of seminal emission. If three emissions were experienced during a three-day period, the man must bring offerings upon his purification.

zavah [pl. **zavos**] – After a woman concludes her seven days of **niddah,** there is an eleven-day period during which any menseslike bleeding renders her a *minor zavah.* If the menstruation lasts for three consecutive days, she is a *major zavah* and must bring offerings upon her purification.

zechiyah – rule which states that one can act as a person's agent without his prior knowledge or consent if the act is clearly advantageous to the beneficiary.

zechus – unqualified benefit.

zerikah [pl. **zerikos**] – throwing; applying the blood of an offering to the Outer **Altar** in the prescribed manner. It is one of the four essential blood **avodos**.

zivah – lit. seepage or flow; the type of discharge which if repeated renders one to be a **zav** or **zavah**.

zomemim] – witnesses proven false through **hazamah**.

zonah – A women who cohabits with a disqualified person attains the legal status of *zonah* and thereby becomes forbidden to marry a **Kohen.zomeim** [pl. **zuz** [pl. **zuzim**] – (a) monetary unit equal to a **dinar;** (b) a coin of that value; (c) the weight of a *zuz* coin.

Tanna [pl. **Tannaim**] – Sage of the Mishnaic period whose view is recorded in a **Mishnah** or **Baraisa.**

Tanna Kamma – the anonymous first opinion of a **Mishnah** or **Baraisa**.

Targum – lit. translation; the Aramaic interpretive translation of Scripture.

techum [pl. **techumim**] – Sabbath boundary; the distance of 2,000 **amos** from a person's Sabbath residence which he is permitted to travel on the Sabbath or **Yom Tov**.

tefach [pl. **tefachim**] – handbreadth; a measure of length equal to the width of four thumbs.

tefillah – (a) prayer; (b) in Talmudic usage, **tefillah** invariably refers to **Shemoneh Esrei**.

tefillin – phylacteries; two black leather casings, each of which contains Torah passages written on parchment. It is a **mitzvah** for adult males to wear one on the head and one on the arm.

temei'ah – female for **tamei**.

Temple – See **Beis HaMikdash**.

Temple Mount – the site of the Holy **Temple.** See **Beis HaMikdash**.

temurah – The Torah forbids a person to even verbally substitute a different animal for an already consecrated sacrificial animal. This is forbidden even if the second animal is superior. If one violates this prohibition, both the animals are sacred. Both the act of substitution and the animal substituted are known as a *temurah.*

tereifah [pl. **tereifos**] – (a) a person, animal or bird that possesses one of a well-defined group of eighteen defects which will certainly cause its death. Any of these defects renders the animal or bird prohibited for consumption even if it was ritually slaughtered; (b) a generic term for all non-kosher food.

terumah [pl. **terumos**] – the first portion of the crop separated and given to a **Kohen,** usually between 1/40 and 1/60 of the total crop. It is separated prior to **maaser,** and upon separation attains a of state sanctity which prohibits it from being eaten by a non-**Kohen,** or by a **Kohen** in a state of **tumah**.

terumah gedolah – See **terumah**.

terumas maaser – the tithe portion separated by the **Levi** from the **maaser rishon** he receives, and given to **Kohen**.

tevel – produce of **Eretz Yisrael** that has become subject to the obligation of **terumah** and **tithes;** it is forbidden for consumption until *terumah* and all tithes have been designated.

Teves – tenth month of the Hebrew calendar.

tevilah – immersion in a **mikveh** for the purpose of purification from **tumah**-contamination.

tevul yom – lit. one who has immersed that day. This is a person who had been rendered ritually impure with a Biblical **tumah** from which he purified himself with immersion in a **mikveh.** A residue of the *tumah* lingers until nightfall of the day of his immersion, leaving him *tamei* in regard to sacrifices, **terumah** and entering the **Temple** Courtyard. A person in this reduced state of *tumah* is known as a *tevul yom.*

Tishah B'Av – lit. the Ninth of Av; the fast day that commemorates the destruction of the First the Second **Beis HaMikdash** and as well as other national tragedies.

Tishrei – seventh month of the Hebrew calendar.

todah [pl. **todos**] – thanksgiving offering brought when a person survives a potentially life-threatening situation. It is unique in that forty loaves of bread accompany it.

toladah [pl. **tolados**] – lit. offspring; subcategory of an **av** (pl. **avos**). See **melachah**.

Torah – the Five Books of Moses; the Chumash or Pentateuch.

Tosefta – a written collection of **Baraisos**.

tumah [pl. **tumos**] – legally defined state of ritual impurity affecting certain people or objects. The strictest level of *tumah, avi avos hatumah* [literally: father of fathers of *tumah*], is limited to a human corpse. The next, and far more common level, is known as *av hatumah,* primary [literally: father] *tumah.* This category includes: one who touched a human corpse; **sheretz,** the carcass of one of the eight species of creeping creatures listed in *Leviticus* 11:29-30; the carcass of a **neveilah,** an animal that died by some means other than a valid ritual slaughter; or one who is a **zav, zavah, niddah** or **metzora**.

An object that is contaminated by an *av hatumah* [primary *tumah*] becomes a *rishon l'tumah* (*first degree of* [acquired] *tumah*). This degree of contamination is also called *v'lad hatumah* (*secondary tumah*) [literally: child (as opposed to *av,* father) of *tumah*]. An object contracting *tumah* from a *rishon* becomes a *sheni l'tumah* (second degree *of* [acquired] *tumah*) – (or *v'lad v'lad hatumah, child of child of tumah*). In the case of *chullin, unsanctified food,* contamination can go no further than a *sheni;* thus, if a *sheni* touches unsanctified food, that food acquires no degree of contamination whatsoever.

Commensurate with the respectively greater degrees of stringency associated with **terumah** and sacrifices, their levels of contamination can go beyond that of *sheni.* Thus, if a *sheni* touches *terumah,* it becomes a *shelishi l'tumah* (third degree of [acquired] *tumah*) but the *tumah* of *terumah* goes no further than this degree. Sacrificial items can go a step further, to *revii l'tumah* (fourth degree of [acquired] *tumah*).

As a general rule, the word **tamei,** *contaminated,* is applied to an object that can convey its *tumah* to another object of its genre. An object that cannot convey its *tumah* in this way is called, **pasul,** (invalid,) rather than *tamei.*

tumas meis – the **tumah** of a human corpse.

tumas midras – See **midras**.

tumas ohel – lit. roof **tumah;** the *tumah* conveyed to objects or persons when they are under the same roof as certain *tumah* conveyors, generally a human corpse.

Twelve Prophets – the final Book of the Prophets which consists of twelve short prophetic works: *Hosea, Joel, Amos, Obadiah, Jonah, Micah, Nahum, Habakkuk, Zephaniah, Haggai, Zechariah, Malachi.*

twofold payment – See double payment.

tzad hashaveh – An exegetical derivation based on the presumption that a law found in two contexts results from characteristics common to both rather than from characteristics unique to each. Any other context possessing these common characteristics is also subject to the common law, even if the third context differs from the first two in regard to their *unique* features.

tzaraas – See **metzora**.

tzitzis – the fringes that by **Torah** law must be placed on a four-cornered garment.

tzon-barzel – lit. iron-sheep; the portion of a woman's dowry assessed prior to the marriage; its value is recorded in the **kesubah.** Should the marriage end, reimbursement is made to the woman at the property's assessed value, even if in the interim it was lost or damaged. Thus, the property's value remains preserved for the wife like *iron.*

unattended corpse – See **meis mitzvah**.

unpaid custodian – a **shomer** who receives no remuneration for his services. He is liable if the object in his care is damaged as a result of his negligence; if it is lost or stolen, he is exempt.

semichah – (a) Rabbinical ordination empowering one to serve as a judge. This ordination stretches back in an unbroken chain to Moses; (b) a rite performed with almost all personal sacrificial offerings. The owner of the offering places both his hands on the top of the animal's head and presses down with all his might. In the case of a **chatas** or an **asham,** he makes his confession during *semichah*. In the case of a **shelamim** or **todah** offering, he praises and thanks God.

semuchin [pl. **semuchim**] – Scriptural juxtaposition. This principle states that two consecutive verses or passages may be compared for purposes of inferring law from one to the other. It is one of the rules of exegesis employed by the Sages.

seven species – See **bikkurim**.

Seventeenth of Tammuz – a fast day. Among the tragedies that occurred on this day were: (a) Moses descended from Mount Sinai and smashed the Tablets of the Ten Commandments when he saw the people worshiping the Golden Calf. (b) Jerusalem's walls were breached by the invading Roman army three weeks before the final destruction of the Second **Temple** (on **Tishah B'Av**).

shaatnez – see **kilayim**.

Shabbos – (a) the Sabbath; (b) the Talmudic tractate that deals with the laws of the Sabbath.

Shacharis – the morning prayer service.

shaos zemaniyos – seasonal or variable hours. According to this reckoning, the day (or night) – regardless of its length – is divided into twelve equal units (hours).

Shavuos – Pentecost; the festival that celebrates the giving of the **Torah** to the Jewish nation at Mount Sinai.

Shechinah – Divine Presence.

shechitah – (a) ritual slaughter; the method prescribed by the **Torah** for slaughtering a kosher animal to make it fit for consumption. It consists of cutting through most of the esophagus and windpipe from the front of the neck with a specially sharpened knife that is free of nicks. (b) One of the four essential blood **avodos**.

shekel [pl. **shekalim, shekels**] – Scriptural coin equivalent to the Aramaic **sela** or four **dinars.** In Mishnaic terminology, the Scriptural half-*shekel* is called a *shekel,* and the Scriptural *shekel* is called by its Aramaic name, **sela**.

shelamim – peace offering; generally brought by an individual on a voluntary basis; part is burnt on the **Altar,** part is eaten by a **Kohen** (and the members of his household) and part is eaten by the owner. It is one of the **kodashim kalim**.

shelichus – See **agency**.

shelishi l'tumah – See **tumah**.

Shemini Atzeres – the eighth and concluding day of the **Succos** celebration. In many respects, it is a **Yom Tov** in its own right.

shemittah – the Sabbatical year, occurring every seventh year, during which the land of **Eretz Yisrael** may not be cultivated.

Shemoneh Esrei – also called **Amidah;** the silent, standing prayer, which is one of the main features of the daily prayer services.

sheni l'tumah – See **tumah**.

sheretz [pl. **sheratzim**] – one of eight rodents or reptiles, listed by the Torah, whose carcasses transmit **tumah.** A *sheretz* is an **av hatumah.** See **tumah**.

Sheva Berachos – (a) The blessing recited under the wedding canopy; (b) the term used for festive meals served during the seven days of rejoicing following the wedding. The blessings which were recited under the wedding canopy are all said at the Grace After Meals of these feasts.

Shevat – eleventh month of the Hebrew calendar.

sheviis – See **shemittah**.

shevuah oaths – a formula with which one may make a self-imposed prohibition. A **shevuah oath** renders actions, in contradistinction to objects, forbidden.

shich'chah – sheaves forgotten in the field during their removal to the threshing floor as well as standing produce that the harvester overlooked. The Torah grants these to the poor. See **leket, pe'ah**.

shitufei mevo'os – incorporation of the alleys; a provision similar to **eruvei chatzeiros,** instituted to permit carrying from a courtyard into an alley on the Sabbath. It merges the different courtyards in a common ownership of a **mavoi**.

sh'liach tzibur – lit. messenger of the congregation; the individual leading the prayer service.

shofar – trumpet formed from the horn of a ram or certain other animals. It is a Biblical obligation to hear the blowing of a *shofar* on **Rosh Hashanah**.

shomer [pl. **shomrim**] – one who has assumed custodial responsibility for another's property.

shtar [pl. **shtaros**] – legal document.

shtei halechem – lit. two loaves; the offering of two wheat loaves that must be brought on **Shavuos.** It is accompanied by two lambs with which it is waved, and whose offering permits it for consumption by the **Kohanim.** In addition to these lambs, the **Torah** mandates another group of offerings to be brought in conjunction with the *shtei halechem,* one of which is the **chatas**.

Shulchan – lit. table; the golden Table for the **lechem hapanim,** located in the **Holy**.

shuman – animal fats that are permitted for consumption. See **cheilev**.

Sifra – lit. the book; the primary collection of Tannaic exegesis, mainly halachic in nature, on the Book of *Leviticus.* It is also known as *Toras Kohanim.*

Sifri (or Sifrei) – lit. the books; the counterpart of the **Sifra;** it expounds on the Books of *Numbers* and *Deuteronomy.*

simta – a public area set aside for temporary use by individuals.

Sivan – third month of the Hebrew calendar.

sotah – an adulteress or a woman whose suspicious behavior has made her suspected of adultery. The Torah prescribes, under specific circumstances, that her guilt or innocence be established by having her drink specially prepared water.

sprinkling – See **hazaah**.

stoning – See **sekilah**.

subverted city – See **ir hanidachas**.

succah – (a) the temporary dwelling in which one must live during the festival of **Succos;** (b) [cap.] the Talmudic tractate that deals with the laws that pertain to the festival of Succos.

Succos – one of the three **pilgrimage festivals;** on Succos one must dwell in a **succah**.

Tabernacle – a portable **Sanctuary** for the sacrificial service used during the forty years of national wandering in the Wilderness and the first fourteen years after entry into **Eretz Yisrael**.

taharah – a halachically defined state of ritual purity; the absence of **tumah**-contamination.

tahor – person or object in a state of **taharah**.

tam – lit. ordinary; term used for a bull the first three times it gores another animal. See **muad**.

tamei – person or object that has been contaminated by **tumah** and that can convey *tumah* to another object of its genre.

tamid – communal **olah,** offered twice daily.

Tammuz – fourth month of the Hebrew calendar.

Paroches – curtain: specifically, the curtain that divided the **Holy** from the **Holy of Holies**.

parsah [pl. **parsaos**] – measure of length equal to eight thousand **amos**.

peace offering – See **shelamim**.

pe'ah – the portion of the crop, generally the corner of the field, that must be left unreaped as a gift to the poor.

peret – individual grapes which fell during harvesting. The Torah grants these to the poor. See **shich'chah, leket** and **pe'ah**.

perutah [pl. **perutos**] – smallest coin used in Talmudic times. In most cases its value is the minimum that is legally significant.

Pesach – Passover; the **Yom Tov** that celebrates the Exodus of the Jewish nation from Egypt.

pesach offering – sacrifice offered on the afternoon of the fourteenth day of **Nissan** and eaten after nightfall. It is one of the **kodashim kalim**.

Pesach Sheni – lit. Second **Pesach;** (a) the fourteenth of **Iyar.** This day fell one month after the **Yom Tov** of Pesach. Any individual who is **tamei** at the time designated for the **pesach offering** must wait till *Pesach Sheni* to bring his offering; (b) a *pesach* offering brought on the fourteenth of Iyar.

pesik reisha – an action that is essentially permitted but has a direct and inevitable consequence that is prohibited.

pesulei kahal – someone who is barred by circumstances of their genealogy from marrying an ordinary Jew.

physical sanctity – See **hekdesh**.

piggul – lit. rejected; an offering rendered invalid by means of an improper intent – by the one performing one of the four essential **avodos** – to eat of it or place it on the **Altar** after its allotted time. The intention must have been present during one of the four blood **avodos.** Consumption of *piggul* is punishable by **kares**.

pikadon – an object deposited with a custodian for safekeeping.

pikuach nefesh – lit. saving a life; a life-threatening situation. All prohibitions (except for murder, immorality and idolatry) are waived, if necessary, in such situations.

pilgrimage festival – the title for the holidays of **Pesach, Shavuos** and **Succos,** when all Jewish males were obligated to appear at the **Beis HaMikdash** in Jerusalem.

plag haminchah – one and a quarter hours before night.

positive commandment – a Torah commandment expressed as a requirement *to do*.

poskim – authoritative decisors of Torah law.

Priestly Blessing – the blessing the **Kohanim** are obligated to confer upon the congregation. It consists of the verses designated for this purpose by the Torah (*Numbers* 6:24-26). It is recited aloud by the **Kohanim**, toward the conclusion of the **Shemoneh Esrei**.

prohibition – a negative commandment, which the Torah expresses as a command *not to do*.

prohibitory law – refers to the category of Torah law which deals with questions of permissible or forbidden status, as opposed to questions of **monetary law.**

Prophets – See **Neviim**.

pundyon – a coin.

purification waters – See **mei chatas**.

R' – Rabbi; specifically a **Tanna,** or **Amora** of **Eretz Yisrael**.

rasha – (a) a wicked person; (b) a person disqualified from serving as a witness by his commission of certain transgressions.

Rebbi – R' Yehudah HaNasi; the redactor of the **Mishnah**.

red cow – See **parah adumah**.

regel – any of the three pilgrimage festivals – **Pesach, Shavuos** and **Succos**.

Reish Gelusa – Exilarch, head of the Babylonian Jewish community; parallels the **Nasi** in **Eretz Yisrael**.

reshus harabim – lit. public domain; any unroofed, commonly used street, public area or highway at least sixteen **amos** wide and open at both ends. According to some, it must be used by at least 600,000 people.

reshus hayachid – lit. private domain; any area measuring at least four **tefachim** by four *tefachim* and enclosed by partitions at least ten *tefachim* high. According to most opinions, it needs to be enclosed only on three sides to qualify as a *reshus hayachid*. Private ownership is not a prerequisite.

resident alien – See **ger toshav**.

revai – fruit produced by a tree in its fourth year. This is consecrated in the same manner as **maaser sheni** and must be eaten in Jerusalem or be redeemed with money which is spent in Jerusalem on food to be eaten there. See **orlah**.

revii l'tumah – see **tumah**.

reviis – a quarter of a **log**.

ribbis – a Talmudic term for interest.

Rishon [pl. **Rishonim**] – a **Torah** authority of the period following the **Geonim** (approx. 1000-1500 C.E.).

rishon l'tumah – first degree of acquired **tumah**. See **tumah**.

Rosh Chodesh – (a) festival celebrating the new month; (b) the first of the month.

Rosh Hashanah – the **Yom Tov** that celebrates the new year. It falls on the first and second days of **Tishrei**.

rov – majority; a principle used in halachah to determine the origin or status of a particular object. An object of undetermined origin or status is assumed to partake of the same origin or status as that of the majority. See also **bitul b'rov**.

rova [pl. **revaim**] – a quarter-**kav** (1/24 of a **se'ah**). This is identical to a log.

Sadducees – heretical sect active during the Second **Temple** era named after Tzaddok, a disciple of Antigenos of Socho. They denied the Divine origin of the **Oral Law** and refused to accept the Sages' interpretation of the **Torah**.

Sages – (a) the collective body of Torah authorities in the Mishnaic era; (b) the anonymous majority opinion in a **Mishnah** or **Baraisa;** (c) [l.c.] Torah scholar and authority.

Sanctuary – a term applied to the Temple building that housed the **Holy** and the **Holy of Holies**.

Sanhedrin – (a) the High Court of Israel; the Supreme Court consisting of seventy-one judges whose decisions on questions of Torah law are definitive and binding on all courts; (b) [l.c.] a court of twenty-three judges authorized to adjudicate capital and corporal cases.

saris – (a) a male who is incapable of maturing sexually; (b) a castrated male.

se'ah – a Mishnaic measure of volume; six **kav**.

Seder [pl. **Sedarim**] – lit. order. (a) The Mishnah is divided into six *sedarim*: *Zeraim* (Plants), *Moed* (Festivals), *Nashim* (Women), *Nezikin* (Damages), *Kodashim* (Sacred Things) and *Taharos* (Ritual Purities); (b) [l.c.] ritual festive meal on **Pesach**.

sefeik sefeika – lit. doubt of a doubt. The term used when the situation under consideration is subject to two separate uncertainties, i.e. to a double doubt.

sekilah – lit. stoning; one of the four forms of death penalty imposed by the court.

sela [pl. **sela'im**] – a silver coin having the weight of 384 grains of barley. This is the equivalent of four **dinars**.

minchah – (a) [cap.] the afternoon prayer service; (b) [pl. **menachos**] a flour offering, generally consisting of fine wheat flour, oil and frankincense, part of which is burnt on the **Altar.** See **kemitzah**.

minyan – quorum of ten adult Jewish males necessary for the communal prayer service and other matters.

Mishkan – predecessor of the **Temple.** See **Tabernacle**.

mishmar [pl. **mishmaros**] – lit. watch; one of the twenty-four watches of **Kohanim** and **Leviim** who served in the Temple for a week at a time on a rotating basis. These watches were subdivided into family groups each of which served on one day of the week.

Mishnah [pl. **Mishnahs**] – (a) the organized teachings of the **Tannaim** compiled by **R' Yehudah HaNasi;** (b) a paragraph of that work.

mitzvah [pl. **mitzvos**] – a **Torah** command, whether of Biblical or Rabbinic origin.

mi'un – By Rabbinic enactment, an underaged orphan girl may be given in marriage by her mother or brothers. She may annul the marriage anytime before reaching majority by declaring, before a **beis din** of three judges, her unwillingness to continue in the marriage. This declaration and process is called *mi'un.*

mixtures of the vineyard – See **kilayim**.

monetary law – law dealing with financial matters rather than matters of ritual prohibition.

monetary sanctity – See **hekdesh**.

movables, movable property – property that is transportable, in contrast to real estate.

muad – lit. warned one. A bull that gores three times and whose owner was duly warned after each incident to take precautions is considered a *muad* bull. The owner must pay full damage for the fourth and all subsequent incidents. See **tam**.

muchzak – one who has physical possession of an object and who is therefore assumed to be in legal possession of it.

mufneh – the superfluity of a word used in a *gezeirah shavah* which makes the derivation impervious to refutation.

muktzeh – lit. set aside; (a) a class of objects which, in the normal course of events, do not stand to be used on the Sabbath or **Yom Tov.** The Rabbis prohibited moving such objects on the Sabbath or *Yom Tov;* (b) an animal set aside to be sacrificed for idolatry.

mum [pl. **mumim]** – physical defects that render a **Kohen** or sacrifice unfit.

mussaf – (a) additional sacrifices offered on the Sabbath, **Rosh Chodesh** or **Yom Tov;** (b) [cap.] the prayer service which is recited in lieu of these sacrifices.

naarah – a girl at least 12 years old who has sprouted a minimum of two pubic hairs. This marks her coming of age to be considered an adult. She is deemed a *naarah* for six months; after that she becomes a **bogeress**.

naarus – the state of being a **naarah**.

Nasi [pl. **Nesiim]** – the Prince. He serves as the head of the **Sanhedrin** and de facto as the spiritual leader of the people.

nasin [f. **nesinah;** pl. **nesinim**] – descendant of the Gibeonites, who deceptively concluded a peace treaty with Joshua (*Joshua* 9:3-27) and converted to Judaism.

nazir [f. **nezirah**] – a person who takes the vow of **nezirus,** which prohibits him to drink wine, eat grapes, cut his hair or contaminate himself with the **tumah** of a corpse.

nedavah – See **donated offering**.

neder – a vow which renders objects, in contradistinction to actions, prohibited. There are two basic categories of vows: (a) restrictive vows; (b) vows to donate to **hekdesh.** See **hekdesh,** see also **donated offering**.

negaim – spots that appear on the skin of a **metzora**.

nesachim – a libation, generally of wine, which is poured upon the **Altar.** It accompanies certain offerings and may be donated separately as well.

neveilah [pl. **neveilos**] – the carcass of an animal that was not slaughtered according to procedure prescribed by the Torah. A *neveilah* may not be eaten. It is an **av hatumah**.

Neviim – Prophets; it consists of the following books: *Joshua, Judges, Samuel, Kings, Jeremiah, Ezekiel, Isaiah,* **Twelve Prophets**.

nezirus – the state of being a **nazir**.

niddah – a woman who has menstruated but has not yet completed her purification process, which concludes with immersion in a **mikveh**.

nidui – a ban. One of the means of punishment available to **beis din** is the *nidui* ban. When *beis din* pronounces a *nidui* upon an offender, the community is enjoined to avoid being in the offender's proximity (within four **amos),** and to refrain from eating and drinking with him. In some instances, further restrictions on the community's contacts with the offender are pronounced. The perpetrator is obligated to conduct himself in most matters like a mourner. In general, the term of a *nidui* is thirty days.

Nissan – first month of the Hebrew calendar.

nisuin – second stage of marriage. It is effected by a procedure called **chupah.** See **kiddushin**.

Noahide laws – the seven commandments given to Noah and his sons, which are binding upon all gentiles. These laws include the obligation to have a body of civil law, and the prohibitions against idolatry, immorality, bloodshed, blasphemy, stealing and robbing, and eating limbs from a live animal.

nossar – part of a **korban** left over after the time to eat it has passed.

oath of modeh bemiktzas – A Biblical oath administered to one who partially admits to a monetary claim.

olah [pl. **olos**] – burnt or elevation offering; an offering which is consumed in its entirety by the **Altar** fire. It is one of the **kodshei kodashim**.

Omer – an obligatory **minchah** offering brought on the sixteenth of **Nissan.** It was forbidden to eat from the new grain crop (**chadash**) before this offering was brought.

onaah – price fraud.

onein [f. **onenes**] [pl. **onenim**] – See **aninus**.

oneiss – one who violates a women.

Oral Sinaitic Law – See **Halachah LeMoshe MiSinai**.

orlah – lit. sealed; fruit that grows on a tree during the first three years after it has been planted (or transplanted). The Torah prohibits any benefit from such fruit.

Outer Altar – the **Altar** that stood in the Courtyard of the **Beis HaMikdash,** to which the blood of most offerings is applied, and on which the offerings are burned.

paid custodian – a **shomer** who receives remuneration for his services. He is obligated to make restitution even in the event of theft or loss; however, he is exempt in the case of loss due to an unavoidable mishap.

parah adumah – lit. red cow. The ashes of the *parah adumah* are mixed with springwater. The resulting mixture is known as **mei chatas** and is used in the purification process of people or objects who have contracted **tumah** from a human corpse.

maaser beheimah – the animal tithe. The newborn kosher animals born to one's herds and flocks are gathered into a pen and made to pass through an opening one at a time. Every tenth animal is designated as **maaser.** It is brought as an offering in the Temple and is eaten by the owner.

maaser of animals – See **maaser beheimah**.

maaser rishon – See **maaser**.

maaser sheni – See **maaser**.

mah matzinu – lit. just as we find; a **binyan av** from one verse. Just as one particular law possesses aspect A and aspect B, so any other law that possesses aspect A should also possess aspect B.

makkas mardus – lashes for rebelliousness. This is the term used for lashes incurred by Rabbinic – rather than Biblical – law.

malkus – the thirty-nine lashes (forty minus one) imposed by the court for violations of Biblical prohibitions, where a more severe punishment is not indicated.

mamzer [pl. **mamzerim**] [f. **mamzeress**] – (a) offspring of most illicit relationships punishable by **kares** or capital punishment; (b) offspring of a *mamzer* or *mamzeress*.

mamzerus – state of being a **mamzer**.

maneh – (a) equivalent to 100 **zuz;** (b) a measure of weight, equal to 17 ounces.

Marcheshvan – eighth month of the Hebrew calendar

matanos [or **matnos kehunah**] – lit. gifts. The Torah commands that we give the right foreleg, jaws and maw of an ox, sheep or goat that are slaughtered (for non-sacrificial purposes) to the **Kohen.** These are referred to as the "gifts."

matzah – unleavened bread; any loaf made from dough that has not been allowed to ferment or rise. One is Biblically obligated to eat *matzah* on the night of the 15th of Nissan.

mavoi – alley; specifically an alley into which courtyards open. See **shitufei mevo'os**.

mayim chayim – living water. Springwater generally has the status of *mayim chayim*. It is so designated because it issues out of the ground with a natural force which makes it "alive" and moving. It is fit to be used for three purposes for which the Torah specifies *mayim chayim*: (a) the immersion of **zavim,** (b) the sprinkling for **metzoraim,** (c) to consecrate therefrom **mei chatas**.

mayim sheuvin – drawn water; water that flows out of a vessel is designated as *sheuvin* and is unfit for use to constitute the forty **se'ah** of a **mikveh**.

mazal – fortune.

mechussar kapparah [pl. **mechussar kippurim**] – lit. lacking atonement; the status accorded to a **tevul yom** in the interim between sunset of the day of his immersion and the time he brings his offerings. During that interval, he retains a vestige of his earlier **tumah** and is thus forbidden to enter the Temple Courtyard or partake of the offerings.

mei chatas – springwater consecrated by the addition of ashes of a **parah adumah.** This was used to purify individuals or objects of **tumas meis**.

me'ilah – unlawfully benefiting from **Temple** property or removing such property from the Temple ownership. As a penalty one must pay the value of the misappropriated item plus an additional one-fifth of the value. He must also bring an **asham** offering.

mefateh – a seducer.

meis mitzvah – See **abandoned corpse**.

meishiv aveidah – lit., one who returns a lost object. Any person stepping forward to return something that would otherwise have been lost to its owner – whether a lost object or a debt he would not have known to claim – is classified as a *meishiv aveidah*.

melachah [pl. **melachos**] – labor; specifically, one of the thirty-nine labor categories whose performance is forbidden by the Torah on the Sabbath and **Yom Tov.** These prohibited categories are known as *avos melachah*. Activities whose prohibition is derived from one of these thirty-nine categories are known as **tolados** (s. *toladah*) – secondary labor.

melikah – the unique manner in which bird offerings were slaughtered. *Melikah* differs from **shechitah** in two respects: (a) The cut is made with the **Kohen's** thumbnail rather than with a knife. (b) The neck is cut from the back rather than from the throat. Only birds for sacrificial purposes may be slaughtered by *melikah;* all others require *shechitah*. See **shechitah**.

melog – a married woman's property in which she retains ownership of the property itself, but her husband enjoys the right of usufruct, i.e. he owns the yield of that property.

menachos – See **minchah**.

Men of the Great Assembly – a group of 120 sages active at the end of the Babylonian exile and during the early years of the Second Temple. They were responsible for the formulation of our prayers and many other enactments.

Menorah – the seven-branched gold candelabrum which stood in the **Holy**.

meshichah – pulling, or otherwise causing an object to move; one of the methods of acquisition used for movable property.

mesirah – handing over; transferring the animal to a buyer by handing him its reins or mane; a means of acquisition used for articles too heavy to be acquired via **meshichah** or **hagbahah**.

meturgeman – (lit. translator). It was customary to employ a translator to explain the Torah readings to those in the congregation who did not understand Hebrew. The translation was presented in Aramaic – the language spoken by the Jews at that time. The **Targum** was recited from memory, not from a written text.

metzora – A *metzora* is a person who has contracted **tzaraas** (erroneously described as leprosy), an affliction mentioned in *Leviticus* (Chs. 13,14). *Tzaraas* manifests itself (on people) as white or light-colored spots on the body.

mezuzah [pl. **mezuzos**] – a small scroll, containing the passages of *Deuteronomy* 6:4-9 and 11:13-21, that is affixed to the right doorpost.

midras – If someone who is **tamei** as a result of a bodily emission (e.g. a **zav, zavah, niddah,** woman who has given birth) sits or leans on a bed, couch or chair, it acquires the same level of **tumah** as the person from whom the *tumah* emanates (i.e. **av hatumah**). This form of *tumah* transmission is called *midras*.

migo – lit. since; a rule of procedure. If one makes a claim that – on its own merits – the court would reject, it nonetheless will be accepted "since" had he wished to tell an untruth he would have chosen a claim that certainly is acceptable to the court.

mikveh – ritualarium; a body of standing water containing at least forty **se'ah.** It is used to purify (by immersion) people and utensils of their **tumah**-contamination. A *mikveh* consists of waters naturally collected, without direct human intervention. Water drawn in a vessel is not valid for a *mikveh*.

mil – 2,000 **amos;** a measure of distance between 3,000 and 4,000 feet.

kebeitzah – an egg's volume.

Kehunah – priesthood; the state of being a **Kohen**.

keifel – See **double payment**.

kemitzah – the first of four essential services of a **minchah** offering. The **Kohen** closes the middle three fingers of his right hand over his palm and scoops out flour from the *minchah* to form the **kometz** that is burned on the **Altar**.

keren – horn. The act of damage that an animal does with destructive intent and which is unusual for animals and their species. This is one of the three primary damages in the case of an ox.

kesef – (a) money; (b) Tyrian currency which is comprised solely of pure silver coins.

kesubah – (a) marriage contract; the legal commitments of a husband to his wife upon their marriage, the foremost feature of which is the payment awarded her in the event of their divorce or his death; (b) document in which this agreement is recorded.

Kesuvim – Hagiographa – Holy Writings. It consists of eleven volumes: *Psalms, Proverbs, Job, Song of Songs, Ruth, Lamentations, Ecclesiastes, Esther, Daniel, Ezra-Nehemiah, Chronicles.*

kezayis – the volume of an olive; minimum amount of food whose consumption is considered "eating."

Kiddush – (a) the benediction recited over wine before the evening and morning meals on the **Sabbath** and **Yom Tov**; (b) sanctification of **mei chatas**.

kiddushin [betrothal] – Jewish marriage consists of two stages: **erusin** and **nisuin.** *Kiddushin* is the procedure which establishes the first stage of marriage [*erusin*].

kilayim – various forbidden mixtures, including: **shaatnez** (cloth made from a blend of wool and linen); cross-breeding of animals; cross-breeding (or side-by-side planting) of certain food crops; working with different species of animals yoked together; and mixtures of the vineyard.

kilei hakerem – forbidden mixtures of the vineyard. See **kilayim**.

kinyan [pl. **kinyanim**] – formal act of acquisition; an action that causes an agreement or exchange to be legally binding.

kinyan agav – lit. acquisition by dint of; the term for the acquisition of movable property by means of the acquisition of land. The **kinyan** used for the land serves for the movable property.

kinyan chalifin – lit. acquisition by exchange. (a) even exchange: an exchange of two items of comparable value, in which each item serves as payment for the other. The acquisition of any one of the items automatically effects the acquisition of the other. (b) uneven exchange: an item of relatively negligible value is given in order to effect the acquisition of the other item. A kerchief or the like is traditionally used.

kinyan chatzeir – the acquisition of movable property by virtue of it being in the premises of the person acquiring it.

kinyan chazakah – See **chazakah (b)**.

kinyan sudar – See **kinyan chalifin (b)**.

Kislev – ninth month of the Hebrew calendar.

kli shareis [pl. **klei shareis**] – service vessel(s); a vessel sanctified for use in the sacrificial service.

kodashim kalim – offerings of lesser holiness (one of the two classifications of sacrificial offerings). They may be eaten anywhere in Jerusalem by any **tahor** person. They include the **todah,** regular **shelamim, bechor, nazir's ram, maaser** and **pesach offerings.** This category of offerings is not subject to the stringencies applied to **kodshei kodashim**.

kodesh – (a) any consecrated object; (b) the anterior chamber of the **Temple** – the **Holy;** (c) portions of sacrificial offerings.

kodshei kodashim – most-holy offerings (one of the two classifications of sacrificial offerings). They may be eaten only in the Temple Courtyard and only by male **Kohanim.** They include the **olah** (which may not be eaten at all), **chatas, asham** and communal **shelamim.** These are subject to greater stringencies than **kodashim kalim**.

Kofer payment – lit. atonement. The court-imposed monetary payment which the owner of a **muad** ox which kills a human must pay.

Kohanim's Courtyard – eleven-**amah**-wide area in the Courtyard of the **Beis HaMikdash** abutting the **Israelite Courtyard** on its east side, and the **Altar** on its west side. It reached across the entire width of the Courtyard from north to south.

Kohen [pl. **Kohanim**] – member of the priestly family descended in the male line from Aaron. The Kohen is accorded the special priestly duties and privileges associated with the **Temple** service and is bound by special laws of sanctity.

Kohen Gadol – High Priest.

kol d'alim g'var – lit. let whoever is stronger prevail. In certain cases where neither litigant advances conclusive proof to support his claim, the court withdraws and allows the stronger party to take possession of the contested property.

kometz [pl. **kematzim**] – See **kemitzah**.

kor – large dry measure; a measure of volume consisting of thirty **se'ah**.

korban – a sacrificial offering brought in the **Beis HaMikdash**.

kri u'ksiv – a word in Scripture written one way but read differently – by special directive to Moses at Sinai.

lashes – See **malkus** and **makkas mardus**.

leaning – See **semichah**.

lechatchilah – (a) before the fact; (b) performance of a **mitzvah** or procedure in the proper manner.

leket – gleanings; one of the various portions of the harvest which the Torah grants to the poor. *Leket* refers to one or two stalks of grain that fall from the reaper when he gathers the harvest. See **shich'chah, pe'ah** and **peret**.

lesech – one half of a **kor**.

Levi [pl. **Leviim**] – male descendant of the tribe of *Levi* in the male line, who is sanctified for auxiliary services in the **Beis HaMikdash.** The *Leviim* were the recipients of **maaser rishon**.

libation – See **nesachim**.

litra – (a) a liquid measure equal to the volume of six eggs; (b) a unit of weight.

log [pl. **lugin**] – a liquid measure equal to the volume of six eggs, between 16 and 21 ounces in contemporary measure.

lulav – See **four species**.

ma'ah [pl. **maos**]– the smallest silver unit in Talmudic coinage. Thirty-two copper **perutos** equal one *ma'ah* and six *ma'ahs* equal a silver **dinar**.

Maariv – the evening prayer service.

maaser [pl. **maasros**] – tithe. It is a Biblical obligation to give two tithes, each known as *maaser,* from the produce of the Land of Israel. The first tithe (**maaser rishon**) is given to a **Levi.** The second tithe (**maaser sheni**) is taken to Jerusalem and eaten there, or redeemed with coins which are then taken to Jerusalem for the purchase of food to be eaten there. In the third and sixth years of the seven-year **shemittah** cycle, the *maaser sheni* obligation is replaced with **maaser ani,** the tithe for the poor.

maaser ani – See **maaser**.

gezeirah shavah – one of the thirteen principles of Biblical hermeneutics. If a similar word or phrase occurs in two otherwise unrelated passages in the **Torah,** the principle of *gezeirah shavah* teaches that these passages are linked to one another, and the laws of one passage are applied to the other. Only those words which are designated by the **Oral Sinaitic Law** for this purpose may serve as a basis for a *gezeirah shavah.*

gifts to the poor – These include **leket, shich'chah, pe'ah, peret, oleilos** and **maaser ani**.

Golden Altar – See **Inner Altar**.

Great Court – See **Sanhedrin**.

hadasim – See **four species**.

hafarah – revocation of a woman's vow by her husband on the grounds that her vow impinges on their marital relationship or that it causes her deprivation.

hagbahah – lifting. One of the methods of acquisition used for movable objects.

halachah [pl. **halachos**] – (a) a **Torah** law; (b) [u.c.] the body of Torah law; (c) in cases of dispute, the position accepted as definitive by the later authorities and followed in practice; (d) a **Halachah LeMoshe MiSinai**.

Halachah LeMoshe MiSinai – laws taught orally to Moses at Sinai, which cannot be derived from the Written Torah.

half-shekel – While the Temple stood, every Jew was required to donate a half-*shekel* annually to fund the purchase of the various communal offerings (including, among others, the daily **tamid** offerings and the holiday **mussaf** offerings).

hanachah – the *setting down* of a transferred article in its new domain; see ***akirah.***

happeh she'assar – term used for the principle that the one who created a prohibition has the authority to remove it.

Hashem – lit. the Name; a designation used to refer to God without pronouncing His Ineffable Name.

hasraah – warning. One does not incur the death penalty or lashes unless he was warned, immediately prior to commission, of the forbidden nature of the crime and the punishment to which he would be liable.

hatarah – annulment of a vow by an expert sage or a group of three competent laymen.

Havdalah – lit. distinction; the blessing recited at the conclusion of the Sabbath.

hazamah – the process by which witnesses are proven false by testimony that places them elsewhere at the time of the alleged incident. Such witnesses are punished with the consequences their testimony would have inflicted upon their intended victim.

Hebrew maidservant – a Jewish girl between the age of six and twelve who has been sold by her father into servitude.

Hebrew servant – a Jewish man who is sold as an indentured servant, generally for a period of six years. He is either sold by the court because he was convicted of stealing and lacks the funds to make restitution, or he sells himself for reasons of poverty.

hechsher l'tumah – rendering a food susceptible to **tumah** contamination by contact with one of seven liquids: water, dew, milk, bee honey, oil, wine or blood.

hefker – ownerless.

hefker beis din hefker – principle which establishes the power of Rabbinic courts to declare property ownerless.

Heichal – See **Beis HaMikdash**.

hekdesh – (a) items consecrated to the **Temple** treasury or as offerings. *Hekdesh* can have two levels of sanctity: **monetary sanctity** and **physical sanctity.** Property owned by the Temple treasury is said to have monetary sanctity. Such property can be redeemed or can be sold by the *hekdesh* treasurers, and the proceeds of the redemption or sale become *hekdesh* in its place. Consecrated items that are fit for the Temple service (e.g. unblemished animals or sacred vessels) are deemed to have physical sanctity; (b) the state of consecration; (c) the **Temple** treasury.

hekeish – an exegetical derivation based on a connection that Scripture makes (often through juxtaposition) between different areas of law. By making this connection, Scripture teaches that the laws that apply to one area can be applied to the other area as well.

hesseis oath – lit. oath of incitement. Oath imposed by the court on one who denies the entire monetary claim made against him. This oath was required by the post-Mishnaic Rabbis on the assumption that a plaintiff would not make a totally frivolous claim.

hin – liquid measure equal to twelve **lugin**.

holachah – one of the four essential blood **avodos.** It involves conveying the blood of the offering to the **Altar**.

Holy – anterior chamber of the **Temple** edifice (**Heichal**) containing the **Shulchan, Inner Altar** and **Menorah**.

Holy Ark – the Ark holding the Tablets of the Ten Commandments and the Torah Scroll written by Moses. It stood in the **Holy of Holies**.

Holy of Holies – interior chamber of the **Temple** edifice (**Heichal**). During most of the First Temple era, it contained the **Holy Ark;** later it was empty of any utensil. Even the **Kohen Gadol** is prohibited from entering there except on **Yom Kippur**.

Inner Altar – the gold-plated Altar which stood in the **Sanctuary.** It was used for the daily incense service and for the blood applications of inner **chataos**.

ir hanidachas – a city in **Eretz Yisrael** in which the majority of the population worshiped idols. Subject to certain conditions, the city is destroyed along with all its property and its guilty inhabitants are beheaded.

Israelite Courtyard – an area in the Temple Courtyard, extending eleven **amos** from the eastern Courtyard wall into the Courtyard, and abutted on its west side by the **Kohanim's Courtyard.** It reached across the entire width of the Courtyard from north to south.

issaron – a dry measure equal to one-tenth of an **ephah** or approximately (depending on the conversion factor) as little as eleven or as much as twenty-one cups.

issur – prohibition.

Iyar – second month of the Hebrew calendar.

Jubilee – See **Yovel**.

kabbalah – (a) term used throughout the Talmud to refer to the books of the **Prophets.** It derives from the Aramaic root – to complain or cry out. It thus refers primarily to the admonitory passages of these books; (b) receiving in a **kli shareis** the blood of a sacrificial animal that is slaughtered; one of the four blood **avodos**.

kal vachomer – lit. light and heavy, or lenient and stringent; an *a fortiori* argument. It is one of the thirteen principles of Biblical hermeneutics. It involves the following reasoning: If a particular stringency applies in a usually lenient case, it must certainly apply in a more serious case; the converse of this argument is also a *kal vachomer.*

kares – excision; Divinely imposed premature death decreed by the **Torah** for certain classes of transgression.

kav [pl. **kabim**] – a measure equal to four **lugin**.

Cutheans – a non-Jewish tribe brought by the Assyrians to settle the part of **Eretz Yisrael** left vacant by the exile of the Ten Tribes. Their subsequent conversion to Judaism was considered questionable and their observance of many laws was lax.

daf [pl. **dafim**] – folio (two sides) in the **Gemara**.

dayyo – lit. it is sufficient; principle which limits the application of a **kal vachomer** argument, for it states: When a law is derived from case A to case B, its application to B cannot exceed its application to A.

death penalty – this refers to a court-imposed death penalty, in contrast to one imposed by Heaven.

decapitated calf – If the body of a murder victim is discovered outside a town in Eretz Yisrael and his murderer is not known, the elders of the **Sanhedrin** must measure the distance to the surrounding towns to determine the town closest to the corpse. The elders of that town must then bring a female calf that was never worked and decapitate it in an untilled valley, in accordance with the procedure outlined *Deuteronomy* 21:1-9.

demai – lit. what is this; produce of **Eretz Yisrael** that is obtained from an unlearned person. By Rabbinic enactment it must be tithed since a doubt exists as to whether its original owner tithed it. However, it is assumed that **terumah** was separated from the produce.

dinar – a coin. The silver content of the coin was equivalent to ninety-six grains of barley. It was worth 1/25 the value of a gold *dinar*.

donated offering – There is a difference between a נֶדֶר, *neder* (vowed offering), and a נְדָבָה, *nedavah* (donated offering). In the case of a *neder*, the vower declares הֲרֵי עָלַי קָרְבָּן, "It is hereby incumbent upon me to bring a sacrifice." He fulfills his vow by later designating a specific animal as the sacrifice and offering it. In the case of a *nedavah*, the vower declares הֲרֵי זוּ קָרְבָּן, "This [animal] is a sacrifice," designating from the very start the particular animal he wishes to bring as an offering. In the case of a *neder*, if the designated animal is lost or dies, the vower must bring another in its place, since he has not yet fulfilled his vow "to bring a sacrifice." In the case of a *nedavah*, however, if anything happens to the designated animal the vower need not replace it since his vow was only to bring "*this* animal."

double payment – a punitive fine. A person convicted of theft is required both to return the stolen object (or its monetary equivalent) and to pay the owner a fine equal to its value. If he stole a sheep or goat and slaughtered or sold it, he pays four times the value of the animal. If he stole an ox and slaughtered or sold it, he pays five times its value.

eglah arufah – see **decapitated calf.**

Elohim – (a) a Name of God; (b) [l.c.] sometimes used to refer to a mortal power or the authority of an ordained judge.

Elul – sixth month of the Hebrew calendar.

emurin – the portions of an animal offering burnt on the **Altar**.

encumbered property – land owned by a debtor at the time he incurred a debt, but which he later sold or gave to a third party. Such land is encumbered by the debt; the creditor can retrieve it from the current owner to satisfy the debt, if the debtor defaults.

ephah [pl. **ephos**] – a measure of volume equal to three **se'ah**.

erech [pl. **arachin**] – a fixed valuation. The *erech* of a person is the amount fixed by the **Torah** for each of eight different groupings classified by age and gender. All individuals included in the same broad grouping have the identical *erech* valuation, regardless of their value on the slave market.

Eretz Yisrael – Land of Israel.

erusin – betrothal, the first stage of marriage. This is effected by the man giving the woman an object of value, in the presence of witnesses, to betroth her. At this point the couple is not yet permitted to have conjugal relations, but is nonetheless considered legally married in most respects and the woman requires a divorce before she can marry again. See **nisuin.**

eruv – popular contraction of **eruvei chatzeiros, eruvei tavshilin** or **eruvei techumin**.

eruvei chatzeiros – a legal device which merges several separate ownerships **(reshus hayachid)** into a single joint ownership. Each resident family of a **chatzeir** contributes food to the *eruv*, which is then placed in one of the dwellings of the *chatzeir*. This procedure allows us to view all the houses opening into the courtyard as the property of a single consortium (composed of all the residents of the courtyard). This permits all the contributing residents of the *chatzeir* to carry items during the Sabbath from the houses into the *chatzeir* and from one house to another.

eruvei tavshilin – the prepared food set aside prior to a **Yom Tov** that falls on Friday to serve as token food for the Sabbath that follows. Once this token food has been set aside, the person is allowed to complete his preparations for Sabbath on *Yom Tov*. Such preparation is generally forbidden otherwise.

eruvei techumin – merging of boundaries; a legal device that allows a person to shift his Sabbath residence from which the 2,000-**amah techum** is measured. This is accomplished by placing a specific amount of food at the desired location before the start of the Sabbath. The place where the food has been placed is then viewed as his Sabbath residence, and his *techum*-limit is measured from there. This does not extend his **techum** Shabbos, but merely shifts the point from which it is measured.

ervah [pl. **arayos**] – (a) matters pertaining to sexual relationships forbidden under penalty of **kares** or death, as enumerated in *Leviticus* Ch. 18; (b) a woman forbidden to a man under pain of one of these penalties.

esrog – see **four species.**

fines – punitive payments that do not bear a strict relation to actual damages.

five grains – wheat, barley, oats, spelt and rye.

forbidden labors of the Sabbath – see **avos melachah**.

forty lashes – see **malkus**.

four species – the four articles of plant-life we are commanded to take and hold in our hands on the festival of Succos. These consist of: (a) **aravos** – willow branches; (b) **esrog** – citron; (c) **hadasim** – myrtle branches; (d) **lulav** – branch of the date palm tree.

Gaon [pl. **Geonim**] – (a) title accorded the heads of the academies in Sura and Pumbedisa, the two Babylonian seats of Jewish learning, from the late 6th to mid-11th centuries C.E. They served as the link in the chain of Torah tradition that joined the **Amoraim** to the **Rishonim;** (b) subsequently used to describe any brilliant Torah scholar.

Gemara – portion of the Talmud which discusses the **Mishnah;** also, loosely, a synonym for the Talmud as a whole.

gematria – the numeric valuation of the Hebrew alphabet.

get [pl. **gittin**] – bill of divorce; the document that – when it is placed in the wife's possession – effects the dissolution of a marriage.

beheimah – domesticated species, livestock. In regard to various laws, the Torah distinguishes between *beheimah,* domestic species, e.g. cattle, sheep, goats; and, **chayah,** wild species, e.g. deer, antelope.

bein haarbayim – lit. between the darkenings. It refers to the hours between the "darkening of the day" and the "darkening of the night." The darkening of the day starts at midday, when the shadows begin to lengthen. The darkening of the night is simply the beginning of the night, after sunset. Thus *bein haarbayim* connotes the afternoon.

bein hashemashos – the twilight period preceding night. The legal status of *bein hashemashos* as day or night is uncertain.

beis din – court; Rabbinical court comprised minimally of three members. Such a court is empowered to rule on civil matters. See also **Sanhedrin**.

beis hamidrash – a **Torah** study hall.

Beis HaMikdash – Holy **Temple** in Jerusalem. The **Temple** edifice comprised (a) the Antechamber or **Ulam**; (b) the **Holy** or **Heichal**; and (c) the **Holy of Holies**. See **Sanctuary**.

beis hapras – a field in which a grave has been plowed over, giving rise to the suspicion that bone fragments have been scattered throughout the field.

bereirah – retroactive clarification. This principle allows for the assignment of a legal status to a person or object whose identity is as yet undetermined, but which will be retroactively clarified by a subsequent choice.

besulah (pl. **besulos**) – a virgin.

bikkurim – the first-ripening fruits of any of the seven species (wheat, barley, grapes, figs, pomegranates, olives, dates), with which the Torah praises Eretz Yisrael. They are brought to the **Temple** where certain rites are performed, and given to the **Kohanim**.

binyan av – one of the thirteen principles of Biblical hermeneutics. This is exegetical derivation based on a logical analogy between different areas of law. Whenever a commonality of law or essence is found in different areas of **Torah** law, an analogy is drawn between them, and the laws that apply to one can therefore be assumed to apply to the others as well.

Bircas HaMazon – the blessings recited after a meal.

Bircas Kohanim – See **Priestly Blessing**.

bitul (or **bitul b'rov**) – the principle of nullification in a majority. Under certain circumstances, a mixture of items of differing legal status assumes the status of its majority component.

bogeress – a girl who has attained the age of 12½ years and is thereupon considered an adult in all respects. See **bagrus**.

Bris Milah – ritual circumcision.

Canaanite slave – a non-Jewish slave owned by a Jew. His term of servitude is for life. While owned by the Jew, he is obligated in all the **mitzvos** incumbent upon a Jewish woman. Upon being freed, he becomes a full-fledged Jew, with a status similar to that of a convert.

chagigah offering – festival offering. Every adult Jewish male is required to bring a *chagigah* offering on the first day of the festivals of **Pesach, Shavuos** and **Succos.** It is one of the **kodashim kalim**, specifically, a type of **shelamim** offering.

chalal [f: **chalalah**] – lit. desecrated. If a **Kohen** cohabits with any woman specifically forbidden to **Kohanim,** the child of that union is a *chalal* who does not possess the sanctity of a *Kohen*. The *chalal* neither enjoys the privileges of the **Kehunah** nor is subject to its restrictions.

chalifin – See **kinyan chalifin**.

chalitzah – See **yibum**.

challah – portion removed from a dough of the **five grains,** given to a **Kohen;** if *challah* is not taken, the dough is **tevel** and may not be eaten. The minimum amount of dough from which *challah* must be separated is the volume-equivalent of 43.2 eggs, which is one **issaron.** Nowadays the *challah* is removed and burned.

chametz – leavened products of the five species of grain. *Chametz* is forbidden on **Pesach**.

Chanukah – Festival of Lights. The holiday that commemorates the Maccabean victory over the Greeks. It begins on the 25th of **Kislev** and lasts for eight days.

chatas [pl. **chataos**] – sin offering; an offering generally brought in atonement for the inadvertent transgression of a prohibition punishable by **kares** when transgressed deliberately. A *chatas* is also brought as one of various purification offerings. It is one of the **kodshei kodashim**.

chatas cow – See **parah adumah**.

chaver [pl. **chaverim**] – (a) one who observes the laws of ritual purity even regarding non-consecrated foodstuffs; (b) a Torah scholar, scrupulous in his observance of **mitzvos**. Regarding tithes, **tumah** and other matters, such as the necessity for **hasraah,** he is accorded a special status.

chayah – See **beheimah**.

chazakah – (a) legal presumption that conditions remain unchanged unless proven otherwise; (b) one of the methods of acquiring real estate; it consists of performing an act of improving the property, such as enclosing it with a fence or plowing it in preparation for planting; (c) "established rights"; uncontested usage of another's property establishes the right to such usage; since the owner registered no protest, acquiescence is assumed; (d) uncontested holding of real property for three years as a basis for claiming acquisition of title from the prior owner.

cheilev – The Torah forbids certain fats of cattle, sheep and goats for human consumption. These are primarily the hind fats (suet) placed on the **Altar.** See **shuman**.

cherem – (a) a vow in which one uses the expression "*cherem*" to consecrate property, placing it under jurisdiction of the Temple; (b) land or property upon which a ban has been declared, forbidding its use to anyone, e.g. the city of Jericho.

cheresh – lit. a deaf person; generally used for a deaf-mute who can neither hear nor speak. A *cheresh* is legally deemed mentally incompetent; his actions or commitments are not legally significant or binding.

Cheshvan – see **Marcheshvan**.

cheskas kashrus – presumption of fitness – the presumption that one who was originally deemed qualified, still is unless proven otherwise.

cheskas mamon – property or money whose ownership is in doubt is presumed to belong to the person in whose possession it is presently found unless proven otherwise.

chilul Hashem – lit. profanation of God's Name. (a) behavior which casts Jews in a negative light; (b) violation of a Torah prohibition done in the presence of ten male Jews.

Chol HaMoed – the Intermediate Days of the festivals of **Pesach** and **Succos**; these enjoy a quasi-**Yom Tov** status.

chullin – lit. profane things; any substance that is not sanctified. See **kodesh**.

chupah – (a) the bridal canopy; (b) a procedure for effecting **nisuin,** the final stage of marriage.

common characteristic – See **tzad hashaveh**.

Glossary

abandoned corpse – a human corpse found with no one to attend to its burial. The Torah obligates the person who finds it to bury it and allows even a **nazir** and **Kohen Gadol** to do so.

Adar – twelfth month of the Hebrew calendar.

Adar Sheni – lit. the second **Adar.** When it is deemed necessary for a leap year to be designated, an extra month is added. This thirteenth month is placed between **Adar** and **Nissan** and is called *Adar Sheni.*

agav – See **kinyan agav**.

agency – the principle that an agent may act as a proxy of a principal and have his actions legally accepted on behalf of the principal.

Aggadah, aggadata – the homiletical teachings of the Sages and all non-halachic Rabbinic literature found in the Talmud.

agunah – lit. a tied women. A woman who cannot remarry because she remains legally bound to her husband.

akirah – the **melachah** of transferring involves the moving of an article from one domain to another. To be Biblically liable one must perform both *akirah,* the *lifting* of the article from its domain of origin, and *hanachah,* the *setting down* of the article in its new domain.

akum – idolater.

Altar – the great *Altar*, which stands in the Courtyard of the **Beis HaMikdash.** Certain portions of every offering are burnt on the *Altar*. The blood of most offerings is applied to the walls of the *Altar*.

amah [pl. **amos**] – cubit; a linear measure equaling six **tefachim.** Opinions regarding its modern equivalent range between 18 and 22.9 inches.

am haaretz [pl. **amei haaretz**] – a common, ignorant person who, possibly, is not meticulous in his observance of **halachah**.

Amora [pl. **Amoraim**] – sage of the **Gemara;** cf. **Tanna**.

amud – one side of the **daf** in the **Gemara**.

aninus – the state of being an **onein.** Upon the death of one's seven closest relatives a person enters a state of mourning. The first stage of the mourning period is called *aninus.* This stage (during which the mourner is known as an *onein*) lasts until the end of the day on which the death occurred. When burial is delayed the Rabbis extend the *aninus* period until the end of that day.

Anshei Knesses HaGedolah – see **Men of the Great Assembly**.

aravos – willow branches. See **four species**.

arayos – See **ervah.**

areiv – guarantor.

arus [f. **arusah**] – one who is betrothed and thereby entered the **erusin** stage of marriage. See **erusin**.

asham [pl. **ashamos**] – guilt offering, an offering brought to atone for one of several specific sins; in addition, a part of certain purification offerings. It is one of the **kodshei kodashim**.

asham talui – an **asham** for doubt. An *asham* offering brought to atone for an uncertain transgression wherever a certain transgression would require a **chatas** to atone.

asheirah – a tree either designated for worship or under which an idol is placed.

asmachta – lit. reliance. (a) a conditional commitment made by a party who does not really expect to have to honor it; (b) a verse cited by the **Gemara** not as a Scriptural basis for the law but rather as an allusion to a Rabbinic law.

assembly – This event took place on the evening following the first day of Succos, in the year following the **shemittah** year. The entire nation would gather in one of the Temple Courtyards to hear the king read the Book of *Deuteronomy.*

Av – (a) fifth month of the Hebrew calendar. (b) l.c. [pl. avos] see **melachah**.

av beis din – chief of the court. This position was second in importance to the **Nasi** who served as head of the **Sanhedrin**.

av [pl. **avos**] **hatumah** – lit. father of **tumah.** See **tumah**.

avi avos hatumah – lit. father of fathers of **tumah.** See **tumah**.

avodah [pl. **avodos**] – the sacrificial service, or any facet of it. There are four critical *avodos* in the sacrificial service. They are **shechitah, kabbalah, holachah** and **zerikah**.

avodah zarah – idol worship, idolatry.

aylonis [pl. **aylonios**] – an adult woman who never developed the physical signs of female maturity. She is therefore assumed to be incapable of bearing children.

azharah – (a) Scriptural warning; the basic prohibition stated in the Torah, which serves to warn the potential sinner against incurring the punishment prescribed for a particular action; (b) term Gemara uses to refer to a negative commandment, the transgression of which is punished by *kares.*

baal keri [pl. **baalei keri**] – one who experienced a seminal emission. He is **tamei** (ritually impure) and must immerse himself in a **mikveh**.

bagrus – the time when a girl becomes a *bogeress* (a full adult), the final legal state of a girl's physical development. A girl automatically becomes a *bogeress* six months after she becomes a **naarah**.

bamah [pl. **bamos**] – lit. high place; altar. This refers to any altar other than the **Altar** of the **Tabernacle** or **Temple**. During certain brief periods of Jewish history, it was permitted to offer sacrifices on a *bamah*. There are two types of *bamah.* The *communal* (or *major*) *bamah* was the altar of the public and was the only *bamah* on which communal offerings could be sacrificed. Private voluntary offerings could be brought even on a *private* (or *minor*) *bamah* which was an altar erected anywhere by an individual for private use.

Baraisa [pl. **Baraisos**] – the statements of **Tannaim** not included by **Rebbi** in the **Mishnah.** R' Chiya and R' Oshaya, the students of Rebbi, researched and reviewed the *Baraisa* and compiled an authoritative collection of them.

bechor – (a) firstborn male child; (b) a firstborn male kosher animal. Such an animal is born with sacrificial sanctity, and must be given to a **Kohen** who then offers it (if unblemished) as a *bechor* sacrifice in the **Temple** and eats its sacred meat. Unlike other sacrifices, the *bechor* is automatically sacred from birth even without designation.

bedek habayis – **Temple** Treasury.

bedi'avad – after the fact. See **lechatchilah**.

Glossary

Scriptural Index

SHOULD NOT PLACE A RICKETY LADDER IN HIS HOUSE?[30] שֶׁנֶּאֱמַר – **FOR IT IS STATED:** ,,וְלֹא־תָשִׂים דָּמִים בְּבֵיתֶךָ'' – ***YOU SHALL NOT PLACE BLOOD IN YOUR HOUSE.***[31]

הדרן עלך אלו נערות

WE SHALL RETURN TO YOU, EILU NE'AROS

NOTES

30. [I.e. even in his own house.] Although it could be argued that these things pose little threat to the members of his household, who are on familiar terms with the dog and who know to beware of the ladder, it is nonetheless forbidden to maintain these hazards [because others who enter the property might be injured] (*Chidushei Aggados Maharsha, Bava Kamma* 15b).

31. *Deuteronomy* 22:8. This quote appears in the Biblical injunction to erect a מַעֲקֶה, *roof-fence.* The verse read in full: *When you build a new house, you shall make a fence for your roof, and you shall not place blood in your house, in case someone should fall from it.* Now, the middle clause of this verse (*and you shall not place blood . . .*) seems redundant, since the verse has already stated the requirement to put up a fence [and the final clause even makes clear the reason for it]. Thus, the middle clause is expounded to add to the first injunction the requirement to remove even hazards that are not primarily a threat to the members of the household (see *Aggados Maharsha* ibid.).

[Since there is a Torah requirement to remove hazards from one's property, the courts use the threat of a ban to force the owner of the vicious animal to fulfill this mitzvah. Even the courts of Babylonia may force him to fulfill his Biblical requirements. *Rosh* to *Bava Kamma* (§20) writes that we do not, however, ban the owner of a *tam* ox that gores, for the case here of the dog is so unusual that it is called כֶּלֶב רַע (*vicious dog*). But certainly we do ban the owner of a *muad* ox until he removes it. See also *Ritva* here.]

הא מני ר' יוסי הגלילי היא דאמר תם משלם חצי כופר [א] ת"ש המית שורי את פלוני או שורו של פלוני הרי זה משלם על פי עצמו מאי לאו בתם לא במועד אבל בתם מאי אינו משלם על פי עצמו אדתני סיפא עבדו של פלוני אינו משלם ע"פ עצמו ניפלוג וניתני בדידה במה דברים אמורים במועד [א] אבל תם אינו משלם על פי עצמו כולה במועד קמיירי ת"ש זה הכלל כל המשלם יותר על מה שהזיק אינו משלם ע"פ עצמו הא פחות ממה שהזיק משלם ע"פ עצמו לא תימא הא פחות ממה שהזיק אלא אימא הא כמה שהזיק משלם ע"פ עצמו אבל פחות מאי אינו משלם ע"פ עצמו ליתני זה הכלל כל שאינו משלם כמה שהזיק אינו משלם על פי עצמו דמשמע פחות ומשמע יתר תיובתא והלכתא פלגא ניזקא קנסא [ב] תיובתא והלכתא אין טעמא מאי איתותב משום דלא קתני כמה שהזיק לא פסיקא ליה כיון דאיכא [א] חצי נזק צרורות דהלכתא גמירי לה דממונא הוא משום הכי לא קתני והשתא דאמרת פלגא ניזקא קנסא [ב] האי כלבא דאכל אימרי ושונרא דאכיל תרנגולי רברבי משונה הוא ולא מגבינן בבבל אבל זוטרי אורחיה הוא ומגבינן [ג] ואי תפס לא מפקינן מיניה ואי אמר אקבעו לי זימנא לארץ ישראל מקבעינן ליה ואי לא אזיל משמתינן ליה בין כך ובין כך משמתינן ליה דאמרינן ליה סליק הזיקך [ג] מדרבי נתן דתניא ר' נתן אומר [ד] מנין שלא יגדל אדם כלב רע בתוך ביתו ולא יעמיד סולם רעוע בתוך ביתו שנאמר [א] ולא תשים דמים בביתך:

הדרן עלך אלו נערות

נערה [ה] שנתפתתה בושתה ופגמה וקנסה של אביה והצער בתפוסה [ו] עמדה בדין עד שלא מת האב הרי הן של אב מת האב הרי הן של אחין לא הספיקה לעמוד בדין עד שמת האב הרי הן של עצמה [ז] עמדה בדין עד שלא בגרה הרי הן של אב מת האב הרי הן של אחין לא הספיקה לעמוד בדין עד שבגרה הרי הן של עצמה רבי שמעון אומר אם לא הספיקה לגבות עד [ח] שמת האב הרי הן של עצמה מעשה

הא מני ר' יוסי הגלילי היא דאמר תם משלם חצי כופר. דדריש להאי נקי לדרשה אחריתי לדמי ולדות אם נגח אשה ויצאו ילדיה הלכך לא הוה ליה לפלוגי בינייהו בכופר וכי תימא הוה ליה לפלוגי דהאי פלגא והאי כוליה ההיא בכלל רישא היא דקתני תם משלם חצי נזק ומועד נזק שלם ותנא בניזקין והוא הדין לכופר: **מאי לאו בתם.** ולי משום דקתני בה המית שורי את פלוני לחיובו כופר ותם ולאו בר כופר הוא הא מני רבי יוסי הגלילי היא: **אדתני עבדו של פלוני כו'.** דלא משכח פטור על פי עצמו אלא בעבד: **ניפלוג בדידה.** בבן חורין ובבהמה נמי הוה מצי לשנויי חילוק ולמיתני דאיכא דלא משלם על פי עצמו: **בד"א.** דמשלם ע"פ עצמו במועד כו': **כולה במועד קמיירי.** במועד אתא לאשמועי' דאף הוא יש בו חילוק דאיכא ביה מידי דלא משלם על פי עצמו ומאי ניהו נגיחת עבד ולי הוה תני דקאמרת הוה שביק נמי לאורחיה דרישא איירי במועד וסיפא ניתני תם ומה לי שבקה תנא לאורחיה גבי ניזק לדלג מבן חורין לעבד מה לי שבקה במזיק ולדלג ממועד לתם: **יתר על מה שהזיק.** כגון נגיחת עבד וכן אונס ומפתה ומוציא שם רע ותשלומי כפל ותשלומי ארבעה וחמשה: **הא פחות ממה שהזיק.** כגון חצי נזק דתם: הכי גרסינן ליתני כל שאינו משלם כמה שהזיק אינו משלם ע"פ עצמו: **והלכתא פלגא ניזקא קנסא.** דהואיל וכל חצי נזק אינו אלא בניזקין דלאו אורחיה לאו על מריה הוה רמיא למינטריה בהכי אלא קנסא הוא כי היכי דלוסיף ביה נטירותא: **טעמא מאי איתותב.** כלומר תיובתא מאי היא: **משום דלא קתני כל שאינו משלם כמה שהזיק אינו משלם על פי עצמו.** דלישתמע מינה נמי חצי נזק הא לאו תיובתא היא: **כיון דאיכא חצי נזק.** דמשתלם בנזקי בהמה במהלכת והתיזה צרורות מתחת רגליה והזיקה דתנן בבבא קמא (דף יז.) דמשלמת חצי נזק וההוא חצי נזק קיימא לן בב"ק דהלכתא גמירי לה מסיני שהוא תולדה של רגל ופטורה ברה"ר כי רגל וניזקי רגל לאו קנסא נינהו אלא ממונא שהרי מועדת מתחילתה וגבי צרורות הוא דאקיל רחמנא וכיון דממונא הוא משלם ע"פ עצמו משום הכי לא פסיקא ליה למיתני כל שאינו משלם כמה שהזיק דהא איכא האי: **דאכיל אימרי.** שחנק טלאים חיים ואכלם: **משונה הוא.** אין דרכו בכך וכל נזק משונה בבהמה הוי תולדה דקרן תמה שאף היא משונה שאין דרכה בכך וחצי נזק הוא דמשלם וכיון דקנסא הוא לא מגבינן ליה בדייני בבל שאין שם סמיכה בזקנים ולא מקרו מומחים וגבי קנס כתיב (שמות כב) ירשיעון אלהים: **אורחיה הוא.** והוו להו נזקי דשן ושן משלמת נזק שלם וממונא הוא וגובין אותו בבבל: **ואי תפס.** ניזק ממונא דמזיק גבי קנסא דחצי נזקו דאין צריך לצעוק לפנינו: **לא מפקינן מיניה.** וגבי פלגא נזקיה: **ואי.** לא תפיס ואמר קמן קבעו לי זמנא בארעא דישראל השיאוהו לילך עמי לדון לפני דייני ארץ ישראל קבעינן ליה: **בין כך ובין כך.** בין שרוצה ניזק לילך לארץ ישראל בין שאינו רוצה: **משמתינן ליה.** למזיק מיהא להרוג אותו כלב ולסלק היזיקיה:

הדרן עלך אלו נערות

נערה שנתפתתה: **והצער בתפוסה.** והצער נמי לאביה באנוסה. בתפוסה לישנא דקרא ותפשה ושכב עמה (דברים כב): **לא הספיקה לעמוד בדין כו'.** כיון דלא עמדה בדין לאו ממון הוא להורישו לבניו ואמרינן לקמן (דף מג.) אין אדם מוריש לבנו זכות שזכתה לו תורה בבתו ויליף לה מקרא: **מת האב.** משעמדה בדין בנערותיה בין בגרה קודם מיתה בין לא בגרה: **הרי הן של אחין.** דכיון דעמדה בדין זכה בהן אב: **ר"ש אומר.** אע"פ שעמדה בדין לא הוי ממון דאב להורישו לבניו עד דמטי לידיה ובגמרא יליף טעמא:

הא מני רבי יוסי הגלילי היא דאמר תם משלם חצי כופר. ולינא שיורא דלאו משום דמועד משלם כופר שלם ותם אינו משלם אלא חצי כופר הא לאו שיורא הוא דהא תנן תם משלם חצי נזק ומועד נזק שלם וכופר בכלל ולא"ת אכתי ליתני דמועד אף כשהוא בסקילה משלם כופר ותם כשהוא בסקילה אינו משלם כופר כלל דהכיאוהו לב"ד וישלם לך דהוא עצמו אינו משלם אלא מגופו כדאמרינן בפרק שור שנגח ד' וה' (ב"ק דף מג. ושם) וי"ל דהך נמי לא הוי שיור דהוי בכלל הא דקתני תם מגופו ומועד מן העלייה [ו] ומיהו תימה דלא אשכחן בהדיא בשום מקום שהיה אומר ר' יוסי הגלילי דתם משלם חצי כופר ולי משום דדריש רבי יוסי הגלילי בפרק שור שנגח ד' וה' (ג"ז שם) נקי מדמי ולדות ולא דריש נקי מחצי כופר מכלל דסבר דחייב ודלמא לעולם סבר דפטור וטעמא משום דפטור מחצי כופר לא איצטריך קרא דכשהשור בסקילה לא שייך כופר דהכיאוהו לב"ד וישלם לך וכשאין השור בסקילה כגון על פי עד אחד או על פי הבעלים פטור מדרבה דאמר התם (דף מג.) שור שהמית בן חורין שלא בכוונה פטור שנאמר השור יסקל וגם בעליו יומת בזמן שהשור בסקילה בעלים משלמין כופר כו' ונראה דס"פ הא מני ר' יוסי הגלילי היא דאמר תם משלם חצי כופר פי' דלא ממעט חצי כופר מנקי ולאו דוקא משלם קאמר אלא היה משלם אם היה לו ממה להשתלם ולשום תנא לא הוה חצי כופר שיור כי אם לרבי אלעזר דדריש נקי מחצי כופר ולית ליה דרבה וכשאין השור בסקילה מועד משלם ותם אינו משלם והא דנקט רבי יוסי הגלילי טפי מרבי עקיבא דדריש נקי מדמי עבד ולדידיה נהי דחצי כופר לא הוי שיור דמי עבד הוי שיור [ז]:

ואי תפס כו'. פר"ת דדוקא אי תפס את המזיק עצמו אבל דבר אחר לא דלענין מזיק עצמו הקילו חכמים שיכול לתופסו דאל"כ יתפוס כל אשר לו ולא נפיק מיניה דאין דנין דיני קנסות ואם נוציא המותר ונשאיר כדי נזק הרי אנו דנין דיני קנסות ודוחק:

הדרן עלך אלו נערות

נערה. לא הספיקה לעמוד בדין עד שמת האב הרי הן של עצמה. תימה תינח קנס אלא בושת ופגם דממונא הוא דאחין בעי למיהוי ושמא מקראי דלעיל דנפקי בושת ופגם איתקוש אהדדי כדפי' לעיל [ז]: לאביה

עין משפט נר מצוה

צו א מיי' פ"ב מהל' נזקי ממון הלכה ז ג סמג עשין סח טוש"ע ח"מ סימן א סעיף א וסי' שצ סעיף ג:
צז ב מיי' פ"ב שם הל' ז ופ"ה מהל' סנהדרין הל' ט סמג עשין נו טור ש"ע שם סי' א סעיף ה וסי' שצ סעיף ו:
צח ג מיי' פ"ה מהל' סנהדרין הלכה יז סמג עשין צז טוש"ע שם סימן א סעיף ה:
צט ד מיי' פי"א מהל' רוצח ושמירת נפש הל' ד סמג עשין עט טוש"ע ח"מ סי' תכז סעיף ז וסמג תמ סעיף ח:
א ה מיי' פ"ב מהלכות נערה בתולה הלכה יד סמג עשין נה טוש"ע אה"ע סי' קנז:
ב ו מיי' שם הל' טו:

תוספות רי"ד

שיוסיף שמירה על שמירתו ת"ש כל המשלם יותר ממה שהזיק אינו משלם ע"פ עצמו. פי' כגון נגיחת העבד וכן אונס ומפתה ומוציא שם רע ותשלומי כפל ותשלומי ד' וה': הא פחות משלם פי' כגון חצי נזק דתם. לא תימא פחות ממה שהזיק אלא אימא הא כמה שהזיק משלם ע"פ עצמו א"ה ליתני זה הכלל כל שאינו משלם כל מה שהזיק משלם ע"פ עצמו דמשמע פחות ומשמע יותר תיובתא. ופסיק תלמודא והלכתא פלגא נזקא קנסא. פי' דהואיל וכל חצי נזק אינו אלא היזקא דלא אורחיה לאו על מרא רמיא לנטורי בהכי אלא קנסא הוא כי היכי דלוסיף ביה נטירותא תיובתא והלכתא אין טעמא מאי איתותב. פי' תיובתיה מאי הוא משום דלא תני הכי כל שאינו משלם (כלו) [כמה שהזיק] ש"מ (בין) חצי נזק (ממונא) הא לאו תיובתא הוא כיון דאיכא חצי נזק צרורות דהל' גמירי לה דממונא הוא ומשלם ע"פ עצמו שהן תולדה דרגל מש"ה לא קתני פי' משום כיון (דאין) [דאיכא] חצי נזק המשתלם [ע"פ עצמו] (כגון) [כגון] בהמה המהלכת והתיזה צרורות מתחת רגליה והזיקו דתנן בבבא קמא דמשלמת חצי נזק והאי חצי נזק ק"ל דהל' גמירי לה דממונא הוא ומשלם ע"פ עצמו שהן תולדה דרגל ופטורים ברה"ר כרגל וניזקי רגל לאו קנסא נינהו א"א ממונא שהרי מועדת בתחלתה דגבי צרורות הוא דאקיל רחמנא. וכיון דממונא הוא משלם ע"פ עצמו מ"ה לא פסיקא ליה למיתני משום דאיכא האי. השתא דאמרת פ"נ קנסא האי כלבא דאכיל אימרא ושונרא דאכיל תרנגולא רברבא משונה הוא. כי אין דרכו בכך וכל נזק משונה בבהמה הוי תולדה דקרן תמה שאין דרכה בכך וחצי נזק הוא שמשלם. וכיון דקנסא הוא לא מגבי' בבבל. פי' בדייני בבל שאין שם סמיכה בזקנים ולא מיקרי אלהים מומחים ובקנס כתיב אשר ירשיעון אלהים. ואי תפיס ניזק ממונא של מזיק גבי קנסא דחצי נזקו ולא מפקי' מיניה. ואי אמר אזמיניה בהדי לדינא בא"י מזמינן ליה. פי' ואי לא תפיס והשתא אמר קמן קבעי לי זמנא בא"י קבעי' לי' ואי לא אזיל משמתינן לי': בין כך ובין כך. פי' בין שרוצה ניזק לילך לא"י בין לא. משמתינן ליה עד דמסלק הזיקיה מביתיה מדר' נתן דתניא אר"נ מנין שלא יגדל אדם כלב רע בתוך ביתו ולא יעמיד סולם רעוע בביתו שנאמר ולא תשים דמים בביתך. ופי' וה"ה נמי לקנס דאונס ומפתה אע"ג דלא מגבי' ליה בבבל אי תפיש לא מפקי' מיניה אבל להזמינו לדין לא"י לא מזמינן ליה שאין עתה ישיבות קבועות שם כאשר היה אז. **וראיתי** בתשובות רב שרירא גאון ז"ל שיש להן קנס ששאלת מהו להגבות שלא יהא חוטא נשכר כיוצא בזה אמרו חכמים אין מגבין קנס קמגבית בבבל שלח לי' חסדא חסדא קנס קמגבית בבבל אלמא הלכתא רווחת היא שאין מגבין קנסות אלא בירושלים ובסנהדרין של כ"ג ותו קאמרי' א"ר נזקי שור באדם ונזקי שור בשור [אין] גובין אותן בבבל אבל אדם באדם ואדם בשור אין מגבין אותו בבבל (ולא) [אך] משום שלא יהא החוטא נשכר נהגו לנדות עד שיפייס וכי נמי חכמים האחרונים לקידוש עד שהוא מפייס בממון או שירבה עליו רעים ויפייסנו בדברים. **ומעשה** בא' שהפיל שינו של חבירו ובא לפני מר רב צמח גאון ז"ל וא"ל דבר קצוב אין אתה חייב לו אלא חייב אתה לפייסו כי אין מחייבין עליך או ממון או בדברים ועכשיו כל דיני קנסות בטלו ומנהג שהנהיג אדונינו מר רב צמח גאון ז"ל אנו נוהגים בו היום בכל קהילות הקודש:

פרק ד נערה שנתפתתה בושתה ופגמה וקנסה לאביה והצער בתפוסה. פי' המורה והצער נמי לאביה כלומר יתירה עליה אונסה שכן יש לה צער ולישנא דקרא נקט ותפשה ושכב עמה עמדה בדין עד שלא מת האב ה"ה של אב מת האב ה"ה של אחין אם לא

מסורת הש"ס

א) [ב"ק טו: מג.], ב) [עירובין י. טו: ב"ק טו:], ג) ב"ק טו: מו, ד) נ"א ר"ש אומר אם לא הספיקה לגבות עד שמת האב הרי הן של עצמה, ה) נ"א שבגרה, ו) [וער' תוס' ב"ק טו: ד"ה הא], ז) [ד' לח: ד"ה יש].

תוספות ישנים

א) [קשה דלא מצי תני הכי דמשמע ע"פ עצמו אינו משלם אבל ע"פ עדים משלם ודלמא לא סבר כר' יוסי הגלילי אלא סבר דאפילו ע"פ עדים אינו משלם חצי כופר ומיהו מהר"ם דמ"מ הוי ליה לפלוגי בדידיה בשורו של פלוני גרידא ולא הוי ליה למינקט עבד. תו"י].

גליון הש"ס

תוס' ד"ה הא מני וכו' ומיהו תימה. עי' תשובת מהרלב"ח סי' פ"ט:

תורה אור השלם

א) כִּי תִבְנֶה בַּיִת חָדָשׁ וְעָשִׂיתָ מַעֲקֶה לְגַגֶּךָ וְלֹא תָשִׂים דָּמִים בְּבֵיתֶךָ כִּי יִפֹּל הַנֹּפֵל מִמֶּנּוּ: [דברים כב, ח]

ליקוטי רש"י

ר' יוסי הגלילי היא דאמר. בפרק שור שנגח את הפרה (לקמן דף מג.) תם משלם חצי כופר ולינא שיורא דלאו משום דהאי משלם כופר שלם והאי לא משלם אלא פלגא כופר לאו שיורא הוא דהא תני לה תם משלם חצי נזק ומועד נזק שלם וכופר בכלל [ב"ק טו.]. **מאי לאו בתם.** דה"ק המית שורי את פלוני שורו של פלוני או פלוני חצי כופר ע"פ עצמו ורבי יוסי הגלילי היא או שורו של פלוני המית משלם ע"פ עצמו ואי חצי נזק אלמא ממונא הוא. **עבדו של פלוני.** לא קנסא הוא דמשלם ל' סלעים ואפילו אינו שוה אלא דינר. **ניפלוג וניתני בדידה.** קמייתא גופיה דהמית שורו של פלוני לפלוני. **כולה במועד קמיירי.** ואיפוקא דמועד בעי לאשמועינן. **יתר על מה שהזיק.** כגון ל' של עבד. **הא פחות.** כגון חצי נזק דתם משלם ע"פ עצמו. **כמה שהזיק.** נזק שלם דמועד. **משום דלא קתני כמה שהזיק.** הא לאו תיובתא היא דלא פסיקא ליה למיתני כמה שהזיק ליהוי משמע דפחות אינו משלם ע"פ עצמו כיון דאיכא חצי נזק צרורות דאינו משלם כמה שהזיק ואפילו הכי משלם ע"פ עצמו דהלכתא גמירי לה דממונא הוא. **אימרי.** כבשים. **תרנגולי רברבי.** תרנגולים וכבשים גדולים דאין דרכן לכך ותחלתו לאו מועד. **משונה הוא.** דאין דרכן בכך והוי תולדה דקרן לשלם חצי נזק.

eat them.[23] Thus, the damage is classified as *shein*[24] damage, for which payment is compensation, וּמַגְבִּינַן – **and we do collect** it in Babylonia.[25]

The Gemara notes that although the Babylonian courts are not empowered to collect the payment of half-damages, there are nevertheless methods for facilitating such payment even in Babylonia:

וְאִי תָּפַס – **But if [the damaged party] seized** property from the owner of the dog or cat, לֹא מַפְּקִינַן מִינֵּיהּ – **we do not take** it **away from him.**[26] וְאִי אָמַר אַקְבְּעוּ לִי זִימְנָא לְאֶרֶץ יִשְׂרָאֵל – **And if [the damaged party] said** to the court, **"Set a date for me to go to Eretz Yisrael** to present the case to a court of ordained judges,"[27] מַקְבְּעִינַן לֵיהּ – **we** [the courts of Babylonia] **set a date for him;** וְאִי לֹא אָזִיל – **and if [the damager] does not go** by that date, מְשַׁמְּתִינַן לֵיהּ – **we place a ban upon him.**[28]

The Gemara continues:

בֵּין כָּךְ וּבֵין כָּךְ מְשַׁמְּתִינַן לֵיהּ – **And either way,** whether the damaged party asks to go to Eretz Yisrael or not, **we place a ban upon [the owner]** of the dog or cat, דְּאַמְרִינַן לֵיהּ סַלֵּיק הֶזֵּיקָךְ – **for we say to him: Remove** (i.e. destroy) **your damaging [animal],**[29] מִדְּרַבִּי נָתָן – **based on** the ruling of **R' Nassan.** דְּתַנְיָא – **For we learned in a Baraisa:** רַבִּי נָתָן אוֹמֵר – **R' NASSAN SAYS:** מִנַּיִן שֶׁלֹּא יְגַדֵּל אָדָם כֶּלֶב רַע בְּתוֹךְ בֵּיתוֹ – **FROM WHERE** do we learn **THAT A PERSON SHOULD NOT RAISE A VICIOUS DOG IN HIS HOUSE,** וְלֹא יַעֲמִיד סוּלָּם רָעוּעַ בְּתוֹךְ בֵּיתוֹ – **AND**

NOTES

kills and eats a sheep, we have no source for considering the owner liable – for nowhere do we find the Torah holding an owner liable for the truly unusual [and thus unexpected] damage of his animals! *Keren* damage is not a precedent for this, because *keren* damage, according to this view, is not uncommon even in a *tam*. Thus, *Tosafos* conclude, if half-damages are compensation, the owner of the dog or cat that attacked and ate a larger animal would not be liable *at all* (even in Eretz Yisrael). This view is shared by *Rashba* to *Bava Kamma* ibid. *Riva,* cited by *Shitah Mekubetzes* to *Bava Kamma* ibid., disputes *Tosafos* and states that even according to the view that the half-damages of *keren* are compensation, *keren* is still defined as an unusual form of damage. Thus, even according to this view, the owner of the dog or cat would be liable. This view is shared by *Ritva* here.]

23. Our texts which read, הַאי כַּלְבָּא דְּאָכַל אִימְרֵי וְשׁוּנְרָא דְּאָכִיל תַּרְנְגוֹלֵי רַבְרְבֵי, which mentions the word רַבְרְבֵי (*large*) with regard to the cat that ate chickens but not with regard to the dog that ate sheep, suggest that the Gemara's distinction between large and small is meant only vis-a-vis the cat that ate chickens. With regard to the dog that ate sheep, however, there is no such distinction, for it is unusual for a dog to choke and eat even small sheep. This is, in fact, the opinion of *Rambam* (*Hil. Nizkei Mamon* 3:7), *Tur* and *Shulchan Aruch,* (*Choshen Mishpat* 391:6). A parallel version of our Gemara, however, appears somewhat different in *Bava Kamma* 15b. *Rashi* ad loc., in explaining that text, states that the Gemara's distinction between large and small refers to the dog that ate sheep as well.

24. Literally: tooth. This refers to damage an animal does through a normal act of eating, and encompasses damage done in the course of any act of normal gratification [e.g. through rubbing itself against an object in order to relieve an itch].

25. The ordinary damage done by an animal [in the pursuit of its food] is classified as *shein,* for which one pays full damages as compensation. Compensation can be collected even by judges who have not been ordained with *semichah* (see *Bava Kamma* 84b); thus, it can be collected even in Babylonia (*Rashi*).

[Strictly speaking, even the collection of ordinary damages requires ordained judges. However, the Rabbis instituted that such damages, as well as other common forms of monetary payments (e.g. loans), may be collected by the unordained judges of Babylonia. In effect, the ordained Sages of Eretz Yisrael commissioned the unordained judges of Babylonia to serve as their surrogates in judging such cases, so that, in the words of the Gemara, "We [the Babylonian judges] carry out the charge of the Sages of Eretz Yisrael" [שְׁלִיחוּתַיְיהוּ קָא עָבְדִינַן]. However, the Rabbis empowered the judges of Babylonia to act on their behalf in cases of compensation but not in cases of penalties (see *Ritva* and Gemara *Bava Kamma* ibid.).]

26. I.e. although the Babylonian courts have no jurisdiction over punitive damages, if the damaged party seizes payment on his own, and therefore does not require the intervention of the court, he may keep the half-damages payment (*Rashi*).

Rabbeinu Tam contends that the courts allow the damaged party to keep what he seized only if he seized the animal that did the damage. For if we were to extend this leniency to other forms of property, there would be nothing to stop the damaged party from seizing much more than the amount of the damage, and the courts, being unable to judge penalty cases, could not retrieve the excess from him [since determining the amount of the "excess" and forcing him to return it would amount to a de facto determination and collection of the penalty] (*Tosafos* ד"ה ואי תפס).

Rabbeinu Tam's view is disputed by *Rosh* (*Bava Kamma* 1:20), who maintains that this would not be tantamount to judging the penalty, because the damaged party has already collected the penalty (by virtue of the law allowing him to keep what he seized). The only issue being decided and enforced by the court is the return of the amount that exceeds the penalty. Since this rightfully belongs to the owner of the dog or cat, retrieving it for him falls within the jurisdiction of the Babylonian court. Thus, *Rosh* maintains, the damaged party can seize any property belonging to the owner of the dog or cat and if the amount of the seizure exceeds half the damages, the courts will intervene to retrieve it.

[From the language of *Rabbeinu Tam,* it seems that the law allowing the damaged party to seize the value of the penalty and retain it is a Rabbinic ordinance. This is also the view of *Rama* (cited by *Rosh* ibid.). However, *Rosh* disputes this, and contends that no special ordinance is needed here; rather, the damaged party may seize the property by right. For, in truth, the owner of the dog or cat owes the damaged party the amount of the penalty, and it is merely the Babylonian courts' lack of authority to judge such cases that prevents him from collecting it through the judicial process. Since the courts are powerless to act for him, the damaged party has the right to enforce the law on his own behalf (עָבִיד אִינִישׁ דִּינָא לְנַפְשֵׁיהּ). See *Kovetz Shiurim* vol. II 13:2,6 for further discussion of *Rosh's* view.]

27. I.e. if the damaged party did not seize property from the owner of the dog or cat, but asked that the court command the damager to go with him before a court of ordained judges in the Land of Israel (*Rashi*).

28. One of the punishments available to a *beis din* is the *shamta* ban. When the court pronounces a *shamta* ban upon an offender, the community is enjoined to avoid being within four *amos* (6-8 feet) of the person, and to refrain from eating and drinking with him. The offender is obligated to conduct himself in most matters like a mourner (e.g. he is forbidden to cut his hair and launder his clothes). In general, a term of *nidui* lasts thirty days (see *Moed Katan* 15-18; *Rambam, Hil. Talmud Torah* 7:2-4). For a more precise definition of *shamta,* see Schottenstein ed. of *Moed Katan,* 16a note 23.

Although there is a general rule that we do not compel a litigant to spend a large sum of money to travel to a distant court (see *Sanhedrin* 32b), that rule applies only when there is a local court able to deal with the matter, even if it is not as well qualified as the more distant court. In our case, however, where the Babylonian courts are not empowered to deal with the claim, the *nizak* can force the *mazik* to go to Eretz Yisrael to have the case tried (*Nimukei Yosef* to *Bava Kamma,* folio 6b ד"ה אמר). [In practice, the threat of having to travel to Eretz Yisrael serves as a goad to force the *mazik* to settle the claim without traveling to Eretz Yisrael; see *Tosafos* to *Bava Kamma* 15b ד"ה ואי.]

29. I.e. we order him – under punishment of a ban – to destroy the vicious animal (*Rashi*). [Thus, if he fails to destroy it within a reasonable time, the ban takes effect against him.]

עין משפט
נר מצוה

צו א מיי' פ"ג מהל' נזקי ממון הלכה ב ז סמג עשין סח טוש"ע ח"מ סימן א סעיף א וסי' של סעיף ג:
צז ב מיי' פ"ג שם הל' ז ופ"ה מהל' סנהדרין הל' ט סמג עשין ב טור ש"ע שם סי' א סעיף א וסי' שלא סעיף ו:
צח ג מיי' פ"ה מהל' סנהדרין הלכה י סמג עשין לז טוש"ע שם סימן א סעיף ה:
צט ד מיי' פ"ה מהל' נזקי ממון הל' ט ופי"א מהל' רוצח הל' ד סמג עשין סו טוש"ע שם סי' תט סעיף ג וסימן תכז סעיף ח:
א ה מיי' פ"ב מהלכות נערה הלכה יד סמג עשין כד טור אה"ע סי' קעז:
ב ו מיי' שם הל' טו:

מסורת הש"ס

א) [ב"ק טו: מג.], ב) [ערכין י. טו: ב"ק טו:], ג) ב"ק טו: מו., ד) נ"א ר"ש אומר אם לא הספיקה לגבות עד שמת האב הרי הן של עצמה, ה) נ"א שבגרה, ו) [ועי' תוס' ב"ק טו: ד"ה הא], ז) [ד' לח: ד"ה יש].

הא מני ר' יוסי הגלילי היא דאמר תם משלם חצי כופר א) ת"ש המית שורי את פלוני או שורו של פלוני הרי זה משלם על פי עצמו מאי לאו בתם לא במועד אבל בתם מאי אינו משלם על פי עצמו אדתני סיפא עבדו של פלוני אינו משלם ע"פ עצמו ניפלוג וניתני בדידה במה דברים אמורים במועד א) אבל תם אינו משלם על פי עצמו כולה במועד קמיירי ת"ש זה הכלל כל המשלם יתר על מה שהזיק אינו משלם ע"פ עצמו הא פחות ממה שהזיק משלם ע"פ עצמו לא תימא הא פחות ממה שהזיק אלא אימא הא כמה שהזיק משלם ע"פ עצמו אבל פחות מאי אינו משלם ע"פ עצמו ליתני זה הכלל כל שאינו משלם כמה שהזיק אינו משלם על פי עצמו דמשמע פחות ומשמע יתר תיובתא והלכתא פלגא ניזקא קנסא ב) תיובתא והלכתא אין טעמא מאי איתותב משום דלא קתני כמה שהזיק לא פסיקא ליה כיון דאיכא א חצי נזק צרורות דהלכתא גמירי לה דממונא הוא משום הכי לא קתני והשתא דאמרת פלגא ניזקא קנסא ב האי כלבא דאכל אימרי ושונרא דאכיל תרנגולי רברבי משונה הוא ולא מגבינן בבבל אבל זוטרי אורחיה הוא ומגבינן ג ואי תפס לא מפקינן מיניה ואי אמר אקבעו לי זימנא לארץ ישראל מקבעינן ליה ואי לא אזיל משמתינן ליה בין כך ובין כך משמתינן ליה דאמרינן ליה סליק היזקך ג) מדרבי נתן דתניא ר' נתן אומר ד מנין שלא יגדל אדם כלב רע בתוך ביתו ולא יעמיד סולם רעוע בתוך ביתו שנאמר א) ולא תשים דמים בביתך:

הדרן עלך אלו נערות

נערה ה שנתפתתה בושתה ופגמה וקנסה של אביה והצער בתפוסה ו עמדה בדין עד שלא מת האב הרי הן של אב מת האב הרי הן של אחין לא הספיקה לעמוד בדין עד שמת האב הרי הן של עצמה ד) עמדה בדין עד שלא בגרה הרי הן של אב מת האב הרי הן של אחין לא הספיקה לעמוד בדין עד שבגרה הרי הן של עצמה רבי שמעון אומר אם לא הספיקה לגבות עד ה) שמת האב הרי הן של עצמה מעשה

הא מני רבי יוסי הגלילי היא דאמר תם משלם חצי כופר. וליכא שיורא דלאי משום דמועד משלם כופר שלם ותם אינו משלם אלא חצי כופר הא לאו שיורא הוא דהא תנן תם משלם חצי נזק ומועד נזק שלם וכופר בכלל וא"ת אכתי ליתני דמועד אף כשהוא בסקילה משלם כופר ותם כשהוא בסקילה אינו משלם כופר כלל דהדיליהו לב"ד וישלם לך דהוא עצמו אינו משתלם אלא מגופו כדאמרינן בפרק שור שנגח ד' וה' (ב"ק דף מג. ושם) וי"ל דהכך נמי לא הוי שיור דהוי בכלל הא דקתני תם מגופו ומועד מן העלייה ומיהו תימה דלא אשכחן בהדיא בשום מקום שהיה אומר ר' יוסי הגלילי דתם משלם חצי כופר ואי משום דדריש רבי יוסי הגלילי בפרק שור שנגח ד' וה' (ג"ז שם) נקי מדמי ולדות ולא דריש נקי מחצי כופר מכלל דסבר דחייב ודלמא לעולם סבר דפטור וטעמא משום דפטור מחצי כופר לא איצטריך קרא דכשהשור בסקילה לא שייך כופר דהדיליהו לב"ד וישלם לך וכשאין השור בסקילה כגון על פי עד אחד או על פי הבעלים פטור מדרבה דאמר התם (דף מג.) שור שהמית בן חורין שלא בכוונה פטור שנאמר השור יסקל וגם בעליו יומת בזמן שהשור בסקילה בעלים משלמין כופר כו' ונראה דה"פ הא מני ר' יוסי הגלילי היא דאמר תם משלם חצי כופר פי' דלא ממעט חצי כופר מנקי ולאו דוקא משלם קאמר אלא היה משלם אם היה לו ממה להשתלם ולשום תנא לא הוה חצי כופר שיור כי אם לרבי אלעזר דדריש נקי מחצי כופר ולית ליה דרבה וכשאין השור בסקילה מועד משלם ותם אינו משלם והא דנקט רבי יוסי הגלילי טפי מרבי עקיבא דדריש נקי מדמי עבד לגלדיה נמי דלחצי כופר לא הוי שיור דמי עבד הוי שיור ו):

ואי תפס כו'. פר"ת דדוקא אי תפס את המזיק עצמו אבל דבר אחר לא דלענין מזיק עצמו הקילו חכמים שיכול לתופסו דאל"כ יתפוס כל אשר לו ולא נפיק מיניה דאין דנין דיני קנסות ואם נוטה המותר ונשאר כדי נזק הרי אנו דנין דיני קנסות ודוחק:

הדרן עלך אלו נערות

נערה. לא הספיקה לעמוד בדין עד שמת האב הרי הן של עצמה. תימה תינח קנס אלא בושת ופגם דממונא הוא דאחין בעי למיהוי ושמא מקראי דלעיל דנפקי בושת ופגם איתקוש אהדדי כדפי' לעיל ז): לאביה

הא מני ר' יוסי הגלילי היא דאמר תם משלם חצי כופר. דדריש להאי נקי לדרשה אחריתי לדמי ולדות אם נגח אשה ויצאו ילדיה הלכך לא הוה ליה לפלוגי בינייהו בכופר וכי תימא הוה ליה לפלוגי דהאי פלגא והאי כוליה ההיא בכלל רישא היא דקתני תם משלם חצי נזק ומועד נזק שלם ותנא בניזקין והוא הדין לכופר: **מאי לאו בתם.** ולאי משום דקתני בה המית שורי את פלוני לחיובו כופר ותם ולאו בר כופר הוא הא מני רבי יוסי הגלילי היא: **אדתני** עבדו של פלוני כו'. דלא אשכח פטור על פי עצמו אלא בעבד: **ניפלוג** בדידה. בבן חורין ובבהמה נמי הוה מצי לשנויי חילוק ולמיתני דאיכא דלא משלם על פי עצמו: **בד"א.** דמשלם ע"פ עצמו במועד כו': **כולה במועד** קמיירי. במועד אתא לאשמועי' דאף הוא יש בו חילוק דאיכא ביה מידי דלא משלם על פי עצמו ומאי ניהו נגיחת עבד ואי הוה תני דקאמרת הוה שביק נמי לאורחיה דרישא איירי במועד וסיפא ניתני תם ומה לי שבקה תנא לאורחיה גבי ניזק דלגלג מבן חורין לעבד מה לי שבקה במזיק ולדלג ממועד לתם: **יתר על מה** שהזיק. כגון נגיחת עבד וכן אונס ומפתה ומוציא שם רע ותשלומי כפל ותשלומי ארבעה וחמשה: **הא פחות** ממה שהזיק. כגון חצי נזק דתם: הכי גרסינן ליתני כל שאינו משלם כמה שהזיק אינו משלם ע"פ עצמו: **והלכתא פלגא ניזקא** קנסא. דהואיל וכל חצי נזק אינו אלא בניזקא דלאו אורחיה לאו על מריה הוה רמיא למינטריה בהכי אלא קנסא הוא כי היכי דלוסיף ביה נטירותא: **טעמא** מאי איתותב. כלומר תיובתא מאי היא: **משום דלא קתני כל שאינו** משלם כמה שהזיק אינו משלם על פי עצמו. דלישתמע מינה נמי חצי נזק הא לאו תיובתא היא: **כיון דאיכא** חצי נזק. דמשתלם בנזקי בהמה במהלכת והתיזה צרורות מתחת רגליה והזיקה דתנן בבבא קמא (דף יז.) דמשלמת חצי נזק ובההוא חצי נזק קיימא לן בב"ק דהלכתא גמירי לה מסיני שהוא תולדה של רגל ופטורה ברה"ר כי רגל וניזקי רגל לאו קנסא נינהו אלא ממונא שהרי מועדת מתחילתה וגבי צרורות הוא דאקיל רחמנא וכיון דממונא הוא משלם ע"פ עצמו משום הכי לא פסיקא ליה למיתני כל שאינו משלם כמה שהזיק דהא איכא האי: **דאכיל אימרי.** שחנק טלאים חיים ואכלם: **משונה** הוא. אין דרכו בכך וכל נזק משונה בבהמה הוי תולדה דקרן תמה שאף היא משונה שאין דרכה בכך וחצי נזק הוא דמשלם וכיון דקנסא הוא לא מגבינן ליה בדייני בבל שאין שם סמיכה בזקנים ולא מקרו מומחים וגבי קנס כתיב (שמות כב) ירשיעון אלהים: **אורחיה הוא.** והוו להו נזקי דשן ושן משלמת נזק שלם וממונא הוא וגובין אותו בבבל: **ואי תפס.** ניזק ממונא דמזיק גבי קנסא דחצי נזקו דאין צריך לצעוק לפנינו: **לא מפקינן** מיניה. וגבי פלגא נזקיה: **ואי.** לא תפיס ואמר קמן קבעו לי זימנא בארעא דישראל השיאוהו לילך עמי לדון לפני דייני ארץ ישראל קבעינן ליה: **בין כך ובין כך.** בין שרוצה ניזק לילך לארץ ישראל בין שאינו רוצה: **משמתינן** ליה. למזיק מיהא להרוג אותו כלב ולסלק היזקיה:

הדרן עלך אלו נערות

נערה שנתפתתה: והצער בתפוסה. והצער נמי לאביה באנוסה. בתפוסה לישנא דקרא ותפשה ושכב עמה (דברים כב): **לא** הספיקה לעמוד בדין כו'. כיון דלא עמדה בדין לאו ממון הוא להורישו לבניו ואמרינן לקמן (דף מג.) אין אדם מוריש לבנו זכות שזכתה לו תורה בבתו ויליף לה מקרא: **מת האב.** משעמדה בדין בנערותיה בין בגרה קודם מיתה בין לא בגרה: **הרי הן של אחין.** דכיון דעמדה בדין זכה בהן אב: **ר"ש אומר.** אע"פ שעמדה בדין לא הוי ממון דאב להורישו לבניו עד דמטי לידיה ובגמרא יליף טעמא:
מעשה

תוספות רי"ד

שיוסיף שמירה על שמירתו ת"ש כל המשלם יתר ממה שהזיק אינו משלם ע"פ עצמו. פי' כגון נגיחת העבד וכן אונס ומפתה ומוציא שם רע ותשלומי כפל ותשלומי ד' וה' הא פחות משלם פי' כגון חצי נזק דתם. לא תימא פחות ממה שהזיק אלא אימא הא כמה שהזיק משלם ע"פ עצמו א"ר ליתני זה הכלל כל שאינו משלם כל מה שהזיק אינו משלם ע"פ עצמו דמשמע פחות ומשמע יותר תיובתא. ופסיק תלמודא והלכתא פלגא נזקא קנסא. פי' דהואיל וכל חצי נזק אינו אלא היזקא דלאו ארחיה לאו על מרא רמיא לאנטורי בהכי אלא קנסא הוא כי היכי דלוסיף ביה נטירותא והלכתא אין טעמא מאי איתותב פי' תיובתיה מאי היא משום דלא קתני כל שאינו משלם [כמה שהזיק] ש"מ נמי חצי נזק [ממונא] הא לאו תיובתא היא כיון דאיכא חצי נזק צרורות דהל' גמירי לה דממונא הוא ומשלם ע"פ עצמו שהן תולדה דרגל כש"ה לא קתני (דאין) [דאיכא] חצי נזק המשתלם [ע"פ עצמו] (כגון) [כגון] בהמה המהלכת והתיזה צרורות מתחת רגליה והזיקה דתנן בבבא קמא דמשלמת חצי נזק והאי חצי נזק קי"ל דהל' גמירי לה דממונא הוא ומשלם ע"פ עצמו שהן תולדה דרגל ופטורים בר"ה כרגל ונזקי רגל לאו קנסא נינהו אלא ממונא שהרי מועדת בתחלתה דגבי צרורות הוא דאקיל רחמנא. וכיון דממונא הוא משלם ע"פ עצמו מ"ה לא פסיקא ליה למיתני כל שאינו משלם דהא איכא האי. והשתא דאמרת פ"נ קנסא האי כלבא דאכיל אימרא ושונרא דאכיל תרנגולא רברבא משונה הוא. פי' אין דרכו בכך וכל נזק משונה בבהמה הוי תולדה דקרן תמה שאין דרכה בכך וחצי נזק הוא שמשלם. וכיון דקנסא הוא לא מגבי' בבבל. פי' בדייני בבל שאין שם סמיכה בזקנים ולא מקרי אלהים מומחים ולגבי קנס כתיב אשר ירשיעון אלהים. ואי תפיס ניזק ממונו של מזיק גבי קנסא דחצי נזקו ולא מפקי' מיניה. ואי אמר אזמיניה בהדי לדינא בא"י מזמנינן לי'. פי' ואי לא תפיס ואמר קמן קבעי לי זמנא בא"י קבעי' לי' ואי לא אזיל משמתינן לי': בין כך ובין כך. פי' בין שרצה ניזק לילך בא"י בין לא. משמתינן ליה עד דמסלק הזיקיה מביתיה מר' נתן דתניא אר"נ מנין שלא יגדל אדם כלב רע בתוך ביתו ולא יעמיד סולם רעוע בתוך ביתו שנאמר ולא תשים דמים בביתך. ופי' וה"ה נמי לקנס דאונס ומפתה אע"ג דלא מגבי' ליה בבבל אי תפיש לא מפקי' מיניה אבל להזמינו לדין לא"י לא מזמינן ליה שאין עתה ישיבות קבועות שם כאשר היה אז. **וראיתי** בתשובות רב צמח גאון ז"ל אלו נערות שיש להן קנס ששאלת מהו להגבות שלא יהא חוטא נשכר כיוצא בזה אמרו חכמים אין מגבין קנס קמגבית קנס בבבל שלח לי' חסדא חסדא קנס קמגבית בבבל אלמא הלכתא רווחת היא שאין מגבין קנסות אלא בירושלים ובסנהדרין של כ"ע ותו קאמרי' א"ר נזקי שור בשור ונזקי שור באדם גובין אותן בבבל אבל אדם באדם ואדם בשור אין מגבין אותו בבבל (ולא) [אך] משום שלא יהא חוטא נשכר ושלא יהיו [בני אדם] פרוצים בניזקין שכיון שהם יודעים שאין מגבין קנסות בבבל שולחים יד זה בזה נהגו חכמים האחרונים לנדותו עד שהוא מפייסו בממון או שירבה עליו רעים ויפייסנו בדברים. **ומעשה** בא' שהפיל שינו של חבירו ובא לפני מר רב צמח גאון ז"ל וא"ל דבר קצוב אני חותך עליך ופייסהו או בממון או בדברים ועכשיו כל דיני קנסות בטלו ומנהג שהנהיג אדונינו מר רב צמח גאון ז"ל אנו נוהגים בו היום בכל קהילות הקודש:

פרק ד נערה שנתפתתה בושתה ופגמה וקנסה לאביה והצער בתפוסה. פי' המורה והצער נמי לאביה כלומר יתירה עליה אנוסה שכן יש לה צער ולישנא דקרא נקט ותפשה ושכב עמה עמדה בדין עד שלא מת האב ה"ה של אב מת האב ה"ה של אחין אם לא

תוספות ישנים

א) [קשה דלא מצי תני הכי דמשמע ע"פ עצמו אינו משלם אבל ע"פ עדים משלם ודלמא לא סבר כר' יוסי הגלילי אלא סבר דאפילו ע"פ עדים אינו משלם חצי כופר ותירץ מהר"ם דמ"מ הוי ליה לפלוגי בדידיה בשורו של פלוני גרידא ולא הוי ליה למינקט עבד. ת"י]

גליון הש"ס

תוס' ד"ה הא מני וכו' ומיהו תימה. עי' תשובת מהרלב"ח סי' ס"ה:

תורה אור השלם

א) כִּי תִבְנֶה בַּיִת חָדָשׁ וְעָשִׂיתָ מַעֲקֶה לְגַגֶּךָ וְלֹא תָשִׂים דָּמִים בְּבֵיתֶךָ כִּי יִפֹּל הַנֹּפֵל מִמֶּנּוּ: [דברים כב, ח]

ליקוטי רש"י

ר' יוסי הגלילי היא דאמר. בפרק שור שנגח את הפרה (לקמן דף מג.) תם משלם חצי כופר וליכא שיורא דלאי משום דהאי משלם כופר שלם והאי משלם חצי כופר ודלמא לאו שיורא הוא דהא תנא ליה תם משלם חצי נזק ומועד נזק שלם וכופר בכלל [ב"ק טו.]. מאי לאו בתם. והכי קאמר המית שורי את פלוני או שורו של פלוני משלם חצי כופר על פי עצמו ואף על גב דתם הוא ור' יוסי הגלילי היא דאמר תם משלם חצי כופר. עבדו של פלוני. דמשלם ל' סלעים ואפילו אינו שוה אלא דינר. ניפלוג וניתני בדידה. קמייתא גופיה דהמית שורי שורו של פלוני. כולה במועד קמיירי. וחילוקים דמועד בעי לאשמועינן. יתר על מה שהזיק. כגון ל' של עבד. הא פחות. כגון חצי נזק דתם משלם ע"פ עצמו. כמה שהזיק. נזק שלם דמועד. משום דלא קתני כמה שהזיק. הא לאו תיובתא היא דלא פסיקא ליה דאיכא חצי נזק צרורות דלאו קנסא הוא ואפילו הכי משלם ע"פ עצמו דהלכתא גמירי לה דממונא הוא. אימרי. כבשים. תרנגולי רברבי. וכבשים גדולים דאין דרכן של כלב וחתול להורגן. משונה הוא. דאין דרכו בכך והוי תולדה דקרן לשלם חצי נזק. ולא

damaged, **what** is indeed the law? אֵינוֹ מְשַׁלֵּם עַל פִּי עַצְמוֹ – That **he does not pay by his own admission?** לִיתְנֵי – But then **let [the Mishnah] state:** זֶה הַכְּלָל כָּל שֶׁאֵינוֹ מְשַׁלֵּם כְּמָה שֶׁהִזִּיק אֵינוֹ מְשַׁלֵּם עַל פִּי עַצְמוֹ – **This is the general rule: Whoever does not pay *as much* as he damaged** does not pay on his own admission, דְּמַשְׁמַע פָּחוֹת וּמַשְׁמַע יָתֵר – **for this would connote both less and more** – i.e. it would imply that one does not pay by his own admission any amount that is either less or more than what he damaged. Since the Mishnah does not word its rule this way, it is evident that the Mishnah means to imply that payments that exceed the amount of the damage are penalties, but those that are less are not penalties. – ? –

The Gemara comments:

תְּיוּבְתָּא – This is indeed **a refutation** of the view that half-damages are a penalty.

The Gemara rules:

וְהִלְכְתָא פַּלְגָא נִיזְקָא קְנָסָא – **And the law is** that **half-damages are a penalty.**[12]

The Gemara asks incredulously:

תְּיוּבְתָּא וְהִלְכְתָא – **A refutation and** yet **the law** follows the refuted view?![13] – ? –

The Gemara answers:

אִין – **Yes,** indeed! טַעְמָא מַאי אִיתּוֹתַב – For **why was [this opinion] refuted?** I.e. what was the refutation? מִשּׁוּם דְּלֹא קָתָנֵי כְּמָה שֶׁהִזִּיק – **Because [the Mishnah] did not state,** "Whoever does not pay **as much as he damaged.**"[14] This is not a refutation, לָא פְּסִיקָא לֵיהּ – since the Tanna did not word the rule this way because **he could not make** it an **absolute** rule.[15] כֵּיוָן דְּאִיכָּא חֲצִי נֶזֶק צְרוֹרוֹת – For **since there are the half-damages of** ***tzroros,***[16] דְּהִלְכְתָא גְּמִירֵי לַהּ דְּמָמוֹנָא הוּא – **concerning which we have learned a law** in the Oral Tradition **that they are a** subcategory of *regel*[17] and a **compensation payment,**[18] מִשּׁוּם הָכִי לֹא קָתָנֵי – **for this reason [the Tanna] could not state** categorically that a payment that is less than the amount of the damage is not paid by one's own admission.[19]

Having established the halachah, the Gemara proceeds to elucidate some practical consequences of it:

וְהַשְׁתָּא דְּאָמַרְתְּ פַּלְגָא נִיזְקָא קְנָסָא – **And now that you have said that the half-damages** of *keren* **are a punitive** payment, הַאי כַּלְבָּא דְּאָכַל אִימְרֵי – then in **this** case of a **dog that** killed and **ate sheep,**[20] וְשׁוּנְרָא דְּאָכִיל תַּרְנְגוֹלֵי רַבְרְבֵי – **or a cat that** killed and **ate large chickens,** מְשׁוּנֶּה הוּא וְלֹא מַגְבִּינַן בְּבָבֶל – **it is** a case of **unusual** damage, for which one pays only half-damages, **and we do not collect it in Babylonia.**[21] [22] אֲבָל זוּטְרֵי אוֹרְחֵיהּ הוּא – **But in** the case of **small ones, it is normal for it** to kill and

NOTES

12. For since the *half-damage* payment is imposed only in cases where the animal inflicts damage through abnormal behavior, the owner [may presume that his animal will not commit such acts, and therefore] is under no obligation to guard against them. Hence, the *half-damages* payment is not a compensatory obligation, but a punitive measure imposed by the Torah so that owners will take special care to guard their oxen from goring others (*Rashi*).

13. How is it possible to rule in favor of this view when we have just refuted it from the wording of our Mishnah?

14. So as to include implicitly the *half-damages* payment as well (*Rashi*).

15. Literally: it was not absolute to him. For even according to the view that the half-damages paid for *keren* are a penalty, there is nevertheless another case of half-damages that is surely compensation, as the Gemara will now explain.

16. Literally: pebbles. As an animal walks, pebbles can fly out from beneath its feet and break utensils lying nearby (*Rashi*). ["Pebbles" is only an example. Included in the category of *tzroros* is any damage that an animal does through a force that it generates, rather than through direct contact between its body and the damaged article. The Mishnah, *Bava Kamma* 17a, teaches that when an animal does damage through *tzroros,* its owner pays only *half-damages.*

17. Literally: foot. This refers to what an animal damages with its foot in the course of its normal walking, and is derived from *Exodus* 22:4. The essential characteristics of *regel* are that the behavior is commonplace for the animal that it damages while it is moving, and that there is no intent to inflict damage with that act. Hence, any damage done by an animal in the course of its normal walking, whether with its foot or with any other part of its body, is included in the category *of regel* (see Mishnah, *Bava Kamma* 17a and Gemara there, 17b). One of the laws of *regel* is that the owner is liable only for damage done in the private domain of the damaged party. If *regel* damage was done in the public domain, the owner is not liable.

18. I.e. there is a *Halachah LeMoshe MiSinai* that teaches that *tzroros* is included in the category of *regel,* and is exempt when done in the public domain. Payment for *regel* damage is most certainly a compensatory payment, not a punitive payment, for the damage is committed in the course of the animal's normal behavior. As such, it is the owner's responsibility to guard against such damage [whether it be actual *regel* or *tzroros*], and therefore by rights the owner who was negligent and did not guard his animal from doing so is liable to full damages. Nevertheless, the Torah was lenient with regard to *tzroros* and reduced the liability to *half-damages.* And since the *half-damages* of *tzroros* are a compensatory payment, they are paid even by the owner's own admission (*Rashi;* cf. *Rashi* to *Bava Kamma* 15b ד״ה משום דלא קתני כמה שהזיק; see also *Rashba* ibid. ד״ה הא דאמרינן).

19. For although the *half-damages* of *keren* are, in fact, a punitive payment and are not paid by the owner's admission, the *half-damages* of *tzroros* are a compensatory payment and are paid by the owner's admission. Hence, our Mishnah could only state, "Whoever pays *more* than what he damaged does not pay by his own admission," since this rule holds true for all cases. Payments for less than the amount of damage, however, are sometimes penalties (which are not paid by one's own admission) and are sometimes compensations (which are paid by one's own admission) [see *Rashi*].

20. I.e. who choked live sheep and ate them (*Rashi*).

21. Acts of unusual damage by an animal are *toldos* (subcategories) of *keren* damage, which likewise is an unusual damage. The owner is therefore liable only to half-damages for them, as long as the animal is a *tam.* Since we have ruled that the half-damages paid by the owner of a *tam* are a penalty, not compensation, courts in Babylonia cannot collect them. For *semichah* [ordination] is given only in Eretz Yisrael, and the collection of punitive damages requires ordained judges [סמוכין], as derived from Scripture's (*Exodus* 22:8) reference to the judges in penalty cases as אֱלֹהִים, a word that connotes special authority (*Rashi*).

[The special ordination known as *semichah* can be given only in Eretz Yisrael. (It originated with Moses, and went from teacher to disciple.) When Roman persecution made it impossible to maintain academies of higher learning there, this type of ordination lapsed (towards the end of the fourth century of the common era). The ancient institution of *semichah* should not be confused with what is today commonly known as "*semichah,*" which is really just a degree attesting that its holder has mastered certain areas of halachah, and which does not entitle its holder to judge those types of cases which required the ancient *semichah.*]

22. [The Gemara prefaces this ruling by saying that it is based on the ruling that half-damages are a penalty. The obvious reason for this is that if half-damages are compensation, we should be able to collect them even in Babylonia, as we do other types of damages. However, *Tosafos* to *Bava Kamma* 15b ד״ה והשתא state that this is not the case. Rather, according to the view that half-damages are compensation, one could not collect for the dog or cat attack even in Eretz Yisrael! For according to this view, *keren* damage is *not* unusual for any ox, even a *tam.* (Indeed, this view holds that the owner of a *tam* should theoretically be liable to pay full damages, as the Gemara explained above, 41a.) But if so, where an animal does damage that is truly unusual [and thus completely unexpected], as in the case of a dog that

הא מני ר' יוסי הגלילי היא דאמר תם משלם חצי כופר [א] ת"ש המית שורי את פלוני או שורו של פלוני הרי זה משלם על פי עצמו מאי לאו בתם לא במועד אבל בתם מאי אינו משלם על פי עצמו אדתני סיפא עבדו של פלוני אינו משלם ע"פ עצמו ניפלוג וניתני בדידה במה דברים אמורים במועד אבל תם אינו משלם על פי עצמו כולה במועד קמיירי ת"ש זה הכלל כל המשלם יתר על מה שהזיק אינו משלם ע"פ עצמו הא פחות ממה שהזיק משלם ע"פ עצמו לא תימא הא פחות ממה שהזיק אלא אימא הא כמה שהזיק משלם ע"פ עצמו אבל פחות מאי אינו משלם ע"פ עצמו ליתני זה הכלל כל שאינו משלם כמה שהזיק אינו משלם על פי עצמו דמשמע פחות ומשמע יתר תיובתא והלכתא פלגא ניזקא קנסא תיובתא והלכתא אין טעמא מאי איתותב משום דלא קתני כמה שהזיק לא פסיקא ליה כיון דאיכא חצי נזק צרורות דהלכתא גמירי לה דממונא הוא משום הכי לא קתני והשתא דאמרת פלגא ניזקא קנסא האי כלבא דאכל אימרי ושונרא דאכיל תרנגולי רברבי משונה הוא ולא מגבינן בבבל אבל זוטרי אורחיה הוא ומגבינן ואי תפס לא מפקינן מיניה ואי אמר אקבעו לי זימנא לארץ ישראל מקבעינן ליה ואי לא אזיל משמתינן ליה בין כך ובין כך משמתינן ליה דאמרינן ליה סליק היזקך מדרבי נתן דתניא ר' נתן אומר מנין שלא יגדל אדם כלב רע בתוך ביתו ולא יעמיד סולם רעוע בתוך ביתו שנאמר [א] ולא תשים דמים בביתך:

הדרן עלך אלו נערות

נערה שנתפתתה בושתה ופגמה וקנסה של אביה והצער בתפוסה עמדה בדין עד שלא מת האב הרי הן של אב מת האב הרי הן של אחין לא הספיקה לעמוד בדין עד שמת האב הרי הן של עצמה עמדה בדין עד שלא בגרה הרי הן של אב מת האב הרי הן של אחין לא הספיקה לעמוד בדין עד שבגרה הרי הן של עצמה רבי שמעון אומר אם לא הספיקה לגבות עד שמת האב הרי הן של עצמה מעשה

רש"י

הא מני ר' יוסי הגלילי היא דאמר תם משלם חצי כופר. דדריש להאי נקי לדרשה אחריתי לדמי ולדות אם נגח אשה ויצאו ילדיה הלכך לא הוה ליה לפלוגי ביניהו בכופר וכי תימא הוה ליה לפלוגי דהאי פלגא והאי כוליה ההיא בכלל רישא היא דקתני תם משלם חצי נזק ומועד נזק שלם ותנא בניזקין והוא הדין לכופר: מאי לאו בתם. ולאו משום דקתני בה המית שורי את פלוני לחיובו כופר ותם נמי לאו בר כופר הוא הא מני רבי יוסי הגלילי היא: אדתני עבדו של פלוני כו'. דלא משכח פטור על פי עצמו אלא בעבד: ניפלוג בדידה. בבן חורין ובבהמה נמי הוה מצי לשנוי חילוק ולמיתני דאיכא דלא משלם על פי עצמו: בד"א. דמשלם ע"פ עצמו במועד כו': כולה במועד קמיירי. במועד אתא לאשמועי' דאף הוא יש בו חילוק דאיכא ביה מידי דלא משלם על פי עצמו ומאי ניהו נגיחת עבד ואי הוה תני תם כדקאמרת הוה שביק נמי לאורחיה דרישא איירי במועד וסיפא ניתני תם ומה לי שבקה תנא לאורחיה גבי ניזק לדלג מבן חורין לעבד מה לי שבקה במזיק ולדלג ממועד לתם: יתר על מה שהזיק. כגון נגיחת עבד וכן אונס ומפתה ומוציא שם רע ותשלומי כפל ותשלומי ארבעה וחמשה: הא פחות ממה שהזיק. כגון חצי נזק דתם: הכי גרסינן ליתני כל שאינו משלם כמה שהזיק אינו משלם ע"פ עצמו: והלכתא פלגא ניזקא קנסא. דהואיל וכל חצי נזק אינו אלא בניזקא דלאו אורחיה לאו על מריה הוה רמיא למינטריה בהכי אלא קנסא הוא כי היכי דלוסיף ביה נטירותא: טעמא מאי איתותב. כלומר תיובתא מאי היא: משום דלא קתני כל שאינו משלם כמה שהזיק אינו משלם על פי עצמו. דלישתמע מינה נמי חצי נזק הא לאו תיובתא היא: כיון דאיכא חצי נזק. דמשתלם בנזקי בהמה במהלכת והתיזה צרורות מתחת רגליה והזיקה דתנן בבבא קמא (דף ח.) דמשלמת חצי נזק ובההיא חצי נזק קיימא לן בב"ק דהלכתא גמירי לה מסיני שהוא תולדה של רגל ופטורה ברה"ר כי רגל וניזקי רגל לאו קנסא נינהו אלא ממונא שהרי מועדת מתחלתה וגבי צרורות הוא דאקיל רחמנא וכיון דממונא הוא משלם ע"פ עצמו משום הכי לא פסיקא ליה למיתני כל שאינו משלם כמה שהזיק דהא איכא האי: דאכיל אימרי. שחנק טלאים חיים ואכלם: משונה הוא. אין דרכו בכך וכל נזק משונה בבהמה הוי תולדה דקרן תמה שלא היא משונה שאין דרכה בכך וחצי נזק הוא דמשלם וכיון דקנסא הוא לא מגבינן ליה בדייני דבבל שאין שם סמיכה בזקנים ולא מקרו מומחים וגבי קנס כתיב (שמות כב) ירשיעון אלהים: אורחיה הוא. והוו להו נזקי דשן ושן משלמת נזק שלם וממונא הוא וגובין אותו בבבל: ואי תפס. ניזק ממונא דמזיק גבי קנסא דלא צריך לצעוק לפנינו: לא מפקינן מיניה. וגבי פלגא נזקיה: ואי לא תפיס ואמר קבעו לי זמנא בארעא דישראל שיאמר לו לילך עמי לדון לפני דייני ארץ ישראל קבעינן ליה: בין כך ובין כך. בין שרוצה ניזק לילך לארץ ישראל בין שאינו רוצה: משמתינן ליה. למזיק מיהא להרוג אותו כלב ולסלק היזיקה:

הדרן עלך אלו נערות

נערה שנתפתתה: והצער בתפוסה. והצער נמי לאביה באנוסה. בתפוסה לישנא דקרא ותפשה ושכב עמה (דברים כב): לא הספיקה לעמוד בדין כו'. כיון דלא עמדה בדין לאו ממון הוא דהא לקמן (דף מג.) אין אדם מוריש לבנו זכות שזכתה לו תורה בבתו ויליף לה מקרא: מת האב. משעמדה בדין בנערותה בין בגרה קודם מיתה בין לא בגרה: הרי הן של אחין. דכיון דעמדה בדין זכה בהן אב: ר"ש אומר. אע"פ שעמדה בדין לא הוי ממון דאב להורישו לבניו עד דמטי לידיה ובגמרא יליף טעמא:

תוספות

הא מני רבי יוסי הגלילי היא דאמר תם משלם חצי כופר. וליכא שיורא דלאו משום דמועד משלם כופר שלם ותם אינו משלם אלא חצי כופר הא לאו שיורא הוא דהא תנן תם משלם חצי נזק ומועד נזק שלם וכופר בכלל וא"ת אכתי ליתני דמועד אף כשהוא בסקילה משלם כופר ותם כשהוא בסקילה אינו משלם כופר כלל דהביאהו לב"ד ויסלם לך דהוא עצמו אינו משתלם אלא מגופו כדאמרינן בפרק שור שנגח ד' וה' (ב"ק דף מב. ושם) וי"ל דהך נמי לא הוי שיור דהוי בכלל הא דקתני תם מגופו ומועד מן העלייה ומיהו תימה דלא אשכחן בהדיא בשום מקום שהיה אומר ר' יוסי הגלילי דתם משלם חצי כופר ולא משום דדריש רבי יוסי הגלילי בפרק שור שנגח ד' וה' (ג"ז שם) נקי מדמי ולדות ולא דריש נקי מחצי כופר מכלל דסבר דחייב ודלמא לעולם סבר דפטור וטעמא משום דפטור מחצי כופר לא איצטריך קרא דכשהשור בסקילה לא שייך כופר דהביאהו לב"ד ויסלם לך וכשאין השור בסקילה כגון על פי עד אחד או על פי הבעלים פטור מדרבה דאמר התם (דף מג.) שור שהמית בן חורין שלא בכוונה פטור שנאמר השור יסקל וגם בעליו יומת בזמן שהשור בסקילה בעלים משלמין כופר כו' ונראה דה"פ הא מני ר' יוסי הגלילי היא דאמר תם משלם חצי כופר פי' דלא ממעט חצי כופר מנקי ולאו דוקא משלם קאמר אלא היה משלם אם היה לו ממה להשתלם ולשום תנא לא הוה חצי כופר שיור כי אם לרבי אלעזר דדריש נקי מחצי כופר ולית ליה דרבה וכשאין השור בסקילה מועד משלם ותם אינו משלם והא דנקט רבי יוסי הגלילי טפי מרבי עקיבא דדריש נקי מדמי עבד לדידיה נמי דחצי כופר לא הוי שיור דמי עבד הוי שיור:

ואי תפס כו'. פר"ת דדוקא אי תפס את המזיק עצמו אבל דבר אחר לא לענין מזיק עצמו הקילו חכמים שיכול לתופסו דאל"כ יתפוס כל אשר לו ולא נפיק מיניה דלאין דנין דיני קנסות ואם נוטה המותר ונשאר כדי נזק הרי אנו דנין דיני קנסות ודוחק:

הדרן עלך אלו נערות

נערה. לא הספיקה לעמוד בדין עד שמת האב הרי הן של עצמה. תימה תינח קנס אלא בושת ופגם דממונא הוא דאחין בעי למיהוי ושמא מקראי דלעיל דנפקי בושת ופגם איתקוש אהדדי כדפי' לעיל לאביה:

הָא מַנִּי – For **who is** the Tanna of **this** Mishnah? רַבִּי יוֹסֵי הַגְּלִילִי הִיא – Quite possibly, **it is R' Yose HaGlili,** דְּאָמַר תָּם מְשַׁלֵּם חֲצִי כּוֹפֶר – **who says** that **a *tam* pays half-*kofer*.**[1] Accordingly, the difference between a *tam* and a *muad* vis-a-vis *kofer* is included in the Mishnah's statement that half-damages are paid in the case of a *tam* and full damages in the case of a *muad*.[2]

The Gemara now attempts a proof from our Mishnah, which rules that a person does not pay a penalty by his own admission:

תָּא שְׁמַע – **Come, learn** a proof from our Mishnah: הֵמִית שׁוֹרִי אֶת פְּלוֹנִי – One who says, "MY OX KILLED SO-AND-SO," אוֹ שׁוֹרוֹ שֶׁל פְּלוֹנִי – or who says, "My ox killed SO-AND-SO'S OX," הֲרֵי זֶה מְשַׁלֵּם עַל פִּי עַצְמוֹ – THIS [PERSON] PAYS BY HIS OWN ADMISSION.[3] מַאי לָאו בְּתָם – **Would** you **not** say that the Mishnah refers here **to a *tam*** and the payment of half-damages?[4] Thus, we see that half-damages are considered compensation, since one pays them even by his own admission. – ? –

The Gemara answers:

לֹא בְּמוּעָד – **No!** The Mishnah refers **to a *muad*** and the payment of full damages, which certainly is compensation.

The Gemara questions this answer:

אֲבָל בְּתָם מַאי – **But in** the case of **a *tam*, what** do you contend is the law? אֵינוֹ מְשַׁלֵּם עַל פִּי עַצְמוֹ – That indeed, **he does not pay on** the basis of **his own admission,** because half-damages are a penalty payment? אַדְּתָנֵי סֵיפָא – If so, then **rather than the last part** of that Mishnah **teaching** the distinction between compensations and penalties with the following case – עַבְדּוֹ שֶׁל פְּלוֹנִי אֵינוֹ מְשַׁלֵּם עַל פִּי עַצְמוֹ – One who says, "My ox killed SO-AND-SO'S SLAVE," DOES NOT PAY BY HIS OWN ADMISSION[5] – נִיפְלוֹג וְנִיתְנֵי בְּדִידָהּ – **let [the Mishnah] differentiate** between them **and teach** that difference **with respect to [the first case]**[6] **itself,** as follows: בַּמֶּה דְּבָרִים אֲמוּרִים – **Concerning what was this** [the Mishnah's first ruling] **said?**[7] בְּמוּעָד – **Concerning a *muad*,** for which damages are a compensation; אֲבָל תָּם אֵינוֹ מְשַׁלֵּם עַל פִּי עַצְמוֹ – **however,** in regard to **a *tam* he does not pay by his own admission,** because half-damages are a penalty.[8] – ? –

The Gemara answers:

כּוּלָּהּ בְּמוּעָד קָמַיירֵי – **The entire [Mishnah] speaks of *muad*;** i.e. the Tanna chose to illustrate the distinction between compensations and penalties in the case of a *muad*.[9]

The Gemara attempts another proof:

תָּא שְׁמַע – **Come, learn** a proof from our Mishnah: זֶה הַכְּלָל – THIS IS THE GENERAL RULE: כָּל הַמְשַׁלֵּם יָתֵר עַל מַה שֶּׁהִזִּיק – WHOEVER PAYS MORE THAN WHAT HE DAMAGED[10] אֵינוֹ מְשַׁלֵּם עַל פִּי עַצְמוֹ – DOES NOT PAY BY HIS OWN ADMISSION.[11] הָא פָּחוֹת מִמַּה שֶּׁהִזִּיק מְשַׁלֵּם עַל פִּי עַצְמוֹ – **This** implies that one who pays ***less* than what he damaged** – such as the half-damages paid by a *tam* – **pays** it even **by his own admission.** Thus, we see that half-damages are compensation! – ? –

The Gemara answers:

לֹא תֵּימָא הָא פָּחוֹת מִמַּה שֶּׁהִזִּיק – **Do not say** that **this** implies that one who pays ***less* than what he damaged** pays by his own admission. אֶלָּא אֵימָא הָא כְּמַה שֶּׁהִזִּיק מְשַׁלֵּם עַל פִּי עַצְמוֹ – **Rather, say** that **this** implies that one who pays ***as much* as he damaged pays by his own admission.**

The Gemara challenges this interpretation:

אֲבָל פָּחוֹת מַאי – **But** in the case of one who pays **less** than what he

NOTES

1. R' Yose HaGlili expounds the verse, *and the owner of the ox shall be absolved,* to teach that the owner of an ox [whether a *tam* or a *muad*] that gores a pregnant woman and causes her to abort her fetus is not liable to pay the value of the fetus. Hence, R' Yose has no verse to exclude the *tam* from paying *half-kofer* (*Rashi;* see also *Tosafos*).

2. [The Gemara does not mean to say that our Mishnah *must* hold like R' Yose HaGlili. The Gemara merely says that since it *could* be following his view, we are not compelled to say that the Mishnah's list is incomplete. Nonetheless, Rav Huna the son of Rav Yehoshua, who holds that half-damages are a penalty, will have to explain that the Mishnah's list is incomplete and that it omits two differences: (a) that in the case of *tam* one does not pay anything based on his own admission, whereas in the case of a *muad* he does; (b) that no *kofer* is paid in the case of a *tam,* whereas full *kofer* is paid in the case of a *muad.* According to him, our Mishnah follows the opinion of the Rabbis who dispute R' Yose HaGlili and rule that there is no *kofer* at all in the case of a *tam.*

However, according to Rav Pappa, who holds that the payment of half-damages is considered compensation (מָמוֹנָא) rather than a penalty, there is certainly no difference between *tam* and *muad* with regard to admission – one pays in either case. This leaves *kofer* as the only possible omission from the Mishnah's list, and a Mishnaic list cannot be incomplete by only one item. Accordingly, Rav Pappa *must* explain our Mishnah according to the opinion of R' Yose HaGlili, that one pays half-*kofer* in the case of a *tam* just as he pays half-damages. Consequently, our Mishnah's list is in fact complete, since it lists half-damages as a difference between *tam* and *muad* (see *Tosafos* ד״ה אי משום כופר, which is cited above, 41a note 47).]

3. He pays *kofer* to the heirs of the person killed, or damages to the owner of the ox that was gored.

4. I.e. half-damages for the ox and half-*kofer* for the person. According to this interpretation, the Mishnah follows the opinion of R' Yose HaGlili, who says that a *tam* pays half-*kofer* (*Rashi*).

[The reason the Gemara considers it more plausible to explain the Mishnah as referring to a *tam* will become evident from the Gemara's next question.]

5. See above, 41a note 10.

6. Where the ox killed a Jew [rather than a slave] or another ox (*Rashi*).

7. I.e. with regard to what case did we say that a person who admits that his ox killed a Jew or an ox pays by his admission? (*Rashi*).

8. Since the point of our Mishnah is to teach that one pays compensation but not a penalty by his own admission, there was no need for the Mishnah to illustrate the latter part of the rule by introducing a new case of damage (the killing of a slave). It would have been more logical for the Mishnah to stay with its original case and illustrate its point by differentiating within that very case between a *tam* and a *muad.* Since the Mishnah does not do so, but resorts to the example of the killing of a slave to find a case of a penalty payment, it is evident that the Mishnah does *not* consider a *tam* to be an example of a penalty payment (see *Rashi*).

9. The Tanna chose to teach us a distinction with regard to a *muad* itself: that there is a case where payment for damage inflicted by even a *muad* is a punitive damage and not paid on the basis of one's admission – viz. when the *muad* kills a slave. And even though this causes the Tanna to introduce a new case of damage (the killing of a slave), had the Tanna followed your suggestion and remained with the case of an ox killing a Jew or another ox and differentiated between a *muad* and a *tam,* he would also be introducing a new case – the case of a *tam* – whereas until now he was discussing a *muad.* Hence, illustrating the distinction between a *tam* and a *muad* in the case of the killing of a Jew or an ox is no finer a distinction than illustrating the distinction between killing a slave and killing a Jew or an ox in the case of a *muad.* [Hence, the fact that the Mishnah, in seeking to illustrate a case where the owner of an ox does not pay by his own admission, chose the case of a *muad* who killed a slave rather than the case of a *tam* who killed a Jew or an ox, does not evince that he holds that the latter pays by his own admission] (*Rashi*).

10. Such as the thirty-*shekel* payment for an ox who killed a slave, the fifty-*shekel* fine for violation and seduction, the one hundred-*shekel* payment imposed on a defamer, and the *double* payment, the *fourfold* payment and the *fivefold* payment imposed on a thief (*Rashi*).

11. For such a payment is by definition a penalty.

הא מני ר' יוסי הגלילי היא דאמר תם משלם חצי כופר א) ת"ש המית את שורי את פלוני או שורו של פלוני הרי זה משלם על פי עצמו מאי לאו בתם לא במועד אבל בתם מאי אינו משלם על פי עצמו אדתני סיפא עבדו של פלוני אינו משלם ע"פ עצמו ניפלוג וניתני בדידה במה דברים אמורים במועד א) אבל תם אינו משלם על פי עצמו כולה במועד קמיירי ת"ש זה הכלל כל המשלם יותר על מה שהזיק אינו משלם ע"פ עצמו הא פחות ממה שהזיק משלם ע"פ עצמו לא תימא הא פחות ממה שהזיק אלא אימא הא כמה שהזיק משלם ע"פ עצמו אבל פחות מאי אינו משלם ע"פ עצמו ליתני זה הכלל כל שאינו משלם כמה שהזיק אינו משלם על פי עצמו דמשמע פחות ומשמע יתר תיובתא והלכתא פלגא ניזקא קנסא ג) תיובתא והלכתא אין טעמא מאי איתותב משום דלא קתני כמה שהזיק לא פסיקא ליה כיון דאיכא א חצי נזק צרורות דהלכתא גמירי לה דממונא הוא משום הכי לא קתני והשתא דאמרת פלגא ניזקא קנסא ב האי כלבא דאכל אימרי ושונרא דאכיל תרנגולי רברבי משונה הוא ולא מגבינן בבבל אבל זוטרי אורחיה הוא ומגבינן ג ואי תפס לא מפקינן מיניה ואי אמר אקבעו לי זימנא לארץ ישראל מקבעינן ליה ואי לא אזיל משמתינן ליה בין כך ובין כך משמתינן ליה דאמרינן ליה סליק הזיקך ז) מדרבי נתן דתניא ר' נתן אומר ד מנין שלא יגדל אדם כלב רע בתוך ביתו ולא יעמיד סולם רעוע בתוך ביתו שנאמר א) ולא תשים דמים בביתך:

הדרן עלך אלו נערות

נערה ה שנתפתתה בושתה ופגמה וקנסה של אביה והצער בתפוסה ו עמדה בדין עד שלא מת האב הרי הן של אב מת האב הרי הן של אחין לא הספיקה לעמוד בדין עד שמת האב הרי הן של עצמה ז) עמדה בדין עד שלא בגרה הרי הן של אב מת האב הרי הן של אחין לא הספיקה לעמוד בדין עד שבגרה הרי הן של עצמה רבי שמעון אומר אם לא הספיקה לגבות עד ח) שמת האב הרי הן של עצמה מעשה

הא מני ר' יוסי הגלילי היא דאמר תם משלם חצי כופר. דדריש להאי נקי לדרשה אחריתי לדמי ולדות אם נגח אשה ואלו ילדיה הלכך לא הוה ליה לפלוגי בינייהו בכופר וכי תימא הוה ליה לפלוגי דהאי פלגא והאי כוליה ההיא בכלל רישא היא דקתני תם משלם חצי נזק ומועד נזק שלם ותנא בניזקין והוא הדין לכופר: **מאי לאו בתם.** ולא משום דקתני בה המית שורי את פלוני לחיובא כופר ותם נמי בר כופר הוא הא מני רבי יוסי הגלילי היא: **אדתני עבדו של פלוני כו'.** דלא משכח פטור על פי עצמו אלא בעבד: **ניפלוג בדידה.** בבן חורין ובבהמה נמי הוה מצי לשנויי חילוק ולמיתני דאיכא דלא משלם על פי עצמו: **בד"א.** דמשלם ע"פ עצמו במועד כו': **כולה במועד קמיירי.** במועד אתא לאשמועינן דאף הוא יש בו חילוק דאיכא ביה מידי דלא משלם על פי עצמו ומאי ניהו נגיחת עבד ואי הוה תני דקאמרת הוה שביק נמי לאורחיה דרישא איירי במועד וסיפא ניתני תם ומה לי שבקה תנא לאורחיה גבי ניזק לדלג מבן חורין לעבד מה לי שבקה במזיק ולדלג ממועד לתם: **יתר על מה שהזיק.** כגון נגיחת עבד וכן אונס ומפתה ומוציא שם רע ותשלומי כפל ותשלומי ארבעה וחמשה: **הא פחות ממה שהזיק.** כגון חצי נזק דתם: הכי גרסינן ליתני כל שאינו משלם כמה שהזיק אינו משלם ע"פ עצמו: **והלכתא פלגא ניזקא קנסא.** דהואיל וכל חצי נזק אינו אלא בניזקא דלאו אורחיה לאו על מריה הוה רמיא למינטריה בהכי אלא קנסא הוא כי היכי דלוסיף ביה נטירותא: **טעמא מאי איתותב.** כלומר תיובתא מאי היא: **משום דלא קתני כל שאינו משלם כמה שהזיק אינו משלם על פי עצמו.** דלישתמע מינה נמי חצי נזק הא לאו תיובתא היא: **כיון דאיכא חצי נזק.** דמשתלם בנזקי בהמה במהלכת והתיזה צרורות מתחת רגליה והזיקה דתנן בבבא קמא (דף יז.) דמשלמת חצי נזק וההוא חצי נזק קיימא לן בב"ק דהלכתא גמירי לה מסיני שהוא תולדה של רגל ופטורה ברה"ר כי רגל וניזקי רגל לאו קנסא נינהו אלא ממונא שהרי מועדת מתחילתה וגבי צרורות הוא דאקיל רחמנא וכיון דממונא הוא משלם ע"פ עצמו משום הכי לא פסיקא ליה למיתני כל שאינו משלם כמה שהזיק דהא איכא האי: **דאכיל אימרי.** שחנק טלאים חיים ואכלם: **משונה הוא.** אין דרכו בכך וכל נזק משונה בבהמה הוי תולדה דקרן תמה שאף היא משונה שאין דרכה בכך וחצי נזק הוא דמשלם וכיון דקנסא הוא לא מגבינן ליה בדייני בבל שאין שם סמיכה בזקנים ולא מקרו מומחים וגבי קנס כתיב (שמות כב) ירשיעון אלהים: **אורחיה הוא.** והוו להו נזקי דשן ושן משלמת נזק שלם וממונא הוא וגובין אותו בבבל: **ואי תפס.** ניזק ממונא דמזיק גבי קנסא דחצי נזקו דאין צריך לצעוק לפנינו: **לא מפקינן מיניה.** וגבי פלגא נזקיה: **ואי.** לא תפיס ואמר קמן קבעו לי זמנא בארעא דישראל השיאוהו לילך עמי לדון לפני דייני ארץ ישראל קבעינן ליה: **בין כך ובין כך.** בין שרוצה ניזק לילך לארץ ישראל בין שאינו רוצה: **משמתינן ליה.** למזיק מיהא להרוג אותו כלב ולסלק היזיקיה:

הדרן עלך אלו נערות

נערה שנתפתתה: והצער בתפוסה. והצער נמי לאביה באנוסה. בתפוסה לישנא דקרא ותפשה ושכב עמה (דברים כב): **לא הספיקה לעמוד בדין כו'.** כיון דלא עמדה בדין לאו ממון הוא להורישו לבניו ואמרינן לקמן (דף מג.) אין אדם מוריש לבנו זכות שזכתה לו תורה בבתו וילפי לה מקרא: **מת האב.** משעמדה בדין בנערותיה בין בגרה קודם מיתה בין לא בגרה: **הרי הן של אחין.** דכיון דעמדה בדין זכה בהן אב: **ר"ש אומר.** אע"פ שעמדה בדין לא הוי ממון דאב להורישו לבניו עד דמטי לידיה ובגמרא יליף טעמא: מעשה

הא מני רבי יוסי הגלילי היא דאמר תם משלם חצי כופר. וליכא שיורא דאי משום דמועד משלם כופר שלם ותם אינו משלם אלא חצי כופר הא לאו שיורא הוא דהא תנן תם משלם חצי נזק ומועד נזק שלם וכופר בכלל וא"ת אכתי ליתני דמועד אף כשהוא בסקילה משלם כופר ותם כשהוא בסקילה אינו משלם כופר כלל דהביאהו לב"ד וישלם לך דהוא עצמו אינו משתלם אלא מגופו כדאמרינן בפרק שור שנגח ד' וה' (ב"ק דף מב. ושם) וי"ל דהך נמי לא הוי שיור דהוי בכלל הא דקתני תם מגופו ומועד מן העלייה ומיהו תימה דלא אשכחן בהדיא בשום מקום שהיה אומר ר' יוסי הגלילי דתם משלם חצי כופר ואי משום דדריש רבי יוסי הגלילי בפרק שור שנגח ד' וה' (ג"ז שם) נקי מדמי ולדות ולא דריש נקי מחצי כופר מכלל דסבר דחייב ודלמא לעולם סבר דפטור וטעמא משום דפטור מחצי כופר לא איצטריך קרא דכשהשור בסקילה לא שייך כופר דהביאהו לב"ד וישלם לך וכשאין השור בסקילה כגון על פי עד אחד או על פי הבעלים פטור מדרבה דאמר התם (דף מג.) שור שהמית בן חורין שלא בכוונה פטור שנאמר השור יסקל וגם בעליו יומת בזמן שהשור בסקילה בעלים משלמין כופר כו' ונראה דה"פ הא מני ר' יוסי הגלילי היא דאמר תם משלם חצי כופר פי' דלא ממעט חצי כופר מנקי ולאו דוקא משלם קאמר אלא היה משלם אם היה לו ממה להשתלם ולשום תנא לא הוה חצי כופר שיור כי אם לרבי אלעזר דדריש נקי מחצי כופר ולית ליה דרבה וכשאין השור בסקילה מועד משלם ותם אינו משלם והא דנקט רבי יוסי הגלילי טפי מרבי עקיבא דדריש נקי מדמי ולדות לדידיה נמי דחצי כופר לא הוי שיור דמי עבד הוי שיור ז):

ואי תפס כו'. פר"ח דדוקא אי תפס את המזיק עצמו אבל דבר אחר לא דלענין מזיק עצמו הקילו חכמים שיכול לתופסו דאל"כ יתפוס כל אשר לו ולא נפיק מיניה דלאו דינין דיני קנסות ואם נוטלה המותר ונשאר כדי נזק הרי אנו דנין דיני קנסות ודוחק:

הדרן עלך אלו נערות

נערה. לא הספיקה לעמוד בדין עד שמת האב הרי הן של עצמה. תימה תינח קנס אלא בושת ופגם דממונא הוא דאחין בעי למיהוי ושמא מקראי דלעיל דנפקי בושת ופגם איתקוש אהדדי כדפי' לעיל ז): לאביה

מסורת הש"ס

א) [ב"ק טו: מג.], ב) [עירובין י. מח: ב"ק טו.], ג) ב"ק טו: מו., ד) נ"ל ר"ש אומר אם לא הספיקה לגבות עד שמת האב הרי הן של עצמה, ה) נ"ל שבגרה, ו) [ועי' תוס' ב"ק טו: ד"ה הא], ז) [ד' לט: ד"ה יש].

תוספות ישנים

גליון הש"ס

תוס' ד"ה הא מני וכו' ומיהו תימה. עי' תשובת מהרלב"ח סי' ס"ה:

תורה אור השלם

א) כִּי תִבְנֶה בַּיִת חָדָשׁ וְעָשִׂיתָ מַעֲקֶה לְגַגֶּךָ וְלֹא תָשִׂים דָּמִים בְּבֵיתֶךָ כִּי יִפֹּל הַנֹּפֵל מִמֶּנּוּ: [דברים כב, ח]

ליקוטי רש"י

תוספות רי"ד

מתני׳ [א]האומר פתיתי את בתו של פלוני משלם בושת ופגם על פי עצמו ואין משלם קנס [ב]האומר גנבתי [א] משלם את הקרן על פי עצמו ואין משלם תשלומי כפל ותשלומי ארבעה וחמשה [ג] [ג]המית שורי את פלוני או שורו של פלוני הרי זה משלם על פי עצמו המית שורי עבדו של פלוני אין משלם ע"פ עצמו [ד]זה הכלל כל המשלם יותר על מה שהזיק אינו משלם ע"פ עצמו: גמ׳ וליתני אנסתי לא מבעיא קאמר לא מבעיא אנסתי דלא קא פגים לה דמשלם בושת ופגם על פי עצמו אבל פתיתי דקא פגים לה אימא לא משלם על פי עצמו קא משמע לן מתניתין דלא כי האי תנא דתניא רבי שמעון בן יהודה אומר משום ר׳ שמעון אף בושת ופגם אינו משלם ע"פ עצמו לפי שלא כל הימנו שיפגום בתו של פלוני אמר ליה רב פפא לאביי ניחא לה לדידה מאי דלמא לא ניחא ליה לאביה ניחא ליה לאביה מאי דלמא לא ניחא להו לבני משפחה ניחא להו לבני משפחה מאי אי אפשר דליכא חד במדינת הים דלא ניחא ליה: האומר גנבתי משלם את הקרן וכו׳: איתמר פלגא ניזקא [ה] רב פפא אמר פלגא ניזקא ממונא רב הונא בריה דרב יהושע אמר [ה]פלגא ניזקא קנסא רב פפא אמר פלגא ניזקא ממונא קסבר סתם שוורים לאו בחזקת שימור קיימי ובדין הוא דמשלם כוליה ורחמנא הוא דחייס עלויה דאכתי לא איעד תורא רב הונא בריה דרב יהושע אמר פלגא ניזקא קנסא קסבר סתם שוורים בחזקת שימור קיימי ובדין הוא דלא לישלם כלל ורחמנא הוא דקנסיה כי היכי דנינטריה לתוריה: סימן הזיק מה והמית כלל: תנן [ו] הניזק והמזיק בתשלומין בשלמא למאן דאמר פלגא ניזקא ממונא היינו דשייך ניזק בתשלומין אלא למ"ד פלגא ניזקא קנסא השתא דלאו דידיה קא שקיל בתשלומין איתיה לא נצרכא אלא לפחת נבילה פחת נבילה תנינא תשלומי נזק [ז]מלמד שהבעלים מטפלין בנבילה חדא בתם וחדא במועד וצריכא דאי אשמועינן תם משום דאכתי לא איעד אבל מועד דאיעד אימא לא ואי אשמועינן מועד משום דקא משלם כוליה אבל תם אימא לא צריכא ת"ש [ח] מה בין תם למועד [ז]שהתם משלם חצי נזק מגופו [ח]ומועד משלם נזק שלם מן העלייה [י] ולא קתני שהתם אינו משלם ע"פ עצמו ומועד משלם ע"פ עצמו [י] תנא ושייר מאי שייר דהאי שייר [ט]חצי כופר אי משום חצי כופר לאו שיורא הוא הא

רש"י

מתני׳ פתיתי. בגמ׳ מפרש אמאי לא תנא אנסתי: ואינו משלם קנס. בבבא קמא [ח] נפקא לן מודה בקנס פטור מאשר ירשיעון אלהים פרט למרשיע את עצמו: המית שורי את פלוני. והריני חייב בכופר: הרי זה משלם ע"פ עצמו. קסבר כופרא ממונא: עבדו של פלוני. והריני חייב שלשים סלע: אינו משלם. דקנס נינהו שאפי׳ אין יפה דינר נותן שלשים: גמ׳ דלא פגים לה. אין לעז של אנוסה גדול כלעז של מפותה וכיון דלאו פגם דילה הוא מהימנין ליה למשקל מיניה בושת ופגם על פיו: אימא לא. נהימניה להחזיק את הלעז: לא כל הימנו. שיוציא עליה לעז מזנה בעיר: ניחא לה לדידה. לשאת את הלעז כדי להשתכר הממון: לא ניחא להו לבני משפחה. וב"ד אין עליהם לעשות דבר להחזיק בושתם: פלגא ניזקא. שחייבה תורה שור תם: [ממונא. ומשלם ע"פ עצמו]: לאו בחזקת שימור קיימי. אם לא ישמרום בעלים שלא יזיקו [אינם בחזקת משתמרים מאליהם שלא יזיקו] אלא מזיקין אפי׳ ניזקא דלאו אורחיה הלכך על מריהו רמיא לנטורינהו וזה שלא שמרו בדין הוא לישלם כולה אלא דרחמנא חס עליה ומיהו מה שמשלם בדין משלם: כי היכי דנינטריה. שיוסיף שמירה על שמירתו: תנן. בבבא קמא: הניזק והמזיק בתשלומין. שניהם מפסידין בדבר כ"ד דהכי קאמר תרוייהו מטו להו בהאי פסידא דניזק מפסיד פלגא ומזיק פלגא: היינו דשייך ניזק בתשלומין. דמפסיד פלגא בממוניה: דלאו דידיה שקיל. דמה שנוטל בחנם נוטל: בתשלומין איתיה. בתמיה: לא נצרכא אלא לפחת נבילה. הא דקתני ניזק בתשלומין לאו בפלגא דקא שביק קאמר אלא בההוא פלגא דקא שקיל ליה רחמנא מפסיד ניזקא נמי דקני ליה רחמנא כל פחת שפחתה נבילה מדמיה משעת מיתה עד שעת העמדה בדין שמין את הנבלה כמה היה יפה השור בחייו וכמה היתה נבילה יפה בשעת מיתה ומשלם החצי אבל מה שהוזלו דמי נבילה משעת מיתה עד שעת מכירה אין המזיק משלם כלום באותו פחת ובבבא קמא (דף י:) יליף לה מקראי ואשמעינן האי מילתא דפחת נבילה הוי: תשלומי נזק מלמד שהבעלים מטפלין בנבילה. תנא דברייתא דריש לישנא דמתניתין דתנן בבבא קמא משלם תשלומי נזק במיטב הארץ ותנא עלה בברייתא דהאי דנקט תנא דמתני׳ תשלומי נזק ולא תנא משלם את הנזק לאשמועינן אתא שהניזק נוטל את נבילתו ומטפל בה ומוכרה והמזיק משלים עליה מה שחייבתו תורה אם תם חצי ואם מועד הכל ותרתי למה ליה לרבי למיתנייהו במתני׳ דבעלים מטפלין בנבילה: דקא משלם כוליה. ודיו בהפסד זה: מגופו. אינו גובה אלא מגוף השור ואם אין בו כדי חצי נזקו יפסיד המותר: מן העלייה. מן המיטב שבנכסי מזיק דגבי תם כתיב (שמות כא) וחצו את כספו ובמועד כתיב (שם) שלם ישלם שור ואם איתא דפלגא ניזקא קנסא ליתני נמי שהתם אינו משלם על פי עצמו ומועד משלם על פי עצמו דלאו בדין משלם שהרי התרו והעידו בו לשמור שורו: שייר חצי כופר. לא שנה כל החילוקים שביניהם שהרי אף יש חילוק זה ביניהם שהמועד שהמית את האדם משלם כופר שלם ותם שהמית אפילו חצי כופר כדינו בניזקין לא משלם דכתיב בעל השור נקי ודרשינן (ב"ק דף מא:) נקי מחצי כופר: הא

תוספות

וליתני אנסתי. דהוי חדוש טפי דפטור אע"ג דמודה שעשה פריצות: רבי שמעון בן יהודה אומר אף בושת ופגם אינו משלם ע"פ עצמו. אור"י דלאי קאי ר"ש בן יהודה אמתניתין דהכא הא דמשמע בריש נערה לקמן (דף מב.) דלר"ש אי דקא תבע בושת ופגם מחייב ליה קרבן שבועה היינו משום דהתם תבעו האב תחלה ואין שייך לומר לאו כל הימנו כו׳ דקאמר הכא ואין צריך לומר דתרי תנאי אליבא דר׳ שמעון (א) ועוד אומר רשב"א דהסיא דלקמן איכא לאוקמי בבת גריס וניחא לה לדידה ולאביה וליכא למימר דלמא איכא חד במדינת הים דלא ניחא ליה ומיהו אי קאי ר׳ שמעון אמתניתין דשבועות דמייתי לקמן בריש נערה (ג"ז שם) ע"כ תרי תנאי אליבא דר׳ שמעון:

[ט] האומר גנבתי כו׳. מוליא ש"ר וינלא בסן ועין לדלא תנא איכא למימר דאמיא בזה הכלל: [י] זה הכלל כל המשלם יותר על מה שהזיק כו׳. ואפילו למ"ד בפרק שור שנגח ארבעה וחמשה (ב"ק דף מ.) דכופר היינו דמי המזיק לא חשיב יותר ממה שהזיק אע"פ שפעמים שוה מזיק יותר מניזק דפדיון נפשו הוא נותן: לא נצרכא אלא לפחת נבילה. אע"ג דלאו דידיה שקיל מ"מ כיון דזכי ליה רחמנא חצי נזק חשבינן ליה בתשלומין מה שפחתה הנבלה והכא לא שייך למימר קרנא דתורך קבירא ביה כדאמרי׳ בהמניח בסופו (ב"ק דף לד.) דהתם ודאי שלא נהרג השור שייך לומר הכי דאין לו למכור שורו בשביל כן שסבור שישביח אבל הכא מיד כשנהרג יש לו למוכרו שידוע שתפחת הנבילה ותסריח: תנינא תשלומי נזק מלמד שהבעלים מטפלים בנבילה כו׳. הכי דייקא לה בבבא קמא (דף י:) חבתי בנזקו לא קתני אלא בתשלומי נזקו כו׳: אי משום חצי כופר לאו שיורא הוא וכו׳. לאו פירכא היא אלא שינויא הוא דלא תיקשי למ"ד פלגא ניזקא ממונא מאי שייר דשייר חצי כופר ומשני לא שייר כלום וחצי כופר לאו שיורא הוא וכן איכא בנזיר בפ׳ ג׳ מינים (דף לח: ושם) גבי אי משום לא יחל לאו שיורא הוא וכן בפרק החליל (סוכה דף נד. ושם) וההוא דהתם מגומגם טפי: הא

מסורת הש"ס

א) ב"ק עד: שבועות לו. וכתובות, ב) ב"ק טו: מג., ג) שם טו. [ושם כל הסוגיא ותוכל עוד שבועות לג.], ד) שם יד:, ה) שם טו., ו) [ואם איתא ליתני נמי הא שהתם כו׳ כצ"ל רש"ל], ז) [סוכה נד. וש"נ], ח) [דף עה.], ט) [שייך לעיל מתני׳], י) [ג"ז שייך לעיל].

הגהות הב"ח

(א) תוס׳ ד"ה ר׳ שמעון וכו׳ דתרי תנאי אליבא דרבי שמעון ומיהו אי קאי ר"ש אמתניתין וכו׳ דר"ש ועוד אומר רשב"א וכו׳ דלא ניחא ליה הס"ד:

ליקוטי רש"י

כל מקום שיש מכר. יש לאביה בה זכיה למכרה בשפחות [לעיל כט.]. כל זמן שהבת קטנה ולאביה זכאי למוכרה. אין קנס. אם נאנסה או נתפתתה אין לאביה חמשים כסף דנערה כתיב (דברים כב) ונתן האיש השוכב עמה לאבי הנערה חמשים כסף. וכל מקום שיש קנס. דהיינו כשהיא נערה. אין מכר. דתניא בערכין (דף כט:) יכול מוכר אדם את בתו כשהיא נערה תלמוד לומר ק"ו ומה מכורה כבר יוצאה עכשיו בסימני נערות שאינה מכורה אינו דין שלא תימכר. אבל חכמים אומרים וכו׳ יש לה קנס. לקטנה וטעמא מפרש בכתובות (דף מ:) כל מקום שנאמר נער בלא ה"א אפילו קטנה במשמע [חולין כו:]. מבת ג׳ שנים ויום אחד. שהיא ראויה לביאה [לעיל שם]. מכר לא. בתמיה והלא קטנה היא עד שתביא שתי שערות [חולין כו:]. אף קנס במקום מכר. ומשום קנס נקט בת שלש אבל למכר מבת יום אחד ועד שתביא שתי שערות [לעיל כט.]. יש לה ואע"פ שיש מכר משתראה לביאה עד שתביא ב׳ שערות ומקדש שתראה לביאה יש מכר ומשתביא שתי שערות ואין קנס ומשתביא שתי שערות עד שתבגר יש קנס ולא מכר ודין בגרות לנערות ששה חדשים [חולין שם]. נערה מלא דיבר הכתוב. בכל מקום כתיב נער וכאן כתיב נערה מלא להוציא את הקטנה [לקמן מד:]. ואם אמת היה הדבר. בעדים והתראה שזנתה לאחר אירוסין. אל פתח בית אביה. ראו גדולים שגדלתם [דברים כב, כא]. אלא כאן נערה. אלא האי דכתיב מלא לא ללמד על עצמו בא ולהוציא את הקטנה דלאו הך דרשה אמעיטא לה קטנה כדאמרינן דלאו בת עונשין אלא ללמד בא על כל נערה שבתורה שכתובין חסר לומר שאף הקטנה במשמע והכי יליף כאן נערה כאן שאי אפשר בקטנה כתיב מלא הא למדת שכל מקום שנכתב חסר אף הקטנה במשמע כגון באונס ומפתה [לקמן מד:]. ראו גדולים שגדלתם, כלומר מבית זה יצאת הנבלה שבו זינתה [לקמן מה.]. [ע"כ שייך לדף מ:] פלגא נזקא ממונא. דקסבר סתם שוורים נגחנים הם ומדינא כולהו בעי לשלומי דהוה ליה למינטריה ורחמנא הוא דחס עליה [סנהדרין ג.]. דין הוא שישלמנו ואינו קנס ונפקא מינה דאי מודה מקמי דאתו סהדי לא מיפטר [ב"ק טו.]. פלגא נזקא קנסא. דסתם שוורים אינם נוגחים ולא היה לבעלים לשמרו כל זמן שלא הועד ולא בעי לשלומי מידי אלא קנסא הוא דקנסיה רחמנא כדי שירבה בשמירת שוורים [סנהדרין שם]. לאו בחזקת שימור קיימי. שרגילין בנגיחה וצריכין שמירה. הניזק והמזיק בתשלומין. משמע דשניהן מפסידי ממון בתשלומין שזה משלם מחצה וזה מפסיד מחצה. היינו דשייך ניזק בתשלומין. כלומר מפסיד ממה שהיה ראוי לו דבעי למשקל כוליה שזה פשע בשורו שלא שמרו. בתשלומין איתיה. בתמיה דמשמע שמפסיד מדינו. לפחת נבילה. דכל פחת נבילה דניזק הוא והיינו דשייך ניזק בתשלומין שאפילו אותו קנס שזיכתה לו תורה אינו נוטל כולו. פחת נבילה תנינא. חבתי בתשלומי נזקו וקתני עלה תשלומי נזק מלמד שהבעלים מטפלים בנבילה ואמרינן לא נצרכא אלא לפחת נבילה. מגופו. ואם אינו שוה חצי נזק מפסיד הניזק דכתיב (שמות כא) וחצו את כספו. מן העלייה. אם אינו שוה כנגד כל הנזק נוטל נכסים מעליות [ב"ק שם]. ואפי׳ אין הנוגח שוה שיעור הנזק דבמועד כתיב (שמות כא) ישלם שור תחת השור ולא כתיב ביה דמגוף הנוגח יפרע [שם טז:]. ולא קתני שהתם וכו׳. אם איתא, דקנסא, ליתני נמי הא, שאני נזקו של תם קנס ואינו משלם ע"פ עצמו ומועד הוי ממון ומשלם ע"פ עצמו [שם טו.]. תנא ושייר. לא חשבינהו לכולהו [סוטה טז.]. מאי שייר דהאי שייר. דלאו אורחא דתנא למתני כל מילי ולשיורי חדא [תענית יג:]. חצי כופר. מועד שהמית את האדם משלם כופר ליורשים ותם אפילו חצי כופר לא משלם [ב"ק שם]. מת האב. משעמד בדין ומת עד שלא הספיק לגבות הרי הוא של אחיה ולא שלה. רבי שמעון אומר אם לא הספיקה לגבות. כי היכי דפליג במתניתין בלא הספיקה לגבות עד שמת האב הכי נמי פליג בלא הספיקה לגבות עד שבגרה דקאמר ת"ק הרי הן של אב ולרבי שמעון הרי הוא של עצמה [לקמן מב.].

עין משפט נר מצוה

פט א מיי׳ פ"ב מהל׳ נערה הל׳ יב ופ"ה מהל׳ סנהדרין הל׳ יד:
צ ב מיי׳ פ"ג מהלכות גניבה הלכה ט סמג עשין עא טור ח"מ סי׳ שמח:
צא ג מיי׳ פ"ה מהלכות סנהדרין הלכה יד סמג עשין ע:
צב ד מיי׳ פ"ב מהל׳ נזקי ממון הל׳ ח:
צג ה מיי׳ פ"ב שם הל׳ ז ופ"ה מהלכות סנהדרין הלכה ט סמג עשין לו טוש"ע ח"מ סי׳ א סעי׳ א:
צד ו ז ח מיי׳ פ"א מהל׳ נזקי ממון הלכה ג סמג עשין סו טוש"ע ח"מ סי׳ שפט סעיף ב ג ד ט:
צה ט מיי׳ פ"י שם הל׳ ב סמג שם:

תוספות רי"ד

מתני׳ האומר פתיתי את בתו של פלוני משלם בושת ופגם ע"פ עצמו ואינו משלם קנס. האומר גנבתי משלם את הקרן ע"פ עצמו ואינו משלם לא תשלומי כפל ולא ד׳ וה׳. המית שורי את פלוני או שורו של פלוני ה"ז משלם על פי עצמו. המית שורי עבדו של פלוני אינו משלם ע"פ עצמו. זה הכלל כל המשלם יותר ממה שהזיק אינו משלם ע"פ עצמו: וליתני אנסתי. לא מבעיא קאמר לא מבעיא אנסתי דלא פגים לה אבל פתיתי דפגים לה אימא לא משלם בושת ופגם ע"פ עצמו קמ"ל: ומתני׳ דלא כי האי תנא דתניא ר"ש בן יהודה אומר משום (רב הונא) [ר"ש] אף בושת ופגם אינו משלם ע"פ עצמו לא כל הימנו שיפגום בתו של פלוני. ואינו משלם קנס ע"פ עצמו כדנפקא לן מאשר ירשיעון אלהים פרט למרשיע את עצמו: ואי קשיא. הכא תנן דבושת הוי ממון ומשלם ע"פ עצמו ובריש פרק המניח אמרי׳ חסדא חסדא קנסא קמגבית בבבל וקרי התם לבושת קנס. תשובה לעולם בושת ממונא הוי לשלם ע"פ עצמו שאין בו שום יתירות אלא שמין לפי המבייש והמתבייש והתם קרי ליה קנסא לומר שאין גובין אותו בבבל דכל מידי דאית ביה חסרון כיס גבינן ליה בבבל אבל בושת דלית ביה חסרון כיס לא גבי׳ לי׳ בבבל כדאמרינן בפרק החובל: המית שורי את פלוני משלם ע"פ עצמו פי׳ דכופרא לאו קנסא הוא דכפי שוי׳ של ניזק משלם ואף למ"ד כפי שויה של מזיק כופרא ממונא הוי ומשלם ע"פ עצמו: המית שורי את עבדו וכו׳. בפרק שור שנגח ד׳ וה׳ מוכיח שאפילו שויה של עבד אינו משלם ע"פ עצמו דכל ל׳ כסף הוו קנסא: זה הכלל וכו׳. איתמר פלגא נזקא שחייבה תורה לשור תם. ר"פ אמר ממונא. פי׳ ומשלם ע"פ עצמו. רב הונא בריה דרב יהושע אמר פלגא נזקא קנסא רב פפא אמר ממונא סתם שוורים לאו בחזקת שימור קיימי. פי׳ אם לא ישמרו בעלים שלא יזיקו אינן בחזקת משתמר מאליהן שלא יזיקו אלא מזיקין אפילו נזקא דלאו אורחיה הלכך על מרייהו רמיא לנטרינהו וזה שלא שמרו בדין הוא דלשלם כוליה. ורחמנא הוא דחס עליה דאכתי לא אייעד תורא. פי׳ ואיהו מה שמשלם בדין משלם. ורב הונא בריה דרב יהושע אמר פלגא נזקא קנסא קסבר סתם שוורים בחזקת שימור קיימי ובדין הוא דלא לשלם כלל ורחמנא הוא דקנסיה כי היכי דנטרינהו לתורי׳. פי׳
שיוסיף

WHEREAS in the case of A *MUAD* ONE PAYS FULL DAMAGES FROM his CHOICE PROPERTY.[43] וְלֹא קָתָנֵי – **And the Mishnah does not teach** that there is a difference שֶׁהַתָּם אֵינוֹ מְשַׁלֵּם עַל פִּי עַצְמוֹ – in **that** in the case of **a *tam* one does not pay on** the basis of **his own admission,** וּמוּעָד מְשַׁלֵּם עַל פִּי עַצְמוֹ – **whereas** in the case of **a *muad*** one **does pay on** the basis of **his own admission.**[44] – ? –

The Gemara rejects the proof:

תָּנָא וְשַׁיֵּיר – **[The Tanna] taught** only some of the differences between a *tam* and a *muad* **and omitted** others. Thus, his failure to list this difference is not probative.

The Gemara questions this answer:

מַאי שַׁיֵּיר דְּהַאי שַׁיֵּיר – **What** else **did [the Tanna] omit** that you may justifiably claim **that he omitted this** difference as well?[45]

The Gemara answers:

שַׁיֵּיר חֲצִי כּוֹפֶר – **He omitted** the payment of **half-*kofer*** in the case of a *tam;* i.e. he left out the rule that when a *tam* kills a person the owner does not even pay half-*kofer,* whereas in the case of a *muad* the owner pays full *kofer.*[46]

The Gemara comments:[47]

אִי מִשּׁוּם חֲצִי כּוֹפֶר – **If it is because** the Mishnah **omits half-*kofer*** that you contend that the Mishnah's list is incomplete – לָאו שִׁיוּרָא הוּא – **that is not** evidence of **an omission.**

NOTES

43. [I.e. the damager's liability is not limited to the ox that inflicted the damage. Hence, even if the damage exceeds the value of the goring ox, the damager is still liable to make restitution with his choicest properties.] With regard to a *muad* ox, the Torah states (ibid v. 36), *He shall pay an ox in place of the ox,* and does not limit the damager's liability to the ox that did the damage [as it does with regard to a *tam*] (*Rashi*).

44. Now, if in fact the payment of *half-damages* for damage inflicted by a *tam* is a punitive payment, then this Mishnah, which states the differences between a *tam* and a *muad,* should state as well that in the case of a *tam* the owner does not pay by his own admission, whereas in the case of a *muad* he does pay by his own admission. For the full damages paid in the case of a *muad* is most certainly a compensatory payment, since the owner was forewarned by the court that his ox has a destructive tendency and needs to be guarded (*Rashi*).

45. While the listing in a Mishnah is not always complete, there is a generally accepted principle that a Tanna would not have omitted only one item (see *Rashi* to *Taanis* 13b ד״ה מאי שייר). Thus, if we are to explain that the Mishnah's list is incomplete, we must show that another difference was omitted.

46. The Mishnah's listing of the differences between a *tam* and a *muad* is, in fact, incomplete. For [in addition to omitting the difference pertaining to liability by one's own admission] it omits the difference between a *tam* and a *muad* vis-a-vis the *kofer* payment (see above, note 6). For in contrast to an ox that inflicts damage (where the owner of a *tam* pays half-damages, as opposed to the owner of a *muad,* who pays full damages), when an ox kills a person the owner of a *muad* pays full *kofer,* whereas the owner of a *tam* does not pay anything – not even half-*kofer.* This is derived from the verse (*Exodus* 21:28), *If a [tam] ox shall gore a man or woman and he shall die, the ox shall be stoned . . . and the owner of the ox shall be absolved,* which the Gemara (*Bava Kamma* 41b) expounds as meaning that he shall be absolved from paying half-*kofer* (*Rashi*).

47. By having demonstrated that the Mishnah omits the difference between a *tam* and a *muad* with regard to *kofer,* we have not only answered Rav Huna the son of R' Yehoshua's position, but we have raised a strong difficulty with Rav Pappa's position (that the *half-damages* are a compensatory payment that is paid by one's own admission). For since the Mishnah omitted the difference of *half-kofer,* and is evidently presenting an incomplete listing, it must have omitted another difference – and presumably it is the difference between *tam* and *muad* with regard to paying on the basis of one's admission. The Gemara therefore demonstrates now that it is not necessarily so that the Mishnah is presenting an incomplete list (*Tosafos*). See also *Ritva;* cf. *Rabbeinu Simchah,* cited by *Ritva.*

מתני' א האומר פתיתי את בתו של פלוני משלם בושת ופגם על פי עצמו ואין משלם קנס ב האומר גנבתי ח) משלם את הקרן על פי עצמו ואין משלם תשלומי כפל ותשלומי ארבעה וחמשה ט) ג המית שורי את פלוני או שורו של פלוני הרי זה משלם על פי עצמו המית שורי עבדו של פלוני אין משלם ע"פ עצמו ד זה הכלל כל המשלם יותר על מה שהזיק אינו משלם ע"פ עצמו: גמ' וליתני אנסתי לא מבעיא קאמר לא מבעיא אנסתי דלא קא פגים לה דמשלם בושת ופגם על פי עצמו אבל פתיתי דקא פגים לה אימא לא משלם על פי עצמו קא משמע לן מתניתין דלא כי האי תנא דתניא רבי שמעון בן יהודה אומר משום ר' שמעון אף בושת ופגם אינו משלם ע"פ עצמו לא כל הימנו שיפגום בתו של פלוני אמר ליה רב פפא לאביי ניחא לה לדידה מאי דלמא לא ניחא ליה לאביה ניחא ליה לאביה מאי דלמא לא ניחא להו לבני משפחה ניחא להו לבני משפחה מאי אי אפשר דליכא חד במדינת הים דלא ניחא ליה: האומר גנבתי משלם את הקרן וכו': איתמר פלגא ניזקא י) רב פפא אמר פלגא ניזקא ממונא רב הונא בריה דרב יהושע אמר ה פלגא ניזקא קנסא רב פפא אמר פלגא ניזקא ממונא קסבר סתם שוורים לאו בחזקת שימור קיימי ובדין הוא דמשלם כוליה ורחמנא הוא דחייס עליה דאכתי לא איעד תורא רב הונא בריה דרב יהושע אמר פלגא ניזקא קנסא קסבר סתם שוורים בחזקת שימור קיימי ובדין הוא דלא לישלם כלל ורחמנא הוא דקנסיה כי היכי דנינטריה לתוריה: סימן היזיק מה והמית כלל: תנן ד) הניזק והמזיק בתשלומין בשלמא למאן דאמר פלגא ניזקא ממונא היינו דשייך ניזק בתשלומין אלא למ"ד פלגא ניזקא קנסא השתא דלאו דידיה קא שקיל בתשלומין איתיה לא נצרכא אלא לפחת נבילה תנינא תשלומי נזק ו מלמד שהבעלים מטפלין בנבילה חדא בתם וחדא במועד וצריכא דאי אשמועינן תם משום דאכתי לא איעד אבל מועד דאיעד אימא לא ואי אשמועינן מועד משום דקא משלם כוליה אבל תם אימא לא צריכא ת"ש ה) מה בין תם למועד ז שהתם משלם חצי נזק מגופו ח ומועד משלם נזק שלם מן העלייה ו) ולא קתני שהתם אינו משלם ע"פ עצמו ומועד משלם ע"פ עצמו ז) תנא ושייר מאי שייר דהאי שייר ט חצי כופר אי משום חצי כופר לאו שיורא הוא הא

רש"י

מתני' פתיתי. בגמ' מפרש אמאי לא תנא אנסתי: ואינו משלם קנס. דבבבא קמא ט) נפקא לן מודה בקנס פטור מאשר ירשיעון אלהים פרט למרשיע את עצמו: המית שורי את פלוני. והרי חייב בכופר: הרי זה משלם ע"פ עצמו. קסבר כופרא ממונא: עבדו של פלוני. והרי חייב שלשים סלע: אינו משלם. דקנס נינהו שאפי' אין יפה דינר נותן שלשים: גמ' דלא פגים לה. אין לעז של אנוסה גדול כלעז של מפותה וכיון דלאו פגם דילה הוא מהימנינן ליה למשקל מיניה בושת ופגם על פיו: אימא לא. נחשדיה להחזיק את הלעז: לא כל הימנו. שיוציא עליה לעז מוזה בעיר: ניחא לה לדידה. לשאת את הלעז כדי להשתכר הממון: לא ניחא להו לבני משפחה. וב"ד אין עליהם לעשות דבר להחזיק בושתם: פלגא ניזקא. שחייבה תורה שור תם: [ממונא. ומשלם ע"פ עצמו]: לאו בחזקת שימור קיימי. אם לא ישמרום בעלים שלא יזיקו [אינם בחזקת משתמרים מאליהם שלא יזיקו] אלא מזיקין אפי' נזיקא דלאו אורחיה הלכך על מריהו רמיא לנטורינהו וזה שלא שמרו בדין הוא לישלם כולה אלא דרחמנא חס עליה ומיהו מה שמשלם בדין משלם: כי היכי דנינטריה. שיוסיף שמירה על שמירתו: תנן. בבבא קמא: הניזק והמזיק בתשלומין. שניהם מפסידין בדבר ס"ד דהכי קאמר תרויהו מטי להו בהאי פסידא דניזק מפסיד פלגא ומזיק פלגא: היינו דשייך ניזק בתשלומין. דמפסיד פלגא בממוניה: דלאו דידיה שקיל. דמה שנוטל בתנס נוטל: בתשלומין איתיה. בתמיה: לא נצרכא אלא לפחת נבילה. הא דקתני ניזק בתשלומין לאו בפלגא דקא שביק קאמר אלא בההיא פלגא ניזקא נמי דקני ליה רחמנא מפסיד כל פחת שפחתה נבילה מדמיה משעת מיתה עד שעת העמדה בדין שמשמין את הנבלה כמה היה יפה השור בחייו וכמה היתה נבילה יפה בשעת מיתה ומשלם החצי אבל מה שהוזלו דמי נבילה משעת מיתה עד שעת מכירה אין המזיק משלם כלום לאותו פחת ובבבא קמא (דף י:) יליף לה מקרא: ואשמעינן האי תנא פחת נבילה דניזק הוי: תשלומי נזק מלמד שהבעלים מטפלין בנבילה. תנא דברייתא דריש לישנא דמתניתין דתנן בבבא קמא משלם תשלומי נזק במיטב הארץ ותנא עלה בברייתא דהאי דנקט תנא דמתני' תשלומי נזק ולא תנא משלם את הנזק לאשמועינן אתא שהניזק נוטל את נבילתו ומטפל בה ומוכרה והמזיק משלים עליה מה שחייבתו תורה אם תם חצי ואם מועד הכל ותרתי למה ליה לרבי למיסתם במתני' דבעלים מטפלין בנבילה: דקא משלם כוליה. ודיו בהפסד זה: מגופו. אינו גובה אלא מגוף השור ואם אין בו כדי חצי נזקו יפסיד המותר: מן העלייה. מן המיטב שבנכסי מזיק דגבי תם כתיב (שמות כא) וחצו את כספו מגופו ובמועד כתיב (שם) שלם ישלם שור ואם איתא דפלגא ניזקא קנסא ניתני נמי שהתם אינו משלם על פי עצמו ומועד משלם על פי עצמו דמועד ודאי בדין משלם שהרי התרו והעידו בו לשמור שורו: שייר חצי כופר. לא שנה כל החילוקים שביניהם שהרי אף יש חילוק זה ביניהם שהמועד שהמית את האדם משלם כופר שלם ותם שהמית אפילו חצי כופר כדינו בניזקין לא משלם דכתיב בעל השור נקי ודרשינן (ב"ק דף מא:) נקי מחצי כופר:

תוספות

וליתני אנסתי. דהוי חדוש טפי לפטור אע"ג דמודה שעשה פריצות: רבי שמעון בן יהודה אומר אף בושת ופגם אינו משלם ע"פ עצמו. תוס' דלאו קאי אר"ש בן יהודה אמתניתין דהכא הא דמשמע בריש נערה לקמן (דף מג.) דלר"ש אי דקא תבע בושת ופגם ומחייב ליה קרבן שבועה היינו משום דהתם תבעו האב תחלה ואין שייך לומר לאו כל הימנו כו' כדקאמר הכא ואין צריך לומר דתרי תנאי אליבא דר' שמעון (א) ועוד אומר רשב"א דההיא דלקמן איכא לאוקמי בבת גרים וניחא לה לדידה ולאביה דליכא למימר דלמא איכא חד במדינת הים דלא ניחא ליה ומיהו אי קאי ר' שמעון אמתניתין דשבועות דמייתי לקמן בריש נערה (ג"ז שם) ע"כ תרי תנאי אליבא דר' שמעון:

ט) האומר גנבתי כו'. מוליא ש"ר ויולא בשן ועין דלא תנא איכא למימר דאתיא בזה הכלל:

י) זה הכלל כל המשלם יותר על מה שהזיק כו'. ואפילו למ"ד בפרק שור שנגח ארבעה וחמשה (ב"ק דף מ.) דכופר היינו דמי המזיק לא חשיב יותר ממה שהזיק אע"פ שפעמים שוה מזיק יותר מניזק דפדיון נפשו הוא נותן:

לא נצרכא אלא לפחת נבילה. אע"ג דלאו דידיה שקיל מ"מ כיון דזכי ליה רחמנא חצי נזק חשבינן ליה בתשלומין מה שפחתה הנבלה והכא לא שייך למימר קרנא דתורך קבירא ביה כדאמרי' בהמניח בסופו (ב"ק דף לד.) דהתם ודאי שלא נהרג השור שייך לומר הכי דאין לו למכור שורו בשביל כן שסבור שישביח אבל הכא מיד כשנהרג יש לו למוכרו שידוע שתפחת הנבילה ותסריח:

תנינא תשלומי נזק מלמד שהבעלים מטפלים בנבילה כו'. הכי דייקא לה בבבא קמא (דף י:) חבתי במזקו לא קתני אלא בתשלומי נזקו כו': אי משום חצי כופר לאו שיורא הוא וכו'. לאו פירכא היא אלא שינויא הוא דלא תיקשי למ"ד פלגא ניזקא ממונא מאי שייר דשייר חצי כופר ומשני לא שייר כלום וחצי כופר לאו שיורא הוא וכן איכא בנזיר בפ' ג' מינים (דף לח: ושם) גבי אי משום לא יחל לאו שיורא הוא וכן בפרק החליל (סוכה דף נד. ושם) והאי דהתם מגומגם טפי: הא

עין משפט נר מצוה

פט א מיי' פ"ב מהל' נערה הל' יב וע"ש מהל' סנהדרין הל' יד:

צ ב מיי' פ"ג מהלכות גניבה הלכה ט סמג עשין עא טור ח"מ סי' שמח:

צא ג מיי' פ"ה מהלכות סנהדרין הלכה יד סמג עשין ע:

צב ד מיי' פ"ב מהל' נזקי ממון הל' ח:

צג ה מיי' פ"ב שם הל' ז ופ"ה מהלכות סנהדרין הלכה ט סמג עשין לו טוש"ע ח"מ סי' א:

צד ו ז ח מיי' פ"א מהל' נזקי ממון הלכה ג סמג עשין סו טוש"ע ח"מ סי' שפט סעיף ב ג ד ט:

צה ט מיי' פ"י שם הל' ז סמג שם:

תוספות רי"ד

מתני' האומר פתיתי את בתו של פלוני משלם בושת ופגם ע"פ עצמו ואינו משלם קנס. האומר גנבתי משלם את הקרן ע"פ עצמו ואינו משלם לא תשלומי כפל ולא ד' וה'. המית שורי את פלוני או שורו של פלוני ה"ז משלם על פי עצמו. המית שורי עבדו של פלוני אינו משלם ע"פ עצמו. זה הכלל כל המשלם יותר ממה שהזיק אינו משלם ע"פ עצמו: וליתני אנסתי. לא מבעיא קאמר לא מבעיא אנסתי דלא פגים לה אבל פתיתי דפגים לה אימא לא משלם בושת ופגם ע"פ עצמו קמ"ל: ומתני' דלא כי האי תנא דתניא ר"ש בן יהודה אומר משום (רב הונא) [ר"ש] אף בושת ופגם אינו משלם על פי עצמו לא כל הימנו שיפגום בתו של פלוני. ואינו משלם קנס ע"פ עצמו כדנפקא לן מאשר ירשיעון אלהים פרט למרשיע את עצמו: ואי קשיא. הכא תנן דבושת הוי ממון ומשלם ע"פ עצמו ובריש פרק המניח אמרי' חסרא חסרא קנסא קמבעית בבבל וקרי התם לבושת קנס. תשובה לעולם בושת ממונא הוי לשלם ע"פ עצמו שאין בו שום יתירות אלא שאין לפי המבייש והמתבייש והתם קרי ליה קנסא לומר שאין גובין אותו בבבל דכל מידי דאית ביה חסרון כיס גבינן ליה בבבל אבל בושת דלית ביה חסרון כיס לא גבי לי' בבבל כדאמרינן בפרק החובל: המית שורי את פלוני משלם ע"פ עצמו פי' דכופרא לאו קנסא הוא דכפי שויו של ניזק הוא ואף למ"ד כפי שויו של מזיק כופרא ממונא הוי ומשלם ע"פ עצמו: המית שורי את עבדו וכו'. בפרק שור שנגח ד' וה' מוכיח שאפילו שויה של עבד אינו משלם ע"פ עצמו דכל ל' כסף הוו קנסא: זה הכלל וכו'. איתמר פלגא נזקא שחייבה תורה לשור תם. ר"פ אמר ממונא. סתם שוורים לאו בחזקת שימור קיימי. פי' אם לא ישמרו בעלים שלא יזיקו אינן בחזקת משתמרי מאיליהן שלא יזיקו אלא מזיקין אפילו נזקא דלאו אורחיה הלכך על מריה רמיא לנטורינהו וזה שלא שמרו בדין הוא דלשלם כוליה. דאכתי לא אייעד תורא. פי' ואיהו מה שמשלם בדין משלם ומשלם ע"פ עצמו. רב הונא בריה דרב יהושע אמר פלגא נזקא קנסא רב פפא אמר ממונא סתם שוורים לאו בחזקת שימור קיימי ובדין הוא דלא לשלם כלל ורחמנא הוא דקנסיה כי היכי דנינטריה לתוריה. פי' שיוסיף

מסורת הש"ס

א) פ"א מבחתי ומברכות, ב) ב"ק טו: מג., ג) שם טו. [ושם כל הסוגיא ומוכר עוד שבועות לג.], ד) שם יד:, ה) שם טו., ו) [ואם איתא ליתני נמי הא שהתם כו' כל"ל רש"ל], ז) [סוכה נד. ושנ"ג], ח) [דף עה.], ט) [שייך לעיל במתני'], י) [ג"ז שייך לעיל].

הגהות הב"ח

(א) תוס' ד"ה ר' שמעון וכו' דתרי תנאי אליבא דרבי שמעון ומיהו אי קאי ר"ש אמתניתין ועוד אומר רשב"א וכו' דלא ניחא ליה הס"ד:

ליקוטי רש"י

כל מקום שיש מכר. יש לאביה בה זכיה להכניס בשפחות [לעיל כט.]. כל זמן שהבת קטנה ולאביה זכאי למוכרה. אין קנס. אם לאנסה או נתפתתה אין לאביה חמשים כסף דבנערה כתיב (דברים כב) ונתן האיש השוכב עמה לאבי הנערה חמשים כסף. וכל מקום שיש קנס. דהיינו כשהיא נערה. אין מכר. דתנא בערכין (דף כט.) יכול ימכור אדם בתו כשהיא נערה אמרת ק"ו ומה מכורה כבר יוצאה עכשיו בסימני נערות שאינה מכורה אינו דין שלא תמכר. אבל חכמים אומרים וכו' יש לה קנס. לקטנה וטעמא מפרש בכתובות (דף מ:) כל מקום שנאמר נער בלא ה"א אפילו קטנה במשמע [חולין כו:]. מבת ג' שנים ויום אחד. שהיא ראויה לביאה [לעיל שם]. מכר לא. בתמיה והלא קטנה היא עד שתביא שתי שערות [חולין כו:]. אף קנס במקום מכר. ומשום קנס נקט בת שלש אבל למכר מבת יום אחד ועד שתביא שתי שערות [לעיל כט.]. יש לה ואע"פ שיש מכר משראויה לביאה עד שתביא ב' שערות וקודם שתביא לביאה יש מכר ואין קנס ומשתביא שתי שערות ועד שתיבגר יש קנס ולא מכר וכן בגרות לנערות שהם מדשים [חולין שם]. נערה מלא דיבר הכתוב. כל מקום כתיב נער וכאן כתיב נערה מלא להוציא את הקטנה [לקמן מד:]. ואם אמת היה הדבר. בעדים והתראה שזנתה לאחר אירוסין. אל פתח בית אביה. הא גדולים [דברים כב, כא]. אלא כאן נערה. אלא הכי דכתיב מלא לא ללמד על עצמו בא והוציא את הקטנה דבלאו הך דרשא אמעיטא לה קטנה כדאמרינן דלאו בת עונשין אלא ללמד בא על כל נערה שבתורה שכתובין חסר לומר שאף הקטנה במשמע והכי יליף כאן נערה כאן שאי אפשר בקטנה כתיב מלא הא למדת שכל מקום שנכתב חסר אף הקטנה במשמע כגון באונס ומפתה [לקמן מד:]. ראו גדולים שגדלתם, כלומר מבית זה יצאת הנבלה שבו זינתה [לקמן מה.]. [ע"כ שייך לדף מ:] פלגא נזקא ממונא. דקסבר סתם שוורים נגחנים הם ומדינא כולהו בעי לשלומי דהוה ליה למינטריה ורחמנא הוא דחס עליה [סנהדרין ג.]. דין הוא שישלמנו ואינו קנס ונפקא מינה דאי מודה מקמי דאתו סהדי לא מיפטר [ב"ק טו.]. פלגא נזקא קנסא. דסתם שוורים אינם נוגחים ולא היה לבעלים לשמרו כל זמן שלא הועד ולא בעי לשלומי מידי אלא קנסא הוא דקנסיה רחמנא כדי שירבה בשמירת שוורים [סנהדרין שם]. לאו בחזקת שימור קיימי. שרגילין בנגיחה וצריכין שמירה. הניזק והמזיק בתשלומין. משמע דשניהן מפסידי ממון בתשלומין שזה משלם מחצה וזה מפסיד מחצה. היינו דשייך ניזק בתשלומין. כלומר מפסיד ממה שהיה ראוי לו דבעי למשקל כוליה שזה פשע בשורו שלא שמרו. בתשלומין איתיה. [illegible] קנס שזיכתה לו תורה אינו נוטל כולו. פחת נבילה תנינא. חבתי בתשלומי נזקו וקתני עלה תשלומי נזק מלמד שהבעלים מטפלים בנבילה [illegible] העלייה. אם אינו שוה כנגד כל הנזק נוטל נכסים מביתו [ב"ק שם]. ואפי' אין הנוגח שוה שיעור הנזק דבמועד כתיב (שמות כא) שלם ישלם [illegible] שחצי נזקו של תם קנס ואינו משלם ע"פ עצמו ומועד הוי ממון ומשלם ע"פ עצמו [שם טו.]. תנא ושייר. לא חשבינהו לכולהו [סוטה [illegible]] [illegible] האדם משלם כופר ליורשים ותם ואפילו חצי כופר לא משלם [ב"ק שם]. מת האב. משעמד בדין ומת עד שלא הספיק לגבות הרי הוא של [illegible] האב הכי נמי פליג בלא הספיקה לגבות עד שבגרה דקאמר ת"ק הרי [illegible]

תְּנַן – **We learned in a Mishnah:**[30] הַנִּיזָּק וְהַמַּזִּיק בְּתַשְׁלוּמִין – Both THE DAMAGED PARTY AND THE DAMAGER ARE involved IN THE PAYMENT.[31] בִּשְׁלָמָא לְמַאן דְּאָמַר פַּלְגָּא נִיזְקָא מָמוֹנָא – Now, **this fits well according to the one who says** that **half-damages is a compensation** payment, הַיְינוּ דְּשַׁיֵּיךְ נִיזָּק בְּתַשְׁלוּמִין – for **this is how the damaged party is involved in the payment.**[32] אֶלָּא לְמַאן דְּאָמַר פַּלְגָּא נִיזְקָא קְנָסָא – **But according to the one who says** that **half-damages is a penalty** payment, in what sense is the damaged party involved in the payment? הַשְׁתָּא דְּלָאו דִּידֵיהּ קָא שָׁקִיל – **Now,** considering that **he is taking** even **that which is not his,**[33] בְּתַשְׁלוּמִין אִיתֵיהּ – **can he** be said to **be** involved **in the payment?!**[34]

The Gemara answers:

לֹא נִצְרְכָא אֶלָּא לְפְחַת נְבֵילָה – No. The Mishnah is referring to an entirely different rule; **it is needed only** with respect **to the depreciation of the carcass** that takes place after the animal's death and before the case comes to court. This loss is borne by the damaged party alone and represents his "share" of the payment.[35]

The Gemara objects:

פְּחַת נְבֵילָה – Are you saying that the Mishnah means to teach the rule regarding **the depreciation of the carcass?** תְּנֵינָא – But that ruling is wholly unnecessary, for **we have** already **learned it in the** first part of that very **Mishnah,** as explained by a Baraisa:[36] תַּשְׁלוּמֵי נֶזֶק – When the Mishnah states[37] that the damager is liable to pay COMPENSATION FOR THE DAMAGE, מְלַמֵּד שֶׁהַבְּעָלִים מְטַפְּלִין בַּנְּבֵילָה – IT TEACHES thereby THAT THE OWNER of the dead animal [i.e. the damaged party] MUST DEAL WITH THE CARCASS. I.e. the owner must take the carcass and sell it, and thus is entitled to recover only the difference between the animal's worth when alive and the carcass' value due to the goring.[38] – ? –

The Gemara answers:

חֲדָא בְּתָם וַחֲדָא בְּמוּעָד – **One** Mishnah teaches this rule **in** the case of **a** ***tam*** **and one** Mishnah teaches it **in** the case of **a** ***muad.*** וּצְרִיכָא – **And** [**both**] teachings **are necessary.** דְּאִי אַשְׁמוּעִינַן תָּם – **For if** [**the Mishnah**] **had taught us** this rule only in the case of **a** ***tam,*** I might have said that it applies only there מִשּׁוּם דְּאַכַּתִּי לֹא אִיַּיעַד – **because** [**the animal**] that gored **had not yet been warned;**[39] אֲבָל מוּעָד דְּאִיַּיעַד אֵימָא לֹא – **but** in the case of **a** ***muad,*** **which has been** fully **warned, I might say** that the damager is liable for the depreciation of the carcass as well. וְאִי אַשְׁמוּעִינַן מוּעָד – **And if** [**the Mishnah**] **had taught us** this rule only in the case of **a** ***muad,*** I might have said that this leniency applies only there מִשּׁוּם דְּקָא מְשַׁלֵּם כּוּלֵּיהּ – **because** [**the owner**] of the goring ox **pays** for **all** [**the damage**];[40] אֲבָל תָּם אֵימָא לֹא – **but** in the case of **a** ***tam,*** where he pays for only half the damage, **I might say that** we do **not** apply this leniency, too. צְרִיכָא – Therefore, [**both**] teachings **were necessary.**

The Gemara attempts to prove from another Mishnah that half-damages are compensation, not a penalty:

תָּא שְׁמַע – **Come, learn** a proof from the following Mishnah:[41] מַה בֵּין תָּם לְמוּעָד – WHAT IS the difference in law BETWEEN A *TAM* AND A *MUAD?* שֶׁהַתָּם מְשַׁלֵּם חֲצִי נֶזֶק מִגּוּפוֹ – It is THAT in the case of A *TAM* ONE PAYS HALF-DAMAGES only FROM THE BODY OF [THE ANIMAL] that damaged,[42] וּמוּעָד מְשַׁלֵּם נֶזֶק שָׁלֵם מִן הָעֲלִיָּיה –

NOTES

30. *Bava Kamma* 14b.

31. The Mishnah there sets forth in cryptic form several rules pertaining to the payment of damages. One of the rules mentioned is: הַנִּיזָּק וְהַמַּזִּיק בְּתַשְׁלוּמִין, *both the damaged party and the damager are* [*involved*] *in the payment.* I.e. both parties suffer part of the loss. The Gemara at this point assumes that this alludes to the payment for half-damages, in which the damaged party suffers half the loss and the damager suffers half the loss (*Rashi*).

32. For according to this view, the ox's owner should by rights have to pay full damages, since he failed to guard his ox properly. Thus, the damaged party is (theoretically) entitled to receive full compensation for his loss. Since he receives only half that amount, he can be said to be involved in the payment, since he is in fact required to forgo half the compensation (see *Rashi* here and to *Bava Kamma* 15a).

33. I.e. that which he does not deserve by right (*Rashi*).

34. To be "involved in the payment" implies that the damaged party is giving up something that should really come to him (*Rashi* to *Bava Kamma* ibid.). But according to the view that the payment is a penalty, the damaged party is not really entitled to receive anything, since the ox's owner is not to blame for the damage done by his ox. Thus, even the half-damages that the *nizak* does receive is nothing more than a gift bestowed upon him by the Torah in order to penalize the *mazik.* Accordingly, the law of half-damages cannot be said to be costing the damaged party anything, since it actually gives him *more* than what he is entitled to, not less.

35. That which the Mishnah teaches that the damaged party is involved in the payment is an allusion not to the half of the damages for which he is not compensated, but to the payment of *half-damages* that he does receive – i.e. the damaged party is involved [i.e. suffers a loss] in the *half-damages* payment itself, which the Torah does award him. For when assessing the damage, we assess the value of the damaged ox prior to its being gored, and the value of the carcass immediately thereafter, and the damager pays half the difference. Now, should the carcass begin to rot and thereby depreciate in value before the case comes to court, that loss is not figured into the valuation of the damage; rather, it is absorbed solely by the damaged party, as derived by the Gemara in *Bava Kamma* (10b). Hence, he does not receive even half of the entire damage, and is *involved* [i.e. shares] in the *half-damages* payment itself. And, accordingly, when the Mishnah states that *"both the damaged party and the damager are involved in the payment,"* it refers not to the law that a *tam* pays for only half the damages, but to the law that the loss suffered on account of the depreciation of the carcass is absorbed totally by the *nizak* (*Rashi*). See *Tosafos* ד״ה לא נצרכא.

36. *Tosefta, Bava Kamma* 1:1, cited in *Bava Kamma* 10b.

37. *Bava Kamma* 2a (see *Rashi* cited in following note; cf. *Tosafos* ד״ה תנינא and *Rashi, Bava Kamma* 15a ד״ה הא תנא ליה רישא; see also Schottenstein ed. of *Bava Kamma,* 10b note 22).

38. The Tanna of the Baraisa is expounding upon the words of the Mishnah: *The damager is liable to pay compensation (tashlumei) for the damage with the choicest of his lands.* The Tanna does not simply state that he is liable to *pay for the damage.* Rather, he states: *to pay compensation (tashlumei) of the damage.* The word תַּשְׁלוּמֵי (*compensation*) is related to הַשְׁלָמָה (*completion*), and connotes "making whole." By couching the statement of liability to include the word תַּשְׁלוּמֵי, the Mishnah teaches that the damaged party must take the carcass and sell it, and the damager need only "make whole" his loss. I.e. the carcass is valued at its worth at the time it was gored and the damager is liable only to make whole the loss by paying for the difference in the animal's value between when it was alive and after it died in the manner prescribed by the Torah: *half-damages* in the case of a *tam* and full damages in the case of a *muad.* The Gemara in *Bava Kamma* (10b) explains that it would be necessary to teach this only where the carcass depreciates in value, from which we derive that the depreciation is absorbed by the damaged party (*Rashi* ibid. 15a ד״ה הא תנא לי׳ and 10b ד״ה אלא לפחת נבילה and ד״ה לא נצרכא). Now, why would it be necessary for Rebbi to state twice in the Mishnah that the damaged party suffers the loss of the depreciation of the carcass? (*Rashi*).

39. The Torah was therefore lenient with the damager and did not hold him liable for the depreciation of the carcass.

40. The Torah therefore considered it sufficient that he pay the actual amount of the loss, and did not burden him further with disposing of the carcass and bearing responsibility for its depreciation (see *Rashi*).

41. *Bava Kamma* 16b.

42. The damaged party can only collect the *half-damage* payment from [the body of] the ox that inflicted the damage itself. If the ox is worth less than half the damages, [the owner need only pay the value of the ox itself and] the damaged party loses the remainder. This is derived from the verse (*Exodus* 21:35) that states: וְחָצוּ אֶת־כַּסְפּוֹ, *and they shall divide its worth* – i.e. the worth of the animal that did the damage; see Mishnah, *Bava Kamma* 34a (*Rashi*).

מתני׳ האומר פתיתי את בתו של פלוני משלם בושת ופגם על פי עצמו ואין משלם קנס. האומר גנבתי משלם את הקרן על פי עצמו ואין משלם תשלומי כפל ותשלומי ארבעה וחמשה. המית שורי את פלוני או שורו של פלוני הרי זה משלם על פי עצמו. המית שורי עבדו של פלוני אין משלם על פי עצמו. זה הכלל כל המשלם יותר על מה שהזיק אינו משלם ע"פ עצמו:

גמ׳ וליתני אנסתי לא מבעיא קאמר לא מבעיא אנסתי דלא קא פגים לה דמשלם בושת ופגם על פי עצמו אבל פתיתי דקא פגים לה אימא לא לישלם על פי עצמו קא משמע לן מתניתין דלא כי האי תנא דתניא רבי שמעון בן יהודה אומר משום ר' שמעון אף בושת ופגם אינו משלם ע"פ עצמו לא כל הימנו שיפגום בתו של פלוני אמר ליה רב פפא לאביי ניחא לה לדידה מאי דלמא לא ניחא ליה לאביה ניחא ליה לאביה מאי דלמא לא ניחא להו לבני משפחה ניחא להו לבני משפחה מאי אי אפשר דליכא חד במדינת הים דלא ניחא ליה:

האומר גנבתי משלם את הקרן וכו': איתמר פלגא ניזקא רב פפא אמר ממונא רב הונא בריה דרב יהושע אמר קנסא. רב פפא אמר פלגא ניזקא ממונא קסבר סתם שוורים לאו בחזקת שימור קיימי ובדין הוא דמשלם כוליה ורחמנא הוא דחייס עליה דאכתי לא איעד. רב הונא בריה דרב יהושע אמר פלגא ניזקא קנסא קסבר סתם שוורים בחזקת שימור קיימי ובדין הוא דלא לישלם כלל ורחמנא הוא דקנסיה כי היכי דנינטריה לתוריה: סימן היזק מה והמית כלל: תנן הניזק והמזיק בתשלומין בשלמא למאן דאמר פלגא ניזקא ממונא היינו דשייך ניזק בתשלומין אלא למ"ד פלגא ניזקא קנסא השתא דלאו דידיה קא שקיל בתשלומין איתיה לא נצרכא אלא לפחת נבילה תנינא תשלומי נזק מלמד שהבעלים מטפלין בנבילה חדא בתם וחדא במועד וצריכא דאי אשמועינן תם משום דאכתי לא איעד אבל מועד דאיעד אימא לא ואי אשמועינן מועד משום דקא משלם כוליה אבל תם אימא לא צריכא. ת"ש ה) מה בין תם למועד ז) שהתם משלם חצי נזק מגופו ח) ומועד משלם נזק שלם מן העלייה י) ולא קתני שהתם אינו משלם ע"פ עצמו ומועד משלם ע"פ עצמו י) תנא ושייר מאי שייר דהאי שייר ט) חצי כופר אי משום חצי כופר לאו שיורא הוא הא

רש"י

מתני׳ פתיתי. בגמ׳ מפרש אמאי לא תנא אנסתי: **ואינו משלם קנס.** דבבבא קמא (דף עה.) נפקא לן מודה בקנס פטור מאשר ירשיעון אלהים פרט למרשיע את עצמו: **המית שורי את פלוני.** והרי חייב בכופר: **הרי זה משלם ע"פ עצמו.** קסבר כופרא ממונא: **עבדו של פלוני.** והרי חייב שלשים סלע: **אינו משלם.** דקנס נינהו שאפי׳ אין יפה דינר נותן שלשים: **גמ׳ דלא פגים לה.** אין לעז של אנוסה גדול כלעז של מפותה וכיון דלאו פגם דילה הוא מהימנינן ליה למשקל מיניה בושת ופגם על פיו: **אימא לא.** נהימניה להחזיק את הלעז: **לא כל הימנו.** שיוציא עליה לעז מזה בעיר: **ניחא לה לדידה.** לשאת את הלעז כדי להשתכר הממון: **לא ניחא להו לבני משפחה.** וב"ד אין עליהם לעשות דבר להחזיק בושתם: **פלגא ניזקא.** שחייבה תורה שור תם: [**ממונא.** ומשלם ע"פ עצמו]: **לאו בחזקת שימור קיימי.** אם לא ישמרום בעלים שלא יזיקו [אינם בחזקת משתמרים מאליהם שלא יזיקו] אלא מזיקין אפי׳ ניזקא דלאו אורחיה הלכך על מרייהו רמיא לנטורינהו וזה שלא שמרו בדין הוא לישלם כולה אלא דרחמנא חס עליה ומיהו מה שמשלם בדין משלם: **כי היכי דנינטריה.** שיוסיף שמירה על שמירתו: **תנן.** בבבא קמא: **הניזק והמזיק בתשלומין.** שניהם מפסידין בדבר בפ"ד דהכי קאמר תרוייהו מטי להו בהאי פסידא דניזק מפסיד פלגא ומזיק פלגא: **היינו דשייך ניזק בתשלומין.** דמפסיד פלגא בממוניה: **דלאו דידיה שקיל.** דמה שנוטל בקנס נוטל: **בתשלומין איתיה.** בתמיה: **לא נצרכא אלא לפחת נבילה.** הא דקתני ניזק בתשלומין לאו בפלגא דקא שביק קאמר אלא בההוא פלגא ניזקא נמי דקני ליה רחמנא מפסיד כל פחת שפחתה נבילה מדמיה משעת מיתה עד שעת העמדה בדין ששמין את הנבלה כמה היה יפה השור בחייו וכמה היתה נבילה יפה בשעת מיתה ומשלם החצי אבל מה שהוזלו דמי נבילה משעת מיתה עד שעת מכירה אין המזיק משלם כלום באותו פחת ובבבא קמא (דף י:) יליף לה מקראי ואשמעינן האי תנא דפחת נבילה דניזק הוי: **תשלומי נזק מלמד שהבעלים מטפלין בנבילה.** תנא דברייתא דריש לישנא דמתניתין דתנן בבבא קמא משלם תשלומי נזק במיטב הארץ ותנא עלה בברייתא דהאי דנקט תנא דמתני׳ תשלומי נזק ולא תנא משלם את הנזק לאשמועינן אתא שהניזק נוטל את נבילתו ומטפל בה ומוכרה והמזיק משלים עליה מה שחייבתו תורה אם תם חצי ואם מועד הכל ותרתי למה ליה לרבי למיסתם במתני׳ דבעלים מטפלין בנבילה: **דקא משלם כוליה.** ודיו בהפסד זה: **מגופו.** אינו גובה אלא מגוף השור ואם אין בו כדי חצי נזקו יפסיד המותר: **מן העלייה.** מן המיטב שבנכסי מזיק דגבי תם כתיב (שמות כא) וחצו את כספו מגופו ובמועד כתיב (שם) שלם ישלם שור ואם איתא דפלגא ניזקא קנסא ליתני נמי שהתם אינו משלם על פי עצמו ומועד משלם על פי עצמו דמועד ודאי בדין משלם שהרי התרו והעידו בו לשמור שורו: **שייר חצי כופר.** לא שנה כל החילוקים שביניהם שהרי אף יש חילוק זה ביניהם שהמועד שהמית את האדם משלם כופר שלם ותם שהמית אפילו חצי כופר כדינו בניזקין לא משלם דכתיב בעל השור נקי ודרשינן (ב"ק דף מא:) נקי מחצי כופר: הא

תוספות

וליתני אנסתי. דהוי חדוש טפי דפטור אע"ג דמודה שעשה פריצות:

רבי שמעון בן יהודה אומר אף בושת ופגם אינו משלם ע"פ עצמו. פר"י דלאו קאי ר"ש בן יהודה אמתניתין דהכא הא דמשמע בריש נערה לקמן (דף מג.) דלר"ש אי דקא תבע בושת ופגם מחייב ליה קרבן שבועה היינו משום דהתם תבעו הוא תחלה ואין שייך לומר לאו כל הימנו כו׳ כדקאמר הכא ואין צריך לומר דתרי תנאי אליבא דר׳ שמעון (א) ועוד אומר רשב"א דההיא דלקמן איכא לאוקמי בבת גרים וניחא לה לדידה ולאביה דליכא למימר דלמא איכא חד במדינת הים דלא ניחא ליה ומיהו אי קאי ר׳ שמעון אמתניתין דשבועות דמייתי לקמן בריש נערה (ג"ש שם) ע"כ תרי תנאי אליבא דר׳ שמעון:

ט) **האומר** גנבתי כו׳. מוציא ש"ר ויוצא בשן ועין דלא תנא איכא למימר דאתיא בזה הכלל:

י) **זה** הכלל כל המשלם יותר על מה שהזיק כו׳. ואפילו למ"ד בפרק שור שנגח ארבעה וחמשה (ב"ק דף מ.) דכופר היינו דמי המזיק לא חשיב יותר ממה שהזיק אע"פ שפעמים שוה מזיק יותר מניזק דפדיון נפשו הוא נותן:

לא נצרכא אלא לפחת נבילה. אע"ג דלאו דידיה שקיל מ"מ כיון דזכי ליה רחמנא חצי נזק חשבינן ליה בתשלומין מה שפחתה הנבלה והכא לא שייך למימר קרנא דתורך קבירא ביה כדאמרי׳ בהמניח בסופו (ב"ק דף לד.) דהתם ודאי שלא נהרג השור שייך לומר הכי דאין לו למכור שורו בשביל כן שסבור שישביח אבל הכא מיד כשנהרג יש לו למוכרו שידוע שתפחת הנבילה ותסריח:

תנינא תשלומי נזק מלמד שהבעלים מטפלים בנבילה כו׳. הכי דייקא לה בבבא קמא (דף י:) חבתי בנזקו לא קתני אלא בתשלומי נזקו כו׳: **אי** משום חצי כופר לאו שיורא הוא וכו׳. לאו פירכא היא אלא שינויא הוא דלא תיקשי למ"ד פלגא ניזקא ממונא מאי שייר דשייר חצי כופר ומשני לא שייר כלום וחצי כופר לאו שיורא הוא וכן איכא בנזיר בפ׳ ג׳ מינים (דף לח: ושם) גבי אי משום הא לא יחל לאו שיורא הוא וכן בפרק החליל (סוכה דף נ: ושם) והוה להתם מגומגם טפי: הא

עין משפט נר מצוה

פט א מיי׳ פ"ב מהל׳ נערה הל׳ יב וע"ש מהל׳ סנהדרין הל׳ יד:

צ ב מיי׳ פ"ג מהלכות גניבה הלכה ט סמג עשין עא טור ח"מ סי׳ שמח:

צא ג מיי׳ פ"ה מהלכות סנהדרין הלכה יד סמג עשין ע:

צב ד מיי׳ פ"ב מהל׳ נזקי ממון הל׳ ח:

צג ה מיי׳ פ"ב שם הל׳ ז ופ"ה מהלכות סנהדרין הלכה ט סמג עשין לו טוש"ע ח"מ סי׳ א סעי׳ ה:

צד ו ז ח מיי׳ פ"א מהל׳ נזקי ממון הלכה ג סמג עשין סו טוש"ע ח"מ סי׳ שפט סעיף ג ד ט:

צה ט מיי׳ פ"י שם הל׳ ג סמג שם:

הגהות הב"ח

(א) תוס׳ ד"ה ר׳ שמעון וכו׳ דתרי תנאי אליבא דרבי שמעון ומיהו אי קאי ר"ש אמתניתין וכו׳ דר"ש ועוד אומר רשב"א וכו׳ דלא ניחא ליה הס"ד:

אֵינוֹ מְשַׁלֵּם עַל פִּי עַצְמוֹ – [A CONFESSED SEDUCER] ALSO DOES NOT PAY for HUMILIATION AND DEPRECIATION BY HIS OWN ADMISSION, לֹא כָּל הֵימֶנּוּ שֶׁיְּפַגֵּם בִּתּוֹ שֶׁל פְּלוֹנִי – for HE IS NOT BELIEVED TO DISCREDIT SO-AND-SO'S DAUGHTER.[17]

The Gemara queries:

אָמַר לֵיהּ רַב פָּפָּא לְאַבַּיֵי – **Rav Pappa said to Abaye:** נִיחָא לָהּ לְדִידָהּ – If **it is acceptable to [the girl]** to suffer the damage to her reputation in order to profit by receiving the payments for humiliation and depreciation, מַאי – **what** is the law according to R' Shimon? Would he still rule that the court does not accept the seducer's admission?

The Gemara answers:

דִּלְמָא לֹא נִיחָא לֵיהּ לְאָבִיהָ – Yes, he would, for **perhaps it is not acceptable to her father.**[18]

The Gemara asks further:

נִיחָא לֵיהּ לְאָבִיהָ – But if **it is acceptable to her father** to bear the embarrassment in order to profit, מַאי – **what** is the law according to R' Shimon?

The Gemara answers:

דִּלְמָא לֹא נִיחָא לְהוּ לִבְנֵי מִשְׁפָּחָה – Even so, the court does not accept the admission, for **perhaps it is not acceptable to the members of** her **family.**[19]

The Gemara persists:

נִיחָא לְהוּ לִבְנֵי מִשְׁפָּחָה – But if **it is acceptable to the members of the family** to bear the embarrassment so that there will be profit, מַאי – **what** is the law according to R' Shimon?

The Gemara answers:

אִי אֶפְשָׁר דְּלֵיכָּא חַד בִּמְדִינַת הַיָּם דְּלֹא נִיחָא לֵיהּ – **It is impossible that there is not one** family member[20] **in a faraway land for whom it is not acceptable.**

The second case of the Mishnah:

הָאוֹמֵר גָּנַבְתִּי מְשַׁלֵּם אֶת הַקֶּרֶן וכו׳ – ONE WHO SAYS, "I STOLE," PAYS THE PRINCIPLE etc.

The Gemara cites an Amoraic dispute in which our Mishnah is brought as a proof:

אִיתְּמַר – **It was stated:** פַּלְגָא נִיזְקָא – Regarding the nature of the **half-damages** that are paid when a *tam* ox inflicts the injury of *keren*[21] – רַב פָּפָּא אָמַר – **Rav Pappa said** פַּלְגָא נִיזְקָא מָמוֹנָא – that the **half-damages** are a **compensation** payment,[22] רַב הוּנָא בְּרֵיהּ דְּרַב יְהוֹשֻׁעַ אָמַר – whereas **Rav Huna the son of Rav Yehoshua said** פַּלְגָא נִיזְקָא קְנָסָא – that the **half-damages** are a **punitive** payment.[23]

The Gemara explains the basis of the dispute:

רַב פָּפָּא אָמַר פַּלְגָא נִיזְקָא מָמוֹנָא – **Rav Pappa said** that the **half-damages** for *keren* are **a compensation** payment because קָסָבַר סְתָם שְׁוָורִים לָאו בְּחֶזְקַת שִׁימּוּר קַיְימֵי – **he holds** that **ordinary oxen are not in a guarded state** with respect to *keren*-type damages.[24] וּבְדִין הוּא דִּמְשַׁלֵּם כּוּלֵּיהּ – **By rights,** therefore, **[the ox's owner] should pay** for **all [the damage],**[25] וְרַחֲמָנָא הוּא דְּחָיֵיס עִלָּוֵיהּ – **but the Merciful One took pity on him** and reduced his liability by half דְּאַכַּתִּי לֹא אִיַּיעַד תּוֹרָא – **because his ox has not yet been warned.**[26] Accordingly, the half that he does pay is considered compensation for the damage done by his ox. רַב הוּנָא בְּרֵיהּ דְּרַב יְהוֹשֻׁעַ אָמַר פַּלְגָא נִיזְקָא קְנָסָא – And **Rav Huna the son of Rav Yehoshua said** that the **half-damages** for *keren* are **a punitive** payment because קָסָבַר סְתָם שְׁוָורִים בְּחֶזְקַת שִׁימּוּר קַיְימֵי – **he holds** that **ordinary oxen are in a guarded state.**[27] וּבְדִין הוּא דְּלֹא לִישַׁלֵּם כְּלָל – **By rights,** therefore, **[the ox's owner] should not have to pay at all,** וְרַחֲמָנָא הוּא דִּקְנָסֵיהּ – **but the Merciful One penalized him,** by requiring him to pay half the damage, כִּי הֵיכִי דְּנִינְטְרֵיהּ לְתוֹרֵיהּ – **in order that he should guard his ox** even further.[28] Thus, the half of the damages that he pays is a punitive payment.

The Gemara now cites a series of Mishnahs as proof that half-damages are compensation, not a penalty, and provides a mnemonic for the ensuing discussion:

סִימָן: הִיזִּיק מַה וְהֵמִית כְּלָל – **A mnemonic: Damage, what, and he killed, rule.**[29]

NOTES

17. I.e. we deny him a judicial venue from which to circulate an evil report in the town that she engages in immoral activities (*Rashi*). [*Shitah Mekubetzes* writes that R' Shimon ben Yehudah argues only in the case of seduction.]

18. I.e. perhaps the girl's father is not willing to have his family's name tarnished in order to receive the payments. Hence, the court does not accept the seducer's admission even though the girl herself wishes to profit financially; see following note.

19. And it is improper for the court to act in a way that would sustain their embarrassment (*Rashi*).

20. See *Shitah Mekubetzes.*

21. Literally: horn. This refers to damage that an animal inflicts intentionally with its horn – i.e. by goring – and is mentioned in *Exodus* 21:35-36. The essential characteristics of *keren* are that it is an abnormal act for most animals and that the animal's intent was to inflict damage. Hence, included in this category is damage that an animal inflicts through pushing, biting, squatting and kicking; see *Bava Kamma* 2b and Mishnah ibid. 15b.

The Torah (ibid.) differentiates in the case of *keren* between a *tam* ox and a *muad* ox. The *tam* [literally: innocent or tame], whose destructive act can be considered an aberration, is liable only for חֲצִי נֶזֶק, *half-damages.* A *muad* [literally: warned], which performs a specific destructive act three times and whose owner is put on notice that his animal has this destructive tendency (see *Bava Kamma* 23b-24b), is liable to pay נֶזֶק שָׁלֵם, *full damages.*

Our Gemara discusses the nature of the unusual payment of *half-damages* prescribed for a *tam.*

22. [I.e. they are a proper payment of damages, not a penalty. Accordingly,] the ox's owner pays the half-damages by his own admission (*Rashi*).

23. And so the ox's owner does not pay them by his own admission.

24. I.e. an ox left to itself cannot be considered guarded against doing *keren* damage. Although it is somewhat of an aberration for a *tam* to inflict damage through *keren,* it cannot be presumed that an ordinary ox is so docile that it will not inflict *keren* damage when left on its own. Hence, its owner has a responsibility to see to it that his ox is guarded from inflicting *keren* damage (*Rashi*).

25. Since he was negligent in not guarding his ox (*Rashi*).

26. [For although the *keren* damage was caused by the owner's negligence, since the animal has a tendency to injure in this manner] this damage is nevertheless somewhat of an aberration and is less common than other forms of damage, such as *shein* and *regel* (see *Shitah Mekubetzes, Bava Kamma* 15a ד״ה פלגא נזקא ממונא; see also *Shitah Mekubetzes* ibid. 15b ד״ה וריב״א אומר and ד״ה כתוב בתוספות).

27. [I.e. since it is an aberration for an ox to gore or do malicious damage, an ox left on its own can be presumed to be docile and thus is considered "guarded" by its own nature against inflicting *keren* damage. Hence, the owner has no obligation to guard it from doing such damage, and should therefore not be held accountable for his failure to do so.]

28. I.e. the Torah imposed a punitive payment of *half-damages* to spur the owner to guard the ox even further. Since it is not totally uncommon for an ordinary ox to inflict *keren* damage, the Torah sees to it that – in addition to its natural "guard" – the owner should safeguard the ox even further (see *Rashi*).

29. The mnemonic is composed of the first words of each of the four Tannaic statements that the Gemara presently cites. [The first word (הִיזִּיק, *damage*) is a paraphrase of the first two words of the first Tannaic statement, which begins with הַנִּיזָּק וְהַמַּזִּיק, *the damaged party and the damager.*]

מתני׳ [א]האומר פתיתי את בתו של פלוני משלם בושת ופגם על פי עצמו ואין משלם קנס [ב]האומר גנבתי [א]משלם את הקרן על פי עצמו ואין משלם תשלומי כפל ותשלומי ארבעה וחמשה [ג]המית שורי את פלוני או שורו של פלוני הרי זה משלם על פי עצמו המית שורי עבדו של פלוני אין משלם ע״פ עצמו [ד]זה הכלל כל המשלם יתר על מה שהזיק אינו משלם ע״פ עצמו: **גמ׳** וליתני אנסתי לא מבעיא קאמר לא מבעיא אנסתי דלא קא פגים לה דמשלם בושת ופגם על פי עצמו אבל פתיתי דקא פגים לה אימא לא משלם על פי עצמו קא משמע לן מתניתין דלא כי האי תנא דתניא רבי שמעון בן יהודה אומר משום ר׳ שמעון אף בושת ופגם אינו משלם ע״פ עצמו לא כל הימנו שיפגום בתו של פלוני אמר ליה רב פפא לאביי ניחא לה לדידה מאי דלמא לא ניחא ליה לאביה ניחא ליה לאביה מאי דלמא לא ניחא להו לבני משפחה ניחא להו לבני משפחה מאי אי אפשר דליכא חד במדינת הים דלא ניחא ליה: האומר גנבתי משלם את הקרן וכו׳: איתמר פלגא ניזקא [ה]רב פפא אמר פלגא ניזקא ממונא רב הונא בריה דרב יהושע אמר [ו]פלגא ניזקא קנסא רב פפא אמר פלגא ניזקא ממונא קסבר סתם שוורים לאו בחזקת שימור קיימי ובדין הוא דמשלם כוליה ורחמנא הוא דחייס עלויה דאכתי לא איעד תורא רב הונא בריה דרב יהושע אמר פלגא ניזקא קנסא קסבר סתם שוורים בחזקת שימור קיימי ובדין הוא דלא לישלם כלל ורחמנא הוא דקנסיה כי היכי דניזדהרו לתוריה: סימן הזיק המית כלל: תנן [ז]הניזק והמזיק בתשלומין בשלמא למאן דאמר פלגא ניזקא ממונא היינו דשייך ניזק בתשלומין אלא למ״ד פלגא ניזקא קנסא השתא דלאו דידיה קא שקיל בתשלומין איתיה לא נצרכא אלא לפחת נבילה פחת נבילה תנינא תשלומי נזק [ח]מלמד שהבעלים מטפלין בנבילה חדא בתם וחדא במועד וצריכא דאי אשמועינן תם משום דאכתי לא איעד אבל מועד דאיעד אימא לא ואי אשמועינן מועד משום דקא משלם כוליה אבל תם אימא לא צריכא ת״ש [ט]מה בין תם למועד [י]שהתם משלם חצי נזק מגופו [ח]ומועד משלם נזק שלם מן העלייה [י]ולא קתני שהתם אינו משלם ע״פ עצמו ומועד משלם ע״פ עצמו [י]תנא ושייר מאי שייר דהאי שייר [ט]חצי כופר אי משום חצי כופר לאו שיורא הוא הא

רש״י

מתני׳ פתיתי. בגמ׳ מפרש אמאי לא תנא אנסתי: **ואינו משלם קנס.** בבבא קמא נפקא לן מודה בקנס פטור מאשר ירשיעון אלהים פרט למרשיע את עצמו: **המית שורי את פלוני.** והרי חייב בכופר: **הרי זה משלם ע״פ עצמו.** קסבר כופרא ממונא: **עבדו של פלוני.** והרי חייב שלשים סלע: **אינו משלם.** דקנס נינהו שאפי׳ אין יפה דינר נותן שלשים: **גמ׳ דלא פגים לה.** אין לעז של אנוסה גדול כלעז של מפותה וכיון דלאו פגם דילה הוא מהימנינן ליה למשקל מיניה בושת ופגם על פיו: **אימא לא.** נהימניה להחזיק את הלעז: **לא כל הימנו.** שיוציא עליה לעז מזנה בעיר: **ניחא לה לדידה.** לשאת את הלעז כדי להשתכר הממון: **לא ניחא להו לבני משפחה.** וב״ד אין עליהם לעשות דבר להחזיק בושתם: **פלגא ניזקא.** שחייבה תורה שור תם: [**ממונא.** ומשלם ע״פ עצמו]: **לאו בחזקת שימור קיימי.** אם לא ישמרום בעלים שלא יזיקו [אינם בחזקת משתמרים מאליהם שלא יזיקו] אלא מזיקין אפי׳ ניזקא דלאו אורחיה הלכך על מריהו רמיא לנטורינהו וזה שלא שמרו בדין הוא לישלם כולה אלא דרחמנא חס עליה ומיהו מה שמשלם בדין משלם: **כי היכי דנינטריה.** שיוסיף שמירה על שמירתו: **תנן.** בבבא קמא: **הניזק והמזיק בתשלומין.** שניהם מפסידין בדבר ס״ד דהכי קאמר תרוייהו מטי להו בהאי פסידא דניזק מפסיד פלגא ומזיק פלגא: **היינו דשייך ניזק בתשלומין.** דמפסיד פלגא בממוניה: **דלאו דידיה שקיל.** דמה שנוטל בתורת קנס נוטל: **בתשלומין איתיה.** בתמיה: **לא נצרכא אלא לפחת נבילה.** הא דקתני ניזק בתשלומין לאו בפלגא דקא שביק קאמר אלא בההוא פלגא דנוטל נמי דקני ליה רחמנא מפסיד כל פחת שפחתה נבילה מדמיה משעת מיתה עד שעת העמדה בדין שמין את הנבלה כמה היה יפה השור בחייו וכמה היתה נבילה יפה בשעת מיתה ומשלם החצי אבל מה שהוזלו דמי נבילה משעת מיתה עד שעת מכירה אין המזיק משלם כלום באותו פחת ובבבא קמא (דף י:) יליף לה מקראי ואשמעינן האי תנא דפחת נבילה דניזק הוי: **תשלומי נזק מלמד שהבעלים מטפלים בנבילה.** תנא דברייתא דריש לישנא דמתניתין דתנן בבבא קמא משלם תשלומי נזק במיטב הארץ ותנא עלה בברייתא דהאי דנקט תנא דמתני׳ תשלומי נזק ולא תנא משלם את הנזק לאשמועינן אתא שהניזק נוטל את נבילתו ומטפל בה ומוכרה והמזיק משלים עליה מה שחייבתו תורה אם תם חצי ואם מועד הכל ותרתי למה ליה לרבי למיתנא במתני׳ דבעלים מטפלין בנבילה: **דקא משלם כוליה.** ודיו בהפסד זה: **מגופו.** אינו גובה אלא מגוף השור ואם אין בו כדי חצי נזקו יפסיד המותר: **מן העלייה.** מן המיטב שבנכסי מזיק דגבי תם כתיב (שמות כא) וחצו את כספו מגופו ובמועד כתיב (שם) שלם ישלם שור ואם איתא דפלגא ניזקא קנסא ליתני נמי שהתם אינו משלם על פי עצמו ומועד משלם על פי עצמו דלמועד ודאי בדין משלם שהרי התרו והעידו בו לשמור שורו: **שייר חצי כופר.** לא שנה כל החילוקים שביניהם שהרי אף יש חילוק זה ביניהם שהמועד שהמית את האדם משלם כופר שלם ותם שהמית אפילו חצי כופר כדינו בניזקין לא משלם דכתיב בעל השור נקי ודרשינן (ב״ק דף מא:) נקי מחצי כופר: הא

תוספות

וליתני אנסתי. דהוי חדוש טפי דפטור אע״ג דמודה שעשה פריצות: **רבי שמעון בן יהודה אומר אף בושת ופגם** אינו משלם ע״פ עצמו. אור״י דלאו קאי ר״ש בן יהודה אמתניתין דהכא הא דמשמע בריש נערה לקמן (דף מב.) דלר״ש אי דקא תבע בושת ופגם מחייב ליה קרבן שבועה היינו משום דהתם תבעו האב תחלה ואין שייך לומר לאו כל הימנו כו׳ כדקאמר הכא ואין צריך לומר דתרי תנאי אליבא דר׳ שמעון (א) ועוד אומר רשב״א דההיא דלקמן איכא לאוקמי בבת גרים וניחא לה לדידה ולאביה דליכא למימר דלמא איכא חד במדינת הים דלא ניחא ליה ומיהו אי קאי ר׳ שמעון אמתניתין דשבועות דמייתי לקמן בריש נערה (ג״ז שם) ע״כ תרי תנאי אליבא דר׳ שמעון:

[ט]**האומר** גנבתי כו׳. מוליא ש״ר ויולא בשן ועין דלא תנא איכא למימר דאתיא בזה הכלל:

[י]**זה** הכלל כל המשלם יותר על מה שהזיק כו׳. ואפילו למ״ד בפרק שור שנגח ארבעה וחמשה (ב״ק דף מ.) דכופר היינו דמי המזיק לא חשיב יותר ממה שהזיק אע״פ שפעמים שוה מזיק יותר מניזק דפדיון נפשו הוא נותן:

לא נצרכא אלא לפחת נבילה. אע״ג דלאו דידיה שקיל מ״מ כיון דזכי ליה רחמנא חצי נזק חשבינן ליה בתשלומין מה שפחתה הנבלה והכא לא שייך למימר קרנא דתורך קבירא ביה כדאמרי׳ בהמניח בסופו (ב״ק דף לד.) דהתם ודאי שלא נהרג השור שייך לומר הכי דאין לו למכור שורו בשביל כן שסבור שישביח אבל הכא מיד כשנהרג יש לו למוכרו שידוע שתפחת הנבילה ותסריח:

תנינא תשלומי נזק מלמד שהבעלים מטפלים בנבילה כו׳. הכי דייקא לה בבבא קמא (דף י:) חבתי בנזקו לא קתני אלא בתשלומי נזקו כו׳: **אי** משום חצי כופר לאו שיורא הוא וכו׳. לאו פירכא היא אלא שינויא הוא דלא תיקשי למ״ד פלגא ניזקא ממונא מאי שייר דשייר חצי כופר ומשני לא שייר כלום וחצי כופר לאו שיורא הוא וכן איכא בנזיר בפ׳ ג׳ מינים (דף לט: ושם) גבי אי משום לא יחל לאו שיורא הוא וכן בפרק החליל (סוכה דף נ: ושם) וההוא דהתם מגומגם טפי: הא

עין משפט נר מצוה

פט א מיי׳ פ״ב מהל׳ נערה הל׳ יב ופ״ה מהל׳ סנהדרין הל׳ יד:
צ ב מיי׳ פ״ג מהלכות גניבה הלכה ט סמג עשין עא טוש״ע ח״מ סי׳ שמח:
צא ג מיי׳ פ״ה מהלכות סנהדרין הלכה יד סמג עשין ע:
צב ד מיי׳ פ״ב מהל׳ נזקי ממון הל׳ ח:
צג ה מיי׳ פ״ב שם הל׳ ז ופ״ה מהלכות סנהדרין הלכה טו סמג עשין לו טוש״ע ח״מ סי׳ ת סעי׳ א:
צד ו ז ח מיי׳ פ״א מהל׳ נזקי ממון הלכה ג סמג עשין סו טוש״ע ח״מ סי׳ שפט סעיף ג ג ד ט:
צה ט מיי׳ פ״י שם הל׳ ג סמג שם:

מסורת הש״ס

א) פ״ק מכתבתי ומכורתי, ב) ב״ק טו. מג. ג) שם טו. [ושם כל הסוגיא ומכר עוד שבועות לב.], ד) שם יד:, ה) שם טו., ו) [סוטה נ.], ז) שם מא., ח) [דף עה.], ט) [שייך לעיל במתני׳], י) [ג״ז שייך לעיל].

הגהות הב״ח

(א) תוס׳ ד״ה ר׳ שמעון וכו׳ דתרי תנאי אליבא דרבי שמעון ומיהו אי קאי ר״ש אמתניתין וכו׳ ועוד אומר רשב״א וכו׳ דלא ניחא ליה הס״ד:

תוספות רי״ד

מתני׳ האומר פתיתי את בתו של פלוני משלם בושת ופגם ע״פ עצמו ואינו משלם קנס. האומר גנבתי משלם את הקרן ע״פ עצמו ואינו משלם לא תשלומי כפל ולא ד׳ וה׳. המית שורי את פלוני או שורו של פלוני ה״ז משלם על פי עצמו. המית שורי עבדו של פלוני אינו משלם ע״פ עצמו. זה הכלל כל המשלם יתר ממה שהזיק אינו משלם ע״פ עצמו: וליתני אנסתי. לא מבעיא קאמר לא מבעיא אנסתי דלא פגים לה אלא אפילו פתיתי דפגים לה דאימא לא משלם בושת ופגם ע״פ עצמו קמ״ל: ומתני׳ דלא כי האי תנא דתניא ר״ש בן יהודה אומר משום (רב הונא) [ר״ש] אף בושת ופגם אינו משלם ע״פ עצמו לא כל הימנו שיפגום בתו של פלוני. ואינו משלם קנס ע״פ עצמו כדנפקא לן מאשר ירשיעון אלהים פרט למרשיע את עצמו: ואי קשיא. הכא תנן דבושת הוי ממון ומשלם ע״פ עצמו ובריש פרק המניח אמרי׳ חסדא חסדא קנסא קמגבית בבבל וקרי התם לבושת קנס. תשובה לעולם בושת ממונא הוי לשלם ע״פ עצמו שאין בו שום יתירות אלא שמין לפי המבייש והמתבייש והתם קרי ליה קנסא לומר שאין גובין אותו בבבל דכל מידי דאית ביה חסרון כיס גבינן ליה בבבל אבל בושת דלית ביה חסרון כיס לא גבי׳ לי׳ בבבל כדאמרינן בפרק החובל: המית שורי את פלוני משלם ע״פ עצמו פי׳ דכופרא לאו קנסא הוא דכפי שוי׳ של ניזק משלם ואף למ״ד כפי שויה של מזיק כופרא ממונא הוי ומשלם ע״פ עצמו: המית שורי את עבדו וכו׳. בפרק שור שנגח ד׳ וה׳ מוכיח שאפילו שויה של עבד אינו משלם ע״פ עצמו דכל ל׳ כסף הוי קנסא: זה הכלל וכו׳. איתמר פלגא נזקא שחייבה תורה לשור תם. ר״פ אמר ממונא. פי׳ ומשלם ע״פ עצמו. רב הונא בריה דרב יהושע אמר פלגא נזקא קנסא רב פפא אמר ממונא סתם שוורים לאו בחזקת שימור קיימי. פי׳ אם לא ישמרו בעלים שלא יזיקו אינן בחזקת משתמר מאליהן שלא יזיקו אלא מזיקין אפילו נזקא דלאו אורחיה הלכך על מרייהו רמיא לנטרינהו וזה שלא שמרו בדין הוא דלשלם כוליה. ורחמנא הוא דחס עליה דאכתי לא אייעד תורא. פי׳ ואיהו מה שמשלם בדין משלם. ורב הונא בריה דרב יהושע אמר פלגא נזקא קנסא קסבר סתם שוורים בחזקת שימור קיימי ובדין הוא דלא לשלם כלל ורחמנא הוא דקנסיה כי היכי דנינטרינהו לתורי׳. פי׳ שיוסיף

ליקוטי רש״י

כל מקום שיש מכר. יש לאביה בה זכיה למוכרה בשפחות [לעיל כט.]. כל זמן שהבת קטנה זכאי למוכרה. אין קנס. אם נאנסה או נתפתתה אין לאביה חמשים כסף דנערה כתיב (דברים כב) ונתן האיש השוכב עמה לאבי הנערה חמשים כסף. וכל מקום שיש קנס. דהיינו בתולה נערה. אין מכר. ... אבל חכמים אומרים וכו׳ יש לה קנס. ... כל מקום שנאמר נער בלא ה״א אפילו קטנה במשמע [חולין כו.]. מבת ג׳ שנים ויום אחד. שהיא ראויה לביאה [לעיל שם]. מכר לא. בתמיה והלא קטנה היא עד שתביא שתי שערות [חולין כו:]. אף קנס במקום מכר. ... נערה בלא דיבר הכתוב. ... ואם אמת היה הדבר. ... אל פתח בית אביה. ... שבמשמע שקטנה חסר לומר שאף הקטנה במשמע והכי יליף כאן נערה כאן שאי אפשר בקטנה כתיב מלא הא למדת שכל מקום שנכתב חסר אף הקטנה במשמע כגון באונס ומפתה [לקמן מ:]. לאו גדולים שגדלתם, כלומר מבית זה יצאת הנבלה שבו זינתה [לקמן מה.]. [ע״כ שייך לדף מ:] **פלגא נזקא ממונא.** דקסבר סתם שוורים נגחנים הם ומדינא כולהו בעי לשלומי דהוה ליה למינטריה ורחמנא הוא דחס עליה [סנהדרין ג.]. דין הוא שישלמנו ואינו קנס ונפקא מינה דאי מודה מקמי דאתו סהדי לא מיפטר [ב״ק טו.]. **פלגא נזקא קנסא.** דסתם שוורים אינם נוגחים ולא היה לבעלים לשמרו כל זמן שלא הועד ולא בעי לשלומי מידי אלא קנסא הוא דקנסיה רחמנא כדי שירבה בשמירת שוורים [סנהדרין שם]. **לאו בחזקת שימור קיימי.** שרגילין בנגיחה וצריכין שמירה. **הניזק והמזיק בתשלומין.** משמע דשניהן מפסידי ממון בתשלומין שזה משלם מחצה וזה מפסיד מחצה. **היינו דשייך ניזק בתשלומין.** כלומר מפסיד ממה שהיה ראוי לו דבעי למשקל כוליה שזה פשע בשורו שלא שמרו. **בתשלומין איתיה.** בתמיה דמשמע שמפסיד מדינו. **לפחת נבילה.** דכל פחת נבילה דניזק הוא והיינו דשייך ניזק בתשלומין שאפילו אותו קנס שזיכתה לו תורה אינו נוטל כולו. **פחת נבילה תנינא.** חבתי בתשלומי נזקו וקתני עלה תשלומי נזק מלמד שהבעלים מטפלים בנבילה ואמרינן לא נצרכא אלא לפחת נבילה. **מגופו.** ואם אינו שוה חצי נזק מפסיד הניזק כדכתיב (שמות כא) וחצו את כספו. **מן העלייה.** אם אינו שוה כנגד כל הנזק נוטל נכסים מיטב [ב״ק שם]. ואפי׳ אין הנוגח שוה שיעור הנזק דבמועד כתיב (שמות כא) ישלם שור תחת השור ולא כתיב ביה דמגוף הנוגח יפרע [שם טז:]. **ולא קתני שהתם וכו׳.** אם איתא, דקנסא. ליתני נמי הא, שחצי נזקו של תם קנס ואינו משלם ע״פ עצמו ומועד הוי ממון ומשלם ע״פ עצמו [שם טו.]. **תנא ושייר.** לא חשבינהו לכולהו [סוטה טז.]. **מאי שייר דהאי שייר.** דלאו אורחא דתנא למתני כל מילי ולשיורי חדא [תענית יג:]. **חצי כופר.** מועד שהמית את האדם משלם כופר ליורשים ותם אפילו חצי כופר לא משלם [ב״ק שם]. **מת האב.** משעמד בדין ומת עד שלא הספיק לגבות הרי הוא של אחיה ולא שלה. **רבי שמעון אומר אם לא הספיקה לגבות.** כי היכי דפליג במתניתין בלא הספיקה לגבות עד שמת האב הכי נמי פליג בלא הספיקה לגבות עד שבגרה דקאמר ת״ק הרי הן של אב ולרבי שמעון הרי הוא של עצמה [לקמן מב:].

Mishnah הָאוֹמֵר פִּתִּיתִי אֶת בִּתּוֹ שֶׁל פְּלוֹנִי – One who says, **"I seduced**[1] **So-and-so's daughter,"** מְשַׁלֵּם בּוֹשֶׁת וּפְגָם עַל פִּי עַצְמוֹ – **pays** for **humiliation and depreciation by his own admission,** וְאֵין מְשַׁלֵּם קְנָס – **but does not pay** the **fine.**[2] הָאוֹמֵר גָּנַבְתִּי – **One who says, "I stole,"** מְשַׁלֵּם אֶת הַקֶּרֶן עַל פִּי עַצְמוֹ – **pays the principle by his own admission,**[3] וְאֵין מְשַׁלֵּם תַּשְׁלוּמֵי כֶּפֶל וְתַשְׁלוּמֵי אַרְבָּעָה וַחֲמִשָּׁה – **but does not pay the double payment**[4] **or the fourfold or fivefold payments.**[5] הֵמִית שׁוֹרִי אֶת פְּלוֹנִי – One who says, **"My ox killed So-and-so,"**[6] אוֹ שׁוֹרוֹ שֶׁל פְּלוֹנִי – **or** "My ox killed **So-and-so's ox,"**[7] הֲרֵי זֶה מְשַׁלֵּם עַל פִּי עַצְמוֹ – **this** person **pays by his own admission.**[8] הֵמִית שׁוֹרִי עַבְדּוֹ שֶׁל פְּלוֹנִי – One who says, **"My ox killed So-and-so's** Canaanite **slave,"**[9] אֵין מְשַׁלֵּם עַל פִּי עַצְמוֹ – **does not pay by his own admission.**[10] זֶה הַכְּלָל – **This is the general rule:** כָּל הַמְשַׁלֵּם יָתֵר עַל מַה שֶּׁהִזִּיק – **Whoever pays more than what he damaged** אֵינוֹ מְשַׁלֵּם עַל פִּי עַצְמוֹ – **does not pay by his own admission.**[11]

Gemara The Gemara asks regarding the first ruling of the Mishnah:

וְלִיתְנֵי אֲנַסְתִּי – **But let [the Tanna] teach** the case of one who says, **"I violated** the daughter of So-and-so"?[12]

The Gemara answers:

לֹא מִבַּעְיָא קָאָמַר – **[The Mishnah] states** its ruling in the **"it is unnecessary"** format,[13] and essentially says: לֹא מִבַּעְיָא אֲנַסְתִּי – **It is unnecessary** to teach with regard to one who says, **"I violated** So-and-so's daughter" – דְּלֹא קָא פָּגִים לָהּ – **where** with his confession **he does not** seriously **discredit [the girl]** – דִּמְשַׁלֵּם בּוֹשֶׁת וּפְגָם עַל פִּי עַצְמוֹ – **that he pays** for **humiliation and depreciation by his own admission.**[14] אֲבָל פִּתִּיתִי – **But** in the case of one who says, **"I seduced** So-and-so's daughter" – דְּקָא פָּגִים לָהּ – **where** with his confession **he does** seriously **discredit her**[15] – אֵימָא לֹא מְשַׁלֵּם עַל פִּי עַצְמוֹ – **I might say** that **he does not pay** for humiliation and depreciation **by his own admission.**[16] קָא מַשְׁמַע לָן – **[The Mishnah]** therefore **informs us** that even in the case of seduction the court extracts payment for humiliation and depreciation on the basis of a confession.

The Gemara notes that our Mishnah's ruling in this matter is not unanimous:

מַתְנִיתִין דְּלֹא כִּי הַאי תַּנָּא – **Our Mishnah is not in accordance with** the opinion of **this Tanna:** דְּתַנְיָא – **For it was taught in a Baraisa:** רַבִּי שִׁמְעוֹן בֶּן יְהוּדָה אוֹמֵר מִשּׁוּם רַבִּי שִׁמְעוֹן – **R' SHIMON BEN YEHUDAH SAYS IN THE NAME OF R' SHIMON:** אַף בּוֹשֶׁת וּפְגָם

NOTES

1. The Gemara will explain why the Mishnah does not state this law with regard to one who confesses to committing violation (*Rashi*).

2. [This and the succeeding rulings in the Mishnah are based on the principle that one pays *compensatory damages* (מָמוֹן) on his own admission but does not pay *punitive damages* (קְנָס, *fines*) on his own admission. One incurs punitive damages (such as the fifty-*shekel* fine for violation and seduction; the double payment (כֶּפֶל) imposed on a thief; the fourfold payment imposed on a thief who steals a sheep and slaughters or sells it; the fivefold payment imposed on a thief who steals an ox and slaughters or sells it; and the thirty-*shekel* payment imposed on the owner of a *muad* ox that kills a slave) only if his crime is established through the testimony of witnesses, not if the perpetrator confesses.] This principle is derived by the Gemara (see *Bava Kamma* 64b and 75a) from the verse that states regarding the double-payment fine imposed on a thief (*Exodus* 22:8): *Whomever the judges find guilty shall pay double to his fellow.* The first part of the phrase implies that the double payment is levied when *the court* finds the accused party guilty [on the basis of witnesses' testimony], not when he declares himself guilty (*Rashi*).

Hence, one who admits to seducing a woman pays for her humiliation and depreciation, since these are מָמוֹן, *compensatory damages.* However, he does not make the fifty-*shekel* payment; since that is a fine, it is not incurred on account of his own admission.

[See *Shitah Mekubetzes* regarding why the Mishnah mentions some fines and leaves out others.]

3. For remitting the principle is a compensatory payment, which is imposed even by one's admission.

4. Which is punitive in nature.

5. If he confesses to having stolen, and slaughtered or sold, a sheep or an ox, respectively (see above, note 2). Some texts of the Mishnah actually read: הָאוֹמֵר גָּנַבְתִּי וְטָבַחְתִּי וּמָכַרְתִּי – *One who says, "I stole and I slaughtered," or "I sold"* (see marginal note; cf. *Rashash*).

6. He confesses that his ox killed a Jew and that he is obliged to pay כֹּפֶר [*kofer,* ransom] to redeem himself from מִיתָה בִּידֵי שָׁמַיִם (*death at the hands of Heaven*) for his neglect, as prescribed in *Exodus* 21:28-31 (see *Rashi*).

7. And therefore I am liable to make restitution for the ox; see *Exodus* ibid. v. 36.

8. Our Tanna holds that *kofer* is a compensatory payment [and so the ox's owner pays by his own admission] (*Rashi*).

[The Gemara elsewhere (*Bava Kamma* 40a and *Makkos* 2b) debates whether the *kofer* payment is מָמוֹנָא, *a compensatory payment,* or כַּפָּרָה, *an atonement payment.* By noting that our Tanna holds that *kofer* is a compensatory payment, *Rashi* seemingly suggests that the other opinion (that *kofer* is an atonement payment) would consider *kofer* a punitive penalty, which one does not pay on his own admission. *Tos. R' Akiva Eiger* (§46) takes issue with *Rashi's* comment on two counts: (a) The Gemara (*Bava Kamma* 41b) clearly states that even according to the opinion that *kofer* is an atonement payment, one *does* pay *kofer* by his own admission. (b) The Gemara (in *Bava Kamma* 40a and *Makkos* 2b) concludes that all agree that *kofer* is, in fact, an atonement payment. How, then, can *Rashi* say that our Tanna holds that *kofer* is compensatory, and how can our Mishnah rule that one pays *kofer* by his own admission if, as *Rashi* seemingly suggests, the one who holds that *kofer* is an atonement payment maintains that one *does not* pay it by his own admission? *Rashash* suggests that *Rashi's* comment here is not in reference to the aforementioned debate regarding whether *kofer* is a compensatory or an atonement payment. Rather, *Rashi* simply means to say that *kofer* is *compensatory* in nature as opposed to *punitive* in nature [even though it is, in fact, an atonement payment] (see *Rashi* to *Bava Kamma* 43b ד״ה והיכי דמי). Cf. *Shitah Mekubetzes* and *Haflaah* for alternative explanations of *Rashi.*]

9. And therefore I am liable to the thirty-*shekel* payment prescribed by *Exodus* 21:32 (*Rashi*).

10. Since an ox's owner pays the thirty *shekels* even when the slave was worth not even a *dinar* (a quarter of a *shekel*), this payment is a fine; hence, one's own admission does not obligate him to remit it (*Rashi*).

11. I.e. wherever the prescribed restitution does not equal the actual damage, that payment is a fine and it is not paid by one's own admission. See Gemara below, 41b.

12. Why does the Mishnah teach these laws of payment only in the case of seduction? Let it teach them also vis-a-vis one who confesses to committing violation (*Ritva,* and *Rashi* to the Mishnah, as explained by *Shitah Mekubetzes;* cf. *Tosafos*).

13. I.e. the Mishnah teaches the more novel ruling (seduction) for emphasis, assuming that the less novel ruling (violation) will be understood.

14. One who admits to having violated does not defame his victim to the extent that one who admits to having seduced her does [since he avers that she participated unwillingly in the illicit act]. Hence, the court readily accepts a violator's admission to extract from him the payments for humiliation and depreciation (*Rashi*), and it was unnecessary for the Mishnah to teach this.

15. By attesting that she participated willingly in the illicit act, he greatly damages her reputation.

16. I.e. the court should not believe him and compel him to pay, for by doing so they are upholding the slander against her (*Rashi*).

The Gemara now explains the dispute between R' Meir and the Rabbis regarding whether minors are entitled to the fines for violation and seduction:

אָמַר רַב חִסְדָּא – Rav Chisda said: **מַאי טַעְמָא דְּרַבִּי מֵאִיר – What is R' Meir's reason** for ruling that a minor is not entitled to the fines?[42] **אָמַר קְרָא ,,וְלוֹ־תִהְיֶה לְאִשָּׁה" – For the verse** in the violation passage **states:**[43] ***and she shall become for him a wife.*** **בִּבְהַוָיָה עַצְמָהּ הַכָּתוּב מְדַבֵּר – Scripture** perforce **speaks of** a woman **who can herself effect becoming** his wife.[44]

The Rabbis' rationale:

וְרַבָּנַן – And the Rabbis, why do they hold that the fines are levied even for a minor? **אָמַר רֵישׁ לָקִישׁ – Reish Lakish said:** **אָמַר קְרָא ,,(נערה) [נַעֲרָ]"[45] – The verse states:** ***naara,*** without the final ה.[46] **אֲפִילּוּ קְטַנָּה בְּמַשְׁמַע** – This unusual spelling indicates that **even a minor is within the meaning** of the verse.[47]

The Gemara relates:

שְׁמָעָהּ רַב פָּפָּא בְּרֵיהּ דְּרַב חָנָן מִבֵּי כְּלוֹחִית – Rav Pappa the son of Rav Chanan from Bei Kelochis heard [Reish Lakish's explanation] of the Rabbis' ruling, **אָזַל אֲמָרָהּ קַמֵּיהּ דְּרַב שִׁימִי בַּר אַשִׁי** – and subsequently **went and stated it in the presence of Rav Shimi bar Ashi.** **אָמַר לֵיהּ – [Rav Shimi bar Ashi] said to him:** **אַתּוּן אַהָא מַתְנִיתוּ לָהּ – You learned [Reish Lakish's dictum] apropos of this** ruling of the Rabbis, that a minor is entitled to the fine. **אֲנַן אַהָא מַתְנִינַן לָהּ – We learned it apropos of this** other teaching: **אָמַר רֵישׁ לָקִישׁ – Reish Lakish said:** **הַמּוֹצִיא שֵׁם רַע עַל הַקְּטַנָּה פָּטוּר – One who defames** his **minor** wife **is exempt,**[48] **שֶׁנֶּאֱמַר ,,וְנָתְנוּ לַאֲבִי הַנַּעֲרָה" – for it is stated:**[49] *And they shall fine him one hundred silver [shekels]* ***and give [them] to the father of the naarah (הַנַּעֲרָה).*** **נַעֲרָה מָלֵא דִּיבֵּר הַכָּתוּב – Scripture** here **mentions a "full** ***naarah.*"**[50]

The Gemara objects:

מַתְקִיף לָהּ רַב אַדָּא בַּר אַהֲבָה – Rav Adda bar Ahavah challenges [this interpretation] of Reish Lakish's "defamer" passage teaching: **טַעְמָא דִּכְתַב רַחֲמָנָא ,,נַעֲרָה" –** You say that **the reason** a minor is excluded from the law of the defamer **is that the Merciful One wrote** the word ***naarah*** fully, with a ה, **הָא לָאו הָכִי – but** had it **not** been written **thus,** **הֲוָה אֲמִינָא אֲפִילּוּ קְטַנָּה –** you imply that **I would have said** that the law applies **even** to **a minor.** **וְהָא כְּתִיב – But it is written:**[51] **,,וְאִם־אֱמֶת הָיָה הַדָּבָר הַזֶּה לֹא־נִמְצְאוּ בְתוּלִים לַנַּעֲרָה וְהוֹצִיאוּ אֶת־הַנַּעֲרָה אֶל־פֶּתַח בֵּית־אָבִיהָ וּסְקָלוּהָ" –** ***But if this matter was true – signs of virginity were not found on the girl***[52] ***– then they shall take the girl out to the entrance of her father's house and stone her –*** **וּקְטַנָּה לָאו בַּת עוֹנָשִׁין הִיא – and a minor is not subject to punishment!?**[53]

Rav Adda bar Ahavah reinterprets Reish Lakish, giving rise to Rav Shimi's statement:

אֶלָּא כָּאן נַעֲרָה – Rather, Reish Lakish is teaching as follows: **Here** in the passage of the defamer, where the Torah perforce refers only to a *naarah,* the Torah writes the word ***naarah*** in full. **הָא כָּל מָקוֹם שֶׁנֶּאֱמַר ,,נַעֲרָ" – This** implies that in **every place where it is stated** ***naara*** (without the final ה),[54] **אֲפִילּוּ קְטַנָּה בְּמַשְׁמַע – even a minor is within the meaning** of the verse.[55]

NOTES

this the Sages reply that a minor is indeed entitled to the fine. Hence, they are saying that] from when a girl is [three years old and] fit for cohabitation until she develops two pubic hairs, there is *also* a fine – i.e. in addition to the right of sale. And from when she develops two pubic hairs until she becomes a *bogeress,* there is a fine but no right of sale, as R' Meir stated (*Rashi*).

42. Although *Deuteronomy* 22:28 (*If a man finds a virgin naarah ... and takes hold of her and lies with her*) specifically mentions a *naarah,* perhaps it means to exclude a *bogeress* and not a minor (*Shitah Mekubetzes*).

43. *Deuteronomy* 22:29.

44. Viz. a woman who has the legal capacity to allow herself to be acquired by the violator as his wife (*Rashi*). Excluded, then, is a minor, who cannot consent to an act of *kiddushin* even when she does not have a father. See *Kovetz Shiurim* §146.

45. Emendation follows *Hagahos HaBach.*

46. The word *naarah* would normally be spelled נַעֲרָה. However, when referring to the violated victim, the Torah (*Deuteronomy* 22:28-29) writes נַעֲרָ, eliminating the final 'ה' (even though the word is still read as if the 'ה' were there).

47. Reish Lakish teaches that wherever the word *naarah* is written deficiently, without the final 'ה', the Torah's intent is to include a girl other than a *naarah* – viz. a minor (see *Rashi* ד"ה אהא מתניתו לה).

48. A מוֹצִיא שֵׁם רַע, *defamer,* is a husband who falsely declares in court that his wife was not a virgin when their marriage was consummated; he claims that she had committed adultery after they were legally married (i.e. after *kiddushin,* which in former times commonly preceded the consummation of the marriage by a significant period of time; see below, 57a), and he produces false witnesses to support his claim. If the witnesses are shown to be false, he must pay a fine of 100 *shekels* to her father, he is liable to lashes, and he may never divorce her against her will (see *Deuteronomy* 22:13-19). Reish Lakish teaches that these penalties are imposed when the wife is a *naarah,* but not when she is a minor.

49. *Deuteronomy* 22:19.

50. Here in the "defamer" passage the word *naarah* appears with its full complement of letters. Hence, the Torah gives no indication that it wishes to include in this law any girl other than the *naarah* herself.

51. Ibid. vs. 20-21.

52. I.e. the witnesses who testified that the girl committed adultery during the interval between her betrothal and marriage, as her husband had charged, were *not* invalidated.

53. I.e. it is self-evident that the passage of the defamer deals exclusively with a *naarah,* for the Torah prescribes the punishment of stoning if the girl is guilty and a minor is not subject to punishment. It is therefore unnecessary to expound the Torah's full spelling of the word *naarah* to prove that the passage of the defamer concerns a *naarah* alone.

54. E.g. in the passages of the violator and the seducer.

55. I.e. the reason the Torah writes the word *naarah* fully in the passage of the defamer is not to teach a law for that selfsame passage (viz. that a minor is excluded from the law of the defamer), for that exclusion is gleaned from the fact that a minor is not subject to punishment. Rather, the full spelling of *naarah* here teaches that elsewhere, where the the word is written without a final 'ה', a minor is included in the law (*Rashi*). This, then, is what Rav Shimi was saying.

עין משפט נר מצוה

פד א מיי' פ"ב מהל' נערה הל' א סמג עשין נד טוש"ע אה"ע סי' קנז סעיף א:
פה ב מיי' שם הל' יב:
פו ג מיי' פ"ג מהלכות אישות הל' יא סמג עשין מח טוש"ע שם סי' לז סעיף א:
פז ד ה מיי' פ"ב מהל' נערה הל' ו ופ"ה מהל' חובל ומזיק הל' ב סמג עשין קנז ועי' טור אה"ע סימן קנז וטור ע"ש ח"מ סימן תכ סעיף טו:
פח ו מיי' פ"ב מהלכות נערה הל' ב סמג לאוין פו ועשין נה טור אה"ע סי' קנז:

גמרא

מעשה מחט שלשים אלא א"ר זירא (א) אילו באו עליה שנים אחד כדרכה ואחד שלא כדרכה יאמרו בעל שלימה חמשים בעל פגומה חמשים א"ל אביי אי הכי גבי עבד נמי יאמרו עבד בריא שלשים עבד מוכה שחין שלשים אלא (ב) אמר אביי אמר קרא (א) תחת אשר עינה הני תחת אשר עינה מכלל דאיכא בושת ופגם רבא אמר אמר קרא (א) ונתן האיש השוכב עמה לאבי הנערה חמשים כסף (ד) הנאת שכיבה נ' מכלל דאיכא בושת ופגם ואימא לדידה (ה) א"ק (ב) בנעוריה בית אביה (ו) כל שבח נעורים לאביה ואלא הא דאמר רב הונא אמר רב (ז) מנין שמעשה הבת לאביה שנאמר (ג) וכי ימכור איש את בתו לאמה מה אמה מעשה ידיה לרבה (ח) אף בת מעשה ידיה לאביה למה לי תיפוק ליה מבנעוריה בית אביה אלא ההיא בהפרת נדרים הוא דכתי' וכי תימא נילף מיניה (ט) ממונא מאיסורא לא ילפינן וכי תימא נילף מקנסא ממונא מקנסא לא ילפינן אלא מסתברא דאביה הוי דאי בעי מסר לה למנוול ומוכה שחין: (י) פגם רואין אותה כאילו היא שפחה נמכרת: היכי שיימינן לה אמר אבוה דשמואל אומדין כמה אדם רוצה ליתן בין שפחה בתולה לשפחה בעולה לשמשו מאי נפקא ליה מינה אלא בין שפחה בעולה לשפחה שאינה בעולה להשיאה לעבדו ולעבדו מאי נפקא ליה מינה (כ) בעבד שיש לו לרבו קורת רוח הימנו:

מתני' (ל) כל מקום שיש מכר אין קנס וכל מקום שיש קנס אין מכר קטנה יש לה מכר ואין לה קנס נערה יש לה קנס ואין לה מכר הבוגרת אין לה לא מכר ולא קנס:

גמ' (מ) אמר רב יהודה אמר רב זו דברי ר"מ אבל חכמים אומרים יש לה קנס במקום מכר דתניא (נ) קטנה מבת יום אחד ועד שתביא שתי שערות יש לה מכר ואין לה קנס משתביא שתי שערות עד שתיבגר יש לה קנס ואין לה מכר דברי ר"מ שהיה ר"מ אומר כ"מ שיש מכר אין קנס וכ"מ שיש קנס אין מכר וחכמים אומרים קטנה מבת ג' שנים ויום אחד ועד שתיבגר יש לה קנס קנס אין מכר לא אימא אף קנס במקום מכר א"ר חסדא מ"ט דר"מ א"ק (א) ולו תהיה לאשה במהוה עצמה הכתוב מדבר ורבנן אמר ר"ל א"ק (ה) נערה אפילו קטנה במשמע שמעה רב פפא בריה דרב חנן מבי כלוחית אזל אמרה קמיה דרב שימי בר אשי א"ל אתון אהא מתניתו לה אנן אהא מתנינן לה אמר ר"ל (ס) (ע) המוציא שם רע על הקטנה פטור שנא' (ד) ונתנו לאבי הנערה נערה מלא דיבר הכתוב מתקיף לה רב אדא בר אהבה טעמא דכתב רחמנא נערה הא לאו הכי הוה אמינא אפילו קטנה והא כתיב (ה) ואם אמת היה הדבר הזה לא נמצאו בתולים לנערה והוציאו את הנערה אל פתח בית אביה וסקלוה וקטנה לאו בת עונשין היא אלא כאן נערה הא כל מקום שנאמר נער אפילו קטנה במשמע:

מתני'

רש"י

מעשה מחט. חייט תופר: אלא אמר רבי זירא. מהכא מסתברא שאין בושת בכלל חמשים דאם כן אין הפרש בין בעל שלימה לבעל פגומה שנבעלה שלא כדרכה והיכן הוא הפרש שביניהם ש"מ גבי בושת כיון שנפגמה ככר אין בושתה רב כשלימה: תחת אשר עינה. גבי חמשים כסף כתיב: מכלל דבושת ופגם. שאינם משום עינוי שהרי ישנן בשאר חובלין אינו בכלל זה. פגם הוא נזק הניסוס נמי בשאר חבלות: ואימא לדידה הוי. דבשלמא קנס כתיב ביה ונתן לאבי הנערה אלא הני ליהוו לדידה: בנעוריה בית אביה. גבי נדרים כתיב ומיהו איכא למשמע מינה דבימי נעוריה תלאה הכתוב בבית אביה: בתו לאמה. הקיש בת לאמה: תיפוק ליה כו'. אלא על כרחך מהתם לא מצי למילף דההוא בהפרת נדרים כתיב: נילף מקנסא. מה קנסה לאביה אף שאר שבח ממון נעורים לאביה: אלא מסתברא. דבושת ופגם דאב הוא שהרי בידו לביישה בבושת בעילה ולפוגמה בפגם בעילה: דאי בעי מסר לה. לקדשה בביאה: למנוול ומוכה שחין. כדתנן לקמן האב זכאי בבתו בקידושי' בכסף ובשטר ובביאה וכיון דבידו ליטול ממון לפוגמה ולביישה בושה זו השתא אפסדיה האי דפגמה: (ט) [מאי נפקא ליה. לכל אדם בבעילתה אם בעולה היא הואיל ולמלאכה קיימא]: ולעבדו מאי נפקא ליה. למריה מינה אם בעולה היא מי קפיד מריה אלא שיהו להן ולדות: קורת רוח. שזהיר בעבודתו ואף הוא רוצה לעשות לו נחת רוח להטעימו טעם בתולה: מתני' כ"מ שיש מכר. לאב בבתו דהיינו בקטנותה: אין לו בה קנס. דאין קנס לקטנה: כל מקום שיש קנס. משהיא נערה: אין מכר. דתניא (ערכין דף כט:) יכול ימכור אדם בתו כשהיא נערה אמרת (ג) מכורה כבר יוצאה עכשיו שאינה מכורה אינו דין שלא תימכר: גמ' זו דברי ר"מ. דאמר אין קנס לקטנה: מבת ג' שנים. שביאתה ביאה ואין בתוליה חוזרין: מכר לא. בתמיה: אף קנס במקום מכר. משתהא ראויה לביאה עד שתביא שתי שערות הוו תרוייהו ומשהביאה שערות עד שתבגר קנס ולא מכר: מאי טעמא דר"מ. דאמר קטנה אין לה קנס: דאמר קרא. גבי קנס ולו תהיה לאשה: במהוה עצמה. במי שיש בידה להקנות עצמו לאישות הכתוב מדבר: אהא מתניתו לה. להא דריש לקיש דאמר כ"מ שנכתב נער בלא ה' וקרינן נערה ללמד על הקטנה בא: שם רע. לא מצאתי לבתך בתולים: פטור. דוענשו אותו מאה כסף ונתנו לאבי הנערה מלא כתיב: אלא כאן נערה. האי דכתיב נערה מלא לאו לגלויי עליה אתא אלא על כל מקום שנאמר נער חסר ויליף הכי כאן שאי אפשר אלא בנערה כתיב נערה מלא וללמדך דכל מקום שנאמר נער אפילו קטנה במשמע:

תוספות

ואימא לדידה. אע"ג דפרישית לעיל (דף לח.) דבושת ופגם הוקשו לקנס וניתן למי שקנס ניתן היינו בתר דקים לן הכא דהוי הכל לאביה: מסתברא דאביה הוי דאי בעי כו'. וא"ת אמאי לא קאמר דאביה הוי מדקא יהיב מפתה כדאמר לקמן בריש נערה (דף מב.) וי"ל דלמא לא יהיב מפתה דקראי דאביי ורבא באונס כתיבי: דאי בעי מסר לה למנוול ומוכה שחין. וממעשה ידיה ליכא למילף דהא מיתוקמא מיניה כדאמרינן בפרק קמא דקדושין (דף ד. ושם) ולא מקדושין דמעלמא קאתו לה ומתרוייהו נמי לא דחבלה דגופה דאתי תימה הכא לא קים לן בושת ופגם דהוי לאביה אלא מכח שיכול לקדשה למנוול ומוכה שחין ואם כן היכי בעי למימר בריש קדושין (דף ג.) גבי קדושי כסף מנא לן דמיקדשה בכסף וקידושין דאביה הן וכי תימא נילף מבושת ופגם הא בושת ופגם גופיה לא קים לן אלא מכח שיכול לקדשה ואומר ר"י דלורחיה דהש"ס דבעי לדחוי אפילו קים לן דבושת ופגם הוי דאביה ממקום אחר (ז) א"נ התם בעי למילף קדושי נערה מבושת ופגם של קטנה ומקדושי קטנה הוה יליף להו אי לאו דהוה אמינא הני מילי קטנה דלית לה יד ונערה אית לה יד כדאמרינן התם לעיל ולהכי קאמר וכי תימא נילף מבושת ופגם דקטנה אע"ג דלהכי אית לה יד כדאמרינן בהחובל (ב"ק דף פז:) יעשה לה סגולה ואפ"ה הוי דאביה ה"נ קדושי נערה ואם (ה) תימי מפרשים דלא קאי אקידושין הא דקאמר ונילף מבושת ופגם אלא אמעשה ידיה דאמרי' התם לעיל הוה אתי שפיר אבל לא משמע הכי ועוד דא"כ הכא נמי ה"ל לאסוקי וכ"ת נילף מבושת ופגם כיון דלמעשה ידיה קאי וכן לקמן בפרק נערה (דף מו:): כמה אדם רוצה ליתן כו' להשיא כו' לעבדו. תימה למה שומא היא זו וכי אשה חשובה ממשפחה גדולה אינה נפסדת בפגימה אלא שוה שפחה הניסת לעבד וי"ל דכל אשה שמין לפי מה שהיא בענין זה כמה אדם רוצה ליתן בין בתולה לבעולה להשיאה לעבדו אשה כזאת הנפגמת והא דנקט שפחה אורחא דמלתא נקט דאין דרך להשיא לעבדו בת מלכים:

הא לאו הכי ה"א אפילו קטנה והכתיב אם אמת היה וכו'. תימה לר"י מה בכך אם קרא איירי בבת עונשין מ"מ מלינו למימר דה"ה קטנה דהא בא על קטנה מאורסה הוי בסקילה לרבנן בפרק ד' מיתות (סנהדרין דף סו:) אע"ג דהאי פרשה דנערה המאורסה בבת עונשין כתיבא (ט) [כדכתיב ואת הנערה על דבר אשר לא צעקה] ותירץ דהתם משום דמסקינן בסמוך כאן נערה הא כל מקום שנאמר נער אפילו קטנה במשמע הלכך מחייבין ליה התם וכולהו עריות ילפי מינה אי נמי דוקא במוציא שם רע סברא הוא לומר דלא מחייב קנס ומלקות אלא בגדולה כיון דקרא איירי בבת עונשין ולא בעלמא משום דמוציא שם רע על הקטנה סברא הוא דפטור דפיתוי קטנה אונס הוא (ל) והוי כמוציא שם רע על הנערה שנאנסה דלא מחייב אבל אין לומר דמסתבר ליה דדוקא בבת עונשין מחייב ליה משום שבא להורגה דבפרק קמא דסנהדרין (דף ח:) בשמעתא דחוששין ללעז משמע דלאו משום דקא גריס לה קטלא מחייב:

וליתני

תוספות ישנים

א) כמו שסיים סבור המקשה וה"ה שאני בושת ופגם לאביה נמי שייך פי' שמתביישים ומלגלגע"מ כמה ולא קים ליה אלא אמר הכא דאי בעי מסר לה למנוול ומוכה שחין דהכתי לא קים ליה שיכול לקדשה. ת"י עה"ג.

הגהות הב"ח

(א) גמ' אמר ר"ל אמר קרא נער: (ב) רש"י ד"ה אין מכר וכו' אמרה קל ואומר מכירה.

תוספות רי"ד

אמר אביי א"ק תחת אשר ענה הני תחת אשר ענה מכלל דאיכא בושת ופגם: רבא אמ' א"ק ונתן האיש השוכב עמה לאבי הנערה נ' כסף. הנאת שכיבה נ' כסף מכלל דאיכא בושת ופגם: ואימא לדידה. כי דדוקא נ' כסף זכה רחמ' לאב אבל בושת ופגם להוי דידה. מסתברא דאבוה הוי מיגו דאי בעי מסר לה למנוול ומוכה שחין: פגם רואים אותה וכו'. היכי שיימינן לה אמר אבוה דשמואל אומדים כמה אדם רוצה ליתן בין שפחה בתולה לשפחה בעולה להשיאה לעבדו שיש לו קורת רוח ממנו: מתני' כל מקום שיש מכר אין קנס וכ"מ שיש קנס אין מכר קטנה יש לה מכר ואין לה קנס נערה יש לה קנס ואין לה מכר בוגרת אין לה לא קנס ולא מכר: אר"י א"ר זו דברי רבי מאיר אבל חכמים אומרים יש קנס במקום מכר: א"ר חסדא מ"ט דר"מ דאמ' קרא ולו תהיה לאשה במהווה עצמה הכתוב מדבר ורבנן אמרי ר"ל קרא נערה ואפילו קטנה במשמע פי' נער כתיב וקרינן נערה מלא:

מסורת הש"ס

א) [ערכין טו.], ב) לעיל לג., ג) לקמן מו: מז. קדושין ג:, ד) [ברכות יט: וש"נ], ה) לעיל כט. חולין כו:, ו) [לעיל לג. חולין כו:], ז) [תוספתא פ"ג ע"ש], ח) לקמן מד: ע"ש, ט) נ"י כ"י, י) [וע"ע תוס' יומא מט: ד"ה שאני ותוס' חולין עה: ד"ה זה בנה], כ) מ"י כ"י, ל) [כלא' יבמות לג: ושם.]

תורה אור השלם

א) וְנָתַן הָאִישׁ הַשֹּׁכֵב עִמָּהּ לַאֲבִי הַנַּעֲרָ חֲמִשִּׁים כָּסֶף וְלוֹ תִהְיֶה לְאִשָּׁה תַּחַת אֲשֶׁר עִנָּהּ לֹא יוּכַל שַׁלְּחָהּ כָּל יָמָיו: [דברים כב, כט]
ב) אֵלֶּה הַחֻקִּים אֲשֶׁר צִוָּה יְיָ אֶת מֹשֶׁה בֵּין אִישׁ לְאִשְׁתּוֹ בֵּין אָב לְבִתּוֹ בִּנְעֻרֶיהָ בֵּית אָבִיהָ: [במדבר ל, יז]
ג) וְכִי יִמְכֹּר אִישׁ אֶת בִּתּוֹ לְאָמָה לֹא תֵצֵא כְּצֵאת הָעֲבָדִים: [שמות כא, ז]
ד) וְעָנְשׁוּ אֹתוֹ מֵאָה כֶסֶף וְנָתְנוּ לַאֲבִי הַנַּעֲרָה כִּי הוֹצִיא שֵׁם רָע עַל בְּתוּלַת יִשְׂרָאֵל וְלוֹ תִהְיֶה לְאִשָּׁה לֹא יוּכַל לְשַׁלְּחָהּ כָּל יָמָיו: [דברים כב, יט]
ה) וְאִם אֱמֶת הָיָה הַדָּבָר הַזֶּה לֹא נִמְצְאוּ בְתוּלִים לַנַּעֲרָ: וְהוֹצִיאוּ אֶת הַנַּעֲרָ אֶל פֶּתַח בֵּית אָבִיהָ וּסְקָלוּהָ אַנְשֵׁי עִירָהּ בָּאֲבָנִים וָמֵתָה כִּי עָשְׂתָה נְבָלָה בְּיִשְׂרָאֵל לִזְנוֹת בֵּית אָבִיהָ וּבִעַרְתָּ הָרָע מִקִּרְבֶּךָ: [דברים כב, כ-כא]

ליקוטי רש"י

ואחד שלא כדרכה. מחילה ולא"כ בא עליה זה כדרכה דאכתי הואי בתולה ואית לה קנס [ויאמרו] זה שבעל פגומה ליתיב בושת כולי האי ויהיב נ' סלעים ואילו בעל בתולה שלימה לא יהיב נמי אלא חמשים אי לאו דהשתא גבי בושת איכא חילוק דיהיב דמי בושת לשלימה טפי מפגומה. מוכה שחין. דהוי בושת דומיא דנבעלה שלא כדרכה. תחת אשר עינה. רישיה דקרא ונתן האיש השוכב עמה לאבי הנערה חמשים כסף וגו' [דברים כב] כסף יתן בשביל קנס העינוי ומדלאיצטריך למכתב הכי מכלל דאיכא מילי אחרינא כגון בושת ופגם דלאו קנסא דעינוי נינהו דבלאו עינוי נמי איכא בושת ופגם היינו נזק שפוה פחות מבתחילה [ערכין טו.]. חמשים כסף נתחדשו (ס"א: נתחייבו) תחת קנס העינוי אבל בושת ופגם מחמת עינוי שמגיע מוגלים לא כלל כאן. השוכב עמה. קרא יתירא הוא לדרשה ונתן לאבי הנערה חמשים כסף. מכלל דאיכא בושת ופגם. דלאו מחמת הנאת שכיבה נינהו שהרי ישנן בשאר חובלים לא כיילינהו בגוייהו חמשים [לעיל לג.]. א"ק בנעוריה בית אביה. הכי דריש לה כל שבנעוריה היא של אביה דכל שבח הבא לה לאביה הוא. לאמה. קרא יתירא הוא ודריש ליה בתו הרי היא לו כאמה ובבתו נערה אשמעי' דאי בקטנה לא איצטריך השתא זבוני מזבין לה מעשה ידיה מבעיא. תיפוק ליה מבנעוריה. אי מיניה הוי מצי למילף אלא על כרחך מדלא יליף מהתם שמעינן מינה לא לשבח נעורים אתיא דלגופיה איצטריך גבי נדרים דקאי עלייהו [קידושין ג:]. אלא ההיא בהפרת נדרים הוא דכתי'. מסקנא דקושיא היא ולא שינויא הוא [לקמן מו:]. וכי תימא נילף. כמון תנדרים ממונא מאיסורא כו' [קידושין שם]. ממונא. קל מאיסורא [ברכות יט:]. וכי תימא נילף. מכסף קנסא שאונס ופתוי לאביה חמשים כסף [קידושין שם]. מקנסא שזיכתה תורה לאב [לקמן שם]. ממונא מקנסא לא ילפינן. שקנס כולו חדוש וכחדוש לא גמרינן [קידושין שם]. דאי בעי מסר לה וכו'. בידו ליטול ממון ולביישה בבושת זה למוסרה לביאת קידושין למנוול ולמוכה שחין [לקמן שם]. שיש בידו לביישה ולפוגמה בשביל ממון שיתנו לו דאי בעי מסר לה למנוול ומוכה שחין דהויא לה בושת ופגם ואנס זה שבא עליה מחסר ממון זה שזילזלה ולא יקפצו עליה תובעין [קידושין שם].

[המשך בדף מא.]

The Gemara answers:

אָמַר אֲבוּהַ דִּשְׁמוּאֵל – **The father of Shmuel said:** אוֹמְדִין כַּמָּה אָדָם רוֹצֶה לִיתֵּן – **We assess how much a person would be willing to give** בֵּין שִׁפְחָה בְּתוּלָה לְשִׁפְחָה בְּעוּלָה – **between** the purchase of **a virgin slavewoman and** the purchase of **a nonvirgin slavewoman,** לְשַׁמְּשׁוֹ – **to serve him.**

The Gemara wonders:

שִׁפְחָה בְּעוּלָה לְשַׁמְּשׁוֹ – **A nonvirgin slavewoman to serve him!?** מַאי נַפְקָא לֵיהּ מִינָּהּ – **What difference does it make to him?**[25]

The Gemara replies:

אֶלָּא בֵּין שִׁפְחָה בְּעוּלָה לְשִׁפְחָה שֶׁאֵינָהּ בְּעוּלָה – **Rather,**[26] we assess the difference in purchase price **between a nonvirgin slavewoman and a virgin slavewoman,** לְהַשִּׂיאָהּ לְעַבְדּוֹ – **for** purposes of **marrying her off to one's slave.**[27]

The Gemara again asks:

וּלְעַבְדּוֹ – **But** even if one purchases the slavewoman **for his slave** to marry, מַאי נַפְקָא לֵיהּ מִינָּהּ – **what difference does it make to him** whether she is a virgin or a nonvirgin?[28]

The Gemara answers:

בְּעֶבֶד שֶׁיֵּשׁ לוֹ לְרַבּוֹ קוֹרַת רוּחַ הֵימֶנּוּ – We are speaking **of a slave whose master has satisfaction from him.**[29]

Mishnah כָּל מָקוֹם שֶׁיֵּשׁ מֶכֶר – In **every place where there is a** law of **sale,**[30] אֵין קְנָס – **there is no fine** for violation or seduction;[31] וְכָל מָקוֹם שֶׁיֵּשׁ קְנָס – **and** in **every place where there is a fine,**[32] אֵין מֶכֶר – **there is no** law of **sale.**[33]

The Mishnah elaborates:

קְטַנָּה יֵשׁ לָהּ מֶכֶר – **A minor is subject to sale** וְאֵין לָהּ קְנָס – **but is not entitled to the fine.** נַעֲרָה יֵשׁ לָהּ קְנָס – **A** ***naarah*** **is entitled to the fine** וְאֵין לָהּ מֶכֶר – **but is not subject to sale.** הַבּוֹגֶרֶת אֵין לָהּ לֹא מֶכֶר וְלֹא קְנָס – **A** ***bogeress*** **is not subject to sale nor is she entitled the fine.**[34]

Gemara אָמַר רַב יְהוּדָה אָמַר רַב – **Rav Yehudah said in the name of Rav:** זוֹ דִּבְרֵי רַבִּי מֵאִיר – **This** Mishnah presents **the opinion of R' Meir.**[35] אֲבָל חֲכָמִים אוֹמְרִים – **But the Sages say:** יֵשׁ לָהּ קְנָס בִּמְקוֹם מֶכֶר – **[A girl] is entitled to the fine** even **where** she is subject to **sale,**[36] דְּתַנְיָא – **for it was taught in a Baraisa:** קְטַנָּה מִבַּת יוֹם אֶחָד וְעַד שֶׁתָּבִיא שְׁתֵּי שְׂעָרוֹת – A MINOR GIRL, FROM the time she is ONE DAY OLD UNTIL SHE GROWS TWO pubic HAIRS,[37] יֵשׁ לָהּ מֶכֶר – IS SUBJECT TO SALE וְאֵין לָהּ קְנָס – BUT IS NOT ENTITLED TO THE FINE. מִשֶּׁתָּבִיא שְׁתֵּי שְׂעָרוֹת עַד שֶׁתִּיבָּגֵר – FROM WHEN [THE GIRL] GROWS TWO pubic HAIRS UNTIL SHE BECOMES A *BOGERESS* and attains full adulthood,[38] יֵשׁ לָהּ קְנָס – SHE IS ENTITLED TO THE FINE וְאֵין לָהּ מֶכֶר – BUT SHE IS NOT SUBJECT TO SALE; דִּבְרֵי רַבִּי מֵאִיר – these are THE WORDS OF R' MEIR, שֶׁהָיָה רַבִּי מֵאִיר אוֹמֵר – FOR R' MEIR USED TO SAY: כָּל מָקוֹם שֶׁיֵּשׁ מֶכֶר – WHEREVER THERE IS a father's right of SALE, אֵין קְנָס – THERE IS NO FINE; וְכָל מָקוֹם שֶׁיֵּשׁ קְנָס – AND WHEREVER THERE IS A FINE, אֵין מֶכֶר – THERE IS NO right of SALE. וַחֲכָמִים אוֹמְרִים – BUT THE SAGES SAY: קְטַנָּה מִבַּת שָׁלֹשׁ שָׁנִים וְיוֹם אֶחָד וְעַד שֶׁתִּיבָּגֵר – A MINOR GIRL, FROM THE AGE OF THREE YEARS AND A DAY[39] UNTIL SHE REACHES FULL ADULTHOOD, יֵשׁ לָהּ קְנָס – IS ENTITLED TO THE FINE if she is violated or seduced.

The Gemara notes that the Sages' statement is silent on the question of whether the father has a right of sale. It thus, in astonishment, asks:

קְנָס אִין מֶכֶר לֹא – Can the Sages mean that the law of **fine – yes,** it applies to a girl of this age; but the father's right of **sale – no,** it does not apply to her? Why, the Torah[40] authorizes a father to sell his daughter as a maidservant until she becomes a *naarah*! – ? –

The Gemara answers:

אֵימָא – The Sages mean to **say** אַף קְנָס בִּמְקוֹם מֶכֶר – that there is **also a fine where** there is **a** right of **sale.**[41]

NOTES

25. What difference is there to one who is purchasing a slavewoman only for her work whether she is a virgin or a nonvirgin? (*Rashi*).

26. [*Shitah Mekubetzes,* citing *Re'ah,* explains that the father of Shmuel stated only that we assess the difference between the purchase prices of a virgin slavewoman and a nonvirgin slavewoman. The Gemara originally understood this to mean the purchase of the slavewoman for work, and so incorporated the word לְשַׁמְּשׁוֹ (*to serve him*) in Shmuel's father's statement. However, having just demonstrated that this could not have been his intent, the Gemara concludes, "Rather, Shmuel's father did *not* say that!"]

27. *Tosafos* question the validity of this assessment: How can we calculate the depreciation of, for example, a *naarah* from a distinguished Jewish family by using virgin and nonvirgin slavewomen as our models? *Tosafos* explain that the Gemara mentions slavewomen only because they are what a master would ordinarily give to his slaves. However, the Gemara means that the value of each girl should be calculated *according to her station,* in these terms of "what a master would pay etc."

28. The master's only interest in purchasing a consort for his slave is that together they will produce offspring [thereby augmenting the master's wealth]. Why, then, would he desire to purchase a virgin? (*Rashi*).

29. This slave performed his tasks conscientiously, giving the master considerable satisfaction. To show his appreciation, the master wishes to give the slave the satisfaction that comes from experiencing conjugal relations with a virgin (*Rashi*).

30. The Torah (*Exodus* 21:7) grants a father the right to sell his minor daughter as a maidservant. [She serves until the end of a six-year term unless she is redeemed earlier; she is married by her master or his son; her master dies, the *Yovel* year intervenes, or she becomes a *naarah* (reaches twelve years of age and shows evidence of two pubic hairs)] Thus, the Mishnah's statement, "(in) every place where there is (a right of) sale," essentially means "as long as a girl is a minor" (*Rashi*).

31. The author of this Mishnah holds that the fines for violation and seduction apply in the case of a *naarah* but not in the case of a minor (*Rashi*).

32. I.e. when she is a *naarah* (*Rashi*).

33. A Baraisa, cited in *Arachin* 29b, derives this law with a *kal vachomer* argument, as follows: If a Jewish maidservant goes free upon becoming a *naarah* [see above, note 30], then certainly her father cannot initially sell her after that time! (*Rashi*).

34. [*Rif* infers from here that a *bogeress* is disqualified from only the fine; nevertheless, she is entitled to restitution for humiliation and depreciation. However, this law applies only in the case of violation. A *bogeress* who was seduced receives nothing, for by consenting to the seduction she waived her rights to these compensatory damages.]

35. Who maintains that a minor is not entitled to the fines for violation and seduction (*Rashi*).

36. [I.e. even when she is a minor and subject to being sold, she is entitled to the fine.]

37. At which point (if she has reached the age of twelve) she becomes a *naarah.*

38. During this period of her development she is classified as a *naarah.*

39. I.e. from when she is deemed legally fit for cohabitation (see *Rashi*).

40. See note 30 above.

41. [The reason the Sages failed to mention the law of sale is not because they hold that a minor cannot be sold. Rather, the Sages were replying to R' Meir's statement, that during the period the father enjoys the right of sale – from birth until she develops pubic hairs – there is no fine. To

ואימא לדידה. אע"ג דפרישית לעיל (דף לט:) דבושת ופגם הוקשו לקנס וניתן למי שקנס ניתן היינו בתר דקים לן הכא דהוי הכל לאביה: **מסתברא** דאביה הוי דאי בעי כו'. וא"ת אמאי לא קאמר דאביה הוי מדקא יהיב מפתה כדאמר לקמן בריש נערה (דף מג.) וי"ל דלמא לא יהיב מפתה דקרא לאבי ורבא באונס כתיבי: **דאי** בעי מסר לה למנוול ומוכה שחין. וממעשה ידיה ליכא למילף דהא מיתזנא מיניה כדאמרינן בפרק קמא דקדושין (דף ד. ושם) ולא מקדושין דמעלמא קאתו לה ומתרוייהו נמי לא דחבלה דגופה שאני תימה דהכא לא קים לן בושת ופגם דהוי לאביה אלא מכח שיכול לקדשה למנוול ומוכה שחין ואם כן היכי בעי למימר בריש קדושין (דף ג:) גבי קדושי כסף מנא לן דמיקדשה בכסף וקידושין דאביה הן וכי תימא נילף מבושת ופגם הא בושת ופגם גופיה לא קים לן אלא מכח שיכול לקדשה ואומר ר"י דאורחיה דהש"ס דבעי לדחוי אפילו קים לן דבושת ופגם הוי דאביה ממקום אחר י) א"נ התם בעי למילף קדושי נערה מבושת ופגם של קטנה ומקדושי קטנה הוה יליף להו אי לאו דהוה אמינא הני מילי קטנה דלית לה יד ונערה אית לה יד כדאמרינן התם לעיל ולהכי קאמר וכי תימא נילף מבושת ופגם דקטנה אע"ג דלהכי אית לה יד כדאמרינן בהחובל (ב"ק דף פז:) יעשה לה סגולה ואפ"ה הוי דאביה ה"נ קדושי נערה ואם א) היינו מפרשים דלא קאי אקדושין הא דקאמר ונילף מבושת ופגם אלא אמעשה ידיה דאייתי התם לעיל הוה אתי שפיר אבל לא משמע הכי ועוד דא"כ הכא נמי ה"ל לאסוקי וכ"ת נילף מבושת ופגם כיון דאמעשה ידיה קאי וכן לקמן בפרק נערה (דף מו:): **כמה** אדם רוצה ליתן כו' להשיא לעבדו. תימה דמה שומא היא זו וכי אשה חשובה ממשפחה גדולה אינה נפסדת בפגמה אלא שוה שפחה הניסת לעבד וי"ל דכל אשה שמין לפי מה שהיא בענין זה כמה אדם רוצה ליתן בין בתולה לבעולה להשיא לעבדו אשה כזאת הנפגמת והא דנקט שפחה אורחא דמלתא נקט דאין דרך להשיא לעבדו בת מלכים:

הא לאו הכי ה"א אפילו קטנה והכתיב אם אמת היה וכו'. תימה לר"י מה בכך אם קרא איירי בבת עונשין מ"מ מצינו למימר דה"ה קטנה דהא בא על קטנה מאורסה הוי בסקילה לרבנן בפרק ד' מיתות (סנהדרין דף סו:) אע"ג דההיא פרשה דנערה המאורסה בבת עונשין כתיבא כ) [כדכתיב ואת הנערה על דבר אשר לא צעקה] ותירץ דהתם משום דמסקינן בסמוך כאן נערה הא כל מקום שנאמר נער אפילו קטנה במשמע הלכך מחייבין ליה התם וכולהו עריות ילפי מינה אי נמי דוקא במוציא שם רע סברא הוא לומר דלא מחייב קנס ומלקות אלא בגדולה כיון דקרא איירי בבת עונשין ולא בעלמא משום דמוציא שם רע על הקטנה סברא הוא דפטור דפיתוי קטנה אונס הוא ל) והוי כמוציא שם רע על הנערה שנאנסה דלא מחייב אבל אין לומר דמסתבר ליה דלוקא בבת עונשין מחייב ליה משום שבא להורגה דבפרק קמא דסנהדרין (דף ח:) בשמעתא דחוששין ללעז משמע דלאו משום דקא גריס לה קטלא מיחייב:

מעשה מחט שלשים אלא א"ר זירא א) אילו באו עליה שנים אחד כדרכה ואחד שלא כדרכה יאמרו בעל שלימה חמשים בעל פגומה חמשים א"ל אביי אי הכי גבי עבד נמי יאמרו עבד בריא שלשים עבד מוכה שחין שלשים אלא ב) אמר אביי אמר קרא א) תחת אשר עינה הני תחת אשר עינה מכלל דאיכא בושת ופגם רבא אמר אמר קרא א) ונתן האיש השוכב עמה לאבי הנערה חמשים כסף א הנאת שכיבה נ' מכלל דאיכא בושת ופגם ואימא לדידה א"ק ב) בנעוריה בית אביה ב כל שבח נעוריה לאביה ואלא הא דאמר רב הונא אמר רב ג) מנין שמעשה הבת לאביה שנאמר ג) וכי ימכור איש את בתו לאמה מה אמה מעשה ידיה לרבה ג אף בת מעשה ידיה לאביה למה לי תיפוק ליה מבנעוריה בית אביה אלא ההיא בהפרת נדרים הוא דכתי' וכי תימא נילף מיניה ד) ממונא מאיסורא לא ילפינן וכי תימא נילף מקנסא ממונא מקנסא לא ילפינן אלא מסתברא דאביה הוי דאי בעי מסר לה למנוול ומוכה שחין: ד פגם רואין אותה כאילו היא שפחה נמכרת: היכי שיימינן לה אמר אבוה דשמואל אומדין כמה אדם רוצה ליתן בין שפחה בתולה לשפחה בעולה לשמשו לשמשו מאי נפקא ליה מינה אלא בין שפחה בעולה לשפחה שאינה בעולה להשיאה לעבדו ולעבדו מאי נפקא ליה מינה ה בעבד שיש לו לרבו קורת רוח הימנו: **מתני'** ה) כל מקום שיש מכר אין קנס וכל מקום שיש קנס אין מכר קטנה יש לה מכר ואין לה קנס נערה יש לה קנס ואין לה מכר הבוגרת אין לה לא מכר ולא קנס: **גמ'** ו) אמר רב יהודה אמר רב זו דברי ר"מ אבל חכמים אומרים יש לה קנס במקום מכר דתניא ז) קטנה מבת יום אחד ועד שתביא שתי שערות יש לה מכר ואין לה קנס משתביא שתי שערות עד שתיבגר יש לה קנס ואין לה מכר דברי ר"מ שהיה ר"מ אומר כ"מ שיש מכר אין קנס וכ"מ שיש קנס אין מכר וחכמים אומרים קטנה מבת ג' שנים ויום אחד ועד שתיבגר יש לה קנס קנס אין מכר לא אימא אף קנס במקום מכר א"ר חסדא מ"ט דר"מ א"ק א) ולו תהיה לאשה במהווה עצמה הכתוב מדבר ורבנן אמר ר"ל א"ק (א) נערה אפילו קטנה במשמע שמעה רב פפא בריה דרב חנן מבי כלוחית אזל אמרה קמיה דרב שימי בר אשי א"ל אתון אהא מתניתו לה אנן אהא מתנינן לה אמר ר"ל ח) המוציא שם רע על הקטנה פטור שנא' ד) ונתנו לאבי הנערה נערה מלא דיבר הכתוב מתקיף לה רב אדא בר אהבה טעמא דכתב רחמנא נערה הא לאו הכי הוה אמינא אפילו קטנה והא כתיב ה) ואם אמת היה הדבר הזה לא נמצאו בתולים לנערה והוציאו את הנערה אל פתח בית אביה וסקלוה וקטנה לאו בת עונשין היא אלא כאן נערה הא כל מקום שנאמר נער אפילו קטנה במשמע: **מתני'**

מעשה מחט. מייט תופר: **אלא אמר רבי זירא.** מהכא מסתברא שאין בושת בכלל חמשים דאם כן אין הפרש בין בעל שלימה לבעל פגומה שנבעלה שלא כדרכה והיכן הוא הפרש שביניהם ש"מ גבי בושת כיון שנפגמה כבר אין בושתה רב כשלימה: **תחת אשר עינה.** גבי חמשים כסף כתיב: **מכלל דבושת ופגם.** שאינם חמשים משום עינוי שהרי ישנן בשאר חובלין אינו בכלל זה. פגם הוא נזק הניזוק נמי בשאר חבלות: **ואימא לדידה הוי.** דבשלמא קנס כתיב ביה ונתן לאבי הנערה אלא הני ליהוו לדידה: **בנעוריה בית אביה.** גבי נדרים כתיב ומיהו איכא למשמע מינה דבימי נעוריה תלאה הכתוב בבית אביה: **בתו לאמה.** הקיש בת לאמה. **תיפוק ליה כו'.** אלא על כרחך מהתם לא מצי למילף דההוא בהפרת נדרים כתיב: **נילף מקנסא.** מה קנסא לאביה אף שאר שבח ממון נעורים לאביה: **אלא מסתברא.** דבושת ופגם לאב הוא שהרי בידו לביישה בבושת בעילה ולפוגמה בפגם בעילה: **דאי בעי מסר לה.** לקדשה בביאה: **למנוול ומוכה שחין.** דלתנן לקמן האב זכאי בבתו בקידושי' בכסף ובשטר ובביאה וכיון דבידו ליטול ממון לפוגמה ולביישה בושה זו השתא אפסדיה האי לפגמה: **מאי נפקא ליה.** לכל אדם אם בעולה היא הואיל ולמלאכה קיימא: **ולעבדו מאי נפקא ליה.** למריה מינה אם בעולה היא מי קפיד מריה אלא שיהו להן ולדות: **קורת רוח.** שזהיר בעבודתו ואף הוא רוצה לעשות לו נחת רוח להטעימו טעם בתולה: **מתני' כ"מ שיש מכר.** לאב בבתו דהיינו בקטנותה: **אין לו בה קנס.** דאין קנס לקטנה: **כל מקום שיש קנס.** משהיא נערה: **אין מכר.** דתניא (ערכין דף כט:) יכול ימכור אדם בתו כשהיא נערה אמרת (ב) מכורה כבר יוצאה עכשיו שאינה מכורה אינו דין שלא תימכר: **גמ' זו דברי ר"מ.** דלאמר אין קנס לקטנה: **מבת שלש שנים.** שביאתה ביאה ואין בתולים חוזרין: **מכר לא.** בתמיה: **אף קנס במקום מכר.** משהתחלה ראויה לביאה עד שתביא שתי שערות הוו תרוייהו ומשהביאה שערות עד שתבגר קנס ולא מכר: **מאי טעמא דר"מ.** דלאמר קטנה אין לה קנס: **דאמר קרא.** גבי קנס ולו תהיה לאשה: **במהווה עצמה.** במי שיש בידה להקנות עצמה לאישות הכתוב מדבר: **אהא מתניתו לה.** להא דריש לקיש לאמר כל מקום שנכתב נער בלא ה' וקרינן נערה ללמד על הקטנה בא: **שם רע.** לא מצאתי לבתך בתולים: **פטור.** דוענשו אותו מאה כסף ונתנו לאבי הנערה מלא כתיב: **אלא כאן נערה.** הא דכתיב נערה מלא לא לגלויי עליה אתא אלא על כל מקום שנאמר נער חסר וילף הכי כאן שאי אפשר אלא בנערה כתיב נערה מלא וללמדך לכל מקום שנאמר נער אפילו קטנה במשמע:

וליתני

עין משפט נר מצוה

פד א מיי' פ"ב מהל' נערה הל' א סמג עשין נד טוש"ע אה"ע סי' קעז סעיף א:

פה ב מיי' שם הל' יד:

פו ג מיי' פ"ג מהלכות אישות הל' יא סמג עשין מח טוש"ע שם סי' לז סעיף א:

פז ד ה מיי' פ"ב מהל' נערה הל' ג ופ"ג מהל' חובל ומזיק הל' ב סמג עשין נד ועי' טור אה"ע סי' קעז סעיף טו:

פח ו מיי' פ"ג מהלכות נערה הל' ב סמג לאוין פז ועשין נה טור אה"ע סי' קעז:

תוספות ישנים

א) כמו ששיה כבור המקשה וכו"ס שאין בושת ופגם לאביה נמי שייך פי' שמתביישים ומצטערים כשהרתה ולכך כמו שפי' שם בקונט' דאי בעי מסר לה למנוול ומוכה שחין דאכתי לא קים ליה שיכול לקדשה. ת"י ע"ג:

הגהות הב"ח

(א) גמ' אמר ר"ל אמר קרא נער: (ב) רש"י ד"ה אין מכר וכו' אמרת ק"ו מכורה:

תוספות רי"ד

אמר אביי א"ק תחת אשר ענה הני תחת אשר ענה מכלל דאיכא בושת ופגם **רבא אמר** א"ק ונתן האיש השוכב עמה לאבי הנערה נ' כסף. הנאת שכיבה נ' כסף מכלל דאיכא בושת ופגם: **ואימא לדידה.** פי' דדוקא נ' כסף זכה רחמנא לאב אבל בושת ופגם להוי דידה. מסתברא דאבוה הוי מיגו דאי בעי מסר לה למנוול ומוכה שחין: **פגם רואין אותה וכו'.** היכי שיימינן לה אמר אבוה דשמואל אומדים כמה אדם רוצה ליתן בין שפחה בתולה לשפחה בעולה להשיאה לעבדו שיש לו קורת רוח ממנו: **מתני' כל מקום שיש** מכר אין קנס וכ"מ שיש קנס אין מכר קטנה יש לה מכר ואין לה קנס נערה יש לה קנס ואין לה מכר בוגרת אין לה לא קנס ולא מכר אר"י אמר רב זו דברי רבי מאיר אבל חכמים אומרים יש קנס במקום מכר א"ר חסדא מ"ט דר"מ דאמר קרא ולו תהיה לאשה במהווה עצמה הכתוב מדבר ורבנן אמרי אמר קרא נערה ואפילו קטנה במשמע פי' נער כתיב וקרינן נערה מלא:

מסורת הש"ס

א) [ערכין טו.], ב) לעיל לג., ג) לקמן מו: מז. קדושין ג., ד) [ברכות יט: וש"נ], ה) [לעיל לט.] חולין כו:], ו) [לעיל לג. חולין כו: תוספתא פ"ג ע"ש], ז) לקמן מד: ע"ש, ח) [וע"ע תוס' יומא מט.], ט) סד"ה שאני ותוס' חולין עח. סד"ה זה בנה], י) תוס' כ"י, כ) [כדאי' יבמות לג: ושם].

תורה אור השלם

א) וְנָתַן הָאִישׁ הַשֹּׁכֵב עִמָּהּ לַאֲבִי הַנַּעֲרָ חֲמִשִּׁים כָּסֶף וְלוֹ תִהְיֶה לְאִשָּׁה תַּחַת אֲשֶׁר עִנָּהּ לֹא יוּכַל שַׁלְּחָהּ כָּל יָמָיו: [דברים כב, כט]

ב) אֵלֶּה הַחֻקִּים אֲשֶׁר צִוָּה יְיָ אֶת מֹשֶׁה בֵּין אִישׁ לְאִשְׁתּוֹ בֵּין אָב לְבִתּוֹ בִּנְעֻרֶיהָ בֵּית אָבִיהָ: [במדבר ל, יז]

ג) וְכִי יִמְכֹּר אִישׁ אֶת בִּתּוֹ לְאָמָה לֹא תֵצֵא כְּצֵאת הָעֲבָדִים: [שמות כא, ז]

ד) וְעָנְשׁוּ אֹתוֹ מֵאָה כֶסֶף וְנָתְנוּ לַאֲבִי הַנַּעֲרָה כִּי הוֹצִיא שֵׁם רָע עַל בְּתוּלַת יִשְׂרָאֵל וְלוֹ תִהְיֶה לְאִשָּׁה לֹא יוּכַל לְשַׁלְּחָהּ כָּל יָמָיו: [דברים כב, יט]

ה) וְאִם אֱמֶת הָיָה הַדָּבָר הַזֶּה לֹא נִמְצְאוּ בְתוּלִים לַנַּעֲרָ: וְהוֹצִיאוּ אֶת הַנַּעֲרָ אֶל פֶּתַח בֵּית אָבִיהָ וּסְקָלוּהָ אַנְשֵׁי עִירָהּ בָּאֲבָנִים וָמֵתָה כִּי עָשְׂתָה נְבָלָה בְּיִשְׂרָאֵל לִזְנוֹת בֵּית אָבִיהָ וּבִעַרְתָּ הָרָע מִקִּרְבֶּךָ: [דברים כב, כ-כא]

ליקוטי רש"י

ואחד שלא כדרכה. מתחלה ואח"כ בא עליה זה כדרכה ולאבי כמו שהוא בתולה ולא לה קנס [ויאמרו] זה שבעל פגומה לגבלה בושת כולי האי יהיב נ' סלעים ואלו בעל בתולה שלימה לא יהיב נמי אלא חמשים אבל השתא גבי בושת איכא חילוק דיהיב דמי בושת לשלימה טפי מפגומה. **מוכה שחין.** דהוי פגום דומיא דנבעלה שלא כדרכה. **תחת אשר עינה.** ריבויא דקרא ונתן האיש השוכב עמה לאבי הנערה חמשים כסף וגו' (דברים כב) דמשמע הני חמשים כסף יתן בשביל קנס העינוי ומדלאיצטריך למכתב הכי מילי אחריתא כגון בושת ופגם דלאו קנסא דעינוי ניהו דבלאו עינוי נמי איכא בושת ופגם היינו נזק ששוה פחות מבתחילה [ערכין טו.]. חמשים כסף נתחדשו (ס"א: נתחייב) תחת קנס העינוי אבל בושת ופגם שהוא בשאר חובלים לא כלל כו'. **השוכב עמה.** קרא יתירא הוא לדרשה ונתן לאבי הנערה חמשים כסף. **מכלל דאיכא בושת ופגם.** דלא מחמת הנאת שכיבה נינהו שהרי ישנן בשאר חובלים לא כיילינהו בגווייהו הכי [לעיל לג.]. **א"ק בנעוריה בית אביה.** הכי דריש לה כל זמן שבנעוריה היא של אביה דכל שבח הבא לה לאביה הוא. **לאמה.** קרא יתירא הוא ודריש ליה בתו הרי היא לו כאמה ובבתו נערה אשמעי' דאי בקטנה לא איצטריך השתא זבוני מזבין לה מעשה ידיה מבעיא. **תיפוק ליה מבנעוריה.** אי מיניה הוי מצי למילף אלא על כרחך מדלא יליף מהתם שמעינן מינה לא לשבח נעורים אתיא דלגופיה איצטריך גבי נדרים דקאי עלייהו [קידושין ג:]. **אלא ההיא בהפרת נדרים הוא דכתי'.** מסקנא דקושיא היא ולא שינויא הוא [לקמן מו:]. **וכי תימא נילף.** ממון מנדרים ממונא מאיסורא כו' [קידושין שם]. **ממונא.** קל מאיסורא [ברכות יט:]. **וכי תימא נילף.** מכסף קנסא שאונס ומפתה לאביה חמשים כסף [קידושין שם]. מקנסא שזיכתה תורה לאב [לקמן שם]. **ממונא מקנסא לא ילפינן.** שהקנס כולו חדוש ומחדוש לא גמרינן [קידושין שם]. **דאי בעי מסר לה וכו'.** בידו ליטול ממון ולביישה בבושת זה למוסרה לביאת קידושין למנוול ולמוכה שחין [לקמן שם]. שיש בידו לביישה ולפוגמה בשביל ממון שיתנו לו דאי בעי מסר לה למנוול ומוכה שחין הלכך לו בושת ופגם ואפילו זה שבא עליה מחסר ממון זה שזלזלה ולא יקפצו עליה תובעין [קידושין שם]. [המשך בדף מא.]

The Gemara rejects this notion:
"אָמַר קְרָא ,,בִּנְעֻרֶיהָ בֵּית אָבִיהָ — The **verse states:**[13] ***in her*** (state of) ***naarus, in her father's house.*** From here it is derived that כָּל שְׁבַח נְעוּרֶיהָ לְאָבִיהָ — **all profits** generated by a girl during **her** ***naarus*** accrue **to her father.**[14] Hence, the "profits" of recompense for humiliation and depreciation go to him and not her.

The Gemara challenges the legitimacy of this exegesis:
וְאֶלָּא הָא דְּאָמַר רַב הוּנָא אָמַר רַב — **But** consider **this** dictum **that Rav Huna said in the name of Rav:** מִנַּיִן שֶׁמַּעֲשֵׂה הַבַּת לְאָבִיהָ — **From where** do we know **that** the fruit of **a daughter's labor** (her earnings) belongs **to her father?** "שֶׁנֶּאֱמַר ,,וְכִי־יִמְכֹּר אִישׁ אֶת־בִּתּוֹ לְאָמָה — **For it is stated:**[15] ***When a father shall sell his daughter as a maidservant.*** The Torah juxtaposes the words *daughter* and *maidservant* to teach an analogy: מָה אָמָה מַעֲשֵׂה יָדֶיהָ לְרַבָּהּ — **Just as** in the case of **a maidservant** the fruit of **the work of her hands** belongs **to her master,** אַף בַּת מַעֲשֵׂה יָדֶיהָ לְאָבִיהָ — so **too,** in the case of **a daughter** the fruit of **the work of her hands** belongs **to her father.** לָמָּה לִי — Now, **why do I need** Rav's exegesis? "תֵּיפּוֹק לֵיהּ מ,,בִּנְעֻרֶיהָ בֵּית אָבִיהָ — **Derive [the law]** that a daughter's earnings belong to her father **from** the verse, ***in her naarus, in her father's house,*** which purportedly teaches that *all* profits generated by a *naarah* accrue to the father!

The Gemara concludes its challenge:
אֶלָּא — **Rather,** the fact that Rav needed to cite another verse demonstrates that his law cannot be derived from *in her naarus, in her father's house,* הַהִיא בַּהֲפָרַת נְדָרִים הוּא דִּכְתִיב — for **it is concerning** only **the annulment of vows that that** verse **is written.**[16] Hence, we cannot derive from it that restitution for the daughter's humiliation and depreciation are paid to the father. — ? —

The Gemara deflects two possible difficulties with this conclusion:
וְכִי תֵּימָא נֵילַף מִינֵּיהּ — **And if you will say** that **we should derive** that a father has the right to her monetary rights **from [the very law]** that he has jurisdiction over his daughter's vows,[17] I shall respond: מָמוֹנָא מֵאִיסּוּרָא לָא יַלְפִינַן — **We cannot derive monetary law from prohibitory law!**[18] וְכִי תֵּימָא נֵילַף מִקְּנָסָא — **And,** further, **if you will say** that **we should derive** that her monetary rights go to the father **from** the law that **the fine** for violation and for seduction go to the father, I shall respond: מָמוֹנָא מִקְּנָסָא לָא יַלְפִינַן — **We cannot derive monetary law from** the laws of **fines!**[19]

The Gemara concedes that there is no Biblical verse that awards the payments for humiliation and depreciation to the girl's father.[20] It therefore takes a different direction:
אֶלָּא מִסְתַּבְּרָא דְּאָבִיהָ הָוֵי — **Rather, it is logical** to say **that [the compensation]** for humiliation and depreciation **is the father's,**[21] דְּאִי בָּעֵי מָסַר לָהּ לִמְנוּוָּל וּמוּכֵּה שְׁחִין — **for if he wishes he can deliver her**[22] **to one who is repulsive or afflicted with boils.**[23]

The Mishnah further stated:
פְּגָם רוֹאִין אוֹתָהּ כְּאִילּוּ הִיא שִׁפְחָה נִמְכֶּרֶת — DEPRECIATION is assessed as follows: WE SEE HER AS IF SHE WERE A SLAVEWOMAN BEING SOLD IN THE MARKETPLACE [and we calculate how much she was worth (prior to the violation) and how much she is worth (now, after the violation)].

The Gemara asks:
הֵיכִי שָׁיְימִינַן לָהּ — **How do we assess [her depreciation]** on the slave market?[24]

NOTES

for the verse states explicitly: *The man who lay with her shall give the father of the girl fifty silver [shekels].* But restitution for humiliation and depreciation [which is common to assaults in general and is not mentioned in this verse (see *Shitah Mekubetzes* ד״ה רבא אמר)] should be made to the victim herself (*Rashi*).

13. *Numbers* 30:17. This verse appears at the conclusion of the passage that details a father's right to annul his *naarah* daughter's vows. The verse states in full: אֵלֶּה הַחֻקִּים אֲשֶׁר צִוָּה ה׳ אֶת־מֹשֶׁה בֵּין אִישׁ לְאִשְׁתּוֹ בֵּין־אָב לְבִתּוֹ בִּנְעֻרֶיהָ בֵּית אָבִיהָ, *These are the decrees that God commanded Moses regarding the relationship between a man and his wife, between a father and his daughter in her naarus, in her father's house.*

14. Although this verse is stated with regard to the annulment of vows, the juxtaposition of בִּנְעֻרֶיהָ, *in her naarus,* and בֵּית אָבִיהָ, *in her father's house,* implies that while she is a *naarah,* she is "in her father's house." That is, she is under her father's jurisdiction, so that all monies (including compensation for her humiliation and depreciation) generated by her while she is a *naarah* belong to her father (see *Rashi* here and to *Kiddushin* 3b).

15. *Exodus* 21:7.

16. Since Rav cites a different verse as the source for his ruling, it is evident that *in her naarus, in her father's house* has implications only for its own context — viz. for the laws of annulling vows (see *Rashi* to *Kiddushin* ibid. ד״ה תיפוק ליה). The verse's teaching is thus a limited one: that a *naarah* is "in her father's house" in the sole sense that he has jurisdiction over annulling her vows. However, we cannot derive from there that the father owns all profits generated by the girl.

17. I.e. granted that *in her naarus, in her father's house* refers only to the annulment of vows and does not imply that profits generated by a *naarah* belong to her father. Nevertheless, derive that the father has the right to her profits from this law that he has jurisdiction over her vows through operation of the exegetical rule of *binyan av* [בִּנְיַן אָב], which states that when the Torah reveals a law in one passage, that law may be applied to all other cases that logically appear to be similar!

18. The rule of *binyan av* (see preceding note) cannot be invoked here, for monetary law is inherently different from prohibitory law; hence, the former can never be derived from the latter. Accordingly, we cannot derive from the father's explicitly endowed jurisdiction over the daughter's vows [which is a prohibitory matter] that he also has control over her profits [which is a monetary matter].

19. The rule of *binyan av* cannot be applied here either, for *monetary law* generally deals with payments tendered as compensation for damages inflicted, or for goods and services rendered. *Penalty payments,* on the other hand, involve amounts set by the Torah, and are not based on the damage caused (see Mishnah and Gemara below, 41a-b).

Penalty payments thus represent a novel subcategory of monetary law, and cannot serve as a source for the derivation of general monetary rules (see *Rashi* to *Kiddushin* 3b ד״ה ממונא מקנסא לא ילפינן; see also above, 34b note 3).

20. We cannot derive it from the aforementioned *When a father shall sell his daughter as a maidservant,* which teaches that a girl's earnings belong to her father, for the award of the earnings is in compensation for the father's supporting his daughter. Here, however, the father has done nothing to deserve receiving the payments for humiliation and depreciation (*Tosafos*).

21. For he has the authority to humiliate her with the humiliation of cohabitation and to depreciate her value with the depreciation of cohabitation [as the Gemara proceeds to explain] (*Rashi*).

22. I.e. he has the authority to give his daughter to someone who will betroth her through cohabitation (*Rashi;* see following note; cf. *Rashash*).

23. [The Mishnah (*Kiddushin* 2a) states that *kiddushin* can be effected in one of three ways: through money, through a document of betrothal, or through cohabitation.] The Mishnah below (46b) states that a father is empowered to betroth his daughter with any of these methods, to whomever he pleases. Hence, a father has the legal right to subject his daughter to a *kiddushin*-by-cohabitation with a repulsive individual — and thereby humiliate and blemish her — in exchange for a sum of money. Thus, when a violator preemptorily humiliates a girl and depreciates her value, he causes the father to lose this potential gain. Logic then dictates that compensation for that loss be paid to the father (*Rashi*).

24. I.e. in what way does her being violated or seduced diminish her value on the slave market? (*Shitah Mekubetzes,* citing *Rashi* above, 40a ד״ה כאילו היא שפחה).

מעשה מחט שלשים אלא א"ר זירא [א]אילו באו עליה שנים אחד כדרכה ואחד שלא כדרכה יאמרו בעל שלימה חמשים בעל פגומה חמשים א"ל אביי אי הכי גבי עבד נמי יאמרו עבד בריא שלשים עבד מוכה שחין שלשים אלא [ב]אמר אביי אמר קרא [א]תחת אשר עינה הני תחת אשר עינה הני מכלל דאיכא בושת ופגם רבא אמר אמר קרא ונתן האיש השוכב עמה לאבי הנערה חמשים כסף הנאת שכיבה נ' מכלל דאיכא בושת ופגם ואימא לדידה א"ק [ב]בנעוריה בית אביה [ג]כל שבח נעוריה לאביה ואלא הא דאמר רב הונא אמר רב [ג]מנין שמעשה הבת לאביה שנאמר [ג]וכי ימכור איש את בתו לאמה מה אמה מעשה ידיה לרבה אף בת מעשה ידיה לאביה למה לי תיפוק ליה מבנעוריה בית אביה אלא ההיא בהפרת נדרים הוא דכתי' וכי תימא נילף מיניה [ד]ממונא מאיסורא לא ילפינן וכי תימא נילף מקנסא ממונא מקנסא לא ילפינן אלא מסתברא דאביה הוי דאי בעי מסר לה למנוול ומוכה שחין: [ה]פגם רואין אותה כאילו היא שפחה נמכרת: היכי שיימינן לה אמר אבוה דשמואל אומדין כמה אדם רוצה ליתן בין שפחה בתולה לשפחה בעולה לשמשו שפחה בעולה לשמשו מאי נפקא ליה מינה אלא בין שפחה בעולה לשפחה שאינה בעולה להשיאה לעבדו ולעבדו מאי נפקא ליה מינה [ו]בעבד שיש לו לרבו קורת רוח הימנו: מתני' [ז]כל מקום שיש מכר אין קנס וכל מקום שיש קנס אין מכר קטנה יש לה מכר ואין לה קנס נערה יש לה קנס ואין לה מכר הבוגרת אין לה לא מכר ולא קנס: גמ' [ח]אמר רב יהודה אמר רב זו דברי ר"מ אבל חכמים אומרים יש לה קנס במקום מכר דתניא [ט]קטנה מבת יום אחד ועד שתביא שתי שערות יש לה מכר ואין לה קנס משתביא שתי שערות עד שתיבגר יש לה קנס ואין לה מכר דברי ר"מ שהיה ר"מ אומר כ"מ שיש מכר אין קנס וכ"מ שיש קנס אין מכר וחכמים אומרים קטנה מבת ג' שנים ויום אחד ועד שתיבגר יש לה קנס קנס אין מכר לא אימא אף קנס במקום מכר א"ר חסדא מ"ט דר"מ א"ק [א]ולו תהיה לאשה במהוה עצמה הכתוב מדבר ורבנן אמר ר"ל א"ק (א) נערה אפילו קטנה במשמע שמעה רב פפא בריה דרב חנן מבי כלוחית אזל אמרה קמיה דרב שימי בר אשי א"ל אתון אהא מתניתו לה אנן אהא מתנינן לה אמר ר"ל [י]המוציא שם רע על הקטנה פטור שנא' [ד]ונתנו לאבי הנערה נערה מלא דיבר הכתוב מתקיף לה רב אדא בר אהבה טעמא דכתב רחמנא נערה הא לאו הכי הוה אמינא אפילו קטנה והא כתיב [ה]ואם אמת היה הדבר הזה לא נמצאו בתולים לנערה והוציאו את הנערה אל פתח בית אביה וסקלוה וקטנה לאו בת עונשין היא אלא כאן נערה הא כל מקום שנאמר נער אפילו קטנה במשמע: מתני'

רש"י

מעשה מחט. חייט תופר: **אלא אמר רבי זירא.** מהכא מסתברא שאין בושת בכלל חמשים דאם כן אין הפרש בין בעל שלימה לבעל פגומה שנבעלה שלא כדרכה והיכן הוא הפרש שביניהם ש"מ גבי בושת כיון שנפגמה כבר אין בושתה רב כשלימה: **תחת אשר עינה.** גבי חמשים כסף כתיב: מכלל דבושת ופגם. שאינם משום עינוי שהרי ישנן בשאר חובלין אינו בכלל זה. פגם הוא נזק הניסוס נמי בשאר חבלות: **ואימא** לדידה הוי. דבשלמא קנס כתיב ביה ונתן לאבי הנערה אלא הני ליהוו לדידה: **בנעוריה בית אביה.** גבי נדרים כתיב ומיהו איכא למשמע מינה דימי נעוריה תלאה הכתוב בבית אביה: **בתו לאמה.** הקיש בת לאמה: **תיפוק ליה כו'.** אלא על כרחך מהתם לא מצי למילף דההוא בהפרת נדרים כתיב: **נילף מקנסא.** מה קנסה לאביה אף שאר שבח ממון נעורים לאביה: **אלא מסתברא.** דבושת ופגם דאב הויא שהרי בידו לביישה בבושת בעילה ולפוגמה בפגם בעילה: **דאי בעי מסר לה.** לקדשה בביאה: **למנוול ומוכה שחין.** כדתנן לקמן האב זכאי בבתו בקידושי' בכסף ובשטר ובביאה וכיון דבידו ליטול ממון לפוגמה ולביישה בושה זו השתא אפסדיה האי דפגמה: [ט][**מאי נפקא ליה.** לכל אדם בבעילתה אם בעולה היא הואיל ולמלאכה קיימא]: **ולעבדו מאי נפקא ליה.** למריה מינה אם בעולה היא מי קפיד מריה אלא שיהו להן ולדות: **קורת רוח.** שזהיר בעבודתו ואף הוא רוצה לעשות לו נחת רוח להטעימו טעם בתולה: **מתני'** כ"מ שיש מכר. לאב בבתו דהיינו בקטנותה: **אין לו בה קנס.** דאין קנס לקטנה: **כל מקום שיש קנס.** משהיא נערה: **אין מכר.** דתניא (ערכין דף כט:) יכול ימכור אדם בתו כשהיא נערה אמרת (ב) מכורה כבר יוצאה עכשיו שאינה מכורה אינו דין שלא תימכר: **גמ'** זו דברי ר"מ. דאמר אין קנס לקטנה: **מבת ג' שנים.** שביאתה ביאה ואין בתוליה חוזרין: **מכר לא.** בתמיה: **אף קנס במקום מכר.** משהיא ראויה לביאה עד שתביא שתי שערות הוו תרוייהו ומשהביאה שערות עד שתבגר קנס ולא מכר: **מאי טעמא דר"מ.** דאמר קטנה אין לה קנס: **דאמר קרא.** גבי קנס ולו תהיה לאשה: **במהוה עצמה.** במי שיש בידה להקנות עצמה לאישות הכתוב מדבר: **אהא מתניתו לה.** להא דריש לקיש דאמר כ"מ שנכתב נער בלא ה' וקרינן נערה ללמד על הקטנה בא: **שם רע.** לא מצאתי לבתך בתולים: **פטור.** דוענשו אותו מאה כסף ונתנו לאבי הנערה מלא כתיב: **אלא כאן נערה.** האי דכתיב נערה מלא לאו לגלויי עליה אתא אלא על כל מקום שנאמר נער חסר ויליף הכי כאן שאי אפשר אלא בנערה כתיב נערה מלא וללמדך דכל מקום שנאמר נער אפילו קטנה במשמע:

תוספות

ואימא לדידה. אע"ג דפרישית לעיל (דף לט:) דבושת ופגם הוקשו לקנס וניתן למי שקנס ניתן היינו בתר דקים לן הכא דהוי הכל לאביה: **מסתברא** דאביה הוי דאי בעי כו'. וא"ת אמאי לא קאמר דאביה הוי מדקא יהיב מפתה כדאמר לקמן בריש נערה (דף מב.) וי"ל דלמא לא יהיב מפתה דקראי דאביי ורבא באונס כתיבי: **דאי** בעי מסר לה למנוול ומוכה שחין. וממעשה ידיה ליכא למילף דהא מיתונא מיניה כדאמרינן בפרק קמא דקדושין (דף ד. ושם) ולא מקדושין דמעלמא קאתו לה ומתרוייהו נמי לא דחבלה דגופה שאני תימה דהכא לא קים לן בושת ופגם דהוי לאביה אלא מכח שיכול לקדשה למנוול ומוכה שחין ואם כן היכי בעי למימר בריש קדושין (דף ג:) גבי קדושי כסף מנא לן דמיקדשה בכסף וקידושין דאביה הן וכי תימא נילף מבושת ופגם הא בושת ופגם גופיה לא קים לן אלא מכח שיכול לקדשה ואומר ר"י דאורחיה דהש"ס דבעי לדחויי אפילו קים לן דבושת ופגם הוי דאביה ממקום אחר [י]א"נ התם בעי למילף קדושי נערה מבושת ופגם של קטנה ומקדושי קטנה הוה יליף להו אי לאו דהוה אמינא הני מילי קטנה דלית לה יד ונערה אית לה יד כדאמרינן התם לעיל ולהכי קאמר וכי תימא נילף מבושת ופגם דקטנה אע"ג דלהכי אית לה יד כדאמרינן בהחובל (ב"ק דף פז:) יעשה לה סגולה ואפ"ה הוי דאביה ה"נ קדושי נערה ואם א) היינו מפרשים דלא קאי אקדושין הא דקאמר ונילף מבושת ופגם אלא אמעשה ידיה דאייתי התם לעיל הוה אתי שפיר אבל לא משמע הכי ועוד דא"כ הכא נמי ה"ל לאסוקי וכ"ת נילף מבושת ופגם כיון דאמעשה ידיה קאי וכן לקמן בפרק נערה (דף מו:): **כמה** אדם רוצה ליתן כו' להשיא לעבדו. תימה דמה שומא היא זו וכי אשה חשובה ממשפחה גדולה אינה נפסדת בפגמה אלא שוה שפחה הניסת לעבד וי"ל דכל אשה שמין לפי מה שהיא בענין זה כמה אדם רוצה ליתן בין בתולה לבעולה להשיא לעבדו אשה כזאת הנפגמת והא דנקט שפחה אורחא דמלתא נקט דאין דרך להשיא לעבדו בת מלכים:

הא לאו הכי ה"א אפילו קטנה והכתיב אם אמת היה וכו'. תימה לר"י מה בכך אם קרא איירי בבת עונשין מ"מ מצינו למימר דה"ה קטנה דהא בא על קטנה מאורסה הוי בסקילה לרבנן בפרק ד' מיתות (סנהדרין דף סו:) אע"ג דההיא פרשה דנערה המאורסה בבת עונשין כתיבא [כ][כדכתיב ואת הנערה על דבר אשר לא צעקה] ותירץ דהתם משום דמסקינן בסמוך כאן נערה הא כל מקום שנאמר נער אפילו קטנה במשמע הלכך מחייבין ליה התם וכולהו עריות ילפי מינה אי נמי דוקא במוציא שם רע סברא הוא לומר דלא מחייב קנס ומלקות אלא בגדולה כיון דקרא איירי בבת עונשין ולא בעלמא משום דמוציא שם רע סברא הוא לפטור קטנה אונס הוא [ל]והוי כמוציא שם רע על הנערה שנאנסה דלא מחייב אבל אין לומר דמסתבר ליה דדוקא בבת עונשין מחייב ליה משום שבא להורגה דבפרק קמא דסנהדרין (דף ח:) בשמעתא דמוסיפין ללעוז משמע דלאו משום דקא גריס לה קטלא מיחייב:

עין משפט נר מצוה

פד א מיי' פ"ב מהל' נערה הל' א סמג עשין נד טוש"ע אה"ע סי' קנז סעיף א:

פה ב מיי' פ"ג מהל' עבדים הל' יד:

פו ג מיי' פ"ג מהלכות אישות הל' יא סמג עשין מח טוש"ע אה"ע סי' לז סעיף א:

פז ד ה מיי' פ"ב מהל' חובל ומזיק הל' ו ופ"א מהל' נערה הל' ב סמג עשין נד ועי' טור אה"ע סימן קנז וטוש"ע ח"מ סימן תכ סעיף טו:

פח ו מיי' פ"ג מהלכות נערה הל' ב סמג לאוין פז ועשין ע טור אה"ע סי' קנז:

תוספות ישנים

א) [כמו שהיה סבור המקשה דה"ם שאני בושת ופגם דלאביה נמי שייך פי' שממשיבים ולמלעטר בעומה ולא כמו שפי' שם בקונט' דאי בעי מסר לה למנוול ומוכה שחין דאכתי לא קים ליה שיכול לקדשה. מ"י עס"ג].

הגהות הב"ח

(א) גמ' אמר ר"ל אמר קרא נער: (ב) רש"י ד"ה אין מכר וכו' אמרת קל וחומר מכורה:

תוספות רי"ד

אמר אביי א"ק תחת אשר ענה הני תחת אשר ענה מכלל דאיכא בושת ופגם **רבא אמר** א"ק ונתן האיש השוכב עמה לאבי הנערה נ' כסף. הנאת שכיבה נ' כסף מכלל דאיכא בושת ופגם: **ואימא לדידה.** פי' דדוקא נ' כסף זכה רחמנא לאב אבל בושת ופגם להוי דידה. מסברא דאבוה הוי מיגו דאי בעי מסר לה למנוול ומוכה שחין: **פגם רואים אותה וכו'.** היכי שיימינן לה אמר אבוה דשמואל אומדים כמה אדם רוצה ליתן בין שפחה בתולה לשפחה בעולה להשיאה לעבדו שיש לו קורת רוח ממנו: **מתני': כל מקום** שיש מכר אין קנס וכ"מ שיש קנס אין מכר קטנה יש לה מכר ואין לה קנס נערה יש לה קנס ואין לה מכר בוגרת לא קנס ולא מכר: אר"י א"ר זו דברי רבי מאיר אבל חכמים אומרים יש קנס במקום מכר א"ר חסדא מ"ט דר"מ דאמר קרא ולו תהיה לאשה במהווה עצמה הכתוב מדבר ורבנן אמר ר"ל אמר קרא נערה ואפילו קטנה במשמע פי' נער כתיב וקרינן נערה מלא:

מסורת הש"ס

א) [ערכין טו.], ב) לעיל לג., ג) לקמן מו: מז. קדושין ג:, ד) [ברכות יט: וש"נ], ה) לעיל כט. חולין כו:, ו) לעיל לו. חולין כו:, ז) [תוספתא פ"ג ע"ש], ח) לקמן מד: ע"ש, ט) כ"י, י) [וע"ע תוס' יומא מט: סד"ה שאני ותוס' חולין עח: סד"ה זה בנה], כ) ת"י כ"י, ל) [מלא' יבמות לג: וקא.].

תורה אור השלם

א) וְנָתַן הָאִישׁ הַשֹּׁכֵב עִמָּהּ לַאֲבִי הַנַּעֲרָ חֲמִשִּׁים כָּסֶף וְלוֹ תִהְיֶה לְאִשָּׁה תַּחַת אֲשֶׁר עִנָּהּ לֹא יוּכַל שַׁלְּחָהּ כָּל יָמָיו: [דברים כב, כט]

ב) אֵלֶּה הַחֻקִּים אֲשֶׁר צִוָּה יְיָ אֶת מֹשֶׁה בֵּין אִישׁ לְאִשְׁתּוֹ בֵּין אָב לְבִתּוֹ בִּנְעֻרֶיהָ בֵּית אָבִיהָ: [במדבר ל, יז]

ג) וְכִי יִמְכֹּר אִישׁ אֶת בִּתּוֹ לְאָמָה לֹא תֵצֵא כְּצֵאת הָעֲבָדִים: [שמות כא, ז]

ד) וְעָנְשׁוּ אֹתוֹ מֵאָה כֶסֶף וְנָתְנוּ לַאֲבִי הַנַּעֲרָה כִּי הוֹצִיא שֵׁם רָע עַל בְּתוּלַת יִשְׂרָאֵל וְלוֹ תִהְיֶה לְאִשָּׁה לֹא יוּכַל לְשַׁלְּחָהּ כָּל יָמָיו: [דברים כב, יט]

ה) וְאִם אֱמֶת הָיָה הַדָּבָר הַזֶּה לֹא נִמְצְאוּ בְתוּלִים לַנַּעֲרָ: וְהוֹצִיאוּ אֶת הַנַּעֲרָ אֶל פֶּתַח בֵּית אָבִיהָ וּסְקָלוּהָ אַנְשֵׁי עִירָהּ בָּאֲבָנִים וָמֵתָה כִּי עָשְׂתָה נְבָלָה בְּיִשְׂרָאֵל לִזְנוֹת בֵּית אָבִיהָ וּבִעַרְתָּ הָרָע מִקִּרְבֶּךָ: [דברים כב, כ-כא]

ליקוטי רש"י

ואחד שלא כדרכה. תחילה ואח"כ בא עליה זה כדרכה דלכתחי הואי בתולה ולית לה קנס [ויאמרו] זה שבעל פגומה דליכא בושת כולי האי יהיב נ' סלעים ואילו בעל בתולה שלימה לא יהיב נמי אלא חמשים אלא השתא גבי בושת איכא חילוק דיהיב דמי בושת לשלימה טפי מפגומה. **מוכה שחין.** דהוי פגום דומיא דנבעלה שלא כדרכה. **תחת אשר עינה.** רישיה דקרא ונתן האיש השוכב עמה לאבי הנערה חמשים כסף וגו' (דברים כב) דמשמע הני חמשים כסף יתן בשביל קנס העינוי ומדאיצטריך למכתב הכי מכלל דמחייב מילי אחרנייתא כגון בושת ופגם דלאו קנסא דעינוי ניהו דבלאו עינוי נמי איכא בושת ופגם והיינו נזק שהוא פחות מבתחילה [ערכין טו.]. חמשים כסף נתחדשו (נ"א: נתחייבו) תחת קנס העינוי אבל בושת ופגם שהוא מתחילה אלו לא כל כך. **השוכב עמה.** קרא יתירא הוא לדרשה ימתא ונתן לאבי הנערה חמשים כסף. **מכלל דאיכא בושת ופגם.** דלאו מחמת הנאת שכיבה שהרי ישנן בשאר חובלים לא כלייתנו בגוייהו דהכי [לעיל לג.]. א"ק **בנעוריה בית אביה.** הכי דריש לה כל זמן שבנעוריה היא של אביה דכל שבח הבא לה לאביה הוא. **לאמה.** קרא יתירא הוא ודריש ליה כמו הרי היא לו כאמה ובבתו נערה משמעי' דאי בקטנה לא איצטריך השתא וזוני מזבין לה מעשה ידיה מבעיא. **תיפוק לה מבנעוריה.** אי מינה הוי מצי למילף אלא על כרחך מהלך ליף מהתם שמעינן מינה לבת נעורים אלא דלגופיה איצטריך גבי נדרים דקאי עלייהו [קידושין ג:]. **אלא ההיא בהפרת נדרים הוא דכתי'.** מקנסא דקודשה היא ולא שיוכא הוא [לקמן מו:]. **ממונא.** כל מאיסורא [ברכות יט.]. **וכי תימא נילף.** מכסף קנסה שאונס ופתוי נותן לאבי הנערה חמשים כסף [קידושין שם]. מקנסא שזיכתה תורה לאב [לקמן שם]. מבון מנדרים ממונא לא ילפינן [קידושין שם]. **ממונא מקנסא לא ילפינן.** שהקנס כולו חדוש ומחדשו לא גמרינן [קידושין שם]. **דאי בעי מסר לה כו'.** בידו ליטול ממון ולביישה ולפוגמה בשביל שהוא מקדשה למנוול ומוכה שחין דהוא לה בושת ופגם ואפשר כי יקפטו עליה תובעין [קידושין שם]. [המשך בדף מא.]

מַעֲשֵׂה מַחַט שְׁלֹשִׁים – **needlework**[1] he also pays **thirty** *shekels*?! In fact, however, a thirty-*shekel* fine is levied in either case, even though there is reason to differentiate.[2] – ? –

The Gemara again attempts to prove that the fifty-*shekel* payment does not include compensation for humiliation and depreciation:

אֶלָּא אָמַר רַבִּי זֵירָא – **Rather, R' Zeira said:** אִילוּ בָּאוּ עָלֶיהָ שְׁנַיִם – **If two** men forcibly **came upon** (i.e. violated) [**a girl**], אֶחָד כְּדַרְכָּהּ וְאֶחָד שֶׁלֹּא כְּדַרְכָּהּ – **one in the natural way and one in the unnatural way** [viz. anal cohabitation],[3] יֹאמְרוּ בָּעַל שְׁלֵימָה חֲמִשִּׁים – **shall they say** that **one who cohabited with a** girl who is **whole**[4] pays **fifty** *shekels* בָּעַל פְּגוּמָה חֲמִשִּׁים – and **the one** here **who cohabited with a blemished** girl[5] also pays **fifty** *shekels*?![6] Obviously not![7]

The Gemara again challenges R' Zeira's reasoning:

אָמַר לֵיהּ אַבַּיֵי – **Abaye said to him:** אִי הָכִי גַּבֵּי עֶבֶד נַמִּי – **If so, with regard to** the thirty-*shekel* fine for **a slave** killed by a *muad* ox, you can **also** ask your question: יֹאמְרוּ עֶבֶד בָּרִיא שְׁלֹשִׁים – **Shall they say,** then, that if **a healthy slave** is killed the ox's owner pays **thirty** *shekels* עֶבֶד מוּכֵּה שְׁחִין שְׁלֹשִׁים – **and** if **a slave who is afflicted with boils** is killed the owner also pays **thirty** *shekels*?! In fact, however, a thirty-*shekel* fine is levied in either case, even though there is reason to differentiate.[8] – ? –

Having refuted R' Zeira's two attempts to prove that the fifty-*shekel* payment does not include compensation for humiliation and depreciation, Abaye offers his own proof:

אֶלָּא אָמַר אַבַּיֵי – **Rather, Abaye said:** אָמַר קְרָא ,,תַּחַת אֲשֶׁר עִנָּהּ" – The **verse states:**[9] *The man who lay with* (i.e. violated) *her shall give the father of the girl fifty silver [shekels]* . . . ***because he had afflicted her.*** הָנֵי תַּחַת אֲשֶׁר עִינָּהּ – The verse states that **these** fifty *shekels* are paid specifically **"because he had afflicted** (i.e. violated) **her."** מִכְּלָל דְּאִיכָּא בּוֹשֶׁת וּפְגַם – **This implies that** in addition to this payment for "affliction" **there is** compensation for **humiliaton and depreciation.**[10]

An alternative proof:

רָבָא אָמַר – **Rava said:** אָמַר קְרָא ,,וְנָתַן הָאִישׁ הַשֹּׁכֵב עִמָּהּ לַאֲבִי הַנַּעֲרָה חֲמִשִּׁים כָּסֶף" – The same **verse states:** ***The man who lay with her shall give the father of the girl fifty silver [shekels].*** הֲנָאַת שְׁכִיבָה חֲמִשִּׁים – The verse states that for **the pleasure of lying** [i.e. cohabiting] with the girl the man pays **fifty** *shekels* to the father. מִכְּלָל דְּאִיכָּא בּוֹשֶׁת וּפְגַם – **This implies that** in addition to this payment for pleasure **there is** compensation for **humiliation and depreciation.**[11]

The Gemara discusses the ownership of these additional payments:

וְאֵימָא לְדִידָהּ – **But say** that the compensations for humiliation and depreciation are paid **to her!?**[12]

NOTES

1. I.e. he sews (*Rashi*).

2. Evidently, there are areas of law where the Torah sets a uniform penalty even though there is actual cause for differentiation between the individual cases. Accordingly, perhaps here too the Torah instituted a uniform penalty, even though there is an obvious difference between the violation of a princess and the violation of a commoner. If so, we can say that the fifty-*shekel* payment for violation (and seduction) is all inclusive.

3. I.e. if one man violated her in the natural way after another man had forcibly engaged in anal relations with her (see *Rashi* to *Arachin* 15a).

[Note: Although anal cohabitation is generally considered cohabitation, it does not render the woman a nonvirgin (see *Rashi* ibid.). Hence, the second violator is liable to pay the fifty-*shekel* fine for the violation of a virgin. However, had the first violator come upon her in the natural way, she would no longer be a virgin and the second violator would not be liable to the fine.]

Tosafos (printed above, 40a) note that, to report the true sequence of events, the Gemara should have stated: *If two people violated her, one in the unnatural way and one in the natural way.* Nevertheless, it is common for the Talmud not to be meticulous about the order of presentation. [See, however, *Arachin* 15a, where the Gemara does arrange R' Zeira's statement in the proper sequence.]

4. I.e. a man who has natural relations with a complete virgin (see note 6 below).

5. I.e. the second violator in R' Zeira's case, who had natural relations with the girl after she was subjected to unnatural relations (see following note).

6. I.e. should the second violator in R' Zeira's case (who violated the girl after she had unnatural relations and had become blemished) pay the same amount as one who violates a girl who had never previously cohabited and thus was whole and unblemished? (see *Rashi* here and to *Arachin* 15a ד״ה אילו באו עליה שנים).

Tos. HaRosh here, and *Tosafos* to *Arachin* ibid. ד״ה אילו, note that in explaining R' Zeira's proof *Rashi* seems to introduce a third violator, one not mentioned in R' Zeira's case. That is, instead of identifying the first violator in the case (the one who has unnatural relations with a complete virgin) as the assailant of an "unblemished" girl, *Rashi* gives us a new case of one who violates a complete virgin. It would thus appear that *Rashi* holds that the fifty-*shekel* fine is imposed only for natural violation (indeed, see *Rashi* to *Sanhedrin* 73b ד״ה משעת הערצה), and so R' Zeira could not claim that the first violator in his case, who violated her unnaturally, pays the full fifty *shekels* (cf. explanation of *Rashi* by *Tos. HaRosh* to *Arachin* ibid., cited by *Shitah Mekubetzes* here). However, *Tosafos* and *Rosh* cite various proofs that the fifty-*shekel* fine is levied even for unnatural violation. Accordingly, they explain that R' Zeira indeed refers to the two violators mentioned in his case.

7. From here we can prove that the fifty-*shekel* payment does not include restitution for humiliation. For if it did, there would be no difference between the violation of a girl who is whole [who has never before suffered even unnatural violation] and the violation of the girl who is blemished by the unnatural violation inflicted by the first violator in R' Zeira's case. But since there is an obvious difference between the two cases, in that the victim who had previously endured anal relations now suffers less humiliation than a completely unblemished girl, logic dictates that the compensation for humiliation is paid separately – i.e. in addition to the fifty-*shekel* payment, which is uniform for all (*Rashi*).

Shitah Mekubetzes ד״ה אלא אר״ז [second explanation] explains that although Abaye has already demonstrated to R' Zeira that there are areas of law where the Torah establishes a uniform penalty even when a reason for differentiation exists, R' Zeira opines that that policy governs only when the differences involve external matters, such as a girl's lineage [royal versus common] or the acquired skills of a slave [gem cutter versus tailor]. However, when the differences involve more sensitive physical matters, such as those between a girl who is blemished and one who is not, logic dictates that the Torah must acknowledge the more profound disparity of suffering and compensate accordingly. Consequently, in those latter cases we can conclude that the fifty-*shekel* payment does not include compensation for humiliation. Cf. *Shitah Mekubetzes'* first explanation (ibid.).

8. Evidently, there are areas of law where the Torah establishes a uniform penalty even though there are *physical* differences (*Shitah Mekubetzes* ibid.). Accordingly, perhaps here too the Torah institutes a uniform penalty, even though there is an obvious difference between a blemished and an unblemished girl. If so, we can say that the fifty-*shekel* payment for violation (and seduction) includes compensation for humiliation and depreciation as well.

9. *Deuteronomy* 22:29.

10. The Torah mandates the fifty-*shekel* payment specifically for the "affliction" of the act of violation. Since humiliation and depreciation are not components of that "affliction," inasmuch as they occur in other types of assault, their compensation is perforce not included in the fifty *shekels* (*Rashi*).

11. See 33a note 11.

12. The Mishnah below (41b) states that the restitution for humiliation and depreciation, as well as the fine, are paid to the girl's father (*Shitah Mekubetzes*). Now, it is understandable that the father receives the fine,

מעשה מחט שלשים אלא א"ר זירא (א) אילו באו עליה שנים אחד כדרכה ואחד שלא כדרכה יאמרו בעל שלימה חמשים בעל פגומה חמשים א"ל אביי אי הכי גבי עבד נמי יאמרו עבד בריא שלשים עבד מוכה שחין שלשים אלא (ג) אמר אביי אמר קרא (א) תחת אשר עינה הני תחת אשר עינה מכלל דאיכא בושת ופגם רבא אמר אמר קרא (א) ונתן האיש השוכב עמה לאבי הנערה חמשים כסף (א) הנאת שכיבה נ' מכלל דאיכא בושת ופגם ואימא לדידה א"ק (ב) בנעוריה בית אביה (ב) כל שבח נעוריה לאביה ואלא הא דאמר רב הונא אמר רב (ג) מנין שמעשה הבת לאביה שנאמר (ג) וכי ימכור איש את בתו לאמה מה אמה מעשה ידיה לרבה (ז) אף בת מעשה ידיה לאביה למה לי תיפוק ליה מבנעוריה בית אביה אלא ההיא בהפרת נדרים הוא דכתי' וכי תימא נילף מיניה (ד) ממונא מאיסורא לא ילפינן וכי תימא נילף מקנסא ממונא מקנסא לא ילפינן אלא מסתברא דאביה הוי דאי בעי מסר לה למנוול ומוכה שחין: (ה) פגם רואין אותה כאילו היא שפחה נמכרת: היכי שיימינן לה אמר אבוה דשמואל אומדין כמה אדם רוצה ליתן בין שפחה בתולה לשפחה בעולה לשמשו שפחה בעולה לשמשו מאי נפקא ליה מינה אלא בין שפחה בעולה לשפחה שאינה בעולה להשיאה לעבדו ולעבדו מאי נפקא ליה מינה (ה) בעבד שיש לו לרבו קורת רוח הימנו: מתני' (ט) כל מקום שיש מכר אין קנס וכל מקום שיש קנס אין מכר קטנה יש לה מכר ואין לה קנס נערה יש לה קנס ואין לה מכר הבוגרת אין לה לא מכר ולא קנס: גמ' (י) אמר רב יהודה אמר רב זו דברי ר"מ אבל חכמים אומרים יש לה קנס במקום מכר דתניא (י) קטנה מבת יום אחד ועד שתביא שתי שערות יש לה מכר ואין לה קנס משתביא שתי שערות עד שתיבגר יש לה קנס ואין לה מכר דברי ר"מ שהיה ר"מ אומר כ"מ שיש מכר אין קנס וכ"מ שיש קנס אין מכר וחכמים אומרים קטנה מבת ג' שנים ויום אחד ועד שתיבגר יש לה קנס קנס אין מכר לא אימא אף קנס במקום מכר א"ר חסדא מ"ט דר"מ א"ק (א) ולו תהיה לאשה במהוה עצמה הכתוב מדבר ורבנן אמר ר"ל א"ק (א) נערה אפילו קטנה במשמע שמעה רב פפא בריה דרב חנן מבי כלוחית אזל אמרה קמיה דרב שימי בר אשי א"ל אתון אהא מתניתו לה אנן אהא מתנינן לה אמר ר"ל (ו) המוציא שם רע על הקטנה פטור שנא' (ד) ונתנו לאבי הנערה נערה מלא דיבר הכתוב מתקיף לה רב אדא בר אהבה טעמא דכתב רחמנא נערה הא לאו הכי הוה אמינא אפילו קטנה והא כתיב (ה) ואם אמת היה הדבר הזה לא נמצאו בתולים לנערה והוציאו את הנערה אל פתח בית אביה וסקלוה וקטנה לאו בת עונשין היא אלא כאן נערה הא כל מקום שנאמר נער אפילו קטנה במשמע: מתני'

מעשה מחט. חייט תופר: אלא אמר רבי זירא. מהכא מסתברא שאין בושת בכלל חמשים דאם כן אין הפרש בין בעל שלימה לבעל פגומה שנבעלה שלא כדרכה והיכן הוא הפרש שביניהם ש"מ גבי בושת כיון שנפגמה כבר אין בושתה רב כשלימה: תחת אשר עינה. גבי חמשים כסף כתיב: מכלל דבושת ופגם. שאינם משום עינוי שהרי ישנן בשאר חובלין אינו בכלל זה. פגם הוא נזק הניסוס נמי בשאר חבלות: ואימא לדידה הוי. דבשלמא קנס כתיב ביה ונתן לאבי הנערה אלא הני ליהוו לדידה: בנעוריה בית אביה. גבי נדרים כתיב ומיהו איכא למשמע מינה דימי נעוריה תלאה הכתוב בבית אביה: בתו לאמה. הקיש בת לאמה: תיפוק ליה כו'. אלא על כרחך מהתם לא מצי למילף דההוא בהפרת נדרים כתיב: נילף מקנסא. מה קנסה לאביה אף שאר שבח ממון נעורים לאביה: אלא מסתברא. דבושת ופגם דאב הוא שהרי בידו לביישה בבושת בעילה ולפוגמה בפגם בעילה: דאי בעי מסר לה. לקדשה בביאה: למנוול ומוכה שחין. כדתנן לקמן האב זכאי בבתו בקידושי' בכסף ובשטר ובביאה וכיון דבידו ליטול ממון לפוגמה ולביישה בושה זו השתא אפסדיה האי דפגמה: (ט) [מאי נפקא ליה. לכל אדם בבעילתה אם בעולה היא הואיל ולמלאכה קיימא]: ולעבדו מאי נפקא ליה. למריה מינה אם בעולה היא מי קפיד מריה אלא שיהו להן ולדות: קורת רוח. שזהיר בעבודתו ואף הוא רוצה לעשות לו נחת רוח להטעימו טעם בתולה: מתני' כ"מ שיש מכר. לאב בבתו דהיינו בקטנותה: אין לו בה קנס. דאין קנס לקטנה: כל מקום שיש קנס. משהיא נערה: אין מכר. דתניא (ערכין דף כט:) יכול ימכור אדם בתו כשהיא נערה אמרת (ב) מכורה כבר יוצאה עכשיו שאינה מכורה אינו דין שלא תימכר: גמ' זו דברי ר"מ. דאמר אין קנס לקטנה: מבת ג' שנים. שביאתה ביאה ואין בתוליה חוזרין: מכר לא. בתמיה: אף קנס במקום מכר. משתהא ראויה לביאה עד שתביא שתי שערות הוו תרוייהו ומשהביאה שערות עד שתבגר קנס ולא מכר: מאי טעמא דר"מ. דאמר קטנה אין לה קנס: דאמר קרא. גבי קנס ולו תהיה לאשה: במהוה עצמה. במי שיש בידה להקנות עצמה לאישות הכתוב מדבר: אהא מתניתו לה. להא דריש לקיש דאמר כ"מ שנכתב נער בלא ה' וקרינן נערה ללמד על הקטנה בא: שם רע. לא מצאתי לבתך בתולים: פטור. דוענשו אותו מאה כסף ונתנו לאבי הנערה מלא כתיב: אלא כאן נערה. האי דכתיב נערה מלא לאו לגלויי עליה אתא אלא על כל מקום שנאמר נער חסר ויליף הכי כאן שאי אפשר אלא בנערה כתיב נערה מלא וללמדך דכל מקום שנאמר נער אפילו קטנה במשמע:

ואימא לדידה. אע"ג דפרישית לעיל (דף לח:) דבושת ופגם הוקשו לקנס וניתן למי שקנס ניתן היינו בתר דקים לן הכא דהוי הכל לאביה: **מסתברא** דאביה הוי דאי בעי כו'. וא"ת אמאי לא קאמר דאביה הוי מדקא יהיב מפתה כדאמר לקמן בריש נערה (דף מב.) וי"ל דלמא לא יהיב מפתה דקראי לאביי ורבא באונס כתיבי: **דאי** בעי מסר לה למנוול ומוכה שחין. וממעשה ידיה ליכא למילף דהא מיתזנא מיניה כדאמרינן בפרק קמא דקדושין (דף ד. ושם) ולא מקדושין דמעלמא קאתו לה ומתרוייהו נמי לא דחבלה דגופה שאני תימה דהכא לא קים לן בושת ופגם דהוי לאביה אלא מכח שיכול לקדשה למנוול ומוכה שחין ואם כן היכי בעי למימר בריש קדושין (דף ג:) גבי קדושי כסף מנא לן דמיקדשה בכסף וקידושין לאביה הן וכי תימא נילף מבושת ופגם הא בושת ופגם גופיה לא קים לן אלא מכח שיכול לקדשה ואומר ר"י דאורחיה דהש"ס דבעי לדחויי אפילו קים לן דבושת ופגם הוי לאביה ממקום אחר (י) א"נ התם בעי למילף קדושי נערה מבושת ופגם של קטנה ומקדושי קטנה הוה יליף להו אי לאו דהוה אמינא הני מילי קטנה דלית לה יד ונערה אית לה יד כדאמרינן התם לעיל ולהכי קאמר וכי תימא נילף מבושת ופגם דקטנה אע"ג דלהכי אית לה יד כדאמרינן בהחובל (ב"ק דף פז:) יעשה לה סגולה ואפ"ה הוי לאביה ה"נ קדושי נערה ואם (א) היינו מפרשים דלא קאי אקדושין הא דקאמר ונילף מבושת ופגם אלא אמעשה ידיה דאייתי התם לעיל הוה אתי שפיר אבל לא משמע הכי ועוד דא"כ הכא נמי ה"ל לאסוקי וכ"ת נילף מבושת ופגם כיון דאמעשה ידיה קאי וכן לקמן בפרק נערה (דף מו:): **כמה** אדם רוצה ליתן כו' להשיא לעבדו. תימה דמה שומא היא זו וכי אשה חשובה ממשפחה גדולה אינה נפסדת בפגמה אלא שוה שפחה הניסת לעבד וי"ל דכל אשה שמין לפי מה שהיא בענין זה כמה אדם רוצה ליתן בין בתולה לבעולה להשיא לעבדו אשה כזאת הנפגמת והא דנקט שפחה אורחא דמלתא נקט דאין דרך להשיא לעבדו בת מלכים:

הא לאו הכי ה"א אפילו קטנה והכתיב אם אמת היה וכו'. תימה לר"י מה בכך אם קרא איירי בבת עונשין מ"מ מצינו למימר דה"ה קטנה דהא בא על קטנה מאורסה הוי בסקילה לרבנן בפרק ד' מיתות (סנהדרין דף סו:) אע"ג דההיא פרשה דנערה המאורסה בבת עונשין כתיבא (כ) [כדכתיב ואת הנערה על דבר אשר לא צעקה] ותירץ דהתם משום דמסקינן בסמוך כאן נערה הא כל מקום שנאמר נער אפילו קטנה במשמע הלכך מחייבין ליה התם וכולהו עריות ילפי מינה אי נמי דוקא במוציא שם רע סברה הוא לומר דלא מחייב קנס ומלקות אלא בגדולה כיון דקרא איירי בבת עונשין ולא בעלמא משום דמוציא שם רע על הקטנה סברה הוא לפטור דפיתוי קטנה אונס הוא (ל) והוי כמוציא שם רע על הנערה שנאנסה דלא מחייב אבל אין לומר דמסתבר ליה לדוקא בבת עונשין מחייב ליה משום שבא להורגה דבפרק קמא דסנהדרין (דף ח:) במשמעות דמוסשין דלאו משום דקא גריס לה קטלא מיחייב:

עין משפט נר מצוה

פד א מיי' פ"ב מהל' נערה הל' ח סמג עשין נד טוש"ע אה"ע סי' קנז סעיף א:
פה ב מיי' שם הל' יד:
פו ג מיי' פ"ד מהלכות אישות הל' יא סמג עשין מח טוש"ע שם סי' לז סעיף ב:
פז ד ה מיי' פ"ב מהל' נערה הל' ו ופ"ה מהל' חובל ומזיק הל' ב סמג עשין נד ועי' טור אה"ע סימן קעז וש"ע שם סימן תכ סעיף טו:
פח ו מיי' פ"ג מהלכות נערה הל' ב סמג לאוין פז ועשין נה טור אה"ע סי' קעז:

תוספות ישנים

א) [כמו שהיה סבור המקשה דס"ד שאני ב"ש ופגם דאביה נמי שייך פי' שמחשיבים ולמטעטר כמ"ש ולא כמו שפי' שם בקהטע' דלאו בעי מסר לה למנוול ומוכה שחין דלכתי לא קים ליה שיכול לקדשה. מ"י עה"ג].

הגהות הב"ח

(א) גמ' אמר ר"ל אמר קרא נער: (ב) רש"י ד"ה אין מכר וכו' אמרת קל וחומר מכרה:

תוספות רי"ד

אמר אביי א"ק תחת אשר ענה הני תחת אשר ענה מכלל דאיכא בושת ופגם רבא אמר א"ק ונתן האיש השוכב עמה לאבי הנערה נ' כסף הנאת שכיבה נ' כסף מכלל דאיכא בושת ופגם: ואימא לדידה. פי' דדוקא נ' כסף זכה רחמנא לאב אבל בושת ופגם להוי דידה. מסתברא דאבוה הוי מיגו דאי בעי מסר לה למנוול ומוכה שחין: פגם רואין אותה וכו'. היכי שיימינן לה אמר אבוה דשמואל אומדים כמה אדם רוצה ליתן בין שפחה בתולה לשפחה בעולה להשיאה לעבדו שיש לו קורת רוח ממנו: מתני' כל מקום שיש מכר אין קנס וכ"מ שיש קנס אין מכר קטנה יש לה מכר ואין לה קנס נערה יש לה קנס ואין לה מכר בוגרת לא קנס ולא מכר אר"י זו דברי רבי מאיר אבל חכמים אומרים יש קנס במקום מכר א"ר חסדא מ"ט דר"מ דאמר קרא ולו תהיה לאשה במהוה עצמה הכתוב מדבר ורבנן אמרי אמר קרא נערה ואפילו קטנה במשמע פי' נער כתיב וקרינן נערה מלא:

מסורת הש"ס

א) [ערכין טו.], ב) לעיל לג., ג) לקמן מו: מז. קדושין ג., ד) [ברכות יט: וש"נ], ה) לעיל כט. חולין כו., ו) [לעיל לו. חולין כו:], ז) לעיל כט. חולין כו: [תוספתא פ"ג ע"ש], ח) לקמן מד: ע"ש, ט) כ"י, י) [וע"ע תוס' יומא מט: סד"ה שאני ותוס' חולין עט. סד"ה זה כנס], כ) ת"י כ"י, ל) [כדאי' יבמות לג: ושם.].

תורה אור השלם

א) וְנָתַן הָאִישׁ הַשֹּׁכֵב עִמָּהּ לַאֲבִי הַנַּעֲרָ חֲמִשִּׁים כָּסֶף וְלוֹ תִהְיֶה לְאִשָּׁה תַּחַת אֲשֶׁר עִנָּהּ לֹא יוּכַל שַׁלְּחָהּ כָּל יָמָיו: [דברים כב, כט]
ב) אֵלֶּה הַחֻקִּים אֲשֶׁר צִוָּה יְיָ אֶת מֹשֶׁה בֵּין אִישׁ לְאִשְׁתּוֹ בֵּין אָב לְבִתּוֹ בִּנְעֻרֶיהָ בֵּית אָבִיהָ: [במדבר ל, יז]
ג) וְכִי יִמְכֹּר אִישׁ אֶת בִּתּוֹ לְאָמָה לֹא תֵצֵא כְּצֵאת הָעֲבָדִים: [שמות כא, ז]
ד) וְעָנְשׁוּ אֹתוֹ מֵאָה כֶסֶף וְנָתְנוּ לַאֲבִי הַנַּעֲרָה כִּי הוֹצִיא שֵׁם רָע עַל בְּתוּלַת יִשְׂרָאֵל וְלוֹ תִהְיֶה לְאִשָּׁה לֹא יוּכַל לְשַׁלְּחָהּ כָּל יָמָיו: [דברים כב, יט]
ה) וְאִם אֱמֶת הָיָה הַדָּבָר הַזֶּה לֹא נִמְצְאוּ בְתוּלִים לַנַּעֲר: וְהוֹצִיאוּ אֶת הַנַּעֲר אֶל פֶּתַח בֵּית אָבִיהָ וּסְקָלוּהָ אַנְשֵׁי עִירָהּ בָּאֲבָנִים וָמֵתָה כִּי עָשְׂתָה נְבָלָה בְּיִשְׂרָאֵל לִזְנוֹת בֵּית אָבִיהָ וּבִעַרְתָּ הָרָע מִקִּרְבֶּךָ: [דברים כב, כ-כא]

ליקוטי רש"י

ואחד שלא כדרכה. תחילה ולאח"כ בא עליה זה כדרכה דלהכי הוא בתולה ואית לה קנס [ויאמרו] זה שבעל פגומה דליכא בושת כולי האי יהיב נ' סלעים ואילו בעל בתולה שלימה לא יהיב נמי אלא חמשים אבל השתא גבי בושת איכא חילוק. מוכה שחין. דהוי פגום דומיא דנבעלה שלא כדרכה. תחת אשר עינה. רישיה דקרא ונתן האיש השוכב עמה לאבי הנערה חמשים כסף ונתן (דברים כב) דמשמע הני חמשים כסף יתן בשביל קנס העינוי ומדאיצטריך למכתב הכי מכלל דמיחייב מילי אחרנייתא כגון בושת ופגם דלאו קנסא דעינוי ניהנו דבלאו עינוי נמי איכא בושת ופגם והיינו נזק שהוא פחות מבתולה [ערכין טו.]. חמשים כסף נתחדשו (ס"א: נתחייבו) מתחת קנס העינוי אבל בושת ופגם הוא בשאר חובלים. השוכב עמה. קרא יתירא הוא לדרשה דמשמע לא נתן לאבי הנערה חמשים כסף. מכלל דאיכא בושת ופגם. דלאו ממעט הנאת שכיבה דהרי ישנן בשאר חובלים לא כליינהו. א"ק בנעוריה בית אביה. הכי דריש לה כל זמן [לעיל לג.].

שבנעוריה היא של אביה דכל שבח הבא לה לאביה הוא. לאמה. קרא יתירא הוא ודרשינן ליה בתו הרי היא לו כאמה ובתו נערה האמה' דאי קטנה לא איצטריך השתא זכותי מזכן לה מעשה ידיה מבעיא. תיפוק ליה מבנעוריה. אי מינה הוי מצי למילף אלא על כרחך מדלא יליף מהתם שמעינן מינה דלא אתא לממונא אלא להפרת נדרים [קידושין ג:]. אלא ההיא בהפרת נדרים הוא דכתי' [קידושין ג.]. וכי תימא נילף. מכסף קנסה מאונס ומפתה דנותנין לאביה חמשים כסף [קידושין שם]. ממונא. קל מאיסורא [קידושין שם]. וכי תימא נילף ממונא מקנסא. מקנסא לא ילפינן [קידושין שם]. דאי בעי מסר לה וכו'. כיון דבידו ליטול ממון לפוגמה ולביישה בושה זו השתא אפסדיה ולא דידה היא ומדקא ממזג הוא להו לגבי דידה ולא יקפלו עליה תובעין [קידושין שם]. [המשך בדף מא.]

להא מילתא נמי ליגמרו מהדדי אמר קרא א) מהר ימהרנה לו לאשה לו מדעתו: כיצד שותה בעציצו כו': אמר רב כהנא אמריתא לשמעתא קמיה דרב זביד מנהרדעא ניתי עשה ונדחה ל"ת אמר לי היכא אמרינן ניתי עשה ונידחי ל"ת כגון מילה בצרעת דלא אפשר לקיומיה לעשה אבל הכא אי אמרה דלא בעינא מי איתיה לעשה כלל: **מתני'** יתומה שנתארסה ונתגרשה ר' אלעזר אומר האונס חייב והמפתה פטור: **גמ'** אמר רבה בר בר חנה אמר ר' יוחנן ר"א בשיטת ר"ע רבו אמרה דאמר יש לה קנס וקנסה לעצמה ממאי מדקתני יתומה ר"א אומר האונס חייב והמפתה פטור יתומה פשיטא אלא הא קמ"ל דנערה שנתארסה ונתגרשה כיתומה מה יתומה לעצמה אף נערה שנתארסה ונתגרשה לעצמה א"ר זירא אמר רבה בר שילא אמר רב המנונא סבא א"ר אדא בר אהבה אמר רב הלכה כר' אלעזר קרי רב עליה דרבי אלעזר טובינא דחכימי: **מתני'** איזהו בושת הכל לפי המבייש והמתבייש פגם רואין אותה כאילו היא שפחה נמכרת בשוק כמה היתה יפה וכמה היא יפה קנס שוה בכל אדם וכל שיש לו קצבה מן התורה שוה בכל אדם: **גמ'** ואימא חמשים סלעים אמר רחמנא מכל מילי א"ר זירא יאמרו בעל בת מלכים חמשים בעל בת הדיוטות חמשים א"ל אביי אי הכי גבי עבד נמי יאמרו עבד נוקב מרגליות שלשים עבד עושה מעשה

רש"י

להא מילתא. שיהיה מפתה נושא על כרחו: **עשה.** לו תהיה לאשה: **ונדחה את לא תעשה.** דאינה ראויה לבא בישראל כגון ממזרת: **מי איתיה לעשה כלל.** השתא נמי מלמדין אותה לומר איני רוצה: **מתני' יתומה שנתארסה ונתגרשה האונס חייב והמפתה פטור.** דכיון דיתומה היא וקנס שלה היא ואמחילתיה דמדעתה נתפתתה לו פטור ובגמרא מפרש דנתארסה ונתגרשה מילתא אחריתי היא ולא איתומה קאי: **גמ' בשיטת ר"ע רבו אמרה.** דאמר במתני' נערה שנתארסה ונתגרשה קנסה לעצמה והך נתארסה ונתגרשה דר' אלעזר כשאביה קיים וקרי לה יתומה משום דפקע זכות אב מינה לגבי קנסה: **ממאי.** דכר"ע סבירא ליה: **מדקתני אונס חייב ומפתה פטור.** אלמא יש לה קנס ולעצמה הלכך מפתה פטור למדעתה עבד ואונס חייב ואפילו אביה קיים דאי יתומה כדקתני פשיטא דמפתה פטור אלא הא קמ"ל כו': **יתומה פשיטא.** מסקנא דמילתא דר' יוחנן היא: **טובינא דחכימי.** מאושר שבחכמים אשרי מתרגמינן טובאי. ר' אלעזר הוא ר' אלעזר בן שמוע ותלמידו של ר"ע היה כדאמרינן ביבמות בהבא על יבמתו (דף סב:) והיה העולם שמם עד שבא ר"ע אצל רבותינו שבדרום ושנה להם ר"מ ור' יהודה ור' יוסי ור"ש ורבי אלעזר בן שמוע: **מתני' הכל לפי המבייש.** אדם בינוני המבייש בושתו קשה מאדם זולל ומאדם חשוב: **והמתבייש.** לפי חשיבותו בושתו: **כאילו היא שפחה.** בגמרא מפרש מאי גריעותא מחמת בעילה: **גמ' יאמרו כו'.** והיכן הוא חילוק שביניהן אלא בושת הלכך יהיב בושת: **גבי עבד.** שנגחו שור שנתנה תורה קצבה ל' שקלים:

תוספות

מהר ימהרנה לו מדעתו. וא"ת ולו תהיה לאשה נידרוש נמי לו מדעתו והא דכתיב לא יוכל לשלחה היינו היכא דכבר נשאה וי"ל דאין סברא שיהיה מדעתו כיון שאם נשאה לא יוכל לשלחה [ועוד ולו תהיה קאי אאשה ולהכי בעינן מדעתה אבל מהר ימהרנה קאי אגברא]: **ניתי עשה ונדחה לא תעשה.** לאו למנקט בה דבר ערוה פריך דהא איכא בה לאו ועשה כדאמרי' בפ"ק דיבמות (דף יא: ושם) לא יוכל בעלה וגו' לרבות סוטה שנסתרה והיינו לאו ודרשינן (סוטה דף כח:) ונטמאה ונטמאה חד לבעל וחד לבועל אלא אשאינה ראויה לקהל פריך וא"ת ומאי פריך וליתי עשה ולידחי ל"ת הא דריש מקרא בהדיא במתני' דבעינן אשה הראויה לו ולמאי דמשני דלא חשיב עשה קשה דמאי איצטריך קרא למעוטי שאינה ראויה לו וי"ל דלאו מיתורא דקרא מפיק ליה במתניתין אלא דולו תהיה לאשה משמע מדעתה והכי ממעט אשה שאינה ראויה לו דהא אי אמרה לא בעינא לית לה מי איתא לעשה כלל הלכך לא חשיב עשה ולא דחי לא תעשה ומ"מ ס"ד דפריך דהשתא היכא דאמרה בעינא ליה ליתי עשה ולידחי ל"ת ומסיק דאפילו אמרה בעינא ליה לא חשיב עשה כיון דלא דמי למילה בצרעת אי נמי מיתורא דקרא דריש ופריך דליתי עשה ולידחי ל"ת ומיתורא דקרא נוקי לחייבי כריתות דלאו קרא הוה סברינן אפי' חייבי כריתות דהואיל ואיתרבו לקנס לעיל בריש פירקין איתרבו נמי לנישואין דקראי משתמעי שפיר דהיכא דאיכא קנס איכא נמי נישואין אי נמי יש לומר דהכי פריך ניתי עשה ונידחי לא תעשה וכי תימא שאני הכא דגלי קרא א"כ ניגמר מהכא בכל דוכתא דלא דחי ומשני דלא חשיב עשה ומ"מ איצטריך קרא דאי לאו קרא הוה חשבינן ליה דלא אפשר לקיים שניהם וחשיב עשה דעיקר מצוה היא לישא כי היכי דאמרינן בפרק ב' דיבמות (דף כא.) דחליצה במקום יבום לאו י) כלום הוא:

כגון מילה בצרעת. א) אומר ר"ת דלסימנא בעלמא נקטיה דהא בקוצץ בהרתו איכא עשה ולא תעשה כדאמרינן בפרק ר' אליעזר דמילה (שבת דף קלב:) ללשון אחד הכתוב בספרים ומהתם לא ילפינן בעלמא דליתי עשה ודחי לא תעשה ועשה דמה למילה שכן נכרתו עליה י"ג בריתות אלא עיקר מילתא מכלאים בציצית וא"ת והא כלאים בציצית אפשר לקיים שניהם שיעשה בטלית צמר חוטין של צמר ואומר ר"י דבטלית של פשתן אי אפשר לקיים שניהם דלא אפשר לקיים מצות תכלת אלא ע"י כלאים דתכלת עמרא הוא וזה אין לנו לומר שיהא אסור ללבוש טלית של פשתן משום דאפשר בשל צמר דאין זה חשוב אפשר והא דאמרי' בפ' התכלת (מנחות דף מ. ושם) כל המטיל תכלת בסדין בירושלים אינו אלא מן המתמיהין ומפרש בגמרא גזירה משום קלא אילן ופריך לא יהיה אלא לבן ומשני אפשר במינו כדריש לקיש דאמר כל מקום שאתה כו' התם ודאי כיון דליכא תכלת אלא הכל לבן מצות לבן אפשר לקיים במינו וא"ת והא אמר התם לעיל ח) חוטי צמר פוטרין בשל פשתן ושל פשתן פוטרין בשל צמר ואמאי פוטרין והא אפשר לקיים שניהם דלבן אפשר במינו ואור"ת דכל ד' חוטין לבן ודאי אסור דאפשר במינו אבל התם קאמר דשני חוטי צמר לבן פוטרים בשל פשתן דמגו דתכלת פטרה שכבר נעשה כלאים ע"י תכלת שבו לבן של צמר נמי פטר ומגו דשני חוטי לבן של צמר פוטרים בשל פשתן שני חוטי לבן של פשתן נמי פוטרין בשל צמר אע"ג דלא נעשה התם כלאים ע"י תכלת שבו וצריך עיון אם שני חוטי לבן של פשתן ושני חוטי לבן של צמר מותר לתת בטלית של צמר או בטלית של פשתן דשמא לא הותרו שני חוטי לבן אלא דווקא במקום תכלת אבל שלא במקום תכלת לא או דלמא לא שנא דהא שני חוטי לבן של פשתן פוטרים בשל צמר אע"ג דהתם תכלת לא מעלה ולא מוריד דע"י אותו תכלת לא נעשה אכתי כלאים ואין להקשות אי שרו שני חוטי לבן בכלאים אפי' אין תכלת עמהן אמאי מטיל תכלת בסדין בירושלים אינו אלא מן המתמיהין יטילו עמו שני חוטי לבן של פשתן דאפילו הוי ההוא תכלת קלא אילן או לבן גמור שרי דאיכא למיגזר שמא יטילו עמו שני חוטי לבן של צמר ויסברו שאותן שני חוטין הצבועין הן תכלת ויהיו כל ד' חוטין לבן של צמר:

[**אי אמרה לא בעינא מי איתיה לעשה כלל.** הקשה הר"ר עזרא אמאי איצטריך קרא בפ"ק דיבמות (דף ה:) דאין עשה דכיבוד דוחה שבת הא ליכא עשה דאי אמר לא בעינא ליכבוד מי איתא לעשה כלל וי"ל דהתם מ"מ מיד כשצוה אב הוי עשה לעשות מצותו ול"נ דהכא גבי דידה ליכא עשה דהא אי בעיא אמרה לא בעינא ליה הלכך אין לה לעבור בלאו משום עשה דידיה דהיא מוזהרת כמותו והשוה הכתוב אשה לאיש כדאמרינן ביש מותרות (יבמות דף פד:). ת"י כ"י]:

הכי גרסינן ממאי מדקתני האונס חייב והמפתה פטור יתומה פשיטא אלא הא קמ"ל כו'. כלומר מדקתני האונס חייב והמפתה פטור ש"מ דיש לה קנס וקנסה לעצמה דאי משום יתומה נקט מפתה פטור פשיטא דפטור דהא מחלה אלא ע"כ לא נקט מפתה פטור אלא משום נערה שנתארסה ונתגרשה ולא נקט יתומה במתני' אלא ליתן טעם אמאי מפתה פטור והלא קנסה לאביה ואשמעי' דהרי היא כיתומה שקנסה לעצמה וא"ת ומנלן הא אדרבה אימא דנקט יתומה למידק טעמא דהויא נמי יתומה הא אינה יתומה אפילו מפתה חייב דקנסה לאביה וי"ל דלית לן למימר לדיוקא אתא כל זמן דנוכל לומר דלגופיה אתא: ט) **אחד** כדרכה ואחד שלא כדרכה. שלא כדרכה ה"ל למינקט ברישא אלא כן דרך הש"ס שאינו חושש כדנקט לעיל (דף לה.) בתנא דבי חזקיה בין מתכוין לשאין מתכוין דה"ל למינקט שאין מתכוין ברישא כדקתני בין שוגג למזיד אלא כן דרך הש"ס במקום שצריך לשנות הן ולאו י): **יאמרו** בעל שלימה חמשים. פירוש הראשון שבא עליה שלא כדרכה דמחייב קנס אפילו שלא כדרכה כדאמרינן בפ"ק דקידושין (דף ט:) באו עליה י' ועדיין היא בתולה כו' פירוש שלא כדרכה וקאמר מודה רבי לענין קנס דכולהו משלמי ובפרק הבא על יבמתו (יבמות דף נט. ושם) גבי ולו תהיה לאשה באשה הראויה לו פרט לאלמנה לכ"ג כו' ופריך היכי דמי אילימא כדרכה תיפוק ליה דהויא לה בעולה אלא לאו שלא כדרכה והכא הוה מצי למינקט שבאו עליה ב' שלא כדרכה וכן בפרק בן סורר (סנהדרין עג:) דמוקי ההיא דאלו נערות שיש להן קנס כגון שבא עליה שלא כדרכה וחזר ובא עליה כדרכה הוה מצי למינקט וחזר ובא עליה שלא כדרכה ומה שקשה על פירוש הקונטרס דהתם פירשנו בהבא על יבמתו (יבמות דף נט.) ובפרק קמא דקידושין (דף ט:):

ואימא

עין משפט נר מצוה

עט א מיי' פ"ג מהל' מילה הלכה ו:
פ ב מיי' פ"ב מהלכות נערה הלכה יד סמג עשין נד טור אה"ע סי' קעז:
פא ג מיי' פ"ב שם הל' ט סמג וטור שם:
פב ד מיי' פ"ב שם הל' ד ומיי' פ"ג מהל' חובל ומזיק הל' ו סמג שם ועשין ע טוש"ע ח"מ סי' תכ סעיף לד:
פג ה מיי' פ"ב מהלכות נערה הל' ג סמג עשין נד טור אה"ע סי' קעז:

תוספות רי"ד

מתני' כיצד שותה בעציצו אפי' היא חיגרת ואפילו סומא אפי' מוכת שחין נמצא בה דבר זימה או שאינה ראויה לבוא בישראל אינו רשאי לקיימה שנאמר ולו תהיה לאשה אשה הראויה לו: **וליתי עשה** ולדחי את ל"ת היכא אמרי' דאתי עשה ודחי את ל"ת כגון מילה בצרעת דא"א לי' לקיומי לעשה אבל הכא אי אמרה לא בעינא ליה ליתא לעשה כלל. פי' המורה והשתא נמי מלמדים אותה לומר איני רוצה וקשה לי להאי פי' דא"כ גבי יבם אמאי אמרינן דאתי עשה ודחי ל"ת כיון דכתיב אם לא יחפוץ נלמדנו לומר איני רוצה ליבם ולא לידחי ואמאי אמרי' התם דדחי מ"ה נ"ל לפרש דמאי דאמר רחמנא גבי אונס ולו תהיה לאשה אינה אלא להפיס דעתה ואי אמרה לא בעינא לי' ליתי' לעשה כלל הלכך לאו כלום הוא עשה למדחי את ל"ת כיון שלא ציוהו הבורא אלא להפיס דעתה אבל מצות יבום רחמנא הוא דרמי עליה דאע"ג דאמרה אשה לא בעינא לא מיעקרא מצות יבום הלכך מצוה דרמי עליה רחמנא הוא ולהכי דחיא את ל"ת ואע"ג דמצי יבם למימר לא בעינא ליבומי כ"א למיחלץ הא אמרי' התם חליצה במקום יבום אינה מצוה: **מתני' יתומה שנתארס'** ונתגרשה ר"א אומר האונס חייב והמפתה פטור. פי' שתי נערות הן יתומות אע"פ שלא נתארסה שקנסה הוא לעצמה כיון שאין לה אב שאין אדם מוריש זכות בתו לבנו. וכן נערה שנתארס' ונתגרש' אע"פ שיש לה אב הרי קנסה לעצמה כר"ע. הלכך האונס חייב ליתן קנסא אבל המפתה פטור דאיהי אחילתיה גביה כיון שנתרצית לו: **אמר רבה בב"ח א"ר י'** ר"א בשיטת ר"ע אמרה דאמר נערה המאורסה יש לה קנס וקנסה לעצמה ממאי מדקתני יתומה פשיטא אלא הא קמ"ל דנערה שנתארס' ונתגרשה ה"ה כיתומה מה יתומה לעצמה אף נערה שנתארסה ונתגרשה לעצמה **אמר ר"א ב"א אמר רב** הלכתא כר"א וקרי ליה רב עליה דר"א טובינא דחכימא. פי' מאושר שבחכמים תרגום אשריך ישראל טובך ישראל: **מתני' איזהו בושת** הכל לפי המבייש והמתבייש. פי' אדם בינוני המבייש בושתו קשה מאדם זולל ומאדם חשוב

והמתבייש פי' לפי חשיבותו בושתו: **פגם** רואים אותה כאילו היא שפחה נמכרת לשוק כמה היתה יפה וכמה היא יפה וקנס שוה בכל אדם וכל שיש לו קצבה מה"ת שוה בכל אדם: ואימא נ' כסף אמר רחמנא מכל מילי. אמר

מסורת הש"ס

א) שבת קלג: ביצה ח. ב) [לעיל לח.] ג) גיטין כו: כריתות יג. ד) [ב"ק פג.] ה) ערכין יד. ו) [לעיל לח.] ז) ב"ק מלוה היא, ח) [דף לט:] ט) שייך לע"ב, י) [ועי' אריכות תוספות בזה בפסחים פה. ועוד ביתר ביאור בסוכה ל. ד"ה אתמר].

תוספות ישנים

א) ולספרים דלא גרסי הכא מילה בצרעת וכלאים בציצית אלא מילה בצרעת לחודיה היינו משום דבכלאים אינו פשוט כל כך דאי אפשר לקיים שניהם. מ"י.

לקוטים מהגר"א

[א] משנה יתומה שנתארסה. נקט כאן שגם זה חילוק בין אונס למפתה:

תורה אור השלם

א) וְכִי יְפַתֶּה אִישׁ בְּתוּלָה אֲשֶׁר לֹא אֹרָשָׂה וְשָׁכַב עִמָּהּ מָהֹר יִמְהָרֶנָּה לּוֹ לְאִשָּׁה: [שמות כב, טו]

ליקוטי רש"י

מהר ימהרנה. יפסוק לה מוהר כמשפט איש לאשתו שכותב לה כתובה וישאנה [שמות כב, טו]. **מילה בצרעת.** מילה דוחה לצרעת. דאתי עשה ודחי לא תעשה דהשמר (לך) דהכי קיימא לן בפרק קמא דיבמות (דף ג:) דאתי עשה ודחי לא תעשה. מילה דוחה וכו' את צרעת כדתניא לקמן ימול בשר ערלתו אפילו במקום בהרת יקוץ [שבת קלב:]. דכתיב (דברים כד) השמר בנגע הצרעת ותניא בקוצץ בהרתו הכתוב מדבר ותניא בגמרא דאם לא הביא כלי במסכת שבת (דף קלב:) ימול בשר ערלתו אפילו במקום בהרת יקוץ [ביצה ח.]. **הכל לפי המבייש.** אדם קל שבייש בושתו מרובה. **והמתבייש.** אדם חשוב שנתבייש בושתו מרובה [ב"ק פג:]. **אמר רחמנא מכל מילי.** ואימא קנס לא ליתיב. **בעל בת הדיוטות כו'.** בתמיה אלא השתא יהיב בושת יש חילוק בין בת מלכים לבת הדיוטות [ערכין יד:]. **נוקב מרגליות.** שעבודתו נוחה לעשות ושכרו מרובה [בכורות כט.]. **שלשים.** שלשים שקלים יתן. גזרת הכתוב הוא בין שהוא שוה אלף זוז בין שאינו שוה אלא דינר והשקל משקלו ד' זוזים שהם חצי אונקיא למשקל הישר של קולוני"א [שמות כא, לב].

things![22] – ? –

The Gemara counters:

אָמַר רַבִּי זֵירָא – R' Zeira said: יאמְרוּ בָּעַל בַּת מְלָכִים חֲמִשִּׁים – Shall they say, then, that if **one has relations with a daughter of kings** he pays **fifty** *shekels* **בָּעַל בַּת הֶדְיוֹטוֹת חֲמִשִּׁים – and** if **he has relations with a daughter of commoners** he also pays **fifty** *shekels*?! Obviously not![23]

The Gemara challenges this reasoning:

אָמַר לֵיהּ אַבַּיֵי – Abaye said to him: אִי הָכִי גַּבֵּי עֶבֶד נַמִּי – If so, with regard to the thirty-*shekel* fine paid for **a slave** killed by a *muad* ox,[24] you can **also** ask your question: **יאמְרוּ עֶבֶד נוֹקֵב מַרְגָּלִיּוֹת שְׁלֹשִׁים – Shall they say,** then, that if one's *muad* ox kills **a slave who cuts gems**[25] he pays **thirty** *shekels* **עֶבֶד עוֹשֶׂה –** and if his *muad* ox kills **a slave who performs**

NOTES

22. Perhaps the Torah does not prescribe compensatory payments for humiliation and depreciation in addition to the fifty-*shekel* fine. Rather, perhaps the fifty *shekels* are a lump-sum payment for all three things.

23. I.e. logic dictates that one who violates a princess should pay more than one who violates a commoner. And since the difference between the two cases lies in the fact that the princess suffers greater humiliation than does the commoner, logic further dictates that the compensation for humiliation is paid separately – i.e. in addition to the fifty-*shekel* payment, which is uniform for all (*Rashi*). [And once we see that the fifty *shekel* payment is not all-inclusive, i.e. that it does not cover a compensation (for humiliation) that is common to other assault cases, we can infer that it also fails to cover compensation for depreciation, which is likewise common to other assault cases (*Shitah Mekubetzes*).]

24. *Exodus* 21:32.

25. [Or is otherwise highly skilled.]

להא מילתא נמי ליגמרו מהדדי אמר קרא א) מהר ימהרנה לו לאשה לו מדעתו: כיצד שותה בעציצו כו': אמר רב כהנא אמריתא לשמעתא קמיה דרב זביד מנהרדעא ניתי עשה ונדחה ל"ת דאמר לי א היכא אמרינן ב) ניתי עשה ונידחי ל"ת כגון מילה בצרעת דלא אפשר לקיומיה לעשה אבל הכא אי אמרה דלא בעינא מי איתיה לעשה כלל: **מתני'** ו יתומה שנתארסה ונתגרשה ר' אלעזר אומר האונס חייב והמפתה פטור: **גמ'** אמר רבה בר בר חנה אמר ר' יוחנן ר"א בשיטת ר"ע רבו אמרה דאמר ג) יש לה קנס וקנסה לעצמה ממאי מדקתני יתומה ר"א אומר האונס חייב והמפתה פטור יתומה פשיטא אלא הא קמ"ל דנערה שנתארסה ונתגרשה כיתומה מה ב יתומה לעצמה אף נערה שנתארסה ונתגרשה לעצמה א"ר זירא אמר רבה בר שילא אמר רב המנונא סבא א"ר אדא בר אהבה אמר רב ג הלכה כר' אלעזר ד) קרי רב עליה דרבי אלעזר טובינא דחכימי: **מתני'** ה) איזהו בושת ד הכל לפי המבייש והמתבייש פגם רואין אותה כאילו היא שפחה נמכרת בשוק כמה היתה יפה וכמה היא יפה ה קנס שוה בכל אדם וכל שיש לו קצבה מן התורה שוה בכל אדם: **גמ'** ואימא ו) חמשים סלעים אמר רחמנא מכל מילי א"ר זירא יאמרו בעל בת מלכים חמשים בעל בת הדיוטות חמשים א"ל אביי אי הכי גבי עבד נמי יאמרו עבד נוקב מרגליות שלשים עבד עושה מעשה

רש"י

להא מילתא. שיהיה מפתה נושא על כרחו: עשה. לו תהיה לאשה: ונדחה את לא תעשה. דאינה ראויה לבא בישראל כגון ממזרת: מי איתיה לעשה כלל. השתא נמי מלמדין אותה לומר איני רוצה: **מתני'** יתומה שנתארסה ונתגרשה האונס חייב והמפתה פטור. דכיון דיתומה היא וקנס שלה היא ואחילתיה דמדעתה נתפתתה לו פטור ובגמרא מפרש דנתארסה ונתגרשה מילתא אחריתי היא ולא איתומה קאי: **גמ'** בשיטת ר"ע רבו אמרה. דאמר במתני' ז) נערה שנתארסה ונתגרשה קנסה לעצמה והכך נתארסה ונתגרשה דר' אלעזר כשאביה קיים וקרי לה יתומה משום דפקע זכות אב מינה לגבי קנסה: ממאי. דכר"ע סבירא ליה: מדקתני אונס חייב ומפתה פטור. אלמא יש לה קנס ולעצמה הלכך מפתה פטור דמדעתה עבד ואונס חייב ואפילו אביה קיים דאי יתומה כדקתני פשיטא דמפתה פטור אלא הא קמ"ל כו': יתומה פשיטא. מסקנא דמילתא דר' יוחנן היא: טובינא דחכימי. מאושר שבחכמים אשרי מתרגמינן טובאי. ר' אלעזר הוא ר' אלעזר בן שמוע ותלמידו של ר"ע היה כדאמרינן ביבמות בהבא על יבמתו (דף סב:) והיה העולם שמם עד שבא ר"ע אצל רבותינו שבדרום ושנה להם ר"מ ור' יהודה ור' יוסי ור"ש ורבי אלעזר בן שמוע: **מתני'** הכל לפי המבייש. אדם בינוני המבייש בושתו קשה מאדם זולל ומאדם חשוב: והמתבייש. לפי חשיבותו בושתו: כאילו היא שפחה. בגמרא מפרש מאי גריעותא מחמת בעילה: **גמ'** יאמרו כו'. והיכן הוא חילוק שביניהן אלא בושת הלכך יהיב בושת: גבי עבד. שנגחו שור שנתנה תורה קצבה ל' שקלים:

תוספות

מהר ימהרנה לו מדעתו. וא"ת ולו תהיה לאשה נידרוש נמי לו מדעתו והא דכתיב לא יוכל לשלחה היינו היכא דכבר נשאה וי"ל דאין סברא שיהיה מדעתו כיון שאם נשאה לא יוכל לשלחה ולו תהיה קאי אאשה ולהכי בעינן מדעתה אבל מהר ימהרנה קאי אגברא]: ניתי עשה ונדחה לא תעשה. לאו אמגלה בה דבר ערוה פריך דהא איכא בה לאו ועשה כדאמרי' בפ"ק דיבמות (דף יא: ושם) לא יוכל בעלה וגו' לרבות סוטה שנסתרה והיינו לאו ודרשינן (סוטה דף כח:) ונטמאה ונטמאה חד לבעל וחד לבועל אלא אמאי אינה ראויה לבא בקהל פריך וא"ת ומאי פריך וליתי עשה ולידחי ל"ת הא דריש מבקרא בהדיא במשנה דבעינן אשה הראויה לו ולמאי דמשני דלא חשיב עשה קשה דמאי איצטריך קרא למעוטי שאינה ראויה לו וי"ל דלאו מיתורא דקרא מפיק ליה במתניתין אלא דולו תהיה לאשה משמע מדעתה להכי ממעט אשה שאינה ראויה לו דהא לא אמרה לא בעינא ליה מי איכא לעשה כלל הלכך לא חשיב עשה לא דחי לא תעשה ומ"מ ס"ד דפריך השתא היכא דאמרה בעינא ליה אי ליתי עשה ולידחי ל"ת ומסיק דאפילו אמרה בעינא ליה לא חשיב עשה דלא דחי למילה בצרעת אי כוי מיתורא דקרא דריש ופריך דליתי עשה ולדחי ל"ת ויתורא דקרא נוקי להכי למיתי כריתות דאי לאו קרא הוה סברינן אפי' חייבי כריתות דהא איל ואתרבו לקנס לעיל בריש פירקין איתרבו נמי לנישואין דקראי משתמעי שפיר היכא דאיכא קנס איכא נמי נישואין אי נמי יש לומר דהכי פריך ניתי עשה ונידחי לא תעשה וכי תימא שאני הכא דגלי קרא א"כ ניגמר מהכא בכל דוכתא דלא דחי ומשני דלא חשיב עשה ומ"מ איצטריך קרא דאי לאו קרא הוה חשבינן ליה דלא אפשר לקיים שניהם וחשיב עשה דעיקר מצוה היא לישא כי היכי דאמרינן בפרק ב' דיבמות (דף כא.) דחליצה במקום יבוס לאו ז) כלום הוא:

כגון מילה בצרעת. א) אומר ר"ת דלסימנא בעלמא נקטיה דהא בקוצץ בהרתו איכא עשה ולא תעשה כדאמרינן בפרק ר' אליעזר דמילה (שבת דף קלב:) ללשון אחד הכתוב בספרים ומהתם לא ילפינן בעלמא דליתי עשה ודחי לא תעשה ועשה דמה למילה שכן נכרתו עליה י"ג בריתות אלא עיקר מילתא מכלאים בציצית וא"ת והא כלאים בציצית אפשר לקיים שניהם שיעשה בטלית צמר חוטין של צמר ואומר ר"י דבטלית של פשתן אי אפשר לקיים שניהם דלא אפשר לקיים מצות תכלת אלא ע"י כלאים דתכלת עמרא הוא וזה אין לנו לומר שיהא אסור ללבוש טלית של פשתן משום דאפשר בשל צמר דאין זה חשוב אפשר והא דאמרי' בפ' התכלת (מנחות דף מ. ושם) כל המטיל תכלת בסדין בירושלים אינו אלא מן המתמיהין ומפרש בגמרא גזירה משום קלא אילן ופריך לא יהיה אלא לבן ומשני אפשר במינו כדריש לקיש דאמר כל מקום שאתה כו' התם ודאי כיון דליכא תכלת אלא הכל לבן מצות לבן אפשר לקיים במינו וא"ת והא אמר התם לעיל ח) חוטי צמר פוטרין בשל פשתן ושל פשתן פוטרין בשל צמר ואמאי פוטרין והא אפשר לקיים שניהם דלבן אפשר במינו ואור"ת דכל ד' חוטין לבן ודאי אסור דאפשר במינו אבל התם קאמר דשני חוטי צמר לבן פוטרים בשל פשתן דמגו דתכלת פטרה שכבר נעשה כלאים ע"י תכלת שבו לבן של צמר נמי פטר ומגו דשני חוטי לבן של צמר פוטרים בשל פשתן שני חוטי לבן של פשתן נמי פוטרין בשל צמר אע"ג דלא נעשה התם כלאים כ"י תכלת שבו וצריך עיון אם שני חוטי לבן של פשתן ושני חוטי לבן של צמר מותר לתת בטלית של צמר או בטלית של פשתן דשמא לא התרו שני חוטי לבן אלא דווקא במקום תכלת אבל שלא במקום תכלת לא או דלמא לא שנא דהא שני חוטי לבן של פשתן פוטרים בשל צמר אע"ג דהתם תכלת לא מעלה ולא מוריד דע"י אותו תכלת לא נעשה אכתי כלאים ואין להקשות אי שרו שני חוטי לבן בכלאים אפי' אי תכלת עמהן אמאי מטיל תכלת בסדין בירושלים אינו אלא מן המתמיהין יטילו עמו שני חוטי לבן של פשתן דאפילו הוי ההוא תכלת קלא אילן או לבן גמור שרי דליכא למיגזר שמא יטילו עמו שני חוטי לבן של צמר ויסברו שאותן שני חוטין הצבועין הן תכלת ויהיו כל ד' חוטין לבן של צמר:

[**אי** אמרה לא בעינא מי איתיה לעשה כלל. הקשה הר"ר עזרא אמאי איצטריך קרא בפ"ק דיבמות (דף ה:) דאין עשה דכיבוד דוחה שבת הא ליכא עשה דאי אמר לא בעינא לכיבוד מי איתא לעשה כלל וי"ל דהתם מ"מ מיד כשצוה אב הוי עשה לעשות מצותו ול"נ דהכא גבי דידה ליכא עשה דהכא אי בעיא אמרה לא בעינא ליה הלכך אין לה לעבור בלאו משום עשה דידיה דהיא מחהרת כמותו והשוה הכתוב אשה לאיש כדאמרינן ביש מותרות (יבמות דף פד:). ת"י כ"י]:

הכי גרסינן ממאי מדקתני האונס חייב והמפתה פטור יתומה פשיטא אלא הא קמ"ל כו'. כלומר מדקתני האונס חייב והמפתה פטור ש"מ דיש לה קנס וקנסה לעצמה דאי משום יתומה נקט מפתה פטור פשיטא דפטור דהא מחלה אלא ע"כ לא נקט מפתה פטור אלא משום נערה שנתארסה ונתגרשה ולא נקט יתומה במתני' אלא ליתן טעם אמאי מפתה פטור והלא קנסה לאביה ואשמעי' דהרי היא כיתומה שקנסה לעצמה וא"ת ומנלן הא אדרבה אימא דנקט יתומה למידק טעמא דהויא נמי יתומה הא אינה יתומה אפילו מפתה חייב דקנסה לאביה וי"ל דלית לן למימר לדיוקא אתא כל זמן דנוכל לומר לגופיה אתא: ט) **אחד** כדרכה ואחד שלא כדרכה. שלא כדרכה ה"ל למינקט ברישא אלא כן דרך הש"ס שאינו חושש כדנקט לעיל (דף לה.) בתנא דבי חזקיה בין מתכוין לשאין מתכוין דה"ל למינקט שאין מתכוין ברישא כדקתני בין שוגג למזיד אלא כן דרך הש"ס במקום שצריך לשנות הן ולאו י): **יאמרו** בעל שלימה חמשים. פירוש הראשון שבא עליה שלא כדרכה דמחייב קנס אפילו שלא כדרכה כדאמרינן בפ"ק דקידושין (דף ט:) באו עליה י' ועדיין היא בתולה כו' פירוש שלא כדרכה וקאמר מודה רבי לענין קנס דכולהו משלמי ובפרק הבא על יבמתו (יבמות דף נט. ושם) גבי ולו תהיה לאשה באשה הראויה לו פרט לאלמנה לכ"ג כו' ופריך היכי דמי אילימא כדרכה תיפוק ליה דהויא לה בעולה אלא לאו שלא כדרכה והכא הוה מצי למינקט שבאו עליה ב' שלא כדרכה וכן בפרק בן סורר (סנהדרין עג:) דמוקי ההיא דאלו נערות שיש להן קנס כגון שבא עליה שלא כדרכה וחזר ובא עליה כדרכה והוה מצי למינקט וחזר ובא עליה שלא כדרכה ומה שקשה על פירוש הקונטרס דהתם פירשנו בהבא על יבמתו (יבמות דף נט.) ובפרק קמא דקידושין (דף ט:): ואימא

תוספות רי"ד

מתני' כיצד שותה בעציצו אפי' היא חיגרת ואפילו סומא אפי' מוכת שחין נמצא בה דבר זימה או שאינה ראויה לבוא בישראל אינו רשאי לקיימה שנאמר ולו תהיה לאשה אשה הראויה לו: **וליתי עשה** ולדחי את ל"ת היכא אמרי' דאתי עשה ודחי את ל"ת כגון מילה בצרעת דא"א לי' לקיומי לעשה אבל הכא אי אמרה לא בעינא ליה ליתא לעשה כלל. פי' המורה והשתא נמי מלמדים אותה לומר איני רוצה וקשה לי להאי פי' דא"כ גבי יבם אמאי אמרינן דאתי עשה ודחי ל"ת כיון דכתיב אם לא יחפוץ נלמדנו לומר איני רוצה ליבם ולא לידחי ואמאי אמרי' התם דדחי מ"ה נ"ל לפרש דמאי דאמר רחמנא גבי אונס ולו תהיה לאשה אינה אלא להפיס דעתה ואי אמרה לא בעינא לי' ליתי' לעשה כלל הלכך לאו כלום הוא עשה למדחי את ל"ת כיון שלא ציוהו הבורא אלא להפיס דעתה אבל מצות יבום רחמנא הוא דרמי עליה דאע"ג דאמרה אשה לא בעינא לא מיעקרא מצות יבום הלכך מצוה דרמי עליה רחמנא הוא ולהכי דחיא את ל"ת ואע"ג דמצי יבם למימר לא בעינא ליבומי כ"א למיחלץ הא אמרי' התם חליצה במקום יבום אינה מצוה: **מתני' יתומה שנתארס'** ונתגרשה ר"א אומר האונס חייב והמפתה פטור. פי' שתי נערות הן יתומות אע"פ שלא נתארסה שקנסה הוא לעצמה כיון שאין לה אב שאין אדם מוריש זכות בתו לבניו. וכן נערה שנתארס' ונתגרש' אע"פ שיש לה אב קנסה לעצמה כר"ע. הלכך האונס חייב ליתן קנס אבל המפתה פטור דאיהי אחילתיה גבה כיון שנתרצית לו: **אמר רבה בב"ח אר"י** ר"א בשיטת ר"ע אמרה דאמר נערה המאורסה יש לה קנס וקנסה לעצמה ממאי מדקתני יתומה פשיטא אלא הא קמ"ל דנערה שנתארס' ונתגרשה ה"ה כיתומה מה יתומה לעצמה אף נערה שנתארסה ונתגרשה לעצמה **אמר ר"א ב"א אמר רב** הלכתא כר"א וקרי ליה רב עליה דר"א טוביינא דחכימא. פי' מאושר שבחכמים תרגום אשריך ישראל טובך ישראל: **מתני' איזהו בושת** הכל לפי המבייש והמתבייש פי' אדם בינוני המבייש בושתו קשה מאדם זולל ומאדם חשוב

עין משפט נר מצוה

עט א מיי' פ"ב מהל' נערה הלכה ו:
פ ב מיי' פ"ב מהלכות נערה הלכה יד סמג עשין נד טור אה"ע סי' קעז:
פא ג מיי' פ"ג שם הל' ט סמג ועור שם:
פב ד מיי' פ"ב שם הל' ד ומיי' פ"ג מהל' חובל ומזיק הל' ב סמג עשין ע טור שם וטוש"ע ח"מ סי' תכ סעיף כד:
פג ה מיי' פ"ב מהלכות נערה הל' ג סמג עשין נד טור אה"ע סי' קעז:

מסורת הש"ס

א) שבת קלג. בילה ח., ב) [לעיל לח.], ג) גיטין כה: כריתות יג., ד) [ב"ק פג:], ה) ערכין יד:, ו) [לעיל לח.], ז) ס"א מלוה היא, ח) [דף לט:], ט) שייך לע"ב, י) [וע"ע תוספות בזה בפסחים פה. ועוד ביאור בקונה כ"ה אמחן].

תוספות ישנים

א) ולספרים דלא גרסי הכא מילה בצרעת וכלאים בציצית אלא מילה בצרעת לחודיה היינו משום דבכלאים אינו פשוט כל כך דלא אפשר לקיים שניהם. ת"י]

ליקוטים מהגר"א

[א] משנה יתומה שנתארסה. נקט כאן שגם זה חילוק בין אונס למפתה:

תורה אור השלם

א) וְכִי יְפַתֶּה אִישׁ בְּתוּלָה אֲשֶׁר לֹא אֹרָשָׂה וְשָׁכַב עִמָּהּ מָהֹר יִמְהָרֶנָּה לּוֹ לְאִשָּׁה: [שמות כב, טו]

ליקוטי רש"י

מהר ימהרנה. יפסוק לה מוהר כמשפט איש לאשתו שכותב לה כתובה ויטאנה [שמות כב, טו]. מילה בצרעת. מילה דוחה צרעת, דלאי עשה דימול ודחי לא תעשה דהשמר [לך] דהכי קיימא לן בפרק קמא דיבמות (דף ג:) דלאו עשה ודחי לא תעשה. מילה דוחה וכו' את הצרעת כדמתא לקוץ ימול בשר ערלתו אפילו במקום בהרת יקוץ [שבת קלב:]. דכתיב (דברים כד) השמר בנגע הצרעת ותניא בקוצץ בהרתו הכתוב מדבר ותניא בגמרא דאם לא הכיא כלי במסכת שבת (דף קלב:) ימול בשר ערלתו אפילו במקום בהרת יקוץ [ביצה ח.]. הכל לפי המבייש. אדם קל שבייש בושתו מרובה. והמתבייש. אדם חשוב בושתו מרובה [ב"ק פג:]. אמר רחמנא מכל מילי. ונופת ופגם לא ליתיב. בעל בת הדיוטות כו'. בתמיה אבל השתא כי יהיב בושת יש חילוק בין בת מלכים לבת הדיוטות [ערכין יד:]. נוקב מרגליות. שעבודתו נוחה לעשות ושכרו מרובה [בכורות כט:]. שלשים. שלשים שקלים קנס, גזרת הכתוב הוא בין שחוה שוה אלף זוז בין שאינו שוה אלא דינר והשקל משקלו ד' זוזים שהם כסף של אוקיא למשקל הישר של קלוני"א [שמות כא, לב].

והמתבייש פי' לפי חשיבותו בושתו: **פגם** רואים אותה כאילו היא שפחה נמכרת לשוק כמה היתה יפה וכמה היא יפה וקנס שוה בכל אדם וכל שיש לו קצבה מה"ת שוה בכל אדם: ואימא נ' כסף אמר רחמנא מכל מילי. אמר

[our Mishnah] states: יְתוֹמָה רַבִּי אֶלְעָזָר אוֹמֵר הָאוֹנֵס חַיָּיב וְהַמְפַתֶּה פָּטוּר — AN ORPHAN ... R' ELAZAR SAYS: THE ONE WHO VIOLATES her IS LIABLE, AND THE ONE WHO SEDUCES her IS EXEMPT. יְתוֹמָה פְּשִׁיטָא — Now, the ruling in the case of **an orphan is obvious!**[13] אֶלָּא הָא קָא מַשְׁמַע לָן — **Rather, [the Mishnah] is teaching us this:** דְּנַעֲרָה שֶׁנִּתְאָרְסָה וְנִתְגָּרְשָׁה כִּיתוֹמָה — **That a *naarah* who was betrothed and divorced** and whose father is still alive **is like an orphan.** מַה יְתוֹמָה לְעַצְמָהּ — That is, **just as** the fine in the case of **an orphan** belongs **to her,** אַף נַעֲרָה שֶׁנִּתְאָרְסָה וְנִתְגָּרְשָׁה לְעַצְמָהּ — so **too,** the fine in the case of **a *naarah* who was betrothed and divorced** belongs **to her.**[14]

The Gemara rules:

אָמַר רַבִּי זֵירָא אָמַר רַבָּה בַּר שֵׁילָא — **R' Zeira said in the name of Rabbah bar Shila,** אָמַר רַב הַמְנוּנָא סָבָא — who said **in the name of Rav Hamnuna the Elder,** אָמַר רַב אַדָּא בַּר אַהֲבָה — who said **in the name of Rav Adda bar Ahavah,** אָמַר רַב — who said **in the name of Rav:** הֲלָכָה כְּרַבִּי אֶלְעָזָר — **The law accords with** the ruling of **R' Elazar.** קָרֵי רַב עֲלֵיהּ דְּרַבִּי אֶלְעָזָר טוּבִינָא דַּחֲכִימֵי — And **Rav proclaimed upon R' Elazar** the title **"most fortunate of sages."**[15]

Mishnah אֵיזֶהוּ בּוֹשֶׁת — **What is** the compensation for **humiliation?** I.e. what are the criteria for determining the amount of payment? הַכֹּל לְפִי הַמְבַיֵּישׁ וְהַמִּתְבַּיֵּישׁ — It is **all according to** the stature of **the humiliater**[16] **and the humiliated.**[17] Both factors must be considered. פְּגָם — **Depreciation** is assessed as follows: רוֹאִין אוֹתָהּ כְּאִילּוּ הִיא שִׁפְחָה נִמְכֶּרֶת בַּשּׁוּק — **We see her as if she were a slavewoman being sold in the marketplace,** כַּמָּה הָיְתָה יָפָה — and we calculate **how much she was worth** prior to the violation וְכַמָּה הִיא יָפָה — **and how much she is worth** now, after the violation.[18] קְנָס שָׁוֶה בְּכָל אָדָם — However, the **fine is the same for every person.**[19] וְכָל שֶׁיֵּשׁ לוֹ קִצְבָה מִן הַתּוֹרָה שָׁוֶה בְּכָל אָדָם — **And every** monetary liability **that has a fixed amount from the Torah is the same for every person.**[20]

Gemara The Gemara questions the legitimacy of requiring a violator and seducer to pay additional compensatory damages:

וְאֵימָא חֲמִשִּׁים סְלָעִים אָמַר רַחֲמָנָא מִכָּל מִילֵּי — **But say** that when **the Merciful One stated** in the Torah that the violator and seducer remit **fifty *selaim*,**[21] it is a payment **for all**

NOTES

or a girl who was betrothed and divorced." Here, however, *Rashi* says that the Mishnah speaks of only one case, and the word "orphan" means not an actual orphan but a יְתוֹמָה בְּחַיֵּי הָאָב, *a girl with the halachic status of orphan during her father's lifetime. Ritva* explains that *Rashi* is actually informing us that R' Elazar uses the word "orphan" to connote *both* an actual orphan and a girl who has the halachic status of an orphan during her father's lifetime, so that the Mishnah should be read as follows: *An orphan,* i.e. both an actual orphan and a girl who has the halachic status of an orphan [with regard to the fine] on account of her *having been betrothed and divorced,* etc. See *Shitah Mekubetzes* ד״ה מתני׳ וד״ה ה״ג ממאי for a lengthy explanation of what prompted *Rashi* to interpret the Mishnah in this manner.

Ritva explains further that *Rashi* equates an actual orphan and a legal orphan only vis-a-vis R' Elazar's ruling that a seducer is not liable to the fine. However, the seducer of a legal orphan must still pay the father for humiliation (בֹּשֶׁת) and depreciation (פְּגָם), since betrothal abrogates his right to receive her fine but not these penalties. [This is also the opinion of *Rambam, Hil. Naarah Besulah* 2:16, and *Ran.* However, *Rosh* (3:5) understands our Mishnah as exempting the seducer from *all* payments. He thus concludes that betrothal abrogates a *naarah's* father's rights not only to the fine, but to the payments for humiliation and depreciation as well. This is also the opinion of *Tosafos* above, 38b ד״ה יש.]

13. If R' Elazar is discussing only the case of an actual orphan (who happened to have been betrothed and divorced), it is obvious that her seducer is exempt from the fine — for there is no living father, and she herself, by acquiescing to the seduction, has waived any right to the fine she might have (see *Rashi*).

14. From R' Elazar's ruling that the violator is liable and the seducer is exempt, it is evident that he holds that the girl under discussion is entitled to the fine and that the fine belongs to her. Indeed, it is for that very reason that the seducer is exempt (for by her acquiescence she waived her right to the fine) and the violator is liable (for she did not waive it). And since R' Elazar bothers to teach that the seducer is exempt from paying the fine, he obviously applies this law even to where the father is still alive [i.e. the word "orphan" stated in the Mishnah must be referring to both an actual orphan and a יְתוֹמָה בְּחַיֵּי הָאָב, *a girl who has the halachic status of orphan during her father's lifetime;* see note 12 above]. For if R' Elazar meant only an actual orphan, it would be unnecessary to teach that the seducer is exempt (for reasons enumerated in the previous note). Rather, the Mishnah must be referring to a *naarah* who was betrothed and divorced and whose father is still alive. Nevertheless, the Mishnah indicates that she is "like an orphan" in the sense that her father's right to the fine has been abrogated on account of her betrothal, and this is consistent with R' Akiva's ruling in the Mishnah on 38a (*Rashi,* as explained by *Shitah Mekubetzes;* see there at length).

15. The "R' Elazar" who authored our Mishnah and is the subject of Rav's praise is R' Elazar ben Shamua, who was a disciple of R' Akiva, as the Gemara relates (*Yevamos* 62b): *R' Akiva had twenty-two thousand pairs of students, all of whom died in one period* [between Pesach and Shavuos; see *Tur, Orach Chaim* §493] etc. *And the world remained desolate [of Torah scholars] until R' Akiva came to our teachers in the South and taught them. [They were] R' Meir, R' Yehudah, R' Yose, R' Shimon and R' Elazar ben Shamua* (*Rashi*). [*Rashi* was bothered by why ruling in accordance with the teaching of R' Akiva, his master, earned R' Elazar the title "most fortunate of sages." Why not confer it upon the teacher himself, R' Akiva? *Rashi* thus explains that the world was devoid of Torah scholarship until R' Akiva came and taught the oral tradition of the Torah (תּוֹרָה שֶׁבְּעַל פֶּה) to these five students. By virtue of the fact that he saved the Oral Law from being forgotten, R' Akiva took the place of Moses for these disciples. Consequently, one who was able to comprehend and rule in accordance with his teachings had, in fact, ruled in accordance with the halachah, and was deserving of the sobriquet "most fortunate of sages" (*Shitah Mekubetzes;* cf. *Ritva* ד״ה קרי רב).]

16. The humiliation inflicted by a person of average stature is more severe than that inflicted by either a worthless or an important person (*Rashi;* cf. *Rashi* to *Bava Kamma* 83b ד״ה הכל לפי המבייש, and see *Rav* to our Mishnah). [*Rashi* presumably means that the actions of a worthless individual carry little weight, while mere involvement with someone of great stature ameliorates the shame he inflicts.] *Ran* concedes that *Rashi's* explanation is applicable to cases of humiliation in general; however, with regard to violation and seduction, the more lowly the assailant, the greater the shame.

17. The greater the stature of the victim, the greater his humiliation (*Rashi*).

18. [And the assailant pays the difference.] The Gemara will explain why violation and seduction diminish her value on the slave market (*Rashi*).

19. A violator or seducer pays fifty silver *shekels* regardless of whether his victim was the daughter of the Kohen Gadol, the daughter of a convert, or a *mamzeress* (*Rambam, Hil. Naarah Besulah* 2:3, from *Arachin* 14b).

20. This general rule refers to the thirty *shekels* one pays when his *muad* ox kills a slave (*Exodus* 21:32); the hundred *shekels* one pays for מוֹצִיא שֵׁם רַע, *defaming* his wife (*Deuteronomy* 22:19); the *erech* valuations prescribed for various age groups and genders (*Leviticus* 27:1-8); and the five *shekels* for פִּדְיוֹן הַבֵּן, *the redemption of the firstborn* (*Numbers* 18:16). Everyone pays these fixed amounts [regardless of the family or social status of the persons involved] (*Meiri*).

21. The Scriptural *shekel* was replaced by the *sela* in the Mishnaic era. The *sela* actually was slightly larger, weighing 1.2 *shekel* (see *Bechoros* 50a; *Tosafos* to *Bava Basra* 90a ד״ה והשקל; and *Rambam, Hil. Shekalim* 1:2).

להא מילתא נמי ליגמרו מהדדי אמר קרא א) מהר ימהרנה לו לאשה לו מדעתו: כיצד שותה בעציצו כו': אמר רב כהנא אמריתא לשמעתא קמיה דרב זביד מנהרדעא ניתי עשה ונדחה ל"ת אמר לי א) היכא אמרינן ב) ניתי עשה ונידחי ל"ת כגון מילה בצרעת דלא אפשר לקיומיה לעשה אבל הכא אי אמרה דלא בעינא מי איתיה לעשה כלל: מתני' ג) יתומה שנתארסה ונתגרשה ר' אלעזר אומר האונס חייב והמפתה פטור: גמ' אמר רבה בר בר חנה אמר ר' יוחנן ר"א בשיטת ר"ע רבו אמרה דאמר ג) יש לה קנס וקנסה לעצמה ממאי מדקתני יתומה ר"א אומר האונס חייב והמפתה פטור יתומה פשיטא אלא הא קמ"ל דנערה שנתארסה ונתגרשה כיתומה מה ב) יתומה לעצמה אף נערה שנתארסה ונתגרשה לעצמה א"ר זירא אמר רבה בר שילא אמר רב המנונא סבא א"ר אדא בר אהבה אמר רב ג) הלכה כר' אלעזר ג) קרי רב עליה דרבי אלעזר טובינא דחכימי: מתני' ד) איזהו בושת ד) הכל לפי המבייש והמתבייש פגם רואין אותה כאילו היא שפחה נמכרת בשוק כמה היתה יפה וכמה היא יפה ה) קנס שוה בכל אדם וכל שיש לו קצבה מן התורה שוה בכל אדם: גמ' ואימא ה) חמשים סלעים אמר רחמנא מכל מילי א"ר זירא יאמרו בעל בת מלכים חמשים בעל בת הדיוטות חמשים א"ל אביי אי הכי גבי עבד נמי יאמרו עבד נוקב מרגליות שלשים עבד עושה מעשה

רש"י

להא מילתא. שיהיה מפתה נושא על כרחו: עשה. לו תהיה לאשה: ונדחה את לא תעשה. דאינה ראויה לבא בישראל כגון ממזרת: מי איתיה לעשה כלל. הכא נמי מלמדין אותה לומר איני רוצה: מתני' יתומה שנתארסה ונתגרשה האונס חייב והמפתה פטור. דכיון דיתומה היא וקנס שלה היא ואחליתיה דמדעתה נתפתתה לו פטור ובגמרא מפרש דנתארסה ונתגרשה מילתא אחריתי היא ולא איתומה קאי: גמ' בשיטת ר"ע רבו אמרה. דאמר במתני' ו) נערה שנתארסה ונתגרשה קנסה לעצמה והכך נתארסה ונתגרשה דר' אלעזר כשאביה קיים וקרי לה יתומה משום דפקע זכות אב מינה לגבי קנסה: ממאי. דכר"ע סבירא ליה: מדקתני אונס חייב ומפתה פטור. אלמא יש לה קנס ולעצמה הלכך מפתה פטור דמדעתה עבד ואונס חייב ואפילו אביה קיים דאי יתומה כדקתני פשיטא דמפתה פטור אלא הא קמ"ל כו': יתומה פשיטא. מסקנא דמילתא דר' יוחנן היא: טובינא דחכימי. מאושר שבחכמים אשרי מתרגמינן טובאי. ר' אלעזר הוא ר' אלעזר בן שמוע ותלמידו של ר"ע היה כדאמרינן ביבמות בהבא על יבמתו (דף סב:) והיה העולם שמם עד שבא ר"ע אצל רבותינו שבדרום ושנה להם ר"מ ור' יהודה ור' יוסי ור"ש ורבי אלעזר בן שמוע: מתני' הכל לפי המבייש. אדם בינוני המבייש בושתו קשה מאדם זולל ומאדם חשוב: והמתבייש. לפי חשיבותו בושתו: כאילו היא שפחה. בגמרא מפרש מאי גריעותא מחמת בעילה: גמ' יאמרו כו'. והיכן הוא חילוק שביניהן אלא בושת הלכך יהיב בושת: גבי עבד. שנגחו שור שנתנה תורה קצבה ל' שקלים:

תוספות

מהר ימהרנה לו מדעתו. וא"ת ולו תהיה לאשה נידרוש נמי לו מדעתו והא דכתיב לא יוכל לשלחה היינו היכא דלכבר נשאה וי"ל דאין סברא שיהיה מדעתו כיון שאם נשאה לא יוכל לשלחה [ועוד ולו תהיה קאי אאשה ולהכי בעינן מדעתה אבל מהר ימהרנה קאי אגברא]: ניתי עשה ונדחה לא תעשה. לאו אמצאת בה דבר ערוה פריך דהא איכא בה לאו ועשה כדאמרי' בפ"ק דיבמות (דף יא. ושם) לא יוכל בעלה וגו' לרבות סוטה שנסתרה והיינו לאו ודרשינן (סוטה דף כח.) ונטמאה ונטמאה חד לבעל וחד לבועל אלא אשאינה ראויה לקהל פריך וא"ת ומאי פריך וליתי עשה ולידחי ל"ת הא דרים מקרא בהדיא במשנה דבעינן אשה הראויה לו ולמאי דמשני דלא חשיב עשה קשה דמאי איצטריך קרא למעוטי שאינה ראויה לו וי"ל דלאו מיתורא דקרא מפיק ליה דממעטינן אלא דולו תהיה לאשה משמע מדעתה ולהכי ממעט אשה שאינה ראויה לו דהא אי אמרה לא בעינא ליה ליתא לעשה כלל הלכך לא חשיב עשה ולא דחי לא תעשה ומ"מ ס"ד דפריך דהשתא היכא דאמרה בעינא ליה איתיה לעשה ולידחי ל"ת ומסיק דאפילו אמרה בעינא ליה לא חשיב עשה דלא דמי למילה בצרעת אי נמי מיתורא דקרא דריש ומפריך דליתי עשה ולדחי ל"ת ויתורא דקרא מוקי לחייבי כריתות דלאו קרא הוה שרינן אפי' חייבי כריתות דהוה לאו ואיתרבו לקנס לעיל בריש פירקין איתרבו נמי לנישואין דקראי משתמעי שפיר דהיכא דאיכא קנס איכא נמי נישואין אי נמי יש לומר דהכי פריך ניתי עשה ונידחי לא תעשה וכי תימא שאני הכא דגלי קרא א"כ ניגמר מהכא בכל דוכתא דלא דחי ומשני דלא חשיב עשה ומ"מ איצטריך קרא דאי לאו קרא הוה חשבינן ליה דלא אפשר לקיים שניהם וחשיב עשה דעיקר מצוה היא לישא כי היכי דאמרינן בפרק ב' דיבמות (דף כ.) דחליצה במקום יבום לאו ז) כלום הוא:

כגון מילה בצרעת. א) אומר ר"ת דלסימנא בעלמא נקטיה דהא בקוצץ בהרתו איכא עשה ולא תעשה כדאמרינן בפרק ר' אליעזר דמילה (שבת דף קלג:) ללשון אחד הכתוב בספרים ומהתם לא ילפינן בעלמא דליתי עשה ודחי לא תעשה ועשה דמה למילה שכן נכרתו עליה י"ג בריתות אלא עיקר מילתא מכלאים בציצית וא"ת והא כלאים בציצית אפשר לקיים שניהם שיעשה בטלית צמר חוטין של צמר ואומר ר"י דבטלית של פשתן אי אפשר לקיים שניהם דלא אפשר לקיים מצות תכלת אלא ע"י כלאים דתכלת עמרא הוא וזה אין לנו לומר שיהא אסור ללבוש טלית של פשתן משום דאפשר בשל צמר דאין זה חשוב אפשר והא דאמרי' בפ' התכלת (מנחות דף מ. ושם) כל המטיל תכלת בסדין בירושלים אינו אלא מן המתמיהין ומפרש בגמרא גזירה משום קלא אילן ופריך לא יהיה אלא לבן ומשני אפשר במינו כדריש לקיש דאמר כל מקום שאתה כו' התם ודאי כיון דליכא תכלת אלא הכל לבן מצות לבן אפשר לקיים במינו וא"ת והא אמר התם לעיל ח) חוטי צמר פוטרין בשל פשתן ושל פשתן פוטרין בשל צמר ואמאי פוטרין והא אפשר לקיים שניהם דלבן אפשר במינו ואור"ת דכל ד' חוטין לבן ודאי אסור דאפשר במינו אבל התם קאמר דשני חוטי צמר לבן פוטרים בשל פשתן דמגו דתכלת פטרה שכבר נעשה כלאים ע"י תכלת שבו לבן של צמר נמי פטר ומגו דשני חוטי לבן של צמר פוטרים בשל פשתן שני חוטי לבן של פשתן נמי פוטרין בשל צמר אע"ג דלא נעשה התם כלאים ע"י תכלת שבו וצריך עיון אם שני חוטי לבן של פשתן ושני חוטי לבן של צמר מותר לתת בטלית של צמר או בטלית של פשתן דשמא לא הותרו שני חוטי לבן אלא דווקא במקום תכלת אבל שלא במקום תכלת לא או דלמא לא שנא דהא שני חוטי לבן של פשתן פוטרים בשל צמר אע"ג דהתם תכלת לא מעלה ולא מוריד דע"י אותו תכלת לא נעשה אכתי כלאים ואין להקשות אי שרו שני חוטי לבן בכלאים אפי' אין תכלת עמהן אמאי מטיל תכלת בסדין בירושלים אינו אלא מן המתמיהין יטילו עמו שני חוטי לבן של פשתן דאפילו הוי ההוא תכלת קלא אילן או לבן גמור שרי דאיכא למיגזר שמא יטילו עמו שני חוטי לבן של צמר ויסברו שאותן שני חוטין הצבועין הן תכלת ויהיו כל ד' חוטין לבן של צמר:

[אי אמרה לא בעינא מי איתיה לעשה כלל. הקשה הר"ר עזרא אמאי איצטריך קרא בפ"ק דיבמות (דף ה:) דאין עשה דכיבוד דוחה שבת הא ליכא עשה דאי אמר לא בעינא לכיבוד מי איתא לעשה כלל וי"ל דהתם מ"מ מיד כשלוה אב הוי עשה לעשות מצותו ול"נ דהכא גבי דידה ליכא עשה דהא אי בעיא אמרה לא בעינא ליה הלכך אין לה לעבור בלאו משום עשה דידיה דהיא מוזהרת כמותו והשוה הכתוב אשה לאיש כדאמרינן בים מותרות (יבמות דף פד:). ת"י כ"י]:

הכי גרסינן ממאי מדקתני האונס חייב והמפתה פטור יתומה פשיטא אלא הא קמ"ל כו'. כלומר מדקתני האונס חייב והמפתה פטור ש"מ דיש לה קנס וקנסה לעצמה דאי משום יתומה נקט מפתה פטור פשיטא דפטור דהא מחלה אלא ע"כ לא נקט מפתה פטור אלא משום נערה שנתארסה ונתגרשה ולא נקט יתומה במתני' אלא ליתן טעם אמאי מפתה פטור והלא קנסה לאביה ואשמעי' דהרי היא כיתומה שקנסה לעצמה וא"ת ומנלן הא אדרבה אימא דנקט יתומה למידק טעמא דהויא נמי יתומה הא אינה יתומה אפילו מפתה חייב דקנסה לאביה וי"ל דלית לן למימר לדיוקא אתא כל זמן דנוכל לומר דלגופיה אתא: ט) אחד כדרכה ואחד שלא כדרכה. שלא כדרכה ה"ל למינקט ברישא אלא כן דרך הש"ס שאינו חושש כדנקט לעיל (דף לה.) בתנא דבי חזקיה בין מתכוין לשאין מתכוין דה"ל למינקט שאין מתכוין ברישא דקתני בין שוגג למזיד אלא כן דרך הש"ס במקום שצריך לשנות הן ולאו י): יאמרו בעל שלימה חמשים. פירוש הראשון שבא עליה שלא כדרכה דמחייב קנס אפילו שלא כדרכה כדאמרינן בפ"ק דקידושין (דף ט:) באו עליה י' ועדיין היא בתולה כו' פירוש שלא כדרכה וקאמר מודה רבי לענין קנס דכולהו משלמי ובפרק הבא על יבמתו (יבמות דף נט. ושם) גבי ולו תהיה לאשה באשה הראויה לו פרט לאלמנה לכ"ג כו' ופריך היכי דמי אילימא כדרכה תיפוק ליה דהויא לה בעולה אלא לאו שלא כדרכה והכא הוה מצי למינקט שבאו עליה ב' שלא כדרכה וכן בפרק בן סורר (סנהדרין עג:) דמוקי ההיא דאלו נערות שיש להן קנס כגון שבא עליה שלא כדרכה וחזר ובא עליה כדרכה הוה מצי למינקט וחזר ובא עליה שלא כדרכה ומה שקשה על פירוש הקונטרס דהתם פירשנו בהבא על יבמתו (יבמות דף נט.) ובפרק קמא דקידושין (דף ט:): ואימא

מסורת הש"ס

א) שבת קלג: ביצה ח, ב) [לעיל לח.], ג) גיטין כו: כריתות יג, ד) ב"ק פג:, ה) ערכין יד:, ו) [לעיל לח.], ז) [דף לט:], ח) מנחות מא, ט) שייך לע"ב, י) [וע' תוספות ...]

תוספות ישנים

א) [ולספרים דלא גרסי הכא מילה בצרעת וכלאים בציצית אלא מילה בצרעת לחודיה היינו משום דבכלאים אינו פשוט כל כך דלא אפשר לקיים שניהם. ת"י].

ליקוטים מהגר"א

[א] משנה יתומה שנתארסה. נקט כאן שגם זה חילוק בין אונס למפתה:

תורה אור השלם

א) וְכִי יְפַתֶּה אִישׁ בְּתוּלָה אֲשֶׁר לֹא אֹרָשָׂה וְשָׁכַב עִמָּהּ מָהֹר יִמְהָרֶנָּה לּוֹ לְאִשָּׁה: [שמות כב, טו]

ליקוטי רש"י

מהר ימהרנה. יפסוק לה מוהר כמשפט איש לאשתו שכותב לה כתובה וישאנה [שמות כב, טו]. מילה בצרעת. מילה דוחה צרעת דלאתי עשה דימול ודחי לא תעשה דהשמר בנגע הצרעת דהכי קיימא לן בפרק קמא דיבמות [דף ז:] ... הכל לפי המבייש. אדם קל שבייש בושתו מרובה. והמתבייש. אדם חשוב שנתבייש בושתו מרובה [ב"ק פג:]. אמר רחמנא מכל מילי ... בעל בת הדיוטות כו'. נוקב מרגליות. שעבודתו נוחה לעשות ושכרו מרובה [בכורות]. שלשים. שקלים ...

עין משפט נר מצוה

עט א מיי' פ"ג מהל' אישות הלכה ו:
פ ב מיי' פ"ב מהלכות נערה הלכה יד סמג עשין נד טור אה"ע סי' קעז:
פא ג מיי' פ"א שם הל' ט סמג שם:
פב ד מיי' פ"ב שם הל' ד ומיי' פ"ג מהל' חובל ומזיק הל' א סמג שם ועשין ע טור שם וטוש"ע ח"מ סי' תכ סעיף כד:
פג ה מיי' פ"ה מהלכות נערה הל' ג סמג עשין נד טור אה"ע סי' קעז:

תוספות רי"ד

מתני' כיצד שותה בעציצו אפי' היא חיגרת ואפילו סומא אפי' מוכת שחין נמצא בה דבר זימה או שאינה ראויה לבוא בישראל אינו רשאי לקיימה שנאמר ולו תהיה לאשה הראויה לו: וליתי עשה ולדחי את ל"ת היכא אמרי' דאתי עשה ודחי את ל"ת כגון מילה בצרעת דא"א לי' לקיומי לעשה אבל הכא אי אמרה לא בעינא ליה ליתא לעשה כלל. המורה והשתא נמי מלמדים אותה לומר איני רוצה וקשה לי להאי פי' דא"כ גבי יבם אמאי אמרינן דאתי עשה ודחי ל"ת כיון דכתיב אם לא יחפוץ נלמדנו לומר איני רוצה ליבם ולא לידחי ואמאי אמרי' התם דחי מ"ה נ"ל לפרש דמאי דאמר רחמנא גבי אונס ולו תהיה לאשה להפיס דעתה ואי אמרה לא בעינא לא ליתי לעשה כלל הלכך לא כלום הוא עשה למדחי את ל"ת כיון שלא ציוהו הבורא אלא להפיס דעתה אבל מצות יבום רחמנא הוא דרמי עליה דאע"ג דאמרה אשה לא בעינא לא מיעקרא מצות יבום הלכך מצוה דרמי עליה רחמנא הוא ולהכי דחיא את ל"ת ואע"ג דמצי יבם למימר לא בעינא ליבומי כ"א לא מיחלץ לה אמרי' התם חליצה במקום יבום אינה מצוה: מתני' יתומה שנתארסה ונתגרשה ר"א אומר האונס חייב והמפתה פטור. פי' שתי נערות הן יתומות אע"פ שלא נתארסה שקנסה הוא לעצמה כיון שאין לה אב שאין אדם מוריש זכות בתו לבניו. וכן נערה שנתארס' ונתגרש' אע"פ שיש לה אב הוי קנסא לעצמה כר"ע. הלכך האונס חייב ליתן קנס אבל המפתה פטור דאיהי אחילתי' גביה כיון שנתרצית לו: אמר רבה בב"ח אר"י ר"א בשיטת ר"ע אמרה דאמר נערה המאורסה יש לה קנס וקנסה לעצמה ממאי מדקתני יתומה פשיטא אלא הא קמ"ל דנערה שנתארסה ונתגרשה ה"ה כיתומה מה יתומה לעצמה אף נערה שנתארסה ונתגרשה לעצמה אמר ר"א אמר רב הלכתא כר"א וקרי ליה רב עליה דר"א טובינא דחכימא. פי' מאושר שבחכמים תרגום אשריך ישראל טובך ישראל: מתני' איזהו בושת הכל לפי המבייש והמתבייש. פי' אדם בינוני המבייש בושתו קשה מאדם זולל ומאדם חשוב

והמתבייש פי' לפי חשיבותו בושתו: פגם רואים אותה כאילו היא שפחה נמכרת לשוק כמה היתה יפה וכמה היא יפה וקנס שוה בכל אדם וכל שיש לו קצבה מה"ת שוה בכל אדם: ואימא נ' כסף אמר רחמנא מכל מילי. אמר

לְהָא מִילְתָא נַמִּי לִיגְמְרוּ מֵהֲדָדֵי – **let them be derived from one another for this matter as well!**[1] – ? –

The Gemara answers:

אָמַר קְרָא – That extrapolation is not possible, for the **verse states** with regard to the seducer: "מָהֹר יִמְהָרֶנָּה לּוֹ לְאִשָּׁה", – *If a man shall seduce a virgin . . . **he shall provide her with a marriage settlement to be a wife for him.***[2] "לוֹ", מִדַּעְתּוֹ – ***For him*** implies **"with his consent."**[3]

The Mishnah stated in explanation of the third distinction between a violator and a seducer:

כֵּיצַד שׁוֹתֶה בַּעֲצִיצוֹ כו' – HOW DOES [A VIOLATOR] DRINK FROM HIS POT? etc. [(However, if . . .) she is unfit to enter (into matrimony) with a Jew,[4] he is not permitted to keep her.]

The Gemara questions this ruling:

אָמַר רַב כַּהֲנָא – **Rav Kahana said:** אַמְרִיתָא לִשְׁמַעְתָּא קַמֵּיהּ דְּרַב זְבִיד מִנְּהַרְדְּעָא – **I stated the** following **argument in the presence of Rav Zevid from Nehardea:** נֵיתֵי עֲשֵׂה וְנִדְחֶה לֹא תַעֲשֶׂה – **Let the positive [commandment] come and override the negative [commandment]!?**[5]

Rav Kahana reports Rav Zevid's response:

אָמַר לִי – **He said to me:** הֵיכָא אַמְרִינַן נֵיתֵי עֲשֵׂה וְנִידְחֵי לֹא תַעֲשֶׂה – **Where do we say, "Let the positive [commandment] come and override the negative [commandment]"?** כְּגוֹן מִילָה בְּצָרַעַת – In cases **like the circumcision** of a foreskin that is afflicted **with *tzaraas*,**[6] דְּלֹא אֶפְשָׁר [דְּלֹא] לְקִיּוּמֵיהּ לַעֲשֵׂה – **where it is impossible** to choose **not**[7] **to fulfill the positive [commandment].**[8] אֲבָל הָכָא – **But here,** although the violator is positively commanded to marry his victim, אִי אָמְרָה דְּלֹא בָּעֵינָא – **if she says that I do not want** him for a husband, מִי אִיתֵיהּ לַעֲשֵׂה כְּלָל – **is there a positive [commandment] at all?!** No![9]

Mishnah The Mishnah presents another difference between the cases of violation and seduction:

יְתוֹמָה שֶׁנִּתְאָרְסָה וְנִתְגָּרְשָׁה – Regarding **an orphan who was betrothed and** then **divorced,** רַבִּי אֶלְעָזָר אוֹמֵר – **R' Elazar says:** הָאוֹנֵס חַיָּיב – **The one who violates** her **is liable** for the fine, וְהַמְפַתֶּה פָּטוּר – **and the one who seduces** her **is exempt.**[10]

Gemara The Gemara identifies the source of the Mishnah's ruling:

אָמַר רַבָּה בַּר בַּר חָנָה אָמַר רַבִּי יוֹחָנָן – **Rabbah bar bar Chanah said in the name of R' Yochanan:** רַבִּי אֶלְעָזָר בְּשִׁיטַת רַבִּי עֲקִיבָא רַבּוֹ אֲמָרָהּ – **R' Elazar stated [this ruling] in [accordance with] the opinion of R' Akiva, his teacher,** דְּאָמַר – **who said**[11] regarding a *naarah* who was betrothed and then divorced: יֵשׁ לָהּ קְנָס וּקְנָסָהּ לְעַצְמָהּ – SHE HAS A right to the FINE, AND HER FINE belongs TO HER.[12] מִמַּאי – **From what** evidence do I say that R' Elazar holds like R' Akiva of the Mishnah? מִדְּקָתָנֵי – **From that which**

NOTES

1. To teach that just as the violator is compelled to marry his victim, so must the seducer (*Rashi*).

2. *Exodus* 22:15. See above, 39b note 17.

3. See *Tosafos; Rabbeinu Yonah,* cited by *Shitah Mekubetzes;* cf. *Ritva.*

4. E.g. if she is a *mamzeress,* whose marriage to an ordinary Jew the Torah prohibits (*Deuteronomy* 23:3): A *mamzer shall not enter the congregation of Hashem* (see above, 39a note 40, and following note).

5. [There is a general principle that where a disparity arises between a positive and a negative commandment, the positive commandment overrides the negative one (עֲשֵׂה דוֹחֶה לֹא תַעֲשֶׂה; see *Yevamos* 3b-6b). Hence,] let the positive commandment that the violator must marry his victim [-וְלוֹ תִהְיֶה לְאִשָּׁה, *and she shall be for him a wife* (*Deuteronomy* 22:29)] override the negative commandment against marrying an unfit woman like a *mamzeress*!? (*Rashi;* see *Tosafos* regarding why *Rashi* explains the Gemara's question as referring to an unfit woman rather than an adulterous one, the previous case in the Mishnah; cf. *Ramban* in first approach).

[The Rishonim have difficulty with the Gemara's question. Since the Mishnah expounds the verse, *and she shall be for him a wife,* as teaching that the violator is commanded to marry his victim only when she is "a wife who is fit *for him,*" there is, in fact, no positive commandment for the violator to marry his victim when she is not legally fit. Hence, how can the Gemara suggest that the positive commandment overrides the negative commandment when there is no positive commandment in our case of *mamzeress* (and the like)?! See *Tosafos* and *Shitah Mekubetzes* for various explanations.]

6. The Torah forbids the removal of skin afflicted with a condition known as *tzaraas* (*Deuteronomy* 24:8). However, to fulfill the positive mitzvah of circumcision (*milah*), one is allowed to remove a *tzaraas*-afflicted foreskin (see *Shabbos* 132b).

Actually, the Gemara (ibid.) established that the passage of *tzaraas* contains both a positive and a negative commandment, which ordinarily a single positive commandment cannot override [*milah* being an exception]. Hence, the Gemara is presenting the case of *milah* and *tzaraas* simply as an example of an absolutely obligatory positive commandment (see note 8 below) overriding an opposing commandment (*Tosafos*).

7. Emendation follows *Shitah Mekubetzes* and accords with variant texts cited in *Dikdukei Soferim HaShalem.* This was the reading of most Rishonim, see there §19.

8. I.e. a person cannot declare that the mitzvah of circumcision does not apply to him.

9. Hence, in all cases of unfit women we instruct the victim to say that she does not want the violator for a husband [so that there is no positive commandment to override the prohibition against marrying a *mamzeress* or the like] (*Rashi*).

It would appear from *Rashi's* explanation of Rav Zevid's response that if the girl insisted that the violator marry her, we would apply the general rule that a positive commandment overrides a negative one and indeed require the violator to marry her. However, the Mishnah states that the violator "is not permitted to keep her," which implies that he is never permitted to marry her.

Rashba, Ritva and *Ran* thus explain the Gemara to mean that the general rule of overriding applies only to positive commandments like circumcision, which are absolutely obligatory. However, since the violator's obligation to marry his victim is so inherently weak that the girl can actually uproot it, it lacks the power to override a negative commandment. Accordingly, even if the victim who is unfit demands that the violator marry her, he is not permitted to do so. See *Ritva* for his interpretation of *Rashi's* opinion, and see *Rashba.* See *Rambam, Hil. Naarah Besulah* 3:5, for what is apparently another interpretation. See also *Tos. Yeshanim* ד"ה אי אמרה and *Kovetz Shiurim* §142.

10. Since she is an orphan, the fine belongs to her; and by acquiescing to the seduction she waived her right to the fine. The Gemara will explain that the Mishnah actually refers to two cases, and means to say: An orphan, ***or*** a girl who was betrothed and divorced etc. (*Rashi*). [*Ritva* here discusses at length the subject of waiving a fine-obligation. See also what *Ran* writes in *Ramban's* name, and see *Mishneh LaMelech* to *Hil. Ishus* 23:1.]

11. In the Mishnah above, 38a (see *Rashi* ד"ה בשיטת רבי עקיבא; see also *Ritva,* who explains that R' Yochanan means to exclude the opinion of R' Akiva of the Baraisa (ibid.), where he states that the fine belongs to the father).

12. I.e. the "orphan who was betrothed and divorced" discussed by R' Elazar actually refers to a girl whose father is still alive (which is R' Akiva's case). R' Elazar calls her an "orphan" because she has the halachic status of an orphan, in that her father's right to the fine has been abrogated (on account of her betrothal, which is R' Akiva's ruling) [*Rashi*].

Ritva notes that *Rashi* here appears to be contradicting his comment on the Mishnah [see note 10 above], that "the Gemara will explain that the Mishnah actually refers to two cases, and means to say: An orphan,

The Gemara now completes its quote of the Baraisa:

מֵת – If [THE VIOLATOR] DIED before his wife, יָצָא כֶּסֶף קְנָסָהּ בִּכְתוּבָּתָהּ – THE MONEY paid for HER FINE SATISFIES the obligation in HER *KESUBAH*.[28] רַבִּי יוֹסֵי בְּרַבִּי יְהוּדָה אוֹמֵר – R' YOSE THE SON OF R' YEHUDAH SAYS: יֵשׁ לָהּ כְּתוּבָּה מָנֶה – SHE HAS the right TO A separate *KESUBAH* award OF A *MANEH*.[29]

The Gemara explains the dispute of the Baraisa:

בְּמַאי קָמִיפַּלְגֵי – **Regarding what** underlying issue **do they argue?** רַבָּנָן סָבְרֵי – **The Rabbis** (i.e. the Tanna Kamma) **hold:** טַעְמָא מַאי תַּקִּינוּ רַבָּנָן כְּתוּבָּה – **What is the reason the Rabbis instituted a *kesubah*** for the ordinary wife?[30] כְּדֵי שֶׁלֹּא תְּהֵא קַלָּה בְּעֵינָיו לְהוֹצִיאָהּ – **So that she should not be easy in [her husband's] eyes to send away** with a bill of divorce. וְהָא לֹא מָצֵי מַפֵּיק לָהּ – **But this** violator **cannot divorce [his wife]!** Hence, there is no need to institute a *kesubah* for her.[31] וְרַבִּי יוֹסֵי בְּרַבִּי יְהוּדָה סָבַר – **But R' Yose the son of R' Yehudah holds** that הָא נַמִי מְצַעֵר לָהּ עַד דְּאָמְרָה הִיא – **this** violator **can also torment [his wife] until she says,** לֹא בָּעֵינָא לָךְ – **"I do not want you."**[32]

The Mishnah stated a third and final distinction between a violator and a seducer:

אוֹנֵס שׁוֹתֶה בַּעֲצִיצוֹ – [THE] VIOLATOR MUST DRINK FROM HIS POT [and the seducer, if he wants to send (her) away, may send (her) away].

The Gemara asks:

אָמַר לֵיהּ רָבָא מִפַּרְזְקְיָא לְרַב אַשִׁי – An Amora named **Rava from** the town of **Parzakya said to Rav Ashi:** מִכְּדֵי מִיגְמַר גָּמְרֵי מֵהֲדָדֵי – **Since** the laws of **[the violator and the seducer] are derived from one another,**[33]

NOTES

28. See note 31 below, where the Baraisa's change of terminology is discussed.

29. [As do other nonvirgins.] R' Yose the son of R' Yehudah disputes both of the Tanna Kamma's rulings, maintaining that whether the marriage ends with divorce (at her insistence) or with the death of the violator, the wife is entitled to a separate *kesubah* award of a *maneh* (see *Shitah Mekubetzes*).

30. See *Tosafos, Shitah Mekubetzes* et al., who discuss our Gemara vis-a-vis those who hold that a *kesubah* is Biblically mandated.

31. The Rishonim explain that this reason, which applies in the case of divorce, teaches that the wording אֵין לָהּ עָלָיו כְּלוּם ("she has no [claim] upon him whatsoever") means that there is no cause for a *kesubah* obligation. The Baraisa changes its terminology in the case of the violator dying, however, to indicate that there is cause for a *kesubah* of a *maneh*, and nevertheless "the money [paid for] her fine satisfies" that obligation (see *Tosafos, Shitah Mekubetzes, Tos, HaRosh, Ritva* et al. for an elaboration of this point).

32. Although a violator cannot divorce his wife against her will, he can nevertheless make her life so miserable that she will demand a divorce. Hence, it was necessary to institute a *kesubah* even for a violator's wife, so that "it should not be easy in his eyes to [utilize this method and ultimately] divorce her."

33. The Gemara above (38a; see note 35 there) establishes a *gezeirah shavah* teaching between the passages of the violator and seducer, whereby we derive that just as the violator pays a fine of fifty coins, so does the seducer; and just as the seducer pays *shekalim*, so too the violator's fifty coins are *shekalim* (*Rashi*).

עין משפט
נר מצוה

עא א מיי' פ"ב מהל' נערה הל' ז סמג עשין נד טור אה"ע סי' קעז:
עב ב מיי' פ"א שם הל' ג סמג וטור שם:
עג ג ד מיי' שם הל' ד:

תוספות רי"ד

והמפתה לכשיוציא וכי אשתו היא אמר אביי אימא לכשלא יכנוס. פי' שתמאן הוא או היא או אבי' דדרשי' לו מדעתו. אבל אם כונס אינו נותן כלום דכתיב מהר ימהרנה לו לאשה ואם מאן ימאן אביה לתתה לו כסף ישקול. תנ"ה אע"פ שאמרו המפתה נותן לכשלא יכנוס בושת ופגם נותן מיד ואחד האונס ואחד המפתה בין היא ובין אביה יכולין לעכב. פי' שלא יכנסנה. בשלמא מפותה כתיב אם מאן ימאן אביה אין לי אלא אביה היא עצמה מנין ת"ל מאן ימאן מ"מ אלא אונס בשלמא איהי דכתיב ולו תהיה לאשה מדעתה אלא אביה מנלן. אביי אמר שלא יהא חוטא נשכר. רבא אמר [ק"ו] הוא מה מפתה שלא עבר אלא ע"ד אביה בין היא בין אביה יכולין לעכב אונס שעבר על דעתה וע"ד אביה לא כ"ש. תניא אע"פ שאמרו האונס נותן מיד לכשהיא יוצאה. פי' כגון שתרצו שניהן בגירושין אין לה עליו כלום. פי' מת יצא כסף קנסה בכתובתה. ר' יוסי ברבי יהודה אומר יש לה כתובה מנה וקי"ל כת"ק והמפתה אם רצה להוציא מוציא מ"ט אמר רב אשי א"ק מהר ימהרנה לו מדעתו פירוש ומאי דתנן אם רצה להוציא אינו מוציא מתפרש אם רצה שלא יכנוס לא יכנוס דפרשנא לכשיוציא דישא:

ליקוטי רש"י

ותפשקי את רגליך. לפי שדימה אותה לזונה דכך דרכה של זונה שיש פיסוק הרגלים [יחזקאל טז, כה]. שיראין. של משי [מנחות לט:]. בת אבא סוראה. כדאמרינן (לעיל ט:) אמרה לי בת אבא סוראה כי נהמא אקושא בחינכי [קידושין נב:]. אין לי. דכול למאן אלא אביה [קידושין מו:]. יצא כסף קנסה בכתובתה. ואין לה כתובה. יש לה כתובה. מנכסיו. מנה. שהיא כבר בעולה. ואע"ג שכבר נתן כסף קנסה לאביה. טעמא מאי תקינו וכו'. כל כתובת אשה משום שלא תהא קלה בעיניו להוציאה תקנוה [לקמן נד.].

אי הכי מפותה נמי. יש לה צער פיסוק רגלים כמו אנוסה ומאי קאמר אין דומה נבעלת באונס לנבעלת ברצון ואמר מורי הרב דודי ז"ל [ו] דאמתני' לא ה"מ למיפרך אמאי אונס חייב כיון שסופה להצטער בכך תחת בעלה דהא אפילו בעולה מצטערת בכך ואע"ג דבא עליה עתה סופה נמי להצטער ולא תרויח כלום [ז] [קצת נראה דאמתני' פריך אמאי מפותה פטור]:

קרע שיראין שלי והפטר. ואע"ג דלא אמרה על מנת לפטור איכא למימר דמחמת הנאת בעילה מחלה לגמרי:

[ח] [**לכשיוציא** אשתו היא. אפי' פיתה לשם אישות מ"מ פריך אשתו היא כיון דאינה צריכה גטן]:

בושת ופגם נותן מיד. אע"ג דאיתקש לקנס היינו לענין שניתן זה למי שזה ניתן אבל יש מקומות שפטור מקנס לגמרי וחייב בבושת ופגם: **אין** לי אלא אביה היא עצמה מנין כו'. (ב) תימה לר"י במאי איירי אי בקטנה או בנערה היאך היא יכולה למאן כיון שהאב רוצה והוא יכול לקדשה בעל כרחה למי שירצה וה"ה לזה ואי בשאין לה אב או שבגרה אחר כך מה צריך קרא תיפוק ליה שיכולה לעכב שלא יהא חוטא נשכר דקאמר אביי בסמוך וכן אביה אמאי צריך קרא לאביי ואומר ר"י דנהי שאינה יכולה לעכב על אביה שלא יקדשנה לו מ"מ מועיל מיאונה לענין שישלם קנס וכן במיאון אביה והא דתניא הכא המפתה לכשלא יכנוס צריך לפרש לכשלא יכנוס מדעתה ומיהו קשה דהכא דרשינן מאם מאן ימאן מ"מ שהיא יכולה לעכב ובפרק נערה (לקמן מד:) דרשינן מינה לרבות יתומה לקנס ור"ל ליכתוב או מאן מאן או ימאן ימאן מאי מאן ימאן ש"מ תרתי ובכה"ג אמרינן במרובה (ב"ק דף סה. ושם) גבי אם המצא תמצא ובהחובל (שם דף פה.) גבי ורפא ירפא ועוד נראה דלאו מיתורא דקרא דריש לה התם דאם כן מאי פריך מינה לרבי יוסי בר' חנינא דפטר מוציא שם רע על היתומה דשאני מפתה דרבי קרא אלא כן הוא עיקר כמו שפירש בקונטרס לקמן דלאו מריבוי דריש אלא ה"פ לרבות יתומה לקנס דדרשינן שיש קנס כשהיא מעכבת והוא הדין דה"מ למימר לרבות בוגרת לקנס כשהיא מעכבת דדוקא בבוגרת או ביתומה יש קנס בעיכוב שלהן אבל כל זמן שלא בגרה תלוי באב והשתא דייק התם שפיר דשמעינן דסבר האי תנא שיש קנס ביתומה ולא ממעטינן ליה מדכתיב לאבי הנערה אע"ג דליכא ריבוי ליתומה כדפירשתי דאיכא לאוקמי קרא לבוגרת:

אלא אונס בשלמא איהו כו'. תימה כיון דאונס ומפתה מיגמר גמירי מהדדי להא מילתא נמי ליגמרו מהדדי כדפריך בסמוך ומאי קאמר אלא אביה מנלן וי"ל דלהאי מילתא לא גמרינן מהדדי דהא מפתה יכול לעכב ואונס שותה בעציצו וה"ה ה"נ אין אביה יכול לעכב וה"נ קאמר אביי בסמוך ורבא לא מסתבר ליה למימר הכי כיון דאיכא ק"ו וא"ת ואיהי גבי אונס אמאי איצטריך למיכתב נילף לאביי מסברא שלא יהא חוטא נשכר ולרבא מק"ו ויש לומר דלו תהיה לאשה אינו מיותר [ט] [דאיצטריך לעשה ולדרשות דלעיל. מהר"ס. א"נ אביי ורבא לא הוו משנו הכי אלא בתר דגלי קרא בהדיא]: **מפתה** דאיהו מצי מעכב. ואפי' פיתה לשם אישות יכול הוא לגרשה:

טעמא מאי תקינו לה רבנן כתובה שלא תהא קלה בעיניו להוציאה. אע"ג דבתולה יש לה כתובה מן התורה וזאת בעולה היא ומיהו תימה דקא פסיק ותני דבכל ענין אין לה כתובה אפילו בא עליה שלא כדרכה ובתולה גמורה היא ויש לה כתובה מן התורה דהא אם בא עליה שני יש לה קנס ולא הוי טעמא שלא תהא קלה בעיניו להוציאה תימה לר"י כיון דטעמא שלא תהא קלה בעיניו להוציאה אלמנה אמאי תקינו לה רבנן כתובה לא היה להם לתקן אלא לגרושה בלבד ואומר ר"י דמתוך שהוצרכו לתקן בגרושה שלא תהא קלה בעיניו להוציאה תקינו נמי לאלמנה משום חינא ומיהו לכתחילה לא היו מתקנים משום חינא קשה לרשב"א הא דתניא בהחובל (ב"ק דף פט. ושם) וכן היא שחבלה בבעלה לא הפסידה כתובתה ופריך אמאי תזבין לכתובתה [י] בטובת הנאה ומתיב ליה בהאי חבלה ומשני הא מני רבי מאיר היא דאמר אסור לאדם שישהא את אשתו בלא כתובה אפילו שעה אחת והשתא כיון דטעמא שלא תהא קלה בעיניו להוציאה תזבין כתובתה על מנת שאם תתאלמן אבל אם יגרשנה יהא לה כתובה דהתם לא שייך משום חינא ואומר ר"י כיון דבשאר נשים שייך חינא אף על גב דבזאת לא שייך לא פלוג רבנן ואסור להשהותה בלא כתובה לר"מ וא"ת ואמאי תני הכא יצא כסף קנסה בכתובתה ליתני מת אין לה עליו כלום דהא לא תקינו רבנן לאלמנה אלא משום גרושה והכא מכח גרושה אין לתקן לזאת דהא לא מצי לגרשה ואור"י דה"נ כיון דשייך בה חינא כמו בשאר אלמנות אין לנו לשנותה משאר אלמנות להכי איצטריך טעמא דילא כסף קנסה בכתובתה ולא חשו במה דאין לה כתובה:

מהר

שסופה להצטער תחת בעלה אמרו לו אינו דומה נבעלת באונס לנבעלת ברצון אלא אמר רב נחמן אמר רבה בר אבוה צער של פיסוק הרגלים וכן הוא אומר ותפשקי את רגליך לכל עובר אי הכי מפותה נמי אמר רב נחמן אמר רבה בר אבוה משל דמפותה למה הדבר דומה לאדם שאמר לחבירו קרע שיראין שלי והפטר שלי דאבוה ניהנו אלא אמר רב נחמן אמר רבה בר אבוה פקחות שבהן אומרות מפותה אין לה צער והא קא חזינן דאית לה אמר אביי אמרה לי אם כמיא חמימי על רישיה דקרחא רבא אמר אמרה לי בת רב חסדא כי ריבדא דכוסילתא רב פפא אמר אמרה לי בת אבא סוראה כי נהמא אקושא בחינכי: האונס נותן מיד המפתה לכשיוציא וכו': לכשיוציא אשתו היא אמר אביי אימא לכשלא יכנוס תניא נמי הכי אע"פ שאמרו המפתה נותן לכשלא יכנוס בושת ופגם נותן מיד ואחד האונס ואחד המפתה בין היא ובין אביה יכולין לעכב בשלמא מפותה כתיב אם מאן ימאן אביה אין לי אלא אביה היא עצמה מנין תלמוד לומר ימאן מכל מקום אלא אונס בשלמא איהי כתיב ולו תהיה מדעתה אלא אביה מנלן אמר אביי שלא יהא חוטא נשכר רבא אמר ק"ו ומה מפתה שלא עבר אלא על דעת אביה בלבד בין היא ובין אביה יכולין לעכב אונס שעבר על דעת אביה ועל דעת עצמה לא כל שכן רבא לא אמר כאביי כיון דקא משלם קנס לאו חוטא נשכר הוא אביי לא אמר כרבא מפתה דאיהו מצי מעכב אביה נמי מצי מעכב אונס דאיהו לא מצי מעכב אביה נמי לא מצי מעכב תניא אידך אע"פ שאמרו אונס נותן מיד כשיוציא הוא אין לה עליו כלום כשיוציא מי מצי מפיק לה אימא כשתצא היא אין לה עליו כלום מת יצא כסף קנסה בכתובתה רבי יוסי ברבי יהודה אומר יש לה כתובה מנה במאי קמיפלגי רבנן סברי טעמא מאי תקינו רבנן כתובה כדי שלא תהא קלה בעיניו להוציאה והא לא מצי מפיק לה ורבי יוסי ברבי יהודה סבר הא נמי מצער לה עד דאמרה היא לא בעינא לך: אונס שותה בעציצו: אמר ליה רבא מפרזקיא לרב אשי מכדי מיגמר גמרי מהדדי להא

שסופה להצטער כו'. ואי חיבוט על גבי קרקע הוא וכי סופה ליחבט על גבי קרקע תחת בעלה: שלי. בתמיה: דאבוה הוא. דהא כל שבח נעורים ילפינן לקמן (דף מו:) לאביה והיאך היא יכולה למחול: ריבדא דכוסילתא. פולטוייר"א דפלמוא"ה בלע"ז: ריבדא. ניקור: כוסילתא. כלי אומן מקיז ואית דגרסי כי תרפתא דסיכורי והיא היא: אמרה לי אם. (א) אומנתו היתה: בת רב חסדא. אשתו של רבא: בת אבא סוראה. דביתהו דרב פפא: נהמא אקושא בחינכי. כלחם קשה שגורר את החיך: אשתו היא. וכי אשתו היא כבר דקאמר לכשיוציא: לכשלא יכנוס. שתמאן היא או אביה או המפתה עצמו: יכולין לעכב. שלא יכניסנה: תהיה. משמע היא מהוה את עצמה לו: מצי מעכב. שאם רצה אינו כונס כדאמרינן לקמן ימהרנה לו מדעתו: אביה נמי לא מצי מעכב. אי לאו שלא יהא חוטא נשכר: אע"פ שאמרו אונס נותן מיד כשיוציאנה אין לה עליו כלום. ולא אמרינן אין קנסה תחת כתובתה שהרי לאביה נותן מיד אלא כסף קנסה הוא כתובתה וכן אם מת יצא כסף קנסה בכתובתה: מי מצי מפיק לה. לא יוכל שלחה כתיב: כשתצא היא. אם יצתה מאליה ותבעה הימנו גט: טעמא מאי תקינו רבנן כתובה. לשאר נשים: מיגמר גמרי מהדדי. אונס ממפתה לשקלים ומפתה מאונס לחמשים: להא

מסורת הש"ס

א) [קדושין לג: וש"נ], ב) קדושין מו., ג) [לעיל יא. וש"נ], ד) לקמן נד., ה) [לעיל יא. לקמן נד. יבמות סט.], ו) [נ"ל דלאמתניתא לא ה"מ כו'. מהרש"א], ז) תוס' כ"י, ח) תוס' כ"י, ט) תוס' כ"י, י) לבעלה בטובת הנאה כצ"ל. מהרש"א.

הגהות הב"ח

(א) רש"י ד"ה אמרה וכו' אומנתו. נ"ב דילדתו אמו ומתה עי' קידושין דף לא ע"ב: (ב) תוס' ד"ה אין לי וכו' תימה. נ"ב עי' פ' האיש מקדש דף מ ע"א ובמ"ש התוס' לשם.

תורה אור השלם

א) אֶל כָּל רֹאשׁ דֶּרֶךְ בָּנִית רָמָתֵךְ וַתְּתַעֲבִי אֶת יָפְיֵךְ וַתְּפַשְּׂקִי אֶת רַגְלַיִךְ לְכָל עוֹבֵר וַתַּרְבִּי אֶת תַּזְנוּתָיִךְ: [יחזקאל טז, כה]

ב) אִם מָאֵן יְמָאֵן אָבִיהָ לְתִתָּהּ לוֹ כֶּסֶף יִשְׁקֹל כְּמֹהַר הַבְּתוּלֹת: [שמות כב, טז]

ג) וְנָתַן הָאִישׁ הַשֹּׁכֵב עִמָּהּ לַאֲבִי הַנַּעֲרָ חֲמִשִּׁים כָּסֶף וְלוֹ תִהְיֶה לְאִשָּׁה תַּחַת אֲשֶׁר עִנָּהּ לֹא יוּכַל שַׁלְּחָהּ כָּל יָמָיו: [דברים כב, כט]

לעזי רש"י

פוצטוויר"א. פירוש ניקור, דקירה. דפלמוא"ה. פירוש של כלי אומן המקיז דם בכתפים (רש"י ע"ז דף כח ע"א) של איזמל להקזת דם.

לְעַכֵּב – **BOTH [THE GIRL] AND HER FATHER CAN PREVENT** the marriage from taking place.[16]

The Gemara digresses to discuss the last ruling of the Baraisa: בִּשְׁלָמָא מְפוּתָּה כְּתִיב – **It is well** to say that in the case of **a seduced girl** both she and her father can reject the marriage, for **it is written,** "אִם־מָאֵן יְמָאֵן אָבִיהָ" – ***If refusing shall her father refuse** to give her to him,*[17] and we learned in a Baraisa:[18] אֵין לִי אֶלָּא אָבִיהָ – Now, if Scripture had not used repetitive language here, **I WOULD HAVE** known **ONLY** that **HER FATHER** can refuse the marriage between the girl and the seducer. הִיא עַצְמָהּ מִנַּיִן – **FROM WHERE** is it known that also **[THE GIRL] HERSELF** can refuse the marriage? תַּלְמוּד לוֹמַר "יְמָאֵן" – **[THE TORAH] STATES, *SHALL HE REFUSE,*** a repetition of *refusing* (מָאֵן) that implies that מִכָּל מָקוֹם – the verse's law applies **IN ALL CASES** – i.e. even when the girl herself is the one that refuses.[19] אֶלָּא אוֹנֵס – **But** in the case of **violation,** בִּשְׁלָמָא אִיהִי – albeit **it is well** to say that **she** is empowered to block the marriage, כְּתִיב "וְלוֹ־תִהְיֶה" – for **it is written** with regard to the violator,[20] ***and she shall be for him** a wife,* מִדַּעְתָּהּ – which implies that she does so **willingly.**[21] אֶלָּא אָבִיהָ מְנָלַן – **But from where do we [know]** that **her father** can likewise prevent her marriage to the violator?

The Gemara offers two answers:

אָמַר אַבַּיֵי – **Abaye said:** שֶׁלֹּא יְהֵא חוֹטֵא נִשְׂכָּר – Logic dictates that he is empowered to do so, **so that the sinner** [i.e. the violator] **will not profit** from his sin.[22] רָבָא אָמַר – **Rava said:** קַל וָחוֹמֶר – The father's power of refusal is derived via the following ***kal vachomer*** argument: וּמָה מְפַתֶּה שֶׁלֹּא עָבַר אֶלָּא עַל דַּעַת אָבִיהָ בִּלְבַד – **Since** in the case of **a seducer, who contravened only the will of her father,** בֵּין הִיא וּבֵין אָבִיהָ יְכוֹלִין לְעַכֵּב – **both [the girl] and her father can prevent** the marriage, אוֹנֵס שֶׁעָבַר עַל דַּעַת אָבִיהָ וְעַל דַּעַת עַצְמָהּ – then in the case of **a violator, who contravened her father's will and [the girl's] will** as well, לֹא כָּל שֶׁכֵּן – **is it not all the more so** that both she and her father can prevent the marriage?!

The Gemara explains why each Amora rejects the argument of the other:

רָבָא לֹא אָמַר כְּאַבַּיֵי – **Rava did not say like Abaye,** and use the logic of "so that the sinner will not profit" to derive the father's power of refusal, כֵּיוָן דְּקָא מְשַׁלֵּם קְנָס – for **since [the violator] pays the** fifty-*shekalim* **fine,** לָאו חוֹטֵא נִשְׂכָּר הוּא – **he is not "a profiting sinner."** אַבַּיֵי לֹא אָמַר כְּרָבָא – And, conversely, **Abaye did not say like Rava** and employ the *kal vachomer* argument, for he could offer the following rebuttal to it: מְפַתֶּה דְּאִיהוּ מָצֵי מְעַכֵּב – In the case of **a seducer, where [the seducer] is able to prevent** the marriage,[23] אָבִיהָ נַמִּי מָצֵי מְעַכֵּב – **her father also can prevent** the marriage. אוֹנֵס דְּאִיהוּ לֹא מָצֵי מְעַכֵּב – However, in the case of **a violator, where [the violator] cannot prevent** the marriage, אָבִיהָ נַמִּי לֹא מָצֵי מְעַכֵּב – **the father also cannot prevent** the marriage.[24]

The Gemara cites a related ruling:

תַּנְיָא אִידָךְ – **It was taught in another Baraisa:** אַף עַל פִּי שֶׁאָמְרוּ אוֹנֵס נוֹתֵן מִיָּד – **EVEN THOUGH THEY SAID** that **A VIOLATOR REMITS** the fifty-*shekalim* fine **IMMEDIATELY,** כְּשֶׁיּוֹצִיא הוּא – **WHEN HE SENDS** her **AWAY** with a bill of divorce, אֵין לָהּ עָלָיו כְּלוּם – **SHE HAS NO** claim **UPON HIM WHATSOEVER** for a separate *kesubah* payment.[25]

The Gemara interrupts its quote of the Baraisa to ask with astonishment:

כְּשֶׁיּוֹצִיא – **When he sends** her **away?!** מִי מָצֵי מַפִּיק לָהּ – **Is he** really **able to divorce her?** Why, the Torah states explicitly:[26] *He* [i.e. the violator] *cannot divorce her all his life!*

The Gemara clarifies the Baraisa's statement:

אֵימָא כְּשֶׁתֵּצֵא הִיא – **Say** the Baraisa means that **when she departs** on her own,[27] אֵין לָהּ עָלָיו כְּלוּם – **she has no** claim **upon him whatsoever.**

NOTES

16. The Rishonim question how the Baraisa can rule that the girl too can prevent the victimizer from marrying her, inasmuch as the father of a minor or a *naarah* can betroth his daughter even against her will. Hence, if the victim's father consents to the marriage, how can she obstruct it? *Tosafos* [first explanation] and *Ritva* here, and *Rashi* to *Kiddushin* 46a ד״ה אמר, explain the Baraisa to mean that the girl's objection is effective to the extent that it can compel a seducer to pay the fine [in the context of the Torah's insistence that the seducer marry her, she has refused, and the fine obligation now devolves; the father's ability to marry her off to this person, even against her will, does not play a role]. Alternatively, *Tosafos* [second explanation; see also *Tosafos* to *Kiddushin* ibid. ד״ה קרא] suggest that the Baraisa speaks of where the girl was orphaned or became a *bogeress* by the time the perpetrator was sued and found guilty by the court. According to this explanation, the Baraisa is saying that both the girl – when she has jurisdiction over her marital affairs (i.e. when she is an orphan or a *bogeress*) – and her father – when he has jurisdiction over her marital affairs (i.e. when she is a minor or a *naarah*) – have the legal capacity to veto the marriage.

17. *Exodus* 22:16. The preceding verse states that a seducer has the option of [exempting himself from paying the fine by] marrying his victim (see below, 40a). Our verse prescribes what happens if the father does not acquiesce to the marriage: אִם־מָאֵן יְמָאֵן אָבִיהָ לְתִתָּהּ לוֹ כֶּסֶף יִשְׁקֹל כְּמֹהַר הַבְּתוּלֹת, *If refusing shall her father refuse to give her* [in marriage] *to him* [the seducer]; *he shall weigh* [pay] *silver in the amount of the settlement* [*made*] *to the virgins.* That is, although the seducer wishes to marry the girl [and exempt himself from the fine], her father is empowered to block the marriage and demand the fine. The Baraisa now expounds the verse's repetitive phraseology – מָאֵן יְמָאֵן, *refuses, he shall refuse.*

18. See *Kiddushin* 46a.

19. [I.e. the repetitive phraseology implies that even when someone else refuses (viz. the girl herself), the same law applies (the marriage is blocked and the fine is paid). Cf. *Rashash.*] See note 16 above regarding her power of refusal.

20. *Deuteronomy* 22:29.

21. The term תִּהְיֶה, *she shall be [for him a wife],* implies that she must effect her "becoming" his wife [by providing the requisite consent] (*Rashi*).

22. [Since prior to the violation the father could have refused to give his daughter in marriage to the future violator (even if the daughter wanted to marry him; see below, 46b), logic dictates that the violator does not after the violation – by dint of his sinning – become obligated to marry the girl against her father's will.] From here we see that the argument, "so that the sinner will not profit," operates on the Biblical level (see *Kovetz Shiurim* §138).

23. The Gemara below (40a) derives exegetically that a seducer cannot be compelled to marry his victim (*Rashi*).

24. [I.e. since it is possible for a victimizer to have the power of refusal in the case of seduction while lacking it in the case of violation, the fact that the father has the power of refusal in the case of seduction cannot serve as the basis for endowing him – by dint of the logic of the *kal vachomer* – with that selfsame power in the case of violation.] Hence, if not for the argument "so that the sinner will not profit," we would not know that the father can prevent the marriage in the case of violation (*Rashi*).

25. I.e. although one might think that the fine for violation does not supplant a *kesubah,* inasmuch as the fine money is paid immediately to the father [in contrast to the *kesubah* award, which is paid to the woman herself (*Shitah Mekubetzes*)], the Baraisa teaches that this is not the case. Rather, there is no *kesubah* obligation [see below] (*Rashi*).

26. *Deuteronomy* ibid.

27. I.e. when she demands a divorce from her husband [in which case the violator is permitted to divorce her] (*Rashi;* see *Shitah Mekubetzes* סוד״ה אע״פ).

עין משפט
נר מצוה

עו א מיי' פי"ג מהל' נערה הל' ז סמג עשין נד טור אה"ע סי' קעז:
עז ב מיי' פ"א שם הל' ג סמג וטור שם:
עח ג ד מיי' שם הל' ד:

שסופה להצטער תחת בעלה אמרו לו אינו דומה נבעלת באונס לנבעלת ברצון אלא אמר רב נחמן אמר רבה בר אבוה צער של פיסוק הרגלים וכן הוא אומר א) ותפשקי את רגליך לכל עובר אי הכי מפותה נמי אמר רב נחמן אמר רבה בר אבוה משל דמפותה למה הדבר דומה לאדם שאמר לחבירו קרע שיראין שלי והפטר שלי דאבוה נינהו אלא אמר רב נחמן אמר רבה בר אבוה פקחות שבהן אומרות מפותה אין לה צער והא קא חזינן דאית לה אמר אביי א) אמרה לי אם כמיא חמימי על רישיה דקרחא רבא אמר אמרה לי בת רב חסדא כי ריבדא דכוסילתא רב פפא אמר אמרה לי בת אבא סוראה כי נהמא אקושא בחינכי: האונס נותן מיד המפתה לכשיוציא וכו': לכשיוציא אשתו היא אמר אביי אימא לכשלא יכנוס תניא נמי הכי אע"פ שאמרו א המפתה נותן לכשלא יכנוס בושת ופגם נותן מיד ואחד ב האונס ואחד המפתה בין היא ובין אביה יכולין לעכב בשלמא מפותה כתיב ב) אם מאן ימאן אביה ג) אין לי אלא אביה היא עצמה מנין תלמוד לומר ימאן מכל מקום אלא אונס בשלמא איהי כתיב ג) ולו תהיה מדעתה אלא אביה מנלן אמר אביי ג) שלא יהא חוטא נשכר רבא אמר ק"ו ומה מפתה שלא עבר אלא על דעת אביה בלבד בין היא ובין אביה יכולין לעכב אונס שעבר על דעת אביה ועל דעת עצמה לא כל שכן רבא לא אמר כאביי כיון דקא משלם קנס לאו חוטא נשכר הוא אביי לא אמר כרבא מפתה דאיהו מצי מעכב אביה נמי מצי מעכב אונס דאיהו לא מצי מעכב אביה נמי לא מצי מעכב תניא אידך אע"פ שאמרו אונס נותן מיד כשיוציא הוא אין לה עליו כלום כשיוציא מי מצי מפיק לה אימא כשתצא היא אין לה עליו כלום ג מת ד) יצא כסף קנסה בכתובתה רבי יוסי ברבי יהודה אומר יש לה כתובה מנה במאי קמיפלגי רבנן סברי ה) טעמא מאי תקינו רבנן כתובה כדי שלא תהא קלה בעיניו להוציאה והא לא מצי מפיק לה ורבי יוסי ברבי יהודה סבר הא נמי מצער לה עד דאמרה היא לא בעינא לך: אונס שותה בעציצו: אמר ליה רבא מפרזקיא לרב אשי מכדי מיגמר גמרי מהדדי להא

רש"י

שסופה להצטער כו'. ואי חיבוט על גבי קרקע הוא וכי סופה ליחבט על גבי קרקע תחת בעלה: שלי. בתמיה: דאבוה הוא. דהא כל שבח נעורים ילפינן לקמן (דף מו:) לאביה והיאך היא יכולה למחול: ריבדא דכוסילתא. פולטוייר"א דפלמוא"ה בלע"ז: ריבדא. ניקור: כוסילתא. כלי אומן מקיז ואית דגרסי כי תרפתא דסיכורי והיא היא: אמרה לי אם. (א) אומנתו היתה: בת רב חסדא. אשתו של רבא: בת אבא סוראה. דביתהו דרב פפא: נהמא אקושא בחינכי. כלחם קשה שגורר את החיך: אשתו היא. וכי אשתו היא כבר דקאמר לכשיוציא: לכשלא יכנוס. שתמאן היא או אביה או המפתה עצמו: יכולין לעכב. שלא יכניסנה: תהיה. משמע היא מהוה את עצמה לו: מצי מעכב. שאם רצה אינו כונס כדאמרינן לקמן ימהרנה לו מדעתו: אביה נמי לא מצי מעכב. אי לאו שלא יהא חוטא נשכר: אע"פ שאמרו אונס נותן מיד כשיוציאנה אין לה עליו כלום. ולא אמרינן אין קנסה תחת כתובתה שהרי לאביה נותן מיד אלא כסף קנסה הוא כתובתה וכן אם מת יצא כסף קנסה בכתובתה: מי מצי מפיק לה. לא יוכל לשלחה כתיב: כשתצא היא. אם יצתה מאליה ותבעה הימנו גט: טעמא מאי תקינו רבנן כתובה. לשאר נשים: מיגמר גמרי מהדדי. אונס ממפתה לשקלים ומפתה מאונס לחמשים: להא

תוספות

אי הכי מפותה נמי. יש לה צער פיסוק רגלים כמו אנוסה ואמאי קאמר אין דומה נבעלת באונס לנבעלת ברצון ואמר מורי הרב דודי ז"ל י) דאמתני' לא ה"מ למיפרך אמאי אונס חייב כיון שסופה להצטער בכך תחת בעלה דהא אפילו בעולה מצטערת בכך ואע"ג דבא עליה עתה סופה נמי להצטער ולא תרויח כלום י) [קצת נראה דאמתני' פריך אמאי מפותה פטור]:

קרע שיראין שלי והפטר. ואע"ג דלא אמרה על מנת לפטור איכא למימר דמחמת הנאת בעילה מחלה לגמרי:

ח) [לכשיוציא אשתו היא. אפי' פיתה לשם אישות מ"מ פריך אשתו היא כיון דאינה צריכה גט]:

בושת ופגם נותן מיד. אע"ג דאיתקש לקנס היינו לענין שניתן זה למי שזה ניתן אבל יש מקומות שפטור מקנס לגמרי וחייב בבושת ופגם: אין לי אלא אביה היא עצמה מנין כו'. (ג) תימה לר"י במאי איירי אי בקטנה או בנערה היאך היא יכולה למאן כיון שהאב רוצה והוא יכול לקדשה בעל כרחה למי שירצה וה"ה לזה ואי בשאין לה אב או שבגרה אחר כך מה צריך קרא תיפוק ליה שיכולה לעכב שלא יהא חוטא נשכר כדקאמר אביי בסמוך וכן אביה אמאי צריך קרא לאביי ואומר ר"י דנהי שאינה יכולה לעכב על אביה שלא יקדשנה לו מ"מ מועיל מיאונה לענין שישלם קנס וכן במיאון אביה והא דתניא הכא המפתה לכשלא יכנוס צריך לפרש לכשלא יכנוס מדעתה ומיהו קשה דהכא דרשינן מאם מאן ימאן מ"מ שהיא יכולה לעכב ובפרק נערה (לקמן מד:) דרשינן מינה לרבות יתומה לקנס וי"ל דליכתוב או מאן מאן או ימאן ימאן מאי מאן ימאן ש"מ תרתי ובכה"ג אמרינן במרובה (ב"ק דף סה. ושם) גבי אם המצא תמצא ובהחובל (שם דף פה.) גבי ורפא ירפא ועוד נראה דלאו מיתורא דקרא דריש לה התם דאם כן מאי פריך מינה לרבי יוסי בר' חנינא דפטר מוציא שם רע על היתומה דשאני מפתה דרבי קרא אלא כן הוא עיקר כמו שפירש בקונטרס לקמן דלאו מריבוי דריש אלא ה"פ לרבות יתומה לקנס דדרשינן שיש קנס כשהיא מעכבת והוא הדין דה"מ למימר לרבות בוגרת לקנס כשהיא מעכבת דדוקא בבוגרת או ביתומה יש קנס בעיכוב שלהן אבל כל זמן שלא בגרה תלוי באב והשתא דייק התם שפיר דשמעינן דסבר האי תנא שיש קנס ביתומה ולא ממעטינן ליה מדכתיב לאבי הנערה אע"ג דליכא ריבוי ליתומה כדפירשתי דאיכא לאוקמי קרא לבוגרת:

אלא אונס בשלמא איהי כו'. תימה כיון דאונס ומפתה מיגמר גמירי מהדדי להא מילתא נמי ליגמרו מהדדי כדפריך בסמוך ומאי קאמר אלא אביה מנלן וי"ל דלהאי מילתא לא גמרינן מהדדי דהא מפתה יכול לעכב ואונס שותה בעציצו וה"ה ה"נ אין אביה יכול לעכב וה"נ קאמר אביי בסמוך ורבא לא מסתבר ליה למימר הכי כיון דאיכא ק"ו וא"ת ואיהי גבי אונס אמאי איצטריך למיכתב נילף לאביי מסברא שלא יהא חוטא נשכר ולרבא מק"ו ויש לומר דלו תהיה לאשה אינו מיותר ט) [דאיצטרי"ך לעשה ולדרשות דלעיל. מהר"ס. א"נ אביי ורבא לא הוו משנו הכי אלא בתר דגלי קרא בהדיא]:

מפתה דאיהו מצי מעכב. ואפי' פיתה לשם אישות יכול הוא לגרשה:

טעמא מאי תקינו לה רבנן כתובה שלא תהא קלה בעיניו להוציאה. אע"ג דבתולה יש לה כתובה מן התורה זאת בעולה היא ומיהו תימה דקא פסיק ותני דבכל ענין אין לה כתובה אפילו בא עליה שלא כדרכה ובתולה גמורה היא ויש לה כתובה מן התורה דהא אם בא עליה שני יש לה קנס ולא הוי טעמא שלא תהא קלה בעיניו להוציאה תימה לר"י כיון דטעמא שלא תהא קלה בעיניו להוציאה אלמנה אמאי תקינו לה רבנן כתובה לא היה להם לתקן אלא לגרושה בלבד ואומר ר"י דמתוך שהוצרכו לתקן בגרושה שלא תהא קלה בעיניו להוציאה תקינו נמי לאלמנה משום חינא ומיהו לכתחילה לא היו מתקנים משום חינא קשה לרשב"א הא דתניא בהחובל (ב"ק דף פט. ושם) וכן היא שחבלה בבעלה לא הפסידה כתובתה ופריך אמאי תוזין לכתובתה י) בטובת הנאה ומתיב ליה בהאי חבלה ומשני הא מני רבי מאיר היא דאמר אסור לאדם שישהא את אשתו בלא כתובה אפילו שעה אחת והשתא כיון דטעמא שלא תהא קלה בעיניו להוציאה תוזין כתובתה על מנת שאם תתאלמן אבל אם יגרשנה יהא לה כתובה דהתם לא שייך משום חינא ואומר ר"י כיון דבשאר נשים שייך חינא אף על גב דבזאת לא שייך לא פלוג רבנן ואסור להשהותה בלא כתובה לר"מ וא"ת ואמאי תני הכא יצא כסף קנסה בכתובתה ליתני מת אין לה עליו כלום דהא לא תקינו רבנן לאלמנה אלא משום גרושה והכא מכח גרושה אין לתקן לזאת דהא לא מצי לגרשה ואור"י דה"נ כיון דשייך בה חינא כמו בשאר אלמנות אין לנו לשנותה משאר אלמנות להכי איצטריך טעמא דילא כסף קנסה בכתובתה ולא חשו במה דאין לה כתובה:

מהר

תוספות רי"ד

והמפתה לכשיוציא וכי אשתו היא. אמר אביי אימא לכשלא יכנוס. פי' שתמאן הוא או היא או אבי' דדרשי' לו מדעתו. אבל אם כנסה אינו נותן כלום דכתיב גבי מפתה מהר ימהרנה לו לאשה ואם מאן ימאן אביה לתתה לו כסף ישקול. תנ"ה אע"פ שאמרו המפתה נותן לכשלא יכנוס בושת ופגם נ"תן מיד אחד האונס ואחד המפתה בין היא בין אביה יכולין לעכב. פי' שלא יכנסנה. בשלמא מפותה כתיב אם כאן ימאן אביה אין לי אלא אביה היא עצמה מנין ת"ל מאן ימאן מ"מ. אלא אונס בשלמא איהי דכתיב ולו תהיה לאשה מדעתה אלא אביה מנלן. אביי אמר שלא יהא חוטא נשכר. רבא אמר (קנס) [ק"ו] ומה מפרה שלא עבר אלא ע"ד אביה בין היא בין אביה יכולין לעכב אונס שעבר על דעתה וע"ד אביה לא כ"ש. תניא אע"פ שאמרו האונס נותן מיד לכשיוציא הוא אין לה עליו כלום. פי' כגון שנתרצו שניהן בגירושין אין לה עליו כלום. מת יצא כסף קנסה בכתובתה. ר' יוסי ברבי יהודה אומר יש לה כתובה מנה וקיי"ל כת"ק והמפתה אם רצה להוציא מוציא מ"ט אמר רב אשי א"ק מהר ימהרנה לו מדעתו פירוש ומאי דתב אם רצה להוציא יוציא מתפרש אם רצה שלא יכנוס כדפי' לכשיוציא דרישא:

ליקוטי רש"י

ותפשקי את רגליך. לפי שדימה אותה לזונה דבר בלשון תשמיש שיש פיסוק הרגלים אפורקישמ"ט בלע"ז [יחזקאל טז, כה]. שיראין. של משי [במדבר לט:]. בת אבא סוראה. חמיו היה וכו' כדאמרינן באלו נערות [לעיל לט.] אמרה לי בת אבא סוראה כי כהמא אקושא בחינכי וכסנהדרין (דף יד:) נמי אמרינן איש ושמי נשים שאין מעלין לכיס אחד כגון רב פפא ובת אבא סוראה [לקמן נב:]. אין לי. יכול אמאן אלא אביה [קידושין מו:]. יצא כסף קנסה בכתובתה. שאין לה כתובה. יש לה כתובה. מנה. מנכסיו. מנה. אם מת ואע"ג שכבר נתן כסף קנסה לאביה. טעמא מאי תקינו וכו'. כל כתובה משום שלא תהא קלה בעיניו להוציאה תקנוה [לקמן נד:].

מסורת הש"ס

א) [קדושין לא: וש"נ], ב) קדושין מו., ג) [לעיל יא. וש"נ], ד) לקמן נד., ה) [לעיל יא. לקמן נד. יבמות פט.], ו) [נ"ל דלמתניתא לא ה"מ כו'. מהרש"א], ז) ת"י כ"י, ח) ת"י כ"י, ט) ת"י כ"י, י) לבעלה בטובת הנאה כצ"ל. מהרש"א.

הגהות הב"ח

(א) רש"י ד"ה אמרה וכו' אומנתו. נ"ב דילדתו אמו ומתה עי' קדושין דף לא ע"ב: (ב) תוס' ד"ה אין לי וכו' תימה. נ"ב עי' פ' האיש מקדש דף מו ע"א ובמ"ש התוס' לשם:

תורה אור השלם

א) אֶל כָּל רֹאשׁ דֶּרֶךְ בָּנִית רָמָתֵךְ וַתְּתַעֲבִי אֶת יָפְיֵךְ וַתְּפַשְּׂקִי אֶת רַגְלַיִךְ לְכָל עוֹבֵר וַתַּרְבִּי אֶת תַּזְנוּתָיִךְ: [יחזקאל טז, כה]

ב) אִם מָאֵן יְמָאֵן אָבִיהָ לְתִתָּהּ לוֹ כֶּסֶף יִשְׁקֹל כְּמֹהַר הַבְּתוּלֹת: [שמות כב, טז]

ג) וְנָתַן הָאִישׁ הַשֹּׁכֵב עִמָּהּ לַאֲבִי הַנַּעֲרָ חֲמִשִּׁים כָּסֶף וְלוֹ תִהְיֶה לְאִשָּׁה תַּחַת אֲשֶׁר עִנָּהּ לֹא יוּכַל שַׁלְּחָהּ כָּל יָמָיו: [דברים כב, כט]

לעזי רש"י

פולטוייר"א. פירוש ניקור, דקירה. דפלמוא"ה. פירוש של כלי אומן המקיז דם (כתפפס) (רש"י ע"ז דף כח ע"א) של אזמל להקזת דם.

שֶׁסּוֹפָהּ לְהִצְטַעֵר תַּחַת בַּעְלָהּ – SHE IS DESTINED TO SUFFER this pain UNDER HER HUSBAND.[1] אָמְרוּ לוֹ – [THE SAGES] SAID TO [R' SHIMON BEN YEHUDAH]: אֵינוֹ דּוֹמֶה נִבְעֶלֶת בְּאוֹנֶס לְנִבְעֶלֶת בְּרָצוֹן – The case of a virgin WHO HAS RELATIONS FORCIBLY IS NOT COMPARABLE TO the case of a virgin WHO HAS RELATIONS WILLINGLY. Hence, a violator does compensate for pain. In any event, from here we see that our Mishnah could not have been speaking of the pain of being thrown down. – ? –

The Gemara offers a different explanation:

אֶלָּא אָמַר רַב נַחְמָן אָמַר רַבָּה בַּר אֲבוּהַּ – **Rather, Rav Nachman said in the name of Rabbah bar Avuha:** צַעַר שֶׁל פִּיסוּק הָרַגְלַיִם – The Mishnah refers to the **pain of** the **separation of [her] legs.**[2] וְכֵן הוּא אוֹמֵר ,,וַתְּפַשְּׂקִי אֶת־רַגְלַיִךְ לְכָל־עוֹבֵר" – **And so it states:**[3] ***and you separated your legs for every passerby.***[4]

The Gemara asks:

אִי הָכִי מְפוּתָּה נַמִּי – **If so, a seduced girl also** should receive compensation for pain. Why does the Mishnah rule otherwise?[5]

The Gemara answers:

אָמַר רַב נַחְמָן אָמַר רַבָּה בַּר אֲבוּהַּ – **Rav Nachman said in the name of Rabbah bar Avuha:** מָשָׁל דִּמְפוּתָּה – **An analogy of the seduced-girl** case will explain why she is not compensated for pain: לְמָה הַדָּבָר דּוֹמֶה – **To what is the matter comparable?** לְאָדָם שֶׁאָמַר לַחֲבֵירוֹ – **To a person who said to his friend,** קְרַע שִׁירָאִין שֶׁלִּי וְהִפָּטֵר – **"Tear my silks and be exempt** from payment."[6]

The Gemara retorts:

שֶׁלִּי – Is this a case of **"my"** financial interests?! דַּאֲבוּהָ נִינְהוּ – Why, **[the damages for her pain] are her father's!**[7] – ? –

The Gemara offers a third and final explanation:

אֶלָּא אָמַר רַב נַחְמָן אָמַר רַבָּה בַּר אֲבוּהַּ – **Rather, Rav Nachman said in the name of Rabbah bar Avuha:** פִּקְחוֹת שֶׁבָּהֶן אוֹמְרוֹת – **The astute ones among [the women] say,** מְפוּתָּה אֵין לָהּ צַעַר – **"A seduced girl has no pain** from separating her legs."

The Gemara objects:

וְהָא קָא חָזֵינַן דְּאִית לָהּ – **But we see** from common experience **that she does have** pain?!

The Gemara deflects the challenge with several versions of essentially one answer:

אָמַר אַבַּיֵי – **Abaye said:** אָמְרָה לִי אֵם – **Mother told me,**[8] כְּמַיָּא חֲמִימֵי עַל רֵישֵׁיהּ דְּקַרְחָא – "The pain a woman experiences is merely **like hot water on the head of a bald person."**[9] רָבָא אָמַר – **Rava said:** אָמְרָה לִי בַּת רַב חִסְדָּא – **The daughter of Rav Chisda**[10] **told me,** כִּי רִיבְדָּא דְּכוּסִילְתָּא – "It feels **like the lancet puncture** of a bloodletter." רַב פָּפָּא אָמַר – **Rav Pappa said:** אָמְרָה לִי בַּת אַבָּא סוּרָאָה – **The daughter of Abba Suraah**[11] **told me,** כִּי נַהֲמָא אַקּוּשָׁא בְּחִינְכֵי – "It feels **like hard bread** rubbing **against [one's] palate."**

The Mishnah stated a second distinction between a violator and a seducer:

הָאוֹנֵס נוֹתֵן מִיָּד הַמְפַתֶּה לִכְשֶׁיּוֹצִיא וכו׳ – THE VIOLATOR REMITS the fifty-*shekalim* fine IMMEDIATELY, AND THE SEDUCER pays it only WHEN HE SENDS HER AWAY **etc.**

The Gemara asks in astonishment:

לִכְשֶׁיּוֹצִיא – **When he sends her away!?** אִשְׁתּוֹ הִיא – **Is she his wife** yet?![12]

The Gemara answers:

אָמַר אַבַּיֵי – **Abaye said:** אֵימָא לִכְשֶׁלֹּא יִכְנוֹס – **Say** the Mishnah means that the seducer pays the fine **when he does not marry** her.[13]

The Gemara offers support for this interpretation:

תַּנְיָא נַמִּי הָכִי – **It was also taught thus in a Baraisa:** אַף עַל פִּי שֶׁאָמְרוּ הַמְפַתֶּה נוֹתֵן לִכְשֶׁלֹּא יִכְנוֹס – EVEN THOUGH THEY SAID that THE SEDUCER REMITS the fine only WHEN HE DOES NOT MARRY her,[14] בּוֹשֶׁת וּפְגָם נוֹתֵן מִיָּד – HE GIVES restitution for HUMILIATION AND DEPRECIATION IMMEDIATELY [i.e. even if he does marry her].[15] וְאֶחָד הָאוֹנֵס וְאֶחָד הַמְפַתֶּה – AND in BOTH THE case of VIOLATION AND the case of SEDUCTION, בֵּין הִיא וּבֵין אָבִיהָ יְכוֹלִין

NOTES

1. Clearly, a husband does not throw his new bride onto the ground before consummating their marriage. Hence, the pain of being thrown down is not the pain a virgin would experience from both a violator and her husband, and so it cannot be the pain to which the Mishnah refers (*Rashi;* cf. *Shitah Mekubetzes* ד״ה וכי תימא).

2. [I.e. the position a woman assumes to receive the male intrinsically involves some pain.]

3. *Ezekiel* 16:25.

4. The prophet speaks disparagingly to the wayward Jewish people: So steeped are you in lewdness that you ignore the pain of cohabitation and "separate your legs for every passerby" (*Ritva*). [However, the plain meaning of the passage suggests that the prophet speaks metaphorically about the people's lusting after idolatry.]

5. This question does not arise regarding the pain of being thrown to the ground, since a seduced girl does not experience that pain. But if the Mishnah refers to the pain of spreading her legs for intercourse, a seduced girl also should be compensated, for she too endures that pain (*Ritva*; see *Ramban,* who asks why she should be compensated, when ultimately she would experience that pain with her husband; cf. *Tosafos,* as explained by *Shitah Mekubetzes* ד״ה אי הכי מפותה).

6. [If someone says to his friend, "Inflict damage upon one of my possessions or inflict pain upon me and be exempt," the perpetrator is exempt from payment (see Mishnah *Bava Kamma* 92a; Gemara ad loc. 93a with *Rashi* ד״ה רבא אמר לפי שאין אדם מוחל על ראשי אבריו; and *Sma* 421:21).] *Tosafos* note that although in our case the girl did not specify that she is exempting the seducer from liability for pain [and generally, when there is no explicit waiver, we assume that the injured party meant only to permit the infliction of damage or pain but did not exempt the perpetrator from payment; see Mishnah ibid.], we presume that she waived her right to payment as well in consideration for the pleasure she derives from the act of cohabitation.

7. The Gemara below (46b) teaches that all income generated by a *naarah* accrues to her father. How, then, can the girl exempt the seducer from financial liability for her pain when the right to that compensation belongs to the father? (*Rashi*). See *Rashba* and *Ritva* for explanations of why Rabbah bar Avuha thought otherwise. See also *Rashash.*

8. Abaye was an orphan. He often quoted the nurse who raised him, referring to her as "Mother" [see *Kiddushin* 31b] (see *Rashi*).

9. The pain a woman experiences [in spreading her legs] during consensual relations is negligible, and is offset by the pleasure she derives (*Talmidei R' Yonah,* cited by *Shitah Mekubetzes* ד״ה פקחות).

10. Rava's own wife [see *Bava Basra* 12b] (*Rashi*).

11. Rav Pappa's own wife [see *Sanhedrin* 14b and below, end of 52b] (*Rashi*).

12. The term לִכְשֶׁיּוֹצִיא, *when he sends her away,* means "divorce." The Gemara argues that its use is inappropriate here, since the seduced girl is not yet his wife (*Rashi*). [The Mishnah cannot be speaking of where the seducer married the girl and then divorces her, for in that case he does not pay the fine (*Ritva*).] See above, 39a note 36. Cf. *Raavad,* cited in *Shitah Mekubetzes.*

13. Either because the girl, her father or the seducer objects to the marriage (*Rashi*). According to *Ritva,* the Gemara means that when the Mishnah states, "When he sends her away," it does not mean "when he sends her away with a bill of divorce." Rather, it means "when he sends her away in court, having declared his unwillingness to marry her."

14. This statement of the Baraisa confirms Abaye's interpretation.

15. Although the Torah levies the fine for seduction only when the seducer does not marry his victim (*Exodus* 22:16), restitution for humiliation and depreciation, a common component of assault cases in general, is imposed regardless of the outcome.

עין משפט
נר מצוה

עו א מיי' פ"ב מהל' נערה הל' ז סמג עשין נד טור אה"ע סי' קעז:
עז ב מיי' פ"א שם הל' ג סמג וטור שם:
עח ג ד מיי' שם הל' ד:

שסופה להצטער תחת בעלה אמרו לו אינו דומה נבעלת באונס לנבעלת ברצון אלא אמר רב נחמן אמר רבה בר אבוה צער של פיסוק הרגלים וכן הוא אומר א) ותפשקי את רגליך לכל עובר אי הכי מפותה נמי אמר רב נחמן אמר רבה בר אבוה משל דמפותה למה הדבר דומה לאדם שאמר לחבירו קרע שיראין שלי והפטר שלי דאבוה נינהו אלא אמר רב נחמן אמר רבה בר אבוה פקחות שבהן אומרות מפותה אין לה צער והא קא חזינן דאית לה אמר אביי א) אמרה לי אם כמיא חמימי על רישיה דקרחא רבא אמר אמרה לי בת רב חסדא כי ריבדא דכוסילתא רב פפא אמר אמרה לי בת אבא סוראה כי נהמא אקושא בחינכי: האונס נותן מיד המפתה לכשיוציא וכו': לכשיוציא אשתו היא אמר אביי אימא לכשלא יכנוס תניא נמי הכי אע"פ שאמרו א המפתה נותן לכשלא יכנוס בושת ופגם נותן מיד ואחד ב האונס ואחד המפתה בין היא ובין אביה יכולין לעכב בשלמא מפותה כתיב ב) אם מאן ימאן אביה ג) אין לי אלא אביה היא עצמה מנין תלמוד לומר ימאן מכל מקום אלא אונס בשלמא איהי כתיב ג) ולו תהיה מדעתה אלא אביה מנלן אמר אביי ו) שלא יהא חוטא נשכר רבא אמר ק"ו ומה מפתה שלא עבר אלא על דעת אביה בלבד בין היא ובין אביה יכולין לעכב אונס שעבר על דעת אביה ועל דעת עצמה לא כל שכן רבא לא אמר כאביי כיון דקא משלם קנס לאו חוטא נשכר הוא אביי לא אמר כרבא מפתה דאיהו מצי מעכב אביה נמי מצי מעכב אונס דאיהו לא מצי מעכב אביה נמי לא מצי מעכב תניא אידך אע"פ שאמרו אונס נותן מיד כשיוציא הוא אין לה עליו כלום כשיוציא מי מצי מפיק לה אימא כשתצא היא אין לה עליו כלום ג מת ז) יצא כסף קנסה בכתובתה רבי יוסי ברבי יהודה אומר יש לה כתובה מנה במאי קמיפלגי רבנן סברי ד טעמא מאי תקינו רבנן כתובה כדי שלא תהא קלה בעיניו להוציאה והא לא מצי מפיק לה ורבי יוסי ברבי יהודה סבר הא נמי מצער לה עד דאמרה היא לא בעינא לך: אונס שותה בעציצו: אמר ליה רבא מפרזקיא לרב אשי מכדי מיגמר גמרי מהדדי להא

רש"י

שסופה להצטער כו'. ואי מיבעט על גבי קרקע הוא וכי סופה ליחבט על גבי קרקע תחת בעלה: שלי. בתמיה: דאבוה הוא. דהא כל שבח נעורים ילפינן לקמן (דף מו:) לאביה והיאך היא יכולה למחול: ריבדא דכוסילתא. פוצטוייר"א דפלמוא"ה בלע"ז: ריבדא. ניקור: כוסילתא. כלי אומן מקיז ואית דגרסי כי תרפתא דסיכורי והיא היא: אמרה לי אם. (א) אומנתו היתה: בת רב חסדא. אשתו של רבא: בת אבא סוראה. דביתהו דרב פפא: נהמא אקושא בחינכי. כלחם קשה שגורר את החיך: אשתו היא. וכי אשתו היא כבר דקאמר לכשיוציא: לכשלא יכנוס. שתמאן היא או אביה או המפתה עצמו: יכולין לעכב. שלא יכניסנה: תהיה. משמע היא מהוה את עצמה לו: מצי מעכב. שאם רצה אינו כונס כדאמרינן לקמן ימהרנה לו מדעתו: אביה נמי לא מצי מעכב. אי לאו שלא יהא חוטא נשכר: אע"פ שאמרו אונס נותן מיד כשיוציאנה אין לה עליו כלום. ולא אמרינן אין קנסה כתובתה שהרי לאביה נותן מיד אלא כסף קנסה הוא כתובתה וכן אם מת יצא כסף קנסה בכתובתה: מי מצי מפיק לה. לא יוכל לשלחה כתיב: כשתצא היא. אם יצתה מאליה ותבעה הימנו גט: טעמא מאי תקינו רבנן כתובה. לשאר נשים: מיגמר גמרי מהדדי. אונס ממפתה לשקלים ומפתה מאונס לחמשים: להא

תוספות

אי הכי מפותה נמי. יש לה צער פיסוק רגלים כמו אנוסה ומאי קאמר אין דומה נבעלת באונס לנבעלת ברצון ואמר מורי הרב דודי ז"ל י) דאמתני' לא ה"מ למיפרך מאי אונס חייב כיון שסופה להצטער בכך תחת בעלה דהא אפילו בעולה מצטערת בכך ואע"ג דבא עליה עתה סופה נמי להצטער ולא תרויח כלום י) [קצת נראה דאמתני' פריך אמאי מפותה פטור]:

קרע שיראין שלי והפטר. ואע"ג דלא אמרה על מנת לפטור איכא למימר דמחמת הנאת בעילה מחלה לגמרי:

ח) [לכשיוציא אשתו היא. ואפי' פיתה לשם אישות מ"מ פריך אשתו היא כיון דאינה גרושה בלא גט:]

בושת ופגם נותן מיד. אע"ג דליתקש לקנס היינו לענין שיתן זה למי שזה ניתן אבל יש מקומות שפטור מקנס לגמרי וחייב בבושת ופגם: אין לי אלא אביה היא עצמה מנין כו'. (ג) תימה לר"י במאי מיירי אי בקטנה או בנערה היאך היא יכולה למאן כיון שהאב רוצה והוא יכול לקדשה בעל כרחה למי שירצה וה"ה לזה ואי בשאין לה אב או שבגרה אחר כך מה צריך קרא מיפוק ליה שיכולה לעכב שלא יהא חוטא נשכר כדקאמר אביי בסמוך וכן אביה אמאי צריך קרא לאביי ואומר ר"י דנהי שאינה יכולה לעכב על אביה שלא יקדשנה לו מ"מ מועיל מיאונה לענין שישלם קנס וכן במיאון אביה והא דתניא הכא המפתה לכשלא יכנוס צריך לפרש לכשלא יכנוס מדעתה ומיהו קשה דהכא דרשינן מאם מאן ימאן מ"מ שהיא יכולה לעכב ובפרק נערה (לקמן מד:) דרשינן מינה לרבות יתומה לקנס וי"ל דליכתוב אי מאן או ימאן ימאן מאן ימאן ש"מ תרתי ובכה"ג אמרינן במרובה (ב"ק דף סה. ושם) גבי אם המצא תמצא ובהחובל (שם דף פה.) גבי ורפא ירפא ועוד נראה דלאו מיתורא דקרא דריש לה התם דאם כן מאי פריך מינה לרבי יוסי בר' חנינא דפטר מוציא שם רע על היתומה דשאני מפתה דרבי קרא אלא כן הוא עיקר כמו שפירש בקונטרס לקמן דלאו מריבוי דריש אלא ה"פ לרבות יתומה לקנס דדרשינן שיש קנס כשהיא מעכבת והוא הדין דה"מ למימר לרבות בוגרת לקנס כשהיא מעכבת דדוקא בבוגרת או ביתומה יש קנס בעיכוב שלהן אבל כל זמן שלא בגרה תלוי באב והשתא דייק התם שפיר דשמעינן דסבר האי תנא שיש קנס ביתומה ולא ממעטינן ליה מדכתיב לאבי הנערה אע"ג דליכא ריבוי ליתומה כדפירשתי דאיכא לאוקמי קרא לבוגרת:

אלא אונס בשלמא איהי כו'. תימה כיון דאונס ומפתה מיגמר גמירי מהדדי להא מילתא נמי ליגמרו מהדדי כדפריך בסמוך ומאי קאמר אלא אביה מנלן וי"ל דלהאי מילתא לא גמרינן מהדדי דהא מפתה יכול לעכב ואונס שותה בעציצו וה"ה ה"נ אין אביה יכול לעכב וה"נ קאמר אביי בסמוך ורבא לא מסתבר ליה למימר הכי כיון דאיכא ק"ו וא"ת ואיהי גבי אונס אמאי איצטריך למיכתב נילף לאביי מסברא שלא יהא חוטא נשכר ולרבא מק"ו ויש לומר דלו תהיה לאשה אינו מיותר ט) [דאיצטריך לעשה ולדרשות דלעיל. מהר"ס. א"נ אביי ורבא לא הוו משנו הכי אלא בתר דגלי קרא בהדיא]: מפתה דאיהו מצי מעכב. ואפי' פיתה לשם אישות יכול הוא לגרשה:

טעמא מאי תקינו לה רבנן כתובה שלא תהא קלה בעיניו להוציאה. אע"ג דבתולה יש לה כתובה מן התורה וזאת בעולה היא ומיהו תימה דקא פסיק ותני דבכל ענין אין לה כתובה אפילו בא עליה שלא כדרכה ובתולה גמורה היא ויש לה כתובה מן התורה דהא אם בא עליה שני יש לה קנס ולא הוי טעמא שלא תהא קלה בעיניו להוציאה תימה לר"י כיון דטעמא שלא תהא קלה בעיניו להוציאה אלמנה אמאי תקינו לה רבנן כתובה לא היה להם לתקן אלא לגרושה בלבד ואומר ר"י דמתוך שהוצרכו לתקן בגרושה שלא תהא קלה בעיניו להוציאה תקינו נמי לאלמנה משום חינא ומיהו לכתחילה לא היו מתקנים משום חינא קשה לרשב"א הא דתניא בהחובל (ב"ק דף פט. ושם) וכן היא שחבלה בבעלה לא הפסידה כתובתה ופריך אמאי תזבין לכתובתה י) בטובת הנאה ומותיב ליה בהאי חבלה ומשני הא מני רבי מאיר היא דאמר אסור לאדם שישהא את אשתו בלא כתובה אפילו שעה אחת והשתא כיון דטעמא שלא תהא קלה בעיניו להוציאה תזבין כתובתה על מנת שאם תתאלמן אבל אם יגרשנה יהא לה כתובה דהתם לא שייך משום חינא ואומר ר"י כיון דבשאר נשים שייך חינא אף על גב דבזאת לא שייך לא פלוג רבנן ואסור להשהותה בלא כתובה לר"מ וא"ת ואמאי תני הכא יצא כסף קנסה בכתובתה ליתני מת אין לה עליו כלום דהא לא תקינו רבנן לאלמנה אלא משום גרושה והכא מכח גרושה אין לתקן לזאת דהא לא מצי לגרשה ואור"י דה"נ כיון דשייך בה חינא כמו בשאר אלמנות אין לנו לשנותה משאר אלמנות להכי איצטריך טעמא דילא כסף קנסה בכתובתה ולא חשו במה דאין לה כתובה:

מהר

תוספות רי"ד

והמפתה לכשיוציא וכי אשתו היא. אמר אביי אימא לכשלא יכנוס. פי' שתמאן הוא או היא או אביה דדרשי' לי' מדעתו. אבל אם כנסה אינו נותן כלום דכתיב גבי מפתה מהר ימהרנה לו לאשה ואם מאן ימאן אביה לתתה לו כסף ישקול. תנ"ה אע"פ שאמרו המפתה נותן לכשלא יכנוס בושת ופגם נותן מיד אחד האונס ואחד המפתה בין היא בין אביה יכולין לעכב. פי' שלא יכנסנה. בשלמא מפותה כתיב אם מאן ימאן אביה אין לי אלא אביה היא עצמה מנין ת"ל מאן ימאן מ"מ. אלא אונס בשלמא איהי דכתיב ולו תהיה לאשה מדעתה אלא אביה מנלן. אביי אמר שלא יהא חוטא נשכר. רבא אמר (שם) [ק"ו] הוא מה מפתה שלא עבר אלא ע"ד אביה בין היא בין אביה יכולין לעכב אונס שעבר על דעתה וע"ד אביה לא כ"ש. תניא אע"כ שאמרו האונס נותן מיד לכשהיא יוצאה. פי' כגון שנתרצו שניהן בגירושין אין לה עליו כלום. מת יצא כסף קנסה בכתובתה. ר' יוסי ברבי יהודה אומר יש לה כתובה מנה וקיי"ל כת"ק והמפתה אם רצה להוציא מוציא מ"ט אמר רב אשי א"ק מהר ימהרנה לו מדעתו פירוש ומאי דהנן אם רצה להוציא יוצא מתפרש אם רצה שלא יכנוס לא יכנוס כדפרישנא לכשיוציא דרישא:

ליקוטי רש"י

ותפשקי את רגליך. לפי שדימה אותה לזונה דבר בלשון תשמיש שיש פיסוק הרגלים איאקיישמ"ש בלע"ז [יחזקאל טז, כה]. שיראין. של משי [מנחות לט:]. בת אבא סוראה. חמיו היה וכו' כדאמרינן באלו נערות (לעיל לט:) אמרה לי בת אבא סוראה כי נהמא אקושא בחינכי ובסנהדרין (דף יד:) נמי אמרינן איש ושתי נשים שאין מטילין לכים אחד כגון רב פפא ובת אבא סוראה [לקמן נב:]. אין לי. דיכול למאן אלא אביה [קידושין מו.]. יצא כסף קנסה בכתובתה. ואין לה כתובה. יש לה כתובה. מנכסיו. מנה. אב מר ואע"ג שכבר נתן כסף קנסה לאביה. טעמא מאי תקינו וכו'. כל כתובת אשה משום שלא תהא קלה בעיניו להוציאה תקנוה [לקמן נד.].

מסורת הש"ס

א) [קדושין לא: וש"נ], ב) קדושין מו., ג) [לעיל יא. וש"נ], ד) לקמן נד., ה) [לעיל יא. לקמן נד. יבמות פט.], ו) [צ"ל דאמתניתא לא ה"מ כו'. מהרש"א], ז) ת"י כ"י, ח) ת"י כ"י, ט) ת"י כ"י, י) לבעלה בטובת הנאה כצ"ל. מהרש"א.

הגהות הב"ח

(א) רש"י ד"ה אמרה וכו' אומנתו. נ"ב דילדתו אמו ומתה עי' קדושין דף לא ע"ב: (ב) תוס' ד"ה אין לי וכו' תימה. נ"ב עי' פ' האיש מקדש דף מ ע"א וכמ"ש התוס' לשם:

תורה אור השלם

א) אֶל כָּל רֹאשׁ דֶּרֶךְ בָּנִית רָמָתֵךְ וַתְּתַעֲבִי אֶת יָפְיֵךְ וַתְּפַשְּׂקִי אֶת רַגְלַיִךְ לְכָל עוֹבֵר וַתַּרְבִּי אֶת תַּזְנוּתָיִךְ: [יחזקאל טז, כה]

ב) אִם מָאֵן יְמָאֵן אָבִיהָ לְתִתָּהּ לוֹ כֶּסֶף יִשְׁקֹל כְּמֹהַר הַבְּתוּלֹת: [שמות כב, טז]

ג) וְנָתַן הָאִישׁ הַשֹּׁכֵב עִמָּהּ לַאֲבִי הַנַּעֲרָ חֲמִשִּׁים כָּסֶף וְלוֹ תִהְיֶה לְאִשָּׁה תַּחַת אֲשֶׁר עִנָּהּ לֹא יוּכַל שַׁלְּחָהּ כָּל יָמָיו: [דברים כב, כט]

לעזי רש"י

פוצטוייר"א. פירוש ניקור, דקירה. דפלמוא"ה. פירוש של כלי אומן המקיז (דם בכתפים) (רש"י ע"ז דף כח ע"א) של איזמל להקזת דם:

מסורת הש"ס

א) יבמות יב: ק: נדה מה. נדרים לה: [תוספתא נדה פ"ב], ב) קדושין עט. נדה סה. ג) נדרים סו: עד: יבמות כט: לקמן מו: קדושין ד, ד) לקמן מב. [לעיל כט:] ו) ב"ק נט. ע"ש, ז) [ע' תוס' יבמות יב: ותוס' נדה יג.], ח) [וע' תוס' נדה סה. ד"ה וכ"ת כו' מייבין הגירסא], ט) מ"י כ"י.

עין משפט נר מצוה

סט א מיי' פ"ב מהל' אישות הל' ג טור ש"ע יו"ד סימן קלד סעיף א בהג"ה:

ע ב מיי' פ"ב מהל' נערה הל' טו סמג עשין נד טור אה"ע סימן קעז:

עא ג מיי' שם הל' טו:

עב ד מיי' פי"א מהל' נדרים הל' ע סמג לאוין רמב טוש"ע י"ד סי' רלד סעיף ה:

עג ה מיי' פ"ב מהלכות נערה הל' ז סמג עשין נד טוש"ע אה"ע סי' קעז סעיף א:

עד ו מיי' פ"א שם הל' ג סמג שם טוש"ע שם סעיף ג:

עה ז מיי' שם הל' ה טוש"ע שם סעי' ד:

גמרא

ומי מעברא והתני רב ביבי קמיה דרב נחמן [א] שלש נשים משמשות במוך אלו הן קטנה ומעוברת ומניקה קטנה שמא תתעבר ותמות מעוברת שמא תעשה עוברה סנדל מניקה שמא תגמול את בנה וימות ואיזוהי קטנה מבת אחת עשרה שנה ויום אחד עד שתים עשרה שנה ויום אחד פחות מיכן ויותר על כן משמשת כדרכה והולכת דברי ר"מ וחכמים אומרים אחת זו ואחת זו משמשת כדרכה והולכת ומן השמים ירחמו משום שנאמר [א] שומר פתאים ה' וכי תימא דאיעברא כשהיא נערה ואולידה כשהיא נערה ובשיתא ירחי מי קא ילדה והאמר שמואל [ג] אין בין נערות לבגרות אלא ששה חדשים וכי תימא בציר הוא דליכא הא טפי איכא הא אלא קאמר אלא הכי קמיבעיא ליה יש בגר בקבר או אין בגר בקבר ולא פקע אב או דלמא אין בגר בקבר ולא פקע אב מר בר רב אשי בעי לה הכי מיתה עושה בגרות או אין עושה בגרות תיקו בעי מיניה רבא מאביי בא עליה ונתארסה מהו א"ל [ב] מי כתיב ונתן לאבי הנערה אשר לא ארוסה ולטעמיך הא דתניא [ג] בא עליה ונשאת לעצמה מי כתיב ונתן לאבי הנערה אשר לא נשואה הכי השתא התם הואיל ובגרות מוציאה מרשות אב ונישואין מוציאין מרשות אב מה בגרות בא עליה ובגרה לעצמה אף נישואין בא עליה ונשאת לעצמה אלא אירוסין מי קא מפקי מרשותא דאב לגמרי הא תנן [ד] נערה המאורסה אביה ובעלה מפירין לה נדריה: מתני' [ה] המפתה נותן שלשה דברים והאונס ארבעה המפתה נותן בושת ופגם וקנס מוסיף עליו אונס שנותן את הצער מה בין אונס למפתה האונס נותן את הצער והמפתה אינו נותן את הצער האונס נותן מיד והמפתה לכשיוציא האונס שותה בעציצו והמפתה אם רצה להוציא מוציא [ו] כיצד שותה בעציצו אפילו היא חיגרת אפי' היא סומא ואפילו היא מוכת שחין [ז] נמצא בה דבר ערוה או שאינה ראויה לבא בישראל אינו רשאי לקיימה שנאמר [ב] [ח] ולו תהיה לאשה אשה הראויה לו: גמ' צער דמאי אמר אבוה דשמואל צער שחבטה על גבי קרקע מתקיף לה רבי זירא אלא מעתה חבטה על גבי שיראין הכי נמי דפטור וכי תימא הכי נמי והתניא ר' שמעון בן יהודה אומר משום רבי שמעון [י] אונס אינו משלם את הצער מפני שסופה

רש"י

ומי מעברא. בקטנות או בנערות כשהיא בת קנס שתלד בנערות: משמשות במוך. מותר להן לשמש במוך ואינן כמשחיתות זרע: שמא יעשה עוברה סנדל. שאם תתעבר עובר שני פוחת השני את לורת (א) הראשון ודומה לסנדל שהוא דג שטוח: שמא תגמול את בנה. מפני שחלב נעכר כשמתעברת ואינו טוב לינוק ולריך להעתיקו משדים וימות: פחות מכאן. מבת אחת עשרה שנה משמשת כדרכה לפי שלא תתעבר: ויותר על כן. על בת שתים עשרה שנה משמשת כדרכה שאם תתעבר לא תמות אלמא בקטנות לא מיעברא שיבלה לכלל לידה דהא ותמות קתני: וכי תימא. מבת שתים עשרה ויום אחד שהגיעו ימי הנעורים נתעברה וילדה בנערות ומתה בנערות הא נמי ליתא דאמר שמואל אין בין נערות לבגרות אלא ששה חדשים מתחילת שתי שערות הויא נערה באותן שתחילת משתים עשרה שנה והלאה ומשתביאם עד שתגדל ששה חדשים ותו לא וממתניתא דקתני מבת שתים עשרה והלך אי מעברא לא מתה במביאה שתי שערות קודם שתתעבר קאמר אבל כל זמן שלא הביאה קטנה היא והאי דנקט מנין שנים משום דבבציר משתים עשרה ויום אחד אפילו הביאה שערות אינו אלא שומא כדאמרינן במסכת נדה וקדושין: ופקע אב. פקעה תביעת אב והכא הלה כמה שבידו שאין בעל דינו קיים וקנס לאו ממון הוא להורישו לאביה בתורת ירושה כל כמה דלא גבתיה: או אין בגר בקבר. לאפקועי תביעת אב: מר בר רב אשי. לא בעי לה בעיא דרבא משום בגר בקבר אלא אם מתה בנערותה מי פקעה כי בגרות דמקמיה או לא ולהאי לישנא דמר בר רב אשי איבעיא דרבא אמרו לעיל מילתא דפשיטא ליה לאביי מיבעיא ליה דרבא דאילו לישנא קמא מפשט פשיטא ליה דרבא דמיתה לא מפקעא ודלא כאביי כל זמן שלא בגרה וכי קא מיבעיא ליה בבגר בקבר קמבעיא ליה אבל במיתה כל זמן שלא בגרה פליג אדאביי ואמר לא מפקעא ומייב: מיתה עושה בגרות. עושה דין בגרות דמפקעא כח אב כי בגרות: מהו. מי הוי לאביה או לעצמה: בגרות מוציאה מרשות אב. דלא מלינו שזכתה לו תורה בבתו אלא מכר בקטנות ושאר שבח כגון קנסה ומעשה ידיה בנערות כדילפינן בפרק נערה (לקמן דף מו:) אבל בבגרות לא אשכחן וכיון דלא זיכתה לו תורה אנן מהיכא תיתי לן לזכותו בשלה: ונשואין מוציאין מרשות אב. כדאשכחן בהפרת נדרים דכל זמן דלא ניסת אביה מיפר ומשניסת אין יכול להפר: בא עליה. כשהיא נערה ובגרה: לעצמה. דכתיב ונתן האיש השוכב עמה לאבי הנערה אם נערה היא בשעת נתינה: אביה ובעלה. ואינו מופר עד שיפרו שניהם: מתני' בושת ופגם. במתני' לקמן מפרש להו: האונס נותן מיד. לאביה אע"פ שכונסה: לכשיוציא. בגמרא פריך הטו אשתו היא ומפרש לה לכשלא יכנוס דאם כנסה אינו נותן קנס כדכתיב מהר ימהרנה לו ואם מאן ימאן וגו' כסף ישקול אבל אונס כתיב ונתן חמשים כסף ולו תהיה לאשה: שותה בעציצו. בכלי שבחר לו לשתות בו כלומר על כרחו ישאנה כדכתיב לא יוכל לשלחה (דברים כב): גמ' שסופה

תוספות

שלש נשים משמשות במוך. פי' בקונטרס מותרות לשמש במוך אע"ג דשאר נשים אסורות משום השחתת זרע ואין נראה לר"ת [י] דהא קטנה ואילונית מותר לשמש בהדייהו ולא הוי השחתת זרע כיון שהוא דרך תשמיש ומפרש ר"ת משמשות לריכות לשמש במוך אחר תשמיש ועלה טובה קמ"ל ולר"י נראה לקיים פי' הקונט' דבריש נדה (דף ג.) משמע שהמוך הוא במעיה כל שעה והוי כמשמש על האבנים ועל העצים ולא דמי למשמש קטנה ואילונית ועוד אפילו היתה נותנת מוך אחר תשמיש אסורה ° דאף על פי שאינה מצווה על פריה ורביה מ"מ אסורה היא להשחית זרע כדמשמע בנדה (דף יג.) דתנן כל היד המרבה לבדוק בנשים משובחת באנשים תיקצץ ומפרש בגמרא משום דנשים לאו בנות הרגשה נינהו משמע דאם היו בנות הרגשה הוו אסירי ויש לדחות דלאו בנות איסור הרגשה נינהו קאמר: וכי תימא בציר הוא כו' והא בלבד קאמר. בקונטרס (בקדושין דף עט.) ל"ג ליה דבלאו בלבד משמע טפי לא [ח]: בא עליה ונתארסה מהו. לרבי עקיבא דמתני' קא מיבעיא ליה דאמר נתארסה ונתגרשה קנסה לעצמה דמי אמרינן כיון שיצאה מרשות האב לענין קנס יהא קנסה לעצמה או דלמא כיון דלענין שאר מילי לא נפקא מרשות האב יהא קנסה לאביה אבל לרבי עקיבא דברייתא פשיטא דקנסה לאביה ולר' יוסי הגלילי נהי דאמר אין לה קנס נמי לא מיבעיא ליה דהא דאין לה קנס לאו משום מיפק מרשותא דאב היא אלא גזירת הכתוב הוא דאין לה קנס ולא נפקא באירוסין כלל מרשות אביה דהא זכאי בקדושיה ובמעשה ידיה אע"ג דנתארסה והא דקא בעי לה סתם ולא קאמר לרבי עקיבא בהדיא מהו משום דהלכה כר' עקיבא מחבירו: הואיל ונישואין מוציאין מרשות אב. פי' בקונט' דילפינן מהפרת נדרים ואע"ג דקי"ל דממונא מאיסורא לא ילפינן ה"מ לאוקמה ברשות אב הוא דלא ילפינן ממונא מאיסורא אבל לאפוקי מרשות אב ילפינן שפיר מהפרת נדרים דבסברא מועטת יש להוציאה מרשות אב ור"י ב"ר אברהם פי' כיון דגלי לן קרא דלאוקמה ברשות אב איסורא וממונא שוין ה"ה לאפוקה [ט] [ור"י מפרש דנישואין מוציאין מרשות אב מדדרשינן איש אמו ואביו תיראו איש סיפק כו' אשה אין סיפק בידה לעשות ולא נהירא דמעשה ידיה אינו לבעל מן התורה]: מה בוגרת בא עליה ובגרה לעצמה. פירוש דהא מלינו בוגרת שיצאה מרשות אב לענין ממון וקשה דה"נ נישואין מוציאין מרשות אב לענין ממון ואמאי לריך למילף מבוגרת ונראה דבא עליה ובגרה לעצמה נפקא לן מונתן לאבי הנערה דדרשינן לאבי הנערה ולא לאבי בוגרת: צער דמאי. קשה לר"י דמאי קא מיבעיא ליה וכי לא ידע הש"ס שיש לער גדול לבתולה בביאה ראשונה וכמה קטנות חולות מזה וכ"ת דמאותו לער פשיטא ליה להש"ס דפטור שהרי סופה להלטער בכך תחת בעלה והא איכא כמה תנאי בהכונס (ב"ק דף נט. ושם) דלא חיישי לכחש גופנא פירוש דבר שסופו להיות כן ונראה לר"י דלער בעילה משום תאות תשמיש אינו בא בשעת תשמיש אלא אחר כך וכל לער החבלה דמחייב היינו אותו לער הבא לו בשעת חבלה אבל מה שבא לו אחר כך מיפטר דגרמא בעלמא הוא הלכך בעי לער דמאי ורשב"א מפרש דפשיטא דלער של בתולים ליכא למימר דע"כ תנא דמתני' חייש לכחש גופנא מדמפתה פטור: אי

תוספות רי"ד

תניא בא עליה ונשאת לעצמה הואיל ובגרות מוציאה מרשות אב. פי' שלא מצינו שזכתה לו תורה בבתו אלא מכר בקטנותה ושאר שבח ממון כגון קנסה ומעשה ידיה בנערות כדילפי' לקמן בפ' נערה ונשואין נמי מוציאין מרשות אב. פירוש כדאשכחן בהפרת נדרים דכ"ז שלא נשאת אביה מפר נדריה ומשנשאת אין יכול להפר. מה בוגרת בא עלי' ובגרה לעצמה דכתיב ונתן האיש השוכב עמה לאבי הנערה. אם היא נערה בשעת נתינה אף נשואין בא עליה ונשאת לעצמה: מתני' המפתה נותן ג' דברים והאונס ד' המפתה נותן בושת ופגם וקנס מוסיף עליו אונס שנותן את הצער מה בין אונס למפתה האונס נותן את הצער והמפתה אין נותן את הצער האונס נותן מיד והמפתה לכשיוציא האונס שותה בעציצו. פי' בכלי שבחר לו לשתות בו כלומר ע"כ ישאנה דכתיב לא יוכל לשלחה כל ימיו והמפתה אם רצה להוציא מוציא. פי' האונס נותן מיד ואע"פ שכונסה שנאמר ונתן האיש השוכב עמה לאבי הנערה חמשים כסף ולו תהיה לאשה. ודרשי' תו לו אתה כופה ולא לה:

ליקוטי רש"י

משמשות במוך. מותרות לתת מוך במקום תשמיש כשהן משמשות כדי שלא יתעברו [יבמות יב:]. תקנתן הוה לשמש במוך שלא יתעברו [נדה מה.]. סנדל. ולד שאין לו לורת פנים וקיימא לן במסכת נדה (דף כה:) אין סנדל שאין עמו ולד משל לאדם שסטר את חבירו והחזיר לורתו לאחוריו דכשהיא מעוברת וחוזרת ומתעברת דוחק האחד את חבירו ופוחת לורתו [יבמות שם]. כשמתעברת תאומים פעמים שאחד דוחק את חבירו ופוחת את לורתו כדאמרינן במכילתין אין סנדל שאין עמו ולד [נדה שם]. עובר שני דוחק את הראשון ופוחת את לורתו בהמפלת (נדה כה:) [יבמות ק:]. שמא תגמול את בנה. אם תתעבר תהא לריכה לגמול את בנה מלהניק כמו ויגמל (בראשית כא) לשון הגדלה [שם יב:]. תפריש את בנה מלהניק מחמת עיבורה [נדה שם]. ואיזוהי קטנה. הראויה להתעבר ולמות [יבמות שם]. שמתעברת ומתה [שם ק:]. מבת אחת עשרה שנה וכו'. פחות מי"א ודאי לא תתעבר ויותר מי"ב אם תתעבר לא תמות [שם יב:]. פחות מכן, אינה לריכה לשמש במוך דודאי לא תתעבר. יתר על כן, אם תתעבר לא תמות [נדה שם]. משמשת כדרכה. בלא מוך [יבמות שם]. אין בין נערות לבגרות אלא ששה חדשים. בלבד כשהביאה סימני נערות אינה שוהה להיות בוגרת אלא ששה חדשים ופעמים שהיא ממהרת לבגור וסימניה ניכרים בדדיה כדתנן במס' נדה (דף מז) פגה בוחל וצמל. וכי תימא בציר הוא דליכא הא טפי איכא הא אלא בלבד קאמר, לא גרס דמהיכא תיסק אדעתין למימר הכי מי קאמר אין בין נערות לבגרות פחות מששה חדשים [קידושין עט. ועי' תוס' כאן וגליון שם]. נערה המאורסה אביה ובעלה וכו'. ולהכי נקט נערה דלוקא נערה שהיא ברשות אביה [דכתיב בנעוריה בית אביה] וכדאמרינן נמי במס' כתובות האב זכאי בקדושי בתו ובמעשה ידיה ובמליאתה ובהפרת נדריה בזמן שהיא נערה ומפיק לה מהאי קרא [נדרים סו:]. דכל זמן שהיא ארוסה אכתי שייך בה אביה [שם עד:]. המפתה. מדבר על לבה עד ששומעת לו וכן תרגומו וארי ישדל, שדול בלשון ארמי כפתוי בלשון עברי [שמות כב, טו]. ופגם. שייך באונס ומפתה והוא במקום נזק דאומדים כמה אדם רוצה ליתן בין שפחה בתולה לבעולה להשיאה לעבדו שיש לו קורת רוח ממנו [ב"ק פד:]. שיראין. של משי [מנחות לט:].

הגהות הב"ח

(א) רש"י ד"ה שמא יעשה עוברה וכו' לורת השני. נ"ב ותוספות פרק המפלת הביאו בשם רש"י שולד אחרון ממעך לורת הראשון וע"ש בד"ה קמ"ל בדף כה מיהו ביבמות דף יב כתב רש"י ז"ל דוחק האחד את חברו ופוחת לורתו משמע לפעמים הראשון גובר ולפעמים השני גובר ופעם פי' כך ופעם פי' כך ואין כאן טעות:

גליון הש"ס

תוס' ד"ה שלש וכו' דאע"פ שאינה מצווה על פריה ורביה. ע' סנהדרין דף נט ע"ב תוד"ה והא:

תורה אור השלם

א) שֹׁמֵר פְּתָאיִם יְיָ דַּלּוֹתִי וְלִי יְהוֹשִׁיעַ: [תהלים קטז, ו]

ב) וְנָתַן הָאִישׁ הַשֹּׁכֵב עִמָּהּ לַאֲבִי הַנַּעֲרָ חֲמִשִּׁים כָּסֶף וְלוֹ תִהְיֶה לְאִשָּׁה תַּחַת אֲשֶׁר עִנָּהּ לֹא יוּכַל שַׁלְּחָהּ כָּל יָמָיו: [דברים כב, כט]

ground before violating her.

The Gemara objects:

מַתְקִיף לָהּ רַבִּי זֵירָא – **R' Zeira challenges [this answer]:** אֶלָּא מֵעַתָּה חֲבָטָהּ עַל גַּבֵּי שִׁירָאִין – **But now, if he threw her down onto silk,** וְכִי הָכִי נַמִּי דְּפָטוּר – **is it indeed so that he is exempt?** תֵּימָא הָכִי נַמִּי – **And if you will say that it is indeed so,** I shall respond: וְהָתַנְיָא – **But it was taught in a Baraisa:** רַבִּי שִׁמְעוֹן בֶּן יְהוּדָה אוֹמֵר מִשּׁוּם רַבִּי שִׁמְעוֹן – R' SHIMON BEN YEHUDAH SAYS IN THE NAME OF R' SHIMON: אוֹנֵס אֵינוֹ מְשַׁלֵּם אֶת הַצַּעַר – A VIOLATOR DOES NOT PAY FOR THE PAIN, מִפְּנֵי – BECAUSE

NOTES

empts any sensation of pain. Hence, since the pain of the penetration is not felt until afterward, the violator should be exempt from paying damages for that pain, inasmuch as an assailant is liable only for pain experienced at the time of the assault. Deferred pain is only an *indirect effect* (גְּרָמָא) of the tortious act, for which there is no liability (*Tosafos*). To what pain, then, does the Mishnah refer?

ומי מעברא והתני רב ביבי קמיה דרב נחמן (א) שלש נשים משמשות במוך אלו הן קטנה ומעוברת ומניקה קטנה שמא תתעבר ותמות מעוברת שמא תעשה עוברה סנדל מניקה שמא תגמול את בנה וימות ואיזוהי קטנה מבת אחת עשרה שנה ויום אחד עד שתים עשרה שנה ויום אחד פחות מיכן ויתר על כן משמשת כדרכה והולכת דברי ר"מ וחכמים אומרים אחת זו ואחת זו משמשת כדרכה והולכת ומן השמים ירחמו משום שנאמר (א) שומר פתאים ה' וכי תימא דאיעברא כשהיא נערה ואולידה כשהיא נערה ובשיתא ירחי מי קא ילדה והאמר שמואל (ב) אין בין נערות לבגרות אלא ששה חדשים וכי תימא בציר הוא דליכא הא טפי איכא הא אלא קאמר אלא הכי קמיבעיא ליה יש בגר בקבר ופקע אב או דלמא אין בגר בקבר ולא פקע אב מר בר רב אשי בעי לה הכי מיתה עושה בגרות או אין עושה בגרות תיקו בעי מיניה רבא מאביי בא עליה ונתארסה מהו א"ל (ג) מי כתיב ונתן לאבי הנערה אשר לא ארוסה ולטעמיך הא דתניא (ד) בא עליה ונשאת לעצמה מי כתיב ונתן לאבי הנערה אשר לא נשואה הכי השתא התם הואיל ובגרות מוציאה מרשות אב ונישואין מוציאין מרשות אב מה בגרות בא עליה ובגרה לעצמה אף נישואין בא עליה ונשאת לעצמה אלא אירוסין מי קא מפקי מרשותא דאב לגמרי הא תנן (ה) נערה המאורסה אביה ובעלה מפירין לה נדריה: **מתני'** (ו) המפתה נותן שלשה דברים והאונס ארבעה המפתה נותן בושת ופגם וקנס מוסיף עליו אונס שנותן את הצער מה בין אונס למפתה האונס נותן את הצער והמפתה אינו נותן את הצער האונס נותן מיד והמפתה לכשיוציא האונס שותה בעציצו והמפתה אם רצה להוציא מוציא (ז) כיצד שותה בעציצו אפי' היא חיגרת אפי' היא סומא ואפילו היא מוכת שחין (ח) נמצא בה דבר ערוה או שאינה ראויה לבא בישראל אינו רשאי לקיימה שנאמר (ב) ולו תהיה לאשה אשה הראויה לו: **גמ'** צער דמאי אמר אבוה דשמואל צער שחבטה על גבי קרקע מתקיף לה רבי זירא אלא מעתה חבטה על גבי שיראין הכי נמי דפטור וכי תימא הכי נמי והתניא ר' שמעון בן יהודה אומר משום רבי שמעון (ט) אונס אינו משלם את הצער מפני שסופה

רש"י

ומי מעברא. בקטנות או בנערות כשהיא בת קנס שתלד בנערות: משמשות במוך. מותר להן לשמש במוך ואינן כמשחיתות זרע: שמא יעשה עוברה סנדל. שאם תתעבר עובר שני פוחת השני את צורת (א) הראשון ודומה לסנדל שהוא דג שדים: שמא תגמול את בנה. מפני שהחלב נעכר כשמתעברת ואינו טוב ליונק ותצטרך להעתיקו משדים וימות: פחות מכאן. מבת אחת עשרה שנה משמשת כדרכה לפי שלא תתעבר: ויתר על כן. על בת שתים עשרה שנה משמשת כדרכה שאם תתעבר לא תמות אלמא בקטנות לא מיעברא שיבא לכלל לידה דהא ותמות קתני: וכי תימא. מבת שתים עשרה ויום אחד שהגיעו ימי הנעורים נתעברה וילדה בנערות ומתה בנערות הא נמי ליתא דאמר שמואל אין בין נערות לבגרות אלא ששה חדשים משתביא שתי שערות הויא נערה באותן שתביא משתים עשרה שנה והלאה ומשתביאם עד שתבגור ששה חדשים ותו לא ומתניתא דקתני מבת שתים עשרה ואילך אי מעברא לא מתה במביאה שתי שערות קודם שתתעבר קאמר אבל כל זמן שלא הביאה קטנה היא והאי דנקט מנין שנים משום דבציר משתים עשרה ויום אחד אפילו הביאה שערות אינו אלא שומא כדאמרינן במסכת נדה ובקדושין: ופקע אב. פקעה תביעת אב וזכה הלה במה שבידו שאין בעל דינו קיים וקנס לאו ממון הוא להורישו לאביה בתורת ירושה כל כמה דלא גבתיה: או אין בגר בקבר. לאפקועי תביעת אב: מר בר רב אשי. לא בעי לה בעיא דרבא משום בגר בקבר אלא אם מתה בנערותה מי פקעה כי בגרות דמחיים או לא ולהאי לישנא דמר בר רב אשי איבעיא דרבא אמרו לעיל מילתא דפשיטא ליה לאביי מיבעיא ליה לרבא דאילו ללישנא קמא מספקא פשיטא ליה לרבא דמיתה לא מפקעא ודלא כאביי כל זמן שלא בגרה וכי קא מיבעיא ליה בבגר בקבר קמבעיא ליה אבל במיתה כל זמן שלא בגרה פליג אדאביי ואמר לא מפקעא וחייב: מיתה עושה בגרות. עושה דין בגרות דמפקעא כח אב כי בגרות: מהו. מי הוי לאביה או לעצמה: בגרות מוציאה מרשות אב. דלא מלינו שזיכתה לו תורה בבתו אלא מכר בקטנות ושאר שבח כגון קנסה ומעשה ידיה בנערות כדילפינן בפרק נערה (לקמן דף מו:) אבל בבגרות לא אשכחן וכיון דלא זיכתה לו תורה אנן מהיכא תיתי לן לזכותו בשלה: ונשואין מוציאין מרשות אב. כדאשכחן בהפרת נדרים דכל זמן דלא ניסת אביה מיפר ומשניסת אין יכול להפר: בא עליה. כשהיא נערה ובגרה: לעצמה. דכתיב ונתן האיש השוכב עמה לאבי הנערה אם נערה היא בשעת נתינה: אביה ובעלה. ואינו מופר עד שיפרו שניהם: מתני' בושת ופגם. במתני' לקמן מפרש להו: האונס נותן מיד. לאביה אע"פ שכונסה: לכשיוציא. בגמרא פריך הוא אשתו היא ומפרש לה לכשלא יכנוס דאם כנסה אינו נותן קנס דכתיב מהר ימהרנה לו ואם מאן ימאן וגו' כסף ישקול אבל אונס כתיב ונתן חמשים כסף ולו תהיה לאשה: שותה בעציצו. בכלי שבחר בו לשתות בו כלומר על כרחו ישאנה כדכתיב לא יוכל לשלחה (דברים כב): **גמ'** שסופה

תוספות

שלש נשים משמשות במוך. פי' בקונטרס מותרות לשמש במוך אע"ג דשאר נשים אסורות משום השחתת זרע ואין נראה לר"ת (ו) דהא קטנה ואילונית מותר לשמש בהדייהו ולא הוי השחתת זרע כיון שהוא דרך תשמיש ומפרש ר"ת משמשות צריכות לשמש במוך אחר תשמיש ועלה טובה קמ"ל ולר"י נראה לקיים פי' הקונט' דבריש נדה (דף ג.) משמע שהמוך הוא במעיה כל שעה והוי כמשמש על האבנים ועל העצים ולא דמי למשמש קטנה ואילונית ועוד אפילו היתה נותנת מוך אחר תשמיש אסורה (ט) דאף על פי שאינה מצווה על פריה ורביה מ"מ אסורה היא להשחית זרע כדמשמע בנדה (דף יג.) דתנן כל היד המרבה לבדוק בנשים משובחת באנשים תיקצץ ומפרש בגמרא משום דנשים לאו בנות הרגשה נינהו משמע דאם היו בנות הרגשה הוו אסירי ויש לדחות דלאו בנות איסור הרגשה נינהו קאמר: **וכי** תימא בציר הוא כו' והא בלבד קאמר. בקונטרס (בקדושין דף עט.) ל"ג ליה דבלאו בלבד משמע טפי לא (ח): **בא** עליה ונתארסה מהו. לרבי עקיבא דמתני' קא מיבעיא ליה דאמר נתארסה ונתגרשה קנסה לעצמה דמי אמרינן כיון שיצאה מרשות האב לענין קנס יהא קנסה לעצמה או דלמא כיון דלענין שאר מילי לא נפקא מרשות האב יהא קנסה לאביה אבל לרבי עקיבא דברייתא פשיטא דקנסה לאביה ולר' יוסי הגלילי נהי דאמר אין לה קנס נמי לא מיבעיא ליה דהא דאין לה קנס לאו משום מיפק מרשותא דאב היא אלא גזירת הכתוב הוא דאין לה קנס ולא נפקא באירוסין כלל מרשות אביה דאב זכאי בקדושיה ובמעשה ידיה אע"ג דנתארסה והא דקא בעי לה סתם ולא קאמר לרבי עקיבא בהדיא מהו משום דהלכה כר' עקיבא מחבירו: **הואיל** ונישואין מוציאין מרשות אב. פי' בקונט' דילפינן מהפרת נדרים ואע"ג דקי"ל דממונא מאיסורא לא ילפינן ה"מ לאוקמה ברשות אב הוא דלא ילפינן ממונא מאיסורא אבל לאפוקי מרשות אב ילפינן שפיר מהפרת נדרים דבסברא מועטת יש להוציאה מרשות אב ור"י ב"ר אברהם פי' כיון דגלי לן קרא דלאוקמה ברשות אב איסורא וממונא שוין ה"ה לאפוקה (י) [ור"י] מפרש דנישואין מוציאין מרשות אב מדדרשינן איש אמו ואביו תיראו איש שיספק כו' אשה אין סיפק בידה לעשות ולא נהירא למעשה ידיה אינו לגבל מן התורה: **מה** בוגרת בא עליה ובגרה לעצמה. פירוש דהא מלינו בוגרת שיצאה מרשות אב לענין ממון וקשה דה"נ נישואין מוציאין מרשות אב ואמאי צריך למילף מבוגרת ונראה דבא עליה ובגרה לעצמה נפקא לן מונתן לאבי הנערה דדרשינן לאבי הנערה ולא לאבי בוגרת:

צער דמאי. קשה לר"י דמאי קא מיבעיא ליה וכי לא ידע הש"ס שיש צער גדול לבתולה בביאה ראשונה וכמה קטנות חולות מזה וכ"ת דמאותו צער פשיטא ליה להש"ס דפטור שהרי סופה להצטער בכך תחת בעלה והא איכא כמה תנאי בהכונס (ב"ק דף נט. ושם) דלא חייבי לכתוב גופנא פירוש דבר שסופו להיות כן ונראה לר"י דצער בעילה משום תאות תשמיש אינו לא בשעת תשמיש אלא אחר כך וכל צער החבלה דמחייב היינו אותו צער הבא לו בשעת חבלה אבל הוא שבא לו אחר כך מיפטר דגרמא בעלמא הוא הלכך בעי צער של בתולים ליכא למימר דע"כ תנא דמתני' חייב לכתוב גופנא מדמפתה פטור: ולמי

מסורת הש"ס

א) יבמות יב: ק: נדה מה. נדרים לה: [תוספתא נדה פ"ב], ב) נדרים סו: ג) קדושין עט. נדה סה., ד) [לעיל כט:], ה) נדרים עג: [לקמן מו: קדושין ד.], ו) [לקמן מב. ע"ש, ז) (עי' תוס' יבמות יב: ותוס' נדה יג.], ח) [ועי' תוס' נדה סה. ד"ה וכ"מ כו' מיישבין הגירסא], ט) מ"י כ"י.

הגהות הב"ח

(א) רש"י ד"ה שמא יעשה עוברה וכו' צורת הסני. נ"ב ותוספות פרק המפלת הביא בשם רש"י שולד אחרון ממעך צורת הראשון ע"ש בד"ה קמ"ל בדף כה מיהו ביבמות דף יב כתב רש"י ז"ל דוחק האחד את חברו ולרמב"ם משמע לפעמים הראשון גורם ולפעמים השני גורם ופעם פי' כך ופעם פי' כך ואין כאן טעות:

גליון הש"ס

תוס' ד"ה שלש וכו' דאע"פ שאינה מצווה על פריה ורביה. עי' סנהדרין דף נט ע"ב תוד"ה והא:

תורה אור השלם

א) שֹׁמֵר פְּתָאִים יְיָ דַּלֹּתִי וְלִי יְהוֹשִׁיעַ: [תהלים קטז, ו]

ב) וְנָתַן הָאִישׁ הַשֹּׁכֵב עִמָּהּ לַאֲבִי הַנַּעֲרָ חֲמִשִּׁים כָּסֶף וְלוֹ תִהְיֶה לְאִשָּׁה תַּחַת אֲשֶׁר עִנָּהּ לֹא יוּכַל שַׁלְּחָהּ כָּל יָמָיו: [דברים כב, כט]

עין משפט נר מצוה

סט א מיי' פ"ב מהל' אישות הל' ב טור ש"ע יו"ד סימן רלד סעיף א בהג"ה:

ע ב מיי' פ"ב מהל' נערה הל' טו סמג עשין נד טור אה"ע סימן קעז:

עא ג מיי' שם הל' טו:

עב ד מיי' פי"א מהל' נדרים הל' ט סמג לאוין רמב טוש"ע י"ד סי' רלד סעיף ה:

עג ה מיי' פ"ב מהלכות נערה הל' ז סמג עשין נד טוש"ע אה"ע סי' קעז סעיף א:

עד ו מיי' פ"א שם הל' ג סמג שם טוש"ע שם סעיף ג:

עה ז מיי' שם הל' ה טוש"ע שם סעי' ד:

תוספות רי"ד

תניא בא עליה ונשאת לעצמה הואיל ובגרות מוציאה מרשות אב. פי' שלא מצינו שזכתה לו תורה בבתו אלא מכר בקטנותה ושאר שבח ממון כגון קנסה ומעשה ידיה בנערות כדילפי' לקמן בפ' נערה ונשואין נמי מוציאין מרשות אב. פירוש כדאשכחן בהפרת נדרים דכ"ז שלא נשאת אביה מפר נדריה ומשנשאת אין יכול להפר. מה בוגרת בא עלי' ובגרה לעצמה דכתיב ונתן האיש השוכב עמה לאבי הנערה. אם היא נערה בשעת נתינה אף נשואין בא עליה ונשאת לעצמה. מתני' המפתה נותן ג' דברים והאונס ד' המפתה נותן בושת ופגם וקנס מוסיף עליו אונס שנותן את הצער מה בין אונס למפתה האונס נותן את הצער והמפתה אין נותן את הצער האונס נותן מיד והמפתה לכשיוציא האונס שותה בעציצו. פי' בכלי שבחר לו לשתות בו כלומר ע"כ ישאנה דכתיב לא יוכל לשלחה כל ימיו והמפתה אם רצה להוציא מוציא. פי' האונס נותן מיד ואע"פ שכונסה שנאמר ונתן האיש השוכב עמה לאבי הנערה חמשים כסף ולו תהיה לאשה. ודרשי' תו לו אתה כופה ולא לה:

ליקוטי רש"י

משמשות במוך. מותרות לתת מוך במקום תשמיש כשהן משמשות כדי שלא יתעברו [יבמות יב:]. תקנתן הוא לשמש במוך שלא יתעברו [נדה מה.]. סנדל. ולד שאין לו צורת פנים וקיימא לן במסכת נדה (דף כה:) אין סנדל שאין עמו ולד של לאחר שמעך את חבירו והחזיר צורתו לאחוריו דכשהיא מעוברת ותחלת ומתעברת דוחק האחד את חבירו ופוחת צורתו [יבמות שם]. כשמתעברת תאומים פעמים שאחד דוחק את חבירו ופוחת את צורתו כדאמרינן במכילתין אין סנדל שאין עמו ולד [נדה שם]. ולר' שני דוחק את הראשון ופוחת את צורתו בהמפלת (נדה כה.) [יבמות יב:]. שמא תגמול את בנה. אם תתעבר תצטרך לגמול את בנה מלהניק כמו ויגמל (בראשית כא) לשון הגדלה [שם יב:]. תפריש את בנה מלהניק מחמת עיבורה [נדה שם]. ואיזוהי קטנה. הראויה

וְנִישּׂוּאִין מוֹצִיאִין מֵרְשׁוּת אָב – **and marriage** (*nesuin*) likewise **removes** her **from the father's jurisdiction,**[26] we can compare the two events and say: מַה בַּגְרוּת בָּא עָלֶיהָ וּבָגְרָה – **Just as** in the case of ***bagrus,* where one violates her** while she is a *naarah* **and she becomes a *bogeress*** before judgment, לְעַצְמָהּ – the fine belongs **to her,**[27] אַף נִישּׂוּאִין בָּא עָלֶיהָ וְנִשֵּׂאת – so, **too,** in the case of **marriage,** where **one violates her** while she is single **and she marries** before judgment, לְעַצְמָהּ – the fine should belong **to her.** אֶלָּא אֵירוּסִין – **But** with regard to **betrothal,** מִי קָא מַפְקֵי מֵרְשׁוּתָא דְּאָב לְגַמְרֵי – **does it remove her from the father's jurisdiction entirely?!** הָא תְּנַן – **Why, we learned in a Mishnah:**[28] נַעֲרָה הַמְאוֹרָסָה – In the case of A BETROTHED *NAARAH,* אָבִיהָ וּבַעְלָהּ מְפִירִין לָהּ נְדָרֶיהָ – both HER FATHER AND HER HUSBAND are needed to ANNUL HER VOWS FOR HER![29]

Mishnah הַמְפַתֶּה נוֹתֵן שְׁלֹשָׁה דְּבָרִים – **The seducer gives** restitution for **three things** וְהָאוֹנֵס אַרְבָּעָה – **and the violator** gives for **four.**[30] הַמְפַתֶּה נוֹתֵן בּוֹשֶׁת וּפְגָם וּקְנָס – **The seducer gives** for **humiliation and depreciation,**[31] **and** pays the **fine;** מוֹסִיף עָלָיו אוֹנֵס – the **violator exceeds him,** שֶׁנּוֹתֵן אֶת הַצַּעַר – in **that he gives** restitution also for **the pain** his victim suffered.[32] מַה בֵּין אוֹנֵס לִמְפַתֶּה – **What** are the various differences **between a violator and a seducer?**[33] הָאוֹנֵס נוֹתֵן אֶת הַצַּעַר – **The violator gives** restitution for **the pain** she suffered, וְהַמְפַתֶּה אֵינוֹ נוֹתֵן אֶת הַצַּעַר – **and the seducer does not give** restitution for **the pain;**[34] הָאוֹנֵס נוֹתֵן מִיָּד – **the violator remits** the fifty-*shekalim* fine **immediately,**[35] וְהַמְפַתֶּה לִכְשֶׁיּוֹצִיא – **and the seducer** pays it only **when he sends her away;**[36] הָאוֹנֵס שׁוֹתֶה בַּעֲצִיצוֹ – **the violator must drink from his pot,**[37] וְהַמְפַתֶּה אִם רָצָה לְהוֹצִיא מוֹצִיא – **and the seducer, if he wants to send** her **away, may send** her **away.**

The Mishnah now elaborates on this last ruling:

כֵּיצַד שׁוֹתֶה בַּעֲצִיצוֹ – **How does [a violator] drink from his pot?**[38] אֲפִילוּ הִיא חִיגֶּרֶת – He must marry her **even though she is lame,** אֲפִילוּ הִיא סוּמָא – or **even though she is blind,** וַאֲפִילוּ הִיא מוּכַּת שְׁחִין – **or even though she is afflicted with boils.** נִמְצָא בָהּ דְּבַר עֶרְוָה – However, if **a lewd matter was discovered involving her,**[39] אוֹ שֶׁאֵינָהּ רְאוּיָה לָבֹא בְּיִשְׂרָאֵל – **or she is unfit to enter the Jewish** congregation,[40] אֵינוֹ רַשַּׁאי לְקַיְּימָהּ – **he is not permitted to keep her,** שֶׁנֶּאֱמַר ,,וְלוֹ־תִהְיֶה לְאִשָּׁה'' – **for it is stated,**[41] ***and she shall be to him a wife,*** אִשָּׁה הָרְאוּיָה לוֹ – which implies that she must be **a woman who is fit *for*** marriage to ***him.***[42]

Gemara The Mishnah taught that a violator must offer compensation for his victim's pain. The Gemara asks: צַעַר דְּמַאי – **For what pain** does he pay?[43]

The Gemara answers:

אָמַר אֲבוּהּ דִּשְׁמוּאֵל – **The father of Shmuel said:** צַעַר שֶׁחֲבָטָהּ עַל גַּבֵּי קַרְקַע – The **pain is that he threw her down onto the**

NOTES

26. As we find with regard to the annulment of her vows — until marriage (*nesuin*) a father is empowered to annul his daughter's vows; afterward he is not (*Rashi*).

27. As derived from the verse (*Deuteronomy* 22:29), *And the man who lay with her shall give to the father of the "naarah" fifty silver [coins],* which implies that if the rape victim is not a *naarah,* but a *bogeress,* at the time of payment, the fine is not paid to the father (*Rashi*).

28. *Nedarim* 66b.

29. Whereas the vows of a *nesuah* [a married woman] are annulled exclusively by her husband, the vows of an *arusah* [a woman who was merely betrothed] can be annulled only when her husband and father act in concert. From this we see that betrothal does not entirely remove a girl from her father's jurisdiction, as marriage does. Hence, only marriage can be compared with *bagrus,* which also removes a girl from her father's jurisdiction entirely. Accordingly, we do not extrapolate additionally from the *bagrus* teaching (see note 27 above) that the father forfeits the fine for violation if his daughter was an *arusah* at the time of payment. Rather, he retains it even there, as Abaye contends.

30. The Gemara below (40b) derives that the fifty-*shekel* payment the Torah prescribes for violation and seduction is purely punitive in nature, and is accompanied by the compensatory damages commonly paid in all assault cases (see Mishnah, *Bava Kamma* 83b). Our Mishnah now delineates the various damages that the assailants pay.

[Although the Mishnah's opening statement, which totals the types of payments for each category of assailant, appears unnecessary, the Tanna's intent is to limit the payments, for he intimates that if the victim became ill on account of her ruptured hymen, the seducer and the violator — unlike other assaulters — do not pay שֶׁבֶת, *indemnity for loss of time from work,* or רִפּוּי, *indemnity for medical expenses* [perhaps because at some point her hymen would be ruptured and she would anyway lose earnings and incur medical expenses; see also *Bircas Avraham*] (*Shitah Mekubetzes;* cf. *Meleches Shlomo*).]

31. These payments are explained in the Mishnah below, 40a (*Rashi*).

32. [I.e. in addition to paying the fine for the act of violation itself and damages for causing humiliation and depreciation, the violator must compensate for the pain he inflicted on his victim. The Gemara will discuss the nature of this pain.]

33. [Since the Tanna already mentioned one distinction — that the seducer pays for three things and the violator pays for four — he now lists all the differences between the laws of the violator and the seducer.]

34. The reason for this distinction will be explained in the Gemara. [Here the Mishnah repeats itself; see *Shitah Mekubetzes* ד״ה מה בין; cf. *Tiferes Yisrael.*]

35. The violator pays the fine to the father immediately — i.e. even if he marries the victim (*Rashi*).

36. The term לִכְשֶׁיּוֹצִיא, *when he sends her away,* generally connotes "divorce." The Gemara notes (below, 39b) that this interpretation is inappropriate here, since a seducer does not pay the fine if he marries the girl (even if he subsequently divorces her), for it is written (*Exodus* 22:14-15): *If a man shall seduce a virgin ... he shall provide her with a marriage settlement as his wife. If her father refuses to give her to him, he shall weigh out silver in the amount of the settlement [made] to the virgins.* Hence, as used here in the Mishnah, the phrase *when he sends her away* perforce means: "when he decides not to marry her" (see 39b note 13). With regard to the violator, however, the Torah states (*Deuteronomy* 22:29): *He shall pay fifty silver [coins]* ***and*** *she shall be for him a wife* (*Rashi*).

37. I.e. from the vessel that he chose for himself to drink from. [*Rambam, Commentary to the Mishnah,* notes that an עָצִיץ is an earthenware pot used for unclean things.] That is, he is compelled to marry his victim, as it is written (ibid.): *She shall be for him a wife ... he cannot divorce her all his life* (*Rashi*).

38. I.e. what are the parameters of this requirement to marry the victim he violated?

39. If she committed adultery after their marriage (*Meiri*).

40. If she was a *mamzeress,* whose marriage to an ordinary Jew is prohibited by a negative commandment, or a first- or second-generation Egyptian or Edomite convert, whose marriage is forbidden by a positive commandment (*Meiri*). *Rambam, Hil. Naarah Besulah* 1:5, includes in this category even those women who are prohibited to marry the violator by Rabbinical decree.

41. *Deuteronomy* 22:29.

42. I.e. she must be legally suitable for marrying him. Excluded, then, are the women mentioned in the preceding notes.

43. Although the rupturing of a virgin victim's hymen is traumatic, the pleasure she inevitably experiences from the cohabitation itself pre-

ומי מעברא והתני רב ביבי קמיה דרב נחמן (א) שלש נשים משמשות במוך אלו הן קטנה ומעוברת ומניקה קטנה שמא תתעבר ותמות מעוברת שמא תעשה עוברה סנדל מניקה שמא תגמול את בנה ואיזוהי קטנה מבת אחת עשרה שנה ויום אחד עד שתים עשרה שנה ויום אחד פחות מיכן ויותר על כן משמשת כדרכה והולכת דברי ר"מ וחכמים אומרים אחת זו ואחת זו משמשת כדרכה והולכת ומן השמים ירחמו משום שנאמר א שומר פתאים ה' וכי תימא דאיעברא כשהיא נערה ואולידה כשהיא בוגרת ובשיתא ירחי מי קא ילדה והאמר שמואל (ג) אין בין נערות לבגרות אלא ששה חדשים וכי תימא בציר הוא דליכא הא טפי איכא הא אלא קאמר אלא הכי קמיבעיא ליה יש בגר בקבר ופקע אב או דלמא אין בגר בקבר ולא פקע אב מר בר רב אשי בעי לה הכי מיתה עושה בגרות או אין עושה בגרות תיקו בעי מיניה רבא מאביי בא עליה ונתארסה מהו א"ל (ג) מי כתיב ונתן לאבי הנערה אשר לא ארוסה ולטעמיך הא דתניא (ג) בא עליה ונשאת לעצמה מי כתיב ונתן לאבי הנערה אשר לא נשואה הכי השתא התם הואיל ובגרות מוציאה מרשות אב ונישואין מוציאין מרשות אב מה בגרות בא עליה ובגרה לעצמה אף נישואין בא עליה ונשאת לעצמה אלא אירוסין מי קא מפקי מרשותא דאב לגמרי הא תנן (ד) נערה המאורסה אביה ובעלה מפירין לה נדריה: **מתני'** (ה) המפתה נותן שלשה דברים והאונס ארבעה המפתה נותן בושת ופגם וקנס מוסיף עליו אונס שנותן את הצער מה בין אונס למפתה האונס נותן את הצער והמפתה אינו נותן את הצער האונס נותן מיד והמפתה לכשיוציא האונס שותה בעציצו והמפתה אם רצה להוציא מוציא (ו) כיצד שותה בעציצו אפילו היא חיגרת אפי' היא סומא ואפילו היא מוכת שחין (ז) נמצא בה דבר ערוה או שאינה ראויה לבא בישראל אינו רשאי לקיימה שנאמר ב ולו תהיה לאשה אשה הראויה לו: **גמ'** צער דמאי אמר אבוה דשמואל צער שחבטה על גבי קרקע מתקיף לה רבי זירא אלא מעתה חבטה על גבי שיראין הכי נמי דפטור וכי תימא הכי נמי והתניא ר' שמעון בן יהודה אומר משום רבי שמעון (י) אונס אינו משלם את הצער מפני שסופה

רש"י

ומי מעברא. בקטנות או בנערות כשהיא בת קנס שהלך בנערות: **משמשות במוך.** מותר להן לשמש במוך ואינן כמשחיתות זרע: **שמא יעשה עוברה סנדל.** שאם תתעבר עובר שני פוחס השני את צורת (א) הראשון ודומה לסנדל שהוא דג שבים: **שמא תגמול את בנה.** מפני שהחלב נעכר כשמתעברת ואינו טוב ליונק ותצטרך להעתיקו משדים וימות: **פחות מכאן.** מבת אחת עשרה שנה משמשת כדרכה לפי שלא תתעבר: **ויותר על כן.** על בת שתים עשרה שנה משמשת כדרכה שאם תתעבר לא תמות אלמא בקטנות לא מיעברא שיהא לכלל לידה דהא ותמות קתני: **וכי תימא.** מבת שתים עשרה ויום אחד שהגיעו ימי הנעורים נתעברה וילדה בנערות ומתה בנערות הא נמי ליתא דאמר שמואל אין בין נערות לבגרות אלא ששה חדשים משתביא שתי שערות הויא נערה באותן שתביא משתים עשרה שנה והלאה ומשתביאם עד שתבגור ששה חדשים ותו לא ומתניתא דקתני מבת שתים עשרה ואילך אי מעברא לא מתה במביאה שתי שערות קודם שתתעבר קאמר אבל כל זמן שלא הביאה קטנה היא והאי דנקט מנין שנים משום דבבציר משתים עשרה ויום אחד אפילו הביאה שערות אינו אלא שומא כדאמרינן במסכת נדה וקדושין: **ופקע אב.** פקעה תביעת אב וזכה הלה במה שבידו שאין בעל דינו קיים וקנס לאו ממון הוא להורישו לאביה בתורת ירושה כל כמה דלא גבתיה: **או אין בגר בקבר.** לאפקועי תביעת אב: **מר בר רב אשי.** לא בעי לה בעיא דרבא משום דבגר בקבר אלא אם מתה בנערותה מי פקעה כי בגרות דמחייס או לא והאי לישנא דמר בר רב אשי אליבא דרבא אמרו לעיל מילתא דפשיטא ליה לאביי מיבעיא ליה לרבא דאילו ללישנא קמא מפשט פשיטא ליה לרבא דמיתה לא מפקעא ודלא כאביי כל זמן שלא בגרה וכי קא מיבעיא ליה בבגר בקבר קמבעיא ליה אבל במיתה כל זמן שלא בגרה פליג אדאביי ואמר לא מפקעא ומיהו: **מיתה עושה בגרות.** עושה דין בגרות דמפקעא כח אב כי בגרות: **מהו.** מי הוי לאביה או לעצמה: **בגרות מוציאה מרשות אב.** דלא מצינו שזכתה לו תורה בבתו אלא מכר בקטנות ושאר שבח כגון קנסה ומעשה ידיה בנערות כדילפינן בפרק נערה (לקמן דף מו:) אבל בבגרות לא אשכחן וכיון דלא זכתה לו תורה אנן מהיכא תיתי לן לזכותו בשלה: **ונשואין מוציאין מרשות אב.** כדאשכחן בהפרת נדרים דכל זמן דלא ניסת אביה מיפר ומשניסת אין יכול להפר: **בא עליה.** כשהיא נערה ובגרה: **לעצמה.** דכתיב ונתן האיש השוכב עמה לאבי הנערה אם נערה היא בשעת נתינה: **אביה ובעלה.** ואינו מופר עד שיפרו שניהם: **מתני' בושת ופגם.** במתני' לקמן מפרש להו: **האונס נותן מיד.** לאביה אע"פ שכונסה: **לכשיוציא.** בגמרא פריך אטו אשתו היא ומפרש לה לכשלא יכנוס דאם כנסה אינו נותן קנס כדכתיב מהר ימהרנה לו ואם מאן ימאן וגו' כסף ישקול אבל אונס כתיב ונתן חמשים כסף ולו תהיה לאשה: **שותה בעציצו.** בכלי שבחר לו לשתות בו כלומר על כרחו ישאנה כדכתיב לא יוכל לשלחה (דברים כב): **גמ'** שסופה

תוספות

שלש נשים משמשות במוך. פי' בקונטרס מותרות לשמש במוך אע"ג דשאר נשים אסורות משום השחתת זרע ואין נראה לר"ת דהא קטנה ואילונית מותר לשמש כהדדיהו ולא הוי השחתת זרע כיון שהוא דרך תשמיש ומפרש ר"ת משמשות צריכות לשמש במוך אחר תשמיש ועלה טובה קמ"ל ולר"י נראה לקיים פי' הקונט' דבריש נדה (דף ג.) משמע שהמוך הוא במעיה כל שעה והוי כמשמש על הלבנים ועל העצים ולא דמי למשמש קטנה ואילונית ועוד אפילו היתה נותנת מוך אחר תשמיש אסורה ח דאף על פי שאינה מצווה על פריה ורביה מ"מ אסורה היא להשחית זרע כדמשמע בנדה (דף יג.) דתנן כל היד המרבה לבדוק בנשים משובחת באנשים תיקצץ ומפרש בגמרא משום דנשים לאו בנות הרגשה נינהו משמע דאם היו בנות הרגשה הוו אסירי ויש לדחות דלאו בנות איסור הרגשה נינהו קאמר: **וכי** תימא בציר הוא כו' והא בלבד קאמר. בקונטרס (בקדושין דף עט.) ל"ג ליה דבלאו בלבד משמע טפי לא ט: **בא** עליה ונתארסה מהו. לרבי עקיבא דממתני' קא מיבעיא ליה דאמר נתארסה ונתגרשה קנסה לעצמה דמי אמרינן כיון שיצאה מרשות האב לענין קנס יהא קנסה לעצמה או דלמא כיון דלענין שאר מילי לא נפקא מרשות האב יהא קנסה לאביה אבל לרבי עקיבא דברייתא פשיטא דקנסה לאביה ולר' יוסי הגלילי נמי דאמר אין לה קנס נמי לא מיבעיא ליה דהא דאין לה קנס לאו משום מיפק מרשותא דאב היא אלא גזירת הכתוב הוא דאין לה קנס ולא נפקא באירוסין כלל מרשות אביה דהא זכאי בקדושיה ובמעשה ידיה אע"ג דנתארסה והא דקא בעי לה אליבא דר"ע ולא קאמר לרבי עקיבא מחבירו משום דהלכה כר' עקיבא מחבירו: **הואיל** ונישואין מוציאין מרשות אב. פי' בקונט' דילפינן מהפרת נדרים ואע"ג דקי"ל דממונא מאיסורא לא ילפינן ה"מ לאוקמה ברשות אב הוא דלא ילפינן ממונא מאיסורא אבל לאפוקי מרשות אב ילפינן שפיר מהפרת נדרים דבסברא מועטת יש להוציאה מרשות אב ור"י ב"ר אברהם פי' כיון דגלי לן קרא דלאוקמה ברשות אב איסורא וממונא שוין ה"ה לאפוקה ט [ור"י מפרש דנישואין מוציאין מרשות אב מדדרשינן איש אמו ואביו תיראו איש סיפק כו' אשה אין סיפק בידה לעשות ולא נהירא דלמעשה ידיה אינו לבעל מן התורה]: **מה** בוגרת בא עליה ובגרה לעצמה. פירוש דהא מלינו בוגרת שיוצאה מרשות אב לענין ממון וקשה דה"נ נישואין מוציאין מרשות אב לענין ממון ואמאי צריך למילף מבוגרת ונראה דבא עליה ובגרה לעצמה נפקא לן מונתן לאבי הנערה דדרשינן לאבי הנערה ולא לאבי בוגרת: **צער** דמאי. קשה לר"י דמאי קא מיבעיא ליה וכי לא ידע הש"ס שיש צער גדול לבתולה בביאה ראשונה וכמה קטנות חולות מזה ור"ת דמאותו צער פשיטא ליה להש"ס דפטור שהרי סופה להצטער בכך תחת בעלה והא איכא כמה תנאי בהכונס (ב"ק דף נט. ושם) דלא חיישי לכחש גופנא פירוש דבר שסופו להיות כן ונראה לר"י דצער בעילה משום תאות תשמיש אינו בא בשעת תשמיש אלא אחר כך וכל צער החבלה דמחייב היינו אותו צער הבא לו בשעת חבלה אבל מה שבא לו אחר כך מיפטר דגרמא בעלמא הוא הלכך בעי צער דמאי ורשב"א מפרש דפשיטא דצער של בתולים ליכא למימר דע"כ תנא דמתני' חייש לכחש גופנא מדמפתה פטור: אי

עין משפט נר מצוה

סט א מיי' פ"ב מהל' איסורי ביאה הל' ג טור ש"ע יו"ד סימן רלד סעיף א בהג"ה:

ע ב מיי' פ"ב מהל' נערה הל' טז סמג עשין נד טור אה"ע סימן קעז:

עא ג מיי' שם הל' טו:

עב ד מיי' פי"א מהל' נדרים הל' ט סמג לאוין רמב טוש"ע י"ד סי' רלד סעיף ה:

עג ה מיי' פ"ב מהלכות נערה הל' ז סמג עשין נד טוש"ע אה"ע סי' קעז סעיף א:

עד ו מיי' פ"א שם הל' ג סמג שם טוש"ע שם סעיף ג:

עה ז מיי' שם הל' ה טוש"ע שם סעי' ד:

תוספות רי"ד

תניא בא עליה ונשאת לעצמה הואיל ובגרות מוציאה מרשות אב. פי' שלא מצינו שזכתה לו תורה בבתו אלא מכר בקטנותה ושאר שבח ממון כגון קנסה ומעשה ידיה בנערות כדילפי' לקמן בפ' נערה ונשואין נמי מוציאין מרשות אב. פירוש כדאשכחן בהפרת נדרים דכ"ז שלא נשאת אביה מפר נדריה ומשנשאת אין יכול להפר. מה בוגרת בא עלי' ובגרה לעצמה דכתיב ונתן האיש השוכב עמה לאבי הנערה. אם היא נערה בשעת נתינה אף נשואין בא עליה ונשאת לעצמה: **מתני' המפתה** נותן ג' דברים והאונס ד' המפתה נותן בושת ופגם וקנס מוסיף עליו אונס שנותן את הצער מה בין אונס למפתה האונס נותן את הצער והמפתה אין נותן את הצער האונס נותן מיד והמפתה לכשיוציא האונס שותה בעציצו. פי' בכלי שבחר לו לשתות בו כלומר ע"כ ישאנה דכתיב לא יוכל לשלחה כל ימיו והמפתה אם רצה להוציא מוציא. פי' האונס נותן מיד ואע"פ שכונסה שנאמר ונתן האיש השוכב עמה לאבי הנערה חמשים כסף ולו תהיה לאשה. ודרשי' לו אתה כופה ולא לה:

ליקוטי רש"י

משמשות במוך. מותרות לתת מוך במקום תשמיש כשהן משמשות כדי שלא יתעברו [יבמות יב:]. מקנחן הוא לשמש במוך שלא יתעברו [נדה מה.]. **סנדל.** ולד שאין לו צורת פנים וקיימא לן במסכת נדה (דף כה:) אין סנדל שאין עמו ולד שלא לאדם שטער את חבירו והחזיר לורתו דכשהיא מעוברת ומתעברת דוחק את חבירו [יבמות שם]. כשמתעברת תאומים פעמים שאחד דוחק את חבירו ופוחס את לורתו כדאמרינן במכילתין אין סנדל שאין עמו ולד [נדה שם]. עובר שני דוחק את הראשון ופוחס את לורתו בהמפלת (נדה כה:) [יבמות קי:]. **שמא תגמול את בנה.** אם תתעבר תהא לריכה לגמול את בנה מלהניק כמו ויגמל (בראשית כא) לשון הבדלה [שם יב:]. תפריש את בנה מלהניק מחמת עיבורה [נדה שם]. **ואיזוהי קטנה.** הראויה

מסורת הש"ס

א) יבמות יב: ק: נדה מה. נדרים לה: [תוספתא נדה פ"ב], ב) קדושין עט. נדה סה., ג) נדרים סו: עד: יבמות כט: לקמן מו: קדושין ד., ד) לקמן מב., ה) [לעיל כט:], ו) ב"ק נט. ע"ש, ז) [עי' תוס' יבמות יב: ותוס' נדה יג.], ח) [עי' תוס' נדה סה. ד"ה וכ"ח כו' מייפין הגירסא], ט) ת"י כ"י.

הגהות הב"ח

(א) רש"י ד"ה שמא יעשה עוברה וכו' צורת הראשון. נ"ב ותוספות פרק המפלת הביאו בשם רש"י שולד אחרון ממעך צורת הראשון ע"ש ובד"ה קמ"ל בדף כה מיהו ביבמות דף יב כתב רש"י ז"ל דוחק האחד את חבירו ופוחס לורתו משמע דלפעמים הראשון גובר ולפעמים השני גובר ופעם פי' כך ופעם פי' כך ואין כאן טעות:

גליון הש"ס

תוס' ד"ה שלש וכו' דאע"פ שאינה מצווה על פריה ורביה. ע' סנהדרין דף נט ע"ב תוד"ה והא.

תורה אור השלם

א) שֹׁמֵר פְּתָאיִם יְיָ דַּלֹּתִי וְלִי יְהוֹשִׁיעַ: [תהלים קטז, ו]

ב) וְנָתַן הָאִישׁ הַשֹּׁכֵב עִמָּהּ לַאֲבִי הַנַּעֲרָ חֲמִשִּׁים כָּסֶף וְלוֹ תִהְיֶה לְאִשָּׁה תַּחַת אֲשֶׁר עִנָּהּ לֹא יוּכַל שַׁלְּחָהּ כָּל יָמָיו: [דברים כב, כט]

להתעבר ולמות [יבמות שם]. שמתעברת ומתה [שם ק:]. **מבת אחת עשרה שנה וכו'.** פחות מי"א ודאי לא תתעבר ויותר מי"ב אם תתעבר לא תמות [שם יב:]. פחות מכן, אינה לריכה לשמש במוך דודאי לא תתעבר. יתר על כן, אם תתעבר לא תמות [נדה שם]. **משמשת כדרכה.** בלא מוך [יבמות שם]. **אין בין נערות לבגרות אלא ששה חדשים.** בלבד כשהביאה סימני נערות אינה שוהה להיות בוגרת אלא ששה חדשים ופעמים שהיא ממהרת לבגור וסימניה ניכרים בדדיה כדתנן במס' נדה (דף מז) פגה בוחל ולמל. **וכי תימא וכו'.** וכי תימא בציר הוא דליכא הא טפי איכא הא אלא בלבד קאמר, לא גרס דמהיכא תיסק אדעתין למימר הכי מי קאמר אין בין נערות לבגרות פחות מששה חדשים [קידושין עט. ועי' תוס' כאן וגליון שם]. **נערה המאורסה אביה ובעלה וכו'.** ולהכי נקט נערה דלדוקא נערה שהיא ברשות אביה [דכתיב בנעוריה בית אביה] וכדאמרינן נמי במס' כתובות האב זכאי בקדושי בתו ובמעשה ידיה ובמציאתה ובהפרת נדריה בזמן שהיא נערה ומפיק לה מהאי קרא [נדרים סו:]. דכל זמן שהיא ארוסה אכתי שייך בה אביה [שם עד:]. **המפתה.** מדבר על לבה עד שנשמעת לו וכן תרגומו ואזי ישתדל, שדול בלשון ארמי כפתוי בלשון עברי [שמות כב, טו]. **ופגם.** שייך באונס ומפתה והוא במקום נזק דאומדים כמה אדם רוצה ליתן בין שפחה בתולה לבעולה להשיאה לעבדו שיש לו קורת רוח ממנו [ב"ק פד:]. **שיראין.** של משי [מנחות לט:].

six months הָא טְפֵי אִיכָּא – **but there can be more,**[15] I shall respond: הָא אֶלָּא קָאָמַר – **But [Shmuel] said "only"** six months![16] – ? –

The Gemara concedes that its first interpretation of Rava's query has been refuted, and now advances a second interpretation:

אֶלָּא הָכִי קָמִיבַּעְיָא לֵיהּ – **Rather, Rava** actually **inquired thus:** יֵשׁ בֶּגֶר בַּקֶּבֶר וּפָקַע אָב – **Is there an attaining of *bagrus* in the grave**[17] **and** so **the father**'s right to the fine for violation **has been abrogated,**[18] אוֹ דִלְמָא – **or perhaps** אֵין בֶּגֶר בַּקֶּבֶר וְלֹא פָּקַע אָב – **there is not an attaining of *bagrus* in the grave and the father**'s right to the fine **has not been abrogated?**[19]

The Gemara presents a different version of Rava's query:

מַר בַּר רַב אַשִׁי בָּעֵי לָהּ הָכִי – **Mar bar Rav Ashi posed the question thus:** מִיתָה עוֹשָׂה בַּגְרוּת – **Does** the *naarah's* **death effect** the same law as does ***bagrus,*** אוֹ אֵין עוֹשָׂה בַּגְרוּת – **or does it not effect** the same law as does ***bagrus*?**[20]

The Gemara concludes:

תֵּיקוּ – **Let [the question] stand** unresolved.

The Gemara presents a related query:

בָּעֵי מִינֵּיהּ רָבָא מֵאַבַּיֵי – **Rava inquired of Abaye:** בָּא עָלֶיהָ וְנִתְאָרְסָה – Where **one raped [a *naarah*] and she became betrothed** before the rapist was sued and found guilty by the court, מַהוּ – **what is [the law]?**[21]

The Gemara answers with a rhetorical question:

אָמַר לֵיהּ – **[Abaye] said to [Rava]** in reply: מִי כְּתִיב וְנָתַן לַאֲבִי הַנַּעֲרָה אֲשֶׁר לֹא אֹרָשָׂה – **Is it then written, "And he** [the violator] **shall give to the father of the *naarah* who was not betrothed"?!**[22]

Rava counters:

וּלְטַעְמֵיךְ – **But according to your reasoning,** הָא דְתַנְיָא – how will you explain **this** ruling **that was taught in a Baraisa:** בָּא עָלֶיהָ וְנִשֵּׂאת – If HE VIOLATED HER AND then SHE MARRIED,[23] לְעַצְמָהּ – the fine belongs TO HER? מִי כְּתִיב וְנָתַן לַאֲבִי הַנַּעֲרָה אֲשֶׁר לֹא נְשׂוּאָה – Now, here too you could ask: Why should the father not receive the fine? **Is it then written, "And he** [the violator] **shall give to the father of the *naarah* who was not married"?!**[24]

Abaye's reply:

הָכִי הַשְׁתָּא – **Now, is this** analogy correct?! הָתָם – **There** in the case of the married daughter the father's disqualification can be derived logically, without an explicit indication in the payment verse, as follows: הוֹאִיל וּבַגְרוּת מוֹצִיאָה מֵרְשׁוּת אָב – **Since *bagrus* removes** a girl **from** her **father's jurisdiction**[25]

NOTES

two pubic hairs and attained *naarus* at the age of twelve years and a day. However, a twelve-year-old girl who has not developed the two pubic hairs remains a minor, who cannot survive a pregnancy. And the reason the girl must also be twelve years and one day to qualify as a *naarah* is because two hairs grown in the pubic region prior to that age are attributable to a mole, and thus are not considered signs of adulthood (*naarus*).

15. And so it is possible for a *naarah* to conceive and give birth nine months later, and yet die afterward while still a *naarah.*

16. I.e. it never takes more than six months to develop from a *naarah* into a *bogeress* . Hence, we see from the aforementioned Baraisa, which states that a "minor" who conceives cannot remain alive to complete her pregnancy, that it is impossible for a girl who died as a *naarah* to have given birth to an heir.

17. The Gemara again defines the case as where a victim died while yet a *naarah* and would have reached the stage of *bagrus* before the court passes judgment on the violator.

18. [The Torah states (*Deuteronomy* 22:29): *The man who lay with her shall give to the father of the naarah fifty silver [coins].* This verse is expounded to teach that the fine is paid only to "the father of the *naarah*" – i.e. and not to the father of a *bogeress* . That is, if the victim became a *bogeress* before the violator was sued and found guilty by the court, the fine is no longer paid to her father; rather, it goes to the girl herself (see Mishnah below, 41b).] Hence, if we say that a violated victim attains the status of a *bogeress* in the grave [see above, 38b note 27], the father's claim to the fine would be abolished and the money would remain in the possession of the violator, since his proper legal adversary – the girl – is no longer living. (Nor can the father inherit the fine, for since the girl never collected it, it is not considered a monetary asset that she can bequeath to her heirs) (*Rashi*). See *Tosafos* above, 38b ד״ה יש בגר and 38b note 33.

19. For he is still classified as "the father of the *naarah,*" who is entitled to the fine.

20. According to Mar bar Rav Ashi, Rava is not concerned about whether a *naarah* attains the status of a *bogeress* in her grave at the conclusion of the six-month period. Rather, he is asking whether we equate the effect of a *naarah's* death with the effect of her becoming a *bogeress* while *still alive.* That is, do we say that just as the father's right to the fine is abrogated when his living daughter becomes a *bogeress* [before the violator is sued and found guilty by court], so too this right is abrogated when the victim dies while yet a *naarah*? (*Rashi*).

Rashi comments that the Gemara's statement above (38b), "A matter that was obvious to Abaye was a subject of inquiry to Rava," applies only to this version of Rava's query. For in the other versions Rava's question was whether the violated victim attains *bagrus after* her death, so that the father loses his claim to the fine on account of her having become a *bogeress* . Implicit in this formulation is that Rava was sure that her death per se does not cause the father to lose his right to the fine – in clear contradiction to Abaye, who maintains that her death alone abrogates the father's rights.

21. Is the fine paid to the father or to the violated victim herself? (*Rashi*). Rava's inquiry is directed to the opinion of R' Akiva of our Mishnah that if one violates a previously betrothed and divorced *naarah* he pays the fine to the victim herself and not to her father [the Gemara does not bother to tell us this, since the halachah always follows R' Akiva's opinion in a dispute with one other colleague (here, R' Yose Haglili), and it is obvious that the question cannot concern R' Akiva's opinion in the Baraisa]. Now, do we say that just as betrothal abrogates a father's right to the fine for any future violation, so too it abrogates his right to collect the fine for a past violation; or do we say that since with regard to other matters [viz. her earnings, "findings" and vows] a father retains his rights in his daughter even after her betrothal, so too he retains his right to collect the fine for a past violation? (*Tosafos*).

22. If the Torah had meant to disqualify the father from receiving the fine even where betrothal occurred after the violation, the phrase *who was not betrothed* would have appeared in the verse that discusses payment (*Deuteronomy* 22:29). By mentioning that conditional phrase in the verse that discusses the act of violation itself [*If a man finds a virgin naarah* ***who was not betrothed*** *and takes hold of her and lies with her* etc. (ibid. v. 28)], the Torah teaches that her being betrothed at the time of payment is irrelevant, and so the fine still accrues to the father (*Pnei Yehoshua* to *Tosafos* ד״ה בא).

23. I.e. she underwent both stages of the matrimonial process – *kiddushin* (betrothal) and *nesuin* (marriage) – before judgment was obtained.

24. [Say that here, too, since the conditional phrase "who was not married" does not appear in the verse that discusses payment, the Torah must be teaching that even her being *married* at the time of payment is irrelevant, and so the payment is made to the father. The Baraisa, however, debunks such reasoning, for it rules that the fine goes to the girl.]

25. The only prerogatives that the Torah expressly grants a father vis-a-vis his daughter are the rights to sell her as a minor and to receive other financial gain, such as the fines for her violation or seduction and her earnings, that accrue when she is a *naarah* (see below, 46b). However, nowhere do we find that the Torah grants the father any rights in his daughter after she becomes a *bogeress* . Given Scripture's refusal to do so, how can we invest him with rights? (*Rashi*).

ומי מעברא והתני רב ביבי קמיה דרב נחמן [א] שלש נשים משמשות במוך אלו הן קטנה ומעוברת ומניקה קטנה שמא תתעבר ותמות מעוברת שמא תעשה עוברה סנדל מניקה שמא תגמול את בנה ותמות ואיזוהי קטנה מבת אחת עשרה שנה ויום אחד עד שתים עשרה שנה ויום אחד פחות מיכן ויותר על כן משמשת כדרכה והולכת דברי ר"מ וחכמים אומרים אחת זו ואחת זו משמשת כדרכה והולכת ומן השמים ירחמו משום שנאמר א) שומר פתאים ה' וכי תימא דאיעברא כשהיא נערה ואולידה כשהיא נערה ובשיתא ירחי מי קא ילדה והאמר שמואל [ג] אין בין נערות לבגרות אלא ששה חדשים וכי תימא בציר הוא דליכא הא טפי איכא הא אלא קאמר אלא הכי קמיבעיא ליה יש בגר בקבר ופקע אב או דלמא אין בגר בקבר ולא פקע אב מר בר רב אשי בעי לה הכי מיתה עושה בגרות או אין עושה בגרות תיקו בעי מיניה רבא מאביי בא עליה ונתארסה מהו א"ל [ג] מי כתיב ונתן לאבי הנערה אשר לא ארוסה ולטעמיך הא דתניא [ג] בא עליה ונשאת לעצמה מי כתיב ונתן לאבי הנערה אשר לא נשואה הכי השתא התם הואיל ובגרות מוציאה מרשות אב ונישואין מוציאין מרשות אב מה בגרות בא עליה ובגרה לעצמה אף נישואין בא עליה ונשאת לעצמה אלא אירוסין מי קא מפקי מרשותא דאב לגמרי הא תנן [ד] נערה המאורסה אביה ובעלה מפירין לה נדריה: מתני' [ה] המפתה נותן שלשה דברים והאונס ארבעה המפתה נותן בושת ופגם וקנס מוסיף עליו אונס שנותן את הצער מה בין אונס למפתה האונס נותן את הצער והמפתה אינו נותן את הצער האונס נותן מיד והמפתה לכשיוציא האונס שותה בעציצו והמפתה אם רצה להוציא מוציא [ו] כיצד שותה בעציצו אפילו היא חיגרת אפי' היא סומא ואפילו היא מוכת שחין [ז] נמצא בה דבר ערוה או שאינה ראויה לבא בישראל אינו רשאי לקיימה שנאמר ב) [ח] ולו תהיה לאשה אשה הראויה לו: גמ' צער דמאי אמר אבוה דשמואל צער שחבטה על גבי קרקע מתקיף לה רבי זירא אלא מעתה חבטה על גבי שיראין הכי נמי דפטור וכי תימא הכי נמי והתניא ר' שמעון בן יהודה אומר משום רבי שמעון [י] אונס אינו משלם את הצער מפני שסופה

רש"י

ומי מעברא. בקטנות או בנערות כשהיא בת קנס שתלד בנערות: משמשות במוך. מותר להן לשמש במוך ואינן כמשחיתות זרע: שמא יעשה עוברה סנדל. שאם תתעבר עובר שני פוחת השני את צורת (א) הראשון ודומה לסנדל שהוא דג שבים: שמא תגמול את בנה. מפני שהחלב נעכר כשמתעברת ואינו טוב ליונק ותצטרך להעתיקו משדים וימות: פחות מכאן. מבת אחת עשרה שנה משמשת כדרכה לפי שלא תתעבר: ויתר על כן. על בת שתים עשרה שנה משמשת כדרכה שאם תתעבר לא תמות אלמא בקטנות לא מיעברא שיבא לכלל לידה דהא ותמות קתני: וכי תימא. מבת שתים עשרה ויום אחד שהגיעו ימי הנעורים נתעברה וילדה בנערות ומתה בנערות הא נמי ליתא דאמר שמואל אין בין נערות לבגרות אלא ששה חדשים משהביאה שתי שערות הויא נערה באותן שתביא משתים עשרה שנה והלאה ומשתביאם עד שתגדל ששה חדשים ותו לא ומתניתא דקתני מבת שתים עשרה ואילך אי מעברא לא מתה מה שתביאה שתי שערות קודם שתתעבר קאמר אבל כל זמן שלא הביאה קטנה היא והאי דנקט מנין שנים משום דבכלל משתים עשרה ויום אחד אפילו הביאה שערות אינו אלא שומא כדאמרינן במסכת נדה ובקדושין: ופקע אב. פקעה תביעת אב וזכה הלה במה שבידו שאין בעל דינו קיים וקנס לאו ממון הוא להורישו לאביו בתורת ירושה כל כמה דלא גבתיה: או אין בגר בקבר. ולאפקועי תביעת אב: מר בר רב אשי. לא בעי לה בעיא דרבא אלא אם מתה בנערותה מי פקעה כי בגרות מחמיס או לא ולהאי לישנא דמר בר רב אשי אליבא דרבא אמרו לעיל מילתא דפשיטא ליה לאביי מיבעיא ליה לרבא דאילו ללישנא קמא מפשט פשיטא ליה לרבא דמיתה לא מפקעא ודלא כאביי כל זמן שלא בגרה וכי קא מיבעיא ליה בבגר בקבר קמבעיא ליה אבל במיתה כל זמן שלא בגרה פליג אדאביי ואמר לא מפקעא וחייב: מיתה עושה בגרות. עושה דין בגרות למפקעא כח אב כי בגרות: מהו. מי הוי לאביה או לעצמה: בגרות מוציאה מרשות אב. דלא מצינו שזיכתה לו תורה בבתו אלא מכר בקטנות ושאר שבח כגון קנסה ומעשה ידיה בנערות כדילפינן בפרק נערה (לקמן דף מו:) אבל בבגרות לא אשכחן וכיון דלא זיכתה לו תורה אנן מהיכא תיתי לן לזכותו בשלה: ונשואין מוציאין מרשות אב. כדאשכחן בהפרת נדרים דלכל זמן דלא ניסת אביה מיפר ומשניסת אין יכול להפר: בא עליה. כשהיא נערה ובגרה: לעצמה. דכתיב ונתן האיש השוכב עמה לאבי הנערה אם נערה היא בשעת נתינה: אביה ובעלה. ואינו מופר עד שיפרו שניהם: מתני' בושת ופגם. במתני' לקמן מפרש להו: האונס נותן מיד. לאביה אע"פ שכונסה: לכשיוציא. בגמרא פריך אטו אשתו היא ומפרש לה לכשלא יכנוס דאם כנסה אינו נותן קנס כדכתיב מהר ימהרנה לו ואם מאן ימאן וגו' כסף ישקול אבל אונס כתיב ונתן חמשים כסף ולו תהיה לאשה: שותה בעציצו. בכלי שבחר לו לשתות בו כלומר על כרחו ישאנה כדכתיב לא יוכל לשלחה (דברים כב): גמ' שסופה

תוספות

שלש נשים משמשות במוך. פי' בקונטרס מותרות לשמש במוך ושאר נשים אסורות משום השחתת זרע ואין נראה לר"ת [ז] דהא קטנה ואילונית מותר לשמש בהדייהו ולא הוי השחתת זרע כיון שהוא דרך תשמיש ומפרש ר"ת משמשות צריכות לשמש במוך אחר תשמיש ועלה טובה קמ"ל ולר"י נראה לקיים פי' הקונט' דבריש נדה (דף ג.) משמע שהמוך הוא במעיה כל שעה והוי כמשמש על האבנים ועל העצים ולא דמי למשמש קטנה ואילונית ועוד אפילו היתה נותנת מוך אחר תשמיש אסורה ° דאף על פי שאינה מצווה על פריה ורביה מ"מ אסורה היא להשחית זרע כדמשמע בנדה (דף יג.) דתנן כל היד המרבה לבדוק בנשים משובחת באנשים תיקצץ ומפרש בגמרא משום דנשים לאו בנות הרגשה נינהו משמע דאם היו בנות הרגשה הוו אסירי ויש לדחות דלאו בנות איסור הרגשה נינהו קאמר: וכי תימא בציר הוא כו' והא בלבד קאמר. בקונטרס (בקדושין דף עט.) ל"ג ליה דבלאו בלבד משמע טפי לא [ח]: בא עליה ונתארסה מהו. לרבי עקיבא דמתני' קא מיבעיא ליה דאמר נתארסה ונתגרשה קנסה לעצמה דמי אמרינן כיון שיצאה מרשות האב לענין קנס יהא קנסה לעצמה או דלמא כיון דלענין שאר מילי לא נפקא מרשות האב יהא קנסה לאביה אבל לרבי עקיבא דברייתא פשיטא דקנסה לאביה ולר' יוסי הגלילי נהי דאמר אין לה קנס נמי לא מיבעיא ליה דהא דאין לה קנס לאו משום מיפק מרשותא דאב היא אלא גזירת הכתוב הוא דאין לה קנס ולא נפקא באירוסין כלל מרשות אביה דאב זכאי בקדושיה ובמעשה ידיה אע"ג דנתארסה והא דקא בעי לה סתם ולא קאמר לרבי עקיבא בהדיא מהו משום דהלכה כר' עקיבא מחבירו: הואיל ונישואין מוציאין מרשות אב. פי' בקונט' דילפינן מהפרת נדרים ואע"ג דקי"ל דממונא מאיסורא לא ילפינן ה"מ לאוקמה ברשות אב הוא דלא ילפינן ממונא מאיסורא אבל לאפוקי מרשות אב ילפינן שפיר מהפרת נדרים דבסברא מועטת יש להוציאה מרשות אב ור"י ב"ר אברהם פי' כיון דגלי לן קרא דלאוקמה ברשות אב איסורא וממונא שוין ה"ה לאפוקה [ט] [ור"י מפרש דנישואין מוציאין מרשות אב מדדרשינן איש אמו ואביו תיראו איש סיפק כו' אשה אין סיפק בידה לעשות ולא נהירא דמעשה ידיה אינו לבעל מן התורה]: מה בוגרת בא עליה ובגרה לעצמה. פירוש דהא מלינו בוגרת שיוצאה מרשות אב לענין ממון וקשה דה"נ נישואין מוציאין מרשות אב לענין ממון ואמאי צריך למילף מבוגרת ונראה דבא עליה ובגרה לעצמה נפקא לן מונתן לאבי הנערה דדרשינן לאבי הנערה ולא לאבי בוגרת: צער דמאי. קשה לר"י דמאי קא מיבעיא ליה וכי לא ידע הש"ס שיש צער גדול לבתולה בביאה ראשונה וכמה קטנות חולות מזה וכ"ת דמאותו צער פשיטא ליה להש"ס דפטור שהרי סופה להצטער בכך תחת בעלה והא איכא כמה תנאי בהכונס (ב"ק דף נט. ושם) דלא חיישי לכחש גופנא פירוש דבר שסופו להיות כן ונראה לר"י דצער בעילה משום תאות תשמיש אינו בא בשעת תשמיש אלא אחר כך וכל צער החבלה דמחייב היינו אותו צער הבא לו בשעת חבלה אבל מה שבא לו אחר כך מיפטר דגרמא בעלמא הוא הלכך בעי צער דמאי ורשב"א מפרש דפשיטא דצער של בתולים ליכא למימר דע"כ תנא דמתני' חייש לכחש גופנא מדמפתה פטור:

אי

עין משפט נר מצוה

סט א מיי' פ"ב מהל' אישות הל' ב טור ש"ע יו"ד סימן רלד סעיף א בהג"ה:
ע ב מיי' פ"ב מהל' נערה הל' טו סמג עשין נד טור אה"ע סימן קנו:
עא ג מיי' שם הל' טו:
עב ד מיי' פי"א מהל' נדרים הל' ט סמג לאוין רמב טוש"ע י"ד סי' רלד סעיף ה:
עג ה מיי' פ"ב מהלכות נערה הל' ז סמג עשין נד טוש"ע אה"ע סי' קנז סעיף א:
עד ו מיי' פ"א שם הל' ג סמג שם טוש"ע שם סעיף ג:
עה ז מיי' שם הל' ה טוש"ע שם סעי' ד:

תוספות רי"ד

תניא בא עליה ונשאת לעצמה הואיל ובגרות מוציאה מרשות אב. פי' שלא מצינו שזכתה לו תורה בבתו אלא מכר בקטנותה ושאר שבח ממון כגון קנסה ומעשה ידיה בנערות כדילפי' לקמן בפ' נערה ונשואין נמי מוציאין מרשות אב. פירוש כדאשכחן בהפרת נדרים דכ"ז שלא נשאת אביה מפר נדריה ומשנשאת אין יכול להפר. מה בוגרת בא עלי' ובגרה לעצמה דכתיב ונתן האיש השוכב עמה לאבי הנערה. אם היא נערה בשעת נתינה אף נשואין בא עליה ונשאת לעצמה: מתני' המפתה נותן ג' דברים והאונס ד' המפתה נותן בושת ופגם וקנס מוסיף עליו אונס שנותן את הצער מה בין אונס למפתה האונס נותן את הצער והמפתה אין נותן את הצער האונס נותן מיד והמפתה לכשיוציא האונס שותה בעציצו. פי' בכלי שבחר לו לשתות בו כלומר ע"כ ישאנה דכתיב לא יוכל לשלחה כל ימיו והמפתה אם רצה להוציא מוציא. פי' האונס נותן מיד ואע"פ שכונסה שנאמר ונתן האיש השוכב עמה לאבי הנערה חמשים כסף ולו תהיה לאשה. ודרשי' תו לו אתה כופה ולא לה:

ליקוטי רש"י

משמשות במוך. מותרות לתת מוך במקום תשמיש כשהן משמשות כדי שלא יתעברו [יבמות יב:]. תקנתן הוה לשמש במוך שלא יתעברו [נדה מה.]. סנדל. ולד שאין לו צורת פנים וקיימא לן במסכת נדה (דף כה:) אין סנדל שאין עמו ולד משל לאדם שסטר את חבירו והחזיר צורתו לאחוריו דכשהיא מעוברת וחוזרת ומתעברת דוחק האחד את חבירו ופוחת צורתו [יבמות שם]. כשמתעברת תאומים פעמים שאחד דוחק את חבירו ופוחת את צורתו כדאמרינן במכילתין אין סנדל שאין עמו ולד [נדה שם]. עובר שני דוחק את הראשון ופוחת את צורתו בהמפלת (נדה כה:) [יבמות ק:]. שמא תגמול את בנה. אם תתעבר תהא צריכה לגמול את בנה מלהניק כמו ויגמל (בראשית כא) לשון הבדלה [שם יב:]. תפריש את בנה מלהניק מחמת עיבורה [נדה שם]. ואיזוהי קטנה. הראויה להתעבר ולמות [יבמות שם]. שמתעברת ומתה [שם ק:]. מבת אחת עשרה שנה וכו'. פחות מי"א ודאי לא תתעבר ויותר מי"ב אם תתעבר לא תמות [שם יב:]. פחות מכן, אינה צריכה לשמש במוך דודאי לא תתעבר. יתר על כן, אם תתעבר לא תמות [נדה שם]. משמשת כדרכה. בלא מוך [יבמות שם]. אין בין נערות לבגרות אלא ששה חדשים. בלבד כשהביאה סימני נערות אינה שוהה להיות בוגרת אלא ששה חדשים ופעמים שהיא ממהרת לבגור וסימניה ניכרים בגדיה כדתנן במס' נדה (דף מז) פגה בוחל וצמל. וכי תימא בציר הוא דליכא הא טפי איכא הא אלא בלבד קאמר, לא גרס דמהיכא תיסק אדעתין למימר הכי מי קאמר אין בין נערות לבגרות פחות משסה חדשים [קידושין עט. ועי' תוס' כאן וגליון שם]. נערה המאורסה אביה ובעלה וכו'. ולהכי נקט נערה דדוקא נערה שהיא ברשות אביה [דכתיב בנעוריה בית אביה] ודאמרינן נמי במס' כתובות האב זכאי בקדושיה ובמעשה ידיה ובמציאתה ובהפרת נדריה בזמן שהיא נערה ומפיק לה מהאי קרא [נדרים סו:]. דכל זמן שהיא ארוסה אכתי שייך בה אביה [שם עד:]. המפתה. מדבר על לבה עד ששומעת לו וכן תרגומו ואמרי ישמעאל, שדול בלשון ארמי כפתוי בלשון עברי [שמות כב, טו]. ופגם. שייך באונס ומפתה והוא במקום נזק דאומדים כמה אדם רוצה ליתן בין שפחה בתולה לבעולה להשיאה לעבדו שיש לו קורת רוח ממנו [ב"ק פד:]. שיראין. של משי [מנחות לט:].

מסורת הש"ס

א) יבמות יב: ק: נדה מה. נדרים לה: [תוספתא נדה פ"ב], ב) קדושין עט. נדה סה., ג) נדרים סו: עד: יבמות כט: [לקמן מו: קדושין ד.], ד) לקמן מב., ה) [לעיל כט:], ו) ב"ק נט: ע"ש, ז) [עי' תוס' יבמות יב: ותוס' נדה יג.], ח) [ועי' תוס' נדה סה. ד"ה וכו' כ"מ מישבין הגירסא], ט) מ"י כ"י.

הגהות הב"ח

(א) רש"י ד"ה שמא יעשה עוברה וכו' צורת השני. נ"ב ובתוספות פרק המפלת הביא בשם רש"י שולד אחרון ממעך צורת הראשונה ע"ש בד"ה קמ"ל בדף כה מיהו ביבמות דף יב כתב רש"י ז"ל דוחק האחד את חבירו ופוחת צורתו משמע לפעמים הראשון גורר ולפעמים השני גורר ופעם פי' כך ופעם פי' כך ואין כאן טעות:

גליון הש"ס

תוס' ד"ה שלש וכו' דאע"פ שאינה מצווה על פריה ורביה. עי' סנהדרין דף נט ע"ב תוד"ה והא:

תורה אור השלם

א) שֹׁמֵר פְּתָאיִם יְיָ דַּלּוֹתִי וְלִי יְהוֹשִׁיעַ: [תהלים קטז, ו]

ב) וְנָתַן הָאִישׁ הַשֹּׁכֵב עִמָּהּ לַאֲבִי הַנַּעֲרָ חֲמִשִּׁים כָּסֶף וְלוֹ תִהְיֶה לְאִשָּׁה תַּחַת אֲשֶׁר עִנָּהּ לֹא יוּכַל שַׁלְּחָהּ כָּל יָמָיו: [דברים כב, כט]

The Gemara questions whether there is any factual basis for such a query:

וּמִי מִעַבְּרָא – And could [a woman who died while a *naarah*] have conceived and given birth prior to her death? **וְהָתָנֵי רַב בִּיבִי קַמֵּיהּ דְּרַב נַחְמָן – But Rav Bivi taught** a Baraisa **in the presence of Rav Nachman: שָׁלֹשׁ נָשִׁים מְשַׁמְּשׁוֹת בְּמוֹךְ –** THREE WOMEN are permitted to COHABIT WITH AN ABSORBENT CLOTH[1] to prevent pregnancy,[2] **אֵלּוּ הֵן –** and THESE ARE THEY: **קְטַנָּה וּמְעוּבֶּרֶת וּמֵנִיקָה –** A MINOR, A PREGNANT WOMAN AND A NURSING WOMAN. **קְטַנָּה שֶׁמָּא תִּתְעַבֵּר וְתָמוּת –** A MINOR is permitted to use a cloth for PERHAPS SHE WILL BECOME PREGNANT AND DIE as a result;[3] **מְעוּבֶּרֶת שֶׁמָּא תֵּעָשֶׂה עוּבָּרָהּ סַנְדָּל –** A PREGNANT WOMAN may use a cloth because PERHAPS she will be impregnated again and HER FETUS WILL BE RENDERED A *SANDAL*;[4] **מֵנִיקָה שֶׁמָּא תִּגְמוֹל אֶת בְּנָהּ –** and A NURSING WOMAN is afforded this leniency since PERHAPS SHE WILL become pregnant and have to WEAN HER first CHILD.[5] **וְאֵיזוֹהִי קְטַנָּה –** AND WHICH girl IS considered A MINOR for purposes of this law?[6] **מִבַּת אַחַת עֶשְׂרֵה שָׁנָה וְיוֹם אֶחָד עַד שְׁתֵּים עֶשְׂרֵה שָׁנָה וְיוֹם אֶחָד –** One FROM THE AGE OF ELEVEN YEARS AND ONE DAY UNTIL TWELVE YEARS AND ONE DAY. **פָּחוֹת מִיכֵּן וְיָתֵר עַל כֵּן –** At an age LESS THAN THIS OR GREATER THAN THIS **מְשַׁמֶּשֶׁת כְּדַרְכָּהּ וְהוֹלֶכֶת –** SHE MUST COHABIT ROUTINELY IN THE USUAL MANNER [i.e. without an absorbent cloth].[7] **דִּבְרֵי רַבִּי מֵאִיר –** These are THE WORDS OF R' MEIR. **וַחֲכָמִים אוֹמְרִים –** BUT THE SAGES SAY: **אַחַת זוֹ וְאַחַת זוֹ מְשַׁמֶּשֶׁת כְּדַרְכָּהּ וְהוֹלֶכֶת –** BOTH THIS one AND THAT one MUST COHABIT ROUTINELY IN THE USUAL MANNER,[8] **וּמִן הַשָּׁמַיִם יְרַחֲמוּ –** AND FROM HEAVEN THEY WILL HAVE MERCY on them,[9] **מִשּׁוּם שֶׁנֶּאֱמַר ,,שֹׁמֵר פְּתָאיִם ה׳ ״ –** SINCE IT IS STATED:[10] *HASHEM PROTECTS THE SIMPLE.*[11] How, then, is it possible for a *naarah* who died to have given birth to an heir?[12]

The Gemara rules out one possible answer:

וְכִי תֵּימָא דְּאִיעַבְּרָא כְּשֶׁהִיא נַעֲרָה וְאוֹלִידָה כְּשֶׁהִיא נַעֲרָה – And if you will say that Rava's case is **where she conceived when she was a *naarah* and gave birth when she was a *naarah*,**[13] I shall respond: **וּבְשִׁיתָּא יַרְחֵי מִי קָא יָלְדָה – And can one give birth in six months?! וְהָאָמַר שְׁמוּאֵל – But Shmuel has said: אֵין בֵּין נְעָרוּת לְבַגְרוּת אֶלָּא שִׁשָּׁה חֳדָשִׁים – There is only six months between *naarus* and *bagrus*!**[14] **וְכִי תֵּימָא בָּצִיר הוּא דְּלֵיכָּא – And if you will say** that Shmuel means **that there is no less** than

NOTES

1. I.e. they may insert a cloth into their vaginal canal prior to having relations to absorb their husbands' semen (*Rashi* here [as explained by *Ri* in *Tosafos*] and explicitly in *Yevamos* 12b ד״ה משמשות במוך; cf. *Rabbeinu Tam,* cited here by *Tosafos*).

2. The ejaculation of semen outside a woman's body is considered הַשְׁחָתַת זֶרַע, *the destruction of seed,* and is a major sin (see *Niddah* 13a). Accordingly, placing an absorbent cloth in a woman's vaginal canal prior to cohabitation is generally prohibited, for then the husband discharges his semen into the cloth rather than into his wife, and that is tantamount to discharging the semen onto the ground. R' Meir rules, however, that since in these three cases conception poses a danger to the woman's life, using an absorbent cloth does not violate the prohibition against destroying seed, and thus is permitted (*Rashi,* as understood by *Ri* in *Tosafos* and by *Ritva* to *Yevamos* 12b ד״ה שלש; see *Teshuvos R' Akiva Eiger* I §71 regarding how *Rashi* was understood by *Ramban, Rashba* and *Nimukei Yosef*).

[*Igros Moshe, Even HaEzer* I §63:2, wonders why indeed R' Meir's leniency is justified. That is, although Biblical prohibitions are generally relaxed when human life is *already* in danger, in these cases there is no threat to life if the couple simply abstains from cohabiting. Hence, the danger that pregnancy poses to these women's lives should prohibit them from engaging in cohabitation rather than permit them to use such a birth-control technique. *Igros Moshe* explains that since it is a mitzvah to have relations with one's wife, and in these cases, due to the danger involved, cohabitation cannot be performed without a cloth, the discharge of semen into the cloth constitutes not הוֹצָאַת זֶרַע לְבַטָּלָה, *discharging seed in vain* (i.e. the destruction of seed), but *discharging semen for the sake of the cohabitation,* which is permitted.]

3. I.e. if she becomes pregnant, she will definitely die (see *Yevamos* 12b and *Ritva* here ד״ה ומי מעברא). A minor is physically incapable of giving birth; if she does conceive, she will most certainly die before giving birth. (As the Gemara will make clear, a girl who conceives while a minor will die from the pregnancy even if it would not come to term until she is an adult.)

4. Should she conceive again, the second fetus would diminish the form of the first, giving it the appearance of a [flat] ocean fish called *sandal* (*Rashi*). [See *Rashi* to *Yevamos* 12b ד״ה סנדל, where he writes that, specifically, the affected fetus would lack facial features. *Bach* here notes that *Rashi's* comment there goes on to imply that either fetus could have this deleterious impact on the other. But see *Ritva* here and *Tosafos* in *Yevamos* ibid. ד״ה שמא תעשה, who hold that it is the first fetus that is damaged.]

See *Kovetz Shiurim* §135, who discusses the mitzvah of saving a life (פִּקּוּחַ נֶפֶשׁ) as it applies to a fetus.

5. If a nursing woman becomes pregnant, her milk becomes turbid and harmful to the child. Hence, she will have to wean him, and he may die (*Rashi*).

6. *Ritva.*

7. A girl less than eleven years old cannot conceive, and a girl over twelve years old will not die if she does. Hence, neither is allowed to use this birth-control device (*Rashi*).

8. [I.e. even the minor, pregnant woman and nursing woman are forbidden to use an absorbent cloth during relations.]

9. And not allow them to conceive (see *Maharam Schif*).

10. *Psalms* 116:6.

11. Although one is generally forbidden to place himself in danger and rely on Heavenly protection, the chances of these three women becoming pregnant are so remote that cohabiting without a cloth is not considered placing oneself in danger. Hence, they are permitted to rely on Heavenly protection and engage in relations in the usual manner. See *Igros Moshe, Even HaEzer* I 63:1, for a lengthy discussion of this concept as it pertains to the issue at hand.

Shitah Mekubetzes cites many Rishonim who note that the verse, *Hashem protects the simple,* merely *allows* one to rely on Heavenly protection when the risk is minimal. It does not, however, *mandate* such reliance. Hence, even though the verse could provide the Sages with a rationale for permitting these women to cohabit without a cloth, it does not support their forbidding the use of a cloth. These Rishonim thus maintain that the dispute between R' Meir and the Sages is not whether these women are permitted to use an absorbent cloth (as *Rashi* understands; see note 1 above), but whether they are required to do so. R' Meir holds that they are required to use a cloth so as not to place their lives in danger, whereas the Sages allow them to rely on Heavenly protection in lieu of a cloth. See *Igros Moshe* ibid. for an explanation of both opinions. See also *Kovetz Shiurim* §136.

12. [In order for a *naarah* to give birth, she would have had to conceive the child as a "minor" (i.e. as per the definition of minor that applies here – viz. a girl between the ages of eleven and twelve), as the Gemara proceeds to demonstrate.] And we see from the Baraisa that it is impossible for a "minor" who conceived to give birth, for the Baraisa states that she will die (*Rashi* ד״ה ויתר על כן).

13. I.e. she conceived after becoming a *naarah* at the age of twelve years and one day, and subsequently gave birth and then died while yet a *naarah* (*Rashi*).

14. The period of *naarus* begins when, after her twelfth birthday, a girl develops two pubic hairs, and it extends for exactly six months, at which time she becomes a *bogeress* (*Rashi*). [Hence, since the gestation period for a human embryo is nine months, had she conceived while a *naarah* she would be a *bogeress* by the time she gives birth.]

Rashi notes that we cannot answer that Rava's query concerns a girl who conceived after reaching the age of twelve years and a day but did not develop two pubic hairs and become a *naarah* until six months later, in which case she becomes a *bogeress* at age thirteen, well after the nine months necessary for her to give birth. For when the Baraisa states that a girl who is older than twelve years and one day can conceive and give birth without dying, it refers to a girl who developed

דְּבָעֵי רָבָא – for Rava inquired: יֵשׁ בֶּגֶר בַּקֶּבֶר אוֹ אֵין בֶּגֶר בַּקֶּבֶר – Is there an attaining of *bagrus* in the grave or is there not an attaining of *bagrus* in the grave?[32]

The Gemara elucidates Rava's query:

יֵשׁ בֶּגֶר בַּקֶּבֶר וְדִבְנָהּ הָוֵי – That is, **is there an attaining of *bagrus* in the grave and** so **[the fine] belongs to her son,**[33] **אוֹ דִלְמָא – or perhaps אֵין בֶּגֶר בַּקֶּבֶר וּדְאָבִיהָ הָוֵי – there is not an attaining of *bagrus* in the grave and [the fine] belongs to her father?**

NOTES

32. If a violated victim died while yet a *naarah* and would have reached the stage of *bagrus* before the court passes judgment on the violator, is she considered a *bogeress* or a *naarah* for purposes of determining the fine's recipient [the Gemara will now explain the ramifications of these two choices]? (*Rashi*). [The Gemara below (39a) teaches that *naarus* begins when a girl becomes twelve years old and has developed two pubic hairs; this stage lasts for six months, at which time the girl attains the state of *bagrus* (full maturity, when she attains complete legal independence). The issue at hand is whether a girl is classified a *bogeress* at the end of this six-month period even if she is no longer alive.]

33. The Mishnah below (41b) teaches that although the fine for violation ordinarily accrues to the victim's father, if the victim becomes a *bogeress* before the violator was sued and found guilty by the court, the father loses his right to the fine and it is awarded to the victim herself. Hence, if we say that at the conclusion of the six-month period a *naarah* attains the status of a *bogeress* even though she is dead, her father would lose his right to the fine at that time, and it would be paid to the violated victim's son (if she has one), who inherits his mother's estate (*Rashi*).

See *Tosafos* et al., who discuss the seeming conflict between the Gemara's assumption that a son would inherit the fine (if her father does lose it) and a ruling taught below (42b) that a person cannot bequeath a fine to his sons (אין אדם מוריש קנס לבניו). See also *Kovetz Shiurim* II §12.

סח א מיי' פ"א מהל' נערה הלכה טו סמג עשין נד טור אה"ע סימן קעז:

אימא בתולה לגזירה שוה ואשר לא אורסה פרט לנערה שנתארסה ונתגרשה מסתברא אשר לא אורסה לגזירה שוה שהרי אני קורא בה נערה בתולה אדרבה בתולה לגזירה שוה שהרי אני קורא בה אשר לא אורסה מסתברא [א] הא אישתני גופה והא לא אישתני גופה ורבי יוסי הגלילי האי סברא מנא ליה נפקא ליה [ג] מדרתניא [א] כסף ישקול כמוהר הבתולות שיהא זה כמוהר הבתולות ומוהר הבתולות כזה קשיא דר"ע אדר"ע תרי תנאי ואליבא דר"ע בשלמא ר"ע דמתני' לא אתיא ג"ש ומפקא ליה לקרא מפשטיה לגמרי אלא לר"ע דברייתא אתיא גזירה שוה ומפקא מפשטיה לגמרי אמר רב נחמן בר יצחק קרי ביה אשר לא ארוסה ארוסה בת סקילה היא ס"ד אמינא הואיל וחידוש הוא שחידשה תורה בקנס אע"ג דמיקטיל משלם ולרבה דאמר [ג] חידוש הוא שחידשה תורה בקנס אע"ג דמיקטיל משלם מאי איכא למימר סבר לה כרבי עקיבא דמתניתין תנו רבנן קנסה למי לאביה ויש אומרים לעצמה אמאי אמר רב חסדא הכא בנערה שנתארסה ונתגרשה עסקינן וקמיפלגי בפלוגתא דר"ע דמתניתין ורבי עקיבא דברייתא [ד] אמר אביי [א] בא עליה ומתה פטור שנאמר [ב] ונתן לאבי הנערה ולא לאבי מתה מלתא דפשיטא ליה לאביי מיבעיא ליה לרבא דבעי רבא יש בגר בקבר או אין בגר בקבר יש בגר בקבר ודבנה הוי או דלמא אין בגר בקבר ודאביה הוי ומי

רש"י

אימא בתולה לגזירה שוה. ולאו למעוטי בעולה ויהא קנס לבעולה: **מסתברא אשר לא אורסה לגזירה שוה.** ואפי' אורסה אית לה קנס: **שהרי אני קורא בה נערה בתולה.** אע"פ שנתארסה ונתגרשה דהא נערה בתולה היא כדכתיב קרא אבל בעולה שאין אני קורא בה נערה בתולה אין לה קנס: **אדרבה בתולה לגזירה שוה.** ולאו למעוטי בעולה דזונות אלא יש לה קנס לבעולה דזונות שהרי אני קורא אותה נערה אשר לא אורסה: **מסתברא.** ארוסה יש לה קנס ובעולה אין לה: **דהא אישתני גופה.** ופגמה אין רב כל כך: **והא.** דנתארסה ונתגרשה לא נשתנה גופה: **הא סברא.** דחמשים כסף דאונס שקלים הן וכסף ישקול דמפתה יהו חמשים: **כמוהר הבתולות.** מנין המפורש אצל אונס דהיינו חמשים: **ומוהר הבתולות.** יהיו שקלים: **כזה.** שכתוב בו ישקול: **קשיא דרבי עקיבא.** דברייתא דאמר קנסה לאביה: **אדרבי עקיבא.** דמתני': **לא אתיא גזירה שוה ומפקא לקרא מפשטיה לגמרי.** דלאו פשטיה לאשמועינן הא ארוסה לעצמה וחד מתרוייהו לאפוקי אי נמי לא מופקי ליכא למיפרך מידי: **אלא לרבי עקיבא דברייתא וכי אתיא גזירה שוה ומפקא מפשטיה לגמרי.** דלא דריש פשטא דאשר לא אורסה כלל ומשוי אורסה כלא אורסה ואם כן מיעקר משמעותיה: **קרי ביה.** בפשטיה אשר לא ארוסה למעוטי ארוסה: **בת סקילה היא.** ומלא יהיה אסון נפקא פטורה מתשלומין: **קנסה למי.** קא סלקא דעתך בסתם אנוסה קאי: **בא עליה ומתה.** לא הספיק האב להעמידו בדין עד שמתה: **יש בגר בקבר.** אם מתה בנערותה עד שלא עמדה בדין והגיע זמן בגרותה בקבר מי חשיב בגר או לא ולקמיה מפרש ואזיל למאי הלכתא: **יש בגר בקבר.** וכי היכי דאם לא הספיקה לעמוד בדין עד שבגרה תנן לקמן בפרק נערה שנתפתתה (דף מא:) דהרי הן לעצמה ולא לאביה והשתא נמי בגר בקבר מפקיע כח האב ובנה ירית לה אם יש לה בן: ומי

תוספות

[**אימא** בתולה לג"ש. ולא נמעט בעולה כדמשמע בסמוך נראה דר"ע דריש ג"ש מקרא לגופיה דהיינו בתולה קמייתא ודקנס ודמפתה אבל הבתולות דריש לבתולות בתולות ולא שייך למידרשיה לג"ש ולא לשום דבר ואיתר נער נערה הנערה וה' דהבתולות חד לחייבי לאוין ועשה וחד לחייבי לאוין וכריתות ואיכא ג' רבויין ה' דהבתולות ונער נערה הנערה חד לכדלעיל וחד לחייבי עשה וחד לחייבי לאוין וכריתות דלא איכא לר"ע חד לגופיה בלא ג"ש א"כ נמעט בעולה מההוא לגופיה ואף על גב דבקנס ליכא אלא חד בתולה לגופיה מגזירה שוה דמפתה יליף בתולה ולא בעולה כי היכי דיליף מפתה מאונס לענין נערה דלא כתיב במפתה. (ת"י כ"י)

אימא בתולה לג"ש. תימה דמקשי ליה דלימא תרוייהו לגופייהו ולא לג"ש ונראה דהש"ס קים ליה דחד מינייהו לגזירה שוה הואיל והמקראות סתומים לענין שקלים וחמשים הלכך פריך ואימא איפכא ולא פריך ואימא תרוייהו לגופייהו וכי האי גוונא איכא פ"ק דסנהדרין (דף ט.) דלאמר ולא את נביא השקר אלא בב"ד של ע' ואחד מה"מ א"ר יוסי בר חנינא אתיא הזדה הזדה מזקן ממרא ופריך הא הזדה כי כתיב בקטלא הוא דכתיב וקטלא בכ"ג אלא אמר ריש לקיש גמר דבר דבר מהמראתו והשתא היכי הוה בעי למילף ולמימר כרבי יוסי ברבי חנינא דלאתיא הזדה הזדה אלא דהוה קים ליה דאיכא ג"ש ולא הוה ידע במאי וקאמר מסברא דלאתיא הזדה הזדה: **מי אתיא גזרה שוה ומפקא ליה מפשטיה לגמרי.** דדיוק הא אורסה הוי עקר וקשה דבריש הערל (יבמות ד' ע.) יליף דערל אסור בתרומה מגזירה שוה דתושב ושכיר מפסח וכתיב תושב ושכיר לא יאכל בו גבי פסח משום גזירה שוה אע"פ שאינו אמת דהא תושב ושכיר אוכלין בפסח כדאמרינן התם דלא קני ליה רביה ומפקי' קרא מפשטיה טפי מהכא ואומר ר"ת דההוא תושב ושכיר מיירי בערלים ולהכי לא יאכל ומוכח דלאו תושב ישראל קאמר דהא לא קני ליה רביה אלא ודאי בערל ומשום הפנאה כתביה [ה]:

ארוסה בת סקילה היא. וא"ת מאי קשיא ליה הא השתא לא נפיק קרא ממשמעותיה ואי לא איצטריך לגופיה כ"ש דניחא טפי דג"ש מופנה ואומר ר"י דהכי פירושו ארוסה בת סקילה היא וכיון דלא איצטריך למידי אלא לגזירה שוה הוה ליה למכתב אשר לא ארוסה בהדיא ואמאי שני למכתב אשר לא אורסה דאיכא למטעי ולמימר הא אורסה לעצמה דבשלמא אי הוה בארוסה שום חידוש הוה אתי שפיר במה ששינה הלשון דאמרינן האי דשנה וכתב אורסה למדרש לגזירה שוה ואתא פשטיה לחידושא אבל השתא למה לי:

לאבי הנערה ולא לאבי מתה. וא"ת דבפרק נערה לקמן (דף מה:) גבי סרחה ולבסוף בגרה תידון בסקילה דרשינן הנערה שהיתה כבר ויש לומר דהתם מעינא דקרא והכא מעינא דקרא והתם ודאי אתיא לחייבה דאי לפוטרה לשתוק קרא מיניה ואנא ידענא דלא הויא בסקילה דלאו נערה היא והכא לחיובא דקנס לא אצטריך דמסברא מחייב אשעת ביאה ואי אפשר לפוטרו בולא כלום הלכך אתא לפוטרו: **יש** בגר בקבר ודבנה הוי. וא"ת היכי מצי למימר שתהא מורשת קנס לבנה הא אין אדם מוריש קנס לבניו כדאמרינן ריש פרק נערה לקמן (דף מג:) ובסמוך נמי אמר יש בגר בקבר ופקע אב ואי אדם מוריש קנס כי יש בגר בקבר נמי לא פקע אב ויהא לו מתורת ירושה ומיהו ההיא דבסמוך יש לדחות דנפקא מינה אם היא חייבת לאחרים דאם יש בגר בקבר פקע אב אע"ג דאדם מוריש קנס דנוטלין בעלי חובות כלום דלא פקע אב והקנס הוא שלו ולא שלה ויש לומר [י] דהכא ה"מ לאקשויי והא אין מורשת קנס לבנה אלא דעדיפא מיניה פריך ור"י מוקי הך בעיא דהכא בבושת ופגם דממונא הוי ויכולה להוריש ואע"ג דתנן בריש נערה (שם מא:) לא הספיקה לעמוד בדין עד שמת האב הרי הן של עצמה ואבושת ופגם נמי קאי מדקתני הרי הן משמע דאין יכול להוריש בושת ופגם ואור"י דלענין זה ודאי איתקוש בושת ופגם לקנס דכתיב תחת אשר ענה מכלל דאיכא בושת ופגם דלמי שזה ניתן זה ניתן אבל למילי אחריני לא איתקוש דהא בושת ופגם משלם ע"פ עצמו וקנס אינו משלם ע"פ עצמו אבל הקשה ריב"ס דאמרינן במרובה (ב"ק דף עא: ושם) א"ל חמשה בקר אמר רחמנא ולא חמשה תאי בקר איתיביה גנב משל אביו וטבח ומכר ואח"כ מת אביו משלם תשלומי ד' וה' והא הכא כיון דמת אביו זכה ליה במנתא דידיה וקתני דמשלם תשלומי ד' וה' ומשני הב"ע שעמד בדין משמע דאי לאו משום דחמשה בקר ולא חמשה תאי בקר הוה אתי ליה שפיר ולא הוה צריך לאוקומי בשעמד בדין אלמא דאדם מוריש קנס לבניו ומיהו יש לדחות דה"מ למימר וליטעמיך אבל קשה דמסיק לנפרא א"ל חמשה בקר אמר רחמנא ואפי' חמשה תאי בקר א"ל מאי שנא רישא ומאי שנא סיפא פירוש דקתני גנב משל אביו ומת ואח"כ טבח ומכר פטור א"ל רישא קרינן ביה וטבחו כולו באיסורא סיפא לא קרינן וטבחו כולו באיסורא משמע דאי קרינן ביה וטבחו כולו באיסורא חייב אע"ג דלא עמד בדין דאדם מוריש קנס לבניו דאי בעמד בדין לא מחייב קנס דשלו הוא טובח ומוכר ותי' ר"י דמיירי דעמד בדין ואמרו חייב אתה ליתן לו דאם הוא טובח אחרי כן חייב כדאמרינן בהגוזל (שם דף קו: ושם) ור"י הלבן תירץ דההיא דפרק נערה איירי לענין קרבן שבועה והכי פירושו דסוגיא דהתם מודינא לך לענין קרבן שבועה דרחמנא פטריה מוכחש בעמיתו בפקדון וכי קאמינא דממון הוי להורישו לבניו שאם יתבעוהו לאחר מיתת אביהן קנס שהיה חייב לאביהן שהעמידו בדין ונתחייב וכפר ונשבע והודה הואיל וכשנפל ליורשין כבר היה ממון שכבר עמד בדין ולא היה יכול להודות ולהפטר א"כ הוי דומיא דפקדון דקרא ומחייב קרבן שבועה איתיביה ר"ש אומר כו' דלאחין הוא ופירוש שאם אינו לאחין איך מתחייב הכופר קרבן שבועה על טענותם והא לאו בעל דברים דידהו הוא אלא ש"מ דלאחין הוא ומסיק כי קאמר רבה דממון הוא להורישו לבניו בשאר קנסות לענין חיוב קרבן שבועה ומסיק דאצטריך וכתש לעמדה בדין ובגרה ואחר כך מתה דמינה קא ירית מכל מקום עיקרו קנס מיקרי לגבי דידה ודידיה ולא דמי לשאר קנסות דמוריש לבניו דלגבי בניו לא הוה קנס כלל ומיהו לשון להורישו לבניו לא משמע כפירוש זה. [ועיין תוספות בבא קמא עב. ד"ה סיפא]:

שלש

תוספות רי"ד

אמר אביי בא עליה ומתה פטור שנאמר ונתן לאבי הנערה ולא לאבי מתה. פי' כגון שלא הספיק האב להעמידו בדין עד שמתה. אבל אם עמד עמו בדין ונתחייב לו אע"פ שמתה [אח"כ] נותן לאביה:

ליקוטי רש"י

כמוהר הבתולות. שהוא קצוב נ' כסף אצל התופש את הבתולה ושוכב עמה באונס שנא' (דברים כב כט) ונתן האיש השוכב עמה לאבי הנערה חמשים כסף [שמות כב, טז]. האמור באונס את הבתולה (דברים כב) קנסו הכתוב נ' כסף בשביל מוהר בתוליה. **שיהא זה כמוהר הבתולות.** הקיש הכתוב קנס המפתה לקנס האונס מה להלן נ' אף כאן נ' מה כסף האמור כאן שקלים דכתיב ישקול אף להלן שקלים דלא תימא מעות [לעיל י.]. בתולה בתולה לג"ש מה כסף האמור באונס חמשים אף מפתה חמשים ומה מפתה שקלים דכתיב ביה ישקול אף חמשים של אונס שקלים קאמר [לעיל כט:]. **חידוש הוא שחידשה תורה בקנס.** כל משפט קנס חידוש הוא הלכך אע"ג דמיקטיל נמי לא מיפטר מיניה [לעיל לד:]. בכל תשלומי קנס שאינו דין אלא גזרת מלך בעלמא וכיון דחידוש הוא וגזירת מוק. **סד"א חידוש.** אימא אע"ג דאיכא בהדה מיתה לשלם [לעיל ע"ב]. **לאבי הנערה.** משמע שהיא קיימת [לעיל כט:].

א) [עי' תוס' לקמן מה. ד"ה דלמא ותוס' יבמות נט. ד"ה הא], ב) לעיל י. [לעיל כט:], ג) [לעיל לד: לה:], ד) לעיל כט:, ה) [ועי' תוס' יבמות ע: ד"ה אלא], ו) נ"ל דהכא נמי.

תורה אור השלם

א) אִם מָאֵן יְמָאֵן אָבִיהָ לְתִתָּהּ לוֹ כֶּסֶף יִשְׁקֹל כְּמֹהַר הַבְּתוּלֹת: [שמות כב, טז]

ב) וְנָתַן הָאִישׁ הַשֹּׁכֵב עִמָּהּ לַאֲבִי הַנַּעֲרָ חֲמִשִּׁים כָּסֶף וְלוֹ תִהְיֶה לְאִשָּׁה תַּחַת אֲשֶׁר עִנָּהּ לֹא יוּכַל שַׁלְּחָהּ כָּל יָמָיו: [דברים כב, כט]

entirely,[18] and this is unacceptable! – ? –

The Gemara answers:

אָמַר רַב נַחְמָן בַּר יִצְחָק – Rav Nachman bar Yitzchak said: קְרִי בֵּיהּ ,,אֲשֶׁר לֹא אֲרוּסָה" – **Read [the verse]** (for purposes of its plain meaning) as if it were written: **"Who *is* not betrothed *(arusah)*."**[19] Accordingly, the verse does serve an exclusionary function – to deny the fine in the case of a girl who is *presently* betrothed.

The Gemara counters:

אֲרוּסָה בַּת סְקִילָה הִיא – But a betrothed girl who commits adultery **is subject to** death by **stoning,** as is her partner![20] Why, then, do we need a verse to teach that the father is not entitled to the fine?[21]

The Gemara answers:

סַלְקָא דַּעְתָּךְ אֲמִינָא – Had the Torah not stated *who is not betrothed* to exclude a girl who is presently betrothed, **it might enter your mind to say** that הוֹאִיל וְחִידּוּשׁ הוּא שֶׁחִידְּשָׁה תּוֹרָה בִּקְנָס – **since it is a novel law that the Torah innovated in [the case of] a fine,** אַף עַל גַּב דְּמִיקְטִיל מְשַׁלֵּם – **one must pay** it **even though he is executed.**[22] Hence, *who is not [presently] betrothed* is needed to teach that the principle that liability to the death penalty exempts one from monetary payment applies even in cases of fines.

The Gemara asks:

וּלְרַבָּה דְּאָמַר – But according to Rabbah, who said that חִידּוּשׁ הוּא שֶׁחִידְּשָׁה תּוֹרָה בִּקְנָס – **it is** indeed **a novel law that the Torah innovated in [the case of] a fine,** אַף עַל גַּב דְּמִיקְטִיל מְשַׁלֵּם – and therefore **even though he is executed he** still **pays,** מַאי אִיכָּא לְמֵימַר – **what is there to say?**[23]

The Gemara answers:

סָבַר לָהּ כְּרַבִּי עֲקִיבָא דְּמַתְנִיתִין – **[Rabbah] holds like** the ruling of **R' Akiva of the Mishnah.**[24]

The Gemara cites a related Tannaic dispute:

תָּנוּ רַבָּנָן – **The Rabbis taught** in a Baraisa: קְנָסָה לְמִי – **TO WHOM DOES [THE VIOLATED VICTIM'S]**[25] **FINE** belong? לְאָבִיהָ – **TO HER FATHER.** וְיֵשׁ אוֹמְרִים – **AND THERE ARE** those **WHO SAY:** לְעַצְמָהּ – It belongs **TO HER.**

The Gemara asks in astonishment:

לְעַצְמָהּ – It belongs **to her!?** אַמַּאי – But **why?!** The Torah expressly states[26] that the fine for violation is paid to the father. – ? –

The Gemara clarifies the case in dispute:

אָמַר רַב חִסְדָּא – Rav Chisda said: הָכָא בְּנַעֲרָה שֶׁנִּתְאָרְסָה וְנִתְגָּרְשָׁה עַסְקִינַן – **Here** in the Baraisa **we are dealing with a *naarah* who was betrothed and divorced,** וְקָמִיפַּלְגֵי בִּפְלוּגְתָּא דְּרַבִּי עֲקִיבָא דְּמַתְנִיתִין וְרַבִּי עֲקִיבָא דִּבְרַיְיתָא – **and [the two Tannaim] are arguing in the dispute between** the ruling of **R' Akiva of the Mishnah**[27] **and** the ruling of **R' Akiva of the Baraisa.**[28]

The Gemara discusses another aspect of the law of the fine for violation:

אָמַר אַבַּיֵי – Abaye said: בָּא עָלֶיהָ וּמֵתָה – **If one violated [a virgin *naarah*] and she died** before the violator was sued by the father and found liable by the court, פָּטוּר – **[the violator] is exempt** from paying the fine, שֶׁנֶּאֱמַר – **for it is stated:** ,,וְנָתַן . . . לַאֲבִי הַנַּעֲרָה" – ***And he*** [the violator] ***shall give . . . to the father of the naarah*** *fifty silver [coins];*[29] וְלֹא לַאֲבִי מֵתָה – the superfluous expression *the naarah* teaches that he pays a fine to the father of the *naarah,* **and not to the father of a deceased girl.**[30]

The Gemara notes:

מִלְּתָא דִּפְשִׁיטָא לֵיהּ לְאַבַּיֵי – **A matter that was obvious to Abaye**[31] מִיבַּעְיָא לֵיהּ לְרָבָא – **was a subject of inquiry to Rava,**

NOTES

18. I.e. the plain meaning of the verse – that the law of the fine is unique to a girl *who was not betrothed* – is totally ignored, for according to the Baraisa's version of R' Akiva ruling there is no difference whatsoever between a girl who was not betrothed and a girl who was previously betrothed (*Rashi*).

19. [The word ארשה, as it appears without vowels in the Torah, can be read in either the past or present tense – as אֹרָשָׂה, ***was*** *betrothed,* or אֲרֻשָׂה, ***is*** *betrothed.* Now, although the Masoretic tradition stipulates that we read אֹרָשָׂה, so that אֲשֶׁר לֹא־אֹרָשָׂה ostensibly denotes a girl *who was not* betrothed, R' Akiva nonetheless maintains that this phrase does not exclude a girl who was previously betrothed and divorced, since it is needed for the *gezeirah shavah* cited above.] And to endow the verse with a simple meaning, we can read it as if it were written: אֲשֶׁר לֹא־אֲרֻשָׂה *[a naarah] who* ***is*** *not betrothed,* which perforce excludes a *naarah* who is *presently* betrothed [whom even R' Akiva of the Baraisa concedes is not entitled to the fine, since the violator is liable to the death penalty] (*Rashi,* as explained by *Shitah Mekubetzes* ד״ה עוד נוכל לתרץ בא״ד ומלשונו של רש״י).

Rashba, Ritva and *Tos. HaRosh* explain that the Gemara is not saying that the reading of the word is actually changed from אֹרָשָׂה to אֲרֻשָׂה. Rather, we should interpret the phrase אֲשֶׁר לֹא־אֹרָשָׂה to mean: *[a naarah] who was not betrothed* [*and remains so*] – to the exclusion of a *naarah* who was betrothed and remains so. See also *Rashash.*

20. [And in our case of violation, where the betrothed girl is blameless and thus not punished for adultery, the violator alone is subject to death by stoning.] Accordingly, he is exempt from paying the fine for violation, since the verse *And there is no fatality* teaches that one who is subject to the death penalty incurs no monetary liability (*Rashi,* from Gemara above, 36b).

21. *Tosafos* take issue with the Gemara's claim that the phrase *who was not betrothed* is unnecessary. The fact that it does not teach us anything new concerning the fine for violation only indicates all the more that the phrase is free and superfluous for the *gezeirah shavah*!

Tosafos thus explain the Gemara's question as follows: If the phrase has no purpose other than for the *gezeirah shavah,* the Torah should have stated explicitly אֲשֶׁר לֹא־אֲרֻשָׂה, *[a naarah] who* ***is*** *not betrothed.* Why does the Torah state instead אֲשֶׁר לֹא־אֹרָשָׂה, *who was not betrothed,* which can be misconstrued as implying that where she was only *previously* betrothed the girl herself receives the fine (or that there is no fine)? Now, it is understandable that if אֲשֶׁר לֹא־אֹרָשָׂה in fact indicates a novel exclusion, it would not be free and superfluous for the *gezeirah shavah,* and the Torah would have to state אֲשֶׁר לֹא־אֹרָשָׂה so that we expound both forms of the word ארשה: אֲרוּשָׂה [as the plain meaning] to denote the exclusion, and אוֹרָשָׂה to denote the *gezeirah shavah.* But if, as you say, אֲשֶׁר לֹא־אֲרוּשָׂה excludes only a girl who is presently betrothed, an exclusion already known from the verse *And there is no fatality,* why take the risk of stating אֲשֶׁר לֹא־אֹרָשָׂה?

22. See above, 38a note 17.

23. How does Rabbah expound the phrase *who is not [presently] betrothed*? He cannot expound it as a Scriptural decree (גְּזֵירַת הַכָּתוּב) that one who violates a betrothed *naarah* is exempt from the fine (unlike other cases of fines), for then we should, in turn, derive from there that liability to the death penalty exempts one from payment in all other cases of fines (see *Pnei Yehoshua*).

24. And the Gemara stated in that version that since the *gezeirah shavah* does not dislodge the verse from its plain meaning entirely (see note 16 above), there is no difficulty.

25. The Gemara's understanding at this point is that the Baraisa refers to an ordinary virgin *naarah* (*Rashi*).

26. *Deuteronomy* 22:29.

27. Which states that the fine belongs to the girl.

28. Which states that the fine belongs to her father.

29. Ibid.

30. See above, 29b note 17.

31. That if a victim of violation dies before her father takes the violator to court, there is no fine.

אימא בתולה לגזירה שוה ואשר לא אורסה פרט לנערה שנתארסה ונתגרשה מסתברא אשר לא אורסה לגזירה שוה שהרי אני קורא בה נערה בתולה אדרבה בתולה לגזירה שוה שהרי אני קורא בה אשר לא אורסה מסתברא [א] הא אישתני גופה והא לא אישתני גופה ורבי יוסי הגלילי האי סברא מנא ליה נפקא ליה [ג] מדתניא [א] כסף ישקול כמוהר הבתולות שיהא זה כמוהר הבתולות ומוהר הבתולות כזה קשיא דר"ע אדר' עקיבא תרי תנאי ואליבא דר"ע בשלמא ר"ע דמתני' לא אתיא ג"ש ומפקא ליה לקרא מפשטיה לגמרי אלא לר"ע דברייתא אתיא גזירה שוה ומפקא מפשטיה לגמרי אמר רב נחמן בר יצחק קרי ביה אשר לא ארוסה ארוסה בת סקילה היא ס"ד אמינא הואיל וחידוש הוא שחידשה תורה בקנס אע"ג דמיקטיל משלם ולרבה דאמר [ג] חידוש הוא שחידשה תורה בקנס אע"ג דמיקטיל משלם מאי איכא למימר סבר לה כרבי עקיבא דמתניתין תנו רבנן קנסה למי לאביה ויש אומרים לעצמה אמאי אמר רב חסדא הכא בנערה שנתארסה ונתגרשה עסקינן וקמיפלגי בפלוגתא דר"ע דמתניתין ורבי עקיבא דברייתא [ד] אמר אביי [א] בא עליה ומתה פטור שנאמר [ב] ונתן לאבי הנערה ולא לאבי מתה מלתא דפשיטא ליה לאביי מיבעיא ליה לרבא דבעי רבא יש בגר בקבר או אין בגר בקבר יש בגר בקבר ודבנה הוי או דלמא אין בגר בקבר ודאביה הוי ומי

רש"י

אימא בתולה לגזירה שוה. ולאו למעוטי בעולה ויהא קנס לבעולה: מסתברא אשר לא אורסה לגזירה שוה. ואפי' אורסה אית לה קנס: שהרי אני קורא בה נערה בתולה. אע"פ שנתארסה ונתגרשה דהא נערה בתולה היא כדכתיב קרא אבל בעולה שאין אני קורא בה נערה בתולה אין לה קנס: אדרבה בתולה לגזירה שוה. ולאו למעוטי בעולה בזנות אלא יש לה קנס לבעולה בזנות שהרי אני קורא אותה נערה אשר לא אורסה: מסתברא. ארוסה יש לה קנס ובעולה אין לה: דהא אישתני גופה. ופגמה אין רב כל כך: והא. דנתארסה ונתגרשה לא נשתנה גופה: הא סברא. דחמשים כסף דאונס שקלים הן וכסף ישקול דמפתה יהו חמשים: כמוהר הבתולות. מנין המפורש אצל אונס דהיינו חמשים: ומוהר הבתולות. יהיו שקלים: כזה. שכתוב בו ישקול: קשיא דרבי עקיבא. דברייתא דאמר קנסה לאביה: אדרבי עקיבא. דמתני': לא אתיא גזירה שוה ומפקא לקרא מפשטיה לגמרי. דאתא פשטיה לאשמועינן הא ארוסה לעצמה וחד מתרוייהו לאפנויי אי נמי לא מופני ליכא למיפרך מידי: אלא לרבי עקיבא דברייתא וכי אתיא גזירה שוה ומפקא מפשטיה לגמרי. דלא דריש פשטא דאשר לא אורסה כלל ומשוי אורסה כלא אורסה ואם כן מיעקר משמעותיה: קרי ביה. בפשטיה אשר לא ארוסה למעוטי ארוסה: בת סקילה היא. ומלא יהיה אסון נפקא פטורא מתשלומין: קנסה למי. קא סלקא דעתך בסתם אנוסה קאי: בא עליה ומתה. לא הספיק האב להעמידו בדין עד שמתה: יש בגר בקבר. אם מתה בנערותה עד שלא עמדה בדין והגיע זמן בגרותה בקבר מי חשיב בגר או לא ולקמיה מפרש ואזיל למאי הלכתא: יש בגר בקבר. וכי היכי דאם לא הספיקה לעמוד בדין עד שבגרה תנן לקמן בפרק נערה שנתפתתה (דף מא:) דהרי הן לעצמה ולא לאביה והשתא נמי בגר בקבר מפקיע כח האב ובנה ירית לה אם יש לה בן: ומי

תוספות

[אימא בתולה לג"ש. ולא נמעט בעולה כדמשמע בסמוך נראה דר"ע דריש ג"ש מקרא דלגופיה דהיינו בתולה קמייתא ודקנס ודמפתה אבל הבתולות דריש לכתובת בתולות ולא שייך למידרשיה לג"ש ולא לשום רבוי ואייתר נער נערה הנערה וה' דהבתולות חד לחייבי לאוין ועשה וחד לחייבי לאוין וכריתות ואיכא ג' רבויין ה' דהבתולות ונער נערה הנערה חד לכדאביי וחד לחייבי עשה וחד לחייבי לאוין וכריתות דאי איכא לר"ע חד לגופיה בלא ג"ש א"כ נמעוט בעולה מההוא דלגופיה ואף על גב דבקנס ליכא אלא חד בתולה דלגופיה מגזירה שוה דמפתה יליף בתולה ולא בעולה כי היכי דיליף מפתה מאונס לענין נערה דלא כתיב במפתה]. (ת"י כ"י):

אימא בתולה לג"ש. תימה דתיקשי ליה דלימא תרוייהו לגופייהו ולא לג"ש ונראה דהש"ס קים ליה דחד מינייהו לגזירה שוה הואיל והמקראות סתומים לענין שקלים וחמשים הלכך פריך ואימא איפכא ולא פריך ואימא תרוייהו לגופייהו וכי האי גוונא איכא פ"ק דסנהדרין (דף טו.) דאמר ולא את נביא השקר אלא בב"ד של ע' ואחד מה"מ א"ר יוסי בר חנינא אתיא הזדה הזדה מזקן ממרא ופריך הא הזדה כי כתיב בקטלא הוא דכתיב וקטלא בכ"ג אלא אמר ריש לקיש גמר דבר דבר מהמראתו והשתא היכי הוה בעי למילף ולמימר רבי יוסי ברבי חנינא דאתיא הזדה הזדה אלא דהוה קים ליה דאיכא ג"ש ולא הוה ידע במאי וקאמר מסברא דאתיא הזדה הזדה: מי אתיא גזרה שוה ומפקא ליה מפשטיה לגמרי. דדיוק הא אורסה הוי שקר וקשה דבריש הערל (יבמות ד' ע.) יליף דערל אסור בתרומה מגזירה שוה דתושב ושכיר מפסח וכתיב תושב ושכיר לא יאכל בו גבי פסח משום גזירה שוה אע"פ שאינו אמת דהא תושב ושכיר אוכלין בפסח כדאמרינן התם דלא קני ליה רביה ומפקי' קרא מפשטיה טפי מהכא ואומר ר"ת דההוא תושב ושכיר איירי בערלים ולהכי לא יאכל ומוכח דלאו תושב ישראל קאמר דהא לא קני ליה רביה אלא ודאי בערל ומשום הפנאה כתביה [ה]:

ארוסה בת סקילה היא. וא"ת מאי קשיא ליה הא השתא לא נפיק קרא ממשמעותיה ואי לא איצטריך לגופיה כ"ש דניחא טפי דג"ש מופנה ואומר ר"י דהכי פירושו ארוסה בת סקילה היא וכיון דלא איצטריך למידי אלא לגזירה שוה הוה ליה למכתב אשר לא ארוסה בהדיא ואמאי שני למכתב אשר לא אורסה דליכא למטעי ולמימר הא אורסה לעצמה דבשלמא אי הוה בארוסה שום חידוש הוה אתי שפיר במה ששינה הלשון דאמרינן האי דשנה וכתב אורסה למדרש לגזירה שוה ואתא פשטיה לחידושא אבל השתא למה לי:

לאבי הנערה ולא לאבי מתה. וא"ת דבפרק נערה לקמן (דף מד:) גבי סרחה ולבסוף בגרה תידון בסקילה דרשינן הנערה שהיתה כבר ויש לומר דהתם מענינא דקרא והכא מענינא דקרא והתם ודאי אתיא לחייבה דאי לפוטרה לשתוק קרא מיניה ואנא ידענא דלא הויא בסקילה דלאו נערה היא והכא לחיובה דקנס לא איצטריך דמסברא מיחייב משעת ביאה ואי אפשר לפוטרו בולא כלום הלכך אתא לפוטרו:

יש בגר בקבר ודבנה הוי. וא"ת היכי מצי למימר שתהא מורשת קנס לבנה הא אין אדם מוריש קנס לבניו כדאמרינן ריש פרק נערה לקמן (דף מב.) ובסמוך נמי אמר יש בגר בקבר ופקע אב ואי אדם מוריש קנס כי יש בגר בקבר נמי לא פקע אב ויהא לו מתורת ירושה ומיהו הכא יש לדחות דנפקא מינה אם היא חייבת לאחרים דאם יש בגר בקבר פקע אב אע"ג דאדם מוריש קנס דטוענין בעלי חובות אבל אם אין בגר בקבר אין טוענין בעלי חובות כלום דלא פקע אב והקנס הוא שלו ולא שלה ויש לומר [ו] דהכא ה"מ לאקשויי והא אין מורשת קנס לבנה אלא דעדיפא מיניה פריך ור"י מוקי הך בעיא בבושת ופגם דממונא הוי ויכולה להוריש ואע"ג דתנן בריש נערה (שם מא:) לא הספיקה לעמוד בדין עד שמת האב הרי הן של עצמה ולבושת ופגם נמי קאי מדקתני הרי הן משמע דאין יכול להוריש בושת ופגם ואור"י דלענין זה ודאי איתקוש בושת ופגם לקנס דכתיב תחת אשר ענה מכלל דאיכא בושת ופגם דלמי שזה ניתן זה ניתן אבל למילי אחריני לא איתקוש דהא בושת ופגם משלם ע"פ עצמו וקנס אינו משלם ע"פ עצמו אבל הקשה ריב"ם דאמרינן במרובה (ב"ק דף עא: ושם) א"ל חמשה בקר אמר רחמנא ולא חמשה תלאי בקר איתיביה גנב משל אביו וטבח ומכר ואח"כ מת אביו משלם תשלומי ד' וה' והא הכא כיון דמת אביו זכה ליה במנתא דידיה וקתני משלם תשלומי ד' וה' ומשני הב"ע שעמד בדין משמע דאי לאו משום דחמשה בקר ולא חמשה תלאי בקר הוה אתי שפיר ולא הוה צריך לאוקומי בשעמד בדין אלמא דאדם מוריש קנס לבניו ומיהו יש לדחות דה"מ למימר וליטעמיך אבל קשה דמסיק לפרקא א"ל חמשה בקר אמר רחמנא ואפי' חמשה תלאי בקר א"ל מאי שנא רישא ומאי שנא סיפא פירוש דקתני רישא גנב משל אביו ומת ואח"כ טבח ומכר פטור א"ל רישא קרינן ביה וטבחו כולו באיסורא סיפא לא קרינן ביה וטבחו כולו באיסורא משמע דאי קרינן ביה וטבחו כולו באיסורא חייב אע"ג דלא עמד בדין דאדם מוריש קנס לבניו דאי בעמד בדין לא מחייב קנס דשלו הוא טובח ומוכר ותי' ר"י דמיירי דעמד בדין ואמרו חייב אתה ליתן לו דאם הוא טובח אחרי כן חייב כדאמרינן בהגוזל (שם דף קו: ושם) ור"י הלבן תירץ דההיא דפרק נערה איירי לענין קרבן שבועה והכי פירושו דסוגיא דהתם מודיענו לך לענין קרבן שבועה דרחמנא פטריה מוכחש בעמיתו בפקדון וכי קאמינא דממון הוי הורישו לבניו אם יתבעוהו לאחר מיתת אביהן קנס שהיה חייב לאביהן שהעמידו בדין ונתחייב וכפר ונשבע והודה הואיל ונפגע ליורשין כבר היה ממון שכבר עמד בדין והיה יכול להודות ולהפטר א"כ הוי דומיא דפקדון דקרא ומחייב קרבן שבועה איתיביה ר"ש אומר כו' דלאחין הוא ואי לאחין איך מתחייב הכופר קרבן שבועה על טענותם והא לאו בעל דברים דידהו הוא אלא ש"מ דלאחין הוא ומסיק כי קאמר רבה דממון הוא להורישו לבניו קאמר ולענין קנסות לענין חיוב קרבן שבועה ומסיק דלאצטריך לעמדה בדין ובגרה ואחר כך מתה דקא ירית מקום שעיקרו קנס מיקרי לגבי דידה ודידיה ולא דמי לשאר קנסות דמוריש לבניו דלגבי בניו לא הוה קנס כלל ומיהו לשון להורישו לבניו לא משמע כפירוש זה. [ועיין תוספות בבא קמא עב. ד"ה סיפא]:

שלש

עין משפט נר מצוה

סח א מיי' פ"ב מהל' נערה הלכה טו סמג עשין נד טור אה"ע סימן קעז:

תוספות רי"ד

אמר אביי בא עליה ומתה פטור שנאמר ונתן לאבי הנערה ולא לאבי מתה. פי' כגון שלא הספיק האב להעמידו בדין עד שמתה. אבל אם עמד עמו בדין ונתחייב לו אע"פ שמתה [אח"כ] נותן לאביה.

ליקוטי רש"י

כמוהר הבתולות. שכתוב כסף ככר אבל התופש את הבתולה ושוכב עמה באונס שנא' (דברים כב כט) ונתן האיש השוכב עמה לאבי הנערה חמשים כסף [שמות כב, טז]. את הבתולה (דברים כב) קנסו הכתוב נ' כסף בשביל מוהר בתולה. שיהא זה כמוהר הבתולות. הקיש הכתוב קנס המפתה לקנס האונס מה להלן נ' אף כאן נ' ומה כסף האמור כאן שקלים אף האמור להלן שקלים [לעיל י.]. בתולה בתולה לג"ש מה כסף האמור באונס חמשים ומה מכתה שקלים דכתיב כאן ישקול אף חמשים של אונס שקלים קאמר [לעיל כט:]. חידוש הוא שחידשה תורה בקנס. כל משפט קנס חידוש הוא הלכך אע"ג דמיקטיל לא מיפטר מיניה [לעיל ל:]. בכל תשלומי קנס שאינו דין אלא גזרת מלך בעלמא וכיון דחידוש הוא וגזירת מלך הוא לא דרשו. אימא אע"ג דאיכא בהדיה מיתה לשלם [לעיל ע"א]. לאבי הנערה. משמע שהיא קיימת [לעיל כט:].

מסורת הש"ס

א) [עי' תוס' לקמן מה. ד"ה דלמא ותוס' יבמות נט. ד"ה הא], ב) לעיל י., ג) [לעיל כט:], ד) לעיל לד:, ה) [ועי' תוס' יבמות ע: ד"ה אלא], ו) נ"ל דהכא נמי.

תורה אור השלם

א) אִם מָאֵן יְמָאֵן אָבִיהָ לְתִתָּהּ לוֹ כֶּסֶף יִשְׁקֹל כְּמֹהַר הַבְּתוּלֹת: [שמות כב, טז]

ב) וְנָתַן הָאִישׁ הַשֹּׁכֵב עִמָּהּ לַאֲבִי הַנַּעֲרָ חֲמִשִּׁים כָּסֶף וְלוֹ תִהְיֶה לְאִשָּׁה תַּחַת אֲשֶׁר עִנָּהּ לֹא יוּכַל שַׁלְּחָהּ כָּל יָמָיו: [דברים כב, כט]

אֵימָא – **Say** instead that "בְּתוּלָה" לִגְזֵירָה שָׁוָה – the common word ***virgin*** is expounded **for the *gezeirah shavah***[1] "וַאֲשֶׁר לֹא אֹרָשָׂה" – **and** the phrase ***who was not betrothed*** teaches with regard to the fine: פְּרָט לְנַעֲרָה שֶׁנִּתְאָרְסָה וְנִתְגָּרְשָׁה – **to the exclusion of a *naarah* who was betrothed and divorced** – i.e. she is indeed excluded from the fine![2] – ? –

The Gemara answers:

מִסְתַּבְּרָא "אֲשֶׁר לֹא אֹרָשָׂה" לִגְזֵירָה שָׁוָה – **It is logical** to expound ***who was not betrothed*** **for the *gezeirah shavah*** and thereby say that even a *naarah* who was betrothed and divorced is entitled to the fine, שֶׁהֲרֵי אֲנִי קוֹרֵא בָּהּ "נַעֲרָה בְתוּלָה" – **for indeed I can apply** the verse, ***a virgin naarah,* to her.**[3]

The Gemara counters:

אַדְּרַבָּה – **On the contrary!** "בְּתוּלָה" לִגְזֵירָה שָׁוָה – It makes sense to expound ***virgin*** **for the *gezeirah shavah*** and thereby say that even a non-virgin[4] is entitled to the fine, שֶׁהֲרֵי אֲנִי קוֹרֵא בָּהּ "אֲשֶׁר לֹא אֹרָשָׂה" – **for indeed I can apply** the verse, ***who was not betrothed,* to her.**[5] – ? –

The Gemara answers:

מִסְתַּבְּרָא – **It is logical** to say that a previously betrothed girl has the fine and a non-virgin does not have it, הָא אִישְׁתַּנֵּי גּוּפָהּ – for **this one's** [the non-virgin's] **body had changed** prior to the violation[6] וְהָא לֹא אִישְׁתַּנֵּי גּוּפָהּ – **and this** other **one's body had not changed.**[7]

The Gemara now inquires regarding R' Yose HaGlili's approach:

וְרַבִּי יוֹסֵי הַגְּלִילִי – **But R' Yose HaGlili,** who has other uses for the word *virgin* and the phrase *who was not betrothed*[8] – הַאי סְבָרָא מְנָא לֵיהּ – **from where does he [derive] this teaching** that the "fifty coins" prescribed as the fine for violation are *shekalim* and the "*shekalim*" prescribed as the fine for seduction are fifty in number?[9]

The Gemara answers:

נַפְקָא לֵיהּ מִדְּתַנְיָא – **He derives it from** that **which was taught in a Baraisa:** "כֶּסֶף יִשְׁקֹל כְּמֹהַר הַבְּתוּלֹת" – The Torah states:[10] ***[THE SEDUCER] SHALL PAY OUT SILVER SHEKALIM IN THE AMOUNT OF THE SETTLEMENT [MADE] TO THE VIRGINS.*** שֶׁיְּהֵא זֶה כְּמוֹהַר הַבְּתוּלוֹת – This teaches **THAT THIS** award for seduction **SHOULD BE LIKE THE SETTLEMENT [MADE] TO THE VIRGINS,**[11] וּמוֹהַר הַבְּתוּלוֹת כָּזֶה – **AND** that **THE MARRIAGE CONTRACT OF THE VIRGINS** shall be paid in *shekalim* coins, **LIKE THIS** award for seduction.[12]

The Gemara now notes an obvious contradiction:

קַשְׁיָא דְּרַבִּי עֲקִיבָא אַדְּרַבִּי עֲקִיבָא – The ruling **of R' Akiva** in the Baraisa[13] **contradicts** the ruling **of R' Akiva** in the Mishnah.[14] – ? –

The Gemara explains:

תְּרֵי תַּנָּאֵי וְאַלִּיבָּא דְּרַבִּי עֲקִיבָא – The conflicting statements of the Mishnah and Baraisa are made by **two** different **Tannaim, and** they disagree **about the opinion of R' Akiva.**

The Gemara now challenges the Baraisa's version of the ruling:

בִּשְׁלָמָא רַבִּי עֲקִיבָא דְּמַתְנִיתִין – Now, **it is well according to** the ruling of **R' Akiva of the Mishnah,** that the fine for violating a previously betrothed *naarah* is paid to the girl and not to her father, לֹא אַתְיָא גְּזֵירָה שָׁוָה וּמַפְקָא לֵיהּ לִקְרָא מִפְּשָׁטֵיהּ לְגַמְרֵי – for according to this version **the *gezeirah shavah***[15] **does not come and dislodge the verse from its plain meaning entirely.**[16] אֶלָּא לְרַבִּי עֲקִיבָא דִּבְרַיְיתָא – **But according to** the ruling of **R' Akiva of the Baraisa,** that in this case too the fine is paid to the father,[17] אַתְיָא גְּזֵירָה שָׁוָה וּמַפְקָא לֵיהּ מִפְּשָׁטֵיהּ לְגַמְרֵי – **the *gezeirah shavah* comes and dislodges the verse from its plain meaning**

NOTES

1. [The common word בְּתוּלָה (*virgin*) appears in both the violation (*Deuteronomy* 22:28) and the seduction (*Exodus* 22:15) passages. Say, then, that the *gezeirah shavah,* which teaches the quantity and type of coin paid as the fine for these two violations, comes from the word *virgin.*] Accordingly, *virgin* is not an exclusionary term, and so a non-virgin would be entitled to the fine for violation (*Rashi*).

2. *Tosafos* question why the Gemara does not ask: Let each term come for its own exclusionary teaching, so that neither is free for the *gezeirah shavah*?! See there for their answer.

Shitah Mekubetzes asks further: How can the Gemara suggest that the *gezeirah shavah* comes from the word *virgin* instead of from the term אשר לא ארשה? *Gezeirah shavah* teachings are a received tradition from Sinai, and no sage may innovate his own. See there for two approaches.

3. The Gemara is saying that we should presume the operative phrase to be נַעֲרָה בְתוּלָה (*virgin naarah*); it includes, then, all girls who fit these requirements, even if they were previously betrothed and divorced (*Rashi*). See *Shitah Mekubetzes* regarding why, at this point in the Gemara, this presumption would be made.

4. Who was never betrothed, and lost her virginity through promiscuous behavior (*Rashi*).

5. The Gemara counters that logic equally dictates that we presume the operative phrase to be ***who was not betrothed;*** it includes, then, all girls who fit this description, even if they are no longer virgins (see *Rashi* and *Shitah Mekubetzes*).

6. Since she lost her virginity prior to the violation the violation, did not blemish her considerably (*Rashi*).

7. [Although the other one had been betrothed and divorced, she was still a virgin at the time of the violation. Hence, she is more deserving of the fine than is a non-virgin.]

8. He expounds *virgin* to exclude a non-virgin from the fine for violation, and *who was not betrothed* to exclude a previously betrothed *naarah.* Hence, neither verse is available for the *gezeirah shavah* teaching.

9. See above, 38a note 35.

10. *Exodus* 22:16, which appears in the seduction passage.

11. I.e. fifty coins in number, as stated expressly in the passage concerning violation [*Deuteronomy* 22:29] (*Rashi;* see above, 29b note 19).

12. For the seduction verse (quoted in the Baraisa) states יִשְׁקֹל (*yishkol*), which indicates that the fine is to be paid in *shekalim* (see *Rashi*).

13. That the fine for violating a previously betrothed and divorced *naarah* is paid to her father (*Rashi*).

14. That the fine is paid to the girl herself.

15. I.e. the fact that R' Akiva expounds *who was not betrothed* for the *gezeirah shavah* rather than use it to exclude a previously betrothed *naarah* from the fine for violation.

16. The verse states that the fine is paid to the father when the victim of violation is *a virgin naarah who was not betrothed.* Although R' Akiva does not use *who was not betrothed* to exclude the case of a previously betrothed girl from the fine itself (since he needs that phrase for the *gezeirah shavah*), he does use it to exclude that case from one aspect of the fine: The phrase teaches that where the girl had been betrothed, the father no longer receives the fine; [rather, she receives it]. Hence, according to the Mishnah's version of R' Akiva's ruling, the "verse" *who was not betrothed* retains some of its implicit exclusionary impact (*Rashi*).

Rashi notes, further, that although according to this version the phrase *who was not betrothed* is not completely free [i.e. superfluous] for the *gezeirah shavah,* since it is needed to exclude the father from receiving the fine, the teaching is still considered a *gezeirah shavah mufneh [mitzad echad],* a *gezeirah shavah* in which *one of its components is free and superfluous* [see above, 32b note 4]. This is because *who is not betrothed* is stated twice, once in the violation passage and again in the seduction passage. Furthermore, even if the *gezeirah shavah* were considered not *mufneh* [free and superfluous] at all, it would nonetheless be a valid *gezeirah shavah,* since no logical argument can be made to differentiate between a violator and a seducer [see ibid.] (*Rashi*).

17. So that the penalty stated in the verse applies in the case of a previously betrothed girl in the very same manner it applies in the case of a girl *who was not betrothed.*

סח א מיי' פ"א מהל' נערה הלכה טו: סמג עשין נד טור אה"ע סימן קעז:

תוספות רי"ד

אמר אביי בא עליה ומתה פטור שנאמר ונתן לאבי הנערה ולא לאבי מתה. פי' כגון שלא הספיק האב להעמידו בדין עד שמתה. אבל אם עמד עמו בדין ונתחייב לו אע"פ שמתה האב[א"כ] נותן לאביה:

ליקוטי רש"י

כמוהר הבתולות. שהוא קצוב נ' כסף אצל התופש את הבתולה דכתיב ונתן האיש השכב עמה לאבי הנערה חמשים כסף [דברים כב, כט]. המאור במאנס את הבתולה [דברים כב] קצוב נ' כסף בבעיל מוהר במוליה. שיהא זה כמוהר הבתולות. הקיש הכתוב קנס המפתה לקנס האונס מה להלן נ' אף כאן נ' ומה כסף האמור כאן שקלים דכתיב ישקול אף להלן שקלים [לעיל י.]. בתולה בתולה לג"ש מה כסף האמור באונס חמשים ומה מפתה שקלים דכתיב ביה ישקול אף אונס חמשים שקלים קאמר [לעיל כט.]. חידוש הוא שחידשה תורה בקנס. כל משפט קנס חידוש הוא הלכך אע"ג דמיקטיל נמי לא מיפטר מיניה [לעיל לד:]. חידוש. שלא לדון בו כשאר דין וגזרה עליו תורה לשלם. ומיהו לא קנס שאינו מתחייב בדין אלא בעמידת בדין. חידוש הוא. אע"ג דאיכא קטלא דהרי אינו משלם. מיתה פטור. לאבי הנערה. משמע שהיא קיימת [לעיל כט.].

אימא בתולה לגזירה שוה ואשר לא אורסה פרט לנערה שנתארסה ונתגרשה מסתברא אשר לא אורסה לגזירה שוה שהרי אני קורא בה נערה בתולה אדרבה בתולה לגזירה שוה שהרי אני קורא בה אשר לא אורסה מסתברא [ה] הא אישתני גופה והא לא אישתני גופה ורבי יוסי הגלילי האי סברא מנא ליה נפקא ליה [ו] מדתניא [א] כסף ישקול כמוהר הבתולות שיהא זה כמוהר הבתולות ומוהר הבתולות כזה קשיא דר"ע אדר"ע תרי תנאי ואליבא דר"ע בשלמא ר"ע דמתני' לא אתיא ג"ש ומפקא ליה לקרא מפשטיה לגמרי אלא לר"ע דברייתא אתיא גזירה שוה ומפקא מפשטיה לגמרי אמר רב נחמן בר יצחק קרי ביה אשר לא ארוסה ארוסה בת סקילה היא ס"ד אמינא הואיל וחידוש הוא שחידשה תורה בקנס אע"ג דמיקטיל משלם ולרבה דאמר [ז] חידוש הוא שחידשה תורה בקנס אע"ג דמיקטיל משלם מאי איכא למימר סבר לה כרבי עקיבא דמתניתין תנו רבנן קנסה למי לאביה ויש אומרים לעצמה אמאי אמר רב חסדא הכא בנערה שנתארסה ונתגרשה עסקינן וקמיפלגי בפלוגתא דר"ע דמתניתין ורבי עקיבא דברייתא [ח] אמר אביי [א] בא עליה ומתה פטור שנאמר [ב] ונתן לאבי הנערה ולא לאבי מתה מלתא דפשיטא ליה לאביי מיבעיא ליה לרבא דבעי רבא יש בגר בקבר או אין בגר בקבר יש בגר בקבר ודבנה הוי או דלמא אין בגר בקבר ודאביה הוי ומי

רש"י

אימא בתולה לגזירה שוה. ולאו למעוטי בעולה והלא קנס לבעולה: מסתברא אשר לא אורסה לגזירה שוה. ואפי' אורסה אית לה קנס: שהרי אני קורא בה נערה בתולה. אע"פ שנתארסה ונתגרשה דהא בעולה שאין אני קורא בה נערה בתולה אין לה קנס: אדרבה בתולה לגזירה שוה. ולאו למעוטי בעולה בזנות אלא יש לה קנס לבעולה בזנות שהרי אני קורא אותה נערה אשר לא אורסה: מסתברא. ארוסה יש לה קנס ובעולה אין לה: דהא אישתני גופה. ופגמא אין רב כל כך: והא. דנתארסה ונתגרשה לא נשתנה גופה: הא סברא. דמחמשים כסף דאונס שקלים הן וכסף ישקול דמפתה יהו חמשים: כמוהר הבתולות. מנין המפורש אצל אונס דהיינו חמשים: ומוהר הבתולות. יהיו שקלים: כזה. שכתוב בו ישקול: קשיא דרבי עקיבא. דברייתא דאמר קנסה לאביה: אדרבי עקיבא. דמתני': לא אתיא גזירה שוה ומפקא לקרא מפשטיה לגמרי. דלאו פשטיה לאשמועינן הא ארוסה לעצמה וחד מתרוייהו לאפנויי אי נמי לא מופני ליכא למיפרך מידי: אלא לרבי עקיבא דברייתא וכי אתיא גזירה שוה ומפקא מפשטיה לגמרי. דלא דריש פשטא דאשר לא אורסה כלל ומשוי אורסה כלא אורסה ואם כן מיעקר משמעותיה: קרי ביה. בפשטיה אשר לא ארוסה למעוטי ארוסה: בת סקילה היא. ומלא יהיה אסון נפקא פטורא מתשלומין: קנסה למי. קא סלקא דעתך בפתח אונסה קאי: בא עליה ומתה. לא הספיק האב להעמידו בדין עד שמתה: יש בגר בקבר. אם מתה בנערותה על שלא עמדה בדין והגיע זמן בגרותה בקבר מי חשיב בגר או לא ולקמיה מפרש ואזיל למאי הלכתא: יש בגר בקבר. וכי היכי דאם לא הספיקה לעמוד בדין עד שבגרה תנן לקמן בפרק נערה שנתפתתה (דף מא:) דהרי הן לעצמה ולא לאביה והשתא נמי בגר בקבר מפקיע כח האב ובנה ירית לה אם יש לה בן: ומי

תוספות

אימא בתולה לג"ש. ולא נמעט בעולה דמשמע בסמוך נראה דר"ע דריש ג"ש מקרא דלגופיה דהיינו בתולה קמייתא דקנס ודמפתה אבל הבתולות דריש לכתובת בתולות ולא שייך למדרשיה לג"ש ולא לשום דבר ואימר נער נערה הנערה וה' דהבתולות חד לחייבי לאוין ועשה וחד לחייבי לאוין וכריתות ומילא ג' רבויין ה' דהבתולות ונער נערה הנערה חד לכלאביי וחד לחייבי עשה וחד לחייבי לאוין וכריתות דאי איכא לר"ע חד לגופיה בלא ג"ש א"כ נמעט בעולה מההוא לגופיה ואף על גב דבקנס ליכא אלא חד בתולה לגופיה מגזירה שוה דמפתה יליף בתולה ולא בעולה כי היכי דיליף מפתה מאונס לענין נערה דלא כתיב במפתה. (תו"י):

אימא בתולה לג"ש. תימה דתיקשי ליה לימא תרוייהו לגופייהו ולא לג"ש ונראה דהש"ס קים ליה דחד מינייהו לגזירה שוה הואיל והמקראות סתומים לענין שקלים וחמשים הלכך פריך ולימא איפכא ולא פריך ולימא תרוייהו לגופייהו וכי האי גוונא איכא פ"ק דסנהדרין (דף טז.) דאמר ולא את נביא השקר אלא בב"ד של ע' ואחד מה"מ א"ר יוסי בר חנינא אתיא הזדה הזדה מזקן ממרא ופריך הא הזדה כי כתיב בקטלה הוא דכתיב וקטלה בכ"ג אלא אמר ריש לקיש גמר דבר דבר מהמראתו והשתא היכי הוה בעי למילף ולמימר רבי יוסי ברבי חנינא דאתיא הזדה הזדה אלא דהוה קים ליה דאיכא ג"ש ולא הוה ידע במאי וקאמר מסברא דאתיא הזדה הזדה: **מי** אתיא גזרה שוה ומפקא ליה מפשטיה לגמרי. דדיוק הא אורסה הוי שקר וקשה דבריש הערל (יבמות ד' ע.) יליף דערל אסור בתרומה מגזירה שוה דתושב ושכיר מפסח וכתיב תושב ושכיר לא יאכל בו גבי פסח משום גזירה שוה אע"פ שאינו אמת דהא תושב ושכיר אוכלין בפסח כדאמרינן התם דלא קני ליה רביה ומפקי' קרא מפשטיה טפי מהכא ואומר ר"ת דההוא תושב ושכיר מיירי בערלים ולהכי לא יאכל ומוכח דלאו תושב ישראל קאמר דהא לא קני ליה רביה אלא ודאי בערל ומשום הפנאה כתביה [ט]:

ארוסה בת סקילה היא. וא"ת מאי קשיא ליה הא השתא לא נפיק קרא ממשמעותיה ואי לא איצטריך לגופיה כ"ש דניחא טפי דג"ש מופנה ואומר ר"י דהכי פירושו ארוסה בת סקילה היא וכיון דלא איצטריך למידי אלא לגזירה שוה הוה ליה למכתב אשר לא ארוסה בהדיא ואמאי שני למכתב אשר לא אורסה דאיכא למטעי ולמימר הא אורסה לעצמה דבשלמא אי הוה בארוסה שום חידוש הוה אתי שפיר במה ששינה הלשון דאמרינן האי דשנה וכתב אורסה למדרש לגזירה שוה ואתא פשטיה לחידושא אבל השתא למה לי: **לאבי** הנערה ולא לאבי מתה. וא"ת דבפרק נערה לקמן (דף מה:) גבי סרחה ולבסוף בגרה תידון בסקילה דרשינן הנערה שהיתה כבר ויש לומר דהתם מעינא דקרא והכא מעינא דקרא והתם ודאי אתיא לחייבה דאי לפוטרה לשתוק קרא מיניה ואנא ידענא דלא הויא בסקילה דלאו נערה היא והכא לחיובא דקנס לא אצטריך דמסברא מיחייב אשעת ביאה ואי אפשר לפוטרו בולא כלום הלכך אתא לפוטרו: **יש** בגר בקבר ודבנה הוי. וא"ת היכי מצי למימר שתהא מורשת קנס לבנה הא אין אדם מוריש קנס לבניו כדאמרינן ריש פרק נערה לקמן (דף מב:) ובסמוך נמי אמר יש בגר בקבר ופקע אב ואי אדם מוריש קנס כי יש בגר בקבר נמי לא פקע אב ויהא לו מתורת ירושה ומיהו ההיא דבסמוך יש לדחות דנפקא מינה אם היא חייבת לאחרים דאם יש בגר בקבר פקע אב אע"ג דאדם מוריש קנס דנוטלין בעלי חובות אבל אם אין בגר בקבר אין נוטלין בעלי חובות כלום דלא פקע אב והקנס הוא שלו ולא שלה ויש לומר [י] דהכא ה"מ לאקשויי והא אין מורשת קנס לבנה אלא דעדיפא מיניה פריך ור"י מוקי הך בעיא דהכא בבושת ופגם דממונא הוי ויכולה להוריש ואע"ג דתנן בריש נערה (שם מא:) לא הספיקה לעמוד בדין עד שמת האב הרי הן של עצמה ואבושת ופגם נמי קאי מדקתני הרי הן משמע דאין יכול להוריש בושת ופגם ואור"י דלענין זה ודאי איתקוש בושת ופגם לקנס דכתיב תחת אשר ענה מכלל דאיכא בושת ופגם דלמי שזה ניתן זה ניתן אבל למילי אחריני לא איתקוש דהא בושת ופגם משלם ע"פ עצמו וקנס אינו משלם ע"פ עצמו אבל הקשה ריב"ם דאמרינן במרובה (ב"ק דף עא: ושם) א"ל חמשה בקר אמר רחמנא ולא חמשה חצאי בקר איתיביה גנב משל אביו וטבח ומכר ואח"כ מת אביו משלם תשלומי ד' וה' והא הכא כיון דמת אביו זכה ליה במנתא דידיה וקתני דמשלם תשלומי ד' וה' ומשני הב"ע שעמד בדין משמע דאי לאו משום דחמשה בקר ולא חמשה חצאי בקר הוה אתי ליה שפיר ולא הוה נריך לאוקומי בשעמד בדין אלמא דאדם מוריש קנס לבניו ומיהו יש לדחות דה"מ למימר וליטעמיך אבל קשה דמסיק לנפרא א"ל חמשה בקר אמר רחמנא ואפי' חמשה חצאי בקר א"ל מאי שנא רישא ומאי שנא סיפא פירוש דקתני גנב משל אביו ומת ואח"כ טבח ומכר פטור א"ל רישא קרינן ביה וטבחו כולו באיסורא סיפא לא קרינן וטבחו כולו באיסורא משמע דאי קרינן ביה וטבחו כולו באיסורא חייב אע"ג דלא עמד בדין דאדם מוריש קנס לבניו דאי בעמד בדין לא מחייב קנס דשלו הוא טובח ומוכר ותי' ר"י דמיירי דעמד בדין ואמרו חייב אתה ליתן לו דאם הוא טובח אחרי כן חייב כדאמרינן בהגוזל (שם דף קו: ושם) ור"י הלבן תירץ דההיא דפרק נערה איירי לענין קרבן שבועה והכי פירושו דסוגיא דהתם מודינא לך לענין קרבן שבועה דרחמנא פטריה מוכחש בעמיתו בפקדון וכי קאמינא דממון הוי להורישו לבניו שאם יתבעוהו לאחר מיתת אביהן קנס שהיה חייב לאביהן שהעמידו בדין ונתחייב וכפר ונשבע והודה הואיל וכשנפל ליורשין כבר היה ממון שכבר עמד בדין ולא היה יכול להודות ולהפטר א"כ הוי דומיא דפקדון דקרא ומחייב קרבן שבועה איתיביה ר"ש אומר כו' דאחין הוא ופירוש שאם אינו לאחין איך מתחייב הכופר קרבן שבועה על טענותם והא לאו בעל דברים דידהו הוא אלא ש"מ דאחין הוא ומסיק כי קאמר רבה דממון הוא להורישו לבניו בשאר קנסות לענין חיוב קרבן שבועה ומסיק דאצטריך וכתש עמדה בדין ובגרה ואחר כך מתה דמינה קא ירית מכל מקום עיקרו קנס מיקרי לגבי דידה ודידיה ולא דמי לשאר קנסות דמוריש לבניו דלגבי בניו לא הוה קנס כלל ומיהו לשון להורישו לבניו לא משמע כפירוש זה. [ועיין תוספות בבא קמא עב. ד"ה סיפא]:

מסורת הש"ס

א) [עי' תוס' לקמן מה. ד"ה דלמא ותוס' יבמות נט. ד"ה הא], ב) לעיל י. [לעיל כט.], ג) [לעיל לד: לה:], ד) לעיל כט:, ה) [עי' תוס' יבמות ע. ד"ה אלא], ו) נ"ל דהכא נמי.

תורה אור השלם

א) אִם מָאֵן יְמָאֵן אָבִיהָ לְתִתָּהּ לוֹ כֶּסֶף יִשְׁקֹל כְּמֹהַר הַבְּתוּלֹת: [שמות כב, טז]

ב) וְנָתַן הָאִישׁ הַשֹּׁכֵב עִמָּהּ לַאֲבִי הַנַּעֲרָ חֲמִשִּׁים כָּסֶף וְלוֹ תִהְיֶה לְאִשָּׁה תַּחַת אֲשֶׁר עִנָּהּ לֹא יוּכַל שַׁלְּחָהּ כָּל יָמָיו: [דברים כב, כט]

שלם

הני מילי היכא דהרגו דרך עלייה ^א^ שלא ניתנה שגגתו לכפרה אבל הרגו דרך ירידה דניתנה שגגתו לכפרה אימא נישקול ממונא מיניה וניפטריה קמ"ל א"ל רבא הא מדתנא דבי חזקיה נפקא ^ו^ דתנא דבי חזקיה ^א^ מכה אדם ומכה בהמה מה מכה בהמה לא חלקת בו בין שוגג למזיד בין מתכוין לשאין מתכוין בין דרך ירידה לדרך עלייה לפוטרו ממון אלא לחייבו ממון אף מכה אדם לא תחלוק בו בין שוגג למזיד • בין מתכוין לשאין מתכוין בין דרך ירידה לדרך עליה לחייבו ממון אלא לפוטרו ממון אלא אמר רמי בר חמא איצטריך ס"ד אמינא ה"מ היכא דסימא את עינו והרגו בה אבל היכא דסימא את עינו והרגו בדבר אחר אימא נישקול ממונא מיניה א"ל רבא הא נמי מאידך תנא דבי חזקיה נפקא ^ג^ דתנא דבי חזקיה ^ב^ עין תחת עין ^ב^ ולא עין ונפש תחת עין אלא אמר רב אשי איצטריך ס"ד אמינא הואיל וחידוש הוא שחידשה תורה בקנס אע"ג דמיקטיל משלם קמ"ל ולרבה דאמר ^ג^ חידוש הוא שחידשה תורה בקנס אע"ג דמיקטיל משלם האי ^ג^ כל חרם מאי עביד ליה סבר לה כתנא קמא דר' חנניא בן עקביא: **מתני'** נערה שנתארסה ונתגרשה רבי יוסי הגלילי אומר אין לה קנס ר"ע אומר ^ד^ יש לה קנס וקנסה לעצמה: **גמ'** מ"ט דר' יוסי הגלילי אמר קרא ^ד^ אשר לא אורשה הא אורסה אין לה קנס ור"ע אשר לא אורשה לאביה הא אורסה לעצמה אלא מעתה נערה ולא בוגרת ה"נ דלעצמה בתולה ולא בעולה ה"נ דלעצמה אלא לגמרי הכא נמי לגמרי אמר לך ר"ע האי לא אורשה מיבעי ליה לכדתניא אשר לא אורשה פרט לנערה שנתארסה ונתגרשה שאין לה קנס דברי ר' יוסי הגלילי ר"ע אומר יש לה קנס וקנסה לאביה והדין נותן הואיל ואביה זכאי בכסף קידושיה ואביה זכאי בכסף קנסה ^ד^ מה כסף קידושיה אע"פ שנתארסה ונתגרשה לאביה אף כסף קנסה אע"פ שנתארסה ונתגרשה לאביה א"כ מה ת"ל אשר לא אורשה מופנה להקיש לו ולדון הימנו ג"ש נאמר כאן אשר לא אורשה ונאמר להלן ^ה^ אשר לא אורשה מה כאן נ' אף להלן נ' ומה להלן שקלים אף כאן שקלים ור"ע מאי חזית דאשר לא אורשה לג"ש ובתולה למעוטי בעולה

הני מילי. דלא תקמו כופר לפטור רוצח מזיד מקטלא: היכא דהרגו. במזיד דרך עלייה שהנפת ידו הכהו מאחריו דכוותה בשוגג לא ניתן לכפרת גלות דכתיב ויפל דרך נפילה: מדתנא דבי חזקיה נפקא. שאין חילוק בין דרך עלייה לדרך ירידה: לחייבו ממון. והוא הדין לפדותו ולא יהיה אסון מיהא איצטריך דאי מהיקישא הוה אמינא אדרבה לאידך גיסא מה מכה בהמה לעולם ישלם אף מכה אדם ישלם והשתא דנפקא לן פטור תשלומין למזיד מלא יהיה אסון על כרחך היקישא לפטור שוגג לדרך עליה: הכי גרסינן **אלא אמר רמי בר חמא** כו'. איצטריך חד מהני קראי לאשמועינן דלא ליעביד ליה תרתי ואף על גב דנפקא לן מולא יהיה אסון: הני מילי. דלא ענשינן ליה בתרתי היכא דסימא את עינו והרגו בה בלאותה מכה ומת: בדבר אחר. במכה אחרת ובבת אחת: אימא. ליענשיה דמי עין ומיתה בשביל הריגה: הא. דסימא עינו והרגו בה: מאידך דבי חזקיה נפקא. דלא תיענשיה: **ולא** עין ונפש תחת עין. מיניה קיימא לן בהחובל דעין תחת עין לאו ממש דלא אמרת ממש דלמאה בהדי דסמינן לעינייה מיית והוה ליה עין ונפש תחת עין מיהו שמעינן מינה דלא תעביד ביה תרתי לא שנא מת בלאותה מכה לא שנא לא מת: **סלקא דעתך אמינא** חידוש הוא שחידשה תורה. בכל תשלומי קנס שאינו דין אלא גזרת מלך בעלמא וכיון דחידוש הוא וגזירת חוק אימא אע"ג דאיכא בהדיה מיתה לשלם: קמ"ל. חד מהנך קראי יתירא שאינו ענין לממון תניהו ענין לקנס: כתנא קמא. ודריש ליה בלאומר ערכו של יוצא ליהרג עלי: **מתני'** שנתארסה ונתגרשה. דאילו ארוסה שלא נתגרשה חייב מיתה ואין שם קנס: אין לה קנס. טעמא מפרש בגמרא וריש דקתני אשת אחיו ואשת אחי אביו דנתארסה ונתגרשה עסקינן וקתני יש להן קנס ר' עקיבא היא: **גמ'** אלא מעתה. לר' עקיבא הא דכתיב נערה למעוטי בוגרת ובתולה למעוטי בעולה: הכי נמי. דלא ממעטו לגמרי ותדרוש נערה לאביה הא בוגרת לעצמה הא לא אשכחן לאשמועינן תנא ומתני בוגרת יש לה קנס ומימא רבי עקיבא היא: וקנסה לאביה. ולקמן מקשינן דר"ע אדר"ע: הואיל ואביה זכאי בכסף קידושיה. שלו הוא בנערותה ולקמן יליף לה בפרק נערה שנתפתתה (דף מו:): מה כסף קידושיה אף על פי שנתארסה ונתגרשה. מאחר כשחזרת ומתקדשת בתוך נערות: לאביה הוי. דהא כל קידושי נערות ילפינן לאביה דגבי קידושין לא כתיב מיעוטא דאשר לא אורסה כי הכא: נאמר כאן. באונס: להלן. במפתה: מה להלן. במפתה שקלים דכתיב ישקול:

הני מילי היכא דהרגו דרך עלייה דלא ניתן שגגתו לכפרה. פירוש לכפרה בידי אדם אע"ג דדרך עלייה קיל טפי מדרך ירידה כדמוכח בפרק אלו הן הגולין (מכות דף ט. ושם) גבי גר תושב גולה ע"י גר תושב וכל חומרי דשמעתין לא תלי אלא במה שלא ניתן לכפרה דאינו מקפיד הש"ס במה שסקילה ושריפה חמורין מהרג וחנק: **אבל** סימא את עינו והרגו בדבר אחר אימא נשקול מיניה ממונא ונקטליה. כך גרס ר"ח דמלא יהיה אסון לא נפקא לן אלא סימא את עינו והרגו בה כי התם שבהכאה אחת הרג את האשה וגם הולדות אבל סימא את עינו והרגו בדבר אחר בבת אחת לא ^א^ להכי איצטריך כל חרם למיפטריה קשה לרשב"א דהא ר' ישמעאל בנו של ר' יוחנן בן ברוקה לא דריש קרא להכי דלא נשקול מיניה ממונא ונקטליה אלא שלא יתן ממון ונפטריה ושמא אילו לא נאמר קאמר כדאשכחן ריש פרק נגמר הדין (סנהדרין דף מג. ושם) וככמה דוכתי ולרשב"א נראה דהכא מסיק אליבא דתנא דבי חזקיה אבל לרבי ישמעאל ודאי לית ליה הא דתנא דבי חזקיה והא דאמר בריש הנחנקין (שם דף פד: ושם) הניחא למאן דאית ליה דתנא דבי חזקיה אלא למאן דלית ליה היקישא למה לי תנא דלית ליה דבי חזקיה היינו רבי ישמעאל ובסמוך דקאמר ולרבה דאמר חידוש הוא שחידשה תורה בקנס כו' סבר לה כת"ק דר' חנניא בן עקביא הוה מצי למימר ס"ל כרבי ישמעאל: **הא** נמי מאידך תנא דבי חזקיה נפקא. לאו מההיא דרשה גופה קאמר דנפקא לן דהא ההיא דרשה לא שייכא כלל לסימא את עינו והרגו בדבר אחר אלא הכי דייק דכי היכי דדרשי' ולא עין ונפש תחת עין ה"נ דרשינן נפש תחת נפש ולא עין ונפש תחת נפש וסימא את עינו והרגו בד"א לא חשיב עין ונפש אלא נפש גריד' דמה שסימא את עינו בשעת הריגה לא חשיב כלום דבלאו הכי היה מת אלא שהמיתו בלער מרובה וא"ת ^ב^ הא מילתא נמי מתנא דבי חזקיה דלעיל נפקא דמה מכה בהמה לא חלקת בין סימא את עינה והרגה בה להורגה בד"א כו' וי"ל דמכה אדם ומכה בהמה משמע ליה בהכאה אחת וא"ת סימא את עינו והרגו בד"א תיפוק ליה דפטור מדמי עין אפי' לא הרג דבשעה שסימא את עינו היה רודף וניתן להצילו בנפשו וי"ל דמיירי בשיכול להצילו באחד מאיבריו שלא ניתן להצילו בנפשו: **אמר** רב אשי איצטריך כו'. תימה דמשמע דאם הרגו וקרע שיראין דידיה דמחייב דליכא למיפטריה לא מקרא דלא יהיה אסון ולא מקרא דנפש תחת נפש דהא הוי ממון ונפש תחת ממון ונפש ולעיל (דף ל:) פטר ^ו^ אביי זר שאכל תרומה משלו וקרע שיראין של חבירו וי"ל דלפי האמת נפקי כולהו מתנא דבי חזקיה וה"פ והא נמי מאידך תנא דבי חזקיה נפקא כלומר ע"כ לא איצטריך כל חרם להכי אלא כולה נפקא לן מתנא דבי חזקיה דפטור דאי הוה צריך קרא למפטריה בלא כל חרם הוה פטרינן ליה מאידך תנא דבי חזקיה וא"ת ולישני דאיצטריך כל חרם להרג חבירו וקרע שיראין וי"ל דכל חרם לא יפדה משמע ליה בממון שבא על ידי אותה חבלה שהמיתה באה על ידה:

סלקא דעתך אמינא חידוש הוא קמ"ל. אע"ג דבמתני' מייתי קרא דלא יהיה אסון והכא מפיק קנס מכל חרם היינו משום דכייל מתניתין כל חייבי מיתות דקתני וכל המתחייב בנפשו כו' אי נמי מתניתין אתיא כתנא קמא דרבי חנניא בן עקביא:

אימא

תוספות ישנים

א) [ולימא למימר דהכא לא קאי אקרא דכל חרם אלא אקרא דלא תקחו כופר דהא דאמר' בסמוך ולרבה דאמר חידוש כו'. ת"י].

ב) [ולפי האמת אע"ג דמלא יהיה אסון נפקי כולהו מדתנא דבי חזקיה איצטריך עין תחת עין ולא עין ונפש תחת עין ונפש תחת נפש לא איצטריך למדרש' ולאו קרא יתירא הוא אלא משמעות דקרא קדריש וליכא למימר לישתוק מלא יהיה אסון ונפש תחת נפש וגם נפיק כולהו מכח היקשא דתנא דבי חזקיה דהכי שמעי' מיניה ממון אחר לא משמע מיתה דסימא את עינו והרגו בדבר אחר לא חשיב גרידא כדמוכח בפנים להכי איצטריך לא יהיה אסון והמקשה שמעי' מיניה אפי' הרג וקרע שיראין מהקישא דתנא דבי חזקיה. ת"י].

גליון הש"ס

גמ' בין מתכוין לשאין מתכוין. עיין לקמן מ ע"א תוד"ה אחד כדרכה.

תורה אור השלם

א) וּמַכֵּה בְהֵמָה יְשַׁלְּמֶנָּה וּמַכֵּה אָדָם יוּמָת: [ויקרא כד, כא]

ב) עַיִן תַּחַת עַיִן שֵׁן תַּחַת שֵׁן יָד תַּחַת יָד רֶגֶל תַּחַת רָגֶל: [שמות כא, כד]

ג) כָּל חֵרֶם אֲשֶׁר יָחֳרַם מִן הָאָדָם לֹא יִפָּדֶה מוֹת יוּמָת: [ויקרא כז, כט]

ד) כִּי יִמְצָא אִישׁ נַעֲרָ בְתוּלָה אֲשֶׁר לֹא אֹרָשָׂה וּתְפָשָׂהּ וְשָׁכַב עִמָּהּ וְנִמְצָאוּ: [דברים כב, כח]

ה) וְכִי יְפַתֶּה אִישׁ בְּתוּלָה אֲשֶׁר לֹא אֹרָשָׂה וְשָׁכַב עִמָּהּ מָהֹר יִמְהָרֶנָּה לּוֹ לְאִשָּׁה: [שמות כב, טו]

מסורת הש"ס: א) לעיל לה. ב"ק לה. סנהדרין עט: פד:, ב) ב"ק פד., ג) [לעיל לד: לה:], ד) [לקמן מ.], ה) [נ"ל רב אשי].

עין משפט נר מצוה

סד א מיי' פ"א מהלכות רוצח ושמירת נפש הל' יג יג סמג עשין עה:

סה ב מיי' פ"א מהל' חובל הלכה ג ג ד סמג עשין ע:

סו ג מיי' פ"ב מהל' נערה הל' טו סמג עשין נד טור אה"ע סימן קעז:

סז ד מיי' פ"ב מהל' אישות הל' יא סמג עשין מח טוש"ע אה"ע סימן לז סעיף א:

תוספות רי"ד

מתני' נערה שנתארסה ונתגרשה ר"י הגלילי אומר אין לה קנס ר"ע אומר יש לה קנס וקנסה לעצמה. מ"ט דר' יוסי אמר קרא אשר לא אורשה הא אורסה אין לה קנס ור"ע אומר אשר לא אורשה לאביה הא אורסה לעצמה. וקי"ל הלכה כר"ע מחבירו. ומתני' דתני הבא על בתו אין לה קנס מפני שמתחייב בנפשו כר"ע אתיא. דהיכי דמי אילימא בבתו השתא אילו בא עליה אחר שקיל איהו קנס. השתא שבא עליה הוא לא כ"ש ובלא מיתה נמי פשיטא דלא משלם קנס. אלא ודאי מתני' בבתו נערה שנתארסה ונתגרשה עסקינן שקנסה לעצמה כר"ע ומפני שנתחייב בנפשו פטור ותדע דסתם מתני' כר"ע אתיא דהא אשת אחיו ואשת אחי אביו דתנן לעיל יש לה קנס לא אתיא אלא כר"ע דבע"כ גירשה או נתאלמנה שאל"כ הו"ל א"א ויש בהן מיתת ב"ד:

ליקוטי רש"י

מכה אדם ומכה בהמה. מכה בהמה ישלמנה ומכה אדם לא ישלם אלא יומת הקיש פטור ממון דמכה אדם לחיוב ממון דמכה בהמה מה מכה בהמה אין לך בו חילוק [לחיוב] [לפטור] אף מכה אדם אין לך בו חילוק [לפטור] [לחיוב] מכה בהמה לעולם חייב דאמרי' בב"ק (דף כו) פצע תחת פצע לחייב על השוגג כמזיד ואונס כרצון [לעיל לה.]. הוקשו יחד דמה מכה בהמה לעולם משלם ואפי' בשוגג כדאמרי' (לעיל דף כו.) אדם מועד לעולם אף מכה אדם דפטוריה קרא מתשלומין דכתיב יומת לעולם פטור ואפילו שוגג הואיל ובמזיד שייכא מיתה [ב"ק לה.]. לכך הוקשו בהאי קרא מכה בהמה ישלמנה ומכה אדם יומת ומשמע בבהמה חייב ממון ובאדם פטור מממון דכתיב בהאי קרא לא אדם והקיש לך הכתוב פטור תשלומין של אדם לחיוב תשלומין של בהמה. לדרך עליה. לא שייך למתני גבי בהמה אלא משום דבאדם אשכחן ביה חילוק בהורג בשוגג דרך ירידה חייב גלות אבל דרך עלייה כהרימו את ידו פטור מגלות דכתיב (במדבר לה) ויפל עליו וימת דרך נפילה בעינן. לפוטרו ממון אלא לחייבו ממון. כלומר לא

חלקת בו שום צד להפטר מן תשלומין אלא בכל צדדין הוא דמחייב דרבינן כל מזיקין בבבא קמא (דף כו:) מפלע תחת פלע לחייב על השוגג כמזיד ועל האונס כרצון ומכה בהמה נזק הוא. אף מכה אדם. אין דין פטור תשלומין הכתוב בו חלוק לשום צד שיתחייב ממון אלא כל שעה פטור ממון בין בשוגג ואין נתכון דפטור ממיתה בין במזיד ונתכון דחייב מיתה [סנהדרין עט:]. לשאין מתכוין. שהכהו בהגבהת ידו או שחתכו בחרבו מלמטה למעלה[לעיל שם]. שהרגו כלאחר יד בהרימו הגרזן דקיימא לן (מכות דף ז.) דפטור מגלות אפ"ה פטור מתשלומין [ב"ק שם]. בין דרך ירידה לדרך עלייה. משום דגבי גלות דהורג בשוגג איכא חילוק בין דרך ירידה לדרך עלייה כדאמרי' במכות (דף ז) כל שבדרך ירידתו גולה דכתיב ויפל עליו עד שיפול כדרך נפילה [לעיל שם]. לחייבו ממון. וה"ה לפדותו שאינו נפדה לעולם לא כשהוא חייב מיתה ולא כשהוא חייב גלות ולא כשהוא פטור מגלות ולא יהיה אסון מיהא וכו' [כנוסחתינו. רש"י מכת"י בשיטמ"ק ועיי"ש]. אלא לפטרו ממון. אלמא פטור ממון לתנא דבי חזקיה [סנהדרין שם]. עין תחת עין. סימא עין חבירו נותן לו דמי עינו כמה שפחתו דמיו למכור בשוק וכן כולם ולא נטילת אבר ממש כמו שדרשו רבותינו בפרק החובל (ב"ק פד) [שמות כא, כד]. חידוש הוא שחידשה תורה בקנס. כל משפט קנס חידוש הוא הלכך אע"ג דמיקטיל נמי לא מיפטר מיניה [לעיל לד: ועי' בשיטמ"ק].

The Gemara asks:

וְרַבִּי עֲקִיבָא מַאי חָזֵית – **But what does R' Akiva see** that compels him to say ד,,אֲשֶׁר לֹא־אֹרָשָׂה" לִגְזֵירָה שָׁוָה – **that** the common phrase ***who was not betrothed*** **is** expounded **for a** ***gezeirah shaveh*** ו,,בְּתוּלָה" לְמַעוּטֵי בְּעוּלָה – **and** the word ***virgin***[36] **is** expounded **to exclude a non-virgin** from the fine?

NOTES

just as the seducer pays *shekalim,* so the violator's fifty silver coins are *shekalim.*

36. *Virgin* appears in both the violation and the seduction passages; see below, 38b note 1.

הני מילי היכא דהרגו דרך עליה א שלא ניתנה שגגתו לכפרה אבל הרגו דרך ירידה דניתנה שגגתו לכפרה אימא נישקול ממונא מיניה וניפטריה קמ"ל א"ל רבא הא מדתנא דבי חזקיה נפקא א) דתנא דבי חזקיה א מכה אדם ומכה בהמה מה מכה בהמה לא חלקת בו בין שוגג למזיד בין מתכוין לשאין מתכוין בין דרך ירידה לדרך עליה לפוטרו ממון אלא לחייבו ממון אף מכה אדם לא תחלוק בו בין שוגג למזיד ב בין מתכוין לשאין מתכוין בין דרך ירידה לדרך עליה לחייבו ממון אלא לפוטרו ממון אלא אמר רמי בר חמא איצטריך ס"ד אמינא ה"מ היכא דסימא את עינו והרגו בה אבל היכא דסימא את עינו והרגו בדבר אחר אימא נישקול ממונא מיניה א"ל רבא הא נמי מאידך תנא דבי חזקיה נפקא ג) דתנא דבי חזקיה ב) עין תחת עין ג ולא עין ונפש תחת עין אלא אמר רב אשי איצטריך ס"ד אמינא הואיל וחידוש הוא שחידשה תורה בקנס אע"ג דמיקטיל משלם קמ"ל ולרבה דאמר ג חידוש הוא שחידשה תורה בקנס אע"ג דמיקטיל משלם האי ג) כל חרם מאי עביד ליה סבר לה כתנא קמא דר' חנניא בן עקביא: **מתני'** נערה שנתארסה ונתגרשה רבי יוסי הגלילי אומר אין לה קנס ר"ע אומר ז) ג יש לה קנס וקנסה לעצמה: **גמ'** מ"ט דר' יוסי הגלילי אמר קרא ד) אשר לא אורשה הא אורסה אין לה קנס ור"ע אשר לא אורשה לאביה הא אורסה לעצמה אלא מעתה נערה ולא בוגרת ה"נ דלעצמה בתולה ולא בעולה ה"נ דלעצמה אלא לגמרי הכא נמי לגמרי אמר לך ר"ע האי לא אורשה מיבעי ליה לכדתניא אשר לא אורשה פרט לנערה שנתארסה ונתגרשה שאין לה קנס דברי ר' יוסי הגלילי ר"ע אומר יש לה קנס וקנסה לאביה והדין נותן הואיל ואביה זכאי בכסף קידושיה ואביה זכאי בכסף קנסה ד מה כסף קידושיה אע"פ שנתארסה ונתגרשה לאביה אף כסף קנסה אע"פ שנתארסה ונתגרשה לאביה א"כ מה ת"ל אשר לא אורשה מופנה להקיש לו ולדון הימנו ג"ש נאמר כאן אשר לא אורשה ונאמר להלן ה) אשר לא אורשה מה כאן נ' אף להלן נ' ומה להלן שקלים אף כאן שקלים ור"ע מאי חזית דאשר לא אורשה לג"ש ובתולה למעוטי בעולה

רש"י

הני מילי. דלא תקנו כופר לפטור רוצח מזיד מקטלא: היכא דהרגו. במזיד דרך עלייה בהנפת ידו הכהו מאחריו דלכוונה בשוגג לא ניתן לכפרת גלות דכתיב ויפל דרך נפילה: מדתנא דבי חזקיה נפקא. שאין חילוק בין דרך עלייה לדרך ירידה: לחייבו ממון. והוא הדין לפדותו ולא יהיה אסון מיהא איצטריך דאי מהיקישא הוה אמינא אדרבה לאידך גיסא מה מכה בהמה לעולם ישלם אף מכה אדם ישלם והשתא דנפקא לן פטור תשלומין למזיד מלא יהיה אסון על כרחך היקישא לפטור שוגג דרך עליה: הכי גרסינן אלא אמר רמי בר חמא כו'. איצטריך חד מהני קראי לאשמועינן דלא ליעביד ביה תרתי ואף על גב דנפקא לן מולא יהיה אסון: הני מילי. דלא ענשינן ליה בתרתי היכא דסימא את עינו והרגו בה באותה מכה ומת: בדבר אחר. במכה אחרת ובעת אחרת: אימא. ניענשיה דמי עין ומיתה בשביל הריגה: הא. דסימא עינו והרגו בה: מאידך דבי חזקיה נפקא. דלא תיענשיה: ולא עין ונפש תחת עין. מיניה קיימא לן בהחובל דעין תחת עין לאו ממש דלאו ממש אמרת ממש דלמא זימנין דסמינן לעיניה מיית והוה ליה עין ונפש תחת עין מהיו שמעינן מינה דלא תעביד ביה תרתי לא שנא מת באותה מכה לא שנא לא מת: סלקא דעתך אמינא חידוש הוא שחידשה תורה. בכל תשלומי קנס שאינו דין אלא גזרת מלך הוא וכיון דחידוש הוא וגזירת חוק אימא אע"ג דליכא בהדיה מיתה לשלם: קמ"ל. חד מהנך קראי יתירא שאינו ענין לממון תניהו ענין לקנס: כתנא קמא. ודריש ליה באומר ערכו של יוצא ליהרג עלי: מתני' שנתארסה ונתגרשה. דלאו ארוסה שלא נתגרשה חייב מיתה ולאו שם קנס: אין לה קנס. טעמא מפרש בגמרא ורישא דקתני אשת אחיו ואשת אחי אביו דנתארסה ונתגרשה עסקינן וקתני יש להן קנס ר' עקיבא היא: גמ' אלא מעתה. לר' עקיבא הא דכתיב נערה למעוטי בוגרת ובתולה למעוטי בעולה: הכי נמי. דלא ממעט לגמרי ומדרוש נערה לאביה הא בוגרת לעצמה הא לא אשכחן דאישתמיט תנא ומתני בוגרת יש לה קנס ונימא רבי עקיבא היא: וקנסה לאביה. ולקמן מקשינן דר"ע אדר"ע: הואיל ואביה זכאי בכסף קידושיה. שלו הוא בנערותה ולקמן יליף לה בפרק נערה שנתפתתה (דף מו:): מה כסף קידושיה אף על פי שנתארסה ונתגרשה. מאחר כשחזרת ומתקדשת בתוך נערות: לאביה הוי. דהא כל קידושי נערות ילפינן לאביה דגבי קידושין לא כתיב מיעוטא דאשר לא אורסה כי הכא: נאמר כאן. באונס: להלן. במפתה: מה להלן. במפתה שקלים דכתיב ישקול:

תוספות

הני מילי היכא דהרגו דרך עלייה דלא ניתן שגגתו לכפרה. פירוש לכפרה בידי אדם אע"ג דלדם קיל טפי מדרך ירידה כדמוכח בפרק אלו הן הגולין (מכות דף ט. ושם) גבי גר תושב גולה ע"י גר תושב וכל הומרי דשמעתין לא הוי אלא במה שלא ניתן לכפרה דלאו מקפיד הש"ס במה שסקילה ושריפה חמורין מהרג וחנק: **אבל** סימא את עינו והרגו בדבר אחר אימא נשקול מיניה ממונא ונקטליה. כך גרס ר"ח דמלא יהיה אסון לא נפקא לן אלא סימא את עינו והרגו בה כי התם שבהכאה אחת הרג את האשה וגם הולדות אבל סימא את עינו והרגו בדבר אחר בבת אחת לא א) להכי איצטריך כל חרם למיפטריה קשה לרשב"א דהא ר' ישמעאל בנו של ר' יוחנן בן ברוקה לא דריש קרא להכי דלא נשקול מיניה ממונא ונקטליה אלא שלא יתן ממון ונפטריה ושמא אילו לא נאמר קאמר כדאשכחן ריש פרק נגמר הדין (סנהדרין דף מג. ושם) ובכמה דוכתי ולרשב"א נראה דהכא מסיק אליבא דתנא דבי חזקיה אבל לרבי ישמעאל ודאי לית ליה הא דתנא דבי חזקיה והא דאמר בריש הכונס (שם דף כב: ושם) הניחא למאן דלית ליה דתנא דבי חזקיה אלא למאן דלית ליה היקישא למה לי תנא דלית ליה דבי חזקיה היינו רבי ישמעאל ובסמוך דקאמר ולרבה דאמר חידוש הוא שחידשה תורה בקנס כו' סבר לה כת"ק דר' חנניא בן עקביא הוה מצי למימר ס"ל כרבי ישמעאל: **הא** נמי מאידך תנא דבי חזקיה נפקא. לאו מההיא דרשה גופה קאמר דנפקא לן דהא ההיא דרשה לא שייכא כלל לסימא את עינו והרגו בדבר אחר אלא הכי דייק דכי היכי דדרשי' ולא עין ונפש תחת עין ה"ה דרשינן נפש תחת נפש ולא עין ונפש תחת נפש וסימא את עינו והרגו בד"א לא חשיב עין ונפש אלא נפש גריד' דמה שסימא את עינו בשעת הריגה לא חשיב כלום דבלאו הכי היה מת אלא שהמיתו בנער מרובה וא"ת ב) הא מילתא נמי מתנא דבי חזקיה דלעיל נפקא דמה מכה בהמה לא חלקת בין סימא את עינה והרגה בה להורגה בד"א כו' וי"ל דמכה אדם ומכה בהמה משמע ליה בהכאה אחת וא"ת סימא את עינו והרגו בד"א תיפוק ליה דפטור מדמי עין אפי' לא הרג דבשעה שסימא את עינו היה רודף וניתן להצילו בנפשו וי"ל דמיירי בשיכול להצילו באחד מאיבריו שלא ניתן להצילו בנפשו: **אמר** רב אשי איצטריך כו'. תימה דמשמע דאם הרגו וקרע שיראין דידיה דמחייב דליכא למיפטריה לא מקרא דלא יהיה אסון ולא מקרא דנפש תחת נפש דהא הוי ממון ונפש תחת ממון ונפש ולעיל (דף ל:) פטר ה) אביי זר שאכל תרומה משלו וקרע שיראין של חבירו וי"ל דלפי האמת נפקי כולהו מתנא דבי חזקיה וה"פ והא נמי מאידך תנא דבי חזקיה נפקא כלומר ע"כ לא איצטריך כל חרם להכי אלא כולה נפקא לן מתנא דבי חזקיה דפטור דאי הוה צריך קרא למפטריה בלא כל חרם הוה פטרינן ליה מאידך תנא דבי חזקיה וא"ת ולישני דאיצטריך כל חרם להרג חבירו וקרע שיראין וי"ל דכל חרם לא יפדה משמע ליה בממון שבא על ידי אותה חבלה שהמיתה באה על ידה: **סלקא** דעתך אמינא חידוש הוא קמ"ל. אע"ג דבמתני' מייתי קרא דלא יהיה אסון והכא מפיק קנס מכל חרם היינו משום דכייל מתניתין כל חייבי מיתות דקתני וכל המתחייב בנפשו כו' אי נמי מתניתין אתיא כתנא קמא דרבי חנניה בן עקביא: תימה

מסורת הש"ס

א) לעיל לה. ב"ק לה. סנהדרין עט: פד:, ב) ב"ק פד., ג) [לעיל לד: לה:], ד) [לקמן ע.], ה) [נ"ל רב אשי]

תוספות ישנים

א) [וליכא למימר דהכא לא קאי אקרא דכל חרם לא יפדה אלא אקרא דלא תקחו כופר דהא אמרי' בסמוך ולרבה דאמר חידוש כו'. ת"י]:
ב) [ולפי האמת יהיה אסון נפקי כולהו מדתנא דבי חזקיה איצטריך עין תחת עין לכדדרשינן ולא עין ונפש תחת עין ולא איצטריך למדרש' ולאו קרא יתירא הוא ולא משמעות דקרא קדריש וליכא למימר דלישתוק מלא יהיה אסון ונפש תחת נפש כולהו מכח היקשא דתנא דבי חזקיה דלכתי לא שמעי' מיניה ממון דמכה אדם דסימא את עינו והרגו בדבר אחר לא חשיב ממון ונפש אלא נפש גרידא כדמוכח בפנים לכך איצטריך לא יהיה אסון ומהשתא שמעי' מינה אפי' הרגו וקרע שיראין מהקישא דתנא דבי חזקיה. ת"י]:

גליון הש"ס

גמ' בין מתכוין לשאין מתכוין. עיין לקמן מ ע"א תוד"ה אחד כדרכה:

תורה אור השלם

א) וּמַכֵּה בְהֵמָה יְשַׁלְּמֶנָּה וּמַכֵּה אָדָם יוּמָת: [ויקרא כד, כא]
ב) עַיִן תַּחַת עַיִן שֵׁן תַּחַת שֵׁן יָד תַּחַת יָד רֶגֶל תַּחַת רָגֶל: [שמות כא, כד]
ג) כָּל חֵרֶם אֲשֶׁר יָחֳרַם מִן הָאָדָם לֹא יִפָּדֶה מוֹת יוּמָת: [ויקרא כז, כט]
ד) כִּי יִמְצָא אִישׁ נַעֲרָ בְתוּלָה אֲשֶׁר לֹא אֹרָשָׂה וּתְפָשָׂהּ וְשָׁכַב עִמָּהּ וְנִמְצָאוּ: [דברים כב, כח]
ה) וְכִי יְפַתֶּה אִישׁ בְּתוּלָה אֲשֶׁר לֹא אֹרָשָׂה וְשָׁכַב עִמָּהּ מָהֹר יִמְהָרֶנָּה לּוֹ לְאִשָּׁה: [שמות כב, טו]

עין משפט נר מצוה

סד א מיי' פ"ו מהלכות רוצח ושמירת נפש הל' יג סמג עשין עה:
סה ב מיי' פ"א מהל' חובל הלכה ג ד סמג עשין ע:
סו ג מיי' פ"ב מהל' נערה הל' טז סמג עשין נד טור אה"ע סימן קעז:
סז ד מיי' פ"ג מהל' אישות הל' יא סמג עשין מח טוש"ע אה"ע סימן לז סעיף א:

תוספות רי"ד

מתני' נערה שנתארסה ונתגרשה ר"י הגלילי אומר אין לה קנס ר"ע אומר יש לה קנס וקנסה לעצמה. מ"ט דר' יוסי אמר קרא אשר לא אורשה הא אורסה אין לה קנס ור"ע אומר אשר לא אורשה לאביה הא אורסה לעצמה. וקי"ל הלכה כר"ע מחבירו. ומתני' דתני הבא על בתו אין לה קנס מפני שמתחייב בנפשו כר"ע אתיא. דהיכי דמי שיתחייב בבתו השתא אילו בא עליה אחר שקיל איהו קנס. השתא שבא עליה הוא לא כ"ש ובלא מיתה נמי פשיטא דלא משלם קנס. אלא ודאי מתני' בבתו נערה שנתארסה ונתגרשה עסקינן שקנסה לעצמה כר"ע ומפני שנתחייב בנפשו פטור ותדע דסתם מתני' כר"ע אתיא דהא אשת אחיו ואשת אחי אביו דתנן לעיל יש לה קנס לא אתיא אלא כר"ע דבע"כ גירשה או נתאלמנה שאל"כ הו"ל א"א ויש בהן מיתת ב"ד:

ליקוטי רש"י

מכה אדם ומכה בהמה. מכה בהמה ישלמנה ומכה אדם לא ישלם אלא יומת הקיש פטור ממון דמכה אדם לחיוב ממון דמכה בהמה מה מכה בהמה אין לך בו חילוק (לחיוב) [לפטור] אף מכה אדם אין לך בו חילוק (לפטור) [לחיוב] מכה בהמה לעולם חייב דאמרי' בב"ק (דף כו.) פצע תחת פצע לחייב על השוגג כמזיד ואונס כרצון [לעיל לה.]. הוקשו יחד דמה מכה בהמה לעולם משלם ואפילו בשוגג כדאמרי' [לעיל דף כו.] אדם מועד לעולם אף מכה אדם דפטריה קרא מתשלומין דכתיב יומת לעולם פטור ואפילו בשוגג הואיל ובמזיד שייכא מיתה [ב"ק לה.]. לכך הוקשו בהאי קרא מכה בהמה ישלמנה ומכה אדם יומת ומשמע בבהמה חייב ממון ובאדם פטור ממון דכתיב בהמה ישלמנה ולא אדם והקיש לך הכתוב פטור תשלומין של אדם לחיוב תשלומין של בהמה. לדרך עליה. לא שייך למתני גבי בהמה אלא משום דבאדם אשכחן ביה חילוק בהורג בשוגג דרך ירידה חייב גלות אבל דרך עלייה בהרימו את ידו פטור מגלות דכתיב (במדבר לה) ויפל עליו וימת דרך נפילה בעינן. לפוטרו ממון אלא לחייבו ממון. כלומר לא

חלקת בו שום צד להפטר מן תשלומין אלא בכל צדדין הוא דמחייב דרבינן כל נזקין בבבא קמא (דף כו:) מפצע תחת פצע לחייב על השוגג כמזיד ועל האונס כרצון ומכה בהמה נזק הוא. אף מכה אדם. אין דין פטור תשלומין הכתוב בו חלוק לשום צד שיתחייב ממון אלא כל שעה פטור [illegible]

not entitled to the fine.[23] רַבִּי עֲקִיבָא אוֹמֵר – **R' Akiva says:** יֵשׁ לָהּ קְנָס – **She is entitled to the fine,** וּקְנָסָהּ לְעַצְמָהּ – **and her fine** belongs **to her.**[24]

Gemara The Gemara seeks to explain the conflicting opinions of the Mishnah:

מַאי טַעְמָא דְּרַבִּי יוֹסֵי הַגְּלִילִי – **What is R' Yose HaGlili's reason** for ruling that a *naarah* who was betrothed and divorced is not entitled to the fine for violation? אָמַר קְרָא – Because the **verse states:**[25] ,,אֲשֶׁר לֹא־אֹרָשָׂה" – *If a man finds a virgin naarah **who was not betrothed** and takes hold of her and lies with her* etc. [he pays a fine]. הָא אוֹרָסָה – **This** implies that if **she *was* betrothed,** אֵין לָהּ קְנָס – **she has no** right to the **fine.** וְרַבִּי עֲקִיבָא – **But R' Akiva holds:** ,,אֲשֶׁר לֹא־אֹרָשָׂה" לְאָבִיהָ – The Torah states that when one violates *a virgin naarah **who was not betrothed*** the fine is paid **to her father;**[26] הָא אוֹרָסָה – **this** implies that if **she *was*** previously **betrothed,** לְעַצְמָהּ – the fine belongs **to her.**[27]

The Gemara challenges R' Akiva's interpretation:

אֶלָּא מֵעַתָּה ,,נַעֲרָה" – **But then,** when the verse states ***naarah,*** וְלֹא בוֹגֶרֶת – which implies **"but not a *bogeress,*"** הָכִי נַמִּי דִּלְעַצְמָהּ – **is it also so that** R' Akiva would say that the fine belongs **to her?!** ,,בְּתוּלָה" וְלֹא בְּעוּלָה – And when the verse states ***a virgin,*** which implies **"but not a non-virgin,"** הָכִי נַמִּי דִּלְעַצְמָהּ – **is it also so that** R' Akiva would say that the fine belongs **to her?!**[28] Certainly not![29] אֶלָּא לְגַמְרֵי – **Rather,** R' Akiva agrees that the words *naarah* and *virgin* come to exclude a *bogeress* and a non-virgin from the fine **altogether.** הָכָא נַמִּי לְגַמְרֵי – **Here too,** let him expound *who was not betrothed* to exclude a previously betrothed *naarah* from the fine **altogether! – ? –**

The Gemara defends R' Akiva's interpretation:

הַאי – אָמַר לָךְ רַבִּי עֲקִיבָא – **R' Akiva would say to you:** ,,לֹא־אֹרָשָׂה" מִיבְּעֵי לֵיהּ לִכְדְתַנְיָא – **This** phrase *who was **not** **betrothed*** cannot exclude a previously betrothed *naarah* from the fine altogether, because **we need it for that** law **which was taught in a Baraisa:** ,,אֲשֶׁר לֹא־אֹרָשָׂה" – The Torah states, *WHO WAS NOT BETROTHED* – פְּרַט לְנַעֲרָה שֶׁנִּתְאָרְסָה וְנִתְגָּרְשָׁה – **TO THE EXCLUSION OF A *NAARAH* WHO WAS BETROTHED AND** then **DIVORCED,** שֶׁאֵין לָהּ קְנָס – **WHO HAS NO** right to the **FINE;** דִּבְרֵי רַבִּי יוֹסֵי הַגְּלִילִי – these are **THE WORDS OF R' YOSE HAGLILI.** רַבִּי עֲקִיבָא אוֹמֵר – But **R' AKIVA SAYS:** יֵשׁ לָהּ קְנָס – **SHE HAS A** right to the **FINE,** וּקְנָסָהּ לְאָבִיהָ – **AND HER FINE** belongs **TO HER FATHER.**[30] וְהַדִּין נוֹתֵן – **AND LOGIC DICTATES** that this is so, הוֹאִיל וְאָבִיהָ זַכַּאי בְּכֶסֶף קִידּוּשֶׁיהָ וְאָבִיהָ זַכַּאי בְּכֶסֶף קְנָסָהּ – for **SINCE HER FATHER IS ENTITLED TO HER *KIDDUSHIN* MONEY**[31] **AND HER FATHER IS ENTITLED TO HER FINE MONEY** as well, the following legal analogy can be made: מַה כֶּסֶף קִידּוּשֶׁיהָ אַף עַל פִּי שֶׁנִּתְאָרְסָה וְנִתְגָּרְשָׁה לְאָבִיהָ – **JUST AS [A *NAARAH'S*] *KIDDUSHIN* MONEY BELONGS TO HER FATHER EVEN THOUGH SHE WAS** previously **BETROTHED AND DIVORCED,**[32] אַף כֶּסֶף קְנָסָהּ אַף עַל פִּי שֶׁנִּתְאָרְסָה וְנִתְגָּרְשָׁה לְאָבִיהָ – so **TOO, HER FINE MONEY BELONGS TO HER FATHER EVEN THOUGH SHE WAS** previously **BETROTHED AND DIVORCED.** אִם כֵּן מַה תַּלְמוּד לוֹמַר ,,אֲשֶׁר לֹא־אֹרָשָׂה" – But **IF SO,** for **WHAT** purpose **DOES THE TORAH STATE,** with regard to the victim of violation, *WHO WAS NOT BETROTHED?* מוּפְנֶה לְהַקִּישׁ לוֹ וְלָדוּן הֵימֶנּוּ גְּזֵירָה שָׁוָה – **[THAT PHRASE] IS FREE**[33] and thus available **TO BE COMPARED WITH AND TO HAVE A *GEZEIRAH SHAVAH* EXPOUNDED FROM IT,** as follows: נֶאֱמַר כָּאן ,,אֲשֶׁר לֹא־אֹרָשָׂה" – **IT IS STATED HERE** regarding the girl who was violated, *WHO WAS NOT BETROTHED,* וְנֶאֱמַר לְהַלָּן ,,אֲשֶׁר לֹא־אֹרָשָׂה" – **AND IT IS STATED THERE**[34] regarding the girl who was seduced, *WHO WAS NOT BETROTHED.* מַה כָּאן חֲמִשִּׁים – The commonality of phrase teaches that **JUST AS HERE** the violator pays **FIFTY** silver coins, אַף לְהַלָּן חֲמִשִּׁים – **THERE ALSO** the seducer pays **FIFTY** silver coins; וּמַה לְהַלָּן שְׁקָלִים – **AND JUST AS THERE** the seducer pays *SHEKALIM,* אַף כָּאן שְׁקָלִים – **HERE ALSO** the violator pays *SHEKALIM.*[35]

NOTES

23. [I.e. although she was only an *arusah* and thus still a virgin *naarah* at the time of the violation, she is nonetheless disqualified from receiving the fine.] The reason for this will be explained in the Gemara (*Rashi*).

Rashi notes that the Mishnah above (29a), which imposes the fine upon one who violates his brother's wife or his father's brother's wife [who was betrothed and divorced prior to *nisuin* – see ad loc. notes 11 and 12], does not follow the view of R' Yose HaGlili in our Mishnah. Rather, it accords with R' Akiva, who maintains that a virgin *naarah* who was betrothed and divorced *is* entitled to the fine.

24. [I.e. although the fine for the violation of a virgin *naarah* is generally awarded to the father, in this case it is awarded to the victim herself; the Gemara will explain why.]

25. *Deuteronomy* 22:28, which speaks of the violation of a virgin *naarah*. [The next verse mandates a fine of fifty *shekels.*]

26. For the following verse (v. 29) states: *And the man who lay with her shall give to the father of the naarah fifty silver [coins].*

27. I.e. the Torah's specifying a girl *who was not betrothed* does not exclude a previously betrothed girl from the fine itself (as R' Yose HaGlili holds); rather, it excludes her only from the law that the fine is paid to her father.

28. I.e. does R' Akiva say also that the Torah's specification of *naarah* and *virgin* does not actually exclude a *bogeress* and a non-virgin from the fine itself, but only teaches that the fine is given to the victim rather than to her father? (*Rashi*).

29. For nowhere do we find a Tannaic opinion stating that a *bogeress* [or a non-virgin] is entitled to the fine, which we could attribute to R' Akiva (*Rashi*).

30. The Gemara below will note the obvious contradiction between R' Akiva's ruling here and his ruling in our Mishnah, where he stated that the fine is paid to the rape victim and not to her father (*Rashi*).

31. [One of the ways of effecting *kiddushin* is by tendering "money." That is, a man acquires a woman to be his betrothed by giving her money or something of value (see *Kiddushin* 2a).] The Gemara below (46b) derives from Scripture that when the woman is a minor or a *naarah,* the money accrues to her father (*Rashi*).

32. The Baraisa speaks of a *naarah* who was betrothed and then divorced and subsequently became betrothed a second time while yet a *naarah.* Here as well the *kiddushin* money belongs to the father, for when the Torah awarded a *naarah's kiddushin* money to her father, it did not specify that the *naarah* be a woman "who was not betrothed," as it did in the passage of the fine for violation. Hence, the father's entitlement to *kiddushin* money exists in *all* cases of *naeros,* even those who had been betrothed once before (*Rashi*).

[Note: The Baraisa refers only to a *naarah* who was betrothed and then divorced *prior to nesuin,* for once a girl becomes a *nesuah* (married) her father loses all rights to her; that is, if she was then divorced while even a minor, the father does not receive her *kiddushin* money if she becomes betrothed again.]

33. I.e. superfluous.

34. *Exodus* 22:15.

35. In the passage of the violator the Torah states (*Deuteronomy* 22:29): *The man who violated her shall give the father of the naarah fifty silver [coins].* The verse does not, however, specify which silver coin should be given. On the other hand, in the passage of the seducer the Torah states (*Exodus* 22:16): *He shall pay out silver.* While the word *yishkol* indicates that the fine is to be paid in *shekalim,* the Torah does not specify how many *shekalim* are to be paid. Nevertheless, the *gezeirah shavah* from the common words *who was not betrothed* links the violator and seducer passages and teaches us to let one instruct as to the other, as follows: Just as the violator pays fifty coins, so does the seducer; and

הני מילי היכא דהרגו דרך עלייה שלא ניתנה שגגתו לכפרה אבל הרגו דרך ירידה דניתנה שגגתו לכפרה אימא נישקול ממונא מיניה וניפטריה קמ"ל א"ל רבא הא מדתנא דבי חזקיה נפקא דתנא דבי חזקיה מכה אדם ומכה בהמה מה מכה בהמה לא חלקת בו בין שוגג למזיד בין מתכוין לשאין מתכוין בין דרך ירידה לדרך עלייה לפוטרו ממון אלא לחייבו ממון אף מכה אדם לא תחלוק בו בין שוגג למזיד בין מתכוין לשאין מתכוין בין דרך ירידה לדרך עליה לחייבו ממון אלא לפוטרו ממון אלא אמר רמי בר חמא איצטריך ס"ד אמינא ה"מ היכא דסימא את עינו והרגו בה אבל היכא דסימא את עינו והרגו בדבר אחר אימא נישקול ממונא מיניה א"ל רבא הא נמי מאידך תנא דבי חזקיה נפקא דתנא דבי חזקיה עין תחת עין ולא עין ונפש תחת עין אלא אמר רב אשי איצטריך ס"ד אמינא הואיל וחידוש הוא שחידשה תורה בקנס אע"ג דמיקטיל משלם קמ"ל ולרבה דאמר חידוש הוא שחידשה תורה בקנס אע"ג דמיקטיל משלם האי כל חרם מאי עביד ליה סבר לה כתנא קמא דר' חנניא בן עקביא:

מתני' נערה שנתארסה ונתגרשה רבי יוסי הגלילי אומר אין לה קנס ר"ע אומר יש לה קנס וקנסה לעצמה:

גמ' מ"ט דר' יוסי הגלילי אמר קרא אשר לא אורשה הא אורסה אין לה קנס ור"ע אשר לא אורשה לאביה הא אורסה לעצמה אלא מעתה נערה ולא בוגרת ה"נ דלעצמה בתולה ולא בעולה ה"נ דלעצמה אלא לגמרי הכא נמי לגמרי אמר לך ר"ע האי לא אורשה מיבעי ליה לכדתניא אשר לא אורשה פרט לנערה שנתארסה ונתגרשה שאין לה קנס דברי ר' יוסי הגלילי ר"ע אומר יש לה קנס וקנסה לאביה והדין נותן הואיל ואביה זכאי בכסף קידושיה ואביה זכאי בכסף קנסה מה כסף קידושיה אע"פ שנתארסה ונתגרשה לאביה אף כסף קנסה אע"פ שנתארסה ונתגרשה לאביה א"כ מה ת"ל אשר לא אורשה מופנה להקיש לו ולדון הימנו ג"ש נאמר כאן אשר לא אורשה ונאמר להלן אשר לא אורשה מה כאן נ' אף להלן נ' ומה להלן שקלים אף כאן שקלים ור"ע מאי חזית דאשר לא אורשה לג"ש ובתולה למעוטי בעולה

רש"י

הני מילי. דלא תקתו קרא לפטור רוצח מזיד מקטלא: היכא דהרגו. במזיד דרך עלייה שהגביה ידו הכהו מאחריו להכותו בשוגג לא ניתן לכפרת גלות כדכתיב ויפל דרך נפילה: מדתנא דבי חזקיה נפקא. שאין חילוק בין דרך עלייה לדרך ירידה: לחייבו ממון. והוא הדין לפדותו ולא יהיה אסון מיהא איצטריך דאי מהיקישא הוה אמינא אדרבה לאידך גיסא מה מכה בהמה לעולם ישלם אף מכה אדם ישלם והשתא דנפקא לן פטור תשלומין למזיד מלא יהיה אסון על כרחך היקישא לפטור שוגג דרך עליה: הכי גרסינן אלא אמר רמי בר חמא כו'. איצטריך חד מהני קראי לאשמועינן דלא לעביד ביה תרתי ואף על גב דנפקא לן מולא יהיה אסון: הני מילי. דלא ענשינן ליה בתרתי היכא דסימא את עינו והרגו בה באותה מכה ומת: בדבר אחר. במכה אחרת ובעת אחת: אימא. ליענשיה דמי עין ומיתה בשביל הסריגה: הא. דסימא עינו והרגו בה: מאידך דבי חזקיה נפקא. דלא תיענשיה: ולא עין ונפש תחת עין. מיניה קיימא לן דהמובל לעין תחת עין לאו ממש דאי אמרת ממש למאי בהדי דקמינן לעייניה מיית והוה ליה עין ונפש תחת עין מיהו שמעינן מינה דלא תעביד ביה תרתי לא שנא מת באותה מכה לא שנא לא מת: סלקא דעתך אמינא חידוש הוא שחידשה תורה. בכל תשלומי קנס שאינו דין אלא גזרת מלך בעלמא וכיון דחידוש הוא וגזירת חוק אימא אע"ג דאיכא בהדיה מיתה לשלם: קמ"ל. חד מהנך קראי יתירא שאינו ענין לממון תניהו ענין לקנס: כתנא קמא. ודריש ליה באומר ערכו של יוצא ליהרג עלי: **מתני'** שנתארסה ונתגרשה. דאילו ארוסה שלא נתגרשה חייב מיתה ואין שם קנס: אין לה קנס. טעמא מפרש בגמרא וריש דקתני אשת אחיו ואשת אחי אביו דנתארסה ונתגרשה עסקינן וקתני יש להן קנס ר' עקיבא היא: **גמ'** אלא מעתה. לר' עקיבא הא דכתיב נערה למעוטי בוגרת ובתולה למעוטי בעולה: הכי נמי. דלא ממעט לגמרי ותדרוש נערה לאביה הא בוגרת לעצמה הא לא אשכחן דאשתמיטיה תנא ומתני בוגרת יש לה קנס ויימא רבי עקיבא היא: וקנסה לאביה. ולקמן מקשינן דר"ע אדר"ע: הואיל ואביה זכאי בכסף קידושיה. שלו הוא בנערותה ולקמן יליף לה בפרק נערה שנתפתתה (דף מו:): מה כסף קידושיה אף על פי שנתארסה ונתגרשה. אמאר כשחוזרת ומתקדשת בתוך נערות: לאביה הוי. דהא כל קידושי נערות ילפינן לאביה דגבי קידושין לא כתיב מיעוטא דאשר לא אורסה כי הכא: נאמר כאן. באונס: להלן. במפתה: מה להלן. במפתה שקלים דכתיב ישקול:

תוספות

הני מילי היכא דהרגו דרך עלייה דלא ניתן שגגתו לכפרה. פירוש לכפרה בידי אדם אע"ג דדרך עלייה קיל טפי מדרך ירידה כדמוכח בפרק אלו הן הגולין (מכות דף ט. ושם) גבי גר תושב גולה ע"י גר תושב וכו' ואומרי' דשמעתין לא תלי אלא במה שלא ניתן לכפרה דאינו מקפיד הש"ס במה שסקילה ושריפה חמורין מהרג וחנק: **אבל** סימא את עינו והרגו בדבר אחר אימא נשקול מיניה ממונא ונקטליה. כך גרס ר"ח דמלא יהיה אסון לא נפקא לן אלא סימא את עינו והרגו בה כי התם שבהכאה אחת הרג את האשה וגם הולדות אבל סימא את עינו והרגו בדבר אחר בבת אחת לא א) להכי איצטריך כל חרם למיפטריה קשה לרשב"א דהא ר' ישמעאל בנו של ר' יוחנן בן ברוקה לא דריש קרא להכי דלא נשקול מיניה ממונא ונקטליה אלא שלא יתן ממון ונפטריה ושמא אילו לא נאמר קאמר כדאשכחן ריש פרק נגמר הדין (סנהדרין דף מג. ושם) וזכמה דוכתי ולרשב"א נראה דהכא מסיק אליבא דתנא דבי חזקיה אבל לרבי ישמעאל ודאי לית ליה הא דתנא דבי חזקיה והא דאמר בריש הנחנקין (שם דף פד: ושם) הניחא למאן דלית ליה דתנא דבי חזקיה אלא למאן דלית ליה היקישא למה לי תנא דלית ליה דבי חזקיה היינו רבי ישמעאל ובסמוך דקאמר ולרבה דאמר חידוש הוא שחדשה תורה בקנס כו' סבר לה כת"ק דר' חנניא בן עקביא הוה מצי למימר ס"ל כרבי ישמעאל: **הא** נמי מאידך תנא דבי חזקיה נפקא. לאו מהאי דרשה גופה קאמר דנפקא לן דהא ההיא דרשה לא שייכא כלל לסימא את עינו והרגו בדבר אחר אלא הכי דייק דכי היכי דדרשי' ולא עין ונפש תחת עין ה"נ דרשינן נפש תחת נפש ולא עין ונפש תחת נפש וסימא את עינו והרגו בד"א לא חשיב עין ונפש אלא נפש גרידא' דמה שסימא את עינו בשעת הריגה לא חשיב כלום דבלאו הכי היה מת אלא שהמיתו בלער מרובה וא"ת ב) הא מילתא נמי מתנא דבי חזקיה דלעיל נפקא דמה מכה בהמה לא חלקת בין סימא את עינה והרגה בה להורגה בד"א כו' וי"ל דמכה אדם ומכה בהמה משמע ליה בהכאה אחת וא"ת סימא את עינו והרגו בד"א תיפוק ליה דפטור מדמי עין אפי' לא הרג דבשעה שסימא את עינו היה רודף וניתן להצילו בנפשו וי"ל דמיירי בשיכול להצילו באחד מאיבריו שלא ניתן להצילו בנפשו: **אמר** רב אשי איצטריך כו'. תימה דמשמע דאם הרגו וקרע שיראין דידיה דמחייב דליכא למיפטריה לא מקרא דלא יהיה אסון ולא מקרא דנפש תחת נפש דהא הוי ממון ונפש תחת ממון ונפש ולעיל (דף ל:) פטר ה) אביי זר שאכל תרומה משלו וקרע שיראין של חבירו וי"ל דלפי האמת נפקי כולהו מתנא דבי חזקיה וה"פ והא נמי מאידך תנא דבי חזקיה נפקא כלומר ע"כ לא איצטריך כל חרס להכי אלא כולה נפקא לן מתנא דבי חזקיה דפטור דאי הוה צריך קרא למפטריה בלא כל חרם הוה פטרינן ליה מאידך תנא דבי חזקיה וא"ת וליטני דאיצטריך כל חרם להרג חבירו וקרע שיראין וי"ל דכל חרם לא יפדה משמע ליה בממון שבא על ידי אותה חבלה שהמיתה באה על ידה: **סלקא** דעתך אמינא חידוש הוא קמ"ל. אע"ג דבמתני' מייתי קרא דלא יהיה אסון והכא מפיק קנס מכל חרם היינו משום דכייל מתניתין כל חייבי מיתות דקתני וכל המתחייב בנפשו כו' אי נמי מתניתין אתיא כתנא קמא דרבי חנניא בן עקביא:

מסורת הש"ס

א) לעיל לה. ב"ק לה. סנהדרין עט. פד:, ב) ב"ק סד., ג) לעיל לד: לה:, ד) לקמן מ., ה) ל"ל רב אשי.

תוספות ישנים

א) וליכא למימר דהכלא קאי אקרא דכל חרם אלא אקרא דלא תקתו כופר דהא אמרי' בסמוך ולרבה דאמר חידוש כו'. מ"י.

ב) ולפי האמת אע"ג דמלא יהיה אסון לא נפקי כולהו מדתנא דבי חזקיה איצטריך עין תחת עין למדרשינן ולא עין ונפש תחת עין אבל לא עין ונפש תחת נפש לא איצטריך למדרשי' ולאו קרא יתירא הוא אלא מפשטיה דקרא קדריש וליכא למימר ליפשוט מלא יהיה אסון ומנפש תחת נפש דיוק כולהו מכח היקשא דתנא דבי חזקיה דלהכי לא שמעי' מיניה ממון למיתה דסימא את עינו והרגו בדבר אחר לא חשיב עין ונפש אלא נפש גרידא כדמוכח בפנים להכי איצטריך לא יהיה אסון והשתא שמעי' מינה אפי' הרג וקרע שיראין מהיקשא דתנא דבי חזקיה. מ"י.

גליון הש"ס

גמ' בין מתכוין לשאין מתכוין. עיין לקמן מ ע"א תוד"ה אחד כדרכה:

תורה אור השלם

א) וּמַכֵּה בְהֵמָה יְשַׁלְּמֶנָּה וּמַכֵּה אָדָם יוּמָת: [ויקרא כד, כא]

ב) עַיִן תַּחַת עַיִן שֵׁן תַּחַת שֵׁן יָד תַּחַת יָד רֶגֶל תַּחַת רָגֶל: [שמות כא, כד]

ג) כָּל חֵרֶם אֲשֶׁר יָחֳרַם מִן הָאָדָם לֹא יִפָּדֶה מוֹת יוּמָת: [ויקרא כז, כט]

ד) כִּי יִמְצָא אִישׁ נַעֲרָ בְתוּלָה אֲשֶׁר לֹא אֹרָשָׂה וּתְפָשָׂהּ וְשָׁכַב עִמָּהּ וְנִמְצָאוּ: [דברים כב, כח]

ה) וְכִי יְפַתֶּה אִישׁ בְּתוּלָה אֲשֶׁר לֹא אֹרָשָׂה וְשָׁכַב עִמָּהּ מָהֹר יִמְהָרֶנָּה לּוֹ לְאִשָּׁה: [שמות כב, טו]

עין משפט נר מצוה

סד א מיי' פ"ו מהלכות רוצח ושמירת נפש הל' יג יג סמג עשין נט.

סה ב מיי' פ"א מהל' חובל הלכה ב ג ד סמג עשין ע.

סו ג מיי' פ"ב מהל' נערה הל' טו סמג עשין נד טור אה"ע סימן קעז.

סז ד מיי' פ"ג מהל' אישות הל' יא סמג עשין מח טוש"ע אה"ע סימן לז סעיף א.

תוספות רי"ד

מתני' נערה שנתארסה ונתגרשה ר' יוסי הגלילי אומר אין לה קנס ר"ע אומר יש לה קנס וקנסה לעצמה. מ"ט דר' יוסי אמר קרא אשר לא אורסה הא אורסה אין לה קנס ור"ע אומר אשר לא אורסה לאביה הא אורסה לעצמה. וקיי"ל הלכה כר"ע מחבירו. ומתני' דתני הבא על בתו אין לה קנס מפני שמתחייב בנפשו כר"ע אתיא. דהיכי דמי שיתחייב בבתו השתא אילו בא עליה אחר שקיל איהו קנס. השתא שבא עליה הוא לא כ"ש ובלא מיתה נמי פשיטא דלא משלם קנס. אלא ודאי מתני' בבתו נערה שנתארסה ונתגרשה עסקינן שקנסה לעצמה כר"ע ומפני שנתחייב בנפשו פטור ותדע דסתם מתני' כר"ע אתיא דהא אשת אחיו ואשת אחי אביו דתנן לעיל יש לה קנס לא אתיא אלא כר"ע דבע"ל גירשה או נתאלמנה שאל"כ הו"ל א"א ויש בהן מיתת ב"ד:

ליקוטי רש"י

[illegible]

[another's] eye and kills him with [that selfsame blow].[9] אֲבָל הֵיכָא דְסִימֵּא אֶת עֵינוֹ – **But where one blinds [another's] eye** with one blow וַהֲרָגוֹ בְּדָבָר אַחֵר – **and kills him with a different [blow],** delivered simultaneously with the first one, אֵימָא נִישְׁקוֹל מָמוֹנָא מִינֵּיהּ – **I would say** that **we should take money from him** to compensate for the eye and also execute him for the murder. Hence, a second verse is needed.[10]

The Gemara rejects this answer as well:

אָמַר לֵיהּ רָבָא – **Rava said to [Rami bar Chama]:** הָא נַמִּי מֵאִידָךְ תַּנָּא דְּבֵי חִזְקִיָּה נָפְקָא – But the law in **this** case **as well is derived from** what **the other** sage **of the academy of Chizkiyah taught,**[11] דְּתָנָא דְּבֵי חִזְקִיָּה – **for [a sage] of the academy of Chizkiyah taught** a Baraisa: "עַיִן תַּחַת עַיִן" – The Torah states, ***AN EYE FOR AN EYE,***[12] וְלֹא עַיִן וְנֶפֶשׁ תַּחַת עַיִן – which implies: **BUT NOT AN EYE AND A LIFE FOR AN EYE.**[13] Hence, another verse is not necessary.[14] **– ? –**

The Gemara offers a new answer:

אֶלָּא אָמַר רַב אַשִׁי – **Rather, Rav Ashi said:** אִיצְטְרִיךְ – **[An extra verse] is** indeed **needed,** סָלְקָא דַּעְתָּךְ אָמֵינָא – for **you might have thought to say** that one incurs no monetary liability while committing a capital offense only in cases of compensatory damages. But with regard to paying a fine, הוֹאִיל וְחִידּוּשׁ הוּא שֶׁחִידְּשָׁה תּוֹרָה בִּקְנָס – **since it is a novel law that the Torah innovated in [the case of] a fine,**[15] אַף עַל גַּב דְּמִיקְטִיל מְשַׁלֵּם – **one must pay** it **even though he is executed.**[16] קָא מַשְׁמַע לָן – **[The Torah]** therefore **informs us** with the extra verse[17] that the payment exemption applies to fines as well.[18]

The Gemara asks:

וּלְרַבָּה דְּאָמַר חִידּוּשׁ הוּא שֶׁחִידְּשָׁה תּוֹרָה בִּקְנָס – **But according to Rabbah, who said** that **it is** indeed **a novel law that the Torah innovated in [the case of] a fine,** אַף עַל גַּב דְּמִיקְטִיל מְשַׁלֵּם – and therefore **even though he is executed he** still **pays,**[19] הַאי "כָּל־חֵרֶם" מַאי עָבִיד לֵיהּ – the original question returns: **What does he do with this** superfluous verse, ***Any condemned one?***[20]

The Gemara answers:

סָבַר לָהּ כְּתַנָּא קַמָּא דְּרַבִּי חֲנַנְיָא בֶּן עֲקַבְיָא – **He holds like the Tanna Kamma of R' Chananya ben Akavya.**[21]

Mishnah נַעֲרָה שֶׁנִּתְאָרְסָה וְנִתְגָּרְשָׁה – In the case of **a *naarah* who was betrothed and** then **divorced** and subsequently was violated,[22] רַבִּי יוֹסֵי הַגְּלִילִי אוֹמֵר – **R' Yose HaGlili says:** אֵין לָהּ קְנָס – **She is**

NOTES

9. I.e. you might have thought that one is exempt from monetary liability only when he inflicts damage and causes death with one action.

10. *You shall not take atonement money* etc. (see note 8 above) is needed to teach that even where the two injuries were caused by separate (yet simultaneous) actions, only the greater penalty is incurred.

11. I.e. another Baraisa from the academy of Chizkiyah teaches that where one both blinds and kills with one blow, he incurs only the greater penalty (*Rashi;* cf. *Tosafos*). Hence, the verse *And there shall be no fatality* etc. is not needed for that teaching, and thus must be coming for the case of two blows, to indicate that even there only the greater penalty is meted out (*Shitah Yeshanah,* cited by *Shitah Mekubetzes* and *Maharam Schif*). Hence, the verse *You shall not take atonement money* is indeed extraneous.

12. *Exodus* 21:24.

13. The Gemara elsewhere (*Bava Kamma* 84a) derives from this inference that the punishment of *an eye for an eye* is not to be taken literally. For if the punishment for one who destroys his fellow's eye is the actual destruction of his own (which is a dangerous procedure), it is possible that the assailant will die while being punished, so that his punishment would entail "a life and an eye for an eye" rather than the *eye for an eye* prescribed by the Torah. And, although the main point of that Gemara's exegesis is that *an eye for an eye* is not to be taken literally, we can derive from there that the assailant receives only one punishment whether or not the blow that destroyed the victim's eye also killed him (*Rashi*).

Tos. HaRosh and *Re'ah* [see also *Ritva* and *Maharam Schif*] note that *Rashi's* explanation is incomplete, for that Gemara's reasoning is only that we must take care not to punish the assailant for more than his crime demands. That is, if he only blinded his victim, we must not impose a punishment that could also cause his death [which he does not deserve]. However, where the assailant did, in fact, both blind and kill his victim, how do we know that we do not punish him for both acts by executing him *and* exacting payment for the eye?

Tos. HaRosh explains that *Rashi* means to say that just as the first *eye* (which refers to the punishment meted out to the assailant) in the phrase *an eye for an eye* is understood to mean "only an eye" (and not an eye and a life), so the second *eye* in the phrase (which refers to the injury inflicted by the assailant) is also understood to mean "only an eye" (and not an eye and a life). Hence, pursuant to the Gemara's exegesis that the verse refers to monetary payment, the verse is expounded as follows: [The value of] an eye [shall be paid as compensation] for an eye – but not for an eye and a life. That is, the value of an eye shall be paid when the assailant only injured an eye, not when he both injured an eye and took the life of his victim – for then the assailant's liability to the death penalty exempts him from payment. See *Ritva* and *Shitah Mekubetzes* for other explanations of *Rashi.*

14. Since *an eye for an eye* implies that liability to the death penalty exempts one from monetary payment when both liabilities are incurred with one blow, the verse *And there shall be no fatality* etc. is now free to extend this ruling to where both liabilities are incurred simultaneously through two blows (see note 11 above). Hence, the verse *You shall not take atonement money for the life of a murderer* is not needed for that purpose, and is indeed extraneous.

15. Compensation is a rational law, for it is logical to require a damager to make whole the damaged party. Fines, such as those paid to the father for violation and seduction, are – on the other hand – decrees of the King [Hashem] (*Rashi*).

16. I.e. we might have thought that since a fine is a novel dictate of the Torah, it is not subject to the general rule that liability to execution exempts one from monetary payment (*Rashi*).

17. Either the verse *You shall not take atonement money for the life of a murderer* or the verse *Any condemned one* (*Rashi*). According to *Maharam* (see note 8 above), *Rashi* actually means *You shall not take* etc.

18. Since the extra verse is not needed to teach that liability to execution exempts one from paying compensatory damages, we assign it to the case of fines, to teach that the exemption applies there as well (*Rashi*).

Ritva asks: Since our Mishnah (36b) speaks of the violation of various forbidden relations, which carries both the death penalty and a fine, it should have quoted *You shall not take atonement money* (instead of *And there shall be no fatality*) as the source for exempting the violator from paying the fine. In his second and preferred answer, *Ritva* explains that since the Tanna's ruling is after all true and there are different verses supporting the general concept, he is not particular which one of them he cites – and this practice is common among Tannaim. Cf. *Tosafos.*

19. Obviously, then, Rabbah does not expound the extra verse to teach that liability to execution exempts one from paying a fine.

20. The Gemara now reverts to its original understanding – that *If there is no fatality* (וְלֹא יִהְיֶה אָסוֹן) teaches that liability to execution exempts monetary [i.e. compensatory] payments, and *You shall not take atonement money* (לֹא־תִקְחוּ כֹפֶר) outlaws atonement payments in capital cases.

21. The Tanna Kamma [cited above, 37b] expounds *Any condemned one* to teach that one who vows to give to the Temple the fixed-valuation of a person going out to be executed is exempt from making that payment [see notes 23-25 there] (*Rashi*).

22. The Mishnah's case is specifically where she was *betrothed and divorced,* for had she not been divorced, the violator would be liable to the death penalty for committing adultery with an *arusah.* Accordingly, he would be exempt from any monetary liability, as we learned in the Mishnah above, 36b (*Rashi*).

הני מילי היכא דהרגו דרך עלייה [א] שלא ניתנה שגגתו לכפרה אבל הרגו דרך ירידה דניתנה שגגתו לכפרה אימא נישקול ממונא מיניה וניפטריה קמ"ל א"ל רבא הא מדתנא דבי חזקיה נפקא (א) דתנא דבי חזקיה א) מכה אדם ומכה בהמה מה מכה בהמה לא חלקת בו בין שוגג למזיד בין מתכוין לשאין מתכוין בין דרך ירידה לדרך עלייה לפוטרו ממון אלא לחייבו ממון אף מכה אדם לא תחלוק בו בין שוגג למזיד ° בין מתכוין לשאין מתכוין בין דרך ירידה לדרך עליה לחייבו ממון אלא לפוטרו ממון אלא אמר רמי בר חמא איצטריך ס"ד אמינא ה"מ היכא דסימא את עינו והרגו בה אבל היכא דסימא את עינו והרגו בדבר אחר אימא נישקול ממונא מיניה א"ל רבא הא נמי מאידך תנא דבי חזקיה נפקא (ב) דתנא דבי חזקיה ב) עין תחת עין [ב] ולא עין ונפש תחת עין אלא אמר רב אשי איצטריך ס"ד אמינא הואיל וחידוש הוא שחידשה תורה בקנס אע"ג דמיקטיל משלם קמ"ל ולרבה דאמר (ג) חידוש הוא שחידשה תורה בקנס אע"ג דמיקטיל משלם האי ג) כל חרם מאי עביד ליה סבר לה כתנא קמא דר' חנניא בן עקביא:

מתני' נערה שנתארסה ונתגרשה רבי יוסי הגלילי אומר אין לה קנס ר"ע אומר (ד) [ג] יש לה קנס וקנסה לעצמה:

גמ' מ"ט דר' יוסי הגלילי אמר קרא ד) אשר לא אורשה הא אורסה אין לה קנס ור"ע אשר לא אורשה לאביה הא אורסה לעצמה אלא מעתה נערה ולא בוגרת ה"נ דלעצמה בתולה ולא בעולה ה"נ דלעצמה אלא לגמרי הכא נמי לגמרי אמר לך ר"ע האי לא אורשה מיבעי ליה לכדתניא אשר לא אורשה פרט לנערה שנתארסה ונתגרשה שאין לה קנס דברי ר' יוסי הגלילי ר"ע אומר יש לה קנס וקנסה לאביה והדין נותן הואיל ואביה זכאי בכסף קידושיה ואביה זכאי בכסף קנסה [ד] מה כסף קידושיה אע"פ שנתארסה ונתגרשה לאביה אף כסף קנסה אע"פ שנתארסה ונתגרשה לאביה א"כ מה ת"ל אשר לא אורשה מופנה להקיש לו ולדון הימנו ג"ש נאמר כאן אשר לא אורשה ונאמר להלן ה) אשר לא אורשה מה כאן נ' אף להלן נ' ומה להלן שקלים אף כאן שקלים ור"ע מאי חזית דאשר לא אורשה לג"ש ובתולה למעוטי בעולה

רש"י

הני מילי. דלא תקחו כופר לפטור רוצח מזיד מקטלא: **היכא דהרגו.** במזיד דרך עלייה בהנפת ידו הכהו מאחריו דלכוותה בשוגג לא ניתן לכפרת גלות כדכתיב ויפל דרך נפילה: **מדתנא דבי חזקיה נפקא.** שאין חילוק בין דרך עלייה לדרך ירידה: **לחייבו ממון.** והוא הדין לפדותו ולא יהיה אסון מיהא איצטריך דאי מהיקישא הוה אמינא אדרבה לאידך גיסא מה מכה בהמה לעולם ישלם אף מכה אדם ישלם והשתא דנפקא לן פטור תשלומין למזיד מלא יהיה אסון על כרחך היקישא לפטור שוגג דרך עלייה: **הכי גרסינן אלא אמר רמי בר חמא כו'.** איצטריך חד מהני קראי לאשמועינן דלא ליעביד ביה תרתי ואף על גב דנפקא לן מולא יהיה אסון: **הני מילי.** דלא ענשינן ליה בתרתי היכא דסימא את עינו והרגו בה באותה מכה ומת: **בדבר אחר.** במכה אחרת ובבת אחת: **אימא.** ניענשיה דמי עין ומיתה בשביל ההריגה: **הא.** דסימא עינו והרגו בה: **מאידך דבי חזקיה נפקא.** דלא תיענשיה: **ולא עין ונפש תחת עין.** מיניה קיימא לן בהחובל דעין תחת עין לאו ממש דאי אמרת ממש דלמא בהדי דסמינן לעיניה מיית והוה ליה עין ונפש תחת עין מיהו שמעינן מינה דלא תעביד ביה תרתי לא שנא מת באותה מכה לא שנא לא מת: **סלקא דעתך אמינא חידוש הוא שחידשה תורה.** בכל תשלומי קנס שאינו דין אלא גזרת מלך בעלמא וכיון דחידוש הוא וגזירת חוק אימא אע"ג דאיכא בהדיה מיתה לשלם: **קמ"ל.** חד מהנך קראי יתירא שאינו ענין לממון תניהו ענין לקנס: **כתנא קמא.** ודריש ליה באומר ערכו של יוצא ליהרג עלי: **מתני' שנתארסה ונתגרשה.** דאילו ארוסה שלא נתגרשה חייב מיתה ואין שם קנס: **אין לה קנס.** טעמא מפרש בגמרא ורישא דקתני אשת אחיו ואשת אחי אביו דבנתארסה ונתגרשה עסקינן וקתני יש להן קנס ר' עקיבא היא: **גמ' אלא מעתה.** לר' עקיבא הא דכתיב נערה למעוטי בוגרת ובתולה למעוטי בעולה: **הכי נמי.** דלא ממעט לגמרי ותדרוש נערה לאביה הא בוגרת לעצמה הא לא אשכחן דאישתמיט תנא ומתני בוגרת יש לה קנס ונימא רבי עקיבא היא: **וקנסה לאביה.** ולקמן מקשינן לר"ע: **הואיל ואביה זכאי בכסף קידושיה.** שלו הוא בנערותה ולקמן יליף לה בפרק נערה שנתפתתה (דף מו:): **מה כסף קידושיה אף על פי שנתארסה ונתגרשה.** מאחר כשחוזרת ומתקדשת בתוך נערות: **לאביה הוי.** דהא כל קידושי נערות ילפינן לאביה דגבי קידושין לא כתיב מיעוטא דאשר לא אורסה כי הכא: **נאמר כאן.** באונס: **להלן.** במפתה: **מה להלן.** במפתה שקלים דכתיב ישקול:

אימא

תוספות

הני מילי היכא דהרגו דרך עלייה דלא ניתן שגגתו לכפרה. פירוש לכפרה בידי אדם אע"ג דדרך עלייה קיל טפי מדרך ירידה כדמוכח בפרק אלו הן הגולין (מכות דף ט. ושם) גבי גר תושב גולה ע"י גר תושב וכל חומרי דשמעתין לא תלי אלא במה שלא ניתן לכפרה דאינו מקפיד הש"ס במה שסקילה ושריפה חמורין מהרג וחנק:

אבל סימא את עינו והרגו בדבר אחר אימא נשקול מיניה ממונא ונקטליה. כך גרס ר"ח דמלא יהיה אסון לא נפקא לן אלא סימא את עינו והרגו בה כי התם שבהכאה אחת הרג את האשה וגם הולדות אבל סימא את עינו והרגו בדבר אחר בבת אחת לא א) והכי איצטריך כל חרם למיפטריה קשה לרשב"א דהא ר' ישמעאל בנו של ר' יוחנן בן ברוקה לא דריש קרא להכי דלא נשקול מיניה ממונא ונקטליה אלא שלא יתן ממון ונפטריה ושמא אילו לא נאמר קאמר כדאשכחן ריש פרק נגמר הדין (סנהדרין דף מג. ושם) ובכמה דוכתי ולרשב"א נראה דהכא מסיק אליבא דתנא דבי חזקיה אבל לרבי ישמעאל ודאי לית ליה הא דתנא דבי חזקיה והא דאמר בריש הנחנקין (שם דף פד: ושם) הניחא למאן דאית ליה דתנא דבי חזקיה אלא למאן דלית ליה היקישא למה לי תנא דלית ליה דבי חזקיה היינו רבי ישמעאל ובסמוך דקאמר ולרבה דאמר חידוש הוא שחידשה תורה בקנס כו' סבר לה כת"ק דר' חנניא בן עקביא הוה מצי למימר ס"ל כרבי ישמעאל:

הא נמי מאידך תנא דבי חזקיה נפקא. לאו מההיא דרשה גופה קאמר דנפקא לן דהא ההיא דרשה לא שייכא כלל לסימא את עינו והרגו בדבר אחר אלא הכי דייק דכי היכי דדרשי' ולא עין ונפש תחת עין ה"נ דרשינן נפש תחת נפש ולא עין הנפש תחת נפש וסימא את עינו והרגו בד"א לא חשיב עין ונפש אלא נפש גרידא דמה שסימא את עינו בשעת הריגה לא חשיב כלום דבלאו הכי היה מת אלא שהמיתו בצער מרובה וא"ת בלא הא מילתא נמי מתנא דבי חזקיה דלעיל נפקא דמה מכה בהמה לא חלקת בין סימא את עינה והרגה בה להורגה בד"א כו' וי"ל דמכה אדם ומכה בהמה משמע ליה בהכאה אחת וא"ת סימא את עינו והרגו בד"א תיפוק ליה דפטור מדמי עין אפי' לא הרג דבשעה שסימא את עינו היה רודף וניתן להצילו בנפשו וי"ל דמיירי בשיכול להצילו באחד מאיבריו שלא ניתן להצילו בנפשו:

אמר רב אשי איצטריך כו'. תימה דמשמע דאם הרגו וקרע שיראין דידיה דמחייב דליכא למיפטריה לא מקרא דלא יהיה אסון ולא מקרא דנפש תחת נפש דהא הוי ממון ונפש תחת ממון ונפש ולעיל (דף ל:) פטר ה) אביי זר שאכל תרומה משלו וקרע שיראין של חבירו וי"ל דלפי האמת נפקי כולהו מתנא דבי חזקיה וה"פ והא נמי מאידך תנא דבי חזקיה נפקא כלומר ע"כ לא איצטריך כל חרם להכי אלא כולה נפקא לן מתנא דבי חזקיה דפטור דאי הוה צריך קרא למפטריה בלא כל חרם הוה פטרינן ליה מאידך תנא דבי חזקיה וא"ת וליטני דאיצטריך כל חרם להרג חבירו וקרע שיראין וי"ל דכל חרם לא יפדה משמע ליה בממון שבא על ידי אותה חבלה שהמיתה באה על ידה:

סלקא דעתך אמינא חידוש הוא קמ"ל. אע"ג דבמתני' מייתי קרא דלא יהיה אסון והכא מפיק קנס מכל חרם היינו משום דכייל מתניתין כל חייבי מיתות דקתני וכל המתחייב בנפשו כו' אי נמי מתניתין אתיא כתנא קמא דרבי חנניא בן עקביא:

אימא

חלקת בו שום לד להפטר מן תשלומין אלא בכל לדין הוא דמחייב דרבינן כל מזקין בבבא קמא (דף כו:) מפלע תחת פלע לחייב על השוגג כמזיד ועל האונס כרצון ומכה בהמה נזק הוא. **אף מכה אדם.** אין דין פטור תשלומין הכתוב בו חלוק לגום לו שיתחייב ממון אלא כל שעה פטור ממון בין בשוגג ואין נתכוון לפטור ממיתה בין במזיד ונתכוון לחייב מיתה [סנהדרין עט:]. **לשאין מתכוין.** אין בו חיוב מיתה באדם. **לדרך עליה.** שהכהו בהגבהת ידו או שהכו בחרבו מלמטה למעלה בהרימו הגרזן דקיימא לן (מכות דף ז.) דפטור מגלות אפ"ה פטור מתשלומין [ב"ק שם]. **בין דרך ירידה לדרך עלייה.** משום דגבי גלות דהורג בשוגג איכא חילוק בין דרך ירידה לדרך עלייה כדאמרי' במכות (דף ז) כל שבדרך ירידתו גולה כדכתיב ויפל עליו עד שיפול כדרך נפילה [לעיל שם]. **לחייבו ממון.** וה"ה לפדותו שאינו נפדה לעולם לא כשהוא חייב מיתה ולא כשהוא חייב גלות ולא כשהוא פטור מגלות ולא יהיה אסון מיהא וכו' [כונסחתינו. רש"י מכות בשיטמ"ק ועיי"ש]. **אלא** ממון לתנא דבי חזקיה [סנהדרין שם]. **עין תחת עין.** סימא עין חבירו נותן לו דמי עינו כמה שפחתו דמיו למכור בשוק וכן כולם ולא נטילת אבר ממש כמו שדרשו רבותינו בפרק החובל (ב"ק פד) [שמות כא, כד]. **חידוש הוא** משפט קנס חידוש הוא הלכך אע"ג דמיקטיל נמי לא מיפטר מיניה [לעיל לד: ועי' בשיטמ"ק].

מסורת הש"ס

א) לעיל לה. ב"ק לה. סנהדרין עט: פד:, ב) ב"ק פד., ג) [לעיל לד: לה:], ד) [לקמן ע.], ה) [צ"ל רב אשי].

תוספות ישנים

א) [וליכא למימר דהכא לא קאי אקרא דכל חרם אלא אקרא דלא תקחו כופר דהא אמרי' בסמוך ולרבה דאמר חידוש כו'. ת"י]:

ב) [ולפי האמת אע"ג דמלא יהיה אסון נפקי כולהו מדתנא דבי חזקיה איצטריך עין תחת עין לכדדרשינן ולא עין ונפש תחת עין אבל לא עין ונפש תחת נפש לא איצטריך למדרשי' ולאו קרא יתירא הוא אלא מפשטיה דקרא קדריש וליכא למימר דלישתוק מלא יהיה אסון ומנפש תחת נפש נפיק כולהו מכח הקישא דתנא דבי חזקיה דאכתי לא שמעי' מיניה ממון אחר בהדי מיתה דסימא את עינו והרגו בדבר אחר לא חשיב ממון ונפש אלא נפש גרידא כדמוכח בפנים להכי איצטריך לא יהיה אסון ומהשתא שמעי' מינה אפי' הרג וקרע שיראין מהקישא דתנא דבי חזקיה. ת"י]:

גליון הש"ס

גמ' בין מתכוין לשאין מתכוין. עיין לקמן מ ע"א תוד"ה אחד כדרכה:

תורה אור השלם

א) וּמַכֵּה בְהֵמָה יְשַׁלְּמֶנָּה וּמַכֵּה אָדָם יוּמָת: [ויקרא כד, כא]

ב) עַיִן תַּחַת עַיִן שֵׁן תַּחַת שֵׁן יָד תַּחַת יָד רֶגֶל תַּחַת רָגֶל: [שמות כא, כד]

ג) כָּל חֵרֶם אֲשֶׁר יָחֳרַם מִן הָאָדָם לֹא יִפָּדֶה מוֹת יוּמָת: [ויקרא כז, כט]

ד) כִּי יִמְצָא אִישׁ נַעֲרָ בְתוּלָה אֲשֶׁר לֹא אֹרָשָׂה וּתְפָשָׂהּ וְשָׁכַב עִמָּהּ וְנִמְצָאוּ: [דברים כב, כח]

ה) וְכִי יְפַתֶּה אִישׁ בְּתוּלָה אֲשֶׁר לֹא אֹרָשָׂה וְשָׁכַב עִמָּהּ מָהֹר יִמְהָרֶנָּה לּוֹ לְאִשָּׁה: [שמות כב, טו]

עין משפט נר מצוה

סד א מיי' פ"ו מהלכות רוצח ושמירת נפש הל' יג יג סמג עשין עה:

סה ב מיי' פ"א מהל' חובל הלכה ב ג ד סמג עשין ע:

סו ג מיי' פ"ב מהל' נערה הל' טז סמג עשין נד טור אה"ע סימן קעז:

סז ד מיי' פ"ג מהל' אישות הל' יא סמג עשין מח טוש"ע אה"ע סימן לז סעיף א:

תוספות רי"ד

מתני' נערה שנתארסה ונתגרשה ר"י הגלילי אומר אין לה קנס ר"ע אומר יש לה קנס וקנס' לעצמה. **מ"ט** דר' יוסי אמר קרא אשר לא אורסה הא אורסה אין לה קנס ור"ע אומר אשר לא אורסה לאביה הא אורסה לעצמה. וקי"ל הלכה כר"ע מחבירו. ומתני' דתני הבא על בתו אין לה קנס מפני שמתחייב בנפשו כר"ע אתיא. דהיכי דמי שיתחייב בבתו השתא אילו בא עליה אחר שקיל איהו קנס. השתא שבא עליה הוא לא כ"ש ובלא מיתה נמי פשיטא דלא משלם קנס. אלא ודאי מתני' בבתו נערה שנתארסה ונתגרשה עסקינן שקנסה לעצמה כר"ע ומפני שנתחייב בנפשו פטור ותדע דסתם מתני' כר"ע אתיא דהא אשת אחיו ואשת אחי אביו דתנן לעיל יש לה קנס לא אתיא אלא כר"ע דבע"כ גירשה או נתאלמנה שאל"כ הו"ל א"א ויש בהן מיתת ב"ד:

ליקוטי רש"י

מכה אדם ומכה בהמה. מכה בהמה ישלמנה ומכה אדם לא ישלם אלא יומת הקיש פטור ממון דמכה אדם לחיוב ממון דמכה בהמה מה מכה בהמה אין לך בו חילוק (לחיוב) [לפטור] אף מכה אדם אין לך בו חילוק (לפטור) [לחיוב] מכה בהמה לעולם חייב דאמרי' בב"ק (דף כו) פלע תחת פלע לחייב על השוגג כמזיד ואונס כרצון [לעיל לה.]. הוקשו יחד דמה מכה בהמה לעולם משלם ואפילו בשוגג כדאמרי' [לעיל דף כו.] לא מכה אדם דפטוריה קרא מתשלומין דכתיב יומת לעולם פטור ואפילו בשוגג הואיל ובמזיד שייך מיתה [ב"ק לה.]. לכך הוקשו בהאי קרא מכה בהמה ישלמנה ומכה אדם יומת ומשמע בבהמה חייב ממון ובאדם פטור ממון דכתיב בהמה ישלמנה אדם והקיש לך הכתוב פטור תשלומין של אדם לחיוב תשלומין של בהמה. **לדרך עליה.** לא שייך למתני גבי בהמה אלא משום דבאדם אשכחן ביה חילוק בהורג בשוגג דדרך ירידה חייב גלות אבל דרך עלייה בהרימו את ידו פטור מגלות (במדבר לה) ויפל עליו וימת לדרך נפילה [מכות ז.]. **לפוטרו ממון אלא לחייבו ממון.** כלומר לא

הָנֵי מִילֵּי – **these words** that bar taking money to redeem an intentional murderer from execution הֵיכָא דַהֲרָגוֹ דֶּרֶךְ עֲלִיָּיה – apply only **where [the murderer] killed [his victim]** with an **upward** blow,[1] שֶׁלֹּא נִיתְּנָה שִׁגְגָתוֹ לְכַפָּרָה – **whose unintentional commission is not given to atonement.**[2] אֲבָל הֲרָגוֹ דֶּרֶךְ יְרִידָה – **But if he killed him** deliberately with a **downward** blow, דְּנִיתְּנָה שִׁגְגָתוֹ לְכַפָּרָה – **whose unintentional commission *is* given to atonement,** אֵימָא נִישְׁקוֹל מָמוֹנָא מִינֵּיהּ וְנִיפְטְרֵיהּ – **I would say** that **we should take money from him and pardon him** from execution. קָא מַשְׁמַע לָן – **[The Torah]** therefore **informs us,** via the verse *Any condemned one,* that atonement payment cannot be made even when one kills deliberately with a downward blow.[3]

The Gemara rejects this answer:

הָא מִדְּתָנָא אֲמַר לֵיהּ רָבָא – **Rava said to [Rami bar Chama]:** דְּבֵי חִזְקִיָּה נָפְקָא – **This** law **is derived from** that **which [a sage] of the academy of Chizkiyah taught,**[4] דְּתָנָא דְּבֵי חִזְקִיָּה – **for [a sage] of the academy of Chizkiyah taught** a Baraisa:[5] ,,מַכֵּה אָדָם . . . וּמַכֵּה בְהֵמָה" – Scripture draws an analogy between ***ONE WHO STRIKES*** [i.e. kills] ***A PERSON*** (the killer is executed and does not pay monetary damages) and ***ONE WHO STRIKES AN ANIMAL*** (he does pay monetary damages). From this analogy we derive: מַה מַּכֵּה בְהֵמָה לֹא חִלַּקְתָּ בּוֹ בֵּין שׁוֹגֵג לְמֵזִיד – **JUST AS** in the case of **ONE WHO STRIKES AN ANIMAL YOU DO NOT DISTINGUISH BETWEEN** an **INADVERTENT** act **AND** a **DELIBERATE** act, בֵּין מִתְכַּוֵּין לְשֶׁאֵין מִתְכַּוֵּין – **BETWEEN** an **INTENTIONAL** act **AND** an **UNINTENTIONAL** act, בֵּין דֶּרֶךְ יְרִידָה לְדֶרֶךְ עֲלִיָּיה – or **BETWEEN** a **DOWNWARD** blow **AND** an **UPWARD** blow, לְפוֹטְרוֹ מָמוֹן – **TO EXEMPT HIM** from paying **MONEY** in any of these cases – אֶלָּא לְחַיְּיבוֹ מָמוֹן – **RATHER,** the verse means **TO OBLIGATE HIM** to pay **MONEY** in all these cases; אַף מַכֵּה אָדָם – so **TOO,** with regard to killing **A PERSON,** לֹא תַחֲלוֹק בּוֹ בֵּין שׁוֹגֵג לְמֵזִיד – **YOU SHOULD NOT DISTINGUISH BETWEEN** an **INADVERTENT** act **AND** a **DELIBERATE** act, בֵּין מִתְכַּוֵּין לְשֶׁאֵין מִתְכַּוֵּין – **BETWEEN** an **INTENTIONAL** act **AND** an **UNINTENTIONAL** act, בֵּין דֶּרֶךְ יְרִידָה לְדֶרֶךְ עֲלִיָּה – or **BETWEEN** a **DOWNWARD** blow **AND** an **UPWARD** blow לְחַיְּיבוֹ מָמוֹן – **TO OBLIGATE HIM** to pay **MONEY** in any of these cases – אֶלָּא לְפוֹטְרוֹ מָמוֹן – **RATHER** you are **TO EXEMPT HIM** from paying **MONEY** in all these cases.[6] – ? –

Rami bar Chama acknowledges that his answer has been refuted, and offers a different one:

אֶלָּא אָמַר רָמִי בַּר חָמָא – **Rather, Rami bar Chama said:** אִיצְטְרִיךְ – **[One]** of the two verses[7] **is needed** to teach that a person incurs no monetary liability while committing a capital offense, even though that law is derived from the third verse – *And there shall be no fatality* etc.[8] סָלְקָא דַעְתָּךְ אֲמִינָא – For **you might have thought to say** that הָנֵי מִילֵּי – **this law** הֵיכָא דְּסִימֵּא אֶת עֵינוֹ וַהֲרָגוֹ בָּהּ – was stated only **where one blinds**

NOTES

1. I.e. he killed him deliberately with a blow delivered by the upward thrust of his arm, coming from behind (*Rashi*).

2. For one is liable to exile (for unintentional homicide) only if he killed the victim with a downward motion, as derived from *Numbers* 35:23: וַיַּפֵּל עָלָיו, *he caused to fall upon him* (*Rashi,* from *Makkos* 7b).

3. *Tosafos* (above, 37b ד״ה מיתות) question why – according to *Rashi,* who counts murder among the "light" capital offenses because its unintentional commission has an atonement through exile (see above, 37b note 37) – three verses are needed to outlaw atonement payments in every situation. [According to *Rashi,* the Gemara previously stated that *You shall not take atonement money for the life of the murderer* bans atonement payments in the case of "light" capital offenses (see *Rashi* above, 37b ד״ה ולא ממילא); [*A*] *condemned one . . . shall not be redeemed* restricts them in the case of "grave" capital offenses; and *Any* [*condemned one . . . shall not be redeemed*], the Gemara now tells us, outlaws them when one murders with a downward blow.] *Tosafos* (as explained by *Rashash,* who claims that *Maharsha's* explanation is unclear) argue that, in *Rashi's* view, murder itself encompasses all possibilities. That is, deliberate killing with a downward blow is a "light" capital offense, since its unintentional commission has an atonement (exile). Deliberate killing with an upward blow is a "grave" capital offense, since its unintentional commission does not have the atonement of exile. Hence, only two verses should be needed to create a universal ban on atonement payments: *You shall not take atonement money* etc. outlaws them in the case of an upward blow (which represents "grave" capital offenses), and [*A*] *condemned one* etc. restricts them in the case of a downward blow ("light" capital offenses) – or the reverse. *Any* [*condemned one* etc.] thus remains superfluous according to Chananya ben Akavya. See *Tosafos* and *Shitah Mekubetzes* for different approaches in our *sugya.*

4. He taught us that there is no difference between an upward and a downward blow [with regard to monetary matters] (*Rashi*).

5. See above, 35a notes 5-12, for a full elucidation of this Baraisa.

6. [I.e. the Torah's juxtaposing the phrases *one who strikes a person* and *one who strikes an animal* teaches that just as in the case of the animal the damager's monetary liability is not affected by how his harmful act was committed (whether deliberately or inadvertently, upward or downward etc.), so too where one killed a human being, his monetary liability is not affected by how the act was committed. For example, we derive from the verse, *And there shall be no fatality, he shall be punished* (monetarily), that one is exempt from any monetary liability arising from an intentional murder, and the aforementioned Scriptural juxtaposition extends that law to the case of an inadvertent murder.] And the juxtaposition further teaches us not to differentiate between an upward and a downward motion with regard to redeeming one's death penalty with atonement money (*Rashi*). [Hence, even if we posit that *You shall not take atonement money for the life of a murderer* was stated regarding a deliberate murder through an upward motion (whose inadvertent commission has no atonement through exile), we would nonetheless know that the atonement-payment ban applies also in the case of a deliberate murder through a downward motion – even though its inadvertent commission does have atonement through exile – for the Baraisa of Chizkiyah's academy teaches that there is no difference between an upward and downward motion with regard to monetary payment. Hence, we already know that the death penalty cannot be redeemed through monetary atonement even where an inadvertent commission of the offense has an atonement. Why, then, is the verse *Any condemned one* necessary?]

Rashi notes that even in light of Chizkiyah's Baraisa, it was necessary for the Mishnah to derive from *And there shall be no fatality, he shall be punished* [monetarily] that one who is liable to execution is exempt from monetary payment. For from the juxtaposition expounded in the Baraisa alone we would have inferred the opposite ruling – viz. that just as one who strikes an animal is always liable to payment, so too one who kills a person is always liable to payment. It is only after we derive from *And there shall be no fatality* etc. that liability to the death penalty exempts one from monetary payment we can say that the juxtaposition teaches that the exemption from monetary liability applies even when the act occurred inadvertently [or] (see *Shitah Mekubetzes* on *Rashi's* text and *Beur* to *Maharam Schif*) with an upward motion.

7. *Any condemned one* etc. (כָּל־חֵרֶם) and *You shall not take atonement money* etc. (לֹא־תִקְחוּ כֹפֶר) [see following note].

8. *Rashi. Maharam* (to *Tosafos* ד״ה אבל) explains *Rashi* to mean that the verse *Any condemned one . . . shall not be redeemed,* which the Gemara contends is extraneous, is actually needed to teach that a person condemned to execution cannot proffer atonement money to redeem his death sentence – and this interpretation indeed concurs with the Baraisa of R' Yishmael the son of R' Yochanan ben Berokah (above, 37b). The verse *You shall not take atonement money for the life of the murderer,* which heretofore we have understood as outlawing atonement payments in capital cases, in fact comes to teach that a murderer is exempt from paying damages if he is to be executed. Although that law is derived also from *And there shall be no fatality* (וְלֹא יִהְיֶה אָסוֹן), Rami bar Chama now argues that both verses are needed to establish it as applying in all cases. [According to Rami's interpretation, the term *atonement money* in the verse *You shall not take atonement money* perforce means money paid to "atone" for damages inflicted simultaneously with the murder (see *Shitah Mekubetzes* above, 37b ד״ה לא תקחו כופר לנפש רוצח בא״ד ולשון כופר היינו כופר השיראין שקרע וכו׳).]

מִנַּיִן – But FROM WHERE do I know that the law applies even to CAPITAL OFFENSES that are LIGHT in the sense THAT THEIR UNINTENTIONAL COMMISSIONS *ARE* GIVEN TO ATONEMENT?[40] תַּלְמוּד לוֹמַר – To teach us this, THE TORAH STATES: ,,כָּל־חֵרֶם" – *"ANY" CONDEMNED ONE*[41] . . . *shall not be redeemed.*[42]

The Gemara objects to this answer:

וְלֹא מִמֵּילָא מִ,,לֹא־תִקְחוּ כֹפֶר" שָׁמְעַתְּ מִינָּהּ – **But do you not, as a matter of course, derive** this **from** the verse, ***You shall not take atonement money*** *for the life of a murderer,*[43] לֹא תִּשְׁקוֹל מָמוֹנָא מִינֵּיהּ וְתִיפַּטְרֵיהּ – which, as explained above, teaches: **Do not take money from [the murderer] and pardon him** from execution?[44] ,,כָּל חֵרֶם" לָמָּה לִי – **Why,** then, **do I [need]** the verse, ***Any condemned one*** etc.? According to Chananya ben Akavya, it is indeed superfluous! – ? –

The Gemara answers:

אָמַר רָמִי בַּר חָמָא – **Rami bar Chama said:** אִיצְטְרִיךְ – In fact, **[*Any condemned one* etc.] is needed,** סַלְקָא דַּעְתָּךְ אֲמִינָא – for if the Torah had stated only *You shall not take atonement money for the life of a murderer,* **you might have thought to say** that

NOTES

chatas-offering is available when they are committed inadvertently (*Rashi,* as explained by the Rishonim; cf. *Shitah Mekubetzes,* who interprets *Rashi* differently).

Tosafos below (38a ד״ה הני) explain that the "grave capital offenses" mentioned in the Baraisa are not those involving the greatest turpitude, for surely the transgressions punishable by stoning [e.g. idolatry, Sabbath desecration] are more heinous than those like kidnaping that are punished by choking (see *Sanhedrin* 49b). Rather, the Baraisa speaks of capital offenses that are "grave" in the specific sense that when committed unintentionally they have no atonement. For since the issue at hand is whether one can exempt himself from the death penalty by atoning for his transgression with a monetary payment, the existence of another method of atonement for a different contingency is more of a determining factor than is the degree of evil inherent in the sin itself.

40. The Baraisa now refers to all capital offenses that carry the *kares* penalty when the perpetrator was not warned by witnesses [and thus cannot be executed by the court]. Examples include idolatry, Sabbath desecration and the forbidden relations, and in each case an unintentional transgression has atonement via a *chatas* offering. The Baraisa refers also to murder, which when committed inadvertently has an atonement through exile in a city of refuge (*Rashi*). The Baraisa thus asks: Since each of these offenses has a method of atonement for the contingency of unintentional commission, how do we know that they *do not* likewise have another method of atonement (viz. monetary payment) for the contingency of intentional commission?

41. See above, note 36.

42. The inclusionary word "any" teaches that *all* individuals "condemned" to execution, even those who – had they committed the same sin unintentionally – could have had an atonement, "shall not be redeemed" [cannot make an atonement payment].

43. *Numbers* 35:31.

44. I.e. the *Numbers* verse itself teaches that atonement payments cannot be made for the intentional violation of a capital offense even when a method of atonement is prescribed for its unintentional violation – for the verse speaks of an intentional murderer and expressly denies him the opportunity to make an atonement payment even though, had he killed unintentionally, he could have achieved atonement through being exiled (*Rashi;* cf. *Tosafos* ד״ה מיתות).

וחדא במיתה ומלקות וצריכא דאי אשמעינן מיתה וממון משום דחדא בגופיה וחדא בממוניה לא עבדינן אבל במיתה ומלקות דאידי ואידי בגופיה אימא מיתה אריכתא היא ונעביד ביה ואי אשמעינן מיתה ומלקות דתרתי בגופיה לא עבדינן אבל מיתה וממון דחדא בגופיה וחדא בממוניה אימא נעביד ביה צריכא א) ולא תקחו כופר לנפש רוצח למה לי ה) דאמר רחמנא א לא תשקול ממונא מיניה ותפטריה מקטלא ב) לא תקחו כופר לנוס אל עיר מקלטו א) למה לי ב דאמר רחמנא לא תשקול ממונא מיניה ותפטריה מן גלות ותרי קראי למה לי חד בשוגג וחד במזיד וצריכי דאי אשמעינן מזיד משום דחמיר איסוריה אבל שוגג דלא חמיר איסוריה אימא לא ואי אשמעינן שוגג משום דליכא איבוד נשמה אבל מזיד דאיכא איבוד נשמה אימא לא צריכא ג) ולארץ לא יכופר לדם אשר שופך בה כי אם בדם שופכו למה לי מבעי ליה לכדתניא ג) מנין ג שאם נתערפה עגלה ואח"כ נמצא ההורג מנין שאין פוטרין אותו שנאמר ולארץ לא יכופר לדם אשר שופך בה וגו' ד) ואתה תבער הדם הנקי מקרבך למה לי מיבעי ליה לכדתניא ג) מנין למומתים בסייף שהוא מן הצואר ת"ל ואתה תבער הדם הנקי מקרבך הוקשו כל שופכי דמים לעגלה ערופה מה להלן מן הצואר ד אף שופכי דמים מן הצואר אי מה ה להלן בקופיץ וממול עורף אף כאן בקופיץ וממול עורף ז אמר רב נחמן אמר רבה בר אבוה אמר קרא ה) ואהבת לרעך כמוך ברור לו מיתה יפה ו) כל חרם אשר יחרם מן האדם לא יפדה למה לי מיבעי ליה לכדתניא ח) מנין ליוצא ליהרג ואמר אחד ערכו עלי מנין ו שלא אמר כלום שנאמר כל חרם אשר יחרם מן האדם לא יפדה יכול אף קודם שנגמר דינו בן ת"ל מן האדם ולא כל האדם ט) ולרבי חנניא בן עקביא דאמר נערך מפני שדמיו קצובין האי כל חרם מאי עביד ליה מיבעי ליה לכדתניא י) רבי ישמעאל בנו של ר' יוחנן בן ברוקה אומר ז לפי שמצינו למומתים בידי שמים שנותנין ממון ומתכפר להן שנאמר ז) אם כופר יושת עליו יכול אף בידי אדם כן ת"ל חרם מן האדם לא יפדה ואין לי אלא מיתות חמורות שלא ניתנה שגגתן לכפרה מיתות קלות שניתנה שגגתן לכפרה מנין ת"ל כל חרם ולא ממילא מלא תקחו כופר שמעת מינה לא תשקול ממונא מיניה ותיפטריה כל חרם ל"ל אמר רמי בר חמא איצטריך ס"ד אמינא הני

רש"י

לא תקחו כופר. משמע נמי אם תהרגנו לא תענשנו ממון: דאמר רחמנא. שבילה הוא דמשנין לאו לאשמעינן דלא תעביד ביה תרתי אלא לאשמועינן בחיוב מיתה לבדה שלא יפדה בממון: לא תקחו כופר לנוס. קא ס"ד לא תעביד ביה תרתי להורג בשוגג גלות וממון: וצריכי דאי אשמעינן מזיד. דלא ליפרוק נפשיה בממון הוה אמינא משום דחמיר איסוריה אבל בשוגג ליפרוק נפשיה בממון מגלות: ואי אשמעינן שוגג. דמשום דאין בגלותו איבוד נשמה להכי לא לפטריה בממון אלא ליגלי: אבל מזיד. משום איבוד נשמה איחור ישקול ממונא ונקיים נפש בישראל: כי אם בדם שופכו. ולא בפדיון ממון למה לי מלא תקחו כופר נפקא: שאין פוטרין אותו. לומר כבר נתכפר בעודו ספק שהעגלה מכפרת על הספק: ואתה תבער. בתר עריפה כתיב: מיתה יפה. בסייף ומלך הסימנים שימות מהר: כל חרם וגו'. משמע לשון חייבי מיתות כמו זובח לאלהים יחרם (שמות כב): ערכו עלי. ואע"פ שערך אינו לפי דמים אלא לפי שנים לא אמר כלום דמעטיה קרא הכא והאי חרם לשון הקדש הוא: שדמיו קצובין. בתורה לפי שנים ולא דמי לאומר דמיו עלי דדמים אין לו אבל ערך יש לו: למומתין בידי שמים. כגון מי שהרג שורו את הנפש דכתיב ביה יומת ולא מיתת בית דין דנפקא לן בסנהדרין (דף טו:) מות יומת המכה רוצח הוא על רציחתו אתה הורגו ואי אתה הורגו על רציחת שורו והאי יומת בידי שמים: יכול אף. חייבי מיתות ב"ד יפדו בממון: חרם מן האדם. אדם שמחויב חרם: אלא מיתות חמורות שלא ניתנה שגגתן לכפרה. כיון דקרא לא פריש כל מיתות מיסתייך אי שדית הך חומרא דאין ממונו מצילו אמיתות חמורות ומאי ניהו כגון העושה חבורה באביו או גונב נפש מישראל שאין כפרה כתובה בשגגתו שאין כרת בזדונו דליחייב חטאת בשגגתו: מיתות קלות. היינו כל מיתות האמורות בהן כרת על זדונו בלא התראה יש כפרה בשגגתה בחטאת כגון עבודת כוכבים ושבת ועריות א"נ רוצח שיש כפרה לשגגתו בגלות: ולא ממילא. שמעת לה מלא תקחו כופר הא גבי רוצח כתיבא וניתנה כפרה לשגגתו ואשמעינן קרא שלא יגאל את עצמו בממון ולמה לי תו כל חרם:

תוספות

וחדא במיתה ומלקות. ורבנן מלקות וממון ומיתה ומלקות תרוייהו נפקי מכדי רשעתו דמשמע אם נתחייב בהדי מלקות מיתה או ממון משום רשעה אחת אתה מחייבו ואע"ג דסמיך ליה ארבעים יכנו לא יוסיף מ"מ אין לנו לומר דילקה ולא ימות כמו שלוקה ואינו משלם דאתגורי איתגור כדפריך בהגזלן (סנהדרין דף פא. ושם) ואע"ג דגבי ממון ומלקות אמרינן דנדון בממון אפילו ממונא קולא התם משום דהם רחמנא אנחבל ה): לא תשקול ממונא מיניה ותפטריה מגלות. קשה לרשב"א דל"ל קרא מתנא דבי חזקיה נפקא דלא חילקת בין שוגג למזיד וכי היכי דבמזיד לא תשקול מיניה ממונא ותפטריה מקטלא אף שוגג לא תשקול מיניה ממונא ותפטריה מגלות ואומר ר"י דלא שייך לאקושי שוגג למזיד כי האי גוונא כיון שאין פדיון שניהם שוה דפדיון של מזיד לפוטרו ממיתה ופדיון של שוגג לפוטרו מגלות: ואח"כ נמצא ההורג. בפירוש החומש פ"ה הך דרשה מואתה תבער דם הנקי ולא עיין כאן ומיהו יש לקיים פירושו דהך סוגיא דשמעתא דמוקמי' ואתה תבער להקיש שופכי דמים לעגלה ערופה אתיא כמאן דאמר חנק חמור כדמוכח בפרק ד' מיתות (שם דף נב:) דלמאן דאמר חנק קל יליף סייף ברוצח מנקום ינקם הלכך לדידיה אייתר ואתה תבער לנערפה העגלה ואח"כ נמצא ההורג וקרא דולארץ לא יכופר דרשינן ליה לכדרבא בפ' בתרא דכריתות (דף כו.) דמייתינן עגלה ערופה אע"פ שעבר יוה"כ עליה: מה להלן בקופיץ וממול עורף. וא"ת ממול עורף מנלן והא וערפו כתיב דמשמע עורף ממש ויש לומר דבפ' עגלה ערופה (סוטה דף מו:) גמר עריפה עריפה מחטאת העוף: הוקשו שופכי דמים כו'. הוה מצי למימר הניחא למ"ד חנק חמור אלא למ"ד חנק קל כו': ברור לו מיתה יפה. ומהאי טעמא לא הוה שמעינן מן הלואר דאם יתחב סכין בלבו הוי נמי מיתה יפה: לפי שמצינו מומתים בידי שמים. דכתיב וגם בעליו יומת דע"כ לא בידי אדם קאמר דכתיב מות יומת המכה רוצח הוא וגו' על רציחתו אתה הורגו כו' אלא ודאי בידי שמים ואף על גב דדרשינן מיניה בפ"ק דסנהדרין (דף טו. ושם) כמיתת בעלים כך מיתת השור היינו מדכתיב יומת ולא כתיב ימות וכ"ת כולה להכי הוא דאתא אם כן ליכתוב השור יסקל כבעלים ולשתוק אי נמי ט) וגם כבעליו יומת הלכך שמע מינה תרתי: יכול אף בידי אדם כן. יש תימה דהיכי בעי למילף מיתה בידי אדם ממיתה בידי שמים י) [ותירץ מהר"ם כיון דאיתקש מיתת שור למיתת בעלים נקיט נמי מיתת בעלים שעל ידי שור]: מיתות קלות שניתן שגגתן לכפרה מנין. פי' בקונט' כגון עבודת כוכבים ושבת וגילוי עריות שניתן שגגתן לכפרה ע"י קרבן וכן רוצח ניתנה שגגתו לכפרה ע"י גלות וקשה דא"כ למסקנא אמאי איצטריך חרם וכל חרם ולא תקחו ג' קראי בלא תקחו כופר ובחרם סגי דחד לדרך עלייה וחד לדרך ירידה שניתן שגגתו לכפרה דהיינו מיתות קלות לפ"ה לכך נראה דמיתות קלות לא חשיב אלא הנהו שניתן שגגתן לכפרה ע"י ממון או ע"י קרבן אבל רוצח לא ניתן שגגתו לכפרה ע"י ממון אלא על ידי גלות וה"פ דברייתא אין לי אלא מיתות חמורות שלא ניתן שגגתן לכפרה ע"י קרבן דהיינו כל מיתות שאין בהן כרת כגון מסית ומדיח ונביא השקר וזקן ממרא ומכה אביו ואמו ומקלל אביו ואמו וגונב נפש ומגדף אליבא דרבנן דאמרי בכריתות (דף ג:) דאין מביא קרבן על שגגתו דכתיב לעושה בשגגה פרט למגדף שאין בו מעשה ורוצח ומיתות קלות כגון עבודת כוכבים ושבת ועריות דיש בהן כרת ומביא קרבן על שגגתן ופריך ולא ממילא שמעת מינה מלא תקחו כופר ומהתם שמעינן כל מיתות חמורות ולמה לי קרא למיתות חמורות אבל למיתות קלות ודאי צריך קרא ומשני דאיצטריך תרי קראי למיתות חמורות חד לדרך עלייה שלא ניתן שגגתו לכפרה כלל וחד לדרך ירידה שניתן שגגתו לכפרה על ידי גלות קשה לרשב"א דמאי איצטריך קרא לחייבי מיתות קלות כגון עבודת כוכבים ושבת ועריות דמה שייך שם כופר למ"ד כופר היינו דמי ניזק ותירץ דרבי ישמעאל בנו של רבי יוחנן בן ברוקה לטעמיה דאמר בפרק שור שנגח ד' וה' (ב"ק דף מ.) ונתן פדיון נפשו דמי מזיק:

הני

עין משפט נר מצוה

נז א מיי' פ"א מהל' רוצח ושמירת נפש הלכה ד סמג לאוין קסא:
נח ב מיי' פ"ה שם הל' א סמג לאוין קסב:
נט ג מיי' פ"י שם הל' ח סמג עשין עח:
ס ד מיי' פט"ו מהל' סנהדרין הלכה ד סמג עשין קג:
סא ה מיי' פ"ט מהל' רוצח הלכה ג סמג עשין עח:
סב ו מיי' פ"א מהל' ערכין הל' יג סמג עשין קכח:
סג ז מיי' פ"י מהלכות נזקי ממון הל' ד סמג עשין סז:

תוספות ישנים

א) [דנפקא לן מתנא דבי חזקיה דלא חילקת בין שוגג למזיד לאמאי הס"ד השתא דבעי למימר קרא לא תשקול מיניה ממונא ונחייביה. מ"י].

תורה אור השלם

א) וְלֹא תִקְחוּ כֹפֶר לְנֶפֶשׁ רֹצֵחַ אֲשֶׁר הוּא רָשָׁע לָמוּת כִּי מוֹת יוּמָת: [במדבר לה, לא]
ב) וְלֹא תִקְחוּ כֹפֶר לָנוּס אֶל עִיר מִקְלָטוֹ לָשׁוּב לָשֶׁבֶת בָּאָרֶץ עַד מוֹת הַכֹּהֵן: [במדבר לה, לב]
ג) וְלֹא תַחֲנִיפוּ אֶת הָאָרֶץ אֲשֶׁר אַתֶּם בָּהּ כִּי הַדָּם הוּא יַחֲנִיף אֶת הָאָרֶץ וְלָאָרֶץ לֹא יְכֻפַּר לַדָּם אֲשֶׁר שֻׁפַּךְ בָּהּ כִּי אִם בְּדַם שֹׁפְכוֹ: [במדבר לה, לג]
ד) וְאַתָּה תְּבַעֵר הַדָּם הַנָּקִי מִקִּרְבֶּךָ כִּי תַעֲשֶׂה הַיָּשָׁר בְּעֵינֵי יְיָ: [דברים כא, ט]
ה) לֹא תִקֹּם וְלֹא תִטֹּר אֶת בְּנֵי עַמֶּךָ וְאָהַבְתָּ לְרֵעֲךָ כָּמוֹךָ אֲנִי יְיָ: [ויקרא יט, יח]
ו) כָּל חֵרֶם אֲשֶׁר יָחֳרַם מִן הָאָדָם לֹא יִפָּדֶה מוֹת יוּמָת: [ויקרא כז, כט]
ז) אִם כֹּפֶר יוּשַׁת עָלָיו וְנָתַן פִּדְיֹן נַפְשׁוֹ כְּכֹל אֲשֶׁר יוּשַׁת עָלָיו: [שמות כא, ל]

מסורת הש"ס

א) ב"ק פג., ב) סוטה מז:, ג) סנהדרין נב:, ד) שם ודף מה. פסחים עה. [ב"ק נא. סוטה מ:], ה) ערכין ו:, ו) [שם], ח) [וע"ע תוס' לעיל לב. ד"ה ולא], ט) ס"א ליכתוב וגם בעליו יומת ותו לא, י) מ"י כ"י.

ליקוטי רש"י

ולא תקחו כופר. לא יפטר בממון [במדבר לה, לא]. לא תקחו כופר לנוס אל עיר מקלטו. למי שנס אל עיר מקלטו שהרג בשוגג אינו נפטר מגלות בממון ליתן כופר לשוב לשבת בארץ בטרם ימות הכהן. לנוס. כמו לנס (בשו"א וקמ"ץ) כמו (מיכה ב) שובי מלחמה ששבו מן המלחמה וכן (צפניה ג) נוגי ממועד וכן (יהושע ה) כי מולים היו כאשר תאמר שוב על מי ששב כבר ומול על מי שמל כבר כן תאמר לנוס על מי שנס כבר וקורהו נוס כלומר מוברח. ואם תאמר לנוס לברוח ותפרשהו לא תקחו כופר למי שיש לו לברוח לפטרו מן הגלות לא ידעתי היאך יאמר לשוב לשבת בארץ הרי עדיין לא נס ומהיכן ישוב [במדבר לה, לב ועי' שיטמ"ק]. ואתה תבער הדם הנקי. מגיד שאם נמצא ההורג אחר שנתערפה העגלה הרי זה יהרג והוא הישר בעיני ה' [דברים כא, ט]. מן הצואר. גרון [סנהדרין נב:]. בקופיץ. סכין גדול שבן לדך עריפה [בכורות י:]. סכין גדול הוא ורוכן אינן לשחיטה אלא לחיתוך בשר ולשבירת עצמות [פסחים ע.]. סכין גדול שקולבין בו בשר [ביצה כח.]. סתם קופיץ הוא סכין של קצבים דומה לקרדומות שלנו [שם לא.]. וממול עורף. מאחרי הפנים דכתיב (דברים כא) וערפו לשון עורף מול הרואה את העורף דהיינו אחורי צואר שרואין את העורף ועורף הוא קטרי"ל שכנגד הפנים דכתיב (ירמיה לב) ויפנו אלי עורף ולא פנים אלמא עורף להדי פנים [סנהדרין שם]. ואהבת לרעך כמוך. אמר רבי עקיבא זה כלל גדול בתורה (ת"כ) [ויקרא יט, יח]. מיתה יפה. ולא תבזהו [סנהדרין מה.]. כל חרם וכו' לא יפדה. מי שהוא ראוי ליחרם וליהרג אינו בכלל פדיון. למומתים בידי שמים. כגון האי דכתיב השור יסקל וגם בעליו יומת והך מיתה ליכא למימר בידי אדם דהא אמרי' בפ"ק דסנהדרין (דף טו:) מות יומת המכה רוצח הוא על רציחתו אתה הורגו ואי אתה הורגו על רציחת שורו [ערכין ו:]. אם כופר יושת עליו. אם זה אינו תלוי והרי הוא כמו (לקמן כב כד) אם כסף תלוה לשון אשר זה משפטו שישיתו עליו בית דין כופר [שמות כא, ל]. שלא ניתנה שגגתן לכפרה. כגון מגדף ומקלל אביו דאם עשה בשוגג אינו בקרבן ולא בגלות. מיתות קלות. כלומר דקלות להך מילתא שניתנה שגגתן לכפרה כגון רוצח דשגגתו גולה ועובד ע"ז ומחלל שבת ובא על הערוה דשגגתו חטאת [ערכין שם].

the verse, ***Any condemned one – who among man has been condemned – shall not be redeemed;*** *he shall be put to death*?[24]

The Gemara answers:

מִיבָּעֵי לֵיהּ לִכְדְתַנְיָא – **We need it for that** law **which was taught in a Baraisa:**[25] מִנַּיִן לַיּוֹצֵא לֵיהָרֵג – FROM WHERE do we know in the case of a person WHO IS GOING OUT TO BE EXECUTED וְאָמַר אֶחָד עֶרְכּוֹ עָלַי – AND ONE other person SAID, "I take UPON MYSELF to give HIS FIXED VALUATION"[26] – מִנַּיִן שֶׁלֹּא אָמַר כְּלוּם – FROM WHERE do we know THAT HE HAS SAID NOTHING?[27] שֶׁנֶּאֱמַר – FOR IT IS STATED: ,,כָּל־חֵרֶם אֲשֶׁר יָחֳרַם מִן־הָאָדָם לֹא יִפָּדֶה'' – *ANY CONSECRATED ONE* (*cherem*) – *WHO AMONG MAN HAS BEEN CONDEMNED* (*yacharam*) – *SHALL NOT BE REDEEMED.*[28] יָכוֹל אַף קוֹדֶם שֶׁנִּגְמַר דִּינוֹ כֵּן – However, IT COULD BE thought that the law is ALSO THUS if the vow was made BEFORE HIS SENTENCE WAS FINALIZED. תַּלְמוּד לוֹמַר – To disabuse us of this notion THE TORAH STATES: ,,מִן־הָאָדָם'' – *FROM A MAN* – וְלֹא כָּל הָאָדָם – which implies: BUT NOT ALL MEN.[29]

The Gemara asks:

וּלְרַבִּי חֲנַנְיָא בֶּן עֲקַבְיָא – **But according to Chananya ben Akavya,** דְּאָמַר נֶעֱרָךְ – **who said**[30] that **[one going out to be executed] can be the subject of a fixed-valuation vow** מִפְּנֵי שֶׁדָּמָיו קְצוּבִין – **because his worth is fixed** in the Torah according to his age and gender and not according to his actual market value,[31] הַאי ,,כָּל־חֵרֶם'' מַאי עָבֵיד לֵיהּ – **what does he do with this** seemingly superfluous verse, ***Any condemned one*** ... *shall not be redeemed*?[32]

The Gemara answers:

מִיבָּעֵי לֵיהּ לִכְדְתַנְיָא – **He needs it for that** law **which was taught in a Baraisa:** רַבִּי יִשְׁמָעֵאל בְּנוֹ שֶׁל רַבִּי יוֹחָנָן בֶּן בְּרוֹקָה אוֹמֵר – R' YISHMAEL THE SON OF R' YOCHANAN BEN BEROKAH SAYS: לְפִי שֶׁמָּצִינוּ לַמּוּמָתִים בִּידֵי שָׁמַיִם – SINCE WE FIND regarding THOSE WHO ARE LIABLE TO DEATH AT THE HANDS OF HEAVEN[33] שֶׁנּוֹתְנִין מָמוֹן וּמִתְכַּפֵּר לָהֶן – THAT THEY GIVE MONEY AND RECEIVE ATONEMENT, שֶׁנֶּאֱמַר ,,אִם־כֹּפֶר יוּשַׁת עָלָיו'' – AS IT IS STATED: *WHEN AN ATONEMENT PAYMENT SHALL BE ASSESSED UPON HIM,*[34] יָכוֹל אַף בִּידֵי אָדָם כֵּן – IT COULD BE thought that the law is ALSO THUS with regard to one who is liable to death AT THE HAND OF MAN.[35] תַּלְמוּד לוֹמַר – To disabuse us of this notion THE TORAH STATES: ,,חֵרֶם . . . מִן־הָאָדָם לֹא יִפָּדֶה'' – *A CONDEMNED ONE... FROM AMONG MAN*[36] *SHALL NOT BE REDEEMED.*[37] וְאֵין לִי אֶלָּא מִיתוֹת חֲמוּרוֹת שֶׁלֹּא נִיתְּנָה שִׁגְגָתָן לְכַפָּרָה – NOW, I HAVE support for establishing this law ONLY vis-a-vis CAPITAL OFFENSES that are GRAVE in the sense THAT[38] THEIR UNINTENTIONAL COMMISSIONS ARE NOT GIVEN TO ATONEMENT.[39] מִיתוֹת קַלּוֹת שֶׁנִּיתְּנָה שִׁגְגָתָן לְכַפָּרָה

NOTES

24. *Leviticus* 27:29. The word חֵרֶם, *cherem,* connotes one who has been *condemned to execution,* as in the verse (*Exodus* 22:19): זֹבֵחַ לָאֱלֹהִים יָחֳרָם, *One who slaughters [offerings] for the gods shall be condemned* (*Rashi*). Hence, this verse appears to be saying that anyone who has been condemned by the court to die shall not be redeemed [with money]. Now, why is this verse necessary, when we already know that law from *You shall not take atonement money for the life of a murderer* [as stated in the Gemara above]?

25. [I.e. this verse is not, as presumed by the questioner, coming to teach that a murderer cannot redeem himself from execution with atonement money, for that law is already known to us. Rather, it is coming to teach the law expounded in the following Baraisa.]

26. There are two types of vows for pledging the worth of a person to the Temple treasury. The first makes reference to the person's דָּמִים, *monetary worth,* while the second mentions his עֵרֶךְ, *fixed valuation.* The fundamental difference between these two types of vows is the method used to determine the subject's value.

A vow of דָּמִים, *monetary value,* obligates the vower to give the market value of the subject of the vow. This is the price the subject would fetch if he or she were sold on the slave market.

The second type of vow makes reference not to the subject's actual worth, but to his עֵרֶךְ, *fixed valuation.* A valuation is the amount established by the Torah (*Leviticus* 27:1-8) for each of eight different groupings that are arranged by age and gender [e.g. fifty *shekel* for a man who is between twenty and sixty years old, ten *shekel* for a woman over sixty years old]. If a person says, "I take upon myself to give my valuation" or "to give the valuation of Reuven," he is assessed the Torah's valuation for the subject's grouping, regardless of the latter's market value.

The Mishnah in *Arachin* 6b states that a vow to give the monetary value of someone condemned by the court to execution has no effect. For since the subject's execution is imminent, he has no market value. There is a Tannaic dispute, however, regarding a vow to give a condemned man's valuation. R' Chananya ben Akavya maintains that the vow is valid, for since a person's valuation is fixed by the Torah according to his age and gender, the condemned man's lack of market value is irrelevant. However, the Tanna Kamma there rules that in this case as well the vow does not take effect. Our Baraisa cites the source for the Tanna Kamma's ruling.

27. I.e. from where do we know that although one's fixed valuation is not based on market value, the vow is nonetheless invalid and the vower has no obligation to pay? (*Rashi*).

28. *Rashi* writes that the word *cherem* (חרם) in this verse means הֶקְדֵּשׁ, *an item consecrated for the Temple.* However, *Rashash* finds this interpretation problematic, since the verse could not then be explained as speaking of a man going out to be executed. *Rashash* thus prefers *Rashi's* own comment in *Arachin* (6b ד״ה כל חרם לא יפדה), where he explains that the words חרם and יָחֳרַם both connote a person condemned to execution, and the words *shall not be redeemed* teach that such a person cannot be involved in a "redemption," i.e. as the subject of a fixed-valuation vow (see *Rashash*).

29. The word מן (*from*) is exclusionary, connoting "from, but not all of, a group." Thus, מִן־הָאָדָם is expounded to teach that the law of the verse – that one who is destined for execution cannot be the subject of a fixed-valuation vow – applies only to *some* of these condemned individuals – viz. only to those whose sentences have been finalized.

30. In the Mishnah in *Arachin* 6b; see note 26 above.

31. And so, even though he cannot be the subject of a monetary-value vow (because he has no market value), he can be the subject of a fixed-valuation vow (*Rashi*).

32. Since R' Chananya ben Akavya does not expound this verse to disqualify one going out to be executed from serving as the subject of a fixed-valuation vow, how does he expound it?

33. E.g. one whose *muad* ox kills a person, for whom the Torah (*Exodus* 21:29) prescribes death: וְגַם־בְּעָלָיו יוּמָת, *and its owner, too, shall die.* This is not, however, a court-imposed death penalty, for the Torah states (*Numbers* 35:21), *The one who struck the blow shall surely die; he is a murderer,* and the Gemara (*Sanhedrin* 15b) derives from there that an assailant is put to death by the court only when *he* himself *is a murderer,* and not when his ox has killed. Hence, the death penalty prescribed in the *Exodus* verse is one that is suffered "at the hands of Heaven" [see above, 30b note 13, regarding what this means] (*Rashi*).

34. *Exodus* 21:30, which discusses a man whose *muad* ox kills a person (see previous note). The entire verse reads: *When an atonement payment shall be assessed upon him, he shall pay* ***as a redemption for his life*** *whatever shall be assessed upon him.*

35. I.e. it might be thought that one who is liable to execution by the court can likewise redeem his life with an atonement payment (*Rashi*).

36. I.e. a man who is liable to condemnation [i.e. execution] (*Rashi*).

37. From execution with an atonement payment.

38. See *Tosafos* below, 38a ד״ה הני; see following note.

39. Since the verse does not explicitly state that the restriction against atonement payments applies to all court executions, it suffices to apply that stringency to the more serious capital cases, such as the wounding of one's father or the kidnaping of an Israelite, for whose inadvertent commission the Torah prescribes no method of atonement. For the general method of atonement for unintentional sins – the bringing of a *chatas*-offering – is available only when the *kares* penalty is also imposed for an intentional commission of the sin [as in, for example, the cases of idolatry and Sabbath desecration, when the perpetrator was not warned by witnesses]. However, capital offenses such as kidnaping etc. do not carry the *kares* penalty, and therefore no atonement via a

וחדא במיתה ומלקות וצריכא דאי אשמעינן מיתה וממון משום דחדא בגופיה וחדא בממוניה לא עבדינן אבל במיתה ומלקות דאידי ואידי בגופיה אימא מיתה אריכתא היא ונעביד ביה ואי אשמעינן מיתה ומלקות דתרתי בגופיה לא עבדינן אבל מיתה וממון דחדא בגופיה וחדא בממוניה אימא נעביד ביה צריכא ולא תקחו כופר לנפש רוצח למה לי דאמר רחמנא לא תשקול ממונא מיניה ותפטריה מקטלא לא תקחו כופר לנוס אל עיר מקלטו למה לי דאמר רחמנא לא תשקול ממונא מיניה ותפטריה מן גלות ותרי קראי למה לי חד בשוגג וחד במזיד וצריכי דאי אשמעינן מזיד משום דחמיר איסוריה אבל שוגג דלא חמיר איסוריה אימא לא ואי אשמעינן שוגג משום דליכא איבוד נשמה אבל מזיד דאיכא איבוד נשמה אימא לא צריכא ולארץ לא יכופר לדם אשר שופך בה כי אם בדם שופכו למה לי מבעי ליה לכדתניא מנין שאם נתערפה עגלה ואח"כ נמצא ההורג מנין שאין פוטרין אותו שנאמר ולארץ לא יכופר לדם אשר שופך בה וגו' ואתה תבער הדם הנקי מקרבך למה לי מיבעי ליה לכדתניא מנין למומתים בסייף שהוא מן הצואר ת"ל ואתה תבער הדם הנקי מקרבך הוקשו כל שופכי דמים לעגלה ערופה מה להלן מן הצואר אף שופכי דמים מן הצואר אי מה להלן בקופיץ וממול עורף אף כאן בקופיץ וממול עורף אמר רב נחמן אמר רבה בר אבוה אמר קרא ואהבת לרעך כמוך ברור לו מיתה יפה כל חרם אשר יחרם מן האדם לא יפדה למה לי מיבעי ליה לכדתניא מנין ליוצא ליהרג ואמר אחד ערכו עלי מנין שלא אמר כלום שנאמר כל חרם אשר יחרם מן האדם לא יפדה יכול אף קודם שנגמר דינו כן ת"ל מן האדם ולא כל האדם ולרבי חנניא בן עקביא דאמר נערך מפני שדמיו קצובין האי כל חרם מאי עביד ליה מיבעי ליה לכדתניא רבי ישמעאל בנו של ר' יוחנן בן ברוקה אומר לפי שמצינו למומתים בידי שמים שנותנין ממון ומתכפר להן שנאמר אם כופר יושת עליו יכול אף בידי אדם כן ת"ל חרם מן האדם לא יפדה ואין לי אלא מיתות חמורות שלא ניתנה שגגתן לכפרה מיתות קלות שניתנה שגגתן לכפרה מנין ת"ל כל חרם ולא ממילא מלא תקחו כופר שמעת מינה לא תשקול ממונא מיניה ותיפטריה כל חרם ל"ל אמר רמי בר חמא איצטריך ס"ד אמינא הני

לא תקחו כופר. משמע נמי אם תהרגנו לא תענשנו ממון: **דאמר רחמנא.** שגיאה הוא למשנין לאו לאשמעינן דלא תעביד ביה תרתי אלא לאשמועינן בחיוב מיתה לבדה שלא יפדה בממון: **לא תקחו כופר לנוס.** קא ס"ד לא תעביד ביה תרתי להורג בשוגג גלות וממון: **וצריכי דאי אשמעינן מזיד.** דלא ליפרוק נפשיה בממון הוה אמינא משום דחמיר איסוריה אבל בשוגג ליפרוק נפשיה בממון מגלות: **ואי אשמעינן שוגג.** דמשום דאין בגלותו איבוד נשמה להכי לא לפטריה בממון אלא ליגלי: **אבל מזיד.** משום איבוד נשמה אימור ניסקול ממונא ונקיים נפש בישראל: **כי אם בדם שופכו.** ולא בפדיון ממון למה לי מלא תקחו כופר נפקא: **שאין פוטרין אותו.** לומר כבר נתכפר בעודו ספק שהעגלה מכפרת על הספק: **ואתה תבער.** בתר עריפה כתיב: **מיתה יפה.** בסייף ומלד הסימנים שימות מהר: **כל חרם וגו'.** משמע לשון חייבי מיתות כמו זובח לאלהים יחרם (שמות כב): **ערכו עלי.** ואע"פ שערך אינו לפי דמים אלא לפי שנים לא אמר כלום דמעטיה קרא הכא והאי חרם לשון הקדש הוא: **שדמיו קצובין.** בתורה לפי שנים ולא דמי לאומר דמיו עלי דדמים אין לו אבל ערך יש לו: **למומתין בידי שמים.** כגון מי שהרג שורו את הנפש דכתיב ביה יומת ולא מיתת בית דין דנפקא לן בסנהדרין (דף טו:) מות יומת המכה רוצח הוא על רציחתו אתה הורגו ואי אתה הורגו על רציחת שורו והאי יומת בידי שמים: **יכול אף.** חייבי מיתות ב"ד יפדו בממון: **חרם מן האדם.** אדם שמחויב חרם: **אלא מיתות חמורות שלא ניתנה שגגתן לכפרה.** כיון דקרא לא פריש כל מיתות מיסתייך אי שדית הך חומרא דאין ממונו מצילו אמיתות חמורות ומאי נינהו כגון העושה חבורה באביו או גונב נפש מישראל שאין כפרה כתובה בשגגתו שאין כרת בזדונו דליחייב חטאת בשגגתו: **מיתות קלות.** היינו כל מיתות האמורות בהן כרת על זדונו בלא התראה יש כפרה בשגגתה בחטאת כגון עבודת כוכבים ושבת ועריות א"נ רוצח שיש כפרה לשגגתו בגלות: **ולא ממילא.** שמעת לה מלא תקחו כופר הא גבי רוצח כתיבא וניתנה כפרה לשגגתו ואשמעינן קרא שלא יציל את עצמו בממון ולמה לי תו כל חרם:

וחדא במיתה ומלקות. ורבנן מלקות וממון ומיתה ומלקות תרוייהו נפקי מכדי רשעתו דמשמע אם נתחייב בהדי מלקות מיתה או ממון משום רשעה אחת אתה מחייבו ולע"ג דסמיך ליה ארבעים יכנו לא יוסיף מ"מ אין לנו לומר דילקה ולא ימות כמו שלוקה ואינו משלם דהתם לאתגורי איתגור לכדפריך בהנשרפים (סנהדרין דף פא. ושם) ולע"ג דגבי ממון ומלקות אמרינן דנדון בממון אפילו ממונא קולא התם משום דתק רחמנא אנחבל ה): **לא** תשקול ממונא מיניה ותפטריה מגלות. קשה לרשב"א דל"ל קרא מתנא דבי חזקיה נפקא דלא חילקת בין שוגג למזיד וכי היכי דבמזיד לא תשקול מיניה ממונא ותפטריה מקטלא אף שוגג לא תשקול מיניה ממונא ותפטריה מגלות ואומר ר"י דלא שייך לאקושי שוגג למזיד כי האי גוונא כיון שאין פדיון שניהם שוה דפדיון של מזיד לפוטרו ממיתה ופדיון של שוגג לפוטרו מגלות:

ואח"כ נמצא ההורג. בפירוש החומש פי' הך דרשה מואתה תבער דם הנקי ולא עיין כאן ומיהו יש לקיים פירושו דהך סוגיא דשמעתא דמוקמי' ואתה תבער להקיש שופכי דמים לעגלה ערופה אתיא כמאן דאמר חנק חמור כדמוכח בפרק ד' מיתות (שם דף נב:) דלמאן דאמר חנק קל יליף סייף ברוצח מנקום ינקם הלכך לדידיה אייתר ואתה תבער לנערפה העגלה ואח"כ נמצא ההורג וקרא דולארץ לא יכופר דרשינן ליה לכדרבא בפ' בתרא דכריתות (דף כו.) דמייתינן עגלה ערופה אע"פ שעבר יוה"כ עליה: **מה** להלן בקופיץ וממול עורף. וא"ת ממול עורף מנלן והא וערפו כתיב דמשמע עורף ממש וי"ל דבפ' עגלה ערופה (סוטה דף מו.) גמר עריפה עריפה מחטאת העוף: **הוקשו** שופכי דמים כו'. הוה מצי למימר דהיינו למ"ד חנק חמור אלא למ"ד חנק קל כו': **ברור** לו מיתה יפה. ומהאי טעמא לא הוה שמעינן מן הכופר דאם יתחב סכין בלבו הוי נמי מיתה יפה: **לפי** שמצינו מומתים בידי שמים. דכתיב וגם בעליו יומת דע"כ לא בידי אדם קאמר דכתיב מות יומת המכה רוצח הוא וגו' על רציחתו אתה הורגו כו' אלא והאי בידי שמים ואף על גב דדרשינן מיניה בפ"ק דסנהדרין (דף טו. ושם) כמיתת בעלים כך מיתת השור היינו מדכתיב יומת ולא כתיב ימות וכ"ת כולה להכי הוא דאתא אם כן ליכתוב השור יסקל כבעלים ולשתוק אי נמי ט) וגם כבעליו יומת הלכך שמע מינה תרתי: **יכול** אף בידי אדם כן. יש תימה דהיכי בעי למילף מיתה בידי אדם ממיתה בידי שמים ט) [ותירץ מהר"ש כיון דלאתקש מיתת שור למיתת בעלים נקיט נמי מיתת בעלים בידי אדם למיתת בעלים שעל ידי שור]:

מיתות קלות שניתן שגגתן לכפרה מנין. פי' בקונט' כגון עבודת כוכבים ושבת וגילוי עריות שניתן שגגתן לכפרה ע"י קרבן וכן רוצח ניתנה שגגתו לכפרה ע"י גלות וקשה דא"כ למסקנא למאי איצטריך חרם וכל חרם ולא תקחו ג' קראי בלא תקחו כופר ובחרם סגי דחד לדרך עליה וחד לדרך ירידה שניתן שגגתן לכפרה דהיינו מיתות קלות לפ"ה לכך נראה דמיתות קלות לא חשיב אלא הנהו שניתן שגגתן לכפרה ע"י ממון או ע"י קרבן אבל רוצח לא ניתן שגגתו לכפרה ע"י ממון אלא על ידי גלות וה"פ דבריתא אין לי אלא מיתות חמורות שלא ניתן שגגתן לכפרה ע"י קרבן דהיינו כל מיתות שאין בהן כרת כגון מסית ונביא השקר וזקן ממרא ומכה אביו ואמו ומקלל אביו ואמו וגונב נפש ומגדף אליבא דרבנן דאמרי בכריתות (דף ג:) דאין מביא קרבן על שגגתו דכתיב לעושה בשגגה פרט למגדף שאין בו מעשה ורוצח ומיתות קלות כגון עבודת כוכבים ושבת ועריות דיש בהן כרת ומביא קרבן על שגגתן ופריך ולא ממילא שמעת מינה מלא תקחו כופר והתם שמעינן כל מיתות חמורות ולמה לי קרא למיתות חמורות אבל למיתות קלות ודאי צריך קרא ומשני דאיצטריך תרי קראי למיתות חמורות חד לדרך עליה וחד לדרך ירידה שניתן שגגתו לכפרה על ידי גלות קשה לרשב"א דמאי איצטריך קרא לחייבי מיתות קלות כגון עבודת כוכבים ושבת ועריות דמה שייך שם כופר למ"ד כופר היינו דמי ניזק ותירץ דרבי ישמעאל בנו של רבי יוחנן בן ברוקה לטעמיה דאמר בפרק שור שנגח ד' וה' (ב"ק דף מ.) וממון פדיון נפשו דמי מזיק:

עין משפט
נר מצוה

נז א מיי' פ"א מהל' רוצח ושמירת נפש הלכה ד סמג לאוין קסב:
נח ב מיי' פ"ה שם הל' א סמג לאוין קסב:
נט ג מיי' פ"י שם הל' ח סמג עשין עח:
ס ד מיי' פט"ו מהל' סנהדרין הלכה ד סמג עשין קז:
סא ה מיי' פ"ט מהל' רוצח הלכה ג סמג עשין עח:
סב ו מיי' פ"א מהל' ערכין הל' יג סמג עשין קמ:
סג ז מיי' פ"י מהלכות נזקי ממון הל' ד סמג עשין סו:

תוספות ישנים

א) [דנפקא לן מתנא דבי חזקיה דלא חלקת בין שוגג למזיד למאי הא"ד השתא דבעי למימר קרא לא תשקול מיניה ממונא ונחייביה. ת"י].

תורה אור השלם

א) וְלֹא תִקְחוּ כֹפֶר לְנֶפֶשׁ רֹצֵחַ אֲשֶׁר הוּא רָשָׁע לָמוּת כִּי מוֹת יוּמָת: [במדבר לה, לא]
ב) וְלֹא תִקְחוּ כֹפֶר לָנוּס אֶל עִיר מִקְלָטוֹ לָשׁוּב לָשֶׁבֶת בָּאָרֶץ עַד מוֹת הַכֹּהֵן: [במדבר לה, לב]
ג) וְלֹא תַחֲנִיפוּ אֶת הָאָרֶץ אֲשֶׁר אַתֶּם בָּהּ כִּי הַדָּם הוּא יַחֲנִיף אֶת הָאָרֶץ וְלָאָרֶץ לֹא יְכֻפַּר לַדָּם אֲשֶׁר שֻׁפַּךְ בָּהּ כִּי אִם בְּדַם שֹׁפְכוֹ: [במדבר לה, לג]
ד) וְאַתָּה תְּבַעֵר הַדָּם הַנָּקִי מִקִּרְבֶּךָ כִּי תַעֲשֶׂה הַיָּשָׁר בְּעֵינֵי יְיָ: [דברים כא, ט]
ה) לֹא תִקֹּם וְלֹא תִטֹּר אֶת בְּנֵי עַמֶּךָ וְאָהַבְתָּ לְרֵעֲךָ כָּמוֹךָ אֲנִי יְיָ: [ויקרא יט, יח]
ו) כָּל חֵרֶם אֲשֶׁר יָחֳרַם מִן הָאָדָם לֹא יִפָּדֶה מוֹת יוּמָת: [ויקרא כז, כט]
ז) אִם כֹּפֶר יוּשַׁת עָלָיו וְנָתַן פִּדְיֹן נַפְשׁוֹ כְּכֹל אֲשֶׁר יוּשַׁת עָלָיו: [שמות כא, ל]

מסורת הש"ס

א) ב"ק פג., ב) סוטה מז., ג) סנהדרין נב., ד) שם ודף מה. פסחים עה. [ב"ק נא. סוטה ח:], ה) ערכין ו., ו) [שם], ז) [שם], ח) [וע"ע תוס' לעיל לג. ד"ה ואין], ט) ס"א ליכתוב וגם בעליו יומת ותו לא, י) ת"י כ"י.

ליקוטי רש"י

ולא תקחו כופר. לא יפטר בממון [במדבר לה, לא]. **לא תקחו כופר לנוס אל עיר מקלטו.** למי שנס אל עיר מקלטו שהרג בשוגג אינו נפטר מגלות בממון ליתן כופר לשוב לשבת בארץ בטרם ימות הכהן. **לנוס.** כמו לנס (בשו"א ובקמ"ץ) כמו (מיכה ב) שובי מלחמה ששבו מן המלחמה וכן (צפניה ג) נוגי ממועד וכן (יהושע ה) כי מולים היו כאשר תאמר שוב על מי ששב כבר ומול על מי שמל כבר כן תאמר לנוס על מי שנס כבר וקורהו נוס כלומר מוברח. ואם תאמר לנוס לברוח ותפרשהו לא תקחו כופר למי שיש לו לברוח לפטרו מן הגלות לא ידעתי היאך יאמר לשוב לשבת בארץ הרי עדיין לא נס ומהיכן ישוב [במדבר לה, לב וער' שיטמ"ק]. **ואתה תבער הדם הנקי.** מגיד שאם נמצא ההורג אחר שנתערפה העגלה הרי זה יהרג והוא הישר בעיני ה' [דברים כא, ט]. **מן הצואר.** גרון [סנהדרין נב:]. **בקופיץ.** סכין גדול שכן דרך עריפה [בכורות י:]. סכין גדול הוא ורוכן אינו לשחיטה אלא לחיתוך בשר ולשבירת עצמות [פסחים ע.]. סכין גדול שקולבין בו בשר [ביצה כח.]. סתם קופיץ הוא סכין של קצבים דומה לקרדומות שלנו [שם לא.]. **וממול עורף.** מאחרי הפנים דכתיב (דברים כא) וערפו לשון עורף מול הרואה את העורף דהיינו אחורי צואר שרואין את העורף ועורף הוא קטרי"ל שכנגד הפנים דכתיב (ירמיה לב) ויפנו אלי עורף ולא פנים אלמא עורף להדי פנים [סנהדרין שם]. **ואהבת לרעך כמוך.** אמר רבי עקיבא זה כלל גדול בתורה (ת"כ) [ויקרא יט, יח]. **מיתה יפה.** ולא תבזהו [סנהדרין מה.]. **כל חרם וכו' לא יפדה.** מי שהוא ראוי ליחרם וליהרג אינו בכלל פדיון. **למומתים בידי שמים.** כגון האי דכתיב השור יסקל וגם בעליו יומת והך מיתה ליכא למימר בידי אדם דהא אמרי' בפ"ק דסנהדרין (דף טו:) מות יומת המכה רוצח הוא על רציחתו אתה הורגו ואי אתה הורגו על רציחת שורו [ערכין ו:]. **אם כופר יושת עליו.** אם זה אינו תלוי והרי הוא כמו (לקמן כב כד) אם כסף תלוה לשון אשר זה משפטו שישיתו עליו בית דין כופר [שמות כא, ל]. **שלא ניתנה שגגתן לכפרה.** כגון מגדף ומקלל אביו דאם עשה בשוגג אינו בקרבן ולא בגלות. **מיתות קלות.** כלומר דקלות להך מילתא שניתנה שגגתן לכפרה כגון רוצח דשגגתו גולה ועובד ע"ז ומחלל שבת ובא על הערוה דשגגתו חטאת [ערכין שם].

his punishment by paying atonement money **because there is no loss of life** for the killer.[8] אֲבָל מֵזִיד – **But** in the case of one who killed **deliberately,** דְּאִיכָּא אִיבּוּד נְשָׁמָה – **where there is a loss of life,**[9] אֵימָא לֹא – **I would say** that the Torah does **not** bar him from redeeming his punishment with atonement money.[10] צְרִיכָא – Therefore, **it was necessary** to state both verses.[11]

The Gemara again cites a seemingly superfluous verse, and asks: ,,וְלָאָרֶץ לֹא־יְכֻפַּר לַדָּם אֲשֶׁר שֻׁפַּךְ־בָּהּ כִּי־אִם בְּדַם שֹׁפְכוֹ'' לָמָּה לִי – **Why do I [need]** the verse, ***and the land will not have atonement for the blood spilled in it except through the blood of the one who spilled it?***[12]

The Gemara answers:

מִבָּעֵי לֵיהּ לִכְדִתַנְיָא – **We need it for that** law **which was taught in a Baraisa:**[13] מִנַּיִן שֶׁאִם נִתְעָרְפָה עֶגְלָה וְאַחַר כָּךְ נִמְצָא הַהוֹרֵג – **FROM WHERE** do we know **THAT IF THE CALF WAS DECAPITATED**[14] **AND AFTERWARD THE MURDERER IS FOUND** – מִנַּיִן שֶׁאֵין פּוֹטְרִין אוֹתוֹ – **FROM WHERE** do we know **THAT WE DO NOT ACQUIT HIM?**[15] שֶׁנֶּאֱמַר – **FOR IT IS STATED:** ,,וְלָאָרֶץ לֹא־יְכֻפַּר לַדָּם אֲשֶׁר־שֻׁפַּךְ בָּהּ'' וגו' – ***AND THE LAND WILL NOT HAVE ATONEMENT FOR THE BLOOD SPILLED IN IT* etc.** [*except through the blood of the one who spilled it*].[16]

The Gemara counters:

,,וּבִעַרְתָּ הַדָּם הַנָּקִי מִקִּרְבֶּךָ'' לָמָּה לִי – But then **why do I [need]** the verse, ***And you shall purge the [spillers of] innocent blood from your midst?***[17]

The Gemara answers:

מִיבָּעֵי לֵיהּ לִכְדִתַנְיָא – **We need it for that** law **which was taught in a Baraisa:** מִנַּיִן לַמּוּמָתִים בְּסַיִיף – **FROM WHERE** do we know **WITH REGARD TO THOSE WHO ARE EXECUTED** by the court **WITH A SWORD**[18] שֶׁהוּא מִן הַצַּוָּאר – **THAT [THEIR DEATH] IS** effected **FROM THE NECK?**[19] תַּלְמוּד לוֹמַר – **THE TORAH STATES** at the conclusion of the passage of the decapitated calf: ,,וְאַתָּה תְּבַעֵר הַדָּם הַנָּקִי מִקִּרְבֶּךָ'' – ***AND YOU SHALL PURGE THE [SPILLERS OF] INNOCENT BLOOD FROM YOUR MIDST.*** הוּקְשׁוּ כָּל שׁוֹפְכֵי דָמִים לְעֶגְלָה עֲרוּפָה – Here **ALL SPILLERS OF BLOOD ARE EXEGETICALLY LINKED TO THE DECAPITATED CALF,**[20] to teach: מַה לְּהַלָּן מִן הַצַּוָּאר – **JUST AS THERE** the death of the calf is effected **FROM THE NECK,** אַף שׁוֹפְכֵי דָמִים מִן הַצַּוָּאר – here **TOO** the death of **SPILLERS OF BLOOD** is effected **FROM THE NECK.**

The Gemara asks:

אִי מַה לְּהַלָּן בְּקוֹפִיץ וּמִמּוּל עוֹרֶף – But **if** we are comparing the execution of a murderer with the decapitation of the calf, we should also say: **Just as there** the calf is killed **with an ax and from the back of the neck,** אַף כָּאן בְּקוֹפִיץ וּמִמּוּל עוֹרֶף – **here too** murderers should be executed **with an ax and from the back of the neck** [which is not the case].[21] – ? –

The Gemara answers:

אָמַר רַב נַחְמָן אָמַר רַבָּה בַּר אֲבוּהָ – **Rav Nachman said in the name of Rabbah bar Avuha:** אָמַר קְרָא – **The verse states:**[22] ,,וְאָהַבְתָּ לְרֵעֲךָ כָּמוֹךָ'' – ***and you shall love your fellow as yourself.*** בְּרוֹר לוֹ מִיתָה יָפָה – This teaches that if your fellow has been condemned to die, **choose for him a favorable death.**[23]

The Gemara cites another seemingly superfluous verse, and asks: ,,כָּל־חֵרֶם אֲשֶׁר יָחֳרַם מִן־הָאָדָם לֹא יִפָּדֶה'' לָמָּה לִי – **Why do I [need]**

NOTES

8. I.e. since this killer's punishment is exile, which does not involve the loss of his life, the Torah does not afford him the option of commuting his punishment with atonement money, and so he must go into exile (*Rashi*).

9. For this killer's punishment is execution.

10. I would say that in order to save a Jewish soul, the Torah does afford the murderer the opportunity to commute his punishment with atonement money (*Rashi*).

11. *Tosafos* (ד"ה לא) ask why, indeed, is *Numbers* 35:32 necessary, given that the Baraisa of Chizkiyah teaches us not to differentiate between an inadvertent and a deliberate murder. Accordingly, we should equate the two and say that just as an intentional killer cannot redeem his prescribed penalty with payment, so too an unintentional killer cannot redeem his prescribed penalty with payment. *Tosafos* answer that on the basis of the juxtaposition expounded by the Baraisa of Chizkiyah we can equate the two types of murder only with regard to the same penalty or the same exemption [e.g. just as a deliberate homicide exempts the perpetrator from monetary liability, so an inadvertent homicide exempts the perpetrator from monetary liability]. We cannot, however, say that just as money does not redeem [an intentional killer] from execution, so money does not redeem [an unintentional killer] from exile, since the very nature of the redemption is different.

12. *Numbers* 35:33. This verse appears after the two verses cited above, which barred the intentional and unintentional killers from redeeming their punishments with atonement money. Verse 33 appears to be saying – in a similar vein – that an intentional killing can be atoned for only through the execution of the murderer. But if so, the verse is unnecessary, for we already know to rule out monetary redemption in that case from verse 31: *You shall not take atonement money for the life of a murderer* (*Rashi*).

13. [I.e. verse 33 is not, as presumed by the questioner, coming to teach that a murderer cannot redeem himself from execution with atonement money, for this is already indicated by *You shall not take atonement money for the life of a murderer*. Rather, it is coming to teach the law expounded in the following Baraisa.]

14. When a murder victim is discovered outside a town in Eretz Yisrael and the killer's identity is unknown, the Torah (*Deuteronomy* 21:1-8) commands that the elders of the town nearest to the body take a calf that was never worked and bring it to a valley whose soil was never tilled, and there decapitate it in a ritual involving their declaration of innocence and a prayer by the Kohanim. The Torah assures (v. 8) that this ritual will effect atonement.

15. For we could argue that since the decapitation of the calf – which effects atonement in cases of uncertainty, where the identity of the murderer is unknown – was performed prior to the discovery of the murderer, it has already effected atonement and so executing the murderer is no longer required (*Rashi*).

16. [The verse teaches that the decapitation ritual's functioning is contingent upon the murderer's identity remaining uncertain. Once it is discovered, the ritual's atoning effect terminates and the murder's execution becomes necessary.]

17. *Deuteronomy* 21:9. The Torah states this verse after delineating the *eglah arufah* (decapitated calf) procedure (*Rashi*), and appears to be saying that even after the decapitation of the calf the court is required to execute the murderer if and when he is discovered (see *Rashi* ad loc., where he indeed interprets the verse thus, and see *Tosafos* ד"ה ואח"כ, who discuss this). However, having just demonstrated that this law is derived from the verse *And the land will not have atonement for the blood spilled in it except through the blood of the one who spilled it,* the Gemara questions why this is necessary (cf. *Maharsha*).

18. One of the four methods of execution available to the court is הֶרֶג [*death by the sword*] (see Mishnah, *Sanhedrin* 49b). This method is reserved for murderers and the people of a subverted city, *ir hanidachas* (see ibid. 76b).

19. And not by (stabbing or) cutting them in half; see *Sanhedrin* 52b.

20. The juxtaposition of this verse, which speaks of the "purging" [i.e. execution] of murderers, to the "decapitated calf" passage indicates that certain details of an execution should be gleaned from the act of decapitation.

21. Rather, they are killed with a sword, from the front.

22. *Leviticus* 19:18.

23. And the thrust of a sword to the throat, where the trachea and esophagus are located, causes a quicker [and thus more favorable] death than does the blow of an ax to the back of the neck (see *Rashi*).

וחדא במיתה ומלקות וצריכא דאי אשמעינן מיתה וממון משום דחדא בגופיה וחדא בממוניה לא עבדינן אבל במיתה ומלקות דאידי ואידי בגופיה אימא מיתה אריכתא היא ונעביד ביה ואי אשמעינן מיתה ומלקות דתרתי בגופיה לא עבדינן אבל מיתה וממון דחדא בגופיה וחדא בממוניה אימא נעביד ביה צריכא ולא תקחו כופר לנפש רוצח למה לי דאמר רחמנא לא תשקול ממונא מיניה ותפטריה מקטלא לא תקחו כופר לנוס אל עיר מקלטו למה לי דאמר רחמנא לא תשקול ממונא מיניה ותפטריה מן גלות ותרי קראי למה לי חד בשוגג וחד במזיד וצריכי דאי אשמעינן מזיד משום דחמיר איסוריה אבל שוגג דלא חמיר איסוריה אימא לא ואי אשמעינן שוגג משום דליכא איבוד נשמה אבל מזיד דאיכא איבוד נשמה אימא לא צריכא ולארץ לא יכופר לדם אשר שופך בה כי אם בדם שופכו למה לי מבעי ליה לכדתניא מנין שאם נתערפה עגלה ואח"כ נמצא ההורג מנין שאין פוטרין אותו שנאמר ולארץ לא יכופר לדם אשר שופך בה וגו' ואתה תבער הדם הנקי מקרבך למה לי מיבעי ליה לכדתניא מנין למומתים בסייף שהוא מן הצואר ת"ל ואתה תבער הדם הנקי מקרבך הוקשו כל שופכי דמים לעגלה ערופה מה להלן מן הצואר אף שופכי דמים מן הצואר אי מה להלן בקופיץ וממול עורף אף כאן בקופיץ וממול עורף אמר רב נחמן אמר רבה בר אבוה אמר קרא ואהבת לרעך כמוך ברור לו מיתה יפה כל חרם אשר יחרם מן האדם לא יפדה למה לי מיבעי ליה לכדתניא מנין ליוצא ליהרג ואמר אחד ערכו עלי מנין שלא אמר כלום שנאמר כל חרם אשר יחרם מן האדם לא יפדה יכול אף קודם שנגמר דינו ת"ל מן האדם ולא כל האדם ולרבי חנניא בן עקביא דאמר נערך מפני שדמיו קצובין האי כל חרם מאי עביד ליה מיבעי ליה לכדתניא רבי ישמעאל בנו של ר' יוחנן בן ברוקה אומר לפי שמצינו למומתים בידי שמים שנותנין ממון ומתכפר להן שנאמר אם כופר יושת עליו יכול אף בידי אדם כן ת"ל חרם מן האדם לא יפדה ואין לי אלא מיתות חמורות שלא ניתנה שגגתן לכפרה מיתות קלות שניתנה שגגתן לכפרה מנין ת"ל כל חרם ולא תקחו ממילא מלא תקחו כופר שמעת מינה לא תשקול ממונא מיניה ותיפטריה כל חרם ל"ל אמר רמי בר חמא איצטריך ס"ד אמינא

הני

וחדא במיתה ומלקות. ורבנן מלקות וממון ומיתה ומלקות תרוייהו נפקי מכדי רשעתו דמשמע אם נתחייב בהדי מלקות מיתה או ממון משום רשעה אחת אתה מחייבו ואע"ג דסמיך ליה ארבעים יכנו לא יוסיף מ"מ אין לנו לומר דילקה ולא ימות כמו שלוקה ואינו משלם דאתגורי איתגור כדפריך בהנשרפים (סנהדרין דף פא. ושם) ואע"ג דגבי ממון ומלקות אמרינן דנדון בממון אפילו ממונא קולא התם משום דהם רחמנא אנחבל: לא תשקול ממונא מיניה ותפטריה מגלות. קשה לרשב"א דל"ל קרא מתנא דבי חזקיה נפקא דלא חילקת בין שוגג למזיד וכי היכי דבמזיד לא תשקול מיניה ממונא ותפטריה מקטלא אף שוגג לא תשקול מיניה ממונא ותפטריה מגלות ואומר ר"י דלא שייך לאקושי שוגג למזיד כי האי גוונא כיון שאין פדיון שניהם שוה דפדיון של מזיד לפוטרו ממיתה ופדיון של שוגג לפוטרו מגלות:

ואח"כ נמצא ההורג. בפירוש החומש פ"ה הך דרשה מואתה תבער דם הנקי ולא עיין כאן ומיהו יש לקיים פירושו דהך סוגיא דשמעתא דמוקמי' ואתה תבער להקיש שופכי דמים לעגלה ערופה אתיא כמאן דאמר חנק חמור כדמוכח בפרק ד' מיתות (שם דף נב:) דלמאן דאמר חנק קל יליף סייף ברוצח מנקום ינקם הלכך לדידיה אייתר ואתה תבער לנערפה העגלה ואח"כ נמצא ההורג וקרא דולארץ לא יכופר דרשינן ליה לכדרבא בפ' בתרא דכריתות (דף כו.) דמייתינן עגלה ערופה אע"פ שעבר יוה"כ עליה: מה להלן בקופיץ וממול עורף. וא"ת ממול עורף מנלן והא וערפו כתיב דמשמע עורף ממש ויש לומר דבפ' עגלה ערופה (סוטה דף מו:) גמר עריפה עריפה מחטאת העוף: הוקשו שופכי דמים כו'. הוה מצי למימר הניחא למ"ד חנק חמור אלא למ"ד חנק קל כו': ברור לו מיתה יפה. ומהאי טעמא לא הוה שמעינן מן הצואר דאם יתחב סכין בלבו הרי נמי מיתה יפה: לפי שמצינו מומתים בידי שמים. דכתיב וגם בעליו יומת דע"כ לא בידי אדם קאמר דכתיב מות יומת המכה רוצח הוא וגו' על רציחתו אתה הורגו כו' אלא והאי בידי שמים ואף על גב דדרשינן מיניה בפ"ק דסנהדרין (דף טו. ושם) כמיתת בעלים כך מיתת השור היינו מדכתיב יומת ולא כתיב ימות וכ"ת כולה להכי הוא דאתא אם כן ליכתוב השור יסקל כבעלים ולשתוק אי נמי (ו) וגם כבעליו יומת הלכך שמע מינה תרתי: יכול אף בידי אדם כן. יש תימה דהיכי בעי למילף מיתה בידי אדם ממיתה בידי שמים (ז) ומיהו מהר"ם כיון דאשתכח מיתת שור למיתת בעלים נקיט נמי מיתת בעלים בידי אדם למיתת בעלים שעל ידי שור: מיתות קלות שניתנה שגגתן לכפרה מנין. פי' בקונט' כגון עבודת כוכבים ושבת וגילוי עריות שניתן שגגתן לכפרה ע"י קרבן וכן רוצח ניתנה שגגתו לכפרה ע"י גלות וקשה דא"כ למסקנא דמאי איצטריך חרם וכל חרם ולא תקחו ג' קראי דלא תקחו כופר ובחרם סגי דחד לדרך עלייה וחד לדרך ירידה שניתן שגגתו לכפרה דהיינו מיתות קלות לפ"ה לכך נראה דמיתות קלות לא חשיב אלא הנהו שניתן שגגתן לכפרה ע"י ממון או ע"י קרבן אבל רוצח לא ניתן שגגתו לכפרה אלא על ידי גלות וה"פ דבריתא אין לי אלא מיתות חמורות שלא ניתן שגגתן לכפרה ע"י קרבן דהיינו כל מיתות שאין בהן כרת כגון מסית ומדיח ונביא השקר וזקן ממרא ומכה אביו ואמו ומקלל אביו ואמו וגונב נפש ומגדף דליכא לרבנן דאמרי בכריתות (דף ג:) דאין מביא קרבן על שגגתו דכתיב לעושה בשגגה פרט למגדף שאין בו מעשה ורוצח ומיתות קלות כגון עבודת כוכבים ושבת ועריות דיש בהן כרת ומביא קרבן על שגגתן ופריך ולא ממילא שמעת מינה מלא תקחו כופר והשתא משמעינן כל מיתות חמורות ולמה לי קרא למיתות חמורות אבל למיתות קלות ודאי לריך קרא ומשני דאיצטריך תרי קראי למיתות חמורות חד לדרך עלייה וחד לדרך ירידה שניתן שגגתו לכפרה על ידי גלות קשה לרשב"א דמאי איצטריך קרא לחייבי מיתות קלות כגון עבודת כוכבים ושבת ועריות למה שייך שם כופר למ"ד כופר דמי ניזק והיכי דרבי ישמעאל בנו של רבי יוחנן בן ברוקה לטעמיה דאמר בפרק שור שנגח ד' וה' (ב"ק דף מ.) ונתן פדיון נפשו דמי מזיק:

הני

נז א מיי' פ"א מהל' רוצח ושמירת נפש הלכה ד סמג לאוין קסב:
נח ב מיי' פ"ה שם הל' ה סמג לאוין קסב:
נט ג מיי' פ"י שם הל' ח סמג עשין עה:
ס ד מיי' פט"ו מהל' סנהדרין הלכה יב סמג עשין קג:
סא ה מיי' פ"ע מהל' רוצח הלכה ג סמג עשין עה:
סב ו מיי' פ"ה מהל' ערכין הל' יג סמג עשין קמ:
סג ז מיי' פ"י מהלכות נזקי ממון הל' ד סמג עשין סו:

תוספות ישנים

א) [דנפקא לן מתנא דבי חזקיה דלא חילקת בין שוגג למזיד לא"ל שם"ד השתא דבעי לגימר קרא לא תשקול מיניה מבזנות ותפטריה. פ"י].

תורה אור השלם

א) וְלֹא תִקְחוּ כֹפֶר לְנֶפֶשׁ רֹצֵחַ אֲשֶׁר הוּא רָשָׁע לָמוּת כִּי מוֹת יוּמָת: [במדבר לה, לא]
ב) וְלֹא תִקְחוּ כֹפֶר לָנוּס אֶל עִיר מִקְלָטוֹ לָשׁוּב לָשֶׁבֶת בָּאָרֶץ עַד מוֹת הַכֹּהֵן: [במדבר לה, לב]
ג) וְלֹא תַחֲנִיפוּ אֶת הָאָרֶץ אֲשֶׁר אַתֶּם בָּהּ כִּי הַדָּם הוּא יַחֲנִיף אֶת הָאָרֶץ וְלָאָרֶץ לֹא יְכֻפַּר לַדָּם אֲשֶׁר שֻׁפַּךְ בָּהּ כִּי אִם בְּדַם שֹׁפְכוֹ: [במדבר לה, לג]
ד) וְאַתָּה תְּבַעֵר הַדָּם הַנָּקִי מִקִּרְבֶּךָ כִּי תַעֲשֶׂה הַיָּשָׁר בְּעֵינֵי יְיָ: [דברים כא, ט]
ה) לֹא תִקֹּם וְלֹא תִטֹּר אֶת בְּנֵי עַמֶּךָ וְאָהַבְתָּ לְרֵעֲךָ כָּמוֹךָ אֲנִי יְיָ: [ויקרא יט, יח]
ו) כָּל חֵרֶם אֲשֶׁר יָחֳרַם מִן הָאָדָם לֹא יִפָּדֶה מוֹת יוּמָת: [ויקרא כז, כט]
ז) אִם כֹּפֶר יוּשַׁת עָלָיו וְנָתַן פִּדְיֹן נַפְשׁוֹ כְּכֹל אֲשֶׁר יוּשַׁת עָלָיו: [שמות כא, ל]

לא תקחו כופר. משמע נמי אם תהרגנו לא תענשנו ממון: דאמר רחמנא. שניא הוא דמשנינן לאו לאשמעינן דלא תעביד ביה תרתי אלא לאשמועינן בחיוב מיתה לבדה שלא יפדה בממון: לא תקחו כופר לנוס. קא ס"ד לא תעביד ביה תרתי להורג בשוגג גלות וממון: וצריכי דאי אשמעינן מזיד. דלא ליפרוק נפשיה בממון הוה אמינא משום דחמיר איסוריה אבל בשוגג ליפרוק נפשיה בממון מגלות: ואי אשמעינן שוגג. דמשום דאין בגלותו איבוד נשמה להכי לא לפטריה בממון אלא ליגלי: אבל מזיד. משום איבוד נשמה אימור נשקול ממונא ונקיים נפש בישראל: כי אם בדם שופכו. ולא בפדיון ממון למה לי מלא תקחו כופר נפקא: שאין פוטרין אותו. לומר כבר נתכפר בעודו ספק שהעגלה מכפרת על הספק: ואתה תבער. בתר עריפה כתיב: מיתה יפה. בסייף ומלך הסימנים שימות מהר: כל חרם וגו'. משמע לשון חייבי מיתות כמו זובח לאלהים יחרם (שמות כב): ערכו עלי. ואע"פ שערך אינו לפי דמים אלא לפי שנים לא אמר כלום דמעטיה קרא הכא והאי חרם לשון הקדש הוא: שדמיו קצובין. בתורה לפי שנים ולא דמי לאומר דמיו עלי דדמים אין לו אבל ערך יש לו: למומתין בידי שמים. כגון מי שהרג שורו את הנפש דכתיב ביה יומת ולא מיתת בית דין דנפקא לן בסנהדרין (דף טו:) מות יומת המכה רוצח הוא על רציחתו אתה הורגו ואי אתה הורגו על רציחת שורו והאי יומת בידי שמים: יכול אף. חייבי מיתות ב"ד יפדו בממון: חרם מן האדם. אדם שמחויב חרם: אלא מיתות חמורות שלא ניתנה שגגתן לכפרה. כיון דקרא לא פריש כל מיתות מיסתייך אי שדית הך חומרא דאין ממונו מצילו אמיתות חמורות ומאי נינהו כגון העושה חבורה באביו או גונב נפש מישראל שאין כפרה כתובה בשגגתו שאין כרת בזדונו לחייב חטאת בשגגתו: מיתות קלות. היינו כל מיתות האמורות שיש בהן כרת על זדונו ובאה התראה יש כפרה בשגגתה בחטאת כגון עבודת כוכבים ושבת ועריות וה"נ רוצח שיש כפרה בשגגתו בגלות: ולא ממילא. שמעת לה מלא תקחו כופר הא גבי רוצח כתיבא וניתנה כפרה לשגגתו ואשמעינן קרא שלא יציל את עצמו בממון ולמה לי תו כל חרם:

א) ב"ק פג:, ב) סוטה מז:, ג) סנהדרין נב:, ד) שם ודף מה. פסחים עה. [ב"ק נא. סוטה ח:], ה) ערכין ו:, ו) [שם], ז) [וע"ע תוס' לעיל לב. ד"ה ואין], ט) פ"א ליכתוב וגם בעליו יומת ותו לא, י) מ"י כ"י.

ליקוטי רש"י

ולא תקחו כופר. לא יפטר בממון [במדבר לה, לא]. לא תקחו כופר לנוס אל עיר מקלטו. למי שנס אל עיר מקלטו שהרג בשוגג אינו נפטר מגלות בממון ליתן כופר לשוב לשבת בארץ בטרם ימות הכהן. לנוס. כמו לנס (בשו"ע וקמ"ץ) כמו (מיכה ב) שובי מלחמה ששבו מן המלחמה וכן (צפניה ג) נוגי ממועד וכן (יהושע ה) כי מולים היו כאשר תאמר שוב על מי ששב כבר ומול על מי שמל כבר כן תאמר לנוס על מי שנס כבר וקורהו נוס כלומר מוברח. ואם תאמר לנוס לברוח ופתרהו לא תקחו כופר למי שיש לו לברוח לפטרו מן הגלות לא ידעתי היאך יאמר לשוב לשבת בארץ הרי עדיין לא נס ומהיכן ישוב [במדבר לה, לב ועי' שיטמ"ק]. ואתה תבער הדם הנקי. מגיד שאם נמצא ההורג אחר שנתערפה העגלה הרי זה יהרג והוא היושר בעיני ה' [דברים כא, ט]. מן הצואר. גרון [סנהדרין נב:]. בקופיץ. סכין גדול שבו חותכין בשר בכבורות י':]. סכין גדול הוא ורוצון אינן בשחיטה אלא לחיתוך בשר ולשבירת עצמות [פסחים ע.]. סכין גדול שקולבין בו בשר [ביצה כח.]. קופץ קופיץ הוא סכין של קצבים דומה לקרדומות שלנו [שם לא.]. וממול עורף. מאחרי הפנים דכתיב (דברים כא) וערפו לשון עורף מול הרואה אשר הם העורף דהיינו אחורי צואר שרואין את העורף ועורף הוא קמו"ל שכנגד הפנים דכתיב (ירמיה לב) ויפנו אלי עורף ולא פנים אלמא עורף לנגד פנים [סנהדרין שם]. ואהבת לרעך כמוך. אמר רבי עקיבא זה כלל גדול בתורה (ת"כ) [ויקרא יט, יח]. ולא ממילא. שמעת לה מלא תקחו כופר יפה. ולא תבוזו [סנהדרין מה.]. כל חרם וכו' לא יפדה. מי שהולך ליהרג ואמר ערכו עלי לא אמר כלום שאינו בכלל פדיון. למומתים בידי שמים. כגון הא דכתיב השור יסקל וגם בעליו יומת והך מיתה ליכא למימר בידי אדם דהא אמרי' בפ"ק דסנהדרין (דף טו:) מות יומת המכה רוצח הוא על רציחתו אתה הורגו ואי אתה הורגו על רציחת שורו [ערכין ו:]. אם כופר יושת עליו. אם זה אינו תלוי והרי הוא כמו (לקמן כב כד) אם כסף תלוה לשון אשר הוא משפטו שישיתו עליו בית דין כופר [שמות כא, ל]. שלא ניתנה שגגתן לכפרה. כגון מגדף ומקלל אביו אין להם קרבן בשוגג אינו בקרבן ולא בגלות. מיתות קלות. כלומר קלות שניתנה שגגתן לכפרה כגון רוצח דשגגתו גולה ועובד ע"ז ומחלל שבת ובא על הערוה דשגגתו חטאת [ערכין שם].

וְחָדָא בְּמִיתָה וּמַלְקוּת – **and one** verse[1] teaches that only the greater penalty is incurred **where** the transgressor is liable to the **death** penalty **and to lashes.**[2]

The Gemara now explains why the principle must be taught in both contexts:

וּצְרִיכָא – **And** both verses are **necessary.** דְּאִי אַשְׁמְעִינַן מִיתָה וּמָמוֹן – **For if [the Torah] had taught us** only where the transgressor is liable to the **death** penalty **and** to **monetary** payment, מִשּׁוּם דְּחָדָא בְּגוּפֵיהּ וְחָדָא בְּמָמוֹנֵיהּ לֹא עָבְדִינַן – I would have thought that there only the greater penalty is given **because we do not administer one** punishment **on [a person's] body and one** punishment **on his property** for the same sinful act, since that would constitute two punishments. אֲבָל בְּמִיתָה וּמַלְקוּת – **But** when one is liable to the **death** penalty **and** to **lashes,** דְּאִידִי וְאִידִי בְּגוּפֵיהּ – **where both** punishments **are** administered **on his body,** אֵימָא מִיתָה אֲרִיכְתָּא הִיא – **I would say** that their joint effect **is** one **long death,** וְנַעֲבִיד בֵּיהּ – **and** so **we should administer** them **to him.**[3] וְאִי אַשְׁמְעִינַן מִיתָה וּמַלְקוּת – **And,** conversely, **if [the Torah] had taught us** this principle only where one is liable to the **death** penalty **and** to **lashes,** דְּתַרְתֵּי בְּגוּפֵיהּ לֹא עָבְדִינַן – I would have thought that there only the greater punishment is given **since we do not administer two** punishments **upon one's body.** אֲבָל מִיתָה וּמָמוֹן – **But** when one is liable to the **death** penalty **and** to **monetary** payment, דְּחָדָא בְּגוּפֵיהּ וְחָדָא בְּמָמוֹנֵיהּ – **where one** punishment **is** administered **on his body and one** punishment **is** administered **on his property,** אֵימָא נַעֲבִיד בֵּיהּ – **I would say** that **we do administer** both punishments **on him.** צְרִיכָא – Therefore, both verses are **necessary.**

The Gemara cites a seemingly superfluous verse, and asks:

,,וְלֹא־תִקְחוּ כֹפֶר לְנֶפֶשׁ רֹצֵחַ'' לָמָּה לִי – **Why do I [need]** the verse, *You shall not take atonement money for the life of a murderer?*[4]

The Gemara answers:

דְּאָמַר רַחֲמָנָא – **Because** there in that verse **the Merciful One** actually **said:** לֹא תִּשְׁקוֹל מָמוֹנָא מִינֵּיהּ וְתִפְטְרֵיהּ מִקְּטָלָא – **Do not take money from him and pardon him from execution.**[5]

The Gemara asks in a similar vein:

,,[וְ]לֹא־תִקְחוּ כֹפֶר לָנוּס אֶל־עִיר מִקְלָטוֹ'' לָמָּה לִי – **Why do I [need]** the verse, *You shall not take atonement money for one who fled to his city of refuge?*[6]

The Gemara answers:

דְּאָמַר רַחֲמָנָא – **Because** there in that verse **the Merciful One** actually **said:** לֹא תִּשְׁקוֹל מָמוֹנָא מִינֵּיהּ וְתִפְטְרֵיהּ מִן גָּלוּת – **Do not take money from him and pardon him from exile.**[7]

The Gemara now asks:

וּתְרֵי קְרָאֵי לָמָּה לִי – **But why do I [need] two verses** to teach that a killer cannot redeem his punishment with atonement money?

The Gemara answers:

חַד בְּשׁוֹגֵג וְחַד בְּמֵזִיד – **One** verse teaches this law **with regard to** a person who kills **unintentionally, and one** verse teaches it **with regard to** a person who kills **deliberately,** וּצְרִיכֵי – **and [both verses] are necessary.** דְּאִי אַשְׁמְעִינַן מֵזִיד – **For if [the Torah] had taught us** only regarding one who killed **deliberately,** מִשּׁוּם דַּחֲמִיר אִיסּוּרֵיהּ – I would have thought that he cannot redeem his punishment with atonement money **because his transgression is grave.** אֲבָל שׁוֹגֵג – **But** in the case of one who killed **unintentionally,** דְּלֹא חֲמִיר אִיסּוּרֵיהּ – **where his transgression is not** as **grave,** אֵימָא לֹא – **I would say** that the Torah does **not** bar him from redeeming his punishment with atonement money. וְאִי אַשְׁמְעִינַן שׁוֹגֵג – **And,** conversely, **if [the Torah] had taught us** only regarding one who killed **unintentionally,** מִשּׁוּם דְּלֵיכָּא אִיבּוּד נְשָׁמָה – I would have thought that he cannot redeem

NOTES

1. *And the judge shall cast him down and lash him . . . in accordance with his wickedness* (see above, 37a note 25).

2. This verse teaches that if one's sinful act involves two transgressions, one punishable by lashes and the other by execution, he shall be punished for only "one wickedness" — i.e. he shall receive the death penalty and not the lashes.

Tosafos explain that the Rabbis also learn the law in that case (death penalty and lashes) from this verse. That is, they understand that if one becomes liable to either monetary payment *or* the death penalty along with lashes, *in accordance with his wickedness* teaches that he is actually punished for only "one wickedness" — i.e. the greater of the two (see *Tosafos*). *Rashba,* on the other hand, explains that the Rabbis do not need this verse for the case of lashes and death. Rather, he derives the law in that case from the other two cases, as follows: If where the penalties are lashes and money, which are not severe, he receives only one punishment, then certainly where the penalties are lashes and death, the latter being severe, he should receive only one punishment. And if you will say that in the case of lashes and death he should receive both penalties because he has committed a grave transgression (as evidenced by his incurring the death penalty), I shall point out the case of money and death, where he receives only one punishment even though he has committed a grave transgression. See *Ritva.* See *R' Akiva Eiger* to *Tosafos.*

3. I.e. since lashes and execution essentially constitute one protracted punishment of the body.

4. *Numbers* 35:31. Like *Exodus* 21:22 (*And there shall be no fatality* etc.), this verse also implies that if a murderer is to be executed, he should not be punished monetarily as well. That is, we should not think that execution alone is an insufficient punishment for murder and that indemnification to the victim's family is also required. Accordingly, the Gemara asks: Why is this verse necessary? Inasmuch as *And there shall be no fatality* etc. exempts the murderer of the mother from paying even an unrelated monetary claim [viz. the value of the fetus], it certainly exempts a murderer from paying a claim for damages from the murder itself (*Rashi,* according to *Shitah Mekubetzes'* first explanation; cf. *Shitah's* second explanation; cf. *Tosafos* to *Bava Kamma* 26a ד״ה עליו).

5. The Gemara answers that our verse is not concerned with exempting a murderer from monetary liability [as the questioner presumed], for that is indeed derived from *And there shall be no fatality* etc. (see preceding note). Rather, the verse comes to teach that a murderer cannot redeem himself from execution by paying atonement money (*Rashi*). [Although the Torah prescribes execution as the punishment for murder, we might have thought that in order to save a Jewish soul (i.e. the life of the murderer) the Torah allows the murderer to redeem himself with atonement money (Gemara below, with *Rashi* ד״ה אבל מזיד; see *Shitah Mekubetzes*).]

6. [*Numbers* 35:32. This verse refers to one who committed unintentional homicide, which is punishable by exile in one of the עָרֵי מִקְלָט, *cities of refuge.*] The questioner presumes that the verse is teaching that one who kills inadvertently shall not be liable to both exile and the payment of damages for the life of his victim (*Rashi;* see note 4 above).

The questioner thus asks: Why is this verse necessary? Inasmuch as *And there shall be no fatality* etc. exempts the intentional killer of the mother from paying even an unrelated monetary claim [viz. the value of the fetus], and since the Baraisa taught in the academy of Chizkiyah (above, 35a) instructs that there is no distinction between an intentional killer and an unintentional killer with respect to monetary exemptions (see *Tos. HaRosh*), it follows that the *Exodus* verse certainly exempts an unintentional killer from paying a claim that arises from the killing itself. Why, then, is the *Numbers* verse needed?

7. The Gemara answers that our verse is not concerned with exempting an unintentional killer from monetary liability [as the questioner presumed], for that is derived from *And there shall be no fatality* etc. and the Baraisa taught in the academy of Chizkiyah (see preceding note). Rather, the verse comes to teach that an unintentional killer cannot redeem himself from exile by paying money instead. [Although the Torah prescribes exile for this killer, we might have thought that since his sin is not as great as that of a murderer, the Torah affords him the possibility of redemption with money (Gemara below, with *Rashi* ד״ה וצריכי דאי וכו׳).]

וחדא במיתה ומלקות וצריכא דאי אשמעינן מיתה וממון משום דחדא בגופיה וחדא בממוניה לא עבדינן אבל במיתה ומלקות דאידי ואידי בגופיה אימא מיתה אריכתא היא ונעביד ביה ואי אשמעינן מיתה ומלקות דתרתי בגופיה לא עבדינן אבל מיתה וממון דחדא בגופיה וחדא בממוניה אימא נעביד ביה צריכא ולא תקחו כופר לנפש רוצח למה לי דאמר רחמנא לא תשקול ממונא מיניה ותפטריה מקטלא לא תקחו כופר לנוס אל עיר מקלטו למה לי דאמר רחמנא לא תשקול ממונא מיניה ותפטריה מן גלות ותרי קראי למה לי חד בשוגג וחד במזיד וצריכי דאי אשמעינן מזיד משום דחמיר איסוריה אבל שוגג דלא חמיר איסוריה אימא לא ואי אשמעינן שוגג משום דליכא איבוד נשמה אבל מזיד דאיכא איבוד נשמה אימא לא צריכא ולארץ לא יכופר לדם אשר שופך בה כי אם בדם שופכו למה לי מבעי ליה לכדתניא מנין שאם נתערפה עגלה ואח"כ נמצא ההורג מנין שאין פוטרין אותו שנאמר ולארץ לא יכופר לדם אשר שופך בה וגו' ואתה תבער הדם הנקי מקרבך למה לי מיבעי ליה לכדתניא מנין למומתים בסייף שהוא מן הצואר ת"ל ואתה תבער הדם הנקי מקרבך הוקשו כל שופכי דמים לעגלה ערופה מה להלן מן הצואר אף שופכי דמים מן הצואר אי מה להלן בקופיץ וממול עורף אף כאן בקופיץ וממול עורף אמר רב נחמן אמר רבה בר אבוה אמר קרא ואהבת לרעך כמוך ברור לו מיתה יפה כל חרם אשר יחרם מן האדם לא יפדה למה לי מיבעי ליה לכדתניא מנין ליוצא ליהרג ואמר אחד ערכו עלי מנין שלא אמר כלום שנאמר כל חרם אשר יחרם מן האדם לא יפדה יכול אף קודם שנגמר דינו כן ת"ל מן האדם ולא כל האדם ולרבי חנניא בן עקביא דאמר נערך מפני שדמיו קצובין האי כל חרם מאי עביד ליה מיבעי ליה לכדתניא רבי ישמעאל בנו של ר' יוחנן בן ברוקה אומר לפי שמצינו למומתים בידי שמים שנותנין ממון ומתכפר להן שנאמר אם כופר יושת עליו יכול אף בידי אדם כן ת"ל חרם מן האדם לא יפדה ואין לי אלא מיתות חמורות שלא ניתנה שגגתן לכפרה מיתות קלות שניתנה שגגתן לכפרה מנין ת"ל כל חרם ולא ממילא מלא תקחו כופר שמעת מינה לא תשקול ממונא מיניה ותיפטריה כל חרם ל"ל אמר רמי בר חמא איצטריך ס"ד אמינא הני

רש"י

לא תקחו כופר. משמע נמי אם תהרגנו לא תענשנו ממון: **דאמר רחמנא.** שניא הוא דמשנינן להו לאשמעינן דלא תעביד ביה תרתי אלא לאשמועינן בחיוב מיתה לבדה שלא יפדה בממון: **לא תקחו כופר לנוס.** קא ס"ד לא תעביד ביה תרתי להורג בשוגג גלות וממון: **וצריכי דאי אשמעינן מזיד.** דלא ליפרוק נפשיה בממון הוה אמינא משום דחמיר איסוריה אבל בשוגג ליפרוק נפשיה בממון מגלות: **ואי אשמעינן שוגג.** דמשום דאין בגלותו איבוד נשמה להכי לא לפטריה בממון אלא ליגלי: **אבל מזיד.** משום איבוד נשמה אימור ניסקול ממונא ונקיים נפש בישראל: **כי אם בדם שופכו.** ולא בפדיון ממון למה לי מלא תקחו כופר נפקא: **שאין פוטרין אותו.** לומר כבר נתכפר בעודו ספק שהעגלה מכפרת על הספק: **ואתה תבער.** בתר עריפה כתיב: **מיתה יפה.** בסייף ומלד הסימנים שימות מהר: **כל חרם וגו'.** משמע לשון חייבי מיתות כמו זובח לאלהים יחרם (שמות כב): **ערכו עלי.** ואע"פ שערך אינו לפי דמים אלא לפי שנים לא אמר כלום דמעטיה קרא הכא והאי חרם לשון הקדש הוא: **שדמיו קצובין.** בתורה לפי שנים ולא דמי לאומר דמיו עלי דדמים אין לו אבל ערך יש לו: **למומתין בידי שמים.** כגון מי שהרג שורו את הנפש דכתיב ביה יומת ולא מיתת בית דין דנפקא לן בסנהדרין (דף טו:) מות יומת המכה רוצח הוא על רציחתו אתה הורגו ואי אתה הורגו על רציחת שורו והאי יומת בידי שמים: **יכול אף.** חייבי מיתות ב"ד יפדו בממון: **חרם מן האדם.** אדם שמחויב חרם: **אלא מיתות חמורות שלא ניתנה שגגתן לכפרה.** כיון דקרא לא פריש כל מיתות מיסתייך אי שדית הך חומרא דאין ממונו מצילו אמיתות חמורות ומאי נינהו כגון העושה חבורה באביו או גונב נפש מישראל שאין כפרה כתובה בשגגתו שאין כרת בזדונו דליחייב חטאת בשגגתו: **מיתות קלות.** היינו כל מיתות האמורות בהן כרת על זדונו בלא התראה יש כפרה בשגגתה בחטאת כגון עבודת כוכבים ושבת ועריות א"נ רוצח שיש כפרה לשגגתו גלות: **ולא ממילא.** שמעת לה מלא תקחו כופר הא גבי רוצח כתיבה וניתנה כפרה לשגגתו ואשמעינן קרא שלא יציל את עצמו בממון ולמה לי תו כל חרם:

תוספות

וחדא במיתה ומלקות. ורבנן מלקות וממון ומיתה ומלקות תרוייהו נפקי מכדי רשעתו דמשמע אם נתחייב בהדי מלקות מיתה או ממון משום רשעה אחת אתה מחייבו ואע"ג דסמיך ליה ארבעים יכנו לא יוסיף מ"מ אין לנו לומר דילקה ולא ימות כמו שלוקה ואינו משלם דאתגורי איתגור כדפריך בהנשרפים (סנהדרין דף פא. ושם) ואע"ג דגבי ממון ומלקות אמרינן דנדון בממון אפילו ממונא קולא התם משום דהם רחמנא אנחבל ח): **לא** תשקול ממונא מיניה ותפטריה מגלות. קשה לרשב"א דל"ל קרא מתנא דבי חזקיה נפקא דלא חילקת בין שוגג למזיד וכי היכי דבמזיד לא תשקול מיניה ממונא ותפטריה מקטלא אף שוגג לא תשקול מיניה ממונא ותפטריה מגלות ואומר ר"י דלא שייך לאקושי שוגג למזיד כי האי גוונא כיון שאין פדיון שניהם שוה דפדיון של מזיד לפוטרו ממיתה ופדיון של שוגג לפוטרו מגלות: **ואח"כ** נמצא ההורג. בפירוש החומש פ"ה הך דרשה מואתה תבער דם הנקי ולא עיין כאן ומיהו יש לקיים פירושו דהך סוגיא דשמעתא דמוקמי' ואתה תבער להקיש שופכי דמים לעגלה ערופה אתיא כמאן דאמר חנק חמור כדמוכח בפרק ד' מיתות (שם דף נג:) דלמאן דאמר חנק קל יליף סייף ברוצח מנקום ינקם הלכך לדידיה אייתר ואתה תבער לנערפה העגלה ואח"כ נמצא ההורג וקרא דולארץ לא יכופר דרשינן ליה לכדרבא בפ' בתרא דכריתות (דף כו.) דמייתינן עגלה ערופה אע"פ שעבר יוה"כ עליה: **מה** להלן בקופיץ וממול עורף. וא"ת ממול עורף מנלן והא וערפו כתיב דמשמע עורף ממש ויש לומר דבפ' עגלה ערופה (סוטה דף מו:) גמר עריפה עריפה מחטאת העוף: **הוקשו** שופכי דמים כו'. הוה מצי למימר הניחא למ"ד חנק חמור אלא למ"ד חנק קל כו': **ברור** לו מיתה יפה. ומהאי טעמא לא הוה שמעינן מן הגואל דאם יתחב סכין בלבו הוי נמי מיתה יפה: **לפי** שמצינו מומתים בידי שמים. דכתיב וגם בעליו יומת דע"כ לא בידי אדם קאמר דכתיב מות יומת המכה רוצח הוא וגו' על רציחתו אתה הורגו כו' אלא ודאי בידי שמים ואף על גב דדרשינן מיניה בפ"ק דסנהדרין (דף טו. ושם) כמיתת בעלים כך מיתת השור היינו מדכתיב יומת ולא כתיב ימות וכ"ת כולה להכי הוא דאתא אם כן ליכתוב השור יסקל כבעלים ולשתוק אי נמי ט) וגם כבעליו יומת הלכך שמע מינה תרתי: **יכול** אף בידי אדם כן. יש תימה דהיכי בעי למילף מיתה בידי אדם ממיתה בידי שמים י) [ותירץ מהר"ס כיון דאיתקש מיתת שור למיתת בעלים נקיט נמי מיתת בעלים בידי אדם למיתת בעלים שעל ידי שור]: **מיתות** קלות שניתן שגגתן לכפרה מנין. פי' בקונט' כגון עבודת כוכבים ושבת וגילוי עריות שניתן שגגתן לכפרה ע"י קרבן וכן רוצח ניתנה שגגתו לכפרה ע"י גלות וקשה דא"כ למסקנא אמאי איצטריך חרם וכל חרם ולא תקחו ג' קראי בלא תקחו כופר ובחרם סגי דחד לדרך עלייה וחד לדרך ירידה שניתן שגגתו לכפרה דהיינו מיתות קלות לפ"ה לכך נראה דמיתות קלות לא חשיב אלא הנהו שניתן שגגתן לכפרה ע"י ממון או ע"י קרבן אבל רוצח לא ניתן שגגתו לכפרה ע"י ממון אלא על ידי גלות וה"פ דברייתא אין לי אלא מיתות חמורות שלא ניתן שגגתן לכפרה ע"י קרבן דהיינו כל מיתות שאין בהן כרת כגון מסית ומדיח ונביא השקר וזקן ממרא ומכה אביו ואמו ומקלל אביו ואמו וגונב נפש ומגדף אליבא דרבנן דאמרי בכריתות (דף ג:) דאין מביא קרבן על שגגתו דכתיב לעושה בשגגה פרט למגדף שאין בו מעשה ורוצח ומיתות קלות כגון עבודת כוכבים ושבת ועריות דיש בהן כרת ומביא קרבן על שגגתן ופריך ולא ממילא שמעת מינה מלא תקחו כופר ומהתם שמעינן כל מיתות ולמה לי קרא למיתות חמורות אבל למיתות קלות ודאי צריך קרא ומשני דאיצטריך תרי קראי למיתות חמורות חד לדרך עלייה שלא ניתן שגגתו לכפרה כלל וחד לדרך ירידה שניתן שגגתו לכפרה על ידי גלות קשה לרשב"א דמאי איצטריך קרא לחייבי מיתות קלות כגון עבודת כוכבים ושבת ועריות דמה שייך שם כופר למ"ד כופר היינו דמי ניזק ותירץ דרבי ישמעאל בנו של רבי יוחנן בן ברוקה לטעמיה דאמר בפרק שור שנגח ד' וה' (ב"ק דף מ.) ונתן פדיון נפשו דמי מזיק:

עין משפט נר מצוה

נז א מיי' פ"א מהל' רוצח ושמירת נפש הלכה ד סמג לאוין קסח:
נח ב מיי' פ"ה שם הל' א סמג לאוין קסח:
נט ג מיי' פ"ו שם הל' יב סמג עשין עה:
ס ד מיי' פט"ו מהל' סנהדרין הלכה ד סמג עשין קב:
סא ה מיי' פ"ט מהל' רוצח הלכה ג סמג עשין עח:
סב ו מיי' פ"א מהל' ערכין הל' יג סמג עשין קכח:
סג ז מיי' פ"י מהלכות נזקי ממון הל' יג סמג עשין סז:

תוספות ישנים

א) [דנפקא לן מתנא דבי חזקיה דלא חילקת בין שוגג למזיד דלמאי קס"ד השתא דבעי למימר קרא לא תשקול מיניה ממונא ותפטריה. ת"י].

תורה אור השלם

א) וְלֹא תִקְחוּ כֹפֶר לְנֶפֶשׁ רֹצֵחַ אֲשֶׁר הוּא רָשָׁע לָמוּת כִּי מוֹת יוּמָת: [במדבר לה, לא]
ב) וְלֹא תִקְחוּ כֹפֶר לָנוּס אֶל עִיר מִקְלָטוֹ לָשׁוּב לָשֶׁבֶת בָּאָרֶץ עַד מוֹת הַכֹּהֵן: [במדבר לה, לב]
ג) וְלֹא תַחֲנִיפוּ אֶת הָאָרֶץ אֲשֶׁר אַתֶּם בָּהּ כִּי הַדָּם הוּא יַחֲנִיף אֶת הָאָרֶץ וְלָאָרֶץ לֹא יְכֻפַּר לַדָּם אֲשֶׁר שֻׁפַּךְ בָּהּ כִּי אִם בְּדַם שֹׁפְכוֹ: [במדבר לה, לג]
ד) וְאַתָּה תְּבַעֵר הַדָּם הַנָּקִי מִקִּרְבֶּךָ כִּי תַעֲשֶׂה הַיָּשָׁר בְּעֵינֵי יְיָ: [דברים כא, ט]
ה) לֹא תִקֹּם וְלֹא תִטֹּר אֶת בְּנֵי עַמֶּךָ וְאָהַבְתָּ לְרֵעֲךָ כָּמוֹךָ אֲנִי יְיָ: [ויקרא יט, יח]
ו) כָּל חֵרֶם אֲשֶׁר יָחֳרַם מִן הָאָדָם לֹא יִפָּדֶה מוֹת יוּמָת: [ויקרא כז, כט]
ז) אִם כֹּפֶר יוּשַׁת עָלָיו וְנָתַן פִּדְיֹן נַפְשׁוֹ כְּכֹל אֲשֶׁר יוּשַׁת עָלָיו: [שמות כא, ל]

מסורת הש"ס

א) ב"ק פג:, ב) סוטה מז., ג) סנהדרין נב:, ד) שם ודף מה. פסחים עה. [ב"ק נא. סוטה ח:], ה) ערכין ו:, ו) [שם], ח) [וע"ע תוס' לעיל לג. ד"ה ולא], ט) ס"א ליכתוב וגם בעליו יומת ותו לא, י) ת"י כ"י.

ליקוטי רש"י

ולא תקחו כופר. לא יפטר בממון [במדבר לה, לא]. **לא תקחו כופר לנוס אל עיר מקלטו.** למי שנס אל עיר מקלטו שהרג בשוגג אינו נפטר מגלות בממון ליתן כופר לשוב לשבת בארץ בטרם ימות הכהן. **לנוס.** כמו לנס (בשו"א וקמ"ץ) כמו (מיכה ב) שובי מלחמה שבטו מן המלחמה וכן (צפניה ג) נוגי ממועד וכן (יהושע ה) כי מולים היו כאשר תאמר שוב על מי ששב כבר ומול על מי שמל כבר כך תאמר לנוס על מי שנס כבר וקורהו נוס כלומר מוברח. ואם תאמר לנוס לברוח ותפרשהו לא תקחו כופר למי שיש לו לברוח לפטרו מן הגלות לא ידעתי היאך יאמר לשוב לשבת בארץ הרי עדיין לא נס ומהיכן ישוב [במדבר לה, לב]. **ואתה תבער הדם הנקי.** מגיד שאם נמצא ההורג אחר שנתערפה העגלה הרי זה יהרג והוא הישר בעיני ה' [דברים כא, ט]. **מן הצואר.** גרון [סנהדרין נב:]. **בקופיץ.** סכין גדול שכן דרך עריפה [בכורות י:]. סכין גדול הוא ורוכן אינו לשחיטה אלא לחתוך בשר ולשבירת עצמות [פסחים ע.]. סכין גדול שקולבין בו בשר [ביצה כח.]. ססס קופיץ הוא סכין של קצבים דומה לקרדומות שלנו [שם לא.]. **וממול עורף.** מאחרי הפנים דכתיב (דברים כא) וערפו ולשון עורף מול הרואה את העורף דהיינו אחורי צואר שרואין את העורף ועורף הוא קטו"ל שכנגד הפנים דכתיב (ירמיה לב) ויפנו אלי עורף ולא פנים אלמא עורף להדי פנים [סנהדרין שם]. **ואהבת לרעך כמוך.** אמר רבי עקיבא זה כלל גדול בתורה (ת"כ) [ויקרא יט, יח]. **מיתה יפה.** ולא תבזהו [סנהדרין מה.]. **כל חרם וכו' לא יפדה.** מי שהוא יוצא ליהרג וליהרג אינו בכלל פדיון. **למומתים בידי שמים.** כגון האי דכתיב השור יסקל וגם בעליו יומת והך מיתה ליכא למימר בידי אדם דהא אמרי' בפ"ק דסנהדרין (דף טו:) מות יומת המכה רוצח הוא על רציחתו אתה הורגו ואי אתה הורגו על רציחת שורו [ערכין ו:]. **אם כופר יושת עליו.** אם זה אינו תלוי והרי הוא כמו (לקמן כב כד) אם כסף תלוה לשון אשר זה משפט ששיתו עליו בית דין כופר [שמות כא, ל]. **שלא ניתנה שגגתן לכפרה.** כגון מגדף ומקלל אביו ואמו שאין עושה בשגגה לא קרבן ולא גלות. **מיתות קלות.** כלומר דקלות לכך קא מילתא שניתנה שגגתן לכפרה כגון רוצח דשגגתו גולה ועובד ע"ז ומחלל שבת ובא על הערוה וגם בעליו חטאת [ערכין שם].

נו א ב ג מיי' פי"א מהל' גירושין הל' כא כב סמג עשין נ טוש"ע אה"ע סימן יג סעיף ה ו:

וסבר רבי יהודה בקדושתה קיימא והתניא הגיורת שנתגיירה וראתה דם ר' יהודה אומר דיה שעתה אר' יוסי אומר הרי היא ככל הנשים ומטמאה מעת לעת ומפקידה לפקידה וצריכה להמתין ג' חדשים דברי ר' יהודה ר' יוסי מתיר ליארס ולינשא מיד א"ל גיורת אשבויה קא רמית גיורת לא מנטרא נפשה שבויה מנטרא נפשה ורמי שבויה אשבויה דתניא הגיורת והשבויה והשפחה שנפדו ושנתגיירו ושנשתחררו יתירות על בנות ג' שנים ויום אחד צריכות להמתין ג' חדשים דברי ר' יהודה ר' יוסי מתיר ליארס ולינשא מיד אשתיק א"ל מידי שמיע לך בהא אמר ליה הכי אמר רב ששת שראוה שנבעלה א"ה מאי טעמא דר' יוסי אמר רבה קסבר ר' יוסי אשה מזנה משמשת במוך שלא תתעבר בשלמא גיורת כיון דדעתה לאיגיורי מנטרא נפשה שבויה נמי דלא ידעה היכא ממטו לה שפחה נמי דשמעה מפי מרה אלא יוצאה בשן ועין מאי איכא למימר וכי תימא כל ממילא לא א"ר יוסי הרי אנוסה ומפותה דממילא ותניא אנוסה ומפותה צריכות להמתין ג' חדשים דברי ר' יהודה ר' יוסי מתיר ליארס ולינשא מיד אלא אמר רבה קסבר ר' יוסי אשה מזנה מתהפכת כדי שלא תתעבר ואידך חיישי' שמא לא נהפכה יפה יפה: שנא' ולא יהיה אסון ענוש יענש וכו': והא מהכא נפקא מהתם נפקא כדי רשעתו משום רשעה אחת אתה מחייבו ואי אתה מחייבו משום שתי רשעיות חדא במיתה וממון וחדא במלקות וממון וצריכא דאי אשמעינן מיתה וממון משום דאיכא איבוד נשמה אבל מלקות וממון דליכא איבוד נשמה אימא לא ואי אשמעינן מלקות וממון משום דלא חמיר איסוריה אבל מיתה וממון דחמיר איסוריה אימא לא צריכא ולרבי מאיר דאמר לוקה ומשלם תרתי למה לי חדא במיתה וממון וחדא

רש"י

וראתה דם. בו ביום: דיה שעתה. ולא גזרו בה טומאת מעת לעת לטמא טהרות שנגעה בהן משעת טבילה עד שעת ראייה דהא אפי' יצא דם זה מאתמול והעמידוהו כותלי בית הרחם שזהו הטעם של מעת לעת בבנות ישראל הלא דם כנענית כדם בהמה ואם תאמר ניחוש שמא משטבלה נעקר ולא מיד טומאה למפרע דרבנן היא והיכא דליכא למיגזר מעת לעת שלא גזור מפקידה לפקידה והיכא דלא גזור מעת לעת לא גזור מפקידה לפקידה: וצריכה להמתין ג' חדשים. שלא תנשא להבחין בין זרע שנזרע בקדושה לזרע שנזרע שלא בקדושה: רבי יוסי מתיר. לקמיה מפרש טעמא: צריכות להמתין. ואף על פי שקטנה אינה מתעברת גזירה קטנה אטו גדולה: משמשת במוך. מוכנת מוך לאחר בעילה ושואבת הזרע: מנטרא נפשה. ומזמנת לה מוך: דלא ידעה היכא ממטו לה. שבאים למוכרה וסברה דלמא ממטו לה לגבי ישראל ופרקו לה ומנטרא נפשה לשמש במוך: אלא יוצאה בשן ועין. שפחה שהכתה את עיניה ויצאה לחירות מנא הוה ידעה מעיקרא דמיפוק לחירות דמנטרא נפשה לזמן מוך לשימושה: כל ממילא. מידי דליכא לאיזדהורי ביה מעיקרא דמיפוק לחירות מודה רבי יוסי: הרי אנוסה דממילא. דלא הוה ידעה ליסלק בה הכי ולזמן לה מוך: מתהפכת. שיצא הזרע ולא יקלוט והא אפילו במידי דממילא מצו למיעבד וכולן עושות כן: משום דאיכא איבוד נשמה. יש לכאן עונש חמור ודיו בכך אם ענשנו לאבד נשמה ליהרג: אימא לא. אין זה עונש יתירה וליעביד ביה תרתי: דלא חמיר איסוריה. לא עבר עבירה חמורה ודיו שתענשנו עונש אחד: לא

תוספות

וסבר רבי יהודה בקדושתה קיימא והתניא הגיורת כו'. קשה להשתא דמדמה גיורת לשבויה א"כ תיקשי ליה מתניתין גופה דר' יהודה לא משוה גיורת לשבויה דתנן ר' יהודה אומר שבויה שנפדית הרי היא בקדושתה משמע דבהנך מודה לתנא קמא ואמר ר"י דמתני' אתי ליה שפיר דמודה בגיורת שאין לה קנס דודאי היא בחזקת בעולה שנבעלה בעוד שלא היה דעתה להתגייר ואפילו אם היה דעתה להתגייר משהיתה בת שלש שנים ויום אחד מ"מ לא מנטרא נפשה כיון דאינה ראויה להתעבר אבל מהך דצריכה להמתין שלשה חדשים אף על גב דדעתה לאיגיורי ומנטרא נפשה אפילו הכי קאמר צריכה להמתין ג' חדשים דלא אפשר לשמור עצמה מן העובדי כוכבים כ"ש שבויה שהיא מסורה בידם: **רבי** יהודה אומר דיה שעתה. פירש הקונטרס כיון דליכא מעת לעת מפקידה לפקידה נמי לא גזור רבנן ורבי יוסי דקאמר ומטמאה מעת לעת לאו דוקא מעת לעת אלא כלומר כבנות ישראל מעת לעת משנתגיירה: **שבויה** מנטרא נפשה. וא"ת והא בקטנה נמי מיירי דלא מנטרא נפשה דהא אינה יודעת לשמור עצמה וקאמר ר"י דבקדושתה קיימא דקתני במתני' יתירה מבת ג' שנים ויום אחד וי"ל דקטנה לגמרי אינה מוסרת עצמה לביאה וכשהיא מוסרת עצמה לביאה קצת היא בת דעת ויודעת לשמור עצמה: **צריכות** להמתין שלשה חדשים דברי ר' יהודה. משמע דאפי' בקטנה שאינה ראויה להתעבר קאמר רבי יהודה דצריכה להמתין מדקאמר יתירות מבנות ג' ויום אחד דגזר קטנה אטו גדולה וקשה לר"י ולרבינו תם דתניא בהחולץ (יבמות דף מב: ושם) הרי שהיתה רדופה לילך לבית אביה או קטנה כו' צריכה להמתין ג' חדשים דברי ר"מ ר' יהודה מתיר ליארס ולינשא מיד אלמא לא גזר רבי יהודה קטנה אטו גדולה וכ"ת דוקא בגיורת ומשוחררת ושבויה גזר טפי כדי להבחין בין זרע שנזרע בקדושה לשנזרע שלא בקדושה זה אין נראה דהא לרבא דמפרש התם לעיל טעם דצריכות להמתין גזירה שמא ישא אחותו מאביו וייבם אשת אחיו מן אמו כו' טפי אית לן למיגזר בקטנה בת ישראל דשייך בה כל הנהו דמפרש התם אבל בגיורת ושבויה ומשוחררת לא שייך שמא ישא אחותו מאביו ועוד דשמואל אית ליה סברא איפכא מדר' יהודה דהא שמואל קאמר בס"פ ד' אחין (שם דף לד: ושם) דכולן צריכות להמתין ג' חדשים חוץ מגיורת ומשוחררת קטנה אבל קטנה בת ישראל צריכה להמתין אלמא בקטנה בת ישראל גזר קטנה אטו גדולה ובגיורת ומשוחררת לא גזר והיינו איפכא מדרבי יהודה ועוד לשמואל בשלמא בקטנה בת ישראל סבר כר"מ אלא בגיורת כמאן לא כרבי יהודה ולא כר' יוסי דלרבי יהודה בין קטנה בין גדולה צריכה להמתין ולרבי יוסי אפי' גדולה אינה צריכה להמתין ומיהו למאי דמוקי להך דהכא בשראוה שנבעלה אתי שפיר כר' יהודה ומצינן למימר דדוקא בראוה שנבעלה קאמר ר' יהודה דגזרי' קטנה אטו גדולה אבל אותה שאינה ודאי בעולה לא ולפי לשון אחרון דהתם לא קשה כלל אע"ג דשמואל איפכא מדרבי יהודה כיון דאין הטעם משום דגזרינן קטנה אטו גדולה דאפילו בגדולה נמי שרי לפי שמתהפכת ואור"י דבס"פ ד' אחין (ג"ז שם לה.) מייתי הך ברייתא דהכא ול"ג בה יתירות מבנות ג' ויום אחד ובתוספתא נמי ל"ג ליה ולפי זה ניחא דמיירי בגדולה אבל בקטנה מודה דאין צריכה להמתין כדקאמר בברייתא דרדופה והשתא שמואל בגיורת כר' יהודה ובבת ישראל כרבי מאיר ואפשר דבגיורת קטנה מודה ר' מאיר דאין צריכה להמתין וללשון אחרון דהתם דאמר שמואל כולן צריכות להמתין חוץ מגיורת ומשוחררת גדולה וקטנה בת ישראל אינה צריכה להמתין בזנות משום דזנות דקטנה לא שכיח אבל בנשואין גזר קטנה אטו גדולה וסבר בגיורת כרבי יוסי ובבת ישראל כר"מ דגזר קטנה אטו גדולה וס"ל דדוקא בנשואין גזר ר"מ ושמא בנשואין מודה ר' יוסי לר"מ ומיהו בזנות ודאי פליג דהא שרי אנוסה ומפותה אפילו גדולה ואית דגרסי בברייתא דרדופה ר' יוסי במקום ר' יהודה ושם פירשנו: **אי** הכי מ"ט דר' יוסי. תימה לר"י דמשמע דמשום דאוקימנא בראוה שנבעלה הוא דקשיא ליה מאי טעמא בלאו הכי נמי תיקשי ליה ברייתא דרבי יוסי דמייתי לקמן דאנוסה ומפותה ולפי הסוגיא נראה דזה המקשה עצמו הוא דמייתי לה ומיהו י"ס דגרסי בסמוך א"ל אביי בשלמא גיורת כיון דדעתה לאיגיורי כו' ולפי גירסא זו אתי שפיר שזה המקשה לא ידע ברייתא דמייתי לקמן דאביי הוא דמייתי לה וכן הוא גירסא בשילהי ד' אחין (ג"ז שם):

אמר רבה קסבר רבי יוסי כו'. אליבא דרבי יוחנן משני דלדידיה דמפרש טעמא דר' יהודה שלא יהא חוטא נשכר לא קשיא מידי [ומיהו רבה לא קאמר אלא דלמא]: **אשה** מזנה מתהפכת. ומהשתא לא קשה אנוסה ומפותה ומיהו יוצאה בשן ועין מודה רבי יוסי דצריכה להמתין דאותה למה תתהפך: **הבא** על בתו. למאי דמוקי מתני' בפרק בן סורר (סנהדרין דף עג: ושם) במפותה צריך לאוקמה בשבא עליה ובגרה כדפרישית לעיל: **ועל** בת אשתו. הוה מצי למיתני אשת אביו וכלתו דהא חשיב נמי עריות דעל ידי קדושין אלא תנא ושייר: **חדא** במלקות וממון. לעיל פירשתי למה לא יליף רשע רשע תימה דדריש החובל (ב"ק דף פג:) פריך הא מיבעי ליה קרא דלא תקחו כופר דלא תשקול מיניה ממונא ותקטליה ומשני ההוא מכדי רשעתו נפקא הוה ליה למימר ההוא מלא יהיה אסון נפקא דכדי רשעתו אתא למלקות וממון וי"ל דהתם טעי כי היכי דטעי הכא מעיקרא לומר דמכדי רשעתו נפקא מיתה וממון [והא דלא פריך האי במלקות וממון כתיב לא חש להקשות משום דהוי מצי לשנויי מלא יהיה אסון נפקא] אי נמי לסימנא בעלמא נקטיה התם: וחדא

ליקוטי רש"י

דיה שעתה. אם ראתה דם די לנו אם תטמא תרומה וטהרות שתגע בהן משעת ראייה ואילך ולא אמרי' כי היכי דהשתא אישתכח דם בבית החיצון אי הות בדקה נמי מקמי הכי הוה אישתכח וכותלי בית הרחם העמידוהו וקיימא לן בפ' יוצא דופן (לקמן דף מ) כל הנשים מטמאות בבית החיצון [נדה ב.]. ככל הנשים. הרואות דם [שבת טו.]. מעת לעת ומפקידה לפקידה. מעת לעת ממעטת על יד מפקידה לפקידה, שאם יש ימים הרבה בין פקידה לפקידה לא מטמאין להו לכולהו טהרות דביני וביני אלא אותם שנתעסקה בהם מאתמול בשעה הזאת וטעמייהו דרבנן מפרש לקמן בגמרא נמצא מעת לעת ממעטת זמן מפקידה לפקידה. ומפקידה לפקידה ממעטת על יד מעת לעת, שאם היה זמן מפקידה לפקידה מועט מזמן מעת לעת הולכין אחריו להקל כגון בדקה עצמה שחרית ומצאתה טהורה וחזרה ובדקה ערבית ומצאתה טמאה דאמרי' לקמן במתני' (דף יא) פעמים צריכה להיות בודקת שחרית ובין השמשות לא מטמאין טהרות של ליל אמש דהא בדקה שחרית ומצאתה טהורה וליכא למימר דהוי דם מאתמול בהאי שעתא אלא הנך טהרות דמבדיקת שחרית ואילך מטמאין דהיינו מפקידה לפקידה [נדה שם]. מפקידה לפקידה, למפרע, בדקה היום ומצאתה טהורה ובדקה לסוף שבוע ומצאתה טמאה חוששין למגעה מבדיקה ראשונה ואילך שמא עם סילוק ידיה ראתה. מעת לעת ממעט על יד מפקידה לפקידה. שני זמנים החכרו בה למפרע להכך אחר הקל שבהן אם מפקידה לפקידה יותר על מעת לעת מעת הכך אחר מעת לעת ואם מעת לעת יותר על מפקידה לפקידה הלך אחר הפקידה [שבת שם]. מנטרא נפשה. ומתקנת מוך בהדה ומזומן לה. אלא יוצאה בשן ועין. דלא הוה ידעת מעיקרא דעתידה להשתחרר לא מיטרחא ומזדהרא לאתויי מוך בהדה. אנוסה. ישראלית והרי אונס ממילא הוא ולאין לה מוך. מתהפכת. ואף יוצאה בשן ועין ליכא דאשתא לאפוקי כיון דהיפוך קל הוא ולאין בו טורח מתהפכת דכל אשה מזנה אינה רוצה להתעבר [יבמות לה.]. דאמר לוקה ומשלם. במסכת מכות (דף ד) מעידים אנו בפלוני שחייב לחבירו מאתים זוז והוזמו לוקין ומשלמין שלא השם המביאו לידי מכות [ב"ק עא.]. שלא המביאו לידי תשלומין מלקות מכאשר זמם וכיון דשני שמות הן חייב על שניהם [לעיל לב:].

מסורת הש"ס

א) יבמות לה. [כל הסוגיא ע"ש], ב) [אין לזה מובן וכן נראה מפירש"י דליתא], ג) [שם איתא אביי], ד) ב"ק פג: מכות ד: יג: [לעיל לב:], ה) [לעיל לג: וש"נ], ו) [שם מב.], ז) [לא גרסינן כצ"ל רש"ל], ח) [שייך לעיל במשנה לו:], ט) [דף כט. ד"ה ועל אשת], י) [ג"ז שייך שם], כ) [לה. ד"ה רבה].

גליון הש"ס

רש"י ד"ה דיה שעתה וכו' לא גזור מפקידה לפקידה. כדאיתא בנדה לו ע"א:

הגהות מהר"ב רנשבורג

אן גמ' ר' יוסי אומר הרי היא ככל הנשים. עי' נדה דף לו ע"א תוד"ה דליכא שכות וכו' והגאון מהרר"ם לא ציינו בש"ס החדשים בהגהותיו:

תורה אור השלם

א) וְכִי יִנָּצוּ אֲנָשִׁים וְנָגְפוּ אִשָּׁה הָרָה וְיָצְאוּ יְלָדֶיהָ וְלֹא יִהְיֶה אָסוֹן עָנוֹשׁ יֵעָנֵשׁ כַּאֲשֶׁר יָשִׁית עָלָיו בַּעַל הָאִשָּׁה וְנָתַן בִּפְלִלִים: [שמות כא, כב]

ב) וְהָיָה אִם בִּן הַכּוֹת הָרָשָׁע וְהִפִּילוֹ הַשֹּׁפֵט וְהִכָּהוּ לְפָנָיו כְּדֵי רִשְׁעָתוֹ בְּמִסְפָּר: [דברים כה, ב]

The Gemara asks:

וְאִידָךְ – **And the other one,** R' Yehudah, why does he require all these women to wait three months before marrying, if pregnancy can be prevented merely by "turning"? Certainly she availed herself of that simple method! – ? –

The Gemara explains R' Yehudah's position:

חָיְישִׁינַן שֶׁמָּא לֹא נֶהֶפְכָה יָפֶה יָפֶה – **We are concerned** that **perhaps she did not turn well,** and thus did not prevent a pregnancy.

The Mishnah concluded:

שֶׁנֶּאֱמַר ,,וְלֹא יִהְיֶה אָסוֹן עָנוֹשׁ יֵעָנֵשׁ וגו׳ " – And anyone who is liable with his life does not pay money, FOR IT IS STATED:[21] *If men shall quarrel and they jolt a pregnant woman and she miscarries, AND THERE SHALL BE NO FATALITY, HE SHALL BE PUNISHED* **etc.**[22]

The Gemara asks:

וְהָא מֵהָכָא נָפְקָא – **But is this** principle that one incurs only the greater of two simultaneously deserved penalties **derived from here?!** מֵהָתָם נָפְקָא – No! **It is derived from there:**[23] ,,כְּדֵי רִשְׁעָתוֹ" – *And the judge shall cast him down and lash him . . .* ***in accordance with his wickedness.*** מִשּׁוּם רִשְׁעָה אַחַת אַתָּה מְחַיְּיבוֹ – The singular form of the word "wickedness" teaches that **you may hold [a transgressor] liable for one wickedness,** וְאִי אַתָּה מְחַיְּיבוֹ מִשּׁוּם שְׁתֵּי רִשְׁעָיוֹת – **but you may not hold him liable for two wickednesses.** That is, you may not subject him to two penalties for one sinful act. – ? –

The Gemara answers:

חֲדָא בְּמִיתָה וּמָמוֹן – **One** verse[24] teaches us this principle **where** the transgressor is liable to the **death** penalty **and** to **monetary** payment, וַחֲדָא בְּמַלְקוּת וּמָמוֹן – **and one** verse[25] teaches it **where** the transgressor is liable to **lashes and** to **monetary** payment.

The Gemara now explains why the principle must be taught in both contexts:

וּצְרִיכָא – **And** both verses are **necessary.** דְּאִי אַשְׁמְעִינַן מִיתָה וּמָמוֹן – **For if [the Torah] had taught us** only where the transgressor is liable to the **death** penalty **and** a **monetary** payment, מִשּׁוּם דְּאִיכָּא אִיבּוּד נְשָׁמָה – I would have thought that there only the greater punishment is given **because there is a loss of life.**[26] אֲבָל מַלְקוּת וּמָמוֹן – **But** when one is liable to **lashes and** a **monetary** payment, דְּלֵיכָּא אִיבּוּד נְשָׁמָה – **where there is no loss of life,** אֵימָא לֹא – **I would say** that we do **not** give only one penalty.[27] וְאִי אַשְׁמְעִינַן מַלְקוּת וּמָמוֹן – **And,** conversely, **if [the Torah] had taught us** the principle only where one is liable to **lashes and** a **monetary** payment, מִשּׁוּם דְּלֹא חָמִיר אִיסּוּרֵיהּ – I would have thought that there only one punishment is given **because his transgression is not** that **grave.**[28] אֲבָל מִיתָה וּמָמוֹן – **But** when one is liable to the **death** penalty **and** a **monetary** payment, דַּחֲמִיר אִיסּוּרֵיהּ – **where his transgression *is* grave,**[29] אֵימָא לֹא – **I would say** that it does **not** suffice for the transgressor to incur only one penalty. צְרִיכָא – Therefore, both verses are **necessary.**[30]

The Gemara asks:

וּלְרַבִּי מֵאִיר – **But according to R' Meir,** דְּאָמַר לוֹקֶה וּמְשַׁלֵּם – **who said**[31] that **one is lashed *and* pays** for the same sinful act, תַּרְתֵּי לָמָּה לִי – **why do I [need] two** verses?[32]

The Gemara answers:

חֲדָא בְּמִיתָה וּמָמוֹן – **One** verse[33] teaches that only the greater penalty is incurred **where** the transgressor is liable to the **death** penalty **and** a **monetary** payment,

NOTES

victim of violation does not wait three months), but also the preceding one (that R' Yose made a general statement exempting "emancipated slavewomen" from waiting three months, which apparently includes even those slavewomen who were emancipated because of a lost tooth or eye). The Gemara is now answering that even though this slavewoman (or victim of violation) did not think to prepare a cloth, she will nonetheless employ the trouble-free method of "turning." Hence, according to R' Yose she is presumed not to be pregnant at the time of her emancipation, and is permitted to marry without waiting the three months (see also *Rashi* to *Yevamos* 35a ד״ה מתהפכת, who states this explicitly).

Ramban, however, finds this interpretation difficult: Why should a slavewoman who has no expectation of being emancipated think to use a birth-control technique?! *Ramban* thus agrees with *Tosafos,* who explain that the Gemara is answering only why a *victim of violation* is presumed not pregnant and is permitted to marry immediately. Accordingly, when R' Yose ruled that an emancipated slavewoman need not wait three months, he was not referring to one whose master knocked out her tooth or eye (see note 16 above).

21. *Exodus* 21:22.

22. [I.e. monetarily, in that he pays the value of the fetus.] The verse thus implies that if there *is* a fatality (i.e. the death of the mother), the assailant is not punished monetarily, but is executed (see *Rashi* to Mishnah above, 36b). See *Rambam, Hil. Naarah Besulah* 1:13, and *Hil. Chovel U'Mazik* 4:5,6 with *Raavad* and commentaries; see also Gemara above, 34b-35a.

23. *Deuteronomy* 25:2, which speaks of the judicial administration of the lashes penalty.

24. *And there shall be no fatality, he shall surely be punished,* which alludes to one who commits murder, a capital offense.

25. *And the judge shall cast him down and lash him ... in accordance with his wickedness,* which speaks of a transgressor who is punished with lashes.

26. I would have thought that since the transgressor incurs the ultimate penalty – the loss of his life – one punishment suffices (*Rashi*).

27. Since lashes is not as severe a punishment, both penalties should be imposed (*Rashi*).

28. Since the transgression he committed is not of the greatest magnitude [as evidenced by the fact that he incurs only lashes], it suffices that he receives only one punishment (*Rashi*).

29. It is, indeed, a capital offense!

30. Regarding which punishment is given in the case of lashes and monetary payment, see above, 32a-33b.

31. In the Mishnah in *Makkos* 4a, cited above, 32b.

32. Since, according to R' Meir, the principle that one incurs only the greater penalty applies only to one who commits a capital offense, why do I need the "lashes" verse?

33. *And there shall be no fatality, he shall surely be punished* (see note 24 above).

וסבר רבי יהודה בקדושתה קיימא והתניא הגיורת שנתגיירה וראתה דם ר' יהודה אומר דיה שעתה א ר' יוסי אומר הרי היא ככל הנשים ומטמאה מעת לעת ומפקידה לפקידה וצריכה להמתין ג' חדשים דברי ר' יהודה ר' יוסי מתיר ליארס ולינשא מיד א"ל גיורת אשבויה קא רמית גיורת לא מנטרא נפשה שבויה מנטרא נפשה ורמי שבויה אשבויה דתניא [א] הגיורת והשבויה והשפחה שנפדו ושנתגיירו ושנשתחררו יתירות על בנות ג' שנים ויום אחד א צריכות להמתין ג' חדשים דברי ר' יהודה ר' יוסי מתיר ליארס ולינשא מיד אשתיק א"ל מידי שמיע לך בהא אמר ליה הכי אמר רב ששת שראוה שנבעלה א"ה מאי טעמא דר' יוסי אמר רבה קסבר ר' יוסי אשה מזנה משמשת במוך שלא תתעבר בשלמא גיורת כיון דדעתה לאיגיורי מנטרא נפשה שבויה נמי דלא ידעה היכא ממטו לה שפחה נמי דשמעה מפי מרה אלא יוצאה בשן ועין מאי איכא למימר וכי תימא כל ממילא לא א"ר יוסי הרי אנוסה [ג] ומפותה דממילא ותניא אנוסה ומפותה צריכות להמתין ג' חדשים דברי ר' יהודה ב ר' יוסי מתיר ליארס ולינשא מיד אלא אמר [ג] רבה קסבר ר' יוסי ג אשה מזנה מתהפכת כדי שלא תתעבר ואידך חיישי' שמא לא נהפכה יפה: שנא' [א] ולא יהיה אסון ענוש יענש וכו': והא מהכא נפקא מהתם נפקא [ב] כדי רשעתו [ד] משום רשעה אחת אתה מחייבו ואי אתה מחייבו משום שתי רשעיות חדא במיתה וממון וחדא במלקות וממון וצריכא דאי אשמעינן מיתה וממון משום דאיכא איבוד נשמה אבל מלקות וממון דליכא איבוד נשמה אימא לא ואי אשמעינן מלקות וממון משום דלא חמיר איסוריה אבל מיתה וממון דחמיר איסוריה אימא לא צריכא ולרבי מאיר [ה] דאמר לוקה ומשלם תרתי למה לי חדא במיתה וממון וחדא

רש"י

וראתה דם. בו ביום: דיה שעתה. ולא גזרו בה טומאת מעת לעת לטמא טהרות שנגעה בהן משעת טבילה עד שעת ראייה דהא אפי' ילא דם זה מאתמול והעמידוהו כותלי בית הרחם שזהו הטעם של מעת לעת בבנות ישראל הלא דם כנענית כדם בהמה ואם תאמר ניחוש שמא משטבלה נעקר ויצא מיד טומאה למפרע דרבנן היא והיכא דליכא למיגזר מעת לעת שלא גזור מפקידה לפקידה והיכא דלא גזור מעת לעת * לא גזור מפקידה לפקידה: וצריכה להמתין ג' חדשים. שלא תנשא להבחין בין זרע הנזרע בקדושה לזרע הנזרע שלא בקדושה: רבי יוסי מתיר. לקמיה מפרש טעמא: צריכות להמתין. ואף על פי שקטנה אינה מתעברת גזירה קטנה אטו גדולה: משמשת במוך. מוכין מוך לאחר בעילה ושואבת הזרע: מנטרא נפשה. ומזמנת לה מוך: דלא ידעה היכא ממטו לה. שבאים למוכרה וסבורה דלמא ממטו לה לגבי ישראל ופרקו לה ומנטרא נפשה לשמש במוך: אלא יוצאה בשן ועין. שפחה שסימא אדוניה את עינה ויצאה לחירות מנא הוה ידעה מעיקרא דתיפוק לחירות דתנטרא נפשה לזמן מוך לשימושה: כל ממילא. מידי דליכא לאזדהורי ביה מעיקרא דתיפוק לחירות מודה רבי יוסי: הרי אנוסה דממילא. דלא הוה ידעה לאיסתקופי בה הכי ותזמן לה מוך: מתהפכת. שילא הזרע ולא יקלוט והא אפילו במידי דממילא נמי לא למיעבד וכולן עושות כן: משום דאיכא איבוד נשמה. יש כאן עונש חמור ודיו בכך אם עונשתו לאבד נשמה ליהרג: אימא לא. אין זה עונש יתירה וליעביד ביה תרתי: דלא חמיר איסוריה. לא עבר עבירה חמורה ודיו שתענשנו עונש אחד: לא

תוספות

וסבר רבי יהודה בקדושתה קיימא והתניא הגיורת כו'. קשה דהשתא למדמה גיורת לשבויה א"כ תיקשי ליה מתניתין גופה דר' יהודה לא משוה גיורת לשבויה דלתנן ר' יהודה אומר שבויה שנפדית הרי היא בקדושתה משמע דבהכך מודה לתנא קמא ואמר ר"י דמתני' אתי ליה שפיר דמודה בגיורת שאין לה קנס דודאי היא בחזקת בעולה שנבעלה בעוד שלא היה דעתה להתגייר ואפילו אם היה דעתה להתגייר משהיתה בת שלש שנים ויום אחד מ"מ לא מנטרה נפשה כיון דאינה ראויה להתעבר אבל מהך דלריכה להמתין שלשה חדשים אף על גב דדעתה לאיגיורי ומנטרא נפשה אפילו הכי קאמר לריכה להמתין ג' חדשים דאי אפשר לשמור עצמה מן העובדי כוכבים כ"ש שבויה שהיא מסורה בידם: רבי יהודה אומר דיה שעתה. פירש הקונטרס כיון דליכא מעת לעת מפקידה לפקידה נמי לא גזור רבנן ורבי יוסי דקאמר ומטמאה מעת לעת לאו דוקא מעת לעת אלא כלומר בתורת מעת לעת מטמאה משנתגיירה: שבויה מנטרא נפשה. וא"ת והא בקטנה נמי מיירי דלא מנטרא נפשה דהא אינה יודעת לשמור עצמה וקאמר ר"י דבקדושתה קיימא דקתני במתני' יתירה מבת ג' שנים ויום אחד וי"ל דקטנה לגמרי אינה מוסרת עצמה לביאה וכשהיא מוסרת עצמה לביאה קלת היא בת דעת ויודעת לשמור עצמה: צריכות להמתין שלשה חדשים דברי ר' יהודה. משמע דאפי' בקטנה שאינה ראויה להתעבר קאמר רבי יהודה דלריכה להמתין מדקאמר יתירות מבנות ג' ויום אחד דגזר קטנה אטו גדולה וקשה לר"י ולרבינו תם דתניא בהחולץ (יבמות דף מב. ושם) הרי שהיתה רדופה לילך לבית אביה או קטנה כו' לריכה להמתין ג' חדשים דברי ר"מ ר' יהודה מתיר ליארס ולינשא מיד אלמא לא גזר רבי יהודה קטנה אטו גדולה וכ"ת דוקא בגיורת ומשוחררת ושבויה גזר טפי כדי להבחין בין זרע שנזרע בקדושה לשנזרע שלא בקדושה זה אין נראה דהא לרבא דמפרש התם לעיל [ו] טעם דלריכות להמתין גזירה שמא ישא אחותו מאביו וייבם אשת אחיו מן אמו כו' טפי אית לן למיגזר בקטנה בת ישראל דשייך בה כל הנהו דמפרש התם אבל בגיורת ושבויה ומשוחררת לא שייך שמא ישא אחותו מאביו ועוד דשמואל אית ליה סברא איפכא מדר' יהודה דהא שמואל קאמר בס"פ ד' אחין (שם דף לד: ושם) דכולן לריכות להמתין ג' חדשים חוץ מגיורת ומשוחררת קטנה אבל קטנה בת ישראל לריכה להמתין אלמא בקטנה בת ישראל גזר קטנה אטו גדולה ובגיורת ומשוחררת לא גזר והיינו איפכא מדרבי יהודה ועוד דשמואל בשלמא בקטנה בת ישראל מלא בגיורת כמאן לא כרבי יהודה ולא כר' יוסי דלרבי יהודה בין קטנה בין גדולה לריכה להמתין ולרבי יוסי אפי' גדולה אינה לריכה להמתין ומיהו למאי דמוקי להך דהכא בשראוה שנבעלה אתי שפיר כר' יהודה ומלינן למימר דדוקא קאמר ר' יהודה דגזרי' קטנה אטו גדולה אבל אותה שאינה ודאי בעולה לא ולפי לשון אחרון דהתם לא קשה כלל אע"ג דשמואל איפכא מדרבי יהודה כיון דאין הטעם משום [ז] דגזרינן קטנה אטו גדולה דאפילו בגדולה נמי שרי לפי שמתהפכת ואור"י דבס"פ ד' אחין (ג"ז שם לה.) מייתי הך ברייתא דהכא ול"ג בה יתירות מבנות ג' ויום אחד ובתוספתא נמי ל"ג ליה ולפי זה ניחא דמיירי בגדולה אבל בקטנה מודה ר' יהודה דאין לריכה להמתין כדקאמר בברייתא דרדופה והשתא שמואל בגיורת כר' יהודה ובבת ישראל כר"מ ואפשר דבגיורת קטנה מודה ר' מאיר דאין לריכה להמתין ולגלון אחרון דהתם דקאמר שמואל כולן לריכות להמתין חוץ מגיורת ומשוחררת גדולה וקטנה בת ישראל אינה לריכה להמתין בזנות משום זנות דקטנה לא שכיח אבל בנשואין גזר קטנה אטו גדולה וסבר בגיורת כרבי יוסי ובבת ישראל כר"מ דגזר קטנה אטו גדולה וס"ל דדוקא בנשואין גזר ר"מ ושמא בנשואין מודה ר' יוסי לר"מ ומיהו בזנות ודאי פליג דהא שרי אנוסה ומפותה אפילו גדולה ולית דגרסי בברייתא דרדופה ר' יוסי במקום ר' יהודה ושם פירשנו: **אי** הכי מ"ט דר' יוסי. תימה לר"י דמשמע דמשום דאוקימנא בראוה שנבעלה הוא דקשיא ליה מאי טעמא דר' יוסי דמייתי לקמן לאנוסה ומפותה ולפי הסוגיא נראה דזה המקשה עצמו הוה דמייתי לה ומיהו י"ס דגרסי בסמוך א"ל אבי בשלמא גיורת כיון דדעתה לאיגיורי כו' ולפי גירסא זו אתי שפיר שזה המקשה לא ידע ברייתא דמייתי לקמן דאביי הוא דמייתי לה וכן הוא גירסא בשילהי ד' אחין (ג"ז שם):

אמר רבה קסבר רבי יוסי כו'. אליבא דרבי יוחנן משני לדידיה דמפרש טעמא דר' יהודה שלא יהא חוטא נשכר לא קשיא מידי [ומיהו רבה לא קאמר אלא לדמאי]: **אשה** מזנה מתהפכת. והשתא לא קשה אנוסה ומפותה ומיהו יוצאה בשן ועין מודה רבי יוסי דלריכה להמתין דאוסה לא ממתין להמתין פ' מתהפך: **הבא** [ח] על בתו. למאי דמוקי מתני' בפרק בן סורר (סנהדרין דף עג: ושם) במפותה לריך לאוקמה בשבא עליה ובגרה כדפרישית לעיל [ט]: **ועל** בת אשתו. הוה מלי למיתני אשת אביו וכלתו דהא חשיב נמי עריות דעל ידי קידושין אלא תנא ושייר: **חדא** במלקות וממון. לעיל [י] פירשתי למה לא יליף רשע רשע מחייבי מיתות: **חדא** במלקות וממון. (ב"ק דף פג:) פריך הא מיבעי ליה קרא דלא תקחו כופר לדלא תשקול מיניה ממונא ותקטליה ומשני מכדי רשעתו נפקא הוה ליה למימר רשעה מאי רשעתו דהכא שמעת מינה דתרתי והתם טעי כי היכי דטעי הכא מעיקרא לומר מכדי רשעתו נפקא מיתה וממון [והא] אסון נפקא לדכי רשעתו אתא למלקות וממון וי"ל דהתם דיליף נפקא מיתה וממון [והא] דלא פריך הכי במלקות וממון כתיב לא תא להקשות משום דהוי מצי לשנויי מלא יהיה אסון נפקא] אי נמי לסימנא בעלמא נקטיה התם:

ליקוטי רש"י

דיה שעתה. אם ראתה דם די לנו אם תטמא תרומה וטהרות שתגע בהן משעת ראייה ואילך ולא אמרי' כי היכי דהשתא איפשתא דם בבית החיצון אף הוא דבדק נמי מקמי הכי הוה איפשתא וכותלי בית הרחם העמידוהו וקיימא לן בפ' יולא דופן (לקמן דף מ) כל הנשים מטמאות בבית החיצון [נדה ב.]. ככל הנשים. הרואות דם [שבת טו.]. מעת לעת ומפקידה לפקידה. מעת לעת ממעטת על יד מפקידה לפקידה, שאם יש ימים הרבה בין פקידה לפקידה לא מטמאינן להו לכולהו טהרות דכיני וכיני אלא אותם שנתעסקה בהם מאתמול בשעה הזאת ועמידיהו דרבנן מפרש לקמן בגמרא נתנלא מעת לעת ממעטת וזמן מפקידה לפקידה ומפקידה לפקידה ממעטת על יד מעת לעת, שאם היה זמן מפקידה לפקידה מועט מזמן מעת לעת אם הולכין אחריו להקל כגון בדקה עלמה שחרית ומלאתה טהורה וחזרה ובדקה ערבית ומלאתה טמאה דאמרי' במתני' (לקמן דף יא) פעמים לריכה להיות בודקת שחרית וביין השמשות לא מטמאינן טהרות של ליל אמש דהא בדקה שחרית ומלאתה טהורה ולילה למימר דהוי דם מאתמול בהאי שעתא אלא הנך טהרות דמבדיקת שחרית ואילך מטמאינן דהיינו מפקידה לפקידה [נדה שם]. מפקידה לפקידה, למפרע, בדקה היום ומלאתה טהורה ובדקה לסוף שבוע ומלאתה טמאה חוששין למגעה מבדיקה ראשונה ואילך טמאה עם קילוק ידיה ראשונה. מעת לעת ממעט על יד מפקידה לפקידה, שאם שני זמנים התכרו זה למפרע הולכין אחר הקל שבהן אם מפקידה לפקידה יותר על מעת לעת הולך אחר מעת לעת ואם מעת לעת יותר על מפקידה לפקידה הולך אחר הפקידה [שבת שם]. מנטרא נפשה. ומזמינת מוך בהדה ומזומן לה. אלא יוצאה בשן ועין. דלא הוה ידעה מעיקרא דעתידה להשתחרר לא מיטרחא ומזדהרה לאחורי מוך בהדה. אנוסה. ישראלית הוי אונס ממילא הוא ואין לה מוך. מתהפכת. ואף יוצאה בשן ועין נמי ליכא השתא למפרך דכיון דהיפוך קל הוא ולא אין כו עורת מתהפכת היא דכל אשה מזנה אינה רולה להתעבר [יבמות לה.]. דאמר לוקה ומשלם. במסכת מכות (דף ד) מעידים אנו בפלוני שחייב לחבירו מאתים זוז ונמלאו זוממין לוקין ומשלמין שלא השם המביאן לידי מכות (ב"ק עא.) שלא השם המביאו לידי מכות הוא המקרא המביאו לידי מלקות אינו מביאו לתשלומין מלקות מלא תענה תשלומין מכאשר זמם וכיון דשני שמות הן חייב על שניהם [לעיל לב:].

מסורת הש"ס

א) יבמות לה. [כל הסוגיא ע"ש], ב) [אין לזה מובן וכן נראה מפירש"י דליתא], ג) [שם איתא אביי], ד) ב"ק פג: מכות ד: יג: [לעיל לב:], ה) [לעיל לג: וש"נ], ו) [שם מב.], ז) [דלא גרסינן כל"ל רש"ל], ח) [שייך לעיל במשנה לו:], ט) [דף כט. ד"ה ועל אחות], י) [ג"ז שייך שם], כ) [לב. ד"ה רבא].

גליון הש"ס

רש"י ד"ה דיה שעתה וכו' לא גזור מפקידה לפקידה. כדאיתא נדה לו ע"א:

הגהות מהר"ב רנשבורג

א] גמ' ר' יוסי אומר הרי היא ככל הנשים. עי' נדה דף לו ע"א תוד"ה דליכא שהות וכו' והגאון מהרי"פ ז"ל לייתי בס"ס החדשים בהגהותיו:

תורה אור השלם

א) וְכִי יִנָּצוּ אֲנָשִׁים וְנָגְפוּ אִשָּׁה הָרָה וְיָצְאוּ יְלָדֶיהָ וְלֹא יִהְיֶה אָסוֹן עָנוֹשׁ יֵעָנֵשׁ כַּאֲשֶׁר יָשִׁית עָלָיו בַּעַל הָאִשָּׁה וְנָתַן בִּפְלִלִים: [שמות כא, כב]

ב) וְהָיָה אִם בִּן הַכּוֹת הָרָשָׁע וְהִפִּילוֹ הַשֹּׁפֵט וְהִכָּהוּ לְפָנָיו כְּדֵי רִשְׁעָתוֹ בְּמִסְפָּר: [דברים כה, ב]

עין משפט נר מצוה

נו א ב ג מיי' פי"א מהל' גירושין הל' כא לאוין סמג עשין נ טוש"ע אה"ע סימן יג סעיף ה ו:

וחדא

marrying;[8] דִּבְרֵי רַבִּי יְהוּדָה – these are the WORDS OF R' YEHUDAH. רַבִּי יוֹסֵי מַתִּיר לֵיאָרֵס וְלִינָּשֵׂא מִיָּד – But R' YOSE PERMITS them TO BECOME BETROTHED AND TO MARRY IMMEDIATELY. Here we see that R' Yehudah does suspect captives of cohabiting, and thus requires them to wait three months after being ransomed. Why, then, does he rule in our Mishnah that a captive is presumed to be a virgin?

The Gemara relates:

אִשְׁתִּיק – **[Rav Yosef] was silent,** unable to answer. אָמַר לֵיהּ – Eventually **he said to [Rav Pappa bar Shmuel]:** מִידִי שְׁמִיעַ לָךְ בְּהָא – **Have you heard anything about this** that would reconcile R' Yehudah's two statements? אָמַר לֵיהּ – **[Rav Pappa bar Shmuel] said to [Rav Yosef]** in reply: הָכִי אָמַר רַב שֵׁשֶׁת – **So said Rav Sheishess:** שֶׁרָאוּהָ שֶׁנִּבְעֲלָה – The Baraisa speaks of **where they** actually **saw her cohabit** with one of her captors.[9]

The Gemara counters:

אִי הָכִי מַאי טַעְמָא דְּרַבִּי יוֹסֵי – **If so, what is R' Yose's reason** for permitting her to marry immediately? Certainly she should wait to see if a child resulted from that union! – ? –

The Gemara answers:

אָמַר רַבָּה – **Rabbah said:** קָסָבַר רַבִּי יוֹסֵי – **R' Yose holds** that אִשָּׁה מְזַנָּה מְשַׁמֶּשֶׁת בְּמוֹךְ שֶׁלֹּא תִתְעַבֵּר – **a woman who is engaged in an illicit act cohabits with** the use of **an** absorbent **cloth so that she does not conceive.**[10] Thus, because there is little fear that she has been impregnated by her captor, R' Yose allows the ransomed captive to marry immediately.

The Gemara objects to this explanation:

בִּשְׁלָמָא גִּיּוֹרֶת – Now, according to your explanation, Rabbah, **it is understandable** that **a convert** need not wait three months before marrying, כֵּיוָן דְּדַעְתָּהּ לְאִיגַּיּוֹרֵי – for **since** in the months prior to her conversion **she has in mind to convert,**[11] מִנְטְרָא נַפְשָׁהּ – **she protects herself** from becoming pregnant by preparing a cloth for immediate use after cohabiting. שְׁבוּיָה נַמִּי – And it is understandable that **a** ransomed **captive also** need not wait three months, דְּלֹא יָדְעָה הֵיכָא מַמְטוּ לָהּ – **for** while in captivity **she does not know where [her captors] are taking her** to be sold.[12] שִׁפְחָה נַמִּי – And it is understandable that **an** emancipated **slavewomen also** need not wait three months, דְּשָׁמְעָה מִפִּי מָרָהּ – **for** while yet in bondage **she hears from her master** that he intends to free her.[13] אֶלָּא יוֹצְאָה בְּשֵׁן וְעַיִן – **But** in the case of a maidservant who **leaves** her master's service **with** the loss of **a tooth or eye,**[14] מַאי אִיכָּא לְמֵימַר – **what is there to say?** She did not anticipate her emancipation, and thus surely did not prepare an absorbent cloth![15] – ? –

The Gemara eliminates one possible answer:

וְכִי תֵימָא – **And if you will say** that כָּל מִמֵּילָא לֹא אָמַר רַבִּי יוֹסֵי – **R' Yose** indeed **did not state** his leniency in **any** case of **unplanned** occurrence,[16] I shall respond: הֲרֵי אֲנוּסָה וּמְפוּתָּה – But **here are** the cases of **[a woman] who was violated and [a woman] who was seduced,**[17] דְּמִמֵּילָא – **which are unplanned** occurrences,[18] וְתַנְיָא – **and** yet **it was taught in a Baraisa:** אֲנוּסָה וּמְפוּתָּה צְרִיכוֹת לְהַמְתִּין שְׁלֹשָׁה חֳדָשִׁים – [A WOMAN] WHO WAS VIOLATED AND [A WOMAN] WHO WAS SEDUCED ARE REQUIRED TO WAIT THREE MONTHS before marrying; דִּבְרֵי רַבִּי יְהוּדָה – these are the WORDS OF R' YEHUDAH. רַבִּי יוֹסֵי מַתִּיר לֵיאָרֵס וְלִינָּשֵׂא מִיָּד – But R' YOSE PERMITS them TO BECOME BETROTHED AND TO MARRY IMMEDIATELY. Here R' Yose rules leniently even though the woman apparently did not prevent impregnation, since the cohabitation was unplanned. – ? –

Rabbah concedes that his explanation of R' Yose's lenient ruling in the case of the slavewoman has been refuted, but offers a different one:

אֶלָּא אָמַר רַבָּה – **Rather, Rabbah said:** קָסָבַר רַבִּי יוֹסֵי – **R' Yose holds** that אִשָּׁה מְזַנָּה מִתְהַפֶּכֶת כְּדֵי שֶׁלֹּא תִתְעַבֵּר – **a woman who is engaged in an illicit act**[19] **turns herself** after cohabiting **so that she does not become pregnant.**[20]

NOTES

8. In order to ascertain whether she is carrying a fetus, and thereby establish its status and patrilineage; see note 4 above.

Rashi notes that although a minor cannot become pregnant, the Rabbis enacted a general prohibition for the sake of older women (in these categories) who can become pregnant. [See Gemara below (60b) and *Tosafos* here ד״ה צריכות.]

9. As a general rule, R' Yehudah presumes that a captive has retained her state of purity. His ruling here, that a captive must wait three months before marrying, applies only when witnesses testify that they actually saw her cohabiting with one of her captors.

[It is unclear whether the Gemara means that witnesses saw her cohabiting even many years or months prior to her release, but nevertheless she lost her presumptive status of purity, or whether they saw her within three months of her release.]

10. After cohabiting she inserts a cloth into her vagina to absorb the semen and prevent pregnancy (*Rashi;* see *Rashi* below, 39a, and to *Yevamos* 12b ד״ה משמשות במוך, where a different definition of "cohabits with a cloth" is given; see also *Tosafos* in both places ד״ה שלש). See *Hagahos Yavetz.*

11. And therefore does not want to become pregnant prior to her conversion; see above, note 6.

12. Hence, she entertains the possibility that her captives will bring her to a Jewish community and she will be ransomed there. Thus anticipating a return to the Jewish people, she will protect herself from becoming pregnant by preparing and using an absorbent cloth (*Rashi*).

13. And so she, too, prepares a cloth to ensure that she does not become pregnant prior to her full-fledged joining of the Jewish people.

14. The Torah (*Exodus* 21:26-27) stipulates that if a master knocks out an eye or tooth of his slave or slavewomen (as well as other appendages; see *Rashi* to verse), he must set that servant free (*Rashi*).

15. [R' Yose stated with a general term that "emancipated slavewomen" need not wait three months. His ruling ostensibly encompasses *all* cases of emancipated slavewomen – i.e. including one who was freed because her master knocked out her eye or tooth.] However, in that case of sudden emancipation the slavewoman did not anticipate her release, and thus had no incentive to use a cloth and protect herself from becoming pregnant (*Rashi*).

16. [Literally: an occurrence that happened on its own.] As here, where the injury to the slavewoman occurred suddenly and unexpectedly, and she had not anticipated her emancipation. In such a case, since she was not using a cloth for birth control, R' Yose would concede that she must wait three months before marrying (*Rashi*).

17. *Mesoras HaShas* deletes the case of the seduced woman, since seduction is obviously a planned act. Also, it apparently did not appear in *Rashi's* text.

18. They did not know in advance what would happen to them, so as to prepare a cloth (*Rashi*).

19. And thus wishes to prevent pregnancy.

20. I.e. she jerks her body so that the semen will drip out of her and not be absorbed into and impregnate her. This birth-control technique can be employed even in cases of unexpected occurrence [when the woman would not have prepared an absorbent cloth], and all women who are engaged in an illicit act use it (*Rashi*).

As we have noted, *Rashi* concludes his comment by noting that according to R' Yose "all women" employ this birth-control technique, which implies that even a slavewoman whose master knocked out her tooth or eye (i.e. who did not anticipate her emancipation at the time she was having physical relations, and thus had never prepared an absorbent cloth) is nonetheless presumed to have employed this readily available method of forceful movements. It is therefore *Rashi's* understanding (as explained by *Ramban* and *Ritva*) that the Gemara now means to answer not only its last challenge to Rabbah (that a

וסבר רבי יהודה בקדושתה קיימא והתניא הגיורת שנתגיירה וראתה דם ר' יהודה אומר דיה שעתה [א]ר' יוסי אומר הרי היא ככל הנשים ומטמאה מעת לעת ומפקידה לפקידה וצריכה להמתין ג' חדשים דברי ר' יהודה ר' יוסי מתיר ליארס ולינשא מיד א"ל גיורת אשבויה קא רמית גיורת לא מנטרא נפשה שבויה מנטרא נפשה ורמי שבויה אשבויה דתניא [א]הגיורת והשבויה והשפחה שנפדו ושנתגיירו ושנשתחררו יתירות על בנות ג' שנים ויום אחד [א]צריכות להמתין ג' חדשים דברי ר' יהודה ר' יוסי מתיר ליארס ולינשא מיד אשתיק א"ל מידי שמיע לך בהא אמר ליה הכי אמר רב ששת שראוה שנבעלה א"ה מאי טעמא דר' יוסי אמר רבה קסבר ר' יוסי אשה מזנה משמשת במוך שלא תתעבר בשלמא גיורת כיון דדעתה לאיגיורי מנטרא נפשה שבויה נמי דלא ידעה היכא ממטו לה שפחה נמי דשמעה מפי מרה אלא יוצאה בשן ועין מאי איכא למימר וכי תימא כל ממילא לא א"ר יוסי הרי אנוסה [ג]ומפותה דממילא ותניא אנוסה ומפותה צריכות להמתין ג' חדשים דברי ר' יהודה [ב]ר' יוסי מתיר ליארס ולינשא מיד אלא אמר [ג]רבה קסבר ר' יוסי [ג]אשה מזנה מתהפכת כדי שלא תתעבר ואידך חיישי' שמא לא נהפכה יפה יפה: שנא' [א]ולא יהיה אסון ענוש יענש וכו': והא מהכא נפקא מהתם נפקא [ב]כדי רשעתו [ד]משום רשעה אחת אתה מחייבו ואי אתה מחייבו משום שתי רשעיות חדא במיתה וממון וחדא במלקות וממון וצריכא דאי אשמעינן מיתה וממון משום דאיכא איבוד נשמה אבל מלקות וממון דליכא איבוד נשמה אימא לא ואי אשמעינן מלקות וממון משום דלא חמיר איסוריה אבל מיתה וממון דחמיר איסוריה אימא לא צריכא ולרבי מאיר [ה]דאמר לוקה ומשלם תרתי למה לי חדא במיתה וממון וחדא

רש"י

וראתה דם. בו ביום: דיה שעתה. ולא גזרו בה טומאת מעת לעת לטמא טהרות שנגעה בהן משעת טבילה עד שעת ראייה דהא אפי' יצא דם זה מאתמול והעמידוהו כותלי בית הרחם שזהו הטעם של מעת לעת בבנות ישראל הלא דם כנענית כדם בהמה ואם תאמר ניחוש שמא משטבלה נעקר ויצא מיד טומאה למפרע דרבנן היא והיכא דאיכא למיגזר מעת לעת שלם גזור מפקידה לפקידה והיכא דלא גזור מעת לעת [ט]לא גזור מפקידה לפקידה: וצריכה להמתין ג' חדשים. שלא תנשא להבחין בין זרע הנזרע בקדושה לזרע הנזרע שלא בקדושה: רבי יוסי מתיר. לקמיה מפרש טעמא: צריכות להמתין. ואף על פי שקטנה אינה מתעברת גזירה קטנה אטו גדולה: משמשת במוך. נותנת מוך לאחר בעילה ושואבת הזרע: מנטרא נפשה. ומזמנת לה מוך: דלא ידעה היכא ממטו לה. שבאים למוכרה וסבורה דלמא ממטו לה לגבי ישראל ופרקו לה ומנטרא נפשה לשמש במוך: אלא יוצאה בשן ועין. שפחה שסימא אדוניה את עינה ויצאה לחירות מנא הוה ידעה מעיקרא דתיפוק לחירות דמנטרא נפשה לזמן מוך לשימושה: כל ממילא. מידי דליכא לאיזדהורי ביה מעיקרא דתיפוק לחירות מודה רבי יוסי: הרי אנוסה דממילא. דלא הוה ידעה ליזהר בה הכי ולזמן לה מוך: מתהפכת. שלא יקלוט והא אפילו במידי דממילא מצו למיעבד וכולן עושות כן: משום דאיכא איבוד נשמה. יש כאן עונש חמור ודיו בכך אם ענשתו לאבד נשמה ליהרג: אימא לא. אין זה עונש יתירה ולעביד ביה תרתי: דלא חמיר איסוריה. לא עבר עבירה חמורה ודיו שתענשנו עונש אחד:

תוספות

וסבר רבי יהודה בקדושתה קיימא והתניא הגיורת כו'. קשה להשתא דמדמה גיורת לשבויה א"כ תיקשי ליה מתניתין גופה דר' יהודה לא משוה גיורת לשבויה דתנן ר' יהודה אומר שבויה שנפדית הרי היא בקדושתה משמע דבהנך מודה לתנא קמא ואמר ר"י דמתני' אתי ליה שפיר דמודה בגיורת שאין לה קנס דודאי היא בחזקת בעולה שנבעלה בעוד שלא היה דעתה להתגייר ואפילו אם היה דעתה להתגייר משהיתה בת שלש שנים ויום אחד מ"מ לא מנטרא נפשה כיון דאינה ראויה להתעבר אבל מהך דצריכה להמתין שלשה חדשים אף על גב דדעתה לאיגיורי ומנטרא נפשה אפילו הכי קאמר צריכה להמתין ג' חדשים דאי אפשר לשמור עצמה מן העובדי כוכבים כ"ש שבויה שהיא מסורה בידם: **רבי** יהודה אומר דיה שעתה. פירש הקונטרס כיון דליכא מעת לעת מפקידה לפקידה נמי לא גזור רבנן ורבי יוסי דקאמר ומטמאה מעת לעת לאו דוקא מעת לעת אלא כלומר כתורת מעת לעת דמטמאה משנתגיירה: **שבויה** מנטרא נפשה. וא"ת והא בקטנה נמי מיירי דלא מנטרא נפשה דהא אינה יודעת לשמור עצמה וקאמר ר"י דבקדושתה קיימא דקתני במתני' יתירה מבת ג' שנים ויום אחד וי"ל דקטנה לגמרי אינה מוסרת עצמה לביאה וכשהיא מוסרת עצמה לביאה קצת היא בת דעת ויודעת לשמור עצמה: **צריכות** להמתין שלשה חדשים דברי ר' יהודה. משמע דאפי' בקטנה שאינה ראויה להתעבר קאמר רבי יהודה דצריכה להמתין מדקאמר יתירות מבנות ג' ויום אחד דגזר קטנה אטו גדולה וקשה לר"י ולרבינו תם דתניא בהחולץ (יבמות דף מב: ושם) הרי שהיתה רדופה לילך לבית אביה או קטנה כו' צריכה להמתין ג' חדשים דברי ר"מ ר' יהודה מתיר ליארס ולינשא מיד אלמא לא גזר רבי יהודה קטנה אטו גדולה וכ"ת דוקא בגיורת ומשוחררת ושבויה גזר טפי כדי להבחין בין זרע שנזרע בקדושה לשנזרע שלא בקדושה זה אין נראה דהא לרבא דמפרש התם לעיל [י]טעם דצריכות להמתין גזירה שמא ישא אחותו מאביו ויבם אשת אחיו מן אמו כו' טפי אית לן למיגזר בקטנה בת ישראל דשייך בה כל הנהו דמפרש התם אבל בגיורת ושבויה ומשוחררת לא שייך שמא ישא אחותו מאביו ועוד דשמואל אית ליה סברא איפכא מדר' יהודה דהא שמואל קאמר בס"פ ד' אחין (שם דף לד: ושם) דכולן צריכות להמתין ג' חדשים חוץ מגיורת ומשוחררת קטנה אבל קטנה בת ישראל צריכה להמתין אלמא בקטנה בת ישראל גזר קטנה אטו גדולה ובגיורת ומשוחררת לא גזר והיינו איפכא מדרבי יהודה ועוד לשמואל בשלמא בקטנה בת ישראל סבר כר"מ אלא בגיורת כמאן לא כרבי יהודה ולא כר' יוסי דלרבי יהודה בין קטנה בין גדולה צריכה להמתין ולרבי יוסי אפי' גדולה אינה צריכה להמתין ומיהו למאי דמוקי להך דהכא בשראוה שנבעלה אתי שפיר כר' יהודה ומצינן למימר דדוקא בראוה שנבעלה קאמר ר' יהודה דגזרי' קטנה אטו גדולה אבל אותה שאינה ודאי בעולה לא ולפי לשון אחרון דהתם לא קשה כלל אע"ג דשמואל איפכא מדרבי יהודה כיון דאין הטעם משום [י]דגזרינן קטנה אטו גדולה דאפילו בגדולה נמי שרי לפי שמתהפכת ואור"י דבס"פ ד' אחין (ג"ז שם לה.) מייתי הך ברייתא דהכא ול"ג בה יתירות מבנות ג' ויום אחד ובתוספתא נמי ל"ג ליה ולפי זה ניחא דמיירי בגדולה אבל בקטנה מודה דאין צריכה להמתין כדקאמר בברייתא דרדופה והשתא שמואל בגיורת כר' יהודה ובבת ישראל כרבי מאיר ואפשר דבגיורת קטנה מודה ר' מאיר דאין צריכה להמתין וללשון אחרון דהתם דאמר שמואל כולן צריכות להמתין חוץ מגיורת ומשוחררת גדולה וקטנה בת ישראל אינה צריכה להמתין בזונות משום דזונות דקטנה לא שכיח אבל בנשואין גזר קטנה אטו גדולה וסבר בגיורת כרבי יוסי ובבת ישראל כר"מ דגזר קטנה אטו גדולה וס"ל דדוקא בנשואין גזר ר"מ ושמא בנשואין מודה ר' יוסי לר"מ ומיהו בזונות ודאי פליג דהא שרי אנוסה ומפותה אפילו גדולה ואית דגרסי בברייתא דרדופה ר' יוסי במקום ר' יהודה וכן פירשנו: **אי** הכי מ"ט דר' יוסי. תימה לר"י דמשמע דמשום דאוקימנא בראוה שנבעלה הוא דקשיא ליה מאי טעמא בלאו הכי נמי תיקשי ליה ברייתא דרבי יוסי דמייתי לקמן דאנוסה ומפותה ולפי הסוגיא נראה דזה המקשה עצמו הוא דמייתי לה ומיהו י"ס דגרסי בסמוך א"ל אביי בשלמא גיורת כיון דדעתה לאיגיורי כו' ולפי גירסא זו אתי שפיר שזה המקשה לא ידע ברייתא דמייתי לקמן דאביי הוא דמייתי לה וכן הוא גירסא בשילהי ד' אחין (ג"ז שם): **אמר** רבה קסבר רבי יוסי כו'. אליבא דרבי יוחנן משני דלדידיה דמפרש טעמא דר' יהודה שלא יהא חוטא נשכר לא קשיא מידי [ומיהו רבה לא קאמר אלא דלמא]: **אשה** מזנה מתהפכת. ומהשתא לא קשה אנוסה ומפותה ומיהו יוצאה בשן ועין מודה רבי יוסי דצריכה להמתין דאותה למה תתהפך: [ח]**הבא** על בתו. למאי דמוקי מתני' בפרק בן סורר (סנהדרין דף עג: ושם) במפותה צריך לאוקמה בשבא עליה ובגרה כדפרישית לעיל [ט]: [י]**ועל** בת אשתו. הוה מצי למיתני אשת אביו וכלתו דהא חשיב נמי עריות דעל ידי קדושין אלא תנא ושייר: **חדא** במלקות וממון. לעיל [כ]פירשתי למה לא יליף רשע רשע תימה דבריש החובל (ב"ק דף פג:) פריך הא מיבעי ליה קרא דלא תקחו כופר דלא תשקול מיניה ממונא ותקטליה ומשני ההוא מכדי רשעתו נפקא הוה ליה למימר ההוא מלא יהיה אסון נפקא דכדי רשעתו אתא למלקות וממון וי"ל דהתם טעי דטעי הכא מעיקרא לומר דמכדי רשעתו נפקא מיתה וממון [והא דלא פריך האי במלקות וממון כתיב לא חש להקשות משום דהוי מצי לשנויי מלא יהיה אסון נפקא] אי נמי לסימנא בעלמא נקטיה התם:

וחדא

מסורת הש"ס

א) יבמות לה. [כל הסוגיא ע"ש], ב) [אין לזה מובן וכן נראה מפירש"י דליתא], ג) [שם איתא אביי], ד) ב"ק פג: מכות ד: יג: [לעיל לב:], ה) [לעיל לב: וש"נ], ו) [שם מב.], ז) [גירסא כל"ל רש"ל], ח) [שייך לעיל במשנה לו:], ט) [דף כט. ד"ה ועל אשת], י) [ג"ז שייך שם], כ) [לה. ד"ה רבא].

עין משפט נר מצוה

נו א ב ג מיי' פ"א מהל' גירושין הל' כה סמג עשין נ טוש"ע אה"ע סימן יג סעיף ה ו:

ליקוטי רש"י

דיה שעתה. אם ראתה דם די לנו אם תטמא תרומה וטהרות שנגעו בהן משעת ראייה ואילך ולא אמרי' כי היכי דהשתא איטמאת דם בבית החיצון אי הוה בדקה נמי מקמי הכי הוה איטמאת וכותלי בית הרחם העמידוהו וקיימא לן בפ' יוצא דופן [לקמן דף מ] כל הנשים מטמאות בבית החיצון [נדה ב.]. ככל הנשים. הרואות דם [שבת טו.]. מעת לעת ומפקידה לפקידה. מעת לעת ממעטת על יד מפקידה לפקידה, שאם יש ימים הרבה בין פקידה לפקידה לא מטמאינן להו לכולהו טהרות דביני ביני אלא אותם שנתעסקה בהם מאתמול בשעה זאת וטעמייהו דרבנן מפרש לקמן בגמרא נמצא מעת לעת ממעטת זמן מפקידה לפקידה. ומפקידה לפקידה ממעטת על יד מעת לעת, שאם היה זמן מפקידה לפקידה מועט מזמן מעת לעת הן הולכין אחריו להקל כגון בדקה עצמה שחרית ומצאתה טהורה וחזרה ובדקה ערבית ומצאתה טמאה דאמרי' לקמן במתני' (דף יא) פעמים שצריכה להיות בודקת שחרית ובין השמשות לא מטמאינן טהרות של ליל אמש דהא בדקה שחרית ומצאתה טהורה וליכא למימר דהוי דם מאתמול בהאי שעתא אלא הנך טהרות דמבדיקת שחרית ואילך מטמאינן דהיינו מפקידה לפקידה [נדה שם]. מפקידה לפקידה, דבקה היום ולמחר, ובדקה היום ומצאתה טהורה ובדקה לסוף שבוע ומצאתה טמאה חוששין למגעה מבדיקה ראשונה ואילך שמא עם סילוק ידיה ראתה. מעת לעת ממעטת על יד מפקידה לפקידה, שני זמנים הללו בה למפרע להלך אחר הקל שבהן אם מפקידה לפקידה יותר על מעת לעת הלך אחר מעת לעת ואם מעת לעת יותר על מפקידה לפקידה הלך אחר הפקידה [שבת שם]. מנטרא נפשה. ממתינה מוך בהדה ומזומן לה. אלא יוצאה בשן ועין. דלא הוה ידעה מעיקרא דעתידה להשתחרר לא מיזדהרה ומזדהרה לאתויי מוך בהדה. אנוסה. ישראלית והרי אותם ממילא הוא ואין לה מוך. מתהפכת. ואף על פי שאלא בשן ועין נמי ליכא השתא למפרך דכיון דהיפוך קל הוא ואין בו טורח מתהפכת היא דכל אשה מזנה אינה רוצה להתעבר [יבמות לה.]. דאמר לוקה ומשלם. במסכת מכות (דף ד) מעידים אנו בפלוני שחייב לחבירו מאתים זוז ונמצאו זוממין לוקין ומשלמין שלא השם המביאו לידי מכות מביאו לידי תשלומין [ב"ק עא.]. שלא השם המביאו לידי מכות כו', המקרא המביאו לידי מלקות אינו מביאו לתשלומין מלקות אלא תענה תשלומין מכאשר זמם וכיון דשני שמות הן חייב על שניהם [לעיל לב:].

גליון הש"ס

רש"י ד"ה דיה שעתה וכו' לא גזור מפקידה לפקידה. כדאיתא נדה לו ע"א:

הגהות מהר"ב רנשבורג

אן גמ' ר' יוסי אומר הרי היא ככל הנשים. עי' נדה דף לו ע"ב תוד"ה ליכא שהות וכו' והגאון מהרצ"ס לא ציינו בש"ס החדשים בהגהותיו:

תורה אור השלם

א) וְכִי יִנָּצוּ אֲנָשִׁים וְנָגְפוּ אִשָּׁה הָרָה וְיָצְאוּ יְלָדֶיהָ וְלֹא יִהְיֶה אָסוֹן עָנוֹשׁ יֵעָנֵשׁ כַּאֲשֶׁר יָשִׁית עָלָיו בַּעַל הָאִשָּׁה וְנָתַן בִּפְלִלִים: [שמות כא, כב]

ב) וְהָיָה אִם בִּן הַכּוֹת הָרָשָׁע וְהִפִּילוֹ הַשֹּׁפֵט וְהִכָּהוּ לְפָנָיו כְּדֵי רִשְׁעָתוֹ בְּמִסְפָּר: [דברים כה, ב]

וְסָבַר רַבִּי יְהוּדָה בִּקְדוּשָּׁתָהּ קַיְימָא – **And does R' Yehudah** really **hold that [a captive] remains in her state of purity** with regard to all issues? וְהָתַנְיָא – **But it was taught** otherwise **in a Baraisa:** הַגִּיּוֹרֶת שֶׁנִּתְגַּיְּירָה וְרָאֲתָה דָּם – In the case of A [FEMALE] CONVERT WHO CONVERTED AND then[1] DISCHARGED uterine BLOOD, רַבִּי יְהוּדָה אוֹמֵר – R' YEHUDAH SAYS: דַּיָּהּ שַׁעְתָּהּ – IT SUFFICES FOR HER to be considered *tamei* from HER TIME of discovering the discharge.[2] רַבִּי יוֹסֵי אוֹמֵר – But R' YOSE SAYS: הֲרֵי הִיא כְּכָל הַנָּשִׁים – SHE IS LIKE ALL other WOMEN, וּמְטַמְּאָה מֵעֵת לְעֵת וּמִפְּקִידָה לִפְקִידָה – AND SHE CONTAMINATES *terumah* and *kodashim* retroactively for TWENTY-FOUR HOURS OR FROM EXAMINATION TO EXAMINATION.[3] The Baraisa now presents another dispute involving the female convert, one that concerns our issue of virgin status: וּצְרִיכָה לְהַמְתִּין שְׁלֹשָׁה חֳדָשִׁים – AND SHE MUST WAIT THREE MONTHS before marrying;[4] דִּבְרֵי רַבִּי יְהוּדָה – these are THE WORDS OF R' YEHUDAH. רַבִּי יוֹסֵי מַתִּיר לֵיאָרֵס וְלִינָּשֵׂא מִיָּד – But R' YOSE PERMITS her TO BECOME BETROTHED AND TO MARRY IMMEDIATELY.[5] Since R' Yehudah requires the convert to wait three months before marrying, we see that he suspects her of having had physical relations up until the moment of her conversion. Accordingly, he should also suspect a captive of cohabiting up until her ransom. Why, in our Mishnah, does he presume her to be a virgin?[6]

The Gemara answers:

אָמַר לֵיהּ – **[Rav Yosef] said to [Rav Pappa bar Shmuel]** in reply: גִּיּוֹרֶת אַשְּׁבוּיָה קָא רָמֵית – **Are you comparing a convert with a captive?!** There is a difference between the two! גִּיּוֹרֶת לֹא מִנַּטְרָא נַפְשָׁהּ – **A convert does not watch herself** prior to her conversion, שְׁבוּיָה מִנַּטְרָא נַפְשָׁהּ – whereas **a captive does watch herself.**[7]

Rav Pappa bar Shmuel points out an inherent contradiction involving the case of a captive itself:

וְרָמֵי שְׁבוּיָה אַשְּׁבוּיָה – **But contrast** R' Yehudah's ruling in the Mishnah regarding **a captive with** his ruling in another Baraisa regarding **a captive!** דְּתַנְיָא – **For it was taught in** that other **Baraisa:** הַגִּיּוֹרֶת וְהַשְּׁבוּיָה וְהַשִּׁפְחָה – CONVERTS, CAPTIVES OR SLAVEWOMEN שֶׁנִּפְדּוּ וְשֶׁנִּתְגַּיְּירוּ וְשֶׁנִּשְׁתַּחְרְרוּ יְתֵירוֹת עַל בְּנוֹת שָׁלֹשׁ שָׁנִים וְיוֹם אֶחָד – WHO WERE RANSOMED, CONVERTED OR WERE EMANCIPATED ABOVE THE AGE OF THREE YEARS AND ONE DAY צְרִיכוֹת לְהַמְתִּין שְׁלֹשָׁה חֳדָשִׁים – MUST WAIT THREE MONTHS before

NOTES

1. On the day of her conversion (*Rashi*).

2. A Jewish woman who discovers a discharge of uterine blood is rendered a *niddah;* the Sages decreed that she is to be considered *tamei* (vis-a-vis contaminating *terumah* and *kodashim* she had contact with) retroactively for the lesser of two periods – either twenty-four hours or until the last time she examined herself and determined that she was *tahor* (see opinion of the Sages in Mishnah, *Niddah* 2a). This stringency is due to the fact that a woman who discharges uterine blood becomes *tamei* the moment the blood leaves the uterus, even before it descends through the vaginal canal to the outside of her body. Thus, if a woman has such a discharge, or even if she just performs an internal examination and finds blood in her vaginal canal, it is possible that she has been *tamei* for some time, for the blood might have left her uterus a while ago and adhered to the walls of the canal. Accordingly, any *terumos* or *kodashim* that she handled since the last examination are deemed "*safek* (i.e. possibly) *tamei.*" The Sages further maintain, however, that the vaginal walls do not retain discharged uterine blood for more than a twenty-four-hour period. Hence, they rule that we render the woman retroactively *tamei* for the lesser of two periods – either twenty-four hours or until her last internal examination (at which time there was no blood).

From a Biblical standpoint, a woman who discovers a discharge is *not* rendered *tamei* retroactively. This is based on the principle of חֲזָקָה (*chazakah,* presumptive status), which teaches that when questions of fact affecting legal issues arise, we preserve the last-known legal status until proof is offered that it has changed; see *Chullin* 10b. It is only by Rabbinic decree that the woman is considered "possibly *tamei*" retroactively with regard to *terumah* and *kodashim* [the Rabbis did not extend their decree of retroactive *tumah* to cases of ordinary food].

In our Baraisa R' Yehudah rules that, furthermore, the Rabbis did not decree retroactive *tumah* in the case of a convert who noticed a uterine discharge within twenty-four hours of her conversion. This is because a non-Jewess does not become *tamei* when she menstruates. Hence, even if we were to concern ourselves with the possibility that her uterine discharge occurred within the past twenty-four hours, she would not be rendered *tamei* on account of that discharge. And although it is possible that the discharge occurred immediately after her conversion took effect, which would justify our rendering her *tamei* retroactively (if not for the entire twenty-four hour period, at least up until the time of her conversion), R' Yehudah maintains that since we cannot implement the Rabbinic decree of retroactive *tumah* in its theoretical entirety (i.e. for a full twenty-four-hours), we do not implement it at all (see *Rashi;* cf. *Shitah Yeshanah,* cited by *Shitah Mekubetzes* ד"ה הגיורת שנתגיירה וראתה דם).

3. R' Yose maintains that although we cannot implement the Rabbinic decree of retroactive *tumah* in its theoretical entirety (for the full twenty-four-hour period), we nevertheless implement it as far back as possible – viz. until the moment of her conversion or until her last internal post-conversion examination (*Ritva* here). [*Ritva's* text apparently lacked the words מֵעֵת לְעֵת in R' Yose's statement. According to our text, *Tosafos* here (ד"ה רבי יהודה) explain that by מֵעֵת לְעֵת the Gemara means "as far back as we can" (i.e. to conversion or to the last post-conversion examination). *Meiri* here implies that R' Yose actually intends a twenty-four-hour period.]

4. Since it takes three months for a pregnancy to become apparent, the convert must wait that amount of time before marrying so that we can ascertain if she is carrying a fetus that was conceived prior to her conversion [in which case it too, regarding certain laws, would be classified a convert] (*Rashi*).

5. R' Yose's reasoning will be explained by the Gemara below (*Rashi*).

6. The Gemara's challenge is difficult to understand. How can it think to equate the cases of a convert and a captive when R' Yehudah himself in our Mishnah differentiates between them, ruling that a captive is presumed to be a virgin who is entitled to the fine for violation, whereas a convert is presumed to be a non-virgin who is not entitled to the fine for violation?

Tosafos answer that the Gemara understands that a convert, prior to deciding to convert, is certainly presumed to have had physical relations, and for that reason R' Yehudah in our Mishnah disqualifies her from receiving the fine for violation. However, the Gemara also understands that from the moment a woman decides to convert she does try to abstain from consensual cohabitation, and does her utmost to protect herself from becoming pregnant prior to joining the Jewish people. Hence, R' Yehudah's ruling in the Baraisa, that the convert must wait three months before marrying because she is *nonetheless* suspected of having had physical relations up until her conversion – i.e. *even though* she had wished to protect herself from cohabitation from the time of her decision to convert – demonstrates that R' Yehudah considers a woman in a non-Jewish society incapable of protecting herself against unwanted physical relations. Accordingly, he should hold that a captive, who is totally subjugated to her non-Jewish captors, is certainly incapable of protecting herself against unwanted physical relations. Why, then, does he not disqualify her from receiving the fine for violation (in the Mishnah)? See also *Ritva.*

7. [Rav Yosef explains that although, in R' Yehudah's view, neither a Jewish captive nor a potential convert is likely to be violated in the non-Jewish environment, a difference exists between the two with regard to consensual physical relations. The Jewish captive, because of her Torah upbringing, will guard herself from immoral behavior, and for that reason R' Yehudah grants her the fine for violation. The potential convert, on the other hand, was raised in a promiscuous society and has subconsciously absorbed its values. Hence, even after her decision to convert, it is possible that she willingly engaged in physical relations. R' Yehudah thus treats her more stringently, requiring her to wait three months.]

teaches that מֵעִיד בָּהּ לֹא יִשָּׂאֶנָּה – **if he** also **testifies about her,** that she was not violated, **he may not marry her!** מִשּׁוּם דְּמֵעִיד בָּהּ לֹא יִשָּׂאֶנָּה – Does it make sense to say that **because [a Kohen]** also **testifies about her** purity **he may not marry her?!**[47] – ? –

The Gemara explains the Baraisa:

הָא לֹא קַשְׁיָא – **This is not difficult.** הָכִי קָאָמַר – **[The Baraisa] is** actually **stating thus:** הַפּוֹדֶה אֶת הַשְּׁבוּיָה וּמֵעִיד בָּהּ יִשָּׂאֶנָּה – **One who ransoms a captive and testifies about her** purity **may marry her.**[48] מֵעִיד בָּהּ כְּדִי – But if **he testifies about her** purity **and nothing else,** לֹא יִשָּׂאֶנָּה – **he may not marry her.**[49]

The Gemara returns to its challenge to R' Yochanan:

מִכָּל מָקוֹם קַשְׁיָא לְרַבִּי יְהוּדָה – **In any event, [R' Yehudah's ruling]** in this Baraisa (that a captive is prohibited even to the Kohen who ransoms her and attests to her purity) **poses a difficulty to** R' Yochanan's understanding of **R' Yehudah** (i.e. that R' Yehudah holds that with regard to all issues a captive retains her presumptive status of virgin). – ? –

The Gemara deflects the challenge:

אָמַר רַב פָּפָּא – **Rav Pappa said:** אֵימָא – **Say** that the Baraisa's text actually reads: רַבִּי יְהוּדָה אוֹמֵר – R' YEHUDAH SAYS: בֵּין כָּךְ וּבֵין כָּךְ יִשָּׂאֶנָּה – EITHER WAY HE MAY MARRY HER.[50]

An alternative reply:

רַב הוּנָא בְּרֵיהּ דְּרַב יְהוֹשֻׁעַ אוֹמֵר – **Rav Huna the son of Rav Yehoshua says:** לְעוֹלָם כִּדְקָתָנֵי – **In truth, [the Baraisa]** is correct **as stated,**[51] רַבִּי יְהוּדָה לְדִבְרֵיהֶם דְּרַבָּנַן קָאָמַר לְהוּ – and here **R' Yehudah** is not espousing his own opinion, but **is responding to [the Rabbis] according to the Rabbis'** own **opinion,** as follows: לְדִידִי בֵּין כָּךְ וּבֵין כָּךְ יִשָּׂאֶנָּה – **According to my [opinion],** that a captive retains her state of purity, **either way he may marry her.**[52] אֶלָּא לְדִידְכוּ – **But according to your [opinion],** that a captive is presumed violated by her captors and is therefore forbidden to marry a Kohen, בֵּין כָּךְ וּבֵין כָּךְ לֹא יִשָּׂאֶנָּה מִבָּעֵי לֵיהּ – you **should have** stated: **"Either way he may not marry her."** The fact that the prospective husband ransomed her should not affect this presumption and render her permitted to him!

The Gemara now defends the Rabbis' position:

וְרַבָּנַן הַפּוֹדֶה אֶת הַשְּׁבוּיָה וּמֵעִיד בָּהּ יִשָּׂאֶנָּה – **But the Rabbis** hold that **one who ransoms a captive and testifies about her** purity **may marry her,** לֹא שָׁדֵי אִינִישׁ זוּזֵי בִּכְדִי – because **one does not throw away** his **money for nothing.**[53] מֵעִיד בָּהּ כְּדִי לֹא יִשָּׂאֶנָּה – But **one who testifies about her** piety **and nothing else may not marry her,** שֶׁמָּא עֵינָיו נָתַן בָּהּ – **for perhaps he set his eyes upon her** and is testifying falsely so that he will be allowed to marry her. According to the Rabbis, then, the act of ransoming is indeed a crucial factor.

The Gemara again challenges R' Yochanan's understanding of R' Yehudah's position:[54]

רָמֵי לֵיהּ רַב פָּפָּא בַּר שְׁמוּאֵל לְרַב יוֹסֵף – **Rav Pappa bar Shmuel pointed out a contradiction to Rav Yosef:**

NOTES

47. If a Kohen who ransoms a captive is permitted to marry her, even without testifying as to her purity, why should his actually testifying to that effect prohibit him from marrying her? (see *Rashi*). See *Tos. HaRashba,* who explain the flow of the Gemara's discussion; see also *Shitah Mekubetzes.*

48. Since he ransomed her in order to marry her, we can presume that he indeed ascertained that she was not violated. For if he were not certain, and it turns out that she was violated, he would have wasted his money [since he would now have to divorce her] (*Rashi*).

49. For perhaps he testified that she was not violated only because he wants to marry her (*Rashi*).

50. [See *Ritva.*] I.e. because as a general rule captives retain their status as virgins, as R' Yochanan understood.

51. I.e. R' Yehudah's ruling should not be emended.

52. I.e. his failure to spend money on her does not alter her presumptive status of virgin.

53. See above, note 48.

54. *Tosafos* ד״ה מכל מקום.

אי דקא טוען טענת דמים הכי נמי הכא במאי עסקינן דקטעין טענת פתח פתוח: סומכוס אומר משום ר"מ סומא אין לה טענת בתולים: מ"ט דסומכוס א"ר זירא מפני שנחבטת על גבי קרקע כולהו נמי חבוטי מיחבטי כולהו רואות ומראות לאמן זו אינה רואה ואינה מראה לאמה: והיוצאת משום שם רע אין לה לא קנס ולא פיתוי: היוצאת משום שם רע בת סקילה היא אמר רב ששת הכי קאמר מי שיצא עליה שם רע בילדותה אין לה לא קנס ולא פיתוי אמר רב פפא ש"מ האי שטרא ריעא לא מגבינן ביה היכי דמי אילימא דנפק קלא עליה דשטרא דזייפא הוא דכוותה הכא דנפק עלה קלא דזנאי והא אמר רבא יצא לה שם מזנה בעיר אין חוששין לה אלא דאתו בי תרי ואמרי לדידהו תבעתנהי באיסורא דכוותה הכא דאתו בי תרי ואמרי לדידהו אמר להו זייפו לי בשלמא התם שכיחי פרוצין אלא הכא אם הוא הוחזק כל ישראל מי הוחזקו הכא נמי כיון דקא מהדר אזיופא אימר זיופי זייף וכתב: מתני' ואלו שאין להן קנס הבא על הגיורת ועל השבויה ועל השפחה שנפדו ושנתגיירו ושנשתחררו יתירות על בנות שלש שנים ויום אחד רבי יהודה אומר שבויה שנפדית הרי היא בקדושתה אע"פ שגדולה הבא על בתו על בת בתו על בת בנו על בת אשתו על בת בנה על בת בתה אין להן קנס מפני שמתחייב בנפשו שמיתתן בידי בית דין וכל המתחייב בנפשו אין משלם ממון שנאמר ואם לא יהיה אסון ענוש יענש: גמ' א"ר יוחנן רבי יהודה ורבי דוסא אמרו דבר אחד רבי יהודה הא דאמרן רבי דוסא דתניא שבויה אוכלת בתרומה דברי ר' דוסא אמר רבי דוסא וכי מה עשה לה ערבי הלז וכי מפני שמיעך לה בין דדיה פסלה מן הכהונה אמר רבה דלמא לא היא עד כאן לא קאמר ר' יהודה הכא אלא שלא יהא חוטא נשכר אבל התם כרבנן סבירא ליה אי נמי עד כאן לא קאמר ר' דוסא התם אלא בתרומה דרבנן אבל קנס דאורייתא כרבנן סבירא ליה אמר ליה אביי וטעמיה דרבי יהודה הכא שלא יהא חוטא נשכר הוא והא תניא ר' יהודה אומר שבויה שנשבית הרי היא בקדושתה אפי' בת עשר שנים כתובתה מאתים והתם מאי שלא יהא חוטא נשכר איכא התם נמי דלמא מימנעי ולא נסבי לה וסבר ר"י בקדושתה קיימה והתניא הפודה את השבויה ישאנה מעיד בה לא ישאנה ר' יהודה אומר בין כך ובין כך לא ישאנה הא גופה קשיא אמרת הפודה את השבויה ישאנה והדר תנא מעיד בה לא ישאנה משום דמעיד בה לא ישאנה הא לא קשיא הכי קאמר הפודה את השבויה ומעיד בה ישאנה מעיד בה כדי לא ישאנה מ"מ קשיא לר' יהודה אמר רב פפא אימא רבי יהודה אומר בין כך ובין כך ישאנה רב הונא בריה דרב יהושע אומר לעולם כדקתני ר' יהודה לדבריהם דרבנן קאמר להו לדידי בין כך ובין כך ישאנה אלא לדידכו בין כך ובין כך לא ישאנה מבעי ליה ורבנן הפודה את השבויה ומעיד בה ישאנה לא שדי איניש זוזי בכדי מעיד בה כדי לא ישאנה שמא עיניו נתן בה רמי ליה רב פפא בר שמואל לרב יוסף וסבר

ה"ג אי דקא טוען טענת דמים הכי נמי הב"ע דקטעין טענת פתח פתוח. אי דקאמר בעלתי ולא מצאתי דם ודאי טענה מעלייתא היא והכא דקתני אין לה טענת בתולים דקטעין ואמר פתח פתוח מצאתי ודם לא בדקתי אם נמצא בה אם לאו בנערה וקטנה טענה היא כדאמרינן בפ"ק ואע"פ שאין יכול לברר דבריו בפנינו אמרינן חזקה אין אדם טורח בסעודה ומפסידה אבל משבגרה אין רחמה צר כבתחילה ודומה לו כאילו פתח פתוח: שנחבטה. ובתוליה נושרין: כולהו רואות. אם נשרו בתוליהן [רואות דם]: ומראות לאמן. ופוסקות עליהן שאין בתולות ואם לא הודיעתו הטעתו: וזו אינה רואה ואינה מראה לאמה. וזה שכנסה בחזקת נחבטת כנסה ואין אדם פוסק עליה ולאו טעות הוא: ריעא. שיצא עליו שם זיוף: אין חוששין לה. אפי' לכהונה: אלא. יצא עליה שם רע היכי דמי כגון בעדים ולא שאמרו עליה שנבעלה דא"כ מאי למימרא הא לאו בתולה היא אלא אמרי לדידהו תבעתנהו לאיסורא הפקירה עצמה לכך ולא שמענו לה: בשלמא התם כו'. היכי גמר רב פפא מינה דלא מגבינן בשטרא כי האי בשלמא התם שכיחי פרוצין וכיון שיש עדים שהיתה מחזרת אחר הזנות הרבה מצאה לה משום הכי אין לה קנס לאחר זמן דלאו בחזקת בתולה הואי: אלא. לגבי שטר: אם הוא הוחזק. לחזור אחר עידי שקר: כל ישראל מי הוחזקו. להיות שומעין לו לזייף: אימר זיופי זייף. הוא עצמו למד לכוין כתב הדומה לכתב ידי עדים שחתם בו: מתני' יתירות על בנות שלש שנים. דכיון דראויות לביאה בחזקת הפקר הן ונבעלות בנכריותן והשבויה בשביתה: ולא יהיה אסון ענוש יענש. הא אם יהיה אסון לא יענש: גמ' שבויה. בת כהן: אוכלת בתרומה. ולא מחזקינן לה בחזקת בעולה לפסול לה המחללה בביאתו: מפני שמיעך לה. כלומר אין נוהגין בהן הפקר לאונסן בבעילה אלא לשחק עמהן: [רבנן פליגי אדרבי דוסא ואמרו יש שבויה אוכלת ויש שאינה אוכלת כיצד האשה שאמרה נשביתי וטהורה אני אוכלת ואם יש עדים שנשבית והיא אומרת טהורה אני אינה אוכלת במסכת עדיות]: אלא בתרומה בזמן הזה דרבנן. דכיון דאפילו נבעלה איסורא דרבנן בעלמא הוא לא גזרו על ספיקה אבל קנס דאפוקי ממונא הוא אימא לך ספק בעולה היא ומספיקא לא מפקינן ממונא: דלמא ממנעי ולא נסבי לה. אי פחתת כתובתה משוית לה בחזקת בעולה ומרחקי לה אפילו ישראל: מעיד בה. קא סלקא דעתין דאפודה קאי שאם היה מעיד בה שלא נבעלה לעובד כוכבים לא ישאנה אם כהן הוא: משום דמעיד בה וכו'. והא אמרו הפודה את השבויה ישאנה: הפודה את השבויה ומעיד בה ישאנה. דאי לאו דקים ליה בגוה לא שדי זוזי בכדי שהרי לישאנה פדאה: מעיד בה כדי לא ישאנה. שמא עיניו נתן בה: ורואה

אי דקא טוען טענת דמים ה"נ כו'. כך גרס בקונטרס ור"ת גריס איפכא כמו שהיה כתוב בספרים אי דקא טוען טענת פתח פתוח ה"נ כו' ולעיל בפ"ק (דף ט. ד"ה האומר) פירשתי קצת וקשה לפי' ר"ת דמפרש למוכת עץ אין לה דמים אבל פתחה נעול אם כן בחנם דחק לשנויי הא ר"ג והא רבי יהושע דה"מ לשנויי הא דקא טוען פתח פתוח הא דקא טוען טענת דמים ושמא לית ליה חזקה דאין אדם טורח בסעודה ומפסידה ולא מהימן בפתח פתוח להפסידה כתובתה אע"ג דקאמר אי דקא טוען פתח פתוח הכי נמי דמשמע דנאמן שמא היינו לאוסרה עליו אבל ברייתא דלעיל משמע דיש להן טענת בתולים לענין כתובה דומיא דקנס:

כולהו רואות ומראות לאמן. פירש הקונטרס ופוסקות עליהן שהן בעולות ואם לא הודיעתו הטעתו וקשה לפירושו דהא אליבא דר"מ קיימינן ור' מאיר אית לי' בפ"ק (דף יג.) דמוכת עץ בין הכיר בה בין לא הכיר בה מאתים ונראה לר"י דה"פ כולהו רואות ומראות לאמן ויודעות שהן מוכת עץ שאמותיהן מגידות להן ולהכי [כשהוא אומר לא מצאתי לבתך בתולים והיא אומרת בתולה הייתי אין לנו לתלות במוכת עץ שא"כ היתה אומרת מוכת עץ אני] וכי לא אמרה מוכת עץ אני יש לה טענת בתולים אבל סומא תלינן שהיא מוכת עץ אע"ג דלא אמרה דאינה יודעת לפי שאינה רואה ואינה מראה לאמה ואין אמה מגדת לה:

היוצאת משום שם רע בת סקילה היא. ופשיטא דלאו בת קנס היא דהא בעולה ודאי היא אבל אין לפרש הואיל ויש חיוב סקילה לא עליה פשיטא דאין לה קנס דקם ליה בדרבה מיניה דהא קתני במתניתין הבא על בתו ולעיל נמי קתני עריות בברייתא:

ואלו שאין להן קנס הגיורת והשבויה כו'. אף על גב דמדאורייתא שבויה לא הויא בחזקת בעולה כדאמרינן בכל דוכתי דשבויה קילו מ"מ אין לה קנס משום גזירה שלא תנהג עצמה כבעולה לכל דבריה:

וכי מה עשה לה ערבי זה. נקט ערבי לפי שהם שטופים בזימה כדאמר בקדושין (דף מט:) עשרה קבין זימה ירדו לעולם ט' נטלו ערביים: משום דמעיד בה לא ישאנה. קס"ד הפודה את השבויה ישאנה בלא עדות קאמר:

מכל מקום קשיא. אליבא דרבי יוחנן פריך וכן כל הנך פירכי דלקמן אבל לרבה דאמר דטעמא דרבי יהודה שלא יהא חוטא נשכר לא קשיא מידי: וסבר

עין משפט נר מצוה

מט א מיי' פי"ז מהל' איסורי ביאה הל' כא טוש"ע אה"ע סי' ו סעיף טז:
נ ב מיי' פ"א מהל' נערה בתולה הל' ט סמג עשין נד טוש"ע שם סי' קעז ס"ד בהג"ה:
נא ג מיי' פכ"ב מהל' עדות הל' ה סמג עשין קי טוש"ע ח"מ סי' לא סעיף ד וסי' מב סעיף א:
נב ד מיי' פ"א מהל' נערה בתולה הל' י סמג עשין נד טור אה"ע סי' קעז:
נג ה מיי' שם הל' יג יד:
נד ו מיי' פ"ו מהל' תרומות הל' יא סמג לאוין רנו:
נה ז ח מיי' פי"ח מהל' איסורי ביאה הל' כ טוש"ע אה"ע סי' ז ס"ג:

תוספות רי"ד

ת"ר יצא עליה ש"ר בילדותה אין לה לא אונס ולא פיתוי אמר ר"פ ש"מ האי שטרא ריעא לא מגבינן בי' פי' שיצא עלי' שם זיוף ה"ד אי נימא דנפיק עלי' קלא דשטר זייפא הוא דכוותה הכא נמי דנפיק עלי' קלא דזנאי והא"ר יצא עליה שם מזנה בעיר אין חוששין לה אפי' לכהונה אלא דאתו בי תרי ואמרו לדידהו תבעתנהי באיסורא פי' אלא יצא עליה ש"ר כגון בעדים שאמרו שנבעלה דא"כ מאי למימרא לאו בתולה היא אלא אמרי לדידהו הכי פרוש והפקירה עצמה לכך ולא שמענו לה דכוותה התם דאתו בי תרי ואמרו לדידהו אמר זייפו לי. בשלמא הכא שכיחי פרוצות פי' דהכא גמר ר"פ מינה דלא מגבי בשטרא כי דאי התם שכיחי פרוצות כיון שיש עדים שהיתה מחזרת אחר זנות הרבה מצאה לה מ"ה אין לה קנס לאחר זמן דלאו בחזקת בתולה הואי אלא התם אם הוא הוחזק כל ישראל מי הוחזקו פי' גבי שטר אם הוא מחזק לחזור אחר עידי שקר כ"ש מי הוחזקו להיות שומעין לו לזייף. התם נמי כיון דמהדר אזיופא אימור זיופי זייף וכתב פי' הוא עצמו למד לכוין כתב הדומה לכתב העדים שחתום בו. והלכך אפי' יש עדים המכירים החתימה ואומרים שחתימות יד העדים הוא לא מגבי' ביה. מתני' ואלו שאין להן קנס. הבא על הגיורת ועל השבויה ועל השפחה שנפדו ושנתגיירו ושנשתחררו יתירות על בנות ג"ש ויום א'. פי' שכיון שראויה לביאה בחזקת הפקר הן ונבעלו בגיותם ר"י אומר שבויה שנשבית ה"ה בקדושתה אע"פ שגדולה. הבא על בתו ועל בת בתו ועל בת בנו על ב"א על בת בנה ועל בת בתה אין להם קנס מפני שנתחייב בנפשו שמיתתן ע"י ב"ד וכל המתחייב בנפשו אינו משלם ממון שנאמר לא יהיה אסון ענוש יענש פי' הא אם יהיה אסון לא יענש ובגמרא פ"ק בזא מהכא נפקא מהתם נפקא פי' מכדי רשעתו. משום רשעה אחת אתה מחייבו ולא משום ב' רשעיות וכו' במיתה וממון וחד"א במלקות וממון וצריכי וכו' ואין הל' כר"י: ת"ר הפודה את השבויה ומעיד בה ישאנה דלא שדא איניש זוזי בכדי. מעיד בה כדי לא ישאנה פי' אם הוא כהן חיישינן שמא עיניו נתן בהו לעלמא שריא:

מסורת הש"ס

א) [ע' היטב תוס' לקמן פה. ד"ה מרגלא ותוס' לקמן לב: ד"ה דילמא ותוס' שבועות מב. ד"ה איפרע ותוס' יבמות קה: ד"ה מרגלא], ב) גיטין פט., ג) [מכות ה:], ד) [ע' תו' לקמן לג. ד"ה הבא], ה) [וע' תו' שם ד"ה ועל], ו) [משום סיומא דמילתא דאמר ר' דוסא וכי מה עשה לה כו' שהביא הש"ס לחזק הענין שפיר גרסי' דתניא], ז) גיטין פא. עדיות פ"ב מ"ו, ח) [נ"ל רבא וע' תוס' לעיל יא: בד"ה אביי לא אמר וע' תוס' לקמן לז. ד"ה אמר רבה קסבר וכו' נע"ש], ט) [תוספתא פרק ג], י) [תוספתא איתא קטנה], כ) [תוס' דיבמות פ"ד], ל) [וכן גירסת הערוך ערך פדא ע"ש], מ) ת"י כ"י.

תוספות ישנים

א) [נ"ל דמצינן לפרש בת סקילה היא דקם ליה בדרבה מיניה ופשיטא דמרישא דברייתא שמעי' לה. מ"י].

תורה אור השלם

א) וְכִי יִנָּצוּ אֲנָשִׁים וְנָגְפוּ אִשָּׁה הָרָה וְיָצְאוּ יְלָדֶיהָ וְלֹא יִהְיֶה אָסוֹן עָנוֹשׁ יֵעָנֵשׁ כַּאֲשֶׁר יָשִׁית עָלָיו בַּעַל הָאִשָּׁה וְנָתַן בִּפְלִלִים: [שמות כא, כב]

ליקוטי רש"י

יצא לה. לאשה פנויה בעיר. שם מזנה. לעובד כוכבים ולעבד שפוסלין אותה מן הכהונה. אין חוששין לה. לאוסרה לכהונה [גיטין פט.]. מפני שמיעך לה. שמשחק עמה לא חיישינן שמא בא עליה [שם פא.].

רַבִּי יְהוּדָה הָא דַּאֲמָרָן – The opinion of **R' Yehudah is this** ruling **that we have** just **stated;**[30] רַבִּי דוֹסָא – and the compatible ruling of **R' Dosa** is that דְּתַנְיָא – **which was taught in a Baraisa:** שְׁבוּיָה אוֹכֶלֶת בִּתְרוּמָה – A former CAPTIVE WOMAN[31] MAY EAT *TERUMAH;*[32] דִּבְרֵי רַבִּי דוֹסָא – these are THE WORDS OF R' DOSA. אָמַר רַבִּי דוֹסָא – R' DOSA EXPLAINED: וְכִי מֶה עָשָׂה לָהּ עַרְבִי הַלָּז – NOW, WHAT DID THIS ARAB captor DO TO HER that would prohibit her from eating *terumah*? וְכִי מִפְּנֵי שֶׁמִּיעֲךְ לָהּ בֵּין דַּדֶּיהָ – BECAUSE HE simply PRESSED AND RUBBED HER BETWEEN HER BREASTS פְּסָלָהּ מִן הַכְּהוּנָּה – DID HE DISQUALIFY HER FROM enjoying the privileges of THE PRIESTHOOD?! Of course not![33]

The Gemara is not convinced that the opinions of R' Yehudah and R' Dosa are fundamentally concordant:

אָמַר רַבָּה – **Rabbah**[34] **said:** דִּלְמָא לֹא הִיא – **Perhaps it is not so** that R' Yehudah and R' Dosa agree, for we could say: עַד כָּאן לֹא קָאָמַר רַבִּי יְהוּדָה הָכָא אֶלָּא שֶׁלֹּא יְהֵא חוֹטֵא נִשְׂכָּר – **Until here does R' Yehudah state here** in the Mishnah that the captive retains her status as a virgin and remains eligible to receive the fines for violation or seduction – i.e. **only so that the sinner should not benefit.**[35] אֲבָל הָתָם כְּרַבָּנָן סְבִירָא לֵיהּ – **But there,** with regard to eating *terumah,*[36] **he holds like the Rabbis,** who maintain that we *do* presume that she was violated in captivity and therefore disqualify her from eating *terumah.* אִי נַמִּי – **Alternatively,** we could say: עַד כָּאן לֹא קָאָמַר רַבִּי דוֹסָא הָתָם אֶלָּא בִּתְרוּמָה דְּרַבָּנָן – **Until here does R' Dosa state there** that we do not presume that the captive was violated – i.e. **only with regard to** the eating of ***terumah* which** nowadays **is** only **Rabbinic.**[37] אֲבָל קְנָס דְּאוֹרַיְיתָא – **But the fine** for violation **is a Biblical** monetary issue, כְּרַבָּנָן סְבִירָא לֵיהּ – and so there **[R' Dosa] holds like the Rabbis,** who rule that she is not entitled to the fine.[38] – ? –

The Gemara now challenges Rabbah's explanation of the rationale for R' Yehudah's ruling in our Mishnah:

וְטַעְמֵיהּ דְּרַבִּי יְהוּדָה הָכָא – אֲמַר לֵיהּ אַבַּיֵי – **Abaye said to [Rabbah]:** – **And is R' Yehudah's reason here** for awarding a captive the fines really שֶׁלֹּא יְהֵא חוֹטֵא נִשְׂכָּר הוּא – **so that the sinner should not benefit?!** וְהָא תַנְיָא – **But it was taught** otherwise **in a Baraisa:** רַבִּי יְהוּדָה אוֹמֵר – R' YEHUDAH SAYS: שְׁבוּיָה שֶׁנִּשְׁבֵּית הֲרֵי הִיא בִּקְדוּשָּׁתָהּ – A CAPTIVE WHO WAS CAPTURED[39] IS still IN HER STATE OF PURITY; אֲפִילּוּ בַּת עֶשֶׂר שָׁנִים כְּתוּבָּתָהּ מָאתַיִם – EVEN if SHE IS TEN YEARS OLD,[40] HER *KESUBAH* award IS TWO HUNDRED *zuz.*[41] וְהָתָם מַאי שֶׁלֹּא יְהֵא חוֹטֵא נִשְׂכָּר אִיכָּא – **And there, what** application of **"so that the sinner should not benefit" exists?**[42]

Rabbah's reply:

הָתָם נַמִּי – **There, too,** there exists a valid reason for R' Yehudah's considering her a virgin: דִּלְמָא מִימְּנְעֵי וְלֹא נָסְבֵי לָהּ – If we were to award this captive only the *kesubah* of a nonvirgin (i.e. one hundred *zuz*), people would see that we presume that she had been violated and **perhaps they will refrain from marrying her.**[43]

The Gemara now challenges R' Yochanan's explanation of R' Yehudah's ruling in our Mishnah:[44]

וְסָבַר רַבִּי יְהוּדָה בִּקְדוּשָּׁתָהּ קַיְּימָה – **And does R' Yehudah** really **hold,** as a general rule, that **[a captive] is** still **in her state of purity?** וְהָתַנְיָא – **But it was taught** otherwise **in a Baraisa:** הַפּוֹדֶה אֶת הַשְּׁבוּיָה יִשָּׂאֶנָּה – ONE[45] WHO RANSOMS A FEMALE CAPTIVE MAY MARRY HER. מֵעִיד בָּהּ לֹא יִשָּׂאֶנָּה – If HE TESTIFIES ABOUT HER that she was not violated, HE MAY NOT MARRY HER.[46] רַבִּי יְהוּדָה אוֹמֵר – R' YEHUDAH SAYS: בֵּין כָּךְ וּבֵין כָּךְ לֹא יִשָּׂאֶנָּה – EITHER WAY HE MAY NOT MARRY HER.

The Gemara digresses from its challenge to R' Yochanan to address the seemingly faulty logic of the Tanna Kamma's opinion:

הָא גּוּפָהּ קַשְׁיָא – **This Baraisa is itself difficult!** אָמַרְתְּ הַפּוֹדֶה אֶת הַשְּׁבוּיָה יִשָּׂאֶנָּה – First **you said** that **one who ransoms a captive may marry her,** וַהֲדַר תָּנָא – **but then [the Baraisa]**

NOTES

30. Viz. his ruling in the Mishnah, that a ransomed captive retains her status as a virgin, and thus is entitled to the fines for violation and seduction.

31. Who is the daughter of a Kohen (*Rashi*) [or the wife of a Kohen (see *Hagahos Yavetz*)].

32. If a Kohen's unmarried daughter, who normally may eat *terumah,* cohabits with a non-Jew, she is rendered a *zonah* and is disqualified from eating *terumah* (or from marrying a Kohen).

R' Dosa rules that a ransomed captive is still permitted to eat *terumah,* for we do not presume that her captors violated her (see *Rashi*).

33. While Arabs [whom R' Dosa mentions because they are especially lascivious (*Tosafos,* citing *Kiddushin* 49b; see *Hagahos Yavetz*)] are depraved enough to fondle their female captives, they will stop short of actual violation. Hence, their captives from priestly families are not disqualified from eating *terumah* or marrying a Kohen (*Rashi*).

The Rabbis (in *Eduyos* 3:6) dispute R' Dosa's unqualified ruling and hold that only in specific cases may these women captives eat *terumah.* That is, if a woman states that she was captured by non-Jews but was not violated, and there are no witnesses to her capture, we believe her and she is permitted to eat *terumah.* If, however, there *are* witnesses to her capture, she is not believed to claim that she was not defiled, and so she is disqualified from eating *terumah* [see above, 22a] (ibid.).

34. *Mesoras HaShas* emends this to "Rava."

35. If the captive were disqualified from receiving the fine, the "sinner" – i.e. the violator or seducer – would "benefit" by not having to pay it.

36. An issue that does not impact any sinner.

37. Nowadays, while the conditions of exile persist, the requirement to separate *terumah* even from grain, wine and oil is only Rabbinic in origin (for reasons, see *Rambam* and *Raavad, Hil. Terumos* 1:26; *Raavad* op. cit. 13:14; *Rashba* to *Yevamos* 82b). Hence, even if the Kohen's daughter was violated by her captors, she would transgress only a Rabbinic prohibition by eating *terumah.* Thus, perhaps R' Dosa maintains that in the case of a captive, where it is uncertain whether she was actually violated, the Rabbis did not impose a prohibition (*Rashi; cf. Tos. HaRosh;* see also *Mitzpeh Eisan*).

38. Since the issue of a fine involves extracting payment, and since wherever there is uncertainty as to financial liability we do not extract payment, the Rabbis admonished us to consider the possibility that she was violated by her captors (*Rashi*).

39. In *Tosefta* the text reads: A minor [girl] who was captured (*Mesoras HaShas*).

40. See *Rashash* regarding why R' Yehudah specifies the age of ten.

41. I.e. she has the status of a virgin, whose *kesubah* is two hundred *zuz,* not the status of a nonvirgin, whose *kesubah* is only one hundred *zuz.*

42. In the case of a *kesubah,* what sinner would benefit if she were presumed a nonvirgin and stripped of her full award? None, for only her husband stands to gain! Hence, we must conclude that R' Yehudah does disagree with the Rabbis, and holds that we presume that a captive has not been violated.

43. Even an Israelite, who is permitted to marry her, will refrain from doing so, seeing that we presume that she is a nonvirgin (*Rashi*).

44. According to R' Yochanan, R' Yehudah awards a captive the fine not to deprive the violator of any benefit, as Rabbah maintains, but because R' Yehudah *generally* presumes that captives are not violated. Consequently, the following Baraisa is adduced as a rebuttal to R' Yochanan only; it poses no difficulty to Rabbah's approach (*Tosafos* ד״ה מכל מקום).

45. Even a Kohen (see *Rashi* below ד״ה מעיד בה).

46. At this point the Gemara understands that this statement relates back to the Baraisa's first ruling, thus teaching that if the "one who ransomed her" also "testified" that she was not violated by her captors, he may not marry her if he is a Kohen (*Rashi*). See *Tos. HaRashba,* cited in following note.

אי דקא טעין טענת דמים הכי נמי הכא במאי עסקינן דקטעין טענת פתח פתוח: סומכוס אומר משום ר"מ סומא אין לה טענת בתולים: מ"ט דסומכוס א"ר זירא מפני שנחבטת על גבי קרקע כולהו נמי חבוטי מיחבטי כולהו רואות ומראות לאמן זו אינה רואה ואינה מראה לאמה: והיוצאת משום שם רע אין לה לא קנס ולא פיתוי: היוצאת משום שם רע בת סקילה היא אמר רב ששת הכי קאמר מי שיצא עליה שם רע בילדותה אין לה לא קנס ולא פיתוי אמר רב פפא ש"מ [א] האי שטרא ריעא לא מגבינן ביה היכי דמי אילימא דנפק קלא עליה דשטרא דזייפא הוא דכוותה הכא דנפק עלה קלא דזנאי והא אמר רבא [ב] יצא לה שם מזנה בעיר אין חוששין לה אלא [ג] דאתו בי תרי ואמרי לדידהו תבעתנהי באיסורא דכוותה הכא [ד] דאתו בי תרי ואמרי לדידהו אמר להו זייפו לי בשלמא התם שכיחי פרוצין אלא הכא [ה] אם הוא הוחזק כל ישראל מי הוחזקו הכא נמי כיון דקא מהדר אזיופא אימר זיופי זייף וכתב: **מתני'** [ו] ואלו שאין להן קנס הבא על הגיורת ועל השבויה ועל השפחה שנפדו ושנתגיירו ושנשתחררו יתירות על בנות שלש שנים ויום אחד רבי יהודה אומר שבויה שנפדית הרי היא בקדושתה אע"פ שגדולה [ז] הבא על בתו על בת בתו על בת בנו [ח] על בת אשתו על בת בנה על בת בתה אין להן קנס מפני שמתחייב בנפשו שמיתתן בידי בית דין וכל המתחייב בנפשו אין משלם ממון שנאמר [א] ואם לא יהיה אסון ענוש יענש: **גמ'** א"ר יוחנן רבי יהודה ורבי דוסא אמרו דבר אחד רבי יהודה הא דאמרן רבי דוסא [ט] דתניא [י] שבויה אוכלת בתרומה דברי ר' דוסא אמר רבי דוסא וכי מה עשה לה ערבי הלז וכי מפני שמיעך לה בין דדיה פסלה מן הכהונה אמר [מ] רבה דלמא לא היא עד כאן לא קאמר ר' יהודה הכא אלא שלא יהא חוטא נשכר אבל התם [י] כרבנן סבירא ליה אי נמי עד כאן לא קאמר ר' דוסא התם אלא בתרומה דרבנן אבל קנס דאורייתא כרבנן סבירא ליה אמר ליה אביי וטעמיה דרבי יהודה הכא שלא יהא חוטא נשכר הוא והא תניא [כ] ר' יהודה אומר [ל] שבויה שנשבית הרי היא בקדושתה אפי' בת עשר שנים כתובתה מאתים והתם מאי שלא יהא חוטא נשכר איכא התם נמי דלמא מימנעי ולא נסבי לה וסבר ר"י בקדושתה קיימה והתניא [ל] הפודה את השבויה ישאנה מעיד בה לא ישאנה ר' יהודה אומר בין כך ובין כך לא ישאנה הא גופה קשיא אמרת הפודה את השבויה ישאנה והדר תנא מעיד בה לא ישאנה הא לא קשיא הכי קאמר הפודה את השבויה ומעיד בה ישאנה מעיד בה כדי לא ישאנה מ"מ קשיא לר' יהודה אמר רב פפא אימא רבי יהודה אומר בין כך ובין כך ישאנה רב הונא בריה דרב יהושע אומר לעולם כדקתני ר' יהודה לדבריהם דרבנן קאמר להו לדידי בין כך ובין כך ישאנה אלא לדידכו בין כך ובין כך לא ישאנה ורבנן [מ] הפודה את השבויה ומעיד בה ישאנה לא שדי איניש זוזי בכדי [מ] מעיד בה כדי לא ישאנה שמא עיניו נתן בה רמי ליה רב פפא בר שמואל לרב יוסף וסבר

רש"י

ה"ג אי דקא טעין טענת דמים הכי נמי הב"ע דקטעין טענת פתח פתוח. אי דקאמר בעלתי ולא מצאתי דם ודאי טענה מעלייתא היא והכא דקתני אין לה טענת בתולים דקטעין ואמר פתח פתוח מצאתי ודם לא בדקתי אם לא נמצא בה אם לאו בנערה וקטנה טענה היא כדאמרינן בפ"ק ואע"פ שאין יכול לברר דבריו בפנינו אמרינן חזקה אין אדם טורח בסעודה ומפסידה אבל משנבגרה אין רחמה צר כבתחלה ודומה לו כאילו פתח פתוח: **שנחבטת.** ובתולים נושרין: **כולהו רואות.** אם נשרו בתוליהן [רואות דם]: **ומראות לאמן.** ופוסקות עליהן שאין בתולות ואם לא הודיעתו הטעתו: **וזו אינה רואה ואינה מראה לאמה.** וזה שכנסה בחזקת בתולה נתכוון לכנסה ואין אדם פוסק עליה ולאו טעות הוא: **ריעא.** שיצא עליו שם זיוף: **אין חוששין לה.** אפי' לכהונה: **אלא.** יצא עליה שם רע היכי דמי כגון בעדים ולא שאמרו עליה שנבעלה דא"כ מאי למימרא הא לאו בתולה היא אלא אמרי לדידהו תבעתנהו לאיסורא הפקירה עצמה לכך ולא שמענו לה: **בשלמא התם כו'.** היכי גמר רב פפא מינה דלא מגבינן בשטרא כי האי בשלמא התם שכיחי פרוצין וכיון שיש עדים שהיתה מחזרת אחר הזנות הרבה מצאה לה משום הכי אין לה קנס לאחר זמן דלאו בחזקת בתולה הוא: **אלא.** גבי שטר: **אם הוא הוחזק.** לחזור אחר עידי שקר: **כל ישראל מי הוחזקו.** להיות שומעין לו לזייף: **אימר זיופי זייף.** הוא עצמו למד לכוין כתב הדומה לכתב ידי עדים שחתם בו: **מתני' יתירות על בנות שלש שנים.** דכיון דראויות לביאה בחזקת הפקר הן ונבעלות בגיותן והשבויה בשביתה: **ולא יהיה אסון ענוש יענש.** הא אם יהיה אסון לא יענש: **גמ' שבויה.** בת כהן: **אוכלת בתרומה.** ולא מחזקינן לה בחזקת בעולה לפסול לה המחללה בביאתו: **מפני שמיעך לה.** כלומר אין נוהגין בהן הפקר לאונסן בבעילה אלא לשחק עמהן: [רבנן פליגי אדרבי דוסא ואמרו יש שבויה אוכלת ויש שאינה אוכלת כיצד האשה שאמרה נשביתי וטהורה אני אוכלת ואם יש עדים שנשבית והיא אומרת טהורה אני אינה אוכלת במסכת עדיות]: **אלא בתרומה בזמן הזה דרבנן.** דכיון דאפילו נבעלה איסורא דרבנן בעלמא הוא לא גזרו על ספיקה אבל קנס דאפוקי ממונא הוא אימא לך ספק בעולה היא ומספיקא לא מפקינן ממונא: **דלמא ממנעי ולא נסבי לה.** אי פחתת כתובתה משוית לה בחזקת בעולה ומרחקי לה אפילו ישראל: **מעיד בה.** קא סלקא דעתין דאפודה קאי שאם היה מעיד בה שלא נבעלה לעובד כוכבים לא ישאנה אם כהן הוא: **משום דמעיד בה וכו'.** והא אמרו הפודה את השבויה ישאנה: **הפודה את השבויה ומעיד בה ישאנה.** דאי לאו דקים ליה בגוה לא שדי זוזי בכדי שהרי לישאנה פדאה: **מעיד בה כדי לא ישאנה.** שמא עיניו נתן בה: ולאתה

תוספות

אי דקא טעין טענת דמים ה"נ כו'. כך גרס בקונטרס ור"ת גריס איפכא [ט] כמו שהיה כתוב בספרים אי דקא טעין טענת פתח פתוח ה"נ כו' ולעיל בפ"ק (דף ט. ד"ה האומר) פירשתי קלת קשה לפי' ר"ת דמפרש דמוכת עץ אין לה דמים אבל פתחה נעול אם כן בתמה דחק לשנויי הא ר"ג והא רבי יהושע דה"מ לשנויי הא דקא טעין פתח פתוח הא דקא טעין טענת דמים ושמא לית ליה חזקה דאין אדם טורח בסעודה ומפסידה ולא מהימן בפתח פתוח להפסידה כתובתה אע"ג דקאמר אי דקא טעין פתח פתוח הכי נמי דמשמע דנאמן שמא היינו לאוסרה עליו אבל ברייתא דלעיל משמע דיש להן טענת בתולים לענין כתובה דומיא דקנס:

כולהו רואות ומראות לאמן. פירש הקונטרס ופוסקות עליהן שהן בעולות ואם לא הודיעתו הטעתו וקשה לפירושו דהא אליבא דר"מ קיימינן ור' מאיר אית לי' בפ"ק (דף יא.) דמוכת עץ בין הכיר בה בין לא הכיר בה מאתים ונראה לר"י דה"פ כולהו רואות ומראות לאמן ויודעות שהן מוכת עץ שאמותיהן מגידות להן ולהכי [ב] כשהוא אומר לא מצאתי לבתך בתולים והיא אומרת בתולה הייתי אין לנו לתלות במוכת עץ שא"כ היתה אומרת מוכת עץ אני וכי לא אמרה מוכת עץ אני יש לה טענת בתולים אבל סומא תלינן שהיא מוכת עץ אע"ג דלא אמרה דאינה יודעת לפי שאינה רואה ואינה מראה לאמה ואין אמה מגדת לה:

היוצאת משום שם רע [א] **בת סקילה היא.** ופשיטא דלאו בת קנס היא דהא בעולה ודאי היא אבל אין לפרש הואיל ויש חיוב סקילה לגב עליה פשיטא דאין לו קנס דקים ליה בדרבה מיניה דהא קתני במתניתין הבא על אחותו ולעיל נמי קתני עריות בברייתא:

ואלו שאין להן קנס הגיורת והשבויה כו'. אף על גב דמדאורייתא שבויה לא הויא בחזקת בעולה כדאמרינן בכל דוכתי דבשבויה הקילו מ"מ אין לה קנס דמשום גזירה שלא תנשא לכהן עשאוה כבעולה לכל דבריה:

וכי מה עשה לה ערבי זה. נקט ערבי לפי שהם שטופים בזימה כדאמר בקדושין (דף מט:) עשרה קבין זימה ירדו לעולם ט' נטלו ערביים: **משום דמעיד בה לא ישאנה.** קס"ד הפודה את השבויה ישאנה בלא עדות קאמר:

מכל מקום קשיא. אליבא דרבי יוחנן פריך וכן כל הנך פירכי דלקמן אבל לרבה דאמר דטעמא דרבי יהודה שלא יהא חוטא נשכר לא קשיא מידי: וסבר

עין משפט נר מצוה

מט א מיי' פי"ז מהל' איסורי ביאה הל' כא טוש"ע אה"ע סי' ו סעיף טו:
נ ב מיי' פ"א מהל' נערה בתולה הל' ט סמג עשין נד טוש"ע שם סי' קע ס"ד בהג"ה:
נא ג מיי' פכ"ב מהל' עדות הל' ה סמג עשין קי טוש"ע ח"מ סי' לא סעיף ד וסי' סג סעיף א:
נב ד מיי' פ"א מהל' נערה בתולה הל' י סמג עשין נד טור אה"ע סי' קעז:
נג ה מיי' שם הל' יג יד:
נד ו מיי' פ"ו מהל' תרומות הל' יא סמג לאוין רנו:
נה ז ח מיי' פי"ח מהל' איסורי ביאה הל' כ טוש"ע אה"ע סי' ז ס"ג:

מסורת הש"ס

א) [ע' היטב תוס' לקמן פה. ד"ה מרענא ותוס' לקמן לב: ד"ה דינא ותוס' שבועות מב. ד"ה איפרע ותוס' יבמות קא: ד"ה מרענא], ב) גיטין פט., ג) [מכות ה:], ד) [ע' תו' לקמן לו. ד"ה הבא], ה) [וע' תו' שם ד"ה ועל], ו) [משום סיומא דמילתא דאמר ר' דוסא וכי מה עשה לה כו' שהביא הש"ס לחזק הענין שפיר גרסי' דתניא], ז) גיטין פא. עדיות פ"ג מ"ו, ח) [צ"ל רבא וע' בתוס' לעיל יא. בד"ה אביי לא אמר וע' תוס' לקמן לו. ד"ה אמר רבה קסבר וכו' לע"ק], ט) [תוספתא פרק ג], י) [בתוספתא איתא קטנה], כ) [תוס' דיבמות פ"ד], ל) [וכן גירסת הערוך ערך פתח ע"ש], מ) ת"י כ"י.

תוספות ישנים

א) [נ"ל דמלינן לפרש בת סקילה היא דקס ליה בדרבה מיניה ופשיטא דמרישא דברייתא שמעי' לה. מ"י].

תורה אור השלם

א) וְכִי יִנָּצוּ אֲנָשִׁים וְנָגְפוּ אִשָּׁה הָרָה וְיָצְאוּ יְלָדֶיהָ וְלֹא יִהְיֶה אָסוֹן עָנוֹשׁ יֵעָנֵשׁ כַּאֲשֶׁר יָשִׁית עָלָיו בַּעַל הָאִשָּׁה וְנָתַן בִּפְלִלִים: [שמות כא, כב]

ליקוטי רש"י

יצא לה. לאשה פנויה בעיר. **שם מזנה.** לעובד כוכבים ולעבד שמולין אותה מן הכהונה. **אין חוששין לה.** לאוסרה לכהונה [גיטין פט.]. **מפני שמיעך לה.** שמשך עמה לא חיישינן שמא בא עליה [שם פא.].

תוספות רי"ד

ת"ר יצא עליה ש"ר בילדותה אין לה לא אונס ולא פיתוי אמר ר"פ ש"מ האי שטרא ריעא לא מגבינן בי' פי' שיצא עלי' שם זיוף ה"ד אי במאי דנפיק עלי' קלא דשטר דזייפא הוא דכוותה הכא נמי דנפיק עלי' קלא דזנאי והא"ר יצא עליה שם מזנה בעיר אין חוששין לה אפי' לכהונה אלא דאתי בי תרי ואמרו לדידהו תבעתהו באיסורא פי' אלא יצא עליה ש"ר ה"ד כגון בעדים דא"כ מאי למימרא הא לאו בתולה היא אלא אמרי לדידהו וכו' פי' והפקירה עצמה לכך ולא שמענו לה דכותה התם דאתי בי תרי ואמרו לדידהו אמר זייפו לי. **בשלמא** הכא שכיחי פריצות פי' היכא גמר ר"פ מינה דלא מגבי' בשטרא כי האי הכא שכיחי פרוצות וכיון שיש עדים שהיתה מחזרת אחר זנות הרבה מצאה לה מ"ה אין לה קנס לאחר זמן דלאו בחזקת בתולה הואי אלא התם אם הוא מוחזק כל ישראל מי הוחזקו פי' בי' שטר אם הוא מוחזק לחזור אחר עידי שקר כ"י מי הוחזקו להיות שומעין לו לזייף. התם נמי כיון דמהדר אזייפא אימ' זיופי זייף וכתב פי' הוא עצמו למד לכוין כתב הדומה לכת"י העדים שחתום בו. והלכך אפי' יש עדים המכירים ואומרים שחתימות יד העדים הוא לא מגבי' ביה: **מתני'** ואלו שאין להן קנס. הבא על הגיורת וע' השבויה ועל השפחה שנפדו ושנתגיירו ושנשתחררו יתירות ע' בנות ג"ש ויום א'. פי' שכיון שראויה לביאה בחזקת הפקר הן ונבעלו בגיותן ור"י אומר שבויה שנשבית ה"ה בקדושתה אע"פ שגדולה. הבא ע' בתו ועל בת בתו ועל בת בנו ועל ב"א ע' בת בתה ועל בת בנה אין להם קנס מפני שנתחייב בנפשו שמיתתו ע"י ב"ד וכל המתחייב בנפשו אינו משלם ממון שנאמר ולא יהיה אסון ענוש יענש פי' הא אם יהיה אסון לא יענש ובגמרא פריך והא מהכא נפקא מהתם נפקא פי' מכדי רשעתו. משום רשעה אחת אתה מחייבו ולא משום ב' רשעיות לא וחדא במיתה וממון וחדא במלקות וממון וצריכי וכו' ואין הל' כר"י: **ת"ר** הפודה את השבויה ומעיד בה ישאנה דלא שדי איניש זוזי בכדי. מעיד בה כדי לא ישאנה פי' אם הוא כהן חיישינן שמא עיניו נתן בהו לעלמא שריא:

בְּאִיסּוּרָא – she once **solicited them for an illicit act,**[14] דִּכְוָותָהּ הָכָא – **so that corresponding to it here** in the case of the suspicious loan document **is** דְּאָתוּ בֵּי תְּרֵי וְאָמְרֵי – **where two** men **came forward and said** that לְדִידְהוּ אָמַר לְהוּ זַיְּיפוּ לִי – **[the holder of the document] said to them, "Forge** a loan document **for me."**

The Gemara argues that this explanation of the document case is untenable, and thereby completes its challenge to Rav Pappa:

בִּשְׁלָמָא הָתָם – But how can the two cases be compared?[15] **It is understandable there** in the case of the soliciting woman that we presume she is no longer a virgin, שְׁכִיחֵי פְּרוּצִין – for **promiscuous men** who would not refuse her **are common.**[16] אֶלָּא הָכָא – **But here** in the case of the loan document, אִם הוּא הוּחְזַק – **if [the document holder] has been established** to be a seeker of false witnesses, כָּל יִשְׂרָאֵל מִי הוּחְזְקוּ – **has all of Israel been established** to be willing accomplices?![17] – ? –

The Gemara defends Rav Pappa's corollary:

הָכָא נַמִּי – **Here, too,** a disqualifying presumption can be made, for כֵּיוָן דְּקָא מְהַדַּר אַזִּיוּפָא – **since** it is known that **[the document holder] was going around after a forgery,** אֵימַר זַיּוּפֵי זַיֵּיף וְכָתַב – **we can say** that eventually, when he found no accomplices, **he himself forged** the signatures of the witnesses **and wrote** the document.[18]

Mishnah וְאֵלּוּ שֶׁאֵין לָהֶן קְנָס – **And these are [the cases of** ***naaros*****] that are not entitled** to **the fine:** הַבָּא עַל הַגִּיוֹרֶת וְעַל הַשְּׁבוּיָה וְעַל הַשִּׁפְחָה – **If one violates a convert, or a** former **captive or** Canaanite **slave girl,** שֶׁנִּפְדּוּ וְשֶׁנִּתְגַּיְּירוּ וְשֶׁנִּשְׁתַּחְרְרוּ – **who were ransomed, or converted or were emancipated** יְתֵירוֹת עַל בְּנוֹת שָׁלֹשׁ שָׁנִים וְיוֹם אֶחָד – when they were **above the age of three years and one day.**[19] רַבִּי יְהוּדָה אוֹמֵר – **R' Yehudah says:** שְׁבוּיָה שֶׁנִּפְדֵּית הֲרֵי הִיא בִּקְדוּשָּׁתָהּ – **A captive who was ransomed is** still **in her state of purity,**[20] אַף עַל פִּי שֶׁגְּדוֹלָה – **even if she is old.**[21]

More women who are not entitled to the fine:

הַבָּא עַל בִּתּוֹ – In the cases of **one who violates his daughter,** עַל בַּת בִּתּוֹ – **his daughter's daughter,** עַל בַּת בְּנוֹ – **his son's daughter,** עַל בַּת אִשְׁתּוֹ – **his wife's daughter,**[22] עַל בַּת בְּנָהּ – **her son's daughter,** עַל בַּת בִּתָּהּ – **or her daughter's daughter,** אֵין לָהֶן קְנָס – **[these women] are not entitled** to **the fine,** מִפְּנֵי שֶׁמִּתְחַיֵּיב בְּנַפְשׁוֹ – **for [the violator] is liable with his life,**[23] שֶׁמִּיתָתָן בִּידֵי בֵית דִּין – **since their death** penalty[24] **is at the hands of the court;**[25] וְכָל הַמִּתְחַיֵּיב בְּנַפְשׁוֹ אֵין מְשַׁלֵּם מָמוֹן – **and anyone who is liable with his life does not pay money,** שֶׁנֶּאֱמַר – **for it is stated:**[26] ,,(ואם לא) [וְלֹא] יִהְיֶה אָסוֹן עָנוֹשׁ יֵעָנֵשׁ'' – *If men shall quarrel and they jolt a pregnant woman and she miscarries* ***and***[27] ***there shall be no fatality, he shall be punished.***[28]

Gemara The Gemara points out a compatibility between two Tannaic statements:

אָמַר רַבִּי יוֹחָנָן – **R' Yochanan said:** רַבִּי יְהוּדָה וְרַבִּי דוֹסָא אָמְרוּ דָּבָר אֶחָד – **R' Yehudah and R' Dosa said one** and the same **thing.**[29]

NOTES

14. I.e. her bad reputation was based not on hearsay, but on the testimony of witnesses. However, it cannot be that they testified that she actually cohabited with them, for then she is obviously a nonvirgin, and it would be unnecessary for the Baraisa to disqualify her from receiving the fines. Rather, the witnesses testified that she merely solicited them for cohabitation, and they refused. Nevertheless, we presume that she propositioned others as well and some of them did not refuse her, and so she loses her presumptive status of virgin and forfeits the fines (*Rashi*).

15. I.e. how can Rav Pappa derive that we do not collect with this document from the Baraisa's ruling that we presume that the soliciting woman is not a virgin? (*Rashi*).

16. And since there are witnesses who say that she was soliciting for non-marital cohabitation, we can presume that she found many who were willing to comply. Hence, she is not entitled to the fines for violation and seduction, for we presume that she is not a virgin (*Rashi;* cf. *Rambam,* cited by *Ran*).

17. [I.e. why should we presume that the two witnesses signed on the document did not act properly?]

18. Although, in fact, we do not presume that witnesses would act improperly, we must consider the possibility that the document holder – after failing to enlist others in his scheme – learned to forge the handwriting of two individuals and then himself wrote and signed the document (*Rashi*), and the "witnesses" later confirmed their signatures (*Ran*); cf. *Rambam, Hil. Eidus* 22:5.

19. Girls over the age of three [in contrast to younger ones; see above, 29a note 8] lose their virginity if they engage in cohabitation.] Converts and emancipated maidservants are presumed to have had physical relations prior to their conversion or emancipation. Similarly, there exists a strong possibility that women captives are violated by their captors. Consequently, the three women mentioned in the Mishnah have lost the presumptive status of virgins, and thus forfeit the fines for violation or seduction that are awarded a virgin *naarah* (*Rashi*).

Note: The case of the ransomed captive differs from those of the convert and emancipated maidservant, in that under Biblical law a former captive is still presumed a virgin (and is permitted, for example, to marry a Kohen) since there is no concrete evidence that she was violated by her captors. Since, however, captors often do violate their female captives, the Rabbis decreed that a ransomed captive be prohibited to a Kohen (see above, 23a, and *Rashi* there ד״ה בשבויה הקילו). In order to ensure that people are not lenient with this prohibition, the Rabbis treated the captive as a nonvirgin with regard to other laws as well – e.g. she is not entitled to the fines for violation and seduction [see also Mishnah above, 11a] (see *Tosafos;* see also *Pnei Yehoshua, R' Akiva Eiger* and *Haflaah* on *Tosafos*).

20. I.e. we presume that she was not violated and thus remains a virgin, who is entitled to the fines for violation and seduction.

21. I.e. older than three years of age.

22. From another marriage (and so the next two cases).

23. In all these cases the violator is liable to the court-imposed capital punishment of שְׂרֵפָה, *burning;* see Mishnah, *Sanhedrin* 75a.

The Rishonim ask why the Mishnah needs this reason for exempting the violator from payment in the case of one who violates his daughter – when the fine goes to him! See *Tos. HaRosh, Ramban, Tosafos* above, 29a ד״ה ועל אשת אחיו, *Shitah Mekubetzes* et al. for discussion and various answers.

24. I.e. the death penalty imposed for violating the aforementioned forbidden relations.

25. [In contrast to the incestuous relations mentioned in the Mishnah above (29a), where the violator is liable only to *kares* (a Divinely imposed death penalty), which does not exempt him from monetary liability.]

26. *Exodus* 21:22.

27. *Rashash* emends the text to read וְלֹא יִהְיֶה אָסוֹן, to accord with Scripture. Our translation follows his emendation. See Gemara below, 37a, where the verse is quoted correctly.

28. [I.e. monetarily, in that he pays the value of the fetus.] The verse thus implies that if there is a fatality, the assailant is not punished monetarily [see above, 35a] (*Rashi*).

29. I.e. both hold that we do not presume that a female captive was violated by her captors.

אי דקא טעין טענת דמים הכי נמי הכא במאי עסקינן דקטעין טענת פתח פתוח: סומכוס אומר משום ר"מ סומא אין לה טענת בתולים: מ"ט דסומכוס א"ר זירא מפני שנחבטת על גבי קרקע כולהו נמי חבוטי מיחבטי כולהו רואות ומראות לאמן וזו אינה רואה ואינה מראה לאמה: והיוצאת משום שם רע אין לה לא קנס ולא פיתוי: היוצאת משום שם רע בת סקילה היא אמר רב ששת הכי קאמר מי שיצא עליה שם רע בילדותה אין לה לא קנס ולא פיתוי אמר רב פפא ש"מ האי שטרא ריעא לא מגבינן ביה היכי דמי אילימא דנפק קלא עליה דשטרא דזייפא הוא דכוותה הכא דנפק עלה קלא דזנאי והא אמר רבא יצא לה שם מזנה בעיר אין חוששין לה אלא דאתו בי תרי ואמרי לדידהו תבעתנהי באיסורא דכוותה הכא דאתו בי תרי ואמרי לדידהו אמר להו זייפו לי בשלמא התם שכיחי פרוצין אלא הכא אם הוא הוחזק כל ישראל מי הוחזקו הכא נמי כיון דקא מהדר אזיופא אימר זיופי זייף וכתב: מתני' ואלו שאין להן קנס הבא על הגיורת ועל השבויה ועל השפחה שנפדו ושנתגיירו ושנשתחררו יתירות על בנות שלש שנים ויום אחד רבי יהודה אומר שבויה שנפדית הרי היא בקדושתה אע"פ שגדולה הבא על בתו על בת בתו על בת בנו על בת אשתו על בת בנה על בת בתה אין להן קנס מפני שמתחייב בנפשו שמיתתן בידי בית דין וכל המתחייב בנפשו אין משלם ממון שנאמר ואם לא יהיה אסון ענוש יענש: גמ' א"ר יוחנן רבי יהודה ורבי דוסא אמרו דבר אחד רבי יהודה הא דאמרן רבי דוסא דתניא שבויה אוכלת בתרומה דברי ר' דוסא אמר רבי דוסא וכי מה עשה לה ערבי הלז וכי מפני שמיעך לה בין דדיה פסלה מן הכהונה אמר רבה דלמא לא היא עד כאן לא קאמר ר' יהודה הכא אלא שלא יהא חוטא נשכר אבל התם כרבנן סבירא ליה אי נמי עד כאן לא קאמר ר' דוסא התם אלא בתרומה דרבנן אבל קנס דאורייתא כרבנן סבירא ליה אמר ליה אביי וטעמיה דרבי יהודה הכא שלא יהא חוטא נשכר הוא והא תניא ר' יהודה אומר שבויה שנשבית הרי היא בקדושתה אפי' בת עשר שנים כתובתה מאתים והתם מאי שלא יהא חוטא נשכר איכא התם נמי דלמא מימנעי ולא נסבי לה וסבר ר"י בקדושתה קיימה והתניא הפודה את השבויה ישאנה מעיד בה לא ישאנה ר' יהודה אומר בין כך ובין כך לא ישאנה הא גופה קשיא אמרת הפודה את השבויה ישאנה והדר תנא מעיד בה לא ישאנה משום דמעיד בה לא ישאנה הא לא קשיא הכי קאמר הפודה את השבויה ומעיד בה ישאנה מעיד בה כדי לא ישאנה מ"מ קשיא לר' יהודה אמר רב פפא אימא רבי יהודה אומר בין כך ובין כך ישאנה רב הונא בריה דרב יהושע אומר לעולם כדקתני ר' יהודה לדבריהם דרבנן קאמר להו לדידי בין כך ובין כך ישאנה אלא לדידכו בין כך ובין כך לא ישאנה מבעי ליה ורבנן הפודה את השבויה ומעיד בה לא שדי איניש זוזי בכדי מעיד בה כדי לא ישאנה שמא עיניו נתן בה רמי ליה רב פפא בר שמואל לרב יוסף וסבר

רש"י

ה"ג אי דקא טעין טענת דמים הכי נמי הב"ע דקטעין טענת פתח פתוח. אי דקאמר בעלתי ולא מצאתי דם ודאי טענה מעלייתא היא והכא דקתני אין לה טענת בתולים דקטעין ואמר פתח פתוח מצאתי ודם לא בדקתי אם נמצא בה אם לאו בנערה וקטנה טענה היא כדאמרינן בפ"ק ואע"פ שאין יכול לברר דבריו בפנינו אמרינן חזקה אין אדם טורח בסעודה ומפסידה אבל משבגרה אין רחמה צר כבתחילה ודומה לו כאילו פתח פתוח: שנחבטה. ובתוליה נושרין: כולהו רואות. אם נשרו בתוליהן [רואות דם]: ומראות לאמן. ופוסקות עליהן שאינן בתולות ואם לא הודיעתו הטעתו: וזו אינה רואה ואינה מראה לאמה. וזה שכנסה בחזקת נחבטת כנסה ואין אדם פוסק עליה ולאו טעות הוא: ריעא. שיצא עליו שם זיוף: אין חוששין לה. אפי' לכהונה: אלא. יצא עליה שם רע היכי דמי כגון בעדים ולא שאמרו עליה שנבעלה דא"כ מאי למימרא הא לאו בתולה היא אלא אמרי לדידהו תבעתנהו לאיסורא הפקירה עצמה לכך ולא שמענו לה: בשלמא התם כו'. היכי גמר רב פפא מינה דלא מגבינן בשטרא כי האי בשלמא התם שכיחי פרוצין וכיון שיש עדים שהיתה מחזרת אחר הזנות הרבה מצאה לה משום הכי אין לה קנס לאחר זמן דלאו בחזקת בתולה הואי: אלא. לגבי שטר: אם הוא הוחזק. לחזור אחר עידי שקר: כל ישראל מי הוחזקו. להיות שומעין לו לזייף: אימר זיופי זייף. הוא עצמו למד לכוין כתב הדומה לכתב ידי עדים שחתם בו: מתני' יתירות על בנות שלש שנים. דכיון דראויות לביאה בחזקת הפקר הן ונבעלות בנכריותן והשבויה בשביתה: ולא יהיה אסון ענוש יענש. הא אם יהיה אסון לא יענש: גמ' שבויה. בת כהן: אוכלת בתרומה. ולא מחזקינן לה בחזקת בעולה לפסול לה המחללה בביאתו: מפני שמיעך לה. כלומר אין נוהגין בהן הפקר לאונסן בבעילה אלא לשחק עמהן: [רבנן פליגי אדרבי דוסא ואמרו יש שבויה אוכלת ויש שאינה אוכלת כיצד האשה שאמרה נשביתי וטהורה אני אוכלת ואם יש עדים שנשבית והיא אומרת טהורה אני אינה אוכלת במסכת עדיות]: אלא בתרומה בזמן הזה דרבנן. דכיון דאפילו נבעלה איסורא דרבנן בעלמא הוא לא גזרו על ספיקה אבל קנס דאפוקי ממונא הוא אימא לך ספק בעולה היא ומספיקא לא מפקינן ממונא: דלמא ממנעי ולא נסבי לה. אי פחתת כתובתה משוית לה בחזקת בעולה ומרחקי לה אפילו ישראל: מעיד בה. קא סלקא דעתך דאפודה קאי שאם היה מעיד בה שלא נבעלה לעובד כוכבים לא ישאנה אם כהן הוא: משום דמעיד בה וכו'. והא אמרו הפודה את השבויה ישאנה: הפודה את השבויה ומעיד בה ישאנה. דאי לאו דקים ליה בגוה לא שדי זוזי בכדי שהרי לישאנה פדאה: מעיד בה כדי לא ישאנה. שמא עיניו נתן בה: ולאותה

תוספות

אי דקא טעין טענת דמים ה"נ כו'. כך גרס בקונטרס ור"ח גריס איפכא כמו שהיה כתוב בספרים אי דקא טעין טענת פתח פתוח ה"נ כו' ולעיל בפ"ק (דף ט. ד"ה האומר) פירשתי קצת קשה לפי' ר"ח דמפרש דמוכת עץ אין לה דמים אבל פתחה נעול אם כן בחנם דחק לשנויי הא ר"ג והא רבי יהושע דה"מ לשנויי הא דקא טעין פתח פתוח הא דקא טעין טענת דמים ושמא לית ליה חזקה דאין אדם טורח בסעודה ומפסידה ולא מהימן בפתח פתוח להפסידה כתובתה אע"ג דקאמר אי דקא טעין פתח פתוח הכי נמי דמשמע דנאמן שמא היינו לאוסרה עליו אבל ברייתא דלעיל משמע דיש להן טענת בתולים לענין כתובה דומיא דקנס:

כולהו רואות ומראות לאמן. פירש הקונטרס ופוסקות עליהן שהן בעולות ואם לא הודיעתו הטעתו וקשה לפירושו דהא אליבא דר"מ קיימינן ור' מאיר אית לי' בפ"ק (דף יג.) דמוכת עץ בין הכיר בה בין לא הכיר בה מאתים ונראה לר"י דה"פ כולהו רואות ומראות לאמן ויודעות שהן מוכת עץ שאמותיהן מגידות להן ולהכי [כשהוא אומר לא מצאתי לבתך בתולים והיא אומרת בתולה הייתי אין לנו לתלות במוכת עץ שא"כ היתה אומרת מוכת עץ אני] וכי לא אמרה מוכת עץ אני יש לה טענת בתולים אבל סומא תלינן שהיא מוכת עץ אע"ג דלא אמרה דאינה יודעת לפי שאינה רואה ואינה מראה לאמה ואין אמה מגדת לה:

היוצאת משום שם רע בת סקילה היא. ופשיטא דלאו בת קנס היא דהא בעולה ודאי היא אבל אין לפרש הואיל ויש חיוב סקילה לבא עליה פשיטא דאין לה קנס דקם ליה בדרבה מיניה דהא קתני במתניתין הבא על בתו ולעיל נמי קתני עריות בברייתא:

ואלו שאין להן קנס הגיורת והשבויה כו'. אף על גב דמדאורייתא שבויה לא הויא בחזקת בעולה כדאמרינן בכל דוכתי דבשבויה הקילו מ"מ אין לה קנס משום גזירה שלא תנשא לכהן עשאוה כבעולה לכל דבריה:

וכי מה עשה לה ערבי זה. נקט ערבי לפי שהם שטופים בזימה כדאמר בקדושין (דף מט:) עשרה קבין זימה ירדו לעולם ט' נטלו ערביים:

משום דמעיד בה לא ישאנה. קס"ד הפודה את השבויה ישאנה בלא עדות קאמר:

מכל מקום קשיא. אליבא דרבי יוחנן פריך וכן כל הנך פירכי דלקמן אבל לרבה דאמר דטעמא דרבי יהודה שלא יהא חוטא נשכר לא קשיא מידי: וסבר

עין משפט נר מצוה

מט א מיי' פי"ח מהל' איסורי ביאה הל' כא טוש"ע אה"ע סי' ו סעיף כו:
נ ב מיי' פ"א מהל' נערה בתולה הל' ט סמג עשין נג טוש"ע שם סי' קכו ס"ד בהג"ה:
נא ג מיי' פכ"ב מהל' עדות הל' ה סמג עשין קי טוש"ע ח"מ סי' לא סעיף ד וסי' סג סעיף א:
נב ד מיי' פ"א מהל' נערה בתולה הל' י סמג עשין נד טור אה"ע סי' קנז:
נג ה מיי' שם הל' יג יד:
נד ו מיי' פ"ו מהל' תרומות הל' יא סמג לאוין רטו:
נה ז ח מיי' פי"ח מהל' איסורי ביאה הל' כ טוש"ע אה"ע סי' ז ס"ג:

תוספות רי"ד

ת"ר יצא עליה ש"ר בילדותה אין לה לא אונס ולא פיתוי אמר ר"פ ש"מ האי שטרא ריעא לא מגבינן בי' פי' שיצא עלי' שם זיוף ה"ד אי נימא דנפיק עלי' קלא דשטר זייפא הוא דכוותה הכא נמי דנפיק עלי' קלא דזנאי והא"ר יצא עליה שם מזנה בעיר אין חוששין לה אפי' לכהונה אלא דאתי בי תרי ואמרו לדידהו תבעינהי באיסורא פי' אלא יצא עליה ש"ר ה"ד כגון בעדים לא שאמרו נבעלה דא"כ מאי למימרא הא לאו בתולה היא אלא אמרי לדידהו וכו' פירוש והפקירה עצמה לכך ולא שמענו לה דכותה בתם דאתי בי תרי ואמרו לדידהו אמר זייפו לי. בשלמא הכא שכיחי פריצות פי' היכא גמר ר"פ מינה דלא מגבי' בשטרא כי האי דתם שכיחי פרוצות וכיון שיש עדים שהיתה מחזרת אחר זנות הרבה מצאה לה מ"ה אין לה קנס לאחר זמן דלאו בחזקת בתולה הואי אלא התם אם הוא מוחזק כל ישראל מי הוחזקו פי' גבי שטר אם הוא מוחזק לחזור אחר עידי שקר כ"י מי הוחזקו להיות שומעי' לו לזייף. התם נמי כיון דמהדר אזייפא איכור זיופי' זייף וכתב פי' הוא עצמו למד לכוין כתב הדומה לכת"י העדים שחתום בו. והילכך אפי' יש עדים המכירים החתימה ואומרים שחתימות יד העדים הוא לא מגבי' ביה: מתני' ואלו שאין להן קנס. הבא על הגיורת ועל השפחה ועל השבויה שנפדו ושנתגיירו ושנשתחררו יתירות על בנות ג"ש ויום א'. פי' שכיון שראויה לביאה בחזקת הפקר הן ונבעלו בגיותן ר"י אומר שבויה שנשבית ה"ה בקדושתה אע"פ שגדולה. הבא על בתו ועל בת בתו על בת בנו ועל ב"א על בת בתה ועל בת בנה אין להם קנס מפני שנתחייב בנפשו שמיתתן ע"י ב"ד וכל המתחייב בנפשו אינו משלם ממון שנאמר ולא יהיה אסון ענוש יענש הא אם יהיה אסון לא יענש ובגמרא פריך והא מהכא נפקא מהתם נפקא פי' מכדי רשעתו משום רשעה אחת אתה מחייבו ולא משום ב' רשעיות חדא במיתה וממון וחדא במלקות וממון וצריכי וכו' ואין הל' כר"י: ת"ר הפודה את השבויה ומעיד בה ישאנה דלא שדא איניש זוזי בכדי. מעיד בה כדי לא ישאנה פי' אם הוא כהן חיישינן שמא עיניו נתן בהו לעלמא שריא:

מסורת הש"ס

א) [ע' היטב תוס' לקמן פה. ד"ה מרענא ותוס' לקמן נב: ד"ה דינא ותוס' שבועות מב. ד"ה איפרע ותוס' יבמות קא: ד"ה מרענא], ב) גיטין פט., ג) [מכות ה:], ד) [ע' תו' לקמן לז. ד"ה הבא], ה) [וע' תו' שם ד"ה ועל], ו) [משום סיומא דמילתא דאמר ר' דוסא וכי מה עשה לה כו' שהביא הש"ס לחזק הענין שפיר גרסי' דתניא], ז) גיטין פא. עדיות פ"ג מ"ו, ח) [נ"ל רבא וע' בתוס' לעיל יא. בד"ה אביי לא אמר וע' תוס' לקמן לז. ד"ה אמר רבה קסבר וכו' לע"ק], ט) [תוספתא פרק ג], י) [בתוספתא איתא קטנה], כ) [תוס' דיבמות פ"ד], ל) [וכן גירסת הערוך ערך פתח ע"ש], מ) ת"י כ"י.

תוספות ישנים

א) [נ"ל דמלינן לפרש בת סקילה היא דקם ליה בדרבה מיניה ופשיטא דמרישא דברייתא שמעי' לה. ת"י].

תורה אור השלם

א) וְכִי יִנָּצוּ אֲנָשִׁים וְנָגְפוּ אִשָּׁה הָרָה וְיָצְאוּ יְלָדֶיהָ וְלֹא יִהְיֶה אָסוֹן עָנוֹשׁ יֵעָנֵשׁ כַּאֲשֶׁר יָשִׁית עָלָיו בַּעַל הָאִשָּׁה וְנָתַן בִּפְלִלִים: [שמות כא, כב]

ליקוטי רש"י

יצא לה. לאשה פנויה בעיר. שם מזנה. לעובד כוכבים ולעבד שפוסלין אותה מן הכהונה. אין חוששין לה. לאוסרה לכהונה [גיטין פט.]. מפני שמיעך לה. שמשחק עמה לא חיישינן שמא בא עליה [שם פא.].

The Gemara resolves the apparent contradiction:

אִי דְקָא טָעִין טַעֲנַת דָּמִים – Regarding a claim of lost virginity, the Baraisa's subject: **If [the husband] made the** specific **claim of** having found no **blood** during the initial cohabitation, **הָכִי נַמִּי – it is indeed so** that he has made a valid claim, for even a virgin *bogeress* discharges the blood of virginity,[1] as Rav's ruling presumed. **הָכָא בְּמַאי עַסְקִינַן – Here** in the Baraisa, however, **with what** specific claim **are we dealing? דְּקָטָעִין טַעֲנַת פֶּתַח פָּתוּחַ – With where [the husband] made the claim of** having found **"an open door."**[2]

The Gemara cites the final clause of the aforementioned Baraisa:

סוּמְכוֹס אוֹמֵר מִשּׁוּם רַבִּי מֵאִיר – SUMCHOS SAYS IN THE NAME OF R' MEIR: סוּמָא אֵין לָהּ טַעֲנַת בְּתוּלִים – A BLIND [WOMAN] CANNOT HAVE against her **A CLAIM OF** lost **VIRGINITY.**

The Gemara explains this opinion:

מַאי טַעְמָא דְסוּמְכוֹס – What is Sumchos' reason for ruling thus? **אָמַר רַבִּי זֵירָא – R' Zeira said: מִפְּנֵי שֶׁנֶּחְבֶּטֶת עַל גַּבֵּי קַרְקַע – Because [a blind girl]** is prone to fall and **strike the ground,** thus rupturing her hymen and losing her blood of virginity.[3]

The Gemara counters:

כּוּלְּהוּ נַמִּי חֲבוּטֵי מִיחַבְּטֵי – All girls as well can fall and **strike** the ground, thus rupturing their hymens.[4] – ? –

The Gemara answers:

כּוּלְּהוּ רוֹאוֹת וּמַרְאוֹת לְאִמָּן – All other **girls,** if they fall and rupture their hymens, **see** that they are bleeding **and show their mothers.**[5] **זוֹ אֵינָהּ רוֹאָה וְאֵינָהּ מַרְאָה לְאִמָּהּ – This** blind girl, however, **does not see** that she is bleeding, **and** so **does not show her mother.**[6]

The Gemara now turns to the final ruling in the Baraisa cited above (35b):

וְהַיּוֹצֵאת מִשּׁוּם שֵׁם רַע – AND [A WOMAN] WHO DEPARTS BECAUSE OF A BAD NAME אֵין לָהּ לֹא קְנָס וְלֹא פִּיתּוּי – HAS NO right to the **FINE** for violation **AND** the fine for **SEDUCTION.**[7]

The Gemara asks:

הַיּוֹצֵאת מִשּׁוּם שֵׁם רַע בַּת סְקִילָה הִיא – A woman who departs her marriage (i.e. was divorced) **because of a bad name is liable to** death by **stoning!** Why is it necessary for the Baraisa to teach us that she is not entitled to the fines for the violation or seduction of a virgin?[8]

The Gemara answers:

אָמַר רַב שֵׁשֶׁת – Rav Sheishess said: הָכִי קָאָמַר – The Baraisa is actually **saying thus: מִי שֶׁיָּצָא עָלֶיהָ שֵׁם רַע בְּיַלְדוּתָהּ – [A woman] regarding whom a bad name went out in her youth**[9] **אֵין לָהּ לֹא קְנָס וְלֹא פִּיתּוּי – has no** right to the **fine** for violation **and** the fine for **seduction,** for we presume her to be a nonvirgin.

The Gemara presents a corollary ruling:

אָמַר רַב פָּפָּא – Rav Pappa said: שְׁמַע מִינָּהּ – Derive from [the Baraisa] הַאי שְׁטָרָא רִיעָא לָא מַגְבִּינַן בֵּיהּ – that we do not collect with this suspicious loan **document.**[10]

The Gemara objects to Rav Pappa's extrapolation (and in the process clarifies Rav Sheishess' interpretation):

הֵיכִי דָּמֵי – What is the case there? **אִילֵימָא דִּנְפַק קָלָא עֲלֵיהּ – If we say that a rumor circulated about it דִּשְׁטָרָא דְזַיְּיפָא הוּא – that it is a forged document, דִּכְווֹתָהּ הָכָא דִּנְפַק עֲלָהּ קָלָא דִזְנַאי – so that corresponding to it here** in our case of the woman **is that a rumor circulated about her that she had premarital relations,**[11] can that really be?! **וְהָא אָמַר רָבָא – But Rava has said: יָצָא לָהּ שֵׁם מְזַנָּה בָּעִיר – If the reputation of "promiscuous woman" attached to [an unmarried woman] in the town,**[12] **אֵין חוֹשְׁשִׁין לָהּ – we pay no heed to it.**[13] **אֶלָּא דְּאָתוּ בֵּי תְרֵי וְאָמְרֵי – Rather,** the Baraisa must be speaking of **where two** men **came forward and said** that **לְדִידְהוּ תְּבָעֲתִנְהִי**

NOTES

1. And therefore the absence of bleeding *is* evidence that she is a nonvirgin.

2. [I.e. the lack of tightness one would normally feel when cohabiting with a woman whose hymen was not previously perforated through cohabitation.] The Baraisa, which stops the husband from claiming nonvirginity and thus preserves the virgin *bogeress' kesubah,* speaks of where the groom did not check the sheets for virginal blood and sues on account of not having experienced tightness during the initial cohabitation. Such a claim, although impossible to prove [in contrast to the claim of no blood, which can be corroborated by producing the unstained sheet], is believed in the case of a bride who is a minor or a *naarah,* for we presume that a person does not take pains to prepare a wedding feast and ruin it by claiming falsely that his bride was a nonvirgin (see above, 10a). A *bogeress,* however, does not exhibit such tightness, even when she is in fact a virgin, for the vagina of the maturing *bogeress* naturally expands and thus feels like "an open door." Hence, the fact of an "open door" does not establish a *bogeress'* nonvirginity (*Rashi; cf. Rabbeinu Chananel,* cited by *Tosafos,* et al.).

3. Hence, the absence of blood during the initial cohabitation is attributed to her injury, and is not a telltale sign of premarital cohabitation.

4. If the counterclaim of injury is available to a blind bride to excuse her lack of virginal blood, it should be available to all brides for that purpose [since falling for anyone is a conceivable occurrence] (see *Ritva*).

5. And their mothers tell them that they have lost their blood of virginity. Hence, if they do not notify their grooms about this condition, their marriages are regarded as having been made under a false pretext, and the grooms may sue to have the *kesubah* awards voided (*Rashi*; see *Tosafos* and *Ritva* for different interpretations). See *Maginei Shlomo* for a novel interpretation of *Rashi's* approach in our *sugya,* which resolves *Tosafos'* difficulty. See also *Beis Aharon.*

6. Having not been told by anyone about the loss of her virginal blood, she is perforce ignorant of the loss. Accordingly, one who marries a blind girl must presume that although he was not notified by his bride that she lost her virginal blood through a fall, such a possibility exists; consequently, their marriage was not made under a pretext, and she is entitled to the *kesubah* (see *Rashi*).

7. As noted above (35b note 38), the Gemara at this point understands that this case involves a woman whose husband brought witnesses who testified that she committed adultery as an *arusah.* The Baraisa teaches that if she is violated or seduced after she "departs" (i.e. after her husband divorces her), she is not entitled to the fine.

8. If we rely on witnesses' testimony regarding her adultery to execute her by stoning, we certainly rely on their testimony to establish that she is no longer a virgin. That is, even if we say that the Baraisa speaks of where the husband divorced his wife **prior to** *nesuin* on account of the witnesses' testimony, so that her loss of virginity definitely was not occasioned by her husband, it is nonetheless obvious that we rely on the witnesses' testimony regarding her adultery to establish her as a nonvirgin, who is not entitled to the fines (*Tosafos,* as explained by *Maharam*).

9. [The exact meaning of this will be discussed in the Gemara below.] See *Haflaah* for how this interpretation conforms with the wording of the Baraisa: וְהַיּוֹצֵאת מִשּׁוּם שֵׁם רַע [literally: one who departs because of a bad name].

10. I.e. with a loan document that is reputed to be forged (*Rashi*). [Rav Pappa infers that just as we give credence to the woman's bad reputation and deny her the fines, so too we give credence to the document's reputation for being forged.]

11. And so when the Baraisa rules that she is not entitled to the fines for violation and seduction, it is in effect stating that we pay heed to those rumors and consider her a nonvirgin.

12. It was rumored that she had relations with an idolater or a slave, which would disqualify her from marrying a Kohen (*Rashi* to *Gittin* 89a).

13. And she is permitted to marry even a Kohen (*Rashi*). Similarly, with regard to our case, we should pay no heed to any bad rumor that circulated about the woman in her youth. Why, then, does the Baraisa disqualify her from receiving the fines?

אי דקא טעין טענת דמים הכי נמי הכא במאי עסקינן דקטעין טענת פתח פתוח: סומכוס אומר משום ר"מ סומא אין לה טענת בתולים: מ"ט דסומכוס א"ר זירא מפני שנחבטת על גבי קרקע כולהו נמי חבוטי מיחבטי כולהו רואות ומראות לאמן זו אינה רואה ואינה מראה לאמה: והיוצאת משום שם רע אין לה לא קנס ולא פיתוי: היוצאת משום שם רע בת סקילה היא אמר רב ששת הכי קאמר מי שיצא עליה שם רע בילדותה אין לה לא קנס ולא פיתוי אמר רב פפא ש"מ האי שטרא ריעא לא מגבינן ביה היכי דמי אילימא דנפק קלא עליה דשטרא דזייפא הוא דכוותה הכא דנפק עלה קלא דזנאי והא אמר רבא יצא לה שם מזנה בעיר אין חוששין לה אלא דאתו בי תרי ואמרי לדידהו תבעתנהו באיסורא דכוותה הכא דאתו בי תרי ואמרי לדידהו אמר להו זייפו לי בשלמא התם שכיחי פרוצין אלא הכא אם הוא הוחזק כל ישראל מי הוחזקו הכא נמי כיון דקא מהדר אזוופא אימר זיופי זייף וכתב: **מתני'** ואלו שאין להן קנס הבא על הגיורת ועל השבויה ועל השפחה שנפדו ושנתגיירו ושנשתחררו יתירות על בנות שלש שנים ויום אחד רבי יהודה אומר שבויה שנפדית הרי היא בקדושתה אע"פ שגדולה הבא על בתו על בת בתו על בת בנו על בת אשתו על בת בנה על בת בתה אין להן קנס מפני שמתחייב בנפשו שמיתתן בידי בית דין וכל המתחייב בנפשו אין משלם ממון שנאמר ואם לא יהיה אסון ענוש יענש: **גמ'** א"ר יוחנן רבי יהודה ורבי דוסא אמרו דבר אחד רבי יהודה הא דאמרן רבי דוסא דתניא שבויה אוכלת בתרומה דברי ר' דוסא אמר רבי דוסא וכי מה עשה לה ערבי הלז וכי מפני שמיעך לה בין דדיה פסלה מן הכהונה אמר רבה דלמא לא היא עד כאן לא קאמר ר' יהודה הכא אלא שלא יהא חוטא נשכר אבל התם כרבנן סבירא ליה אי נמי עד כאן לא קאמר ר' דוסא התם אלא בתרומה דרבנן אבל קנס דאורייתא כרבנן סבירא ליה אמר ליה אביי וטעמיה דרבי יהודה הכא שלא יהא חוטא נשכר הוא והא תניא ר' יהודה אומר שבויה שנשבית הרי היא בקדושתה אפי' בת עשר שנים כתובתה מאתים והתם מאי שלא יהא חוטא נשכר איכא התם נמי דלמא מימנעי ולא נסבי לה וסבר ר"י בקדושתה קיימה והתניא הפודה את השבויה ישאנה מעיד בה לא ישאנה ר' יהודה אומר בין כך ובין כך לא ישאנה הא גופה קשיא אמרת הפודה את השבויה ישאנה והדר תנא מעיד בה לא ישאנה משום דמעיד בה לא ישאנה הא לא קשיא הכי קאמר הפודה את השבויה ומעיד בה ישאנה מעיד בה כדי לא ישאנה מ"מ קשיא לר' יהודה אמר רב פפא אימא רבי יהודה אומר בין כך ובין כך ישאנה רב הונא בריה דרב יהושע אומר לעולם כדקתני ר' יהודה לדבריהם דרבנן קאמר להו לדידי בין כך ובין כך ישאנה אלא לדידכו בין כך ובין כך לא ישאנה מבעי ליה ורבנן הפודה את השבויה ומעיד בה ישאנה לא שדי איניש זוזי בכדי מעיד בה כדי לא ישאנה שמא עיניו נתן בה רמי ליה רב פפא בר שמואל לרב יוסף וסבר

ה"ג אי דקא טעין טענת דמים הכי נמי הב"ע דקטעין טענת פתח פתוח. אי דקאמר בעלתי ולא מצאתי דם ודאי טענה מעלייתא היא והכא דקתני אין לה טענת בתולים דקטעין ואמר פתח פתוח מצאתי ודם לא בדקתי אם נמצא בה אם לאו בנערה וקטנה טענה היא כדאמרינן בפ"ק ואע"פ שאין יכול לברר דבריו בפניו אמרינן חזקה אין אדם טורח בסעודה ומפסידה אבל משבגרה אין רחמה צר כבתחילה ודומה לו כאילו פתח פתוח: שנחבטה. ובתוליה נושרין: כולהו רואות. אם נשרו בתוליהן [רואות דם]: ומראות לאמן. ופוסקות עליהן שאין בתולות ואם לא הודיעתו הטעתו: וזו אינה רואה ואינה מראה לאמה. וזה שכנסה בחזקת נחבטת כנסה ואין אדם פוסק עליה ולאו טעות הוא: ריעא. שיצא עליו שם זיוף: אין חוששין לה. אפי' לכהונה: אלא. יצא עליה שם רע היכי דמי כגון בעדים ולא שאמרו עליה שנבעלה דא"כ מאי למימרא הא לאו בתולה היא אלא אמרי לדידהו תבעתנהו לאיסורא הפקירה עצמה לכך ולא שמענו לה: בשלמא התם כו'. היכי גמר רב פפא מינה דלא מגבינן בשטרא כי האי בשלמא התם שכיחי פרוצין וכיון שיש עדים שהיתה מחזרת אחר הזנות הרבה מצאה לה משום הכי אין לה קנס לאחר זמן דלאו בחזקת בתולה הואי: אלא. לגבי שטר: אם הוא הוחזק. לחזור אחר עדי שקר: כל ישראל מי הוחזקו. להיות שומעין לו לזייף: אימר זויפי זייף. הוא עצמו למד לכוין כתב הדומה לכתב ידי עדים שחתם בו: מתני' יתירות על בנות שלש שנים. דכיון דראויות לביאה בחזקת הפקר הן ונבעלות בנכריותן והשבויה בשבויתה: ולא יהיה אסון ענוש יענש. הא אם יהיה אסון לא יענש: גמ' שבויה. בת כהן: אוכלת בתרומה. ולא מחזקינן לה בחזקת בעולה לפסול לה המחללה בביאתו: מפני שמיעך לה. כלומר אין נוהגין בהן הפקר לאונסן בבעילה אלא לשחק עמהן: [רבנן פליגי אדרבי דוסא ואמרו יש שבויה אוכלת ויש שאינה אוכלת כיצד האשה שאמרה נשביתי וטהורה אני אוכלת ואם יש עדים שנשבית והיא אומרת טהורה אני אינה אוכלת במסכת עדיות]: אלא בתרומה בזמן הזה דרבנן. דכיון דאפילו נבעלה איסורא דרבנן בעלמא הוא לא גזרו על ספיקה אבל קנס דאפוקי ממונא הוא אימא לך ספק בעולה היא ומספיקא לא מפקינן ממונא: דלמא ממנעי ולא נסבי לה. אי פחתת כתובתה משוית לה בחזקת בעולה ומרחקי לה אפילו ישראל: מעיד בה. קא סלקא דעתין דאפודה קאי שאם היה מעיד בה שלא נבעלה לעובד כוכבים לא ישאנה אם כהן הוא: משום דמעיד בה וכו'. והא אמרו הפודה את השבויה ישאנה: הפודה את השבויה ומעיד בה ישאנה. דאי לאו דקים ליה בגוה לא שדי זוזי בכדי שהרי לישאנה פדאה: מעיד בה כדי לא ישאנה. שמא עיניו נתן בה:
ולאתה

אי דקא טעין טענת דמים ה"נ כו'. כך גרס בקונטרס ור"ח גריס איפכא [א] כמו שהיה כתוב בספרים אי דקא טעין טענת פתח פתוח ה"נ כו' ולעיל בפ"ק (דף ט. ד"ה האומר) פירשתי קצת קשה לפי' ר"ח דמפרש דמוכת עץ אין לה דמים אבל פתחה נעול אם כן בחנם דחק לשנויי הא ר"ג והא רבי יהושע דה"מ לשנויי הא דקא טעין פתח פתוח הא דקא טעין טענת דמים ושמא לית ליה חזקה דאין אדם טורח בסעודה ומפסידה ולא מהימן בפתח פתוח להפסידה כתובתה אע"ג דקאמר אי דקא טעין פתח פתוח הכי נמי דמשמע דנאמן שמא היינו לאוסרה עליו אבל ברייתא דלעיל משמע דיש להן טענת בתולים לענין כתובה דומיא דקנס:

כולהו רואות ומראות לאמן. פירש הקונטרס ופוסקות עליהן שהן בעולות ואם לא הודיעתו הטעתו וקשה לפירושו דהא אליבא דר"מ קיימינן ור' מאיר אית לי' בפ"ק (דף יג.) דמוכת עץ בין הכיר בה בין לא הכיר בה מאתים ונראה לר"י דה"פ כולהו רואות ומראות לאמן ויודעות שהן מוכת עץ שאמותיהן מגידות להן ולהכי [מ] [כשהוא אומר לא מצאתי לבתך בתולים והיא אומרת בתולה הייתי אין לנו לתלות במוכת עץ שא"כ היתה אומרת מוכת עץ אני] וכי לא אמרה מוכת עץ אני יש לה טענת בתולים אבל סומא תלינן שהיא מוכת עץ אע"ג דלא אמרה דאינה יודעת לפי שאינה רואה ואינה מראה לאמה ואין אמה מגדת לה:

היוצאת משום שם רע א) בת סקילה היא. ופשיטא דלאו בת קנס היא דהא בעולה ודאי היא אבל אין לפרש הואיל ויש חיוב סקילה לבא עליה פשיטא דאין לה קנס דקם ליה בדרבה מיניה דהא קתני במתניתין הבא על בתו ולעיל נמי קתני עריות בברייתא:

ואלו שאין להן קנס הגיורת והשבויה כו'. אף על גב דמדאורייתא שבויה לא הויא בחזקת בעולה כדאמרינן בכל דוכתי דבשבויה הקילו מ"מ אין לה קנס דמשום גזירה שלא תנשא לכהן עשאוה כבעולה לכל דבריה:

וכי מה עשה לה ערבי זה. נקט ערבי לפי שהם שטופים בזימה כדאמר בקדושין (דף מט:) עשרה קבין זימה ירדו לעולם ט' נטלו ערביים:

משום דמעיד בה לא ישאנה. קס"ד הפודה את השבויה ישאנה בלא עדות קאמר:

מכל מקום קשיא. אליבא דרבי יוחנן פריך וכן כל הנך פירכי דלקמן אבל לרבה דאמר דטעמא דרבי יהודה שלא יהא חוטא נשכר לא קשיא מידי:
וסבר

עין משפט נר מצוה

מט א מיי' פי"ז מהל' איסורי ביאה הל' כא טוש"ע אה"ע סי' ו סעיף טו:

נ ב מיי' פ"א מהל' נערה בתולה הל' ט סמג עשין נד טוש"ע שם סי' קעז ס"ד בהג"ה:

נא ג מיי' פכ"ב מהל' עדות הל' ה סמג עשין קי טוש"ע ח"מ סי' מב סעיף ד וסי' סג סעיף א:

נב ד מיי' פ"א מהל' נערה בתולה הל' י סמג עשין נד טור אה"ע סי' קעז:

נג ה מיי' שם הל' יג יד:

נד ו מיי' פ"ו מהל' תרומות הל' יא סמג לאוין רנו:

נה ז ח מיי' פי"ח מהל' איסורי ביאה הל' כ טוש"ע אה"ע סי' ז ס"ג:

תוספות רי"ד

ת"ר יצא עליה ש"ר בילדותה אין לה לא אונס ולא פיתוי אמר ר"פ ש"מ האי שטרא ריעא לא מגבינן בי' פי' שיצא עלי' שם זיוף ה"ד אי נימא דנפיק עלי' קלא דשטר זייפא הוא דכוותה הכא נמי דנפיק עלי' קלא דזנאי והא"ר יצא עליה שם מזנה בעיר אין חוששין לה אפי' לכהונה אלא דאתי בי תרי ואמרו לדידהו תבעתהי באיסורא פי' אלא יצא עליה ש"ר ה"ד כגון בעדים לא שאמרו נבעלה דא"כ מאי למימרא הא לאו בתולה היא אלא אמרי לדידהו וכו' פירוש והפקירה עצמה לכך ולא שמענו לה דכוותה התם דאתי בי תרי ואמרו לדידהו אמר זייפו לי. **בשלמא** הכא שכיחי פריצות פי' היכא גמר ר"פ מינה דלא מגבי' בשטרא כי האי התם שכיחי פרוצות וכיון שיש עדים שהיתה מחזרת אחר זנות הרבה מצאה לה מ"ה אין לה קנס לאחר זמן דלאו בחזקת בתולה הואי אלא התם אם הוא מוחזק כל ישראל מי הוחזקו פי' גבי שטר אם הוא מוחזק לחזור אחר עדי שקר כ"י מי הוחזקו להיות שומעי' לו לזייף. התם נמי כיון דמהדר אזייפא אימור זיופי' זייף וכתב פי' הוא עצמו למד לכוין כתב הדומה לכת"י העדים שחתום בו. והילכך אפי' יש עדים המכירים החתימה ואומרים שחתימות יד העדים הוא לא מגבי' ביה: **מתני'** ואלו שאין להן קנס. הבא על הגיורת ועל השבויה ועל השפחה שנפדו ושנתגיירו ושנשתחררו יתירות על בנות ג"ש ויום א'. פי' שכיון שראויה לביאה בחזקת הפקר הן ונבעלו בגיותם ר"י אומר שבויה שנשבית ה"ה בקדושתה אע"פ שגדולה. הבא על בתו ועל בת בתו ועל בת בנו ועל ב"א על בת בתה ועל בת בנה אין להם קנס מפני שנתחייב בנפשו שמיתתו ע"י ב"ד וכל המתחייב בנפשו אינו משלם ממון שנאמר ולא יהיה אסון ענוש יענש פי' הא אם יהיה אסון לא יענש ובגמרא פריך והא מהכא נפקא מהתם נפקא פי' מכדי רשעתו. משום רשעה אחת אתה מחייבו ולא משום ב' ומשני חדא במיתה וממון וחדא במלקות וממון וצריכי וכו' ואין הל' כר"י: ת"ר הפודה את השבויה ומעיד בה ישאנה דלא שדא איניש זוזי בכדי. מעיד בה כדי לא ישאנה פי' אם הוא כהן חיישינן שמא עיניו נתן בהו לעלמא שריא:

מסורת הש"ס

א) [ע' היטב תוס' לקמן פה. ד"ה מרענא ותוס' לקמן לב: ד"ה דיגא ותוס' שבועות מב. ד"ה איסרא ותוס' יבמות קח: ד"ה מרענא], ב) גיטין סט., ג) [מכות ה:], ד) [ע' תו' לקמן לג. ד"ה הבא], ה) [וע' תו' שם ד"ה וע"ן], ו) [משום קיומא דמילתא דאמר ר' דוסא וכו' מה עשה לה כו' שהביא הש"ס לחזק הענין שפיר גרסי' דתניא], ז) גיטין פא. עדיות פ"ג מ"ו, ח) [נ"ל רבא וע' בתוס' לעיל יא. בד"ה אבל לא אמר וע' תוס' לקמן לג. ד"ה אמר רבה קסבר וכו' לע"ע], ט) [תוספתא פרק ג], י) [תוספתא איתא קטנה], כ) תוס' דיבמות פ"ד, ל) [וכן גירסת הערוך ערך פתח ע"ש], מ) ח"י כ"י.

תוספות ישנים

א) [נ"ל דמצינן לפרש בת סקילה היא דקם ליה בדרבה מיניה ופשיטא דמרישא דברייתא שמעי' לה. מ"י].

תורה אור השלם

א) וְכִי יִנָּצוּ אֲנָשִׁים וְנָגְפוּ אִשָּׁה הָרָה וְיָצְאוּ יְלָדֶיהָ וְלֹא יִהְיֶה אָסוֹן עָנוֹשׁ יֵעָנֵשׁ כַּאֲשֶׁר יָשִׁית עָלָיו בַּעַל הָאִשָּׁה וְנָתַן בִּפְלִלִים: [שמות כא, כב]

ליקוטי רש"י

יצא לה. לאשה פנויה בעיר. שם מזנה. לעובד כוכבים ולעבד שפוסלין אותה מן הכהונה. אין חוששין לה. לאוסרה לכהונה [גיטין פט.]. מפני שמיעך לה. שמשחק עמה לא חיישינן שמא בא עליה [שם פא.].

עריות ממש שניות מדברי סופרים כיון דמדאורייתא חזיא ליה אמאי אין להן קנס אלא עריות [א]חייבי מיתות בית דין שניות חייבי כריתות אבל חייבי לאוין יש להן קנס ומני [א] שמעון התימני היא איכא דאמרי עריות חייבי מיתות ב"ד וחייבי כריתות שניות חייבי לאוין מני [ב] ר"ש בן מנסיא היא: הממאנת אין לה לא קנס ולא פיתוי הא קטנה בעלמא אית לה מני רבנן היא דאמרי [ג] קטנה יש לה קנס אימא סיפא איילונית אין לה לא קנס ולא פיתוי אתא לר"מ דאמר [ד] קטנה אין לה קנס והא מקטנותה יצתה לבגר רישא רבנן וסיפא ר"מ וכ"ת כולה ר"מ היא ובממאנת סבר לה כרבי יהודה ומי סבר לה והתניא [ה] עד מתי הבת ממאנת [ב]עד שתביא שתי שערות דברי ר"מ [ו] ר' יהודה אומר עד שירבה שחור על הלבן אלא ר' יהודה היא ובקטנה סבר לה כר"מ ומי סבר לה והאמר רב יהודה אמר רב [ז] זו דברי ר"מ ואם איתא זו דברי ר"מ ור' יהודה מיבעי ליה האי תנא סבר לה כר"מ בחדא ופליג עליה בחדא רפרם אמר מאי ממאנת הראויה למאן וליתני קטנה קשיא: איילונית אין לה לא קנס ולא פיתוי ורמינהי החרשת והשוטה והאיילונית יש להן קנס ויש להן טענת בתולים והא מאי רומיא הא ר"מ הא רבנן ודקארי לה מאי קארי לה משום דאית ליה למירמא אחריתי עילויה [ג]החרשת והשוטה והבוגרת ומוכת עץ אין להן טענת בתולים [ד]הסומא ואיילונית יש להן טענת בתולים סומכוס אומר משום ר"מ סומא אין לה טענת בתולים אמר רב ששת לא קשיא הא [ח] רבן גמליאל והא ר' יהושע אימר דשמעת ליה לרבן גמליאל היכא דקא טענה איהי היכא דלא קא טענה איהי מי שמעת ליה כיון דאמר ר"ג מהימנא [ט] כגון זו [א] פתח פיך לאלם הוא: והבוגרת אין לה טענת בתולים: והאמר רב [י] [ה]בוגרת נותנין לה לילה הראשון

אי

רש"י

עריות ממש. המפורש באחרי מות והן בכריתות: **שניות.** שגזרו חכמים על שניות להן להרחיק מן העבירה כגון אם אמו ואם אביו ושאר עריות השנויות בפרק ב' דיבמות (דף כא.): **כיון דשניות חזיין ליה מדאורייתא.** קרינן ביה ולו תהיה לאשה: **אמאי אין לה קנס.** בשלמא בעריות איכא למימר כשמעון התימני דלית ליה נערה נערה הנערה אלא שניות קשיא: **שמעון התימני.** בריש פירקין דאמר אשה שיש בה הויה: **ר"ש בן מנסיא.** דאמר אשה הראויה לקיימה: **רבנן היא.** דפליגי אדר"מ בריש פירקין: **ובממאנת סבר לה כר' יהודה.** דאמר נערה ממאנת והכי תידוק מינה נערה ממאנת אין לה קנס הא נערה בעלמא יש לה קנס: **עד שתביא שתי שערות.** ומשהביאה אינה ממאנת ואפילו לא בעל לאחר מיכן: **רבי יהודה אומר.** אם לא בעל לאחר שגדלה ממאנת: **עד שירבה שחור על הלבן.** וגמרא מפרש שתי שערות שוכבות ונראה כמו שירבה השחור: **אלא ר' יהודה היא.** ובממאנת נערה קאמרינן דאין לה קנס ולא תדוק הא קטנה יש לה קנס וגבי אילונית דתנא נמי אין לה קנס משום דבקטנה סבר כר"מ וזו מקטנותה יצאה לבגר: **זו דברי כו'.** לקמן בפרקין (דף מ:): **סבר לה כר' מאיר.** דקטנה אין לה קנס משום הכי אין קנס באילונית: **ופליג עליה.** בממאנת ואמר עד שירבה השחור וכי תנא הממאנת אין לה קנס למאן הראויה למאן יש לה קנס בנערה קאמר: **מאי ממאנת הראויה למאן.** כלומר כל קטנה קאמר וכולה ר"מ היא: **ויש להן טענת בתולים.** להפסידה כתובה: **הא ר"מ.** דאמר קטנה אין לה קנס ואילונית מקטנותה יצתה לבגר: **ודקארי לה מאי קארי לה.** מי שהשיב תשובה זו בבית המדרש מה עלתה על רוחו ולא סבירא ליה דאיכא לאוקמינהו כר"מ ורבנן: **משום דאית ליה למירמא אחריתא עליה.** לא הביאה לבית המדרש אלא לפי שיש להשיב אחרת על זו חרשת ושוטה אחרשת ושוטה: **בוגרת.** בתוליה כלים מאליהן: **הא רבן גמליאל.** דאמר בפ"ק (דף יב:) היא אומרת משאירסתני נאנסתי נאמנת הכא נמי אין לה טענת בתולים להפסידה כתובתה דאמרינן אי הוה פקחת לטעון הוה טענה משאירסתני נאנסתי ומהימנא: **הא רבי יהושע.** דאמר לא מפיה אנו חיין הכא יש לה טענת בתולים דאי נמי הוה טענה קמן לא מהימנינן לה: **נותנין לה לילה הראשון.** ובועל כמה בעילות ותלינן כל דמים של אותו הלילה בדם בתולים אלמא אית לה דם בתולים לבוגרת דאי לא לא הוה בעי למיתב לה אלא בעילת מצוה וכיון דאית לה בתולים היכא דבעל ולא מצא דם תפסיד כתובתה דהא כנסה בחזקת בתולה ומצאה בעולה:

ה"ג

תוספות

[אבל חייבי לאוין יש להן קנס ומני שמעון התימני היא. לא הוה מצי למימר מני רבי נחוניא היא דלדידיה לא הוה קרי להו שניות שהרי משוה חייבי כריתות לחייבי מיתות ב"ד והא דלא קאמר הא מני רבי עקיבא ועריות חייבי מיתות ושניות חייבי כריתות וחייבי לאוין אלא דניחא ליה לאוקמי אפי' כרבנן דאמרי קידושין תופסין ועוד משום דקאמר בלישנא קמא מני שמעון התימני היא קאמר נמי באיכא דאמרי מני רבי שמעון בן מנסיא היא דהוי בר פלוגתיה דשמעון התימני]:

עד שירבה השחור כו'. אית דלא גרסי על הלבן משום דאמרינן בפרק בא סימן (נדה דף נב. ושם) לא שירבה ממש אלא כדי שיהו שתי שערות שוכבות ונראה כמו שירבה שחור ועל הלבן משמע יותר מן הלבן ור"ח פירש על הלבן שהשערות סמוך לבשר הם שחורים ובראשם לבנים [ג]: **זו** דברי ר"מ. אמתניתין דלקמן (דף מ:) דכל מקום שיש מכר אין קנס קאמר לה רב יהודה:

ואם איתא זו דברי ר"מ ורבי יהודה מיבעי ליה. ואע"ג דרבי יונתן ור' יאשיה סבירא להו כר"מ בס"פ ד' מיתות (סנהדרין סו: ושם) לפי' ר"ת דפי' עד שיהיו שניהם שוין במיתה אחת ואפי' לפ"ה דמפרש בני עונשין מ"מ ר' יאשיה כר' מאיר סבירא ליה דלית ליה הא דדרשי רבנן לקמן (דף מ:) כאן נערה כו' דהא פטר קטנה מאורסה מ"מ לא קאמר זו דברי ר"מ ור' יאשיה דלא פריך הכא זו דברי ר"מ ורבי יהודה מיבעי ליה אלא משום דרבי יהודה בר פלוגתיה דר"מ והוי בכלל חכמים דפליגי עליה ולהכי אם איתא דלא פליג ה"ל למימר זו דברי ר"מ ור' יהודה אבל קשה דה"ל למימר הא מני ר' יאשיה היא ובממאנת סבר לה כר' יהודה:

וליתני קטנה קשיא. אע"ג דהוי תני קטנה לא הוה מצי למימר דלית לה קנס מ"מ תני נמי אילונית דה"א דוקא קטנה שיש לה ימים שתהיה נערה אין לה קנס ותימה לר"י אמאי לא משני דלהגן אורחיה קמ"ל דעד מתי הבת ממאנת עד שתביא שתי שערות:

החרשת והשוטה כו' אין להן טענת בתולים. פי' בקונטרס דאי הוה פקחת לטעון הוה טענה משאירסתני נאנסתי וקשה לר"י דהיכי טענינן לה הכי מספק לאפוקי ממונא כיון דאיהי לא טענה דחזקת גופה איתרעי דהוי שור שחוט לפניך אבל חזקת ממון לא איתרע ומיהו מביא ר"י ראיה לפי' הקונטרס דאמר בפ' המדיר (לקמן עו: ושם) לא הוגלד פי המכה המוציא מחבירו עליו הראיה ומפרש דאפי' לא יהיב טבח דמי על הטבח להביא ראיה שברשות המוכר נטרפה והא דמפרש רב אשי למתני' דהמדיר דהיו בה מומין ועודה בבית אביה על האב להביא ראיה רישא מנה לאבא בידך סיפא מנה לי בידך לא מטעם דברי ושמא ברי עדיף כדמשמע לפום ריהטא דא"כ הוה קשה דהיכי טענינן לה הכי אלא כדפי' התם בקונטרס רישא מנה לאבא בידך דלגבי האב לא מהני חזקת הגוף דבתו דהכתובה היא באירוסין של אב סיפא מנה לי בידך לגבי דידה מהני חזקת הגוף דידה וכן צריך לפרש דאי מטעם ברי קאמר התם אמאי קאמר דעודה בבית אביה על האב להביא ראיה דמשנתארסה נולדו בה מומין אמאי צריך להביא ראיה כיון דאמר ברי לי דבכל ענין משמע דצריך להביא ראיה אפילו אב אמר ברי לי ולר"י נראה לפרש הכא דאין להן טענת בתולים לפי שבחזקת מוכת עץ היא ואע"ג דכולהו נמי תבועי מתבען מ"מ שאר נשים יש להן טענת בתולים מדלא קאמרי שהן מוכת עץ אבל הנך חרשת ושוטה דלא מצי אמרי בחזקת מוכת עץ נשאות וכן נראה דברוב ספרים ל"ג לעיל בברייתא אלא החרשת והשוטה והאילונית יש להן קנס ותו לא ואין כתוב ברוב ספרים ויש להן טענת בתולים ולפר"י פריך שפיר דמדקאמר יש להן קנס אלמא לא חשבינן להו בחזקת מוכת עץ אבל לפי' הקונטרס מאי קפריך הכא נמי בחזקת בתולות חשבינן להו דהא אמרינן השתא [א] דמשנתארסה נאנסה ורשב"א [ב] הקשה לפר"י דאמאי לא משני הא דקתני אין להן טענת בתולים כר"מ דאמר בפ"ק (לעיל יג.) מוכת עץ בין הכיר בה בין לא הכיר בה מאתים והא דקתני יש להן טענת בתולים [ג] כרבנן דאמרי כתובתן מנה וכי תימא משום דקתני חרשת דומיא דאילונית הא ע"כ אילונית גופה לא הפסידה כתובתה לגמרי דהא רב ששת דמשני הא ר"ג הא ר' יהושע סבירא ליה כפ"ק (דף יא:) כנסה בחזקת בתולה ונמצאת בעולה יש לה כתובה מנה:

מסורת הש"ס

א) [לעיל כט.], ב) [שם], ג) [לעיל כט. וש"נ], ד) [שם], ה) חולין כו:, ו) יבמות יב: ב"ב קנו: נדה נב., ז) [לקמן מ:], ח) [לעיל יב:], ט) [ב"ב מא. גיטין לז:], י) נדה סד:, כ) [וע' תוס' ב"ב קנו. ותוס' חולין כו: ד"ה עד].

תוספות ישנים

א) [ולמאן דמפרש התם משום כאן נתלה וכלאן היה צ"ל דהכא איירי כגון שיצא קול שמשנתארסה נאנסה דאי לאו הכי הוי לן למימר כיון שבבית אביה נאנסה שמעיקרא נאנסה כדאמר התם גבי מומין. מ"י]:

ב) [נראה דלא מצי למימר הא ר"מ דהא ר"מ פליג בסיפא א"כ קמא בר פלוגתיה תנא אחרינא הוא. מ"י]:

ג) [ולכאורה נראה דלא מצי לשנויי קמייתא כרבנן דכתובתה מנה דמ"מ תקשי אמאי יש לה קנס כיון שהיא בחזקת מוכת עץ. מ"י]:

תורה אור השלם

א) פְּתַח פִּיךָ לְאִלֵּם אֶל דִּין כָּל בְּנֵי חֲלוֹף: [משלי לא, ח]

עין משפט נר מצוה

מד א מיי' פ"א מהל' נערה בתולה הל' יא יג סמג עשין כד טור אה"ע סי' קעז:

מה ב מיי' פי"א מהל' גירושין הל' ד סמג עשין נ טוש"ע אה"ע סי' קנה סעי' יג:

מו ג מיי' פי"א מהל' אישות הלכה ג ד ח סמג עשין מח טוש"ע שם סי' סז סעיף ה [וברב אלפס פ"א דמכילתין דף סו.]:

מז ד מיי' שם טוש"ע שם סעי' ו:

מח ה מיי' פ"ה מהל' איסורי ביאה הל' יט סמג לאוין קיא [וברב אלפס שם]:

תוספות רי"ד

תנו רבנן החרשת והשוטה והבוגרת ומוכ"ע אין להם קנס וא"ל טענת בתולים פי' להפסידן כתובתן חרשת ושוטה לא דאמרי' אי הוו פקחות לטעון הוו טענו כל חדא וחדא משאירסתני נאנסתי ומהימן בוגרת נמי לא שבתולי' כלין מאליהן האיילונית והסומא יש להן ט"ב פי' א) ודוקא דקא טעין טענת פ"פ אבל אי טעין טענת דמים ל"ל דבוגרת כלין בתוליה. אבל פתח נעול יש לה (והרב אומר היפך טענות דמים יש לה טענות פ"פ אין לה):

חשק שלמה על תוס' רי"ד

א) הך פי' קאי אבוגרת ונראה דצ"ל פי' ודווקא דקא טעין טענת דמים אבל אי טעין טענת פ"פ טענתו טענה דבוגרת כלו בתוליה וכו'.

ליקוטי רש"י

אתא לר"מ דאמר קטנה אין לה קנס. שהבא עליה אינו חייב קנס [לעיל כט.]. **ואיילונית** הואיל ואין לה שערות קטנה היא בימים שהיתה ראויה לנערות. **והא מקטנותה יצתה לבגר.** דנערות בסימנים תלוין וזו שאין לה סימנים חשבינן כל ימי קטנותה קטנה ובימי נערות בוגרת וזו וזו לר"מ אין לה קנס [יבמות פ.]. לפי שאין קנס אלא לנערה וזו שלא תביא שערות לעולם כל כ' שנה היא בחזקת קטנה ומשם ואילך בוגרת [לעיל לה:]. **עד שירבה שחור.** שיקיף אותו מקום בשער ובמסכת נדה (דף נב:) מפרש לא שירבה ממש אלא שיהו שתי שערות ארוכות שוכבות ונראה כמו שריבה השחור [חולין כו:]. שיהיו שם שערות הרבה [יבמות יב:]. במסכת נדה מפרש עד שירבו השערות ויהיו שוכבות ונראה כמו שהרבה השחור ולא גרס על הלבן [רשב"ם ב"ב קנו.]. ול"ג על הלבן כלומר שישחיר אותו מקום משערות הרבה [נדה נב. ועי' שיטמ"ק]. **בוגרת נותנין לה לילה הראשון.** ואפי' לב"ה דאמרי בהגיע זמנה לראות ארבעה הני מילי נערה דמשיגיעו ימי הנעורים הוי זמנה אבל בוגרת לילה הראשון ותו לא [נדה סד:].

לָהּ – **why** indeed **did he ask?** [28]

The Gemara answers:

מִשּׁוּם דְּאִית לֵיהּ לְמִירְמָא אַחֲרִיתֵי עִילָוֵיהּ – The student who cited the second Baraisa in the academy did so **because he had another** Baraisa **to contrast with it.**[29]

The Gemara presents the contradiction that the questioner had in mind:

הַחֵרֶשֶׁת וְהַשּׁוֹטָה וְהַבּוֹגֶרֶת וּמוּכַּת עֵץ – We learned in another Baraisa: **A DEAF-MUTE WOMAN, A DERANGED WOMAN, A *BOGERESS* AND [A WOMAN] INJURED BY A PIECE OF WOOD:**[30] אֵין לָהֶן טַעֲנַת בְּתוּלִים – **A CLAIM OF CONCERNING THEIR VIRGINITY CANNOT BE MADE AGAINST THEM.**[31] הַסּוּמָא וְאַיילוֹנִית יֵשׁ לָהֶן טַעֲנַת בְּתוּלִים – But **A BLIND [WOMAN] AND AN *AYLONIS,* A CLAIM CONCERNING THEIR VIRGINITY CAN BE MADE AGAINST THEM.** סוּמְכוּס אוֹמֵר מִשּׁוּם רַבִּי מֵאִיר – **SUMCHOS SAYS IN THE NAME OF R' MEIR:** סוּמָא – **A BLIND [WOMAN]** – אֵין לָהּ טַעֲנַת בְּתוּלִים – **A CLAIM CONCERNING HER VIRGINITY CANNOT BE MADE AGAINST HER.** Unlike the second Baraisa, this Baraisa rules that a deaf-mute and a deranged woman *cannot* be legally deprived of their *kesubah* award. — ? —

The Gemara resolves the problem:

אָמַר רַב שֵׁשֶׁת – **Rav Sheishess said:** לֹא קַשְׁיָא – **[This] is not difficult.** הָא רַבָּן גַּמְלִיאֵל – **This** Baraisa that shields the deaf-mute and deranged woman from forfeiture **is** the opinion of **Rabban Gamliel,**[32] וְהָא רַבִּי יְהוֹשֻׁעַ – **and this** Baraisa that exposes them to forfeiture **is** the opinion of **R' Yehoshua.**[33]

The Gemara challenges this answer:

אֵימַר דִּשְׁמַעַתְּ לֵיהּ לְרַבָּן גַּמְלִיאֵל – **Say that you heard Rabban Gamliel** stating that a woman is shielded from forfeiting her *kesubah* הֵיכָא דְּקָא טָעֲנָה אִיהִי – **when she** actually **claims** that she was violated. הֵיכָא דְּלֹא קָא טָעֲנָה אִיהִי – However, **where she does not** so **claim,** מִי שְׁמַעַתְּ לֵיהּ – **did you hear [Rabban Gamliel]** stating that she is similarly protected?[34]

The Gemara responds:

אִין – That **indeed** is Rabban Gamliel's position, כֵּיוָן דְּאָמַר רַבָּן גַּמְלִיאֵל מְהֵימְנָא – for **since Rabban Gamliel says** that **she is believed** when she does claim violation, כְּגוֹן זוּ ,,פְּתַח־פִּיךָ לְאִלֵּם" הוּא – **a case such as this** invokes the principle of ***"Open your mouth on behalf of the mute."***[35]

The Gemara discusses one of the rulings of the aforementioned Baraisa, which stated:

וְהַבּוֹגֶרֶת. . . אֵין לָהּ טַעֲנַת בְּתוּלִים – **A *BOGERESS*... A CLAIM CONCERNING HER VIRGINITY CANNOT BE MADE AGAINST HER.**[36]

The Gemara cites a conflicting opinion:

וְהָאָמַר רַב בּוֹגֶרֶת נוֹתְנִין לָהּ לַיְלָה הָרִאשׁוֹן – **But Rav has stated:** – **We give a** virgin ***bogeress*** **the entire first night.**[37] The Baraisa's ruling is ostensibly predicated on the assumption that a virgin *bogeress* lacks virginal blood, whereas Rav's ruling presumes that she has it. — ? —

NOTES

28. [Literally: and the one who involved it, why did he involve it?] Did he not himself realize that one Baraisa was authored by R' Meir and the other by the Rabbis, so that there is no contradiction? See *Rashi* with *Shitah Mekubetzes.*

29. I.e. the student knew that the second Baraisa was not really a contradiction to the first one. Rather, his entire purpose in citing the second Baraisa was to contrast its "virginity claim" ruling in the cases of deaf-mute and deranged women with a parallel ruling in a third Baraisa, as the Gemara now explains (see *Rashi* with *Shitah Mekubetzes*).

In the text of many Rishonim only the phrase יֵשׁ לָהֶן קְנָס, *they have [a right to the] fine,* appears. See *Ramban, Shitah Mekubetzes* et al. for how they understand our *sugya.*

30. See 11a note 29.

31. The hymen of a *bogeress* disintegrates by itself (*Rashi*). Hence, the absence of the signs of virginity (see note 25 above) is not probative.

[The Mishnah above (11a) cites a dispute between R' Meir and the Sages regarding whether a woman whose hymen was ruptured by a piece of wood, rather than through premarital relations, is entitled to the two hundred *zuz* of a virgin's *kesubah* or to the one hundred *zuz* of a non-virgin's *kesubah.* All agree, however, that even if the groom was unaware of her ruptured hymen at the time of the marriage, he cannot later claim that the marriage was predicated on a mistaken assumption [that her hymen was whole] and sue to deprive her of her *kesubah* (see Gemara ad loc.); this is because she did not have premarital relations. The reasons for the other women's immunity to *kesubah* forfeiture will be explained in the following Gemara.]

32. Rabban Gamliel ruled in the Mishnah above (12b) that if a husband finds that his wife is not a virgin and she claims that she was violated after *kiddushin,* she is believed and does not forfeit her *kesubah.* Hence, Rabban Gamliel would also hold that a bride who is deaf or deranged cannot lose her *kesubah* on account of a lost-virginity claim, for we say that had she been mentally competent, she might have claimed that she was violated after *kiddushin* and she would have been believed (*Rashi;* cf. *Tosafos*).

33. R' Yehoshua ruled in the Mishnah (ibid.) that a bride is *not* believed to say that she was violated after *kiddushin,* and so her husband may divorce her without paying her *kesubah* award. Hence, R' Yehoshua would hold that a bride who is deaf or deranged *can* lose her *kesubah* on account of a lost-virginity claim, for even if she were mentally competent to claim that she was violated after *kiddushin,* she would not be believed (*Rashi*).

34. [The dispute between Rabban Gamliel and R' Yehoshua in the aforementioned Mishnah involves whether we believe the wife's version of how her virginity was lost. In our case, however, the wife does not offer any explanation for her condition. Perhaps here Rabban Gamliel agrees with R' Yehoshua, who holds that we must entertain the possibility that she cohabited prior to *kiddushin* and thus is not entitled to her *kesubah.*]

35. *Proverbs* 31:8. Scripture charges people to speak up on behalf of anyone who cannot do so for himself — either because he is mentally disabled, as in our cases of the deaf-mute and deranged brides, or because he is legally disabled by his ignorance of the law or the circumstances of a case. [This verse is the source for a court's advancing certain claims on behalf of orphans (who are not knowledgeable about their father's business affairs) and other such cases; see *Bava Basra* 23a and 41a; see also *Rashi* below, 87a ד״ה מנכסים; see *Chazon Ish, Even HaEzer* 82:21, for parameters of this law.]

36. [The hymen of a *bogeress* disintegrates naturally when she matures, and so it is presumed that her virginal blood was discharged as well. Hence, the absence of bleeding during the couple's initial cohabitation does not prove that the bride had premarital relations; see note 31 above.]

37. I.e. if one's bride is a virgin *bogeress,* the couple may cohabit repeatedly the entire first night even though she is discharging blood. For since she is a virgin, we presume that any bleeding she experiences throughout the night is דַּם בְּתוּלִים, *blood of virginity,* rather than דַּם נִדָּה, *blood of menstruation* [which would render her a *niddah,* who is prohibited to her husband].

Rav evidently maintains that a *bogeress* has blood of virginity, for if not we must conclude that she is menstruating and prohibit her from cohabiting a second time (see, however, *Hagahos Poras Yosef*). And since a virgin *bogeress* does have blood of virginity, the absence of blood during the initial marital cohabitation would indicate that the bride had premarital relations, and so she should forfeit her *kesubah* award (*Rashi*).

עריות ממש שניות מדברי סופרים כיון דמדאורייתא חזיא ליה אמאי אין להן קנס אלא עריות א) חייבי מיתות בית דין שניות חייבי כריתות אבל חייבי לאוין יש להן קנס ומני ב) שמעון התימני היא איכא דאמרי עריות חייבי מיתות ב"ד וחייבי כריתות שניות חייבי לאוין מני ר"ש בן מנסיא היא: הממאנת אין לה לא קנס ולא פיתוי הא קטנה בעלמא אית לה מני רבנן היא דאמרי ג) קטנה יש לה קנס אימא סיפא איילונית אין לה לא קנס ולא פיתוי אתא לר"מ דאמר ד) קטנה אין לה קנס והא מקטנותה יצתה לבגר רישא רבנן וסיפא ר"מ וכ"ת כולה ר"מ היא ובממאנת סבר לה כרבי יהודה ומי סבר לה והתניא ה) עד מתי הבת ממאנת עד שתביא שתי שערות דברי ר"מ ו) ר' יהודה אומר עד שירבה שחור על הלבן אלא ר' יהודה היא ובקטנה סבר לה כר"מ ומי סבר לה והאמר רב יהודה אמר רב ז) זו דברי ר"מ ואם איתא זו דברי ר"מ ור' יהודה מיבעי ליה האי תנא סבר לה כר"מ בחדא ופליג עליה בחדא רפרם אמר מאי ממאנת הראויה למאן וליתני קטנה קשיא: איילונית אין לה לא קנס ולא פיתוי ורמינהי החרשת והשוטה והאיילונית יש להן קנס ויש להן טענת בתולים והא מאי רומיא הא ר"מ הא רבנן ודקארי לה מאי קארי לה משום דאית ליה למירמא אחריתי עילויה ח) החרשת והשוטה והבוגרת ומוכת עץ אין להן טענת בתולים ט) הסומא ואיילונית יש להן טענת בתולים סומכוס אומר משום ר"מ סומא אין לה טענת בתולים אמר רב ששת לא קשיא הא רבן גמליאל והא ר' יהושע אימר דשמעת ליה לרבן גמליאל היכא דקא טענה איהי היכא דלא קא טענה איהי מי שמעת ליה כיון דאמר ר"ג מהימנא כגון זו א) פתח פיך לאלם הוא: והבוגרת אין לה טענת בתולים: והאמר רב י) בוגרת נותנין לה לילה הראשון

אי

עריות ממש. המפורש בלאחרי מות והן בכריתות: **שניות.** שגזרו חכמים על שניות להן להרחיק מן העבירה כגון אם אמו ואם אביו ושאר עריות השנויות בפרק ב' דיבמות (דף כא.): **כיון דשניות חזיין ליה מדאורייתא.** קרינן ביה ולו תהיה לאשה: **אמאי אין לה קנס.** בשלמא בעריות איכא למימר כשמעון התימני דלית ליה נערה הנערה אלא שניות קשיא: **שמעון התימני.** בריש פירקין דאמר אשה שיש בה הויה: **ר"ש בן מנסיא.** דאמר אשה הראויה לקיימה: **רבנן היא.** דפליגי אדר"מ בריש פירקין: **ובממאנת סבר לה כר' יהודה.** דאמר נערה ממאנת והכי תדוק מינה נערה ממאנת אין לה קנס הא נערה בעלמא יש לה קנס: **עד שתביא שתי שערות.** ומשהביאה אינה ממאנת ואפילו לא בעל לאחר מיכן: **רבי יהודה אומר.** אם לא בעל לאחר שגדלה ממאנת: **עד שירבה שחור על הלבן.** וכולה מפרש שתי שערות שוכבות ונראה כמו שירבה השחור: **אלא ר' יהודה היא.** ובממאנת נערה אשמעינן דאין לה קנס ולא תדוק הא קטנה יש לה קנס וגבי איילונית דתנא נמי אין לה קנס משום דבקטנה סבר כר"מ או מקטנותה יצאת לבגר: **זו דברי כו'.** לקמן בפרקין (דף מ:) **סבר לה כר' מאיר.** דקטנה אין לה קנס משום הכי אין קנס באיילונית: **ופליג עליה.** בממאנת ואמר עד שירבה השחור וכי תנא הממאנת אין לה קנס הא הראויה למאן יש לה קנס בנערה קאמר: **מאי ממאנת הראויה למאן.** כלומר כל קטנה קאמר וכולה ר"מ היא: **ויש להן טענת בתולים.** להפסידה כתובה: **הא ר"מ.** דאמר קטנה אין לה קנס ואיילונית מקטנותה יצאה לבגר: **ודקארי לה מאי קארי לה.** מי שהשיב תשובה זו בבית המדרש מה עלתה על רוחו ולא סבירא ליה דאיכא לאוקמינהו כר"מ ורבנן: **משום דאית ליה למירמא אחריתא עליה.** לא הביאה לבית המדרש אלא לפי שיש להשיב אחרת על זו חרשת ושוטה אחרשת ושוטה: **בוגרת.** בתולים כלים מאליהן: **הא רבן גמליאל.** דאמר בפ"ק (דף יב:) היא אומרת משארסתני נאנסתי נאמנת הכא נמי אין לה טענת בתולים להפסידה כתובה דאמרינן אי הוה פקחת אי הוה טוענת משארסתני נאנסתי ומהימנא: **הא רבי יהושע.** דאמר לא מפיה אנו חיין הכא יש לה טענת בתולים דאי נמי הוה טוענת קמן לא מהימנינן לה: **נותנין לה לילה הראשון.** ובועל כמה בעילות ותולין כל דמים של אותו הלילה בדם בתולים אלמא אית לה דם בתולים לבוגרת דאי לא לא הוה בעי למיתב לה אלא בעילת מצוה וכיון דאית לה בתולים היכא דבעל ולא מצא דם תפסיד כתובתה דהא כנסה בחזקת בתולה ומצאה בעולה: ה"ג

[אבל חייבי לאוין יש להן קנס ומני שמעון התימני היא. לא הוה מצי למימר מני רבי נחוניא היא דלדידיה לא הוה קרי להו שניות שהרי משוה חייבי כריתות לחייבי מיתות ב"ד והא דלא קאמר הא מני רבי עקיבא ועריות חייבי מיתות ושניות חייבי כריתות וחייבי לאוין אלא דניחא ליה לאוקמי אפי' כרבנן דאמרי קידושין תופסין ועוד משום דקאמר בלישנא קמא מני שמעון התימני היא קאמר נמי בהאי לישנא דאמרי מני רבי שמעון בן מנסיא היא דהוי בר פלוגתיה דשמעון התימני]:

עד שירבה השחור כו'. אית דלא גרסי על הלבן משום דאמרינן בפרק בא סימן (נדה דף נב. ושם) לא שירבה ממש אלא כדי שיהו שתי שערות שוכבות ונראה כמו שירבה שחור ועל הלבן משמע יותר מן הלבן ור"ת פירש על הלבן שהשערות סמוך לבשר הם שחורים ובראשם לבנים: **זו** דברי ר"מ. אמתניתין דלקמן (דף מ:) דכל מקום שיש מכר אין קנס קאמר לה רב יהודה:

ואם איתא זו דברי ר"מ ורבי יהודה מיבעי ליה. ואע"ג דרבי יונתן ור' יאשיה סבירא להו כר"מ בפ"ב [ד'] מיתות (סנהדרין סו: ושם) לפי' ר"ת דפי' עד שיהיו שניהם שוין במיתה אחת ואפי' לפ"ה דמפרש בני עונשין מ"מ ר' יאשיה כר' מאיר סבירא ליה דלית ליה הא דדרשי רבנן לקמן (דף מ:) כאן נערה כו' דהא פטר קטנה מאורסה מ"מ לא קאמר זו דברי ר"מ ור' יאשיה דלא פריך הכא זו דברי ר"מ ורבי יהודה מיבעי ליה אלא משום דרבי יהודה בר פלוגתיה דר"מ והוי בכלל חכמים דפליגי עליה ולהכי אם איתא דלא פליג ה"ל למימר זו דברי ר"מ ור' יהודה אבל קשה דה"ל למימר הא מני ר' יאשיה היא ובממאנת סבר לה כר' יהודה:

וליתני קטנה קשיא. אע"ג דהוי תני קטנה דאין לה קנס מ"מ תני נמי איילונית דה"א דוקא קטנה שיש לה נערות אין לה קנס ותימה לר"י אמאי לא משני לאשמועינן קמ"ל דעד מתי הבת ממאנת עד שתביא שתי שערות:

החרשת והשוטה כו' אין להן טענת בתולים. פי' בקונטרס דאי הוה פקחת לטעון הוה טוענה משארסתני נאנסתי וקשה לר"י דהיכי טענינן לה הכי מספק לאפוקי ממונא כיון דאיהי לא טענה דחזקת גופה איתרעי דהוי שור שחוט לפניך אבל חזקת ממון לא איתרע ומיהו מביא ר"י ראיה לפי' הקונטרס דאמר בפ' המדיר (לקמן עו: ושם) לא הוגלד פי המכה המוציא מחבירו עליו הראיה ומפרש דאפי' לא יהיב טבח דמי על הטבח להביא ראיה שברשות המוכר נטרפה והא דמפרש רב אשי למתני' דהמדיר דהיו בה מומין ועודה בבית אביה על האב להביא ראיה רישא מנה לאבא בידך סיפא מנה לי בידך לא מטעם דברי ושמא ברי עדיף כדמשמע לפום ריהטא דא"כ הוה קשה דהיכי טענינן לה הכי אלא כדפי' התם בקונטרס רישא מנה לאבא בידך דלגבי האב לא מהני חזקת הגוף דבתו דהכתובה היא באירוסין של אב סיפא מנה לי בידך דלגבי דידה מהני חזקת הגוף דידה וכן צריך לפרש דלאי מטעם ברי קאמר התם אמאי קאמר דעודה בבית אביה על האב להביא ראיה דמשנתארסה נולדו בה מומין אמאי צריך להביא ראיה כיון דאמר ברי לי דבכל ענין משמע דצריך להביא ראיה אפילו אב אמר ברי לי ולר"י נראה לפרש הכא דאין להן טענת בתולים לפי שבחזקת מוכת עץ היא ואע"ג דכולהו נמי חבוטי מחבטן מ"מ שאר נשים יש להן טענת בתולים מדלא קאמרי שהן מוכת עץ אבל הנך חרשת ושוטה דלא מצי אמרי בחזקת מוכת עץ נשאות וכן נראה דברוב ספרים ל"ג לעיל בברייתא אלא החרשת והשוטה והאילונית יש להן קנס ותו לא ואין כתוב ברוב ספרים ויש להן טענת בתולים ולפר"י פריך שפיר דמדקאמר יש להן קנס אלמא לא חשבינן להו בחזקת מוכת עץ אבל לפי' הקונטרס מאי קפריך הכא נמי בחזקת בתולות חשבינן להו דהא אמרינן השתא א) דמשנתארסה נאנסה ורשב"א ב) הקשה לפר"י דלמאי לא משני הא דקתני אין להן טענת בתולים כר"מ דאמר בפ"ק (לעיל יא.) מוכת עץ בין לא הכיר בה מאתים והא דקתני יש להן טענת בתולים ג) כרבנן דאמרי כתובתן מנה וכי תימא משום דקתני חרשת דומיא דאיילונית הא ע"כ איילונית גופה לא הפסידה כתובתה לגמרי דהא רב ששת דמשני הא ר"ג הא ר' יהושע סבירא ליה בפ"ק (דף יא:) כנסה בחזקת בתולה ומצאת בעולה יש לה כתובה מנה:

מסורת הש"ס

א) [לעיל כט.], ב) [שם], ג) [שם], ד) [לעיל כט. וש"נ], ה) חולין כו:, ו) יבמות יב: ב"ב קנו:, ז) נדה נב., ח) [לקמן מ:], ט) [לעיל יב:], ט) [ב"ב מא. גיטין לז.], י) נדה סד., כ) [וע' תוס' ב"ב קנו. ותוס' חולין כו: ד"ה עד].

תוספות ישנים

א) ולמאן דמפרש התם משום כאן נמצא וכאן היה צ"ל דהכא איירי כגון שיצא קול שמשנתארסה נאנסה דלאו לא הכי הוי לן למימר כיון שבבית אביה נאנסה שמעיקרא נאנסה כדאמר התם גבי מומין. מ"י:

ב) נראה דלא מצי למימר הא ר"מ דהא ר"מ פליג בסיפא א"כ מנא קמא בר פלוגתיה מנא אחריתא הוא. מ"י:

ג) ולכאורה נראה דלא מצי לשנויי קמייתא כרבנן דכתובתה מנה דמ"מ מקשי אמאי יש לה קנס כיון שהיא בחזקת מוכת עץ. מ"י:

תורה אור השלם

א) פְּתַח פִּיךָ לְאִלֵּם אֶל דִּין כָּל בְּנֵי חֲלוֹף: [משלי לא, ח]

עין משפט נר מצוה

מד א מיי' פ"א מהל' נערה בתולה הל' יא יג סמג עשין כד טור אה"ע סי' קעז:

מה ב מיי' פי"א מהל' גירושין הל' ז סמג עשין נ טוש"ע אה"ע סי' קנה סעי' יג:

מו ג מיי' פ"א מהל' אישות הלכה ג ד ח סמג עשין מח טוש"ע שם סי' סח סעיף ה [וברב אלפס פ"ב דמכילתין דף טו.]:

מז ד מיי' שם טוש"ע שם סעי' ו:

מח ה מיי' פ"ה מהל' איסורי ביאה הל' יג סמג לאוין קיא [וברב אלפס שם]:

תוספות רי"ד

תנו רבנן החרשת והשוטה והבוגרת ומוכ"ע אין להם קנס וא"ל טענת בתולים פי' להפסידן כתובתן חרשת ושוטה לא דאמרי' אי הוו פקחות לטענן הוו טוענו כל חדא וחדא משאירסתני נאנסתי ומהימן בוגרת נמי לא שבתולי' כלין מאליהן האיילונית והסומא יש להן טענת פ"פ א) דוקא דקא טעין טענת פ"פ אבל אי טעין טענת דמים ל"ל דבוגרת כלין בתוליה. אבל פתח נעול אי טעין ליה (והרב אומר היפך טענות דמים יש לה טענות פ"פ אין לה:)

חשק שלמה על תוס' רי"ד

א) כך פי' קאי אבוגרת ונראה דל"ל פי' ודווקא דקא טעין טענת דמים אבל אי טעין טענת פ"פ טענתו טענה דבוגרת כלו בתוליה וכו'.

ליקוטי רש"י

אתא לר"מ דאמר קטנה אין לה קנס. שהבא עליה אינו חייב קנס [לעיל כט.]. **ואיילונית** הואיל ואין לה שערות קטנה היא בימים שהיתה ראויה לנערות. **והא מקטנותה יצתה לבגר.** דנערות בסימנים תלוין וזו שאין לה סימנים חשבינן כל ימי קטנותה קטנה ובימי נערות בוגרת וזו חזו לר"מ אין לה קנס [יבמות פ.]. לפי שאין קנס אלא לנערה וזו שלא תביא שערות לעולם כל כ' שנה היא בחזקת קטנה ומשם ואילך בוגרת [לעיל לה:]. **עד שירבה שחור.** שיוקף אותו מקום בשער ובמסכת נדה (דף נב:) מפרש לא שירבה ממש אלא שיהו שתי שערות ארוכות שוכבות ונראה כמו שריבה השחור [חולין כו:]. שיהיו שם שערות הרבה [יבמות יב:]. במסכת נדה מפרש עד שירבו השערות ויהיו שוכבות ונראה כמו שהרבה השחור ולא גרס על הלבן [רשב"ם ב"ב קנו.]. ול"נ על הלבן כלומר שישחיר אותו מקום משערות הרבה [נדה נב. ועי' שיטמ"ק]. **בוגרת נותנין לה לילה הראשון.** ואפי' לב"ש דאמרי בהגיע זמנה לראות ארבעה הני מילי נערה דמשייעיה ימי הנעורים הוי זמנה אבל בוגרת לילה ראשון אין לא [נדה סד:].

MEIR. רַבִּי יְהוּדָה אוֹמֵר – But R' YEHUDAH SAYS: עַד שֶׁיִּרְבֶּה שָׁחוֹר עַל הַלָּבָן – She may declare her refusal UNTIL THE BLACK appears ABUNDANT UPON THE WHITE.[16] The Baraisa expressly indicates that R' Meir disagrees with R' Yehudah. – ? –

The Gemara offers another explanation of the authorship of the Baraisa:

אֶלָּא רַבִּי יְהוּדָה הִיא – **Rather,** say that **[the Baraisa] is** following **R' Yehudah,** who holds that a *naarah* may declare her refusal,[17] וּבִקְטַנָּה סָבַר לָהּ כְּרַבִּי מֵאִיר – **and with regard to** the fine of **a minor girl [R' Yehudah] holds like R' Meir** – i.e. that she is not entitled to the fine.[18]

The Gemara challenges this approach as well:

וּמִי סָבַר לָהּ – **And does [R' Yehudah]** really **hold [that view]?**[19] וְהָאָמַר רַב יְהוּדָה אָמַר רַב – **But** the Amora **Rav Yehudah has said in the name of Rav:**[20] זוֹ דִּבְרֵי רַבִּי מֵאִיר – **This** Mishnah, which states that a minor girl is not entitled to a fine, **is the opinion of R' Meir** [but the Sages maintain that a minor girl *is* entitled to a fine]. וְאִם אִיתָא – **And if it were true** that R' Yehudah also holds that a minor girl is not entitled to a fine, זוֹ דִּבְרֵי רַבִּי מֵאִיר וְרַבִּי יְהוּדָה מִיבָּעֵי לֵיהּ – **[Rav] should have** said: **"This** Mishnah **is the opinion of R' Meir *and* R' Yehudah."** The omission indicates that R' Yehudah, in fact, disagrees with R' Meir on this issue.[21] – ? –

Having successfully demonstrated that the Baraisa could not have been authored by either R' Meir or R' Yehudah, the Gemara concludes:

הַאי תַּנָּא סָבַר לָהּ כְּרַבִּי מֵאִיר בַּחֲדָא – **This Tanna** who authored the Baraisa is neither R' Meir nor R' Yehudah; rather, he is a third Tanna, who **holds like R' Meir on one** issue[22] וּפְלִיג עֲלֵיהּ בַּחֲדָא – **and disagrees with him on one** other.[23]

The Gemara suggests an alternative answer:

רָפְרָם אָמַר – **Rafram said:** מַאי מְמָאֶנֶת – **What** does the Baraisa mean by **"[a girl] who declares her refusal"?** הָרְאוּיָה לְמָאֵן – It means **[a girl] who is fit to declare her refusal.**[24]

The Gemara retorts:

וְלִיתְנֵי קְטַנָּה – **But** if that is the intent, **let [the Baraisa] state** simply **"a minor girl,"** rather than the somewhat ambiguous "a girl who is fit to declare her refusal"!? – ? –

The Gemara concedes:

קַשְׁיָא – **[This]** is indeed **difficult.**

The Gemara turns to the Baraisa's third statement, and notes a contradiction:

אַיְילוֹנִית אֵין לָהּ לֹא קְנָס וְלֹא פִּיתּוּי – The Baraisa stated: AN *AYLONIS* HAS NO right to the FINE for violation AND the fine for SEDUCTION. וּרְמִינְהִי – **But contrast this** with the following Baraisa: הַחֵרֶשֶׁת וְהַשּׁוֹטָה וְהָאַיְילוֹנִית – A DEAF-MUTE WOMAN, A DERANGED WOMAN AND AN *AYLONIS* יֵשׁ לָהֶן קְנָס – HAVE a right to THE FINE for violation, וְיֵשׁ לָהֶן טַעֲנַת בְּתוּלִים – AND can HAVE against them A CLAIM OF lost VIRGINITY.[25] – ? –

The Gemara retorts:

וְהָא מַאי רוּמְיָא – **But what contradiction does this pose?** The answer is obvious: הָא רַבִּי מֵאִיר – **This** Baraisa that disqualifies an *aylonis* from receiving the fine **is** the opinion of **R' Meir,**[26] הָא רַבָּנָן – whereas **this** Baraisa that awards it to her **is** the opinion of **the Rabbis.**[27]

The Gemara concedes that the answer is obvious, and asks:

וּדְקָאָרֵי לָהּ – **And the one who asked [this question],** מַאי קָאָרֵי

NOTES

marries an orphan girl in a Rabbinically sanctioned marriage, their marriage attains Biblical status when they cohabit after she attains adulthood. For since at that point she is eligible to effect Biblical *kiddushin* on her own, we presume that they cohabit with the intent of doing so. (בִּיאָה, *cohabitation* is one of the methods that can effect *kiddushin* – see *Kiddushin* 2a and below, 73a.) Hence, it would be superfluous and misleading for R' Meir to say that a girl cannot declare her refusal after she developed two pubic hairs *and* cohabited with her husband, for in that case the marriage has attained Biblical stature and only a Rabbinically sanctioned marriage can be annulled through a declaration of refusal. *Rashi* thus remarks that R' Meir's ruling applies even where they did not cohabit after she reached adulthood, in which case their marriage remains only Rabbinically sanctioned; nevertheless, R' Meir rules that once she attains adulthood, she cannot declare her refusal to annul the marriage.]

16. If she did not cohabit with her husband after attaining adulthood [so that her marriage remains only Rabbinically sanctioned], she may declare her refusal and annul her marriage even after she develops two pubic hairs and reaches adulthood (*Rashi*).

"The black" refers to her pubic hair and "the white" to her skin. The Gemara (*Niddah* 52a) explains that this does not mean that she must actually develop hairs over most of the pubic area, but that the two hairs must be long enough so that when they lie flat on the skin, they appear to blacken most of the pubic area (see *Rashi* and *Tosafos*).

17. And so the Baraisa's disqualification of a girl that declares refusal from receiving the fines does not imply that ordinary minors are entitled to them; see note 13 above (*Rashi*).

18. And, accordingly, the Baraisa rules that an *aylonis,* who passes directly from minority into *bagrus,* is not entitled to the fine; see note 11 above (*Rashi*).

19. That a minor girl is not entitled to these fines.

20. With reference to the Mishnah below, 40b (*Rashi*).

21. *Tosafos* ד״ה ואם איתא note that the question is precisely predicated on R' Yehudah's position, for he is always R' Meir's disputant and would normally be included in the "Sages" who argue with R' Meir in the Mishnah.

22. He concurs with R' Meir that a minor is not entitled to the fines, and therefore rules that an *aylonis* does not receive them (*Rashi*).

23. In contradistinction to R' Meir, this Tanna holds that even a *naarah* may declare her refusal – i.e. until "the black [appears] abundant upon the white." Consequently, when the Baraisa rules that a girl who declares her refusal is not entitled to the fine, which implies that other girls of her age *are* entitled, it refers to a *naarah* (*Rashi;* see *Ritva*).

Rambam rules that a minor is entitled to the fine, but an *aylonis* is not (see *Hil. Naarah Besulah* 1:8,9). The commentators seek to explain *Rambam's* ruling and how he understands our *sugya;* see *Maharik* 138, *Kesef Mishneh* to ibid. 1:9, *Yam Shel Shlomo* 3:7, *Or Same'ach* et al.

24. I.e. it does not mean a girl who actually declared her refusal, which would carry the implication that other girls of her age [who according to R' Meir would be ordinary minors] *are* entitled to the fine. Rather, it means a girl who is fit to declare her refusal – which is tantamount to saying *any* minor, inasmuch as only minors are fit to declare a refusal. Accordingly, in this clause the Baraisa is indeed stating that a minor is not entitled to the fine, and the entire Baraisa was authored by R' Meir (*Rashi*).

25. If one marries any of these three categories of women and discovers, after their first cohabitation, that she is not a virgin, he may sue to divorce her without paying her *kesubah,* as is the case with other brides whose husbands find them to be nonvirgins (see *Rashi*). [One ascertains that his bride is not a virgin by the absence of bleeding during their initial intercourse or by the discovery of an "open entrance" – i.e. by the failure to experience the tightness one normally feels when cohabiting with a woman whose hymen was not previously perforated through cohabitation. See above, 9a ff.]

In any case, the second Baraisa's ruling (that an *aylonis* is entitled to the fine for violation) contradicts the first Baraisa's ruling (that an *aylonis* is not entitled to it).

26. Who maintains that only a *naarah* is entitled to the fine for violation, so that an *aylonis,* who goes from minority to *bagrus* without ever passing through the *naarus* stage, is never eligible to receive the fine (*Rashi*).

27. Who maintain that a minor girl also is entitled to the fine for violation, so that as long as an *aylonis* is considered a minor (i.e. until the age of twenty), she is entitled to the fine.

עריות ממש שניות מדברי סופרים כיון דמדאורייתא חזיא ליה אמאי אין להן קנס אלא עריות [א]חייבי מיתות בית דין שניות חייבי כריתות אבל חייבי לאוין יש להן קנס ומני [ה]שמעון התימני היא איכא דאמרי עריות חייבי מיתות ב"ד וחייבי כריתות שניות חייבי לאוין מני [ו]ר"ש בן מנסיא היא: הממאנת אין לה לא קנס ולא פיתוי הא קטנה בעלמא אית לה מני רבנן היא דאמרי [ג]קטנה יש לה קנס אימא סיפא איילונית אין לה לא קנס ולא פיתוי אתא לר"מ דאמר [ד]קטנה אין לה קנס והא מקטנותה יצתה לבגר רישא רבנן וסיפא ר"מ וכ"ת כולה ר"מ היא ובממאנת סבר לה כרבי יהודה ומי סבר לה והתניא [ה]עד מתי הבת ממאנת [ב]עד שתביא שתי שערות דברי ר"מ [ו]ר' יהודה אומר עד שירבה שחור על הלבן אלא ר' יהודה היא ובקטנה סבר לה כר"מ ומי סבר לה והאמר רב יהודה אמר רב [ז]זו דברי ר"מ ואם איתא זו דברי ר"מ ור' יהודה מיבעי ליה האי תנא סבר לה כר"מ בחדא ופליג עליה בחדא רפרם אמר מאי ממאנת הראויה למאן וליתני קטנה קשיא: איילונית אין לה לא קנס ולא פיתוי ורמינהי החרשת והשוטה והאיילונית יש להן קנס ויש להן טענת בתולים והא מאי רומיא הא ר"מ הא רבנן ודקארי לה מאי קארי לה משום דאית ליה למירמא אחריתי עילויה [ג]החרשת והשוטה והבוגרת ומוכת עץ אין להן טענת בתולים [ד]הסומא ואיילונית יש להן טענת בתולים סומכוס אומר משום ר"מ סומא אין לה טענת בתולים אמר רב ששת לא קשיא הא [ח]רבן גמליאל והא ר' יהושע אימר דשמעת ליה לרבן גמליאל היכא דקא טוענה איהי היכא דלא קא טוענה איהי מי שמעת ליה אין כיון דאמר ר"ג מהימנא [ט]כגון זו [א]פתח פיך לאלם הוא: והבוגרת אין לה טענת בתולים: והאמר רב [י]ה[ה]בוגרת נותנין לה לילה הראשון

אי

עריות ממש. המפורש באחרי מות והן בכריתות: **שניות.** שגזרו חכמים על שניות להן להרחיק מן העבירה כגון אם אמו ואם אביו ושאר עריות השנויות בפרק ב' דיבמות (דף כא.): **כיון דשניות חזיין ליה מדאורייתא.** קרינן ביה ולו תהיה לאשה: **אמאי אין לה קנס.** בשלמא בעריות איכא למימר כשמעון התימני דלית ליה נערה נערה הנערה אלא שניות קשיא: **שמעון התימני.** בריש פירקין דאמר אשה שיש בה הויה: **ר"ש בן מנסיא.** דאמר אשה הראויה לקיימה: **רבנן היא.** דפליגי אדר"מ בריש פירקין: **ובממאנת סבר לה כר' יהודה.** דאמר נערה ממאנת והכי מדוק מינה נערה ממאנת אין לה קנס הא נערה בעלמא יש לה קנס: **עד שתביא שתי שערות.** ומשהביאה אינה ממאנת ואפילו לא בעל לאחר מיכן: **רבי יהודה אומר.** אם לא בעל לאחר שגדלה ממאנת: **עד שירבה שחור על הלבן.** ובגמ' מפרש שתי שערות שוכבות ונראה כמו שירבה השחור: **אלא ר' יהודה היא.** ובממאנת נערה אשמעינן דאין לה קנס ולא תדוק הא קטנה יש לה קנס וגבי איילונית דתנא נמי אין לה קנס משום דבקטנה סבר כר"מ וזו מקטנותה יצאה לבגר: **זו דברי כו'.** לקמן בפרקין (דף מ:): **סבר לה כר' מאיר.** דקטנה אין לה קנס משום הכי אין קנס באיילונית: **ופליג עליה.** בממאנת ואמר עד שירבה השחור וכי תנא הממאנת אין לה קנס הא הראויה למאן יש לה קנס בנערה קאמר: **מאי ממאנת הראויה למאן.** כלומר כל קטנה קאמר וכולה ר"מ היא: **ויש להן טענת בתולים.** להפסידה כתובה: **הא ר"מ.** דאמר קטנה אין לה קנס ואיילונית מקטנותה יצתה לבגר: **ודקארי לה מאי קארי לה.** מי שהשיב תשובה זו בבית המדרש מה עלתה על רוחו ולא סבירא ליה דהיכא לאוקמינהו כר"מ ורבנן: **משום דאית ליה למירמא אחריתא עליה.** לא הביאה לבית המדרש אלא לפי שיש להשיב משנה אחרת על זו חרשת ושוטה אחרשת ושוטה: **בוגרת.** בתוליה כלים מאליהן: **הא רבן גמליאל.** דאמר בפ"ק (דף יב:) היא אומרת משאירסתני נאנסתי נאמנת הכא נמי אין לה טענת בתולים להפסידה כתובתה דאמרינן אי הוה פקחת לטעון הוה טענה משאירסתני נאנסתי ומהימנא: **הא רבי יהושע.** דאמר לא מפיה אנו חיין הכא יש לה טענת בתולים דאי נמי הוה טענה קמן לא מהימנינן לה: **נותנין לה לילה הראשון.** ובועל כמה בעילות ותלינן כל דמים של אותו הלילה בדם בתולים אלמא אית לה דם בתולים לבוגרת דאי לא לא הוה בעי למיתב לה אלא בעילת מצוה וכיון דאית לה בתולים היכא דבעל ולא מצא דם תפסיד כתובתה דהא כנסה בחזקת בתולה ומצאה בעולה:

ה"ג

אבל חייבי לאוין יש להן קנס ומני שמעון התימני היא. לא הוה מצי למימר מני רבי נחוניא היא דלדידיה לא הוה קרי להן שניות שהרי משוה חייבי כריתות לחייבי מיתות ב"ד והא דלא קאמר הא מני רבי עקיבא ועריות חייבי מיתות ושניות חייבי כריתות וחייבי לאוין אלא דניחא ליה לאוקמי אפי' כרבנן דאמרי קידושין תופסין ועוד משום דקאמר בלישנא קמא מני שמעון התימני היא קאמר נמי בהאי לישנא דלאמר מני רבי שמעון בן מנסיא היא דהוי בר פלוגתיה דשמעון התימני:

עד שירבה השחור כו'. אית דלא גרסי על הלבן משום דאמרינן בפרק בא סימן (נדה דף נב. ושם) לא שירבה ממש אלא כדי שיהו שתי שערות שוכבות ונראה כמו שירבה שחור ועל הלבן משמע יותר מן הלבן ור"ח פירש על הלבן שהשערות סמוך לבשר הם שחורים ובראשם לבנים[ז]: **זו דברי ר"מ.** ממתניתין דלקמן (דף מ:) דכל מקום שיש מכר אין קנס קאמר לה רב יהודה:

ואם איתא זו דברי ר"מ ורבי יהודה מיבעי ליה. ואע"ג דרבי יונתן ור' יאשיה סבירא להו כר"מ בס"פ ד' מיתות (סנהדרין סו: ושם) לפי' ר"ת דפי' עד שיהיו שניהם שוין במיתה אחת ואפי' לפ"ה דמפרש בני עונשין מ"מ ר' יאשיה כר' מאיר סבירא ליה דלית ליה הא דדרשי רבנן לקמן (דף מ:) כאן נערה כו' דהא פטר קטנה מאורסה מ"מ לא קאמר זו דברי ר"מ ור' יאשיה דלא פריך הכא זו דברי ר"מ ורבי יהודה מיבעי ליה אלא משום דרבי יהודה בר פלוגתיה דר"מ והוי בכלל חכמים דפליגי עליה והכי אם איתא דלא פליג ה"ל למימר זו דברי ר"מ ור' יהודה אבל קשה דה"ל למימר הא מני ר' יאשיה היא ובממאנת סבר לה כר' יהודה:

וליתני קטנה קשיא. אע"ג דהוי תני קטנה דאין לה קנס מ"מ תני נמי איילונית דה"א דוקא קטנה שיש לה נערות אין לה קנס ותימה לר"י אמאי לא משני דלהגב אורחיה קמ"ל דעד מתי הבת ממאנת עד שתביא שתי שערות:

החרשת והשוטה כו' אין להן טענת בתולים. פי' בקונטרס דאי הוה פקחת לטעון הוה טענה משאירסתני נאנסתי וקשה לר"י דהיכי טענינן לה הכי מספק לאפוקי ממונא כיון דאיהי לא טענה דחזקת גופה איתרעי דהוי שור שחוט לפניך אבל חזקת ממון לא איתרע ומיהו מביא ר"י ראיה לפי' הקונטרס דאמר בפ' המדיר (לקמן עו: ושם) לא הוגלד פי המכה המוציא מחבירו עליו הראיה ומפרש דאפי' לא יהיב טבח דמי על הטבח להביא ראיה שברשות המוכר נטרפה והא דמפרש רב אשי למתני' דהמדיר דהיו בה מומין ועודה בבית אביה על האב להביא ראיה רישא מנה לאבא בידך סיפא מנה לי בידך לא מטעם דברי ושמא ברי עדיף כדמשמע לפום ריהטא דא"כ הוה קשה דהיכי טענינן לה הכי אלא כדפי' התם בקונטרס רישא מנה לאבא בידך דלגבי האב לא מהני חזקת הגוף דבתו דהכתובה היא באירוסין של אב סיפא מנה לי בידך דלגבי דידה מהני חזקת הגוף דידה וכן צריך לפרש דלאי מטעם ברי קאמר התם אמאי קאמר דעודה בבית אביה על האב להביא ראיה דמשנתארסה נולדו בה מומין אמאי צריך להביא ראיה כיון דאמר ברי לי דבכל ענין משמע דצריך להביא ראיה אפילו אב אמר ברי לי ולר"י נראה לפרש הכא דאין להן טענת בתולים לפי שבחזקת מוכת עץ היא ואע"ג דכולהו נמי חבוטי מחבטן מ"מ שאר נשים יש להן טענת בתולים מדלא קאמרי שהן מוכת עץ אבל הנך חרשת ושוטה דלא מצי אמרי בחזקת מוכת עץ נשאות וכן נראה דגרוס ספרים ל"ג לעיל בברייתא אלא החרשת והשוטה והאילונית יש להן קנס ותו לא ואין כתוב ברוב ספרים ויש להן טענת בתולים ולפר"י פריך שפיר דמדקאמר יש להן קנס אלמא לא חשבינן להו בחזקת מוכת עץ אבל לפי' הקונטרס מאי קפריך הכא נמי בחזקת בתולות חשבינן להו דהא אמרינן השתא א) דמשנתארסה נאנסה ורשב"א ב) הקשה לפר"י דאמאי לא משני הא דקתני אין להן טענת בתולים כר"מ דאמר בפ"ק (לעיל יג.) מוכת עץ בין הכיר בה בין לא הכיר בה מאתים והא דקתני יש להן טענת בתולים ג) כרבנן דאמרי כתובתן מנה וכי תימא משום דקתני חרשת דומיא דאיילונית הא ע"כ איילונית גופה לא הפסידה כתובתה לגמרי דהא רב ששת דמשני הא ר"ג הא ר' יהושע סבירא ליה בפ"ק (דף יא:) כנסה בחזקת בתולה ונמצאת בעולה יש לה כתובה מנה:

אי

עין משפט
נר מצוה

מד א מיי' פ"א מהל' נערה בתולה הל' יא יג סמג עשין כד טור אה"ע סי' קעז:

מה ב מיי' פ"א מהל' גירושין הל' ד סמג עשין נ טוש"ע אה"ע סי' קנה סעי' יב:

מו ג מיי' פ"א מהל' אישות הלכה ג ד ח סמג עשין מח טוש"ע שם סי' מז סעיף ה [וברב אלפס פ"א דמכילתין דף סו.]:

מז ד מיי' שם טוש"ע שם סעי' ו:

מח ה מיי' פ"ה מהל' איסורי ביאה הל' יט סמג לאוין קיא [וברב אלפס שם]:

תוספות רי"ד

תנו רבנן החרשת והשוטה והבוגרת ומוכ"ע אין להם קנס וא"ל טענת בתולים פי' להפסידן כתובתן חרשת ושוטה לא דאמרי' אי הוו פקחות לטעון הוו טענו כל חדא וחדא משאירסתני נאנסתי ומהימן בוגרת נמי לא שבתולי' כלין מאליהן האיילונית והסומא יש להן ט"ב פי' א) ודוקא דקא טעין טענת פ"פ אבל אי טעין טענת דמים ל"ל דבוגרת כלין בתוליה. אבל פתח נעול יש לה (והרב אומר היפך טענות דמים יש לה טענות פ"פ אין לה):

חשק שלמה
על תוס' רי"ד

א) הך פי' קאי אבוגרת ונראה דל"ל פי' ודווקא דקא טעין טענת דמים אבל אי טעין טענת פ"פ טענתו טענה דבוגרת כלו בתוליה וכו'.

ליקוטי רש"י

אתא לר"מ דאמר קטנה אין לה קנס. שהבא עליה אינו חייב קנס [לעיל כט.]. **ואיילונית** הואיל ואין לה שערות קטנה היא בימים שהיתה ראויה לנערות. **והא מקטנותה יצתה לבגר.** דנערות בסימנים תלוין וזו שאין לה סימנים חשבינן כל ימי קטנותה קטנה ובימי נערות בוגרת וזו וזו לר"מ אין לה קנס [יבמות פ.]. לפי שאין קנס אלא לנערה וזו שלא תביא שערות לעולם כל כ' שנה היא בחזקת קטנה ומשם ואילך בוגרת [לעיל לה:]. **עד שירבה שחור.** שיוקף אותו מקום בשער ובמסכת נדה (דף נב:) מפרש לא שירבה ממש אלא שיהו שתי שערות ארוכות שוכבות ונראה כמו שרבה השחור [חולין כו:]. שיהיו שם שערות הרבה [יבמות יב:]. במסכת נדה מפרש עד שירבו השערות ויהיו שוכבות ונראה כמו שהרבה השחור ולא גרס על הלבן [רשב"ם ב"ב קנו.]. ול"ג על הלבן כלומר שישחיר אותו מקום משערות הרבה [נדה נב. ועי' שיטמ"ק]. **בוגרת נותנין לה לילה הראשון.** ואפי' לב"ה דאמרי בהגיע זמנה לראות ארבעה הני מילי נערה דמשיגיעו ימי הנעורים הוי זמנה אבל בוגרת לילה הראשון ותו לא [נדה סד:].

מסורת הש"ס

א) [לעיל כט.], ב) [שם], ג) [שם], ד) [לעיל כט. וש"נ], ה) חולין כו:, ו) יבמות יב: ב"ב קנו: נדה נב., ז) [לקמן מ:], ח) [לעיל יב:], ט) [ב"ב מא. גיטין לז:], י) נדה סד:, כ) [וע' תוס' ב"ב קנו. ותוס' חולין כו: ד"ה עד].

תוספות ישנים

א) [ולמאן דמפרש התם משום כאן נמצא וכאן היה צ"ל דהכא איירי כגון שיצא קול שמשנתארסה נאנסה דאי לאו הכי הוי לן למימר כיון שבבית אביה נאנסה שמעיקרא נאנסה כדאמר התם גבי מומין. ת"י]:

ב) [נראה דלא מצי למימר הא ר"מ דהא ר"מ פליג בסיפא א"כ תנא קמא בר פלוגתיה תנא אחרינא הוא. ת"י]:

ג) [ולכאורה נראה דלא מצי לשנויי קמייתא כרבנן דכתובתה מנה דמ"מ תקשי אמאי יש לה קנס כיון שהיא בחזקת מוכת עץ. ת"י]:

תורה אור השלם

א) פְּתַח פִּיךָ לְאִלֵּם אֶל דִּין כָּל בְּנֵי חֲלוֹף: [משלי לא, ח]

עֲרָיוֹת מַמָּשׁ – *arayos,* literally,[1] שְׁנִיּוֹת מִדִּבְרֵי סוֹפְרִים – and secondary *arayos* means the relatives forbidden **by Rabbinic decree,**[2] you will be confronted with the following difficulty: כֵּיוָן דְּמִדְּאוֹרַיְיתָא חַזְיָא לֵיהּ – **Since they** [i.e. the girls who are secondary *arayos* to the violator] **are Biblically fit to** marry **[the violator],**[3] אַמַּאי אֵין לָהֶן קְנָס – **why are they not entitled to the fine?**[4] אֶלָּא עֲרָיוֹת – **Rather,** when the Baraisa says ***arayos,*** חַיָּיבֵי מִיתוֹת בֵּית דִּין – it refers to **those** relatives for which the violator is **liable to court-imposed execution** by cohabiting with them,[5] שְׁנִיּוֹת – and when the Baraisa says **secondary** ***arayos,*** חַיָּיבֵי כְּרֵיתוֹת – it refers to **those** relatives for which the violator is **liable to *kares*** by cohabiting with them.[6] אֲבָל חַיָּיבֵי לָאוִין – **But those** girls for which the violator is **liable for** violating **a prohibition** by cohabiting with them יֵשׁ לָהֶן קְנָס – **are entitled to the fine** (since the Baraisa does not list them among those who are *not* entitled). וּמַנִּי – **And** accordingly, **whose** authorship **is** reflected in **[the Baraisa]?** שִׁמְעוֹן הַתִּימְנִי הִיא – **It is** a Baraisa authored by **Shimon HaTimni.**[7]

An alternative explanation of the Baraisa:

אִיכָּא דְּאָמְרֵי – **There are those who say:** עֲרָיוֹת – When the Baraisa says ***arayos,*** חַיָּיבֵי מִיתוֹת בֵּית דִּין וְחַיָּיבֵי כְּרֵיתוֹת – it refers to **those** relatives for which the violator is **liable to court-imposed execution** by cohabiting with them **and** to **those** relatives for which the violator is **liable to *kares*** by cohabiting with them. שְׁנִיּוֹת – And when it says **secondary** *arayos,* חַיָּיבֵי לָאוִין – it refers to **those** girls for which the violator is **liable for** violating **a prohibition** by cohabiting with them. מַנִּי – And accordingly, **whose** authorship **is** reflected in **[this Baraisa]?** רַבִּי שִׁמְעוֹן בֶּן מְנַסְיָא הִיא – **It is** a Baraisa authored by **R' Shimon ben Menasya.**[8]

The Gemara turns to the Baraisa's second statement:

הַמְּמָאֶנֶת אֵין לָהּ לֹא קְנָס וְלֹא פִּיתּוּי – [A MINOR GIRL] WHO DECLARES HER REFUSAL to continue in her marriage HAS NO right to the FINE for violation AND the fine for SEDUCTION.

The Gemara discusses the authorship of the Baraisa:

הָא קְטַנָּה בְּעָלְמָא אִית לָהּ – **This** ruling implies that **an ordinary minor girl does have** a right to the fine for violation.[9] מַנִּי – **Whose** ruling **is it?** רַבָּנַן הִיא – **It is** the ruling of **the Rabbis,** דְּאָמְרֵי קְטַנָּה יֵשׁ לָהּ קְנָס – who say[10] that **a minor girl has a** right to the **fine.**

The Gemara objects:

אֵימָא סֵיפָא – But **consider the latter clause** of the Baraisa: אַיְילוֹנִית אֵין לָהּ לֹא קְנָס וְלֹא פִּיתּוּי – AN *AYLONIS* HAS NO right to the FINE for violation OR the fine for SEDUCTION. אָתָא לְרַבִּי מֵאִיר – Now, **[this clause] follows R' Meir,** דְּאָמַר קְטַנָּה אֵין לָהּ קְנָס – **who said** that **a minor girl has no** right to the **fine,** וְהָא מִקַּטְנוּתָהּ יָצְתָה לְבַגֵּר – **and this** girl **went out from** the state of **minority** directly **into** the state of ***bagrus.***[11] רֵישָׁא רַבָּנַן – But can **the first segment** of the Baraisa represent the opinion of **the Rabbis** וְסֵיפָא רַבִּי מֵאִיר – **and the latter segment** of the same Baraisa represent the opinion of **R' Meir?!** Obviously not! Who, then, is the author of the Baraisa?

The Gemara eliminates one possible answer:

וְכִי תֵּימָא כּוּלָּהּ רַבִּי מֵאִיר הִיא – **And if you will say** that **the entire [Baraisa]** is authored by **R' Meir,** who holds that a minor girl is not entitled to the fine,[12] וּבִמְמָאֶנֶת סָבַר לָהּ כְּרַבִּי יְהוּדָה – **and with regard to [a girl] who declares her refusal** to continue in her marriage **[R' Meir] holds like R' Yehudah,** who – as we shall now see – maintains that even a *naarah* may declare her refusal,[13] I shall respond to you: וּמִי סָבַר לָהּ – **And does [R' Meir]** really **hold [that view]?**[14] וְהָתַנְיָא – **But it was taught** otherwise **in a Baraisa:** עַד מָתַי הַבַּת מְמָאֶנֶת – UNTIL WHEN CAN A GIRL DECLARE HER REFUSAL and annul her Rabbinically sanctioned marriage? עַד שֶׁתָּבִיא שְׁתֵּי שְׂעָרוֹת – UNTIL SHE DEVELOPS TWO pubic HAIRS.[15] דִּבְרֵי רַבִּי מֵאִיר – These are the WORDS OF R'

NOTES

1. [I.e. as it is generally understood; namely,] the incestuous relations prohibited by force of *kares,* enumerated in *Leviticus* 18:6 ff. which carry the *kares* penalty [see above, 35b note 31] (*Rashi*).

2. That is, the more distant relatives whose unions are not considered incestuous from a Biblical standpoint, but were forbidden by the Rabbis as a protective measure to ensure that no one marries a Biblically forbidden *ervah*. Examples of these *sheniyos* are one's mother's mother, or one's father's mother, and the other relatives enumerated in the Baraisa, *Yevamos* 21a (*Rashi*).

3. And thus we can apply the verse stated with regard to the violator (*Deuteronomy* 22:29): *and she shall be for him a wife* (*Rashi*).

4. Granted, we could explain why the Baraisa rules [in contradiction of our Mishnah, 29a] that actual *arayos* are not entitled to the fine, by saying that the Baraisa is authored by Shimon HaTimni (cited above, 29b), who excludes *arayos* from receiving the fine because we cannot apply in their case the verse *and she shall be for him a wife.* But why does the Baraisa exclude secondary *arayos* from the fine, when they are indeed Biblically fit to marry the violator? (*Rashi*).

5. Those enumerated in the Mishnah, *Sanhedrin* 53a, 75a, 76b and 84b.

6. See Mishnah, *Kereisos* 2a.

7. Above (29b), Shimon HaTimni expounds the verse *and she shall be for him a wife* to teach that a violated girl is entitled to the fine only if she can *become* her attacker's wife – i.e. she is a girl in whom his *kiddushin* would take effect. Thus, only girls prohibited to the attacker by force of *kares* are excluded, since *kiddushin* cannot take effect in those prohibited on pain of *kares* [see 29b note 29]. But a girl forbidden to the attacker only by force of a prohibition, which does *not* preclude the effectiveness of his *kiddushin,* is entitled to the fine (see *Rashi*).

8. Above (29b), R' Shimon ben Menasya expounds the verse *and she shall be for him a wife* to teach that a violated girl is entitled to the fine only if she can *remain* her attacker's wife [see 29b note 30]. Hence, the verse excludes from the fine even a girl prohibited to the attacker only by force of a prohibition. For although she is fit to *become* his wife, she is not fit to *remain* his wife (see *Rashi*).

9. The accepted opinion is that an orphan girl who was given in marriage by her mother or brothers [see above, 35b note 34] can declare her refusal and annul her marriage only while she is still a minor [and the Baraisa's case is where she was violated immediately after the annulment, while she was still a minor (see *Ritva* above, 35b ד״ה הממאנת)]. Hence, from the Baraisa's disqualifying her from receiving the fines for violation and seduction because she was married and thus lost the legal presumption of being a virgin, we can infer that other minor girls who are virgins are entitled to these fines (see *Rashi* above, 35b ד״ה הממאנת ;וד״ה אין לה קנס; cf. *Tosafos* and *Ramban* ibid. ד״ה הממאנת).

10. In the Baraisa cited above, 29a, where they argue with R' Meir (*Rashi*).

11. The Baraisa ruled that an *aylonis* is not entitled to the fines for violation and seduction because it follows the view of R' Meir, who maintains the fines are unique to a *naarah.* Thus, since an *aylonis* passes directly from minority to *bagrus* and never enters the *naarah* stage, she is not entitled to these fines [see above, 35b note 37]. However, according to the Rabbis, who maintain that a minor girl *is* entitled to the fines, an *aylonis* may receive them until the age of twenty, when she reaches the *bagrus* stage [see ibid.].

12. Which explains the Baraisa's ruling regarding an *aylonis.*

13. And, accordingly, we are not forced to say that when the Baraisa discusses a girl declaring refusal to her marriage, it refers to a minor, which implies that other minors are entitled to the fine. Rather, we can now say that the Baraisa's case of a girl declaring refusal involves a *naarah,* which implies only that other *naaros* are entitled to the fine (*Rashi*).

14. That a *naarah* may declare her refusal and annul her marriage.

15. But once she develops two pubic hairs and attains *naarus,* she can no longer declare her refusal and annul her marriage, even if her husband did not cohabit with her after she became a *naarah* (*Rashi*). [When one

IS NOT ENTITLED TO THE FINE for violation NOR TO the fine for SEDUCTION.

The Gemara explains the Baraisa:

מַאי עֲרָיוֹת וּמַאי שְׁנִיּוֹת לַעֲרָיוֹת – **What** does the Baraisa mean by ***arayos*** **and what** does it mean by **secondary *arayos*?** אִילֵימָא עֲרָיוֹת – **If you say** that ***arayos*** means

NOTES

concerning her that she was not a virgin [and the accusation was proven true by witnesses who testified that she had committed adultery as an *arusah*]. The Gemara below (36b) will raise the question as to why the Baraisa must teach us that she is not entitled to the fine, when she is in fact liable to stoning [see below, 36b note 8, where this question of the Gemara is explained] (*Rashi*).

סוף סוף לאו בר תשלומין הוא (א) לא צריכא דבהדי דמחייה קרע שיראין דיליה א"ל רב חייא לרבא ולתנא דבי חזקיה דאמר מכה אדם ומכה בהמה ממאי דבחול כתיב וליכא לאיפלוגי דלמא בשבת כתיב דבבהמה גופה איכא לאיפלוגי לא ס"ד דכתיב א ומכה בהמה ישלמנה ומכה אדם יומת היכי דמי אי דלא אתרו ביה מכה אדם אמאי יומת אלא פשיטא דאתרו ביה ואי בשבת מכה בהמה ישלמנה אלא לאו בחול א"ל רב פפא לאביי ב לרבה דאמר חידוש הוא שחידשה תורה בקנס ואף על גב דמיקטיל משלם מתניתין כמאן מוקים לה אי כר"מ קשיא בתו אי כרבי נחוניא בן הקנה קשיא אחותו אי כר' יצחק קשיא ממזרת הניחא אי סבר לה כר' יוחנן הוא נמי מתרץ לה כר' יוחנן אלא אי סבר כר"ל היכי מתרץ לה על כרחך כר' יוחנן ס"ל א"ל רב מתנא לאביי לר"ל דאמר בפירוש ריבתה תורה חייבי מלקיות כחייבי מיתות מאן תנא דפליג עליה דרבי נחוניא בן הקנה אי ר"מ אי רבי יצחק: ת"ר עריות ושניות לעריות אין להן לא קנס ולא פיתוי א הממאנת אין לה לא קנס ולא פיתוי איילונית אין לה לא קנס ולא פיתוי והיוצאת משום שם רע אין לה לא קנס ולא פיתוי מאי עריות ומאי שניות לעריות אילימא עריות

עריות

רש"י

סוף סוף. האי לא תחלוק בו לחייבו ממון טעמא משום דאין בו כדי תשלומין ולא משום היקישא אבל הכא דיש בה שוה פרוטה אימא תחלוק: לא צריכא. להכי איתקש: דבהדי דמחייה קרע שיראין וכו'. כלומר ואשמועינן דלוקה משום חבלה ופטור מתשלומי קריעה לא שנא התרו בו ולא שנא לא התרו דלא לקי פטור מתשלומין מהיקישא דלא תחלוק: ממאי דבחול כתיב. דפשיטא ליה דמכה בהמה בין שוגג בין מזיד חייב לשלם: דלמא בשבת כתיב. ועל כרחך אשוגג כתיב קרא דאי במזיד הו"ל מתחייב בנפשו ופטור מן התשלומין: איכא לאיפלוגי. בין שוגג למזיד: לא ס"ד. דבשבת כתיב ובשוגג: ואי בשבת מכה בהמה ישלמנה. בתמיה: אלא לאו בחול. דליכא לפלוגי ואיתקש לה מכה אדם שלא תחלוק בו ואפי' אינו חייב מיתה: לרבה דאמר. לרבי מאיר חדוש הוא כו': מתניתין כמאן מוקים. לשנויי רומיא דרמינן עלה דאלו הן הלוקין וקיימא לן דאין לוקה ומשלם: אי כר' מאיר. דאמר לוקה ומשלם ולטעמיה ר"ל לקיש: קשיא בתו. דבשלמא לריש לקיש לאוקמה להכא דגנב וטבח בשבת בטובח על ידי אחר אבל בטובח על ידי עצמו לא משלם לא קשיא דמת ומשלם לית ליה לר' מאיר אפי' בקנס אלא לרבה קשיא בתו דקנס הוא וקתני מתניתין פטור: ואי כר' נחוניא בן הקנה. דאית ליה נמי לוקה ומשלם כר' מאיר מדקאמר יום הכפורים כשבת יה"כ הוא דפטור מתשלומין ומשום כרת דאית ביה ומג"ש דאסון אסון אבל משום לאו ומלקות דאית ביה לא פטר ומתניתין נמי דאית ליה לוקה ומשלם דידיה הוא ומת ומשלם לית ליה אפי' בקנס: קשיא אחותו. נהי נמי דמשום מלקות לא פטר ליה ליפטריה משום כרת: ואי כרבי יצחק. תוקמה דאמר במסכת מכות (דף יד.) אין חייבי כריתות בכלל מלקות מ' ולית ליה האי דאלו הן הלוקין הבא על אחותו ומשום הכי חייבין בתשלומין: קשיא ממזרת. דהכל מודים שהוא במלקות וקתני אית לה קנס: הניחא אי סבר. רבה כר' יוחנן כשלא התרו בו דמשלם דחייבי מלקיות שוגגין ודבר אחר חייב: איהו נמי. מוקי למתני' בשלא התרו בו כר' יוחנן: אלא אי סבר לה. בממון ומלקות דאפי' לא התרו בו פטור מממון ופליג אדרבי יוחנן וכל שכן אדעולא דאמר אפילו התרו בו משלם ממון ואינו לוקה: היכי מתרץ לה. לא כר' יוחנן ולא כעולא ולא כריש לקיש: על כרחך. אי סבירא ליה בממון ומלקות דלוקה ואינו משלם כרבי יוחנן סבירא ליה בשוגגים דמשלם ממון ומוקי לה בשלא התרו בו: לריש לקיש דאמר בפירוש ריבתה תורה כו'. דחייבי מלקיות שוגגין פטורין מלשלם: מאן תנא דפליג אדר' נחוניא. ומחייב תשלומין בחייבי כריתות כגון ההיא דשבועות ושהדליק גדיש ביה"כ חייבין בפרק שבועת העדות (שבועות לג.) ומתני' דהכא דקנסה באחותו ונהי נמי דלית ליה אסון למיפטריה משום כרת ליפטריה משום לאו בין התרו בו בין לא התרו בו דאין כרת בלא לאו חוץ מפסח ומילה דבשלמא ר' יוחנן מוקי לה אפילו כרבנן דפליגי עליה דרבי מאיר דאמרי אין לוקה ומשלם והני בשלא התרו בו אלא לריש לקיש כמאן מוקי לה: אי רבי מאיר. דאמר לוקה ומשלם: אי רבי יצחק. דאמר לא שייך מלקות בחייבי כריתות וג"ש דאסון אסון לית ליה ובמאי ליפטר הילכך מתניתין דהכא על כרחך ר"מ היא ולא רבי יצחק משום דקשיא ממזרת אבל ההיא דשבועות בין כר"מ בין כרבי יצחק: עריות ושניות. לקמן מפרש להו: קנס. דאנוסה: פיתוי. דמפותה: הממאנת. בבעלה כגון יתומה קטנה שהשיאתה אמה ומיאנה בבעלה: אין לה קנס. שאינה בחזקת בתולה הואיל וניסת: איילונית. שאין לה סימני נערות לעולם ואינה יולדת לשון איל זכר דוכרניתא דלא ילדה (לעיל דף יא.): אין לה קנס. לפי שאין קנס אלא לנערה וזו שלא תביא שערות לעולם כל כ' שנה היא בחזקת קטנה ומשם ואילך בוגרת: והיוצאת משום שם רע. קס"ד שלא מצא לה בעלה בתולים ולקמן פריך בת סקילה היא:

עריות

תוספות

אם אינו ענין להכאה שיש בה שוה פרוטה. וא"ת והא איצטריך להכי דמהכא נפקא לן חובל בחברו לתשלומין בריש החובל (ב"ק פג: ושם) וי"ל דהך סוגיא כאידך תנאי דהתם דמפקי החובל בחברו לתשלומין מקרא אחרינא: דלמא בשבת כתיב דבבהמה גופה כו'. וא"ת א"כ היקישא למה לי וי"ל דאתיא לבין דרך ירידה לדרך עלייה דלא שייך לפלוגי גבי שבת: אלא לאו בחול. וא"ת בחול נמי מלינן למימר דבהדי דמחייה לבהמה הרג את האדם ולא אתרו ביה משום אדם ואפי' בשבת נמי מלינן למימר דאתרו ביה משום בהמה ולא אתרו בו משום שבת וי"ל דמ"מ ילפינן שפיר דמה מכה בהמה לא חלקת בין שוגג בהכאתה למזיד בהכאתה אף אדם לא תחלוק בו בין מזיד בהכאתו לשוגג בהכאתו אע"ג הואיל ומכה אדם איירי באתרו ביה מכה בהמה נמי איירי בכל ענין דאתרו ביה והכי לא מצי איירי בשבת ולא בהרג אדם עמה: מתניתין כמאן מוקי לה. א) תימה מיקשי ליה לרב פפא גופיה דאיהו סבר לעיל (דף לד:) כרבה דאמר היתה פרה גנובה לו כו' ועוד קשה לישני כעולא דמאי דפירש בקונ' דלא סבר כריש לקיש דחייבי מלקיות שוגגין פטורין כ"ש דפליג אדעולא זה אינו נראה דלמא בממון אחר סבר כריש לקיש אבל בממונא דבההוא מילתא גופיה משלם ממון ומיפטר ממלקות מג"ש דתחת תחת ב) ונראה דרב פפא אפי' סבר כר"ל מצי לשנויי כדעולא כדפרישית אבל לאביי פריך שפיר דלית ליה דעולא דהא מוקי לעיל תחת לדרשא אחרינא והכי קשיא ליה אי ס"ל כר"ל מתני' כמאן מוקי לה: אי כר' נחוניא קשיא אחותו. לא מצי למימר קשיא ממזרת ואחותו דע"כ כר"מ ס"ל מדנקט יום הכפורים כשבת וה"ל למימר יו"ט כשבת וכ"ש יום הכפורים אלא ודאי ס"ל או כר"מ דאמר לוקה ומשלם או כר' יצחק דאמר אין מלקות בחייבי כריתות הלכך לא נקט יו"ט דמיניה לא הוה שמעינן יוה"כ שאין בו מלקות וכיון דלא קאי כרבנן לא מוקמי ליה כרבי יצחק אלא כר"מ ולא תיקשי ממזרת: אי כרבי יצחק קשיא ממזרת. לא הוצרך לומר אי כרבנן לדלידהו קשיא ממזרת ואחותו ולא מצי למימר נמי דמתני' כרבי עקיבא דסבר עדים זוממין קנסא ואית ליה לוקה ומשלם ולית ליה מת ומשלם דלרבי עקיבא מלינן למימר דלא גמר עדים זוממין ממועלה ש"ר אע"ג דהוי קנסא מקנסא כדפרי' לעיל (דף לג. ד"ה דאין) ואית ליה שפיר כרבנן דלוקה ואינו משלם: מאן תנא דפליג עליה דרבי נחוניא אי ר' מאיר אי רבי יצחק. תימה דלריש לקיש בהדיא פליג ר"מ ארבי נחוניא דהא מוקים מתני' כר"מ וקתני דיש קנס בחייבי כריתות וי"ל דידע שפיר דר"מ פליג עליה אלא דק"ל דרבנן לא מלינן למימר דפליגי עליה אבל לר' יוחנן אתי שפיר: לא קנס ולא פיתוי. אית דגרס ולא אונס משום דפיתוי נמי קנס הוא ואומר ר"י דגרסי' ליה דשייך למיקרי לאונס קנס טפי מלפיתוי משום דאונס שותה בעציצו (לקמן דף לט:): הממאנת אין לה לא קנס. פירש בקונט' לפי שהיא בחזקת בעולה וקשה לר"י דא"כ היכי דייק לקמן הא קטנה בעלמא אית לה דלמא ה"ק הממאנת אין לה קנס אם בא עליה כשהיא נערה הא נערה בעלמא אית לה ומיהו אין להקשות אמאי נקט ממאנת ה"ל למינקט כל אשה שניסת ונתגרשה דהא איכא למ"ד לקמן (דף לח.) דאפי' אם נתארסה ונתגרשה אין לה קנס ונראה לר"י דה"פ אין לה לא קנס ולא פיתוי אם אנסה בעלה או פיתה אותה כשהיתה תחתיו קודם מיאון אע"ג דכשמיאנה איגלאי מילתא שלא היתה אשתו והשתא דייק שפיר לקמן הא קטנה בעלמא אית לה אבל קשה לר"י מהא דקאמר בסמוך וכ"ת כולה ר"מ היא ובממאנת סבר לה כרבי יהודה והשתא כיון דאיירי שבא עליה כשהיא נערה שוב אינה יכולה למאן למודה רבי יהודה כשבעל כדאמר בפרק בא סימן (נדה נב. ושם) ותירץ ר"י דמיירי כשפירש בהדיא שאינו בועל לשם קידושין ועוד דפיתוי ואונס לאו לשם קידושין הוא דבההיא לא מודה רבי יהודה: ולא פיתוי. קשה לרשב"א אמאי נקט פיתוי למאי דמוקי לה בסמוך בנערה הא כל נערה מפותה אין לה קנס דמחלה אפי' נערה שאינה ממאנת ויש לומר דנקט אין לה פיתוי אגב דנקט באידך:

אבל

עין משפט נר מצוה

מג א מיי' פ"א מהל' נערה בתולה הל' ט סמג עשין כד טור אה"ע סי' קנז:

ליקוטי רש"י

שיראין. של משי [מנחות לט:]. חידוש הוא שחידשה תורה בקנס. בכל תשלומי קנס שאינו דין אלא גזרת מלך בעלמא וכיון דחידוש הוא וגזירת חוק אימא אע"ג דאיכא בהדיה מיתה לשלם [לקמן לח.]. כל משפט קנס חידוש הוא הלכך אע"ג דמיקטיל נמי לא מיפטר מיניה [לעיל לד:].

מסורת הש"ס

א) [לעיל לד: לקמן לח.].

תוספות ישנים

א) [לרב פפא לא שייך למיפרך דהא לא פריך לנפשיה משום דידע דסבר כר' יוחנן דלא דריש ג"ש דרשע ודמכה וכ"מ קלת דקאמר הי מכה. ת"י]: ב) לפי' ר"י דלעיל אתי שפיר דרשב"ל מוקי לה כר"מ אבל רבה כמאן מוקי לה אי כר' נחוניא קשיא אחותו דלדידיה אחותו לית לה קנס דחד ריבויא מוקי לחייבי לאוין וחד ליבמה לשוק אי כדפי' רשב"א לעיל קשיא אחותו דאי נוקי חד קרא לחייבי כריתות א"כ חייבי מיתות נמי ולמה שהביא מהר"מ לעיל בתום' אתי טפי שפיר אי ר' יצחק קשיא ממזרת דלדידיה מוקמינן חד לחייבי עשה וחד לחייבי כריתות הניחא אי סבר לה כר' יוחנן אלא אי סבר כרשב"ל דחייבי מלקות שוגגין פטורין א"כ איצטריך תרי ריבויי חד לחייבי עשה וחד לחייבי לאוין והא דלא קאמר אי כרבנן קשיא אחותו משום דעיקר קושיא כבר הקשה לרבנן לעיל והא קי"ל דאין לוקה ומשלם ולכך לא חזר והקשה. ת"י עה"ג:

הגהות הב"ח

(א) גמ' תשלומין הוא (לא צריכא) תא"מ ונ"ב ס"א הא לא קשיא:

תורה אור השלם

א) וּמַכֵּה בְהֵמָה יְשַׁלְּמֶנָּה וּמַכֵּה אָדָם יוּמָת: [ויקרא כד, כא]

According to Reish Lakish, who says that **"the Torah has explicitly included those liable to lashes** in the law of exemption from monetary liability **just like those liable to** the **death** penalty," and thus one who commits a lashes-bearing sin is exempt from monetary payment even if he acted inadvertently and does not actually receive lashes, מַאן תַּנָּא דְּפָלִיג עֲלֵיהּ דְּרַבִּי נְחוּנְיָא בֶּן הַקָּנָה – **who is the Tanna who argues with R' Nechunya ben HaKanah** and maintains that liability to *kares* does *not* exempt one from monetary liability?[25]

The Gemara answers:

אִי רַבִּי מֵאִיר – It is **either R' Meir,** who maintains that one can receive lashes and pay money for the same crime,[26] אִי רַבִּי יִצְחָק – **or R' Yitzchak,** who maintains that *kares*-bearing prohibitions are *not* punishable by lashes.[27]

The Gemara cites a Baraisa that enumerates certain girls who are not entitled to the fines for violation and seduction:

תָּנוּ רַבָּנַן – **The Rabbis taught in a Baraisa:** עֲרָיוֹת וּשְׁנִיּוֹת לַעֲרָיוֹת – Girls who are prohibited to the violator or seducer as *ARAYOS*[28] OR as SECONDARY *ARAYOS*[29] אֵין לָהֶן לֹא קְנָס – ARE NOT ENTITLED TO THE FINE for violation, וְלֹא פִּיתּוּי – NOR TO the fine for SEDUCTION.[30] הַמְמָאֶנֶת – A GIRL WHO DECLARES HER REFUSAL to continue with her Rabbinically ordained marriage[31] אֵין לָהּ לֹא קְנָס וְלֹא פִּיתּוּי – IS NOT ENTITLED TO THE FINE for violation NOR TO the fine for SEDUCTION.[32] אַיְילוֹנִית – AN *AYLONIS*[33] אֵין לָהּ לֹא קְנָס וְלֹא פִּיתּוּי – IS NOT ENTITLED TO THE FINE for violation NOR TO the fine for SEDUCTION.[34] וְהַיּוֹצֵאת מִשּׁוּם שֵׁם רַע – AND A WOMAN WHO WAS DIVORCED BECAUSE OF A BAD NAME[35] אֵין לָהּ לֹא קְנָס וְלֹא פִּיתּוּי –

NOTES

25. Though R' Nechunya ben HaKanah holds that liability to *kares* does exempt one from liability to monetary payment, we find that the Tanna of the Mishnah in *Shevuos* (33a) argues, and maintains that one who ignites a stack of grain on Yom Kippur [and thus incurs liability to *kares*] *is* liable to pay for the stack. And similarly, the Tanna of our Mishnah argues with R' Nechunya ben HaKanah, and maintains that one who violates his sister, etc., though liable to *kares,* is obligated to pay the fine. Now, granted that these Tannaim do not subscribe to the *gezeirah shavah* of *ason, ason* (R' Nechunya's source for exempting the one who becomes liable to *kares* from monetary payment), let them exempt the sinner from the payment of money on the basis of the lashes inherent in the prohibition itself (against desecrating Yom Kippur or violating one's sister)! For according to Reish Lakish, one who commits a lashes-bearing transgression is exempt from monetary payment even if he was *not* warned that he would receive lashes, and thus does not actually receive them.

Now, according to R' Yochanan, there is no difficulty in explaining why these Mishnahs impose monetary payment even in the face of a lashes-bearing transgression. R' Yochanan could say that these Mishnahs follow even the view of the Rabbis who argue with R' Meir and hold that one does not receive lashes and pay money for the same crime. For according to R' Yochanan, the Rabbis hold this view only in cases where the sinner is *actually* subject to lashes (viz. where he was warned). Thus, he can explain that the Mishnah in *Shevuos* (which rules that one who ignites a grain stack on Yom Kippur must pay for it) and our Mishnah (which rules that one who violates his sister must pay the fine) are dealing with situations in which the sinner was *not* warned that he would receive lashes. But according to Reish Lakish, who maintains that an act which carries the lashes penalty exempts one from monetary payment even when the act was committed inadvertently, who can the author of these Mishnahs possibly be? (see *Rashi*).

26. Accordingly, the fact that one who commits a *kares*-bearing sin is liable to lashes does not serve to exempt him from monetary payment.

27. And there is thus no lashes penalty to exempt one who commits a *kares*-bearing sin from monetary payment (*Rashi*).

Thus, according to Reish Lakish, the Tanna who disputes R' Nechunya ben HaKanah and does not exempt one who commits a *kares*-bearing sin from monetary payment would have to be either R' Meir or R' Yitzchak. Since this Tanna does not subscribe to the *gezeirah shavah* of *ason, ason* to exempt the sinner on the basis of the *kares* penalty, and holds either that one *can* receive lashes and pay money for the same crime, or that there are no lashes altogether for a *kares*-bearing sin, there is nothing to exempt the one who commits the *kares*-bearing sin from monetary payment (see *Rashi*).

As stated, the only Tannaim who would dispute R' Nechunya ben HaKanah's exemption of one who commits a *kares*-bearing sin are (according to Reish Lakish) R' Meir and R' Yitzchak. Our Mishnah, though, could be authored only by R' Meir (who holds that one can receive lashes and pay money for the same crime). R' Yitzchak's view, however (as pointed out by the Gemara above), would not account for why our Mishnah rules that one who violates a *mamzeress* must pay the fine. The Mishnah in *Shevuos,* on the other hand, can be attributed either to R' Meir or R' Yitzchak (*Rashi*).

28. [*Arayos* (singular: *ervah*) is the term generally used to denote the relatives that the Torah prohibits one to marry on pain of *kares.* They are enumerated in *Leviticus* 18:6 ff.] The Gemara below will discuss the sense in which this term is used here (*Rashi*).

29. [The term שְׁנִיּוֹת לַעֲרָיוֹת, *secondary arayos,* generally refers to more distant relatives, which are not forbidden in marriage from the Biblical standpoint, but are Rabbinically forbidden, as a protective measure to ensure that no one shall come to marry a Biblically forbidden *ervah.*] The Gemara below will discuss the sense in which this term is used here (*Rashi*).

30. [See *Tosafos* and *Shitah Mekubetzes,* who discuss why the Baraisa refers to the fine for violation simply as קְנָס, *fine,* and to the fine for seduction as פִּיתּוּי, *seduction.*]

31. The reference is to a fatherless girl who was married off by her mother or brothers while she was still a minor, and then declared her refusal to remain with her husband.

Biblically, a minor girl can be married off only by her father [see below, 46b]. The Rabbis, however, instituted that the mother or brother of an orphaned minor girl shall be empowered to marry her off, so that she not be abused by unscrupulous men. This marriage has no standing, though, on the Biblical level. Together with their institution of marriage for the orphaned minor girl, however, the Rabbis also instituted that she be able, before reaching majority, to annul the marriage through מִאוּן, *mi'un* (refusal) – her declaration before a *beis din* of three judges that she is unwilling to continue in the marriage. This *mi'un* serves to annul the marriage retroactively from its inception, and accordingly no *get* is needed.

Our Baraisa is discussing a girl who annulled her marriage by declaring her refusal and was then either violated or seduced (see *Rashi*).

32. For only virgins are entitled to these fines, and since this girl was previously married, she is presumed to be a nonvirgin (*Rashi*).

33. An *aylonis* is a woman who does not develop the physical signs of *naarus* [i.e. the two pubic hairs that signal physical maturity] and exhibits certain male characteristics, including an underdeveloped reproductive system. The word אַיְלוֹנִית stems from אַיִל, *a ram* (a male sheep), and she is so called because she is like a male in that she cannot bear children (*Rashi*; see above, 11a).

34. The Tanna of this Baraisa holds that the fines for violation and seduction pertain only to a *naarah,* not to a minor or *bogeress* [see above, 29a and below, 40b]. A woman who exhibits characteristics of an *aylonis* is classified as a minor until the age of twenty, at which point she is classified as a *bogeress.* She is never classified as a *naarah,* for she never develops pubic hairs. Hence, the fines for violation and seduction, which are unique to a *naarah,* are inapplicable to the *aylonis* (see *Rashi*).

35. [The Torah (*Deuteronomy* 22:13 ff.) states: *If a man marries a wife and cohabits with her and hates her and he makes a wanton accusation against her, spreading a "bad name" against her* etc. The Torah refers here to a husband who accuses his new wife of not being a virgin and brings witnesses that she committed adultery after *kiddushin* but prior to *nisuin.* The Torah proceeds to state that if the accusation is proven to be false, the husband receives lashes and pays the father of the bride one hundred *shekels,* and he must keep her as his wife forever (i.e. he may never divorce her against her will). On the other hand, if she is found to be guilty as charged, she is put to death by stoning.]

The Gemara at this point understands that by the term "a woman who was divorced for a bad name," the Baraisa refers to the woman referred to in the aforementioned verse, whose husband spread a "bad name"

עין משפט
נר מצוה

מג א מיי' פ"א מהל' נערה בתולה הל' ט סמג עשין כד טור אה"ע סי' קעז:

סוף סוף לאו בר תשלומין הוא (א) לא צריכא דבהדי דמחייה קרע שיראין דיליה א"ל רב חייא לרבא ולתנא דבי חזקיה דאמר מכה אדם ומכה בהמה ממאי דבחול כתיב וליכא לאיפלוגי דלמא בשבת כתיב דבבהמה גופה איכא לאיפלוגי לא ס"ד דכתיב א) ומכה בהמה ישלמנה ומכה אדם יומת היכי דמי אי דלא אתרו ביה מכה אדם אמאי יומת אלא פשיטא דאתרו ביה ואי בשבת מכה בהמה ישלמנה אלא לאו בחול א"ל רב פפא לאביי (א) לרבה דאמר חידוש הוא שחידשה תורה בקנס ואף על גב דמיקטיל משלם מתניתין כמאן מוקים לה אי כר"מ קשיא בתו אי כרבי נחוניא בן הקנה קשיא אחותו אי כר' יצחק קשיא ממזרת הניחא אי סבר לה כר' יוחנן הוא נמי מתרץ לה כר' יוחנן אלא אי סבר כר"ל היכי מתרץ לה על כרחך כר' יוחנן ס"ל א"ל רב מתנא לאביי לר"ל דאמר בפירוש ריבתה תורה חייבי מלקיות כחייבי מיתות מאן תנא דפליג עליה דרבי נחוניא בן הקנה אי ר"מ אי רבי יצחק: ת"ר עריות ושניות לעריות אין להן לא קנס ולא פיתוי א הממאנת אין לה לא קנס ולא פיתוי איילונית אין לה לא קנס ולא פיתוי והיוצאת משום שם רע אין לה לא קנס ולא פיתוי מאי עריות ומאי שניות לעריות אילימא עריות עריות

סוף סוף. הא לא תחלוק בו לחייבו ממון טעמא משום דאין בו כדי תשלומין ולא משום היקישא אבל היכא דיש בה שוה פרוטה אימא תחלוק: לא צריכא. להכי איתקש: דבהדי דמחייה קרע שיראין וכו'. כלומר ואשמועינן דלוקה משום חבלה ופטור מתשלומי קריעה לא שנא התרו בו ולא שנא לא התרו דלא לקי פטור מתשלומין מהיקישא דלא תחלוק: ממאי דבחול כתיב. דפשיטא ליה דמכה בהמה בין שוגג בין מזיד חייב לשלם: דלמא בשבת כתיב. ועל כרחך אשוגג כתיב קרא דאי במזיד הו"ל מתחייב בנפשו ופטור מן התשלומין: איכא לאיפלוגי. בין שוגג למזיד: לא ס"ד. דבשבת כתיב ובשוגג: ואי בשבת מכה בהמה ישלמנה. בתמיה: אלא לאו בחול. דליכא לפלוגי ואיתקש לה מכה אדם שלא תחלוק בו ואפי' אינו חייב מיתה: לרבה דאמר. לרבי מאיר חדוש הוא כו': מתניתין כמאן מוקים. לשנויי רומיא דרמינן עלה דאלו הן הלוקין וקיימא לן דאין לוקה ומשלם: אי כר' מאיר. דאמר לוקה ומשלם וכדשנינהו ריש לקיש: קשיא בתו. דבשלמא לריש לקיש דאוקמה להיא דגנב וטבח בשבת בטובח על ידי אחר אבל בטובח על ידי עצמו לא משלם לא קשיא דמת ומשלם לית ליה לר' מאיר אפי' בקנס אלא לרבה קשיא בתו דקנס הוא וקתני מתניתין פטור: ואי כר' נחוניא בן הקנה. דאית ליה נמי לוקה ומשלם כר' מאיר מדקאמר יום הכפורים כשבת יה"כ הוא דפטור מתשלומין ומשום כרת דאית ביה ומג"ש דאסון אסון אבל משום לאו ומלקות דאית ביה לא פטר ומתניתין נמי דאית ליה לוקה ומשלם דידיה הוא ומת ומשלם לית ליה אפי' בקנס: קשיא אחותו. נהי נמי דמשום מלקות לא פטר ליה ליפטריה משום כרת: ואי כרבי יצחק. תוקמה דאמר במסכת מכות (דף יד.) אין חייבי כריתות בכלל מלקות מ' ולית ליה האי דאלו הן הלוקין הבא על אחותו ומשום הכי חייבין בתשלומין: קשיא ממזרת. דהכל מודים שהוא במלקות וקתני אית לה קנס: הניחא אי סבר. רבה כר' יוחנן כשלא התרו בו דמשלם דחייבי מלקיות שוגגין ודבר אחר חייב: איהו נמי. מוקי למתני' בשלא התרו בו כר' יוחנן: אלא אי סבר לה. בממון ומלקות דאפי' לא התרו בו פטור מממון ופליג אדרבי יוחנן וכל שכן אדעולא דאמר אפילו התרו בו משלם ממון ואינו לוקה: היכי מתרץ לה. לא כר' יוחנן ולא כעולא ולא כריש לקיש: על כרחך. אי סבירא ליה בממון ומלקות דלוקה ואינו משלם כרבי יוחנן סבירא ליה בשוגגים דמשלם ממון ומוקי לה בשלא התרו בו: לריש לקיש דאמר בפירוש ריבתה תורה כו'. דחייבי מלקיות שוגגין פטורין מלשלם: מאן תנא דפליג אדר' נחוניא. ומחייב תשלומין בחייבי כריתות כגון ההיא דשבועות ושהדליק גדיש ביה"כ חייבין בפרק שבועת העדות (שבועות לג.) ומתני' דהכא דקנסה באחותו ונהי נמי דלית ליה אסון אסון למיפטריה משום כרת ליפטריה משום לאו בין התרו בו בין לא התרו בו דאין כרת בלא לאו חוץ מפסח ומילה דבשלמא ר' יוחנן מוקי לה אפילו כרבנן דפליגי עליה דרבי מאיר דאמרי אין לוקה ומשלם והני בשלא התרו בו אלא לריש לקיש כמאן מוקי לה: אי רבי מאיר. דאמר לוקה ומשלם: אי רבי יצחק. דאמר לא שייך מלקות בחייבי כריתות וג"ש דאסון אסון לית ליה ובמאי ליפטר הילכך מתניתין דהכא על כרחך ר"מ היא ולא רבי יצחק משום דקשיא ממזרת אבל ההיא דשבועות בין כר"מ בין כרבי יצחק: עריות ושניות. לקמן מפרש להו: קנס. דאנוסה: פיתוי. דמפותה: הממאנת. בבעלה כגון יתומה קטנה שהשיאתה אמה ומיאנה בבעלה: אין לה קנס. שאינה בחזקת בתולה הואיל וניסת: איילונית. שאין לה סימני נערות לעולם ואינה יולדת לשון איל זכר דוכרניתא דלא ילדה (לעיל דף יא.): אין לה קנס. לפי שאין קנס אלא לנערה וזו שלא תביא שערות לעולם כל כ' שנה היא בחזקת קטנה ומשם ואילך בוגרת: והיוצאת משום שם רע. קס"ד שלא מצא לה בעלה בתולים ולקמן פריך בת סקילה היא:

אם אינו ענין להכאה שיש בה שוה פרוטה. וא"ת והא איצטריך להכי דמהכא נפקא לן חובל בחברו לתשלומין בריש החובל (ב"ק פג: ושם) וי"ל דהך סוגיא כאידך תנאי דהתם דמפקי החובל בחברו לתשלומין מקרא אחרינא: דלמא בשבת כתיב דבבהמה גופה כו'. וא"ת א"כ היקישא למה לי וי"ל דאתיא לבין דרך ירידה לדרך עלייה דלא שייך לפלוגי גבי שבת: אלא לאו בחול. וא"ת בחול נמי מלינן למימר דבהדי דמחייה לבהמה הרג את האדם ולא אתרו ביה משום אדם ואפי' בשבת נמי מלינן למימר דאתרו ביה משום בהמה ולא אתרו בו משום שבת וי"ל דמ"מ ילפינן שפיר דמה מכה בהמה לא חלקת בין שוגג בהכאתה למזיד בהכאתה אף אדם לא תחלוק בו בין מזיד בהכאתו לשוגג בהכאתו א"כ הואיל ומכה אדם איירי באתרו ביה מכה בהמה נמי איירי בכל ענין דאתרו ביה ולהכי לא מצי איירי בשבת ולא בהרג אדם עמה: מתניתין כמאן מוקי לה. א) תימה תיקשי ליה לרב פפא גופיה דאיהו סבר לעיל (דף לד:) כרבה דאמר היתה פרה גנובה לו כו' ועוד קשה לישני כעולא דמאי דפירש בקונ' דאי סבר כריש לקיש דחייבי מלקיות שוגגין פטורין כ"ש דפליג אדעולא זה אינו נראה דלמא בממון אחר סבר כריש לקיש אבל בממונא דההוא מילתא גופיה משלם ממון ומיפטר ממלקות מג"ש דתחת תחת ב) ונראה דרב פפא אפי' סבר כר"ל מצי לשנויי כדעולא כדפרישית אבל לאביי פריך שפיר דלית ליה דעולא דהא מוקי לעיל תחת לדרשא אחרינא ולהכי קשיא ליה אי ס"ל כר"ל מתני' כמאן מוקי לה: אי כר' נחוניא קשיא אחותו. לא מצי למימר קשיא ממזרת ואחותו דע"כ כר"מ ס"ל מדנקט יום הכפורים כשבת וה"ל למימר יו"ט כשבת וכ"ש יום הכפורים אלא ודאי ס"ל או כר"מ דאמר לוקה ומשלם או כר' יצחק דאמר אין מלקות בחייבי כריתות הלכך לא נקט יו"ט דמיניה לא הוה שמעינן יוה"כ שאין בו מלקות וכיון דלא הוי כרבנן לא מוקמי ליה כרבי יצחק אלא כר"מ ולא תיקשי ממזרת: אי כרבי יצחק קשיא ממזרת. לא הוצרך לומר אי כרבנן דלדידהו קשיא ממזרת ואחותו ולא מצי למימר נמי דמתני' כרבי עקיבא דסבר עדים זוממין קנסא ואית ליה לוקה ומשלם ולית ליה מת ומשלם דלרבי עקיבא מלינן למימר דלא גמר עדים זוממין ממוציא ש"ר אע"ג דהוי קנסא מקנסא כדפרי' לעיל (דף לג. ד"ה דאין) ואית ליה שפיר כרבנן דלוקה ואינו משלם: מאן תנא דפליג עליה דרבי נחוניא אי ר' מאיר אי רבי יצחק. תימה דלריש לקיש בהדיא פליג ר"מ ארבי נחוניא דהא מוקים מתני' כר"מ וקתני דיש קנס בחייבי כריתות וי"ל דידע שפיר דר"מ פליג עליה אלא דק"ל דרבנן לא מלינן למימר דפליגי עליה אבל לר' יוחנן אתי שפיר: לא קנס ולא פיתוי. אית דגרס ולא אונס משום דפיתוי נמי קנס הוא ואומר ר"י דגרסי' ליה דשייך למיקרי לאונס קנס טפי מלפיתוי משום דאונס שותה בעציצו (לקמן דף לט.):

הממאנת אין לה לא קנס. פירש בקונט' לפי שהיא בחזקת בעולה וקשה לר"י דא"כ היכי דייק לקמן הא קטנה בעלמא אית לה דלמא ה"ק הממאנת אין לה קנס אם בא עליה כשהיא נערה הא נערה בעלמא אית לה ומיהו אין להקשות אמאי נקט ממאנת ה"ל למינקט כל אשה שניסת ונתגרשה דהא איכא למ"ד לקמן (דף לח.) דאפי' אם נתארסה ונתגרשה אין לה קנס ונראה לר"י דה"פ אין לה לא קנס ולא פיתוי אם אנסה בעלה או פיתה אותה כשהיתה תחתיו קודם מיאון אע"ג דכשמיאנה איגלאי מילתא שלא היתה אשתו והשתא דייק שפיר לקמן הא קטנה בעלמא אית לה אבל קשה לר"י מהא דקאמר בסמוך וכ"ת כולה ר"מ היא ובממאנת סבר לה כרבי יהודה והשתא כיון דאיירי שבא עליה בעלה כשהיא נערה שוב אינה יכולה למאן דמודה רבי יהודה כשבעל כדאמר בפרק בא סימן (נדה נב. ושם) ותירץ ר"י דמיירי כשפירש בהדיא שאינו בועל לשם קידושין ועוד דפיתוי ואונס לאו לשם קידושין הוא דבההיא לא מודה רבי יהודה:

ולא פיתוי. קשה לרשב"א אמאי נקט פיתוי למאי דמוקי לה בסמוך בנערה הא כל נערה מפותה אין לה קנס דמחלה אפי' נערה שאינה ממאנת ויש לומר דנקט אין לה פיתוי אגב דנקט באידך:

ליקוטי רש"י

שיראין. של משי [מנחות לט:]. חידוש הוא שחידשה תורה בקנס. בכל תשלומי קנס שאינו דין אלא גזרת מלך בעלמא וכיון דחדוש הוא וגזירת חוק איכא אע"ג דאיכא בהדיה מיתה משלם [לקמן לח.]. כי מכפט קנס חידוש הוא הלכך אע"ג דמיקטיל נמי לא מיפטר מיניה [לעיל לד:].

מסורת הש"ס

א) [לעיל לד: לקמן לח.].

תוספות ישנים

א) [לרב פפא לא שייך למיפרך דהא לא פריך לנפשיה משום דידע דסבר כר' יוחנן דלא דריש ג"ש דרשע ודמכה וכ"מ קלא דקאמר הי מכה. ת"י]: ב) לפי' ר"י דלעיל אתי שפיר דרשב"ל מוקי לה כר"מ אבל רבה כמאן מוקי לה אי כר' נחוניא קשיא אחותו דלדידיה אחותו לית לה קנס דחד ריבויא מוקי לחייבי לאוין וחד ליבמה לשוק אי כדפי' רשב"א לעיל קשיא אחותו דאי נוקי חד קרא לחייבי כריתות א"כ חייבי מיתות נמי ולמה שהביא מהר"מ לעיל בתוס' אתי טפי שפיר אי ר' יצחק קשיא ממזרת דלדידיה מוקמינן חד לחייבי עשה וחד לחייבי כריתות הניחא אי סבר לה כר' יוחנן אלא אי סבר כרשב"ל דחייבי מלקות שוגגין פטורין א"כ איצטריך תרי ריבויי חד לחייבי עשה וחד לחייבי לאוין והא דלא קאמר אי כרבנן קשיא אחותו משום דעיקר קושיא ככר הקשה לרבנן לעיל והא קי"ל דאין לוקה ומשלם ולכך לא חזר והקשה. ת"י עה"ג:

הגהות הב"ח

(א) גמ' תשלומין הוא (לא צריכא) תא"מ ונ"ב ס"א הא לא קשיא:

תורה אור השלם

א) וּמַכֵּה בְהֵמָה יְשַׁלְּמֶנָּה וּמַכֵּה אָדָם יוּמָת: [ויקרא כד, כא]

and since a fine is by its very nature a novelty, **even though he is executed, he** still **pays** the fine,"[10] מַתְנִיתִין כְּמַאן מוֹקִים לָהּ – as being **in accordance with whom does he interpret our Mishnah?**[11] אִי כְּרַבִּי מֵאִיר – **If** Rabbah interprets our Mishnah as being **in accordance with R' Meir,** who holds that one can receive lashes and pay money for the same crime,[12] קַשְׁיָא בִּתּוֹ – then the Mishnah's ruling[13] that one who violates **his daughter** is exempt from the fine **is difficult.**[14] אִי כְּרַבִּי נְחוּנְיָא בֶּן הַקָּנָה – **If** Rabbah interprets our Mishnah as being **in accordance with R' Nechunya ben HaKanah,** who holds with R' Meir that one can receive lashes and pay money for the same crime,[15] קַשְׁיָא אֲחוֹתוֹ – then the Mishnah's ruling that one who violates **his sister** is liable to the fine **is difficult.**[16] אִי כְּרַבִּי יִצְחָק – **If** Rabbah interprets our Mishnah as being **in accordance with R' Yitzchak,**[17] who argues with the Mishnah in *Makkos* 13a, and maintains that transgressions which carry the *kares* penalty do *not* carry the lashes penalty,[18] קַשְׁיָא מַמְזֶרֶת – then the Mishnah's ruling that one who violates **a *mamzeress*** is liable to the fine **is difficult.**[19] הָנִיחָא אִי סָבַר לָהּ כְּרַבִּי יוֹחָנָן – Now, **all is well if [Rabbah] holds with R' Yochanan,**[20] הוּא נַמִּי מְתָרֵץ לָהּ כְּרַבִּי יוֹחָנָן – for then **[Rabbah], too, can explain [our Mishnah] as** did **R' Yochanan.**[21] אֶלָּא אִי סָבַר כְּרֵישׁ לָקִישׁ – **But if [Rabbah] holds with Reish Lakish,**[22] הֵיכִי מְתָרֵץ לָהּ – **how does he explain our Mishnah?**[23]

The Gemara concludes:

עַל כָּרְחָךְ כְּרַבִּי יוֹחָנָן סְבִירָא לֵיהּ – **You are,** thus, **forced** to conclude **that [Rabbah] holds with R' Yochanan.**[24]

The Gemara asks:

אָמַר לֵיהּ רַב מַתְנָא לְאַבַּיֵי – **Rav Masna said to Abaye:** לְרֵישׁ לָקִישׁ דְּאָמַר בְּפֵירוּשׁ רִיבְּתָה תּוֹרָה חַיָּיבֵי מַלְקִיּוֹת כְּחַיָּיבֵי מִיתוֹת –

NOTES

10. I.e. although there is a general principle that liability to death exempts one from monetary liability, a fine, being an extrajudicial decree, is not subject to the general exemptions from monetary liability. Hence, liability to the death penalty does *not* exempt one from paying a fine.

11. In order to resolve the contradiction between our Mishnah (which states that one who violates his sister pays the fine) and the Mishnah in *Makkos* (which rules that one who cohabits with his sister receives lashes) (*Rashi*).

12. [As he states in the Mishnah, *Makkos* 4a (see above, 33b note 18).] This is the resolution presented above (33b) by Reish Lakish (*Rashi*).

13. Below, 36b.

14. Although Reish Lakish was able to answer that our Mishnah is authored by R' Meir, Rabbah cannot do so. For Reish Lakish (above, 33b) explained R' Meir's ruling in the Baraisa (that a thief is liable to the fourfold or fivefold penalty when the stolen animal was slaughtered on the Sabbath) as pertaining to where the thief slaughters the animal through his agent, and thus does not incur liability to the death penalty for Sabbath desecration. If, however, the thief himself had slaughtered the animal on the Sabbath, even R' Meir would exempt him from payment. For although R' Meir holds that one can receive lashes and pay money for the same crime, he agrees that one does not receive the death penalty and pay money for the same crime – even if that payment is a fine [e.g. the fourfold or fivefold penalty for slaughtering a stolen animal or the fifty-*shekel* fine for forcible violation]. Hence, our Mishnah's ruling that one who violates his daughter is exempt from the fine is compatible with the view of R' Meir.

Rabbah, though, explained above (34a-b) that R' Meir's ruling in the Baraisa applies even where the thief himself slaughters the stolen animal on the Sabbath. Even though he is liable to the death penalty, he must pay the fourfold or fivefold penalty, because liability to the death penalty does not exempt one from monetary *fines.* Accordingly, Rabbah cannot ascribe the authorship of our Mishnah to R' Meir. For our Mishnah rules that the death penalty one incurs for violating his daughter *does* exempt him from paying the *fine* of fifty *shekels*! (see *Rashi*).

15. That R' Nechunya ben HaKanah holds that one can receive lashes and pay money for the same crime can be deduced from his ruling (above, 30a) that desecrating Yom Kippur exempts one from monetary payment as does Sabbath desecration, because Yom Kippur desecration, too, subjects one to *kares* – a premature death at the hands of Heaven. For he derives through the *gezeirah shavah* of *ason, ason* that liability to death at the hands of Heaven exempts one from payment just like liability to a court-imposed death sentence. Now, if an act that carries the lashes penalty exempts one from payment, why must R' Nechunya ben HaKanah exempt the one who desecrates Yom Kippur from monetary payment on account of his liability to *kares*? Let him exempt the sinner simply on account of his having committed an offense that carries the lashes penalty! Evidently, R' Nechunya ben HaKanah must hold with R' Meir that one can receive lashes and pay money for the same crime; therefore, R' Nechunya exempts the Yom Kippur desecrator from monetary payment only because of the *kares* to which he is liable. And accordingly, our Mishnah, which rules that the violator pays the fine even where he is liable to lashes [but not in cases where he is liable to the death penalty, such as where he violates his daughter], could in fact be the opinion of R' Nechunya ben HaKanah, who maintains that one can receive lashes and pay money for the same crime, but one cannot receive the death penalty and pay money for the same crime, even when the payment is a fine (*Rashi*).

16. For although his liability to lashes for this crime does not exempt him from the fine for violation, R' Nechunya ben HaKanah would nevertheless exempt him from the fine on account of his liability to *kares* (*Rashi*).

17. *Makkos* 13b.

18. The Mishnah in *Makkos* 13a states that prohibitions which carry the *kares* penalty carry the lashes penalty as well, and accordingly rules that one who cohabits with his sister, his father's sister, his mother's sister, his wife's sister, his brother's wife, his father's brother's wife, or a *niddah,* receives lashes, even though these acts carry the *kares* penalty as well. This led to the Gemara's difficulty as to how our Mishnah can impose the fine for violating any of these women, in light of the principle that one cannot receive lashes and pay money for the same crime. If, however, our Mishnah is authored by R' Yitzchak, who maintains that transgressions which carry the *kares* penalty do *not* carry a lashes penalty, then the difficulty is resolved. [For one who cohabits with these women is *not* subject to lashes. Nor would R' Yitzchak hold with R' Nechunya ben HaKanah that *kares* itself exempts the sinner from monetary payment] (*Rashi*).

19. For everyone – even R' Yitzchak – agrees that one who cohabits with a *mamzeress* is liable to lashes [and not *kares*]. Yet, our Mishnah rules that the violator pays the fine in this case (*Rashi*).

20. Who maintains (above, 35a) that only one who is *actually* subject to lashes is exempt from paying money, but one who commits a lashes-bearing offense inadvertently or without being warned by witnesses is *not* exempt from paying the money (*Rashi*).

21. [Above, 32b.] That our Mishnah, which imposes the fine for the violation of girls forbidden on pain of lashes, is referring to where the one who violated them was *not* warned that he would receive lashes (*Rashi*).

22. Who maintains (above, 35a) that one who violates a lashes-bearing prohibition is exempt from paying money even if he was *not* warned. Accordingly, Rabbah would not agree with R' Yochanan [who explains that the Tanna of our Mishnah does not exempt the sinner from monetary payment where he was not warned about the lashes]. And he certainly would not agree with Ulla, who explains (above, 32a) that in cases of dual penalty, the monetary liability supersedes the lashes penalty [and thus resolves the contradiction between the two Mishnahs by interpreting the Mishnah in *Makkos* as referring to where there was no monetary liability] (see *Rashi*).

23. Since he cannot explain our Mishnah either as R' Yochanan did, nor as Ulla did, nor as Reish Lakish [see note 14] did (*Rashi*).

24. That is, if you assume that Rabbah [unlike Ulla] holds the generally accepted view that where there is liability to lashes and monetary payment, it is the lashes that supersedes the payment, then he must hold with R' Yochanan that the lashes exempts from monetary payment only where the sinner was warned and is thus actually subject to lashes. Accordingly, Rabbah would resolve the contradiction between the two Mishnahs by explaining (as R' Yochanan does) that our Mishnah, which imposes the fine on those who violate girls forbidden to them on pain of lashes, refers to where the violator was not warned that he would be subject to lashes (*Rashi*).

סוף סוף לאו בר תשלומין הוא (א) לא צריכא דבהדי דמחייה קרע שיראין דיליה א"ל רב חייא לרבא ולתנא דבי חזקיה דאמר מכה אדם ומכה בהמה ממאי דבחול כתיב וליכא לאיפלוגי דלמא בשבת כתיב דבבהמה גופה איכא לאיפלוגי לא ס"ד דכתיב א) ומכה בהמה ישלמנה ומכה אדם יומת היכי דמי אי דלא אתרו ביה מכה אדם אמאי יומת אלא פשיטא דאתרו ביה ואי בשבת מכה בהמה ישלמנה אלא לאו בחול א"ל רב פפא לאביי א) לרבה דאמר חידוש הוא שחידשה תורה בקנס ואף על גב דמיקטיל משלם מתניתין כמאן מוקים לה אי כר"מ קשיא בתו אי כרבי נחוניא בן הקנה קשיא אחותו אי כר' יצחק קשיא ממזרת הניחא אי סבר לה כר' יוחנן הוא נמי מתרץ לה כר' יוחנן אלא אי סבר כר"ל היכי מתרץ לה על כרחך כר' יוחנן ס"ל א"ל רב מתנא לאביי לר"ל דאמר בפירוש ריבתה תורה חייבי מלקיות כחייבי מיתות מאן תנא דפליג עליה דרבי נחוניא בן הקנה אי ר"מ אי רבי יצחק: ת"ר עריות ושניות לעריות אין להן לא קנס ולא פיתוי א הממאנת אין לה לא קנס ולא פיתוי איילונית אין לה לא קנס ולא פיתוי והיוצאת משום שם רע אין לה לא קנס ולא פיתוי מאי עריות ומאי שניות לעריות אילימא עריות עריות

רש"י

סוף סוף. האי לא תחלוק בו לחייבו ממון טעמא משום דאין בו כדי תשלומין ולא משום היקישא אבל היכא דיש בה שוה פרוטה אימא תחלוק: לא צריכא. להכי איתקש: דבהדי דמחייה קרע שיראין וכו'. כלומר ואשמועינן דלוקה משום חבלה ופטור מתשלומי קריעה לא שנא התרו בו ולא שנא לא התרו דלא לקי פטור מתשלומין מהיקישא דלא תחלוק: ממאי דבחול כתיב. דפשיטא ליה דמכה בהמה בין שוגג בין מזיד חייב לשלם: דלמא בשבת כתיב. ועל כרחך אשוגג כתיב קרא דאי במזיד הו"ל מתחייב בנפשו ופטור מן התשלומין: איכא לאיפלוגי. בין שוגג למזיד: לא ס"ד. דבשבת כתיב ובשוגג: ואי בשבת מכה בהמה ישלמנה. בתמיה: אלא לאו בחול. דליכא לפלוגי ואיתקש לה מכה אדם שלא תחלוק בו ואפי' אינו חייב מיתה: לרבה דאמר. לרבי מאיר חדוש הוא כו': מתניתין כמאן מוקים. לשנויי רומיא דרמינן עלה דאלו הן הלוקין וקיימא לן דאין לוקה ומשלם: אי כר' מאיר. דאמר לוקה ומשלם וכדשנינהו ריש לקיש: קשיא בתו. דבשלמא לריש לקיש דאוקמה להאי דגנב וטבח בשבת בטובח על ידי אחר אבל בטובח על ידי עצמו לא משלם לא קשיא דמת ומשלם לית ליה לר' מאיר אפי' בקנס אלא לרבה קשיא בתו דקנס הוא וקתני מתניתין פטור: ואי כר' נחוניא בן הקנה. דאית ליה נמי לוקה ומשלם כר' מאיר מדקאמר יום הכפורים כשבת יה"כ הוא דפטור מתשלומין ומשום כרת דאית ביה ומג"ש דאסון אסון אבל משום לאו ומלקות דאית ביה לא פטר ומתניתין נמי דאית ליה לוקה ומשלם דידיה הוא ומת ומשלם לית ליה אפי' בקנס: קשיא אחותו. נהי נמי דמשום מלקות לא פטר ליה ליפטר·ה משום כרת: ואי כרבי יצחק. תוקמה דאמר במסכת מכות (דף יד.) אין חייבי כריתות בכלל מלקות מ' ולית ליה האי דאלו הן הלוקין הבא על אחותו ומשום הכי חייבין בתשלומין: קשיא ממזרת. דהכל מודים שהוא במלקות וקתני אית לה קנס: הניחא אי סבר. רבה כר' יוחנן כשלא התרו בו דמשלם דחייבי מלקיות שוגגין ודבר אחר חייב: איהו נמי. מוקי למתני' בשלא התרו בו כר' יוחנן: אלא אי סבר לה. בממון ומלקות דאפי' לא התרו בו פטור מממון ופליג אדרבי יוחנן וכל שכן אדעולא דאמר אפילו התרו בו משלם ממון ואינו לוקה: היכי מתרץ לה. לא כר' יוחנן ולא כעולא ולא כריש לקיש: על כרחך. אי סבירא ליה בממון ומלקות דלוקה ואינו משלם כרבי יוחנן סבירא ליה בשוגגים דמשלם ממון ומוקי לה בשלא התרו בו: לריש לקיש דאמר בפירוש ריבתה תורה כו'. דחייבי מלקיות שוגגין פטורין מלשלם: מאן תנא דפליג אדר' נחוניא. ומחייב תשלומין בחייבי כריתות כגון ההיא דשבועות ושהדליק גדיש ביה"כ חייבין בפרק שבועת העדות (שבועות לג.) ומתני' דהכא דקנסה באחותו ונהי נמי דלית ליה אסון אסון למיפטריה משום כרת ליפטריה משום לאו בין התרו בו בין לא התרו בו דאין כרת בלא לאו חוץ מפסח ומילה דבשלמא ר' יוחנן מוקי לה אפילו כרבנן דפליגי עליה דרבי מאיר דאמרי אין לוקה ומשלם והני בשלא התרו בו אלא לריש לקיש כמאן מוקי לה: אי רבי מאיר. דאמר לוקה ומשלם: אי רבי יצחק. דאמר לא שייך מלקות בחייבי כריתות וג"ש דאסון אסון לית ליה ובמאי ליפטר הילכך מתניתין דהכא על כרחך ר"מ היא ולא רבי יצחק משום דקשיא ממזרת אבל ההיא דשבועות בין כר"מ בין כרבי יצחק: עריות ושניות. לקמן מפרש להו: קנס. דאנוסה: פיתוי. דמפותה: הממאנת. בבעלה כגון יתומה קטנה שהשיאתה אמה ומיאנה בבעלה: אין לה קנס. שאינה בחזקת בתולה הואיל וניסת: איילונית. שאין לה סימני נערות לעולם ואינה יולדת לשון איל זכר דוכרניתא דלא ילדה (לעיל דף יא.): אין לה קנס. לפי שאין קנס אלא לנערה וזו שלא תביא שערות לעולם כל כ' שנה היא בחזקת קטנה ומשם ואילך בוגרת: והיוצאת משום שם רע. קס"ד שלא מצא לה בעלה בתולים ולקמן פריך בת סקילה היא:

עריות

תוספות

אם אינו ענין להכאה שיש בה שוה פרוטה. וא"ת והא איצטריך להכי דמהכא נפקא לן חובל בחברו לתשלומין בריש החובל (ב"ק פג: ושם) וי"ל דהך סוגיא כאידך תנאי דהתם דמפקי החובל בחברו לתשלומין מקרא אחרינא: דלמא בשבת כתיב דבבהמה גופה כו'. וא"ת א"כ היקישא למה לי וי"ל דאתיא לבין דרך ירידה לדרך עלייה דלא שייך לפלוגי גבי שבת: אלא לאו בחול. וא"ת בחול נמי מצינן למימר דבהדי דמחייה לבהמה הרג את האדם ולא אתרו ביה משום אדם ואפי' בשבת נמי מצינן למימר דאתרו ביה משום בהמה ולא אתרו בו משום שבת וי"ל דמ"מ ילפינן שפיר דמה מכה בהמה לא חלקת בין שוגג בהכאתה למזיד בהכאתה אף אדם לא תחלוק בו בין מזיד בהכאתו לשוגג בהכאתו א"נ הו"ל ומכה אדם איירי באתרו ביה ומכה בהמה נמי איירי בכל ענין דאתרו ביה ולהכי לא מצי איירי בשבת ולא בהרג אדם עמה: מתניתין כמאן מוקי לה. א) תימה תיקשי ליה לרב פפא גופיה דאיהו סבר לעיל (דף לד:) כרבה דאמר היתה פרה גנובה לו כו' ועוד קשה דלישני כעולא דמאי פריך בקונ' דאי סבר כריש לקיש דחייבי מלקיות שוגגין פטורין כ"ש דפליג אדעולא זה אינו נראה דלמא בממון אחר סבר כריש לקיש אבל בממונא דההוא מילתא גופיה משלם ממון ומיפטר ממלקות מג"ש דתחת תחת ב) ונראה דרב פפא אפי' סבר כר"ל מצי לשנויי כעולא כדפרישית אבל לאביי פריך שפיר דלית ליה דעולא דהא מוקי לעיל תחת לדרשא אחרינא ולהכי קשיא ליה אי ס"ל כר"ל מתני' כמאן מוקי לה: אי כר' נחוניא קשיא אחותו. לא מצי למימר ממזרת ואחותו דע"כ כר"מ ס"ל מדנקט יום הכפורים כשבת והו"ל למימר יו"ט כשבת וכ"ש יום הכפורים אלא ודאי ס"ל או כר"מ דאמר לוקה ומשלם או כר' יצחק דאמר אין מלקות בחייבי כריתות הלכך לא נקט יו"ט דמיניה לא הוה שמעינן יוה"כ שאין בו מלקות וכיון דלא הוי כרבנן לא מוקמי ליה כרבי יצחק אלא כר"מ ולא תיקשי ממזרת: אי כרבי יצחק קשיא ממזרת. לא הוצרך לומר אי כרבנן קשיא ממזרת ואחותו ולא מצי למימר נמי דמתני' כרבי עקיבא דסבר עדים זוממין קנסא ואית ליה לוקה ומשלם ולית ליה מת ומשלם לדרבי עקיבא מצינן למימר דלא גמר עדים זוממין ממוציא ש"ר אע"ג דהוי קנסא מקנסא כדפרי' לעיל (דף לב. ד"ה דאין) ואית ליה שפיר כרבנן דלוקה ואינו משלם: מאן תנא דפליג עליה דרבי נחוניא אי ר' מאיר אי רבי יצחק. תימה דלר"ל נקיש בהדיא פליג ר"מ ארבי נחוניא דהא מוקים מתני' כר"מ וקתני דיש קנס בחייבי כריתות וי"ל דידע שפיר דר"מ פליג עליה אלא דק"ל דרבנן לא מצינן למימר דפליגי עליה אבל לר' יוחנן אתי שפיר: לא קנס ולא פיתוי. אית דגרס ולא אונס משום דפיתוי נמי קנס הוא ואומר ר"י דגרסי' ליה דשייך למיקרי לאונס קנס טפי מלפיתוי משום דאונס שותה בעציצו (לקמן דף לט:):

הממאנת אין לה לא קנס. פירש בקונט' לפי שהיא בחזקת בעולה וקשה לר"י היכי דייק לקמן הא קטנה בעלמא אית לה דלמא ה"ק הממאנת אין לה קנס אם בא עליה כשהיא נערה הא בעלמא אית לה ומיהו אין להקשות אמאי נקט ממאנת ה"ל למינקט כל אשה שניסת ונתגרשה דהא איכא למ"ד לקמן (דף לח.) דאפי' אם נתארסה ונתגרשה אין לה קנס ונראה לר"י דה"פ אין לה לא קנס ולא פיתוי אם אנסה בעלה או פיתה אותה כשהיתה תחתיו קודם מיאון אע"ג דכשמיאנה איגלאי מילתא שלא היתה אשתו והשתא דייק שפיר לקמן הא קטנה בעלמא אית לה אבל קשה לר"י מהא דקאמר בסמוך וכ"ת כולה ר"מ היא וממאנת סבר לה כרבי יהודה והשתא כיון דאיירי שבא עליה בעלה כשהיא נערה שוב אינה יכולה למאן דמודה רבי יהודה כשבעל כדאמר בפרק בא סימן (נדה נב. ושם) ותירץ ר"י דמיירי כשפירש בהדיא שאינו בועל לשם קידושין ועוד דפיתוי ואונס לאו לשם קידושין הוא דבהא לא מודה רבי יהודה:

ולא פיתוי. קשה לרשב"א אמאי נקט פיתוי למאי דמוקי לה בסמוך בנערה הא כל נערה מפותה אין לה קנס דמחלה אפי' נערה שאינה ממאנת ויש לומר דנקט אין לה פיתוי אגב דנקט באידך:

אבל

עין משפט נר מצוה

מג א מיי' פ"א מהל' נערה בתולה הל' ט סמג עשין כד טור אה"ע סי' קעז:

ליקוטי רש"י

שיראין. של משי [מנחות לט:]. חידוש הוא שחידשה תורה בקנס. בכל תשלומי קנס שאינו דין אלא גזרת מלך בעלמא וכיון דחידוש הוא וגזירת חוק אימא אע"ג דאיכא בהדיה מיתה לשלם [לקמן לח.]. כל משפט קנס חידוש הוא הלכך אע"ג דמיקטיל נמי לא מיפטר מיניה [לעיל לד:].

מסורת הש"ס

א) [לעיל לד: לקמן לח.].

תוספות ישנים

א) [לרב פפא לא שייך למיפרך דהא לא פריך לנפשיה משום דידע דסבר כר' יוחנן דלא דריש ג"ש דרשע ודמכה וכ"מ קלת דקאמר הי מכה. ת"י]:

ב) לפי' ר"י דלעיל אתי שפיר דרשב"ל מוקי לה כר"מ אבל רבה כמאן מוקי לה אי כר' נחוניא קשיא אחותו דלדידיה אחותו לית לה קנס דחד ריבויא מוקי לחייבי לאוין וחד ליבמה לשוק אי כדפי' רשב"א לעיל קשיא אחותו דאי נוקי חד קרא לחייבי כריתות א"כ חייבי מיתות נמי ולמה שהביא מהר"מ לעיל בתוס' אתי טפי שפיר אי ר' יצחק קשיא ממזרת דלדידיה מוקמינן חד לחייבי עשה וחד לחייבי כריתות הניחא אי סבר לה כר' יוחנן אלא אי סבר כרשב"ל דחייבי מלקות שוגגין פטורין א"כ איצטריך תרי ריבויי חד לחייבי עשה וחד לחייבי לאוין והא דלא קאמר אי כרבנן קשיא אחותו משום דעיקר קושיא כבר הקשה לרבנן לעיל והא קי"ל דאין לוקה ומשלם ולכך לא חזר והקשה. ת"י עה"ג:

הגהות הב"ח

(א) גמ' תשלומין הוא (לא צריכא) תא"מ ונ"ב ס"א הא לא קשיא:

תורה אור השלם

א) וּמַכֵּה בְהֵמָה יְשַׁלְּמֶנָּה וּמַכֵּה אָדָם יוּמָת: [ויקרא כד, כא]

The Gemara asks:

סוֹף סוֹף – But **in the final analysis,** one can still not derive from this juxtaposition that committing an offense which carries the lashes penalty exempts one from monetary payment in all instances,[1] לָאו בַּר תַּשְׁלוּמִין הוּא – for since the verse is discussing a blow that does not amount to a *perutah* in damages, **he is not subject to payment** altogether![2] – ? –

The Gemara answers:

לֹא צְרִיכָא – **This is not** a difficulty. **It is** only **necessary** to explain that the purpose of the juxtaposition is for the case דִּבַהֲדֵי דְּמַחְיֵיהּ קָרַע שִׁירָאִין דִּילֵיהּ – **where together with striking him, he** also **ripped his silks.**[3]

The Gemara returns to discuss the Baraisa taught in the academy of Chizkiyah, cited above on 35a:

אָמַר לֵיהּ רַב חִיָּיא לְרָבָא: וּלְתַנָּא דְּבֵי חִזְקִיָּה דְּאָמַר – **Rav Chiya said to Rava: But according to the Tanna of the academy of Chizkiyah, who says** "מַכֵּה אָדָם", "וּמַכֵּה בְהֵמָה" – that the juxtaposition of ***one who strikes*** (and kills) ***a person*** and ***one who strikes an animal*** teaches us that just as one who strikes an animal is always liable to payment, whether he did so deliberately or inadvertently, so too is one who kills a person always exempt from payment, מִמַּאי דִּבְחוֹל כְּתִיב וְלֵיכָּא לְאִיפְּלוּגֵי – **on the basis of what** does he presume that **[the verse] is written with regard to** one who strikes an animal on **a weekday and it is** thus **not possible to distinguish** between a deliberate and inadvertent act?[4] דִּלְמָא בְּשַׁבָּת כְּתִיב – **Perhaps [the verse] is written with regard to** one who strikes an animal on **the Sabbath,** דְּבִבְהֵמָה גּוּפָהּ אִיכָּא לְאִיפְּלוּגֵי – **where** in the case of striking **an animal itself, it is possible**[5] **to distinguish** between a deliberate and inadvertent act![6] – ? –

The Gemara answers:

לֹא סָלְקָא דַּעְתָּךְ – **It should not enter your mind** to say that the verse refers to where he struck the animal on the Sabbath and inadvertently. דִּכְתִיב, "וּמַכֵּה בְהֵמָה יְשַׁלְּמֶנָּה וּמַכֵּה אָדָם יוּמָת" – **For it is written** in that verse: ***One who strikes an animal shall pay for it, and one who strikes*** (and kills) ***a person shall be put to death.*** הֵיכִי דָּמֵי – Now, **what is the case** with which this verse is dealing? אִי דְּלָא אַתְרוּ בֵּיהּ – **If** it is dealing with **where witnesses did not warn him** that his act would make him liable to the death penalty, מַכֵּה אָדָם אַמַּאי יוּמָת – then **why** in the case of **one who strikes** and kills **a person is he put to death?** אֶלָּא פְּשִׁיטָא דְּאַתְרוּ בֵּיהּ – **Rather, it is obvious** that the verse deals with **where witnesses warned him** that his act would make him liable to the death penalty. וְאִי בְּשַׁבָּת מַכֵּה בְהֵמָה יְשַׁלְּמֶנָּה – **And if** the verse refers to where the acts of striking the animal and the person were done **on the Sabbath,** as you propose, would the verse state that **one who strikes an animal shall pay for it?**[7] אֶלָּא לָאו בְּחוֹל – **Rather,** must you **not** conclude that the verse refers to where the striking of the animal occurred **on a weekday?**[8] Certainly you must conclude so.

The Gemara now considers the view of Rabbah, whose opinion regarding R' Meir's view was cited above, 34a-b:

אָמַר לֵיהּ רַב פַּפָּא לְאַבַּיֵי: לְרַבָּה דְּאָמַר חִידּוּשׁ הוּא שֶׁחִידְּשָׁה תּוֹרָה בִּקְנָס וְאַף עַל גַּב דְּמִיקְטִיל מְשַׁלֵּם – **Rav Pappa said to Abaye: According to Rabbah, who says**[9] that R' Meir holds **"it is a novelty that the Torah innovated in** the imposition of **a fine,**

NOTES

1. Without distinguishing between whether the offense was committed deliberately or inadvertently.

2. I.e. granted that the juxtaposition (one who strikes his fellow a blow whose injury does not amount to a *perutah,* and one who strikes an animal) states, in effect, that one who strikes his fellow a blow that does not amount to a *perutah* in damages is always exempt from payment — even when he is not subjected to lashes — we still cannot derive from this that the same applies in other cases where one inadvertently commits an act that carries the lashes penalty. For in this source case there is nothing at all to pay, since the injury amounted to less than a *perutah.* Where, however, one incurs a monetary liability of a *perutah,* perhaps we do distinguish between where the sinner is actually subjected to lashes and where he is not, and do not exempt him from payment when the transgression was committed inadvertently (see *Rashi;* cf. *Rashash*).

3. [If the Torah meant the case in which the assailant merely struck his fellow a blow that does not amount to a *perutah* in damages, we would then learn nothing from the juxtaposition of that case to the case of one who strikes an animal. If we are to take this juxtaposition to be significant, the verse must refer to where together with that blow (which does not inflict a *perutah's* worth of damage) that assailant ripped his victim's silks. In that case, if the assailant was warned that he would be liable to lashes for striking the blow (for violating *he shall not add*), he would receive lashes and not pay for the silks, since in cases of liability to both monetary payment and lashes the law is that one receives lashes and does not pay the money. (*Ritva* notes that although the Gemara [32b] explains that in the case of חוֹבֵל בַּחֲבֵירוֹ, *one who wounds his fellow,* the Torah decrees that the payment of money supersedes the lashes, that applies only where the money is paid *for the wounding.* In the present case, however, where the money is to be paid for property damage [the silks] and there is no payment for wounding, the usual law prevails that the penalty of lashes supersedes the payment of money.)] And the juxtaposition of the verses teaches us that just as in the case of one who strikes an animal, there is no difference between advertence and inadvertence, etc., so too in the case of one who strikes his fellow (viz. a blow that does not inflict a *perutah's* worth of damage) and rips his silks, there is no difference between advertence and inadvertence, etc. In either case, the fact that the crime is one that bears the penalty of lashes exempts the sinner from simultaneous monetary liability, even if he was not warned and thus does not receive lashes (see *Rashi*).

4. [If the striking of the animal is done on a weekday (and there is thus no Sabbath desecration to exempt the striker from monetary liability), it is not possible to distinguish between whether the striking was done deliberately or inadvertently. For a person is liable for damages that he inflicts regardless of whether or not he inflicted them deliberately (see 35a note 9).]

The Tanna of this Baraisa, in taking for granted that one who strikes an animal is always liable to payment regardless of whether the act was committed deliberately or inadvertently, evidently presumes that the verse refers to where the act was committed on a weekday. [For had it been committed on the Sabbath, there would be a distinction — see note 6.] The Gemara now challenges this presumption (see *Rashi*).

5. [The word אִיכָּא, *it is possible,* seems imprecise. For if the verse is discussing one who strikes an animal on the Sabbath, we *must* distinguish between a deliberate and an inadvertent act; see following note (see *Shitah Mekubetzes* ד״ה דילמא).]

6. If the verse (which states that one who strikes an animal must pay for it) refers to one who strikes an animal on the Sabbath, we are forced to say that he did so inadvertently. For had he done so deliberately, he would be liable to the death penalty for desecrating the Sabbath, and thus *exempt* from payment (*Rashi*). [And accordingly, the verse would be stating — in contradiction to the Baraisa taught in the academy of Chizkiyah — that one who incurs a monetary liability while inadvertently committing a capital offense (e.g. Sabbath desecration) is *liable* to payment.]

7. Since he was warned that striking the animal on the Sabbath would make him liable to the death penalty, he is actually liable to it and therefore certainly exempt from payment!

8. In which case he is always liable to payment, regardless of whether he did so deliberately or inadvertently. Hence, the juxtaposition to *one who strikes a person* teaches us not to distinguish in that case either between where the act was done deliberately or inadvertently, and thus we derive that a capital crime exempts one from payment even when he is not actually subjected to the death penalty (*Rashi*).

9. In explanation of R' Meir's ruling in the Baraisa cited on 33b that a thief who slaughters the stolen animal on the Sabbath is liable to the fourfold or fivefold penalty, even though his act of slaughtering makes him liable to the death penalty for Sabbath desecration.

סוף סוף לאו בר תשלומין הוא (א) לא צריכא דבהדי דמחייה קרע שיראין דיליה א"ל רב חייא לרבא ולתנא דבי חזקיה דאמר מכה אדם ומכה בהמה ממאי דבחול כתיב וליכא לאיפלוגי דלמא בשבת כתיב דבבהמה גופה איכא לאיפלוגי לא ס"ד דכתיב א) ומכה בהמה ישלמנה ומכה אדם יומת היכי דמי אי דלא אתרו ביה מכה אדם אמאי יומת אלא פשיטא דאתרו ביה ואי בשבת מכה בהמה ישלמנה אלא לאו בחול א"ל רב פפא לאביי א) לרבה דאמר חידוש הוא שחידשה תורה בקנס ואף על גב דמיקטיל משלם מתניתין כמאן מוקים לה אי כר"מ קשיא בתו אי כרבי נחוניא בן הקנה קשיא אחותו אי כר' יצחק קשיא ממזרת הניחא אי סבר לה כר' יוחנן הוא נמי מתרץ לה כר' יוחנן אלא אי סבר כר"ל היכי מתרץ לה על כרחך כר' יוחנן ס"ל א"ל רב מתנא לאביי לר"ל דאמר בפירוש ריבתה תורה חייבי מלקיות כחייבי מיתות מאן תנא דפליג עליה דרבי נחוניא בן הקנה אי ר"מ אי רבי יצחק: ת"ר עריות ושניות לעריות אין להן לא קנס ולא פיתוי א הממאנת אין לה לא קנס ולא פיתוי איילונית אין לה לא קנס ולא פיתוי והיוצאת משום שם רע אין לה לא קנס ולא פיתוי מאי עריות ומאי שניות לעריות אילימא עריות

עריות

סוף סוף. האי לא תחלוק בו לחייבו ממון טעמא משום דאין בו כדי תשלומין ולא משום היקישא אבל היכא דיש בה שוה פרוטה אימא תחלוק: לא צריכא. להכי איתקש: דבהדי דמחייה קרע שיראין וכו'. כלומר ואשמועינן דלוקה משום חבלה ופטור מתשלומי קריעה לא שנא התרו בו ולא שנא לא התרו דלא לקי פטור מתשלומין מהיקישא דלא תחלוק: ממאי דבחול כתיב. דפשיטא ליה דמכה בהמה בין שוגג בין מזיד חייב לשלם: דלמא בשבת כתיב. ועל כרחך בשוגג כתיב קרא דאי במזיד הו"ל מתחייב בנפשו ופטור מן התשלומין: איכא לאיפלוגי. בין שוגג למזיד: לא ס"ד. דבשבת כתיב ובשוגג: ואי בשבת מכה בהמה ישלמנה. בתמיה: אלא לאו בחול. דליכא לפלוגי ואיתקש לה מכה אדם שלא תחלוק בו ואפי' אינו חייב מיתה: לרבה דאמר. לרבי מאיר חדוש הוא כו': מתניתין כמאן מוקים. לשנויי רומיא דרמינן עלה דאלו הן הלוקין וקיימא לן דאין לוקה ומשלם: אי כר' מאיר. דאמר לוקה ומשלם ולדמינהו ריש לקיש: קשיא בתו. דבשלמא לריש לקיש לאוקמא להכיא דגנב וטבח בשבת בטובח על ידי אחר אבל בטובח על ידי עצמו לא משלם לא קשיא דמת ומשלם לית ליה לר' מאיר אפי' בקנס אלא לרבה קשיא בתו דקנס הוא וקתני מתניתין פטור: ואי כר' נחוניא בן הקנה. דאית ליה נמי לוקה ומשלם כר' מאיר מדקאמר יום הכפורים כשבת יה"כ הוא לפטור מתשלומין ומשום כרת דאית ביה ומג"ש דאסון אסון אבל משום לאו ומלקות דאית ביה לא פטר ומתניתין נמי דאית ליה לוקה ומשלם דידיה הוא ומת ומשלם לית ליה אפי' בקנס: קשיא אחותו. נהי נמי דמשום מלקות לא פטר ליה ליפטריה משום כרת: ואי כרבי יצחק. תוקמה דאמר במסכת מכות (דף יג.) אין חייבי כריתות בכלל מלקות מ' ולית ליה האי דלאו הן הלוקין הבא על אחותו ומשום הכי חייבין בתשלומין: קשיא ממזרת. דהכל מודים שהוא במלקות וקתני אית לה קנס: הניחא אי סבר. רבה כר' יוחנן בשלא התרו בו משלם דחייבי מלקות שוגגין ודבר אחר חייב: איהו נמי. מוקי למתני' בשלא התרו בו כר' יוחנן: אלא אי סבר לה. בממון ומלקות דאפי' לא התרו בו פטור מממון ופליג אדרבי יוחנן וכל שכן אדעולא דאמר אפילו התרו בו משלם ממון ואינו לוקה: היכי מתרץ לה. לא כר' יוחנן ולא כעולא ולא כריש לקיש: על כרחך. אי סבירא ליה בממון ומלקות דלוקה ואינו משלם כרבי יוחנן סבירא ליה בשוגגים דמשלם ממון ומוקי לה בשלא התרו בו: לריש לקיש דאמר בפירוש ריבתה תורה כו'. דחייבי מלקיות שוגגין פטורין מלשלם: מאן תנא דפליג אדר' נחוניא. ומחייב תשלומין בחייבי כריתות כגון הבא על אחותו ומתניתין דהכא ושהדליק גדיש ביה"כ חייבין בפרק שבועת העדות (שבועות לג.) וממתני' דהכא דקנסא באחותו ונהי נמי דלית ליה אסון אסון ליפטריה משום כרת ליפטריה משום לאו בין התרו בו בין לא התרו בו דאין כרת בלא לאו חוץ מפסח ומילה דבשלמא ר' יוחנן מוקי לה אפילו כרבנן דפליגי עליה דרבי מאיר דאמרי אין לוקה ומשלם והני בשלא התרו בו אלא לריש לקיש כמאן מוקי לה: אי רבי מאיר. דאמר לוקה ומשלם: אי רבי יצחק. דאמר לא שייך מלקות בחייבי כריתות וג"ש דאסון אסון לית ליה ובמאי ליפטר הילכך מתניתין דהכא על כרחך ר"מ היא ולא רבי יצחק משום דקשיא ממזרת אבל ההיא דשבועות בין כר"מ בין כרבי יצחק: עריות ושניות. לקמן מפרש להו: קנס. לאונסה: פיתוי. למפותה: הממאנת. בבעלה כגון יתומה קטנה שהשיאתה אמה ומיאנה בבעלה: אין לה קנס. שאינה בחזקת בתולה הואיל ונשאת: איילונית. שאין לה סימני נערות לעולם ואינה יולדת לשון איל זכר דוכרניתא דלא ילדה (לעיל דף יא.): אין לה קנס. לפי שאין קנס אלא לנערה וזו שלא תביא שערות לעולם כל כ' שנה היא בחזקת קטנה ומשם ואילך בוגרת: והיוצאת משום שם רע. קס"ד שלא מצא לה בעלה בתולים ולקמן פריך בת סקילה היא:

עריות

אם אינו ענין להכאה שיש בה שוה פרוטה. וא"ת והא אילטריך להכי דמהכא נפקא לן חובל בחברו לתשלומין בריש החובל (ב"ק פג: ושם) וי"ל דהך סוגיא כאידך תנאי דהתם דמפקי החובל בחברו לתשלומין מקרא אחרינא: דלמא בשבת כתיב דבבהמה גופה כו'. וא"ת א"כ היקישא למה לי וי"ל דאתיא לבין דרך ירידה לדרך עלייה דלא שייך לפלוגי גבי שבת: אלא לאו בחול. וא"ת בחול נמי מצינן למימר דבהדי דמחייה לבהמה הרג את האדם ולא אתרו ביה משום אדם ואפי' בשבת נמי מצינן למימר דאתרו ביה משום בהמה ולא אתרו בו משום שבת וי"ל דמ"מ ילפינן שפיר דמה מכה בהמה לא חלקת בין שוגג בהכאתה למזיד בהכאתה אף אדם לא תחלוק בו בין מזיד בהכאתו לשוגג בהכאתו א"נ הואיל ומכה אדם איירי באתרו ביה מכה בהמה נמי איירי בכל ענין דאתרו ביה ולהכי לא מצי איירי בשבת ולא בהרג אדם עמה: מתניתין כמאן מוקי לה. א) תימה תיקשי ליה לרב פפא גופיה דאיהו סבר לעיל (דף לד:) כרבה דאמר היתה פרה גנובה לו כו' ועוד קשה דלישני כעולא דמאי דפירש בקונ' דאי סבר כריש לקיש דחייבי מלקיות שוגגין פטורין כ"ש דפליג אדעולא זה אינו נראה דלמא בממון אחר סבר כריש לקיש אבל בממונא דבההוא מילתא גופיה משלם ממון ומיפטר ממלקות מג"ש דתחת תחת ב) ונראה דרב פפא אפי' סבר כר"ל מצי לשנויי כדעולא כדפרישית אבל לאביי פריך שפיר דלית ליה דעולא דהא מוקי לעיל תחת לדרשא אחרינא ולהכי קשיא ליה אי ס"ל כר"ל מתני' כמאן מוקי לה: אי כר' נחוניא קשיא אחותו. לא מצי למימר קשיא ממזרת ואחותו דע"כ כר"מ ס"ל מדנקט יום הכפורים כשבת וה"ל למימר יו"ט כשבת וכ"ש יום הכפורים אלא ודאי ס"ל או כר"מ דאמר לוקה ומשלם או כר' יצחק דאמר אין מלקות בחייבי כריתות הלכך לא נקט יו"ט דמיניה לא הוה שמעינן יוה"כ שאין בו מלקות וכיון דלא הוי כרבנן לא מוקמי ליה כרבי יצחק אלא כר"מ ולא תיקשי ממזרת: אי כרבי יצחק קשיא ממזרת. לא הוצרך לומר אי כרבנן דלדידהו קשיא ממזרת ואחותו ולא מצי למימר נמי דמתני' כרבי עקיבא דסבר עדים זוממין קנסא ואית ליה לוקה ומשלם ולית ליה מת ומשלם דלרבי עקיבא מצינן למימר דלא גמר עדים זוממין ממוליא ש"ר אע"ג דהוי קנסא מקנסא כדפרי' לעיל (דף לג. ד"ה דאין) ואית ליה שפיר כרבנן דלוקה ואינו משלם: מאן תנא דפליג עליה דרבי נחוניא אי ר' מאיר אי רבי יצחק. תימה דלריש לקיש בהדיא פליג ר"מ ארבי נחוניא דהא מוקים מתני' כר"מ וקתני דיש קנס בחייבי כריתות וי"ל דידע שפיר דר"מ פליג עליה אלא דק"ל דרבנן לא מצינן למימר דפליגי עליה אבל לר' יוחנן אתי שפיר: לא קנס ולא פיתוי. אית דגרס ולא אונס משום דפיתוי נמי קנס הוא ואומר ר"י דגרסי' ליה דשייך למיקרי לאונס קנס טפי מלפיתוי משום דאונס שותה בעציצו (לקמן דף לט.): הממאנת אין לה לא קנס. פירש בקונט' לפי שהיא בחזקת בעולה וקשה לר"י דא"כ היכי דייק לקמן הא קטנה בעלמא אית לה דלמא ה"ק הממאנת אין לה קנס אם בא עליה כשהיא נערה הא נערה בעלמא אית לה ומיהו אין להקשות אמאי נקט ממאנת ה"ל למינקט כל אשה שניסת ונתגרשה דהא איכא למ"ד לקמן (דף לח.) דאפי' אם נתארסה ונתגרשה אין לה קנס ונראה לר"י דה"פ אין לה לא קנס ולא פיתוי אם אנסה בעלה או פיתה אותה כשהיתה תחתיו קודם מיאון אע"ג דכשמיאנה איגלאי מילתא שלא היתה אשתו והשתא דייק שפיר לקמן הא קטנה בעלמא אית לה אבל קשה לר"י מהא דקאמר בסמוך וכ"ת כולה ר"מ היא וממאנת סבר לה כרבי יהודה והשתא כיון דאיירי שבא עליה בעלה כשהיא נערה שוב אינה יכולה למאן דמודה רבי יהודה כשבעל כדאמר בפרק בא סימן (נדה נב. ושם) ותירץ ר"י דמיירי כשפירש בהדיא שאינו בועל לשם קידושין ועוד דפיתוי ואונס לאו לשם קידושין הוא דבההיא לא מודה רבי יהודה: ולא פיתוי. קשה לרשב"א אמאי נקט פיתוי למאי דמוקי לה בסמוך בנערה הא כל נערה מפותה אין לה קנס דמחלה אפי' נערה שאינה ממאנת וי"ל דנקט אין לה פיתוי אגב דנקט באידך:

אבל

עין משפט
נר מצוה

מג א מיי' פ"א מהל' נערה בתולה הל' ט סמג עשין כד טור אה"ע סי' קעז:

ליקוטי רש"י

שיראין. של משי [בבבות לט:]. חידוש הוא שחידשה תורה בקנס. בכל תשלומי קנס שאינו דין אלא גזרת מלך בעלמא וכיון דחידוש הוא וגזירת חוק איתא כע"ג לאיכא בהדיה מיתה משלם [לקמן לח.]. כל משפט קנס חידוש הוא שלכך אע"ג דמיקטיל נמי לא מיפטר מיניה [לעיל לד:].

מסורת הש"ס

א) [לעיל לד: לקמן לח.]

תוספות ישנים

א) [לרב פפא לא שייך למיפרך דהא לא פריך לנפשיה משום דידע דסבר כר' יוחנן דלא דריש ג"ש דרשע ודמכה וכו"מ קלת דקאמר הי מכה. מ"י]: ב) לפי' ר"י דלעיל אתי שפיר דרשב"ל מוקי לה כר"מ אבל רבה כמאן מוקי לה אי כר' נחוניא ליכא לה קנס דהד לאין ומשום כרת והיה ליבמה לשוק אי כדפי' רשב"א לעיל קשיא אחותו דלא נוקי חד קרא לחייבי כריתות אלא בחייבי מיתות נמי ולמה שכתב מהר"מ לעיל בתוס' אתי נמי שפיר אי ר' יצחק קשיא ממזרת דהא מוקמינן מה לחייבי עשה ומה לחייבי כריתות הניחא אי סבר כר' יוחנן אלא אי סבר כרשב"ל לחייבי מלקות שוגגין פטורין א"כ אילטריך תרי ריבויי חד לחייבי עשה וחד לחייבי לאוין והא דלא קאמר מי כרבנן קשיא אחותו משום דעיקר קושיא כבר הקשה לרבנן לעיל והא ק"ל דאין לוקה ומשלם ולכך לא חזר והקשה. מ"י עכ"ג:

הגהות הב"ח

(א) גמ' תשלומין הוא לא צריכא. תא"מ ונ"ב ס"א הא לא קשיא:

תורה אור השלם

א) וּמַכֵּה בְהֵמָה יְשַׁלְּמֶנָּה וּמַכֵּה אָדָם יוּמָת: [ויקרא כד, כא]

מאי לאו אסון ממש לא דין אסון איכא דאמרי איתיביה רבי יוחנן לר"ל א) ולא יהיה אסון ענוש יענש מאי לאו דין אסון לא אסון ממש אמר רבא ומי איכא למ"ד חייבי מיתות שוגגין חייבים והא תנא א) דבי חזקיה ב) *מכה אדם ומכה בהמה מה מכה בהמה לא חילקת בו בין בשוגג בין במזיד בין מתכוין לשאין מתכוין בין דרך ירידה לדרך עלייה לפוטרו ממון אלא לחייבו ממון אף מכה אדם לא תחלוק בו בין בשוגג בין במזיד בין מתכוין לשאין מתכוין בין דרך ירידה לדרך עלייה לחייבו ממון אלא לפוטרו ממון אלא כי אתא רבין אמר ב חייבי מיתות שוגגין כולי עלמא לא פליגי דפטורין כי פליגי בחייבי מלקות שוגגין ודבר אחר ג רבי יוחנן אמר חייב חייבי מיתות איתקוש חייבי מלקיות לא איתקוש ריש לקיש אמר פטור בפירוש ריבתה תורה חייבי מלקיות כחייבי מיתות היכן ריבתה תורה ג) אמר אביי אתיא ג) רשע ד) רשע רבא אמר אתיא מכה מכה אמר ליה רב פפא לרבא ג) הי מכה אילימא ב) ומכה בהמה ישלמנה ומכה אדם יומת האי בקטלא כתיב אלא האי מכה ה) מכה נפש בהמה ישלמנה נפש תחת נפש וסמיך ליה ו) ואיש כי יתן מום בעמיתו [כאשר עשה כן יעשה לו] והאי לאו מכה היא אנן הכאה הכאה קאמרינן והא כי כתיב בחובל בחבירו הוא דכתיב וחובל בחבירו בר תשלומין הוא אם אינו ענין להכאה שיש בה שוה פרוטה ד תנהו ענין להכאה שאין בה שוה פרוטה

סוף

רש"י

מאי לאו אסון ממש. אם לא מתה האשה יענש הנוגף בדמי ולדות הא אם מתה לא יענש ואפי' לא התרו בו וקשיא לר' יוחנן: **לא דין אסון.** הכי קאמר קרא אם אין משפט מות לנוגף כגון שלא מתה האשה או מתה ולא התרו בו ענוש יענש: **מכה אדם ומכה בהמה.** מכה בהמה ישלמנה ומכה אדם לא ישלם אלא יומת הקיש פטור ממון דמכה אדם לחיוב ממון דמכה בהמה מה מכה בהמה אין לך בו חילוק ד) לחיוב אף מכה אדם אין לך בו חילוק ה) לפטור מכה בהמה לעולם חייב דאמרי' בב"ק (דף כו:) פצע תחת פצע לחייב על השוגג כמזיד ואונס כרצון: **שאין מתכוין.** אין בו חיוב מיתה באדם: **דרך עלייה.** שהכהו בהגבהת ידו או שחתכו בחרבו מלמטה למעלה: **בין דרך ירידה לדרך עלייה.** משום דגבי גלות דהורג בשוגג איכא חילוק בין דרך ירידה לדרך עלייה כדאמרי' במכות (דף ז:) כל שבדרך ירידתו גולה דכתיב ויפל עליו עד שיפול כדרך נפילה: **כולי עלמא לא פליגי דפטור.** מדתנא דבי חזקיה: **חייבי מיתות איתקוש.** למכה בהמה: **אתיא רשע רשע.** נאמר בחייבי מיתות אשר הוא רשע למות ונאמר בחייבי מלקות והיה אם בן הכות הרשע: **רבא אמר אתיא מכה מכה.** דמלקות נמי איתקוש למכה בהמה ולאו מגזרה שוה דחייבי מיתות ילפינן: **ואיש כי יתן מום בעמיתו כאשר עשה כן יעשה לו.** והאי יעשה לו מלקות קאמר ולקמן פריך והא חובל בחבירו בתשלומין ולא מלקות: **והאי.** מלקות לאו מכה כתיב אלא כי יתן מום ומאי אתיא מכה מכה דקאמר רבא: **הכאה הכאה קאמרינן.** ומום ע"י הכאה הוא ניתן: **וחובל בחבירו בר תשלומין הוא.** והיכי מוקמת ליה את במלקות ופטור ממון: **אם אינו ענין.** האי קרא: **להכאה שיש בה שוה פרוטה.** ולתשלומין דהא מקרא דבתריה ילפינן דכתיב כיה כן ינתן בו דבר הניתן מיד ליד: **תנהו ענין.** להאי כן יעשה לו: **להכאה שאין בה שוה פרוטה.** ולמלקות ואיתקיש למכה בהמה שלא תחלוק בו:

סוף

תוספות

מאי לאו אסון ממש. אע"ג דסיפיה דקרא דאם אסון יהיה ע"כ היינו דין אסון כדכתיב ונתת נפש וגו' מ"מ לא יהיה אסון הוה משמע ליה אסון ממש אי נמי אם אסון יהיה נמי בכי למימר דהוי אסון ממש ודריש ונתת נפש וגו' היינו ממון: **ומי** איכא למאן דאמר חייבי מיתות שוגגין דיבין והא תנא דבי חזקיה וכו'. וא"ת והא אמרינן בפ' הנשרפין (סנהדרין עט: שם) תנא דבי חזקיה מפקא מדרבי ומפקא מדרבנן אלמא פליגי תנאי אתנא דבי חזקיה וי"ל דלענין ממון אחר אית להו לכולהו היקישא דתנא דבי חזקיה ולא פליגי עליה א) אלא במאי דקתני בין מתכוין לשאינו מתכוין דמשמע בין מתכוין להרוג האשה בין אין מתכוין להורגה אלא להרוג את חבירו והרגה דבכל ענין פטור מדמי האשה דלענין ממון אחר כבר תנא דלא תחלוק בין שוגג בין מזיד והיינו דמפקא מדרבי ומדרבנן דלר' נתכוין להרג את זה והרג את זה חייב ממון ורבנן חייב מיתה ולתנא דבי חזקיה פטור ממיתה וממון אבל קשה לרבינו יצחק דבריש הנחנקין (שם פד:) אמרינן הניחא למאן דאית ליה דתנא דבי חזקיה אבל למאן דלית ליה כו' משמע דאיכא תנא דפליג ואומר רבינו יצחק דהיינו רבי חגא מדרומא דאייתי מתניתא בידיה כדאמרינן בפרק שור שנגח ארבעה וחמשה (ב"ק מג. ושם) דשני אנשים כי נתכוונו זה לזה אע"פ שיש אסון באשה יענשו בדמי ולדות אלמא לית ליה היקישא דבין שוגג למזיד והא דקאמר מי איכא למאן דאמר כו' היינו משום דתנא דבי חזקיה עיקר שהיה שונה ברייתות של רבי חייא שהיה אביו כדמוכח בסוף פרק הבא על יבמתו (יבמות סה:) והן עיקר ומותבינן תיובתא מינייהו ולרשב"א נראה דמשום הכי קא פריך ליה מתנא דבי חזקיה משום דרבי יוחנן מוקי מתניתין (לעיל לג:) בשלא התרו בו וקתני סיפא דחייבי מיתות פטורין ° א"כ מתני' סברה דחייבי מיתות שוגגין פטורי דאי סיפא מיירי בשהתרו בו ליפלוג בחייבי מלקיות גופייהו והוה מצי למיפרך ממתני' אלא דלא מצי למיפרך אלא מדיוקא ולהכי פריך ליה מתנא דבי חזקיה ומתניתין סמיך ולפי זה מצינן למימר דמפקא מדרבי ורבנן בכולה מילתא ועוד אומר רשב"א דר' ישמעאל בנו של רבי יוחנן בן ברוקה לקמן בפירקין (דף לז:) י) הוא תנא דלית ליה דתנא דבי חזקיה וצריך לומר דלתנא דבי חזקיה לא יהיה אסון היינו אסון ממש וקרא דאם אסון יהיה היינו דין אסון כגון שנתכוין לה פטור ממיתה וממון ולתנא דבי חזקיה א"נ לא קאי קרא דאסון אאשה אלא אחברו שנתכוין לו ולא איירי קרא שנתכוין להרוג את זה והרג את זה ובפ' הנשרפין דדייק לר"ש דפטר נתכוין להרוג את זה והרג את זה היכי מפרש קראי הוה מצי למימר כדפרישית אלא אליבא דר"א דאמר קראי בנתכוין להרוג את זה והרג את זה דייק: **אף** מכה אדם לא תחלוק בו כו'. וקרא דלא יהיה אסון דאשמעינן דלא ישלם דמי ולדות בהדי מיתה והא נמי דדרשינן בשילהי פרק כילד הרגל (ב"ק כו.) עליו ולא על האדם דלא תשקול מיניה ממונא ותקטליה על הרציחה לחוד וקרא דלא תקחו דדרשינן מיניה דלא תשקול ממונא מיניה ונפטריה אצטריכו כולהו דלא מצי למילף מהיקישא דתנא דבי חזקיה כדפירש בקונטרס לקמן (דף לח.) דממכה בהמה לא מצי למילף פטור ממון דאדרבה חיוב היה לו למילף דמכה בהמה חייב להכי איצטריך למכתב כולהו והכי ילפינן מה מכה בהמה לא חלקת במה שכתוב בו דהיינו חיוב דבכל עניין חייב אף מכה אדם כל עניני פטור ממון שכתוב בו לא תחלוק בין שוגג בין מזיד ובין דרך עלייה לדרך ירידה ושוגג למזיד היינו ממון אחר בהדי מיתה ודרך עלייה וירידה בכל ענין לא תשקול ממונא מיניה ונפטריה כדאמרינן לקמן ומתכוין לשאין מתכוין לענין דמי האשה: **רבא** אמר אתיא מכה מכה. תימה לרבא לית ליה הכא גזרה שוה דרשע רשע וכן ר' יוחנן ולקמן (דף לז.) נמי מצרכינן חד קרא למיתה וממון וחד למלקות וממון ולא ילפינן מלקות וממון ממיתה וממון בגזרה שוה דרשע רשע וסתמא דהש"ס דריש ליה בפ"ק דמכות (דף ה:) גבי אין עדים זוממין נהרגין עד שיגמר הדין על פיהן דאמרינן חייבי מלקיות מנין אתיא רשע רשע וברייתא נמי איכא בר"פ אחד דיני ממונות (סנהדרין לג: ושם) גבי דיני נפשות מחזירין לזכות אבל לא לחובה דאמרינן חייבי מלקיות מנין אתיא רשע רשע תניא נמי הכי כו' ור' יהודה נמי דריש ליה בהחובל (ב"ק פו: ושם) גבי וכן היה ר"י פוטרו פירוש את הסומא מחייבי גליות ומחייבי מלקיות ומחייבי מיתות ב"ד וגמר התם חייבי מיתות ב"ד מרוצח רוצח וחייבי מלקיות אתיא רשע רשע ורבנן דפליגי עליה התם לאו משום דלית להו רשע רשע אלא משום דמחייבי ליה כחייבי מיתות ב"ד וי"ל דרבא ור' יוחנן אית להו ב) בכ"מ גז"ש דרשע רשע בדבר שהוא בגוף המלקות אבל הכא לענין פטור ממון שהוא עם המלקות וכן לקמן לא ילפינן רשע רשע וטעמא משום דקרא מוכח דרשע כתיב לענין מלקות והיה אם בן הכות הרשע והא דדריש מכה מכה משום דמכה גבי תשלומין כתיב שנאמר מכה בהמה ישלמנה ואביי אית ליה גזרה שוה דרשע רשע בכ"מ וסוגיא דלקמן כרבא ודלא כאביי ואביי מוקי קרא במיתה ומלקות כר"מ דלמלקות וממון לא צריך קרא דאתיא רשע רשע ואם תאמר ר' יוחנן אמאי לא דריש מכה מכה הא ברייתא היא בריש החובל (שם פג: ושם) וי"ל דסבר כאידך תנאי דהתם דלא דרשי מכה מכה אלא ילפי מאידך קראי דלאו עין תחת עין ממש: **וכתיב** ואיש כי יתן מום וגו'. אית דגרסי וסמיך ליה ולא מגזרה שוה יליף אלא מסמוכין וכן משמע קצת מדשביק קרא דמכה בהמה ישלמנה ונקיט קרא אחרינא ומיהו מדפריך בריש החובל (שם פ:) מאי חזית דילפת ממכה בהמה נילף ממכה אדם משמע דגזרה שוה הוא והא דהדר ביה מקרא קמא משום דאיצטריך למהדר ממכה אדם ולאתויי כי יתן מום בעמיתו הדר ביה נמי ממכה בהמה ישלמנה ומייתי מכה נפש בהמה דסמיך ליה אי נמי משום דאיצטריך קרא קמא לכדתנא דבי חזקיה ולמאן דלית ליה נמי איצטריך מה מכה בהמה לרפואה פטור אף מכה אדם כו' כדאמרינן בריש הנחנקין (סנהדרין פד: ושם): **אם**

ליקוטי רש"י

משלמין פרעון שלא יהוו לישנו במקום אבוהון ואשלה משלמין. **אבל ארישא.** דמתה כדרכה לא דלא אמרינן דמשתעבדי נכסים דלה לאבי חיוב אונסין בו השואל עד שעת מיתה וכלה כי אשתעבד ליתמה לשואל והרי לא קבול עליהון מידי [ב"ק שם]. **חייבי מיתות שוגגין וחייבי מלקיות שוגגין ודבר אחר.** מתכוין (קלו) [קאמר] חייבי מיתות שוגגין ודבר אחר עבד עבירה בלא התראה דאינו נהרג ... [remaining lines of this column not legible in this scan]

(במדבר לה) ויפל עליו וימת דרך נפילה בעינן. **לפוטרו ממון אלא לחייבו ממון.** כלומר לא חלקת בו לתשלומין אלא בכל לדין הוא דמחייב דרבינן כל מזיקין בבבא קמא (דף כו:) מפלע תחת פלע לחייב על השוגג כמזיד ועל האונס כרצון ומכה בהמה נזק הוא. **אף מכה אדם.** אין דין פטור תשלומין הכתוב בו חלוק לשום צד שיתחייב ממון בין בשוגג ואין נתכוון לפטור ממיתה בין במזיד ונתכוון לחייב מיתה [סנהדרין עט:]. **לדרך עלייה.** דרימו הגרון דקיימא לן (מכות דף ז:) דפטור מגלות אפ"ה פטור מתשלומין [ב"ק שם]. **אלא לפטרו ממון.** למתנא דבי חזקיה [סנהדרין שם]. **ומכה בהמה ישלמנה.** למעלה דבר בהורג בהמה וכאן דבר במכה אדם יומת. אפילו לא הרגו אלא עשה בו חבורה שלא נאמר כאן נפש ובמכה אביו ואמו דבר הכתוב ובא להקישו למכה בהמה מה מכה בהמה מחיים אף מכה אביו ואמו מחיים פרט למכה לאחר מיתה לפי שמצינו שהמקללו לאחר מיתה חייב הוצרך לומר במכה שפטור ומה בבהמה בחבלה שאם אין חבלה אין תשלומין אף מכה אביו ואמו אינו חייב עד שיעשה בהם חבורה [ויקרא כד, כא]. **בקטלא כתיב.** ותשלומין אין שם. **הכאה הכאה קאמרינן.** אע"ג דקראי לא דמו גמרינן ג"ש כדתנא דבי ר' ישמעאל ושב הכהן ובא הכהן עירובין (דף נא.) ומכה אדם דקתני הכא הכאה הוא דקאמר ומכי יתן מום גמר דמום ע"י הכאה בא [ב"ק פד.].

מסורת הש"ס

א) לקמן לח. ב"ק לה. סנהדרין עט: פד:, ב) [סנהדרין י: וש"נ], ג) ב"ק לב. ד) ס"א לפטור, ה) ס"א לחיוב, ו) [ועיין לקמן תוס' לח. ד"ה אבל סימא].

תוספות ישנים

א) [וטעמא דרבי דדריש ונתת ממון וגו' ממון ורבנן דרשי נפש ממש ואפ"ה לא מצי לאוקמי היקשא לאין ממון אבל לענין שוגג ומזיד כולהו אית להו היקשא. ת"י]. ב) ובפ' קמא דסנהדרין דקאמר מ"ט דר' ... [remainder not legible in this scan]

עין משפט נר מצוה

מ א ב מיי' פ"א מהל' נערה בתולה הל' יג ופ"ד מהל' חובל הל' ו סמג עשין ע טוש"ע ח"מ סי' תכד סעיף ד:

מא ג מיי' פ"א מהל' נערה בתולה הל' יא ופ"ג מהל' גניבה הל' א סמג עשין עג:

מב ד מיי' פ"ד מהל' חובל הל' ט ופ"ה הל' ג סמג עשין ע טוש"ע ח"מ סי' תכ סעי' ב:

גליון הש"ס

תוס' ד"ה ומי איכא וכו' א"כ מתני' סברה. כעין זה בב"מ דף מ ע"ב תוס' ד"ה מנהיג לתודיה:

תורה אור השלם

א) וְכִי יִנָּצוּ אֲנָשִׁים וְנָגְפוּ אִשָּׁה הָרָה וְיָצְאוּ יְלָדֶיהָ וְלֹא יִהְיֶה אָסוֹן עָנוֹשׁ יֵעָנֵשׁ כַּאֲשֶׁר יָשִׁית עָלָיו בַּעַל הָאִשָּׁה וְנָתַן בִּפְלִלִים: [שמות כא, כב]

ב) וּמַכֵּה בְהֵמָה יְשַׁלְּמֶנָּה וּמַכֵּה אָדָם יוּמָת: [ויקרא כד, כא]

ג) וְלֹא תִקְחוּ כֹפֶר לְנֶפֶשׁ רֹצֵחַ אֲשֶׁר הוּא רָשָׁע לָמוּת כִּי מוֹת יוּמָת: [במדבר לה, לא]

ד) וְהָיָה אִם בִּן הַכּוֹת הָרָשָׁע וְהִפִּילוֹ הַשֹּׁפֵט וְהִכָּהוּ לְפָנָיו כְּדֵי רִשְׁעָתוֹ בְּמִסְפָּר: [דברים כה, ב]

ה) וּמַכֵּה נֶפֶשׁ בְּהֵמָה יְשַׁלְּמֶנָּה נֶפֶשׁ תַּחַת נָפֶשׁ: [ויקרא כד, יח]

ו) וְאִישׁ כִּי יִתֵּן מוּם בַּעֲמִיתוֹ כַּאֲשֶׁר עָשָׂה כֵּן יֵעָשֶׂה לּוֹ: [ויקרא כד, יט]

תוספות רי"ד

א"ר ומי איכא למ"ד חייבי מיתות שוגגין חייבין והתנא דבי חזקי' מכה אדם ומכה בהמה מה מכה בהמה לא חלקת בה בין בשוגג בין במזיד בין מתכוין לשאינו מתכוין בין דרך ירידה לדרך עלייה לפוטרו ממון אלא לחייבו ממון אף מכה אדם לא חלקת בו בין בשוגג בין במזיד בין מתכוין לאינו מתכוין בין דרך ירידה לדרך עלייה לחייבו ממון אלא לפוטרו ממון. פי' המורה (מכה אדם) מכה בהמה ישלמנה ומכה אדם לא ישלם אלא יומת הקיש פטור ממון דמכה אדם לחיוב ממון דמכה בהמה. מה מכה בהמה אין לך בו חילוק לפטור מלשלם דאדם מועד לעולם בין ער ובין ישן בין שוגג בין מזיד אף מכה אדם אין לך בו חילוק לחיובא ומכה בהמה לעולם חייב דאמרי' בב"ק פצע תחת פצע לחייב השוגג כמזיד ואונס כרצון פי' שאין מתכוין אין בו חיוב מיתה באדם פי' דרך עלי' שהכהו בהגבהת ידו או בחרבו ממטה למעלה פי' בין דרך עליה וכו' משום דגבי גלות דהורג בשוגג איכא חילוק בין דרך ירידה לדרך עלייה. כדאמרי' במס' מכות כל שבדרך ירידתו גולה דכתיב ויפל עליו עד שיפול בדרך נפילה: **אלא כי אתא רבין אמר** ח"מ שוגגין דכ"ע לא פליגי דפטירי פי' מדתנא דבי חזקי' כי פליגי בחייבי מלקות שוגגים וד"א ר"י אמר חייבי מיתות איתקוש [חייבי מלקות לא איתקוש] ור"ל אמר פטור בפירוש רבתה תורה חייבי מלקות כחייבי מיתות היכן ריבתה אביי אמר רשע רשע פי' נאמר בחייבי מיתות אשר הוא רשע למות ונאמר בח"מ והי' אם בן הכות הרשע. **רבא אמר** אתיא מכה מכה פי' דחייבי מלקות נמי איתקש למכה בהמה ולא מג"ש דח"מ ילפינן וקי"ל כר"י:

Rava answers:

אֲנַן הַכָּאָה הַכָּאָה קָאָמְרִינַן – **We mean to say** that the Torah juxtaposes the act of **striking** a person and the act of **striking** an animal, not that the identical terms are used in both contexts.[24]

The Gemara asks:

וְהָא כִּי כְּתִיב בְּחוֹבֵל בַּחֲבֵירוֹ הוּא דִּכְתִיב – **But that** verse **is written with regard to one who wounds his fellow,** וְחוֹבֵל בַּחֲבֵירוֹ בַּר תַּשְׁלוּמִין הוּא – **and one who wounds his fellow is subject to payment,** not lashes![25] – ? –

The Gemara answers:

אִם אֵינוֹ עִנְיָן לְהַכָּאָה שֶׁיֵּשׁ בָּהּ שָׁוֶה פְּרוּטָה – **If it** [the verse *so shall be done to him*] **has no application to** (i.e. it is not needed to teach anything regarding) the case of one who strikes his fellow **a blow that amounts to a *perutah*** in damages,[26] תְּנֵהוּ עִנְיָן לְהַכָּאָה שֶׁאֵין בָּהּ שָׁוֶה פְּרוּטָה – **apply it** instead **to** the case of one who strikes his fellow **a blow that does not amount to a *perutah*** in damages.[27]

NOTES

24. Although the second verse does not actually state the expression *one who strikes,* it does speak of the inflicting of a wound, which is done through striking [and this too can be expounded as a *gezeirah shavah*] (*Rashi*).

25. [As taught above on 32b.] How, then, can you say that when the verse states *as he did, so shall be done to him,* it means that he shall be punished with lashes and be exempt from payment [see note 22]? (*Rashi*).

26. [A *perutah's* worth of damages is the minimum that is subject to payment – see 32b note 13.] *As he did, so shall be done to him* (verse 19) is not needed to teach that one who wounds his fellow pays damages. For that law is taught in the verse that follows (*Leviticus* 24:20): כַּאֲשֶׁר יִתֵּן מוּם בָּאָדָם כֵּן יִנָּתֶן בּוֹ, *as one inflicts a wound in a person so shall be "given" in him,* which the Gemara above (32b) expounds to mean monetary payment, since the word *given* implies "something given from hand to hand" – i.e. monetary payment (*Rashi*).

27. And the verse (by stating *so shall be done to him*) teaches that he is liable to lashes [and not to payment, as there has not been a *perutah's* worth of damages inflicted]. Thus, verse 19 is indeed expounded as referring to a lashes-bearing offense for which there is no payment of damages. And since this verse is juxtaposed to verse 18, which states: *And one who mortally strikes an animal . . .,* we derive that just as in the case of one who strikes an animal we do not distinguish between one who did so deliberately or inadvertently with regard to monetary liability, so too in the case of one who strikes his fellow a blow whose injury does not amount to a *perutah,* which is a lashes-bearing offense, we do not distinguish between one who did so deliberately or inadvertently with regard to being *exempt* from monetary liability (see *Rashi*).

מאי לאו אסון ממש לא דין אסון איכא דאמרי איתיביה רבי יוחנן לר"ל א) ולא יהיה אסון ענוש יענש מאי לאו דין אסון לא אסון ממש אמר רבא ומי איכא למ"ד חייבי מיתות שוגגין חייבים והא תנא דבי חזקיה ב) מכה אדם ומכה בהמה מה מכה בהמה לא חילקת בו בין בשוגג בין במזיד בין מתכוין לשאין מתכוין בין דרך ירידה לדרך עליה לפוטרו ממון אלא לחייבו ממון אף מכה אדם לא תחלוק בו בין בשוגג בין במזיד בין מתכוין לשאין מתכוין בין דרך ירידה לדרך עליה לחייבו ממון אלא לפוטרו ממון אלא כי אתא רבין אמר חייבי מיתות שוגגין כולי עלמא לא פליגי דפטורין כי פליגי בחייבי מלקות שוגגין ודבר אחר רבי יוחנן אמר חייב חייבי מיתות איתקוש חייבי מלקות לא איתקוש ריש לקיש אמר פטור בפירוש ריבתה תורה חייבי מלקות כחייבי מיתות היכן ריבתה תורה אמר אביי אתיא ג) רשע ד) רשע רבא אמר אתיא מכה מכה אמר ליה רב פפא לרבא הי מכה אילימא ומכה בהמה ישלמנה ומכה אדם יומת האי בקטלא כתיב אלא האי מכה ה) מכה נפש בהמה ישלמנה נפש תחת נפש וסמיך ליה ו) ואיש כי יתן מום בעמיתו [כאשר עשה כן יעשה לו] והאי לאו מכה היא אנן הכאה הכאה קאמרינן והא כי כתיב בחובל בחבירו הוא דכתיב וחובל בחבירו בר תשלומין הוא אם אינו ענין להכאה שיש בה שוה פרוטה תנהו ענין להכאה שאין בה שוה פרוטה סוף

רש"י

מאי לאו אסון ממש. אם לא מתה האשה יענש הנוגף בדמי ולדות הא אם מתה לא יענש ואפי' לא התרו בו וקשיא לר' יוחנן: **לא דין אסון.** הכי קאמר קרא אם אין משפט מות לנוגף כגון שלא מתה האשה או מתה ולא התרו בו ענוש יענש: **מכה אדם ומכה בהמה.** מכה בהמה ישלמנה ומכה אדם לא ישלם אלא יומת הקיש פטור ממון דמכה אדם לחיוב ממון דמכה בהמה מה מכה בהמה אין לך בו חילוק לחיוב אף מכה אדם אין לך בו חילוק לפטור מכה בהמה לעולם חייב דאמרי' בב"ק (דף כו.) פצע תחת פצע לחייב על השוגג כמזיד ואונס כרצון: **שאין מתכוין.** אין בו חיוב מיתה באדם: **דרך עלייה.** שהכהו בהגבהת ידו או שחתכו בחרבו מלמטה למעלה: **בין דרך ירידה לדרך עלייה.** משום דגבי גלות דהורג בשוגג איכא חילוק בין דרך ירידה לדרך עלייה כדאמרי' במכות (דף ז:) כל שבדרך ירידתו גולה דכתיב ויפל עליו עד שיפול כדרך נפילה: **כולי עלמא לא פליגי דפטור.** מדתנא דבי חזקיה: **חייבי מיתות איתקוש.** למכה בהמה: **אתיא רשע רשע.** נאמר בחייבי מיתות אשר הוא רשע למות ונאמר בחייבי מלקות והיה אם בן הכות הרשע: **רבא אמר אתיא מכה מכה.** דמלקות נמי איתקוש למכה בהמה ולאו מגזרה שוה דחייבי מיתות ילפינן: **ואיש כי יתן מום בעמיתו כאשר עשה כן יעשה לו.** והאי מלקות הוא והא חובל בחבירו בתשלומין ולא מלקות: **והאי.** מלקות לאו מכה כתיב אלא מום ומאי אתיא מכה מכה דקאמר רבא: **הכאה הכאה קאמרינן.** ומום ע"י הכאה הוא ניתן: **וחובל בחבירו בר תשלומין הוא.** והיכי מוקמת ליה את במלקות ופטור ממון: **אם אינו ענין.** האי קרא: **להכאה שיש בה שוה פרוטה.** ולתשלומין דהא מקרא דבתריה ילפינן דכתיב ביה כן ינתן בו דבר הניתן מיד ליד: **תנהו ענין.** להאי כן יעשה לו: **להכאה שאין בה שוה פרוטה.** ולמלקות ואיתקיש למכה בהמה שלא תחלוק בו: סוף

תוספות

מאי לאו אסון ממש. אע"ג דסיפיה דקרא דאם אסון יהיה ע"כ היינו דין אסון דכתיב ונתת נפש וגו' מ"מ לא יהיה אסון הוה משמע ליה אסון ממש אי נמי אם אסון יהיה נמי בעי למימר דהוי אסון ממש ודריש ונתת נפש וגו' היינו ממון: **ומי** איכא למאן דאמר חייבי מיתות שוגגין חייבין והא תנא דבי חזקיה וכו'. וא"ת והא אמרינן בפ' הנשרפין (סנהדרין עט: ושם) תנא דבי חזקיה מפקא מדרבי ומפקא מדרבנן אלמא פליגי תנאי אתנא דבי חזקיה וי"ל דלענין ממון אחר אית להו לכולהו היקישא דתנא דבי חזקיה ולא פליגי עליה א) אלא במאי דקתני בין מתכוין לשאינו מתכוין דמשמע בין מתכוין להרוג האשה בין אין מתכוין להורגה אלא להרוג את חבירו והרגה דבכל ענין פטור מדמי האשה דלענין ממון אחר כבר תנא דלא תחלוק בין שוגג בין מזיד והיינו דמפקא מדרבי ומדרבנן דלר' נתכוין להרוג את זה והרג את זה חייב ממון ולרבנן חייב מיתה ולתנא דבי חזקיה פטור ממיתה וממון אבל קשה לרבינו יצחק דבריש הנחנקין (שם פד:) אמרינן הניחא למאן דלית ליה דתנא דבי חזקיה אלא למאן דלית ליה כו' משמע דאיכא תנא דפליג ואומר רבינו יצחק דהיינו רבי תנא מדרומאה דאייתי מתניתא בידיה כדאמרינן בפרק שור שנגח ארבעה וחמשה (ב"ק מג. ושם) דשני אנשים כי נתכוונו זה לזה אע"פ שיש אסון באשה יענשו בדמי ולדות אלמא לית ליה היקישא דבין שוגג למזיד והא דקאמר מי איכא למאן דאמר כו' היינו משום דתנא דבי חזקיה עיקר שהיה שונה ברייתות של רבי חייא שהיה אביו כדמוכח בסוף פרק הבא על יבמתו (יבמות סה:) והן עיקר ומותבינן תיובתא מינייהו ולרשב"א נראה דמשום הכי קא פריך ליה מתנא דבי חזקיה משום דרבי יוחנן מוקי מתניתין (לעיל לג:) בשלא התרו בו וקתני סיפא דחייבי מיתות פטורין ° א"כ מתני' סברה דחייבי מיתות שוגגין פטורין דאי סיפא מיירי בשהתרו בו ליפלוג בחייבי מלקות גופייהו והוה מצי למיפרך ממתני' אלא דלא מצי למיפרך אלא מדיוקא ולהכי פריך ליה מתנא דבי חזקיה ומתניתין סמיך ולפי זה מצינן למימר דמפקא מדרבי ורבנן בכולה מילתא ועוד אומר רשב"א דר' ישמעאל בנו של רבי יוחנן בן ברוקה לקמן בפירקין (דף לז:) ו) הוא תנא דלית ליה דתנא דבי חזקיה וצריך לומר דלתנא דבי חזקיה לא יהיה אסון היינו אסון ממש וקרא דאם אסון יהיה היינו דין אסון כגון שנתכוין לאשה דאם לא נתכוין לה פטור ממיתה וממון לתנא דבי חזקיה א"כ לא קאי קרא דאסון אאשה אלא אחברו שנתכוין לו ולא איירי קרא שנתכוין להרוג את זה והרג את זה ובפ' הנשרפין דדייק לר"ש דפטר נתכוין להרוג את זה והרג את זה היכי מפרש קראי הוה מצי למימר כדפרישית אלא אליבא דר"א דאמר קראי בנתכוין להרוג את זה והרג את זה דייק:

אף מכה אדם לא תחלוק בו כו'. וקרא דלא יהיה אסון דאשמעינן דלא ישלם דמי ולדות בהדי מיתה והא נמי דדרשינן בשילהי פרק כילד הרגל (ב"ק כו.) עליו ולא על האדם דלא תשקול מיניה ממונא ותקטליה על הרליחה לחוד וקרא דלא תקחו דדרשינן מיניה דלא תשקול ממונא מיניה ונפטריה אצטריכו כולהו דלא מצי למילף מהיקישא דתנא דבי חזקיה כדפירש בקונטרס לקמן (דף לח.) דממכה בהמה לא מצי למילף פטור ממון דאדרבה חיוב היה לו למילף דמכה בהמה חייב להכי איצטריך למכתב כולהו והכי ילפינן מה מכה בהמה לא חלקת במה שכתוב בו דהיינו חיוב דבכל ענין חייב אף מכה אדם כל ענייני פטור ממון שכתוב בו לא תחלוק בין שוגג בין מזיד ובין דרך עלייה לדרך ירידה ושוגג למזיד היינו ממון אחר בהדי מיתה ודרך עלייה וירידה בכל ענין לא תשקול ממונא מיניה ונפטריה כדאמרינן לקמן ומתכוין לשאין מתכוין לענין דמי האשה: **רבא** אמר אתיא מכה מכה. תימה לרבא לית ליה הכא גזרה שוה דרשע רשע וכן ר' יוחנן ולקמן (דף לז.) נמי מצרכינן חד קרא למיתה וממון וחד למלקות וממון ולא ילפינן מלקות וממון ממיתה וממון בגזרה שוה דרשע רשע וסתמא דהש"ס דריש ליה בפ"ק דמכות (דף ה:) גבי אין עדים זוממין נהרגין עד שיגמר הדין על פיהן דאמרינן חייבי מלקיות מנין אתיא רשע רשע וברייתא נמי איכא בר"פ אחד דיני ממונות (סנהדרין לג: ושם) גבי דיני נפשות מחזירין לזכות אבל לא לחובה דאמרינן חייבי מלקיות מנין אתיא רשע רשע תניא נמי הכי כו' ור' יהודה נמי דריש ליה בהחובל (ב"ק פו: ושם) גבי וכן היה ר"י פוטרו פירוש את הסומא מחייבי גליות ומחייבי מלקיות ומחייבי מיתות ב"ד וגמר התם חייבי מיתות ב"ד מרוצח רוצח וחייבי מלקיות אתיא רשע רשע ורבנן דפליגי עליה התם לאו משום דלית להו רשע רשע אלא משום דמחייבי ליה כחייבי מיתות ב"ד וי"ל דרבא ור' יוחנן אית להו ב) בכ"מ גז"ש דרשע רשע בדבר שהוא בגוף המלקות אבל הכא לענין פטור ממון שהוא עם המלקות וכן לקמן לא ילפינן רשע רשע וטעמא משום דקרא מוכח דרשע כתיב לענין מלקות והיה אם בן הכות הרשע והא דדריש מכה מכה משום דמכה גבי תשלומין כתיב שנאמר מכה בהמה ישלמנה ואביי אית ליה גזרה שוה דרשע רשע בכ"מ וסוגיא דלקמן כרבא ודלא כאביי ואביי מוקי קרא במיתה ומלקות כר"מ דלמלקות וממון לא צריך קרא דאתיא רשע רשע ואם תאמר ר' יוחנן אמאי לא דריש מכה מכה הא ברייתא היא בריש החובל (שם פג: ושם) וי"ל דסבר כאידך תנאי דהתם דלא דרשי מכה מכה אלא ילפי מאידך קראי דלאו עין תחת עין ממש: **וכתיב** ואיש כי יתן מום וגו'. אית דגרסי וסמיך ליה ולא מגזרה שוה יליף אלא מסמוכין וכן משמע קצת מדשביק קרא דמכה בהמה ישלמנה ונקיט קרא אחרינא ומיהו מדפריך בריש החובל (שם פג:) מאי חזית דילפת ממכה בהמה נילף ממכה אדם משמע דגזרה שוה הוא והא דהדר ביה מקרא קמא משום דאיצטריך למהדר ממכה אדם ולאתויי כי יתן מום בעמיתו הדר ביה נמי ממכה בהמה ישלמנה ומייתי מכה נפש בהמה דסמיך ליה אי נמי משום דאיצטריך קרא קמא לכדתנא דבי חזקיה ולמאן דלית ליה נמי איצטריך מה מכה בהמה לרפואה פטור אף מכה אדם כו' כדאמרינן בריש הנחנקין (סנהדרין פד: ושם): אם

מסורת הש"ס

א) לקמן לח. ב"ק לה. סנהדרין עט: פד:, ב) [סנהדרין עט: וש"נ], ג) ב"ק פו., ד) ס"א לפטור, ה) ס"א לחיוב, ו) [ועיין לקמן תוס' לח. ד"ה אבל מימא].

תוספות ישנים

א) [וטעמא דרבי דדריש ונתת נפש וגו' ממון ורבנן דרשי נפש ממש ולהכי לא מצי לאוקמי קושיא לאין מתכוין אבל לענין שוגג ומזיד כולהו אית להו הקישא. ב) ובפ' קמא דסנהדרין דקאמר מ"ט דר' עקיבא דאמר מלקות בכ"ג אביי אמר אתיא רשע רשע רבא אמר אתיא מכה מכה עומדת לא משום דלית ליה כו' אלא משום דס"ל כדאמרי' בפ"ק דמכות [illegible] עה"ג.]

ליקוטי רש"י

[illegible]

עין משפט נר מצוה

מ א ב מיי' פ"א מהל' נערה בתולה הל' יג ופ"ד מהל' חובל הל' ז סמג עשין ע טוש"ע ח"מ סי' תכג סעיף ד:

מא ג מיי' פ"א מהל' נערה בתולה הל' יא ופ"ג מהל' גניבה הל' א סמג עשין עד:

מב ד מיי' פ"ד מהל' חובל הל' ט ופ"ה הל' ג סמג עשין ע טוש"ע ח"מ סי' תכ סעי' ב:

גליון הש"ס

תוס' ד"ה ומי איכא וכו' **א"כ** מתני' סברה. כעין זה בב"מ דף ח ע"ב תוס' ד"ה מנהיג לחודיה:

תורה אור השלם

א) וְכִי יִנָּצוּ אֲנָשִׁים וְנָגְפוּ אִשָּׁה הָרָה וְיָצְאוּ יְלָדֶיהָ וְלֹא יִהְיֶה אָסוֹן עָנוֹשׁ יֵעָנֵשׁ כַּאֲשֶׁר יָשִׁית עָלָיו בַּעַל הָאִשָּׁה וְנָתַן בִּפְלִלִים: [שמות כא, כב]

ב) וּמַכֵּה בְהֵמָה יְשַׁלְּמֶנָּה וּמַכֵּה אָדָם יוּמָת: [ויקרא כד, כא]

ג) וְלֹא תִקְחוּ כֹפֶר לְנֶפֶשׁ רֹצֵחַ אֲשֶׁר הוּא רָשָׁע לָמוּת כִּי מוֹת יוּמָת: [במדבר לה, לא]

ד) וְהָיָה אִם בִּן הַכּוֹת הָרָשָׁע וְהִפִּילוֹ הַשֹּׁפֵט וְהִכָּהוּ לְפָנָיו כְּדֵי רִשְׁעָתוֹ בְּמִסְפָּר: [דברים כה, ב]

ה) וּמַכֵּה נֶפֶשׁ בְּהֵמָה יְשַׁלְּמֶנָּה נֶפֶשׁ תַּחַת נָפֶשׁ: [ויקרא כד, יח]

ו) וְאִישׁ כִּי יִתֵּן מוּם בַּעֲמִיתוֹ כַּאֲשֶׁר עָשָׂה כֵּן יֵעָשֶׂה לּוֹ: [ויקרא כד, יט]

תוספות רי"ד

א"ר ומי איכא למ"ד חייבי מיתות שוגגין חייבין והתנא דבי חזקי' מכה אדם ומכה בהמה ישלמנה מה מכה בהמה לא חלקת בה בין בשוגג בין במזיד בין מתכוין לאינו מתכוין בין דרך ירידה לדרך עליה לפוטרו ממון אלא לחייבו ממון אף מכה אדם לא חלקת בו בין שוגג למזיד בין מתכוין לא"מ בין דרך ירידה לד"ע לחייבו ממון אלא לפוטרו ממון. פי' המורה (מכה אדם) מכה בהמה ישלמנה ומכה אדם לא ישלם אלא יומת הקיש פטור ממון דמכה אדם לחיוב ממון דמכה בהמה. מה מכה בהמה אין לך בו חילוק לפטור מלשלם דאדם מועד לעולם בין ער ובין ישן בין שוגג בין מזיד אף מכה אדם אין לך בו חילוק לחיוב ומכה בהמה לעולם חייב דאמרי' בב"ק פצע תחת פצע לחייב השוגג כמזיד ואונס כרצון פי' שאין מתכוין אין בו חיוב מיתה באדם פי' דרך עלי' שהכהו בהגבהת ידו או בחרבו ממטה למעלה פי' בין דרך עליה וכו' משום דגבי גלות דהורג בשוגג איכא חילוק בין דרך ירידה לדרך עלייה. כדאמרי' במס' מכות כל שבדרך ירידתו גולה דכתיב ויפל עליו עד שיפול בדרך נפילה: **אלא כי אתא רבין אמר** ח"מ שוגגין דכ"ע לא פליגי דפטירי פי' מדתנא דבי חזקי' כי פליגי בחייבי מלקות שוגגים וד"א ר"י אמר חייבי מיתות איתקוש [חייבי מלקות לא איתקוש] ור"ל אמר פטור בפירוש רבתה תורה חייבי מלקות כחייבי מיתות היכן ריבתה אביי אמר רשע רשע פי' נאמר אשר הוא רשע למות ונאמר בח"מ והי' אם בן הכות הרשע. **רבא אמר** אתיא מכה מכה פי' דחייבי מלקות נמי איתקש למכה בהמה ולא מג"ש דח"מ ילפינן וקי"ל כר"י:

ליקוטי רש"י

(במדבר לה) ויפל עליו וימת דרך נפילה בעינן. **לפוטרו ממון אלא לחייבו ממון.** כלומר לא חלקת בו תשלומין אלא בכל לדין הוא דמחייב דרבינן כל נזקין בבבא קמא (דף כו:) מפלע תחת פלע לחייב על השוגג [illegible] ומכה בהמה נזק הוא. **אף מכה אדם.** אין דין פטור תשלומין הכתוב בו חלוק לשום לד שיתחייב ממון בין בשוגג ואין נתכוון לפטור ממיתה בין במזיד ונתכוון לחייב מיתה [סנהדרין עט:]. **לדרך עלייה.** [illegible] הגרון דקיימא לן (מכות דף ז:) דפטור מגלות אפ"ה פטור מתשלומין [ב"ק שם]. **אלא לפטרו ממון** לתנא דבי חזקיה [סנהדרין שם]. **ומכה בהמה ישלמנה.** למעלה דבר בהורג בהמה וכאן דבר [illegible] **מכה אדם יומת.** אפילו לא הרגו אלא עשה בו חבורה שלא נאמר כאן נפש ובמכה אביו ואמו דבר הכתוב ובא להקישו למכה בהמה מה מכה בהמה מחיים אף מכה אביו ואמו מחיים פרט למכה לאחר מיתה לפי [illegible] במכה שפטור ומה בבהמה בחבלה שאם אין חבלה אין תשלומין אף מכה אביו ואמו אינו חייב עד שיעשה בהם חבורה [ויקרא כד, כא]. **בקטלא כתיב.** ותשלומין אין שם. **הכאה הכאה קאמרינן.** אע"ג דקראי כדתנא דבי ר' ישמעאל ושב הכהן ובא הכהן עירובין (דף נא.) ומכה אדם דקתני הכא הכאה הוא דקאמר ומכי יתן מום גמר דמום ע"י הכאה בא [ב"ק פג:].

OBLIGATE HIM to pay **MONEY** in any of these cases, אֶלָּא לְפוֹטְרוֹ מָמוֹן – **RATHER** you are **TO EXEMPT HIM** from paying **MONEY** in all these cases.[12] Thus, a Baraisa states explicitly that an act that bears the death penalty exempts from monetary payment even in cases where the sinner cannot be executed. How, then, could Rav Dimi report that R' Yochanan does *not* exempt the sinner from payment where the sinner cannot be executed?

The Gemara concedes that Rav Dimi's version of the dispute between R' Yochanan and Reish Lakish is thus refuted, and therefore presents a different version of that dispute:

אֶלָּא כִּי אֲתָא רָבִין אָמַר – **Rather, when Ravin came** from Eretz Yisrael to Bavel **he reported** the views of R' Yochanan and Reish Lakish as follows: חַיָּיבֵי מִיתוֹת שׁוֹגְגִין – With regard to **those acting inadvertently who** commit acts for which they **would be liable to** the **death** penalty had they acted deliberately, כּוּלֵּי עָלְמָא לֹא פְּלִיגֵי דִּפְטוּרִין – **all** – both R' Yochanan and Reish Lakish – **agree that they are exempt** from monetary liability incurred simultaneously.[13] כִּי פְּלִיגֵי – **When do they disagree?** בְּחַיָּיבֵי מַלְקוֹת שׁוֹגְגִין וְדָבָר אַחֵר – **With** regard to **those acting inadvertently who** commit acts for which they **would be liable to lashes** had they acted deliberately, **and** who simultaneously incur liability to **something else,** i.e. to monetary payment. רַבִּי יוֹחָנָן אָמַר – **R' Yochanan says:** חַיָּיב – **He is liable** to make the monetary payment. חַיָּיבֵי מִיתוֹת אִיתְקוּשׁ – For only **those who** commit acts for which they **are liable to** the **death** penalty where they act deliberately **are compared** to one who strikes an animal, and are thus *always* exempt from payment. חַיָּיבֵי מַלְקִיּוֹת לֹא אִיתְקוּשׁ – But **those who** commit acts for which they **are liable to lashes** where they act deliberately **are not compared** to one who strikes an animal. Thus, they are not *always* exempt from monetary payment.[14] רֵישׁ לָקִישׁ אָמַר – But **Reish Lakish says:** פָּטוּר – **He,** too, is **exempt.** בְּפֵירוּשׁ רִיבְּתָה תּוֹרָה חַיָּיבֵי מַלְקִיּוֹת כְּחַיָּיבֵי מִיתוֹת – For **the Torah has explicitly included those liable to lashes** in the law of exemption from monetary liability **just like those liable to** the **death** penalty.[15]

The Gemara inquires:

הֵיכָן רִיבְּתָה תּוֹרָה – **Where did the Torah include** them in this law?

The Gemara answers:

אַבַּיֵי אָמַר – **Abaye said:** אַתְיָא ,,רָשָׁע" ,,רָשָׁע" – **It is derived from** a *gezeirah shavah* linking the expressions ***guilty, guilty.***[16] רָבָא אָמַר – **Rava says:** אַתְיָא ,,מַכֵּה" ,,מַכֵּה" – **It is derived from** the Torah's juxtaposition of ***one who strikes*** (stated with regard to an offense punishable by lashes) to ***one who strikes an animal.***[17]

The Gemara asks:

אָמַר לֵיהּ רַב פָּפָּא לְרָבָא – **Rav Pappa said to Rava:** הֵי ,,מַכֵּה" – **Which** comparison of ***one who strikes*** do you mean? אִילֵימָא ,,וּמַכֵּה בְהֵמָה יְשַׁלְּמֶנָּה וּמַכֵּה אָדָם יוּמָת" – **If you** mean to **say** the one in the verse: ***And one who strikes an animal shall pay for it, and one who strikes a person shall be put to death,***[18] הַאי בִּקְטָלָא כְּתִיב – why, **that** verse **is written with regard to murder,** not with regard to a lashes-bearing offense![19] אֶלָּא הַאי ,,מַכֵּה" – **Rather,** you are certainly referring to **this** following comparison regarding ***one who strikes:*** ,,[וּ]מַכֵּה נֶפֶשׁ־בְּהֵמָה יְשַׁלְּמֶנָּה נֶפֶשׁ תַּחַת נָפֶשׁ" – The verse states: ***[And] one who mortally strikes an animal life shall pay for it, a life for a life,***[20] וּסְמִיךְ לֵיהּ – **and adjacent to it** is written:[21] ,,וְאִישׁ כִּי־יִתֵּן מוּם בַּעֲמִיתוֹ [כַּאֲשֶׁר עָשָׂה כֵּן יֵעָשֶׂה לּוֹ"] – ***And if a man inflicts a wound in his fellow [as he did so shall be done to him].***[22] וְהַאי לָאו ,,מַכֵּה" הִיא – **But this** latter verse, while it might indeed deal with a lashes-bearing offense, **is not** a verse that uses the expression ***one who strikes!***[23] – ? –

NOTES

therefore, notes that although with regard to liability to exile there is a distinction between killing through a downward or an upward motion, there is no such distinction with regard to the exemption from monetary liability (*Rashi*).

12. The Torah's juxtaposition of *one who strikes a person* and *one who strikes an animal* teaches that just as in the case of one who inflicts damage on an animal, the law regarding damages is uniform, regardless of how the act was committed, so too in the case of one who kills a person. Thus, since we derive from the verse *if there is no fatality, he shall be punished [monetarily]* that one is exempt from paying for a monetary liability incurred in the course of an intentional murder [or while committing any other capital offense], the aforementioned juxtaposition teaches that the same applies in the case of an inadvertent murder [or any other capital offense committed inadvertently] (see *Rashi* below, 38a ד״ה לחייבו ממון and *Tosafos* here ד״ה אף).

13. As derived by the Baraisa taught in the academy of Chizkiyah, just cited (*Rashi*).

14. When they act deliberately, they are exempt from payment because of the verse *in accordance with his wickedness,* which teaches that one cannot receive lashes and be required to pay money for the same crime (above, 32b). But when they act inadvertently, and thus do not receive lashes, they are not exempt from payment. For we do not have a verse indicating that the law regarding damages for those who violate a lashes-bearing offense must be uniform.

15. This special Scriptural inclusion (which the Gemara will cite below) teaches that just as acts carrying the death penalty exempt from monetary liability even when committed inadvertently, so too do acts carrying the lashes penalty exempt from monetary liability even when committed inadvertently.

16. With regard to a capital offense, the verse states (*Numbers* 35:31): וְלֹא־תִקְחוּ כֹפֶר לְנֶפֶשׁ רֹצֵחַ אֲשֶׁר־הוּא רָשָׁע לָמוּת, *And you shall not accept ransom for the life of a murderer who is "guilty" to be put to death.* With regard to lashes, the verse states (*Deuteronomy* 25:2): וְהָיָה אִם־בִּן הַכּוֹת הָרָשָׁע, *And it shall be if the "guilty" one deserves lashes* (*Rashi*). Therefore, just as a capital offense exempts one from payment, regardless of whether the offense was committed deliberately or inadvertently (as derived by comparison to "one who strikes an animal"), so too does a lashes-bearing offense exempt one from payment, regardless of whether the offense was committed deliberately or inadvertently.

17. I.e. we do not have to derive the exemption in the case of lashes-bearing offenses from a *gezeirah shavah* to capital offenses, which in turn are compared to "one who strikes an animal," as Abaye does. Rather, lashes-bearing offenses themselves are directly compared to the striking of an animal (*Rashi*).

18. *Leviticus* 24:21.

19. True, this verse compares "one who strikes a person" to "one who strikes an animal." But the "one who strikes a person" in this verse is a reference to murder, which is a capital offense, not a lashes-bearing offense!

20. Ibid. v. 18.

21. In the very next verse – v. 19.

22. I.e. just as he inflicted a wound in his fellow, so shall lashes be inflicted in him (*Rashi;* see end of note). [Thus, the "one who strikes an animal" in the previous verse is compared to the one who commits the lashes-bearing offense of striking his fellow in this verse. Just as one who strikes an animal must *always* pay the damages (regardless of whether the act was deliberate or inadvertent), so too is one who commits a lashes-bearing offense *always* exempt from monetary payment (regardless of whether the act was deliberate or inadvertent).]

The Gemara below will object that *so shall be done to him* apparently refers to the payment of money, not the penalty of lashes [since one who wounds his fellow pays and does not receive lashes] (*Rashi*).

23. The word מַכֵּה, *one who strikes,* is not mentioned in this latter verse. Rather, the verse states וְאִישׁ כִּי־יִתֵּן מוּם, *And if a man inflicts a wound.* Hence, if Rava, was, in fact, referring to the juxtaposition of these two verses, what is the meaning of his statement that the law is derived from the Torah's juxtaposition of *one who strikes* and *one who strikes*? (*Rashi*).

מאי לאו אסון ממש לא דין אסון איכא דאמרי איתיביה רבי יוחנן לר"ל א) ולא יהיה אסון ענוש יענש מאי לאו דין אסון לא אסון ממש אמר רבא ומי איכא למ"ד חייבי מיתות שוגגין חייבים והא תנא א) דבי חזקיה ב) מכה אדם ומכה בהמה מה מכה בהמה לא חילקת בו בין בשוגג בין במזיד בין מתכוין לשאין מתכוין בין דרך ירידה לדרך עלייה לפוטרו ממון אלא לחייבו ממון אף מכה אדם לא תחלוק בו בין בשוגג בין במזיד בין מתכוין לשאין מתכוין בין דרך ירידה לדרך עלייה לחייבו ממון אלא לפוטרו ממון אלא כי אתא רבין אמר ב חייבי מיתות שוגגין כולי עלמא לא פליגי דפטורין כי פליגי בחייבי מלקות שוגגין ודבר אחר ג רבי יוחנן אמר חייב חייבי מיתות איתקוש חייבי מלקיות לא איתקוש ריש לקיש אמר פטור בפירוש ריבתה תורה חייבי מלקות כחייבי מיתות היכן ריבתה תורה ג) אמר אביי אתיא ג) רשע ד) רשע רבא אמר אתיא מכה מכה אמר ליה רב פפא לרבא ה) הי מכה אילימא ב) ומכה בהמה ישלמנה ומכה אדם יומת האי בקטלא כתיב אלא האי מכה ה) מכה נפש בהמה ישלמנה נפש תחת נפש וסמיך ליה ו) ואיש כי יתן מום בעמיתו [כאשר עשה כן יעשה לו] והאי לאו מכה היא אנן הכאה הכאה קאמרינן והא כי כתיב בחובל בחבירו הוא דכתיב וחובל בחבירו בר תשלומין הוא אם אינו ענין להכאה שיש בה שוה פרוטה ד תנהו ענין להכאה שאין בה שוה פרוטה

סוף

רש"י

מאי לאו אסון ממש. אם לא מתה האשה יענש הנוגף בדמי ולדות הא אם מתה לא יענש ואפי' לא התרו בו וקשיא לר' יוחנן: לא דין אסון. הכי קאמר קרא אם אין משפט מות לנוגף כגון שלא מתה האשה או מתה ולא התרו בו ענוש יענש: מכה אדם ומכה בהמה. מכה בהמה ישלמנה ומכה אדם לא ישלם אלא יומת הקיש פטור ממון דמכה אדם לחיוב ממון דמכה בהמה מה מכה בהמה אין לך בו חילוק ד) לחיוב אף מכה אדם אין לך בו חילוק ה) לפטור מכה בהמה לעולם חייב דאמרי' בב"ק (דף כו:) פצע תחת פצע לחייב את השוגג כמזיד ואונס כרצון: שאין מתכוין. אין בו חיוב מיתה באדם: דרך עלייה. שהכהו בהגבהת ידו או שהכהו בחרבו מלמטה למעלה: בין דרך ירידה לדרך עלייה. משום דגבי גלות להורג בשוגג איכא חילוק בין דרך ירידה לדרך עלייה כדאמרי' במכות (דף ז:) כל שבדרך ירידתו גולה דכתיב ויפל עליו עד שיפול לדרך נפילה: כולי עלמא לא פליגי דפטור. מדתנא דבי חזקיה: חייבי מיתות איתקוש. למכה בהמה: אתיא רשע רשע. נאמר בחייבי מיתות אשר הוא רשע למות ונאמר בחייבי מלקות והיה אם בן הכות הרשע: רבא אמר אתיא מכה מכה. דמלקות נמי איתקוש למכה בהמה ולאו מגזרה שוה דחייבי מיתות ילפינן: ואיש כי יתן מום בעמיתו כאשר עשה כן יעשה לו. מלקות קאמר ולקמן פריך והא חובל בחבירו בר תשלומין הוא: והאי. מלקות לאו מכה כתיב אלא כי יתן מום ומאי אתיא מכה מכה דקאמר רבא: הכאה הכאה קאמרינן. ומום ע"י הכאה הוא ניתן: וחובל בחבירו בר תשלומין הוא. והיכי מוקמת ליה את במלקות ופטור ממון: אם אינו ענין. האי קרא: להכאה שיש בה שוה פרוטה. ולתשלומין דהא מקרא דבתריה ילפינן דכתיב ביה כן ינתן בו דבר הניתן מיד ליד: תנהו ענין. להאי כן יעשה לו: להכאה שאין בה שוה פרוטה. ולמלקות ואיתקיש למכה בהמה שלא תחלוק בו:

סוף

תוספות

מאי לאו אסון ממש. אע"ג דסיפיה דקרא דאם אסון יהיה ע"כ היינו דין אסון כדכתיב ונתת נפש וגו' מ"מ לא יהיה אסון הוה משמע ליה אסון ממש אי נמי אם אסון יהיה נמי בעי למימר דהוי אסון ממש ודריש ונתת נפש וגו' היינו ממון: ומי איכא למאן דאמר חייבי מיתות שוגגין חייבין והא תנא דבי חזקיה וכו'. וא"ת והא אמרינן בפ' הנשרפין (סנהדרין עט: ושם) תנא דבי חזקיה מפקא מדרבי ומפקא מדרבנן אלמא פליגי תנאי אתנא דבי חזקיה וי"ל דלענין ממון אחר אית להו לכולהו היקישא דתנא דבי חזקיה ולא פליגי עליה א) אלא במאי דקתני בין מתכוין לשאינו מתכוין דמשמע בין מתכוין להרוג האשה בין אין מתכוין להורגה אלא להרוג את חברו והרגה דבכל ענין פטור מדמי האשה דלענין ממון אחר כבר תנא דלא תחלוק בין שוגג בין מזיד והיינו דמפקא מדרבי ומדרבנן דלר' נתכוין להרוג את זה והרג את זה חייב ממון ולרבנן חייב מיתה ולתנא דבי חזקיה פטור ממיתה וממון אבל קשה לרבינו יצחק דבריש הנחנקין (שם פד:) אמרינן הניחא למאן דאית ליה דתנא דבי חזקיה אלא למאן דלית ליה כו' משמע דאיכא תנא דפליג ואומר רבינו יצחק דהיינו רבי חגא מדרומא דאייתי מתניתא בידיה כדאמרינן בפרק שור שנגח ארבעה וחמשה (ב"ק מב. ושם) דשני אנשים כי נתכוונו זה לזה אע"פ שיש אסון באשה יענשו בדמי ולדות אלמא לית ליה היקישא דבין שוגג למזיד והא דקאמר מי איכא למאן דאמר כו' היינו משום דתנא דבי חזקיה עיקר שהיה שונה ברייתות של רבי חייא שהיה אביו כדמוכח בסוף פרק הבא על יבמתו (יבמות סה:) והן עיקר ומותבינן תיובתא מינייהו ולרשב"א נראה דמשום הכי קא פריך ליה מתנא דבי חזקיה משום דרבי יוחנן מוקי מתניתין (לעיל לג:) בשלא התרו בו וקתני סיפא דחייבי מיתות פטורין ° א"כ מתני' סברה דחייבי מיתות שוגגין פטורין דאי סיפא מיירי בשהתרו בו ליפלוג בחייבי מלקיות גופייהו והוה מצי למיפרך ממתני' אלא דלא מצי למיפרך אלא מדיוקא ולהכי פריך ליה מתנא דבי חזקיה ומתניתין סמיך ולפי זה מצינן למימר דמפקא מדרבי ורבנן בכולה מילתא ועוד אומר רשב"א דר' ישמעאל בנו של רבי יוחנן בן ברוקה לקמן בפירקין (דף לז:) ו) הוא תנא דלית ליה דתנא דבי חזקיה לא יהיה אסון היינו אסון ממש וקרא דאם אסון יהיה היינו דין אסון כגון שנתכוין לאשה דאם לא נתכוין לה פטור ממיתה וממון לתנא דבי חזקיה א"כ לא קאי קרא דאסון אאשה אלא אחברו שנתכוין לו ולא איירי קרא שנתכוין להרוג את זה והרג את זה ובפ' הנשרפין דדייק לר"ש דפטר נתכוין להרוג את זה והרג את זה היכי מפרש קראי הוה מצי למימר כדפרישית אלא אליבא דר"א דאמר קראי בנתכוין להרוג את זה והרג את זה דייק:

אף מכה אדם לא תחלוק בו כו'. וקרא דלא יהיה אסון דאשמעינן דלא ישלם דמי ולדות בהדי מיתה והא נמי דדרשינן בשילהי פרק כיצד הרגל (ב"ק כו.) עליו ולא על האדם דלא תשקול מיניה ממונא ותקטליה על הרציחה לחוד וקרא דלא תקחו כופר דדרשינן מיניה דלא תשקול ממונא מיניה ונפטריה אצטריכו כולהו דלא מצי למילף מהיקישא דתנא דבי חזקיה כדפירש בקונטרס לקמן (דף לח.) דממכה בהמה לא מצי למילף פטור ממון דאדרבה חיוב היה לו למילף דמכה בהמה חייב להכי איצטריך למכתב כולהו והכי ילפינן מה מכה בהמה לא חלקת במה שכתוב בו דהיינו חיוב דבכל ענין חייב אף מכה אדם כל עניני פטור ממון שכתוב בו לא תחלוק בין שוגג בין מזיד ובין דרך עלייה לדרך ירידה ושוגג למזיד היינו ממון אחר בהדי מיתה ודרך עלייה וירידה בכל ענין לא תשקול ממונא מיניה ונפטריה כדאמרינן לקמן ומתכוין לשאין מתכוין לענין דמי האשה: רבא אמר אתיא מכה מכה. תימה לרבא לית ליה הכא גזרה שוה דרשע רשע וכן ר' יוחנן ולקמן (דף לז.) נמי מצרכינן חד קרא למיתה וממון וחד למלקות וממון ולא ילפינן מלקות וממון ממיתה וממון בגזרה שוה דרשע רשע וסתמא דהש"ס דריש ליה בפ"ק דמכות (דף ה:) גבי אין עדים זוממין נהרגין עד שיגמר הדין על פיהן דאמרינן חייבי מלקיות מנין אתיא רשע רשע וברייתא נמי איכא בר"פ אחד דיני ממונות (סנהדרין לג: ושם) גבי דיני נפשות מחזירין לזכות אבל לא לחובה דאמרינן חייבי מלקיות מנין אתיא רשע רשע תניא נמי הכי כו' ור' יהודה נמי דריש ליה בהחובל (ב"ק פו: ושם) גבי וכן היה ר"י פוטרו פירוש את הסומא מחייבי גליות ומחייבי מלקיות ומחייבי מיתות ב"ד וגמר התם חייבי מיתות ב"ד מרוצח רוצח וחייבי מלקיות אתיא רשע רשע ורבנן דפליגי עליה התם לאו משום דלית להו רשע רשע אלא משום דמחייבי ליה כחייבי מיתות ב"ד וי"ל דרבא ור' יוחנן אית להו ב) בכ"מ גז"ש דרשע רשע בדבר שהוא בגוף המלקות אבל הכא לענין פטור ממון שהוא עם המלקות וכן לקמן לא ילפינן רשע רשע וטעמא משום דקרא מוכח דרשע כתיב לענין מלקות והיה אם בן הכות הרשע והא דדריש מכה מכה משום דמכה גבי תשלומין כתיב שנאמר מכה בהמה ישלמנה ואביי אית ליה גזרה שוה דרשע רשע בכ"מ וסוגיא דלקמן כרבא ודלא כאביי ואביי מוקי קרא במיתה ומלקות כר"מ דלמלקות וממון לא צריך קרא דאתיא רשע רשע ואם תאמר ר' יוחנן אמאי לא דריש מכה מכה הא ברייתא היא בריש החובל (שם פג: ושם) וי"ל דסבר כאידך תנאי דהתם דלא דרשי מכה מכה אלא ילפי מאידך קראי דלאו עין תחת עין ממש: וכתיב ואיש כי יתן מום וגו'. אית דגרסי וסמיך ליה ולא מגזרה שוה יליף אלא מסמוכין וכן משמע קצת מדפריך קרא דמכה בהמה ישלמנה ונקיט קרא אחרינא ומיהו מדפריך בריש החובל (שם פג:) מאי חזית דילפת ממכה בהמה נילף ממכה אדם משמע דגזרה שוה הוא והא דהדר ביה מקרא קמא משום דאיצטריך למהדר ממכה אדם ולאתויי כי יתן מום בעמיתו הדר ביה נמי ממכה בהמה ישלמנה ומייתי מכה נפש בהמה דסמיך ליה אי נמי משום דאיצטריך קרא קמא לכדתנא דבי חזקיה ולמאן דלית ליה נמי איצטריך מה מכה בהמה לרפואה פטור אף מכה אדם כו' כדאמרינן בריש הנחנקין (סנהדרין פד: ושם):

אם

מסורת הש"ס

א) לקמן לח. ב"ק לה. סנהדרין עט: פד:, ב) [סנהדרין י: וש"נ], ג) ב"ק פג:, ד) ס"א לפטור, ה) ס"א לחיוב, ו) [ועיין לקמן תוס' לח. ד"ה אבל סימא].

תוספות ישנים

א) [וטעמא דרבי דדריש ונתת וגו' ממון ורבנן דרשי נפש ממש ולהכי לא מצי לאוקמי הקישא לאין מתכוין אבל לענין שוגג ומזיד כולהו אית להו הקישא. ת"י].

ב) וכפ' קמא דסנהדרין דקאמר מ"ט דר' ישמעאל דאמר מלקות בכ"ג אביי אמר אתיא רשע רשע רבא אמר מלקות תחת מיתה עומדת לא משום דלית ליה כו' אלא משום דא"צ כדאמר בפ"ק דמכות גבי ואין משלשין במכות וגבי מחזירים לזכות לא בעי למימר דתחת מיתה עומדת דשאני במיתה דוקא משום דכתיב ושפטו העדה והצילו. ת"י עה"ג.

ליקוטי רש"י

משלמין פרעון שלם דהוו איננו במקום אבוהון והואיל והן אכלוה משלמין. אבל ארישא. דמתה כדרכה לא דלא אמרינן אשתעבוד נכסים דלא רמי חיוב אונסין על השואל עד שעת אונסין והכא כי אתניסא ליתיה לשואל והני לא קבול עלייהו מידי [ב"ק שם]. חייבי מיתות שוגגין וחייבי מלקיות שוגגין ודבר אחר. אתרוייהו (קאי) [קאמר] חייבי מיתות שוגגין ודבר אחר עבר עבירה בלא התראה דהיינו שוגג ויש בה דין מיתה אם היו מתרים בו ויש בה עוד חיוב דבר אחר כגון מלקות שהתרו בו למלקות כי הא דאמרן או יש בה חיוב ממון. ר' יוחנן אמר חייב. באותו דבר אחר שעם המיתה הואיל ואינו נהרג וכן חייבי מלקיות שוגגין ודבר אחר שעבר עבירה שיש בה מלקות וממון כגון אכל מעשר שני של חבירו בגבולין או נבלה וטרפה של חבירו ולא התרו בו למלקות [חולין פא:].

[ע"כ שייך לדף לד:]

והא תנא דבי חזקיה. בבבא קמא [בסמנים] (דף לה.) לפטור חייבי מיתות שוגגין מן התשלומין מה מכה בהמה לא חלקת בו וכו' [סנהדרין פד:]. מכה אדם ומכה בהמה. הוקשו יחד דמה מכה בהמה לעולם משלם ואפי' בשוגג כדאמרי' (לעיל דף כו.) אדם מועד לעולם אף מכה אדם דפטריה קרא מתשלומין דכתיב יומת לעולם פטור ואפילו בשוגג הואיל ובמזיד שייכא מיתה [ב"ק לה.]. לכך הוקשו בהאי קרא מכה בהמה ישלמנה ומכה אדם יומת ומשמע בבהמה חייב ממון ובאדם פטור מממון דכתיב בהמה ישלמנה ולא אדם והקיש לך הכתוב פטור תשלומין של אדם לחיוב תשלומין של בהמה. לדרך עלייה. לא שייך למתני גבי בהמה אלא משום דבאדם אשכחן ביה חילוק בהורג בשוגג דרך ירידה חייב גלות אבל דרך עלייה בהרימו את ידו פטור מגלות דכתיב (במדבר לה) ויפל עליו וימת דרך נפילה בעינן. לפוטרו ממון אלא לחייבו ממון. כלומר לא חלקת בו שום צד להפטר מן תשלומין אלא בכל לדין הוא דמחייב דרבינן כל נזקין בבבא קמא (דף כו:) מפצע תחת פצע לחייב על השוגג כמזיד ועל האונס כרצון ומכה בהמה נזק הוא. אף מכה אדם. אין דין פטור תשלומין הכתוב בו חלוק לשום צד שיתחייב ממון אלא כל שעה פטור ממון בין בשוגג ואין נתכוון לפטור ממיתה בין במזיד ונתכוון דחייב מיתה [סנהדרין עט:]. לדרך עלייה. שהרגו כלאחר יד בהרימו הגרזן דקיימא לן (מכות דף ז:) דפטור מגלות אפ"ה פטור מתשלומין [ב"ק שם]. אלא לפטרו ממון. אלמא פטור ממון לתנא דבי חזקיה [סנהדרין שם]. ומכה בהמה ישלמנה. למעלה דבר בהורג בהמה וכאן דבר בעושה בה חבורה. ומכה אדם יומת. אפילו לא הרגו אלא עשה בו חבורה שלא נאמר כאן נפש ובמכה אביו ואמו דבר הכתוב ובא להקישו למכה בהמה מה מכה בהמה מחיים אף מכה אביו ואמו מחיים פרט למכה לאחר מיתה לפי שמצינו שהמקללו לאחר מיתה חייב הוצרך לומר במכה שפטור ומה בבהמה בחבלה שאם אין חבלה אין תשלומין אף מכה אביו ואמו אינו חייב עד שיעשה בהם חבורה [ויקרא כד, כא]. בקטלא כתיב. ותשלומין אין שם. הכאה הכאה קאמרינן. אע"ג דקראי לא דמו גמרינן ג"ש כדתנא דבי ר' ישמעאל ושב הכהן ובא הכהן עירובין (דף נא.) ומכה אדם דקתני הכא הכאה הוא דקאמר ומכי יתן מום גמר דמום ע"י הכאה בא [ב"ק פג:].

עין משפט נר מצוה

מ א ב מיי' פ"א מהל' נערה בתולה הל' יג ופ"ד מהל' חובל הל' ז סמג עשין ע טוש"ע ח"מ סי' תכב סעיף ד:

מא ג מיי' פ"א מהל' נערה בתולה הל' יא ופ"ג מהל' גניבה הל' א סמג עשין עא:

מב ד מיי' פ"ד מהל' חובל הל' ט ופ"ה הל' ג סמג עשין ע טוש"ע ח"מ סי' תכ סעי' ג:

גליון הש"ס

תוס' ד"ה ומי איכא וכו' א"כ מתני' סברה. כעין זה בכ"מ דף מ ע"ב תוס' ד"ה מנהיג למודיה:

תורה אור השלם

א) וְכִי יִנָּצוּ אֲנָשִׁים וְנָגְפוּ אִשָּׁה הָרָה וְיָצְאוּ יְלָדֶיהָ וְלֹא יִהְיֶה אָסוֹן עָנוֹשׁ יֵעָנֵשׁ כַּאֲשֶׁר יָשִׁית עָלָיו בַּעַל הָאִשָּׁה וְנָתַן בִּפְלִלִים: [שמות כא, כב]

ב) וּמַכֵּה בְהֵמָה יְשַׁלְּמֶנָּה וּמַכֵּה אָדָם יוּמָת: [ויקרא כד, כא]

ג) וְלֹא תִקְחוּ כֹפֶר לְנֶפֶשׁ רֹצֵחַ אֲשֶׁר הוּא רָשָׁע לָמוּת כִּי מוֹת יוּמָת: [במדבר לה, לא]

ד) וְהָיָה אִם בִּן הַכּוֹת הָרָשָׁע וְהִפִּילוֹ הַשֹּׁפֵט וְהִכָּהוּ לְפָנָיו כְּדֵי רִשְׁעָתוֹ בְּמִסְפָּר: [דברים כה, ב]

ה) וּמַכֵּה נֶפֶשׁ בְּהֵמָה יְשַׁלְּמֶנָּה נֶפֶשׁ תַּחַת נָפֶשׁ: [ויקרא כד, יח]

ו) וְאִישׁ כִּי יִתֵּן מוּם בַּעֲמִיתוֹ כַּאֲשֶׁר עָשָׂה כֵּן יֵעָשֶׂה לּוֹ: [ויקרא כד, יט]

תוספות רי"ד

א"ר ומי איכא למ"ד חייבי מיתות שוגגין חייבין והתנא דבי חזקי' מכה אדם ומכה בהמה ישלמנה מה מכה בהמה לא חלקת בה בין בשוגג בין במזיד בין מתכוין לאינו מתכוין בין דרך ירידה לדרך עלייה לפוטרו ממון אלא לחייבו ממון אף מכה אדם לא חלקת בו בין שוגג למזיד בין מתכוין לא"מ בין דרך ירידה לד"ע לחייבו ממון אלא לפוטרו ממון. פי' המורה (מכה אדם) מכה בהמה ישלמנה ומכה אדם לא ישלם אלא יומת הקיש פטור ממון דמכה אדם לחיוב ממון דמכה בהמה. מה מכה בהמה אין לך בו חילוק לפטור מלשלם דאדם מועד לעולם בין ער ובין ישן בין שוגג בין מזיד אף מכה אדם אין לך בו חילוק לחיובא ומכה בהמה לעולם חייב דאמרי' בב"ק פצע תחת פצע לחייב השוגג כמזיד ואונס כרצון פי' שאין מתכוין אין בו חיוב מיתה באדם פי' דרך עלי' שהכהו בהגבהת ידו או בחרבו מממטה למעלה פי' בין דרך עליה וכו' משום דגבי גלות ההורג בשוגג איכא חילוק בין דרך ירידה לדרך עלייה. כדאמרי' במס' מכות כל שבדרך ירידתו גולה דכתיב ויפל עליו עד שיפול בדרך נפילה: אלא כי אתא רבין אמר ח"מ שוגגין דכ"ע לא פליגי דפטירי פי' מדתנא דבי חזקי' כי פליגי בחייבי מלקות שוגגים וד"א ר"י אמר חייבי מלקות לא איתקוש [חייבי מלקות לא איתקוש] ור"ל אמר פטור בפירוש רבתה תורה חייבי מלקות כחייבי מיתות היכן ריבתה אביי אמר רשע רשע פי' נאמר בחייבי מיתות אשר הוא רשע למות ונאמר בח"מ והי' אם בן הכות הרשע. רבא אמר אתיא מכה מכה פי' דחייבי מלקות נמי איתקש למכה בהמה ולא מג"ש דח"מ ילפינן וקי"ל כר"י:

מַאי לַאו אָסוֹן מַמָּשׁ – **Is this not** a reference to **a fatality in the literal sense?**[1]

R' Yochanan's reply:

לֹא – **No!** דִּין אָסוֹן – The verse refers to **a judgment of fatality** (i.e. the death penalty) against the one who struck the woman.[2]

The Gemara presents a converse version of the preceding discussion:

אִיכָּא דְּאָמְרֵי – **There are those who say** that the aforementioned discussion went as follows: אֵיתִיבֵיהּ רַבִּי יוֹחָנָן לְרֵישׁ לָקִישׁ – **R' Yochanan challenged Reish Lakish** from the following verse: "וְלֹא יִהְיֶה אָסוֹן עָנוֹשׁ יֵעָנֵשׁ" – *If men shall quarrel and they jolt a pregnant woman and she miscarries* ***and there shall be no fatality, he shall be punished [monetarily],*** i.e. he pays the value of the fetus. מַאי לַאו דִּין אָסוֹן – **Is this not** a reference to **a judgment of fatality** against the one who struck the woman?[3]

Reish Lakish's reply:

לֹא – **No!** It refers to אָסוֹן מַמָּשׁ – **a fatality in the literal sense.**[4]

The Gemara asks:

אָמַר רָבָא – **Rava said:** וּמִי אִיכָּא לְמַאן דְּאָמַר חַיָּיבֵי מִיתוֹת שׁוֹגְגִין חַיָּיבִים – **But is there anyone who says** that **those acting unintentionally who** commit acts for which they **would be liable to** the **death** penalty had they acted deliberately **are liable** to pay for a monetary liability incurred simultaneously? וְהָא תָּנָא דְּבֵי חִזְקִיָּה – **Why, it was taught in a Baraisa in the academy of Chizkiyah:** "מַכֵּה אָדָם" "וּמַכֵּה בְהֵמָה" – The Torah draws an analogy between ***ONE WHO STRIKES*** and kills ***A PERSON*** (who is executed and does not pay damages) ***AND ONE WHO STRIKES*** and kills ***AN ANIMAL*** (who does pay monetary damages).[5] From this analogy it is derived that מַה מַכֵּה בְהֵמָה לֹא חִילַּקְתָּ בּוֹ בֵּין בְּשׁוֹגֵג בֵּין בְּמֵזִיד – JUST AS in the case of ONE WHO STRIKES AN ANIMAL YOU DO NOT DISTINGUISH BETWEEN an INADVERTENT act[6] AND a DELIBERATE act, בֵּין מִתְכַּוֵּין לְשֶׁאֵין מִתְכַּוֵּין – BETWEEN an INTENTIONAL act AND an UNINTENTIONAL act,[7] בֵּין דֶּרֶךְ יְרִידָה לְדֶרֶךְ עֲלִיָּיה – or BETWEEN a DOWNWARD blow AND an UPWARD blow,[8] לְפוֹטְרוֹ מָמוֹן – TO EXEMPT HIM from paying MONEY in any of these cases, אֶלָּא לְחַיְּיבוֹ מָמוֹן – RATHER, the verse means TO OBLIGATE HIM to pay MONEY in all these cases;[9] אַף מַכֵּה אָדָם – so TOO, in regard to ONE WHO STRIKES A PERSON, לֹא תַחֲלוֹק בּוֹ בֵּין בְּשׁוֹגֵג בֵּין בְּמֵזִיד – YOU DO NOT DISTINGUISH BETWEEN an INADVERTENT act AND a DELIBERATE act, בֵּין מִתְכַּוֵּין לְשֶׁאֵין מִתְכַּוֵּין – BETWEEN an INTENTIONAL act AND an UNINTENTIONAL act,[10] בֵּין דֶּרֶךְ יְרִידָה לְדֶרֶךְ עֲלִיָּיה – or BETWEEN a DOWNWARD blow AND an UPWARD blow,[11] לְחַיְּיבוֹ מָמוֹן – TO

NOTES

1. I.e. the verse apparently means [see end of note 2] that if the woman does not die, the one who struck her pays for the fetus, implying that if she *does* die, then he does *not* pay for the fetus – even if he was not warned and would thus not be executed in any case. This shows, then, that an act bearing the death penalty exempts from monetary payment, even if the death penalty cannot be carried out in this particular instance, which contradicts R' Yochanan! (*Rashi*).

2. [In contrast to Reish Lakish (who maintains that the verse refers to a "fatality" occurring to the woman), R' Yochanan maintains that the verse refers to a "fatality" occurring to the the one who struck her – i.e. his being sentenced to death for murder.] Thus, the verse is saying that if the one who struck her is not sentenced to death – either because the woman was not killed or because he was not warned – he shall be liable to pay for the value of the fetus (*Rashi;* see also *Ritva*). [Thus, even though he committed an act of murder, for which he would have been executed had he been warned, he pays the value of the fetus, since he was *not* warned and does *not* actually receive the death penalty.]

[One could ask: As explained, the essential difference between Reish Lakish and R' Yochanan is whether the verse refers to the fatality of the woman or that of the one who struck her. Why, then, does the Gemara express this as a contrast between fatality being "literal" or meaning "a judgment of fatality"? Even R' Yochanan understands "fatality" to be *literal,* except that it refers not to the woman but to the one who struck her! Perhaps, the answer is that according to Reish Lakish, the essential point is whether or not the woman actually dies as a result of her injuries. According to R' Yochanan, however, the essential point is whether or not the one who struck her is *sentenced* to death, not whether the execution has been carried out. For even if the death sentence has not been carried out, the murderer is exempt from monetary payment because he has become actually *liable* to death.]

[It should be noted that the next verse (*Exodus* 21:23) states: *But if there shall be a fatality, then you shall give a life for a life* (i.e. if the woman dies, the one who struck her shall be executed for murder). Now, according to R' Yochanan's interpretation, "there being a fatality" in the second verse indeed exactly parallels "there not being a fatality" in the first verse. For in the second verse, where the Torah states that the one who struck her shall be executed, it means that he *was* warned and there is thus a judgment of death against him. This exactly parallels "there not being a fatality" in the first verse, which R' Yochanan takes to mean that the one who struck her was *not* warned and thus cannot be executed; he then pays for the fetus, even if the mother was killed. According to Reish Lakish's interpretation, however, the parallel is not exact. For whereas in the second verse the meaning is that the one who struck her was warned and is sentenced to death, in the first verse it means not only that he was not warned, but that the woman did not die altogether! For if the woman does die, then the one who struck her does *not* pay for the fetus (according to Reish Lakish), since the very act of murder exempts from monetary payment, even if the murderer is not actually liable to death. This would seem to make R' Yochanan's interpretation the more plausible one. Nevertheless, Reish Lakish, in issuing his challenge to R' Yochanan, assumes his own interpretation to be the more plausible one, since the simple meaning of the verse is indeed that the "fatality" referred to is the inadvertent death of the woman, not the judgment of death against the one who struck her (see *Ritva;* see also *Tosafos*).]

3. See note 2. This version initially assumes R' Yochanan's interpretation to be the more plausible one, since it is only according to that interpretation that "there being a fatality" in the second verse exactly parallels "there not being a fatality" in the first [as explained in note 2] (see *Ritva*).

4. See note 1.

5. *Leviticus* 24:21. The Torah states: וּמַכֵּה בְהֵמָה יְשַׁלְּמֶנָּה וּמַכֵּה אָדָם יוּמָת, *And one who strikes an animal shall pay for it, and one who strikes a person shall be put to death* [i.e. and *not* pay]. The Torah in this verse compares the exemption from monetary liability for one who kills a person to the liability to payment incurred by one who strikes an animal. This comparison teaches that just as one who strikes an animal is *always* liable to payment (see below, note 9), so too, one who kills a man is *always* exempt from payment (see below, note 12), as the Baraisa proceeds to explain (*Rashi*).

6. [I.e. where he did not intend to strike an animal altogether.]

7. [I.e. where he intended to strike one animal, but struck another animal instead; see *Sanhedrin* 79b.]

8. The distinction between an upward motion and a downward motion is relevant only to the inadvertent killing of a person (see below, note 11). It is mentioned here (in regard to injury caused to an animal) only to stylistically complement its mention below in the context of killing a person (see *Rashi* to *Sanhedrin* ibid. ד״ה דרך עלייה).

9. The Gemara, *Bava Kamma* 26b, expounds the verse (*Exodus* 21:25) *a wound for a wound* to teach that a person who inflicts damage [e.g. one who strikes an animal] is liable to pay whether he did so deliberately or inadvertently, willingly or unwillingly (*Rashi* above ד״ה מכה אדם ומכה בהמה).

10. [I.e. where he intended to kill one person, but killed another person instead, in which case, the Tanna of this Baraisa maintains that] the murderer is exempt from the death penalty (*Rashi;* see *Tosafos* ד״ה ומי and *Sanhedrin* ibid.).

11. E.g. he killed him by lifting his hand or by cutting him with a sword in an upward motion.

One is liable to exile (for inadvertent homicide) only if he killed the victim through a downward motion. This is derived from the verse (*Numbers* 35:23): וַיַּפֵּל עָלָיו, *and he caused to fall upon him.* The Baraisa,

with regard to the latter part of his ruling.[29] מַאן דְּמַתְנֵי לַהּ אַרֵישָׁא כָּל שֶׁכֵּן אַסֵּיפָא – **The one who teaches it with regard to the first part certainly** applies it **to the latter part** as well.[30] וּפְלִיגָא דְּרַב פָּפָּא – **Moreover,** according to this understanding, **this** ruling of Rava **disputes that of Rav Pappa.**[31] וּמַאן דְּמַתְנֵי לַהּ אַסֵּיפָא – **But the one who teaches it with regard to the latter part** applies it *only* to the latter part, אֲבָל אַרֵישָׁא לֹא – **but with regard to the first part,** it does **not** apply,[32] וְהַיְינוּ דְּרַב פָּפָּא – **and** accordingly **this** ruling of Rava **is** identical to the teaching **of Rav Pappa.**[33]

Having concluded the lengthy discussion engendered by Reish Lakish's way of reconciling our Mishnah with the Mishnah in *Makkos,*[34] the Gemara considers why Reish Lakish did not adopt instead the reconciliation of the Mishnahs proposed by R' Yochanan:[35]

בִּשְׁלָמָא רַבִּי יוֹחָנָן לֹא אָמַר כְּרֵישׁ לָקִישׁ – **It is understandable that R' Yochanan does not say as Reish Lakish** does, דְּקָא מוֹקִים לַהּ כְּרַבָּנָן – **for** with his answer **[R' Yochanan] interprets [the Mishnah]** as being the opinion of **the Rabbis.**[36] אֶלָּא רֵישׁ לָקִישׁ מַאי טַעְמָא לֹא אָמַר כְּרַבִּי יוֹחָנָן – **But why does Reish Lakish not say as R' Yochanan** does?

The Gemara answers:

אָמַר לָךְ – **[Reish Lakish] would say to you** כֵּיוָן דְּאִילּוּ אַתְרוּ בֵּיהּ פָּטוּר – that according to the Rabbis, **since if [the witnesses] would warn him** that he would be subject to lashes should he proceed and cohabit with his sister, **he would be exempt** from paying the fine, כִּי לֹא אַתְרוּ בֵּיהּ נַמִּי פָּטוּר – **when they do not warn him, he is also exempt.**[37]

The Gemara notes:

וְאַזְדוּ לְטַעְמַיְיהוּ – **And** in this matter **they** [Reish Lakish and R' Yochanan] **are consistent with their opinions** stated elsewhere. דְּכִי אֲתָא רַב דִּימִי אָמַר – **For when R' Dimi came** from Eretz Yisrael to Bavel, **he reported** the following discussion: חַיָּיבֵי מִיתוֹת שׁוֹגְגִין וְחַיָּיבֵי מַלְקִיּוֹת שׁוֹגְגִין וְדָבָר אַחֵר – With regard to **those acting inadvertently**[38] **who** commit acts for which they **would be liable to** the **death** penalty had they acted deliberately, or **those acting inadvertently**[38] **who** commit acts for which they **would be liable to lashes** had they acted deliberately, **and** who simultaneously incur liability to **something else,** i.e. to monetary payment, רַבִּי יוֹחָנָן אָמַר – **R' Yochanan says:** חַיָּיב – **He is liable** to pay the money. וְרֵישׁ לָקִישׁ אָמַר – **But Reish Lakish says:** פָּטוּר – **He is exempt** from paying the money.

The Gemara explains:

רַבִּי יוֹחָנָן אָמַר חַיָּיב – **R' Yochanan says that he is liable** to pay, דְּהָא לֹא אַתְרוּ בֵּיהּ – **for indeed they did not warn him;** thus, he is not actually subject to lashes.[39] רֵישׁ לָקִישׁ אָמַר פָּטוּר – **Reish Lakish says that he is exempt** from paying, כֵּיוָן דְּאִילּוּ אַתְרוּ בֵּיהּ פָּטוּר – for **since if they would warn him, he would be exempt** from monetary payment, כִּי לֹא אַתְרוּ בֵּיהּ נַמִּי פָּטוּר – **when they do not warn him, he is also exempt.**[40]

Reish Lakish presents a challenge to R' Yochanan:

אֵיתִיבֵיהּ רֵישׁ לָקִישׁ לְרַבִּי יוֹחָנָן – **Reish Lakish challenged R' Yochanan** from the following verse:[41] ,,וְלֹא יִהְיֶה אָסוֹן עָנוֹשׁ יֵעָנֵשׁ'' – *If men shall quarrel and they jolt a pregnant woman and she miscarries* ***and there shall be no fatality, he shall be punished [monetarily],*** i.e. he pays the value of the fetus.

NOTES

29. In the latter part of his ruling, Rava said that if the heirs (assuming the cow had belonged to their father) slaughtered the cow and ate its meat, they must pay the lender only the value of meat at the cheap rate. Rava now states that if, however, their father left them real property, they must pay full market value for the cow [from that real property]. For they should have taken care [to investigate whether the cow was actually their father's before slaughtering it] (*Rashi*).

Ramban and other Rishonim find difficulty with *Rashi's* explanation. If the heirs are in fact considered negligent for not investigating before slaughtering the cow, they should be liable to pay the full market price even when the father does *not* leave any real property! [*Ramban* therefore explains (as do *Tosafos*) that the reason for this ruling is not that the *heirs* are considered negligent (as *Rashi* states) but rather that the *father* is considered to have been negligent in not informing his heirs at the time of his death that the cow was not his. And since this negligence caused the subsequent slaughter of the cow by his heirs, he (and his estate) incurs liability to pay for the eventual slaughter from the moment of the negligence.] See *Shitah Mekubetzes* for several defenses of *Rashi*.

30. If the father's estate is liable to pay even if the cow dies after his death, because liability for all future unavoidable mishaps is incurred at the time the borrower takes possession, certainly the estate is liable where the heirs themselves slaughtered the cow and ate its meat.

31. For Rav Pappa said above that one who borrows a cow and slaughters it on the Sabbath is exempt from payment, because his liability to payment is incurred simultaneously with his liability to Sabbath desecration at the time of the slaughter — *not* at the moment that he borrows it (*Rashi*). Accordingly, in Rava's case, Rav Pappa would rule that where the cow died on its own, the owner could not collect from the father's estate even if he left real property.

32. For according to this way of understanding Rava, he says nothing about liability being incurred at the time of borrowing. It is only in the latter case, where the liability is on account of negligence (see above, note 29), that the heirs must pay from the real property left by their father.

33. Who said that the borrower incurs no liability at the time of borrowing. Accordingly, Rav Pappa would rule here that if the cow died on its own, the heirs do not pay even if their father left them real property. For a borrower's liability is incurred at the time of the unavoidable mishap, and in the present case the borrower (viz. the father) was no longer alive to incur any liability (see *Rashi*).

34. On 33b, Reish Lakish explained that the Mishnah in *Makkos* (which prescribes lashes for one who cohabits with his sister) reflects the view of R' Meir, who says that one *can* receive lashes and be required to pay money for the same crime.

35. R' Yochanan had explained (32b) that one who commits a crime for which there is liability to both lashes and monetary payment ordinarily receives the lashes and does not pay. Nevertheless, our Mishnah rules that one who violates his sister pays the fine, because it refers to where he was not warned that he would receive lashes. Since he does not receive the lashes in this case, he pays the fine.

36. Who hold that one cannot receive lashes and be required to pay money for the same crime. And it is indeed preferable to establish the Mishnah as following the majority view of the Rabbis, rather than the minority view of R' Meir, who holds that one *can* receive lashes and be required to pay money for the same crime.

37. [For his monetary liability was incurred simultaneously with an act that *bears* the penalty of lashes, even if those lashes will not actually be administered in this particular instance.]

Thus, Reish Lakish maintains that R' Yochanan's resolution is untenable. For even if our Mishnah discusses a case in which the violator was *not* warned about lashes, the Rabbis would hold that he does not pay the fine.

38. I.e. without being warned (*Rashi*). [*Rashi* means to say that the law stated below *also* refers to a case where they committed the act deliberately but without being warned. For in either case — actual inadvertence or lack of warning — they will not receive the physical punishment for their transgression.]

39. The only reason to exempt him from payment is that we cannot administer two penalties for one crime (above, 32b). Accordingly, where they did *not* warn him and he does *not* receive lashes, we require him to pay, for we are then subjecting him to only one penalty (see *Rashi*).

40. The Gemara below (35a) will present the source for Reish Lakish's view in this matter (*Rashi*).

41. *Exodus* 21:22.

עין משפט
נר מצוה

לה א מיי' פ"ג מהל' גנבה הל' יג סמג לאוין קנ:
לו ב מיי' פ"ב שם הל' ד סמג שם:
לז ג ד מיי' פ"א מהל' שאלה הל' ג סמג עשין פט טוש"ע ח"מ סימן שמ סעיף ד:
לח ה מיי' שם הל' ה ופמג שם טוש"ע שם סי' שמא סעיף ג:
לט ו ז מיי' שם טוש"ע שם סעי' ד:

ור' מאיר א) לוקה ומשלם אית ליה מת ומשלם לית ליה ושאני הני דחידוש הוא שחידשה תורה בקנס אע"ג דמיקטיל משלם ואזדא רבה לטעמיה דאמר רבה היה גדי גנוב לו וטבחו בשבת חייב שכבר נתחייב בגניבה קודם שיבא לידי איסור שבת היה גנב וטבח בשבת פטור שאם אין גניבה אין טביחה ואין מכירה ואמר רבה היה גדי גנוב לו וטבחו במחתרת חייב שכבר נתחייב בגניבה קודם שיבא לידי איסור מחתרת א גנב וטבח במחתרת פטור שאם אין גניבה אין טביחה ואין מכירה וצריכא דאי אשמעינן שבת משום דאיסורה איסור עולם אבל מחתרת דאיסור שעה הוא אימא לא ואי אשמעינן מחתרת משום ב) דמחתרתו זו היא התראתו אבל שבת דבעיא התראה אימא לא צריכא אמר רב פפא ג) היתה פרה גנובה לו וטבחה בשבת חייב שכבר נתחייב בגניבה קודם שיבא לידי איסור שבת ב היתה פרה שאולה לו וטבחה בשבת פטור אמר ליה רב אחא בריה דרבא לרב אשי רב פפא פרה אתא לאשמועינן אמר ליה רב פפא שאולה אתא לאשמועינן סלקא דעתך אמינא הואיל ואמר רב פפא ד) ג משעת משיכה הוא דאתחייב ליה במזונותיה הכא נמי ד משעת שאלה אתחייב באונסיה קא משמע לן ה) אמר רבא ה הניח להן אביהן פרה שאולה משתמשין בה כל ימי שאלתה מתה אין חייבין באונסה ו כסבורין של אביהם היא וטבחוה ואכלוה אן משלמין ו) דמי בשר בזול הניח להן אביהן אחריות נכסים חייבין לשלם איכא דמתני לה ארישא ואיכא דמתני לה אסיפא מאן דמתני לה ארישא כל שכן אסיפא ופליגא דרב פפא ומאן ז דמתני לה אסיפא אבל ארישא לא והיינו דרב פפא בשלמא ר' יוחנן לא אמר כריש לקיש דקא מוקים לה כרבנן אלא ריש לקיש מ"ט לא אמר כר' יוחנן אמר לך כיון דאילו אתרו ביה פטור כי לא אתרו ביה נמי פטור ז) ואזדו לטעמייהו דכי אתא רב דימי אמר חייבי מיתות שוגגין וחייבי מלקיות שוגגין ודבר אחר ר' יוחנן אמר חייב וריש לקיש אמר פטור ר' יוחנן אמר חייב דהא לא אתרו ביה ר"ל אמר פטור כיון דאילו אתרו ביה פטור כי לא אתרו ביה נמי פטור איתיביה ר"ל לרבי יוחנן א) ולא יהיה אסון ענוש יענש מאי

ורבי מאיר לוקה ומשלם אית ליה מת ומשלם לית ליה ושאני הני. משמע דלרבי מאיר לית ליה לוקה ומשלם אף בממון שאינו קנס וכן משמע בהשוכר את הפועלים (ב"מ צא.) שהבאתי לעיל ותימה דבפ"ק דמכות (ד' ד:) קאמר עולא טעמא דרבי מאיר דאמר עדים זוממין לוקין ומשלמין משום דגמר ממוציא שם רע ופריך מה למוציא שם רע שכן קנס סבר לה כר' עקיבא דאמר עדים זוממין קנס הוא משמע דבממון אינו לוקה ומשלם ויש לומר דודאי אי עדים זוממין הוי ממונא לא הוה גמר ממוציא ש"ר שכן הוא קנס אלא הוה דרשינן מכדי רשעתו שאינו לוקה ומשלם אבל השתא דסבר עדים זוממין קנסא וגמר ממוציא שם רע לוקין ומשלמין ע"כ מוקי כדי רשעתו במיתה ומלקות כיון דכדי רשעתו לא הוי במלקות וממון מהשתא בכל דוכתא לוקה ומשלם דמהיכא נמעיט שלא ילקה וישלם: **דאמר** רבה היה גדי גנוב לו. אליבא דרבי מאיר קאמר ולא משום דסבר הכי: **משום** דאיסורו איסור עולם כו'. שאם חלל שבת לאחר השבת יעידו עליו ויהרגוהו אבל מחתרת אע"פ שמתחייב בנפשו בעודו במחתרת מ"מ אחר שילא תו לא הוי בר קטלא ולא הוי דומיא דאם יהיה אסון: **אבל** שבת דבעי התראה אימא לא. תימה דעיקר קים ליה בדרבה מיניה ברליחה כתיב דבעינן התראה ועוד דשבת ומחתרת תרווייהו תנניי דבפרק המניח (ב"ק דף לד:) תנן והוא שהדליק את הגדיש בשבת פטור מפני שנידון בנפשו ומחתרת נמי תנינא בפרק בן סורר (סנהדרין עב.) היה בא במחתרת ושיבר את החבית אם אין לו דמים פטור ונראה דהכא עביד צריכותא אמאי דקנס מיקטיל ומשלם וה"ק משום דחמיר איסוריה והוה אמינא דהתם דווקא הוא דליחייב קנס עם המיתה וכה"ג עביד צריכותא לקמן (דף לז.) גבי לא יהיה אסון וכדי רשעתו דמשום דחמור הוי אמרינן דלעביד ביה תרתי אבל קשה למאי דפרישית דרבה אליבא דרבי מאיר קאמר אם כן היכי קאמר אבל שבת דבעיא התראה אימא לא מיקטיל ומשלם והא עיקר מילתיה דרבי מאיר גבי שבת תניא לעיל ומצינן למימר דרבה אשמועינן דשייך קים ליה בדרבה מיניה אע"ג דבשעה דמתחייב עדיין הממון בעין לא הוה לן למימר קים ליה בדרבה מיניה כדאמר רבה גופיה בפרק בן סורר (סנהדרין עב. ושם) אמר ט) רבה מסתברא מילתיה דרב כששיבר דליתנהו אבל ליתנהו לא אפ"ה כיון דטבח אחרי כן מיפטר על הגנבה והא דפטור אגנבה אף על גב דבאותה שעה הוי בעין עביד צריכותא: **מתה** אין חייבין באונסין. אבל בגנבה ואבדה נראה לר"י שהן חייבין דהואיל ונהנין דמשתמשין בה והכי (א) אמר בהשואל (ב"מ צז. ושם): **אבל** ארישא לא והיינו דרב פפא. דלא אמרינן משעת שאלה חייב באונסין וא"ת אם כן בסיפא נמי בשטבחוה אמאי משלמין כשהניח להן אביהן אחריות נכסים הא לא נתחייב האב וי"ל דהתם פשע בה האב שהיה לו לומר לבניו שאינה שלו הלכך מחיים פשע בה ונתחייב בה באותה שעה ונשתעבדו נכסיו:

ור' מאיר. בעלמא בתשלומי ממון לית ליה מת ומשלם והכא תשלומי ארבעה וחמשה קנס הם וכל משפט קנס חידוש הוא הלכך אע"ג דמיקטיל נמי לא מיפטר מיניה ולקמן פריך לרבה אליבא דרבי מאיר קשיא בתו דמתניתין נמי קנס הוא וקא פטר ליה אבתו: **היה גדי גנוב לו.** גנב גדי בחול ונתחייב הקרן וטבחו בשבת דלא אתי עליה חיובא דממון באיסור שבת אלא חיוב קנס: **חייב.** ד' וה' דקנס חידוש הוא ורבה סבירא ליה כרבי מאיר: **גנב וטבח בשבת.** דחיוב ממון דקרן אתא עליה באיסור שבת: **פטור.** דקיימא לן אין מת ומשלם וכיון דאקרן לא מיחייב קנס נמי לא משלם דתשלומי ד' וה' אמר רחמנא ולא תשלומי שלשה וארבעה ולא סבירא לן כרבי נתן דאמר (שבת דף לז.) אי נושא את עצמו אי נמי בכפות: **שאם אין גניבה.** כלומר שמאחר שפטור על הקרן משום מיתה: **אין טביחה ואין מכירה.** אינו מחויב קנס כדפירשתי דתשלומי ארבעה וחמשה כתיב ולא תשלומי שלשה וארבעה: **מחתרת.** שחתר בית והוליאו: **וטבחו במחתרת.** עלמה דההיא שעתא בר קטלא הוא אי הוה אשכחיה בעל הבית כדכתיב (שמות כב) אין לו דמים: **משום דאסוריה איסור עולם.** כל זמן שיעידו עליו שחילל שבת ימיתוהו בית דין הלכך חמירא מיתה דילה לפוטרו מממון: **דאיסור שעה.** אי לא משכח ליה ההיא שעתא תו לא מיקטיל: **היתה פרה שאולה לו וטבחה בשבת פטור.** דההיא שעתא דקא טבח לה גזיל לה ממרה ומיתה וממון באין כאחד ולא גרסינן שאם אין גניבה אין טביחה ואין מכירה דגבי שואל לא שייך לא כפל ולא ארבעה וחמשה שהרי חייב בקרן לעולם אפילו טוען טענת גנב ואין קנס אלא או בגנב או בשומר חנם הפוטר עצמו בטוען טענת גנב שאומר נגנבה: **פרה אתא לאשמועינן.** בתמיה מה למדנו ממנה שלא למדנו מגדי דקאמר רבה: **שאולה אתא לאשמועינן.** דטובחה בשבת פטור: **ס"ד אמינא הואיל ואמר רב פפא.** בהשוכר את הפועלים: **הכא נמי.** נימא משעת שאלה רמיא עליה חיוב קרן וכי טבחה בשבת ליחייב: **קמ"ל.** כיון דכל כמה דאיתא הדרא בעינא ההיא שעתא דקא טבח לה קא גזיל לה: **כל ימי שאלתה.** כל ימי משך הזמן ששאלה אביהן מן הבעלים: **אין חייבין באונסה.** דאינהו לאו שואלין נינהו עלה: **דמי בשר בזול.** כל זוזא חשבינן בארבעה דנקי הכי אמרינן בפרק מי שמת (ב"ב קמו:) והעור יחזירו לבעלים: **אחריות נכסים.** קרקעות: **איכא דמתני ארישא.** להאי הניח להן אביהן אחריות נכסים חייבין לשלם ואמרינן דחייבין באונסין דאישתעבוד נכסים דאבוהון מחיים משעת שאלה: **כ"ש אסיפא.** כשטבחוה ואכלוה: **ופליגא דרב פפא.** דאמר לעיל ההיא שעתא דמטו לה אונסין הוא דאתי חיובא עליה ולא משעת שאלה: **ואיכא דמתני לה אסיפא.** היכא דטבחוה אם הניח להן אביהן אחריות נכסים משלמין תשלומי מעליא ולא בזול דאיבעי להו למידק: **אבל ארישא.** אם מתה לא מיחייבי לשלומי ולא אמרינן אישתעבוד נכסי דאבוהון משעת שאלה: **והיינו דרב פפא.** דאמר לעיל לא אמרינן משעת שאלה רמו עליה תשלומין אלא משעת אונסין ואילך וההיא שעתא ליתיה לשואל דליחייב: **בשלמא רבי יוחנן.** דמוקי מתניתין בשלא התרו בו: **לא אמר כריש לקיש.** דאוקמיה כר' מאיר: **כי לא אתרו ביה נמי פטור.** הואיל ואיכא לד מלקות: **שוגגין.** שלא התרו בהן: **ודבר אחר.** ממון ואכולה מילתא קאי כלומר חייבי מיתות או חייבי מלקיות שוגגין וממון: **ר' יוחנן אומר חייב.** בתשלומין: **דהא לא אתרו ביה.** ואין אתה מחייבו אלא משום רשעה אחת דממון: **כי לא אתרו ביה נמי פטור.** ולקמן יליף טעמא: מאי

מסורת הש"ס

א) [לעיל דף לג: וש"נ], ב) [סנהדרין עב.], ג) ב"ק קיב., ד) ב"מ לא., ה) ב"ק קיב., ו) ב"ק שם [ב"מ מג: ב"ב קמו:], ז) חולין פא., ח) [דף לג. ד"ה ועולא], ט) [בסנהדרין שם איתא רבא].

ליקוטי רש"י

לוקה ומשלם. במסכת מכות (דף ד.) מעידים אנו בפלוני שחייב לחבירו מאתים זוז ונמצאו זוממין לוקין ומשלמין שלא השם המביאן לידי מכות מביאן לידי תשלומין [ב"ק עא.].

הגהות הב"ח

(א) תוס' ד"ה מתה וכו' והכי אמרי' בהשואלין דף צה ע"א:

הגהות מהר"ב רנשבורג

אן גמ' משלמין דמי בשר בזול. עי' רש"י ד"ה דמי בשר וכו' ורשב"ם ב"ב דף קמו ע"ב ד"ה ושמין להם וכו':

תורה אור השלם

א) וְכִי יִנָּצוּ אֲנָשִׁים וְנָגְפוּ אִשָּׁה הָרָה וְיָצְאוּ יְלָדֶיהָ וְלֹא יִהְיֶה אָסוֹן עָנוֹשׁ יֵעָנֵשׁ כַּאֲשֶׁר יָשִׁית עָלָיו בַּעַל הָאִשָּׁה וְנָתַן בִּפְלִלִים: [שמות כא, כב]

תוספות רי"ד

אמר רבא הניח להן אביהם פרה שאולה משתמשי' בה כל ימי שאלה. מתה אין חייבים באונסיה פי' שלא שאלו הן ולא קבלו עליהן אונסים. כסבורין של אביהן היא טבחוה ואכלוה משלמי' דמי בשר בזול. פי' כל זוזי בארבע דנקא והעור יחזירו לבעלים. ואם הניח להן אביהן אחריות נכסים פי' קרקעות חייבים לשלם משום דאישתעבוד נכסים. פי' נכסי דאבוהון מחיים: כי אתא רב דימי אמר חייבי מיתות שוגגין וד"א ר"י אמר חייב ור"ל אמר פטור ר"י אמר חייב דהא לא התרו בו ואי אתה מחייבו אלא משום רשעה אחת ור"ל אמר פטור פי' הואיל ואיכא צד מלקות:

חשק שלמה על תוס' רי"ד

א) נ"ל כיון דאילו אתרו ביה פטור כי לא אתרו ביה נמי פטור פי' וכו'.

מתכלה קרנה סוו לבו ג' לגאון וד' לבקר. ולא היה לי לב להבין את מושל שטעם זה אין צריך לכאן שהרי אין קנס בשואל הטובח ואפילו אמרינן כרב פפא דעד השתא קם ברשותא דמרה אפילו הכי גזלן נעשה עליה ולא גנב שאין דין גנב...

[המשך בדף לה.]

The Gemara asks:

אָמַר לֵיהּ רַב אַחָא בְּרֵיהּ דְּרָבָא לְרַב אַשִׁי – **Rav Acha the son of Rava said to Rav Ashi:** רַב פָּפָּא פָּרָה אָתָא לְאַשְׁמוּעִינַן – **Is Rav Pappa coming to teach us** that Rabbah's ruling regarding a stolen goat pertains to **a** stolen **cow** as well?[18]

The Gemara answers:

אָמַר לֵיהּ – **[Rav Ashi] said to him:** רַב פָּפָּא שְׁאוּלָה אָתָא לְאַשְׁמוּעִינַן – **Rav Pappa is coming to teach us** the law of the **borrowed** cow.[19] סַלְקָא דַעְתָּךְ אָמֵינָא – For **you might have thought to say** that הוֹאִיל וְאָמַר רַב פָּפָּא – **since Rav Pappa said,** מִשְּׁעַת מְשִׁיכָה הוּא דְּאִתְחַיֵּיב לֵיהּ בִּמְזוֹנוֹתֶיהָ – **"It is from the time that [the borrower] pulls** the cow out of the owner's domain **that [the borrower] is obligated in its food allotment,"**[20] הָכָא נַמִּי – **here, too,** מִשְּׁעַת שְׁאֵלָה אִתְחַיֵּיב בְּאוֹנְסֶיהָ – **from the time that he borrows** the cow, prior to his incurring liability for desecrating the Sabbath at the time of the slaughter, **he becomes liable** to pay **for its unavoidable mishaps.**[21] קָא מַשְׁמַע לָן – **[Rav Pappa]** therefore **informs us** otherwise.[22]

The Gemara cites a related ruling.

אָמַר רָבָא – **Rava said:** הִנִּיחַ לָהֶן אֲבִיהֶן פָּרָה שְׁאוּלָה – **If their father** died and **left for them a cow that he had borrowed,** מִשְׁתַּמְּשִׁין בָּהּ כָּל יְמֵי שְׁאֵלָתָהּ – **they may use it for the duration of the days** for which **it was borrowed** by their father from the owner.[23] מֵתָה אֵין חַיָּיבִין בְּאוֹנְסָהּ – **If it died,** however, **they are not liable** to pay **for the unavoidable mishap that befell it.**[24] כִּסְבוּרִין שֶׁל אֲבִיהֶם הִיא וּטְבָחוּהָ וַאֲכָלוּהָ – **If they thought** that **it was their father's** cow **and they slaughtered it and ate it,** מְשַׁלְּמִין דְּמֵי בָשָׂר בְּזוֹל – **they pay** the lender **the value of** the cow's **meat** when sold **at the cheap rate.**[25] הִנִּיחַ לָהֶן אֲבִיהֶן אַחֲרָיוּת נְכָסִים – **If their father left for them real property,** i.e. land or houses,[26] חַיָּיבִין לְשַׁלֵּם – **they are liable to pay.**[27]

The Gemara cites two explanations of what Rava meant by this last statement, "If their father left for them real property, they are liable to pay":

אִיכָּא דְּמַתְנֵי לָהּ אַרֵישָׁא – **There are those who teach it** as being made **with regard to the first part** of his ruling.[28] וְאִיכָּא דְּמַתְנֵי לָהּ אַסֵּיפָא – **And there are those who teach it** as being made

NOTES

cow itself; he is not liable to the fivefold penalty. Hence, Rav Pappa's statement exempting the borrower from payment because the slaughter occurred on the Sabbath is referring to the borrower's obligation to pay for the cow itself, not to any fivefold payment, which is not relevant to a borrower altogether. [See, however, *Rambam, Hil. Geneivah* 3:4, who evidently had in his text the clause deleted by *Rashi.* See also *Rambam* ibid. 4:10 with *Raavad, Kesef Mishneh* and *Or Same'ach.*]

18. I.e. what is Rav Pappa teaching us that we do not already know from the statement of the earlier Amora (Rabbah)? Rabbah stated already that if one steals a goat during the week and slaughters it on the Sabbath, he is liable to the fourfold payment. Is it necessary for Rav Pappa to teach that Rabbah's ruling regarding a goat pertains to a cow as well? (*Rashi*).

19. [I.e. Rav Pappa's main point is the *second* part of his statement – that one who slaughters the *borrowed* cow on the Sabbath is exempt from payment. The first part of his statement (regarding one who slaughters a stolen cow) is made only in order to contrast the exemption of the one who slaughters the *borrowed* cow with the liability of one who slaughters the *stolen* one.]

20. *Bava Metzia* 91a. The Gemara there cites a Baraisa that discusses a case in which a farmer hired or borrowed his fellow's animal to thresh grain. The Baraisa rules that if the farmer muzzles the animal, not only does he incur lashes for transgressing the prohibition against muzzling an animal while it threshes [see *Deuteronomy* 25:4], but he must also pay the animal's owner the amount of produce that the animal would have eaten in the course of threshing. The Gemara there questions how he can be liable to both lashes and payment in light of the principle that one does not receive lashes and pay money for the same crime. To this, Rav Pappa answers that the borrower did not become subject to the two liabilities simultaneously. For he became liable to feed the cow as soon as he took possession of her [by pulling her out of the owner's domain]. If he subsequently muzzles her while she threshes, he does not pay for depriving her of the food *at that time,* but rather for failing to discharge the financial obligation to feed her that he undertook when he took possession of her initially.

21. I.e. I would say that the borrower's liability to pay for any unavoidable mishaps (אונס) is incurred not at the time of the mishap. Rather, from the moment he takes possession of the animal, he becomes liable to return either it or its value to the owner. Hence, although he slaughtered it on the Sabbath, he would nevertheless be liable to payment – not for slaughtering it, but on account of the liability he incurred when he took possession of it (see *Rashi*).

22. For since as long as the animal is alive it is fit to be returned to its owner, it is only at the time that the borrower slaughters it – when he in effect robs it from its owner – that he incurs liability to payment. Consequently, when he slaughters it on the Sabbath, he is exempt from payment, since his liability to payment is incurred simultaneously with his liability for Sabbath desecration (see *Rashi*).

23. For they inherit their father's right to use it during the period for which he borrowed it (*Rashba* and *Ritva*).

24. For since they themselves did not borrow it, they are not encumbered with the liabilities of a "borrower" (see *Rashi*).

[*Rosh, Bava Kamma* 10:1 rules that this law pertains only to where the owner leaves it in their possession without making any stipulations. The owner does, however, have the right to demand that they either accept upon themselves liability for unavoidable mishaps or return the cow. See *Shulchan Aruch, Choshen Mishpat* 341:3.]

25. The cheap rate is two-thirds of the market value [see *Bava Basra* 146b]. They must also return the cow's hide to the lender (*Rashi*). They are not liable to pay the full price of meat, for had they known that they would have to pay for it, they might not have eaten meat (*Rashi* to *Bava Kamma* 112a). [Since the heirs had no idea that they were destroying someone else's property, they cannot be held liable as *damagers* (מַזִּיק); see *Tosafos* to *Bava Kamma* 27b ד״ה ושמואל. Hence, their only monetary liability is to pay for the *benefit* that they derived from the meat; see above, 30b note 19. We assess this benefit at two-thirds the market price. We cannot assess their benefit at full market price, for perhaps they would not have chosen to eat meat had they known that they would have to pay for it. Since, however, it is common for people who would otherwise not eat meat to eat it if it is available at two-thirds the market price, we may presume that they too would have done so (see *Sma* 341:11).]

26. [Literally: possessions that have responsibility. I.e. property upon which a lien for monetary liability takes effect.] When one incurs a debt and that debt is recorded in a legal document, a lien automatically takes effect on any real property owned by the debtor at that time. Even if the debtor subsequently sells the property, the lien is not voided. Should the debtor default on his obligation, the creditor can seize the real property from the buyer to satisfy the debt. For this reason, real property (land and houses) is said to have "responsibility." Since it will always be there (unlike movable property), the lender relies on real property for surety (see *Rashi* to *Kiddushin* 26a ד״ה שיש להם אחריות).

Similarly, when one incurs a monetary liability as a שׁוֹאֵל, *borrower,* a lien takes effect on his real property, and hence, even if he dies and his possessions are transferred to his heirs, the lienholder may seize the property to satisfy the obligation.

27. The Gemara will now explain what this means.

28. In the first part of his ruling, Rava said that if the cow dies, the heirs (who are not encumbered with the liabilities of a "borrower") are not liable to pay for this unavoidable mishap. Rava now states that if, however, their father left them real property, they are indeed liable to pay for the unavoidable mishap. For, in Rava's view, at the moment a borrower takes possession of the borrowed item, he incurs liability to payment for any future unavoidable mishap [see above, note 21]. Thus, their father, who *was* a "borrower," became liable to pay for the unavoidable mishap when he took possession of the cow, and a lien for this liability took effect on his real property at that time. Hence, although the actual mishap occurred after his death (at which point he can no longer *become* liable), the real property that he left can be seized by the lender to satisfy the liability incurred by the father at the time of the initial borrowing (see *Rashi*).

עין משפט
נר מצוה

לה א מיי' פ"ג מהל' גנבה הל' ג סמג לאוין קנ:
לו ב מיי' שם הל' ד סמג שם:
לז ג ד מיי' פ"א מהל' שאלה הל' ד סמג עשין פג טוש"ע ח"מ סימן שמ סעיף ד:
לח ה מיי' שם הל' ה וסמג שם טוש"ע שם סימן שמב סעיף ג:
לט ו ז מיי' שם טוש"ע שם סעי' ד:

ור' מאיר לוקה ומשלם אית ליה מת ומשלם לית ליה ושאני הני דחידוש הוא שחידשה תורה בקנס אע"ג דמיקטיל משלם ואזדא רבה לטעמיה דאמר רבה היה גדי גנוב לו וטבחו בשבת חייב שכבר נתחייב בגניבה קודם שיבא לידי איסור שבת גנב וטבח בשבת פטור שאם אין גניבה אין טביחה ואין מכירה ואמר רבה היה גדי גנוב לו וטבחו במחתרת חייב שכבר נתחייב בגניבה קודם שיבא לידי איסור מחתרת גנב וטבח במחתרת פטור שאם אין גניבה אין טביחה ואין מכירה וצריכא דאי אשמעינן שבת משום דאיסורה איסור עולם אבל מחתרת דאיסור שעה הוא אימא לא ואי אשמעינן מחתרת משום דמחתרתו זו היא התראתו אבל שבת דבעיא התראה אימא לא צריכא אמר רב פפא היתה פרה גנובה לו וטבחה בשבת חייב שכבר נתחייב בגניבה קודם שיבא לידי איסור שבת היתה פרה שאולה לו וטבחה בשבת פטור אמר ליה רב אחא בריה דרבא לרב אשי רב פפא פרה אתא לאשמועינן אמר ליה רב פפא שאולה אתא לאשמועינן סלקא דעתך אמינא הואיל ואמר רב פפא משעת משיכה הוא דאתחייב ליה במזונותיה הכא נמי משעת שאלה אתחייב באונסיה קא משמע לן אמר רבא הניח להן אביהן פרה שאולה משתמשין בה כל ימי שאלתה מתה אין חייבין באונסה כסבורין של אביהם היא וטבחוה ואכלוה משלמין דמי בשר בזול הניח להן אביהן אחריות נכסים חייבין לשלם איכא דמתני לה ארישא ואיכא דמתני לה אסיפא מאן דמתני לה ארישא כל שכן אסיפא ופליגא דרב פפא ומאן דמתני לה אסיפא אבל ארישא לא והיינו דרב פפא בשלמא ר' יוחנן לא אמר כריש לקיש דקא מוקים לה כרבנן אלא ריש לקיש מ"ט לא אמר כר' יוחנן אמר לך כיון דאילו אתרו ביה פטור כי לא אתרו ביה נמי פטור ואזדו לטעמייהו דכי אתא רב דימי אמר חייבי מיתות שוגגין וחייבי מלקיות שוגגין ודבר אחר ר' יוחנן אמר חייב וריש לקיש אמר פטור ר' יוחנן אמר חייב דהא לא אתרו ביה ר"ל אמר פטור כיון דאילו אתרו ביה פטור כי לא אתרו ביה נמי פטור איתיביה ר"ל לרבי יוחנן [א] ולא יהיה אסון ענוש יענש מאי

ורבי מאיר לוקה ומשלם אית ליה מת ומשלם לית ליה ושאני הני. משמע דרבי מאיר אית ליה לוקה ומשלם אף בממון שאינו קנס וכן משמע בהשוכר את הפועלים (ב"מ צא.) שהבאתי לעיל ותימה דבפ"ק דמכות (דף ד:) קאמר עולא טעמא דרבי מאיר דאמר עדים זוממין לוקין ומשלמין משום דגמר ממוציא שם רע ופריך מה למוציא שם רע שכן קנס סבר לה כר' עקיבא דאמר עדים זוממין קנס הוא משמע דבממון אינו לוקה ומשלם ויש לומר דודאי אי עדים זוממין הוי ממונא לא הוה גמר ממוציא ש"ר שכן הוא קנס אלא הוה דרשינן מכדי רשעתו שאינו לוקה ומשלם אבל השתא דסבר עדים זוממין קנסא וגמר ממוציא שם רע דלוקין ומשלמין ע"כ מוקי כדי רשעתו במיתה ומלקות כיון דכדי רשעתו לא הוי במלקות וממון מהשתא בכל דוכתא לוקה ומשלם דמהיכא נפקא שלא ילקה וישלם: **דאמר** רבה היה גדי גנוב לו. אליבא דרבי מאיר קאמר ולא משום דסבר הכי: **משום** דאיסורו איסור עולם כו'. שאם חלל שבת לאחר השבת יעידו עליו ויהרגוהו אבל מחתרת אע"פ שמתחייב בנפשו בעודו במחתרת מ"מ אחר שילא תו לא הוי בר קטלא ולא הוי דומיא דאם יהיה אסון: **אבל** שבת דבעי התראה אימא לא. תימה דעיקר קים ליה בדרבה מיניה בגליה כתיב דבעינן התראה ועוד דשבת ומחתרת תרוייהו תנינהו דבפרק המניח (ב"ק דף לד:) תנן והוא שהדליק את הגדיש בשבת פטור מפני שנדון בנפשו ומחתרת נמי תנינא בפרק בן סורר (סנהדרין עב.) היה בא במחתרת ושיבר את החבית אם יש לו דמים פטור ונראה דהכא עביד לריכותא אמאי דבקנס מיקטיל ומשלם וה"ק משום דחמיר איסוריה והוה אמינא דהתם דחוקה הוא לחייב קנס עם המיתה והכ"ג עביד לריכותא לקמן (דף לז.) גבי לא יהיה אסון וכדי רשעתו משום דחמור הוי אמרינן לעביד ביה תרתי אבל קשה למאי דפרישית דרבה אליבא דרבי מאיר קאמר אם כן היכי קאמר אבל שבת דבעיא התראה אימא לא מיקטיל ומשלם והא עיקר מילתיה דרבי מאיר גבי שבת תניא לעיל ומלינן למימר דרבה אשמועינן דשייך קים ליה בדרבה מיניה אע"ג דבשעה דמתחייב עדיין הממון בעין לא הוה לן למימר קים לי' בדרבה מיניה כדאמר רבה גופיה בפרק בן סורר (סנהדרין עב. ושם) אמר [ט] רבה מסתברא מילתיה דרב כשיבר דליתנהו אבל נטל דאיתנהו לא אפ"ה כיון דטבח אחרי כן מיפטר על הגנבה והאה דפטור אגנבה אף על גב דבאותה שעה הוי בעין עביד לריכותא:

מתה אין חייבין באונסין. אבל בגנבה ואבדה נראה לר"י שהן חייבין דהואיל והנין דמשתמשין בה והכי (א) אמר בהשואל (ב"מ צו. ושם): **אבל** ארישא לא והיינו דרב פפא. דלא אמרינן משעת שאלה חייב באונסין וא"ת אם כן בסיפא נמי בשטבחוה אמאי משלמין כשהניח להן אביהן אחריות נכסים הא לא נתחייב בהן האב וי"ל דהתם פשע בה האב שהיה לו לומר לבניו שאינה שלו הלכך מחייב פשע בה ונתחייב בה באותה שעה ונשתעבדו נכסיו:

ור' מאיר. בעלמא בתשלומי ממון לית ליה מת ומשלם והכא תשלומי ארבעה וחמשה קנס הם וכל משפט קנס חידוש הוא הלכך אע"ג דמיקטיל נמי לא מיפטר מיניה ולקמן פריך רבה אליבא דרבי מאיר קשיא כמו דמתניתין נמי קנס הוא וקא פטר ליה אבנו: **היה גדי גנוב לו.** גנב גדי בחול ונתחייב הקרן וטבחו בשבת דלא אתי עליה חיובא דממון באיסור שבת אלא חיוב קנס: **חייב.** ד' וה' דקנס חידוש הוא ורבה סבירא ליה כרבי מאיר: **גנב וטבח בשבת.** דחיוב ממון דקרן לא אתא עליה באיסור שבת: **פטור.** דקיימא לן אין מת ומשלם וכיון דלקרן לא מיחייב קנס נמי לא משלם דתשלומי ד' וה' אמר רחמנא ולא תשלומי שלשה וארבעה ולא סבירא לן כרבי נתן דאמר (שבת דף לג.) אי נושא את עצמו אי נמי בכפות: **שאם אין גניבה.** כלומר שמאחר שפטור על הקרן משום מיתה: **אין טביחה ואין מכירה.** אינו מחויב קנס כדפירשתי דתשלומי ארבעה וחמשה כתיב ולא תשלומי שלשה וארבעה: **מחתרת.** שחתר בית והוציאו: **וטבחו במחתרת.** עצמה דההיא שעתא בר קטלא הוא אי הוה אשכחיה בעל הבית כדכתיב (שמות כב) אין לו דמים: **משום דאסוריה איסור עולם.** כל זמן שיעידו עליו שחילל שבת ימיתוהו בית דין הלכך חמירא מיתה דילה לפוטרו ממנון: **דאיסור שעה.** אי לא משכח ליה ההיא שעתא תו לא מיקטיל: **היתה פרה שאולה לו וטבחה בשבת פטור.** דההיא שעתא דקא טבח לה גזיל לה ממרה ומיתה וממון באין כאחד ולא גרסינן שאם אין גניבה אין טביחה ואין מכירה דגבי שואל לא שייך לא כפל ולא ארבעה וחמשה שהרי חייב בקרן לעולם אפילו טוען טענת גנב ואין קנס אלא או בגנב או בשומר חנם הפוטר עצמו בטוען טענת גנב שאומר נגנבה: **פרה אתא לאשמועינן.** בתמיה מה למדנו ממנה שלא למדנו מגדי דקאמר רבה: **שאולה אתא לאשמועינן.** דטובחה בשבת פטור: **ס"ד אמינא הואיל ואמר רב פפא.** בהשוכר את הפועלים: **הכא נמי.** נימא משעת שאלה רמיא עליה חיוב קרן וכי טבחה בשבת ליחייב: **קמ"ל.** כיון דכל כמה דאיתא הדרא בעינא ההיא שעתא דקא טבח לה קא גזיל לה: **כל ימי שאלתה.** כל ימי משך הזמן ששאלה אביהן מן הבעלים: **אין חייבין באונסה.** דאינהו לאו שואלין נינהו עלה: **דמי בשר בזול.** כל זוזא חשבינן בארבעה דנקי הכי אמרינן בפרק מי שמת (ב"ב קמו:) והעור יחזירו לבעלים: **אחריות נכסים.** קרקעות: **איכא דמתני ארישא.** להאי הניח להן אביהן אחריות נכסים חייבין לשלם ואמרינן דחייבין באונסין דאישתעבוד נכסים דאבוהון מחיים משעת שאלה: **כ"ש אסיפא.** כשטבחוה ואכלוה: **ופליגא דרב פפא.** דאמר לעיל ההיא שעתא דמטו לה אונסין הוא דאתי חיובא עליה ולא משעת שאלה: **ואיכא דמתני לה אסיפא.** היכא דטבחוה אם הניח להן אביהן אחריות נכסים משלמין תשלומי מעליא ולא בזול דאיבעי להו למידק: **אבל ארישא.** אם מתה לא מיחייבי לשלומי ולא אמרינן אישתעבוד נכסי דאבוהון משעת שאלה: **והיינו דרב פפא.** דאמר לעיל לא אמרינן משעת שאלה רמו עליה תשלומין אלא משעת אונסין ואילך וההיא שעתא ליתיה לשואל דליחייב: **בשלמא רבי יוחנן.** דמוקי מתניתין בשלא התרו בו: **לא אמר כריש לקיש.** דאוקמיה כר' מאיר: **כי לא אתרו ביה נמי פטור.** הואיל ואיכא צד מלקות: **שוגגין.** שלא התרו בהן: **ודבר אחר.** ממון ואכולה מילתא קאי כלומר חייבי מיתות שוגגין וחייבי מלקיות שוגגין וממון: **ר' יוחנן אומר חייב.** בתשלומין: **דהא לא אתרו ביה.** ואין אתה מחייבו אלא משום רשעה אחת דממון: **כי לא אתרו ביה נמי פטור.** ולקמן יליף טעמא: מאי

הגהות הב"ח

(א) תוס' ד"ה מתה וכו' והכי אמר בהשואל דף פא ע"א:

הגהות מהר"ב רנשבורג

אן גמ' כשלבין דמי בשר בזול. כו' רש"י ד"ה דמי בשר וכו' ועשב"ם בב"ב דף קמו ע"ב בד"ה ובמין להם וכו':

תורה אור השלם

א) וְכִי יִנָּצוּ אֲנָשִׁים וְנָגְפוּ אִשָּׁה הָרָה וְיָצְאוּ יְלָדֶיהָ וְלֹא יִהְיֶה אָסוֹן עָנוֹשׁ יֵעָנֵשׁ כַּאֲשֶׁר יָשִׁית עָלָיו בַּעַל הָאִשָּׁה וְנָתַן בִּפְלִלִים: [שמות כא, כב]

חשק שלמה על ת"ס רי"ד

א) נ"ל כיון דאילו אתרו ביה פטור כי לא אתרו ביה נמי פטור וכו'.

מסורת הש"ס

א) [לעיל דף לג: וש"נ], ב) [סנהדרין עב.], ג) ב"ק קיב., ד) ב"מ לא., ה) ב"ק קיב., ו) ב"ק [ס.] ב"מ מג: ב"ב קמו:, ז) חולין פא., ח) [דף לג. ד"ה ושולא], ט) [בסנהדרין שם איתא רבא].

ליקוטי רש"י

מַחְתֶּרֶת – **for he has already become liable for** committing **theft before he comes to the point of** liability to death for **the tunneling prohibition.**[8] גָּנַב וְטָבַח בְּמַחְתֶּרֶת פָּטוּר – If, however, **he** both **stole and slaughtered** the goat **while tunneling, he is exempt** from any monetary payment, שֶׁאִם אֵין גְּנֵיבָה אֵין טְבִיחָה וְאֵין מְכִירָה – **because if there is no** liability for the **theft** itself, **there is no** liability for the **slaughter nor** for the **sale.**[9]

The Gemara comments:

וּצְרִיכָא – **And it was necessary for Rabbah** to teach both of these rulings. דְּאִי אַשְׁמְעִינַן שַׁבָּת – **For had he taught** only the ruling regarding **the Sabbath,**[10] we might have thought that only there does his liability to death exempt him from payment, מִשּׁוּם דְּאִיסּוּרֵהּ אִיסּוּר עוֹלָם – **because** the liability to death incurred on account of **its prohibition is everlasting.**[11] אֲבָל מַחְתֶּרֶת דְּאִיסּוּר שָׁעָה הוּא – **But** in the case of **tunneling, where** the liability to death incurred on account of **its prohibition is** but **temporary,**[12] אֵימָא לֹא – **I would say** that his liability to death does **not** exempt him from payment.[13] וְאִי אַשְׁמְעִינַן מַחְתֶּרֶת – **And if,** on the other hand, **he had taught** only the ruling regarding **tunneling,** we might have thought that only there does his liability to death exempt him from payment, מִשּׁוּם דְּמַחְתַּרְתּוֹ זוֹ הִיא הַתְרָאָתוֹ – **because the tunneling of [a burglar] is** in place of **his** legal **warning.**[14] אֲבָל שַׁבָּת דְּבָעֵיָא הַתְרָאָה – **But** in the case of the **Sabbath, where a warning is required** in order to execute him, אֵימָא לֹא – **I would say** that his liability to death does **not** exempt him from payment.[15] צְרִיכָא – Therefore, **it was necessary** for Rabbah to teach both rulings.

The Gemara cites a related ruling:

אָמַר רַב פָּפָּא – **Rav Pappa said:** הָיְתָה פָּרָה גְּנוּבָה לוֹ וּטְבָחָהּ בְּשַׁבָּת – If **one had** in his possession **a cow stolen by him** before the Sabbath and **he** then **slaughtered it on the Sabbath,** חַיָּיב – **he is liable** for the fivefold payment. שֶׁכְּבָר נִתְחַיֵּיב בִּגְנֵיבָה קוֹדֶם שֶׁיָּבֹא לִידֵי אִיסּוּר שַׁבָּת – **For he has already become liable for** committing **theft before he comes to the point of** transgressing **the Sabbath prohibition.**[16] הָיְתָה פָּרָה שְׁאוּלָה לוֹ וּטְבָחָהּ בְּשַׁבָּת – If, however, **one had** in his possession **a borrowed cow and he slaughtered it on the Sabbath,** פָּטוּר – **he is exempt** from monetary liability.[17]

NOTES

owner's home to burglarize it. He then slaughtered the goat while "tunneling" and thus while he was subject to the "death penalty" for "tunneling." [See next note.]

8. Since his liability for compensation of the principal is incurred while not under the threat of death, he is liable to pay that principal. And he is also liable to pay the additional fine for "slaughter," though incurred under the threat of death while tunneling, because the death penalty does not (according to this view) exempt one from paying a fine (as explained above, note 4).

[*Shitah Mekubetzes* ד״ה ורש״י ז״ל כתב understands *Rashi's* explanation of the case to be that the thief entered the house without "tunneling" (i.e. he entered in a way that does not render him liable to death), stole the goat (becoming liable to pay compensation for theft), and only then tunneled his way out (coming under the threat of death), during which time he slaughtered the goat. Accordingly, we would apparently have to say that *Rashi* follows the view of *Raavad, Hil. Geneivah* 9:11, that one may kill "a burglar who is tunneling" even if he is in the process of *leaving* the house. *Rambam* (ibid.), however, maintains that once the burglar has turned around to leave, he may not be killed, since the life of the homeowner is no longer in danger. See *Shitah Mekubetzes* for a suggested reconciliation of *Rashi's* explanation with the view of *Rambam.*]

9. Since the thief is not liable for the theft itself, which he committed under a "death penalty" while "tunneling," he cannot be liable for the additional punitive payment either, even though the latter is a fine. For the Torah prescribes a *four* fold penalty for the slaughter of the goat, not a *three* fold one (see above, note 6).

10. I.e. the case in which the theft is done through an act of Sabbath desecration.

11. The liability to the death penalty that one incurs on account of Sabbath desecration remains upon him forever – even after he concludes the act. Whenever witnesses come and testify to his act of Sabbath desecration, he will be executed by the court. Perhaps, then, it is only a death penalty of this severity that can exempt one from monetary liability (see *Rashi*).

12. The Torah permits the homeowner to kill the burglar only during the course of the burglary. But he may not kill the burglar afterwards (see *Rashi*).

13. For perhaps a temporary liability to death is not considered severe enough to exempt one from payment.

14. I.e. the homeowner may kill the tunneling burglar even though the burglar was not warned that his act makes him liable to execution (see *Rashi, Sanhedrin* 72b ד״ה זו היא התראתו for the source for this law). Hence, "his tunneling," which is what subjects him to execution, serves in place of the "warning" that subjects other capital offenders to the death penalty. In this regard, then, the burglar's liability to death is *more* severe than liability to death in other instances (where an actual warning is required).

15. Thus, we might have thought that only liability to the death penalty for being a burglar in a tunnel, which is administered without warning, is severe enough to exempt from monetary liability for the theft. But the death penalty for Sabbath desecration, which requires a warning, is not severe enough to exempt from monetary liability for the theft (*Rashi,* as understood by *Ramban* and *Rashba;* cf. *Tosafos*).

[*Tosafos* find difficulty with *Rashi's* approach. The Mishnah in *Bava Kamma* 34b states explicitly that an act of Sabbath desecration exempts one from monetary liability. Similarly, the Mishnah in *Sanhedrin* 72a states explicitly that liability to death as a "burglar in a tunnel" exempts one from monetary liability. How, then, can the Gemara say that had Rabbah not taught both rulings, we might have thought that these death penalties do not exempt one from monetary liability? *Ritva* cites a defense of *Rashi's* approach: In Rabbah's cases, the exemption from paying compensatory damages results in a further exemption from paying the multiple fine as well [see above, notes 6 and 8], even though the death penalty generally does *not* exempt one from a fine (in Rabbah's view). The Mishnahs cited by *Tosafos,* however, speak only of exempting one from monetary damages where no fines are involved. On the basis of those Mishnahs alone, then, one might have thought that the death penalty for Sabbath desecration or tunneling does *not* exempt one from compensatory damages where this will in effect exempt him from a fine as well. Hence, it was necessary for Rabbah to teach that both Sabbath desecration and tunneling exempt from compensatory damages even where this will result in an exemption from fines as well.]

16. Just as Rabbah ruled above in the case of a goat – see note 4. [The penalty for slaughtering a goat one has stolen is a fourfold payment. For slaughtering a cow the payment is fivefold.]

17. Unlike a thief, who incurs liability for the stolen item at the moment he steals it, a שׁוֹאֵל, *a borrower,* does *not* incur liability for the borrowed item (should it become unreturnable to the lender) at the time that he borrows it. [For although a borrower is liable even for unavoidable mishaps from the moment that he borrows the item, he is not liable to actual payment until the mishap occurs (*Rashi* to *Bava Kamma* 112a ד״ה היתה פרה שאולה לו וטבחה בשבת; see below).] Thus, his liability to pay for the slaughtered cow is incurred at the time that he slaughters it, at which point he robs the owner of its use. Hence, his liability both to payment and for Sabbath desecration are incurred simultaneously (*Rashi*).

[*Rashi* to *Bava Kamma* ibid. cites the Talmudic text of his teachers, in which this statement of Rav Pappa concludes with the clause: שֶׁאִם אֵין גְּנֵיבָה אֵין טְבִיחָה וְאֵין מְכִירָה, *because if there is no liability for theft there is no liability for slaughter nor for sale.* This text implies that had the borrower slaughtered the cow during the week, he would be liable to the fivefold penalty. *Rashi* here and in *Bava Kamma* contends that this concluding clause is a corruption of the text and should be deleted. For only a thief and an unpaid custodian (who keeps the animal for himself and exempts himself from payment by swearing that it was stolen) are liable to the twofold, fourfold or fivefold payments [see *Bava Kamma* 63b]. A borrower who slaughters the borrowed cow, however, is technically not a גַּנָּב, *thief,* and is liable only to pay compensation for the

ור' מאיר (א) לוקה ומשלם אית ליה מת ומשלם לית ליה ושאני הני דחידוש הוא שחידשה תורה בקנס אע"ג דמיקטיל משלם ואזדא רבה לטעמיה דאמר רבה היה גדי גנוב לו וטבחו בשבת חייב שכבר נתחייב בגניבה קודם שיבא לידי איסור שבת גנב וטבח בשבת פטור שאם אין גניבה אין טביחה ואין מכירה ואמר רבה היה גדי גנוב לו וטבחו במחתרת חייב שכבר נתחייב בגניבה קודם שיבא לידי איסור מחתרת (א)גנב וטבח במחתרת פטור שאם אין גניבה אין טביחה ואין מכירה וצריכא דאי אשמעינן שבת משום דאיסורה איסור עולם אבל מחתרת דאיסור שעה הוא אימא לא ואי אשמעינן מחתרת משום (ב) דמחתרתו זו היא התראתו אבל שבת דבעיא התראה אימא לא צריכא אמר רב פפא (ג) היתה פרה גנובה לו וטבחה בשבת חייב שכבר נתחייב בגניבה קודם שיבא לידי איסור שבת (ב)היתה פרה שאולה לו וטבחה בשבת פטור אמר ליה רב אחא בריה דרבא לרב אשי רב פפא פרה אתא לאשמועינן אמר ליה רב פפא שאולה אתא לאשמועינן סלקא דעתך אמינא הואיל ואמר רב פפא (ד) (ג)משעת משיכה הוא דאתחייב ליה במזונותיה הכא נמי (ד)משעת שאלה אתחייב באונסיה קא משמע לן (ה) אמר רבא (ה)הניח להן אביהן פרה שאולה משתמשין בה כל ימי שאלתה מתה אין חייבין באונסה (ו)כסבורין של אביהם היא וטבחוה ואכלוה (א) משלמין (ז) דמי בשר בזול הניח להן אביהן אחריות נכסים חייבין לשלם איכא דמתני לה ארישא ואיכא דמתני לה אסיפא מאן דמתני לה ארישא כל שכן אסיפא ומאן (ז)דמתני לה אסיפא אבל ארישא לא והיינו דרב פפא בשלמא ר' יוחנן לא אמר כריש לקיש דקא מוקים לה כרבנן אלא ריש לקיש מ"ט לא אמר כר' יוחנן אמר לך כיון דאילו אתרו ביה פטור כי לא אתרו ביה נמי פטור (י) ואזדו לטעמייהו דכי אתא רב דימי אמר חייבי מיתות שוגגין וחייבי מלקיות שוגגין ודבר אחר ר' יוחנן אמר חייב וריש לקיש אמר פטור ר' יוחנן אמר חייב דהא לא אתרו ביה ר"ל אמר פטור כיון דאילו אתרו ביה פטור כי לא אתרו ביה נמי פטור איתיביה ר"ל לרבי יוחנן (א) ולא יהיה אסון ענוש יענש מאי

ור' מאיר. בעלמא בתשלומי ממון לית ליה מת ומשלם והכא תשלומי ארבעה וחמשה קנס הם וכל משפט קנס חידוש הוא הלכך אע"ג דמיקטיל נמי לא מיפטר מיניה ולקמן פריך לרבה אליבא דרבי מאיר קשיה בתו דממתינין נמי קנס הוא וקא פטר ליה אבתו: היה גדי גנוב לו. גנב גדי בחול ונתחייב הקרן וטבחו בשבת דלא אתי עליה חיובא דממון באיסור שבת אלא חיוב קנס: חייב. ד' וה' דקנס חידוש הוא ורבה סבירא ליה כרבי מאיר: גנב וטבח בשבת. דחיוב ממון דקרן אתא עליה באיסור שבת: פטור. דקיימא לן אין מת ומשלם וכיון דאקרן לא מיחייב קנס נמי לא משלם דתשלומי ד' וה' אמר רחמנא ולא תשלומי שלשה וארבעה ולא סבירא לן כרבי נתן דאמר (שבת דף לג:) מי נושא את עצמו אי נמי בכפות: שאם אין גניבה. כלומר שמאחר שפטור על הקרן משום מיתה: אין טביחה ואין מכירה. אינו מחויב קנס דכפילתי דתשלומי ארבעה וחמשה כתיב ולא תשלומי שלשה וארבעה: מחתרת. שמחתר בית והוליכו וטבחו במחתרת. עלמא דהכיא שעתא בר קטלא הוא אי הוה משכחיה בעל הבית כדכתיב (שמות כב) אין לו דמים: משום דאסורה איסור עולם. כל זמן שיעידו עליו שחילל שבת ימיתוהו בית דין הלכך חמירא מיתה דילה לפוטרו מממון: דאיסור שעה. אי לא משכח ליה ההיא שעתא תו לא מיקטיל: היתה פרה שאולה לו וטבחה בשבת פטור. דההיא שעתא דקא טבח לה הוא גזיל ממרה ומיתה וממון באין כאחד ולא גרסינן שאם אין גניבה אין טביחה ואין מכירה דגבי שואל לא שייך לא כפל ולא ארבעה וחמשה שהרי חייב בקרן לעולם אפילו טוען טענת גנב ואין קנס אלא בגנב או בשומר חנם הפוטר עצמו בטוען טענת גנב שאמר נגנבה: פרה אתא לאשמועינן. בתמיה מה למדנו ממנה שלא למדנו מגדי דקאמר רבה: שאולה אתא לאשמועינן. דטובחה בשבת פטור: ס"ד אמינא הואיל ואמר רב פפא. בהשוכר את הפועלים: הכא נמי. נימא משעת שאלה רמיא עליה חיוב קרן וכי טבחה בשבת ליחייב: קמ"ל. כיון דכל כמה דאיתא הדרא בעינא ההיא שעתא דקא טבח לה קא גזיל לה: כל ימי שאלתה. כל ימי משך הזמן ששאלה אביהן מן הבעלים: אין חייבין באונסה. דאינהו לאו שואלין נינהו עלה: דמי בשר בזול. כל זוזא חשבינן בארבעה דנקי הכי אמרינן בפרק מי שמת (ב"ב קמו:) והעור יחזירו לבעלים: אחריות נכסים. קרקעות: איכא דמתני ארישא. להאי הניח להן אביהן אחריות נכסים חייבין לשלם ואמרינן דחייבין באונסין דאישתעבוד נכסים דאבוהון מחיים משעת שאלה: כ"ש אסיפא. כשטבחוה ואכלוה: ופליגא דרב פפא. דאמר לעיל ההיא שעתא דמטו לה אונסין הוא דאתי חיובא עליה ולא משעת שאלה: ואיכא דמתני לה אסיפא. היכא דטבחוה אם הניח להן אביהן אחריות נכסים משלמין תשלומי מעליא ולא בזול דאיבעי להו למידק: אבל ארישא. אי מתה לא מיחייבי לשלומי ולא אמרינן אישתעבוד נכסי דאבוהון משעת שאלה: והיינו דרב פפא. דאמר לעיל לא אמרינן משעת שאלה רמו עליה תשלומין אלא משעת אונסין ואילך וההיא שעתא ליתיה לשואל דליחייב: בשלמא רבי יוחנן. דמוקי מתניתין בשלא התרו בו: לא אמר כריש לקיש. דאוקמיה כר' מאיר: כי לא אתרו ביה נמי פטור. הואיל ואיכא לד מלקות: שוגגין. שלא התרו בהן: ודבר אחר. ממון ואכולה מילתא קאי כלומר חייבי מיתות שוגגין וממון או חייבי מלקיות שוגגין וממון: ר' יוחנן אומר חייב. בתשלומין: דהא לא אתרו ביה. ואין אתה מחייבו אלא משום רשעה אחת דממון: כי לא אתרו ביה נמי פטור. ולקמן יליף טעמא: מאי

ורבי מאיר לוקה ומשלם אית ליה מת ומשלם לית ליה ושאני הני. משמע דרבי מאיר אית ליה לוקה ומשלם אף בממון שאינו קנס וכן משמע בהשוכר את הפועלים (ב"מ צא.) שהבאתי לעיל ותימה דבפ"ק דמכות (ד' ד:) קאמר עולא טעמא דרבי מאיר דאמר עדים זוממין לוקין ומשלמין משום דגמר ממוציא שם רע ופריך מה למוציא שם רע שכן קנס קסבר לה כר' עקיבא דאמר עדים זוממין קנס הוא משמע דבממון אינו לוקה ומשלם ויש לומר דודאי אי עדים זוממין הוי ממונא לא הוה גמר ממוציא ש"ר שכן הוא קנס אלא הוה דרשינן מכדי רשעתו שאינו לוקה ומשלם אבל השתא דקסבר עדים זוממין קנסא וגמר ממוציא שם רע דלוקין ומשלמין ע"כ מוקי כדי רשעתו במיתה ומלקות כיון דכדי רשעתו לא הוי במלקות וממון והשתא בכל דוכתא לוקה ומשלם דמהיכא נמעיט שלא ילקה וישלם: דאמר רבה היה גדי גנוב לו. אליבא דרבי מאיר קאמר ולא משום דסבר הכי:

משום דאיסורו איסור עולם כו'. שאם חלל שבת לאחר השבת יעידו עליו ויהרגוהו אבל מחתרת אע"פ שמתחייב בנפשו בעודו במחתרת מ"מ אחר שילא מן לא הוי בר קטלא ולא הוי דומיא דאם יהיה אסון:

אבל שבת דבעי התראה אימא לא. תימה דעיקר קים ליה בדרבה מיניה ברציחה כתיב דבעינן התראה ועוד דשבת ומחתרת תרוייהו תנהני דבפרק המניח (ב"ק לד:) תנן והוא שהדליק את הגדיש בשבת פטור מפני שנידון בנפשו ומחתרת נמי תניא בפרק בן סורר (סנהדרין עב.) היה בא במחתרת ושיבר את החבית אם יש לו דמים פטור ונראה דהכא עביד לריבותא דאמאי דבקנס מיקטיל ומשלם וה"ק משום דחמיר איסוריה והוה אמינא דהתם דווקא הוא דליחייב קנס עם המיתה והכא"ג עביד לריבותא דלקמן (דף לו.) גבי לא יהיה אסון וכדי רשעתו דמשום דתמור הוי אמרינן דלעביד ביה תרתי אבל קשה דאמאי דפרישית דרבה אליבא דרבי מאיר קאמר אם כן היכי קאמר אבל שבת דבעיא התראה אימא לא מיקטיל ומשלם והא עיקר מילתיה דרבי מאיר גבי שבת תניא לעיל ומאין למימר דרבה אשמועינן דשייך קים ליה בדרבה מיניה אע"ג דבשעה דמתחייב עדיין הממון בעין לא הוה לן למימר קים לי' בדרבה מיניה כדאמר רבה גופיה בפרק בן סורר (סנהדרין עב. ושם) אמר (ט) רבה מסתברא מילתיה דרב כששיבר דליתנהו אבל נטל דאיתנהו לא אפ"ה כיון דטבח אחרי כן מיפטר על הגנבה והא דפטור אגנבה אף על גב דבאותה שעה הוי בעין עביד לריבותא:

מתה אין חייבין באונסין. אבל בגנבה ואבדה נראה לר"י שהן חייבין דהואיל ונהנין דמשתמשין בה והכי (א) אמר בהשואל (ב"מ לו. ושם): אבל ארישא לא והיינו דרב פפא. דלא אמרינן משעת שאלה חייב באונסין וא"ת אם כן בסיפא נמי בשטבחוה אמאי משלמין כשהניח להן אביהן אחריות נכסים הא לא נתחייב בהן האב וי"ל דהתם פשע בה האב שהיה לו לומר לבניו שאינה שלו הלכך מחיים פשע בה ונתחייב בה באותה שעה ונשתעבדו נכסיו:

עין משפט נר מצוה

לה א מיי' פ"ט מהל' גנבה הל' יב סמג לאוין קס:

לו ב מיי' פ"ג שם הל' ד סמג שם:

לז ג ד מיי' פ"א מהל' שאלה הל' ד סמג עשין פט טוש"ע ח"מ סימן שמ סעיף ה:

לח ה מיי' שם הל' ה וסמג שם טוש"ע שם סעיף ו:

לט ו ז מיי' שם טוש"ע שם סעי' ז:

הגהות הב"ח

(א) תוס' ד"ה מתה וכו' והכי אמרי' בהשואלין דף פא ע"א:

הגהות מהר"ב רנשבורג

אן גמ' משלמין דמי בשר בזול. עי' רש"י ד"ה דמי בשר וכו' עי' ב"ב דף קמו ע"ב ד"ה ושמין להם וכו':

תורה אור השלם

א) וְכִי יִנָּצוּ אֲנָשִׁים וְנָגְפוּ אִשָּׁה הָרָה וְיָצְאוּ יְלָדֶיהָ וְלֹא יִהְיֶה אָסוֹן עָנוֹשׁ יֵעָנֵשׁ כַּאֲשֶׁר יָשִׁית עָלָיו בַּעַל הָאִשָּׁה וְנָתַן בִּפְלִלִים: [שמות כא, כב]

תוספות רי"ד

אמר רבא הניח להן אביהן פרה שאולה משתמשין בה כל ימי שאלה. מתה אין חייבים באונסה כו' שלא שאלו הן ולא קבל' עליהן אונסים. כסבורין של אביהן היא טבחוה ואכלוה משלמין דמי בשר בזול. פי' כל זוז בארבע דנקא והעור יחזירו לבעלים. ואם הניח להן אביהן אחריות נכסים. פי' קרקעות דחייבי לשלם משום דאישתעבד נכסיה. פי' נכסי דאבוהון מחיים משעת שאלה: כי אתא רב דימי אמר חייבי מיתות שוגגין וד"א. פי' ממון או חייבי מלקות שוגגין וד"א ר"י אמר חייב בתשלומין ור"ל אמר פטור ר"י אמר חייב דהא לא התרו ביה פי' ואי אתה מחייבו אלא משום רשעה א' ממון ור"ל אמר פטור כי אתרו בי' נמי פטור פי' הואיל ואיכא צד מלקות:

חשק שלמה על תוס' רי"ד

א) נ"ל כיון דאילו אתרו ביה פטור כי לא אתרו ביה נמי פטור פי' וכו':

מסורת הש"ס

א) [לעיל דף לג: וש"נ], ב) [סנהדרין עב.], ג) ב"ק קיא., ד) ב"מ לא., ה) ב"ק קיב., ו) ב"מ מב: ז) ב"ב קמו:, ח) [דף לג. ד"ה ועולא], ט) [בסנהדרין שם איתא רבה]

ליקוטי רש"י

לוקה ומשלם. במסכת מכות (דף ד.) מעידים אנו בפלוני שחייב לחבירו מאתים זוז ונמצאו זוממין לוקין ומשלמין שלא השם המביאן לידי מכות מביאן לידי תשלומין [ב"ק עא.]. הוא חידוש שחידשה תורה בקנס. בכל תשלומי קנס שאינו דין אלא גזרת מלך בעלמא וכיון דחידוש הוא וגזירת חוק אימא אע"ג דאיכא בהדיה מיתה לשלם [לקמן לח. עיי"ש בשיטמ"ק]. שאם אין גניבה אין טביחה ואין מכירה. עי' להלן בד"ה היתה פרה שאולה. זו היא התראתו. שאין לריך התראה אחרת [illegible] פירש לנו רבינו שאם אין גניבה אחר שפטור מן הקרן משום דקם ליה בדרבה מיניה אין טביחה קנס נמי לא משלם ואף על גב דחידוש הוא ואין מיתה פוטרתו הכא דליכא קרן פטור דתשלומי ארבעה וחמשה אמר רחמנא ולא תשלומי ג' וד' וכי מדלית

מסכת קרנא הוו לה ג' לצאן וד' לבקר. ולא היה לי לב להבין את מושל שטעם זה אין צריך לכאן שהרי אין קנס בשואל הטובח ואפילו אמרינן כרב פפא דעד השתא קם ברשותא דמרה אפילו הכי גזלן נעשה עליה ולא גנב שאין דין גנב אלא בטוען טוענת גנב והוא שומ' חנם. וכי גרם ליה בכתובות גרסינן ליה ובמלתא [דרבה] דאמר התם גנב וטבח בשבת פטור שאם אין גניבה כו' דהתם בגנב עצמו קאי וליכא למיפטריה מקנסא אלא משום האי טעמא אבל בדרב פפא ליכא למגרסא לא התם ולא הכא ואילו למילתא דרב פפא איתמר התם גבי מלתא [דרבה] איגרסא נמי אגב שטפא בדרב פפא ותשובות רב האי גאון מסייעא לי. אין חייבין באונסה. דלא קבילו עלייהו נטירותא. דמי בשר בזול. כל זוזא חשבינא בארבע דנקי וכן כל היכא דתני בזול והיינו שני שלישי דמים וכולהו דמי לא נשלמו דאי הוו ידעי דבעו שלומי לא הוו אכלי בשרא והעור יחזירנו כמות שהוא [ב"ק קיב.]. ולא ישלם כל דמי השור כמות שהוא חי אלא העור יחזיר לבעלים והבשר שמין וישלם שני שלישים זוזי מיהא משלם בזול כל זוזא שהוא שש מעה כסף חשבינן בארבעה דנקי בפרק מי שמת [ב"מ מב:]. לפחות שליש מדמיו שבענין זה שמין כל מחזירין אוכלים הנאכלים מתחלה שלא לדעת חזרה שאילו היה יודע שצריך להחזיר לא היה אוכל משלו ומיהו אמרו (ב"ק דף כ.) גבי אכלה מתוך הרחבה משלמת מה שנהנית דמי שעורים בזול או דמי עמיר בזול וכן (כתובות דף לד:) גבי הניח להם אביהם פרה שאולה שטבחוה ואכלוה משלמין דמי בשר בזול ומהכא פשטינן לכל בזול דהיינו כל זוזא חשבינן ואמרי' לשלומי בארבעה דנקי ארבע מעות דהיינו שני חלקי דינר שהרי שש מעה כסף דינר ודנקא היא מעה [רשב"ם ב"ב קמו:]. איכא דמתני לה. להא [דהניח] להן אביהן אחריות נכסים חייבין. ארישא. דקאמר מתה אין הניח להן אביהן קרקעות חייבין לשלם דאשתעבוד נכסים מחיים דאבוהון דקסבר רבא חיוב אונסים משעת שאלה מוטל על השואל ופליגא דרב פפא דאמר (לקמן) לא רמי חיוב אונסים אשואל עד שעה שתיאנס [ב"ק קיב.]. ואיכא דמתני לה אסיפא. היכא דטבחוה אם הניח להן אביהן אחריות נכסים משלמין תשלומי מעליא ולא בזול דאיבעי ליה למידק [רש"י מכת"י בשיטמ"ק עיי"ש]. טבחוה ואכלוה משלמים דמי בשר בזול ואם הניח להן אביהן קרקע [המשך בדף לה.]

וְרַבִּי מֵאִיר לוֹקֶה וּמְשַׁלֵּם אִית לֵיהּ מֵת וּמְשַׁלֵּם לֵית לֵיהּ – And still you can say that **R' Meir** generally **holds** only that **one can receive lashes and pay** for the same crime, but **he does not hold** that **one can be put to death and pay** for the same crime. **וְשָׁאנֵי הָנֵי – And** why, then, does the thief pay if he slaughters on the Sabbath or for idol worship? Because **these cases are different, דְּחִידּוּשׁ הוּא שֶׁחִידְּשָׁה תּוֹרָה בִּקְנָס – for it is a novelty that the Torah innovated in** the imposition of **a fine.**[1] **אַף עַל גַּב דְּמִיקְטִיל מְשַׁלֵּם** – And since a fine is by its very nature a novelty, **even though he is executed, he** still **pays** the fine.[2]

The Gemara notes:

וְאַזְדָא רַבָּה לְטַעְמֵיהּ – And Rabbah, in presenting this explanation, **is consistent with his reasoning** stated elsewhere. **דְּאָמַר רַבָּה – For Rabbah** also **said: הָיָה גְּדִי גָּנוּב לוֹ וּטְבָחוֹ בְּשַׁבָּת –** If **one had** in his possession **a goat stolen by him** before the Sabbath, **and he slaughtered it on the Sabbath,**[3] **חַיָּיב – he is liable** for the fourfold payment. **שֶׁכְּבָר נִתְחַיֵּיב בִּגְנֵיבָה קוֹדֶם שֶׁיָּבֹא לִידֵי אִיסּוּר שַׁבָּת – For he has already become liable for** committing **theft before he comes to the point of** transgressing **the Sabbath prohibition.**[4] **גָּנַב וְטָבַח בְּשַׁבָּת פָּטוּר –** If, however, **he** both **stole and slaughtered** the goat **on the Sabbath,**[5] **he is exempt** from any monetary payment, **שֶׁאִם אֵין גְּנֵיבָה אֵין טְבִיחָה וְאֵין מְכִירָה – because if there is no** liability for the **theft** itself, **there is no** liability for the **slaughter nor** for the **sale.**[6] **וְאָמַר רַבָּה – And Rabbah** also **said: הָיָה גְּדִי גָּנוּב לוֹ וּטְבָחוֹ בְּמַחְתֶּרֶת –** If **one had** in his possession **a goat stolen by him,** and **he** then **slaughtered it while tunneling,**[7] **חַיָּיב – he is liable** for the fourfold penalty, **שֶׁכְּבָר נִתְחַיֵּיב בִּגְנֵיבָה קוֹדֶם שֶׁיָּבֹא לִידֵי אִיסּוּר**

NOTES

1. I.e. by their very natures, fines, such as the fourfold and fivefold payments for slaughtering a stolen animal, are not logically imperative payments of compensation, but rather extrajudicial penalties imposed as punitive measures (see *Rashi* here and below, 38a ד״ה סד״א חידוש הוא שחידשה תורה).

2. Although R' Meir holds the general principle that liability to death exempts one from monetary liability, the fourfold and fivefold payments, being extrajudicial measures, are not governed by the general rules of monetary liability, such as exemption in the face of liability to death (see *Rashi* loc. cit.).

The Gemara below (35b) will ask that if so, R' Meir cannot be the author of our Mishnah, which states further that one who violates his daughter is exempt from paying the fine. For the fine for violating a virgin, too, is a novelty of the Torah, and as such should *not* be subject to the general exemption from monetary liability in the face of capital liability (*Rashi*).

3. [The fourfold payment for slaughtering a goat one has stolen consists of the principal (which is a regular compensatory payment for the theft of the item) plus the כֶּפֶל, *keifel* (the punitive fine equal to the principal that applies to cases of theft in general even when the thief must return the stolen object intact) plus an additional two-times the principal as a punitive fine for slaughtering the goat. (See, however, *Kuntres HaBeurim, Bava Kamma* §59 and *Maasei Chiyah, Bava Kamma* §20.)]

In Rabbah's case, the thief stole the goat before the Sabbath, and thus did not incur any death penalty simultaneously with his liability to pay restitution for the principal (*Rashi*).

4. Since his liability to pay restitution for the principal came about without simultaneous liability to the death penalty, he must make that payment [as well as the *keifel* payment]. And he must make as well the additional payment for slaughtering the goat on the Sabbath, even though that payment *did* come about simultaneously with liability to the death penalty for desecrating the Sabbath. For Rabbah holds the view of R' Meir (as Rabbah explains it) that simultaneous liability to the death penalty does *not* exempt the sinner from *fines* that he incurs, since fines are extrajudicial novelties of the Torah (*Rashi;* cf. *Tosafos* ד״ה דאמר). [Rabbah states that the underlying reason for liability in this case is that "he has already become liable for theft before he comes to the point of the Sabbath prohibition." For had he become liable for theft through an act of Sabbath desecration, he would not be liable to any payments whatsoever, as Rabbah states next.]

5. I.e. he stole it through an act of Sabbath desecration [such as "transferring" – see next note], in which case his liability to the death penalty exempts him from the compensatory payment for the goat itself (*Rashi*).

6. In this case, there is no monetary liability for the theft itself, which was accomplished through an act of Sabbath desecration. [Even R' Meir, who maintains that incurring the death penalty does not exempt one from paying a *fine,* agrees that it exempts one from a *compensatory* liability.] Hence, the thief is not liable to pay the compensatory payment for the goat itself. And since he is exempt from the compensatory payment for the goat itself, he cannot be liable for the additional "three goats" to be paid as a fine. For the Torah prescribes that a "fourfold" payment be made for the slaughter or sale of the goat, not that a "*three*fold" payment be made. [And similarly, in the case of an ox, the Torah prescribes a "fivefold" payment, not a "*four*fold" one] (see *Rashi*).

Rashi understands that the act of Sabbath desecration to which Rabbah refers is the *melachah* of הוֹצָאָה, *transferring;* i.e. the thief stole the goat by transferring it from the private domain of the owner to the public domain. *Rashi,* therefore, notes that Rabbah does not hold R' Nassan's ruling (*Shabbos* 94a) that one is not liable for carrying a live animal because "a live animal carries itself." Alternatively, *Rashi* explains that Rabbah refers to where the goat was tied up, in which case the live animal cannot carry itself and even R' Nassan agrees that one is liable for carrying it on the Sabbath.

[As mentioned, *Rashi* explains that the Sabbath desecration referred to by Rabbah is the *melachah* of *transferring.* Now, the Gemara above (31a) cited a Baraisa that distinguishes between where the thief stole a purse on the Sabbath by "lifting" (in which case the act of theft *precedes* the Sabbath desecration) and where he stole it by "pulling" (in which case they are simultaneous). Accordingly, *Rashi* here apparently refers to where the thief stole the goat by "pulling" it out of the owner's domain (see *Ramban* and *Ritva;* see *Rashba,* who raises several difficulties with this approach). *Rashba* suggests that *Rashi* refers to where the thief "lifted" the goat and in a case where R' Avin's principle that "lifting is needed for the act of transfer" is applicable (see above, 31a). In a departure from *Rashi's* explanation, *Ramban* and *Rashba* suggest that Rabbah does not refer to where the thief removed the goat from the owner's domain at all, but rather to where the goat entered into the property of the thief on its own, and the thief proceeded to slaughter it for his own personal use. In this case, the slaughter itself serves as the act of theft. Thus, his liability to pay compensation for the theft itself is incurred simultaneously with his liability to the death penalty for desecrating the Sabbath through the *melachah* of *slaughter.*]

[Actually, where the theft itself occurred through an act of Sabbath desecration (e.g. the *melachah* of *transferring*), the thief should not be liable to any monetary payment for slaughter even if he later slaughtered the animal *on a weekday.* For "if there is no liability for the theft itself, there is no liability for the slaughter or sale." Why, then, does Rabbah speak only of a case in which one stole *and slaughtered* on the Sabbath? *Ritva* cites *Rashi* (not found in our editions of *Rashi*) as answering that where the animal was slaughtered on a weekday, the thief would be liable to the fourfold or fivefold payment, since the act of slaughter itself would constitute a new act of theft. See also *Chidushei R' Akiva Eiger.*]

7. The Torah states (*Exodus* 22:1): אִם־בַּמַּחְתֶּרֶת יִמָּצֵא הַגַּנָּב וְהֻכָּה וָמֵת אֵין לוֹ דָּמִים, *If the thief is discovered while tunneling in and he is struck and dies, there is no blood-guilt on his account.* In this verse, the Torah permits a homeowner to kill the burglar who tunnels into his house. [The reason for this permit is that a burglar is well aware that the occupant of the house will stand up against him and defend his belongings, and the burglar is thus prepared to kill the occupant should the occupant confront him. The occupant is therefore permitted to kill the burglar in self-defense (see *Sanhedrin* 72a with *Rashi*). Any other bystander may kill the burglar as well – see *Rambam, Hil. Geneivah* 9:7.] The Mishnah, *Sanhedrin* 72a, applying the principle of קָם לֵיהּ בִּדְרַבָּה מִינֵּיהּ, *he stands liable to the penalty greater [than payment],* rules that the thief's liability to the "death penalty" [at the hands of the homeowner] while he is tunneling serves to exempt him from paying for any property damage he does during the break-in.

In Rabbah's case, the thief had already stolen the goat (and became liable to pay compensation for theft) before he "tunneled" into the

עין משפט נר מצוה

לה א מיי׳ פ״ט מהל׳ גנבה הל׳ יג סמג לאוין קסו:
לו ב מיי׳ פ״ב שם הל׳ ד סמג שם:
לז ג ד מיי׳ פ״א מהל׳ שאלה הל׳ ב סמג עשין פט טוש״ע ח״מ סימן שמ סעיף ד:
לח ה מיי׳ שם הל׳ ה ופ״ג שם טוש״ע שם סי׳ שמא סעיף ג:
לט ו ז מיי׳ שם טוש״ע שם סעי׳ ד:

מסורת הש״ס

א) [לעיל דף לג: וש״נ], ב) [סנהדרין עב:], ג) ב״ק קיב., ד) ב״מ לא., ה) ב״ק קיב., ו) ב״ק שם [כ״מ ב״מ מג.], ז) [ב״ק קיב.], ח) חולין פא., ט) [דף לג. ד״ה ועולא], י) [סנהדרין שם איתא רבא].

ור׳ מאיר לוקה ומשלם אית ליה מת ומשלם לית ליה ושאני הני דחידוש הוא שחידשה תורה בקנס אע״ג דמקטיל משלם ואזדא רבה לטעמיה דאמר רבה היה גדי גנוב לו וטבחו בשבת חייב שכבר נתחייב בגניבה קודם שיבא לידי איסור שבת גנב וטבח בשבת פטור שאם אין גניבה אין טביחה ואין מכירה ואמר רבה היה גדי גנוב לו וטבחו במחתרת חייב שכבר נתחייב בגניבה קודם שיבא לידי איסור מחתרת גנב וטבח במחתרת פטור שאם אין גניבה אין טביחה ואין מכירה וצריכא דאי אשמעינן שבת משום דאיסורה איסור עולם אבל מחתרת דאיסור שעה הוא אימא לא ואי אשמעינן מחתרת משום דמחתרתו זו היא התראתו אבל שבת דבעיא התראה אימא לא צריכא אמר רב פפא היתה פרה גנובה לו וטבחה בשבת חייב שכבר נתחייב בגניבה קודם שיבא לידי איסור שבת היתה פרה שאולה לו וטבחה בשבת פטור אמר ליה רב אחא בריה דרבא לרב אשי רב פפא פרה אתא לאשמועינן אמר ליה רב פפא שאולה אתא לאשמועינן סלקא דעתך אמינא הואיל ואמר רב פפא משעת משיכה הוא דאתחייב ליה במזונותיה הכא נמי משעת שאלה אתחייב באונסיה קא משמע לן אמר רבא הניח להן אביהן פרה שאולה משתמשין בה כל ימי שאלתה מתה אין חייבין באונסה כסבורין של אביהם היא וטבחוה ואכלוה משלמין דמי בשר בזול הניח להן אביהן אחריות נכסים חייבין לשלם איכא דמתני לה ארישא ואיכא דמתני לה אסיפא מאן דמתני לה ארישא כל שכן אסיפא ופליגא דרב פפא ומאן דמתני לה אסיפא אבל ארישא לא והיינו דרב פפא בשלמא ר׳ יוחנן לא אמר כריש לקיש דקא מוקים לה כרבנן אלא ריש לקיש מ״ט לא אמר כר׳ יוחנן אמר לך כיון דאילו אתרו ביה נמי פטור כי לא אתרו ביה נמי פטור ואזדו לטעמייהו דכי אתא רב דימי אמר חייבי מיתות שוגגין וחייבי מלקיות שוגגין ודבר אחר ר׳ יוחנן אמר חייב וריש לקיש אמר פטור ר׳ יוחנן אמר חייב דהא לא אתרו ביה ר״ל אמר פטור כיון דאילו אתרו ביה פטור כי לא אתרו ביה נמי פטור איתיביה ר״ל לרבי יוחנן ולא יהיה אסון ענוש יענש מאי

ורבי מאיר לוקה ומשלם אית ליה מת ומשלם לית ליה ושאני הני. משמע דלרבי מאיר אית ליה לוקה ומשלם אף בממון שאינו קנס וכן משמע בהשוכר את הפועלים (ב״מ צא.) שהבאתי לעיל ותימה דבפ״ק דמכות (ד׳ ד:) קאמר עולא טעמא דרבי מאיר דאמר עדים זוממין לוקין ומשלמין משום דגמר ממוציא שם רע ופריך מה למוציא שם רע שכן קנס סבר לה כר׳ עקיבא דאמר עדים זוממין קנס הוא משמע דבממון אינו לוקה ומשלם ויש לומר דודאי אי עדים זוממין הוי ממונא לא הוה גמר ממוציא ש״ר שכן קנס הוא אלא הוה דרשינן מכדי רשעתו שאינו לוקה ומשלם אבל השתא דסבר עדים זוממין קנסא וגמר ממוציא שם רע דלוקין ומשלמין ע״כ מוקי כדי רשעתו במיתה ומלקות כיון דכדי רשעתו לא הוי בין מלקות וממון מהשתא בכל דוכתא לוקה ומשלם דמהיכא נמעיט שלא ילקה וישלם: **דאמר** רבה היה גדי גנוב לו. אליבא דרבי מאיר קאמר ולא משום דסבר הכי: **משום** דאיסורה איסור עולם כו׳. שאם חלל שבת לאחר השבת יעידו עליו ויהרגוהו אבל מחתרת אע״פ שמתחייב בנפשו בעודו במחתרת מ״מ אחר שילך תו לא הוי בר קטלא ולא הוי דומיא דאם יהיה אסון: **אבל** שבת דבעי התראה אימא לא. תימה דעיקר קים ליה בדרבה מיניה ברציחה כתיב דבעינן התראה ועוד דשבת ומחתרת תרוייהו תנינהו דבפרק המניח (ב״ק דף לד:) תנן והוא שהדליק את הגדיש בשבת פטור מפני שנידון בנפשו ומחתרת נמי תנינא בפרק בן סורר (סנהדרין עב.) היה בא במחתרת ושיבר את החבית אם יש לו דמים פטור ונראה דהכא עביד צריכותא אמאי דבקנס מיקטיל ומשלם וה״ק משום דחמיר איסוריה והוה אמינא דהתם דווקא הוא דליחייב קנס עם המיתה וכה״ג עביד צריכותא לקמן (דף לז.) גבי לא יהיה אסון וכדי רשעתו דמשום דחמור הוי אמרינן לעביד ביה תרתי אבל קשה למאי דפרישית דרבה אליבא דרבי מאיר קאמר אם כן היכי קאמר אבל שבת דבעיא התראה אימא לא מיקטיל ומשלם והא עיקר מילתיה דרבי מאיר גבי שבת תניא לעיל ומנלן למימר דרבה אשמועינן דשייך קים ליה בדרבה מיניה אע״ג דבשעה דמתחייב עדיין הממון בעין לא הוה לן למימר קים לי׳ בדרבה מיניה כדאמר רבה גופיה בפרק בן סורר (סנהדרין עב. ושם) אמר רבה מסתברא מילתיה דרב כששיבר דליתנהו אבל נטל דאיתנהו לא אע״פ כיון דנעשה אחרי כן מיפטר על הגנבה והא דפטור אגנבה אף על גב דבשעתה שעה הוי בעין עביד צריכותא:

מתה אין חייבין באונסין. אבל בגנבה ואבדה נראה לר״י שהן חייבין דהואיל ונהנו משתמשין בה והכי (א) אמר בהשואל (ב״מ צו. ושם): **אבל** ארישא לא והיינו דרב פפא. דלא אמרינן משעת שאלה חייב באונסין וא״ת אם כן בסיפא נמי כשטבחוה אמאי משלמין כשהניח להן אביהן אחריות נכסים הא לא נתחייב בהן האב וי״ל דהתם פשע בה האב שהיה לו לומר לבניו שאינה שלו הלכך מחייב פשע בה ונתחייב בה באותה שעה ושתעבדו נכסיו:

ור׳ מאיר. בעלמא בתשלומי ממון לית ליה מת ומשלם והכא תשלומי ארבעה וחמשה קנס הם וכל משפט קנס חידוש הוא הלכך אע״ג דמיקטיל נמי לא מיפטר מיניה ולקמן פריך לרבה אליבא דרבי מאיר קשיא בתו דמתניתין נמי קנס הוא וקא פטר ליה אבתו: **היה גדי גנוב לו.** גנב גדי בחול ומתחייב הקרן וטבחו בשבת דלא אתי עליה חיובא דממון באיסור שבת אלא חיוב קנס: **חייב.** ד׳ וה׳ דקנס חידוש הוא ורבה סבירא ליה כרבי מאיר: **גנב וטבח בשבת.** דחיוב ממון דקרן אתא עליה באיסור שבת: **פטור.** דקיימא לן אין מת ומשלם וכיון דלקרן לא מיחייב קנס נמי לא משלם דתשלומי ד׳ וה׳ אמר רחמנא ולא תשלומי שלשה וארבעה ולא סבירא לן כרבי נתן דאמר (שבת דף לד.) מי עושה את עצמו אי נמי בכפות: **שאם אין גניבה.** כלומר שמאחר שפטור על הקרן משום מיתה: **אין טביחה ואין מכירה.** אינו מחויב קנס דכפילתא לתשלומי ארבעה וחמשה כתיב ולא תשלומי שלשה וארבעה: **מחתרת.** שמחתר בית והוליאו וטבחו במחתרת. עלמא דהריגה דשעתא בר קטלא הוא אי הוה אשכחיה בעל הבית כדכתיב (שמות כב) אין לו דמים: **משום דאסוריה איסור עולם.** כל זמן שיעידו עליו שחילל שבת ימיתוהו בית דין הלכך חמירא מיתה דיליה לפוטרו ממממון: **דאיסור שעה.** אי לא משכח ליה ההיא שעתא תו לא מיקטיל: **היתה פרה שאולה לו וטבחה בשבת פטור.** דההיא שעתא דקא טבח לה קא גזיל לה ממרה ומיתה וממון בהדי הדדי אתו עליה וגרסינן שאם אין גניבה אין טביחה ואין מכירה דגבי שואל לא שייך לא כפל ולא ארבעה וחמשה שהרי חייב בקרן לעולם אפילו טוען טענת גנב ואין קנס אלא אם בגנב או בשומר חנם הספיר עצמו בטוען טענת גנב שלומר נגנבה: **פרה אתא לאשמועינן.** בתמיה מה למדנו ממנה שלא למדנו מגדי דקאמר רבה: **שאולה אתא לאשמועינן.** דטובחה בשבת פטור: **ס״ד אמינא הואיל ואמר רב פפא.** בהשוכר את הפועלים: **הכא נמי.** נימא משעת שאלה רמיא עליה וקנאה לכן וכי טבחה בשבת לחייב: **קמ״ל.** כיון דלכל כמה דאיתא הדרא בעינא ההיא שעתא דקא טבח לה קא גזיל לה: **כל ימי שאלתה.** כל ימי משך הזמן ששאלה אביהן מן הבעלים: **אין חייבין באונסה.** דאינהו לאו שואלין נינהו עלה: **דמי בשר בזול.** כל זוזא חשבינן בארבעה דנקי הכי אמרינן בפרק מי שמת (ב״ב קמו:) והשור יחזירו לבעלים: **אחריות נכסים.** קרקעות: **איכא דמתני ארישא.** להאי הניח להן אביהן אחריות נכסים חייבין לשלם ואמרינן דחייבין באונסין דאשתעבוד נכסים דאבוהון מחיים משעת שאלה: **כ״ש אסיפא.** כשטבחוה ואכלוה: **ופליגא דרב פפא.** דאמר לעיל ההיא שעתא דטבח לה אונסין הוא דלאו חיובא עליה ולא משעת שאלה: **ואיכא דמתני לה אסיפא.** היכא דטבחוה אם הניח להן אביהן אחריות נכסים משלמין תשלומי מעליא ולא בזול דאיבעי להו למידק: **אבל ארישא.** אם מתה לא מיחייבי לשלומי אי לא אמרינן אישתעבוד נכסי דאבוהון משעת שאלה: **והיינו דרב פפא.** דאמר לעיל לא אמרינן משעת שאלה רמו עליה תשלומין אלא משעת אונסין ואילך והאיתא בעינא ליתיה לשואל לחייב: **בשלמא רבי יוחנן.** דמוקי מתניתין בשלא התרו בו: **לא אמר כריש לקיש.** דלוקמיה כר׳ מאיר: **כי לא אתרו ביה נמי פטור.** הואיל ואיכא לד מלקות שוגגין. שלא התרו בהן: **ודבר אחר.** ממון ואכלה חלבא קאי כלומר חייבי מיתות שוגגין וממון או חייבי מלקיות שוגגין וממון: **ר׳ יוחנן אומר חייב.** בתשלומין: **דהא לא אתרו ביה.** ולא אתא מיחייבו אלא משום רשעה אחת דממון: **כי לא אתרו ביה נמי פטור.** ולקמן יליף טעמא:

ליקוטי רש״י

לוקה ומשלם. במסכת מכות (דף ד.) מעידים אנו בפלוני שחייב למוריו מלקות וזו ונמצאו זוממין לוקין ומשלמין שלא השם המכיאן לידי מכות ומביאן לידי תשלומין [ב״ק עא.]. **שחידשה תורה** בקנס. כל תשלומי קנס שאינו לפי גזלת היזק בעלמא וכיון לחידוש הוא וגזירת חוק איתא אע״ג דאיכא בהדיה מיתה משלם [לקמן לח. עיי״ש בשיטמ״ק]. **שאם אין גניבה אין טביחה ואין מכירה.** ע׳ לכהן בד״ה היתה פרה שאולה. **זו היא התראתו.** אין לריך התראה אחרת אלא הורגו מיד כיון דערים ומסר נפשיה לחתור ולדעתם דהכי קאמר אחו דאי קאי לאפאי קטילנא ליה ומורה בויה כיון לרודף הוא אין לריך התראה אבל מלילין אותו בנפשו אבל נכנס לאלול וגנב ולא דרך הפספח אינו הורגו אם שיתרו בו בעדים חזו דקיימא לאפך וקטילנא לך ווה יקבל עליו התראה ויאמר יודע אני ועל מנת כן אני עושה שאם תעמוד לנגדי אהרוג אותך אבל בלא התראה לא דלזלמא לא לדעתא דנפשות קא אתי אלא לדעתא דממונא ובא לנזדאו ועל לדעתא דאי קאי באפאי ליפוק [סנהדרין עב.]. **היתה פרה גנובה לו.** כלומר גנב פרה מערב שבת וטבח בשבת חייב אף בתשלומין ארבעה וחמשה שהרי נתחייב בקרן קודם שיבא לידי איסור סקילה ואף על גב דקנסא לא אתי עליה עד דנחבוה כו׳ **שאולה לו** מקנסא משום חיוב מיתה דאמר בגלו נערות (כתובות דף לד:) קנס חידוש הוא שחידשה תורה הלכך אע״ג דמקטיל משלם. **היתה פרה שאולה לו וטבחה בשבת פטור.** מן הכל דלא אמרינן משעת שאלה מחייב ליה קרנא וקמה ליה ברשותיה אפילו להתחייב באונסין ואע״ג דלאו בכל שעה מדיך אלה דלגוליה ואיסור שבת וגניבה באין כאחד ונפטר מן הקרן משום דקם ליה בדרבה מיניה וקנס ליכא דהא אין כאן כפל ולא ארבעה וחמשה אלא בגנב או שומר אבדה או מכית בעלים או בשומר חנם שאמר נגנבה לפטור עלמו בטענת גנב ושואל ששכר ושוכר שאין יכולין להפטר בטענת גנב אין כפל כדאמר בכמה דוכתי לא משום נשבעה גנב ואמר גנב שבעתו שלוחא כמו לשתא מיהו איכא למימר מכירה לא ממר בה כי. שאם אין גניבה אין טביחה ואין מכירה לא ההל גרם ליה לשוכר ליה ולכן בכתובות ובכן פירש לנו רבינו אחר שאין גניבה אין טביחה ואין מכירה ואין הלכה כתנן מה שהיה ואיך שלוחא על לא התרה היכא דליכא קרן פטור מתשלומי ארבעה וחמשה משום דתשלומי ד׳ וה׳ ולא מדבר

הגהות הב״ח

(א) תוס׳ ד״ה מתה וכו׳ והכי אמרי׳ בהשואל דף צו ע״א:

הגהות כהר״ב רנשבורג

א] גמ׳ משלמין דמי בשר בזול. עי׳ רש״י ד״ה דכי כשר וכו׳ ורשב״ם בב״ב דף קמו ע״ב כד״ה ושמין להם וכו׳:

תורה אור השלם

א) וְכִי יִנָּצוּ אֲנָשִׁים וְנָגְפוּ אִשָּׁה הָרָה וְיָצְאוּ יְלָדֶיהָ וְלֹא יִהְיֶה אָסוֹן עָנוֹשׁ יֵעָנֵשׁ כַּאֲשֶׁר יָשִׁית עָלָיו בַּעַל הָאִשָּׁה וְנָתַן בִּפְלִלִים: [שמות כא, כב]

תוספות רי״ד

אמר רבא הניח להן אביהם פרה שאולה משתמשין בה כל ימי שאלה. מתה אי חייבים באונסיה פי׳ שהא שאולה הן ולא קבלו עליהן אונסים. כסבורין של אביהן היא וטבחוה ואכלוה משלמין דמי בשר בזול. פי׳ כל זוזי בארבע דנקי דהכי אמרינן לבעלים. ואם הניח להן אביהן אחריות נכסים. פי׳ קרקעות חייבים לשלם משום דאשתעבדי נכסיה. פי׳ נכסי דאבוהון מחיים משעת שאלה: **כי אתא רב דימי** אמר חייבי מיתות שוגגין ודא. פי׳ ממון או דחייבי מלקות שוגגין וד׳ ר״י אמר חייב בתשלומין ור״ל אמר פטור ר״י אמר חייב דהא לא התרו ביה פי׳ ואי אתה מחייבו אלא משום רשעה אחת. ור״ל אמר פטור אי אתרו בי׳ נמי פטור פי׳ הואיל ואיכא צד מלקות:

חשק שלמה על תוס׳ רי״ד

א) נ״ל כיון דאילו אתרו ביה פטור כי לא אתרו ביה נמי פטור וכו׳

מהכא קרנא הוו לגו ג׳ לגמרי לבקר. ולא היה לו לב להבין לא זכה בה מפני אין קנס בשואל לפי שהשתא אין קנס ברשותו ולקורא כב פפא משום דהא בעל הבית גזלן כנש הוא שמור חנס. וכי גרש ליה בכתובות גרסינן ליה ובמכלתא [דרבה] דאמר התם גנב וטבח בשבת פטור שאם אין גניבה כו׳ דהתם בגנב עלמו [...] כדרב פפא לאשמועינן מלתא כדרב פפא [...] אין חייבין באונסה [...] דמי בשר בזול [...] והדר אמרינן [...] איכא דמתני לה [...] ואיכא דמתני לה אסיפא [...] ואי לא הניח להן אביהן קרקע (המשך בדף לה.)

ר' שמעון היא א) דאמר א שחיטה שאינה ראויה
לא שמה שחיטה התינח עבודת כוכבים ושור
הנסקל אלא שחיטת שבת שחיטה ראויה
היא דתנן ב) ב השוחט בשבת וביום הכפורים
אע"פ שמתחייב בנפשו שחיטתו כשרה סבר
לה כר' יוחנן הסנדלר ג) דתניא ד) המבשל
בשבת בשוגג יאכל במזיד לא יאכל דברי ר"מ
ר' יהודה אומר ג בשוגג יאכל למוצאי שבת
במזיד לא יאכל עולמית רבי יוחנן הסנדלר
אומר בשוגג יאכל למוצאי שבת לאחרים ולא
לו במזיד לא יאכל עולמית לא לו ולא לאחרים
מאי טעמא דרבי יוחנן הסנדלר כדדריש ר'
חייא אפיתחא דבי נשיאה א) ושמרתם את
השבת כי קדש היא לכם מה קודש אסור
באכילה אף מעשה שבת אסורין באכילה אי
מה קודש אסור בהנאה אף מעשה שבת
אסור בהנאה ת"ל לכם שלכם יהא יכול אפילו
בשוגג ת"ל א) מחלליה מות יומת במזיד אמרתי
לך ולא בשוגג פליגי בה רב אחא ורבינא חד
אמר מעשה שבת דאורייתא וחד אמר דרבנן
מאן דאמר דאורייתא כדאמרן מאן דאמר
דרבנן אמר קרא קדש היא ה) היא קודש ד ואין
מעשיה קודש ולמאן דאמר דרבנן מאי
טעמייהו דרבנן דפטרי כי קא פטרי רבנן
אשארא טובח לעבודת כוכבים א) כיון דשחט
ביה פורתא איתסר ליה אידך כי קא טבח לאו
דמריה קא טבח אמר רבא ו) באומר בגמר
זביחה הוא עובדה שור הנסקל לאו דידיה הוא
דקטבח אמר רבה הכא במאי עסקינן כגון
שמסרו לשומר והזיק בבית שומר ונגמר דינו
בבית שומר וגנבו גנב מבית שומר ורבי מאיר
סבר לה כר' יעקב וסבר לה כר"ש סבר
לה כר' יעקב ז) דאמר אף משנגמר דינו
החזירו שומר לבעליו מוחזר וסבר לה
כר"ש ח) דאמר ה דבר הגורם לממון כממון דמי
רבה אמר לעולם בטובח על ידי עצמו
ור'

רבי שמעון. בפרק מרובה ובכסוי הדם ובאותו ואת בנו: התינח עבודת כוכבים. דזבחי מתים אסורים וכן שור הנסקל דמשנגמר דינו אסור בהנאה כדאמרינן בב"ק (דף מא.) ובפסחים (דף כב:) ממשמע שנאמר סקול יסקל איני יודע שהוא נבלה ונבילה כו': בשוגג יאכל. אפי' בו ביום: במזיד לא יאכל. הוא לעולם אבל אחרים ישראלים אוכלים: ר' יהודה אומר בשוגג יאכל. הוא למוצאי שבת ולא בו ביום דקנסינן שוגג אטו מזיד: במזיד לא יאכל. הוא עולמית אלא אחרים: בדרבי יוחנן הסנדלר גרסינן יאכל: לאחרים. לישראל: לא לו ולא לאחרים. ישראל אבל מוכרו ונותנו לעובדי כוכבים: מ"ט דר' יוחנן הסנדלר. דאמר מעשה שבת אסורין באכילה: יכול אפילו בשוגג. תאסר באכילה אם שגג בבישול שלא ידע שהוא שבת: מחלליה וגו'. היכא דאיכא חיוב מיתה אסרי באכילה כי קודש: במזיד אמרתי. שהוא אסור כקודש דהא גבי חיוב מיתה כתיב ולא בשוגג: מעשה שבת. במזיד אסורין מן התורה באכילה לר' יוחנן הסנדלר: מ"ט דרבנן. דפליגי אדרבי מאיר ופטרי מקנס ארבעה וחמשה הואיל ונטובח על ידי אחר אוקימתא הא שחיטה ראויה היא מדאורייתא: אשארא. אעבודת כוכבים ואשור הנסקל: כיון דשחט ביה פורתא איתסר ליה. דאמר מר (חולין דף מ.) היתה בהמת חבירו רבוצה לפני עבודת כוכבים כיון ששחט בה סימן אחד אסרה: לאו דמריה קא טבח. דהא איתסרא עליה ומיחבא דתשלומי ארבעה וחמשה טביחה כתיב בהו ועד גמר שחיטה לא מיחייב ומקמי דמטי גמר שחיטה איתסרא בהנאה על בעליה ומההיא שעתא אפסדה מיניה דלאי איתא לא הדרא בעינא ולאו דמריה היא: באומר בגמר זביחה הוא עובדה. לעבודת כוכבים אינו עובד לעבודת כוכבים עד גמר זביחה: פלוגתא דר' יעקב בבבא קמא: החזירו שומר לבעליו מוחזר. דאמר ליה תורא אשלמת לי תורא אשלימית לך: כממון דמי. והאי נמי אע"ג דלאו שוי מידי גורם לממון הוא דכי ליתא בעי לשלומי ליה תורא מעליא: דר' שמעון בבבא קמא בפרק מרובה קדשים שחייב באחריותן משלם ארבעה וחמשה משום דגורם לממון הוא ואע"ג דהקדש לאו ממון בעלים הוא והקדש לא שייך קנס דרעהו כתיב: רבה גרסינן בכולהו ותדע מדאמר לקמן א"ל רב פפא לאביי לרבה דאמר אידוש הוא כו' ואם איתא דרבא גרסינן הא רב פפא תלמידו של רבא היה כדאמר לקמן אמר ליה רב פפא לרבה הי מכה מאי שנא דשבקיה לרבה ולא שייליה [לתרוצי שמעתיה] ושייליה לאביי [שמעתא דרבא] אלא רבה גרסינן ורב פפא לא היה בימיו ושייל לאביי שהיה תלמידו של רבה: רבה אמר לעולם בטובח בעצמו ור'

רבי שמעון היא דאמר שחיטה שאינה ראויה לא שמה שחיטה. תימה דעד כאן לא פליגי רבנן התם גבי אותו ואת בנו אלא כדמפרש התם בחולין (דף פה.) טעמא דנין שחיטה משחיטה פירוש משחוטי חוץ ואין דנין שחיטה מטביחה אבל הכא גבי תשלומי ד' וה' דכתיב טביחה אית לן למילף טביחה מטביחה ולא שמה שחיטה ואור"י דאיכא למימר דנין דבר הנאמר בסיני מדבר הנאמר בסיני ואין דנין דבר הנאמר בסיני מטבוח טבח והכן שלא נאמר בסיני והתם נמי ה"מ למימר הכי אלא דלאו דליה סיועא אחריתא א"נ י"ל דצריך סיועא דהתם דנין שחיטה משחיטה דלאי הוה כתיב טביחה גבי אותו ואת בנו הוה ילפינן הכא והתם מטבוח טבח והכן טביחה מטביחה אע"ג דלא נאמרה בסיני דהוי בדדמי מדנילף טביחה משחיטה דלא דמי אע"ג דנאמרה בסיני אבל השתא דכתיב שחיטה גבי אותו ואת בנו דנין שחיטה משחיטה ולפינן נמי השתא מטביחה דד' וה' ואיפכא ליכא למימר דנין טביחה דתשלומי ד' וה' מטביחה ולמילף מהתם משחיטה דאותו ואת בנו דכיון דשקולים הן ואיכא למילף הכי ואיכא למילף הכי אית לן למימר דנין דבר הנאמר בסיני ממה שנאמר בסיני ט): המבשל בשבת בשוגג יאכל. פי' בו ביום ואפילו הוא כדמוכח בפ' כירה (שבת לח.) דבעו מרבי חייא בר אבא שכח קדירה על גבי כירה ובשלה בשבת כו' עד המבשל בשבת כו' בשוגג יאכל ולאותו שבת קא בעי התם אי אסיר גזרה שלא יאמר שוכח אני במזיד לא יאכל פירוש בין הוא בין אחרים בו ביום אבל במוצאי שבת לדידיה נמי שרי דהא בפ' קמא דחולין (דף טו. ושם) אההיא מתני' דהשוחט בשבת וביה"כ אע"פ שמתחייב בנפשו שחיטתו כשרה פריך ונוקמא במזיד ור' מאיר ומשני לא סלקא דעתין דקתני שבת דומיא דיה"כ מה יה"כ לא שנא שוגג ול"ש מזיד והשתא אי לאחרים שרי בו ביום לפרוך ממזיד גופיה מה יוה"כ לא שנא לו ולא שנא לאחרים כו' ואי לדידיה אסור אף למוצאי שבת הוה ליה למימר שחיטתו כשרה קתני ל"ש לו לא שנא לאחרים כדקאמר התם על ר' יוחנן הסנדלר ועוד דא"כ היינו מזיד דר' יהודה כמו שאפרש ומדאצטריך לרבי יהודה לאפוקי מזיד במילתיה משמע דפליג נמי אמזיד: **בשוגג** יאכל במוצאי שבת. שוגג דר' יהודה הוי כמו שפירשתי מזיד דר"מ דהא מוקי התם מתני' דהשוחט בשבת כוותיה: **במזיד** לא יאכל עולמית. הוא אבל אחרים אוכלים דאי אחרים נמי לא יאכלו עולמית היינו מזיד דרבי יוחנן הסנדלר כללא דמילתא מזיד דרבי מאיר שוגג דרבי יהודה מזיד דרבי יהודה שוגג דרבי יוחנן הסנדלר: **אמר** קרא לכם. וא"ת ולא לכתוב לא קדש ולא לכם ואנא ידענא דאסירי באכילה מלא תאכל כל תועבה דכל שתעבתי לך הרי הוא בבל תאכל וי"ל דאי מהתם ה"א בין שוגג בין מזיד להכי איצטריך למכתב הכא למסמכיה למחלליה לומר במזיד אמרתי לך ולא בשוגג: **היא** קדש ואין מעשיה קודש. ואין להקשות דלא לכתוב לא היא ולא קדש דהוה אסורה באכילה מכל אשר תיעבתי לך והכי אמרי' בהדיא בפ' כל הבשר (חולין קטו. ושם): **מאי** טעמא דרבנן דפטרי. לא בעי למימר דלא דרשי או ותחת לרבות את השליח דלא ניחא ליה למימר דפליגי בשליח: **כי** קא פטרי רבנן אשארא. וא"ת אמאי אצטריך למתני כלל טבח בשבת דאפי' בשחיטה שאינה ראויה מחייב ר"מ כ"ש הא דשחיטה ראויה היא וי"ל דזו אף זו קתני: **כיון** דשחט בה פורתא אסרה ואידך כו'. וא"ת כל טובח נמי לאו דמריה קא טבח דמכי שחט פורתא קניא בשינוי אלא ע"כ בהכי חייב רחמנא והכא נמי לא שנא ואור"י דלא חשיב שינוי לקנותה בכך: **סבר** לה כר"ש דאמר דבר הגורם לממון כו'. וא"ת ואמאי לא קאמר דר"מ לטעמיה דדאין דינא דגרמי (ב"ק ק.) גבי מקדש תבואת חבירו או שורף שטרות חבירו (שם לח:) וכ"ש דמחייב בדבר הגורם לממון כדאמר התם בהגוזל (שם לח:) דלמא עד כאן לא קאמר ר"ש אלא בדבר שעיקרו ממון אבל שטר דאין גופו ממון לא וי"ל דאיכא למימר נמי איפכא דעד כאן לא קאמר ר"מ אלא בשורף שטרות של חבירו או מקדש תבואת חבירו שהוא ממון הראוי לכל העולם אבל שור הנסקל אין ראוי אלא לזה השומר שיפטור עצמו וי"מ דמשום הכי קאמר ס"ל כר"ש משום דר"ש קאמר דבר הגורם לממון הוי ממון לענין תשלומי ד' וה' דלהכי תני ליה במרובה (שם עח:) ואילו ר' מאיר לא חזינא דמחייב בדינא דגרמי אלא קרן אבל לא לחייב לשלם על ידו תשלומי ד' וה' ועוד אומר ריצ"א דמשום דינא דגרמי לא מחייב אלא מדרבנן כדמוכח בסוף הכונס (שם סב.) י):

ורבי

מסורת הש"ס

א) קדושין נז. [ב"ק עא. חולין פ. פה.], ב) חולין יד. ב"ק עא, ג) [משום פלוגתא דר"מ ור"י הסנדלר ליתא במשנה שפיר גרסי' דתניא], ד) ב"ק עא. חולין טו. גיטין נג. ביצה יז. תרומות פ"ב מ"ג שבת לח. [תוספתא דשבת פ"ג], ה) [חולין קטו.], ו) [ב"ק עא. ע"ז לד: חולין מ:], ז) ב"ק מה. עא: נח:, ח) ב"ק שם פסחים כט: שבועות לב. לג. [ב"ק קח:], ט) [וע"ע תוס' ב"ק עא. ד"ה איסורא ותוס' חולין פה. ד"ה דנין], י) [וע' תוס' ב"ק נג. ד"ה חמור עוד שם עא. ד"ה וסבר].

תוספות ישנים

א) ופריך אפי' למ"ד ישנה לשחיטה מתחלה ועד סוף כדאמרי' במרובה וטבחו כולו בעינן ה"נ וטבחו כולו בעינן. ת"י עס"ג:

תורה אור השלם

א) וּשְׁמַרְתֶּם אֶת הַשַּׁבָּת כִּי קֹדֶשׁ הִוא לָכֶם מְחַלְלֶיהָ מוֹת יוּמָת כִּי כָּל הָעֹשֶׂה בָהּ מְלָאכָה וְנִכְרְתָה הַנֶּפֶשׁ הַהִוא מִקֶּרֶב עַמֶּיהָ: [שמות לא, יד]

עין משפט נר מצוה

לא א מיי' (פ' יג הל' ה) ופ"ד מהל' שחיטה הל' י ופ"ב מהל' גניבה הל' ח סמג עשין סד ועא ולאוין קמט טוש"ע יו"ד סימן כז סעיף ח וסי' כח סעיף ז וטור ח"מ סימן שנ:
לב ב מיי' פ"א מהל' שחיטה הל' כט סמג עשין סג טוש"ע יו"ד סי' יא סעיף ב:
לג ג ד מיי' פ"ו מהל' שבת הל' כג סמג לאוין סה טוש"ע א"ח סימן שיח סעיף א:
לד ה מיי' פ"ז מהל' חובל הל' ז טוש"ע ח"מ סי' שפו סעי' ג:

ליקוטי רש"י

[תחילת לקוטי רש"י ששייך לכאן נדפס בדף לג:] במזיד לא יאכל. בו ביום והוא הדין לאחרים ואיידי דתנא רישא בדידיה תנא נמי סיפא בדידיה והכי איבעי לן לפרושי בהכל שוחטין [ב"ק שם]. דאיכא איסורא לא יאכל בו ביום עד שתחשך ובכדי שיעשו והוא הדין לאחרים נמי דאסור למיכליה בו ביום דטעמא משום דלא נמטייה הנאה מאיסורא הוא וכי שהי לאורתא בכדי שיעשו לא מטי לו הנאה מיניה ואיידי דתנא רישא בדידיה דאשמעינן רבותא להתירא תנא נמי סיפא בדידיה [חולין שם]. בשול שבת מאבות מלאכות הוא ואיסור סקילה הוא הלכך קנסוה רבנן למזיד [ביצה יז:]. ר' יהודה אומר בשוגג יאכל. הוא בעצמו למוצאי שבת ובו ביום לא הוא ולא אחרים ואיידי דבעי למיתנא סיפא בדידיה תנא נמי ברישא בדידיה [ב"ק שם]. ולא בשבת וה"ה לאחריני דאע"ג דבשוגג מיחייב סקילה ליכא עבירה מיהא איכא ובעינן בכדי שיעשו דלא נימטייה הנאה מעבירה ואיידי דבעי למתני סיפא לא יאכל עולמית בדידיה אבל לאחריני שרי דלאיהו דעבד איסורא קנסוה רבנן אבל אחריני לא תנא רישא נמי בדידיה [חולין שם]. במזיד לא יאכל. הוא עולמית אבל אחרים אוכלים [ב"ק שם]. רבי יוחנן הסנדלר אומר בשוגג יאכל למוצאי שבת. בכדי שיעשו כר' יהודה דמשוי ליה עבירה אף בשוגג ועדיפא מדרבי יהודה דאילו רבי יהודה שרי ליה לאורתא אפי' לדידיה דלא קנים שוגג אטו מזיד ורבי יוחנן קנים שוגג אטו מזיד הלכך איהו דעבד איסורא קנסו רבנן אחריני דלא עבדי איסורא לא קנסו אלא בכדי שיעשו ימתינו דלא ניתהני מעבירה. במזיד לא יאכל עולמית כו'. לאו משום קנסא הוא דהא אחריני לא עבוד איסורא אלא מקראי יליף לה רבי יוחנן בכתובות באלו נערות (דף לד.) ובב"ק בפרק מרובה (דף עא.) ושמרתם את השבת כי קדש וגו' מה קדש אסור באכילה אף מעשה שבת אסורים באכילה יכול אפילו בשוגג ת"ל מחלליה מות יומת במזיד אמרתי ולא בשוגג [חולין שם]. יכול אפילו בשוגג. יאסר באכילה. במזיד אמרתי לך. קודש הוא היכא דשייך דין מיתה ולא בשוגג [ב"ק שם]. פליגי בה רב אחא ורבינא

חד אמר וכו'. בכל התורה כולה, כל היכא דחזית פלוגתייהו ואיתמר סתמא חד אמר לקולא וחד אמר לחומרא ולא פירש מי המקיל ומי המחמיר דע שרב אחא לחומרא ורבינא לקולא והלכתא כרבינא בכולהו כדברי המקיל [פסחים עד:]. מעשה שבת דאורייתא. אסורין באכילה [ב"ק שם]. כיון דשחט בה פורתא איתסר. משום זבחי מתים [ב"ק שם]. בגמר זביחה הוא עובדה. לעבודת כוכבים. כר' יעקב. שמסרו לשומר. החזירו שומר לבעליו מוחזר. דבר הגורם לממון כממון דמי. שאע"פ שאינו שוה כלום גורם לממון הוא שהרי קיים שהשומר פוטר את עצמו בו ואם לא יחזירנו ישלם דמיו [שם].

The Gemara answers:

אָמַר רָבָא – Rava said: **בְּאוֹמֵר בִּגְמַר זְבִיחָה הוּא עוֹבְדָהּ** – The Baraisa refers to **where [the slaughterer] says** that **he** means to **worship [the idol]** only **with the completion of the slaughtering.** Thus, the animal does not become an idolatrous sacrifice until the end of the slaughtering, and it therefore remains permissible and in the possession of the original owner until the end of the slaughter, at which point the thief becomes liable to the fourfold or fivefold penalty.

The Gemara asks further:

שׁוֹר הַנִּסְקָל – In the Baraisa's case of one who slaughters **an ox** condemned **to be stoned,** why is the thief liable, according to R' Meir, to the fourfold or fivefold penalty altogether? **לָאו דִּידֵיהּ הוּא דְּקָטָבַח** – **It is not** the animal **of the** original **[owner] that he is slaughtering!**[29] – ? –

The Gemara answers:

אָמַר רַבָּה – Rabbah said: **הָכָא בְּמַאי עָסְקִינַן** – **What are we dealing with here?** **כְּגוֹן שֶׁמְּסָרוֹ לְשׁוֹמֵר** – **With a case in which he** [the owner of the ox] **had given it to a custodian,** **וְהִזִּיק בְּבֵית שׁוֹמֵר וְנִגְמַר דִּינֵיהּ בְּבֵית שׁוֹמֵר** – **and it damaged** [i.e. it killed a person] **while in the house of the custodian** [i.e. while in his custody] **and its verdict** sentencing it to death **was reached while in the house of the custodian** [i.e. while in his custody], **וּגְנָבוֹ גַּנָּב מִבֵּית שׁוֹמֵר** – **and the thief** then **stole it from the house of the custodian.** **וְרַבִּי מֵאִיר סָבַר לָהּ כְּרַבִּי יַעֲקֹב** – **And R' Meir holds with R' Yaakov,** **וְסָבַר לָהּ כְּרַבִּי שִׁמְעוֹן** – **and he holds with R' Shimon.**

The Gemara explains:

סָבַר לָהּ כְּרַבִּי יַעֲקֹב – **[R' Meir] holds with R' Yaakov,** **דְּאָמַר אַף מִשֶּׁנִּגְמַר דִּינוֹ** – **who says: Even after the verdict** sentencing the animal to death **is reached,** **הֶחֱזִירוֹ שׁוֹמֵר לִבְעָלָיו מוּחְזָר** – **if the custodian returned it to its owner,** it is deemed **returned.**[30] **וְסָבַר לָהּ כְּרַבִּי שִׁמְעוֹן** – **And [R' Meir]** also **holds with R' Shimon,** **דְּאָמַר דָּבָר הַגּוֹרֵם לְמָמוֹן כְּמָמוֹן דָּמֵי** – **who says: Something that can cause** a benefit of **money is considered as money.**[31]

The Gemara cites an alternative explanation for R' Meir's ruling in the Baraisa that the thief is liable to the fourfold or fivefold penalty when the animal is slaughtered on the Sabbath or for idol worship:

רַבָּה אָמַר – Rabbah says: **לְעוֹלָם בְּטוֹבֵחַ עַל יְדֵי עַצְמוֹ** – **In fact,** you can say, as originally thought, that the Baraisa refers to **where [the thief] himself slaughters** the stolen animal.

NOTES

Rashi). [*Rashi's* intent is unclear. Possibly, he means that the fourfold or fivefold penalty for slaughter applies only where it is the act of slaughter that deprives the owner of his stolen animal. In the present case, however, the owner is already deprived of his animal *before* the act of slaughter is complete, since the animal became forbidden for all benefit and would not be returned to him immediately upon the initial cut. Hence, "it is not the owner's animal that he is slaughtering" – i.e. it is not his slaughter that deprives the owner of his animal. (See *Meiri* here, and *Kovetz Shiurim, Bava Kamma* §37.) *Rashash* (to *Bava Kamma* 71b) explains the Gemara to mean simply that something which has no value cannot be "owned" by anyone; hence, one who slaughters a stolen animal that is forbidden for benefit has not slaughtered an animal "belonging" to the original owner. (The matter of whether one can "own" that which has no value, however, is a dispute among Rishonim – see *Ritva* to *Succah* 35b ד״ה ושל ערלה; see also *Kuntres* of *Rivash,* printed at the end of his Responsa, and *Marcheshes* 1:1.)]

29. [For it has already become prohibited for benefit at the moment it is condemned to stoning, and there should thus be no liability for "slaughtering the owner's animal" – see preceding note.]

[This question of the Gemara would seem to contradict the view of *Rabbeinu Tam* (cited by *Tosafos* to *Sanhedrin* 79b-80a et al.) that a condemned ox is not forbidden for benefit while it is still alive. A digest of various resolutions offered by the Acharonim can be found in *Otzar Mefarshei HaTalmud* to *Bava Kamma* 71b (Vol. 3 pp. 563-564).]

30. The Gemara in *Bava Kamma* (45a) cites a dispute regarding an ox that killed a person and was sentenced to death while in the care of a custodian (due to his failure to guard the animal properly). The Rabbis maintain that since the ox is now worthless, the custodian must compensate the ox's owner for the loss of the ox that he suffered on account of the custodian's negligence. R' Yaakov, however, maintains that the custodian can simply return the live ox in its present state of worthlessness and be exempt from payment, for he can say to the owner, "You gave me an ox and I am returning to you an ox." See the Gemara there for the underlying reasons of both opinions (see *Rashi*).

31. The law is that כֶּפֶל, *the twofold payment [for theft],* and the fourfold or fivefold payment are not paid for *hekdesh* property. For the Torah states in the context of these payments רֵעֵהוּ, *his fellow,* which teaches that a thief is liable for these payments only when he steals an item that belongs to "his fellow," not when he steals an item that belongs to *hekdesh.* Nevertheless, R' Shimon maintains (*Bava Kamma* 74b) that if a person vowed to bring a sacrifice and then designated one of his animals as the sacrifice [in which case the law is that if the animal that he designated is lost or dies, he is responsible to bring another animal as a sacrifice in its stead; see *Megillah* 8a], a thief who steals that animal is liable to the twofold and fourfold or fivefold payment to the original owner, even though he has stolen a sacrificial animal that belongs to *hekdesh.* R' Shimon's logic is that although the consecrated animal is no longer the property of its owner, it is nonetheless something that *causes* him a monetary benefit; that is, he benefits monetarily by its existence (in that he does not have to bring a different animal as his sacrifice) and suffers loss by its nonexistence (in that he must replace the sacrifice). In this sense, the consecrated animal is indeed considered "his" property, and the multiple payments associated with the theft of an item belonging to one's "fellow" are therefore applicable (see *Rashi*).

Accordingly, if we combine the view of R' Yaakov [that returning the forbidden ox intact to the owner exempts the custodian from liability] with the view of R' Shimon [that "something that can cause money is considered as money"], the following emerges in the case of an animal that killed and was condemned while in the custody of a custodian and was then stolen from his house and slaughtered: Although the animal is forbidden for benefit when it is stolen and slaughtered, it is "owned" by the custodian, since it "causes him money," as he could free himself of liability to the owner by returning the live animal intact. Hence, the thief who steals and slaughters it has stolen an animal from the custodian and has slaughtered it while still "owned" by the custodian. Thus, he must make the fourfold or fivefold payment to the custodian. The Baraisa refers to such a case, and R' Meir rules that the thief is subject to the fourfold of fivefold payment, because he holds both the view of R' Yaakov and the view of R' Shimon.

ר' שמעון היא דאמר שחיטה שאינה ראויה לא שמה שחיטה התינח עבודת כוכבים ושור הנסקל אלא שחיטת שבת שחיטה ראויה היא דתנן השוחט בשבת וביום הכפורים אע"פ שמתחייב בנפשו שחיטתו כשרה סבר לה כר' יוחנן הסנדלר דתניא המבשל בשבת בשוגג יאכל במזיד לא יאכל דברי ר"מ ר' יהודה אומר בשוגג יאכל למוצאי שבת במזיד לא יאכל עולמית רבי יוחנן הסנדלר אומר בשוגג יאכל למוצאי שבת לאחרים ולא לו במזיד לא יאכל עולמית לא לו ולא לאחרים מאי טעמא דרבי יוחנן הסנדלר כדדריש ר' חייא אפיתחא דבי נשיאה ושמרתם את השבת כי קדש היא לכם מה קודש אסור באכילה אף מעשה שבת אסורין באכילה אי מה קודש אסור בהנאה אף מעשה שבת אסור בהנאה ת"ל לכם שלכם יהא יכול אפילו בשוגג ת"ל מחלליה מות יומת במזיד אמרתי לך ולא בשוגג פליגי בה רב אחא ורבינא חד אמר מעשה שבת דאורייתא וחד אמר דרבנן מאן דאמר דאורייתא כדאמרן מאן דאמר דרבנן אמר קרא קדש היא היא קודש ואין מעשיה קודש ולמאן דאמר דרבנן מאי טעמייהו דרבנן דפטרי כי קא פטרי רבנן אשארא טובח לעבודת כוכבים כיון דשחט ביה פורתא איתסר ליה אידך כי קא טבח לאו דמריה קא טבח לאו באומר בגמר זביחה הוא עובדה שור הנסקל לאו דידיה הוא דקטבח אמר רבה הכא במאי עסקינן כגון שמסרו לשומר והזיק בבית שומר ונגמר דינו בבית שומר וגנבו גנב מבית שומר ורבי מאיר סבר לה כר' יעקב וסבר לה כר"ש סבר לה כר' יעקב דאמר אף משנגמר דינו החזירו שומר לבעליו מוחזר וסבר לה כר"ש דאמר דבר הגורם לממון כממון דמי רבה אמר לעולם בטובח על ידי עצמו ור'

רש"י

רבי שמעון. בפרק מרובה ובכסוי הדם ובאותו ואת בנו: התינח עבודת כוכבים. דזבחי מתים אסורים וכן שור הנסקל דמשנגמר דינו אסור בהנאה כדאמרינן בב"ק (דף מא.) ובפסחים (דף כב:) ממשמע שנאמר סקול יסקל איני יודע שהוא נבילה ונבילה כו': בשוגג יאכל. אפי' בו ביום: במזיד לא יאכל. הוא לעולם אבל אחרים ישראלים אוכלים: ר' יהודה אומר בשוגג יאכל. הוא למוצאי שבת ולא בו ביום דקנסינן שוגג אטו מזיד: במזיד לא יאכל. הוא עולמית אלא אחרים: בדרבי יוחנן הסנדלר גרסינן יאכל: לאחרים. לישראל: לא לו ולא לאחרים. ישראל אבל מוכרו ונותנו לעובדי כוכבים: מ"ט דר' יוחנן הסנדלר. דאמר מעשה שבת אסורין באכילה: יכול אפילו בשוגג. תאסר באכילה אם שגג בבישול שלא ידע שהוא שבת: מחלליה וגו'. היכא דאיכא חיוב מיתה אסירי באכילה כי קודש: במזיד אמרתי. שהוא אסור כקודש דהא גבי חיוב מיתה כתיב ולא בשוגג: מעשה שבת. במזיד אסורין מן התורה באכילה כר' יוחנן הסנדלר: מ"ש דרבנן. דפליגי אדרבי מאיר ופטרי מקנס ארבעה וחמשה הואיל ובטובח על ידי אחר אוקימתא הא שחיטה ראויה היא מדאורייתא: אשארא. אעבודת כוכבים ואשור הנסקל: כיון דשחט ביה פורתא איתסר ליה. דאמר מר (חולין דף מ.) היתה בהמת חבירו רבוצה לפני עבודת כוכבים כיון ששחט בה סימן אחד אסרה: לאו דמריה קא טבח. דהא איתסרא עליה ומיחייב דתשלומי ארבעה וחמשה טביחה כתיב בהו ועד גמר שחיטה לא מיחייב ומקמי דמטי גמר שחיטה איתסרא בהנאה על בעליה ומההיא שעתא אפסדה מיניה דאי מיתא לא הדרא בעינא ולאו דמריה היא: באומר בגמר זביחה הוא עובדה. לעבודת כוכבים אינו עובד לעבודת כוכבים עד גמר זביחה: פלוגתא דר' יעקב בבבא קמא: החזירו שומר לבעליו מוחזר. דאמר ליה תורא אשלמת לי תורא אשלימית לך: כממון דמי. והאי נמי אע"ג דלא שוי מידי גורם לממון הוא דכי ליתא בעי לשלומי ליה תורא מעליא: דר' שמעון בבבא קמא בפרק מרובה קדשים שחייב באחריותן משלם ארבעה וחמשה משום דגורם לממון הוא ואע"ג דהקדש לאו ממון בעלים הוא והקדש לא שייך קנס דרעהו כתיב: רבה גרסינן בכולהו ותדע מדאמר לקמן א"ל רב פפא לאביי לרבה דאמר חידוש הוא כו' ואם איתא דרבא גרסינן הא רב פפא תלמידו של רבא היה כדאמר לקמן אמר ליה רב פפא לרבא הי מכה מאי שנא דשבקיה לרבא ולא שייליה [לתרוצי שמעתיה] ושייליה לאביי [שמעתא דרבא] אלא רבה גרסינן ורב פפא לא היה בימיו ושייל לאביי שהיה תלמידו של רבה: רבה אמר לעולם בטובח בעצמו ור'

תוספות

רבי שמעון היא דאמר שחיטה שאינה ראויה לא שמה שחיטה. תימה דעד כאן לא פליגי רבנן התם גבי אותו ואת בנו אלא כדמפרש התם בחולין (דף פה.) טעמא דנין שחיטה משחיטה פירוש משחוטי חוץ ואין דנין שחיטה מטביחה אבל הכא גבי תשלומי ד' וה' דכתיב טביחה אית לן למילף טביחה מטביחה ולא שמה שחיטה ואור"י דאיכא למימר דנין דבר הנאמר בסיני מדבר הנאמר בסיני ואין דנין דבר הנאמר בסיני מטבוח טבח והכן שלא נאמר בסיני והתם נמי ה"מ למימר הכי אלא דלא ליה שינויא אחרינא א"נ י"ל דלריך שינויא דהתם דנין שחיטה משחיטה דלא הוה כתיב טביחה גבי אותו ואת בנו הוה ילפינן הכא והתם מטבוח טבח והכן טביחה מטביחה אע"ג דלא נאמרה בסיני דהוי בדדמי מדנילף טביחה משחיטה דלא דמי אע"ג דנאמרה בסיני אבל השתא דכתיב שחיטה גבי אותו ואת בנו דנין שחיטה משחיטה ולפינן נמי השתא לטביחה דד' וה' ואיכא למימר דנין טביחה דתשלומי ד' וה' מטביחה ולמילף מהתם משחיטה דאותו ואת בנו דכיון דשקולים הן ואיכא למילף הכי ואיכא למילף הכי אית לן למימר דנין דבר הנאמר בסיני ממה שנאמר בסיני:

המבשל בשבת בשוגג יאכל. פי' בו ביום ואפילו הוא כדמוכח בפ' כירה (שבת לח.) דבעו מרבי חייא בר אבא שכח קדירה על גבי כירה ובשלה בשבת כו' עד המבשל בשבת כו' בשוגג יאכל ולאותו שבת קא בעי התם אי אסיר גזרה שלא יאמר שוכח אני במזיד לא יאכל פירוש בין הוא בין אחרים בו ביום אבל במוצאי שבת לדידיה נמי שרי דהא בפ' קמא דחולין (דף טו. ושם) אההיא מתני' דהשוחט בשבת וביוה"כ אע"פ שמתחייב בנפשו שחיטתו כשרה פריך ונוקמה במזיד ור' מאיר ומשני לא סלקא דעתין דקתני שבת דומיא דיוה"כ מה יוה"כ לא שנא שוגג ול"ש מזיד והשתא אי לאחרים שרי בו ביום לפרוך ממזיד גופיה מה יוה"כ לא שנא לו ולא שנא לאחרים כו' ואי לדידיה אסור אף למוצאי שבת הוה ליה למימר שחיטתו כשרה קתני ל"ש לו לא שנא לאחרים כדקאמר התם על ר' יוחנן הסנדלר ועוד דא"כ היינו מזיד דר' יהודה כמו שאפרש ומדאצטריך לרבי יהודה לאפוקי מזיד במילתיה משמע דפליג נמי אמזיד: בשוגג יאכל במוצאי שבת. שוגג דר' יהודה הוי כמו שפירשתי מזיד דר"מ דהא מוקי התם מתני' דהשוחט בשבת כוותיה: במזיד לא יאכל עולמית. הוא אבל אחרים אוכלים דאי אחרים נמי לא יאכלו עולמית היינו מזיד דרבי יוחנן הסנדלר כללא דמילתא מזיד דרבי מאיר שוגג דרבי יהודה מזיד דרבי יהודה שוגג דרבי יוחנן הסנדלר: אמר קרא לכם. וא"ת ולא לכתוב לא קדש ולא לכם ואנא ידענא דאסירי באכילה מלא תאכל כל תועבה כל שתעבתי לך הרי הוא בבל תאכל וי"ל דאי מהתם ה"א בין שוגג בין מזיד להכי איצטריך למכתב הכא למסמכיה למחלליה לומר במזיד אמרתי לך ולא בשוגג: היא קדש ואין מעשיה קודש. ואין להקשות דלא לכתוב לא היא ולא קדש דהוה אסורה באכילה מכל אשר תיעבתי לך והכי אמרי' בהדיא בפ' כל הבשר (חולין קטו. ושם): מאי טעמא דרבנן דפטרי. לא בעי למימר דלא דרשי או ותחת לרבות את השליח דלא ניחא ליה למימר דפליגי בשליח: כי קא פטרי רבנן אשארא. וא"ת אמאי אצטריך למתני כלל טבח בשבת דאפי' בשחיטה שאינה ראויה מחייב ר"מ כ"ש הא דשחיטה ראויה היא וי"ל דזו אף זו קתני: כיון דשחט בה פורתא אסרה ואידך כו'. וא"ת כל טובח נמי לאו דמריה קא טבח דמכי שחט פורתא קניא בשינוי אלא ע"כ בהכי חייב רחמנא והכא נמי לא שנא ואור"י דלא חשיב שינוי לקנותה בכך: סבר לה כר"ש דאמר דבר הגורם לממון כו'. וא"ת ואמאי לא קאמר דר"מ לטעמיה דדאין דינא דגרמי (ב"ק ק.) גבי מקדש תבואת חבירו או שורף שטרות חבירו (שם לח:) וכ"ש דמחייב בדבר הגורם לממון כדאמר התם בהגוזל (שם לח:) דלמא עד כאן לא קאמר ר"ש אלא בדבר שעיקרו ממון אבל שטר דאין גופו ממון לא וי"ל דאיכא למימר נמי איפכא דעד כאן לא קאמר ר"מ אלא בשורף שטרות של חבירו או מקדש תבואת חבירו שהוא ממון הראוי לכל העולם אבל שור הנסקל אין ראוי אלא לזה השומר שיפטור עצמו וי"מ דמשום הכי קאמר ס"ל כר"ש משום דר"ש קאמר דבר הגורם לממון הוי ממון לענין תשלומי ד' וה' דלהכי תני ליה במרובה (שם עח:) ואילו ר' מאיר לא חזינא דמחייב בדינא דגרמי אלא קרן אבל לחייב לשלם על ידו תשלומי ד' וה' לא חזינא ועוד אומר ריצב"א דמשום דינא דגרמי לא מחייב אלא מדרבנן כדמוכח בסוף הכונס (שם סב.) :

ורבי

מסורת הש"ס

א) קדושין נו. [ב"ק עא. חולין פה. פה.], ב) חולין יד. ב"ק עא., ג) [משום פלוגתא דר"י ור"י הסנדלר דליתא במשנה שפיר גרסי' דתניא], ד) ב"ק עא. חולין טו. גיטין נג: כילה יח: תרומות פ"ב מ"ג שבת לח. [תוספתא דשבת פ"ג], ה) [חולין קטו.], ו) [ב"ק עא: ע"ז לד: חולין מ:], ז) ב"ק מה. עא. לח., ח) ב"ק שם פסחים כט: שבועות לב. לג. [ב"ק קה:], ט) [וע"ע תוס' ב"ק עא: ד"ה איסורא ותוס' חולין פה. ד"ה דנין], י) [וע' תוס' ב"ק נד. ד"ה תמור עוד שם עא: ד"ה ופכר].

תוספות ישנים

א) ופריך אפי' למ"ד ישנה לשחיטה מתחלה ועד סוף כדאמרי' במרובה וטבחו כולו בעינן ה"נ וטבחו כולו בעינן. ת"י עה"ג].

תורה אור השלם

א) וּשְׁמַרְתֶּם אֶת הַשַּׁבָּת כִּי קֹדֶשׁ הִוא לָכֶם מְחַלְלֶיהָ מוֹת יוּמָת כִּי כָּל הָעֹשֶׂה בָהּ מְלָאכָה וְנִכְרְתָה הַנֶּפֶשׁ הַהִוא מִקֶּרֶב עַמֶּיהָ: [שמות לא, יד]

עין משפט נר מצוה

לא א מיי' (פ' יב הל' ה) ופי"ב מהל' גניבה הל' י ופ"ב מהל' שחיטה הל' ח סמג עשין סג ועשין ע ולאוין קמט טוש"ע י"ד סימן טו סעיף ט וסי' כח סעיף ז וטור ח"מ סימן שנ:
לב ב מיי' פ"ג מהל' שחיטה הל' כו סמג עשין סג טוש"ע י"ד סי' יח סעיף ג:
לג ג ד מיי' פ"ו מהל' שבת הל' כג סמג לאוין סה טוש"ע א"ח סימן שיח סעיף א:
לד ה מיי' פ"ו מהל' חובל הל' ז טוש"ע ח"מ סי' שפו סעי' ג:

ליקוטי רש"י

[תחילת לקוטי רש"י ששייך לכאן נדפס בדף לג:] במזיד לא יאכל. בו ביום והוא הדין לאחרים ולדידיה דתנא רישא בדידיה תנא נמי סיפא בדידיה והכי איבעי לן לפרושי בהכל שוחטין [ב"ק שם]. דאיכא איסורא לא יאכל בו ביום עד שתחשך ובכדי שיעשו והוא הדין לאחרים נמי דלאסור למיכליה בו ביום דטעמא משום דלא נמטייה הנאה מאיסורא הוא וכי שהי לאורתא בכדי שיעשו לא מטי לו הנאה מיניה ולדידיה דתנא רישא בדידיה דלאשמעינן רבותא להתירא תנא נמי סיפא בדידיה [חולין שם]. בשוגג. שבת מאבות מלאכות ואיסור סקילה הוא הלכך קנסוה רבנן במזיד [ביצה יז:]. ר' יהודה אומר בשוגג יאכל. הוא בעצמו למוצאי שבת וגו בו ביום לא הוא ולא אחרים ולידיה דבעי למיתנא סיפא בדידיה תנא נמי ברישא בדידיה [ב"ק שם]. ולא בשבת וה"ה לאחרים דאע"ג דבשוגג חיוב סקילה ליכא עבירה מיהא איכא ובעינן בכדי שיעשו דלא לימטייה הנאה מעבירה ולידיה דבעי למתני סיפא לא יאכל עולמית בדידיה תנא נמי בדידיה אבל לאחרים שרי דאיסורא קנסוהו רבנן ולא לאחרים ולא תנא רישא נמי בדידיה [חולין שם]. במזיד לא יאכל. עולמית אבל אחרים אוכלים [ב"ק שם]. רבי יוחנן הסנדלר אומר בשוגג יאכל למוצאי שבת. בכדי שיעשו כר' יהודה דמשוי ליה עבירה אף בשוגג ודפליג מדרבי יהודה דלאו רבי יהודה שרי ליה לאורתא אפי' לדידיה דלא קניס שוגג אטו מזיד ורבי יוחנן קניס שוגג אטו מזיד הלכך לדידיה דעבד איסורא קנסו רבנן אחריני דלא עבדי איסורא לא קנסו בכדי שיעשו ימתינו דלא ניתהני מעבירה. במזיד לא יאכל עולמית כו'. לא משום קנסא הוא דהא אחריני לא עבוד איסורא אלא מקראי יליף לה רבי יוחנן בכתובות באלו נערות (דף לד.) ובב"ק בפרק מרובה (דף עא.) ושמרתם את השבת כי קדש וגו' מה קדש אסור באכילה אף מעשה שבת אסורים באכילה יכול אפילו בשוגג ת"ל מחלליה מות יומת במזיד ולא בשוגג [חולין שם]. יכול אפילו בשוגג. יאסר באכילה. במזיד אמרתי לך. קודש הוא היכא דיש מיתה ולא בשוגג [ב"ק שם]. פליגי בה רב אחא ורבינא

חד אמר וכו'. בכל התורה כולה, כל היכא דחזית פלוגתייהו ואיתמר סתמא חד אמר לחומרא וחד אמר לקולא ולא פירש מי המיקל ומי המחמיר דע שרב אחא לחומרא ורבינא לקולא והלכתא כבולן כדברי המיקל [פסחים עד:]. מעשה שבת דאורייתא. אסורין באכילה [ב"ק שם]. כיון דשחט בה פורתא איתסר. משום זבחי מתים דקא סלקא דעתך ישנה לשחיטה מתחילה ועד סוף ומתחילתה נאסרה משום זבחי מתים ולענין כולו בעינן כדאמרינן לקמן כי גמר לה לאו דמריה קטבח שכבר אבדה ממנו קודם שחיטה ונאסרה עליו והוה ליה כמו שהשליכה לאור קודם שחיטה דמשלם קרן וכפל ותו לא [עי' תוס' דב"ק שם ובפירש"י דע שם ובת"י כאן]. בגמר זביחה הוא עובדה. לע"ז הוא עובד בגמר זביחה ולא בתחילה. שמסרו לשומר. קודם שהזיק והזיק בבית שומר כו'. כר' יעקב. בשילהי שור שנגח ד' וה'. מוחזר. ואומר לו שאע"פ שאינו שוה כלום גורם לממון הוא דכל זמן שהוא קיים שומר פוטר את עצמו בו ואם יאבד ישלם דמיו [שם:].

DELIBERATELY, [THE FOOD] MAY NEVER BE EATEN – לֹא לוֹ וְלֹא לַאֲחֵרִים – **NEITHER BY HIM NOR BY OTHER [JEWS].**[14]

The Gemara explains:

מַאי טַעְמָא דְּרַבִּי יוֹחָנָן הַסַּנְדְּלָר – **What is the reason of R' Yochanan HaSandlar** for prohibiting any Jew to partake of the deliberately cooked food ever? כִּדְדָרִישׁ רַבִּי חִיָּיא אַפִּיתְחָא דְּבֵי נְשִׂיאָה – It is **as R' Chiya expounded at the entrance to the house of the** ***Nasi:*** "וּשְׁמַרְתֶּם אֶת־הַשַּׁבָּת כִּי קֹדֶשׁ הוּא לָכֶם" – The Torah states:[15] ***And you shall observe the Sabbath, for it is consecrated for you.*** By referring to the Sabbath as "consecrated," the verse compares the Sabbath to an item consecrated for the Temple: מַה קוֹדֶשׁ אָסוּר בַּאֲכִילָה – **Just as a consecrated item is forbidden for consumption,** אַף מַעֲשֵׂה שַׁבָּת אֲסוּרִין בַּאֲכִילָה – **so too are the products of** a forbidden **Sabbath** labor **forbidden for consumption.**[16] אִי מַה קוֹדֶשׁ אָסוּר בַּהֲנָאָה – **If** so, let us also say that **just as a consecrated item is forbidden** not only for consumption but **for benefit** as well, אַף מַעֲשֵׂה שַׁבָּת אָסוּר בַּהֲנָאָה – **so too is the product of** a forbidden **Sabbath** labor **forbidden for benefit** as well. תַּלְמוּד לוֹמַר "לָכֶם" – To dispel this notion **[The Torah] states:** *it is consecrated* ***for you.*** שֶׁלָּכֶם יְהֵא – This implies that Sabbath produce **shall be yours** to use, i.e. it is permitted for benefit.[17] יָכוֹל אֲפִילוּ בְּשׁוֹגֵג – **It might be** thought that the produce of Sabbath labor is forbidden for consumption **even** when the labor was performed **inadvertently.**[18] תַּלְמוּד לוֹמַר – To dispel this notion **[The Torah] states** further in the verse:[19] "מְחַלְלֶיהָ מוֹת יוּמָת" – ***its desecrators shall be put to death,*** בְּמֵזִיד אָמַרְתִּי לְךָ וְלֹא בְשׁוֹגֵג – indicating that what **I have said to you** earlier in the verse (that the product of Sabbath desecration is forbidden like a consecrated item) **is with regard to a deliberate** act of Sabbath desecration, **and not with regard to an inadvertent** act of Sabbath desecration.[20]

The Gemara cites a dispute regarding R' Yochanan HaSandlar's position:

פְּלִיגֵי בָהּ רַב אַחָא וְרָבִינָא – **Rav Acha and Ravina argue regarding it:** חַד אָמַר מַעֲשֵׂה שַׁבָּת דְּאוֹרַיְיתָא – **One says** that the prohibition against consuming the **product of Sabbath** labor **is,** according to R' Yochanan HaSandlar, a **Biblical** prohibition. וְחַד אָמַר דְּרַבָּנָן – **And one says** that the prohibition against consuming the product of Sabbath labor is, according to R' Yochanan HaSandlar, only **Rabbinical.**

The Gemara explains:

מַאן דְּאָמַר דְּאוֹרַיְיתָא – The source for **the one who says that it is** a **Biblical** prohibition כְּדַאֲמָרָן – **is as we have said** above – namely, the verse: *And you shall observe the Sabbath, for it is consecrated for you . . .*, as expounded by R' Chiya. מַאן דְּאָמַר דְּרַבָּנָן – The source for **the one who says that it is** only **Rabbinical** is אָמַר קְרָא "קֹדֶשׁ הוּא" – that **the verse** in fact **states:** *And you shall observe the Sabbath, for* ***"it" is consecrated.*** הִיא קוֹדֶשׁ וְאֵין מַעֲשֶׂיהָ קוֹדֶשׁ – This implies that **it** [the Sabbath] itself **is consecrated, but its products are not consecrated.**[21]

The Gemara asks:

וּלְמַאן דְּאָמַר דְּרַבָּנָן מַאי טַעְמַיְיהוּ דְּרַבָּנָן דְּפָטְרֵי – **But according to the one who says** that the prohibition stated by R' Yochanan HaSandlar against consuming the product of a Sabbath labor **is** only **Rabbinic, what is the reason of the Rabbis who exempt** the thief from paying the fourfold or fivefold penalty when the stolen animal was slaughtered by his agent on the Sabbath?[22]

The Gemara answers:

כִּי קָא פָּטְרֵי רַבָּנָן אַשְּׁאָרָא – According to this view (that R' Yochanan HaSandlar forbids the product of a Sabbath labor only Rabbinically), **when the Rabbis** in the Baraisa **exempt** the thief from the fourfold or fivefold payment, they are **referring** only **to the other** two **[cases]** mentioned by R' Meir.[23]

The Gemara raises other questions with respect to the Baraisa:[24]

טוֹבֵחַ לַעֲבוֹדַת כּוֹכָבִים – In the case of **one who slaughters for idol worship,** why is the thief liable, according to R' Meir, to the fourfold or fivefold penalty altogether?[25] כֵּיוָן דְּשָׁחַט בֵּיהּ פּוּרְתָּא – **Once he cuts it a little,** אִיתְּסַר לֵיהּ – **it becomes forbidden** as an idolatrous offering.[26] אִידָךְ כִּי קָא טָבַח – Hence, **when he cuts the rest** of the amount required to complete his act of slaughter,[27] לַאו דְּמָרֵיהּ קָא טָבַח – **it is not** the animal **of the** original **owner that he is slaughtering!**[28] – ? –

NOTES

14. The food may, however, be sold or given to a non-Jew (*Rashi*).

15. *Exodus* 31:14 states: *And you shall observe the Sabbath, for it is consecrated for you; its desecrators shall be put to death . . .*

16. Thus, the food cooked on the Sabbath becomes *intrinsically* forbidden, and may not be eaten by a Jew even if enough time has elapsed so that he does not *benefit* from the fact that it was cooked on the Sabbath.

17. [Thus, it may be sold or given to a non-Jew (see above, note 14).]

18. [I.e. it might be thought that the Torah's comparison of the product of Sabbath labor to a consecrated item pertains even to the product of an *inadvertent* Sabbath labor.]

19. See note 15.

20. Only a *deliberate* Sabbath desecrator is put to death. Thus, we see that this verse refers specifically to *deliberate* desecration, not to inadvertent desecration.

21. Thus, this very verse indicates that only the Sabbath itself – and not the product of its labors – is consecrated. The verse cannot, then, mean that the product of a Sabbath labor is Biblically forbidden.

22. Since the slaughter renders the animal fit for consumption on the Biblical level, all (even R' Shimon) would agree that it is deemed an act of "slaughter" and would obligate the thief in the fourfold or fivefold payment! (see *Rashi*).

23. I.e. the case of the animal that was slaughtered for idol worship and the case of the ox that was condemned to stoning (*Rashi*). Only in those cases, where the agent's slaughter is unfit, do the Rabbis exempt the thief from fourfold or fivefold payment. They agree, however, that in the first case mentioned by R' Meir – where the thief's agent slaughtered the stolen animal on the Sabbath – the thief is liable to the fourfold or fivefold payment.

24. [The questions that follow are relevant regardless of how the Baraisa is explained – either as referring to where the thief slaughtered the animal himself or where he did so through an agent.]

25. *Rashba.*

26. The Gemara in *Chullin* (40a) states that one who slaughters an animal as an offering to an idol renders the animal an idolatrous offering forbidden for all benefit as soon as "he cuts one pipe" in the animal's throat, even though he has not yet done a complete act of slaughter (*Rashi*). [The expression "one pipe" is not specific. The reference is to the slightest cut – even if less than one pipe is cut (see *Rashi* there ד״ה היתה בהמת חבירו and Gemara there 40b).]

27. The "slaughter" of an animal requires the cutting of a majority of the animal's two pipes (i.e. the windpipe and the food-pipe), and it is only when that majority is cut that the thief becomes liable to the fourfold or fivefold payment for "slaughtering" the stolen animal; see next note.

28. For it has already become prohibited to the owner.

The Torah prescribes the fourfold or fivefold penalty for the *slaughter* of the animal, and liability, therefore, cannot take effect until the slaughter is complete. In the present case, however, the animal has already been rendered prohibited for benefit to its owner prior to the conclusion of the act of slaughter (see above, note 26). And it is from that point (before the slaughter is complete) that the owner has been deprived of his animal, for even were the slaughter not to be completed, the animal itself would no longer be returned [rather, the thief would have to pay the owner its value]; thus, it is "not the owner's" (see

רבי שמעון היא דאמר שחיטה שאינה ראויה לא שמה שחיטה. קשיא לשיטתו לר' שמעון היא דאמר **שחיטה שאינה ראויה** לא שמה שחיטה התינח עבודת כוכבים ושור הנסקל אלא שחיטת שבת שחיטה ראויה היא דתנן השוחט בשבת וביום הכפורים אע"פ שמתחייב בנפשו שחיטתו כשרה סבר לה כר' יוחנן הסנדלר דתניא המבשל בשבת בשוגג יאכל במזיד לא יאכל דברי ר"מ ר' יהודה אומר בשוגג יאכל למוצאי שבת במזיד לא יאכל עולמית רבי יוחנן הסנדלר אומר בשוגג יאכל למוצאי שבת לאחרים ולא לו במזיד לא יאכל עולמית לא לו ולא לאחרים מאי טעמא דרבי יוחנן הסנדלר כדדריש ר' חייא אפיתחא דבי נשיאה ושמרתם את השבת כי קדש היא לכם מה קודש אסור באכילה אף מעשה שבת אסורין באכילה אי מה קודש אסור בהנאה אף מעשה שבת אסור בהנאה ת"ל לכם שלכם יהא יכול אפילו בשוגג ת"ל מחלליה מות יומת במזיד אמרתי לך ולא בשוגג פליגי בה רב אחא ורבינא חד אמר מעשה שבת דאורייתא וחד אמר דרבנן מאן דאמר דאורייתא כדאמרן מאן דאמר דרבנן אמר קרא קדש היא היא קודש ואין מעשיה קודש ולמאן דאמר דרבנן מאי טעמייהו דרבנן דפטרי כי קא פטרי רבנן אשארא טובח לעבודת כוכבים כיון דשחט ביה פורתא איתסר ליה אידך כי קא טבח לאו דמריה קא טבח אמר רבא באומר בגמר זביחה הוא עובדה שור הנסקל לאו דידיה הוא דקטבח אמר רבה הכא במאי עסקינן כגון שמסרו לשומר והזיק בבית שומר ונגמר דיניה בבית שומר וגנבו גנב מבית שומר ורבי מאיר סבר לה כר' יעקב וסבר לה כר"ש סבר לה כר' יעקב דאמר אף משנגמר דינו החזירו שומר לבעליו מוחזר וסבר לה כר"ש דאמר דבר הגורם לממון כממון דמי רבה אמר לעולם בטובח על ידי עצמו ור'

רש"י

רבי שמעון. בפרק מרובה ובכסוי הדם ובאותו ואת בנו: התינח עבודת כוכבים. דזבחי מתים אסורים וכן שור הנסקל משנגמר דינו אסור בהנאה כדאמרינן בב"ק (דף מא.) ובפסחים (דף כב:) ממשמע שנאמר סקול יסקל איני יודע שהוא נבילה ונבילה כו': בשוגג יאכל. אפי' בו ביום: במזיד לא יאכל. הוא לעולם אבל אחרים ישראלים אוכלים: ר' יהודה אומר בשוגג יאכל. הוא למוצאי שבת ולא בו ביום דקנסינן שוגג אטו מזיד: במזיד לא יאכל. הוא עולמית אלא אחרים: בדרבי יוחנן הסנדלר גרסינן יאכל: לאחרים. ישראל: לא לו ולא לאחרים. ישראל אבל מוכרו ונותנו לעובדי כוכבים: מ"ט דר' יוחנן הסנדלר. דאמר מעשה שבת אסורין באכילה: יכול אפילו בשוגג. תאסר באכילה אם שגג בבישול שלא ידע שהוא שבת: מחלליה וגו'. היכא דאיכא חיוב מיתה אסירי באכילה כי קודש: במזיד אמרתי. שהוא אסור כקודש דהא גבי חיוב מיתה כתיב ולא בשוגג: מעשה שבת. במזיד אסורין מן התורה באכילה לר' יוחנן הסנדלר: מ"ט דרבנן. דפליגי אדרבי מאיר ופטרי מקנס ארבעה וחמשה הואיל ובטובח על ידי אחר אוקימתא הא שחיטה ראויה היא מדאורייתא: אשארא. אעבודת כוכבים ואשור הנסקל: כיון דשחט ביה פורתא איתסר ליה. דאמר מר (חולין דף מ.) היתה בהמת חבירו רבוצה לפני עבודת כוכבים כיון ששחט בה סימן אחד אסרה: לאו דמריה קא טבח. דהא איתסרא עליה ומיחייב בתשלומי ארבעה וחמשה טביחה כתיב בהו ועד גמר שחיטה לא מיחייב ומקמי דמטי גמר שחיטה איתסרא בהנאה על בעליה ומהשתא שעתא אפסדה מיניה דלאו איהו לא הדרא בעינא ולאו למריה היא: באומר בגמר זביחה הוא עובדה. לעבודת כוכבים אינו עובד לעבודת כוכבים עד גמר זביחה: פלוגתא דר' יעקב בבבא קמא: החזירו שומר לבעליו מוחזר. דאמר ליה תורא אשלמת לי תורא אשלימית לך: כממון דמי. והאי נמי אע"ג דלא שוי מידי גורם לממון הוא דכי ליתא בעי לשלומי ליה תורא מעליא: דר' שמעון בבבא קמא בפרק מרובה קדשים שחייב באחריותן משלם ארבעה וחמשה משום דגורם לממון הוא ואע"ג דהקדש לאו ממון בעלים הוא והקדש לא שייך קנס דרעהו כתיב: רבה גרסינן בכולהו ותדע מדאמר לקמן א"ל רב פפא לאביי לרבה דאמר חידוש הוא כו' ואם איתא דרבא גרסינן הא רב פפא תלמידו של רבא היה כדאמר לקמן אמר ליה רב פפא לרבא הי מכה מאי שנא דשבקיה לרבא ולא שייליה [לתרולי שמעתיה] ושייליה לאביי [שמעתא דרבא] אלא רבה גרסינן ורב פפא לא היה בימיו ושייל לאביי שהיה תלמידו של רבה: רבה אמר לעולם בטובח בעצמו ור'

תוספות

רבי שמעון היא דאמר שחיטה שאינה ראויה לא שמה שחיטה. תימה לעד לכאן לא פליגי רבנן התם גבי אותו ואת בנו אלא כדמפרש התם בחולין (דף פה.) טעמא דנין שחיטה מבשחיטה פירוש משחוטי חוץ ואין דנין שחיטה מטביחה אבל הכא גבי תשלומי ד' וה' דכתיב טביחה אית לן למילף טביחה מטביחה ולא שמה שחיטה ואור"י דאיכא למימר דנין דבר שנאמר בסיני מדבר שנאמר בסיני וכן דנין דבר שנאמר בסיני מטבח ותבוח והכן שלא נאמר בסיני והתם נמי ה"מ למימר הכי אלא דלית ליה שניה אחרינא א"נ י"ל דצריך שינוי דהתם דנין שחיטה משחיטה דאי הוה כתיב טביחה גבי אותו ואת בנו הוה ילפינן הכא והתם מטבוח טבח והכן טביחה מטביחה אע"ג דלא נאמרה בסיני דהוי בדדמי מדנילף טביחה משחיטה דלא דמי אע"ג דנאמרה בסיני אבל השתא דכתיב שחיטה גבי אותו ואת בנו דנין שחיטה משחיטה ולפינן נמי השתא אטביחה דד' וה' ולפסלה ליכא למימר דנין טביחה דתשלומי ד' וה' מטביחה ומלמד מהתם משחיטה דאותו ואת בנו דלוכה דיון דשקולים הן ואיכא למילף הכי ואיכא למילף הכי אית לן למימר דנין דבר הנאמר בסיני ממה שנאמר בסיני:

המבשל בשבת בשוגג יאכל. פי' ב"ב בו ביום ואפילו הוא כדמוכח בפ' כירה (שבת לח.) דבעו מרבי חייא בר אבא שכח קדירה על גבי כירה ובשלה בשבת כו' עד המבשל בשבת כו' בשוגג יאכל ולאותו שבת קא בעי התם אי אסיר גזרה שלא יאמר שוכח אני במזיד לא יאכל פירוש בין הוא בין אחרים בו ביום אבל במוצאי שבת לדידיה נמי שרי דהא בפ' קמא דחולין (דף טו. ושם) אההיא מתני' דהשוחט בשבת וביוה"כ אע"פ שמתחייב בנפשו שחיטתו כשרה פריך ונוקמא במזיד ור' מאיר ומשני לא סלקא דעתין דקתני שבת דומיא דיוה"כ מה יוה"כ לא שנא שוגג ול"ש מזיד והשתא אי לאחרים שרי בו ביום לפרוך ממזיד גופיה מה יוה"כ לא שנא לו ולא שנא לאחרים כו' ואי לדידיה אסור אף למוצאי שבת הוה ליה למימר שחיטתו כשרה קתני ל"ש לו לא שנא לאחרים כדקאמר התם על ר' יוחנן הסנדלר ועוד דא"כ היינו מזיד דר' יהודה כמו שאפרש ומדאצטריך לרבי יהודה לאפוקי מזיד במילתיה משמע דפליג נמי אמזיד: **בשוגג** יאכל במוצאי שבת. שוגג דר' יהודה הוי כמו שפירשתי מזיד דר"מ דהא מוקי התם מתני' דהשוחט בשבת כוותיה: **במזיד** לא יאכל עולמית. הוא אבל אחרים אוכלים דאי אחרים נמי לא יאכלו עולמית היינו מזיד דרבי יוחנן הסנדלר כללא דמילתא מזיד דרבי מאיר שוגג דרבי יהודה מזיד דרבי יהודה שוגג דרבי יוחנן הסנדלר: **אמר** קרא לכם. וא"ת ולא לכתוב לא קדש ולא לכם ואנא ידענא דאסירי באכילה מלא תאכל כל תועבה תעבתי לך הרי הוא בבל תאכל וי"ל דאי מהתם ה"א בין שוגג בין מזיד להכי איצטריך למכתב הכא למסמכיה למחלליה לומר במזיד אמרתי לך ולא בשוגג: **היא** קדש ואין מעשיה קודש. ואין להקשות דלא לכתוב לא היא ולא קדש דהוה אסורה באכילה מכל אשר תיעבתי לך והכי אמרי' בהדיא בפ' כל הבשר (חולין קטו. ושם): **מאי** טעמא דרבנן דפטרי. לא בעי למימר דלא דרשי או ותחת לרבות את השליח דלא ניחא ליה למימר דפליגי בשליח: **כי** קא פטרי רבנן אשארא. וא"ת אמאי אצטריך למתני כלל טבח בשבת דאפי' בשחיטה שאינה ראויה מחייב ר"מ כ"ש הא דשחיטה ראויה היא וי"ל דזו אף זו קתני: **כיון** דשחט בה פורתא אסרה ואידך כו'. וא"ת כל טובח נמי לאו דמריה קא טבח דמכי שחט פורתא קניא בשינוי אלא ע"כ בהכי חייב רחמנא והכא נמי לא שנא ואור"י דלא חשיב שינוי לקנותה בכך: **סבר** לה כר"ש דאמר דבר הגורם לממון כו'. וא"ת ואמאי לא קאמר דר"מ לטעמיה דדאין דינא דגרמי (ב"ק ק.) גבי מקדש תבואת חבירו או שורף שטרות חבירו (שם לח:) וכ"ש דמחייב בדבר הגורם לממון כדאמר התם בהגוזל (שם לח:) דלמא עד כאן לא קאמר ר"ש אלא בדבר שעיקרו ממון אבל שטר דאין גופו ממון לא וי"ל דאיכא למימר נמי איפכא דעד כאן לא קאמר ר"מ אלא בשורף שטרות של חבירו או מקדש תבואת חבירו שהוא ממון הראוי לכל העולם אבל שור הנסקל אין ראוי אלא לזה השומר שיפטור עצמו וי"מ דמשום הכי קאמר ס"ל כר"ש משום דר"ש קאמר דבר הגורם לממון הוי ממון לענין תשלומי ד' וה' דלהכי תני ליה במרובה (שם עא:) ואילו ר' מאיר לא חזינא דמיחייב בדינא דגרמי אלא הרן אבל לחייב לשלם על ידו תשלומי ד' וה' לא חזינא ועוד אומר ריצב"א דמשום דינא דגרמי לא מחייב אלא מדרבנן כדמוכח בסוף הכונס (שם סב.):

ורבי

חד **אמר וכו'**. בכל התורה כולה, כל היכא דחזית פלוגתייהו ואיתמר סתמא חד אמר לקולא וחד אמר לחומרא ולא פירש מי המיקל ומי המחמיר דע שרב אחא לחומרא ורבינא לקולא והלכתא כוותיה כדברי המיקל [פסחים עד:]. **מעשה שבת דאורייתא**. אסורין באכילה [ב"ק שם]. **כיון דשחט בה פורתא איתסר**. משום זבחי מתים דקא סלקא דעתך ישנה לשחיטה מתחילה ועד סוף ומתחילתה נאסרה משום זבחי מתים ולענין כולו בעינן כדאמרינן לקמן כי גמר לה לאו דמריה קטבח שכבר אבדה ממנו קודם שחיטה ונאסרה עליו והוה ליה כמו שהשליכה לאור קודם שחיטה דמשלם קרן וכפל ותו לא [עי' תוס' ב"ק שם ובפירש"י שם]. **באומר בגמר זביחה הוא עובדה**. לע"ז לא עובד בגמר זביחה ולא לפני כן. **כר' יעקב**. בשלה שור שנגח ד' וה'. **מוחזר**. קודם שנגמר דינו הוא החזירו לבעליו, מוחזר. ולומר לו הרי שלך לפניך נמצאת שאע"פ שאינו שוה כלום גורם לממון הוא שאם זמן לא הוי השור קיים שומר פוטר את עצמו בו ואם יאבד לשלם דמיו [שם ב:].

א) קדושין נז. [ב"ק עא. חולין פ. פה.], ב) חולין יד. ב"ק עא., ג) [משום פלוגתא דר"מ ור"י הסנדלר ליתא במשנה שפיר גרסי' **דתניא**], ד) ב"ק עא. חולין טו. גיטין נג: בילה יז: תרומות פ"ב מ"ג שבת לח. [תוספתא דשבת פ"ג], ה) [חולין קטו.], ו) [ב"ק עא: לד: חולין מ:], ז) ב"ק מה. עא: לח., ח) ב"ק שם פסחים כט: שבועות לג. לג. [ב"ק קה.], ט) [וע"ע תוס' ב"ק עא: ד"ה איסורא ותוס' חולין פה. ד"ה דנין], י) [וע' תוס' ב"ק נד. ד"ה תמור עוד שם עא: ד"ה וסבר].

תוספות ישנים

א) ופריך אפי' למ"ד ישנה לשחיטה מתחלה ועד סוף כדאמרי' במרובה וטבחו כולו בעינן וטבחו כולו בעינן. מ"י עה"ג.

תורה אור השלם

א) וּשְׁמַרְתֶּם אֶת הַשַּׁבָּת כִּי קֹדֶשׁ הִוא לָכֶם מְחַלְלֶיהָ מוֹת יוּמָת כִּי כָּל הָעֹשֶׂה בָהּ מְלָאכָה וְנִכְרְתָה הַנֶּפֶשׁ הַהִוא מִקֶּרֶב עַמֶּיהָ: [שמות לא, יד]

עין משפט נר מצוה

לא א מיי' (פ' יב הל' ה) ופי"ב מהל' שחיטה הל' י ופ"ב מהל' גניבה הל' ח סמג עשין סד ועי' ולאוין קמט טוש"ע י"ד סימן טז סעיף ט ופי' ט כת סעיף יד וטור ח"מ סימן שנ:

לב ב מיי' פ"א מהל' שחיטה הל' כט סמג עשין סג טוש"ע י"ד סי' יא סעיף ב:

לג ג ד מיי' פ"ו מהל' שבת הל' כג סמג לאוין סה טוש"ע א"ח סימן שיח סעיף א:

לד ה מיי' פ"ג מהל' מוכל הל' ז טוש"ע ח"מ סי' שפו סעי' ב:

ליקוטי רש"י

[תחילת לקוטי רש"י שייך לכאן נדפס בדף לג:]

במזיד לא יאכל. בו ביום והוא הדין לאחרים ולאידך דתנא רישא בדידיה תנא נמי סיפא בדידיה והכי איבעי לן לפרושי בהכל שוחטין [ב"ק שם]. דאיכא איסורא לא יאכל בו ביום עד שתחשך ובכדי שיעשו והוא הדין לאחרים נמי דאסור למיכליה בו ביום דטעמא משום דלא נמטייה הנאה מאיסורא הוא וכי שרי לאורתא בכדי שיעשו לא מטי ליה הנאה מיניה ולאידך דתנא רישא בדידיה דלאשמעינן רבותא להתירא תנא נמי סיפא בדידיה [חולין שם]. בשוגג שבת מלאכות מלאכה הוא ואיסור סקילה הוא הלכך קנסוה רבנן במזיד [ביצה יז.]. **ר' יהודה אומר בשוגג יאכל.** הוא עצמו למוצאי שבת ובו ביום לא הוא ולא אחרים ולאידך דבעי לאיתנא סיפא בדידיה תנא נמי רישא בדידיה [ב"ק שם]. ולא בשבת והכי נמי לאחריני אף בשוגג ובדפסיק מדרבי יהודה דאילו רבי יהודה שרי ליה לאורתא אפי' לדידיה דלא קנים שוגג אטו מזיד ורבי יוחנן קנים שוגג אטו מזיד הלכך קיהו דעבד איסורא קנסו רבנן אחריני דלא עבדי איסורא לא קנסו אלא בכדי שיעשו ימתינו דלא ניהנו מעבירה. **במזיד לא יאכל עולמית כו'.** לאו משום קנסא הוא דהא אחריני לא עבוד איסורא אלא מקראי יליף לה כר' יוחנן כתובות בפלוגתא בהלו נערות (דף לד.) ובב"ק בפרק מרובה (דף עא.) ושמרתם את השבת כי קדש וגו' מה קדש אסור באכילה יכול אסורים באכילה יכול אפילו בשוגג ת"ל מחלליה מות יומת במזיד ולא בשוגג [חולין שם]. **יכול אפילו בשוגג.** יאסר באכילה. **במזיד אמרתי לך.** קודש הוא היכא דשייך ביה מיתה ולא היכא דלא שייך [ב"ק שם]. **פליגי בה רב אחא ורבינא**.

רַבִּי שִׁמְעוֹן הִיא דְּאָמַר – **It is** an opinion authored by **R' Shimon, who says:**[1] שְׁחִיטָה שֶׁאֵינָהּ רְאוּיָה לֹא שְׁמָהּ שְׁחִיטָה – **A slaughter that is not fit,** i.e. that does not render the animal fit for consumption, **is not termed "a slaughter."**[2]

The Gemara persists:

הָתֵינַח עֲבוֹדַת כּוֹכָבִים וְשׁוֹר הַנִּסְקָל – **This** explanation of why the Sages exempt the thief from the fourfold or fivefold payment **is satisfactory** with regard to the case in which the animal was slaughtered for **idol worship** and the case of the **ox** condemned **to be stoned.**[3] אֶלָּא שְׁחִיטַת שַׁבָּת שְׁחִיטָה רְאוּיָה הִיא – **But** this does not explain why the Sages exempt the thief from the fourfold or fivefold penalty in the Baraisa's first case, where the agent slaughtered the animal on the Sabbath, for **a slaughter** performed **on the Sabbath is a valid slaughter!** דִּתְנַן – **For we learned in a Mishnah:**[4] הַשּׁוֹחֵט בְּשַׁבָּת וּבְיוֹם הַכִּפּוּרִים – IF ONE SLAUGHTERS an animal ON THE SABBATH OR ON YOM KIPPUR, אַף עַל פִּי שֶׁמִּתְחַיֵּיב בְּנַפְשׁוֹ – EVEN THOUGH HE IS LIABLE TO PAY WITH HIS LIFE,[5] שְׁחִיטָתוֹ כְּשֵׁרָה – HIS act of SLAUGHTER IS VALID, and the animal is fit for consumption. – ? –

The Gemara answers:

סָבַר לָהּ כְּרַבִּי יוֹחָנָן הַסַּנְדְּלָר – In regard to a slaughter performed on the Sabbath, **he** [the author of the Sages' view in the Baraisa] **holds with R' Yochanan HaSandlar,** who forbids the slaughtered animal for consumption.[6] דְּתַנְיָא – **For it was taught in a Baraisa:** הַמְבַשֵּׁל בְּשַׁבָּת – IF ONE transgresses and COOKS food ON THE SABBATH, בְּשׁוֹגֵג יֹאכַל – if he did so INADVERTENTLY,[7] HE MAY EAT[8] what he cooked; בְּמֵזִיד לֹא יֹאכַל – if he did so DELIBERATELY, intentionally disregarding the Torah's law, HE MAY NOT EAT what he cooked;[9] דִּבְרֵי רַבִּי מֵאִיר – these are THE WORDS OF R' MEIR. רַבִּי יְהוּדָה אוֹמֵר – R' YEHUDAH SAYS: בְּשׁוֹגֵג יֹאכַל לְמוֹצָאֵי שַׁבָּת – If he did so INADVERTENTLY, HE MAY EAT the food AFTER THE SABBATH DEPARTS (i.e. on Saturday night);[10] בְּמֵזִיד לֹא יֹאכַל עוֹלָמִית – if he did so DELIBERATELY, HE MAY NOT EAT the food EVER.[11] רַבִּי יוֹחָנָן הַסַּנְדְּלָר אוֹמֵר – R' YOCHANAN HASANDLAR SAYS: בְּשׁוֹגֵג יֵאָכֵל לְמוֹצָאֵי שַׁבָּת – If he did so INADVERTENTLY, [THE FOOD] MAY BE EATEN AFTER THE DEPARTURE OF THE SABBATH לַאֲחֵרִים וְלֹא לוֹ – BY OTHER [JEWS],[12] BUT NOT BY HIM.[13] בְּמֵזִיד לֹא יֵאָכֵל עוֹלָמִית – If he did so

NOTES

1. In *Bava Kamma* 71a and in *Chullin* 80a, 81a, 85b (*Rashi*).

2. In *Chullin* 85a, R' Shimon derives through Biblical exegesis that wherever the Torah refers to "slaughter" it refers to a slaughter that renders the animal fit for consumption. Hence, R' Shimon maintains that the Biblical prohibition against slaughtering a mother animal and her offspring on the same day (*Leviticus* 22:28) and the Biblical command to cover the blood of a slaughtered beast or bird do not apply if the slaughter did not render the animal permissible for consumption. Thus, for example, if the slaughtered beast was found to suffer from a defect that renders it a *tereifah* and prohibited for consumption, its blood does not require covering. Similarly, in the case of an animal, it would be permitted to slaughter the offspring on the same day. And similarly, the fourfold or fivefold payment for stealing and "slaughtering" a sheep or an ox does not apply if the slaughter does not render the animal permissible for consumption, e.g. if it was slaughtered for idol worship or if it had been condemned to stoning; see next note.

Thus, the "Sages" in the Baraisa, who dispute R' Meir and exempt the thief from the fourfold or fivefold payment, are none other than R' Shimon, who exempts the thief because the slaughter done by his agent was "a slaughter that is unfit."

3. An animal slaughtered for idol worship is forbidden for consumption or any other benefit (see *Avodah Zarah* 29b). And an ox slaughtered after it was condemned to stoning by the court is forbidden for consumption or any other benefit [see *Pesachim* 22b and *Bava Kamma* 41a] (*Rashi*). Thus, the slaughter of these stolen animals is indeed an unfit slaughter, and that would account for why the Sages exempt the thief from the fourfold or fivefold payment.

4. *Chullin* 14a.

5. One who performs a *melachah* (such as "slaughter") on the Sabbath is liable to the death penalty; if he performs it on Yom Kippur, he is liable to *kares* (Mishnah, *Megillah* 7b).

6. Thus, the agent's slaughter of the animal on the Sabbath is unfit, and the thief does not pay the fourfold or fivefold payment.

7. I.e. he did not realize that it was the Sabbath or that his act of cooking was forbidden on the Sabbath.

8. Even on the Sabbath itself (*Rashi*). For this Tanna (R' Meir) does not penalize one for benefiting from his sin when the sin was committed unintentionally (see *Rashi* to *Chullin* 15a; see also *Gittin* 53b).

9. We penalize him that he never partake of this food. Other Jews, however, may eat the food [even on the Sabbath itself; see *Shitah Mekubetzes'* explanation of *Rashi*] (*Rashi;* cf. *Tosafos* ד״ה המבשל and *Rashi* to *Chullin* 15a לא יאכל).

10. But he may not eat it on the Sabbath itself, because – in R' Yehudah's view – we penalize in the case of inadvertent acts on account of deliberate acts [so that a person should not cook deliberately on the Sabbath and say that he did so inadvertently (see *Rashba*)] (*Rashi;* see following note).

[*Shitah Mekubetzes* deduces that according to *Rashi,* others are permitted to eat the food even on the Sabbath itself. For since the reason we prohibit the food on the Sabbath itself is that we penalize in the case of inadvertent acts on account of deliberate acts, others, who did nothing wrong, cannot be penalized and would be permitted to eat the food even on the Sabbath itself. Cf. *Tosafos* here, and *Rashi* to *Chullin* ibid. ד״ה ר׳ יהודה אומר בשוגג יאכל למוצאי שבת.]

11. He may never eat the food, but others may do so (*Rashi*). That is, others may eat the food after the Sabbath [in contrast to the one who cooked the food itself, whom we penalize and forbid to partake from the food ever]. They are, however, forbidden to eat the food on the Sabbath itself. For R' Yehudah [in contrast to R' Meir – see above, note 9] maintains that it is forbidden for anyone to benefit from a deliberate act of Sabbath desecration. Hence, on the Sabbath itself, the food is forbidden even for others, for others would not have been able to eat the food on the Sabbath itself had it not been cooked on the Sabbath. After the Sabbath, however, once enough time has passed on Saturday night that the food could have been cooked permissibly, it is permitted for others to eat the food. For, at that point, they would no longer be benefiting from the fact that the food was cooked on the Sabbath, since they could have the same benefit even if the cooking of the food had not begun until after the Sabbath (see *Shitah Mekubetzes'* explanation of *Rashi*).

[*Rashba* asks: Since R' Yehudah maintains that we penalize the deliberate transgressor by forbidding him to partake of the food ever, and he also maintains that we penalize in the case of inadvertent acts on account of deliberate acts (see preceding note), the inadvertent transgressor should likewise be penalized and be forbidden to partake of the food ever! Why does R' Yehudah rule that the inadvertent transgressor *may* eat the food after the Sabbath? *Rashba* answers that since we penalize in the case of inadvertent acts only in order to deter a person from doing the act deliberately and claiming that he did so inadvertently (see preceding note), we need not make both penalties identical. Rather, this limited penalty, which eliminates the benefit gained by cooking on the Sabbath, is a sufficient deterrent.]

12. Whereas R' Yehudah forbids benefiting from an act of Sabbath desecration only if the act was *deliberate* (see above, notes 10 and 11), R' Yochanan HaSandlar forbids benefiting from such an act even if it was *inadvertent.* Thus, even in the case of inadvertent transgression, R' Yochanan HaSandlar prohibits any Jew to eat the cooked food until enough time has passed after the Sabbath for the food to have been cooked permissibly (see *Rashi,* and *Shitah Mekubetzes* cited above in notes 10 and 11; cf. *Rashi* to *Chullin* ibid. ד״ה ר׳ יהודה אומר בשוגג יאכל במוצ״ש and ד״ה ר׳ יוחנן הסנדלר אומר בשוגג יאכל למוצ״ש; see also *Pnei Yehoshua* here).

13. Whereas R' Yehudah differentiates between the penalty imposed on the deliberate offender and the one imposed on the inadvertent offender (see above note 11), R' Yochanan HaSandlar penalizes them equally and forbids even the inadvertent offender from ever partaking of the food he cooked. Other people, however, whom we have no reason to penalize, may eat it after the Sabbath once enough time has passed for the food to have been cooked permissibly (see *Rashi* to *Chullin* ibid.).

Baraisa: ,,אוֹ״ לְרַבּוֹת אֶת הַשָּׁלִיחַ – The word *OR* is superfluous to teach us TO INCLUDE slaughter or sale through AN AGENT in the law of liability to the fourfold or fivefold payment.[31] דְּבֵי חִזְקִיָּה תָּנָא – **The academy of Chizkiyah taught in a Baraisa:** ,,תַּחַת״ לְרַבּוֹת אֶת הַשָּׁלִיחַ – The word *INSTEAD* is superfluous to teach us TO INCLUDE slaughter or sale through AN AGENT in the law of liability to the fourfold or fivefold payment.[32]

The Gemara above answered that R' Meir agrees that one who incurs the death penalty is exempt from monetary liability incurred simultaneously, and R' Meir's ruling in the Baraisa that a thief is liable to the fourfold or fivefold penalty when the animal was slaughtered on the Sabbath or for idol worship pertains only to cases in which it was slaughtered through the thief's agent. The Gemara, now, raises an objection:

מַתְקִיף לָהּ מַר זוּטְרָא – **Mar Zutra objected to this:** מִי אִיכָּא מִידִי – **Can there be such a thing** דְּאִילוּ עָבֵד אִיהוּ לֹא מִיחַיַּיב – **that if he does it himself he is not liable,** וְעָבִיד שָׁלִיחַ וּמִחַיַּיב – **yet** his **agent does it and he** ***is*** **liable?**[33]

The Gemara answers:

אִיהוּ לַאו מִשּׁוּם דְּלֹא מִיחַיַּיב – **He** is exempt when he slaughters it himself **not because he is not liable,** אֶלָּא מִשּׁוּם דְּקָם לֵיהּ בִּדְרַבָּה מִינֵּיהּ – **but because he is subject to the penalty greater than [payment].**[34]

The Gemara asks further:

אִי בְּטוֹבֵחַ עַל יְדֵי אַחֵר – **If** the Baraisa in which R' Meir rules that the thief is liable to the fourfold or fivefold penalty when the animal was slaughtered on the Sabbath or for idol worship refers to **where he slaughtered** it **through another person,** מַאי טַעֲמַיְיהוּ דְּרַבָּנַן דְּפָטְרִי – then **what is the reason of the Rabbis who** dispute R' Meir and **exempt** the thief from payment?[35]

The Gemara answers:

מַאן חֲכָמִים – **Who** is the author of the opinion attributed by the Baraisa to **the Sages?**

NOTES

31. The verse states: ,,וּטְבָחוֹ אוֹ״ מְכָרוֹ, *and slaughters it* ***or*** *sells it* . . . (the entire verse is cited above, note 22). The simple meaning of the phrase is that the thief is liable if he either slaughters *or* sells the animal. The word אוֹ, *or,* however, is considered superfluous, since the verse could have conveyed the same idea in one word by writing וּמְכָרוֹ. [According to the academy of R' Yishmael, the *vav* prefix can have the meaning of "or"] (see *Tosafos, Bava Kamma* 71a ד״ה או לרבות את השליח).

32. The verse states: חֲמִשָּׁה בָקָר יְשַׁלֵּם ,,תַּחַת״ הַשּׁוֹר, *five cattle he shall pay "instead" of the ox.* The word תַּחַת is superfluous, for the Torah could have written simply יְשַׁלֵּם בַּשּׁוֹר, *he shall pay for the ox* (*Rashi*).

33. If the thief himself had slaughtered it on the Sabbath or for idol worship, he would not be liable to the fourfold or fivefold payment, for he would be liable to execution (see *Rashi*). How, then, can he be liable if his agent slaughters it in this manner? There is a rule that one cannot accomplish through an agent that which he could not accomplish personally! (see *Kiddushin* 23b and *Nedarim* 35b).

34. That is, in essence he *is* liable to the fourfold or fivefold payment when he slaughters it himself, and it is only because of the rule that *he is subject to the penalty greater than it* that he does not make actual payment (*Rashi*). [And when he slaughters it through his agent and is thus not subject to any greater penalty that would exempt him from actual payment, he remains liable to the payment.]

35. If the Baraisa refers to where the thief slaughtered the animal himself and R' Meir rules that he is obligated to payment despite the fact that he is simultaneously liable to execution, then we can understand the view of the Sages: They subscribe to the rule that *he is subject to the penalty greater than it.* But if the Baraisa refers to where the thief slaughtered the animal through an agent, then why do the Sages exempt the thief from payment?

[*Shitah Mekubetzes* presents various reasons why the Gemara does not answer simply that the Sages reject the expositions cited above and maintain that the general principle that one is not liable for a transgression committed by his agent applies to the fourfold or fivefold payment as well. See also *Tosafos* below, 34a ד״ה מאי.]

כז א מיי' פ"ד מהל' רוצח ושמירת נפש הל' ג: כח ב ג מיי' פ"א מהל' גניבה הל' ו: כט ד מיי' פ"ב שם הל' ו: ל ה מיי' פ"ג שם ה"ג:

ליקוטי רש"י

אילמלי נגדוה וכו' פלחו לצלמא. במתניה [רש"י בשיטמ"ק בשם רשב"א]. **אלא לרבי דאמר.** התם נתכוון להרוג את זה והרג את זה אינו נהרג אלא משלם דמי אשה ואע"ג דלא אתרו ביה אבל התרו ביה אימא לך לוקה ואינו משלם [רש"י כת"י משיטמ"ק]. **ממון.** דמי האשה יתן ליורשיה [סנהדרין עט.]. **על משענתו.** על בוריו וכחו [שמות כא, יט]. מתרגמינן על בוריה שנתרפא לגמרי ונשען על כחו. **וכי תעלה על דעתך.** למה לי למימר ונקה המכה מיתה [סנהדרין עח:]. **ונקה המכה וכו' שחובשין אותו.** ... **שבתו.** בטול מלאכתו ... **ורפא ירפא.** כתרגומו ישלם שכר הרופא [ב"ק פ"ה] [שמות שם]. **ריש לקיש אמר.** ... **רבי מאיר היא.** ... **גנב וטבח בשבת.** ... **שור הנסקל.** ... **חוטא וזה מתחייב.** ... **מה מכירה.** ... **אף טביחה.** ... משלם תשלומי ד' וה'. **תנא או.** לרבות אפילו שליח. **תחת לרבות.** תחת השור תחת השה, דחד מינייהו יתירה הוא ודרוש לרבות שאם מינה שליח תחתיו לטבוח חייב הגנב [קידושין מג.]. **עבד איהו לא מיחייב.** קנס דהא מיקטל [רש"י משיטמ"ק עיי"ש] ליה לאו משום דלא מיחייב אלא משום דקם ליה בדרבה מיניה [ב"ק שם]. **מאן חכמים.** כלומר מאן נינהו ומאי טעמייהו [גיטין כב.]. [מכאן שייך לדף לד.] **ר' שמעון היא.** דאמר לענין כיסוי הדם (חולין דף פה.) ואותו ואת בנו (שם דף פ.) ותשלומי ארבעה וחמשה (ב"ק דף עא.) שחיטה שאינה ראויה לאכילה לא שמיה שחיטה וכל חיוב ואיסור הבא ע"י שחיטה אינו חל עליה [קידושין נח.]. כדתנן בפרקין (ב"ק ע.) רבי שמעון פוטר בשני אלו. **התינח עבודת כוכבים ושור הנסקל.** איסורי הנאה נינהו דאמר במסכת ע"ז (דף נד.) אע"פ שאמרו המשתחוה לבהמת חבירו לא אסרה עשה בה מעשה אסרה [ב"ק עא.]. **וביום הכפורים** מתחייב כרת [חולין יד.]. **המבשל בשבת.** בידים דאיכא חיובא דאורייתא [שבת לח.]. **בשוגג יאכל.** אפי' הוא עצמו ואפילו בו ביום [ב"ק שם]. הוא עצמו וכו ביום ואין צריך להמתין עד הערב בכדי שיעשו דהא דאמרינן בעלמא לערב בכדי שיעשו לית ליה לר"מ אלא היכא דעבד ישראל איסורא ובמזיד דאיכא חיובא דלא נמטייה הנאה מאיסורא אבל בשוגג לא [חולין טו.].

דלמא מלקות חמור דאמר רב אילמלי נגדוה לחנניה מישאל ועזריה פלחו לצלמא א"ל רב סמא בריה דרב אסי לרב אשי ואמרי לה רב סמא בריה דרב אשי לרב אשי ולא שני לך בין הכאה שיש לה קצבה להכאה שאין לה קצבה מתקיף לה רב יעקב מנהר פקוד הניחא לרבנן דאמרי נפש ממש אלא לרבי דאמר ממון מאי איכא למימר אלא אמר רב יעקב מנהר פקוד משמיה דרבא מהכא א) אם יקום והתהלך בחוץ על משענתו ונקה המכה וכי תעלה על דעתך שזה מהלך בשוק וזה נהרג אלא מלמד שחובשין אותו ואי מית קטלינן ליה ואי לא מית שבתו יתן ורפא ירפא היכי דמי אי דלא אתרו ביה אמאי מיקטיל אלא פשיטא דאתרו ביה ומותרה לדבר חמור מותרה לדבר הקל ואמר רחמנא א) שבתו יתן ורפא ירפא מתקיף לה רב אשי ממאי דמותרה לדבר חמור הוי מותרה לדבר הקל דלמא לא הוי ואם תמצא לומר הוי ממאי דמיתה חמורה דלמא מלקות חמור דאמר רב אילמלי נגדוה לחנניה מישאל ועזריה פלחו לצלמא א"ל רב סמא בריה דרב אסי לרב אשי ואמרי לה רב סמא בריה דרב אשי לרב אשי ולא שני לך בין הכאה שיש לה קצבה להכאה שאין לה קצבה מתקיף לה רב מרי ממאי דבמזיד ונקה מקטלא דלמא בשוגג ונקה מגלות קשיא: ריש לקיש אמר הא מני רבי מאיר היא דאמר לוקה ומשלם אי רבי מאיר אפי' בתו נמי וכי תימא ר' מאיר לוקה ומשלם אית ליה מת ומשלם לית ליה ולא והתניא גנב וטבח בשבת גנב וטבח לעבודת כוכבים גנב שור הנסקל וטבחו ב) משלם תשלומי ארבעה וחמשה דברי רבי מאיר וחכמים פוטרין הא איתמר עלה אמר רבי יעקב א"ר יוחנן ואמרי לה אמר רבי ירמיה אמר ר' שמעון בן לקיש ר' אבין ורבי אילעא וכל חבורתא משמיה דרבי יוחנן אמרי בטובח על ידי אחר וכי זה חוטא וזה מתחייב אמר רבא אמר רחמנא ב) וטבחו או מכרו מה מכירה על ידי אחר אף טביחה על ידי אחר דבי רבי ישמעאל תנא או לרבות את השליח דבי חזקיה תנא ב) תחת לרבות את השליח מתקיף לה מר זוטרא מי איכא מידי דאילו עבד איהו לא מיחייב ועביד שליח ומחייב איהו לאו משום דלא מיחייב אלא משום דקם ליה בדרבה מיניה אי בטובח על ידי אחר מאי טעמייהו דרבנן דפטרי מאן חכמים רבי

נגדוה. יסורין: ולא שני לך כו'. יסורי המלכות הכאה שאין לה קצבה היא אבל מלקות יש לה קצבה ארבעים: **הניחא לרבנן דאמרי.** בסנהדרין באלו הן הנשרפים (עט.) נתכוון להרוג את זה והרג את זה חייב והאי ונתת נפש תחת נפש ממש קאמר אית לן למידק ואוקמי קרא בשהתרו בו ולמילף דאע"ג דאיכא התראה יענש ממון כשאין שם מיתה: **אלא לרבי דאמר.** התם נתכוון להרוג את זה והרג את זה אינו נהרג אלא משלם דמי האשה ליורשיה אם כן אפשר לאוקמי קרא בשלא התרו בו ומשום הכי כי אין אסון משלם דמי ולדות וכי יש אסון משלם דמי אשה אבל אתרו ביה אימא לך לוקה ואינו משלם: **מאי איכא למימר.** מהיכא תיתי חובל בחבירו לתשלומין ואף כשהתרו בו: **על משענתו.** כדמתרגמינן על בוריו ששב לכחו ולאיתנו הראשון: **אלא מלמד שחובשין אותו.** לא נאמר מקרא זה אלא ללמדך דהיכא דהכהו ולא מת ונפל למשכב יחבשו את המכה ההוא בבית האסורין עד שנראה אם יקום והתהלך בחוץ אז ונקה המכה מכלל דעד השתא לא יצא מידי בית דין אלא נחבש: **ואי מיית קטלינן ליה.** [כיון דאמרת חובשין מכלל דאי מיית ניזק קטלינן ליה להאי דאי לאו לקטלא למאי חבשינן ליה: **לדבר חמור.** מיתה: **לדבר הקל.** מלקות דלא יוסיף דחובל ולא מת]: **ואמר רחמנא.** להיכא דלא מת דאיכא ממון ומלקות נידון בממון דכתיב שבתו יתן: **ממאי.** דהאי והכה איש את רעהו במזיד קא משתעי והאי ונקה דילפינן מיניה חבישה ונקה מקטלא קאמר דתשמע מינה דאי מיית קטלינן ליה ועל כרחין בהתרו בו: **דלמא בשוגג.** משתעי ולא התרו בו וחבישה לאו לקטלא ונקה נמי לאו לקטלא אלא מגלות דערי מקלט וחבישה דילפינן מינה לגלות קאמר ומשום הכי כי נקה מגלות ישלם ממון אבל היכא דאתרו ביה אימא לך דכי לא מיית לוקה ואינו משלם: **ריש לקיש** מהדר אשינויא דרומיא דרמינן בריש שמעתין מתני' דמכות אדכתובות: **הא מני.** מתניתין דקתני בא על אחותו נותן קנס ר"מ היא דאמר לעיל לוקה ומשלם שלא השם המביאו לידי מכות מביאו לידי תשלומין: **אפי' בתו נמי.** דמיקטיל עלה לישלם דהא לא סבירא ליה לר"מ דפטור משום דרבה מיניה ואמאי תנן מתני' הבא על בתו פטור מן הקנס: **וטבח בשבת.** איכא חיוב מיתה וכן לעבודת כוכבים: **שור הנסקל.** לקמן פריך הא לא שוה מידי: **בטובח על ידי אחר.** הגנב צוה לשלוחו לשחוט: **וכי.** שליח חוטא ושולח מתחייב קנס דארבעה וחמשה והא קיימא לן בקדושין (מג:) אין שליח לדבר עבירה: **מכירה** אי אפשר אלא ע"י אחר שהלוקח לוקחו ממנו: **תחת השור.** מצי למכתב ישלם בשור: **עבד איהו לא מיחייב.** דהא מיקטיל: **לאו משום דלא מיחייב הוא.** דחיובא רמיא עליה אלא משום דקם ליה בדרבה מיניה:
רבי

ודלמא מלקות חמור. הוה מצי לשנויי מסתברא מיתה חמורה שכן ניתנה לאנשי עיר הנידחת כדאמרי' בפ"ד מיתות (סנהדרין נ.): **אילמלי נגדוה לחנניה מישאל ועזריה הוו פלחי לצלמא.** תימה מנלן (א) דהא אמרי' בהרואה (ברכות סא:) כשהוליכו את ר"ע אמר כל ימי הייתי מצטער על פסוק זה אימתי יבא לידי ואקיימנו בכל נפשך אלמא משמע דבכל נפשך מיירי אפי' היו מייסרין את האדם ביסורין קשין דומיא דר' עקיבא שהיו מסרקין בשרו במסרקי ברזל וכ"ש לנגודי ואור"ת דאותו צלם לא היה עבודת כוכבים ממש אלא היה עשוי לכבוד המלך ולעפ"כ היה בו קידוש השם ולכך מסרו עצמן למיתה והיינו דכתיב (דניאל ג) לאלהך לית אנן פלחין ולצלם דהבא די אקימת לא נסגוד משמע שהצלם לא היה תופס באלהות ומיהו פלחו לצלמא משמע שהצלם היה עבודת כוכבים מדקאמר פלחו ח):

דלמא בשוגג ונקה מגלות. תימה לר"י היכי שייך גלות אם מת אחר שחבשוהו ב' או שלשה ימים הא אמרינן במי שאחזו (גיטין ע: ושם) שחט בו שנים או רוב שנים הרי זה אינו גולה דחיישינן שמא הרוח בלבלתו וטעמא דגבי גלות אשכחן מילי טובא לפטור כגון דרך עלייה דגבי מיתה אין חילוק בין דרך עלייה לדרך ירידה הכי נמי גבי גלות בעינן שימות מיד דכתיב ויפל עליו וימות משמע מיד ולאע"ג דגבי מיתה נמי כתיב מכה איש ומת וי"ל דמשכחת לה בביתא דשישא דלא חיישינן שמא הרוח בלבלתו כדאמרינן התם אי נמי דוקא בשחט בו רוב שנים חיישינן שמא הרוח בלבלתו דבקל הרוח מבלבלו אבל בשאר חבלות אין הרוח מזיק כל כך שיכולין לשמור יפה מבלבול רוח לכרוך על המכה שום דבר ול"ת היכי מיתוקם קרא בשוגג הא כתיב שבת בקרא רק שבתו יתן וגו' ובשוגג לא מיחייב כדאמרינן בס"פ כילד הרגל (ב"ק כו: ושם) דמרבה מפצע תחת פצע לחייב על השוגג כמזיד נזק אבל לא ד' דברים וי"ל דמשכחת לה בהוסיף לו רצועה אחת דאמר בהמניח (שם לב:) דגולה ואם לא מת חייב בד' דברים ולא דמי לשאר שוגג או כגון שנכנס לחנותו של נגר ט) (שלא) ברשות דמוכח התם לרב פפא דשייך ביה גלות וד' דברים או נפל מן הגג ברוח מצויה דחייב בד' דברים כדאמרי' בסוף כילד הרגל (שם כז.) ומסתברא דאם מת דגולה ועוד דאפשר דהוי שוגג על המיתה ומזיד על החבלה י):

גנב שור הנסקל וטבחו משלם תשלומי ד' וה'. תימה דתיקשי מהכא לריש לקיש דאמר בפ' מרובה (שם עו: ושם) כל היכא דליתיה במכירה ליתיה בטביחה והכא שור הנסקל ליתיה במכירה וי"ל דהתם קדשים תמירי דליתנהו כלל במכירה אבל שור הנסקל אם ימכרנו לעובד כוכבים אין תופס דמיו ולר"ת שאומר דאין שור הנסקל * נאסר מחיים ניחא:

לאו משום דלא מיחייב כו'. אע"ג דהכא אפי' לצאת ידי שמים אינו חייב דדוקא בממון הוא דאמר רבא בהשוכר את הפועלים (ב"מ צא. ושם) אתנן אסרה תורה אפי' בא על אמו דמיחייב בבא לצאת ידי שמים אבל קנס לא מיחייב אלא ע"פ ב"ד כדאמרי' אשר ירשיעון אלהים פרט למרשיע עצמו מ"מ ניחא דכיון שהיה ראוי להתחייב אם לא היה מתחייב בנפשו מתחייב נמי אממון ע"י שליח כיון שאינו מתחייב בנפשו:
רבי

מסורת הש"ס

א) [סנהדרין דף עט.], ב) [שם], ג) שם עח: [תוס' דב"ק פ"ט], ד) [לקמן לד: לז.], ה) ב"ק עא. ב"מ צא:, ו) קדושין מג. ב"ק עא. [עט.], ז) ערכין פג. וש"נ, ח) [וע"ע תוס' פסחים נג: ד"ה מה ראו ותוס' ע"ז ג. ד"ה שלא], ט) רש"ל מ"ז, י) [וע"ע תוס' יבמות קכ: ד"ה אלא וד"ה מיישינן ותוס' גיטין ע: ובשבועות לד. ד"ה ע"פ].

הגהות הב"ח

(א) תוס' ד"ה אילמלי כו' מנלן ועוד דהא:

גליון הש"ס

תוס' ד"ה גנב וכו' נאסר מחיים ניחא. עי' זבחים דף עא ע"א תוס' ד"ה (בעמוד הקודם) אפי'.

תורה אור השלם

א) אִם יָקוּם וְהִתְהַלֵּךְ בַּחוּץ עַל מִשְׁעַנְתּוֹ וְנִקָּה הַמַּכֶּה רַק שִׁבְתּוֹ יִתֵּן וְרַפֹּא יְרַפֵּא: [שמות כא, יט]

ב) כִּי יִגְנֹב אִישׁ שׁוֹר אוֹ שֶׂה וּטְבָחוֹ אוֹ מְכָרוֹ חֲמִשָּׁה בָקָר יְשַׁלֵּם תַּחַת הַשּׁוֹר וְאַרְבַּע צֹאן תַּחַת הַשֶּׂה: [שמות כא, לז]

Above (31b-32a), the Gemara pointed out an apparent contradiction between our Mishnah (which states that one who violates his sister pays the fine) and the Mishnah in *Makkos* (which states that one who cohabits with his sister receives lashes). The Gemara presented the resolutions of Ulla (32a) and R' Yochanan (32b). The Gemara now presents a third resolution — that of Reish Lakish: **רֵישׁ לָקִישׁ אָמַר – Resh Lakish says: הָא מַנִּי – Whose** authorship **is** reflected in **this** Mishnah of ours, which prescribes the fine for one who violates his sister?[17] **רַבִּי מֵאִיר הִיא – It is** a Mishnah authored by **R' Meir, דְּאָמַר לוֹקֶה וּמְשַׁלֵּם – who says** that **one can pay and receive lashes** for the same crime.[18]

The Gemara counters:

אִי רַבִּי מֵאִיר אֲפִילוּ בִּתּוֹ נַמִּי – If our Mishnah is indeed the opinion of **R' Meir,** then **even** one who violates **his daughter** should **also** pay the fine![19] Why, then, does our Mishnah rule below[20] that one who violates his daughter is exempt from paying the fine?

The Gemara anticipates a possible answer:

וְכִי תֵּימָא רַבִּי מֵאִיר לוֹקֶה וּמְשַׁלֵּם אִית לֵיהּ מֵת וּמְשַׁלֵּם לֵית לֵיהּ – And perhaps you will say in reply to this question that **R' Meir holds** only that **one can receive lashes and pay** for the same crime, but **he does not hold** that **one can be put to death and pay** for the same crime.[21] **וְלֹא – But** does he **not** hold that one can be executed and assessed monetary liability for the same crime? **וְהָתַנְיָא – Why, we learned in a Baraisa:**[22] **גָּנַב וְטָבַח בְּשַׁבָּת – If ONE STOLE** a sheep or ox **AND SLAUGHTERED** it **ON THE SABBATH;**[23] **גָּנַב וְטָבַח לַעֲבוֹדַת כּוֹכָבִים** – or if **ONE STOLE** a sheep or ox **AND SLAUGHTERED** it **FOR IDOL WORSHIP;**[24] **גָּנַב שׁוֹר הַנִּסְקָל וּטְבָחוֹ** – or if **ONE STOLE AN OX** that is condemned **TO BE STONED**[25] **AND SLAUGHTERED IT; מְשַׁלֵּם תַּשְׁלוּמֵי אַרְבָּעָה וַחֲמִשָּׁה – HE MUST PAY** the **FOURFOLD OR FIVEFOLD PAYMENTS. דִּבְרֵי רַבִּי מֵאִיר – These** are **THE WORDS OF R' MEIR.**[26] **וַחֲכָמִים פּוֹטְרִין – BUT THE SAGES EXEMPT** him. Evidently, R' Meir indeed holds that one who simultaneously incurs liability to the death penalty and to payment is subjected to both penalties! — ? —

The Gemara answers:

הָא אִיתְּמַר עֲלָהּ – Why, it was stated regarding [that Baraisa]: אָמַר רַבִּי יַעֲקֹב אָמַר רַבִּי יוֹחָנָן – R' Yaakov said in the name of R' Yochanan — **וְאָמְרֵי לָהּ – or, as others report it: אָמַר רַבִּי יִרְמְיָה אָמַר רַבִּי שִׁמְעוֹן בֶּן לָקִישׁ – R' Yirmiyah said in the name of R' Shimon ben Lakish רַבִּי אָבִין וְרַבִּי אִילְעָא וְכָל חֲבוּרְתָא מִשְּׁמֵיהּ דְּרַבִּי יוֹחָנָן אָמְרֵי** — that **R' Avin and R' Il'a and the entire group say in the name of R' Yochanan:**[27] **בְּטוֹבֵחַ עַל יְדֵי אַחֵר – The** Baraisa is dealing with **where he slaughtered** it **through** the agency of **another person.**[28]

The Gemara questions this explanation of the Baraisa:

וְכִי זֶה חוֹטֵא וְזֶה מִתְחַיֵּיב – But can it be that **this one** [the agent] **sins** by slaughtering the stolen animal, **and this** other **one** [the thief] **is liable** for the fourfold or fivefold payment?[29] How, then, can you say that the Baraisa, which states that the thief is liable to the fourfold or fivefold penalty, is discussing a case in which someone else slaughtered the animal for him?

The Gemara answers:

אָמַר רָבָא – Rava said: While it is true that in general one is not liable for a transgression committed by his agent, the fourfold and fivefold payment is an exception to this rule. **אָמַר רַחֲמָנָא – For the Merciful One says** in His Torah with regard to the fourfold or fivefold payment: **"וּטְבָחוֹ אוֹ מְכָרוֹ"** – *If a man steals an ox or sheep* ***and slaughters it or sells it.*** By juxtaposing the acts of slaughtering and selling, the verse indicates a comparison between the two acts: **מַה מְּכִירָה עַל יְדֵי אַחֵר – Just as** the thief brings about the **sale** of the animal only **through** the involvement of **another person** besides himself (i.e. through the buyer),[30] **אַף טְבִיחָה עַל יְדֵי אַחֵר – so too** is he liable if he brings about the **slaughter** of the animal **through another person** besides himself (i.e. through his agent).

The Gemara presents alternative ways of deriving a thief's liability for his agent's slaughter of the stolen animal:

דְּבֵי רַבִּי יִשְׁמָעֵאל תָּנָא – The academy of R' Yishmael taught in a

NOTES

17. *Rashi.*

18. In *Makkos* 4a (cited by the Gemara above, 32b), R' Meir states that *zomemim* who testify falsely in a monetary matter receive lashes *and* pay their intended victim what they sought to deprive him of, "for the Scriptural verse that makes them liable for lashes is not the one that makes them liable for payment" [see above, 32b note 17] (*Rashi*). [Here, too, R' Meir would hold that the one who violates his *naarah* sister receives lashes because of the verse (*Leviticus* 18:9): *The nakedness of your sister . . . you shall not uncover,* and makes payment because of another verse (*Deuteronomy* 22:29): *and the man who lay with her shall give the father of the girl fifty silver [shekels].*]

19. Although he is liable to the death penalty for cohabiting with his daughter (see *Sanhedrin* 75a), he should nevertheless pay the fine for violation, for R' Meir does not hold that one is exempt from payment by virtue of having also incurred a more severe penalty [see Gemara below] (*Rashi*).

20. 36b.

21. For in the case of liability to both execution and monetary payment, R' Meir would apply the principle of קָם לֵיהּ בִּדְרַבָּה מִינֵּיהּ, *he is subject to the penalty greater than [payment].*

22. This Baraisa deals with the law stated in *Exodus* 21:37: *If a man steals an ox or a sheep and slaughters it or sells it, five cattle he shall pay instead of the ox and four sheep instead of the sheep.* (Although we have translated the word שֶׂה used in the verse as *sheep,* the word actually denotes both sheep and goats.)

23. *Slaughtering* is one of the thirty-nine *melachos* forbidden on the Sabbath (see Mishnah, *Shabbos* 73a). Accordingly, one who slaughters on the Sabbath is liable to the death penalty for desecrating the Sabbath.

24. One who slaughters an animal as an offering to an idol is liable to the death penalty for idol worship (*Exodus* 22:19, *Sanhedrin* 60b).

25. [This is an ox condemned to die through "stoning" for having killed a person or for having been involved in an act of bestiality. Such an animal is forbidden for all benefit. The Gemara below will ask why one is liable for stealing and slaughtering such an animal if it has no value (see *Rashi*).

26. Apparently, R' Meir rules that he pays this fourfold and fivefold penalty even when he slaughtered the animal on the Sabbath, or for idol worship, in which case he is simultaneously liable for the death penalty as well.

27. [*Dikdukei Soferim, Bava Kamma* 71a §4 finds difficulty with this text, for R' Shimon ben Lakish was older than R' Avin and R' Il'a and would thus probably not be quoting them. See the alternative text cited by *Dikdukei Soferim* there.]

28. I.e. the thief did not slaughter it himself, but rather instructed his agent to slaughter it for him (*Rashi*). Hence, the thief did not commit the capital offense [of slaughtering on the Sabbath or of slaughtering for idol worship] and thus does not incur the death penalty. That is the case in which R' Meir maintains that he is liable for the fourfold or fivefold penalty. R' Meir agrees, however, that one who *does* incur the death penalty is exempt from monetary payment for that crime because of the rule that *he is subject to the penalty greater than [payment].* And that is why he can be the author of our Mishnah, which states (below, 36a) that one who violates his daughter, etc. does not pay the fine.

29. How can it be that the thief must pay for the act of slaughter done by his agent? Why, we have a principle that אֵין שָׁלִיחַ לִדְבַר עֲבֵירָה, *there is no agency to commit an act of transgression* (see *Kiddushin* 42b); that is, a person commissioned to commit a transgression is not considered to be acting as an agent of the principal but rather to be acting on his own. If the agent indeed carries out the transgression, it is he who is responsible for the misdeed, and not the principal who commissioned him (see *Rashi*).

30. It is impossible for the thief to carry out a sale without another party — namely, the buyer who buys it from him (*Rashi*).

עין משפט נר מצוה

כז א מיי' פ"ד מהל' רוצח ושמירת נפש הל' ג:
כח (ב) ג מיי' פ"ו מהל' גניבה הל' ו:
כט ד מיי' פ"ג שם הל' ב: ל ה מיי' פ"ג שם הל' ג:

ליקוטי רש"י

אילמלי נגדוה וכו' פלחו לצלמא. כמיתה [רש"י בשיטמ"ק בשם רשב"א]. אלא לרבי דאמר. התם נתכוון להרוג את זה והרג את זה אינו נהרג אלא משלם דמי האשה ואע"ג דאתרו ביה אימא לך לוקה ואינו משלם [רש"י כת"י בשיטמ"ק]. ממון. דמי האשה יתן ליורשיה [סנהדרין עט.]. על משענתו. על בוריו וכחו [שמות כא, יט]. [illegible]

דלמא מלקות חמור דאמר רב אילמלי נגדוה לחנניה מישאל ועזריה פלחו לצלמא א"ל רב סמא בריה דרב אסי לרב אשי ואמרי לה רב סמא בריה דרב אשי לרב אשי ולא שני לך בין הכאה שיש לה קצבה להכאה שאין לה קצבה מתקיף לה רב יעקב מנהר פקוד הניחא לרבנן [א]דאמרי נפש ממש אלא לרבי דאמר [ב]ממון מאי איכא למימר אלא אמר רב יעקב מנהר פקוד משמיה דרבא מהכא [א]אם יקום והתהלך בחוץ על משענתו ונקה המכה [ג]וכי תעלה על דעתך שזה מהלך בשוק וזה נהרג אלא מלמד שחובשין אותו ואי מית קטלינן ליה ואי לא מית שבתו יתן ורפא ירפא היכי דמי אי דלא אתרו ביה אמאי מיקטיל אלא פשיטא דאתרו ביה ומותרה לדבר חמור מותרה לדבר הקל ואמר רחמנא [א]שבתו יתן ורפא ירפא מתקיף לה רב אשי ממאי דמותרה לדבר חמור הוי מותרה לדבר הקל דלמא לא הוי ואם תמצא לומר הוי ממאי דמיתה חמורה דלמא מלקות חמור דאמר רב אילמלי נגדוה לחנניה מישאל ועזריה פלחו לצלמא א"ל רב סמא בריה דרב אסי לרב אשי ואמרי לה רב סמא בריה דרב אשי לרב אשי ולא שני לך בין הכאה שיש לה קצבה להכאה שאין לה קצבה אלא מתקיף לה רב מרי ממאי דבמזיד ונקה מקטלא דלמא בשוגג ונקה מגלות קשיא: ריש לקיש אמר הא מני רבי מאיר היא [ד]דאמר לוקה ומשלם אי רבי מאיר אפי' בתו נמי וכי תימא ר' מאיר לוקה ומשלם אית ליה מת ומשלם לית ליה ולא והתניא גנב וטבח בשבת גנב וטבח לעבודת כוכבים גנב שור הנסקל וטבחו [ב]משלם תשלומי ארבעה וחמשה דברי רבי מאיר וחכמים פוטרין הא איתמר עלה אמר רבי יעקב א"ר יוחנן ואמרי לה אמר רבי ירמיה אמר ר' שמעון בן לקיש ר' אבין ורבי אילעא וכל חבורתא משמיה דרבי יוחנן אמרי [ג]בטובח על ידי אחר וכי זה חוטא וזה מתחייב אמר רבא אמר רחמנא [ב]וטבחו או מכרו [ד]מה מכירה על ידי אחר אף טביחה על ידי אחר דבי רבי ישמעאל תנא או לרבות את השליח דבי חזקיה תנא [ב]תחת לרבות את השליח [ו]מתקיף לה מר זוטרא מי איכא מידי דאילו עבד איהו לא מיחייב ועביד שליח ומחייב איהו לאו משום דלא מיחייב [ה]אלא משום דקם ליה בדרבה מיניה אי בטובח על ידי אחר מאי טעמייהו דרבנן דפטרי [ז]מאן חכמים רבי

ודלמא מלקות חמור. הוה מצי לשנויי מסתברא מיתה חמורה שכן ניתנה לאנשי עיר הנידחת כדאמרי' בפ"ד מיתות (סנהדרין נ.): אילמלי נגדוה לחנניה מישאל ועזריה הוו פלחי לצלמא. תימה מנא לן (א) דהא אמרי' בהרואה (ברכות סא:) כשהוציאו את ר"ע אמר כל ימי הייתי מצטער על פסוק זה אימתי יבא לידי ואקיימנו בכל נפשך אלמא משמע דבכל נפשך מיירי אפי' היו מייסרין את האדם ביסורין קשין דומיא דר' עקיבא שהיו מסרקין בשרו במסרקי ברזל וכ"ש לנגודי ואור"ת דאותו צלם לא היה עבודת כוכבים ממש אלא היה עשוי לכבוד המלך ואעפ"כ היה בו קידוש השם ולכך מסרו עצמן למיתה והיינו דכתיב (דניאל ג) לאלהך לית אנן פלחין ולצלם דהבא די אקימת לא נסגוד משמע שהצלם לא היה תופס באלהות ומיהו פלחו לצלמא משמע שהצלם היה עבודת כוכבים מדקאמר פלחו [ח]: דלמא בשוגג ונקה מגלות. תימה לר"י היכי שייך גלות אם מת אחר שחבשוהו ג' או שלשה ימים הא אמרינן במי שאחזו (גיטין ע: ושם) שחט בו שנים או רוב שנים הרי זה אינו גולה דחיישינן שמא הרוח בלבלתו וטעמא דגבי גלות אשכחן מילי טובא דפטור כגון דרך עלייה דגבי מיתה אין חילוק בין דרך עלייה לדרך ירידה הכי נמי גבי גלות בעינן שימות מיד כדכתיב ויפל עליו וימות משמע מיד ואע"ג דגבי מיתה נמי כתיב מכה איש ומת וי"ל דמשכחת לה בביאה דשיא דלא חיישינן שמא הרוח בלבלתו כדאמרינן התם אי נמי דוקא בשחט בו רוב שנים חיישינן שמא הרוח בלבלתו דבקל הרוח מבלבלו אבל בשאר חבלות אין הרוח מזיק כל כך שיכולין לשמור יפה מבלבול רוח לכרוך על המכה שום דבר וא"ת היכי מיתוקם קרא בשוגג הא כתיב שבת בקרא רק שבתו יתן וגו' ובשוגג לא מיחייב כדאמרינן בס"פ כילד הרגל (ב"ק כו: ושם) דמרבה מפצע תחת פצע לחייב על השוגג כמזיד נזק אבל לא ד' דברים וי"ל דמשכחת לה בהוסיף לו רצועה אחת דאמר בהמניח (שם לג:) דגולה ואם לא מת חייב בד' דברים ולא דמי לשאר שוגג או כגון שנכנס לחנותו של נגר [ט] (שלא) ברשות דמוכח התם לרב פפא דשייך ביה גלות וד' דברים או נפל מן הגג ברוח מצויה דחייב בד' דברים כדאמרי' בסוף כילד הרגל (שם כ.) ומסתברא דאם מת דגולה ועוד דאפשר דהוי שוגג על המיתה ומזיד על החבלה [י]: גנב שור הנסקל וטבחו משלם תשלומי ד' וה'. תימה דתיקשי מהכא לריש לקיש דאמר בפ' מרובה (שם עז: ושם) כל היכא דליתיה במכירה ליתיה בטביחה והכא שור הנסקל ליתיה במכירה וי"ל דהתם קדשים קאמרי דליתנהו כלל במכירה אבל שור הנסקל אם ימכרנו לעובד כוכבים אין תופס דמיו ולר"ת שאומר דאין שור הנסקל ° נאסר מחיים ניחא: לאו משום דלא מיחייב כו'. אע"ג דהכא אפי' לצאת ידי שמים אינו חייב דלוקא בממון הוא דאמר רבא בהשוכר את הפועלים (ב"מ צא. ושם) אתנן אסרה תורה אפי' בא על אמו דמיחייב בבא לצאת ידי שמים אבל קנס לא מיחייב אלא ע"פ ב"ד כדאמרי' אשר ירשיעון אלהים פרט למרשיע עצמו מ"מ ניחא דכיון שהיה ראוי להתחייב אם לא היה מתחייב בנפשו מתחייב נמי אממון ע"י שליח כיון שאינו מתחייב בנפשו:

נגדוה. יסורין: ולא שני לך כו'. יסורי המלכות הכאה שאין לה קצבה היא אבל מלקות יש לה קצבה ארבעים: הניחא לרבנן דאמרי. בסנהדרין באלו הן הנשרפים (עט.) נתכוון להרוג את זה והרג את זה חייב והאי ונתת נפש ממש קאמר אית לן למידק ואוקמי קרא בשהתרו בו ולמילף דאע"ג דאיכא התראה יענש ממון כשאין שם מיתה: אלא לרבי דאמר. התם נתכוון להרוג את זה והרג את זה אינו נהרג אלא משלם דמי האשה ליורשיה אם כן אפשר לאוקמי קרא בשלא התרו בו ומשום הכי כי אין אסון משלם דמי ולדות וכי יש אסון משלם דמי אשה אבל אתרו ביה אימא לך לוקה ואינו משלם: מאי איכא למימר. מהיכא תיתי חובל בחבירו לתשלומין ואף כשהתרו בו: על משענתו. כדמתרגמינן על בוריו ששב לכחו ולאיתנו הראשון: אלא מלמד שחובשין אותו. לא נאמר מקרא זה אלא ללמדך דהיכא דהכהו ולא מת ונפל למשכב יחבשו את המכה ההוא בבית האסורין עד שנראה אם יקום והתהלך בחוץ אז ונקה המכה מכלל דעד השתא לא יצא מידי בית דין אלא נחבש: ואי מיית קטלינן ליה. [כיון דאמרת חובשין מכלל דאי מיית ניזק קטלינן ליה להאי דאי לאו לקטלא למאי חבשינן ליה: לדבר חמור. מיתה: לדבר הקל. מלקות דלא יוסיף דחובל ולא מת]: ואמר רחמנא. להיכא דלא מת דאיכא ממון ומלקות נידון בממון דכתיב שבתו יתן: ממאי. דהאי והכה איש את רעהו במזיד קא משתעי והאי ונקה דילפינן מיניה חבישה ונקה מקטלא קאמר דתשמע מינה דאי מיית קטלינן ליה ועל כרחין בהתרו בו: דלמא בשוגג. משתעי ולא התרו בו וחבישה לאו לקטלא ונקה נמי לאו לקטלא אלא מגלות דערי מקלט וחבישה דילפינן מינה לגלות קאמר ומשום הכי כי נקה מגלות ישלם ממון אבל היכא דאתרו ביה אימא לך דכי לא מיית לוקה ואינו משלם: ריש לקיש מהדר אשינויא דרומיא דרמינן בריש שמעתין מתני' דמכות אדכתובות: הא מני. מתניתין דקתני בא על אחותו נותן קנס ר"מ היא דאמר לעיל לוקה ומשלם שלא השם המביאו לידי מכות מביאו לידי תשלומין: אפי' בתו נמי. דמיקטיל עלה לישלם דהא לא סבירא ליה לר"מ דפטור משום דרבה מיניה ואמאי תנן מתני' הבא על בתו פטור מן הקנס: וטבח בשבת. איכא חיוב מיתה וכן לעבודת כוכבים: שור הנסקל. לקמן פריך הא לא שוה מידי: בטובח על ידי אחר. הגנב לוה לשלוחו לשחוט: וכי. שליח חוטא ושולח מתחייב קנס דארבעה וחמשה והא קיימא לן בקדושין (מב:) אין שליח לדבר עבירה: מכירה אי אפשר אלא ע"י אחר שהלוקח לוקחו ממנו: תחת השור. מצי למכתב ישלם בשור: עבד איהו לא מיחייב. דהא מיקטיל: לאו משום דלא מיחייב הוא. דחיובא רמיא עליה אלא משום דקם ליה בדרבה מיניה:
רבי

מיקטל [רש"י משיטמ"ק עיי"ש]. איהו לאו משום דלא מיחייב. כי עביד איהו [דפטרינן] ליה לאו משום דלא מיחייב אלא משום דקם ליה בדרבה מיניה [ב"ק שם]. מאן חכמים. טעמייהו [גיטין כב.]. [מכאן שייך לדף לד.] ר' שמעון היא. דאמר לענין כיסוי הדם (חולין דף פה.) ואותו ואת בנו (שם דף פ.) ותשלומי ארבעה וחמשה (ב"ק דף עא.) שחיטה שאינה ראויה שחיטה ילא חיוב ואיסור הבא ע"י שחיטה אינו חל עליה [קידושין נח.]. כדתנן בפרקין (ב"ק ע.) רבי שמעון פוטר בשני אלו. התינח עבודת כוכבים ושור הנסקל. איסורי הנאה (דף נד.) אע"פ שאמרו המשתחוה לבהמת חבירו לא אסרה עשה בה מעשה אסרה [ב"ק עא.]. וביום הכפורים מתחייב כרת [חולין יד.]. המבשל בשבת. בידים דאיכא חיובא בשוגג יאכל. אפי' הוא עצמו ואפילו בו ביום [ב"ק שם]. הוא עצמו וכו ביום ואין צריך להמתין עד הערב בכדי שיעשו דהא דאמרינן בעלמא לערב בכדי שיעשו לית ליה לר"מ אלא היכא דעבד ישראל איסורא ובמזיד דאיכא חיובא דלא נמטייה הנאה מאיסורא אבל בשוגג לא [חולין טו.].

מסורת הש"ס

א) [סנהדרין דף עט.], ב) [שם], ג) שם עח: [תוס' דב"ק פ"ט], ד) [לקמן לד. לו.], ה) ב"ק עא. ב"מ לא., ו) קדושין מג. ב"ק עא. [עט.], ז) ב"ק ע. [ערכין ...], ח) [וע"ע תוס' פסחים נג: ד"ה מה ראוי ותוס' ע"ז ג. ד"ה שלא], ט) רש"א מ"ז, י) [וע"ע תוס' יבמות קכ: ד"ה אלא וד"ה מיסיון ותוס' גיטין ע: ובשבועות לג. ד"ה ע"פ].

הגהות הב"ח

(א) תוס' ד"ה אילמלי כו' מנא לן ועוד דהא:

גליון הש"ס

תוס' ד"ה גנב וכו' נאסר מחיים ניחא. עי' זבחים דף עא ע"א תוס' ד"ה (בעמוד הקודם) אפי':

תורה אור השלם

א) אִם יָקוּם וְהִתְהַלֵּךְ בַּחוּץ עַל מִשְׁעַנְתּוֹ וְנִקָּה הַמַּכֶּה רַק שִׁבְתּוֹ יִתֵּן וְרַפֹּא יְרַפֵּא: [שמות כא, יט]

ב) כִּי יִגְנֹב אִישׁ שׁוֹר אוֹ שֶׂה וּטְבָחוֹ אוֹ מְכָרוֹ חֲמִשָּׁה בָקָר יְשַׁלֵּם תַּחַת הַשּׁוֹר וְאַרְבַּע צֹאן תַּחַת הַשֶּׂה: [שמות כא, לז]

absolved.[9] *Only for his loss of work*[10] *shall he pay, and he shall provide for healing.*[11] וְכִי תַעֲלֶה עַל דַּעְתָּךְ שֶׁזֶּה מְהַלֵּךְ בַּשּׁוּק וְזֶה נֶהֱרָג – **Now,** why did the Torah have to state that if the victim recovers, the assailant is absolved and not executed? **Would it enter your mind** to say **that this one** [the victim] **is walking** about **in the street and this one** [the assailant] **is executed?!** Surely, it is obvious that the assailant cannot be executed for murder if his victim recovers! אֶלָּא מְלַמֵּד שֶׁחוֹבְשִׁין אוֹתוֹ – **Rather, this** verse **teaches that we imprison [the assailant]** until the fate of the victim is determined:[12] וְאִי מִית קָטְלִינַן לֵיהּ – **And if [the victim]** eventually **dies** from his wounds, **we execute [the assailant];**[13] וְאִי לֹא מִית ,,שִׁבְתּוֹ יִתֵּן וְרַפֹּא יְרַפֵּא" – **and if he** recovers and **does not die,** then the assailant is released from prison, but ***for his loss of work he shall pay, and he shall provide for his healing.*** הֵיכִי דָּמֵי – Now, **what is the case?** אִי דְּלֹא אַתְרוּ בֵּיהּ – **If they did not warn him** that striking and killing his adversary would subject him to the death penalty, אַמַּאי מִיקְטִיל – **why is he executed** if the victim eventually dies? אֶלָּא פְּשִׁיטָא דְּאַתְרוּ בֵּיהּ – **Rather, it is obvious that they did warn him;** וּמוּתְרֶה לְדָבָר חָמוּר מוּתְרֶה לְדָבָר הַקַּל – **and** the rule is that **one who is warned for a severe matter is** deemed **warned for a lenient matter.**[14] Thus, the warning that striking and killing his adversary would subject him to the death penalty serves also as a warning that striking and *wounding* his adversary would subject him to lashes. וְאָמַר רַחֲמָנָא – **Yet, the Merciful One states** in His Torah that in the event the victim does not die, and his assailant is thus liable to both payment and lashes, ,,שִׁבְתּוֹ יִתֵּן וְרַפֹּא יְרַפֵּא" – ***for his loss of work he shall pay, and he shall provide for his healing.*** Evidently, even when an assailant could be liable to lashes for striking his fellow, he pays compensation and does not receive lashes.

The Gemara objects:

מַתְקִיף לָהּ רַב אַשִׁי – **Rav Ashi objected to this** (as above): מִמַּאי דְּמוּתְרֶה לְדָבָר חָמוּר הָוֵי מוּתְרֶה לְדָבָר הַקַּל – **On what basis** do you assume that **one who is warned for a severe matter is** deemed **warned for a lenient matter?** דִּלְמָא לֹא הָוֵי – **Perhaps,** he **is not** deemed warned for the lenient matter! וְאִם תִּמְצָא לוֹמַר הָוֵי – **And** even **if you were to** conclude and **say** that one who is warned for a severe penalty **is** deemed warned for the lenient penalty, מִמַּאי דְּמִיתָה חֲמוּרָה – **on the basis of what** do you assume **that** the **death** penalty **is the more severe** penalty? דִּלְמָא מַלְקוֹת חָמוּר – **Perhaps lashes is the more severe** penalty! דְּאָמַר רַב – **For Rav said:** אִילְמָלֵי נַגְדוּהָ לַחֲנַנְיָה מִישָׁאֵל וַעֲזַרְיָה – **"Had they whipped Chananyah, Mishael and Azaryah,** פָּלְחוּ לְצַלְמָא – **they would have worshiped the statue."** Evidently, the torture inflicted by lashes is worse than death. And accordingly, lashes is a more severe punishment than death. – ? –

The Gemara answers this last objection (as above):

אָמַר לֵיהּ רַב סַמָּא בְּרֵיהּ דְּרַב אַסִּי לְרַב אַשִׁי – **Rav Samma the son of Rav Assi said to Rav Ashi,** וְאָמְרֵי לָהּ רַב סַמָּא בְּרֵיהּ דְּרַב אַשִׁי לְרַב אַשִׁי – **and some say** that it was **Rav Samma the son of Rav Ashi** who **said to Rav Ashi:** וְלֹא שָׁנֵי לָךְ בֵּין הַכָּאָה שֶׁיֵּשׁ לָהּ קִצְבָה לְהַכָּאָה שֶׁאֵין לָהּ קִצְבָה – **But is there no difference to you between a beating that has a limit and a beating that does not have a limit?** Rav refers to a beating without limit. It is that kind of unending torture that would have eventually made Chananyah, Mishael and Azaryah yield and that is worse than death. The finite thirty-nine lashes that the court administers for violating a prohibition (such as the prohibition against striking one's fellow), however, is certainly a punishment less severe than death.

The Gemara proceeds with another objection to Rav Yaakov's source:

מַתְקִיף לָהּ רַב מָרִי – **Rav Mari objected to this:** מִמַּאי דִּבְמֵזִיד ,,וְנִקָּה" מִקְּטָלָא – **On what basis** do you assume that the verse is referring to one **who** meant to kill **intentionally** and that the Torah thus means to say that if the victim recovers the assailant is ***absolved*** **from** liability to **execution?**[15] דִּלְמָא בְּשׁוֹגֵג ,,וְנִקָּה" מִגָּלוּת – **Perhaps,** the verse refers to **one who acted unintentionally,** and the Torah means to say that if the victim recovers the assailant is ***absolved*** **from** liability to **exile?**[16]

The Gemara concedes:

קַשְׁיָא – **It is difficult.** This is indeed a valid objection to the aforementioned proof.

NOTES

9. Apparently, this means that he shall be absolved from liability to execution for murder.

10. I.e. for the victim's loss of earnings during the time that he was bedridden and unable to work.

11. I.e. for the victim's medical expenses.

12. The verse is not coming to teach that the assailant is not executed if the victim recovers, for that is obvious. Rather, it comes to teach that when one assaults someone and the victim does not die but is bedridden on account of his wounds, we imprison the assailant (lest he flee) until we see that the victim has recovered and goes about in the street. The Torah states that the assailant is absolved only *after* the victim recovers, to teach that prior to the victim's recovery, the assailant remains in custody (*Rashi*).

13. This is evident from the fact that we imprison him. For if we would not execute the assailant even in the event that the victim were to eventually die of his wounds, what would be the purpose in imprisoning the assailant pending the victim's recuperation? (*Rashi*). [See *Shitah Mekubetzes* ד"ה מהכא אם יקום והתהלך, who discusses why the execution of the assailant must be derived from the fact that we imprison him rather than from the simple meaning of the verse itself.]

14. See 33a note 38.

15. Which would indicate that if the victim does die, the assailant is executed, which proves that the verse discusses a case in which the assailant was warned (see *Rashi*).

16. That is, perhaps the assailant was not warned [and thus cannot be executed]. And the purpose of imprisoning him is *not* to ensure that he does not flee and evade execution; and similarly, the Torah's statement that the assailant is *absolved* does *not* mean that he is absolved from liability *to execution.* Rather, it means that he is absolved from liability to the exile the Torah imposes on one who kills inadvertently (see *Numbers* 35:11 and *Makkos* ch. 2). And the reason we imprison the assailant until the victim recovers is to ensure that, in the event the victim dies, the assailant will not flee and evade exile. And it is only in this case [where the assailant was *not* warned] that the Torah states that if the victim recovers, the assailant pays for the victim's lost wages and medical expenses. In a case, however, where the assailant was warned that he would be subject to execution [which serves as well as a warning for lashes should the victim not die], we could say that if the victim does not die, the assailant is punished with lashes rather than with payment (see *Rashi*).

[*Shitah Yeshanah* (cited by *Shitah Mekubetzes* ד"ה והקשה מורי) asks: How we can say that the assailant is placed under arrest to ensure that he will be exiled for killing unintentionally. The Torah is obviously discussing a situation in which the assailant struck his victim intentionally, as it is stated: *If men quarrel and one strikes his fellow* etc. Even if we say that the assailant did not mean to actually kill his victim, he did mean to strike and injure him. Thus, he would be considered a שׁוֹגֵג קָרוֹב לְמֵזִיד, *an unintentional [murderer] bordering on the intentional,* who is not liable to exile; see *Bava Kamma* 32b. *Shitah Yeshanah* answers that the Gemara means to say that the verse might refer to where men were quarreling and one of them, while attempting to strike his opponent a nonlethal blow, struck and killed a passerby instead. Though the murderer would be considered "unintentional bordering on intentional" had the blow struck its intended victim, with regard to the passerby, whom he did not intend to strike altogether, he is considered an "unintentional murderer," who is liable to exile.]

עין משפט
נר מצוה

כז א מיי' פ"ד מהל' רוצח ושמירת נפש הל' ה:
כח ב ג מיי' פ"ג מהל' גניבה הל' ג:
כט ד מיי' פ"ג שם הל' י:
ל ה מיי' פ"ג שם הל' ג:

דלמא מלקות חמור דאמר רב אילמלי נגדוה לחנניה מישאל ועזריה פלחו לצלמא א"ל רב סמא בריה דרב אסי לרב אשי ואמרי לה רב סמא בריה דרב אשי לרב אשי ולא שני לך בין הכאה שיש לה קצבה להכאה שאין לה קצבה מתקיף לה רב יעקב מנהר פקוד הניחא לרבנן [ה] דאמרי נפש ממש אלא לרבי דאמר [ג] ממון מאי איכא למימר אלא אמר רב יעקב מנהר פקוד משמיה דרבא מהכא [א] אם יקום והתהלך בחוץ על משענתו ונקה המכה [ג] וכי תעלה על דעתך שזה מהלך בשוק וזה נהרג [א] אלא מלמד שחובשין אותו ואי מית קטלינן ליה ואי לא מית שבתו יתן ורפא ירפא היכי דמי אי דלא אתרו ביה אמאי מיקטיל אלא פשיטא דאתרו ביה ומותרה לדבר חמור מותרה לדבר הקל ואמר רחמנא [א] שבתו יתן ורפא ירפא מתקיף לה רב אשי ממאי דמותרה לדבר חמור הוי מותרה לדבר הקל דלמא לא הוי ואם תמצא לומר הוי ממאי דמיתה חמורה דלמא מלקות חמור דאמר רב אילמלי נגדוה לחנניה מישאל ועזריה פלחו לצלמא א"ל רב סמא בריה דרב אסי לרב אשי ואמרי לה רב סמא בריה דרב אשי לרב אשי ולא שני לך בין הכאה שיש לה קצבה להכאה שאין לה קצבה מתקיף לה רב מרי ממאי דבמזיד ונקה מקטלא דלמא בשוגג ונקה מגלות קשיא: ריש לקיש אמר הא מני רבי מאיר היא [ד] דאמר לוקה ומשלם אי רבי מאיר אפי' בתו נמי וכי תימא ר' מאיר לוקה ומשלם אית ליה מת ומשלם לית ליה והתניא גנב וטבח בשבת גנב וטבח לעבודת כוכבים גנב שור הנסקל וטבחו [ב] משלם תשלומי ארבעה וחמשה דברי רבי מאיר וחכמים פוטרין הא איתמר עלה אמר רבי יעקב א"ר יוחנן ואמרי לה אמר רבי ירמיה אמר ר' שמעון בן לקיש ר' אבין ורבי אילעא וכל חבורתא משמיה דרבי יוחנן אמרי [ג] בטובח על ידי אחר וכי זה חוטא וזה מתחייב אמר רבא אמר רחמנא [ב] וטבחו או מכרו [ה] מה מכירה על ידי אחר אף טביחה על ידי אחר דבי רבי ישמעאל תנא או לרבות את השליח דבי חזקיה תנא [ב] תחת לרבות את השליח [ו] מתקיף לה מר זוטרא מי איכא מידי דאילו עבד איהו לא מיחייב ועביד שליח ומחייב איהו לאו משום דלא מיחייב [ה] אלא משום דקם ליה בדרבה מיניה אי בטובח על ידי אחר מאי טעמייהו דרבנן דפטרי [ז] מאן חכמים רבי

נגדוה. יסורין: ולא שני לך כו'. יסורי המלכות הכאה שאין לה קצבה היא אבל מלקות יש לה קצבה ארבעים: הניחא לרבנן דאמרי. בסנהדרין באלו הן הנשרפים (עט.) נתכוון להרוג את זה והרג את זה חייב והאי ונתת נפש תחת נפש ממש קאמר אית לן למידק ואוקמי קרא בשהתרו בו ולמילף דאע"ג דאיכא התראה יענש ממון כשאין שם מיתה: אלא לרבי דאמר. התם נתכוון להרוג את זה והרג את זה אינו נהרג אלא משלם דמי האשה ליורשיה אם כן אפשר לאוקמי קרא בשלא התרו בו ומשום הכי כי אין אסון משלם דמי ולדות וכי יש אסון משלם דמי אשה אבל אתרו ביה אימא לך לוקה ואינו משלם: מאי איכא למימר. מהיכא תיתי חובל בחבירו לתשלומין ואף כשהתרו בו: על משענתו. כדמתרגמינן על בוריו שבא לכחו ולאיתנו הראשון: אלא מלמד שחובשין אותו. לא נאמר מקרא זה אלא ללמדך דהיכא דהכהו ולא מת ונפל למשכב יחבשו את המכה ההוא בבית האסורין עד שנראה אם יקום והתהלך בחוץ אז ונקה המכה מכלל דעד השתא לא יצא מידי בית דין אלא נחבש: ואי מיית קטלינן ליה. [כיון דאמרת חובשין מכלל דאי מיית ניזק קטלינן ליה להאי דאי לאו לקטלא למאי חבשינן ליה: לדבר חמור. מיתה: לדבר הקל. מלקות דלא יוסיף דחובל ולא מת]: ואמר רחמנא. להיכא דלא מת דאיכא ממון ומלקות נידון בממון דכתיב שבתו יתן: ממאי. דהאי והכה איש את רעהו במזיד קא משתעי והאי ונקה דילפינן מיניה חבישה ונקה מקטלא קאמר דתשמע מינה דאי מיית קטלינן ליה ועל כרחין בהתרו בו: דלמא בשוגג. משתעי ולא התרו בו וחבישה לאו לקטלא ונקה נמי לאו לקטלא אלא מגלות דערי מקלט וחבישה דילפינן מינה לגלות קאמר ומשום הכי כי נקה מגלות ישלם ממון אבל היכא דאתרו ביה אימא לך דכי לא מיית לוקה ואינו משלם: ריש לקיש מהדר אשינויא דרומיא דרמינן בריש שמעתין מתני' דמכות אדכתובות: הא מני. מתניתין דקתני בא על אחותו נותן קנס ר"מ היא דאמר לעיל לוקה ומשלם שלא השם המביאו לידי מכות מביאו לידי תשלומין: אפי' בתו נמי. דמיקטיל עלה לישלם דהא לא סבירא ליה לר"מ דפטור משום דרבה מיניה ואמאי תנן מתני' הבא על בתו פטור מן הקנס: וטבח בשבת. איכא חיוב מיתה וכן לעבודת כוכבים: שור הנסקל. לקמן פריך הא לא שוה מידי: בטובח על ידי אחר. הגנב צוה לשלוחו לשחוט: וכי. שליח חוטא ושולח מתחייב קנס דארבעה וחמשה והא קיימא לן בקדושין (מג:) אין שליח לדבר עבירה: מכירה אי אפשר אלא ע"י אחר שהלוקח לוקחו ממנו: תחת השור. מצי למכתב ישלם בשור: עבד איהו לא מיחייב. דהא מיקטיל: לאו משום דלא מיחייב הוא. דחיובא רמיא עליה אלא משום דקם ליה בדרבה מיניה:

ודלמא מלקות חמור. הוה מצי לשנויי מסתברא מיתה חמורה שכן ניתנה לאנשי עיר הנידחת כדאמרי' בפ"ד מיתות (סנהדרין נ.): אילמלי נגדוה לחנניה מישאל ועזריה הוו פלחי לצלמא. תימה מנא לן (א) דהא אמרי' בברכות (ברכות סא:) כשהוציאו את ר"ע אמר כל ימי הייתי מצטער על פסוק זה אימתי יבא לידי ואקיימנו בכל נפשך אלמא משמע דבכל נפשך איירי אפי' היו מייסרין את האדם ביסורין קשין דומיא דר' עקיבא שהיו מסרקין בשרו במסרקי ברזל וכ"ש לנגודי ואור"ת דאותו צלם לא היה עבודת כוכבים ממש אלא היה עשוי לכבוד המלך ואעפ"כ היה בו קידוש השם ולכך מסרו עצמן למיתה והיינו דכתיב (דניאל ג) לאלהך לית אנן פלחין ולצלם דהבא די אקימת לא נסגוד משמע שהצלם לא היה תופס באלהות ומיהו פלחו לצלמא משמע שהצלם היה עבודת כוכבים מדקאמר פלחו [ח]: דלמא בשוגג ונקה מגלות. תימה לר"י היכי שייך גלות אם מת אחר שחבשוהו ב' או שלשה ימים הא אמרינן במי שאחזו (גיטין ע: ושם) שחט בו שנים או רוב שנים הרי זה אינו גולה דחיישינן שמא הרוח בלבלתו וטעמא דגבי גלות אשכחן מילי טובא דפטור כגון דרך עלייה דגבי מיתה אין חילוק בין דרך עלייה לדרך ירידה הכי נמי גבי גלות בעינן שימות מיד כדכתיב ויפל עליו וימות משמע מיד ואע"ג דגבי מיתה נמי כתיב מכה איש ומת וי"ל דמשכחת לה בביאה דשישא דלא חיישינן שמא הרוח בלבלתו כדאמרינן התם אי נמי דוקא בשחט בו רוב שנים חיישינן שמא הרוח בלבלתו דבקל הרוח מבלבלו אבל בשאר חבלות אין הרוח מזיק כל כך שיכולין לשמור יפה מבלבול רוח לכרוך על המכה שום דבר וא"ת היכי מיתוקם קרא בשוגג הא כתיב שבת בקרא רק שבתו יתן וגו' ובשוגג לא מיחייב כדאמרינן בס"פ כילד הרגל (ב"ק כו: ושם) דמרבה מפצע תחת פצע לחייב על השוגג כמזיד נזק אבל לא ד' דברים וי"ל דמשכחת לה בהוסיף לו רצועה אחת דאמר בהמניח (שם לב:) דגולה ואם לא מת חייב בד' דברים ולא דמי לשאר שוגג או כגון שנכנס לחנותו של נגר [ט] (שלא) ברשות דמוכח התם לרב פפא דשייך ביה גלות וד' דברים או נפל מן הגג ברוח מצויה דחייב בד' דברים כדאמרי' בסוף כילד הרגל (שם כז.) ומסתברא דאם מת דגולה ועוד דאפשר דהוי שוגג על המיתה ומזיד על החבלה [י]: גנב שור הנסקל וטבחו משלם תשלומי ד' וה'. תימה דתיקשי מהכא לריש לקיש דאמר בפ' מרובה (שם עו: ושם) כל היכא דליתיה במכירה ליתיה בטביחה והכא שור הנסקל ליתיה במכירה וי"ל דהתם קדשים חמירי דליתנהו כלל במכירה אבל שור הנסקל אם ימכרנו לעובד כוכבים אין תופס דמיו ולר"ת שאומר דאין שור הנסקל [ט] נאסר מחיים ניחא: לאו משום דלא מיחייב כו'. אע"ג דהכא אפי' לצאת ידי שמים אינו חייב דדוקא בממון הוא דאמר רבא בהשוכר את הפועלים (ב"מ צא. ושם) אתנן אסרה תורה אפי' בא על אמו דמיחייב בנפשו אבל קנס לא מיחייב אלא ע"פ ב"ד כדאמרי' אשר ירשיעון אלהים פרט למרשיע עצמו מ"מ ניחא דכיון שהיה ראוי להתחייב אם לא היה מתחייב בנפשו מתחייב נמי אממון ע"י שליח כיון שאינו מתחייב בנפשו:

ליקוטי רש"י

אילמלי נגדוה וכו' פלחו לצלמא. בממיה [רש"י בשיטמ"ק בשם רשב"א]. אלא לרבי דאמר. התם נתכוון להרוג את זה והרג את זה אינו נהרג אלא משלם דמי אשה ואע"ג דלא אתרו ביה אבל אתרו ביה אימא לך לוקה ואינו משלם [רש"י כת"י משטמ"ק]. ממון. דמי האשה יתן ליורשיה [סנהדרין עט.]. על משענתו. על בוריו וכחו [שמות כא, יט]. מתרגמינן על בוריה שנתרפא לגמרי ונשען על כחו. וכי תעלה על דעתך. למה לי למימר ונקה המכה מיתה [סנהדרין עח:]. ונקה המכה וכו' שחובשין אותו. וכי תעלה על דעתך שיהרג זה שלא הרג אלא למדך כאן שחובשים אותו עד שנראה אם יתרפא זה וכן משמעו כשקם זה והולך על משענתו אז נקה המכה אבל עד שלא יקום זה לא נקה המכה [שמות שם]. אם אמדוהו למיתה חובשין את המכה שלא יברח עד שנראה אם ימות אם לאו להכי אתי ונקה המכה דמשמע לשיקום ונקה מכלל דעד השתא חבוש הוא [סנהדרין שם]. שבתו. בטול מלאכתו מחמת החולי אם קטע ידו או רגלו רואין בטול מלאכתו מחמת החולי כאילו הוא שומר קשואין שהרי אף לאחר החולי אינו ראוי למלאכת יד ורגל והוא כבר נתן לו מתן נזקו דמי ידו או רגלו כמשאמר יד תחת יד רגל תחת רגל. ורפא ירפא. כתרגומו ישלם שכר הרופא [ב"ק פה.] [שמות שם]. ריש לקיש אמר. ר"ל מהדר אקושיא דרמינן בריש שמעתין מתני' דמכות אדכתובות [רש"י כת"י משיטמ"ק עיי"ש]. רבי מאיר היא. במסכת מכות מעידים אנו פלוני שחייב לחבירו מאתים זוז ונמצאו זוממין לוקין ומשלמין שלא השם המביאו לידי מכות מביאו לידי תשלומין. גנב וטבח בשבת. ואע"ג דאיכא חיוב מיתה. גנב שור הנסקל. אע"ג דאיסורי הנאה הוא ולא חייב ובלתני לקמן טעמא. וכי זה חוטא וזה מתחייב. אין שליח לדבר עבירה שאין שליח שולחו אלא הרי הוא כגונב עצמו ולא מאליו [קידושין מב:]. דאמרינן דברי הרב ודברי התלמיד דברי מי שומעין ולא היה לו לעשות [ב"מ י.]. מה מכירה. אינה מתקיימת אלא ע"י אחר הגנב מוכר והלוקח לוקח. אף טביחה. אפילו טבחה שליח מתחייב הגנב בתשלומי ד' וה'. תנא או. לרבות אפילו שליח. תחת. לרבות. פתח השור תחת השה, דחד מיניהו יתירה הוא ודרש לרבות שאם טבח מינה שליח מתחייב [קידושין מג.]. עבד איהו לא מיחייב. קנס דהא מיקטל [רש"י משיטמ"ק עיי"ש]. איהו לאו משום דלא מיחייב. כי עביד איהו [דפטרינן] ליה לאו משום דלא מיחייב אלא משום דקם ליה בדרבה מיניה [ב"ק שם]. מאן חכמים. כלומר מאן נינהו ומאי טעמייהו [גיטין כב.]. [מכאן שייך לדף לד.] ר' שמעון היא. דאמר לענין כיסוי הדם (חולין דף פה.) ואותו ואת בנו (שם דף פ.) ותשלומי ארבעה וחמשה (ב"ק דף עא.) שחיטה שאינה ראויה לאכילה לא שמה שחיטה וכל חיוב ואיסור הבא ע"י שחיטה אינו חל עליה [קידושין נח.]. כדתנן בפרקין (ב"ק ע.) רבי שמעון פוטר בשני אלו. התינח עבודת כוכבים ושור הנסקל. איסורי הנאה ע"ז (דף נד.) אע"פ שאמרו המשתחוה לבהמת חבירו לא אסרה עשה בה מעשה אסרה [ב"ק עא.]. וביום הכפורים מתחייב כרת [חולין יד.]. המבשל בשבת. בידים דאיכא חיובא בשוגג יאכל. אפי' הוא עצמו ואפילו בו ביום [ב"ק שם]. הוא עצמו ובו ביום ואין צריך להמתין עד הערב בכדי שיעשו דהא דאמרינן בעלמא לערב בכדי שיעשו לית ליה לר"מ אלא היכא דעבד ישראל איסורא ובמזיד דאיכא חיובא דלא נמטייה הנאה מאיסורא אבל בשוגג לא [חולין טו.].

מסורת הש"ס

א) [סנהדרין דף עט.], ב) [שם], ג) שם עח. [תוס' דב"ק פ"ט], ד) [לקמן לד. לו.], ה) ב"ק עא. ב"מ צא., ו) קדושין מג. ב"ק עא. [עט.], ז) [עירובין פג. וש"נ], ח) [וע"ע תוס' פסחים עג: ד"ה מה לאו ותוס' ע"ז ג. ד"ה שלא], ט) רש"ל מ"ז, י) [וע"ע תוס' יבמות קכ: ד"ה אלא וד"ה חיישינן ותוס' גיטין ע: ובשבועות לד. ד"ה ע"פ].

הגהות הב"ח

(א) תוס' ד"ה אלמלי כו' מנא לן ועוד דהא:

גליון הש"ס

תוס' ד"ה גנב וכו' נאסר מחיים ניחא. עי' זבחים דף עא ע"א תוס' ד"ה (בעמוד הקודם) אפי'.

תורה אור השלם

א) אִם יָקוּם וְהִתְהַלֵּךְ בַּחוּץ עַל מִשְׁעַנְתּוֹ וְנִקָּה הַמַּכֶּה רַק שִׁבְתּוֹ יִתֵּן וְרַפֹּא יְרַפֵּא: [שמות כא, יט]

ב) כִּי יִגְנֹב אִישׁ שׁוֹר אוֹ שֶׂה וּטְבָחוֹ אוֹ מְכָרוֹ חֲמִשָּׁה בָקָר יְשַׁלֵּם תַּחַת הַשּׁוֹר וְאַרְבַּע צֹאן תַּחַת הַשֶּׂה: [שמות כא, לז]

דִּלְמָא מַלְקוּת חָמוּר – Perhaps lashes is the more severe penalty![1] **דְּאָמַר רַב – For Rav said: אִילְמָלֵי נַגְדּוּהָ לַחֲנַנְיָה מִישָׁאֵל וַעֲזַרְיָה – "Had they whipped Chananyah, Mishael and Azaryah, פָּלְחוּ לְצַלְמָא – they would have worshiped the statue."**[2] Evidently, the torture inflicted by lashes is worse than death. And accordingly, lashes is a more severe punishment than death. – ? –

The Gemara answers this last objection:

אָמַר לֵיהּ רַב סַמָּא בְּרֵיהּ דְּרַב אַסִּי לְרַב אַשִׁי – Rav Samma the son of Rav Assi said to Rav Ashi, וְאָמְרֵי לָהּ רַב סַמָּא בְּרֵיהּ דְּרַב אַשִׁי לְרַב אַשִׁי – and some say that it was **Rav Samma the son of Rav Ashi** who **said to Rav Ashi: וְלֹא שָׁנֵי לָךְ בֵּין הַכָּאָה שֶׁיֵּשׁ לָהּ קִצְבָה לְהַכָּאָה שֶׁאֵין לָהּ קִצְבָה – But is there no difference to you between a beating that has a limit and a beating that does not have a limit?** Rav refers to a beating without limit. It is that kind of unending torture that would have eventually made Chananyah, Mishael and Azaryah yield and that is worse than death. The finite thirty-nine lashes that the court administers for violating a prohibition (such as the prohibition against striking one's fellow), however, is certainly a punishment less severe than death.

The Gemara proceeds with another objection to Rav Shisha the son of Rav Idi's source for punishing one who strikes his fellow with the monetary penalty rather than with lashes:

מַתְקִיף לָהּ רַב יַעֲקֹב מִנְּהַר פְּקוֹד – Rav Yaakov from Nehar Pekod objected to it as follows: **הָנִיחָא לְרַבָּנָן דְּאָמְרֵי נֶפֶשׁ מַמָּשׁ – This** source **is fine according to the Rabbis, who say** that the verse *you shall give a life for a life* refers to **an actual life,** and accordingly the verse must be discussing a situation in which the assailant was warned.[3] **אֶלָּא לְרַבִּי דְּאָמַר מָמוֹן – But according to Rebbi, who says** that *and you shall give a life for a life* refers to the payment of **money** as compensation for the life that was taken,[4] and the verse might thus refer to where the assailant was *not* warned,[5] **מַאי אִיכָּא לְמֵימַר – what is there to say?** How can you derive from here that in the case of an assailant who *was* warned and is thus liable to both money and lashes, the law is that he pays instead of receiving lashes?[6]

Having refuted Rav Shisha's source, R' Yaakov offers an alternative source:

אֶלָּא אָמַר רַב יַעֲקֹב מִנְּהַר פְּקוֹד מִשְּׁמֵיהּ דְּרָבָא – Rather, Rav Yaakov from Nehar Pekod said in the name of Rav: מֵהָכָא – We can derive that one who wounds his fellow is liable to payment rather than to lashes (even when he was warned in advance) **from the following** verse:[7] "אִם־יָקוּם וְהִתְהַלֵּךְ בַּחוּץ עַל־מִשְׁעַנְתּוֹ וְנִקָּה הַמַּכֶּה" – *If men quarrel and one strikes his fellow with a stone or a fist, and he does not die but falls into bed:* ***If he gets up and goes about outside under his own strength,***[8] ***the assailant shall be***

NOTES

1. [*Ritva* (cited also in *Shitah Mekubetzes*) writes that death is undoubtedly the more severe penalty from a *legal* standpoint. The Gemara here means only that a person might be more ready to forfeit his life in order to kill his adversary than to suffer extended lashes in order to strike his adversary. Thus, the warning against the death penalty for murder might not be sufficient as a warning against lashes for assault.]

2. Chapter 3 of the Book of *Daniel* recounts Nebuchadnezzar's construction of an enormous golden statue and his ultimatum that Chananyah, Mishael and Azaryah bow to it or be cast into a fiery furnace. They remained steadfast in their refusal to bow, and they were cast into the furnace and miraculously saved.

Rav states that although they were ready to sacrifice their lives in sanctification of God's Name, they would have yielded had they been tortured.

[Some Rishonim understand Rav to mean that although the Torah obligates one to sacrifice his life rather than bow to an idol (see *Pesachim* 25a), it does *not* obligate him to endure torture – which is worse than death – to that end (*R' Eliezer,* cited by *Shitah Mekubetzes* ד״ה ובקונטרסין כתוב). *Tosafos,* however, maintain that the Biblical obligation to suffer death rather than worship idols does include the obligation to withstand torture as well. *Rabbeinu Tam,* therefore, opines that the statue was not actually an idol, but a monument erected for the king's glory. Thus, the law did not require that they sacrifice their lives or endure torture rather than bow to it. (Nevertheless, because this promotion of a mortal king's honor perforce diminished the King of kings' honor – and indeed this was the wicked Nebuchadnezzar's intent – forfeiting their lives for the sanctification of God's Name was justified; see *Chidushei Rabbeinu David* and *Chidushei HaRan* to *Pesachim* 53b; cf. *Shitah Mekubetzes* here ד״ה וז״ל הרא״ה תלמידו בא״ד ור״ת ז״ל וכו׳.) According to this understanding, Rav is saying that although they were ready to go beyond the strict dictates of the law and sacrifice their lives rather than bow before this particular statue, they would not have maintained their pious resolve in this matter in the face of torture. (*Tosafos* note, however, that Rav's expression פָּלְחוּ לְצַלְמָא, *they would have "worshiped" the statue,* implies that the bowing would indeed have constituted actual idol worship.)]

[Other solutions to this difficulty are found in the Rishonim: *Rashba* (cited also in *Shitah Mekubetzes*) quotes *Rashi* (absent from our editions of *Rashi*) as explaining Rav's statement as an interrogative: "Would Chananyah, Mishael and Azaryah have, God forbid, bowed to the statue even had they been whipped?" Accordingly, Rav is saying in effect that they would *not* have bowed *even* if tortured. Rav's comment nonetheless indicates that torture is worse than death. Others explain that Rav meant his statement only as an exaggerated possibility. That is, it is conceivable that Chananyah, Mishael and Azaryah would have been unable to remain steadfast in the face of torture, although the law would indeed have required them to do so (see *Ramban,* first approach, and *R' Crescas*).]

3. Rav Shisha's proof is based on the view of the Rabbis (*Sanhedrin* 79a), who maintain that one who intends to kill one person and instead kills another is liable to execution, and the Torah's command that if the woman dies *you shall give a life for a life* means that you shall execute the murderer [though he did not intend to kill the woman but rather his adversary]. For according to that view, the verse must refer to where the assailant was warned (or else he could not be put to death), and still the Torah states that *if there will be no fatality, he shall be punished [monetarily]* [and *not* receive lashes for violating *he shall not add*] (*Rashi*).

4. This interpretation of Rebbi is cited in *Sanhedrin* loc. cit. According to Rebbi, one who intends to kill one person and kills another instead is *not* liable to execution. In Rebbi's view, the verse *and you shall give a life for a life* (where the assailant struck and killed the pregnant woman rather than his adversary) means that the assailant must pay the "value" of the woman to her heirs (*Rashi*).

5. Monetary penalty can be imposed without prior warning.

6. Since according to Rebbi the Torah is not prescribing the death penalty in the case where the woman dies, we are no longer compelled to say that the verse is discussing a case where the assailant was warned. Hence, we can say that the Torah is speaking only about a case where he was not warned. That is: Only where he was not warned does the Torah say that if the woman does not die the assailant pays for the miscarriage, and if she does die he pays the value of the woman. But when he was warned, he indeed receives lashes and does not pay compensation (*Rashi*).

[*Rashi's* comment that where the assailant was warned he would receive lashes and not pay seems puzzling. After all, we are now discussing the view of Rebbi, who holds that one who intends to kill one person but kills another is not executed. Similarly, Rebbi would apparently hold that one who intends to strike one person but strikes another does not receive lashes. (He must pay compensation, though, because intent is not a factor in liability to pay compensation for damage that one inflicts.) Thus, *Rashi* should apparently have explained that even if the assailant was warned, he would pay and not receive lashes (see *Chidushei R' Akiva Eiger*). *Kovetz Shiurim* (§116) answers that according to *Rashi,* Rebbi absolves the assailant who intended a different victim only from the death penalty (for murder). But Rebbi would indeed agree that one who intends to strike one person and strikes another instead is liable to lashes (for striking his fellow). See there for the reason for this distinction.]

7. *Exodus* 21:18-19.

8. The word מִשְׁעַנְתּוֹ is rendered by Targum as בּוּרְיֵהּ, *his strength.* I.e. if the victim makes a complete recovery and regains "his former strength" (*Rashi*).

עין משפט נר מצוה

כז א מיי' פ"ד מהל' רוצח ושמירת נפש הל' ה:
כח ב ג מיי' פ"א מהל' גניבה הל' ו:
כט ד מיי' שם הל' ז:
ל ה מיי' פ"ג שם הל' ג:

מסורת הש"ס

א) [סנהדרין דף עט.], ב) [שם], ג) שם עח: [תוס' ד"ק פ"ט], ד) [לקמן לד: לז.] ב"ק עא. ב"מ לא., ה) קדושין מג. ב"ק עא. [עט.], ו) ב"ק עא., ז) [עירובין סב. וש"נ], ח) [וע"ע תוס' פסחים מג: ד"ה מה לאו ותוס' מ"ז ג. ד"ה שלא], ט) רש"א מ"ז, י) [וע"ע תוס' יבמות קכ: ד"ה אלא וד"ה חיישינן ותוס' גיטין ע: ובשבועות לג. ד"ה ע"פ].

דלמא מלקות חמור דאמר רב אילמלי נגדוה לחנניה מישאל ועזריה פלחו לצלמא א"ל רב סמא בריה דרב אסי לרב אשי ואמרי לה רב סמא בריה דרב אשי לרב אשי ולא שני לך בין הכאה שיש לה קצבה להכאה שאין לה קצבה מתקיף לה רב יעקב מנהר פקוד הניחא לרבנן ה) דאמרי נפש ממש אלא לרבי דאמר ו) ממון מאי איכא למימר אלא אמר רב יעקב מנהר פקוד משמיה דרבא מהכא א) אם יקום והתהלך בחוץ על משענתו ונקה המכה ז) וכי תעלה על דעתך שזה מהלך בשוק וזה נהרג א) אלא מלמד שחובשין אותו ואי מית קטלינן ליה ואי לא מית שבתו יתן ורפא ירפא היכי דמי אי דלא אתרו ביה אמאי מיקטיל אלא פשיטא דאתרו ביה ומותרה לדבר חמור מותרה לדבר הקל ואמר רחמנא א) שבתו יתן ורפא ירפא מתקיף לה רב אשי ממאי דמותרה לדבר חמור הוי מותרה לדבר הקל דלמא לא הוי ואם תמצא לומר הוי ממאי דמיתה חמורה דלמא מלקות חמור דאמר רב אילמלי נגדוה לחנניה מישאל ועזריה פלחו לצלמא א"ל רב סמא בריה דרב אסי לרב אשי ואמרי לה רב סמא בריה דרב אשי לרב אשי ולא שני לך בין הכאה שיש לה קצבה להכאה שאין לה קצבה מתקיף לה רב מרי ממאי דבמזיד ונקה מקטלא דלמא בשוגג ונקה מגלות קשיא: ריש לקיש אמר הא מני רבי מאיר היא ז) דאמר לוקה ומשלם אי רבי מאיר אפי' בתו נמי וכי תימא ר' מאיר לוקה ומשלם אית ליה מת ומשלם לית ליה ולא והתניא גנב וטבח בשבת גנב וטבח לעבודת כוכבים גנב שור הנסקל וטבחו ב) משלם תשלומי ארבעה וחמשה דברי רבי מאיר וחכמים פוטרין הא איתמר עלה אמר רבי יעקב א"ר יוחנן ואמרי לה אמר רבי ירמיה אמר ר' שמעון בן לקיש ר' אבין ורבי אילעא וכל חבורתא משמיה דרבי יוחנן אמרי ח) בטובח על ידי אחר וכי זה חוטא וזה מתחייב אמר רבא אמר רחמנא ב) וטבחו או מכרו ט) מה מכירה על ידי אחר אף טביחה על ידי אחר דבי רבי ישמעאל תנא או לרבות את השליח דבי חזקיה תנא ב) תחת לרבות את השליח י) מתקיף לה מר זוטרא מי איכא מידי דאילו עבד איהו לא מיחייב ועביד שליח ומחייב איהו לאו משום דלא מיחייב ה) אלא משום דקם ליה בדרבה מיניה אי בטובח על ידי אחר מאי טעמייהו דרבנן דפטרי י) מאן חכמים רבי

רש"י

נגדוה. יסורין: ולא שני לך כו'. יסורי המלכות הכאה שאין לה קצבה היא אבל מלקות יש לה קצבה ארבעים: הניחא לרבנן דאמרי. בסנהדרין באלו הן הנשרפים (עט.) נתכוון להרוג את זה והרג את זה חייב והאי ונתת נפש ממש קאמר אית לן למידק ואוקמי קרא בשהתרו בו ולמילף דאע"ג דאיכא התראה יענש ממון כשאין שם מיתה: אלא לרבי דאמר. התם נתכוון להרוג את זה והרג את זה אינו נהרג אלא משלם דמי האשה ליורשיה אם כן אפשר לאוקמי קרא בשלא התרו בו ומשום הכי כי אין אסון משלם דמי ולדות וכי יש אסון משלם דמי אשה אבל אתרו ביה אימא לך לוקה ואינו משלם: מאי איכא למימר. מהיכא תיתי חובל בחבירו לתשלומין ואף כשהתרו בו: על משענתו. כדמתרגמינן על בוריו שבא לכחו ולאיתנו הראשון: אלא מלמד שחובשין אותו. לא נאמר מקרא זה אלא ללמדך דהיכא דהכהו ולא מת ונפל למשכב יחבשו את המכה הסוה בבית האסורין עד שנראה אם יקום והתהלך בחוץ אז ונקה המכה מכלל דעד השתא לא יצא מידי בית דין אלא נחבש: ואי מיית קטלינן ליה. [כיון דאמרת חובשין מכלל דאי מיית ניזק קטלינן ליה להאי דאי לאו לקטלא למאי חבשינן ליה:] לדבר חמור. מיתה: לדבר הקל. מלקות דלא יוסיף דחובל ולא מת: ואמר רחמנא. להיכא דלא מת דליכא ממון ומלקות נידון בממון דכתיב שבתו יתן: ממאי. דהאי והכה איש את רעהו במזיד קא משתעי והאי ונקה דילפינן מיניה חבישה ונקה מקטלא קאמר דתשמע מינה דאי מיית קטלינן ליה ועל כרחין בהתרו בו: דלמא בשוגג. משתעי ולא התרו בו וחבישה לאו לקטלא ונקה נמי לאו מקטלא אלא מגלות דעדי מקלט וחבישה דילפינן מיניה לגלות קאמר ומשום הכי כי נקה מגלות ישלם ממון אבל היכא דאתרו ביה אימא לך דכי לא מיית לוקה ואינו משלם: ריש לקיש מהדר אשינויא דרומיא דרמינן ברייתא שמעתין מתני' דמכות אדכתובות: הא מני. מתניתין דקתני בא על אחותו נותן קנס ר"מ היא דאמר לעיל לוקה ומשלם שלא הכתוב המביאו לידי מכות מביאו לידי תשלומין: אפי' בתו נמי. דמיקטיל עלה לישלם דהא לא סבירא ליה לר"מ דפטור משום דרבה מיניה ואמאי תנן מתני' הבא על בתו פטור מן הקנס: וטבח בשבת. איכא חיוב מיתה וכן לעבודת כוכבים: שור הנסקל. לקמן פריך הא לא שוה מידי: בטובח על ידי אחר. הגנב לוה לשלוחו לשחוט: וכי. שליח חוטא ושולח מתחייב קנס דארבעה וחמשה והא קיימא לן בקדושין (מג:) אין שליח לדבר עבירה: מכירה אי אפשר אלא ע"י אחר שהלוקח לוקחו ממנו: תחת השור. מצי למכתב ישלם בשור: עבד איהו לא מיחייב. דהא מיקטיל: לאו משום דלא מיחייב הוא. דחיובא רמיא עליה אלא משום דקם ליה בדרבה מיניה:

רבי

תוספות

ודלמא מלקות חמור. הוה מצי לשנויי מסתברא מיתה חמורה שכן ניתנה לאנשי עיר הנדחת כדאמרי' בפ"ד מיתות (סנהדרין נ.): אילמלי נגדוה לחנניה מישאל ועזריה הוו פלחי לצלמא. תימה מנא לן (א) דהא אמרי' בהרואה (ברכות סא:) כשהוציאו את ר"ע להריגה אמר כל ימי הייתי מצטער על פסוק זה אימתי יבא לידי ואקיימנו בכל נפשך אלמא משמע דבכל נפשך מיירי אפי' היו מייסרין את האדם ביסורין קשין דומיא דר' עקיבא שהיו מסרקין בשרו במסרקי ברזל וכ"ש לנגודי ואור"ת דאותו צלם לא היה עבודת כוכבים ממש אלא היה עשוי לכבוד המלך ואעפ"כ היה בו קידוש השם ולכך מסרו עצמן למיתה והיינו דכתיב (דניאל ג) לאלהך לית אנן פלחין ולצלם דהבא די הקימת לא נסגוד משמע שהצלם לא היה תופס באלהות ומיהו פלחו לצלמא משמע שהצלם היה עבודת כוכבים מדקאמר פלחו (ה):

דלמא בשוגג ונקה מגלות. תימה לר"י היכי שייך גלות אם מת אחר שחבשוהו ג' או ארבעה ימים הא אמרינן במי שאחזו (גיטין ע: ושם) שחט בו שנים או רוב שנים הרי זה אינו גולה דחיישינן שמא הרוח בלבלתו וטעמא דגבי גלות אשכחן מילי טובא דפטור כגון דרך עלייה לגבי מיתה אין חילוק בין דרך עלייה לדרך ירידה הכי נמי גבי גלות בעינן שימות מיד דכתיב ויפל עליו וימות משמע מיד ואע"ג דגבי מיתה נמי כתיב מכה איש ומת וי"ל דמשכחת לה בגיסא דשיפא דלא חיישינן שמא הרוח בלבלתו כדאמרינן התם אי נמי דוקא בשחט בו רוב שנים חיישינן שמא הרוח בלבלתו דבקל הרוח מבלבלו אבל בשאר מכות אין הרוח מזיק כל כך שיכולין לשמור יפה מבלבול רוח לכרוך על המכה שום דבר וא"ת היכי מיתוקם קרא בשוגג הא כתיב בקרא רק שבתו יתן וגו' ובשוגג לא מיחייב כדאמרינן בס"פ כיצד הרגל (ב"ק כו: ושם) דמרבה מפצע תחת פצע לחייב על השוגג כמזיד נזק אבל לא ד' דברים וי"ל דמשכחת לה בהוסיף לו רצועה אחת דאמר בהמניח (שם לג:) דגולה ואם לא מת חייב בד' דברים ולא דמי לשאר שוגג או כגון שנכנס לחנותו של נגר (ו) (שלא) ברשות דמוכח התם לרב פפא דשייך ביה גלות וד' דברים או נפל מן הגג ברוח מצויה דחייב בד' דברים כדאמרי' בסוף כיצד הרגל (שם כז.) ומסתברא דאם מת דגולה ועוד דאפשר דהוי שוגג על המיתה ומזיד על החבלה (ז): גנב שור הנסקל וטבחו משלם תשלומי ד' וה'. תימה דתיקשי מהכא לריש לקיש דאמר בפ' מרובה (שם עו: ושם) כל היכא דליתיה במכירה ליתיה בטביחה והכא שור הנסקל ליתיה במכירה וי"ל דהתם קדשים קאמר דליתנהו כלל במכירה אבל שור הנסקל אם ימכרנו לעובד כוכבים אין תופס דמיו ולר"ת שאומר דאין שור הנסקל ° נאסר מחיים ניחא: לאו משום דלא מיחייב כו'. אע"ג דהכא אפי' לצאת ידי שמים אינו חייב דדוקא בממון הוא דאמר רבא בהשוכר את הפועלים (ב"מ צא. ושם) אתנן אסרה תורה אפי' בא על אמו דמיחייב בבא לצאת ידי שמים אבל קנס לא מיחייב אלא ע"פ ב"ד כדאמרי' אשר ירשיעון אלהים פרט למרשיע עצמו מ"מ ניחא דכיון שהיה ראוי להתחייב אם לא היה מתחייב בנפשו מתחייב נמי אממון ע"י שליח כיון שאינו מתחייב בנפשו:

רבי

ליקוטי רש"י

אילמלי נגדוה וכו' פלחו לצלמא. בתמיה [רש"י בשיטמ"ק בשם רשב"א]. אלא לרבי דאמר. התם נתכוון להרוג את זה והרג את זה אינו נהרג אלא משלם דמי אשה ואע"ג דלא אתרו ביה אבל אתרו ביה אימא לך לוקה ואינו משלם [רש"י כת"י בשיטמ"ק]. ממון. דמי האשה יתן ליורשיה [סנהדרין עט.]. על משענתו. על בוריו וכחו [שמות כא, יט]. מתרגמינן על בוריה שנתרפא לגמרי ועומד על כחו. וכי תעלה על דעתך. [illegible] ונקה המכה [סנהדרין עח:]. ונקה המכה וכו' שחובשין אותו. [illegible] שבתו. [illegible] ורפא ירפא. [illegible] ריש לקיש אמר. [illegible] רבי מאיר היא. [illegible] גנב וטבח בשבת. [illegible] גנב שור הנסקל. [illegible] חוטא וזה מתחייב. [illegible] מה מכירה. [illegible] אף טביחה. [illegible] תנא או. לרבות אפילו שליח. תחת לרבות. [illegible] עבד איהו לא מיחייב. [illegible] דהא מיקטיל [רש"י משיטמ"ק עיי"ש]. איהו לאו משום דלא מיחייב. כי עביד איהו [דפטרינן] ליה לאו משום דלא מיחייב אלא משום דקם ליה בדרבה מיניה [ב"ק שם]. מאן חכמים. מאי טעמייהו [גיטין כב.]. [מכאן שייך לדף לד.] ר' שמעון היא. דאמר לענין כיסוי הדם (חולין דף פה.) ואותו ואת בנו (שם דף פ.) ותשלומי ארבעה וחמשה (ב"ק דף עא.) שחיטה שאינה ראויה שחיטה וכל חיוב ואיסור הבא ע"י שחיטה אינו חל עליה [קידושין נח.]. כדתנן בפרקין (ב"ק ע.) רבי שמעון פוטר בשני אלו. התינח עבודת כוכבים ושור הנסקל. איסורי הנאה ע"ז (דף נד.) אע"פ שאמרו המשתחוה לבהמת חבירו לא אסרה עשה בה מעשה אסרה [ב"ק עא.]. וביום הכפורים מתחייב כרת [חולין יד.]. המבשל בשבת. בידים דאיכא חיובא בשוגג יאכל. אפי' הוא עצמו וכו ביום [ב"ק שם]. הוא עצמו ואפילו בו ביום ואין צריך להמתין עד הערב בכדי שיעשו דהא דאמרינן בעלמא לערב בכדי שיעשו לית ליה לר"מ אלא היכא דעבד ישראל איסורא ובמזיד דאיכא חיובא דלא נמטייה הנאה מאיסורא אבל בשוגג לא [חולין טו.].

הגהות הב"ח

(א) תוס' ד"ה אילמלי כו' מנא לן ועוד דהא:

גליון הש"ס

תוס' ד"ה גנב וכו' נאסר מחיים ניחא. עי' זבחים דף עא ע"א תוס' ד"ה (בעומד הקודש) אפי':

תורה אור השלם

א) אִם יָקוּם וְהִתְהַלֵּךְ בַּחוּץ עַל מִשְׁעַנְתּוֹ וְנִקָּה הַמַּכֶּה רַק שִׁבְתּוֹ יִתֵּן וְרַפֹּא יְרַפֵּא: [שמות כא, יט]

ב) כִּי יִגְנֹב אִישׁ שׁוֹר אוֹ שֶׂה וּטְבָחוֹ אוֹ מְכָרוֹ חֲמִשָּׁה בָקָר יְשַׁלֵּם תַּחַת הַשּׁוֹר וְאַרְבַּע צֹאן תַּחַת הַשֶּׂה: [שמות כא, לז]

חובל בחבירו נמי א"כ בטלת א) לא יוסיף פן יוסיף עדים זוממין נמי א"כ בטלת ב) והיה אם בן הכות הרשע אלא עדים זוממין אפשר לקיומה בבן גרושה ובן חלוצה חובל בחבירו נמי איכא לקיומה כגון שהכהו הכאה שאין בה שוה פרוטה אחותו נמי איכא לקיומה באחותו בוגרת (א) אמר לך ר' יוחנן האי תחת אשר ענה מיבעי ליה לכדאביי דאמר אביי אמר קרא ג) תחת אשר ענה האי תחת אשר ענה מכלל דאיכא בושת ופגם ועולא נפקא ליה מדרבא דאמר רבא אמר קרא ג) ונתן האיש השוכב עמה לאבי הנערה חמשים כסף הנאת שכיבה חמשים מכלל דאיכא בושת ופגם רבי אליעזר אומר עדים זוממין ממונא משלמי ומילקא לא לקי משום דלאו בני התראה נינהו אמר רבא תדע ניתרי בהו איתת ניתרי בהו מעיקרא אמרי אישתלין ניתרי בהו בשעת מעשה פרשי ולא מסהדי ניתרי בהו לבסוף מאי דהוה הוה מתקיף לה אביי וניתרי בהו בתוך כדי דבור מתקיף לה רב אחא בריה דרב איקא וניתרי בהו מעיקרא ונרמז בהו רמוזי הדר אמר אביי לאו מילתא היא דאמרי אי סלקא דעתך עדים זוממין צריכין התראה כי לא מתרינן בהו לא קטלינן להו מי איכא מידי דאינהו בעו קטיל בלא התראה ואינהו בעו התראה הא בעינן ד) ועשיתם לו כאשר זמם לעשות לאחיו וליכא מתקיף לה רב סמא בריה דרב ירמיה אלא מעתה בן גרושה ובן חלוצה דלא מכאשר זמם קא מיתרבי ליבעי התראה אמר קרא ה) משפט אחד יהיה לכם משפט השוה לכולכם רב שישא בריה דרב אידי אמר חובל בחבירו נמי ממונא משלם ומילקא לא לקי מהכא ו) וכי ינצו אנשים ונגפו אשה הרה ויצאו ילדיה ואמר רבי אלעזר במצות שבמיתה הכתוב מדבר דכתיב ז) ואם אסון יהיה ונתת נפש תחת נפש היכי דמי אי דלא אתרו ביה אמאי מיקטיל אלא פשיטא דאתרו ביה ומותרה לדבר חמור הוי מותרה לדבר הקל ואמר רחמנא ולא יהיה אסון ענוש יענש מתקיף לה רב אשי ממאי דמותרה לדבר חמור הוי מותרה לדבר הקל דלמא לא הוי אם תמצא לומר הוי ממאי דמיתה חמורה דלמא

רש"י

ופרכינן חובל בחבירו דעל כרחך בממון נידון תקשי בטלת לאו דלא יוסיף פן יוסיף שהוא אזהרה למכה את חבירו: **והיה אם בן הכות.** במסכת מכות (דף ב:) מוקמינן לה בעדים זוממין: **אלא.** על כרחך כיון דרבייה קרא לתשלומין איכא לאוקמא לעונש מלקות דלאו דידיה במעידין אנו את איש פלוני כהן שהוא בן גרושה דליכא לאוקמי כאשר זמם ולומר יהא הוא בן גרושה תחתיו אלא סופג את הארבעים והכי תנן במסכת מכות וחובל בחבירו נמי מוקמינן ליה בשאין בה שוה פרוטה בכל חמשה דברים שבה כגון שלא פיחתו מכספו וממלאכתו וריפוי לא הוצרך ולא צער היה בה ובשוטה שאין לה בושת והכא נמי באחותו מצית לאוקמי מלקות דידה בבוגרת אבל נערה לישלם ולא לילקי הואיל וריבתה גזירה שוה דתחת תחת לתשלומין: **לכדאביי.** בשילהי פירקין דפרכינן ואימא חמשים אמר רחמנא מכל מילי ושני אביי חמשים כסף נתחדשו תחת קנס העינוי אבל בושת ופגם שהוא בשאר חובלים לא כלל כאן: **השוכב עמה.** קרא יתירא הוא לדרשה נימא ונתן לאבי הנערה חמשים כסף: **מכלל דבושת ופגם.** דלאו מחמת הנאת שכיבה נינהו שהרי ישנן בשאר חובלים לא כיילינהו בגוייהו דהני: **רבי אלעזר אומר עדים זוממין דממונא משלמי ולא לקו.** לא צריכי קרא דסברא היא דמלקות לא שייך בהו: **דלאו בני התראה נינהו.** קודם עדות כדמפ' רבא ואזיל הלכך אי איכא למענשינהו לא תענשינהו אלא ממון דאין עונש הגוף בלא התראה ואע"ג דגבי בן גרושה ובן חלוצה ענשינן להו מלקות בלא התראה התם גזירת הכתוב דאשכחן בהו מלקות בהדיא והיה אם בן הכות ומוקמינן לקרא במידי דלא מצית למענשינהו מכאשר זמם אבל היכא דמצית למיעבד בהו הזמה לא שייך בהו מלקות: **תדע.** שאי אפשר להתרות בהם: **מעיקרא.** יום או שעה קודם שיעידו העדות: **אמרי אישתלין.** שכחנו ההתראה הרי שבטלה ההתראה: **פרשי ולא מסהדי.** אפילו אמת הואיל ואנו חשודים בעיניכם מה לנו ולצרה: **לבסוף.** לאחר שהעידו: **מאי דהוה הוה.** דכיון שהגיד אינו חוזר ומגיד ואינן יכולין לחזור: **וניתרי בהו בתוך כדי דבור.** לאחר שהעידו דתוך כדי דבור כדבור דמי ויכולים לחזור: **תוך כדי דבור.** כדי שאילת שלום: **ונרמז רמוזי.** בשעת העדות נרמוז להם רמזים על ההתראה להזכירם ובלשון רך שלא יקפידו: **לאו מילתא היא דאמרי.** שיהו עדים זוממין צריכין התראה: ה"ג דאינהו בעו למיקטל בלא התראה ואינהו בעו התראה כו': **כאשר זמם.** והם זממו להרוג את זה בעדותן שלא היה ולא נברא ולא התרו בו ההתראה שהעידו עליה: **אלא מעתה.** דהאי דלא בעו התראה משום כאשר זמם הוא מלקות של זוממי עדות בן גרושה ובן חלוצה: **דלאו מכאשר זמם אתי.** עונש דידהו שהרי לא זממו להלקותו אלא לחללו: **משפט השוה.** וכיון דרוב זוממין לאו בני התראה נינהו הני נמי לא בעו התראה: **במצות שבמיתה.** שמתכוין היה להורגו: **הכתוב מדבר.** דכתיב אם אסון יהיה שמתה האשה ונתת נפש ואע"פ שלא נתכוון אלא לחבירו ואשמעינן נתכוון להרוג את זה והרג את זה חייב: **אי דלא אתרו ביה.** אם תמיתנו תהרג: **לדבר חמור.** מיתה: **הוי מותרה לדבר הקל.** שאם יכנו ולא ימות ילקה ואפילו הכי אמר רחמנא דכי אין שם חיוב מיתה יענש דמי ולדות ואף על גב דאיכא התראה למלקות אלמא משלם ואינו לוקה:

תוספות

אלא אפשר לקיומי בבן גרושה או בבן חלוצה. ואם תאמר אמאי לקו אעדות דבן גרושה הא הוי עדות שאין אתה יכול להזימה וי"ל דלא חשיב עדות שאין אתה יכול להזימה אלא במעידין על הטרפה דאי אפשר לקיומי בשום דבר לא במיתה ולא במלקות דגברא קטילא בעו למיקטל אבל הכא נתקיימה הזמה במלקות ז): **מיבעי** ליה לכדאביי. ואם תאמר כיון דאיצטריך תחת להך דרשה א"כ מנא לן מיטב וי"ל דיליף מנתינה או מכסף:

ועולא נפקא ליה מדרבא. משמע דרבא סבר כעולא דרבי יוחנן גופיה הוה דריש כעולא אי לאו משום דמיבעי ליה לכדאביי וקשה לרשב"א דבפרק השוכר את הפועלים (ב"מ צא. ושם) משמע בהדיא דסבר כרבי יוחנן גבי חוסם פרה ודש בה לוקה ומשלם דמוקי לה אביי כרבי מאיר ורבא אמר לעולם כרבנן ואתנן אסרה תורה אפי' בא על אמו פירוש ומשלם לצאת ידי שמים משמע דבדין לוקה ואינו משלם ולמאי דפרישי' לעיל דלמסקנא דווקא בהני תלת אית ליה לעולא דממונא משלם ולא לקי אתי שפיר דבעלמא סבר כרבי יוחנן דלוקה ואין משלם כדדריש רבי יוחנן וסמיך ליה ארבעים יכנו:

ניתרי בהו מעיקרא כו'. ואם תאמר תיפוק ליה דהויא התראת ספק דאין אנו יודעין אם מעידים שקר ויש לומר דהתראת ספק לא הויא אלא כגון אל תותיר שאף למותרה עצמו הוא ספק שסבור שעדיין יש שהות ביום אבל הכא המותרין יודעין שמעידין שקר:

וניתרי בהו בתוך כדי דבור. ואם תאמר היכי מצי תו הדרי בהו והא בהתראה איכא טפי מכדי דבור שהוא כדי שאילת שלום ויש לומר דכל זמן שעסוקים באותו דבר חשיב הכל תוך כדי דבור כדאמרינן במכות (דף ו.) דאפי' מעידין מאה כל אחד תוך כדי דבור של חבירו חשובין כולן תוך כדי דבור של ראשון ואם נמצא אחד מהן קרוב או פסול עדותן בטילה:

אלא פשיטא דאתרו ביה. וא"ת היכי משלם ממון אפי' כי אין אסון הא כיון דמתכוין להרוג הוי ליה רודף ומתחייב בנפשו וקים ליה בדרבה מיניה וי"ל בשיכולין להצילו באחד מאבריו והכי אמרינן בבן סורר (סנהדרין דף עד.):

ממאי דמותרה לדבר חמור הוי מותרה לדבר הקל דלמא לא הוי. אין לומר דטעמא משום דאהריגה הוא דקיבל התראה דניחא ליה ליהרג על מנת שיהרוג שונאו דתמות נפשי עם פלשתים הוא דקאמר אבל לא ניחא ליה להכות את חבירו על מנת שילקוהו דהא אמתני' דפרק הנשרפין (סנהדרין ד' עט:) דקתני דחייבי מיתות שנתערבו ידונו בקלה וקאמר בגמ' (שם דף פ:) ש"מ מותרה לדבר חמור הוי מותרה לדבר הקל והתם פשיטא דכיון דהתרו בו לסקילה וקבל כ"ש שאם התרו בו חנק על אותו דבר עצמו שהיה מקבל ואפ"ה בעי למימר דמותרה לדבר חמור לא הוי מותרה לדבר הקל אלא יש לומר דגזירת הכתוב הוא דבעינן שיתיר עצמו לאותה מיתה בין קלה בין חמורה:

ודלמא

נגדוה

מסורת הש"ס

א) לקמן מ., ב) [נ"ל אליעזר], ג) [ב"ק פג: פד. סנהדרין כח.], ד) סנהדרין עב. עט. [ועי' על הגליון מ"ש בשם התוס' ע"ש], ה) [סנהדרין ט:], ו) ס"א כסף נתחדשו תחת, ז) [ועיין תוס' מכות ב. ד"ה מעידין וכו' ביתר ביאור].

תורה אור השלם

א) אַרְבָּעִים יַכֶּנּוּ לֹא יֹסִיף פֶּן יֹסִיף לְהַכֹּתוֹ עַל אֵלֶּה מַכָּה רַבָּה וְנִקְלָה אָחִיךָ לְעֵינֶיךָ: [דברים כה, ג]

ב) וְהָיָה אִם בִּן הַכּוֹת הָרָשָׁע וְהִפִּילוֹ הַשֹּׁפֵט וְהִכָּהוּ לְפָנָיו כְּדֵי רִשְׁעָתוֹ בְּמִסְפָּר: [דברים כה, ב]

ג) וְנָתַן הָאִישׁ הַשֹּׁכֵב עִמָּהּ לַאֲבִי הַנַּעֲרָ חֲמִשִּׁים כָּסֶף וְלוֹ תִהְיֶה לְאִשָּׁה תַּחַת אֲשֶׁר עִנָּהּ לֹא יוּכַל שַׁלְּחָהּ כָּל יָמָיו: [דברים כב, כט]

ד) וַעֲשִׂיתֶם לוֹ כַּאֲשֶׁר זָמַם לַעֲשׂוֹת לְאָחִיו וּבִעַרְתָּ הָרָע מִקִּרְבֶּךָ: [דברים יט, יט]

ה) מִשְׁפַּט אֶחָד יִהְיֶה לָכֶם כַּגֵּר כָּאֶזְרָח יִהְיֶה כִּי אֲנִי יְיָ אֱלֹהֵיכֶם: [ויקרא כד, כב]

ו) וְכִי יִנָּצוּ אֲנָשִׁים וְנָגְפוּ אִשָּׁה הָרָה וְיָצְאוּ יְלָדֶיהָ וְלֹא יִהְיֶה אָסוֹן עָנוֹשׁ יֵעָנֵשׁ כַּאֲשֶׁר יָשִׁית עָלָיו בַּעַל הָאִשָּׁה וְנָתַן בִּפְלִלִים: [שמות כא, כב]

ז) וְאִם אָסוֹן יִהְיֶה וְנָתַתָּה נֶפֶשׁ תַּחַת נָפֶשׁ: [שמות כא, כג]

עין משפט נר מצוה

כה א מיי' פי"ח מהל' עדות הל' ד סמג עשין קי טור ח"מ סי' לח:

כו ב ג מיי' פי"ט מהל' סנהדרין הלכה ג [דין דמותרה לדבר חמור לא מלאתי במיי' שם מבואר רק כשהתרו בו בשתי מיתות ספק דהוי התראה והיינו דהוי כמקבל עליו בין מיתה חמורה כגון סקילה ובין קלה אבל כשהתרו בו בחמורה לבד לא נתבאר שם ועי' בתוספות דהכא סד"ה ממאי וכו' דגזירת הכתוב הוא וכו']:

הגהות הב"ח

(א) גמ' אמר לך ר"י. נ"ב ס"א אלא ר' יוחנן:

גליון הש"ס

גמ' אמר קרא משפט אחד. עיין מכות דף ד ע"ב ברש"י ד"ה עדים זוממין א"צ התראה ולע"ק:

ליקוטי רש"י

תחת אשר ענה. גבי חמשים כסף כתיב. **מכלל דאיכא בושת ופגם.** שאינם משום עינוי שהרי ישנן בשאר חבלות אינו בכלל זה. פגם הוא נזק הניזוקים נמי בשאר חבלות [לקמן מ:]. דמשמע הכי חמשים כסף יתן בשביל קנס העינוי ומדאיצטריך למכתב הכי מכלל דמיחייב מילי אחרנייתא כגון בושת ופגם דלאו קנסא לעינוי נינהו דבלאו עינוי נמי איכא בושת ופגם והיינו נזק שווה פחות מבתחילה. **תחת אשר עינה.** רישיה דקרא ונתן האיש השוכב עמה לאבי הנערה חמשים כסף וגו' (דברים כב) [ערכין טו.]. **אמר קרא משפט אחד וכו'.** עדים זוממין אין צריכין התראה. בכתובות אמרינן טעמא באלו נערות (דף לג.) נתרי בהו איתת כו' אבל כל שאר עונשין בכ"ד מטה צריכין התראה [מכות ד: עי' גהש"ס]. **וכי ינצו אנשים.** זה עם זה ונתכוין להכות את חבירו והכה את האשה. **ונגפו.** אין נגיפה אלא לשון דחיפה והכאה כמו (תהלים צא יב) פן תגוף באבן רגלך (ירמיה יג טז) ובטרם יתנגפו רגליכם (ישעיה ח יד) ולאבן נגף [שמות כא, כב]. **במצות שבמיתה.** שהוא מתכוין להרוג את חבירו והכה את האשה הכתוב מדבר. **דכתיב ואם וכו'.** ואי לא מתכוין להרוג דשוגג הוא אמאי מקטיל לאו שמע מינה במתכוין [סנהדרין עד.]. ואי לא נתכוון להרוג היאך מקטיל כי איכוון מיהא חייב אע"ג דלא נתכוון אלא לחבירו דהא כתיב וכי ינצו אנשים וגו' [שם עט.]. **ואם אסון יהיה.** באשה. **ונתת נפש תחת נפש.** רבותינו חולקין בדבר יש אומרים נפש ממש ויש אומרים ממון אבל לא נפש ממש שהמתכוין להרוג את זה והרג את זה פטור ממיתה ומשלם ליורשיו דמיו כמו שהיה נמכר בשוק [שמות כא, כג].

The Gemara objects:

מַתְקִיף לָהּ רַב סַמָּא בְּרֵיהּ דְּרַב יִרְמְיָה – **Rav Samma the son of Rav Yirmiyah objected to this:** אֶלָּא מֵעַתָּה – **But accordingly,**[27] בֶּן גְּרוּשָׁה וּבֶן חֲלוּצָה – *zomeim* witnesses who testified that a certain Kohen is **the son of a divorcee or the son of a** ***chalutzah,***[28] דְּלָא מ,,כַּאֲשֶׁר זָמַם" קָא מִיתְרַבֵּי – **who are not included** in their punishment of lashes **by virtue of** the verse *you shall do to him **as he conspired,***[29] but rather by virtue of the verse *it will be if the wicked one is subject to lashes,* לִיבָּעֵי הַתְרָאָה – **should require a warning** in order to receive lashes! – ? –

The Gemara answers:

אָמַר קְרָא ,,מִשְׁפַּט אֶחָד יִהְיֶה לָכֶם" – **The verse states:**[30] ***One law shall be for you.*** מִשְׁפָּט הַשָּׁוֶה לְכוּלְּכֶם – This teaches that **the law is the same for all of you.**[31]

The Gemara now presents an alternative source as well for the ruling that one who wounds his fellow pays money rather than receive lashes:[32]

רַב שִׁישָׁא בְּרֵיהּ דְּרַב אִידִי אָמַר – **Rav Shisha the son of Rav Idi says:** חוֹבֵל בַּחֲבֵירוֹ נַמִּי מָמוֹנָא מְשַׁלֵּם וּמִילְקָא לֹא לָקֵי מֵהָכָא – **One who wounds his fellow, too,**[33] **pays money and does not receive lashes, based on the following:**[34] ,,וְכִי־יִנָּצוּ אֲנָשִׁים וְנָגְפוּ אִשָּׁה הָרָה וְיָצְאוּ יְלָדֶיהָ" – The verse states: ***If men shall quarrel and they jolt a pregnant woman and she miscarries.***[35] וְאָמַר רַבִּי אֶלְעָזָר – **And R' Elazar said** in explanation of this verse: בְּמַצּוּת שֶׁבְּמִיתָה הַכָּתוּב מְדַבֵּר – **Scripture** here **is discussing a fight to the death,** i.e. a fight in which the combatant was trying to kill his fellow, דִּכְתִיב ,,וְאִם־אָסוֹן יִהְיֶה וְנָתַתָּה נֶפֶשׁ תַּחַת נָפֶשׁ" – **as** is evident from that which **is written** in the very next verse: ***And if there shall be a fatality*** [i.e. if the woman is killed] ***then you shall give a life for a life,*** i.e. the murderer shall be executed even though he did not intend to kill the woman but his adversary.[36] הֵיכִי דָמֵי – Now, **what is the case?** אִי דְּלָא אַתְרוּ בֵּיהּ – **If they did not warn him** that striking and killing his opponent would subject him to the death penalty, אַמַּאי מִיקְטִיל – then **why is he executed?**[37] אֶלָּא פְּשִׁיטָא דְּאַתְרוּ בֵּיהּ – **Rather, it is obvious that they did warn him** that striking and killing would subject him to the death penalty. וּמוּתְרֶה לְדָבָר חָמוּר הָוֵי מוּתְרֶה לְדָבָר הַקַּל – **And** the rule is that **one who is warned for a severe matter is** deemed **warned for a lenient matter.**[38] Thus, the warning that striking and killing his adversary would subject him to the death penalty serves also as a warning that striking and *wounding* his adversary would subject him to lashes.[39] וְאָמַר רַחֲמָנָא – **Yet, the Merciful One** states in His Torah: ,,וְלֹא יִהְיֶה אָסוֹן עָנוֹשׁ יֵעָנֵשׁ" – ***If there will be no fatality, he shall be punished [monetarily].***[40] Thus, we have a situation in which an assailant becomes liable to the dual penalty of payment and lashes,[41] and the Torah states that he pays the money [and does not receive lashes].[42]

The Gemara objects:

מַתְקִיף לָהּ רַב אַשִׁי – **Rav Ashi objected to this:** מִמַּאי דְּמוּתְרֶה לְדָבָר חָמוּר הָוֵי מוּתְרֶה לְדָבָר הַקַּל – **On what basis** do you assume that **one who is warned for a severe matter is** deemed **warned for a lenient matter?** דִּלְמָא לֹא הָוֵי – **Perhaps** he **is not** deemed warned for the lenient matter![43] אִם תִּמְצָא לוֹמַר הָוֵי – And even **if you were to** conclude and **say** that one who is warned for a severe penalty **is** deemed warned for the lenient penalty, מִמַּאי דְּמִיתָה חֲמוּרָה – **on the basis of what** do you assume **that** the **death** penalty **is the more severe** penalty?

NOTES

27. I.e. if the basis of not requiring a warning for witnesses is that the Torah's mandate to *do to him as he conspired* precludes this (*Rashi*).

28. As we learned above, such witnesses do not receive a reciprocal punishment, but rather lashes (see note 5).

29. For they did not conspire to subject him to lashes, but to render him a *chalal* (*Rashi*).

30. *Leviticus* 24:22.

31. [Accordingly, there must be one law for all *zomemim.*] And since most *zomemim* do not require warning [as their punishment is mandated by the verse *you shall to him as he conspired*], so, too, *zomemim* who testified that a Kohen is the son of a divorcee do not require a warning either (*Rashi*).

32. Even when he was warned that striking his fellow would subject him to lashes.

33. [I.e. just as an alternative source was presented for the law cited above that *zomemim* pay and do not receive lashes, so too is there an alternative source for the law cited above that one who wounds his fellow and is subject to the dual penalty of compensation and lashes pays the compensation rather than receive the lashes.]

34. And not on the basis of the verse cited above on 32b: *so shall be "given" in him.*

35. *Exodus* 21:22. The verse in its entirety reads: וְכִי־יִנָּצוּ אֲנָשִׁים וְנָגְפוּ אִשָּׁה הָרָה וְיָצְאוּ יְלָדֶיהָ וְלֹא יִהְיֶה אָסוֹן עָנוֹשׁ יֵעָנֵשׁ כַּאֲשֶׁר יָשִׁית עָלָיו בַּעַל הָאִשָּׁה וְנָתַן בִּפְלִלִים, *If men shall quarrel and they jolt a pregnant woman and she miscarries, if there will be no fatality* [i.e. the woman does not die], *he [who struck the woman] shall be punished as the husband of the woman shall cause to be assessed against him, and he shall give [compensation] by order of judges.*

36. And this verse teaches that if someone strikes a blow intending to kill one person and the blow falls upon and kills someone else, the murderer is liable to the death penalty for willful murder (*Rashi*). If, however, the killer had not intended to kill anyone, he could not be given the death penalty. Thus, the verse's imposition of the death penalty indicates that the killer had indeed intended to kill someone.

[There is, though, a Tanna who holds that intent to kill someone other than the actual victim is *not* sufficient for imposition of the death penalty. That Tanna explains this verse differently – see *Sanhedrin* 79a, and below, 33b.]

37. Certainly, a murderer cannot be executed without having been warned.

38. I.e. a warning to a person that his contemplated act might result in the death penalty is certainly sufficient to punish him with lashes if his act results in a mere violation of a prohibition and not in a capital offense. [The Gemara is presently assuming that there is such a rule – an assumption that the Gemara below will call into question.]

39. For violating the prohibition against hitting one's fellow; see above, note 2.

40. [See note 35 for a full citation of the verse.] That is, he must pay the value of the offspring that the woman miscarried [see Mishnah, *Bava Kamma* 48b as to how this is assessed].

41. He is liable to payment for killing the offspring, and to lashes for striking the woman [thereby violating the prohibition *he shall not add* – see above, note 2].

42. [For he cannot receive lashes in addition to paying the money, since the verse states *according to his wickedness* – see above, 32b.]

43. Perhaps a punishment cannot be administered unless the sinner has accepted upon himself that particular punishment. And although the sinner accepted upon himself a more severe penalty, the court is not empowered to administer any other penalty – even a less severe one (see *Tosafos*).

חובל בחבירו נמי א"כ בטלת [א] לא יוסיף פן יוסיף עדים זוממין נמי א"כ בטלת [ב] והיה אם בן הכות הרשע אלא עדים זוממין אפשר לקיומה בבן גרושה ובן חלוצה חובל בחבירו נמי איכא לקיומה כגון שהכהו הכאה שאין בה שוה פרוטה אחותו נמי איכא לקיומה באחותו בוגרת (א) אמר לך ר' יוחנן האי תחת אשר עינה מיבעי ליה לכדאביי [ה] דאמר אביי אמר קרא [ג] תחת אשר עינה האי תחת אשר עינה מכלל דאיכא בושת ופגם ועולא נפקא ליה מדרבא דאמר רבא אמר קרא [ג] ונתן האיש השוכב עמה לאבי הנערה חמשים כסף הנאת שכיבה חמשים מכלל דאיכא בושת ופגם רבי [ו] אליעזר אומר עדים זוממין ממונא משלמי ומילקא לא לקי משום [א] דלאו בני התראה נינהו אמר רבא תדע ניתרי בהו איתרו בהו מעיקרא [ב] אמרי אישתלין ניתרי בהו בשעת מעשה פרשי ולא מסהדי ניתרי בהו לבסוף מאי דהוה הוה מתקיף לה אביי וניתרי בהו בתוך כדי דבור מתקיף לה רב אחא בריה דרב איקא וניתרי בהו מעיקרא ונרמוז בהו רמוזי הדר אמר אביי לאו מילתא היא דאמרי אי סלקא דעתך עדים זוממין צריכין התראה כי לא מתרינן בהו לא קטלינן להו מי איכא מידי דאינהו בעו קטיל בלא התראה ואינהו בעו התראה הא בעינן [ד] ועשיתם לו כאשר זמם לעשות לאחיו וליכא מתקיף לה רב סמא בריה דרב ירמיה אלא מעתה בן גרושה ובן חלוצה דלא מכאשר זמם קא מיתרבי ליבעי התראה * אמר קרא [ה] משפט אחד יהיה לכם [ג] משפט השוה לכולכם רב שישא בריה דרב אידי אמר חובל בחבירו נמי ממונא משלם ומילקא לא לקי מהכא [ו] וכי ינצו אנשים ונגפו אשה הרה ויצאו ילדיה ואמר רבי אלעזר [ד] במצות שבמיתה הכתוב מדבר דכתיב [ז] ואם אסון יהיה ונתת נפש תחת נפש היכי דמי אי דלא אתרו ביה אמאי מיקטיל אלא פשיטא דאתרו ביה [ה] ומותרה לדבר חמור הוי מותרה לדבר הקל ואמר רחמנא [ו] ולא יהיה אסון ענוש יענש מתקיף לה רב אשי ממאי דמותרה לדבר חמור הוי מותרה לדבר הקל דלמא לא הוי אם תמצא לומר הוי ממאי דמיתה חמורה דלמא

דלמא

רש"י

ופרכינן חובל בחבירו דעל כרחך בממון נידון תקשי בטלת לאו דלא יוסיף פן יוסיף שהוא אזהרה למכה את חבירו: **והיה אם בן הכות.** במסכת מכות (דף ג:) מוקמינן לה בעדים זוממין: **אלא.** על כרחך כיון דרבייה קרא לתשלומין איכא לאוקמא לעונש מלקות דלאו דידיה במעידין אנו את איש פלוני כהן שהוא בן גרושה דליכא לאוקמי כאשר זמם ולומר יעשה הוא בן גרושה תחתיו אלא סופג את הארבעים והכי תנן במסכת מכות וחובל בחבירו נמי מוקמינן ליה בשאין בה שוה פרוטה בכל חמשה דברים שבה כגון שלא פיחתו מכספו וממלאכתו וריפוי לא הוצרך ולא צער היה בה ובשוטה שאין לה בושת והכא נמי באחותו מצית לאוקמי מלקות דידיה בבוגרת אבל נערה לישלם ולא ליל(ק)י הואיל וריבתה גזירה שוה דתחת תחת לתשלומין: **לכדאביי.** בשילהי פירקין דפרכינן ואימא חמשים אמר רחמנא מכל מילי ושני אביי חמשים [ו] כסף נאמר דשו תחת קנס העינוי אבל בושת ופגם שהוא בשאר חובלים לא כלל כאן: **השוכב עמה.** קרא יתירא הוא לדרשה נימא ונתן לאבי הנערה חמשים כסף: **מכלל דבושת ופגם.** דלאו מחמת הנאת שכיבה נינהו שהרי ישנן בשאר חובלים לא כיילינהו בגוייהו דהני: **רבי אלעזר אומר עדים זוממין דממונא משלמי ולא לקו.** לא צריך קרא לסברא היא למלקות לא שייך בהו: **דלאו בני התראה נינהו.** קודם עדות דמפ' רבא ואזיל הלכך אי איכא למענשינהו לא מענשינהו אלא ממון דאין עונש הגוף בלא התראה ואע"ג דגבי בן גרושה ובן חלוצה ענשינן להו מלקות בלא התראה התם גזירת הכתוב דאשכחן בהו מלקות בהדיא והיה אם בן הכות ומוקמינן לקרא במידי דלא מצית למענשינהו מכאשר זמם אבל היכא דמצית למיעבד בהו זומה לא שייך בהו מלקות: **תדע.** שאי אפשר להתרות בהם: **מעיקרא.** יום או שעה קודם שיעידו העדות: **אמרי אישתלין.** שכחנו ההתראה הרי שבטלה ההתראה: **פרשי ולא מסהדי.** אפילו אמת הואיל ואנו חשודים בעיניכם מה לנו ולצרה: **לבסוף.** לאחר שהעידו: **מאי דהוה הוה.** דכיון שהגיד אינו חוזר ומגיד ואין יכולין לחזור: **וניתרי בהו בתוך כדי דבור.** לאחר שהעידו דתוך כדי דבור כדבור דמי ויכולים לחזור: **תוך כדי דבור.** כדי שאילת שלום: **ורמוז רמוזי.** בשעת העדות נרמוז להם רמזים על ההתראה להזכירם ובלשון רך שלא יקפידו: **לאו מילתא היא דאמרי.** שיהו עדים זוממין צריכין התראה: ה"ג דאינהו בעו למיקטל בלא התראה ואינהו בעו התראה הם: **כאשר זמם.** והם זממו להרוג את זה בעדותן שלא היה ולא נהרג ולא התרו בו התראה שהעידו עליה: **אלא מעתה.** דהאי לאו בעו התראה משום כאשר זמם הוא מלקות של זוממי עדות בן גרושה ובן חלוצה: **דלאו מכאשר זמם אתי.** עונש דידהו שהרי לא זממו להלקותו אלא לחללו: **משפט השוה.** וכיון דרוב זוממין לאו בני התראה נינהו הני נמי לא בעו התראה: **במצות שבמיתה.** שמתכוין היה להורגו: **הכתוב מדבר.** דכתיב אם אסון יהיה שמתה האשה ונתת נפש ואע"פ שלא נתכוון אלא לחבירו ולאשמעינן נתכוון להרוג את זה והרג את זה חייב: **אי דלא אתרו ביה.** אם המיתה מתרה: **לדבר חמור.** מיתה: **הוי מותרה לדבר הקל.** שאם יכנו ולא ימות ילקה ואפילו הכי אמר רחמנא דכי אין שם מיתה חייב ממון ענש דמי ולדות ואף על גב דאיכא התראה למלקות אלמא משלם ואינו לוקה:

נגדוה

תוספות

אלא אפשר לקיומי בבן גרושה או בבן חלוצה. ואם תאמר אמאי לקו אעדות דבן גרושה הא הוי עדות שאין אתה יכול להזימה ויש לומר דלא חשיב עדות שאין אתה יכול להזימה אלא במעידין על הטרפה דלאי אפשר לקיומי בשום דבר לא במיתה ולא במלקות דגברא קטילא בעו למיקטל אבל הכא נתקיימה הזמה במלקות [ז]: **מיבעי ליה לכדאביי.** ואם תאמר כיון דאיצטריך תחת להך דרשה א"כ מנא לן מיטב וי"ל דיליף מנתינה או מכסף: **ועולא נפקא ליה מדרבא.** משמע דרבא סבר כעולא דרבי יוחנן גופיה הוה דריש כעולא אי לאו משום דמיבעי ליה לכדאביי וקשה לרשב"א דבפרק השוכר את הפועלים (ב"מ צא. ושם) משמע בהדיא דסבר כרבי יוחנן גבי חוסם פרה ודש בה לוקה ומשלם דמוקי לה אביי כרבי מאיר ורבא אמר לעולם כרבנן ואתנן אסרה תורה אפי' בא על אמו פירוש ומשלם לצאת ידי שמים משמע דבדין לוקה ואינו משלם ולמאי דפירשי' לעיל דלמסקנא דווקא בהני תלת אית ליה לעולא דממונא משלם ולא לקי אתי שפיר דבעלמא סבר כרבי יוחנן דלוקה ואין משלם כדדריש רבי יוחנן וסמיך ליה ארבעים יכנו: **ניתרי בהו מעיקרא כו'.** ואם תאמר תיפוק ליה דהויא התראת ספק דאין אנו יודעין אם מעידים שקר ויש לומר דהתראת ספק לא הויא אלא כגון אל תותיר שאף למותרה עצמו הוא ספק שסבור שעדיין יש שהות ביום אבל הכא המותרין יודעין שמעידין שקר: **וניתרי בהו בתוך כדי דבור.** ואם תאמר היכי מצי תו הדרי בהו והא בהתראה איכא טפי מכדי דבור שהוא כדי שאילת שלום ויש לומר דכל זמן שעסוקים באותו דבר חשיב הכל תוך כדי דבור כדאמרינן במכות (דף ו.) דאפי' מעידין מאה כל אחד תוך כדי דבור של חבירו חשובין כולן תוך כדי דבור של ראשון ואם נמצא אחד מהן קרוב או פסול עדותן בטילה: **אלא פשיטא דאתרו ביה.** וא"ת היכי משלם ממון אפי' כי אין אסון הא כיון דמתכוין להרוג הוי ליה רודף ומתחייב בנפשו וקים ליה בדרבה מיניה וי"ל בשיכולין להצילו באחד מאבריו והכי אמרינן בבן סורר (סנהדרין דף עד.): **ממאי דמותרה לדבר חמור הוי מותרה לדבר הקל דלמא לא הוי.** אין לומר דטעמא משום דלהתרגה הוא דקיבל התראה דניחא ליה ליהרג על מנת שיהרוג שונאו דתמות נפשי עם פלשתים הוא דקאמר אבל לא ניחא ליה להכות את חבירו על מנת שילקוהו דהא אמתני' דפרק הנשרפין (סנהדרין ד' עט:) דקתני דחייבי מיתות שנתערבו ידונו בקלה וקאמר בגמ' (שם דף פ:) ש"מ מותרה לדבר חמור הוי מותרה לדבר הקל והתם פשיטא דכיון דהתרו בו לסקילה וקבל כ"ש שאם התרו בו חנק על אותו דבר עצמו שהיה מקבל ואפ"ה בעי למימר דמותרה לדבר חמור לא הוי מותרה לדבר הקל אלא יש לומר דגזירת הכתוב הוא דבעינן שיתיר עצמו למיתה בין קלה בין חמורה:

ודלמא

מסורת הש"ס

א) לקמן מ., ב) [ג"ל אלעזר], ג) [ב"ק פג: פד. סנהדרין כח.], ד) סנהדרין עד. עט. [וע"ש על הגליון מ"ש בשם התוס' עט], ה) [סנהדרין פ:], ו) ס"א כסף נתחייבו תחת, ז) [ועיין תוס' מכות ג. ד"ה מעידין וכו' ביתר ביאור].

תורה אור השלם

א) אַרְבָּעִים יַכֶּנּוּ לֹא יֹסִיף פֶּן יֹסִיף לְהַכֹּתוֹ עַל אֵלֶּה מַכָּה רַבָּה וְנִקְלָה אָחִיךָ לְעֵינֶיךָ: [דברים כה, ג]

ב) וְהָיָה אִם בִּן הַכּוֹת הָרָשָׁע וְהִפִּילוֹ הַשֹּׁפֵט וְהִכָּהוּ לְפָנָיו כְּדֵי רִשְׁעָתוֹ בְּמִסְפָּר: [דברים כה, ב]

ג) וְנָתַן הָאִישׁ הַשֹּׁכֵב עִמָּהּ לַאֲבִי הַנַּעֲרָ חֲמִשִּׁים כָּסֶף וְלוֹ תִהְיֶה לְאִשָּׁה תַּחַת אֲשֶׁר עִנָּהּ לֹא יוּכַל שַׁלְּחָהּ כָּל יָמָיו: [דברים כב, כט]

ד) וַעֲשִׂיתֶם לוֹ כַּאֲשֶׁר זָמַם לַעֲשׂוֹת לְאָחִיו וּבִעַרְתָּ הָרָע מִקִּרְבֶּךָ: [דברים יט, יט]

ה) מִשְׁפַּט אֶחָד יִהְיֶה לָכֶם כַּגֵּר כָּאֶזְרָח יִהְיֶה כִּי אֲנִי יי אֱלֹהֵיכֶם: [ויקרא כד, כב]

ו) וְכִי יִנָּצוּ אֲנָשִׁים וְנָגְפוּ אִשָּׁה הָרָה וְיָצְאוּ יְלָדֶיהָ וְלֹא יִהְיֶה אָסוֹן עָנוֹשׁ יֵעָנֵשׁ כַּאֲשֶׁר יָשִׁית עָלָיו בַּעַל הָאִשָּׁה וְנָתַן בִּפְלִלִים: [שמות כא, כב]

ז) וְאִם אָסוֹן יִהְיֶה וְנָתַתָּה נֶפֶשׁ תַּחַת נָפֶשׁ: [שמות כא, כג]

עין משפט נר מצוה

כה א מיי' פי"ח מהל' עדות הל' ד סמג עשין קי טור ח"מ סי' לח:

כו ב ג מיי' פי"ב מהל' סנהדרין הלכה ב [דין דמותרה לדבר חמור לא מצאתי במיי' שם מבואר רק כשהתרו בו בסתם מיתה פסק דהוי התראה והיינו דהוי כמקבל עליו בין מיתה חמורה כגון סקילה ובין קלה אבל כשהתרו בו בחמורה לבד לא נתבאר שם ועי' בתוספות דהכא סד"ה ממאי וכו' דגזירת הכתוב הוא וכו']:

הגהות הב"ח

(א) גמ' אמר לך ר"י. נ"ב ס"א אלא ר' יוחנן:

גליון הש"ס

גמ' אמר קרא משפט אחד. עיין מכות דף ד ע"ב ברש"י ד"ה עדים זוממין א"צ התראה ולע"ק:

ליקוטי רש"י

תחת אשר עינה. גבי חמשים כסף כתיב. **מכלל דאיכא בושת ופגם.** שאינם משום עינוי שהרי ישנן בשאר חובלין אינו בכלל זה. פגם הוא נזק הנישום נמי בשאר חבלות [לקמן מ:]. דמשמע הכי חמשים כסף יתן בשביל קנס העינוי ומדאיצטריך למכתב הכי מכלל דמיחייב מילי אחרנייתא כגון בושת ופגם דלאו קנסא דעינוי נינהו דבלאו עינוי נמי איכא בושת ופגם היינו נזק ששוה פחות מבתחילה. **תחת אשר עינה.** רישיה דקרא ונתן האיש השוכב עמה לאבי הנערה חמשים כסף וגו' (דברים כב) [ערכין טו.]. **אמר קרא משפט אחד וכו'.** עדים זוממין אין צריכין התראה. בכתובות אמרינן טעמא באלו נערות (דף לג.) נתרי בהו אימת כו' אבל כל שאר עונשין בב"ד של מטה צריכין התראה [מכות ד: עי' גהש"ס]. **וכי ינצו אנשים.** זה עם זה ונתכוין להכות את חבירו והכה את האשה. **ונגפו.** אין נגיפה אלא לשון דחיפה והכאה כמו (תהלים לא יב) פן תגוף באבן רגלך (ירמיה יג טז) ובטרם יתנגפו רגליכם (ישעיה ח יד) ולאבן נגף [שמות כא, כב]. **במצות שבמיתה.** שהוא מתכוין להרוג את חבירו והכה את האשה הכתוב מדבר. **דכתיב ואם וכו'.** ואי לא מתכוין להרוג דשוגג הוא אמאי מקטיל אלא לאו שמע מינה במתכוין [סנהדרין עד.]. ואי לא נתכוון להרוג היאך מקטיל וכי איתכוון מיהא חייב אע"ג דלא נתכוון אלא לחבירו דהא כתיב וכי ינצו אנשים וגו' [שם עט.]. **ואם אסון יהיה.** באשה. **ונתת נפש תחת נפש.** רבותינו חולקין בדבר יש אומרים נפש ממש ויש אומרים ממון אבל לא נפש ממש שהמתכוין להרוג את זה והרג את זה פטור ממיתה ומשלם ליורשיו דמיו כמו שהיה נמכר בשוק [שמות כא, כג].

payment for **"the benefit of lying"** with her is **fifty** *shekels,* מִכְּלָל דְּאִיכָּא בּוֹשֶׁת וּפְגָם – **implying that there is** also a requirement for him to pay compensation **for humiliation and depreciation.**[14]

The Gemara above (32b) expounded the verse *a hand for a hand* to teach that *zomemim* who are liable to payment and lashes pay rather than receive lashes. The Gemara now suggests an alternative basis for that law:

עֵדִים זוֹמְמִין [אֶלְעָזָר] (אליעזר) רַבִּי אוֹמֵר – **R' Elazar**[15] **says:** מָמוֹנָא מְשַׁלְּמֵי וּמִילְקָא לֹא לָקֵי – ***Zomemim*** **witnesses pay the money and do not receive lashes** מִשּׁוּם דְּלַאו בְּנֵי הַתְרָאָה נִינְהוּ – **because they are not subject to** receiving a **warning** prior to their transgression.[16] אָמַר רָבָא – **Rava said:** תֵּדַע – **Know** that it is so:[17] נִיתְרֵי בְּהוּ אֵימַת – For **when shall we warn them?** נִיתְרֵי בְּהוּ מֵעִיקָרָא – **Shall we warn them** a day or an hour **before** they testify? אָמְרֵי אִישְׁתְּלַיְין – **They will say, "We forgot** the warning"![18] נִיתְרֵי בְּהוּ בִּשְׁעַת מַעֲשֶׂה – **Shall we warn them at the time of the act,** i.e. immediately before they testify? פָּרְשֵׁי וְלֹא מַסְהֲדֵי – **They will withdraw and not testify!**[19] נִיתְרֵי בְּהוּ לְבַסּוֹף – **Shall we warn them in the end,** after they testify?[20] מַאי דַּהֲוָה הֲוָה – **What was, was!**[21]

The Gemara objects that there are indeed possible ways to warn them:

מַתְקִיף לָהּ אַבָּיֵי – **Abaye objected to this:** וְנִיתְרֵי בְּהוּ בְּתוֹךְ כְּדֵי דִּבּוּר – **But let us warn them** after they testify, **within the time it takes to make an utterance!**[22] מַתְקִיף לָהּ רַב אַחָא בְּרֵיהּ דְּרַב אִיקָא – And **Rav Acha the son of Rav Ika,** too, **objected to this:** וְנִיתְרֵי בְּהוּ מֵעִיקָּרָא וּנְרַמֵּז בְּהוּ רַמּוּזֵי – **But let us warn them beforehand and hint to them** discreetly at the time that they give their testimony![23] – ? –

Abaye, however, reconsiders his position:

הֲדַר אָמַר אַבָּיֵי – **Abaye then said:** לָאו מִילְּתָא הִיא דְּאָמְרִי – **That which I said is not** correct.[24] אִי סָלְקָא דַּעְתָּךְ עֵדִים זוֹמְמִין צְרִיכִין הַתְרָאָה – For **if it should enter your mind that** ***zomemim*** **witnesses require a warning,** כִּי לֹא מַתְרִינַן בְּהוּ לֹא קָטְלִינַן לְהוּ – then it would emerge that **when we do not warn them, we do not kill them.** But can this be so? מִי אִיכָּא מִידֵי דְּאִינְהוּ בָּעוּ קְטִיל בְּלֹא הַתְרָאָה – **Can there be such a thing that they wanted to kill** their victim **without** his receiving a **warning,**[25] וְאִינְהוּ בָּעוּ הַתְרָאָה – **and they require a warning** in order to be executed? הָא בְּעִינַן ,,וַעֲשִׂיתֶם לוֹ כַּאֲשֶׁר זָמַם לַעֲשׂוֹת לְאָחִיו'' וְלֵיכָּא – **Why, we need** to implement the verse: ***And you shall do to him as he conspired to do to his brother,*** **and it is lacking!**[26]

NOTES

14. He pays the fifty *shekels* for being "the man who lay with her," i.e. for the benefit he derived from lying with her, not for humiliation and depreciation, which are common to assaults in general and are not payments specifically "for lying with her" (see *Rashi*).

15. Emendation follows *Mesoras HaShas.*

16. I.e. it is not possible to warn them before they give testimony, as Rava proceeds to demonstrate. Therefore, given the choice between punishing them monetarily or with lashes, logic dictates that we punish them monetarily. For we generally do not subject a sinner to physical punishment unless he was warned prior to his transgression. Hence, imposing the monetary penalty [which never requires prior warning] takes precedence (*Rashi*). Now, it is true that in the case of *zomemim* who testify that a Kohen is the son of a divorcee or a *chalutzah,* we *do* subject them to lashes even though they were not warned. That case, however, is an exception [to the general rule that we do not impose physical punishment without prior warning] on account of a special Scriptural decree. For we find that the Torah does prescribe lashes for *zomemim* in the verse: *And if it will be that the wicked one is liable to lashes* [see above, note 4]. Hence, we apply that verse in a situation where we cannot apply the punishment of *and you shall do to him as he conspired* ... [e.g. where they testified that a Kohen is the son of a divorcee; see above, note 5]. However, in a situation where we *can* apply the punishment of *and you shall do to him as he conspired* ... [e.g. where they testified falsely that someone owes two hundred *zuz*], it is that punishment which supersedes the punishment of lashes [since lashes are less appropriate, as he did not receive a warning] (*Rashi;* see *Maharsha* and *Maharam Schif*).

17. That it is not possible to give warning to *zomemim* witnesses (*Rashi*).

18. In order for a warning to be legally effective, it must immediately precede the transgression. Otherwise, the sinner can claim that by the time he committed the act he had forgotten the warning (see *Sanhedrin* 40b with *Rashi* ד״ה המית בתוך כדי דיבור). Hence, if we were to warn witnesses a day or an hour prior to their testimony [that they will be punished if they are found to be *zomemim*], the warning would be ineffective (*Rashi*).

19. If we were to warn witnesses immediately before they give testimony that they will be punished if they testify falsely, they will refrain from testifying even truthfully. For they will say, "If you consider us suspect, why should we bother testifying altogether?" (*Rashi;* cf. *Ritva*).

20. *Rashi.* [That is: Shall we warn them, after they testify, to retract any false testimony they may have given, as adhering to such testimony would subject them to punishment as *zomemim*? (see next note).]

21. Once witnesses give testimony, they cannot retract or alter their testimony (*Rashi;* see above, 18b, with *Rashi* there ד״ה כיון שהגיד שוב אינו חוזר ומגיד).

22. "The time it takes to make an utterance" is the length of time it takes to utter a greeting (*Rashi*). [*Rashi* appears to be referring to a simple greeting, i.e. the time it takes to say, שָׁלוֹם עָלֶיךָ, *shalom alecha* ("peace unto you"). The Gemara *Makkos* 6b, however, defines "the time it takes to make an utterance" as the length of time it takes for a student to greet his teacher, i.e. [שָׁלוֹם עָלֶיךָ רַבִּי [וּמוֹרִי, *shalom alecha rabbi [u-mori]* ("peace unto you my teacher [and master]"). See *Bava Kamma* 73b and *Rashbam, Bava Basra* 129b ד״ה תוך כדי דבור. See also *Mishnah Berurah* 206:12.

A statement is not considered completed until "the time of an utterance" elapses after the conclusion of the statement. Hence, although witnesses cannot retract or alter testimony that was already given, they may do so within the time it takes to issue an utterance, since their testimony will not yet have been completed when they retract it (see *Rashi*). Hence, we could warn them immediately after they issue their testimony that they will be punished as *zomemim* if they do not retract any false testimony that they may have given.

[*Tosafos* ask that by the time we complete the warning the time of an utterance will already have elapsed. How, then, will they be able to retract their testimony? *Tosafos* answer that since the court *began* its warning before the time of an utterance has elapsed, the testimony of the witnesses is still considered to be in progress, and may be altered or retracted until the time of an utterance elapses after the warning is completed.]

23. I.e. immediately prior to their testimony, we will remind them of the warning that was issued earlier. This will legally serve the purposes of "warning immediately prior to the act," and at the same time will not, if done tactfully, provoke them to refrain from testifying (*Rashi*).

24. I.e. while it is indeed possible to warn the witnesses within the time of an utterance following their testimony, the fact remains that *zomemim* do *not* require warning, as R' Elazar had asserted (see *Rashi*). Now, Abaye had not actually said that the witnesses *do* require warning. Nevertheless, the clear implication of his objection to Rava was that since it *is* possible to warn them (within the time of an utterance following their testimony), there is no basis for R' Elazar's assertion (based as it was on Rava's reasoning) that they do *not* require warning, and the implication was that the law would be that they do indeed require warning. Thus, Abaye now states that he retracts that position, and concedes that R' Elazar's basic statement (that *zomemim* do not require warning) is indeed correct (see *Ritva*).

25. Though they indeed testify that they warned the alleged sinner that he would be subject to the death penalty [for they could not otherwise conspire to kill him with their testimony], we now know that their testimony regarding him was a complete fabrication, and thus they never did warn him (see *Rashi*).

26. *Deuteronomy* 19:19. Thus, the mandate that *you shall do to him as he conspired to do to his brother* precludes requiring that the *zomemim* be warned in order to be punished.

חובל בחבירו נמי א"כ בטלת לא יוסיף פן יוסיף עדים זוממין נמי א"כ בטלת והיה אם בן הכות הרשע אלא עדים זוממין אפשר לקיומה בבן גרושה ובן חלוצה חובל בחבירו נמי איכא לקיומה כגון שהכהו הכאה שאין בה שוה פרוטה אחותו נמי איכא לקיומה באחותו בוגרת אמר לך ר' יוחנן האי תחת אשר עינה מיבעי ליה לכדאביי דאמר אביי אמר קרא תחת אשר עינה האי תחת אשר עינה מכלל דאיכא בושת ופגם ועולא נפקא ליה מדרבא דאמר רבא אמר קרא ונתן האיש השוכב עמה לאבי הנערה חמשים כסף הנאת שכיבה חמשים מכלל דאיכא בושת ופגם רבי אליעזר אומר עדים זוממין ממונא משלמי ומילקא לא לקי משום דלאו בני התראה נינהו אמר רבא תדע ניתרי בהו מעיקרא אימת ניתרי בהו מעיקרא אמרי אישתלין ניתרי בהו בשעת מעשה פרשי ולא מסהדי ניתרי בהו לבסוף מאי דהוה הוה מתקיף לה אביי וניתרי בהו בתוך כדי דבור מתקיף לה רב אחא בריה דרב איקא וניתרי בהו מעיקרא ונרמוז בהו רמוזי הדר אמר אביי לאו מילתא היא דאמרי אי סלקא דעתך עדים זוממין צריכין התראה כי לא מתרינן בהו לא קטלינן להו מי איכא מידי דאינהו בעו התראה ואינהו בעו התראה הא קטיל בלא התראה בעינן ועשיתם לו כאשר זמם לעשות לאחיו וליכא מתקיף לה רב סמא בריה דרב ירמיה אלא מעתה בן גרושה ובן חלוצה דלא מכאשר זמם קא מיתרבי ליבעי התראה אמר קרא משפט אחד יהיה לכם משפט השוה לכולכם רב שישא בריה דרב אידי אמר חובל בחבירו נמי ממונא משלם ומילקא לא לקי מהכא וכי ינצו אנשים ונגפו אשה הרה ויצאו ילדיה ואמר רבי אלעזר במצות שבמיתה הכתוב מדבר דכתיב ואם אסון יהיה ונתת נפש תחת נפש היכי דמי אי דלא אתרו ביה אמאי מיקטיל אלא פשיטא דאתרו ביה ומותרה לדבר חמור הוי מותרה לדבר הקל ואמר רחמנא ולא יהיה אסון ענוש יענש מתקיף לה רב אשי ממאי דמותרה לדבר חמור הוי מותרה לדבר הקל דלמא לא הוי אם תמצא לומר הוי ממאי דמיתה חמורה דלמא

רש"י

ופרכינן חובל בחבירו דעל כרחך בממון נידון תקשי בטלת לאו דלא יוסיף פן יוסיף שהוא אזהרה למכה את חבירו: **והיה אם בן הכות.** במסכת מכות (דף ב:) מוקמינן לה בעדים זוממין: **אלא.** על כרחך כיון דרבייה קרא לתשלומין איכא לאוקמא לעונש מלקות דלאו דידיה במעידין אנו את איש פלוני כהן שהוא בן גרושה דליכא לאוקמי כאשר זמם ולומר יהא הוא בן גרושה תחתיו אלא סופג את הארבעים והכי תנן במסכת מכות וחובל בחבירו נמי מוקמינן ליה בשאין בה שוה פרוטה בכל חמשה דברים שבה כגון שלא פיחתו מכספו וממלאכתו וריפוי לא הוצרך ולא צער היה בה ובשוטה שאין לה בושת והכא נמי באחותו מלית לאוקמי מלקות דידה בבוגרת אבל נערה לישלם ולא לילקי הואיל וליכתה גזירה שוה דתחת תחת לתשלומין: **לכדאביי.** בשילהי פירקין דפרכינן ולימא חמשים אמר רחמנא מכל מילי ושני אביי חמשים כסף נתחדשו תחת קנס העינוי אבל בושת ופגם שהוא בשאר חובלים לא כלל כאן: **השוכב עמה.** קרא יתירה הוא לדרשה נימא ונתן לאבי הנערה חמשים כסף: **מכלל דבושת ופגם.** דלאו מחמת הנאת שכיבה נינהו שהרי ישנן בשאר חובלים לא כיילינהו בגוייהו הכי: **רבי אלעזר אומר עדים זוממין דממונא משלמי ולא לקו.** לא צריכי קרא דסברא היא דמלקות לא שייך בהו: **דלאו בני התראה נינהו.** קודם עדות כדמפ' רבא ואזיל הלכך אי איכא למענשינהו לא מענשינהו אלא ממון דאין עונש הגוף בלא התראה ואע"ג דגבי בן גרושה ובן חלוצה ענשינן להו מלקות בלא התראה התם גזירת הכתוב דאשכחן בהו מלקות בהדיא והיה אם בן הכות ומוקמינן לקרא במידי דלא מלית למענשינהו מכאשר זמם אבל היכא דמלית למיעבד בהו זמה לא שייך בהו מלקות: **תדע.** שאי אפשר להתרות בהם: **מעיקרא.** יום או שעה קודם שיעידו העדות: **אמרי אישתלין.** שכחנו ההתראה הרי שבטלה ההתראה: **פרשי ולא מסהדי.** אפילו אמת הואיל ואנו חשודים בעיניכם מה לנו ולצרה: **לבסוף.** לאחר שהעידו: **מאי דהוה הוה.** דכיון שהגיד אינו חוזר ומגיד ואינן יכולין לחזור: **וניתרי בהו בתוך כדי דבור.** לאחר שהעידו דתוך כדי דבור כדבור דמי ויכולים לחזור: **תוך כדי דבור.** כדי שאילת שלום: **ונרמוז רמוזי.** בשעת העדות נרמוז להם רמזים על ההתראה להזכירם ובלשון רך שלא יקפידו: **לאו מילתא היא דאמרי.** שיהו עדים זוממין צריכין התראה: ה"ג דאינהו בעו למיקטל בלא התראה ואינהו בעו התראה כו': **כאשר זמם.** והם זממו להרוג את זה בעדותן שלא היה ולא נברא ולא התרו בו ההתראה שהעידו עליה: **אלא מעתה.** דהאי דלא בעו התראה משום כאשר זמם הוא מלקות של זוממי עדות בן גרושה ובן חלוצה: **דלאו מכאשר זמם אתי.** עונש דידהו שהרי לא זממו להלקותו אלא לחללו: **משפט השוה.** וכיון דרוב זוממין לאו בני התראה נינהו הני נמי לא בעו התראה: **במצות שבמיתה.** שמתכוין היה להורגו: **הכתוב מדבר.** דכתיב אם אסון יהיה שמתה האשה ונתת נפש ואע"פ שלא נתכוון אלא לחבירו ואשמעינן נתכוון להרוג את זה והרג את זה חייב: **אי דלא אתרו ביה.** אם תמיתנו תהרג: **לדבר חמור.** מיתה: **הוי מותרה לדבר הקל.** שאם יכנו ולא ימות ילקה ואפילו הכי אמר רחמנא דכי אין שם חיוב מיתה יענש דמי ולדות ואף על גב דאיכא התראה למלקות אלמא משלם ואינו לוקה:

תוספות

אלא אפשר לקיומי בבן גרושה או בבן חלוצה. ואם תאמר אמאי לא קאי אעדות דבן גרושה הא הוי עדות שאין אתה יכול להזימה וי"ל דלא חשיב עדות שאין אתה יכול להזימה אלא במעידין על הטרפה דלאו אפשר לקיומי בשום דבר לא במיתה ולא במלקות דגברא קטילא קטלו בעו למיקטל אבל הכא נתקיימה הזמה במלקות: **מיבעי** ליה לכדאביי. ואם תאמר כיון דאיצטריך תחת להך דרשה א"כ מנא לן מיטב וי"ל דיליף מנגיחה או מכסף:

ועולא נפקא ליה מדרבא. משמע דרבא סבר כעולא דרבי יוחנן גופיה הוה דריש כעולא אי לאו משום דמיבעי ליה לכדאביי וקשה לרשב"א דבפרק השוכר את הפועלים (ב"מ צא. ושם) משמע בהדיא דסבר כרבי יוחנן גבי חוסם פרה ודש בה לוקה ומשלם דמוקי לה אביי כרבי מאיר ורבא אמר לעולם כרבנן ולאו אסרה תורה אפי' על ממו פירוש ומשלם לצאת ידי שמים משמע דדין לוקה ואינו משלם ולמאי דפרישי' לעיל דלמסקנא דווקא בהני תלת אית ליה לעולא דממונא משלם ולא לקי אתי שפיר דבעלמא סבר כרבי יוחנן דלוקה ואין משלם כדדריש רבי יוחנן וסמיך ליה ארבעים יכנו:

ניתרי בהו מעיקרא כו'. ואם תאמר מיפוק ליה דהויא התראת ספק דאין אנו יודעין אם מעידים שקר ויש לומר דהתראת ספק לא הויא אלא כגון אל תותיר שאף למותרה עצמו הוא ספק שסבור שעדיין יש שהות ביום אבל הכא המותרין יודעין שמעידין שקר:

וניתרי בהו בתוך כדי דבור. ואם תאמר היכי מצי תו הדרי בהו והא בהתראה איכא טפי מכדי דבור שהוא כדי שאילת שלום ויש לומר דכל זמן שעסוקים באותו דבר חשיב הכל תוך כדי דבור כדאמרינן במכות (דף ו.) דאפי' מעידין מאה כל אחד תוך כדי דבור של חבירו חשובין כולן תוך כדי דבור של ראשון ואם נמצא אחד מהן קרוב או פסול עדותן בטילה:

אלא פשיטא דאתרו ביה. וא"ת היכי משלם ממון אפי' כי אין אסון הא כיון דמתכוין להרוג הוי ליה רודף ומתחייב בנפשו וקים ליה בדרבה מיניה וי"ל בשיכולין להצילו באחד מאבריו והכי אמרינן בבן סורר (סנהדרין דף עד.):

ממאי דמותרה לדבר חמור הוי מותרה לדבר הקל דלמא לא הוי. אין לומר דטעמא משום דלאהריגה הוא דקיבל התראה דניחא ליה ליהרג על מנת שיהרוג שונאו דתמות נפשי עם פלשתים הוא דקאמר אבל לא ניחא ליה להכות את חבירו על מנת שילקוהו דהא אמתני' דפרק הנשרפין (סנהדרין ד' עט:) דקתני דחייבי מיתות שנתערבו ידונו בקלה וקאמר בגמ' (שם דף פ:) ש"מ מותרה לדבר חמור הוי מותרה לדבר הקל והתם פשיטא דכיון דהתרו בו לסקילה וקבל כ"ש שאם התרו בו חנק על אותו דבר עצמו שהיה מקבל ואפ"ה בעי למימר דמותרה לדבר חמור לא הוי מותרה לדבר הקל אלא יש לומר דגזירת הכתוב הוא דבעינן שיתיר עצמו לאותה מיתה בין קלה בין חמורה: ודלמא

נגדוה

מסורת הש"ס

א) לקמן מ., ב) [נ"ל אלעזר], ג) [ב"ק פג: פד. סנהדרין כח.], ד) סנהדרין עד. עט. [וע"ע על הגליון מ"ש בשם התוי"ט], ה) [סנהדרין פ:], ו) ס"ל כסף נתחדשו חמש, ז) [ועיין תוס' מכות ב. ד"ה מעידין וכו' ביתר ביאור].

תורה אור השלם

א) אַרְבָּעִים יַכֶּנּוּ לֹא יֹסִיף פֶּן יֹסִיף לְהַכֹּתוֹ עַל אֵלֶּה מַכָּה רַבָּה וְנִקְלָה אָחִיךָ לְעֵינֶיךָ: [דברים כה, ג]

ב) וְהָיָה אִם בִּן הַכּוֹת הָרָשָׁע וְהִפִּילוֹ הַשֹּׁפֵט וְהִכָּהוּ לְפָנָיו כְּדֵי רִשְׁעָתוֹ בְּמִסְפָּר: [דברים כה, ב]

ג) וְנָתַן הָאִישׁ הַשֹּׁכֵב עִמָּהּ לַאֲבִי הַנַּעֲרָ חֲמִשִּׁים כָּסֶף וְלוֹ תִהְיֶה לְאִשָּׁה תַּחַת אֲשֶׁר עִנָּהּ לֹא יוּכַל שַׁלְּחָהּ כָּל יָמָיו: [דברים כב, כט]

ד) וַעֲשִׂיתֶם לוֹ כַּאֲשֶׁר זָמַם לַעֲשׂוֹת לְאָחִיו וּבִעַרְתָּ הָרָע מִקִּרְבֶּךָ: [דברים יט, יט]

ה) מִשְׁפַּט אֶחָד יִהְיֶה לָכֶם כַּגֵּר כָּאֶזְרָח יִהְיֶה כִּי אֲנִי יְיָ אֱלֹהֵיכֶם: [ויקרא כד, כב]

ו) וְכִי יִנָּצוּ אֲנָשִׁים וְנָגְפוּ אִשָּׁה הָרָה וְיָצְאוּ יְלָדֶיהָ וְלֹא יִהְיֶה אָסוֹן עָנוֹשׁ יֵעָנֵשׁ כַּאֲשֶׁר יָשִׁית עָלָיו בַּעַל הָאִשָּׁה וְנָתַן בִּפְלִלִים: [שמות כא, כב]

ז) וְאִם אָסוֹן יִהְיֶה וְנָתַתָּה נֶפֶשׁ תַּחַת נָפֶשׁ: [שמות כא, כג]

עין משפט נר מצוה

כה א מיי' פי"ח מהל' עדות הל' ב סמג עשין קי טור ח"מ סי' לח:

כו ב ג מיי' פי"ב מהל' סנהדרין הלכה ב [דין דמותרה לדבר חמור לא מלאתי בהרמב"ם ושם מבואר רק כשהתרו בו בפסק מה פסק דהוי התראה והיינו דהוי כמקבל עליו בין מיתה חמורה כגון סקילה ובין קלה אבל כשהתרו בו בחמורה לבד לא נתבאר שם וע' בתוספות דהכא בד"ה ממאי וכו' דגזירת הכתוב הוא וכו']:

הגהות הב"ח

(א) גמ' אמר לך ר"י. נ"ב ס"א אלא ר' יוחנן:

גליון הש"ס

גמ' אמר קרא משפט אחד. עיין מכות דף ד ע"ב ברש"י ד"ה עדים זוממין א"צ התראה ועג"ק:

ליקוטי רש"י

תחת אשר עינה. גבי חמשים כסף כתיב. **מכלל דאיכא בושת ופגם.** שאינם משום עינוי שהרי ישנן בשאר חובלין ואינו בכלל זה. פגם הוא נזק הניזוק בשאר חבלות [לקמן מ:]. דמשמע הני חמשים כסף יתן בשביל קנס העינוי ומדאיצטריך למכתב הכי מכלל דמיחייב מילי אחריניתא כגון בושת ופגם דלאו קנסא דעינוי נינהו דלאו עינוי נמי איכא בושת ופגם היינו נזק שהוא פחות מבתולתה. **תחת אשר עינה.** רישיה דקרא ונתן האיש השוכב עמה לאבי הנערה חמשים כסף וגו' [ערכין טו.]. **אמר קרא משפט אחד וכו'.** עדים זוממין אין צריכין התראה. בכתובות אמרינן טעמא באלו נערות (דף לג.) נתרי בהו אימת כו' אבל כל שאר עושין בב"ד מיתה צריכין התראה [מכות ד: ע' גהש"ס]. **וכי ינצו אנשים.** זה עם זה ונתכוין להכות את חבירו והכה את האשה. **ונגפו.** אין נגיפה אלא לשון דחיפה והכאה כמו (תהלים צא יב) פן תגוף באבן רגלך (ירמיה יג טז) ובטרם יתנגפו רגליכם (ישעיה ח יד) ולאבן נגף [שמות כא, כב]. **במצות שבמיתה.** שהוא מתכוין להרוג את חבירו והכה את האשה הכתוב מדבר. **דכתיב ואם וכו'.** ואי לא מתכוין להרוג דשוגג הוא אמאי מקטיל לאו שמע מינה במתכוין [סנהדרין עד.]. ואי לא נתכוון להרוג היאך מקטיל וכי איתכוון מיהא חייב אע"ג דלא נתכוון אלא לחבירו דהא כתיב וכי ינצו אנשים וגו' [שם עט.]. **ואם אסון יהיה.** באשה. **ונתת נפש תחת נפש.** רבותינו חולקין בדבר יש אומרים נפש ממש ויש אומרים ממון אבל לא נפש ממש שהמתכוין להרוג את זה והרג את זה פטור ממיתה ומשלם ליורשיו דמיו כמה שהיה נמכר בשוק [שמות כא, כג].

The Gemara counters:

חוֹבֵל בַּחֲבֵירוֹ נַמִּי – But in the case of one who wounds his fellow, too, you could make the same argument: אִם כֵּן בַּטַּלְתָּ ,,לֹא יֹסִיף פֶּן־יֹסִיף'' – **If so,** that the assailant pays and does not receive lashes,[1] **you have nullified the verse:** *Forty [lashes] he shall strike him,* ***he shall not add; lest he*** *strike him* ***an additional . . .***[2] עֵדִים זוֹמְמִין נַמִּי – And similarly, in the case of the ***zomemim* witnesses, too,** you could make the same argument: אִם כֵּן בַּטַּלְתָּ ,,וְהָיָה אִם־בִּן הַכּוֹת הָרָשָׁע'' – **If so,** that the witness pays and does not receive lashes,[3] **you have nullified the verse:** ***And if it will be that the wicked one is liable to lashes.***[4] אֶלָּא עֵדִים זוֹמְמִין אֶפְשָׁר לְקַיּוּמָהּ בְּבֶן גְּרוּשָׁה וּבֶן חֲלוּצָה – **Rather,** you must say about the verse decreeing lashes on ***zomemim* witnesses** that **it is possible to fulfill it in** a case where they testify to disqualify a Kohen by saying that he is **the son of a divorced woman or the son of a *chalutzah*.**[5] חוֹבֵל בַּחֲבֵירוֹ נַמִּי – Similarly, you must say about the verse decreeing lashes on **one who wounds his fellow, too,** אִיכָּא לְקַיּוּמָהּ כְּגוֹן שֶׁהִכָּהוּ הַכָּאָה שֶׁאֵין בָּהּ שָׁוֶה פְּרוּטָה – that **it can be fulfilled in a case where he struck him a blow that does not amount to a *perutah*** in damages.[6] אֲחוֹתוֹ נַמִּי – Similarly, you may say about the verse decreeing lashes on one who cohabits with **his sister, too,** אִיכָּא לְקַיּוּמָהּ בַּאֲחוֹתוֹ בּוֹגֶרֶת – that **it can be fulfilled in** the case of **his sister** who is **a *bogeress*.**[7] – ? –

The Gemara concedes this objection, and must therefore provide a different reason to account for why R' Yochanan does not expound the *gezeirah shavah* of *tachas, tachas* as Ulla does: אָמַר לָךְ רַבִּי יוֹחָנָן – Rather,[8] **R' Yochanan would say to you** that הַאי ,,תַּחַת אֲשֶׁר עִנָּהּ'' – **this** verse ***"tachas" that he violated her*** is not superfluous and free for the *gezeirah shavah*,[9] for מִיבְּעֵי לֵיהּ לִכְדַאֲבַיֵּי – **he needs it for the** following **exposition of Abaye.** דְּאָמַר אַבַּיֵּי – **For Abaye said:** אָמַר קְרָא ,,תַּחַת אֲשֶׁר עִנָּהּ'' – **The verse states:**[10] *And the man who lay with her shall give the father of the naarah fifty silver [coins] . . .* ***"tachas" he violated her.*** הַאי ,,תַּחַת אֲשֶׁר עִנָּהּ'' – **This** expression ***"tachas" he violated her,*** which means literally: *"in place of" that which he violated her,* מִכְּלָל דְּאִיכָּא בּוֹשֶׁת וּפְגָם – **implies that there is** also a requirement for him to pay compensation **for humiliation and depreciation.**[11]

The Gemara must therefore explain why Ulla does not require the expression *tachas* for Abaye's exposition:

וְעוּלָּא – **And Ulla?** How does he derive that the violator is subject to the other assault penalties, in addition to the fifty-*shekel* fine? נָפְקָא לֵיהּ מִדְּרָבָא – **He derives it from that** derivation **of Rava.**[12] דְּאָמַר רָבָא – **For Rava said:** אָמַר קְרָא ,,וְנָתַן הָאִישׁ הַשֹּׁכֵב עִמָּהּ לַאֲבִי הַנַּעֲרָה חֲמִשִּׁים כָּסֶף'' – **The verse states:** ***And the man who lay with her shall give the father of the naarah fifty silver [coins].*** הֲנָאַת שְׁכִיבָה חֲמִשִּׁים – The apparently unnecessary expression, *"the man who lay with her,"*[13] indicates that his

NOTES

1. As must indeed be so [since (as the Gemara states above) the Torah states a special verse to teach this] (*Rashi*).

2. *Deuteronomy* 25:3. This prohibition against striking one's fellow [see above, 32a note 14 (*Rashi*)] subjects the transgressor to lashes. But according to your line of reasoning, the law that he pays and does not receive lashes in effect nullifies the force of this prohibition by removing from it the penalty of lashes. Yet, it is undoubtedly so that the assailant pays and does not receive lashes (see note 1). Does this not, then, show that your line of reasoning is flawed?

3. [As must indeed be so since (as the Gemara states above) the Torah states a special verse to teach this.]

4. Ibid. v. 2. The Gemara in *Makkos* 2b interprets this as referring to *zomemim* witnesses (*Rashi*), and the verse thus states that they are liable to lashes. But according to your line of reasoning, the law that they pay and do not receive lashes nullifies this other verse, which states that they *do* receive lashes. Does this not, then, show that your line of reasoning is flawed?

5. A Kohen is forbidden by Biblical law to marry a divorcee and by Rabbinic law to marry a *chalutzah*. [A *chalutzah* is a woman whose husband died childless, and who then received *chalitzah* from his brother, who chose to free her from the levirate bond with *chalitzah* rather than marry her in *yibum* – see Deuteronomy 25:5-10.] In the event that a Kohen does marry a divorcee or a *chalutzah*, the children born from this forbidden union are disqualified to serve as Kohanim (*chalalim*). Hence, *zomemim* who testify that a Kohen is the son of a divorcee or a *chalutzah* are conspiring to disqualify him from serving as a Kohen. Nevertheless, the Mishnah in *Makkos* 2a rules that we cannot punish them by rendering them *chalalim* ["as they had conspired to do to their fellow"]; rather, they receive lashes (*Rashi*).

Thus, the special verse (*a hand for a hand*) forces us to say that in cases of dual penalty the *zomemim* witnesses pay and do not receive lashes. This in turn forces us to apply the verse *And if it will be that the wicked one is liable to lashes* to cases in which there is no monetary penalty, such as where the *zomemim* testified that a Kohen is the son of a divorcee or a *chalutzah*.

6. I.e. where the total monetary liability for all five things usually payable in cases of assault does not amount to a *perutah*. That is, the victim of the assault did not diminish in value on account of the assault, he was not laid off from work, he did not require medical attention, he suffered no pain, and he was mentally deranged and thus did not suffer humiliation (*Rashi*).

Thus, the special verse (*so shall be "given" in him*) forces us to say that in cases of dual penalty, the assailant pays and does not receive lashes. This in turn forces us to explain the penalty of lashes prescribed by the verse *he shall not add* . . . as referring to a case in which the total compensation would amount to less than a *perutah*.

7. [And he seduces rather than violates her – see above, 32a] in which case there is no monetary liability (*Rashi*). Thus, the Gemara argues that the verse *the nakedness of your sister . . . you shall not uncover* does not force R' Yochanan to reject Ulla's application of the *gezeirah shavah* of *tachas, tachas*. Rather, *tachas, tachas* should teach us that where there is a dual penalty the rapist pays and does not receive lashes (as Ulla indeed maintains), and we would then have to restrict the lashes inherent in the verse *the nakedness of your sister . . . you shall not uncover* to cases in which no monetary payment is incurred. Why, then, does R' Yochanan not agree with Ulla?

8. *Hagahos HaBach* §1 cites editions in which the word אֶלָּא, *rather,* appears in the text [as is usually the case when the Gemara means to retract a previous explanation].

9. [As explained above (see 32b note 4), the law that a violator pays instead of receiving lashes can be derived from the law that one who wounds his fellow pays instead of receiving lashes only through a *gezeirah shavah* that is *mufneh* (i.e. based on a superfluous expression). If, however, R' Yochanan needs that expression for some other exposition, the *gezeirah shavah* is not *mufneh*, and he cannot then use it to teach that the rapist pays instead of receiving lashes.]

10. *Deuteronomy* 22:29.

11. The Mishnah below (39a) states that the violator, in addition to paying the fifty-*shekel* fine, is liable to pay compensation for humiliation, depreciation and the pain he caused his victim. The Gemara (40a) asks that perhaps the Torah prescribed the fifty-*shekel* payment as compensation for all of the above liabilities. To this Abaye replied that the verse states that the fifty-*shekel* payment is *"in place of" that which he violated her;* i.e. it is a penalty for the act of violation itself, and not for humiliation, depreciation and pain, which are liabilities common to assaults in general (*Rashi*). [Generally, an assailant pays for five things: נֶזֶק, *depreciation;* צַעַר, *pain;* רִפּוּי, *healing;* שֶׁבֶת, *lost time from work;* and בּוֹשֶׁת, *humiliation* (see 32a note 16). In the case of violation, the payments for medical expense and lost time from work do not apply (see below, 39a note 30). The other three payments – depreciation (called here פְּגָם), pain and humiliation – however, are applicable.]

12. Thereby leaving the expression *tachas* superfluous to establish a *gezeirah shavah* that is *mufneh*.

13. For the verse could have written simply וְנָתַן לַאֲבִי הַנַּעֲרָה, *and he shall give to the father of the naarah*, and this would obviously mean that it is the violator who must pay. Hence, the words הָאִישׁ הַשֹּׁכֵב עִמָּהּ, *the man who lay with her,* are superfluous (*Rashi*).

The Gemara now elaborates on what it said above, that in the case of wounding, too, the Torah has specifically stated a verse to make the assailant liable to compensation rather than to lashes:

חובֵל בַּחֲבֵירוֹ נַמִּי – And with regard to **one who wounds his fellow, too,** the Torah states an expansive verse to make him liable to payment,[23] as follows: מִכְּדִי – **Now,** let us see: כְּתִיב ,,כַּאֲשֶׁר עָשָׂה כֵּן יֵעָשֶׂה לוֹ'' – **It is written:** *And if a man inflicts a wound in his fellow, **as he did so shall be done to him.***[24] ,,כֵּן יִנָּתֶן בּוֹ'' לָמָּה לִי – **Why** then **do I need** the Torah to say in the very next verse: *. . . just as he gave a wound in a person, **so shall be given in him**?*[25] דָּבָר שֶׁיֵּשׁ בּוֹ נְתִינָה – It must be that the Torah teaches us that he is liable for **something that entails "giving."** וּמַאי נִיהוּ – **And what is that?** מָמוֹן – **Money,** which is "given" as payment.[26]

The Gemara asks:

וְרַבִּי יוֹחָנָן מַאי טַעְמָא לֹא אָמַר כְּעוּלָּא – **And what is the reason that R' Yochanan does not say as Ulla** does?[27]

The Gemara answers:

אִם כֵּן בִּטַּלְתָּ ,,עֶרְוַת אֲחוֹתְךָ . . . לֹא תְגַלֵּה'' – R' Yochanan reasons that **if so,** i.e. if you expound the *gezeirah shavah* as teaching that one who violates or seduces his sister pays money rather than receive lashes, **you will have nullified** the verse: ***The nakedness of your sister . . . you shall not uncover!***[28]

NOTES

hand – indicating that *they pay money,* and thus cannot receive lashes! To answer this difficulty, *Tosafos* offer an entirely different explanation of the Gemara; see, however, *Ritva* at length.]

23. Even in a case where he was warned that striking his fellow would make him subject to lashes (*Tosafos;* see below, note 26).

24. *Leviticus* 24:19. [The reference here is to *monetary* compensation for the wound inflicted: I.e. just as he caused his victim to lose the value of a limb, so too shall he be deprived of the value of a limb, by paying compensation to his victim.]

25. Ibid. v. 20. These words seem superfluous, a mere reiteration of what was stated previously.

26. [The Gemara already knew that כֵּן יִנָּתֶן בּוֹ, *so shall be given in him,* was a reference to the payment of money (see note 24). The Gemara's main point here is not to demonstrate that *so shall be given in him* refers to money, but rather to explain that the Torah's emphasis that the assailant pays money indicates that he does so even if he also is liable to lashes for his sin. This would not be known from the verse *as he did so shall be done to him,* since we could interpret that verse as referring to a case in which he is not liable to lashes, such as where he was not warned that he would be subject to lashes. The otherwise superfluous verse, however, teaches that he pays *even* where he would also be subject to lashes. And since he pays, he cannot receive lashes, as a dual penalty is excluded by the verse *according to his wickedness.*]

27. I.e. why does R' Yochanan not expound, as does Ulla, the *gezeirah shavah* of *tachas, tachas* to derive that wherever one becomes liable to both money and lashes, he pays the money and does not receive lashes? (*Rashi*). [The *gezeirah shavah* of *tachas, tachas* is expounded in several places in the Talmud (albeit with regard to different contexts; see, for example *Bechoros* 12a), and was certainly accepted by R' Yochanan. Hence, the Gemara questions why R' Yochanan does not expound it with regard to the present context as well, as Ulla does (see *Tosafos*).]

28. *Leviticus* 18:9. Inherent in a prohibition is that the transgressor is punished with lashes. Hence, were we to expound the *gezeirah shavah* of *tachas, tachas* to teach that one who violates or seduces his sister is liable to payment rather than to lashes, we would in effect be nullifying the force of the "prohibition" against cohabiting with one's sister (with respect to lashes; of course, the *kares* penalty applies). [The Gemara below will reject this argument.] R' Yochanan, therefore, finds it preferable not to expound *tachas, tachas* with regard to violation as Ulla does, but rather for some other matter [such as the one expounded in *Bechoros* 12a] (see *Tosafos*).

אלא עולא תחת תחת גמר כתיב הכא (א) תחת אשר ענה וכתיב התם (ב) עין תחת עין מה התם ממונא משלם מילקא לא לקי אף כל היכא דאיכא ממונא ומלקות ממונא משלם מילקא לא לקי ורבי יוחנן אמר אפי' תימא אחותו נערה כאן שהתרו בו כאן שלא התרו בו אלמא קסבר רבי יוחנן כל היכא דאיכא ממון ומלקות ואתרו ביה מילקא לקי ממונא לא משלם מנא ליה לר' יוחנן הא אמר קרא (ג) כדי רשעתו משום רשעה אחת אתה מחייבו ואי אתה מחייבו משום שתי רשעיות וסמיך ליה (ד) ארבעים יכנו והרי חובל בחבירו דאיכא ממון ומלקות ממונא משלם מילקא לא לקי וכי תימא הני מילי היכא דלא אתרו ביה אבל אתרו ביה מילקא לקי ממונא לא משלם והאמר ר' אמי א"ר יוחנן הכהו הכאה שאין בה שוה פרוטה לוקה היכי דמי אי דלא אתרו ביה אמאי לוקה אלא פשיטא דאתרו ביה וטעמא דלית בה שוה פרוטה הא אית בה שוה פרוטה ממונא משלם מילקא לא לקי כדאמר רבי אילעא בפירוש ריבתה תורה עדים זוממין לתשלומין הכא נמי בפירוש ריבתה תורה חובל בחבירו לתשלומין והיכא איתמר דר' אילעא אהא מעידין אנו את איש פלוני שחייב לחבירו מאתים זוז ונמצאו זוממין לוקין ומשלמין שלא השם המביאו לידי מכות מביאו לידי תשלומין דברי ר"מ וחכמים אומרים כל המשלם אינו לוקה ונימא כל הלוקה אינו משלם א"ר אילעא בפירוש ריבתה תורה עדים זוממין לתשלומין היכן ריבתה תורה מכדי כתיב (ה) ועשיתם לו כאשר זמם לעשות לאחיו (ו) יד ביד למה לי דבר הניתן מיד ליד ומאי ניהו ממון חובל בחבירו נמי מכדי כתיב (ז) כאשר עשה כן יעשה לו (ח) כן ינתן בו למה לי דבר שיש בו נתינה ומאי ניהו ממון ורבי יוחנן מ"ט לא אמר כעולא אם כן בטלת (ט) ערות אחותך לא תגלה חובל

רש"י

תחת תחת גמר. וגזירה שוה מופנה היא ולמדין ואין משיבין: **אפי' תימא.** ההיא דמכות באחותו נערה וכשהתרו בו דאיכא ממון ומלקות ואשמעינן דלקי ולא משלם ומתניתין דכתובות בשלא התרו בו דליכא מלקות: **וסמיך ליה ארבעים יכנו.** דהיכא דאיכא שתי רשעיות ניעבד ביה הכא: **בפירוש ריבתה.** לקמיה מפרש היכא: **שלא השם המביאו לידי מכות כו'.** המקרא המביאו לידי מלקות אינו מביאו לתשלומין מלקות מלא תענה תשלומין מכאשר זמם וכיון דשני שמות הן חייב על שניהם: **נימא כל הלוקה אינו משלם.** ונידרייה במלקות מאי שנא ממון דפשיטא להו: **יד ביד.** דסמיך ליה לא תחוס עינך נפש בנפש וגו': **כן ינתן.** כאשר יתן מום באדם וגו': **מאי טעמא לא אמר כעולא.** דגמר גזירה שוה לעונשו ממון ולא מלקות לכל חייבי ממון ומלקות: **אם כן.** דפטרת בא על אחותו ממלקות בטלת לאו שבה שעונש לאו במלקות: ופרכינן:

תוספות

יש במינו אב הטומאה יותר מככר שהרי יש בו שום כלי שהוא אב הטומאה כגון כלי עץ אבל שום אוכל אינו נעשה אב הטומאה ועל שני הפירושים קשה לרשב"א דנימא התם אוכל ראשון יוכיח שאין במינו אב הטומאה ומטמא תרומה אף אני אביא שני וכי תימא מה לאוכל ראשון שכן עושה שני בחולין טבול יום יוכיח וליכא למיפרך נמי השתא שכן משונה דאין כאן שום שינוי ונראה לפרש גבי חמור דהתם לפי שבאין מכח אב הטומאה דטבול יום וכלי חרס ואוכל ראשון כולם נגעו באב הטומאה מה שאין כן בשני דלא נגע אלא בראשון ור"ת מפרש דגבי עדים זוממין שייך לא חמור משום דאותו לא חמור של חובל יכול להיות בעדים זוממין אם העידו על אחד שחבל בחבירו והוזמו דמשלמין חמשה דברים מה שרצו לחייבו ולא הקל יש לפרש שכן לאו דבחובל ועדים זוממין אין בהן כרת אלא לאו גרידא ולא נגמר מינייהו חייבי כריתות וכן בפ"ק דמכות (דף ד:) דיליף ממוציא שם רע ועדים זוממין דלאו שאין בו מעשה לוקין עליו ופריך מה להצד השוה שבהם שכן לא חמור יש לפרש כי הכא לרבינו תם ולרבינו יצחק ובפרק כיצד צולין (פסחים דף עז.) גבי במועדו ואפילו בטומאה דאמר אי כתב בתמיד שכן כליל ואי כתב בפסח שכן כרת בתרווייהו שכן יש בהן לא חמור התם יש שום פירכא אחריתי דלא מצינו למילף במה הצד ולא חש הש"ס לפרשה ובטעם מועט מסתלק לומר דצריכי: **אלא** עולא תחת תחת גמר. מצינו למימר לפי מסקנא זו דלא קאמר עולא דממונא משלם ולא לקי אלא בהנהו תלת דגלי בהו קרא וליכא למימר דילפינן לעולא בכל דוכתא מתחת נתינה ישלם כסף דמהאי גזירה שוה ילפינן מיטב בכולהו דדוקא לענין מיטב נתקבל שהוא גוף התשלומין דאם לא כן תקשי לר' יוחנן ולאביי דפליגי אעולא דלאו מי לית להו גזירה שוה לענין מיטב והכא לעולא אייתר ליה האי תחת למיפטר ממלקות מגזירה שוה דחובל בחבירו הלכך צריך לומר לקמן לעולא דנפקא ליה בושת ופגם מדרבא:

[**מנא** ליה לר"י הא. וא"ת לעיל בעי מנא ליה לעולא דממונא משלם ולא לקי כו' והשתא בעי איפכא וי"ל דהכא משום ג"ש דתחת תחת קאמר מנ"ל לר"י דלא דרשינן ג"ש להכי דג"ש זו נתקבלה לכ"ע בבכורות (דף יב.) לגבי בכור:]

שלא השם המביאו לידי מלקות מביאו כו'. פירש בקונטרס משום דממון ומלקות אתו מתרי קראי מלקות מלא תענה וממון מועשיתם לו כאשר זמם וקשה דכ"ש דאי הוו כתיבי בחד קרא שילקה וישלם שהיה לוקה ומשלם ומיהו שמא יש לפרש לפ"ה משום דממון ומלקות אתו מתרי קראי אין לנו לבטל פסוק אחד לגמרי ולקיים האחר אבל אם היו באים שניהם מועשיתם לו כאשר זמם כגון שהעידו על אחד שהוציא שם רע על אשתו דבאין לחייבו ממון ומלקות אין לוקין ומשלמין ואין נראה לר"י דלא מסתבר שלא יהו חיידין ממון ומלקות בכה"ג כיון שרצו לחייבו שניהם ונראה לר"י לפרש שלא השם המביאו לידי מכות כו' כלומר שהתשלומין לא נכתבו בסמוך למלקות דאם היה כתוב באותו פסוק עצמו לא תענה ואם ענה ועשיתם לו כאשר זמם אז ודאי הוה אמינא דה"ל לאו שניתק לעשה ולא ילקה עליו אבל עתה שנכתב רחוק זה מזה לא הוי ניתק לעשה ולא דמי ללאו דגזילה דחשיב ליה ניתק לעשה בפ' בתרא דמכות (דף טז.) ובשלוח הקן (חולין קמא.) אע"ג דעשה דוהשיב את הגזילה לא כתיב אצל לאו דלא תגזול דהתם ודאי ע"כ הוא ניתק לעשה שהרי עוקר גזילה מתחת ידו אבל קרא דועשיתם לו כאשר זמם אינו עוקר הלאו דלא תענה דעל ידי שאנו עושין לו כאשר זמם אינו נעקר עדותו אלא ע"י שהוזם הלכך לא חשבינן ליה ניתק לעשה כיון שלא נכתב אחריו סמוך לו והר"ר שלמה מדרוי"ש מפרש שלא השם המביאו לידי מכות דהיינו לא תענה מביאו לידי תשלומין פי' אינו בא להיות אזהרה לענוש תשלומין כדאמרינן במכות דממון לא בעי אזהרה ועוד דר' מאיר נפקא ליה אזהרה לכאשר זמם מוכל ישראל ישמעו ויראו ולא יוסיפו כדאמרינן בפ"ק דמכות (דף ד:) שאם היה צריך לא תענה לאזהרת ממון אז לא היה לוקה עליו דמחד לאו לא הוה ענשינן ליה ממון ומלקות:

ה) [כדמשמע בפ"ק דמכות אההיא דתנן מעידין אנו באיש פלוני שחייב מלקות מ' לוקים שמונים ארבעים משום לא תענה וארבעים מועשיתם לו כאשר זמם ואי מלא תענה וחכ"א אין סופג אלא מ' ורבנן האי לא תענה מאי עבדי ליה מיבעיא להו לאזהרת עדים זוממים ור"מ אזהרה נפקא ליה מוכל ישראל וגו' משמע דאי לאו קרא אחרינא לאזהרה מלא תענה לא הוה ענשינן ליה תרי מלקיות ולרבנן אע"ג דלא תענה לא צריך לאזהרת ממון מ"מ אינו לוקה ומשלם משום כדי רשעתו ולא לקי לרבנן אלא כשמעידים שהוא בן גרושה דליכא כאשר זמם ואע"ג דלא תענה לאו שאין בו מעשה ועוד דניתן לאזהרת מיתת ב"ד הכא גלי קרא דלקי מוהיה אם בן הכות הרשע:]

מכדי כתיב ועשיתם לו כאשר זמם יד ביד למה לי. וליכא למימר דלמה לי יד ביד דמועשיתם לו כאשר זמם משמע בהדיא ממון דכמו שהיה רוצה לחייבו ממון כן יתחייב לו ממון דמצינו למימר דכאשר זמם איירי במיתה ומלקות אבל בממון מילקא לקי ממונא לא משלם ומיהו קשה לישנא דמכדי כתיב ועשיתם לו כו' יד ביד למה לי דמשמע דמייתורא דלא איצטריך לגופיה הוא דמפיק ליה והא אפילו לא מייתר יד ביד משמע שפיר ממון דליכא לפרושי יד ביד ממש כדנפקא לן בהחובל (ב"ק דף פג: ופד.) מעין תחת עין ועוד הא דקאמר גבי חובל בחבירו כן ינתן בו למה לי דבר הניתן מיד ליד ומאי ניהו ממון אימא הני מילי היכא דלא אתרו ביה דמכן ינתן בו נפקא בהחובל נזק ולא מכאשר עשה אבל היכא דאתרו ביה אימא דמילקא לקי ונראה לר"י דהך סוגיא אתיא כמאן דמפיק התם עין תחת עין ממון מקרא דיד ביד והיינו דקאמר מכדי כתיב ועשיתם לו כאשר זמם ואי ס"ד עין תחת עין ממש א"כ יד ביד בעדים זוממין למה לי מכאשר זמם נפקא אלא אייתר יד ביד למידרש דבר הניתן מיד ליד דהיינו ממון אבל אי לא אייתר הוה אמינא יד ביד ממש: (א) **חובל** בחבירו מכדי כתיב כאשר עשה כן יעשה לו. דמשמע ממון כדאוכחן מייתורא דיד ביד כדפרישית וא"כ כן ינתן בו למה לי והא ליכא למימר דאתא להיכא דלא אתרו ביה דמיד ביד נפקא אלא ע"כ לא איצטריך אלא היכא דאתרו ביה ומיהו הא לא קשיא ליה אמאי איצטריך כאשר עשה וגו' דנשנה כאן לשום טורך כדאמרינן כל פרשה שנאמרה ונישנית כו' אבל כן ינתן בו למה חזר ושנה שתי פעמים אלא לומר לך דבר הניתן מיד ליד להיכא דאתרו ביה והוא הדין דהוה מצי למימר מכדי כתיב יד ביד כן ינתן בו למה לי: **ורבי** יוחנן מ"ט לא אמר כעולא. והא ליכא למימר דלא שמיע ליה גזירה שוה דתחת תחת דהא ילפינן לה בבכורות גבי בכור ובכמה מקומות: **אם** כן בטלת ערות אחותך לא תגלה. וא"ת כל לאו שאין בו מעשה ולאו הניתק לעשה ביטלנו הלאו כיון שאין לוקין עליו הא לאו מילתא היא דההיא לאו בר מלקות הוא אבל הכא דשייך ביה מלקות לית לן למידרש גזירה שוה לאפוקי מלקות מיניה כיון דאיכא לאוקומי גז"ש אמילתא אחריתי:

אלא

מסורת הש"ס

א) לקמן לו. ב"ק פג: מכות ד: יג., ב) סנהדרין פה. מכות ט., ג) מכות ד., ד) [ב"ק ה.], ה) ת"י כ"י, ו) ס"א יד תחת יד ממש, ז) [דף יב. נז.].

הגהות הב"ח

(א) תוס' ד"ה מכדי וד"ה חובל בחבירו נמי מכדי הד"א:

ליקוטי רש"י

עין תחת עין. סימא עין חבירו נותן לו דמי עינו כמה שפחתו דמיו למכור בשוק וכו' ולא נטילת אבר ממש כמו שדרשו רבותינו בפרק החובל (ב"ק פג:) [שמות כא, כד]. **שאין בה שוה פרוטה.** שאם יש בה תשלומי פרוטה משלם ואינו לוקה דילפינן בכתובות באלו נערות בפירוש ריבתה תורה חובל בחבירו לתשלומין וכי אין בה שוה פרוטה לוקה שעבר על לא תוסיף פן יוסיף (דברים כה) [מכות ט.]. **שלא השם המביאן לידי מכות מביאן לידי תשלומין.** מלקות משום לא תענה ותשלומין משום כאשר זמם. **כל המשלם אינו לוקה.** דכתיב כדי רשעתו משום רשעה אחת אתה מחייבו ואי אתה מחייבו משום שתי רשעיות ובמסכת כתובות (דף לב:) מקשינן ונימא כל הלוקה אינו משלם וילקו כל הזוממין ולא ישלמו ומשנינן בפירוש רבתה תורה עדים זוממין לתשלומין ויליף לה התם [שם ד.]. **כן ינתן בו.** פירשו רבותינו שאינו נתינת מום ממש אלא תשלומי ממון שמין אותו כעבד לכך כתיב בו לשון נתינה דבר הנתון מיד ליד [ויקרא כד, כ].

עין משפט נר מצוה

כב א מיי' פי"ח מהל' סנהדרין הל' ד סי' קלא טוש"ע ח"מ סימן תכ סעיף ג:

כג ב מיי' פ"ד מהל' חובל ומזיק הל' ט סמג עשין ע טוש"ע ח"מ סימן תכ סעיף ג:

כד ג מיי' פי"ח מהל' עדות הל' א סמג עשין קי טור ח"מ סי' לח:

תורה אור השלם

א) וְנָתַן הָאִישׁ הַשֹּׁכֵב עִמָּהּ לַאֲבִי הַנַּעֲרָ חֲמִשִּׁים כָּסֶף וְלוֹ תִהְיֶה לְאִשָּׁה תַּחַת אֲשֶׁר עִנָּהּ לֹא יוּכַל שַׁלְּחָהּ כָּל יָמָיו: [דברים כב, כט]

ב) עַיִן תַּחַת עַיִן שֵׁן תַּחַת שֵׁן יָד תַּחַת יָד רֶגֶל תַּחַת רָגֶל: [שמות כא, כד]

ג) וְהָיָה אִם בִּן הַכּוֹת הָרָשָׁע וְהִפִּילוֹ הַשֹּׁפֵט וְהִכָּהוּ לְפָנָיו כְּדֵי רִשְׁעָתוֹ בְּמִסְפָּר: [דברים כה, ב]

ד) אַרְבָּעִים יַכֶּנּוּ לֹא יֹסִיף פֶּן יֹסִיף לְהַכֹּתוֹ עַל אֵלֶּה מַכָּה רַבָּה וְנִקְלָה אָחִיךָ לְעֵינֶיךָ: [דברים כה, ג]

ה) וַעֲשִׂיתֶם לוֹ כַּאֲשֶׁר זָמַם לַעֲשׂוֹת לְאָחִיו וּבִעַרְתָּ הָרָע מִקִּרְבֶּךָ: [דברים יט, יט]

ו) וְלֹא תָחוֹס עֵינֶךָ נֶפֶשׁ בְּנֶפֶשׁ עַיִן בְּעַיִן שֵׁן בְּשֵׁן יָד בְּיָד רֶגֶל בְּרָגֶל: [דברים יט, כא]

ז) וְאִישׁ כִּי יִתֵּן מוּם בַּעֲמִיתוֹ כַּאֲשֶׁר עָשָׂה כֵּן יֵעָשֶׂה לּוֹ: [ויקרא כד, יט]

ח) שֶׁבֶר תַּחַת שֶׁבֶר עַיִן תַּחַת עַיִן שֵׁן תַּחַת שֵׁן כַּאֲשֶׁר יִתֵּן מוּם בָּאָדָם כֵּן יִנָּתֶן בּוֹ: [ויקרא כד, כ]

ט) עֶרְוַת אֲחוֹתְךָ בַת אָבִיךָ אוֹ בַת אִמֶּךָ מוֹלֶדֶת בַּיִת אוֹ מוֹלֶדֶת חוּץ לֹא תְגַלֶּה עֶרְוָתָן: [ויקרא יח, ט]

תוספות ר"ד

ור"י אמר אפילו תימא באחותו נערה. כאן שהתרו בו כאן שלא התרו בו אלמא קסבר ר"י כל היכא דאיכא ממון ומלקות מילקא לקי ממונא לא משלם פי' המורה. אפילו תימא ההיא דמכות באחותו נערה וכשהתרו בו דאיכא ממון ומלקות דלקי ולא משלם. ומתני' דהכא בשלא אתרו בי' דליכא מלקות כ"א ממון.

The Gemara anticipates a possible answer:

וְכִי תֵּימָא הָנֵי מִילֵּי הֵיכָא דְּלָא אַתְרוּ בֵּיהּ – **And perhaps you will say** in defense of R' Yochanan that **these things** (that the assailant pays the one he has injured) apply only **when they did not warn him** that he would be liable to lashes for striking his fellow; אֲבָל אַתְרוּ בֵּיהּ – but if **they warned him,** מִילְקָא לָקֵי מָמוֹנָא לֹא מְשַׁלֵּם – then indeed **he receives lashes** and **does not pay the money.** וְהָאָמַר רַבִּי אַמִּי אָמַר רַבִּי יוֹחָנָן – **Why,** this cannot be R' Yochanan's view, for **R' Ami said in the name of R' Yochanan:** הִכָּהוּ הַכָּאָה שֶׁאֵין בָּהּ שָׁוֶה פְּרוּטָה לוֹקֶה – If **he struck [his fellow] a blow that does not amount to a** *perutah* in damages, **he receives lashes.** הֵיכִי דָּמֵי – Now, **what is the circumstance** in which this ruling applies? אִי דְּלָא אַתְרוּ בֵּיהּ – **If they did not warn him** that he would be liable to lashes for striking his fellow, אַמַּאי לוֹקֶה – then **why** indeed **does he receive lashes?** אֶלָּא פְּשִׁיטָא דְּאַתְרוּ בֵּיהּ – **Rather, it is obvious** that the reference is to **where they did warn him,** וְטַעְמָא דְּלֵית בָּהּ שָׁוֶה פְּרוּטָה – **and** nevertheless, **the reason** R' Yochanan rules that he receives lashes and does not pay **is that [the injury] does not amount to a** *perutah.*[13] הָא אִית בָּהּ שָׁוֶה פְּרוּטָה – **But had it amounted to a** *perutah,* מָמוֹנָא מְשַׁלֵּם מִילְקָא לֹא לָקֵי – then **he would pay the money** and **not receive lashes!**[14] – ? –

The Gemara answers:

כִּדְאָמַר רַבִּי אִילְעָא – The case of wounding one's fellow is an exception to the general rule. For just **as R' Ila'a said:** בְּפֵירוּשׁ רִיבְּתָה תּוֹרָה עֵדִים זוֹמְמִין לְתַשְׁלוּמִין – **The Torah has explicitly included** *zomemim* **witnesses** in the obligation **to** make **payment;**[15] הָכָא נַמִּי בְּפֵירוּשׁ רִיבְּתָה תּוֹרָה חוֹבֵל בַּחֲבֵירוֹ לְתַשְׁלוּמִין – **here too, the Torah has explicitly included one who wounds his fellow** in the obligation **to** make **payment.**[15]

The Gemara presents the context in which R' Ila'a made his statement:

וְהֵיכָא אִיתְּמַר דְּרַבִּי אִילְעָא – **And where** was **Rav Ila'a's** statement **said?** אַהָא – It was said **with regard to this** following Mishnah:[16] מְעִידִין אָנוּ אֶת אִישׁ פְּלוֹנִי – If witnesses said, "WE TESTIFY ABOUT THIS MAN שֶׁחַיָּיב לַחֲבֵירוֹ מָאתַיִם זוּז – THAT HE OWES HIS FELLOW TWO HUNDRED *ZUZ,*" וְנִמְצְאוּ זוֹמְמִין – AND THEY WERE FOUND TO BE *ZOMEMIM,* לוֹקִין וּמְשַׁלְּמִין – THEY RECEIVE LASHES for their false testimony, AND THEY PAY their victim the amount they conspired to make him lose; שֶׁלֹּא הַשֵּׁם הַמְבִיאָן לִידֵי מַכּוֹת מְבִיאָן לִידֵי תַּשְׁלוּמִין – FOR THE SCRIPTURAL VERSE THAT MAKES THEM LIABLE FOR LASHES IS NOT THE ONE THAT MAKES THEM LIABLE FOR PAYMENT. I.e. the Biblical verse that mandates the penalty of lashes for false testimony is not the one which dictates the reciprocal punishment of *zomemim* witnesses.[17] Since the respective penalties derive from two different verses, both are carried out. דִּבְרֵי רַבִּי מֵאִיר – [THESE ARE] THE WORDS OF R' MEIR. וַחֲכָמִים אוֹמְרִים – BUT THE SAGES SAY: כָּל הַמְשַׁלֵּם אֵינוֹ לוֹקֶה – WHOEVER PAYS DOES NOT RECEIVE LASHES, i.e. a person cannot be liable to both lashes and monetary payment for the same crime; and since the *zomeim* witness pays money, he does not receive lashes. And the following question was asked regarding the Sages' ruling: וְנֵימָא כָּל הַלוֹקֶה אֵינוֹ מְשַׁלֵּם – **But let [the Sages] say** instead that **whoever receives lashes does not pay?**[18] אָמַר רַבִּי אִילְעָא – In response to this question **R' Ila'a said:** בְּפֵירוּשׁ רִיבְּתָה תּוֹרָה עֵדִים זוֹמְמִין לְתַשְׁלוּמִין – **The Torah has explicitly included** *zomemim* **witnesses** in the obligation **to** make **payment** even where this will exclude them from the penalty of lashes.

The Gemara elaborates:

הֵיכָן רִיבְּתָה תּוֹרָה – **Where did the Torah include** the *zomemim* witnesses in the obligation to make payment, to the exclusion of lashes? מִכְּדִי – **Now,** let us see: כְּתִיב ,,וַעֲשִׂיתֶם לוֹ כַּאֲשֶׁר זָמַם לַעֲשׂוֹת לְאָחִיו" – **It is written** regarding the *zomeim* witness:[19] ***And you shall do to him as he conspired to do to his brother.*** ,,יָד בְּיָד" לָמָּה לִי – **Why** then **do I need** the Torah to state as well: ***a hand for a hand?***[20] דָּבָר הַנִּיתָּן מִיָּד לְיָד – To teach that he is liable to **something which is given from hand to hand.**[21] וּמַאי נִיהוּ – **And what is that?** מָמוֹן – **Money,** which changes hands when it is paid.[22]

NOTES

32a (ד״ה חובל בחבירו). Thus, we see that the assailant pays money [and accordingly he cannot receive lashes].

13. [A *perutah* is the minimum threshold for payment. Any liability of less than a *perutah* is considered too insignificant to require payment.]

14. R' Yochanan specifies that the assailant receives lashes only if the injury did not amount to a *perutah.* Obviously, his reasoning is that if the injury did amount to a *perutah* or more, the assailant would have to pay money and thus he would *not* receive lashes. We see, then, that R' Yochanan agrees that in the case of wounding one's fellow, the law is that the assailant pays the money and does not receive lashes. Accordingly, our question remains: Why is it that R' Yochanan holds that in general lashes supersedes payment, yet in the case of wounding, payment supersedes lashes?

15. As the Gemara will demonstrate shortly.

16. *Makkos* 4a.

17. The witnesses are liable to lashes for having transgressed the prohibition stated in *Exodus* 20:13: *You shall not bear false witness;* and are liable to payment on account of the verse stated in *Deuteronomy* 19:19 regarding the *zomeim* witness: *You shall do to him as he conspired to do to his brother* (*Rashi*).

18. Granted the Sages hold that the verse *according to his wickedness* precludes dual penalties even if each derives from a different verse, why do they decide in the case of the *zomeim* witness that the payment of money supersedes the lashes and not the reverse? (see *Rashi*).

19. *Deuteronomy* 19:19.

20. Ibid. v. 21. After stating in verse 19: *And you shall do to him as he conspired to do to his brother,* the Torah states in verse 21: *Your eye shall have no pity [upon the zomeim witness]; a life for a life . . . a hand for a hand . . .* (*Rashi*). Isn't *a hand for a hand* already included in *and you shall do to him as he conspired?*

21. [An exposition that renders יָד בְּיָד as *[from] a hand "into" a hand.*]

22. Thus, the Torah requires *zomemim* to pay money, even though they should also be liable to lashes for false testimony. Hence, we see that where *zomemim* incur liability to both money and lashes, they pay the money and do not receive lashes (since a *dual* penalty is excluded by the verse *according to his wickedness*). [And we cannot say that the verse requiring payment (*a hand for a hand*) refers only to where the *zomemim* were not warned regarding the lashes, since – as the Gemara states on 33a – *zomemim* do not require a warning in order to receive physical punishment.]

There seems to be a difficulty here. Why did the Gemara have to prove that *zomemim* pay money from the verse *a hand for a hand*? Why not simply prove it from the very first verse itself: *And you shall do to him as he conspired . . .,* which would seem to include that if they conspired to deprive their victim of money, then they shall pay money – even though they should also be liable to lashes for false testimony! *Tosafos* answer that the first verse might have been interpreted as referring only to where the witnesses conspired to have their victim put to death. Only then do we "do to them as they conspired." But where they conspired to make him liable to money, I would say that they receive lashes and do not pay money. Therefore, the Gemara must resort to a proof from the next verse *a hand for a hand.* [*Tosafos,* however, point out another difficulty: The Gemara's terminology indicates that the point is proven from the *superfluity* of the verse *a hand for a hand* (which induces us to interpret it as referring to "something given from hand to hand"). But why isn't the point already evident from the simple meaning of *a hand for a hand*? For, as we know, the witnesses could not have conspired to actually have their victim's hand cut off (for no testimony would yield that result). Rather, this clause means that if they conspired to make Reuven pay the value of a hand to Shimon (by testifying that Reuven had cut off Shimon's hand), so too must they pay to Reuven the value of a

אלא עולא תחת תחת גמר כתיב הכא א) תחת אשר ענה וכתיב התם ב) עין תחת עין מה התם ממונא משלם מילקא לא לקי אף כל היכא דאיכא ממונא ומלקות ממונא משלם מילקא לא לקי רבי יוחנן אמר אפי' תימא אחותו נערה כאן שהתרו בו כאן שלא התרו בו אלמא קסבר רבי יוחנן כל היכא דאיכא ממון ומלקות ואתרו ביה מילקא לקי ממונא לא משלם מנא ליה לר' יוחנן הא אמר קרא ג) כדי רשעתו משום רשעה אחת אתה מחייבו ואי אתה מחייבו משום שתי רשעיות וסמיך ליה ד) ארבעים יכנו והרי חובל בחבירו דאיכא ממון ומלקות וממונא משלם מילקא לא לקי וכי תימא הני מילי היכא דלא אתרו ביה אבל אתרו ביה מילקא לקי ממונא לא משלם והאמר ר' אמי א"ר יוחנן הכהו הכאה שאין בה שוה פרוטה לוקה היכי דמי אי דלא אתרו ביה אמאי לוקה אלא פשיטא דאתרו ביה וטעמא דלית בה שוה פרוטה הא אית בה שוה פרוטה ממונא משלם מילקא לא לקי כדאמר רבי אילעא בפירוש ריבתה תורה עדים זוממין לתשלומין הכא נמי בפירוש ריבתה תורה חובל בחבירו לתשלומין והיכא איתמר דר' אילעא אהא מעידין אנו את איש פלוני שחייב לחבירו מאתים זוז ונמצאו זוממין לוקין ומשלמין שלא השם המביאן לידי מכות מביאן לידי תשלומין דברי ר"מ וחכמים אומרים כל המשלם אינו לוקה ונימא כל הלוקה אינו משלם א"ר אילעא בפירוש ריבתה תורה עדים זוממין לתשלומין היכן ריבתה תורה מכדי כתיב ה) ועשיתם לו כאשר זמם לעשות לאחיו ו) יד ביד למה לי דבר הניתן מיד ליד ומאי ניהו ממון חובל בחבירו נמי מכדי כתיב ז) כאשר עשה כן יעשה לו ח) כן ינתן בו למה לי דבר שיש בו נתינה ומאי ניהו ממון ורבי יוחנן מ"ט לא אמר כעולא אם כן בטלת ט) ערות אחותך לא תגלה

חובל

רש"י

תחת תחת גמר. וגזירה שוה מופנה היא ולמדין ולאין משיבין: **אפי' תימא.** היכא למכות באחותו נערה וכשהתרו בו דאיכא ממון ומלקות ולאשמעינן דלקי ולא משלם ומתניתין דכתובות בשלא התרו בו דליכא מלקות: **וסמיך ליה ארבעים יכנו.** להיכא דאיכא שתי רשעיות ניעבד ביה הלכה: **בפירוש ריבתה.** לקמיה מפרש היכא: **שלא השם המביאו לידי מכות כו'.** המקרא המביאו לידי מלקות אינו מביאו לתשלומין מלקות מלא תענה תשלומין מכאשר זמם וכיון דשני שמות הן חייב על שניהם: **נימא כל הלוקה אינו משלם.** ונלפינייה במלקות מאי שנא ממון דפשיטא להו: **יד ביד.** דסמיך ליה לא תחוס עינך נפש בנפש וגו': **כן ינתן.** כאשר יתן מום באדם וגו': **מאי טעמא לא אמר כעולא.** דגמר גזירה שוה לעונשו ממון ולא מלקות לכל חייבי ממון ומלקות: **אם כן.** דפטרת בא על אחותו ממלקות בטלת לאו שבה שעונש לאו במלקות:

תוספות

יש במינו לא הטומאה יותר מככר שהרי יש בו טוס כלי שהוא לא הטומאה כגון כלי עץ אבל טוס אוכל אינו נעשה לא הטומאה ועל שני הפירושים קשה לרשב"א דנימא התם אוכל ראשון יוכיח שאין במינו לא הטומאה ומטמא תרומה אף אני אביא שני וכי תימא מה לאוכל ראשון שכן עושה שני בחולין טבול יום יוכיח וליכא למיפרך נמי השתא שכן משונה דאין כאן טוס שיעור ונראה לפרש לא חמור דהתם לפי שבאין מכח לא הטומאה דטבול יום וכלי חרס ואוכל ראשון כולם נגעו בלא הטומאה מה שאין כן בשני דלא נגע אלא בראשון ור"ת מפרש דגבי עדים זוממין שייך לא חמור משום דאותו לא חמור של אוכל יכול להיות בעדים זוממין אם העידו על אחד שאכל בחבירו והוחזו דמשלמין חמשה דברים מה שרצו לחייבו ולד הקל יש לפרש שכן לאו דבחובל ועדים זוממין אין בהן כרת אלא לאו גרידא ולא נגמר מינייהו חייבי כריתות וכן בפ"ק דמכות (דף ד:) דיליף ממוציא שם רע ועדים זוממין דלאו שאין בו מעשה לוקין עליו ופריך מה להצד השוה שבהם שכן לא חמור יש לפרש כי הכא לרבינו תם ולרבינו יצחק ובפרק כיצד צולין (פסחים דף עז.) גבי מועדו ואפילו בטומאה דלאמר לא כתב בתמיד שכן כליל ולאי כתב בפסח שכן כרת בתרוייהו שכן יש בהן לא חמור התם יש טוס פירכא אחריתי דלא מצינו למילף במה הצד ולא תם הש"ס לפרשה ובטעם מועט מסתלק לומר דלריכי: **אלא** עולא תחת תחת גמר. מצינו למימר לפי מסקנא זו דלא קאמר עולא דממונא משלם ולא לקי אלא בהנהו תלת דגלי בהו קרא וליכא למימר דילפינן לעולא בכל דוכתא מתחת נתינה ישלם כסף דמהאי גזירה שוה ילפינן[ז] מיטב בכולהו דדוקא לענין מיטב נתקבל שהוא גוף התשלומין דאם לא כן תקשי לר' יוחנן ולאביי דפליגי אעולא דאטו מי לית להו גזירה שוה לענין מיטב והכא לעולא אייתר ליה האי תחת למיפטר ממלקות מגזירה שוה דחובל בחבירו הלכך צריך לומר לקמן לעולא דנפקא ליה בושת ופגם מדרבא:

[**מנא** ליה לר"י הא. וא"ת לעיל בעי מנא ליה לעולא דממונא משלם ולא לקי כו' והשתא בעי איפכא וי"ל דהכא משום ג"ש דתחת תחת קאמר מנ"ל לר"י דלא דרשינן ג"ש להכי דג"ש זו נתקבלה לכ"ע בבכורות (דף יז.) לגבי בכור]:

שלא השם המביאו לידי מלקות מביאו כו'. פירש בקונטרס משום דממון ומלקות אתו מתרי קראי מלקות מלא תענה וממון מועשיתם לו כאשר זמם וקשה דכ"ש דאי הוו כתיבי בחד קרא שילקה וישלם שהיה לוקה ומשלם ומיהו שמא יש לפרש לפ"ה משום דממון ומלקות אתו מתרי קראי אין לנו לבטל פסוק אחד לגמרי ולקיים האחר אבל אם היו באים שניהם מועשיתם לו כאשר זמם כגון שהעידו על אחד שהוציא שם רע על אשתו דבאין לחייבו ממון ומלקות אין לוקין ומשלמין ואין נראה לר"י דלא מסתבר שלא יהו חייבין ממון ומלקות בכה"ג כיון שרצו לחייבו שניהם ונראה לר"י לפרש שלא השם המביאו לידי מכות כו' כלומר שהתשלומין לא נכתבו בסמוך למלקות דאם היה כתוב באותו פסוק עצמו לא תענה ואם ענה ועשיתם לו כאשר זמם או ודאי הוה אמינא דה"ל לאו שניתק לעשה ולא ילקה עליו אבל עתה שנכתב רחוק זה מזה לא הוי ניתק לעשה ולא דמי ללאו דגזילה דחשיב ליה ניתק לעשה בפ' בתרא דמכות (דף טז.) ובשלוח הקן (חולין קמא.) אע"ג דעשה דוהשיב את הגזילה לא כתיב אלל לאו דלא תגזול דהתם ודאי ע"כ הוא ניתק לעשה שהרי עוקר גזילה מתחת ידו אבל קרא דועשיתם לו כאשר זמם אינו עוקר הלאו דלא תענה דעל ידי שאנו עושין לו כאשר זמם אינו נעקר עדותו אלא ע"י שהוזם הלכך לא חשבינן ליה ניתק לעשה כיון שלא נכתב אחריו סמוך לו והר"ר שלמה מדרוי"ש מפרש שלא השם המביאו לידי מכות דהיינו לא תענה מביאו לידי תשלומין פי' אינו בא להיות אזהרה לענוש תשלומין כדאמרינן במכות דממון לא בעי אזהרה ועוד דר' מאיר נפקא ליה אזהרה לכאשר זמם מוכל ישראל ישמעו ויראו ולא יוספו כדאמרינן בפ"ק דמכות (דף ד:) שאם היה צריך לא תענה לאזהרת ממון אז לא היה לוקה עליו דמחד לאו לא הוה ענשינן ליה ממון ומלקות:

ה) [כדמשמע בפ"ק דמכות אההיא דתנן מעידין אנו באיש פלוני שחייב מלקות מ' לוקים שמונים א' מועשיתם כאשר זמם וא' מלא תענה וחכ"א אין סופג אלא מ' ורבנן האי לא תענה מאי עבדי ליה מיבעיא להו לאזהרת עדים זוממים ור"מ אזהרה נפקא ליה מוכל ישראל וגו' משמע דאי לאו קרא אחרינא לאזהרה מלא תענה לא הוה ענשינן ליה תרי מלקיות ולרבנן אע"ג דלא תענה לא צריך לאזהרת ממון מ"מ אינו לוקה ומשלם משום כדי רשעתו ולא לקי לרבנן אלא כשמעידים שהוא בן גרושה דליכא כאשר זמם ואע"ג דלא תענה לאו שאין בו מעשה ועוד דניתן לאזהרת מיתת ב"ד הכא גלי קרא דלקי מוהיה אם בן הכות הרשע]:

מכדי כתיב ועשיתם לו כאשר זמם יד ביד למה לי. וליכא למימר דלמה לי יד ביד דמועשיתם לו כאשר זמם משמע בהדיא ממון דכמו שהיה רוצה לחייבו ממון כן יתחייב לו ממון דמצינו למימר דכאשר זמם מיירי במיתה ומלקות אבל בממון מילקא לקי ממונא לא משלם ומיהו קשה לישנא דמכדי כתיב ועשיתם לו כו' יד ביד למה לי דמשמע דמייתורא דלא איצטריך לגופיה הוא דמפיק ליה והא אפילו לא מייתר יד ביד משמע שפיר ממון דליכא לפרושי יד ביד ממש כדנפקא לן בהחובל (ב"ק דף פג: ופד.) מעין תחת עין ועוד הא דקאמר גבי חובל בחבירו כן ינתן בו למה לי דבר הניתן מיד ליד ומאי ניהו ממון אימא הני מילי היכא דלא אתרו ביה דמכן ינתן בו נפקא בהחובל נזק ולא מכאשר עשה אבל היכא דאתרו ביה אימא דמילקא לקי ונראה לר"י דהך סוגיא אתיא כמאן דמפיק התם עין תחת עין ממון מקרא דיד ביד והיינו דקאמר מכדי כתיב ועשיתם לו כאשר זמם ואי ס"ד ו) עין תחת עין ממש א"כ יד ביד בעדים זוממין למה לי מכאשר זמם נפקא אלא אייתר יד ביד למידרש דבר הניתן מיד ליד דהיינו ממון אבל אי לא אייתר הוה אמינא יד ביד ממש: (א) **חובל** בחבירו מכדי כתיב כאשר עשה כן יעשה לו. דמשמע ממון כדאוכחן מייתורא דיד ביד כדפרישית וא"כ כן ינתן בו למה לי והא ליכא למימר דאתא להיכא דלא אתרו ביה דמיד ביד נפקא אלא ע"כ לא איצטריך אלא היכא דאתרו ביה ומיהו הא לא קשיא ליה אמאי איצטריך כאשר עשה וגו' דנשנה כאן לשום צורך כדאמרינן כל פרשה שנאמרה ונישנית כו' אבל כן ינתן בו למה חזר ושנה שתי פעמים אלא לומר לך דבר הניתן מיד ליד להיכא דאתרו ביה והוא הדין דהוה מצי למימר מכדי כתיב יד ביד כן ינתן בו למה לי: **ורבי** יוחנן מ"ט לא אמר כעולא. והא ליכא למימר דלא שמיע ליה גזירה שוה דתחת תחת דהא ילפינן לה בבכורות[ז] גבי בכור ובכמה מקומות: **אם** כן בטלת ערות אחותך לא תגלה. וא"ת כל לאו שאין בו מעשה ולאו הניתק לעשה ביטלנו הלאו כיון שאין לוקין עליו הא לאו מילתא היא דההיא לאו בר מלקות הוא אבל הכא דשייך ביה מלקות לית לן למידרש גזירה שוה לאפוקי מלקות מיניה כיון דאיכא לאוקמי גז"ש אמילתא אחריתי:

אלא

עין משפט נר מצוה

כב א מיי' פי"כ מהל' סנהדרין הל' ד סי' קלא טוש"ע ח"מ סימן תכ סעיף ג:

כג ב מיי' פ"ד מהל' חובל ומזיק הל' ט סמג עשין ע טוש"ע ח"מ סימן תכד סעיף ג:

כד ג מיי' פי"ח מהל' עדות הל' א סמג עשין קי טור ח"מ סי' לח:

תורה אור השלם

א) וְנָתַן הָאִישׁ הַשֹּׁכֵב עִמָּהּ לַאֲבִי הַנַּעֲר חֲמִשִּׁים כָּסֶף וְלוֹ תִהְיֶה לְאִשָּׁה תַּחַת אֲשֶׁר עִנָּהּ לֹא יוּכַל שַׁלְּחָהּ כָּל יָמָיו: [דברים כב, כט]

ב) עַיִן תַּחַת עַיִן שֵׁן תַּחַת שֵׁן יָד תַּחַת יָד רֶגֶל תַּחַת רָגֶל: [שמות כא, כד]

ג) וְהָיָה אִם בִּן הַכּוֹת הָרָשָׁע וְהִפִּילוֹ הַשֹּׁפֵט וְהִכָּהוּ לְפָנָיו כְּדֵי רִשְׁעָתוֹ בְּמִסְפָּר: [דברים כה, ב]

ד) אַרְבָּעִים יַכֶּנּוּ לֹא יֹסִיף פֶּן יֹסִיף לְהַכֹּתוֹ עַל אֵלֶּה מַכָּה רַבָּה וְנִקְלָה אָחִיךָ לְעֵינֶיךָ: [דברים כה, ג]

ה) וַעֲשִׂיתֶם לוֹ כַּאֲשֶׁר זָמַם לַעֲשׂוֹת לְאָחִיו וּבִעַרְתָּ הָרָע מִקִּרְבֶּךָ: [דברים יט, יט]

ו) וְלֹא תָחוֹס עֵינֶךָ נֶפֶשׁ בְּנֶפֶשׁ עַיִן בְּעַיִן שֵׁן בְּשֵׁן יָד בְּיָד רֶגֶל בְּרָגֶל: [דברים יט, כא]

ז) וְאִישׁ כִּי יִתֵּן מוּם בַּעֲמִיתוֹ כַּאֲשֶׁר עָשָׂה כֵּן יֵעָשֶׂה לּוֹ: [ויקרא כד, יט]

ח) שֶׁבֶר תַּחַת שֶׁבֶר עַיִן תַּחַת עַיִן שֵׁן תַּחַת שֵׁן כַּאֲשֶׁר יִתֵּן מוּם בָּאָדָם כֵּן יִנָּתֶן בּוֹ: [ויקרא כד, כ]

ט) עֶרְוַת אֲחוֹתְךָ בַת אָבִיךָ אוֹ בַת אִמֶּךָ מוֹלֶדֶת בַּיִת אוֹ מוֹלֶדֶת חוּץ לֹא תְגַלֶּה עֶרְוָתָן: [ויקרא יח, ט]

תוספות רי"ד

ור"י אמר אפילו תימא באחותו נערה. כאן שהתרו בו כאן שלא התרו בו אלמא קסבר ר"י כל היכא דאיכא ממון ומלקות מילקא לקי ממונא לא משלם פי' המורה. אפילו תימא ההיא דמכות באחותו נערה וכשהתרו בו דאיכא ממון ומלקות דלקי ולא משלם. ומתני' דהכא בשלא אתרו בי' דליכא מלקות כ"א ממון.

מסורת הש"ס

א) לקמן לו. ב"ק פג: מכות ד: יג:, ב) סנהדרין פה. מכות ט., ג) מכות ד., ד) [ב"ק ה.], ה) ת"י כ"י, ו) ס"א יד תחת יד ממש, ז) [דף יז. נז.].

הגהות הב"ח

(א) תוס' ד"ה מכדי וד"ה חובל בחבירו נמי מכדי הד"א:

ליקוטי רש"י

עין תחת עין. סימא עין חבירו נותן לו דמי עינו כמה שפחתו דמיו למכור בשוק וכו' ולא נטילת אבר ממש כמו שדרשו רבותינו בפרק החובל (ב"ק פג:) [שמות כא, כד]. **שאין בה שוה פרוטה.** שאם יש בה תשלומי פרוטה משלם ואינו לוקה דילפינן בכתובות באלו נערות בפירוש ריבתה תורה חובל בחבירו לתשלומין וכי אין בה שוה פרוטה לוקה שעבר על לא תוסיף פן יוסיף (דברים כה) [מכות ט.]. **שלא השם המביאן לידי מכות מביאן לידי תשלומין.** מלקות משום לא תענה ותשלומין משום כאשר זמם. **כל המשלם אינו לוקה.** דכתיב כדי רשעתו משום רשעה אחת אתה מחייבו ואי אתה מחייבו משום שתי רשעיות ובמסכת כתובות (דף לב:) מקשינן ונימא כל הלוקה אינו משלם וילקו כל הזוממין ולא ישלמו ומשנינן בפירוש רבתה תורה עדים זוממין לתשלומין ויליף לה התם [שם ד.]. **כן ינתן בו.** פירשו רבותינו שאינו נתינת מום ממש אלא תשלומי ממון שמין אותו כעבד לכך כתיב בו לשון נתינה דבר הנתון מיד ליד [ויקרא כד, כ].

The Gemara concedes this objection and offers another source for Ulla's rule that in cases of dual penalty, one pays money and does not receive lashes:

אֶלָּא עוּלָּא ,,תַּחַת'' ,,תַּחַת'' גָּמַר – **Rather, Ulla derives** this rule through a *gezeirah shavah* that links the word ***"tachas"*** written in the context of violation with the word ***"tachas"*** written in the context of wounding one's fellow. כְּתִיב הָכָא ,,תַּחַת אֲשֶׁר עִנָּהּ'' – **It is written here,** with regard to the violator: ***"tachas" he violated her.***[1] וּכְתִיב הָתָם ,,עַיִן תַּחַת עַיִן'' – **And it is written there,** with regard to one who strikes and wounds his fellow: ***an eye "tachas" an eye.***[2] מָה הָתָם מָמוֹנָא מְשַׁלֵּם מִילְקָא לֹא לָקֵי – **Just as there,** in the case of the one who wounds his fellow, **he pays money** and **does not receive lashes,**[3] אַף כָּל הֵיכָא דְּאִיכָּא מָמוֹנָא וּמַלְקוֹת – **so too, wherever there is** liability to both **money and lashes** [such as where one violates his sister], מָמוֹנָא מְשַׁלֵּם מִילְקָא לֹא לָקֵי – the law is that **he pays money** and **does not receive lashes.**[4]

The Gemara cites an alternative solution to the apparent contradiction between our Mishnah (which states that one who violates his sister is liable to the fine) and the Mishnah in *Makkos* (which states that one who cohabits with his sister receives lashes):

רַבִּי יוֹחָנָן אָמַר – **R' Yochanan says:** אֲפִילוּ תֵּימָא אֲחוֹתוֹ נַעֲרָה – **You can even say** that the Mishnah in *Makkos* is also dealing with **his sister** who is **a *naarah,*** who is generally entitled to a fine,[5] and still it does not contradict our Mishnah, which states that one pays the fine for violating his sister who is a *naarah.* כָּאן שֶׁהִתְרוּ בּוֹ – For **here,** in *Makkos,* the Mishnah refers to **where they warned him** that he would be liable to lashes for cohabiting with his sister,[6] כָּאן שֶׁלֹּא הִתְרוּ בּוֹ – whereas **here,** in our Mishnah, it refers to **where the witnesses did not warn him** that he would be liable to lashes for cohabiting with his sister.[7]

The Gemara comments:

אַלְמָא קָסָבַר רַבִּי יוֹחָנָן – **Evidently, R' Yochanan holds** that כָּל הֵיכָא דְּאִיכָּא מָמוֹן וּמַלְקוֹת וְאַתְרוּ בֵּיהּ – **wherever there is** liability to both **money and lashes, and they warned him** that his sin would make him liable to lashes, מִילְקָא לָקֵי מָמוֹנָא לֹא מְשַׁלֵּם – the law is that **he receives lashes** and **does not pay the money.**

The Gemara asks:

מְנָא לֵיהּ לְרַבִּי יוֹחָנָן הָא – **From where does R' Yochanan know this?**

The Gemara answers:

אָמַר קְרָא ,,כְּדֵי רִשְׁעָתוֹ'' – **The verse states** regarding the administering of lashes: *And the judge shall cast him down and lash him . . .* ***in accordance with his wickedness.***[8] The singular form of the word "wickedness" teaches that מִשּׁוּם רִשְׁעָה אַחַת אַתָּה מְחַיְּיבוֹ – **you may hold him liable** (i.e. punish him) **for one wickedness,** וְאִי אַתָּה מְחַיְּיבוֹ מִשּׁוּם שְׁתֵּי רִשְׁעָיוֹת – **but you may not hold him liable for two wickednesses,** i.e. you may not subject him to two penalties — to payment and to lashes — for one crime.[9] וּסְמִיךְ לֵיהּ ,,אַרְבָּעִים יַכֶּנּוּ'' – **And adjacent to [this verse]** it states: ***Forty [lashes] he shall strike him.***[10]

The Gemara challenges R' Yochanan's position that wherever there is liability to payment and lashes, the sinner receives lashes and does not pay:

וַהֲרֵי חוֹבֵל בַּחֲבֵירוֹ – **But there is** the case of **one who wounds his fellow,** דְּאִיכָּא מָמוֹן וּמַלְקוֹת – **where there is** liability to both **money and lashes,**[11] מָמוֹנָא מְשַׁלֵּם מִילְקָא לֹא לָקֵי – and the law is that **he pays the money** and **does not receive lashes!**[12] — ? —

NOTES

1. *Deuteronomy* 22:29 states: וְלוֹ־תִהְיֶה לְאִשָּׁה תַּחַת אֲשֶׁר עִנָּהּ, *and she shall become his wife in place of [tachas] that which he violated her.*

2. *Exodus* 21:24 states that the assailant shall pay *an eye in place of [tachas] an eye.* [The reference is to monetary payment, as explained by the Gemara in *Bava Kamma* 83b ff.]

3. See 32a note 15.

4. The clause *because [tachas] he violated her* is superfluous, making the *gezeirah shavah* one that is *mufneh* — based on a *free* or *superfluous* term. And the rule regarding a *gezeirah shaveh mufneh* is that "we derive laws from it and we do not raise objections," i.e. even if a logical argument can be made that the two contexts are not comparable, the *gezeirah shavah* serves to compare them (*Rashi*). Hence, although logical arguments can be made that the rule of "paying instead of receiving lashes" found in the case of one who wounds his fellow — be that rule a stringency or a leniency — cannot be applied to the case of one who violates his sister (as the Gemara above demonstrates), the *gezeirah shavah* nevertheless serves to apply that rule to the case of one who violates his sister. [Actually, there is a dispute whether the rule that objections cannot be raised against a *gezeirah shavah mufneh* applies even to a *gezeirah shavah* that is *mufneh* on only one side (as in our case, where only the *tachas* stated with regard to violation is superfluous, and not the *tachas* stated with regard to wounding — see *Ritva*) — see *Niddah* 22b. However, all would agree here that objections cannot be raised against this *gezeirah shavah,* since there is nothing else to be expounded from the superfluous *tachas* (see *Shitah Mekubetzes* ד״ה וז״ל הריטב״א ז״ל אלא עולא).]

The Gemara's language here (אַף כָּל הֵיכָא, *so too, wherever . . .*) suggests that the *gezeirah shavah* serves to apply the rule that one pays money instead of receiving lashes to *all* situations of dual penalty, not just to the case of violation included in the *gezeirah shavah. Tosafos* ד״ה אלא, however, suggest that according to the present explanation of Ulla's source, Ulla might indeed extend the rule of "payment rather than lashes" only to the case of violation, which is included in the *gezeirah shavah,* but not to other cases of dual penalty. [See also *Ritva,* who cites *Tosafos* as emending the Gemara text to read: אַף הָכָא דְּאִיכָּא מָמוֹנָא וּמַלְקוּת, *so too, "here," where there is both money and lashes . . .* According to this reading, the Gemara is limiting extension of this rule to the specific case included in the *gezeirah shavah* — namely, the case of violation.] From *Rashi* below ד״ה מאי טעמא, however, it would seem that even now the Gemara understands Ulla as extending the rule of "payment rather than lashes" to all situations of dual penalty. See *Tos. Yeshanim* 32a ד״ה ועוד פר״ת בא״ד נילף מקנס וחובל ועדים זוממים, who suggest that in light of this *gezeirah shavah,* a new צַד הַשָּׁוֶה, *derivation from the common characteristic,* can be expounded using all *three* contexts — wounding, violation and *zomemim* — and this new derivation is *not* subject to the challenge presented by the Gemara above to the previous צַד הַשָּׁוֶה. [As to why our *Tosafos* might hold that the צַד הַשָּׁוֶה from all three might be insufficient, see *Pnei Yehoshua* to *Tosafos* here and *Beis Yaakov* to *Tosafos* 32a ד״ה אלמא, passage beginning בא״ד ולתרץ נראה דהנה דברי התוס׳ הכא שכתבו שיכולין ללמוד מהנך שלשה וכו׳.]

5. I.e. in contrast to Ulla, who maintained that the Mishnah in *Makkos* must be dealing with a woman who is not entitled to any monetary payment.

6. Hence, he incurs liability to both payment and lashes, and the Mishnah there thus teaches us that where there is a dual penalty, he receives the lashes and does not pay the money.

7. Hence, he is not liable to lashes (*Rashi*), and he remains subject to the other penalty — the payment of the fine.

8. *Deuteronomy* 25:2.

9. [This is the source for the rule that one cannot both receive lashes *and* pay money for the same crime, which is the premise on which the *sugya* until now has been based (see 32a note 1). The Gemara mentions it here explicitly in order to show how it is juxtaposed to the *next* verse, which is the basis for R' Yochanan's opinion, as the Gemara will now demonstrate.]

10. [Ibid. v. 3.] Thus, the first verse (*according to his wickedness . . .*) teaches that we subject him to only one of the two penalties, but does not indicate which. The next verse states *Forty [lashes] he shall strike him,* indicating that the one penalty to which we subject him is lashes and not monetary payment (see *Rashi*).

11. See 32a note 14.

12. For the Torah states in *Exodus* 21:18-19: *If men quarrel and one hits his fellow . . . he shall pay for his lost time [from work]* etc. (see *Rashi* to

אלא עולא תחת תחת גמר כתיב הכא (א) תחת אשר ענה וכתיב התם (ב) עין תחת עין מה התם ממונא משלם מילקא לא לקי אף כל היכא דאיכא ממונא ומלקות ממונא משלם מילקא לא לקי רבי יוחנן אמר אפי' תימא אחותו נערה כאן שהתרו בו כאן שלא התרו בו אלמא קסבר רבי יוחנן כל היכא דאיכא ממון ומלקות ואתרו ביה מילקא לקי ממונא לא משלם מנא ליה לר' יוחנן הא אמר קרא (ג) כדי רשעתו משום רשעה אחת אתה מחייבו ואי אתה מחייבו משום שתי רשעיות וסמיך ליה (ד) ארבעים יכנו והרי חובל בחבירו דאיכא ממון ומלקות ממונא משלם מילקא לא לקי וכי תימא הני מילי היכא דלא אתרו ביה אבל אתרו ביה לקי ממונא לא משלם והאמר ר' אמי א"ר יוחנן הכהו הכאה שאין בה שוה פרוטה לוקה היכי דמי אי דלא אתרו ביה אמאי לוקה אלא פשיטא דאתרו ביה וטעמא דלית בה שוה פרוטה הא אית בה שוה פרוטה ממונא משלם מילקא לא לקי כדאמר רבי אילעא בפירוש ריבתה תורה עדים זוממין לתשלומין הכא נמי בפירוש ריבתה תורה חובל בחבירו לתשלומין והיכא איתמר דר' אילעא אהא מעידין אנו את איש פלוני שחייב לחבירו מאתים זוז ונמצאו זוממין לוקין ומשלמין שלא השם המביאן לידי מכות מביאן לידי תשלומין דברי ר"מ וחכמים אומרים כל המשלם אינו לוקה ונימא כל הלוקה אינו משלם א"ר אילעא בפירוש ריבתה תורה עדים זוממין לתשלומין היכן ריבתה תורה מכדי כתיב (ה) ועשיתם לו כאשר זמם לעשות לאחיו (ו) יד ביד למה לי דבר הניתן מיד ליד ומאי ניהו ממון חובל בחבירו נמי מכדי כתיב (ז) כאשר עשה כן יעשה לו (ח) כן ינתן בו למה לי דבר שיש בו נתינה ומאי ניהו ממון ורבי יוחנן מ"ט לא אמר כעולא אם כן בטלת (ט) ערות אחותך לא תגלה

חובל

רש"י

תחת תחת גמר. וגזירה שוה מופנה היא ולמדין ואין משיבין: אפי' תימא. הסיא למכות באחותו נערה וכשהתרו בו דאיכא ממון ומלקות ואשמעינן דלקי ולא משלם ומתניתין דכתובות בשלא התרו בו דליכא מלקות: וסמיך ליה ארבעים יכנו. דהיכא דאיכא שתי רשעיות ניעבד ביה הכאה: בפירוש ריבתה. לקמיה מפרש היכא: שלא השם המביאו לידי מכות כו'. המקרא המביאו לידי מלקות אינו מביאו לתשלומין מלקות מלא תענה תשלומין מכאשר זמם וכיון דשני שמות הן חייב על שניהם: נימא כל הלוקה אינו משלם. ונידייניה במלקות מאי שנא ממון דפשיטא להו: יד ביד. דסמיך ליה לא תחוס עינך נפש בנפש וגו': כן ינתן. כאשר יתן מום באדם וגו': מאי טעמא לא אמר כעולא. דגמר גזירה שוה לעונשו ממון ולא מלקות לכל חייבי ממון ומלקות: אם כן. דפטרת בא על אחותו ממלקות בטלת לאו שבה שעונש לאו במלקות:

ופרכינן

תוספות

יש במינו אב הטומאה יותר מככר שהרי יש בו שום כלי שהוא אב הטומאה כגון כלי עץ אבל שום אוכל אינו נעשה אב הטומאה ועל שני הפירושים קשה לרשב"א דנימא התם אוכל ראשון יוכיח שאין במינו אב הטומאה ומטמא תרומה אף אני אביא שני וכי תימא מה לאוכל ראשון שכן עושה שני בחולין טבול יום יוכיח וליכא למיפרך נמי השתא שכן משנה דאין כאן שום שינוי ונראה לפרש לא תמור דהתם לפי שבאין מכח אב הטומאה דטבול יום וכלי חרס ואוכל ראשון כולם נגעו באב הטומאה מה שאין כן בשני דלא נגע אלא בראשון ור"ת מפרש דגבי עדים זוממין שייך לא תמור משום דאותו לא תמור של אוכל יכול להיות בעדים זוממין אם העידו על אחד שאכל בחבירו והחמו למשלמין חמשה דברים מה שרצו לחייבו ולא הקל יש לפרש שכן לאו דבהוכל ועדים זוממין אין בהן כרת אלא לאו גרידא ולא נגמר מינייהו חייבי כריתות וכן בפ"ק דמכות (דף ד:) דיליף ממוציא שם רע ועדים זוממין דלאו שאין בו מעשה לוקין עליו ופריך מה להלל השוה שבהם שכן לא תמור יש לפרש כי הכא אלא תס ולרבינו יצחק ובפרק כילד צולין (פסחים דף עז.) גבי במועדו ואפילו בטומאה דאמר אי כתב בתמיד שכן כליל ואי כתב בפסח שכן כרת בתרויהו שכן יש בהן לא תמור התם יש שום פירכא אחריתי דלא מצינו למילף במה הצד ולא חש הש"ס לפרשה ובטעם מועט מסתלק לומר דלריכי: **אלא** עולא תחת תחת גמר. מצינו למימר לפי מסקנא זו דלא קאמר עולא דממונא משלם ולא לקי אלא בהנהו תלת דגלי בהו קרא וליכא למימר דילפינן לעולא בכל דוכתא מתחת נתינה ישלם כסף דמהאי גזירה שוה ילפינן[ז] מיטב בכולהו דדוקא לענין מיטב נתקבל שהוא גוף התשלומין דאם לא כן תקשי לר' יוחנן ולאביי דפליגי אעולא דאטו מי לית להו גזירה שוה לענין מיטב והכא לעולא אייתר ליה האי תחת למיפטר ממלקות מגזירה שוה דחובל בחברו הלכך לריך לומר לקמן לעולא דנפקא ליה בושת ופגם מדרבא:

[**מנא** ליה לר"י הא. וא"ת לעיל בעי מנא ליה לעולא דממונא משלם ולא לקי כו' והשתא בעי איפכא וי"ל דהכא משום ג"ש דתחת תחת קאמר מנ"ל לר"י דלא דרשינן ג"ש להכי דג"ש זו נתקבלה לכ"ע בבכורות (דף יב.) לגבי בכור]:

שלא השם המביאו לידי מלקות מביאו כו'. פירש בקונטרס משום דממון ומלקות אתו מתרי קראי מלקות מלא תענה וממון מועשיתם לו כאשר זמם וקשה דכ"ש דאי הוו כתיבי בחד קרא שילקה וישלם שהיה לוקה ומשלם ומיהו שמא יש לפרש לפ"ה משום דממון ומלקות אתו מתרי קראי אין לנו לבטל פסוק אחד לגמרי ולקיים האחר אבל אם היו באים שניהם מועשיתם לו כאשר זמם כגון שהעידו על אחד שהוציא שם רע על אשתו דבאין לחייבו ממון ומלקות אין לוקין ומשלמין ואין נראה לר"י דלא מסתבר שלא יהו חייבין ממון ומלקות בכה"ג כיון שרצו לחייבו שניהם ונראה לר"י לפרש שלא השם המביאו לידי מכות כו' כלומר שהתשלומין לא נכתבו בסמוך למלקות דאם היה כתוב באותו פסוק עצמו לא תענה ואם ענה ועשיתם לו כאשר זמם אז ודאי הוה אמינא דה"ל לאו שניתק לעשה ולא ילקה עליו אבל עתה שנכתב רחוק זה מזה לא הוי ניתק לעשה ולא דמי ללאו דגזילה דחשיב ליה ניתק לעשה בפ' בתרא דמכות (דף טז.) ובשלוח הקן (חולין קמא.) אע"ג דעשה דוהשיב את הגזילה לא כתיב אצל לאו דלא תגזול דהתם ודאי ע"כ הוא ניתק לעשה שהרי עוקר גזילה מתחת ידו אבל קרא דועשיתם לו כאשר זמם אינו עוקר הלאו דלא תענה דעל ידי שאנו עושין לו כאשר זמם אינו נעקר עדותו אלא ע"י שהוזם הלכך לא חשבינן ליה ניתק לעשה כיון שלא נכתב אחריו סמוך לו והר"ר שלמה מדרוי"ש מפרש שלא השם המביאו לידי מכות דהיינו לא תענה מביאו לידי תשלומין פי' אינו בא להיות אזהרה לענוש תשלומין כדאמרינן במכות דממון לא בעי אזהרה ועוד דר' מאיר נפקא ליה אזהרה לכאשר זמם מוכל ישראל ישמעו ויראו ולא יוסיפו כדאמרינן בפ"ק דמכות (דף ד:) שאם היה לריך לא תענה לאזהרת ממון אז לא היה לוקה עליו דמחד לאו לא הוה ענשינן ליה ממון ומלקות:

[ה] [כדמשמע בפ"ק דמכות אההיא דתנן מעידין אנו באיש פלוני שחייב מלקות מ' לוקים שמונים א' מועשיתם כאשר זמם וא' מלא תענה וחכ"א אין סופג אלא מ' ורבנן האי לא תענה מאי עבדי ליה מיבעיא להו לאזהרת עדים זוממים ור"מ אזהרה נפקא ליה מוכל ישראל וגו' משמע דאי לאו קרא אחרינא לאזהרה מלא תענה לא הוה ענשינן ליה תרי מלקיות ולרבנן אע"ג דלא תענה לא צריך לאזהרת ממון מ"מ אינו לוקה ומשלם משום כדי רשעתו ולא לקי לרבנן אלא כשמעידים שהוא בן גרושה דליכא כאשר זמם ואע"ג דלא תענה לאו שאין בו מעשה ועוד דניתן לאזהרת מיתת ב"ד הכא גלי קרא דלקי מוהיה אם בן הכות הרשע]:

מכדי כתיב ועשיתם לו כאשר זמם יד ביד למה לי. וליכא למימר דלמה לי יד ביד דמועשיתם לו כאשר זמם משמע בהדיא ממון דכמו שהיה רוצה לחייבו ממון כן יתחייב לו ממון דמצינו למימר דכאשר זמם איירי במיתה ומלקות אבל בממון מילקא לקי ממונא לא משלם ומיהו קשה לישנא דמכדי כתיב ועשיתם לו כו' יד ביד למה לי דמשמע דמייתורא דלא איצטריך לגופיה הוא דמפיק ליה והא אפילו לא מייתר יד ביד משמע שפיר ממון דליכא לפרושי יד ביד ממש כדנפקא לן בהחובל (ב"ק דף פג: ופד.) מעין תחת עין ועוד הא דקאמר גבי חובל בחבירו כן ינתן בו למה לי דבר הניתן מיד ליד ומאי ניהו ממון אימא הני מילי היכא דלא אתרו ביה דמכן ינתן בו נפקא בהחובל נזק ולא מכאשר עשה אבל היכא דאתרו ביה אימא דמילקא לקי ונראה לר"י דהך סוגיא אתיא כמאן דמפיק התם עין תחת עין ממון מקרא דיד ביד והיינו דקאמר מכדי כתיב ועשיתם לו כאשר זמם ואי ס"ד[י] עין תחת עין ממש א"כ יד ביד בעדים זוממין למה לי מכאשר זמם נפקא אלא אייתר יד ביד למידרש דבר הניתן מיד ליד דהיינו ממון אבל אי לא אייתר הוה אמינא יד ביד ממש: (א) **חובל** בחבירו מכדי כתיב כאשר עשה כן יעשה לו. דמשמע ממון כדאוכחן מייתורא דיד ביד כדפרישית וא"כ כן ינתן בו למה לי והא ליכא למימר דאתא להיכא דלא אתרו ביה דמיד ביד נפקא אלא ע"כ לא איצטריך אלא היכא דאתרו ביה ומיהו הא לא קשיא ליה אמאי איצטריך כאשר עשה וגו' דנשנה כאן לשום דורך כדאמרינן כל פרשה שנאמרה ונישנית כו' אבל כן ינתן בו למה חזר ושנה שתי פעמים אלא לומר לך דבר הניתן מיד ליד להיכא דאתרו ביה והוא הדין דהוה מצי למימר מכדי כתיב יד ביד כן ינתן בו למה לי: **ורבי** יוחנן מ"ט לא אמר כעולא. והא ליכא למימר דלא שמיע ליה גזירה שוה דתחת תחת דהא ילפינן לה בבכורות[י] גבי בכור ובכמה מקומות: **אם** כן בטלת ערות אחותך לא תגלה. וא"ת כל לאו שאין בו מעשה ולאו הניתק לעשה ביטלנו הלאו כיון שאין לוקין עליו הא לאו מילתא היא דההיא לאו בר מלקות הוא אבל הכא דשייך ביה מלקות לית לן למידרש גזירה שוה לאפוקי מלקות מיניה כיון דאיכא לאוקומי גז"ש אמילתא אחריתי:

אלא

עין משפט נר מצוה

כב א מיי' פ"כ מהל' סנהדרין הל' ד סי' קלא טוש"ע ח"מ סימן תכ סעיף ג:

כג ב מיי' פ"ד מהל' חובל ומזיק הל' ט סמג עשין ע טוש"ע ח"מ סימן תכ סעיף ג:

כד ג מיי' פי"ח מהל' עדות הל' א סמג עשין קי טור ח"מ סי' לח:

תורה אור השלם

א) וְנָתַן הָאִישׁ הַשֹּׁכֵב עִמָּהּ לַאֲבִי הַנַּעֲרָ חֲמִשִּׁים כָּסֶף וְלוֹ תִהְיֶה לְאִשָּׁה תַּחַת אֲשֶׁר עִנָּהּ לֹא יוּכַל שַׁלְּחָהּ כָּל יָמָיו: [דברים כב, כט]

ב) עַיִן תַּחַת עַיִן שֵׁן תַּחַת שֵׁן יָד תַּחַת יָד רֶגֶל תַּחַת רָגֶל: [שמות כא, כד]

ג) וְהָיָה אִם בִּן הַכּוֹת הָרָשָׁע וְהִפִּילוֹ הַשֹּׁפֵט וְהִכָּהוּ לְפָנָיו כְּדֵי רִשְׁעָתוֹ בְּמִסְפָּר: [דברים כה, ב]

ד) אַרְבָּעִים יַכֶּנּוּ לֹא יֹסִיף פֶּן יֹסִיף לְהַכֹּתוֹ עַל אֵלֶּה מַכָּה רַבָּה וְנִקְלָה אָחִיךָ לְעֵינֶיךָ: [דברים כה, ג]

ה) וַעֲשִׂיתֶם לוֹ כַּאֲשֶׁר זָמַם לַעֲשׂוֹת לְאָחִיו וּבִעַרְתָּ הָרָע מִקִּרְבֶּךָ: [דברים יט, יט]

ו) וְלֹא תָחוֹס עֵינֶךָ נֶפֶשׁ בְּנֶפֶשׁ עַיִן בְּעַיִן שֵׁן בְּשֵׁן יָד בְּיָד רֶגֶל בְּרָגֶל: [דברים יט, כא]

ז) וְאִישׁ כִּי יִתֵּן מוּם בַּעֲמִיתוֹ כַּאֲשֶׁר עָשָׂה כֵּן יֵעָשֶׂה לּוֹ: [ויקרא כד, יט]

ח) שֶׁבֶר תַּחַת שֶׁבֶר עַיִן תַּחַת עַיִן שֵׁן תַּחַת שֵׁן כַּאֲשֶׁר יִתֵּן מוּם בָּאָדָם כֵּן יִנָּתֶן בּוֹ: [ויקרא כד, כ]

ט) עֶרְוַת אֲחוֹתְךָ בַת אָבִיךָ אוֹ בַת אִמֶּךָ מוֹלֶדֶת בַּיִת אוֹ מוֹלֶדֶת חוּץ לֹא תְגַלֶּה עֶרְוָתָן: [ויקרא יח, ט]

תוספות רי"ד

ור"י אמר אפילו תימא באחותו נערה. כאן שהתרו בו כאן שלא התרו בו אלמא קסבר ר"י כל היכא דאיכא ממון ומלקות מילקא לקי ממונא לא משלם פי' המורה. אפילו תימא ההיא דמכות באחותו נערה וכשהתרו בו דאיכא ממון ומלקות לקי ולא משלם. ומתני' דהכא בשלא אתרו בי' דליכא מלקות כ"א ממון.

מסורת הש"ס

א) לקמן לו. ב"ק פג:, ב) מכות ד: יג., ג) סנהדרין פה. מכות ט., ג) מכות ד., ד) [ב"ק ה.], ה) ח"מ כ"י, ו) ס"א יד תחת יד ממש, ז) [דף יב. נו.]

הגהות הב"ח

(א) תוס' ד"ה חובל בחבירו נמי מכדי הד"א:

ליקוטי רש"י

עין תחת עין. ממון עין חבירו נותן לו דמי עינו כמה שפחתו דמיו למכור בשוק וכו' ולא נטילת אבר ממש כמו שדרשו רבותינו בפרק החובל (ב"ק פג:) [שמות כא, כד]. שאין בה שוה פרוטה. שאם יש בה שוה פרוטה משלם ואינו לוקה דילפינן בכתובות באלו נערות בפירוש ריבתה תורה חובל בחבירו לתשלומין וכי אין בה שוה פרוטה לוקה שעבר על לא יוסיף [דברים כה] [מכות ט.]. שלא השם המביאן לידי מכות מביאן לידי תשלומין. מלקות משום לא תענה ותשלומין משום כאשר זמם. כל המשלם אינו לוקה. דכתיב כדי רשעתו משום רשעה אחת אתה מחייבו ואי אתה מחייבו משום שתי רשעיות ובמסכת כתובות (דף לב:) מקשינן ונימא כל הלוקה אינו משלם ולילקו כל הזוממין ולא ישלמו ומשנינן בפירוש ריבתה תורה עדים זוממין לתשלומין ויליף לה התם [שם ד.]. כן ינתן בו. פירשו רבותינו שאינו נתינת מום ממש אלא תשלומי ממון שמין אותו כעבד לכך כתיב בו לשון נתינה דבר הנתון מיד ליד [ויקרא כד, כ].

וקיימא לן דאינו לוקה ומשלם אמר עולא לא קשיא כאן באחותו נערה כאן באחותו בוגרת אחותו בוגרת נמי הא איכא [א]בושת ופגם [ב]בשוטה והא איכא [ג]צערא במפותה השתא דאתית להכי אפי' תימא אחותו נערה ביתומה ומפותה אלמא קסבר עולא כל היכא דאיכא ממון ומלקות ממונא משלם מילקא לא לקי מנא ליה לעולא הא גמר מחובל בחבירו מה חובל בחבירו דאיכא ממון ומלקות ממונא משלם מילקא לא לקי אף כל היכא דאיכא ממון ומלקות ממונא משלם מילקא לא לקי מה לחובל בחבירו שכן חייב בחמשה דברים ואי ממונא לקולא שכן הותר מכללו בבית דין אלא גמר מעדים זוממין מה עדים זוממין דאיכא ממון ומלקות ממונא משלם מילקא לא לקי אף כל היכא דאיכא ממון ומלקות ממונא משלם מילקא לא לקי [ד]מה לעדים זוממין שכן אינן צריכים התראה ואי ממונא לקולא הוא שכן לא עשו מעשה אלא גמר מתרווייהו מה הצד השוה שבהן דאיכא ממון ומלקות ממונא משלם מילקא לא לקי אף כל היכא דאיכא ממון ומלקות ממונא משלם מילקא לא לקי מה להצד השוה שבהן [א] שכן יש בהן צד חמור ואי ממונא לקולא הוא שכן יש בהן צד הקל אלא

מתני' באחותו נערה. דאיכא קנס וסבירא ליה דממונא משלם ולא לקי והאיל דמכות בבוגרת דאין לה קנס: **בושת ופגם.** דגבי קנס הוא דבעינן נערה אבל בושת ממונא הוא: **ופגם.** כלומר היא שפחה נמכרת בשוק כמה פיחתה מדמיה להשיאה לעבד שיש לרבו קורת רוח הימנו כדלקמן (דף מ:) והא בבוגרת נמי איתא: **בשוטה.** שאין לה בושת ודמים למכור בשוק נמי אין לה: **והא איכא צערא.** דהכי תנן במתניתין המפתה נותן בושת ופגם וקנס מוסיף עליו האונס שנותן את הצער: **במפותה.** דאין לה צער כדאמרי' לקמן בפירקין (ד' לט:) פקחות שבהן אומרות מפותה אין לה צער: **ביתומה.** שקנסה ובושתה ופגמה שלה: **ומפותה.** כיון שהכל שלה אין כאן חיוב ממון דהא עבדא מדעתה ואחולי אחלה גביה: שוטה לא גרסי' דבפקחת נמי אין שום חיוב ממון במפותה יתומה: **קסבר עולא.** דאוקי מתני' דמכות בבוגרת ולא אוקמה למתני' דהכא בשלא התרו בו שמעת מינה אפי' אתרו ביה נמי ממונא משלם ולא לקי: **חובל בחבירו.** איכא מלקות דלא יוסיף (דברים כה) וממונא משלם כדכתיב (שמות כא) שבתו יתן ואפילו אתרו ביה נמי מרבי ליה לקמן בשמעתין בהדיא לתשלומין: **מה לחובל בחבירו.** דין הוא לידון בממון שהוא חמור ממלקות שכן יש בו חומר אחר: **שחייב בחמשה דברים.** נזק צער ריפוי שבת ובושת: **ואי ממונא לקולא הוא.** וא"ת ממון קל מן המלקות ואין זו תשובה שהשבנו דכ"ש בעלמא מה זה שחמור להתחייב בחמשה דברים נדון בקלה שבשני חיובין שבהן ק"ו לשאר חייבי ממון הקלין שידונו בממון הקל איכא למיפרך מה לחובל בחבירו שכן הותר מכללו בב"ד דניתן רשות לב"ד להלקותו תאמר בשאר חייבי ממון כגון קנס דאונס ומפתה שלא הותרו מכללן בב"ד: **אלא גמר מעדים זוממים.** במה מלינו: **דאיכא ממון.** דכאשר זמם: **ומלקות.** דלא תענה: **ממונא משלם.** לקמן יליף לה בשמעתין: **שכן אין צריכין התראה.** ונענשין במיתה או במלקות או בממון ודין הוא שידונו בחמורה כי איכא תרתי: **ואי ממונא קולא הוא.** אשכחן בהן צד הקל ודין הוא שידונו בקלה: **שכן לא עשו מעשה.** אלא בדיבורא בעלמא מיענשי: **מתרווייהו.** כי פרכת מה לחובל בחבירו שכן חייב בחמשה דברים עדים זוממין יוכיחו מה לעדים זוממין שכן אין צריכין התראה חובל יוכיח וחזר הדין: תחת

וקיימא לן דאינו לוקה ומשלם. נראה לר"י דלא פריך [א] אמתני' להתם אמאי לוקה דהא פשיטא דמשכחת לה מלקות בלא קנס כגון בוגרת ומפותה או בעולה אלא אמתניתין קשיא ליה אמאי משלם קנס כיון דאיכא מלקות ואפילו בלא אתרו ביה מ"ינן למימר דס"ד דמקשה דחייבי מלקות שוגגים פטורים מן התשלומין וכשני עולא דמתניתין אפילו בהתרו בו דממונא משלם ולא לקי ורבי יוחנן משני דמיירי בלא התרו בו ואזיל לטעמיה דאית ליה דחייבי מלקיות שוגגים חייבין בתשלומין: **דאין** לוקה ומשלם. תימה דבפ"ק דמכות (דף ד: ושם) משמע דבקנס לוקה ומשלם דקאמר אפלוגתא דר' מאיר ורבנן דמעידין אנו באיש פלוני שחייב לחברו מאתים זוז בשלמא רבנן פי' טעמייהו משום רשעה אחת כו' אלא ר"מ מ"ט גמר ממוציא שם רע מה למוציא שם רע שכן קנס קסבר ר"מ עדים זוממין נמי קנסא משמע דלרבנן לא ילפינן ממוציא שם רע משום דסברי דעדים זוממין ממונא אבל קנסא ילפינן שפיר ממוציא שם רע דלוקה ומשלם ועולא גופיה דדחיק הכא לשנויי כאן באחותו נערה הוא דמסיק התם הכי וליכא למימר דמבושת ופגם שהן ממון פריך דהא מדמשני כאן באחותו בוגרת משמע דלאו מבושת ופגם פריך דא"כ לא הוה משני מידי וי"ל כיון דלרבנן דר' מאיר עדים זוממין לאו קנסא הוא ולכך לא ילפינן ממוציא שם רע אלא אין לוקין ומשלמין מכדי רשעתו דהשתא אית לן למילף מכל דוכתין מעדים זוממין ולא ממוציא שם רע דכל מלקיות ילפינן ממלקות דעדים זוממין דסמיך ליה לא דחסימה דארבעים יכנו בעדים זוממין כתיב ולפי שמפורש בהן מלקות ילפינן כולהו לאוי דליהוי דומין ללאו דחסימה דסמיך ליה וכי היכי דעדים זוממין אין לוקין ומשלמין בכל ענין בין בממון בין בקנס דמקרא מלא דבר הכתוב כדי רשעתו משום רשעה אחת אתה מחייב כו' אפילו נתחייבו קנס כגון בשעה שהעידו טבחו או מכרו שור של גניבה הם או אחרים בשבילם הכי נמי בכל מלקיות ועוד תירץ ריצב"א דרבנן נמי מלו סברי דעדים זוממין קנסא ומ"מ לא ילפינן ממוציא שם רע משום דכדי רשעתו משמע בממון ומלקות אבל לר"מ משום בנין אב דמוציא שם רע מוקי כדי רשעתו למיתה ומלקות ומפיק ליה ממשמעותיה אי נמי טעמא דרבנן כדמפרש בירושלמי דמ[ו]ציא שם רע חידוש הוא דבדיבור גרידא מיחייב דאע"ג דעדים זוממין נמי בדיבורייהו מיחייבי מ"מ לא הוי חידוש כולי האי דע"י דבורם היה נפסד אבל במוציא שם רע לא איתעבד מעשה בדבורו אלא ע"י עדים וכן משמע לקמן (דף לה:) דאפילו עדים זוממין קנסא אין לוקה ומשלם קנס דאמר ולרבה דאמר לר"מ חידוש הוא שחידשה תורה בקנס מתני' במאי מוקים לה ואמאי לא מוקים לה כר' עקיבא דס"ל בפ' קמא דב"ק (דף ה.) עדים זוממין קנסא הוא דלדידיה לא שמעינן דאית ליה מת ומשלם אלא משמע דאין שום תנא דסבר לוקה ומשלם אלא רבי מאיר לחודיה: **אלמא** קסבר עולא כל היכא דאיכא ממון ומלקות ממונא משלם מילקא לא לקי. וא"ת מנא ליה להש"ס דלמא בעלמא סבר דמילקא לקי וממונא לא משלם והכא דוקא הוא דמשלם ממונא דגלי קרא כדאמרינן לעיל (דף כט:) [נ]ערה נערה הנערה ואין לומר כמו שפירש ר"ת דאי ס"ל דבעלמא מילקא לקי ולא משלם הוה ליה לאוקומי מתני' דמכות (דף יג.) [נ]מי באחותו נערה ובהתרו בו ומתני' בשלא התרו בו אלא ודאי סבר דבעלמא נמי ממונא משלם ולא לקי ולהכי לא הוה מצי לאוק[מ]י מתניתין דמכות באחותו נערה דאין זה דיוק דאיכא למימר דעולא סבר לה כריש לקיש דלא בעי לשנויי כאן בהתרו בו כאן שלא התרו בו כדאמרינן לקמן דאין חילוק לדידיה דאית ליה דחייבי מלקיות שוגגין פטורין מן התשלומין בין התרו בו בין לא התרו בו ואי מרבינן לקנס מקרא בלא התרו ה"ה התרו ונראה לר"י דע"כ ס"ל ממונא משלם מילקא לא לקי מדמרבינן מחד קרא חייבי לאוין ומחד חייבי כריתות דאי בעלמא מילקא לקי דלמא חד לחייבי עשה וחד לחייבי לאוין אע"ג דבעלמא לוקה ואינו משלם [ב] אבל חייבי כריתות לא משום דבעינן אשה שיש בה הויה וכדרבנן דאמרי קדושין תופסין בחייבי לאוין:

[ג] [ועוד פי' ר"ת דדייק דממונא משלם מדפריך בוגרת והא איכא בושת ופגם ומשני בשוטה ולא משני דלוקה ואינו משלם אלא ודאי סבר דבעלמא נמי ממונא משלם ולא לקי וקשה דאין נראה שיהא זה מדברי עולא אלא תלמודא הוא דקאמר ליה ועוד מדמסיק אלא [עולא] תחת תחת גמר משמע דבקנס גופיה בעי קרא דממונ[א] משלם ואמאי לא שמעינן מנער נערה הנערה ועוד מאי קאמר מנ"ל לעולא נימא דיליף בושת ופגם מקנס דרבי קרא וכ"ת מקנס לא ילפינן נילף מקנס וחובל ועדי[ם] זוממים ועוד כיון דאבושת ופגם קאי מאי קאמר בסמוך מה לחובל שכן חייב בד' דברים אטו בושת לאו חובל הוא וכמה עניני חבלות שאין בהן כל ה' דברים כ[ד]אמר בהחובל. ומיהו ריב"ס פי' דהכי פריך מה ללאו דחובל שכן פעמים יש בו כל ה' דברים תאמר בלאו דערות אחותך לא תגלה שלעולם אין בו כל ה' דברים ופי' ר"י נראה עיקר]:

ואי ממונא קולא הוא. וא"ת איתגורי איתגור שנידון בקלה דהכי פריך בפרק הנשרפין (סנהדרין דף פא.) גבי מי שנתחייב שתי מיתות וי"ל דשאני הכא דחס רחמנא אממונא של נחבל: **שכן** יש בהן צד חמור. קשה דא"כ לא נלמד עוד מהצד השוה בשום מקום דאכולהו איכא למיפרך או צד חמור או צד קל ונראה לר"י דהכא פריך הכי שכן יש בהן צד חמור משונה כי ההיא דבפרק ד' מיתות (שם דף סו.) מה להצד השוה שבהן שכן משונין גבי דיין נשיא וחרש דהכא חמשה דברים שאין צריכין התראה הוי צד חמור יותר משאר דברים וצד הקל נמי הוי קולא יתירא בחובל שהותר מכללו שמותר לחבול בחבירו וכן עדים זוממין לא עשו מעשה הוי קולא יתירא דאפילו למ"ד עקימת שפתים הוי מעשה הא אמרי' בסנהדרין (דף סה: ושם) שאני עדים זוממין הואיל וישנן בראיה [ג] ובפרק כשם (סוטה כט:) יש לפרש נמי דפריך גבי טבול יום וכלי חרס מה להצד השוה שבהן שכן צד חמור דקרי צד חמור משונה כלי חרס שמטמא מאוירו וכבול יום נמי יש לפרש בדוחק שקורא צד חמור מה שנעשה אב הטומאה במגע שלא היה נראה שיהיה שום דבר אב הטומאה אלא אב כן טומאה יוצאה מגופו ועוד יש לומר דצד חמור דהתם היינו דאיכא למפרך שכן במינו אב הטומאה דנהי דכלי חרס אינו נעשה אב מכל מקום יש

מסורת הש"ס

א) פסחים עז. סוטה כט: מכות ד:, ב) ת"י כ"י.

תוספות ישנים

א) [נראה דאיכא דאמתני' לא קשיא ליה הא דמשלם דהא רבי קרא חייבי לאוין וכריתות לתשלומין אלא אהאיא מתני' קשיא ליה אמאי לוקה דמשמע ליה דאיירי התם בנערה דומיא דמתני' ומיהו איכא למימר דפריך אמתני' אמאי משלם וחייבי כריתות כדפי' ר"י בסמוך. ת"י].

ב) [ורשב"א נמי לא אוקמי כרבנן משום חייבי כריתות. ולר"י דאמר מלקי לקי כר' סבר ממונא קולא דאי מודה וכי מאגורי אתגור. והשתא א"ש דקאמר מנ"ל הא דע"כ מדמוקי חד לחייבי כריתות נפקא ליה בעלמא דממונא משלם ולא לקי ולפי המסקנא דגמר תחת תחת לאיצטריך קרא לחייבי עשה דאי לאו ההוא קרא הוה דרשי תחת אחריני ולאיך לחייבי כריתות. ת"י].

ג) הג"ה עיקר חיובא בא ע"י הראיה שמעידין שראו ורואים לית בה מעשה. לשון רש"י.

עין משפט נר מצוה

יח א מיי' פ"ב מהלכות נערה הלכה יא טור אה"ע סימן קעז:

יט ב מיי' פ"ג מהל' חובל ומזיק הל' ד ופ"ב מהל' נערה הל' יא טור שם טוש"ע ח"מ סי' תכ סעיף לז:

כ ג מיי' פ"א שם הלכה ב סמג עשין ע טור אה"ע שם:

כא ד מיי' פי"ח מהל' עדות הלכה ד סמג עשין קי טור ח"מ סי' לח:

תוספות רי"ד

דמכות בבוגרת ולא אוקי מתני' דהכא בשלא היתרו בו ש"מ אפילו איתרו ביה נמי ממונא משלם וכו': **אמר עולא** ל"ק כאן באחותו נערה כאן באחותו בוגרת אחותו נערה דאיכא קנס משלם ולא לקי. בוגרת דליכא קנס לקי פי' המורה מתני' דהכא בנערה. ומתני' דמכות בבוגרת. אלמא קסבר עולא כל היכא דאיכא ממון ומלקות ממונא משלם ומילקי לא לקי דגמיר לה מחובל בחבירו ומעדים זוממין דממונא משלם ומילקי לא לקי. פי' חובל בחבירו איכא מלקות בלא יוסיף פן יוסיף. וממונא משלם כדכתיב רק שבתו יתן ואפי' אתרו בי' נמי עדים זוממין נמי (במה) מצינו דאיכא ממון דכאשר זמם ומלקות מלא תענה:

ליקוטי רש"י

באחותו נערה. משהביאה שתי שערות עד שתבגר והם ששה חדשים שבין נערות לבגרות [לעיל כט.]. **ופגם.** שייך באונס ומפתה והוא במקום נזק דאומדים כמה אדם רוצה ליתן בין שפחה בתולה לבעולה להשיאה לעבדו שיש לו קורת רוח ממנו [ב"ק פד:]. **מה לחובל בחבירו שכן חייב בחמשה דברים.** כל חובלין חייבין רפואה משא"כ בבועל בתולה שהרי אינה צריכה רפואה והיינו דקא פריך מה לחובל כו' אבל ממה שיש בחובל כגון שבת שאינו בבועל בתולה לא הוה מצי למפרך שיש גם בהרבה חובלים שאין חייבין שבת ואפילו הכי ממונא משלמי ולא לקי. **שכן יש בהן צד חמור.** דחובל חייב בה' דברים ועדים זוממין אין צריכין התראה [גליון מכות רש"י ישן בשיטמ"ק]. **שכן יש בהן צד הקל.** דחובל הותר מכללו ועדים זוממין לא עשו מעשה [רש"י מריטב"א].

money is considered to be **a leniency** over receiving lashes,[23] we can object to the derivation as follows: שֶׁכֵּן לֹא עָשׂוּ מַעֲשֶׂה – What comparison can you make to *zomemim* witnesses, **who indeed did not commit an** actual **act?**[24]

The Gemara concedes that Ulla could not have derived his rule from the *zomemim* witnesses alone, and suggests a third approach: אֶלָּא גָּמַר מִתַּרְוַיְיהוּ – **Rather, he derives it from both of them** together – from the case of one who wounds his fellow *and* from the case of *zomemim* witnesses – as follows: מַה הַצַּד הַשָּׁוֶה שֶׁבָּהֶן – **Just as their common characteristic** is that they are cases דְּאִיכָּא מָמוֹן וּמַלְקוּת – **where there is** liability to both **money and lashes,** מָמוֹנָא מְשַׁלֵּם מִילְקָא לֹא לָקֵי – and the law is that **he** [the transgressor] **pays the money** and **does not receive lashes,** אַף כָּל הֵיכָא דְּאִיכָּא מָמוֹן וּמַלְקוּת – **so too, wherever there is** liability to both **money and lashes,** מָמוֹנָא מְשַׁלֵּם מִילְקָא לֹא לָקֵי – the law is that **he pays the money** and **does not receive lashes.**[25]

Still, the Gemara objects:

מַה לְהַצַּד הַשָּׁוֶה שֶׁבָּהֶן שֶׁכֵּן יֵשׁ בָּהֶן צַד חָמוּר – **What** comparison can you make **to their common characteristic when indeed** they also share the common characteristic[26] that **they have a stringent aspect?**[27] וְאִי מָמוֹנָא לְקוּלָּא הוּא – **And if** the payment of **money is** considered to be **a leniency** over receiving lashes,[28] we can object to the aforementioned derivation as follows: שֶׁכֵּן יֵשׁ בָּהֶן צַד הַקַּל – What comparison can you make to their common characteristic **when indeed** they also share the common characteristic[29] that **they have a lenient aspect?**[30]

NOTES

23. [And thus when the Torah states that the assailant pays money instead of receiving lashes, it is being lenient with him.] Accordingly, the fact that the *zomeim* witness is punished without prior warning does not undermine Ulla's use of this case as a model, but in fact *strengthens* it: For if even in the case of *zomemim,* where there is the stringency that the witness is punished without prior warning, the Torah is lenient and states that he pays money instead of receiving lashes, certainly in other cases of dual penalty, where there is no special stringency imposed on the sinner, the law would be that he is subject to the lenient penalty of paying money and not to lashes (see above, note 17).

24. The *zomeim* transgression is weaker (relative to other prohibitions) in that it does not involve a physical act but merely speech (*Rashi;* see *Tosafos* ד״ה שכן יש בהן צד חמור). How, then, can Ulla extrapolate from the fact that the *zomeim* witness pays money instead of receiving lashes that the same applies in *all* cases of dual penalties? Perhaps it is only in the case of transgressing the weaker false-witness prohibition that the Torah is lenient and rules that he pays rather than receive lashes. But one who transgresses a regular prohibition involving a physical act would indeed, in cases of dual penalty, receive the more severe penalty of lashes instead of paying money!

25. Since we find both in the case of one who wounds his fellow and in the case of the *zomeim* witness that there is dual liability and the sinner pays instead of receiving lashes, we can derive that the same applies in every situation where there is liability to both. For we can no longer say that this law might be linked to the fact that the sinner must pay five things, since it applies to the *zomeim* witness, who does *not* pay the five things. Similarly, we can no longer say that this law might be linked to the fact that the sinner need not be forewarned, since it applies to the assailant, who must be forewarned in order to be subject to lashes (*Rashi*). [The foregoing assumes that the payment of money is deemed to be the severer penalty. The same line of reasoning, however, applies even if we take lashes to be the severer penalty: We can no longer say that the lenient law of payment instead of lashes might be linked to the fact that the prohibition is weak in that there are exceptions in the case of *beis din* (as in the case of assault) for this weakness is not found in the case of *zomemim.* Similarly, we can no longer say that the lenient law might be linked to the weakness that the crime does not involve a physical act (as in the case of *zomemim*), since this weakness is not found in the case of assault.]

[This method of derivation from "both of them together" is called a צַד הַשָּׁוֶה, *the common characteristic.* The derivation presumes that a law found in two contexts results from characteristics common to both rather than from characteristics unique to each. Therefore, once we isolate the characteristics common to the two contexts, we can conclude that any other context possessing these characteristics is also subject to the common law, even if this third context differs from the first two in regard to their *unique* features. In the present situation, the strength or weakness found in the case of assault is not shared by the case of *zomemim,* and vice versa. Hence, we attribute the fact that the sinner pays instead of receiving lashes to the features *common* to both cases – namely, that they are cases involving liability to both payment and lashes, and the law is that the sinner pays and does not receive lashes.]

26. Not found in other instances where there is liability to both payment and lashes, such as the case of one who violates his sister.

27. [Again, the starting assumption is that the payment of money is deemed to be the severer penalty.] Although the cases of assault and *zomemim* do not share the *same* stringency, they both nevertheless possess unique stringencies (liability to pay five things in the case of assault, and punishment despite the lack of forewarning in the case of *zomemim*). Perhaps, then, the stringency that the sinner pays instead of receiving lashes is linked to the fact that in both source cases there is a stringent aspect. [On the surface, this line of argument seems to be applicable in every case of צַד הַשָּׁוֶה, *derivation by the common characteristic,* and thus contradicted by the very existence of such a method of derivation. See, however, note 30 below.]

28. [In which case the common aspect of stringency would only serve to *strengthen* Ulla's derivation (see above, notes 17 and 23).]

29. Not found in other instances where there is liability to both payment and lashes, such as the case of one who violates his sister.

30. Although the cases of assault and *zomemim* do not share the *same* leniency, they both nevertheless possess unique weaknesses (an exception to the prohibition with regard to *beis din* in the case of assault, and the absence of a physical act in the case of *zomemim*). Perhaps, then, the leniency that the sinner pays instead of receiving lashes is linked to the fact that in both source cases there is a lenient aspect.

Tosafos find difficulty with the Gemara's objection. The basic premise of the צַד הַשָּׁוֶה derivation is that each stringency [or leniency] unique to each individual case cannot be the determining factor for the common rule. If we are to say, as the Gemara appears to be saying, that the fact that each one has a stringent (or lenient) aspect is in itself considered a common characteristic, it would never be possible to derive anything through a צַד הַשָּׁוֶה! *Tosafos* suggest that our Gemara does not mean to say simply that they share the common characteristic of having a stringent aspect, but rather that they share the common characteristic of having an *unusual* stringent aspect. The liability to pay five things and punishment without being forewarned are stringent aspects that are not found anywhere else in the Torah. Similarly, they share the common characteristic of having an *unusual* lenient aspect. A prohibition being permitted in the case of *beis din* and the absence of a physical act are weaknesses not common to other offenses punishable by the court. (See also *Ritva* and *Maharam Schif* for other resolutions to the difficulty raised by *Tosafos.*)

וקיימא לן דאינו לוקה ומשלם אמר עולא לא קשיא כאן באחותו נערה כאן באחותו בוגרת אחותו בוגרת נמי הא איכא [א] בושת ופגם [ב] בשוטה והא איכא [ג] צערא במפותה השתא דאתית להכי אפי' תימא אחותו נערה ביתומה ומפותה אלמא קסבר עולא כל היכא דאיכא ממון ומלקות ממונא משלם מילקא לא לקי מנא ליה לעולא הא גמר מחובל בחבירו מה חובל בחבירו דאיכא ממון ומלקות ממונא משלם מילקא לא לקי אף כל היכא דאיכא ממון ומלקות ממונא משלם מילקא לא לקי מה לחובל בחבירו שכן חייב בחמשה דברים ואי ממונא לקולא שכן הותר מכללו בבית דין אלא גמר מעדים זוממין מה עדים זוממין דאיכא ממון ומלקות ממונא משלם מילקא לא לקי אף כל היכא דאיכא ממון ומלקות ממונא משלם מילקא לא לקי [ד] מה לעדים זוממין שכן אינן צריכים התראה ואי ממונא לקולא הוא שכן לא עשו מעשה אלא גמר מתרוייהו מה הצד השוה שבהן דאיכא ממון ומלקות ממונא משלם מילקא לא לקי אף כל היכא דאיכא ממון ומלקות ממונא משלם מילקא לא לקי מה להצד השוה שבהן [א] שכן יש בהן צד חמור ואי ממונא לקולא הוא שכן יש בהן צד הקל אלא

מתני' באחותו נערה. דליכא קנס וסבירא ליה דממונא משלם ולא לקי והיא דמכות בבוגרת דלאין לה קנס: **בושת ופגם.** דגבי קנס הוא דבעינן נערה אבל בושת ממונא הוא: **ופגם.** כאילו היא שפחה נמכרת בשוק כמה פיחתה מדמיה להשיאה לעבד שיש לרבו קורת רוח הימנו כדלקמן (דף מ:) והא בבוגרת נמי איתא: **בשוטה.** שאין לה בושת ודמים לסמוך בשוק נמי אין לה: **והא איכא צערא.** דהכי תנן במתניתין המפתה נותן בושת ופגם וקנס והאונס מוסיף עליו שהאונס שנותן את הצער: **במפותה.** דאין לה צער כדאמרי' לקמן בפירקין (ד' לט:) פקחות שבהן אומרות מפותה אין לה צער: **ביתומה.** שקנסה ובושתה ופגמה שלה: **ומפותה.** כיון שהכל שלה אין כאן חיוב ממון דהא עבדא מדעתה ואחולי אחלה גביה: שוטה לא גרסי' דבפקחת נמי אין שום חיוב ממון במפותה יתומה: **קסבר עולא.** דלוקי מתני' דמכות בבוגרת ולא אוקמה למתני' דהכא בשלא התרו בו שמעת מינה אפי' אתרו ביה נמי ממונא משלם ולא לקי: **חובל בחבירו.** איכא מלקות דלא יוסיף (דברים כה) וממונא משלם כדכתיב (שמות כא) שבתו יתן ואפילו אתרו ביה נמי מרבי ליה לקמן בשמעתין בהדיא לתשלומין: **מה לחובל בחבירו.** דין הוא לידון בממון שהוא חמור ממלקות שכן יש בו חומר אחר: **שחייב בחמשה דברים.** נזק צער ריפוי שבת ובושת: **ואי ממונא לקולא הוא.** וא"ת ממון קל מן המלקות ואין זו תשובה שהשבנו לכ"ש בעלמא מה זה שחמור להתחייב בחמשה דברים נדון בקלה שבשני חיובין שבהן ק"ו לשאר חייבי ממון הקלין שידונו בממון הקל איכא למיפרך מה לחובל בחבירו שכן הותר מכללו בב"ד דניתן רשות לב"ד להלקותו תאמר בשאר חייבי ממון כגון קנס דאונס ומפתה שלא הותרו מכללן בב"ד: **אלא גמר מעדים זוממים.** במה מצינו: **דאיכא ממון.** דכאשר זמם: **ומלקות.** דלא תענה: **ממונא משלם.** לקמן יליף לה בשמעתין: **שכן אין צריכין התראה.** ועונשין במיתה או במלקות או בממון ודין הוא שידונו בחמורה כי איכא תרתי: **ואי ממונא קולא הוא.** אשכחן בהן צד הקל ודין הוא שידונו בקלה: **שכן לא עשו מעשה.** אלא בדיבורא בעלמא מיענשי: **מתרוייהו.** כי פרכת מה לחובל בחבירו שכן חייב בחמשה דברים עדים זוממין יוכיחו מה לעדים זוממין שכן אין צריכין התראה חובל יוכיח וחזר הדין: תחת

וקיימא לן דאינו לוקה ומשלם. נראה לר"י דלא פריך א) אמתני' דהכא אמאי לוקה דהא פשיטא דמשכחת לה מלקות בלא קנס כגון בוגרת ומפותה או בעולה אלא אמתניתין קשיא ליה אמאי משלם קנס כיון דאיכא מלקות ואפילו בלא אתרו ביה מצינן למימר דס"ד דמקשה דחייבי מלקיות שוגגים פטורים מן התשלומין ומשני עולא דמתניתין אפילו בהתרו בו דממונא משלם ולא לקי ורבי יוחנן משני דמיירי בלא התרו בו ואזיל לטעמיה דאית ליה דחייבי מלקיות שוגגים חייבין בתשלומין: **דאין** לוקה ומשלם. תימה דבפ"ק דמכות (דף ד: ושם) משמע דבקנס לוקה ומשלם דקאמר אפלוגתא דר' מאיר ורבנן דמעידין אנו באיש פלוני שחייב לחבירו מאתים זוז בשלמא רבנן כי טעמייהו משום רשעה אחת אתה כו' אלא ר"מ מ"ט גמר ממוציא שם רע מה למוציא שם רע שכן קנס קסבר ר"מ עדים זוממין נמי קנסא משמע דלרבנן לא ילפינן ממוציא שם רע משום דסברי דעדים זוממין ממונא אבל קנסא ילפינן שפיר ממוציא שם רע דלוקה ומשלם ועולא גופיה דדחיק הכא לשנויי כאן באחותו נערה הוא דמסיק התם הכי וליכא למימר דמבושת ופגם שהן ממון פריך הא מדמשני כאן באחותו בוגרת משמע דלאו מבושת ופגם פריך דא"כ לא הוה משני מידי וי"ל כיון דלרבנן דר' מאיר עדים זוממין לאו קנסא הוא ולכך לא ילפינן ממוציא שם רע אלא אין לוקין ומשלמין מכדי רשעתו השתא אית לן למילף בכל דוכתין מעדים זוממין ולא ממוציא שם רע דכל מלקיות ילפינן ממלקות דעדים זוממין דסמיך ליה לאו לחסימה דארבעים יכנו בעדים זוממין כתיב ולפי שמפורש בהן מלקות ילפינן כולהו לאו דליהוי דומיא דחסימה דסמיך ליה וכי היכי דעדים זוממין אין לוקין ומשלמין בכל ענין בין בממון בין בקנס דמקרא מלא דבר הכתוב כדי רשעתו משום רשעה אחת אתה מחייבו כו' אפילו נתחייבו קנס כגון בשעה שהעידו טבחו או מכרו שור של גניבה הם או אחרים בשבילם הכי נמי בכל מלקיות ועוד תירץ ריצב"א דרבנן נמי מצו סברי דעדים זוממין קנסא ומ"מ לא ילפינן ממוציא שם רע משום דכדי רשעתו משמע בממון ומלקות אבל לר"מ משום בנין אב דמוציא שם רע מוקי כדי רשעתו למיתה ומלקות ומפיק ליה ממשמעותיה אי נמי טעמא דרבנן כדמפרש בירושלמי דמוציא שם רע חידוש הוא דבדיבור גרידא מחייב דאע"ג דעדים זוממין נמי בדיבורייהו מיחייבי מ"מ לא הוה חידוש כולי האי דע"י דבורם היה נפסק אבל במוציא שם רע לא איתעבד מעשה בדבורו אלא ע"י עדים וכן משמע לקמן (דף מה:) דלאפילו עדים זוממין קנסא אין לוקה ומשלם קנס דלאמר ולרבה דאמר לר"מ חידוש הוא שחידשה תורה בקנס מתני' במאי מוקים לה ואמאי לא מוקים לה כר' עקיבא דס"ל בפ' קמא דב"ק (דף ה.) עדים זוממין קנסא הוא דלדידיה לא שמעינן דאית ליה מת ומשלם אלא משמע דליכא שום תנא דסבר לוקה ומשלם אלא רבי מאיר לחודיה: **אלמא** קסבר עולא כל היכא דאיכא ממון ומלקות ממונא משלם מילקא לא לקי. וא"ת מנא ליה להש"ס דלמא בעלמא סבר דמילקא לקי וממונא לא משלם והכא דוקא הוא דמשלם דגלי קרא כדאמרינן לעיל (דף כט:) נערה הנערה ואין לומר כמו שפירש ר"ת דאי ס"ל דבעלמא מילקא לקי ולא משלם הוה ליה לאוקומי מתני' דמכות (דף יג.) נמי באחותו נערה ובהתרו בו ומתני' בשלא התרו בו דבעלמא נמי ממונא משלם ולא לקי והכי לא הוה מצי לאוקומי מתניתין דמכות באחותו נערה דאין זה דיוק דאיכא למימר דעולא סבר לה כריש לקיש דלא בעי לשנויי כאן בהתרו בו כאן שלא התרו בו כדאמרינן לקמן דאין חילוק לדידיה דאית ליה דחייבי מלקיות שוגגין פטורין מן התשלומין בין התרו בו בין לא התרו בו ואי מרבינן לקנס מקרא בלא התרו ה"ה התרו ונראה לר"י דע"כ ס"ל ממונא משלם מילקא לא לקי מדמרבינן מחד קרא חייבי לאוין ומחד חייבי כריתות דאי בעלמא מילקא לקי דלמא חד לחייבי עשה וחד לחייבי לאוין אע"ג דבעלמא לוקה ואינו משלם ב) אבל חייבי כריתות לא משום דבעינן אשה שיש בה הויה וכדרבנן דאמרי קדושין תופסין בחייבי לאוין:

ג) [ועוד פי' ר"ת דדייק דממונא משלם מדפריך בוגרת והא איכא בושת ופגם ומשני בשוטה ולא משני דלוקה ואינו משלם אלא ודאי סבר דבעלמא נמי ממונא משלם ולא לקי וקשה דאין נראה שיהא זה מדברי עולא אלא תלמודא הוא דקאמר ליה ועוד מדמסיק אלא [עולא] תחת תחת גמר משמע דבקנס גופיה בעי קרא דממונא משלם ואמאי לא שמעינן מנער נערה הנערה ועוד מאי קאמר מנ"ל לעולא נימא דיליף בושת ופגם מקנס דרבי קרא וכ"ת מקנס לא ילפינן נילף מקנס וחובל ועדים זוממים ועוד כיון דלאבושת ופגם קאי מאי קאמר בסמוך מה לחובל שכן חייב בד' דברים אטו בושת לאו חובל הוא וכמה ענייני חבלות שאין בהן כל ה' דברים כדאמר בהחובל. ומיהו ריב"ס פי' דהכי פריך מה ללאו דחובל שכן פעמים יש בו כל ה' דברים תאמר בלאו דערות אחותך לא תגלה שלעולם אין בו כל ה' דברים ופי' ר"י נראה עיקר]:

ואי ממונא קולא הוא. וא"ת איתגורי איתגור שנידון בקלה דהכי פריך בפרק הנשרפין (סנהדרין דף פא.) גבי מי שנתחייב שתי מיתות וי"ל דשאני הכא דחס רחמנא אממונא של נחבל: **שכן** יש בהן צד חמור. קשה דא"כ לא נלמד עוד מהצד השוה בשום מקום דאכולהו איכא למיפרך או צד חמור או צד קל ונראה לר"י דהכא פריך הכי שכן יש בהן צד חמור משונה כי ההיא דבפרק ד' מיתות (שם דף סו.) מה להצד השוה שבהן שכן משונין גבי דיין נשיא וחרש דהכא חמשה דברים שאין צריכין התראה הוי צד חמור יותר משאר דברים וצד הקל נמי הוי קולא יתירא בחובל שהותר מכללו שמותר לחבול בחבירו וכן עדים זוממין לא עשו מעשה הוי קולא יתירא ואפילו למ"ד עקימת שפתים הוי מעשה הא אמרי' בסנהדרין (דף סה: ושם) שאני עדים זוממין הואיל וישנן בראיה ג) ובפרק כשם (סוטה כט:) יש לפרש נמי דפריך גבי טבול יום וכלי חרס מה להצד השוה שבהן שכן צד חמור דקרי צד חמור משונה כלי חרס שמטמא באוירו וטבול יום נמי יש לפרש בדוחק שקורא צד חמור מה שנעשה אב הטומאה במגע שלא היה נראה שיהיה שום דבר אב הטומאה אלא אם כן טומאה יוצאה מגופו ועוד יש לומר דצד חמור דהתם היינו דאיכא למפרך שכן במינו אב הטומאה דנהי דכלי חרס אינו נעשה אב מכל מקום יש

מסורת הש"ס

א) [פסחים עז. סוטה כט: מכות ד:], ב) ת"י כ"י.

תוספות ישנים

א) [נראה איפכא דאמתני' לא קשיא ליה הא דמשלם דהא רבי קרא חייבי לאוין וכריתות דמשלמין אלא אההיא מתני' קשיא ליה אמאי לוקה דמשמע ליה דאיירי התם בנערה דומיא דמתני' ומיהו איכא למימר דפריך אמתני' אמאי משלם בחייבי כריתות כדפי' ר"י בסמוך. ת"י]:

ב) [ורשב"ל נמי לא אוקמי כרבנן משום חייבי כריתות. ולר"י דאמר מלקי לקי כו' דסבר ממונא קילא דאי חומרא וכי אתגורי אתגור. והשתא א"ש דקאמר מנ"ל הא דע"כ מדמוקי חד לחייבי כריתות נפקא ליה בעלמא דממונא משלם ולא לקי ולפי המסקנא דגמר תחת איצטריך קרא לחייבי עשה דאי לאו ההוא קרא הוי דרשי תחת לדרשא אחריתי ואידך לחייבי כריתות. ת"י]:

ג) הג"ה עיקר חיובא בא ע"י הראיה שמעידין שראו וראיה לית בה מעשה. לשון רש"י:

עין משפט נר מצוה

יח א מיי' פ"ב מהלכות נערה הלכה יא טור אה"ע סימן קעז:

יט ב מיי' פ"ג מהל' חובל ומזיק הל' ד ופ"ב מהל' נערה הל' יא טור שם טוש"ע ח"מ סי' תכ סעיף לז:

כ ג מיי' פ"א שם הלכה ב סמג עשין ע טור אה"ע שם:

כא ד מיי' פי"ח מהל' עדות הלכה ד סמג עשין קי טור ח"מ סי' לח:

תוספות רי"ד

דמכות בבוגרת ולא אוקי מתני' דהכא בשלא היתרו בו ש"מ אפילו איתרו ביה נמי ממונא משלם וכו': **אמר עולא** ל"ק כאן באחותו נערה כאן באחותו בוגרת אחותו נערה דאיכא קנס משלם ולא לקי. בוגרת דליכא קנס לקי פי' המורה מתני' דהכא בנערה. ומתני' דמכות בבוגרת. אלמא קסבר עולא כל היכא דאיכא ממון ומלקות ממונא משלם מילקי לא לקי דגמיר לה מחובל בחבירו ומעדים זוממין דממונא משלם ומילקי לא לקי. פי' חובל בחבירו איכא מלקות בלא יוסיף פן יוסיף. וממונא משלם כדכתיב רק שבתו יתן ואפי' אתרו בי' נמי עדים זוממין נמי (במה) מצינו דאיכא ממון דכאשר זמם ומלקות מלא תענה:

ליקוטי רש"י

באחותו נערה. משהביאה שתי שערות עד שתבגר והם ששה חדשים שבין נערות לבגרות [לעיל כט.]. **ופגם.** שייך באונס ומפתה והוא במקום נזק דאומדים כמה אדם רוצה ליתן בין שפחה בתולה לבעולה להשיאה לעבדו שיש לו קורת רוח ממנו [ב"ק פד:]. **מה לחובל בחבירו שכן חייב בחמשה דברים.** כל חובלין חייבין רפואה משא"כ בבועל בתולה שהרי אינה צריכה רפואה והיינו דקא פריך מה לחובל כו' אבל ממה שיש בחובל כגון שבת שאינו בבועל בתולה לא הוה מצי למפרך שיש גם בהרבה חובלים שאין חייבין שבת ואפילו הכי ממונא משלמי ולא לקי. **שכן יש בהן צד חמור.** דחובל חייב בה' דברים ועדים זוממין אין צריכין התראה [גליון מכת' רש"י ישן בשיטמ"ק]. **שכן יש בהן צד הקל.** דחובל הותר מכללו ועדים זוממין לא עשו מעשה [רש"י מריטב"א].

lashes, מָמוֹנָא מְשַׁלֵּם מִילְקָא לֹא לָקֵי – the law is that **he pays the money** and **does not receive lashes.**[12]

The Gemara asks:

מְנָא לֵיהּ לְעוּלָּא הָא – **From where does Ulla know this?**[13]

The Gemara answers:

גָּמַר מֵחוֹבֵל בַּחֲבֵירוֹ – **He derives** it **from** the law regarding **one who wounds his fellow.** מָה חוֹבֵל בַּחֲבֵירוֹ – **Just as** in the case of **one who wounds his fellow,** דְּאִיכָּא מָמוֹן וּמַלְקוּת – **where there is** liability to both **money and lashes,**[14] מָמוֹנָא מְשַׁלֵּם מִילְקָא לֹא לָקֵי – the law is that **he pays the money** and **does not receive lashes,**[15] אַף כָּל הֵיכָא דְּאִיכָּא מָמוֹן וּמַלְקוּת – **so too, wherever there is** liability to both **money and lashes,** מָמוֹנָא מְשַׁלֵּם מִילְקָא לֹא לָקֵי – the law is that **he pays the money** and **does not receive lashes.**

The Gemara objects to the derivation from the case of wounding:

מָה לְחוֹבֵל בַּחֲבֵירוֹ שֶׁכֵּן חַיָּיב בַּחֲמִשָּׁה דְּבָרִים – **What** comparison can you make **to one who wounds his fellow, where indeed he is liable** to pay **for five things?**[16] וְאִי מָמוֹנָא לְקוּלָּא – **And if** you deem that the payment of **money is a leniency** over receiving lashes,[17] we can object to the derivation as follows: שֶׁכֵּן הוּתַּר מִכְּלָלוֹ בְּבֵית דִּין – What comparison can you make to the prohibition against wounding one's fellow, **where indeed there is a release from its general rule** of prohibition – the release being **in** regard to **the court?**[18]

The Gemara concedes that Ulla could not have derived his rule from the law regarding one who wounds his fellow, and suggests another source:

אֶלָּא גָּמַר מֵעֵדִים זוֹמְמִין – **Rather, [Ulla] derives** his rule **from** the law regarding ***zomemim* witnesses.**[19] מָה עֵדִים זוֹמְמִין – **Just as** in the case of ***zomemim* witnesses,** דְּאִיכָּא מָמוֹן וּמַלְקוּת – in a case **where there is** liability to both **money and lashes,**[20] מָמוֹנָא מְשַׁלֵּם מִילְקָא לֹא לָקֵי – the law is that **he** [the *zomeim* witness] **pays money** and **does not receive lashes,**[21] אַף כָּל הֵיכָא דְּאִיכָּא מָמוֹן וּמַלְקוּת – **so too, wherever there is** liability to both **money and lashes,** מָמוֹנָא מְשַׁלֵּם מִילְקָא לֹא לָקֵי – the law is that **he pays the money** and **does not receive lashes.**

The Gemara objects to this source as well:

מָה לְעֵדִים זוֹמְמִין שֶׁכֵּן אֵינָן צְרִיכִים הַתְרָאָה – **What** comparison can you make **to *zomemim* witnesses, who indeed do not need a warning?**[22] וְאִי מָמוֹנָא לְקוּלָּא הוּא – **And if** the payment of

NOTES

12. For Ulla interprets the Mishnah in *Makkos* as referring to a *bogeress* [in which case there is no monetary payment, and that is why the sinner receives lashes]. And he does not interpret our Mishnah [as R' Yochanan does on 32b] as referring to where the sinner did not receive a warning [and thus cannot receive lashes (see 30b note 42), so he pays the fine] (see *Rashi*).

13. How does Ulla know that in cases of dual penalty, monetary payment supersedes lashes? Why not say that, to the contrary, lashes supersedes monetary payment?

14. The Torah (*Deuteronomy* 25:3) states that when the court agent administers lashes to a sinner: *Forty [lashes] shall he strike him, he shall not add.* The clause *he shall not add* represents a prohibition against striking another person – even one who is liable to *malkus* – more lashes than warranted, and most certainly serves as a prohibition against striking a person who is not liable to lashes altogether. Thus, one who wounds his fellow is subject to lashes for transgressing the prohibition of *he shall not add* (see *Rashi*, Gemara below, 33a, and *Rambam, Hil. Chovel U'Mazik* 5:1). He is also subject to paying his victim compensation, as stated in *Exodus* 21:18-19: *If men quarrel and one hits his fellow . . . he shall pay for his lost time [from work]* etc. (*Rashi*).

15. For the Gemara below (32b) derives that the verse *he shall pay* [see preceding note] refers even to where the assailant was warned that he would transgress a prohibition by striking the victim (*Rashi*). Thus, he is indeed fit to be lashed, and still the verse says that *he shall pay* [and *not* be lashed, in accordance with the rule that one cannot be lashed *and* pay – see above, note 1].

16. [The Gemara's starting assumption is that the payment of money is deemed to be a more severe penalty than lashes. Thus, when the Torah indicates in the case of wounding one's fellow that the assailant pays money instead of receiving lashes, the Torah is imposing a stringency on him. Accordingly, the Gemara asks that] perhaps the stringency of being subject to the monetary penalty instead of lashes applies only to the case of wounding one's fellow, which has another stringency in that the sinner must pay compensation for five things: נֶזֶק, *depreciation;* צַעַר, *pain;* רִפּוּי, *healing;* שֶׁבֶת, *lost time from work;* and בּוֹשֶׁת, *humiliation* [see Mishnah, *Bava Kamma* 83b] (*Rashi*).

17. [And thus when the Torah states that the assailant pays money instead of receiving lashes, it is being lenient with him. *Tosafos* explain that although logic would dictate that one who is liable to two penalties should be punished with the more severe penalty, it is possible that the Torah chose to punish him with the less severe monetary punishment so that the victim should receive compensation.] Accordingly, the fact that the assailant must pay for five things does not undermine Ulla's use of this case as a model, but in fact *strengthens* it: For if even in the case of wounding, where there is the stringency that the assailant must pay five things, the Torah is lenient and states that he pays money instead of receiving lashes, certainly in other cases of dual penalty, where there is no special stringency imposed on the sinner, the law would be that he is subject to the lenient penalty of paying money and not to lashes (*Rashi*).

18. Although the Torah prohibits one to hit his fellow, it is permitted for the *beis din* to administer lashes. Hence, the prohibition against hitting one's fellow has a weakness (relative to other prohibitions) in that the prohibition is not universal, as it does not apply to *beis din* when they administer lashes [see *Ritva*, cited in *Shitah Mekubetzes* ד״ה שכן הותר מכללו; see, though, *Chidushei Chasam Sofer, Mahadura Basra* from year 5573]. How, then, can Ulla extrapolate from the fact that the assailant pays money instead of receiving lashes that the same applies in *all* cases of dual penalties? Perhaps it is only in the case of transgressing the weaker prohibition against wounding one's fellow that the Torah is lenient and rules that one pays rather than receive lashes. But one who transgresses a universal prohibition that bears a dual penalty, such as one who violates his sister (cohabiting with one's sister is never permitted), would indeed receive the more severe penalty of lashes instead of paying money! (see *Rashi* and *Chochmas Shlomo*).

19. *Zomemim* (sing. *zomeim*) are witnesses who are proven false by other testimony that places them elsewhere at the time of the alleged incident (see *Deuteronomy* 19:16-21). For example, one set of witnesses testifies that someone borrowed two hundred *zuz* from his friend at a particular time and place. A second set of witnesses then testifies that the first witnesses were at that time together with them in a different location and thus could not possibly have witnessed it. The Torah decrees that in such a case the second witnesses are believed and the first witnesses, known as *zomemim* ["conspiring"] witnesses, are punished with whatever punishment they conspired to have imposed. (In our example, they would have to pay two hundred *zuz* to the defendant, the one who they alleged had borrowed the money.)

20. I.e. where the *zomemim* had testified that their victim was subject to a financial liability (as in the example presented in the previous note). In that case the *zomemim* are liable to pay that money to their victim, and are liable to lashes for transgressing the prohibition (*Exodus* 20:13): *You shall not bear false witness* [see Mishnah, *Makkos* 4a] (*Rashi*).

21. As derived by the Gemara below [32b] (*Rashi*).

22. [Again, the Gemara's starting assumption is that the payment of money is deemed to be a more severe penalty than lashes.] *Zomemim* are punished – either with death, lashes or monetary fine, depending on the case – even if they were not warned that false testimony is forbidden and would result in such penalties [for reasons that the Gemara will elaborate below, 33a]. Perhaps, then, just as the Torah made them subject to the stringency of punishment without warning, so too did it make them subject to the stringency of receiving the severer penalty of paying money instead of lashes (*Rashi;* see *Rashash*).

א) [פסחים עו. סוטה כט:] מכות ד:, ב) מ"ו כ"י.

יח א מיי' פ"ב מהלכות נערה הלכה יא טור אה"ע סימן קעז:
יט ב מיי' פ"ב מהל' חובל ומזיק הל' ד ופ"ב מהל' נערה הל' יא טור שם טוש"ע ח"מ סי' תכ סעיף לז:
כ ג מיי' פ"א שם הלכה ב סמג עשין ע טור אה"ע שם:
כא ד מיי' פי"ח מהל' עדות הלכה ד סמג עשין קי טור ח"מ סי' לח:

וקיימא לן דאינו לוקה ומשלם אמר עולא לא קשיא כאן באחותו נערה כאן באחותו בוגרת אחותו בוגרת נמי הא איכא [א] בושת ופגם [ב] בשוטה והא איכא [ג] צערא במפותה השתא דאתית להכי אפי' תימא אחותו נערה ביתומה ומפותה אלמא קסבר עולא כל היכא דאיכא ממון ומלקות ממונא משלם מילקא לא לקי מנא ליה לעולא הא גמר מחובל בחבירו מה חובל בחבירו דאיכא ממון ומלקות ממונא משלם מילקא לא לקי אף כל היכא דאיכא ממון ומלקות ממונא משלם מילקא לא לקי מה לחובל בחבירו שכן חייב בחמשה דברים ואי ממונא לקולא שכן הותר מכללו בבית דין אלא גמר מעדים זוממין מה עדים זוממין דאיכא ממון ומלקות ממונא משלם מילקא לא לקי אף כל היכא דאיכא ממון ומלקות ממונא משלם מילקא לא לקי [ד] מה לעדים זוממין שכן אינן צריכים התראה ואי ממונא לקולא הוא שכן לא עשו מעשה אלא גמר מתרוייהו מה הצד השוה שבהן דאיכא ממון ומלקות ממונא משלם מילקא לא לקי אף כל היכא דאיכא ממון ומלקות ממונא משלם מילקא לא לקי מה להצד השוה שבהן [ה] שכן יש בהן צד חמור ואי ממונא לקולא הוא שכן יש בהן צד הקל אלא

מתני' באחותו נערה. דאיכא קנס וסבירא ליה דממונא משלם ולא לקי והיא דמכות בבוגרת דאין לה קנס: בושת ופגם. דגבי קנס הוא דבעינן נערה אבל בושת ממונא הוא: ופגם. כאילו היא שפחה נמכרת בשוק כמה פיחתה מדמיה להשיאה לעבד שיש לרבו קורת רוח הימנו כדלקמן (דף מ:) והא בבוגרת נמי איתא: בשוטה. שאין לה בושת ודמים למכור בשוק נמי אין לה: והא איכא צערא. דהכי תנן במתניתין המפתה נותן בושת ופגם וקנס מוסיף עליו האונס שנותן את הצער: במפותה. דאין לה צער כדאמרי' לקמן בפירקין (ד' לט:) פקחות שבהן אומרות מפותה אין לה צער: ביתומה. שקנסה ובושתה ופגמה שלה: ומפותה. כיון שהכל שלה אין כאן חיוב ממון דהא עבדא מדעתה ואחולי אחלה גביה: שוטה לא גרסי' דבפקחת נמי אין שום חיוב ממון במפותה יתומה: קסבר עולא. דאוקי מתני' דמכות בבוגרת ולא אוקמה למתני' דהכא בשלא התרו בו שמעת מינה אפי' אתרו ביה נמי ממונא משלם ולא לקי: חובל בחבירו. איכא מלקות דלא יוסיף (דברים כה) וממונא משלם כדכתיב (שמות כא) שבתו יתן ואפילו אתרו ביה נמי מרבי ליה לקמן בשמעתין בהדיא לתשלומין: מה לחובל בחבירו. דין הוא לידון בממון שהוא חמור ממלקות שכן יש בו חומר אחר: שחייב בחמשה דברים. נזק צער ריפוי שבת ובושת: ואי ממונא לקולא הוא. וא"ת ממון קל מן המלקות ואין זו תשובה שהשבנו דכ"ש בעלמא מה זה שחמור להתחייב בחמשה דברים נדון בקלה שבשני חיובין שבהן ק"ו לשאר חייבי ממון הקלין שידונו בממון הקל איכא למיפרך מה לחובל בחבירו שכן הותר מכללו בב"ד דניתן רשות לב"ד להלקותו תאמר בשאר חייבי ממון כגון קנס דאונס ומפתה שלא הותרו מכללן בב"ד: אלא גמר מעדים זוממים. במה מצינו: דאיכא ממון. דכאשר זמם: ומלקות. דלא תענה: ממונא משלם. לקמן יליף לה בשמעתין: שכן אין צריכין התראה. ונענשין במיתה או במלקות או בממון ודין הוא שידונו בחמורה כי איכא תרתי: ואי ממונא קולא הוא. אשכחן בהן צד הקל ודין הוא שידונו בקלה: שכן לא עשו מעשה. אלא בדיבורא בעלמא מיענשי: מתרווייהו. כי פרכת מה לחובל בחבירו שכן חייב בחמשה דברים עדים זוממין יוכיחו מה לעדים זוממין שכן אין צריכין התראה חובל יוכיח וחזר הדין:
תחת

וקיימא לן דאינו לוקה ומשלם. נראה לר"י דלא פריך א) אמתני' דהכא אמאי לוקה דהא פשיטא דמשכחת לה מלקות בלא קנס כגון בוגרת ומפותה או בעולה אלא אמתניתין קשיא ליה אמאי משלם קנס כיון דאיכא מלקות ואפילו בלא אתרו ביה מלינן למימר דס"ד דמקשה דחייבי מלקיות שוגגים פטורים מן התשלומין ומשני עולא דמתניתין אפילו בהתרו בו דממונא משלם ולא לקי ורבי יוחנן משני דמיירי בלא התרו בו ואזיל לטעמיה דאית ליה דחייבי מלקיות שוגגים חייבין בתשלומין: דאין לוקה ומשלם. תימה דבפ"ק דמכות (דף ד: ושם) משמע דבקנס לוקה ומשלם דקאמר אפלוגתא דר' מאיר ורבנן דמעידין אנו באיש פלוני שחייב לחברו מאתים זוז בשלמא רבנן כי טעמייהו משום רשעה אחת כו' אלא ר"מ מ"ט גמר ממוציא שם רע מה למוציא שם רע שכן קנס קסבר ר"מ עדים זוממין נמי קנסא משמע דלרבנן לא ילפינן ממוציא שם רע משום דסברי דעדים זוממין ממונא אבל קנסא ילפינן שפיר ממוציא שם רע דלוקה ומשלם ועולא גופיה דדחיק הכא לשנויי כאן באחותו נערה הוא דמסיק התם הכי וליכא למימר דמבושת ופגם שהן ממון פריך דהא מדמשני כאן באחותו בוגרת משמע דלאו מבושת ופגם פריך דא"כ לא הוה משני מידי וי"ל כיון דלרבנן דר' מאיר עדים זוממין לאו קנסא הוא ולכך לא ילפינן ממוציא שם רע אלא אין לוקין ומשלמין מכדי רשעתו דהשתא אית לן למילף בכל דוכתין מעדים זוממין ולא ממוציא שם רע דכל מלקיות ילפינן ממלקות דעדים זוממין דסמיך ליה לאו דחסימה דארבעים יכנו בעדים זוממין כתיב ולפי שמפורש בהן מלקות ילפינן כולהו לאו דליהוי דומין ללאו דחסימה דסמיך ליה וכי היכי דעדים זוממין אין לוקין ומשלמין בכל ענין בין בממון בין בקנס דמקרא מלא דבר הכתוב כדי רשעתו משום רשעה אחת אתה מחייבו כו' אפילו נתחייבו קנס כגון בשעה שהעידו טבחו או מכרו שור של גניבה הם או אחרים בשבילם הכי נמי בכל מלקות ועוד תירץ ריצב"א דרבנן נמי מלו סברי דעדים זוממין קנסא ומ"מ לא ילפינן ממוציא שם רע משום דכדי רשעתו משמע בממון ומלקות אבל לר"מ משום בנין אב דמוציא שם רע מוקי כדי רשעתו למיתה ומלקות ומפיק ליה ממשמעותיה אי נמי טעמא דרבנן כדמפרש בירושלמי דמוציא שם רע חידוש הוא דבדיבור גרידא מיחייב דאע"ג דעדים זוממין נמי בדיבורייהו מיחייבי מ"מ לא הוי חידוש כולי האי דע"י דבורם היה נפסד אבל במוציא שם רע לא איתעבד מעשה בדבורו אלא ע"י עדים וכן משמע לקמן (דף לג:) דאפילו עדים זוממין קנסא אין לוקה ומשלם קנס דאמר ולרבה דאמר לר"מ חידוש הוא שחידשה תורה בקנס מתני' במאי מוקים לה ואמאי לא מוקים לה כר' עקיבא דס"ל בפ' קמא דב"ק (דף ה.) עדים זוממין קנסא הוא דלדידיה לא שמעינן דאית ליה מת ומשלם אלא משמע דאין שום תנא דסבר לוקה ומשלם אלא רבי מאיר לחודיה: אלמא קסבר עולא כל היכא דאיכא ממון ומלקות ממונא משלם מילקא לא לקי. וא"ת מנא ליה להש"ס דלמא בעלמא סבר דמילקא לקי וממונא לא משלם והכא דוקא הוא דמשלם ממונא דגלי קרא כדאמרינן לעיל (דף כט:) נערה נערה הנערה ואין לומר כמו שפירש ר"ת דאי ס"ל דבעלמא מילקא לקי ולא משלם הוה ליה לאוקומי מתני' דמכות (דף יג.) נמי באחותו נערה ובהתרו בו ומתני' בשלא התרו בו אלא ודאי סבר דבעלמא נמי ממונא משלם ולא לקי ולהכי לא הוה מצי לאוקומי מתניתין דמכות באחותו נערה דאין זה דיוק דאיכא למימר דעולא סבר לה כר"ש לקיש דלא בעי לשנויי כאן בהתרו בו כאן שלא התרו בו כדאמרינן לקמן דאין חילוק לדידיה דאית ליה דחייבי מלקיות שוגגין פטורין מן התשלומין בין התרו בו בין לא התרו בו ואי מרבינן לקנס מקרא בלא התרו ה"ה התרו ונראה לר"י דע"כ ס"ל ממונא משלם מילקא לא לקי מדמרבינן מחד קרא חייבי לאוין ומחד חייבי כריתות דאי בעלמא מילקא לקי דלמא חד לחייבי עשה וחד לחייבי לאוין אע"ג דבעלמא לוקה ואינו משלם ב) אבל חייבי כריתות לא משום דבעינן אשה שיש בה הויה וכדרבנן דאמרי קדושין תופסין בחייבי לאוין:

ג) [ועוד פי' ר"ת דדייק דממונא משלם מדפריך בוגרת והא איכא בושת ופגם ומשני בשוטה ולא משני דלוקה ואינו משלם אלא ודאי סבר דבעלמא נמי ממונא משלם ולא לקי וקשה דאין נראה שיהא זה מדברי עולא אלא תלמודא הוא דקאמר ליה ועוד מדמסיק אלא [עולא] תחת תחת גמר משמע דבקנס גופיה בעי קרא דממונא משלם ואמאי לא שמעינן מנער נערה הנערה ועוד מאי קאמר מנ"ל לעולא נימא דיליף בושת ופגם מקנס דרבי קרא וכ"ת מקנס לא ילפינן נילף מקנס וחובל ועדים זוממים ועוד כיון דאבושת ופגם קאי מאי קאמר בסמוך מה לחובל שכן חייב בד' דברים אטו בושת לאו חובל הוא וכמה ענייני חבלות שאין בהן כל ה' דברים כדאמר בהחובל. ומיהו ריב"ס פי' דהכי פריך מה ללאו דחובל שכן פעמים יש בו כל ה' דברים תאמר בלאו דערות אחותך לא תגלה שלעולם אין בו כל ה' דברים ופי' ר"י נראה עיקר]:

ואי ממונא קולא הוא. וא"ת איתגורי איתגור שנידון בקלה דהכי פריך בפרק הנשרפין (סנהדרין דף פא.) גבי מי שנתחייב שתי מיתות וי"ל דשאני הכא דהס רחמנא אממונא של נחבל: שכן יש בהן צד חמור. קשה דא"כ לא נלמד עוד מהצד השוה בשום מקום דאכולהו איכא למיפרך או צד חמור או צד קל ונראה לר"י דהכא פריך הכי שכן יש בהן צד חמור משונה כי ההיא דבפרק ד' מיתות (שם דף סו.) מה להצד השוה שבהן שכן משונין גבי דיין נשיא וחרש דהכא חמשה דברים שאין צריכין התראה הוי צד חמור יותר משאר דברים וצד הקל נמי הוי קולא יתירא בחובל שהותר מכללו שמותר לחבול בחבירו וכן עדים זוממין לא עשו מעשה הוי קולא יתירא ואפילו למ"ד עקימת שפתים הוי מעשה הא אמרי' בסנהדרין (דף סה: ושם) שאני עדים זוממין הואיל וישנן בראיה ג) ובפרק כשם (סוטה כט:) יש לפרש נמי דפריך גבי טבול יום וכלי חרס מה להצד השוה שבהן שכן צד חמור דקרי צד חמור משונה כלי חרס שמטמא באוירו וטבול יום נמי יש לפרש בדוחק שקורא צד חמור מה שנעשה אב הטומאה במגע שלא היה נראה שיהיה שום דבר אב הטומאה אלא אם כן טומאה יוצאה מגופו ועוד יש לומר דלצד חמור דהתם היינו דאיכא למפרך שכן במינו אב הטומאה דנהי דכלי חרס אינו נעשה אב מכל מקום
יש

תוספות ישנים

א) [נראה איפכא דלמתני' לא קשיא ליה הא דמשלם דהא רבי קרא חייבי לאוין וכריתות דמשלמין אלא אההיא מתני' קשיא ליה אמאי לוקה דמשמע ליה דחייבי מלקות דוקא בנערה דומיא דמתני' ומיהו איכא למימר דפריך אמתני' אמאי משלם בחייבי כריתות כדפי' ר"י בסמוך. ת"י]:

ב) [ורשב"ל נמי לא אוקמי כרבנן משום חייבי כריתות. ולר"י דאמר מלקי לקי כר' דסבר ממונא קילא דאי סומכא וכי אתגורי אתגור. והשתא א"ש דקאמר מנ"ל הא דע"כ דמוקי הך לחייבי כריתות נפקא ליה בעלמא דממונא משלם ולא לקי ולפי המסקנא דגמר תחת אלעריך קרא לחייבי עשה דאי לאו הכי קרא הוי דרכי תחת לדרשא אחריתי ולידך לחייבי כריתות. ת"י]:

ג) הגה"ה עיקר מיהא בלא ע"י הרלוה שמעידין שרלו ורליה לית בה מעשה. לשון רש"י:

תוספות רי"ד

דמכות בבוגרת ולא אוקי מתני' דהכא בשלא התרו בו ש"מ אפילו איתרו ביה נמי ממונא משלם וכו': אמר עולא ל"ק כאן באחותו נערה כאן באחותו בוגרת אחותו נערה דאיכא קנס משלם ולא לקי. בוגרת דליכא קנס לקי פי' המורה מתני' דהכא בנערה. ומתני' דמכות בבוגרת. אלמא קסבר עולא כל היכא דאיכא ממון ומלקות ממונא משלם ומילקי לא לקי. פי' חובל בחבירו דממון משלם ומעדים זוממין דממונא משלם ומילקי לא לקי. פי' חובל בחבירו איכא מלקות בלא יוסיף פן יוסיף. וממונא משלם כדכתיב רק שבתו יתן ואפי' אתרו בי' נמי עדים זוממין נמי (במה) מצינו דאיכא ממון דכאשר זמם ומלקות מלא תענה:

ליקוטי רש"י

באחותו נערה. משהביאה שתי שערות עד שתבגר והם ששה חדשים שבין נערות לבגרות [לעיל כט.]. ופגם. שייך לאונס ומפתה והוא במקום נזק דאומדים כמה אדם רוצה ליתן בין שפחה בתולה לבעולה להשיאה לעבדו שיש לו קורת רוח ממנו [ב"ק פד:]. מה לחובל בחבירו שכן חייב בחמשה דברים. כל חובלין חייבין רפואה משא"כ בבועל בתולה שהרי אינה צריכה רפואה והיינו דקא פריך מה לחובל כו' אבל מאחר שיש לחובל כו' כגון שבת שאינו בבועל בתולה לא הוה מצי למפרך שיש גם בהכרה חובלים שאינן חייבין שבת ואפילו הכי ממונא משלמי ולא לקי. שכן יש בהן צד חמור. דמחובל חייב בה' דברים ועדים זוממין אין צריכין התראה [גליון מכה רש"י ישן בשיטמ"ק]. שכן יש בהן צד הקל. דחובל הותר מכללו ועדים זוממין לא עשו מעשה [רש"י מריטב"א].

וְקַיְימָא לַן דְּאֵינוֹ לוֹקֶה וּמְשַׁלֵּם – Now, it has been established for us that one does not receive lashes and pay money for the same crime.[1] Thus, our Mishnah, which states that one pays the fine for violating these women, is ruling in effect that he does *not* receive lashes for cohabiting with them. And conversely, the Mishnah in *Makkos,* which states that he receive lashes for cohabiting with them, is ruling in effect that he does *not* pay the fine![2] – ? –

The Gemara answers:

אָמַר עוּלָּא – Ulla said: לֹא קַשְׁיָא – There is no difficulty. כָּאן בַּאֲחוֹתוֹ נַעֲרָה – Here, in our Mishnah, we are dealing **with** one who forcibly violates **his sister** who is **a *naarah,*** where the fine for violation is applicable.[3] **כָּאן בַּאֲחוֹתוֹ בּוֹגֶרֶת – There,** in *Makkos,* the Mishnah is dealing **with** one who cohabits with **his sister** who is **a *bogeress,*** in which case the fine for violation is not applicable.[4]

The Gemara asks:

אֲחוֹתוֹ בּוֹגֶרֶת נַמִי הָא אִיכָּא בּוֹשֶׁת וּפְגָם – But in the case of one who violates **his sister who is a *bogeress,* too, there is** monetary liability for **humiliation and depreciation!**[5] Why, then, does the Mishnah in *Makkos* rule that he receives lashes? He should pay the compensatory damages and *not* receive lashes! – ? –

The Gemara answers:

בְּשׁוֹטָה – The Mishnah there is dealing **with a mentally deranged girl.**[6]

The Gemara asks:

וְהָא אִיכָּא צַעֲרָא – But even so, **there is** still monetary liability for the physical **pain** she suffers when she is violated![7] – ? –

The Gemara answers:

בִּמְפוּתָּה – The Mishnah in *Makkos* is dealing **with one** [i.e. a *bogeress*] **who is** not violated but **seduced,** in which case she does not suffer physical pain.[8]

In light of this last answer, the Gemara remarks:

הַשְׁתָּא דְּאָתֵית לְהָכִי – Now that you have come to this conclusion that the Mishnah in *Makkos* (which subjects one who cohabits with his sister to lashes) must be dealing with a case of seduction rather than violation, **אֲפִילּוּ תֵּימָא אֲחוֹתוֹ נַעֲרָה – you can even say** that the Mishnah there refers to **his sister** who is **a *naarah,*** as originally thought,[9] **בִּיתוֹמָה וּמְפוּתָּה** – by explaining that it is dealing **with an orphan**[10] **who is seduced.** In the case of a mentally competent orphan *naarah* who is seduced, there is no monetary liability whatsoever,[11] and the seducer therefore receives lashes for transgressing the prohibition.

Having concluded Ulla's resolution of the contradiction between the two Mishnahs, the Gemara comments:

אַלְמָא קָסָבַר עוּלָּא – Evidently, Ulla holds that **כָּל הֵיכָא דְּאִיכָּא מָמוֹן וּמַלְקוֹת – wherever there is** liability to both **money and**

NOTES

1. I.e. a person cannot be subjected to both lashes (*malkus*) and monetary liability for the same crime.

The Gemara below (32b and 37a; see also *Makkos* 4b) derives this rule from the verse (*Deuteronomy* 25:2): *And the judge shall cast him down and lash him . . . in accordance with his wickedness.* The word *wickedness,* which is in the singular form, indicates that "you may punish him for one wickedness, but you may not punish him for two wickednesses," i.e. you (the court) cannot impose two kinds of penalty for the same act (*Rashi,* printed at the end of 31b).

2. See, though, *Tosafos* and *Tos. Yeshanim.*

3. Therefore, he pays the money and does not receive lashes.

4. [See above, 29a note 2.] Since there is no monetary penalty in that case, he receives lashes for transgressing the prohibition against cohabiting with one's sister.

According to Ulla, both Mishnahs agree that when one commits a crime punishable by both lashes and a monetary penalty, we give him the monetary penalty and not lashes. Thus, in the case of our Mishnah (where he violates his sister who is a *naarah*), both penalties are applicable, and he pays and does not receive lashes. In the case of the Mishnah in *Makkos* (where his sister is a *bogeress*), however, only the lashes penalty is applicable; hence, he receives lashes (see *Rashi*).

5. One who violates a *bogeress,* though he does not pay the fine, does pay for her humiliation and depreciation (*Rashi*), which are compensatory damages common to all victims of assault (see Mishnah, *Bava Kamma* 83b, and Mishnah below, 39a).

[The פְּגָם, *depreciation,* in this case refers to the reduction in her value brought about by the fact that she is no longer a virgin. It is measured by calculating the reduction in value that the loss of virginity would cause to an analogous slave girl at the slave market. A nonvirgin slave-girl is indeed worth less, since a slave owner who wants to reward his loyal slave with a wife will pay a premium for a virgin slave girl; see below, 40b (*Rashi*).]

6. A mentally deranged girl is not humiliated by the assault [for she is deranged, which is already the greatest humiliation (see *Ritva*)]. Nor does she have any value on the slave market (*Rashi;* see, however, *Rashash*). [Hence, the violator has no liability for humiliation or depreciation, and – because she is a *bogeress* – no liability to a fine. Since he is not subject to any monetary punishment, he is punished with lashes for transgressing the prohibition against cohabiting with one's sister.]

7. For we learn below in the Mishnah (39a) that a victim of violation receives monetary compensation for pain [just like other victims of assault – see Mishnah, *Bava Kamma* 83b] (*Rashi*). Even a deranged victim suffers pain. Hence, the violator would be punished monetarily and not receive lashes!

8. [The Mishnah below (39a) indicates that a seducer does not pay his "victim" for physical pain, for] as the Gemara below (39b) states: Astute women say that seduction does not cause physical pain to the girl (*Rashi*).

Previously, the Gemara explained that the Mishnah in *Makkos* is referring to a girl who is a *bogeress* as well as mentally deranged. Apparently, the Gemara now is simply supplying the additional factor that she was seduced rather than violated. The Mishnah, then, refers to one who seduces a mentally deranged *bogeress.* Thus, the seducer does not pay a fine (because she is no longer a *naarah*), nor for pain (since she was seduced), nor for humiliation and depreciation (since she is deranged). Since he is not subject to any monetary penalty, he receives lashes (see *Shitah Mekubetzes, Oz VeHadar* edition [addendum from manuscript] ד״ה והאיכא צערא, in explanation of *Rashi*).

Alternatively, the Gemara is now retracting its previous assertion that the Mishnah in *Makkos* deals with a mentally deranged girl. (Some texts indeed read "אֶלָּא" בִּמְפוּתָּה, *"Rather," with one who is seduced.*) And the Gemara is now explaining that the Mishnah refers to one who seduces a mentally competent *bogeress.* For a *bogeress* is a fully independent adult, whose father no longer has any rights to her income. Thus, any fine or compensatory damages that would accrue to her would belong to her rather than to her father. And since she willingly consents to the seduction, she thereby waives any claim to monetary compensation (which she would *not* be empowered to do if that compensation would belong to her father) – see below, note 11. Thus, the seducer does not pay a fine (since she is no longer a *naarah;* moreover, she has waived all monetary claims), nor for pain (since she was seduced, and thus does not suffer pain; moreover, she has waived all monetary claims), nor for humiliation and depreciation (since she has waived all monetary claims). Since he is not subject to any monetary penalty, he receives lashes (see *Shitah Mekubetzes, Oz VeHadar* edition [addendum from manuscript] ד״ה וז״ל שיטה ישנה, in explanation of *Rashi;* see also *Re'ah, R' Crescas* and *Rashash*).

9. And it is no longer necessary to explain that the reference is to a *bogeress.*

10. I.e. her father died, in which case any payment given for her violation or seduction would accrue to her rather than to her father (see *Rashi;* see next note).

11. For by her voluntary consent to the seduction, she has waived all claims to the monetary liabilities (fine, humiliation and depreciation) that would theoretically accrue to her (see *Rashi*). [Where the *naarah's* father is alive, however, and is the recipient of the fine and the payments for humiliation and depreciation, her consent does not free the seducer from monetary liability, since she has no power to waive her father's rights.]

as being in **the owner's domain.**[38] סֵיפָא לְרָבִינָא לֹא קַשְׁיָא – **The last clause** of the Mishnah[39] **does not pose a difficulty to Ravina,** הוֹצָאָה דוּמְיָא דְהַגְבָּהָה לֹא אַמְרִינַן – for in his view, **we do not say** that the case of **"taking out"** must be **similar to** the case of **"lifting."**[40]

The Gemara cites the clause of the Mishnah that reads:
הַבָּא עַל אֲחוֹתוֹ וְעַל אֲחוֹת אָבִיו כו׳ – If ONE VIOLATES HIS SISTER, OR HIS FATHER'S SISTER, **etc.** [or his mother's sister, or his wife's sister, or his brother's wife, or his father's brother's wife, or a *niddah,* they are entitled to the fine].

The Gemara notes a seeming contradiction between this ruling and that of another Mishnah:
וּרְמִינְהוּ – **But contrast** this Mishnah with another one and see the contradiction between **them.** For another Mishnah states:[41] אֵלּוּ הֵן הַלּוֹקִין – THESE ARE THE ONES WHO RECEIVE LASHES for transgressing a prohibition:[42] הַבָּא עַל אֲחוֹתוֹ – ONE WHO COHABITS WITH HIS SISTER, וְעַל אֲחוֹת אָבִיו – OR WITH HIS FATHER'S SISTER, וְעַל אֲחוֹת אִמּוֹ – OR WITH HIS MOTHER'S SISTER, וְעַל אֲחוֹת אִשְׁתּוֹ – OR WITH HIS WIFE'S SISTER, וְעַל אֵשֶׁת אָחִיו – OR WITH HIS BROTHER'S WIFE, וְעַל אֵשֶׁת אֲחִי אָבִיו – OR WITH HIS FATHER'S BROTHER'S WIFE, וְעַל הַנִּדָּה – OR WITH A *NIDDAH.*[43]

NOTES

38. I.e. the Mishnah uses the term רְשׁוּת בְּעָלִים, *owner's domain,* not in the sense of the owner's *physical* domain (his house in contrast to the public domain), but rather in the sense of the owner's *dominion.* Thus, the Mishnah is saying that if the thief was pulling the animal and it died while still under the owner's dominion – i.e. before the thief pulled it into a place where the *kinyan* of *meshichah* is effective, thereby taking it under his own dominion and out of the owner's – he is not liable (see *Ritva*).

39. Which juxtaposes "taking out" and "lifting."

40. He holds that the fact that they are juxtaposed does not indicate that pulling, too, refers to where the thief took the animal into his own physical domain. It might rather refer to where he simply pulled it into the public domain.

41. *Makkos* 13a.

42. If they were first warned [that the act they were about to do is prohibited by a negative command and is punishable with lashes] (*Rashi*).

43. All these acts are prohibited by negative commands [see *Leviticus* 18:9-19] and are thus punishable with lashes.

פטור אדרתני היה מגרר ויוצא מגרר ויוצא פטור נפלוג וניתני בדידה במה דברי' אמורים בעומד לפוש אבל לכתף פטור אלא הא מני בן עזאי היא דאמר מהלך כעומד דמי אבל זורק מאי פטור ניפלוג [וניתני] בדידה במה דברים אמורים במהלך אבל זורק פטור מגרר ויוצא איצטריכא ליה ס"ד אמינא אין דרך הוצאה בכך קמ"ל ובמאי אי ברברבי אורחיה הוא אי בזוטרי לאו אורחיה הוא אלא במיצעי ודאפקיה להיכא אי דאפקיה לרה"ר איסור שבת איכא איסור גניבה ליכא אי דאפקיה לרשות היחיד איסור גניבה איכא איסור שבת ליכא לא צריכא דאפקיה לצידי רשות הרבים וכמאן אי כר' אליעזר דאמר צידי רה"ר כרה"ר דמו איסור שבת איכא איסור גניבה ליכא אי כרבנן דאמרי צידי רה"ר לאו כרה"ר דמו איסור גניבה איכא איסור שבת ליכא לעולם כר' אליעזר וכי אמר ר"א צידי רה"ר כרה"ר דמו הני מילי לענין חיובא דשבת דזימנין דדחקי רבים ועיילי להתם אבל לענין מיקנא קני מ"ט דהא לא שכיחי רבים רב אשי אמר כגון שצירף ידו למטה משלשה וקיבלו כדרבא דאמר רבא ידו של אדם חשובה לו כארבעה על ארבעה רב אחא מתני הכי רבינא מתני לעולם דאפקיה לרה"ר וברה"ר נמי קנה ותרווייהו בדיוקא דהא מתני' קמיפלגי דתנן היה מושכו ויוצא ומת ברשות בעלים פטור הגביהו או שהוציאו מרשות בעלים ומת חייב רבינא דייק מרישא רב אחא דייק מסיפא רבינא דייק מרישא היה מושכו ויוצא ומת ברשות בעלים פטור טעמא דמת ברשות בעלים הא הוציאו מרשות בעלים ומת חייב רב אחא דייק מסיפא הגביהו או שהוציאו הוצאה דומיא דהגבהה מה הגבהה דאתי לרשותיה אף הוצאה נמי דאתי לרשותיה לרב אחא קשיא רישא לרבינא קשיא סיפא רישא לרב אחא לא קשיא כמה דלא אתי לרשותיה רשות בעלים קרינא ביה סיפא לרבינא לא קשיא הוצאה דומיא דהגבהה לא אמרינן: הבא על אחותו ועל אחות אביו כו': ורמינהו אלו הן הלוקין הבא על אחותו ועל אחות אביו ועל אחות אמו ועל אחות אשתו ועל אשת אחיו ועל אשת אחי אביו ועל הנדה וקיימא

פטור. מתשלומין דאתי עליה חיוב שבת מחמת הגבהה ראשונה שבה נקנה לו הכיס ומיתה ותשלומין באין כאחד: ניפלוג בדידה. במגביה עצמו אינו יכול לשנות בו חיוב ופטור: אלא. לא תוקמא כשעמד ואפ"ה חיוב שבת דעקירה לאו מחמת עקירה ראשונה דהגבהה אתיא ליה אלא בעקירת גופו של פסיעה אחרונה כשיוצא מן הבית ובן עזאי היא: דאמר. בפ"ק דשבת: מהלך כעומד דמי. ועקירת כל פסיעה הויא עקירה והנחת הרגל היא הנחה הלכך קניה משעת הגבהה וחיוב מיתה בפסיעה בתרייתא קא אתיא ליה: אבל זורק מאי. הגביהו וזרקו: פטור. מתשלומין דאתיא ליה חיוב שבת ע"י חיוב הגבהה דמי ליתא עקירה אחריתי: אין דרך הוצאה בכך. ולאו כאן חיוב שבת: ובמאי. איצטריך לאשמועינן דדרך הוצאה בכך: אי ברברבי. כיס גדול שיש בו משוי להגביהו: אורחיה הוא. לגררו ופשיטא דהוצאה היא: לאו אורחיה הוא. ולאמי חייב משום שבת: איסור גניבה ליכא. דמשיכה בלא הגבהה קמ"ל דלא קניא ברה"ר: לרשות היחיד. לרשותו שהיתה סמוכה לחצר הבעלים: צידי רה"ר. סמוך לבתים שנותנין להלן מן הבתים אבנים ומכשולין להרחיק מיכוך העגלות ומלותן חיפופי ולפנים קרי ליה צידי רה"ר: פלוגתא דרבי אליעזר ורבנן בעירובין בפרק כל גגות: דהא לא שכיחי רבים. והוי ליה כסימטא דתיקון בה משיכה: רב אשי אמר. מגרר ויוצא דקאמר פטור לעולם ברשות הרבים ודקשיא לך איסור גניבה ליכא: כגון שצירף ידו. השניה לפחות משלשה סמוך לקרקע ובידו אחת גוררה ונפלה לתוך חברתה וידו קניא ליה: כדרבא דאמר רבא ידו של אדם חשובה. לענין הנחת שבת כמקום ארבעה על ארבעה וכי היכי דלענין שבת חשוב מקום לענין מיקנא נמי חשוב מקום למיקני כאילו הגביהה למעלה משלשה ומיהו ברשות היחיד לא אגבהה דלתיקני ליה מקמי דליתי חיוב שבת עליה וביאתה לרה"ר וקנייתה באין כאחד והכי משני כשצירף דלא תיהוי הגבהה ברשות היחיד דקתני מגרר ויוצא: רב אחא מתני הכי. כדאמרן דמשיכה ברשות הרבים לא קני ומוקים לה כשצירף ידו וקיבלה לתוכה: היה מושכו. בגונב בהמה ברשות בעלים קאי בפרק מרובה: ומת. השור: ברשות הבעלים פטור. הגנב מלשלם כלום דלא קני להתחייב באונסין: הגביהו. אפי' ברשות הבעלים: הא הוציאו. כל היכא דאפקיה ואפי' לרה"ר: אלו הן הלוקין. אם התרו בהן: וקיימא לן דאין לוקה ומשלם. דנפקא לן לקמן מכדי רשעתו משום רשעה אחת אתה מחייבו ואי אתה מחייבו משום שתי רשעיות: מתני'

מהלך כעומד דמי. ומעביר ארבע אמות דחייב ברה"ר הלכתא גמירי לה כדאמרינן בהזורק (שבת דף צו:) ולא ילפינן מינה דהתם מקום מיוחד הוא אבל בן עזאי מיירי במהלך מחנות לפלטיא דרך סטיו שהוא מקום פטור ובירושלמי פריך לבן עזאי היכי משכחת מעביר ד"א ברה"ר דמיחייב ומשני בקופץ: אבל זורק מאי פטור ליפלוג וליתני בדידה. משום הכי חשיב זורק בדידה טפי ממגרר משום דבמוציא ובזורק בשניהם בא בהגבהה הקנין קודם שיבא חיוב הוצאה אבל במגרר ההוצאה והקנין באין כאחד: מגרר ויוצא איצטריך ליה. לעיל דפריך ליפלוג בין לפוש ובין לכתף לא בעי לשנויי הכי משום דלכתף פטור נראה לו חידוש טפי מחידוש דמגרר ועוד דהכא לא הוי לגמרי בדידה אבל לעיל דהוי ממש בדידה לא שייך לשנויי הכי: אי דאפקיה לרה"ר איסור גניבה ליכא. אף על גב דאיכא למ"ד בפ"ק דב"מ (דף י. ושם) דד' אמות קונות לו לאדם אפילו ברה"ר ה"מ גבי מציאה דלא ליתו לאינצויי ונגבו משום עיגונא אבל גנב לא תקינו שיקנו לו ד' אמות: אלא במיצעי. תימה לר"י דבפרק הספינה (ב"ב דף פו. ושם) גבי דברים שדרכן להגביהן אין נקנין במשיכה אלא בהגבהה ופריך מהגונב כיס דבר הגבהה הוא ומשני במידי דבעי מיתנא משמע דאי הוה אמר דבר הגבהה נמי נקנה במשיכה הוה אתי ליה שפיר אפילו בזוטרי ולאמאי הא על כרחך לא מצי איירי בזוטרי דא"כ היכי מיחייב לענין שבת בגרירה דאין דרך הוצאה בכך וי"ל דאפשר שיהא דרך הוצאה בכך אפילו בזוטרי כגון שמוציאו דרך מחתרת דדרכו בגרירה ואינו נקנה אלא בהגבהה א"נ הוה מצי למימר ולטעמיך ולא פריך וכן דרך הש"ס בכמה מקומות: רב אשי אמר כגון שצירף ידו למטה מג' וקיבלה וכדרבא. פירש בקונטרס דקאי אמאי דפריך לעיל איסור גניבה ליכא והשתא משני דאיכא נמי איסור גניבה כדרבא וקשה לר"י חדא דמה ענין חשיבות מקום ד' לענין שבת לקנין ועוד דאין צריך שום ראיה להביא דקניא ליה ידו דפשיטא דונתן בידה אמר רחמנא כדפרישית לעיל ועוד א) דלאמאי לא מוקי אפילו כשצירף ידו למעלה מג' כגון שהאסקופה גבוהה ג' דליכא הגבהה ברה"י והוה מייתי מדרבא אקנין ואשבת ונראה כגירסת הספר שמצא ר"י בן רבינו מאיר בספרי אשכנז דגרס אי נמי כדרבא וכולה מילתא אשבת קאי כשצירף ידו למטה מג' דאע"ג דלא חשיבא לענין שבת הנחה אלא על גבי מקום ד' איכא הכא חיוב שבת כשצירף ידו למטה מג' דלמטה מג' לא בעינן מקום ד' דכלבוד דמי ב) וכמונחת אארעא דמיא אי נמי אפי' צירף ידו למעלה מג' וכדרבא דידו חשובה כד' על ד' ור"ת ל"ג דאמר רבא ידו של אדם אלא וכדרבא ותו לא ואתא לשנויי דמגרר ויוצא איצטריך ליה לאשמועינן דאגד יד לא שמיה אגד והא מייתי כדרבא דאמר בהמצניע (שבת דף צב.) דאגד יד לא שמיה אגד ומיירי כשהוא נשאר בפנים והוציא ידו אחת ובאחרת מגרר לתוכה ודוקא צירף למטה מג' דלמעלה משלשה שמיה אגד דבתר גופו גרירא [ולפי' קמא קשה דלשנויא קמא לית ליה דרבא וכולהו מתנייתא דשבת וכן ר' יוחנן (שבת ה.) אתו כרבא]: וברשות הרבים נמי קנה. והא דאמר בהמוכר את הספינה (ב"ב פד:) דאביי ורבא דאמרי תרוייהו דמשיכה לא קניא ברה"ר אומר ר"י דלא פליגי אדרבינא דהכא דהא דקאמר דקני היינו לענין להתחייב באונסין אבל אינו קונה שיהא שלו לגמרי וריב"א נראה לו דפליג דהא במרובה (ב"ק דף עט. ושם) גבי נתנה לבכורות בנו דקתני סיפא איכא נמי למידק כמו שמדקדק כאן והתם לענין משיכה דקנין איירי ללשון ראשון שפי' בקונט' ואפילו ללשון שני הא מוכח התם בגמ' (דף סה.) שאין לגנב להתחייב אלא במשיכה הראויה לקנין: ורמינהי אלו הן הלוקין הבא על אחותו. ארישא דמתניתין הוה מצי למיפרך דקתני הבא על הממזרת יש לה קנס והתם קתני דלקי עלה אלא נטר הכא עד הבא על אחותו למיפרך מרישא דמתניתין דהתם דחייבי לאוין שנויין שם בתר חייבי כריתות והיה צריך להביא כל המשנה עד הבא על הממזרת:

עין משפט נר מצוה

יג א מיי' פ"ד מהל' מכירה הלכה ד טוש"ע ח"מ סימן קצח סעיף יד:
יד ב מיי' פי"ג מהל' שבת הלכה טו:
טו ג מיי' פ"ג מהל' גניבה הלכה ב טור ח"מ סימן שנא:
טז ד ה מיי' פ"ב מהל' גניבה הל' ט סמג עשין עא טוש"ע ח"מ סי' שמח סעיף ד:
יז ו מיי' פי"ט מהל' סנהדרין הלכה ד:

תוספות רי"ד

ובמאי. פי' במאי איצטריך לאשמועינן דדרך הוצאה בכך אי בגדול שיש בו משוי להגביה אורחיה הוא לגוררו ופשיטא דהוצאה היא ואי בזוטרא לאו אורחי' הוא ואמאי חייב משום שבת א) גניבה ליכא דמשיכה בלא הגבהה לא קניא ברה"ר אלא במיצעי. פי' אם היה הכיס קטן שדרכו להוציאו בהגבהה והוציאו בגרירה פטור לענין שבת דהוצאה כלאחר יד הוא. וגם לענין קני' נמי אמרינן בפ' המוכר את הספינה דברים שדרכן להגביהן אינן נקנים אלא בהגבהה לא במשיכה ומוקמי' להא דתני היה מגרר ויוצא במידי דצריך מיתנא. ודאפקיה היכא אי דאפקי' לרה"ר איסור שבת איכא איסור גניבה ליכא פי' (אי) דמשיכה [אינה] קונה ברה"ר ואי דאפקה לרה"י איסור גניבה איכא איסור שבת ליכא ר"א אמר כגון שצירף ידו למטה מג' וקבלה. פי' מכי נפלה לתוך ידו איכא איסור גניבה שידו קונה לו ואיכא איסור שבת שכל פחות מג' כלבוד דמי וכאילו נחה ברשות הרבים דמי פי' המורה: לעולם הא דקתני מגרר ויוצא פטור לעולם דאפקיה לרה"ר ודלך איסור גניבה ליכא איכא ודאי כגון שצירף ידו השנית לפחות משלשה סמוך לקרקע ובידו האחת גוררה והפילה לתוך ידו חברתה וידו קונה לו כדרבא דאמר ידו של אדם חשובה לו כד' על ד' פי' לענין הנחת שבת חשיבא מקום לענין מיקנא נמי חשיב מקום למקני' כאילו הגביה למעלה מג' מיהו ברה"י לא אגביה דלקני' מקמי דליתי חיוב שבת עלי' וביאתה לרה"ר וקנייתה באין כאחד והכי משני כשצירף דלא תהוי הגבהה ברשות היחיד כדקתני (מגביה) [מגרר] ויוצא. א"נ כדרבא ג) דאמר ידו של אדם חשובה לו כד' על ד' פי' ראע"פ שהיתה למעלה מג' יש בה איסור שבת דידו של אדם חשובה לו כד' על ד' ולענין שבת בעינן שיעשה הנחה ע"ג מקום חשוב שיש בו ד' על ד' והיד היא חשובה כד' על ד': רב אחא מתני הכי פי' כדאמרי' דמשיכ' ברה"ר לא קניא ומוקי לה כשצירף ידו וקבלה לתוכה. רבינא מתני לעולם דאפקיה לרה"ר וברה"ר נמי קני. פי' דמשיכה ברה"ר קנה.

מסורת הש"ס

א) [שבת ה. עירובין לח.], ב) שבת ו. עירובין לד, ג) שבת ה., ד) ב"ק עט., ה) מכות יג., ו) [ביתר ביאור כתבו תוס' שבת ה: ד"ה בשלמא], ז) ח"מ כ"י.

תוספות ישנים

א) [ור' אליהו פי' כגון שהאסקופה כרמלית ולהכי צריך כשצירף ידו למטה מג' מגגב האסקופה דאי בתוך ג' לארעא הוי כרמלית כמו אסקופה עלמא ולא מחייב. מ"י]. ב) [ורש"י דפי' דצריך הגבהה הא דאמרי' בהמניח (דף כט:) כשספסה בפחות מג' וקאמר דקני הא פי' התם בקונט' משום דהוי הפקר ואיכא למ"ד דפי' הכונה דהפקר קני וסיפוי מבואות דאמר שצריך שיגביה טפח התם נמי בעירוב הקילו. מ"י].

גליון הש"ס

תוס' ד"ה רב אשי וכו' דקניא ליה ידו. עי' בב"ק כט ע"ב תוד"ה אלא אמר רב אשי:

ליקוטי רש"י

זוטרי. קטנים [שבת קנה.]. איסור גניבה ליכא. ברשות הרבים לאו מקום קנייה היא [שבת צא.]. לצידי רשות הרבים. סמם לידי רשות הרבים איכא חיפופי וטולין יתידות אבנים גדולות סמוך לכותל שלא יזיקוהו קרונות והחזה אויר שבינייהו לכותל קרי לידי רשות הרבים [עירובין צד.]. לענין גניבה מיקנא קני ולענין שבת הוי רשות הרבים כרבי אליעזר [רשב"ם פו.]. כגון שצירף ידו למטה משלשה וקיבלו. וצריך ידו למטה משלשה וקבלה לתוכה כל ארבעה והרי הוא לו כמלרו ועע"ש שאין כאן הגבהה והכי מוקים לה בכתובות [סנהדרין עב.]. ברה"ר סמוך לאסקופת הבית [רשב"ם ב"ב פה.]. וידו של אדם חשובה לו כד' על ד' וקניא ליה ולא בעינן לגבי רה"ר לגבי קנייה ויש כאן [איסור] שבת וגניבה כאחד והך קנייה לאו משום הגבהה היא אלא משיכה לתוך ידו שהרי ידו סמוכה לתוך ג' לקרקע [שם פו.]. היה. גנב מושכו ויוצא פטור מכלום (ס"מ). מכלל, הגביהו. אפי' ברשות בעלים שהרי הגבהה קונה בכל מקום במסכת קידושין (דף כה:) [ב"ק עט.]. אלו הן הלוקין. אלו לאו דוקא דתנא ושייר לוקין טובא אלא תנא חייבי כריתות לאשמועינן דיש מלקות בחייבי כריתות [מכות יג.].

ואע"ג דקיי"ל דכל היכא דפליגי רב אחא ורבינא הלכתא כרבינא. הכא הלכתא כר"א משום דקיימו כוותיה אביי ורבא בפרק המוכר את הספינה ואמרי שאין משיכה קונה ברה"ר. ותלמודא נמי מקשה ממילתיה וקיי"ל שאין התלמוד מקשה אלא מהלכה פסוקה: הבא על אחותו וכו'. ורמינהו אלו הן הלוקין הבא על אחותו וכו' וקיי"ל דאין לוקה ומשלם. פי' דנפקא לן מכדי רשעתו משום רשעה א' אתה מחייבו ולא משום ב' רשעיות. פי' המורה והא דאוקי מתני'

חשק שלמה על תוס' רי"ד א) ממיכת איסור גניבה ליכא עד ברה"ר שייך להלן. ב) גירסת רבינו א"נ כדרבא וכ"ה בתוס' בד"ה רב אשי בשם הריב"ם.

The Gemara presents the resolutions of other Amoraim: רַב אַחָא מַתְנֵי הָכִי – **Rav Acha teaches** (i.e. explains) **the Baraisa** in **this** same **way** that Rav Ashi teaches it.[28] רָבִינָא מַתְנֵי – **Ravina,** however, **teaches it** as follows: לְעוֹלָם דְּאַפְּקֵיהּ לִרְשׁוּת הָרַבִּים – **In fact,** as originally assumed, the Baraisa refers to **where he took [the purse] out to** the floor of **the public domain,** and not into his hand. וּבִרְשׁוּת הָרַבִּים נַמִּי קָנָה – **And** this constitutes an act of theft because **[*meshichah*] effects acquisition even in the public domain.**[29]

The Gemara explains this dispute about whether *meshichah* into the public domain is an effective *kinyan:*

וְתַרְוַיְיהוּ בְּדִיּוּקָא דְּהָא מַתְנִיתִין קָמִיפַּלְגֵי – **And both** Rav Acha (who maintains that *meshichah* into the public domain is ineffective) and Ravina (who maintains that it is effective) **argue with regard to the inference** that is to be drawn **from this** following **Mishnah.** I.e. their respective positions are rooted in the respective inferences they draw from the following Mishnah. דִּתְנַן – **For we learned in a Mishnah:**[30] הָיָה מוֹשְׁכוֹ וְיוֹצֵא וּמֵת בִּרְשׁוּת בְּעָלִים – If [THE THIEF] WAS in the process of PULLING [THE ANIMAL] OUT of the owner's domain, AND IT DIED while still IN THE OWNER'S DOMAIN, פָּטוּר – HE IS NOT LIABLE to pay for it.[31] הִגְבִּיהוֹ – If, however, HE LIFTED IT while it was still in the owner's domain,[32] אוֹ שֶׁהוֹצִיאוֹ מֵרְשׁוּת בְּעָלִים – OR HE TOOK IT OUT OF THE OWNER'S DOMAIN,[33] וָמֵת – AND then IT DIED, after he had performed the *kinyan* to it, חַיָּיב – HE IS LIABLE to pay for it.[34] רָבִינָא דָּיֵיק מֵרֵישָׁא – **Ravina infers** his ruling that *meshichah* is effective in the public domain **from the** Mishnah's **first clause,** רַב אַחָא דָּיֵיק מִסֵּיפָא – whereas, **Rav Acha infers** his ruling that *meshichah* is ineffective in the public domain **from the** Mishnah's **latter clause.**

The Gemara explains:

רָבִינָא דָּיֵיק מֵרֵישָׁא – **Ravina infers** his ruling **from the first clause** as follows: הָיָה מוֹשְׁכוֹ וְיוֹצֵא וּמֵת בִּרְשׁוּת בְּעָלִים פָּטוּר – The first clause states: If [THE THIEF] WAS PULLING [THE ANIMAL] OUT of the owner's domain, AND IT DIED while still IN THE OWNER'S DOMAIN, HE IS NOT LIABLE. טַעְמָא דְּמֵת בִּרְשׁוּת בְּעָלִים – This implies that **the** only **reason** he is not liable is **that it died** while still **in the owner's domain,** הָא הוֹצִיאוֹ מֵרְשׁוּת בְּעָלִים וָמֵת חַיָּיב – **but had he taken it out of the owner's domain, and** then **it died, he would be liable** in all cases, even if he had pulled it into a public domain.[35] רַב אַחָא דָּיֵיק מִסֵּיפָא – **Rav Acha,** on the other hand, **infers** his ruling **from the latter clause** as follows: הִגְבִּיהוֹ אוֹ שֶׁהוֹצִיאוֹ – The latter clause states that the thief is liable if HE LIFTED IT while it was still in the owner's domain, OR HE TOOK IT OUT ... הוֹצָאָה דּוּמְיָא דְּהַגְבָּהָה – The Mishnah presents the case of **"taking out"** together with – and thus **similar to** – the case of **"lifting,"** from which we learn that מָה הַגְבָּהָה דְּאָתֵי לִרְשׁוּתֵיהּ – **just as** in the case of **"lifting"** the Mishnah is referring to **where [the animal] came into [the thief's] domain,** אַף הוֹצָאָה נַמִּי דְּאָתֵי לִרְשׁוּתֵיהּ – **so too** in the case of **"taking out"** (i.e. pulling the animal out) the Mishnah is **also** referring to **where [the animal] came into [the thief's] domain.**[36]

Since both inferences indeed seem valid, the Gemara asks: לְרַב אַחָא קַשְׁיָא רֵישָׁא – **The first clause** of the Mishnah (from which Ravina infers that *meshichah* into the public domain *is* effective) **poses a difficulty to Rav Acha,** לְרָבִינָא קַשְׁיָא סֵיפָא – while **the last clause** of the Mishnah (from which Rav Acha infers that *meshichah* into the public domain is *not* effective) **poses a difficulty to Ravina!** – ? –

The Gemara explains how each one would resolve the difficulty confronting his position:

רֵישָׁא לְרַב אַחָא לֹא קַשְׁיָא – **The first clause** of the Mishnah[37] **does not pose a difficulty to Rav Acha,** כַּמָּה דְּלֹא אָתֵי לִרְשׁוּתֵיהּ רְשׁוּת בְּעָלִים קָרֵינָא בֵּיהּ – for he will explain that **as long as [the animal] has not come into [the thief's] domain, we refer to it**

NOTES

just as with regard to the laws of the Sabbath, a hand has the significance of a "separate and distinct location," so too is it considered "a separate and distinct location" with regard to the laws of *kinyan,* as if he had lifted his hand three *tefachim* above the ground (*Rashi*).

[*Rashi's* intent would seem to be as follows: Ordinarily, anything within three *tefachim* of the ground is considered to be subordinate to the ground. Rava's teaching regarding a person's hand, however, indicates that the hand is considered a place that is separate and distinct from the ground even when it is within three *tefachim* of the ground. Hence, the hand can function as the person's "courtyard" even when it is within three *tefachim* of the ground, and the person thus acquires the object that he draws into his hand (see *Rashi* to *Sanhedrin* 72a ד״ה היה מגרר ויוצא, *Rashbam* to *Bava Basra* 86a ד״ה שהרי איסור שבת ואיסור גניבה באין כאחד, *Shitah Mekubetzes* here ד״ה רב אשי אמר and *Dvar Avraham* 21:23; cf. *Rashba* here, who explains *Rashi's* intent differently).]

[Though Rava's statement was made with regard to *hanachah, Rashi* implies that the statement is introduced here *only* to account for why the purse's entry into his second hand constitutes an act of *kinyan,* and *not* to account for why it constitutes a *hanachah.* Perhaps, this is because it would be deemed a *hanachah* in the public domain in any event, since the hand into which it comes is positioned within three *tefachim* of the floor of the public domain (see *Re'ah* and *Ritva,* citing *Rashi*).]

Thus, liability for desecrating the Sabbath and for theft occur simultaneously with the entry of the purse into the thief's other hand. For at that moment, the act of theft is committed, and the *hanachah* of the purse in the public domain is complete [since the person and his hand are both in the public domain – see Mishnah, *Shabbos* 2a]. Rav Ashi had to say that the thief's other hand was within three *tefachim* of the ground. For had the other hand been higher, then the thief would have had to lift the purse three *tefachim* in order to get it into his other hand. In that case, the act of theft would have occurred first (with the *hagbahah* of the purse three *tefachim*), whereas liability for desecrating the Sabbath would not have been incurred until the purse comes to rest in the thief's other hand (see *Rashi* and *Ritva*).

28. Namely, that the Baraisa indeed means that he dragged the purse into the public domain, and though *meshichah* there is ineffective, it refers to where he received the purse in his other hand, which was positioned within three *tefachim* of the ground of the public domain (*Rashi*).

29. Unlike your assumption above (see above, note 11).

[Even Ravina might deem *meshichah* to be a *kinyan* in the public domain only with regard to theft (and the thief's consequent liability for the stolen article), but not with regard to the normal acquisition of an article from its owner (see *Tosafos*).]

30. *Bava Kamma* 79a. The Mishnah, discussing a thief who steals an animal from its owner's domain, teaches the point at which the thief "acquires" the animal and becomes liable for whatever happens to it subsequently.

31. For although he "pulled" the animal, *meshichah* is ineffective in the owner's domain. Hence he does not "acquire" it to become liable for unavoidable mishaps such as the natural death of the animal [see above, 30b note 17] (see *Rashi*).

32. Thus, he has performed to it the *kinyan* of *hagbahah,* which is effective even in the owner's domain (see above, 31a note 15).

33. And thus performed to it the *kinyan* of *meshichah.*

34. For the animal died after the thief had performed a *kinyan* to it, thereby "acquiring" it with regard to liability for any subsequent damage or mishap.

35. This shows that *meshichah* into the public domain is effective.

36. E.g. where he "pulled" the animal into a *simta* – see above, notes 11 and 24.

37. Which implies that when the thief "pulls" the animal, he is free from liability only if the animal dies while yet *in the owner's domain,* but not if it dies after he pulled it out into the public domain.

פטור אדתני היה מגרר ויוצא פטור נפלוג וניתני בדידה במה דברי' אמורים בעומד לפוש אבל לכתף פטור אלא הא מני [א] בן עזאי היא דאמר מהלך כעומד דמי אבל זורק מאי פטור ניפלוג [וניתני] בדידה במה דברים אמורים במהלך אבל זורק פטור מגרר ויוצא איצטריכא ליה ס"ד אמינא אין דרך הוצאה בכך קמ"ל ובמאי אי ברברבי אורחיה הוא אי בזוטרי לאו אורחיה הוא אלא במיצעי ודאפקיה להיכא אי דאפקיה לרה"ר איסור שבת איכא איסור גניבה ליכא אי דאפקיה לרשות היחיד איסור גניבה איכא איסור שבת ליכא לא צריכא דאפקיה לצידי רשות הרבים וכמאן אי כר' אליעזר דאמר [ב] צידי רה"ר כרה"ר דמו איסור שבת איכא איסור גניבה ליכא אי כרבנן דאמרי צידי רה"ר לאו כרה"ר דמו איסור גניבה איכא איסור שבת ליכא לעולם כר' אליעזר וכי אמר ר"א צידי רה"ר כרה"ר דמו הני מילי לענין חיובא דשבת דזימנין דדחקי רבים ועיילי להתם [א] אבל לענין מיקנא קני מ"ט דהא לא שכיחי רבים רב אשי אמר כגון שצירף ידו למטה משלשה וקיבלו כדרבא דאמר רבא [ג] [ב] ידו של אדם חשובה לו כארבעה על ארבעה רב אחא מתני הכי רבינא מתני לעולם דאפקיה לרה"ר [ג] וברה"ר נמי קנה ותרווייהו בדיוקא דהא מתני' קמיפלגי דתנן [ד] [ד] היה מושכו ויוצא ומת ברשות בעלים פטור הגביהו או שהוציאו מרשות בעלים ומת חייב רבינא דייק מרישא רב אחא דייק מסיפא רבינא דייק מרישא היה מושכו ויוצא ומת ברשות בעלים פטור טעמא דמת ברשות בעלים [ה] הא הוציאו מרשות בעלים ומת חייב רב אחא דייק מסיפא הגביהו או שהוציאו הוצאה דומיא דהגבהה מה הגבהה דאתי לרשותיה אף הוצאה נמי דאתי לרשותיה לרב אחא קשיא רישא לרבינא קשיא סיפא רישא לרב אחא לא קשיא כמה דלא אתי לרשותיה רשות בעלים קרינא ביה סיפא לרבינא לא קשיא הוצאה דומיא דהגבהה לא אמרינן: הבא על אחותו ועל אחות אביו כו': ורמינהו [ה] [ו] אלו הן הלוקין הבא על אחותו ועל אחות אביו ועל אחות אמו ועל אחות אשתו ועל אשת אחיו ועל אשת אחי אביו ועל הנדה וקיימא

רש"י

פטור. מתשלומין דלאו עליה חיוב שבת מחמת הגבהה ראשונה שבה נקנה לו הכיס ומיתה ותשלומין באין כאחד: ניפלוג בדידה. במגביה עצמו יכול לשנות בו חיוב ופטור: אלא. לא תוקמה כשעמד ואפ"ה חיוב שבת דעקירה לאו מחמת עקירה ראשונה דהגבהה אתיא ליה אלא בעקירת גופו של פסיעה אחרונה כשיוצא מן הבית ובן עזאי היא: דאמר. בפ"ק דשבת: מהלך כעומד דמי. ועקירת כל פסיעה הויא עקירה והנחת הרגל היא הנחה הלכך קניה משעת הגבהה וחיוב מיתה בפסיעה בתרייתא קא אתיא ליה: אבל זורק מאי. הגביהו וזרקו: פטור. מתשלומין דאתיא ליה חיוב שבת ע"י חיוב הגבהה דתו ליתא עקירה אחריתי: אין דרך הוצאה בכך. ואין כאן חיוב שבת: ובמאי. איצטריך לאשמועינן דדרך הוצאה בכך: אי ברברבי. כיס גדול שיש בו משוי להגביהו: אורחיה הוא. לגררו ופשיטא דהוצאה היא: לאו אורחיה הוא. ואמאי חייב משום שבת: איסור גניבה ליכא. דמשיכה בלא הגבהה קס"ד דלא קניא ברה"ר: לרשות היחיד. לרשותו שהיתה חצירו סמוכה לחצר הבעלים: צידי רה"ר. סמוך לבתים שנותנין להלן מן הבתים אבנים ומכשולין להרחיק חיכוך העגלות ומאותן חיפופי ולפנים קרי לידי רה"ר: פלוגתא דרבי אליעזר ורבנן בעירובין בפרק כל גגות: דהא לא שכיחי רבים. והוי ליה כסימטא דתיקון בה משיכה: רב אשי אמר. מגרר ויוצא דקאמר פטור לעולם ברשות הרבים ודקשיא לך איסור גניבה ליכא: כגון שצירף ידו. השניה לפחות משלשה סמוך לקרקע ובידו אחת גיררה ונפלה לתוך חברתה וידו קניא ליה: כדרבא דאמר רבא ידו של אדם חשובה. לענין הנחת שבת כמקום ארבעה על ארבעה וכי היכי דלענין שבת חשוב מקום לענין מיקנא נמי חשוב מקום למיקני כאילו הגביהה למעלה משלשה ומיהו ברשות היחיד לא אגבהה דתיקני ליה מקמי דליתי חיוב שבת עליה וביאתה לרה"ר וקנייתה באין כאחד ולהכי משני כשצירף דלא תיהוי הגבהה ברשות היחיד כדקתני מגרר ויוצא: רב אחא מתני הכי. כדאמרן דמשיכה ברשות הרבים לא קני ומוקים לה כשצירף ידו וקיבלה לתוכה: היה מושכו. בגונב בהמה ברשות בעלים קאי בפרק מרובה: ומת. השור: ברשות הבעלים פטור. הגנב מלשלם כלום דלא קני להתחייב באונסין: הגביהו. אפי' ברשות הבעלים: הא הוציאו. כל היכא דאפקיה ואפי' לרה"ר: אלו הן הלוקין. אם התרו בהן: וקיימא לן דאין לוקה ומשלם. דנפקא לן לקמן מכדי רשעתו משום רשעה אחת אתה מחייבו ואי אתה מחייבו משום שתי רשעיות: מתני'

תוספות

מהלך כעומד דמי. ומעביר ארבע אמות דחייב ברה"ר הלכתא גמירי לה כדאמרינן בהזורק (שבת דף צו:) ולא ילפינן מינה דהתם מקום חיובא הוא אבל בן עזאי מיירי במהלך מחנות לפלטיא דרך סטיו שהוא מקום פטור וירושלמי פריך לבן עזאי היכי משכחת מעביר ד"א ברה"ר דמיחייב ומשני בקופץ[ו]: אבל זורק מאי פטור ליפלוג וליתני בדידה. משום הכי חשיב זורק בדידה טפי ממגרר משום דבמוציא וזורק בשניהם בא בהגבהה הקנין קודם שיבא חיוב הוצאה אבל במגרר ההוצאה והקנין באין כאחד: מגרר ויוצא איצטריך ליה. לעיל דפריך דליפלוג בין לפוש ובין לכתף לא בעי לשנויי הכי משום דלכתף פטור נראה לו חידוש טפי מחידוש דמגרר [ז] [ועוד דהכא לא הוי לגמרי בדידה אבל לעיל דהוי ממש בדידה לא שייך לשנויי הכי]: אי דאפקיה לרה"ר איסור גניבה ליכא. אף על גב דאיכא למ"ד בפ"ק דב"מ (דף י. ושם) דד' אמות קונות לו לאדם אפילו ברה"ר ה"מ גבי מציאה דלא ליתו לאינצויי ובגט משום עיגונא אבל לגנב לא תקינו שיקנו לו ד' אמות: אלא במיצעי. תימה לר"י דבפרק הספינה (ב"ב דף פו. ושם) גבי דברים שדרכן להגביהן אין נקנין במשיכה אלא בהגבהה ופריך מהגונב כיס דבר הגבהה הוא ומשני במידי דבעי מיתנא משמע דאי הוה אמר דבר הגבהה נמי נקנה במשיכה הוה אתי ליה שפיר אפילו בזוטרי ואמאי הא על כרחך לא מצי איירי בזוטרי דא"כ היכי מיחייב לענין שבת בגרירה דאין דרך הוצאה בכך וי"ל דאפשר שיהא דרך הוצאה בכך אפילו בזוטרי כגון שמוציאו דרך מחתרת דדרכו בגרירה ואינו נקנה אלא בהגבהה אי נמי הוה מצי למימר ולטעמיך ולא פריך וכן דרך הש"ס בכמה מקומות: רב אשי אמר כגון שצירף ידו למטה מג' וקיבלה וכדרבא. פירש בקונטרס דקאי אמאי דפריך לעיל איסור גניבה ליכא והשתא משני דאיכא נמי איסור גניבה כדרבא וקשה לר"י חדא דמה ענין חשיבות מקום ד' דלענין שבת לקנין ועוד דאין צריך שום ראיה להביא [ה] דקניא ליה ידו דפשיטא דונתן בידה אמר רחמנא כדפרישית לעיל ועוד א) דלמאי לא מוקי אפילו כשצירף ידו למעלה מג' כגון שהאסקופה גבוהה ג' דליכא הגבהה ברה"י והוה מייתי מדרבא לקנין ולשבת ונראה כגירסת הספר שמצא ר"י בן רבינו מאיר בספרי אשכנז דגרס אי נמי כדרבא וכולה מילתא דשבת קאי כשצירף ידו למטה מג' דלא"ג דלא חשיבא לענין שבת הנחה אלא על גבי מקום ד' איכא הכא חיוב שבת כשצירף ידו למטה מג' דלמטה מג' לא בעינן מקום ד' דכלבוד דמי ב) וכמונחת אארעא דמיא אי נמי אפי' ליכא ידו למעלה מג' וכדרבא דידו חשובה כד' על ד' ור"ת ל"ג דאמר רבא ידו של אדם אלא וכדרבא ותו לא ואתא לשנויי דמגרר ויוצא איצטריך ליה לאשמועינן דאגד יד לא שמיה אגד והשתא מיירי כדרבא דאמר בהמצניע (שבת דף צב.) דאגד יד לא שמיה אגד ומיירי כשהוא נשאר בפנים והוציא ידו אחת ובאחרת מגרר לתוכה ודוקא צירף למטה מג' דלמעלה משלשה שמיה אגד דבתר גופו גרירה [ולפי' קמא קשה לשנויא קמא לית ליה דרבא וכולהו מתניתא דשבת וכן ר' יוחנן (שבת ה.) אתו כרבא]: וברשות הרבים נמי קנה. והא דאמר בהמוכר את הספינה (ב"ב פד:) דאביי ורבא דאמרי תרוייהו דמשיכה לא קניא אלא בסימטא אומר ר"י דלא פליגי אדרבינא דהכא דקאמר דקני היינו לענין להתחייב באונסין אבל אינו קונה שיהא שלו לגמרי וריב"א נראה לו דפליגי דהא במרובה (ב"ק דף עט. ושם) גבי נתנה לבכורות בנו דקתני סיפא איכא נמי לדיוק כמו שמדקדק כאן והתם לענין משיכה דקנין איירי ללשון ראשון שפי' שם בקונט' ואפילו ללשון שני הא מוכח התם בגמ' (דף פא.) שאין לגנב להתחייב אלא במשיכה הראויה לקנין: ורמינהי אלו הן הלוקין הבא על אחותו. תימה למתמיהין הוה מצי למיפרך דקתני הבא על הממזרת יש לה קנס והתם תני לאו ביה דלקי עליה אלא עולה עד הבא על אחותו או למיפרך מרישא דמתניתין דהתם דחייבי לאוין שנויין שם בתר חייבי כריתות והיה צריך להביא כל המשנה עד הבא על הממזרת:

ואע"ג דקי"ל דכל היכא דפליגי רב אחא ורבינא הלכתא כרבינא. הכא הלכתא כר"א משום דקיימו כוותיה אביי ורבא בפרק המוכר את הספינה ואמרי שאין משיכה קונה ברה"ר. ותלמודא נמי מקשה מילתיה וקי"ל שאין התלמוד מקשה אלא אם מהלכה פסוקה: הבא על אחותו וכו'. ורמינהו אלו הן הלוקין הבא על אחותו וכו' וקי"ל דאין לוקה ומשלם. פי' דנפקא לן מכדי רשעתו משום רשעה א' אתה מחייבו ולא משום ב' רשעיות. פי' המורה והא דאוקי מתני'

חשק שלמה על תוס' רי"ד א) מתיבת איסור גניבה ליכא עד ברה"ר שייך להלן. ב) נ"ל דצ"ל ולית ליה. ג) גירסת רבינו ל"ג כדרבא וכ"ה בתוס' בד"ה רב אשי בשם הריב"ם.

עין משפט נר מצוה

יג א מיי' פ"ד מהל' מכירה הלכה ד טוש"ע ח"מ סימן קצח סעיף יד:
יד ב מיי' פי"ג מהל' שבת הלכה טו:
טו ג מיי' פ"ג מהל' גניבה הלכה ב טוש"ע ח"מ סימן שנא:
טז ד ה מיי' פ"ב מהל' גניבה הל' טו סמג עשין עא טוש"ע ח"מ סי' שמח סעיף ד:
יז ו מיי' פי"ט מהל' סנהדרין הלכה ד:

תוספות רי"ד

ובמאי. פי' ובמאי איצטריך לאשמועינן דדרך הוצאה בכך אי בגדול שיש בו משוי להגביה אורחיה הוא לגוררו ופשיטא דהוצאה היא ואי בזוטרא לאו אורחיה הוא ואמאי חייב משום שבת (איסור א) גניבה ליכא דמשיכה בלא הגבהה לא קניא ברה"ר) אלא במציעי. פי' אם היה הכיס קטן שדרכו להוציאו בהגבהה והוציאו בגרירה פטור לענין שבת דהוצאה כלאחר יד הוא. גם לענין קני' נמי אמרינן בפ' המוכר את הספינה דדברים שדרכן להגביהן אינן נקנים אלא בהגבהה לא במשיכה ומוקמי' להא דתני היה מגרר ויוצא במידי דצריך מיתנא. ודאפקוה היכא אי דאפקי' לרה"ר איסור שבת איכא איסור גניבה ליכא פי' (אין) דמשיכה [אינה] קונה ברה"ר ואי דאפקה לרה"י איסור גניבה איכא איסור שבת ליכא ר"א אבר כגון שצירף ידו למטה מג' וקבלה. פי' מכי נפלה לתוך ידו איכא איסור גניבה שידו קונה לו ואיכא איסור שבת שכל פחות מג' כלבוד דמי וכאילו נחה ברשות הרבים דמי פי' המורה: לעולם הא דקתני מגרר ויוצא פטור לעולם דאפקיה לרה"ר

מסורת הש"ס

א) [שבת ה: עירובין מח.] ב) שבת ו. עירובין לד. ג) שבת ה. ד) ב"ק עט. ה) מכות יג. ו) [ציל דבשבת ליתא]

תוספות ישנים

א) [ור' אליהו פי' כגון שהאסקופה כרמלית ולהכי לריך כשלירף ידו למטה מג' ...]

גליון הש"ס

תוס' ד"ה רב אשי וכו' דקניא ליה ידו. עי' בב"ק כט ע"ב תוד"ה אלא אמר רב אשי:

ליקוטי רש"י

זוטרי. קטנים [שבת קנה.]. איסור גניבה ליכא. דרשות הרבים לאו מקום קנייה היא [שבת צא:]. לצידי רשות הרבים. ... אלו הן הלוקין. ...

דְּאַפְּקִיהּ לִרְשׁוּת הָרַבִּים – **If he took it out into the public domain,** אִיסּוּר שַׁבָּת אִיכָּא אִיסּוּר גְּנֵיבָה לֵיכָּא – **there is** a transgression of **the Sabbath prohibition,** but **there is no** transgression of the **theft prohibition.**[11] אִי דְּאַפְּקִיהּ לִרְשׁוּת הַיָּחִיד – And **if he took it out into a private domain** of his own,[12] אִיסּוּר גְּנֵיבָה אִיכָּא אִיסּוּר שַׁבָּת לֵיכָּא – **there is** a transgression of **the theft prohibition,**[13] but **there is no** transgression of the **Sabbath prohibition!**[14] – ? –

The Gemara answers:

לֹא צְרִיכָא – This is **no** difficulty. **It is** only **necessary** to say that the Baraisa refers to דְּאַפְּקִיהּ לִצְדֵי רְשׁוּת הָרַבִּים – **where he took [the purse] out to the sides of the public domain.**[15]

The Gemara asks:

וּכְמַאן – **But in accordance with whom** does this Baraisa hold in regard to the legal status of "the sides of the public domain"? אִי כְּרַבִּי אֱלִיעֶזֶר – **If** the Baraisa holds **in accordance with R' Eliezer,** דְּאָמַר צִידֵי רְשׁוּת הָרַבִּים כִּרְשׁוּת הָרַבִּים דָּמוּ – **who says**[16] that **"the sides of the public domain are** legally **like the public domain** itself,"[17] אִיסּוּר שַׁבָּת אִיכָּא אִיסּוּר גְּנֵיבָה לֵיכָּא – then when he drags the purse from the house into the sides of the public domain, **there is** a transgression of **the Sabbath prohibition,** but **there is no** transgression of the **theft prohibition.**[18] אִי כְּרַבָּנָן – And **if** the Baraisa holds **in accordance with the Rabbis,** דְּאָמְרֵי צִידֵי רְשׁוּת הָרַבִּים לָאו כִּרְשׁוּת הָרַבִּים דָּמוּ – **who say**[19] that **"the sides of the public domain are not** legally **like the public domain** itself,"[20] אִיסּוּר גְּנֵיבָה אִיכָּא אִיסּוּר שַׁבָּת לֵיכָּא – **there is** a transgression of **the theft prohibition,**[21] but **there is no** transgression of the **Sabbath prohibition.**[22] – ? –

The Gemara answers:

לְעוֹלָם כְּרַבִּי אֱלִיעֶזֶר – **In fact,** the Baraisa holds **in accordance with R' Eliezer,** who says that the sides of the public domain are like the public domain itself. וְכִי אָמַר רַבִּי אֱלִיעֶזֶר צִידֵי רְשׁוּת הָרַבִּים כִּרְשׁוּת הָרַבִּים דָּמוּ – **But when R' Eliezer said that the sides of the public domain are like the public domain,** הָנֵי מִילֵּי לְעִנְיַן חִיּוּבָא דְּשַׁבָּת – **these words** were said **with regard to liability** for the desecration **of the Sabbath,** דְּזִימְנִין דְּדָחֲקֵי רַבִּים וְעָיְילֵי לְהָתָם – **for at times** (when there is heavy traffic in the main thoroughfare) **the public are crowded and enter there** [into the sides of the public domain].[23] אֲבָל לְעִנְיַן מִיקְנָא – **But with regard to acquisition** through *meshichah,* קָנֵי – R' Eliezer agrees that **the acquisition takes effect** when the item is pulled into the sides of the public domain. מַאי טַעְמָא – **What is the reason** for this? דְּהָא לֹא שְׁכִיחֵי רַבִּים – **For the public are not commonly** there.[24]

An alternative explanation, which does not require us to say that the Baraisa refers to where the thief dragged the purse into the sides of the public domain:[25]

רַב אַשִׁי אָמַר – **Rav Ashi says:** The Baraisa is indeed dealing with where he dragged the purse into the public domain. And as regards your question that there would then be no act of theft, since *meshichah* into the public domain is ineffective, I will answer that the Baraisa speaks כְּגוֹן שֶׁצֵּירַף יָדוֹ לְמַטָּה מִשְּׁלֹשָׁה וְקִיבְּלוֹ – **in a case where [the thief],** dragging the purse with one hand into the public domain, **brought his** other **hand close** to the ground **to** a point **below** the height of **three** *tefachim* from the ground of the public domain,[26] **and received [the purse]** into that hand, allowing the purse to come to rest there. כִּדְרָבָא – And this dragging of the purse into his other hand constitutes a valid *kinyan* (and thus an act of theft) even in the public domain **in accordance** with the teaching **of Rava.** דְּאָמַר רָבָא – **For Rava said:** יָדוֹ שֶׁל אָדָם חֲשׁוּבָה לוֹ כְּאַרְבַּע עַל אַרְבַּע – **A person's hand is as significant to him as** an area of **four by four** *tefachim.*[27]

NOTES

11. The Gemara here holds that the *kinyan* of *meshichah* ("pulling") is ineffective in a public domain (*Rashi*). [The reason for this would be that the *kinyan* of *meshichah* is defined as the pulling or drawing of the object *into one's domain* – either one's actual domain or one that is his for purposes of acquisition, such as a *simta* (a recessed area off the public thoroughfare; see below, note 24).] Thus, in this case, where he did not lift the purse and perform *hagbahah,* but rather dragged it and performed *meshichah,* he would not be liable for theft by pulling it into the public domain.

12. In a case where, for example, his own courtyard was adjacent to that of the purse's owner (*Rashi*), and he dragged the purse from the owner's courtyard directly into his own courtyard.

13. [For he "acquires" the purse by pulling it into his own domain.]

14. For he has transferred the purse from one private domain to another, which is not Biblically forbidden under any circumstances.

15. Where houses border on a public thoroughfare, it is common to place boulders and other obstacles in the public domain to serve as a buffer that prevents the wagons from banging into the walls of the houses. The space between this line of obstructions and the houses is called "the sides of the public domain" (*Rashi;* see, though, *Shabbos* 6a and *Tosafos* there ד״ה היכא דאיכא חיפופי).

By dragging the purse from the house into the sides of the public domain, the person desecrates the Sabbath and commits theft simultaneously. The Gemara will now ask how this is so.

16. *Eruvin* 94a.

17. And one who carries from a private domain into "the sides of the public domain" has performed the *melachah* of *transferring.*

18. For *meshichah* is ineffective in a public domain (see note 11). Why, then, does the Baraisa state that he is exempt from liability for theft "for the Sabbath prohibition and the theft occur simultaneously," when he did not commit an act of theft altogether?

19. *Eruvin* ibid.

20. But are rather considered a less public area.

21. Since *meshichah* into a little-used public area, such as a *simta* [see below, note 24] is effective.

22. Since he did not transfer the purse from the private domain into a full-fledged public domain. How, then, can the Baraisa state that he is exempt from liability for theft on account of his liability to the death penalty for desecrating the Sabbath?

23. [See *Rashi* printed alongside *Rif, Eruvin* 94a (folio 31a).] Since these sides are sometimes used as a public thoroughfare, R' Eliezer maintains that they are considered to be a full-fledged public domain with regard to the Sabbath laws.

24. And hence, this area is treated as a *simta,* where *meshichah* is effective (*Rashi*).

[A *simta* is a quiet, recessed area close to the public domain, to which people who must discuss transactions with clear thought withdraw to escape the hubbub and commotion of the marketplace (*Rashi* below, 84b). Since the traffic of the public thoroughfare spills over into the *simta* only occasionally, it is not treated as a true public thoroughfare, and therefore any individual who happens to be there can legally use it as his domain for purposes of *meshichah.* Since the sides of the public domain, too, are traversed by the public only occasionally, *meshichah* is effective there as well.]

25. And thus we need not assert that the Baraisa follows specifically the view of R' Eliezer.

26. We have followed *Rashi's* understanding of the expression שֶׁצֵּירַף יָדוֹ, as explained by *Maharam Schif.* [See there for the explanation of this clause according to *Tosafos* and according to the *Tur.*]

27. Generally, an object is considered in a state of rest with regard to the laws of the Sabbath only when it is placed on an area that is four *tefachim* by four *tefachim* wide. Hence, placing an item on a narrower area would not constitute a *hanachah* (see *Shabbos* 5a). Rava (ibid.) teaches that a person's hand has the significance of an area four *tefachim* by four *tefachim* wide, and hence placing an object in one's hand *does* constitute a *hanachah.* [Now, by saying that one's hand has the significance of an area four *tefachim* by four *tefachim,* Rava indicates that it is considered a separate and distinct location (see *Rashi* to *Shabbos* 6a ד״ה אדם עומד על האסקופה).] The Gemara here reasons that

פטור אדתני היה מגרר ויוצא מגרר ויוצא פטור נפלוג וניתני בדידה במה דברי אמורים בעומד לפוש אבל לכתף פטור אלא הא מני [א] בן עזאי היא דאמר מהלך כעומד דמי אבל זורק מאי פטור ניפלוג [וניתני] בדידה במה דברים אמורים במהלך אבל זורק פטור מגרר ויוצא איצטריכא ליה ס"ד אמינא אין דרך הוצאה בכך קמ"ל ובמאי אי ברברבי אורחיה הוא אי בזוטרי לאו אורחיה הוא אלא במיצעי ודאפקיה להיכא אי דאפקיה לרה"ר איסור שבת איכא איסור גניבה ליכא אי דאפקיה לרשות היחיד איסור גניבה איכא איסור שבת ליכא לא צריכא דאפקיה לצידי רשות הרבים וכמאן אי כר' אליעזר דאמר [ב] צידי רה"ר כרה"ר דמו איסור שבת איכא איסור גניבה ליכא אי כרבנן דאמרי צידי רה"ר לאו כרה"ר דמו איסור גניבה איכא איסור שבת ליכא לעולם כר' אליעזר וכי אמר ר"א צידי רה"ר כרה"ר דמו הני מילי לענין חיובא דשבת דזימנין דדחקי רבים ועיילי להתם [א] אבל לענין מיקנא קני מ"ט דהא לא שכיחי רבים רב אשי אמר כגון שצירף ידו למטה משלשה וקיבלו כדרבא דאמר רבא [ג] ידו של אדם חשובה לו כארבעה על ארבעה רב אחא מתני הכי רבינא מתני לעולם דאפקיה לרה"ר [ג] וברה"ר נמי קנה ותרוייהו בדיוקא דהא מתני' קמיפלגי דתנן [ד] היה מושכו ויוצא ומת ברשות בעלים פטור הגביהו או שהוציאו מרשות בעלים ומת חייב רבינא דייק מרישא רב אחא דייק מסיפא רבינא דייק מרישא היה מושכו ויוצא ומת ברשות בעלים פטור טעמא דמת ברשות בעלים [ה] הא הוציאו מרשות בעלים ומת חייב רב אחא דייק מסיפא הגביהו או שהוציאו הוצאה דומיא דהגבהה מה הגבהה דאתי לרשותיה אף הוצאה נמי דאתי לרשותיה לרב אחא קשיא רישא לרבינא קשיא סיפא רישא לרב אחא לא קשיא כמה דלא אתי לרשותיה רשות בעלים קרינא ביה סיפא לרבינא לא קשיא הוצאה דומיא דהגבהה לא אמרינן: הבא על אחותו ועל אחות אביו כו': ורמינהו [ה] [ו] אלו הן הלוקין הבא על אחותו ועל אחות אביו ועל אחות אמו ועל אחות אשתו ועל אשת אחיו ועל אשת אחי אביו ועל הנדה וקיימא

רש"י

פטור. מתשלומין דלאי עליה חיוב שבת מחמת הגבהה ראשונה שבה נקנה לו הכיס ומיתה ותשלומין באין כאחד: ניפלוג בדידה. במגביה עלמו יכול לשנות בו חיוב ופטור: אלא. לא תוקמה כשעמד ואפ"ה חיוב שבת דעקירה לאו מחמת עקירה ראשונה דהגבהה אתיא ליה אלא בעקירת גופו של פסיעה אחרונה כשיולא מן הבית ובן עזאי היא: דאמר. בפ"ק דשבת: מהלך כעומד דמי. ועקירת כל פסיעה הויא עקירה והנחת הרגל היא הנחה הלכך קניה משעת הגבהה וחיוב מיתה בפסיעה בתרייתא קא אתיא ליה: אבל זורק מאי. הגביהו וזרקו: פטור. מתשלומין דאתיא ליה חיוב שבת ע"י חיוב הגבהה דמו ליתא עקירה אחריתי: אין דרך הוצאה בכך. ולאו כאן חיוב שבת: ובמאי. אילטריך לאשמועינן דדרך הוצאה בכך: אי ברברבי. כיס גדול שיש בו משוי להגביהו: אורחיה הוא. לגררו ופשיטא דהוצאה היא: לאו אורחיה הוא. ולמאי חייב משום שבת: איסור גניבה ליכא. דמשיכה בלא הגבהה קסבר דלא קניא ברה"ר: לרשות היחיד. לרשותו שהיתה אצלו סמוכה לחצר הבעלים: צידי רה"ר. סמוך לבתים שנותנין להלן מן הבתים אבנים ומכשולין להרחיק חיכוך העגלות ומאותן חיפופי ולפנים קרי לידי רה"ר: פלוגתא דרבי אליעזר ורבנן בעירובין בפרק כל גגות: דהא לא שכיחי רבים. והוי ליה כסימטא דתיקון בה משיכה: רב אשי אמר. מגרר ויולא דקאמר פטור לעולם ברשות הרבים ודקשיא לך איסור גניבה ליכא: כגון שצירף ידו. השניה לפחות משלשה סמוך לקרקע ובידו אחת גיררה ונפלה לתוך חברתה וידו קניא ליה: כדרבא דאמר רבא ידו של אדם חשובה. לענין הנחת שבת כמקום ארבעה על ארבעה וכי היכי דלענין שבת חשוב מקום לענין מיקנא נמי חשוב מקום למיקני כאילו הגביהה למעלה משלשה ומיהו ברשות היחיד לא אגבהה דתיקני ליה מקמי דליתי חיוב שבת עליה וביאתה לרה"ר וקנייתה באין כאחד ולהכי משני כשלירף דלא תיהוי הגבהה ברשות היחיד כדקתני מגרר ויולא: רב אחא מתני הכי. כדאמרן דמשיכה ברשות הרבים לא קני ומוקים לה כשלירף ידו וקיבלה לתוכה: היה מושכו. בגונב בהמה ברשות בעלים קאי בפרק מרובה: ומת. השור: ברשות הבעלים פטור. הגנב מלשלם כלום דלא קני להתחייב באונסין: הגביהו. אפי' ברשות הבעלים: הא הוציאו. כל היכא דאפקיה ואפי' לרה"ר: אלו הן הלוקין. אם התרו בהן: וקיימא לן דאין לוקה ומשלם. דנפקא לן לקמן מכדי רשעתו משום רשעה אחת אתה מחייבו ואי אתה מחייבו משום שתי רשעיות:

מתני'

תוספות

מהלך כעומד דמי. ומעביר ארבע אמות דחייב ברה"ר הלכתא גמירי לה כדאמרינן בזורק (שבת דף צו:) ולא ילפינן מינה דהתם מקום חיובא הוא אבל בן עזאי מיירי במהלך מחנות לפלטיא דרך סטיו שהוא מקום פטור ובירושלמי פריך לבן עזאי היכי משכחת מעביר ד"א ברה"ר דמיחייב ומשני בקופץ [ו]: אבל זורק מאי פטור ליפלוג וליתני בדידה. משום הכי חשיב זורק בדידה טפי ממגרר משום דמוצא וזורק בשניהם בא בהגבהה הקנין קודם שיבא חיוב הוצאה אבל במגרר ההוצאה והקנין באין כאחד: מגרר ויוצא איצטריך ליה. לעיל דפריך ליפלוג בין לפוש ובין לכתף לא בעי לשנויי הכי משום דלכתף פטור נראה לו חידוש טפי מחידוש דמגרר [ז] [ועוד דהכא לא הוי לגמרי בדידה אבל לעיל דהוי ממש בדידה לא שייך לשנויי הכי]: אי דאפקיה לרה"ר איסור גניבה ליכא. אף על גב דאיכא למ"ד בפ"ק דב"מ (דף י. ושם) דד' אמות קונות לו לאדם אפילו ברה"ר ה"מ גבי מציאה דלא ליתו לאינצויי ובגט משום עיגונא אבל לגנב לא תקינו שיקנו לו ד' אמות: אלא במיצעי. תימה לר"י דבפרק הספינה (ב"ב דף פו. ושם) גבי דברים שדרכן להגביהן אין נקנין במשיכה אלא בהגבהה ופריך מהגונב כיס דבר הגבהה הוא ומשני במידי דבעי מיתנא משמע דאי הוה אמר דבר הגבהה אי נמי נקנה במשיכה הוה אתי ליה שפיר אפילו בזוטרי ולמאי הא על כרחך לא מלי איירי בזוטרי דא"כ היכי מיחייב לענין שבת בגרירה דאין דרך הוצאה בכך וי"ל דאפשר שיהא דרך הוצאה בכך אפילו בזוטרי כגון שמוליאו דרך מחתרת דדרכו בגרירה ואינו נקנה אלא בהגבהה אי נמי הוה מלי למימר ולטעמיך ולא פריך וכן דרך הש"ס בכמה מקומות: רב אשי אמר כגון שצירף ידו למטה מג' וקיבלה וכדרבא. פירש בקונטרס דקאמר דפריך לעיל איסור גניבה ליכא והשתא משני דאיכא נמי איסור גניבה כדרבא וקשה לר"י חדא דמה ענין חשיבות מקום ד' לענין שבת לקנין ועוד דאין לריך שום ראיה להביא [ט] דקניא ליה ידו דפשיטא דונתן בידה אמר רחמנא כדפרישית לעיל ועוד א) דלמאי לא מוקי אפילו כשלירף ידו למעלה מג' כגון שהאסקופה גבוהה ג' דליכא הגבהה ברה"י והוה מייתי מדרבא אקנין ואשבת ונראה כגירסת הספר שמלא ר"י בן רבינו מאיר בספרי אשכנז דגרס אי נמי כדרבא וכולה מילתא אשבת קאי כשלירף ידו למטה מג' דאע"ג דלא חשיבא לענין שבת הנחה אלא על גבי מקום ד' איכא הכא חיוב שבת כשלירף ידו למטה מג' דלמטה מג' לא בעינן מקום ד' דכלבוד דמי ב) וכמונחת אארעא דמיא אי נמי אפי' לירף ידו למעלה מג' וכדרבא דידו חשובה כד' על ד' ור"ת ל"ג דאמר רבא ידו של אדם אלא וכדרבא ותו לא ואתא לשנויי דמגרר ויולא אילטריך ליה לאשמועינן דאגד יד לא שמיה אגד והא מייתי כדרבא דאמר בהמלניע (שבת דף לב.) דאגד יד לא שמיה אגד ומיירי כשהוא נשאר בפנים והוליא ידו אחת ובאחרת מגרר לתוכה ודוקא לירף למטה מג' דלמעלה משלשה שמיה אגד דבתר גופו גרירא [ולפי' קמא קשה לשנויא קמא לית ליה דרבא וכולהו מתנייתא דשבת וכן ר' יוחנן (שבת ה.) אתו כרבא]: וברשות הרבים נמי קנה. והא דאמר בהמוכר את הספינה (ב"ב פד:) דאביי ורבא דאמרי תרוייהו דמשיכה לא קניא ברה"ר אומר ר"י דלא פליגי אדרבינא דהכא דהא דקאמר דקני היינו לענין להתחייב באונסין אבל אינו קונה שיהא שלו לגמרי וריצב"א נראה לו דפליג דהא במרובה (ב"ק דף עט. ושם) גבי נתנה לבכורות בנו דקתני סיפא איכא נמי למידק כמו שמדקדק כאן והתם לענין משיכה דקנין איירי ללשון ראשון שפי' שם בקונט' ואפילו ללשון שני הא מוכח התם בגמ' (דף סה.) שאין לגנב להתחייב אלא במשיכה הראויה לקנין: ורמינהי אלו הן הלוקין הבא על אחותו. ארישא דמתניתין הוה מלי למיפרך דקתני הבא על הממזרת יש לה קנס והתם קתני דלקי עלה אלא נטר הכא עד הבא על אחותו למיפרך מרישא דמתניתין דהתם דחייבי לאוין שנויין שם בתר חייבי כריתות והיה לריך להביא כל המשנה עד הבא על הממזרת:

עין משפט נר מצוה

יג א מיי' פ"ד מהל' מכירה הלכה ד טוש"ע ח"מ סימן קצז סעיף יד:
יד ב מיי' פי"ג מהל' שבת הלכה טו:
טו ג מיי' פ"ג מהל' גניבה הלכה ג טור ש"ע ח"מ סימן שנא:
טז ד ה מיי' פ"ג מהל' גניבה הל' טו סמג עשין עא טוש"ע ח"מ סי' שמח סעיף ד
יז ו מיי' פי"ט מהל' סנהדרין הלכה א:

תוספות רי"ד

ובמאי. פי' ובמאי איצטריך לאשמועינן דדרך הוצאה בכך אי בגדול שיש בו משוי להגביה אורחיה הוא לגוררו ופשיטא דהוצאה היא ואי בזוטרא לאו אורחי' הוא ובמאי חייב משום שבת (איסור א) גניבה ליכא דמשיכה בלא הגבהה לא קניא ברה"ר) אלא במיצע. פי' אם היה הכיס קטן שדרכו להוציאו בהגבהה והוציאו בגרירה פטור לענין שבת דהוצאה כלאחר יד הוא. וגם לענין קני' נמי אמרינן בפ' המוכר את הספינה דדברים שדרכן להגביהן אינן נקנים אלא בהגבהה לא במשיכה ומוקמי להא דתני היה מגרר ויוצא במידי דצריך מיתנא. ודאפקוה היכא אי דאפקי' לרה"ר איסור שבת איכא איסור גניבה ליכא פי' (אי) דמשיכה [אינה] קונה ברה"ר ואי דאפקה לרה"י איסור גניבה איכא איסור שבת ליכא ר"א אמר כגון שצירף ידו למטה מג' וקבלה. פי' מכי נפלה לתוך ידו איכא איסור גניבה שידו קונה לו ואיכא איסור שבת שכל פחות מג' כלבוד דמי וכאילו נחה ברשות הרבים דמי פי' המורה: לעולם הא דקתני מגרר ויוצא פטור לעולם דאפקה לרה"ר ודק' לך איסור גניבה ליכא ודאי כגון שצירף ידו השנית לפחות מג' סמוך לקרקע ובידו האחת גיררה והפילה לתוך יד חברתה וידו של אדם קניא ליה כדרבא דאמר ידו של אדם חשובה לו כד' על ד'. פי' לענין הנחת שבת וכי היכי דלענין שבת חשיבא מקום לענין מיקנא נמי חשיב מקום למיקני כאילו הגביה למעלה מג' מיהו ברה"י לא אגבה דתיקני לי' מקמי דליתי חיוב שבת עלי' ויציאתה וביאתה לרה"ר וקנייתה באין כא' ולהכי משני כשצירף דלא תהוי הגבהה ברשות היחיד כדקתני היה (מכניס) [מגרר] ויוצא. א"נ כדרבא ג) דאמר ידו של אדם חשובה לו כד' על ד'. פי' ואע"פ שהיתה למעלה מג' יש בה איסור שבת דידו של אדם פי' לענין שבת בעינן שיעשה הנחה ע"ג מקום חשוב שיש בו ד' על ד' והיד היא חשובה כד' על ד': רב אחא מתני הכי פי' כדאמרי' דמשיכ' ברה"ר לא קניא ומוקי לה כשצירף ידו וקבלה לתוכה. רבינא מתני לעולם דאפקיה לרה"ר וברה"ר נמי קני. פי' דמשיכה ברה"ר קונה.
ואע"ג דקיי"ל דכל הכא דפליגי רב אחא ורבינא הלכתא כרבינא. הכא הלכתא כר"א משום דקיימו כוותיה אביי ורבא בפרק המוכר את הספינה ואמרי שאין משיכה קונה ברה"ר. ותלמודא נמי מקשה ממילתיה וקיי"ל שאין התלמוד מקשה אלא מהלכה כסוקד: הבא על אחותו וכו'. ורמינהו אלו הן הלוקין הבא על אחותו וכו' וקי"ל דאין לוקה ומשלם. פי' דנפקא לן מכדי רשעתו משום רשעה א' אתה מחייבו ולא משום ב' רשעיות. פי' המורה והא דאוקי מתני'

חשק שלמה על תוס' רי"ד א) מתיבת איסור גניבה ליכא עד ברה"ר שייך להלן. ב) גירסת רבינו א"נ כדרבא וכ"ה בתוס' בד"ה רב אשי בשם הריב"ס.

מסורת הש"ס

א) [שבת ה: עירובין לח.], ב) שבת ו. עירובין לד., ג) שבת ה., ד) ב"ק עט., ה) מכות יג., ו) [ביאור כתבו תוס' שבת ה: ד"ה בשלמא], ז) מ"י כ"י.

תוספות ישנים

א) [ור' אליהו פי' כגון שהאסקופה כרמלית ולהכי צריך כשצירף ידו למטה מג' מגג האסקופה דאי בתוך ג' לראשה הוי כרמלית כמו אסקופה עצמה ולא מחייב. מ"ר]: ב) [ור"ש הפי' דלריך הגבהה הא דאמרי' בהמניח (דף כט:) בשהפכה בפמות מג' וקאמר דקני הא התם בקונט' משום דהוי הפקר ואיכא למ"ד דאפי' הבעה בהפקר קני ושותפי מבואות לאמר שצריך שיגביה טפח התם נמי בעירוב הקילו. מ"ר].

גליון הש"ס

תוס' ד"ה רב אשי וכו' דקניא ליה ידו. עי' בב"ק כט ע"ב תוד"ה אלא אמר רב אשי:

ליקוטי רש"י

זוטרי. קטנים [שבת קנה.]. איסור גניבה ליכא. דרשות הרבים לאו מקום קנייה היא [שבת צא.]. לצידי רשות הרבים. סמוך לצידי רשות הרבים איכא חיפופי נועצין יתידות ואבנים גדולות סמוך לכותל שלא יזיקום קרונות והחיכוך אויר שביניהם לכותל קרי לידי רשות הרבים [עירובין צד.]. לענין גניבה מיקנא קני ולענין שבת הוי רשות הרבים כרבי אליעזר [רשב"ם שם]. כגון שצירף ידו למטה משלשה וקיבלו. ולירף ידו למטה משלשה וקיבלה בידו דידו חשובה לו כארבעה על ארבעה והרי הוא לו כמלוי ואע"פ שאין כאן הגבהה והכי מוקים לה בכתובות [סנהדרין עב.]. ברה"ר סמוך לאסקופת הבית [רשב"ם ב"ב פה.]. ידו של אדם חשובה לו כד' על ד' וקניא ליה ולא בעלה לגבי רה"ר לגבי קנייה יש כאן [איסור] שבת וגניבה באין כאחד והכן ע"י קנין לא משום הגבהה היא אלא משיכה לתוך ידו שהרי ידו סמוכה בתוך ג' לקרקע [שם פו.]. היה. הגנב מושכו ויולא פטור מכלום (ס"א: מכפל). הגביהו. אפי' ברשות בעלים שהרי הגבהה קונה בכל מקום במסכת קדושין (דף כה:) [ב"ק עט.]. אלו הן הלוקין. אלו לאו דוקא דתנא ושייר לוקין טובא אלא תנא חייבי כריתות לאשמועינן דיש מלקות בחייבי כריתות [מכות יג.].

פָּטוּר — The law would be (as you have just stated) that **he is exempt** from payment.[1] אַדְתָּנֵי הָיָה מְגָרֵר וְיוֹצֵא מְגָרֵר וְיוֹצֵא פָּטוּר — If so, instead of teaching in the end of the Baraisa the contrasting case of: If HE WAS DRAGGING it OUT, DRAGGING it OUT, HE IS EXEMPT from liability for his theft, נִפְלוֹג וְנִיתְנֵי בְּדִידָהּ — **[the Tanna] should teach a distinction** between liability and non-liability **in that very case** of a thief who *lifts* the purse, as follows: בַּמֶּה דְּבָרִים אֲמוּרִים — **When are these things said** (that the thief is liable for payment when he lifts the purse inside the house, and then stops before leaving the house)? בְּעוֹמֵד לָפוּשׁ — **When he stops to rest.** אֲבָל לְכַתֵּף פָּטוּר — **But** when he stops only **to adjust** the load **on his shoulder, he is exempt** from payment for the purse. The fact that the Tanna had to introduce a completely different case (namely, where he *dragged* the purse outside) to illustrate nonliability for theft implies that in the original case (i.e. where he *lifted* the purse and then stopped before leaving the house), he is always liable for theft — even if he stopped only to adjust his load.[2] — ? —

The Gemara accepts this objection and therefore reconciles the Baraisa with R' Avin's ruling in a different manner:

אֶלָּא הָא מַנִּי — **Rather,** we must say (as you have proven) that the Baraisa rules the thief who lifts the purse liable to pay in all cases — even if he did not stop at all during the course of the transfer. Nevertheless, this does not contradict R' Avin's ruling that one is exempt from monetary liability from the time that he performs the *akirah.* For we can say that **this** Baraisa is authored **by whom?** בֶּן עַזַּאי הִיא — **It is** a Baraisa authored by **Ben Azzai,** דְּאָמַר מְהַלֵּךְ כְּעוֹמֵד דָּמֵי — **who says** that **walking is tantamount to standing.**[3]

The Gemara challenges this answer as well:

אֲבָל זוֹרֵק — **But** according to this answer, if **he** lifts the purse and, continuing the motion, **throws** it out of the house into the public domain, rather than walking with it, מַאי — **what** would be the law? פָּטוּר — The law would be that **he is exempt** from liability for theft.[4] נִיפְלוֹג [וְנִיתְנֵי] בְּדִידָהּ — If so, then instead of teaching in the end of the Baraisa the case of "if he was dragging it out . . .," to illustrate the contrasting case of nonliability, **[the Tanna] should teach a distinction** between liability and non-liability **in that very case** of a thief who *lifts* the purse, as follows: בַּמֶּה דְּבָרִים אֲמוּרִים — **When are these things said** (that the thief is liable for payment when he lifts the purse)? בִּמְהַלֵּךְ — **When he** then **walks** out with the purse into the public domain. אֲבָל זוֹרֵק פָּטוּר — **But** when **he** then **throws** it into the public domain, **he is exempt** from paying for the purse. — ? —

The Gemara answers:

מְגָרֵר וְיוֹצֵא אִיצְטְרִיכָא לֵיהּ — True, the Tanna could have made that distinction instead. **But he considered it** more **necessary** to teach that the thief is not liable for theft where **he was dragging it out.** For had the Tanna not taught that, סַלְקָא דַּעְתָּךְ אָמִינָא — **you might have thought to say** that the thief is liable for theft in that case because אֵין דֶּרֶךְ הוֹצָאָה בְּכָךְ — **this is not a normal way of transporting** a purse. Thus, he would not be liable for desecrating the Sabbath,[5] and as a result he *would* be liable to pay for the theft of the purse.[6] קָא מַשְׁמַע לָן — Therefore, **[the Tanna] informs us** that dragging a purse *is* a normal method of transport, and hence the thief is liable for desecrating the Sabbath and exempt from payment for the theft.[7]

The Gemara asks:

וּבְמַאי — **And with what** kind of purse are we dealing in this Baraisa, that the Tanna found it necessary to teach that dragging it is considered a normal method of transport? אִי בְּרַבְרְבֵי — **If** we are dealing **with large [purses]** that are too heavy to lift and carry, אוֹרְחֵיהּ הוּא — then **[dragging it] is** obviously **its normal method** of transport, and there would be no need for the Tanna to teach us this. אִי בְּזוּטְרֵי — And **if** we are dealing **with small [purses],** לָאו אוֹרְחֵיהּ הוּא — then **[dragging it] is** certainly ***not* its normal method** of transport, and the Tanna's ruling (that one who drags it outside into the public domain is liable for desecrating the Sabbath) would simply not be true![8] — ? —

The Gemara answers:

אֶלָּא בְּמִיצְעֵי — **Rather,** we must be dealing **with midsized [purses].**[9]

The Gemara asks further:

וּדְאַפְּקֵיהּ לְהֵיכָא — **And to where did he take it out?**[10] אִי

NOTES

1. For then his eventual liability for desecrating the Sabbath comes on account of the *akirah* he performed by initially lifting the purse (see 31a note 23), and his liability for theft and for desecration of the Sabbath are thus incurred simultaneously (*Rashi*).

2. The Tanna evidently wishes to draw a contrast between a case involving liability and one in which there is no liability. If it were possible to draw such a contrast within the first case itself, the Tanna would surely have done so, rather than introduce a different case. Since the Tanna *does* introduce a new case to illustrate nonliability, it is evident that the first case always involves liability.

[*Tosafos* (31a ד״ה אבל לכתף) point out that the Gemara did not really have to preface its question with the statement that the thief would be exempt if he stopped only to adjust his load. Even if the law were that stopping to adjust a load is a *hanachah* no different from stopping to rest, the question would remain: If in the first part of the Baraisa liability for theft exists only where the thief came to a halt before leaving the house (as the Gemara above asserts), then why did the Tanna have to introduce a completely new case (dragging) to illustrate nonliability? Let him illustrate the case of non-liability using the first case (lifting) but where the thief did *not* halt before leaving the house!]

3. In *Shabbos* 5b, Ben Azzai considers a person who takes, say, ten steps to have started and stopped ten times. Each time he places his foot upon the ground he is considered to have placed his body down and made a *hanachah,* and each time he lifts his foot he is considered to have lifted his body and made an *akirah.*

Accordingly, in this Baraisa's case, the thief's liability for desecrating the Sabbath is not on account of the *akirah* that he made when he lifted the purse, for that *akirah* was terminated by his very next step, which constituted a *hanachah* in the private domain. Rather, his act of transfer begins with the last step he takes before leaving the house with the purse, for that step is the *akirah* for which he is liable for desecrating the Sabbath. His liability for theft, however, occurred earlier, with his initial lifting of the purse (see *Rashi*).

4. For his lifting of the purse is both the act of theft and the *akirah* of the act of *transfer* for which he is liable for desecrating the Sabbath (see *Rashi*).

5. One is liable for performing a *melachah* on the Sabbath only if he performs it in the manner that it is normally performed. A *melachah* performed in an abnormal manner, though, is not Biblically prohibited (although it is still Rabbinically prohibited). See Schottenstein edition of Tractate *Shabbos,* General Introduction, Section II e.

6. Since there is no death penalty in this case to exempt him.

7. The Tanna considered teaching us this ruling more important than showing a distinction in the first case itself.

[The question arises as to why the Gemara did not similarly defend the first explanation proposed above (that the Baraisa refers to where the thief halted before walking out of the house with the purse). There too, the Gemara could apparently have said that rather than show a distinction in the first case itself, the Tanna preferred to teach us the novel ruling that dragging a purse is a normal mode of transport. See *Tosafos* ד״ה מגרר, who present two answers to this question.]

8. See above, note 5.

9. And the Tanna must teach us that dragging is considered a normal method of transporting such purses.

10. I.e. into what type of domain did he drag the purse, that the *kinyan* of theft and desecration of the Sabbath occur simultaneously?

פטור אדתני היה מגרר ויוצא מגרר ויוצא פטור נפלוג וניתני בדידה במה דברי' אמורים בעומד לפוש אבל לכתף פטור אלא הא מני א) בן עזאי היא דאמר מהלך כעומד דמי אבל זורק מאי פטור ניפלוג [וניתני] בדידה במה דברים אמורים במהלך אבל זורק פטור מגרר ויוצא איצטריכא ליה ס"ד אמינא אין דרך הוצאה בכך קמ"ל ובמאי אי ברברבי אורחיה הוא אי בזוטרי לאו אורחיה הוא אלא במיצעי ודאפקיה להיכא אי דאפקיה לרה"ר איסור שבת איכא איסור גניבה ליכא אי דאפקיה לרשות היחיד איסור גניבה איכא איסור שבת ליכא לא צריכא דאפקיה לצידי רשות הרבים וכמאן אי כר' אליעזר דאמר ב) צידי רה"ר כרה"ר דמו איסור שבת איכא איסור גניבה ליכא אי כרבנן דאמרי צידי רה"ר לאו כרה"ר דמו איסור גניבה איכא איסור שבת ליכא לעולם כר' אליעזר וכי אמר ר"א צידי רה"ר כרה"ר דמו הני מילי לענין חיובא דשבת דזימנין דדחקי רבים ועיילי להתם אבל לענין מיקנא קני מ"ט דהא לא שכיחי רבים רב אשי אמר כגון שצירף ידו למטה משלשה וקיבלו כדרבא דאמר רבא ג) ידו של אדם חשובה לו כארבעה על ארבעה רב אחא מתני הכי רבינא מתני לעולם דאפקיה לרה"ר וברה"ר נמי קנה ותרוייהו בדיוקא דהא מתני' קמיפלגי דתנן ד) היה מושכו ויוצא ומת ברשות בעלים פטור הגביהו או שהוציאו מרשות בעלים ומת חייב רבינא דייק מרישא רב אחא דייק מסיפא רבינא דייק מרישא היה מושכו ויוצא ומת ברשות בעלים פטור טעמא דמת ברשות בעלים ה) הא הוציאו מרשות בעלים ומת חייב רב אחא דייק מסיפא הגביהו או שהוציאו הוצאה דומיא דהגבהה מה הגבהה דאתי לרשותיה אף הוצאה נמי דאתי לרשותיה לרב אחא קשיא רישא לרבינא קשיא סיפא רישא לרב אחא לא קשיא כמה דלא אתי לרשותיה רשות בעלים קרינא ביה סיפא לרבינא לא קשיא הוצאה דומיא דהגבהה לא אמרינן: הבא על אחותו ועל אחות אביו כו': ורמינהו ו) אלו הן הלוקין הבא על אחותו ועל אחות אמו ועל אחות אשתו ועל אשת אחיו ועל אשת אחי אביו ועל הנדה וקיימא

רש"י

פטור. מתשלומין דאתי עליה חיוב שבת מחמת הגבהה ראשונה שבה נקנה לו הכיס ומיתה ותשלומין באין כאחד: ניפלוג בדידה. במגביה עצמו יכול לשנות בו חיוב ופטור: אלא. לא תוקמה כשעומד ואפ"ה חיוב שבת דעקירה לאו מחמת עקירה ראשונה דהגבהה אתיא ליה אלא בעקירת גופו של פסיעה אחרונה כשיוצא מן הבית ובן עזאי היא: דאמר. בפ"ק דשבת: מהלך כעומד דמי. ועקירת כל פסיעה הויא עקירה והנחת הרגל היא הנחה הלכך קניה משעת הגבהה וחיוב מיתה בפסיעה בתרייתא קא אתיא ליה: אבל זורק מאי. הגביהו וזרקו: פטור. מתשלומין דאתיא ליה חיוב שבת ע"י חיוב הגבהה דתו ליתא עקירה אחריתי: אין דרך הוצאה בכך. ואין כאן חיוב שבת: ובמאי. איצטריך לאשמועינן דדרך הוצאה בכך: אי ברברבי. כיס גדול שיש בו משוי להגביהו: אורחיה הוא. לגררו ופשיטא דהוצאה היא: לאו אורחיה הוא. ואמאי חייב משום שבת: איסור גניבה ליכא. דמשיכה בלא הגבהה קס"ד דלא קניא ברה"ר: לרשות היחיד. לרשותו שהיתה חצירו סמוכה לחצר הבעלים: צידי רה"ר. סמוך לבתים שנותנין להלן מן הבתים אבנים ומכשולין להרחיק חיכוך העגלות ומאותן חיפופי ולפנים קרי צידי רה"ר: פלוגתא דרבי אליעזר ורבנן בעירובין בפרק כל גגות: דהא לא שכיחי רבים. והוי ליה כסימטא דמיקנן בה משיכה: רב אשי אמר. מגרר ויוצא דקאמר פטור לעולם ברשות הרבים ודקשיא לך איסור גניבה ליכא: כגון שצירף ידו. השניה לפחות משלשה סמוך לקרקע ובידו אחת גיררה ונפלה לתוך חברתה וידו קניא ליה: כדרבא דאמר רבא ידו של אדם חשובה. לענין הנחת שבת כמקום ארבעה על ארבעה וכי היכי דלענין שבת חשוב מקום לענין מיקנא נמי חשוב מקום למיקני כאילו הגביהה למעלה משלשה ומיהו ברשות היחיד לא אגבהה דתיקני ליה מקמי דליתי חיוב שבת עליה וביאתה לרה"ר וקנייתה באין כאחד ולהכי משני כשצירף דלא תיהוי הגבהה ברשות היחיד כדקתני מגרר ויוצא: רב אחא מתני הכי. כדאמרן דמשיכה ברשות הרבים לא קני ומוקים לה כשצירף ידו וקיבלה לתוכה: היה מושכו. בגונב בהמה ברשות בעלים קאי בפרק מרובה: ומת. השור: ברשות הבעלים פטור. הגנב מלשלם כלום דלא קני להתחייב באונסין: הגביהו. אפי' ברשות הבעלים: הא הוציאו. כל היכא דאפקיה ואפי' לרה"ר: אלו הן הלוקין. אם התרו בהן: וקיימא לן דאין לוקה ומשלם. דנפקא לן לקמן מכדי רשעתו משום רשעה אחת אתה מחייבו ואי אתה מחייבו משום שתי רשעיות: מתני'

תוספות

מהלך כשעומד דמי. ומעביר ארבע אמות דחייב ברה"ר הלכתא גמירי לה כדאמרינן בהזורק (שבת דף צו:) ולא ילפינן מינה דהתם מקום חיובא הוא אבל בן עזאי מיירי במהלך מחנות לפלטיא דרך סטיו שהוא מקום פטור ובירושלמי פריך לבן עזאי היכי משכחת מעביר ד"א ברה"ר דמיחייב ומשני בקופץ ז): אבל זורק מאי פטור ליפלוג וליתני בדידה. משום הכי חשיב זורק בדידה טפי ממגרר משום דבמוליא וזורק בשיהס בא בהגבהה הקנין קודם שיבא חיוב הוצאה אבל במגרר ההוצאה והקנין באין כאחד: מגרר ויוצא איצטריך ליה. לעיל דפריך דליפלוג בין לפוש ובין לכתף לא בעי לשנויי הכי משום דלכתף פטור נראה לו חידוש טפי מחידוש דמגרר ז) [ועוד דהכא לא הוי לגמרי בדידה אבל לעיל דהוי ממש בדידה לא שייך לשנויי הכי]: אי דאפקיה לרה"ר איסור גניבה ליכא. אף על גב דאיכא למ"ד בפ"ק דב"מ (דף י. ושם) דד' אמות קונות לו לאדם אפילו ברה"ר ה"מ גבי מציאה דלא ליתו לאינצויי ובגט משום עיגונא אבל לגנב לא תקינו שיקנו לו ד' אמות: אלא במיצעי. תימה לר"י דבפרק הספינה (ב"ב דף פו. ושם) גבי דברים שדרכן להגביהן אין נקנין במשיכה אלא בהגבהה ופריך מהגונב כיס דבר הגבהה הוא ומשני במידי דבעי מיתנא משמע דאי הוה אמר דבר הגבהה נמי נקנה במשיכה הוה אתי ליה שפיר אפילו בזוטרי ואמאי הא על כרחך לא מצי איירי בזוטרי דא"כ היכי מיחייב לענין שבת בגרירה דאין דרך הוצאה בכך וי"ל דאפשר שיהא דרך הוצאה בכך אפילו בזוטרי כגון שמוליאו דרך מתחרת דדרכו בגרירה ואינו נקנה אלא בהגבהה אי נמי הוה מצי למימר ולטעמיך ולא פריך וכן דרך הש"ס בכמה מקומות: רב אשי אמר כגון שצירף ידו למטה מג' וקיבלה וכדרבא. פירש בקונטרס דקאי אמאי דפריך לעיל איסור גניבה ליכא והשתא משני דאיכא נמי איסור גניבה כדרבא וקשה לר"י חדא דמה ענין חשיבות מקום ד' דלענין שבת לקנין ועוד דאין צריך שום ראיה להביא דקניא ליה ידו דפשיטא דונתן בידה אמר רחמנא כדפרישית לעיל ועוד א) דאמאי לא מוקי אפילו כשצירף ידו למעלה מג' כגון שהאסקופה גבוהה ג' דליכא הגבהה ברה"י והוה מייתי מדרבא אקנין ואשבת ונראה כגירסת הספר שמצא ר"י בן רבינו מאיר בספרי אשכנז דגרס אי נמי כדרבא וכולה מילתא אשבת קאי כשצירף ידו למטה מג' דאע"ג דלא חשיבא לענין שבת הנחה אלא על גבי מקום ד' איכא הכא חיוב שבת כשצירף ידו למטה מג' דלמטה מג' לא בעינן מקום ד' דכלבוד דמי ב) וכמונחת אארעא דמיא אי נמי אפי' צירף ידו למעלה מג' וכדרבא דידו חשובה כד' על ד' ור"ת ל"ג דאמר רבא ידו של אדם אלא וכדרבא ותו לא ואתא לשנויי דמגרר ויוצא איצטריך ליה לאשמועינן דאגד יד לא שמיה אגד והא מייתי כדרבא דאמר בהמצניע (שבת דף צב.) דאגד יד לא שמיה אגד ומיירי כשהוא נשאר בפנים והוציא ידו אחת ובאחרת מגרר לתוכה ודוקא צירף למטה מג' דלמעלה משלשה שמיה אגד דבתר גופו גרירא [ולפי' קמא קשה דלשנויא קמא לית ליה דרבא וכולהו מתנייתא דשבת וכן ר' יוחנן (שבת ה.) אתו כרבא]: וברשות הרבים נמי קנה. והא דאמר בהמוכר את הספינה (ב"ב פד:) דאביי ורבא דאמרי תרוייהו דמשיכה לא קניא ברה"ר אומר ר"י דלא פליגי אדרבינא דהכא דהא דקאמר דקני היינו לענין להתחייב באונסין אבל אינו קונה שיהא שלו לגמרי וריב"א נראה לו דפליג דהא במרובה (ב"ק דף עט. ושם) גבי נתנה לבכורות בנו דקתני סיפא איכא נמי למידק כמו שמדקדק כאן והתם לענין משיכה דקנין איירי ללשון ראשון שפי' שם בקונט' ואפילו ללשון שני הא מוכח התם בגמ' (דף סה.) שאין לגנב להתחייב אלא במשיכה הראויה לקנין: ורמינהי אלו הן הלוקין הבא על אחותו. ארישא דמתניתין הוה מצי למיפרך דקתני הבא על הממזרת יש לה קנס והתם קתני דלקי עלה אלא נטר הכא עד הבא על אחותו למיפרך מרישא דמתניתין דהתם דחייבי לאוין שניין שם בתר חייבי כריתות והיה צריך להביא כל המשנה עד הבא על הממזרת:

עין משפט נר מצוה

יג א מיי' פ"ד מהל' מכירה הלכה ד טוש"ע ח"מ סימן קצח סעיף יד:

יד ב מיי' פי"א מהל' שבת הלכה טו:

טו ג מיי' פ"ג מהל' גניבה הלכה ב ופרק ב' טוש"ע ח"מ סימן שנא:

טז ד ה מיי' פ"ב מהל' גניבה הל' ט סמג עשין עא טוש"ע ח"מ סי' שמח סעיף ד:

יז ו מיי' פי"ט מהל' סנהדרין הלכה א:

תוספות רי"ד

ובמאי. פי' ובמאי איצטריך לאשמועינן דדרך הוצאה בכך בגדול שיש בו משוי להגביה אורחיה הוא לגוררו ופשיטא דהוצאה היא ואי בזוטרא לאו אורחיה הוא ואמאי חייב משום שבת. איסור גניבה ליכא דמשיכה בלא הגבהה לא קניא ברה"ר אלא במיצעי. פי' אם היה הכיס קטן שדרכו להוציא בהגבהה והוציאו בגרירה פטור לענין שבת דהוצאה כלאחר יד הוא. וגב לענין קני' נמי אמרינן בפ' המוכר את הספינה דברים שדרכן להגביהן אינן נקנים אלא בהגבהה לא במשיכה הלכך הא דתני היה מגרר ויוצא במידי דצריך פיתנא. ודאפקיה להיכא אי דאפקי' לרה"ר איסור שבת איכא איסור גניבה ליכא פי' אי דכשהיה [אינה] קונה ברה"ר ואי דאפקה לרה"י איסור גניבה איכא איסור שבת ליכא ר"א אמר כגון שצירף ידו למטה מג' וקיבלה. פי' מכי נפלה לתוך ידו איכא איסור גניבה שידו קונה לו ואיכא איסור שבת שכל פחות מג' כלבוד דמי ואילו נחה ברשות הרבים דמי פי' המורה: לעולם הא דקתני מגרר ויוצא פטור לר"א ורבינא דקשיא לך איסור גניבה ליכא איכא ודאי כגון שצירף ידו השנית לפחות מג' סמוך לקרקע ובידו האי גררה והפילה לתוך יד חברתה וידו של אדם קני' ליה כדרבא דאמר רבא ידו של אדם חשובה לו כד' על ד'. פי' לענין הנחת שבת כמו מקום ד' על ד' וכי היכי דלענין שבת חשיבא מקום לענין מיקנא נמי חשיב מקום לפיקני' כאילו הגביה למעלה מג' מיהו ברה"י לא אגביה דתיקני לי' מקמי דליתי חיוב שבת עלי' וביאתה לרה"ר וקנייתה באין כאחד ולהכי משני כשצירף דלא תהוי הגבהה ברשות היחיד דקתני היה [מגרר] ויוצא. א"נ כדרבא ב) דאמר ידו של אדם חשובה לו כד' על ד'. פי' ואע"פ שהיתה למעלה מג' יש בה איסור שבת דידו של אדם פי' לענין שבת בענין שישבה בגופו ע"ג מקום חשוב שיש בו ד' על ד' דידו חשובה כד' על ד': רב אחא מתני הכי פי' כדאמרי' המשיכה ברה"ר לא קניא ומוקי לה כשצירף ידו וקבלה לתוכה. רבינא מתני לעולם דאפקיה לרה"ר וברה"ר נמי קני. פי' המשיכה ברה"ר קונה.

ואע"ג דקיי"ל דכל היכא דפליגי רב אחא ורבינא הלכתא כרבינא. הכא הלכתא כר"א משום דקיימו כוותיה אביי ורבא בפרק המוכר את הספינה ואמרי שאין משיכה קונה ברה"ר. ותלמודא נמי מקשה ממילתיה וקיי"ל שאין התלמוד מקשה אלא מהלכה פסוקה: הבא על אחותו וכו'. ורמינהו אלו הן הלוקין הבא על אחותו וכו' וקיי"ל דאין לוקה ומשלם. פי' דנפקא לן מכדי רשעתו משום רשעה א' אתה מחייבו ולא משום ב' רשעיות. פי' המורה והא דאוקי מתני'

חשק שלמה על תוס' רי"ד א) מחיבת איסור גניבה ליכא עד ברה"ר שייך להלן. ב) גירסת רבינו א"נ כדרבא וכ"ה בתוס' בד"ה רב אשי בשם הריב"ס.

מסורת הש"ס

א) [שבת קנג: עירובין לח.], ב) שבת ו. עירובין לד., ג) שבת ה., ד) ב"ק עט., ה) מכות יג., ו) [ביאור כתבו תוס' שבת ה: ד"ה בשלמא], ז) מ"כ.

תוספות ישנים

א) [ור' אליהו פי' כגון שהאסקופה כרמלית ולהכי צריך שצירף ידו למטה מג' מגג האסקופה דאי בתוך ג' לראשה הוי כרמלית כמו אסקופה עצמה ולא מחייב. מ"י]. ב) [ורש"י פי' דלריך הגבהה הא דאמרי' בהמניח (דף כט:) כשהספינה בפחות מג' וקאמר דקני אף פי' התם בקונט' משום דהוי הפקר ואיכא למ"ד דאפי' הכונה בהפקר קני ושיתופי מבואות דאמר שצריך שיגביה טפח התם נמי בעירוב קפידא. מ"י].

גליון הש"ס

תוס' ד"ה רב אשי וכו' דקניא ליה ידו. עי' בב"ק כט ע"ב תוד"ה אלא אמר רב אשי:

ליקוטי רש"י

זוטרי. קטנים [שבת קנה.]. איסור גניבה ליכא. ברשות הרבים לאו מקום קנייה היא [שבת צא:]. לצידי רשות הרבים. סמוך לצדי רשות הרבים איכא חיפופי נועצין יתדות אבנים גדולות סמוך לכותל שלא יזיקוהו קרונות והסוס אויר שביניהם לכותל קרי צידי רשות הרבים [עירובין צד.]. לענין גניבה מיקנא קני ולענין שבת הוי רשות הרבים כרבי אליעזר [רשב"ם פו.]. כגון שצירף ידו למטה משלשה וקיבלו. ולכך ידו למטה משלשה וקבלה בידו דידו חשובה לו כארבעה על ארבעה והרי הוא לו כאלו נח וכי שאין כאן הגבהה והכי מוקים לה בכתובות [סנהדרין עב.]. ברה"ר סמוך לאסקופת הבית [רשב"ם ב"ב פה.]. ידו של אדם חשובה לו כד' על ד' וקנייה ליה אלא כולה לגבי רה"ר לגבי קנייה ויש כאן [איסור] שבת וגניבה באין כאחד וכאן כלאחד שלא הוסיף משום הגבהה היא אלא משיכה לתוך ידו שהרי ידו סמוכה בתוך ג' לקרקע [שם פו.]. היה. הגנב. מושכו ויוצא פטור מכלום (ס"א: מכפל). הגביהו. אפי' ברשות בעלים שהרי הגבהה קונה בכל מקום במסכת קדושין (דף כה:) [ב"ק עט.]. אלו הן הלוקין. אלו לאו דוקא דתנא ושייר דלוקין טובא אלא תנא חייבי כריתות לאשמועינן דיש מלקות בחייבי כריתות [מכות יג.].

וקרע שיראין של חבירו גופא אמר רב חסדא מודה רבי נחוניא בן הקנה בגונב חלבו של חבירו ואכלו שהוא חייב שכבר נתחייב בגנבה קודם שיבא לידי איסור חלב לימא פליגא דרבי אבין דאמר רבי אבין א) אהזורק חץ מתחילת ארבע לסוף ארבע וקרע שיראין בהליכתו פטור שעקירה צורך הנחה היא הכא נמי הגבהה צורך אכילה היא הכי השתא התם אי אפשר להנחה בלא עקירה הכא אפשר לאכילה בלא הגבהה דאי בעי ב) גחין ואכיל אי נמי התם אי בעי לאהדורה לא מצי מהדר לה הכא מצי מהדר לה מאי איכא בין האי לישנא להאי לישנא איכא בינייהו המעביר סכין ברה"ר וקרע שיראין בהליכתו להך לישנא דאמרת אי אפשר להנחה בלא עקירה הכא נמי אי אפשר להנחה בלא עקירה להך לישנא דאמרת לא מצי מהדר לה הכא מצי מהדר לה גופא אמר רבי אבין הזורק חץ מתחלת ארבע לסוף ארבע וקרע שיראין בהליכתו פטור שעקירה צורך הנחה היא מתיב רב ביבי בר אביי ג) בהגונב כיס בשבת חייב שכבר נתחייב בגניבה קודם שיבא לידי איסור סקילה גהיה מגרר ויוצא פטור שהרי איסור שבת וגניבה באין כאחד ואמאי הכא נמי לימא הגבהה צורך הוצאה היא הכא במאי עסקינן כגון שהגביהו על מנת להצניעו ונמלך עליו והוציאו וכי האי גוונא מי חייב והאמר רב שימון אמר רבי אמי אמר רבי יוחנן ד) דהמפנה חפצים מזוית לזוית ונמלך עליהם והוציאן פטור שלא היתה עקירה משעה ראשונה לכך לא תימא ע"מ להצניעו אלא אימא ע"מ להוציאו הכא במאי עסקינן ה) הכשעמד עמד למאי אי לכתף אורחיה הוא אלא בעומד לפוש אבל לכתף מאי פטור

רש"י

וקרע שיראים. בשעה שבולעה ואע"ג דמיתה לאו משום ממונא דניזק אתיא ליה מיפטר וסבירא ליה לרב אשי מיתה לזה ותשלומין לזה פטור: שעקירה צורך הנחה היא. הלכך אע"ג דחיוב ממון מקמי הנחה אתיא ליה פטור הואיל ובין עקירה והנחה אתיא ליה מיתה ותשלומין באין כאחד שעקירה צורך הנחה היא ומההיא שעתא אתחלה לה מלאכה: דאי בעי גחין. למטה מג' טפחים ואכיל ובציר מג' לאו הגבהה היא: לא מצי לאהדורה. משזרק את החץ הלכך משעת עקירה סופו לקרוע לו שיראין: הכא מצי מהדר ליה. הלכך לא אמרי' משעת הגבהה אתחלה לה אכילה: המעביר סכין. בידו בהליכה: הגונב כיס בשבת. הגביהו ברשות הבעלים והוציאו לרה"ר: חייב. בתשלומין אף על פי שנהרג: שכבר נתחייב בגניבה. לשלם דהגבהה קונה בכל מקום וקמה לה ברשותיה אף להתחייב באונסים: היה מגרר ויוצא. שלא הגביהו ברשות הבעלים ולא קנאו אלא בהוצאה מרשות הבעלים פטור שאיסור שבת כו': ואמאי. כי הגביהו ברשות הבעלים וקנאו אמאי חייב נימא משעת הגבהה אתחלה לה הוצאה: וכה"ג מי חייב. משום שבת: לכך. להוציאו: לא תימא בהגביהו ע"מ להצניעו אלא הגביהו ע"מ להוציאו. ודקשיא לך נימא הגבהה צורך הוצאה היא: הכא במאי עסקינן כשעמד. ועמידתו היא הנחה לעקירה ראשונה ואין חיוב שבת באה לו ע"י עקירת חפץ הראשונה אלא ע"י עקירת גופו שעוקר עצמו אחר העמידה על מנת להוציא ועקירת גופו כעקירת חפץ: אורחיה הוא. ואין עמידתו הנחה לבטל עקירה ראשונה ממלאכת שבת:

תוספות

והוא שהדליק את הגדיש בשבת פטור מפני שנידון בנפשו והיינו מיתה לזה משום שבת ותשלומין לזה משום גדיש אלא על כרחך חשיב מיתה ותשלומין לאחד הואיל ולא מתחייב מיתה בשביל אדם אלא לשמים וה"נ אכילת תרומה וקריעת שיראין הוי מיתה ותשלומין לאחד ור"י רצה ליישב פי' הקונט' דחשיב הכא מיתה לזה ותשלומין לזה לפי שהן ב' מעשים אכילת תרומה וקריעת שיראין וכן פלוני בא על בתו של פלוני הם ב' עדיות שהיו יכולין להעיד עליו בלא הבת ועל הבת בלא עליו פלוני בא על נערה המאורסה פלונית זינתה אבל מדליק גדיש הכל בא על מעשה אחד ולכך חשיב מיתה ותשלומין לאחד ואין נראה לרשב"א דהא אמר רב יוסף בפ"ק דסנהדרין (דף ט: ושם) הביא הבעל עדים שזינתה והביא האב עדים והזימום לעדי הבעל עדי הבעל נהרגים ואין משלמין ממון חזר והביא הבעל עדים והזימום לעדי האב עדי האב נהרגין ומשלמין ממון ממון לזה פירוש לבעל שרצו להפסידו כתובה ונפשות לעדים והתם על הזמה אחת בא להם הכל ונראה לר"ת דרבא דוקא גבי עדים זוממים אית ליה דממון לזה ונפשות לזה חייב משום דבעינן שתתקיים הזמה כלפי כל אחד ומיהו ממון ונפשות בחד גברא פטור כיון דמתקיים בו קצת הזמה אבל בעלמא מודה רבא דממון לזה ונפשות לזה פטור דהא גבי סמוך לו ועבד כפות לו דתנן פטור ומוקמינן בפרק כילד הרגל (ב"ק דף כב: ושם) בגדי דחד ועבדא דחד ועוד דרבא גופיה אית ליה בפרק בן סורר ומורה (סנהדרין דף עד.) דרודף ששבר כלים בין של נרדף בין של כל אדם פטור אע"ג דהוי מיתה לנרדף ותשלומין לבעל הכלים ומיהו התם גבי רודף רבה גרס כדמוכח בהגוזל בתרא (ב"ק דף קיז:) ובפ"ק דסנהדרין (דף י.) הוי רבא ועוד אומר ר"ת דע"כ לכ"ע מיתה לזה ותשלומין לזה פטור דהא קים ליה בדרבה מיניה דפטור נפקא לן מלא יהיה אסון וגו' והתם הוי מיתה לאשה ותשלומין לבעל שהולדות שלו ואומר ר"י דאינה ראיה דהתם כיון שהולדות הן בגוף האשה חשיב מיתה ותשלומין לאחד תדע דבפרק בן סורר ומורה (שם דף עד.) בעי לחייב כשאין אסון באשה אף ע"ג דניתן להצילו בנפשו דבמלות שבמיתה הכתוב מדבר משום דהוי מיתה לזה שרצה להורגו ותשלומין לבעל ואפי' הכי כשיש אסון פטור והיינו משום דחשיב מיתה ותשלומין לאחד לפי שהן בגוף האשה כדפרישית וריב"א אומר דבכל מקום מיתה לזה ותשלומין לזה חייב ועבד כפות לו ורודף שאני דניתן להציל לכל אדם וחייב מיתה לכל העולם [אף לבעל העבד ולבעל הכלים] ולהכי חשיב מיתה ותשלומין לאחד ואע"ג דמעיקרא בפרק בן סורר (ג"ז שם) חשיב רודף מיתה לזה ותשלומין לזה לפי המסקנא דקאמר אלא לא שנא חזר בו מאותה סברא וה"פ אלא לא שנא משום דהוי מיתה ותשלומין לאחד [והכא חשיב מיתה ותשלומין לאחד כמו במדליק גדיש]: **שעקירה** צורך הנחה היא. קשה דאמרינן במרובה (ב"ק דף ע:) גבי גנב ומכר בשבת דפטור כגון דאמר ליה זרוק גניבותיך לחצרי ותיקני לי חצרי גניבותיך ופריך מכי מטי לאויר חצירו קנה ומתחייב בנפשו משום שבת לא הוי עד שתנוח ומאי פריך והא עקירה צורך הנחה היא כדאמר הכא ולפר"ת אתי שפיר דפירש דאי אפשר לניסוך בלא הגבהה ואפ"ה קאמר רב מנסך ממש בהניזקין (גיטין דף נב: ושם) ולא קא מפטר משום דקים ליה בדרבה מיניה כדרבי ירמיה דמשעת הגבהה קונה ומתחייב בנפשו לא הוי עד שעת ניסוך והשתא רבי ירמיה לית ליה דהגבהה צורך ניסוך היא וה"ה דלית ליה דעקירה צורך הנחה היא ולא הוה מפליג בין מצי לאהדורי ללא מצי לאהדורי תדע ללישנא דאי אפשר להנחה בלא עקירה אמאי נקט רבי אבין זרק חץ לינקוט מעביר אלא ודאי כי הדדי נינהו ומאן דפליג אמעביר פליג נמי אזורק ואליבא דרבי ירמיה פריך במרובה (ב"ק דף ע: ושם) אבל אם אפשר לניסוך בלא הגבהה לא פליג רבי ירמיה אדרבי אבין ובהגוזל בתרא (שם דף קיז.) משמע קצת דרבי ירמיה פליג אדרבי אבין גבי חזרו לומר אף המנסך דקאמר התם מעיקרא סבור כדרבי אבין ולבסוף סבור כדרבי ירמיה [ומיהו יש לדחות דמעיקרא סבור דדמיא לדרבי אבין ולבסוף סבור דדמיא לדר' ירמיה]: **דאי** בעי גחין ואכיל. פי' בקונט' למטה מג' דלא הויא הגבהה וקשה לר"י דמה שייך הגבהה בדבר שהוא תופס בידו או בפיו דונתן בידה אמר רחמנא ואמרינן בגיטין (דף עח.) זרק לתוך קלתה מגורשת קשורה אע"פ שאינה תלויה אע"ג דמיירי ברשות הבעל ואפי' מאן דבעי התם תלויה אינו מצריך שתהא גבוה ג' אלא נראה לר"י א) דה"פ דאי בעי גחין ואכיל אם הוא בראש קנה יכול הוא לשחות ולתוחבה עד בית בליעתו אע"ג דבהך אכילה אינו עושה כן והויא הגבהה זו לצורך אכילה מ"מ הואיל ויכול להתחייב בלא הגבהה לאו צורך אכילה היא וה"ה דה"מ למימר דאפשר לאכילה בלא הגבהה כגון אם תחבה לו חבירו: **הכא** נמי נימא הגבהה צורך הוצאה היא. ללישנא דאי בעי לאהדורי לא מצי מיהדר א] לא פריך מידי אבל ללישנא דאי אפשר להנחה בלא עקירה פריך דהכא נמי אי אפשר להנחה בלא הגבהה אע"ג דאפשר בגרירה כך לי עקירה זו כמו עקירה אחרת דמ"מ האיסור מתחיל משעת הגבהה דאם היה אחר עושה עקירה לא היה מתחייב בהנחה נמצא עקירה גורמת החיוב ועד שעת הנחה מושך החיוב: **נימא** הגבהה צורך הוצאה היא. תימה לפר"ת דהגבהה קונה פחות משלשה טפחים ו) מאי פריך והא כיון דקנאה קודם התחלת העקירה דעקירה לא הויא עד שיגביה שלשה דלמטה משלשה הוי כלבוד כדאמרינן בהמוציא (שבת דף פ. ושם) העביר חצי גרוגרת דרך עליה חייב ואם כן דין הוא שיתחייב כמו לבן עזאי דאמר מהלך כעומד דמי דחייב לפי שקנאה קודם שהתחיל העקירה ואומר רשב"א דמשמע ליה בכל ענין גונב כיס אפילו מונח על גבי מקל שהוא גבוה שלשה טפחים שבא הקנין והעקירה בבת אחת: **שהגביהו** על מנת להצניעו ונמלך להוציאו. ואם תאמר וכיון דסלקא דעתיה השתא דמיחייב אהך הוצאה אם כן הדרא קושיא לדוכתין לצורך הוצאה היא ויש לומר דסלקא דעתין הא דנמלך והוציאו הוי עקירה שניה: **אבל** לכתף מאי פטור כו'. אפילו הוי לכתף חייב הוי מצי למיפרך ליפלוג בדידיה בין עמד ללא עמד כלל:

מסורת הש"ס

א) ב"ק קז., ב) [מנחות ע.], ג) ב"ב פ. סנהדרין עב. שבת לה: תוספתא דב"ק פ"ט, ד) שבת ה: עירובין כ: ע"ש, ה) [וע"ע תוס' עירובין עט: ד"ה צריך ותוס' קדושין כו. ד"ה אי נמי ותוס' ב"ק כט: ד"ה אלא].

גליון הש"ס

גמרא הגונב כיס בשבת. עיין ירושלמי ב"ק פ"ג הלכה ד:

הגהות מהר"ב רנשבורג

א] תוס' ד"ה הכא וכו' לא פריך מידי. ע' מ"ש בשם הרש"א דלכך לישנא נמי פריך ולדבריו נ"ל דרב ביבי בר אביי המותיב לית ליה איכא בינייהו דעביד הש"ס לעיל בסמוך. ועי' הרש"ש ושיטה מקובצת בשם הרמב"ן והרשב"א וקרובים דבריהם לדברי זה ברור ודו"ק:

ליקוטי רש"י

שיראין. של משי [מנחות לט:]. הזורק חץ. בשבת. שעקירה צורך הנחה. דכיון דבין עקירה להנחה קרע נמצא מעשה עקירה [קריעה] באין כאחד ולא אמרינן משעת [עקירה] [קריעה] חייב ממון ומתחייב בנפשו לא הוי עד שעת הנחת חץ [ב"ק קז.]. הגונב כיס בשבת חייב. בתשלומין ואע"פ שנדון בנפשו שכבר נתחייב בגניבה בשעה שהגביה הכיס בבית הבעלים [שבת צא.]. שהגביהו וקנאו בהגבהה חייב להחזיר ואע"ג שהוציאו אחר כך לרשות הרבים ונתחייב בהוצאתו מיתה [סנהדרין עב.]. בתשלומין ליכא למימר קם ליה בדרבה מיניה ליכא הכא שתי רשעיות ביחד [רשב"ם ב"ב פו.]. שכבר נתחייב בגניבה וכו'. ובשביל חיוב מיתה הבא עליו לאחר מכאן אינו נפטר מן התשלומין [סנהדרין שם]. משעת הגבהה דהגבהה בכל מקום קונה ואיסור שבת ליכא עד שעת הוצאה [רשב"ם ב"ב שם]. היה מגרר ויוצא. שלא קנאה בהגבהה אלא בהוצאה מבית הבעלים [שבת שם]. שלא הגביהו ולא קנאו בתוך הבית אלא כשיוצא לרשות הרבים קנאו בשנוי רשות שהוציאו מרשות הבעלים [סנהדרין שם]. בקרקע דהגבהה ליכא ולא קני ליה אלא בשינוי רשות שימשכנו לרשותו. פטור. מן התשלומין דקם ליה בדרבה מיניה וכתיב כדי רשעתו [דברים כה] משום רשעה אחת אתה מחייבו ואי אתה מחייבו משום שתי רשעיות. שהרי איסור שבת וגניבה באין כאחד. דבשעת הוצאה תוך קנייה ומתחייב בסקילה [רשב"ם ב"ב שם]. שלא היתה עקירה כו'. ליכא עקירה אלא עקירה ראשונה והיא לא היתה על מנת להוציא והנחה והתורה לא חייבה אלא מלאכת מחשבת וגמרינן ממשכן ובמשכן לא עשו מלאכתן אלא במחשבה אבל לא יודע שהוא שבת או כסבור שמלאכה זו מותרת [שבת ה:]. ובשבת מלאכת מחשבת אסרה תורה שנתכוין לכך אלא שנגע בשבת כסבור שהיום חול או מלאכה זו מותרת אבל כי לא נתכוין פטור מתעסק [עירובין כ:]. לכתף. לתקן משאו על כתפיו לאו עמידה היא. לפוש. לנוח הסיא הויא עמידה ועקירה דבתרה הוי עקירה [שבת שם].

עין משפט נר מצוה

י א מיי' פ"ג מהל' גניבה הלכה ב:

יא ב ג מיי' שם טוש"ע ח"מ סימן שנא:

יב ד ה מיי' פי"ג מהל' שבת הלכה יב:

תוספות ישנים

א) [וכן רוצה לומר הספר התם מתחיל האיסור משעת עקירה הכא אין האיסור מתחיל אלא משעת אכילה דאי בעי גחין ואכיל ליה בלא הגבהה אבל באם לא היה אפשר בלא הגבהה היה מתחיל נמי האיסור משעת הגבהה. מ"י].

תוספות רי"ד

א"ר אבין הזורק חץ מתחילת ד' לסוף ד' וקרע שיראין בהליכתו פטור שעקירה צורך הנחה היא. פי' ומההיא שעתא אתחלה לה מלאכה והלכך אע"ג דחיוב ממון מקמי הנחה אתיא ליה פטור הואיל א) וכן עקיר להנחה אתיא לה מיתה ותשלומין באין כאחד ולא תימא תשלומין קדמי למיתה: תניא הגונב כיס בשבת חייב. פי' חייב בתשלומין אע"פ שנהרג שכבר נתחייב בגניבה קודם שיבוא לידי איסור שבת פי' דמשעה דאגבהה קניא שהגבהה קונה בכ"מ אפילו ברה"ר. ופי' אף להתחייב באונסים מתחייב בנפשו לא הוי עד דמפיק ליה היה מגרר ויוצא פירוש שלא הגביהו ברשות הבעלים ולא קנאה אלא בהוצאה מרשות בעלים פטור. שהרי איסור שבת ואיסור גניבה באין כא'. בפ' בן סורר ומורה מוקי לה כגון דשדייה בנהרא שאין הכיס בעין שאם הוא בעין א"י לזכות בו אלא בעל הכיס בא ונוטלו. ע"ש בפסקי.

חשק שלמה על תוס' רי"ד

א) נראה דצ"ל הואיל דהא דקא עקיר להנחה אתיא לה הוי לה מיתה ותשלומין וכו'.

The Gemara answers:

הָכָא בְּמַאי עַסְקִינַן – **What are we dealing with here?** כְּגוֹן שֶׁהִגְבִּיהוּ עַל מְנָת לְהַצְנִיעוֹ – **With a case in which he lifted [the purse] with intent to put it away** inside the house, וְנִמְלַךְ עָלָיו וְהוֹצִיאוֹ – **and** then **he reconsidered and took it outside** into the public domain.[19]

The Gemara challenges this explanation of the Baraisa:

וְכִי הַאי גַּוְונָא מִי חַיָּיב – **But in such a case, is he** indeed **liable** for desecrating the Sabbath? וְהָאָמַר רַב סִימוֹן אָמַר רַבִּי אַמִי אָמַר רַבִּי יוֹחָנָן – **Why, Rav Simone said in the name of R' Ami, who said in the name of R' Yochanan:** הַמְפַנֶּה חֲפָצִים מִזָּוִית לְזָוִית – **If one was moving things from** one **corner to** another **corner** within a private domain without any intention of taking them outside, וְנִמְלַךְ עֲלֵיהֶם וְהוֹצִיאָן – **and** then, after picking them up, **reconsidered and took them outside** into the public domain,[20] פָּטוּר – **he is not liable** for desecrating the Sabbath. שֶׁלֹּא הָיְתָה עֲקִירָה מִשָּׁעָה רִאשׁוֹנָה לְכָךְ – **For the** ***akirah*** **was not originally** performed **for this** purpose.[21] Hence, our Baraisa, which states that he *is* liable for desecrating the Sabbath (albeit after the time he becomes liable for theft) cannot be discussing a case in which he lifted the purse with the intent to put it away inside rather than to take it outside. – ? –

The Gemara retracts and answers instead:

לֹא תֵּימָא עַל מְנָת לְהַצְנִיעוֹ – **Do not say that** he lifted the purse **with intent to put it away** inside the house (as was said before), for there would then be no liability for desecrating the Sabbath at all. אֶלָּא אֵימָא עַל מְנָת לְהוֹצִיאוֹ – **Rather say** that he indeed lifted the purse **with intent to take it outside** into the public domain, in which case the initial lifting of the purse would constitute an *akirah.* Nevertheless, he is not exempt from liability for the theft he committed with that lifting. הָכָא בְּמַאי עַסְקִינַן – For **what are we dealing with here?** כְּשֶׁעָמַד – With a case **where he stood still** momentarily, while yet inside the house, before continuing to carry the purse into the public domain.[22]

The Gemara elaborates on the circumstances of this case:

עָמַד לְמַאי – **For what** purpose **did he stop?** אִי לְכַתֵּף – **If** he stopped **to adjust** the load **on his shoulder,** אוֹרְחֵיהּ הוּא – **it is normal to do so!**[23] אֶלָּא בְּעוֹמֵד לָפוּשׁ – **Rather,** it must be that we are dealing with **when he stops to rest.**[24]

The Gemara challenges this explanation:

אֲבָל לְכַתֵּף – **But** according to this answer, if he stops only **to adjust** the load **on his shoulder,** מַאי – **what** would be the law?

NOTES

Ramban's second approach in ד״ה הא.]

[It is true that even the first version applies R' Avin's principle only when it is *impossible* to perform the *hanachah* without the *akirah* (see above, note 8). And here, in the case of the purse, it is *possible* to perform the *melachah* of *transferring* without "lifting" the purse, but by dragging it, as in the second case of the Baraisa. Nevertheless, the fact that it is impossible to perform the *melachah* without *some* sort of *akirah* – be it "lifting" *or* "dragging" – serves to make us consider the *melachah* as having begun with the *akirah,* regardless of which method of *akirah* is used (*Tosafos*).]

19. [Since the "lifting" of the purse was not done with the intent of transferring the purse to another domain, it does not constitute an *akirah;* see below, note 21.] The Gemara at this point is of the opinion that his subsequent reconsideration and taking out of the purse constitutes the necessary *akirah* for the act of *transfer* for which the Baraisa holds him liable (see *Tosafos* and *Tos. HaRosh*). Hence, although the *melachah* of *transferring* [with its exemption from monetary liability] begins with the *akirah,* it does not exempt him from liability for the theft, since liability for the theft was incurred with the "lifting," which was *prior* to the *akirah.*

20. After beginning to walk to the other corner, he changed his mind and carried the items out into the public domain (see *Rashi, Shabbos* 5b ד״ה היה טעון; see also *She'eilos U'Teshuvos Nefesh Chayah* §6 and 7).

21. One is not Biblically liable for any *melachah* on the Sabbath unless all its essential components were performed for purposes of the *melachah.* This is one of the aspects of the Sabbath principle that מְלֶאכֶת מַחֲשֶׁבֶת אָסְרָה תּוֹרָה, *the Torah prohibited only calculated labor.* Since lifting the object (i.e the *akirah*) is an essential component of the *melachah* of *transferring,* no Biblical liability is incurred unless the object was lifted with the intention of carrying it to the other domain. Where the person lifted the object intending merely to carry it within his own domain (even if he changed his mind after beginning to walk and transferred the object to the other domain), he is not liable, for he did not have the requisite intent at the time of the *akirah* (see *Rashi* to *Shabbos* ibid. ד״ה אינו חייב עד שיעמוד).

[We see from R' Yochanan's ruling absolving the person from liability that where the original *akirah* was done without intent to transfer, the subsequent reconsideration to transfer does *not* constitute a new *akirah,* unlike our assumption above – see note 19.]

22. When one comes to a halt, any object that he is carrying is considered to be in a state of *hanachah* even though it has not been set down on the ground. Similarly, when he begins to walk again, he in effect performs an *akirah* to the object he is carrying, even though it was in his hand the whole time (see *Shabbos* 3b). In the present case, then, the thief's coming to a halt inside the house after lifting the purse constitutes the *hanachah* for (and termination of) that original *akirah.* His beginning to walk again (with the intent to carry the purse outside) constitutes a new *akirah* (*Rashi*), and it is this new *akirah* that begins the act of transfer for which he is liable for desecrating the Sabbath. Thus, he is not exempt for paying for his theft. For the theft was committed with his initial lifting of the purse, whereas his act of Sabbath desecration did not begin until later, when he resumed walking after he had stopped.

23. In the course of transporting a load, it is normal to stop in order to adjust it. Hence, one who stops for that purpose is still considered to be in transit, and his stopping does not constitute a *hanachah.* Accordingly, if the thief lifted the purse with the intent of transferring it into the public domain, and then stopped to adjust his load, his stopping would not terminate the original *akirah* of lifting the purse (*Rashi*). His act of transfer, then, *would* begin with the original lifting of the purse, and he would be exempt from liability for the theft committed with that lifting.

24. In that case, his original *akirah* is terminated. And his resumption of walking constitutes a new *akirah,* which begins his act of transfer.

וקרע שיראין של חבירו גופא אמר רב חסדא מודה רבי נחוניא בן הקנה בגונב חלבו של חבירו ואכלו שהוא חייב שכבר נתחייב בגנבה קודם שיבא לידי איסור חלב לימא פליגא דרבי אבין דאמר רבי אבין [א] הזורק חץ מתחילת ארבע לסוף ארבע וקרע שיראין בהליכתו פטור שעקירה צורך הנחה היא הכא נמי הגבהה צורך אכילה היא הכי השתא התם אי אפשר להנחה בלא עקירה הכא אפשר לאכילה בלא הגבהה דאי בעי [ג] גחין ואכיל אי נמי התם אי בעי לאהדורה לא מצי מהדר לה הכא מצי מהדר לה מאי איכא בין האי לישנא להאי לישנא איכא בינייהו המעביר סכין ברה"ר וקרע שיראין בהליכתו להך לישנא דאמרת אי אפשר להנחה בלא עקירה הכא נמי אי אפשר להנחה בלא עקירה להך לישנא דאמרת לא מצי מהדר לה הכא מצי מהדר לה גופא אמר רבי אבין הזורק חץ מתחלת ארבע לסוף ארבע וקרע שיראין בהליכתו פטור שעקירה צורך הנחה היא מתיב רב ביבי בר אביי [ב] [ב] הגונב כיס בשבת חייב שכבר נתחייב בגניבה קודם שיבא לידי איסור סקילה [ג] היה מגרר ויוצא פטור שהרי איסור שבת וגניבה באין כאחד ואמאי הכא נמי לימא הגבהה צורך הוצאה היא הכא במאי עסקינן כגון שהגביהו על מנת להצניעו ונמלך עליו והוציאו וכי האי גוונא מי חייב והאמר רב שמעון אמר רבי אמי אמר רבי יוחנן [ז] [ד] המפנה חפצים מזוית לזוית ונמלך עליהם והוציאן פטור שלא היתה עקירה משעה ראשונה לכך לא תימא ע"מ להצניעו אלא אימא ע"מ להוציאו הכא במאי עסקינן [ה] כשעמד עמד למאי אי לכתף אורחיה הוא אלא בעומד לפוש אבל לכתף מאי פטור

רש"י

וקרע שיראים. בשעה שבולעה ואע"ג דמיתה לאו משום ממונא דניזק אתיא ליה מיפטר וסבירא ליה לרבא אשי מיתה לזה ותשלומין לזה פטור: **שעקירה צורך הנחה היא.** הלכך אע"ג דחיוב ממון מקמי הנחה אתיא ליה פטור הואיל ובין עקירה והנחה אתיא ליה מיתה ותשלומין באין כאחד שעקירה לורך הנחה היא ומההיא שעתא אתחלה לה מלאכה: **דאי בעי גחין.** למטה מג' טפחים ואכיל ובליר מג' לאו הגבהה היא: **לא מצי לאהדורה.** משזרק את החץ הלכך משעת עקירה סופו לקרוע לו שיראין: **הכא מצי מהדר ליה.** הלכך לא אמרי' משעת הגבהה אתחלה לה אכילה: **המעביר סכין.** בידו בהליכה: **הגונב כיס בשבת.** הגביהו ברשות הבעלים והוליאו לרה"ר: **חייב.** בתשלומין אף על פי שנהרג: **שכבר נתחייב בגניבה.** לשלם דהגבהה קונה בכל מקום וקמה לה ברשותיה אף להתחייב באונסים: **היה מגרר ויוצא.** שלא הגביהו ברשות הבעלים ולא קנאו אלא בהוצאה מרשות הבעלים פטור שאיסור שבת כו': **ואמאי.** כי הגביהו ברשות הבעלים וקנאו אמאי חייב נימא משעת הגבהה אתחלה לה הוצאה: **וכה"ג מי חייב.** משום שבת: **לכך.** להוציאו: **לא תימא בהגביהו ע"מ להצניעו אלא הגביהו ע"מ להוציאו.** ודקשיא לך נימא הגבהה צורך הוצאה היא: **הכא במאי עסקינן כשעמד.** ועמידתו היא הנחה לעקירה ראשונה ואין חיוב שבת בזה לו ע"י עקירת חפץ הראשונה אלא ע"י עקירת גופו שעוקר עלמו אחר העמידה על מנת להוליא ועקירת גופו כעקירת חפץ. ואין עמידתו הנחה אורחיה הוא. ולבטל עקירה ראשונה ממלאכת שבת: **פטור**

תוספות

והוא שהדליק את הגדיש בשבת פטור מפני שנידון בנפשו והיינו מיתה לזה משום שבת ותשלומין לזה משום גדיש אלא על כרחך חשיב מיתה ותשלומין לאחד הואיל ולא מתחייב מיתה בשביל אדם אלא לשמים וה"נ אכילת תרומה וקריעת שיראין הוי מיתה ותשלומין לאחד ור"י רלה ליישב פי' הקונט' דחשיב הכא מיתה לזה ותשלומין לזה לפי שהן ב' מעשים אכילת תרומה וקריעת שיראין וכן פלוני בא על בתו של פלוני הם ב' עדיות שהיו יכולין להעיד עליו בלא הבת ועל הבת בלא עליו פלוני בא על נערה המאורסה פלונית וזינתה אבל מדליק גדיש הכל בא על מעשה אחד ולכך חשיב מיתה ותשלומין לאחד ואין נראה לרשב"א דהא אמר רב יוסף בפ"ק דסנהדרין (דף ט: ושם) הביא הבעל עדים שזינתה והביא האב עדים והזימום לעדי הבעל נהרגים ואין משלמין ממון חזר והביא הבעל עדים והזימום לעדי האב עדי האב נהרגין ומשלמין ממון ממון לזה פירוש לבעל שרצו להפסידו כתובה ונפשות לעדים והתם על הזמה אחת בא להם הכל ונראה לר"ת דרבא דוקא גבי עדים זוממים אית ליה דממון לזה ונפשות לזה חייב משום דבעינן שתתקיים הזמה כלפי כל אחד ומיהו ממון ונפשות בחד גברא פטור כיון דמתקיים בו קלת הזמה אבל בעלמא מודה רבא דממון לזה ונפשות לזה פטור דהא גדי סמוך לו ועבד כפות לו דתנן פטור ומוקמינן בפרק כילד הרגל (ב"ק דף כב: ושם) בגדי דחד ועבדא דחד ועוד דרבא גופיה אית ליה בפרק בן סורר ומורה (סנהדרין דף עד.) דרודף ששבר כלים בין של נרדף בין של כל אדם פטור אע"ג דהוי מיתה לנרדף ותשלומין לבעל הכלים ומיהו התם גבי רודף רבה גרס כדמוכח בהגוזל בתרא (ב"ק דף קיז:) ובפ"ק דסנהדרין (דף י.) הוי רבא ועוד אומר ר"ת דע"כ לכ"ע מיתה לזה ותשלומין לזה פטור דהא קים ליה בדרבה מיניה דפטור נפקא לן מלא יהיה אסון וגו' והתם הוי מיתה לאשה ותשלומין לבעל שהולדות שלו ואומר ר"י דאינה ראיה דהתם כיון שהולדות הן בגוף האשה חשיב מיתה ותשלומין לאחד תדע דבפרק בן סורר ומורה (שם דף עד.) בעי לחייב כשאין אסון באשה אף ע"ג דניתן להצילו בנפשו דמלות שבמיתה הכתוב מדבר משום דהוי מיתה לזה שרצה להורגו ותשלומין לבעל ואפי' הכי כשיש אסון פטור והיינו משום דחשיב מיתה ותשלומין לאחד לפי שהן בגוף האשה כדפרישית וריב"א אומר דבכל מקום מיתה לזה ותשלומין לזה חייב ועבד כפות לו ורודף שאני דניתן להציל לכל אדם וחייב מיתה לכל העולם [אף לבעל העבד ולבעל הכלים] ולהכי חשיב מיתה ותשלומין לאחד ואע"ג דמעיקרא בפרק בן סורר (ג"ז שם) חשיב רודף מיתה לזה ותשלומין לזה לפי המסקנא דקאמר אלא לא שנא חזר בו מאותה סברא וה"פ אלא לא שנא משום דהוי מיתה ותשלומין לאחד [והכא חשיב מיתה ותשלומין לאחד כמו במדליק גדיש]: **שעקירה** צורך הנחה היא. קשה דאמרינן במרובה (ב"ק דף ע:) גבי גנב ומכר בשבת דפטור כגון דאמר ליה זרוק גניבותיך לחצרי ותיקני לי חצירי גניבותיך ופריך מכי מטי לאויר חצירו קנה ומתחייב בנפשו משום שבת לא הוי עד שתנוח ומאי פריך והא עקירה צורך הנחה היא כדאמר הכא ולפר"ת אתי שפיר דפירש דאי אפשר לניסוך בלא הגבהה ואפ"ה קאמר רב מנסך ממש בהניזקין (גיטין דף נב: ושם) ולא קא מפטר משום דקים ליה בדרבה מיניה כדרבי ירמיה דמשעת הגבהה קונה ומתחייב בנפשו לא הוי עד שעת ניסוך והשתא רבי ירמיה לית ליה דהגבהה צורך ניסוך היא וה"ה דלית ליה דעקירה צורך הנחה היא ולא הוה מפליג בין מצי לאהדורי ללא מצי לאהדורי תדע ללישנא דאי אפשר להנחה בלא עקירה אמאי נקט רבי אבין זרק חץ לינקוט מעביר אלא ודאי כי הדדי נינהו ומאן דפליג אמעביר פליג נמי אזורק ואליבא דרבי ירמיה פריך במרובה (ב"ק דף ע: ושם) אבל אם אפשר לניסוך בלא הגבהה לא פליג רבי ירמיה אדרבי אבין ובהגוזל בתרא (שם דף קיז.) משמע קצת דרבי ירמיה פליג אדרבי אבין גבי חזרו לומר אף המנסך דקאמר התם מעיקרא סבור כדרבי אבין ולבסוף סבור כדרבי ירמיה [ומיהו יש לדחות דמעיקרא סבור דדמיא לדרבי אבין ולבסוף סבור דדמיא לדר' ירמיה]: **דאי** בעי גחין ואכיל. פי' בקונט' למטה מג' דלא הויא הגבהה וקשה לר"י דמה שייך הגבהה בדבר שהוא תופס בידו או בפיו דונתן בידה אמר רחמנא ואמרינן בגיטין (דף עח.) זרק לתוך קלתה מגורשת קשורה אע"פ שאינה תלויה אע"ג דמיירי ברשות הבעל ואפי' מאן דבעי התם תלויה אינו מצריך שתהא גבוה ג' אלא נראה לר"י א) דה"פ דאי בעי גחין ואכיל אם הוא ברא קנה יכול הוא לשחות ולתוחבה עד בית בליעתו אע"ג דבהך אכילה אינו עושה כן והויא הגבהה זו לצורך אכילה מ"מ הואיל ויכול להתחייב בלא הגבהה לאו צורך אכילה היא וה"ה דה"מ למימר דאפשר לאכילה בלא הגבהה כגון אם תחבה לו חבירו: **הכא** נמי נימא הגבהה צורך הוצאה היא. ללישנא דאי בעי לאהדורי לא מצי מיהדר א) לא פריך מידי אבל ללישנא דאי אפשר להנחה בלא עקירה פריך דהכא נמי אי אפשר להנחה בלא הגבהה אע"ג דאפשר בגרירה כך לי עקירה זו כמו עקירה אחרת דמ"מ האיסור מתחיל משעת הגבהה דאם היה אחר עושה עקירה לא היה מתחייב בהנחה נמלא עקירה גורמת החיוב ועד שעת הנחה מושך החיוב: **נימא** הגבהה צורך הוצאה היא. תימה לפר"ת דהגבהה קונה פחות משלשה טפחים ה) מאי פריך והא כיון דקנאה קודם התחלת העקירה דעקירה לא הויא עד שיגביה שלשה דלמטה משלשה הוי כלבוד כדאמרינן בהמוליא (שבת דף פ. ושם) העביר תאי גרוגרת דרך עליה חייב ואם כן דין הוא שיתחייב כמו לבן עזאי דאמר מהלך כעומד דמי דחייב לפי שקנאה קודם שהתחיל העקירה ואומר רשב"א דמשמע ליה בכל ענין גונב כיס אפילו מונח על גבי מקל שהוא גבוה שלשה טפחים שבא הקנין והעקירה בבת אחת: **שהגביהו** על מנת להצניעו ונמלך להוציאו. ואם תאמר וכיון דסלקא דעתיה השתא דמיחייב אהך הוצאה אם כן הדרא קושיא לדוכתין דלורך הוצאה היא ויש לומר דסלקא דעתין הא דנמלך והוציאו הוי עקירה שניה: **אבל** לכתף מאי פטור כו'. אפילו הוי לכתף חייב הוי מצי למיפרך דליפלוג בדידיה בין עמד ללא עמד כלל:

עין משפט נר מצוה

י א מיי' פ"ג מהל' גניבה הלכה ב:
יא ב ג מיי' שם טוש"ע ח"מ סימן שנא:
יב ד ה מיי' פי"ג מהל' שבת הלכה יב:

תוספות ישנים

א) [וכן רוצה לומר הספר התם מתחיל האיסור משעת עקירה הכא אין האיסור מתחיל אלא משעת אכילה דאי בעי גחין ואכיל ליה בלא הגבהה אבל באם לא היה אפשר בלא הגבהה היה מתחיל נמי האיסור משעת הגבהה. ת"י]:

תוספות רי"ד

א"ר אבין הזורק חץ מתחילת ד' לסוף ד' וקרע שיראין בהליכתו פטור שעקירה צורך הנחה היא. פי' ומההיא שעתא אתחלה לה מלאכה והלכך אע"ג דחיוב ממון מקמי הנחה אתיא ליה פטור הואיל א) וכן עקיר להנחה אתיא לה מיתה ותשלומין באין כאחד ולא תימא תשלומין קדמי למיתה: **תניא** הגונב כיס בשבת חייב. פי' חייב בתשלומין אע"פ שנהרג שכבר נתחייב בגניבה קודם שיבוא לידי איסור שבת פי' דמשעה דאגבהה קניא שהגבהה קונה בכ"מ אפילו ברה"ר. ופי' אף להתחייב באונסים מתחייב בנפשו לא הוי עד דמפיק ליה היה מגרר ויוצא פירוש שלא הגביהו ברשות הבעלים ולא קנאה אלא בהוצאה מרשות בעלים פטור. שהרי איסור שבת ואיסור גניבה באין כא'. בפ' בן סורר ומורה מוקי לה כגון דשדייה בנהרא שאין הכיס בעין שאם הוא בעין א"י לזכות בו אלא בעל הכיס בא ונוטלו. ע"ש בפסקי:

חשק שלמה על תוס' רי"ד

א) נראה דצ"ל הואיל דהא דקא עקיר להנחה אתיא לה הוי לה מיתה ותשלומין וכו'.

מסורת הש"ס

א) ב"ק קיז. ג) [מנחות ע.], ג) ב"ב פו. סנהדרין עב. שבת צא: תוספתא דב"ק פ"ט, ז) שבת ה. עירובין כ: ע"ש, ה) [וע"ע תוס' עירובין כ. ד"ה לריך ותוס' קדושין כו. ד"ה אי נמי ותוס' ב"ק כט: ד"ה אלא].

גליון הש"ס

גמרא הגונב כיס בשבת. עיין ירושלמי ב"ק פ"ג הלכה ד:

הגהות מהר"ב רנשבורג

א] תוס' ד"ה הכא וכו' לא פריך מידי. עי' פ"י בשם הרא"ש דלהך לישנא נמי פריך ולדבריו צ"ל דרב ביבי בר אביי המותיב לית ליה אלא כלישנא דעביד הש"ס לעיל בסמוך. וע"ש הרא"ש ושיטה מקובצת בשם הרמב"ן והרא"ה וקרובים דבריהם לדברי הרב כרור ודו"ק:

ליקוטי רש"י

שיראין. של משי [מנחות לט:]. **הזורק חץ.** בשבת. **שעקירה צורך הנחה.** דכיון דבין עקירה להנחה קרע נמלא מעשה שבת ומעשה [עקירה] [קריעה] באין כאחד ולא אמרינן משעת (עקירה) [קריעה] חייב ממון ומתחייב בנפשו לא הוי עד שעת הנחת חץ [ב"ק קיז.]. **הגונב כיס בשבת חייב.** בתשלומין ואע"פ שנידון בנפשו שכבר נתחייב בגניבה שכבר קנאו בהגבהה מבית הבעלים [שבת צא.]. שהגביהו וקנאו בהגבהה חייב לשלם ואע"ג שהוציאו אחר כך לרשות הרבים ונתחייב בהוצאתו מיתה [סנהדרין עב.]. בתשלומין דליכא למימר קם ליה בדרבה מיניה דהכא שתי רשעיות ביחד [רשב"ם ב"ב פו.]. **שכבר נתחייב בגניבה וכו'.** בשביל חיוב מיתה הבא עליו לאחר מכאן אינו נפטר מן התשלומין [סנהדרין שם]. משעת הגבהה דהגבהה בכל מקום קונה ואיסור שבת ליכא עד שעת הוצאה [רשב"ם ב"ב שם]. **היה מגרר ויוצא.** שלא הגביהו אלא גררו בהוצאה מבית הבעלים [שבת שם]. שלא הגביהו ולא קנאו בתוך הבית אבל כשיוצא לרשות הרבים קנאו בשינוי רשות כשהוציאו מרשות הבעלים [סנהדרין שם]. בקרקע דהגבהה ליכא ולא קני ליה אלא בשינוי רשות שמשכהו לרשותו. **פטור.** מן התשלומין דקם ליה בדרבה מיניה וכתיב כדי רשעתו [דברים כה] משום רשעה אחת אתה מחייבו ואי אתה מחייבו משום שתי רשעיות. **שהרי איסור שבת וגניבה באין כאחד.** דבשעת הוצאה מתוך קנייה ומתחייב בסקילה [רשב"ם ב"ב שם]. **שלא היתה עקירה כו'.** ליכא עקירה ראשונה והיא לא היתה על מנת לאפוקי לא מיחייב אלא מלאכת מחשבת אסרה תורה וגמרינן ממשכן שיתכוין לעשות המלאכה אבל כי לא יודע שהוא שבת או כסבור שמלאכה זו מותרת [שבת ה:], ובשבת מלאכת מחשבת אסרה תורה נתכוין לכך אלא שגג בשבת כסבור שהיום חול או מלאכה זו מותרת אבל כי לא נתכוין פטור מתעסק [עירובין כ:]. **לכתף.** לתקן משאו על כתיפו לאו עמידה היא. **לפוש.** לנוח ההיא הויא עמידה ועקירה דבתרה הוי עקירה [שבת שם].

The Gemara analyzes the difference between these two versions:

מַאי אִיכָּא בֵּין הַאי לִישָּׁנָא לְהַאי לִישָּׁנָא – **What is** the practical difference **between this version and that version?**

The Gemara answers:

אִיכָּא בֵּינַיְיהוּ – **There is** a practical difference **between them** in the case of הַמַּעֲבִיר סַכִּין בִּרְשׁוּת הָרַבִּים וְקָרַע שִׁירָאִין בַּהֲלִיכָתוֹ – **one who transports a knife** by carrying it in his hand four *amos* **in the public domain and tears** someone else's **silks as he moves** with the knife. לְהָךְ לִישָּׁנָא דְּאָמְרַתְּ אִי אֶפְשָׁר לְהַנָּחָה בְּלֹא עֲקִירָה – **According to this version** in **which you said** that the reason he is exempt from paying for the silks torn by the arrow is that **it is impossible to** have **a** ***hanachah*** **without an** ***akirah,*** הָכָא נַמִּי – **here too,** he is exempt from paying for the silks torn by the knife, אִי אֶפְשָׁר לְהַנָּחָה בְּלֹא עֲקִירָה – because **it is impossible to** have **a** ***hanachah*** **without an** ***akirah.***[11] לְהָךְ לִישָּׁנָא דְּאָמְרַתְּ לֹא מָצֵי מַהֲדַר לָהּ – But **according to this version** in **which you said** that the reason he is exempt from paying for the silks torn by the arrow is that **he cannot draw back [the arrow]** after it was shot, הָכָא מָצֵי מַהֲדַר לָהּ – **here,** in the case of the knife, he would have to pay for the silks, because **he can draw back [the knife].**[12]

The Gemara focuses on R' Avin's statement:

גּוּפָא – **The text itself** stated: אָמַר רַבִּי אָבִין – **R' Avin said:** הַזּוֹרֵק חֵץ מִתְּחִלַּת אַרְבַּע לְסוֹף אַרְבַּע – **If one shoots an arrow** in the public domain **from the beginning of** a **four-*amah*** stretch **to the end of** the **four-*amah*** stretch וְקָרַע שִׁירָאִין בַּהֲלִיכָתוֹ – **and the [arrow] tears** someone else's **silks as it travels,** פָּטוּר – **he is exempt** from paying for the silks, שֶׁעֲקִירָה צוֹרֶךְ הַנָּחָה הִיא – **because** the ***akirah*** of the arrow **is a prerequisite of** its ***hanachah.***

The Gemara presents a challenge:

מַתְקִיף רַב בִּיבִי בַּר אַבַּיֵּי – **Rav Bivi bar Abaye challenged** R' Avin's ruling from the following Baraisa: הַגּוֹנֵב כִּיס בְּשַׁבָּת – ONE WHO STEALS A PURSE ON THE SABBATH from someone's house and then carries it into a public domain[13] חַיָּיב – IS LIABLE to pay for the stolen purse, even though he is also liable to the death penalty for desecrating the Sabbath.[14] שֶׁכְּבָר נִתְחַיֵּיב בִּגְנֵיבָה – FOR HE HAS ALREADY BECOME LIABLE FOR committing THEFT[15] קוֹדֶם שֶׁיָּבֹא לִידֵי אִיסוּר סְקִילָה – BEFORE HE COMES TO THE point of transgressing THE PROHIBITION that carries the penalty OF STONING (i.e. Sabbath desecration).[16] הָיָה מְגָרֵר וְיוֹצֵא מְגָרֵר וְיוֹצֵא – If, however, HE WAS DRAGGING it OUT, DRAGGING it OUT, i.e. he did not lift the purse in the owner's house, but rather dragged the purse from the house into the street, פָּטוּר – HE IS EXEMPT from liability for his theft, שֶׁהֲרֵי אִיסוּר שַׁבָּת וּגְנֵיבָה בָּאִין כְּאֶחָד – FOR INDEED in this case the transgression of THE SABBATH PROHIBITION AND THE THEFT OCCUR SIMULTANEOUSLY.[17]

Rav Bivi concludes his challenge:

וְאַמַּאי – **But why,** in the Baraisa's first case, where he first lifts up the purse and then takes it out, is he liable to payment? Granted that the liability for theft is incurred when he picks up the purse, prior to his liability for desecrating the Sabbath (which is incurred only after he takes the purse outside), nevertheless, הָכָא נַמִּי לֵימָא הַגְבָּהָה צוֹרֶךְ הוֹצָאָה הִיא – **here too, let us say** that the **lifting** of the purse **is a prerequisite of** the act of **transfer!**[18] – ? –

NOTES

rather that at the time of the release, *the hanachah of the arrow* is inevitable. For once the *hanachah* is inevitable, then the *melachah* has already begun, and there can be no liability for the tearing of the silks that occurs in the course of the *melachah's* completion! (see *Maharam Schif* and *Rashash*). Perhaps *Rashi* understands the innovation of this second version to be that the mere occurrence of monetary liability during the commission of an act that *results* in the death penalty is not sufficient to exempt the person from monetary liability because of *he stands liable to the greater penalty.* Rather, the monetary liability must occur at the time the person *becomes liable* to the death penalty. Hence, the one who shoots the arrow is exempt from paying for the silks because he becomes liable to the death penalty upon his release of the arrow (at which point the completion of the *melachah* is inevitable) and that is the very moment at which he would incur liability for the silks as well because their tearing, too, is inevitable. (See *Meiri. Maharam Schif* suggests this as a possible way of explaining *Rashi,* but he concludes that it does not seem that *Rashi* meant this. See *Shitah Mekubetzes* ד״ה אי נמי התם אי בעי לאהדורי וכו׳ for a different way of explaining *Rashi.* See also the explanation of *Rashi* proposed by *R' Aharon Kotler,* cited in the *Ginzei HaOhel* section of *Ohel Avraham* to *Kesubos.*)]

11. True, the death penalty is not incurred until the knife comes to rest, which is after the liability for tearing the silks occurs. Nevertheless, he is exempt from paying for the silks, since he tore them during the commission of the *melachah* for which he eventually incurs the death penalty (see above, note 5).

12. [According to the explanation suggested in note 10, the meaning is as follows: Since he can draw back the knife at any time, the *melachah* and the tearing of the silks are not inevitable from the time of the *akirah.* Hence, liability for the silks occurs when they are torn, and the death penalty occurs later, with the *hanachah.* And his later liability to the death penalty cannot exempt him from his earlier incurrence of monetary liability.]

13. I.e. he lifted the purse while he was in the owner's house and then carried it out into the public domain [and set it down] (*Rashi*).

14. For *transferring* an object from a private domain (the house) into a public domain (the street), making an *akirah* in the one domain and a *hanachah* in the other (see above, note 2).

15. By "lifting" the purse. For *hagbahah* [lifting] constitutes a *kinyan* [act of acquisition] in all places [even in the domain of the original owner]. Hence, as soon as the thief "lifts" the purse in the owner's house, he has committed an act of theft (see above, 30b note 17), which places the purse in his domain even with regard to being liable for damage that occurs to it through אוֹנֶס, *unavoidable mishap* (*Rashi*).

16. The desecration of the Sabbath does not occur until he takes the purse outside into the public domain and performs a *hanachah* (see above, note 2).

17. In this case the thief did not perform *hagbahah* in the owner's house. He therefore does not become liable for theft until he drags the purse out of the owner's house [and thereby "acquires" it through the *kinyan* of *meshichah* (pulling), which does not take effect until he pulls it into the public domain – see Gemara below, 31b], at which point he becomes liable for desecrating the Sabbath as well. Hence, he is exempt from payment (*Rashi*).

18. I.e. let us say that his act of *transferring* the purse from the private domain to the public domain begins with the lifting (the *akirah*) of the purse, and that he is therefore exempt from liability for the theft of the purse, which is incurred at that time (see *Rashi*). [The "lifting" of the purse, which constitutes the *akirah,* is a prerequisite of the *transfer* of the purse from the private domain to the public domain, just as the *akirah* of the arrow (its release) is a prerequisite of the *hanachah* in R' Avin's case. Hence, just as in R' Avin's case, the *melachah,* with its capacity to exempt from monetary liability, is considered as having begun with the *akirah* because the *akirah* is needed for the *hanachah,* so too in the case of the purse, the *melachah,* with its capacity to exempt from monetary liability, should be considered as having begun with the "lifting," for the "lifting" (the *akirah*) is needed for the *transfer.*]

Tosafos note that Rav Bivi is *not* asking his question according to the second version above, which states that the principle of "the *akirah* is the prerequisite of the *hanachah*" is applied only when the completion of the *hanachah* is inevitable at the time of the *akirah.* For, according to that version, R' Avin's principle would not apply in the case of the purse, since at the time of the "lifting" (the *akirah*) it is still possible for the thief not to follow through with the act of *transfer.* Rather, Rav Bivi's question is directed only at the first version, which applies R' Avin's principle even in cases where at the time of the *akirah* it is still possible that the *melachah* will not be consummated (e.g. where one tears silk while *carrying* a knife four *amos* in the public domain). [Cf.

וקרע שיראין של חבירו גופא אמר רב חסדא מודה רבי נחוניא בן הקנה בגונב חלבו של חבירו ואכלו שהוא חייב שכבר נתחייב בגנבה קודם שיבא לידי איסור חלב לימא פליגא דרבי אבין דאמר רבי אבין [א] הזורק חץ מתחילת ארבע לסוף ארבע וקרע שיראין בהליכתו פטור שעקירה צורך הנחה היא הכא נמי הגבהה צורך אכילה היא הכי השתא התם אי אפשר להנחה בלא עקירה הכא אפשר לאכילה בלא הגבהה דאי בעי [ג] גחין ואכיל אי נמי התם אי בעי לאהדורה לא מצי מהדר לה הכא מצי מהדר לה מאי איכא בין האי לישנא להאי לישנא איכא בינייהו המעביר סכין ברה"ר וקרע שיראין בהליכתו להך לישנא דאמרת אי אפשר להנחה בלא עקירה הכא נמי אי אפשר להנחה בלא עקירה להך לישנא דאמרת לא מצי מהדר לה הכא מצי מהדר לה גופא אמר רבי אבין הזורק חץ מתחלת ארבע לסוף ארבע וקרע שיראין בהליכתו פטור שעקירה צורך הנחה היא מתיב רב ביבי בר אביי [ב] הגונב כיס בשבת חייב שכבר נתחייב בגניבה קודם שיבא לידי איסור סקילה [ג] היה מגרר ויוצא מגרר ויוצא פטור שהרי איסור שבת וגניבה באין כאחד ואמאי הכא נמי לימא הגבהה צורך הוצאה היא הכא במאי עסקינן כגון שהגביהו על מנת להצניעו ונמלך עליו והוציאו וכי האי גוונא מי חייב והאמר רב סימון אמר רבי אמי אמר רבי יוחנן [ד] המפנה חפצים מזוית לזוית ונמלך עליהם והוציאן פטור שלא היתה עקירה משעה ראשונה לכך לא תימא ע"מ להצניעו אלא אימא ע"מ להוציאו הכא במאי עסקינן [ה] כשעמד עמד למאי אי לכתף אורחיה הוא אלא בעומד לפוש אבל לכתף מאי פטור

רש"י

וקרע שיראים. בשעה שבולעה ואע"ג דמיתה לאו משום ממונא דניזק אתיא ליה מיפטר וסבירא ליה לרב אשי מיתה לזה ותשלומין לזה פטור: **שעקירה צורך הנחה היא.** הלכך אע"ג דחיוב ממון מקמי הנחה אתיא ליה פטור הואיל ובין עקירה והנחה אתיא ליה מיתה ותשלומין באין כאחד שעקירה צורך הנחה היא ומההיא שעתא אתחלה לה מלאכה: **דאי בעי גחין.** למטה מג' טפחים ואכיל ובציר מג' לאו הגבהה היא: **לא מצי לאהדורה.** משזרק את החץ הלכך משעת עקירה סופו לקרוע לו שיראין: **הכא מצי מהדר ליה.** הלכך לא אמרי' משעת הגבהה אתחלה לה אכילה: **המעביר סכין.** בידו בהליכה: **הגונב כיס בשבת.** הגביהו ברשות הבעלים והוציאו לרה"ר: **חייב.** בתשלומין אף על פי שנהרג: **שכבר נתחייב בגניבה.** לשלם דהגבהה קונה בכל מקום וקמה לה ברשותיה אף להתחייב באונסים: **היה מגרר ויוצא.** שלא הגביהו ברשות הבעלים ולא קנאו אלא בהוצאה מרשות הבעלים פטור שאיסור שבת כו': **ואמאי.** כי הגביהו ברשות הבעלים וקנאו אמאי חייב נימא משעת הגבהה אתחלה לה הוצאה: **וכה"ג מי חייב.** משום שבת: **לכך.** להוציאו: **לא תימא בהגביהו ע"מ להצניעו אלא הגביהו ע"מ להוציאו.** ודקשיא לך נימא הגבהה צורך הוצאה היא: **הכא במאי עסקינן כשעמד.** ועמידתו היא הנחה לעקירה ראשונה ואין חיוב שבת בא לו ע"י עקירת חפץ הראשונה אלא ע"י עקירת גופו שעוקר עצמו אחר העמידה על מנת להוציא ועקירת גופו כעקירת חפץ: **אורחיה הוא.** ואין עמידתו הנחה לבטל עקירה ראשונה ממלאכת שבת: פטור

תוספות

והוא שהדליק את הגדיש בשבת פטור מפני שנידון בנפשו והיינו מיתה לזה משום שבת ותשלומין לזה משום גדיש אלא על כרחך חשיב מיתה ותשלומין לאחד הואיל ולא מתחייב מיתה בשביל אדם אלא לשמים וה"נ אכילת תרומה וקריעת שיראין הוי מיתה ותשלומין לאחד ור"י רצה ליישב פי' הקונט' דחשיב הכא מיתה לזה ותשלומין לזה לפי שהן ב' מעשים אכילת תרומה וקריעת שיראין וכן פלוני בא על בתו של פלוני הם ב' עדיות שהיו יכולין להעיד עליו בלא הבת ועל הבת בלא עליו פלוני בא על נערה המאורסה פלונית זינתה אבל מדליק גדיש הכל בא על מעשה אחד ולכך חשיב מיתה ותשלומין לאחד ואין נראה לרשב"א דהא אמר רב יוסף בפ"ק דסנהדרין (דף ט: ושם) הביא הבעל עדים שזינתה והביא האב עדים והזימום לעידי הבעל עידי הבעל נהרגים ואין משלמין ממון חזר והביא הבעל עדים והזימום לעידי האב עדי האב נהרגין ומשלמין ממון ממון לזה פירוש לבעל שרצו להפסידו כתובה ונפשות לעדים והתם על הזמה אחת בא להם הכל ונראה לר"ת דרבא דוקא גבי עדים זוממים אית ליה דממון לזה ונפשות לזה חייב משום דבעינן שתתקיים הזמה כלפי כל אחד ומיהו ממון ונפשות בחד גברא פטור כיון דמתקיים בו קלת הזמה אבל בעלמא מודה רבא דממון לזה ונפשות לזה פטור דהא גדי סמוך לו ועבד כפות לו דתנן פטור ומוקמינן בפרק כילד הרגל (ב"ק דף כב: ושם) בגדי דחד ועבדא דחד ועוד דרבא גופיה אית ליה בפרק בן סורר ומורה (סנהדרין דף עד.) דרודף ששבר כלים בין של נרדף בין של כל אדם פטור אע"ג דהוי מיתה לנרדף ותשלומין לבעל הכלים ומיהו התם גבי רודף רבה גרס כדמוכח בהגוזל בתרא (ב"ק דף קיז:) ובפ"ק דסנהדרין (דף י.) הוי רבא ועוד אומר ר"ת דע"כ לכ"ע מיתה לזה ותשלומין לזה פטור דהא קים ליה בדרבה מיניה דפטור נפקא לן מלא יהיה אסון וגו' והתם הוי מיתה לאשה ותשלומין לבעל שהולדות שלו ואומר ר"י דאינה ראיה דהתם כיון שהולדות הן בגוף האשה חשיב מיתה ותשלומין לאחד תדע דבפרק בן סורר ומורה (שם דף עד.) בעי לחייב כשאין אסון באשה אף ע"ג דניתן להצילו בנפשו דבמלות שבמיתה הכתוב מדבר משום דהוי מיתה לזה שרצה להורגו ותשלומין לבעל ואפי' הכי כשיש אסון פטור והיינו משום דחשיב מיתה ותשלומין לאחד לפי שהן בגוף האשה כדפרישית וריב"א אומר דבכל מקום מיתה לזה ותשלומין לזה חייב ועבד כפות לו ורודף שאני דניתן להציל לכל אדם וחייב מיתה לכל העולם [אף לבעל העבד ולבעל הכלים] ולהכי חשיב מיתה ותשלומין לאחד ואע"ג דמעיקרא בפרק בן סורר (ג"ז שם) חשיב רודף מיתה לזה ותשלומין לזה לפי המסקנא דקאמר אלא לא שנא חזר בו מאותה סברא וה"פ אלא לא שנא משום דהוי מיתה ותשלומין לאחד [והכא חשיב מיתה ותשלומין לאחד כמו במדליק גדיש]: **שעקירה** צורך הנחה היא. קשה דאמרינן במרובה (ב"ק דף ע:) גבי גנב ומכר בשבת דפטור כגון דאמר ליה זרוק גניבותיך לחצרי ותיקני לי חצירי גניבותיך ופריך מכי מטי לאויר חצירו קנה ומתחייב בנפשו משום שבת לא הוי עד שתנוח ומאי פריך והא עקירה צורך הנחה היא כדאמר הכא ולפר"ת אתי שפיר דפירש דאי אפשר לניסוך בלא הגבהה ואפ"ה קאמר רב מנסך ממש בהניזקין (גיטין דף נב: ושם) ולא קא מפטר משום דקים ליה בדרבה מיניה כדרבי ירמיה דמשעת הגבהה קונה ומתחייב בנפשו לא הוי עד שעת ניסוך והשתא רבי ירמיה לית ליה דהגבהה צורך ניסוך היא וה"ה דלית ליה דעקירה צורך הנחה היא ולא הוה מפליג בין מצי לאהדורי ללא מצי לאהדורי תדע ללישנא דאי אפשר להנחה בלא עקירה אמאי נקט רבי אבין זרק חץ לינקוט מעביר אלא ודאי כי הדדי נינהו ומאן דפליג אמעביר פליג נמי אזורק ואליבא דרבי ירמיה פריך במרובה (ב"ק דף ע: ושם) אבל אם אפשר לניסוך בלא הגבהה לא פליג רבי ירמיה אדרבי אבין ובהגוזל בתרא (שם דף קיז.) משמע קצת דרבי ירמיה פליג אדרבי אבין גבי חזרו לומר אף המנסך דקאמר התם מעיקרא סבור כדרבי אבין ולבסוף סבור כדרבי ירמיה [ומיהו יש לדחות דמעיקרא סבור דדמיא לדרבי אבין ולבסוף סבור דדמיא לדר' ירמיה]: **דאי** בעי גחין ואכיל. פי' בקונט' למטה מג' דלא הויא הגבהה וקשה לר"י דמה שייך הגבהה בדבר שהוא תופס בידו או בפיו דונתן בידה אמר רחמנא ואמרינן בגיטין (דף עח.) זרק לתוך קלתה מגורשת קשורה אע"פ שאינה תלויה אע"ג דמיירי ברשות הבעל ואפי' מאן דבעי התם תלויה אינו מצריך שתהא גבוה ג' אלא נראה לר"י א) דה"פ דאי בעי גחין ואכיל אם הוא ברשות קנה יכול הוא לשחות ולתוחבה עד בית בליעתו אע"ג דבהכי אכילה אינו עושה כן והואיל הגבהה זו לצורך אכילה מ"מ הואיל ויכול להתחייב בלא הגבהה לאו צורך אכילה היא וה"ה דה"מ למימר דאפשר לאכילה בלא הגבהה כגון אם תחבה לו חבירו: **הכא** נמי נימא הגבהה צורך הוצאה היא. ללישנא דאי בעי לאהדורי לא מצי מיהדר א] לא פריך מידי אבל ללישנא דאי אפשר להנחה בלא עקירה פריך דהכא נמי אי אפשר להוצאה בלא הגבהה אע"ג דאפשר בגרירה כך לי עקירה זו כמו עקירה אחרת דמ"מ האיסור מתחיל משעת הגבהה דאם היה אחר עושה עקירה לא היה מתחייב בהנחה נמצא עקירה גורמת החיוב ועד שעת הנחה מושך החיוב: **נימא** הגבהה צורך הוצאה היא. תימה לפר"ת דהגבהה קונה פחות משלשה טפחים [ה] מאי פריך והא כיון דקנאה קודם התחלת העקירה דעקירה לא הויא עד שיגביה שלשה דלמטה משלשה הוי כלבוד כדאמרינן בהמוציא (שבת דף פ. ושם) העביר תאני גרוגרת דרך עליה אי הוא חייב ואם כן דין הוא שיתחייב כמו לבן עזאי דאמר מהלך כעומד דמי דחייב לפי שקנאה קודם שהתחיל העקירה ואומר רשב"א דמשמע ליה בכל ענין גונב כיס אפילו מונח על גבי מקל שהוא גבוה שלשה טפחים שבא הקנין והעקירה בבת אחת: **שהגביהו** על מנת להצניעו ונמלך להוציאו. ואם תאמר וכיון דלסלקא דעתיה השתא דמיתחייב אהך הוצאה אם כן הדרא קושיא לדוכתין דלצורך הוצאה היא ויש לומר דלסלקא דעתין הא דנמלך והוציאו הוי עקירה שניה: **אבל** לכתף מאי פטור כו'. אפילו הוי לכתף חייב הוי מצי למיפרך ליפלוג בדידיה בין עמד ללא עמד כלל:

עין משפט נר מצוה

י א מיי' פ"ג מהל' גניבה הלכה ב:
יא ב ג מיי' שם טוש"ע ח"מ סימן שנא:
יב ד ה מיי' פי"ג מהל' שבת הלכה יג:

תוספות ישנים

א) [וכן] רוצה לומר הספר התם מתחיל האיסור משעת עקירה הכא אין האיסור מתחיל אלא משעת אכילה דאי בעי גחין ואכיל ליה בלא הגבהה אבל באם לא היה אפשר בלא הגבהה היה מתחיל נמי האיסור משעת הגבהה. תו"י.

תוספות רי"ד

א"ר אבין הזורק חץ מתחילת ד' לסוף ד' וקרע שיראין בהליכתו פטור שעקירה צורך הנחה היא. פי' ומההיא שעתא אתחלה לה מלאכה והלכך אע"ג דחיוב ממון מקמי הנחה אתיא ליה פטור הואיל א) וכן עקיר להנחה אתיא לה מיתה ותשלומין באין כאחד ולא תימא תשלומין קדמי למיתה: תניא הגונב כיס בשבת חייב. פי' חייב בתשלומין אע"פ שנהרג שכבר נתחייב בגניבה קודם שיבא לידי איסור שבת פי' דמשעה דאגבהה קניא שהגבהה קונה בכ"מ אפילו ברה"ר. ופי' אף להתחייב באונסים מתחייב בנפשו לא הוי עד דמפיק ליה היה מגרר ויוצא פירוש שלא הגביהו ברשות הבעלים ולא קנאה אלא בהוצאה מרשות בעלים פטור. שהרי איסור שבת ואיסור גניבה באין כא'. בפ' בן סורר ומורה מוקי לה כגון דשדייה בנהרא שאין הכיס בעין שאם הוא בעין א"י לזכות בו אלא בעל הכיס בא ונוטלו. ע"ש בפסקי:

חשק שלמה על תוס' רי"ד

א) נראה דצ"ל הואיל דהא דקא עקיר להנחה אתיא לה הוי לה מיתה ותשלומין וכו'.

מסורת הש"ס

א) ב"ק קיז., ב) [מנחות לט.], ג) ב"ב ל. סנהדרין עב. שבת לא: תוספתא דב"ק פ"ט, ד) שבת ה: עירובין כ:, ה) [ע"ע תוס' עירובין עט: ד"ה גליף ותוס' קדושין כו: ד"ה אי נמי ותוס' ב"ק כט: ד"ה אלא].

גליון הש"ס

גמרא הגונב כיס בשבת. עיין ירושלמי ב"ק פ"ג הלכה ד:

הגהות מהר"ב רנשבורג

א] תוס' ד"ה הכא וכו' לא פריך מידי. עי' פ"י בשם הרא"ש דלכך לישנא נמי פריך ולדברי נ"ל דרב ביבי בר אביי המותיב ליה ליה אליבא דעביד חד ... ועי' בשמו ... וקרובים הדברים לדברי ... :

ליקוטי רש"י

שיראין. של משי [מנחות לט:]. הזורק חץ. בשבת. שעקירה צורך הנחה. דכיון דבין עקירה להנחה קרע נמצא מעשה (עקירה) [קריעה] באין כאחד ולא אמרינן משעת (עקירה) [קריעה] חייב ממון ומתחייב בנפשו לא הוי עד שעת הנחת חץ [ב"ק קיז.]. הגונב כיס בשבת חייב. בתשלומין ואע"פ שנידון בנפשו שכבר נתחייב בגניבה בשעה שהגביה הכיס בבית הבעלים [שבת צא.]. היה מגרר ויוצא. שלא הגביהו ברשות הבעלים ולא קנאו אלא בהוצאה מרשות הבעלים פטור. שהרי איסור שבת וגניבה באין כאחד. שבת חייב הוצאה ממלאכת שבת אבל ...

שנתכוין לכך אלא שגג בשבת כסבור שהיום חול או מלאכה זו מותרת אבל כי לא נתכוין פטור מתעסק [עירובין כ:]. לכתף. לתקן משאו על כתפיו אין זו עמידה היא. לפוש. לנוח הוא הוי עמידה ועקירה דבתרה הוי עקירה [שבת שם].

וְקָרַע שִׁירָאִין שֶׁל חֲבֵירוֹ – **and** simultaneously (as he swallowed the *terumah*) **tore the silks of his fellow.**[1]

The Gemara focuses on the statement of Rav Chisda cited above:

גּוּפָא – **The text itself** stated: אָמַר רַב חִסְדָּא – **Rav Chisda said:** מוֹדֶה רַבִּי נְחוּנְיָא בֶּן הַקָּנָה – **R' Nechunya ben HaKanah agrees** בְּגוֹנֵב חֶלְבּוֹ שֶׁל חֲבֵירוֹ וַאֲכָלוֹ – **in** the case of **one who steals the *cheilev* belonging to his fellow and eats it** שֶׁהוּא חַיָּיב – **that he is liable** to pay the owner for the *cheilev,* even though he is also liable to *kares* for eating it, שֶׁכְּבָר נִתְחַיֵּיב בִּגְנֵיבָה – **because he has already become liable for** committing **theft** קוֹדֶם שֶׁיָּבֹא לִידֵי אִיסּוּר חֵלֶב – **before he comes to the point of** transgressing **the prohibition against** eating ***cheilev.***

The Gemara points out an apparent contradiction between Rav Chisda's statement and that of another Amora:

לֵימָא פְּלִיגָא דְּרַבִּי אָבִין – **Let us say** that **this** statement of Rav Chisda **disputes that of R' Avin.** דְּאָמַר רַבִּי אָבִין – **For R' Avin said:** הַזּוֹרֵק חֵץ מִתְּחִילַּת אַרְבַּע לְסוֹף אַרְבַּע – **If one shoots an arrow** in the public domain **from the beginning of** a **four-*amah*** stretch **to the end of** the **four-*amah*** stretch[2] וְקָרַע שִׁירָאִין בַּהֲלִיכָתוֹ – **and the [arrow] tears** someone else's **silks as it travels,** פָּטוּר – **he is exempt** from paying for the silks, שֶׁעֲקִירָה צוֹרֶךְ הֲנָחָה הִיא – **because** the ***akirah*** of the arrow **is a prerequisite of** its ***hanachah.***[3] That is, although the arrow tears the silks prior to its subsequent coming to rest on the ground, and the moment of monetary liability for tearing the silks thus precedes the moment of liability to capital punishment for desecrating the Sabbath,[4] it is nevertheless considered that these liabilities were incurred simultaneously, since the *akirah* (i.e. the shooting of the arrow) inevitably results for the *hanachah.*[5] הָכָא נַמִּי הַגְבָּהָה צוֹרֶךְ אֲכִילָה הִיא – **Here too,** argues the Gemara, we should say that the **lifting** of the *cheilev* **is a prerequisite of** the **eating.**[6] – ? –

The Gemara answers:

הָכִי הַשְׁתָּא – **Now,** is **this** a comparison? הָתָם אִי אֶפְשָׁר לְהַנָּחָה בְּלֹא עֲקִירָה – **There,** in the case of the arrow, **it is impossible to** have **a *hanachah* without an *akirah.***[7] הָכָא אֶפְשָׁר לַאֲכִילָה בְּלֹא הַגְבָּהָה – **Here,** however, **it is possible to eat** the *cheilev* **without lifting** it. דְּאִי בָּעֵי גָּחִין וְאָכִיל – **For if he wants, he can bend down and eat** it.[8]

An alternative version of the distinction:

אִי נַמִּי – **Alternatively,** we can differentiate between the two cases in the following manner: הָתָם אִי בָּעֵי לְאַהֲדוּרָה – **There,** in the case of the arrow, **if he wishes to draw back [the arrow]** after he shoots it, לֹא מָצֵי מַהְדַּר לָהּ – **he cannot draw it back.**[9] הָכָא מָצֵי מַהְדַּר לָהּ – **Here,** however, **he can draw back [the *cheilev*]** after he lifts it.[10]

NOTES

1. [Rav Ashi maintains that when the Gemara above said that the difference between Abaye and Rava emerges where a non-Kohen eats *terumah,* it refers to monetary liability for *incidental* damages, not for the *terumah,* which belongs to the eater himself. For if the *terumah* would indeed belong to someone else, then both Abaye and Rava would agree that the eater is subject to monetary liability for the *terumah,* which is incurred *prior* to the swallowing that makes him liable to "death at the hand of Heaven."]

[Rava rules in *Sanhedrin* 10a that liability to the death penalty does not exempt from simultaneous monetary liability where the two liabilities are for crimes against different people. Evidently,] Rav Ashi, who exempts the eater of his own *terumah* from paying for another person's torn silks, [disputes this and] holds that the exemption applies even where the two liabilities are for crimes against different people (*Rashi;* see, however, *Tosafos,* who suggest various ways of reconciling Rav Ashi's explanation here with the ruling of Rava in *Sanhedrin*).

2. הוֹצָאָה, *taking out* or *transferring,* is one of the thirty-nine *melachos* forbidden on the Sabbath. It includes transferring an item between a private domain and public domain, as well as transferring it a distance of four *amos* in the public domain. The penalty for doing the forbidden *melachah* is the court-imposed death penalty of "stoning."

3. One is liable for *transferring* only when the transfer begins with his עֲקִירָה, *removal* [of the object from its state of rest], and ends with his הֲנָחָה, *placement* [of that object in a state of rest]. In the present case, the release of the arrow constitutes the *akirah* (for that is the point at which it is being *removed* from its state of rest in his hand), and its subsequent coming to rest on the ground four *amos* away at the end of its flight constitutes the *hanachah.*

4. Liability for the silks is incurred at the moment the arrow tears through them. Liability for desecrating the Sabbath is not incurred until the arrow comes to rest on the ground, when the three conditions of *akirah,* transferring four *amos,* and *hanachah* are fulfilled.

5. I.e. one cannot incur liability for the *hanachah* without performing an *akirah.* Hence, the forbidden *melachah* actually begins with the *akirah* [and ends with the *hanachah*]. And since the liability for tearing the silks is incurred between the *akirah* and the *hanachah* — during the extended act of *melachah* that makes him liable to capital punishment — he is exempt from paying for the silks (see *Rashi*).

6. One cannot eat *cheilev* unless he first lifts it and places it into his mouth. Hence, if we follow R' Avin's line of reasoning, the act of eating the *cheilev* actually begins with the person's lifting of the *cheilev* and ends with his swallowing it. Accordingly, he would not be liable for the theft of the *cheilev,* even though it occurs at the time he lifts the *cheilev* (see above, 30b note 17), prior to his swallowing it. For the theft of the *cheilev* does occur simultaneously with the *beginning* of the extended act of eating that makes him liable to *kares.*

7. Hence, the *akirah* is considered the beginning of the act of *transferring* for which he is liable to capital punishment.

8. I.e. he can lower his head to within three *tefachim* of the ground and eat the *cheilev* there, in which case the taking of the *cheilev* to put it into his mouth would not constitute an act of *hagbahah* [lifting] (see *Rashi*). [*Rashi* is following his opinion in *Kiddushin* 26a ד״ה בחבילי זמורות, that an act of lifting does not constitute the *kinyan* of *hagbahah* unless the item is lifted at least three *tefachim* off the ground (*Rashba*).]

[Thus, the act of "eating" does not require a prior act of *hagbahah* (or any other act of *kinyan*). Accordingly, even if one *does* "lift" food to eat it, the act of eating does not begin with the act of *kinyan,* but rather with the actual eating of the food. In Rav Chisda's case, then, where one stole the *cheilev* (by lifting it three *tefachim*) and then ate it, he is liable to pay for the theft, since that liability was incurred with the "lifting," which was *prior* to the beginning of the act of "eating" *cheilev* for which he is liable to *kares.*]

[Other Rishonim dispute *Rashi's* contention that *hagbahah* requires the height of three *tefachim,* and maintain that one *tefach* is sufficient (see *Rashba* and *R' Crescas*). Some, therefore, explain that our Gemara means that one can lower his head to within a *tefach* of the ground to eat the food (*R' Crescas*). Others maintain that taking an item into one's hand or mouth constitutes a *kinyan* even without lifting the item (and thus a *kinyan* would seem to be a prerequisite for the act of eating). Accordingly, they explain the Gemara's intent here differently (*Tosafos, Rashba*). See *Meiri, Shitah Mekubetzes* and *Pnei Yehoshua* for various defenses of *Rashi's* position. See also *Dvar Avraham,* cited below, 31b note 27.]

9. Therefore, at the time of the *akirah* (the release of the arrow) it is definite that the silk will be torn (*Rashi;* see next note).

10. Therefore, we do not say that the act of eating [for which he is liable to *kares*] begins from when he "lifts" the *cheilev* [which is the time that he becomes liable for theft] (*Rashi*).

[Apparently, this second version means to say that even if one could *not* eat without first lifting the food, you could not compare the case of eating *cheilev* to the case of shooting an arrow on the Sabbath. For in the case of the arrow, the *melachah* (for which the person is eventually liable to death) begins with the release of the arrow because at that point the act is irreversible. In the case of eating, however, the act is reversible until the person actually swallows the *cheilev;* hence, you cannot say that the act for which the eater eventually becomes liable to death begins with the lifting of the *cheilev.* Accordingly, however, *Rashi* ד״ה לא מצי לאהדורה (see note 9) should not have emphasized that at the time of the arrow's release the *tearing of the silks* is inevitable, but

inserted deeply, to a point from where **he cannot return it,**[25] **אַמַּאי חַיָּיב – why is he liable?**[26]

The Gemara answers:

לֹא צְרִיכָא – There is **no** difficulty. **It is necessary** only to say that we are dealing with a case **דְּמָצֵי לְאַהֲדוּרָה עַל יְדֵי הַדְּחָק** – where it was thrust into his throat to a point from **where he can return it with difficulty.**[27]

An alternative solution:[28]

רַב פָּפָּא אָמַר – Rav Pappa says: כְּגוֹן שֶׁתָּחַב לוֹ חֲבֵירוֹ מַשְׁקִין שֶׁל תְּרוּמָה לְתוֹךְ פִּיו – We are dealing in a case **where his fellow thrust a beverage of *terumah* into his mouth.**[29]

Another alternative solution:

רַב אַשִׁי אָמַר – Rav Ashi says: בְּזָר שֶׁאָכַל תְּרוּמָה מִשֶּׁלּוֹ – We are dealing **with a non-Kohen who ate his own *terumah,***[30]

NOTES

who inserted the *terumah* into his throat – who is liable for *theft.* [This way of understanding *Rashi* would coincide with the view of *Ritzba* (cited above, note 19), that voluntarily holding someone else's item in one's mouth does constitute "theft."] See also *Ritva,* who likewise maintains that the liability for not bringing the *terumah* back up is for theft.

[*Rashi* says at the end that the one who thrust it into the eater's throat did not actually do anything and thus owes nothing to the Kohen. Besides the stated exemption of the one who thrust the *terumah* into the eater's throat, these comments also indicate that had the one who thrust it into the eater's throat become liable to the Kohen, the eater himself would *not* be liable. *Chidushei R' Akiva Eiger* points out, however, that the Gemara in *Bava Kamma* 111a seems to contradict *Rashi* on both points. For the Gemara there states that if one person steals food and a second person comes along and eats the stolen food, the original owner has the option of collecting from either the thief or from the one who ate the food. Similarly, reasons *R' Akiva Eiger,* the one who thrust the *terumah* into the eater's throat *should* be liable to the Kohen, and this should *not* exempt the eater himself from liability! See *Imrei Moshe* 33:3 for an explanation and defense of *Rashi's* position.]

25. [In which case his monetary liability would be limited to the amount he benefited from eating the *terumah.*]

26. Why is he liable to "death at the hand of Heaven" for eating *terumah*? He was forced to eat it, and one is not punished for a transgression that he was forced to commit! (*Rashi*). Accordingly, Abaye would not exempt him from paying what he benefited from the *terumah,* since he does not incur the punishment of death at all. [See *Tosafos,* who discuss why the Gemara did not answer that the *terumah* was thrust into the eater's throat with his consent.]

[Actually, the Gemara below (35a) states that one is exempt from a monetary liability incurred while committing a capital *offense* even if the act was committed בְּשׁוֹגֵג, *inadvertently,* in which case there is no actual liability to capital *punishment.* Similarly, in this case, the commission of the *offense* bearing the penalty of "death at the hand of Heaven" should exempt the eater from payment even though he is not actually liable to the *punishment* of "death at the hand of Heaven" (since he committed the offense against his will). *R' Akiva Eiger* suggests that *Rashi* is following his view stated in *Pesachim* 32a ד״ה כרבי נחוניא בן הקנה (see *Maharsha* there), that the *offense* exempts from monetary liability even if committed inadvertently only in the case of capital offenses that bear the penalty of מִיתַת בֵּית דִּין, *court-imposed execution.* R' Nechunya ben HaKanah's rule that a Heavenly death penalty also exempts from payment, however, applies only to one who actually *incurs* the penalty of death at the hands of Heaven through deliberate transgression. Inadvertent commission of the *offense,* however, does not exempt him. (See *Shitah Mekubetzes* here ד״ה זר שאכל את התרומה for a rationale of this distinction; cf. *Tosafos* here ד״ה זר and to *Pesachim* 29a ד״ה רבי נחוניא.) Alternatively, *R' Akiva Eiger* suggests that even if inadvertent transgression (שׁוֹגֵג) would exempt from payment, transgression *against one's will* (אֹנֶס) would not exempt. Acts committed בְּשׁוֹגֵג, *inadvertently,* although not punishable by death, are nevertheless considered "acts of capital offense," and thus exempt from payment. Acts committed בְּאֹנֶס, *against one's will,* on the other hand, are not considered "acts of capital offense" at all, and thus do not exempt from payment.]

27. When the food is inserted to that point, it becomes repulsive. Thus, even if he had brought it back up and spit it out, it would have been repulsive and unfit for use by the owner. Therefore, he cannot be held liable for "theft" on account of keeping the *terumah* in his throat and opting not to bring it back up (see above, note 24), for his failure to do so in this case is not what deprives the owner of its use. Hence, his only monetary liability would be to pay for "the benefit derived by his throat and digestive system" from the owner's property [see above, note 19], a liability that he incurs *simultaneously* with his liability to "death at the hand of Heaven" when he *voluntarily* swallows the *terumah* that he could have spit out (see *Rashi*).

[Actually, if the *terumah* was worth absolutely nothing to the owner before it is swallowed, the one who swallowed it would not have to pay for the benefit he received even if there was no penalty of death was incurred. We must say, therefore, that the *terumah* remains minimally fit, say, for the owner's dog, so that it has some residual value, albeit less than a *perutah's* worth. In this case, there is no liability for theft (since it is worth less than a *perutah*), but there is liability for the full amount of the benefit enjoyed, even though it exceeds the loss sustained by the owner (see *Tosafos* and *Tos. HaRosh,* based on *Bava Kamma* 20b).]

28. Which does not require us to adopt the forced explanation that the other fellow thrust the *terumah* down the eater's *throat* (*Rashi*). Rather, we can remain with the original [and more plausible] suggestion that he thrust it simply into the eater's mouth.

29. A beverage becomes repulsive to others as soon as it enters one's mouth. Therefore, he cannot be held liable for keeping the beverage in his mouth and not spitting it out, for it is already useless to the owner (see note 27). Hence, his only liability to the owner is to pay for "the benefit derived by his throat and digestive system" [see note 19], a liability he incurs *simultaneously* with his liability to "death at the hand of Heaven" when he voluntarily swallows the *terumah* beverage.

30. Such as where he inherited *terumah* from his mother's father, who was a Kohen (*Meiri; Haflaah*).

עין משפט
נר מצוה

ח א מיי' פ"ו מהלכות תרומות הל' ו סמג לאוין רכו:

ט ב מיי' פ"ג מהלכות גניבה הלכה ד סמג עשין עא טוש"ע ח"מ סימן שנ:

דין ארבע מיתות לא בטלו מי שנתחייב סקילה או נופל מן הגג או חיה דורסתו ומי שנתחייב שריפה או נופל בדליקה או נחש מכישו ומי שנתחייב הריגה או נמסר למלכות או ליסטים באין עליו ומי שנתחייב חנק או טובע בנהר או מת בסרונכי אלא איפוך אריא וגנבי בידי שמים צינים ופחים בידי אדם רבא אמר טעמא דרבי נחוניא בן הקנה מהכא א) ואם העלם יעלימו עם הארץ את עיניהם מן האיש ההוא בתתו מזרעו למולך ושמתי אני את פני באיש ההוא ובמשפחתו והכרתי אותו אמרה תורה כרת שלי כמיתה שלכם מה מיתה שלכם פטור מן התשלומין אף כרת שלי פטור מן התשלומין מאי איכא בין רבא לאביי איכא בינייהו זר שאכל תרומה לאביי [א] פטור ולרבא חייב ולאביי פטור והאמר רב חסדא מודה ר' נחוניא בן הקנה [ב] בגונב חלבו של חבירו ואכלו שהוא חייב שכבר נתחייב בגניבה קודם שבא לידי איסור חלב אלמא דמעידנא דאגביה קנייה מתחייב בנפשו א) לא הוה עד דאכיל ליה הכא נמי בעידנא דאגביה קנייה מתחייב בנפשו לא הוי עד דאכיל ליה הכא במאי עסקינן כגון שתחב לו חבירו לתוך פיו סוף סוף כיון דלעסיה קנייה מתחייב בנפשו לא הוי עד דבלעה כגון [ה] שתחב לו לתוך בית הבליעה היכי דמי אי דמצי לאהדורה ניהדר אי לא מצי לאהדורה אמאי חייב לא צריכא דמצי לאהדורה ע"י הדחק רב פפא אמר כגון שתחב לו חבירו משקין של תרומה לתוך פיו רב אשי אמר בזר שאכל תרומה משלו וקרע

רש"י

דין ד' מיתות. עונש דוגמתם: נופל מן הגג. דומה לנסקל שדוחפין אותו מבית הסקילה לארץ דגבוה ב' קומות היה כדאמרי' בנגמר הדין (סנהדרין דף מה.): חיה דורסתו. אף מפילו לארץ והורגו בדריסה: נחש מכישו. והאש שורפו: נמסר למלכות. והן מתיזין ראשו בסייף כי כן דרך המומתין על ידיהן וזו היא מיתת סייף: סרונכי. אסכרה והוא בגרון מלנ"ט: מן האיש ההוא. שהוא חייב מיתת ב"ד: ושמתי אני את פני והכרתי. למדנו שהכרת במקום מיתה וחילופה: זר שאכל תרומה. במזיד הוא במיתה בידי שמים ולא בכרת. כרת הוא שזרעו נכרתין דכתיב (ויקרא כ) ערירים יהיו: לאביי פטור. מתשלומין דנפקא ליה מאסון בידי שמים וכל אסון משמע בין במיתה בין בכרת: ולאביי פטור. במיתה נמי דמיתה בידי שמים פוטרת מתשלומין אבל היכא דלאכיל תרומה דגזולה מי מיפטר הא כיון דלהגבהה קניה וחייב בתשלומין ואפילו תישרף ומתחייב בנפשו לא הוי עד דלאכיל לה: שתחב לו חבירו. דלא להגבהה ולא קניה ולא מיחייב בתשלומין אלא בבליעתו מתחייב דמי הניית מעיו ולא דמי כולה וההיא שעתא חיוב מיתה נמי איכא: איבעי ליה לאהדורה. וכי לא אהדרה מההיא שעתא איהו מזיק לה דלראשון לאו מידי עבד ולא נתחייב לכהן כלום: ואי דלא מצי לאהדורה אמאי חייב. מיתה אנוס הוא: ע"י הדחק. דאי נמי אהדרה ממאסה ולא חזיא לבעלים הלכך מגזל לא גזלה אמאי קא מחייבת ליה בתשלומין אהנאת גרונו ומעיו ההיא שעתא חיוב מיתה איכא: משקין של תרומה. ולא תדחקה לשנויה בבית הבליעה אלא מכיון שתחבה לתוך פיו אימאסא לה ולא מצית לאחיובי משום גזילה דהא לא חזיא למידי אלא אהניית גרונו ומעיו מיחייב ומיתה ותשלומין באים כאחד: וקרע

תוספות

דין ד' מיתות לא בטלו. וא"ת והא אמר בהשוכר את הפועלים (ב"מ צא:) בהמוא דזקפוהו אע"פ שהיה חייב סקילה שבעלו הוא ובנו נערה המאורסה וי"ל בשבעל בנו תחלה ואח"כ הוא דהוי בעולה והרי הוא בחנק אבל קשה דחזינן כמה עבריינים ועובדי עבודת כוכבים שמתים על מטותם ויש לומר דע"י תשובה הקב"ה מיקל ולפעמים מוחל לגמרי או זכות תולה לו ואינו נפרע ממנו בחייו ובפ' אחד דיני ממונות (סנהדרין דף לז: וסם) דפריך והא בר נחש הוא לפי שהחמיר עליו יותר: זר שאכל תרומה לאביי פטור. והוא הדין לאוכל תרומה בשוגג והזיד במעילה לרבי דאמר במיתה (פסחים דף לג.) דחייב גזירת הכתוב הוא וא"ת לאביי דפטר חייבי מיתות בידי שמים אי ר' נחוניא ס"ל כרבי דאמר הזיד במעילה במיתה אמאי תניא בפרק כל שעה (פסחים דף כט. וסם) האוכל חמץ של הקדש במועד יש אומרים לא מעל ואמרינן מאן י"א רבי נחוניא בן הקנה והא כיון דגלי רחמנא גבי הקדש דלא שייך קים ליה (א) דאם לא כן אין לך אדם שמועל בהקדש א"כ בפסח נמי דאיכא כרת ליחייב ולא הוה לן למימר דקים ליה בדרבה מיניה וי"ל במיתה דהקדש דוקא גלי רחמנא דלא אמרינן דקים ליה בדרבה מיניה אבל התם דהוי פסח דאיכא כרת לא גלי קרא א"כ הא דתנן התם (סם דף לב:) האוכל תרומת חמץ בפסח בשוגג משלם קרן וחומש ובמזיד פטור מן התשלומין ומדמי עצים ומפרש בגמ' במזיד פטור דקים ליה בדרבה מיניה כרבי נחוניא והשתא בשוגג נמי ליפטר משום כרת דפסח דלפי' בשוגג אמרי' דקים ליה בדרבה מיניה כדאמרינן לקמן בפירקין (דף לה.) אלא ע"כ משום דגלי רחמנא במיתה דתרומה בשוגג דלא אמרינן קים ליה בדרבה מיניה וה"ה כי איכא כרת ולא אמרינן דוקא במיתה דגלי גלי אבל כי איכא כרת לא וי"ל דשאני שוגג דתרומה משום דתשלומין דידיה כפרה ולא ממונא כדאמרינן במסכת תרומות (פ"ו מ"א) דאם רצה כהן למחול אינו יכול למחול משום דלא הוי ממון אלא כפרה ואפילו אוכל תרומת עצמו דלא גזל מידי משלם כפרה לעצמו וחומש לכהן ולכך לא שייך קים ליה בדרבה מיניה לפוטרו מכפרה אבל קרן וחומש של הקדש אינו משום כפרה אלא משלם ממון שגזל הקדש ותדע דבתרומה חייב משום דכפרה הוא ולא משום כיון דגלי גלי דהא לרבא דלא פטר במיתה מטעם דקים ליה בדרבה מיניה מאי טעמא לא מיפטר אוכל תרומת חמץ בפסח אלא ודאי משום כפרה הוא ב) וא"ת והא דתנן בפרק נושאין (יבמות דף לט:) כהנת שנתערב ולדה בולד שפחתה ושחררו זה את זה וכן ספק בן תשעה לראשון או בן ז' לאחרון דאמרינן אם אכלו בתרומה אין משלמין קרן וחומש ואמאי כיון דכפרה הוא ליחייבו מספק וי"ל דודאי צריכין להפריש אבל אין נותנין לכהן ולפי זה צריך לומר שהכפרה תלויה בהפרשה והא דאין הכהן יכול למחול היינו לענין שלא יהיה צריך להפריש אבל לאחר שהפריש יכול למחול לו שיהא שלו: ולאביי פטור והאמר רב חסדא כו'. הכי נמי הוה מצי לאקשויי אמתניתין דכל שעה (פסחים דף לא:) דקתני פטור מן התשלומין לפי מה דמוקמינן לה כרבי נחוניא בן הקנה: אי דמצי לאהדורה ניהדרה. וכי לא מיהדר חייב דמיתה לא פטרה ליה דלא אתיא עד דבלע לגמרי: ואי דלא מצי לאהדורה אמאי חייב. פירש בקונטרס אמאי חייב מיתה וקשה לר"י דלוקי כגון שמרצונו מניח לו לתחוב דהשתא ודאי חייב מיתה אע"ג דלא מצי לאהדורה וממון נמי לא מיחייב כיון דלא מצי לאהדורה אלא על הנאת גרונו ומעיו וההיא שעתא קים ליה בדרבה מיניה ונראה לר"י דה"פ אמאי חייב ממון והרי הוא לא גזלו ואהנאתו לא מיחייב דאע"ג דאמרי' (ב"ק דף קיא:) גזל ולא נתייאשו הבעלים ובא אחר ואכלו רצה מזה גובה כו' היינו דוקא לפי שהדבר הגזול ישנו בעולם בשעה שזה שני גוזלו אבל הכא דבשעה שזה נהנה ממנו כבר הוא אבוד מן העולם שהוא במקום דלא אפשר לאהדוריה אין לו על השני כלום ג) וריצב"א מפרש כשיטת רש"י ופשיטא ליה להש"ס דאיירי כשתוחב לו בע"כ דכשתוחב לו מרצונו מיד כשמשים בפיו ולא אהדרה קנאה מיד להתחייב באונסין ואין באין כאחד דמסתמא מניחה בפיו ואח"כ תוחב לו באצבעו או בכוס ואת"ל שהוא בראש הכוס מתחלתו ועד גמר בית הבליעה מ"מ קונה אותו בפיו להתחייב באונסים אע"ג דיכול לנתקו ולהביאו אצלו ◦ דדוקא לענין הגט אמרי' היכא דיכול לנתקו דלא הוי גט משום דבעינן כריתות והא אגידא ביה אבל לענין זכיה אשכחן בפ"ק דב"מ (דף ט. וסם) טלית חציה על גבי קרקע וחציה על גבי העמוד והגביה חציה שעל גבי קרקע דלא קני מטעם שיכול לנתקה ולהביאה אצלו וכיון שאינו זוכה מטעם זה ה"ה דאינו מגרע זכיית האחר שהוא מונח בתוך ידו או בתוך פיו מטעם זה ועוד דלכל הפחות קונה מחצה כמו שנים שהגביהו מציאה ולכך פשיטא ליה להש"ס דבאונס מיירי וה"פ אנוס הוא ופטור ממיתה וממון דאין סהדי דלא ניחא ליה באכילת איסור: לא צריכא דמצי לאהדורה על ידי הדחק. והשתא ליכא למימר דניהדרה דאין מרויחין בעלים בכך דכבר נמאסו הלכך ליכא חיוב ממון אלא ע"י הנאת מעיו ואז באין כאחד ואע"ג שחבירו גזלה הואיל ויכול להחזירה הויא כמו שהיא בעין והרי הוא בולעה ונהנה בה ואם תאמר והא אמרינן בפרק בהמה המקשה (חולין דף עא.) גבי טומאה בלועה [דלא מטמאה לא משום דלא חזיא דנהי דבפניו לא חזיא] שלא בפניו מיחזא חזיא א"כ אי הוה מהדר לה הויא חזיא וי"ל כגון דמעיקרא לא הוי בה כי אם שוה פרוטה או מעט יותר ועתה שנתקלקלה קצת אינה שוה פרוטה ואפילו אי זה נהנה וזה לא חסר פטור ◦ מ"מ כיון דשוין כל שהוא אז מיחייב בכל כדאמרינן התם (ב"ק דף כ:) משום דא"ל את גרמת לי היקפא יתירתא מיחייב בכל הנאה או משום שחרוריתא דאשיתא מיחייב לכולי עלמא בכל וריצב"א פי' דמיירי אפי' באוכלין דלא מאיסי וכיון דתחב לו בבית הבליעה ובלע ונהנה מיד חשוב באין כאחת אע"פ שאין כאחד ממש כדאשכחן בסוף פרק ד' אחין (יבמות דף לג. וסם) דמפרש בעל מום ששמש בטומאה דאתו בהדי הדדי כגון שחתך אצבעו בסכין טמאה אע"פ שאי אפשר שלא יגע בסכין קודם שיחתוך ד): רב אשי אמר בזר שאכל תרומה משלו וקרע שיראים כו'. פ"ה דסבירא ליה לרב אשי דמיתה לזה ותשלומין לזה פטור ופליג אדרבא דאמר בפרק קמא דסנהדרין (דף י. וסם) פלוני בא על בת פלוני והוזמו נהרגין ומשלמין ממון לזה ונפשות לזה ב) פי' ממון לבת שרצו להפסיד לה כתובתה ונפשות לזה שאומר שבא עליה ואין נראה ה) דאי חשיב אכילת תרומה וקריעת שיראין ממון לזה ונפשות לזה א"כ תקשי ליה לרבא הא דתנן בהמניח את הכד (ב"ק דף לד: וסם)

והוא

גליון הש"ס

תוס' ד"ה ואי וכו' דדוקא לענין הגט. תמוה לי הא בהדיא איתא כן בב"מ ז ע"א ולעג"ג: ד"ה לא צריכא וכו' מ"מ כיון דשוין כל שהוא. עי' ב"ק דף כ ע"ב תוד"ה הא איתהנית:

ליקוטי רש"י

דין ארבע מיתות. דין שמים שהיא דוגמתו [סוטה ח:]. פורענות בידי שמים הדומה למיתה שהוא מחויב בה [סנהדרין לז:]. נופל מן הגג. דומיא דסקילה דתנן (סנהדרין דף מה.) בית הסקילה היה גבוה שתי קומות אחד מן העדים בא ודוחפו כו' [סוטה שם]. דומיא דסקילה כדתנן לקמן (דף מה:) בית הסקילה היתה גבוהה שתי קומות וקומה שלו הרי כאן שלש [סנהדרין שם]. חיה דורסתו. אף דורסו בצפרניו ומפילו לארץ וגם זה דוכה לנסקל [סוטה שם]. נחש מכישו. דקלי לה זיהרא ארס של נחש שורפו [סנהדרין שם]. נמסר למלכות. ומיתת מלכות מתיזין את ראשו בסייף והרג נמי סייף הוא כדאמרינן בסנהדרין (דף נב.) [סוטה שם]. ליסטים באין עליו. שדרכן להרגו בסייף [סנהדרין שם]. בסרונכי. בומנל"ט והוא חולי בגרונו [סוטה שם]. חולי ששמו אשטרנגליו"ן הוא בו"ן מלנטן [יומא פד.]. ואם העלם יעלימו. אם סוף שיעלימו בדבר אחד סוף שיעלימו בדברים הרבה אם העלימו סנהדרי קטנה סוף שיעלימו סנהדרי גדולה [ויקרא כ, ד]. למולך. ע"ז היא שמה מולך והיא עבודתה שמוסר בנו לכומרים ועושין שתי מדורות גדולות ומעבירין את הבן ברגליו בין שתי מדורות האש [שם יח, כא]. ובמשפחתו. אמר ר' שמעון וכי משפחה מה חטאה אלא ללמדך שאין לך משפחה שיש בה מוכס שאין כולם מוכסים שכולם מחפין עליו. והכרתי אותו. למה נאמר לפי שנאמר ובמשפחתו יכול יהיו כל המשפחה בהכרת תלמוד לומר אותו אותו בהכרת ולא כל המשפחה בהכרת [שם כ, ה]. ולאביי פטור. במיתה נמי דמיתה בידי שמים פוטרת מתשלומין אבל היכא דלאכיל תרומה דגזולה מי מיפטר... הקדש לא דקי בהדדי דאמרינן [קידושין דף נב.]. גזל ולא נתייאשו הבעלים שניהם אינם יכולים להקדישו זה לפי שאינו שלו וזה לפי שאינו ברשותו מיהו מחייב משעת הגבהה באחריותו [רש"י מכתב יד ישן בשיטמ"ק].

מסורת הש"ס

א) [עי' תוס' ב"ק כב: ד"ה הא], ב) [פי' ממון לבת שרצו להפסידו כתובה כל"ל מהרש"א].

תוספות ישנים

א) וא"ת כיון דלעסיה נתקלקל והיאך חייב תו עלה כדאמר פ"ק דכריתות [דף ז.] כהן שסך שמן של תרומה בן בתו ישראל מתעגל בו ואינו חושש וי"ל דהתם ודאי נתקלקל שכבר נגמרה כל הנאתו אבל הכא לא נגמרה כל הנאתו בלעיסה לחודיה. מ"י. ב) [ועוד יש להוכיח דכפרה הוי מדפטרינן לאביי מזיד בתרומה ואע"ג דגלי רחמנא גבי שוגג דלא אמרי' קים ליה בדרבה מיניה בתרומה אלא ודאי משום כפרה הוא ויש לדחות דשאני שוגג דתרומה לפי שאלמנו שהוא חמור משלם חומש. מ"י]. ג) [פי' ריצב"א לא יתחייב בשמוך דקאמר אי בעי גמין ואכיל. מ"י]. ד) [ור"ח פירש כיון שהוא במקום דלא מצי לאהדורי אלא ע"י הדחק כבר נהנה גרונו ואין כאחד ואי"ת והיאך יתחייב ממון כיון שתחב לו בתוך פיו וי"ל כיון דמצי לאהדורה ע"י הדחק ולא הדרה ניחא ליה בהנאה זו. מ"י]. ה) [ועוד דלכאורה מאי איכא בין רבא לאביי לאפוקי אי הוי סבר רבא דליליף מאסון הוי מיחייב כיון דהוי ממון לזה ונפשות לזה. מ"י].

הגהות הב"ח

(א) תוס' ד"ה זר וכו' קים ליה בדרבה מיניה דאם:

לעזי רש"י

מלנ"ט. פירוש אסכרה, מין חולי הגרון המחנק (מוסף הערוך ערך אסכרה ועיין רש"י שבת דף לג סוע"א):

תורה אור השלם

א) וְאִם הַעְלֵם יַעְלִימוּ עַם הָאָרֶץ אֶת עֵינֵיהֶם מִן הָאִישׁ הַהוּא בְּתִתּוֹ מִזַּרְעוֹ לַמֹּלֶךְ לְבִלְתִּי הָמִית אֹתוֹ: וְשַׂמְתִּי אֲנִי אֶת פָּנַי בָּאִישׁ הַהוּא וּבְמִשְׁפַּחְתּוֹ וְהִכְרַתִּי אֹתוֹ וְאֵת כָּל הַזֹּנִים אַחֲרָיו לִזְנוֹת אַחֲרֵי הַמֹּלֶךְ מִקֶּרֶב עַמָּם: [ויקרא כ, ד-ה]

The Gemara asks:

וּלְאַבַּיֵי פָּטוּר – **But** is it indeed so that **according to Abaye,** R' Nechunya ben HaKanah rules a non-Kohen who eats *terumah* exempt from paying for the *terumah*? וְהָאָמַר רַב חִסְדָּא – **Why, Rav Chisda said:** מוֹדֶה רַבִּי נְחוּנְיָא בֶּן הַקָּנָה – **R' Nechunya ben HaKanah agrees** בְּגוֹנֵב חֶלְבּוֹ שֶׁל חֲבֵירוֹ וַאֲכָלוֹ – **in** the case of **one who steals the *cheilev* belonging to his fellow and eats it** שֶׁהוּא חַיָּיב – **that he is liable** to pay the owner for the *cheilev,* even though he is also liable to *kares* for eating it,[16] שֶׁכְּבָר נִתְחַיֵּיב בִּגְנֵיבָה – **because he has already become liable for** committing **theft** קוֹדֶם שֶׁבָּא לִידֵי אִיסּוּר חֵלֶב – **before he comes to the point of** transgressing **the prohibition against** eating ***cheilev.*** The Gemara elaborates: אַלְמָא דְּמֵעִידָּנָא דְּאַגְבְּיהּ קַנְיֵיהּ – **Evidently,** the reasoning is that **from the moment that he lifted [the *cheilev*]** with the intent to "steal" it by eating it, **he "acquired" it** as stolen property, making him liable to pay for it.[17] מִתְחַיֵּיב בְּנַפְשׁוֹ לֹא הֲוָה עַד דְּאָכִיל לֵיהּ – But **he is not liable** to pay **with his life** [i.e. *kares*] for eating *cheilev* **until he** actually **eats it.** Thus, since the monetary liability is incurred prior to the *kares* liability, rather than simultaneously with it, he is liable to both penalties.[18] הָכָא נָמֵי – Similarly, **here too,** in the case of the non-Kohen eating a Kohen's *terumah,* בְּעִידָּנָא דְּאַגְבְּיהּ קַנְיֵיהּ – **at the moment that he lifted it** with the intent to "steal" it by eating it, **he "acquired" it as stolen property,** and is liable to pay for it. מִתְחַיֵּיב בְּנַפְשׁוֹ לֹא הֲוֵי עַד דְּאָכִיל לֵיהּ – But **he is not liable** to pay **with his life** [i.e. "death at the hand of Heaven"] **until he** actually **eats it.** And since the monetary liability is incurred prior to the liability to "death at the hand of Heaven," rather than simultaneously with it, he should be liable to both penalties – even according to Abaye who maintains that according to R' Nechunya ben HaKanah "death at the hand of Heaven" *does* have the capacity to exempt one from monetary liability! – ? –

The Gemara answers:

הָכָא בְּמַאי עַסְקִינַן – **What** case **are we dealing with here,** when we say that the difference between Abaye and Rava is where a non-Kohen eats *terumah*? כְּגוֹן שֶׁתָּחַב לוֹ חֲבֵירוֹ לְתוֹךְ פִּיו – We are dealing **in a case where his fellow thrust** the *terumah* **into his mouth.**[19]

The Gemara asks:

סוֹף סוֹף – **Even so,**[20] כֵּיוָן דִּלְעָסֵיהּ קַנְיֵיהּ – **as soon as he chewed [the *terumah*]** he **"acquired" it** as stolen property,[21] and is liable to pay for it; מִתְחַיֵּיב בְּנַפְשׁוֹ לֹא הֲוֵי עַד דְּבָלְעָהּ – but **he was not liable** to pay **with his life** for eating *terumah* **until he** actually **ate** (i.e. swallowed) **it.** And since the monetary liability is incurred prior to the liability to "death at the hand of Heaven," he should not be exempt from paying for the *terumah*! – ? –

The Gemara answers:

כְּגוֹן שֶׁתָּחַב לוֹ לְתוֹךְ בֵּית הַבְּלִיעָה – Modify the preceding answer and say that we are dealing **in a case where [his fellow] thrust** the *terumah* directly **into his throat.**[22]

The Gemara analyzes this last answer:

הֵיכִי דָּמֵי – **What** exactly **is the case?** How deep into his throat was it thrust? אִי דְּמָצֵי לְאַהֲדוּרָהּ – **If** it was not thrust too deeply, so **that he is able to bring it back up** and spit it out, נִיהֲדַר – then **let him bring it back up!** And if he opts not to do so, he is liable to monetary payment from that moment,[23] whereas he does not become liable to "death at the hand of Heaven" until the later point at which he actually swallows it. Hence, he would be liable to payment.[24] אִי לָא מָצֵי לְאַהֲדוּרָהּ – **And if** it was

NOTES

16. One who eats *cheilev* is liable to *kares,* as stated in *Leviticus* 7:25.

17. At the moment that he picks up someone else's *cheilev* with the intent to eat it, he has committed an act of theft, which makes him liable to pay for it even if it is then destroyed by fire [through no fault of his own] (see *Rashi* above ד״ה ולאביי פטור). [Generally, the criteria for establishing an act of theft are the same as for establishing any other type of acquisition. Whatever act constitutes a *kinyan* (act of acquisition) for a particular item (that is ownerless or being transferred by its owner) also constitutes an act of theft if done to the item with intent to steal. Hence, the liability for theft is incurred as soon as he picks up the *cheilev,* for in doing so he has performed the *kinyan* of *hagbahah* (*lifting*).]

18. The exemption of קָם לֵיהּ בִּדְרַבָּה מִינֵּיהּ, *he is subject only to the greater penalty,* does not apply here, since the two liabilities take effect at different times.

19. The non-Kohen eater thus did not "lift" and "acquire" the *terumah* as stolen property [see end of note]. In such a case, though the eater would not have to pay the full value of the food [since he did not steal it], he ordinarily would have to pay the value of the benefit he derives from swallowing the food (known as "the benefit derived by his throat and digestive system"). [When one benefits at the expense of another, he is obligated to pay for the benefit that he derived – even if he did not commit an act of theft (גְּנֵיבָה) or damage (נֶזֶק); see *Bava Kamma* 20a זה נהנה וזה חסר.] Here, however, since his monetary liability to pay for his benefit is incurred only at the time that he swallows his food, at which time he is simultaneously liable to "death at the hand of Heaven" for eating *terumah,* he would be exempt from payment according to Abaye (*Rashi*).

[As explained at the beginning of the note, the *terumah* does not become "stolen" by the eater simply by virtue of its being inside his mouth. According to *Ritzba* (cited by *Tosafos* ד״ה ואי, in explanation of *Rashi's* approach) this applies only where the other person *forcibly* stuffed the *terumah* into the eater's mouth against the latter's will. If, however, this had been done with the eater's consent, he would indeed be deemed a thief who has "acquired" the *terumah* immediately through its very presence in his mouth. Others, however, maintain that theft requires an *act* of acquisition; the mere presence of an article in one's "domain" does not make it stolen, even if it is the intent of the domain's owner to steal it. Accordingly, our Gemara might refer even to where the *terumah* was thrust into the eater's mouth willingly. Even then, he is not a thief, since he has not performed an *act* of acquisition (see *Ri* in *Tosafos* loc. cit. and *Shitah Mekubetzes* ד״ה ואי לא מצי לאהדורה; *Shitah Mekubetzes* below, 31a ד״ה והתוספות ז״ל שלנו הקשו על פרש״י, in explanation of *Rashi; Ketzos HaChoshen* §348 and *Kovetz Shiurim* §98). See also *Meiri* here ד״ה מכיון שביארנו.]

20. Literally: in the end.

21. [According to *Ritzba* (cited at the end of note 19), the Gemara here would mean that even though it was stuffed into his mouth against his will, his chewing of it demonstrates his consent to steal it and he therefore "acquires" it through its presence in his mouth. According to the other view cited there, the chewing of the *terumah* that is in his "domain" constitutes an *act* of acquisition. (See *Ritva* below, 34b ד״ה פטור שאיסור שבת, *Nesivos HaMishpat* 34:5 and *Hagahos Baruch Taam* to *Mekor Chaim* 454:1.)]

22. [So that he swallows it directly, without first chewing it.]

23. See next note.

24. *Rashi* explains: At the moment that he does not bring it back up, he is considered to be damaging it, whereas the fellow who thrust it into the eater's throat did not actually do anything [to the *terumah,* as he placed it at a point where it did not have to be swallowed] and thus is under no liability whatsoever to the Kohen who owned the *terumah.*

A simple reading of *Rashi* would suggest that in this case the eater's liability is for *damaging* the *terumah* [מַזִּיק] rather than for *theft.* Hence, he cannot be held liable under the laws of theft, but he can be held liable under the laws of *damages,* for by keeping the food in his mouth, he renders it repulsive and unfit to be eaten by its owner.

Rashi's wording below in ד״ה על ידי הדחק and in ד״ה משקין של תרומה, however, suggests that the liability for opting not to bring it back up is, in fact, for *theft* [see below, notes 27 and 29]. Accordingly, when *Rashi* here says that by opting not to bring the *terumah* back up "he is *damaging* it," *Rashi* would not mean that his liability actually falls under the law of "damages," but only that it is *he* who is causing the loss of the *terumah* to its owner, and thus it is *he* – rather than the one

דין ארבע מיתות לא בטלו מי שנתחייב סקילה או נופל מן הגג או חיה דורסתו ומי שנתחייב שריפה או נופל בדליקה או נחש מכישו ומי שנתחייב הריגה או נמסר למלכות או ליסטים באין עליו ומי שנתחייב חנק או טובע בנהר או מת בסרונכי אלא איפוך אריא וגנבי בידי שמים צינים ופחים בידי אדם רבא אמר טעמא דרבי נחוניא בן הקנה מהכא א) ואם העלם יעלימו עם הארץ את עיניהם מן האיש ההוא בתתו מזרעו למולך ושמתי אני את פני באיש ההוא ובמשפחתו והכרתי אותו אמרה תורה כרת שלי כמיתה שלכם מה מיתה שלכם פטור מן התשלומין אף כרת שלי פטור מן התשלומין מאי איכא בין רבא לאביי איכא בינייהו זר שאכל תרומה לאביי [א] פטור ולרבא חייב ולאביי פטור והאמר רב חסדא מודה ר' נחוניא בן הקנה [ב] בגונב חלבו של חבירו ואכלו שהוא חייב שכבר נתחייב בגניבה קודם שבא לידי איסור חלב אלמא דמעידנא דאגביה קנייה מתחייב בנפשו א) לא הוה עד דאכיל ליה הכא נמי בעידנא דאגביה קנייה מתחייב בנפשו לא הוי עד דאכיל ליה הכא במאי עסקינן כגון שתחב לו חבירו לתוך פיו סוף סוף כיון דלעסיה קנייה מתחייב בנפשו לא הוי עד דבלעה כגון ה) שתחב לו לתוך בית הבליעה היכי דמי אי דמצי לאהדורה ניהדר אי לא מצי לאהדורה אמאי חייב לא צריכא דמצי לאהדורה ע"י הדחק רב פפא אמר כגון שתחב לו חבירו משקין של תרומה לתוך פיו רב אשי אמר בזר שאכל תרומה משלו וקרע

רש"י

דין ד' מיתות. עונש דוגמתם: נופל מן הגג. דומה לנסקל שדוחפין אותו מבית הסקילה לארץ דגבוה ב' קומות היה כדאמרי' בנגמר הדין (סנהדרין דף מה.): חיה דורסתו. הרי מפילו לארץ והורגו בדריסה: נחש מכישו. והארס שורפו: נמסר למלכות. והן מתיזין ראשו בסייף כי כן דרך המומתין על ידיהן והיא מיתת סייף: סרונכי. אסכרה והוא בגרון מלנ"ט: מן האיש ההוא. שהוא חייב מיתת ב"ד: ושמתי אני את פני והכרתי. למדנו שהכרת במקום מיתה וחילופה: זר שאכל תרומה. במזיד הוא במיתה בידי שמים ולא בכרת. כרת הוא חלבו ונענשין דכתיב (ויקרא כ) ערירים יהיו: לאביי פטור. מתשלומין דנפקא ליה מאסון בידי שמים וכל אסון במשמע בין במיתה בין בכרת: ולאביי פטור. בתמיה נהי נמי דמיתה בידי שמים פוטרת מתשלומין אבל היכא דאכיל תרומה דגזולה מי מיפטר הא כיון דאגבהה קניה וחייב בתשלומין ואפילו תישרף ומתחייב בנפשו לא הוי עד דאכיל לה: שתחב לו חברו. דלא אגבהה ולא קניה ולא מיחייב בתשלומין אלא בבליעתו מתחייב דמי הנאת מעיו ולא דמי כולה וההיא שעתא שעת חיוב מיתה הוא נמי היכא: איבעי ליה לאהדורה. וכי לא אהדרה מההיא שעתא איהו מזיק לה דלראשון לאו מידי עבד ולא נתחייב לכהן כלום: ואי דלא מצי לאהדורה אמאי חייב. מיתה אנוס הוא: ע"י הדחק. דאי נמי אהדרה ממאסה ולא חזיא לבעלים הלכך מגזל לא גזלה אלא קא מחייבת ליה בתשלומין אהנאת גרונו ומעיו וההיא שעתא חיוב מיתה היא: משקין של תרומה. ולא תדחקה לשנויה בבית הבליעה אלא מכיון שתחב לתוך פיו לאימאסא לה ולא מצית לאוקימי משום גזילה דהא לא חזיא למידי אלא אהניית גרונו ומעיו מיחייב ומיתה ותשלומין באים כאחד: וקרע

תוספות

דין ד' מיתות לא בטלו. וא"ת והא אמר בהשוכר את הפועלים (ב"מ צא:) בההוא דזקפוהו אע"פ שהיה חייב סקילה שבעלו הוא וכנו נערה המאורסה וי"ל בשבעל בנו תחלה ואח"כ הוא דהוי בעולה והרי הוא בחנק אבל קשה דחזינן כמה עבריינים ועובדי עבודת כוכבים שמתים על מטותם ויש לומר דע"י תשובה הקב"ה מיקל ולפעמים מוחל לגמרי או זכות תולה לו ואינו נפרע ממנו בחייו ובפ' אחד דיני ממונות (סנהדרין דף לז: ושם) דפריך והא בר נחש הוא לפי שהמחמיר עליו יותר: זר שאכל תרומה לאביי פטור. ואוכל תרומה בשוגג והזיד במעילה לרבי דאמר במיתה (פסחים דף לג.) דמייב גזירת הכתוב הוא וא"ת לאביי דפטר חייבי מיתות בידי שמים אי ר' נחוניא ס"ל כרבי דאמר הזיד במעילה במיתה אמאי תניא בפרק כל שעה (פסחים דף לב. ושם) האוכל חמץ של הקדש במועד יש אומרים לא מעל ואמרינן מאן י"א רבי נחוניא בן הקנה והא כיון דגלי רחמנא גבי הקדש דלא שייך קים ליה (א) דאם לא כן אין לך אדם שמועל בהקדש א"כ בפסח נמי דאיכא כרת ליחייב ולא הוה לן למימר דקים ליה בדרבה מיניה וכ"ת במיתה הקדש דוקא גלי רחמנא דלא אמרינן דקים ליה בדרבה מיניה אבל התם דהוי בפסח דאיכא כרת לא גלי קרא א"כ הא דתנן התם (שם דף לב:) האוכל תרומת חמץ בפסח בשוגג משלם קרן וחומש במזיד פטור מן התשלומין ומפרש בגמ' במזיד פטור דקים ליה בדרבה מיניה כרבי נחוניא והשתא בשוגג נמי ליפטור משום כרת דפסח דלפי' בשוגג אמרי' דקים ליה בדרבה מיניה כדאמרינן לקמן בפירקין (דף לה.) אלא ע"כ משום דגלי רחמנא במיתה דתרומה בשוגג דלא אמרינן קים ליה בדרבה מיניה וה"ה כי איכא כרת ולא אמרינן דוקא במיתה דגלי גלי אבל כי איכא כרת לא וי"ל דשאני שוגג דתרומה משום דתשלומין דידיה כפרה ולא ממונא כדאמרינן במסכת תרומות (פ"ו מ"א) דאם רצה כהן למחול אינו יכול למחול משום דלא הוי ממון אלא כפרה ואפילו אוכל תרומת עצמו דלא גזל מידי משלם כפרה לעצמו וחומש לכהן ולכך לא שייך קים ליה בדרבה מיניה לפוטרו מכפרה אבל קרן וחומש של הקדש אינו משום כפרה אלא משלם ממון שגזל הקדש ותדע דבתרומה חייב משום דכפרה הוא ולא משום כיון דגלי גלי דהא לרבא דלא פטר במיתה מטעם דקים ליה בדרבה מיניה מאי טעמא לא מיפטר אוכל תרומת חמץ בפסח אלא ודאי משום כפרה הוא ב) וא"ת והא דתנן בפרק נושאין (יבמות דף צט:) כהנת שנתערב ולדה בולד שפחתה ושחררו זה את זה וכן ספק בן תשעה לראשון או בן ז' לאחרון דאמרינן אם אכלו בתרומה אין משלמין קרן וחומש ואמאי כיון דכפרה הוא ליחייבו מספק וי"ל דודאי צריכין להפריש אבל אין נותנין לכהן ולפי זה צריך לומר שהכפרה תלויה בהפרשה והא דאין הכהן יכול למחול היינו לענין שלא יהיה צריך להפריש אבל לאחר שהפריש יכול למחול לו שיהא שלו: ולאביי פטור והאמר רב חסדא כו'. הכי נמי הוה מצי לאקשויי אמתניתין דכל שעה (פסחים דף לא:) דקתני פטור מן התשלומין לפי מה דמוקמינן לה כרבי נחוניא בן הקנה: אי דמצי לאהדורה ניהדרה. וכי לא מיהדר חייב דמיתה לא פטרה ליה דלא אתיא עד דבלע לגמרי: ואי דלא מצי לאהדורה אמאי חייב. פירש בקונטרס אמאי חייב מיתה וקשה לר"י דלוקי כגון שמרצונו מניח לו לתחוב דהשתא ודאי חייב מיתה אע"ג דלא מצי לאהדורה וממון נמי לא מיחייב כיון דלא מצי לאהדורה אלא על הנאת גרונו ומעיו וההיא שעתא קים ליה בדרבה מיניה ונראה לר"י דה"פ אמאי חייב ממון והרי הוא לא גזלו והנאתו לא מיחייב דאע"ג דאמרי' (ב"ק דף קיא:) גזל ולא נתייאשו הבעלים ובא אחר ואכלו רצה מזה גובה כו' היינו דוקא לפי שהדבר הגזול ישנו בעולם בשעה שזה שני גוזלו אבל הכא דבשעה שזה נהנה ממנו כבר הוא אבוד מן העולם שהוא במקום דלא אפשר לאהדוריה אין לו על השני כלום ג) וריצב"א מפרש כשיטת רש"י ופשיטא ליה להש"ס דאיירי כשתוחב לו בע"כ דכשתוחב לו מרצונו מיד כשמשים בפיו ולא אהדרה קנאה מיד להתחייב באונסין ואין באין כאחד דמסתמא מניחה בפיו ואח"כ תוחב לו באצבעו או בכוס ואת"ל שהוא בראש הכוס מתחלתו ועד גמר בית הבליעה מ"מ קונה אותו בפיו להתחייב באונסים אע"ג דיכול לנתקו ולהביאו אצלו ◦ דדוקא לענין הגט אמרי' היכא דיכול לנתקו דלא הוי גט משום דבעינן כריתות והא אגידא ביה אבל לענין זכיה אשכחן בפ"ק דב"מ (דף ט. ושם) טלית תליה על גבי קרקע ותליה על גבי העמוד והגביה תליה שעל גבי קרקע דלא קני מטעם שיכול לנתקה ולהביאה אצלו וכיון שאינו זוכה מטעם זה ה"ה דאינו מגרע זכיית האחר שהוא מונח בתוך ידו או בתוך פיו מטעם זה ועוד דלכל הפחות קונה מחצה כמו שנים שהגביהו מציאה ולכך פשיטא ליה להש"ס דבאונס איירי וה"פ אנוס הוא ופטור ממיתה וממון דאנן סהדי דלא ניחא ליה באכילת איסור: לא צריכא דמצי לאהדורה על ידי הדחק. והשתא ליכא למימר דניהדרה דאין מרויחין בעלים בכך דכבר נמאסו הלכך ליכא חיוב ממון אלא ע"י הנאת מעיו ואז באין כאחד ואע"ג שחבירו גזלה הואיל ויכול להחזירה הויא כמו שהיא בעין והרי הוא בולעה ונהנה בה ואם תאמר והא אמרינן בפרק בהמה המקשה (חולין דף עא.) גבי טומאה בלועה [דלא מטמאה לא משום דלא חזיא דנהי דבפניו לא חזיא] שלא בפניו מיחזא חזיא א"כ אי הוה מהדר לה הויא חזיא וי"ל כגון דמעיקרא לא הוי בה כי אם שוה פרוטה או מעט יותר ועתה שנתקלקלה קצת אינה שוה פרוטה ואפילו אי זה נהנה וזה לא חסר פטור ◦ מ"מ כיון דשוין כל שהוא אז מיחייב בכל כדאמרינן התם (ב"ק דף כ:) משום דא"ל את גרמת לי היקפא יתירתא מיחייב בכל הנאה או משום שחרוריתא דאשיתא מיחייב לכולי עלמא בכל וריצב"א פי' דמיירי אפי' באוכלין דלא מאיסי וכיון דתחב לו בבית הבליעה ובלע ונהנה מיד חשוב באין כאחת אע"פ שאין כאחד ממש כדאשכחן בסוף פרק ד' אחין (יבמות דף לג. ושם) דמפרש בעל מום ששמש בטומאה דאתו בהדי הדדי כגון שחתך אצבעו בסכין טמאה אע"פ שאי אפשר שלא יגע בסכין קודם שיחתוך ד): רב אשי אמר בזר שאכל תרומה משלו וקרע שיראים כו'. פ"ה דסבירא ליה לרב אשי דמיתה לזה ותשלומין לזה פטור ופליג אדרבא דאמר בפרק קמא דסנהדרין (דף י. ושם) פלוני בא על בת פלוני והוחמו נהרגין ומשלמין ממון לזה ונפשות לזה ה) פי' ממון לבת שרצו להפסיד לה כתובתה ונפשות לזה שאומר שבא עליה ואין נראה ה) דאי חשיב אכילת תרומה וקריעת שיראין ממון לזה ונפשות לזה א"כ תקשי ליה לרבא הא דתנן בהמניח את הכד (ב"ק דף לד: ושם) והוא

עין משפט נר מצוה

ח א מיי' פ"י מהלכות תרומות הל' ו סמג לאוין רמו:
ט ב מיי' פ"ג מהלכות גניבה הלכה ב סמג עשין על טוש"ע ח"מ סימן שנ:

גליון הש"ס

תוס' ד"ה ואי וכו' דדוקא לענין הגט. תמוה לי הא הדיא איתא כן בב"מ דף י ע"א ולע"ג: ד"ה לא צריכא וכו' מ"מ כיון דשוין כל שהוא. עי' בב"ק דף כ ע"ב תוד"ה הא ליתנהו:

ליקוטי רש"י

דין ארבע מיתות. דין שמים שהיא דוגמתו [סוטה ח:]. מובעות בידי שמים הדומה למיתה שהוא מחויב [סנהדרין לז:]. נופל מן הגג. דומיא דסקילה דתנן (סנהדרין דף מה.) בית הסקילה היה גבוה שתי קומות אחד מן העדים דוחפו כו' [סוטה שם]. דומיא דסקילה כדתנן לקמן [דף מה:] בית הסקילה היתה גבוהה שתי קומות וקומה שלו שהרי כאן שלש [סנהדרין שם]. חיה דורסתו. הרי דורסו ומפילו לארץ וגם זה דומה לנסקל [סוטה שם]. נחש מכישו. דקלי ליה זיהרא הארס שלו כאש שורפו [סנהדרין שם]. נמסר למלכות. ומיתת מלכות מתיזין את ראשו בסייף והרגו נמי סייף הוא כדאמרינן בסנהדרין (דף נב.) [סוטה שם]. ליסטים באין עליו. שהרגו בסייף [סנהדרין שם]. בסרונכי. בולמו"ס והוא חולי גרונו [סוטה שם]. חולי שמתו אסטרנגולי"ן הוא בו"ן מלנגו"ן [יומא פד.]. ואם העלם יעלימו. אם העלימו בדבר אחד סוף שיעלימו בדברים הרבה אם העלימו בהדר קטנה סוף שיעלימו בסנהדרי גדולה [ויקרא כ, ד]. למולך. ע"א היא ששמה מולך חו הוא עבודתה שמוסר בנו לכומרים ועושין שתי מדורות גדולות ומעבירין את הבן ברגליו בין שתי המדורות האש [שם יח, כא]. ובמשפחתו. אמר ר' שמעון וכי משפחה מה חטאה ללמדך שאין לך משפחה שיש בה מוכס שאין כולם מוכסין שכולם מחפין עליו. והכרתי אותו. למה נאמר לפי שנאמר ובמשפחתו יכול יהיו כל המשפחה בהכרת תלמוד לומר אותו אותו בהכרת ולא כל המשפחה כולה ביסורין [שם כ, ה]. ולאביי פטור. בתמיה נהי נמי דמיתה בידי שמים פוטרת מתשלומין אבל היכא דאכיל תרומה דגזולה מי מיפטר הא לבנין הקדש לא קאי כדפרשינן [קידושין דף נג.]. גזל ולא נתייאשו הבעלים אינם יכולים להקדיש זה לפי שאינם שלו וזה לפי שאינם ברשותו מיהו מחייב משעת הגבהה באחריותה [רש"י מכות ישן בשיטמ"ק].

מסורת הש"ס

א) [עי' תוס' בבא קמא ד"ה הא], ב) [פי' ממון לבת שרצו להפסידו כתובה כצ"ל מהרש"א].

תוספות ישנים

א) וא"ת כיון דלעסו ליה נתקלקל והיאך חייב הוא עלה כדאמר פ"ק דכריתות [דף ז.] כהן שסך שמן של תרומה בתו ישראל מתעגל בו ואינו חושש וי"ל דהתם ודאי הוא נתקלקל שכבר נגמרה כל הנאתו אבל הכא לא נגמרה כל הנאתו בלעיסה לחודיה. ת"י]. ב) [ועוד יש לומר דכפרה הוי מדסתרי' לאביי מזיד בתרומה ואע"ג דגלי רחמנא גבי שוגג דלא אמרי' קים ליה בדרבה מיניה בתרומה אלא ודאי משום כפרה הוא ויש לדחות דשאני שוגג דתרומה לפי שאינו שוגג גמור משלם חומש. ת"י]. ג) [פי' ריצב"א לא יתיישב בסמוך דקאמר אי בעי גמין ואכיל. ת"י]. ד) [ור"ח פירש כיון שהוא במקום דלא מצי לאהדורי אלא אם כן הדחק ככר נהנה גרונו ובלען כאחד ואי"ת והיאך יתחייב ממון והא כיון שתחבו לו באונס ויש לומר כיון דמצי לאהדורה ע"י הדחק ולא הדרה ניחא ליה בהנאה זו. ת"י]. ה) [ועוד דלאמתי אמי איכא בין רבא לאביי אי הוי סבר רבא דליף מאסון אסון הוי מיחייב ממון לזה ונפשות לזה. ת"י].

הגהות הב"ח

(א) תוס' ד"ה זר וכו' קים ליה בדרבה מיניה דאם:

לעזי רש"י

מלנ"ט. פירוש אסכרה, מין חולי הגרון המחנק (מוסף הערוך ערך אסכרה ועיין רש"י שבת דף לג סוע"א).

תורה אור השלם

א) וְאִם הַעְלֵם יַעְלִימוּ עַם הָאָרֶץ אֶת עֵינֵיהֶם מִן הָאִישׁ הַהוּא בְּתִתּוֹ מִזַּרְעוֹ לַמֹּלֶךְ לְבִלְתִּי הָמִית אֹתוֹ: וְשַׂמְתִּי אֲנִי אֶת פָּנַי בָּאִישׁ הַהוּא וּבְמִשְׁפַּחְתּוֹ וְהִכְרַתִּי אֹתוֹ וְאֵת כָּל הַזֹּנִים אַחֲרָיו לִזְנוֹת אַחֲרֵי הַמֹּלֶךְ מִקֶּרֶב עַמָּם: [ויקרא כ, ד - ה]

דִּין אַרְבַּע מִיתוֹת לֹא בָּטְלוּ – the equivalent **punishment of the four** types of **executions has not ceased.**[1]

The Gemara returns to its citation of the Baraisa, which explains in what form the four capital punishments continue to be administered:

מִי שֶׁנִּתְחַיֵּיב סְקִילָה – ONE WHO IS DESERVING OF death by STONING אוֹ נוֹפֵל מִן הַגָּג אוֹ חַיָּה דוֹרַסְתּוֹ – EITHER FALLS FROM A ROOF OR IS TRAMPLED BY A WILD BEAST.[2] וּמִי שֶׁנִּתְחַיֵּיב שְׂרֵיפָה – AND ONE WHO IS DESERVING OF death by BURNING[3] אוֹ נוֹפֵל בִּדְלֵיקָה אוֹ נָחָשׁ מַכִּישׁוֹ – EITHER FALLS INTO A FIRE OR IS BITTEN BY A SNAKE.[4] וּמִי שֶׁנִּתְחַיֵּיב הֲרִיגָה – AND ONE WHO IS DESERVING OF death by BEHEADING אוֹ נִמְסַר לַמַּלְכוּת אוֹ לִיסְטִים בָּאִין עָלָיו – IS EITHER HANDED OVER TO THE AUTHORITIES OR ATTACKED BY BANDITS.[5] וּמִי שֶׁנִּתְחַיֵּיב חֶנֶק – AND ONE WHO IS DESERVING OF death by STRANGULATION אוֹ טוֹבֵעַ בַּנָּהָר אוֹ מֵת בִּסְרוּנְכִי – EITHER DROWNS IN A RIVER OR DIES OF QUINSY.[6] Now, it is evident from this Baraisa that death at the hand of a wild beast or bandits is a direct Heavenly retribution for one's sins.[7] How, then, does Rav Adda refer to such death as "death at the hand of man"?

The Gemara answers:

אֶלָּא אֵיפוּךְ – **Rather, reverse** the wording of Rav Adda bar Ahavah's question, so that he is saying that אַרְיָא וְגַנָּבֵי בִּידֵי שָׁמַיִם – death by **a lion or bandits is at the hand of Heaven,**[8] צִינִּים וּפַחִים בִּידֵי אָדָם – and through exposure to **cold and heat is at the hand of man.**[9]

The Gemara cites a different source for R' Nechunya ben HaKanah's ruling:

רָבָא אָמַר – **Rava says:** טַעְמָא דְּרַבִּי נְחוּנְיָא בֶּן הַקָּנָה מֵהָכָא – **The reason of R' Nechunya ben HaKanah** for ruling as he does **is based on the following** verse:[10] "וְאִם הַעְלֵם יַעְלִימוּ עַם הָאָרֶץ אֶת־עֵינֵיהֶם מִן־הָאִישׁ הַהוּא בְּתִתּוֹ מִזַּרְעוֹ לַמֹּלֶךְ ... – ***But if the people of the land avert their eyes from that man when he gives from his offspring to the Molech,*** *and do not put him to death,*[11] וְשַׂמְתִּי אֲנִי אֶת־פָּנַי בָּאִישׁ הַהוּא וּבְמִשְׁפַּחְתּוֹ וְהִכְרַתִּי אֹתוֹ" – ***then I shall concentrate My attention upon that man and upon his family and I shall cut him off . . .***[12] Thus, God says that if the people of the land do not implement the court-imposed death penalty of stoning, I will punish him with *kares.* אָמְרָה תוֹרָה – **The Torah** thus in effect **states** in the name of God: כָּרֵת שֶׁלִּי כְּמִיתָה שֶׁלָּכֶם – **My** ***kares*** punishment **is like your death** penalty, which it replaces. מָה מִיתָה שֶׁלָּכֶם פָּטוּר מִן הַתַּשְׁלוּמִין – Accordingly, **just as** in the case of **your** court-imposed **death** penalty, **he is exempt from payment** for damages done simultaneously with the act that made him liable to death, אַף כָּרֵת שֶׁלִּי פָּטוּר מִן הַתַּשְׁלוּמִין – **so too,** in the case of **My** ***kares*** punishment, **he is exempt from payment** for damages done simultaneously with the act that made him liable to death.

The Gemara asks:

מַאי אִיכָּא בֵּין רָבָא לְאַבָּיֵי – **What** practical difference **is there between** the reasons offered by **Rava and Abaye?**

The Gemara answers:

אִיכָּא בֵּינַיְיהוּ – **There is** a practical difference **between them** in the case of זָר שֶׁאָכַל תְּרוּמָה – **a non-Kohen who ate** ***terumah,*** for which the penalty is not *kares* but death at the hand of Heaven.[13] לְאַבָּיֵי פָּטוּר – **According to Abaye,** R' Nechunya ben HaKanah would rule that **he is exempt** from paying for the *terumah,*[14] וּלְרָבָא חַיָּיב – **whereas according to Rava,** R' Nechunya ben HaKanah would rule that **he is liable** to pay for the *terumah.*[15]

NOTES

1. I.e. although a Sanhedrin could not nowadays sentence a guilty person to the capital punishment prescribed for his crime, nevertheless, God may punish him by causing him to be killed in a similar way (see *Rashi* and *Tosafos*).

2. In execution by סְקִילָה, *stoning,* the convict is pushed from an elevation to the ground below. Only if he survives this fall are stones actually thrown at him (see Mishnah, *Sanhedrin* 45a). Hence, in the post-Temple era, Divine Providence brings about an analogous punishment by causing the one deserving of stoning to be killed by falling off a roof or by being thrown to the ground by a wild animal (see *Rashi*).

3. In execution by שְׂרֵפָה, *burning,* molten lead is poured down the convict's throat, burning him internally (see Mishnah, *Sanhedrin* 52a).

4. And the snake venom kills him by "burning" him internally (see *Rashi*).

5. Such a person dies either at the hand of bandits, who kill their victims with a sword, or at the hands of the authorities, who execute by beheading (see *Rashi* here and to *Sanhedrin* 37b ד״ה ליסטין באין עליו).

6. *Rashi,* as rendered by *Targum HaLaaz.* This disease can so constrict the throat that the person cannot breathe and suffocates.

7. [Actually, the Gemara could have proven that lions and thieves come upon a person by Heavenly decree by inference from the first Baraisa cited, which states: *All is in the hand of Heaven except for cold and heat,* indicating that anything other than cold and heat – including death at the hand of a lion or bandits – *is* in the hand of Heaven. The Gemara, however, chooses to prove its point by citing the Baraisa of R' Chiya, where the point is stated explicitly (*Shitah Mekubetzes* to 30a ד״ה ותו אריא וגנבי and *Maharsha* there; cf. *Maharam Schif* there).]

8. As stated in the Baraisa taught by R' Chiya.

9. On account of his negligence, as stated in the first Baraisa.

[Thus, what Rav Adda bar Ahavah actually asked was: On the basis of what do you assume that Jacob warned his sons about death by a lion or bandits, which is at the hand of Heaven? Perhaps he warned about death through exposure to heat and cold, which is at the hand of man!]

10. *Leviticus* 20:4-5.

11. By stoning, as prescribed earlier in verse 2: *Any man . . . who shall give of his offspring to Molech shall be put to death; the people of the land shall pelt him with stones.*

12. *"I shall cut him off"* refers to *kares.*

13. A non-Kohen who intentionally eats *terumah* is subject to the penalty known technically as מִיתָה בִּידֵי שָׁמַיִם, *death at the hand of Heaven,* a lesser form of Divinely imposed death than *kares.* For in the case of *kares,* the sinner's children are also affected, as stated in *Leviticus* 20:21: *They shall be childless* (*Rashi* [see also verse 20 there]).

[Other Rishonim dispute *Rashi* on this point and maintain that dying childless is not a universal feature of *kares* (see *Tosafos* to *Shabbos* 25a ד״ה כרת and *Ramban* to *Leviticus* 18:29). Some maintain that whereas *kares* causes death between the ages of fifty and fifty-nine, "death at the hand of Heaven" does not take effect until one's sixtieth year (see *Moed Katan* 28a with *Tosafos* ד״ה מת וד״ה ומיתה; cf. *Yerushalmi* cited by *Tosafos* to *Shabbos* 25a loc. cit.). Others maintain that *kares* atones only for one who repents; one who does not repent will be further punished for his sin after death. "Death at the hand of Heaven," however, atones for the sin even without repentance (*Rav* to *Sanhedrin* 9:6). See also *Rabbeinu Bachya* to *Leviticus* 18:29 for a lengthy discussion of the penalty of *kares.*]

At any rate, the non-Kohen who has eaten *terumah* has simultaneously incurred "death at the hand of Heaven" for eating the *terumah,* as well as monetary liability for destroying the property of the Kohen [where the *terumah* had already been given to a specific Kohen – see *Haflaah* ד״ה עוד נלע״ד (in his comments to *Tosafos* ד״ה ולאביי)].

14. According to Abaye, R' Nechunya ben HaKanah derives that whatever form of death Jacob meant by the term *ason* serves to exempt the sinner from simultaneous liability to monetary payment. Since Jacob certainly was concerned about *any* form of death – even lesser forms than *kares* – even "death at the hand of Heaven" serves to exempt from monetary payment (see *Rashi*).

15. According to Rava, R' Nechunya ben HaKanah derives only that "My *kares* punishment" is the equivalent of the court-administered death penalty. Hence, there is no basis to say that a lesser form of death, such as "death at the hand of Heaven," should exempt from monetary payment.

דין ארבע מיתות לא בטלו מי שנתחייב סקילה או נופל מן הגג או חיה דורסתו ומי שנתחייב שריפה או נופל בדליקה או נחש מכישו ומי שנתחייב הריגה או נמסר למלכות או ליסטים באין עליו ומי שנתחייב חנק או טובע בנהר או מת בסרונכי אלא איפוך אריא וגנבי בידי שמים צינים ופחים בידי אדם רבא אמר טעמא דרבי נחוניא בן הקנה מהכא א) ואם העלם יעלימו עם הארץ את עיניהם מן האיש ההוא בתתו מזרעו למולך ושמתי אני את פני באיש ההוא ובמשפחתו והכרתי אותו אמרה תורה כרת שלי כמיתה שלכם מה מיתה שלכם פטור מן התשלומין אף כרת שלי פטור מן התשלומין מאי איכא בין רבא לאביי איכא בינייהו זר שאכל תרומה לאביי (א) פטור ולרבא חייב ולאביי פטור והאמר רב חסדא מודה ר' נחוניא בן הקנה ב בגונב חלבו של חבירו ואכלו שהוא חייב שכבר נתחייב בגניבה קודם שבא לידי איסור חלב אלמא דמעידנא דאגביה קנייה מתחייב בנפשו א) לא הוה עד דאכיל ליה הכא נמי בעידנא דאגביה קנייה מתחייב בנפשו לא הוי עד דאכיל ליה הכא במאי עסקינן כגון שתחב לו חבירו לתוך פיו סוף סוף כיון דלעסיה קנייה מתחייב בנפשו לא הוי עד דבלעה כגון ב) שתחב לו לתוך בית הבליעה היכי דמי אי דמצי לאהדורה ניהדר אי לא מצי לאהדורה אמאי חייב לא צריכא דמצי לאהדורה ע"י הדחק רב פפא אמר כגון שתחב לו חבירו משקין של תרומה לתוך פיו רב אשי אמר בזר שאכל תרומה משלו וקרע

רש"י

דין ד' מיתות. עונש דוגמתם: נופל מן הגג. דומה לנסקל שדוחפין אותו מבית הסקילה לארץ דגבוה ב' קומות היה כדאמרי' בנגמר הדין (סנהדרין דף מה.): חיה דורסתו. ארי מפילו לארץ והורגו בדריסה: נחש מכישו. והארס שורפו: נמסר למלכות. והן מתיזין ראשו בסייף כי כן דרך המומתין על ידיהן וזו היא מיתת סייף: סרונכי. אסכרא והוא בגרון מלנ"ט: מן האיש ההוא. שהוא חייב מיתת ב"ד: ושמתי אני את פני והכרתי. למדנו שהכרת במקום מיתה וחילופה: זר שאכל תרומה. במזיד הוא במיתה בידי שמים ולא בכרת. כרת הוא ערירי ונענשין דכתיב (ויקרא כ) ערירים יהיו: לאביי פטור. מתשלומין דנפקא ליה מאסון בידי שמים וכל אסון במשמע בין במיתה בין בכרת: ולאביי פטור. בתמיה נהי נמי דמיתה בידי שמים פוטרת מתשלומין אבל היכא דאכיל תרומה דגזולה מי מיפטר הא כיון דלאגבהה קניה וחייב בתשלומין ואפילו מישרף ומתחייב בנפשו לא הוי עד דאכיל לה: שתחב לו חברו. דלא אגבהה ולא קניה ולא מיחייב בתשלומין אלא בבליעתו מתחייב דמי הנאית מעיו ולא דמי גזלה וההיא שעתא שעת חיוב מיתה נמי היא: איבעי ליה לאהדורה. וכי לא אהדרה מההיא שעתא איהו מזיק לה דראשון לאו מידי עבד ולא נתחייב לכהן כלום: ואי דלא מצי לאהדורה אמאי חייב. מיתה אנוס הוא: ע"י הדחק. דאי נמי אהדרה ממאסה ולא חזיא לבעלים הלכך מגזל לא גזלה אמאי קא מחייבת ליה בתשלומין אהנאת גרונו ומעיו ההיא שעתא חיוב מיתה היא: משקין של תרומה. ולא תדקדק לשנויה בבית הבליעה אלא מכיון שמתחבה לתוך פיו איממסה לה ולא מצית לאחיובי משום גזלה דהא לא חזיא לאו מידי אלא אהנאית גרונו ומעיו מיחייב ומיתה ותשלומין באים כאחד: וקרע

תוספות

דין ד' מיתות לא בטלו. וא"ת והא אמר בהשוכר את הפועלים (ב"מ פג:) בההוא דזקפוהו אע"פ שהיה חייב סקילה שבעלו הוא ובנו נערה המאורסה וי"ל בשבעל בנו תחלה ואח"כ הוא דהוי בעולה והרי הוא בחנק אבל קשה דחזינן כמה עבריינים ועובדי עבודת כוכבים שמתים על מטותם ויש לומר דע"י תשובה הקב"ה מיקל ולפעמים מוחל לגמרי או זכות תולה לו ואינו נפרע ממנו בחייו ובפ' אחד דיני ממונות (סנהדרין דף לז: ושם) דפריך והא בר נחש הוא לפי שהתמיר עליו יומר: זר שאכל תרומה לאביי פטור. והוא אוכל תרומה בשוגג והזיד במעילה לרבי דאמר במיתה (פסחים דף לג.) דחייב גזירת הכתוב הוא וא"ת לאביי דפטר חייבי מיתות בידי שמים אי ר' נחוניא ס"ל כרבי דאמר הזיד במעילה במיתה אמאי הזיד בפרק כל שעה (פסחים דף כט. ושם) האוכל חמץ של הקדש במועד יש אומרים לא מעל ואמרינן מאן י"א רבי נחוניא בן הקנה והא כיון דגלי רחמנא גבי הקדש דלא שייך קים ליה (א) דאם לא כן אין לך אדם שמועל בהקדש א"כ בפסח נמי דאיכא כרת ליחייב ולא הוה לן למימר דקים ליה בדרבה מיניה וכ"ת במיתה דהקדש דוקא גלי רחמנא דלא אמרינן דקים ליה בדרבה מיניה אבל התם דהוי בפסח דאיכא כרת לא גלי קרא א"כ הא דתנן התם (שם דף לג:) האוכל תרומת חמץ בפסח בשוגג משלם קרן וחומש במזיד פטור מן התשלומין ומפרש בגמ' במזיד פטור דקים ליה בדרבה מיניה כרבי נחוניא והשתא בשוגג נמי ליפטר משום כרת דפסח דלפי' בשוגג אמרי' דקים ליה בדרבה מיניה כדאמרינן לקמן בפירקין (דף לה.) אלא ע"כ משום דגלי רחמנא במיתה דתרומה בשוגג דלא אמרינן קים ליה בדרבה מיניה וה"ה כי איכא כרת ולא אמרינן דוקא במיתה דגלי גלי אבל כי איכא כרת לא וי"ל דשאני שוגג דתרומה משום דתשלומין דידיה כפרה ולא ממונא כדאמרינן במסכת תרומות (פ"ו מ"א) דאם רצה כהן למחול אינו יכול למחול משום דלא הוי ממון אלא כפרה ואפילו אוכל תרומת עצמו דלא גזל מידי משלם כפרה לעצמו וחומש לכהן ולכך לא שייך קים ליה בדרבה מיניה לפוטרו מכפרה אבל קרן וחומש של הקדש אינו משום כפרה אלא משלם ממון שגזל הקדש ותדע דבתרומה חייב משום דכפרה הוא ולא משום כיון דגלי גלי דהא לרבא דלא פטר במיתה מטעם דקים ליה בדרבה מיניה מאי טעמא לא מיפטר אוכל תרומת חמץ בפסח אלא ודאי משום כפרה הוא ב) וא"ת והא דתנן בפרק נושאין (יבמות דף לט:) כהנת שנתערב ולדה בולד שפחתה ושחררו זה את זה וכן ספק בן תשעה לראשון או בן ז' לאחרון דאמרינן אם אכלו בתרומה אין משלמין קרן וחומש ואמאי כיון דכפרה הוא ליחייבו מספק וי"ל דודאי צריכין להפריש אבל אין נותנין לכהן ולפי זה צריך לומר שהכפרה תלויה בהפרשה והא דאין הכהן יכול למחול היינו לענין שלא יהיה צריך להפריש אבל לאחר שהפריש יכול למחול לו שיהא שלו: **ולאביי** פטור והאמר רב חסדא כו'. הכי נמי הוה מצי לאקשויי אמתניתין דכל שעה (פסחים דף לא:) דקתני פטור מן התשלומין לפי מה דמוקמינן לה כרבי נחוניא בן הקנה: **אי** דמצי לאהדורה ניהדרה. וכי לא מיהדר חייב דמיתה לא פטרה ליה דלא אתיא עד דבלע לגמרי: **ואי** דלא מצי לאהדורה אמאי חייב. פירש בקונטרס אמאי חייב מיתה וקשה לר"י דלוקי כגון שמרצונו מניח לו לתחוב דהשתא ודאי חייב מיתה אע"ג דלא מצי לאהדורה וממון נמי לא מיחייב כיון דלא מצי לאהדורה אלא על הנאת גרונו ומעיו וההיא שעתא קים ליה בדרבה מיניה ונראה לר"י דה"פ אמאי חייב ממון והרי הוא לא גזלו ואהנאתו לא מיחייב דאע"ג דאמרי' (ב"ק דף קיא:) גזל ולא נתייאשו הבעלים ובא אחר ואכלו רצה מזה גובה כו' היינו דוקא לפי שהדבר הגזול ישנו בעולם בשעה שזה שני גזלו אבל הכא דבשעה שזה נהנה ממנו כבר הוא אבוד מן העולם שהוא במקום דלא אפשר לאהדוריה אין לו על השני כלום ג) וריצב"א מפרש כשיטת רש"י ופשיטא ליה להש"ס דאיירי כשתוחב לו בע"כ דכשתוחב לו מרצונו מיד כשמשים בפיו ולא אהדרה קנאה מיד להתחייב באונסין ואין באין כאחד דמסתמא מניחה בפיו ואח"כ תוחב לו באצבעו או בכוס ואת"ל שהוא בראש הכוס מתחלתו ועד גמר בית הבליעה מ"מ קונה אותו בפיו להתחייב באונסים אע"ג דיכול לנתקו ולהביאו אצלו ° דדוקא לענין הגט אמרי' היכא דיכול לנתקו דלא הוי גט משום דבעינן כריתות והא אגידא ביה אבל לענין זכיה אשכחן בפ"ק דב"מ (דף ט. ושם) טלית חציה על גבי קרקע וחציה על גבי העמוד והגביה חציה שעל גבי קרקע דלא קני מטעם שיכול לנתקה ולהביאה אצלו וכיון שאינו זוכה מטעם זה ה"ה דאינו מגרע זכיית האחר שהוא מונח בתוך ידו או בתוך פיו מטעם זה ועוד דלכל הפחות קונה מחלה כמו שנים שהגביהו מציאה ולכך פשיטא ליה להש"ס דבאונס מיירי וה"פ אנוס הוא ופטור ממיתה וממון דאנן סהדי דלא ניחא ליה באכילת איסור: **לא** צריכא דמצי לאהדורה על ידי הדחק. והשתא ליכא למימר דניהדרה דאין מרויחין בעלים בכך דכבר נמאסו הלכך ליכא חיוב ממון אלא ע"י הנאת מעיו ואז באין כאחד ואע"ג שחבירו גזלה הואיל ויכול להחזירה הויא כמו שהיא בעין והרי הוא בולעה ונהנה בה ואם תאמר והא אמרינן בפרק בהמה המקשה (חולין דף עא.) גבי טומאה בלועה [דלא מטמאה לא משום דלא חזיא דנהי דבפניו לא חזיא] שלא בפניו מיחזא חזיא א"כ אי הוה מהדר לה הויא חזיא וי"ל כגון דמעיקרא לא הוי בה כי אם שוה פרוטה או מעט יותר ועתה שנתקלקלה קצת אינה שוה פרוטה ואפילו אי זה נהנה חזה לא חסר פטור ° מ"מ כיון דשוין כל שהוא אז מיחייב בכל כדאמרינן התם (ב"ק דף כ:) משום דא"ל את גרמת לי היקפא יתירתא מיחייב בכל הנאה או משום שחרוריתא דאשיתא מיחייב לכולי עלמא בכל וריצב"א פי' דמיירי אפי' באוכלין דלא מאיסי וכיון דתחב לו בבית הבליעה ובלע ונהנה מיד חשוב באין כאחת אע"פ שאין כאחד ממש כדאשכחן בסוף פרק ד' אחין (יבמות דף לג. ושם) דמפרש בעל מום ששמש בטומאה דאתו בהדי הדדי כגון שחתך אצבעו בסכין טמאה אע"פ שאי אפשר שלא יגע בסכין קודם שיחתוך ד): **רב** אשי אמר בזר שאכל תרומה משלו וקרע שיראים כו'. פ"ה דסבירא ליה לרב אשי דמיתה לזה ותשלומין לזה פטור ופליג אדרבא דאמר בפרק קמא דסנהדרין (דף י. ושם) פלוני בא על בת פלוני והחמו נהרגין ומשלמין ממון לזה ונפשות לזה ג) פי' ממון לבת שרצו להפסיד לה כתובתה ונפשות לזה שאומר שבא עליה ואין נראה ה) דאי חשיב אכילת תרומה וקריעת שיראין ממון לזה ונפשות לזה א"כ תקשי ליה לרבא הא דתנן בהמניח את הכד (ב"ק דף לד: ושם)

והוא

עין משפט נר מצוה

ח א מיי' פ"י מהלכות תרומות הל' ו סמג לאוין רנו:

ט ב מיי' פ"ב מהלכות גניבה הלכה ד סמג עשין עא טוש"ע ח"מ סימן שנ:

גליון הש"ס

תוס' ד"ה ואי וכו' דדוקא לענין הגט. תמוה לי הא בדידה איתא כן בב"מ ז ע"א ולע"ג: ד"ה לא צריכא וכו' מ"מ כיון דשוין כל שהוא. עי' ב"ק דף כ ע"ב תוד"ה הא אמהני:

ליקוטי רש"י

דין ארבע מיתות. דין שמים בהיא דוגמתו [סוטה ח:]. פורענות בידי שמים הדומה למיתה שהוא מחויב בה [סנהדרין לז:]. נופל מן הגג. דומיא דסקילה דתנן (סנהדרין דף מה.) בית הסקילה היה גבוה שתי קומות אחד מן העדים בא ודחפו כו' [סוטה שם]. דומיא דסקילה כדתנן לקמן (דף מה:) בית הסקילה היתה גבוהה שתי קומות וקתני אלו הרי כאן שלש [סנהדרין שם]. חיה דורסתו. ארי דורסו בצפרניו ומפילו לארץ וגם זה דומה לנסקל [סוטה שם]. נחש מכישו. דקלי ליה זיהרא ארס של נחש שורפו [סנהדרין שם]. נמסר למלכות. ומיתר מלכות מתיזין את ראשו בסייף והרג נמי סייף הוא כדאמרינן בסנהדרין (דף נב.) [סוטה שם]. ליסטים באין עליו. שדרכן להרגו בסייף [סנהדרין שם]. בסרונכי. בומלנ"ט והוא חולי בגרונו [סוטה שם]. חולי ששמו אשטרנגלי"ן הוא בו"ן מלנט[יומא פד.]. ואם העלם יעלימו. אם העלימו בדבר אחד סוף שיעלימו בדברים הרבה אם העלימו סנהדרי קטנה סוף שיעלימו סנהדרי גדולה [ויקרא כ, ד]. למולך. ע"ז היא ששמה מולך וזו היא עבודתה שמוסר בנו לכמרים ועושין שתי מדורות גדולות ומעבירין את הבן ברגליו בין שתי מדורות האש [שם יח, כא]. ובמשפחתו. אמר ר' שמעון וכי משפחה מה חטאה אלא לומדך שאין לך משפחה שיש בה מוכס שאין כולם מוכסין כולם מחפין עליו. והכרתי אותו. למה נאמר לפי שנאמר ובמשפחתו יכול יהיו כל המשפחה בהכרת תלמוד לומר אותו אותו בהכרת ולא כל המשפחה בהכרת אלא ביסורין [שם כ, ה]. ולאביי פטור. בתמיה נהי נמי דמיתה בידי שמים פוטרת מתשלומין אבל היכא דאכיל תרומה דגזולה מי מיפטר ואע"ג דלבנין ההקדש לא קני ברשותיה כדאמרינן (קידושין דף נב:) גזל ולא נתייאשו הבעלים שניהם אינם יכולים להקדיש זה לפי שאינו שלו וזה לפי שאינו ברשותו מיהו מחייב משעת הגבהה באחריותה [רש"י מכתי"ק בשיטמ"ק].

מסורת הש"ס

א) [עי' תוס' בבא קמא כ: ד"ה הא], ב) [פי' ממון לאב שרצו להפסידו כתובה כצ"ל מהרש"א].

תוספות ישנים

א) [וא"ת כיון דלעס ליה נתקלקל והיאך חייב תו עלה כדאמר פ"ק דכריתות [דף ז.] כהן שסך שמן של תרומה בן בתו ישראל מתעגל בו ואינו חושש וי"ל דהתם ודאי נתקלקל שכבר נגמרה כל הנאתו אבל הכא לא נגמרה כל הנאתו בלעיסה לחודיה. ת"י]:

ב) [ועוד יש להוכיח דכפרה הוי מדפטרי' לאביי מזיד בתרומה ואע"ג דגלי רחמנא גבי שוגג דלא אמרי' קים ליה בדרבה מיניה במיתה דתרומה אלא ודאי משום כפרה הוא ויש לדחות דשאני שוגג דתרומה לפי שמצינו שהוא חמור שמשלם חומש. ת"י]:

ג) [פי' ריצב"א לא יתיישב בסמוך דקאמר אי בעי גחין ואכיל. ת"י]:

ד) [ור"ת פירש כיון שהוא במקום דלא מצי לאהדורי אלא ע"י הדחק כבר נהנה גרונו ובאין כאחד וא"ת והיאך יתחייב ממון כיון שתחב לו באונס וי"ל כיון דמצי לאהדורה ע"י הדחק ולא הדרה ניחא ליה בהנאה זו. ת"י]:

ה) [ועוד דאכתי מאי איכא בין רבא לאביי דלאפי' אי הוי סבר רבא דיליף מאסון אסון הוי מיחייב כיון דהוי ממון לזה ונפשות לזה. ת"י].

הגהות הב"ח

(א) תוס' ד"ה זר וכו' קים ליה בדרבה מיניה דאם:

לעזי רש"י

מלנ"ט. פירוש אסכרה, מין חולי הגרון המחנק (מוסף הערוך ערך אסכרה ועיין רש"י שבת דף לג סוע"א):

תורה אור השלם

א) וְאִם הַעְלֵם יַעְלִימוּ עַם הָאָרֶץ אֶת עֵינֵיהֶם מִן הָאִישׁ הַהוּא בְּתִתּוֹ מִזַּרְעוֹ לַמֹּלֶךְ לְבִלְתִּי הָמִית אֹתוֹ: וְשַׂמְתִּי אֲנִי אֶת פָּנַי בָּאִישׁ הַהוּא וּבְמִשְׁפַּחְתּוֹ וְהִכְרַתִּי אֹתוֹ וְאֵת כָּל הַזֹּנִים אַחֲרָיו לִזְנוֹת אַחֲרֵי הַמֹּלֶךְ מִקֶּרֶב עַמָּם: [ויקרא כ, ד - ה]

חייבי עשה מצרי ואדומי הניחא לר' ישבב אי לאפוקי מטעמא דר' סימאי קאתי שפיר אלא אי טעמא דנפשיה קאמר כל שאין לו ביאה בישראל הולד ממזר ואפי' חייבי עשה מאי בינייהו * איכא בינייהו בעולה לכ"ג ומ"ש דהוה ליה עשה שאינו שוה בכל אמר רב חסדא הכל מודים בבא על הנדה שמשלם קנס למ"ד יש בה הויה הא נמי יש בה הויה למ"ד ראויה לקיימה הא נמי ראויה לקיימה ולאפוקי מדרבי נחוניא בן הקנה דתניא א) רבי נחוניא בן הקנה היה עושה את יום הכפורים כשבת לתשלומין מה שבת מתחייב בנפשו ופטור מן התשלומין אף יום הכפורים מתחייב בנפשו ופטור מן התשלומין מ"ט דר' נחוניא בן הקנה אמר אביי נאמר א) אסון בידי אדם ונאמר ב) אסון בידי שמים א מה אסון האמור בידי אדם פטור מן התשלומין אף אסון האמור בידי שמים פטור מן התשלומין מתקיף לה רב אדא בר אהבה ממאי דכי קא מזהר להו יעקב לבניה על צינים ופחים דבידי שמים נינהו דלמא על אריא וגנבי דבידי אדם נינהו אטו יעקב אהא אזהר אהא לא אזהר יעקב על כל מילי אזהר וצינים פחים בידי שמים נינהו והתניא ב) הכל בידי שמים חוץ מצינים פחים שנאמר ג) צינים פחים בדרך עיקש שומר נפשו ירחק מהם ותו אריא וגנבי בידי אדם נינהו ג) והאמר רב יוסף וכן תני רבי חייא מיום שחרב בית המקדש אף על פי שבטלו סנהדרין ארבע מיתות לא בטלו לא בטלו הא בטלו להו אלא דין

רש"י

חייבי עשה מצרי ואדומי. בתוך שלשה דורות דכתיב (דברים כג) דור שלישי יבא להם דור שני לא ולאו הבא מכלל עשה עשה: הניחא. אי רבי ישבב האי כל שאין לו היתר ביאה דקאמר אליבא דר"ע לאו כללא כייל אלא לאפוקי מדרבי סימאי לחודיה אתא ואחייבי לאוין הוא דפליג לאוסופי חייבי לאוין ד) בכהונה אבל שום חייבי עשה לא הוסיף: שפיר. מצינו למימר איכא בינייהו דשמעון התימני ור"ש בן מנסיא חייבי עשה: אלא. אי לאו אדרבי סימאי קאי וטעמא דנפשיה קאמר בשם ר"ע שכל שאין לו היתר ביאה באשה זו הולד ממזר מאי איכא למימר: בעולה לכ"ג. שאין בה לאו דאלמנות וגירושין אלא עשה דבתולה יקח (ויקרא כא) ולא בעולה וא"ת יש כאן לאו דזונה לא אשכחן תנא דאמר פנוי הבא על הפנויה עשאה זונה אלא ר' אלעזר ה) (א) ולית הלכתא כוותיה ואין זונה אלא הנבעלת לפסול לה ובבעולה שלא כדרכה איירי דאי כדרכה תו ליכא קנס: ומאי שנא. האי עשה מאחר עשה דמודה ביה ר"ע: דהוה ליה עשה שאינו שוה בכל. שאינו נוהג אלא בכ"ג אבל עשה דמצרי ואדומי נוהג בכל הקהל: הא נמי יש בה הויה. המקדש אשה בימי נדותה מקודשת: ולאפוקי מדר' נחוניא. מתני' דמחייב תשלומין לבא על אחותו ואע"פ שמתחייב כרת בביאתו מפקא מדר' נחוניא: את יום הכפורים כשבת. לפטור המדליק את הגדיש ביום הכפורים כאילו הדליקו בשבת: מה שבת. שהוא מיתת ב"ד: פטור מן התשלומין. כדתנן במתני' גבי בא על בתו וילף לה מולא יהיה אסון ענוש יענש: אף יום הכפורים. שהוא בכרת חיוב נפש הוא זה ופטור מן התשלומין: אסון בידי אדם. ולא יהיה אסון דמשתעי במיתת ב"ד למימר דהיכא דליכא מיתת ב"ד משלם דמי ולדות: אסון בידי שמים. וקראהו אסון: צינים פחים. קור וחום: בידי שמים. אם באים פורעניות על האדם גזירת המלך הוא: חוץ מצינים ופחים. שפעמים שבאין בפשיעה: בידי אדם נינהו. שלא מגזירת מלך: דין

תוספות

אי לאפוקי מדרבי סימאי קאתי. תימה תיפשוט דרבי ישבב טעמא דנפשיה קאמר אליבא דמ"ד בפ"ק דיבמות (דף יג. ושם) הבא על יבמתו וחזר ובא אחד מן האחים על צרתה בעשה דהא תנן בפרק ר"ג (יבמות דף נ.) ר"ג אומר דאין בעילה אחר בעילה א"כ רבי ישבב טעמא דנפשיה קאמר והוי התם כר' ישבב דלאין קידושין תופסין בחייבי עשה והכי אין אחר בעילה כלום כדאמר התם בגמרא ו) ממתני' דלאין אחר חליצה כלום אמר רב הונא אמר רב זו דברי ר"ע דאמר דאין קידושין תופסין בחייבי לאוין ומשמע הכא אליבא דר"ע מספקא ליה אי טעמא דנפשיה קאמר אי לאו לכך נראה לר"ת דגרסי' בפ"ק דיבמות (דף יא.) חד אמר בלאו ובלא זה מוכיח ר"ח בההיא שמעתא דל"ג בעשה וכן בפר"ה דהיינו לאו שלכך לאחת דאמר קרא אשר לא יבנה כיון שלא בנה שוב לא יבנה אחרת ה"נ כיון שבנה שוב יבמה לא יבנה אחרת:

איכא בינייהו בעולה לכ"ג. פי' בקונט' בעולה שלא כדרכה וקשה דפלוגתא דר"מ ורבי אלעזר היא בפרק הבא על יבמתו (יבמות דף נט. ושם) אי כשירה לכ"ג וה"ל למימר ולר"מ דאמר כשירה לכ"ג מאי איכא למימר כדקאמר ולר"ע דאמר כו' ואור"י דמר"ע פריך שפיר כדי לאוקומי ר"ש בן מנסיא שהוא בתרא כר"ע שהיה רבו אבל בהא לא חייש אי פליג ר"מ אר"ש בן מנסיא ור"ח פי' דהכא לא מיירי בבעולה מאחר אלא בכ"ג שאנס בתולה גמורה ולא חשיבה ראויה לקיימה אע"ג דאמר בהבא על יבמתו ז) אנוסת עצמו ומפותת עצמו לא ישא ואם נשא נשוי מ"מ כיון דלכתחלה לא ישא לא חשיבה ראויה לקיימה דהאי לא ישא הוי מן התורה אף ע"ג דאם נשא נשוי ה"נ אמר בוגרת ומוכת עץ לא ישא ואם נשא נשוי אע"ג דהוי מן התורה כדמוכח התם ועוד דקאמר התם ח) מתיב רבא ולו תהיה לאשה באשה הראויה לו פרט אלמנה לכ"ג היכי דמי אילימא בכדרכה מאי איריא משום אלמנה תיפוק ליה דהויא לה בעולה משמע דבעולת עצמו אסורה לו מן התורה ור"ת לא פירש כן:

הכל מודים בבא על הנדה שמשלם קנס. תימה לר"י מנלן דר"ש בן מנסיא מודה בה דלמא כר' נחוניא בן הקנה ס"ל דחייבי כריתות פטורים מן התשלומין ומיהו ר"ש התימני ע"כ לית ליה דר' נחוניא מדאיצטריך למעוטי חייבי כריתות מולו תהיה לאשה אשה שיש בה הויה דע"כ לא איצטריך למעוטי אלא חייבי כריתות דחייבי לאוין ס"ל בסוף החולץ (יבמות דף מט. ושם) דאית בהו הויה אבל מר"ש בן מנסיא קשה מנלן דלית ליה דר' נחוניא ועוד אפי' ר"ש התימני דלמא אית ליה דר' נחוניא ואיצטריך למעוטי מולו תהיה לאשה יבמה לשוק דאין קידושין תופסין בה לכ"ע כדאמר בהאשה רבה (שם דף צב: ושם) וי"ל דרב חסדא ס"ל דאין שום תנא סובר כרבי נחוניא ולה"ק ולאפוקי כו' ובקונט' פירש דאמתני' קאי דמפקא מדר' נחוניא ותימה מנ"ל דמפקא מיניה דלמא מודה ר' נחוניא דחייבי כריתות יש להן קנס דרבינהו קרא חד לחייבי לאוין וחד לחייבי כריתות ולר"ע ניחא דמפקא מתני' מדר' נחוניא דכיון דאין קידושין תופסין בחייבי לאוין איכא לאוקומי הנך תרי ריבויי חד לחייבי עשה וחד לחייבי לאוין אבל חייבי כריתות לר' נחוניא לא א) ונראה לרשב"א לתרץ ב) דע"כ מפקא מתני' מר' נחוניא דלר' נחוניא אין חילוק בין חייבי כריתות לחייבי מיתות ב"ד או מאסון אסון או כדדריש רבא כרת שלי כמיתה שלכם ואם יש קנס לר' נחוניא בחייבי כריתות יש ג"כ בחייבי מיתות ב"ד ומתני' קתני בא על בתו פטור: הכל בידי שמים חוץ מצינים פחים. והא דאמרי' (שבת דף לב.) לעולם אל יעמוד אדם במקום סכנה אלמא יכול לשמור עצמו מן הפורענות וכן קיר נטוי דאסור לעבור תחתיו התם מן הפשיעה יכול לשמור עצמו דהא ודאי שבידו להמית עצמו אבל כשמביאין עליו מן השמים באונס אי אפשר לו לשמור אבל צינים פחים לעולם אל יבואו עליו באונס אם רוצה ליזהר וא"ת והא דרשינן (ב"מ דף קז:) והסיר ה' ממך כל חולי זה צינה אלמא דבידי שמים הוא וי"ל דהיינו שיחם הקב"ה עולמו או יתן לו מלבושים ולא יצטרך ליזהר וא"ת והא פחים בידי שמים הוא כדאמרי' בבראשית רבה בפרשה ט"ו א"ל אנטונינוס לרבי צלי עלי א"ל רחמנא שיזבך מצינתא א"ל דא צלותא היא יתיר חד כסו וצינתא אזלא א"ל תשתזב משרבא א"ל הא כדו צלותא דכתיב אין נסתר מחמתו וי"ל דקרא כתיב בעוברי דרכים או במלחמה כדרך שהמלכים עושים דבדרך אין אדם יכול ליזהר מן החום אבל אם רוצה לישב בביתו יכול להזהר שישב בבית של אבנים או יכנס במרתף ויש מפרשים דצינים פחים חדא מילתא היא כלומר צינים שהם פחים לאדם לשון פח ומוקש ואינו כן דבפ"ק דמסכת ע"ז (דף ג: ושם) מייתי לה [אהא דכתיב ותעשה אדם כדגי הים מה] דגים שבים כיון שקדרה עליהן חמה מיד מתים [אף בני אדם כיון שקדרה עליהם חמה מיד מתים] והא דאמר (ברכות דף לג:) הכל בידי שמים חוץ מיראת שמים אין ענינו לכאן דהתם קאי על הולד במעי אמו (נדה טז:) שגוזרין אם יהא עני או עשיר גבור או חלש טפש או חכם אבל צדיק ורשע לא ט) והכא מיירי במאורעות הבאות על האדם ג): מיום שחרב בית כו'. וא"ת אמאי לא נקט מ' שנה קודם שחרב בהמ"ק דמ' שנה קודם חורבן גלתה סנהדרין כו' שלא דנו דיני נפשות וי"ל דלפעמים לצורך שעה היו חוזרין סנהדרין ללשכת הגזית ולהכי לא פסיקא ליה למיתני מ' שנה קודם חורבן וא"ת א"כ מאי פריך בפרק היו בודקין (סנהדרין דף מא.) גבי מעשה ובדק ר' יוחנן בן זכאי בעוקצי תאנים ופריך מי הוה בסנהדרין והא תניא כל שנותיו של רבן יוחנן בן זכאי מאה ועשרים שנה מ' עסק בפרקמטיא ומ' למד ומ' לימד ותניא מ' שנה קודם חורבן גלתה סנהדרין כו' והשתא מאי קשיא ליה כיון דלפעמים היו חוזרין ודנין וי"ל דרבן יוחנן בן זכאי דבדק בעוקצי תאנה מעשה דרציחה היה ומשום דיני נפשות דרציחה לא היו חוזרין לעולם דעיקרם לא גלו אלא משום רציחה דחזו דנפישי רוצחים כדאמרינן בפ"ק דמסכת ע"ז (דף ח: ושם) וי"מ דלהכי נקט משחרב בהמ"ק משום דקודם לכן אע"פ שגלו היו בגדי כהונה מכפרים על מזיד דלא אתרו ביה כדאמרינן בפרק יש בערכין (ערכין דף טז. ושם) ואין נראה דהא בימי שמעון בן שטח היו בגדי כהונה והיה דין ארבע מיתות כדאמרינן בפרק אחד דיני ממונות (סנהדרין דף לז: ושם) אר"ש בן שטח אראה בנחמה אם לא ראיתי אחד שרץ אחר חברו לחורבה וכו' לא זז משם עד שנשכו נחש ופריך והאי בר נחש הוא והא תני ר' חייא אע"פ שבטלו סנהדרין כו' ועוד אמר (מכות י:) מרשעים יצא רשע כו' ד) והתם בזמן שבהמ"ק קיים איירי מדקאמר ונמצא זה מת וזה גולה י): דין

מסורת הש"ס

א) [תוספתא ב"ק פ"ז] שבועות לג. מגילה ז: פסחים כט. לב. [תוספתא דמגילה פ"א], ב) ב"מ קז: ב"ב קמד: ע"ש ע"ז ג: ע"ש, ג) סוטה ח. סנהדרין לז: ע"ש, ד) ל"ל דכהונה, ה) [יבמות סא:], ו) דף נב:, ז) [יבמות דף נט:], ח) [דף נט. ושם ד"ה אילימא], ט) [וע"ע תוס' מגילה כה. ד"ה הכל ותוס' נדה טז: ד"ה הכל], י) [וע"ע תוס' סוטה ח: ד"ה מכפרים].

תוספות ישנים

א) ומהר"ר אומר כי מלא בתוספתא פרק אלו נערות ר' נחוניא אומר הבא על אחותו ועל אחות אביו אין להם קנס וכן היה עושה רבי נחוניא בן הקנה יוה"כ כשבת: ב) ול"נ לתרץ דע"כ מפקא מתני' דלר' אליעזר לאוקמי חד לחייבי לאוין וחד לחייבי עשה דאיכא דלא מוקמי להו לגבי יבמה לשוק אבל חייבי כריתות קים ליה בדרבה מיניה וכי תימא לקמן בפירקין אי כרבי נחוניא קשיא אחותו משמע דבחייבי כריתות לא מוקמינן כוותיה: ג) ולא דמי לשבת דאמר לשמור עצמו על כרחך אחת מי שאין לו דרך לפרנס עצמו אלא אם הולך בדרך לר"י מקום שאין שם סכנה ועל כרחך עד"מ לענין אחר מיירי וגרסי' ע"כ אחת מי שאין לו עליו כמו המסתכן בפסיעות ולחזור ולילך: ד) ומיהו אפשר לומר דפעמים שלא היו מכפרים לא פסיקא ליה:

עין משפט נר מצוה

ז א (מיי' פ"א מהלכות נערה הלכה יג ופ"ג מהלכות גניבה הלכה ב טוש"ע ח"מ סי' שנא):

תוספות רי"ד

מתני' דלא כר"נ בן הקנה. פירוש מתני' דמחייב קנס לבא על אחותו ואע"פ שמתחייב כרת בביאתו. דתניא ר"נ [בן הקנה] היה עושה יוה"כ כשבת לתשלומין. פי' לפטור המדליק את הגדיש ביוה"כ כאילו הדליקו בשבת מה שבת שהוא מיתת ב"ד פטור מתשלומין כדתנן מתני' לקמן בבא על בתו ודלפי' לה מולא יהי' אסון. אף יוה"כ שהוא בכרת מתחייב בנפשו ופטור מן התשלומין. מ"ט דר"נ ב"ה. אמר אביי נאמר אסון בידי שמים. פי' וקראהו אסון ונאמר אסון בידי אדם ואם אסון יהיה מה אסון הנאמר בידי אדם פטור מן התשלומין. פי' דמשתעי במיתת ב"ד למימר היכא דליכא מיתת ב"ד משלם דמי וולדות. אף אסון האמור בידי שמים פטור מן התשלומין:

ליקוטי רש"י

חייבי עשה מצרי ואדומי. קודם ג' דורות דכתיב (דברים כג) דור שלישי יבא להם ולא שני ולאו הבא מכלל עשה עשה [יבמות מט.]. אי לאפוקי מטעמא דר' סימאי קאתי. ולא להוסיף אלא אחייבי לאוין דכהונה אבל במצרי ואדומי תוך ג' דורות שהן חייבי עשה מודה דקידושין תופסין לו בה [קידושין סח.]. אי לאו כללא הוא אלא לאפוקי מדרבי סימאי דמפיק חד מחייבי לאוין אתי ואשמועי' דכל חייבי לאוין עושה ר"ע ממזרין [שם סח.]. אלא אי טעמא דנפשיה קאמר. ולאו לאפוקי מדר' סימאי למודיה אתי לאפלוגי אחייבי לאוין דכהונה לחודייהו אלא כלל הוא בידו שכל ביאה שיש בעבירה הולד ממזר [שם סד.]. ובכללא כייל ולאו מדרבי סימאי לחודיה פליג אלא אשמעינן דכל שביאתו לאיסור הולד ממזר. בעולה לכ"ג. דעשה הוא דכתיב (ויקרא כא) אשה בבתוליה יקח ולא בעולה ולאו הבא מכלל עשה עשה וליכא לאוקמי הא זונה היא או אלמנה או גרושה דבעולה פנויה לא זונה היא כדתנן ביבמות (דף סא.) אין זונה אלא גיורת ומשוחררת ושנבעלה בעילת זנות וביאתו איסור לפסול לה. ומ"ש. האי עשה מחייבי עשה דמצרי ואדומי. שאינו שוה בכל. שאינו נוהג אלא בכ"ג הילכך קיל [שם סח.]. את יום הכפורים כשבת. המדליק גדיש ביום הכפורים ומתחייב כרת פטור מן התשלומין כאילו הדליקו בשבת שהוא מתחייב בנפשו מיתת בית דין דפשיטא לן דפטור מלשלם דכתיב (שמות כא) ולא יהיה אסון ענוש יענש שאף יום הכיפורים שמתחייב מיתה בידי שמים אסון הוא דכתיב (בראשית מב) וקראהו אסון הלכך פטור מלשלם והכי פרשינן לה באלו נערות [פסחים כט.]. המתחייב כרת פטור מן התשלומין ויליף טעמא מאסון אסון והוא הדין למתחייב מיתת שמים כגון זר אוכל תרומה מזיד [שם לב.]. אף יום הכפורים מתחייב בנפשו. דאיסור כרת כמיתת ב"ד דמי. ופטור מן התשלומין. אם הדליק גדישו של חבירו ביום הכפוריסת שאין תשלומין אלא חיוב מיתה שנאמר ולא יהיה אסון ענש יענש (שמות כא) הא אם יהיה אסון לא יענש [מגילה ז:]. הכל בידי שמים. מחושים ומכאובות הבאים לאדם כולם על ידי גזירת שמים. חוץ מצינים פחים. צנים צנה פחים חולי הבא ע"י חום כמו (שיר השירים ב) עד שיפוח היום [ע"ז ג:]. קור הנופח [ב"מ קז:]. לישנא דקרא צנים פחים בדרך עקש הצנה והקור פחים כמו (במדבר לג) לצנינים בצדיכם ובאו עליך הוצן (יחזקאל כ"ג) ל' גדודים ולסטים. ויש מפרשים צנים פחים קור וחום [רשב"ם ב"ב קמד:]. צינים פחים בדרך עיקש. המעקש דרכיו כלומר יסורים מוכנים לו. שומר נפשו ירחק מהם. שמיישר מעשיו ינצל מהם [משלי כב, ה].

הגהות הב"ח

(א) רש"י ד"ה בעולה וכו' אלא ר' אלעזר ולית. נ"ב וביבמות (דף ס"א ע"ב) מסיק דלאו אליבא דר"א משכחת לה בממאנת ע"ש:

גליון הש"ס

גמ' איכא בינייהו בעולה לכ"ג. עי' פסחים מא ע"ב תוד"ה אכל:

תורה אור השלם

א) וְכִי יִנָּצוּ אֲנָשִׁים וְנָגְפוּ אִשָּׁה הָרָה וְיָצְאוּ יְלָדֶיהָ וְלֹא יִהְיֶה אָסוֹן עָנוֹשׁ יֵעָנֵשׁ כַּאֲשֶׁר יָשִׁית עָלָיו בַּעַל הָאִשָּׁה וְנָתַן בִּפְלִלִים: [שמות כא, כב]

ב) וַיֹּאמֶר לֹא יֵרֵד בְּנִי עִמָּכֶם כִּי אָחִיו מֵת וְהוּא לְבַדּוֹ נִשְׁאָר וּקְרָאָהוּ אָסוֹן בַּדֶּרֶךְ אֲשֶׁר תֵּלְכוּ בָהּ וְהוֹרַדְתֶּם אֶת שֵׂיבָתִי בְּיָגוֹן שְׁאוֹלָה: [בראשית מב, לח]

ג) צִנִּים פַּחִים בְּדֶרֶךְ עִקֵּשׁ שׁוֹמֵר נַפְשׁוֹ יִרְחַק מֵהֶם: [משלי כב, ה]

death **at the hand of Heaven, one is exempt from payment** for damages done simultaneously.[21]

The Gemara objects:

מַתְקִיף לָהּ רַב אַדָּא בַּר אַהֲבָה – Rav Adda bar Ahavah objected to this: מִמַּאי דְּכִי קָא מַזְהַר לְהוּ יַעֲקֹב לִבְנֵיהּ – On the basis of what do you assume **that when Jacob warns his sons** about the possibility of an *ason* (fatality) befalling Benjamin, **עַל צִינִּים וּפַחִים דְּבִידֵי שָׁמַיִם נִינְהוּ** – he is referring **to** death on account of exposure to the **cold and heat, which are at the hand of Heaven?**[22] **דִּלְמָא עַל אַרְיָא וְגַנָּבֵי דְּבִידֵי אָדָם נִינְהוּ – Perhaps** he is referring **to** death at the hand of **a lion or thieves, which are "at the hand of man."**[23] And if so, the aforementioned *gezeirah shavah* cannot teach that *kares,* which is at the hand of Heaven, exempts one from monetary liability! – ? –

The Gemara replies:

אָטוּ יַעֲקֹב אַהָא אַזְהַר אַהָא לֹא אַזְהַר – Did Jacob warn only **about this** type of death [at the hand of man] but **not warn about this** type of death [at the hand of Heaven]? **יַעֲקֹב עַל כָּל מִילֵי אַזְהַר** – JACOB WARNED ABOUT ALL THINGS, i.e. most certainly he was concerned about *any* form of death befalling Benjamin – whether at the hand of man or at the hand of Heaven. Hence, the term *ason* that he used encompasses both types of fatalities. And accordingly, the aforementioned *gezeirah shavah* can indeed teach that death at the hand of Heaven, such as *kares,* exempts one from monetary liability.

The Gemara now digresses to address Rav Adda bar Ahavah's characterization of death on account of cold and heat as "death at the hand of Heaven," and of death by a lion or thieves as "death at the hand of man." The Gemara asks:

וְצִינִּים פַּחִים בִּידֵי שָׁמַיִם נִינְהוּ – But are deaths on account of exposure to the **cold and heat** considered **"death at the hand of Heaven"? וְהָתַנְיָא – Why, it was taught in a Baraisa: הַכֹּל בִּידֵי שָׁמַיִם חוּץ מִצִּינִּים פַּחִים** – ALL manner of misfortune IS IN THE HAND OF HEAVEN[24] EXCEPT FOR sicknesses brought on by exposure to COLD AND HEAT.[25] **שֶׁנֶּאֱמַר ,,צִנִּים פַּחִים בְּדֶרֶךְ עִקֵּשׁ שׁוֹמֵר נַפְשׁוֹ יִרְחַק מֵהֶם''** – FOR IT IS STATED: *COLD AND HEAT ARE IN THE PATH OF THE PERVERSE; ONE WHO GUARDS HIS SOUL WILL DISTANCE HIMSELF FROM THEM.*[26] **וְתוּ אַרְיָא וְגַנָּבֵי בִּידֵי אָדָם נִינְהוּ – And furthermore,** are deaths at the hand of **a lion or thieves** considered **"death at the hand of man"?**[27] **וְהָאָמַר רַב יוֹסֵף – Why, Rav Yosef said, וְכֵן תָּנֵי רַבִּי חִיָּיא – and so, too, did R' Chiya teach a Baraisa** that states: **מִיּוֹם שֶׁחָרַב בֵּית הַמִּקְדָּשׁ** – FROM THE DAY THAT THE TEMPLE WAS DESTROYED, **אַף עַל פִּי שֶׁבָּטְלוּ סַנְהֶדְרִין** – EVEN THOUGH THE Great SANHEDRIN HAS CEASED to function in its traditional place in the Temple, **אַרְבַּע מִיתוֹת לֹא בָּטְלוּ** – THE FOUR types of EXECUTIONS administered by the Sanhedrin HAVE NOT CEASED.[28]

The Gemara interrupts to seek a clarification:

לֹא בָּטְלוּ – [Executions] have not ceased? הָא בָּטְלוּ לְהוּ – But surely they have ceased, as the Great Sanhedrin no longer sits in the Temple![29] – ? –

The Gemara explains:

אֶלָּא – Rather, the Baraisa means that

NOTES

21. I.e. just as incurring the death penalty exempts the sinner from monetary liability incurred simultaneously, so too does incurring death at the hand of Heaven, such as *kares,* exempt him.

22. Only if we assume that Jacob was concerned specifically with "death at the hand of Heaven" can we interpret the word *ason* used in this context to mean such death, and thus – through *gezeirah shavah* – to compare death at the hand of Heaven (*kares*) to death at the hand of man (execution by the court) with regard to exempting one from monetary liability.

[The Gemara at this point is of the opinion that death from exposure to the elements, such as cold and heat (which are phenomena that have no independent will), is considered to be death by direct Divine decree, even if the person was negligent in exposing himself to those elements.]

23. [I.e. not by direct Divine decree, but rather by the operation of forces to which God has granted a measure of independent will. (See *Rashi* below ד״ה בידי אדם נינהו.) Rav Adda bar Ahavah's point is that the *ason* mentioned by Jacob might *not* refer to death by direct Divine decree (such as *kares*).]

24. I.e. any misfortune that befalls a person is on account of a Heavenly decree (*Rashi*).

25. Which, at times, are the result of one's own negligence (*Rashi;* cf. *Tosafos*).

26. *Proverbs* 22:5. This verse shows that sickness due to cold or heat can be the result of one's negligence, rather than on account of a direct Heavenly decree.

27. I.e. *not* the result of direct Divine decree? (*Rashi;* see above, note 23).

28. The Torah prescribes four different methods of execution for different capital offenses: סְקִילָה שְׂרֵיפָה הֶרֶג וָחֶנֶק, *stoning, burning, beheading and strangulation;* see Mishnah, *Sanhedrin* 49b.

29. The Gemara (*Sanhedrin* 41a) states that no Sanhedrin can sentence a person to death unless the Great Sanhedrin is functioning in the Chamber of Hewn Stone in the *Beis HaMikdash* (see *Rashi* ad loc.). How, then, can Rav Yosef and the Baraisa state that capital punishment remains in effect after the destruction of the *Beis HaMikdash*?

ז א (מיי' פ"א מהלכות נערה הלכה יג ופ"ב מהלכות גניבה הלכה ג טוש"ע ח"מ סי' שנא):

חייב עשה מצרי ואדומי הניחא לר' ישבב אי לאפוקי מטעמא דר' סימאי קאתי שפיר אלא אי טעמא דנפשיה קאמר כל שאין לו ביאה בישראל הולד ממזר ואפי' חייבי עשה מאי בינייהו * איכא בינייהו בעולה לכ"ג ומ"ש דהוה ליה עשה שאינו שוה בכל אמר רב חסדא הכל מודים בבא על הנדה שמשלם קנס למ"ד יש בה הויה הא נמי יש בה הויה למ"ד ראויה לקיימה הא נמי ראויה לקיימה ולאפוקי מדרבי נחוניא בן הקנה דתניא א) רבי נחוניא בן הקנה היה עושה את יום הכפורים כשבת לתשלומין מה שבת מתחייב בנפשו ופטור מן התשלומין אף יום הכפורים מתחייב בנפשו ופטור מן התשלומין מ"ט דר' נחוניא בן הקנה אמר אביי נאמר א) אסון בידי אדם ונאמר ב) אסון בידי שמים *מה אסון האמור בידי אדם פטור מן התשלומין אף אסון האמור בידי שמים פטור מן התשלומין מתקיף לה רב אדא בר אהבה ממאי דכי קא מזהר להו יעקב לבניה על צינים ופחים דבידי שמים נינהו דלמא על אריא וגנבי דבידי אדם נינהו אטו יעקב אהא אזהר אהא לא אזהר יעקב על כל מילי אזהר וצינים פחים בידי שמים נינהו והתניא ג) הכל בידי שמים חוץ מצינים פחים שנאמר ג) צינים פחים בדרך עיקש שומר נפשו ירחק מהם ותו אריא וגנבי בידי אדם נינהו ג) והאמר רב יוסף וכן תני רבי חייא מיום שחרב בית המקדש אף על פי שבטלו סנהדרין ארבע מיתות לא בטלו לא בטלו הא בטלו להו אלא
דין

רש"י

חייבי עשה מצרי ואדומי. בתוך שלשה דורות דכתיב (דברים כג) דור שלישי יבא להם דור שני לא ולאו הבא מכלל עשה עשה: הניחא. אי רבי ישבב האי כל שאין לו היתר ביאה קאמר אליבא דר"ע לאו כללא כייל אלא לאפוקי מדרבי סימאי לחודיה אתא ומחייבי לאוין הוא דפליג לאתויי חייבי לאוין ד) בכהונה אבל שום חייבי עשה לא הוסיף: שפיר. מצינו למימר איכא בינייהו דשמעון התימני ור"ש בן מנסיא חייבי עשה: אלא. אי לאו אדרבי סימאי קאי וטעמא דנפשיה קאמר בשם ר"ע שכל שאין לו היתר ביאה באשה זו הולד ממזר מאי איכא למימר: בעולה לכ"ג. שאין בה לאו דאלמנות וגירושין אלא עשה דבתולה יקח (ויקרא כא) ולא בעולה וא"ת יש כאן לאו דזונה לא שכיחא דאמר פנוי הבא על הפנויה עשאה זונה אלא ר' אלעזר ה) (א) ולית הלכתא כוותיה ואין זונה אלא הנבעלת לפסול לה ובעולה שלא כדרכה איירי דלאו כדרכה תו ליכא קנס: ומאי שנא. האי עשה משאר עשה דמודה ביה ר"ע: דהוה ליה עשה שאינו שוה בכל. שאינו נוהג אלא בכ"ג אבל עשה דמצרי ואדומי נוהג בכל הקהל: הא נמי יש בה הויה. המקדש אשה בימי נדותה מקודשת: ולאפוקי מדר' נחוניא. מתני' דמחייב תשלומין לבא על אחותו ואע"פ שמתחייב כרת בביאתו מפקא מדר' נחוניא: את יום הכפורים כשבת. לפטור המדליק את הגדיש ביום הכפורים כאילו הדליקו בשבת: מה שבת. שהוא מיתת ב"ד: פטור מן התשלומין. כדתנן במתני' גבי בא על בתו וילפינן לה מולא יהיה אסון ענוש יענש: אף יום הכפורים. שהוא בכרת חיוב נפש הוא זה ופטור מן התשלומין: אסון בידי אדם. ולא יהיה אסון דמשתעי במיתת ב"ד למימר דהיכא דליכא מיתת ב"ד משלם דמי ולדות: אסון בידי שמים. וקראהו אסון: צינים פחים. קור וחום: בידי שמים. אם באים פורעניות על האדם הכל גזירת המלך הוא: חוץ מצינים ופחים. פעמים שבאין בפשיעה: בידי אדם נינהו. שלא מגזירת מלך:
דין

תוספות

אי לאפוקי מדרבי סימאי קאתי. תימה מיפשט פשיטא דרבי ישבב טעמא דנפשיה קאמר אליבא דמ"ד בפ"ק דיבמות (דף יג. ושם) הבא על יבמתו וחזר ובא אחד מן האחים על צרתה בעשה דהא תנן בפרק ר"ג (יבמות דף נ.) ר"ג אומר אין גט אחר גט ולא בעילה אחר בעילה וא"ר ישבב טעמא דנפשיה קאמר והיינו התם כר' ישבב דאין קידושין תופסין בחייבי עשה ולהכי אין אחר בעילה כלום כדאמר התם בגמרא ו) ואמתני' דאין אחר חליצה כלום אמר רב הונא אמר רב זו דברי ר"ע דאמר דאין קידושין תופסין בחייבי לאוין ומסתמא הכא אליבא דר"ע מספקא ליה אי טעמא דנפשיה קאמר אי לאו לכך נראה לר"ת דגרסי' בפ"ק דיבמות (דף יג.) חד אמר בלאו וחד אמר בעשה ולא זה מוכיח ר"ת בההיא שמעתא דל"ג בעשה וכן פר"ח דהיינו לאו שהלך לאחת דאמר קרא אשר לא יבנה כיון שלא בנה שוב לא יבנה אחרת וה"נ כיון שבנה שוב יבמה לא יבנה אחרת:

איכא בינייהו בעולה לכ"ג. פי' בקונט' בעולה שלא כדרכה וקשה דפלוגתא דר"מ ורבי אלעזר היא בפרק הבא על יבמתו (יבמות דף נט. ושם) אי כשירה לכ"ג וה"ל למימר ולר"מ דאמר כשירה לכ"ג מאי איכא למימר דקאמר ולר"ע דאמר כו' ואור"י דמר"ע פריך שפיר כדי לאוקומי ר"ש בן מנסיא שהוא בתרא כר"ע שהיה רבו אבל הכא לא חיים אי פליג ר"מ אר"ש בן מנסיא ור"מ פי' דלא איירי בבעולה שלא כדרכה אלא בכ"ג שאנס בתולה גמורה ולא חשיבה ראויה לקיימה אע"ג דאמר בהבא על יבמתו ח) אנוסת עצמו ומפותת עצמו לא ישא ואם נשא נשוי מ"מ כיון דלכתחלה לא ישא לא חשיבה ראויה לקיימה דהאי לא ישא הוי מן התורה אף ע"ג דאם נשא נשוי ה"נ אמר בוגרת ומוכת עץ לא ישא ואם נשא נשוי אע"ג דהוי מן התורה כדמוכח התם ועוד דקאמר התם ט) מתיב רבא ולו תהיה לאשה באשה הראויה לו פרט לאלמנה לכ"ג היכי דמי אילימא בדרכה מאי איריא משום אלמנה תיפוק ליה דהויא לה בעולה אלא משמע דבעולת עצמו אסורה לו מן התורה ור"ת לא פירש כן:

הכל מודים בבא על הנדה שמשלם קנס. תימה לר"י מנלן דר"ש בן מנסיא מודה בה דלמא כר' נחוניא בן הקנה ס"ל דחייבי כריתות פטורים מן התשלומין ומיהו ר"ש התימני ע"כ לית ליה דר' נחוניא מדאיצטריך למעוטי חייבי כריתות מולו תהיה לאשה שיש בה הויה דע"כ לא איצטריך למעוטי אלא חייבי כריתות דחייבי לאוין ס"ל בסוף החולץ (יבמות דף מט. ושם) דלית בהו הויה אבל מר"ש בן מנסיא קשה מנלן דלית ליה דר' נחוניא ועוד אפי' ר"ש התימני דלמא אית ליה דר' נחוניא ואיצטריך למעוטי מולו תהיה לאשה יבמה לשוק דאין קידושין תופסין בה לכ"ע כדאמר בהאשה רבה (שם דף צב: ושם) וי"ל דרב חסדא ס"ל דאין שום תנא סובר כרבי נחוניא וה"ק ולאפוקי כו' ובקונט' פירש דאמתני' קאי דמפקא מדר' נחוניא ותימה מנ"ל דמפקא מתני' מדר' נחוניא דלמא מודה ר' נחוניא דחייבי כריתות יש להן קנס כדרבינהו קרא חד לחייבי לאוין וחד לחייבי כריתות ולר"ע ניחא דמפקא מתני' מדר' נחוניא דכיון דאין קידושין תופסין בחייבי לאוין איכא לאוקומי הנך תרי ריבויי חד לחייבי עשה וחד לחייבי לאוין אבל חייבי כריתות לר' נחוניא לא א) ונראה לרשב"א לתרץ דע"כ מפקא מדר' נחוניא דלר' נחוניא אין חילוק בין חייבי כריתות לחייבי מיתות ב"ד ומתני' קתני בא על בתו פטור: הכל בידי שמים חוץ מצינים פחים. והא דאמרי' (שבת דף לב.) לעולם אל יעמוד אדם במקום סכנה אלמא יכול לשמור עצמו מן הפורענות וכן קיר נטוי דאסור לעבור תחתיו התם מן הפשיעה יכול לשמור עצמו דהא ודאי שבידו להמית עצמו אבל כשמביאין עליו מן השמים באונס אי אפשר לו לשמור אבל צינים פחים לעולם אל יבואו עליו באונס אם רוצה ליזהר וא"ת והא דרשינן (ב"מ דף קז:) והסיר ה' ממך כל חולי זה צינה אלמא דבידי שמים הוא וי"ל דהיינו שיחם הקב"ה עולמו או יתן לו מלבושים ולא יצטרך ליזהר וא"ת והא פחים בידי שמים הוא כדאמרי' בבראשית רבה בפרשה ט"ו א"ל אנטונינוס לרבי צלי עלי א"ל רחמנא שיזבן מצינתא א"ל דא צלותא היא יתיר חד כסו וצינתא אזלא א"ל תשתזב משרבא א"ל הא כדו צלותא דכתיב אין נסתר מחמתו וי"ל דקרא כתיב בעוברי דרכים או במלחמה כדרך שהמלכים עושים דבדרך אין אדם יכול ליזהר מן החום אבל אם רוצה לישב בביתו יכול להזהר שישב בבית של אבנים או יכנס במרתף ויש מפרשים צנים פחים חדא מילתא היא כלומר צנים שהם פחים לאדם לשון פח ומוקש ואינו כן דבפ"ק דמסכת ע"ז (דף ג: ושם) מייתי לה [אהא דכתיב ותעשה אדם כדגי הים מה] דגים שבים כיון שקדרה עליהן חמה מיד מתים [אף בני אדם כיון שקדרה עליהם חמה מיד מתים] והא דאמר (ברכות דף לג:) הכל בידי שמים חוץ מיראת שמים אין ענינו לכאן דהתם קאי על הולד במעי אמו (נדה טז:) שגוזרין אם יהא עני או עשיר גבור או חלש טפש או חכם אבל צדיק ורשע לא ט) והכא איירי במאורעות הבאות על האדם ג): מיום שחרב בית כו'. וא"ת אמאי לא נקט מ' שנה קודם שחרב בהמ"ק דמ' שנה קודם חורבן גלתה סנהדרין כו' שלא דנו דיני נפשות וי"ל דלפעמים לצורך שעה היו חוזרין סנהדרין ללשכת הגזית ולהכי לא פסיקא ליה למיתני מ' שנה קודם חורבן וא"ת א"כ מאי פריך בפרק היו בודקין (סנהדרין דף מא.) גבי מעשה ובדק ר' יוחנן בן זכאי בעוקצי תאנים ופריך מי הוה בסנהדרין והא תניא כל שנותיו של רבן יוחנן בן זכאי מאה ועשרים שנה מ' עסק בפרקמטיא ומ' למד ומ' לימד ותניא מ' שנה קודם חורבן גלתה סנהדרין כו' והשתא מאי קשיא ליה כיון דלפעמים היו חוזרין ודנין וי"ל דרבן יוחנן בן זכאי דבדק בעוקצי תאנה אמעשה דרציחה היה ומשום דיני נפשות דרציחה לא היו חוזרין לעולם דעיקרם לא גלו אלא משום רציחה דחזו דנפישי רוצחים כדאמרינן בפ"ק דמסכת ע"ז (דף ח: ושם) וי"מ דלהכי נקט משחרב בהמ"ק משום דקודם לכן אע"פ שגלו היו בגדי כהונה מכפרים על מזיד דלא אתרו ביה כדאמרינן בפרק יש בערכין (ערכין דף טז. ושם) ואין נראה דהא בימי שמעון בן שטח היו בגדי כהונה והיה דין ארבע מיתות כדאמרינן בפרק אחד דיני ממונות (סנהדרין דף לז: ושם) אר"ש בן שטח אראה בנחמה אם לא ראיתי אחד שרץ אחר חברו לחורבה וכו' לא זז משם עד שנשכו נחש ופריך והאי בר נחש הוא והא תני ר' חייא אע"פ שבטלו סנהדרין כו' ועוד אמר (מכות י:) מרשעים יצא רשע כו' ד) והתם בזמן שבהמ"ק קיים איירי מדקאמר ונמצא זה מת וזה גולה י):
דין

תוספות רי"ד

מתני' דלא כר"נ בן הקנה. פירוש מתני' דמחייב קנס לבא על אחותו ואע"פ שמתחייב כרת בביאתו. דתניא ר"נ [בן הקנה] היה עושה יוה"כ כשבת לתשלומין. פי' לפטור המדליק את הגדיש ביוה"כ כאילו הדליקו בשבת שהיא מיתת ב"ד פטור מתשלומין כדתנן מתני' לקמן בבא על בתו וילפי' לה מולא יהיה אסון. אף יוה"כ שהוא בכרת מתחייב בנפשו ופטור מן התשלומין. מ"ט דר"נ ב"ה. אמר אביי נאמר אסון בידי שמים. פי' וקראהו אסון ונאמר אסון בידי אדם ואם אסון יהיה מה אסון הנאמר בידי אדם פטור מן התשלומין. פי' דמשתעי במיתת ב"ד למימר היכא דליכא מיתת ב"ד משלם דמי ולדות. אף אסון האמור בידי שמים פטור מן התשלומין:

ליקוטי רש"י

חייבי עשה מצרי ואדומי. קודם ג' דורות דכתיב (דברים כג) דור שלישי יבא להם ולא שני ולאו הבא מכלל עשה עשה [יבמות מט.].

תוספות ישנים

א) [ומשה"מ אומר כי מלא בתוספתא פרק אלו נערות ר"ש בן מנסיא אומר הבא על אחותו ועל אחות אביו כו' אין להם קנס וכן היה עושה ר"נ בן הקנה יוה"כ כשבת.

הגהות הב"ח

(א) רש"י ד"ה בעולה וכו' אלא לר' אלעזר וליתא. נ"ב וביבמות ע"ב מסיק דאף אליבא דר"א משכחת לה בהאנוסה ע"ש:

גליון הש"ס

גמ' איכא בינייהו בעולה לכ"ג. עי' פסחים דף ע"ב תוד"ה אבל:

תורה אור השלם

א) וְכִי יִנָּצוּ אֲנָשִׁים וְנָגְפוּ אִשָּׁה הָרָה וְיָצְאוּ יְלָדֶיהָ וְלֹא יִהְיֶה אָסוֹן עָנוֹשׁ יֵעָנֵשׁ כַּאֲשֶׁר יָשִׁית עָלָיו בַּעַל הָאִשָּׁה וְנָתַן בִּפְלִלִים: [שמות כא, כב]

ב) וַיֹּאמֶר לֹא יֵרֵד בְּנִי עִמָּכֶם כִּי אָחִיו מֵת וְהוּא לְבַדּוֹ נִשְׁאָר וּקְרָאָהוּ אָסוֹן בַּדֶּרֶךְ אֲשֶׁר תֵּלְכוּ בָהּ וְהוֹרַדְתֶּם אֶת שֵׂיבָתִי בְּיָגוֹן שְׁאוֹלָה: [בראשית מב, לח]

ג) צִנִּים פַּחִים בְּדֶרֶךְ עִקֵּשׁ שׁוֹמֵר נַפְשׁוֹ יִרְחַק מֵהֶם: [משלי כב, ה]

מסורת הש"ס

א) [תוספתא ב"ק פ"ו] שבועות לג. פסחים כט. לג. [תוספתא דמגילה פ"א], ב) ב"מ קז:, ג) סוטה ח: סנהדרין לז:

הכפורים מתחייב בנפשו. דאיסור כרת כמיתת ב"ד דמי. ופטור מן התשלומין. אם הדליק גדישו של חבירו ביום הכפורים שאין תשלומין אלא חיוב מיתה שנאמר ולא יהיה אסון ענוש יענש (שמות כא) הא אם יהיה אסון לא … בידי שמים. פורענות ומכאובות הבאים לאדם כולם על ידי גזרת שמים. חוץ מצינים פחים. צנים צנה פחים חולי הבא ע"י חום כמו (שיר השירים ב) עד שיפוח היום [ע"ז ג:]. קור הנופח [ב"מ קז:]. לישנא דקרא צנים פחים בדרך … בידו הדבר תלוי להשמר מן הצנה ויש מפרשים צנים פחים קור וחום [רשב"ם ב"ב קמד:]. צינים פחים בדרך עיקש. כמו (במדבר לג) לצנינים בצדיכם ובאו עליך הוצן (יחזקאל כ"ג) ל' גדודים ולסטים. צנים פחים … המעקש דרכיו כלומר יסורים מוכנים לו. שומר נפשו ירחק מהם. שמיישר מעשיו ינצל מהם [משלי כב, ה].

The Gemara notes that while Shimon HaTimni and R' Shimon ben Menasya disagree with the Tanna of our Mishnah in regard to the granting of the fine to some of the unfit girls listed in the Mishnah, they agree with him in regard to one of them:

אָמַר רַב חִסְדָּא – **Rav Chisda said:** הַכֹּל מוֹדִים בְּבָא עַל הַנִּדָּה שֶׁמְּשַׁלֵּם קְנָס – **All** [Shimon HaTimni and R' Shimon ben Menasya] **agree in** regard to **one who violates** a girl while she is **a *niddah* that he pays the fine.**[10] לְמַאן דְּאָמַר יֵשׁ בָּהּ הֲוָיָה – For **according to the one** [Shimon HaTimni] **who says** that the *oneiss* pays the fine only if the girl is **one who has** the possibility of **"being"** his wife (i.e. a woman with whom his *kiddushin* would take effect), הָא נַמִּי יֵשׁ בָּהּ הֲוָיָה – **this** *niddah,* **too, has** the possibility of **"being"** his wife.[11] לְמַאן דְּאָמַר רְאוּיָה לְקַיְּימָהּ – And **according to the one** [R' Shimon ben Menasya] **who says** that the *oneiss* pays the fine only if the girl is **one who is fit** for him **to keep her** as his wife, הָא נַמִּי רְאוּיָה לְקַיְּימָהּ – **this** *niddah,* **too, is fit** for him **to keep her** as his wife.[12]

The Gemara notes that our Mishnah, in addition to rejecting the opinions of Shimon HaTimni and R' Shimon ben Menasya, also rejects the opinion of R' Nechunya ben HaKanah:

וּלְאַפּוּקֵי מִדְּרַבִּי נְחוּנְיָא בֶּן הַקָּנָה – **And** our Mishnah, which applies the fine even where the *oneiss* incurs *kares* for violating the girl,[13] also serves **to exclude** the opinion **of R' Nechunya ben HaKanah.** דְּתַנְיָא – **For it was taught in a Baraisa:** רַבִּי נְחוּנְיָא בֶּן הַקָּנָה הָיָה עוֹשֶׂה אֶת יוֹם הַכִּפּוּרִים כְּשַׁבָּת לְתַשְׁלוּמִין – **R' NECHUNYA BEN HAKANAH WOULD TREAT YOM KIPPUR LIKE THE SABBATH IN REGARD TO MONETARY PAYMENT.**[14] מַה שַּׁבָּת – **JUST AS** one who desecrates **THE SABBATH** while simultaneously committing an act for which there is monetary liability מִתְחַיֵּיב בְּנַפְשׁוֹ וּפָטוּר מִן הַתַּשְׁלוּמִין – **IS LIABLE** to pay **WITH HIS LIFE**[15] **AND IS EXEMPT FROM PAYMENT,**[16] אַף יוֹם הַכִּפּוּרִים – **SO TOO,** one who desecrates **YOM KIPPUR** while simultaneously committing an act for which there is monetary liability מִתְחַיֵּיב בְּנַפְשׁוֹ וּפָטוּר מִן הַתַּשְׁלוּמִין – **IS LIABLE** to pay **WITH HIS LIFE**[17] **AND IS EXEMPT FROM PAYMENT.**[18]

The Gemara explains:

מַאי טַעְמָא דְּרַבִּי נְחוּנְיָא בֶּן הַקָּנָה – **What is the reason of R' Nechunya ben HaKanah** for ruling this way? אָמַר אַבַּיֵי – **Abaye said:** נֶאֱמַר "אָסוֹן" בִּידֵי אָדָם – The word ***ason*** (fatality) **is stated** with regard to death **at the hand of man,** i.e. a court-imposed death penalty,[19] וְנֶאֱמַר "אָסוֹן" בִּידֵי שָׁמַיִם – **and** the word ***ason*** (fatality) **is stated** with regard to death **at the hand of Heaven.**[20] מַה "אָסוֹן" הָאָמוּר בִּידֵי אָדָם פָּטוּר מִן הַתַּשְׁלוּמִין – **Just as** in the case of ***ason* stated** with regard to death **at the hand of man, one is exempt from payment** for damages done simultaneously, אַף "אָסוֹן" הָאָמוּר בִּידֵי שָׁמַיִם פָּטוּר מִן הַתַּשְׁלוּמִין – **so too,** in the case of ***ason* stated** with regard to

NOTES

Yesheivav *might* agree that a Kohen Gadol can effect marriage with a nonvirgin, it has not shown why R' Yesheivav *must* agree that this is so. *Rashba* (to the end of 29b), however, indicates why R' Yesheivav *must* agree: For if R' Yesheivav would hold that even the union of a Kohen Gadol and a nonvirgin produces a *mamzer,* then there would be no case of *chalal,* as all women forbidden to a Kohen would then produce *mamzerim*! Since the Torah does state that there is an instance in which the child of the Kohen Gadol and a woman forbidden to him is a *chalal* and *not* a *mamzer* [see Baraisa on 29b citing R' Simai], it must at least apply in the case of a Kohen Gadol and a nonvirgin, which is the least severe case of women prohibited to a Kohen.

[Alternatively, as stated in *Kiddushin* 68a, the verse *If a man has two wives, one beloved and one despised ...* (*Deuteronomy* 21:15) indicates that there must be some woman who can be a man's "wife" yet "despised" (that is, her marriage to her husband is despised in the eyes of Heaven – i.e. forbidden). Thus, R' Yesheivav must agree that the least forbidden of all women (a nonvirgin to a Kohen Gadol) can "become" the wife of the man to whom she is forbidden (see Gemara there, where this reasoning is indeed applied to R' Yesheivav's view). See *Chidushei R' Akiva Eiger* here ד״ה שם בגמרא איכא בינייהו בעולה לכה״ג. Yet another answer to this question emerges from his comments in ד״ה שם גמרא ומ״ש בעולה לכ״ג.]

10. Even though cohabiting with a *niddah* is prohibited on pain of *kares,* and both Shimon HaTimni and R' Shimon ben Menasya agree that, generally, a girl prohibited to the *oneiss* on pain of *kares* is *not* entitled to the fine. The case of *niddah,* however, is an exception.

11. For if one betroths a woman during the days that she is a *niddah,* the *kiddushin* takes effect [as derived by the Gemara in *Yevamos* 49b] (*Rashi*).

12. [Obviously, one is not obligated to divorce his wife when she becomes a *niddah;* they need only abstain from relations until she purifies herself from her *niddah* state.]

13. For our Mishnah states that one who violates his sister [or other girls for which he incurs *kares* for cohabiting with them] is subject to the fine (*Rashi*).

14. The law is that one who burns someone else's stack of grain on the Sabbath is not liable to pay for the damage [since he has simultaneously incurred the death penalty for desecrating the Sabbath, and thus is liable only to the more severe penalty – see note 16]. R' Nechunya ben HaKanah similarly exempts from payment one who burns the stack on Yom Kippur, even though the penalty for desecrating Yom Kippur is *kares* and not execution (see *Rashi*).

15. One who desecrates the Sabbath deliberately is liable to execution by stoning (see *Exodus* 31:14 and *Numbers* 15:35).

16. The Mishnah below (36b) states that one who violates his daughter is exempt from the fine. For his act of cohabiting with his daughter has made him subject to execution by the court. And whoever is subject to execution for an act is exempt from any financial penalty incurred simultaneously. For it is stated (*Exodus* 21:22): ...,וְלֹא יִהְיֶה אָסוֹן עָנוֹשׁ יֵעָנֵשׁ *and there is no fatality, he shall be punished [monetarily].* The verse deals with two men who are fighting and one of them inadvertently strikes a pregnant woman, causing her to miscarry. The Torah specifies that he pays compensation for the fetus *only* if the woman does not die. The implication, then, is that if the woman dies as a result of her injuries, so that the crime becomes a capital offense, the murderer is exempt from paying compensation for the fetus, since he incurs the court-imposed death penalty for murder [see below, 34b-35a]. From this we derive the principle that *one is subject only to the greater penalty* [קָם לֵיהּ בִּדְרַבָּה מִינֵּיהּ]; that is, when one incurs a monetary liability simultaneously with a court-imposed death penalty, he is subject only to the greater penalty [execution], and is not subject to the lesser penalty [monetary payment] (see *Rashi*). For this reason, one who burns someone else's stack of grain on the Sabbath is exempt from paying for the damage.

17. One who desecrates Yom Kippur is liable to the Divinely imposed premature death of *kares* (see *Leviticus* 23:30).

18. That is, even though the penalty for desecrating Yom Kippur is not execution but *kares* [which is considered a lesser penalty], *kares,* too, is deemed to be "payment with one's life" in this regard, and the desecrater is not liable to monetary payment (*Rashi*).

Thus, our Mishnah, which exempts the sinner from monetary payment only where he incurs the court-administered death penalty (see end of Mishnah on 29a; Mishnah below, 36b), but not where he incurs only *kares,* excludes the view of R' Nechunya ben HaKanah, who exempts from monetary payment even in the case of *kares.*

19. According to Abaye, R' Nechunya ben HaKanah interprets the word *"ason"* in the clause וְלֹא יִהְיֶה אָסוֹן עָנוֹשׁ יֵעָנֵשׁ, *and there is no fatality (ason), he shall be punished [monetarily]* (see note 16), as referring to the fatality of the *assailant* [see 35a notes 1 and 2]. That is, if the assailant is not liable to death at the hand of the court for murder, then he pays for the fetus [implying that where the assailant *is* subject to death at the hand of the court, he does *not* pay for the fetus] (*Rashi,* as understood by *Ramban, Rashba, Chidushei HaRan* and *R' Crescas* to beginning of 30b).

20. In *Genesis* 42:38, Jacob tells his sons that he refuses to allow Benjamin to travel to Egypt lest *an "ason" befall him on the way,* i.e. lest he die. This does not refer to any court-imposed death, but rather to death by "accident" – i.e. by the hand of Heaven.

חייבי עשה מצרי ואדומי הניחא לר' ישבב אי לאפוקי מטעמא דר' סימאי קאתי שפיר אלא אי טעמא דנפשיה קאמר כל שאין לו ביאה בישראל הולד ממזר ואפי' חייבי עשה מאי בינייהו ° איכא בינייהו בעולה לכ"ג ומ"ש דהוה ליה עשה שאינו שוה בכל אמר רב חסדא הכל מודים בבא על הנדה שמשלם קנס למ"ד יש בה הויה הא נמי יש בה הויה למ"ד ראויה לקיימה הא נמי ראויה לקיימה ולאפוקי מדרבי נחוניא בן הקנה דתניא [א] רבי נחוניא בן הקנה היה עושה את יום הכפורים כשבת לתשלומין מה שבת מתחייב בנפשו ופטור מן התשלומין אף יום הכפורים מתחייב בנפשו ופטור מן התשלומין מ"ט דר' נחוניא בן הקנה אמר אביי נאמר [א] אסון בידי אדם ונאמר [ב] אסון בידי שמים [א] מה אסון האמור בידי אדם פטור מן התשלומין אף אסון האמור בידי שמים פטור מן התשלומין מתקיף לה רב אדא בר אהבה ממאי דכי קא מזהר להו יעקב לבניה על צינים ופחים דבידי שמים נינהו דלמא על אריא וגנבי דבידי אדם נינהו אטו יעקב אהא אזהר אהא לא אזהר יעקב על כל מילי אזהר וצינים פחים בידי שמים נינהו והתניא [ג] הכל בידי שמים חוץ מצינים פחים שנאמר [ג] צינים פחים בדרך עיקש שומר נפשו ירחק מהם ותו אריא וגנבי בידי אדם נינהו [ג] והאמר רב יוסף וכן תני רבי חייא מיום שחרב בית המקדש אף על פי שבטלו סנהדרין ארבע מיתות לא בטלו לא בטלו הא בטלו להו אלא

דין

רש"י

חייבי עשה מצרי ואדומי. בתוך שלשה דורות דכתיב (דברים כג) דור שלישי יבא להם דור שני ולא ולאו הבא מכלל עשה עשה: **הניחא.** אי רבי ישבב האי כל שאין לו היתר ביאה דקאמר אליבא דר"ע לאו כללא כייל אלא לאפוקי מדרבי סימאי דמוקי לה לחייבי כריתות אתא ולחייבי לאוין הוא דפליג לאוסופי חייבי לאוין [ז] בכהונה אבל שום חייבי עשה לא הוסיף: **שפיר.** מצינו למימר איכא בינייהו דשמעון התימני ור"ש בן מנסיא חייבי עשה: **אלא.** אי לאו אדרבי סימאי קאי וטעמא דנפשיה קאמר בשם ר"ע כל שאין לו היתר ביאה באשה זו הולד ממזר מאי איכא למימר: **בעולה לכ"ג.** שאין בה לאו ללאלמנות וגירושין אלא עשה דבתולה יקח (ויקרא כא) ולא בעולה וא"ת יש כאן לאו דזונה לא אשכחן תנא דאמר פנוי הבא על הפנויה עשאה זונה אלא ר' אלעזר [ח] (א) ולית הלכתא כוותיה ואין זונה אלא הנבעלת לפסול לה ובבעולה שלא כדרכה איירי דלא כדרכה תו ליכא קנס: **ומאי שנא.** האי עשה מאשר עשה דמודה ביה ר"ע: **דהוה ליה עשה שאינו שוה בכל.** שאינו נוהג אלא בכ"ג אבל עשה דמצרי ואדומי נוהג בכל הקהל: **הא נמי יש בה הויה.** המקדש אשה בימי נדותה מקודשת: **ולאפוקי מדר' נחוניא.** מתני' דמחייב תשלומין לבא על אחותו ואע"פ שמתחייב כרת בביאתו מפקא מדר' נחוניא: **את יום הכפורים כשבת.** לפטור המדליק את הגדיש ביום הכפורים כאילו הדליקו בשבת: **מה שבת.** שהוא מיתת ב"ד: **פטור מן התשלומין.** כדתנן במתני' גבי בא על בתו וכו' וילפי' לה מולא יהיה אסון ענוש יענש: **אף יום הכפורים.** שהוא בכרת חיוב נפש הוא וזה ופטור מן התשלומין: **אסון בידי אדם.** ולא יהיה אסון דמשתעי במיתת ב"ד למימר דהיכא דליכא מיתת ב"ד משלם דמי ולדות: **אסון בידי שמים.** וקראהו אסון: **צינים פחים.** קור וחום: **בידי שמים.** אם באים פורענות על האדם גזירת המלך הוא: **חוץ מצינים ופחים.** שפעמים שבאין בפשיעה: **בידי אדם נינהו.** שלא מגזירת מלך:

דין

תוספות

אי לאפוקי מדרבי סימאי קאתי. תימה תיפשוט דרבי ישבב טעמא דנפשיה קאמר אליבא דמ"ד בפ"ק דיבמות (דף יג. ושם) הבא על יבמתו וחזר ובא אחד מן האחים על צרתה עשה דהא תנן בפרק ר"ג (יבמות דף נ.) ר"ג אומר דאין בעילה אחר בעילה א"כ רבי ישבב טעמא דנפשיה קאמר והוי התם כר' ישבב דאין קידושין תופסין בחייבי עשה והלכך אין אחר בעילה כלום כדאמר התם בגמרא [י] מתני' דאין אחר חליצה כלום אמר רב הונא אמר רב זו דברי ר"ע דאמר דאין קידושין תופסין בחייבי לאוין ומסתמא הכא אליבא דר"ע מספקא ליה אי טעמא דנפשיה קאמר אי לאו לכך נראה לר"ת דגרסי' בפ"ק דיבמות (דף יא.) חד אמר בלאו ובלא זה מודה ר"מ בהשיא שמעתא דלכ"ג עשה וכן פר"ח דהיינו לאו שחלץ לאחת דאמר קרא אשר לא יבנה כיון שלא בנה שוב לא יבנה אחרת ה"נ כיון שבנה שוב לא יבנה אחרת:

איכא בינייהו בעולה לכ"ג. פי' בקונט' בעולה שלא כדרכה וקשה דפלוגתא דר"מ ורבי אלעזר היא בפרק הבא על יבמתו (יבמות דף נט. ושם) אי כשירה לכ"ג וי"ל למימר ולר"מ דאמר כשירה לכ"ג מאי איכא למימר דקאמר ולר"ע דאמר כו' ואור"י דמר"ע פריך שפיר כדי לאוקומי ר"ש בן מנסיא שהוא בתרא כר"ע שהיה רבו אבל בהא לא חייש אי פליג ר"מ אר"ש בן מנסיא ור"מ פי' דהכא לא איירי בבעולה מאחר אלא בכ"ג שאנס בתולה גמורה ולא חשיבה ראויה לקיימה אע"ג דאמר בהבא על יבמתו [ט] אנוסת עצמו ומפותת עצמו לא ישא ואם נשא נשוי מ"מ כיון דלכתחלה לא ישא לא חשיבה ראויה לקיימה דהאי לא ישא הוי מן התורה אף ע"ג דאם נשא נשוי ה"נ אמר בוגרת ומוכת עץ לא ישא ואם נשא נשוי אע"ג דהוי מן התורה כדמוכח התם ועוד דקאמר התם [פ] מתיב רבא ולו תהיה לאשה באשה הראויה לו פרט אלמנה לכ"ג היכי דמי אילימא בכדרכה מאי איריא משום אלמנה תיפוק ליה דהויא לה בעולה משמע דבעולת עצמו אסורה לו מן התורה ור"ת לא פירש כן:

הכל מודים בבא על הנדה שמשלם קנס. תימה לר"י מנלן דר"ש בן מנסיא מודה בה דלמא כר' נחוניא בן הקנה ס"ל דחייבי כריתות פטורים מן התשלומין ומיהו ר"ש התימני ע"כ לית ליה דר' נחוניא מדאיצטריך למעוטי חייבי כריתות מולו תהיה לאשה אשה שיש בה הויה דע"כ לא איצטריך למעוטי אלא חייבי כריתות דחייבי לאוין ס"ל בסוף החולץ (יבמות דף מט. ושם) דאית בהו הויה אבל מר"ש בן מנסיא קשה מנלן דלית ליה דר' נחוניא ועוד אפי' ר"ש התימני דלמא אית ליה דר' נחוניא ואיצטריך למעוטי מולו תהיה לאשה יבמה לשוק דאין קידושין תופסין בה לכ"ע כדאמר בהאשה רבה (שם דף צב: ושם) וי"ל דרב חסדא ס"ל דאין שום תנא סובר כרבי נחוניא ולה"ק ולאפוקי כו' ובקונט' פירש דאמתני' קאי דמפקא מדר' נחוניא ותימה מנ"ל דמפקא מיניה דלמא מודה ר' נחוניא דחייבי כריתות יש להן קנס דרבינהו קרא חד לחייבי לאוין וחד לחייבי כריתות ולר"ע ניחא דמפקא מתני' מדר' נחוניא דכיון דאין קידושין תופסין בחייבי לאוין איכא לאוקומי הנך תרי ריבויי חד לחייבי עשה וחד לחייבי לאוין אבל חייבי כריתות לר' נחוניא לא [א] ונראה לרשב"א לתרץ [ב] דע"כ מפקא מתני' מר' נחוניא דלר' נחוניא אין חילוק בין חייבי כריתות לחייבי מיתות ב"ד או מאסון אסון או כדדריש רבא כרת שלי כמיתה שלכם ואם יש קנס לר' נחוניא בחייבי כריתות יש ג"כ בחייבי מיתות ב"ד ומתני' קתני בא על בתו פטור: **הכל** בידי שמים חוץ מצינים פחים. והא דאמרי' (שבת דף לב.) לעולם אל יעמוד אדם במקום סכנה אלמא יכול לשמור עצמו מן הפורענות וכן קיר נטוי דאסור לעבור תחתיו התם מן הפשיעה יכול לשמור עצמו דהא ודאי שבידו להמית עצמו אבל כשמביאין עליו מן השמים באונס אי אפשר לו לשמור אבל צינים פחים לעולם אל יבואו עליו באונס אם רוצה ליזהר וא"ת והא דרשינן (ב"מ דף קז:) והסיר ה' ממך כל חולי זה צינה אלמא דבידי שמים הוא וי"ל דהיינו שיתם הקב"ה עולמו או יתן לו מלבושים ולא יצטרך ליזהר וא"ת והא פחים בידי שמים הוא כדאמרי' בבראשית רבה בפרשה ט"ו א"ל אנטונינוס לרבי צלי עלי א"ל רחמנא שיזבך מצינתא א"ל דא צלותא היא יתיר חד כסו וצינתא אזלא א"ל תשתזב משרבא א"ל הא כדו צלותא דכתיב אין נסתר מחמתו וי"ל דקרא כתיב בעוברי דרכים או במלחמה כדרך שהמלכים עושים דבדרך אין אדם יכול ליזהר מן החום אבל אם רוצה לישב בביתו יכול להזהר שישב בבית של אבנים או יכנס במרתף ויש מפרשים דצינים פחים חדא מילתא היא כלומר צינים שהם פחים לאדם לשון פח ומוקש ואינו כן דבפ"ק דמסכת ע"ז (דף ג: ושם) מייתי לה [אהא דכתיב ותעשה אדם כדגי הים מה] דגים שבים כיון שקדרה עליהן חמה מיד מתים [אף בני אדם כיון שקדרה עליהם חמה מיד מתים] והא דאמר (ברכות דף לג:) הכל בידי שמים חוץ מיראת שמים אין ענינו לכאן דהתם קאי על הולד במעי אמו (נדה טז:) שגוזרין אם יהא עני או עשיר גבור או חלש טפש או חכם אבל צדיק ורשע לא [ט] והכא איירי במאורעות הבאות על האדם [ג]: **מיום** שחרב בית כו'. וא"ת אמאי לא נקט מ' שנה קודם שחרב בהמ"ק דמ' שנה קודם חורבן גלתה סנהדרין כו' שלא דנו דיני נפשות וי"ל דלפעמים לצורך שעה היו חוזרין סנהדרין ללשכת הגזית ולהכי לא פסיקא ליה למיתני מ' שנה קודם חורבן וא"ת א"כ מאי פריך בפרק היו בודקין (סנהדרין דף מא.) גבי מעשה ובדק ר' יוחנן בן זכאי בעוקצי תאנים ופריך מי הוה בסנהדרין והא תניא כל שנותיו של רבן יוחנן בן זכאי מאה ועשרים שנה מ' עסק בפרקמטיא ומ' למד ומ' לימד ותניא מ' שנה קודם חורבן גלתה סנהדרין כו' והשתא מאי קשיא ליה כיון דלפעמים היו חוזרין ודנין וי"ל דרבן יוחנן בן זכאי דבדק בעוקצי תאנה אמעשה דרציחה היה ומשום דיני נפשות דרציחה לא היו חוזרין לעולם דעיקרם לא גלו אלא משום רציחה דחזו דנפישי רוצחים כדאמרינן בפ"ק דמסכת ע"ז (דף ח: ושם) וי"מ דלהכי נקט משחרב בהמ"ק משום דקודם לכן אע"פ שגלו היו בגדי כהונה מכפרים על מזיד דלא אתרו ביה כדאמרינן בפרק יש בערכין (ערכין דף טז. ושם) ואין נראה דהא בימי שמעון בן שטח היו בגדי כהונה והיה דין ארבע מיתות כדאמרינן בפרק אחד דיני ממונות (סנהדרין דף לז: ושם) אר"ש בן שטח אראה בנחמה אם לא ראיתי אחד שרץ אחר חברו לחורבה וכו' לא זז משם עד שנשכו נחש ופריך והאי בר נחש הוא והא תני ר' חייא אע"פ שבטלו סנהדרין כו' ועוד אמר (מכות י:) מרשעים יצא רשע כו' [ד] והתם בזמן שבהמ"ק קיים איירי מדקאמר ונמצא זה מת וזה גולה [י]:

דין

מסורת הש"ס

א) [תוספתא ב"ק פ"ז שבועות לג. מגילה ז: פסחים כט. לג. [תוספתא פ"ה], ב) כ"מ קז: ב"ב קמד: ע"ש ע"ז ג: ע"ש, ג) סוטה מ: סנהדרין לז: ע"ש, ד) צ"ל דכהונה, ה) [יבמות נט:], ו) דף נג:, ז) [יבמות דף נג.], ח) [דף נט. ושם ד"ה חייבי], ט) [ע"ש תוס' מגילה ז. ד"ה הכל ותוס' נדה טז:], י) [וע"ע תוס' סוטה מ: ד"ה מכפרים].

עין משפט נר מצוה

ז א (מיי' פ"א מהלכות נערה הלכה יג ופ"ג מהלכות גניבה הלכה ב טוש"ע ח"מ סי' שנא):

תוספות רי"ד

מתני' דלא כר"נ בן הקנה. פירוש מתני' דמחייב קנס לבא על אחותו ואע"פ שמתחייב כרת בביאתו. דתניא ר"נ [בן הקנה] היה עושה יוה"כ כשבת לתשלומין. פי' לפטור המדליק את הגדיש ביוה"כ כאילו הדליקו בשבת מה שבת שהיא מיתת ב"ד פטור מתשלומין כדתנן מתני' לקמן בבא על בתו וילפי' לה מולא יהי' אסון. אף יוה"כ שהוא בכרת מתחייב בנפשו ופטור מן התשלומין. מ"ט דר"נ ב"ה. אמר אביי נאמר אסון בידי שמים. פי' וקראהו אסון ונאמר אסון בידי אדם ואם אסון יהיה מה אסון הנאמר בידי אדם פטור מן התשלומין. פי' דמשתעי במיתת ב"ד למימר היכא דליכא מיתת ב"ד משלם דמי ולדות. אף אסון האמור בידי שמים פטור מן התשלומין:

תוספות ישנים

א) ומהר"מ אומר כי תלא בתוספתא פרק אלו נערות ר' נחוניא אומר הבא על אחותו ועל אחות אביו כו' אין להם קנס כן היה עושה רבי נחוניא בן הקנה יוה"כ כשבת: ב) ול"נ לתרץ דע"כ מפקא מתני' מר' נחוניא דלר"ע איצטריך לאוקומי חד לחייבי לאוין ועשה וחד לחייבי כריתות לשוק אבל חייבי כריתות קים ליה בדרבה מיניה וכ"מ לקמן בפירקין אי כרבי נחוניא קשיא אחותו משמע דבחייבי כריתות לא מתוקמא כוותיה. מ"י: ג) והא דתנן (פ"ד דאבות) אל כרחך אתה חי היינו שאין לך אדם שמתה להרוג עצמו ואינו הגון לר"י דע"כ אתה חי לעתיד קאמר וגרסי' ע"כ אתה מת ואתה חי וכו' כמו כן התמים להחיות והמתים לדון. מ"י: ד) ומיהו אפשר לומר לפי שלפעמים היו מכפרים לא פסיקא ליה. מ"י:

ליקוטי רש"י

חייבי עשה מצרי ואדומי. קודם ג' דורות דכתיב (דברים כג) דור שלישי יבא להם ולא שני ולאו הבא מכלל עשה עשה [יבמות מט.]. אי לאפוקי מטעמא דר' סימאי קאתי. ולא להוסיף על חייבי לאוין דכהונה אבל מצרי ואדומי תוך ג' דורות שהן חייבי עשה מודה דקידושין תופסין בה [קידושין סח:]. אי לאו כללא הוא אלא לאפוקי מדרבי סימאי דמפיק חד מחייבי לאוין אתי ולאשמועי' דהכל חייבי לאוין עושה ר"ש ממזר [שם סח.]. אלא אי טעמא דנפשיה קאמר. ולאו לאפוקי מדר' סימאי אתי לאפלוגי אחייבי לאוין דכהונה לחודייהו אתי אלא כל ביאה שהיא בעבירה הולד ממזר [שם סד:]. וכללא כייל ולאו אדרבי סימאי לחודיה פליג אלא אשמעינן כל שביאתו באיסור הולד ממזר. בעולה לכ"ג. דעשה הוא דכתיב (ויקרא כא) אשה בבתוליה יקח ולא בעולה ולאו הבא מכלל עשה עשה וליכא לאקשויי הא זונה היא אלא אלמנה או גרושה דבעולה פנויה לאו זונה היא לכדתנן ביבמות (דף סא.) אין זונה אלא גיורת ומשוחררת ושנבעלה בעילת זנות וביאת איסור לפסול לה. ומ"ש. האי עשה מחייבי עשה למצרי ואדומי. שאינו שוה בכל. שאינו נוהג אלא בכ"ג הילכך קיל [שם סח.]. את יום הכפורים כשבת. המדליק גדיש ביום הכפורים ומתחייב כרת פטור מן התשלומין כאילו הדליקו בשבת שהוא מתחייב בנפשו מיתת בית דין דפשיטא לן דפטור מלשלם דכתיב (שמות כא) ולא יהיה אסון ענוש יענש הא אם יהיה אסון לא יענש אף יום הכפורים שמתחייב כרת שהוא מיתה בידי שמים פטור מלשלם וגמרי אסון אסון קרי שנאמר (בראשית מב) וקראהו אסון הלכך בידי שמים פטור מלשלם והכי פרשינן לה באלו נערות (פסחים כט.). המתחייב כרת פטור מן התשלומין ויליף טעמא מאסון אסון והוא הדין למתחייב מיתה בידי שמים כגון האוכל תרומה מזיד [שם לב.]. אף יום

הגהות הב"ח

(א) רש"י ד"ה בעולה וכו' אלא ר' אלעזר וליח. נ"ב וביבמות בש"ס ע"ב מסיק דאף אליבא דר"א משכחת לה בממאנת ע"ש:

גליון הש"ס

גמ' איכא בינייהו בעולה לכ"ג. עי' פסחים מא ע"ב תוד"ה הכל:

תורה אור השלם

א) וְכִי יִנָּצוּ אֲנָשִׁים וְנָגְפוּ אִשָּׁה הָרָה וְיָצְאוּ יְלָדֶיהָ וְלֹא יִהְיֶה אָסוֹן עָנוֹשׁ יֵעָנֵשׁ כַּאֲשֶׁר יָשִׁית עָלָיו בַּעַל הָאִשָּׁה וְנָתַן בִּפְלִלִים: [שמות כא, כב]

ב) וַיֹּאמֶר לֹא יֵרֵד בְּנִי עִמָּכֶם כִּי אָחִיו מֵת וְהוּא לְבַדּוֹ נִשְׁאָר וּקְרָאָהוּ אָסוֹן בַּדֶּרֶךְ אֲשֶׁר תֵּלְכוּ בָהּ וְהוֹרַדְתֶּם אֶת שֵׂיבָתִי בְּיָגוֹן שְׁאוֹלָה: [בראשית מב, לח]

ג) צִנִּים פַּחִים בְּדֶרֶךְ עִקֵּשׁ שׁוֹמֵר נַפְשׁוֹ יִרְחַק מֵהֶם: [משלי כב, ה]

הכפורים מתחייב בנפשו. דאיסור כרת כמיתת ב"ד דמי. ופטור מן התשלומין. אם הדליק גדישו של חבירו ביום הכפורים שאין תשלומין אלא חיוב מיתה שנאמר ולא יהיה אסון ענש יענש (שמות כא) הא אם יהיה אסון לא יענש [מגילה ז:]. הכל בידי שמים. מתחלואות ומכאובות הבאים לאדם כולם על ידי גזירת שמים. חוץ מצינים פחים. צנים לנה פחים חולי הבא ע"י חום כמו (שיר השירים ב) עד שיפוח היום [ע"ז ג:]. קור הנופח [ב"מ קז:]. לישנא דקרא צנים פחים בדרך עקש הצנה והחום ומוקש בדרך עקש שבידו הדבר תלוי להשמר מהם. צנים פחים הם טמונים בדרכי המעקש דרכיו כלומר יסורים מוכנים לו. שומר נפשו ירחק מהם. המשמר מעשיו יגלל מהם [משלי כב, ה].

חַיָּיבֵי עֲשֵׂה מִצְרִי וַאֲדוֹמִי – when the victim is one of **those** for which the *oneiss* is **liable for** violating **a positive command** by cohabiting with them, such as where the girl is a first- or second-generation **Egyptian or Edomite** convert and the *oneiss* is a native Jew.[1] Since the union of a native Jew and an Egyptian convert is not prohibited by a negative command, their *kiddushin* is effective even according to R' Yesheivav's understanding of R' Akiva.[2] Hence, the fine would be applicable according to the exposition of Shimon HaTimni (since she can *become* his wife), but not according to that of R' Shimon ben Menasya (since she cannot *remain* his wife, as they are forbidden to one another by force of a positive command).

The Gemara asks, however, that the foregoing would resolve the matter only according to one way of understanding R' Yesheivav's statement:

הָנִיחָא לְרַבִּי יְשֵׁבָב אִי לְאַפּוּקֵי מִטַּעְמָא דְּרַבִּי סִימַאי קָאָתֵי – **Now, all is well according to R' Yesheivav, if he is coming** simply **to preclude the view of R' Simai.**[3] **שַׁפִּיר** – **It is** then **correct** to say that there is a difference between Shimon HaTimni and R' Shimon ben Menasya with regard to a native Jew who violates an Egyptian or Edomite convert.[4] **אֶלָּא אִי טַעְמָא דְּנַפְשֵׁיהּ קָאָמַר** – **But if it is his own** general **articulation** of R' Akiva's opinion that **[R' Yesheivav] is saying,** rather than a response to R' Simai's statement, then R' Yesheivav's statement must be taken at face value to mean, literally, **כָּל שֶׁאֵין לוֹ בִּיאָה בְּיִשְׂרָאֵל** – that if ***any*** man **among Jews who does not have** the permit of **cohabitation** with a particular woman does cohabit with her and produce a child, **הַוָּלָד מַמְזֵר** – **the child is a *mamzer,*** **וַאֲפִילּוּ חַיָּיבֵי עֲשֵׂה** – **and,** as such, the statement encompasses **even those** for which he is **liable for** transgressing only **a positive command** by cohabiting with them.[5] **מַאי בֵּינַיְיהוּ** – Accordingly, **what** practical difference **is there between them** [the interpretations of Shimon HaTimni and R' Shimon ben Menasya]? For according to this interpretation of R' Akiva, *kiddushin* does not take effect even between a native Jew and an Egyptian or Edomite convert.[6] Thus, there would be no fine for a native Jew's violation of such a convert even according to the interpretation of Shimon HaTimni! – ? –

The Gemara answers:

אִיכָּא בֵּינַיְיהוּ בְּעוּלָה לְכֹהֵן גָּדוֹל – Even so, **there is** a practical difference **between them** when the victim is forbidden to the *oneiss* by force of the positive command prohibiting **a nonvirgin to a Kohen Gadol,**[7] in which case even R' Yesheivav agrees that the child is not a *mamzer* and *kiddushin* can take effect.[8] Hence, the fine would be applicable according to the interpretation of Shimon HaTimni (since she is fit to "become" the wife of the *oneiss*), but not according to the interpretation of R' Shimon ben Menasya (since she is not fit to *remain* his wife).

The Gemara asks:

וּמַאי שְׁנָא – **And why is** the positive command prohibiting a nonvirgin to a Kohen Gadol **different** than the other unions prohibited by force of a positive command (i.e. the Egyptian and Edomite), where R' Yesheivav maintains that (according to R' Akiva) the child *is* a *mamzer* and the *kiddushin* does *not* take effect?

The Gemara answers:

דַּהֲוָה לֵיהּ עֲשֵׂה שֶׁאֵינוֹ שָׁוֶה בַּכֹּל – The positive command forbidding a nonvirgin to a Kohen Gadol is different, **for it is a positive command that is not common to all.**[9]

NOTES

1. The Torah (*Deuteronomy* 23:9) states that the third-generation offspring of an Egyptian or Edomite convert is permitted to marry into the general community of Israel. This implies that a first- or second-generation Egyptian or Edomite convert is prohibited from marrying a native Jew. Since this prohibition is not stated explicitly as a prohibition but derived only by inference from a positive statement, it has only the [lesser] force of a positive command [מִצְוַת עֲשֵׂה], and not the [greater] force of a prohibition [מִצְוַת לֹא תַעֲשֶׂה] (see *Rashi*).

2. For it is possible to say that R' Yesheivav's understanding of R' Akiva extends R' Akiva's ruling only to all who are prohibited *by force of a prohibition* – even a widow to a Kohen Gadol – but not to those who are forbidden simply by the force of a positive command (see Gemara further).

3. R' Yesheivav can be understood in one of two ways. His comments might have been completely independent, or they might have been in response to R' Simai's statement. If they were in response to R' Simai's statement, then they would be understood in the following context: R' Akiva said that a *mamzer* is the child of any union forbidden by force of a prohibition (see 29b note 34). R' Simai asserted that R' Akiva agrees that the child of a Kohen and a woman forbidden to a Kohen is not a *mamzer.* R' Yesheivav then disagrees: According to R' Akiva, a *mamzer* is produced by "*any* Jew who does not have the permit to cohabit with that particular woman" – even a Kohen who cohabits with a woman forbidden to a Kohen. [That is, R' Yesheivav means "any" only in the context of R' Simai's statement. Whereas R' Simai states that the union of a Kohen and a woman forbidden to a Kohen is an exception to R' Akiva's rule that the product of a union forbidden by force of *a prohibition* is a *mamzer,* R' Yesheivav argues that it is *not* an exception. Rather, in *any* union between those forbidden to one another by force of *a prohibition,* the child is a *mamzer*] (see *Rashi*).

4. For even R' Yesheivav agrees that R' Akiva does *not* deem the offspring of that union to be a *mamzer.* Hence, it is a union in which *kiddushin* would be effective, and the victim could thus "become" her attacker's wife.

5. For R' Yesheivav's statement in and of itself speaks only about the lack of permit of cohabitation, and those forbidden by force of a positive command indeed lack the permit of cohabitation.

6. Since the making of a *mamzer* and the possibility of effecting *kiddushin* are interdependent, as explained above (29b note 39).

7. I.e. where a Kohen Gadol violated a girl who was never married but who had previously cohabited with a man. Since she was never married, she is not prohibited to the Kohen Gadol by force of the prohibitions against his marrying a widow or divorcee (*Leviticus* 21:14). She is, however, forbidden to him by force of the positive command (ibid. verse 13): *And he [the Kohen Gadol] shall marry a woman in her virginity,* which implies that he may *not* marry a nonvirgin [even if she was never married; and a prohibition inferred from a positive command has only the force of a positive command] (*Rashi*).

[Though a זוֹנָה, *zonah* (harlot), is indeed forbidden to a Kohen by force of a prohibition (see ibid. verses 7 and 14), it is only the lone opinion of the Tanna R' Elazar that nonmarital cohabitation with a potentially suitable marriage partner gives the woman the legal status of a *zonah.* The prevailing opinion is that the *zonah* of this prohibition is specifically a woman who cohabited with a man Biblically forbidden to her, not a woman who merely cohabited out of wedlock (*Rashi*). We must also say that the Gemara means that the girl had previously lost her virginity through *unnatural* intercourse. For if she had lost it through natural cohabitation, then she would not be a virgin with regard to the fine, and thus would not be entitled to the fine altogether (*Rashi*). Unnatural intercourse renders a woman a "nonvirgin" with respect to unfitness to marry a Kohen Gadol (see the opinion of R' Elazar and R' Shimon cited in *Yevamos* 59a), but not with respect to the fine for her subsequent violation (see *Kiddushin* 10a), with regard to which she remains classified as a "virgin" (*Shitah Mekubetzes*). See, however, *Tosafos* and *Rabbeinu Chananel* cited there.]

8. For reasons that the Gemara will explain shortly.

9. In contrast to the positive commands prohibiting an Egyptian or Edomite convert, which pertain to all Jews, the positive command prohibiting a nonvirgin pertains only to a Kohen Gadol (*Rashi*). Thus, it is a less severe restriction [and *kiddushin* takes effect] (see *Rashi* to *Kiddushin* 68a ד״ה שאינו שוה בכל). [Possibly, this is alluded to in R' Yesheivav's words, "If any man *among Jews* (בְּיִשְׂרָאֵל) does not have the permit of cohabitation with a particular woman ...," indicating that he is referring to unions that are forbidden to Jews in general, rather than to a specific class, such as a Kohen Gadol.]

Actually, one could ask that while the Gemara has shown why R'

does not have the permit of **cohabitation** with a particular woman[41] does cohabit with her and produce a child, **הַוָּלָד מַמְזֵר – the child is a *mamzer,*"**[42] **מַאי בֵּינַיְיהוּ – what** practical difference **is there between them** [the interpretations of Shimon HaTimni and R' Shimon ben Menasya]? Since, according to R' Yesheivav, R' Akiva's ruling that the child of a union prohibited by a simple prohibition is a *mamzer* encompasses even the union of a widow and a Kohen Gadol,[43] it follows that *kiddushin* cannot take effect between them.[44] Hence, a widow violated by a Kohen Gadol would not be entitled to the fine even according to the exposition of Shimon HaTimni. What practical difference, then, emerges from R' Shimon ben Menasya expounding *she shall "be" to him a wife* differently?[45]

The Gemara answers:

אִיכָּא בֵּינַיְיהוּ – There is a practical difference **between them**

NOTES

41. *Rashi* to *Kiddushin* 64a.

42. R' Yesheivav protested that R' Akiva was needlessly increasing the number of *mamzerim* among the Jewish people (*Rashi*). [For R' Akiva considers a child a *mamzer* even if the parents' union was prohibited by a simple prohibition, whereas all other Tannaim consider the child a *mamzer* only if the union was forbidden on pain of *kares* or execution (see *Yevamos* 49a).]

It is evident from the way R' Yesheivav cites R' Akiva's view ("any among Jews who does not have the permit . . .") that he understands R' Akiva to rule the child a *mamzer* even in the case of a Kohen Gadol who marries a widow (see *Rashi,* and Gemara below).

43. See preceding note.

44. See note 39.

45. See note 35.

עין משפט נר מצוה

ד א מיי' פ"א מהלכות נערה הל' טו סמג עשין נד טוש"ע אה"ע סי' קעז:
ה ב מיי' שם הל' ח:
ו ג מיי' שם הל' ה:

מסורת הש"ס

א) [לקמן לג.], ב) [לקמן לח:], ג) [לעיל י. לקמן לח:], ד) [לקמן לג.], ה) [יבמות ט: וש"נ], ו) [יבמות סט. קידושין סד. סח.], ז) [לקמן לג:], ח) [דף ה:], ט) מ"י כ"י.

אף קנס במקום מכר והני בני קנסא נינהו ואמאי איקרי כאן (א) ולו (ו) תהיה לאשה אשה הראויה לו אמר ריש לקיש (א) נערה נערה הנערה חד לגופיה וחד לאתויי חייבי לאוין וחד לאתויי חייבי כריתות רב פפא אמר (ג) בתולה (ד) בתולות הבתולות חד לגופיה וחד לאתויי חייבי לאוין וחד לאתויי חייבי כריתות ורב פפא מ"ט לא אמר כר"ל ההוא מיבעי ליה לכדאביי (ג) דאמר אביי *בא עליה ומתה פטור שנאמר (א) ונתן לאבי הנערה לאבי נערה ולא לאבי מתה וריש לקיש מ"ט לא אמר כרב פפא ההוא מיבעי ליה לגזירה שוה דתניא (ד) כסף ישקול כמוהר הבתולות (ג) שיהא זה כמוהר הבתולות ומוהר הבתולות כזה וריש לקיש נמי מיבעי ליה לכדאביי ורב פפא נמי מיבעי ליה לגזירה שוה אלא שיתא קראי כתיבי נערה נערה הנערה בתולה בתולות הבתולות תרי לגופיהו חד לכדאביי וחד לגזירה שוה אייתרו ליה תרי חד לאתויי חייבי לאוין וחד לאתויי חייבי כריתות ולאפוקי מהאי תנא דתניא ולו תהיה לאשה (ה) שמעון התימני אומר אשה שיש בה הויה רבי שמעון בן מנסיא אומר (ג) אשה הראויה לקיימה מאי בינייהו אמר ר' זירא ממזרת ונתינה איכא בינייהו למאן דאמר יש בה הויה הא נמי יש בה הויה למאן דאמר ראויה לקיימה הא אינה ראויה לקיימה ולרבי עקיבא דאמר (ו) אין קידושין תופסין בחייבי לאוין מאי בינייהו איכא בינייהו אלמנה לכהן גדול כרבי סימאי דתניא רבי סימאי אומר (ז) מן הכל עושה רבי עקיבא ממזרין חוץ מאלמנה לכהן גדול שהרי אמרה תורה (ה) לא יקח ולא יחלל חילולין הוא עושה ואין עושה ממזרין ולרבי ישבב דאמר בואו ונצוח על עקיבא בן יוסף שהיה אומר כל שאין לו ביאה בישראל הולד ממזר מאי בינייהו איכא בינייהו חייבי

רש"י

אף קנס במקום מכר. ומשום קנס נקט בת שלש אבל למכר מבת יום אחד ועד שתביא שתי שערות: ואמאי. יש להן קנס לנערות פסולות: איקרי כאן כו'. למתני' מקשי: ה"ג נערה נערה הנערה. באונס כתיב כי ימצא איש נערה בתולה וגו' וכתיב בתריה ונתן האיש השוכב עמה לאבי הנערה ודרשינן נערה יתירה וה"א יתירה להנערה דמלי למיכתב ונתן לאביה: חד לגופיה. לכשרה: בתולה בתולות הבתולות. במפתה כתיב וכי יפתה איש בתולה וקרא אחרינא בתריה כסף ישקול כמוהר הבתולות ומלי למיכתב כמוהר בתולות הא תלת דדרשינן ה' יתירה ובתולות דמלי למיכתב כמוהר ולשתוק: ההוא מיבעי ליה. ההוא הנערה הא דלא כתיב ונתן לאביה מיבעי ליה לכדאביי שאם לא הספיק האב להעמידו בדין עד שמתה פטור: לאבי הנערה. משמע שהיא קיימת: מיבעי ליה לג"ש. בתולה דכתיב גבי מפתה מיבעי ליה לג"ש בתולה בתולה לג"ש מה כסף האמור באונס חמשים אף מפתה חמשים ומה מפתה שקלים דכתיב בה ישקול אף חמשים של אונס שקלים קאמר: כמוהר הבתולות. חמשים כסף המפורשים במאנס את הבתולה: שיהא זה. חמשים כמוהר הבתולות: ומוהר הבתולות. יהיו שקלים כזה: וחד לג"ש. ותהי מופנה מלד אחד ולמידים הימנה: ולאפוקי מהאי תנא. מתני' דקתני יש קנס לממזרת ולאחותו ולאפוקי מהאי תנא: שיש בה הויה. שקדושין תופסין לו בה פרט לאחותו ולכל חייבי כריתות דילפינן בקדושין שאין קדושין תופסין בהן בפרק שלישי (דף סז:) ומשמע ליה תהיה לשון הויית קדושין ור"ש בן מנסיא משמע ליה תהיה לשון קיום: הא נמי אית בה הויה. דקדושין תופסין בחייבי לאוין והכא יליף לה: ולר"ע דאמר אין קדושין תופסין בחייבי לאוין. ביבמות בהחולץ (דף מד:) בבריית' המחזיר גרושתו ר"ע אומר אין לו בה קדושין: מאי בינייהו. משום ר"ש בן מנסיא קא פריך לה דאילו שמעון התימני שמעינן ליה ביבמות (דף מט.) דפליג עליה דר"ע בהא דתנן איזהו ממזר כל שאר בשר שהוא בלא יבא דברי ר"ע שמעון התימני אומר כל שחייבין עליו כרת בידי שמים אלא לר"ש בן מנסיא קא בעינן לה אי ס"ל כר"ע מאי איכא בין משמעותא דתהיה לשון קיום למשמעות דשמעון התימני אי נמי משמע ליה לר"ש בן מנסיא לשון הויה אימעיטא לה ממזר ומה בין ראויה לקיימה ליש בה הויה: אלמנה לכהן גדול. דמודה בה ר"ע שקדושין תופסין לו בה ואע"פ שהיא בלאו וכרבי סימאי והוא הדין גרושה להדיוט: מן הכל. כל הנולדים מחייבי לאוין: לא יקח. וסמיך ליה ולא יחלל זרעו מדין כהונה הוא מחללו ולא שם ממזרים עליהם: בואו ונצוח על עקיבא בן יוסף. שמרבה ממזרים בישראל חנם: שהוא אומר כל שאין לו ביאה בישראל. הבא על אשה שאין לו בה היתר ביאה הולד ממזר אפי' אלמנה לכ"ג נמי:

תוספות

נערה נערה הנערה. פי' רבינו חננאל דמחד נערה דריש כולה מלתא נער נערה הנערה ואין נראה לר"ת דלא כתיב נערה מלא בה"א אלא ההוא דמוציא שם רע לחודיה כדמוכח בסוף פרקין ועוד הקשה רבינו יצחק מה צריך חד לגופה הא גופה הא איכא נערה אחרינא בפרשה אלא פי' הקונטרס עיקר:

בתולה בתולות הבתולות. כאן נמי פר"ח דמחד קרא נפקי כולהו ואין נראה דלא צריך חד לגופיה דבתולה אחרינא כתיב:

וחד לאיתויי חייבי לאוין. הקשה ר"י בן רבינו מאיר אכתי נימא חד לאתויי חייבי עשה וחד לאתויי חייבי לאוין ואכתי חייבי כריתות מנא לן ותירץ דלחייבי לאוין ועשה לא צריך אלא חד קרא דהא אי לאו דכתיב ולו תהיה לאשה דמשמע שיש בה הויה וראויה לקיימה לא הוה צריך קרא לרבויינהו הלכך מחד ריבויא מרבינן אין ראויה לקיימה דהיינו חייבי עשה וחייבי לאוין כיון דאית בהו הויה ואידך ריבויא לחייבי כריתות ולמאן דאמר אין קדושין תופסין בחייבי לאוין הוי חד ריבויא לחייבי עשה ואידך לחייבי לאוין וחייבי כריתות וא"ת ולשתוק מלו תהיה לאשה ולא יצטרך להנך ריבויי וי"ל דאיצטריך למידרש ולו תהיה לאשה מדעתה (ז):

אייתרו להו תרי כו'. וחד ריבויא כתב באונס וחד במפתה וא"ת ומנא לן דחד לאתויי חייבי כריתות אימא דתרוייהו אתו לרבויי חייבי לאוין וחד לאונס וחד למפתה וי"ל דלהא לא צריך דמגזרה שוה ילפינן אונס ומפתה מהדדי:

ת"י [ולאפוקי מהאי תנא. פי' תנא דברייתא אבל מפיק מתרוייהו תנאי שמחכרים בברייתא]:

ולרבי עקיבא דאמר כו'. ואף ע"ג דר"ש התימני פליג בהדיא אר' עקיבא בהחולץ (יבמות דף מד. ודף מט.) הכא לר"ש בן מנסיא פריך דאי סבר כר"ע מאי בינייהו פי' בינו לר"ש התימני דמדנקט ראויה לקיימה ולא נקט שיש בה הויה משמע דיש שאין ראויה לקיימה ויש בה הויה:

חילולין הוא עושה ואינו עושה ממזרים. משמע דהא בהא תליא דכיון דלא הוי ממזר קדושין תופסין וכן משמע בפרק החולץ (שם דף מה:) מה אשת אב דלא תפסי בה קדושין והוולד ממזר כו' [ור"ע נמי משום דיליף בהחולץ דיש ממזר מחייבי לאוין קאמר דאין קדושין תופסין בחייבי לאוין] ותימה דלרבי יהושע אע"ג דאין ממזר מחייבי כריתות כדיליף בשילהי החולץ (שם דף מט.) מודה דאין קדושין תופסין בחייבי כריתות כדפריך ס"פ ר"ג ביבמות (דף נג. ושם) איצטריך לאשמעינן דאין קדושין תופסין בחייבי כריתות ובפ' החולץ (שם דף מד: ושם) קאמר לרבי יהושע פגום מיהא הוי מחייבי כריתות משום דעשאה זונה חונה לא הויא אלא מהנהו דלא תפסי בה קדושין כדמוכח בתמורה (דף כט: ושם) וקאמרינן נמי בהחולץ (יבמות דף מד: ושם) הכל מודים בכותי ועבד הבא על בת ישראל הוולד ממזר מאן הכל מודים שמעון התימני דאע"ג דאמר אין ממזר מחייבי לאוין ה"מ חייבי לאוין דתפסי בהו קידושין אבל כותי ועבד כו' ולא קאמר מאן הכל מודים ר' יהושע דאע"ג דאמר אין ממזר מחייבי כריתות ה"מ חייבי כריתות דתפסי בהו קדושין כו' אלמא דלר' יהושע אין קדושין תופסין בחייבי כריתות ואפ"ה לא הוי ממזר ולהכי לא מצי למימר דמודה בכותי ועבד ויש לומר דלר"ש התימני ולר"ע ודאי הא בהא תליא דליכא מידי דלא תפסי בה קדושין והוולד כשר רק שהוא דומה לאשת אב אבל לר' יהושע אע"ג דאין קדושין תופסין בחייבי כריתות כדילפי' בסוף האומר (קדושין סח. ושם) לא הוי ממזר אלא מחייבי מיתות ב"ד כדיליף ר' יהושע בסוף החולץ (יבמות מט. ושם) אבל קשה דא"כ לר' יהושע אין קדושין תופסין באלמנה לכ"ג לרבא דאמר בפ"ק דתמורה (דף ד: ושם) כל דאמר רחמנא לא תעביד אי עביד לא מהני דהתם (ח) פריך ליה והרי אלמנה לכ"ג דקאמר רחמנא לא יקח ותנן כל מקום שיש קדושין ויש עבירה כגון אלמנה לכ"ג כו' ומשני אמר לך רבא שאני התם דא"ק לא יחלל חלולין הוא עושה ואינו עושה ממזרים ולר' יהושע ליכא לשנויי הכי וא"ת בקדושין בסוף האומר (דף סז: ושם) כי מסכה דלא תפסי קדושין באשת אב הא לכתחלה הא דיעבד אמאי לא יליף מינה דכל היכא דהוי ממזר לא תפסי בה קדושין כיון דהא בהא תליא כדפירשנו וי"ל דהכתי לא שמעינן ממזרות בשאר חייבי כריתות כל כמה דלא מייתי התם היקישא דר' יונה דמלא יקח ולא יגלה דאיירי באשת אב ובשומרת יבם של אביו לא שמעינן מינה ממזרות באשת איש ובאחות אשה דיש היתר לאיסורן וכל דכוותייהו אבל לבסוף דמייתי היקישא דרבי יונה התם איכא למילף בעלמא כדפירשנו:

ט) וכן משמע בפרק ד' מיתות דליכא מאן דפליג דבחייבי כריתות לא תפסי קדושין וט"ו נשים דפוטרות צרותיהן מן החליצה ואי קדושין תופסין בחייבי כריתות א"כ היו עולין לחליצה כמו חייבי לאוין כדאמר התם בפ"ב מסתברא חייבי לאוין תפסי בהו קדושין ולכך עולין לחליצה והיא מתני' אתיא ככ"ע דהא קאמר עלה דבפלוגתא לא קא מיירי:

מאי בינייהו. תימה אמאי לא קאמר איכא בינייהו סוטה שאירסה וזינתה תחתיו שלא כדרכה וגירשה דלית בה הויה לכ"ע כדאמרינן בסוף החולץ הכל מודים בבא על הסוטה שאין הוולד ממזר):

תוספות רי"ד

לה קנס: ומקשינן אמאי' קרי כאן ולו תהיה לאשה אשה הראויה לו. פי' באשה הראויה לו יתן קנס מקיים בה ולו תהיה לאשה. אבל באשה שאינה ראויה לו דלא מקיים בה ולו תהיה לאשה גם מן הקנס יהא פטור. אר"ל נער נערה הנערה. חד לגופיה. פי' לכשרה. וחד לאתויי חייבי לאוין. וחד לאתויי חייבי כריתות. [illegible]

ליקוטי רש"י

[illegible]

תורה אור השלם

א) וְנָתַן הָאִישׁ הַשֹּׁכֵב עִמָּהּ לַאֲבִי הַנַּעֲרָ חֲמִשִּׁים כָּסֶף וְלוֹ תִהְיֶה לְאִשָּׁה תַּחַת אֲשֶׁר עִנָּהּ לֹא יוּכַל שַׁלְּחָהּ כָּל יָמָיו: [דברים כב, כט]

ב) כִּי יִמְצָא אִישׁ נַעֲרָ בְתוּלָה אֲשֶׁר לֹא אֹרָשָׂה וּתְפָשָׂהּ וְשָׁכַב עִמָּהּ וְנִמְצָאוּ: [דברים כב, כח]

ג) וְכִי יְפַתֶּה אִישׁ בְּתוּלָה אֲשֶׁר לֹא אֹרָשָׂה וְשָׁכַב עִמָּהּ מָהֹר יִמְהָרֶנָּה לּוֹ לְאִשָּׁה: [שמות כב, טו]

ד) אִם מָאֵן יְמָאֵן אָבִיהָ לְתִתָּהּ לוֹ כֶּסֶף יִשְׁקֹל כְּמֹהַר הַבְּתוּלֹת: [שמות כב, טז]

ה) אַלְמָנָה וּגְרוּשָׁה וַחֲלָלָה זֹנָה אֶת אֵלֶּה לֹא יִקָּח כִּי אִם בְּתוּלָה מֵעַמָּיו יִקַּח אִשָּׁה: וְלֹא יְחַלֵּל זַרְעוֹ בְּעַמָּיו כִּי אֲנִי יְיָ מְקַדְּשׁוֹ: [ויקרא כא, יד - טו]

[illegible] בניו ממזרים [יבמות מט.]. שהרי אמרה תורה לא יקח. וסמיך ליה ולא יחלל זרעו בעמיו למשמע [illegible] שמחוללין מן הכהונה ואינו עושה ממזרין וכיון דאין הולד ממזר ש"מ ס"ל קידושין תופסין בחייבי [illegible]

[illegible] הולד ממזר כדתנן בפרקין (לעיל סו) כל שאין לה קידושין עליו הולד ממזר [קידושין סד.]. ולא יחלל. הא אם נשא אחת מן הפסולות זרעו הימנה חלל מדין קדושת כהונה [ויקרא כא, טו]. בואו ונצוח על עקיבא בן יוסף. [illegible] כל שאין לו ביאה בישראל הולד ממזר. [illegible]

אָמַר רַבִּי זֵירָא – R' Zeira said: מַמְזֶרֶת וּנְתִינָה אִיכָּא בֵּינַיְיהוּ – There is a practical difference between them when the victim is a *mamzeress* or a *nesinah*, who is prohibited to the *oneiss* by force of a prohibition,[31] but who would legally be his wife should he perform *kiddushin* to her. לְמַאן דְּאָמַר יֵשׁ בָּהּ הֲוָיָה – According to the one (Shimon HaTimni) who says that the fine is contingent on the victim being one who has the possibility of "being" the wife of the *oneiss*, הָא נַמִּי יֵשׁ בָּהּ הֲוָיָה – this *mamzeress* or *nesinah*, too, is entitled to the fine, because she has the possibility of "being" his wife.[32] לְמַאן דְּאָמַר רְאוּיָה לְקַיְּימָהּ – But according to the one (R' Shimon ben Menasya) who says that the fine is contingent on the victim being one who is fit for him to keep her as his wife, הָא אֵינָהּ רְאוּיָה לְקַיְּימָהּ – this *mamzeress* or *nesinah* is not entitled to a fine, because she is not fit for him to keep her as his wife.[33]

The Gemara asks:

וּלְרַבִּי עֲקִיבָא דְּאָמַר אֵין קִידּוּשִׁין תּוֹפְסִין בְּחַיָּיבֵי לָאוִין – And according to R' Akiva, who says that *kiddushin* do not take effect on women for whom one is liable for violating a prohibition by cohabiting with them,[34] מַאי בֵּינַיְיהוּ – what is the practical difference between them?[35]

The Gemara answers:

אִיכָּא בֵּינַיְיהוּ אַלְמָנָה לְכֹהֵן גָּדוֹל כְּרַבִּי סִימַאי – There is a practical difference between them when the victim is forbidden to the *oneiss* by force of the commandment prohibiting a widow to a Kohen Gadol,[36] and in accordance with R' Akiva's view as interpreted by R' Simai. דְּתַנְיָא – For it was taught in a Baraisa: רַבִּי סִימַאי אוֹמֵר – R' SIMAI SAYS: מִן הַכֹּל עוֹשֶׂה רַבִּי עֲקִיבָא מַמְזֵרִין – A child born FROM ANY union forbidden by force of a prohibition R' AKIVA DEEMS A *MAMZER*, חוּץ מֵאַלְמָנָה לְכֹהֵן גָּדוֹל – EXCEPT FOR the child of a union forbidden because she is A WIDOW married TO A KOHEN GADOL. And why is this prohibition an exception? שֶׁהֲרֵי אָמְרָה תּוֹרָה – FOR THE TORAH STATES regarding the Kohen Gadol: "לֹא יִקָּח... וְלֹא־יְחַלֵּל" – *HE SHALL NOT TAKE* a widow for a wife... *AND HE SHALL NOT PROFANE* his *offspring*.[37] חִילּוּלִין הוּא עוֹשֶׂה – The juxtaposition of these phrases indicates that if the Kohen Gadol *does* take a widow as his wife, HE MAKES the children of that union "PROFANED" (*chalalim*),[38] וְאֵין עוֹשֶׂה מַמְזֵרִין – BUT HE DOES NOT MAKE them *MAMZERIM*. Since the verse thus indicates that the offspring of this forbidden union are not *mamzerim*, we can conclude that a Kohen Gadol's *kiddushin* to a widow are effective despite the fact that she is forbidden to him by force of a prohibition.[39] Hence, according to the exposition of Shimon HaTimni, a virgin widow violated by a Kohen Gadol is entitled to the fine, since she could "be" his wife. According to the exposition of R' Shimon ben Menasya, however, she is not entitled to the fine, since he is not permitted to keep her as a wife.[40]

The Gemara asks:

וּלְרַבִּי יְשֵׁבָב דְּאָמַר – And according to R' Yesheivav, who says: בּוֹאוּ וְנִצְוַח עַל עֲקִיבָא בֶּן יוֹסֵף – Come, let us shout in protest against Akiva the son of Yosef (R' Akiva), שֶׁהָיָה אוֹמֵר – who used to say, כָּל שֶׁאֵין לוֹ בִּיאָה בְּיִשְׂרָאֵל – "If any man among Jews who

NOTES

Shimon HaTimni, who extends the fine even to a girl that the *oneiss* may not *keep* as his wife, as long as his *kiddushin* would take effect and *make* her his wife.]

31. But not on pain of *kares*. [According to the view that a *nesinah* is *not* Biblically forbidden (see 29a note 5), *nesinah* might be mentioned here simply because it is commonly paired in legal formulations with *mamzeress* (see *Tosafos* to 29a ד״ה הבא על הנתינה).]

32. For [according to the prevailing view] *kiddushin* performed to a woman forbidden by force of a simple prohibition is legally effective; see *Kiddushin* 67b-68a (*Rashi*).

33. Though his *kiddushin* to her would be effective in making her his wife, he would be forbidden to keep her as his wife.

[Thus, both Shimon HaTimni and R' Shimon ben Menasya agree that an *oneiss* pays no fine to a girl forbidden to him on pain of *kares*, as she is not fit even to *be* his wife. They argue only whether he pays a fine to a girl who is fit to *be* but not to *remain* his wife.) Our Mishnah, then, which rules that he pays the fine even to a girl forbidden to him on pain of *kares*, accords neither with Shimon HaTimni nor with R' Shimon ben Menasya. The Gemara above, then, which states that our Mishnah excludes the opinion of "this Tanna" (singular), refers not to the Tannaim mentioned in the Baraisa, but to the Tanna who authored the Baraisa that cites the two opinions (*Tosafos Yeshanim* [printed with *Tosafos*]).]

34. R' Akiva holds that even if a woman is forbidden to a man by force of a simple prohibition without *kares*, his *kiddushin* in her are ineffective (see *Rashi*, citing *Yevamos* 44b).

35. According to R' Akiva, we can no longer say that the difference between Shimon HaTimni's interpretation of *she shall be to him a wife* (that she must be able to *become* his wife) and R' Shimon ben Menasya's interpretation (that she must be able to *remain* his wife) emerges in the case of a *mamzeress* or *nesinah*. For according to R' Akiva, a *mamzeress* or *nesinah* is neither fit to become nor remain the wife of the *oneiss*. Hence, both Tannaim would agree that she is not entitled to the fine.

Rashi notes that the Gemara's question is *not* directed at Shimon HaTimni. For Shimon HaTimni (see *Yevamos* 49a) explicitly disputes R' Akiva's position in this matter and maintains that *kiddushin* in a woman forbidden by force of a simple prohibition *are* effective (see below, note 39). Thus, how Shimon HaTimni interprets *she shall be to him a wife* clearly affects how he rules in the case of a *mamzeress* or *nesinah*: Since he interprets "being a wife" as "*becoming* a wife," he would rule that a *mamzeress* or *nesinah* is entitled to the fine. Would he have interpreted "being" as "remaining," he would rule that a *mamzeress* or *nesinah* is *not* entitled to the fine. The Gemara's question is rather directed at R' Shimon ben Menasya, whose opinion regarding the effectiveness of *kiddushin* on a woman forbidden by force of a simple prohibition is unknown. And the Gemara is asking: If R' Shimon ben Menasya holds the view of R' Akiva in this matter, then the case of *mamzeress* or *nesinah* cannot be what prompted R' Shimon ben Menasya to interpret *she shall "be" to him a wife* differently than Shimon HaTimni. For even if R' Shimon ben Menasya had interpreted "being" as *becoming* (as Shimon HaTimni does), a *mamzeress* and *nesinah* would be excluded from the fine (since *kiddushin* on a woman forbidden by force of a simple prohibition are ineffective)!

36. That is, where a Kohen Gadol violated a virgin widow (whose husband died without consummating the marriage).

37. *Leviticus* 21:14-15.

38. A *chalal* is the child of a Kohen and a woman forbidden to him (e.g. a divorcee, or — in the case of a Kohen Gadol — even a widow). The *chalal* does not have the sanctity of a Kohen, but he is otherwise an untainted Jew and may marry any Jewess. [A *mamzer*, however, may marry a convert, but not a native Jewess (other than a *mamzeress*).]

39. There is a principle that if the prohibition of a union prevents *kiddushin* from being effective, the offspring of their union will be a *mamzer* (see Mishnah, *Kiddushin* 66b). A corollary of this principle is that where the child of a union is not a *mamzer*, then the prohibition of that union does not prevent *kiddushin* from being effective (see *Tosafos* ד״ה חילולין and *Rashi* to *Kiddushin* 64a ד״ה שהרי אמרה תורה אלמנה לא יקח).

Here, the Gemara applies this corollary to prove that R' Akiva recognizes the *kiddushin* done by a Kohen Gadol to a widow. The Gemara cites R' Simai's statement to establish that R' Akiva considers the child of such a union to be a *chalal* rather than a *mamzer*, and it follows, therefore, that the *kiddushin* of the parents would be effective.

40. By the same token, the Gemara could have said that the practical difference emerges where an ordinary Kohen violated a divorced virgin. There, too, R' Akiva (according to R' Simai) agrees that their union does not produce *mamzerim* and, by extension, that *kiddushin* are effective. Hence, she would be entitled to the fine according to the exposition of Shimon HaTimni, but not according to that of R' Shimon ben Menasya (see *Rashi* ד״ה אלמנה לכהן גדול).

אף קנס במקום מכר והני בני קנסא נינהו ואמאי איקרי כאן א) ולו [א] תהיה לאשה אשה הראויה לו אמר ריש לקיש ב) נערה א) נערה הנערה חד לגופיה וחד לאתויי חייבי לאוין וחד לאתויי חייבי כריתות רב פפא אמר ג) בתולה ד) בתולות הבתולות חד לגופיה וחד לאתויי חייבי לאוין וחד לאתויי חייבי כריתות ורב פפא מ"ט לא אמר כר"ל ההוא מיבעי ליה לכדאביי ה) דאמר אביי א באעליה ומתה פטור שנאמר א) ונתן לאבי הנערה נערה ולא לאבי מתה וריש לקיש מ"ט לא אמר כרב פפא ההוא מיבעי ליה לגזירה שוה דתניא ו) כסף ישקול כמוהר הבתולות ב שיהא זה כמוהר הבתולות ומוהר הבתולות כזה וריש לקיש נמי מיבעי ליה לכדאביי ורב פפא נמי מיבעי ליה לגזירה שוה אלא שיתא קראי כתיבי נערה נערה הנערה בתולה בתולות הבתולות תרי לגופייהו חד לכדאביי וחד לגזירה שוה אייתרו ליה תרי חד לאתויי חייבי לאוין וחד לאתויי חייבי כריתות ולאפוקי מהאי תנא דתניא ולו תהיה לאשה ז) שמעון התימני אומר אשה שיש בה הויה רבי שמעון בן מנסיא אומר ג אשה הראויה לקיימה מאי בינייהו אמר ר' זירא ממזרת ונתינה איכא בינייהו למאן דאמר יש בה הויה הא נמי יש בה הויה למאן דאמר ראויה לקיימה הא אינה ראויה לקיימה ולרבי עקיבא דאמר ח) אין קידושין תופסין בחייבי לאוין מאי בינייהו איכא בינייהו אלמנה לכהן גדול כרבי סימאי דתניא רבי סימאי אומר ט) מן הכל עושה רבי עקיבא ממזרין חוץ מאלמנה לכהן גדול שהרי אמרה תורה ה) לא יקח ולא יחלל חילולין הוא עושה ואין עושה ממזרין ולרבי ישבב דאמר בואו ונצוח על עקיבא בן יוסף שהיה אומר כל שאין לו ביאה בישראל הולד ממזר מאי בינייהו איכא בינייהו חייבי

רש"י

אף קנס במקום מכר. ומשום קנס נקט בת שלש אבל למכר מבת יום אחד ועד שתביא שתי שערות: ואמאי. יש להן קנס לנערות פסולות: איקרי כאן כו'. אמתני' מקשי: ה"ג נערה נערה הנערה. באונס כתיב כי ימצא איש נערה בתולה וגו' וכתיב בתריה ונתן האיש השוכב עמה לאבי הנערה ודרשינן נערה יתירה וה"א יתירה דהנערה דמלי למיכתב ונתן לאביה: חד לגופיה. לכשרה: בתולה בתולות הבתולות. במפתה כתיב וכי יפתה איש בתולה וקרא אחרינא בתריה כסף ישקול כמוהר הבתולות ומלי למיכתב כמוהר בתולות הא תלת דדרשינן ה' יתירה ובתולות דמלי למיכתב כמוהר ולשתוק: ההוא מיבעי ליה. ההוא הנערה הא דלא כתיב ונתן לאביה מיבעי ליה לכדאביי שאם לא הספיק האב להעמידו בדין עד שמתה פטור: לאבי הנערה. משמע שהיא קיימת: מיבעי ליה לג"ש. בתולה דכתיב גבי מפתה מיבעי ליה לג"ש בתולה בתולה לג"ש מה כסף האמור באונס חמשים אף מפתה חמשים ומה מפתה שקלים דכתיב ביה ישקול אף חמשים של אונס שקלים קאמר: כמוהר הבתולות. חמשים כסף המפורשים באונס את הבתולה: שיהא זה. חמשים כמוהר הבתולות: ומוהר הבתולות. יהיו שקלים מה: וחד לג"ש. ותהי מופנה מלד אחד ולמידים הימנה: ולאפוקי מהאי תנא. מתני' דקתני יש קנס לממזרת ולאחותו לאפוקי מהאי תנא: שיש בה הויה. שקדושין תופסין לו בה פרט לאחותו ולכל חייבי כריתות דילפינן בפרק שלישי (דף סז:) [קדושין] דאין קדושין תופסין בהן ומשמע ליה תהיה לשון קדושין הוות קדושין ור"ש בן מנסיא משמע ליה תהיה לשון קיום: הא נמי אית בה הויה. דקדושין תופסין בחייבי לאוין והכא יליף לה: ולר"ע דאמר אין קדושין תופסין בחייבי לאוין. ביבמות בהחולץ (דף מד.) בברייתא המחזיר גרושתו ר"ע אומר אין לו בה קדושין: מאי בינייהו. משום ר"ש בן מנסיא קא פריך לה דאילו שמעון התימני שמעינן ליה ביבמות (דף מט.) דפליג עליה דר"ע בהא דתנן איזהו ממזר כל שאר בשר שהוא בלא יבא דברי ר"ע שמעון התימני אומר כל שחייבין עליו כרת בידי שמים אלא לר"ש בן מנסיא קא בעינן לה אי ס"ל כר"ע מאי איכא בין משמעותא דתהיה לשון קיום למשמעות דשמעון התימני אי נמי משמע ליה לר"ש בן מנסיא לשון הויה אימעיטא לה ממזר ומה בין ראויה לקיימה ליש בה הויה: אלמנה לכהן גדול. דמודה בה ר"ע שקדושין תופסין לו בה ואע"פ שהיא בלאו וכרבי סימאי והוא הדין גרושה להדיוט: מן הכל. כל הנולדים מחייבי לאוין: לא יקח. וסמיך ליה ולא יחלל זרעו מדין כהונה הוא מחללו ולא שם ממזרים עליהם: בואו ונצוח על עקיבא בן יוסף. שמרבה ממזרים בישראל אנס: שהוא אומר כל שאין לו ביאה בישראל. הבא על אשה שאין לו בה היתר ביאה הולד ממזר אפי' אלמנה לכ"ג נמי:

תוספות

נערה נערה הנערה. פי' רבינו חננאל דמחד נערה דריש כולה מלתא נער נערה הנערה ואין נראה לר"ת דלא כתיב נערה מלא בה"א אלא ההוא דמוציא שם רע לתחייה כדמוכח בסוף פרקין ועוד הקשה רבינו יצחק מה צריך חד לגופה הא איכא נערה אחרינא בפרשה אלא פי' הקונטרס עיקר:

בתולה בתולות הבתולות. כאן נמי פר"ח דמחד קרא נפקי כולהו ואין נראה דלא צריך חד לגופיה דבתולה אחרינא כתיב:

וחד לאתויי חייבי לאוין. הקשה ר"י בן רבינו מאיר אלמאי נימא חד לאתויי חייבי עשה וחד לאתויי חייבי לאוין ולאתויי חייבי כריתות מנא לן ומיהך דלחייבי לאוין ועשה לא צריך אלא חד קרא דהא אי לאו דכתיב ולו תהיה לאשה דמשמע שיש בה הויה וראויה לקיימה לא הוה צריך קרא לרבויינהו הלכך מחד ריבויא מרבינן אין ראויה לקיימה דהיינו חייבי עשה וחייבי לאוין כיון דאית בהו הויה ואידך ריבויא לחייבי כריתות ולמאן דאמר אין קדושין תופסין בחייבי לאוין הוי חד ריבויא לחייבי עשה ואידך לחייבי לאוין וחייבי כריתות וא"ת ולשתוק מנו תהיה לאשה ולא יצטרך להכי ריבויי וי"ל דאיצטריך למידרש ולו תהיה לאשה מדעתה:

אייתרו להו תרי כו'. וחד ריבויא כתב באונס וחד במפתה וא"ת ומנא לן לחד לאתויי חייבי כריתות אימא לרבויי חייבי לאוין וחד לאונס וחד למפתה וי"ל דלהא לא צריך דמגזרה שוה ילפינן אונס ומפתה מהדדי:

ולאפוקי מהאי תנא. פי' תנא דברייתא אבל מתני' מפיק מתרוייהו תנאי שמחכרים בברייתא:

ולרבי עקיבא דאמר כו'. ואף ע"ג דר"ש התימני פליג בהדיא אר' עקיבא בהחולץ (יבמות דף מד. ודף מט.) הכא לר"ש בן מנסיא פריך דלא סבר כר"ע מאי בינייהו פי' בינו לר"ש התימני דמדנקט ראויה לקיימה ולא נקט שיש בה הויה משמע דיש שאין ראויה לקיימה ויש בה הויה:

חילולין הוא עושה ואינו עושה ממזרים. משמע דהא בהא תליא דכיון דלא הוי ממזר קדושין תופסין וכן משמע בפרק החולץ (שם דף מה:) מה אשת אב דלא תפסי בה קדושין והוולד ממזר כו' [ור"ע נמי משום דיליף בהחולץ דיש ממזר מחייבי לאוין קאמר דאין קדושין תופסין בחייבי לאוין] ותימה דלרבי יהושע אע"ג דאין ממזר מחייבי כריתות כדיליף בשילהי החולץ (שם דף מט.) מודה דאין קדושין תופסין בחייבי כריתות כדפריך ס"פ ר"ג ביבמות (דף נג. ושם) איצטריך לאשמעינן דאין קדושין תופסין בחייבי כריתות ובפ' החולץ (שם דף מד: ושם) קאמר דלרבי יהושע פגום מיהא הוי מחייבי כריתות משום דעשאה זונה וזונה לא הויא אלא מהנהו דלא תפסי בה קדושין כדמוכח בתמורה (דף כט: ושם) וקאמרינן נמי בהחולץ (יבמות דף מד: ושם) הכל מודים בכותי ועבד הבא על בת ישראל הוולד ממזר מאן הכל מודים שמעון התימני דאע"ג דאמר אין ממזר מחייבי לאוין ה"מ חייבי לאוין דתפסי בהו קדושין אבל כותי ועבד כו' ולא קאמר מאן הכל מודים ר' יהושע דאע"ג דאמר אין ממזר מחייבי כריתות ה"מ חייבי כריתות דתפסי בהו קדושין כו' אלמא דלר' יהושע אין קדושין תופסין בחייבי כריתות ואפ"ה לא הוי ממזר ולהכי לא מצי למימר דמודה בכותי ועבד ויש לומר דלר"ש התימני ולר"ע ודאי הא בהא תליא דליכא מידי דלא תפסי בה קדושין והוולד כשר רק שהוא דומה לאשת אב אבל לר' יהושע אע"ג דאין קדושין תופסין בחייבי כריתות כדילפי' בסוף האומר (קדושין סח. ושם) לא הוי ממזר אלא מחייבי מיתות ב"ד כדיליף ר' יהושע בסוף החולץ (יבמות מט. ושם) אבל קשה דא"כ לר' יהושע אין קדושין תופסין באלמנה לכ"ג לרבא דאמר בפ"ק דתמורה (דף ד: ושם) כל דאמר רחמנא לא תעביד אי עביד לא מהני דהתם [פ] פריך ליה והרי אלמנה לכ"ג דקאמר רחמנא לא יקח ותנן כל מקום שיש קדושין ויש עבירה כגון אלמנה לכ"ג כו' ומשני אמר לך רבא שאני התם דא"ק לא יחלל חלולין הוא עושה ואינו עושה ממזרים ולר' יהושע ליכא לשנויי הכי וא"ת בקדושין בסוף האומר (דף סז: ושם) כי משכח דלא תפסי קדושין באשת אב מאי פריך התם ואימא תרוייהו באשת אב הא לכתחלה הא דיעבד אמאי לא יליף מינה דכל היכא דהוי ממזר לא תפסי בה קדושין כיון דהא בהא תליא כדפירשנו וי"ל דאכתי לא שמעינן ממזרות בשאר חייבי כריתות כל כמה דלא מייתי התם היקישא דר' יונה דמלא יקח ולא יגלה דאיירי באשת אב ובשומרת יבם של אביו לא שמעינן מינה ממזרות באשת איש ובאחות אשה דיש היתר לאיסורן וכל דכוותייהו אבל לבסוף דמייתי היקישא דרבי יונה התם איכא למילף בעלמא כדפירשנו: ט) (וכן משמע בפרק ד' מיתות דליכא מאן דפליג דבחייבי כריתות לא תפסי קדושין וט"ו נשים דפוטרות צרותיהן מן החליצה ואי קדושין תופסין בחייבי כריתות א"כ היו עולין לחליצה כמו חייבי לאוין כדאמר התם בפ"ב מסתברא חייבי לאוין תפסי בהו קדושין ולכך עולין לחליצה והיאך מתני' אתיא ככ"ע דהא קאמר עלה דבפלוגתא לא קא מיירי:)

מאי בינייהו. תימה אמאי לא קאמר איכא בינייהו סוטה שאירסה וזינתה תחתיו שלא כדרכה וגירשה דלאית בה הויה לכ"ע כדאמרינן בסוף החולץ הכל מודים בבא על הסוטה שאין הוולד ממזר):

עין משפט נר מצוה

ד א מיי' פ"א מהלכות נערה הל' טו סמג עשין נד טוש"ע אה"ע סי' קעז:
ה ב מיי' שם הל' א:
ו ג מיי' שם הל' ה:

תוספות רי"ד

לה קנס: ומקשינן אמתני' קרי כאן ולו תהיה לאשה אשה הראוי' לו. פי' באשה הראויה לו יתן קנס דמקיים בה ולו תהיה לאשה. אבל באשה שאינה ראויה לו דלא מקיים בה ולו תהיה לאשה בם מן הקנס יהא פטור. אר"ל נער נערה הנערה. חד לגופיה. פי' לכשירה. וחד לאתויי חייבי לאוין. וחד לאתויי חייבי כריתות. פי' גבי אונס כתיב וכי ימצא איש נערה בתולה. וכתיב בתרי' ונתן האיש השוכב עמה לאבי הנערה דהו"ל למיכתב לאביה וקרא יתירה הוא. ודרשי' נערה וה' דהנערה תרי קראי יתירי חד לרבויי חייבי לאוין וחד לאתויי חייבי כריתות. האי לשיא והא בפ"ב דיבמות תנן כלל אמרו ביבמה כל שאיסורה איסור ערוה (קדושה) לא חולצת ולא מתיבמת עד אסור קדושה אלמנה לכ"ג גרושה וחלוצה לכהן הדיוט [חולצת ולא מתיבמת]. ומקשה בגמ' ואמאי אין מתיבמת ליתי עשה וידחה את ל"ת. ותירץ רבא גזירה ביאה ראשונה אטו ביאה שניה. ותנ"ה אם בעלו קנו בביאה ראשונה ואסור לקיימם בביאה שניה. ופי' אלא מוציא בגט שכבר פרחה מצות יבמה בביאה ראשונה. ואע"ג דמצי למיחלץ. אמרי' התם חליצה במקום ייבום אינה מצוה. והרם נמי כתיב ולקחה לו לאשה ויבמה. דאיכא למימר באשה הראויה לו. ואפ"ה אתי עשה ודחי את ל"ת וה"נ ליתי עשה דולו תהיה לאשה ולידחי את ל"ת ואע"פ שהיא ממזרת יקחנה לו לאשה דהאי ולו תהיה לאשה עשה הוא כדאמרי' בפ' אלו הן הלוקין בהלכה ד' טמא שאכל את הקודש אונס שגירש. אם ישראל הוא מחזיר ואינו לוקה. והוי לאו שניתק לעשה דהאי ולו תהיה לאשה קאי אכל ימיו דכל ימיו בעמוד והחזר קאי. וכיון דעשה הוא ליתי ולדחי את ל"ת ואמאי דרשי' אשה הראויה לו. ולקמן בפירקין (דף כ ע"א) מקשה לה ר"כ ומתרץ לה:

מסורת הש"ס

א) [לקמן לט.], ב) לקמן לח:, ג) [לעיל י. לקמן לח:], ד) [לקמן לו.], ה) [יבמות י: ושם נסמן], ו) [יבמות סט.] קידושין סד. סח., ז) [לקמן לט:], ח) [דף ה:], ט) ת"י כ"י.

תורה אור השלם

א) וְנָתַן הָאִישׁ הַשֹּׁכֵב עִמָּהּ לַאֲבִי הַנַּעֲרָ חֲמִשִּׁים כָּסֶף וְלוֹ תִהְיֶה לְאִשָּׁה תַּחַת אֲשֶׁר עִנָּהּ לֹא יוּכַל שַׁלְּחָהּ כָּל יָמָיו: [דברים כב, כט]

ב) כִּי יִמְצָא אִישׁ נַעֲרָ בְתוּלָה אֲשֶׁר לֹא אֹרָשָׂה וּתְפָשָׂהּ וְשָׁכַב עִמָּהּ וְנִמְצָאוּ: [דברים כב, כח]

ג) וְכִי יְפַתֶּה אִישׁ בְּתוּלָה אֲשֶׁר לֹא אֹרָשָׂה וְשָׁכַב עִמָּהּ מָהֹר יִמְהָרֶנָּה לּוֹ לְאִשָּׁה: [שמות כב, טו]

ד) אִם מָאֵן יְמָאֵן אָבִיהָ לְתִתָּהּ לוֹ כֶּסֶף יִשְׁקֹל כְּמֹהַר הַבְּתוּלֹת: [שמות כב, טז]

ה) אַלְמָנָה וּגְרוּשָׁה וַחֲלָלָה זֹנָה אֶת אֵלֶּה לֹא יִקָּח כִּי אִם בְּתוּלָה מֵעַמָּיו יִקַּח אִשָּׁה: וְלֹא יְחַלֵּל זַרְעוֹ בְּעַמָּיו כִּי אֲנִי יְיָ מְקַדְּשׁוֹ: [ויקרא כא, יד - טו]

ליקוטי רש"י

אימא אף קנס. יש לה ואע"פ שיש מכר משתראה לביאה עד שתביא ב' שערות וקודם שתראה לביאה יש מכר ואין קנס ומשתביא שתי שערות ועד שתיבגר יש קנס ולא מכר ובין בגרות לנערות ששה חדשים [חולין כו:]. בא עליה ומתה. לא הספיק האב להעמידו בדין עד שמתה [לקמן לח:]. כמוהר הבתולות. שהוא קצוב נ' כסף אצל התופס את הבתולה ושוכב עמה באונס שנא' (דברים כב כט) ונתן האיש השוכב עמה לאבי הנערה חמשים כסף [שמות כב, טז]. האמור במאנס את הבתולה (דברים כב) קנסו הכתוב נ' כסף בשביל מוהר בתוליה. שיהא זה כמוהר הבתולות. הקיש הכתוב קנס המפתה לקנס האונס מה להלן נ' אף כאן נ' ומה כסף האמור כאן שקלים דכתיב ישקול אף להלן שקלים דלא תימא מעות [לעיל י.]. ומוהר הבתולות כזה. שכתוב בו ישקול לקמן לח:]. שיתא קראי כתיבי. בתולה דכתיב באונס דהא כתיב כי ימצא איש נערה בתולה לא קא חשיב דאצטריך להיקשא דכמוהר הבתולות במשמע שיהא זה כמוהר הבתולות הנזכרת גבי אונס ואי לא הוה כתיב ביה בתולה לא הוה ידעינן מאיזו בתולה קאי [גליון רש"י ישן משיטמ"ק]. ולרבי עקיבא וכו'. דאמר ביבמות שאין קידושין תופסין בחייבי לאוין דקתני (שם דף נ:) חלץ ועשה בה מאמר אין לאחר חליצה כלום כלומר אין המאמר תופס בה דקס ליה השתא בולא יבנה ואמר בגמ' (שם דף נב:) תניא רבי אומר אין הדברים הללו אמורים אלא לדברי ר"ע שהיה עושה חלוצה כערוה [קידושין סח.]. אין קידושין תופסין לאשה האסורה על המקדשה בלאו ורבנן פליגי עליה ואמרי בחייבי כריתות הוא דלא תפסי אבל בחייבי לאוין תפסי [סוטה יח:]. מאי בינייהו. משום ר"ש בן מנסיא קא פריך לה דאילו שמעון התימני שמעינן ליה ביבמות (דף מט.) דפליג עליה דר"ע בהא דתנן איזהו ממזר כל שאר בשר שהוא בלא יבא דברי ר"ע שמעון התימני אומר כל שחייבין עליו כרת בידי שמים [ע"כ ברש"י מכת"י המדויקים בשיטמ"ק עיי"ש מה שהוקשה לו בנוסח שלנו]. (איכא בינייהו) אלמנה לכהן גדול. בההוא הוא דתפסי קידושי דגלי רחמנא בה דאין הולד ממזר אלא חלל [קידושין סח.]. ואפי' לר"ע דאע"ג דחייבי לאוין היא מודה ר' עקיבא דקידושין תופסין לו בה [שם סד.]. חוץ מאלמנה לכהן גדול. שעושה חללין ולא ממזרי' מדקאמר חוץ מאלמנה אלמא אפי' חייבי לאוין שלא מחמת קורבה מרבה כגון מחזיר גרושתו משניסאת וכגון נתינה לישראל דקיימא בלא תתחתן בם (דברים ז) ומשבעה אומות הוא וכגון עמוני שנשא בת ישראל בניו ממזרים [יבמות מט.]. שהרי אמרה תורה לא יקח. וסמיך ליה ולא יחלל זרעו בעמיו דמשמע חללין הוא עושה זרעו שמחוללין מן הכהונה ואינו עושה ממזרין וכיון דאין הולד ממזר ש"מ ס"ל קידושין תופסין בחייבי לאוין דכהונה דאי אין קידושין תופסין הוי הולד ממזר כדתנן בפרקין (לעיל כט) כל שאין לה קידושין עליו הולד ממזר [קידושין סד.]. ולא יחלל. הא אם נשא אחת מן הפסולות זרעו הימנה חלל מדין קדושת כהונה [ויקרא כא, טו]. בואו ונצוח על עקיבא בן יוסף. שפוסל הרבה [קידושין סח.]. כל שאין לו ביאה בישראל הולד ממזר. כל איש בישראל שאין ביאתו מותרת באשה שיבא עליה הולד שנולד מאותה ביאה ממזר [קידושין סד.]. כל ביאה בישראל שאין לו היתר בה הולד ממזר שם סח.].

The Gemara asks:

וְרֵישׁ לָקִישׁ מַאי טַעְמָא לֹא אָמַר כְּרַב פָּפָּא – **And what is the reason that Reish Lakish does not say as Rav Pappa** does? Why does Reish Lakish not derive the entitlement of prohibited girls to the fine by expounding the superfluous word *ha-besulos,* as Rav Pappa does?

The Gemara answers:

הַהוּא מִיבָּעֵי לֵיהּ לִגְזֵירָה שָׁוָה – **He needs that** word *ha-besulos* **for a** ***gezeirah shavah,***[18] as taught in the Baraisa. דְּתַנְיָא – **For it was taught in a Baraisa:** "כֶּסֶף יִשְׁקֹל כְּמֹהַר הַבְּתוּלֹת" – The verse states regarding the *mefateh:* ***HE SHALL PAY OUT SILVER SHEKALIM IN THE AMOUNT OF THE SETTLEMENT [MADE] TO THE VIRGINS.***[19] שֶׁיְּהֵא זֶה כְּמוֹהַר הַבְּתוּלוֹת – This teaches **THAT THIS** award for seduction **SHALL BE LIKE THE SETTLEMENT [MADE] TO THE VIRGINS,**[20] וּמוֹהַר הַבְּתוּלוֹת כָּזֶה – **AND THAT THE SETTLEMENT [MADE] TO THE VIRGINS** shall be **LIKE THIS** award for seduction.[21]

The Gemara asks:

וְרֵישׁ לָקִישׁ נַמִּי מִיבָּעֵי לֵיהּ לְכִדְאַבַּיֵי – **But Reish Lakish also needs it** [the word *ha-naarah*] **to** expound it **in accordance with the** exposition **of Abaye,** וְרַב פָּפָּא נַמִּי מִיבָּעֵי לֵיהּ לִגְזֵירָה שָׁוָה – **and Rav Pappa also needs it** [the word *ha-besulos*] **for a** ***gezeirah shavah*****!** I.e. these expositions of *ha-naarah* and *ha-besulos* are surely accepted by both Reish Lakish and Rav Pappa. Where, then, do they find the superfluity needed to teach that the fines apply even to girls that are forbidden to the *oneiss* or *mefateh?*

The Gemara answers:

אֶלָּא שִׁיתָּא קְרָאֵי כְּתִיבֵי – **Rather,**[22] **there are six Scriptural expressions written** that might be expounded: "נַעֲרָה", "נַעֲרָה", "הַנַּעֲרָה", "בְּתוּלָה", "בְּתוּלוֹת", "הַבְּתוּלֹת" – ***naarah, naarah, ha-naarah,*** and ***besulah, besulos, ha-besulos.*** תְּרֵי לְגוּפַיְיהוּ – **Two** of these six expressions[23] **are needed for themselves,** i.e. to teach the basic law that one who violates or seduces a *naarah* who is a virgin (*besulah*) pays fifty *shekels.* חַד לְכִדְאַבַּיֵי – **One** of the *naarah* expressions **is needed to** expound it **in accordance with** the exposition **of Abaye.** וְחַד לִגְזֵירָה שָׁוָה – **And one** expression (*besulos*) **is needed for the** ***gezeirah shavah.***[24] אִיַּיתְּרוּ לֵיהּ תְּרֵי – **Two** expressions thus **remain** available for exposition.[25] חַד לְאַתּוּיֵי חַיָּיבֵי לָאוִין – **One** is expounded **to include those** girls for which the *oneiss* or *mefateh* is **liable for** violating **a prohibition** by cohabiting with them, וְחַד לְאַתּוּיֵי חַיָּיבֵי כְּרֵיתוֹת – **and one** is expounded **to include those** girls for which the *oneiss* or *mefateh* is **liable to** ***kares*** for cohabiting with them.[26]

After presenting the Scriptural source for the Mishnah's ruling that the *oneiss* fine applies even where the girl is forbidden to her attacker by force of a prohibition or on pain of *kares,* the Gemara notes:

וּלְאַפּוּקֵי מֵהַאי תַּנָּא – **And** our Mishnah, which states the *oneiss* fine for these unfit girls,[27] serves **to exclude** the opinion of **this Tanna** who teaches the following Baraisa. דְּתַנְיָא – **For it was taught in a Baraisa:** "וְלוֹ־תִהְיֶה לְאִשָּׁה" – The Torah states with regard to the victim of an *oneiss:* ***AND SHE SHALL BE TO HIM A WIFE.*** שִׁמְעוֹן הַתִּימְנִי אוֹמֵר – **SHIMON HATIMNI**[28] **SAYS:** אִשָּׁה שֶׁיֵּשׁ בָּהּ הֲוָיָה – This teaches that the *oneiss* pays the fine only when his victim is **A WOMAN WHO HAS** the possibility of **"BEING"** his wife, i.e. a woman in whom his *kiddushin* would take effect.[29] רַבִּי שִׁמְעוֹן בֶּן מְנַסְיָא אוֹמֵר – **R' SHIMON BEN MENASYA SAYS:** אִשָּׁה הָרְאוּיָה לְקַיְּימָהּ – This teaches that he pays the fine only when his victim is **A WOMAN WHO IS FIT** for him **TO KEEP HER** as his wife.[30]

The Gemara explains:

מַאי בֵּינַיְיהוּ – **What is** the practical difference **between them?**

NOTES

18. The superfluous *"besulos"* stated with regard to the *mefateh* (see above, note 10) is needed to establish a *gezeirah shavah* between the context of *mefateh* and the context of *oneiss,* where the Torah also states *"besulah"* (*Deuteronomy* 22:28). This compares the two contexts and allows what is specified in the one to be applied to the other. In the case of *oneiss,* the Torah states (*Deuteronomy* 22:29) that the fine is חֲמִשִּׁים כָּסֶף, *fifty [units of] silver,* but does not specify what the unit is. In the case of *mefateh,* the Torah states (*Exodus* 22:16): כֶּסֶף יִשְׁקֹל, *he shall pay out silver shekalim,* but does not specify how many. The *gezeirah shavah* tells us to derive the one context from the other. Just as the amount in the case of *oneiss* is fifty, so too in the case of *mefateh.* And just as the unit in the case of *mefateh* is the *shekel,* so too in the case of *oneiss.* In both cases, then, the amount is fifty *shekalim* (see *Rashi*).

[Here, the two contexts are derived from one another through a *gezeirah shavah.* In the Baraisa cited next as a support, however, the derivation seems to be, rather, a *hekeish* (comparison). See *Shitah Mekubetzes* ד״ה ההוא מבעי ליה, who discusses this.]

19. *Exodus* 22:16. [*The amount of the settlement [made] to the virgins* is the fifty silver coins stated in *Deuteronomy* 22:29 regarding the fine paid for violating a virgin (see *Rashi* above to 10a ד״ה כמוהר הבתולות, and note 6 there).]

20. I.e. fifty coins (see note 18).

21. I.e. in units of *shekalim* (see note 18).

22. [The expression אֶלָּא, *rather,* indicates a retraction of a previously stated explanation. We no longer explain that Reish Lakish and Rav Pappa are at odds with one another. Rather, they complement one another. It is the combination of both expositions that allows us to derive that the fine applies even where the girl is forbidden in marriage to the *oneiss* or *mefateh,* as the Gemara proceeds to explain.]

23. I.e. one *naarah* expression and one *besulah* expression.

24. A *gezeirah shavah* requires that at least one of the two words establishing the link be superfluous [see *Niddah* 22b]. Hence, we require a superfluous *besulah* expression to establish the *gezeirah shavah,* and we cannot establish it on the basis of the word *besulah* stated in the beginning of the *mefateh* passage (*If a man will seduce a besulah . . .*), which is needed "for itself" [to teach that the fine for seduction pertains only to a virgin] (*Rashi,* as explained by *Shitah Mekubetzes* ד״ה ורש״י ז״ל לקמן; see *Shitah Mekubetzes's* in-depth explanation of *Rashi*).

25. I.e. the *"ha"* of *ha-naarah* and the *"ha"* of *ha-besulos.*

26. We do not need one expression to include girls forbidden by an ordinary prohibition for the case of *oneiss,* and another expression to include them for the case of *mefateh,* because the laws of *oneiss* and *mefateh* are derived one from the other. Hence, one expression suffices to include such girls for both the fines of *oneiss* and *mefateh,* and the remaining expression serves to include for both cases even girls prohibited on pain of *kares* (*Tosafos*).

27. Such as a *mamzeress* or one's sister (*Rashi*).

28. Shimon was from the city of Timnah, mentioned in *Judges* 14:1 in the story of Samson (*Rashi* to *Beitzah* 21a and to *Taanis* 19a; cf. *Seder HaDoros*).

29. This excludes his sister or any girl prohibited to him on pain of *kares.* For, as derived by the Gemara in *Kiddushin* (67b), *kiddushin* cannot take effect between a man and a woman forbidden to one another on pain of *kares.* [A woman's being forbidden to a man in marriage and the marriage being legally recognized are two different things. It may be that a woman is forbidden to a man, yet her marriage to him is recognized and requires the dissolution of a *get.* In the case of a woman forbidden to a man on pain of *kares,* however, the marriage is null and void.] Shimon HaTimni understands the term תִהְיֶה, *she "shall be,"* in this verse as referring to her *being* his wife in a legal sense, viz. that *kiddushin* would take effect (*Rashi*). [We find the term *"being"* used to connote *marriage* in a legal sense in the verse: וְהָיְתָה לְאִישׁ אַחֵר, *and she will "be" [married] to another man* (*Deuteronomy* 24:2).] Since a girl prohibited to the *oneiss* on pain of *kares* cannot "be" his wife, Shimon HaTimni excludes her from entitlement to the fine as well.

30. R' Shimon ben Menasya understands the term תִהְיֶה, *she "shall be,"* in this verse as denoting a continuous state of being, i.e. she must be one who may remain with him as his wife (*Rashi*). Accordingly, this verse excludes even a girl with whom *kiddushin* would take effect, if the *oneiss* would be forbidden to *keep* her as his wife. [This is in contrast to

עין משפט נר מצוה

ד א מיי' פ"א מהלכות נערה הל' טו סמג עשין נג טור אה"ע סי' קעז:
ה ב מיי' שם הל' א:
ו ג מיי' שם הל' ה:

אף קנס במקום מכר והני בני קנסא נינהו ואמאי איקרי כאן א) ולו ו) תהיה לאשה אשה הראויה לו אמר ריש לקיש א) נערה ב) נערה הנערה חד לגופיה וחד לאתויי חייבי לאוין וחד לאתויי חייבי כריתות רב פפא אמר ג) בתולה ד) בתולות הבתולות חד לגופיה וחד לאתויי חייבי לאוין וחד לאתויי חייבי כריתות ורב פפא מ"ט לא אמר כר"ל ההוא מיבעי ליה לכדאביי ג) דאמר אביי א*בא עליה ומתה פטור שנאמר א) ונתן לאבי הנערה לאבי נערה ולא לאבי מתה וריש לקיש מ"ט לא אמר כרב פפא ההוא מיבעי ליה לגזירה שוה דתניא ג) ד) כסף ישקול כמוהר הבתולות ה) שיהא זה כמוהר הבתולות ומוהר הבתולות כזה וריש לקיש נמי מיבעי ליה לכדאביי ורב פפא נמי מיבעי ליה לגזירה שוה אלא שיתא קראי כתיבי נערה נערה הנערה בתולה בתולות הבתולות תרי לגופייהו חד לכדאביי וחד לגזירה שוה אייתרו ליה תרי חד לאתויי חייבי לאוין וחד לאתויי חייבי כריתות ולאפוקי מהאי תנא דתניא ולו תהיה לאשה ו) שמעון התימני אומר אשה שיש בה הויה רבי שמעון בן מנסיא אומר ג*אשה הראויה לקיימה מאי בינייהו אמר ר' זירא ממזרת ונתינה איכא בינייהו למאן דאמר יש בה הויה הא נמי יש בה הויה למאן דאמר ראויה לקיימה הא אינה ראויה לקיימה ולרבי עקיבא דאמר ח) אין קידושין תופסין בחייבי לאוין מאי בינייהו איכא בינייהו אלמנה לכהן גדול כרבי סימאי דתניא רבי סימאי אומר ו) מן הכל עושה רבי עקיבא ממזרין חוץ מאלמנה לכהן גדול שהרי אמרה תורה ה) לא יקח ולא יחלל חילולין הוא עושה ואין עושה ממזרין ולרבי ישבב דאמר בואו ונצוח על עקיבא בן יוסף שהיה אומר כל שאין לו ביאה בישראל הולד ממזר מאי בינייהו איכא בינייהו חייבי

רש"י

אף קנס במקום מכר. ומשום קנס נקט בת שלש אבל למכר מבת יום אחד ועד שתביא שתי שערות: ואמאי. יש להן קנס לנערות פסולות: איקרי כאן כו'. ממתני' מקשי: ה"ג נערה נערה הנערה. באונס כתיב כי ימצא איש נערה בתולה וגו' וכתיב בתריה ונתן האיש השוכב עמה לאבי הנערה ודרשינן נערה יתירה וה"א יתירה דהנערה דמצי למיכתב ונתן לאביה: חד לגופיה. לכשרה: בתולה בתולות הבתולות. במפתה כתיב וכי יפתה איש בתולה וקרא אחרינא בתריה כסף ישקול כמוהר הבתולות ומצי למיכתב כמוהר בתולות הא תלת דדרשינן ה' יתירה ובתולות דמצי למיכתב כמוהר ולשתוק: ההוא מיבעי ליה. ההוא הנערה הא דלא כתיב ונתן לאביה מיבעי ליה לכדאביי שאם לא הספיק האב להעמידו בדין עד שמתה פטור: לאבי הנערה. משמע שהיא קיימת: מיבעי ליה לג"ש. בתולה דכתיב גבי מפתה מיבעי ליה לג"ש בתולה בתולה לג"ש מה כסף האמור באונס חמשים אף מפתה חמשים ומה האמור במפתה שקלים דכתיב כסף ישקול אף חמשים של אונס שקלים קאמר: כמוהר הבתולות. חמשים כסף המפורשים במאנס את הבתולה: שיהא זה. חמשים כמוהר הבתולות: ומוהר הבתולות. יהיו שקלים כזה: וחד לג"ש. ותהי מופנה מצד אחד ולמדים הימנה: ולאפוקי מהאי תנא. מתני' דקתני יש קנס לממזרת ולאחותו ולאפוקי מהאי תנא: שיש בה הויה. שקדושין תופסין בה לאפוקי כל חייבי כריתות דילפינן בקדושין שאין קדושין תופסין בהן בפרק שלישי (דף סז:) ומשמע ליה תהיה לשון קדושין הווית ור"ש בן מנסיא משמע ליה תהיה לשון קיום: הא נמי אית בה הויה. דקדושין תופסין בחייבי לאוין והתם יליף לה: ולר"ע דאמר אין קדושין תופסין בחייבי לאוין. ביבמות בהחולץ (דף מד:) בברייתא המחזיר גרושתו ר"ע אומר אין לו בה קדושין: מאי בינייהו. משום ר"ש בן מנסיא קא פריך לה דאילו שמעון התימני שמעינן ליה ביבמות (דף מט.) דפליג עליה דר"ע בהא דתנן איזהו ממזר כל שאר בשר שהוא בלא יבא דברי ר"ע שמעון התימני אומר כל שחייבין עליו כרת בידי שמים אלא לר"ש בן מנסיא קא בעינן לה אי ס"ל כר"ע מאי איכא בין משמעותא דתהיה לשון קיום למשמעות דשמעון התימני אי נמי משמע ליה לר"ש בן מנסיא לשון הויה אימעיטא לה ממזר ומה בין ראויה לקיימה ליש בה הויה: אלמנה לכהן גדול. דמודה בה ר"ע שקדושין תופסין לו בה ואע"פ שהיא בלאו וכרבי סימאי והוא הדין גרושה להדיוט: מן הכל. כל הנולדים מחייבי לאוין: לא יקח. וסמיך ליה ולא יחלל זרעו מדין כהונה הוא מחללו ולא שם ממזרים עליהם: בואו ונצוח על עקיבא בן יוסף. שמרבה ממזרים בישראל חנם: שהוא אומר כל שאין לו ביאה בישראל. הבא על אשה שאין לו בה היתר ביאה הולד ממזר אפי' אלמנה לכ"ג נמי:

תוספות

נערה נערה הנערה. פי' רבינו חננאל דמחד נערה דריש כולה מלתא נער נערה הנערה ואין נראה לר"ת דלא כתיב נערה מלא בה"א אלא ההוא דמוציא שם רע לחודיה כדמוכח בסוף פרקין ועוד הקשה רבינו יצחק מה צריך חד לגופה הא איכא נערה אחרינא בפרשה אלא פי' הקונטרס עיקר: בתולה בתולות הבתולות. כאן נמי פר"ח דמחד קרא נפקי כולהו ואין נראה דלא צריך חד לגופיה דבתולה אחרינא כתיב: וחד לאיתויי חייבי לאוין. הקשה ר"י בן רבינו מאיר אכתי נימא חד לאתויי חייבי עשה וחד לאתויי חייבי לאוין ואכתי חייבי כריתות מנא לן ותירץ דלחייבי לאוין ועשה לא צריך אלא חד קרא דהא אי לאו דכתיב ולו תהיה לאשה דמשמע שיש בה הויה וראויה לקיימה לא הוה צריך קרא לרבויינהו הלכך מחד ריבויא מרבינן אין ראויה לקיימה דהיינו חייבי עשה וחייבי לאוין כיון דאית בהו הויה ואידך ריבויא לחייבי כריתות ולמאן דאמר אין קדושין תופסין בחייבי לאוין הוי חד ריבויא לחייבי עשה ואידך לחייבי לאוין וחייבי כריתות וא"ת ולשתוק מלו תהיה לאשה ולא יצטרך להנך ריבויי וי"ל דאיצטריך למידרש ולו תהיה לאשה מדעתה ז): אייתרו להו תרי כו'. וחד ריבויא כתב באונס וחד במפתה וא"ת ומנא לן דחד לאתויי חייבי כריתות אימא דתרוייהו אתו לרבויי חייבי לאוין וחד לאונס וחד למפתה וי"ל דלהא לא צריך דמגזרה שוה ילפינן אונס ומפתה מהדדי: ח) [ולאפוקי מהאי תנא. פי' תנא דברייתא אבל מפיק מתרוייהו תנאי שמוזכרים בברייתא]: ולרבי עקיבא דאמר כו'. ואף ע"ג דר"ש התימני פליג בהדיא אר' עקיבא בהחולץ (יבמות דף מד. ודף מט.) הכא לר"ש בן מנסיא פריך דאי סבר כר"ע מאי בינייהו פי' בינו לר"ש התימני דמדנקט ראויה לקיימה ולא נקט שיש בה הויה משמע דיש שאין ראויה לקיימה ויש בה הויה: חילולין הוא עושה ואינו עושה ממזרים. משמע דהא בהא תליא דכיון דלא הוי ממזר קדושין תופסין וכן משמע בפרק החולץ (שם דף מה:) מה אשת אב דלא תפסי בה קדושין והוולד ממזר כו' [ור"ע נמי משום דיליף בהחולץ דיש ממזר מחייבי לאוין קאמר דאין קדושין תופסין בחייבי לאוין] ותימה דלרבי יהושע אע"ג דאין ממזר מחייבי כריתות כדיליף בשילהי החולץ (שם דף מט.) מודה דאין קדושין תופסין בחייבי כריתות כדפריך ס"פ ר"ג ביבמות (דף נג. ושם) איצטריך לאשמעינן דאין קדושין תופסין בחייבי כריתות ובפ' החולץ (שם דף מד: ושם) קאמר לרבי יהושע פגום מיהא הוי מחייבי כריתות משום דעשאה זונה וזונה לא הויא אלא מהנהו דלא תפסי בה קדושין כדמוכח בתמורה (דף כט: ושם) וקאמרינן נמי בהחולץ (יבמות דף מד: ושם) הכל מודים בכותי ועבד הבא על בת ישראל הוולד ממזר מאן הכל מודים שמעון התימני דאע"ג דאמר אין ממזר מחייבי לאוין ה"מ חייבי לאוין דתפסי בהו קדושין אבל כותי ועבד כו' ולא קאמר מאן הכל מודים ר' יהושע דאע"ג דאמר אין ממזר מחייבי כריתות ה"מ חייבי כריתות דתפסי בהו קדושין כו' אלמא דלר' יהושע אין קדושין תופסין בחייבי כריתות ואפ"ה לא הוי ממזר ולהכי לא מצי למימר דמודה בכותי ועבד ויש לומר דלר"ש התימני ולר"ע ודאי הא בהא תליא דליכא מידי דלא תפסי בה קדושין והוולד כשר רק שהוא דומה לאשת אב אבל לר' יהושע אע"ג דאין קדושין תופסין בחייבי כריתות כדילפי' בסוף האומר (קדושין סח. ושם) לא הוי ממזר אלא מחייבי מיתות ב"ד כדיליף ר' יהושע בסוף החולץ (יבמות מט. ושם) אבל קשה דא"כ לר' יהושע אין קדושין תופסין באלמנה לכ"ג לרבא דאמר בפ"ק דתמורה (דף ד: ושם) כל דאמר רחמנא לא תעביד אי עביד לא מהני דהתם ח) פריך ליה והרי אלמנה לכ"ג דקאמר רחמנא לא יקח ותנן כל מקום שיש קדושין ויש עבירה כגון אלמנה לכ"ג כו' ומשני אמר לך רבא שאני התם דא"ק לא יחלל חלולין הוא עושה ואינו עושה ממזרים ולר' יהושע ליכא לשנויי הכי וא"ת בקדושין בסוף האומר (דף סז: ושם) כי משכח דלא תפסי קדושין באשת אב מאי פריך התם ואימא תרוייהו באשת אב הא לכתחלה הא דיעבד אמאי לא יליף מינה דכל היכא דהוי ממזר לא תפסי בה קדושין כיון דהא בהא תליא כדפירשנו וי"ל דאכתי לא שמעינן ממזרות בשאר חייבי כריתות כל כמה דלא מייתי התם היקישא דר' יונה דמלא יקח ולא יגלה דאיירי באשת אב ובשומרת יבם של אביו לא שמעינן מינה ממזרות באשת איש ובאחות אשה דיש היתר לאיסורן וכל דכוותייהו אבל לבסוף דמייתי היקישא דרבי יונה התם איכא למילף בעלמא כדפירשנו: ט) (וכן משמע בפרק ד' מיתות דליכא מאן דפליג דבחייבי כריתות לא תפסי קדושין וט"ו נשים דפוטרות צרותיהן מן החליצה ואי קדושין תופסין בחייבי כריתות א"כ היו עולין לחליצה כמו חייבי לאוין כדאמר התם בפ"ב מסתברא חייבי לאוין תפסי בהו קדושין ולכך עולין לחליצה והיא מתני' אתיא ככ"ע דהא קאמר עלה דבפלוגתא לא קא מיירי: מאי בינייהו. תימה אמאי לא קאמר איכא בינייהו סוטה שאירסה וזינתה תחתיו שלא כדרכה וגירשה דלית בה הויה לכ"ע כדאמרינן בסוף החולץ הכל מודים בבא על הסוטה שאין הוולד ממזר):

תוספות רי"ד

לה קיס: ומקשינן אמתני' פי' כאן ולו תהיה לאשה אשה הראויה לו. פי' באשה הראויה לו יתן קנס דמקיים בה ולו תהיה לאשה. אבל באשה שאינה ראויה לו דלא מקיים בה ולו תהיה לאשה פטור. א"ל נער נערה הנערה. חד לגופיה. פי' לכשירה. וחד לאתויי חייבי לאוין. וחד לאתויי חייבי כריתות. פי' גבי אונס כתיב וכי ימצא איש נערה בתולה. וכתיב בתר' ונתן האיש השוכב עמה לאבי הנערה דהו"ל למיכתב לאביה וקרא יתירה הוא. ודרשי' נערה וה' דהנערה תרי קראי יתירי חד לרבויי חייבי לאוין וחד לאתויי חייבי כריתות. ומי קשיא והא בפ"ב דיבמות תנן כלל אמרו ביבמה כל שאיסורה איסור ערוה (קדושה) לא חולצת ולא מתיבמת עד אסור קדושה אלמנה לכ"ג גרושה וחלוצה להדיוט חולצת ולא מתייבמת. ומקשה בגמ' ואמאי אין מתייבמת ליתי עשה וידחה את ל"ת. ותירץ רבא גזירה ביאה ראשונה אטו ביאה שניה. אע"ג דכי אתי בעלו קנו בביאה ראשונה ואסור לקיימה בביאה שניה. ופי' אלא אוקיה בגט שכבר פרחה מצוה יבמה בביאה ראשונה. אע"ג דמצי למיחלץ. אמרי' התם חליצה במקום יבום אינה מצוה. התם נמי כתיב ולקחה לו לאשה ויבמה. דאיכא למימר באשה הראויה לו. ואפ"ה אתי עשה ודחי את ל"ת וה"נ ליתי עשה דולו תהיה לאשה ולידחי את ל"ת ואע"פ שדיא ממזרת יקנסה לו לאשה דהאי ולו תהיה לאשה עשה הוא כדאמרי' בפ' אלו הן הלוקין בהלוקח זר טמא שאכל את הקודש אונס שגירש. אם ישראל הוא מחזיר ואינו לוקה. והוי לאו שבתקו לעשה דהאי ולו תהיה לאשה קאי אכל ימיו דכל יומיו בעמוד והחזר קאי. כיון דעשה הוא לידי לידחי את ל"ת ואמאי דרשי' אשה הראויה לו. ולקמן בפירקין [דף מ"א] מקשה לה ר"ב ומתרץ לה:

תורה אור השלם

א) וְנָתַן הָאִישׁ הַשֹּׁכֵב עִמָּהּ לַאֲבִי הַנַּעֲרָ חֲמִשִּׁים כָּסֶף וְלוֹ תִהְיֶה לְאִשָּׁה תַּחַת אֲשֶׁר עִנָּהּ לֹא יוּכַל שַׁלְּחָהּ כָּל יָמָיו: [דברים כב, כט]

ב) כִּי יִמְצָא אִישׁ נַעֲרָ בְתוּלָה אֲשֶׁר לֹא אֹרָשָׂה וּתְפָשָׂהּ וְשָׁכַב עִמָּהּ וְנִמְצָאוּ: [דברים כב, כח]

ג) וְכִי יְפַתֶּה אִישׁ בְּתוּלָה אֲשֶׁר לֹא אֹרָשָׂה וְשָׁכַב עִמָּהּ מָהֹר יִמְהָרֶנָּה לּוֹ לְאִשָּׁה: [שמות כב, טו]

ד) אִם מָאֵן יְמָאֵן אָבִיהָ לְתִתָּהּ לוֹ כֶּסֶף יִשְׁקֹל כְּמֹהַר הַבְּתוּלֹת: [שמות כב, טז]

ה) אַלְמָנָה וּגְרוּשָׁה וַחֲלָלָה זֹנָה אֶת אֵלֶּה לֹא יִקָּח כִּי אִם בְּתוּלָה מֵעַמָּיו יִקַּח אִשָּׁה: וְלֹא יְחַלֵּל זַרְעוֹ בְּעַמָּיו כִּי אֲנִי יְיָ מְקַדְּשׁוֹ: [ויקרא כא, יד - טו]

מסורת הש"ס

א) [לקמן לט.], ב) [לקמן לח:], ג) [לעיל י. לקמן לח:], ד) [לקמן לו.], ה) [יבמות י: ושם נסמן], ו) [יבמות סט.] קידושין סד. סח., ז) [לקמן לט:], ח) [דף ה:], ט) תו"כ.

ליקוטי רש"י

אימא אף קנס. לם לה ואע"פ שיש מכר משתראה לביאה עד שתביא ב' שערות וקודם שתראה לביאה יש מכר ואין קנס ומשתביא שתי שערות ועד שיבגרו יש קנס ולא מכר וכן בגרות לנערות שהם חדשים [חולין כו:]. בא עליה ומתה. לא הספיק האב להעמידו בדין עד שמתה [לקמן לח:]. כמוהר הבתולות. שהוא קצוב ב' כסף אלא שהוא מן הבתולות וסוכל עמה באונס שנאמר (דברים כב) ונתן האיש השוכב עמה לאבי הנערה חמשים כסף [שמות כב, טז]. האמור באונס את הבתולה (דברים כב) קנסו הכתוב נ' כסף בשביל מוהר בתולים. שיהא זה כמוהר הבתולות. קנס המפתה לקנס האונס מה להלן נ' אף כאן נ' ומה כסף האמור כאן שקלים דכתיב ישקול אף להלן שקלים [לעיל י.]. ומוהר הבתולות כזה. שכתוב בו ישקול [לקמן לח:]. שיתא קראי כתיבי. באונס ומפתה דכתיב ביה נערה וכתיב כי ימצא איש נערה בתולה לא קא משני לאצטרוכי לכמוהר הבתולות במשמע שיהא זה כמוהר הבתולות הנזכרת גבי אונס ולא זה הוא כתיב ביה בתולה לא הוה ידעינן אלמו בתולה קאי [גליון רש"י ישן משיטמ"ק]. ולרבי עקיבא וכו'. דאמר ביבמות שאין קדושין תופסין בחייבי לאוין (דף דקתני (שם דף כ:) חלוק ועשה בה מאמר אין לאחר חליצה כלום כלומר אין המאמר תופס בה דקס ליה השתא בלא יבנה ואמר בגמ' (שם דף נב:) תניא רבי אומר אין הדברים הללו אמורים אלא לדברי ר"ע שהיה עושה חלוצה כערוה [קידושין סח.]. אין קדושין תופסין לאשה האסורה לו המקדשה בלאו ולכן פליגי עליה ואמרי בחייבי כריתות הוא דלא תפסי אבל בחייבי לאוין תפסי [סוטה יח:]. מאי בינייהו. משום ר"ש בן מנסיא קא פריך לה דאילו שמעון התימני שמעינן ליה ביבמות (דף מט.) דפליג עליה דר"ע בהא דתנן איזהו ממזר כל שאר בשר שהוא בלא יבא דברי ר"ע שמעון התימני אומר כל שחייבין עליו כרת בידי שמים בר"א ברש"י מכתב"י המדויקים בשיטמ"ק עיי"ש מה שהוקשה לו בנוסח שלנו]. (איכא בינייהו) אלמנה לכהן גדול. בהכהן הוא דתפסי קידושי דגלי רחמנא בה דאין הולד ממזר אלא חלל [קידושין סח.]. ואפי' לר"ע דאע"ג דחייבי לאוין היא מודה ר' עקיבא דקידושין תופסין לו בה [שם סד.] חוץ מאלמנה לכהן גדול. שעושה חללין ולא ממזרי' מדקאמר חוץ מאלמנה אלמא אפי' חייבי לאוין שלא מחמת מרבה כגון ממזר משניאה וכגון לישראל דקיימא תחתתן בם (דברים ז) ומשבעה אומות הוא וכגון עמוני שנשא בת ישראל

אַף קְנָס בִּמְקוֹם מֶכֶר – There is **also a fine where there is** a right of **sale.**[1]

The Gemara addresses the Mishnah's ruling that the fine applies even where the *oneiss* is forbidden to marry his victim. The Gemara asks:

וְהָנֵי בְּנֵי קְנָסָא נִינְהוּ – **But are these** *ne'aros* indeed **eligible to** receive **a fine?** וְאַמַּאי – **But why** should they be eligible to receive the fine? אִיקְרֵי כָּאן – **Read** (i.e. apply) **here** the verse: ,,וְלוֹ־תִהְיֶה לְאִשָּׁה" – ***And she shall be to him a wife,***[2] אִשָּׁה הָרְאוּיָה לוֹ – which implies that we are dealing specifically with **a woman who is** legally **fit for** marriage to **him!**[3] – ? –

The Gemara answers:

אָמַר רֵישׁ לָקִישׁ – **Reish Lakish said:** ,,נַעֲרָה" ,,נַעֲרָה" ,,הַנַּעֲרָה" – The Torah states: ***naarah, naarah, ha-naarah.***[4] חַד לְגוּפֵיהּ – **One** expression[5] **is** needed **for itself,** i.e. to teach the basic law that the fine for violation applies to one who violates a *naarah.*[6] וְחַד לְאַתּוּיֵי חַיָּיבֵי לָאוִין – **And one** expression[7] **is** expounded **to include those** girls for which the *oneiss* is **liable for** violating **a prohibition** by cohabiting with them. וְחַד לְאַתּוּיֵי חַיָּיבֵי כְרֵיתוֹת – **And one** expression[8] **is** expounded **to include those** girls for which the *oneiss* is **liable to *kares*** for cohabiting with them.[9]

An alternative answer:

רַב פָּפָּא אָמַר – **Rav Pappa says:** ,,בְּתוּלָה" ,,בְּתוּלוֹת" ,,הַבְּתוּלֹת" – The Torah states: ***besulah, besulos, ha-besulos.***[10] חַד לְגוּפֵיהּ – **One** expression[11] **is** needed **for itself,** i.e. to teach the basic law that the fine for seduction applies to one who seduces a virgin. וְחַד לְאַתּוּיֵי חַיָּיבֵי לָאוִין – **And one** expression[12] **is** expounded **to include those** girls for which the *mefateh* is **liable for** violating **a prohibition** by cohabiting with them. וְחַד לְאַתּוּיֵי חַיָּיבֵי כְּרֵיתוֹת – **And one** expression[13] **is** expounded **to include those** girls for which the *mefateh* is **liable to *kares*** for cohabiting with them.[14]

The Gemara asks:

וְרַב פָּפָּא מַאי טַעְמָא לֹא אָמַר כְּרֵישׁ לָקִישׁ – **And what is the reason that Rav Pappa does not say as Reish Lakish** does? Why does Rav Pappa not derive the entitlement of unfit girls to the fine by expounding the superfluous word *ha-naarah,* as Reish Lakish does?

The Gemara answers:

הַהוּא מִיבְּעֵי לֵיהּ לִכְדְאַבַּיֵּי – **He needs that** word *ha-naarah*[15] **to** expound it **in accordance with** the exposition **of Abaye.** דְּאָמַר אַבַּיֵּי – **For Abaye said:** בָּא עָלֶיהָ וּמֵתָה פָּטוּר – **If he violated her and she died** before he was sued and found liable by the court, **he is exempt** from paying the fine. שֶׁנֶּאֱמַר ,,וְנָתַן... לַאֲבִי הַנַּעֲרָה" – **For it is stated: *And he shall give . . . to the father of the naarah*** *fifty silver [coins];*[16] לַאֲבִי נַעֲרָה וְלֹא לַאֲבִי מֵתָה – the superfluous expression *the naarah* teaches that he pays a fine **to the father of the *naarah,* but not to the father of a deceased girl.**[17]

NOTES

1. The Sages are responding to R' Meir's statement that during the period that the father enjoys the right of sale (from birth until she grows two pubic hairs) there is no fine. To this the Sages reply that a minor *is* entitled to the fine. Hence, from when she is three years old (and thus legally fit for cohabitation) until she grows two pubic hairs, there is also a fine – *in addition to the right of sale.* And from when she grows two pubic hairs until she becomes a *bogeress,* there is a fine but no right of sale. (See *Rashi* to 40b ד״ה אף קנס במקום מכר.)

[*Rashi* notes that although the intent of the Sages (as has been explained) is to say that this period – from age three until the growth of two pubic hairs – occasions both the father's right of sale *and* the fine for violation or seduction, they do not mean to exclude the period prior to three years old from the right of sale. Rather, they specify the period from three years old onward because it is only then that the fine is awarded. (For cohabitation with a girl less than three is not legally regarded as cohabitation (see above, 29a note 27); hence, her violation or seduction would not be deemed an act of violation or seduction.)]

2. *Deuteronomy* 22:29.

3. For if his victim is a girl who is forbidden to him in marriage, he cannot fulfill the obligation *and she shall be to him a wife* stated in the passage (since the positive command to marry her would not supersede the prohibition against doing so – see Gemara below, 40a). Hence, I would say that since the mitzvah to marry the victim does not apply, the fine does not apply either (see *Ritva;* cf. *Tosafos,* end of ד״ה וחד לאיתויי and *Kovetz Shiurim* §86).

4. In the verses regarding the *oneiss* (cited in the preceding note), the Torah states: *If a man will find a "naarah" . . . then the man who lay with her shall give the father of "the naarah" fifty silver [coins] . . .* Having already stated that the victim was a *naarah,* it would have sufficed for the Torah to state simply: *then the man who lay with her shall give "her" father.* The superfluous word הַנַּעֲרָה, *the naarah,* is therefore expounded, with the core word *"naarah"* and the prefix *"the"* being expounded separately (*Rashi*). It is thus as if the Torah wrote the expression *"naarah"* here three times: once at the beginning of the verse, and two more times with the superfluous word *ha-naarah.*

5. I.e. the expression: *If a man will find a "naarah."*

6. [But not if she has already become a *bogeress.*] I would know, though, only that the fine applies where the *naarah* is legally fit to be married to the *oneiss* (see *Rashi*).

7. I.e. the superfluous *naarah* mentioned in the phrase *the father of the "naarah."*

8. I.e. the *ha* prefix of the expression *the father of "the" naarah.*

9. The two latter cases are thus included in the law subjecting the *oneiss* to a fine despite the fact that he is forbidden to marry his victim.

[A single superfluous expression would have served to include only "those liable for violating a prohibition," who – though forbidden in marriage to the *oneiss* – would nonetheless be legally married to him should he in fact marry them (see below, note 32). We would not, however, know that "those liable to *kares*" are included, since they would not be legally deemed married to him even if he did marry them (see below, note 29). Hence, a second inclusive expression is needed to include "those liable to *kares*" in the law (see *Tosafos*).]

10. Rav Pappa is referring to the passage written with regard to a seducer (*mefateh*), where the Torah states (*Exodus* 22:15-16): *If a man will seduce a virgin (besulah) who was not betrothed and lie with her . . . he shall weigh out silver in the amount of the marriage contract of the virgins (ha-besulos).* Both the *ha* prefix and the core word *besulos* at the end of the verse are superfluous. For the Torah could have stated *in the amount of the award [for the violation] of virgins (besulos),* deleting the prefix *ha* (the). Or, the Torah could have omitted the word *ha-besulos* entirely, and stated simply: *he shall weigh out silver in the amount of the marriage contract.* The Gemara, therefore, expounds both the core word *besulos* and the prefix *ha* separately (*Rashi*).

11. I.e. the expression: *If a man will seduce "a virgin."*

12. I.e. the superfluous *virgins* mentioned in the phrase *in the amount of the marriage contract of the "virgins."*

13. I.e. the *ha* prefix of the expression *the marriage contract of "the" virgins.*

14. The two latter cases are thus included in the law subjecting the *mefateh* despite the fact that he is forbidden to marry her (see above, note 9).

Although these expressions are stated with regard to the *mefateh,* the laws derived from them are applied to the *oneiss* as well, for the laws of the *oneiss* and the *mefateh* are derivable from one another (see *Tosafos* ד״ה איתרו and *Shitah Mekubetzes* ד״ה וכתבו הקונטריסין).

15. In the verse *and he shall give to the father of the naarah (ha-naarah),* a word that the Torah could have omitted by stating simply *her father* (*Rashi;* see above, note 4).

16. *Deuteronomy* 22:29.

17. The expression הַנַּעֲרָה, *the naarah,* implies the *naarah* as she was originally [earlier in the narrative] – i.e. alive (see *R' Crescas*).

[Since Rav Pappa subscribes to Abaye's exposition, he does not have the expression *ha-naarah* available to teach that the fine applies even where the *oneiss* is forbidden to marry the girl. Rather, he must derive that the fine applies to such a girl from *besulah, besulos, ha-besulos* stated with regard to *mefateh.*]

אף קנס במקום מכר והני בני קנסא נינהו ואמאי איקרי כאן א) ולו ו) תהיה לאשה אשה הראויה לו אמר ריש לקיש נערה א) נערה הנערה חד לגופיה וחד לאתויי חייבי לאוין וחד לאתויי חייבי כריתות רב פפא אמר ג) בתולה ד) בתולות הבתולות חד לגופיה וחד לאתויי חייבי לאוין וחד לאתויי חייבי כריתות ורב פפא מ"ט לא אמר כר"ל ההוא מיבעי ליה לכדאביי ה) דאמר אביי א באו עליה ומתה פטור שנאמר א) ונתן לאבי הנערה לאבי נערה ולא לאבי מתה וריש לקיש מ"ט לא אמר כרב פפא ההוא מיבעי ליה לגזירה שוה דתניא ג) כסף ישקול כמוהר הבתולות ב) שיהא זה כמוהר הבתולות ומוהר הבתולות כזה וריש לקיש נמי מיבעי ליה לכדאביי ורב פפא נמי מיבעי ליה לגזירה שוה אלא שיתא קראי כתיבי נערה נערה הנערה בתולה בתולות הבתולות תרי לגופייהו חד לכדאביי וחד לגזירה שוה אייתרו ליה תרי חד לאתויי חייבי לאוין וחד לאתויי חייבי כריתות ולאפוקי מהאי תנא דתניא ולו תהיה לאשה ז) שמעון התימני אומר אשה שיש בה הויה רבי שמעון בן מנסיא אומר ג אשה הראויה לקיימה מאי בינייהו אמר ר' זירא ממזרת ונתינה איכא בינייהו למאן דאמר יש בה הויה הא נמי יש בה הויה למאן דאמר ראויה לקיימה הא אינה ראויה לקיימה ולרבי עקיבא דאמר ח) אין קידושין תופסין בחייבי לאוין מאי בינייהו איכא בינייהו אלמנה לכהן גדול כרבי סימאי דתניא רבי סימאי אומר י) מן הכל עושה רבי עקיבא ממזרין חוץ מאלמנה לכהן גדול שהרי אמרה תורה ה) לא יקח ולא יחלל חילולין הוא עושה ואין עושה ממזרין ולרבי ישבב דאמר בואו ונצוח על עקיבא בן יוסף שהיה אומר כל שאין לו ביאה בישראל הולד ממזר מאי בינייהו איכא בינייהו

חייבי

רש"י

אף קנס במקום מכר. ומשום קנס נקט בת שלש אבל למכר מבת יום אחד ועד שתביא שתי שערות: ואמאי. יש להן קנס לנערות פסולות: איקרי כאן כו'. מתני' מקשי: ה"ג נערה נערה הנערה. באונס כתיב כי ימצא איש נערה בתולה וגו' וכתיב בתריה ונתן האיש השוכב עמה לאבי הנערה ודרשינן נערה יתירה וה"א יתירה להנערה דמלי למיכתב ונתן לאביה: חד לגופיה. לכשרה: בתולה בתולות הבתולות. במפתה כתיב וכי יפתה איש בתולה וקרא אחרינא בתריה כסף ישקול כמוהר הבתולות ומלי למיכתב כמוהר בתולות הא תלת דדרשינן ה' יתירה ובתולות דמלי למיכתב כמוהר ולשתוק: ההוא מיבעי ליה. ההוא הנערה הא דלא כתיב ונתן לאביה מיבעי ליה לכדאביי שאם לא הספיק האב להעמידו בדין עד שמתה פטור: לאבי הנערה. משמע שהיא קיימת: מיבעי ליה לג"ש. בתולה דכתיב גבי מפתה מיבעי ליה לג"ש בתולה בתולה לג"ש מה כסף האמור באונס חמשים אף מפתה חמשים ומה האמור במפתה שקלים דכתיב ביה ישקול אף חמשים של אונס שקלים קאמר: כמוהר הבתולות. חמשים כסף המפורשים במאנס את הבתולה: שיהא זה. חמשים כמוהר הבתולות: ומוהר הבתולות. יהיו שקלים כזה: וחד לג"ש. ותרי מופנה מצד אחד ולמידים הימנה: ולאפוקי מהאי תנא. מתני' דקתני יש קנס לממזרת ולאחותו לאפוקי מהאי תנא: שיש בה הויה. שקדושין תופסין לו בה פרט לאחותו ולכל חייבי כריתות דילפינן בקדושין שאין קדושין תופסין בהן בפרק שלישי (דף סז:) ומשמע ליה תהיה לשון קדושין הוויות ור"ש בן מנסיא משמע ליה תהיה לשון קיום: הא נמי אית בה הויה. דקדושין תופסין בחייבי לאוין והתם יליף לה: ולר"ע דאמר אין קדושין תופסין בחייבי לאוין. ביבמות בהחולץ (דף מד:) בברייתא המחזיר גרושתו ר"ע אומר אין לו בה קדושין: מאי בינייהו. משום ר"ש בן מנסיא קא פריך לה דאילו שמעון התימני שמעינן ליה ביבמות (דף מט.) דפליג עליה דר"ע בהא דתנן איזהו ממזר כל שאר בשר שהוא בלא יבא דברי ר"ע שמעון התימני אומר כל שחייבין עליו כרת בידי שמים אלא לר"ש בן מנסיא קא בעינן לה אי ס"ל כר"ע מאי איכא בין משמעותא דתהיה לשון קיום למשמעות דשמעון התימני אי נמי משמע ליה לר"ש בן מנסיא לשון הויה אימעיטא לה ממזר ומה בין ראויה לקיימה ליש בה הויה: אלמנה לכהן גדול. דמודה בה ר"ע שקדושין תופסין לו בה ואע"פ שהיא בלאו וכרבי סימאי והוא הדין גרושה להדיוט: מן הכל. כל הנולדים מחייבי לאוין: לא יקח. וסמיך ליה ולא יחלל זרעו מדין כהונה הוא מחללו ולא שם ממזרים עליהם: בואו ונצוח על עקיבא בן יוסף. שמרבה ממזרים בישראל חנם: שהוא אומר כל שאין לו ביאה בישראל. הבא על אשה שאין לו בה היתר ביאה הולד ממזר אפי' אלמנה לכ"ג נמי:

תוספות

נערה נערה הנערה. פי' רבינו חננאל דמחד נערה דריש כולה מלתא נער נערה הנערה ואין נראה לר"ת דלא כתיב נערה מלא בה"א אלא ההוא דמוציא שם רע לחודיה כדמוכח בסוף פרקין ועוד הקשה רבינו יצחק מה צריך חד לגופיה הא איכא נערה אחרינא בפרשה אלא פי' הקונטרס עיקר:

בתולה בתולות הבתולות. כאן נמי פר"ח דמחד קרא נפקי כולהו ואין נראה דלא צריך חד לגופיה דבתולה אחרינא כתיב:

וחד לאתויי חייבי לאוין. הקשה ר"י בן רבינו מאיר אלמאי ניימא חד לאתויי חייבי עשה וחד לאתויי חייבי לאוין ולאלתמי חייבי כריתות מנא לן ומיצרך דלחייבי לאוין ועשה לא צריך אלא חד קרא דהא אי לאו דכתיב ולו תהיה לאשה משמע שיש בה הויה ולאו לקיימה לא הוה צריך קרא לרבוייהו הלכך מחד ריבויא מרבינן אין ראויה לקיימה דהיינו חייבי עשה וחייבי לאוין כיון דאית בהו הויה ואידך ריבויא לחייבי כריתות ולמאן דאמר אין קדושין תופסין בחייבי לאוין הוי חד ריבויא לחייבי עשה ואידך לחייבי לאוין וחייבי כריתות וא"ת ולשתוק מלו תהיה לאשה ולא יצטרך להכך ריבויי וי"ל דאיצטריך למידרש ולו תהיה לאשה מדעתה ז):

אייתרו להו תרי כו'. וחד ריבויא כתב באונס וחד במפתה וא"ת ומנא לן דחד לאתויי חייבי כריתות אימא לרבויי חייבי לאוין וחד לאונס וחד למפתה וי"ל דהא לא צריך דמגזרה שוה ילפינן אונס ומפתה מהדדי: [ולאפוקי מהאי תנא. פי' תנא דברייתא אבל מפיק מתרווייהו תנאי שמחברים בברייתא]:

ולרבי עקיבא דאמר כו'. ואע"ג דר"ש התימני פליג בהדיא אר' עקיבא בהחולץ (יבמות דף מד. ודף מט.) הכא לר"ש בן מנסיא פריך דאי סבר כר"ע מאי בינייהו פי' בינו לר"ש התימני דמדנקט ראויה לקיימה ולא נקט שיש בה הויה משמע דיש שאין ראויה לקיימה ויש בה הויה:

חילולין הוא עושה ואינו עושה ממזרים. משמע דהא בהא תליא דכיון דלא הוי ממזר קדושין תופסין וכן משמע בפרק החולץ (שם דף מה:) מה אשת אב דלא תפסי בה קדושין והוולד ממזר כו' [ור"ע נמי משום דיליף בהחולץ דיש ממזר מחייבי לאוין קאמר דאין קדושין תופסין בחייבי לאוין] ותימה דלרבי יהושע אע"ג דאין ממזר מחייבי כריתות כדיליף בשילהי החולץ (שם דף מט.) מודה דאין קדושין תופסין בחייבי כריתות כדפריך ס"פ ר"ג ביבמות (דף נג. ושם) איצטריך לאשמעינן דאין קדושין תופסין בחייבי כריתות ובפ' החולץ (שם דף מד: ושם) קאמר דלרבי יהושע פגום מיהא הוי מחייבי כריתות משום דעשאה זונה וזונה לא הויא אלא מהנהו דלא תפסי בה קדושין כדמוכח בתמורה (דף כט: ושם) וקאמרינן נמי בהחולץ (יבמות דף מד: ושם) הכל מודים בכותי ועבד הבא על בת ישראל הוולד ממזר מאן הכל מודים שמעון התימני דאע"ג דאמר אין ממזר מחייבי לאוין דתפסי בהו קדושין אבל כותי ועבד כו' ולא קאמר מאן הכל מודים ר' יהושע דאע"ג דאמר אין ממזר מחייבי כריתות ה"מ חייבי כריתות דתפסי בהו קדושין כו' אלמא דלר' יהושע אין קדושין תופסין בחייבי כריתות ואפ"ה לא הוי ממזר ולהכי לא מצי למימר דמודה בכותי ועבד ויש לומר דלר"ש התימני ולר"ע ודאי הא בהא תליא דליכא מידי דלא תפסי בה קדושין והוולד כשר רק שהוא דומה לאשת אב אבל לר' יהושע אע"ג דאין קדושין תופסין בחייבי כריתות כדילפי' בסוף האומר (קדושין סח. ושם) לא הוי ממזר אלא מחייבי מיתות ב"ד כדיליף ר' יהושע בסוף החולץ (יבמות מט. ושם) אבל קשה דא"כ לר' יהושע אין קדושין תופסין באלמנה לכ"ג לרבא דאמר בפ"ק דתמורה (דף ד: ושם) כל דאמר רחמנא לא תעביד אי עביד לא מהני דהתם ח) פריך ליה והרי אלמנה לכ"ג דקאמר רחמנא לא יקח ותנן כל מקום שיש קדושין ויש עבירה כגון אלמנה לכ"ג כו' ומשני אמר לך רבא שאני התם דא"ק לא יחלל חלולין הוא עושה ואינו עושה ממזרים ולר' יהושע ליכא לשנויי הכי וא"ת בקדושין בסוף האומר (דף סו: ושם) כי משכח דלא תפסי קדושין באשת אב מאי פריך התם ואימא תרוייהו באשת אב הא לכתחלה הא דיעבד אמאי לא יליף מינה דכל היכא דהוי ממזר לא תפסי בה קדושין כיון דהא בהא תליא כדפירשנו וי"ל דהכתי לא שמעינן ממזרות בשאר חייבי כריתות כל כמה דלא מייתי התם היקישא דר' יונה דמלא יקח ולא יגלה דאיירי באשת אב ובשומרת יבם של אביו לא שמעינן מינה ממזרות באשת איש ובאחות אשה דיש היתר לאיסורן וכל דכוותייהו אבל לבסוף דמייתי היקישא דרבי יונה התם איכא למילף בעלמא כדפירשנו:

ט) (וכן משמע בפרק ד' מיתות דליכא מאן דפליג דבחייבי כריתות לא תפסי קדושין וט"ו נשים דפוטרות צרותיהן מן החליצה ואי קדושין תופסין בחייבי כריתות א"כ היו עולין לחליצה כמו חייבי לאוין כדאמר התם בפ"ב מסתברא חייבי לאוין תפסי בהו קדושין ולכך עולין לחליצה והיא מתני' אתיא כר"ע דהא קאמר עלה דפלוגתא לא קא מיירי:) מאי בינייהו. תימה אמאי לא קאמר איכא בינייהו סוטה שאיסורה [illegible] הויה כר"ע [illegible] הכל מודים בסוטה שאין הולד ממזר:)

עין משפט נר מצוה

ד א מיי' פ"א מהלכות נערה הל' טו סמג עשין נד טור אה"ע סי' קעז:
ה ב מיי' שם הל' ו:
ו ג מיי' שם הל' ה:

תוספות רי"ד

לה קנס: ומקשינן אמתני' קרי כאן ולו תהיה לאשה אשה הראויה לו. פי' באשה הראויה לו יתן קנס דמקיים בה ולו תהיה לאשה. אבל באשה שאינה ראויה לו דלא מקיים בה ולו תהיה לאשה גם מן הקנס יהא פטור. אר"ל נער נערה הנערה. חד לגופיה. פי' לכשירה. וחד לאתויי חייבי לאוין. וחד לאתויי חייבי כריתות. פי' גבי אונס כתיב כי ימצא איש נערה בתולה. וכתיב בתריה ונתן האיש השוכב עמה לאבי הנערה [illegible] יתירה הוא. ודרשי' נערה וה' דהנערה תרי יתירי חד לחייבי לאוין וחד לאתויי חייבי כריתות. ואי קשיא [illegible]

תורה אור השלם

א) וְנָתַן הָאִישׁ הַשֹּׁכֵב עִמָּהּ לַאֲבִי הַנַּעֲרָ חֲמִשִּׁים כָּסֶף וְלוֹ תִהְיֶה לְאִשָּׁה תַּחַת אֲשֶׁר עִנָּהּ לֹא יוּכַל שַׁלְּחָהּ כָּל יָמָיו: [דברים כב, כט]
ב) כִּי יִמְצָא אִישׁ נַעֲרָ בְתוּלָה אֲשֶׁר לֹא אֹרָשָׂה וּתְפָשָׂהּ וְשָׁכַב עִמָּהּ וְנִמְצָאוּ: [דברים כב, כח]
ג) וְכִי יְפַתֶּה אִישׁ בְּתוּלָה אֲשֶׁר לֹא אֹרָשָׂה וְשָׁכַב עִמָּהּ מָהֹר יִמְהָרֶנָּה לּוֹ לְאִשָּׁה: [שמות כב, טו]
ד) אִם מָאֵן יְמָאֵן אָבִיהָ לְתִתָּהּ לוֹ כֶּסֶף יִשְׁקֹל כְּמֹהַר הַבְּתוּלֹת: [שמות כב, טז]
ה) אַלְמָנָה וּגְרוּשָׁה וַחֲלָלָה זֹנָה אֶת אֵלֶּה לֹא יִקָּח כִּי אִם בְּתוּלָה מֵעַמָּיו יִקַּח אִשָּׁה: וְלֹא יְחַלֵּל זַרְעוֹ בְּעַמָּיו כִּי אֲנִי יְיָ מְקַדְּשׁוֹ: [ויקרא כא, יד - טו]

מסורת הש"ס

א) [לקמן לט.], ב) [לקמן לח:], ג) [לעיל י. לקמן לח:], ד) [לקמן לו.], ה) [יבמות יז: ושם נסמן], ו) [יבמות סט.] קידושין סד. סח., ז) [לקמן לג:], ח) [דף ה:], ט) ת"י כ"י.

ליקוטי רש"י

אימא אף קנס. יש לה ואע"פ שיש מכר משתראה לביאה עד שתביא ב' שערות וקודם שתראה לביאה יש מכר ואין קנס ומשתביא שתי שערות ועד שתיבגר יש קנס ולא מכר ובין גבגרות לנערות ששה חדשים [חולין כו:]. בא עליה ומתה. לא הספיק האב להעמידו בדין עד שמתה [לקמן לח:]. כמוהר הבתולות. שהוא קצוב נ' כסף אלא להתופס את הבתולה ושוכב עמה באונס שנאמר (דברים כב) ונתן האיש השוכב עמה לאבי הנערה חמשים כסף [שמות כב, טו]. והאמור במאנס את הבתולה (דברים כב) קנסו הכתוב נ' כסף בשביל מוהר בתוליה. שיהא זה כמוהר הבתולות. [illegible] [לעיל י.]. ומוהר הבתולות כזה. [illegible] [לקמן לח:]. שיתא קראי כתיבי. [illegible] [גליון רש"י ישן משיטמ"ק]. ולרבי עקיבא וכו'. [illegible] מאי בינייהו. [illegible] איכא בינייהו אלמנה לכהן גדול. [illegible] חוץ מאלמנה לכהן גדול. [illegible]

כנוי ממזרים [יבמות מט.]. שהרי אמרה תורה לא יקח. וסמיך ליה ולא יחלל זרעו בעמיו דמשמע חללין הוא עושה וזרעו שמחוללין מן הכהונה ואינו עושה ממזרין וכיון דלאו ממזר ש"מ קידושין תופסין בחייבי לאוין [illegible] ולא יחלל. [illegible] כל שאין לו ביאה בישראל הולד ממזר. [illegible] בואו ונצוח על עקיבא בן יוסף. [illegible] [קידושין סח.].

אלו ^(א) נערות שיש להן קנס הבא על הממזרת ועל הנתינה ועל הכותית הבא על הגיורת ועל השבויה ועל השפחה שנפדו ושנתגיירו ושנשתחררו פחותות מבנות שלש שנים ויום אחד ^(ב) הבא על אחותו ועל אחות אביו ועל אחות אמו ועל אחות אשתו ועל אשת אחיו ועל אשת אחי אביו ועל הנדה יש להם קנס אע"פ שהן בהכרת אין בהן מיתת בית דין: גמ' הני נערות פסולות אית להו קנס כשירות לא הכי קאמר אלו נערות פסולות שיש להם קנס הבא על הממזרת ועל הנתינה ועל הכותית: נערה אין קטנה לא מאן תנא אמר רב יהודה אמר רב רבי מאיר היא דתניא ^(ג) קטנה מבת יום אחד ועד שתביא שתי שערות יש לה מכר ^(ד) ואין לה קנס ומשתביא שתי שערות ועד שתיבגר יש לה קנס ואין לה מכר דברי רבי מאיר שהיה רבי מאיר אומר כל מקום שיש מכר אין קנס וכל מקום שיש קנס אין מכר ^(ג) וחכמים אומרים קטנה מבת שלש שנים ויום אחד ועד שתיבגר ^(ה) יש לה קנס קנס אין מכר לא אימא אף

רש"י

אלו נערות. דוקא נערה משהביאה שתי שערות עד שתבגר והם ששה חדשים שבין נערות לבגרות אבל קטנה ובוגרת אין להם קנס: שיש להן קנס. אם אנסה אדם נותן לאביה חמשים כסף דכתיב ונתן האיש השוכב וגו' (דברים כב): הבא על הממזרת. בגמרא פריך אבל כשירות לא ומשני פסולות אילטריכא ליה לאשמועינן: נתינה. מן הגבעונים והיא אסורה לקהל דדוד גזר עליהם כדאמרינן ביבמות (ד' עח:) ועל שם ויתנם יהושע חוטבי עצים ושואבי מים וגו' (יהושע ט) קרי להו נתינים: כותית. קסבר גירי אריות הן וישנן בלאו לא תתחתן בם (דברים ז): ועל השבויה. ישראלית שנפדית פחותה מבת שלש שנים דבחזקת בתולה היא שאפי' נבעלה בשביה בתוליה חוזרים: ועל אשת אחיו. שנתקדשה לו לאחיו וגירשה שאין בה מיתה אלא כרת: ועל אשת אחי אביו. שנתקדשה לו וגירשה: אע"פ שהן בהכרת הרי אין בהם מיתת ב"ד. וכרת לא פטר ליה מן התשלומין: גמ' ר"מ היא. כדמייתי ברייתא לקמיה: יש לה מכר. יש לאביה בה זכייה למכרה לשפחות: ואין לה קנס. שהבא עליה אינו חייב קנס: ואין לה מכר. כדתניא (ערכין דף כט:) יכול ימכור אדם את בתו כשהיא נערה אמרת ק"ו מכורה כבר יוצאה עכשיו שאינה מכורה אינו דין שלא תמכר: מבת ג' שנים ויום אחד. שהיא ראויה לביאה: מכר לא. בתמיה: אף

תוספות

אלו נערות. הבא על הנתינה. פי' בקונטרס לדוד גזר עליהם שלא לבא בקהל והיינו משום עבדות כדאמרינן בהערל (יבמות עח: ושם) ואין נראה לר"ת דהא משמע בגמרא (ע"ב) דנתינה הויא דאורייתא דקאמר ממזרת ונתינה איכא בינייהו למ"ד ראויה לקיימה כו' משמע דהויא דאורייתא דהא בקראי פליגי וברים יש מותרות (שם דף פה: ושם) אמרינן ממזרת ונתינה איכא בינייהו מ"ד דאורייתא הא נמי דאורייתא ועוד דתנן (מכות דף יג.) אלו הן הלוקין ממזרת ונתינה לישראל משמע דלקי עלה מדאורייתא דומיא דכל הנך דחשיב התם ומיהו איכא למימר דכל הנהו נקט נתינה אגב ממזרת וכן לריך לומר ע"כ לרבא למאי דס"ד בהערל (יבמות דף עו. ושם) דגיורותן לית להו איסור חתנות ומ"מ אין נראה לר"ת פירושו דהא מסיק רבא בהערל (ג"ז שם) דגירותן אית להו איסור חתנות וכל היכא דחשיב נתינה בהדי ממזרת איירי בגירות כמו הכא דבנכריותה לית לה קנס כדאמרינן לעיל בפ"ק (דף יא. ושם) יהבינן לה קנס ואזלה ואכלה בנכריותה וכן בקדושין בפרק האומר (דף סו:) תנן כל מקום שיש קדושין ויש עבירה כגון ממזרת ונתינה כו' ועוד לפירוש הקונטרס כיון דעבדות ממש גזר עליהו שמתוך כך נאסרו לבוא בקהל משום לא יהיה קדש א"כ אמאי יש לה קנס הא תנן בהדיא במתניתין דשפחה אין לה קנס ואי משום דנתינה מנטרא נפשה הא אמרינן בירושלמי דשפחה אפילו משומרת אין לה קנס ועוד דתנן בפרק עשרה יוחסין (שם דף סט.) דחרורי ונתיני מותרים לבא זה בזה ואמאי והא חרורי אסירי בשפחה כדתנן (גיטין דף מג.) לישא שפחה אינו יכול ומיהו הא י"ל דלאו ממש גזר עליהו עבדות לאסור בלא יהיה קדש ונראה לר"ת דנתינה אסורה דאורייתא משום לא תתחתן כדמסיק רבא בהערל (יבמות דף עו. ושם) ודוד לא גזר עליהו אלא שיעבוד ולאו לאוסרן בבנות ישראל דהא אסירי וקיימי מלאו דלא תתחתן אלא כדי שלא יטמעו בישראל והא דגזור בהו טפי מבשאר פסולי קהל משום דהוו אומה שלימה והא דקאמר התם ^(י) כל מי שיש בו שלשה סימנים הללו ראוי לידבק בהן לא לישא מהן אלא להיות בן חורין כמותן וכן הא דקאמר התם ^(ז) בימי רבי בקשו להתיר נתינים א"ר אם חלקנו נתיר חלק מזבח מי יתיר לא שהיו רוצים להתירם לבא בקהל דהא מדאורייתא אסירי אלא בקשו לפטרן מעבדות להיות בני חורין ואמר להו רבי דאין יכולין להפקיע חלק מזבח ואע"ג דקיימא לן ^(ח) דהפקר ב"ד היה הפקר היינו לצורך אבל זה אינו צורך כל כך ומיהו בירושלמי משמע כפי' הקונט' בפ' עשרה יוחסין דקאמר התם נתינים יהושע ריחקם כלום ריחקם אלא משום פסול משפחה דא"ת משום פסול עבדות אלא מעתה הבא על הנתינה לא יהיה לה קנס משמע משום דיהושע גזר עליהם נפסלו מלבא בקהל וגזרת יהושע ודוד הכל גזירה אחת היא כדמוכח בהערל (שם דף עט.) ומיהו בירושלמי איכא למימר דסבר כמו שהיה ס"ד דרבא מעיקרא בהערל דגירותן לית להו איסור חתנות ועוד י"ל דריחקן היינו שלא יטמעו בהן והא דאמרינן בהאומר בקדושין (דף סח: ושם) נכרית מנא לן דלא תפסי בה קדושין דכתיב לא תתחתן בם אומר ר"ת דאסיפיה דקרא סמיך ובתו לא תקח לבנך אבל רישיה דקרא מיירי בגירות וכענין זה מצינו בהערל (יבמות דף עז.) דפריך גבי בני שאול והכתיב לא יומתו אבות על בנים וע"כ לא פריך אלא מסיפא דקרא אע"ג דרישא דקרא מוקמינן ליה לפסול קרובים לעדות בפרק החובל (ב"ק דף פח.) ובפרק זה בורר (סנהדרין דף כז:) ^(ט): ועל הכותית. פירש בקונטרס דקסבר כותים גירי אריות הן וישנן בלאו דלא תתחתן והו לפי שיטתו כדסלקא דעתין מעיקרא בהערל (יבמות דף עו. ושם) דבנכרותן אית להו איסור חתנות ומה שפי' דקסבר כותים גירי אריות הן ל"נ לרבינו יצחק בן רבינו מאיר דא"כ עובדת כוכבים היא ועובדת כוכבים אין לה קנס כדפריך בפ"ק (לעיל יא.) יהבינן לה קנס ואזלה ואכלה בנכריותה ועוד דבגמרא מוקי מתני' כר"מ ור"מ אית ליה דגירי אמת הן ואע"ג דכולה מתניתין לא אתיא כר"מ דהא בתו אמר בגמרא דלא אתיא כוותיה מ"מ בהא דסבר דגירי אמת הן אתיא כוותיה דהא בשור שנגח ד' וה' (ב"ק דף לח: ושם) מסקינן דשור ישראל שנגח שור של כותי פטור משום דקנס הוא דקניס רבי מאיר בממונם אע"ג דמן הדין חייב דגירי אמת הם ופריך ממתני' דהכא דכותית יש לה קנס ואי ס"ד דקנס הוא שקנס ר"מ בממונם ה"נ לקנוס כו' אלמא דמתניתין דהכא סברה דגירי אמת הן וא"ת אם כן מאי קמ"ל פשיטא דיש לה קנס דישראלית גמורה היא וי"ל דס"ד דלא יהבינן לה קנס שלא יטמעו בהן ^(א) וא"ת למ"ד בפרק עשרה יוחסין (קדושין דף עו.) דפסול כותים משום דעבד ושפחה נטמעו בהן אמאי יש לה קנס נימא לה אייתי ראיה דלאו שפחה את ושקילי לשמואל דאמר (ב"ק דף מו:) אין הולכין בממון אחר הרוב ואפילו לרב אי דאזיל איהו גבה ה"ל קבוע וכל קבוע כמחצה על מחצה דמי ויש לומר דכל אחת מוקמינן לה אחזקת אבהתא שהיו כותים אע"ג דלענין פסול לא מוקמינן לה אחזקתה לענין קנס מוקמינן להו שלא יהא חוטא נשכר ^(ב) ^(י) ואם תאמר ואמאי לא חשיב נמי אלמנה לכ"ג גרושה וחלוצה לכהן הדיוט וי"ל דבפסול כהונה לא קמיירי והא דלא תני מצרי ואדומי משום שיש להם היתר [א"נ לא חשיב אלא חייבי לאוין] אבל קשה דליתני מחזיר גרושתו משניסת ונבעלה שלא כדרכה ואע"ג דאמרי' בפ' עשרה יוחסין (קדושין עח.) הכל מודים שאם בעל ולא קידש שאינו לוקה מ"מ לר"ע דאמר אין קדושין תופסין במחזיר גרושתו ליתני ועוד הוה מצי למיתני יבמה לשוק [ועבד הבא על הכותית הולד ממזר ויש לה קנס. ת"י] וי"ל דתנא ושייר ואע"ג דבפ"ק דקדושין (דף טז:) דייק תנא תני אלו ואת אמרת תנא ושייר הכא דתני בסיפא ואלו שאין להם קנס לא שייך למידק הכי כדאשכחן בפרק המזבח מקדש (זבחים דף פד.) דקתני ואלו פסולן בקדש ואלו שאין פסולן בקדש ומשייר ברישא ובסיפא ^(כ) ועי"ל דהכא לא חשיב אלא פסולי קהל: והבא על הגיורת. חילקן לשנות חייבי לאוין לחודייהו וגיורת ומשוחררת דכשירות הן לחודייהו וחייבי כריתות לחודייהו משום דבעי למיתני סיפא אע"פ שהם בהכרת כו' אבל באלו הן הלוקין (מכות יג.) לא תני אלא הבא אחד על כולם: ועל אשת אחיו. פר"ח דפריך בירושלמי אשת אחיו ולא יבמה היא לו וזקוקה לו ומה קנס וכרת שייך בה ומשני בשיש לו בנים מאשה אחרת ואיירי במת מן האירוסין והוא הדין דהוה מצי לאוקמה כשגירשה וקשה לר"י ב"ר אברהם לרב פפא דמוקי הך מתניתין במפותה בפרק בן סורר (סנהדרין דף עג. ושם) תקשי דהיכי מצי לאוקומי הכי הא נתארסה ונתגרשה קנסה לעצמה (לקמן דף לח.) וכיון דלעצמה מפותה אין לה קנס כדאמרינן בגמרא (לקמן מ.) וברים נערה משום דמדעתה עבדה וכ"ת דקסבר תנא דמתניתין כר"ע דברייתא דקנסה לאביה הוי אם כן אכתי ^(ג) תיקשי ליה סיפא דקתני (שם לו:) הבא על בתו פטור משום דקם ליה בדרבה מיניה תיפוק ליה דקנסה לאביה הוי דאי לעצמה תיקשי ליה דמחלה וממה נפשך תקשי סיפא ומיהו בירושלמי מוקי לה כשבא עליה עד שלא מת ומת והוא הדין עד שלא בגרה ובגרה ולמאי דאמר בירושלמי דמפותה אינו פטור אלא מבושת ופגם אבל קנס אינה יכולה למחול אתי שפיר ומיהו בש"ס דידן משמע דאין לה אפי' קנס דמוקי הא דאלו הן הלוקין לקמן בגמ' (דף לב.) ביתומה ומפותה שאין לה קנס: נערה אין קטנה לא. תימה מנא ליה דלמא לא אתי למעוטי אלא בוגרת דהא משמע ^(ד) בס"פ ארבע מיתות (סנהדרין דף סו:) גבי הא דתנן אינו חייב אלא עד שתהא נערה בתולה מאורסה דלא הוה תני אלא על נערה בתולה כו' הוה מוקמינן לה אפילו כרבנן ולא הוה אתי למעוטי קטנה אלא בוגרת ותירץ ריצב"א ^(ה) דאסיפא דמתניתין סמיך דתנן (לקמן דף מ:) כל מקום שיש מכר אין קנס:

מסורת הש"ס

א) לעיל יא. ב"ק לח., ב) סנהדרין דף עג., ג) [תוספתא פ"ג ע"ש] לקמן מ: חולין כו., ד) [לקמן לו.], ה) [לקמן לו.], ו) [דף עט.], ז) שם., ח) [שם פט:], ט) [ועי' תוס' יבמות עט. ד"ה ונתיניס ותוס' ע"ז לו: ד"ה דכתיב], י) [ועי' תוס' ב"ק לח: ד"ה ועל הכותית], כ) [עי' תוס' יבמות פד: ד"ה אלא ותוס' זבחים פד. ד"ה הלן ותוס' שבועות לט. ד"ה ואלו נאמרין ותוס' שם מד: ד"ה כל הנשבעין ותוס' שבת עה: ד"ה חסר אחת].

תוספות ישנים

א) א"נ היא גופא קמ"ל דגירי אמת הן. ת"י: ב) ועבד הבא על הכותית הולד ממזר ויש לה קנס. ת"י: ג) אבל ליכא לאוקמי הבא על בתו אחר שנכנסה לחופה ולא נבעלה וגירשה דא"כ בלאו הכי אין לה קנס כיון דמוקי לה במפותה דמחלה וא"ל דסיפא בא על בתו לא איירי במפותה אלא באנוסה א"כ בתנם נקט בא על בתו דחייבי כריתות נמי אין לה קנס כיון דניתנה להצילה בנפשו דמשום הכי מוקי לה התם במפותה: ד) דפריך עד שתהא נערה אינו חייב אלא על נערה מבעי ליה. ת"י:

ליקוטי רש"י

שיש להן קנס. נ' כסף אם יאנסו. הבא על הממזרת. ואע"ג דלא קרינן ביה ולו תהיה לאשה שהרי אינה ראויה לקיימה אפילו הכי יש לה קנס [לעיל יא.]. ועל הנתינה. נתינים, גבעונים שנתגיירו בערמה בימי יהושע ונתנם עבדים לחוטבי עצים ושואבי מים [יבמות עח:]. הבא על אחותו. כלומר אפילו בא על אחותו דלא קרינא בה ולו תהיה לאשה אפילו הכי קרינא בה ונתן האיש השוכב עמה דלאתרבי מקראי בכתובות (דף כט:) ואע"ג דחייב כרת לא מפטר מתשלומין [סנהדרין עג:]. כל מקום שיש מכר. כל זמן שהבת קטנה ואביה זכאי למוכרה. כלומר לא נתפתחה אין לאביה חמשים כסף דנערה כתיב (דברים כב) ונתן האיש השוכב עמה לאבי הנערה חמשים כסף. וכל מקום שיש קנס. דהיינו כשהיא נערה. אין מכר. דתניא בערכין (דף כט:) יכול ימכור אדם את בתו כשהיא נערה אמרת ק"ו ומה מכורה כבר יוצאה עכשיו בסימני נערות שאינה מכורה אינו דין שלא תימכר. וחכמים וכו' יש לה קנס. לקטנה וטעמא מפרש בכתובות (דף מ:) כל מקום שנאמר נערה אפילו קטנה במשמע. מכר לא. במתמיה והלא קטנה היא עד שתביא שתי שערות [חולין כו:].

עין משפט נר מצוה

א א מיי' פ"א מהל' נערה הלכה י סמג עשין נד טור אה"ע סי' קעז:
ב ב מיי' פ"ד מהל' עבדים הלכה א סמג עשין פה:
ג ג מיי' פ"א מהלכות נערה הלכה ח סמג עשין נד טוש"ע אה"ע סי' קעז סעיף א בהג"ה:

גליון הש"ס

תוס' ד"ה נערה וכו' דאסיפא דמתני' סמיך. עי' נדה מד ע"ב תוס' ד"ה שלשים יום:

תוספות רי"ד

אלו נערות שיש להן קנס. פי' אנסה אדם נותן לאביה נ' כסף כדכתיב ונתן האיש וגו'. הבא על הממזרת ועל הנתינה ועל הכותית על הגיורת ועל השבויה. פי' ישראלית שנשבית. ועל השפחה. שנפדו ושנתגיירו ושנשתחררו פחותות מבנות ג"ש ויום אחד. הבא על אחותו ועל אחות אביו ועל אחות אמו ועל אחות אשתו ועל אשת אחיו ועל אשת אחי אביו ועל הנדה יש להן קנס. אע"פ שהן בכרת אין בהן מיתת ב"ד. פי' דוקא נערה ולא בוגרת וקטנה. שהבוגרת כלו בתוליה ואין להם קנס. וקטנה הויא כעין א) שמדמעת וחוזרת ומדמעת. ונערה היא מבת י"ב שנים ויום אחד אם הביאה ב' שערות וממתנת ששה חדשים אחר שהביאה ב' שערות והיא בוגרת שאין בין נערות לבוגרת אלא ו' חדשים בלבד. נתינה היא מן הגבעונים ע"ש ויתנם יהושע חוטבי עצים ושואבי מים. ומשום צד עבדות הן אסורות. והכותיות קסבר גירי אמת הן ומ"ה יש להן קנס. שאילו היו גירי אריות הויא לה עובדת כוכבים. ואין קנס לעובדת כוכבים אלא שהכותים פסולים כדתנן בעשרה יוחסין אלו הן הספיקות שתוקי ואסופי וכותי. והתם מפרש טעמא למה הן הכותים פסולין. ועל אשת אחיו. כגון שקידש את הבתולה וגירשה. א"נ שמת ויש לו בן מאשה אחרת דקיימי עליה בכרת אע"פ שהן בהכרת אין הכרת פוטרו מן התשלומין אלא מיתת ב"ד: נערה אין קטנה לא. דהיינו קודם שתביא ב' שערות. מאן תנא אר"י א"ר ר"מ הוא דתניא קטנה ב) מבת ג' שנים ויום אחד. פירוש שמזמן זה היא ראויה לביאה ועד שתביא ב' שערות יש לה מכר ואין לה קנס. ומשתביא ב' שערות ועד שתבגר יש לה קנס ואין לה מכר דברי ר"מ שהיה ר"מ אומר כ"מ שיש מכר אין קנס וכל מקום שיש קנס אין מכר. וחכ"א קטנה מבת ג' שנים ויום אחד עד שתבגר יש לה מכר ויש

חשק שלמה על תוס' רי"ד

א) דברי רבינו אינו מובן דהך סברא אמרינן בנדה (מ"ה) לענין קטנה פחותה מבת שלש דבתולים חוזרין אבל משמע הא ס"ל דלאין קטנה כלל רק נערה ול"ע. ב) ולפנינו בגמ' הגירסא בדברי ר"מ מבת יום אחד וגירסת רבינו ל"ע.

קְנָס – **SHE IS ENTITLED TO A FINE** if she is violated or seduced, וְאֵין לָהּ מֶכֶר – **BUT SHE IS NOT SUBJECT TO SALE.**[24] דִּבְרֵי רַבִּי מֵאִיר – These are **THE WORDS OF R' MEIR.** שֶׁהָיָה רַבִּי מֵאִיר אוֹמֵר – **FOR R' MEIR USED TO SAY:** כָּל מָקוֹם שֶׁיֵּשׁ מֶכֶר – **WHEREVER THERE IS** a father's right of **SALE,**[25] אֵין קְנָס – **THERE IS NO FINE** for violation or seduction; וְכָל מָקוֹם שֶׁיֵּשׁ קְנָס – **AND WHEREVER THERE IS THE FINE,**[26] אֵין מֶכֶר – **THERE IS NO** right of **SALE.** וַחֲכָמִים אוֹמְרִים – **BUT THE SAGES SAY:** קְטַנָּה מִבַּת שָׁלֹשׁ שָׁנִים וְיוֹם אֶחָד וְעַד שֶׁתִּיבָּגֵר – **A MINOR GIRL, FROM THE AGE OF THREE YEARS AND A DAY**[27] **UNTIL SHE REACHES FULL ADULTHOOD,** יֵשׁ לָהּ קְנָס – **IS ENTITLED TO THE FINE** if she is violated or seduced.

Thus, we have a Tannaic dispute as to whether there is a fine in the case of a minor girl, with R' Meir holding that there is none. Accordingly, R' Meir is the author of our Mishnah, which also holds that view.

Having cited this Baraisa, the Gemara questions the statement of the Sages, who say only that a girl between the age of three and full adulthood is entitled to the fine, and omit any reference to her sale: קְנָס אֵין מֶכֶר לֹא – Do the Sages really mean that the law of **fine – yes,** it applies to a girl this age; but the father's right of **sale – no,** it does not apply to her? Why, the law of sale applies specifically to a minor girl who has not grown two hairs![28] – ? –

The Gemara answers:

אֵימָא – **Say** that the Sages mean:

NOTES

24. Once a girl becomes a *naarah,* her father can no longer sell her, as derived by a Baraisa in *Arachin* 29b from a *kal vachomer:* If a girl already sold by her father goes free upon becoming a *naarah* [see above, note 21], is it not certain that a girl who has not been sold can no longer be sold once she becomes a *naarah*? (*Rashi*).

25. I.e. when the girl is a minor.

26. I.e. when the girl is a *naarah.*

27. This is the age at which a girl is deemed [physically] fit for cohabitation (*Rashi*). [Cohabitation with a girl less than three years old is not legally regarded as cohabitation; see Mishnah *Niddah* 44b.]

28. See above, notes 21 and 24.

אלו א) נערות שיש להן קנס הבא על הממזרת ועל הנתינה ועל הכותית הבא על הגיורת ועל השבויה ועל השפחה שנפדו ושנתגיירו ושנשתחררו פחותות מבנות שלש שנים ויום אחד ב) הבא על אחותו ועל אחות אביו ועל אחות אמו ועל אחות אשתו ועל אשת אחיו ועל אשת אחי אביו ועל הנדה יש להם קנס אע"פ שהן בהכרת אין בהן מיתת בית דין: **גמ'** הני נערות פסולות אית להו קנס כשירות לא הכי קאמר אלו נערות פסולות שיש להם קנס הבא על הממזרת ועל הנתינה ועל הכותית: נערה אין קטנה לא מאן תנא אמר רב יהודה אמר רב רבי מאיר היא דתניא ג) קטנה מבת יום אחד ועד שתביא שתי שערות יש לה מכר ד) ואין לה קנס ומשתביא שתי שערות ועד שתיבגר יש לה קנס ואין לה מכר דברי רבי מאיר שהיה רבי מאיר אומר כל מקום שיש מכר אין קנס וכל מקום שיש קנס אין מכר ה) וחכמים אומרים קטנה מבת שלש שנים ויום אחד ועד שתיבגר ו) יש לה קנס קנס אין מכר לא אימא אף

אלו נערות. דוקא נערה משהביאה שתי שערות עד שתבגר והם ששה חדשים שבין נערות לבגרות אבל קטנה ובוגרת אין להם קנס: שיש להן קנס. אם אנסה אדם נותן לאביה חמשים כסף כדכתיב ונתן האיש השוכב וגו' (דברים כב): הבא על הממזרת. בגמרא פריך אבל כשירות לא ומשני פסולות איצטריכא ליה לאשמועינן: נתינה. מן הגבעונים והיא אסורה לקהל לדוד גזר עליהם כדאמרינן ביבמות (ד' עט.) ועל שם ויתנם יהושע חוטבי עצים ושואבי מים וגו' (יהושע ט) קרי להו נתינים: כותית. קסבר גירי אריות הן וישנן בלאו לא תתחתן בם (דברים ז): ועל השבויה. ישראלית שנפדית פחותה מבת שלש שנים דבחזקת בתולה היא שאפי' נבעלה בשביה בתולה חוזרים: ועל אשת אחיו. שנתקדשה לו לאחיו וגירשה שאין בה מיתה אלא כרת: ועל אשת אחי אביו. שנתקדשה לו וגירשה: אע"פ שהן בהכרת הרי אין בהם מיתת ב"ד. וכרת לא פטר ליה מן התשלומין כדמיימי בריימא לקמיה: גמ' ר"מ היא. כדמייתי לקמיה: יש לה מכר. יש לאביה בה זכייה למוכרה לשפחות: ואין לה קנס. שהבא עליה אינו חייב קנס: ואין לה מכר. כדתניא (ערכין דף כט.) יכול ימכור אדם את בתו כשהיא נערה אמרת ק"ו מכורה כבר יוצאה עכשיו שאינה מכורה אינו דין שלא תמכר: מבת ג' שנים ויום אחד. שהיא ראויה לביאה: מכר לא. בתמיה: אף

אלו נערות. הבא על הנתינה. פי' בקונטרס לדוד גזר עליהם שלא לבא בקהל והיינו משום עבדות כדאמרינן בהערל (יבמות עח. ושם) ואין נראה לר"ת דהא משמע בגמרא (ע"ב) דנתינה הויא דאורייתא דקאמר ממזרת ונתינה איכא בינייהו למ"ד דאיתא לקיימה כו' משמע דהויא דאורייתא דהא בקרא פליגי ובריש יש מותרות (שם דף פה:) אמרינן ממזרת ונתינה איכא בינייהו מ"ד דאורייתא הא נמי דאורייתא ועוד דתנן (מכות דף יג.) אלו הן הלוקין ממזרת ונתינה לישראל משמע דלקי עלה מדאורייתא דומיא דכל הנך דחשיב התם ומיהו איכא למימר דבכל הנהו נקט נתינה אגב ממזרת וכן לריך לומר ע"כ לרבא למאי דס"ד בהערל (יבמות דף עו. ושם) דבגירותן לית להו איסור חתנות ומ"מ אין נראה לר"ת פירושו דהא מסיק רבא בהערל (ג"ז שם) דבגירותן אית להו איסור חתנות וכל היכא דחשיב נתינה בהדי ממזרת איירי בגירות כמו הכא דבנכריותה לית לה קנס כדאמרינן לעיל בפ"ק (דף יא. ושם) יהבינן לה קנס ואזלה ואכלה בנכריותה וכן בקדושין בפרק האומר (דף סו:) תנן כל מקום שיש קדושין ויש עבירה כגון ממזרת ונתינה כו' ועוד לפירוש הקונטרס כיון דעבדות ממש גזר עליהו שמתוך כך נאסרו לבוא בקהל משום לא יהיה קדש א"כ אמאי יש לה קנס הא תנן בהדיא במתניתין דשפחה אין לה קנס ואי משום דנתינה

מנטרא נפשה הא אמרינן בירושלמי דשפחה אפילו משומרת אין לה קנס ועוד דתנן בפרק עשרה יוחסין (שם דף סט.) דחרורי ונתיני מותרים לבא זה בזה ואמאי והא חרורי אסירי בשפחה כדתנן (גיטין דף מא.) לישא שפחה אינו יכול ומיהו הא י"ל דלאו ממש גזר עליהו עבדות לאסור בלא יהיה קדש ונראה לר"ת דנתינה אסורה דאורייתא משום לא תתחתן כדמסיק רבא בהערל (יבמות דף עו. ושם) ודוד לא גזר עליהו אלא שיעבוד ולאו לאוסרן בבנות ישראל דהא אסירי וקיימי מלאו דלא תתחתן אלא כדי שלא יטמעו בישראל והא דגזר בהו טפי מבשאר פסולי קהל משום דהוו אומה שלימה והא דקאמר התם ז) כל מי שיש בו שלשה סימנים הללו ראוי לידבק בהן לא לישא מהן אלא להיות בן חורין כמותן וכן הא דקאמר התם ח) בימי רבי בקשו להתיר נתינים א"ר אם חלקנו נתיר חלק מזבח מי יתיר לא שהיו רוצים להתירם לבא בקהל דהא מדאורייתא אסירי אלא בקשו לפטרן מעבדות להיות בני חורין ואמר להו רבי דאין יכולין להפקיע חלק מזבח ואע"ג דקיימא לן ט) דהפקר ב"ד היה הפקר היינו לצורך אבל זה אינו צורך כל כך ומיהו בירושלמי משמע כפי' הקונט' בפ' עשרה יוחסין דקאמר התם נתינים יהושע ריחקם כלום ריחקם אלא משום פסול משפחה דא"ת משום פסול עבדות אלא מעתה הבא על הנתינה לא יהיה לה קנס משמע משום דיהושע גזר עליהם נפסלו מלבא בקהל וגזרת יהושע ודוד הכל גזירה אחת היא כדמוכח בהערל (שם דף עט.) ומיהו בירושלמי איכא למימר דסבר כמו שהיה ס"ד דרבא מעיקרא בהערל דבגירותן לית להו איסור חתנות ועוד י"ל דריחקן היינו שלא יטמעו בהן והא דאמרינן בהאומר בקדושין (דף סח: ושם) נכרית מנא לן דלא תפסי בה קדושין דכתיב לא תתחתן בם אומר ר"ת דאסיפיה דקרא סמיך ובתו לא תקח לבנך אבל רישיה דקרא מיירי בגירות וכענין זה מלינו בהערל (יבמות דף עט.) דפריך גבי בני שאול והכתיב לא יומתו אבות על בנים וע"כ לא פריך אלא מסיפא דקרא איש בחטאו יומתו דרישא דקרא מוקמינן ליה לפסול קרובים לעדות בפרק החובל (ב"ק דף פח.) ובפרק זה בורר (סנהדרין דף כז:) ט): **ועל** הכותית. פירש בקונטרס דקסבר כותים גירי אריות הן וישנן בלאו דלא תתחתן וזהו לפי שיטתו כדסלקא דעתין מעיקרא בהערל (יבמות דף עו. ושם) דבנכרותן אית להו איסור חתנות ומה שפי' דקסבר כותים גירי אריות הן ל"נ לרבינו יצחק בן רבינו מאיר דא"כ עובדת כוכבים היא ועובדת כוכבים אין לה קנס כדפריך בפ"ק (לעיל יא.) יהבינן לה קנס ואזלה ואכלה בנכריותה ועוד דבגמרא מוקי מתני' כר"מ ור"מ אית ליה דגירי אמת הן ואע"ג דכולה מתניתין לא אתיא כר"מ דהא בתו אמר בגמרא דלא אתיא כוותיה מ"מ בהא דסבר דגירי אמת הן אתיא כוותיה דהא בשור שנגח ד' וה' (ב"ק דף לח: ושם) מסקינן דשור ישראל שנגח שור של כותי פטור משום דקנס הוא דקניס רבי מאיר בממונם אע"ג דמן הדין חייב דגירי אמת הם ופריך ממתני' דהכא דכותית יש לה קנס ואי ס"ד דקנס הוא שקנס ר"מ בממונם ה"נ לקנוס כו' אלמא דמתניתין דהכא סברה דגירי אמת הן וא"ת אם כן מאי קמ"ל פשיטא דיש לה קנס דישראלית גמורה היא וי"ל דס"ד דלא יהבינן לה קנס שלא יטמעו בהן א) וא"ת למ"ד בפרק עשרה יוחסין (קדושין דף עו.) דפסול כותים משום דעבד ושפחה נטמעו בהן אמאי יש לה קנס נימא לה אייתי ראיה דלאו שפחה את ושקילי לשמואל דאמר (ב"ק דף מו:) אין הולכין בממון אחר הרוב ואפילו לרב אי דאזיל איהו גבה ה"ל קבוע וכל קבוע כמחצה על מחצה דמי ויש לומר דכל אחת מוקמינן לה אחזקת אבהתא שהיו כותים אע"ג דלענין פסול לא מוקמינן להו שלא יהא חוטא נשכר ב) י) ואם תאמר ואמאי לא חשיב נמי אלמנה לכ"ג גרושה וחלוצה לכהן הדיוט וי"ל דבפסול כהונה לא קמיירי והא דלא תני מצרי ואדומי משום שיש להם היתר [א"כ לא חשיב אלא חייבי לאוין] אבל קשה דליתני מחזיר גרושתו משניסת ונבעלה שלא כדרכה ואע"ג דאמרי' בפ' עשרה יוחסין (קדושין עח.) הכל מודים שאם בעל ולא קידש שאינו לוקה מ"מ לר"ע דאמר אין קדושין תופסין במחזיר גרושתו ליתני ועוד הוה מצי למיתני יבמה לשוק [ועבד הבא על הכותית הולד ממזר ויש לה קנס. ת"י] וי"ל דתנא ושייר ואע"ג דבפ"ק דקדושין (דף טז:) דייק תנא תני אלו ואת אמרת תנא ושייר הכא דתני בסיפא ואלו שאין להם קנס לא שייך למידק הכי כדאשכחן בפרק המזבח מקדש (זבחים דף פד.) דקתני ואלו פסולן בקדש ואלו שאין פסולן בקדש ומשייר ברישא ובסיפא כ) ועי"ל דהכא לא חשיב אלא פסולי קהל: **והבא** על הגיורת. חילקן לשנות חייבי לאוין לחודייהו וגיורת ומשוחררת דכשירות הן לחודייהו וחייבי כריתות לחודייהו משום דבעי למיתני סיפא אע"פ שהם בהכרת כו' אבל באלו הן הלוקין (מכות יג.) לא תני אלא הבא אחד על כולם: **ועל** אשת אחיו. פר"ח דפריך בירושלמי אשת אחיו ולא יבמה היא לו וזקוקה לו ומה קנס וכרת שייך בה ומשני בשיש לו בנים מאשה אחרת ואיירי במת מן האירוסין והוא הדין דהוה מצי לאוקמה כשגירשה וקשה לר"י ב"ר אברהם לרב פפא דמוקי הך מתניתין במפותה בפרק בן סורר (סנהדרין דף עג. ושם) תקשי דהיכי מצי לאוקומי הכי הא נתארסה ונתגרשה קנסה לעצמה (לקמן דף לח.) וכיון דלעצמה מפותה אין לה קנס כדאמרינן בגמרא (לקמן מ.) ובריש נערה משום דמדעתה עבדה וכ"ת דקסבר תנא דמתניתין כר"ע דברייתא דקנסה לאביה הוי אם כן אכתי ג) תיקשי ליה סיפא דקתני (שם לו:) הבא על בתו פטור משום דקם ליה בדרבה מיניה תיפוק ליה דקנסה לאביה הוי דאי לעצמה תיקשי ליה דמחלה וממה נפשך תקשי סיפא ומיהו בירושלמי מוקי לה כשבא עליה עד שלא מת ומת והוא הדין עד שלא בגרה ובגרה ולמאי דאמר בירושלמי דמפותה אינו פטור אלא מבושת ופגם אבל קנס אינה יכולה למחול אתי שפיר ומיהו בש"ס דידן משמע דאין לה אפי' קנס דמוקי הא דאלו הן הלוקין לקמן בגמ' (דף לב.) ביתומה ומפותה שאין לה קנס: **נערה** אין קטנה לא. תימה מנא ליה דלמא לא אתי למעוטי אלא בוגרת דהא משמע ד) בס"פ ארבע מיתות (סנהדרין דף סו:) גבי הא דתנן אינו חייב אלא עד שתהא נערה בתולה מאורסה דאי הוה תני אלא על נערה בתולה כו' הוה מוקמינן לה אפילו כרבנן ולא הוה אתי למעוטי קטנה אלא בוגרת ותירץ ריצב"א ה) דאסיפא דמתניתין סמיך דתנן (לקמן דף מ:) כל מקום שיש מכר אין קנס:

גליון הש"ס

תוס' ד"ה נערה וכו' דאסיפא דמתני' סמיך. עי' נדה מד ע"ב תוס' ד"ה שלשים יום:

תוספות רי"ד

אלו נערות שיש להן קנס. פי' אנסה אדם נותן לאביה נ' כסף כדכתיב ונתן האיש וגו'. הבא על הממזרת ועל הנתינה ועל הכותית על הגיורת ועל השבויה. פי' ישראלית שנשבית. ועל השפחה. שנפדו ושנתגיירו ושנשתחררו פחותות מבנות ג"ש ויום אחד. הבא על אחותו ועל אחות אביו ועל אחות אמו ועל אחות אשתו ועל אשת אחיו ועל אשת אחי אביו ועל הנדה יש להן קנס. אע"פ שהן בכרת אין בהן מיתת ב"ד. פי' דוקא נערה ולא בוגרת וקטנה. שהבוגרת כלו בתוליה ואין להם קנס. וקטנה הויא כעין א) שמדמעת וחוזרת ומדמעת. ונערה היא מבת י"ב שנים ויום אחד אם הביאה ב' שערות וממתנת ששה חדשים אחר שהביאה ב' שערות והיא בוגרת שאין בין נערות לבוגרת אלא ו' חדשים בלבד. נתינה היא מן הגבעונים ע"ש ויתנם יהושע חוטבי עצים ושואבי מים. ומשום צד עבדות הן אסורות. והכותיות קסבר גירי אמת הן ומ"ה יש להן קנס. שאילו היו גירי אריות הויא לה עובדת כוכבים. ואין קנס לעובדת כוכבים אלא שהכותים פסולים כדתנן בעשרה יוחסין אלו הן הספיקות שתוקי ואסופי וכותי. והתם מפרש טעמא למה הן הכותים פסולין: ועל אשת אחיו. כגון שקידש את הבתולה וגירשה. א"נ שמת ויש לו בן מאשה אחרת דקיימי עליה בכרת אע"פ שהן בהכרת אין הכרת פוטרו מן התשלומין אלא מיתת ב"ד: נערה אין קטנה לא. דהיינו קודם שתביא ב' שערות. מאן תנא אר"י א"ר ר"מ הוא דתניא קטנה ב) מבת ג' שנים ויום אחד. פירוש שמזמן זה היא ראויה לביאה ועד שתביא ב' שערות יש לה מכר ואין לה קנס. ומשתביא ב' שערות ועד שתבגר יש לה קנס ואין לה מכר דברי ר"מ שהיה ר"מ אומר כ"מ שיש מכר אין קנס וכל מקום שיש קנס אין מכר. וחכ"א קטנה מבת ג' שנים ויום אחד עד שתבגר יש לה מכר ויש

חשק שלמה על תוס' רי"ד

א) דברי רבינו אינו מובן דהך סברא דאמרינן כנדה לענין קטנה פחותה מבת שלש דבתוליה חוזרין אבל מתני' הא ס"ל דאין קנס בקטנה כלל רק נערה ול"ע. ב) לפנינו בגמ' הגירסא כדברי ר"מ מבת יום אחד וגירסת רבינו ל"ע.

תוספות ישנים

א) א"נ היא גופא קמ"ל דגירי אמת הן. מ"י: ב) ועבד הבא על הכותית הולד ממזר ויש לה קנס. מ"י: ג) אבל ליכא לאוקמי הכא על בתו כשנתארסה לחופה ולא נבעלה וגירשה דא"כ בלאו הכי אין לה קנס כיון דמפותה דמחלה וא"ל דמיפלג על בתו לא איירי אלא באנוסה א"כ בתנא נקט בה לא על בתו לא תרבינן חייבי כריתות נמי אין לה קנס כיון דינתנה להלוה בנפשה דמשום הכי מוקי לה התם במפותה: ד) דפריך עד שתהא נערה אינו חייב אלא על נערה מבעי ליה. מ"י:

ליקוטי רש"י

שיש להן קנס. נ' כסף אם יאנסו. הבא על הממזרת. ואע"ג דלא קרינן ביה ולו תהיה לאשה שהרי אינה ראויה לקיימה אפילו הכי יש לה קנס [לעיל יא.]. ועל הנתינה. נתינים, גבעונים שנתגיירו בערמה בימי יהושע ונתנם עבדים לחוטבי עצים ושואבי מים [יבמות עח:]. הבא על אחותו. כלומר אפילו בא על אחותו דלא קרינא בה ולו תהיה לאשה אפילו הכי קרינא ביה ונתן האיש השוכב עמה לאבי הנערה חמשים כסף. ואע"ג דחייב כרת לא מפטר מתשלומין [סנהדרין עג.]. כל מקום שיש מכר. כלומר בזמן שהבת קטנה ולאביה זכאי למוכרה. אין קנס. אם נאנסה או נתפתתה אין לאביה חמשים כסף דנערה כתיב (דברים כב) ונתן האיש השוכב עמה לאבי הנערה חמשים כסף. וכל מקום שיש קנס. דהיינו כשהיא נערה. אין מכר. דתניא בערכין (דף כט.) יכול ימכור אדם בתו כשהיא נערה אמרת ק"ו ומה מכורה כבר יוצאה עכשיו בסימני נערות שאינה מכורה אינו דין שלא תמכר. וחכמים וכו' יש לה קנס. לקטנה ונערה. מפרש בכתובות (דף מ.) כל מקום שנאמר נער נער בלא ה"א אפילו קטנה במשמע. מכר לא. בתמיה. והלא קטנה היא עד שתביא שתי שערות [חולין כו:].

מסורת הש"ס

א) לעיל יא. ב"ק לח., ב) סנהדרין דף עג:, ג) [תוספתא פ"ג ע"ש] לקמן מ: חולין כו:, ד) [לקמן לו.], ה) [לקמן לו.], ו) [דף עט.], ז) שם:, ח) [שם פט:], ט) [ועי' תוס' יבמות עט. ד"ה ונתינים ותוס' ע"ז לו: ד"ה דכתיב], י) [ועי' תוס' ב"ק לח. ד"ה ועל הכותית], כ) [עי' תוס' יבמות פד: ד"ה אלא ותוס' זבחים פד. ד"ה הכא ותוס' שבועות לג. ד"ה ואלו נאמרין ותוס' שם מד: ד"ה כל הנשבעין ותוס' שבת עה: ד"ה חסר אחת].

עין משפט נר מצוה

א א מיי' פ"א מהל' נערה הלכה י סמג עשין נד טור אה"ע סי' קעז:

ב ב מיי' פ"ד מהל' עבדים הלכה א סמג עשין פה:

ג ג מיי' פ"א מהלכות נערה הלכה ח סמג עשין נד טוש"ע אה"ע סי' קעז סעיף א בהג"ה:

the age of three years and one day, he must pay the fine.[9]

The third group:

הַבָּא עַל אֲחוֹתוֹ – **If one violates his sister**[10] וְעַל אֲחוֹת אָבִיו – **or his father's sister** וְעַל אֲחוֹת אִמּוֹ – **or his mother's sister**[11] וְעַל אֲחוֹת אִשְׁתּוֹ – **or his wife's sister**[12] וְעַל אֵשֶׁת אָחִיו – **or his brother's wife**[13] וְעַל אֵשֶׁת אֲחִי אָבִיו – **or his father's brother's wife**[14] וְעַל הַנִּדָּה – **or a *niddah*,**[15] יֵשׁ לָהֶם קְנָס – **they are entitled to a fine.** אַף עַל פִּי שֶׁהֵן בְּהִכָּרֵת אֵין בָּהֶן מִיתַת בֵּית דִּין – **For even though they are** girls for whom the violator is **subject to *kares*, they are not** girls for whom he is **subject to court-imposed execution.**[16]

Gemara The Gemara asks: הָנֵי נְעָרוֹת פְּסוּלוֹת אִית לְהוּ קְנָס – Can the Mishnah really be saying that only **these unfit *ne'aros* are entitled to a fine,** כְּשֵׁירוֹת לֹא – but **those** *ne'aros* **who are fit** are **not?**[17]

The Gemara answers:

הָכִי קָאָמַר – **This** is what [**the Tanna**] **is saying:** אֵלּוּ נְעָרוֹת פְּסוּלוֹת שֶׁיֵּשׁ לָהֶם קְנָס – **These are the unfit *ne'aros* who are entitled to a fine:** הַבָּא עַל הַמַּמְזֶרֶת וְעַל הַנְּתִינָה וְעַל הַכּוּתִית – **If one violates a *mamzeress*, or a *nesinah* or a Cuthean,** etc.[18]

The Gemara draws an inference from the Mishnah:

נַעֲרָה אִין – The Mishnah states that a ***naarah*** – **yes,** she is entitled to the fine; קְטַנָּה לֹא – but **a minor** – **no,** she is not entitled to it. מַאן תַּנָּא – **Who is** then **the Tanna** of our Mishnah?[19] אָמַר רַב יְהוּדָה אָמַר רַב – **Rav Yehudah said in the name of Rav:** רַבִּי מֵאִיר הִיא – **It is** a Mishnah authored by **R' Meir.** דְּתַנְיָא – **For it was taught in a Baraisa:** קְטַנָּה מִבַּת יוֹם אֶחָד וְעַד שֶׁתָּבִיא שְׁתֵּי שְׂעָרוֹת – A MINOR GIRL, FROM the time she is ONE DAY OLD UNTIL SHE GROWS TWO pubic HAIRS,[20] יֵשׁ לָהּ מֶכֶר – IS SUBJECT TO SALE,[21] וְאֵין לָהּ קְנָס – BUT IS NOT ENTITLED TO A FINE if she is violated or seduced.[22] וּמִשֶּׁתָּבִיא שְׁתֵּי שְׂעָרוֹת וְעַד שֶׁתִּיבָּגֵר – AND FROM WHEN SHE GROWS TWO pubic HAIRS UNTIL SHE BECOMES A *BOGERESS* and attains full adulthood,[23] יֵשׁ לָהּ

NOTES

9. Gentile girls and Canaanite slave girls are generally assumed not to be virgins because they tend to be promiscuous. Similarly, there is a strong probability that heathen captors violate their women captives. Hence, when a gentile girl converts to Judaism, or a Canaanite slave girl is emancipated (thereby becoming a full-fledged Jewess), or a captured Jewish girl is freed, she is assumed to be a non-virgin and would thus not be awarded any fine if violated. [As mentioned above (note 2), the Torah imposes the *oneiss* fine specifically for a virgin *naarah.*] A girl's cohabitation prior to the age of three, however, does not remove her virgin status, since her hymen will regenerate. Accordingly, our Mishnah states that if the conversion, emancipation or freeing of the captive took place before the girl turned three, she *is* considered to be a virgin, and is awarded the *oneiss* fine if violated (see *Rashi*).

10. The Mishnah now lists virgin *ne'aros* forbidden to the *oneiss* on pain of *kares,* but not on pain of execution.

One who cohabits with his sister incurs *kares,* as stated in *Leviticus* 20:17.

11. These, too, are forbidden to a man on pain of *kares*. The prohibition is stated in *Leviticus* 18:12,13, and the *kares* penalty in verse 29 ibid.

12. I.e. while his wife is still alive (even if he has divorced her). The prohibition for this is stated in *Leviticus* 18:18, and the *kares* penalty in verse 29 ibid. [After one's wife has died, however, he is permitted to marry her sister (see *Yevamos* 49a).]

13. I.e. where the brother betrothed her with *erusin* and then divorced her without consummating the marriage (see *Rashi*). A brother's wife (even if she is subsequently divorced or widowed) is forbidden on pain of *kares* (see *Leviticus* 18:16 and 29), except where the law of *yibum* applies [which requires the brother of one who has died without child to marry the widow of the deceased – see *Deuteronomy* 25:5].

[The Mishnah cannot mean that the violator's brother had consummated the marriage, for she would then no longer be a virgin, and the fine would not be applicable. Nor could it mean that she was still married to the brother, for she would then be a married woman, whose violation is punishable by execution (in which case the fine is not applicable, as stated below, 36b). Neither does *Rashi* say that the husband had *died* before consummating the marriage, for he would then have died childless, making his wife bound to the *oneiss* for *yibum,* in which case there is certainly no penalty (*Shitah Mekubetzes*). Actually, though, the Mishnah could refer to where the husband died, but was survived by a child from a different woman. In that case, *yibum* would not apply; the young widow would still be a virgin entitled to the fine, and would be forbidden to the *oneiss* on pain of *kares* (see *Tosafos,* citing *Rabbeinu Chananel* and *Yerushalmi*).]

14. I.e. where the father's brother betrothed her with *erusin* and then divorced her without consummating the marriage (*Rashi*). One's father's brother's wife (even if she is subsequently divorced or widowed) is forbidden on pain of *kares* (see *Leviticus* 18:14 and 29).

[Actually, in this case *Rashi* could have said that the father's brother had *died* (for one does not perform *yibum* to his uncle's wife). Nevertheless, *Rashi* keeps his explanation of this case parallel to the preceding case, where it is indeed simpler to explain that she was divorced (as seen there).]

15. I.e. a woman who has menstruated but not immersed herself in the *mikveh* after waiting the requisite number of days. Cohabitation with her is forbidden on pain of *kares* (see *Leviticus* 18:19 and 29; ibid. 20:18).

16. The Mishnah below (36b) teaches that one who commits a capital offense is exempt from minor penalties [such as the fifty-*shekel* fine for violation] incurred simultaneously. Hence, one might have thought that the same applies where one commits a *kares*-bearing offense [such as violating a girl forbidden to him on pain of *kares*] and he would be exempt from the fifty-*shekel* fine. The Mishnah, therefore, teaches that the rule that "one incurs only the greater penalty" applies only where the greater penalty is a court-imposed [death] penalty, not where it is merely the *kares* penalty. Hence, although the *oneiss* is subject to *kares,* he is nevertheless liable to the fine (see *Rashi*).

17. The Mishnah's statement: *These are the ne'aros who are entitled to a fine* . . . followed by its subsequent listing only of *ne'aros* who are somehow unfit seems to indicate that a *naarah* who is completely fit is *not* entitled to the fine (see *Ritva*). But this is surely not the case!

[The term פסולות generally refers to those who are *disqualified.* Now, while the bulk of the *ne'aros* listed in the Mishnah are indeed disqualified from marriage to the *oneiss,* the Mishnah's list also includes girls who were captured and redeemed prior to the age of three, who are not disqualified from marriage even for a Kohen. Hence, we must say that the Gemara uses the term פסולות here to denote that the *ne'aros* are *unfit* or *tainted* – either because they are forbidden in marriage to the *oneiss,* or because they have engaged in prior sexual activity, albeit prior to the age of three (see *Ramban;* see also *Rashba, Ritva* et al.).]

18. I.e. the Mishnah's opening statement means: These are the *ne'aros* who are entitled to a fine even though there is reason to think that they are *not* entitled to it (see *Rashi* to the Mishnah ד״ה הבא על הממזרת). But there was no reason for the Tanna to say anything about perfectly fit *ne'aros,* for it is obvious that the Torah's imposition of a fine applies in their case.

19. The Torah (*Deuteronomy* 22:28-29) states: *If a man finds a virgin "naarah" . . . and seizes her and lies with her and they are discovered, then the man who lay with her shall give the father of the naarah fifty silver [coins]* . . . Who is the Tanna of our Mishnah who maintains that the Torah's specification of *"naarah"* excludes not only a *bogeress* (a full adult) but a minor as well?

20. See above, note 1.

21. The Torah (*Exodus* 21:7) grants a father the right to sell his minor daughter as a maidservant (*Rashi*). She serves for six years unless she is redeemed earlier, is married by her master or his son, her master dies, the *Yovel* year intervenes, or she becomes a *naarah.*

22. Since she is not yet a *naarah.*

23. This is the period during which she is a *naarah;* see above, note 1.

אלו ‎נערות שיש להן קנס הבא על הממזרת ועל הנתינה ועל הכותית הבא על הגיורת ועל השבויה ועל השפחה שנפדו ושנתגיירו ושנשתחררו פחותות מבנות שלש שנים ויום אחד הבא על אחותו ועל אחות אביו ועל אחות אמו ועל אחות אשתו ועל אשת אחיו ועל אשת אחי אביו ועל הנדה יש להם קנס אע"פ שהן בהכרת אין בהן מיתת בית דין: **גמ'** הני נערות פסולות אית להו קנס כשירות לא הכי קאמר אלו נערות פסולות שיש להם קנס הבא על הממזרת ועל הנתינה ועל הכותית: נערה אין קטנה לא מאן תנא אמר רב יהודה אמר רב רבי מאיר היא דתניא קטנה מבת יום אחד ועד שתביא שתי שערות יש לה מכר ואין לה קנס ומשתביא שתי שערות ועד שתיבגר יש לה קנס ואין לה מכר דברי רבי מאיר שהיה רבי מאיר אומר כל מקום שיש מכר אין קנס וכל מקום שיש קנס אין מכר וחכמים אומרים קטנה מבת שלש שנים ויום אחד ועד שתיבגר יש לה קנס קנס אין מכר לא אימא אף

רש"י

אלו נערות. דוקא נערה משתביאה שתי שערות עד שתבגר והם ששה חדשים שבין נערות לבגרות אבל קטנה ובוגרת אין להם קנס: שיש להן קנס. אם אנסה אדם נותן לאביה חמשים כסף כדכתיב ונתן האיש השוכב וגו' (דברים כב): הבא על הממזרת. בגמרא פריך אבל כשירות לא ומשני פסולות איצטריכא ליה לאשמועינן: נתינה. מן הגבעונים והיא אסורה לקהל דדוד גזר עליהם כדאמרינן ביבמות (דף עח:) ועל שם ויתנם יהושע חוטבי עצים ושואבי מים וגו' (יהושע ט) קרי להו נתינים: כותית. קסבר גירי אריות הן וישנן בלאו לא תתחתן בם (דברים ז): ועל השבויה. ישראלית שנפדית פחותה מבת שלש שנים דבחזקת בתולה היא שאפי' נבעלה בשביה בתולה חוזרים: ועל אשת אחיו. שנתקדשה לו לאחיו וגירשה שאין בה מיתה אלא כרת: ועל אשת אחי אביו. שנתקדשה לו וגירשה: אע"פ שהן בהכרת הרי אין בהם מיתת ב"ד. וכרת לא פטר ליה מן התשלומין: גמ' ר"מ היא. כדמייתי ברייתא לקמיה: יש לה מכר. יש לאביה בה זכייה למכרה לשפחות: ואין לה קנס. שהבא עליה אינו חייב קנס: ואין לה מכר. כדתניא (ערכין דף כט:) יכול ימכור אדם את בתו כשהיא נערה אמרת ק"ו מכורה כבר יוצאה עכשיו שאינה מכורה אינו דין שלא תמכר: מבת ג' שנים ויום אחד. שהיא ראויה לביאה: מכר לא. בתמיה: אף

תוספות

אלו נערות. הבא על הנתינה. פי' בקונטרס דדוד גזר עליהם שלא לבא בקהל והיינו משום עבודות כדאמרינן בהערל (יבמות עח. ושם) ולאו נראה לר"ת דהא משמע בגמרא (ע"ב) דנתינה הויא דאורייתא דקאמר ממזרת ונתינה איכא בינייהו למ"ד לאוי לקיימה כו' משמע דהויא דאורייתא דהא בקרא פליגי וכריש יש מותרות (שם דף פה: ושם) אמרינן ממזרת ונתינה איכא בינייהו מ"ד דאורייתא הא נמי דאורייתא ועוד דתנן (מכות דף יג.) אלו הן הלוקין ממזרת ונתינה לישראל משמע דלקי עלה מדאורייתא דומיא דכל הנך דחשיב התם ומיהו איכא למימר דכל הנהו נקט נתינה אגב ממזרת וכן צריך לומר ע"כ לרבא למאי דס"ד בהערל (יבמות דף עו. ושם) דבגירותן לית להו איסור חתנות ומ"מ אין נראה לר"ת פירושו דהא מסיק רבא בהערל (ג"ז שם) דבגירותן אית להו איסור חתנות וכל היכא דחשיב נתינה בהדי ממזרת איירי בגירות כמו הכא דבנכריותה לית לה קנס כדאמרינן לעיל בפ"ק (דף יא. ושם) יהבינן לה קנס ואזלה ואכלה בנכריותה וכן בקדושין בפרק האומר (דף סו:) תנן כל מקום שיש קדושין ויש עבירה כגון ממזרת ונתינה כו' ועוד לפירוש הקונטרס כיון דעבדות ממש גזר עליהו שמתוך כך נאסרו לבוא בקהל משום לא יהיה קדש א"כ אמאי יש לה קנס הא תנן בהדיא במתניתין דשפחה אין לה קנס ואי משום דנתינה מנטרא נפשה הא אמרינן בירושלמי דשפחה אפילו משומרת אין לה קנס ועוד דתנן בפרק עשרה יוחסין (שם דף סט.) דחרורי ונתיני מותרים לבא זה בזה ואמאי והא חרורי אסירי בשפחה כדתנן (גיטין דף מא.) לישא שפחה אינו יכול ומיהו הא י"ל דלאו ממש גזר עלייהו עבדות לאסור בלא יהיה קדש ונראה לר"ת דנתינה אסורה דאורייתא משום לא תתחתן כדמסיק רבא בהערל (יבמות דף עו. ושם) ודוד לא גזר עלייהו אלא שיעבוד ולאו לאוסרן בבנות ישראל דהא אסירי וקיימי מלאו דלא תתחתן אלא כדי שלא יטמעו בישראל והא דגזר בהו טפי מבשאר פסולי קהל משום דהוו אומה שלימה והא דקאמר התם ט) כל מי שיש בו שלשה סימנים הללו ראוי לידבק בהן לא לישא מהן אלא להיות בן חורין כמותן וכן הא דקאמר התם י) בימי רבי בקשו להתיר נתינים א"ר אם חלקנו נתיר חלק מזבח מי יתיר לא שהיו רוצים להתירם לבא בקהל דהא מדאורייתא אסירי אלא בקשו לפטרן מעבדות להיות בני חורין ואמר להו רבי דאין יכולין להפקיע חלק מזבח ואע"ג דקיימא לן כ) דהפקר ב"ד היה הפקר היינו לצורך אבל זה אינו צורך כל כך ומיהו בירושלמי משמע כפי' הקונט' בפ' עשרה יוחסין דקאמר התם נתינים יהושע ריחקם כלום ריחקם אלא משום פסול משפחה דא"ת משום פסול עבדות אלא מעתה הבא על הנתינה לא יהיה לה קנס משמע משום דיהושע גזר עליהם נפסלו מלבא בקהל וגזרת יהושע ודוד הכל גזירה אחת היא כדמוכח בהערל (שם דף עט.) ומיהו בירושלמי איכא למימר דסבר כמו שהיה ס"ד דרבא מעיקרא בהערל דבגירותן לית להו איסור חתנות ועוד י"ל דריחקן היינו שלא יטמעו בהן והא דאמרינן בהאומר בקדושין (דף סח: ושם) נכרית מנא לן דלא תפסי בה קדושין דכתיב לא תתחתן בם אומר ר"ת דאסיפיה דקרא סמיך ובתו לא תקח לבנך אבל רישיה דקרא מיירי בגירות וכענין זה מצינו בהערל (יבמות דף עט.) דפריך גבי בני שאול והכתיב לא יומתו אבות על בנים וע"כ לא פריך אלא מסיפא דקרא איש בחטאו יומתו דרישא דקרא מוקמינן ליה לפסול קרובים לעדות בפרק החובל (ב"ק דף פח.) ובפרק זה בורר (סנהדרין דף כז:) ט): **ועל** הכותית. פירש בקונטרס דקסבר כותים גירי אריות הן וישנן בלאו דלא תתחתן והוו לפי שיטתו כדסלקא דעתין מעיקרא בהערל (יבמות דף עו. ושם) דבנכריותן אית להו איסור חתנות ומה שפי' דקסבר כותים גירי אריות הן ל"נ לרבינו יצחק בן רבינו מאיר דא"כ עובדת כוכבים היא ועובדת כוכבים אין לה קנס כדפריך בפ"ק (לעיל יא.) יהבינן לה קנס ואזלה ואכלה בנכריותה ועוד דבגמרא מוקי מתני' כר"מ ור"מ אית ליה דגירי אמת הן ואע"ג דכולה מתניתין לא אתיא כר"מ דהא בתו אמר בגמרא דלא אתיא כוותיה מ"מ בהא דסבר דגירי אמת הן אתיא כוותיה דהא בשור שנגח ד' וה' (ב"ק דף לח: ושם) מסקינן דשור ישראל שנגח שור של כותי פטור משום דקנס הוא דקניס רבי מאיר בממונם אע"ג דמן הדין חייב דגירי אמת הם ופריך ממתני' דהכא דכותית יש לה קנס ואי ס"ד דקנס הוא שקנס ר"מ בממונם ה"נ לקנוס כו' אלמא דמתניתין דהכא סברה דגירי אמת הן וא"ת אם כן מאי קמ"ל פשיטא דיש לה קנס דישראלית גמורה היא וי"ל דס"ד דלא יהבינן לה קנס שלא יטמעו בהן א) וא"ת למ"ד בפרק עשרה יוחסין (קדושין דף עו.) דפסול כותים משום דעבד ושפחה נטמעו בהן אמאי יש לה קנס נימא לה אייתי ראיה דלאו שפחה את ושקילי לשמואל דאמר (ב"ק דף מו:) אין הולכין בממון אחר הרוב ואפילו לרב אי דאזיל איהו גבה ה"ל קבוע וכל קבוע כמחצה על מחצה דמי ויש לומר דכל אחת מוקמינן לה אחזקת אבהתא שהיו כותים אע"ג דלענין פסול לא מוקמינן לה אחזקתה לענין קנס מוקמינן להו שלא יהא חוטא נשכר ב) י) ואם תאמר ואמאי לא חשיב נמי אלמנה לכ"ג גרושה וחלוצה לכהן הדיוט וי"ל דבפסול כהונה לא קמיירי והא דלא תני מצרי ואדומי משום שיש להם היתר [א"נ לא חשיב אלא חייבי לאוין] אבל קשה דליתני מחזיר גרושתו משניסת ונבעלה שלא כדרכה ואע"ג דאמרי' בפ' עשרה יוחסין (קדושין עח.) הכל מודים שאם בעל ולא קידש שאינו לוקה מ"מ לר"ע דאמר אין קדושין תופסין במחזיר גרושתו ליתני ועוד הוה מצי למיתני יבמה לשוק [ועבד הבא על הכותית הולד ממזר ויש לה קנס. ת"י] וי"ל דתנא ושייר ואע"ג דבפ"ק דקדושין (דף טז:) דייק תנא תני אלו ואת אמרת תנא ושייר הכא דתני בסיפא ואלו שאין להם קנס לא שייך למידק הכי כדאשכחן בפרק המזבח מקדש (זבחים דף פד.) דקתני ואלו פסולן בקדש ואלו שאין פסולן בקדש ומשייר ברישא ובסיפא כ) ועי"ל דהכא לא חשיב אלא פסולי קהל: **והבא** על הגיורת. חילקן לשנות חייבי לאוין לחודייהו וגיורת ומשוחררת דכשירות הן לחודייהו וחייבי כריתות לחודייהו משום דבעי למיתני סיפא אע"פ שהם בהכרת כו' אבל באלו הן הלוקין (מכות יג.) לא תני אלא הבא אחד על כולם: **ועל** אשת אחיו. פר"ח דפריך בירושלמי אשת אחיו ולא יבמה היא לו חקוקה לו ומה קנס וכרת שייך בה ומשני בשיש לו בנים מאשה אחרת ואיירי במת מן האירוסין והוא הדין דהוה מצי לאוקמה כשגירשה וקשה לר"י ב"ר אברהם לרב פפא דמוקי הך מתניתין במפותה בפרק בן סורר (סנהדרין דף עד. ושם) תקשי דהיכי מצי לאוקומי הכי הא נתארסה ונתגרשה קנסה לעצמה (לקמן דף לח.) וכיון דלעצמה מפותה אין לה קנס כדאמרינן בגמרא (לקמן מ.) ובריש נערה משום דמדעתה עבדה וכ"ת דקסבר תנא דמתניתין כר"ע דברייתא דקנסה לאביה הוי אם כן אכתי ג) תיקשי ליה סיפא דקתני (שם לו:) הבא על בתו פטור משום דקם ליה בדרבה מיניה תיפוק ליה דקנסה לאביה הוי דאי לעצמה תיקשי ליה דמחלה וממה נפשך תקשי סיפא ומיהו בירושלמי מוקי לה כשבא עליה עד שלא מת ומת והוא הדין עד שלא בגרה ובגרה ולמאי דאמר בירושלמי דמפותה אינו פטור אלא מבושת ופגם אבל קנס אינה יכולה למחול אתי שפיר ומיהו בש"ס דידן משמע דאין לה אפי' קנס דמוקי הא דאלו הן הלוקין לקמן בגמ' (דף לב.) ביתומה ומפותה שאין לה קנס: **נערה** אין קטנה לא. תימה מנא ליה דלמא לא אתי למעוטי אלא בוגרת דהא משמע ד) בפ"ס ארבע מיתות (סנהדרין דף סו:) גבי הא דתנן אינו חייב אלא עד שתהא נערה בתולה מאורסה דאי הוה תני אלא על נערה בתולה כו' הוה מוקמינן לה אפילו כרבנן ולא הוה אתי למעוטי קטנה אלא בוגרת ותירץ ריצב"א ה) דאסיפא דמתניתין סמיך דתנן (לקמן דף מ:) כל מקום שיש מכר אין קנס:

עין משפט נר מצוה

א א מיי' פ"א מהל' נערה הלכה י סמג עשין נד טוש"ע אה"ע סי' קעז:

ב ב מיי' פ"ד מהל' עבדים הלכה א סמג עשין פה:

ג ג מיי' פ"א מהלכות נערה הלכה ח סמג עשין נד טוש"ע אה"ע סי' קעז סעיף א בהג"ה:

גליון הש"ס

תוס' ד"ה נערה וכו' דאסיפא דמתני' סמיך. עי' נדה מד ע"ב תוס' ד"ה שלשים יום:

תוספות רי"ד

אלו נערות שיש להן קנס. פי' אנסה אדם נותן לאביה נ' כסף כדכתיב ונתן האיש וגו'. הבא על הממזרת ועל הנתינה ועל הכותית על הגיורת ועל השבויה. פי' ישראלית שנשבית. ועל השפחה. שנפדו ושנתגיירו ושנשתחררו פחותות מבנות ג"ש ויום אחד. הבא על אחותו ועל אחות אביו ועל אחות אמו ועל אחות אשתו ועל אשת אחיו ועל אשת אחי אביו ועל הנדה יש להן קנס. אע"פ שהן בכרת אין בהן מיתת ב"ד. **פי'** דוקא נערה ולא בוגרת וקטנה. שהבוגרת כלו בתוליה ואין להם קנס. וקטנה הויא כעין א) שמדמעת וחוזרת ומדמעת. ונערה היא מבת י"ב שנים ויום אחד אם הביאה ב' שערות וממתנת ששה חדשים אחר שהביאה ב' שערות והיא בוגרת שאין בין נערות לבוגרת אלא ו' חדשים בלבד. **נתינה** היא מן הגבעונים ע"ש ויתנם יהושע חוטבי עצים ושואבי מים. ומשום צד עבדות הן אסורות. והכותיות קסבר גירי אמת הן ומ"ה יש להן קנס. שאילו היו גירי אריות הויא לה עובדת כוכבים. ואין קנס לעובדת כוכבים אלא שהכותים פסולים כדתנן בעשרה יוחסין אלו הן הספיקות שתוקי ואסופי וכותי. והתם מפרש טעמא למה הן הכותים פסולין: **ועל** אשת אחיו. כגון שקידש את הבתולה וגירשה. א"נ שמת ויש לו בן מאשה אחרת דקיימי עליה בכרת אע"פ שהן בהכרת אין הכרת פוטרו מן התשלומין אלא מיתת ב"ד: **נערה** אין קטנה לא. דהיינו קודם שתביא ב' שערות. מאן תנא אר"י א"ר ר"מ הוא דתניא קטנה ב) מבת ג' שנים ויום אחד. פירוש שמזמן זה היא ראויה לביאה ועד שתביא ב' שערות יש לה מכר ואין לה קנס. ומשתביא ב' שערות ועד שתבגר יש לה קנס ואין לה מכר דברי ר"מ שהיה ר"מ אומר כ"מ שיש מכר אין קנס וכל מקום שיש קנס אין מכר. וחכ"א קטנה מבת ג' שנים ויום אחד עד שתבגר יש לה מכר ויש

חשק שלמה על תוס' רי"ד

א) דברי רבינו אינו מובן דהך סברא דאמרינן בנדה (מ"ה) לענין קטנה פחותה מבת ג' דבתולים חוזרין ... ס"ל דלאו קנס בקטנה רק בנערה וצ"ע. ב) לפנינו בגמ' הגירסא בדברי ר"מ מבת יום אחד וגירסת רבינו צ"ע.

מסורת הש"ס

א) לעיל יא. ב"ק לח., ב) סנהדרין דף עג., ג) [תוספתא פ"ג ע"ש] לקמן מ: חולין כו., ד) [לקמן לו.], ה) [לקמן לו.], ו) [דף עט.], ז) [שם סט.], ח) [שם סט.] [וע' תוס' יבמות עט. ד"ה ונתינים ותוס' ע"ז לו: ד"ה דכתיב], י) [וע' תוס' ב"ק לח. ד"ה ועל הכותית], כ) [ע' תוס' יבמות פד: ד"ה אלו ותוס' זבחים פד. ד"ה הלן ותוס' שבועות לג. ד"ה ואלו נאמרין ותוס' מד. ד"ה כל הנשבעין ותוס' שבת עה. ד"ה ספר אחד].

תוספות ישנים

א) א"נ היא גופה קמ"ל דגירי אמת הן. מ"י. ב) ועבד הבא על הכותית הולד ממזר ויש לה קנס. מ"י. ג) אבל איכא לאוקמי הכא על בתו אחר שנתקדשה לחופה ולא נבעלה וגירשה דא"כ בלאו הכי אין לה קנס כיון דמפותה דמחלה וי"ל דסיפא בא על בתו לא איירי במפותה א"כ באנוסה בא על כל דבר ומחייבי כריתות נמי אין קנס כיון דניתנה להצילה בנפשו דמשום הכי מוקי לה התם במפותה: ד) דפריך עד שתהא נערה אינו חייב אלא על נערה מבעי ליה. מ"י.

ליקוטי רש"י

שיש להן קנס. נ' כסף אם יאנסו. הבא על הממזרת. ואע"ג דלא קרינן ביה ולו תהיה לאשה שהרי אינה ראויה לקיימה אפילו הכי יש לה קנס [לעיל יא.]. ועל הנתינה. נתינים, גבעונים שנתגיירו בערמה בימי יהושע ונתנם לחוטבי עצים ושואבי מים [יבמות עח.]. הבא על אחותו. כלומר אפילו בא על אחותו דלאו קרינא בה ולו תהיה לאשה אפילו הכי קרינא ביה ונתן האיש השוכב עמה דאמרי מקראי בכתובות (דף כט.) [דמייר דכר לא מפטר מתשלומין [סנהדרין עג.]. כל מקום שיש מכר. יש לאביה מכר קטנה ואביה זכאי למוכרה. אין קנס. אם נאנסה או נתפתתה אין לאביה חמשים כסף דנערה כתיב. מכר לא. בתמיה. והלא קטנה היא עד שתביא שתי שערות [חולין כו.].

Chapter Three

Mishnah אֵלּוּ נְעָרוֹת שֶׁיֵּשׁ לָהֶן קְנָס – **These are the *ne'aros*[1] who are entitled to the fine** stipulated by the Torah for a woman who is violated.[2] The Mishnah proceeds to enumerate three groups.

The first group:

הַבָּא עַל הַמַּמְזֶרֶת – **If one violates[3] a *mamzeress*[4]** וְעַל הַנְּתִינָה – **or a *nesinah*[5]** וְעַל הַכּוּתִית – **or a Cuthean,[6]** he must pay the fine.[7]

The second group:

הַבָּא עַל הַגִּיּוֹרֶת וְעַל הַשְּׁבוּיָה וְעַל הַשִּׁפְחָה – **If one violates a convert or a captive[8] or a** Canaanite **slave girl,** שֶׁנִּפְדּוּ וְשֶׁנִּתְגַּיְּירוּ וְשֶׁנִּשְׁתַּחְרְרוּ פְּחוּתוֹת מִבְּנוֹת שָׁלֹשׁ שָׁנִים וְיוֹם אֶחָד – **who were ransomed, converted, or emancipated under**

NOTES

1. The three stages of legal development through which a girl passes are: קַטְנוּת, *katnus* (minority), נַעֲרוּת, *naarus* and בַּגְרוּת, *bagrus* (adulthood). After passing through the minority stage, she enters the state of *naarus*. *Naarus* is contingent on two factors – she must be twelve years (and one day) old and have sprouted at least two pubic hairs. This state (*naarus*) is of short duration. At the age of 12 ½ she achieves the final stage of adulthood, called *bagrus* (see *Rashi*). [A girl in the *naarus* state is called a *naarah* (plural: *ne'aros*). A girl in the *bagrus* state is called a *bogeress*.]

2. The reference is to the fifty-*shekel* fine that the Torah (*Deuteronomy* 22:28-29) imposes on a man who forcibly violates an unmarried *naarah* who is a virgin. [The rapist is called an אוֹנֵס, *oneiss*.] He pays this fine to the girl's father [in most cases; there are, however, some exceptions, in which the fine is given to the girl herself – see below, 38a and 40a] (*Rashi*). [The Torah also requires that the *oneiss* wed the girl he has violated (if she so desires).] These fifty *shekels* are punitive damages, and are in addition to the compensatory damages he is liable to as in any case of assault; see Mishnah, *Bava Kamma* 83b, and Mishnah below, 39a.

[As *Rashi* has explained, the Mishnah refers to the fine imposed in the case of a *naarah's* rape. Now, the Torah also states a fine in the case of one who seduces an unmarried virgin *naarah* (*Exodus* 22:15-16; see below, 29b). [The seducer is called a מְפַתֶּה, *mefateh*.] Our Mishnah, however, cannot be referring to the *mefateh's* fine. For our Mishnah mentions certain *ne'aros* whose fathers do not have legal rights to their daughters' punitive damages [e.g. the convert and the freed maid], in which case the damages are awarded to the *ne'aros* themselves. But in cases of seduction (in contrast to violation), the damages would *not* be awarded to the girl herself, since her ultimate consent to the seduction would constitute a waiver of her rights to payment. Thus, the punitive damages in our Mishnah must be referring to damages for violation rather than for seduction (see *Pnei Yehoshua*).]

[The Gemara will present a Tannaic dispute as to whether this fine applies in the case of a minor girl. All agree, however, that it does not apply in the case of a *bogeress*.] Our Mishnah's statement that *these are the "ne'aros" who are entitled to a fine* indicates that in the view of our Tanna, the fine is applicable *only* in the case of a *naarah,* but not in the case of a minor girl or a *bogeress* (*Rashi,* based on Gemara below; cf. *Tosafos* below ד"ה נערה).

3. Literally: cohabits with. [As explained in the previous note, the Mishnah is dealing with violation rather than with seduction.]

4. A *mamzeress* (fem. of *mamzer*) is the offspring of illicit relations that are punishable by *kares* (see *Yevamos* 49a). The Torah (*Deuteronomy* 23:3) prohibits a regular Israelite from cohabiting with a *mamzeress*. [The Mishnah proceeds to list only girls that are somehow unfit to marry. The Gemara will explain that this does not mean to exclude girls who are perfectly fit. Rather, it is specifically those who are unfit that the Mishnah had to list, in order to teach that *even* they are entitled to punitive damages from the *oneiss* (*Rashi;* see note 7).]

5. The *nesinim* (sing.: *nasin* [masc.]; *nesinah* [fem.]) are the Giveonites, a Canaanite people that lived in the land of Canaan at the time of Joshua's conquest. As related in *Joshua* 9:3-27, the Giveonites feared the Israelite conquerors, who had already destroyed Jericho and Ai (and who were bidden to destroy all the Canaanite peoples). The Giveonites therefore posed as travelers from a distant land and approached Joshua and the elders of Israel to establish a treaty with them. They succeeded in eliciting from Joshua a treaty guaranteeing their safety, backed by a solemn oath taken by the elders. The Giveonites subsequently circumcised themselves and converted to Judaism. Their ruse was soon discovered, but to avoid a public desecration of God's Name, the treaty was honored and the Giveonites spared. Scripture (ibid. verse 27) states, however, that: וַיִּתְּנֵם יְהוֹשֻׁעַ בַּיּוֹם הַהוּא חֹטְבֵי עֵצִים וְשֹׁאֲבֵי מַיִם, *And Joshua "assigned" them on that day to be woodcutters and water drawers* . . . Hence, they are called נְתִינִים, *assigned ones* (see *Rashi*).

Because of the cruel nature later exhibited by the *nesinim,* King David issued a ban forbidding Jews to intermarry with them (see *Rashi,* and *Yevamos* 78b-79a). [This ban had originally been issued by Joshua himself, to be in force for as long as the Temple stood. King David then made the ban permanent (see *Yevamos* ibid. and *Rambam, Hil. Isurei Biah* 12:22-24; cf. *Tosafos* to *Yevamos* 79a ד"ה ונתינים).]

[The prohibition against intermarriage with the *nesinim* is thus Rabbinic, not Biblical. *Tosafos* ד"ה אלו נערות, however, disagree, and maintain that the *nesinim* – as descendants of the Canaanite nations – are *Biblically* forbidden in marriage even after their conversion to Judaism, on the basis of the prohibition: לֹא תִתְחַתֵּן בָּם, *you shall not intermarry with them* (*Deuteronomy* 7:3 – see note 7). According to *Tosafos,* the thrust of King David's decree (*Yevamos* 79a) was only to extend their *servitude* for all time; their intermarriage with Jews, though, was in any case Biblically forbidden. Other Rishonim contend that only first-generation Canaanite converts are Biblically forbidden to intermarry with Jews; their children, however, are permitted to marry ordinary Jews, because nowhere does the Torah state that the prohibition applies to subsequent generations, as the Torah does state in the case of Egyptian or Edomite converts. According to this view, King David's decree against them prohibited intermarriage even with later-generation *nesinim* (see *Ramban* and *Ran* here, and *Ramban* to *Yevamos* 78b; see also *Maggid Mishneh* to *Rambam* ibid.).]

6. The Cutheans were one of the nations brought by the Assyrian king Shalmanesser to settle the part of Eretz Yisrael left desolate by the exile of the Ten Tribes (*II Kings* 17:24-41). An outbreak of attacks by lions motivated the Cuthean immigrants to convert to Judaism out of fear that they were being punished for not observing the religion of the land, but they still did not relinquish all their pagan beliefs and practices (ibid.). There is a Tannaic dispute as to whether their conversion was valid or not (see *Kiddushin* 75b).

Our Mishnah [which finds it necessary to state that a Cuthean girl is entitled to the fine] holds the view that the Cuthean conversion was invalid. Hence, cohabiting with a Cuthean is Biblically forbidden by force of the prohibition (*Deuteronomy* 7:3): *You shall not intermarry with them* (*Rashi;* cf. *Tosafos* cited in the next note). [Had our Mishnah been of the opinion that Cutheans are genuine converts, however, there would be no novelty in its ruling that a Cuthean girl is awarded the fine.]

7. [Our Mishnah teaches that] although the *oneiss* is forbidden to marry the *mamzeress, nesinah* or Cuthean, and thus the command that the *oneiss* marry his victim cannot apply, the fine, nonetheless, *does* apply (see Gemara below, 29b).

[*Tosafos* object to *Rashi's* comments regarding the Cuthean. For if the Cuthean girl is legally deemed to be a non-Jewess, then she would not be awarded any fine, for there is no fine imposed in the case of a non-Jewish girl, as stated by the Gemara above, 11a. Moreover, the Gemara in *Bava Kamma* (38b) implies that our Mishnah here considers Cutheans to be *genuine* converts. *Tosafos* therefore explain (based on *Bava Kamma* 38b; see there) that our Mishnah is authored by R' Meir, who considers the Cutheans to be genuine converts, yet who imposes certain monetary penalties on the Cutheans in order to discourage their intermarriage with the main body of Jews. And our Mishnah teaches that the Rabbis did *not* penalize the Cutheans by depriving their daughters of the *oneiss* fine, so that the *oneiss* not profit from his criminal behavior. See also *Ramban.*]

8. I.e. a Jewish girl who had been captured by non-Jews and then freed; see next note.

the death penalty is not actually administered (e.g. where one committed the capital offense inadvertently, or where he was not warned that his act would subject him to the death penalty).[8] According to some, the exemption of *he stands liable* ... applies even when the "death penalty" is but *kares,* [9] and – according to others – even if it is but "death at the hand of Heaven."[10]

In the case of lashes and monetary liability, too, the view of the majority of the Sages is that the sinner can be punished with only one of the penalties.[11] The Amoraim dispute whether in such cases the general rule is that the lashes penalty supersedes the monetary penalty, or that the monetary penalty supersedes the lashes penalty.[12] Also, it is an Amoraic dispute whether the rule that lashes supersedes the monetary penalty applies even when the lashes penalty is not actually administered (e.g. where one committed the lashes-bearing offense inadvertently, or where he was not warned that his act would subject him to lashes).[13]

NOTES

8. Baraisa taught in the academy of Chizkiyah, cited on 35a.

9. R' Nechunya ben HaKanah (30a) as explained by Rava (see below, 30b).

10. R' Nechunya ben HaKanah, as explained by Abaye (see ibid.).

11. *Makkos* 4a-b; below, 32a-b. The view of R' Meir, however, is that one can receive lashes and pay money for the same crime (*Makkos* ibid.; below, 32b, 33b and 34b).

12. Below, 32a-b.

13. Below, 35a.

Chapter Three

Introduction

❧ אוֹנֵס, *Violator, and* מְפַתֶּה, *Seducer*

This chapter deals with the various liabilities incurred by one who violates or seduces a virgin *naarah.*[1] The violator is known as an אוֹנֵס, *oneiss,* and the seducer is known as a מְפַתֶּה, *mefateh.*

With regard to the violator, the Torah states:[2] כִּי־יִמְצָא אִישׁ נַעֲרָ בְתוּלָה אֲשֶׁר לֹא־אֹרָשָׂה וּתְפָשָׂהּ וְשָׁכַב עִמָּהּ וְנִמְצָאוּ. וְנָתַן הָאִישׁ הַשֹּׁכֵב עִמָּהּ לַאֲבִי הַנַּעֲרָ חֲמִשִּׁים כָּסֶף וְלוֹ־תִהְיֶה לְאִשָּׁה תַּחַת אֲשֶׁר עִנָּהּ לֹא־יוּכַל שַׁלְּחָהּ כָּל־יָמָיו, *And if a man will find a virgin naarah who was not betrothed, and takes hold of her and lies with her, and they are discovered. Then the man who lay with her shall give the father of the naarah fifty silver [coins], and she shall be his wife, because he violated her, he cannot divorce her all his life.* In addition to the fine, the violator must pay her for pain, humiliation and depreciation.[3] He must marry her (if she and her father so desire) and may never divorce her against her will.

With regard to the seducer, the Torah states:[4] וְכִי־יְפַתֶּה אִישׁ בְּתוּלָה אֲשֶׁר לֹא־אֹרָשָׂה וְשָׁכַב עִמָּהּ מָהֹר יִמְהָרֶנָּה לּוֹ לְאִשָּׁה. אִם־מָאֵן יְמָאֵן אָבִיהָ לְתִתָּהּ לוֹ כֶּסֶף יִשְׁקֹל כְּמֹהַר הַבְּתוּלֹת, *And if a man shall seduce a virgin who was not betrothed and lie with her, he shall provide her with a marriage settlement as his wife. If her father refuses to give her to him, he shall weigh out silver in the amount of the settlement [made] to the virgins.* In addition, the seducer must pay her for humiliation and depreciation.[5] The seducer is not *obligated* to marry the girl. If he refuses to marry her (or if she or her father refuses him), he pays the fine stipulated by the Torah. If he does marry her, he does not pay the fine; rather he writes for her the *kesubah* to which virgins are entitled. Also, he is permitted to subsequently divorce her.[6]

❧ Dual Penalties

A large portion of this chapter is devoted to the law in situations where a person becomes liable simultaneously to two penalties — either the death penalty and monetary liability (or lashes), or lashes and monetary liability.

In the case of the death penalty and monetary liability (or lashes), the operative principle is קָם לֵיהּ בִּדְרַבָּה מִינֵּיהּ, *he stands liable to the [penalty] greater than it.* That is, his being subject to the death penalty exempts him from monetary liability (or lashes) that is simultaneously incurred.[7] This exemption applies even if

NOTES

1. When a girl sprouts two pubic hairs after reaching the age of twelve, she is a *naarah.* She remains in this state for six months, after which she becomes a *bogeress* (see 29a note 1).

2. *Deuteronomy* 22:28-29.

3. Mishnah, 39a. The depreciation is the difference between the amount a virgin and nonvirgin slavegirl would fetch at the slave market (see 32a note 5). These payments, too, are generally given to the girl's father.

4. *Exodus* 22:15-16.

5. Mishnah, 39a. There is no payment for pain, however, since the seduced girl does not suffer any pain (see below, 39b).

6. See below, 39a ff.; *Rambam, Hil. Naarah Besulah* 1:3.

7. See Gemara below, and *Chullin* 81b.

From the Gemara in *Bava Metzia* 91a (as explained by *Rashi* there ד״ה רבא אמר and other Rishonim), it emerges that this exemption serves only to prevent the courts from enforcing the monetary obligation, but the person remains "obligated by the laws of Heaven" to pay it. Moreover, according to *Rashi* (ibid.), if the aggrieved party seizes the assets of the offender to satisfy this obligation, the courts cannot remove those seized assets from him. See *Ketzos HaChoshen* 28:1.

AND A EULOGIZING SPOT IN THIS PLACE."

A dissenting view:

רַבִּי יוֹחָנָן בֶּן בְּרוֹקָא אוֹמֵר – R' YOCHANAN BEN BEROKA SAYS: נֶאֱמָנִים – THEY ARE BELIEVED.

The Gemara asks:

רַבִּי יוֹחָנָן בֶּן בְּרוֹקָא אַהֵייא – **Regarding which** ruling **is R' Yochanan ben Beroka** stating his opposition? אִילֵימָא אַסֵּיפָא – **If you will say it is regarding the** Baraisa's **final** ruling, which disallows testimony establishing one's right of way in the field of another, or his right to use the field for standing and eulogizing – this cannot be! אַפּוּקֵי מָמוֹנָא הוּא – For **this is** an instance of **exacting money,** and we do not exact money on the basis of this subpar testimony. אֶלָּא אַרֵישָׁא – **Rather,** then, he disagrees **regarding the** Baraisa's **earlier** ruling, which states: וְכוּלָּם – AND regarding ALL [THESE WITNESSES], אִם הָיָה עוֹבֵד כּוֹכָבִים וְנִתְגַּיֵּיר – IF THEY WERE GENTILES WHO CONVERTED, עֶבֶד וְנִשְׁתַּחְרֵר – or SLAVES WHO WERE FREED, and they are testifying on the basis of past memories, אֵין נֶאֱמָנִין – THEY ARE NOT BELIEVED. It is regarding these witnesses that the Baraisa states: רַבִּי יוֹחָנָן בֶּן בְּרוֹקָא אוֹמֵר – R' YOCHANAN BEN BEROKA SAYS: נֶאֱמָנִין – THEY ARE BELIEVED.

Having established the subject of the dispute, the Gemara attempts to uncover the underlying reasoning:

בְּמַאי קָמִיפַּלְגֵי – **In what** issue **do they disagree?**

The Gemara explains:

תַּנָּא קַמָּא סָבַר – **The Tanna Kamma holds** that we must assume כֵּיוָן דְּעוֹבֵד כּוֹכָבִים הוּא – that **since he was a gentile** at the time of witnessing, לֹא הֲוָה דָּיֵיק – **he was not precise** in his observations. וְרַבִּי יוֹחָנָן בֶּן בְּרוֹקָא סָבַר – **But R' Yochanan ben Beroka holds** כֵּיוָן דְּדַעְתֵּיהּ לְאִיגַּיּוּרֵי – that **since he was of a mind to convert,** מֵידָק הֲוָה דָּיֵיק – **he was precise** in his observations even as a gentile, so as to be able to testify after converting.[28]

The Gemara examines another of this Baraisa's rulings:

מַאי קְצָצָה – **What is a** ***ketzatzah*****?** דְּתָנוּ רַבָּנָן – It is **as our Rabbis have taught in a Baraisa:** כֵּיצַד קְצָצָה – HOW IS A *KETZATZAH* performed? אֶחָד מִן הָאַחִין שֶׁנָּשָׂא אִשָּׁה שֶׁאֵינָהּ הוֹגֶנֶת לוֹ – If ONE OF THE BROTHERS of a family MARRIES A WOMAN WHO IS UNFIT FOR HIM,[29] בָּאִין בְּנֵי מִשְׁפָּחָה – THE MEMBERS OF THE FAMILY COME, וּמְבִיאִין חָבִית מְלֵיאָה פֵּירוֹת – AND THEY BRING A BARREL FULL OF FRUIT, וְשׁוֹבְרִין אוֹתָהּ בְּאֶמְצַע רְחָבָה – AND THEY BREAK IT IN MIDDLE OF THE public SQUARE,[30] וְאוֹמְרִים – AND THEY SAY: אַחֵינוּ בֵּית יִשְׂרָאֵל שְׁמָעוּ – "OUR BROTHERS, THE HOUSE OF ISRAEL, HEAR YE! אָחִינוּ פְּלוֹנִי נָשָׂא אִשָּׁה שֶׁאֵינָהּ הוֹגֶנֶת לוֹ – OUR BROTHER, SO-AND-SO, MARRIED A WOMAN WHO IS UNFIT FOR HIM, וּמִתְיָירְאִים אָנוּ שֶׁמָּא יִתְעָרֵב זַרְעוֹ בְּזַרְעֵינוּ – AND WE FEAR LEST HIS SEED BECOME MIXED WITH OUR SEED.[31] בּוֹאוּ וּקְחוּ לָכֶם דּוּגְמָא לְדוֹרוֹת – COME AND TAKE FOR YOUSELVES A TOKEN FOR GENERATIONS,[32] שֶׁלֹּא יִתְעָרֵב זַרְעוֹ בְּזַרְעֵינוּ – SO THAT HIS SEED WILL NOT BECOME MIXED WITH OUR SEED." וְזוֹ הִיא קְצָצָה שֶׁהַתִּינוֹק נֶאֱמָן לְהָעִיד עָלֶיהָ – AND THIS IS THE *KETZATZAH* REGARDING WHICH A CHILD IS TRUSTED TO TESTIFY when he becomes an adult.[33]

הדרן עלך האשה שנתארמלה

WE SHALL RETURN TO YOU, HA'ISHAH SHENISARMELAH

NOTES

28. And likewise in the case of a freed slave. For one who plans to free his slave will generally inform him beforehand; therefore, a slave too will be precise in his observations (*Ritva; Yad David,* cited in *Ohel Avraham;* see *Yevamos* 35a).

29. I.e. she is of tainted lineage (*Ran*), which means that there exists a suspicion that she is of those to whom marriage is forbidden; e.g. a *mamzeress,* who is forbidden to any Jew, or a *chalalah,* who is forbidden to a Kohen (see *Beis Yosef* and *Bach* to *Even HaEzer* §2; *Beis Shmuel, Even HaEzer* 2:1).

30. *Aruch* (ע׳ קץ [ו׳]) connects קְצָצָה, *ketzatzah,* to the root קץ, which connotes "shards." Presumably, the reference here is to the broken pieces of the barrel; see also *Maharshal*. For other interpretations of the word, see *Maharsha; Hagahos Zeev ben Aryeh,* printed in back of the standard Gemara.

31. [I.e. lest his offspring intermarry with ours and render them unfit. Alternatively, they feared that people would confuse his offspring with theirs and assume that the taint that affects his offspring affects theirs as well.]

32. I.e. take some fruit, and let the act serve as a token and a remembrance for all generations that the offspring of this individual are of tainted lineage (see *Rashi*). *Maharsha* explains that the reason the remembrance was made with fruit was to evoke interest from the children, for their memories are the keenest, and they will long remember the events of the day. Since children love fruit, fruit was used.

[*Ritva* cites *Yerushalmi* here, who states that if the brother later divorces the unfit wife, or if she dies, the family must negate the *ketzatzah* publicly (provided there were no children), since the taint has now been removed.]

33. Here, as in the testimony concerning a genealogically unfit family (see note 22), the testimony concerns a *ketzatzah* performed because of a Kohen who married a woman unfit for him. It establishes the remaining members' status with regard to consumption of Rabbinical *terumah* only (*Rambam, Eidus* 14:3). Furthermore, *Ran* maintains that here too, as previously, this testimony is effective only in clarifying a previous suspicion. Thus, the Baraisa discusses a Kohanic family upon whom there already lies a suspicion of unfitness. However, we do not know which part of the family is affected; the witness' report of the *ketzatzah* he experienced as a child clarifies that the suspicion falls only upon the family of one of the brothers, but not upon the families of all the other brothers. His recollection serves only to permit the other brothers to partake of Rabbinical *terumah;* it does not return to them all other Kohanic privileges. Cf. *Raavad,* quoted in *Ran.*

עין משפט
נר מצוה

קכז א מיי' פי"ב מהל' תרומות הלכה כב:
קכח ב ג מיי' פ"ו מהל' קרבן פסח הל' ח:
קכט ד מיי' פכ"ח מהל' שבת הלכה יט טוש"ע א"ח סי' שצט סעי' יא:
קל ה מיי' פי"ד מהל' עדות הלכה ג סמג לאוין רט טוש"ע ח"מ סי' לה סעי' ו:
קלא ו מיי' שם הלכה ד וטוש"ע שם סעי' ז:
קלב ז מיי' שם הלכה ג טוש"ע אה"ע סי' ג סעי' א בהג"ה:

אפוטרופוס (א) או שהניח תפילין בפני רבו או שקרא שלשה פסוקים בבית הכנסת הרי זה לא יצא לחירות התם דאיקרי עבד מדעתו כי קאמרינן דקא נהיג ביה מנהג בנים: לטבול לאכול בתרומה: בתרומה דרבנן: ושהיה חולק עמנו על הגורן: ודלמא עבד כהן הוא תנן כמאן דאמר (א) אין חולקין תרומה לעבד אלא אם כן רבו עמו דתניא (ב) אין חולקין תרומה לעבד אלא אם כן רבו עמו דברי רבי יהודה רבי יוסי אומר יכול הוא שיאמר אם כהן אני תנו לי בשביל עצמי ואם עבד כהן אני תנו לי בשביל רבי במקומו של רבי יהודה (ג) היו מעלין מתרומה ליוחסין במקומו של רבי יוסי לא היו מעלין מתרומה ליוחסין תניא (ד) א"ר אלעזר ברבי יוסי מימי לא העדתי פעם אחת העדתי והעלו עבד לכהונה על פי העלו סלקא דעתך (ה) השתא ומה בהמתן של צדיקים (ו) אין הקב"ה מביא תקלה על ידם צדיקים עצמם לא כ"ש אלא בקשו להעלות עבד לכהונה על פי חזא באתריה דרבי יוסי ואזל ואסהיד באתריה דרבי יהודה: ושהמקום הזה בית הפרס הוא: מ"ט בית הפרס דרבנן (ז) דאמר רב יהודה אמר שמואל (ב) מנפח אדם בית הפרס והולך (ח) ורב יהודה בר אמי משמיה דרב יהודה אמר (ג) בית הפרס שנידש טהור מאי טעמא אי אפשר לעצם כשעורה שלא נידש ברגל: (ד) ועד כאן היינו באין בשבת: קסבר תחומין דרבנן: ואין נאמן לומר דרך היה לפלוני במקום הזה מעמד ומספד היה לפלוני במקום הזה: מאי טעמא אפוקי ממונא לא מפקינן תנו רבנן (ט) (ה) נאמן התינוק לומר כך אמר לי אבא משפחה זו טהורה משפחה זו טמאה טהורה וטמאה סלקא דעתך אלא משפחה זו כשרה ומשפחה זו פסולה ושאכלנו בקצצה של בת פלוני לפלוני ושהיינו מוליכים חלה ומתנות לפלוני כהן על ידי עצמו אבל לא על ידי אחר (ו) וכולן אם היה עובד כוכבים ונתגייר עבד ונשתחרר אין נאמנים ואין נאמן לומר דרך היה לפלוני במקום הזה מעמד ומספד היה לפלוני במקום הזה ר' יוחנן בן ברוקא אומר נאמנים ר' יוחנן בן ברוקא אהייא אילימא אסיפא אפוקי ממונא הוא אלא ארישא וכולם אם היה עובד כוכבים ונתגייר עבד ונשתחרר אין נאמנין ר' יוחנן בן ברוקא אומר נאמנין במאי קמיפלגי ת"ק סבר כיון דעובד כוכבים הוא לא הוה דייק ורבי יוחנן בן ברוקא סבר כיון דדעתיה לאיגיורי מידק הוה דייק מאי קצצה דתנו רבנן כיצד קצצה (ז) אחד מן האחין שנשא אשה שאינה הוגנת לו באין בני משפחה ומביאין חבית מליאה פירות ושוברין אותה באמצע רחבה ואומרים אחינו בית ישראל שמעו אחינו פלוני נשא אשה שאינה הוגנת לו ומתייראים אנו שמא יתערב זרעו בזרעינו בואו וקחו לכם דוגמא לדורות שלא יתערב זרעו בזרעינו וזו היא קצצה שהתינוק נאמן להעיד עליה:

הדרן עלך האשה שנתארמלה

רש"י

אפוטרופוס. מסר נכסיו בידו להכניס ולהוציא לסחורה: הרי זה לא יצא לחירות. ולא אמרינן אי לאו דשחרריה לא הוה יזיף מיניה ולא הוה שביק ליה לנהוג מנהג בן חורין ושמעינן מינה דיש עבד שלומד תורה: בתרומה דרבנן. כגון תרומת חוצה לארץ או פירות המניחנו להני דהאכילו על פיהם: הכי גרסינן דתניא שאין חולקין תרומה לעבד כו'. ורישא דברייתא כהנת שנתערב ולדה בוולד שפחתה שניהן יוצאין לגורן ונוטלין חלק אחד שאין חולקין תרומה לעבד כו' הלכך אי אזיל חד מינייהו לא פלגינן ליה דלמא אתי לאחזוקי בכהן ודלמא האי ניהו העבד: במקומו של ר' יהודה. משום הכי אמר אין חולקין: בהמתן של צדיקים. חמורו של רבי פנחס בן יאיר בהכל שוחטין (חולין ז.): חזא באתריה דרבי יוסי. שחלקו לו תרומה בגורן: ואסהיד באתריה דרבי יהודה. ושם לא היו חולקין תרומה לעבדי כהנים: בית הפרס. החורש את הקבר הרי זה עושה בית הפרס מאה אמה שכן שיערו שהמחרישה מוליכה את עצמות המת ודלמא נגע או הסיט המהלך בו את עצם כשעורה שמטמא במגע ובמשא: מנפח אדם בית הפרס. וסומך על כך שאם יש עצם רואהו ואע"ג דמאהיל לא חיישינן דאין עצם כשעורה מטמא באהל עד דאיכא שדרה או גולגולת שלמה או רוב בנין או רוב מנין: שנידש. דישה רבה ברגלים הרבה: טהור. דתלינן לקולא ואמרינן כל העצמות נכתתו לפחות מכשיעור דלמא חששא דרבנן בעלמא הוא: נאמן התינוק. להעיד בגודלו מה שראה בקוטנו: טמאה וטהורה סלקא דעתך. מה טומאה וטהרה יש לומר במשפחות: בקצצה. לקמן מפרש לה: של בת פלוני לפלוני. כשנשאה פלוני את בת פלוני: ושהיינו מוליכין כו' על ידי עצמו. אם כך העיד התינוק על ידי היה אבא שולח לו חלה ומתנות: אם היה עובד כוכבים ונתגייר. והעיד משנתגייר שראה את אלה בגיותו אינו נאמן: דוגמא. אות וסימן זכרון לדורות הבאים:

הדרן עלך האשה שנתארמלה

תוספות

תנן כמאן דאמר אין חולקין לעבד כו'. ואם תאמר והא לא קאמר רבי יהודה דאין חולקין אלא בתרומה דאורייתא דמעלין ממנה ליוחסין אבל מתני' דמוקמינן בתרומה דרבנן דאין מעלין ממנה ליוחסין מודה דחולקין לעבד בלא רבו ואם כן אמאי מקשי ודלמא עבד כהן הוא ולאו מלתא היא דמתניתין איירי שפיר שמעיד שחלק לו תרומה דאורייתא אלא שאינו נאמן להאכילו אלא בתרומה דרבנן:

ומה בהמתן של צדיקים. מפורש במקום אחר (גיטין דף ז. (ט)):

ושהמקום הזה בית הפרס. ולא יותר ולא לטהר:

(י) מנפח. דלדעבד אם עשה כבר טהרות אבל דבדיקה לכתחלה מפרש במשנה (אהלות פי"ח מ"ד) כיצד בודקין (כ): בית הפרס דרבנן. נראה דאפי' במקום הקבר מקילין כמו בשאר שדה ואין לומר דמקום הקבר מטמא באהל ומביא רבינו יצחק ראיה מדתניא בפ"ק דמועד קטן (דף ה:) מלא שדה מלויינת ואינו יודע מה טיבה יש בה אילנות בידוע שנחרש בה קבר אין בה אילנות בידוע שאבד בה קבר ומאי נפקא מינה כיון שעתה אינו יודע מקום הקבר בין נחרש בין אבד אלא שמע מינה דמקום הקבר טהור כשנחרש ובית הפרס להכי הוי דרבנן משום דהוי ספק טומאה ברשות הרבים אע"ג דבעלמא טיהרו חכמים ספק טומאה ברה"ר היינו היכא שהטומאה מבוררת ולא נולד הספק אלא במקרא ופעם אחרת לא יטמא כיון שמקום הטומאה ידוע אבל הכא שלעולם השדה בספק לא רצו לטהר אע"ג דמדאורייתא טהור:

תוספות רי"ד

עדי' צריך בעדות הינומא כדתנן אם יש עדים שיצאה בהינומא וראשה פרוע וכל היכא דבעי' שני עדים בעינן שיהא גדול עמו שלא יעידו שניהם על ראיית קטנותן ושהיה איש פ' יוצא מבית הספר. פי' כשהיינו להדים יחד עם תינוקת בבית רבן ומחזיקי' לכהונה בראיית קטנות ולא בעי' הכא גדול עומד עמו. שמעלים לכהונה ע"פ ע"א. ובגמרא מפרש בתרומה דרבנן כגון תרומות ח"ל או פירות יהימנהו רבנן בדרבנן. ה"נ בגודלו מעיד על מה שראה בקוטנו אבל הקטן אינו מעיד שאע"פ שמעלים בתרומ' ע"פ ע"א דוקא גדול אבל קטן לא וכן עבד ואשה לא רבן שיהו נאמנים בכהונה כדתנן גבי שבוי' וא"א במת בעלה הלכ' אי' הקטן נאמן בכהונה והא נאמן בשבוי' ומר בעלך ולא תימא כ"מ שע"א נאמן גם עבד ואשה נאמנים שהרי במת בעלך יש תנא שהיה מכשיר ע"א ולא היה מכשיר אשה וקרוב כדתנן בפ' בתרא דיבמות. ר"א אומר אין משיאין את אשה ע"פ ע"א ר"ע אומר לא ע"פ אשה ולא ע"פ קרובים אלמא אע"ג דפליג ר"ע על ר"א ומכשיר בע"א. הא אמר לא ע"פ אשה ולא ע"פ קרובים א"כ אינו דן כלל להכשיר עבד ואשה במקום שע"א נאמן אלא היכא דתנן תני היכא דלא תנן לא תני. ובמקום שעבד ואשה נאמנים גם הקטן נאמן. ומקשה דלמא עבד הוא מסייע ליה לריב"ל דאריב"ל אסור לו לאדם שילמוד את עבדו תורה כתיבי לוה ממנו רבו או שנשאו רבו אפוטרופוס. פי' מסר כל נכסיו בידו להכניס ולהוציא בסחורה או שהניח תפילין בפני רבו או שקרא שלשה פסוקים בבה"כ ה"ז לא יצא לחירות. פי' לא אומרים אי לאו דשחרריה לא הוה יזיף מיניה ולא הוי שביק ליה לנהוג [מנהג] ב"ד. ש"מ דיש עבד שלומד תורה התם דאיקרי עבד מדעתיה. וכי קאמרינן דקא נהוג בי' מנהג בנים: ושהיה חולק עמנו בגורן ולידוש דילמא עבד כהן הוא תנן כמאן דאמר אין חולקין תרומה לעבד אא"כ רבו עמו דברי ר' יהודה ר"י אומר יכול הוא שיאמר אם כהן אני תנו לי בשביל עצמי ואם אני עבד כהן תנו לי בשביל רבי ובמקומו של ר' יוסי לא היה מעלים מתרומה ליוחסים: ושהמקום הזה בית הפרס. פי' הכי תנן בפ' בתרא דאהלות החורש את הקבר ה"ז עושה בית הפרס עד כמה הוא עושה מלא המענה ק' אמה בית ארבעת קבין. פי' החורש אנו חוששים שמא המחרישה פזרה עצמות המת ועצם כשעורה ממנו מטמא במגע ובמשא אבל לא באהל פי' עד דאיכא שדרה או גולגולת שלמים או רוב מנין או רוב בנין ואנו חוששים שמא פזרה שברי עצמות מן הקבר ועד ק' אמה שאם חרש מן הקבר לצד מזרח מונה מן הקבר ק' אמה ועושה אותה בית הפרס והנכנס טמא שמא נגע או היסט עצם כשעורה שהוא מכוסה בעפר ולאו אדעתיה ואלו ק' אמה המונה אותם מרובעין שהן ק' על ק' שיביאו ארבעת סאין. שרסאה הוא נ' על נ' ולמה אנו מחמירים כ"כ ולא נעשה אלא ק' אמה ברוחב הקבר שהמחרישה מוליכה את העצמות אלא אנו חוששים שמא הוליכה והחזירה ועוד הוליכה שדרך החורש לחרוש התלם ולחרוש עוד בצידו עד שיחרוש כל השדה לפיכך החמירו והחזיקו חכמים כל ק' וק' במזרחו של קבר בבית הפרס ומפרש דבית הפרס דרבנן. פי' ומ"ה האמינו בו ראיית הקטן וכשמעיד להקל ולא להחמיר כגון שהיו יודעים השדה שנחרש בה קבר אבל לא היו מכירים מקום הקבר שימדדו משם ק' אמה ובא זה ומעיד שזה המקום הוא בית הפרס ולא יותר ומשום דבית הפרס הוא חששא בעלמא דרבנן. הימנוהו רבנן בדרבנן. ולא להחמיר שאם לא היו יודעים שהוא בית הפרס וזה מעיד אני זוכר שהי' בית הפרס ומחזיקי' בחזקת טומאה למה תולה הטעם משום דבית הפרס דרבנן. השתא בדרבנן נאמן לאחזוקי איסורא כ"ש בדאורייתא. אלא לאו ש"מ להקל מעיד. וע"כ היינו באין בשבת קסבר תחומין דרבנן. ומ"ה האמינוהו ראיית הקטן: אבל אינו נאמן לומר דרך היה לפלוני במקום הזה שהיה הולך משם לשדהו. או מעמד ומספד הי' לפלוני במקום הזה שהיה מספיד שם את מתו ושהיה עושה שם מעמד ומושב למתו כשהיו חוזרים מבית הקברות. מ"ט אפוקי ממונא הוא ולא מפקי' ממונא ע"פ ראיית הקטן. עיין ברפ"ק דפסחים:

מסורת הש"ס

א) [עיין תוס' לקמן לו. ד"ה אבל], ב) יבמות לט., ג) [שם ע"ש], ד) גיטין ז. חולין ה: ו. ז. [יבמות לט:], ה) [עיין תוס' יבמות שם ד"ה ס"ד השתא וכו'], ו) ברכות יט: עירובין ל: פסחים לב: מ"ק ה: חגיגה כה: בכורות כט. נדה נז., ז) [ברכות יט: ע"ש], ח) [תוספתא פרק ג], ט) [ד"ה השתא ותוס' שבת יב: ד"ה ר' נתן ותוס' חולין ה: ד"ה לדיקים ותוס' פסחים קו: ד"ה אישתלאי], י) שייך אחר ד"ה בית הפרס, כ) [ועי' היטב תוס' פסחים לב: ד"ה מאי בודקין ועוד תוס' בכורות כט. ד"ה היכי אזיל].

גליון הש"ס

גמ' היו מעלין מתרומה ליוחסין. עיין ברכות דף טז ע"ב תוס' ד"ה אין עומדין:

ליקוטי רש"י

שדיקדקה המחרישה את העצמות ומגלגלתן. פרס. לשון דבר שבור ופרוס על שם שנפרסו העצמות [נדה נז.]. מעמד ומספד. למת כשנושאין את המת לקוברו היו יושבין שבע פעמים לבכות את המת והרוצה לסופדו יספוד והכי תניא (ב"ב ק:) אין פוחתין משבעה מעמדות ומושבות למת כגון עמדו יקרים עמודו שבו יקרים שבו [מגילה כג:]. בחזירתן מן הקבר הולכין מעט ויושבין לנחם האבל או להרבות לער על המת שמת ולהרבות בבכי ולתת איש אל לבו לשוב בתשובה כי חיי האדם הבל ועומדין והולכין מעט וחוזרין ויושבין מעט כך עושין ז' פעמים כדי לתת אל לבם שחיי האדם הבל והיינו דמפרש לקמיה כנגד שבעה הבל הבלים שכתובין בראש ספר קהלת כן נראה הטעם בעיני וראיתי כתוב מפני שהשדים מתלוים עם החוזרים מבית הקברות לכך תקנו מעמדות ומושבות כדי שבתוך כך יסתלקו השדים מעליהן ולא נהירא דא"כ יהיו עושין כן בכ"מ ולקמן אמרינן דבמנהגא תליא מילתא ועוד מאי כנגד הבל הבלים. היאך עבדי, היאך היו רגילין לעשות במקום שנהגו. עמדו יקרים, לאחר שישבו מעט היה הממונה אומר להן עמדו ולכו אל מקום אחר כך נראה בעיני [רשב"ם ב"ב ק:]. דרוב נשים. שבעולם שנישאות לבעל בתולות הן [רשב"ם ב"ב צב:]. [ע"כ שייך לע"א]

אפוטרופוס. על נכסיו דאי לאו דשחרריה לא הוה חשיב ליה [גיטין מ.]. שהניח תפילין בפני רבו. אין דרך עבד להניח תפילין דמ"ע שהזמן גרמא היא דלילה לאו זמן תפילין הוא [גיטין מ.]. אין חולקין תרומה לעבד אלא אם כן רבו עמו. אם באו שניהם על הגורן נותנים להם אבל זה בלא זה אין חולקין להם דקסבר אין חולקין תרומה לעבד אא"כ רבו עמו דלמא אתי לאסוקי ליוחסין דסברי כהן הוא. אם כהן אני כו'. אספק כהן וספק עבד קאי כי מתניתין. היו מעלין מתרומה ליוחסין. לאו מאכילתה אלא מחלוקה הלכך אין חולקין לו דלא ליתי לאסוקי ליוחסין [יבמות צט:]. השתא בהמתן וכו'. היאך יגרום שום שטן לפני צדיקים ע"י שוגג שום דבר עון. אין הקב"ה מביא תקלה על ידם. שתאכל הבהמה דבר האסור לה [חולין ה:]. בית הפרס. [מלא] מעני מענה מלא אחד של מאה אמה [מו"ק ה:]. בית הפרס דרבנן. דלא מטמא אלא מדרבנן והוא שדה שנחרש בו קבר וחשו חכמים שמא לדלדלו כלי המחרישה את העצמות והדורס עליהן מסיטן ועצם כשעורה מטמא במגע ובמשא ולא באהל [ברכות יט:]. הוא שדה שנחרש בה קבר כדתנן (אהלות פי"ז מ"א) החורש בית הקבר הרי זה עושה בית הפרס מלא מענה מאה אמה וגזור רבנן שמא כיתתה מחרישה את העצמות ופיזרתן באורך המענה ויש כאן עצם כשעורה ויעבור ויסיטנו ועצם כשעורה מטמאה במגע ובמשא דהיינו היסט [פסחים צב:]. שדה שנחרש בה קבר ואוקמי רבנן (על) [כל] סביבות הקבר מאה אמה בספק טומאה שדיקדקה המחרישה את העצמות ומגלגלתן. פרס. לשון דבר שבור ופרוס על שם שנפרסו העצמות [נדה נז.]. מנפח אדם. לפניו שאם היה שם עצם יראנו דאי לדאורייתא הוא לא הוינן מזלזלין ביה כולי האי למיסמך אנפיחה והך בדיקה לעושה פסח איפשרי ולא לאוכלי תרומה כדאמרינן בחומר בקדש (חגיגה דף כה:) [ברכות יט:]. דכולה ספיקא משום עצמות היא ועצמות בלא בשר אינו מטמא באהל וכשמנפח לפני רגליו אם יש שם עצם גדול נראה מאליו ועצם קטן נראה בנפיחה ואינו מסיטו ברגליו [עירובין ל:]. מנפחו בפיו ואם יש עצם גדול יראנו ועצם כשעורה נדחה בנפיחתו ואהל אין מטמאו דהא אין טומאת אהל בעצמות אלא רוב בנין ורוב מנין [פסחים שם]. היה הולך לעשות פסחו ובית הפרס של שדה שנחרש בו קבר מפסיקו בודקו בנפיחה ואם יש עצם כשעורה רואהו ונשמט ממנו ועצם כשעורה אינו מטמא באהל אלא במגע ובמשא לפיכך בודק בנפיחה שלא יסיטנו ברגלו [חגיגה כה:]. דבשר ליכא ועצם כשעורה לא מטמא אלא במגע ובמשא הלכך מנפח כדי שלא יגעו רגליו בו והולך [נדה שם]. שנידש. בדריסת רגלי בני אדם [עירובין שם]. ברגל וזו היא בדיקתו בודק אם נידש או לא נידש [חגיגה שם]. ברגלי אדם שהרגלים נושאים את העצמות ושוקקום [נדה שם]. טהור. שדריסת הרגלים העבירתן והבא לעשות פסחו יבדוק אם נידש ויעבור אבל לאכילת תרומה לא סמכינן עלה שיכול להמתין ובית הפרס מדבריהם ולא העמידום במקום כרת דפסח [פסחים שם]. שככר נידשו עצמות שבו ונפחתו מכשעורה [עירובין שם]. שאי אפשר לעצם כשעורה שלא יהא נידש ברגל ובית הפרס אין בו שום ספק אלא משום עצם כשעורה דבית הפרס היינו שדה שנחרש בו קבר [בכורות כט.]. ואין בודקין לאוכלי תרומה, אין סומכין על בדיקה זו דכיון דאין זמן קבוע לאכילה ימתין שבעה ימים ויזה שלישי ושביעי ויטבול אבל גבי פסח הואיל ובית הפרס דרבנן לא העמידו דבריהם במקום כרת [חגיגה שם]. תחומין דרבנן. דרבנן בעלמא ניינהו שגזרו עליהן לאחר מתן תורה [יומא סו:]. אסמכוה רבנן תחומין אקראי ואפי' למאן דאמר תחומין דרבנן כדאמרינן בעירובין (דף נא.) ילפינן מקום ממקום ומקום מניסה כו' [שבת לד.].

מעמד ומספד. לאחר כשנושאין את המת לקוברו היו יושבין שבע פעמים לבכות את המת והרוצה לסופדו יספוד והכי תניא (ב"ב ק:) אין פוחתין משבעה מעמדות ומושבות למת כגון עמדו יקרים עמודו שבו יקרים שבו [מגילה כג:]. בחזירתן מן הקבר הולכין מעט ויושבין לנחם האבל או להרבות לער על המת שמת ולהרבות בבכי ולתת איש אל לבו לשוב בתשובה כי חיי האדם הבל ועומדין והולכין מעט וחוזרין ויושבין מעט כך עושין ז' פעמים כדי לתת אל לבם שחיי האדם הבל והיינו דמפרש לקמיה כנגד שבעה הבל הבלים שכתובין בראש ספר קהלת כן נראה הטעם בעיני וראיתי כתוב מפני שהשדים מתלוים עם החוזרים מבית הקברות לכך תקנו מעמדות ומושבות כדי שבתוך כך יסתלקו השדים מעליהן ולא נהירא דא"כ יהיו עושין כן בכ"מ ולקמן אמרינן דבמנהגא תליא מילתא ועוד מאי כנגד הבל הבלים. היאך עבדי, היאך היו רגילין לעשות במקום שנהגו. עמדו יקרים, לאחר שישבו מעט היה הממונה אומר להן עמדו ולכו אל מקום אחר כך נראה בעיני [רשב"ם ב"ב ק:].

מִשְּׁמֵיהּ דְּרַב יְהוּדָה אָמַר – **And Rav Yehudah bar Ami said in the name of Rav Yehudah:** בֵּית הַפְּרָס שֶׁנִּידַּשׁ טָהוֹר – **A *beis hapras* that was trampled** by many people **is *tahor.*** Therefore, one on the way to offer the *pesach* sacrifice must check whether it is sufficiently trampled; if it is, he may traverse it. מַאי טַעְמָא – **What is the reason** that a trampled *beis hapras* may be traversed? אִי אֶפְשָׁר לְעֶצֶם כִּשְׂעוֹרָה שֶׁלֹּא נִידַּשׁ בָּרֶגֶל – For **it is impossible that a bone the size of a barley grain** would remain, and **would not have been trampled** until it is less than that size.[18] Therefore, we may assume that no fragments of sufficient size to generate *tumah* remain in the field.

We see that although we do not know with certainty whether fragments larger than a barley grain remain, we assume that none do. This is evidence that *beis hapras* is a Rabbinic decree; otherwise, we would not rely upon this assumption.[19]

The Mishnah stated:

וְעַד כָּאן הָיִינוּ בָּאִין בְּשַׁבָּת – AND WE WOULD COME UNTIL HERE ON THE SABBATH.

With this testimony, the witness establishes the Sabbath *techum* of a city. The Gemara explains why he is believed:

קָסָבַר תְּחוּמִין דְּרַבָּנָן – **We hold** that the laws of ***techumin* are** of **Rabbinic** origin.[20] Therefore, this ordinarily invalid testimony suffices.

The Mishnah stated:

וְאֵין נֶאֱמָן לוֹמַר – HOWEVER, [A PERSON] IS NOT TRUSTED TO SAY: דֶּרֶךְ הָיָה לִפְלוֹנִי בְּמָקוֹם הַזֶּה – "SO-AND-SO HAD A PATH IN THIS PLACE. מַעֲמָד וּמִסְפֵּד הָיָה לִפְלוֹנִי בְּמָקוֹם הַזֶּה – SO-AND-SO HAD A STANDING SPOT AND A EULOGIZING SPOT IN THIS PLACE."

The Gemara asks:

מַאי טַעְמָא – **What is the reason** that he is not believed to testify from childhood memory regarding these facts?

The Gemara answers:

אַפּוּקֵי מָמוֹנָא לֹא מַפְקִינַן – It is because **we do not exact money** on the basis of such testimony. Since he is endeavoring to establish a monetary claim with this testimony, it cannot be based upon childhood memory.

The Gemara cites a Baraisa that enumerates other instances in which the Rabbis accepted testimony based on one's childhood memories:

תָּנוּ רַבָּנָן – **Our Rabbis have taught in a Baraisa:** נֶאֱמָן הַתִּינוֹק לוֹמַר – A CHILD IS TRUSTED TO SAY:[21] כָּךְ אָמַר לִי אַבָּא – "THUS DID FATHER SAY TO ME: מִשְׁפָּחָה זוֹ טְהוֹרָה מִשְׁפָּחָה זוֹ טְמֵאָה – 'THIS FAMILY IS *TAHOR;* THIS other FAMILY IS *TAMEI.*'"

The Gemara interrupts:

טְהוֹרָה וּטְמֵאָה סָלְקָא דַּעְתָּךְ – **Can it enter your mind** that the Baraisa reads ***tahor* and *tamei*?** There are no issues of *taharah* and *tumah* that pertain to families. – ? –

The Gemara therefore emends the Baraisa:

אֶלָּא מִשְׁפָּחָה זוֹ כְּשֵׁרָה וּמִשְׁפָּחָה זוֹ פְּסוּלָה – **Rather,** read the Baraisa thus: "THIS FAMILY IS genealogically FIT; THIS other FAMILY IS genealogically UNFIT."[22]

The Gemara returns to the Baraisa:

וְשֶׁאָכַלְנוּ בִּקְצָצָה שֶׁל בַּת פְּלוֹנִי לִפְלוֹנִי – A child is trusted to say: "AND I remember THAT WE ATE OF THE *KETZATZAH*[23] distributed upon the marriage OF THE DAUGHTER OF SO-AND-SO TO SO-AND-SO, וְשֶׁהָיִינוּ מוֹלִיכִים חַלָּה וּמַתָּנוֹת לִפְלוֹנִי כֹּהֵן – AND THAT WE WOULD BRING *CHALLAH* AND the Kohanic GIFTS TO THE KOHEN SO-AND-SO."[24]

The Baraisa qualifies the clause concerning Kohanic gifts:

עַל יְדֵי עַצְמוֹ אֲבָל לֹא עַל יְדֵי אַחֵר – He is trusted in this testimony only if the gifts were delivered BY HIMSELF, BUT NOT if they were delivered BY ANOTHER.[25]

The Baraisa presents a related law:

וְכוּלָּן – AND regarding ALL [THESE WITNESSES]: אִם הָיָה עוֹבֵד כּוֹכָבִים וְנִתְגַּיֵּיר – IF THEY WERE GENTILES WHO CONVERTED, עֶבֶד וְנִשְׁתַּחְרֵר – or SLAVES WHO WERE FREED,[26] and they are testifying on the basis of past memories, אֵין נֶאֱמָנִים – THEY ARE NOT BELIEVED.[27]

The Baraisa returns to the laws of one testifying from childhood memory:

וְאֵין נֶאֱמָן לוֹמַר – AND HE IS NOT TRUSTED TO SAY: דֶּרֶךְ הָיָה לִפְלוֹנִי בְּמָקוֹם הַזֶּה – "SO-AND-SO HAD A PATH IN THIS PLACE. מַעֲמָד וּמִסְפֵּד הָיָה לִפְלוֹנִי בְּמָקוֹם הַזֶּה – SO-AND-SO HAD A STANDING SPOT

NOTES

who passes over it; a *beis hapras,* however, contains only bone fragments (see *Rashi, Eruvin* 30b ד״ה מנפח).]

18. For the constant tramping of many feet will ensure that any bone chips will be reduced to less than the measure of a grain of barley, the smallest measure at which they generate corpse *tumah* (*Rashi* here and to *Eruvin* 30b ד״ה טהור). Alternatively, the heavy traffic will inevitably push to the side any bone fragments that lie in the path (*Rashi, Pesachim* ibid. ד״ה שנידש).

19. For were this a Biblical law, we would not rely upon the assumption that blowing and trampling will remove the *tumah* (see *Rashi* here and to *Berachos* 19b ד״ה מנפח אדם).

20. See *Rambam, Eidus* 14:3 with *Kesef Mishneh;* see also *Kovetz Shiurim* §77.

21. I.e. once he reaches adulthood he is trusted to testify regarding what he saw as a child (*Rashi;* see *Ran;* cf. *Raavad,* quoted in *Ran;* cf. also *Ritva*).

22. I.e. one family is of unblemished lineage; the other is of tainted lineage.

Rambam (*Eidus* 14:3) states that this testimony concerns Kohanic families. The family designated as genealogically fit is permitted to partake of Rabbinical *terumah* (see above, note 6). *Ran* explains that testimony based on childhood memory can neither taint the reputation of a family traditionally held to be unblemished, nor remove the taint from one traditionally held to be blemished. The Baraisa's case concerns a family of Kohanim upon whom there already lies a suspicion of genealogical taint. The purpose of the testimony is to clarify which members of the family are actually blemished; thus, the witness testifies that it is "this family" (meaning one segment of the larger family) that is unfit, whereas "this other family" (meaning another segment of the same extended family) is genealogically fit. Since it is not clear that the suspicion extends to the entire family, one testifying on the basis of youthful recollection is believed to clarify which part of the family is fit and which is not. However, he is believed only with regard to permitting the family that is fit to partake of Rabbinical *terumah;* with regard to any other Kohanic prerogative, they remain under suspicion. Cf. *Raavad,* quoted in *Ran.*

23. The Gemara will soon define *"ketzatzah."*

24. [*Challah* is the portion separated from a batch of dough and given to the Kohen, as required in *Numbers* 15:20,21. "The Kohanic gifts" refer to the forelegs, jaws and abomasums of animals. One separates these parts from every kosher beast he slaughters and presents them to the Kohen, as stated in *Deuteronomy* 18:3.]

25. I.e. if he testifies that his father would send the gifts with him, he is believed to identify the recipient as a Kohen (with regard to permitting him to partake of Rabbinical *terumah*), but if he testifies that his father would send them with another, he is not believed to do so (*Rashi*). For unless he was personally involved, we fear that his observations were less than precise (*Ran*).

26. Literally: If he was a gentile who converted, or a slave who was freed.

27. [I.e. even though in the cases enumerated, an adult Jew is believed to testify regarding what he observed as a child,] a gentile who converted is not believed to testify regarding that which he saw as a gentile (*Rashi*), nor is a slave who was freed believed to testify regarding that which he saw as a slave (*Ran*). The Gemara will give the reason shortly.

אפוטרופוס או שהניח תפילין בפני רבו או שקרא שלשה פסוקים בבית הכנסת הרי זה לא יצא לחירות התם דאיקרי עבד מדעתו כי קאמרינן דקא נהיג ביה מנהג בנים: לטבול לאכול בתרומה: בתרומה דרבנן: ושהיה חולק עמנו על הגורן: ודלמא עבד כהן הוא תנן כמאן דאמר אין חולקין תרומה לעבד אלא אם כן רבו עמו דתניא אין חולקין תרומה לעבד אלא אם כן רבו עמו דברי רבי יהודה רבי יוסי אומר יכול הוא שיאמר אם כהן אני תנו לי בשביל עצמי ואם עבד כהן אני תנו לי בשביל רבי במקומו של רבי יהודה היו מעלין מתרומה ליוחסין במקומו של רבי יוסי לא היו מעלין מתרומה ליוחסין תניא א"ר אלעזר ברבי יוסי מימי לא העדתי פעם אחת העדתי והעלו עבד לכהונה על פי העלו סלקא דעתך השתא ומה בהמתן של צדיקים אין הקב"ה מביא תקלה על ידם צדיקים עצמם לא כ"ש אלא בקשו להעלות עבד לכהונה על פי חזא באתריה דרבי יוסי ואזל ואסהיד באתריה דרבי יהודה: ושהמקום הזה בית הפרס הוא: מ"ט בית הפרס דרבנן דאמר רב יהודה אמר שמואל מנפח אדם בית הפרס והולך ורב יהודה בר אמי משמיה דרב יהודה אמר בית הפרס שנידש טהור מאי טעמא אי אפשר לעצם כשעורה שלא נידש ברגל: ועד כאן היינו באין בשבת: קסבר תחומין דרבנן: ואין נאמן לומר דרך היה לפלוני במקום הזה מעמד ומספד היה לפלוני במקום הזה: מאי טעמא אפוקי ממונא לא מפקינן תנו רבנן נאמן התינוק לומר כך אמר לי אבא משפחה זו טהורה ומשפחה זו טמאה וטמאה סלקא דעתך אלא משפחה זו כשרה ומשפחה זו פסולה ושאכלנו בקצצה של בת פלוני לפלוני ושהיינו מוליכים חלה ומתנות לפלוני כהן על ידי עצמו אבל לא על ידי אחר וכולן אם היה עובד כוכבים ונתגייר עבד ונשתחרר אין נאמנים ואין נאמן לומר דרך היה לפלוני במקום הזה מעמד ומספד היה לפלוני במקום הזה רבי יוחנן בן ברוקא אומר נאמנים ר' יוחנן בן ברוקא אהייא אילימא אסיפא אפוקי ממונא הוא אלא ארישא וכולם אם היה עובד כוכבים ונתגייר עבד ונשתחרר אין נאמנין ר' יוחנן בן ברוקא אומר נאמנין במאי קמיפלגי ת"ק סבר כיון דעובד כוכבים הוא לא הוה דייק ורבי יוחנן בן ברוקא סבר כיון דדעתיה לאיגיורי מידק הוה דייק מאי קצצה דתנו רבנן כיצד קצצה אחד מן האחין שנשא אשה שאינה הוגנת לו באין בני משפחה ומביאין חבית מליאה פירות ושוברין אותה באמצע רחבה ואומרים אחינו בית ישראל שמעו אחינו פלוני נשא אשה שאינה הוגנת לו ומתייראים אנו שמא יתערב זרעו בזרעינו בואו וקחו לכם דוגמא לדורות שלא יתערב זרעו בזרעינו וזו היא קצצה שהתינוק נאמן להעיד עליה:

הדרן עלך האשה שנתארמלה

אפוטרופוס. מסר נכסיו בידו להכניס ולהוציא לסחורה: **הרי זה לא יצא לחירות.** ולא אמרינן אי לאו דשחרריה לא הוה יזיף מיניה ולא הוה שביק ליה לנהוג מנהג בן חורין ושמעינן מינה דיש עבד שלומד תורה: **בתרומה דרבנן.** כגון תרומת חוצה לארץ או פירות המנינהו להכי להאכילו על פיהם: **הכי גרסינן דתניא שאין חולקין תרומה לעבד כו'.** ורישא דברייתא כהנת שנתערב ולדה בולד שפחתה שניהן יוצאין לגורן ונוטלין חלק אחד שאין חולקין תרומה לעבד כו' הלכך אי אזיל חד מינייהו לא פלגינן ליה דלמא אתי לאחזוקי בכהן ודלמא האי ניהו העבד: **במקומו של ר' יהודה.** משום הכי אמר אין חולקין: **בהמתן של צדיקים.** חמורו של רבי פנחס בן יאיר בהכל שוחטין (חולין ז.): **חזא באתריה דרבי יוסי.** שחלקו לו תרומה בגורן: **ואסהיד באתריה דרבי יהודה.** ושם לא היו חולקין תרומה לעבדי כהנים: **בית הפרס.** החורש את הקבר הרי זה עושה בית הפרס מאה אמה שכך שיערו שהמחרישה מוליכת את עצמות המת ודלמא נגע או הסיט המהלך בו את עצם כשעורה שמטמא במגע ובמשא: **מנפח אדם בית הפרס.** וסומך על כך שאם יש עצם רואהו ואע"ג דמאהיל לא חיישינן דאין עצם כשעורה מטמא באהל עד דאיכא שדרה או גולגולת שלמה או רוב בנין או רוב מנין: **שנידש.** דישה רבה ברגלים הרבה: **טהור.** דתלינן לקולא ואמרינן כל העצמות נכתתו לפחות מכשיעור אלמא חששא דרבנן בעלמא הוא: **נאמן התינוק.** להעיד בגודלו מה שראה בקוטנו: **טמאה וטהורה סלקא דעתך.** מה טומאה וטהרה יש לומר במשפחות: **בקצצה.** לקמן מפרש לה: **של בת פלוני לפלוני.** כשנשאת פלוני את בת פלוני: **ושהיינו מוליכין כו' על ידי עצמו.** אם כך העיד התינוק על ידי היה אבא שולח לו חלה ומתנות: **אם היה עובד כוכבים ונתגייר.** והעיד משנתגייר שראה את אלה בגיותו אינו נאמן: **דוגמא.** אות וסימן וזכרון לדורות הבאים:

הדרן עלך האשה שנתארמלה

תנן כמאן דאמר אין חולקין לעבד כו'. ואם תאמר והא לא קאמר רבי יהודה דאין חולקין אלא בתרומה דאורייתא דמעלין ממנה ליוחסין אבל מתני' דאוקימנא בתרומה דרבנן דאין מעלין ממנה ליוחסין מודה דחולקין לעבד בלא רבו ואם כן אכתי תקשי ודלמא עבד כהן הוא ולאו מלתא היא דמתניתין איירי שפיר שמעיד שחלק לו תרומה דאורייתא אלא שאינו נאמן להאכילו אלא בתרומה דרבנן:

ומה בהמתן של צדיקים. מפורש במקום אחר (גיטין דף ז.):

ושהמקום הזה בית הפרס. ולא יוכל ולא לטהר:

מנפח. דליעבד אם עשה כבר טהרות אבל בדיקה לכתחלה מפרש במשנה (אהלות פי"ח מ"ד) כילד בודקין: **בית הפרס דרבנן.** נראה לפי' במקום הקבר מקילין כמו בשאר שדה ואין לומר דמקום הקבר מטמא באהל ומביא רבינו יצחק ראיה מדתניא בפ"ק דמועד קטן (דף ה:) מצא שדה מצויינת ואינו יודע מה טיבה יש בה אילנות בידוע שנחרש בה קבר אין בה אילנות בידוע שאבד בה קבר ומאי נפקא מינה כיון שעתה אינו יודע מקום הקבר בין נחרש בין אבד אלא שמע מינה דמקום הקבר טהור כשנחרש ובית הפרס לכך הוי דרבנן משום דהוי ספק טומאה ברשות הרבים אע"ג דבעלמא טיהרו חכמים ספק טומאה ברה"ר היינו היכא שהטומאה מבוררת ולא נולד הספק אלא בתחלה ופעם אחרת לא יטמא כיון שמקום הטומאה ידוע אבל הכא שלעולם השדה בספק לא רצו לטהר אע"ג דמדאורייתא טהור:

הדרן עלך האשה שנתארמלה

עין משפט נר מצוה

קכז א מיי' פי"ב מהל' תרומות הלכה כב:

קכח ב ג מיי' פ"ו מהל' קרבן פסח הל' ח:

קכט ד מיי' פכ"ח מהל' שבת הלכה יט טוש"ע א"ח סי' שלט סעי' יב:

קל ה מיי' פי"ד מהל' עדות הלכה ג סמג לאוין רע טוש"ע ח"מ סי' לה סעי' ו:

קלא ו מיי' שם הלכה ד וטוש"ע שם סעי' ז:

קלב ז מיי' שם הלכה ג טוש"ע אה"ע סי' ג סעי' א בהג"ה:

תוספות רי"ד

עדי' צריך בעדות הינומא כדתנן אם יש עדים שיצאה בהינומא וראשה פרוע וכל היכא דבעי' שני עדים בעינן שיהא גדול עמו שלא יעיד שניהם על ראיית קטנות: **ושהיה** איש פ' יוצא מבית הספר. פי' כשהיינו למדים יחד עם תינוקות בבית רבן ומחזיקי' לכהונה בראיית קטנות ולא בעי' הכא גדול עומד עמו. שמעלים לכהונה ע"פ ע"א. ובגמרא מפרש בתרומה דרבנן כגון תרומות ח"ל או פירות והימנוהו רבנן בדרבנן. וה"ה בגודלו מעיד על מה שראה בקוטנו אבל דקטן אינו מעיד שאע"פ שמעלים בתרומ' ע"פ ע"א דוקא גדול אבל קטן לא וכן עבד ואשה לא תנן שיהו נאמנים בכהונה כדתנן גבי שבוי' וא"א במת בעלה הלכך אין הקטן נאמן בכהונה והוא נאמן בשבוי' ומת בעלך ולא תימא כ"מ שע"א נאמן גם עבד ואשה נאמנים שהרי במת בעלך יש תנא שהיה מכשיר ע"א ולא היה מכשיר אשה וקרוב כדתנן בפ' בתרא דיבמות. ר"א אומר אין משיאין את אשה ע"פ ע"א ר"ע אומר לא ע"פ אשה ולא ע"פ קרובים אלמא אע"ג דפליג ר"ע על ר"א ומכשיר בע"א. הא אמר לא ע"פ אשה ולא ע"פ קרובים א"כ אינו דין כלל להכשיר עבד ואשה במקום שע"א נאמן אלא היכא דתנן תנן היכא דלא תנן לא תנן. ובמקום שעבד ואשה נאמנים גם הקטן נאמן. ומקשה דלמא עבד הוא מסייע ליה לריב"ל דאריב"ל אסור לו לאדם שילמוד את עבדו תורה מיתיבי לוה ממנו רבו או שעשאו רבו אפוטרופוס. פ' מסר כל נכסיו בידו להכניס ולהוציא בסחורה או שהניח תפילין בפני רבו או שקרא שלשה פסוקים בבה"כ ה"ז לא יצא לחירות. פי' לאו אמרים אי לאו דשחרריה לא הוה יזיף מיניה ולא הוי שביק ליה לנהוג [מנהג] ב"ח. ש"מ דיש עבד שלומד תורה דאיקרי עבד מדעתיה. וכי קאמרינן דקא נהוג בי' מנהג בנים: **ושהיה** חולק עמנו בגורן ולחוש דילמא עבד כהן הוא תנן כמ"ד אין חולקין תרומה לעבד אא"כ רבו עמו דברי ר' יהודה ר"י אומר יכול הוא שיאמר אם כהן אני תנו לי בשביל עצמי ואם אני עבד כהן תנו לי בשביל רבי ובמקומו של ר' יוסי לא היה מעלים מתרומה ליוחסים: **ושהמקום** הזה בית הפרס. פי' הכי תנן בפ' בתרא דאהלות החורש את הקבר ה"ז עושה בית הפרס עד כמה הוא עושה מלא המענה ק' אמה בית ארבעת קבין. פי' החורש אנו חוששים שמא המחרישה פזרה עצמות המת ועצם כשעורה ממנו מטמא במגע ובמשא אבל לא באהל פי' עד דאיכא שדרה או גולגולת שלמים או רוב מנין או רוב בנין ואנו חוששים שמא פזרה שברי עצמות מן הקבר ועד ק' אמה שאם חרש מן הקבר לצד מזרח מונה מן הקבר ק' אמה ועושה אותה בית הפרס והנכנס שמא נגע או היסט עצם כשעורה שהוא מכוסה בעפר ולאו אדעתיה ואלו ק' אמה המונה אותם מרובעין שהן ק' על ק' שיביאו ארבעת סאין. שהסאה הוא נ' על נ' ולמה אנו מחמירים כ"כ ולא נעשה אלא ק' אמה ברוחב הקבר שהמחרישה מוליכה את העצמות אלא אנו חוששים שמא הוליכה והחזירה ועוד הוליכה שדרך החורש לחרוש התלם ולחרוש עוד בצידו עד שיחרוש כל השדה לפיכך החמירו והחזיקו חכמים כל ק' וק' במזרחו של קבר בבית הפרס ומפרש דבית הפרס דרבנן. פי' ומ"ה האמינו בו ראיית הקטן וכשמעיד להקל ולא להחמיר כגון שהיו יודעים השדה שנחרש בה קבר אבל לא היו מכירים מקום הקבר שימדדו משם ק' אמה ובא זה והעיד שזה המקום הוא בית הפרס ולא יותר ומשום דבית הפרס הוא חששא בעלמא דרבנן. הימנוהו רבנן בדרבנן. ולא להחמיר שאם לא היו יודעים שהוא בית הפרס וזה מעיד אני זוכר שהי' בית הפרס ומחזיק' בחזקת טומאה למה תולה הטעם משום דבית הפרס דרבנן. השתא בדרבנן נאמן לאחזוקי איסורא כ"ש בדאורייתא. אלא לאו ש"מ להקל מעיד. וע"כ היינו באין בשבת קסבר תחומין דרבנן. ומ"ה האמינוהו ראיית הקטן: **אבל** אינו נאמן לומר דרך היה לפלוני במקום הזה שהיה הולך משם לשדהו. א) מעמד ומספד הי' לפלוני במקום הזה שהיה מספיד שם את מתו ושהיה עושה שם מעמד ומושב למתו כשהיו חוזרים מבית הקברות. מ"ט אפוקי ממונא הוא ולא מפקי' ממונא ע"פ ראיית הקטן. עיין ברפ"ק דפסחים:

מסורת הש"ס

א) [עיין תוס' לקמן לו. ד"ה אבל], ב) יבמות לט., ג) [שם ע"ש], ד) גיטין ז. חולין ה: ו. ז. [יבמות לט:], ה) [עיין תוס' יבמות שם ד"ה ס"ד השתא וכו'], ו) ברכות יט: עירובין ל: פסחים לב: מ"ק ה: חגיגה כה: בכורות כט. נדה נז., ז) [ברכות יט: ע"ש], ח) [תוספתא פרק ג], ט) [ד"ה השתא ותוס' שבת יב: ד"ה ר' נתן ותוס' חולין ה: ד"ה לדיקים ותוס' פסחים קו: ד"ה אישתלאי], י) שייך אחר ד"ה בית הפרס, כ) [ועי' היטב תוס' פסחים לב: ד"ה מאי בודקין ועוד תוס' בכורות כט. ד"ה היכי אזיל].

גליון הש"ס

גמ' היו מעלין מתרומה ליוחסין. עיין ברכות דף טז ע"ב תוס' ד"ה אין עומדין:

ליקוטי רש"י

שדיקדקה המחרישה את העצמות ומגלגלתן. **פרס.** לשון דבר שבור ופרוס על שם שנפרסו העצמות [נדה נז.]. **מעמד ומספד.** למת כשנושאין את המת לקוברו היו יושבין שבע פעמים לבכות את המת והרוצה לסופדו יספוד והכי תניא (ב"ב ק:) אין פוחתין משבעה מעמדות ומושבות למת כגון עמדו יקרים עמודו שבו יקרים שבו [מגילה כג:]. בחזירתן מן הקבר הולכין מעט ויושבין לנחם האבל או להרבות צער על המת שמת ולהרבות בבכי ולתת איש אל לבו לשוב בתשובה כי חיי האדם הבל ועומדין והולכין מעט וחוזרין ויושבין מעט כך עושין ז' פעמים כדי לתת אל לבם שחיי האדם הבל והיינו דמפרש לקמיה כנגד שבעה הבל הבלים שכתובין בראש ספר קהלת כן נראה הטעם בעיני וראיתי כתוב מפני שהשדים מתלוים עם החוזרים מבית הקברות לכך תקנו מעמדות ומושבות כדי שבתוך כך יסתלקו השדים מעליהן ולא נהירא דא"כ יהיו עושין כן בכ"מ ולקמן אמרינן דבמנהגא תליא מילתא ועוד מאי כנגד הבל הבלים. היאך עבדי, היאך היו רגילין לעשות במקום שנהגו. עמדו יקרים, לאחר שישבו מעט היה הממונה אומר להן עמדו ולכו אל מקום אחר כך נראה בעיני [רשב"ם ב"ב ק:]. **דרוב נשים.** שבעולם שנישאות לבעל בתולות הן [רשב"ם ב"ב צב:]. [ע"כ שייך לע"א]

אפוטרופוס. על נכסיו דאי לאו דשחרריה לא הוה חשיב ליה [גיטין מ.]. **שהניח תפילין בפני רבו.** אין דרך עבד להניח תפילין דמ"ע שהזמן גרמא היא דלילה לאו זמן תפילין הוא [גיטין מ.]. **אין חולקין תרומה לעבד אלא אם כן רבו עמו.** אם באו שניהם על הגורן נותנים לזה אבל זה בלא זה אין חולקין להם דקסבר אין חולקין תרומה לעבד אא"כ רבו עמו דלמא אתי לאסוקי ליוחסין דסברי כהן הוא. **אם כהן אני כו'.** אספק כהן וספק עבד קאי כי מתניתין. **היו מעלין מתרומה ליוחסין.** לאו מאכילתה אלא מחלוקה הלכך אין חולקין לו דלא ליתי לאסוקי ליוחסין [יבמות צט:]. **השתא בהמתן וכו'.** היאך יגרום שום שטן לפני צדיקים ע"י שוגג שום דבר עון. **אין הקב"ה מביא תקלה על ידם.** שתאכל הבהמה דבר האסור לה [חולין ה:]. **בית הפרס.** [מלא] חצי מענה תלם אחד של מאה אמה [מו"ק ה:]. **בית הפרס דרבנן.** דלא מטמא אלא מדרבנן והוא שדה שנחרש בו קבר וחשו חכמים שמא דלדלו כלי המחרישה את העצמות והדורס עליהן מסיטן ועצם כשעורה מטמא במגע ובמשא ולא באהל [ברכות יט:]. הוא שדה שנחרש בה קבר דתנן (אהלות פי"ז מ"א) החורש בית הקבר הרי זה עושה בית הפרס מלא מענה מאה אמה וגזור רבנן שמא כיתתה מחרישה את העצמות ופיזרתן באורך המענה ויש כאן עצם כשעורה ויעבור ויסיטנו ועצם כשעורה מטמאה במגע ובמשא דהיינו היסט [פסחים צב:]. שדה שנחרש בה קבר ואוקמי רבנן (על) [כל] סביבות הקבר מאה אמה בספק טומאה שדיקדקה המחרישה את העצמות ומגלגלתן. **פרס.** לשון דבר שבור ופרוס על שם שנפרסו העצמות [נדה נז.]. **מנפח אדם.** לפניו שאם יש שם עצם יראנו דאי לדאורייתא הוא לא הוינן מזלזלינן ביה כולי האי למיסמך אנפיחה והך בדיקה לעושה פסח איתמרי ולא לאוכלי תרומה כדאמרינן בחומר בקדש (חגיגה דף כה:) [ברכות יט:]. דכולה ספיקא משום עצמות היא ועצמות בלא בשר אינו מטמא באהל וכשמנפח לפני רגליו אם יש שם עצם גדול נראה מאליו ועצם קטן נראה בנפיחה ואינו מסיטו ברגליו [עירובין ל:]. מנפחו בפיו ואם יש עצם גדול יראנו ועצם כשעורה נדחה בנפיחתו ואהל אין מטמאו דהא אין טומאת אהל בעצמות אלא רוב בנין ורוב מנין [פסחים שם]. היה הולך לעשות פסחו ובית הפרס של שדה שנחרש בו קבר מפסיקו בודקו בנפיחה ואם יש עצם כשעורה רואהו ונשמט ממנו ועצם כשעורה אינו מטמא באהל אלא במגע ובמשא לפיכך בודק בנפיחה שלא יסיטנו ברגלו [חגיגה כה.]. דבשר ליכא ועצם כשעורה לא מטמא אלא במגע ובמשא הלכך מנפח כדי שלא יגעו רגליו בו והולך [נדה שם]. **שנידש.** בדריסת רגלי בני אדם [עירובין שם]. ברגל זו היא בדיקתו בודק אם נידש או לא נידש [חגיגה שם]. ברגלי אדם שהרגלים נושאים את העצמות ושוחקים [נדה שם]. **טהור.** שדריסת הרגלים העבירתן והבא לעשות פסחו יבדוק אם נידש ויעבור אבל לאכילת תרומה לא סמכינן עלה שיכול להמתין ובית הפרס מדבריהם ולא העמידום במקום כרת דפסח [פסחים שם]. שכבר נידשו עצמות שבו ונפחתו מכשעורה [עירובין שם]. שאי אפשר לעצם כשעורה שלא יהא נידש ברגל ובית הפרס אין בו שום ספק אלא משום עצם כשעורה דבית הפרס היינו שדה שנחרש בו קבר [בכורות כט.]. ואין בודקין לאוכלי תרומה, אין סומכין על בדיקה זו דכיון דאין זמן קבוע לאכילה ימתין שבעה ימים ויזה שלישי ושביעי ויטבול אבל גבי פסח הואיל ובית הפרס דרבנן לא העמידו דבריהם במקום כרת [חגיגה שם]. **תחומין דרבנן.** דרבנן בעלמא ניהו שגזרו עליהן לאחר מתן תורה [יומא סו:]. אסמכוה רבנן תחומין אקראי ואפי' למאן דאמר תחומין דרבנן כדאמרינן בעירובין (דף נא.) ילפינן מקום ממקום ומקום מניסה כו' [שבת לד.]. **מעמד ומספד.** למת כשנושאין את המת לקוברו היו יושבין שבע פעמים לבכות את המת והרוצה לסופדו יספוד והכי תניא (ב"ב ק:) אין פוחתין משבעה מעמדות ומושבות למת כגון עמדו יקרים עמודו שבו יקרים שבו [מגילה כג:]. בחזירתן מן הקבר הולכין מעט ויושבין לנחם האבל או להרבות צער על המת שמת ולהרבות בבכי ולתת איש אל לבו לשוב בתשובה כי חיי האדם הבל ועומדין והולכין מעט וחוזרין ויושבין מעט כך עושין ז' פעמים כדי לתת אל לבם שחיי האדם הבל והיינו דמפרש לקמיה כנגד שבעה הבל הבלים שכתובין בראש ספר קהלת כן נראה הטעם בעיני וראיתי כתוב מפני שהשדים מתלוים עם החוזרים מבית הקברות לכך תקנו מעמדות ומושבות כדי שבתוך כך יסתלקו השדים מעליהן ולא נהירא דא"כ יהיו עושין כן בכ"מ ולקמן אמרינן דבמנהגא תליא מילתא ועוד מאי כנגד הבל הבלים. היאך עבדי, היאך היו רגילין לעשות במקום שנהגו. עמדו יקרים, לאחר שישבו מעט היה הממונה אומר להן עמדו ולכו אל מקום אחר כך נראה בעיני [רשב"ם ב"ב ק:].

tributed to a person of uncertain status unless his master was present, lest people assume that he is of untainted Kohanic lineage. בִּמְקוֹמוֹ שֶׁל רַבִּי יוֹסֵי – **In R' Yose's locale,** however, לֹא הָיוּ מַעֲלִין מִתְּרוּמָה לְיוּחֲסִין – **they would not elevate** someone **from** the status of those to whom ***terumah*** is distributed **to** the status of **the genealogically fit.** R' Yose therefore perceived no danger in permitting the distribution of *terumah* to this individual.[12]

A related Baraisa:

תַּנְיָא – **It has been taught in a Baraisa:** אָמַר רַבִּי אֶלְעָזָר בְּרַבִּי יוֹסֵי – R' ELAZAR THE SON OF R' YOSE SAID: מִיָּמַי לֹא הֵעַדְתִּי – IN ALL MY DAYS, I had NEVER TESTIFIED regarding any person's fitness to receive *terumah.* פַּעַם אַחַת הֵעַדְתִּי – Then, ONE TIME I DID TESTIFY that I had observed *terumah* distributed to a certain individual at the granary, וְהֶעֱלוּ עֶבֶד לִכְהוּנָּה עַל פִּי – AND it transpired that THEY ELEVATED A SLAVE TO THE KEHUNAH (priesthood) BECAUSE OF MY WORDS!

The Gemara wonders at this:

הֶעֱלוּ סָלְקָא דַּעְתָּךְ – **Can it** even **enter your mind that they** actually **elevated** the slave because of R' Elazar's testimony? הַשְׁתָּא וּמַה בְּהֶמְתָּן שֶׁל צַדִּיקִים – Consider **now, if** with **the animals of the righteous,** אֵין הַקָּדוֹשׁ בָּרוּךְ הוּא מֵבִיא תַּקָּלָה עַל יָדָם – **the Holy One, Blessed is He, does not bring** about **a transgression through them,**[13] צַדִּיקִים עַצְמָם לֹא כָּל שֶׁכֵּן – then through **the righteous themselves, is it not certain** that he does not bring about a transgression? R' Elazar could not possibly have been the cause of a slave being elevated to the Kehunah! – ? –

Because of this difficulty, the Gemara emends the Baraisa:

אֶלָּא בִּקְשׁוּ לְהַעֲלוֹת עֶבֶד לִכְהוּנָּה עַל פִּי – **Rather,** the Baraisa reads: THEY *ATTEMPTED* TO ELEVATE A SLAVE TO THE KEHUNAH BECAUSE OF MY WORDS. In the end, though, the slave's true identity was discovered, and there was no transgression.

The Gemara explains how this came to pass:

חֲזָא בְּאַתְרֵיהּ דְּרַבִּי יוֹסֵי – **He** (i.e. R' Elazar) **observed** *terumah* distributed to the slave at a granary **in R' Yose's locale,** where they distribute *terumah* to the slaves of Kohanim without their masters present, וְאָזַל וְאַסְהִיד בְּאַתְרֵיהּ דְּרַבִּי יְהוּדָה – **and he went and testified in R' Yehudah's locale,** where they do not distribute *terumah* to slaves unless their masters are present. Those of R' Yehudah's locale assumed, in accordance with their practice, that this must be a Kohen of unblemished lineage. They were therefore prepared to elevate him to the Kehunah.

The Mishnah stated:

וְשֶׁהַמָּקוֹם הַזֶּה בֵּית הַפְּרָס הוּא – AND THAT THIS PLACE IS A *BEIS HAPRAS.*[14]

The Gemara asks:

מַאי טַעְמָא – **What is the reason** that we accept this person's testimony regarding the boundaries of a *beis hapras*?

The Gemara explains:

בֵּית הַפְּרָס דְּרַבָּנָן – It is because the decree of ***beis hapras*** **is** of **Rabbinic** origin.[15] The Rabbis decreed corpse *tumah* upon a field containing a plowed-over grave (a *beis hapras*) because of the possibility that fragments of bone were scattered throughout the field.

The Gemara proves that this is no more than a Rabbinic decree:

דְּאָמַר רַב יְהוּדָה אָמַר שְׁמוּאֵל – **For Rav Yehudah said in the name of Shmuel,** regarding the checking required of one who must traverse a *beis hapras* in order to bring his *pesach* offering:[16] מְנַפֵּחַ אָדָם בֵּית הַפְּרָס וְהוֹלֵךְ – **A person blows on** the ground of **the *beis hapras* and walks** through it. This ensures that he will not touch or move a bit of bone.[17] וְרַב יְהוּדָה בַּר אַמִי

NOTES

our Mishnah's witness testifies that the person in question shared in the distribution of Biblical *terumah,* his testimony is effective *only* in permitting this person to partake of Rabbinical *terumah.* It does not permit him to partake of Biblical *terumah,* and certainly does not render him a genealogically fit Kohen (*Tosafos;* see *Ran*).]

12. [For this would not cause anyone to assume that he is of untainted lineage.]

13. This refers to the incident described in *Chullin* (7a-b), in which the donkey of R' Pinchas ben Yair would not eat untithed produce (*Rashi;* see *Ritva*).

14. A *beis hapras* is a field containing a grave that has been plowed over (see *Oholos* 18:2-4). The Rabbis feared that the plowing will have scattered fragments of bone throughout the field; such fragments, if they are the size of a grain of barley or larger, can generate corpse *tumah.* The Rabbis therefore decreed that one who passes within a hundred *amos* (cubits) of the grave in any direction is contaminated with corpse *tumah* because of the possibility that he touched or moved a bit of bone. They reckoned one hundred *amos* to be the distance that the plowshare would spread the bone fragments (*Rashi*).

The case of our Mishnah concerns a field that was known to contain a plowed-over grave; the grave's precise location, however, was forgotten. As a result, every inch of the field must be considered *tamei* because of doubt. The object of the testimony is to remove the doubt from some of the field by identifying the *beis hapras* area. This person testifies, based on his childhood memories, that the *beis hapras* area extended only so far, but no further (see *Ran* to the Mishnah; *Tosafos* here; cf. *Re'ah; Meiri,* first explanation).

15. Because the *tumah* is only Rabbinic, and because the exact boundaries of the *beis hapras* are in doubt, the Rabbis permitted the *tahor* areas to be identified by testimony based on childhood recollection (see *Ran* ibid.; see previous note). However, this testimony cannot remove the *tumah* from a place that has been traditionally held to be a *beis hapras* (*Ran;* cf. *Raavad,* quoted there), nor can it confer *beis hapras* status upon an area that has been traditionally held to be *tahor* (*Ran;* cf. *Re'ah; Meiri,* first explanation).

[By Biblical law the field does not generate *tumah,* as it is unlikely that the plowshare dug deeply enough into the ground to reach a buried corpse. The Rabbis, however, placed a stringency upon this field, and decreed that it be treated as if strewn with fragments of bone (*Tosafos, Moed Katan* 5b ד״ה מנפח אדם). The name בֵּית הַפְּרָס (*beis hapras*) derives from the root פרס, meaning *broken* or *fragmented;* the term refers to the bones that may have been plowed through and broken (*Rashi* to *Niddah* 57a ד״ה פרס; cf. *Rambam, Oholos* 17:1).]

16. Rav Yehudah (and Rav Yehudah bar Ami) is explaining a Mishnah in *Oholos* (18:4) which states that one confronted with a *beis hapras* while on his way to make the *pesach* offering may "check" the *beis hapras* and proceed. Each of them puts forward another method of checking (see *Pesachim* 92b and *Chagigah* 25b with *Rashi; Tosafos, Pesachim* ibid.; cf. *Tosafos* here; *Bechoros* 29a ד״ה היכי אזיל).

17. As stated above, the reason a *beis hapras* renders one *tamei* is because of the possibility that it is strewn with bone fragments. The Rabbis feared that one walking through the field would acquire corpse *tumah* either by coming into contact with a fragment, or by moving it with his foot. [The former is a form of contact-generated *tumah* (מַגָּע); the latter a form of carrying *tumah* (מַשָּׂא).] Therefore, with each step, one must blow on the ground before him [with a bellows – see *Meiri* to *Chagigah* 25b]. We assume that the blowing will cause any minute fragments to move; he will notice them, and avoid treading upon them (*Rashi* here and to *Chagigah* ibid., *Berachos* 19b; see *Rashi* to *Eruvin* 30b and *Pesachim* 92b).

Blowing will alert one only to bone chips lying on the surface of the field, not to those buried beneath the ground. Nevertheless, it suffices, for our one concern is that he might touch or move the fragment with his foot. Although a corpse contaminates one who forms a "roof" (*ohel*) over it with his body, we are not troubled by the possibility that one traversing the *beis hapras* will pass over a buried bit of bone. For *ohel tumah* is a consideration only if a majority of the corpse's bones remain extant, or if the large bones that make up the greater part of a person's frame (see *Oholos* 3:1) or the entire skull or spine remain extant. A *beis hapras,* however, contains only small bits of bone at worst. Therefore, as long as one ensures that the path he treads is free of visible bone fragments, he may pass through the field (see *Rashi* here and to *Pesachim* ibid. ד״ה מנפח; see *Moed Katan* 5b with *Rashi*). [Of course, if an olive's measure of the corpse's *flesh* remains, it *will* contaminate one

אפוטרופוס או שהניח תפילין בפני רבו או שקרא שלשה פסוקים בבית הכנסת הרי זה לא יצא לחירות התם דאיקרי עבד מדעתו כי קאמרינן דקא נהיג ביה מנהג בנים: לטבול לאכול בתרומה: בתרומה דרבנן: ושהיה חולק עמנו על הגורן: ודלמא עבד כהן הוא תנן כמאן דאמר אין חולקין תרומה לעבד אלא אם כן רבו עמו דתניא אין חולקין תרומה לעבד אלא אם כן רבו עמו דברי רבי יהודה רבי יוסי אומר יכול הוא שיאמר אם כהן אני תנו לי בשביל עצמי ואם עבד כהן אני תנו לי בשביל רבי במקומו של רבי יהודה היו מעלין מתרומה ליוחסין במקומו של רבי יוסי לא היו מעלין מתרומה ליוחסין תניא א"ר אלעזר ברבי יוסי מימי לא העדתי פעם אחת העדתי והעלו עבד לכהונה על פי העלו סלקא דעתך השתא ומה בהמתן של צדיקים אין הקב"ה מביא תקלה על ידם צדיקים עצמם לא כ"ש אלא בקשו להעלות עבד לכהונה על פי חזא באתריה דרבי יוסי ואזל ואסהיד באתריה דרבי יהודה: ושהמקום הזה בית הפרס הוא: מ"ט בית הפרס דרבנן דאמר רב יהודה אמר שמואל מנפח אדם בית הפרס והולך ורב יהודה בר אמי משמיה דרב יהודה אמר בית הפרס שנידש טהור מאי טעמא אי אפשר לעצם כשעורה שלא נידש ברגל: ועד כאן היינו באין בשבת: קסבר תחומין דרבנן: ואין נאמן לומר דרך היה לפלוני במקום הזה מעמד ומספד היה לפלוני במקום הזה: מאי טעמא אפוקי ממונא לא מפקינן תנו רבנן נאמן התינוק לומר כך אמר לי אבא משפחה זו טהורה משפחה זו טמאה טמאה סלקא דעתך אלא משפחה זו כשרה ומשפחה זו פסולה ושאכלנו בקצצה של בת פלוני לפלוני ושהיינו מוליכים חלה ומתנות לפלוני כהן על ידי עצמו אבל לא על ידי אחר וכולן אם היה עובד כוכבים ונתגייר עבד ונשתחרר אין נאמנים ואין נאמן לומר דרך היה לפלוני במקום הזה מעמד ומספד היה לפלוני במקום הזה ר' יוחנן בן ברוקא אומר נאמנים ר' יוחנן בן ברוקא אהייא אילימא אסיפא אפוקי ממונא הוא אלא ארישא וכולם אם היה עובד כוכבים ונתגייר עבד ונשתחרר אין נאמנין ר' יוחנן בן ברוקא אומר נאמנין במאי קמיפלגי ת"ק סבר כיון דעובד כוכבים הוא לא הוה דייק ורבי יוחנן בן ברוקא סבר כיון דדעתיה לאיגיורי מידק הוה דייק מאי קצצה דתנו רבנן כיצד קצצה אחד מן האחין שנשא אשה שאינה הוגנת לו באין בני משפחה ומביאין חבית מליאה פירות ושוברין אותה באמצע רחבה ואומרים אחינו בית ישראל שמעו אחינו פלוני נשא אשה שאינה הוגנת לו ומתייראים אנו שמא יתערב זרעו בזרעינו בואו וקחו לכם דוגמא לדורות שלא יתערב זרעו בזרעינו וזו היא קצצה שהתינוק נאמן להעיד עליה:

הדרן עלך האשה שנתארמלה

רש"י

אפוטרופוס. מסר נכסיו בידו להכנים ולהוציא לסחורה: הרי זה לא יצא לחירות. ולא אמרינן אי לאו דשחרריה לא הוה יזיף מיניה ולא הוה שביק ליה לנהוג מנהג בן חורין ושמעינן מינה דיש עבד שלומד תורה: בתרומה דרבנן. כגון תרומת חוצה לארץ או פירות המניינהו להני להאכילו על פיהם: הכי גרסינן דתניא שאין חולקין תרומה לעבד כו'. ורישא דברייתא כהנת שנתערב וולדה בוולד שפחתה שניהן יוצאין לגורן ונוטלין חלק אחד שאין חולקין תרומה לעבד כו' הלכך אי אזיל חד מינייהו לא פלגינן ליה דלמא אתי לאחזוקי בכהן ודלמא האי ניהו העבד: במקומו של ר' יהודה. משום הכי אמר אין חולקין: בהמתן של צדיקים. חמורו של רבי פנחס בן יאיר בהכל שוחטין (חולין ז.): חזא באתריה דרבי יוסי. שחלקו לו תרומה בגורן: ואסהיד באתריה דרבי יהודה. ושם לא היו חולקין תרומה לעבדי כהנים: בית הפרס. החורש את הקבר הרי זה עושה בית הפרס מאה אמה שכך שיערו שהמחרישה מולכת את עצמות המת ודלמא נגע או הסיט המהלך בו את עצם כשעורה שמטמא במגע ובמשא: מנפח אדם בית הפרס. וסומך על כך שאם יש עצם רואהו ואע"ג דמאהיל לא חיישינן דאין עצם כשעורה מטמא באהל עד דאיכא שדרה או גולגולת שלמה או רוב בנין או רוב מנין: שנידש. דישה רבה ברגלים הרבה: טהור. דתלינן לקולא ואמרינן כל העצמות נכתתו לפחות מכשיעור אלמא חששא דרבנן בעלמא הוא: נאמן התינוק. להעיד בגודלו מה שראה בקוטנו: טמאה וטהורה סלקא דעתך. מה טומאה וטהרה יש לומר במשפחות: בקצצה. לקמן מפרש לה: של בת פלוני לפלוני. כשנשא פלוני את בת פלוני: ושהיינו מוליכין כו' על ידי עצמו. אם כך העיד התינוק על ידי היה אבא שולח לו חלה ומתנות: אם היה עובד כוכבים ונתגייר. והעיד משנתגייר מראה את אלה בנכרותו אינו נאמן: דוגמא. אות וסימן וזכרון לדורות הבאים:

הדרן עלך האשה שנתארמלה

תוספות

תנן כמאן דאמר אין חולקין לעבד כו'. ואם תאמר והא לא קאמר רבי יהודה דאין חולקין אלא בתרומה דאורייתא דמעלין ממנה ליוחסין אבל מתני' דאוקמינן בתרומה דרבנן דאין מעלין ממנה ליוחסין מודה דחולקין לעבד בלא רבו ואם כן אכתי תקשי ודלמא עבד כהן הוא ולאו מלתא היא דמתניתין איירי שפיר שמעיד שחלק לו תרומה דאורייתא אלא שאינו נאמן להאכילו אלא בתרומה דרבנן:

ומה בהמתן של צדיקים. מפורש במקום אחר (גיטין דף ז. ט)):

ושהמקום הזה בית הפרס. ולא יותר וצא לטהר:

י) מנפח. בדיעבד אם עשה כבר טהרות אבל בדיקה לכתחלה מפרש במשנה (אהלות פי"ח מ"ד) כילד בודקין כ):

בית הפרס דרבנן. נראה דאפי' במקום הקבר מקילין כמו בשאר שדה ואין לומר דמקום הקבר מטמא באהל ומביא רבינו יצחק ראיה מדתניא בפ"ק דמועד קטן (דף ה:) מצא שדה מצויינת ואינו יודע מה טיבה יש בה אילנות בידוע שנחרש בה קבר אין בה אילנות בידוע שאבד בה קבר ומאי נפקא מינה כיון שעתה אינו יודע מקום הקבר בין נחרש בין אבד אלא שמע מינה דמקום הקבר טהור כשנחרש ובית הפרס להכי הוי דרבנן משום דהוי ספק טומאה ברשות הרבים אע"ג דבעלמא טיהרו חכמים ספק טומאה ברה"ר היינו היכא שהטומאה מבוררת ולא נולד הספק אלא באקראי ופעם אחרת לא יטמא כיון שמקום הטומאה ידוע אבל הכא שלעולם השדה בספק לא רצו לטהר אע"ג דמדאורייתא טהור:

הדרן עלך האשה שנתארמלה

עין משפט נר מצוה

קכז א מיי' פי"ב מהל' תרומות הלכה כב:
קכח ב ג מיי' פ"ו מהל' קרבן פסח הל' ח:
קכט ד מיי' פ"ב מהל' שבת הלכה יט טוש"ע א"ח סי' שצו סעי' יב:
קל ה מיי' פי"ד מהל' עדות הלכה ג סמג לאוין רטו טוש"ע ח"מ סי' לה סעי' ו:
קלא ו מיי' שם הלכה ד וטוש"ע שם סעי' ז:
קלב ז מיי' שם הלכה ג טוש"ע אה"ע סי' ב סעי' א בהג"ה:

תוספות רי"ד

עדי' צריך בעדות הינומא כדתנן אם יש עדים שיצאה בהינומא וראשה פרוע וכל היכא דבעי' שני עדים בעינן שיהא גדול עמו שלא יעיד שניהם על ראיית קטנות: ושהיה איש פ' יוצא בבית הספר. פי' כשהיה לומדים יחד עם תינוקות בבית רבן ומחזיקי' להההיה בראיית קטנות ולא בעי' הכא גדול עומד עמו. שמעלים לכהונה ע"פ ע"א. ובגמרא מפרש בתרומה דרבנן כגון תרומות ח"ל או פירות והימנוהו רבנן בדרבנן. וכי בגידלו מעיד על מה שראה בקוטנו אבל קטן אינו מעיד שמעלים בתרומ' ע"פ ע"א דוקא גדול אבל קטן לא וכן עבד ואשה לא תנן שיהו נאמנים בכהונה כדתנן גבי שבויי' וא"כ במת בעלה הלכך אין הקטן נאמן בכהונה והוא נאמן בשבוי' ומת בעלך ולא תימא כ"מ שע"א נאמן גם עבד ואשה נאמנים שהרי במת בעלך יש הבא שהיה מכשיר ע"א ר"א היה מכשיר אשה ר"ע כדתנן בפ' בתרא דיבמות. ר"א אומר אין משיאין את אשה ע"פ ע"א ר"ע אומר לא ע"פ אשה ולא ע"פ קרובים אלמא אע"ג דפליג ר"ע ע' ר"א ומכשיר ע"א. דא אמר לא ע"פ אשה ולא ע"פ קרובים א"כ אינו כן כלל להכשיר עבד ואשה במקום שע"א נאמן אלא היכא דתנן תנן היכא דלא תנן לא תנן. במקום שעבד ואשה נאמנים גם הקטן נאמן. ומקשה דלמא עבד הוא מסייע ליה לריב"ל דאריב"ל אסור לו לאדם שילמוד את עבדו תורה מותיבי לה ממנו רבו או שעשאו רבו אפוטרופוס. פי' מסר כל נכסיו בידו להכניס ולהוציא בסחורה או שהניח תפלין בפני רבו או שקרא שלשה פסוקים בבה"כ הה"ז לא יצא לחירות. פי' לאו אמרים אי לאו דשחררי' לא הוה יזיף מיניה ולא הוי שביק ליה לנהוג מנהג ב"ח. ש"מ דיש עבד שלומד תורה התם דאיקרי עבד מדעתיה. וכי קאמרינן דקא נהוג בי' מנהג בנים: ושהיה חולק עמנו בגורן וליחוש דילמא עבד כהן הוא תנן אין חולקין תרומה לעבד אא"כ רבו עמו דברי ר' יהודה ר"י אומר יכול הוא שיאמר אם כהן אני תנו לי בשביל עצמי ואם אני עבד כהן תנו לי בשביל רבי ובמקומו של ר' יוסי לא היה מעלים מתרומה ליוחסין: ושהמקום הזה בית הפרס. פי' הכי תנן בפ' בתרא דאהלות החורש את הקבר ה"ז עושה בית הפרס עד כמה הוא עושה מלא המענה ק' אמה בית ארבעת קבין. פי' החורש אנו חוששים שמא המחרישה פזרה עצמות המת ועצם כשעורה ממנו מטמא במגע ובמשא אבל לא באהל פי' עד דאיכא שדרה או גולגולת שלמים או רוב מנין או רוב בנין ואנו חוששים שמא פזרה שברי עצמות מן הקבר ועד ק' אמה שאם חרש מן הקבר לצד מזרח מונה מן הקבר ק' אמה ועושה אותה בית הפרס והנכנס טמא שמא נגע או היסט עצם כשעורה שהוא מכוסה בעפר ולאו אדעתיה ואלו ק' אמה המונה אותם מרובעין שהן ק' על ק' שיביאו ארבעת קבין. שכשאה הוא נ' על נ' ולמה אנו מחמירים כ"כ ולא נעשה אלא ק' אמה ברוחב הקבר שהמחרישה מוליכה את העצמות אלא אנו חוששים שמא הוליכה והחזירה ועוד הוליכה שדרך החורש לחרוש התלם ולחרוש עוד בצידו עד שיחרוש כל השדה לפיכך החמירו והחזיקו חכמים כל ק' וק' במזרחו של קבר בבית הפרס ומפרש דבית הפרס דרבנן. פי' ומ"ה האמינו בו ראיית הקטן וכשמעידי להקל ולא להחמיר כגון שהיו יודעים השדה שנחרש בה קבר אבל לא היו מכירים מקום הקבר שימדדו משם ק' ולא להחמיר שאם העיד שזה המקום הוא בית הפרס ולא יותר ומשום דבית הפרס הוא חששא בעלמא דרבנן. הימנוהו רבנן בדרבנן. ולא להחמיר שאם לא היו יודעים שהוא בית הפרס וזה מעיד אני זוכר שהי' בית הפרס ומחזיקי' בחזקת טומאה למה תולה הטומאה משום דבית הפרס דרבנן. השתא בדרבנן נאמן לאחזוקי איסורא כ"ש בדאורייתא. אלא לאו ש"מ להקל מעיד. וע"כ היינו באין בשבת קסבר תחומין דרבנן. ומ"ה האמינוהו ראיית הקטן: אבל אינו נאמן לומר דרך היה לפלוני במקום הזה שהיה הולך משם לשדהו. או מעמד ומספד הי' לפלוני במקום הזה שהיה מספיד שם את מתו ושהיה עושה שם מעמד ומושב למתו כשחוזרים מבית הקברות. מ"ט אפוקי ממונא הוא ולא מפקי' ממונא ע"פ ראיית הקטן. עיין ברפ"ק דפסחים:

מסורת הש"ס

א) [עיין תוס' לקמן לו. ד"ה אלא], ב) יבמות צט., ג) [שם ע"ש], ד) גיטין ז. חולין ה: ו. ז., ה) [עיין תוס' יבמות שם ד"ה השתא ותוס'], ו) ברכות יט: עירובין ל: פסחים צב: מ"ק ה: חגיגה כה: בכורות כט. נדה נז., ז) [ברכות יט: ע"ש], ח) [תוספתא פרק ג], ט) [ד"ה השתא ותוס' שבת יב: ד"ה ר' נתן ותוס' חולין ה: ד"ה צדיקים ותוס' פסחים קו: ד"ה אישתלאי], י) שייך אחר ד"ה בית הפרס, כ) [ועי' היטב תוס' פסחים לב: ד"ה מאי בודקין ועוד תוס' בכורות כט. ד"ה היכי אזיל].

גליון הש"ס

גמ' היו מעלין מתרומה ליוחסין. עיין ברכות דף טו ע"ב תוס' ד"ה אין עומדין:

ליקוטי רש"י

שדיקדקה המחרישה את העצמות ומגלגלתן. פרס. לשון דבר שבור ופרוס על שם שנפרסו העצמות [נדה נז.]. מעמד ומספד. למת כשנושאין את המת לקוברו היו יושבין שבע פעמים לבכות את המת והרוצה לסופדו יספוד והכי תניא (ב"ב ק:) אין פוחתין משבעה מעמדות ומושבות למת כגון עמדו יקרים עמודו שבו יקרים שבו [מגילה כג:]. בחזירתן מן הקבר הולכין מעט ויושבין לנחם האבל או להרבות צער על המת שמת ולהרבות בבכי ולתת איש אל לבו לשוב בתשובה כי חיי האדם הבל ועומדין והולכין מעט וחוזרין ויושבין מעט כך עושין ז' פעמים כדי לתת אל לבם שחיי האדם הבל והיינו דמפרש לקמיה שבעה הבלים שכתובין בספר קהלת כן נראה הטעם בעיני וראיתי כתוב מפני שהשדים מתלוים עם החוזרים מבית הקברות לכך תקנו מעמדות ומושבות כדי שבתוך כך יסתלקו השדים מעליהן ולא נהירא דא"כ יהיו עושין כן בכ"מ ולקמן אמרינן דמנהגא תליא מילתא ועוד מאי כנגד הבל הבלים. היאך עבדי, היאך היו רגילין לעשות במקום שנהגו. עמדו יקרים, לאחר שישבו מעט היה הממונה אומר להן עמדו ולכו אל מקום אחר כך נראה בעיני [רשב"ם ב"ב ק:]. דרוב נשים. שבעולם שנישאות לבעל בתולות הן [רשב"ם ב"ב צב:]. [ע"כ שייך לע"א]

אפוטרופוס. על נכסיו דאי לאו דשחרריה לא הוה חשיב ליה [גיטין מ.]. שהניח תפילין בפני רבו. אין דרך עבד להניח תפילין דמ"ע שהזמן גרמא היא דלילה לאו זמן תפילין הוא [גיטין מ.]. אין חולקין תרומה לעבד אלא אם כן רבו עמו. אם באו נותנים לגם אבל זה בלא זה אין חולקין להם דקסבר אין חולקין תרומה לעבד אא"כ רבו עמו דלמא אתי לאסוקי ליוחסין דסברי כהן הוא. אם כהן אני כו'. אספק כהן וספק עבד קאי כי מתניתין. היו מעלין מתרומה ליוחסין. … מחלוקה הלכך אין חולקין לו דלא ליתי לאסוקי ליוחסין [יבמות צט:]. השתא בהמתן וכו'. היאך יגרום שום … ע"י שוגג שום דבר עון. אין הקב"ה מביא תקלה על ידם. שתאכל הבהמה דבר האסור לה [חולין ה …] [מלא] חצי מענה תלם אחד של מאה אמה [מו"ק ה:]. בית הפרס דרבנן. דלא מטמא אלא מדרבנן והוא שד… וחשו חכמים שמא דלדלו כלי המחרישה את העצמות והדורס עליהן מסיטן ועצם כשעורה מטמא במגע … [ברכות יט:]. הוא שדה שנחרש בה קבר כדתנן (אהלות פי"ז מ"א) החורש בית הקבר הרי זה עושה בית הפרס … אמה וגזור רבנן שמא כיתתה מחרישה את העצמות ופיזרתן באורך המענה ויש כאן עצם כשעורה ויעבור ויסיט… מטמאה במגע ובמשא דהיינו היסט [פסחים צב:]. שדה שנחרש בה קבר ואוקמי רבנן (על) [כל] סביבות הקבר … טומאה שדיקדקה המחרישה את העצמות ומגלגלתן. פרס. לשון דבר שבור ופרוס על שם שנפרסו העצמות [נדה נז.]. מנפח אדם. לפניו שאם היה שם עצם יראהו דאי דאורייתא הוא לא הוינן מזלזלינן ביה כולי האי למיסמך אנפיחה … פסח איטתרי ולא לאוכלי תרומה כדאמרינן בחומר בקדש (חגיגה דף כה:) [ברכות יט:]. דכולה ספיקא … ועצמות בלא בשר אינו מטמא באהל וכשמנפח לפני רגליו אם יש שם עצם גדול נראה מאליו ועצם קטן … מסיטו ברגליו [עירובין ל:]. מנפחו בפיו ואם יש עצם גדול יראנו ועצם כשעורה נדחה בנפיחתו ואהל אין … טומאת אהל בעצמות אלא רוב בנין ורוב מנין [פסחים שם]. היה הולך לעשות פסחו ובית הפרס של שדה שנחרש … בודקו בנפיחה ואם יש עצם כשעורה רואהו ונשמט ממנו ועצם כשעורה אינו מטמא באהל אלא במגע ובמ… בנפיחה שלא יסיטנו ברגלו [חגיגה כה:]. דבשר ליכא ועצם כשעורה לא מטמא אלא במגע ובמשא הלכך מנפח כו והולך [נדה שם]. שנידש. בדריסת רגלי בני אדם [עירובין שם]. ברגל וזו היא בדיקתו בודק אם נידש או לא נידש [חגיגה שם]. ברגלי אדם שהרגלים נושאים את העצמות ושחקום [נדה שם]. טהור. שדריסת הרגלים העבירתן והבא לעשות פסח … לא סמכינן עלה שיכול להמתין ובית הפרס מדבריהם ולא העמידום במקום כרת דפסח [פסחים שם]. שכבר נידשו עצמות שבו ונפחתו מכשעורה [עירובין שם]. שאי אפשר לעצם כשעורה שלא יהא נידש ברגל ובית הפרס … דבית הפרס היינו שדה שנחרש בו קבר [בכורות כט.]. ואין בודקין לאוכלי תרומה, אין סומכין על בדיקה זו דכיון דאין זמן קבוע לאכילה ימתין שבעה ימים ויזה שלישי ושביעי ויטבול אבל גבי פסח הואיל ובית הפרס … [חגיגה שם]. תחומין דרבנן. דרבנן בעלמא ניהו שגזרו עליהן לאחר מתן תורה [יומא סו:]. אסמכוה רבנן תחומין אקראי ואפי' למאן דאמר תחומין דרבנן כדאמרינן בעירובין (דף נא.) ילפינן מקום ממקום ומקום מניס … שנושאין את המת לקוברו היו יושבין שבע פעמים לבכות את המת והרוצה לסופדו יספוד והכי תניא (ב"ב ק:) אין פוחתין משבעה מעמדות ומושבות למת כגון עמדו יקרים עמודו שבו יקרים שבו [מגילה כג:]. בחזירתן … אבל או להרבות צער על המת שמת ולהרבות בבכי ולתת איש אל לבו לשוב בתשובה כי חיי האדם הבל ועומדין והולכין מעט וחוזרין ויושבין מעט כך עושין ז' פעמים כדי לתת אל לבם שחיי האדם הבל והיינו דמפרש לקמיה … בספר קהלת כן נראה הטעם בעיני וראיתי כתוב מפני שהשדים מתלוים עם החוזרים מבית הקברות לכך תקנו מעמדות ומושבות כדי שבתוך כך יסתלקו השדים מעליהן ולא נהירא דא"כ יהיו עושין כן בכ"מ ולקמן אמרינן … מילתא ועוד מאי כנגד הבל הבלים. היאך עבדי, היאך היו רגילין לעשות במקום שנהגו. עמדו יקרים, לאחר שישבו מעט היה הממונה אומר להן עמדו ולכו אל מקום אחר כך נראה בעיני [רשב"ם ב"ב ק:].

אַפּוֹטְרוֹפּוֹס – AN ADMINISTRATOR over his property, to buy and sell merchandise on his behalf,[1] אוֹ שֶׁהֵנִיחַ תְּפִילִּין בִּפְנֵי רַבּוֹ – OR IF HE DONNED TEFILLIN IN FRONT OF HIS MASTER,[2] אוֹ שֶׁקָּרָא שְׁלֹשָׁה פְּסוּקִים בְּבֵית הַכְּנֶסֶת – OR IF HE READ THREE Torah VERSES IN THE SYNAGOGUE,[3] הֲרֵי זֶה לֹא יָצָא לְחֵירוּת – it is still possible that HE WAS NOT SET FREE.[4] These actions do not necessarily indicate that he is a freeman.

We see from this Baraisa that even a slave will sometimes study Torah. How can R' Yehoshua ben Levi rule differently?

The Gemara answers:

הָתָם דְּאִיקְּרִי עֶבֶד מִדַּעְתּוֹ – Over there, the Baraisa discusses **a slave who read** the verses **on his own. כִּי קָאָמְרִינַן – When we said** our law, however, **דְּקָא נָהִיג בֵּיהּ מִנְהַג בָּנִים – it was** regarding **one who treats [the slave] as sons are treated,** i.e. he teaches him Torah. It is this which R' Yehoshua ben Levi forbids.[5] Since in the Mishnah's case the person in question had been *taught* Torah, it is clear that he is not a slave.

The Mishnah stated:

לִטְבּוֹל לֶאֱכוֹל בִּתְרוּמָה – TO IMMERSE himself in order TO EAT *TERUMAH.*

The purpose of this testimony is to prove that this individual is a Kohen, and is thus permitted to consume *terumah.* The Gemara therefore explains:

בִּתְרוּמָה דְּרַבָּנָן – This testimony renders him permitted **with regard to Rabbinical *terumah*** only,[6] but not with regard to Biblical *terumah.* For on the Biblical level, testimony based on childhood memory is worthless. However, the Rabbis accepted it where it pertains to Rabbinic law.[7]

The Mishnah stated:

וְשֶׁהָיָה חוֹלֵק עִמָּנוּ עַל הַגּוֹרֶן – AND THAT HE WOULD DIVIDE *terumah* WITH US AT THE GRANARY.

The Gemara questions the efficacy of this testimony:

וְדִלְמָא עֶבֶד כֹּהֵן הוּא – But perhaps he is the slave of a Kohen, and receives *terumah* on account of his master.[8] How does this testimony prove that he is himself a Kohen?

The Gemara answers:

תְּנַן כְּמַאן דְּאָמַר – Our Mishnah taught its law **in accordance with the one who says אֵין חוֹלְקִין תְּרוּמָה לְעֶבֶד אֶלָּא אִם כֵּן רַבּוֹ עִמּוֹ** – that **we do not distribute *terumah* to a slave unless his master is with him. דְּתַנְיָא – For it has been taught in a Baraisa,** regarding one who we know may eat *terumah,* and who is now demanding a portion, but about whom it is not certain whether he is a Kohen or the slave of a Kohen:[9] אֵין חוֹלְקִין תְּרוּמָה לְעֶבֶד אֶלָּא אִם כֵּן רַבּוֹ עִמּוֹ – WE DO NOT DISTRIBUTE *TERUMAH* TO A SLAVE UNLESS HIS MASTER IS WITH HIM. Therefore, this person of doubtful status may not come alone to the granary and receive *terumah,* for he may be a slave. דִּבְרֵי רַבִּי יְהוּדָה – THESE ARE THE WORDS OF R' YEHUDAH.[10] רַבִּי יוֹסֵי אוֹמֵר – R' YOSE SAYS: יָכוֹל הוּא שֶׁיֹּאמַר – HE IS ABLE TO come alone to the granary and SAY: אִם כֹּהֵן אֲנִי תְּנוּ לִי בִּשְׁבִיל עַצְמִי – "IF I AM A KOHEN, GIVE ME *terumah* ON MY OWN ACCOUNT, וְאִם עֶבֶד כֹּהֵן אֲנִי תְּנוּ לִי בִּשְׁבִיל רַבִּי – AND IF I AM THE SLAVE OF A KOHEN, GIVE ME ON ACCOUNT OF MY MASTER!"

Our Mishnah follows the opinion of R' Yehudah. Accordingly, testimony that this person shared in the division of *terumah* at the granary is tantamount to testimony that he is not a slave. Perforce, he is a Kohen.

Having cited this Baraisa, the Gemara explains the reasoning underlying the dispute:

בִּמְקוֹמוֹ שֶׁל רַבִּי יְהוּדָה – In R' Yehudah's locale, הָיוּ מַעֲלִין מִתְּרוּמָה לְיוּחֲסִין – they would elevate someone **from** the status of those to whom ***terumah*** is distributed **to** the status of **the genealogically fit.**[11] Therefore, he did not permit *terumah* to be dis-

NOTES

1. One would not usually appoint his slave to the prestigious position of administrator of his property (see *Rashi, Gittin* 40a ד״ה אפוטרופוס). Perhaps, then, his doing so demonstrates that this is not a slave, but a freeman.

2. A slave generally does not don tefillin. [For a slave, like a woman, is not obligated to perform positive commandments that are dependent upon time (מִצְוֹת עֲשֵׂה שֶׁהַזְּמַן גְּרָמָן, e.g. succah; *lulav*).] Included in this category is the tefillin obligation, which applies only by day, not by night (*Rashi, Gittin* ibid. ד״ה שהניח תפילין בפני רבו). Perhaps, then, the fact that this slave donned tefillin in front of his master [and his master remained silent (see *Rambam, Avodim* 8:17)] constitutes proof that he has been freed.

3. [I.e. he was called to the Torah for an *aliyah* and he read the minimum number of verses. This might give rise to the notion that he was freed, because it is considered disrespectful to the congregation for a slave to be called up for an *aliyah* (see *Rama* to *Orach Chaim* 282:3; see *Hagahos Yavetz*).]

4. I.e. the fact that the master borrowed money from him [entrusted him with his property] and permitted him to engage in the practices of freemen does not constitute proof that he set him free (*Rashi;* cf. *Rambam, Avodim* 8:17,18; *Meiri*).

5. R' Yehoshua ben Levi feared that if this young slave would be treated as a regular Jew, people would assume that he actually was a Jew, and would allow him to marry a Jewish woman, which is forbidden (*Ran*).

6. Such as the *terumah* taken from the produce of certain countries outside of Eretz Yisrael, or the *terumah* taken from certain fruits and vegetables even in Eretz Yisrael, both of which are the product of Rabbinic obligation. Testimony based on youthful recollection will permit the consumption of Rabbinical *terumah* [which is prohibited to a non-Kohen by Rabbinic decree only] (*Rashi;* see *Rashba*). It will not, however, permit the consumption of Biblical *terumah.*

[By Biblical law, *terumah* is taken from the produce of Eretz Yisrael only. However, the Rabbis decreed that the produce of certain countries near Eretz Yisrael is also liable to *terumah* (see *Rambam, Terumos* 1:1). By Biblical law, *terumah* is taken only from the five species of grain, and from grapes and olives (or wine and oil). By Rabbinic decree, it is taken also from other sorts of fruits and vegetables (see 25a note 4).

7. See 28a note 19.

8. See 28a note 34.

9. The Baraisa discusses a case in which the infant son of a Kohen's wife was confused with the son of his slavewoman, and now it is not known which is which. The status of each, then, is uncertain; he may be a Kohen, or he may be the slave of a Kohen (*Rashi;* see *Tosefta, Yevamos* 12:4).

10. Although each of these boys may partake of *terumah* – the Kohen by Kohanic right, the slave because he is the slave of a Kohen – R' Yehudah does not permit either of them to come alone to the granary to receive a portion. For one of them is certainly a slave, and R' Yehudah holds that we do not distribute *terumah* to a slave unless his master is present. [Rather, both must come together, so that no matter which one is the slave, his master will be with him.] The reason R' Yehudah requires the presence of the master is so that people will not take the fact that this person receives *terumah* as evidence that he is a full-fledged Kohen, as the Gemara will explain (*Rashi*).

11. I.e. they elevate those to whom *terumah* is distributed at the granary. However, they do not elevate those who merely *partake* of *terumah* (*Rashi, Yevamos* 99b ד״ה היו מעלין; see also *Rashi* above, 24b ד״ה במעלין מתרומה ליוחסין and note 20 there).

[*Rashi* (25b ד״ה להשיא אשה), explains that the fact that he shares in *terumah* demonstrates that he is neither a *nasin* nor a *mamzer* (both of whom are forbidden to marry Jewish women). However, other Rishonim maintain that the purpose of this elevation is to confer upon him the status of a genealogically fit Kohen (see 24a note 12; see also the forthcoming Gemara, regarding the testimony of R' Elazar the son of R' Yose).]

[It must be noted that although our Mishnah follows the opinion of R' Yehudah, it does not mean that testimony based on childhood memory will elevate a Kohen to the status of genealogical fitness. Even though

עין משפט
נר מצוה

קכז א מיי' פי"ב מהל' תרומות הלכה כב:
קכח ב ג מיי' פ"ו מהל' קרבן פסח הל' ח:
קכט ד מיי' פכ"ח מהל' שבת הלכה יט טוש"ע א"ח סי' שלט סעי' יט:
קל ה מיי' פי"ד מהל' עדות הלכה ג סמג לאוין רט טוש"ע ח"מ סי' לה סעי' ו:
קלא ו מיי' שם הלכה ד וטוש"ע שם סעי' ז:
קלב ז מיי' שם הלכה ג טוש"ע אה"ע סי' ב סעי' א בהג"ה:

מסורת הש"ס

א) [עיין תוס' לקמן לו. ד"ה אבל], ב) יבמות לט., ג) [שם ע"ש], ד) גיטין ז. חולין ה: ו. ז. [יבמות לט:], ה) [עיין תוס' יבמות שם ד"ה ס"ד השתא וכו'], ו) ברכות יט: עירובין ל: פסחים לב: מ"ק ה: חגיגה כה: בכורות כט. נדה נז., ז) [ברכות יט: ע"ש], ח) [תוספתא פרק ג], ט) [ד"ה השתא ותוס' שבת יב: ד"ה ר' נתן ותוס' חולין ה: ד"ה לדיקים ותוס' פסחים קו: ד"ה אישתלאי], י) שייך אחר ד"ה בית הפרס, כ) [ועי' היטב תוס' פסחים לב: ד"ה מאי בודקין ועוד תוס' בכורות כט. ד"ה היכי אזיל].

גליון הש"ס

גמ' היו מעלין מתרומה ליוחסין. עיין ברכות דף טז ע"ב תוס' ד"ה אין עומדין:

אפוטרופוס [א] או שהניח תפילין בפני רבו או שקרא שלשה פסוקים בבית הכנסת הרי זה לא יצא לחירות התם דאיקרי עבד מדעתו כי קאמרינן דקא נהיג ביה מנהג בנים: לטבול לאכול בתרומה: בתרומה דרבנן: ושהיה חולק עמנו על הגורן: ודלמא עבד כהן הוא תנן כמאן דאמר א אין חולקין תרומה לעבד אלא אם כן רבו עמו דתניא [ב] אין חולקין תרומה לעבד אלא אם כן רבו עמו דברי רבי יהודה רבי יוסי אומר יכול הוא שיאמר אם כהן אני תנו לי בשביל עצמי ואם עבד כהן אני תנו לי בשביל רבי במקומו של רבי יהודה [ה] היו מעלין מתרומה ליוחסין במקומו של רבי יוסי לא היו מעלין מתרומה ליוחסין תניא [ג] א"ר אלעזר ברבי יוסי מימי לא העדתי פעם אחת העדתי והעלו עבד לכהונה על פי העלו סלקא דעתך [ד] השתא ומה בהמתן של צדיקים [ה] אין הקב"ה מביא תקלה על ידם צדיקים עצמם לא כ"ש אלא בקשו להעלות עבד לכהונה על פי חזא באתריה דרבי יוסי ואזל ואסהיד באתריה דרבי יהודה: ושהמקום הזה בית הפרס הוא: מ"ט בית הפרס דרבנן [ו] דאמר רב יהודה אמר שמואל ב מנפח אדם בית הפרס והולך [ז] ורב יהודה בר אמי משמיה דרב יהודה אמר ג בית הפרס שנידש טהור מאי טעמא אי אפשר לעצם כשעורה שלא נידש ברגל: ד ועד כאן היינו באין בשבת: קסבר תחומין דרבנן: ואין נאמן לומר דרך היה לפלוני במקום הזה מעמד ומספד היה לפלוני במקום הזה: מאי טעמא אפוקי ממונא לא מפקינן תנו רבנן [ח] ה נאמן התינוק לומר כך אמר לי אבא משפחה זו טהורה וזו טמאה טמאה סלקא דעתך אלא משפחה זו כשרה ומשפחה זו פסולה ושאכלנו בקצצה של בת פלוני לפלוני ושהיינו מוליכים חלה ומתנות לפלוני כהן על ידי עצמו אבל לא על ידי אחר ו וכולן אם היה עובד כוכבים ונתגייר עבד ונשתחרר אין נאמנים ואין נאמן לומר דרך היה לפלוני במקום הזה מעמד ומספד היה לפלוני במקום הזה רבי יוחנן בן ברוקא אומר נאמנים ר' יוחנן בן ברוקא אהייא אילימא אסיפא אפוקי ממונא הוא אלא ארישא וכולם אם היה עובד כוכבים ונתגייר עבד ונשתחרר אין נאמנין ר' יוחנן בן ברוקא אומר נאמנין במאי קמיפלגי ת"ק סבר כיון דעובד כוכבים הוא לא הוה דייק ורבי יוחנן בן ברוקא סבר כיון דדעתיה לאיגיורי מידק הוה דייק מאי קצצה דתנו רבנן כיצד קצצה ז אחד מן האחין שנשא אשה שאינה הוגנת לו באין בני משפחה ומביאין חבית מליאה פירות ושוברין אותה באמצע רחבה ואומרים אחינו בית ישראל שמעו אחינו פלוני נשא אשה שאינה הוגנת לו ומתייראים אנו שמא יתערב זרעו בזרעינו בואו וקחו לכם דוגמא לדורות שלא יתערב זרעו בזרעינו וזו היא קצצה שהתינוק נאמן להעיד עליה:

הדרן עלך האשה שנתארמלה

תוספות

תנן כמאן דאמר אין חולקין לעבד כו'. ואם תאמר והא לא קאמר רבי יהודה דאין חולקין אלא בתרומה דאורייתא דמעלין ממנה ליוחסין אבל מתני' דאוקמינן בתרומה דרבנן דאין מעלין ממנה ליוחסין מודה דחולקין לעבד בלא רבו ואם כן אכתי תקשי ודלמא עבד כהן הוא ולאו מלתא היא דמתניתין איירי שפיר שמעיד שחלק לו תרומה דאורייתא אלא שאינו נאמן להאכילו אלא בתרומה דרבנן:

ומה בהמתן של צדיקים. מפורש במקום אחר (גיטין דף ז. [ט]):

ושהמקום הזה בית הפרס. ולא יותר וצא לטהר:

[י] **מנפח.** בדיעבד אם עשה כבר טהרות אבל בדיקה לכתחלה מפרש במשנה (אהלות פי"ח מ"ד) כיצד בודקין [כ]: **בית** הפרס דרבנן. נראה דאפי' במקום הקבר מקילין כמו בשאר שדה ואין לומר דמקום הקבר מטמא באהל ומביא רבינו יצחק ראיה מדתניא בפ"ק דמועד קטן (דף ה:) מצא שדה מצויינת ואינו יודע מה טיבה יש בה אילנות בידוע שנחרש בה קבר אין בה אילנות בידוע שאבד בה קבר ומאי נפקא מינה כיון שעתה אינו יודע מקום הקבר בין נחרש בין אבד אלא שמע מינה דמקום הקבר טהור כשנחרש ובית הפרס להכי הוי דרבנן משום דהוי ספק טומאה ברשות הרבים אע"ג דבעלמא טיהרו חכמים ספק טומאה ברה"ר היינו היכא שהטומאה מבוררת ולא נולד הספק אלא באקראי ופעם אחרת לא יטמא כיון שמקום הטומאה ידוע אבל הכא שלעולם השדה בספק לא רצו לטהר אע"ג דמדאורייתא טהור:

הדרן עלך האשה שנתארמלה

רש"י

אפוטרופוס. מסר נכסיו בידו להכניס ולהוציא לסחורה: **הרי זה לא יצא לחירות.** ולא אמרינן אי לאו דשחרריה לא הוה יזיף מיניה ולא הוה שביק ליה לנהוג מנהג בן חורין ושמעינן מינה דיש עבד שלומד תורה: **בתרומה דרבנן.** כגון תרומת חוצה לארץ או פירות המנינהו להכי להאכילו על פיהם: **הכי גרסינן דתניא שאין חולקין** תרומה לעבד כו'. ורישא דברייתא כהנת שנתערב וולדה בוולד שפחתה שניהן יוצאין לגורן ונוטלין חלק אחד שאין חולקין תרומה לעבד כו' הלכך אי אזיל חד מינייהו לא פלגינן ליה דלמא אתי לאחזוקי בכהן ודלמא האי ניהו העבד: **במקומו של ר' יהודה.** משום הכי אמר אין חולקין: **בהמתן של צדיקים.** חמורו של רבי פנחס בן יאיר בהכל שוחטין (חולין ז.): **חזא באתריה דרבי יוסי.** שחלקו לו תרומה בגורן: **ואסהיד באתריה דרבי יהודה.** ושם לא היו חולקין תרומה לעבדי כהנים: **בית הפרס.** החורש את הקבר הרי זה עושה בית הפרס מאה אמה שכך שיערו שהמחרישה מולכת את עצמות המת ודלמא נגע או הסיט המהלך בו את עצם כשעורה שמטמא במגע ובמשא: **מנפח אדם בית הפרס.** וסומך על כך שאם יש עצם רואהו ואע"ג דמאהיל לא חיישינן דאין עצם כשעורה מטמא באהל עד דאיכא שדרה או גולגולת שלמה או רוב בנין או רוב מנין: **שנידש.** דישה רבה ברגלים הרבה: **טהור.** דתלינן לקולא ואמרינן כל העצמות נכתתו לפחות מכשיעור אלמא חששא דרבנן בעלמא הוא: **נאמן התינוק.** להעיד בגודלו מה שראה בקוטנו: **טמאה וטהורה סלקא דעתך.** מה טומאה וטהרה יש לומר במשפחות: **בקצצה.** לקמן מפרש לה: **של בת פלוני לפלוני.** כשנשא פלוני את בת פלוני: **ושהיינו מוליכין** כו' **על ידי עצמו.** אם כך העיד התינוק על ידי היה אבא שולח לו חלה ומתנות: **אם היה עובד כוכבים ונתגייר.** והעיד משנתגייר שראה את אלה בנכריותו אינו נאמן: **דוגמא.** אות וסימן וזכרון לדורות הבאים:

הדרן עלך האשה שנתארמלה

ואם היה כהן לא תדור עמו במבוי ואמרו כפר קטן זה היה מעשה ואמרו כפר קטן נידון (א) כשכונה מי נדחה מפני מי ת"ש דתניא היא נדחית מפניו ואין הוא נדחה מפניה ואם היתה חצר שלה הוא נדחה מפניה איבעיא להו היתה חצר של שניהם מהו ת"ש היא נדחית מפניו במאי עסקינן אילימא בחצר שלו פשיטא ואלא בחצר שלה והתניא אם היתה חצר שלה הוא נדחה מפניה אלא לאו כי האי גוונא דלמא דאגיר מיגר מאי הוי עלה ת"ש הנה ה' מטלטלך טלטלה גבר ואמר רב טלטולי דגברא קשין מדאיתתא ת"ר לוה הימנה בנכסי אביה אינה נפרעת אלא ע"י אחר אמר רב ששת ואי אתו לקמן לדינא לא מזדקקינן להו רב פפא אמר שמותי משמתינן להו רב הונא בריה דרב יהושע אמר נגודי (ב) נמי מנגדינן להו אמר רב נחמן תנא באבל רבתי בד"א שנתגרשה מן הנשואין אבל כשנתגרשה מן האירוסין נפרעת ע"י עצמה שאין לבו גס בה ההוא ארוס וארוסתו דאתו לקמיה דרבא יתיב רב אדא בר מתנא קמיה אוקי רבא שלוחא בינתייהו א"ל רב אדא בר מתנא והאמר רב נחמן תנא באבל רבתי כו' א"ל קא חזינן דקא גייסי בהדדי איכא דאמרי לא אוקי רבא שליח בינתייהו א"ל רב אדא בר מתנא ניקום מר שלוחא בינתייהו א"ל והא [אמר] רב נחמן תנא באבל רבתי כו' א"ל ה"מ היכא דלא גייסי בהדדי אבל הני קא חזינא להו דגייסי בהדדי: **מתני'** ואלו נאמנין להעיד בגודלן מה שראו בקוטנן נאמן אדם לומר זה כתב ידו של אבא וזה כתב ידו של רבי וזה כתב ידו של אחי זכור הייתי בפלונית שיצאה בהינומא וראשה פרוע ושהיה איש פלוני יוצא מבית הספר לטבול לאכול בתרומה ושהיה חולק עמנו על הגורן והמקום הזה בית הפרס ועד כאן היינו באין בשבת אבל אין אדם נאמן לומר דרך היה לפלוני במקום הזה מעמד ומספד היה לפלוני במקום הזה: **גמ'** אמר רב הונא בריה דרב יהושע והוא שיש גדול עמו וצריכא דאי אשמעינן אביו משום דשכיח גביה אבל רבו לא ואי אשמעינן רבו משום דאית ליה אימתיה דרביה אבל אביו לא ואי אשמעינן הני תרתי אביו דשכיח גביה ורבו דאית ליה אימתיה אבל אחיו דלית ליה לא הא ולא הא אימא לא קמ"ל כיון דקיום שטרות מדרבנן הימנוהו רבנן בדרבנן: זכור הייתי בפלונית שיצאה בהינומא וראשה פרוע: מאי טעמא כיון דרוב נשים בתולות נישאות גלוי מלתא בעלמא הוא: ושהיה איש פלוני יוצא מבית הספר לטבול לאכול בתרומה: ודלמא עבד כהן הוא מסייע ליה לר' יהושע בן לוי דאמר ר' יהושע בן לוי אסור לאדם שילמד את עבדו תורה ולא והתניא לוה הימנו רבו או שעשאו רבו אפוטרופוס

רש"י

ואם היה כהן. אפילו לא נסת: לא תדור עמו במבוי. שמא יבא עליה וכהן אסור בגרושה אבל ישראל כל זמן שלא נסת תדור בשכונתו: ולמאר רב גרס ומהאי קרא שמעינן לה: לוה הימנה. בהיותה תחתיו: בנכסי אביה. שהיו בידה נכסי מלוג ובכהן שגירש את אשתו קא מיירי: אינה נפרעת. הימנו ע"י עצמה שלא יקרבו בדברים: באבל רבתי. מסכתא היא וקורין אותה שמחות וזו היא משנה ראשונה שלה הגוסס הרי הוא כחי לכל דבריו: ארוס וארוסתו. כהן היה: והאמר רב נחמן תנא באבל רבתי. דמן האירוסין נפרעת על ידי עצמה: דגייסי בהדדי. מכירין זה את זה ברמיזות וקריצות בלע"ז פריוו"ץ: **מתני'** זה כתב ידו של אבא. ומקיימין השטר על פיו אע"פ שמת אביו בעוד זה קטן: שיצאת בהינומא. והוא סימן שניסת בתולה וכתובתה מאתים כדאמרינן בריש פירקין: יוצא מבית הספר. כשהיינו למידין תינוקות בבית רבן וכולהו מפרש טעמא בגמרא: אבל אין נאמנין כו'. דלאפוקי ממונא הוא ובעינן עדות מעלייתא וכתובה היינו טעמא לדרוב נשים בתולות נישאות: מעמד ומספד. מקום היה לו כאן להספיד מתיו כשמוליכין לבית קברות שלו ולעשות שם מעמדות ומושבות שהיו עושין שבעה למת: רבי יוחנן בן ברוקא אומר נאמנים. לא גרסינן ליה במתני' אלא בברייתא ולא אדרך מעמד ומספד קאי: **גמ'** דשכיח גביה. ונתן עיניו בקטנותו בכתב יד אביו: קיום שטרות מדרבנן. דמדאורייתא לא בעינן קיום לאמר ר"ל (לעיל דף יח:) עדים החתומים על השטר נעשה כמי שנחקרה עדותן בב"ד: הימנוהו רבנן בדרבנן. בדבר שהוא מדבריהם האמינוהו ואין זה עוקר דבר מן התורה הם אמרו והם אמרו הם הצריכו קיום העדות והם הכשירו בו את אלו: גלוי מלתא בעלמא הוא. כלומר אין הדבר צריך עדות אלא לפרסם שילא הדין לאור בלא גמגום:

תוספות

ואם היה כהן לא תדור עמו במבוי א). דכיון דפנויה היא קיל ליה אבל אם נישאת אין צריך להרחיק אלא כדי שכונה דהיינו ג' בתים כדאמרינן בסוף פרק קמא דע"ז (דף כא.) דכיון דנישאת אמירה ליה אפי' לכהן: **כפר** קטן נידון (ג) כשכונה. וטעמא לפי שאין בני אדם מצוין שם ורגיל יותר לבא אצלה ודווקא כפר קטן אבל כפר בינוני לא: **רב** הונא אמר נגודי מנגדינן להו. נראה לר"ת דלרב הונא נמי משמתינן וגם מנגדין שכל אחד מחמיר מחבירו ואם הוא אומר לנגדין ליה בלא שמתא הוה מיקל טפי כדאמרינן במועד קטן (דף יז.) ובפרק מקום שנהגו (פסחים נב.) במערבא כי מחייב איניש נגידא מרבנן מימנו אנגידא ולא מימנו אשמתא: **אלו** נאמנין להעיד בגודלן מה שראו בקוטנן. משמע דבקוטנן לא מהימן אפילו בדרבנן דהא מוקי לה בגמרא בתרומה דרבנן וקשה לריב"א דאמר בפ"ק דפסחים (דף ד: ושם) דנאמנים על בדיקת חמץ אפי' נשים ועבדים וקטנים ופריך מידי משמע אית בהו ומשני הואיל ובדיקת חמץ דרבנן הימנוהו רבנן בדרבנן וי"ל דהתם היינו טעמא משום דבדיקת חמץ הוא בידו לכן נאמן אפילו קטן דהכל קשה היכא דבידו אפי' דלאורייתא אשה מהימנא דבפרק המדיר (לקמן דף עב. ושם) תנן (ד) ונקולה לה חלה וניקור מעשים בכל יום שאנו סומכין עליהן וי"ל דבירושלמי מפרש דבדיקת חמץ הוא טורח ונשים עצלניות הן ולהכי אי לאו דבדיקת חמץ דרבנן לא הוו מהימני: **והוא** שיש גדול עמו. ° לא קאי אתרומה דבתרומה סגי בלא' כיון דאין מעלין מתרומה דרבנן ליוחסין להכי מוקי לה בתרומה דרבנן בתרומה דאורייתא כיון דסבר תנא דידן דמעלין ממנה ליוחסין כדאמרינן לקמן אינו נאמן אפי' יש גדול עמו הלכך בתרומה סגי בלאיהו לחודיה וכל היכא דבעינן תרי מדרבנן סגי בהוא ואחר: **קיום** שטרות דרבנן. תימה כיון דמדאורייתא אפילו אין עדים שיכירו חתימת העדים השטר כשר א"כ כל אדם שירצה יזייף ויכתוב ויחתום מה שירצה ויגבה ממנו והכא אור"י ז) דאיכא למימר כגון שלוה מודה שכתבו וטוען שהוא פרוע וקסבר האי תנא דמודה בשטר שכתבו צריך לקיימו והאי קיום הוי ודאי מדרבנן אי נמי כגון שנתקיים משדה אחת או משתי שדות ויולא מתחת ידי עצמו דאמר לעיל (דף כ.) דחיישינן שמא זייף ומיהו בריש גיטין (דף ג. ושם) מוכח דאפילו היכא דאין מכירין החתימה כלל הוי מדאורייתא כמי שנחקרה עדותן בב"ד: **ודלמא** עבד כהן הוא. פי' ועכשיו נשתחרר ונוטל שלא כדין וקשה לרבינו יצחק דבפ' נושאין על האנוסה (יבמות דף צט: ושם) מפרש הש"ס הא דאין חולקין תרומה לעבד משום דלמא אתי לאסוקיה ליוחסין מה צריך להאי טעמא הוה ליה למימר דאין חולקין אפי' אין מעלין שמא ישאל גם אחר שישתחרר כדפריך הכא הש"ס וכן מפרש התם הש"ס דאין חולקין לאשה בלא בעלה משום גרושה ומאי טעמא נמי דמאן דאמר חולקין וי"ל דלא שכיחא כולי האי שישאל תרומה אחר שישתחרר לא בתורת עבד ולא בתורת כהן כי ירא פן יבדקוהו ויתברר שהוא עבד ויוציאו עליו קול עבדות ולא חיישינן נמי פן ימכרנו רבו לישראל וישאל תרומה שהרי מזונותיו על רבו ואין אדם חוטא ולא לו וכולי האי לא חיישינן שמא יאמר לו רבו ישראל לאי מעשה ידיך במזונותיך:

תנן

מסורת הש"ס

א) סנהדרין כו, ג) [מס' שמחות פ"ב], ג) [בערוך ערך עמד גורס ומושב], ד) [לעיל כא:], ה) [לעיל יח. ב"ב לב:], ו) גיטין מ, ז) [ע' תוס' לעיל יט. ד"ה מודה].

הגהות הב"ח

(א) גמ' כפר קטן נידון כמבוי מי: (ב) שם נגודי מנגדינן כל"ל ותיבת נמי נמחק: (ג) תוס' ד"ה כפר קטן נידון כמבוי וטעמא: (ד) ד"ה אלו כו' דבפרק המדיר תנן ואינה קולה לה:

גליון הש"ס

תוס' ד"ה והוא וכו' לא קאי אתרומה. ע' עירובין דף נט ע"א תוס' ד"ה אפילו עבד:

תורה אור השלם

א) הִנֵּה יְיָ מְטַלְטֶלְךָ טַלְטֵלָה גָּבֶר וְעֹטְךָ עָטֹה: [ישעיה כב, יז]

תוספות ישנים

א) [מגלתי דאם רשות הרבים מפסיק מבית לבית שרי. ח"ן].

לעזי רש"י

פריוו"ץ. פירוש מכירין זה את זה ברמיזות וקריצות (ועיין רש"י עירובין דף מו ע"א ד"ה גם בה):

ליקוטי רש"י

טלטלה גבר. כהדין תרנגולא דמטלטל מאתר לאתר ורבותינו אמרו טלטולא דגברא קשה מדאיתתא [ישעיה כב, יז]. **שמותי משמתינן.** מנדים [ע"פ קידושין ע.]. **נגודי מנגדינן.** מייסרים [ע"פ ב"מ פו.]. **בפלונית שיצאה.** מבית אביה לבית בעלה כשנכנסה לחופה. **בהינומא.** קריטא, לעיף על ראשה משורבב על עיניה כמו שעושין במקומינו ופעמים שמנמנמת בתוכו מתוך שאין עיניה מגולין ולכך נקרא הינומא על שם תנומה [לעיל יז:]. קלתא דמנמנמת ביה כלתא או ראשה פרוע בשוק בשעת כניסה לחופה שכן דרך הנישאות בתולות [רשב"ם ב"ב צב:]. נערה המאורסה היו רגילין לעשות לה חופה של הדס בכניסתה לחופה וקורין לה הינומא כדאמרינן בכתובות (דף טו:) שילאתה בהינומא וראשה פרוע [ברכות נו:]. **וראשה פרוע.** איטרייאלד"ה שערה על כתיפיה כך היו נוהגין להוליא את הבתולות מבית אביהן לבית החתונה [לעיל טו:]. **בית הפרס.** לא מטמא אלא מדרבנן והוא שדה שנחרש בו קבר ואמרו חכמים שמא דלדלו כלי המחרישה את העצמות והדורס עליהן מסיטן ועלם כשעורה מטמא במגע ובמשא ולא באהל [ברכות יט:]. הוא שדה שנחרש בה קבר כדתנן (אהלות פי"ז מ"א) החורש בית הקבר הרי זה עושה בית הפרס מלא מענה מאה אמה וגזור רבנן שמא כיתתה מחרישה את העצמות ופיזרתן באורך המענה ויש כאן עלם כשעורה ויעבור ויסיטנו ועלם כשעורה מטמאה במגע ובמשא דהיינו היסט [פסחים צב:]. שדה שנחרש בה קבר ואוקמי רבנן (על) [כל] סביבות הקבר מאה אמה בספק טומאה [המשך בע"ב]

עין משפט נר מצוה

קיח א ב ג מיי' פכ"א מהל' איסורי ביאה הלכה כז סמג לאוין קכז טוש"ע אה"ע סימן ו סעיף ז וסימן קיט סעיף יא:
קיט ד מיי' שם טוש"ע שם סי' קיט ס"ח:
קכ ה ו מיי' שם טוש"ע שם סעיף ט:
קכא ז ח מיי' שם טוש"ע שם סעיף י:
קכב ט י מיי' פי"ז מהל' עדות הלכ' א ופי"ד הלכה ג סמג לאוין רטו טוש"ע ח"מ סי' לה סעיף ד ה ו וסי' מו סעי' ח [וברב אלפס עוד ביבמות פ"ג דף י ע"ב]:
קכג כ מיי' פט"ו מהל' אישות הלכה כה סמג עשין מח טוש"ע אה"ע סי' לו סעיף טו:
קכד ל מיי' פ"כ מהל' אסורי ביאה הלכ' טו טוש"ע שם סי' ג' סעיף ה:
קכה מ מיי' פ"ח מהל' עבדים הלכה יח טוש"ע י"ד סי' רסז סעיף עא:
קכו נ מיי' שם הלכה יז טוש"ע שם סעיף ע:

תוספות רי"ד

ת"ש המגרש את אשתו לא תנשא בשכונתו. פי' לפי שמכרת ברמיזותו ובקריצותו ושמא יבואו לידי עבירה. ואם היה כהן לא תדור עמו במבוי. פי' שמא יבוא עליה וכהן אסור בגרושה [אם היה כפר קטן] זה היה מעשה ואמרו כפר קטן נידון כשכונה: **איבעי' להו** מי נדחה בפני מי ת"ש דתניא היא נדחת מפניו והוא אינו נדחה מפניה. ואם היתה חצר שלה הוא נדחה מפניה **איבעיא להו** היתה חצר של שניהם מהו. **ת"ש** היא נדחית מפניו דטלטולא דגברא קשה מדאיתתא: **ת"ר** לוה ממנה בנכסי אביה. פי' בעודה תחתיו שהי' בידה נכסי מלוג ובכהן שגירש את אשתו מיירי ה"ז אינה נפרעת אלא על ידי שליח. פי' ולא ע"י עצמה שלא יתקרבו בדבריהם. א"ר ששת כי אתו לקמן לא מזדקקינן להו. ר"פ אמר שמותי משמתינן להו ר"ה ברי' דר"י אמר נגידי נמי מנגדינן להו. **אמר ר"נ** תנא באבל רבתי פי' מסכתא היא וקרי' אותה מס' שמחות ומשנה ראשונה שלה זו היא הגוסס הרי הוא כחי לכל דבריו בד"א בשנתגרשה מן הנשואין אבל נתגרשה מן האירוסין נפרעת ע"י עצמה שאין לבו גס בה. ההוא ארוס וארוסתו דאתו קמי' דרבא אוקי רבא שליח בינייהו. פי' בפניו היו הוה יתיב ר"א ב"מ קמי'. א"ל למה ליה למר כולי האי והאר"נ תנא באבל רבתא וכו'. א"ל ה"מ היכי דלא גיסי אהדדי הכא הא חזינא דגיסי אהדדי. פי' שמכירין זא"ז ברמיזות ובקריצות: **מתני' ואלו נאמנין** להעיד בגודלן על מה שראו בקוטנן. פי' אע"ג דבעינן ראי' והגדה בכשרות הכא נאמנים על ראיית קטנותם משום דהוה מדרבנן ודוקא להעיד בגודלן על מה שראו בקוטנן אבל להעיד בקטנותם לא פי' שאם יאמר הקטן זה כת"י של אבא אין משגיחין בדבריו אבל כשהגדיל ומעיד על ראיית קטנותו אמרי' אי לאו דקים לי' שפיר לא הוה מסהיד בגודלו. נאמן אדם לומר זה כת"י של אבא זה כת"י של רבי זה כת"י של אחי. פי' ומקיימים השטר על פיו. ואע"פ שמתו בעוד זה קטן. שנמצא שמעיד עכשיו כשהוא גדול על ראיית קטנותו נאמן הוא משום דקיום שטרות דרבנן. זכור אני באשת פ' שיצאת בהינומא וראשה פרוע פי' והוא סימן שנשאת בתולה וכתובתה מאתים כדאמרינן בריש פירקן. ושהיה איש פ' יוצא מבית הספר לטבול לתרומתו ושהיה חולק עמנו בגורן ושהמקום הזה הוא בית הפרס אבל אינו נאמן לומר דרך הי' לאיש פלוני במקום הזה מעמד ומספד הי' לפלוני במקום הזה. פי' דאפוקי ממונא הוא ובעי' עדות מעלייתא והיינו טעמא דכתובה דרוב נשים בתולות נשאות: **אמר ר"ה ברי' דר"י** והוא שיש גדול עמו. פי' דשני עדים צריך להעיד על חתימ' שהיא שלהן כדאמר לעיל דע"כ לא פליגי רבנן עלי' דר' אלא בז"א זה כתבי אבל זה כתב חבירי מודו רבנן דבעינן שנים עדים על כל חתימה וחתימה והכא אמר ר"ה דוקא ראיית קטן א' הכשירו ולא ראיית שני קטנים שאם היו שניהם מעידין בגודלן על מה שראו בקוטנן אינן נאמנים אלא בעי' שיהא א' גדול מעיד על ראיית קטנותו. וצריכא דאי אשמעינן אביו משום דשכיח גבי' פי' ונותן עיניו בקטנותו מכתב יד אביו אבל רבו אימא לא ואי אשמעינן רבו משום דאית ליה אימתי' דרביה אבל אביו אימא לא ואי אשמעינן הני תרתי אביו משום דשכיח גבי' ורבו משום דא"ל אימתי' אבל אחיו דלא הא ולא הא אימא לא קמ"ל. כיון דקיום שטרות דרבנן. פי' דמדאורייתא לא בעי קיום דאר"ל עדים החתומים ע"ה נעשה כמי שנחקרה עדותן בב"ד הימנוה רבנן בדרבנן פי' בדבר שהוא מדבריהם האמינוהו. ואין זה עוקר דבר מן התורה אלא הם אמרו והם אמרו. הם הצריכו העדות והם הכשירו בו את אלו ודוקא בהלו רגיל בהן הוא נאמן אבל על כתב נכרים אינו נאמן להעיד על ראיות קטנותו דדילמא לא קים ליה שפיר ואפילו אמר אני ראיתי כשחתם בשטר זה אין ראיית הקטן עדות עד שיאמר כי אני מכיר בחתימתו ודוקא הקרוב מעיד על חתימת הקרוב ואין זה נוגע בעדותו שאין מגיע לקרובו שום הנאה והפסד אלא למלוה וללוה מגיעים. אבל אם היו העדים קרובים למלוה או ללוה או שהי' שניהם קרובים זל"ז אינן נאמנים להעיד על החתימה שאין מוציאין ממון ע"פ קרובים. ואע"ג דקיום שטרות דרבנן וראיית קטן הוא דהכשירו בהן חכמים. אבל לא עדות קרובים: **זכור** הייתי וכו' מ"ט כיון דרוב נשים בתולות נשאות גלוי מילתא בעלמא הוא על הרוב. פי' אע"ג דבמידי דממונא לאו מהימן דלאו עליה בלחוד סמכי אלא על הרוב. וה"ה דבעינן נמי הכא והוא שיש גדול עמו ששני

regarding his father's handwriting as well. וְאִי אַשְׁמְעִינַן הָנֵי תַּרְתֵּי – **And if [the Mishnah] would have informed us** only that he is trusted with regard to the handwriting of **these two,** and not with regard to the handwriting of his brother, I might say that אָבִיו דִּשְׁכִיחַ גַּבֵּיהּ – in the case of **his father, it is because he frequented him** as a child, וְרַבּוֹ דְּאִית לֵיהּ אֵימְתֵיהּ – and in the case of **his teacher, it is because he was in awe of him.** אֲבָל אָחִיו – **But** in the case of **his brother,** דְּלֵית לֵיהּ לֹא הָא וְלֹא הָא – **whose** handwriting **he has neither this** reason **nor that** reason to recognize, אֵימָא לֹא – **I will say** that he is **not** believed. קָא מַשְׁמַע לָן – **[The Mishnah]** therefore **informs us** that כֵּיוָן דְּקִיּוּם שְׁטָרוֹת מִדְּרַבָּנָן – **since certification of documents is** required **by Rabbinic law** only,[29] הֵימְנוּהוּ רַבָּנָן בִּדְרַבָּנָן – **the Rabbis granted him trust regarding a Rabbinic law.**[30]

The Mishnah stated:
זָכוּר הָיִיתִי בִּפְלוֹנִית שֶׁיָּצְאָה בְּהִינוּמָא וְרֹאשָׁהּ פָּרוּעַ – I REMEMBER REGARDING SO-AND-SO THAT SHE WENT OUT of her father's house on the way to her wedding WITH A VEIL AND with HER HAIR DOWN.

The point of this testimony is to prove that this woman was a virgin at her wedding, and should receive the full *kesubah* payment. Accordingly, the Gemara asks:

מַאי טַעְמָא – **What is the reason** he is believed regarding this? Since the purpose of this testimony is to exact money, he should not be believed.[31] – ? –

The Gemara answers:

כֵּיוָן דְּרוֹב נָשִׁים בְּתוּלוֹת נִישָּׂאוֹת – **Since the majority of women marry as virgins,** we may rely upon the majority to award this woman the full payment. גִּלּוּי מִלְּתָא בְּעָלְמָא הוּא – Accordingly, **[this testimony] simply reveals** to the public that the court's majority-based ruling is in fact correct.[32] Since his testimony does not decide the matter, it is accepted.

The Mishnah stated:
וְשֶׁהָיָה אִישׁ פְּלוֹנִי יוֹצֵא מִבֵּית הַסֵּפֶר לִטְבּוֹל לֶאֱכוֹל בִּתְרוּמָה – AND THAT SO-AND-SO WOULD GO OUT OF THE SCHOOLHOUSE TO IMMERSE himself in order TO EAT *TERUMAH.*

This testimony is meant to prove that this person is a Kohen. The Gemara questions its efficacy:

וְדִלְמָא עֶבֶד כֹּהֵן הוּא – **But perhaps [this person] is** only **the** Canaanite **slave of a Kohen,** and is eating *terumah* because of his master.[33] How does this testimony prove that he himself is a Kohen?

The Gemara answers:

מְסַיֵּיע לֵיהּ לְרַבִּי יְהוֹשֻׁעַ בֶּן לֵוִי – Clearly, **[this Mishnah] supports** the ruling of **R' Yehoshua ben Levi.** דְּאָמַר רַבִּי יְהוֹשֻׁעַ בֶּן לֵוִי – **For R' Yehoshua ben Levi said:** אָסוּר לְאָדָם שֶׁיְּלַמֵּד אֶת עַבְדּוֹ תּוֹרָה – **It is forbidden for a person to teach his** Canaanite **slave Torah.** The fact, then, that this person was studying Torah in the schoolhouse with the others is proof that he is not a slave.[34]

The Gemara questions R' Yehoshua ben Levi's ruling:[35]

וְלֹא – **And** is it true that a person may **not** teach his slave Torah? וְהָתַנְיָא – **But it has been taught in a Baraisa:** לָוָה הֵימֶנּוּ רַבּוֹ – If [A SLAVE'S] MASTER BORROWED money FROM HIM,[36] אוֹ שֶׁעֲשָׂאוֹ רַבּוֹ – OR if HIS MASTER APPOINTED HIM

NOTES

29. By Biblical law, confirmation of the signatures on a contract is unnecessary, as Reish Lakish states (above, 18b): עֵדִים הַחֲתוּמִים עַל הַשְּׁטָר נַעֲשָׂה כְּמִי שֶׁנֶּחְקְרָה עֵדוּתָן בְּבֵית דִּין, *Witnesses signed on a contract are treated as if their testimony was examined in beis din* [and accepted] (*Rashi*). We assume that a person would not have the audacity to forge signatures on a contract (see *Rashi, Gittin* 3a ד״ה נעשה כמי; but see *Tosafos* here; see also *Pnei Yehoshua* here).

30. I.e. since certification is required by Rabbinic decree only, the acceptance of these ordinarily invalid witnesses is not a negation of Biblical law. Since it was the Rabbis who established the need for this testimony, it is they who set its guidelines (*Rashi*).

[*Ritva* suggests that this individual is believed to testify not only regarding the handwriting of his brother, but also regarding the handwriting of any person at all, even one unrelated to him. For the Gemara stated that there is nothing about one's relationship with one's brother that would enhance one's memory of his handwriting. Presumably, then, there is no difference between testifying regarding the handwriting of one's brother or the handwriting of any other person. However, *Rosh* maintains that one is believed only regarding a brother's handwriting, not regarding the handwriting of others (see also *Meiri*).]

31. [In accordance with the Mishnah's final clause, which disallows testimony based on youthful recollection where the purpose is to establish a monetary claim (see *Rashi* to the Mishnah).]

32. See *Rashi; Ran; Tosafos, Bava Basra* 92b ד״ה וזו.

33. I.e. perhaps he was *then* the slave of a Kohen and ate *terumah* at that time because of his master. Now, however, he is clearly a freeman. For were he still a slave, this person's testimony would be irrelevant, since a slave may eat *terumah* on account of his master (see *Tosafos; Shitah Mekubetzes* to 28b ד״ה ושהיה חולק; see *Ritva* to 28b for another approach).

[The slave of a Kohen is permitted to eat *terumah;* see *Leviticus* 22:11.]

34. It emerges that the proof to this person's Kohanic status is not simply his consumption of *terumah,* but also his study of Torah. One who studied Torah cannot be a slave. Therefore, his consumption of *terumah* stands as proof that he is a Kohen.

35. See *Shitah Mekubetzes* ד״ה ולא והתניא.

36. Ordinarily, a master would not borrow money from his slave, but would simply take it [because whatever a slave owns belongs to his master] (*Meiri* to *Gittin* 40a). Perhaps, then, the fact that the master did borrow money proves that this slave was set free.

ואם היה כהן לא תדור עמו במבוי אם היה כפר קטן זה היה מעשה ואמרו כפר קטן נידון (א) כשכונה מי נדחה מפני מי ת"ש דתניא [א]היא נדחית מפניו ואין הוא נדחה מפניה ואם היתה חצר שלה הוא נדחה מפניה איבעיא להו היתה חצר של שניהם מהו ת"ש היא נדחית מפניו במאי עסקינן אילימא בחצר שלו פשיטא ואלא בחצר שלה והתניא אם היתה חצר שלה הוא נדחה מפניה אלא לאו כי האי גוונא [ב]דלמא דאגיר מיגר מאי הוי עלה ת"ש [א]הנה ה' מטלטלך טלטלה גבר (א) ואמר רב [ג]טלטולי דגברא קשין מדאיתתא ת"ר [ד]לוה הימנה בנכסי אביה אינה נפרעת אלא ע"י אחר אמר רב ששת ואי אתו לקמן לדינא לא מזדקקינן להו רב פפא אמר [ה]שמותי משמתינן להו רב הונא בריה דרב יהושע אמר [ו]נגודי (ב) נמי מנגדינן להו אמר רב נחמן תנא [ז]באבל רבתי בד"א שנתגרשה מן הנשואין [ח]אבל כשנתגרשה מן האירוסין נפרעת ע"י עצמה שאין לבו גס בה ההוא ארוס וארוסתו דאתו לקמיה דרבא יתיב רב אדא בר מתנא קמיה אוקי רבא שלוחא בינתיהו א"ל רב אדא בר מתנא והאמר רב נחמן תנא באבל רבתי כו' א"ל קא חזינן דקא גייסי בהדדי איכא דאמרי לא אוקי רבא שליח בינתיהו א"ל רב אדא בר מתנא ניקום מר שלוחא בינתייהו א"ל והא [אמר] רב נחמן תנא באבל רבתי כו' א"ל ה"מ היכא דלא גייסי בהדדי אבל הני קא חזינא להו דגייסי בהדדי: **מתני'** ואלו נאמנין להעיד בגודלן מה שראו בקוטנן [ט]נאמן אדם לומר זה כתב ידו של אבא וזה כתב ידו של רבי וזה כתב ידו של אחי זכור הייתי בפלונית שיצאה בהינומא וראשה פרוע ושהיה איש פלוני יוצא מבית הספר לטבול לאכול בתרומה ושהיה חולק עמנו על הגורן והמקום הזה בית הפרס ועד כאן היינו באין בשבת אבל אין אדם נאמן לומר דרך היה לפלוני במקום הזה מעמד [י]ומספד היה לפלוני במקום הזה: **גמ'** אמר רב הונא בריה דרב יהושע [כ]והוא שיש גדול עמו וצריכא דאי אשמעינן אביו משום דשכיח גביה אבל רבו לא ואי אשמעינן רבו משום דאית ליה אימתיה דרביה אבל אביו לא ואי אשמעינן הני תרתי אביו דשכיח גביה ורבו דאית ליה אימתיה אבל אחיו דלית ליה לא הא ולא הא אימא לא קמ"ל כיון [ל]דקיום שטרות מדרבנן הימנוהו רבנן בדרבנן: [מ]זכור הייתי בפלונית שיצאה בהינומא וראשה פרוע: מאי טעמא [נ]כיון דרוב נשים בתולות נישאות גלוי מלתא בעלמא הוא: [ס]ושהיה איש פלוני יוצא מבית הספר לטבול לאכול בתרומה: ודלמא עבד כהן הוא מסייע ליה לר' יהושע בן לוי דאמר ר' יהושע בן לוי [ע]אסור לאדם שילמד את עבדו תורה ולא והתניא [פ]לוה הימנו רבו או שעשאו רבו אפוטרופוס

רש"י

ואם היה כהן. אפילו לא ניסת: **לא תדור עמו במבוי.** שמא יבא עליה וכהן אסור בגרושה אבל ישראל כל זמן שלא ניסת תדור בשכונתו: **ואמר רב** גרס ומהאי קרא שמעינן לה: **לוה הימנה.** בהיותה תחתיו: **בנכסי אביה.** שהיו בידה נכסי מלוג ובכהן שגירש את אשתו קא מיירי: **אינה נפרעת.** הימנו ע"י עצמה שלא יקרבו לדברים: **באבל רבתי.** מסכתא היא וקורין אותה שמחות וזו היא משנה ראשונה שלה הגוסס הרי הוא כחי לכל דבריו: **ארוס וארוסתו.** כהן היה: **והאמר רב נחמן תנא באבל רבתי.** דמן האירוסין נפרעת על ידי עצמה: **דגייסי בהדדי.** מכירין זה את זה ברמיזות וקריצות בלע"ז פריווי"ץ: **מתני' זה כתב ידו של אבא.** ומקיימין השטר על פיו אע"פ שמת אביו בעוד זה קטן: **שיצאת בהינומא.** והוא סימן שניסת בתולה וכתובתה מאתים כדאמרינן בריש פירקין: **יוצא מבית הספר.** כשהיינו למדין תינוקות בבית רבן וכולהו מפרש טעמא בגמרא: **אבל אין נאמנין כו'.** דלאפוקי ממונא הוא ובעינן עדות מעלייתא וכתובה היינו טעמא דרוב נשים בתולות ניסאות: **מעמד ומספד.** מקום היה לו כאן להספיד מתיו כשמוליכן לבית קברות שלו ולעשות שם מעמדות ומושבות שהיו עושין שבעה למת: **רבי יוחנן בן ברוקא אומר נאמנים.** לא גרסינן ליה במתני' אלא בברייתא ולא אדרך מעמד ומספד קאי: **גמ' דשכיח גביה.** ונתן עיניו בקטנותו בכתב יד אביו: **קיום שטרות מדרבנן.** דמדאורייתא לא בעינן קיום דאמר ר"ל (לעיל דף יח:) עדים החתומים על השטר נעשה כמי שנחקרה עדותן בב"ד: **הימנוהו רבנן בדרבנן.** בדבר שהוא מדבריהם האמינו ואין זה עוקר דבר מן התורה הם אמרו והם אמרו הם הצריכו קיום העדות והם הכשירו בו את אלו: **גלוי מלתא בעלמא הוא.** כלומר אין הדבר צריך עדות אלא לפרסם שילא הדין לאור בלא גמגום:

אפוטרופוס

תוספות

ואם היה כהן לא תדור עמו במבוי א). דכיון דפנויה היא קיל ליה אבל אם ניסאת אין צריך להרחיק אלא כדי שכונה דהיינו ג' בתים כדאמרינן בסוף פרק קמא דע"ז (דף כא.) דכיון דניסאת חמירא ליה אפי' לכהן: **כפר** קטן נידון (ג) כשכונה. וטעמא לפי שאין בני אדם מצוין שם ורגיל יותר לבא אצלה ודווקא כפר קטן אבל כפר בינוני לא: **רב** הונא אמר נגודי מנגדינן להו. נראה לר"ת דלרב הונא נמי משמתינן וגם מנגדין שכל אחד מחמיר מחבירו ואם הוא אומר דנגדינן ליה בלא שמתא הוה מיקל טפי כדאמרינן במועד קטן (דף יז.) ובפרק מקום שנהגו (פסחים נב.) במערבא כי מחייב צורבא מרבנן מימנו אנגידא ולא מימנו אשמתא: **אלו** נאמנין להעיד בגודלן מה שראו בקוטנן. משמע דבקוטנן לא מהימן אפילו בדרבנן דהא מוקי לה בגמרא בתרומה דרבנן וקשה לריב"א דאמר בפ"ק דפסחים (דף ד: ושם) דנאמנים על בדיקת חמץ אפי' נשים ועבדים וקטנים ופריך מידי משנא אית בהו ומשני הואיל ובדיקת חמץ דרבנן הימנוהו רבנן בדרבנן וי"ל דהתם היינו טעמא משום דבדיקת חמץ הוא בידו לכן נאמן אפילו קטן בדרבנן אבל קשה דהיכא דבידו אפי' בדאורייתא אשה מהימנא דבפרק המדיר (לקמן דף עב. ושם) תנן (ד) וקולה לה חלה ובניקור מעשים בכל יום שאנו סומכין עליהן וי"ל דבירושלמי מפרש דבדיקת חמץ הוא טורח ונשים עצלניות הן ולהכי אי לאו דבדיקת חמץ דרבנן לא הוו מהימני: **והוא** שיש גדול עמו. ה) לא קאי אתרומה דבתרומה סגי בלא' כיון דאין מעלין מתרומה דרבנן ליוחסין דלהכי מוקי לה בתרומה דרבנן דבתרומה דאורייתא כיון דסבר תנא דידן דמעלין ממנה ליוחסין כדאמרינן לקמן אינו נאמן אפי' יש גדול עמו הלכך בתרומה סגי באיהו לחודיה וכל היכא דבעינן תרי מדרבנן סגי בהוא ואחר: **קיום** שטרות דרבנן. תימה כיון דמדאורייתא אפילו אין עדים שיכירו חתימת העדים השטר כשר א"כ כל אדם שירצה יזייף ויכתוב ויחתום מה שירצה ויגבה ממנו והכא אור"י ו) דליכא למימר כגון שלוה מודה שכתבו וטוען שהוא פרוע וקסבר האי תנא דמודה בשטר שכתבו צריך לקיימו והאי קיום הוי ודאי מדרבנן אי נמי כגון שנתקיים משדה אחת או משתי שדות ויולא מחמת ידי עלמו דאמר לעיל (דף כ.) דחיישינן שמא זייף ומיהו בריש גיטין (דף ג. ושם) מוכח דאפילו היכא דאין מכירין החתימה כלל הוי מדאורייתא כמי שנחקרה עדותן בב"ד: **ודלמא** עבד כהן הוא. פי' ועכשיו נשתחרר ונוטל שלא כדין וקשה לרבינו יצחק דבפ' נושאין על האנוסה (יבמות דף צט: ושם) מפרש הש"ס הא דאין חולקין תרומה לעבד משום דלמא אתי לאסוקיה ליוחסין מה צריך להאי טעמא הוה ליה למימר דאין חולקין אפי' אין מעלין שמא ישאל גם אחר שישתחרר כדפריך הכא הש"ס וכן מפרש התם הש"ס דאין חולקין לאשה בלא בעלה משום גרושה ומאי טעמא נמי דמאן דאמר חולקין וי"ל דלא שכיחא כולי האי שישאל תרומה אחר שישתחרר לא בתורת עבד ולא בתורת כהן כי ירא פן יבדקוהו ויתברר שהוא עבד ויוציאו עליו קול עבדות ולא חיישינן נמי פן ימכרנו רבו לישראל וישאל תרומה שהרי מזונותיו על רבו ואין אדם חוטא ולא לו וכולי האי לא חיישינן שמא יאמר לו רבו ישראל לאי מעשה ידיך במזונותיך:

תנן

א) סנהדרין כו., ב) [מס' שמחות פ"ב], ג) [בערוך ערך עמד גורס ומושב], ד) [לעיל כא:], ה) [לעיל עח. ב"ב כג:], ו) גיטין מ., ז) [ע' תוס' לעיל יט. ד"ה מודה].

הגהות הב"ח

(א) גמ' כפר קטן נידון כשכונה מי: (ב) שם נגודי מנגדינן כצ"ל ותיבת נמי נמחק: (ג) תוס' ד"ה כפר קטן נידון כשכונה וטעמא: (ד) ד"ה אלו כו' דבפרק המדיר תנן ואינה קולה לה:

גליון הש"ס

תוס' ד"ה והוא וכו' לא קאי אתרומה. ע' עירובין דף נט ע"ב תוס' ד"ה אפילו עבד:

תורה אור השלם

א) הִנֵּה יְיָ מְטַלְטֶלְךָ טַלְטֵלָה גָּבֶר וְעֹטְךָ עָטֹה: [ישעיה כב, יז]

תוספות ישנים

א) [מלשון דאם רשות הרבים מפסיק מבית לבית שרי. ת"י].

לעזי רש"י

פריוויי"ץ. פירוש מכירין זה את זה ברמיזות וקריצות (ועיין רש"י עירובין דף מ ע"א ד"ה גם כה).

ליקוטי רש"י

טלטלה גבר. כהדין תרנגולא דמטלטל מאתר לאתר ורבותינו אמרו טלטולא דגברא קשה מדאיתתא [ישעיה כב, יז]. **שמותי משמתינן.** מנדים [ע"פ קידושין ע.]. **נגודי מנגדינן.** מייסרים [ע"פ ב"מ כח.]. **בפלונית שיצאה.** מבית אביה לבית בעלה כשנכנסה לחופה. **בהינומא.** קריתא, צעיף על ראשה משורבב על עיניה כמו שעושין בתוקמיו ופעמים שמנמנמת בתוכו מתוך שאין עיניה מגולין ולכך נקרא הינומא על שם תנומה [לעיל יז:]. קלתא דמנמנמת ביה כלתא או ראשה פרוע בשוק כשהיא נכנסה לחופה שכן דרך הנישאות בתולות [רשב"ם ב"ב צב:]. נערה המאורסה היו רגילין לעשות לה חופה של הדס בכניסתה לחופה וקורין לה הינומא כדאמרינן בכתובות (דף טו:) שיצאתה בהינומא וראשה פרוע [ברכות נו:]. **וראשה פרוע.** אלטויילד"ה שערה על כתפיה כך היו נוהגין להוציא את הבתולות מבית אביהן לבית החתונה [לעיל טו:]. **בית הפרס.** לא מטמא אלא מדרבנן והוא שדה שנחרש בו קבר ואשו חכמים שמא דלדלו כלי המחרישה את העצמות והדורס עליהן מסיטן ועצם כשעורה מטמא במגע ובמשא ולא באהל [ברכות יט:]. הוא שדה שנחרש בה קבר כדתנן (אהלות פי"ז מ"א) החורש בית הקבר הרי זה עושה בית הפרס מלא מענה מאה אמה וגזור רבנן שמא כיתתה מחרישה את העצמות ופיזרתן בתוך המענה ויש כאן עצם כשעורה ויעבור ויסיטנו ועצם כשעורה מטמאה במגע ובמשא דהיינו היסט [פסחים צב:]. שדה שנחרש בה קבר ואוקמי רבנן (על) [כל] סביבות הקבר מאה אמה בספק טומאה [המשך בע"ב]

עין משפט נר מצוה

קיח א ב ג מיי' פכ"א מהל' איסורי ביאה הלכה כ סמג לאוין קח טוש"ע אה"ע סימן ו סעיף ז וסימן קיט סעיף יא:
קיט ד מיי' שם טוש"ע שם סי' קיט סעיף ט:
קכ ה ו מיי' שם טוש"ע שם סעיף י:
קכא ז ח מיי' שם טוש"ע שם סעיף י:
קכב ט י מיי' פ"ו מהל' עדות הלכ' ג ופי"ד הלכה ג סמג לאוין רעו טוש"ע ח"מ סי' לה סעיף ד ה ו וסי' מט [וברב אלפס עוד ביבמות פ"ג דף י ע"ב]:
קכג כ מיי' פט"ז מהל' אישות הלכה כה סמג עשין מח טוש"ע אה"ע סי' לו סעיף טו:
קכד ל מיי' פ"כ מהל' איסורי ביאה הלכ' טו טוש"ע שם סי' ג סעיף ה:
קכה מ מיי' פ"ח מהל' עבדים הלכה יח טוש"ע יו"ד סי' רמז סעיף עא:
קכו נ מיי' שם הלכה יח טוש"ע שם סעיף עב:

תוספות רי"ד

ת"ש המגרש את אשתו לא תנשא בשכונתו. פי' לפי שמכרת ברמיזותו ובקריצותו ושמא יבואו לידי עבירה. ואם היה כהן לא תדור עמו במבוי. פי' שמא יבוא עליה וכהן אסור בגרושה [אם היה כפר קטן] זה היה מעשה ואמרו כפר קטן נידון כשכונה: **איבעי' להו** מי נדחה בפני מי ת"ש דתניא היא נדחת מפניו והוא אינו נדחה מפניה. ואם היתה חצר שלה הוא נדחה מפניה. **איבעיא להו** היתה חצר של שניהם מהו. **ת"ש** היא נדחית מפניו דטלטולא דגברא קשה מדאיתתא. **ת"ר** לוה ממנה בנכסי אביה. פי' בעודה תחתיו שהי' בידה נכסי מלוג ובכהן שגירש את אשתו מיירי הו"ז אינה נפרעת אלא על ידי שליח. פי' ולא ע"י עצמה שלא יתקרבו לדבריהם. א"ר ששת כי אתו לקמן לא מזדקקינן להו. ר"פ אמר שמותי משמתינן להו ר"ה ברי' דר"י אמר נגודי נמי מנגדינן להו. **אמר ר"נ** תנא באבל רבתי פי' מסכתא היא וקרי' אותה מס' שמחות ומשנה ראשונה שלה זו היא הגוסס הרי הוא כחי לכל דבריו בד"א שנתגרשה מן הנשואין אבל נתגרשה מן האירוסין נפרעת ע"י עצמה שאין לבו גס בה. ההוא ארוס וארוסתו דאתו קמי' דרבא אוקי רבא שליח ביניהו. פי' בפניו היו ההוא יתיב ר"א ב"מ קמי'. א"ל למה ליה למר כולי האי והאר"נ תנא באבל רבתא וכו'. א"ל ה"מ היכי דלא גיסי אהדדי הכא הא חזינא דגיסי אהדדי. פי' שמכירין זא"ז ברמיזות ובקריצות: **מתני' ואלו נאמנין** להעיד בגודלן על מה שראו בקוטנן. פי' אע"ג דבעינן ראי' והגדה בכשרות הכא נאמנים על ראיית קטנותם משום דהוה מדרבנן ודוקא להעיד בגודלן על מה שראו בקוטנן אבל להעיד בקטנותם לא פי' שאם יאמר הקטן זה כת"י של אבא אין משגיחין בדבריו דאמרי' אין ממש בדבריו אבל כשהגדיל ומעיד על ראיית קטנותו אמרי' אי לאו דקים לי' שפיר לא הוה מסהיד בגודלו. נאמן אדם לומר זה כת"י של אבא זה כת"י של רבי זה כת"י של אחי. פי' ומקיימים השטר על פיו. ואע"פ שמתו בעוד זה קטן. שנמצא שמעיד עכשיו כשהוא גדול על ראיית קטנותו נאמן הוא משום דקיום שטרות דרבנן. זכור אני באשת פ' שיצאת בהינומא וראשה פרוע פי' והוא סימן שנשאת בתולה וכתובתה מאתים כדאמרינן בריש פירקין. ושהיה איש פ' יוצא מבית הספר לטבול לתרומתו ושהיה חולק עמנו בגורן ושהמקום הזה הוא בית הפרס אבל אינו נאמן לומר דרך הי' לאיש פלוני במקום הזה מעמד ומספד הי' לפלוני במקום הזה. פי' דאפוקי ממונא הוא ובעי' עדות מעלייתא והיינו טעמא דכתובה דרוב נשים בתולות נשאות: **אמר ר"ה ברי' דר"י** והוא שיש גדול עמו. פי' דשני עדים צריך להעיד על חתימ' שהיא שלהן כדאמר לעיל דע"כ לא פליגי רבנן עלי' דר' אלא בז"א זה כתבי אבל זה כתב חבירי מודו רבנן דבעינן שנים עדים על כל חתימה וחתימה והכא אמר ר"ה דוקא ראיית קטן א' הכשירו ולא ראיית שני קטנים שאם היו שניהם מעידין בגודלן על מה שראו בקוטנן אינן נאמנים אלא בעי' שיהא א' גדול מעיד על ראיית קטנותו. וצריכא דאי אשמעינן אביו משום דשכיח גבי' פי' ונותן עיניו בקטנותו מכתב יד אביו אבל רבו אימא לא ואי אשמעינן רבו משום דאית ליה אימתי' דרביה אבל אביו אימא לא ואי אשמעינן הני תרתי אביו משום דשכיח גבי' ורבו משום דא"ל אימתי' אבל אחיו דלא הא ולא הא אימא לא קמ"ל. כיון דקיום שטרות דרבנן.

Mishnah The previous Mishnah cited a case in which the Rabbis permitted the testimony of ordinarily invalid witnesses. This Mishnah continues with further instances in which they permitted such testimony. וְאֵלּוּ נֶאֱמָנִין לְהָעִיד בְּגוֹדְלָן – **And these** (i.e. those testifying regarding the forthcoming issues) **are trusted to testify during their adulthood** מַה שֶּׁרָאוּ בְּקוֹטְנָן – regarding **what they saw when they were minors.**[18] נֶאֱמָן אָדָם לוֹמַר – **A person is trusted to say:** זֶה כְּתַב יָדוֹ שֶׁל אַבָּא – **"This** handwriting on this contract **is the handwriting of Father,** וְזֶה כְּתַב יָדוֹ שֶׁל רַבִּי – **and this is the handwriting of my teacher,** וְזֶה כְּתַב יָדוֹ שֶׁל אָחִי – **and this is the handwriting of my brother."**[19] זָכוּר הָיִיתִי בִּפְלוֹנִית – **"I remember regarding So-and-so,** שֶׁיָּצְאָה בְּהִינוּמָא וְרֹאשָׁהּ פָּרוּעַ – **that she went out** of her father's house on the way to her wedding **with a veil and** with **her hair down,**[20] וְשֶׁהָיָה אִישׁ פְּלוֹנִי יוֹצֵא מִבֵּית הַסֵּפֶר לִטְבּוֹל לֶאֱכוֹל בִּתְרוּמָה – **and that So-and-so would go out of the schoolhouse to immerse** himself in order **to eat *terumah,***[21] וְשֶׁהָיָה חוֹלֵק עִמָּנוּ עַל הַגּוֹרֶן – **and that he would divide** *terumah* **with us at the granary,** וְהַמָּקוֹם הַזֶּה בֵּית הַפְּרָס – **and** that **this place is a *beis hapras,***[22] וְעַד כָּאן הָיִינוּ בָּאִין בְּשַׁבָּת – **and** that **we would come until here on the Sabbath."**[23]

אֲבָל אֵין אָדָם נֶאֱמָן לוֹמַר – **However, a person is not trusted to say:** דֶּרֶךְ הָיָה לִפְלוֹנִי בְּמָקוֹם הַזֶּה – **"So-and-so had a path in this place."**[24] מַעֲמָד וּמִסְפֵּד הָיָה לִפְלוֹנִי בְּמָקוֹם הַזֶּה – **So-and-so had a standing spot and a eulogizing spot in this place."**[25] Since the purpose in these cases is to establish a monetary claim, valid testimony is required. Testimony based upon youthful recollection is not accepted.[26]

Gemara The Mishnah above (on 27a) permitted ordinarily invalid testimony in the cases enumerated. The Gemara now qualifies the permit:

אָמַר רַב הוּנָא בְּרֵיהּ דְּרַב יְהוֹשֻׁעַ – **Rav Huna the son of Rav Yehoshua said:** וְהוּא שֶׁיֵּשׁ גָּדוֹל עִמּוֹ – **And this** permit **is** applicable only **if there is an adult** (i.e. one who came by this knowledge as an adult) testifying **with him.**[27]

The Gemara focuses on the three rulings that concern validation of handwriting seen in one's youth:

וּצְרִיכָא – **And it is necessary** for the Mishnah to cite all three rulings. דְּאִי אַשְׁמְעִינַן אָבִיו – **For if [the Mishnah] would have informed us** only that he is trusted regarding **his father's** handwriting, I might say that the reason is מִשּׁוּם דִּשְׁכִיחַ גַּבֵּיהּ – **because he presumably frequented [his father]** as a child, and is therefore sure to recognize his handwriting. אֲבָל רַבּוֹ – **But** with regard to **his teacher's** handwriting, לֹא – perhaps he is **not** believed. The Mishnah must therefore teach that he is trusted regarding his teacher's handwriting also. וְאִי אַשְׁמְעִינַן רַבּוֹ – **And if [the Mishnah] would have informed us** only that he is trusted regarding **his teacher's** handwriting, I might say the reason is מִשּׁוּם דְּאִית לֵיהּ אֵימְתֵיהּ דְּרַבֵּיהּ – **because he was in awe of his teacher;** consequently, his teacher's handwriting was deeply impressed upon his memory.[28] אֲבָל אָבִיו – **But** with regard to **his father's** handwriting, לֹא – perhaps he is **not** believed. The Mishnah must therefore teach that he is trusted

NOTES

18. For testimony to be valid it must be delivered by one who was legally fit to act as a witness from the moment of witnessing until the testimony. Although one who testifies regarding that which he saw in his childhood is in violation of this rule, since the witnessing took place during a period in which he was not fit (i.e. his minority), he is still permitted to act as a witness in the cases set forth below (*Ritva;* cf. *Ramban, Milchamos Hashem* to 21b, folio 8b in the *Rif*). For in all these cases, the testimony concerns Rabbinic law only, and the Rabbis chose to allow testimony of this sort (see Gemara).

19. He thus confirms the validity of the contract. He is trusted to say this even if his father [or his teacher or brother] died while he was yet a minor (*Rashi*). [A person is believed to identify the handwriting of a relative (see *Shitah Mekubetzes*).]

20. [I.e. her usual hairpieces were removed and] her hair was allowed to fall free to her shoulders. This was the manner in which virgins were customarily brought from their father's homes to their weddings (*Rashi* to Mishnah 15b ד״ה ראשה פרוע). The purpose of this testimony is to prove that she was a virgin at her wedding, and should therefore now receive the full two hundred-*zuz kesubah* payment (*Rashi*).

[Our translation of הִינוּמָא as "veil" follows one explanation in the Gemara on 17b; according to the other explanation, הִינוּמָא is a bridal canopy fashioned of myrtles. It was customarily used in escorting a virgin bride to her wedding.]

21. When as children we would be studying in our teacher's house [he would leave to purify himself through immersion, so as to partake of *terumah,* which may not be eaten by one in a state of *tumah.* Clearly, he is a Kohen] (*Rashi*).

22. A *beis hapras* is a field wherein a grave has been plowed over and which, by Rabbinic decree, contaminates those who traverse it. The purpose of this testimony is to limit the size of the *beis hapras* by saying that it extends only this far and no further (see *Tos. Yom Tov;* see 28b, notes 14 and 15).

23. With these words, he establishes the *techum* (Sabbath boundary) of a particular city. The *techum* is the 2,000-*amah* (cubit) boundary assigned each individual or city at the onset of the Sabbath, beyond which one is prohibited from traveling on the Sabbath by Rabbinic law (see Gemara 28b).

24. I.e. he had the privilege of traversing the field of another in order to reach his own field or vineyard (*Meiri*). The purpose of this testimony is to establish his right of way in the other's field.

25. I.e. this person would halt the funeral processions of the members of his family in this spot [which belongs to another] to eulogize them, and, [after the burial] would pause in this spot to perform the customary seven standings and sittings (*Rashi;* see *Bava Basra* 100b with *Rashbam* ד״ה משבעה מעמדות ומושבות). Thus, this testimony establishes this person's right to use this spot for these purposes.

26. Although the testimony that a woman was married as a virgin is also intended to establish a monetary claim, it is nevertheless accepted. For in that case, the law is not really decided by his testimony, but by the fact that a majority of women marry as virgins, as the Gemara will explain (*Rashi*).

27. The requirement to have an adult testify with this individual applies only to those of the Mishnah's cases which require the testimony of *two* witnesses. These are the cases in which one attests to another's handwriting and to the fact that a particular woman was a virgin at marriage. Although in these cases the Mishnah allows testimony based on childhood memory, it does not allow *both* witnesses to offer such testimony. At least one of the witnesses must have come by this knowledge as an adult. In the Mishnah's other cases, however [i.e. *terumah; beis hapras; techum*], only a single witness is needed. This means that if an adult were to join the childhood witness, the testimony would stand on the strength of the adult alone. The other witness would be accomplishing nothing. The Mishnah, however, includes these cases among those in which testimony based on childhood memory is accepted! Clearly, this witness testifies alone in these cases, without the participation of an adult (*Ritva; Rosh;* cf. *Raavad,* cited in *Rashba;* cf. *Meiri;* cf. *Tosafos, Eruvin* 59a ד״ה אפי׳ עבר; see *Tos. R' Akiva Eiger* to the Mishnah §35).

28. It is natural for a young boy in awe of his teacher to try to emulate him. As part of this attempt, he will study his teacher's handwriting, and make an effort to imitate it. The memory of his teacher's handwriting is thus deeply ingrained in the boy (*Shitah Mekubetzes* ד״ה משום דאית ליה; see *Rashash* for another approach).

ואם היה כהן לא תדור עמו במבוי אם היה כפר קטן זה היה מעשה ואמרו כפר קטן נידון (א) כשכונה מי נדחה מפני מי ת"ש דתניא [א] היא נדחית מפניו ואין הוא נדחה מפניה ואם היתה חצר שלה הוא נדחה מפניה איבעיא להו היתה חצר של שניהם מהו ת"ש היא נדחית מפניו במאי עסקינן אילימא בחצר שלו פשיטא ואלא בחצר שלה והתניא אם היתה חצר שלה הוא נדחה מפניה אלא לאו כי האי גוונא [ב] דלמא דאגיר מיגר מאי הוי עלה ת"ש [א] הנה ה' מטלטלך טלטלה גבר [ו] ואמר רב [ג] טלטולי דגברא קשין מדאיתתא ת"ר [ד] לוה הימנה בנכסי אביה אינה נפרעת אלא ע"י אחר אמר רב ששת ואי אתו לקמן לדינא לא מזדקקינן להו רב פפא אמר [ה] שמותי משמתינן להו רב הונא בריה דרב יהושע אמר [ו] נגודי (ב) נמי מנגדינן להו אמר רב נחמן תנא [ג] באבל רבתי בד"א שנתגרשה מן הנשואין [ז] אבל כשנתגרשה מן האירוסין נפרעת ע"י עצמה שאין לבו גס בה ההוא ארוס וארוסתו דאתו לקמיה דרבא יתיב רב אדא בר מתנא קמיה אוקי רבא שלוחא בינתייהו א"ל רב אדא בר מתנא והאמר רב נחמן תנא באבל רבתי כו' א"ל קא חזינן דקא גייסי בהדדי איכא דאמרי לא אוקי רבא שליח בינתיהו א"ל רב אדא בר מתנא ניקום מר שלוחא בינתיהו א"ל והא [אמר] רב נחמן תנא באבל רבתי כו' א"ל [ח] ה"מ היכא דלא גייסי בהדדי אבל הני קא חזינא להו דגייסי בהדדי: מתני' ואלו נאמנין להעיד בגודלן מה שראו בקוטנן [ט] נאמן אדם לומר זה כתב ידו של אבא וזה כתב ידו של רבי וזה כתב ידו של אחי זכור הייתי בפלונית שיצאה בהינומא וראשה פרוע ושהיה איש פלוני יוצא מבית הספר לטבול לאכול בתרומה ושהיה חולק עמנו על הגורן והמקום הזה בית הפרס ועד כאן היינו באין בשבת אבל אין אדם נאמן לומר דרך היה לפלוני במקום הזה מעמד [ג] ומספד היה לפלוני במקום הזה: גמ' אמר רב הונא בריה דרב יהושע [י] והוא שיש גדול עמו וצריכא דאי אשמעינן אביו משום דשכיח גביה אבל רבו לא ואי אשמעינן רבו משום דאית ליה אימתיה דרביה אבל אביו לא ואי אשמעינן הני תרתי אביו דשכיח גביה ורבו דאית ליה אימתיה אבל אחיו דלית ליה לא הא ולא הא אימא לא קמ"ל כיון [ד] דקיום שטרות מדרבנן הימנוהו רבנן בדרבנן: [ב] זכור הייתי בפלונית שיצאה בהינומא וראשה פרוע: מאי טעמא [ה] כיון דרוב נשים בתולות נישאות גלוי מלתא בעלמא הוא: [ו] ושהיה איש פלוני יוצא מבית הספר לטבול לאכול בתרומה: ודלמא עבד כהן הוא מסייע ליה לר' יהושע בן לוי דאמר ר' יהושע בן לוי [ט] אסור לאדם שילמד את עבדו תורה ולא והתניא [י] לוה הימנו רבו או שעשאו רבו אפוטרופוס

רש"י

ואם היה כהן. אפילו לא ניסת: **לא תדור עמו במבוי.** שמא יבא עליה וכהן אסור בגרושה אבל ישראל כל זמן שלא ניסת תדור בשכונתו: **ואמר רב** גרס ומהאי קרא שמעינן לה: **לוה הימנה.** בעודה תחתיו: **בנכסי אביה.** שהיו בידה נכסי מלוג ובכהן שגירש את אשתו קא מיירי: **אינה נפרעת.** הימנו ע"י עצמה שלא יקרבו לדברים: **באבל רבתי.** מסכתא היא וקורין אותה שמחות וזו היא משנה ראשונה שלה הגוסס הרי הוא כחי לכל דבריו: **ארוס וארוסתו.** כהן היה: **והאמר רב נחמן תנא באבל רבתי.** דמן האירוסין נפרעת על ידי עצמה: **דגייסי בהדדי.** מכירין זה את זה ברמיזות וקריצות בלע"ז פריוויי"ץ: **מתני' זה כתב ידו של אבא.** ומקיימין השטר על פיו אע"פ שמת אביו בעוד זה קטן: **שיצאת בהינומא.** והוא סימן שניסת בתולה וכתובתה מאתים כדאמרינן בריש פירקין: **יוצא מבית הספר.** כשהיינו למידין תינוקות בבית רבן ובכולהו מפרש טעמא בגמרא: **אבל אין נאמנין כו'.** דלאפוקי ממונא הוא ובעינן עדות מעליותא וכתובה היינו טעמא דרוב נשים בתולות נישאות: **מעמד ומספד.** מקום היה לו כאן להספיד מתיו כשמוליכין לבית קברות שלו ולעשות שם מעמדות ומושבות שהיו עושין שבעה למת: **רבי יוחנן בן ברוקא אומר נאמנים.** לא גרסינן ליה במתני' אלא בברייתא ולא אדרך מעמד ומספד קאי: **גמ' דשכיח גביה.** ונתן עיניו בקטנותו בכתב יד אביו: **קיום שטרות מדרבנן.** דמדאורייתא לא בעינן קיום דאמר ר"ל (לעיל דף יח:) עדים החתומים על השטר נעשה כמי שנחקרה עדותן בב"ד: **הימנוהו רבנן בדרבנן.** בדבר שהוא מדבריהם האמינוהו ואין זה עוקר דבר מן התורה הם אמרו והם אמרו הם הצריכו קיום העדות והם הכשירו בו את אלו: **גלוי מלתא בעלמא הוא.** כלומר אין הדבר צריך עדות אלא לפרסם שילא הדין לאור בלא גמגום:

אפוטרופוס

תוספות

ואם היה כהן לא תדור עמו במבוי (א). דכיון דפנויה היא קיל ליה אבל אם ניסאת אין צריך להרחיק אלא כדי שכונה דהיינו ג' בתים כדאמרינן בסוף פרק קמא דמ"ק (דף כח.) דכיון דניסאת חמירא ליה אפי' לכהן: **כפר** קטן נידון (ג) כשכונה. וטעמא לפי שאין בני אדם מצוין שם ורגיל יותר לבא אצלה ודווקא כפר קטן אבל כפר בינוני לא: **רב הונא** אמר נגודי מנגדינן להו. נראה לר"ת דלרב הונא נמי משמתינן וגם מנגדין שכל אחד מחמיר מחבירו ואם הוא אומר דנגדינן ליה בלא שמתא הוה מיקל טפי כדאמרינן במועד קטן (דף יז.) ובפרק מקום שנהגו (פסחים נב.) במערבא כי מחייב איניש לצורבא מרבנן מימנו אנגידא ולא מימנו אשמתא: **אלו** נאמנין להעיד בגודלן מה שראו בקוטנן. משמע דבקוטנן לא מהימן אפילו בדרבנן דהא מוקי לה בגמרא בתרומה דרבנן וקשה לריב"א דאמר בפ"ק דפסחים (דף ד: ושם) דנאמנים על בדיקת חמץ אפי' נשים ועבדים וקטנים ופריך מידי משמא אית בהו ומשני הואיל ובדיקת חמץ דרבנן הימנוהו רבנן בדרבנן וי"ל התם משום דבדיקת חמץ הוא בידו לכן נאמן אפילו קטן בדרבנן אבל קשה דהיכא דבידו אפי' דלאורייתא אשה מהימנא דבפרק המדיר (לקמן דף עב. ושם) תנן (ד) וקולה לה חלה ובניקור מעשים בכל יום שאנו סומכין עליהן וי"ל דבירושלמי מפרש דבדיקת חמץ הוא טורח ונשים עצלניות הן ולהכי אי לאו דבדיקת חמץ דרבנן לא הוו מהימני: **והוא** שיש גדול עמו. לא קאי אתרומה דבתרומה סגי בלא' כיון דאין מעלין מתרומה דרבנן ליוחסין להכי מוקי לה בתרומה דרבנן דבתרומה דאורייתא כיון דסבר תנא דידן דמעלין ממנה ליוחסין כדאמרינן לקמן אינו נאמן אפי' יש גדול עמו הלכך בתרומה סגי באיהו לחודיה וכל היכא דבעינן תרי מדרבנן סגי בהוא ואחר: **קיום** שטרות דרבנן. תימה כיון דמדאורייתא אפילו אין עדים שיכירו חתימת העדים השטר כשר א"כ כל אדם שירצה יזייף ויכתוב ויחתום מה שירצה ויגבה ממנו והכא אור"י (ו) דאיכא למימר כגון שלוה מודה שכתבו וטוען שהוא פרוע וקסבר האי תנא דמודה בשטר שכתבו צריך לקיימו והאי קיום הוי ודאי מדרבנן אי נמי כגון שנתקיים משדה אחת או משתי שדות ויוצא מתחת ידי עצמו דאמר לעיל (דף כ.) דחיישינן שמא זייף ומיהו בריש גיטין (דף ג. ושם) מוכח דאפילו היכא דאין מכירין החתימה כלל הוי מדאורייתא כמי שנחקרה עדותן בב"ד: **ודלמא** עבד כהן הוא. פי' ועכשיו נשתחרר ונוטל שלא כדין וקשה לרבינו יצחק דבפ' נושאין על האנוסה (יבמות דף לט: ושם) מפרש הש"ס הא דאין חולקין תרומה לעבד משום דלמא אתי לאסוקיה ליוחסין מה צריך להאי טעמא הוה ליה למימר דאין חולקין אפי' אין מעלין שמא ישאל גם אחר שישתחרר כדפריך הכא הש"ס וכן מפרש התם הש"ס דאין חולקין לאשה בלא בעלה משום גרושה ומאי טעמא נמי דמאן דאמר חולקין וי"ל דלא שכיחא כולי האי שישאל תרומה אחר שישתחרר לא בתורת עבד ולא בתורת כהן כי ירא פן יבדקוהו ויתברר שהוא עבד ויוציאו עליו קול עבדות ולא חיישינן נמי פן ימכרנו רבו לישראל וישאל תרומה שהרי מזונותיו על רבו ואין אדם חוטא ולא לו וכולי האי לא חיישינן שמא יאמר לו רבו ישראל לאי מעשה ידיך במזונותיך:

תנן

מסורת הש"ס

א) סנהדרין כו., ב) [מס' שמחות פ"ב], ג) [בערוך ערך עמד גורס ומושבין], ד) [לעיל כח.], ה) [לעיל כח. ב"ב לב:], ו) גיטין ה., ז) [עי' תוס' לעיל יז. ד"ה מוחין].

הגהות הב"ח

(א) גמ' כפר קטן נידון כמבוי מי: (ב) שם נגודי מנגדינן כצ"ל ותיבת נמי נמחק: (ג) תוס' ד"ה כפר קטן נידון כמבוי וטעמא: (ד) ד"ה אלו כו' דבפרק המדיר תנן ואינה קולה לה:

גליון הש"ס

תוס' ד"ה והוא וכו' לא קאי אתרומה. עי' עירובין דף נט ע"א תוס' ד"ה אפילו עבד:

תורה אור השלם

א) הִנֵּה יְיָ מְטַלְטֶלְךָ טַלְטֵלָה גָּבֶר וְעֹטְךָ עָטֹה: [ישעיה כב, יז]

תוספות ישנים

א) [מלתא דאם רשות הרבים מפסיק מבית לבית שרי. ת"י].

לעזי רש"י

פריווי"ץ. פירוש מכירין זה את זה ברמיזות וקריצות (ועיין רש"י עירובין דף מו ע"א ד"ה גם בה):

ליקוטי רש"י

טלטלה גבר. כהדין תרנגולא דמטלטל מאתר לאתר ורבותינו אמרו טלטולא דגברא קשה מדאיתת' [ישעיה כב, יז]. **שמותי משמתינן.** מנדים [ע"פ קידושין ע.]. **נגודי מנגדינן.** מייסרים [ע"פ ב"מ פו.]. **בפלונית שיצאה.** מבית אביה לבית בעלה כשנכנסה לחופה. **בהינומא.** קריתא, לעיף על ראשה משורבב על עיניה כמו שעושין במקומינו ופעמים שמנמנמת בתוכו מתוך שאין עיניה מגולין ולכך נקרא הינומא על שם תנומה [לעיל יז:]. קלתא דמנמנמא ביה כלתא או ראשה פרוע בשוק בשעת כניסה לחופה שכן דרך הנישאות בתולות [רשב"ם ב"ב צב:]. נערה המאורסה היו רגילין לעשות לה חופה של הדס בכניסתה לחופה וקורין לה הינומא כדאמרינן בכתובות (דף טו:) שילאתה בהינומא וראשה פרוע [ברכות נו:]. **וראשה פרוע.** אישטייליד"ה שערה על כתפיה כך היו נוהגין להוציא את הבתולות מבית אביהן לבית החתונה [לעיל טו:]. **בית הפרס.** לא מטמא אלא מדרבנן והוא שדה שנחרש בו קבר וחשו חכמים שמא דלדלו כלי המחרישה את העצמות והדורש עליהן מסיטן ועצם כשעורה מטמא במגע ובמשא ולא באהל [ברכות יט:]. הוא שדה שנחרש בה קבר כדתנן (אהלות פי"ז מ"א) החורש בית הקבר הרי זה עושה בית הפרס מלא מענה מאה אמה וגזור רבנן שמא כיתתה מחרישה את העצמות ופיזרתן באורך המענה ויש כאן עצם כשעורה ויעבור ויסיטנו ועצם כשעורה מטמאה במגע ובמשא דהיינו היסט [פסחים צב:]. שדה שנחרש בה קבר ואוקמי רבנן (על) [כל] סביבות הקבר מאה אמה בספק טומאה [המשך בע"ב]

עין משפט נר מצוה

קיח א ב ג מיי' פכ"א מהל' איסורי ביאה הלכה כח סמג לאוין קכו טוש"ע אה"ע סימן יו סעיף ז וסימן קיט סעיף יא: קיט ד מיי' שם טוש"ע שם סי' קיט ס"ח: קכ ה ו מיי' שם טוש"ע שם סעיף ט: קכא ז ח מיי' שם טוש"ע שם סעיף י: קכב ט י מיי' פ"ו מהל' עדות הלכ' א ופ"ד הלכה ג סמג לאוין רטו טוש"ע ח"מ סי' לה סעיף ד ה וסי' מו סעי' ט [וברב אלפס עוד ביבמות פ"ג דף י ע"ב]: קכג כ מיי' פט"ו מהל' אישות הלכה כה סמג עשין מח טוש"ע אה"ע סי' סו סעיף טו: קכד ל מיי' פ"ג מהל' איסורי ביאה הלכ' טו טוש"ע שם סי' ג' סעיף ה: קכה מ מיי' פ"ח מהל' עבדים הלכה יח טוש"ע י"ד סי' רסז סעיף עא: קכו נ מיי' שם הלכה יח טוש"ע שם סעיף ע:

תוספות רי"ד

ת"ש המגרש את אשתו לא תנשא בשכונתו. פי' לפי שמכרת ברמיזותו ובקריצותו ושמא יבואו לידי עבירה. ואם היה כהן לא תדור עמו במבוי. פי' שמא יבוא עליה וכהן אסור בגרושה [אם היה כפר קטן] זה היה מעשה ואמרו כפר קטן נידון כשכונה: **איבעי' להו** מי נדחה בפני מי ת"ש דתניא היא נדחת מפניו והוא אינו נדחה מפניה. ואם היתה חצר שלה הוא נדחה מפניה **איבעיא להו** היתה חצר של שניהם מהו. **ת"ש** היא נדחית מפניו דטלטולא דגברא קשה מדאיתתא: **ת"ר** לוה ממנה בנכסי אביה. פי' בעודה תחתיו שהי' בידה נכסי מלוג ובכהן שגירש את אשתו מיירי ה"ז אינה נפרעת אלא על ידי שליח. פי' ולא ע"י עצמה שלא יתקרבו בדבריהם. א"ר ששת כי אתו לקמן לא מזדקקינן להו. ר"פ אמר שמותי משמתינן להו ר"ה ברי' דר"י אמר נגידי נמי מנגדינן להו. **אמר ר"נ** תנא באבל רבתי פי' מסכתא היא וקרי' אותה מס' שמחות ומשנה ראשונה שלה זו היא הגוסס הרי הוא כחי לכל דבריו בד"א בשנתגרשה מן הנשואין אבל נתגרשה מן האירוסין נפרעת ע"י עצמה שאין לבו גס בה. ההוא ארוס וארוסתו דאתו קמי' דרבא אוקי רבא שליח בינייהו. פי' בפניו היו הוה יתיב ר"א ב"מ קמי'. א"ל למה ליה למר כולי האי והאר"נ תנא באבל רבתא וכו'. א"ל ה"מ היכי דלא גיסי אהדדי הכא הא חזינא דגיסי אהדדי. פי' שמכירין זא"ז ברמיזות ובקריצות: **מתני' ואלו נאמנין** להעיד בגודלן על מה שראו בקוטנן. פי' אע"ג דבעינן ראי' והגדה בכשרות הכא נאמנים על ראיית קטנותם משום דהוה מדרבנן ודוקא להעיד בגודלן על מה שראו בקוטנן אבל להעיד בקטנותם לא פי' שאם יאמר הקטן זה כת"י של אבא אין משגיחין בדבריו דאמרי' אין ממש בדבריו אבל כשהגדיל ומעיד על ראיית קטנותו אמרי' אי לאו דקים לי' שפיר לא הוה מסהיד בגודלו. נאמן אדם לומר זה כת"י של אבא זה כת"י של רבי זה כת"י של אחי. פי' ומקיימים השטר על פיו. ואע"פ שמתו בעוד זה קטן. שנמצא שמעיד עכשיו כשהוא גדול על ראיית קטנותו נאמן הוא משום דקיום שטרות דרבנן. זכור אני באשת פ' שיצאת בהינומא וראשה פרוע פי' והוא סימן שנשאת בתולה וכתובתה מאתים כדאמרינן בריש פירקן. ושהיה איש פ' יוצא מבית הספר לטבול לתרומתו ושהיה חולק עמנו בגורן ושהמקום הזה הוא בית הפרס אבל אינו נאמן לומר דרך הי' לאיש פלוני במקום הזה מעמד ומספד הי' לפלוני במקום הזה. פי' דאפוקי ממונא הוא ובעי' עדות מעלייתא והיינו טעמא דכתובה דרוב נשים בתולות נשאות: **אמר ר"ה ברי' דר"י** והוא שיש גדול עמו. פי' דשני עדים צריך להעיד על חתימ' שהיא שלהן כדאמר לעיל דע"כ לא פליגי רבנן עלי' דר' אלא בז"א זה כתבי אבל זה כתב חבירי מודו רבנן דבעינן שנים עדים על כל חתימה וחתימה והכא אמר ר"ה דוקא ראיית קטן א' הכשירו ולא ראיית שני קטנים שאם היו שניהם מעידין בגודלן על מה שראו בקוטנן אינן נאמנים אלא בעי' שיהא א' גדול מעיד על ראיית קטנותו. וצריכא דאי אשמעינן אביו משום דשכיח גבי' פי' ונותן עיניו בקטנותו מכתב יד אביו אבל רבו אימא לא ואי אשמועינן רבו משום דאית ליה אימתי' דרביה אבל אביו אימא לא ואי אשמעינן הני תרתי אביו משום דשכיח גבי' ורבו משום דא"ל אימתי' אבל אחיו דלא הא ולא הא אימא לא קמ"ל. כיון דקיום שטרות דרבנן. פי' דמדאורייתא לא בעי קיום דאר"ל עדים החתומים ע"ה נעשה כמי שנחקרה עדותן בב"ד הימנוה רבנן בדרבנן פי' בדבר שהוא מדבריהם האמינוהו. ואין זה עוקר דבר מן התורה אלא הם אמרו והם אמרו. הם הצריכו העדות והם הכשירו בו את אלו ודוקא באלו שהוא רגיל בהן הוא נאמן אבל על כתב נכרים אינו נאמן להעיד על ראיות קטנותו דדילמא לא קים ליה שפיר ואפילו אמר אני ראיתי כשחתם בשטר זה אין ראיית הקטן עדות עד שיאמר כי אני מכיר בחתימתו ודוקא הקרוב מעיד על חתימת הקרוב ואין זה נוגע בעדותו שאין מגיע לקרובו שום הנאה והפסד אלא למלוה וללוה מגיעים. אבל אם היו העדים קרובים למלוה או ללוה או שהי' שניהם קרובים זל"ז אינן נאמנים להעיד על החתימה שאין מוציאין ממון ע"פ קרובים. ואע"ג דקיום שטרות דרבנן ראיית קטן הוא דהכשירו בהן חכמים. אבל לא עדות קרובים: **זכור** הייתי וכו' מ"ט כיון דרוב נשים בתולות נשאות גלוי מילתא בעלמא הוא לברר הדבר. פי' אע"ג דבמידי דממונא לאו מהיכן דלאו עליה בלחוד סמכי אלא על הרוב. וה"ה דבעינן נמי הכא והוא שיש גדול עמו ששני

The Gemara answers:

תָּא שְׁמַע – **Come, hear** a proof. The verse states:[7] ,,הִנֵּה ה׳ מְטַלְטֶלְךָ טַלְטֵלָה גָּבֶר" – ***Behold, Hashem will cause you to wander the wandering of a man.*** וְאָמַר רַב – **And Rav said:** Why does the verse stress the wandering of "a man"? טִלְטוּלֵי דְּגַבְרָא קָשִׁין מִדְּאִיתְּתָא – Because **the wandering of a man is a greater hardship than that of a woman.**[8] Therefore, it stands to reason that she should be the one displaced, for she will find it a lesser hardship than he.

Having cited one law concerning a Kohen who divorces his wife, the Gemara now cites another:[9]

תָּנוּ רַבָּנָן – **The Rabbis have taught in a Baraisa:** לָוָה הֵימֶנָּה בְּנִכְסֵי אָבִיהָ – If while they were married [THE KOHEN] BORROWED FROM [HIS WIFE] money from HER FATHER'S POSSESSIONS, אֵינָהּ נִפְרַעַת אֶלָּא עַל יְדֵי אַחֵר – SHE MAY NOT COLLECT the debt FROM HIM after the divorce EXCEPT THROUGH the agency of ANOTHER, lest their discussions reawaken a sense of intimacy and lead them to sin.[10]

A related law:

אָמַר רַב שֵׁשֶׁת – **Rav Sheishess said:** וְאִי אָתוּ לְקַמָּן לְדִינָא לֹא מִזְדַּקְקִינַן לְהוּ – **And if they** (i.e. a Kohen and his divorcee) **come before us for judgment** without benefit of an intermediary,[11] **we do not attend to them,** for we view their association as illicit. רַב פָּפָּא אָמַר – **Rav Pappa said:** שַׁמּוּתֵי מְשַׁמְּתִינַן לְהוּ – **We** even **excommunicate them.** רַב הוּנָא בְּרֵיהּ דְּרַב יְהוֹשֻׁעַ אָמַר – **Rav Huna the son of Rav Yehoshua said:** נַגּוּדֵי נַמִּי מְנַגְּדִינַן לְהוּ – **We also punish them with lashes.**[12]

The Gemara qualifies the foregoing ruling:

אָמַר רַב נַחְמָן – **Rav Nachman said:** תָּנָא בְּאֵבֶל רַבָּתִי – **The Baraisa in *Eivel Rabbasi*[13] has taught:** בַּמֶּה דְּבָרִים אֲמוּרִים – WHEN ARE THESE WORDS SAID, i.e. that a Kohen's divorcee may not collect from her former husband without an intermediary?[14] שֶׁנִּתְגָּרְשָׁה מִן הַנִּשּׂוּאִין – WHEN THEY WERE DIVORCED AFTER *NISUIN.* אֲבָל כְּשֶׁנִּתְגָּרְשָׁה מִן הָאֵירוּסִין – BUT IF THEY WERE DIVORCED AFTER *ERUSIN,* נִפְרַעַת עַל יְדֵי עַצְמָהּ – SHE MAY COLLECT ON HER OWN. שֶׁאֵין לִבּוֹ גַס בָּהּ – FOR in that case, HE IS NOT yet FAMILIAR WITH HER; therefore, we do not fear that their association will lead to sin.[15]

The Gemara cites an incident concerning this ruling:

הַהוּא אָרוּס וַאֲרוּסָתוֹ דְּאָתוּ לְקַמֵּיהּ דְּרָבָא – **There was this certain couple** (i.e. a Kohen and his wife) **who had undergone *erusin*** and then divorced **who came before Rava** regarding a monetary dispute, without using an intermediary. יָתֵיב רַב אַדָּא בַּר מַתְנָא קַמֵּיהּ – **Rav Adda bar Masna was sitting before [Rava]** at that time, אוֹקֵי רָבָא שְׁלוּחָא בֵּינָתַיְיהוּ – and **Rava appointed him the intermediary between them.** אָמַר לֵיהּ רַב אַדָּא בַּר מַתְנָא – **Rav Adda bar Masna said to [Rava]:** וְהָאָמַר רַב נַחְמָן תָּנָא בְּאֵבֶל רַבָּתִי כו׳ – **But Rav Nachman said** that **the Baraisa in *Aivel Rabasi* has taught** [that if they were divorced after *erusin* she may collect on her own] **etc.** Why, then, do you require a go-between? אָמַר לֵיהּ – **[Rava] said to him:** קָא חָזֵינַן דְּקָא גָּיְיסֵי בַּהֲדָדֵי – **Behold, we see that they are familiar with one another.**[16] Since their association may thus bring them to sin, they require an intermediary.[17]

Another version of this incident:

אִיכָּא דְּאָמְרֵי – **There are those who say** that the incident occurred in this manner. לֹא אוֹקֵי רָבָא שָׁלִיחַ בֵּינָתַיְיהוּ – **Rava did not appoint an intermediary between them,** אָמַר לֵיהּ רַב אַדָּא בַּר מַתְנָא – whereupon **Rav Adda bar Masna said to him:** נֵיקוּם מַר שְׁלוּחָא בֵּינָתַיְיהוּ – **Let the master appoint an intermediary between them.** אָמַר לֵיהּ – **[Rava] said to him:** וְהָא [אָמַר] רַב נַחְמָן תָּנָא בְּאֵבֶל רַבָּתִי כו׳ – **But Rav Nachman said** that **the Baraisa in *Eivel Rabbasi* has taught etc.** אָמַר לֵיהּ – **[Rav Adda]** then **said to [Rava]:** הָנֵי מִילֵּי הֵיכָא דְּלָא גָּיְיסֵי בַּהֲדָדֵי – **These words** were said **where they are not familiar with one another.** אֲבָל הָנֵי קָא חָזֵינָא לְהוּ דְּגָיְיסֵי בַּהֲדָדֵי – **But these** two – **behold, we see that they are familiar with one another.** Therefore, an intermediary is necessary.

NOTES

7. *Isaiah* 22:17.

8. See *Maharsha, Sanhedrin* 26a.

9. *Rashi;* cf. *Rambam, Isurei Biah* 21:27 with *Maggid Mishneh;* cf. also *Ran.*

10. [Property that a woman brings into her marriage from her father's house (with the exception of her dowry that is written into the *kesubah*) or inherits during her marriage is known as *melog* property (נִכְסֵי מְלוֹג). This property remains her own, but is set aside for the husband's use throughout the marriage. In the event of divorce, it is returned to the woman.] This Baraisa discusses the case of a Kohen who borrows *melog* money from his wife and then divorces her (see *Rashi*). She may not collect it herself, but must appoint an intermediary to collect it for her.

[Of course, the same applies regarding her *kesubah* payment (or any other debt that her former husband owes her). The Baraisa discusses a loan made from *melog* property because it is the most common case, since the *kesubah* is usually paid at the time of the divorce (*Shitah Mekubetzes* ד״ה ת״ר לוה).]

11. See *Beis Yosef, Even HaEzer* §119 ד״ה ומ״ש משמתינן להו.

12. I.e. in addition to excommunicating them, we punish them with lashes (*Ritva*). [Some versions of Rav Huna's ruling do not include the word נַמִּי, *also. Tosafos* nevertheless state that Rav Huna is not disagreeing with Rav Pappa. Rather, he is *adding* lashes to excommunication (see also *Ran,* first explanation). Others say that he *is* disagreeing with Rav Pappa. He holds that they receive lashes but are not excommunicated (*Ran,* second explanation).]

Ritva states that in this case it is the responsibility of the woman to appoint someone her intermediary. It is not the responsibility of the man. See *Ritva* for his reasoning.

13. *Eivel Rabbasi* is one of the minor Talmudic tractates (מַסֶּכְתּוֹת קְטַנּוֹת). [It is concerned primarily with the laws of death, burial and mourning.] The first Baraisa in the tractate begins with the words הַגּוֹסֵס הֲרֵי הוּא כְּחַי לְכָל דְּבָרָיו, *one near death is as a live person in all his matters.* However, unlike many other tractates (e.g. *Beitzah; Megillah*), this one is not named after its opening word [or subject], in which case it would be called Tractate *HaGoseis,* but is named Tractate *Semachos* ("Rejoicings"), in euphemistic reference to its contents (*Rashi,* as explained by *Shitah Mekubetzes* ד״ה באבל רבתי; see *Mira Dachya,* printed in *Asifas Zekeinim,* for another explanation). The reason it is not named *HaGoseis,* which means "one near death" is because we do not wish to refer to a tractate with a word of ill-omen (*Shitah Mekubetzes* ibid.).

[In referring to the first Baraisa in *Aivel Rabbasi, Rashi* employs the term "Mishnah." This is puzzling, for it is generally agreed that the minor tractates are made up of Baraisos, not Mishnahs. However, it is not uncommon for *Rashi* to call a Baraisa a Mishnah; see, for example, *Rashi* to *Shabbos* 140b ד״ה אידי; see also *Rashi* to *Succah* 28a ד״ה משנה.]

14. See *Rashi* ד״ה והאמר רב נחמן.

15. [Marriage is accomplished in two stages. The first is known as *erusin* or *kiddushin;* the second as *nisuin.* After *erusin,* the marriage is complete in many respects; however, with *nisuin,* the groom formally brings the bride into his home. Since the Rabbis prohibit a couple to cohabit until after *nisuin* is performed (see *Rambam, Ishus* 10:1), intimacy grows between them only after that point (see *Hagahos Yavetz*).]

16. For we see that they recognize each other's private gestures and signals (*Rashi*), and are not shy with one another (*Rabbeinu Yehonasan,* cited in *Shitah Mekubetzes*).

17. [However, they were not liable to the sanctions mentioned above, since they had not undergone *nisuin.*]

ואם היה כהן לא תדור עמו במבוי ואמרו כפר קטן זה היה מעשה ואמרו כפר קטן נידון (א) כשכונה מי נדחה מפני מי ת"ש דתניא [א] היא נדחית מפניו ואין הוא נדחה מפניה ואם היתה חצר שלה הוא נדחה מפניה איבעיא להו היתה חצר של שניהם מהו ת"ש היא נדחית מפניו במאי עסקינן אילימא בחצר שלו פשיטא ואלא בחצר שלה והתניא אם היתה חצר שלה הוא נדחה מפניה אלא לאו כי האי גוונא [ב] דלמא דאגיר מיגר מאי הוי עלה ת"ש [א] הנה ה' מטלטלך טלטלה גבר [א] ואמר רב [ג] טלטולי דגברא קשין מדאיתתא ת"ר [ד] לוה הימנה בנכסי אביה אינה נפרעת אלא ע"י אחר אמר רב ששת ואי אתו לקמן לדינא לא מזדקקינן להו רב פפא אמר [ה] שמותי משמתינן להו רב הונא בריה דרב יהושע אמר [ו] נגודי (ג) נמי מנגדינן להו אמר רב נחמן תנא [ז] באבל רבתי בד"א שנתגרשה מן הנשואין [ח] אבל כשנתגרשה מן האירוסין נפרעת ע"י עצמה שאין לבו גס בה ההוא ארוס וארוסתו דאתו לקמיה דרבא יתיב רב אדא בר מתנא קמיה אוקי רבא שלוחא בינתייהו א"ל רב אדא בר מתנא והאמר רב נחמן תנא באבל רבתי כו' א"ל קא חזינן דקא גייסי בהדדי איכא דאמרי לא אוקי רבא שליח בינתייהו א"ל רב אדא בר מתנא ניקום מר שלוחא בינתייהו א"ל והא [אמר] רב נחמן תנא באבל רבתי כו' א"ל [ח] ה"מ היכא דלא גייסי בהדדי אבל הני קא חזינא להו דגייסי בהדדי: **מתני'** ואלו נאמנין להעיד בגודלן מה שראו בקוטנן [ט] נאמן אדם לומר זה כתב ידו של אבא וזה כתב ידו של רבי וזה כתב ידו של אחי זכור הייתי בפלונית שיצאה בהינומא וראשה פרוע ושהיה איש פלוני יוצא מבית הספר לטבול לאכול בתרומה ושהיה חולק עמנו על הגורן והמקום הזה בית הפרס ועד כאן היינו באין בשבת אבל אין אדם נאמן לומר דרך היה לפלוני במקום הזה מעמד [י] ומספד היה לפלוני במקום הזה: **גמ'** אמר רב הונא בריה דרב יהושע [י] והוא שיש גדול עמו וצריכא דאי אשמעינן אביו משום דשכיח גביה אבל רבו לא ואי אשמעינן רבו משום דאית ליה אימתיה דרביה אבל אביו לא ואי אשמעינן הני תרתי אביו דשכיח גביה ורבו דאית ליה אימתיה אבל אחיו דלית ליה לא הא ולא הא אימא לא קמ"ל כיון [ז] דקיום שטרות מדרבנן הימנוהו רבנן בדרבנן: [כ] זכור הייתי בפלונית שיצאה בהינומא וראשה פרוע: מאי טעמא [ה] כיון דרוב נשים בתולות נישאות גלוי מלתא בעלמא הוא: [ל] ושהיה איש פלוני יוצא מבית הספר לטבול לאכול בתרומה: ודלמא עבד כהן הוא מסייע ליה לר' יהושע בן לוי דאמר ר' יהושע בן לוי [מ] אסור לאדם שילמד את עבדו תורה ולא והתניא [ו] [נ] לוה הימנו רבו או שעשאו רבו אפוטרופוס

רש"י

ואם היה כהן. אפילו לא ניסת: לא תדור עמו במבוי. שמא יבא עליה וכהן אסור בגרושה אבל ישראל כל זמן שלא ניסת תדור בשכונתו: ואמר רב גרם ומהאי קרא שמעינן לה: לוה הימנה. בהיותה תחתיו: בנכסי אביה. שהיו בידה נכסי מלוג ובכהן שגירש את אשתו קא מיירי: אינה נפרעת. הימנו ע"י עצמה שלא יקרבו בדברים: באבל רבתי. מסכתא היא וקורין אותה שמחות וזו היא משנה ראשונה שלה הגוסס הרי הוא כחי לכל דבריו: ארוס וארוסתו. כהן היה: והאמר רב נחמן תנא באבל רבתי. דמן האירוסין נפרעת על ידי עצמה: דגייסי בהדדי. מכירין זה את זה ברמיזות וקריצות בלע"ז פריווי"ן: **מתני'** זה כתב ידו של אבא. ומקיימין השטר על פיו אע"פ שמת אביו בעוד זה קטן: שיצאת בהינומא. והוא סימן שניסת בתולה וכתובתה מאתים כדאמרינן בריש פירקין: יוצא מבית הספר. כשהיינו למדין תינוקות בבית רבן וכולהו מפרש טעמא בגמרא: אבל אין נאמנין כו'. דלפסוקי ממונא הוא ובעינן עדות מעליותא וכתובה היינו טעמא דרוב נשים בתולות נישאות: מעמד ומספד. מקום היה לו כהן להספיד מתיו כשמוליכין לבית קברות שלו ולעשות שם מעמדות ומושבות שהיו עושין שבעה למת: רבי יוחנן בן ברוקא אומר נאמנים. לא גרסינן ליה במתני' אלא בברייתא ולא אלדך מעמד ומספד קאי: **גמ'** דשכיח גביה. ונתן עיניו בקטנותו בכתב יד אביו: קיום שטרות מדרבנן. דמדאורייתא לא בעינן קיום דאמר ר"ל (לעיל דף יח:) עדים החתומים על השטר נעשה כמי שנחקרה עדותן בב"ד: הימנוהו רבנן בדרבנן. בדבר שהוא מדבריהם האמינו ואין זה עוקר דבר מן התורה הם אמרו והם אמרו הם הצריכו קיום העדות והם הכשירו בו את אלו: גלוי מלתא בעלמא הוא. כלומר אין הדבר צריך עדות אלא לפרסם שילא הדין לאור בלא גמגום:

אפוטרופוס

תוספות

ואם היה כהן לא תדור עמו במבוי [א]. דכיון דפנויה היא קיל ליה אבל אם נישאת אין צריך להרחיק אלא כדי שכונה דהיינו ג' בתים כדאמרינן בסוף פרק קמא דע"ז (דף כא.) דכיון דנישאת תמירא ליה אפי' לכהן: **כפר** קטן נידון (ג) כשכונה. וטעמא לפי שאין בני אדם מצוין שם ורגיל יותר לבא אצלה ודווקא כפר קטן אבל כפר בינוני לא: **רב** הונא אמר נגודי מנגדינן להו. נראה לר"ת דלרב הונא נמי משמתינן וגם מנגדינן שכל אחד מחמיר מחבירו ואם הוא אומר דנגדינן ליה בלא שמתא הוה מיקל טפי כדאמרינן במועד קטן (דף יז.) ובפרק מקום שנהגו (פסחים נב.) במערבא כי מחייב צורבא מרבנן מימנו אנגידא ולא מימנו אשמתא: **אלו** נאמנין להעיד בגודלן מה שראו בקטנן. משמע דבקטנותן לא מהימן אפילו בדרבנן דהא מוקי לה בגמרא בתרומה דרבנן וקשה לריב"א דאמר בפ"ק דפסחים (דף ד: ושם) דנאמנים על בדיקת חמץ אפי' נשים ועבדים וקטנים ופריך מידי איריא כהו ומשני הואיל ובדיקת חמץ דרבנן הימנוהו רבנן בדרבנן וי"ל דהתם היינו טעמא משום דבדיקת חמץ הוא בידו לכן נאמן אפילו קטן בדרבנן אבל קשה דהיכא דבידו אפי' בדאורייתא אשה מהימנא דבפרק המדיר (לקמן דף עב. ושם) תנן (ד) וקוצה לה חלה וניקור מעשים בכל יום שאנו סומכין עליהן וי"ל דבירושלמי מפרש דבדיקת חמץ הוא טורח ונשים עצלניות הן ולהכי אי לאו דבדיקת חמץ דרבנן לא הוו מהימני:

והוא שיש גדול עמו. ° לא קאי אתרומה דבתרומה סגי בלא כיון דאין מעלין מתרומה דרבנן ליוחסין להכי מוקי לה בתרומה דרבנן דבתרומה דאורייתא כיון דסבר תנא דידן דמעלין ממנה ליוחסין כדאמרינן לקמן אינו נאמן אפי' יש גדול עמו הלכך בתרומה סגי בלאיהו לחודיה וכל היכא דבעינן תרי מדרבנן סגי בהוא ואחר: **קיום** שטרות דרבנן. תימה כיון דמדאורייתא אפילו אין עדים שיכירו חתימת העדים השטר כשר א"כ כל אדם שירצה יזייף ויכתוב ויחתום מה שירצה ויגבה ממנו והכא אור"י [ז] דאיכא למימר כגון שלוה מודה שכתבו וטוען שהוא פרוע וקסבר האי תנא דמודה בשטר שכתבו צריך לקיימו והאי קיום הוי ודאי מדרבנן אי נמי כגון שנתקיים מצדה אחת או משתי שדות ויוצא מתחת ידי עצמו דאמר לעיל (דף כ.) דחיישינן שמא זייף ומיהו בריש גיטין (דף ג. ושם) מוכח דאפילו היכא דאין מכירין החתימה כלל הוי מדאורייתא כמי שנחקרה עדותן בב"ד:

ודלמא עבד כהן הוא. פי' ועכשיו נשתחרר ונוטל שלא כדין וקשה לרבינו יצחק דבפ' נושאין על האנוסה (יבמות דף צט: ושם) מפרש הש"ס הא דאין חולקין תרומה לעבד משום דלמא אתי לאסוקיה ליוחסין מה צריך להאי טעמא הוה ליה למימר דאין חולקין אפי' אין מעלין שמא ישאל גם אחר שישתחרר כדפריך הכא הש"ס וכן מפרש התם הש"ס דאין חולקין לאשה בלא בעלה משום גרושה ומאי טעמא נמי דמאן דאמר חולקין וי"ל דלא שכיחא כולי האי שישאל תרומה אחר שישתחרר לא בתורת עבד ולא בתורת כהן כי ירא פן יבדקוהו ויתברר שהוא עבד ויוציאו עליו קול עבדות ולא חיישינן נמי פן ימכרנו רבו לישראל וישאל תרומה שהרי מזונותיו על ישראל ולא הוא ולכולי האי לא חיישינן שמא יאמר לו רבו לישראל לאי מעשה ידיך במזונותיך:

תנן

וְאִם הָיָה כֹּהֵן – AND IF [THE HUSBAND] WAS A KOHEN, לֹא תָּדוּר עִמּוֹ בְּמָבוֹי – SHE MAY NOT DWELL WITH HIM IN A *MAVOI,* even if she has not remarried.[1] אִם הָיָה כְּפָר קָטָן – IF IT WAS A SMALL VILLAGE in which they dwelt – זֶה הָיָה מַעֲשֶׂה וְאָמְרוּ – THIS ONCE OCCURRED, AND [THE SAGES] SAID: כְּפָר קָטָן נִידּוֹן כִּשְׁכוּנָה – A SMALL VILLAGE IS JUDGED AS A NEIGHBORHOOD. Accordingly, a woman who has remarried may not dwell in the same small village as her former husband.[2]

We see from this Baraisa that a woman divorced from a Kohen may not dwell even in the same *mavoi* as her former husband, and certainly not in the same courtyard. Thus, Abaye's inquiry is resolved.

The Gemara asks:

מִי נִדְחֶה מִפְּנֵי מִי – **Who is displaced by whom?** Must she leave the courtyard or must he?

The Gemara offers a proof:

תָּא שְׁמַע – **Come, hear** a proof. דְּתַנְיָא – **For it has been taught in a Baraisa:** הִיא נִדְחֵית מִפָּנָיו – SHE IS DISPLACED BY HIM, וְאֵין הוּא נִדְחֶה מִפָּנֶיהָ – AND HE IS NOT DISPLACED BY HER.[3] וְאִם הָיְתָה חָצֵר שֶׁלָּהּ – BUT IF IT WAS HER COURTYARD,[4] הוּא נִדְחֶה מִפָּנֶיהָ – HE IS DISPLACED BY HER.

The Gemara cites an inquiry:

אִיבַּעְיָא לְהוּ – **They inquired:** הָיְתָה חָצֵר שֶׁל שְׁנֵיהֶם מַהוּ – **If it was the courtyard of both of them,**[5] **what is [the law]?** Who is displaced?

The Gemara brings a proof:

תָּא שְׁמַע – **Come, hear** a proof. The Baraisa stated in its first clause: הִיא נִדְחֵית מִפָּנָיו – SHE IS DISPLACED BY HIM. בְּמַאי עַסְקִינַן – **With what are we dealing** here? אִילֵימָא בְּחָצֵר שֶׁלּוֹ פְּשִׁיטָא – **If you will say** we are dealing **with his courtyard, it is obvious** that it is she who is displaced! Surely the Baraisa would not bother to state something so elementary. וְאֶלָּא בְּחָצֵר שֶׁלָּהּ – **Rather, then,** you will say that we are dealing **with her courtyard.** וְהָתַנְיָא – **But it has been taught in the** final clause of this **Baraisa:** אִם הָיְתָה חָצֵר שֶׁלָּהּ הוּא נִדְחֶה מִפָּנֶיהָ – IF IT WAS HER COURTYARD, HE IS DISPLACED BY HER. Clearly, the Baraisa's first clause is not discussing her courtyard. אֶלָּא לָאו כִּי הַאי גַּוְונָא – **Is it not** evident, **then,** that we are dealing with **this sort of case,** where they both own houses in the courtyard? Seemingly, it is. Thus, the inquiry is resolved, for this Baraisa rules that in this case she is displaced by him.

The Gemara deflects this proof:

דִּלְמָא דַּאֲגִיר מֵיגַר – No, **perhaps** we are dealing here with a case **where they are** both **renting** houses in the courtyard, but not where they both own houses there.[6]

Having deflected the proof, the Gemara returns to its question:

מַאי הֲוֵי עֲלָהּ – **What was decided regarding this [matter]?**

NOTES

1. A Kohen is prohibited to cohabit with any divorcee, even his former wife. The Rabbis feared that if the divorced couple would dwell in a single *mavoi,* their proximity might lead them to sin. In the case of a Yisrael, however, there is no prohibition forbidding him to cohabit with a divorcee. Therefore, he is permitted to reside [even] in the same neighborhood as his former wife, so long as she has not remarried (*Rashi;* see *Haflaah;* see note 2).

[A *mavoi* is an alleyway into which courtyards open, and which opens onto the public domain (רְשׁוּת הָרַבִּים). All the courtyards of her former husband's *mavoi* are off limits to a woman divorced from a Kohen.] Note that the Baraisa is discussing a closed *mavoi* (i.e. one open only on one end). It would be permissible, however, for a Kohen and his former wife to reside together in an open *mavoi* (i.e. one open on both ends to the public domain), for large numbers of people pass through such a *mavoi;* therefore, the danger that the couple will sin is considerably reduced (*R' Yaakov MiOrleans,* cited in *Ran*).

2. The Rishonim disagree on several points concerning this Baraisa, as follows:

Tosafos (based on *Avodah Zarah* 21a) give the measure of a "neighborhood" (שְׁכוּנָה) as three houses. This means that a woman divorced from a Yisrael may not reside within three houses of her former husband if she has remarried. The unmarried divorcee of a Kohen, however, has an even more stringent law, for she may not reside anywhere in her former husband's *mavoi,* notwithstanding that it certainly contains more than three houses. The reason her law is more stringent than that of the remarried divorcee of a Yisrael is that the prohibition forbidding cohabitation with a married woman is more stringent than that forbidding a Kohen to cohabit with a divorcee. As a rule, people will be more careful regarding greater sins than lesser ones; therefore, the greater sin requires less guarding (see *Ram HaKohen,* cited in *Ran,* for another rationale). According to this reasoning, the law of a woman divorced from a Kohen changes once she remarries. For the greater sin of cohabiting with a married woman now applies; therefore she need leave only the neighborhood, not the *mavoi* (see *Tosafos; Pnei Yehoshua; Mishneh LaMelech, Isurei Biah* 21:27). *Rosh* and *Ran* maintain, however, that a neighborhood is *larger* than a *mavoi.* Accordingly, the unmarried divorcee of a Kohen, who is displaced only from the husband's *mavoi,* has a *less* stringent law than a woman divorced from a Yisrael and then remarried, who may not reside anywhere in his neighborhood. The reason the Kohen's divorcee is treated less stringently is that the prohibition forbidding her to the Kohen is less stringent than that forbidding a married woman to a man other than her husband; these Rishonim reason that it therefore does not warrant such stringent safeguards. According to these Rishonim too, the law of a Kohen's wife changes if she remarries, for she must now leave even his neighborhood, in accordance with the Baraisa's first clause (see *Pnei Yehoshua; Mishneh LaMelech* ibid.). *Rashi* does not state his view on this issue; however, *Mishneh LaMelech* (ibid.) infers from *Rashi* that he agrees with *Tosafos* that a neighborhood is smaller than a *mavoi* (cf., however, *Pnei Yehoshua*).

An outgrowth of this difference of opinion is a dispute regarding the Baraisa's reasoning in judging a small village as a neighborhood. *Ran,* who holds that a "neighborhood" is a comparatively large place, explains that the reason a small village shares its law is because it is of similar size. *Tosafos,* however, are compelled to explain this ruling differently, since even a small village certainly contains more than three houses. They maintain that a small village is judged as a neighborhood because people rarely pass through it. Accordingly, there is greater danger that the couple will come to sin (see *Kikayon DeYonah*).

Another area of disagreement concerns the status of a woman who was divorced from a Yisrael, but who has *not* yet remarried. *Rambam* (*Isurei Biah* 21:27) and *Ran* hold that she is prohibited to reside in her former husband's courtyard (but not in his *mavoi* or neighborhood). *Ritva* and *Ram HaKohen* (cited in *Ran*) maintain that there is no reason whatsoever to forbid this woman to reside near her former husband. Therefore, she may reside even in his courtyard. As for *Rashi,* he says only that she may reside in his neighborhood, but does not discuss the law of his courtyard. At first, *Mishneh LaMelech* (ibid.) takes this to mean that she is forbidden to reside in his courtyard; however, he later retracts, on the basis of *Ritva* and *Smag,* who imply that according to *Rashi* this woman may reside wherever she pleases. See *Mishneh LaMelech* for discussion; see also *Haflaah.*

3. The redundancy, *and he is not displaced by her,* teaches that even if her new quarters are distant from her present dwelling and his would be close by, it is she, not he, who must move (*Ritva*).

4. I.e. if it is she who owns the house in the courtyard in which they reside (see *Ritva*).

5. I.e. if they each owned a house in the courtyard (*Ritva*).

6. According to this answer, the Baraisa's first clause, *she is displaced by him,* teaches that when they are both renting in the courtyard, she must leave, even though she would appear to have equal rights in the courtyard. Now, it would seem logical for the law to be the same in a courtyard in which both *own* property, since both have equal rights there too; however, it is not so. For whatever reason exists to displace a woman who is renting in a courtyard may not suffice to evict her from property she *owns* there. Therefore, the law of a courtyard in which the couple owns property cannot be derived from the law of one in which they merely rent (*Ritva*).

his **divorcee?** הָתָם הוּא דְּבִשְׁבוּיָה הֵקִילוּ – One might say that **over there** (i.e. in the case of R' Zecharyah's wife) **this** was permitted **because [the Rabbis] were lenient regarding a captive woman,**[34] אֲבָל הָכָא לֹא – **but here** (i.e. in the case of a Kohen's divorcee) it is **not** permissible for her to dwell in his courtyard.[35] אוֹ דִּלְמָא לֹא שְׁנָא – **Or perhaps it makes no difference,** and a Kohen's divorcee is also permitted to dwell in the same courtyard as her former husband.

The Gemara offers a proof:

תָּא שְׁמַע – **Come, hear** a proof: דְּתַנְיָא – **For it has been taught in a Baraisa:** הַמְגָרֵשׁ אֶת אִשְׁתּוֹ – If ONE DIVORCES HIS WIFE, לֹא תִנָּשֵׂא בִּשְׁכוּנָתוֹ – SHE SHOULD NOT REMARRY and dwell IN HIS (i.e. the first husband's) NEIGHBORHOOD.[36]

NOTES

marriage because of the danger that their proximity could lead them to sin.]

34. For there is a real possibility that she was never even violated, and thus never became forbidden to her husband (see *Rashi* 23a ד״ה בשבויה הקילו; *Rashbam, Bava Basra* 135a ד״ה אם הקילו בשבויה; *Ritva* here). Perhaps, then, it is for this reason that the Rabbis, despite forbidding her to cohabit with her husband, were lenient in allowing them to live at close quarters.

35. Lest their proximity lead them to sin.

[A Kohen is forbidden to cohabit with a divorcee [and he may not remarry his divorced wife] – see *Leviticus* 21:7.]

36. For having been intimate with him, she knows his private gestures and signals, and we fear they may come to sin (*Rashi*).

[In this clause the Baraisa discusses a Yisrael, not a Kohen. The differences between the law of a woman divorced from a Yisrael and one divorced from a Kohen as regards their living at close quarters will be discussed on 28a, note 2. [A Yisrael may remarry his divorced wife unless she married another person (with *nisuin*) in the interim (and was then widowed or divorced).] See there also for a halachic definition of שְׁכוּנָה, *neighborhood.*]

מה לי לשקר או דלמא לא אמרינן ומאי שנא מההוא מעשה דההוא גברא דאגר ליה חמרא לחבריה א"ל לא תיזיל באורחא דנהר פקוד דאיכא מיא זיל באורחא דנרש דליכא מיא ואזל איהו באורחא דנהר פקוד ומית חמרא אתא לקמיה דרבא א"ל אין באורחא דנהר פקוד אזלי מיהו לא הוו מיא אמר רבא מה לי לשקר אי בעי א"ל באורחא דנרש אזלי ואמר ליה אביי מה לי לשקר במקום עדים לא אמרינן הכי השתא התם ודאי איכא עדים דאיכא מיא הכא ודאי איטמי חששא הוא ובמקום חששא אמרינן: אם יש עדים אפילו עבד ואפילו שפחה נאמנין: ואפילו שפחה דידה מהימנא ורמינהו לא תתיחד עמו אלא ע"פ עדים ואפילו ע"פ עבד וע"פ שפחה חוץ משפחתה מפני שלבה גס בשפחתה אמר רב פפי בשבויה הקילו רב פפא אמר הא בשפחה דידיה הא בשפחה דידה ושפחה דידיה לא מהימנא הא קתני אין אדם מעיד על עצמו הא שפחה דידיה מהימנא שפחתה נמי כעצמה דמי רב אשי אמר הא והא בשפחה דידה ושפחה מיחזא חזיא ושתקה התם דשתיקתה מתירתה לא מהימנא הכא דשתיקתה אוסרתה מהימנא השתא נמי אתיא ומשקרא תרתי לא עבדה כי הא דמרי בר איסק אתא ליה אחא מבי חוזאה א"ל פלוג לי בנכסי דאבא א"ל לא ידענא לך אתא לקמיה דרב חסדא א"ל שפיר קאמר לך דכתיב ויכר יוסף את אחיו והם לא הכירוהו מלמד שיצא בלא חתימת זקן ובא בחתימת זקן א"ל זיל אייתי סהדי דאחוה את א"ל אית לי סהדי ומסתפינו מיניה דגברא אלמא הוא א"ל לדידיה זיל (א) אייתינהו את דלאו אחוך הוא א"ל דינא הכי המוציא מחבירו עליו הראיה א"ל הכי דאינא לך ולכולהו אלמי חברך השתא נמי אתו ומשקרי תרתי לא עבדי לימא כתנאי זו עדות איש ואשה תינוק ותינוקת אביה ואמה ואחיה ואחותה אבל לא בנה ובתה לא עבדה ושפחתה ותניא אידך הכל נאמנין להעיד חוץ מהימנה ובעלה דרב פפי ודרב אשי תנאי היא דרב פפא [מי] לימא תנאי היא אמר לך רב פפא כי תניא ההיא במסיחה לפי תומה כי הא דכי אתא רב דימי אמר רב חנן קרטיגנאה משתעי מעשה בא לפני רבי יהושע בן לוי ואמרי לה רבי יהושע בן לוי משתעי מעשה בא לפני רבי באדם אחד שהיה מסיח לפי תומו ואמר אני ואמי נשבינו לבין העובדי כוכבים יצאתי לשאוב מים דעתי על אמי ללקט עצים דעתי על אמי והשיאה ר' לכהונה על פיו: **מתני'** אמר ר' זכריה בן הקצב המעון הזה לא זזה ידה מתוך ידי משעה שנכנסו עובדי כוכבים לירושלים ועד שיצאו אמרו לו אין אדם מעיד על עצמו: **גמ'** תנא ואעפ"כ יחד לה בית בחצרו וכשהיא יוצאה יוצאה בראש בניה וכשהיא נכנסת נכנסת בסוף בניה בעי אביי מהו לעשות בגרושה כן התם הוא דבשבויה הקילו אבל הכא לא או דלמא לא שנא ת"ש דתניא המגרש את אשתו לא תנשא בשכונתו ואם

רש"י

מה לי לשקר. אי בעיא אמרה נחבאתי: **במקום עדים.** דאכן סהדי דכל שעתא איכא מיא: **ודאי איטמי.** בתמיה: **לא תתייחד עמו.** במסכת גיטין היא שכיב מרע שכתב ומסר גט לאשתו על מנת שאם מת יהא גט למפרע ולא תיזקק לחליצה לא תתייחד עמו שמא יבא עליה והוה ליה גט ישן ותנן בית הלל אוסרין לפטור בגט ישן ואיזהו גט ישן כל שנתייחד עמה מאחר שכתבו לה וטעמא גזירה שמא יאמרו גיטה קודם לבנה: **ואפילו על פי עבד.** דייה כעבד שהיה עמה: **שלבה גס בשפחתה.** ותשמש בפניה: **רב אשי אמר הא והא בשפחה דידה.** והיינו טעמא דבמתני' מהימנא והתם לא מהימנא דשפחה דידה מיחזא חזיא בקלקול גבירתה ושתקה: **התם.** גבי גט: **דשתיקותה מתירתה.** שאינה צריכה שתעיד לומר לא שמשה אלא שתאמר לא הייתי עמה: **לא מהימנא.** להיות זו מותרת על ידה דאי נמי חזיא לא מסהדא: **הכא.** גבי שבויה: **דשתיקותה.** דשפחה: **אוסרתה.** לגבירתה דכל כמה שאינה מעידה לומר טהורה היא מחזקין לה בטמאה כי מסהדא ואמרה טהורה היא מהימנא לשקורי לאו אורחא אלא למשתק: **השתא נמי.** כיון (ב) דרחמא לה לגבירתה או דדחלה מינה אתיא ומשקרא ואמרה טהורה היא: **תרתי לא עבדא.** חדא למשתק בקלקולה ועוד למיתי ולשקר: **אחא מבי חוזאה.** שהלך אביו שם והוליכו עמו וגדלו שם ומת אביו וחזר לעירו ותבע חלקו בנכסי אביו: **א"ל.** רב חסדא להוהוא אחא: **שפיר קאמר לך.** שאינו מכירך לפי שיצאת בלא חתימת זקן [ובאת בחתימת זקן]: **ויכר יוסף את אחיו.** שכשפירש מהן כבר היו חתומי זקן: **א"ל.** רב חסדא למרי: **זיל (ג) אייתינהו את.** להנהו סהדי המכירין אותו ויעידון שאינו בן אביך: **השתא נמי.** כיון דדחלי מיניה אתו ומשקרי: **תרתי לא עבדי.** חדא לשתקי מלהעיד אמת וחדא למסהדי שיקרא: **לימא כתנאי.** שפחתה אי מהימנא אי לא: **זו עדות.** של שבויה הכל כשרים בה איש ואשה תינוק ותינוקת: **חוץ מהימנה.** היא עצמה: **דרב פפי ודרב אשי.** דאמרו לעיל שפחה דידה מהימנא: **ודאי תנאי היא.** על כרחך יאמרו אכן דאמרי כי מתניתא בתרייתא מדקשיא להו קמייתא: **דרב פפא.** דאמר לא מהימנא: **מי לימא תנאי היא.** כלומר לדחוק הוא לומר אלא דאמרי כי מתניתא קמייתא או יוכל לתרץ מתניתא בתרייתא נמי כוותיה למימר שפחתה כעצמה דמי והרי היא בכלל חוץ מהימנה דקתני בה או תירוצא אחרינא: **אמר לך רב פפא כי תניא ההיא.** דקתני הכל נאמנים ואפילו שפחה דידה במסיחה לפי תומה: **רב חנא קרטיגנאה משתעי.** רב חנן דמן קרטיגי היה מספר מעשה זה: **מתני' המעון הזה.** שבועה היא: **גמ' ואעפ"כ.** שאסרו עליו לפי שכהן היה: **כשהיא יוצאה.** והוא בחצר: **יוצאה בראש בניה.** שיהו הבנים עמהם שלא יתייחדו: **וכשהיא נכנסת נכנסת בסוף בניה.** כדי שלא יהא הוא והיא בחצר והבנים מבחוץ: **בגרושה.** כהן שגירש את אשתו מהו לדור עמו בחצר: **לא תנשא בשכונתו.** לפי שמכירה ברמיזותיו וקריצותיו שמא יבואו לידי עבירה:

תוספות

לא תתיחד עמו אלא בעדים. פירש בקונטרס משום גט ישן ולא פירש לטעמיה דפירש בגיטין (דף עג.) דמהיום אם מתי מגורשת למפרע משעת נתינה ולא תתיחד עמו משום חשש קידושין כמו המגרש אשתו ולנה עמו בפונדקי בית הלל אומרים צריכה הימנו גט שני (שם דף פא.) [ולא שייך גט ישן כלל לפירוש דהתם] וכן משמע התם בגמרא אבל לרבינו תם דמפרש מה היא בזמן הימים קאי אמהיום אם מתי ונעשה כאומר מעת שאני בעולם שאין דעתו לגרשה אע"פ שאומר מהיום אלא שעה אחת לפני מיתתו הוי טעמא משום גט ישן ובתוספתא משמע כפי' רבינו תם:

שפיר קאמר לך דכתיב ויכר יוסף. זה שבא נולד כאן והלך עם אביו למדינת הים ועתה כשחזר ואמר לא ידענא לך מיחזי כשקרא כי היה לו לידע אם הוא אחיו אם לאו כיון שמכירו קודם להכי קאמר רב חסדא דשפיר קאמר ליה שאינו מכירו כדאשכחן ביוסף: **אמר** ליה אית לי סהדי ומסתפינו מיניה דאיניש אלמא הוא. נראה לר"י דמיירי שהביא עדים ואומרים אותו עדות שאתה שואל לא נאמר (ד) לך כלום עליו דרגלים לדבר שהוא אלא אמר ליה זיל כו' פי' לך הבא אותם עדים עצמם שירצו להעיד (ה) עליך שיעידו שאינו אחיך או שיאמרו שאינם יודעים אם הוא אחיך אם לאו וקאמר השתא נמי כיון שירצו ממנו יעקרו לומר אינו אחיו או שאין יודעין אם הוא אחיו אבל אם אין רגלים לדבר אין נראה כלל שיהא נאמן לומר דגברא אלמא הוא דאם לא כן כל אדם יאמר על חבירו שהוא גברא אלמא ויביא הוא עדים ואם לא יביא יפסיד ועוד דקאמר השתא נמי אתו ומסהדי אטו משום דמסתפו מיניה הני סהדי מסתפו מיניה כולי עלמא:

תרתי לא עבדי. שישתקו ולא יעידו האמת ועוד שיאמרו שקר וכן גבי שפחה:

במסיחה לפי תומה. ואפילו הכי היא ובעלה אינן נאמנין אע"ג דיוחנן אוכל חלות (לעיל דף כו.) היה נאמן על עצמו במסיח לפי תומו הני מילי לתרומה אבל הכא מעלה עשו ביוחסין [ואומר ר"י דמסיח לפי תומו אינו כשר אלא לעדות אשה או דרבנן כדאמר ביבמות והכא בשבויה הקילו] ואם

עין משפט נר מצוה

קח א מיי' פ"ד מהל' שכירות הלכה ג סמג עשין פט טוש"מ סימן סט:
קט ב מיי' פי"ח מהל' איסורי ביאה הלכ' כח טוש"ע אה"ע סי' ו סעיף י:
קי ג מיי' פ"ח מהל' גירושין הל' ו סמג עשין נ טוש"ע שם סימן קמח סעיף ב:
קיא ד מיי' פי"ח מהל' איסורי ביאה הלכ' יט סמג לאוין קכט טוש"ע שם סימן ז סעיף ב:
קיב ה מיי' פ"ג מהל' עדות הלכה ב סמג עשין קט טוש"ע ח"מ סי' כח סעיף ה:
קיג ו מיי' פי"ח מהל' איסורי ביאה הל' יט טוש"ע אה"ע סי' סעיף ב:
קיד ז מיי' שם הלכה יח טוש"ע שם סעיף א:
קטו ח מיי' שם הלכה יט טוש"ע שם סעיף ב:
קטז ט מיי' שם הלכה כה טוש"ע שם סעיף ט:
קיז י מיי' פכ"א שם הלכה כו סמג לאוין קכו טוש"ע אה"ע סי' ו סעיף ז וסי' קיט סעיף ז:

הגהות הב"ח

(א) גמ' זיל אייתי את: (ב) רש"י ד"ה השתא (דרחמא לה לגבירתה או) תא"מ ונ"ב ס"א לאן זה: (ג) ד"ה זיל אייתי את: (ד) תוס' ד"ה אמר וכו' לא נאמר כלום דרגלים כצ"ל ותי' לך ותי' עליו נמחק: (ה) בא"ד להעיד שיעידו כצ"ל ותי' עליך נמחק:

הגהות מהר"י לנדא

א] תוספות ד"ה במסיחה. אלא לעדות אשה כדאמר ביבמות והכא בשבויה דרבנן דקילו כצ"ל:

תורה אור השלם

א) וַיַּכֵּר יוֹסֵף אֶת אֶחָיו וְהֵם לֹא הִכִּרֻהוּ: [בראשית מב, ח]

תוספות רי"ד

איפשיטא ולקולא עבדי' בעי ר"א לא נחבאתי ולא נטמאתי מהו מי אמרינן מה לי לשקר במקום חששא אי לא. ולא איפשטא ולקולא עבדי': **ואם** יש להן עדים אפילו עבד ואפילו שפחה ואפילו שפחה דידה מהימני ורמינהו לא תתיחד עמו אלא בעדים אפילו עבד ואפילו שפחה חוץ משפחתה מפני שלבה גס בשפחתה. פי' גבי שכ"מ שנתן גט לאשתו דחיישינן שמא יבוא עליה ותהי' צריכה גט שני שאין אדם עושה בעילתו בעילת זנות. **ואסיק** ר"א הא והא בשפחה דידה ושפחתה מיחזא ושתקה התם דשתיקותא מתירתה לא מהימנא והכא דשתיקתה אוסרתה מהימנא השתא נמי אתיא ומשקרא תרתי לא עבדי. פי' חדא ששותקת מלהעיד האמת ועוד שתעיד שקר. **תנא** זו עדות כשר איש ואשה תינוק ותינוקת אביה ואמה אחיה ואחותה אבל לא בתה ובנה. פי' זו עדות של שבויה כל אלו כשרין להעיד ואם הבן מסיח ל"ת ואומר אני ואמי נשבינו לבין העובדי כוכבים ויצאתי לשאוב מים וללקט עצים ודעתי על אמי והשיאה ר' לכהונה על פיו. פי' מסיח ל"ת יקרא כ"ז שלא בא לפני ב"ד להעיד אלא מספר עם חבירו. והשומעים מפיו מגידים לב"ד וכ"מ שהעבד ואשה נאמנים גם הקטן נאמן ולגבי מת בעלך שעבד ואשה נאמנים כדתנן החזקו להיות משיאים עד מפי עד (עד) מפי שפחה הקטן נמי נאמן כדתנן התם ר"י אומר אפילו שמע מן התינוקות אומרים הרי אנו הולכים לספוד ולקבור את איש פ' והשתא השומע מן התינוקות מעיד תינוקות עצמן לא כ"ש: **[מתני'] א"ר זכריה וכו'.** תנא אע"פ. פי' אע"פ שאסרה לו לפי שהיה כהן יחד לה בית בחצירו כשהיא יוצאה יוצאה בראש בניה וכשהיא נכנסת נכנסת בסוף בניה. ופי' כדי שלא יתייחדו. **בעי אביי** מהו לעשות כן בגרושה. פי' לדור עמה בחצר התם בשבויה היקילו אבל הכא לא. א"ד ל"ש.

מסורת הש"ס

א) [קדושין סד: וש"נ], ב) בכורות לו. ב"מ פא:, ג) [צ"ל רבה ועי' תוס' בכורות לו. ד"ה ואמר], ד) [ב"ב לג: קדושין סד: ושם נסמן], ה) גיטין עג., ו) [לעיל כג: וש"נ], ז) ב"מ לט: ע"ש, ח) שם יבמות פח., ט) צ"ל ומסתפו. יעב"ץ, י) ב"ק קיד:, כ) [פי' נשבע שבועה במקדש. ערוך וכן פי' רשב"ם בב"ב קסו.], ל) [תוספתא פרק ג], מ) [שמחות פ"ב ע"ש], נ) [ועיין היטיב תוס' גיטין עג. ד"ה לא], ס) כ"י כ"י, ע) [כל זה מבואר בסוגיא ב"ק קיד:].

ליקוטי רש"י

במקום עדים. דאכן סהדי שאין אותו הדרך בלא מים [ב"מ פא:]. **לא תתיחד עמו.** זה שנתן גט ואמר לה מהיום אם מתי לא תתייחד עמו שמא יבא עליה דאיכא למ"ד חיישינן שמא בעל לשם קדושין וצריכה גט שני ולמאן דלא חיים נמי מ"מ פנויה היא ואסור להתייחד עם הפנויה [גיטין עג.]. **בשבויה הקילו.** דחששא בעלמא הוא דאיכא שמא נבעלה לעובד כוכבים ונפסלה לכהונה [לעיל כג.]. דספיקא בעלמא היא [ב"ק קיד:]. דהרבה הקילו בה חכמים במסכת כתובות דאפי' אשה ועבד ואחד נאמנין לומר טהורה וטעמא דבשביל שנתייחדה בין השבאין אין לנו לאסרה שהרי סתם אשה משמרת עצמה מזנות ואוקמה אחזקתה ואיסור קל הוא אם נישאת לכהן [רשב"ם ב"ב קלה.]. **אתא ליה אחא מבי חוזאה.** שהלך אביו לבי חוזאי ונשא שם אשה וילדה לו את זה וחזר מרי לכאן וירד לנכסי אביו ובא זה אחריו לזמן מרובה ותבע חלקו. **שפיר קאמר לך.** שאינו מכירך ואין זה רמאות שכשיצא מאצלך לא היה לך חתימת זקן ועכשיו באת בחתימת זקן. **ויכר יוסף את אחיו.** שכשיצא מהם היו כולם חתומי זקן והם לא הכירוהו שיצא מאצלם בלא חתימת זקן ובא בחתימת זקן [ב"מ לט:]. **ומסתפינו.** ומתיראים [ע"פ מעילה יז:]. **דלאו אחוך הוא.** אותם עדים שיש לו לזה שבאו משם ומכירין בו מי הוא ואם הוא אחיו ויעידו שאינו בן אביך או בקש עדים אחרים. **תרתי לא עבדי.** עשו אחת שישתקו אבל שתים לא יעשו לא דיין שישתקו ולא יעידו האמת אלא גם שיעידו שקר [ב"מ שם]. **והשיאה ר' לכהונה.** ואע"ג דלאורייתא היא משום זונה דאורייתא [ב"ק קיד:]. **המעון הזה.** בבית המקדש נשבע [רשב"ם קסו.].

Pappa's [opinion], which is that the slavewoman may not testify, the matter is less clear — [מִי] לֵימָא תַּנָּאֵי הִיא — **must he say** that **[the slavewoman's testimony] is** the subject of **a Tannaic dispute,** or can he somehow reconcile the two Baraisos?[26]

The Gemara answers:

אָמַר לָךְ רַב פָּפָּא — **Rav Pappa will say to you:** כִּי תַּנְיָא הַהִיא — **In what case was this** second **Baraisa taught?** בְּמְסִיחָה לְפִי תוּמָּהּ — **In the case of one who speaks casually,**[27] without awareness of legal ramifications. Under these circumstances, even a woman's own slavewoman is believed. כִּי הָא — And **this is like** the ruling issued in **this** following **[incident],** דְּכִי אֲתָא רַב דִּימִי אֲמַר — **for when Rav Dimi came** to Babylonia from Eretz Yisrael, **he said:** רַב חָנָן קַרְטִיגְנָאָה מִשְׁתָּעֵי — **Rav Chanan of Carthage related** מַעֲשֶׂה בָּא לִפְנֵי רַבִּי יְהוֹשֻׁעַ בֶּן לֵוִי — that **an incident came before R' Yehoshua ben Levi,** וְאָמְרֵי לָהּ — **and others quote** Rav Dimi as saying רַבִּי יְהוֹשֻׁעַ בֶּן לֵוִי מִישְׁתָּעֵי — that it was **R' Yehoshua ben Levi** who **related** מַעֲשֶׂה בָּא לִפְנֵי רַבִּי — that **an incident came before Rebbi** בְּאָדָם אֶחָד שֶׁהָיָה מֵסִיחַ לְפִי תוּמּוֹ וְאָמַר — **regarding a certain person who was speaking casually and said,** אֲנִי וְאִמִּי נִשְׁבֵּינוּ לְבֵין הָעוֹבְדֵי כּוֹכָבִים — **"My mother and I were taken captive amongst the idolaters.** יָצָאתִי לִשְׁאוֹב מַיִם — When **I would go out to draw water,** דַּעְתִּי עַל אִמִּי — **my mind was on my mother.** לְלַקֵּט עֵצִים — When I would go out **to gather wood,** דַּעְתִּי עַל אִמִּי — **my mind was on my mother.** I kept a constant watch on her, and thus ensured that they did not violate her." וְהִשִּׂיאָהּ רַבִּי לִכְהוּנָּה עַל פִּיו — **And Rebbi permitted her to marry a Kohen on** the strength of **his words.**

This incident teaches that even one who would not usually be believed to testify that a particular woman was not violated is believed if he is speaking casually.[28] Accordingly, the Baraisa that implies that a woman's own slavewoman is believed to give such testimony can be interpreted as discussing testimony delivered in a casual manner.[29] The other Baraisa, however, which bars her from testifying, is speaking of a slavewoman aware of the effect of her words. Thus, according to Rav Pappa, the Baraisos might very well be in accord.

Mishnah

Having ruled that one may not testify on his own behalf, the Mishnah now cites an incident that illustrates this ruling:

אָמַר רַבִּי זְכַרְיָה בֶּן הַקַּצָּב — **R' Zecharyah ben HaKatzav said** regarding his wife, who underwent the siege and occupation of Jerusalem: הַמָּעוֹן הַזֶּה — I swear by **this Dwelling Place!**[30] לֹא זָזָה יָדָהּ מִתּוֹךְ יָדִי — **Her hand did not leave mine** מִשָּׁעָה שֶׁנִּכְנְסוּ עוֹבְדֵי כּוֹכָבִים לִירוּשָׁלַיִם וְעַד שֶׁיָּצְאוּ — **from the moment the idolaters entered Jerusalem until they left.** I can confirm that she was not violated! אָמְרוּ לוֹ — **They said to him:** אֵין אָדָם מֵעִיד עַל עַצְמוֹ — **A person cannot testify on his own behalf.**[31]

Gemara

The Gemara cites a Baraisa concerning this incident:

תָּנָא — **A Baraisa has taught:** וְאַף עַל פִּי כֵן — AND EVEN SO, i.e. even though R' Zecharyah ben HaKatzav was forbidden to cohabit with his wife,[32] יִיחֵד לָהּ בַּיִת בַּחֲצֵרוֹ — HE was permitted to SET ASIDE A HOUSE FOR HER IN HIS COURTYARD.[33] וּכְשֶׁהִיא יוֹצְאָה יוֹצְאָה בְּרֹאשׁ בָּנֶיהָ — AND WHEN SHE WOULD LEAVE, SHE WOULD LEAVE BEFORE HER CHILDREN, so that she would not be alone with R' Zecharyah, וּכְשֶׁהִיא נִכְנֶסֶת נִכְנֶסֶת בְּסוֹף בָּנֶיהָ — AND WHEN SHE WOULD ENTER, SHE WOULD ENTER AFTER HER CHILDREN, for the same reason. [Although they were permitted to dwell in the same courtyard, they took precautions to never be alone with each other.]

The Gemara presents an inquiry:

בָּעֵי אַבָּיֵי — **Abaye inquired:** מַהוּ לַעֲשׂוֹת בִּגְרוּשָׁה כֵּן — **What is [the law]** with regard **to** whether a Kohen may **do the same with**

NOTES

26. Rav Pappa ruled that a woman's own slavewoman is not believed to testify that she was not violated during the occupation of the city. His ruling accords perfectly with that of the first Baraisa cited; the question is whether the second Baraisa, which appears to imply the opposite, can also be interpreted to accord with Rav Pappa's ruling, or whether Rav Pappa is compelled to say that the two Baraisos are in conflict.

One of the ways by which the second Baraisa might be brought into conjunction with the first has been explained in the Gemara above, which states that according to Rav Pappa a woman's slavewoman is comparable to her mistress. According to this reasoning, when the (second) Baraisa states that the woman herself is not believed to testify, it in effect refers to her slavewoman too, who is included in the term "herself." Thus, with regard to the law of a slavewoman, the two Baraisos are in perfect accord (*Rashi*).

[The Gemara will decide that Rav Pappa *can* in fact reconcile the Baraisos. Interestingly, though, the resolution it offers is not the tentative one presented by *Rashi* here. For discussion of why the Gemara does not give *Rashi's* solution, see *Rashba; Ritva; Maharsha; Haflaah.* For why *Rashi* presents an original solution in place of that offered by the Gemara, see *Pnei Yehoshua.*]

27. Literally: talking in her innocence.

28. In the instance related by R' Yehoshua ben Levi, the person would not have been believed if not for the fact that he had been speaking casually — either because he was testifying for a relative, or because he was a minor (see *Bava Kamma* 114b). See *Shulchan Aruch, Even HaEzer* 7:1 with commentaries, and *Gra* there §2.

29. It thus emerges that according to Rav Pappa's interpretation of the Baraisa, the woman herself and her husband are not believed to say that she was not violated even when they are speaking casually. See *Tosafos; Rashba; Ritva* for discussion.

[Several Acharonim ask: Why didn't the Gemara resolve the original contradiction between our Mishnah and the Mishnah in *Gittin* by saying that our Mishnah is dealing with testimony offered casually, regarding which even a slavewoman is believed? For discussion, see *Maharsha; Pnei Yehoshua; Kikayon DeYonah; Chasam Sofer; Haflaah.*]

30. I.e. the Holy Temple (*Aruch* ע׳ מעון; see *Tos. Yom Tov*). Alternatively, he swore by the fifth of the seven Heavens, which is called מָעוֹן, or "Dwelling Place" (*Maharsha;* see *Chagigah* 12b).

31. Testimony given on behalf of one's wife is regarded as testimony given on one's own behalf, in accordance with the Talmudic formula of אשתו כגופו, *one's wife is as oneself* — see *Berachos* 24b; *Bechoros* 35b (*Shitah Mekubetzes* ד״ה לא זוה; see *Tos. R' Akiva Eiger's* interpretation of *Rashi*). Alternatively, the reason this is regarded as testimony on the husband's own behalf is because he stands to gain from it, for it will permit him to remain with his wife (see *Nimukei Yosef;* see *Tos. R' Akiva Eiger's* interpretation of *Rav*). See *Emes LeYaakov.*

[Some Acharonim point out that there were certainly many hiding places in Jerusalem. Accordingly, R' Zecharyah ben HaKatzav's wife should have been believed to say that she was not violated on the strength of a "What reason do I have to lie" argument (see beginning of this *amud*), since she could have claimed that she hid herself throughout the occupation. For discussion of the question, see *Binyan Yechezkel,* printed in *Asifas Zekeinim; Tosafos Chadashim* to the Mishnah.]

32. R' Zecharyah ben HaKatzav was a Kohen. Since he was not trusted to testify that his wife had not been violated, he was forbidden to cohabit with her (*Rashi*). [For other interpretations of the phrase "And even so," see *Shitah Mekubetzes* ד״ה תנא וד״ה ובלקוטי הגאונים.]

33. I.e. she remained his wife, and was permitted to dwell in the same courtyard as he (*Meiri*). [The Rabbis did not require him to end the

עין משפט נר מצוה

קח א מיי' פ"ד מהל' שכירות הלכה ו סמג עשין פט טוש"ח סימן סט:
קט ב מיי' פי"ח מהל' איסורי ביאה הל' כח טוש"ע אה"ע סי' ז סעיף י:
קי ג מיי' פ"ח מהל' גירושין הל' ג סמג עשין נ טוש"ע שם סימן קמח סעיף ג:
קיא ד מיי' פי"ח מהל' איסורי ביאה הל' יט סמג לאוין קכא טוש"ע שם סימן ז סעיף ג
קיב ה מיי' פ"ג מהל' עדות הלכה יב סמג עשין קט טוש"ע ח"מ סי' כח סעיף ה:
קיג ו מיי' פ"ח מהל' איסורי ביאה הל' יט טוש"ע אה"ע סי' ז סעיף ג:
קיד ז מיי' שם הלכה יח טוש"ע שם סעיף ס:
קטו ח מיי' שם הלכה יט טוש"ע שם סעיף ג:
קטז ט מיי' שם הלכה כה טוש"ע שם סעיף ט:
קיז י מיי' פכ"א שם הלכה כו סמג לאוין קמ טוש"ע אה"ע סי' ו סעיף ז וסי' קיט סעיף ז:

הגהות הב"ח

(א) גמ' זיל אייתי את: (ב) רש"י ד"ה השתא (דרחמא לה לגבירתה או) תא"מ ונ"ב ס"א אין זה: (ג) ד"ה זיל אייתי את: (ד) תוס' ד"ה אמר כו' לא נאמר כלום דרגלים כצ"ל ותיבת לך נמחק: (ה) בא"ד להעיד שיעידו כצ"ל ותי' עליך נמחק:

הגהות מהר"ר לנדא

אז תוספות ד"ה במסיחה. אלא לעדות אשה כדאמר ביבמות והכא בשבויה דרבנן הקילו כצ"ל:

תורה אור השלם

א) וַיַּכֵּר יוֹסֵף אֶת אֶחָיו וְהֵם לֹא הִכִּרֻהוּ: [בראשית מב, ח]

תוספות רי"ד

איפשיטא ולקולא עבדי' בעי ר"א לא נחבאתי ולא נטמאתי מהו מי אמרינן מה לי לשקר במקום חששא אי לא ולא איפשטא ולקולא עבדי': ואם יש להן עדים אפילו עבד ואפילו שפחה מהימני ורמינהו לא תתיחד עמו אלא בעדים אפילו עבד ואפילו שפחה חוץ משפחתה מפני שלבה גס בשפחתה. פי' גבי שכ"מ שנתן גט לאשתו דחיישינן שמא יבוא עליה והוי' צריכה גט שני שאין אדם עושה בעילתו בעילת זנות. ואסיק ר"א הא בשפחה דידיה והא בשפחה דידה ושפחה מיחזא חזיא ושתקה. התם דשתיקה מתירתה לא מהימנא והכא דשתיקתה אוסרתה מהימנא השתא נמי אתיא ומשקרא תרתי לא עבדי. פי' חדא ששותקת מלהעיד האמת ועוד שתעיד שקר. תנא זו עדות כשר איש ואשה תינוק ותינוקת אביה ואמה אחיה ואחיותה אבל לא בתה ובנה. פי' זו עדות של שבויה כל אלו כשרין להעיד ואם הבן מסיח ל"ת ואומר אני ואמי נשבינו לבין העובדי כוכבים ויצאתי לשאוב מים וללקוט עצים ודעתי על אמי והשיאה ר' לכהונה על פיו. פי' מסיח ל"ת יקרא כ"ז שלא בא לפני ב"ד להעיד אלא מספר עם חבירו. והשומעים מפיו מגידים לב"ד וכ"מ שהעבד ואשה נאמנים גם הקטן נאמן ולגבי מת בעלך שעבד ואשה נאמנים כדתנן החזקנו להיות משיאים עד מפי עד (צד) פפי שפחה הקטן נמי נאמן כדתנן התם ר"י אומר אפילו שמע מן התינוקות אומרים הרי אנו הולכים לספוד ולקבור את איש פ' והשתא השומע מן התינוקות מעיד תינוקות עצמן לא כ"ש: [מתני'] א"ר זכריה וכו'. תנא אע"פ. פי' אע"פ שאסרוה ל' לפי שהיה כהן יחד לה בית בחצירו כשהיא יוצאה יוצאה בראש בניה וכשהיא נכנסת נכנסת בסוף בניה. ופי' כדי שלא יתייחדו. בעי אביי מהו לעשות כן בגרושה. פי' לדור עמה בחצר התם בשבויה היקילו אבל הכא לא. א"ד ל"ש.

תוספות

לא תתיחד עמו אלא בעדים. פירש בקונטרס משום גט ישן ולא פירש לטעמיה דפירש בגיטין (דף עג.) דכמהיום אם מתי מגורשת למפרע משעת נתינה ולא תתיחד עמו משום חשש קידושין כמו המגרש אשתו ולנה עמו בפונדקי בית הלל אומרים צריכה הימנו גט שני (שם דף פא.) [ולא שייך גט ישן כלל לפירוש דהתם] וכן משמע התם בגמרא אבל לרבינו תם דמפרש מה היא באותן הימים קאי אמהיום אם מתי ונעשה כאומר מעת שאני בעולם שאין דעתו לגרשה אע"פ שאומר מהיום אלא שעה אחת לפני מיתתו הוי טעמא משום גט ישן ובתוספתא משמע כפי' רבינו תם:

שפיר קאמר לך דכתיב ויכר יוסף. זה שבא נולד כאן והלך עם אביו למדינת הים ועתה כשחזר ואמר לא ידענא לך מיחזי כשיקרא כי היה לו לידע אם הוא אחיו אם לאו כיון שמכירו קודם להכי קאמר רב חסדא דשפיר קאמר ליה שאינו מכירו כדאשכחן ביוסף:

אמר ליה אית לי סהדי ומסתפינו מיניה דאיניש אלמא הוא. נראה לר"י דמיירי שהביא עדים ואומרים אותו עדות שאתה שואל לא נאמר (ד) לך כלום עליו דרגלים לדבר שהוא אלם אמר ליה זיל כו' פי' לך הבא אותם עדים עצמם שיראים להעיד (ה) עליך שיעידו שאינו אחיך או שיאמרו שאינם יודעים אם הוא אחיך אם לאו וקאמר השתא נמי כיון שיראים ממנו ישקרו לומר אינו אחיו או שאין יודעין אם הוא אחיו אבל אם אין רגלים לדבר אין נראה כלל שיהא נאמן לומר דגברא אלמא הוא דאם לא כן כל אדם יאמר על חבירו שהוא גברא אלמא ויביא הוא עדים ואם לא יביא יפסיד ועוד דקאמר השתא נמי אתו ומסהדי אטו משום דמסתפו מיניה הני סהדי מסתפו מיניה כולי עלמא:

תרתי לא עבדי. שישתקו ולא יעידו האמת ועוד שיאמרו שקר וכן גבי שפחה:

במסיחה לפי תומה. ואפילו הכי היא ובעלה אינן נאמנין אע"ג דיוחנן אוכל תלות (לעיל דף כו.) היה נאמן על עצמו במסיח לפי תומו הני מילי לתרומה אבל הכא מעלה עשו ביוחסין ס) ואומר ר"י דמסיח לפי תומו אינו כשר אלא לעדות אשה אז דרבנן כדאמר ביבמות והכא בשבויה הקילו ע): ולאם

גמרא

א) מה לי לשקר או דלמא לא אמרינן ומאי שנא מההוא מעשה דההוא גברא ב) דאגר ליה חמרא לחבריה א"ל לא תיזיל באורחא דנהר פקוד דאיכא מיא זיל באורחא דנרש דליכא מיא ואזל איהו באורחא דנהר פקוד ומית חמרא אתא לקמיה דרבא א"ל אין באורחא דנהר פקוד אזלי מיהו לא הוו מיא אמר רבא מה לי לשקר אי בעי א"ל באורחא דנרש אזלי ואמר ליה אביי ד) מה לי לשקר במקום עדים לא אמרינן הכי השתא התם ודאי איכא עדים דאיכא מיא הכא ודאי איטמי חששא הוא ובמקום חששא אמרינן: אם יש עדים אפילו עבד ואפילו שפחה נאמנין: ואפילו שפחה דידה מהימנא ורמינהי ג) לא תתייחד עמו אלא ע"פ עדים ואפילו ע"פ עבד וע"פ שפחה חוץ משפחתה מפני שלבה גס בשפחתה אמר רב פפי ו) בשבויה הקילו רב פפא אמר ה) הא בשפחה דידיה הא בשפחה דידה ושפחה דידה לא מהימנא הא קתני אין אדם מעיד על עצמו הא שפחה דידה מהימנא שפחתה נמי כעצמה דמי רב אשי אמר הא והא בשפחה דידה ושפחה מיחזא חזיא ושתקה התם דשתיקתה מתירתה לא מהימנא הכא דשתיקתה אוסרתה מהימנא השתא נמי אתיא ומשקרא תרתי לא עבדה ז) כי הא דמרי בר איסק אתא ליה אחא מבי חוזאה א"ל פלוג לי בנכסי דאבא א"ל לא ידענא לך אתא לקמיה דרב חסדא א"ל שפיר קאמר לך דכתיב א) ויכר יוסף את אחיו והם לא הכירוהו ח) מלמד שיצא בלא חתימת זקן ובא בחתימת זקן א"ל זיל אייתי סהדי דאחוה את א"ל אית לי סהדי ט) ומסתפינו מיניה דגברא אלמא הוא א"ל לדידיה זיל (א) אייתינהו את דלאו אחוך הוא א"ל דינא הכי המוציא מחבירו עליו הראיה א"ל ל) הכי דאינא לך ולכולהו אלמי חברך השתא נמי אתו ומשקרי תרתי לא עבדי לימא כתנאי זו עדות איש ואשה תינוק ותינוקת אביה ואמה ואחיה ואחותה אבל לא בנה ובתה לא עבדה ושפחתה ותניא אידך הכל נאמנין להעיד חוץ מהימנה ובעלה מאי לאו דרב פפי ודרב אשי

תנאי היא דרב פפא [מי] לימא תנאי היא אמר לך רב פפא כי תניא ההיא במסיחה לפי תומה כי הא דכי אתא רב דימי אמר רב חנן קרטיגנאה משתעי מעשה בא לפני רבי יהושע בן לוי ואמרי לה רבי יהושע בן לוי מישתעי מעשה בא לפני רבי באדם אחד שהיה מסיח לפי תומו ואמר אני ואמי נשבינו לבין העובדי כוכבים יצאתי לשאוב מים דעתי על אמי ללקט עצים דעתי על אמי והשיאה ר' לכהונה על פיו: **מתני'** אמר ר' זכריה בן הקצב המעון הזה לא זזה ידה מתוך ידי משעה שנכנסו עובדי כוכבים לירושלים ועד שיצאו אמרו לו אין אדם מעיד על עצמו: **גמ'** תנא ואעפ"כ ייחד לה בית בחצרו וכשהיא יוצאה יוצאה בראש בניה וכשהיא נכנסת נכנסת בסוף בניה בעי אביי מהו לעשות בגרושה כן התם הוא דבשבויה הקילו אבל הכא לא או דלמא לא שנא ת"ש דתניא המגרש את אשתו לא תנשא בשכונתו ואם

רש"י

מה לי לשקר. אי בעיא אמרה נחביתי: במקום עדים. דאנן סהדי דכל שעתא איכא מיא: ודאי איטמי. בתמיה: לא תתייחד עמו. במסכת גיטין היא שכיב מרע שכתב ומסר גט לאשתו על מנת שאם מת יהא גט למפרע ולא תיזקק לחליצה לא תתייחד עמו שמא יבא עליה והוה ליה גט ישן ותנן בית הלל אוסרין לפטור בגט ישן ואיזהו גט ישן כל שנתייחד עמה מאחר שכתבו לה וטעמא גזירה שמא יאמרו גיטה קודם לבנה: ואפילו על פי עבד. דייה בעבד שהיה עמה: שלבה גס בשפחתה. ותשמש בפניה: רב אשי אמר הא והא בשפחה דידה. והיינו טעמא דבמתני' מהימנא והתם לא מהימנא דשפחה דידה מיחזא חזיא בקילקול גבירתה ושתקה: התם. גבי גט: דשתיקותה מתירתה. שאינה צריכה שתעיד לומר לא שמשה אלא שתאמר אני הייתי עמה: לא מהימנא. להיות זו מותרת על ידה דאי נמי חזיא לא מסהדא: הכא. גבי שבויה: דשתיקותה. דשפחה: אוסרתה. לגבירתה דכל כמה שאינה מעידה לומר טהורה היא מחזקינן לה בטומאה כי מסהדא ואמרה טהורה היא מהימנא דלשקורי לאו אורחא אלא למשתק: השתא נמי. כיון (ב) דרחמא לה לגבירתה או דדחלה מינה אתיא ומשקרא ואמרה טהורה היא: תרתי לא עבדא. חדא למשתק בקלקולה ועוד דתיתי ותשקר: אחא מבי חוזאה. שהלך אביו שם והוליכו עמו וגדלו שם ומת אביו וחזר לעירו ותבע חלקו בנכסי אביו: א"ל. רב חסדא להוא אחא: שפיר קאמר לך. שאינו מכירך לפי שיצאת בלא חתימת זקן [ובאת בחתימת זקן]: ויכר יוסף את אחיו. שכשפירש מהן כבר היו חתומי זקן: א"ל. רב חסדא למרי: זיל (ג) אייתינהו את. להנהו סהדי המכירין אותו ויעידו שאינו בן אביך: השתא נמי. כיון דדחלי מיניה אתו ומשקרי: תרתי לא עבדי. חדא דשתקי מלהעיד אמת וחדא דמסהדי שיקרא: לימא כתנאי. שפחתה אי מהימנא אי לא: זו עדות. עדות זו של שבויה הכל כשרים בה איש ואשה תינוק ותינוקת: חוץ מהימנה. היא עצמה: דרב פפי ורב אשי. דאמרו לעיל שפחה דידה מהימנה: ודאי תנאי היא. על כרחך יאמרו אלו דאמרי' כי מתניתא בתרייתא מדקשיא להו קמייתא: דרב פפא. דאמר לא מהימנה: מי לימא תנאי היא. כלומר דחוק הוא לומר אלא דאמרי כי מתניתא קמייתא או יוכל לתרץ מתניתא בתרייתא נמי כוותיה למימר שפחתה כעצמה דמי והרי היא בכלל חוץ מהימנה דקתני בה או תירוצא אחרינא: אמר לך רב פפא כי תניא ההיא. דקתני הכל נאמנים ואפילו שפחה דידה במסיחה לפי תומה: רב חנא קרטיגנאה משתעי. רב חנן דמן קרטיגי היה מספר מעשה זה: מתני' המעון הזה. שבועה היא: גמ' ואעפ"כ. שאסרו עליו לפי שכהן היה: כשהיא יוצאה. והוא בחצר: יוצאה בראש בניה. שיהו הבנים עמהם שלא יתייחדו: וכשהיא נכנסת נכנסת בסוף בניה. כדי שלא יהא הוא והיא בחצר והבנים מבחוץ: בגרושה. כהן שגירש את אשתו מהו לדור עמו בחצר: לא תנשא בשכונתו. לפי שמכירה ברמיזותיו וקריצותיו שמא יבואו לידי עבירה: ואם

מסורת הש"ס

א) [קדושין סד: וש"נ], ב) בכורות לו. ב"מ פא., ג) [ל"ל רבה ועי' תוס' בכורות לו. ד"ה ולמר], ד) [ב"ב לג: קדושין סד: ושם נסמן], ה) גיטין עג., ו) [לעיל כג: וש"נ], ז) ב"מ לט: ע"ש, ח) שם יבמות פח., ט) [ל"ל ומסתפו. יעב"ץ], י) ב"ק קיד:, כ) [פי' נשבע שבועה במקדש. ערוך ועיין פי' רשב"ם בב"ב קסו.], ל) [תוספתא פרק ג], מ) [שמות פ"ב ע"ש], נ) [ועיין היטיב תוס' גיטין עג. ד"ה לא], ס) ב"י ע"ע, ע) [כל זה מבואר בסוגיא ב"ק קיד:].

ליקוטי רש"י

במקום עדים. דאנן סהדי שאין אותו הדרך בלא מים [ב"מ פא.]. לא תתייחד עמו. זה שנתן גט ואמר לה מהיום אם מתי לא תתייחד עמו שמא יבא עליה ותיבעל לשם קידושין ותיבעי גט שני ולמאן דלא חייש נמי מ"מ פנויה היא ואסור להתייחד עם הפנויה [גיטין עג.]. בשבויה הקילו. דמשתא בעלמא הוא דאיכא שמא נבעלה לעובד כוכבים ונפסלה לכהונה [לעיל כג.] דספיקא בעלמא היא [ב"ק קיד:]. דהרבה הקילו בה חכמים במסכת כתובות דלפי' אשה ועבד ואחד נאמנין לומר טהורה וטעמא דבשבויה שנתיחדה בין העובדי כוכבים אין לנו לאסרה שהרי סתם אשה משמרת עצמה מזנות ואיסור קל הוא אם ניתנה לכהן [רשב"ם ב"ב קלה.]. אתא ליה אחא מבי חוזאה. שהלך אביו לבי חוזאי ונשא שם אשה והוליד לו את זה והזר מרי לכאן וירד לנכסי אביו ובא זה ואמר לו אחיך אני ותן לי חלקי. שפיר קאמר לך. שאינו מכירך וזה רמאות שבשלא מגדלו לא היה לך חתימת זקן ועכשיו באת חתום זקן. ויכר יוסף את אחיו. שכשנפל מהם היו כולם חתומי זקן והם לא הכירוהו שלא מגדלים בלא חתימת זקן ובא בחתימת זקן ולא ומסתפינו [ע"פ מעילה יז:]. דלאו אחוך הוא. שיש לו לזה שבאו מסה ומכירין בו מי הוא הבאים אתה ויעידו לך שאינו בן אביך או בקש עדים אחרים. תרתי לא עבדי. יעשו אחת שישתקו אבל שתים לא יעשו לא דיין שישתקו ולא יעידו האמת אלא גם שיעידו שקר [ב"מ שם]. והשיאה ר' לכהונה. ואע"ג דאוריתא היא משום זונה לאוריתא היא משום זונה [ב"ק קיד:]. המעון הזה. בבית המקדש נשבע [רשב"ם קסו.].

and claim that her mistress was not violated when in fact she was! — ? —

The Gemara answers:

תַּרְתֵּי לֹא עָבְדָה — We may assume that **she will not perform two** wrongs; i.e. to both keep silent regarding her mistress' violation and to testify falsely regarding it.[17] כִּי הָא דְּמָרִי בַּר אִיסַק — And **this is like** the ruling issued in **this [incident] concerning Mari bar Isak,** וְאָמְרֵי לָהּ חָנָא בַּר אִיסַק — **and some say** concerning **Chana bar Isak.** אֲתָא לֵיהּ אַחָא מִבֵּי חוֹזָאָה — In that case, **his brother came from Bei Chozaah,** where he had been taken by their father as a young child.[18] In the interim, this brother had grown into a young man, and the father had died. אָמַר לֵיהּ — **[The brother] said to [Mari bar Isak]:** פְּלוֹג לִי בְּנִכְסֵי דְּאַבָּא — **"Divide Father's possessions with me."** אָמַר לֵיהּ — **[Mari] said to him:** לֹא יָדַעְנָא לָךְ — **"I do not recognize you.** I do not know whether you are my brother." אֲתָא לְקַמֵּיהּ דְּרַב חִסְדָּא — **[The brother] came before Rav Chisda,** and complained about Mari's reply.[19] אָמַר לֵיהּ — **[Rav Chisda] said to [the brother]:** שַׁפִּיר קָאָמַר לָךְ — **"[Mari] has spoken properly to you.** His claim that he does not recognize you is not a pretext, but is genuine.[20] דִּכְתִיב — **For it is written:**[21] "וַיַּכֵּר יוֹסֵף אֶת־אֶחָיו וְהֵם לֹא הִכִּרֻהוּ" — ***And Joseph recognized his brothers, but they did not recognize him.*** מְלַמֵּד שֶׁיָּצָא בְּלֹא חֲתִימַת זָקָן — **This teaches that he left** them **without the mark of a beard,** וּבָא בַּחֲתִימַת זָקָן — **but came** back to them **with the mark of a beard.** They therefore did not recognize him. Likewise your brother Mari — since you left him as a child, and now return as a bearded man, he cannot be expected to know you."[22] אָמַר לֵיהּ — **[Rav Chisda]** continued, and **said to [the brother]:** זִיל אַיְיתֵי סָהֲדֵי דְּאָחוּהָ אַתְּ — **"Go bring witnesses that you are his brother."** אָמַר לֵיהּ — **[The brother] said to [Rav Chisda]:** אִית לִי סָהֲדֵי וּמִסְתַּפְּינוּ מִינֵּיהּ — **"I have witnesses, but they are afraid of [Mari],** דְּגַבְרָא אַלָּמָא הוּא — **for he is a powerful man.** They fear he will harm them, and therefore refuse to testify." אָמַר לֵיהּ לְדִידֵיהּ — Upon hearing this, **[Rav Chisda] said to [Mari]:** זִיל אַיְיתִינְהוּ אַתְּ דְּלָאו אָחוּךְ הוּא — **"You go** then **and bring** these very witnesses, and have them testify **that he is not your brother.** Otherwise, you will be obliged to share the inheritance with him."[23] אָמַר לֵיהּ — **[Mari] said to [Rav Chisda]:** דִּינָא הָכִי — **"Is this the law?** הַמּוֹצִיא מֵחֲבֵירוֹ עָלָיו הָרְאָיָה — The rule is that **the one who wishes to exact** money **from his fellow bears the burden of proof.** Since I am in possession of the inheritance, and he wishes to take it from me, let him provide proof that he is entitled to it!" אָמַר לֵיהּ — **[Rav Chisda] said to him:** הָכִי דָּאִינְנָא לָךְ וּלְכוּלְּהוּ אַלָּמֵי חַבְרָךְ — "Yes, **thus do we rule regarding you, and all** other **powerful ones like you,** who use their power to intimidate witnesses!"[24]

The Gemara asks:

הַשְׁתָּא נַמִּי — But **even now** that we have required Mari to bring the witnesses, אָתוּ וּמְשַׁקְּרֵי — perhaps **they will come and lie,** out of fear of Mari, and say that this person is in fact not his brother. What did Rav Chisda gain with his ruling?

The Gemara explains:

תַּרְתֵּי לֹא עָבְדֵי — Rav Chisda assumed that **they would not perform two** wrongs out of fear; i.e. to both remain silent and to testify falsely.

We see that it does not follow that those who will withhold testimony will also testify falsely. Likewise, then, regarding a woman's slavewoman: She is suspect to conceal information damaging to her mistress, but is not suspect to testify falsely. Thus, Rav Ashi's resolution of the contradiction between the two Mishnahs stands.[25]

Having cited an Amoraic dispute regarding the veracity of a woman's own slavewoman, the Gemara now suggests that it is the subject of a Tannaic dispute as well:

לֵימָא כְּתַנָּאֵי — **Let us say that this is** the subject of **a Tannaic dispute.** For one Baraisa teaches: זוּ עֵדוּת — THIS TESTIMONY that permits a captive woman to her husband may be offered by anyone at all — אִישׁ וְאִשָּׁה — MAN OR WOMAN; תִּינוֹק וְתִינוֹקֶת — MALE CHILD OR FEMALE CHILD; אָבִיהָ וְאִמָּהּ — [THE WOMAN'S] FATHER OR HER MOTHER; וְאָחִיהָ וַאֲחוֹתָהּ — HER BROTHER OR HER SISTER. אֲבָל לֹא בְּנָהּ וּבִתָּהּ — HOWEVER, NOT by HER SON OR HER DAUGHTER לֹא עַבְדָּהּ וְשִׁפְחָתָהּ — and NOT by HER SLAVE OR HER SLAVEWOMAN. וְתַנְיָא אִידָךְ — **And it has been taught in another Baraisa:** הַכֹּל נֶאֱמָנִין לְהָעִיד — ALL ARE BELIEVED TO TESTIFY regarding a captive woman, חוּץ מֵהֵימֶנָּה וּבַעְלָהּ — EXCEPT FOR the woman HERSELF AND HER HUSBAND. This implies that her slavewoman *is* believed to testify. Thus, these Baraisos contradict one another.

דְּרַב פַּפִּי וּדְרַב אַשִׁי תַּנָּאֵי הִיא — Now, **Rav Pappi's and Rav Ashi's** shared **[opinion]** compels them to say that **this** matter **is** the subject of **a Tannaic dispute.** For they permit a woman's slavewoman to testify regarding her mistress, and are consequently in direct opposition to the first Baraisa. They can justify their stance only by saying that they follow the second Baraisa; perforce, the two Baraisos disagree. דְּרַב פָּפָּא — However, according to **Rav**

NOTES

17. See *Rashi; Ritva;* see *Chidushei R' Akiva Eiger.*

18. Their father had taken this brother with him to Bei Chozaah as a young boy and had raised him there. The brother now returned to his birthplace and demanded his share of the father's possessions (*Rashi; Tosafos;* cf. *Rashi, Bava Metzia* 39b ד״ה אתא ליה אחא).

19. The brother claimed that Mari's answer was an obvious lie, for how could he possibly fail to recognize a brother that he once knew? (*Tosafos;* see *Ritva*).

20. See *Tosafos* here; *Rashi, Bava Metzia* ibid. ד״ה שפיר קאמר לך; *Hagahos Yavetz* here.

21. *Genesis* 42:8.

22. Rav Chisda's answer implies that if Mari's brother *would* have been bearded when he left home, Mari would have been expected to recognize him now. Accordingly, his claim of nonrecognition would have been viewed as a ploy, and he would have been compelled to split the inheritance with the plaintiff. However, *Tosafos* (to *Bava Metzia* ibid. ד״ה שיצא) point out that if Mari would have refuted the plaintiff directly by stating that he is definitely not his brother, he would have been believed, whether or not his brother had been bearded when he left. It was only because he did not refute him, but simply stated that he did not know whether this was his brother, that he was obliged to give a persuasive reason for not knowing. The growth of a beard during the brother's absence provided that reason (see also *Ritva* here; see *Haflaah*).

23. Rav Chisda ruled that the witnesses would have to testify that this individual is not Mari's brother. It would not suffice to say that they do not know whether he is his brother. For perhaps it is fear of Mari that leads them to say this (*Rashi,* as explained by *Kesef Mishneh, Eidus* 3:12; see also *Kikayon D'Yonah;* cf. *Tosafos* ד״ה אמר ליה with *Haflaah*). If these witnesses would not testify on Mari's behalf, he would be required to bring others who would (*Rashi, Bava Metzia* ibid. ד״ה דלאו אחוך הוא; cf. *Ritva* here).

24. However, this rule is invoked only if the court has independent knowledge of the defendant's reputation as an intimidator. Otherwise, every plaintiff could relieve himself of the burden of proof simply by claiming that his witnesses are afraid of the defendant! (*Kesef Mishneh* ibid., explaining *Rashi;* cf. *Tosafos*).

25. This is Rav Ashi's opinion. However, Rav Pappa holds that regular witnesses are not comparable to slavewomen. Witnesses will not testify falsely out of fear. Slavewomen, however, because of their enormous affinity for their mistresses, are suspect to testify falsely on their mistresses' behalf. Therefore, they are not trusted (see *Nimukei Yosef*).

מה לי לשקר או דלמא לא אמרינן ומאי שנא מההוא מעשה דההוא גברא דאגר ליה חמרא לחבריה א"ל לא תיזיל באורחא דנהר פקוד דאיכא מיא זיל באורחא דנרש דליכא מיא ואזל איהו באורחא דנהר פקוד ומית חמרא אתא לקמיה דרבא א"ל אין באורחא דנהר פקוד אזלי מיהו לא הוו מיא אמר רבא מה לי לשקר אי בעי א"ל באורחא דנרש אזלי ואמר ליה אביי מה לי לשקר במקום עדים לא אמרינן הכי השתא התם ודאי איכא עדים דאיכא מיא הכא ודאי איטמי חששא הוא ובמקום חששא אמרינן: אם יש עדים אפילו עבד ואפילו שפחה נאמנין: ואפילו שפחה דידה מהימנא ורמינהי לא תתייחד עמו אלא ע"פ עדים ואפילו ע"פ עבד וע"פ שפחה חוץ משפחתה מפני שלבה גס בשפחתה אמר רב פפי בשבויה הקילו רב פפא אמר הא בשפחה דידה הא בשפחה דידיה ושפחה דידה לא מהימנא הא קתני אין אדם מעיד על עצמו הא שפחה דידה מהימנא שפחתה נמי כעצמה דמי רב אשי אמר הא והא בשפחה דידה ושפחה מיחזא חזיא ושתקה התם דשתיקתה מתירתה לא מהימנא הכא דשתיקתה אוסרתה מהימנא השתא נמי אתיא ומשקרא תרתי לא עבדה כי הא דמרי בר איסק ואמרי לה חנא בר איסק אתא ליה אחא מבי חוזאה א"ל פלוג לי בנכסי דאבא א"ל לא ידענא לך אתא לקמיה דרב חסדא א"ל שפיר קאמר לך דכתיב ויכר יוסף את אחיו והם לא הכירהו מלמד שיצא בלא חתימת זקן ובא בחתימת זקן א"ל זיל אייתי סהדי דאחוה את א"ל אית לי סהדי ומסתפינו מיניה דגברא אלמא הוא א"ל לדידיה זיל (א) אייתינהו את דלאו אחוך הוא א"ל דינא הכי המוציא מחבירו עליו הראיה א"ל הכי דאיננא לך ולכולהו אלמי חברך השתא נמי אתו ומשקרי תרתי לא עבדי לימא כתנאי זו עדות איש ואשה תינוק ותינוקת אביה ואמה ואחיה ואחותה אבל לא בנה ובתה לא עבדה ושפחתה ותניא אידך הכל נאמנין להעיד חוץ מהימנה ובעלה דרב פפי ודרב אשי תנאי היא דרב פפא [מי] לימא תנאי היא אמר לך רב פפא כי תניא ההיא במסיחה לפי תומה כי הא דכי אתא רב דימי אמר רב חנן קרטיגנאה משתעי מעשה בא לפני רבי יהושע בן לוי ואמרי לה רבי יהושע בן לוי מישתעי מעשה בא לפני רבי באדם אחד שהיה מסיח לפי תומו ואמר אני ואמי נשבינו לבין העובדי כוכבים יצאתי לשאוב מים דעתי על אמי ללקט עצים דעתי על אמי והשיאה ר' לכהונה על פיו: **מתני'** אמר ר' זכריה בן הקצב המעון הזה לא זזה ידה מתוך ידי משעה שנכנסו עובדי כוכבים לירושלים ועד שיצאו אמרו לו אין אדם מעיד על עצמו: **גמ'** תנא ואעפ"כ ייחד לה בית בחצרו וכשהיא יוצאה יוצאה בראש בניה וכשהיא נכנסת נכנסת בסוף בניה בעי אביי מהו לעשות בגרושה כן התם הוא דבשבויה הקילו אבל הכא לא או דלמא לא שנא ת"ש דתניא המגרש את אשתו לא תנשא בשכונתו ואם

רש"י

לא תתיחד עמו אלא בעדים. פירש בקונטרס משום גט ישן ולא פירש לטעמיה דפירש בגיטין (דף עג.) דמהיום אם מתי מגורשת למפרע משעת נתינה ולא תתיחד עמו משום חשש קידושין כמו המגרש אשתו ולנה עמו בפונדקי בית הלל אומרים צריכה הימנו גט שני (שם דף פא.) [ולא שייך גט ישן כלל לפירוש דהתם] וכן משמע התם בגמרא אבל לרבינו תם דמפרש מה היא באותן הימים קאי אמהיום אם מתי ונעשה כאומר מעת שאני בעולם שאין דעתו לגרשה אע"פ שאומר מהיום אלא שעה אחת לפני מיתתו הוי טעמא משום גט ישן ובתוספתא משמע כפי' רבינו תם:

שפיר קאמר לך דכתיב ויכר יוסף. זה שבא נולד כאן והלך עם אביו למדינת הים ועתה כשחזר ואמר לא ידענא לך מיחזי כשיקרא כי היה לו לידע אם הוא אחיו אם לאו כיון שמכירו קודם לכן להכי קאמר רב חסדא לשפיר קאמר ליה שאינו מכירו כדאשכחן ביוסף: **אמר** ליה אית לי סהדי ומסתפינו מיניה דאיניש אלמא הוא. נראה לר"י דמיירי שהביא עדים ואומרים אותו עדות שאתה שואל לא נאמר (ד) לך כלום עליו דרגלים לדבר שהוא אלא אמר ליה זיל כו' פי' לך הבא אותם עדים עצמם שירצה להעיד (ה) עליך שיעידו שאינו אחיך או שיאמרו שאינם יודעים אם הוא אחיך אם לאו וקאמר השתא נמי כיון שירצה ממנו שיקרו לומר אינו אחיו או שאין יודעין אם הוא אחיו אבל אם אין רגלים לדבר אין נראה כלל שיהא נאמן לומר דגברא אלמא הוא דאם לא כן כל אדם יאמר על חבירו שהוא גברא אלמא ויביא הוא עדים ואם לא יביא יפסיד ועוד דקאמר השתא נמי אתו ומסהדי אטו משום דמסתפו מיניה הני סהדי מסהדי כולי עלמא:

תרתי לא עבדי. שישתקו ולא יעידו האמת ועוד שיאמרו שקר וכן גבי שפחה:

במסיחה לפי תומה. ואפילו הכי היא ובעלה אינן נאמנין אע"ג דיוחנן אוכל חלות (לעיל דף כו.) היה נאמן על עצמו במסיח לפי תומו הני מילי לתרומה אבל הכא מעלה עשו ביוחסין [אומר ר"י דמסיח לפי תומו אינו כשר אלא לעדות אשה אז דרבנן כדאמר ביבמות והכא בשבויה הקילו]:

ואם

תוספות

מה לי לשקר. אי בעיא אמרה נתבעתי: במקום עדים. דאנן סהדי דכל שעתא איכא מיא: ודאי איטמי. בתמיה: **לא תתייחד עמו.** במסכת גיטין היא שכיב מרע שכתב ומסר גט לאשתו על מנת שאם מת יהא גט למפרע ולא תיזקק לחליצה לא תתייחד עמו שמא יבא עליה והוה ליה גט ישן ותנן בית הלל אוסרין לפטור בגט ישן ואיכא גט ישן כל שנתייחד עמה מאחר שכתבו לה וטעמא גזירה שמא יאמרו גיטה קודם לבנה. **ואפילו על פי עבד.** דייה בעבד שהיה עמה: **שלבה גס בשפחתה.** ותשמש בפניה: **רב אשי אמר הא והא בשפחה דידה.** והיינו טעמא דבמתני' מהימנא והתם לא מהימנא דשפחה דידה מיחזא חזיא בקלקול גבירתה ושתקה: **התם.** גבי גט: **דשתיקותה מתירתה.** שאינה צריכה שתעיד לומר לא שמשה אלא שתאמר לא הייתי עמה: **לא מהימנא.** להיות זו מותרת על ידה דלא נמי חזיא לא מסהדא: **הכא.** גבי שבויה: **דשתיקותה. דשתיקותה. אוסרתה.** לגבירתה דכל כמה שאינה מעידה לומר טהורה היא מחזקינן לה בטמאה כי מסהדא ואמרה טהורה היא מהימנא לשקורי לאו אורחא אלא למשתק: **השתא נמי.** כיון (ג) דרמאה לה לגבירתה או דדחלה מינה אתיא ומשקרא ואמרה טהורה היא: **תרתי לא עבדא.** חדא למשתק בקלקולה ועוד דמיתי ותשקר: **אחא מבי חוזאה.** שהלך אביו שם והוליכו עמו וגדלו שם ומת אביו וחזר לעירו ותבע חלקו בנכסי אביו: **א"ל.** רב חסדא להלוה אחא: **שפיר קאמר לך.** שאינו מכירך לפי שיצאת בלא חתימת זקן [ובאת בחתימת זקן]: **ויכר יוסף את אחיו.** שכשפירש מהן כבר היו חתומי זקן: **א"ל.** רב חסדא למר' זיל (ג) **אייתינהו את.** להנהו סהדי המכירין אותו ויעידון שאינו בן אביך השתא נמי. כיון דדחלי מיניה אתו ומשקרי: **תרתי לא עבדי.** חדא דשתקי מלהעיד אמת וחדא דמסהדי שיקרא: **לימא כתנאי.** שפחתה אי מהימנא אי לא: **עדות.** זו של שבויה הכל כשרים בה איש ואשה תינוק ותינוקת: **חוץ מהימנה.** היא עצמה: **דרב פפי ורב אשי.** דאמרו לעיל שפחה דידה מהימנה: **ודאי תנאי היא.** על כרחך יאמרו אנן דאמרי' כי מתניתא בתרייתא מדקשיא להו קמייתא: **דרב פפא.** דאמר לא מהימנה: **מי לימא תנאי היא.** כלומר דחוק הוא לומר אנא דאמרי כי מתניתא קמייתא או יוכל לתרץ מתניתא בתרייתא נמי כוותיה למימר שפחתה כעצמה דמי והרי היא בכלל חוץ מהימנה דקתני בה או תירולא אחרינא: **אמר לך רב פפא כי תניא ההיא.** דקתני הכל נאמנים ואפילו שפחה דידה במסיחה לפי תומה: **רב חנא קרטיגנאה משתעי.** רב חנן דמן קרטיגי היה מספר מעשה זה: **מתני'** המעון הזה. שבועה היא: **גמ' ואעפ"כ.** שאסרו עליו לפי שכהן היה: **כשהיא יוצאה.** והוא בחצר: **יוצאה בראש בניה.** שיהו הבנים עמהם שלא יתייחדו: **וכשהיא נכנסת נכנסת בסוף בניה.** כדי שלא יהא הוא והיא בחצר והבנים מבחוץ: **בגרושה.** כהן שגירש את אשתו מהו לדור עמו בחצר: **לא תנשא בשכונתו.** לפי שמכירה ברמיזותיו וקריצותיו שמא יבואו לידי עבירה:

ואם

עין משפט נר מצוה

קח א מיי' פי"ד מהל' שחיטות הלכה ב סמג עשין פט טוש"ע חו"מ סימן קצט: קט ב מיי' פ"ט מהל' איסורי ביאה הל' כח טוש"ע אה"ע סי' ז סעיף י: קי ג מיי' פ"ח מהל' גירושין הל' ב סמג עשין נ טוש"ע שם סימן קמט סעיף ג: קיא ד מיי' פי"ח מהל' איסורי ביאה הל' יט סמג לאוין קכו טוש"ע שם סימן ו סעיף ב: קיב ה מיי' פ"ה מהל' עדות הלכה יב סמג עשין קט טוש"ע ח"מ סי' כח סעיף ה: קיג ו מיי' פי"ח מהל' איסורי ביאה הל' יט טוש"ע אה"ע סי' ז סעיף ב: קיד ז מיי' שם הלכה יח טוש"ע שם סעיף א: קטו ח מיי' שם הלכה כ טוש"ע שם סעיף ב: קטז ט מיי' שם הלכה כא טוש"ע שם סעיף ט: קיז י מיי' פכ"א שם הלכה כח סמג לאוין קכו טוש"ע אה"ע סי' קיט סעיף ז וסי' קיט סעיף ח:

הגהות הב"ח

(א) גמ' זיל אייתי את: (ב) רש"י ד"ה השתא (דרמאה לה לגבירתה או) תא"מ ונ"ב פ"א לא זו: (ג) ד"ה זיל אייתי את: (ד) תוס' ד"ה אמר וכו' לא נאמר כלום דרגלים כו' ל"ל יתי' לך ותי' עליו נמחק: (ה) באיד להעיד שיעידו כצ"ל ותיבת עליך נמחק:

הגהות מהר"י לנדא

אן תוספות ד"ה במסיחה. אלא לעדות אשה כדאמר ביבמות והכא בשבויה דרבנן הקילו כצ"ל:

תורה אור השלם

א) וַיַּכֵּר יוֹסֵף אֶת אֶחָיו וְהֵם לֹא הִכִּרֻהוּ: [בראשית מב, ח]

תוספות רי"ד

איפשיטא ולקולא עבדי' בעי ר"א לא נתבעתי ולא נטמאתי מהו מי אמרינן מה לי לשקר במקום חששא אי לא. ולא איפשטא ולקולא עבדי': ואם יש להן עדים אפילו עבד ואפילו שפחה ואפילו שפחה דידה מהימנו ורמינהו לא תתיחד עמו אלא בעדים אפילו עבד ואפילו שפחה חוץ משפחתה מפני שלבה גס בשפחתה. פי' גבי שכ"מ שנתן גט לאשתו דחיישינן שמא יבוא עליה והוי צריכה גט שני שאין אדם עושה בעילתו בעילת זנות. ואסיק ר"א הא והא בשפחה דידה ושפחה מיחזא ושתקה הרם דשתיקותא מתירתה לא מהימנא והכא דשתיקותה אוסרתה מהימנא השתא נמי אתיא ומשקרא תרתי לא עבדי. פי' חדא שתשתוק מלהעיד האמת ועוד שתעיד שקר. **תנא** זו עדות כשר איש ואשה תינוק ותינוקת אביה ואמה אחיה ואחיותה אבל לא בתה ובנה. פי' זו עדות של שבויה כל אלו כשרין להעיד ואם הבן מסיח ל"ת ואומר אני ואמי נשבינו לבין העובדי כוכבים ויצאתי לשאוב מים וללקוט עצים ודעתי על אמי והשיאה ר' לכהונה על פיו. פי' מסיח ל"ת יקרא כ"ז שלא בא לפני ב"ד להעיד אלא מספר עם חבירו. והשומעים מפיו מגידים לב"ד וכ"מ שהעבד ואשה נאמנים כדתנן הזקן לחיות משיאים על מפי ע"ו (עד) מפי שפחה הקטן נמי נאמן כדתנן התם ר"י אומר אפילו שמע מן התינוקות אומרים הרי אנו הולכים לספוד ולקבור את איש פ' והשתא השומע מן התינוקות מעיד תינוקות עצמן לא כ"ש: **[מתני'] א"ר זכריה וכו'**. תנא אע"פ. פי' אע"פ שאסורה לו לפי שהיה כהן לא יחד לה בית בחצרו כשהיא יוצאה יוצאה בראש בניה ונכנסת נכנסת בסוף בניה. פי' לדור עמה בחצר כדי שלא יתיחדו. **בעי אביי** מהו לעשות כן בגרושה. התם השבויה הקילו אבל הכא לא. א"ד ל"ש.

מסורת הש"ס

א) [קדושין סד: וש"נ], ב) בכורות לו. ב"מ פג., ג) [ל"ל רבה ועי' תוס' בכורות לו. ד"ה ולאו], ד) [ב"ב לג: קדושין סד:], ה) גיטין עג., ו) [לעיל כג: וש"נ], ז) ב"מ לט: ע"ש, ח) שם יבמות פח., ט) ל"ל ומסתפו. יעב"ץ, י) ב"ק קיד:, כ) [ל"ל נשבע שבועה במקדש. ערוך וכן פי' רשב"ם ב"ב קכ.], ל) [תוספתא פרק ג], מ) [שמחות פ"ב ע"ש], נ) [ועיין היטיב תוס' גיטין עג. ד"ה לא], ס) ג"י כ"י, ע) [כל זה מבואר בסוגיא ב"ק קיד:].

ליקוטי רש"י

במקום עדים. דאנן סהדי שאין אותו הדרך בלא מים [ב"מ פא:]. **לא תתייחד עמו.** זה שנתן גט ואמר לה זה גיטך אם מתי לא תתייחד עמו שמא יבא עליה דאיכא למ"ד חיישינן שמא בעל לשם קדושין וצריכה גט שני ולמאן דלא חיישינן נמי מ"מ פנויה היא ואסור לתתיחד עם הפנויה [גיטין עג.]. **בשבויה הקילו.** דחששא בעלמא הוא דאיכא שמא נבעלה לעובד כוכבים ונפסלה לכהונה [לעיל כג.] דספיקא בעלמא היא [ב"ק קיד:]. הכרעה הקילו בה חכמים במסכת כתובות דלפי' אשה ועבד אחד נאמנין לומר טהורה וטעמא דבשבויה הקילו [ב"ב קלה.]. **ויכר יוסף את אחיו.** כשפירש מהן כבר היו חתומי זקן: **אתא ליה אחא מבי חוזאה.** שהלך אביו לבי חוזאי ונשא שם אשה וילדה לו את זה וחזר מרי לכאן וירד לנכסי אביו ובא זה ואמר לאחיו למאן מרובה ותבע חלקו. **שפיר קאמר לך.** שאינו מכירך ולאין זה רמאות שבשעה שהלך לא היה לך חתימת זקן ועכשיו באת בחתימת זקן. **ויכר יוסף את אחיו.** שבשעה שנפרד מהם היו כולם תמומי זקן והם לא הכירוהו שלא היה מלאלם בלא חתימת זקן ובא בחתימת זקן [ב"מ לט:]. ומתיראים [ע"פ מעלה יז.]. **דלאו אחוך הוא.** אותם עדים שיש לזה שבאו לומר שאינו אחיך ושמא ומכירין בו מי הוא כנאים אתה ויעידו שאינו בן אביך או בקש עדים אחרים. **תרתי לא עבדי.** ישתקו אחד שישתקו אבל שמים לא יעשו לא לדין שישתקו ולא יעידו האמת אלא גם שיעידו שקר [ב"ק שם]. **והשיאה ר' לכהונה.** ואע"ג דאיסורא דאורייתא היא משום זונה [ב"ק קיד:]. **המעון הזה.** נשבע בבית המקדש [רשב"ם קכ.].

WOMAN suffices, חוּץ מִשִּׁפְחָתָהּ – WITH THE EXCEPTION OF [THE WOMAN'S] OWN personal SLAVEWOMAN, מִפְּנֵי שֶׁלִּבָּהּ גַּס בְּשִׁפְחָתָהּ – FOR SHE IS on FAMILIAR terms WITH HER OWN SLAVEWOMAN, and will not hesitate to cohabit before her. If she did seclude herself with her husband and her slavewoman, the divorce contract should not be used, for we suspect that the husband and wife cohabited during the period of seclusion.[8]

Now, the reason a woman is not afraid to cohabit before her slavewoman is that she trusts the woman's loyalty, and knows that she will not reveal her mistress' indiscretions to others. This means that a slavewoman cannot be trusted to testify truthfully regarding her mistress' personal activities.[9] Seemingly, this contradicts the inference of our Mishnah – that such a woman is believed to testify that her mistress was not violated. – ? –

The Gemara answers:

אָמַר רַב פַּפִּי – Rav Pappi said: בִּשְׁבוּיָה הֵקִילוּ – **In the case of a captive** (i.e. in our Mishnah's case) **[the Rabbis] were lenient,** and gave credence to the testimony of a woman's own slavewoman.[10]

A second answer:

רַב פָּפָּא אָמַר – **Rav Pappa said:** הָא בְּשִׁפְחָה דִּידָהּ – **This** other **[Mishnah] is** dealing **with *her* slavewoman** (i.e. the wife's), who is indeed not believed regarding her mistress' personal activities. הָא בְּשִׁפְחָה דִּידֵיהּ – **This [Mishnah]** (i.e. ours), however, **is** dealing **with *his* slavewoman** (i.e. the husband's), who is trusted to testify that her master's wife was not violated.[11] The testimony of a captive woman's own slavewoman, however, would not suffice to permit her to her husband.

The Gemara questions Rav Pappa's ruling:

וְשִׁפְחָה דִּידָהּ לֹא מְהֵימְנָא – **And is her own slavewoman not trusted** to permit her to her husband? הָא קָתָנֵי אֵין אָדָם מֵעִיד עַל עַצְמוֹ – **But [the Rabbis] have taught in our Mishnah:** A PERSON MAY NOT TESTIFY ON HIS OWN BEHALF.[12] הָא שִׁפְחָה דִּידָהּ מְהֵימְנָא – **This implies that her slavewoman *is* believed** to testify on her behalf.[13] – ? –

The Gemara answers:

שִׁפְחָתָהּ נַמִּי כְּעַצְמָהּ דָּמֵי – **Her slavewoman is comparable to herself** (i.e. to her mistress).[14] When she testifies, it is as if the mistress herself is testifying. Thus, when the Mishnah states that a person cannot testify on his own behalf, it includes a slavewoman's testimony on her mistress' behalf.

Having digressed to question Rav Pappa's ruling, the Gemara now returns to the contradiction posed between the two Mishnahs, and offers a third resolution:

רַב אַשִׁי אָמַר – **Rav Ashi said:** הָא וְהָא בְּשִׁפְחָה דִּידָהּ – Both **this [Mishnah] and that [Mishnah] are** dealing **with *her* slavewoman.** וְשִׁפְחָה מִיחְזָא חָזְיָא וְשָׁתְקָה – **However,** it is the tendency of **a slavewoman** that she simply **sees and keeps silent;** she does not, however, testify falsely on her mistress' behalf. הָתָם דִּשְׁתִיקָתָהּ מַתִּירָתָהּ לֹא מְהֵימְנָא – Therefore, **over there** (in *Gittin*), **where [the slavewoman's]** mere **silence permits [the mistress]** to marry another on the strength of this divorce contract, **she is not trusted.** For when it comes to withholding information damaging to her mistress, she is suspect. הָכָא דִּשְׁתִיקָתָהּ אוֹסַרְתָּהּ מְהֵימְנָא – But **here** (in our Mishnah), **where [the slavewoman's] silence prohibits [her mistress]** to her husband and her testimony permits her, **she is trusted** to testify. For she is not suspect to deliver false testimony.[15]

The Gemara questions this assumption:

הַשְׁתָּא נַמִּי – But **even now,** i.e. in the case where her testimony is required, אַתְיָא וּמְשַׁקְרָא – perhaps **she *will* come and lie,**[16]

NOTES

8. This Mishnah discusses a childless man on the verge of death. He does not wish his wife to fall to his brother in *yibum* (the levirate marriage of the widow of one's childless brother, who is prohibited from marrying any but her husband's brother, the *yavam*), so he presents her with a divorce contract (a *get*), and specifies that on the day he dies, the divorce should take effect retroactively from one hour prior to his death. In this way she is protected, for at the moment of death she is a divorcee, and thus does not fall to *yibum*. The Mishnah rules that in the period between the giving of the divorce and the husband's death, the husband and wife should not be alone, lest they engage in cohabitation. If he does seclude himself with his wife, he renders the *get* (i.e. the divorce contract) a גֵּט יָשָׁן, or "old *get*," and Beis Hillel rule (on *Gittin* 79b) that an "old *get*" may not be used (*Rashi*, as explained by *Ritva*; see *Pnei Yehoshua* to *Tosafos, Gittin* 73b ד״ה אמר רבא; see also *Yad David* ms., cited in *Ohel Avraham*; cf. *Tosafos; Meiri*).

Any *get* will be branded an "old *get*" if the husband and wife are alone with each other at any time between the writing of the *get* and its transmission to the woman. The reason behind the "old *get*" decree is the fear that while secluded they will cohabit, and a child will be born of the act. In later years it may come to pass that people, seeing that the *get* predates the child's conception, will forget that time elapsed between the writing of the *get* and its transmission to the woman, and will assume that this child was conceived *after* the divorce, out of wedlock. So as to prevent the attachment of this stigma to the child, the Rabbis decreed that an "old *get*" should not be used (*Rashi*). In our case, the *get* is actually *given* to the woman prior to her seclusion with her husband. Nevertheless, the seclusion renders the *get* an "old" one, since it takes place before the *get* takes effect, leaving room for the aforementioned error (see *Ritva*).

[*Tosafos* note that *Rashi* to *Gittin* (73a ד״ה לא תתיחד עמו) explains this Mishnah differently than *Rashi* does here. For approaches in resolving the contradiction, see *Shitah Mekubetzes* ד״ה ועוד הקשו; *Pnei Yehoshua; Chasam Sofer*.]

9. See *Rashba*.

10. In the case of any captive woman there exists a real possibility that no molestation took place (see *Rashbam, Bava Basra* 135a ד״ה אם הקילו בשבויה). The decree that requires her to leave her Kohen husband is based on no more than a strong suspicion that she was violated (see *Rashi* 23a ד״ה בשבויה הקילו). Therefore, the Rabbis were lenient in permitting the testimony of usually invalid witnesses, such as the captive's own slavewoman.

11. According to Rav Pappa, the superfluous phrase, *a person is not believed* [to testify] *on his own behalf*, teaches the law of his slavewoman, not hers. Although a man's slavewoman is certainly biased toward his interests, her bias works to ensure that she will testify truthfully regarding his wife, for it is not in a man's best interests to remain married to a woman who is forbidden to him (*Shitah Mekubetzes* ד״ה רב פפא; see above, note 5).

12. These words paraphrase our Mishnah. The Mishnah actually reads וְאֵין נֶאֱמָן אָדָם עַל יְדֵי עַצְמוֹ, *a person is not believed* [to testify] *on his own behalf* (see *Shitah Mekubetzes* ד״ה רב פפא אמר; but see Mishnah below; *Shitah Mekubetzes* ד״ה ויש אומרים שפחתה; *Rashash; Nimukei HaGrib* to *Maharsha*).

13. Although Rav Pappa has interpreted the Mishnah's inference as referring to the *husband's* slavewoman, not the wife's (see note 11), the Gemara is troubled. For simply understood, the statement *a person is not believed* [to testify] *on his own behalf* implies that *any* outsider, even the wife's slavewoman, *is* believed (*Shitah Mekubetzes* ד״ה רב פפא).

14. I.e. her devotion to and sympathy for her mistress renders her suspect of lying to protect her mistress (see *Nimukei Yosef;* see note 30). When this Mishnah makes reference to "a person," it also intends those devoted to the person.

15. In the case in *Gittin,* the slavewoman needs to say only that she was present during the meeting between husband and wife. It is not necessary for her to explicitly testify that they did not cohabit. Since if they did cohabit she would withhold the information, she cannot act as a witness to permit the use of the *get*. In our case, however, the slavewoman must state explicitly that her mistress was not violated; otherwise, we assume that she was. Therefore, she is trusted to testify, for while slavewomen will withhold information, they usually will not lie (*Rashi*).

16. I.e. although a slavewoman is not usually suspect of lying, perhaps she will do so in this case, out of love for or fear of her mistress (see *Rashi;* see *Hagahos HaBach* §2).

מה לי לשקר או דלמא לא אמרינן ומאי שנא מההוא מעשה דההוא גברא דאגר ליה חמרא לחבריה א"ל לא תיזיל באורחא דנהר פקוד דאיכא מיא זיל באורחא דנרש דליכא מיא ואזל איהו באורחא דנהר פקוד ומית חמרא אתא לקמיה דרבא א"ל אין באורחא דנהר פקוד אזלי מיהו לא הוו מיא אמר רבא מה לי לשקר אי בעי א"ל באורחא דנרש אזלי ואמר ליה אביי מה לי לשקר במקום עדים לא אמרינן הכי השתא התם ודאי איכא עדים דאיכא מיא הכא ודאי איטמי חששא הוא ובמקום חששא אמרינן: אם יש עדים אפילו עבד ואפילו שפחה נאמנין: ואפילו שפחה דידה מהימנא ורמינהי לא תתיחד עמו אלא ע"פ עדים ואפילו ע"פ עבד וע"פ שפחה חוץ משפחתה מפני שלבה גס בשפחתה אמר רב פפי בשבויה הקילו רב פפא אמר הא בשפחה דידה הא בשפחה דידיה ושפחה דידיה לא מהימנא הא קתני אין אדם מעיד על עצמו הא שפחה דידה מהימנא שפחתה נמי כעצמה דמי רב אשי אמר הא והא בשפחה דידה ושפחה מיחזא חזיא ושתקה התם דשתיקתה מתירתה לא מהימנא הכא דשתיקתה אוסרתה מהימנא השתא נמי אתיא ומשקרא תרתי לא עבדא כי הא דמרי בר איסק ואמרי לה חנא בר איסק אתא ליה אחא מבי חוזאה א"ל פלוג לי בנכסי דאבא א"ל לא ידענא לך אתא לקמיה דרב חסדא א"ל שפיר קאמר לך דכתיב ויכר יוסף את אחיו והם לא הכירוהו מלמד שיצא בלא חתימת זקן ובא בחתימת זקן א"ל זיל אייתי סהדי דאחוה את א"ל אית לי סהדי ומסתפינו מיניה דגברא אלמא הוא א"ל לדידיה זיל (א) אייתינהו את דלאו אחוך הוא א"ל דינא הכי המוציא מחבירו עליו הראיה א"ל הכי דאיננא לך ולכולהו אלמי חברך השתא נמי אתו ומשקרי תרתי לא עבדי לימא כתנאי זו עדות איש ואשה תינוק ותינוקת אביה ואמה ואחיה ואחותה אבל לא בנה ובתה ועבדה ושפחתה ותניא אידך הכל נאמנין להעיד חוץ מהימנה ובעלה דרב פפי ודרב אשי תנאי היא דרב פפא [מי] לימא תנאי היא אמר לך רב פפא כי תניא ההיא במסיחה לפי תומה כי הא דכי אתא רב דימי אמר רב חנן קרטיגנאה משתעי מעשה בא לפני רבי יהושע בן לוי ואמרי לה רבי יהושע בן לוי משתעי מעשה בא לפני רבי באדם אחד שהיה מסיח לפי תומו ואמר אני ואמי נשבינו לבין העובדי כוכבים יצאתי לשאוב מים ודעתי על אמי וללקט עצים דעתי על אמי והשיאה ר' לכהונה על פיו: **מתני'** אמר ר' זכריה בן הקצב המעון הזה לא זזה ידה מתוך ידי משעה שנכנסו עובדי כוכבים לירושלים ועד שיצאו אמרו לו אין אדם מעיד על עצמו: **גמ'** תנא ואעפ"כ ייחד לה בית בחצרו וכשהיא יוצאה יוצאה בראש בניה וכשהיא נכנסת נכנסת בסוף בניה בעי אביי מהו לעשות בגרושה כן התם הוא דבשבויה הקילו אבל הכא לא או דלמא לא שנא ת"ש דתניא המגרש את אשתו לא תנשא בשכונתו ואם

תוספות

לא תתיחד עמו אלא בעדים. פירש בקונטרס משום גט ישן ולא פירש לטעמיה דפירש בגיטין (דף עג.) דכמהיום אם מתי מגורשת למפרע משעת נתינה ולא תתיחד עמו משום חשש קידושין כמו המגרש אשתו ולנה עמו בפונדקי בית הלל אומרים צריכה הימנו גט שני (שם דף פא.) [ולא שייך גט ישן כלל לפירוש דהתם] וכן משמע התם בגמרא אבל רבינו תם מפרש מה היא באותן הימים קאי אמהיום אם מתי ונעשה כאומר מעת שאני בעולם שאין דעתו לגרשה אע"פ שאומר מהיום אלא שעה אחת לפני מיתתו הוי טעמא משום גט ישן ובתוספתא משמע כפי' רבינו תם:

שפיר קאמר לך דכתיב ויכר יוסף. זה שבא נולד כאן והלך עם אביו למדינת הים ועתה כשחזר ואמר לא ידענא לך מיחזי כשיקרא כי היה לו לידע אם הוא אחיו אם לאו כיון שמכירו קודם שהלך קאמר רב חסדא דשפיר קאמר ליה שאינו מכירו כדאשכחן ביוסף: **אמר** ליה אית לי סהדי ומסתפינו מיניה דאיניש אלמא הוא. נראה לר"י דמיירי שהביא עדים ואומרים אותו עדות שאתה שואל לא נאמר (ד) לך כלום עליו דרגלים לדבר שהוא אלם אמר ליה זיל כו' פי' לך הבא אותם עדים עצמם שיראים להעיד (ה) עליך שיעידו שאינו אחיך או שיאמרו שאינם יודעים אם הוא אחיך אם לאו וקאמר השתא נמי כיון שיראים ממנו ישקרו לומר אינו אחיו או שאינן יודעין אם הוא אחיו אבל אם אין רגלים לדבר אין נראה כלל שיהא נאמן לומר דגברא אלמא הוא דאם לא כן כל אדם יאמר על חבירו שהוא גברא אלמא ויביא הוא עדים ואם לא יביא יפסיד ועוד דקאמר השתא נמי אתו ומסהדי אטו משום דמסתפו מיניה הני סהדי מסתפו מיניה כולי עלמא:

תרתי לא עבדי. שישתקו ולא יעידו האמת ועוד שיאמרו שקר וכן גבי שפחה:

במסיחה לפי תומה. ואפילו הכי היא ובעלה אין נאמנין אע"ג דיוחנן אוכל חלות (לעיל דף כו.) היה נאמן על עצמו במסיח לפי תומו הני מילי לתרומה אבל הכא מעלה עשו ביוחסין [ואומר ר"י דמסיח לפי תומו אינו כשר אלא לעדות אשה אן דרבנן כדאמר ביבמות והכא בשבויה הקילו]:

ואם

רש"י

מה לי לשקר. אי בעיא אמרה לא נחבאתי: במקום עדים. דאנן סהדי דכל שעתא איכא מיא: ודאי איטמי. בתמיה: לא תתייחד עמו. במסכת גיטין היא שכיב מרע שכתב ומסר גט לאשתו על מנת שאם מת יהא גט למפרע ולא תיזקק ליבם לחליצה לא תתייחד עמו שמא יבא עליה והוה ליה גט ישן ותנן בית הלל אוסרין לפטור בגט ישן ואיזהו גט ישן כל שנתייחד עמה מאחר שכתבו לה וטעמא גזירה שמא יאמרו גיטה קודם לבנה: ואפילו על פי עבד. דייה בעבד שהיה עמה: שלבה גס בשפחתה. ותשמש בפניה: רב אשי אמר הא והא בשפחה דידה. והיינו טעמא דבמתני' מהימנא והתם לא מהימנא דשפחה דידה מיחזא חזיא בקילקול גבירתה ושתקה: התם. גבי גט: דשתיקותה מתירתה. שאינה צריכה שתעיד לומר לא שמשה אלא שתאמר אני הייתי עמה: לא מהימנא. להיות זו מותרת על ידה דאי נמי חזיא לא מסהדא: הכא. גבי שבויה: דשתיקותה. דשפחה: אוסרתה. לגבירתה דכל כמה שאינה מעידה לומר טהורה היא מחזקינן לה בטמאה כי מסהדא ואמרה טהורה היא מהימנא דלשקורי לאו אורחא אלא למשתק: השתא נמי. כיון (ב) דרחמא לה לגבירתה או דדחלה מינה אתיא ומשקרא ואמרה טהורה היא: תרתי לא עבדא. חדא למשתק בקלקולה ועוד דתיתי ותשקר: אחא מבי חוזאה. שהלך אביו שם והוליכו עמו וגדלו שם ומת אביו וחזר לעירו ותבע חלקו בנכסי אביו: א"ל. רב חסדא להההוא אחא: שפיר קאמר לך. שאינו מכירך לפי שיצאת בלא חתימת זקן [ובאת בחתימת זקן]: ויכר יוסף את אחיו. שכשפירש מהן כבר היו חתומי זקן: א"ל. רב חסדא למרי: זיל (ג) אייתינהו את. להנהו סהדי המכירין אותו ויעידו שאינו בן אביך: השתא נמי. כיון דדחלי מיניה אתו ומשקרי: תרתי לא עבדי. חדא דשתקי מלהעיד אמת וחדא דמסהדי שיקרא: לימא כתנאי. שפחתה אי מהימנא אי לא: זו עדות. עדות זו של שבויה הכל כשרים בה איש ואשה תינוק ותינוקת: חוץ מהימנה. היא עצמה: דרב פפי ורב אשי. דאמרו לעיל שפחה דידה מהימנה: ודאי תנאי היא. על כרחך יאמרו אנן דאמרי' כי מתניתא בתרייתא מדקשיא להו קמייתא: דרב פפא. דאמר לא מהימנה: מי לימא תנאי היא. כלומר דחוק הוא לומר אנא דאמרי כי מתניתא קמייתא או יוכל לתרץ מתניתא בתרייתא נמי כוותיה למימר שפחתה כעצמה דמי והרי היא בכלל חוץ מהימנה דקתני בה או תירוצא אחרינא: אמר לך רב פפא כי תניא ההיא. דקתני הכל נאמנים ואפילו שפחה דידה במסיחה לפי תומה: רב חנא קרטיגנאה משתעי. רב חנן דמן קרטיגי היה מספר מעשה זה: מתני' המעון הזה. שבועה היא: גמ' ואעפ"כ. שאסרו עליו לפי שכהן היה: כשהיא יוצאה. והוא בחצר: יוצאה בראש בניה. שיהו הבנים עמהם שלא יתייחדו: וכשהיא נכנסת נכנסת בסוף בניה. כדי שלא יהא הוא והיא בחצר והבנים מבחוץ: בגרושה. כהן שגירש את אשתו מהו לדור עמו בחצר: לא תנשא בשכונתו. לפי שמכירה ברמיזותיו וקריצותיו שמא יבואו לידי עבירה: ואם

עין משפט נר מצוה

קח א מיי' פ"ד מהל' שכירות הלכה ב סמג עשין פט טוש"ע חו"מ סימן שז:

קט ב מיי' פי"ח מהל' איסורי ביאה הל' כח סמג לאוין קכו טוש"ע אה"ע סי' ז סעיף ג:

קי ג מיי' פ"ח מהל' גירושין הל' ג סמג עשין נ טוש"ע שם סימן קמט סעיף ג:

קיא ד מיי' פי"ח מהל' איסורי ביאה הל' כ סמג לאוין קכו טוש"ע שם סימן ז סעיף ג:

קיב ה מיי' פי"ב מהל' עדות הלכה י' סמג עשין קט טוש"ע ח"מ סי' כח סעיף ה:

קיג ו מיי' פי"ח מהל' איסורי ביאה הל' יט טוש"ע אה"ע סי' ז סעיף ו:

קיד ז מיי' שם הלכה יח טוש"ע שם סעיף ח:

קטו ח מיי' שם הלכה כ טוש"ע שם סעיף כ:

קטז ט מיי' שם הלכה כה טוש"ע שם סעיף יב:

קיז י מיי' פ"א שם הלכה כ סמג לאוין קכו טוש"ע אה"ע סי' קיט סעיף ז וסי' קיז סעיף ט:

הגהות הב"ח

(א) גמ' זיל אייתי את: (ב) רש"י ד"ה השתא (דרחמא לה לגבירתה או) תא"מ ונ"ב ס"א לא: (ג) ד"ה זיל אייתי את: (ד) תוס' ד"ה אמר וכו' לא נאמר כלום דרגלים כל"ל ותי' עליו נמחק: (ה) בא"ד שאעיד שיעידו כל"ל ותי' עליך נמחק:

הגהות מהר"י לנדא

אן תוספות ד"ה במסיחה. אלא לעדות אשה כדאמר ביבמות והכא בשבויה דרבנן הקילו כצ"ל:

תורה אור השלם

א) וַיַּכֵּר יוֹסֵף אֶת אֶחָיו וְהֵם לֹא הִכִּרֻהוּ: [בראשית מב, ח]

תוספות רי"ד

איפשיטא ולקולא עבדי'. בעי ר"א לא נחבאתי ולא נטמאתי מהו מי אמרי' מה לי לשקר במקום חששא אי לא. ולא איפשטא ולקולא עבדי'. ואם יש להן עדים אפילו עבד ואפילו שפחה ואפילו שפחה דידה מהימנה לא תתיחד עמו אלא בעדים אפילו עבד ואפילו שפחה חוץ משפחתה מפני שלבה גס בשפחתה. פי' גבי שכ"מ שנתן גט לאשתו דחיישינן שמא יבוא עליה ותהי' צריכה גט שני שאין אדם עושה בעילתו בעילת זנות. ואסיק ר"א הא והא בשפחה דידה שפחתה מיחזא ושתקה התם דשתיקותא מתירתה לא מהימנא והכא דשתיקתה אוסרתה מהימנא השתא נמי אתיא ומשקרא תרתי לא עבדי. פי' חדא שותקת מלהעיד האמת ועוד שתעיד שקר. תנא זו עדות כשר איש ואשה תינוקת ותינוק אביה ואמה אחיה ואחיותה אבל לא בתה ובנה. פי' זו עדות של שבויה כל אלו כשרין להעיד ואם הבן מסיח ל"ת ואומר אני ואמי נשבינו לבין העובדי כוכבים ויצאתי לשאוב מים וללקוט עצים ודעתי על אמי והשיאה ר' לכהונה על פיו. פי' מסיח ל"ת יקרא כ"ז שלא בא לפני ב"ד להעיד אלא מספר עם חבירו. והשומעים מפיו מגידים לב"ד וכ"מ שהעבד ואשה נאמנים גם הקטן נאמן ולגבי מת בעלך שעבד ואשה נאמנים כדתנן החזקנו להיות משיאים עד מפי עד (כד) מפי שפחה הקטן נמי נאמן כדתנן התם ר"י אומר אפילו שמע מן התינוקות אומרים הרי אנו הולכים לספוד ולקבור את איש פ' והשתא השומע מן התינוקות מעיד תינוקות עצמן לא כ"ש: **[מתני'] א"ר זכריה וכו'.** תנא אע"פ. פי' אע"פ שאסרה לו לפי שהיה כהן יחד לה בית בחצירו כשהיא יוצאה יוצאה בראש בניה וכשהיא נכנסת נכנסת בסוף בניה. ופי' כדי שלא יתייחדו. **בעי אביי** מהו לעשות כן בגרושה. פי' לדור עמה בחצר התם בשבויה היקילו אבל הכא לא. א"ד ל"ש.

מסורת הש"ס

א) [קדושין סד: וש"נ], ב) בכורות לו. ב"מ פא., ג) [ג"ל רבה ועי' תוס' בכורות לו. ד"ה ולימר], ד) [ב"ב לג: קדושין סד:], ה) גיטין עג., ו) [לעיל כג: וש"נ], ז) ב"מ לט: ע"ש, ח) שם יבמות פח., ט) ג"ל ומסתפו. יעב"ץ, י) ב"ק קיד., כ) [פי' נשבע שבועה במקדש. ערוך וכן פי' רשב"ם בב"ב קסו.], ל) [תוספתא פרק ג], מ) [שמחות פ"ב ע"ש], נ) [ועיין היטיב תוס' גיטין עג. ד"ה לא], ס) ב"ב כ"ב, ע) [כל זה מבואר בסוגיא ב"ק קיד:].

ליקוטי רש"י

במקום עדים. דאנן סהדי שאין אותו הדרך בלא מים [ב"מ פא:]. לא תתייחד עמו. זה שנתן גט ואמר לה מהיום אם מתי לא תתייחד עמו שמא יבא עליה דאיכא למ"ד חיישינן שמא בעל לשם קדושין וצריכה גט שני ולמאן דלא חייש נמי מ"מ פנויה היא ואסור להתייחד עם הפנויה [גיטין עג.]. בשבויה הקילו. דחששא בעלמא הוא דאיכא שמא נבעלה לעובד כוכבים ונפסלה לכהונה [לעיל כג.]. דספיקא בעלמא היא [ב"ק קיד:]. דהרבה הקילו בה חכמים במסכת כתובות דאפי' אשה ועד אחד נאמנין לומר טהורה וטעמא דבשביל שנתייחדה בין השבאין אין לנו לאסרה שהרי סתם אשה משמרת עצמה מזנות ואוקמה אחזקתה ואיסור קל הוא אם נישאת לכהן [רשב"ם ב"ב קלה.]. אתא ליה אחא מבי חוזאה. שהלך אביו לבי חוזאי ונשא שם אשה וילדה לו את זה וחזר מרי לכאן וירד לנכסי אביו ובא זה אחריו לזמן מרובה ותבע חלקו. שפיר קאמר לך. שאינו מכירך ואין זה רמאות שכשיצא מאצלך לא היה לך חתימת זקן ועכשיו באת בחתימת זקן. ויכר יוסף את אחיו. שכשיצא מהם היו כולם חתומי זקן והם לא הכירוהו שיצא מאצלם בלא חתימת זקן ובא בחתימת זקן [ב"מ לט:]. ומסתפינו. ומתיראים [ע"פ מעילה יז:]. דלאו אחוך הוא. אותם עדים שיש לו לזה שבאו משם ומכירין בו מי הוא הביאם אתה ויעידו שאינו בן אביך או בקש עדים אחרים. תרתי לא עבדי. יעשו אחת שישתקו אבל שתים לא יעשו לא דיין שישתקו ולא יעידו האמת אלא גם שיעידו שקר [ב"מ שם]. והשיאה ר' לכהונה. ואע"ג דאיסורא דאורייתא היא משום זונה [ב"ק קיד:]. המעון הזה. בבית המקדש נשבע [רשב"ם קסו.].

מַה לִּי לְשַׁקֵּר – the legal argument of **"What [reason] do I have to lie,"** in which case the woman would be believed? **אוֹ דִּלְמָא לֹא אָמְרִינַן** – **Or perhaps we do not apply** this argument in this instance.[1]

The Gemara asks:

וּמַאי שְׁנָא מֵהַהוּא מַעֲשֶׂה דְּהַהוּא גַּבְרָא – **And how is this different from the incident** that occurred **with a certain man** **דַּאֲגַר לֵיהּ חֲמָרָא לְחַבְרֵיהּ** – **who rented a donkey to his fellow?** **אָמַר לֵיהּ** – In that case, **[the owner] said to [the renter]:** **לֹא תֵּיזִיל בְּאוֹרְחָא דִּנְהַר פְּקוֹד דְּאִיכָּא מַיָּא** – **Do not go on the road by the Pekod River, where there is water** that might sweep the donkey away. **זִיל בְּאוֹרְחָא דְּנֶרֶשׁ דְּלֵיכָּא מַיָּא** – Instead, **go on the Neresh road, where there is no water.** **וְאָזַל אִיהוּ בְּאוֹרְחָא דִּנְהַר פְּקוֹד וּמִית חֲמָרָא** – Now, this [fellow] disobeyed the owner's instructions, and **went on the road by the Pekod River, and the donkey died.** **אָתָא לְקַמֵּיהּ דְּרָבָא אָמַר לֵיהּ** – **He came before Rava,** and **he said to him:** **אִין בְּאוֹרְחָא דִּנְהַר פְּקוֹד אַזְלִי** – **Yes, I did go on the road by the Pekod River;** **מִיהוּ לֹא הֲווּ מַיָּא** – **however, there was no water** there, and the donkey died of other causes (for which the renter would not be liable). **אָמַר רָבָא** – **Rava said:** **מַה לִּי לְשַׁקֵּר** – In this case, we apply the argument of **"What [reason] do I have to lie."** **אִי בָּעֵי אָמַר לֵיהּ בְּאוֹרְחָא דְּנֶרֶשׁ אַזְלִי** – For **had [this fellow] wished** to lie, **he could have said to [the owner], "I went on the Neresh road."** Since he admitted that he used the Pekod River route, it is clear that he is not interested in lying. Therefore, we must believe him when he says that there was no water there. **וְאָמַר לֵיהּ אַבַּיֵי** – **And Abaye said to [Rava]** regarding this ruling: **מַה לִּי לְשַׁקֵּר בִּמְקוֹם עֵדִים לֹא אָמְרִינַן** – **We do not apply** the argument of **"What [reason] do I have to lie" in the face of witnesses** that testify otherwise. The incidence of water on the Pekod River route is so high that we consider its presence to be certain, as if witnesses had testified to it. Therefore, this argument cannot be adduced, and the renter is not believed.[2]

We see that we do not apply this legal argument in the face of an incontrovertible fact. Thus, it cannot serve to validate the testimony of the woman who states that she was at large during the occupation but was not violated.[3] Rav Ashi's inquiry is thus resolved.

The Gemara rejects this resolution:

הָכִי הַשְׁתָּא – Now, is **this** a comparison? **הָתָם וַדַּאי אִיכָּא עֵדִים דְּאִיכָּא מַיָּא** – **Over there,** in the case of the donkey, **there definitely exist "witnesses"** that "testify" **that there is water** on the Pekod River road. **הָכָא וַדַּאי אִיטַּמִּי** – **Here,** however, in the case of the woman who testified, **was she definitely violated?** Of course not! **חֲשָׁשָׁא הוּא** – **It is** no more than **a suspicion,** **וּבִמְקוֹם חֲשָׁשָׁא אָמְרִינַן** – **and in the case of a** mere **suspicion, we do apply** the argument of "What reason do I have to lie." Therefore, the woman should be believed.[4]

The Mishnah stated:

אִם יֵשׁ עֵדִים אֲפִילוּ עֶבֶד וַאֲפִילוּ שִׁפְחָה נֶאֱמָנִין – BUT IF THEY HAVE WITNESSES who testify that they were not molested, EVEN A SLAVE or EVEN A SLAVEWOMAN, THESE witnesses ARE BELIEVED.

The Gemara states:

וַאֲפִילוּ שִׁפְחָה דִּידָהּ מְהֵימְנָא – From the Mishnah we see that **even [a woman's] own slavewoman is believed** to testify that she was not molested during the occupation of the city.[5]

The Gemara questions this:

וּרְמִינְהִי – **But contrast [this ruling with the ruling of this Mishnah]** in Tractate *Gittin,*[6] and note the contradiction: **לֹא תִּתְיַיחֵד עִמּוֹ** – SHE (i.e. a woman under the shadow of a pending divorce) MAY NOT SECLUDE HERSELF WITH [HER HUSBAND] (lest they cohabit) **אֶלָּא עַל פִּי עֵדִים** – UNLESS they are IN THE PRESENCE OF WITNESSES,[7] before whom they will not engage in intimacies. **וַאֲפִילוּ עַל פִּי עֶבֶד וְעַל פִּי שִׁפְחָה** – AND EVEN THE PRESENCE OF A mere SLAVE OR THE PRESENCE OF A mere SLAVE-

NOTES

1. [The argument of "What reason do I have to lie" (or *migo*) assumes that a person would rather enter a stronger claim than a weaker one. The fact, then, that the person does enter the weaker claim lends credibility to his testimony. For had he wished to lie he would have offered the better lie.]

The two sides of Rav Ashi's inquiry are as follows: The woman could simply have claimed that she hid herself during the occupation, and she would have been believed. Since she could have made this strong claim, she should be believed regarding her weaker claim – i.e. that she did not hide herself but was not violated (*Rashi*). On the other hand, she may have had a reason to avoid claiming that she hid herself, in which case her failure to make this claim provides no proof of her integrity. *Ritva* (to 27a and here) explains that the inquiry concerns a hiding place that can hold only a single person. (This inquiry thus flows naturally from the previous one, which concerns an identical case.) In this case, most women would be embarrassed to state that they hid themselves there, since the claim is highly unlikely, and they do not wish to expose themselves before Beis Din as dissemblers. Accordingly, Rav Ashi wonders if perhaps the woman's ability to make this claim does not prove her credibility in this case, since she *does* have considerable reason to employ the weaker claim (see also *Re'ah;* see *Chasam Sofer;* cf. *Shitah Yeshanah,* cited in *Shitah Mekubetzes* ד״ה ה״ג בקצת ספרים).

2. It was known that there was water on the Pekod River road at all times. This was considered certain, just as if it had been testified to by witnesses (*Rashi*). Thus, the claim of the renter that there was no water there is tantamount to a claim that runs counter to the testimony of witnesses. Such a claim is unacceptable, even when backed by the "What reason do I have to lie" argument. Therefore, the renter is liable for the death of the donkey.

[Now, in *Bava Basra* (33b) the Gemara states that Rava and Abaye agree that this argument cannot be used in the face of witnesses. How, then, can Rava state here that this argument does prevail against witnesses? To avoid this difficulty, some Rishonim emend our Gemara to read Rabbah instead of Rava (see *Tosafos, Bechoros* 36a ד״ה ואמר רבא; see also *Tosafos, Bava Basra* 31a ד״ה אמר רבה; see also *Ritva* here). (This fits well with the Gemara in *Bava Basra* 31a, in which a similar dispute between Rabbah and Abaye appears.) Alternatively, Rava holds that the presumption of water on the Pekod River road is not strong enough to qualify as "the testimony of witnesses," for although water is usually found there, the road is *occasionally* dry. Accordingly, the "What reason do I have to lie" argument should prevail (see *Ritva,* first explanation).]

3. At this point, the Gemara believes that any woman who remained at large in the city is presumed to have been definitely violated. The presumption is so strong that it has the force of the testimony of witnesses (see *Re'ah;* cf. *Ritva*).

[This presumption is based upon the statement made in the Gemara above (13b) that the majority of idolaters are wanton in such matters (רוֹב עוֹבְדֵי כוֹכָבִים פְּרוּצִים בַּעֲרָיוֹת); accordingly, we presume that they definitely violated this woman (see *Pnei Yehoshua;* see *Rashi* 13b ד״ה לוז יש עדים וד״ה פרוצים בעריות).]

4. [The Gemara now recognizes that the woman's mere presence in the city does not classify her as one who has positively been violated. Rather, she is prohibited to her husband only because of a *suspicion* that this took place. The "What reason do I have to lie" argument lends credibility to her claim that she remained unmolested.]

5. This is known from the Mishnah's next phrase, וְאֵין נֶאֱמָן אָדָם עַל יְדֵי עַצְמוֹ, *a person is not believed* [to testify] *on his own behalf.* This law appears to be self-evident, for the Mishnah has already stated that witnesses are needed, thus clearly implying that one's own testimony does not suffice. The Gemara therefore understands this phrase to imply that any outsider, even one's own slavewoman, is believed to testify on one's behalf (*Shitah Mekubetzes* ד״ה ואפי׳ שפחה וד״ה רב פפא; see Gemara below with notes 11 and 12).

6. 73a.

7. Although the Mishnah uses the plural "witnesses," one witness is enough, as is evident from the Mishnah's next clause – see *Bach, Even HaEzer* §7 ד״ה לפיכך.

לא תתיחד עמו אלא בעדים. פירש בקונטרס משום גט ישן ולא פירש לטעמיה דפירש בגיטין (דף עג.) דמהיום אם מתי מגורשת למפרע משעת נתינה ולא תתיחד עמו משום חשש קידושין כמו המגרש אשתו ולנה עמו בפונדקי בית הלל אומרים צריכה הימנו גט שני (שם דף פא.) [ולא שייך גט ישן כלל לפירוש דהתם] וכן משמע התם בגמרא אבל לרבינו תם דמפרש מה היא באותן הימים קאי אמהיום אם מתי ונעשה כאומר מעת שאני בעולם שאין דעתו לגרשה אע"פ שאומר מהיום אלא שעה אחת לפני מיתתו הוי טעמא משום גט ישן ובתוספתא משמע כפי' רבינו תם:

שפיר קאמר לך דכתיב ויכר יוסף. זה שבא נולד כאן והלך עם אביו למדינת הים ועתה כשחזר ואמר לא ידענא לך מיחזי כשיקרא כי היה לו לידע אם הוא אחיו אם לאו כיון שמכירו קודם להכי קאמר רב חסדא דשפיר קאמר ליה שאינו מכירו כדאשכחן ביוסף:

אמר ליה אית לי סהדי ומסתפינו מיניה דאיניש אלמא הוא. נראה לר"י דמיירי שהביא עדים ואומרים אותו עדות שאתה שואל לא נאמר (ד) לך כלום עליו דרגלים לדבר שהוא אלם אמר ליה זיל כו' פי' לך הבא אותם עדים עצמם שיראים להעיד (ה) עליך שיעידו שאינו אחיך או שיאמרו שאינם יודעים אם הוא אחיך אם לאו וקאמר השתא נמי כיון שיראים ממנו ישקרו לומר אינו אחיו או שאינן יודעין אם הוא אחיו אבל אם אין רגלים לדבר אין נראה כלל שיהא נאמן לומר דגברא אלמא הוא דאם לא כן כל אדם יאמר על חבירו שהוא גברא אלמא ויביא הוא עדים ואם לא יביא יפסיד ועוד דקאמר השתא נמי אתו ומסהדי אטו משום דמסתפו מיניה הני סהדי מסתפו מיניה כולי עלמא:

תרתי לא עבדי. שישתקו ולא יעידו האמת ועוד שיאמרו שקר וכן גבי שפחה:

במסיחה לפי תומה. ואפילו הכי היא ובעלה אינן נאמנין אע"ג דיוחנן אוכל חלות (לעיל דף כו.) היה נאמן על עצמו במסיח לפי תומו הני מילי לתרומה אבל הכא מעלה עשו ביוחסין [אומר ר"י דמסיח לפי תומו אינו כשר אלא לעדות אשה אן דרבנן כדאמר ביבמות והכא בשבויה הקילו]: ואם

מה לי לשקר או דלמא לא אמרינן ומאי שנא מההוא מעשה דההוא גברא דאגר ליה חמרא לחבריה א"ל לא תיזיל באורחא דנהר פקוד דאיכא מיא זיל באורחא דנרש דליכא מיא ואזל איהו באורחא דנהר פקוד ומית חמרא אתא לקמיה דרבא א"ל אין באורחא דנהר פקוד אזלי מיהו לא הוו מיא אמר רבא מה לי לשקר אי בעי א"ל באורחא דנרש אזלי ואמר ליה אביי מה לי לשקר במקום עדים לא אמרינן הכי השתא התם ודאי איכא עדים דאיכא מיא הכא ודאי איטמי חששא הוא ובמקום חששא אמרינן: אם יש עדים אפילו עבד ואפילו שפחה נאמנין: ואפילו שפחה דידה מהימנא ורמינהי לא תתייחד עמו אלא ע"פ עדים ואפילו ע"פ עבד וע"פ שפחה חוץ משפחתה מפני שלבה גס בשפחתה אמר רב פפי בשבויה הקילו רב פפא אמר הא בשפחה דידה הא בשפחה דידיה ושפחה דידיה לא מהימנא הא קתני אין אדם מעיד על עצמו הא שפחה דידה מהימנא שפחתה נמי כעצמה דמי רב אשי אמר הא והא בשפחה דידה ושפחה מיחזא חזיא ושתקה התם דשתיקתה מתירתה לא מהימנא הכא דשתיקתה אוסרתה מהימנא השתא נמי אתיא ומשקרא תרתי לא עבדה כי הא דמרי בר איסק ואמרי לה חנא בר איסק אתא ליה אחא מבי חוזאה א"ל פלוג לי בנכסי דאבא א"ל לא ידענא לך אתא לקמיה דרב חסדא א"ל שפיר קאמר לך דכתיב ויכר יוסף את אחיו והם לא הכירוהו מלמד שיצא בלא חתימת זקן ובא בחתימת זקן א"ל זיל אייתי סהדי דאחוה את א"ל אית לי סהדי ומסתפינו מיניה דגברא אלמא הוא א"ל לדידיה זיל אייתינהו את דלאו אחוך הוא א"ל דינא הכי המוציא מחבירו עליו הראיה א"ל הכי דאיננא לך ולכולהו אלמי חברך השתא נמי אתו ומשקרי תרתי לא עבדי לימא כתנאי זו עדות איש ואשה תינוק ותינוקת אביה ואמה ואחיה ואחותה אבל לא בנה ובתה לא עבדה ושפחתה ותניא אידך הכל נאמנין להעיד חוץ מהימנה ובעלה דרב פפי ודרב אשי תנאי היא דרב פפא [מי] לימא תנאי היא אמר לך רב פפא כי תניא ההיא במסיחה לפי תומה כי הא דכי אתא רב דימי אמר רב חנן קרטיגנאה משתעי מעשה בא לפני רבי יהושע בן לוי ואמרי לה רבי יהושע בן לוי מישתעי מעשה בא לפני רבי באדם אחד שהיה מסיח לפי תומו ואמר אני ואמי נשבינו לבין העובדי כוכבים יצאתי לשאוב מים דעתי על אמי ללקט עצים דעתי על אמי והשיאה ר' לכהונה על פיו: **מתני'** אמר ר' זכריה בן הקצב המעון הזה לא זזה ידה מתוך ידי משעה שנכנסו עובדי כוכבים לירושלים ועד שיצאו אמרו לו אין אדם מעיד על עצמו: **גמ'** תנא ואעפ"כ ייחד לה בית בחצרו וכשהיא יוצאה יוצאה בראש בניה וכשהיא נכנסת נכנסת בסוף בניה בעי אביי מהו לעשות בגרושה כן התם הוא דבשבויה הקילו אבל הכא לא או דלמא לא שנא ת"ש דתניא המגרש את אשתו לא תנשא בשכונתו ואם

מה לי לשקר. אי בעיא אמרה נחביתי: במקום עדים. דאנן סהדי דכל שעתא איכא מיא: ודאי איטמי. בתמיה: לא תתייחד עמו. במסכת גיטין היא שכיב מרע שכתב ומסר גט לאשתו על מנת שאם מת יהא גט למפרע ולא תיזקק לחליצה לא תתייחד עמו שמא יבא עליה והוה ליה גט ישן ותנן בית הלל אוסרין לפטור בגט ישן ואיזהו גט ישן כל שנתייחד עמה מאחר שכתבו לה וטעמא גזירה שמא יאמרו גיטה קודם לבנה: ואפילו על פי עבד. דייה בעבד שהיה עמה: שלבה גס בשפחתה. ותשמש בפניה: רב אשי אמר הא והא בשפחה דידה. והיינו טעמא דבמתני' מהימנא והתם לא מהימנא דשפחה דידה מיחזא חזיא בקילקול גבירתה ושתקה: התם. גבי גט: דשתיקותה מתירתה. שאינה צריכה שתעיד לומר לא שמשה אלא שתאמר אני הייתי עמה: לא מהימנא. להיות זו מותרת על ידה דאי נמי חזיא לא מסהדא: הכא. גבי שבויה: דשתיקותה. דשפחה: אוסרתה. לגבירתה דכל כמה שאינה מעידה לומר טהורה היא מחזקינן לה בטומאה כי מסהדא ואמרה טהורה היא מהימנא דלשקורי לאו אורחא אלא למשתק: השתא נמי. כיון (ג) דרמאה לה לגבירתה או דדחלה מינה אתיא ומשקרא ואמרה טהורה היא: תרתי לא עבדא. חדא למשתק בקלקולה ועוד דמיתי ותשקר: אחא מבי חוזאה. שהלך אביו שם והוליכו עמו וגדלו שם ומת אביו וחזר לעירו ותבע חלקו בנכסי אביו: א"ל. רב חסדא להההוא אחא: שפיר קאמר לך. שאינו מכירך לפי שיצאת בלא חתימת זקן [ובאת בחתימת זקן]: ויכר יוסף את אחיו. שכשפירש מהן כבר היו חתומי זקן: א"ל. רב חסדא למרי זיל (ג) אייתינהו את. להנהו סהדי המכירין אותו ויעידו שאינו בן אביך: השתא נמי. כיון דדחלי מיניה אתו ומשקרי: תרתי לא עבדי. חדא דשתקי מלהעיד אמת וחדא דמסהדי שיקרא: לימא כתנאי. שפחתה אי מהימנא אי לא: זו עדות. עדות זו של שבויה הכל כשרים בה איש ואשה תינוק ותינוקת: חוץ מהימנה. היא עצמה: דרב פפי ורב אשי. דאמרו לעיל שפחה דידה מהימנא: ודאי תנאי היא. על כרחך יאמרו אנן דאמרי' כי מתניתא בתרייתא מדקשיא להו קמייתא: דרב פפא. דאמר לא מהימנא: מי לימא תנאי היא. כלומר דחוק הוא לומר אנא דאמרי כי מתניתא קמייתא או יוכל לתרץ מתניתא בתרייתא נמי כוותיה למימר שפחתה כעצמה דמי והרי היא בכלל חוץ מהימנה דקתני בה או תירוצא אחרינא: אמר לך רב פפא כי תניא ההיא. דקתני הכל נאמנים ואפילו שפחה דידה במסיחה לפי תומה: רב חנא קרטיגנאה משתעי. רב חנן דמן קרטיגי היה מספר מעשה זה: מתני' המעון הזה. שבועה היא: גמ' ואעפ"כ. שאסרו עליו לפי שכהן היה: כשהיא יוצאה. והוא בחצר: יוצאה בראש בניה. שיהו הבנים עמהם שלא יתייחדו: וכשהיא נכנסת נכנסת בסוף בניה. כדי שלא יהא הוא והיא בחצר והבנים מבחוץ: בגרושה. כהן שגירש את אשתו מהו לדור עמו בחצר: לא תנשא בשכונתו. לפי שמכירה ברמיזותיו וקריצותיו שמא יבואו לידי עבירה: ואם

עין משפט נר מצוה

קח א מיי' פ"ד מהל' שכירות הלכה ג סמג עשין פט טוש"ע ח"מ סימן סט:
קט ב מיי' פי"ח מהל' איסורי ביאה הל' כח טוש"ע אה"ע סי' ז סעיף י:
קי ג מיי' פ"ח מהל' גירושין הל' ב סמג עשין נ טוש"ע שם סימן קמח סעיף ב:
קיא ד מיי' פי"ח מהל' איסורי ביאה הל' יט סמג לאוין קכא טוש"ע שם סימן ז סעיף ב:
קיב ה מיי' פ"ג מהל' עדות הלכה יב סמג עשין קט טוש"ע ח"מ סי' כח סעיף ה:
קיג ו מיי' פי"ח מהל' איסורי ביאה הל' יט טוש"ע אה"ע סי' ז סעיף ב:
קיד ז מיי' שם הלכה יח טוש"ע שם סעיף א:
קטו ח מיי' שם הלכה יט טוש"ע שם סעיף ב:
קטז ט מיי' שם הלכה כה טוש"ע שם סעיף ט:
קיז י מיי' פכ"א שם הלכה כ סמג לאוין קכו טוש"ע אה"ע סי' ו סעיף ז וסי' קיט סעיף ז:

הגהות הב"ח

(א) גמ' זיל אייתי את: (ב) רש"י ד"ה השתא (דרמאה לה לגבירתה או) תא"מ וע"ב ס"פ אד וכו': (ג) ד"ה זיל אייתי את: (ד) תוס' ד"ה אמר וכו' לא נאמר כלום דרגלים כל"ל ותי' עליו נמחק: (ה) בא"ד להעיד שיעידו כל"ל ותי' עליך נמחק:

הגהות מהר"ץ לנדא

אן תוספות ד"ה במסיחה. אלא לעדות אשה כדאמר ביבמות והכא בשבויה דרבנן הקילו כצ"ל:

תורה אור השלם

א) וַיַּכֵּר יוֹסֵף אֶת אֶחָיו וְהֵם לֹא הִכִּרֻהוּ: [בראשית מב, ח]

תוספות רי"ד

איפשיטא וקולא עבדי' בעי ר"א לא נחבאתי ולא נטמאתי מהו מי אמרינן מה לי לשקר במקום חששא אי לא. ולא איפשטא ולקולא עבדי': ואם יש להן עדים אפילו עבד ואפילו שפחה ואפילו שפחה דידה מהימני ורמינהו לא תתיחד עמו אלא בפני עדים אפילו עבד ואפילו שפחה חוץ משפחתה מפני שלבה גס בשפחתה. פי' גבי שכיב מרע שנתן גט לאשתו דחיישינן שמא יבוא עליה ותהיה צריכה גט שני שאין אדם עושה בעילתו בעילת זנות. ואסיק ר"א הא והא בשפחה דידה ושפחתה מיחזא ושתקת התם דשתיקותא מתירתה לא מהימנא והכא דשתיקתה אוסרתה מהימנא השתא נמי אתיא ומשקרא תרתי לא עבדי. פי' דדא ששותקת מלהעיד האמת ועוד שתעיד שקר. תנא

מסורת הש"ס

א) [קדושין סד: וש"נ], ב) בכורות לו. ב"מ פא:, ג) [נ"ל רבה ועי' תוס' בכורות לו. ד"ה ואמר], ד) [ב"ב לב: קדושין סד: ושם נסמן], ה) גיטין עג., ו) [לעיל כג: וש"נ], ז) ב"מ לט: ע"ש, ח) שם יבמות פח., ט) נ"ל ומסתפו. יעב"ץ, י) ב"ק קיד:, כ) [פי' נשבע שבועה במקדש. ערוך וכן פי' רשב"ם בב"ב קסו.], ל) [תוספתא פרק ג], מ) [שמחות פ"ב ע"ש], נ) [ועיין היטיב תוס' גיטין עג. ד"ה לא], ס) נ"י כ"י, ע) [כל זה מבואר בסוגיא ב"ק קיד:].

ליקוטי רש"י

במקום עדים. דאנן סהדי שאין אותו הדרך בלא מים [ב"מ פא:]. לא תתייחד עמו. זה שנתן גט ואמר לה מהיום אם מתי לא תתייחד עמו שמא יבא עליה דאיכא למ"ד מיעין שמא בעל לשם קדושין וצריכה גט שני ולמאן דלא חייש נמי מ"מ פגויה היא ואסור להתייחד עם הפגויה [גיטין עג.]. בשבויה הקילו. דספיקא בעלמא היא ספק נבעלה לעובד כוכבים ונפסלה לכהונה [לעיל כג.]. אתא ליה אחא מבי חוזאה. שהלך אביו לבי חוזאי ונשא שם אשה וילדה לו בן ומת זה וחזר מרי לכאן ויורד לנכסי אביו ובא זה ואחריו לומר מרובה ותובע חלקו. שפיר קאמר לך. שאינו מכירך ואין זה רמאות שכשיצא מאצלך לא היה לך חתימת זקן ועכשיו באת בחתימת זקן. ויכר יוסף את אחיו. שכשיצא מהם היו כולם חתומי זקן והם לא הכירוהו שיצא מאצלם בלא חתימת זקן ובא בחתימת זקן [ב"מ לט:]. ומסתפינו. ומתיראים [ע"פ מעילה יז.]. דלאו אחוך הוא. אותם עדים שיש לזה לומר שאינו אחיך ומכירין בו מי הוא הביאם הנה ויעידו שאינו בן אביך או בקש עדים אחרים. תרתי לא עבדי. ישנו אחת שישתקו אבל שמים לא יעשו לא דיין שישתקו ולא יעידו האמת אלא גם שיעידו שקר [ב"ק שם]. והשיאה ר' לכהונה. ואע"ג דאוריתא היא לאוריתא היא משום זונה [ב"ק קיד:]. המעון הזה. בבית המקדש נשבע [רשב"ם קסו.].

עצים ודעתי על אמי והשיאה ר' לכהונה על פיו. פי' מסיח לפי תומו כ"ש שלא בא לפני ב"ד להעיד אלא מספר עם חבירו. והשומעים מפי מגידים לב"ד וכי מ"ש שהעיד בפני ב"ד ולא נאמן ולגבי עדות אשה נאמנים כדתנן הוחזקו להיות משיאים עד מפי עד (כד) מפי שפחה הקטן נמי נאמן כדתנן התם ר"י אומר אפילו שמע מן התינוקות אומרים הרי אנו הולכים לספוד ולקבור את איש פ' והשתא השומע מן התינוקות מעיד תינוקות עצמן לא כ"ש: [מתני'] א"ר זכריה וכו'. תנא אע"פ. פי' אע"פ שאסרה לו לפי שהיה כהן יחד לה בית בחצירו כשהיא יוצאה יוצאה בראש בניה וכשהיא נכנסת נכנסת בסוף בניה. ופי' כדי שלא יתייחדו. בעי אביי מהו לעשות כן בגרושה. פי' לדור עמה בחצר אחת התם בשבויה הקילו אבל הכא לא. א"ד ל"ש.

ועוד שתעיד שקר. תנא זו עדות כשר איש ואשה תינוק ותינוקת אביה ואמה אחיה ואחיותה אבל לא בתה ובנה. פי' זו עדות של שבויה כל אלו כשרין להעיד ואם הבן מסיח ל"ת ואומר אני ואמי נשבינו לבין העובדי כוכבים ויצאתי לשאוב מים וללקוט עצים ודעתי על אמי והשיאה ר' לכהונה על פיו. פי' מסיח ל"ת יקרא כ"ז שלא בא לפני ב"ד להעיד אלא מספר עם חבירו.

הורהנה. למדעת וכיון דהגיע זמן ולא נפדית הרי היא של עובדי כוכבים דליטיהם משום הכי בעינן עדים מעידין אותה שלא נסתרה: **נחבשה.** דליכא נחלטת להם לא בעינן עדים הואיל ועל ידי ממון הוא: **ואיכא דרמי לה מרמא.** לא מתני לה להא דרב שמואל בר רב יצחק אפירושא למתניתין בלשון לא שנו אלא רמי מירמא מתניתין וברייתא אהדדי ועלה שני רב שמואל חילוק בין יד ישראל תקיפה ליד העובדי כוכבים תקיפה: **הני נשי דגנבי.** שבעליהן ניתלין ודרך המלכות להפקיר ביתם ונשיהן: **בן דונאי.** רוצח היה ואלעזר שמו כדאמרינן בפ' עגלה ערופה (סוטה מז.) אבל נשי דגנבי הגונבים ממון לא מפקרי: **מתני' כרכום.** מצור מתרגמינן כרכומא (דברים כ): **פסולות.** אסורות לבעליהן דאשת כהן אסורה באונס: **גמ' בלשת.** חיל על שם שמחפשים כל המטמונים: **לבעול יש פנאי.** דתקיף להו ילריהו: **רבי יצחק בן אלעזר אמר.** אף בבעילה פעמים שהן מותרות: **כרכום של אותה מלכות.** אינו רוצה להשחית את בני העיר וכשכובש עיר הסמוך לממשלתו שומרה והיא לו למס עובד: **משמרות.** מקום מעמד השומרים שהעמיד המלך שלא יוכל אדם לאנשי העיר: **דמהדר למתא כו'.** שמו סביבות העיר שלשלות ברזל שישמיעו קול בהכשל איש רץ עליהם וכלבים ואווזים זועקין: **וגווזא.** מקלות וקיסמין להכשל בהן: **ולא קשיא ליה מידי.** לא חיים למיעקר איניש יחידאה ולבעול הואיל ואין הדבר הפקר: **ומאי שנא משני שבילין.** דכיון דבא לשאול עליו ועל חבירו אמר רבי יוסי טמאין הכא נמי לכולהו שרינן כי הדדי: **אחד טמא.** שיש בו קברות מפסיק כל רחבו ואין ידוע איזהו הטמא אבל כך מוחזקים באחד מהן: **ועשה טהרות.** נגע בטהרות: **טהורים.** דכל חד כי אתי לקמן תלינן ליה למימר בטהור הלך דהוה ליה ספק טומאה ברה"ר וספיקו טהור: **טמאין.** דהיכי נימא להו טהורים אתם חד מינייהו ודאי בטומאה אזל: **בבת אחת.** באו לשאול בבת אחת: **הכא נמי כו'.** ור' יהודה ור' יוסי הלכה כר' יוסי: מה

הורהנה אין נחבשה לא הוא הדין אפילו נחבשה [ה] **ומעשה שהיה כך היה איכא דאמרי אמר רבא אף אנן נמי תנינא** [ג] **העיד רבי יוסי הכהן ורבי זכריה בן הקצב על בת ישראל שהורהנה באשקלון וריחקוה בני משפחתה ועדיה מעידים עליה שלא נסתרה ושלא נטמאה ואמרו חכמים אם אתם מאמינים שהורהנה האמינו שלא נסתרה ושלא נטמאה ואם אין אתם מאמינים שלא נסתרה ושלא נטמאה אל תאמינו שהורהנה והא אשקלון דעל ידי ממון הוה וטעמא דעדים מעידין אותה הא אין עדים מעידין אותה לא מאי לאו לא שנא הורהנה ולא שנא נחבשה לא הורהנה שאני איכא דרמי לה מירמא תנן על ידי ממון מותרת לבעלה ורמינהו העיד רבי יוסי כו' והא אשקלון דע"י ממון וקתני טעמא דעדים מעידים אותה הא אין עדים מעידין אותה לא ומשני אמר רב שמואל בר רב יצחק לא קשיא כאן שיד ישראל תקיפה על עובדי כוכבים כאן שיד עובדי כוכבים תקיפה על עצמן: על ידי נפשות אסורה וכו': אמר רב כגון** (א) **נשי גנבי ולוי אמר** [א] **כגון אשתו של בן דונאי אמר חזקיה והוא שנגמר דינן להריגה ורבי יוחנן אמר** [ב] **אע"פ שלא נגמר דינן להריגה: מתני'** [ג] **עיר שכבשוה** [ד] **כרכום כל כהנות שנמצאו בתוכה פסולות** [ד] **ואם יש להן עדים אפילו עבד אפי' שפחה הרי אלו נאמנין ואין נאמן אדם על ידי עצמו: גמ' ורמינהו** [ה] **בלשת שבאה לעיר בשעת שלום חביות פתוחות אסורות סתומות מותרות בשעת מלחמה אלו ואלו מותרות לפי שאין פנאי לנסך אמר רב מרי לבעול יש פנאי לנסך אין פנאי רבי יצחק בר אלעזר משמיה דחזקיה אמר כאן** [ו] **בכרכום של אותה מלכות כאן בכרכום של מלכות אחרת של אותה מלכות נמי אי אפשר דלא** (ג) **ערק חד מינייהו אמר רב יהודה אמר שמואל כשמשמרות רואות זו את זו אי אפשר דלא ניימא פורתא אמר רבי לוי** [ז] **כגון דמהדר לה למתא שושילתא וכלבא וגווזא ואווזא אמר רבי אבא בר זבדא פליגי בה רבי יהודה נשיאה ורבנן חד אמר כאן בכרכום של אותה מלכות כאן בכרכום של מלכות אחרת ולא קשיא ליה ולא מידי וחד קשיא ליה כל הני ומשני כגון דמהדר ליה למתא שושילתא וכלבא וגווזא ואווזא אמר רב אידי בר אבין אמר ר' יצחק בר אשיאן** [ח] **אם יש שם מחבואה אחת מצלת על הכהנות כולן בעי רבי ירמיה אינה מחזקת אלא אחת מהו מי אמרינן** [ט] **כל חדא וחדא היינו הא או דלמא לא אמרינן ומאי שנא משני** [י] **שבילין אחד טמא ואחד טהור והלך באחד מהן ועשה טהרות ובא חבירו והלך בשני ועשה טהרות רבי יהודה אומר אם נשאל זה בפני עצמו וזה בפני עצמו טהורות שניהם כאחת טמאות ר' יוסי אומר בין כך ובין כך טמאין ואמר רבא ואיתימא ר' יוחנן** [י] **בבת אחת דברי הכל טמאין בזה אחר זה דברי הכל טהורים לא נחלקו אלא בבא לישאל עליו ועל חבירו מר מדמי ליה לבבת אחת ומר** [כ] **מדמי ליה לבזה אחר זה והכא נמי כיון דשרי להו לכולהו כבת אחת דמי הכי השתא התם ודאי איכא טומאה הכא מי יימר דאיטמי בעי רב אשי אמרה לא נחבאתי ולא נטמאתי מהו מי אמרינן מה**

כאן בכרכום של אותה מלכות. פי' שיושבין בטח לפי שאין אחריהן מחנה ויש להם פנאי לנסך ולבעול אבל בלשת של מלכות אחרת שאימת מלכות שבאו בגבולה עליהם אין להן פנאי וכן פי' ר"ח ור"ת וכן מוכח בירושלמי ופריך כרכום של אותה מלכות אי אפשר דלא ערקא חדא מינייהו והוה לן למשריינהו לכולהו ולמיתלי לקולא דבשבויה הקילו דלאמרינן בסמוך אם יש מחבואה אחת מצלת על כל הכהנות כולן אע"ג דמספקא לן באינה מחזקת אלא אחת הכא פשיטא לן דשרו דהתם לא ודאי נחבאת אבל הכא ודאי ערקא ולפי' הקונטרס קשה טובא חדא דפריך נתלי לחומרא וגבי מחבואה תלינן לקולא ועוד דמה מתרץ מהדר למתא כו' ואין אדם נכנס לשם והא קתני בלשת שנכנסה לעיר ועוד כיון דלהסית דע"ז פריך הוה ליה למימר אי אפשר דלא ערק חד מינייהו ונסך ועוד דהתם מפרש טעמא לפי שאין פנאי לנסך וליה ליה טעמא לפי שאין כרכוס של אותה מלכות רוצה להשחית את בני העיר [ועוד מאי שנא שעת מלחמה משעת שלום] ויש ליישב לפי שיטת הקונטרס דרבי יצחק בן אלעזר לא אתי לשנויי מתני' אהסית דע"ז אלא את ליה סיועא דרב מרי ומתניתין דהתם נמי בכרכוס של מלכות אחרת ולא בא אלא לפרושי מתניתין וכן משמע בפרק במרה דע"ז (דף עא.) דפריך התם ממתניתין דהכא אמתניתין דבלשת ולא מייתי התם דרבי יצחק: **והלך** באחד מהם ועשה טהרות. להכי נקט ועשה טהרות דלענין האדם אלו מוקיקים שניהם לטבול ולהזות פן יבואו לידי טומאה ודאי אם יגעו שניהם בככר אחד לכך קאמר להו זילו טבילו דהא נהרא קמייכו ועוד דמשום דבעי למתני[ז] סיפא זה וטבל טהור הלך בשני ועשה טהרות הרי אלו טהורות ואלו תלויות קיימות הראשונים אלו ואלו תלויות ואם לא טהר ביניתים הראשונות תלויות והשניות ישרפו [ח]:

ואם נשאל זה בפני עצמו וזה בפני עצמו טהורות. לא שיאכלם אדם אחד דאם כן יאכל ודאי טומאה דהכי אמרינן בשבועות בפ"ב (דף יט.) הלך בראשון ולא נכנס בשני ונכנס חייב דטמא הוא ממה נפשך: **בבא** לישאל עליו ועל חבירו. אין לפרש שבא לישאל בבת אחת דהתם מודו כולי עלמא דטמאות מכל שכן דבאו לישאל שניהם בבת אחת אלא איירי שאל על עצמו וטהרוהו ואח"כ בא לישאל על חבירו דמר מדמי ליה לבת אחת כיון ששאל על שניהם במעמד אחד ומר מדמי ליה לזה אחר זה כיון שטיהרוהו קודם והכא נמי כיון דשרו לכולהו כבת אחת דמי אף על פי שאין בא לפנינו אלא על אחת מ"מ הדבר ידוע לכל שהרבה כהנות היו והוי כאילו בא לישאל על כולם בבת אחת והכא מודו כ"ע ונחנס דחק בקונטרס לפרש כר' יוסי: לא

קב א ב מיי' פי"ח מהל' איסורי ביאה הלכה ל טוש"ע אה"ע סימן ז סעיף יא בהג"ה:

קג ג מיי' פי"ח מהל' א"ב הלכה כו טור ש"ע שם סעיף :

קד ד מיי' שם הל' יט טוש"ע שם סעיף א:

קה ה מיי' פי"ב מהל' מאכלות אסורות הלכה כד סמג לאוין קמח טוש"ע י"ד סי' קכט סעיף יב:

קו ו ז ח ט מיי' פי"ח מהל' איסורי ביאה הלכה כח כט טוש"ע אה"ע סי' ז סעיף י:

קז י כ מיי' פי"ט מהל' אבות הטומאה הלכה כ:

הגהות הב"ח

(א) גמ' כגון הני נשי דגנבי: (ב) שם דלא (ערק) תז"מ. ונ"ב ס"א עקר וכן משמע מפרש"י:

גליון הש"ס

רש"י ד"ה בלשת וכו' שמחפשין. כי כפסוק ויחפש ברלשית מ"ד התרגום ובלש:

תוספות רי"ד

ומפקרי לה. **הד** ע"י נפשות א"ר כגון נשי דגנבי אמר חזקיה והוא שנגמר דינם להריגה פי' שבעליהן נתלו ודרך המלכות להפקיר טפס נשיהם ור"י אמר אעפ"י שלא נגמר דינן להריגה. והל' כחזקיה דהוא רביה דר' יוחנן: **עיר שכבשוה כרכום.** פי' חיל הצרים עליה. מצור תרגומו כרכום כל כהנות שבתוכה פסולו' לבעליהן פי' דבחזקת שנבעלו קיימו ואנוסה אסורה לכהן ואם יש להן עדים שלא נבעלו אפילו עבד אפילו שפחה הרי אלו נאמנים ואין אדם נאמן ע"י עצמו לא האשה להעיד על עצמה ולא הבעל להעיד על אשתו **ורמינהו** בולשת שנכנסה לעיר. פי' חיל ונקרא כן ע"ש שמחפשים את כל המטמוניות תרגום ויחפש ובלש בזמן שלום חביות פתוחות אסורות וסתומות מותרות בשעת מלחמה אלו ואלו מותרות לפי שאין פנאי לנסך. **אמר** ר"מ לנסך אין פנאי לבעול יש פנאי דיצרא דעבירה תקיף מיין נסך ר"י בן אלעזר משמיה דחזקי' אמר כאן בכרכום של אותה מלכות אינן יראים ויש להם פנאי לבעול ולנסך. אבל של מלכות אחרת יראים [שמא] יבוא חיל מאיזה מלכות לעזור להן וממהרים לשלול ולהבריח ואין להן פנאי לא לבעול ולא לנסך. **א"ר** אידי ב"א אר"י ב"א אם יש שם מחבואה א' [מצלת] על כל הכהנות ומותרות כלן: **בעי ר"י** אם אינה מחזקת אלא א' מהן מהו. מי אמרינן כל חדא וחדא היינו האי א"ד לא אמרינן ולא איפשיטא

ליקוטי רש"י

כאן שניהם בימד הוה מסקינן ליה ומוקמינן ליה אחזקיה קמייתא דמוחזק בה בלאו דכהן הוא וגלוליות לא מיישכין ורשב"ג כו' נתן. **ובפלוגתא דהני תנאי.** ר' נתן ורבנן. **דתניא אין עדותן מצטרפת.** אין לריך כהן בהאי מחלוקת דרבי יהושע בן קרחה ורבנן אלא כך היא ברייתא שלמה בשלישה זה בורר ומשום גררת דשיפת נקט רישא. **אפי' בזה אחר זה.** אחד אומר ביום ראשון לוה פלוני מפלוני מנה ואחד אומר ביום שני דמ"מ אמנה קא מסהדי ות"ק סבר אמנה דקא מסהיד האי לא קא מסהיד האי וה"ל לגבי מנה תלי עדות ועטמייהו מפרש שפיר בסנהדרין מקרא ומסברא. **ואין עדותן וכו' עד שיעידו שניהם כאחד.** להתקבל בב"ד ואפי' רלו שניהם כאחד על שעידו כל אחד בפני ב"ד ופלוגתא אחריתי היא ולא ר' יהושע ולא ר' אלעזר ורשב"ג בפלוגתא דר"נ ורבנן פליגי [שם לב.]. לספוק הדין על פיהם. וקמת לא קאי אלא ר' יהושע בן קרחה קאמר לה [סנהדרין ל.]. **על ידי ממון.** שהיתה מייבת ממון. **מותרת לבעלה.** דקסבר לי בעילה כי מו לא פרע כי בעילה מידי. **על ידי נפשות.** להריגה. **אסורה לבעלה.** היכלה דלא מירתת להפסיד ממונו אפקורי מפקר לה וממישגין שמא נבעלה לאחד מהן ברלון ואית דמוקרי לה בשמא כהן דמיתסרא באונס ולאשון עיקר דבכתובות (דף כו) מוכח דבאשת ישראל קאי [ע"ז כג.].

[ע"כ שייך לדף כו:]

כל כהנות שנמצאו בתוכה פסולות. לבעליהן דאשת כהן אסורה אף באונס אבל אשת ישראל לא [ע"ז עא.]. **אפילו עבד אפי' שפחה.** דבשבויה הקלינו חכמים על אחד להקל ואפילו עבד או שפחה כדקתני מתני' אם יש להן עדים אפילו עבד כו' [לעיל כג:]. **בלשת.** חילות גיים הבא לעיר על שם שמחפשין ובולשים את העיר קרי לה בולשת [שבת מא.]. חיל על שם שמחפשין ומוחרין קרי להו בולשת כדמתרגמינן (בראשית לא) ויחפש ובלש [ע"ז ע:]. בולשת חיל שמחפשין ובוחזין כדמתרגמינן ויחפש ובלש [נדה יג.]. **בשעת שלום.** כגון שהוא של אותה מלכות [שבת שם]. **לפי שאין פנאי לנסך.** הא הכא דשעת מלחמה היא

מסורת הש"ס

א) [עירובין סה: וש"נ], ב) עדיות פרק ח מ"ב, ג) ע"ז עא., ד) [בערוך איתא ברקום בקו"ף], ה) שם ע: שבת מא. נדה יג., ו) טהרות פ"ה מ"ה פסחים י., ז) [למימנא סיפא כרישא כל"ל. מהרש"א], ח) [וע"ע תוס' פסחים י. ד"ה הלך].

ולא לבעול. **לנסך אין פנאי.** דילך הניסוך לא תקיף להו וטרודין במלחמה [ע"ז עא.]. **ניימא.** מנמנמת [סנהדרין ז.]. **אחד טמא.** קבר מוטל בו לרחבו וממלא את כולו ואין עובר בו שלא יאהיל. **והלך באחד מהן ועשה טהרות.** נגע וקתני אחרות דיש פנאי לבעול. **ובא חבירו והלך בשני.** יודעין הן שבשביל שהלך זה לא הלך זה להשתא ודאי אחד מהן טמא. **אם נשאל.** כל אחד לחכם ספקו בפני עצמו. **טהורות.** ואין בית דין יכול לטמאו דקיימא לן בספק טומאה ברשות הרבים ספקו טהור. **בבת אחת** והוראה אחת יש לנו לומר טמאין או טהורין אי אפשר לנו לומר להם טהורים אתם שהרי האחד ודאי טמא. **בזה אחר זה דברי הכל טהורים.** אע"פ שכל אחד אומר לפנינו כך היה המעשה שלי ושל חבירי אבל איני נשאל אלא על עליו ועל חבירו וכו' לבבת אחת. מה תאמר על שניהם לפניך לריך אתה הוראה אחת לשניהם או טמאין אתם או טהורין אתם והרי אין אתה יכול לומר טהורין אתם. **ומר מדמי ליה** וכו'. הואיל ואין כאן שואל אלא אחד משיבין לו טהור אתה שהרי אחת ביאה הוא ומעלמו יבין שאף חבירו כמוהו אבל כששניהן שואלין בתוך כדי דיבור לריך אתה להשיב לשניהן כאחד [פסחים י.].

The Gemara presents another inquiry relating to a city with a hiding place:

בָּעֵי רַב אַשִׁי – Rav Ashi inquired: אָמְרָה לֹא נֶחְבֵּאתִי וְלֹא נִטְמֵאתִי מַהוּ – If [a particular woman] said, "I did not hide myself, but I was not violated," מִי אַמְרִינַן – do we apply[42]

NOTES

that a woman was violated. Even R' Yose would agree, then, that there is no difficulty in ruling all the wives permitted to their husbands.]

[Although the Gemara comes to no conclusion regarding Rav Yirmiyah's question, *Rif* rules that even if the hiding place holds only a single woman, all the women of the city are permitted to Kohanim. For elucidation, see *Rosh; Ritva; Ran.*]

42. Literally, *do we say,* and likewise on 27b.

מסורת הש"ס

א) [עירובין סה: וש"נ], ב) עדיות פרק ח מ"ב, ג) ע"ז עא., ד) [בערוך איתא כרקום בקו"ף], ה) שם ע: שבת מא. נדה יג., ו) טהרות פ"ה מ"ה פסחים י., ז) [למיתנא סיפא כרישא כצ"ל. מהרש"א], ח) [וע"ע תוס' פסחים י. ד"ה הלך].

הורהנה אין נחבשה לא הוא הדין אפילו נחבשה [א] ומעשה שהיה כך היה איכא דאמרי אמר רבא אף אנן נמי תנינא [ב] העיד רבי יוסי הכהן ורבי זכריה בן הקצב על בת ישראל שהורהנה באשקלון וריחקוה בני משפחתה ועדיה מעידים עליה שלא נסתרה ושלא נטמאה ואמרו חכמים אם אתם מאמינים שהורהנה האמינו שלא נסתרה ושלא נטמאה ואם אין אתם מאמינים שלא נסתרה ושלא נטמאה אל תאמינו שהורהנה והא אשקלון דעל ידי ממון הוה וטעמא דעדים מעידין אותה הא אין עדים מעידין אותה לא מאי לאו לא שנא הורהנה ולא שנא נחבשה לא הורהנה שאני איכא דרמי לה מירמא תנן על ידי ממון מותרת לבעלה ורמינהו העיד רבי יוסי כו' והא אשקלון דע"י ממון וקתני טעמא דעדים מעידים אותה הא אין עדים מעידין אותה לא ומשני אמר רב שמואל בר רב יצחק לא קשיא כאן שיד ישראל תקיפה על עובדי כוכבים כאן שיד עובדי כוכבים תקיפה על עצמן: על ידי נפשות אסורה וכו': אמר רב כגון (א) נשי גנבי ולוי אמר [א] כגון אשתו של בן דונאי אמר חזקיה והוא שנגמר דינן להריגה ורבי יוחנן אמר [ב] אע"פ שלא נגמר דינן להריגה: מתני' [ג] עיר שכבשוה [ד] כרכום כל כהנות שנמצאו בתוכה פסולות [ה] ואם יש להן עדים אפילו עבד אפי' שפחה הרי אלו נאמנין ואין נאמן אדם על ידי עצמו: גמ' ורמינהו [ו] בלשת שבאה לעיר בשעת שלום חביות פתוחות אסורות סתומות מותרות בשעת מלחמה אלו ואלו מותרות לפי שאין פנאי לנסך אמר רב מרי לבעול יש פנאי לנסך אין פנאי רבי יצחק בר אלעזר משמיה דחזקיה אמר כאן [ז] בכרכום של אותה מלכות כאן בכרכום של מלכות אחרת של אותה מלכות נמי אי אפשר דלא (ב) ערק חד מינייהו אמר רב יהודה אמר שמואל כשמשמרות רואות זו את זו אי אפשר דלא ניימא פורתא אמר רבי לוי [ז] כגון דמהדר לה למתא שושילתא וכלבא וגווזא ואווזא אמר רבי אבא בר זבדא פליגי בה רבי יהודה נשיאה ורבנן חד אמר כאן בכרכום של אותה מלכות כאן בכרכום של מלכות אחרת ולא קשיא ליה ולא מידי וחד קשיא ליה כל הני ומשני כגון דמהדר ליה למתא שושילתא וכלבא וגווזא ואווזא אמר רב אידי בר אבין אמר ר' יצחק בר אשיאן [ח] אם יש שם מחבואה אחת מצלת על הכהנות כולן בעי רבי ירמיה אינה מחזקת אלא אחת מהו מי אמרינן [ט] כל חדא וחדא היינו הא או דלמא לא אמרינן ומאי שנא משני [י] שבילין אחד טמא ואחד טהור והלך באחד מהן ועשה טהרות ובא חבירו והלך בשני ועשה טהרות רבי יהודה אומר אם נשאל זה בפני עצמו וזה בפני עצמו טהורות שניהם כאחת טמאות ר' יוסי אומר בין כך ובין כך טמאין ואמר רבא ואיתימא ר' יוחנן [כ] בבת אחת דברי הכל טמאין בזה אחר זה דברי הכל טהורים לא נחלקו אלא בבא לישאל עליו ועל חבירו מר מדמי ליה לבבת אחת ומר [ל] מדמי ליה לבזה אחר זה והכא נמי כיון דשרי להו לכולהו כבת אחת דמי הכי השתא התם ודאי איכא טומאה הכא מי יימר דאיטמי בעי רב אשי אמרה לא נחבאתי ולא נטמאתי מהו מי אמרינן מה

הורהנה. למדעת וכיון דהגיע זמן ולא נפדית הרי היא של עובדי כוכבים בדיניהם משום הכי בעינן עדים מעידין אותה שלא נסתרה: נחבשה. דאינה נחלטת להם לא בעינן עדים הואיל ועל ידי ממון הוא: ואיכא דרמי לה מרמא. לא מתני לה להא דרב שמואל בר רב יצחק אפירושא דמתניתין בלשון לא שנו אלא רמי מירמא מתניתין וברייתא אהדדי ועלה שני רב שמואל חילוק בין יד ישראל תקיפה ליד העובדי כוכבים תקיפה: הני נשי דגנבי. שבעליהן ניתלין ודרך המלכות להפקיר ביתם ונשיהן: בן דונאי. רוצח היה ואלעזר שמו כדאמרינן בפ' עגלה ערופה (סוטה מז.) אבל נשי דגנבי הגונבים ממון לא מפקרי: מתני' כרכום. מצור מתרגמינן כרכומא (דברים כ): פסולות. אסורות לבעליהן דאשת כהן אסורה באונס: גמ' בלשת. חיל על שם [ט] שמחפשים כל המטמונים: לבעול יש פנאי. דתקיף להו יצרייהו: רבי יצחק בן אלעזר אמר. אף בבעילה פעמים שהן מותרות: כרכום של אותה מלכות. אינו רוצה להשחית את בני העיר וכשכובש עיר הסמוך לממשלתו שומרה והיא לו לעם עובד: משמרות. מקום מעמד השומרים שהעמיד המלך שלא יקבל אדם באנשי העיר: דמהדר למתא כו'. שמו סביבות העיר שלשלות ברזל שישמיעו קול בהכשל איש רגל עליהם וכלבים ואווזים זועקין: וגווזא. מקלות וקיסמין להכשל בהן: ולא קשיא ליה מידי. לא חיש למיעקר איניש יחידאה ולבעול הואיל ואין הדבר הפקר: ומאי שנא משני שבילין. דכיון דבא לשאול עליו ועל חבירו אמר רבי יוסי טמאין הכא נמי לכולהו סרינן כי הדדי: אחד טמא. שיש בו קברות מפסיק כל רחבו ואין ידוע איזהו הטמא אבל כך מוחזקים באחד מהן: ועשה טהרות. נגע בטהרות: טהורים. דכל חד כי אתי לקמן תלינן ליה למימר בטהור הלך דהוה ליה ספק טומאה בר"ה וספיקו טהור: טמאין. דהיכי נימא להו טהורים אתם חד מינייהו ודאי בטומאה הלך: בבת אחת. באו לשאול בבת אחת: הכא נמי כו'. ור' יהודה ור' יוסי הלכה כר' יוסי: מה

כאן בכרכום של אותה מלכות. פי' שיושבין בטח לפי שאין אחריהן מחנה ויש פנאי לנסך ולבעול אבל בלשת של מלכות אחרת שאימת מלכות שבאו בגבולה עליהם אין להן פנאי וכן פי' ר"ח ור"ת וכן מוכח בירושלמי ופריך כרכום של אותה מלכות אי אפשר דלא ערקא חדא מינייהו והוה לן למשרינהו לכולהו ולמיתלי לקולא דבשבויה הקילו כדאמרינן בסמוך אם יש מחבואה אחת מצלת על כל הכהנות כולן אע"ג דמספקא לן בשינה מחזקת אלא אחת הכא פשיטא לן דשרו דהתם לא ודאי נחבאת אבל הכא ודאי ערקא ולפי' הקונטרס קשה טובא חדא דפריך נתלי לחומרא ובשבי מחבואה תלינן לקולא ועוד דמה מתרץ דמהדר למתא כו' ואין אדם נכנס לשם והא קתני בלשת שנכנסה לעיר ועוד כיון דאההיא דע"ז פריך הוה ליה למימר אי אפשר דלא ערק חד מינייהו ונסך ועוד דהתם מפרש טעמא לפי שאין פנאי לנסך ולית ליה טעמא לפי שאין כרכום של אותה מלכות רוצה להשחית את בני העיר [ועוד מאי שנא שעת מלחמה משעת שלום] ויש ליישב לפי שיטת הקונטרס דרבי יצחק בן אלעזר לא אתי לשנויי מתני' דההיא דע"ז דלא אית ליה שינויא דרב מרי ומתניתין דהתם נמי בכרכום של מלכות אחרת ולא בא אלא לפרושי מתניתין וכן משמע בפרק בתרא דע"ז (דף עא.) דפריך התם ממתניתין דהכא ולא מייתי התם לדרבי יצחק:

והלך באחד מהן ועשה טהרות. להכי נקט ועשה טהרות דלענין האדם אנו מזקיקים שניהם לטבול ולהזות פן יבואו לידי טומאה ודאי אם יגעו שניהם בככר אחד לכך אומר להו זילו טבילו דהא נהרא קמייכו ועוד דמשום דבעי למתני [ז] סיפא הזה וטבל טהור הלך בשני ועשה טהרות הרי אלו טהורות ואם קיימות הראשונים אלו ואלו תלויות ואם לא טהר בינתים הראשונות תלויות והשניות ישרפו [ח]:

ואם נשאל זה בפני עצמו וזה בפני עצמו טהורות. לא שיאכלם אדם אחד דאם כן יאכל ודאי טומאה דהכי אמרינן בשבועות בפ"ב (דף יט.) הלך בראשון ולא נכנס ובשני ונכנס חייב דטמא הוא ממה נפשך: **בבא** לישאל עליו ועל חבירו. אין פרש שבא לישאל בבת אחת דהתם מודו כולי עלמא דטמאות מכל שכן דבאו לישאל שניהם בבת אחת אלא מיירי ששאל על עצמו וטהרוהו ואח"כ בא לישאל על חבירו דמר מדמי ליה לבת אחת כיון ששאל על שניהם במעמד אחד ומר מדמי ליה לזה אחר זה כיון שטיהרוהו קודם והכא נמי כיון דשרו לכולהו כבת אחת דמי אף על פי שאין באו לפנינו אלא על אחת מ"מ הדבר ידוע לכל שהרבה כהנות הי' והוי כאילו באו לישאל על כולם בבת אחת והכא מודו כ"ע ובחנם דחק בקונטרס לפרש כר' יוסי: לא

ליקוטי רש"י

באו שניהם ביחד הוה מסקינן ליה ומוקמינן ליה אחזקיה קמייתא דמוחזק לן באבוה דכהן הוא ולזילותא לא חיישינן ורשב"ג כר' נתן. ובפלוגתא דהני תנאי. ר' נתן ורבנן. דתניא אין עדותן מצטרפת. אין צריך כאן בהאי מחלוקת דרבי יהושע בן קרחה ורבנן אלא כך היא ברייתא שלימה בשילהי זה בורר ומשום גררא דסיפא נקט רישא. אפי' בזה אחר זה. אחד אומר ביום ראשון לוה פלוני מפלוני מנה ואחד אומר ביום שני ראיתיו גם אני שלוה ממנו דמ"מ אמנה קא מסהדי ות"ק סבר אמנה דקא מסהיד האי לא קא מסהיד האי וה"ל לגבי מנה חצי עדות וטעמייהו מפרש שפיר בסנהדרין מקרא ומסברא. ואין עדותן וכו' עד שיעידו שניהם כאחד. להתקבל בב"ד ואפי' ראו שניהם כאחד עד שיעידו שניהם כאחד בפני ב"ד ופלוגתא אחריתי היא ולא ר' יהושע בן קרחה קאמר לה ור' אלעזר ורשב"ג בפלוגתא דר"נ ורבנן פליגי [שם לב.]. לפסוק הדין על פיהם. וסתמא הוא ולא ר' יהושע בן קרחה קאמר לה [סנהדרין ל.]. על ידי ממון. שהיתה חייבת ממון. מותרת לבעלה. דסבר אי בעילנא לה תו לא פרע לי בעלה מידי. על ידי נפשות. שנתחייבה הריגה. אסורה לבעלה. היכא דלא מירתת להפסד ממונו אפקורי מפקר לה וחיישינן שמא נבעלה לאחד מהן ברצון ואית דמוקמי לה באשת כהן דמיתסרא באונס וראשון עיקר דבכתובות (דף כו) מוכח דבאשת ישראל קאי [ע"ז כג.]. [ע"כ שייך לדף כו:] כל כהנות שנמצאו בתוכה פסולות. לבעליהן דאשת כהן אסורה אף באונס אבל אשת ישראל לא [ע"ז עא.]. אפילו עבד אפי' שפחה. דבשבויה האמינו חכמים עד אחד להקל ואפילו עבד או שפחה כדקתני מתני' אם יש להן עדים אפילו עבד כו' [לעיל כג:]. בלשת. חיילות גיים הבא לעיר על שם שמחפשין ובולשים את העיר קרי לה בולשת [שבת מא.]. חיל על שם שמחפשין ומותרין קרי להו בולשת כדמתרגמינן (בראשית לא) ויחפש ובלש [ע"ז ע:]. בולשת חיל שמחפשין ובוחין כדמתרגמינן ויחפש ובלש [נדה יג.]. בשעת שלום. כגון שהוא של אותה מלכות [שבת שם]. לפי שאין פנאי לנסך. הא הכא דשעת מלחמה היא וקתני אסורות דיש פנאי לבעול. לנסך אין פנאי. דילך הניסוך לא תקיף להו יצרייהו כל כך ועוד דטרידי במלחמה [ע"ז עא.]. ניימא. מתנמנמת [סנהדרין ז.]. אחד טמא. קבר מוטל בו לרחבו וממלא את כולו ואין עובר בו שלא יאהיל. והלך באחד מהן ועשה טהרות. נגע בטהרות אחר כך. ובא חבירו והלך בשני. ויודעין הן שבשביל שהלך זה לא הלך זה דהשתא ודאי אחד מהן טמא. אם נשאל. כל אחד לחכם בפני עצמו. טהורות. ואין בית דין יכול לטהרו דקדימה לו בספק טומאה ברשות הרבים ספקו טהור. שניהם כאחת. הואיל והוראה אחת היא לשניהם כאחד ודאי אחד מהן טמא ואין יכולים לטהר את שניהם. עליו ועל חבירו. בזה אחר זה אבל שאל על עצמו תחלה ואח"כ בא לישאל על חבירו דמר מדמי ליה לבבת אחת וכו'. הואיל ואין כאן שואל אלא אחד מטהרין לו טהור ולחבירו לא שכן אחד שואל עליהם ואינו יכול לטהר את שניהם [פסחים י.].

עין משפט נר מצוה

קב א ב מיי' פי"ח מהל' איסורי ביאה הלכה ל טוש"ע אה"ע סימן ז סעיף יא בהג"ה:
קג ג מיי' פי"ח מהל' א"ב הלכה כו טור ש"ע שם סעיף י:
קד ד מיי' שם הל' יט טוש"ע שם סעיף א:
קה ה מיי' פי"ב מהל' מאכלות אסורות הלכה כד סמג לאוין קמח טוש"ע י"ד סי' קכט סעיף יב:
קו ו ז ח ט מיי' פי"ח מהל' איסורי ביאה הלכה מ כח כט טוש"ע אה"ע סי' ז סעיף י:
קז י כ מיי' פי"ט מהל' אבות הטומאה הלכה ב:

הגהות הב"ח

(א) גמ' כגון הני נשי דגנבי: (ב) שם דלא (ערק) תז"מ. ונ"ב ס"א עקר וכן משמע מפרש"י:

גליון הש"ס

רש"י ד"ה בלשת וכו' שמחפשין. כי בפסוק ויחפש בראשית מ"ד התרגום ובלש:

תוספות רי"ד

ומפקרי לה. ה"ד ע"י נפשות א"ר כגון נשי דגנבי אמר חזקיה והוא שנגמר דינם להריגה פי' שבעליהן נתלו ודרך המלכות להפקיר טפם ונשיהם ור"י אמר אעפ"י שלא נגמר דינן להריגה. והל' כחזקיה דהוא רביה דר' יוחנן: עיר שכבשוה כרכום. פי' חיל הצרים עליה. מצור תרגומו כרכום כל כהנות שבתוכה פסולו' לבעליהן פי' דבחזקת שנבעלו קיימו ואנוסה אסורה לכהן ואם יש להן עדים שלא נבעלו אפילו עבד אפילו שפחה הרי אלו נאמנים ואין אדם נאמן ע"י עצמו לא האשה להעיד על עצמה ולא הבעל להעיד על אשתו ורמינהו בולשת שנכנסה לעיר. פי' חיל ונקרא כן ע"ש שמחפשים את כל המטמוניות תרגום ויחפש ובלש בזמן שלום חביות פתוחות אסורות וסתומות מותרת בשעת מלחמה אלו ואלו מותרות לפי שאין פנאי לנסך. אמר ר"מ לנסך אין פנאי לבעול יש פנאי דיצרא דעבירה תקיף מיין נסך ר"י בן אלעזר משמיה דחזקי' אמר כאן בכרכום של אותה מלכות אינן יראים ויש להם פנאי לבעול ולנסך. אבל של מלכות אחרת יראים [שמא] יבוא חיל מאיזה מלכות לעזור להן וממהרים לשלול ולהבריח ואין להן פנאי לא לבעול ולא לנסך. א"ר אידי ב"א אר"י ב"א אם יש שם מחבואה א' [מצלת] על כל הכהנות ומותרות כלן: בעי ר"י אם אינה מחזקת אלא א' מהן מהו. מי אמרינן כל חדא וחדא היינו האי א"ד לא אמרינן ולא איפשיטא

The Gemara presents an inquiry:

בָּעֵי רַבִּי יִרְמְיָה – **Rav Yirmiyah inquired:** אֵינָהּ מַחֲזֶקֶת אֶלָּא אַחַת מַהוּ – **If [the hiding place] cannot contain more than a single woman, what is [the law]?** מִי אָמְרִינַן כָּל חֲדָא וַחֲדָא הַיְינוּ הָא – **Do we say** regarding **each and every one** of the women, **"This is the one** who made use of the hiding place," in which case all the women of the city would be permitted? אוֹ דִּלְמָא לֹא אָמְרִינַן – **Or perhaps we do not say** this, but suspect each woman of having been violated.

The Gemara asks:

וּמַאי שְׁנָא מִשְּׁנֵי שְׁבִילִין – **But how is this different from** the case mentioned in the following Mishnah:[31] If there were TWO PATHS, אֶחָד טָמֵא וְאֶחָד טָהוֹר – ONE *TAMEI* due to a grave across it AND ONE *TAHOR,* וְהָלַךְ בְּאֶחָד מֵהֶן וְעָשָׂה טְהָרוֹת – AND SOMEONE WALKED DOWN ONE OF THEM AND then DEALT WITH (i.e. touched) *TAHOR* FOOD, וּבָא חֲבֵירוֹ – AND HIS FELLOW CAME וְהָלַךְ בַּשֵּׁנִי וְעָשָׂה טְהָרוֹת – AND WALKED DOWN THE SECOND [PATH] AND then DEALT WITH other *TAHOR* FOOD.[32] רַבִּי יְהוּדָה אוֹמֵר – R' YEHUDAH SAYS: אִם נִשְׁאַל זֶה בִּפְנֵי עַצְמוֹ וְזֶה בִּפְנֵי עַצְמוֹ – IF EACH OF THEM INQUIRED about his status ON HIS OWN, טְהוֹרוֹת – THEY ARE both *TAHOR,* because of doubt.[33] שְׁנֵיהֶם כְּאַחַת – If BOTH inquired about their status TOGETHER, טְמֵאוֹת – THEY ARE both *TAMEI.* For a sage cannot simultaneously rule two people *tahor* when one of them is definitely *tamei.*[34] רַבִּי יוֹסֵי אוֹמֵר – But R' YOSE SAYS: בֵּין כָּךְ וּבֵין כָּךְ טְמֵאִין – EITHER WAY THEY ARE both *TAMEI.* וְאָמַר רָבָא – **And Rava said** regarding this Mishnah, וְאִיתֵּימָא רַבִּי יוֹחָנָן – **and some say it was R' Yochanan:** בְּבַת אַחַת דִּבְרֵי הַכֹּל טְמֵאִין – If the two individuals come **together, everyone agrees that they are** both *tamei.* For the sage must rule regarding both of them, and he cannot simultaneously rule them *tahor.* בְּזֶה אַחַר זֶה דִּבְרֵי הַכֹּל טְהוֹרִים – If they come **one after the other, everyone agrees that they are** both *tahor.* For the sage rules regarding each separately, and each is *tahor* because of doubt.[35] לֹא נֶחְלְקוּ אֶלָּא בְּבָא לִישָּׁאֵל עָלָיו וְעַל חֲבֵירוֹ – The disagreement is only in a case **where one comes to inquire about himself and about his fellow.**[36] מַר מְדַמֵּי לֵיהּ לְבְבַת אַחַת – **The one master** (i.e. R' Yose) **compares it to** a case of them coming **together,** since the ruling must be made regarding both of them. וּמַר מְדַמֵּי לֵיהּ לְבְזֶה אַחַר זֶה – **But the other master** (i.e. R' Yehudah) **compares it to** a case of them coming **one after the other,** for the ruling can be made for one and not the other.[37]

We see that according to R' Yose, even when the two individuals do not actually come at once, a single *tahor* ruling cannot encompass them both, since one of them is definitely *tamei.*

וְהָכָא נַמִּי – **Here too, then,** כֵּיוָן דְּשָׁרֵי לְהוּ לְכוּלְּהוּ – **since they are** simultaneously **permitting all of [these women]** to their husbands even though some of them have definitely been violated,[38] כְּבַת אַחַת דָּמֵי – **it is comparable to** the case of the two people coming **together.**[39]

It emerges that according to R' Yose, these women remain forbidden to their husbands. Since it is a rule that in a dispute between R' Yehudah and R' Yose, we follow R' Yose,[40] the inquiry is resolved.

The Gemara rejects this resolution:

הָכִי הַשְׁתָּא – **Now, is this** a comparison? הָתָם וַדַּאי אִיכָּא טוּמְאָה – **Over there,** i.e. in the case of the two paths, **there is definitely** ***tumah*** on one of the paths. Since one of the travelers is positively *tamei,* we cannot simultaneously rule them both *tahor.* הָכָא מִי יֵימַר דְּאִיטַּמִּי – **Here,** however, in the case of the Kohanic wives, **who says that** any of **them were** actually **violated** in the first place? Since they may all in reality be permitted, there is no difficulty in issuing a ruling to that effect.[41]

NOTES

31. *Tohoros* 5:5.

32. The grave stretched across the width of one of the paths so that it was impossible to walk by without passing over it and being contaminated. Since they know that they walked down different paths, it is clear that one of them definitely became *tamei* (*Rashi* to *Pesachim* 10a ד״ה היינו שני שבילין וד״ה והלך בשני).

33. The rule is that when there is an uncertainty concerning *tumah* in a public domain, it is presumed to be *tahor* [סָפֵק טוּמְאָה בִּרְשׁוּת הָרַבִּים טָהוֹר] (see *Sotah* 28a-b). Since each one's *tumah* is in doubt, when he comes by himself before the sage, the sage must rule him *tahor* (*Rashi*).

The reason the Mishnah discusses the person's status in regard to the *tahor* food he touched and not simply in regard to the person himself is because even if we rule both people *tahor* out of doubt, they must still purify themselves, so that they will not both touch the *same* person or object and render it definitely *tamei.* The Mishnah therefore discusses their status only in regard to *tahor* food they touched *before* coming to the sage (*Tosafos;* see *Tosafos, Pesachim* ibid. ד״ה הלך באחד; cf. *Shitah Mekubetzes* ד״ה והלך באחד מהן).

34. Where both ask their question at the same time, the sage is forced to answer both at once. He cannot tell them that they are both *tahor* because one of them definitely walked down the *tamei* path and became contaminated [thus, to say that both are *tahor* would give the appearance of an untruth; *Mishneh LaMelech, Avos HaTumah* 19:2]. Consequently, he has no choice but to say that both are *tamei* (*Rashi*). [Although this too cannot be true, it does not appear as an untruth because both people might be considered *tamei* out of doubt and thus be required to act stringently.]

This stringency is a Rabbinic enactment. At the Biblical level both people could be ruled *tahor* even if they came together (*Tosafos, Pesachim* ibid. ד״ה בבת אחת).

[*Rashi* (*Pesachim* ibid. ד״ה ר׳ יהודה) writes that when R' Yehudah says that the two people asked their questions together he means that they asked them one immediately after the other (תּוֹךְ כְּדֵי דִבּוּר, *within the time of an utterance*). See *Mishneh LaMelech, Avos HaTumah* 19:2 for a discussion of this point.]

35. Even if each, in relating the incident, tells the sage about his fellow also, he still can be ruled *tahor,* provided that he is *asking* about his own status only (*Rashi, Pesachim* ibid. ד״ה בזה אחר זה).

36. I.e. he asks for a ruling about his friend's status as well as his own (*Rashi, Pesachim* ibid. ד״ה עליו ועל חבירו; cf. *Tosafos* here).

37. R' Yehudah reasons that since only one person has come before him, the sage can tell him that he is *tahor* without mentioning the ruling for the friend. This person will then understand on his own that the same reasoning would apply to his fellow without the sage having said this explicitly. [Thus, although he will conclude that both are *tahor,* the sage will not actually have *said* anything that could be perceived as an untruth.] But R' Yose holds that since the sage was asked regarding both at once, then even if he addresses the ruling to only one of them, it is regarded as if both had asked and he ruled both *tahor.* Even though he mentioned only one explicitly, the ruling is understood to apply to both; thus, it is as though he mentioned both explicitly (*Rashi, Pesachim* ibid. ד״ה עליו ועל חבירו וד״ה ר׳ יהודה מדמי, as explained by *Shitah Mekubetzes* here ד״ה הכא נמי).

38. The Gemara now believes that an unprotected woman in the city will definitely be violated (*Ran*). It follows that since the hiding place holds only one person, the others were certainly violated.

39. Although the city's Kohanic wives do not all come together to the sage, his ruling for one of them is regarded as a ruling for all of them. [This is because the suspicion fell upon all of them together (unlike in the case of two paths). Therefore, there is really only one halachic question here. When he answers it for one, he has in effect answered it for all.] According to R' Yose, this is comparable to a case in which all of them come at once (*Rashi,* and *Ritva* explaining *Rashi;* cf. *Tosafos*). Since some were definitely violated (as the Gemara believes at this point – see *Ran*), the sage cannot rule them permitted. [R' Yehudah, however, holds that a ruling issued regarding one person is not regarded as having been issued regarding the others as well, *even if* it is understood to apply to them.]

40. *Rashi;* see *Eruvin* 46b.

41. [The Gemara now realizes that there is no clear presumption

הורהנה אין נחבשה לא הוא הדין אפילו נחבשה ומעשה שהיה כך היה איכא דאמרי אמר רבא אף אנן נמי תנינא העיד רבי יוסי הכהן ורבי זכריה בן הקצב על בת ישראל שהורהנה באשקלון וריחקוה בני משפחתה ועדיה מעידים עליה שלא נסתרה ושלא נטמאה ואמרו חכמים אם אתם מאמינים שהורהנה האמינו שלא נסתרה ושלא נטמאה ואם אין אתם מאמינים שלא נסתרה ושלא נטמאה אל תאמינו שהורהנה והא אשקלון דעל ידי ממון הוה וטעמא דעדים מעידין אותה הא אין עדים מעידין אותה לא מאי לאו לא שנא הורהנה ולא שנא נחבשה לא הורהנה שאני איכא דרמי לה מירמא תנן על ידי ממון מותרת לבעלה ורמינהו העיד רבי יוסי כו' והא אשקלון דע"י ממון וקתני טעמא דעדים מעידים אותה הא אין עדים מעידין אותה לא ומשני אמר רב שמואל בר רב יצחק לא קשיא כאן שיד ישראל תקיפה על עובדי כוכבים כאן שיד עובדי כוכבים תקיפה על עצמן: על ידי נפשות אסורה וכו': אמר רב כגון (א) נשי גנבי ולוי אמר כגון אשתו של בן דונאי אמר חזקיה והוא שנגמר דינן להריגה ורבי יוחנן אמר אע"פ שלא נגמר דינן להריגה:

מתני' עיר שכבשוה כרכום כל כהנות שנמצאו בתוכה פסולות ואם יש להן עדים אפילו עבד אפי' שפחה הרי אלו נאמנין ואין נאמן אדם על ידי עצמו:

גמ' ורמינהו בלשת שבאה לעיר בשעת שלום חביות פתוחות אסורות סתומות מותרות בשעת מלחמה אלו ואלו מותרות לפי שאין פנאי לנסך אמר רב מרי לבעול יש פנאי לנסך אין פנאי רבי יצחק בר אלעזר משמיה דחזקיה אמר כאן בכרכום של אותה מלכות כאן בכרכום של מלכות אחרת ושל מלכות אחרת נמי אי אפשר דלא (ב) ערק חד מינייהו אמר רב יהודה אמר שמואל כשמשמרות רואות זו את זו אי אפשר דלא ניימא פורתא אמר רבי לוי כגון דמהדר לה למתא שושילתא וכלבא וגווזא ואווזא אמר רבי אבא בר זבדא פליגי בה רבי יהודה נשיאה ורבנן חד אמר כאן בכרכום של אותה מלכות כאן בכרכום של מלכות אחרת ולא קשיא ליה ולא מידי וחד קשיא ליה כל הני ומשני כגון דמהדר ליה למתא שושילתא וכלבא וגווזא ואווזא אמר רב אידי בר אבין אמר ר' יצחק בר אשיאן אם יש שם מחבואה אחת מצלת על הכהנות כולן בעי רבי ירמיה אינה מחזקת אלא אחת מהו מי אמרינן כל חדא וחדא היינו הא או דלמא לא אמרינן ומאי שנא משני שבילין אחד טמא ואחד טהור והלך באחד מהן ועשה טהרות ובא חבירו והלך בשני ועשה טהרות רבי יהודה אומר אם נשאל זה בפני עצמו וזה בפני עצמו טהורות שניהם כאחת טמאות ר' יוסי אומר בין כך ובין כך טמאין ואמר רבא ואיתימא ר' יוחנן בבת אחת דברי הכל טמאין בזה אחר זה דברי הכל טהורים לא נחלקו אלא בבא לישאל עליו ועל חבירו מר מדמי ליה לבבת אחת ומר מדמי ליה לבזה אחר זה והכא נמי כיון דשרי להו לכולהו כבת אחת דמי הכי השתא התם ודאי איכא טומאה הכא מי יימר דאיטמי בעי רב אשי אמרה לא נחבאתי ולא נטמאתי מהו מי אמרינן מה

רש"י

הורהנה. דמלעת וכיון דהגיע זמן ולא נפדית הרי היא של עובדי כוכבים בדיניהם משום הכי בעינן עדים מעידין אותה שלא נסתרה: נחבשה. דאינה נחלטת להם לא בעינן עדים הואיל ועל ידי ממון הוא: ואיכא דרמי לה מרמא. לא מתני לה להא דרב שמואל בר רב יצחק אפירושא דמתניתין בלשון לא שנו אלא רמי מירמא מתניתין וברייתא אהדדי ועלה שני רב שמואל חילוק בין יד ישראל תקיפה ליד העובדי כוכבים תקיפה: הני נשי דגנבי. שבעליהן ניתלין ודרך המלכות להפקיר ביתם ונשיהן: בן דונאי. רולח היה ואלעזר שמו כדאמרינן בפ' עגלה ערופה (סוטה מז.) אבל נשי דגנבי הגונבים ממון לא מפקרי: מתני' כרכום. מלור מתרגמינן כרכומא (דברים כ): פסולות. אסורות לבעליהן דאשת כהן אסורה באונס: גמ' בלשת. חיל על שם שמחפשים כל המטמונים: לבעול יש פנאי. דתקיף להו ילרייהו: רבי יצחק בן אלעזר אמר. אף בבעילה פעמים שהן מותרות: כרכום של אותה מלכות. אינו רולה להשחית את בני העיר וכשכובש עיר הסמוך לממשלתו שומרה והיא לו למס עובד: משמרות. מקום מעמד השומרים שהעמיד המלך שלא יחבל אדם באנשי העיר: דמהדר למתא כו'. שמו סביבות העיר שלשלות ברזל שישמיעו קול בהכשל איש רץ עליהם וכלבים ואווזים זועקין: וגווזא. מקלות וקיסמין להכשל בהן: ולא קשיא ליה מידי. לא חייש למיעקר איניש יחידאה ולבעול הואיל ואין הדבר הפקר: ומאי שנא משני שבילין. דכיון דבא לשאול עליו ועל חבירו אמר רבי יוסי טמאין הכא נמי לכולהו שרינן כי הדדי: אחד טמא. שיש בו קברות מפסיק כל רחבו ואין ידוע איזהו הטמא אבל כך מוחזקים באחד מהן: ועשה טהרות. נגע בטהרות: טהורים. דכל חד כי אתי לקמן תלינן ליה למימר בטהור הלך דהוה ליה ספק טומאה בר"ה וספיקו טהור: טמאין. דהיכי נימא להו טהורים אתם חד מינייהו ודאי בטומאה אזל: בבת אחת. באו לשאול בבת אחת: הכא נמי כו'. וכר' יוסי: מה

תוספות

כאן בכרכום של אותה מלכות. פי' שיושבין בטח לפי שאין להם פנאי לנסך ולבעול אבל בלשת של מלכות אחרת שאימת מלכות שבאו בגבולה עליהם אין להן פנאי וכן פי' ר"ח ור"ת וכן מוכח בירושלמי ופריך כרכום של אותה מלכות אי אפשר דלא ערקא חדא מינייהו והוה לן למשרינהו לכולהו ולמיפלי לקולא דבשבויה הקילו כדאמרינן בסמוך אם יש מחבואה אחת מצלת על כל הכהנות כולן אע"ג דמספקא לן בדאינה מחזקת אלא אחת הכא פשיטא לן דשרו דהתם לא ודאי נחבאת אבל הכא ודאי ערקא ולפי' הקונטרס קשה טובא חדא דפריך נתלי לחומרא וגבי מחבואה תלינן לקולא ועוד דמה מתרץ דמהדר למתא כו' ואין אדם נכנס לשם והא קתני בלשת שנכנסה לעיר ועוד כיון דאהיא דע"ז פרק הוה ליה למימר אי אפשר דלא ערק חד מינייהו ונסך ועוד דהתם מפרש טעמא לפי שאין פנאי לנסך ולית ליה טעמא לפי שאין כרכום של אותה מלכות רולה להשחית את בני העיר [ועוד מאי שנא שעת מלחמה משעת שלום] ויש ליישב לפי שיטת הקונטרס דרבי יצחק בן אלעזר לא אתי לשנויי מתני' אההיא דע"ז אלא אית ליה שינויא דרב מרי ומתניתין דהתם נמי בכרכום של מלכות אחרת ולא בא אלא לפרושי מתניתין וכן משמע בפרק בתרא דע"ז (דף עא.) דפריך התם ממתניתין דהכא אמתניתין דבלשת ולא מייתי התם דרבי יצחק:

והלך באחד מהם ועשה טהרות. להכי נקט ועשה טהרות דלענין האדם אנו מזקיקים שניהם לטבול ולהזות פן יבואו לידי טומאה ודאי אם יגעו שניהם בככר אחד לכך אומר להו זילו טבלו דהא נהרא קמייכו ועוד דמשום דבעי למתני סיפא הזה וטבל טהור הלך בשני ועשה טהרות הרי אלו טהורות ואם קיימות הראשונים אלו ואלו תלויות ואם לא טהר בינתים הראשונות תלויות והשניות ישרפו:

ואם נשאל זה בפני עצמו וזה בפני עצמו טהורות. לא שיאכלם אדם אחד דאם כן יאכל ודאי טומאה דהכי אמרינן בשבועות בפ"ב (דף יט.) הלך בראשון ולא נכנס בשני ונכנס חייב דטמא הוא ממה נפשך: **בבא** לישאל עליו ועל חברו. אין לפרש שבא לישאל בבת אחת דהתם מודו כולי עלמא דטמאות מכל שכן דבאו לישאל שניהם בבת אחת אלא מיירי ששאל על עצמו וטהרוהו ואח"כ בא לישאל על חבירו דמר מדמי ליה לבת אחת כיון ששאל על שניהם במעמד אחד ומר מדמי ליה לזה אחר זה כיון שטיהרוהו קודם והכא נמי כיון דשרו לכולהו כבת אחת דמי אף על פי שאין בא לפנינו אלא על אחת מ"מ הדבר ידוע לכל שהרבה כהנות היו והרי כאילו בא לישאל על כולם בבת אחת והכא מודו כ"ע ובחנם דחק בקונטרס לפרש כר' יוסי:

לא

מסורת הש"ס

א) [עירובין סה: וש"נ], ב) עדיות פרק ח מ"ב, ג) ע"ז עא. ד) [ערוך איתא כרכום בקו"ף], ה) סוטה מז. ו) שבת מה. ע"ז עא., ז) טהרות פ"ה מ"ה פסחים י., ח) [ל"ל כתוספתא מהרש"א], ט) [ע"ע תוס' פסחים י. ד"ה הלך].

ליקוטי רש"י

כגון אשתו של בן דונאי. לא נגמר דינן להריגה. כרכום. כולשת חיל. בלשת. חיל שמחפשין וכולשין את כל הטמונים [ע"ז ע:]. כולשת חיל שמחפשין ובוחנין כדמתרגמינן (בראשית לא) ויחפש ובלש [נדה יג.]. בשעת שלום. כגון שהוא של אותה מלכות [שבת שם]. לפי שאין פנאי לנסך. הא הכא דשעת מלחמה היא.

עין משפט נר מצוה

קב א ב מיי' פי"ח מהל' איסורי ביאה הלכה ל טוש"ע אה"ע סימן ז סעיף יא בהג"ה:

קג ג מיי' פי"ח מהל' א"ב הלכה כו טור ש"ע שם סעיף י:

קד ד מיי' שם הל' יט טוש"ע שם סעיף א:

קה ה מיי' פי"ג מהל' מאכלות אסורות הלכה כד סמג לאוין קמח טוש"ע י"ד סי' קכט סעיף יב:

קו ו ז ח ט מיי' פי"ח מהל' איסורי ביאה הלכה כח כט טוש"ע אה"ע סי' ז סעיף י:

קז י כ מיי' פי"ט מהל' אבות הטומאה הלכה ב:

הגהות הב"ח

(א) גמ' כגון הני נשי דגנבי: (ב) שם דלא (ערק) תז"מ. ונ"ב ס"א עקר וכן משמע מפרש"י:

גליון הש"ם

רש"י ד"ה בלשת וכו' שמחפשין. כי בפסוק ויחפש ברלשית ת"ה התרגום ובלש:

תוספות רי"ד

ומפקרי לה. ה"ד ע"י נפשות א"ר כגון הני נשי דגנבי אמר חזקיה והוא שנגמר דינם להריגה פי' שבעליהן נתלו ודרך המלכות להפקיר טפם ונשיהם ור"י אמר אעפ"י שלא נגמר דינן להריגה. והל' כחזקיה דהוא רביה דר' יוחנן: עיר שכבשוה כרכום. פי' חיל הצרים עליה. מצור תרגומו כרכום כל כהנות שבתוכה פסולו' לבעליהן פי' דבחזקת שנבעלו קיימו ואנוסה אסורה לכהן ואם יש להן עדים שלא נבעלו אפילו עבד אפילו שפחה הרי אלו נאמנים ואין אדם נאמן ע"י עצמו לא האשה להעיד על עצמה ולא הבעל להעיד על אשתו ורמינהו בולשת שנכנסה לעיר. פי' חיל ונקרא כן ע"ש שמחפשים את כל המטמוניות תרגום ויחפש ובלש בזמן שלום חביות פתוחות אסורות וסתומות מותרת בשעת מלחמה אלו ואלו מותרות לפי שאין פנאי לנסך. אמר ר"מ לנסך אין פנאי לבעול יש פנאי דיצרא דעבירה תקיף מיין נסך ר"י בן אלעזר משמיה דחזקי' אמר כאן בכרכום של אותה מלכות אינן יראים ויש להם פנאי לבעול ולנסך. אבל של מלכות אחרת יראים [שמא] יבוא חיל מאיזה מלכות לעזור להן וממהרים לשלול ולהבריח ואין להן פנאי לא לבעול ולא לנסך. א"ר אידי ב"א אר"י ב"א אם יש שם מחבואה א' [מצלת] על כל הכהנות ומותרות כלן: בעי ר"י אם אינה מחזקת אלא א' מהן מהו. מי אמרינן כל חדא וחדא היינו האי א"ד לא אמרינן ולא איפשיטא

וקתני אסורות דיש פנאי לבעול. לנסך אין פנאי. דילר הניסוך לא תקיף להו וערודין במלחמה [ע"ז עא.]. ניימא. מנמנמת [סנהדרין ז.]. אחד טמא. קבר מוטל בו לרחבו וממלא את כולו ואין עובר בו שלא יאהיל. והלך באחד מהן ועשה טהרות. נגע בטהרות אחר כך. ובא חבירו והלך בשני. יודעין הן שבשביל שהלך זה לא הלך זה דהשתא ודאי אחד מהן טמא. טהורות. ואין בית דין יכול לטמאו כדקיימא לן בספק טומאה ברשות הרבים ספקו טהור. שניהם כאחת. הואיל והוראה אחת יש לנו לומר טמאין או טהורין אי אפשר לנו לומר להם טהורים אתם שהרי האחד ודאי טמא. בזה אחר זה דברי הכל טהורים. אע"פ שכל אחד אומר לפנינו כך היה המעשה שלי ושל חבירי אבל איני נשאל אלא על עצמי מה תהא עלי. עליו ועל חבירו וכו' לבבת אחת. מה תהא על שנינו ר' יוסי מדמי להו לבת אחת ואף על פי שאין שניהן לפניך לריך אתה הוראה אחת לשניהן או טמאין אתם או טהורין אתם והרי אין אתה יכול לומר טהורין אתם. ומר מדמי ליה וכו'. הואיל ואין כאן שואל אלא אחד משיבין לו טהור אתה שהרי ספק ביאה הוא ומעלמו יבין שאף חבירו כמוהו אבל כששניהן שואלין בתוך כדי דיבור לריך אתה להשיב לשניהן כאחד [פסחים י.].

that they violated the women of the vanquished city?

The Gemara answers:

אָמַר רַב מָרִי – Rav Mari said: לִבְעוֹל יֵשׁ פְּנַאי – To engage in cohabitation there is time; לְנַסֵּךְ אֵין פְּנַאי – to pour libations to idols **there is no time.** The pull of sensual desire is such that the soldiers make time for it even in the midst of war. Idol worship, however, exerts a far lesser pull upon them.[23] Therefore, while the city's wine is safe, its women are not.

Having drawn a distinction between women and wine, the Gemara now demonstrates that in some cases, the city's women may also be presumed safe from the occupying soldiers:[24]

רַבִּי יִצְחָק בַּר אֶלְעָזָר מִשְּׁמֵיהּ דְּחִזְקִיָּה אָמַר – R' Yitzchak bar Elazar said in the name of Chizkiyah: Sometimes, the women of the city *are* permitted to Kohanim. **כָּאן בְּכַרְכּוֹם שֶׁל אוֹתָהּ מַלְכוּת – The case** in which they are permitted **concerns the siege-army of this** very **kingdom** of which the city is a part.[25] In this case, the occupiers wish to retain the loyalty of the city's inhabitants. Therefore, they do not oppress them; to the contrary, they set a guard about the city, to protect the residents from the depredations of their soldiers. Hence, the women of the city are safe from harm. **כָּאן בְּכַרְכּוֹם שֶׁל מַלְכוּת אַחֶרֶת – The case** in which they are forbidden **concerns the siege-army of a different kingdom.** In this case, the army is unconcerned with the welfare of the city's inhabitants, and its soldiers are therefore suspect of pillage and rape. Consequently, we must fear that the occupiers violated the women of the city.

The Gemara asks:

שֶׁל אוֹתָהּ מַלְכוּת נַמִּי – But **even** in the case of the army **of this kingdom, אִי אֶפְשָׁר דְּלָא עָרַק חַד מִינַּיְיהוּ – it is impossible that** at least **one of them will not elude** the guard and enter the city.[26] Accordingly, the women of the place should be forbidden to Kohanim, on the suspicion that they were violated by a soldier who eluded the guard. – ? –

The Gemara answers:

אָמַר רַב יְהוּדָה אָמַר שְׁמוּאֵל – Rav Yehudah said in the name of Shmuel: כְּשֶׁמִּשְׁמָרוֹת רוֹאוֹת זוֹ אֶת זוֹ – We are speaking of a case in which **the positions of the guards are within sight of one another,** so that no one can slip through unobserved. Therefore, the city is safe.

The Gemara protests:

אִי אֶפְשָׁר דְּלָא נָיְימָא פּוּרְתָּא – But **it is impossible that** one of the guards **will not doze for a while!** During that interval, a marauder might enter the city. – ? –

The Gemara answers:

אָמַר רַבִּי לֵוִי – R' Levi said: כְּגוֹן דְּמַהֲדַר לָהּ לְמָתָא שׁוּשִׁילְתָּא וְכַלְבָּא וְגַוְוזָא וְאַוְוזָא – It is a case where they surrounded the city with chains, dogs, spikes and geese. The spikes impede potential intruders, and the chains, dogs and geese warn the guards of their approach.[27] When these precautions are taken, we are assured that no intrusion took place.

The Gemara cites an Amoraic dispute regarding the need for these extreme measures:

אָמַר רַבִּי אַבָּא בַּר זַבְדָּא – R' Abba bar Zavda said: פְּלִיגֵי בָהּ רַבִּי יְהוּדָה נְשִׂיאָה וְרַבָּנָן – R' Yehudah Nesiah and the Rabbis disagreed regarding this [issue]. חַד אָמַר – One of them **said: כָּאן בְּכַרְכּוֹם שֶׁל אוֹתָהּ מַלְכוּת – "The case** in which they are permitted **concerns the siege-army of this kingdom; כָּאן בְּכַרְכּוֹם שֶׁל מַלְכוּת אַחֶרֶת – the case** in which they are prohibited **concerns the siege-army of a different kingdom," וְלָא קַשְׁיָא לֵיהּ וְלָא מִידֵּי – and he had no difficulties at all!** He was not in the least troubled by the possibility that a single intruder might find his way into the city and violate a woman. **וְחַד קַשְׁיָא לֵיהּ כָּל הָנֵי – But** the other **one, he had all these difficulties** mentioned above; i.e. that one person might elude the guards, and that one of the guards might doze momentarily. **וּמְשַׁנֵּי כְּגוֹן דְּמַהֲדַר לֵיהּ לְמָתָא שׁוּשִׁילְתָּא וְכַלְבָּא וְגַוְוזָא וְאַוְוזָא – And he answered: It is a case where they surrounded the city with chains, dogs, spikes and geese.**

We see that while one Amora finds these measures necessary, the other does not. He holds that provided the city was guarded, we need not be concerned for the possibility that a single marauder eluded the guards and entered the city.[28]

The Gemara sets forth a means by which the decree on the Kohanim's wives might be averted:

אָמַר רַב אִידִי בַּר אָבִין אָמַר רַבִּי יִצְחָק בַּר אַשְׁיָאן – Rav Idi bar Avin said in the name of R' Yitzchak bar Ashyan: אִם יֵשׁ שָׁם מַחֲבוֹאָה אַחַת – If there exists in the city even **a single hiding place,**[29] **מַצֶּלֶת עַל הַכֹּהֲנוֹת כּוּלָּן – it saves all the wives of Kohanim** in the city from the consequences of this decree. For we assume that they made use of the hiding place, and were not molested.[30]

NOTES

23. *Rashi* here and to *Avodah Zarah* 71a ד"ה לנסך אין פנאי.

24. *Rashi,* as explained by *Tosafos, Ritva, Ran; Rambam,* as explained by *Ran;* cf. *Rach* and *Rabbeinu Tam,* quoted in *Tosafos; Ritva* et al.

25. I.e. this city adjoins the kingdom from which the army comes. Generally, the army's objective in this case is not to lay waste to the city, but to make it into a vassal state, from which tribute can be exacted (*Rashi;* cf. *Rach* and *Rabbeinu Tam* ibid.; *Rambam, Isurei Biah* 18:29).

26. *Rashi;* cf. *Rach,* cited in *Ran; Rambam* ibid. §26,27.

27. The chains clank when a runner stumbles over them, and the dogs and geese begin barking and honking at the approach of intruders (*Rashi*).

28. This Amora is of the opinion that as long as the city is not open to the army we will not prohibit the women, even if a single soldier *is* able to enter (*Rashi*).

29. Such as a secret tunnel dug beneath the ground, where the invaders will not usually search (see *Shiltei HaGiborim*).

30. [There is some question among the authorities as to whether a woman must make an explicit claim that she hid herself and was not molested, or whether we simply issue a permit to all the women of the city on the assumption that they made use of the hiding place. For discussion, see *Rif* with *Ran; Rambam, Isurei Biah* 18:28; *Rashi* 27b ד"ה מה לי; *Re'ah* here; *Meiri* here; *Chasam Sofer,* bottom of the *amud.* See below, note 33.]

[*Ramban* (quoted in *Shitah Mekubetzes* ד"ה הא אמרינן) focuses on the term, "even a *single* hiding place." He asks: If it is a hiding place large enough for all the women in town, what difference does it make that it is the only one? And if the point is that although it is *not* large enough for everyone, it nonetheless serves to render them all permitted, how can the Gemara below inquire as to the law of a hiding place that holds only a single woman? If a place that holds only a portion of the city's women permits them all, so too should a place that holds only a solitary woman! *Ramban* answers that the hiding place is actually large enough for all the women of the city. The fact that it is the only place is significant because one might assume that in this situation the women would not be permitted, either because it is unlikely that everyone will be able to reach a single hiding place in time, or because the large number of women converging on a single spot creates a tumult and causes the hideaway to become known. The Gemara must therefore make it clear that even a single hiding place causes all the Kohanic wives in town to remain permitted to their husbands. Alternatively, we are dealing with a place that holds only a portion of the women. Nevertheless, the Gemara below must inquire regarding a place that can contain only a single woman. For everyone knows that the place can hold only one person; therefore, permitting all the Kohanic wives will give the appearance of untruthfulness. Perhaps, then, we do not permit everyone on the basis of this hideaway. This is the point of the Gemara's following inquiry (see also *Re'ah;* see also *Haflaah*).]

הורהנה אין נחבשה לא הוא הדין אפילו נחבשה א) ומעשה שהיה כך היה איכא דאמרי אמר רבא אף אנן נמי תנינא ב) העיד רבי יוסי הכהן ורבי זכריה בן הקצב על בת ישראל שהורהנה באשקלון וריחקוה בני משפחתה ועדיה מעידים עליה שלא נסתרה ושלא נטמאה ואמרו חכמים אם אתם מאמינים שהורהנה האמינו שלא נסתרה ושלא נטמאה ואם אין אתם מאמינים שלא נסתרה ושלא נטמאה אל תאמינו שהורהנה והא אשקלון דעל ידי ממון הוה וטעמא דעדים מעידין אותה הא אין עדים מעידין אותה לא מאי לאו לא שנא הורהנה ולא שנא נחבשה לא הורהנה שאני איכא דרמי לה מירמא תנן על ידי ממון מותרת לבעלה ורמינהו העיד רבי יוסי כו' והא אשקלון דע"י ממון וקתני טעמא דעדים מעידים אותה הא אין עדים מעידין אותה לא ומשני אמר רב שמואל בר רב יצחק לא קשיא כאן שיד ישראל תקיפה על עובדי כוכבים כאן שיד עובדי כוכבים תקיפה על עצמן: על ידי נפשות אסורה וכו': אמר רב כגון (א) נשי גנבי ולוי אמר א כגון אשתו של בן דונאי אמר חזקיה והוא שנגמר דינן להריגה ורבי יוחנן אמר ב אע"פ שלא נגמר דינן להריגה: **מתני'** ג עיר שכבשוה ד) כרכום כל כהנות שנמצאו בתוכה פסולות ד ואם יש להן עדים אפילו עבד אפי' שפחה הרי אלו נאמנין ואין נאמן אדם על ידי עצמו: **גמ'** ורמינהו ה) בלשת שבאה לעיר בשעת שלום חביות פתוחות אסורות סתומות מותרות בשעת מלחמה אלו ואלו מותרות לפי שאין פנאי לנסך אמר רב מרי לבעול יש פנאי לנסך אין פנאי רבי יצחק בר אלעזר משמיה דחזקיה אמר כאן ו בכרכום של אותה מלכות כאן בכרכום של מלכות אחרת של אותה מלכות נמי אי אפשר דלא (ג) ערק חד מינייהו אמר רב יהודה אמר שמואל כשמשמרות רואות זו את זו אי אפשר דלא ניימא פורתא אמר רבי לוי ז כגון דמהדר לה למתא שושילתא וכלבא וגווזא ואווזא אמר רבי אבא בר זבדא פליגי בה רבי יהודה נשיאה ורבנן חד אמר כאן בכרכום של אותה מלכות כאן בכרכום של מלכות אחרת ולא קשיא ליה ולא מידי וחד קשיא ליה כל הני ומשני כגון דמהדר ליה למתא שושילתא וכלבא וגווזא ואווזא אמר רב אידי בר אבין אמר ר' יצחק בר אשיאן ח אם יש שם מחבואה אחת מצלת על הכהנות כולן בעי רבי ירמיה אינה מחזקת אלא אחת מהו מי אמרינן ט כל חדא וחדא היינו הא או דלמא לא אמרינן ומאי שנא משני י שבילין אחד טמא ואחד טהור והלך באחד מהן ועשה טהרות ובא חבירו והלך בשני ועשה טהרות רבי יהודה אומר אם נשאל זה בפני עצמו וזה בפני עצמו טהורות שניהם כאחת טמאות ר' יוסי אומר בין כך ובין כך טמאין ואמר רבא ואיתימא ר' יוחנן ל בבת אחת דברי הכל טמאין בזה אחר זה דברי הכל טהורים לא נחלקו אלא בבא לישאל עליו ועל חבירו מר מדמי ליה לבבת אחת ומר מ מדמי ליה לבזה אחר זה והכא נמי כיון דשרי להו לכולהו כבת אחת דמי הכי השתא התם ודאי איכא טומאה הכא מי יימר דאיטמי בעי רב אשי אמרה לא נחבאתי ולא נטמאתי מהו מי אמרינן מה

רש"י

הורהנה. דמעת וכיון דהגיע זמן ולא נפדית הרי היא של עובדי כוכבים בדיניהם משום הכי בעינן עדים מעידין אותה שלא נסתרה: נחבשה. דאינה נחלטת להם לא בעינן עדים הואיל ועל ידי ממון הוא: ואיכא דרמי לה מרמא. לא מתני לה להא דרב שמואל בר רב יצחק אפירושא דמתניתין בלשון לא שנו אלא רמי מירמא מתניתין וברייתא אהדדי ועלה שני רב שמואל חילוק בין יד ישראל תקיפה ליד העובדי כוכבים תקיפה: הני נשי דגנבי. שבעליהן ניתלין ודרך המלכות להפקיר ביתם ונשיהן: בן דונאי. רוצח היה ואלעזר שמו כדאמרינן בפ' עגלה ערופה (סוטה מז.) אבל נשי דגנבי הגונבים ממון לא מפקרי: **מתני'** כרכום. מצור מתרגמינן כרכומא (דברים כ): פסולות. אסורות לבעליהן דאשת כהן אסורה באונס: **גמ'** בלשת. חיל על שם שמחפשים כל המטמונים: לבעול יש פנאי. דתקיף להו יצרייהו: רבי יצחק בן אלעזר אמר. אף בבעילה פעמים שהן מותרות: כרכום של אותה מלכות. אינו רוצה להשחית את בני העיר וכשכובש עיר הסמוך לממשלתו שומרה והיא לו למס עובד: משמרות. מקום מעמד השומרים שהעמיד המלך שלא יחבל אדם באנשי העיר: דמהדר למתא כו'. שמו סביבות העיר שלשלות ברזל שישמיעו קול בהכשל איש רץ עליהם וכלבים ואווזים זועקין: וגווזא. מקלות וקיסמין להכשל בהן: ולא קשיא ליה מידי. לא חייש למיעקר איניש יחידאה ולבעול הואיל ואין הדבר הפקר: ומאי שנא משני שבילין. דכיון דבא לשאול עליו ועל חבירו אמר רבי יוסי טמאין הכא נמי לכולהו שרינן כי הדדי: אחד טמא. שיש בו קברות מפסיק כל רחבו ואין ידוע איזהו הטמא אבל כך מוחזקים באחד מהן: ועשה טהרות. נגע בטהרות: טהורים. דכל חד כי אתי לקמן תלינן ליה למימר בטהור הלך דהוה ליה ספק טומאה בר"ה וספיקו טהור: טמאין. דהיכי נימא להו טהורים אתם חד מינייהו ודאי בטמא אזל: בבת אחת. באו לשאול בבת אחת: הכא נמי כו'. ור' יהודה ור' יוסי הלכה כר' יוסי:

מה

וקתני אסורות דיש פנאי לבעול. לנסך אין פנאי. דיצר הניסוך לא תקיף להו וטרודין במלחמה [ע"ז עא.]. ניימא. מנמנמת [סנהדרין ז.]. אחד טמא. קבר מוטל בו לרחבו וממלא את כולו ואין עובר בו שלא יאהיל. והלך באחד מהן ועשה טהרות. נגע בטהרות אחר כך. ובא חבירו והלך בשני. יודעין הן שבשביל שהלך זה לא הלך זה דהשתא ודאי אחד מהן טמא. אם נשאל. כל אחד לחכם ספקו בפני עצמו. טהורות. ואין בית דין יכול לטמאו דקיימא לן בספק טומאה ברשות הרבים ספקו טהור. שניהם כאחת. הואיל והוראה אחת יש לנו לומר טמאין או טהורין אי אפשר לנו לומר להם טהורים אתם שהרי האחד ודאי טמא. בזה אחר זה דברי הכל טהורים. אע"פ שכל אחד אומר לפנינו כך היה המעשה שלי ושל חבירי אבל איני נשאל אלא על עצמי מה תהא עלי. עליו ועל חבירו וכו' לבבת אחת. מה תהא על שנינו ר' יוסי מדמי להו לבת אחת ואף על פי שאין שניהן לפניך צריך אתה הוראה אחת לשניהן או טמאין אתם או טהורין אתם והרי אין אתה יכול לומר טהורין אתם. ומר מדמי ליה וכו'. הואיל ואין כאן שואל אלא אחד משיבין לו טהור אתה שהרי ספק ביאה הוא ומעצמו יבין שאף חבירו כמוהו אבל כששניהן שואלין בתוך כדי דיבור צריך אתה להשיב לשניהן כאחד [פסחים י.].

תוספות

כאן בכרכום של אותה מלכות. פי' שיושבין בטח לפי שאין אחריהן מחנה ויש פנאי לנסך ולבעול אבל בלשת של מלכות אחרת שאימת מלכות שבאו בגבולה עליהם אין להן פנאי וכן פי' ר"ח ור"ת וכן מוכח בירושלמי ופריך כרכום של אותה מלכות אי אפשר דלא ערקא חדא מינייהו והוה לן למשרינהו לכולהו ולמיתלי לקולא דבשבויה הקילו כדאמרינן בסמוך אם יש מחבואה אחת מצלת על כל הכהנות כולן אע"ג דמספקא לן באינה מחזקת אלא אחת הכא פשיטא לן דשרו דהתם לא ודאי נחבאת אבל הכא ודאי ערקא ולפי' הקונטרס קשה טובא חדא דפריך נתלי לחומרא וגבי מחבואה תלינן לקולא ועוד דמה מתרץ דמהדר למתא כו' ואין אדם נכנס לשם והא קתני בלשת שנכנסה לעיר ועוד כיון דאההיא דע"ז פריך הוה ליה למימר אי אפשר דלא ערק חד מינייהו ונסך ועוד דהתם מפרש טעמא לפי שאין פנאי לנסך ולית ליה טעמא לפי שאין כרכום של אותה מלכות רוצה להשחית את בני העיר [ועוד מאי שנא שעת מלחמה משעת שלום] ויש ליישב לפי שיטת הקונטרס דרבי יצחק בן אלעזר לא אתי לשנויי מתני' אההיא דע"ז אלא אית ליה שינויא דרב מרי ומתניתין דהתם נמי בכרכום של מלכות אחרת ולא בא אלא לפרושי מתניתין וכן משמע בפרק בתרא דע"ז (דף עא.) דפריך התם ממתניתין דהכא אמתניתין דבלשת ולא מייתי התם דרבי יצחק:

והלך באחד מהם ועשה טהרות. להכי נקט ועשה טהרות לענין האדם אנו מזקיקים שניהם לטבול ולהזות פן יבואו לידי טומאה ודאי אם יגעו שניהם בככר אחד לכך אומר להו זילו טבילו דהא נהרא קמייכו ועוד דמשום דבעי למתני ז) סיפא הזה וטבל טהור הלך בשני ועשה טהרות הרי אלו טהורות ואם קיימות הראשונים אלו ואלו תלויות ואם לא טהר בינתים הראשונות תלויות והשניות ישרפו ח):

ואם נשאל זה בפני עצמו וזה בפני עצמו טהורות. לא שיאכלם אדם אחד דאם כן יאכל ודאי טומאה דהכי אמרינן בשבועות בפ"ב (דף יט.) הלך בראשון ולא נכנס בשני ונכנס חייב דטמא הוא ממה נפשך: **בבא** לישאל עליו ועל חברו. אין לפרש שבא לישאל בבת אחת דהתם מודו כולי עלמא דטמאות מכל מקום דבא לישאל שניהם בבת אחת אלא מיירי שאל על עצמו וטהרוהו ואח"כ בא לישאל על חבירו דמר מדמי ליה לבת אחת כיון ששאל על שניהם במעמד אחד ומר מדמי ליה לזה אחר זה כיון שטיהרוהו קודם והכא נמי כיון דשרו לכולהו כבת אחת דמי אף על פי שאין בא לפנינו אלא על אחת מ"מ הדבר ידוע לכל שהרבה כהנות היו והוי כאילו בא לישאל על כולם בבת אחת והכא מודו כ"ע ומנס דחק בקונטרס לפרש כר' יוסי: לא

מסורת הש"ס

א) [עירובין סה: וש"נ], ב) עדיות פרק ח מ"ב, ג) ע"ז עא., ד) [בערוך איתא כרקום בקו"ף], ה) שם ע: שבת מא. נדה יג., ו) טהרות פ"ה מ"ה פסחים י., ז) [למיתנא סיפא כרישא כצ"ל. מהרש"א], ח) [וע"ע תוס' פסחים י. ד"ה הלך].

ליקוטי רש"י

באו שניהם ביחד הוה מסקינן ליה ומוקמינן ליה אחזקה קמייתא דמוחזק לן באבוה דכהן הוא ולזילותא לא חיישינן ורשב"ג כר' נתן. ובפלוגתא דהני תנאי. ר' נתן ורבנן. דתניא אין עדותן מצטרפת. אין צריך כאן בהאי מחלוקת דרבי יהושע בן קרחה ורבנן אלא כך היא ברייתא שלימה בשילהי זה בורר ומשום גרירא דסיפא נקט רישא. אפי' בזה אחר זה. אחד אומר ביום ראשון לוה פלוני מפלוני מנה ואחד אומר ביום שני ראיתי גם אני שלוה ממנו דמ"מ אמנה קא מסהדי ות"ק סבר אמנה דקא מסהיד האי לא קא מסהיד האי וה"ל לגבי מנה אלו עדות וטעמייהו מפרש שפיר בסנהדרין מקרא ומסברא. ואין עדותן וכו' עד שיעידו שניהם כאחד. להתקבל בב"ד ואפי' ראו שניהם כאחד עד שיעידו שניהם כאחד בפני ב"ד ופלוגתא אחריתי היא ולא ר' יהושע בן קרחה קאמר לה ור' אלעזר ורשב"ג בפלוגתא דר"נ ורבנן פליגי [שם לב.]. לפסוק הדין על פיהם. וסתמא הוא ולא ר' יהושע בן קרחה קאמר לה [סנהדרין ל.]. על ידי ממון. שהיתה חייבת ממון. מותרת לבעלה. דסבר אי בעילנא לה תו לא פרע לי בעלה מידי. על ידי נפשות. שנתחייבה הריגה. אסורה לבעלה. היכא דלא מירתת להפסיד ממונו אפקורי מפקר לה ומיישינן שמא נבעלה לאחד מהן ברצון ואית דמוקמי לה באשת כהן דמיתסרא באונס ולאשון עיקר דבכתובות (דף כו) מוכח דבאשת ישראל קאי [ע"ז כג.].

[ע"כ שייך לדף כו:]

כל כהנות שנמצאו בתוכה פסולות. לבעליהן דאשת כהן אסורה אף באונס אבל אשת ישראל לא [ע"ז עא.]. אפילו עבד אפי' שפחה. דבשבויה האמינו חכמים עד אחד להקל ואפילו עבד או שפחה כדקתני מתני' אם יש להן עדים אפילו עבד כו' [לעיל כג:]. בלשת. חיילות גיים הבא לעיר על שם שמחפשין ובולשים את העיר קרי לה בולשת [שבת מא.]. חיל על שם שמחפשין ומוזרין קרי להו בולשת כדמתרגמינן (בראשית לא) ויחפש ובלש [ע"ז ע:]. בולשת חיל שמחפשין ובוחזין כדמתרגמינן ויחפש ובלש [נדה יג.]. בשעת שלום. כגון שהוא של אותה מלכות [שבת שם]. לפי שאין פנאי לנסך. הא הכא דשעת מלחמה היא

עין משפט נר מצוה

קב א ב מיי' פי"ח מהל' איסורי ביאה הלכה ל טוש"ע אה"ע סימן ז סעיף יא בהג"ה:
קג ג מיי' פי"ח מהל' א"ב הלכה כו טור ש"ע שם סעיף י:
קד ד מיי' שם הל' יט טוש"ע שם סעיף א:
קה ה מיי' פי"ב מהל' מאכלות אסורות הלכה כד סמג לאוין קמח טוש"ע י"ד סי' קכט סעיף יב:
קו ו ז ח ט מיי' פי"ח מהל' איסורי ביאה הלכה כו כח כט טוש"ע אה"ע סי' ז סעיף י:
קז י כ מיי' פי"ט מהל' אבות הטומאה הלכה ג:

הגהות הב"ח

(א) גמ' כגון הני נשי דגנבי: (ג) שם דלא (ערק) מז"מ. ונ"ב ס"א עקר וכן משמע מפרש"י:

גליון הש"ס

רש"י ד"ה בלשת וכו' שמחפשין. כי בפסוק ויחפש בראשית מ"ד התרגום ובלש:

תוספות רי"ד

ומפקרי לה. ה"ד ע"י נפשות א"ר כגון נשי דגנבי אמר חזקיה והוא שנגמר דינם להריגה פי' שבעליהן נתלו ודרך המלכות להפקיר טפם ונשיהם ור"י אמר אעפ"י שלא נגמר דינן להריגה. והל' כחזקיה דהוא רביה דר' יוחנן: **עיר שכבשוה כרכום.** פי' חיל הצרים עליה. מצור תרגומו כרכום כל כהנות שבתוכה פסולו' לבעליהן פי' דבחזקת שנבעלו קיימו ואנוסה אסורה לכהן ואם יש להן עדים שלא נבעלו אפילו עבד אפילו שפחה הרי אלו נאמנים ואין אדם נאמן ע"י עצמו לא האשה להעיד על עצמה ולא הבעל להעיד על אשתו **ורמינהו** בולשת שנכנסה לעיר. פי' חיל ונקרא כן ע"ש שמחפשים את כל המטמוניות תרגום ויחפש ובלש בזמן שלום חביות פתוחות אסורות וסתומות מותרת בשעת מלחמה אלו ואלו מותרות לפי שאין פנאי לנסך. **אמר** ר"מ לנסך אין פנאי לבעול יש פנאי דיצרא דעבירה תקיף מיין נסך ר"י בן אלעזר משמיה דחזקי' אמר כאן בכרכום של אותה מלכות אינן יראים ויש להם פנאי לבעול ולנסך. אבל של מלכות אחרת יראים [שמא] יבוא חיל מאיזה מלכות לעזור להן וממהרים לשלול ולהבריח ואין להן פנאי לא לבעול ולא לנסך. **א"ר** אידי ב"א אר"י ב"א אם יש שם מחבואה א' [מצלת] על כל הכהנות ומותרות כלן: **בעי ר"י** אם אינה מחזקת אלא א' מהן מהו. מי אמרינן כל חדא וחדא היינו האי א"ד לא אמרינן ולא איפשיטא

to any who wish to exploit them. Since all make free with such women, they are forbidden to their husbands.[8]

A dissenting view:

וְלֵוִי אָמַר – **But Levi said:** כְּגוֹן אִשְׁתּוֹ שֶׁל בֶּן דּוּנַאי – **Such as the wife of Ben Dunai,** who was a murderer.[9] It is only the wives of murderers who are abandoned to any who wish to exploit them, not the wives of thieves. Since the idolaters do not make free with the wives of thieves, they remain permitted to their husbands.[10]

The Gemara cites a dispute regarding the wives of these criminals:

אָמַר חִזְקִיָּה – **Chizkiyah said:** וְהוּא שֶׁנִּגְמַר דִּינָן לַהֲרִיגָה – **And this is** the case only **if they** (i.e. the husbands of these women) **were** actually **sentenced to death.** But if their verdict has not yet been handed down, their wives are permitted to them.[11] וְרַבִּי יוֹחָנָן אָמַר – **But R' Yochanan said:** אַף עַל פִּי שֶׁלֹּא נִגְמַר דִּינָן לַהֲרִיגָה – **Even if they were not** yet **sentenced to death,** their wives are forbidden to them.[12]

Mishnah This Mishnah sets forth the status of women captured by an enemy army:

עִיר שֶׁכְּבָשׁוּהָ כַּרְכּוֹם – Concerning **a city vanquished by a siege-army:** כָּל כֹּהֲנוֹת שֶׁנִּמְצְאוּ בְתוֹכָהּ פְּסוּלוֹת – **All wives of Kohanim found therein are unfit,** i.e. they are forbidden to their husbands,[13] for we fear that they were violated by soldiers of the occupying army.[14] וְאִם יֵשׁ לָהֶן עֵדִים – **But if they have witnesses** who testify that they were not molested,[15] אֲפִילוּ עֶבֶד אֲפִילוּ שִׁפְחָה – **even a slave** or **even a slavewoman,** הֲרֵי אֵלּוּ נֶאֱמָנִין – **these** witnesses **are believed,** and the woman in question is permitted to her husband.[16] וְאֵין נֶאֱמָן אָדָם עַל יְדֵי עַצְמוֹ – **However, a person is not believed** to testify **on his own behalf.** Therefore, if a woman states that she was not violated, she is not believed.

Gemara The Gemara questions our Mishnah's ruling on the basis of another Mishnah:

וּרְמִינְהוּ – **But contrast [our Mishnah with this Mishnah]:**[17] בַּלֶּשֶׁת שֶׁבָּאָה לָעִיר – Concerning A TROOP[18] THAT CAME TO A CITY: בִּשְׁעַת שָׁלוֹם – If they came IN PEACETIME,[19] חָבִיּוֹת פְּתוּחוֹת אֲסוּרוֹת – THE city's OPEN BARRELS of wine ARE PROHIBITED, for we suspect that the soldiers used them to pour libations to their idols, סְתוּמוֹת מוּתָּרוֹת – but THE SEALED [BARRELS] ARE PERMITTED.[20] בִּשְׁעַת מִלְחָמָה אֵלּוּ וְאֵלּוּ מוּתָּרוֹת – If they came IN WARTIME, both THESE AND THOSE[21] ARE PERMITTED, לְפִי שֶׁאֵין פְּנַאי לְנַסֵּךְ – FOR THERE IS NO TIME then for the soldiers TO POUR LIBATIONS.[22]

We see that during war, soldiers are preoccupied with fighting, and do not take time for other pursuits. Why, then, do we suspect

NOTES

8. For we fear they submitted willingly to one of their violators (see *Rashi* to the Mishnah and note 17 there).

Rashi to the Mishnah states that the case of a woman imprisoned on capital charges concerns a woman who is herself sentenced to death. However, we see from this Gemara that it also concerns the wife of one sentenced to death (see *Shitah Mekubetzes* to the Mishnah; see also *Meiri*). For an explanation of why *Rashi* there focuses on a woman who is herself sentenced to death, see *Shitah Mekubetzes* ibid.

9. This was a murderer well known in Mishnaic times. The Mishnah in *Sotah* 47a gives his full name as Elazar ben Dunai (*Rashi*).

10. *Rashi* is careful to state that in this context, the word "thieves" refers to those who steal money. Presumably, he means to exclude those who "steal" human beings (i.e. kidnapers), who, while named "thieves" (גַּנָּבִים) in the Torah (see *Exodus* 20:13), are not whom Levi intends here. Rather, under the idolaters' law, the wives of kidnapers are treated like the wives of murderers.

11. For until the final sentence is actually handed down, governmental protection is not withdrawn from them, so people fear to mistreat them (*Ritva*).

12. Chizkiyah and R' Yochanan do not take sides between Rav and Levi. Rather, Chizkiyah and R' Yochanan's dispute applies whether the Mishnah speaks only of the wives of murderers, or even of the wives of thieves (*Ritva*).

13. *Rashi; see Haflaah; Chidushei R' Akiva Eiger.*

14. And the law is that even forcible violation prohibits the wives of Kohanim to their husbands (*Rashi*).

[This decree also affects women who are not wives of Kohanim, for they are forbidden thereafter to marry Kohanim. The Mishnah specifies the wives of Kohanim to demonstrate the stringency of the decree – not only are the women of this city forbidden to marry Kohanim, but even those already *married* to Kohanim must leave them (*Ritva; see Rosh*).]

15. I.e. they testify that they were together with a particular woman throughout the occupation, and at no time was she molested (*Meiri*).

[Although the Mishnah uses the plural "witnesses," a single witness is actually sufficient, as we learned above, on 23b (see *Meiri*).]

16. Slaves and slavewomen are generally unfit as witnesses. However, the decree forbidding these wives to their husbands is of Rabbinic origin, and the Rabbis chose to allow the testimony of these witnesses as it pertains to their decree. *Meiri* explains that captured women tend to make themselves repulsive to their captors. This makes it less likely that they will be violated; the Rabbis were therefore lenient with them with regard to the qualifications of their witnesses (see *Kiddushin* 12b; see also above, 23a note 20). See *Ritva,* who excludes certain types of invalid witness from this leniency.

[There is no difference between male and female slaves as regards their general unfitness as witnesses. Therefore, it is puzzling that the Mishnah finds it necessary to mention both. For a possible explanation, see *Emes LeYaakov*.]

17. *Avodah Zarah* 70b.

18. A marauding troop is called a בַּלֶּשֶׁת because it searches out the hidden treasures of the city it is plundering. In Aramaic, the root בלש connotes the act of searching; see *Targum Onkelos* to *Genesis* 44:12 (*Rashi;* see *Gilyon HaShas*).

19. I.e. if soldiers of the kingdom of which this city is a part came during peacetime (*Rashi, Shabbos* 41a ד״ה בשעת שלום). [Even "friendly" soldiers will forcibly requisition provisions from their countrymen (see *Meiri*).]

20. [The Torah prohibits one to derive benefit from wine that was used to pour libations to idols; see *Avodah Zarah* 29b; *Rambam, Maachalos Asuros* 11:1. Wine that was exposed to idolaters is forbidden by Rabbinic decree because of the possibility that it was used for idolatrous purposes.] This Mishnah rules that when a troop passes through a city during peacetime, the wine in open barrels (i.e. barrels that were open before the troop arrived, or were found open after their passage) is prohibited, because the soldiers had access to it, and we fear they used it to pour libations. Sealed barrels, however, are permitted, because it is clear that their wine was not used for libations. Although the barrels *could* have been broken into and resealed, we may assume that the soldiers were not afraid to be caught plundering and would not have bothered to reseal the barrels (*Ran, Avodah Zarah* 70b; *Meiri* here). [Barrels that were left covered, but not sealed, and are found in the same condition after the troop's passage, are forbidden, for we assume that the soldiers used the wine and then replaced the covers. Even though they are not afraid to be caught plundering, they will normally replace the covers out of habit (*Ran* ibid.).]

21. I.e. both open barrels and sealed ones.

22. In wartime, even the wine in the open barrels is permitted, because the soldiers are too preoccupied with the concerns of war to perform libations. [However, if previously sealed barrels are found open after the troop's passage, their wine is prohibited, for we must assume that the soldiers made use of it for libations (*Ran, Avodah Zarah* ibid.).]

הורהנה אין נחבשה לא הוא הדין אפילו נחבשה [א] ומעשה שהיה כך היה איכא דאמרי אמר רבא אף אנן נמי תנינא [ג] העיד רבי יוסי הכהן ורבי זכריה בן הקצב על בת ישראל שהורהנה באשקלון וריחקוה בני משפחתה ועדיה מעידים עליה שלא נסתרה ושלא נטמאה ואמרו חכמים אם אתם מאמינים שהורהנה האמינו שלא נסתרה ושלא נטמאה ואם אין אתם מאמינים שלא נסתרה ושלא נטמאה אל תאמינו שהורהנה והא אשקלון דעל ידי ממון הוה וטעמא דעדים מעידין אותה הא אין עדים מעידין אותה לא מאי לאו לא שנא הורהנה ולא שנא נחבשה לא הורהנה שאני איכא דרמי לה מירמא תנן על ידי ממון מותרת לבעלה ורמינהו העיד רבי יוסי כו' והא אשקלון דע"י ממון וקתני טעמא דעדים מעידים אותה הא אין עדים מעידין אותה לא ומשני אמר רב שמואל בר רב יצחק לא קשיא כאן שיד ישראל תקיפה על עובדי כוכבים כאן שיד עובדי כוכבים תקיפה על עצמן: על ידי נפשות אסורה וכו': אמר רב כגון (א) נשי גנבי ולוי אמר [א] כגון אשתו של בן דונאי אמר חזקיה והוא שנגמר דינן להריגה ורבי יוחנן אמר [ב] אע"פ שלא נגמר דינן להריגה: **מתני'** [ג] עיר שכבשוה [ד] כרכום כל כהנות שנמצאו בתוכה פסולות [ה] ואם יש להן עדים אפילו עבד אפי' שפחה הרי אלו נאמנין ואין נאמן אדם על ידי עצמו: **גמ'** ורמינהו [ו] בלשת שבאה לעיר בשעת שלום חביות פתוחות אסורות סתומות מותרות בשעת מלחמה אלו ואלו מותרות לפי שאין פנאי לנסך אמר רב מרי לבעול יש פנאי לנסך אין פנאי רבי יצחק בר אלעזר משמיה דחזקיה אמר כאן [ז] בכרכום של אותה מלכות כאן בכרכום של מלכות אחרת של אותה מלכות נמי אי אפשר דלא (ב) ערק חד מינייהו אמר רב יהודה אמר שמואל כשמשמרות רואות זו את זו אי אפשר דלא ניימא פורתא

אמר רבי לוי [ז] כגון דמהדר לה למתא שושילתא וכלבא וגווזא ואווזא אמר רבי אבא בר זבדא פליגי בה רבי יהודה נשיאה ורבנן חד אמר כאן בכרכום של אותה מלכות כאן בכרכום של מלכות אחרת ולא קשיא ליה ולא מידי וחד קשיא ליה כל הני ומשני כגון דמהדר ליה למתא שושילתא וכלבא וגווזא ואווזא אמר רב אידי בר אבין אמר ר' יצחק בר אשיאן [ח] אם יש שם מחבואה אחת מצלת על הכהנות כולן בעי רבי ירמיה אינה מחזקת אלא אחת מהו מי אמרינן [ט] כל חדא וחדא היינו הא או דלמא לא אמרינן ומאי שנא משני [י] שבילין אחד טמא ואחד טהור והלך באחד מהן ועשה טהרות ובא חבירו והלך בשני ועשה טהרות רבי יהודה אומר אם נשאל זה בפני עצמו וזה בפני עצמו טהורות שניהם כאחת טמאות ר' יוסי אומר בין כך ובין כך טמאין ואמר רבא ואיתימא ר' יוחנן [כ] בבת אחת דברי הכל טמאין בזה אחר זה דברי הכל טהורים לא נחלקו אלא בבא לישאל עליו ועל חבירו מר מדמי ליה לבבת אחת ומר [כ] מדמי ליה לבזה אחר זה והכא נמי כיון דשרי להו לכולהו כבת אחת דמי הכי השתא התם ודאי איכא טומאה הכא מי יימר דאיטמי בעי רב אשי אמרה לא נחבאתי ולא נטמאתי מהו מי אמרינן מה

רש"י

הורהנה. למלעט וכיון להגיע זמן ולא נפדית הרי היא של עובדי כוכבים לדיניהם משום הכי בעינן עדים מעידין אותה שלא נסתרה: **נחבשה.** דלאיה נתלטת להם לא בעינן עדים הואיל ועל ידי ממון הוא: **ואיכא דרמי לה מרמא.** לא מתני לה להא דרב שמואל בר רב יצחק אפירושא דמתניתין בלשון לא שנו אלא רמי מירמא מתניתין ובריתא אהדדי ועלה שני רב שמואל חילוק בין יד ישראל תקיפה ליד העובדי כוכבים תקיפה: **הני נשי דגנבי.** שבעליהן ניתלין ודרך המלכות להפקיר ביתם ונשיהן: **בן דונאי.** רולח היה ואלעזר שמו כדאמרינן בפ' עגלה ערופה (סוטה מז.) אבל נשי דגנבי הגוזלים ממון לא מפקרי: **מתני' כרכום.** מצור מתרגמינן כרכומא (דברים כ): **פסולות.** אסורות לבעליהן דאשת כהן אסורה באונס: **גמ' בלשת.** חיל על שם ° שמחפשים כל המטמונים: **לבעול יש פנאי.** דתקיף להו יצרייהו: **רבי יצחק בן אלעזר אמר.** אף בבעילה פעמים שהן מותרות: **כרכום של אותה מלכות.** אינו רוצה להשחית את בני העיר וכשכובש עיר הסמוך לממשלתו שומרה והיא לו לשם עובד: **משמרות.** מקום מעמד השומרים שהעמיד המלך שלא יקבל אדם באנשי העיר: **דמהדר למתא כו'.** שמו סביבות העיר שלשלות ברזל שישמיעו קול בהכשל איש רך עליהם וכלבים ואווזים זועקין: **וגווזא.** מקלות וקיסמין להכשל בהן: **ולא קשיא ליה מידי.** לא חייש למיעקר איניש יחידאה ולבעול הואיל ואין הדבר הפקר: **ומאי שנא משני שבילין.** דכיון דבא לשאול עליו ועל חבירו אמר רבי יוסי טמאין הכא נמי לכולהו שרינן כי הדדי: **אחד טמא.** שיש בו קברות מפסיק כל רחבו ואין ידוע איזהו הטמא אבל כך מוחזקים באחד מהן: **ועשה טהרות.** נגע בטהרות: **טהורים.** דכל חד כי אתי לקמן תלינן ליה למימר בטהור הלך דהוה ליה ספק טומאה בר"ה וספיקו טהור: **טמאין.** דהיכי נימא להו טהורים אתם חד מינייהו ודאי בטמא אזל: **בבת אחת.** באו לשאול בבת אחת: **הכא נמי כו'.** ור' יהודה ור' יוסי הלכה כר' יוסי:

תוספות

כאן בכרכום של אותה מלכות. פי' שיושבין בעת לפי שאין אחריהן מחנה ויש פנאי לנסך ולבעול אבל בלשת של מלכות אחרת שאימת מלכות שבאו בגבולה עליהם אין להן פנאי וכן פי' ר"ח ור"ת וכן מוכח בירושלמי ופריך כרכום של אותה מלכות אי אפשר דלא ערקה חדא מינייהו והוה לן למשריינהו לכולהו ולמיתלי לקולא דבשבויה הקילו כדאמרינן בסמוך אם יש מחבואה אחת מצלת על כל הכהנות כולן אע"ג דמספקא לן באיזה מחזקת אלא אחת הכא פשיטא לן דשרו דהתם לא ודאי נחבאה אבל הכא ודאי ערקה ולפי' הקונטרס קשה טובא חדא דפריך נתלי לחומרא וגבי מחבואה תלינן לקולא ועוד דמה מתרץ למהדר למתא כו' ואין אדם נכנס לשם והא קתני בלשת שנכנסה לעיר ועוד כיון דאההיא דע"ז פריך הוה ליה למימר אי אפשר דלא ערק חד מינייהו ונסך ועוד דהתם מפרש טעמא לפי שאין פנאי לנסך ולית ליה טעמא לפי שאין כרכום של אותה מלכות רוצה להשחית את בני העיר [ועוד מאי שנא שעת מלחמה משעת שלום] ויש ליישב לפי שיטת הקונטרס דרבי יצחק בן אלעזר לא אתי לשנויי מתני' אההיא דע"ז אלא אית ליה סיגויא דרב מרי ומתניתין דהתם נמי בכרכום של מלכות אחרת ולא בא אלא לפרושי מתניתין וכן משמע בפרק בתרא דע"ז (דף עא.) דפריך התם ממתניתין דהכא אמתניתין דבלשת ולא מייתי התם דרבי יצחק:

והלך באחד מהם ועשה טהרות. להכי נקט ועשה טהרות לענין האדם אנו מזקיקים שניהם לטבול ולהזות פן יבואו לידי טומאה ודאי אם יגעו שניהם בככר אחד לכך אומר להו זילו טבילו דהא נהרא קמייכו ועוד דמשום דבעי למתני [ז] סיפא הזה וטבל טהור הלך בשני ועשה טהרות הרי אלו טהורות ואם קיימות הראשונים אלו ואלו תלויות ואם לא טהר בינתים הראשונות תלויות והשניות ישרפו [ח]:

ואם נשאל זה בפני עצמו וזה בפני עצמו טהורות. לא שיאכלם אדם אחד דאם כן יאכל ודאי טומאה דהכי אמרינן בשבועות בפ"ב (דף יט.) הלך בראשון ולא נכנס בשני ונכנס חייב דטמא הוא ממה נפשך: **בבא** לישאל עליו ועל חברו. אין לפרש שבא לישאל בבת אחת דהתם מודו כולי עלמא דטמאות מכל שכן דבאו לישאל שניהם בבת אחת אלא איירי ששאל על עצמו וטהרוהו ואח"כ בא לישאל על חבירו דמר מדמי ליה לבת אחת כיון ששאל על שניהם במעמד אחד ומר מדמי ליה לזה אחר זה כיון שטיהרוהו קודם והכא נמי כיון דשרו לכולהו כבת אחת דמי אף על פי שאין בא לפנינו אלא על אחת מ"מ הדבר ידוע לכל שהרבה כהנות היו והוי כאילו בא לישאל על כולם בבת אחת והכא מודו כ"ע ובחנם דחק בקונטרס לפרש כר' יוסי:

לא

מסורת הש"ס

א) [עירובין סה: וש"נ], ב) עדיות פרק ח מ"ב, ג) ע"ז עא., ד) [בערוך איתא כרקום בקו"ף], ה) שם ע: שבת מא. נדה יג., ו) טהרות פ"ה מ"ה פסחים י., ז) [למיתנא סיפא כרישא כצ"ל. מהרש"א], ח) [וע"ע תוס' פסחים י. ד"ה הלך].

ליקוטי רש"י

באו שניהם ביחד הוה מסקינן ליה ומוקמינן ליה אחזקיה קמייתא דמוחזק לן באבוה דכהן הוא ולזילותא לא חיישינן ורשב"ג כר' נתן. **ובפלוגתא דהני תנאי.** ר' נתן ורבנן. **דתניא אין עדותן מצטרפת.** אין צריך כאן בהאי מחלוקת דרבי יהושע בן קרחה ורבנן אלא כך היא ברייתא שלימה בשילהי זה בורר ומשום גררא דסיפא נקט רישא. **אפי' בזה אחר זה.** אחד אומר ביום ראשון לוה פלוני מפלוני מנה ואחד אומר ביום שני ראיתיו גם אני שלוה ממנו דמ"מ אמנה קא מסהדי ות"ק סבר אמנה דקא מסהיד האי לא קא מסהיד האי וה"ל לגבי מנה חצי עדות וטעמייהו מפרש שפיר בסנהדרין מקרא ומסברא. **ואין עדותן וכו' עד שיעידו שניהם כאחד.** להתקבל בב"ד ואפי' ראו שניהם כאחד עד שיעידו שניהם כאחד בפני ב"ד ופלוגתא אחריתי היא ולא ר' יהושע בן קרחה קאמר לה ור' אלעזר ורשב"ג בפלוגתא דר"נ ורבנן פליגי [שם לב.]. **לפסוק הדין על פיהם.** וסתמא הוא ולא ר' יהושע בן קרחה קאמר לה [סנהדרין ל.]. **על ידי ממון.** שהיתה חייבת ממון. **מותרת לבעלה.** דסבר אי בעילנא לה תו לא פרע לי בעלה מידי. **על ידי נפשות.** שנתחייבה הריגה. **אסורה לבעלה.** היכא דלא מירתת להפסד ממונו לאפקורי מפקר לה ותיישינן שמא נבעלה לאחד מהן ברצון ולית דמוקמי לה באשת כהן דמיתסרא באונס ולא עיקר דבכתובות (דף כו) מוכח דבאשת ישראל קאי [ע"ז כג.]. [ע"כ שייך לדף כו:]

כל כהנות שנמצאו בתוכה פסולות. לבעליהן דאשת כהן אסורה אף באונס אבל אשת ישראל לא [ע"ז עא.]. **אפילו עבד אפי' שפחה.** דבשבויה האמינו חכמים עד אחד להקל ואפילו עבד ואפילו שפחה כדקתני מתני' אם יש להן עדים אפילו עבד כו' [לעיל כג.]. **בלשת.** חיילות גייס הבא לצור על העיר שם שמחפשין את העיר קרי להו בולשת [שבת מא.]. חיל על שם שמחפשין ומתרגמינן להו בולשת כדמתרגמינן (בראשית לא) ויחפש ובלש [ע"ז ע:]. בולשת חיל שמחפשין ובוזזין כדמתרגמינן ויחפש ובלש [נדה יג.]. **בשעת שלום.** כגון שבאה של אותה מלכות [שבת שם]. **לפי שאין פנאי לנסך.** הא הכא דשעת מלחמה היא

עין משפט נר מצוה

קב א ב מיי' פי"ח מהל' איסורי ביאה הלכה ל טוש"ע אה"ע סימן ז סעיף יא בהג"ה:

קג ג מיי' פי"ח מהל' א"ב הלכה כו טור ש"ע שם סעיף י:

קד ד מיי' שם הל' יט טוש"ע שם סעיף א:

קה ה מיי' פי"ג מהל' מאכלות אסורות הלכה כד סמג לאוין קמח טוש"ע י"ד סי' קכט סעיף יב:

קו ו ז ח ט מיי' פי"ח מהל' איסורי ביאה הלכה כז כח כט טוש"ע אה"ע סי' ז סעיף י:

קז י כ מיי' פי"ט מהל' אבות הטומאה הלכה ג:

הגהות הב"ח

(א) גמ' כגון הני נשי דגנבי: (ב) שם דלא (ערק) תז"מ. ונ"ב ס"א עקר וכן משמע מפרש"י:

גליון הש"ס

רש"י ד"ה בלשת וכו' שמחפשין. כי בפסוק ויחפש ברא**שית מ"ד התרגום ובלש:

תוספות רי"ד

ומפקרי לה. **ה"ד** ע"י נפשות א"ר כגון נשי דגנבי אמר חזקיה והוא שנגמר דינם להריגה פי' שבעליהן נתלו ודרך המלכות להפקיר טפם ונשיהם ור"י אמר אעפ"י שלא נגמר דינן להריגה. והל' כחזקיה דהוא רביה דר' יוחנן: **עיר שכבשוה כרכום.** פי' חיל הצרים עליה. מצור תרגומו כרכום כל כהנות שבתוכה פסולו' לבעליהן פי' דבחזקת שנבעלו קיימו ואנוסה אסורה לכהן ואם יש להן עדים שלא נבעלו אפילו עבד אפילו שפחה הרי אלו נאמנים ואין אדם נאמן ע"י עצמו לא האשה להעיד על עצמה ולא הבעל להעיד על אשתו **ורמינהו** בולשת שנכנסה לעיר. פי' חיל ונקרא כן ע"ש שמחפשים את כל המטמוניות תרגום ויחפש ובלש בזמן שלום חביות פתוחות אסורות וסתומות מותרת בשעת מלחמה אלו ואלו מותרות לפי שאין פנאי לנסך. **אמר** ר"מ לנסך אין פנאי לבעול יש פנאי דיצרא דעבירה תקיף מיין נסך ר"י בן אלעזר משמיה דחזקי' אמר כאן בכרכום של אותה מלכות אינן יראים ויש להם פנאי לבעול ולנסך. אבל של מלכות אחרת יראים [שמא] יבוא חיל מאיזה מלכות לעזור להן וממהרים לשלול ולהבריח ואין להן פנאי לא לבעול ולא לנסך. **א"ר** אידי ב"א אר"י ב"א אם יש שם מחבואה א' [מצלת] על כל הכהנות ומותרות כלן: **בעי ר"י** אם אינה מחזקת אלא א' מהן מהו. מי אמרינן כל חדא וחדא היינו האי א"ד לא אמרינן ולא איפשיטא

וקתני אסורות דיש פנאי לבעול. **לנסך אין פנאי.** דילר היניסוך לא תקיף להו וטרודין במלחמה [ע"ז עא.]. **ניימא.** מתנמנמת [סנהדרין ז.]. **אחד טמא.** קבר מוטל בו לרחבו וממלא את כולו ואין עובר בו שלא יאהיל. **והלך באחד מהן ועשה טהרות.** נגע בטהרות אחר כך. **ובא חבירו והלך בשני.** יודעין הן שבשביל שהלך זה לא הלך זה דהשתא ודאי אחד מהן טמא. **אם נשאל.** כל אחד לאכס ספקו בפני עצמו. **טהורות.** ואין בית דין יכול לטמאו דקיימא לן בספק טומאה ברשות הרבים ספקו טהור. **שניהם כאחת.** הואיל ובהוראה אחת יש לנו לומר טמאין או טהורין אי אפשר לנו לומר להם טהורים אתם שהרי האחד ודאי טמא. **בזה אחר זה דברי הכל טהורים.** אע"פ שכל אחד אומר לפנינו כך היה המעשה שלי ושל חבירי אבל איני נשאל אלא על עצמי מה תהא עלי. **עליו ועל חבירו וכו' לבבת אחת.** מה תהא על שנינו ר' יוסי מדמי להו לבת אחת ואף על פי שאין שניהן לפניך צריך אתה הוראה אחת לשניהן או טמאין אתם או טהורין אתם והרי אין אתה יכול לומר טהורין אתם. **ומר מדמי ליה וכו'.** הואיל ואין כאן שואל אלא אחד משיבין לו טהור אתה שהרי ספק ביאה הוא ומעצמו יבין שאף חבירו כמוהו אבל כששניהן שואלין בתוך כדי דיבור צריך אתה להשיב לשניהן כאחד [פסחים י.].

הוּרְהֲנָה אִין – that if **she pledged herself – yes,** she requires witnesses to render her permissible, נֶחְבְּשָׁה לֹא – but if **she was imprisoned** against her will – **no,** she does not require witnesses.[1] We see that even in a place where the idolaters are in power, a woman imprisoned because of a monetary matter is assumed not to have been violated. This contradicts the statement of Rav Shmuel bar Rav Yitzchak. – ? –

The Gemara rejects Rava's inference:

הוּא הַדִּין אֲפִילוּ נֶחְבְּשָׁה – Really **this same law applies even** when **she was imprisoned** against her will; וּמַעֲשֶׂה שֶׁהָיָה כָּךְ הָיָה – **however, the incident that occurred, occurred this way,** i.e. with a woman who pledged herself.[2] Nothing may be inferred from the fact that the Mishnah does not discuss the case of a woman who was imprisoned.

The Gemara cites an alternative version of Rava's comment, in which he does not challenge Rav Shmuel bar Rav Yitzchak's statement, but supports it:

אִיכָּא דְּאָמְרִי – **There are those who say:** אָמַר רָבָא – **Rava said:** אַף אֲנַן נַמִּי תָּנֵינָא – **We too have learned this in a Mishnah:** הֵעִיד רַבִּי יוֹסֵי הַכֹּהֵן וְרַבִּי זְכַרְיָה בֶּן הַקַּצָּב עַל בַּת יִשְׂרָאֵל שֶׁהוּרְהֲנָה בְּאַשְׁקְלוֹן – R' YOSE THE KOHEN AND R' ZECHARYAH BEN HAKATZAV TESTIFIED REGARDING A JEWISH WOMAN WHO PLEDGED HERSELF to idolaters IN ASHKELON, וְרִיחֲקוּהָ בְּנֵי מִשְׁפַּחְתָּהּ – AND WHOSE FAMILY therefore DISTANCED HER. וְעֵדֶיהָ מְעִידִים עָלֶיהָ שֶׁלֹּא נִסְתְּרָה וְשֶׁלֹּא נִטְמְאָה – HOWEVER, HER WITNESSES TESTIFIED REGARDING HER THAT SHE DID NOT SECLUDE HERSELF with AND WAS NOT VIOLATED by her creditors. וְאָמְרוּ חֲכָמִים – AND THE SAGES SAID: אִם אַתֶּם מַאֲמִינִים שֶׁהוּרְהֲנָה – IF YOU BELIEVE THAT SHE PLEDGED HERSELF, הַאֲמִינוּ שֶׁלֹּא נִסְתְּרָה וְשֶׁלֹּא נִטְמְאָה – YOU MUST BELIEVE THAT SHE DID NOT SECLUDE HERSELF AND WAS NOT VIOLATED. וְאִם אֵין אַתֶּם מַאֲמִינִים שֶׁלֹּא נִסְתְּרָה וְשֶׁלֹּא נִטְמְאָה – AND IF YOU DO NOT BELIEVE THAT SHE DID NOT SECLUDE HERSELF AND WAS NOT VIOLATED, אַל תַּאֲמִינוּ שֶׁהוּרְהֲנָה – YOU MAY NOT BELIEVE THAT SHE PLEDGED HERSELF!

Rava develops his proof:

וְהָא אַשְׁקְלוֹן דְּעַל יְדֵי מָמוֹן הֲוָה – **Now** this incident in **Ashkelon was** one in which she was imprisoned **because of a monetary matter.**[3] וְטַעְמָא דְּעֵדִים מְעִידִין אוֹתָהּ – **Still, the reason** she is permitted **is because witnesses testify regarding her** that she was not violated. הָא אֵין עֵדִים מְעִידִין אוֹתָהּ לֹא – **But if no witnesses would testify regarding her,** she would **not** be permitted. מַאי לָאו לֹא שְׁנָא הוּרְהֲנָה וְלֹא שְׁנָא נֶחְבְּשָׁה – Now **is it not** implied in this Mishnah that **no matter whether she pledged herself or whether she was imprisoned** against her will, she is permitted only if witnesses testify on her behalf? Seemingly, it is.[4] Accordingly, this Mishnah constitutes proof that in a place where idolaters are their own masters, a woman imprisoned because of monetary matters is forbidden to her husband, as Rav Shmuel bar Rav Yitzchak stated.

Rava's proof is rejected:

לֹא הוּרְהֲנָה שָׁאנִי – **No, [a woman] who pledged herself is different,** since she is by their law the idolater's property. One imprisoned against her will, however, is not his property.[5] Therefore, she may well be permitted to her husband, even in a place where the idolaters are in power.

The Gemara now cites another version of Rav Shmuel bar Rav Yitzchak's statement, in which he does not qualify the ruling of our Mishnah, but resolves a contradiction between our Mishnah and the Mishnah cited above:[6]

אִיכָּא דְּרָמֵי לָהּ מִירְמָא – **There were those who posed it as a contradiction,** as follows: תְּנַן – **We have learned in our Mishnah:** עַל יְדֵי מָמוֹן מוּתֶּרֶת לְבַעְלָהּ – If it is BECAUSE OF A MONETARY MATTER, SHE IS PERMITTED TO HER HUSBAND. וּרְמִינְהוּ – **But contrast [our Mishnah with this other Mishnah],** which states: הֵעִיד רַבִּי יוֹסֵי כו׳ – R' YOSE THE KOHEN AND R' ZECHARYAH BEN HAKATZAV TESTIFIED etc. וְהָא אַשְׁקְלוֹן דְּעַל יְדֵי מָמוֹן – **Now** this incident in **Ashkelon was** one in which she was imprisoned **because of a monetary matter.** וְקָתָנֵי טַעְמָא דְּעֵדִים מְעִידִים אוֹתָהּ – **Still, the Mishnah teaches** that **the reason** she is permitted **is because witnesses testify regarding her** that she was not violated. הָא אֵין עֵדִים מְעִידִין אוֹתָהּ לֹא – **But if no witnesses would testify regarding her,** she would **not** be permitted, despite being imprisoned for monetary reasons. This seems to contradict our Mishnah.[7] וּמְשַׁנֵּי – **And they answered** thus: אָמַר רַב שְׁמוּאֵל בַּר רַב יִצְחָק – **Rav Shmuel bar Rav Yitzchak said:** לֹא קַשְׁיָא – **There is no difficulty.** כָּאן שֶׁיַּד יִשְׂרָאֵל תַּקִּיפָה עַל עוֹבְדֵי כּוֹכָבִים – **Here** (i.e. in our Mishnah) we are speaking of a place **where the hand of Israel is mighty over the idolaters.** כָּאן שֶׁיַּד עוֹבְדֵי כּוֹכָבִים תַּקִּיפָה עַל עַצְמָן – **Here** (i.e. in the other Mishnah) we are speaking of a place **where the hand of the idolaters is mighty over themselves.** Where the idolaters are ruled by Jews, a woman imprisoned because of a monetary matter is permitted to her husband; where they rule themselves, she is not.

The Mishnah stated:

עַל יְדֵי נְפָשׁוֹת אֲסוּרָה וכו׳ – If it is BECAUSE OF A CAPITAL CRIME, SHE IS FORBIDDEN [to her husband] etc.

The Gemara elaborates:

אָמַר רַב – **Rav said:** כְּגוֹן נְשֵׁי גַּנָּבֵי – **Such as the wives of thieves.** Under the law of the idolaters, the husbands of these women are hanged, and their wives and property are abandoned

NOTES

1. The Gemara now assumes that the Mishnah in *Eduyos* deliberately discusses the case of a woman who pledged herself to idolaters, and not that of a woman imprisoned by them. [The assumption is that the Mishnah does this in order to teach the difference between the two cases, as follows:] One who pledges herself does so willingly; if the debt is not paid, she becomes the lawful property of the creditor (under the laws of the idolaters). [Since he is free to do with her as he wishes,] we assume that she was violated unless witnesses testify otherwise. A woman imprisoned against her will, however, is not by law the chattel of her jailer. Therefore, as long as her imprisonment is only for monetary reasons, she remains permitted to her husband, notwithstanding that she is in a place where the idolaters rule over Israel (*Rashi; Ritva*). This seems to contradict Rav Shmuel bar Rav Yitzchak's ruling.

2. The Gemara now recognizes that there is no difference between a woman who pledged herself and one who was imprisoned. In a place where idolaters are in power, both require witnesses. The Mishnah did not deliberately choose to discuss a woman who pledged herself – that was simply the way the incident occurred. For an understanding of why the Gemara originally did see significance in the Mishnah's choice of topic, see *Shitah Mekubetzes* (end of 26b); *Pnei Yehoshua* here.

3. [I.e. the repayment of the debt for which she pledged herself.]

4. According to this version of Rava's comment, Rava sees no difference between a woman who pledged herself and one who was imprisoned.

5. The Gemara now realizes that there *is* reason to differentiate between the two women; see note 1.

6. It is worth noting that *Rashi* (ד״ה ואיכא) refers to the Mishnah in *Eduyos* as a Baraisa. It is not uncommon for the Rishonim to do this; see, for example, *Rashi* to *Sanhedrin* 48a ד״ה אזכיה ולא צר ביה; *Tosafos* to *Yoma* 6b ד״ה סיפא. *Rashash* to *Nedarim* (26b) suggests that when a Mishnah in one tractate is quoted in another, the Rishonim refer to it in this manner; see *Margaliyos HaYam, Sanhedrin* ibid. §14 in this vein.

7. In this version of the exchange, the Gemara clearly does not recognize any difference between a woman who pledged herself and one who was imprisoned (see *Shitah Mekubetzes* ד״ה איכא דרמי לה).

TESTIFIED REGARDING A JEWISH WOMAN WHO PLEDGED HERSELF to idolaters **IN ASHKELON,**[23] וְרִיחֲקוּהָ בְּנֵי מִשְׁפַּחְתָּהּ – **AND WHOSE FAMILY** therefore **DISTANCED HER.**[24] וְעֵדֶיהָ מְעִידִים אוֹתָהּ שֶׁלֹּא נִסְתְּרָה וְשֶׁלֹּא נִטְמְאָה – **HOWEVER, HER WITNESSES**[25] **TESTIFIED REGARDING HER THAT SHE DID NOT SECLUDE HERSELF** with **AND WAS NOT VIOLATED** by her creditors. וְאָמְרוּ לָהֶם חֲכָמִים – **AND THE SAGES SAID TO THEM** (i.e. to her family): The witnesses testifying that she pledged herself are the very ones testifying that she was not violated; אִם אַתֶּם מַאֲמִינִים שֶׁהוּרְהֲנָה – therefore, **IF YOU BELIEVE THAT SHE PLEDGED HERSELF,** הַאֲמִינוּ שֶׁלֹּא נִסְתְּרָה וְשֶׁלֹּא נִטְמְאָה – **YOU MUST BELIEVE THAT SHE DID NOT SECLUDE HERSELF AND WAS NOT VIOLATED.** וְאִם אִי אַתֶּם מַאֲמִינִים שֶׁלֹּא נִסְתְּרָה וְשֶׁלֹּא נִטְמְאָה – **AND IF YOU DO NOT BELIEVE THAT SHE DID NOT SECLUDE HERSELF AND WAS NOT VIOLATED,** אַל תַּאֲמִינוּ שֶׁהוּרְהֲנָה – **YOU MAY NOT BELIEVE THAT SHE PLEDGED HERSELF!** Either way, you may not distance her.[26]

Rava draws an inference from this Mishnah:

וְהָא אַשְׁקְלוֹן דְּיַד עוֹבְדֵי כּוֹכָבִים תַּקִּיפָה עַל עַצְמָן – **Now Ashkelon** is a place **where the hand of the idolaters is mighty over themselves.**[27] וְקָתָנֵי – **Yet,** by choosing to discuss the case of a woman who pledged herself, **[this Mishnah] teaches**

NOTES

23. I.e. she pledged herself as security for a debt (*Rashi*); the loan was not paid, and she became the property of her creditors (see *Rashi* to 27a ד״ה הורהנה).

24. This woman was married into a family of Kohanim. [They suspected her of having been violated by her creditors. This would render her a *zonah* (i.e. a woman who engaged in certain forbidden sexual relationships), and thus forbidden to a Kohen.] They therefore distanced her by forbidding her to marry other members of the family, i.e. Kohanim [in the event her husband would die] (*Mordechai*).

25. I.e. the witnesses who testified that she had pledged herself (*Rashi*).

26. These were not ordinary, valid witnesses, but were slaves or slavewomen, whose testimony is generally invalid. It was for this reason that the woman's family did not trust them regarding her permissibility (*Ritva; Rashba* et al.). Although such witnesses *are* believed to testify regarding the permissibility of a captive [שְׁבוּיָה] (see Mishnah 27a), a woman who pledged herself to an idolater is more likely to be violated, since she cannot be counted on to make herself repulsive to the idolaters, as can a captive woman. Also, since a woman who pledged herself is by law the chattel of her creditor (see 27a note 1), it is more likely that he molested her. For these reasons, the family assumed that these subpar witnesses would not suffice. Nevertheless, the Sages commanded that their testimony be heeded. For in this case we depend entirely upon their testimony to prohibit the woman; since their words are the sole source of the suspicion regarding her, we are compelled to believe them when they state that she was not violated (*Rashba;* see *Tos. R' Akiva Eiger* to *Eduyos* ibid.). This reasoning is often expressed in Mishnaic terms as הַפֶּה שֶׁאָסַר הוּא הַפֶּה שֶׁהִתִּיר, *The mouth that prohibited is the very mouth that permitted* (see above, 16a; 22a).

27. For Ashkelon was [originally] a part of Philistia, and the Philistines always remained strong there. Furthermore, this incident took place after [the greater part of] Israel was exiled [and the Jews no longer held sway over the Philistines] (*Rashi;* see *Ritva;* see *Tos. Yom Tov* to *Eduyos* ibid.).

עין משפט נר מצוה

צט א מיי' פ"ד מהל' עדות הלכה ד סמג עשין קט טוש"ע ח"מ סימן ל סעיף ו:
ק ב מיי' שם פ"כ מהל' איסורי ביאה הל' טו סמג שם טוש"ע ח"מ סי' ל סעיף ט וטוש"ע אה"ע סי' ג סעיף ז:
קא ג ד מיי' פי"ח מהל' איסורי ביאה הל' ל סמג לאוין קכא טוש"ע אה"ע סימן ז סעיף יא:

מסורת הש"ס

א) ב"ב לב, ב) ג"ז שם ודף קסה: סנהדרין ל. גיטין לג: [תוספתא סנהדרין פרק ה], ג) ע"ז כג, ד) עדיות פ"ח מ"ב, ה) [שם:]:

ואסקיניה [א] ואתו בי תרי ואמרי בן גרושה ובן חלוצה הוא ואחתיניה ואתא עד אחד ואמר ידענא ביה דכהן הוא ודכולי עלמא מצטרפין לעדות והכא במיחש לזילותא דבי דינא קמיפלגי תנא קמא סבר כיון דאחתיניה לא מסקינן ליה חיישינן לזילותא דבי דינא ורשב"ג סבר אנן אחתינן ליה ואנן מסקינן ליה ולזילותא דבי דינא לא חיישינן מתקיף לה רב אשי אי הכי אפי' תרי ותרי נמי אלא אמר רב אשי במצטרפין לעדות קמיפלגי [ג] ובפלוגתא דהני תנאי דתניא אין עדותן מצטרפת עד שיראו שניהם כאחד ר' יהושע בן קרחה אומר [א] אפי' בזה אחר זה ואין עדותן מתקיימת בב"ד עד שיעידו שניהם כאחד ר' נתן אומר [ב] שומעין דבריו של זה היום וכשיבא חבירו למחר שומעין דבריו:

מתני' [ג] האשה שנחבשה בידי עובדי כוכבים על ידי ממון מותרת לבעלה על ידי נפשות אסורה לבעלה:

גמ' אמר רב שמואל בר רב יצחק [ד] לא שנו אלא שיד ישראל תקיפה על עובדי כוכבים אבל יד עובדי כוכבים תקיפה על עצמן אפילו על ידי ממון אסורה לבעלה מתיב רבא [ה] העיד רבי יוסי הכהן ור' זכריה בן הקצב על בת ישראל שהורהנה באשקלון וריחקוה בני משפחתה ועדיה מעידים אותה שלא נסתרה ושלא נטמאה ואמרו להם חכמים אם אתם מאמינים שהורהנה האמינו שלא נסתרה ושלא נטמאה ואם אי אתם מאמינים שלא נסתרה ושלא נטמאה אל תאמינו שהורהנה והא אשקלון דיד עובדי כוכבים תקיפה על עצמן וקתני הורהנה

רש"י

ואסקיניה. דבמקום קול הוי חד מהימן: **ודכולי עלמא.** בין לר' אלעזר בין לר"ש: **מצטרפין.** שני עדים המעידים זה שלא בפני זה בשאר עדות: **דחיישינן לזילותא דבי דינא.** שהורידוהו שני פעמים ועכשיו יעלוהו ויבטלו דבריהם והיינו דקאמר ר' אלעזר למאחר שהורדוהו ע"פ העוררין אין מעלין ע"פ עד זה השני אע"פ שיש לצרפו עם האחר: **ואנן מסקינן ליה.** ולאי קשיא תרי ותרי נינהו אוקי תרי לבהדי תרי ואוקמינן אחזקיה קמייתא דלאסקיניה ע"פ עד הראשון שהוא נאמן דהא אכתי אין עוררין דקול לאו עוררין הוא: **אפילו תרי.** אתו בהדי הדדי נמי בפעם שניה לרבי אלעזר לא מסקינן ליה: **עד שיראו שניהם כאחד.** את העדות לאפוקי אחד אומר בפני הלווה ואחד אומר בפני הודה לו עליו: **ואין עדותן מתקיימת.** להתקבל בב"ד ואפי' ראו שניהן כאחד ופלוגתא אחריתי היא ולאו ר' יהושע בן קרחה קאמר לה ורבי אלעזר ורבן שמעון בפלוגתא דרבי נתן ורבנן פליגי: **מתני' ע"י ממון מותרת לבעלה.** דמרתתי להפסיד ממונן ולאין מפקירין אותה: **ע"י נפשות.** שהיתה נידונת למות: **אסורה לבעלה.** דהואיל ונוהגין בה הפקר חוששין שמא נתרצתה לאחד מהן: **גמ' לא שנו.** דע"י ממון מותרת לבעלה: **אלא שיד ישראל תקיפה על העובדי כוכבים.** ויראים לעשות שלא כדין שמא יפסידו ממונם: **שהורהנה.** נתמשכנה: **ועדיה.** אותן שהעידו שהורהנה: **והא אשקלון.** דארץ פלשתים היא ועוד ככר גלו ישראל: הורהנה

תוספות

ואסקיניה. וא"ת ולמאן דחייש לזילותא דבי דינא היכי אסקוהו כיון דלאחתיניה מחמת הקול וליכא למימר דליכא זילותא דבי דינא אלא היכא שהורידוהו שני פעמים כדמוכח בחזקת הבתים (ב"ב דף לג.) וי"ל דליכא זילותא דבי דינא אלא היכא שהורידוהו ע"י עדות אבל בהורדה שע"י הקול ליכא זילותא דב"ד ואע"ג דאמרינן (גיטין דף פא.) גבי גרושה לכהן דלא מבטלינן קלא היינו משום דלית ליה תקנתא אבל הכא דאי לא מסקינן ליה לעולם פסול מבטלינן א) אי נמי בתרומה דרבנן הקילו: **אנן אחתינן ליה אנן מסקינן ליה.** פי' בקונטרס אע"ג דתרי ותרי נינהו אוקי תרי להדי תרי ואוקי גברא אחזקתיה וקשה לר"י דבפרק האומר בקדושין (דף סו. ושם) קאמר גבי ינאי היכי דמי אילימא דתרי אמרי אשתבאי ותרי אמרי לא אשתבאי מאי חזית דסמכת אהני סמוך אהני ואמאי קאמר ויבוקש הדבר ולא נמצא והתם פי' בקונטרס דלא אמרי' אוקי תרי בהדי תרי ואוקי גברא אחזקיה דהא לא באו להעיד על אמו אלא על ינאי ולו לא היה חזקת כשרות ואין נראה לר"י דחזקת האם מהניא גם לינאי כדמשמע הכא ואמרינן נמי לעיל בפ"ק (דף יג. ושם) לדברי המכשיר בה מכשיר בבתה ואפילו מאן דפסל בבתה היינו משום דמעלה עשו גבי זנות וגם אין לומר כמו שתירץ ר"ת דליכא למימר התם אוקמינן אחזקה לפי שכל הנשים היו בחזקת שבויות דא"כ היכי מייתי מינה ראיה על אשתו שזינתה בעד אחד דשאני התם דכל הנשים בחזקת שבויות אבל אשתו זינתה היא בחזקת היתר ונראה לר"י דתרי ותרי ספיקא דרבנן הוא ומדרבנן החמירו דלא מוקמינן לה אחזקה והכא בתרומה דרבנן הקילו ובפרק בכל מערבין (עירובין דף לה.) גבי תרומה ונטמאה כו' ספק הרי זה חמר גמל דברי ר"מ ומוקי לה ה) רבה ורב יוסף בשתי כתי עדים הא דלא מוקמינן לה אחזקתה דלא נטמאת אע"ג דתרומה בזמן הזה דרבנן היינו משום דערובי תחומין דאורייתא לר"מ אי נמי שאני התם דאיכא ריעותא דהרי נטמאת לפניך ולא אמרינן השתא הוא דאיטמי אע"ג דגבי מקוה אמרינן השתא הוא דחסר ואתאי (נדה דף ב:) הכא דאיכא שתי כתי עדים לא אמרינן השתא הוא דאיטמי ובשנים אומרים מת ושנים אומרים לא מת דאמרינן לעיל (דף כב:) לא תנשא ולא מוקמינן לה אחזקה אשת איש היינו משום דחזקה דאשה דייקא ומנסבא מרעה לה לחזקת אשת איש אע"ג דבשנים אומרים מת אמרינן בהאשה רבה (יבמות פח:) דמותרת לחזור לו וכיון דליכא חומרא בסוף לא דייקא מ"מ הכא כיון דמכחישין זה את זה איכא חומרא ובשנים אומרים נתגרשה ושנים אומרים לא נתגרשה דאמרינן נמי לא תנשא אע"ג דלא דייקא וליכא נמי חזקה דאין האשה מעיזה פניה דשלא בפני בעלה מעיזה וכ"ש היכא דמסייעין לה עדים ויש לומר דמכל מקום דייקא לפי שיראה שיוזמו עדיה או יפסלו אותם בגזלנותא ובהאשה רבה (שם נג: ושם) גבי בעו מיניה מרב ששת עד אחד ביבמה מהו כו' אמר להו תניתוה אמרו לה מת בנך ואחר כך מת בעליך ונתייבמה ואח"כ אמרו לה חילוף הדברים תצא והולד ראשון והאחרון ממזר היכי דמי אילימא תרי ותרי מאי חזית דסמכת אהני לאסרי ליבם סמוך אהני דשרו לה וקשה דמאי פריך והא אית לן לאוקמי אחזקה דאסורה ליבם שמת בעלה תחלה כדאמרינן בפרק ארבעה אחין (שם דף כח. ושם) גבי נפל הבית עליו ועל בת אחיו כו' ועוד כיון דתרי ותרי ספיקא דרבנן הוא יש לאוסרה כדאמרינן גבי ינאי והתם לא דייקא כדאמרינן התם זימנין דרחמא ליה ליבם וי"ל דמ"מ מהני דיוקא דידה לענין דמרעה ליה לחזקת איסור ליבם והא דפריך נמי התם כו' ועוד ממזר ספק ממזר הוא אע"ג דבחזקת איסור ליבם היא מ"מ לא הוי ממזר ודאי דמהני דיוקא דידה כדפרשינן ועוד כיון דתרי ותרי ספיקא דרבנן אין לנו להעמידה על חזקתה ולהתירו בממזרת ורבינו יצחק בר ברוך פי' דלא אמרינן בכל הני אוקמא אחזקה לפי שהשנים שמוציאים אותו מחזקתו של היתר הם מעידים תחלה ומיד כשהעידו יצא מחזקתו ע"י עדותן ותו לא אמרינן אוקמא אחזקה ולהכי פריך לעיל מאי שנא רישא ומאי שנא סיפא דשנים שאומרים נתקדשה העידו תחלה ובשנים אומרים נתגרשה אע"פ שהם העידו תחלה מ"מ היתה בחזקת אשת איש וכן ההיא דהאשה רבה ודינאי שנים המוציאין אותו מחזקתו באו תחלה ואין נראה לרבינו יצחק דהא הכא בשמעתין מוקמינן ליה אחזקה אע"ג דככר פסלוהו השנים והוציאוהו מחזקתו ואין סברא שיועיל מה שעד אחד המכשיר העיד קודם ב) ועוד דרב אשי משמע דבעי למימר דאפילו אתו שניהם לבסוף דמסקינן ליה: **על** ידי ממון מותרת לבעלה. נראה דמותרת אפילו לבעלה כהן דלא חיישינן אפי' לאונסא משום דמרתתי להפסיד ממונם ולא דמי לשבויה וכן מוכח בגמרא דקאמר לא שנו אלא שיד ישראל תקיפה על העובדי כוכבים אבל יד העובדי כוכבים תקיפה על עצמן אפילו ע"י ממון אסורה לבעלה ועל כרחן היינו לכהונה מדקאמרי אף אנן נמי תנינא מההיא דריחקוה בני משפחתה והא לא שייך אלא לכהונה דבישראל לא שייך וריחקוה בני משפחתה דאינה אסורה אלא לבעלה ועוד ראיה דתנן בפ' שני דמסכת ע"ז (דף כב.) אין מעמידין בהמה בפונדקאות של עובדי כוכבים מפני שחשודים על הרביעה ורמינהו לוקחין מהן בהמה לקרבן לא קשיא הא לכתחלה והא דיעבד ומנא תימרא דשני בין לכתחלה כו' דתנן לא תתייחד אשה עמהם מפני שחשודים על העריות ורמינהו האשה שנחבשה ע"י עובדי כוכבים ע"י ממון מותרת לבעלה אלא ש"מ שני לן בין לכתחלה לדיעבד משמע דאין לחוש כלל שנבעלה דאי מותרת לבעלה ישראל קאמר דלא חיישינן שמא נתרצת אבל לבעלה ג) כהן אסורה דחיישינן שמא נאנסה א"כ לא הוה מייתי מידי: **ועל** ידי נפשות אסורה לבעלה. היינו אפילו לבעלה ישראל דחיישינן שמא נתרצת כדי למצא חן שלא יהרגוה דאי לבעלה כהן קאמר ואסורה שמא נאנסה א"כ הוה ליה למימר אסורה לכהונה אלא ודאי אפילו לבעלה ישראל אסורה וא"ת לנועות ליסתרו דקודם לכן מסרן נפשייהו כדמשמע בריש מכילתין (דף ג:) גבי כל הנשאת ברביעי תיבעל להגמון ואין לומר דהכא חיישינן על כל אחת שמא אינה נועה ואפילו נראית נועה שמא אינה: כאן

תוספות ישנים

א) אי נמי אחתיניה לאו דוקא אלא שירד מעצמו. ת"י:
ב) [ואומר ריצב"א דרב אשי נמי מוקי לה כשבא עד אחד המכשיר קודם שנים הפוסלים אבל בבאו שנים הפוסלים תחלה ואח"כ באו שנים המכשירים בזה אחר זה לא בעי לאוקמי דהא לא הוי קרי במתני' ע"פ עד אחד דכיון דכי אתי עד אחד אין ממש בדבריו עד שבא האחר]. ת"י:
ג) [ונקט רישא לבעלה אגב סיפא ובגמ' נמי נקט לבעלה אגב מתני'. ת"י]:

ליקוטי רש"י

ואחתיניה. דאמר במקום שנים אין דבריו כלום. **ואתא עד אחד.** לבסוף ואמר דכהן גמור הוא והוו להו שנים מכשירין. **ודכולי עלמא.** בין רבי אלעזר בין רשב"ג מצטרפים עדים המעידים זה שלא בפני זה בשאר עדות וה"נ יש לנו לצרף מן הדין עד ראשון ועד אחרון המכשירין ונכשירנו לזה אם לא מפני זילותא דבי דינא כדמפרש ואזיל. **תנא קמא סבר כיון דאחתיניה.** על פי ב' עוררין ובדין הורדנוהו דבכל מקום האמינה תורה שנים תו לא ליסקי ליה על פי עד אחד זה השני אף על פי שיש לצרפו עם הראשון ולהכשירו לזה דאוקי תרי לבהדי תרי ואוקי גברא אחזקיה דכשרות קמייתא דהוה מוחזק לן בכהונה דכהן הוא וגם הכשרנוהו תחלה על פי עד אחד קודם שבאו עוררין. **חיישינן לזילותא דבי דינא.** שהורידוהו על פי עוררין ועכשיו [יעלוהו] ויבטלו דבריהם והיכי קאמר ר' אלעזר לעיל אין מעלין ע"פ עד אחד הבא לבסוף בזמן שיש עליו עוררין שיש הפוסלין אותו הלכך לא מהני עד שני הבא לבסוף להכשירו להצטרף עם הראשון המכשיר דאיכא למימר תרי מכשירי ותרי פוסלין ואוקי גברא אחזקיה ויהיה כשר אפי' הכי לא מסקינן ליה משום זילותא דבי דינא ולא דמי דהוי מעיקרא על פי עד אחד הבא לבסוף [אמ] הקול לאו זילותא דבי דינא הוא דלאחתיניה בשביל קול [מעלה] בעלמא הוא ולכי לחזור ולהעלותו אחר שיבדקו הדבר הלכך כי הדר מסקי ליה ליכא זילותא אבל כשהורדנוהו על פי עדים מן הדין הורדנוהו וכי הדר מסקי איכא זילותא [רשב"ם ב"ב לב:]. שמא יגלגלו הבריות על ב"ד על שסותרין את דינייהם ודמי לחוכא ואיטלולא [שם לא:]. **ואנן מסקינן ליה.** ולאי קשיא תרי ותרי נינהו ואמאי מסקינן ליה והא הוי ספק תריץ אוקי תרי לבהדי תרי ואוקמיה אחזקיה קמייתא דלאסקוהו

על פי עד ראשון שהיה נאמן דהא אכתי אין עוררין דקול לאו עוררין הוא. **אי הכי וכו'.** דר' אלעזר חייש לזילותא דבי דינא מאי איריא עד הבא לבסוף דהתם אין מעלין משום זילותא כדקתני מתני' אין מעלין על פי עד אחד בזמן שיש עליו עוררין הא על פי שנים מעלין אפילו תרי אתו בהדי הדדי נמי בפעם שניה לרבי אלעזר לא מסקינן ליה. **במצטרפין לעדות קמיפלגי.** לר' אלעזר אין מצרפין עד אחרון עם הראשון הואיל ולא העידו שניהם כאחד כרבנן דפליגי אדרבי נתן אבל אם [המשך בדף כז.]

תוספות רי"ד

דכהן הוא ואסקיני' פי' דע"א נאמן להכחיש את הקול. ואתו בי תרי עוררים ואמרו בן גרושה ובן חלוצה הוא ואחתיני'. ואתא ע"א ואמר ידענא בי' דכהן הוא ר"א סבר הכא [כיון] דאיכא עוררים תרי דפסלו לי' אין מעלין לכהונה ע"פ ע"א שמכשירו ואע"ג דאיכא ע"א קמא שהכשיר כיון שלא העידו יחד בב"ד אין מצטרפים ורשב"ג סבר אע"פ שיש עוררים מעלין ע"פ ע"א זה שמכשירו שמצטרפים אותו עם הראשון ואמרי' אוקי תרי לבהדי תרי ואוקי גברא אחזקתיה. **ואי קשיא** והא אמרת לעיל דבתרי ותרי דהוא ספק תורה ל"א אוקי גברא אחזקתיה יש לתרץ ודאי באיסור תורה אמרינן הכי והכא בתרומה דרבנן והכי מוקמי' לה לקמן בשילהי פירקין והלכך מקילין בה ואמרי' אוקי תרי לבהדי תרי ואוקי גברא אחזקתיה. ובפלוגתא דתניא. אין עדיות מצטרפין עד שיראו שניהם כאחד כדברי ר"א) ר"י [בן קרחה] אומר אפילו בזה אח"ד פי' לאפוקי ז"א בפני הלוה לו וז"א בפני הודה לו שמה שראה זה לא ראה זה. ואע"ג דבמנה חד מסהדי לתחייב לא מצטרפי. ירד"ל מצטרפין: ואין עדותן מתקיימת בב"ד עד שיעידו שניהם כאח' ר"נ אומר שומעין דבריו של זה היום ולכשיבוא חבירו למחר שומעין דבריו ור"א כת"ק ורשב"ג כר"נ וקי"ל דהלכה כר"נ [בן קרחה] שעדותן מצטרפות אע"פ שלא ראו שניהם כאחד. והל' נמי כר"נ שעדותן מתקיימת בב"ד אע"פ שלא העידו שניהם כאחד: **מתני' האשה** שנחבשה בידי עובדי כוכבים. ע"י ממון מותרת לבעלה ע"י נפשות אסורה. עיר שכבשוה כרכום כל כהנות שבתוכה פסולות. ואם יש להן עדים אפי' עבד אפי' שפחה הרי אלו נאמנין שאין אדם נאמן ע"י עצמו. א"ר זכריה בן הקצב המעון הזה לא זזה ידה מתוך ידי משעה שנכנסו עובדי כוכבים לירושלים ועד שיצאו א"ל אין אדם נאמן על ידי עצמו. פי' באשת כהן מיירי דאי באשת ישראל אפילו ע"י נפשות מותרת דאנוסה היא ומדפישא בכהנות רישא נמי בכהנות הלכך ע"י ממון מותרת לבעלה דבעו' דלמא מפסדי ממונא לא אנסו לה אבל ע"י נפשות דלא מירתתי אנסו לה. והכורה ... הפקר חוששים שמא נתרצתה לא' מה' ומשמע דאסורה לישראל

ואינו נ"ל דא"כ בשבויי' נאמר כן ונאסור אותה על בעלה ישראל. והאיך מתנה אדם לאשתו אם תשתבאי אפרקינך ואותבינך לי לאינתו. א"ו אע"פ שמפקירים אותה לא חיישינן שמא מתרצת אלא הכל הוא באונס. וכך פי' גם ר"ח ז"ל אסורה לבעלה כהן: **המעון הזה.** הוא. **א"ר שמואל ברבי יצחק** ל"ש פי' שע"י ממון מותרת אלא שיד ישראל תקיפה על עובדי כוכבים פי' שיראים משישראל אבל יד עובדי כוכבים תקיפה על ישראל אפילו על ידי ממון אסורה דלא מירתתי

וְאֵין עֵדוּתָן מִתְקַיֶּימֶת בְּבֵית דִּין – And THE TESTIMONY OF [TWO WITNESSES], even if they testify about the same event, CANNOT BE SUSTAINED IN COURT עַד שֶׁיָּעִידוּ שְׁנֵיהֶם כְּאֶחָד – UNLESS THE TWO OF THEM TESTIFY AS ONE (i.e. together). רַבִּי נָתָן אוֹמֵר – But R' NASSAN SAYS: שׁוֹמְעִין דְּבָרָיו שֶׁל זֶה הַיּוֹם – WE LISTEN TO THE WORDS OF THIS witness TODAY, וּכְשֶׁיָּבֹא חֲבֵירוֹ לְמָחָר – AND WHEN HIS FELLOW COMES to testify TOMORROW, שׁוֹמְעִין דְּבָרָיו – WE LISTEN TO HIS WORDS, and we combine their testimonies.[12] R' Elazar and Rabban Shimon ben Gamliel dispute this same point: R' Elazar sides with the Rabbis (i.e. the unnamed first opinion) and Rabban Shimon concurs with R' Nassan.[13]

Mishnah הָאִשָּׁה שֶׁנֶּחְבְּשָׁה בִּידֵי עוֹבְדֵי כוֹכָבִים – Concerning **a woman who is imprisoned in the hands of idolaters:** עַל יְדֵי מָמוֹן – If it is **because of a monetary matter,**[14] מוּתֶּרֶת לְבַעְלָהּ – **she is permitted to her husband** upon her release. For the idolaters will not violate a woman jailed for these reasons, lest by doing so they forfeit their money.[15] עַל יְדֵי נְפָשׁוֹת – However, if it is **because of a capital crime,**[16] אֲסוּרָה לְבַעְלָהּ – **she is forbidden to her husband** upon her release. For idolaters make free with women sentenced to death, and we fear that she therefore submitted to one of them willingly.[17]

Gemara The Gemara qualifies the Mishnah's first clause: אָמַר רַב שְׁמוּאֵל בַּר רַב יִצְחָק אָמַר רַב – **Rav Shmuel bar Rav Yitzchak said in the name of Rav:** לֹא שָׁנוּ – **[The Rabbis] did not teach** that a woman imprisoned because of a monetary matter is permitted אֶלָּא שֶׁיַּד יִשְׂרָאֵל תַּקִּיפָה עַל עוֹבְדֵי כוֹכָבִים – **except when the hand of Israel is mighty over the idolaters.**[18] אֲבָל יַד עוֹבְדֵי כוֹכָבִים תַּקִּיפָה עַל עַצְמָן – **But** when **the hand of the idolaters is mighty over themselves,** i.e. when they rule over Israel,[19] אֲפִילוּ עַל יְדֵי מָמוֹן – **even** a woman imprisoned **because of a monetary matter** אֲסוּרָה לְבַעְלָהּ – **is forbidden to her husband.** For when the idolaters are their own masters, they do not fear being made to forfeit their money. Therefore, they will violate even women imprisoned for monetary reasons.[20]

This stipulation is challenged:

מָתִיב רָבָא – **Rava challenged** it on the basis of a Mishnah:[21] הֵעִיד רַבִּי יוֹסֵי הַכֹּהֵן וְרַבִּי זְכַרְיָה בֶּן הַקַּצָּב עַל בַּת יִשְׂרָאֵל שֶׁהוּרְהֲנָה בְּאַשְׁקְלוֹן – R' YOSE THE KOHEN AND R' ZECHARYAH BEN HAKATZAV[22]

NOTES

12. [See *Sanhedrin* 30a-31a for discussion of this dispute.]

13. See note 8. According to this approach, R' Elazar's statement in our Mishnah should be understood as follows: When do we say that a single witness (i.e. two witnesses who testify separately and thus have the status of only one witness) does not suffice to elevate someone to the Kehunah? Where he is contradicted by two challengers. But if there are no challengers, a single witness does suffice (even if there is no other single witness at all). Rabban Shimon ben Gamliel then responded that even where there are two challengers, what you, R' Elazar, refer to as a "single witness" (i.e. two witnesses who testify separately) does elevate someone to the Kehunah (*Ran*).

14. I.e. she owes the idolaters money (*Rashi, Avodah Zarah* 23a ד״ה ע״י ממון).

15. They fear that if they unlawfully violate her, they will be penalized with forfeiture of the money she owes them. Therefore, they do not make free with her (*Rashi* here and to the Gemara). [Regardless of whether her husband is a Kohen or an Israelite, she is permitted to him. Although a Kohen's wife who is violated even against her will is forbidden to her husband, in this case we may assume that she was not violated at all. This is the opinion of the majority of Rishonim – see *Tosafos* and *Ritva* here. However, some Rishonim understand *Rashi* (in *Avodah Zarah* ibid. ד״ה תרע) to be limiting this ruling to the wife of an Israelite – see *Tosafos, Avodah Zarah* ibid. ד״ה על ידי ממון; *Mordechai* here; *Shitah Mekubetzes* here ד״ה וכתוב בקונטריסין; see *Pnei Yehoshua* for discussion.]

16. I.e. if she was sentenced to death (*Rashi;* see 27a note 8).

17. [See next note.] I.e. we fear that having been continually molested by any who might wish to exploit her, she may at some point during her ordeal have submitted willingly to one of her violators (*Rashi;* see *Shitah Yeshanah,* quoted in *Shitah Mekubetzes* ד״ה וכתוב בקונטריסין for another explanation). [Willful submission is regarded as adultery, and renders a married woman forbidden to her husband (see *Sotah* 2a, 27b-28a). Generally, we do not compel a woman to leave her husband on suspicion of adultery unless she was warned by her husband against secluding herself with a particular man and she disobeyed him (קִינּוּי וּסְתִירָה). However, this applies to a woman suspected of adultery with a Jew. A woman under the control of idolaters [is more likely to have been violated], and is therefore treated more stringently. She must leave her husband even in the absence of these criteria (*Beis Shmuel, Even HaEzer* 7:23).]

[Our translation follows *Rashi,* who states that we suspect this woman of willful submission to her jailers. According to *Rashi,* it makes no difference whether the husband is a Kohen or a Yisrael – either way, she is forbidden to him, since she is suspect of having submitted willingly. However, many Rishonim (see, for example, *Ritva; Ramban; Rashba*) are troubled by the Gemara's ruling on 51b which states that women captured by invaders or bandits are *not* suspect of willing participation in their violation. These Rishonim therefore explain that the Mishnah's second clause is discussing the wife of a Kohen, who becomes forbidden to her husband even if *forcibly* violated. Since the idolaters are known to make free with a woman imprisoned on capital charges, she becomes forbidden to her Kohen husband, *despite* having been entirely unwilling. A Yisrael's wife imprisoned for a capital crime, however, remains permitted to her husband, for such a woman does not become forbidden unless she submits willfully, and we do not suspect Jewish women of willful submission. It seems that *Rashi* differentiated somehow between the case of a captured woman (שְׁבוּיָה) and our Mishnah's case of an imprisoned woman. However, the distinction is unclear; see *Ramban* at length, who proposes various possibilities, but rejects them all. *Tosafos* take a third view. They agree that the Mishnah discusses the wife of a Yisrael. They maintain that the reason she (unlike a captive) is suspect of willful submission to her violator is because she is sentenced to death, and we fear that she will submit willingly in the hope of influencing her jailers to spare her life.]

18. For when they are ruled by Jews, they fear to treat the woman unlawfully, lest they forfeit their money (*Rashi*). [Of course, even when ruled by Jews, the idolaters are not expected to do more than treat the woman in accordance with their *own* laws. It is for this reason that a woman sentenced to death is forbidden to her husband even if the idolaters are ruled by Jews. For notwithstanding their inferior position, the woman is abandoned to all comers, in accordance with the law of the idolaters (*Shitah Mekubetzes* to Mishnah ד״ה לא שנו; see 27a).]

19. The term תַּקִּיפָה עַל עַצְמָן, *mighty over themselves,* is used euphemistically. The Gemara really means that they rule over Israel [but does not wish to direct words of ill omen towards Israel] (*Meiri*).

20. *Shitah Mekubetzes* (ד״ה נמצא לפי זה) writes that according to *Rashi,* even the wife of an Israelite must leave her husband if imprisoned by idolaters for monetary reasons at a time when the idolaters rule over Israel. For idolaters unchecked by the possibility of financial loss will make free even with such prisoners, and will allow them to be molested by any who wish to exploit them. We fear that a woman who undergoes this might at some point during her ordeal submit willingly to one of her violators. Therefore, she must leave her husband who is a Yisrael. However, other Rishonim maintain that only the wife of a Kohen must leave her husband in this case, not the wife of a Yisrael (see *Tosafos; Ramban; Ritva* et al.).

21. *Eduyos* 8:2.

22. *Aruch* ע׳ קצב translates this name as "R' Zecharyah the son of the butcher."

עין משפט
נר מצוה

צט א מיי' פ"ד מהל' עדות הלכה ד סמג עשין קט טוש"ע ח"מ סימן ל סעיף ו:
ק ב מיי' שם ופ"כ מהל' איסורי ביאה הל' טו סמג שם טוש"ע ח"מ סי' ל סעיף ט וטוש"ע אה"ע סי' ג סעיף ז:
קא ג ד מיי' פי"ח מהל' איסורי ביאה הלכ' ל סמג לאוין קכא טוש"ע אה"ע סימן ז סעיף יא:

תוספות ר"ד

דכהן הוא ואסקינ' פי' דע"א נאמן להכריש את הקול. ואתו בי תרי עוררים ואמרו בן גרושה ובן חלוצה הוא ואחתיני'. ואתא ע"א ואמר ידענא בי' דכהן הוא ר"א סבר הכא [כיון] דאיכא עוררים תרי דפסלו לי' אי מעלין לכהונה ע"פ ע"א שמכשירו ואע"ג דאיכא ע"א קמא שהכשירו כיון שלא העידו יחד בב"ד אין מצטרפים ורשב"ג סבר אע"פ שיש עוררים מעלין ע"פ ע"א זה שמכשירו שמצטרפים אותו עם הראשון ואמרי' אוקי תרי לבהדי תרי ואוקי גברא אחזקתיה. ואי קשיא והא אמרת לעיל דבתרי ותרי דהוא ספק תורה ל"א אוקי גברא אחזקתיה יש לתרץ דהאי באיסור תורה אמרינן הכי והכא בתרומה דרבנן והכי מוקמי' לה לקמן בשילהי פירקין והלכך מקלין בה ואמרי' אוקי תרי לבהדי תרי ואוקי גברא אחזקתיה. ובפלוגתא דתניא. אין עדיות מצטרפין עד שיראו שניהם כאחד (דברי ר"א) ר"י [בן קרחה] אומר אפילו בזה אח"ז פי' לאפוקי ז"א בפני בלוה לו וז"א בפני הודה לו שמה שראה זה לא ראה זה. ואע"ג דבמנה חד מסהדי לת"ק לא מצטרפי. ולר"י מצטרפו: ואין עדותן מתקיימת בב"ד עד שיעידו שניהם כאחד ר"נ אומר שומעין דבריו של זה היום ולכשיבוא חבירו למחר שומעין דבריו ואתי ר"א כת"ק רשב"ג כר"נ וקי"ל דהלכה כר"י [בן קרחה] שעדותן מצטרפות אע"פ שלא ראו שניהן כאחד. והל' נמי כר"נ שעדותן מתקיימת בב"ד ואף על פי שלא העידו כאחד: מתני' האשה שנחבשה בידי עובדי כוכבים. ע"י ממון מותרת לבעלה ע"י נפשות אסורה. עיר שכבשוה כרכום כל כהנות שבתוכה פסולות. ואם יש להן עדים אפי' עבד אפי' שפחה הרי אלו נאמנין שאין אדם נאמן ע"י עצמו. א"ר זכרה בן הקצב המעון הזה לא זזה ידה מתוך ידי משעה שנכנסו עובדי כוכבים לירושלים ועד שיצאו א"ל אין אדם נאמן על ידי עצמו. פי' באשת כהן מיירי דאי באשת ישראל אפילו ע"י נפשות מותרת דאנוסה היא וכדסיפא בכהנות רישא נמי בכהנות הלכך ע"י ממון מותרת לבעלה דמירתתי דלמא מפסדי ממונא ולא אנסו לה אבל ע"י נפשות דלא מירתתי אנסו לה. המורה פי' הואיל ונוהגים בה הפקר חוששים שמא נתרצת לא' מהן ומשמע שהיא אסורה לישראל ואינו נ"ל דא"כ גם בשבוי' נאמר כן ונאסור אותה על בעלה ישראל. והאיך מתנה אדם לאשתו אם תשתבאי אפרקינך ואותבינך לי לאינתו. א"י אע"פ שמפקירים אותה לא חיישינן שמא מתרצת אלא הכל הוא באונס. וכך פי' גם ר"ח ז"ל אסורה לבעלה כהן: המעון הזה. פי' שבועה הוא. א"ר שמואל ברבי יצחק ל"ש פי' שע"י ממון מותרת אלא שיד ישראל תקיפה על עובדי כוכבים פי' שירא"ם מישראל אבל יד עובדי כוכבים תקיפה על ישראל אפילו על ידי ממון אסורה דלא מירתתי

ואסקיניה ואתו בי תרי ואמרי בן גרושה ובן חלוצה הוא ואחתיניה ואתא עד אחד ואמר ידענא ביה דכהן הוא ודכולי עלמא מצטרפין לעדות והכא במיחש לזילותא דבי דינא קמיפלגי תנא קמא סבר כיון דאחתיניה לא מסקינן ליה חיישינן לזילותא דבי דינא ורשב"ג סבר אנן אחתינן ליה ואנן מסקינן ליה ולזילותא דבי דינא לא חיישינן מתקיף לה רב אשי אי הכי אפי' תרי ותרי נמי אלא אמר רב אשי במצטרפין לעדות קמיפלגי ובפלוגתא דהני תנאי דתניא אין עדותן מצטרפת עד שיראו שניהם כאחד ר' יהושע בן קרחה אומר אפי' בזה אחר זה ואין עדותן מתקיימת בב"ד עד שיעידו שניהם כאחד ר' נתן אומר שומעין דבריו של זה היום וכשיבא חבירו למחר שומעין דבריו:

מתני' האשה שנחבשה בידי עובדי כוכבים על ידי ממון מותרת לבעלה על ידי נפשות אסורה לבעלה:

גמ' אמר רב שמואל בר רב יצחק אמר רב לא שנו אלא שיד ישראל תקיפה על עובדי כוכבים אבל יד עובדי כוכבים תקיפה על עצמן אפילו על ידי ממון אסורה לבעלה מתיב רבא העיד רבי יוסי הכהן ור' זכריה בן הקצב על בת ישראל שהורהנה באשקלון וריחקוה בני משפחתה ועדיה מעידים אותה שלא נסתרה ושלא נטמאה ואמרו להם חכמים אם אתם מאמינים שהורהנה האמינו שלא נסתרה ושלא נטמאה ואם אי אתם מאמינים שלא נסתרה ושלא נטמאה אל תאמינו שהורהנה והא אשקלון דיד עובדי כוכבים תקיפה על עצמן וקתני הורהנה

רש"י

ואסקיניה. דבמקום קול הוי חד מהימן: ודכולי עלמא. בין לר' אלעזר בין לר"ש: מצטרפין. שני עדים המעידים זה שלא בפני זה בשאר עדיות: דחיישינן לזילותא דבי דינא. שהורידוהו שני פעמים ועכשיו יעלוהו ויבטלו דבריהם והיינו דקאמר ר' אלעזר דמאחר שהורידוהו ע"פ העוררין אין מעלין ע"פ עד זה השני אע"פ שיש לצרפו עם האחר: ואנן מסקינן ליה. ואי קשיא תרי ותרי ניהו אוקי תרי להדי תרי ואוקמינן אחזקיה קמייתא דאסקיניה ע"פ עד הראשון שהוא נאמן דהא אכתי אין עוררין קול לאו עוררין הוא: אפילו תרי. אתו בהדי הדדי נמי בפעם שניה לרבי אלעזר לא מסקינן ליה: עד שיראו שניהם כאחד. את העדות לאפוקי אחד אומר בפני הלווהו ואחד אומר בפני הודה לו עליו: ואין עדותן מתקיימת. להתקבל בב"ד ואפי' ראו שניהן כאחד ופלוגתא אחריתי היא ולאו ר' יהושע בן קרחה קאמר לה ורבי אלעזר ורבן שמעון בפלוגתא דרבי נתן ורבנן פליגי: מתני' ע"י ממון מותרת לבעלה. דמרתתי להפסיד ממונן ואינן מפקירין אותה: ע"י נפשות. שהיתה נידונת למות: אסורה לבעלה. דהואיל ונוהגין בה הפקר חוששין שמא נתרצתה לאחד מהן: גמ' לא שנו. דע"י ממון מותרת לבעלה: אלא שיד ישראל תקיפה על העובדי כוכבים. וירא לעשות שלא כדין שמא יפסידו ממונם: שהורהנה. נתמשכנה: ועדיה. אותן שהעידו שהורהנה: והא אשקלון. דלאכן פלשתים היא ועוד כבר גלו ישראל:

תוספות

ואסקיניה. וא"ת ולמאן דחייש לזילותא דבי דינא היכי אסקוהו כיון דאחתיניה מחמת הקול וליכא למימר דליכא זילותא דבי דינא אלא היכא שהורידוהו שתי פעמים כדמוכח בחזקת הבתים (ב"ב דף לב.) וי"ל דליכא זילותא דבי דינא אלא היכא שהורידוהו ע"י עדות אבל בהורדה שע"י הקול ליכא זילותא דב"ד ואע"ג דאמרינן (גיטין דף פא.) גבי גרושה לכהן דלא מבטלים קלא היינו משום דלית ליה תקנתא אבל הכא דאי לא מסקינן ליה לעולם פסול מבטלין א) אי נמי בתרומה דרבנן הקילו: אנן אחתינן ליה ואנן מסקינן ליה. פי' בקונטרס אע"ג דתרי ותרי ניהו אוקי תרי להדי תרי ואוקי גברא אחזקתיה וקשה לר"י דבפרק האומר בקדושין (דף סו. ושם) קאמר גבי ינאי היכי דמי אילימא דתרי אמרי אשתבאי ותרי אמרי לא אשתבאי מאי חזית דסמכת אהני פירוש אהני דאמרו לא אשתבאי סמוך אהני ואמאי קאמר ויבוקש הדבר ולא נמצא והתם פי' בקונטרס דלא אמרי' אוקי תרי בהדי תרי ואוקי גברא אחזקיה דהא לא באו להעיד על אמו אלא על ינאי ולו לא היה חזקת כשרות ואין נראה לר"י דחזקת האם מהניא גם לינאי כדמשמע הכא ואמרינן נמי לעיל בפ"ק (דף יג. ושם) לדברי המכשיר בה מכשיר בבתה ואפילו מאן דפסל בבתה היינו משום דמעלה עשו גבי זנות וגם אין לומר כמו שתירץ ר"ת דליכא למימר התם אוקמינן אחזקה לפי שכל הנשים היו בחזקת שבויות דא"כ היכי מייתי מינה ראיה על אשתו שזינתה בעד אחד דשאני התם דכל הנשים בחזקת שבויות אבל אשתו זינתה היא בחזקת היתר ונראה לר"י דתרי ותרי ספיקא דרבנן הוא ומדרבנן החמירו דלא מוקמינן לה אחזקה והכא בתרומה דרבנן הקילו ובפרק בכל מערבין (עירובין דף לה.) גבי תרומה ונטמאה כו' ספק הרי זה חמר גמל דברי ר"מ ומוקי לה ה) רבה ורב יוסף בשתי כתי עדים הא דלא מוקמינן לה אחזקתה דלא נטמאת אע"ג דתרומה בזמן הזה דרבנן היינו משום דערובי תחומין דאורייתא לר"מ אי נמי שאני התם דאיכא ריעותא דהרי נטמאת לפניך ולא אמרינן השתא הוא דאיטמי אע"ג דגבי מקוה אמרינן השתא הוא דחסר ואתאי (נדה דף ב:) הכא דאיכא שתי כתי עדים לא אמרינן השתא הוא דאיטמי ובשנים אומרים מת ושנים אומרים לא מת דאמרינן לעיל (דף כב:) לא תנשא ולא מוקמינן לה אחזקת אשת איש היינו משום דחזקה דאשה דייקא ומנסבא מרעה לה לחזקת אשת איש אע"ג דבשנים אומרים מת אמרינן בהאשה רבה (יבמות פח:) דמותרת לחזור לו וכיון דליכא חומרא בסוף לא דייקא מ"מ הכא כיון דמכחישין זה את זה איכא חומרא ובשנים אומרים נתגרשה ושנים אומרים לא נתגרשה דאמרינן נמי לא תנשא אע"ג דלא דייקא וליכא נמי חזקה דאין האשה מעיזה פניה דשלא בפני בעלה מעיזה וכ"ש היכא דמסייעין לה עדים ויש לומר דמכל מקום דייקא לפי שירא שיזומו עדיה או יפסלו אותם בגזלנותא ובהאשה רבה (שם צג: ושם) גבי בעו מיניה מרב ששת עד אחד ביבמה מהו כו' אמר להו תניתוה אמרו לה מת בנך ואחר כך מת בעליך ונתייבמה ואח"כ אמרו לה חילוף הדברים תצא והולד ראשון והאחרון ממזר היכי דמי אילימא תרי ותרי מאי חזית דסמכת אהני דאסרי ליבם סמוך אהני דשרו לה וקשה דמאי פריך והא אית לן לאוקמי אחזקה דאסורה ליבם שמת בעלה תחלה כדאמרינן בפרק ארבעה אחין (שם דף לא. ושם) גבי נפל הבית עליו ועל בת אחיו כו' ועוד כיון דתרי ותרי ספיקא דרבנן הוא יש לאוסרה כדאמרינן גבי ינאי והתם לא דייקא כדאמרינן ליה ליבם וי"ל דמ"מ מהני דיוקא דידה לענין דמרעה ליה לחזקת איסור ליבם והא דפריך נמי התם כו' ועוד ממזר ספק ממזר הוא אע"ג דבחזקת איסור ליבם היא מ"מ לא הוי ממזר ודאי דמהני דיוקא דידה כדפרשינן ועוד כיון דתרי ותרי ספיקא דרבנן אין לנו להעמידה על חזקתה ולהתירו בממזרת ורבינו יצחק בר ברוך פי' דלא אמרינן בכל הני אוקמא אחזקה לפי שהשנים שמוציאים אותו מחזקתו של היתר הם מעידים תחלה ומיד כשהעידו יצא מחזקתו ע"י עדותן ותו לא אמרינן אוקמא אחזקה ולהכי פריך לעיל מאי שנא רישא ומאי שנא סיפא דשנים שאומרים נתקדשה העידו תחלה ובשנים אומרים נתגרשה אע"פ שהם העידו תחלה מ"מ היתה בחזקת אשת איש וכן ההיא דהאשה רבה ודינאי שנים המוציאין אותו מחזקתו באו תחלה ואין נראה לרבינו יצחק דהא הכא בשמעתין מוקמינן ליה אחזקה אע"ג דכבר פסלוהו השנים והוציאוהו מחזקתו ואין סברא שיועיל מה שעד אחד המכשיר העיד קודם ב) ועוד דרב אשי משמע דבעי למימר דאפילו אתו שניהם לבסוף דמסקינן ליה: על ידי ממון מותרת לבעלה. נראה דמותרת אפילו לבעלה כהן דלא חיישינן אפי' לאונסא משום דמרתתי להפסיד ממונם ולא דמי לשבויה וכן מוכח בגמרא דקאמר לא שנו אלא שיד ישראל תקיפה על העובדי כוכבים אבל יד העובדי כוכבים תקיפה על עצמן אפילו ע"י ממון אסורה לבעלה ועל כרחן היינו לכהונה מדקאמרי אף אנן נמי תנינא מההיא דריחקוה בני משפחתה והא לא שייך אלא לכהונה דבישראל לא שייך וריחקוה בני משפחתה דאינה אסורה אלא לבעלה ועוד ראיה דתנן בפ' שני דמסכת ע"ז (דף כב.) אין מעמידין בהמה בפונדקאות של עובדי כוכבים מפני שחשודים על הרביעה ורמינהו לוקחין מהן בהמה לקרבן לא קשיא הא לכתחלה והא דיעבד ומנא תימרא דשני בין לכתחלה כו' דתנן לא תתייחד אשה עמהם מפני שחשודים על העריות ורמינהו האשה שנחבשה ע"י עובדי כוכבים ע"י ממון מותרת לבעלה אלא ש"מ שני לן בין לכתחלה לדיעבד משמע דאין לחוש כלל שנבעלה דאי מותרת לבעלה ישראל קאמר דלא חיישינן שמא נתרצת אבל לבעלה ג) כהן אסורה דחיישינן שמא נאנסה א"כ לא הוה מייתי מידי: ועל ידי נפשות אסורה לבעלה. היינו אפילו לבעלה ישראל דחיישינן שמא נתרצת כדי למצא חן שלא יהרגוה דאי לבעלה כהן קאמר ואסורה שמא נאנסה א"כ הוה ליה למימר אסורה לכהונה אלא ודאי אפילו לבעלה ישראל אסורה וא"ת לנועות ליסתרו דקודש לכן מסרן נפשייהו כדמשמע בריש מכילתין (דף ג:) גבי כל הנשאת ברביעי תיבעל להסר תחלה וצריך לומר דהכא חיישינן על כל אחת שמא אינה לנועה ואפילו נראית לנועה שמא אינה:
כהן

מסורת הש"ס

א) ב"ב לב., ב) ג"ז שם ודף קסה: סנהדרין ל. גיטין לג: [תוספתא סנהדרין פרק ה], ג) ע"ז כג., ד) עדיות פ"ח מ"ב, ה) [שם:]

תוספות ישנים

א) אי נמי אחתיניה לאו דוקא אלא שיורד מעצמו. מ"י: ב) [ואומר ריב"א דרב אשי נמי מוקי לה כשבא עד אחד המכשיר קודם שנים הפוסלים אבל כשבאו שנים הפוסלים תחלה ואח"כ באו שנים המכשירים בזה אחר זה לא בעי לאוקמי דהא לא הוי קרי במתני' ע"פ עד אחד דכיון דבי אתו עד אחד אין ממש בדבריו עד שבא האחר. מ"י]: ג) [ונקט רישא לבעלה אגב סיפא ובגמ' נמי נקט לבעלה אגב מתני'. מ"י]

ליקוטי רש"י

ואחתיניה. דאתא במקום שנים אין דבריו כלום. ואתא עד אחד. לבסוף ואמר דכהן גמור הוא והוו להו שנים מכשירין. ודכולי עלמא. בין לר' אלעזר בין לרשב"ג מצטרפים עדים המעידים זה שלא בפני זה בשאר עדות והכא יש לנו לצרף מן הדין עד ראשון ועד אחרון המכשירין ונכשירו לזה אם לא מפני זילותא דבי דינא כדמפרש ואזיל. תנא קמא סבר כיון דאחתיניה. על פי ב' עוררין ודנין הורדנוהו לכל מקום האמור תורה שנים לא ליסקו ליה על פי עד אחד זה השני אף על פי שיש לצרפו עם הראשון ולהכשירו לזה דאוקי תרי בהדי תרי ואוקי גברא אחזקיה דכשרות קמייתא דהוה מוחזק בן בתחלה דכהן הוא ולא כשבאו תחלה על פי עד אחד קודם שבאו עוררין. חיישינן לזילותא דבי דינא. שהורידוהו על פי עוררין ועכשיו [יעלוהו] ויבטלו דבריהם והיינו דקאמר ר' אלעזר אין מעלין ע"פ עד אחד הבא לבסוף דזמן שיש עליו עוררין שנים הפוסלין אותו הלכך לבסוף מהני עד שני הבא לבסוף להכשירו להצטרף עם הראשון המכשיר דאע"ג דאיכא למימר אוקי תרי מכשירין בהדי תרי פוסלין ואוקי גברא אחזקיה ויהיה כשר אפי' הכי לא מסקינן ליה משום זילותא דבי דינא והאי דאמרינן אחזקיה מעיקרא על פי עד אחד הבא לבסוף [לאו] הקול לאו זילותא דבי דינא הוא דמאי דאמר דאחתיה כשהוכיחו כל קול [מעלה] בעלמא הוא ודכי לחזור ולהעלותו אחר שירדהו הלכך כי הדר מסקי ליה ליכא זילותא אבל כשהורידוהו עדים על פי שנים מן הדין הורידוהו וכי הדר מסקי להו איכא זילותא [רשב"ם ב"ב לב.]. שמא יגלגלו דבריהם כאילו על פי שנים העידוהו ודחיו לאסור להחזיקו ולבסוף יפסלו [... לא:]. ואנן מסקינן ליה. ולא קשיא תרי ותרי ניהו ואמאי מסקינן ליה והא הוי ספק אוקי תרי בהדי תרי ואוקמיה אחזקיה קמייתא דאסקיניה

על פי עד ראשון שהיה נאמן דהא אכתי אין עוררין דקול לאו עוררין הוא. אי הכי וכו'. דר' אלעזר היא מאי איריא עד הבא לבסוף דהתם אין מעלין משום זילותא כדקתני מתני' אין מעלין על פי עד אחד דזמן על פי שנים מעלין אפילו תרי אתו בהדי הדדי נמי בפעם שניה לרבי אלעזר לא מסקינן ליה. במצטרפין לעדות קמיפלגי. לר' אלעזר אין מצרפין עד הראשון עם האחרון הואיל ולא העידו שניהם כאחד דכרבנן פליגי אדרבי נתן [השמטה מדף כז.]

וְאַסְקִינֵיה – **and [the court] elevated him** to his original status based on this testimony.[1] וְאָתוּ בֵּי תְּרֵי – **Subsequently, two witnesses came** forward, וְאָמְרֵי בֶּן גְּרוּשָׁה וּבֶן חֲלוּצָה הוּא – **and said that he is the son of a divorcee or a *chalutzah,*** וְאַחְתִּינֵיה – **and [the court]** once again **demoted him** from the Kehunah based on their testimony.[2] וְאָתָא עֵד אֶחָד – **Then a** *second* **single witness came** forward, וְאָמַר יָדַעְנָא בֵּיהּ דְּכֹהֵן הוּא – **and** also **said, "I know that he is a** [qualified] **Kohen,"** thereby corroborating the testimony of the first witness.

The Gemara now explains the reasoning behind the dispute: וּדְכוּלֵּי עָלְמָא מִצְטָרְפִין לְעֵדוּת – **And all**[3] **agree that** ordinarily **we combine the testimonies** of two witnesses, although they were offered separately.[4] וְהָכָא בְּמֵיחַשׁ לְזִילוּתָא דְּבֵי דִינָא קָמִיפְלְגֵי – **But here they dispute whether we are concerned for disgrace of the court** that may result if we promote him once again. תַּנָּא קַמָּא סָבַר – **The Tanna Kamma** (i.e. R' Elazar) **holds** כֵּיוָן דְּאַחְתִּינֵיה – **that since [the court] demoted him,** לֹא מַסְקִינַן לֵיהּ – **we do not elevate him** once again, חָיְישִׁינַן לְזִילוּתָא דְּבֵי דִינָא – because **we are concerned for disgrace of the court.**[5] וְרַבָּן שִׁמְעוֹן בֶּן גַּמְלִיאֵל סָבַר – **But Rabban Shimon ben Gamliel holds** אֲנַן אַחְתִּינַן לֵיהּ וַאֲנַן מַסְקִינַן לֵיהּ – that although **we** originally **demoted him, we** now **elevate him** based on the new evidence,[6] וְלִזִילוּתָא דְּבֵי דִינָא לֹא חָיְישִׁינַן – **and we are not concerned for disgrace of the court.**

The Gemara objects to this interpretation of the dispute: מַתְקִיף לָהּ רַב אָשֵׁי – **Rav Ashi challenged [this explanation]:** אִי הָכִי – **If so,** that R' Elazar is concerned for disgrace of the court, why does he speak of a case in which the final testimony was that of only one witness? אֲפִילּוּ תְּרֵי וּתְרֵי נַמִּי – **Even if two** witnesses testified together **after** the previous **two** witnesses had caused the man to be demoted, R' Elazar would **also** not re-elevate the man to the Kehunah, out of concern for the court's reputation![7]

Rav Ashi therefore advances another explanation: אֶלָּא אָמַר רַב אָשֵׁי – **Rather, Rav Ashi said:** בְּמִצְטָרְפִין לְעֵדוּת קָמִיפְלְגֵי – **They disagree as to whether we combine the testimonies** of two witnesses who testified separately.[8]

Rav Ashi introduces a Baraisa which records two disputes regarding testimony, the second of which parallels his explanation of the dispute between R' Elazar and Rabban Shimon ben Gamliel:

וּבִפְלוּגְתָּא דְּהָנֵי תַּנָּאֵי – **And** R' Elazar and Rabban Shimon ben Gamliel align themselves **with** the opinions in **the dispute between the following Tannaim.** דְּתַנְיָא – **For it was taught in a Baraisa:** אֵין עֵדוּתָן מִצְטָרֶפֶת – THE TESTIMONIES OF [TWO WITNESSES] CANNOT BE COMBINED, עַד שֶׁיִּרְאוּ שְׁנֵיהֶם כְּאֶחָד – UNLESS THEY BOTH SEE AS ONE, i.e. they both testify about the same event.[9] רַבִּי יְהוֹשֻׁעַ בֶּן קָרְחָה אָמַר – But R' YEHOSHUA BEN KORCHAH SAYS: אֲפִילּוּ בְּזֶה אַחַר זֶה – Their testimonies may be combined EVEN if they testify about different events that took place ONE FOLLOWING THE OTHER.[10]

The second dispute in the Baraisa:[11]

NOTES

1. Because even a single witness is believed to counter a rumor (*Rashi;* see, however, *Ritva*).

2. Because a single witness is ineffective when opposed by two (*Rashbam* to *Bava Basra* 32a ד״ה ואחתיניה). [The demotion in this case is qualitatively different from the demotion effected by the rumor (see 26a note 32).]

3. R' Elazar and Rabban Shimon ben Gamliel (*Rashi;* see *Shitah Mekubetzes* ד״ה ודכולי עלמא).

4. That is, if two single witnesses each testify at different sessions of the court, we do not treat each one's testimony as having been given by single witnesses; rather, they are combined to carry the weight of testimony given by a set of two witnesses. In this case, combining the testimonies of the two individual witnesses would create the testimony of a pair who attest to the man's status as a qualified Kohen. This pair would offset the testimony of the pair who claim that he is unfit for the Kehunah. A doubt is thus created which can be resolved by the prevailing *chazakah.* The *chazakah* of this man is the state of Kehunah that he enjoyed after the first witness asserted that he was a qualified Kohen. [Although that witness' testimony was preceded by a rumor claiming that he was not a Kohen, a rumor is not of sufficient import to establish a status of *chazakah* (see 26a note 32).] Hence, if the two single witnesses do combine to form a pair, the end result ought to be the re-elevation of this man to the Kehunah on the basis of his *chazakah* (*Rashi* ד״ה ואנן מסקינן ליה with *Pnei Yehoshua*).

Other Rishonim, however, argue that since this first witness was subsequently contradicted by two other witnesses, he cannot create a *chazakah* (see *Ran*). Rather, the relevant *chazakah* is the presumption of Kehunah enjoyed by the father of this man, which was transmitted to the son (see *Tosafos,* who apparently had a different reading of *Rashi* [see *Mahashal*]; *Rashba, Ritva* et al.; see *Shitah Mekubetzes* ד״ה עוד כתב רש״י ז״ל). [For elaboration on the significance of the father's *chazakah* in this case, see *R' Shimon Shkop* §10; *Chazon Ish* 2:25; *Kovetz Shiurim, Bava Basra* §132.]

[The Rishonim ask: The rule is that where a doubt is created by two conflicting pairs of witnesses, we do not follow a *chazakah* that would result in a leniency (see 22b note 7). How, then, can we rely on a *chazakah* to promote this man to the Kehunah? For discussion of this problem, see *Tosafos* ד״ה אנן, *Ran* et al.]

5. Since he was demoted twice, it would disgrace the court to reinstate him once again and rescind their previous decisions. According to this interpretation of the dispute, R' Elazar's statement in the Mishnah is understood as follows: We do not raise a man to the Kehunah based on the testimony of a *second* single witness (although his testimony combines with that of another single witness) in an instance where two challengers have *already* caused his removal, due to concern for the ridicule that such a re-elevation might generate (*Rashi;* cf. *Tosafos* ד״ה ואסקיניה, *Ritva;* see *Pnei Yehoshua*).

6. See note 4.

7. The words of the Mishnah, "We do not raise . . . on the word of *one* witness," imply that if *two* witnesses would testify, their testimony would indeed be effective in establishing this man as a Kohen. But, Rav Ashi argues, according to the explanation just offered, the number of witnesses is irrelevant. Even if *two* new witnesses testify (after the man had been demoted on account of the previous pair's testimony), we would still not re-elevate him to the Kehunah, lest that harm the court's reputation (*Rashi;* see *Rashbam* to *Bava Basra* 32a ד״ה מאי אריא; see also *Re'ah*). [See *Rashash* for an explanation of the Gemara's previous approach in light of this problem.]

8. That is, R' Elazar holds that since they did not testify as a unit, the first and last witnesses cannot be combined, so the Kohen remains in his deposed state due to the testimony of the two challengers. Rabban Shimon ben Gamliel, on the other hand, maintains that the last witness combines with the first to oppose the incriminating testimony. Thus they create an impasse, which results in the elevation of the Kohen to his former status (see note 4). Neither opinion, however, is concerned for possible ridicule of the court. Thus, if two supporting witnesses would come forward together (after the incriminating pair), all would agree that the Kohen's original status would be restored (*Rashbam* ibid. ד״ה והכא בלצרף).

9. If, for example, one testifies that he witnessed a loan and the other testifies that he heard the borrower admit to that loan, they do not combine to form the minimum of two witnesses required to establish monetary liability (*Rashi*).

10. Thus, in the example given above (previous note) the witnesses would indeed establish monetary liability. [See *Sanhedrin* 30a for the reasons of each Tanna; and see 30b (ibid.) for two different explanations of the dispute.]

Although this part of the Baraisa has no bearing on our Gemara, it is included here because the Gemara wishes to quote the Baraisa in its entirety (*Rashbam* to *Bava Basra* ibid. ד״ה דתניא; cf. *Shitah Mekubetzes* ד״ה ובפלוגתא).

11. The following words are not a continuation of R' Yishmael ben Korchah's statement; they pertain to a different dispute (*Rashi*).

עין משפט נר מצוה

צט א מיי' פ"ז מהל' עדות הלכה ד סמג עשין קט טוש"ע ח"מ סימן ל סעיף ו:

ק ב מיי' שם ופ"כ מהלכ' איסורי ביאה הל' טו סמג שם טוש"ע ח"מ סי' ל סעיף ט וטוש"ע אה"ע סי' ג סעיף ז:

קא ג ד מיי' פי"ח מהל' איסורי ביאה הלכ' ל סמג לאוין קכא טוש"ע אה"ע סימן ז סעיף יא:

מסורת הש"ס

א) ב"ב לב., ב) ג"ז שם ודף קסה: סנהדרין ל. גיטין לג: [תוספתא סנהדרין פרק ה], ג) ע"ז כג., ד) עדיות פ"ח מ"ב, ה) [שם:]:

גמרא

ואסקיניה א) ואתו בי תרי ואמרי בן גרושה ובן חלוצה הוא ואחתיניה ואתא עד אחד ואמר ידענא ביה דכהן הוא ודכולי עלמא מצטרפין לעדות והכא במיחש לזילותא דבי דינא קמיפלגי תנא קמא סבר כיון דאחתיניה לא מסקינן ליה חיישינן לזילותא דבי דינא ורשב"ג סבר אנן אחתינן ליה ואנן מסקינן ליה ולזילותא דבי דינא לא חיישינן מתקיף לה רב אשי אי הכי אפי' תרי ותרי נמי אלא אמר רב אשי במצטרפין לעדות קמיפלגי ב) ובפלוגתא דהני תנאי דתניא אין עדותן מצטרפת עד שיראו שניהם כאחד ר' יהושע בן קרחה אמר אפי' בזה אחר זה ואין עדותן מתקיימת בב"ד עד שיעידו שניהם כאחד ר' נתן אומר שומעין דבריו של זה היום וכשיבא חבירו למחר שומעין דבריו:

מתני' ג) האשה שנחבשה בידי עובדי כוכבים על ידי ממון מותרת לבעלה על ידי נפשות אסורה לבעלה:

גמ' אמר רב שמואל בר רב יצחק אמר רב לא שנו אלא שיד ישראל תקיפה על עובדי כוכבים אבל יד עובדי כוכבים תקיפה על עצמן אפילו על ידי ממון אסורה לבעלה מתיב רבא ד) העיד רבי יוסי הכהן ור' זכריה בן הקצב על בת ישראל שהורהנה באשקלון וריחקוה בני משפחתה ועדיה מעידים אותה שלא נסתרה ושלא נטמאה ואמרו להם חכמים אם אתם מאמינים שהורהנה האמינו שלא נסתרה ושלא נטמאה ואם אי אתם מאמינים שלא נסתרה ושלא נטמאה אל תאמינו שהורהנה והא אשקלון דיד עובדי כוכבים תקיפה על עצמן וקתני הורהנה

רש"י

ואסקיניה. דבמקום קול הוי חד מהימן: **ודכולי עלמא.** בין לר' אלעזר בין לרשב"ג: **מצטרפין.** שני עדים המעידים זה שלא בפני זה כשאר עדיות: **דחיישינן לזילותא דבי דינא.** שהורידוהו שני פעמים ועכשיו יעלוהו ויבטלו דבריהם והיינו דקאמר ר' אלעזר למאחר שהורדנוהו ע"פ העוררין אין מעלין ע"פ עד זה השני אע"פ שיש לצרפו עם האחר: **ואנן מסקינן ליה.** ואי קשיא תרי ותרי נינהו אוקי תרי לבהדי תרי ואוקמינן אחזקיה קמייתא דאסקיניה ע"פ עד הראשון שהוא נאמן דהא אכתי אין עוררין דקול לאו עוררין הוא: **אפילו תרי.** אתו בהדי הדדי נמי בפעם שניה לרבי אלעזר לא מסקינן ליה: **עד שיראו שניהם כאחד.** את העדות לאפוקי אחד אומר בפני הלווהו ואחד אומר בפני הודה לו עליו: **ואין עדותן מתקיימת.** להתקבל בב"ד ואפי' ראו שניהן כאחד ופלוגתא אחריתי היא ולאו ר' יהושע בן קרחה קאמר לה ורבי אלעזר ורבן שמעון בפלוגתא דרבי נתן ורבנן פליגי: **מתני' ע"י ממון מותרת לבעלה.** דמרתתי להפסיד ממונן ואינן מפקירין אותה: **ע"י נפשות.** שהיתה נידונת למות: **אסורה לבעלה.** דהואיל ונוהגין בה הפקר חוששין שמא נתרצתה באחד מהן: **גמ' לא שנו.** דע"י ממון מותרת לבעלה: **אלא שיד ישראל תקיפה על העובדי כוכבים.** ויראים לעשות שלא כדין שמא יפסידו ממונם: **שהורהנה.** נתמשכנה: **ועדיה.** אותן שהעידו שהורהנה: **והא אשקלון.** דארץ פלשתים היא ועוד כבר גלו ישראל:

הורהנה

תוספות

ואסקיניה. וא"ת ולמאן דחייש לזילותא דבי דינא היכי אסקוהו כיון דלאחתיניה מחמת הקול וליכא למימר דליכא זילותא דבי דינא אלא היכא שהורידוהו שתי פעמים כדמוכח בחזקת הבתים (ב"ב דף לב.) וי"ל דליכא זילותא דבי דינא אלא היכא שהורידוהו ע"י עדות אבל בהורדה שע"י הקול ליכא זילותא דב"ד ואע"ג דאמרינן (גיטין דף פא.) גבי גרושה לכהן דלא מבטלינן קלא היינו משום דלית ליה תקנתא אבל הכא דאי לא מסקינן ליה לעולם פסול מבטלינן א) אי נמי בתרומה דרבנן הקילו: **אנן אחתינן ליה ואנן מסקינן ליה.** פי' בקונטרס אע"ג דתרי ותרי נינהו אוקי תרי לבהדי תרי ואוקי גברא אחזקתיה וקשה לר"י דבפרק האומר בקדושין (דף סו. ושם) קאמר גבי ינאי היכי דמי אילימא דתרי אמרי אשתבאי ותרי אמרי לא אשתבאי מאי חזית דסמכת אהני סמוך אהני ופירש התם בקונטרס דלא אמרי' אוקי תרי בהדי תרי ואוקי גברא אחזקיה דהא לא באו להעיד על אמו אלא על ינאי ולו לא היה חזקת כשרות ואין נראה לר"י דחזקת האם מהניא גם לינאי כדמשמע הכא ואמרינן נמי לעיל בפ"ק (דף יג. ושם) לדברי האומר בה מכשיר בבתה ואפילו מאן דפסל בבתה היינו משום דמעלה עשו גבי זנות וגם אין לומר כמו שתירץ ר"ח דליכא למימר התם אוקמינן אחזקה לפי שכל הנשים היו בחזקת שבויות דא"כ היכי מייתי מינה ראיה על אשתו שזינתה בעד אחד דשאני התם דכל הנשים בחזקת שבויות אבל אשתו זינתה היא בחזקת היתר ונראה לר"י דתרי ותרי ספיקא דרבנן הוא ומדרבנן החמירו דלא מוקמינן לה אחזקה והכא בתרומה דרבנן הקילו ובפרק בכל מערבין (עירובין דף לה.) גבי תרומה וטמאה כו' ספק הרי זה חמר גמל דברי ר"מ ומוקי לה ה) רבה ורב יוסף בשתי כתי עדים הא דלא מוקמינן לה אחזקה דלא נטמאת אע"ג דתרומה בזמן הזה דרבנן היינו משום דערובי תחומין דאורייתא לר"מ אי נמי שאני התם דליכא ריעותא דהרי נטמאת לפניך ולא אמרינן השתא הוא דאיטמי אע"ג דגבי מקוה אמרינן השתא הוא דחסר ואתאי (נדה דף ג:) הכא דליכא שתי כתי עדים לא אמרינן השתא הוא דאיטמי ובשנים אומרים מת ושנים אומרים לא מת דאמרינן לעיל (דף כב:) לא תנשא ולא מוקמינן לה אחזקת אשת איש היינו משום חזקה דאשה דייקא ומנסבא מרעה לה לחזקת אשת איש אע"ג דבשנים אומרים מת אמרינן בהאשה רבה (יבמות פז:) דמותרת לחזור לו וכיון דליכא בסוף לא דייקא מ"מ הכא כיון דמכחישין זה את זה איכא מותרת ובשנים אומרים נתגרשה ושנים אומרים לא נתגרשה דאמרינן נמי לעיל דלא תנשא אע"ג דלא דייקא וליכא נמי חזקה דלאין דאשה מעיזה פניה בפני בעלה לאו היכא דמכחישין לה עדים ויש לומר דמכל מקום דייקא לפי שירא שיחזו עדיה או יפסלו אותם בגזלנותא ובהאשה רבה (שם פח. ושם) גבי בעו מיניה מרב ששת עד אחד ביבמה מהו כו' אמר להו תניתוה אמרו לה מת בנך ואחר כך מת בעליך ונתייבמה ואח"כ אמרו לה חילוף הדברים תצא והולד ראשון והאחרון ממזר היכי דמי אילימא תרי ותרי מאי חזית דסמכת אהני דאמרי ליבם סמוך אהני דשרו לה וקשה דמאי פריך והא איא לן לאוקמי אחזקה דאסורה ליבם שמת בעלה תחלה כדאמרינן בפרק ארבעה אחין (שם דף לא. ושם) גבי נפל הבית עליו ועל בת אחיו כו' ועוד כיון דתרי ותרי ספיקא דרבנן הוא יש לאוסרה כדאמרינן גבי ינאי והתם לא דייקא כדאמרינן התם זימנין דרחמא ליה ליבם וי"ל דמ"מ מהני דיוקא דידה לענין מרעה ליה לחזקת איסור ליבם והא דפריך נמי התם כו' ועוד ממזר ספק ממזר הוא ואע"ג דבחזקת איסור ליבם היא מ"מ לא הוי ממזר ודאי דמהני דיוקא דידה כדפרשינן ועוד כיון דתרי ותרי ספיקא דרבנן אין לנו להעמידה על חזקתה ולהתירו בממזרת ורבינו יצחק בר ברוך פי' דלא אמרינן בכל הני אוקמא אחזקה לפי שהשנים שמוציאים אותו מחזקתו של היתר הם מעידים תחלה ומיד כשהעידו יצא מחזקתו ע"י עדותן ותו לא אמרינן אוקמא אחזקה והכי פריך לעיל מאי שנא רישא ומאי שנא סיפא דשנים שאומרים נתקדשה העידו תחלה ובשנים אומרים נתגרשה אע"פ שהם העידו תחלה מ"מ היתה בחזקת אשת איש וכן ההיא דהאשה רבה ודינאי שנים המוציאין אותו מחזקתו באו תחלה ואין נראה לרבינו יצחק דהא הכא בשמעתין מוקמינן ליה אחזקה אע"ג דכבר פסלוהו השנים והוציאוהו מחזקתו ואין סברא שיועיל מה שעד אחד המכשיר העיד קודם ב) ועוד דרב אשי משמע דבעי למימר דאפילו אתו שניהם לבסוף דמסקינן ליה: **על ידי ממון מותרת לבעלה.** נראה דמותרת אפילו לבעלה כהן דלא חיישינן אפי' לאונסא משום דמרתתי להפסיד ממונס ולא דמי לשבויה וכן מוכח בגמרא דקאמר לא שנו אלא שיד ישראל תקיפה על העובדי כוכבים אבל יד העובדי כוכבים תקיפה על עצמן אפילו ע"י ממון אסורה לבעלה ועל כרחן היינו לכהונה מדקאמרי אף אנן נמי תנינא מההיא דריחקוה בני משפחתה והא לא שייך אלא לכהונה דבישראל לא שייך וריחקוה בני משפחתה דאינה אסורה אלא לבעלה ועוד ראיה דתנן בפ' שני דמסכת ע"ז (דף כב.) אין מעמידין בהמה בפונדקאות של עובדי כוכבים מפני שחשודים על הרביעה ורמינהו לוקחין מהן בהמה לקרבן לא קשיא הא לכתחלה והא דיעבד ומנא תימרא דשני בין לכתחלה כו' דתנן לא תתייחד אשה עמהם מפני שחשודים על העריות ורמינהו האשה שנחבשה ע"י עובדי כוכבים ע"י ממון מותרת לבעלה אלא ש"מ שני לן בין לכתחלה לדיעבד משמע דאין לחוש כלל שנבעלה דאי מותרת לבעלה ישראל קאמר דלא חיישינן שמא נתרצת אבל לבעלה ג) כהן אסורה דחיישינן שמא נאנסה א"כ לא הוה מייתי מידי: **ועל ידי נפשות אסורה לבעלה.** היינו אפילו לבעלה ישראל דחיישינן שמא נתרצת כדי למצא חן שלא יהרגנה דאי לבעלה כהן קאמר ואסורה שמא נאנסה א"כ הוה ליה למימר אסורה לכהונה אלא ודאי אפילו לבעלה ישראל אסורה וא"ת נגועות לישתרו דקודם לכן מסרן נפשייהו כדמשמע בריש מכילתין (דף ג:) גבי כל הנשאת ברביעי תיבעל להשר תחלה וצריך לומר דהכא חיישינן על כל אחת שמא אינה נגועה ואפילו נראית נגועה שמא אינה:

כהן

תוספות ישנים

א) אי נמי אחתיניה לאו דוקא אלא שירד מעצמו. ת"י:

ב) [ואומר ריצב"א דרב אשי נמי מוקי לה כשבא עד אחד המכשיר קודם שנים הפוסלים אבל בבאו שנים הפוסלים תחלה ואח"כ באו שנים המכשירים בזה אחר זה לא בעי לאוקמי דהא לא הוי קרי במתני' ע"פ עד אחד דכיון דכי אתי עד אחד אין ממש בדבריו עד שבא האחר]. ת"י:

ג) [ונקט רישא לבעלה אגב סיפא ובגמ' נמי נקט לבעלה אגב מתני'. ת"י]:

תוספות רי"ד

דכהן הוא ואסקיני' פי' דע"א נאמן להכחיש את הקול. ואתו בי תרי עוררים ואמרו בן גרושה ובן חלוצה הוא ואחתיני'. ואתא ע"א ואמר ידענא בי' דכהן הוא ר"א סבר הכא [כיון] דאיכא עוררים תרי דפסלו לי' אין מעלין לכהונה ע"פ ע"א שמכשירו ואע"ג דאיכא ע"א קמא שהכשירו כיון שלא העידו יחד בב"ד אין מצטרפים ורשב"ג סבר אע"פ שיש עוררים מעלין ע"פ ע"א זה שמכשירו שמצטרפים אותו עם הראשון ואמרי' אוקי תרי לבהדי תרי ואוקי גברא אחזקתיה. ואי קשיא והא אמרת לעיל דבתרי ותרי דהוא ספק תורה לא אוקי גברא אחזקתיה יש לתרץ דודאי באיסור תורה אמרינן הכי והכא בתרומה דרבנן והכי מוקמי' לה לקמן בשלהי פירקין והלכך מקלינן בה ואמרי' אוקי תרי לבהדי תרי ואוקי גברא אחזקתיה. ובפלוגתא דתנאי. אין עדות מצטרפין עד שיראו שניהם כאחד (דברי ר"א) ר"י [בן קרחה] אומר אפילו בזה אחר זה פי' לאפוקי ד"א בפני לוה ו' בפני הודה לו ... שמה שראה זה לא ראה זה. ואע"ג דבמנה חד מסהדי לת"ק לא מצטרפי. ואין עדותן מתקיימת בב"ד עד שיעידו שניהם כאחד ר"נ אומר שומעין דבריו של זה היום ולכשיבוא חבירו למחר שומעין דבריו ואתי ר"א כת"ק ורשב"ג כר"י [בן קרחה] שעדותן מצטרפת אע"פ שלא ראו שניהן כאחד. והל' נמי כר"נ שעדותן מתקיימת בב"ד ואף על פי שלא העידו כאחד: מתני' האשה שנחבשה בידי עובדי כוכבים. ע"י ממון מותרת לבעלה ע"י נפשות אסורה. עיר שכבשה כרכום כל כהנות בתוכה פסולות. ואם יש להן עדים ואפי' עבד ואפי' שפחה הרי אלו נאמנין שאין אדם נאמן ע"י עצמו. א"ר זכריה בן הקצב המעון הזה לא זזה ידה מתוך ידי משעה שנכנסו עובדי כוכבים לירושלים ועד שיצאו א"ל אין אדם נאמן על ידי עצמו. פי' באשת כהן מיירי דאי באשת ישראל אפילו ע"י נפשות מותרת דאנוסה היא ודרישא בכהנות הלכך ע"י ממון מותרת לבעלה דמירתתי דלמא מפסדי ממונא ולא אבל ע"י נפשות ... פי' הואיל ונוהגים בה הפקר חוששים שמא נתרצת לא' מהן ומשמע שהיא אסורה לישראל ואינו נ"ל דא"כ גב בשבורי נאמר כן ונאסור אותה על בעלה ישראל. והאיך מתנה אדם לאשתו אם תשתבאי אפרקינך ואותבינך לי לאינתו. א"ר אבא מפקידים אותה לא חיישינן שמא מתרצת אלא הכל הוא באונס. וכך פי' גם ר"ח ז"ל אסורה לבעלה כהן: המעון הזה. פי' שבועה הוא. א"ר שמואל ברבי יצחק ל"ש פי' שע"י ממון מותרת אלא שיד ישראל תקיפה על עובדי כוכבים פי' שירים מישראל אבל יד עובדי כוכבים תקיפה על ישראל אפילו על ידי ממון אסורה דלא מירתתי

ליקוטי רש"י

ואחתיניה. דאחד במקום שנים אין דבריו כלום. **ואתא עד אחד.** לבסוף ואמר דכהן גמור הוא והוו להו שנים מכשירין. **ודכולי עלמא.** בין רבי אלעזר בין רשב"ג מצטרפים עדים המעידים זה שלא בפני זה בשאר עדות וה"נ לגבי לצרף מן הדין עד ראשון ועד אחרון המכשירין וכנגדן לא ... דבי דינא כדמפרש ואזיל. **תנא קמא סבר כיון דאחתיניה.** על פי ב' עוררין ודנין הורדוהו ...

על פי עד ראשון שהיה נאמן דהא אכתי אין עוררין דקול לאו עוררין הוא. **אי הכי וכו'.** דר' אלעזר מאי איריא עד הבא לבסוף דהתם אין מעלין משום זילותא כדקתני מתני' אין מעלין על פי עד אחד בזמן שיש עליו עוררין ... על פי שנים מעלין אפילו תרי אתו בהדי הדדי נמי בפעם שניה לרבי אלעזר לא מסקינן ליה. **במצטרפין.** לר' אלעזר אין מצרפין עד אחרון עם הראשון הואיל ולא העידו שניהם כאחד כרבנן דפליגי אדרבי נתן ...

במסיח לפי תומו כי הא דאמר רב יהודה אמר שמואל מעשה באדם אחד שהיה מסיח לפי תומו ואמר זכורני כשאני תינוק ומורכב על כתיפו של אבא והוציאוני מבית הספר והפשיטוני את כותנתי והטבילוני לאכול בתרומה לערב ור' חייא מסיים בה וחבירי בדילין ממני והיו קורין אותי יוחנן אוכל חלות והעלהו רבי לכהונה על פיו תניא ר"ש בן אלעזר אומר כשם שתרומה חזקה לכהונה כך מעשר ראשון חזקה לכהונה והחולק בבית דין אינה חזקה מעשר ראשון דלוי הוא כר"א בן עזריה דתניא תרומה לכהן מעשר ראשון ללוי דברי ר"ע ר"א בן עזריה אומר מעשר ראשון אף לכהן אימור דאר"א בן עזריה אף לכהן לכהן ולא ללוי מי אמר אין בתר דקנסינהו עזרא ודלמא איקרו ויהבו ליה אמר רב חסדא הכא במאי עסקינן כגון דמוחזק לן באבוה דהאי דכהן הוא ונפק עליה קלא דבן גרושה ובן חלוצה הוא וחלקו ליה לדידיה מעשר בבית הגרנות לוי דלאו לוי הוא מאי איכא למימר בן גרושה או בן חלוצה הוא לא מיבעיא למאן דאמר מעשר ראשון אסור לזרים דלא הוו יהבי ליה אלא אפילו למ"ד מעשר ראשון מותר לזרים הני מילי למיספק להו אבל בתורת חלוקה לא יהבי ליה והחולק בבית דין אינה חזקה אי בבית דין לא הויא חזקה היכא הויא חזקה אמר רב ששת הכי קאמר החולק תרומה בנכסי אביו עם אחיו בבית דין אינה חזקה פשיטא מהו דתימא מדהנך לאכילה האי נמי לאכילה קמ"ל הנך לאכילה האי לזבוני: רבי יהודה אומר אין מעלין לכהונה על פי עד אחד וכו': רשב"ג היינו רבי אליעזר וכי תימא ערער חד איכא בינייהו דרבי אליעזר סבר ערער חד ורשב"ג סבר ערער תרי [א] והאמר רבי יוחנן דברי הכל אין ערער פחות משנים אלא הכא במאי עסקינן דמוחזק לן באבוה דהאי דכהן הוא ונפק עליה קלא דבן גרושה או בן חלוצה הוא ואחתיניה ואתא עד אחד ואמר ידענא ביה דכהן הוא ואסקיניה

רש"י

והטבילוני. מפני שסתם תינוק מטפח באשפות ושרלים מלוין שם: לערב. דצריך הערב שמש: והחולק בב"ד. קא ס"ד שעל פי ב"ד הקבוע בעיר היו חולקין לו תרומה בבית הגרנות ולקמיה פריך אי בב"ד לא הוי חזקה היכא הויא חזקה: בתר דקנסינהו עזרא. ללוים דלא ליתבו להו כדאמרי' ביבמות בפ' יש מותרות (דף פו:): לוי דלאו לוי הוא. כלומר בלוי ליכא לספוקי דהא אביו כהן: למ"ד כו'. פלוגתא היא ביבמות (שם): בנכסי אביו כו' אינה חזקה. להשבית מעליו קול היוצא על אמו שהיא גרושה והוא חלל: פשיטא. דהא אפי' הוא חלל יורש את אביו: רבן שמעון היינו רבי אליעזר. דהא ודאי במקום שיש עוררין לא אמר רבן שמעון לליהוי חד נאמן וכי אמר מעלין במקום שאין עוררין קאמר: דר"א סבר ערער חד. הוי ערער ואין אחד נאמן עליו להכשירו: ונפק עליה קלא. קול בעלמא ולא עדות: ואחתיניה. מן הכהונה עד שיבדקו את הדבר שמעלה הוא לכהונה:

תוספות

במסיח לפי תומו. וא"ת ומנ"ל דהכי הוא דלמא ר' חייא העלה בן על פי אביו במסיח לפי תומו ורבי העלה אח ע"פ אחיו אפי' בלא מסיח ואר"י דמסתמא דמאי דקתני בברייתא מילתא דרבי עשה רבי מעשה ועוד דאי אפשר דרבי העלה אח ע"פ אחיו ללויה אפילו בלא מסיח דהתם אין שייך לומר שבידו להאכילו מעשר למ"ד מעשר ראשון מותר לזרים: מבית הספר. נקט שלא לומר שהוא עבד כדאמר בסוף פירקין (לקמן דף כח.): אין בתר דקנסינהו עזרא. ולר"ע דקודם קנסא הוי דוקא ללוי בתר קנסא אף לכהנים אבל לר"א בן עזריה דמקמי קנסא הוי אף לכהן בתר קנסא הוי לכהן דוקא והא דמעשר ראשון חזקה לכהונה אתיא כר' אלעזר בן עזריה ולא כר"ע ויש שמוחקין אין ומפרשים דהא דקאמר בתר דקנסינהו עזרא הוי אפי' לר"ע דבתר קנסא הוי לכ"ע לכהן דוקא והוי כמו אלא ושיבוש הוא בידם דהא בכמה מקומות מוכיח דמעשר ראשון ללוי אף בתר קנסא כדתנן בפ' כל הגט (גיטין דף ל.) המלוה מעות את הכהן ואת הלוי להיות מפריש עליהן כו' וכן התם בגמרא ישראל שאמר לבן לוי כור מעשר לאביך בידי ובפ' הזרוע (חולין קלא: ושם) פריך מעשר ראשון דלוי הוא וכן בכמה מקומות והיינו כר"ע ועוד דלמ"ד קנסא לעניים היכי הוי חזקה לכהונה דאליבא דר"ע פליגי בס"פ יש מותרות (יבמות פו: ושם) דאיכא למ"ד קנסא לכהנים ואיכא למ"ד לעניים לר' אלעזר בן עזריה הוי דוקא לכהן ואפי' לעשירים כמו קודם קנסא דלא קנסא עזרא שהרי עלו ולמ"ד קנסא לעניים משמע התם דוקא לעניים ולא לכהנים עשירים אפי' בימי טומאה דלית ליה דבימי טומאה עניים הוו ועניים דהתם אין לפרש עניי לוים דוקא ולא עניי ישראל וכהנים דא"כ נשתכרו עניי לוים במה שלא עלו ועוד דמשמע התם אילו הוו כהנים בימי טומאתם עניים לכ"ע הוו שקלי אע"ג דלענין חלוקת מעשר הוו כישראל דללוי ולא לכהן קאמר אלא לעניים בין עניי כהנים בין עניי לוים ולמ"ד מעשר ראשון מותר לזרים שקלי אפילו עניי ישראל אבל למ"ד אסור לזרים אין נראה שיתנן לעניי ישראל כדי שימכרו דמילתא דאתי לידי תקלה לא אתקינו רבנן דאיכא למיחש דלמא אתי למיכליה [כדאמר בסמוך לא מיבעיא לר"מ דאמר אסור לזרים כו'] ולר"ע לא הפקיע עזרא את הלוים מכל וכל להשוותן לישראל והכהנים שלא יטלו עשירים לוים אלא עניי לוים בתורת עניות אלא ללוים בין עניים בין עשירים היו חולקים לעולם כדמוכח בכל הנהו שהבאתי שהיו נוטלין בתורת לוית ועוד דר"ג בספינה שנתן מעשר ראשון לר' יהושע בן חנניא (מעשר שני פ"ה מ"ט) אי בתורת עניות יהיב ליה אמאי לא יהב ליה נמי מעשר עני שהרי מעשר עני נתן לר"ע ומיהו יש לדחות דלעולם בתורת עניות נתן לו ומה שלא נתן לו מעשר עני לפי שהיו לו מאתים זוז דאינו נוטל במעשר עני כדתנן במסכת פאה (פ"ח מ"ח) אבל מעשר ראשון יטול אפי' יש לו מאתים זוז דהא איכא למ"ד דאפי' כהנים עשירים בימי טומאה עניים נינהו ועוד דלא רצה ליתן כל מתנותיו לעני אחד: בתר דקנסינהו עזרא. לא אשכחן בהדיא בקרא דקנסינהו רק מלינו בעזרא (נחמיה י) והיה הכהן בן אהרן עם הלוים בעשר הלוים ואיכא למימר דה"ק כשיבאו הלוים לחלוק בבית הגרנות יבאו הכהנים עמהם ומיהו לר"א בן עזריה דבתר קנסא דוקא לכהן לא משמע מהאי קרא דליכא למימר עם הלוים דקאמר קרא היינו לקבל מהם מעשר ראשון משלהם דהא משלהם לא קנסם עזרא כדמוכח בפרק הזרוע (חולין קלא:) וי"ל דלר"א בן עזריה לא נמנעו הלוים מכל וכל מלילך לבית הגרנות לחלוק במעשר כדאמר בסמוך דלמא איקרי ויהיב ליה כל שכן בימי עזרא שעדיין לא פשט הקנס שהיו הולכים בבית הגרנות ולכך נאמר שילכו הכהנים עם הלוים ולמ"ד קנסא לעניים הא דכתיב והיה הכהן היינו בכהן עני ומשום דכהנים עניים שכיחי טפי לפי שאין כל כך עסוקים במלאכה אלא בעבודת בית המקדש וגם אין להם קרקעות נקט כהן וה"ה עניי ישראל למ"ד מעשר ראשון מותר לזרים וה"ר יוסף פירש מדכתיב (במלאכי ג) הביאו את כל המעשר אל בית האוצר דבית האוצר היא לשכה שתיקן עזרא לתת שם תרומת הכהנים כדכתיב בעזרא (נחמיה י) וכיון שאומר להביא שם המעשר א"כ של כהנים הוא וקיימא לן (מגילה דף טו.) דמלאכי זה עזרא ולמ"ד לעניים נקט אל בית האוצר משום דכהנים עניים שכיחי טפי כדפרישית אי נמי אל בית האוצר לא ליתן לכהנים אלא לחלק לעניים וה"ר אלחנן הקשה דבסוף עזרא משמע שהמעשר היה ללוים דכתיב ואדע כי מניות הלוים לא נתנה (להם) ויברחו איש לשדהו הלוים והמשוררים כו' משמע שהלוים והמשוררים היו חולקים וצריך לומר דזה היה מקמי דקנסינהו עזרא אך קראי לא מוכחי הכי: והאמר רבי יוחנן דברי הכל אין ערער כו'. נראה לר"י דר' יוחנן עיקר דבריו על משנתנו והכי לא קא משני הכא ה"מ היכא דליכא חזקה דכשרות כו' כדמשני בפרק עשרה יוחסין (קדושין דף עג:) ואם תאמר והואיל ואמתני' קאי היכי פריך מיניה התם ובפרק קמא דגיטין (דף ט.) גבי גט דלמא הא דקאמר ר' יוחנן דלא מהני ערער דחד היינו היכא דאיכא עד אחד דמכשר דקתני מעלין לכהונה על פי עד אחד ויש לומר דהש"ס ידע דר' יוחנן אמסקנא דיבר דבתחלה היה קול ואח"כ בא עד אחד להכשירו והסיר הקול ואתו בי תרי ואמרי דבן גרושה ובן חלוצה הוא דבכי האי גוונא א"ר יוחנן דבעינן שנים אע"ג דהעד שהכשיר והקול כמאן דליתנהו דמי שהרי העד גרוע מן הקול אי לאו משום חזקה דמסייע ליה לבטל הקול שהרי הקול פוסל והעד אינו פוסל לרבי יוחנן: אין ערער פחות משנים. לאפוקי חד דלא הוי ערער אבל קול נמי פוסל בתחלה בתרומה קודם שבא העד המכשיר: ואתא עד אחד ואמר ידענא ביה דכהן הוא. לא בעי למימר דפליגי אי מעלין ע"פ עד אחד כשהקול פוסל דפשיטא ליה להש"ס דלא פסיל קול לכ"ע כיון דאיכא עד וחזקה ועוד דקול לא הוי קרי עוררין:

ואסקיניה

מסורת הש"ס

א) ב"ק קיד:, ב) ב"ב פא: יבמות פו. חולין קלא., ג) [יבמות עד: פה: פו.], ד) [שם פו.], ה) ב"ב לב. קדושין עג: גיטין ט., ו) מ"ב כ"ז, ז) [וע"ע תוס' שם וב"ב לב.]

הגהות מהר"ב רנשבורג

א] גמ' האמר ר' יוחנן דברי הכל אין ערער פחות משנים. עי' תוס' ד"ה והאמר ובחדושי הר"ן בחולין פא ע"א ד"ה וקשיא לן:

ליקוטי רש"י

והטבילוני. לפי שדרכו של תינוק לטפח בשרצים ובטומאות. בדילין ממני. מפני תרומתי [ב"ק קיד:]. מעשר ראשון אף לכהן. דבכ"ד מקומות נקראו כהנים לוים הלכך אע"ג דבמעשר ראשון לוי כתיבא ביה כהנים נמי משתמעי [חולין קלא:]. ומשמע ליה לר' אלעזר בן עזריה לוים דקרא אף כהנים במשמע דבעשרים וארבעה מקומות נקראו כהנים לוים [רשב"ם ב"ב פא:]. בתר דקנסינהו עזרא. ביבמות (דף פו:) אמר מפני מה קנסו לוים במעשר מפני שלא עלו בימי עזרא דכתיב ואבינה בעם ובכהנים ומבני לוי לא מצאתי שם אבל מקרא מפורש לא מצאתי שקנסם אבל דוגמא יש לדבר שכתוב בעזרא (נחמיה י) בסופו והיה הכהן בן אהרן עם הלוים (במעשר) [בעשר] הלוים למדנו שלא האמינום על תרומת מעשר ולא היו חולקין להן מעשר בגורן אלא (דקנסינהו) בפני הכהנים [חולין קלא:]. ערער חד איכא בינייהו. והא דקתני בזמן שיש עליו עוררין היינו עד אחד הפוסלו ומכחיש עד אחד המכשירו [רשב"ם ב"ב לא:]. ורשב"ג סבר ערער תרי. בעינן אבל במקום ערער אחד הוי עד אחד נאמן להכשירו. האמר רבי יוחנן. לא איתפרש היכא קאי. ואחתיניה. מן הכהונה עד שיבדקו את הדבר שמעלה היא בכהונה וכל זה יתור לשון הוא בלא צורך דבלא קול נמי מיוקמא שמעתתא שפיר בעד אחד מכשיר מעיקרא ועד אחד בסוף ושנים עדים עוררים בינתים כדמפרש ואזיל אלא משום הכי נקט ליה דבעי למימר ואתא עד אחד ואמר דכהן גמור הוא ואסקיניה דלמאי אתא עד אחד להכשירו אלא אם כן יצא עליו פסלות קודם לכן [שם לב.].

עין משפט נר מצוה

צד א מיי' פ"כ מהל' איסורי ביאה הל' יד סמג לאוין קטז טוש"ע אה"ע סימן ג סעיף א:

צה ב מיי' פ"ו מהל' תרומות הלכה א סמג לאוין רכד:

צו ג מיי' פ"א מהל' מעשר הלכה ד:

צז ד מיי' פ"כ מהל' איסורי ביאה הלכה טו טוש"ע אה"ע סימן ג סעיף ו:

צח ה מיי' שם הלכה יב:

תוספות רי"ד

רשב"ג אומר וכו'. רשב"ג היינו ת"ק פי' ר"א שאין לומר שבמקום עוררין קאמר רשב"ג דמעלין לכהונה ע"פ עד אחד אלא במקום שאין עוררין והת"ק נמי כר"א. ואסיק רב אשי דבמצטרפין לעדות קמיפלגי ובמקום שיש עוררין. והכא במאי עסקינן במוחזק לן באבוה דהאי דכהן הוא. ונפק עלי' [קלא] דבן גרושה ובן חלוצה הוא ואחתיני' פי' עד שנבדוק הקול אם הוא אמת אם לאו ואתא עד אחד ואמר ידענא ביה

The Mishnah continued: "R' Elazar says . . . where there are no challengers we raise a man to the Kehunah based on the word of one witness. Rabban Shimon ben Gamliel says . . . we raise a man to the Kehunah based on the word of one witness."

The Gemara asks:

רַבָּן שִׁמְעוֹן בֶּן גַּמְלִיאֵל הַיְינוּ רַבִּי (אליעזר) [אֶלְעָזָר][24] – **Rabban Shimon ben Gamliel is** saying **the same as R' Elazar,** for Rabban Shimon could not possibly mean that one witness is believed against challengers![25]

The Gemara suggests and immediately rejects one answer:

וְכִי תֵּימָא עִרְעָר חַד אִיכָּא בֵּינַיְיהוּ – **And if you will say** that **the difference between them is** in an instance where there is only **a single challenger,** דְּרַבִּי (אליעזר) [אֶלְעָזָר][26] סָבַר עִרְעָר חַד – **for R' Elazar holds** that **a challenge is** valid even if raised by only **one** witness,[27] וְרַבָּן שִׁמְעוֹן בֶּן גַּמְלִיאֵל סָבַר עִרְעָר תְּרֵי – **while Rabban Shimon ben Gamliel holds** that **a challenge** requires **two** witnesses to be effective,[28] this is not so. הָאָמַר רַבִּי יוֹחָנָן – **Why, R' Yochanan has said:** דִּבְרֵי הַכֹּל אֵין עִרְעָר פָּחוֹת מִשְּׁנַיִם – **All agree that a challenge is not** effective if made by **fewer than two** witnesses![29]

The Gemara explains the dispute:

אֶלָּא הָכָא בְּמַאי עָסְקִינַן – **Rather, what** case **are we dealing with here?** דְּמוּחְזָק לָן בַּאֲבוּהָ דְּהַאי דְּכֹהֵן הוּא – **Where it had been established that the father of this man was a Kohen,** thereby entitling him to the privileges of the Kehunah. וְנָפַק עֲלֵיהּ קָלָא – **And** then **a rumor**[30] **emerged about him** דְּבֶן גְּרוּשָׁה אוֹ בֶּן חֲלוּצָה הוּא – **that he was the son of a divorcee or the son of a** ***chalutzah,***[31] וְאַחְתִּינֵיהּ – **and [the court] demoted him** from the Kehunah until the matter could be investigated.[32] וְאָתָא עֵד אֶחָד – **Then a single witness came** forward, וְאָמַר יָדַעְנָא בֵּיהּ דְּכֹהֵן הוּא – **and said, "I know that he is a** [qualified] **Kohen,"**

NOTES

24. [Emendation based on *Rashash;* see also *Dikdukei Soferim HaShalem* §26. The Mishnah on 24b, the parallel passage in *Bava Basra* 31b-32a and the Rishonim here (see *Rashi* on 26b) all refer to this Tanna as R' Elazar.]

25. At first glance, it would seem that Rabban Shimon ben Gamliel holds that we elevate a man to the Kehunah on the testimony of one witness even if two witnesses ("challengers") assert that he is ineligible. However, this cannot be, because one witness certainly does not supersede two. Rather, Rabban Shimon ben Gamliel means that one witness can effect the elevation when he is *unopposed* by challengers. But then his opinion is identical with R' Elazar's (*Rashi*).

26. See note 24.

27. R' Elazar's statement in the Mishnah would then be understood as follows: A single witness' testimony is sufficient to promote a man to the Kehunah if there are no challengers at all. Even a single challenger, however, is sufficient to negate the testimony (*Ritva*). [It is Tannaitic style to use the plural noun עוֹרְרִין, *challengers,* even in reference to a single person (*Ritva*).]

28. I.e. if only one challenger contests the man's Kohanic status, we believe the single witness who testified that he is a Kohen (*Ritva*). Thus, when Rabban Shimon says, "We raise [a man] to the Kehunah based on the word of one witness," he means that the witness supersedes a single challenger.

A Tannaic opinion recorded later in a Mishnah or Baraisa typically goes beyond the scope of the preceding opinion (see *Bava Basra* 93b). Hence, in this case, it can be assumed that R' Elazar (whose opinion is recorded first) holds that a single witness can establish someone as a Kohen only if there are no challengers at all, whereas Rabban Shimon ben Gamliel maintains that he overrides a single challenger (*Ritva*). [See *Birkas Avraham,* who explains this version of the dispute; see also *Shitah Mekubetzes.*]

29. It is not clear in what context R' Yochanan made his statement (*Ritva; Rashbam* to *Bava Basra* 32a ד״ה והא אמר ר׳ יוחנן). Regardless, the Gemara assumes that it pertains to our discussion as well.

Some Rishonim suggest that R' Yochanan made his declaration regarding this Mishnah; his words "all agree" refer to R' Elazar and Rabban Shimon ben Gamliel (*Tosafos, Ritva, Ran* et al.; cf. *Ramban's* first approach; see *Pnei Yehoshua*).

At any rate, R' Yochanan's statement teaches in our context that if someone was assumed to be a Kohen (see *Tosafos, Ritva* and the contination of the Gemara), he is not demoted unless *two* witnesses testify against him. Should only one witness claim that he is not a Kohen, he still retains his Kohanic status (see *Birkas Avraham,* who explains why this is a novel point). Hence, when R' Elazar says in our Mishnah that a single witness who testifies that someone is a Kohen does not override "challengers," he must refer to a challenge raised by two (*Tosafos* and *Ritva*).

30. This refers to a mere rumor that was not brought to the attention of the court in a formal manner (see *Rashi;* see also *Shitah Mekubetzes* ד״ה ורש״י ז״ל; cf. *Ritva*).

31. See note 15.

32. Although the Gemara mentioned above that a challenge raised by fewer than two witnesses is ineffective, this refers to a *permanent* removal. Even a rumor, however, can effect a *temporary* removal, which remains in force until the matter is clarified. This extra caution is exercised in an effort to keep the Kehunah free of blemished lineage (see *Rashi*).

מסורת הש"ס

א) ב"ק קיד., ב) ב"ב פא: יבמות פו. חולין קלא., ג) [יבמות עד: פה: פו.], ד) [שם פו.], ה) ב"ב לג. קדושין עג: גיטין ט., ו) ת"י כ"י, ז) [ועי' תוס' שם וב"ב לג.].

הגהות מהר"ב רנשבורג

א] גמ' האמר ר' יוחנן דברי הכל אין ערער פחות משנים. עי' תוס' ד"ה והאמר ובחדושי הר"ן בחולין פא ע"א ד"ה וקשיא לן:

ליקוטי רש"י

והטבילוני. לפי שדרכו של תינוק לטפח בשרצים ובטומאות. בדילין ממני. מפני תרומתי [ב"ק קיד:]. מעשר ראשון אף לכהן. דבכ"ד מקומות נקראו כהנים לוים הלכך אע"ג דבמעשר ראשון לוי כתיבא ביה כהנים נמי משתמעי [חולין קלא:]. ומשמע ליה לר' אלעזר בן עזריה לוים דקרא אף כהנים במשמע דבעשרים וארבעה מקומות נקראו כהנים לוים [רשב"ם ב"ב פא:]. בתר דקנסינהו עזרא. ביבמות (דף פו:) אמר מפני מה קנסו לוים במעשר מפני שלא עלו בימי עזרא דכתיב ואבינה בעם ובכהנים ומבני לוי לא מצאתי שם אבל מקרא מפורש לא מצאתי שקנסם אבל דוגמא יש לדבר שכתוב בעזרא (נחמיה י) בסופו והיה הכהן בן אהרן עם הלוים (במעשר) [בעשר] הלוים למדנו שלא האמינום על תרומת מעשר ולא היו חולקין להן מעשר בגורן אלא (דקנסינהו) בפני הכהנים [חולין קלא:]. ערער חד איכא בינייהו. והא דקתני בזמן שיש עליו עוררין היינו עד אחד הפוסלו ומכחיש עד אחד המכשירו [רשב"ם ב"ב לא:]. ורשב"ג סבר ערער תרי. בעינן אבל במקום ערער אחד הוי עד אחד נאמן להכשירו. האמר רבי יוחנן. לא איתפרש היכא קאי. ואחתיניה. מן הכהונה עד שיבדקו את הדבר שמעלה היא בכהונה וכל זה יתור לשון הוא בלא צורך דבלא קול נמי מיתוקמא שמעתתא שפיר בעד אחד מכשיר מעיקרא ועד אחד בסוף ושנים עדים עוררים בינתים כדמפרש ואזיל אלא משום הכי נקט ליה דבעי למימר ואתא עד אחד ואמר דכהן גמור הוא ואסקיניה דלמאי אתא עד אחד להכשירו אלא אם כן יצא עליו פסלות קודם לכן [שם לב.].

עין משפט נר מצוה

צד א מיי' פ"כ מהל' איסורי ביאה הלכ' יד סמג לאוין קכב טוש"ע אה"ע סימן ג סעיף א:
צה ב מיי' פ"ו מהל' תרומות הלכה א סמג לאוין רכד:
צו ג מיי' פ"א מהל' מעשר הלכה ד:
צז ד מיי' פ"כ מהל' איסורי ביאה הלכה טז טוש"ע אה"ע סימן ג סעיף ו:
צח ה מיי' שם הלכה יג:

תוספות רי"ד

רשב"ג אומר וכו'. רשב"ג היינו ת"ק פי' ר"א שאין לומר שבמקום עוררין קאמר רשב"ג דמעלין לכהונה ע"פ עד אחד אלא במקום שאין עוררין והת"ק נמי ר"א. ואסיק רב אשי דבמצטרפין לעדות קמיפלגי ובמקום שיש עוררין. והכא במאי עסקינן במוחזק לן באבוה דהאי דכהן הוא. ונפק עלי' [קלא] דבן גרושה ובן חלוצה הוא ואחתיני'. פי' עד שנבדוק הקול אם הוא אמת אם לאו ואתא עד אחד ואמר ידענא ביה

גמרא

במסיח לפי תומו כי הא דאמר רב יהודה אמר שמואל [א]מעשה באדם אחד שהיה מסיח לפי תומו ואמר זכורני כשאני תינוק ומורכב על כתיפו של אבא והוציאוני מבית הספר והפשיטוני את כותנתי והטבילוני לאכול בתרומה לערב ור' חייא מסיים בה וחבירי בדילין ממני והיו קורין אותי יוחנן אוכל חלות והעלהו רבי לכהונה על פיו תניא ר"ש בן אלעזר אומר כשם שתרומה חזקה לכהונה כך מעשר ראשון חזקה לכהונה והחולק בבית דין אינה חזקה מעשר ראשון דלוי הוא כר"א בן עזריה דתניא [ב]תרומה לכהן מעשר ראשון ללוי דברי ר"ע ר"א בן עזריה אומר מעשר ראשון אף לכהן אימור דאמר ר"א בן עזריה אף לכהן לכהן ולא ללוי מי אמר [ג]אין בתר דקנסינהו עזרא ודלמא איקרו ויהבו ליה אמר רב חסדא הכא במאי עסקינן [ד]כגון דמוחזק לן באבוה דהאי דכהן הוא ונפק עליה קלא דבן גרושה ובן חלוצה הוא וחלקו ליה לדידיה מעשר בבית הגרנות לוי דלאו לוי הוא מאי איכא למימר בן גרושה או בן חלוצה הוא לא מיבעיא למאן דאמר [ג]מעשר ראשון אסור לזרים דלא הוו יהבי ליה אלא אפילו למ"ד [ד]מעשר ראשון מותר לזרים הני מילי למיספק להו אבל בתורת חלוקה לא יהבי ליה והחולק בבית דין אינה חזקה אי בבית דין לא הויא חזקה היכא הויא חזקה אמר רב ששת הכי קאמר [ה]החולק תרומה בנכסי אביו עם אחיו בבית דין אינה חזקה פשיטא מהו דתימא מדהנך לאכילה האי נמי לאכילה קמ"ל הנך לאכילה האי לזבוני: רבי יהודה אומר אין מעלין לכהונה על פי עד אחד וכו': רשב"ג היינו רבי אליעזר וכי תימא ערער חד איכא בינייהו דרבי אליעזר סבר ערער חד ורשב"ג סבר ערער תרי [א] והאמר רבי יוחנן דברי הכל [ו]אין ערער פחות משנים אלא הכא במאי עסקינן דמוחזק לן באבוה דהאי דכהן הוא ונפק עליה קלא דבן גרושה או בן חלוצה הוא ואחתיניה ואתא עד אחד ואמר ידענא ביה דכהן הוא ואסקיניה

רש"י

והטבילוני. מפני שסתם תינוק מטפח בגללים ושרצים מצויין שם: לערב. לצריך הערב שמש: והחולק בב"ד. קא ס"ד שעל פי ב"ד הקבוע בעיר היו חולקין לו תרומה בבית הגרנות ולקמיה פריך אי בב"ד לא הוי חזקה היכא הוי חזקה: בתר דקנסינהו עזרא. ללוים דלא ליתבו להו כדאמרי' ביבמות בפ' יש מותרות (דף פו:): לוי דלאו לוי הוא. כלומר בלוי ליכא לספוקי דהא אביו כהן: למ"ד כו'. פלוגתא היא ביבמות (שם): בנכסי אביו כו' אינה חזקה. להשבית מעליו קול היוצא על אמו שהיא גרושה והוא חלל: פשיטא. דהא אפי' הוא חלל יורש את אביו: רבן שמעון היינו רבי אליעזר. דהא ודאי במקום שיש עוררין לא אמר רבן שמעון דליהוי חד נאמן וכי אמר מעלין במקום שאין עוררין קאמר: דר"א סבר ערער חד. הוי ערער ואין אחד נאמן עליו להכשירו: ונפק עליה קלא. קול בעלמא ולא עדות: ואחתיניה. מן הכהונה עד שיבדקו את הדבר שמעלה הוא לכהונה: ואסקיניה

תוספות

במסיח לפי תומו. וא"ת ומנ"ל דהכי הוא דלמא ר' חייא העלה בן על פי אביו במסיח לפי תומו ורבי העלה את ע"פ אחיו אפי' בלא מסיח ואר"י דמסתמא דמלתי דקתני בברייתא מילתא דרבי עשה רבי מעשה ועוד דלא אפשר דרבי העלה את ע"פ אחיו ללויה אפילו בלא מסיח דהתם אין שייך לומר שבידו להאכילו מעשר למ"ד מעשר ראשון מותר לזרים: מבית הספר. נקט שלא לומר שהוא עבד כדאמר בסוף פירקין (לקמן דף כח.): אין בתר דקנסינהו עזרא. ולר"ע דקודם קנסא הוי דוקא ללוי בתר קנסא אף לכהנים אבל לר"א בן עזריה דמקמי קנסא הוי אף לכהן בתר קנסא הוי לכהן דוקא והא דמעשר ראשון חזקה לכהונה אתיא כר' אלעזר בן עזריה ולא כר"ע ויש שמוחקין אין ומפרשים דהא דקאמר בתר דקנסינהו עזרא הוי אפי' לר"ע דבתר קנסא הוי לכ"ע לכהן דוקא והוי כמו אלא ושיבוש הוא בידם דהא בכמה מקומות מוכיח דמעשר ראשון ללוי אף בתר קנסא כדתנן בפ' כל הגט (גיטין דף ל.) המלוה מעות את הכהן ואת הלוי להיות מפריש עליהן כו' וכן התם בגמרא ישראל שאמר לבן לוי כור מעשר לאביך בידי ובפ' הזרוע (חולין קלא: ושם) פריך מעשר ראשון ללוי הוא וכן בכמה מקומות והיינו כר"ע ועוד דלמ"ד קנסא לעניים היכי הוי חזקה לכהונה דאליבא דר"ע פליגי בפ"ב יש מותרות (יבמות פו: ושם) דאיכא למ"ד קנסא לכהנים ואיכא למ"ד לעניים דלר' אלעזר בן עזריה הוי דוקא לכהן ואפי' לעשירים כמו קודם קנסא דלא קנסא לעניים שהרי עלו ולמ"ד קנסא לעניים משמע התם דוקא לעניים ולא לכהנים עשירים אפי' בימי טומאה דלית ליה דבימי טומאה עניים הוו ועניים דהתם אין לפרש עניי לויים דוקא ולא עניי ישראל וכהנים דא"כ נשתכרו עניי לויים במה שלא עלו ועוד דמשמע התם אלו הוו כהנים בימי טומאתם עניים לכ"ע הוו שקלי אע"ג דלענין חלוקת מעשר הוו כישראל דללוי ולא לכהן קאמר אלא לעניים בין עניי כהנים בין עניי לויים ולמ"ד מעשר ראשון מותר לזרים שקלי אפילו עניי ישראל אבל למ"ד אסור לזרים אין נראה שיתנו לעניי ישראל כדי למוכרו דמילתא דאתי לידי תקלה לא אתקינו רבנן דאיכא למיחש דלמא אתי למיכליה [כדאמר בסמוך לא מיבעיא לר"מ דאמר אסור לזרים כו'] ולר"ע לא הפקיע עזרא את הלויים מכל וכל להשוותן לישראל והכהנים שלא יטלו עשירים לויים אלא עניי לויים בתורת עניות אלא ללויים בין עניים בין עשירים היו חולקים לעולם כדמוכח בכל הנהו שהבאתי שהיו נוטלין בתורת לויות ועוד דר"ג בספינה שנתן מעשר ראשון לר' יהושע בן חנניא (מעשר שני פ"ה מ"ט) אי בתורת עניות יהיב ליה אמאי לא יהב ליה נמי מעשר עני שהרי מעשר עני נתן לר"ע ומיהו יש לדחות דלעולם בתורת עניות נתן לו ומה שלא נתן לו מעשר עני לפי שהיו לו מאתים זוז דאינו נוטל במעשר עני כדתנן במסכת פאה (פ"ח מ"ח) אבל מעשר ראשון יטול אפי' יש לו מאתים זוז דהא איכא למ"ד דאפי' כהנים עשירים בימי טומאה עניים נינהו ועוד דלא רצה ליתן כל מתנותיו לעני אחד: בתר דקנסינהו עזרא. לא אשכחן בהדיא בקרא דקנסינהו רק מצינו בעזרא (נחמיה י) והיה הכהן בן אהרן עם הלוים בעשר הלוים ואיכא למימר דה"ק כשיבאו הלוים לחלוק בבית הגרנות יבאו הכהנים עמהם ומיהו לר"א בן עזריה דבתר קנסא דוקא לכהן לא משמע מהאי קרא דליכא למימר עם הלוים דקאמר קרא היינו לקבל מהם מעשר ראשון משלהם דהא משלהם לא קנסם עזרא כדמוכח בפרק הזרוע (חולין קלא:) וי"ל דלר"א בן עזריה לא נמנעו הלוים מכל וכל מלילך לבית הגרנות לחלוק במעשר כדאמר בסמוך דלמא איקרי ויהיב ליה כל שכן בימי עזרא שעדיין לא פשט הקנס שהיו הולכים בבית הגרנות ולכך נאמר שילכו הכהנים עם הלוים ולמ"ד קנסא לעניים הא דכתיב והיה הכהן היינו בכהן עני ומשום דכהנים עניים שכיחי טפי לפי שאין כל כך עסוקים במלאכה אלא בעבודת בית המקדש וגם אין להם קרקעות נקט כהן וה"ה עניי ישראל למ"ד מעשר ראשון מותר לזרים וה"ר יוסף פירש מדכתיב (מלאכי ג) הביאו את כל המעשר אל בית האוצר דבית האוצר היא לשכה שתיקן עזרא לתת שם תרומת הכהנים כדכתיב בעזרא (נחמיה י) וכיון שאומר להביא שם המעשר א"כ של כהנים הוא וקיימא לן (מגילה דף טו.) דמלאכי זה עזרא ולמ"ד לעניים נקט אל בית האוצר משום דכהנים עניים שכיחי טפי כדפרישית אי נמי אל בית האוצר לא ליתן לכהנים אלא לחלק לעניים וה"ר אלחנן הקשה דבסוף עזרא משמע שהמעשר היה ללוים דכתיב ואדע כי מניות הלוים לא נתנה (להם) ויברחו איש לשדהו הלוים והמשוררים כו' משמע שהלוים והמשוררים היו חולקים וצריך לומר דזה היה מקמי דקנסינהו עזרא אך קראי לא מוכחי הכי: והאמר רבי יוחנן דברי הכל אין ערער כו'. נראה לר"י דר' יוחנן עיקר דבריו על משנתנו ולהכי לא קא משני הכא ה"מ היכא דליכא חזקה דכשרות כו' כדמשני בפרק עשרה יוחסין (קדושין דף עג:) ואם תאמר והואיל ומתני' קאי היכי פריך מיניה התם ובפרק קמא דגיטין (דף ט.) גבי גט דלמא הא דקאמר ר' יוחנן דלא מהני ערער דחד היינו היכא דאיכא עד אחד דמכשר דקתני מעלין לכהונה על פי עד אחד ויש לומר דהש"ס ידע דר' יוחנן אמסקנא דיבר דבתחלה היה קול ואח"כ בא עד אחד להכשירו והסיר הקול ואתו בי תרי ואמרי דבן גרושה ובן חלוצה הוא דבכי האי גוונא א"ר יוחנן דבעינן שנים אע"ג דהעד שהכשיר והקול כמאן דליתנהו דמי שהרי העד גרוע מן הקול אי לאו משום חזקה דמסייע ליה לבטל הקול שהרי הקול פוסל והעד אינו פוסל לרבי יוחנן [ז]: אין ערער פחות משנים. לאפוקי חד דלא הוי ערער אבל קול נמי פוסל בתחלה בתרומה קודם שבא העד המכשיר: ואתא עד אחד ואמר ידענא ביה דכהן הוא. לא בעי למימר דפליגי אי מעלין ע"פ עד אחד כשהקול פוסל דפשיטא ליה להש"ס דלא פסיל קול לכ"ע כיון דאיכא עד וחזקה ועוד דקול לא הוי קרי עוררין:

ואסקיניה

The Gemara still questions how receiving *maaser rishon* proves Kohanic status:

וְדִלְמָא אִיקְרוּ וִיהָבוּ לֵיהּ – **But perhaps they** (i.e. the owners of produce) **happened to give** *maaser rishon* **to [a Levi].**[14] So, even after Ezra's decree, how can we be certain that the recipient of *maaser rishon* is a Kohen?

The Gemara answers:

אָמַר רַב חִסְדָּא – **Rav Chisda said:** הָכָא בְּמַאי עָסְקִינַן – **What** case **are we dealing with here?** כְּגוֹן דְּמוּחְזָק לָן בַּאֲבוּהָ דְּהַאי דְּכֹהֵן הוּא – **The case is where it had been established that the father of this man is a Kohen,** וְנָפַק עֲלֵיהּ קָלָא דְּבֶן גְּרוּשָׁה וּבֶן חֲלוּצָה הוּא – **but a rumor emerged** which stated **that he was the son of a divorcee or the son of** ***chalutzah*** (i.e. he is a *chalal,* who has the status of a Yisrael),[15] וְחָלְקוּ לֵיהּ לְדִידֵיהּ מַעֲשֵׂר בְּבֵית הַגְּרָנוֹת – **and they distributed** ***maaser rishon*** **to him at the granaries.** In this case, we can be certain that he is a Kohen, because what other possibility is there? לֵוִי – Should we consider that he is **a Levi?** דְּלָאו לֵוִי הוּא – But we know **that he is not a Levi,** since his father is a Kohen. מַאי אִיכָּא לְמֵימַר – **What is there to say?** בֶּן גְּרוּשָׁה אוֹ בֶּן חֲלוּצָה הוּא – That he might be **the son of a divorcee or the son of a** ***chalutzah*** (i.e. a *chalal*). That possibility too can be discounted, because *maaser rishon* would not be distributed to a *chalal.* לֹא מִיבַּעְיָא לְמַאן דְּאָמַר מַעֲשֵׂר רִאשׁוֹן אָסוּר לְזָרִים – **It is not necessary** to state **according to the one who says that** ***maaser rishon*** **is prohibited to a Yisrael**[16] that this man is not a *chalal,* דְּלֹא הֲווּ יָהֲבֵי לֵיהּ – **for** if he were **they would not have given** *maaser rishon* **to him.**[17] אֶלָּא אֲפִילּוּ לְמַאן דְּאָמַר מַעֲשֵׂר רִאשׁוֹן מוּתָּר לְזָרִים – **But even according to the one who says that** ***maaser rishon*** **is permitted to a Yisrael,** we can still be sure that this man is not a *chalal,* הָנֵי מִילֵּי לְמִיסְפַּק לְהוּ – because **that opinion** states only that it is permitted **to give** *maaser rishon* **to [a Yisrael] to eat;** אֲבָל בְּתוֹרַת חֲלוּקָּה לֹא יָהֲבֵי לֵיהּ – **however, they would not give it to [a Yisrael] in the manner of** formal **distribution.**[18]

The Gemara quotes from a Baraisa cited above:

וְהַחוֹלֵק בְּבֵית דִּין אֵינָהּ חֲזָקָה – **BUT ONE WHO DIVIDES** *terumah* **UNDER** the auspices of **A COURT** does **NOT** enjoy **A PRESUMPTION** of **Kehunah.**

The Gemara asks:

אִי בְּבֵית דִּין לֹא הָוְיָא חֲזָקָה – **If** the distribution of *terumah* **under** the auspices of **a court** does **not** establish **a presumption** of Kehunah, הֵיכָא הָוְיָא חֲזָקָה – **where** does **it** establish **a presumption** of Kehunah?[19]

The Gemara answers by reinterpreting the Baraisa:

אָמַר רַב שֵׁשֶׁת – **Rav Sheishess said:** הָכִי קָאָמַר – **This is what it means:** הַחוֹלֵק תְּרוּמָה בְּנִכְסֵי אָבִיו עִם אֶחָיו בְּבֵית דִּין – **If one divides** ***terumah*** that is **in the property of his** deceased **father with his brothers in court,** אֵינָהּ חֲזָקָה – he does **not** enjoy **a presumption** of Kehunah.[20]

The Gemara asks:

פְּשִׁיטָא – That is **obvious!** After all, even a *chalal* inherits his father.[21] So why would the Baraisa need to teach that this person is not assumed to be a Kohen?

The Gemara answers:

מַהוּ דְּתֵימָא מִדְּהָנָךְ לַאֲכִילָה – **You might have said** that **since those** (i.e. the other brothers) are taking *terumah* from the property of their father **for** the sake of **consumption,** הַאי נַמִּי לַאֲכִילָה – **this** brother **is also** taking it **for** the sake of **consumption.**[22] קָא מַשְׁמַע לָן – **[The Baraisa]** therefore **informs us** that this is not necessarily so, הָנָךְ לַאֲכִילָה – because although **those** other brothers are taking it **for** the sake of **consumption,** הַאי לְזַבּוּנֵי – **this** brother could be taking it **for** the purpose of **selling** it to a Kohen.[23]

The Gemara quotes from our Mishnah (23b):

רַבִּי יְהוּדָה אוֹמֵר – **R' YEHUDAH SAYS:** אֵין מַעֲלִין לִכְהוּנָּה עַל פִּי עֵד אֶחָד וכו׳ – **WE DO NOT ELEVATE** a man **TO THE KEHUNAH BASED ON THE TESTIMONY OF ONE WITNESS etc.**

NOTES

and other commentaries).]

14. Even after Ezra's decree it is still permitted to distribute *maaser rishon* to a Levi if no Kohen is present (*Meiri;* see also *Tosafos* ד״ה בתר).

15. The Torah forbids a Kohen to wed a divorcee (*Leviticus* 21:7). The Rabbis additionally forbade him to marry a *chalutzah* [a woman who performed *chalitzah* (see 10b note 20)], because she resembles a divorcee in that a prescribed procedure released her from her attachment to a man (see *Yevamos* 24a). If a Kohen fathers a son through one of these women, that son is a *chalal,* who is disqualified from the Kehunah and has the status of a Yisrael (see note 17).

16. Literally: a stranger. [The word זָר, *stranger,* is often used to denote a non-Kohen. Here, however, it refers to one who is neither a Kohen nor a Levi.]

The Tanna R' Meir is of the opinion that *maaser rishon* may be eaten only by Leviim and Kohanim, and not by Yisraelim (*Yevamos* 85b-86a).

17. For a *chalal* does not enjoy even the status of a Levi; rather, he is a Yisrael. [Although the Kohanim belong to the tribe of Levi (and the disqualification of *chalalus* does not apply to Leviim), nevertheless, a disqualified son of a Kohen does not become a "Levi." In this respect, the Kohanim are treated as a separate category, rather than a special group of Leviim. Hence, if one is disqualified from the Kehunah, he is treated as an ordinary Yisrael (see *Kovetz Shiurim;* see also *Dvar Avraham* vol. II 23:1 and *Minchas Chinuch,* end of §395).]

18. Although, according to this opinion, a Yisrael may eat *maaser rishon,* he certainly has no right to be allocated a portion of it. *Maaser rishon* is the property of Leviim (or Kohanim) and may be distributed only to them. A Yisrael is allowed to eat *maaser rishon* only if he was given permission to do so by the Levi (or Kohen) to whom it was distributed. Hence, if the son of a Kohen formally received *maaser rishon* when it was distributed at the granaries, he must be a qualified Kohen, and not a *chalal,* who has the status of a Yisrael.

The Gemara has thus explained the Baraisa's ruling (namely, that *maaser rishon* provides evidence of Kohanic status) by limiting it to this specific case, where *maaser rishon* was distributed to a Kohen's son who was suspected of being a *chalal.* Consequently, it is no longer necessary to say that the Baraisa follows the view of R' Elazar ben Azaryah (after Ezra's decree), who holds that *maaser rishon* is given only to Kohanim. Since there is no possibility of this man being a Levi, the Baraisa could also follow the opinion of R' Akiva (after the decree) or R' Elazar ben Azaryah (even before the decree), according to which *maaser rishon* is given to both Kohanim and Leviim (see *Re'ah* and *Pnei Yehoshua;* cf. *Shitah Mekubetzes* ד״ה הב״ע).

19. See note 9.

20. [Thus, the Baraisa does not refer to the distribution of *terumah* at the granaries. Rather, it refers to the division by a court of the *terumah* in a Kohen's estate among sons who were born to him from different wives.] A rumor circulated about one of the sons stating that his mother was a divorcee and he is therefore a *chalal.* The Baraisa teaches that his participation in the division of the *terumah* does not dispel the rumor (*Rashi;* see *Ritva* for an alternative approach).

21. [Although he may not eat the *terumah* he inherits, it is still of value to him insofar as he can sell it to a Kohen.]

22. It is degrading for *terumah* to be given to a *chalal* [because it then has to be resold]. Hence, if this man were indeed a *chalal,* the court would have allocated all the *terumah* to the other brothers, and nonsacred property of corresponding value to him (*Ritva, Tos. HaRosh*). The fact that he received a share of the *terumah* thus proves that he is a Kohen, who is allowed to eat *terumah* just as they are.

23. Perhaps there was considerably more *terumah* than non-sacred property in the estate. Therefore, even if one of the heirs was a *chalal,* it would have been impossible to allocate all the *terumah* to the other brothers and only nonsacred items to him (*Ritva*). He consequently had to receive some of the *terumah* for him to sell to a Kohen.

במסיח לפי תומו כי הא דאמר רב יהודה אמר שמואל [א] מעשה באדם אחד שהיה מסיח לפי תומו ואמר זכורני כשאני תינוק ומורכב על כתיפו של אבא והוציאוני מבית הספר והפשיטוני את כותנתי והטבילוני לאכול בתרומה לערב ור' חייא מסיים בה וחבירי בדילין ממני והיו קורין אותי יוחנן אוכל חלות והעלהו רבי לכהונה על פיו תניא ר"ש בן אלעזר אומר כשם שתרומה חזקה לכהונה כך מעשר ראשון חזקה לכהונה והחולק בבית דין אינה חזקה מעשר ראשון דלוי הוא כר"א בן עזריה דתניא [ב] תרומה לכהן מעשר ראשון ללוי דברי ר"ע ר"א בן עזריה אומר מעשר ראשון אף לכהן אימור דאר"א בן עזריה אף לכהן לכהן ולא ללוי מי אמר [ג] אין בתר דקנסינהו עזרא ודלמא איקרו ויהבו ליה אמר רב חסדא הכא במאי עסקינן [ד] כגון דמוחזק לן באבוה דהאי דכהן הוא ונפק עליה קלא דבן גרושה ובן חלוצה הוא וחלקו ליה לדידיה מעשר בבית הגרנות לוי דלאו לוי הוא מאי איכא למימר בן גרושה או בן חלוצה הוא לא מיבעיא למאן דאמר [ג] מעשר ראשון אסור לזרים דלא הוו יהבי ליה אלא אפילו למ"ד [ד] מעשר ראשון מותר לזרים הני מילי למיספק להו אבל בתורת חלוקה לא יהבי ליה והחולק בבית דין אינה חזקה אי בבית דין לא הויא חזקה היכא הויא חזקה אמר רב ששת הכי קאמר [ה] החולק תרומה בנכסי אביו עם אחיו בבית דין אינה חזקה פשיטא מהו דתימא מדהנך לאכילה האי נמי לאכילה קמ"ל הנך לאכילה האי לזבוני: רבי יהודה אומר אין מעלין לכהונה על פי עד אחד וכו': רשב"ג היינו רבי אליעזר וכי תימא ערער חד איכא בינייהו דרבי אליעזר סבר ערער חד ורשב"ג סבר ערער תרי א] האמר רבי יוחנן דברי הכל [ו] אין ערער פחות משנים אלא הכא במאי עסקינן דמוחזק לן באבוה דהאי דכהן הוא ונפק עליה קלא דבן גרושה או בן חלוצה הוא ואחתיניה ואתא עד אחד ואמר ידענא ביה דכהן הוא ואסקיניה

רש"י

והטבילוני. מפני ששם תינוק מטפח בטומאות ושרצים מצויין שם: לערב. דצריך הערב שמש: והחולק בב"ד. קא ס"ד שעל ב"ד הקבוע בעיר היו חולקין לו תרומה בבית הגרנות ולקמיה פריך אי בב"ד לא הוי חזקה היכא הויא חזקה: בתר דקנסינהו עזרא. ללוים דלא ליתבו להו כדאמרי' ביבמות בפ' יש מותרות (דף פו:): לוי דלאו לוי הוא. כלומר בלוי ליכא לספוקי דהא אביו כהן: למ"ד כו'. פלוגתא היא ביבמות (שם): בנכסי אביו כו' אינה חזקה. להשבית מעליו קול היוצא על אמו שהיא גרושה והוא חלל: פשיטא. דהא אפי' הוא חלל יורש את אביו: רבן שמעון היינו רבי אליעזר. דהא ודאי במקום שיש עוררין לא אמר רבן שמעון דליהוי חד נאמן וכי אמר מעלין במקום שאין עוררין קאמר: דר"א סבר ערער חד. הוי ערער ואין אחד נאמן עליו להכשירו: ונפק עליה קלא. קול בעלמא ולא עדות: ואחתיניה. מן הכהונה עד שיבדקו את הדבר שמעלה הוא לכהונה: ואסקיניה

תוספות

במסיח לפי תומו. וא"ת ומנ"ל דהכי הוה דלמא ר' חייא העלה בן על פי אביו במסיח לפי תומו ורבי יוחנן אחיו אפי' בלא מסיח ואר"י דמסתמא דמאי דקתני בברייתא מילתא דרבי עשה רבי מעשה ועוד דלא אפשר דרבי העלה את ע"פ אחיו ללויה אפילו בלא מסיח דהתם אין שייך לומר שבידו להאכילו מעשר למ"ד מעשר ראשון אסור לזרים: מבית הספר. נקט שלא לומר שהוא עבד כדאמר בסוף פירקין (לקמן דף כח.): אין בתר דקנסינהו עזרא. ולר"ע דקודם קנסא הוי דוקא ללוי בתר קנסא אף לכהנים אבל לר"א בן עזריה דמקמי קנסא הוי אף לכהן בתר קנסא הוי לכהן דוקא והא דמעשר ראשון חזקה לכהונה אתיא כר' אלעזר בן עזריה ולא כר"ע ויש שמוחקין אין ומפרשים דהא דקאמר בתר דקנסינהו עזרא הוי אפי' לר"ע דבתר קנסא הוי לכ"ע לכהן דוקא והוי כמו אלא ושיבוש הוא בידם דהא בכמה מקומות מוכיח דמעשר ראשון ללוי אף בתר קנסא כדתנן בפ' כל הגט (גיטין דף ל.) המלוה מעות את הכהן ואת הלוי להיות מפריש עליהן כו' וכן התם בגמרא ישראל שאמר לבן לוי כור מעשר לאביך בידי ובפ' הזרוע (חולין קלא: ושם) פריך מעשר ראשון דלוי הוא וכן בכמה מקומות והיינו כר"ע ועוד דלמ"ד קנסא לעניים היכי הוי חזקה לכהונה דאליבא דר"ע פליגי בס"פ יש מותרות (יבמות פו: ושם) דאיכא למ"ד קנסא לכהנים ואיכא למ"ד לעניים דלר' אלעזר בן עזריה הוי דוקא לכהן ואפי' לעשירים כמו קודם קנסא דלא קנסם עזרא שהרי עלו ולמ"ד קנסא לעניים משמע התם דוקא לעניים ולא לכהנים עשירים אפי' בימי טומאה דלית ליה דבימי טומאה עניים הוו ועניים דהתם אין לפרש עניי לויים דוקא ולא עניי ישראל וכהנים דא"כ נשתכרו עניי לויים במה שלא עלו ועוד דמשמע התם אילו הוו כהנים בימי טומאתם עניים לכ"ע הוו שקלי אע"ג דלענין חלוקת מעשר הוו כישראל דללוי ולא לכהן קאמר אלא לעניים בין עניי כהנים בין עניי לויים ולמ"ד מעשר ראשון מותר לזרים שקלי אפילו עניי ישראל אבל למ"ד אסור לזרים אין נראה שינתן לעניי ישראל כדי למוכרו דמילתא דאתי לידי תקלה לא אתקינו רבנן דאיכא למיחש דלמא אתי למיכליה [כדאמר בסמוך לא מיבעיא לר"מ דאמר אסור לזרים כו'] ולר"ע לא הפקיע עזרא את הלויים מכל וכל להשוותן לישראל וכהנים שלא יטלו עשירים לויים אלא עניי לויים בתורת עניות אלא ללויים בין עניים בין עשירים היו חולקים לעולם כדמוכח בכל הנהו שהבאתי שהיו נוטלין בתורת לויות ועוד דר"ג בספינה שנתן מעשר ראשון לר' יהושע בן חנניה (מעשר שני פ"ה מ"ט) אי בתורת עניות יהיב ליה אמאי לא יהב ליה נמי מעשר עני שהרי מעשר עני נתן לר"ע ומיהו יש לדחות דלעולם בתורת עניות נתן לו ומה שלא נתן לו מעשר עני לפי שהיו לו מאתים זוז דאינו נוטל במעשר עני כדתנן במסכת פאה (פ"ח מ"ח) אבל מעשר ראשון יטול אפי' יש לו מאתים זוז דהא איכא למ"ד דאפי' כהנים עשירים בימי טומאה עניים נינהו ועוד דלא רצה ליתן כל מתנותיו לעני אחד: **בתר** דקנסינהו עזרא. לא אשכחן בהדיא בקרא דקנסינהו רק מלינו בעזרא (נחמיה י) והיה הכהן בן אהרן עם הלויים בעשר הלוים ואיכא למימר דה"ק כשיבאו הלוים לחלוק בבית הגרנות יבאו הכהנים עמהם ומיהו לר"א בן עזריה דבתר קנסא דוקא לכהן לא משמע מהאי קרא דליכא למימר עם הלוים דקאמר קרא היינו לקבל מהם מעשר ראשון משלהם דהא משלהם לא קנסם עזרא כדמוכח בפרק הזרוע (חולין קלא:) וי"ל דלר"א בן עזריה לא נמנעו הלוים מכל וכל מלילך לבית הגרנות לחלוק במעשר כדאמר בסמוך דלמא איקרי ויהיב ליה כל שכן בימי עזרא שעדיין לא פשט הקנס שהיו הולכים בבית הגרנות ולכך נאמר שילכו הכהנים עם הלוים ולמ"ד קנסא לעניים הא דכתיב והיה הכהן היינו בכהן עני ומשום דכהנים עניים שכיחי טפי לפי שאין כל כך עסוקים במלאכה אלא בעבודת בית המקדש וגם אין להם קרקעות נקט כהן וה"ה עניי ישראל למ"ד מעשר ראשון מותר לזרים וה"ר יוסף פירש מדכתיב (במלאכי ג) הביאו את כל המעשר אל בית האוצר דבית האוצר היה לשכה שתיקן עזרא לתת שם תרומת הכהנים כדכתיב בעזרא (נחמיה י) וכיון שאומר להביא שם המעשר א"כ של כהנים הוא וקיימא לן (מגילה דף טו.) דמלאכי זה עזרא ולמ"ד לעניים נקט אל בית האוצר משום דכהנים עניים שכיחי טפי כדפרישית אי נמי אל בית האוצר לא ליתן לכהנים אלא לחלק לעניים וה"ר אלחנן הקשה דבסוף עזרא משמע שהמעשר היה ללוים דכתיב ואדע כי מניות הלוים לא נתנה (להם) ויברחו איש לשדהו הלוים והמשוררים כו' משמע שהלוים והמשוררים היו חולקים וצריך לומר דזה היה מקמי דקנסינהו עזרא אך קראי לא מוכחי הכי: **והאמר** רבי יוחנן דברי הכל אין ערער כו'. נראה לר"י דר' יוחנן עיקר דבריו על משנתנו ולהכי לא קא משני הכא ה"מ היכא דליכא חזקה דכשרות כו' כדמשני בפרק עשרה יוחסין (קדושין דף עג:) ואם תאמר והואיל ואמתני' קאי היכי פריך מיניה התם ובפרק קמא דגיטין (דף ט.) גבי גט דלמא הא דקאמר ר' יוחנן דלא מהני ערער דחד היינו היכא דאיכא עד אחד דמכשר דקתני מעלין לכהונה על פי עד אחד ויש לומר דהש"ס ידע דר' יוחנן אמסקנא דיבר דבתחלה היה קול ואח"כ בא עד אחד להכשירו ולהסיר הקול ואתו בי תרי ואמרי דבן גרושה ובן חלוצה הוא דבכי האי גוונא א"ר יוחנן דבעינן שנים אע"ג דהעד שהכשיר והקול כמאן דליתנהו דמי שהרי העד גרוע מן הקול אי לאו משום חזקה דמסייע ליה לבטל הקול שהרי הקול פוסל והעד אינו פוסל לרבי יוחנן: **אין** ערער פחות משנים. לאפוקי חד דלא הוי ערער אבל קול נמי פוסל בתחלה בתרומה קודס שבא העד המכשיר: **ואתא** עד אחד ואמר ידענא ביה דכהן הוא. לא בעי למימר דפליגי אי מעלין ע"פ עד אחד כשהקול פוסל דפשיטא ליה להש"ס דלא פסיל קול לכ"ע כיון דאיכא עד וחזקה ועוד דקול לא הוי קרי עוררין: ואסקיניה

עין משפט נר מצוה

צד א מיי' פ"כ מהל' איסורי ביאה הלכה יד סמג לאוין קטז טוש"ע אה"ע סימן ג סעיף א:
צה ב מיי' פ"ו מהל' תרומות הלכה א סמג לאוין רכד:
צו ג מיי' פ"א מהל' מעשר הלכה ד:
צז ד מיי' פ"כ מהל' איסורי ביאה הלכה טו טוש"ע אה"ע סימן ג סעיף ו:
צח ה מיי' שם הלכה יג:

תוספות רי"ד

רשב"ג אומר וכו'. רשב"ג היינו ת"ק פי' ר"א שאין לומר שבמקום עוררין קאמר רשב"ג דמעלין לכהונה ע"פ עד אחד אלא במקום שאין עוררין וה"ק נמי ר"א. ואסיק רב אשי דבמצטרפין לעדות קמיפלגי ובמקום שיש עוררין. והכא במאי עסקינן במוחזק לן באבוה דהאי דכהן הוא ונפק עלי' [קלא] דבן גרושה ובן חלוצה הוא ואחתיני'. פי' עד שנבדוק הקול אם הוא אמת אם לאו ואתא עד אחד ואמר ידענא ביה

מסורת הש"ס

א) ב"ק קיד:, ב) ב"ב פא: יבמות פו. חולין קלא:, ג) [יבמות עד: פה: פו.], ד) [שם פו.], ה) ב"ב לב. קדושין עג: גיטין ט., ו) ת"י כ"י, ז) [וע"ע תוס' שם וב"ב לב.].

הגהות מהר"ב רנשבורג

א] גמ' האמר ר' יוחנן דברי הכל אין ערער פחות משנים. עי' תוס' ד"ה והאמר ובחדושי הר"ן בחולין פא ע"א ד"ה וקשיא לן:

ליקוטי רש"י

והטבילוני. לפי שדרכו של תינוק לטפח בשרצים ובטומאות. בדילין ממני. מפני תרומתי [ב"ק קיד:]. מעשר ראשון אף לכהן. דבכ"ד מקומות נקראו כהנים לוים הלכך אע"ג דבמעשר ראשון לוי כתיבא ביה כהנים נמי משתמעי [חולין קלא:]. ומשמע ליה לר' אלעזר בן עזריה לוים דקרא אף כהנים במשמע דבעשרים וארבעה מקומות נקראו כהנים לוים [רשב"ם ב"ב פא:]. בתר דקנסינהו עזרא. ביבמות (דף פו:) אמר מפני מה קנסו לוים במעשר מפני שלא עלו בימי עזרא דכתיב ואבינה בעם ובכהנים ומבני לוי לא מצאתי שם אבל מקרא מפורש לא מצאתי שקנסם אבל דוגמא יש לדבר שכתוב בעזרא (נחמיה י) בסופו והיה הכהן בן אהרן עם הלוים (במעשר) [בעשר] הלוים למדנו שלא האמינום על תרומת מעשר ולא היו חולקין להן מעשר בגורן אלא (דקנסינהו) בפני הכהנים [חולין קלא:]. ערער חד איכא בינייהו. והא דקתני בזמן שיש עליו עוררין היינו עד אחד הפוסלו ומכחיש עד אחד המכשירו [רשב"ם ב"ב לא:]. ורשב"ג סבר ערער תרי. בעינן אבל במקום ערער אחד הוי עד אחד נאמן להכשירו. האמר רבי יוחנן. לא איתפרש היכא קאי. ואחתיניה. מן הכהונה עד שיבדקו את הדבר שמעלה היא בכהונה וכל זה יתור לשון הוא בלא צורך דבלא קול נמי מיתוקמא שמעתתא שפיר בעד אחד מכשיר מעיקרא ועד אחד בסוף ושנים עדים עוררים בינתים כדמפרש ואזיל אלא משום הכי נקט ליה דבעי למימר ואתא עד אחד ואמר דכהן גמור הוא ואסקיניה דלמאי אתא עד אחד להכשירו אלא אם כן יצא עליו פסלות קודם לכן [שם לב.].

The Gemara answers:

בְּמֵסִיחַ לְפִי תוּמוֹ – R' Chiya refers to an instance **where [the brother] is talking casually.**[1] In that case the brother's report is accepted even though he is a relative.[2]

The Gemara gives an example of casual speech that establishes a person's lineage:

כִּי הָא דְּאָמַר רַב יְהוּדָה אָמַר שְׁמוּאֵל – It is **like that which Rav Yehudah said in the name of Shmuel:** מַעֲשֶׂה בְּאָדָם אֶחָד שֶׁהָיָה מֵסִיחַ לְפִי תוּמוֹ וְאָמַר – **It once happened that a certain man was talking casually, and he said,** זְכוּרַנִי כְּשֶׁאֲנִי תִּינוֹק וּמוּרְכָּב עַל כְּתֵיפוֹ שֶׁל אַבָּא – **"I remember when I was a child and** [young enough to be] **riding on my father's shoulder** וְהוֹצִיאוּנִי מִבֵּית הַסֵּפֶר – **that they took me out of school,**[3] וְהִפְשִׁיטוּנִי אֶת כּוּתָּנְתִּי – **removed my tunic** וְהִטְבִּילוּנִי לֶאֱכוֹל בִּתְרוּמָה לָעֶרֶב – **and immersed me** in a *mikveh* so that I would be able **to eat** ***terumah* at night."**[4] וְרַבִּי חִיָּיא מְסַיֵּים בָּהּ – **And R' Chiya concluded it,** i.e. he reported that the man continued as follows: וַחֲבֵירַי בְּדֵילִין מִמֶּנִּי וְהָיוּ קוֹרִין אוֹתִי יוֹחָנָן אוֹכֵל חַלּוֹת – **"And my friends would keep away from me and call me 'Yochanan the** ***challah* eater.'** "[5] וְהֶעֱלָהוּ רַבִּי לִכְהוּנָּה עַל פִּיו – **And Rebbi elevated him to the Kehunah based on his** own **word.**[6]

The Gemara discusses yet another basis for identifying someone as a Kohen:

תַּנְיָא – **It was taught in a Baraisa:** רַבִּי שִׁמְעוֹן בֶּן אֶלְעָזָר אוֹמֵר – **R' SHIMON BEN ELAZAR SAYS:** כְּשֵׁם שֶׁתְּרוּמָה חֲזָקָה לִכְהוּנָּה – **JUST AS** the distribution[7] of ***TERUMAH*** establishes **A PRESUMPTION OF KEHUNAH,** כָּךְ מַעֲשֵׂר רִאשׁוֹן חֲזָקָה לִכְהוּנָּה – **SO** does the distribution of ***MAASER RISHON*** establish **A PRESUMPTION OF KEHUNAH.**[8] וְהַחוֹלֵק בְּבֵית דִּין אֵינָהּ חֲזָקָה – **BUT ONE WHO DIVIDES** *terumah* **UNDER** the auspices of **A COURT** does **NOT** enjoy **A PRESUMPTION** of Kehunah.[9]

The Gemara questions the Baraisa's ruling about *maaser rishon*:

מַעֲשֵׂר רִאשׁוֹן דְּלֵוִי הוּא – But ***maaser rishon* is** the entitlement **of a Levi!** So how can receiving *maaser rishon* prove Kohanic status?

The Gemara answers:

כְּרַבִּי אֶלְעָזָר בֶּן עֲזַרְיָה – This is **in accordance with** the opinion of **R' Elazar ben Azaryah,** דְּתַנְיָא – **for it was taught in a Baraisa:** תְּרוּמָה לְכֹהֵן – ***TERUMAH*** must be given **TO A KOHEN** מַעֲשֵׂר רִאשׁוֹן לְלֵוִי – and ***MAASER RISHON*** must be given **TO A LEVI;**[10] דִּבְרֵי רַבִּי עֲקִיבָא – these are **THE WORDS OF R' AKIVA.** רַבִּי אֶלְעָזָר בֶּן עֲזַרְיָה אוֹמֵר – But **R' ELAZAR BEN AZARYAH SAYS:** מַעֲשֵׂר רִאשׁוֹן אַף לְכֹהֵן – ***MAASER RISHON*** may be given **ALSO TO A KOHEN.**[11]

The Gemara objects:

אֵימוּר דְּאָמַר רַבִּי אֶלְעָזָר בֶּן עֲזַרְיָה אַף לְכֹהֵן – But one could **say that R' Elazar ben Azaryah holds** that *maaser rishon* may ***also*** be given to a Kohen.[12] לְכֹהֵן וְלֹא לְלֵוִי מִי אָמַר – **Did he say** that it may be given only **to a Kohen, and not to a Levi?** He surely holds that it may be given to both Kohanim and Leviim. Thus, how can he maintain that receiving *maaser rishon* is evidence of Kohanic status?

The Gemara answers:

אִין – **Yes!** This is indeed R' Elazar ben Azaryah's opinion בָּתַר דִּקְנַסִינְהוּ עֶזְרָא – **after Ezra penalized [the Leviim],** for Ezra punished the Leviim by decreeing that *maaser rishon* be given only to Kohanim and not to them.[13] Therefore, one who receives *maaser rishon* nowadays can be assumed to be a Kohen.

NOTES

1. Literally: talking in one's innocence. This expression denotes words that are uttered in a casual manner, without awareness of their legal ramifications. Since such speech is not consciously intended to bring benefit or loss to anyone, it is sometimes deemed more reliable than formal testimony.

2. The Gemara is answering that in fact R' Chiya does not differentiate between a father and a brother on halachic grounds. The case in which he ruled just happened to involve two brothers. If a father would mention casually that his son was a Kohen, R' Chiya would accept his word as well.

[According to this answer, there is no longer any compelling reason to assert that it was Rebbi who elevated a son to the Kehunah based on the word of his father. Perhaps it was R' Chiya who issued that ruling and it was a case of casual speech (and Rebbi ruled in the other case concerning two brothers). The Gemara, however, prefers to attribute to Rebbi the ruling in the incident concerning the father and son, because it corresponds to Rebbi's statement in the Baraisa that a father is believed about his son (see *Tosafos;* see also *Pnei Yehoshua*).]

3. This point is needed to show that he was not a Kohen's slave. Since it is forbidden to teach one's slave Torah, a slave would not have been attending school (*Tosafos,* from Gemara below, 28a; see note 34 there).

4. Young boys are presumed to be *tamei* because they play in piles of garbage where *sheratzim* are found. [*Sheratzim* are the eight creeping creatures listed in *Leviticus* 11:29-30 which convey *tumah* when dead] (*Rashi;* cf. *Ritva*). A *tamei* person may not eat *terumah* until nightfall following his immersion in a *mikveh.*

5. [*Challah* is a form of *terumah.*] His friends distanced themselves from him to avoid contaminating his *terumah* (see *Rashi* to *Bava Kamma* 114b בדילין ממני). [See *Birkas Avraham,* who explains R' Chiya's point in stating that these words were added.]

6. Rebbi relied on this man's casual talk only to let him eat Rabbinic, as opposed to Biblical, *terumah* (*Ritva,* from *Bava Kamma* 114b). *Rambam,* however, implies that he was allowed even to eat Biblical *terumah* and recite the Priestly Blessing [which also involves a Biblical prohibition, as explained above, 24b note 21] (*Hil. Isurei Biah* 20:13-14; see *Beis Shmuel, Even HaEzer* 3:6 and *Chazon Ish* ibid. 2:10).

7. Based on *Tosefta* 3:1, cited by *Mareh Kohen.*

8. The Gemara will ask how one who receives *maaser rishon,* which is apparently an entitlement of the Leviim (see note 10), can be assumed to be a Kohen.

9. This apparently means that he was allocated *terumah* when it was distributed at the granaries under the supervision of the local established court. Based on this understanding of the Baraisa, the Gemara will ask why he is not assumed to be a Kohen. If this does not suffice to establish Kohanic status, what does? (*Rashi*).

10. For regarding *maaser rishon* the Torah states (*Numbers* 18:26): *And to the Leviim shall you speak* etc. (*Yevamos* 86b).

11. According to R' Elazar ben Azaryah, when the previously cited verse mentions "Leviim," it refers not only to the Leviim, but to the Kohanim as well, who are also descended from Levi. (In his view, this is one of the twenty-four instances in which Scripture refers to Kohanim by their Levitic origin.) He therefore maintains that both Leviim and Kohanim are entitled to *maaser rishon* (*Yevamos* ibid.).

12. The Gemara's wording implies that the authors of the Gemara had a different version of the Baraisa, in which the word אַף, *also,* does not appear (*Shitah Mekubetzes* סד"ה רבי אלעזר). This is indeed the version of the Baraisa as it appears in *Yevamos* 86a-b. The Gemara's argument ("say that R' Elazar ben Azaryah holds that *maaser rishon* may *also* be given to a Kohen") is based not on the Baraisa, but on the verse (*And to the Leviim* etc.), which certainly does not *exclude* Leviim (see *Rashi* ibid., top of 86b).

13. Ezra punished the Leviim because they did not join a contingent that he led from Babylonia to Eretz Yisrael, as recorded in *Ezra* 8:15 (*Yevamos* ibid.). This punishment took the form of a decree which mandated that *maaser rishon* not be given to the Leviim at all, but only to the Kohanim (*Rashi,* from *Yevamos* ibid.).

The preceding follows the view of R' Elazar ben Azaryah. According to R' Akiva, who holds that *maaser rishon* was initially given only to Leviim, Ezra decreed that it may be given to Kohanim as well [thereby depriving the Leviim of part of the nation's *maaser rishon*]. The Baraisa cited earlier, which rules that one who receives *maaser rishon* can be assumed to be a Kohen, reflects the opinion of R' Elazar ben Azaryah (*Tosafos* ד"ה אין, *Rashba, Re'ah* et al.). [Some other Rishonim, though, give different explanations of Ezra's penalty according to R' Akiva (see *Ritva;* see also *Rambam, Hil. Maaser* 1:4 with *Kesef Mishneh*

MARRY A WOMAN of untainted lineage, **לֹא תַאֲמִינוּ לֶאֱכוֹל בִּתְרוּמָה** – **YOU SHOULD NOT BELIEVE HIM TO** the extent of **LETTING HIM EAT** ***TERUMAH*****!** **אָמַר לוֹ** – **[REBBI] REPLIED TO [R' CHIYA]:** **אֲנִי מַאֲמִינוֹ לְהַאֲכִילוֹ בִּתְרוּמָה** – **I BELIEVE [THE FATHER] TO** the extent of **LETTING [HIS SON] EAT** ***TERUMAH,*** **שֶׁבְּיָדוֹ לְהַאֲכִילוֹ בִּתְרוּמָה** – **BECAUSE IT IS IN HIS POWER TO GIVE HIM** ***TERUMAH*** **TO EAT;**[22] **וְאֵינִי מַאֲמִינוֹ לְהַשִּׂיאוֹ אִשָּׁה** – **BUT I DO NOT BELIEVE HIM TO** the extent of **ALLOWING HIM TO MARRY A WOMAN** of untainted lineage, **שֶׁאֵין בְּיָדוֹ לְהַשִּׂיאוֹ אִשָּׁה** – **BECAUSE IT IS NOT IN HIS POWER TO MARRY HIM OFF TO A WOMAN** of untainted lineage. At any rate, Rebbi rules in this Baraisa that a father can establish his son as a Kohen at least with respect to eating *terumah.*

The Gemara accepts the proof from this Baraisa:

תִּסְתַּיֵּים – **Let it be determined** that Rebbi (and not R' Chiya) was the one who ruled that a father is believed to testify that his son is a Kohen.

The Gemara draws an inference from this conclusion:

וּמִדְּרַבִּי הֶעֱלָה בֵּן עַל פִּי אָבִיו לִכְהוּנָּה – **And since** it was **Rebbi** who **elevated a son to the Kehunah based on the word of his father,** **רַבִּי חִיָּיא הֶעֱלָה אָח עַל פִּי אָחִיו לִלְוִיָּה** – it must have been **R' Chiya** who **elevated a brother to the status of a Levi based on the word of his brother.**

The Gemara questions R' Chiya's opinion:

וְרַבִּי חִיָּיא – **But** how are we to understand the opinion of **R' Chiya?** **מַאי שְׁנָא בֵּן דְּלֹא** – **What is different** about **a son** which dictates **that** testimony about him **not** be accepted?[23] **דְּקָרוֹב הוּא אֵצֶל אָבִיו** – Surely it is **because he is related to his father.** **אָח נַמִּי קָרוֹב הוּא אֵצֶל אָחִיו** – But **a brother too is related to his brother!** So why does R' Chiya reject testimony about a son but accept testimony about a brother?

NOTES

Baraisa cited on 24a; see, however, *Chazon Ish, Even HaEzer* 2:7 (ד״ה והנה מבואר). Therefore, R' Chiya's statement must be understood as follows: If you accept the testimony of the father on his own in regard to *terumah,* then you should accept his testimony together with that of another witness in regard to genealogy (see *Tosafos* ד״ה נאמן [א]; see, however, *Pnei Yehoshua* who objects that this answer is inadequate). For other approaches, see *Ramban, Rashba, Re'ah* and *Ritva.*

22. The "father" is a Kohen, to whom everyone gives *terumah* (*Rashi;* cf. *Ramban*). He can then give his *terumah* to his son. Since he has this power, he is believed to say that his son is a Kohen (at least with respect to eating *terumah*) although they are related. [See the difficulties with this approach raised by *Tosafos, Tos. Yeshanim* et al.; see also *Ramban,* as explained by *Ritva.* For a general discussion of the logic of בְּיָדוֹ ("in his power"), see *Birkas Avraham* and *Beis Aharon.*]

23. As R' Chiya ruled in the Baraisa.

לאו כולהו סלוק ת"ש חזקה לכהונה נשיאות כפים וחילוק גרנות ועדות עדות חזקה היא אלא לאו הכי קאמר נשיאות כפים כי עדות מה עדות ליוחסין אף נשיאות כפים ליוחסין לא עדות הבאה מכח חזקה כחזקה [א] כי ההוא דאתא לקמיה דרבי אמי א"ל מוחזקני בזה שהוא כהן א"ל מה ראית אמר ליה שקרא ראשון בבית הכנסת בחזקת שהוא כהן או בחזקת שהוא גדול שקרא אחריו לוי והעלהו ר' אמי לכהונה על פיו ההוא דאתא לקמיה דרבי יהושע בן לוי אמר ליה [ב] מוחזקני בזה שהוא לוי אמר ליה מה ראית אמר ליה שקרא שני בבית הכנסת בחזקת שהוא לוי או בחזקת שהוא גדול שקרא לפניו כהן והעלהו רבי יהושע בן לוי ללויה על פיו ההוא דאתא לקמיה דריש לקיש אמר ליה מוחזקני בזה שהוא כהן א"ל מה ראית [א"ל] שקרא ראשון בבית הכנסת א"ל ראיתיו שחילק על הגרנות אמר לו ר' אלעזר ואם אין שם גורן בטלה כהונה זימנין הוו יתבי קמיה דר' יוחנן אתא כי הא מעשה לקמיה א"ל ריש לקיש ראיתיו שחילק על הגורן א"ל ר' יוחנן ואם אין שם גורן בטלה כהונה [ד] הדר חזייה לר"א בישות אמר שמעת מילי [ג] דבר נפחא ולא אמרת לן משמיה רבי ור' חייא חד העלה בן ע"פ אביו לכהונה וחד העלה אח ע"פ אחיו ללויה תסתיים דר' העלה בן ע"פ אביו לכהונה דתניא [ג] הרי שבא ואמר בני זה וכהן הוא נאמן להאכילו בתרומה ואינו נאמן להשיאו אשה דברי רבי אמר לו ר' חייא אם אתה מאמינו להאכילו בתרומה תאמינו להשיאו אשה ואם אי אתה מאמינו להשיאו אשה לא תאמינו לאכול בתרומה א"ל אני מאמינו להאכילו בתרומה שבידו להאכילו בתרומה ואיני מאמינו להשיאו אשה שאין בידו להשיאו אשה תסתיים ומדרבי העלה בן ע"פ אביו לכהונה ר' חייא העלה אח ע"פ אחיו ללויה ורבי חייא מאי שנא בן דלא דקרוב הוא אצל אביו אח נמי קרוב הוא אצל אחיו

במסיח

עדות הבאה מכח חזקה. פי' שאנו יודעין שהוא כהן מחמת הקורא אחריו שמוחזק לן שהוא לוי: **שקרא** אחריו לוי. לפירוש ר"י הלוי שפירש בגיטין (נט: ושם) אם אין שם כהן נתפרדה חבילה שיקרא ישראל גדול לפני לוי יש לפרש הכא שקרא אחריו לוי קטן מישראל שקרא אחריו: **שקרא** לפניו כהן. פירוש פעם אחת: **הרי** שאמר בני זה וכהן הוא. מדנקט בני זה וכהן הוא משמע שאינו ידוע לנו אם הוא בנו והוא בא להעיד שהוא בנו ושהוא כהן שאינו בן גרושה דאי ידוע לנו שהוא בנו הוה ליה למינקט בני זה כהן בלא וי"ו ותימה א"כ יהא נאמן לכולי עלמא לתרומה וליוחסין במגו דאי בעי אמר אינו בנו וי"ל דאע"ג דליכא מגו לא מהימן לדבריו קרוב הוא כדאמרינן בהחולץ (יבמות דף מז. ושם) לדבריך כותי אתה ואין עדות לכותי ואין אדם נאמן לפסול את בנו ואע"ג דרבי קאמר בסמוך אני מאמינו להאכילו בתרומה שהרי בידו להאכילו בתרומה אלמא אע"ג דקרוב הוא לדבריו נאמן במגו התם ודאי מהימנינן ליה משום דאית ליה מגו אפי' ידעינן שהוא בנו אבל האי מגו לא הוה דידעינן שהוא בנו ליכא מגו: **נאמן** להאכילו בתרומה. פירוש אע"ג דליכא אלא הוא שהוא קרוב דקסבר רבי אין מעלין מתרומה ליוחסין ואין נאמן להשיאו אשה פירוש להצטרף עם אחר להשיאו אשה כיון שהוא קרוב והשתא אתי שפיר הא דאמר ר' חייא אם אתה מאמינו יחידי להאכילו בתרומה אע"פ שהוא קרוב האמינהו עם אחר להשיאו אשה אבל אין לפרש דאין נאמן יחידי להשיאו אשה דפשיטא דאינו נאמן והכא לא הוה אמר רבי חייא האמינהו לישא דלא מיסתמיט שום תנא למימר דעד אחד כשר ליוחסין והא נמי אין לפרש דנאמן עם אחר להאכילו בתרומה דאי הוה צריך שני עדים בתרומה א"כ הוה סבר דמעלין מתרומה ליוחסין ואם כן היכי מכשיר קרוב כיון דאינו נאמן להשיאו אשה וא"ת כיון דסבירא ליה דאין מעלין מתרומה ליוחסין אם כן היכי מוקמינן בהגזל בתרא (ב"ק קיד:) ההיא דרבי דלקמן במסיח לפי תומו ונאמן בתרומה דרבנן אבל בתרומה דאורייתא לא מהימן והא לרבי כיון דס"ל דאין מעלין מתרומה ליוחסין אם כן ס"ל דמעלין מתרומה דרבנן לתרומה דאורייתא כדמשמע לעיל דכל היכא דאכיל בתרומה דרבנן אכיל נמי בתרומה דאורייתא וי"ל דהאי דמצרכינן למימר לעיל דמעלין מתרומה דרבנן לחלה דאורייתא או איפכא היינו משום דלא תקשי למ"ד אין מעלין מנשיאות כפים ליוחסין אבל רב אשי בהגזל אפשר דסבירא ליה כמ"ד מעלין ועוד נראה דלכולי עלמא בין למאן דאמר מעלין מתרומה ליוחסין בין למאן דאמר אין מעלין מעלין מתרומת דגן תירוש ויצהר של א"י ואפי' היא דרבנן לחלה דאורייתא כיון שבזמן המקדש הויא דאורייתא אבל תרומת פירות או תרומת חו"ל אין מעלין לכ"ע אפי' לתרומת דגן תירוש ויצהר של א"י דרבנן דדוקא בתרומת א"י או חלה דאורייתא בסוריא אמר מעלין מדרבנן לדאורייתא אבל לא בבבל וההיא דהגזל בתרא איירי בתרומת פירות או חוצה לארץ וכן מתני' דלקמן דנאמנים להעיד בגודלן מה שראו בקוטנן ומוקי לה בתרומה דרבנן היינו בתרומת פירות או חוצה לארץ ולמ"ד מעלין מתרומה ליוחסין אפי' מתרומת דגן תירוש ויצהר דא"י אפילו היא דרבנן מעלין דהא ר' יוסי ס"ל בפ' יוצא דופן (נדה מו:) תרומה בזמן הזה דרבנן ודוקא משום דקסבר חולקין תרומה לעבד בלא רבו הוא דאית ליה דאין מעלין הא אי הוה סבר דאין חולקין הוה מודה דמעלין והא דאמר לעיל מעיקרא אכול בתרומה דרבנן א) ולבסוף אכול בתרומה דאורייתא לא מכח שהיו אוכלין בגולה קדשי הגבול אוכלין בתרומה דאורייתא אלא משום שהיו נושאים כפים בגולה שמעלין מנשיאות כפים לתרומה דאורייתא אע"ג דהרי אתם בחזקתכם במה הייתם אוכלין בגולה כו' משמע שמכח אכילה היה מתירו אין לחוש בכך ולההוא לישנא דקאמר בתרומה דרבנן אכול בדאורייתא לא אכול מה שלא העלם מנשיאות כפים לתרומה דאורייתא היינו משום דריע חזקייהו: **נאמן** להאכילו בתרומה. הקשה ריב"ס דתנן בפרק עשרה יוחסין (קדושין דף עט: ושם) מי שהלך הוא ואשתו למדינת הים וכשחזר הביא עמו בנים ומתה אשתו צריך להביא ראיה על בניו ואינו נאמן להאכילם בתרומה כדמוכח התם בגמ' דתניא התם הביא ראיה על הגדולים א"צ ראיה על הקטנים ואמר רשב"ל עלה לא שנו אלא בקדשי הגבול אבל ליוחסין לא והיכי קאמר רבי הכא דאב נאמן להאכילו בתרומה ותירץ דרבי תנא הוא ופליג ור"ת אומר דההיא דקדושין אתיא כר' יהודה דאמר אין מעלין לכהונה ע"פ עד אחד וקדשי הגבול דהתם היינו לכל דבר קדושה כגון תרומה ונשיאות כפים ויוחסין והא דקאמר התם ב) אבל ליוחסין לא היינו יוחסין לקורבה כגון לסקול ולשרוף על ידו כדמסיק התם ר' יוחנן אמר אף ליוחסין ואזדא ר' יוחנן לטעמיה דאמר סוקלין על החזקות ד) [א"נ הכא באשתו עמו דאין צריך להביא ראיה כדאמר התם]: **שבידו** להאכילו בתרומה. ג) תימה איך נאמין אותו על תרומה בהאי מגו הא אין בידו להאכילו אחר מיתה וא"כ אין זה מגו כמו שמצינו ביש נוחלין (ב"ב קכח.) גבי בכור ובפרק בתרא דקדושין (דף עח:) דתניא יכיר יכירנו לאחרים מכאן אמר רבי יהודה נאמן אדם לומר זה בני בכור כו' למאי הלכתא אי לתת לו פי שנים אילו בעי למיתב ליה מתנה מי לא יהיב ליה לא צריכא בנכסים שנפלו לו כשהוא גוסס אלמא אי לאו קרא לא הוה נאמן לפי שאין בידו וי"ל דלא דמי דהכא כיון דנאמן להאכילו בחייו משום דבידו סברא הוא דנאמן אפילו לאחר מיתה:

במסיח

לאו כולהו סלוק. רובן נשארו בבבל דכתיב כל הקהל כאחד ארבע רבוא (עזרא ב): ועדות. אם באו עדים שהוא כהן שמכירין את אביו ואת אמו: ועדות חזקה היא. בתמיה וכי עדות חזקה קרי ליה: עדות הבאה מכח חזקה כחזקה. העדות נקבל ונאכילו בתרומה כאילו ראינוה אנן לאותה חזקה שזה העיד: **או בחזקת שהוא גדול.** כדאמרינן בעלמא ג) (גיטין דף נט:) רב קרי בכהני ואע"ג דלאו כהן הוה: **שקרא אחריו לוי.** ואי לאו כהן הוא אין לוי קורא אחריו דאמרינן במסכת גיטין (שם) אם אין שם כהן נתפרדה חבילה ומפרשינן דאין לוי קורא במקום שאין כהן ויש מפרשים נתפרדה החבילה שבמקום שאין כהן אם רוצה ישראל לקרות לפני לוי קורא ודוקא דאין שם כהן אבל היכא דאיכא כהן לא נתפרדה החבילה ולא יקרא ישראל גדול לפני לוי והכא כהן אחר הוה התם הלכך אי לאו דהאי כהן הוה לא הוה לוי קרי אבתריה: **שקרא לפניו כהן.** ואי לאו דהאי לוי הוא לא היה קורא שני אלא שלישי שנים כהנים היו קורין לפניו והוא שלישי דהכי אמרינן במסכת גיטין אם אין שם לוי קורא כהן במקומו: **ללויה.** לתת לו מעשר ראשון: **ואם אין שם גורן.** אם אין שם זורעי תבואה במקומו: **זימנין.** פעם אחרת: **הדר.** ריש לקיש: **חזייה לרבי אלעזר בישות.** החזיר פניו ונסתכל ברבי אלעזר בעין רעה שהבין שמפי ר' יוחנן שמע לשון זה וכשאמר לשון זה לא אמרה בשם רבי יוחנן לפיכך לא קיבלה הימנו: **להשיאו אשה.** שמא ממזר או נתין הוא: **שיש בידו להאכילו תרומה.** שהרי הוא כהן והכל חולקין לו תרומה:

והטבילוני

עין משפט נר מצוה

צב א ב מיי' פ"כ מהל' איסורי ביאה הלכ' יא:
צג ג מיי' שם הלכה ה:

תוספות רי"ד

ת"ש חזקה לכהונה נשיאות כפים וחילוק גרנות ועדות. פי' המורה אם באו עדים ואומרים שהוא כהן וכהן שמכירים את אביו ואת אמו ועדות חזקה הוא בתמיה ה"ק עדות הבא מכח חזקה כחזקה. פי' כההוא דאתא לקמיה דר"א אמר מוחזקני בזה שהוא כהן א"ל מה ראית א"ל שקרא ראשון בבה"כ א"ל בחזקת שהוא כהן או בחזקת שהוא גדול פי' בחכמה כדאמרינן בעלמא רב קרי בכהני ואע"ג דלא הוה כהן א"ל שקרא אחריו לוי פי' דאי לאו דכהן הוא אין לוי קורא אחריו ואמרינן בהניזקין אין שם כהן נתפרדה החבילה כלומר איבד לוי את זכותו והעלהו ר"א לכהונה ע"פ: **ההוא דאתא** לקמיה דר"ל א"ל מוחזקני בזה שהוא כהן א"ל מה ראית [א"ל] שקרא ראשון בבה"כ. א"ל ראית שחלק על הגורן א"ל ר"א ואם אין שם גורן בטלה דכהונה. פי' המורה אם אין זורעים במקומו. **(אר"י) תניא** הרי שבא ואמר בני זה כהן הוא נאמן שהאכילו בתרומה ואינו נאמן להשיאו אשה דברי רבי א"ל ר"ח אם אתה מאמינו להאכילו בתרומה האמינהו לדשיאו אשה. ואם אינך מאמינו להשיאו אשה אל תאמינהו להאכילו בתרומה. א"ל רבי אני מאמינו שהאכילו תרומה שכן בידו להאכילו תרומה ואיני מאמינו לדשיאו אשה שכן אין בידו להשיאו אשה:

ליקוטי רש"י

הדר חזייה לר"א בישות. החזיר ר"ש לקיש את פניו ונסתכל ברבי אלעזר בפנים זועפות שהבין ריש לקיש שמשמע ר' אלעזר דבר זה מפי רבי יוחנן וכשאמרה לו לא אמרה בשמו [מכות ה:]. **דבר נפחא.** ר' יוחנן דמקרי בר נפחא בכולא הש"ס כמו (ב"מ דף פה:) מאן פייל בר נפחא נראה למורי דלאו של ר' יוחנן הוי נפחא ולהכי מיקרי בר נפחא ואית דמפרשי בר נפחא על שם יופיו [סנהדרין צו.]. **תסתיים.** תתפרש אמיתו של דבר [מגילה יד:].

מסורת הש"ס

א) [מכות ה:], ב) [פירושו תמצא ברש"י סנהדרין צו. ד"ה טבא וכו' אביו של ר"י וכו' על שם יפיו], ג) [מגילה כב.], ד) [ועיין היטב תוס' קדושין פ. ד"ה לא שנו].

תוספות ישנים

א) [ולפ"ז גרסינן לעיל שפיר כי מסקינן מתרומה ליוחסין הנ"מ בתרומה דאורייתא כו' ומ"מ אינו סותר ראייתו דהשתא נמי יכול לומר דאי לא תימא הכי היכי הוי פרשי ידייהו הא אתו לאסוקינהו לתרומה דאורייתא ועוד דהשתא להאי פירושא פשיטא ליה לתלמודא דאין מעלין מתרומה דרבנן דס"ל אפי' לדאורייתא וכ"ש ליוחסין לאב"א ע"כ אינו ראיה ואין חוזר מדבריו דמעיקרא לא הביא ראיה מתרומה אלא משום דאכיל מדאורייתא. ת"י]:

ב) [דליכא למימר ליוחסין להשיאו אשה דהא לרבי יהודה במקום שנאמן להאכילו תרומה נאמן גם להשיאו אשה דמעלין מתרומה ליוחסין. ת"י]:

ג) [ועוד קשה לר"י דאין זה מיגו טוב שאם יוליכנו בגורן ויתן לו חלקו הרי יפסיד והשתא דקאמר שהוא כהן נוטל כל אחד חלקו ואין לפרש שבידו להאכילו בתרומה בשעה שהעיד שהיה יכול לומר אינו בני וכהן הוא דא"כ להשיאו אשה נמי נימא הכי. בתוס' לא תירץ והתירוץ שבפנים מלאחין]: ת"י:

The Gemara now discusses similar evidence regarding a Levi: הַהוּא דְאָתָא לְקַמֵּיהּ דְּרַבִּי יְהוֹשֻׁעַ בֶּן לֵוִי – **A certain man came before R' Yehoshua ben Levi** אָמַר לֵיהּ – **and said to him** about a third party: מוּחְזְקַנִי בָּזֶה שֶׁהוּא לֵוִי – **"I presume that this man is a Levi."** אָמַר לֵיהּ – **[R' Yehoshua ben Levi] asked him:** מָה רָאִיתָ – **"What did you see** that makes you think so?" אָמַר לֵיהּ – **He answered him:** שֶׁקָּרָא שֵׁנִי בְּבֵית הַכְּנֶסֶת – "I saw **that he read second** from the Torah **in the synagogue."** בְּחֶזְקַת שֶׁדּוּא לֵוִי אוֹ בְּחֶזְקַת שֶׁהוּא גָּדוֹל – R' Yehoshua ben Levi asked further: "But did he read second **in the capacity of a Levi or in the capacity of a great man?"**[9] שֶׁקָּרָא לְפָנָיו כֹּהֵן – The witness answered: "I know that he read second in the capacity of a Levi **because a Kohen read** from the Torah **before him."**[10] וְהֶעֱלָהוּ רַבִּי יְהוֹשֻׁעַ בֶּן לֵוִי לִלְוִיָּה עַל פִּיו – **And R' Yehoshua ben Levi elevated him to the status of a Levi based on [the witness'] word.**[11]

Another instance of testimony based on the Torah reading: הַהוּא דְאָתָא לְקַמֵּיהּ דְּרֵישׁ לָקִישׁ – **A certain man came before Reish Lakish** אָמַר לֵיהּ – **and said to him** about a third party: מוּחְזְקַנִי בָּזֶה שֶׁהוּא כֹּהֵן – **"I presume that this man is a Kohen."** אָמַר לֵיהּ – **[Reish Lakish] asked him:** מָה רָאִיתָ – **"What did you see** that makes you say this?" [אָמַר לֵיהּ] – **He answered him:** שֶׁקָּרָא רִאשׁוֹן בְּבֵית הַכְּנֶסֶת – "I saw **that he read first** from the Torah **in the synagogue."** אָמַר לֵיהּ – **[Reish Lakish] asked him** further: רְאִיתִיו שֶׁחִילֵּק עַל הַגְּרָנוֹת – **"Did you see him**[12] **dividing** ***terumah*** **at the granaries?"**[13] אָמַר לוֹ רַבִּי אֶלְעָזָר – Upon hearing Reish Lakish's question, **R' Elazar said to him:** וְאִם אֵין שָׁם גּוֹרֶן בָּטְלָה כְּהוּנָּה – **"And if there is no granary, the Kehunah would be abolished?!"**[14]

The narrative continues:

זִימְנִין הֲווּ יָתְבֵי קַמֵּיהּ דְּרַבִּי יוֹחָנָן – **Another time, they** [Reish Lakish and R' Elazar] **were sitting before R' Yochanan.** אָתָא כִּי הָא מַעֲשֶׂה לְקַמֵּיהּ – **A similar case was brought before [R' Yochanan].** That is, a witness testified that someone was a Kohen on the basis of having seen him read first from the Torah in a synagogue. אָמַר לֵיהּ רֵישׁ לָקִישׁ – **Reish Lakish asked [the witness]:** רְאִיתִיו שֶׁחִילֵּק עַל הַגּוֹרֶן – **"Did you see him**[15] **dividing** ***terumah*** **at the granary?"** אָמַר לֵיהּ רַבִּי יוֹחָנָן – **R' Yochanan said to [Reish Lakish]:** וְאִם אֵין שָׁם גּוֹרֶן בָּטְלָה כְּהוּנָּה – **"And if there is no granary, the Kehunah would be abolished?!"** הֲדַר חַזְיֵיהּ לְרַבִּי אֶלְעָזָר בִּישׁוּת – **[Reish Lakish]** then **turned and looked at R' Elazar crossly,** אָמַר שָׁמַעְתְּ מִילֵּי דְּבַר נַפָּחָא – **saying, "You heard** these **words of Bar Napacha** (i.e. R' Yochanan)[16] וְלָא אָמַרְתְּ לָן מִשְּׁמֵיהּ – **and you did not say them to me in his name."**[17]

Further cases of testimony regarding a person's status as a Kohen or Levi:

רַבִּי וְרַבִּי חִיָּיא – **Rebbi and R' Chiya** gave rulings in different cases: חַד הֶעֱלָה בֵּן עַל פִּי אָבִיו לִכְהוּנָּה – **One elevated a son to the Kehunah based on the word of his father,** וְחַד הֶעֱלָה אָח עַל פִּי אָחִיו לִלְוִיָּה – **and** the other **one elevated a brother to the status of a Levi based on the word of his brother.**[18]

The Gemara identifies the author of the first ruling:

תִּסְתַּיֵּים דְּרַבִּי הֶעֱלָה בֵּן עַל פִּי אָבִיו לִכְהוּנָּה – **Let it be determined that Rebbi** was the one who **elevated a son to the Kehunah based on the word of his father.** דְּתַנְיָא – **For it was taught in a Baraisa:** הֲרֵי שֶׁבָּא וְאָמַר בְּנִי זֶה וְכֹהֵן הוּא – If SOMEONE CAME AND SAID, "THIS IS MY SON AND HE IS A KOHEN," נֶאֱמָן לְהַאֲכִילוֹ בִּתְרוּמָה – HE IS BELIEVED TO the extent of LETTING HIM EAT *TERUMAH*,[19] וְאֵינוֹ נֶאֱמָן לְהַשִּׂיאוֹ אִשָּׁה – BUT HE IS NOT BELIEVED TO the extent of ALLOWING HIM TO MARRY A WOMAN of untainted lineage.[20] דִּבְרֵי רַבִּי – These are THE WORDS OF REBBI. אָמַר לוֹ רַבִּי חִיָּיא – R' CHIYA SAID TO HIM: אִם אַתָּה מַאֲמִינוֹ לְהַאֲכִילוֹ בִּתְרוּמָה – IF YOU BELIEVE [THE FATHER] TO the extent of LETTING [HIS SON] EAT *TERUMAH*, תַּאֲמִינוֹ לְהַשִּׂיאוֹ אִשָּׁה – YOU SHOULD BELIEVE HIM TO the extent of LETTING HIM MARRY A WOMAN of untainted lineage.[21] וְאִם אִי אַתָּה מַאֲמִינוֹ לְהַשִּׂיאוֹ אִשָּׁה – AND IF YOU DO NOT BELIEVE HIM TO the extent of ALLOWING HIM TO

NOTES

9. Perhaps there was no Levi in the synagogue, in which case the privilege of reading second is awarded to the most prominent Yisrael present (*Rashi,* according to *Rashash;* see next note).

10. The Gemara refers to an instance in which *two* Kohanim are present in the synagogue. In that case it is impossible for a Yisrael to read second, because even if no Levi is present, the other Kohen reads second in the Levi's place (and if a Levi is present, *he* reads second). Hence, the witness knew that the second reader could not have been a Yisrael (*Rashi,* according to *Rashash*).

The commentators note that *Rashi* does not follow the conclusion of the Gemara in *Gittin* 59b, which states that if no Levi is in the synagogue, a single Kohen reads *both* of the first two passages. This is so even where another Kohen is available to read the second passage (see *Maharsha, Rashash* and *Hagahos Yavetz*).

11. The consequence of this ruling was that he was entitled to receive *maaser rishon* (the first tithe), which is given to the Leviim (*Rashi*).

12. The text of *Tos. Rid* reads ראיתו, *you saw him* (instead of ראיתיו, *I saw him*). See *Rashash.*

13. [According to Reish Lakish, reading from the Torah first does not suffice to prove someone's Kohanic status. Rather, the person must be seen receiving *terumah* when the owners of produce distribute it at their granaries.]

14. That is, if a Kohen lives in a place where produce is not grown (*Rashi*), he would be unable to prove his Kohanic status!

This would be true, however, only in a place that lacks established courts, where recital of the Priestly Blessing is not a proof of Kehunah. Furthermore, it must be a small town or village, where distribution of the Kohanic gifts (foreleg, cheeks and stomach) also fails to provide proof [see above, 25a] (*Ritva*).

15. See note 12.

16. *Bar Napacha* means "son of a blacksmith" and is a reference to R' Yochanan, whose father was a blacksmith (*Rashi* to *Sanhedrin* 96a ד״ה טבא, first explanation).

17. Reish Lakish was upset with R' Elazar for not having told him that he had heard these words from their teacher, R' Yochanan. Had R' Elazar told him that this was R' Yochanan's opinion, Reish Lakish would have accepted it (*Rashi*), and he would not have repeated his mistake in front of R' Yochanan (*Ritva*).

R' Elazar, however, felt that since he was a primary disciple of R' Yochanan, everyone knew that his opinions were based on R' Yochanan's, and there was no reason for him to say so (*Ritva,* based on *Yevamos* 96b).

18. It was not known who gave which ruling.

19. One witness suffices to establish that someone is a Kohen with respect to letting him eat *terumah* [according to the view that a Kohen who eats *terumah* is not elevated to the level of the genealogically fit] (*Tosafos;* see 24b with notes 10-12). Rebbi teaches that even a father can testify about his son, although they are related. The reason for this leniency is stated in a Baraisa below.

20. For he might be a *mamzer* or *nasin* (*Rashi;* see 24a note 12; see also *Shitah Mekubetzes* סד״ה תו and *Pnei Yehoshua* on *Tosafos* [א] ד״ה נאמן; see also *Beis Aharon*).

A father is not believed in this regard even if he testifies together with another (unrelated) witness. Although two witnesses are believed in matters of genealogy, a father cannot serve as one of them since, as a relative, he is ineligible to give testimony (see *Tosafos;* cf. *Pnei Yehoshua*). [See also *Kovetz He'aros* to *Yevamos* 65:1-5 and *Birkas Avraham,* who discuss the disqualification of a relative as it relates to matters of prohibition.]

21. It is difficult to understand the analogy drawn by R' Chiya between *terumah* and genealogy, for in the case of *terumah* one witness possibly suffices, whereas genealogical matters require two witnesses (see the

לאו כולהו סלוק ת"ש חזקה לכהונה נשיאות כפים וחילוק גרנות ועדות עדות חזקה היא אלא לאו הכי קאמר נשיאות כפים כי עדות מה עדות ליוחסין אף נשיאות כפים ליוחסין לא עדות הבאה מכח חזקה כחזקה [א]כי ההוא דאתא לקמיה דרבי אמי א"ל מוחזקני בזה שהוא כהן א"ל מה ראית א"ל שקרא ראשון בבית הכנסת בחזקת שהוא כהן או בחזקת שהוא גדול שקרא אחריו לוי והעלהו ר' אמי לכהונה על פיו ההוא דאתא לקמיה דרבי יהושע בן לוי אמר ליה [ב]מוחזקני בזה שהוא לוי אמר ליה מה ראית אמר ליה שקרא שני בבית הכנסת בחזקת שהוא לוי או בחזקת שהוא גדול שקרא לפניו כהן והעלהו רבי יהושע בן לוי ללויה על פיו ההוא דאתא לקמיה דריש לקיש אמר ליה מוחזקני בזה שהוא כהן א"ל מה ראית [א"ל] שקרא ראשון בבית הכנסת א"ל ראיתו שחילק על הגרנות אמר לו ר' אלעזר ואם אין שם גורן בטלה כהונה זימנין הוו יתבי קמיה דר' יוחנן אתא כי הא מעשה לקמיה א"ל ריש לקיש ראיתיו שחילק על הגורן א"ל ר' יוחנן ואם אין שם גורן בטלה כהונה [א] הדר חזייה לר"א בישות אמר שמעת מילי [ב]דבר נפחא ולא אמרת לן משמיה רבי ור' חייא חד העלה בן ע"פ אביו לכהונה וחד העלה אח ע"פ אחיו ללויה תסתיים דר' העלה בן ע"פ אביו לכהונה דתניא [ג]הרי שבא ואמר בני זה וכהן הוא נאמן להאכילו בתרומה ואינו נאמן להשיאו אשה דברי רבי אמר לו ר' חייא אם אתה מאמינו להאכילו בתרומה תאמינו להשיאו אשה ואם אי אתה מאמינו להשיאו אשה לא תאמינו לאכול בתרומה א"ל אני מאמינו להאכילו בתרומה שבידו להאכילו בתרומה ואיני מאמינו להשיאו אשה שאין בידו להשיאו אשה תסתיים ומדרבי העלה בן ע"פ אביו לכהונה ר' חייא העלה אח ע"פ אחיו ללויה ורבי חייא מאי שנא בן דלא דקרוב הוא אצל אביו אח נמי קרוב הוא אצל אחיו

במסיח

רש"י

לאו כולהו סלוק. רובן נשארו בבבל דכתיב כל הקהל כאחד ארבע רבוא (עזרא ב): ועדות. אם באו עדים שהוא כהן שמכירין את אביו ואת אמו: ועדות חזקה היא. בתמיה וכי עדות חזקה קרי ליה: עדות הבאה מכח חזקה כחזקה. העדות נקבל ונאכילו בתרומה כאילו ראינוה אנן לאותה חזקה שזה העיד: או בחזקת שהוא גדול. כדאמרינן בעלמא [ג](גיטין דף נט:) רב קרי בכהני ואע"ג דלאו כהן הוה: שקרא אחריו לוי. ואי לאו כהן הוא אין לוי קורא אחריו דאמרינן במסכת גיטין (שם) אם אין שם כהן נתפרדה חבילה ומפרשינן דאין לוי קורא במקום שאין כהן ויש מפרשים נתפרדה החבילה שבמקום שאין כהן אם רוצה ישראל לקרות לפני לוי קורא ודוקא דאין שם כהן אבל היכא דאיכא כהן לא נתפרדה החבילה ולא יקרא ישראל גדול לפני לוי והכא כהן אחר הוה התם הלכך אי לאו דהאי כהן הוה לא הוה לוי קרי אבתריה: שקרא לפניו כהן. ואי לאו דהאי לוי הוא לא היה קורא שני אלא שלישי שנים כהנים היו קורין לפניו והוא שלישי דהכי אמרינן במסכת גיטין אם אין שם לוי קורא כהן במקומו: ללויה. לתת לו מעשר ראשון: ואם אין שם גורן. אם אין שם זורעי תבואה במקומו: זימנין. פעם אחרת: הדר. ריש לקיש: חזייה לרבי אלעזר בישות. החזיר פניו ונסתכל ברבי אלעזר בעין רעה שהבין שמפי ר' יוחנן שמע לשון זה וכשאמר לשון זה לא אמרה בשם רבי יוחנן לפיכך לא קיבלה הימנו: להשיאו אשה. שמא ממזר או נתין הוא: שיש בידו להאכילו תרומה. שהרי הוא כהן והכל חולקין לו תרומה:

והטבילוני

תוספות

עדות הבאה מכח חזקה. פי' שאנו יודעין שהוא כהן מחמת הקורא אחריו שמוחזק לן שהוא לוי: שקרא אחריו לוי. לפירוש ר"י הלוי שפירש בגיטין (נט:) אם אין שם כהן נתפרדה חבילה שיקרא ישראל גדול לפני לוי יש לפרש הכא שקרא אחריו לוי קטן מישראל שקרא אחריו:

שקרא לפניו כהן. פירוש פעם אחת: הרי שאמר בני זה וכהן הוא. מדנקט בני זה וכהן הוא משמע שאינו ידוע לנו אם הוא בנו והוא בא להעיד שהוא בנו ושהוא כהן שאינו בן גרושה דאי ידוע לנו שהוא בנו הוה ליה למינקט בני זה כהן בלא וי"ו ותימה א"כ יהא נאמן לכולי עלמא לתרומה וליוחסין במגו דאי בעי אמר אינו בנו וי"ל דאע"ג דאיכא מגו לא מהימן לדבריו קרוב הוא כדאמרינן בהחולץ (יבמות דף מז. ושם) לדבריך כותי אתה ואין עדות לכותי ואין אדם נאמן לפסול את בנו ואע"ג דרבי קאמר בסמוך אני מאמינו להאכילו בתרומה שהרי בידו להאכילו בתרומה אלמא אע"ג דקרוב הוא לדבריו נאמן במגו התם ודאי מהימנינן ליה משום דאית ליה מגו אפי' ידעינן שהוא בנו אבל האי מגו אי הוה ידעינן שהוא בנו ליכא מגו:

נאמן להאכילו בתרומה. פירוש אע"ג דליכא אלא הוא שהוא קרוב דקסבר רבי אין מעלין מתרומה ליוחסין ואין נאמן להשיאו אשה פירוש להצטרף עם אחר להשיאו אשה כיון שהוא קרוב והשתא אתי שפיר הא דאמר ר' חייא אם אתה מאמינו יחידי להאכילו בתרומה אע"פ שהוא קרוב האמינהו עם אחר להשיאו אשה אבל אין לפרש דאין נאמן יחידי להשיאו אשה דפשיטא דאינו נאמן ובהא לא הוה אמר רבי חייא האמינהו לישא דלא משתמיט שום תנא למימר דעד אחד כשר ליוחסין ובהא נמי אין לפרש דנאמן עם אחר להאכילו בתרומה דאי הוה צריך שני עדים בתרומה א"כ הוה סבר דמעלין מתרומה ליוחסין ואם כן היכי מכשיר קרוב כיון דאינו נאמן להשיאו אשה וא"ת כיון דסבירא ליה דאין מעלין מתרומה ליוחסין אם כן היכי מוקמינן בהגוזל בתרא (ב"ק קד:) הסיא דרבי דלקמן במסיח לפי תומו ונאמן בתרומה דרבנן אבל בתרומה דאורייתא לא מהימן והא לרבי כיון דס"ל דאין מעלין מתרומה ליוחסין אם כן ס"ל דמעלין מתרומה דרבנן לתרומה דאורייתא כדמשמע לעיל דכל היכא דאכיל בתרומה דרבנן אכיל נמי בתרומה דאורייתא וי"ל דהאי דמצרכינן למימר לעיל דמעלין מתרומה דרבנן לחלה דאורייתא או איפכא היינו משום דלא תקשי למ"ד אין מעלין מנשיאות כפים ליוחסין אבל רב אשי בהגוזל אפשר דסבירא ליה כמ"ד מעלין ועוד נראה דלכולי עלמא בין למאן דאמר מעלין מתרומה ליוחסין בין למאן דאמר אין מעלין אין מעלין מתרומת דגן תירוש ויצהר של א"י ואפי' היא דרבנן לחלה דאורייתא כיון שבזמן המקדש הויא דאורייתא אבל תרומת פירות או תרומת חו"ל אין מעלין לכ"ע אפי' לתרומת דגן תירוש ויצהר של א"י דרבנן דדוקא בתרומת א"י או חלה דאורייתא בסוריא אמר מעלין מדרבנן לדאורייתא אבל לא בבבל והסיא דהגוזל בתרא איירי בתרומת פירות או חוצה לארץ וכן מתני' דלקמן דנאמנים להעיד בגדלן מה שראו בקוטנן ומוקי לה בתרומה דרבנן היינו בתרומת פירות או חוצה לארץ ולמ"ד מעלין מתרומה ליוחסין אפי' מתרומת דגן תירוש ויצהר דא"י אפילו היא דרבנן מעלין דהא ר' יוסי ס"ל בפ' יוצא דופן (נדה מו:) תרומה בזמן הזה דרבנן ודוקא משום דקסבר חולקין תרומה לעבד בלא רבו הוא דאית ליה דאין מעלין הא אי הוה סבר דאין חולקין הוה מודה דמעלין והא דאמר לעיל מעיקרא אכול בתרומה דרבנן [א] ולבסוף אכול בתרומה דאורייתא לא מכח שהיו אוכלין בגולה קדשי הגבול אוכלין בתרומה דאורייתא אלא משום שהיו נושאים כפים בגולה שמעלין מנשיאות כפים לתרומה דאורייתא אע"ג דהרי אתם בחזקתכם במה שהייתם אוכלין בגולה כו' משמע שמכח אכילה היה מתירו אין לחוש בכך והשתא לישנא דקאמר בתרומה דרבנן אכול בדאורייתא לא אכול מה שלא העלם מנשיאות כפים לתרומה דאורייתא היינו משום דריע חזקייהו: נאמן להאכילו בתרומה. הקשה ריב"ם דתנן בפרק עשרה יוחסין (קדושין דף עט: ושם) מי שהלך הוא ואשתו למדינת הים ובא הוא ואשתו ובניו ואמר אשתו זו ובניו אלו אין צריך להביא ראיה על בניו ואינו נאמן להאכילם בתרומה כדמוכח התם בגמ' דמייתי התם הביא ראיה על הגדולים א"צ ראיה על הקטנים ואמר רשב"ל עלה לא שנו אלא בקדשי הגבול אבל ליוחסין לא והיכי קאמר רבי הכא דלא נאמן להאכילו בתרומה ומירץ דרבי תנא הוא ופליג ור"ת אומר דהסיא דקדושין מיירי כר' יהודה דאמר אין מעלין לכהונה ע"פ עד אחד וקדשי הגבול היינו לכל דבר קדושה היינו תרומה ונשיאות כפים ויוחסין והא דקאמר התם [ב] אבל ליוחסין לא היינו יוחסין לקורבה כגון לטמא לקבור ולירש על ידו כדמסיק התם ר' יוחנן אמר אף ליוחסין ואזלא ר' יוחנן לטעמיה דאמר חולקין על החזקות [ד] [א"כ הכא באשתו עמו לא צריך להביא ראיה כדאמר התם]: שבידו להאכילו בתרומה. [ג] תימה איך נאמין אותו על תרומה בהאי מגו הא אין בידו להאכילו אחר מיתה וא"כ אין זה מגו כמו שמצינו בים ונוחלין (ב"ב קכז:) גבי בכור ובפרק בתרא דקדושין (דף עח:) דתניא יכיר יכירנו לאחרים מכאן נאמן אדם לומר זה בני בכור כו' למאי הלכתא לא אמר לתת לו פי שנים אלו בעי למיתב ליה מתנה מי לא יהיב ליה לא צריכא בנכסים שנפלו לו כשהוא גוסס אלמא אי לאו קרא לא הוה נאמן לפי שאין בידו וי"ל דלא דמי דהכא כיון דנאמן להאכילו בחייו משום דבידו סברא הוא דנאמן אפילו לאחר מיתה:

במסיח

עין משפט נר מצוה

צב א ב מיי' פ"כ מהל' איסורי ביאה הלכ' א:
צג ג מיי' שם הלכה ה:

תוספות רי"ד

ת"ש חזקה לכהונה נשיאות כפים וחילוק גרנות ועדות. פי' המורה אם באו עדים ואמרים שהוא כהן וכגון שמכירים את אביו ואת אמו ועדות חזקה הוא בתמיה ה"ק עדות הבא מכח חזקה כחזקה. פי' כההוא דאתא לקמיה דר"א אמר מוחזקני בזה שהוא כהן א"ל מה ראית א"ל שקרא ראשון בבה"כ א"ל בחזקת שהוא כהן או בחזקת שהוא גדול פי' בחכמה כדאמרינן בעלמא רב קרי בכהני ואע"ג דלא הוה כהן א"ל שקרא אחריו לוי פי' דאי לאו דכהן הוא אין לוי קורא אחריו ואמרינן בהניזקין אין שם כהן נתפרדה החבילה כלומר איבד לוי את זכותו והעלהו ר"א לכהונה ע"פ: ההוא דאתא לקמיה דר"ל א"ל מוחזקני בזה שהוא כהן א"ל מה ראית [א"ל] שקרא ראשון בבה"כ. א"ל ראית שחלק על הגורן א"ל ר"א ואם אין שם גורן בטלה הכהונה. פי' המורה אם אין זורעים במקומו. (אר"י) תניא הרי שבא ואמר בני זה כהן הוא נאמן להאכילו בתרומה ואינו נאמן להשיאו אשה דברי רבי א"ל ר"ח אם אתה מאמינו להאכילו בתרומה האמינהו להשיאו אשה. ואם אינך מאמינו להשיאו אשה אל תאמינהו להאכילו בתרומה. א"ל רבי אני מאמינו להאכילו תרומה שכן בידו להאכילו תרומה. ואיני מאמינו להשיאו אשה שכן אין בידו להשיאו אשה:

ליקוטי רש"י

הדר חזייה לר"א בישות. החזיר ר"ל לקיש את פניו ונסתכל ברבי אלעזר בפנים זועפות שהבין ר"ל שמע ר' אלעזר דבר זה מפי רבי יוחנן וכשאמרה לו לא אמרה בשמו [מכות ה:]. דבר נפחא. ר' יוחנן דמקרי בר נפחא בכולא הש"ס כמו (ב"מ דף פה:) מאן עייל בר נפחא נראה למורי דאבי של ר' יוחנן הוי נפחא ולהכי מיקרי בר נפחא ואית דמפרשי בר נפחא על שם יופיו [סנהדרין צו.]. תסתיים. תתפרש אמיתו של דבר [מגילה יד:].

מסורת הש"ס

א) [מכות ה:], ב) [פירושו תמצא ברש"י סנהדרין צו. ד"ה טבא וכו' אביו של ר"י וכו' על שם יפיו], ג) [מגילה כב.], ד) [ועיין היטב תוס' קדושין פ. ד"ה לא שנו].

תוספות ישנים

א) [ולפ"ז גרסינן לעיל שפיר כי מסקינן מתרומה ליוחסין הנ"מ בתרומה דאורייתא כו' ומ"מ אינו סותר ראייתו דהשתא נמי יכול לומר דאי לא תימא הכי היכי הוי פרסי ידייהו הא אתו לאסוקינהו לתרומה דאורייתא ועוד דהשתא להאי פירושא פשיטא ליה לתלמודא דאין מעלין מתרומה דרבנן דמ"ל אפי' לדאורייתא וכ"ש ליוחסין לאב"א ע"כ אינו ראיה ואין חוזר מדבריו דמעיקרא לא הביא ראיה מתרומה אלא משום דאכיל מדאורייתא. ת"י]:
ב) [דליכא למימר ליוחסין להשיאו אשה דהא לרבי יהודה במקום שנאמן להאכילו תרומה נאמן גם להשיאו אשה דמעלין מתרומה ליוחסין. ת"י]:
ג) [ועוד קשה לר"י דאין זה מיגו טוב שאם יוליכנו בגורן ויתן לו חלקו הרי יפסיד והשתא דקאמר שהוא כהן נוטל כל אחד חלקו ואין לפרש שבידו להאכילו בתרומה בשעה שהעיד שהיה יכול לומר אינו בני וכהן הוא ואין כהן הוא נאמן להשיאו אשה נמי נימא הכי. בתוס' ... ואין לומר ... והתירוץ שבפנים מלאתין]: ת"י:

לָאו כּוּלְּהוּ סְלוּק – **not all of them went up.**[1] Thus, the Biblical obligation of *challah* does not apply nowadays.[2]

The Gemara again attempts to prove that one who recites the Priestly Blessing is assumed to be genealogically fit:

תָּא שְׁמַע – **Come, learn** a proof from the following Baraisa: חֲזָקָה לִכְהוּנָּה – **A PRESUMPTION OF KEHUNAH** can be established by testifying about a man that נְשִׂיאוּת כַּפַּיִם – he recited **THE PRIESTLY BLESSING,** וְחִילּוּק גְּרָנוֹת – or that he received *terumah* in the **DISTRIBUTION** of *terumah* **AT GRANARIES,** וְעֵדוּת – **OR** by giving **TESTIMONY** about his parents.[3]

The Gemara develops its proof by first questioning the Baraisa: עֵדוּת חֲזָקָה הִיא – How can it say that **testimony** creates only **"a presumption** of Kehunah"? Why, testimony is absolute proof of Kehunah!

The Gemara answers:

אֶלָּא לָאו הָכִי קָאָמַר – **Rather, is this not what [the Baraisa] is teaching:** נְשִׂיאוּת כַּפַּיִם כִּי עֵדוּת – **The Priestly Blessing is like testimony.** מָה עֵדוּת לְיוּחֲסִין – **Just as testimony** establishes him as a Kohen even **with respect to genealogy,** אַף נְשִׂיאוּת כַּפַּיִם לְיוּחֲסִין – **so too the Priestly Blessing** establishes him as a Kohen even **with respect to genealogy.**[4]

The Gemara rejects this proof:

לֹא – **No!** That is not necessarily what the Baraisa means. עֵדוּת הַבָּאָה מִכֹּחַ חֲזָקָה כַּחֲזָקָה – Rather, it could mean that **testimony based on a presumption is tantamount to the presumption** itself.[5]

The Gemara gives an example:

כִּי הַהוּא דְּאָתָא לְקַמֵּיהּ דְּרַבִּי אַמִי – This is **like** the case in which **a certain man came before R' Ami** אָמַר לֵיהּ – **and said to him** about a third party: מוּחְזְקַנִי בָּזֶה שֶׁהוּא כֹּהֵן – **"I presume that this man is a Kohen."** אָמַר לֵיהּ – **[R' Ami] asked him:** מָה רָאִיתָ – **"What did you see** that makes you think so?" אָמַר לֵיהּ – **He answered [R' Ami]:** שֶׁקָּרָא רִאשׁוֹן בְּבֵית הַכְּנֶסֶת – "I saw **that he read first** from the Torah **in the synagogue."** בְּחֶזְקַת שֶׁהוּא כֹּהֵן אוֹ בְּחֶזְקַת שֶׁהוּא גָּדוֹל – R' Ami asked further: "But did he read first **in the capacity of a Kohen or in the capacity of a great man?"**[6] שֶׁקָּרָא אַחֲרָיו לֵוִי – The witness answered: "I know that he read first in the capacity of a Kohen **because a Levi read after him."**[7] וְהֶעֱלָהוּ רַבִּי אַמִי לִכְהוּנָּה עַל פִּיו – **And R' Ami elevated him to the Kehunah based on [the witness'] word.**[8]

NOTES

1. When Ezra led the return to Eretz Yisrael, the majority of the Jewish people remained in Babylonia. Scripture states (*Ezra* 2:64) about the returnees: *The entire congregation together was forty-two thousand three hundred and sixty* (*Rashi;* see *Ran* to *Megillah* folio 1a ד״ה ויש; cf. *Ramban* ibid. ד״ה וכשעיינתי).

2. Rav Huna cites the fact that most Jews lived outside Eretz Yisrael in Ezra's time because the same was presumably true in his day as well. The Biblical mitzvah of *challah* requires the presence of all (or most) Jews in Eretz Yisrael, as is evident from the Baraisa cited previously. Therefore, *challah* nowadays is only a Rabbinic, and not a Biblical, obligation even in Eretz Yisrael. [This is the accepted halachah (*Rambam, Hil. Isurei Biah* 20:3; *Shulchan Aruch, Yoreh Deah* 322:2). Regarding the status of *terumah* nowadays, see *Rambam, Hil. Terumos* 1:1,26; *Tur* and *Shulchan Aruch* ibid. 331:2.]

3. I.e. witnesses testify that his father was a Kohen and his mother was fit to be married to a Kohen (see *Rashi*).

4. The Baraisa should not be understood as meaning that "testimony" is another one of the things that establish a "presumption of Kehunah." Rather, the Baraisa mentions "testimony" – which is a model example of evidence that proves genealogical fitness – together with recital of the Priestly Blessing in order to teach that the Priestly Blessing also proves genealogical fitness.

[Since the Baraisa lists the distribution of *terumah* as well, it apparently holds that this too suffices to establish genealogical fitness (see *Melo HaRo'im* and *Hagahos Radal*).]

5. The Gemara now proposes that "testimony" does not mean that two witnesses testify about a person's parents. Rather, it means that if witnesses testify to having seen an activity that establishes a presumption of Kehunah [e.g. recital of the Priestly Blessing], the judges accept their testimony as though they had seen the activity themselves. Thus, the judges may rely on it to allow the person in question to eat *terumah* (*Rashi*). [*Rashi* specifies *terumah* because the Gemara currently holds that the factors listed in the Baraisa do not suffice to establish genealogical fitness.]

It is difficult, however, to see what novel point is taught by the Baraisa according to *Rashi's* explanation (*Tos. HaRosh;* see *Kovetz Shiurim* §68). [Furthermore, according to *Rashi's* explanation, the example provided next in the Gemara does not appear to be appropriate (*Poras Yosef;* see also the objection raised by *Maharsha*).] Other Rishonim therefore take a different approach. In their opinion, "testimony based on a presumption" means that witnesses testify to having seen someone engage in an activity which indicates that he is a Kohen only if an additional presumption is made (as in the example that follows). The Baraisa teaches that although such testimony is incomplete in itself it is nevertheless acceptable (*Tosafos, Tos. HaRosh*).

6. The Gemara in *Megillah* (22a) relates that Rav read first from the Torah although he was not a Kohen (*Rashi;* see *Ritva*).

As a rule, the first person to read from the Torah must be a Kohen, the second a Levi and the third a Yisrael (Mishnah, *Gittin* 59a). If, however, there is no Kohen in the synagogue, or if the only Kohen is an *am haaretz,* the privilege of reading first is awarded to the greatest Torah scholar present (*Ritva;* cf. *Hagahos Chochmas Manoach*). Thus, the fact that someone reads first from the Torah does not absolutely prove that he is a Kohen.

[Nowadays, the prevalent custom is to have a Kohen read first even if he is an *am haaretz* and there is a an outstanding (non-Kohen) Torah scholar present (see *Shulchan Aruch, Orach Chaim* 135:4).]

7. The Gemara in *Gittin* (59b) states that if no Kohen is present [or if he is an *am haaretz*], the normal sequence is rejected (נִתְפָּרְדָה הַחֲבִילָה, *the bundle is unraveled*). This is understood as meaning that a Levi may not read at all; rather, only Yisraelim are allowed to read (*Rashi,* as explained by *Ritva;* cf. *Beis Yosef, Orach Chaim* 135:6 ד״ה מצאתי כתוב and *Rashbam* cited by *Ritva*). Therefore, if a Levi does read subsequently from the Torah, it is evident that the first reader was a Kohen.

Alternatively, the Gemara in *Gittin* means that if no Kohen is present [or if he is an *am haaretz*], a Levi merely loses his *precedence* over a Yisrael. That is, the privileges of reading are distributed to those present according to their respective levels of scholarship, regardless of whether they are Kohanim or Leviim. In our case, it was known that a Yisrael was present who was a greater scholar than the Levi who read second. Hence, the first reader must have been a Kohen, because otherwise the honor of reading second would have been awarded not to the Levi, but to the scholarly Yisrael (*Rashi,* as emended by *Rashash* [cf. *Maharsha*]; *Tosafos, Ritva* et al.).

[Regarding the current practice where no Kohen is present, see *Beis Yosef* ibid., *Darchei Moshe* ibid. §6 and *Mishnah Berurah* ibid. §23.]

8. That is, R' Ami permitted him to eat *terumah* (*Meiri;* see note 5; cf. *Tosafos* on 24b ד״ה חד; see also *Haflaah*). [It is difficult to understand why this particular example was chosen to illustrate the idea of "testimony based on a presumption" as it was explained by *Rashi* (see note 5). According to *Tosafos,* however, the point is that although the witness' testimony would have been worthless without the presumption that the second reader was a Levi, the testimony is nevertheless accepted.]

We see from the Gemara that one who reads first from the Torah can be assumed to be a Kohen at least with regard to eating *terumah.* Accordingly, a person should not be allowed to read first from the Torah unless he can prove that he is a Kohen. [One witness, however, suffices to furnish such proof, since the only halachic ramification is permission to eat *terumah* and not a declaration of genealogical fitness] (*Ritva; Rambam, Hil. Isurei Biah* 20:13; *Shulchan Aruch, Even HaEzer* 3:1). Other Rishonim, though, maintain that nowadays, when no one eats *terumah* in any event, the privilege of reading first can be given to whoever claims to be a Kohen even if he cannot prove it (*R' Moshe HaKohen,* cited by *Ran; Ramah, Even HaEzer* ibid.; see also *Chasam Sofer*).

עין משפט נר מצוה

צב א ב מיי' פ"כ מהל' איסורי ביאה הלכ' יא:
צג ג מיי' שם הלכה ה:

תוספות רי"ד

ת"ש חזקה לכהונה נשיאות כפים וחילוק גרנות ועדות. פי' המורה שהוא כהן ובאו עדים ואומרים שהוא כהן ומכירים את אביו ואת אמו ועדות חזקה הוא בתמיה ה"ק עדות הבאה מכח חזקה כחזקה. פי' בההוא דאתא לקמיה דר"א אמר מוחזקני בזה שהוא כהן א"ל מה ראית א"ל שקרא ראשון בבה"כ א"ל בחזקת שהוא כהן או בחזקת שהוא גדול פי' בחכמה כדאמרינן בעלמא רב קרי בכהני ואע"ג דלא הוה כהן א"ל שקרא אחריו לוי פי' אי לאו דכהן הוא אין לוי קורא אחריו ואמרינן בהניזקין אין שם כהן נתפרדה החבילה כשמר איבד לוי את זכותו והעלהו ר"א לכהונה כ"פ: ההוא דאתא לקמיה דר"ל א"ל מוחזקני בזה שהוא כהן א"ל מה ראית [א"ל] שקרא ראשון בבה"כ. א"ל ראיו שחלק על הגורן א"ל ר"א ואם אין שם גורן בטלה הכהונה. פי' המורה אם אין זורעים במקומו. (אר"י) תניא הרי שבא ואמר בני זה כהן הוא נאמן להאכילו בתרומה ואינו נאמן להשיאו אשה. ואמר רבי אר"ח אם אתה מאמינו להאכילו בתרומה האמינהו להשיאו אשה. ואם אינך מאמינו להשיאו אשה אל תאמינהו להאכילו בתרומה. א"ל רבי אני מאמינו להאכילו תרומה שכן בידו להאכילו תרומה. ואיני מאמינו להשיאו אשה שכן אין בידו להשיאו אשה:

ליקוטי רש"י

הדר חזייה לר"א בישות. החזיר ריש לקיש את פניו ונסתכל ברבי אלעזר בפנים זועפות שהבין ריש לקיש ששמע ר' אלעזר דבר זה מפי רבי יוחנן וכשאמרו לו לא אמרה בשמו [מכות ה:]. דבר נפחא. ר' יוחנן דמקרי בר נפחא בכולא הש"ס כמו [ב"מ דף פה:] מאן עייל בר נפחא נראה למורי דאביו של ר' יוחנן הוי נפחא ולהכי מיקרי בר נפחא ואית דמפרשי בר נפחא על שם יופיו [סנהדרין צו.]. תסתיים. תתפרש אמיתו של דבר [מגילה יד:].

לאו כולהו סלוק ת"ש חזקה לכהונה נשיאות כפים וחילוק גרנות ועדות עדות חזקה היא אלא לאו הכי קאמר נשיאות כפים כי עדות מה עדות ליוחסין אף נשיאות כפים ליוחסין לא עדות הבאה מכח חזקה כחזקה א כי ההוא דאתא לקמיה דרבי אמי א"ל מוחזקני בזה שהוא כהן א"ל מה ראית אמר ליה שקרא ראשון בבית הכנסת בחזקת שהוא כהן או בחזקת שהוא גדול שקרא אחריו לוי והעלהו ר' אמי לכהונה על פיו ההוא דאתא לקמיה דרבי יהושע בן לוי אמר ליה ב מוחזקני בזה שהוא לוי אמר ליה מה ראית אמר ליה שקרא שני בבית הכנסת בחזקת שהוא לוי או בחזקת שהוא גדול שקרא לפניו כהן והעלהו רבי יהושע בן לוי ללויה על פיו ההוא דאתא לקמיה דריש לקיש א"ל מוחזקני בזה שהוא כהן א"ל מה ראית [א"ל] שקרא ראשון בבית הכנסת א"ל ראיתיו שחילק על הגרנות אמר לו ר' אלעזר ואם אין שם גורן בטלה כהונה זימנין הוו יתבי קמיה דר' יוחנן אתא כי הא מעשה לקמיה א"ל ריש לקיש ראיתיו שחילק על הגורן א"ל ר' יוחנן ואם אין שם גורן בטלה כהונה א הדר חזייה לר"א בישות אמר שמעת מילי ג דבר נפחא ולא אמרת לן משמיה רבי ור' חייא חד העלה בן ע"פ אביו לכהונה וחד העלה אח ע"פ אחיו ללויה תסתיים דר' העלה בן ע"פ אביו לכהונה דתניא ג הרי שבא ואמר בני זה וכהן הוא נאמן להאכילו בתרומה ואינו נאמן להשיאו אשה דברי רבי אמר לו ר' חייא אם אתה מאמינו להאכילו בתרומה תאמינו להשיאו אשה ואם אי אתה מאמינו להשיאו אשה לא תאמינו לאכול בתרומה א"ל אני מאמינו להאכילו בתרומה שבידו להאכילו בתרומה ואיני מאמינו להשיאו אשה שאין בידו להשיאו אשה תסתיים ומדרבי העלה בן ע"פ אביו לכהונה ר' חייא העלה אח ע"פ אחיו ללויה ורבי חייא מאי שנא בן דלא דקרוב הוא אצל אביו אח נמי קרוב הוא אצל אחיו

במסיח

רש"י

לאו כולהו סלוק. רובן נשארו בבבל דכתיב כל הקהל כאחד ארבע רבוא (עזרא ב): ועדות. אם באו עדים שהוא כהן שמכירין את אביו ואת אמו: ועדות חזקה היא. בתמיה וכי עדות חזקה קרי ליה: עדות הבאה מכח חזקה כחזקה. העדות נקבל ונאכילו בתרומה כאילו ראינוה אנן לאותה חזקה שזה העיד: או בחזקת שהוא גדול. כדאמרינן בעלמא ג (גיטין דף נט:) רב קרי בכהני ואע"ג דלאו כהן הוה: שקרא אחריו לוי. ואי לאו כהן הוא אין לוי קורא אחריו דאמרינן במסכת גיטין (שם) אם אין שם כהן נתפרדה חבילה ומפרשינן דאין לוי קורא במקום שאין כהן ויש מפרשים נתפרדה החבילה שבמקום שאין כהן אם רוצה ישראל לקרות לפני לוי קורא ודוקא דאין שם כהן אבל היכא דאיכא כהן לא נתפרדה החבילה ולא יקרא ישראל גדול לפני לוי והכא כהן אחר הוה התם הלכך אי לאו דהאי כהן הוה לא הוה לוי קרי אבתריה: שקרא לפניו כהן. ואי לאו דהאי לוי הוא לא היה קורא שני אלא שלישי שנים כהנים היו קורין לפניו והוא שלישי דהכי אמרינן במסכת גיטין אם אין שם לוי קורא כהן במקומו: ללויה. לתת לו מעשר ראשון: ואם אין שם גורן. אם אין שם זורעי תבואה במקומו: זימנין. פעם אחרת: הדר. ריש לקיש: חזייה לרבי אלעזר בישות. החזיר פניו ונסתכל ברבי אלעזר בעין רעה שהבין שמפי ר' יוחנן שמע לשון זה וכשאמר לשון זה לא אמרה בשם רבי יוחנן לפיכך לא קיבלה הימנו: להשיאו אשה. שמא ממזר או נתין הוא: שיש בידו להאכילו תרומה. שהרי הוא כהן והכל חולקין לו תרומה:

והטבילוני

מסורת הש"ס

א) [מכות ה:], ב) [פירושו תמצא ברש"י סנהדרין לו. ד"ה טבא וכו' אביו של ר"י וכו' על שם יפיו], ג) [מגילה כב.], ד) [ועיין היטב תוס' קדושין פ. ד"ה לא שנו].

תוספות ישנים

א) [ולפ"ז גרסינן לעיל שפיר כי מסקינן מתרומה ליוחסין הנ"מ בתרומה דאורייתא כו' ומ"מ אינו סותר ראייתו דהשתא נמי יכול לומר דאי לא תימא הכי היכי הוי פרסי ידייהו הא אתו לאסוקינהו לתרומה דאורייתא ועוד דהשתא להאי פירושא פשיטא ליה לתלמודא דאין מעלין מתרומה דרבנן דמ"ל אפי' לדאורייתא וכ"ש ליוחסין לאב"א ע"כ אינו ראיה ואין חוזר מדבריו דמעיקרא לא הביא ראיה מתרומה אלא משום דאכיל מדאורייתא. ת"י]:

ב) [דליכא למימר ליוחסין להשיאו אשה דהא לרבי יהודה במקום שנאמן להאכילו תרומה נאמן גם להשיאו אשה דמעלין מתרומה ליוחסין. ת"י]:

ג) [ועוד קשה לר"י דאין זה מיגו טוב שאם יוליכנו בגורן ויתן לו חלקו הרי יפסיד והשתא דקאמר שהוא כהן נוטל כל אחד חלקו ואין לפרש שבידו להאכילו בתרומה בשעה שהעיד שהיה יכול לומר אינו בני וכהן הוא דא"כ להשיאו אשה נמי נימא הכי. בתוס' לא תירץ והתירוץ שבפנים מצאתי]: ת"י:

תוספות

עדות הבאה מכח חזקה. פי' שאנו יודעין שהוא כהן מחמת הקורא אחריו שמוחזק לן שהוא לוי: שקרא אחריו לוי. לפירוש ר"י הלוי שפירש בגיטין (נט: ושם) אם אין שם כהן נתפרדה חבילה שיקרא ישראל גדול לפני לוי יש לפרש הכא שקרא אחריו לוי קטן מישראל שקרא אחריו:

שקרא לפניו כהן. פירוש פעם אחת: הרי שאמר בני זה וכהן הוא. מדנקט בני זה וכהן הוא משמע שאינו ידוע לנו אם הוא בנו והוא בא להעיד שהוא בנו ושהוא כהן שאינו בן גרושה דאי ידוע לנו שהוא בנו מה הוה ליה למינקט בני זה כהן בלא וי"ו ותימה דר"ח יהא נאמן לכולי עלמא לתרומה וליוחסין במגו דאי בעי אמר אינו בנו וי"ל דאע"ג דליכא מגו לא מהימן לדבריו דקרוב הוא כדאמרינן בהחולץ (יבמות דף מז. ושם) לדבריך כותי אתה ואין עדות לכותי ואין אדם נאמן לפסול את בנו ואע"ג דרבי קאמר בסמוך אני מאמינו להאכילו בתרומה שהרי בידו להאכילו בתרומה אלמא אע"ג דקרוב הוא לדבריו נאמן במגו התם ודאי מהימנינן ליה משום דאית ליה מגו אפי' ידעינן שהוא בנו אבל האי מגו לא הוה ידעינן שהוא בנו ליכא מגו: נאמן להאכילו בתרומה. פירוש אע"ג דליכא אלא הוא שהוא קרוב דקסבר רבי אין מעלין מתרומה ליוחסין ואין נאמן להשיאו אשה פירוש להצטרף עם אחר להשיאו אשה כיון שהוא קרוב והשתא אתי שפיר הא דאמר ר' חייא אם אתה מאמינו יחידי להאכילו בתרומה אע"פ שהוא קרוב האמינהו עם אחר להשיאו אשה אבל אין לפרש דאין נאמן יחידי להשיאו אשה דפשיטא דאינו נאמן והא לא הוה אמר רבי חייא האמינהו לישא דלא משתמיט שום תנא למימר דעד אחד כשר ליוחסין והא נמי אין לפרש דנאמן עם אחר להאכילו בתרומה דאי הוה צריך שני עדים בתרומה א"כ הוה סבר דמעלין מתרומה ליוחסין ואם כן היכי מכשיר קרוב כיון דאינו נאמן להשיאו אשה וא"ת כיון דסבירא ליה דאין מעלין מתרומה ליוחסין אם כן היכי מוקמינן בהגוזל בתרא (ב"ק קיד:) ההיא דרבי דלקמן במסיח לפי תומו ונאמן בתרומה דרבנן אבל בתרומה דאורייתא לא מהימן והא לרבי כיון דס"ל דאין מעלין מתרומה ליוחסין אם כן ס"ל דמעלין מתרומה דרבנן לתרומה דאורייתא כדמשמע לעיל דכל היכא דאכיל בתרומה דרבנן אכיל נמי בתרומה דאורייתא וי"ל דהאי דמצרכינן למימר לעיל דמעלין מתרומה דרבנן לחלה דאורייתא או איפכא היינו משום דלא תקשי למ"ד אין מעלין מנשיאות כפים ליוחסין אבל רב אשי בהגוזל אפשר דסבירא ליה כמ"ד מעלין ועוד נראה דלכולי עלמא בין למאן דאמר מעלין מתרומה ליוחסין בין למאן דאמר אין מעלין מעלין מתרומת דגן תירוש ויצהר של א"י ואפי' היא דרבנן לחלה דאורייתא כיון שבזמן המקדש הויא דאורייתא אבל תרומת פירות או תרומת חו"ל אין מעלין לכ"ע אפי' לתרומת דגן תירוש ויצהר של א"י דרבנן דדוקא בתרומת א"י או חלה דאורייתא בסוריא אמר מעלין מדרבנן לדאורייתא אבל לא בבבל וההיא דהגוזל בתרא איירי בתרומת פירות או חוצה לארץ וכן מתני' דלקמן דנאמנים להעיד בגודלן מה שראו בקוטנן ומוקי לה בתרומה דרבנן היינו בתרומת פירות או חוצה לארץ ולמ"ד מעלין מתרומה ליוחסין אפי' מתרומת דגן תירוש ויצהר דא"י אפילו היא דרבנן מעלין דהא ר' יוסי ס"ל בפ' יוצא דופן (נדה מו:) תרומה בזמן הזה דרבנן ודוקא משום דקסבר חולקין תרומה לעבד בלא רבו הוא דאית ליה דאין מעלין הא אי הוה סבר דאין חולקין הוה מודה דמעלין והא דאמר לעיל מעיקרא אכול בתרומה דרבנן א) ולבסוף אכול בתרומה דאורייתא לא מכח שהיו אוכלין בגולה קדשי הגבול אוכלין בתרומה דאורייתא אלא משום שהיו נושאים כפים בגולה שמעלין מנשיאות כפים לתרומה דאורייתא אע"ג דהרי אתם בחזקתכם במה הייתם אוכלין בגולה כו' משמע שמכח אכילה היה מתירו אין לחוש בכך ולהכי לישנא דקאמר בתרומה דרבנן אכול בדאורייתא לא אכול מה שלא העלם מנשיאות כפים לתרומה דאורייתא היינו משום דריע חזקייהו: **נאמן** להאכילו בתרומה. הקשה ריב"ס דתנן בפרק עשרה יוחסין (קדושין דף עט: ושם) מי שילא הוא ואשתו למדינת הים וכשחזר הביא עמו בנים ומתה אשתו צריך להביא ראיה על בניו ואינו נאמן להאכילם בתרומה כדמוכח התם בגמ' דתניא התם הביא ראיה על הגדולים א"צ ראיה על הקטנים ואמר רשב"ל עלה לא שנו אלא בקדשי הגבול אבל ליוחסין לא והיכי קאמר רבי הכא דאב נאמן להאכילו בתרומה ותירץ דרבי תנא הוא ופליג ור"ת אומר דההיא דקדושין אתיא כר' יהודה דאמר אין מעלין לכהונה ע"פ עד אחד וקדשי הגבול דהתם היינו לכל דבר קדושה כגון תרומה ונשיאות כפים ויוחסין והא דקאמר התם ב) אבל ליוחסין לא היינו יוחסין לקורבה כגון לסקול ולשרוף על ידו כדמסיק התם ר' יוחנן אמר אף ליוחסין ואזדא ר' יוחנן לטעמיה דאמר סוקלין על החזקות ד) [א"כ הכא באשתו עמו דאין צריך להביא ראיה כדאמר התם]: **שבידו** להאכילו בתרומה. ג) תימה איך נאמין אותו על תרומה בהאי מגו הא אין בידו להאכילו אחר מיתה וא"כ אין זה מגו כמו שמצינו ביש נוחלין (ב"ב קכח.) גבי בכור ובפרק בתרא דקדושין (דף עח:) דתניא יכיר יכירנו לאחרים מכאן נאמן אדם לומר זה בני בכור כו' למאי הלכתא אי לתת לו פי שנים אילו בעי למיתב ליה מתנה מי לא יהיב ליה לא צריכא בנכסים שנפלו לו כשהוא גוסס אלמא אי לאו קרא לא הוה נאמן לפי שאין בידו וי"ל דלא דמי דהכא כיון דנאמן להאכילו בחייו משום דבידו סברא הוא דנאמן אפילו לאחר מיתה:

במסיח

ואלא מאי גדולה חזקה מעיקרא אכול בתרומה דרבנן השתא אכול בתרומה דאורייתא ואי בעית אימא השתא נמי בתרומה דרבנן אכול בתרומה דאורייתא לא אכול וכי מסקינן מתרומה ליוחסין בתרומה דאורייתא בתרומה דרבנן לא מסקינן ואלא מאי גדולה חזקה דאע"ג דאיכא למיגזר משום תרומה דאורייתא לא גזרינן ובתרומה דאורייתא לא אכול והא כתיב אשר לא יאכלו מקדש הקדשים מקדש הקדשים הוא דלא אכול הא בתרומה דאורייתא אכול ה"ק לא במידי דאיקרי קדש דכתיב וכל זר לא יאכל קדש ולא במידי דאיקרי קדשים דכתיב ובת כהן כי תהיה לאיש זר היא בתרומת הקדשים לא תאכל ואמר מר במורם מן הקדשים לא תאכל ת"ש חזקה לכהונה נשיאות כפים בבבל ואכילת חלה בסוריא וחילוק מתנות בכרכין קתני מיהת נשיאות כפים מאי לאו ליוחסין לא לתרומה והא דומיא דאכילת חלה קתני מה אכילת חלה ליוחסין אף נשיאות כפים ליוחסין לא אכילת חלה גופה לתרומה קסבר חלה בזמן הזה דרבנן ותרומה דאורייתא ומסקינן מחלה דרבנן לתרומה דאורייתא וכדאפיך להו רב הונא בריה דרב יהושע לרבנן ת"ש חזקה לכהונה נשיאות כפים וחילוק גרנות בא"י ובסוריא ובכל מקום שלשלוחי ראש חודש מגיעין נשיאות כפים ראיה אבל לא חילוק גרנות ובבל כסוריא רשב"ג אומר אף אלכסנדריא של מצרים בראשונה מפני שבית דין קבועין שם קתני מיהת נשיאות כפים מאי לאו ליוחסין לא לחלה הא דומיא דחילוק גרנות קתני מה חילוק גרנות ליוחסין אף נשיאות כפים ליוחסין לא חילוק גרנות גופה לחלה וקסבר תרומה בזמן הזה דרבנן וחלה דאורייתא ומסקינן מתרומה דרבנן לחלה דאורייתא וכדאשכחינהו רב הונא בריה דרב יהושע לרבנן דאמר רב הונא בריה דרב יהושע אשכחתינהו לרבנן בבי רב דיתבי וקאמרי אפילו למאן דאמר תרומה בזמן הזה דרבנן חלה דאורייתא שהרי ז' שכיבשו וז' שחילקו נתחייבו בחלה ולא נתחייבו בתרומה ואמינא להו אנא אדרבה אפילו למ"ד תרומה בזמן הזה דאורייתא חלה דרבנן דתניא בבואכם אל הארץ אי בבואכם יכול משנכנסו לה שנים ושלשה מרגלים ת"ל בבואכם בביאת כולכם אמרתי ולא בביאת מקצתכם וכי אסקינהו עזרא

לאו

רש"י

ואלא מאי גדולה חזקה. דקאמר ר' יוסי למה לנו [לחוש] להשבית חזקתם כי מה יש לחוש לבטלה: בתרומה דרבנן. שהרי בגולה היו שאין שם תרומה מן התורה דכל מצוה שהיא תלויה בארץ אינה נוהגת אלא בארץ כדאמרינן בקידושין (דף לו:): ואיבעית אימא השתא נמי בתרומה דרבנן אכול. תרומת פירות האילן וירק: דאורייתא. דגן תירוש ויצהר לא אכול ומש"ה לא קשיא למ"ד מעלין מתרומה ליוחסין דכי מסקינן ליוחסין מתרומה דאורייתא כו': דאיכא למיגזר משום תרומה דאורייתא. שהרי לארץ באו ומצויה שם תרומה גמורה דאורייתא מה שלא היה מצוי להם בגולה ויש לחוש פן יאכלום בה: לא במידי דאקרי קדש. והיינו תרומה: וכל זר לא יאכל קדש. בתרומה משתעי דכתיב בפרשה לעיל מיניה ובא השמש וטהר ואחר יאכל מן הקדשים ואוקמינן בתרומה ביבמות בהערל (דף עד:): ולא במידי דאקרי קדשים. אפילו חזה ושוק של שלמים הנאכלים לנשי כהנים ולעבדיהם: ואמר מר. ביבמות בפרק יש מותרות בבת כהן שניסת לישראל ונעשית אלמנה וגרושה וזרע אין לה שחוזרת לתרומת אביה ואינה חוזרת לחזה ושוק וילפינן לה מהאי קרא כי תהיה לאיש זר היא בתרומת הקדשים לא תאכל עוד: חזקה לכהונה. להעיד עליו שהוא כהן: נשיאות כפים בבבל. הרואהו נושא כפיו בבבל מעיד עליו בכל מקום שהוא כהן ומקבלין הימנו לפי שיש שם ישיבה וב"ד קבוע בודקין אחר נושאי כפים אבל אכילת חלה בסוריא אינה חזקה דחולה בארץ לאו דאורייתא תרומה דיליה ולא קפדי כולי האי: ואכילת חלה בסוריא. היא ארם צובה שכיבשה דוד ומיכרה לא"י וקסבר האי תנא כיבוש יחיד שמיה כיבוש וחלתה ותרומתה דאורייתא וקס"ד תנא חלה וה"ה לתרומה: וחילוק מתנות. הזרוע והלחיים והקיבה: בכרכין. ואע"ג דלאיסורן אין איסור לזרים הואיל וכרכים מקום שווקין הן ומצויין בו עוברים ושבים המכירין בו אי לאו דכהן הוא לא מחליף נפשיה: לא לתרומה. הרואהו נושא כפיו בבבל או אוכל חלה בסוריא והעיד עליו בא"י מקבלין עדותו להאכילו תרומה אבל לא ליוחסין: מה אכילת חלה. עדות חזקתה: ליוחסין. דאי לתרומה פשיטא היא גופה תרומה היא וכבר הוחזק בה: ומסקינן מחלה דרבנן כו'. דאי לאו כהן הוא לא הוו ספו ליה חלה גזירה משום תרומה: וכדאפיך. לקמן מפרש: נשיאות כפים וחילוק גרנות. דתרומה: בא"י. נושאי כפים דאיכא ב"ד קבועין ובדקי וחילוק גרנות קס"ד השתא לתרומה בזמן הזה דאורייתא וכיון דעון מיתה איכא מסקינן מינה ליוחסין: בסוריא וכ"מ ששלוחי א"י מגיעין. להודיע לגולה יום שקידשו ב"ד את החדש לעשות פסח בזמנו דהיינו היושבים בתוך מהלך חמשה עשר יום: נשיאות כפים ראיה. לפי שב"ד קבוע שם שמקבל שליחות החדש של ב"ד הגדול: אבל לא חילוק גרנות. דתרומה דידהו לאו דאורייתא ובסוריא נמי האי תנא סבר כיבוש יחיד לא שמיה כיבוש ופלוגתא דתנאי היא בהך מילתא (ע"ז דף כא.): בבי רב. בית המדרש קרי בי רב: נתחייבו בחלה. דכתיב בבואכם אל הארץ ותניא בספרי ר' ישמעאל אומר שינה הכתוב ביאה זו מכל ביאות שבתורה שבכולן נאמר כי תבאו וכאן נאמר בבואכם ללמדך שכיון שנכנסו לה נתחייבו: ולא נתחייבו בתרומות ומעשרות. דכתיב דגנך תבואת זרעך המיוחדת לך (ה) ועוד שהרי תלה הכתוב המעשר במנין שנות השמטה דכתיב בשנה השלישית שנת המעשר ושמטות לא מנו אלא משכבשו וחילקו כדאמרינן בסדר עולם ובמסכת ערכין (דף יב:): הכי גרסינן אי בבואכם יכול משנכנסו לה שנים ושלשה מרגלים תלמוד לומר בבואכם בביאת כולכם כו'. והכי פירושו כיון דשינה הכתוב ביאה זו לכתוב בה בבואכם ולא כתב כי תבאו יכול משנכנסו לה מרגלים ת"ל כו':

תוספות

ואלא מאי גדולה חזקה. בשלמא אי אין מעלין ניחא הא דגדולה חזקה אע"ג דליכא למיחש לב"ד טועין שיעלו מן נשיאות כפים לקדשי קדשים (ט) [ואע"ג דבלא חזקה מעלין לתרומה ע"פ עד אחד ולא חיישינן לב"ד טועין שמא יעלו ליוחסין השתא סבר המקשן דיוחסין חמירא ולא אתו למיטעי כמו לקדשי קדשים] אבל השתא דאמרת טעמא דריע חזקייהו ולא חיישינן דלמא אתי לאסוקי כיון דלא אתי למטעי מאי גדולה חזקה: או דלמא אפילו למ"ד אין מעלין ה"מ תרומה דמתאכלא בצינעה כו'. תימה מה תולה באכילה והא פשיטא דלכ"ע אין מעלין מאכילת תרומה ליוחסין דהא איכא למיחש דלמא עבד כהן הוא אלא בחלוקת תרומה (א) בגורן הוא דפליגי אם מעלים ליוחסין אם לאו ובמעלין מתרומה ליוחסין לא איפליגו בה תנאי בהדיא אלא דתליא הא פלוגתא בפלוגתא אם חולקין תרומה לעבד בלא רבו אם לאו למ"ד חולקין אין מעלין דדלמא עבד הוא והכי איבעי ליה למימר הכא אפילו למ"ד אין מעלין ה"מ תרומה דחולקין לעבד בלא רבו ואיכא למיחש דלמא עבד הוא אבל נשיאו' כפים לעולם אימא לך דמעלין דאין עבד נושא כפיו: [נ"ל דשפיר נקט דמתאכלא בצינעא דלמ"ד מעלין מאכילת תרומה נמי מעלין ובענין דליכא למיחש שהוא עבד שיצא מבית הספר וטעמא כיון דעון מיתה הוא חיישינן שמא יעלוהו ליוחסין ולכך איצטריך שני עדים להאכילו בתרומה ולכך נמי אין חולקין לעבד אלא א"כ רבו עמו ומ"ד אין מעלין אע"ג דעון מיתה הוא לא חיישינן להכי שמא יעלוהו כיון דבצנעא הויא אכילת תרומה וכן חלוקה אבל נשיאות כפים דאיפרסם איבעיא ליה אי חיישינן שמא יעלוהו משום דאי לאו דכהן הוא לא הוה חציף כולי האי ולא הוי מצי למנקט כמו שכתבו התוס' אפילו למ"ד אין מעלין משום דאיכא למיחש דלמא עבד הוא דלא תליא בהכי דאפילו היכא דליכא למיחש דלמא עבד הוא אין מעלין כמו ביוצא מבית הספר או שמעידין עליו שאינו עבד ואדרבה הא דחולקין לו בלא רבו היינו משום דאין מעלין ועיקר טעמא דפלוגתייהו משום מעלין ואין מעלין דאי לאו הכי קשה באיזה סברא פליגי כמו שהקשו לעיל] (ת"י):

וכי מסקינן מתרומה ליוחסין ה"מ בדאורייתא כו'. רבינו יצחק בן רבינו מאיר לא גרים לה דהא איבעית אימא רב נחמן קאמר לה ואי גרסי' לה א"כ היה סותר בעצמו ראיה שהביא דאי לא תימא הכי למ"ד מעלין מתרומה ליוחסין הא אתי לאסוקי אלא טעמא משום דריע חזקייהו ואין זו סוגיית הש"ס אם לא יאמר ולאו מילתא היא דאמרי ובפ' עשרה יוחסין (קדושין סט:) גרסינן לה ואגב שיטפא דהתם שיבשו לכותבה כאן: לא במידי דאיקרי קדש. וא"ת תרומה נמי איקרי קדשים דכתיב ובא השמש וטהר ואחר יאכל מן הקדשים וההוא קרא איירי בתרומה להעריב שמשו אוכל בתרומה וי"ל דודאי גבי טמא תרומה מיקרי קדשים אבל הכא אאכילת זר קאמר דלא אשכחן קדשים גבי אכילת זר: נשיאות כפים בבבל. דוקא נשיאות כפים ולא אכילת חלה ואע"ג דבסוריא נמי הוי מדרבנן אין מדקדקין בבבל כמו בסוריא דסבר האי תנא כיבוש יחיד שמיה כיבוש ואכילת חלה בסוריא ה"ה נשיאות כפים כדמוכח לקמן: לא חילוק גרנות גופה לחלה וקסבר תרומה כו'. וא"ל דפליגי הנך ברייתות בפלוגתא דרב הונא בריה דרב יהושע ורבנן דאי לאו הכי בחד מהנך ברייתות ממה נפשך איכא למידק דמעלין מנשיאות כפים ליוחסין ופליגי נמי דלברייתא קמייתא אכילת חלה בסוריא חזקה לתרומה וכל שכן דאכילת תרומה דאורייתא דהויא חזקה לאכילת חלה דרבנן ובברייתא שניה קתני דחילוק גרנות דהיינו תרומה בסוריא לא הויא חזקה לחלה:

עדות

לאו

מסורת הש"ס

א) יבמות פח. פז. קדושין סט:, ב) [עיין תוס' שבת י: ד"ה הכא], ג) [תוספתא פאה פ"ד], ד) נדה מז., ה) [ב"מ פט.], ו) [בנדה מז. וכן בב"מ פט. איתא בהלה דברים מרוויחין], ז) [עיין תוס' נדה מז. ד"ה ל"ג אלו נאמר], ח) [ועיין רש"י בנדה מז. וב"מ פט. מפרש בכל מקום טעם אחר], ט) נ"י כ"י.

הגהות הב"ח

(א) תד"ה או דלמא כו' אלא בחלוקת תרומה וכו'. נ"ב וכן פרש"י יבמות דף צט ע"ב:

תורה אור השלם

א) וַיֹּאמֶר הַתִּרְשָׁתָא לָהֶם אֲשֶׁר לֹא יֹאכְלוּ מִקֹּדֶשׁ הַקֳּדָשִׁים עַד עֲמֹד כֹּהֵן לְאוּרִים וּלְתֻמִּים: [עזרא ב, סג]

ב) וְכָל זָר לֹא יֹאכַל קֹדֶשׁ תּוֹשַׁב כֹּהֵן וְשָׂכִיר לֹא יֹאכַל קֹדֶשׁ: [ויקרא כב, י]

ג) וּבַת כֹּהֵן כִּי תִהְיֶה לְאִישׁ זָר הִוא בִּתְרוּמַת הַקֳּדָשִׁים לֹא תֹאכֵל: [ויקרא כב, יב]

ד) דַּבֵּר אֶל בְּנֵי יִשְׂרָאֵל וְאָמַרְתָּ אֲלֵהֶם בְּבֹאֲכֶם אֶל הָאָרֶץ אֲשֶׁר אֲנִי מֵבִיא אֶתְכֶם שָׁמָּה: [במדבר טו, יח]

עין משפט נר מצוה

פז א מיי' פ"כ מהל' איסורי ביאה הלכה א ופ"ו מהל' תרומות ה"ב:
פח ב מיי' פ"כ מהל' איסורי ביאה הל' ד:
פט ג מיי' שם הלכה יא טוש"ע אה"ע סימן ג סעיף ב:
צ ד מיי' שם הלכה ג ופ"א מהל' תרומות ה"א סמג עשין מג טוש"ע י"ד סימן שלא סעיף ב:
צא ה מיי' פ"כ מהל' איסורי ביאה הלכה ג סמג עשין קמ טוש"ע י"ד סי' שכב סעיף ג:

ליקוטי רש"י

[התחלת ליקוטי רש"י ששייך לכאן נדפס בדף כד:]

ולא במידי דאיקרי קדשים. חזה ושוק של שלמים דאשכחן דאיקרי קדשים [קידושין סט:]. לאיש זר. ללוי וישראל [ויקרא כב, יב]. במורם מן הקדשים. חזה ושוק [קידושין שם]. לא תאכל. ואפילו זרע אין לה ושבה אל בית אביה חוזרת לתרומה ואינה חוזרת לחזה ושוק [שם ע.]. [illegible]

אַדְּרַבָּה – **On the contrary!** אֲפִילּוּ לְמַאן דְּאָמַר תְּרוּמָה בַּזְּמַן הַזֶּה דְּאוֹרַיְיתָא – **Even according to the one who says that nowadays *terumah* is Biblical,**[30] חַלָּה דְּרַבָּנָן – ***challah* is Rabbinic.** דְּתַנְיָא – **For it was taught in a Baraisa:** "בְּבֹאֲכֶם אֶל־הָאָרֶץ" – Scripture states that you must separate *challah* *UPON YOUR COMING INTO THE LAND.*[31] אִי "בְּבֹאֲכֶם" – SINCE it states *UPON YOUR COMING,* יָכוֹל מִשֶּׁנִּכְנְסוּ לָהּ שְׁנַיִם וּשְׁלֹשָׁה מְרַגְּלִים – IT MIGHT HAVE BEEN thought that the obligation of *challah* begins ONCE TWO OR THREE SPIES HAVE ENTERED [THE LAND].[32] תַּלְמוּד לוֹמַר "בְּבֹאֲכֶם" – [THE TORAH] therefore STATES: *UPON "YOUR" COMING,* which teaches: בְּבִיאַת כּוּלְּכֶם אָמַרְתִּי – It is only UPON THE ENTRY OF *ALL* OF YOU that I [God] SAID you must separate *challah,* וְלֹא בְּבִיאַת מִקְצָתְכֶם – AND NOT UPON THE ENTRY OF only SOME OF YOU.[33] The verse thus conveys that all (or most) Jews must be in Eretz Yisrael for the *challah* requirement to apply.

Rav Huna the son of R' Yehoshua concludes his proof: וְכִי אַסְקִינְהוּ עֶזְרָא – **And when Ezra took up [the returnees]** from Babylonia to Eretz Yisrael,

NOTES

the entry of the Jewish people to Eretz Yisrael, because the Torah commands that *challah* be taken: בְּבֹאֲכֶם אֶל־הָאָרֶץ, *Upon your coming into the Land* (*Numbers* 15:18). Now, in all other instances the Torah expresses entry into the Land in terms of "when" you enter – e.g. כִּי תָבֹאוּ, *when you come,* or כִּי יְבִיאֲךָ, *when He will bring you.* The passage concerning *challah* is unique in that the Torah states "upon" your entry. From this choice of expression, *Sifri* deduces that the mitzvah of *challah* took effect immediately upon their entry into Eretz Yisrael. This is in contrast to the obligation of *terumah,* which did not begin until after the Jews had conquered and apportioned the Land (fourteen years later). We derive this from the Torah's command (*Deuteronomy* 18:4) that *terumah* be separated from *your grain, your wine and your [olive] oil,* which implies that it must be entirely *yours,* and that was not the case until after the Land had been apportioned (*Rashi*). [See *Rashi* for a source as to why the obligation of *maaser* did not take effect immediately (see also *Rashi* to *Bava Metzia* 89a and to *Niddah* 47a).]

It is thus evident that the Biblical mitzvah of *challah* is not dependent on the Land's sanctification [for Joshua did not sanctify the Land until after it had been conquered and apportioned (see *Responsa of Shaagas Aryeh HaChadashos* §8)]. Therefore, this Biblical obligation should apply nowadays as well, even according to the opinion that the second sanctification of the Land (under Ezra) ceased at the time of the Second Temple's destruction (*Chazon Ish, Even HaEzer* 135; *Shaagas Aryeh* ibid.; see *Turei Even* to *Megillah* 10a). [For *Rambam's* view on these matters, see, *Hil. Terumos* 1:26 with commentaries; *Mishneh LaMelech* on *Hil. Maachalos Asuros* 10:11 and *Chidushei Rabbeinu Chaim HaLevi* on *Hil. Terumos* 1:10.]

30. This opinion holds that Ezra's sanctification of the Land remained in effect even after the destruction of the Second Temple (*Ritva;* see note 28).

31. *Numbers* 15:18 (see note 29).

32. Since the Torah wrote בְּבֹאֲכֶם, *upon your coming,* to indicate that the obligation of *challah* takes effect immediately (see note 29) one might have thought that it begins as soon as just a few Jews have entered the Land (*Rashi*).

33. The possessive suffix כֶם, *your,* indicates that it must be *your* coming (i.e. the coming of the entire nation, to whom this commandment was addressed) that effects the obligation of *challah* (see *Torah Temimah* to *Numbers* ibid. §32; see also *Tosafos* to *Niddah* 47a ד״ה ל״ג אילו לא וד״ה לא כולהו).

ואלא מאי גדולה חזקה מעיקרא אכול בתרומה דרבנן השתא אכול בתרומה דאורייתא ואי בעית אימא השתא נמי בתרומה דרבנן אכול בתרומה דאורייתא לא אכול וכי מסקינן מתרומה ליוחסין בתרומה דאורייתא בתרומה דרבנן לא מסקינן ואלא מאי גדולה חזקה דאע"ג דאיכא למיגזר משום תרומה דאורייתא לא גזרינן ובתרומה דאורייתא לא אכול והא כתיב א) אשר לא יאכלו מקדש הקדשים מקדש הקדשים הוא דלא אכול הא בתרומה דאורייתא אכול ה"ק לא במידי דאיקרי קדש דכתיב ב) וכל זר לא יאכל קדש ולא במידי דאיקרי קדשים דכתיב ג) ובת כהן כי תהיה לאיש זר היא בתרומת הקדשים לא תאכל ואמר מר במורם מן הקדשים לא תאכל ת"ש חזקה לכהונה נשיאות כפים בבבל ואכילת חלה בסוריא וחילוק מתנות בכרכין קתני מיהת נשיאות כפים מאי לאו ליוחסין לא לתרומה והא דומיא דאכילת חלה קתני מה אכילת חלה ליוחסין אף נשיאות כפים ליוחסין לא אכילת חלה גופה לתרומה קסבר חלה בזמן הזה דרבנן ותרומה דאורייתא ומסקינן מחלה דרבנן לתרומה דאורייתא וכדאפיך להו רב הונא בריה דרב יהושע לרבנן ת"ש חזקה לכהונה נשיאות כפים וחילוק גרנות בא"י ובסוריא ובכל מקום ששלוחי ראש חודש מגיעין נשיאות כפים ראיה אבל לא חילוק גרנות ובבל כסוריא רשב"ג אומר אף אלכסנדריא של מצרים בראשונה מפני שבית דין קבועין שם קתני מיהת נשיאות כפים מאי לאו ליוחסין לא לחלה הא דומיא דחילוק גרנות קתני מה חילוק גרנות ליוחסין אף נשיאות כפים ליוחסין לא חילוק גרנות גופה לחלה קסבר תרומה בזמן הזה דרבנן וחלה דאורייתא ומסקינן מתרומה דרבנן לחלה דאורייתא וכדאשכחינהו רב הונא בריה דרב יהושע לרבנן דאמר רב הונא בריה דרב יהושע אשכחתינהו לרבנן בבי רב דיתבי וקאמרי אפילו למאן דאמר תרומה בזמן הזה דרבנן חלה דאורייתא שהרי ז' שכיבשו וז' שחילקו נתחייבו בחלה ולא נתחייבו בתרומה ואמינא להו אנא אדרבה אפילו למ"ד תרומה בזמן הזה דאורייתא חלה דרבנן דתניא ד) בבואכם אל הארץ אי בבואכם יכול משנכנסו לה שנים ושלשה מרגלים ת"ל בבואכם בביאת כולכם אמרתי ולא בביאת מקצתכם וכי אסקינהו עזרא לאו

ואלא מאי גדולה חזקה. דקאמר ר' יוסי למה לנו [לחוש] להסבית חזקתם כי מה יש לחוש לבטלה: **בתרומה דרבנן.** שהרי בגולה היו שאין שם תרומה מן התורה דכל מצוה שהיא תלויה בארץ אינה נוהגת אלא בארץ כדאמרינן בקידושין (דף לו:): **ואיבעית אימא השתא נמי בתרומה דרבנן אכול.** תרומת פירות האילן וירק: **דאורייתא.** דגן תירוש ויצהר לא אכול ומש"ה לא קשיא למ"ד מעלין מתרומה ליוחסין דכי מסקינן ליוחסין מתרומה דאורייתא כו': **דאיכא למיגזר משום תרומה דאורייתא.** שהרי לארץ באו ומצאו שם תרומה גמורה דאורייתא מה שלא היה מצוי להם בגולה ויש לחוש פן יאכילום בה: **לא במידי דאקרי קדש.** והיינו תרומה: **וכל זר לא יאכל קדש.** בתרומה משתעי דכתיב בפרשה לעיל מיניה ובא השמש וטהר ואחר יאכל מן הקדשים ואוקמינן בתרומה ביבמות בהערל (דף עד:): **ולא במידי דאקרי קדשים.** אפילו חזה ושוק של שלמים הנאכלים לנשי כהנים ולעבדיהם: **ואמר מר.** ביבמות בפרק יש מותרות בבת כהן שניסת לישראל ונעשית אלמנה וגרושה וזרע אין לה שחוזרת לתרומת אביה ואינה חוזרת לחזה ושוק ויליף לה מהאי קרא כי תהיה לאיש זר היא בתרומת הקדשים לא תאכל עוד: **חזקה לכהונה.** להעיד עליו שהוא כהן: **נשיאות כפים בבבל.** הרואהו נושא כפיו בבבל מעיד עליו בכל מקום שהוא כהן ומקבלין הימנו לפי שיש שם ישיבה וב"ד קבוע בודקין אחר נושאי כפים אבל אכילת חלה ותרומה אינה חזקה דחולה לארץ לאו דאורייתא תרומה דיליה ולא קפדי כולי האי: **ואכילת חלה בסוריא.** היא ארם צובה שכיבשה דוד וחיברה לא"י וקסבר האי תנא כיבוש יחיד שמיה כיבוש וחלתה ותרומתה דאורייתא וקס"ד תנא חלה וה"ה לתרומה: **וחילוק מתנות.** הזרוע והלחיים: **בכרכין.** ואע"ג דלאיסורן אין איסור לזרים הואיל וכרכים מקום שווקין הן ומצויין בו עוברים ושבים המכירין בו אי לאו דכהן הוא לא מחליף נפשיה: **לא לתרומה.** הרואהו נושא כפיו בבבל או אוכל חלה בסוריא והעיד עליו בא"י מקבלין עדותו להאכילו תרומה אבל לא ליוחסין: **מה אכילת חלה.** עדות חזקתה: **ליוחסין.** דאי לתרומה פשיטא היא גופה תרומה היא וכבר הוחזק בה: **ומסקינן מחלה דרבנן כו'.** דאי לאו כהן הוא לא הוו ספו ליה חלה גזירה משום תרומה: **וכדאפיך.** לקמן מפרש: **נשיאות כפים וחילוק גרנות.** לתרומה: **בא"י.** נושאי כפים דאיכא ב"ד קבועין ובדקי וחילוק גרנות קס"ד השתא דתרומה בזמן הזה דאורייתא וכיון דעון מיתה היא מסקינן מינה ליוחסין: **בסוריא וכ"מ ששלוחי א"י מגיעין.** להודיע לגולה יום שקידשו ב"ד את החדש לעשות פסח בזמנו דהיינו היושבים בתוך מהלך חמשה עשר יום: **נשיאות כפים ראיה.** לפי שב"ד קבוע שם שמקבלין שליחות החדש של ב"ד הגדול: **אבל לא חילוק גרנות.** דתרומה דידהו לאו דאורייתא ובסוריא נמי האי תנא סבר כיבוש יחיד לא שמיה כיבוש ופלוגתא דתנאי היא בהך מילתא (ע"ז דף כא.): **בבי רב.** בית המדרש קרי בי רב: **נתחייבו בחלה.** דכתיב בבואכם אל הארץ ותניא בספרי ר' ישמעאל אומר שינה הכתוב ביאה זו מכל ביאות שבתורה שבכולן נאמר כי תבאו כי יביאך ולכאן בבואכם ללמדך שמיד שנכנסו לה נתחייבו: **ולא נתחייבו בתרומות ומעשרות.** דכתיב דגנך תבואת זרעך המיוחדת לך ועוד שהרי תלה הכתוב המעשר במנין שנות השמטה דכתיב בשנה השלישית שנת המעשר ושמטות לא מנו אלא משכבשו וחלקו כדאמרינן בסדר עולם ובמסכת ערכין (דף יב:): **הכי גרסינן אי בבואכם יכול משנכנסו לה שנים ושלשה מרגלים תלמוד לומר בבואכם בביאת כולכם כו'.** והכי פירושו כיון דשינה הכתוב ביאה זו לכתוב בה בבואכם ולא כתב כי תבאו יכול משנכנסו לה מרגלים ת"ל כו':

ואלא מאי גדולה חזקה. בשלמא אי אין מעלין ניחא הא דגדולה חזקה אע"ג דאיכא למיחש לב"ד טועין שיעלו מן נשיאות כפים לקדשי קדשים [ואע"ג דבלא חזקה מעלין לתרומה ע"פ עד אחד ולא חיישינן לב"ד טועין שמא יעלו ליוחסין השתא סבר המקשן דיוחסין חמירא ולא אתו למיטעי כמו לקדשי קדשים] אבל השתא דאמרת טעמא דריע חזקייהו ולא חיישינן דלמא אתי לאסוקי כיון דלא אתי למטעי מאי גדולה חזקה: **או** דלמא אפילו למ"ד אין מעלין ה"מ תרומה דמתאכלא בצינעה כו'. תימה מה תולה באכילה והא פשיטא דלכ"ע אין מעלין מאכילת תרומה ליוחסין דהא איכא למיחש דלמא עבד כהן הוא אלא בחלוקת תרומה (א) בגורן הוא דפליגי אם מעלים ליוחסין אם לאו ובמעלין מתרומה ליוחסין לא איפליגו בה תנאי בהדיא אלא דתליא הא פלוגתא בפלוגתא אם חולקין תרומה לעבד בלא רבו אם לאו למ"ד חולקין אין מעלין דדלמא עבד הוא והכי איבעי ליה למיתר הכא אפילו למ"ד אין מעלין ה"מ תרומה דחולקין לעבד בלא רבו ואיכא למיחש דלמא עבד הוא אבל נשיאו' כפים לעולם אימא לך דמעלין דאין עבד נושא כפיו: [נ"ל דשפיר נקט דמתאכלא בצינעא דלמ"ד מעלין מאכילת תרומה נמי מעלין ובעינן דליכא למיחש שהוא עבד שילא מבית הספר וטעמא כיון דעון מיתה הוא חיישינן שמא יעלוהו ליוחסין ולכך איצטריך בי עדים להאכילו בתרומה ולכך נמי אין חולקין לעבד אלא א"כ רבו עמו ומ"ד אין מעלין אע"ג דעון מיתה הוא לא חייש להכי שמא יעלוהו כיון דבצנעא הויא אכילת תרומה וכן חלוקה אבל נשיאות כפים דאיפרסם איבעיא ליה אי חיישינן שמא יעלוהו משום דאי לאו דכהן הוא לא הוה חציף כולי האי ולא הוי מצי למנקט כמו שכתבו התוס' אפילו למ"ד אין מעלי' משום דאיכא למיחש דלמא עבד הוא דלא תליא בהכי דאפילו היכא דליכא למיחש דלמא עבד הוא אין מעלין כמו ביוצא מבית הספר או שמעידין עליו שאינו עבד ואדרבה הא דחולקין לו בלא רבו היינו משום דאין מעלין ועיקר טעמא דפלוגתייהו משום מעלין ואין מעלין דאי לאו הכי קשה באיזה סברא פליגי כמו שהקשו לעיל] (ת"י): **וכי** מסקינן מתרומה ליוחסין ה"מ בדאורייתא כו'. רבינו יצחק בן רבינו מאיר לא גרים לה דהא איבעית אימא רב נחמן קאמר לה ואי גרסי' לה א"כ היה סותר בעצמו ראיה שהביא דאי לא תימא הכי למ"ד מעלין מתרומה ליוחסין הא אתי לאסוקי אלא טעמא משום דריע חזקייהו ואין זו סוגיית הש"ס אם לא יאמר ולאו מילתא היא דאמרי ובפ' עשרה יוחסין (קדושין סט:) גרסינן לה ואגב שיטפא דהתם שיבשו לכותבה כאן: **לא** במידי דאיקרי קדש. וא"ת תרומה נמי איקרי קדשים דכתיב ובא השמש וטהר ואחר יאכל מן הקדשים וההוא קרא איירי בתרומה וי"ל דודאי גבי טמא תרומה מיקרי קדשים אבל הכא לאכילת זר קאמר דלא אשכחן קדשים גבי אכילת זר: **נשיאות** כפים בבבל. דוקא נשיאות כפים ולא אכילת חלה ואע"ג דבסוריא נמי הוי מדרבנן אין מדקדקין בבבל כמו בסוריא דסבר האי תנא כיבוש יחיד שמיה כיבוש ואכילת חלה בסוריא ה"ה נשיאות כפים כדמוכח לקמן: **לא** חילוק גרנות גופה לחלה וקסבר תרומה כו'. וי"ל דפליגי הנך ברייתות בפלוגתא דרב הונא בריה דרב יהושע ורבנן דאי לאו הכי בחד מהנך ברייתות ממה נפשך איכא למידק דמעלין מנשיאות כפים ליוחסין ופליגי נמי דלברייתא קמייתא אכילת חלה בסוריא חזקה לתרומה וכל שכן דאכילת תרומה דאורייתא דהויא חזקה לחלה דרבנן ובברייתא שניה קתני חילוק גרנות בסוריא דהיינו תרומה בסוריא לא הויא חזקה לחלה:

עדות

מסורת הש"ס

א) יבמות סח. קדושין סט:, ב) [עיין תוס' שבת י: ד"ה יהבה], ג) [תוספתא פאה פ"ד], ד) נדה מז., ה) [ב"מ פט. וכן בנ"מ פט. איתא במעשר ועי' פרש"י הכלה לגרים תרויהו], ו) [עיין תוס' נדה מז. ד"ה לא נאמר], ח) [ועיין רש"י בנדה מז. וב"מ פט. מפרש בכל מקום טעם אחר], ט) ג"י.

הגהות הב"ח

(א) תד"ה או דלמא כו' אלא בחלוקת תרומה וכו'. נ"ב וכן פרש"י יבמות דף עט ע"ב:

תורה אור השלם

א) וַיֹּאמֶר הַתִּרְשָׁתָא לָהֶם אֲשֶׁר לֹא יֹאכְלוּ מִקֹּדֶשׁ הַקֳּדָשִׁים עַד עֲמֹד כֹּהֵן לְאוּרִים וּלְתֻמִּים: [עזרא ב, סג]

ב) וְכָל זָר לֹא יֹאכַל קֹדֶשׁ תּוֹשַׁב כֹּהֵן וְשָׂכִיר לֹא יֹאכַל קֹדֶשׁ: [ויקרא כב, י]

ג) וּבַת כֹּהֵן כִּי תִהְיֶה לְאִישׁ זָר הִוא בִּתְרוּמַת הַקֳּדָשִׁים לֹא תֹאכֵל: [ויקרא כב, יב]

ד) דַּבֵּר אֶל בְּנֵי יִשְׂרָאֵל וְאָמַרְתָּ אֲלֵהֶם בְּבֹאֲכֶם אֶל הָאָרֶץ אֲשֶׁר אֲנִי מֵבִיא אֶתְכֶם שָׁמָּה: [במדבר טו, יח]

עין משפט נר מצוה

פז א מיי' פ"כ מהל' איסורי ביאה הלכה א ופ"ו מהל' תרומות ה"ב:
פח ב מיי' פ"כ מהל' איסורי ביאה הלכ' ד:
פט ג מיי' שם הלכה יא טוש"ע אה"ע סימן ג סעיף ב:
צ ד מיי' שם הלכה ג ופ"א מהל' תרומות ה"א סמג עשין קמ טוש"ע י"ד סימן שלא סעיף ב:
צא ה מיי' פ"כ מהל' איסורי ביאה הלכה ג סמג עשין קמ טוש"ע י"ד סי' שכב סעיף ב:

ליקוטי רש"י

[התחלת ליקוטי רש"י ששייך לכאן נדפס בדף כד:]
ולא במידי דאיקרי קדשים. חזה ושוק של שלמים דאשכחן דאיקרי קדשים [קידושין סט:]. **לאיש זר.** ללוי וישראל [ויקרא כב, יב]. **במורם מן הקדשים.** חזה ושוק [קידושין שם]. **לא תאכל.** ואפילו זרע אין לה ושבה אל בית אביה חוזרת לתרומה ואינה חוזרת לחזה ושוק [שם ע.]. כשהיא חוזרת לבית אביה במיתת הבעל וזרע אין לה אינה חוזרת לחזה ושוק של שלמים לאכול כשאר אחיות האוכלות כדכתי' אתה ובניך ובנותיך (ויקרא י) [יבמות סח:]. מדהוה מצי למכתב בקדשים וכתב בתרומת למורם הוא דאתא והאי לא תאכל לעולם הוא ולא תימא ביושבת תחת בעלה ישראל כדמשמע קרא ובת כהן כי תהיה לאיש זר כו' דהא אוקימנא להאי קרא בפרק אלמנה (לעיל דף סח.) בנבעלה לפסול לה כגון נתין וממזר וחלל שפסיל עולמית והכנת דמנסבלה לזר דלא הלכה מושבה אל בית אביה ילפינן מכלל דמעיקרא אכלה ומילתא דרב חסדא מכתרומה נפקא לה דכולה קרא לנבעלה לפסול לה אתא לאוכוחי בקדשים לא תאכל מאי בתרומת שמע מינה הכי קאמר יש לך אחרת שאוכלת בקדשים כגון תרומה ואינה אוכלת במורם ואי זו זו חוזרת דסמיך לה ובת כהן כי תהיה אלמנה וגרושה והכי תרגומה להא מילתא בפרק אלמנה (לעיל סח:) [שם סח.]. **נתחייבו בחלה ולא נתחייבו וכו'.** (ספרי פ' שלח) דכתיב בבואכם אל הארץ שינה הכתוב ביאה זו מכל ביאות שבתורה שנאמר בהן כי תבאו ולכאן נאמר בבואכם שמשנכנסו לארץ נתחייבו בחלה אבל במעשר לא נתחייבו עד שירשו וישבו דכתיב עשר תעשר וכתיב בתריה במקום אשר יבחר עד שנבחרה שילה לא נתחייבו והיינו לאחר כיבוש וחילוק דכתיב ביהושע וכל ימי כיבוש וחילוק היה אהל מועד בגלגל ארבע עשרה שנים כדאמר [בזבחים] (דף קיח:) [ב"מ פט.]. דכתיב בחלה (במדבר טו) בבואכם אל הארץ והרי באו. ולא נתחייבו במעשר דבמעשר כתיב (דברים יד) תבואת זרעך עד שיהא כל אחד ואחד מכיר את שלו [נדה מז.]. **בבואכם אל הארץ.** משונה ביאה זו מכל ביאות שבתורה שבכולן נאמר כי תבא כי תבאו כי יביאך למדות זו מזו וכיון שפרט לך הכתוב באחת מהן שאינה אלא לאחר ירושה וישיבה אף כולן כן אבל זו נאמר בה בבואכם משנכנסו ואכלתם מלחמה נתחייבו בחלה [במדבר טו, יח].

this is in accordance with how Rav Huna the son of R' Yehoshua reversed the position of **the Rabbis,** as narrated below.[20]

The Gemara again attempts to prove that one who recites the Priestly Blessing is assumed to be genealogically fit:

תָּא שְׁמַע – **Come, learn** a proof from the following Baraisa: חֲזָקָה לִכְהוּנָּה – A PRESUMPTION OF KEHUNAH can be established by testifying about a man that נְשִׂיאוּת כַּפַּיִם וְחִילּוּק גְּרָנוֹת בְּאֶרֶץ יִשְׂרָאֵל – he recited THE PRIESTLY BLESSING OR that he received *terumah* in the DISTRIBUTION OF *terumah* at GRANARIES IN ERETZ YISRAEL.[21] וּבְסוּרְיָא וּבְכָל מָקוֹם שֶׁשְּׁלוּחֵי רֹאשׁ חוֹדֶשׁ מַגִּיעִין – IN SURIA AND WHEREVER THE MESSENGERS OF ROSH CHODESH WOULD REACH,[22] נְשִׂיאוּת כַּפַּיִם רְאָיָה אֲבָל לֹא חִילּוּק גְּרָנוֹת – THE PRIESTLY BLESSING IS A PROOF BUT the DISTRIBUTION OF *terumah* at THE GRANARIES IS NOT.[23] וּבָבֶל כְּסוּרְיָא – AND BABYLONIA IS treated LIKE SURIA in this regard.[24] רַבָּן שִׁמְעוֹן בֶּן גַּמְלִיאֵל אוֹמֵר – RABBAN SHIMON BEN GAMLIEL SAYS: אַף אֲלֶכְּסַנְדְּרִיָּא שֶׁל מִצְרַיִם בָּרִאשׁוֹנָה – ALSO treated like Suria was ALEXANDRIA OF EGYPT IN FORMER TIMES, מִפְּנֵי שֶׁבֵּית דִּין קְבוּעִין שָׁם – BECAUSE COURTS[25] WERE ESTABLISHED THERE.[26] קָתָנֵי מִיהַת נְשִׂיאוּת כַּפַּיִם – **At any rate, [the Baraisa] teaches** that one who recites the **Priestly Blessing** is assumed to be a Kohen. מַאי לָאו לְיוּחֲסִין – **Does** this **not** mean that he is assumed to be a Kohen even **with respect to genealogy?**

The Gemara rejects the proof:

לֹא לְחַלָּה – **No!** Perhaps it means that he is assumed to be a Kohen only **with respect to** ***challah.***

The Gemara defends the proof:

הָא דּוּמְיָא דְּחִילּוּק גְּרָנוֹת קָתָנֵי – **But [the Baraisa] mentioned** the Priestly Blessing in a manner which implies that it is **analogous to** the **distribution of** *terumah* at the **granaries.**[27] This indicates that מָה חִילּוּק גְּרָנוֹת לְיוּחֲסִין – **just as** the **distribution of** *terumah* at the **granaries** proves that he is a Kohen even **with respect to genealogy,** אַף נְשִׂיאוּת כַּפַּיִם לְיוּחֲסִין – **so too the Priestly Blessing** proves that he is a Kohen even **with respect to genealogy.**

The Gemara finally rejects the proof:

לֹא חִילּוּק גְּרָנוֹת גּוּפָהּ לְחַלָּה – **No!** The **distribution of** *terumah* at the **granaries itself** necessarily proves only that he is a Kohen **with respect to** ***challah.*** And if you will ask why evidence is needed to let him eat *challah* when he is already eating *terumah,* the answer is: קָסָבַר תְּרוּמָה בַּזְּמַן הַזֶּה דְּרַבָּנַן – **[The Tanna of this Baraisa] holds that nowadays** ***terumah*** **is** required only according to **Rabbinic** law וְחַלָּה דְּאוֹרַיְיתָא – **while** ***challah*** **is** required according to **Biblical** law. וּמַסְּקִינַן מִתְּרוּמָה דְּרַבָּנַן לְחַלָּה דְּאוֹרַיְיתָא – **And** thus the Baraisa's point is that **we elevate** a Kohen who eats **Rabbinic** ***terumah*** **to** the level of being allowed to eat **Biblical** ***challah.***

The Gemara supports the notion that even if nowadays *terumah* is only Rabbinic, *challah* is Biblical:

וְכִדְאַשְׁכְּחִינְהוּ רַב הוּנָא בְּרֵיהּ דְּרַב יְהוֹשֻׁעַ לְרַבָּנַן – **And** this accords with the opinion of the Rabbis, **as** recorded in the incident **where Rav Huna the son of R' Yehoshua found the Rabbis.** דְּאָמַר רַב הוּנָא בְּרֵיהּ דְּרַב יְהוֹשֻׁעַ – **For Rav Huna the son of R' Yehoshua said:** אַשְׁכַּחְתִּינְהוּ לְרַבָּנַן בְּבֵי רַב דְּיָתְבֵי וְקָאָמְרֵי – **I found the Rabbis in the study hall sitting and saying:** אֲפִילּוּ לְמַאן דְּאָמַר תְּרוּמָה בַּזְּמַן הַזֶּה דְּרַבָּנַן – **Even according to the one who says** that **nowadays** ***terumah*** is only **Rabbinic,**[28] חַלָּה דְּאוֹרַיְיתָא – ***challah*** **is** nevertheless **Biblical.** שֶׁהֲרֵי שֶׁבַע שֶׁכִּבְּשׁוּ וְשֶׁבַע שֶׁחִילְּקוּ – **For,** in the time of Joshua, during **the seven** years **that [the Jewish people] conquered** Eretz Yisrael **and the seven** years **that they apportioned** it among the tribes, נִתְחַיְּיבוּ בְּחַלָּה וְלֹא נִתְחַיְּיבוּ בִּתְרוּמָה – **they were obligated in** the mitzvah of ***challah*** **but they were not obligated in** the mitzvah of ***terumah.***[29] וַאֲמִינָא לְהוּ אֲנָא – **But I** [Rav Huna] **said to them:**

NOTES

were not investigated at all (*Rashash,* based on *Rashi*). For a different approach, see *Tosafos* ד״ה נשיאות כפים (with *Maharsha*), *Ramban, Rashba* et al.]

20. The Gemara below relates that Rav Huna the son of R' Yehoshua heard the Rabbis say that nowadays *terumah* is required only at the Rabbinic level, whereas *challah* is required under Biblical law. Upon hearing this, Rav Huna argued that the reverse is true. Thus, our Gemara, which states that nowadays *terumah* is Biblical and *challah* is Rabbinic, accords with Rav Huna's response to the Rabbis.

21. One who recites the Priestly Blessing in Eretz Yisrael can be assumed to be a Kohen, because the courts there check the Kohanic status of those who recite the Priestly Blessing. [The Baraisa will soon state that this is true in Suria and Babylonia as well.] And one who receives *terumah* in Eretz Yisrael is also assumed to be a Kohen. [This applies only in Eretz Yisrael.] The Gemara initially supposes that this is because even nowadays the *terumah* of Eretz Yisrael is a Biblical obligation; therefore, a non-Kohen would not eat it lest he become liable to death at the hand of Heaven (*Rashi*).

22. During most of the Talmudic era the beginning of the month (Rosh Chodesh) was not fixed by a static calendar, but by the actual sighting of the new moon. Witnesses who saw the first phase of the new moon would report their observation to the Great Sanhedrin in Jerusalem, which would then declare that day to be Rosh Chodesh. Messengers were then sent to communities in the Diaspora to inform them of the court's decision so that they would know, for example, on which day to observe Pesach. Since Pesach begins on the fifteenth of Nissan, the messengers traveled only to those communities that could be reached by that date (*Rashi*).

23. In each community located within a fifteen-day journey of Jerusalem there were established courts which accepted the messengers sent by the Great Sanhedrin. As mentioned above, established courts would also investigate the Kohanic status of those who recite the Priestly Blessing. Therefore, one who recites the Priestly Blessing in these communities can be assumed to be a Kohen. However, eating *terumah* there does not prove Kohanic status, because *terumah* outside Eretz Yisrael is not a Biblical requirement (*Rashi*).

This Tanna evidently does not consider Suria to be part of Eretz Yisrael (*Rashi;* see note 13). In this point, he disagrees with the Tanna of the previous Baraisa (see *Tosafos* ד״ה לא).

24. Although the court's messengers did not reach Babylonia, it was nevertheless treated in this regard like the communities near Eretz Yisrael. This was because there were courts in Babylonia that investigated the Kohanic status of those who recite the Priestly Blessing.

25. The texts of *Rashba* and *Ritva* read בָּתֵּי דִינִין, *courts* (plural).

26. After the destruction of the First Temple, Alexandria became a major center of Jewish life (see *Succah* 51b with *Rashi* ד״ה סטיו כפול). Several centuries later, the Alexandrian community was slaughtered by a Roman emperor (see *Gittin* 57b and *Succah* 51b note 32 [Schottenstein ed.]).

At the time of this Baraisa's composition, this law was no longer applicable since the courts of Alexandria had already ceased to function. The Tanna nevertheless adds this point to teach that in any place where a court is established, as in Alexandria, we can assume that those who recite the Priestly Blessing were investigated for their Kohanic status (*Ritva*).

27. See note 15.

28. When the Jews returned to Eretz Yisrael from the Babylonian exile, Ezra sanctified the Land anew. There is a question whether Ezra sanctified the Land forever or only until the destruction of the Second Temple. If the sanctification ended at the time of the destruction, then the mitzvah of *terumah* (as well as the other mitzvos applicable to the land and its produce) also ceased at that time. These mitzvos however, were perpetuated by Rabbinic decree.

29. [The text of *Rashi* reads: תְּרוּמוֹת וּמַעַשְׂרוֹת, *terumah and maaser.* The Gemara elsewhere (*Bava Metzia* 89a, *Niddah* 47a) mentions only *maaser.* Evidently, *terumah* and *maaser* are the same in this regard (see previous note).]

The obligation to separate *challah* began to apply immediately upon

ואלא מאי גדולה חזקה מעיקרא אכול בתרומה דרבנן השתא אכול בתרומה דאורייתא ואי בעית אימא א השתא נמי בתרומה דרבנן אכול בתרומה דאורייתא לא אכול ב וכי מסקינן מתרומה ליוחסין בתרומה דאורייתא בתרומה דרבנן לא מסקינן ואלא מאי גדולה חזקה דאע"ג דאיכא למיגזר משום תרומה דאורייתא לא גזרינן ובתרומה דאורייתא לא אכול והא כתיב א) אשר לא יאכלו מקדש הקדשים מקדש הקדשים הוא דלא אכול הא בתרומה דאורייתא אכול ה"ק לא במידי דאיקרי קדש דכתיב ב) וכל זר לא יאכל קדש ולא במידי דאיקרי קדשים דכתיב ג) ובת כהן כי תהיה לאיש זר היא בתרומת הקדשים לא תאכל ואמר מר ח) במורם מן הקדשים לא תאכל ת"ש חזקה לכהונה נשיאות כפים בבבל ואכילת חלה בסוריא ט) וחילוק מתנות בכרכין קתני מיהת נשיאות כפים מאי לאו ליוחסין ג לא לתרומה והא דומיא דאכילת חלה קתני מה אכילת חלה ליוחסין אף נשיאות כפים ליוחסין לא אכילת חלה גופה לתרומה קסבר חלה בזמן הזה דרבנן ותרומה דאורייתא ומסקינן מחלה דרבנן לתרומה דאורייתא וכדאפיך להו רב הונא בריה דרב יהושע לרבנן ת"ש ג) חזקה לכהונה נשיאות כפים וחילוק גרנות בא"י ובסוריא ובכל מקום שלוחי ראש חודש מגיעין נשיאות כפים ראיה אבל לא חילוק גרנות ובבל כסוריא רשב"ג אומר אף אלכסנדריא של מצרים בראשונה מפני שבית דין קבוע שם קתני מיהת נשיאות כפים מאי לאו ליוחסין לא לחלה הא דומיא דחילוק גרנות קתני מה חילוק גרנות ליוחסין אף נשיאות כפים ליוחסין לא חילוק גרנות גופה לחלה ד קסבר תרומה בזמן הזה דרבנן וחלה דאורייתא ומסקינן מתרומה דרבנן לחלה דאורייתא וכדאשכחינהו רב הונא בריה דרב יהושע לרבנן ד) דאמר רב הונא בריה דרב יהושע אשכחתינהו לרבנן בבי רב דיתבי וקאמרי אפילו למאן דאמר תרומה בזמן הזה דרבנן חלה דאורייתא שהרי ה) ז' שכיבשו וז' שחילקו נתחייבו בחלה ולא נתחייבו ו) בתרומה ואמינא להו אנא אדרבה אפילו למ"ד תרומה בזמן הזה דאורייתא חלה ה דרבנן דתניא ד) בבואכם אל הארץ אי ז) בבואכם יכול משנכנסו לה שנים ושלשה מרגלים ת"ל בבואכם בביאת כולכם אמרתי ולא בביאת מקצתכם וכי אסקינהו עזרא לאו

רש"י

ואלא מאי גדולה חזקה. דקאמר ר' יוסי למה לנו [למחוש] להשבית חזקתם כי מה יש לנו לחוש לבטלה: **בתרומה דרבנן.** שהרי בגולה היו שאין שם תרומה מן התורה דכל מצוה שהיא תלויה בארץ אינה נוהגת אלא בארץ כדאמרינן בקידושין (דף לו:): **ואיבעית אימא השתא נמי בתרומה דרבנן אכול.** תרומת פירות האילן וירק: **דאורייתא.** דגן תירוש ויצהר לא אכול ומש"ה לא קשיא למ"ד מעלין מתרומה ליוחסין דכי מסקינן ליוחסין מתרומה דאורייתא כו': **דאיכא למיגזר משום תרומה דאורייתא.** שהרי לארץ באו ומצויה שם תרומה גמורה דאורייתא מה שלא היה מצוי להם בגולה ויש לחוש פן יאכילום בה: **לא במידי דאקרי קדש.** והיינו תרומה: **וכל זר לא יאכל קדש.** בתרומה משתעי דכתיב בפרשה לעיל מיניה ובא השמש וטהר ואחר יאכל מן הקדשים ואוקמינן בתרומה ביבמות בהערל (דף עד:): **ולא במידי דאקרי קדשים.** אפילו חזה ושוק של שלמים הנאכלים לנשי כהנים ולעבדיהם: **ואמר מר.** ביבמות בפרק יש מותרות בבת כהן שניסת לישראל ונעשית אלמנה וגרושה וזרע אין לה שחוזרת לתרומת אביה ואינה חוזרת לחזה ושוק ויליף לה מהאי קרא כי תהיה לאיש זר היא בתרומת הקדשים לא תאכל עוד: **חזקה לכהונה.** להעיד עליו שהוא כהן: **נשיאות כפים בבבל.** הרואהו נושא כפיו בבבל מעיד עליו בכל מקום שהוא כהן ומקבלין הימנו לפי שיש שם ישיבה וב"ד קבוע בודקין אחר נושאי כפים אבל אכילת חלה ותרומה אינה חזקה דמוקי לה בארץ לאו לדאורייתא תרומה דיליה ולא קפדי כולי האי: **ואכילת חלה בסוריא.** היא ארם צובה שכיבשה דוד וחיברה לא"י וקסבר האי תנא כיבוש יחיד שמיה כיבוש והאי חלה ותרומתה לדאורייתא וקס"ד תנא חלה וה"ה לתרומה: **וחילוק מתנות.** הזרוע והלחיים: **בכרכין.** ואע"ג דאיסורן אין איסור לזרים הואיל וכרכים מקום שווקין הן ומצויין בו עוברים ושבים המכירין בו אי לאו דכהן הוא לא מחליף נפשיה: **לא לתרומה.** הרואהו נושא כפיו בבבל אוכל הוא חלה דוודאי בסוריא והעיד עליו בא"י מקבלין עדותו להאכילו תרומה אבל לא ליוחסין: **מה אכילת חלה.** עדות מוקמת: **ליוחסין.** דאי לתרומה פשיטא היא גופה תרומה היא וכבר הוחזק בה: **ומסקינן מחלה דרבנן כו'.** דאי לאו כהן הוא לא הוו ספו ליה חלה גזירה משום תרומה: **וכדאפיך.** לקמן מפרש: **נשיאות כפים וחילוק גרנות.** לתרומה: **בא"י.** נושאי כפים דאיכא ב"ד קבועין ובדקי וחילוק גרנות קס"ד השתא לתרומה בזמן הזה דאורייתא וכיון דעון מיתה איכא מסקינן מינה ליוחסין: **בסוריא וכ"מ ששלוחי א"י מגיעין.** להודיע לגולה יום שקידשו ב"ד את החדש לעשות פסח בזמנו דהיינו היושבים בתוך מהלך חמשה עשר יום: **נשיאות כפים ראיה.** לפי שב"ד קבוע שם שמקבל שליחות החדש של ב"ד הגדול: **אבל לא חילוק גרנות.** דתרומה דידהו לאו לדאורייתא ובסוריא נמי האי תנא סבר כיבוש יחיד לא שמיה כיבוש ופלוגתא דתנאי היא בהך מילתא (ע"ז דף כא.): **בבי רב.** בית המדרש קרי בי רב: **נתחייבו בחלה.** דכתיב בבואכם אל הארץ ותניא בספרי ר' ישמעאל אומר שינה הכתוב ביאה זו מכל ביאות שבתורה שבכולן נאמר כי תבאו כי יביאך וכאן בבואכם ללמדך שכיון שנכנסו לה נתחייבו: **ולא נתחייבו בתרומות ומעשרות.** דכתיב דגנך תבואת זרעך המיוחדת לך ט) ועוד שהרי תלה הכתוב המעשר במנין שנות השמטה דכתיב בשנה השלישית שנת המעשר ושמטות לא מנו אלא משכבשו וחילקו כדאמרינן בסדר עולם ובמסכת ערכין (דף יב:): **הכי גרסינן אי בבואכם יכול משנכנסו לה שנים ושלשה מרגלים תלמוד לומר בבואכם בביאת כולכם כו'.** והכי פירושו כיון דשינה הכתוב ביאה זו לכתוב בה בבואכם ולא כתב כי תבאו יכול משנכנסו לה מרגלים ת"ל כו':

תוספות

ואלא מאי גדולה חזקה. בשלמא אי אין מעלין ניחא הא דגדולה חזקה אע"ג דאיכא למיחש לב"ד טועין שיעלו מן נשיאות כפים לקדשי קדשים ט) ואע"ג דבלא חזקה מעלין לתרומה ע"פ עד אחד ולא חיישינן לב"ד טועין שמא יעלו ליוחסין השתא סבר המקשן דיוחסין חמירא ולא אתו למיטעי כמו לקדשי קדשים [אבל] השתא דאמרת טעמא דר"ע חזקייהו ולא חיישינן דלמא אתי לאסוקי כיון דלא אתי למטעי מאי גדולה חזקה: (לעיל) **או דלמא אפילו למ"ד אין מעלין ה"מ תרומה דמתאכלא בצינעה כו'.** תימה מה תולה באכילה והא פשיטא לכ"ע אין מעלין מאכילת תרומה ליוחסין דהא איכא למיחש דלמא עבד כהן הוא אלא מחלוקת תרומה (א) בגורן הוא דפליגי אם מעלים ליוחסין אם לאו ומעלין מתרומה ליוחסין לא איפליגו בה תנאי בהדיא אלא דתליא הא פלוגתא בפלוגתא אם חולקין תרומה לעבד בלא רבו אם לאו למ"ד חולקין אין מעלין דלמא עבד הוא והכי איבעי ליה למימר הכא אפילו למ"ד אין מעלין ה"מ תרומה דחולקין לעבד בלא רבו ואיכא למיחש דלמא עבד הוא אבל נשיאו' כפים לעולם אימא לך דמעלין דאין עבד נושא כפיו: [נ"ל דשפיר נקט דמתאכלא בצינעא דלמ"ד מעלין מאכילת תרומה נמי מעלין ובענין דליכא למיחש שהוא עבד שילא מביא הספר וטעמא כיון דעון מיתה הוא חיישי' שמא יעלוהו ליוחסין ולכך איצטריך שני עדים להאכילו בתרומה ולכך נמי אין חולקין לעבד אלא א"כ רבו עמו ומ"ד אין מעלין אע"ג דעון מיתה הוא לא חייש להכי שמא יעלוהו כיון דבצנעא הויא אכילת תרומה וכן חלוקה אבל נשיאות כפים דאיפרסם איבעיא ליה אי חיישינן שמא יעלוהו משום דאי לאו דכהן הוא לא הוה חליף כולי האי ולא הוי מצי למנקט כמו שכתבו התוס' אפילו למ"ד אין מעלין משום דאיכא למיחש דלמא עבד הוא דלא תליא בהכי דאפילו היכא דליכא למיחש דלמא עבד הוא אין מעלין כמו ביולא מביא הספר או שמעידין עליו שאינו עבד ואדרבה הא דחולקין לו בלא רבו היינו משום דאין מעלין ועיקר טעמא דפלוגתייהו משום מעלין ואין מעלין דאי לאו הכי קשה באיזה סברא פליגי כמו שהקשו לעיל] (ת"י): **וכי מסקינן מתרומה ליוחסין ה"מ בדאורייתא כו'.** רבינו יצחק בן רבינו מאיר לא גרים לה דהא איבעית אימא רב נחמן קאמר לה ואי גרסי' לה א"כ היה סותר בעצמו ראיה שהביא דאי לא תימא הכי מ"ד מעלין מתרומה ליוחסין הא אתי לאסוקי אלא טעמא משום דריע חזקייהו ואין זו סוגיית הש"ס אם לא יאמר ולאו מילתא היא דאמרי ובפ' עשרה יוחסין (קדושין סט:) גרסינן לה ואגב שיטפא דהתם שיבשו לכתבה כאן: **לא במידי דאיקרי קדש.** וא"ת תרומה נמי איקרי קדשים דכתיב ובא השמש וטהר ואחר יאכל מן הקדשים וההוא קרא איירי בתרומה דהעריב שמשו אוכל בתרומה וי"ל דודאי גבי טמא תרומה מיקרי קדשים אבל הכא אאכילת זר קאמר דלא אשכחן קדשים גבי אכילת זר: **נשיאות כפים בבבל.** דוקא נשיאות כפים ולא אכילת חלה ואע"ג דבסוריא נמי הוי מדרבנן אין מדקדקין בבבל כמו בסוריא דסבר האי תנא כיבוש יחיד שמיה כיבוש ואכילת חלה בסוריא ה"ה נשיאות כפים כדמוכח לקמן: **לא חילוק גרנות גופה לחלה וקסבר תרומה כו'.** וי"ל דפליגי הנך ברייתות בפלוגתא דרב הונא בריה דרב יהושע ורבנן דאי לאו הכי בחד מהנך ברייתות כמה נפשך איכא למידק דמעלין מנשיאות כפים ליוחסין ופליגי נמי דלברייתא קמייתא אכילת חלה בסוריא חזקה לתרומה וכל שכן דאכילת תרומה דאורייתא דהויא חזקה לאכילת חלה דרבנן ובברייתא שניה קתני דחילוק גרנות דהיינו תרומה בסוריא לא הויא חזקה לחלה:

עדות

מסורת הש"ס

א) יבמות סח: פז. קדושין סט:, ב) [עיין תוס' שבת י: ד"ה יהיבנא], ג) תוספתא פאה פ"ד, ד) נדה מז., ה) [ב"מ פט.], ו) [כנדה מז. וכן בב"מ פט. איתא במעשר ועי' פרש"י דהכא דגרים תרווייהו], ז) [עיין תוס' נדה מו: ד"ה ל"ג אילו נאמר], ח) [ועיין רש"י נדרים מז. וב"מ פט. מפרש בכל מקום טעם אחר], ט) נ"י כ"י.

הגהות הב"ח

(א) תד"ה או דלמא כו' אלא בחלוקת תרומה וכו'. נ"ב וכן פרש"י יבמות דף נט ע"ב:

תורה אור השלם

א) וַיֹּאמֶר הַתִּרְשָׁתָא לָהֶם אֲשֶׁר לֹא יֹאכְלוּ מִקֹּדֶשׁ הַקֳּדָשִׁים עַד עֲמֹד כֹּהֵן לְאוּרִים וּלְתֻמִּים: [עזרא ב, סג]

ב) וְכָל זָר לֹא יֹאכַל קֹדֶשׁ תּוֹשַׁב כֹּהֵן וְשָׂכִיר לֹא יֹאכַל קֹדֶשׁ: [ויקרא כב, י]

ג) וּבַת כֹּהֵן כִּי תִהְיֶה לְאִישׁ זָר הִוא בִּתְרוּמַת הַקֳּדָשִׁים לֹא תֹאכֵל: [ויקרא כב, יב]

ד) דַּבֵּר אֶל בְּנֵי יִשְׂרָאֵל וְאָמַרְתָּ אֲלֵהֶם בְּבֹאֲכֶם אֶל הָאָרֶץ אֲשֶׁר אֲנִי מֵבִיא אֶתְכֶם שָׁמָּה: [במדבר טו, יח]

עין משפט נר מצוה

פז א מיי' פ"כ מהל' איסורי ביאה הלכה א ופ"ו מהל' תרומות ה"ב:
פח ב מיי' פ"כ מהל' איסורי ביאה הלכ' ד:
פט ג מיי' שם הלכה יא טוש"ע אה"ע סימן ג סעיף ב:
צ ד מיי' שם הלכה ג ופ"א מהל' תרומות ה"א סמג עשין מג טוש"ע י"ד סימן שלא סעיף ב:
צא ה מיי' פ"כ מהל' איסורי ביאה הלכה ג סמג עשין קמ טוש"ע י"ד סי' שכב סעיף ב:

ליקוטי רש"י

[התחלת ליקוטי רש"י ששייך לכאן נדפס בדף כד:]

ולא במידי דאיקרי קדשים. חזה ושוק של שלמים דאשכחן דאיקרי קדשים [קידושין סט:]. **לאיש זר.** ללוי וישראל [ויקרא כב, יג]. **במורם מן הקדשים.** חזה ושוק [קידושין שם]. **לא תאכל.** ואפילו זרע אין לה ושבה אל בית אביה חוזרת לתרומה ואינה חוזרת לחזה ושוק [שם ע.]. כשהיא חוזרת לבית אביה במיתת הבעל וזרע אין לה אינה חוזרת לחזה ושוק של שלמים לאכול כשאר אחיות האוכלות כדכתי' אתה ובניך ובנותיך (ויקרא י) [יבמות סח:]. מדהוה מצי למכתב בקדשים וכתב בתרומת למורם הוא דאתא והאי לא תאכל לעולם הוא ולא תימא ביושבת תחת בעלה ישראל כדמשמע קרא ובת כהן כי תהיה לאיש זר כו' דהא אוקימנא להאי קרא בפרק אלמנה (לעיל דף סח.) בנבעלה לפסול לה כגון נתין וממזר וחלל שפסיל עולמית והכנת דמנסבא לזר דלא אכלה מושבה אל בית אביה ילפינן מכלל דמעיקרא לא אכלה ומילתיה דרב חסדא מבתרומות נפקא דא"כ דכולה קרא לנבעלה לפסול לה אתא ליכתוב בקדשים לא תאכל מאי בתרומת שמע מינה הכי קאמר יש לך אחרת שאוכלת בקדשים כגון תרומה ואינה אוכלת במורם ואי זו זו חוזרת דסמיך לה ובת כהן כי תהיה אלמנה והכי תרילנא להא מילתא בפרק אלמנה (לעיל סח:) [שם פז.]. **נתחייבו בחלה ולא נתחייבו וכו'.** (ספרי פ' שלח) דכתיב בבואכם אל הארץ שינה הכתוב ביאה זו מכל ביאות שבתורה שנאמר בהן כי תבואו וכאן נאמר בבואכם משנכנסו לארץ נתחייבו בחלה אבל במעשר לא נתחייבו אלא לאחר ירושה וישיבה דכתיב עשר תעשר וכתיב בתריה במקום אשר יבחר עד שנבחרה שילה לא נתחייבו והיינו לאחר כיבוש וחילוק דכתיב ביהושע וכל ימי כיבוש וחילוק היה אהל מועד בגלגל ארבע עשרה שנים כדאמר [בזבחים] (דף קיח:) [ב"מ פט.]. דכתיב בחלה (במדבר טו) בבואכם אל הארץ והרי באו. ולא נתחייבו במעשר דבמעשר כתיב (דברים יד) תבואת זרעך עד שיביא כל אחד ואחד את שלו [נדה מז.]. **בבואכם אל הארץ.** משונה ביאה זו מכל ביאות שבתורה שבכולן נאמר כי תבא לפיכך כולן למדות זו מזו וכיון שפרט לך הכתוב באחת מהן שאינה אלא לאחר ירושה וישיבה אף כולן כן אבל זו נאמר בה בבואכם משנכנסו בה ואכלו מלחמה נתחייבו בחלה [במדבר טו, יח].

The Gemara attempts to prove that one who recites the Priestly Blessing is assumed to be genealogically fit:

תָּא שְׁמַע – **Come, learn** a proof from the following Baraisa: חֲזָקָה לִכְהוּנָּה – A PRESUMPTION OF KEHUNAH can be established by testifying about a man that נְשִׂיאוּת כַּפַּיִם בְּבָבֶל – he recited THE PRIESTLY BLESSING IN BABYLONIA,[12] וַאֲכִילַת חַלָּה בְּסוּרְיָא – OR that he engaged in THE CONSUMPTION OF *CHALLAH* IN SURIA,[13] וְחִילּוּק מַתָּנוֹת בִּכְרַכִּין – OR that he was a recipient in THE DISTRIBUTION OF Kohanic GIFTS IN CITIES.[14] קָתָנֵי מִיהַת נְשִׂיאוּת כַּפַּיִם – **At any rate, [the Baraisa] teaches** that one who recites **the Priestly Blessing** is assumed to be a Kohen. מַאי לָאו לְיוּחֲסִין – **Does** this **not** mean that he is assumed to be a Kohen even **with respect to genealogy?**

The Gemara refutes the proof:

לֹא לִתְרוּמָה – **No!** Perhaps it means that he is assumed to be a Kohen only **with respect to *terumah.***[15]

The Gemara defends the proof:

וְהָא דוּמְיָא דַּאֲכִילַת חַלָּה קָתָנֵי – **But [the Baraisa] mentioned** the Priestly Blessing in a manner which implies that it is **analogous to the consumption of *challah.***[16] This indicates that מָה אֲכִילַת חַלָּה לְיוּחֲסִין – **just as consumption of** *challah* proves that he is a Kohen even **with respect to genealogy,**[17] אַף נְשִׂיאוּת כַּפַּיִם לְיוּחֲסִין – **so too the Priestly Blessing** proves that he is a Kohen even **with respect to genealogy.**

The Gemara finally rejects the proof:

לֹא אֲכִילַת חַלָּה גּוּפָהּ לִתְרוּמָה – **No!** The consumption of ***challah* itself** necessarily proves only that he is a Kohen **with respect to *terumah.*** And if you will ask why evidence is needed to let him eat *terumah* when he is already eating *challah,* the answer is: קָסָבַר חַלָּה בַּזְּמַן הַזֶּה דְּרַבָּנָן – **[The Tanna of this Baraisa] holds** that ***challah* nowadays is** required only according to **Rabbinic** law, וּתְרוּמָה דְּאוֹרַיְיתָא – **while *terumah* is** required according to **Biblical** law.[18] וּמַסְּקִינַן מֵחַלָּה דְּרַבָּנָן לִתְרוּמָה דְּאוֹרַיְיתָא – **And** thus the Tanna's point is that **we elevate** a Kohen who eats **Rabbinic *challah* to** the level of being allowed to eat **Biblical *terumah.***[19] וּכְדְאַפִּיךְ לְהוּ רַב הוּנָא בְּרֵיהּ דְּרַב יְהוֹשֻׁעַ לְרַבָּנָן – **And**

NOTES

cial meat, which is permitted even to the women and servants in a Kohen's household (*Rashi*).

12. If witnesses saw a man recite the Priestly Blessing in Babylonia, they can testify anywhere [even in Eretz Yisrael] that he is a Kohen and their testimony will be accepted. This is because there were established courts in Babylonia that would investigate the Kohanic status of those who recited the Priestly Blessing. Hence, one who recites the Priestly Blessing there can be assumed to have been investigated and found to be genealogically fit (*Rashi*). [It is a Biblical transgression for a non-Kohen to recite the Priestly Blessing (see 24b note 21).]

The Gemara above (24b) stated that the reason why a Kohen who recited the Priestly Blessing can be assumed to be genealogically fit is that he would not be so insolent as to perform this public act if he were not actually a Kohen. However, that is true only in a locale with an established court: In that case we assume that if the court had not permitted him to recite the Priestly Blessing, he would not have the impudence to do so in public. But we would not make such an assumption in a place that lacked a court (*Pnei Yehoshua*).

13. *Challah* is the portion due the Kohen that must be separated from dough made of the five species of grain (listed in *Challah* 1:1). In most respects, *challah* shares the same laws as *terumah* (see *Numbers* 15:17-21).

Suria (or Aram Tzovah) was conquered by King David and annexed to the Land of Israel (*Rashi*). [The entire nation was not united behind King David's conquest of Suria, as it was behind Joshua's conquest of Eretz Yisrael proper. David conquered Suria for only his own purposes, whereas Joshua's conquest of Eretz Yisrael — which took place before the land was divided — was for the sake of all the people (see *Rashi* to *Gittin* 8b ד״ה כיבוש יחיד; see also *Rashi* to *Avodah Zarah* 20b ד״ה סוריא; cf. *Tosafos* on *Gittin* 8a ד״ה כיבוש).]

Considering that Suria was conquered "by an individual," Tannaim debate whether it is part of Eretz Yisrael (see *Gittin* 8b, 47a, *Avodah Zarah* 21a). This Baraisa reflects the view that it *is* included in Eretz Yisrael, and thus its produce is subject to the requirements of *challah* at the Biblical level. Therefore, one who eats *challah* in Suria can be assumed to be a Kohen [for a non-Kohen would not eat Biblical *challah* in light of the fact that the penalty for doing so is death at the hand of Heaven]. The Gemara initially assumes that the same applies to *terumah* (*Rashi*).

In Babylonia, though, the consumption of *challah* (or *terumah*) does not serve as evidence of Kohanic status, because it is not mandatory in Babylonia under Biblical law (*Rashi*); it is required there only by Rabbinic decree.

Recital of the Priestly Blessing in Suria is also evidence of Kohanic status (see the Baraisa cited below). [Although the Baraisa specifies Babylonia in reference to the Priestly Blessing, it does not mean to exclude Suria. Rather, its intent is that *even* in Babylonia, where consumption of *challah* does not prove Kohanic status, the Priestly Blessing is nevertheless a valid proof.]

14. Whenever a kosher domesticated animal is slaughtered, the Kohen is entitled to receive the right foreleg, the jaw and the abomasum (the fourth or true digestive stomach in ruminants) as one of the twenty-four Kohanic gifts (*Deuteronomy* 18:3). The obligation to give these parts, which are often referred to simply as מַתָּנוֹת, *gifts,* applies even outside Eretz Yisrael (see *Yoreh Deah* 61:21 regarding the present practice).

These portions possess no sanctity and a non-Kohen is allowed to eat them (provided he has the Kohen's permission). The mitzvah of giving them, however, is fulfilled only by giving them to a Kohen. It can be assumed, therefore, that only a Kohen would take them when they are being distributed in a city. Since cities attract many visitors who come to participate in its markets, a non-Kohen would not dare take these gifts in a city for fear that he might be exposed by a visitor who recognizes him (*Rashi;* see *Melo HaRo'im*). [This applies only in cities, such as those in Babylonia or Suria, where there are established courts (*Hagahos Radal;* see end of note 12).]

15. If one saw a man recite the Priestly Blessing in Babylonia (or eat *challah* in Suria) and testified to that effect in Eretz Yisrael, the court will allow him to eat *terumah.* However, such testimony does not suffice for him to be declared genealogically fit (*Rashi*).

[This answer is valid only according to the opinion that a Kohen who eats *terumah* is *not* assumed to be genealogically fit. Otherwise, this man would be forbidden even to eat *terumah* lest, upon being seen eating *terumah,* he will be promoted further to the status of the genealogically fit (see *Ramban, Rashba* and *Maharsha*).]

16. By listing the two together, the Baraisa indicates that both carry the same weight.

17. The Baraisa surely does not mean that consumption of *challah* serves only as evidence to let him eat *terumah.* It goes without saying that a person who is already eating *challah* may also eat the *terumah,* since *challah* itself is a form of *terumah.* Rather, the Baraisa must mean that a Kohen who eats *challah* is qualified even with respect to genealogical matters (*Rashi*).

18. These rulings are explained below.

19. If he were not a Kohen, he would not have been given even [Rabbinic] *challah* for fear that he might consequently come to be given [Biblical] *terumah* (*Rashi*). Thus, the Gemara argues, even the consumption of Rabbinic *challah* provides evidence of Kohanic status that suffices to let him eat a Biblical portion. [We are not afraid that this might lead to him being declared genealogically fit, because, according to the Gemara's current position, even consumption of Biblical *challah* or *terumah* (or recital of the Priestly Blessing) cannot be used as proof of genealogy fitness.]

[An apparent difficulty: If the Baraisa considers the consumption of Rabbinic *challah* to be evidence of Kohanic status, why does it specify that one who eats *challah* in *Suria* is assumed to be a Kohen? The same should be true wherever *challah* is a Rabbinic requirement, including Babylonia! One answer given is that in Suria, where Biblical *terumah* is available, there are grounds for concern that one who eats Rabbinic *challah* might come to be given Biblical *terumah.* Hence, a person would not have been given even Rabbinic *challah* unless he was known to be a Kohen. In Babylonia, however, where no such concern existed because Biblical *terumah* was unavailable in any event, those who ate *challah*

ואלא מאי גדולה חזקה מעיקרא אכול בתרומה דרבנן השתא אכול בתרומה דאורייתא ואי בעית אימא השתא נמי בתרומה דרבנן אכול בתרומה דאורייתא לא אכול וכי מסקינן מתרומה ליוחסין בתרומה דאורייתא בתרומה דרבנן לא מסקינן ואלא מאי גדולה חזקה דאע"ג דאיכא למיגזר משום תרומה דאורייתא לא גזרינן ובתרומה דאורייתא לא אכול והא כתיב [א] אשר לא יאכלו מקדש הקדשים מקדש הקדשים הוא דלא אכול הא בתרומה דאורייתא אכול ה"ק לא במידי דאיקרי קדש דכתיב [ב] וכל זר לא יאכל קדש ולא במידי דאיקרי קדשים דכתיב [ג] ובת כהן כי תהיה לאיש זר היא בתרומת הקדשים לא תאכל ואמר מר במורם מן הקדשים לא תאכל ת"ש חזקה לכהונה נשיאות כפים בבבל ואכילת חלה בסוריא וחילוק מתנות בכרכין קתני מיהת נשיאות כפים מאי לאו ליוחסין לא לתרומה והא דומיא דאכילת חלה קתני מה אכילת חלה ליוחסין אף נשיאות כפים ליוחסין לא אכילת חלה גופה קסבר חלה בזמן הזה דרבנן ותרומה דאורייתא ומסקינן מחלה דרבנן לתרומה דאורייתא וכדאפיך להו רב הונא בריה דרב יהושע לרבנן ת"ש חזקה לכהונה נשיאות כפים וחילוק גרנות בא"י ובסוריא ובכל מקום ששלוחי ראש חודש מגיעין נשיאות כפים ראיה אבל לא חילוק גרנות ובבל כסוריא רשב"ג אומר אף אלכסנדריא של מצרים בראשונה מפני שבית דין קבועין שם קתני מיהת נשיאות כפים מאי לאו ליוחסין לא לחלה הא דומיא דחילוק גרנות קתני מה חילוק גרנות ליוחסין אף נשיאות כפים ליוחסין לא חילוק גרנות גופה לחלה קסבר תרומה בזמן הזה דרבנן וחלה דאורייתא ומסקינן מתרומה דרבנן לחלה דאורייתא וכדאשכחינהו רב הונא בריה דרב יהושע לרבנן דאמר רב הונא בריה דרב יהושע אשכחתינהו לרבנן בבי רב דיתבי וקאמרי אפילו למאן דאמר תרומה בזמן הזה דרבנן חלה דאורייתא שהרי ז' שכיבשו וז' שחילקו נתחייבו בחלה ולא נתחייבו בתרומה ואמינא להו אנא אדרבה אפילו למ"ד תרומה בזמן הזה דאורייתא חלה דרבנן דתניא [ד] בבואכם אל הארץ אי בבואכם יכול משנכנסו לה שנים ושלשה מרגלים ת"ל בבואכם בביאת כולכם אמרתי ולא בביאת מקצתכם וכי אסקינהו עזרא לאו

רש"י

ואלא מאי גדולה חזקה. דקאמר ר' יוסי למה לנו [לחוש] להשבית חזקתם כי מה יש לחוש לבטלה: בתרומה דרבנן. שהרי בגולה היו שאין שם תרומה מן התורה דכל מצוה שהיא תלויה בארץ אינה נוהגת אלא בארץ כדאמרינן בקידושין (דף לו:): ואיבעית אימא השתא נמי בתרומה דרבנן אכול. תרומת פירות האילן וירק: דאורייתא. דגן תירוש ויצהר לא אכול ומש"ה לא קשיא למ"ד מעלין מתרומה ליוחסין דכי מסקינן ליוחסין מתרומה דאורייתא כו': דאיכא למיגזר משום תרומה דאורייתא. שהרי לארץ באו ומצויה שם תרומה גמורה דאורייתא מה שלא היה מצוי להם בגולה ויש לחוש פן יאכילום בה: לא במידי דאקרי קדש. והיינו תרומה: וכל זר לא יאכל קדש. בתרומה משתעי דכתיב בפרשה לעיל מיניה ובא השמש וטהר ואחר יאכל מן הקדשים ואוקמינן בתרומה ביבמות בהערל (דף עד:): ולא במידי דאקרי קדשים. אפילו חזה ושוק של שלמים הנאכלים לנשי כהנים ולעבדיהם: ואמר מר. ביבמות בפרק יש מותרות בבת כהן שניסת לישראל ונעשית אלמנה וגרושה וזרע אין לה שחוזרת לתרומת אביה ואינה חוזרת לחזה ושוק וילפינן לה מהאי קרא כי תהיה לאיש זר היא בתרומת הקדשים לא תאכל עוד: חזקה לכהונה. להעיד עליו שהוא כהן: נשיאות כפים בבבל. הרואהו נושא כפיו בבבל מעיד עליו בכל מקום שהוא כהן ומקבלין הימנו לפי שיש שם ישיבה וב"ד קבוע בודקין אחר נושאי כפים אבל אכילת חלה ותרומה אינה חזקה דחוצה לארץ לאו דאורייתא תרומה דיליה ולא קפדי כולי האי: ואכילת חלה בסוריא. היא ארם צובה שכיבשה דוד וחיברה לא"י וקסבר האי תנא כיבוש יחיד שמיה כיבוש וחלתה ותרומתה דאורייתא וקס"ד תנא חלה וה"ה לתרומה: וחילוק מתנות. הזרוע והלחיים: בכרכין. ואע"ג דאיסורן אין איסור לזרים הואיל וכרכים מקום שווקין הן ומצויין בו עוברים ושבים המכירין בו אי לאו דכהן הוה לא מחליף נפשיה: לא לתרומה. הרואהו נושא כפיו בבבל או אוכל חלה דווקא בסוריא והעיד עליו בא"י מקבלין עדותו להאכילו תרומה אבל לא ליוחסין: מה אכילת חלה. עדות חזקתה: ליוחסין. דאי לתרומה פשיטא היא גופה תרומה היא וכבר הוחזק בה: ומסקינן מחלה דרבנן כו'. דאי לאו כהן הוא לא הוו ספו ליה חלה גזירה משום תרומה: וכדאפיך. לקמן מפרש: נשיאות כפים וחילוק גרנות. לתרומה: בא"י. נושאי כפים דאיכא ב"ד קבועין ובדקי וחילוק גרנות קס"ד השתא דתרומה בזמן הזה דאורייתא וכיון דעון מיתה איכא מסקינן מינה ליוחסין: בסוריא וכ"מ ששלוחי א"י מגיעין. להודיע לגולה יום שקידשו ב"ד את החדש לעשות פסח בזמנו דהיינו היושבים בתוך מהלך חמשה עשר יום: נשיאות כפים ראיה. לפי שב"ד קבוע שם שמקבל שליחות החדש של ב"ד הגדול: אבל לא חילוק גרנות. דתרומה דידהו לאו דאורייתא ובסוריא נמי האי תנא סבר כיבוש יחיד לא שמיה כיבוש ופלוגתא דתנאי היא בהך מילתא (ע"ז דף כא.): בבי רב. בית המדרש קרי בי רב: נתחייבו בחלה. דכתיב בבואכם אל הארץ ותניא בספרי ר' ישמעאל אומר שינה הכתוב ביאה זו מכל ביאות שבתורה שבכולן נאמר כי תבאו כי יביאך וכאן בבואכם ללמדך שכיון שנכנסו לה נתחייבו: ולא נתחייבו בתרומות ומעשרות. דכתיב דגנך תבואת זרעך המיוחדת לך ועוד שהרי תלה הכתוב המעשר במנין שנות השמטה דכתיב בשנה השלישית שנת המעשר ושמטות לא מנו אלא משכבשו וחילקו כדאמרינן בסדר עולם ובמסכת ערכין (דף יב:): הכי גרסינן אי בבואכם יכול משנכנסו לה שנים ושלשה מרגלים תלמוד לומר בבואכם בביאת כולכם כו'. והכי פירושו כיון דשינה הכתוב ביאה זו לכתוב בה בבואכם ולא כתב כי תבאו יכול משנכנסו לה מרגלים ת"ל כו':

תוספות

ואלא מאי גדולה חזקה. בשלמא אי אין מעלין ניחא הא דגדולה חזקה אע"ג דאיכא למיחש לב"ד טועין שיעלו מן נשיאות כפים לקדשי קדשים [ואע"ג דבלא חזקה מעלין לתרומה ע"פ עד אחד ולא חיישינן לב"ד טועין שמא יעלו ליוחסין השתא סבר המקשן דיוחסין חמירא ולא אתו למיטעי כמו לקדשי קדשים] אבל השתא דאמרת טעמא דריע חזקייהו ולא חיישינן דלמא אתי לאסוקי כיון דלא אתי למטעי מאי גדולה חזקה: או דלמא אפילו למ"ד אין מעלין ה"מ תרומה דמתאכלא בצינעה כו'. תימה מה תולה באכילה והא פשיטא דלכ"ע אין מעלין מאכילת תרומה ליוחסין דהא איכא למיחש דלמא עבד כהן הוא אלא בחלוקת תרומה (א) בגורן הוא דפליגי אם מעלים ליוחסין אם לאו ובמעלין מתרומה ליוחסין לא איפליגו בה תנאי בהדיא אלא דתליא הא פלוגתא בפלוגתא אם חולקין תרומה לעבד בלא רבו אם לאו למ"ד חולקין אין מעלין דדלמא עבד הוא והכי איבעי ליה למימר הכא אפילו למ"ד אין מעלין ה"מ תרומה דחולקין לעבד בלא רבו ואיכא למיחש דלמא עבד הוא אבל נשיאו' כפים לעולם אימא לך דמעלין דאין עבד נושא כפיו: [נ"ל דספיר נקט דמתאכלא בצינעא דלמ"ד מעלין מאכילת תרומה נמי מעלין ובענין דליכא למיחש שהוא עבד שילא מבית הספר וטעמא כיון דעון מיתה הוא חיישינן שמא יעלוהו ליוחסין ולכך אילטריך שני עדים להאכילו בתרומה ולכך נמי אין חולקין לעבד אלא א"כ רבו עמו ומ"ד אין מעלין אע"ג דעון מיתה הוא לא חיים להכי שמא יעלוהו כיון דבצנעא הויא אכילת תרומה וכן חלוקה אבל נשיאות כפים דאיפרסם איבעיא ליה אי חיישינן שמא יעלוהו משום דאי לאו דכהן הוא לא הוה חליף כולי האי ולא הוי מצי למנקט כמו שכתבו התוס' אפילו למ"ד אין מעלין משום דאיכא למיחש דלמא עבד הוא דלא תליא בהכי דאפילו היכא דליכא למיחש דלמא עבד הוא אין מעלין כמו ביוצא מבית הספר או שמעידין עליו שאינו עבד ואדרבה הא דחולקין לו בלא רבו היינו משום דאין מעלין ועיקר טעמא דפלוגתייהו משום מעלין ואין מעלין דאי לאו הכי קשה באיזה סברא פליגי כמו שהקשו לעיל] (ת"י): וכי מסקינן מתרומה ליוחסין ה"מ בדאורייתא כו'. רבינו יצחק בן רבינו מאיר לא גרים לה דהא איבעית אימא רב נחמן קאמר לה ואי גרסי' לה א"כ היה סותר בעצמו ראיה שהביא דאי לא תימא הכי למ"ד מעלין מתרומה ליוחסין הא אתי לאסוקי אלא טעמא משום דריע חזקייהו ואין זו סוגיית הש"ס אם לא יאמר ולאו מילתא היא דאמרי ובפ' עשרה יוחסין (קדושין סט:) גרסינן לה ואגב שיטפא דהתם שיבשו לכותבה כאן: לא במידי דאיקרי קדש. וא"ת תרומה נמי איקרי קדשים דכתיב ובא השמש וטהר ואחר יאכל מן הקדשים וההוא קרא איירי בתרומה דהעריב שמשו אוכל בתרומה וי"ל דודאי גבי טמא תרומה מיקרי קדשים אבל הכא אאכילת זר קאמר דלא אשכחן קדשים גבי אכילת זר: נשיאות כפים בבבל. דוקא נשיאות כפים ולא אכילת חלה ואע"ג דבסוריא נמי הוי מדרבנן אין מדקדקין בבבל כמו בסוריא דסבר האי תנא כיבוש יחיד שמיה כיבוש ואכילת חלה בסוריא ה"ה נשיאות כפים כדמוכח לקמן: לא חילוק גרנות גופה לחלה וקסבר תרומה כו'. וצ"ל דפליגי הנך ברייתות בפלוגתא דרב הונא בריה דרב יהושע ורבנן דאי לאו הכי בחד מהנך ברייתות ממה נפשך איכא למידק דמעלין מנשיאות כפים ליוחסין ופליגי נמי דלברייתא קמייתא אכילת חלה בסוריא חזקה לתרומה וכל שכן דאכילת תרומה דאורייתא דהויא חזקה לחלה דרבנן ולברייתא שניה קתני חילוק גרנות דהיינו תרומה בסוריא לא הויא חזקה לחלה:

מסורת הש"ס

א) יבמות סח: פז. קדושין סט:, ב) [עיין תוס' שבת י"ד: ד"ה והכהנ], ג) תוספתא פאה פ"ד, ד) נדה מו., ה) [ב"מ פט.], ו) [בנדה מו. וכן בב"מ פט. איתא במעשר ועי' פרש"י הכלל דגרים תרוויהון], ז) [עיין תוס' נדה מו. ד"ה ל"ג אילו נאמר], ח) [ועיין רש"י בנדה מו. וב"מ פט. מפרש בכל מקום טעם אחר], ט) נ"י כ"י.

הגהות הב"ח

(א) תד"ה או דלמא כו' אלא בחלוקת תרומה וכו'. נ"ב וכן פרש"י יבמות דף צט ע"ב:

תורה אור השלם

א) וַיֹּאמֶר הַתִּרְשָׁתָא לָהֶם אֲשֶׁר לֹא יֹאכְלוּ מִקֹּדֶשׁ הַקֳּדָשִׁים עַד עֲמֹד כֹּהֵן לְאוּרִים וּלְתֻמִּים: [עזרא ב, סג]

ב) וְכָל זָר לֹא יֹאכַל קֹדֶשׁ תּוֹשַׁב כֹּהֵן וְשָׂכִיר לֹא יֹאכַל קֹדֶשׁ: [ויקרא כב, י]

ג) וּבַת כֹּהֵן כִּי תִהְיֶה לְאִישׁ זָר הִוא בִּתְרוּמַת הַקֳּדָשִׁים לֹא תֹאכֵל: [ויקרא כב, יב]

ד) דַּבֵּר אֶל בְּנֵי יִשְׂרָאֵל וְאָמַרְתָּ אֲלֵהֶם בְּבֹאֲכֶם אֶל הָאָרֶץ אֲשֶׁר אֲנִי מֵבִיא אֶתְכֶם שָׁמָּה: [במדבר טו, יח]

עין משפט נר מצוה

פז א מיי' פ"כ מהל' איסורי ביאה הלכה א ופ"ו מהל' תרומות ה"ג:
פח ב מיי' פ"כ מהל' איסורי ביאה הל' ד:
פט ג מיי' שם הלכה יא טוש"ע אה"ע סימן ג סעיף ג:
צ ד מיי' שם הלכה ג ופ"א מהל' תרומות ה"א סמג עשין קמג טוש"ע י"ד סימן שלא סעיף ג:
צא ה מיי' פ"כ מהל' איסורי ביאה הלכה ג סמג עשין קמ טוש"ע י"ד סי' שכב סעיף ג:

ליקוטי רש"י

[התחלת ליקוטי רש"י ששייך לכאן נדפס בדף כד:]

ולא במידי דאיקרי קדשים. חזה ושוק של שלמים דאשכחן דאיקרי קדשים [קידושין סט.]. לאיש זר. לוי וישראל [ויקרא כב, יב]. במורם מן הקדשים. חזה ושוק [קידושין שם]. לא תאכל. ואפילו זרע אין לה ושבה אל בית אביה חוזרת לתרומה ואינה חוזרת לחזה ושוק [שם ע.]. כשהיא חוזרת לבית אביה במיתת הבעל וזרע אין לה אינה חוזרת לחזה ושוק של שלמים לאכול כשאר אחיות האוכלות לבכורי אתה ובניך ובנותיך (ויקרא י) [יבמות פח:]. מדהוה מצי למכתב בקדשים וכתב בתרומת למורם הוא דאתא והאי לא תאכל לעולם הוא ולא תימא כשזרע בעלה ישראל כדמשמע קרא ובת כהן כי תהיה לאיש זר כו' דהא אוקימנא להאי קרא בפרק אלמנה (לעיל דף סח.) בנבעלה לפסול לה כגון נתין וממזר וחלל שפסלו עולמית וכהנת דמנסבא לזר לא אכלה מושבה אל בית אביה ילפינן מכלל דמעיקרא לא אכלה ומילתיה דרב חסדא מבתרומות נפקא דלא דכולה קרא לנבעלה לפסול לה אתא ליתמו בקדשים לא תאכל מאי בתרומות שמע מינה הכי קאמר יש לך אחרת שאוכלת בקדשים כגון תרומה ואינה אוכלת במורם ואי זו חוזרת דסמיך לה ובת כהן כי תהיה אלמנה וגרושה ולהא מילתא בפרק אלמנה (לעיל סח:) [שם סח.]. נתחייבו בחלה ולא נתחייבו וכו'. (ספרי פ' שלח) דכתיב בבואכם אל הארץ שינה הכתוב ביאה זו מכל ביאות שבתורה שנאמר בהן כי תבואו וכאן נאמר בבואכם משנכנסו לארץ נתחייבו בחלה אבל במעשר לא נתחייבו אלא לאחר ירושה וישיבה דכתיב עשר תעשר וכתיב בתריה במקום אשר יבחר עד שנבחרה שילה לא נתחייבו והיינו לאחר כיבוש וחילוק דכתיב ביהושע וכל ימי כיבוש וחילוק היה אהל מועד בגלגל ארבע עשרה שנה כדאמר [זבחים] (דף קיח:) [ב"מ פט.]. בחלה (במדבר טו) בבואכם אל הארץ והכי בלאו. ולא נתחייבו במעשר דכתיב עשר תעשר (דברים יד) תבואת זרעך עד שיביא כל אחד ואחד את שלו [נדה מו.]. בבואכם אל הארץ. משונה ביאה זו מכל ביאות שבתורה שבכולן נאמר כי תבא וכיון שפרט לך הכתוב באחת מהן שאינה לאחר ירושה וישיבה אף כולן כן אבל כאן נאמר בה משנכנסו ואכלו מלחמה נתחייבו בחלה [במדבר טו, יח].

The Gemara asks:

וְאֶלָּא מַאי גְּדוֹלָה חֲזָקָה – **But** if this is the basis of Hatirshasa's ruling, **what** did R' Yose mean when he said, **"Great is** the power of ***chazakah*"?** Since there was no reason to prohibit *terumah* to these questionable Kohanim, why is the fact that Hatirshasa allowed them to continue eating *terumah* an exceptional example of the rule of *chazakah*?[1]

The Gemara answers:

מֵעִיקָּרָא אָכוּל בִּתְרוּמָה דְּרַבָּנָן – **Originally, they could eat** only **Rabbinic *terumah,***[2] since that was the only *terumah* available in Babylonia; הַשְׁתָּא אָכוּל בִּתְרוּמָה דְּאוֹרַיְיתָא – but **now,** in Eretz Yisrael, **they could eat** even **Biblical *terumah,*** i.e. the *terumah* of Eretz Yisrael.[3]

The Gemara offers an alternative approach to the question of why Hatirshasa was not afraid that if these questionable Kohanim eat *terumah* they will be elevated to the status of the genealogically fit:

וְאִי בָּעֵית אֵימָא – **Or, if you prefer, say** that הַשְׁתָּא נַמִּי בִּתְרוּמָה דְּרַבָּנָן אָכוּל – **even now,** in Eretz Yisrael, **they could eat** only **Rabbinic *terumah,*** בִּתְרוּמָה דְּאוֹרַיְיתָא לֹא אָכוּל – and **they could not eat Biblical *terumah.***[4] וְכִי מַסְּקִינַן מִתְּרוּמָה לְיוּחֲסִין – **And when do we elevate** someone who eats ***terumah* to the** status of the **genealogically fit?** בִּתְרוּמָה דְּאוֹרַיְיתָא – Only **when** he eats **Biblical *terumah.*** בִּתְרוּמָה דְּרַבָּנָן לֹא מַסְּקִינַן – **When** he eats **Rabbinic *terumah,*** however, **we do not elevate** him **to the** status of the **genealogically fit.** Thus, there was no danger that these questionable Kohanim would be declared genealogically fit.

The Gemara asks:

וְאֶלָּא מַאי גְּדוֹלָה חֲזָקָה – **But** if they were permitted to eat only Rabbinic *terumah,* we return to our earlier question: **What is** meant by the statement, **"Great is** the power of ***chazakah*"?**[5]

The Gemara answers that reliance on their *chazakah* was still extraordinary in this case, for the following reason:

דְּאַף עַל גַּב דְּאִיכָּא לְמִיגְזַר מִשּׁוּם תְּרוּמָה דְּאוֹרַיְיתָא – **Because even though there was** reason **to decree** a ban on their eating Rabbinic *terumah,* **to forestall** the possibility of their eating **Biblical *terumah,*** לֹא גָּזְרִינַן – **we** (i.e. Hatirshasa) **did not decree** such a ban.[6]

The Gemara challenges the assertion that they were not permitted to eat Biblical *terumah*:

וּבִתְרוּמָה דְּאוֹרַיְיתָא לֹא אָכוּל – **Now, did they not** have permission to **eat Biblical *terumah*** in Eretz Yisrael? וְהָא כְּתִיב – **But it is written:**[7] ,,אֲשֶׁר לֹא־יֹאכְלוּ מִקֹּדֶשׁ הַקֳּדָשִׁים'' – *And Hatirshasa instructed them **that they not eat of the holy of holies,*** which implies the following: מִקֹּדֶשׁ הַקֳּדָשִׁים הוּא דְּלֹא אָכוּל – **It is** only **of the holy of holies** (i.e. sacrificial food) **that they may not eat,** הָא בִּתְרוּמָה דְּאוֹרַיְיתָא אָכוּל – **but they may eat everything** else of lesser sanctity, including Biblical *terumah*! – **?** –

The Gemara answers:

הָכִי קָאָמַר – **This is what [Hatirshasa]** meant when he **said** that they could not eat *the holy of holies:* לֹא בְּמִידֵי דְּאִיקְּרֵי קֹדֶשׁ – He meant that they may **not** eat **that which is called *holy,***[8] meaning *terumah,* דִּכְתִיב ,,וְכָל־זָר לֹא־יֹאכַל קֹדֶשׁ'' – **as it is written:** ***And no non-Kohen may eat the holy.***[9] וְלֹא בְּמִידֵי דְּאִיקְּרֵי קֳדָשִׁים – **And** they may **not** eat **that which is called *holies,*** meaning sacrificial food, דִּכְתִיב ,,וּבַת־כֹּהֵן כִּי תִהְיֶה לְאִישׁ זָר הִוא בִּתְרוּמַת הַקֳּדָשִׁים לֹא תֹאכֵל'' – **as it is written:** ***And if a Kohen's daughter marries a non-Kohen she shall not eat of that which is separated from the holies,***[10] וְאָמַר מַר – **and the master has taught** that this means: בְּמוּרָם מִן הַקֳּדָשִׁים לֹא תֹּאכַל – **That which is separated from the sacrificial offerings she may not eat.**[11]

NOTES

1. R' Yose did not say, "Where [in Scripture] do we see the application of the rule of *chazakah?*" but rather, "Great is the power of *chazakah.*" This choice of words implies that the rule of *chazakah* permits whatever was allowed previously even after the grounds for prohibition have *increased* (*Rashi* to *Kiddushin* 69b ד״ה ואלא). In this case, however, the reason for prohibiting these Kohanim to eat *terumah* was not stronger in Eretz Yisrael than it was in Babylonia, since even in Eretz Yisrael their status would not be improperly enhanced as a result.

The Gemara is not specifically challenging the answer just given (namely, that these Kohanim would not be promoted to the level of the genealogically fit *because* their Kohanic status was known to be flawed). Rather, this question also pertains to the opinion that one who eats *terumah* is *never* assumed to be genealogically fit (*Rashi,* according to *Re'ah;* cf. *Tosafos* and *Rashba;* see also *Melo HaRo'im* and *Hagahos Radal*).

2. *Terumah* from crops grown in Babylonia is required only by Rabbinic law (*Rambam, Hil. Terumos* 1:1). Any commandment pertaining to the land or its produce is limited to Eretz Yisrael, as the Mishnah in *Kiddushin* (36b) states (*Rashi*).

3. Thus, *chazakah* extended their Kohanic privileges beyond what they had originally been. [It was within the power of *chazakah* to effect this change, because their previous abstinence from Biblical *terumah* did not stem from doubts about their Kohanic status, but rather from the nonavailability of such *terumah* (see *Melo HaRo'im*).]

4. The Biblical requirement of *terumah* is limited even in Eretz Yisrael to grain, wine and olive oil, while the *terumah* requirement for other fruits as well as for vegetables is only Rabbinic (*Rashi*). [Others consider the *terumah* requirement for all fruits Biblical (see *Rambam, Hil. Terumos* 2:1, and *Kesef Mishneh* there). All agree, however, that *terumah* from vegetables is only a Rabbinic requirement.]

5. [Previously, the Gemara solved this difficulty by explaining that their *chazakah* allowed them to go from eating Rabbinic *terumah* to eating Biblical *terumah.* At this point, however, the Gemara holds that they remained limited to Rabbinic *terumah.*]

6. Since Biblical *terumah* was available in Eretz Yisrael, it would be reasonable to forbid the questionable Kohanim to eat even Rabbinic *terumah* there in order to avoid the possibility of their eating Biblical *terumah.* This was unlike the situation in Babylonia, where Biblical *terumah* was not available in any event (*Rashi*). Hatirshasa thus had to rely on the power of *chazakah* to allow them to retain their permission to eat Rabbinic *terumah,* although the grounds for prohibition had increased (see note 1).

7. *Ezra* 2:63.

8. The phrase *the holy of holies* is taken as referring not to a single category of sacred food, but to two categories: one called *holy* and the other called *holies.*

9. *Leviticus* 22:10. The context of this verse indicates that the topic is *terumah,* not sacrificial offerings. An earlier verse states: *And [when] the sun sets, he will then be tahor, and afterwards he may eat from the holy things* (ibid. v. 7). [The chapter speaks of a variety of *tumah*-contaminated people, among them a *metzora* and *zav.* For these two types of *tumah,* one must not only immerse himself in a *mikveh* to become *tahor,* but must also bring offerings.] Thus, when the verse states that he can eat *the holy things* after sunset — even though he will not bring the sacrifices for his *tumah* until the following day — the verse must be speaking of a type of sacred food permitted to someone after immersion (and sunset) but before the bringing of his offerings. This can refer only to *terumah,* since sacrificial food is forbidden to him until after his offerings have been brought (*Rashi* here and to *Kiddushin* 69b).

10. Ibid. 22:12.

11. This refers to the breast and thigh of a *shelamim* sacrifice, which are *separated* from the offering and given to a Kohen and his household to eat. The verse teaches that if a Kohen's daughter marries a non-Kohen and becomes widowed or divorced without bearing him any children, although she may return to her father's house and eat *terumah* there as she did before, she may not resume eating sacrificial foods (see *Yevamos* 87a).

From this verse we see that the term *holies* refers to the breast and thigh of the *shelamim* sacrifice. Hatirshasa thus meant that the questionable Kohanim could not partake even of this lowest level of sacrifi-

hands[31] to recite the Priestly Blessing, **they could be elevated** to the status of the genealogically fit! What then was accomplished by forbidding them to eat sacrificial foods?[32] Obviously, then, we do not elevate someone who recites the Priestly Blessing to the level of the genealogically fit.

The Gemara refutes this proof:

שָׁאנִי הָכָא דְּרִיעַ חֶזְקַיְיהוּ – That situation **was different because their status was** widely known to be **flawed.** Since other Kohanim were seen eating sacrificial foods, whereas these Kohanim were not, it was widely known that their Kohanic status was tainted. Hence, although they recited the Priestly Blessing, there was no danger that they would be raised to the level of the genealogically fit. But in the case of other people, whose Kohanic status is not known to be flawed,[33] recitation of the Priestly Blessing can indeed be taken as proof of genealogical fitness.

The Gemara supports this refutation:

דְּאִי לֹא תֵּימָא הָכִי – For if you do not say this (namely, that their Kohanic status was widely known to be flawed), **לְמַאן דְּאָמַר מַעֲלִין מִתְּרוּמָה לְיוּחֲסִין – according to the one who says** that **we elevate** a Kohen who eats ***terumah*** **to** the status of **the genealogically fit,** how could Hatirshasa allow these questionable Kohanim to continue eating *terumah*? **כֵּיוָן דְּאָכְלֵי בִּתְרוּמָה אָתֵי לְאַסּוּקִינְהוּ – Once they** are seen **eating *terumah* they will come to be elevated** to the status of the genealogically fit! **אֶלָּא לַאו מִשּׁוּם דְּרִיעַ חֶזְקַיְיהוּ – Rather, is it not** clear that this was not a concern **because their status was** widely known to be **flawed?**

NOTES

31. See note 17.

32. Once they have been established as genealogically pure Kohanim, they would be given sacrificial foods (based on *Rashi;* cf. *Ramban*).

33. E.g. in the current era, when there are no sacrifices [and thus failure to eat sacrificial food is not indicative of anything] (*Rashba;* see *Rashi*).

עין משפט נר מצוה

פד א ב ג ד מיי' פי"ג מהל' משכב ומושב הלכה כג:
פה ה מיי' פ"כ מהל' איסורי ביאה הל"ב ט טוש"ע אה"ע סי' ב סעיף ג:
פו ו מיי' שם הלכה ד והלכה יח:

תוספות רי"ד

לן דחלל הוא. אבל לא ישא אשה כשרה ואפי' בתו של כ"ג. והא ק"ל דלא הוחזרו כשרות להנשא לפסולים. וצ"ל לפרש דהאי דאמר להשיאו אשה לאו להשיא לו אשה. אלא להשיא מנשיו כהונה. כגון אלמנתו ובתו דמספקינן ליה בחלל. ובת חלל ואלמנות חלל הן פסולות לכהונה: איבעיא להו מהו להעלות משטרות ליוחסין. פי' אילימא דכתיב בי' אני פלוני כהן חתמתי עד מאן קמסהיד עלויה. לא צריכא דכתיב בי' אני פ' לויתי מנה מפלוני וחתימו סהדי א"ד אמנה שבשטר קמסהדי או דלמא אכולה מילתא מסהדי. ר"ה ור"ח ח"א מעלין וח"א אין מעלין. והלכתא כדברי המקיל. ואילו כתבו שני עדים פ' כהן לוה מפלוני דליכא מאן דפליג דודאי מעלין. דהא עדים מעידים כי הוא כהן א). איבעי' להו מהו להעלות מכהונה ליוחסין.

חשק שלמה על תוס' רי"ד

א) וכ"כ הר"ן בשם הרא"ה ז"ל ע"ש ובזה מיושב קושית תוס' ד"ה אמנה מה שהקשו מגט פשוט וכו' ועי' בש"ך חו"מ סי' מ"ט ס"ק ט"ו.

תורה אור השלם

א) וּמִבְּנֵי הַכֹּהֲנִים בְּנֵי חֳבַיָּה בְּנֵי הַקּוֹץ בְּנֵי בַרְזִלַּי אֲשֶׁר לָקַח מִבְּנוֹת בַּרְזִלַּי הַגִּלְעָדִי אִשָּׁה וַיִּקָּרֵא עַל שְׁמָם: אֵלֶּה בִּקְשׁוּ כְתָבָם הַמִּתְיַחְשִׂים וְלֹא נִמְצָאוּ וַיְגֹאֲלוּ מִן הַכְּהֻנָּה: וַיֹּאמֶר הַתִּרְשָׁתָא לָהֶם אֲשֶׁר לֹא יֹאכְלוּ מִקֹּדֶשׁ הַקֳּדָשִׁים עַד עֲמֹד כֹּהֵן לְאוּרִים וּלְתֻמִּים: [עזרא ב, סא - סג]

גמרא

הכא נמי בשכלי אומנותו בידו והיכא אתמר דרבי חמא בר עוקבא אהא דתנן [א] הקדר שהניח קדירותיו וירד לשתות (ג מים מן היאור) הפנימיות טהורות והחיצונות טמאות והתניא אלו ואלו טמאות אמר רבי חמא בר עוקבא [ב] בשכלי אומנותו בידו מפני שיד הכל ממשמשת בהן והתניא אלו ואלו טהורות א"ר חמא בר עוקבא [ג] בשאין כלי אומנותו בידו ואלא הא דתנן הפנימיות טהורות והחיצונות טמאות היכי משכחת לה [ד] דסמיכא לרשות הרבים ומשום חיפופי רשות הרבים ואיבעית אימא ר' יהודה ורבנן במעלין מתרומה ליוחסין קמיפלגי איבעיא להו מהו להעלות משטרות ליוחסין היכי דמי אילימא דכתיב ביה אני פלוני כהן חתמתי עד מאן קא מסהיד עילויה לא צריכא דכתיב ביה אני פלוני כהן לויתי מנה מפלוני וחתימו סהדי מאי אמנה שבשטר קא מסהדי או דלמא אכולה מילתא קא מסהדי רב הונא ורב חסדא חד אמר מעלין וחד אמר [ה] אין מעלין איבעיא להו מהו להעלות מנשיאות כפים ליוחסין ותיבעי למ"ד מעלין מתרומה ליוחסין ותיבעי למ"ד אין מעלין תיבעי למ"ד מעלין הני מילי תרומה דעון מיתה היא אבל נשיאות כפים דאיסור עשה לא או דלמא לא שנא תיבעי למ"ד אין מעלין הני מילי תרומה דמיתאכלא בצנעא אבל נשיאות כפים דבפרהסיא אי לאו כהן הוא כולי האי לא מחציף איניש נפשיה או דלמא לא שנא רב חסדא ורבי אבינא חד אמר מעלין וחד אמר [ו] אין מעלין א"ל רב נחמן בר יצחק לרבא מהו להעלות מנשיאות כפים ליוחסין א"ל פלוגתא דרב חסדא ורבי אבינא הלכתא מאי א"ל אנא מתניתא ידענא דתניא ר' יוסי אומר [ז] גדולה חזקה שנאמר א) ומבני הכהנים בני חביה בני הקוץ בני ברזילי אשר לקח מבנות ברזילי הגלעדי אשה ויקרא על שמם אלה בקשו כתבם המתיחשים ולא נמצאו ויגאלו מן הכהונה ויאמר התרשתא להם אשר לא יאכלו מקדש הקדשים עד עמוד כהן לאורים ד) ותומים אמר להם הרי אתם בחזקתכם במה הייתם אוכלים בגולה בקדשי הגבול אף כאן בקדשי הגבול ואי סלקא דעתך מעלין מנשיאות כפים ליוחסין הני כיון דפרסי ידייהו אתי לאסוקינהו שאני הכא דריע חזקייהו דאי לא תימא הכי למאן דאמר מעלין מתרומה ליוחסין כיון דאכלי בתרומה אתי לאסוקינהו אלא לאו משום דריע חזקייהו

ואלא

רש"י

בשכלי אומנותו בידו. חמר המביא תבואה למכור היה נושא בידו כלי היכר של מכירה כגון מחק שמוחקין בה המדה והמביא להשמיע אינו נושא בידו כלי אומנות מכר והכא כגון שכלי אומנותו בידו של זה המזלזל את שלו דאין סהדי שלמוכרה הביאה הלכך אין זה אלא גומל וזה יעיד עליו בכרך שלפניהם: הקדר. שהוא תגר: הפנימיות טהורות. כולה מתרלא ואולא לקמיה: בשכלי אומנותו בידו. להיכר שהוא נושאן למוכרן: ממשמשת בהן. לבדוק וליקח: ומשום חיפופי רשות הרבים. שנותנים בני אדם אבנים גדולות או יתדות אצלי רה"ר להרחיק העגלות מלהזיק את הכתלים ומתוך שהן דוחקות את רה"ר וזה הניח קדירותיו אצלם דחק גם הוא את הדרך והעוברין שם מתחככין בהן ובגדיהן עוברין על פני אוירן ובגדי עם הארץ טמאים הם ומטמאים את הסילוניות: במעלין מתרומה ליוחסין. רבי יהודה סבר הרואה שמאכילין תרומה לאדם בחזקת כהן מעיד עליו בכל מקום שהוא כהן ומעלין אותו ליוחסין הלכך אם תאכילהו תרומה הרי אתה מביאו להשיאו אשה וטעמיה לאו משום גומלין הוא ורבנן סברי אין מעלין מתרומה ליוחסין: דאיסור מיתה. אם זר הוא לא היה אוכל תרומה שהוא עון מיתה: דאיסור עשה. כה תברכו (במדבר ו) אתם ולא זרים ולאו הבא מכלל עשה עשה: גדולה חזקה. שאין ב"ד יכולין להוציא דבר מחזקתו: בקשו כתבם המתיחשים. שיהו כהנים כשרים לפי שהתחתנו כהנים בגולה בגויי הארץ וילדו להם בנים כדכתיב בספר עזרא והם חללים הוצרכו הנולדים בגולה להתייחס כשעלו מן הגולה לשרת בבנין שני: ויגאלו. נפסלו מלשון לחם מגואל (מלאכי א): התרשתא. הוא נחמיה בן חכליה וכן כתוב בספר עזרא (נחמיה ח): עד עמוד כהן לאורים וגו'. כאדם (א) שאומר לחבירו עד שיבא המשיח דאורים ותומים לא הוו במקדש שני שנחסרו חמשה דברים כדאמרינן בסדר יומא (דף כא:): מקדשי הקדשים. דוקא מקדשי המקדש פסלינהו אבל תרומה שהיו רגילין בה בגולה לא אסר עלייהו משום דהוחזקו בה: קדשי הגבול. תרומה שהיא נוהגת בגבולין חוץ למקדש ולירושלים: אף כאן בקדשי הגבול. ומדאמר רבי יוסי גדולה חזקה ש"מ נשיאות כפים נמי לא אסר עלייהו שהרי הוחזקו בה בגבולין: ואי סלקא דעתך כו' אתי לאסוקינהו. ומה הועילו בתקנתם: שאני הכא. דליכא למיחש לאסוקינהו דהא ריע חזקייהו שהרי הכל רואין שאר כהנים אוכלין קדשי המקדש והם אינן אוכלין יש כאן היכר גדול שיש בהן צד פסול אבל שאר בני אדם כגון בזמן הזה לעולם מעלין מנשיאות כפים ליוחסין: [ה] [דאי לא תימא הכי. דעל דא סמיך שיש בהן היכר תרומה נמי תקשי למ"ד מעלין מתרומה ליוחסין]:

ואלא

תוספות

בשכלי אומנותו בידו. פירש רבינו חננאל זה שאומר עליו שהוא כהן יש בידו כלים שמשמשין בהן בטהרה כגון כלי גללים כלי אבנים כלי אדמה שאין מקבלין טומאה שכל הרואה כלים הללו בידו מתרחק ממנו מלטמאותו ודומה שהוא כהן ולכך האמינוהו חכמים:

ואיבעית אימא רבי יהודה ורבנן במעלין מתרומה ליוחסין קמיפלגי. ולא אתא לשנויי אלא קשיא דרבי יהודה אדרבי יהודה אבל לרבנן אדרבנן לעולם צריך לתרץ בשכלי אומנותו בידו והקשה הר' שמואל מוואלדין ומעיקרא היכי בעי למימר לטעמא דר"י משום גומלין והא בלא גומלים ע"כ סבר רבי יהודה בשילהי פרקין (לקמן דף כח.) דמעלין מתרומה ליוחסין ותירץ ר"י דמעיקרא ס"ד דלאו טעמא משום גומלים לא היינו מפקידים את הכהן מן התרומה כדי לומר מעלין כיון דמן הדין ראוי לחלוק ע"פ חבירו ולדרבה קודם היינו אומרים אין מעלין אע"ג דגבי עבד אמר לקמן לרבי יהודה דאין חולקין לו תרומה משום דמעלין התם אין כל כך חששה בהפסד של עבד זה אם אין חולקין לו תרומה בלא רבו וא"ת ובלאו סברא פליגי לימרו תרויהו דמעלין ולצטרך שני עדים בתרומה או לימרו תרויהו דלא מעלין ולא יצטרך אלא עד אחד בתרומה וי"ל דבהא פליגי דמר סבר חיישינן שמא יעלו מתרומה ליוחסין לפיכך הצריכו שני עדים ומר סבר דלא חיישינן א):

אמנה שבשטר קמסהדי. וא"ת ואי לאו אכולה מילתא קמסהדי א"כ עדים חתמי אע"ג דלא ידעי אי כהן הוא אי לאו ואם כן הא דתנן בגט פשוט (ב"ב דף קעג.) שני יוסף בן שמעון הדרין בעיר אחת אם היו משולשין יכתבו כהן ומה מועיל כיון שעדים חותמין אע"פ שאין מכירים בו אם הוא כהן והרי הוא יכול להעריס ולכתוב שטר אחר בשם חבירו כהן ויוציא ממון מחבירו כהן וי"ל דהיכא דהוחזקו שני יוסף בן שמעון ודאי אכולא מילתא קא מסהדי כי או הן צריכין לידע אם בן כהן הוא והתם ודאי מעלין משטרות ליוחסין והכא מיבעיא לן היכא דלא הוחזקו: חד אמר מעלין. ואם תאמר ומאי לא חשיב ליה בהדי הנך דתנן בעשרה יוחסין (קדושין דף עו. ושם) אין בודקין מן המזבח ולמעלה ולא מדוכן כו' וי"ל דהנך דשטרות מלתא דפשיטא היא דלכון דאכולא מלתא קמסהדי א"כ הוי עדות גמור ולכך לא קא חשיב עדים וא"ת ומאי לא חשיב תרומה ונשיאות כפים למ"ד מעלין ואור"ת דתרומה בכלל מזבח ונשיאות כפים בכלל דוכן אע"ג דההוא דוכן היינו שיר כדמשמע התם בגמרא מ"ד מעלין הוה מוקי לה נמי בדוכן כהנים שבגבולים ומיהו קשה אמאי לא חשיב ס"ת שקרא בחזקת כהן כדלקמן ויש לומר דאיכא למימר דתנא ושייר כולהו ובספר הישר פירש ר"ת דלאו בעבודת מזבח ממש איירי אלא כגון הפסט וניתוח דברים הכשרים בזרים דלא היו מניחין לעשות אותם אלא למיוחסין מן המשיאין לכהונה אבל מילי דכהונה כגון תרומה ונשיאות כפים וס"ת לא איצטריך למתני: שאני הכא דריע חזקייהו. פי' בקונטרס שהכל רואים שאר כהנים אוכלין שאר קדשי מזבח ואלו אין אוכלין וק"ק דמ"מ תיקשי למ"ד מעלין אמאי לא אסקינהו לקדשי מזבח וליוחסין ונראה לר"ת דריע חזקייהו היינו שהיו מיחסים אותם אחר בני ברזילי שהיה ישראל ועוד שלא מצאו כתבם והיכא דאיתרע חזקה אין מעלין לכ"ע אבל קשה דפריך מעיקרא אתי לאסוקינהו הוה ליה למיפרך אמאי נגאלו כלל מן הכהונה ויש לומר דשפיר הוה ידע דריע חזקייהו ומשום הכי לא אסקינהו אלא דהוה ס"ד דלאע"ג דריע חזקייהו איכא למיחש דלמא אתי לאסוקינהו לבסוף שלא ידעו שלא מצאו כתבם:

ואלא

מסורת הש"ס

א) טהרות פרק ז משנה א, ב) [משנה ליתא], ג) קדושין סט:, ד) [ל"ל ולתומים], ה) נ"י כ"י.

תוספות ישנים

א) [ועוד דלה ר"י לפרש טעמא דמ"ד מעלין כדי שיהו עדים מצוין ליוחסין וחוזר בו משום דלא משמע הכי במסוך דקאמר ה"מ תרומה דעון מיתה. ת"י עה"ג]:

הגהות הב"ח

(א) רש"י ד"ה עד עמוד כו' כאדם שאומר. נ"ב הוא בפ' עגלה ערופה דף מח ע"ב:

ליקוטי רש"י

במעלין מתרומה ליוחסין. הרואה כהן אוכל בתרומה במקומו אין צריך לבדוק אחריו ביוחסין ונושא כהן בתו. גדולה חזקה. יש לסמוך עליה יפה. בקשו כתבם המתיחשים. כתב יחוסן. התרשתא. נחמיה בן חכליה קרוי כן בספר עזרא ובגמרת ירושלמי נמצא שם שהיה משקה מלך היה צריך לשתות קודש שלא יחשדוהו שמא הטיל סם המות במשקה המלך התירו לו יין של עובדי כוכבים לשתות לכך נקרא התרשתא. מקדש הקדשים. מדכתיב מקדש הקדשים שמעינן דלא אסרי בתרומה אלא מקדשי המקדש. אמר להם. תרומה איני יכול לאסור עליכם מפני מוחזקתם שהוחזקתם בגולה לאכלה. בקדשי הגבול. תרומה הנאכלת בכל מקום. כיון דאכלי בתרומה אתי לאסוקינהו. ומאי לא חש לה נחמיה דלא לאסוקינהו. דריע חזקייהו. לא איצטריך למיחש להאי דכיון דשאר כהנים אוכלים קדשי המקדש והם נגאלו מהם הורע חזקתם ויש בהם היכר ולא אתי לאסוקינהו [קידושין שם].

[מכאן שייך לדף כה.] ואלא. כיון דליכא למגזר מידי. מאי גדולה חזקה. דאמר רבי יוסי מאי רבותא לא היה לו לומר אלא מנין מחזקה כו' מדקאמר גדולה רבותא אשמועינן דאע"ג דאיכא לד איסור השתא טפי מעיקרא מסמכין עלה. בתרומה דרבנן. תרומת חוץ לארץ. בתרומה דאורייתא. משבאו לארץ. השתא נמי בתרומה דרבנן. היא דאכול כדמעיקרא ומאי ניהו תרומת פירות וירק. בתרומה דאורייתא. דגן תירוש ויצהר לא אכול. וכל זר לא יאכל קדש. כל אותו הענין מדבר בתרומה ולא בקדשים דכתיב ובא השמש וטהר ואחר יאכל מן הקדשים וליכא לאוקמי אלא בתרומה שמחוסר כפורים מותר בה.

אֲבָל נְשִׂיאוּת כַּפַּיִם – But regarding the **Priestly Blessing,** דְּאִיסּוּר עֲשֵׂה – **which is forbidden** to a non-Kohen only **by a positive commandment,**[21] לֹא – perhaps we do **not** elevate him. אוֹ דִּלְמָא לֹא שְׁנָא – **Or perhaps there is no difference** between *terumah* and the Priestly Blessing, and we elevate him in either case. תִּיבָּעֵי לְמַאן דְּאָמַר אֵין מַעֲלִין – **You may** also **ask** this question **according to the one who says** that **we do *not* elevate** a Kohen who eats *terumah,* הָנֵי מִילֵּי תְּרוּמָה דְּמִיתְאַכְלָא בְּצִנְעָא – for perhaps **this ruling** applies *only* with respect to ***terumah,* which is eaten in private.** Therefore, a person might eat *terumah* even if he is not a Kohen.[22] אֲבָל נְשִׂיאוּת כַּפַּיִם דִּבְפַרְהֶסְיָא – **But** regarding the **Priestly Blessing, which is** recited **publicly,** אִי לָאו כֹּהֵן הוּא – **if [this person]** were **not** truly **a Kohen,** כּוּלֵּי הַאי לֹא מַחֲצִיף אִינָשׁ נַפְשֵׁיהּ – **he would not be so insolent** as to make this public display of priestly status. אוֹ דִּלְמָא לֹא שְׁנָא – **Or perhaps there is no difference** between *terumah* and the Priestly Blessing, and we do not elevate him in either case.

The Gemara rules on the question of whether we elevate a Kohen who recites the Priestly Blessing to the status of the genealogically fit:

רַב חִסְדָּא וְרַבִּי אֲבִינָא – **Rav Chisda and R' Avina** disagree about this matter: חַד אָמַר מַעֲלִין – **One says that we elevate** him, וְחַד אָמַר אֵין מַעֲלִין – **and one says that we do not elevate** him.

The Gemara cites an exchange between Amoraim regarding this question:

אָמַר לֵיהּ רַב נַחְמָן בַּר יִצְחָק לְרָבָא – **Rav Nachman bar Yitzchak asked Rava:** מַהוּ לְהַעֲלוֹת מִנְּשִׂיאוּת כַּפַּיִם לְיוּחֲסִין – **"What is [the law]** as **to** whether we **elevate** a Kohen who recites **the Priestly Blessing to** the status of the **genealogically fit?"** אָמַר לֵיהּ – **[Rava] answered him:** פְּלוּגְתָּא דְּרַב חִסְדָּא וְרַבִּי אֲבִינָא – "This is the subject of **a dispute between Rav Chisda and R' Avina."** הִלְכְתָא מַאי – Rav Nachman bar Yitzchak asked further: **"What is the law?"** אָמַר לֵיהּ – **[Rava] answered him:** אֲנָא מַתְנִיתָא יָדַעְנָא – **I know a Baraisa** that can be used to decide the matter, דְּתַנְיָא – **for it was taught in a Baraisa:** רַבִּי יוֹסֵי אוֹמֵר – **R' YOSE SAID:** גְּדוֹלָה חֲזָקָה – **GREAT IS** the power of ***CHAZAKAH,***[23] שֶׁנֶּאֱמַר – **FOR IT IS STATED:**[24] "וּמִבְּנֵי הַכֹּהֲנִים בְּנֵי חֲבַיָּה בְּנֵי הַקּוֹץ בְּנֵי בַרְזִלַּי אֲשֶׁר לָקַח מִבְּנוֹת בַּרְזִלַּי הַגִּלְעָדִי אִשָּׁה וַיִּקָּרֵא עַל־שְׁמָם – ***OF THE CHILDREN OF THE KOHANIM: THE CHILDREN OF HOVAIAH, THE CHILDREN OF HAKKOTZ [AND] THE CHILDREN OF BARZILLAI, [EACH OF WHOM] HAD TAKEN A WIFE FROM THE DAUGHTERS OF BARZILLAI THE GILEADITE AND BECAME KNOWN BY THEIR NAME.***[25] אֵלֶּה בִקְשׁוּ כְתָבָם הַמִּתְיַחְשִׂים וְלֹא נִמְצָאוּ וַיְגֹאֲלוּ מִן־הַכְּהֻנָּה – ***THESE SEARCHED FOR THEIR GENEALOGICAL RECORD, BUT THEY COULD NOT BE FOUND, AND THEY WERE DISQUALIFIED FROM THE KEHUNAH.***[26] וַיֹּאמֶר הַתִּרְשָׁתָא לָהֶם אֲשֶׁר לֹא־יֹאכְלוּ מִקֹּדֶשׁ הַקֳּדָשִׁים עַד עֲמֹד כֹּהֵן לְאוּרִים (ותומים) [וּלְתֻמִּים]" – ***AND HATIRSHASA***[27] ***INSTRUCTED THEM THAT THEY NOT EAT OF THE HOLY OF HOLIES UNTIL THERE ARISES A KOHEN TO [ADMINISTER] THE URIM VETUMIM.***[28]

The last verse states that Hatirshasa warned them "not [to] eat of the *holy of holies,"* a term that refers to the sacrificial portions. This implies that, despite their questionable status, they remained permitted to eat *terumah,* whose sanctity is less than that of sacrificial meat. R' Yose explains why:

אָמַר לָהֶם – [HATIRSHASA] SAID TO THEM: הֲרֵי אַתֶּם בְּחֶזְקַתְכֶם – YOU REMAIN WITH YOUR PREVIOUS STATUS (*chazakah*). בַּמֶּה הֱיִיתֶם אוֹכְלִים בַּגּוֹלָה – WHAT type of sanctified food DID YOU EAT as Kohanim IN THE EXILE? בְּקָדְשֵׁי הַגְּבוּל – THE HOLY THINGS OF THE PROVINCES, i.e. *terumah.*[29] אַף כָּאן בְּקָדְשֵׁי הַגְּבוּל – Accordingly, HERE TOO in Eretz Yisrael, you may continue to eat THE HOLY THINGS OF THE PROVINCES, i.e. *terumah,* but you may not eat of "the holy of holies," i.e. sacrificial food, which is reserved for Kohanim of untainted lineage.[30]

Since R' Yose explains Hatirshasa's instruction to be based on maintaining the status quo ("Great is *chazakah*"), these questionable Kohanim were evidently also allowed to continue reciting the Priestly Blessing as they had in the Diaspora. Based on this premise, Rava develops the proof he seeks to infer from this Baraisa:

וְאִי סַלְקָא דַּעְתָּךְ מַעֲלִין מִנְּשִׂיאוּת כַּפַּיִם לְיוּחֲסִין – **Now, if you should think that we elevate** a Kohen who recites **the Priestly Blessing to** the status of **the genealogically fit,** how could they be allowed to recite the Priestly Blessing? הָנֵי כֵּיוָן דְּפָרְסֵי יְדַיְיהוּ אָתֵי לְאַסּוּקִינְהוּ – **Once these** Kohanim are seen **spreading their**

NOTES

21. In its preface to the Priestly Blessing, the Torah states (*Numbers* 6:23): כֹּה תְבָרְכוּ, *So you* [the Kohanim] *shall bless.* By addressing this commandment specifically to the Kohanim, the verse implies that non-Kohanim are prohibited to administer the blessing. Since this prohibition stems from a positive commandment, it too has the status of a positive commandment (*Rashi;* cf. *Tosafos, Shabbos* 118b ד״ה אילו, cited by *Rama, Orach Chaim* 128:1; see *Pnei Yehoshua, Chasam Sofer* et al.; see also the commentaries on *Shulchan Aruch* ibid.).

22. [Here too, the Gemara implies that it is the *eating* of the *terumah* that matters. See note 20.]

23. That is, a court may not change the current status of a person or object [in the absence of compelling evidence] (*Rashi*). This is explained further in the Gemara on 25a.

24. *Ezra* 2:61-63. This chapter identifies those who participated in the first wave of return from the Babylonian exile to Eretz Yisrael.

25. The "children of Barzillai" were men from other families who had married Barzillai's daughters (*Rashi* ad loc.).

26. Some members of the Kehunah had, during the exile, married women from among the gentile nations in which they resided. The children of these marriages [between Kohanim and converts] were *chalalim.* Thus, before being allowed to serve in the Second Temple, the Kohanim had to document their genealogies to demonstrate their fitness to serve. The Kohanim of these three families were unable to do so (*Rashi;* see, however, *Rashash*).

27. This was Nehemiah ben Chachaliah [author of the book of *Nehemiah*], as is evident from *Nehemiah* 8:9 (*Rashi*). The *Yerushalmi* explains the basis of this cognomen. As the wine steward of the Persian emperor, Darius II (*Nehemiah* 2:1), Nehemiah had to drink from the wine he served to demonstrate that he had not poisoned it. Although the wine of idolaters is forbidden by Rabbinical law, the Sages permitted him to drink it because of the extraordinary circumstance in which he found himself. Hence, the name Hatirshasa, which means *hatir* [permission] *shasa* [drink] (*Rashi* to *Kiddushin* 69b ד״ה התרשתא).

28. The *Urim VeTumim* was a parchment bearing the Ineffable Name of God that was inserted into the breastplate worn by the Kohen Gadol. When a request for Divine instruction was put to it, the letters engraved on the breastplate's precious stones would glow, spelling out the Divine message (*Rashi* to *Exodus* 28:30; see *Ramban* ad loc. and *Ritva* to *Yoma* 73b ד״ה הא דאמרי׳). The *Urim VeTumim* disappeared during the destruction of the First Temple and was never restored in the Second Temple. Thus, Nehemiah's statement was an expression that was the equivalent of saying, "when the Messiah comes" (*Rashi,* from *Sotah* 48b).

29. *Terumah* is called "the holy things of the provinces" because it may be eaten outside Jerusalem [in contrast to sacrificial foods, which may be eaten only in the Temple or Jerusalem] (*Rashi*).

30. This decision was based on the rule of *chazakah.* During the period of the exile, the members of these three families had been assumed to be Kohanim, and they were given *terumah* (which, by Rabbinic law, was required in Babylonia as well). When upon their return to Eretz Yisrael, their status as Kohanim came into question, the doubt was treated by maintaining the status quo. They were allowed to continue eating *terumah* as they had in the Diaspora, but they were barred from eating the meat of sacrifices in the newly restored Temple.

הכא נמי בשכלי אומנותו בידו והיכא איתמר דרבי חמא בר עוקבא אהא דתנן [א] [א]הקדר שהניח קדירותיו וירד לשתות (ג) מים מן היאור) הפנימיות טהורות והחיצונות טמאות והתניא אלו ואלו טמאות אמר רבי חמא בר עוקבא [ב]בשכלי אומנותו בידו מפני שיד הכל ממשמשת בהן והתניא אלו ואלו טהורות א"ר חמא בר עוקבא [ב]בשאין כלי אומנותו בידו ואלא הא דתנן הפנימיות טהורות והחיצונות טמאות היכי משכחת לה [ד]דסמיכא לרשות הרבים ומשום חיפופי רשות הרבים ואיבעית אימא ר' יהודה ורבנן במעלין מתרומה ליוחסין קמיפלגי איבעיא להו מהו להעלות משטרות ליוחסין היכי דמי אילימא דכתיב ביה אני פלוני כהן חתמתי עד מאן קא מסהיד עילויה לא צריכא דכתיב ביה אני פלוני כהן לויתי מנה מפלוני וחתימו סהדי מאי אמנה שבשטר קא מסהדי או דלמא אכולה מילתא קא מסהדי רב הונא ורב חסדא חד אמר מעלין וחד אמר [ה]אין מעלין איבעיא להו מהו להעלות מנשיאות כפים ליוחסין ותיבעי למ"ד מעלין מתרומה ליוחסין ותיבעי למ"ד אין מעלין תיבעי למ"ד מעלין הני מילי תרומה דעון מיתה היא אבל נשיאות כפים דאיסור עשה לא או דלמא לא שנא תיבעי למ"ד אין מעלין הני מילי תרומה דמיתאכלא בצנעא אבל נשיאות כפים דבפרהסיא אי לאו כהן הוא כולי האי לא מחציף איניש נפשיה או דלמא לא שנא רב חסדא ורבי אבינא חד אמר מעלין וחד אמר [ו]אין מעלין א"ל רב נחמן בר יצחק לרבא מהו להעלות מנשיאות כפים ליוחסין א"ל פלוגתא דרב חסדא ורבי אבינא הלכתא מאי א"ל אנא מתניתא ידענא דתניא ר' יוסי אומר [ג]גדולה חזקה שנאמר [א]ומבני הכהנים בני חביה בני הקוץ בני ברזילי אשר לקח מבנות ברזילי הגלעדי אשה ויקרא על שמם אלה בקשו כתבם המתיחשים ולא נמצאו ויגאלו מן הכהונה ויאמר התרשתא להם אשר לא יאכלו מקדש הקדשים עד עמוד כהן לאורים [ז]ותומים אמר להם הרי אתם בחזקתכם במה הייתם אוכלים בגולה בקדשי הגבול אף כאן בקדשי הגבול ואי סלקא דעתך מעלין מנשיאות כפים ליוחסין הני כיון דפרסי ידייהו אתי לאסוקינהו שאני הכא דריע חזקייהו דאי לא תימא הכי למאן דאמר מעלין מתרומה ליוחסין כיון דאכלי בתרומה אתי לאסוקינהו אלא לאו משום דריע חזקייהו
ואלא

רש"י

בשכלי אומנותו בידו. חמר המביא תבואה למכור היה נושא בידו כלי היכר של מכירה כגון מחק שמוחקין בו המדה והמביאה להצניע אינו נושא בידו כלי אומנות מכר והכא כגון שכלי אומנותו בידו של זה המזלזל את שלו דאמן סהדי שלמוכרה הביאה הלכך אין זה אלא גומל וזה יעיד עליו בכרך שלפניהם: הקדר. שהוא חבר: הפנימיות טהורות. כולה מתרלא ואזלא לקמיה: בשכלי אומנותו בידו. להיכר שהוא נושאן למוכרן: ממשמשת בהן. לבדוק וליקח: ומשום חיפופי רשות הרבים. שנותנים בני אדם אבנים גדולות או יתדות לצידי רה"ר להרחיק העגלות מלהזיק את הכתלים ומתוך שהן דוחקות את רה"ר וזה הניח קדירותיו אצלם דחק גם הוא את הדרך והעוברין שם מתחככין בהן ובגדיהן עוברין על פני אורן ובגדי עם הארץ טמאים הם ומטמאים את החיצוניות: במעלין מתרומה ליוחסין. רבי יהודה סבר הרואה שמאכילין תרומה לאדם בחזקת כהן מעיד עליו בכל מקום שהוא כהן ומעלין אותו ליוחסין הלכך אם תאכילהו תרומה הרי אתה מביאו להשיאו אשה וטעמיה לאו משום גומלין הוא ורבנן סברי אין מעלין מתרומה ליוחסין: דאיסור מיתה. אם זר הוא לא היה אוכל תרומה שהוא עון מיתה: דאיסור עשה. כה תברכו (במדבר ו) אתם ולא זרים ולאו הבא מכלל עשה עשה: גדולה חזקה. שאין ב"ד יכולין להוציא דבר מחזקתו: בקשו כתבם המתיחשים. שיהו כהנים כשרים לפי שהתחתנו כהנים בגולה בגויי הארץ וילדו להם בנים כדכתיב בספר עזרא והם חללים הוצרכו הנולדים בגולה להתייחס כשעלו מן הגולה לשרת בבנין שני: ויגאלו. נפסלו מלשון לחם מגואל (מלאכי א): התרשתא. הוא נחמיה בן חכליה וכן כתוב בספר עזרא (נחמיה ח): עד עמוד כהן לאורים וגו'. כאדם (א) שאומר לחבירו עד שיבא המשיח דאורים ותומים לא הוו במקדש שני שנחסרו חמשה דברים כדאמרינן בסדר יומא (דף כא:): מקדשי הקדשים. דוקא מקדשי המקדש פסלינהו אבל תרומה שהיו רגילין בה בגולה לא אסר עלייהו משום דהוחזקו בה: קדשי הגבול. תרומה שהיא נוהגת בגבולין חוץ למקדש ולירושלים: אף כאן בקדשי הגבול. ומדאמר רבי יוסי גדולה חזקה ש"מ נשיאות כפים נמי לא אסר עלייהו שהרי הוחזקו בה בגבולין: ואי סלקא דעתך כו' אתו לאסוקינהו. ומה הועילו בתקנתם: שאני הכא. דליכא למיחש דליסוקינהו דהא ריע חזקייהו שהרי הכל רואין שאר כהנים אוכלין קדשי המקדש והם אינן אוכלין יש כאן היכר גדול שיש בהן צד פסול אבל שאר בני אדם כגון בזמן הזה לעולם מעלין מנשיאות כפים ליוחסין: [ח][דאי לא תימא הכי. דעל דא סמיך שיש בהן היכר תרומה נמי תקשי למ"ד מעלין מתרומה ליוחסין]:
ואלא

תוספות

בשכלי אומנותו בידו. פירש רבינו חננאל זה שאומר עליו שהוא כהן יש בידו כלים שמשמשין בהן בטהרה כגון כלי גללים כלי אבנים כלי אדמה שאין מקבלין טומאה שכל הרואה כלים הללו בידו מתרחק ממנו מלטמאותו ודומה שהוא כהן ולכך האמינוהו חכמים:

ואיבעית אימא רבי יהודה ורבנן במעלין מתרומה ליוחסין קמיפלגי. ולא אתא לשנויי אלא קשיא דרבי יהודה אדרבי יהודה אבל דרבנן אדרבנן לעולם צריך לתרץ בשכלי אומנותו בידו והקשה הר' שמואל מוורדין ומעיקרא היכי בעי למימר דטעמא דר"י משום גומלין והא בלא גומלים ע"כ סבר רבי יהודה בשילהי פרקין (לקמן דף כח:) דמעלין מתרומה ליוחסין ומירך ר"י דמעיקרא ס"ד דלאו טעמא משום גומלים לא היינו מפסידים את הכהן מן התרומה כדי לומר מעלין כיון דמן הדין ראוי לחלוק ע"פ חבירו ולהכי קודם היינו אומרים אין מעלין אע"ג דגבי עבד אמר לקמן לרבי יהודה דאין חולקין לו תרומה משום דמעלין התם אין כל כך חששא בהפסד של עבד זה אם אין חולקין לו תרומה בלא רבו וא"ת ובלאו הכי פליגי לימרו תרויהו דמעלין ונצטרך שני עדים בתרומה או לימרו תרויהו דלא מעלין ולא יצטרך אלא עד אחד בתרומה וי"ל דהכא פליגי דמר סבר חיישינן שמא יעלו מתרומה ליוחסין לפיכך הצריכו שני עדים ומר סבר דלא חיישינן א):

אמנה שבשטר קמסהדי. וא"ת ולאו אכולה מילתא קמסהדי א"כ עדים חתמי אע"ג דלא ידעי אי כהן הוא אי לאו ואם כן הא דתנן בגט פשוט (ב"ב דף קסב.) שני יוסף בן שמעון הדרין בעיר אחת אם היו משולשין יכתבו כהן ומה מועיל כיון שעדים חותמין אע"פ שאין מכירים בו אם הוא כהן והרי הוא יכול להערים ולכתוב שטר אחר בשם חבירו כהן ויוציא ממון מחבירו כהן וי"ל דהיכא דהוחזקו שני יוסף בן שמעון ודאי אכולה מילתא קא מסהדי כי אז הן צריכין לידע אם בן כהן הוא והכא מיירי במשטרות ליוחסין והכא מיבעיא לן היכא דלא הוחזקו: חד אמר מעלין. ואם תאמר ואמאי לא חשיב ליה בהדי הנך דתנן בעשרה יוחסין (קדושין דף עו. וסם) אין בודקין מן המזבח ולמעלה ולא מדוכן כו' וי"ל דהך דשטרות מלתא דפשיטא היא דכיון דאכולה מלתא קמסהדי א"כ הוי עדות גמור ולכך לא קא חשיב עדים וא"ת ואמאי לא חשיב תרומה ונשיאות כפים למ"ד מעלין ואור"ת דתרומה בכלל מזבח ונשיאות כפים בכלל דוכן אע"ג דההוא דוכן היינו שיר כדמשמע התם בגמרא מ"ד מעלין הוה מוקי לה נמי בדוכן כהנים שבגבולים ומיהו קשה אמאי לא חשיב ס"ת שקרא בחזקת כהן כדלקמן ויש לומר דליכא למימר דתנא ושייר כולהו ובספר הישר פירש ר"ת דלאו בעבודת מזבח ממש איירי אלא כגון הפשט וניתוח דברים הכשרים בזרים דלא היו מניחין לעשות אותם אלא למיוחסין מן המשיאין לכהונה אבל מילי דכהונה כגון תרומה ונשיאות כפים וס"ת לא איצטריך למתני: שאני הכא דריע חזקייהו. פי' בקונטרס שהכל רואים שאר כהנים אוכלין שאר קדשי מזבח ואלו אין אוכלין וק"ק דמ"מ תיקשי למ"ד מעלין אמאי לא אסקינהו לקדשי מזבח וליוחסין ונראה לר"ת דריע חזקייהו היינו שהיו מיחסים אותם אחר בני ברזילי שהיה ישראל ועוד שלא מצאו כתבם והיכא דאיתרע חזקה אין מעלין לכ"ע אבל קשה דפריך מעיקרא אתי לאסוקינהו הוה ליה למיפרך אמאי נגאלו כלל מן הכהונה ויש לומר דשפיר הוה ידע דריע חזקייהו ומשום הכי לא אסקינהו אלא דהוה ס"ד דאע"ג דריע חזקייהו איכא למיחש דלמא אתי לאסוקינהו לבסוף שלא ידעו שלא מצאו כתבם:
ואלא

עין משפט נר מצוה

פד א ב ג ד מיי' פי"ב מהל' משכב ומושב הלכה כג:
פה ה מיי' פ"כ מהל' איסורי ביאה הלכ' ט טוש"ע אה"ע סי' ג סעיף ב:
פו ו מיי' שם הלכה ד והלכה יא:

תוספות ר"ד

לן דחלל הוא. אמאי לא ישא אשה כשרה ואפי' בתו של כ"ה. והא קי"ל דלא הוזהרו כשרות להנשא לפסולים. וי"ל לפרש דהאי דאמר להשיאו אשה לאו להשיאו לו אשה. אלא להשיא מנשיו לכהונה. כגון אלמנתו ובתו דמספקינן ליה בחלל. ובת חלל ואלמנת חלל הן פסולות לכהונה: **איבעיא להו** מהו להעלות משטרות ליוחסין. פי' אילימא דכתיב בי' אני פלוני כהן חתמתי עד מאן קמסהיד עלויה. לא צריכא דכתיב בי' אני פ' כהן לויתי מנה מפלוני ודחתימו סהדי אמנה שבשטר קא מסהדי א"ד אכולה מילתא מסהדי. **ר"ה ור"ח** ח"א מעלין וח"א אין מעלין. והלכתא כדברי המיקל. ואילו כתבו שני עדים פ' כהן לוה כפלוני דליכא מאן דפליג דודאי מעלין. דהא עדים כעידים כי הוא כהן א). **איבעי'** להו מהו להעלות מכהונה ליוחסין.

חשק שלמה על תוס' ר"ד

א) וכ"כ הר"ן כאן בשם הרא"ה ז"ל כ"ש ובזה מיושב קושית תוס' ד"ה אמנה מה שהקשו מפ' גט פשוט ותו"ק ועי' בש"ך חו"מ סי' מ"ט ס"ק ט"ו

תורה אור השלם

א) וּמִבְּנֵי הַכֹּהֲנִים בְּנֵי חֳבַיָּה בְּנֵי הַקּוֹץ בְּנֵי בַרְזִלַּי אֲשֶׁר לָקַח מִבְּנוֹת בַּרְזִלַּי הַגִּלְעָדִי אִשָּׁה וַיִּקָּרֵא עַל שְׁמָם: אֵלֶּה בִּקְשׁוּ כְתָבָם הַמִּתְיַחְשִׂים וְלֹא נִמְצָאוּ וַיְגֹאֲלוּ מִן הַכְּהֻנָּה: וַיֹּאמֶר הַתִּרְשָׁתָא לָהֶם אֲשֶׁר לֹא יֹאכְלוּ מִקֹּדֶשׁ הַקֳּדָשִׁים עַד עֲמֹד כֹּהֵן לְאוּרִים וּלְתֻמִּים: [עזרא ב, סא-סג]

מסורת הש"ס

א) טהרות פרק ז משנה א, ב) [משנה ליתא], ג) קדושין סט., ד) [נ"ל ולתומים], ה) נ"י כ"י.

תוספות ישנים

א) [ועוד הוה ר"י לפרש טעמא דמ"ד מעלין כדי שיהו עדים מצויין ליוחסין וחזר בו משום דלא משמע הכי בסמוך דקאמר ה"מ תרומה דעון מיתה. תו"י עמ"ג]:

הגהות הב"ח

(א) רש"י ד"ה עד עמוד כו' כאדם שאומר. נ"ב הוא בפ' עגלה ערופה דף מח ע"ב:

ליקוטי רש"י

במעלין מתרומה ליוחסין. הרואה כהן אוכל בתרומה במקומו אין צריך לבדוק אחריו ביוחסין ונושא כהן כמו. גדולה חזקה. יש לסמוך עליה יפה. בקשו כתבם המתיחשים. כתב יחוסם. התרשתא. נחמיה בן חכליה קרוי כן בספר עזרא ובגמרת ירושלמי נמצא שעל שם שהיה משקה למלך היה צריך לשתות קודם שלא ימצאוהו שמא הטיל סם המות במשקה המלך התירו לו יין של עובדי כוכבים לשתות לכך נקרא התרשתא. מקדש הקדשים. מדכתיב מקדש הקדשים שמעינן דלא אסרי בתרומה אלא מקדשי המקדש. אמר להם. תרומה איני יכול לאסור עליכם מפני מוחזקתם שהוחזקתם בכבל לאכלה. בקדשי הגבול. תרומה הנאכלת בכל מקום. כיון דאכלי בתרומה אתי לאסוקינהו. ואמאי לא חש לה נחמיה דלא לאסוקינהו. דריע חזקייהו. לא איצטריך למיחש להכי דכיון דאמר כהנים אוכלים בקדשי המקדש והם לא אוכלין מהם ויש בהם היכר ולא אתי לאסוקינהו [קידושין שם]. [מכאן שייך לדף כה.] ואלא. כיון דליכא למגזר מידי. מאי גדולה חזקה. דאמר רבי יוסי מאי רבותא לא היה לו לומר אלא מנין מוחזק כו' מדקאמר גדולה רבותא שמעינן דאע"ג דליכא לד איסור השתא עפוי מעיקרא סמכינן עלה. בתרומה דרבנן. תרומת חוץ לארץ. תרומה דאורייתא. משבאו לארץ. השתא נמי בתרומה דרבנן. היא דליכא למעיקרא ומאי ניהו תרומת פירות וירק. בתרומה דאורייתא. דגן ותירוש ויצהר לא אכול. וכל זר לא יאכל קדש. כל אותו הענין מדבר בתרומה ולא בקדשים דכתיב וכל הקדשים ... מן הקדשים ... אלא בתרומה ... כפורים מותר בה.

his genealogical fitness. Consequently, a single witness suffices to let someone eat *terumah.*[12]

The Gemara discusses whether another form of evidence suffices to establish a Kohen's genealogical purity:

אִיבַּעְיָא לְהוּ – They asked: מַהוּ לְהַעֲלוֹת מִשְּׁטָרוֹת לְיוּחֲסִין – **What is [the law]** as **to** whether we **elevate** someone who is called a Kohen in **documents to** the status of **the genealogically fit?**[13]

The Gemara clarifies the question:

הֵיכִי דָּמֵי – What is the case? אִילֵימָא דִּכְתִיב בֵּיהּ – **If you say that it is written in [the document],** אֲנִי פְּלוֹנִי כֹּהֵן חָתַמְתִּי עֵד – **"I So-and-so Kohen signed as a witness,"** מַאן קָא מַסְהִיד עִילָוֵיהּ – **who is testifying about him** that he is a Kohen? He merely signed himself as a Kohen without any verification. לֹא צְרִיכָא דִּכְתִיב בֵּיהּ – Rather, **[the question] is warranted only where it is written in [the document],** אֲנִי פְּלוֹנִי כֹּהֵן לָוִיתִי מָנֶה מִפְּלוֹנִי – **"I So-and-so Kohen borrowed a *maneh* from So-and-so,"** וַחֲתִימוּ סָהֲדֵי – **and witnesses signed** on the document. Thus, the question is as follows: מַאי – **What** is the scope of the witnesses' testimony? אַמָּנֶה שֶׁבַּשְּׁטָר קָא מַסְהֲדֵי – **Are they testifying** only **about the** loan of the ***maneh*** that is recorded **in the document?**[14] אוֹ דִלְמָא אַכּוּלָּהּ מִילְּתָא קָא מַסְהֲדֵי – **Or perhaps they are testifying about everything** in the document, including its description of the borrower as a Kohen.[15]

The Gemara cites two opinions:

רַב הוּנָא וְרַב חִסְדָּא – **Rav Huna and Rav Chisda disagree** about this matter: חַד אָמַר מַעֲלִין – **One said that we do elevate** someone who is called a Kohen in **documents to** the status of **the genealogically fit,** וְחַד אָמַר אֵין מַעֲלִין – **and one said that we do not elevate** him.

Another inquiry of this nature:

אִיבַּעְיָא לְהוּ – They asked: מַהוּ לְהַעֲלוֹת מִנְּשִׂיאוּת כַּפַּיִם לְיוּחֲסִין – **What is [the law]** as **to** whether we **elevate** a Kohen who recites **the Priestly Blessing**[16] **to** the status of **the genealogically fit?**[17]

The Gemara relates this inquiry to a dispute mentioned above:

תִּיבָּעֵי לְמַאן דְּאָמַר מַעֲלִין מִתְּרוּמָה לְיוּחֲסִין – **You may ask** this question **according to the one who says** that **we elevate** a Kohen who eats ***terumah*** **to** the status of **the genealogically fit,** וְתִיבָּעֵי לְמַאן דְּאָמַר אֵין מַעֲלִין – and **you may** also **ask** this question **according to the one who says** that **we do not elevate** him.[18]

The Gemara explains:

תִּיבָּעֵי לְמַאן דְּאָמַר מַעֲלִין – **You may ask** this question **according to the one who says** that **we do elevate** a Kohen who eats *terumah,* הָנֵי מִילֵּי תְּרוּמָה – for perhaps **this ruling** is true *only* with respect to eating ***terumah,*** דַּעֲוֹן מִיתָה הִיא – **which,** in the case of a non-Kohen, **is a sin** punishable **by death** at the hand of Heaven.[19] In view of the sin's gravity, it can be assumed that a person would not eat *terumah* unless he were truly a Kohen.[20]

NOTES

eat *terumah* unless two witnesses testify that he is a Kohen (see *Rashi*).

According to this explanation of R' Yehudah's view, in the case where two men testify that the other is a Kohen, the reason why he disqualifies their testimony (even with respect to *terumah*) has nothing to do with suspicions of collusion. Rather, his reason is that a single witness just does not suffice for this purpose (*Rashi*). Hence, there is no contradiction between R' Yehudah's ruling here and his ruling in the case of tithing (24a), where he does not consider suspicions of collusion sufficient grounds to disqualify testimony.

12. Since no consequences of more serious import will result from allowing him to eat *terumah,* a single witness suffices for this purpose in accordance with the rule: עֵד אֶחָד נֶאֱמָן בְּאִיסּוּרִין, *a single witness is believed with regard to prohibitions* (*Ritva*).

The Gemara's purpose here is only to resolve the contradiction between the rulings of R' Yehudah. It has not addressed the contradiction between the ruling of the Rabbis in this case (where they do not suspect collusion) and their ruling in the case of tithing (where they do suspect collusion). To resolve this problem, we must still rely on the answer given previously (end of 24a) that the Rabbis suspect collusion in the case of tithing only because the speaker is carrying the tools of his trade, which provide clear evidence of his duplicity (*Tosafos;* see *Ritva;* cf. *Pnei Yehoshua* and *Rashash*).

13. If someone is given the title of a Kohen in a document (e.g. Reuven ben Yaakov the Kohen), can that be used as evidence that he is a Kohen with respect to genealogical fitness?

14. That is, since the borrower's Kohanic status is not relevant to the purpose of the document, the witnesses might have signed it without first ascertaining that he is indeed a Kohen (*Rashba*). Consequently, the document provides no evidence at all about this person's status as a Kohen. It cannot be used even to permit him to eat *terumah* (*Ritva;* cf. *Shach, Choshen Mishpat* 49:15; *Haflaah* on *Tosafos* ד״ה אמנה; see *Ran* citing *Re'ah*).

15. According to this position, witnesses are expected to realize that the title of "Kohen" might be needed for purposes of identification. Therefore, the witnesses of this document would not have signed it unless they had verified that this person was truly a Kohen (see *Rashba*). [See *Chazon Ish, Even HaEzer* 2:13,14 at length, see also *Ketzos HaChoshen* 28:6.]

16. The Kohanim are commanded to bless Israel, as stated in *Numbers* 6:22-27. Since they raise their hands during its recitation, the blessing is referred to as נְשִׂיאַת כַּפַּיִם, which literally means "raising of the hands." It is also known as בִּרְכַּת כֹּהֲנִים, *Birkas Kohanim* (the Priestly Blessing).

17. If witnesses testify that they saw someone recite the Priestly Blessing, does their testimony suffice to establish him as genealogically pure?

[According to the notion that recital of the Priestly Blessing *can* be used as evidence of genealogical fitness, two witnesses would be required to let someone recite the Priestly Blessing in the first place. According to the opposing view, one witness would suffice. This is the same idea as that discussed above (note 11) in the context of *terumah* (*Ramban, Rashba;* see *Ritva*).]

18. That is, the evidence provided by *terumah* and the evidence provided by the Priestly Blessing have contrasting strengths and weaknesses, as the Gemara will explain. Therefore, regardless of how one rules on the issue of whether *terumah* can be used as proof of genealogical fitness, it is still questionable whether the Priestly Blessing satisfies this purpose.

19. The penalty of death at the hands of Heaven for a non-Kohen who eats *terumah* is not written explicitly, but is derived exegetically from the verse that prohibits consuming *terumah* while *tamei.* That verse reads, in part (*Leviticus* 22:9): וְלֹא־יִשְׂאוּ עָלָיו חֵטְא וּמֵתוּ בוֹ, *and they* [i.e. those who eat *terumah* while *tamei*] *shall not bear a transgression thereby, and die because of it.* It is followed by the verse prohibiting a non-Kohen to eat *terumah,* which reads: וְכָל־זָר לֹא־יֹאכַל קֹדֶשׁ, *And no non-Kohen may eat the holy.* The juxtaposition of verses teaches that the penalty of death — written regarding the consumption of *terumah* by one who is *tamei* — applies as well to its consumption by a non-Kohen (*Rashi* to *Pesachim* 32b ד״ה מאן שמעת ליה, from *Sanhedrin* 83b).

20. Therefore, if someone is seen eating *terumah,* we can assume that he is genealogically fit. Since this is so, *two* witnesses are needed to let someone eat *terumah* in the first place, as explained in note 11 (*Ramban, Rashba;* see the opinion of *Rabbeinu Tam* cited by the Rishonim here).

[The Gemara here implies that it is the *eating* of *terumah* that establishes someone as a genealogically fit Kohen (see *Rashi;* cf. *Melo HaRo'im*). It was demonstrated above, however, that the *receiving* of *terumah* is the essential factor, because even a Kohen's slave could eat *terumah* (see note 8). Thus, it seems that both factors are required. To rule out the possibility of his being a slave, he must be seen receiving *terumah.* On the other hand, if he is seen only receiving *terumah,* he might be a Yisrael whom a Kohen appointed to fetch *terumah* for him. That possibility is discounted by seeing him eat *terumah,* which a non-Kohen would be afraid to do in view of the gravity of the transgression (see *Hagahos Yavetz* to *Tosafos* on 25a ד״ה או דלמא).]

הכא נמי בשכלי אומנותו בידו והיכא אתמר דרבי חמא בר עוקבא אהא דתנן [א] הקדר שהניח קדירותיו וירד לשתות (ג מים מן היאור) הפנימיות טהורות והחיצונות טמאות והתניא אלו ואלו טמאות אמר רבי חמא בר עוקבא [ב] בשכלי אומנותו בידו מפני שיד הכל ממשמשת בהן והתניא אלו ואלו טהורות א"ר חמא בר עוקבא [ג] בשאין כלי אומנותו בידו ואלא הא דתנן הפנימיות טהורות והחיצונות טמאות היכי משכחת לה [ד] דסמיכא לרשות הרבים ומשום חיפופי רשות הרבים ואיבעית אימא ר' יהודה ורבנן במעלין מתרומה ליוחסין קמיפלגי איבעיא להו מהו להעלות משטרות ליוחסין היכי דמי אילימא דכתיב ביה אני פלוני כהן חתמתי עד מאן קא מסהיד עילויה לא צריכא דכתיב ביה אני פלוני כהן לויתי מנה מפלוני וחתימו סהדי מאי אמנה שבשטר קא מסהדי או דלמא אכולה מילתא קא מסהדי רב הונא ורב חסדא חד אמר מעלין וחד אמר [ה] אין מעלין איבעיא להו מהו להעלות מנשיאות כפים ליוחסין תיבעי למ"ד מעלין מתרומה ליוחסין ותיבעי למ"ד אין מעלין תיבעי למ"ד מעלין הני מילי תרומה דעון מיתה היא אבל נשיאות כפים דאיסור עשה לא או דלמא לא שנא תיבעי למ"ד אין מעלין הני מילי תרומה דמיתאכלא בצנעא אבל נשיאות כפים דבפרהסיא אי לאו כהן הוא כולי האי לא מחציף איניש נפשיה או דלמא לא שנא רב חסדא ורבי אבינא חד אמר מעלין וחד אמר [ו] אין מעלין א"ל רב נחמן בר יצחק לרבא מהו להעלות מנשיאות כפים ליוחסין א"ל פלוגתא דרב חסדא ורבי אבינא הלכתא מאי א"ל אנא מתניתא ידענא דתניא ר' יוסי אומר [ז] גדולה חזקה שנאמר א) ומבני הכהנים בני חביה בני הקוץ בני ברזילי אשר לקח מבנות ברזילי הגלעדי אשה ויקרא על שמם אלה בקשו כתבם המתיחשים ולא נמצאו ויגאלו מן הכהונה ויאמר התרשתא להם אשר לא יאכלו מקדש הקדשים עד עמוד כהן לאורים [ד] ותומים אמר להם הרי אתם בחזקתכם במה הייתם אוכלים בגולה בקדשי הגבול אף כאן בקדשי הגבול ואי סלקא דעתך מעלין מנשיאות כפים ליוחסין הני כיון דפרסי ידייהו אתי לאסוקינהו שאני הכא דריע חזקייהו דאי לא תימא הכי למאן דאמר מעלין מתרומה ליוחסין כיון דאכלי בתרומה אתי לאסוקינהו אלא לאו משום דריע חזקייהו ואלא

רש"י

בשכלי אומנותו בידו. חמר המביא תבואה למכור היה נושא בידו כלי היכר של מכירה כגון מחק שמוחקין בה המדה והמביא להצניע אינו נושא בידו כלי אומנות מכר והכא כגון שכלי אומנותו בידו של זה המוזל את שלו דלאו סהדי שלמוכרה הביאה הלכך אין זה אלא גומל וזה יעיד עליו בככך שלפניהם: **הקדר.** שהוא חבר: **הפנימיות טהורות.** כולה מתרלא ואזלא לקמיה: **בשכלי אומנותו בידו.** להיכר שהוא נושאן למוכרן: **ממשמשת בהן.** לבדוק וליקח: **ומשום חיפופי רשות הרבים.** שנותנים בני אדם אבנים גדולות או יתדות לגדר רה"ר להרחיק העגלות מלהזיק את הכתלים ומתוך שהן דוחקות את רה"ר זה הניח קדירותיו אצלם לתקן גם הוא את הדרך והעוברין שם מתחככין בהן ובגדיהן עוברין על פני אורין ובגדי עם הארץ טמאים הם ומטמאים את החיצוניות: **במעלין מתרומה ליוחסין.** רבי יהודה סבר הרואה שמאכילין תרומה לאדם בחזקת כהן מעיד עליו בכל מקום שהוא כהן ומעלין אותו ליוחסין הלכך אם מאכילהו תרומה הרי אתה מביא להשיאו אשה וטעמיה לאו משום גומלין הוא ורבנן סברי אין מעלין מתרומה ליוחסין: **דאיסור מיתה.** אם זר הוא לא היה אוכל תרומה שהוא עון מיתה: **דאיסור עשה.** כה תברכו (במדבר ו) אתם ולא זרים ולאו הבא מכלל עשה עשה: **גדולה חזקה.** שאין ב"ד יכולין להוציא דבר מחזקתו: **בקשו כתבם המתיחשים.** שיהו כהנים כשרים לפי שהתחתנו כהנים בגולה בגויי הארץ וילדו להם בנים כדכתיב בספר עזרא והם חללים הוצרכו הנולדים בגולה להתייחס כשעלו מן הגולה לשרת בבנין שני: **ויגאלו.** נפסלו מלשון לחם מגואל (מלאכי א): **התרשתא.** הוא נחמיה בן חכליה וכן כתוב בספר עזרא (נחמיה ח): **עד עמוד כהן לאורים וגו'.** כאדם (א) שאומר לחבירו עד שיבא המשיח דאורים ותומים לא הוו במקדש שני שנחסרו חמשה דברים כדאמרינן בסדר יומא (דף כא:): **מקדשי הקדשים.** דוקא מקדשי המקדש פסלינהו אבל תרומה שהיו רגילין בה בגולה לא אסר עליהו משום שהוחזקו בה: **קדשי הגבול.** תרומה שהיא נוהגת בגבולין חוץ למקדש ולירושלים: **אף כאן בקדשי הגבול.** ומדאמר רבי יוסי גדולה חזקה ש"מ נשיאות כפים נמי לא אסר עליהו שהרי הוחזקו בה בגבולין: **ואי סלקא דעתך כו' אתו לאסוקינהו.** ומה הועילו בתקנתם: **שאני הכא.** דליכא למיחש לאסוקינהו דהא ריע חזקייהו שהרי הכל רואין שאר כהנים אוכלין קדשי המקדש והם אינן אוכלין יש כאן היכר גדול שיש בהן צד פסול אבל שאר בני אדם כגון בזמן הזה לעולם מעלין מנשיאות כפים ליוחסין: [ה] [דאי לא תימא הכי. דעל לא סמיך שיש בהן היכר תרומה נמי תקשי למ"ד מעלין מתרומה ליוחסין]:

ואלא

תוספות

בשכלי אומנותו בידו. פירש רבינו חננאל זה שאומר עליו שהוא כהן יש בידו כלים שמשמשין בהן בטהרה כגון כלי גללים כלי אבנים כלי אדמה שאין מקבלין טומאה שכל הרואה כלים הללו בידו מתרחק ממנו מלטמאותו ודומה שהוא כהן ולכך האמינוהו חכמים:

ואיבעית אימא רבי יהודה ורבנן במעלין מתרומה ליוחסין קמיפלגי. ולא אתא לשנויי אלא קושיא דרבי יהודה אדרבי יהודה אבל לרבנן אדרבנן לעולם צריך לתרץ בשכלי אומנותו בידו וקשה הר"ר שמואל מוואלדין ומעיקרא היכי בעי למימר דטעמא דר"י משום גומלין והא בלא גומלים ע"כ סבר רבי יהודה בשילהי פרקין (לקמן דף כח:) דמעלין מתרומה ליוחסין ותירץ ר"י דמעיקרא ס"ד דלאו טעמא משום גומלים לא היינו מפקידים את הכהן מן התרומה כדי לומר מעלין כיון דמן הדין ראוי לחלוק ע"פ חבירו ולהכי קודם היינו אומרים אין מעלין אע"ג דגבי עבד אמר לקמן לרבי יהודה דאין חולקין לו תרומה משום דמעלין התם אין כל כך חששא בהפסד של עבד זה אם אין חולקין לו תרומה בלא רבו ומ"מ ובלאו סברא פליגי לימרו תרויהו דמעלין ונצטרך שני עדים בתרומה או לימרו תרויהו דלא מעלין ולא יצטרך אלא עד אחד בתרומה וי"ל דהכא פליגי דמר סבר חיישינן שמא יעלו מתרומה ליוחסין לפיכך הצריכו שני עדים ומר סבר דלא חיישינן א):

אמנה שבשטר קמסהדי. ומ"ת ואי לאו אכולה מילתא קמסהדי א"כ עדים חתמי אע"ג דלא ידעי אי כהן הוא אי לאו ואם כן הא דתנן בגט פשוט (ב"ב דף קסב.) שני יוסף בן שמעון הדרין בעיר אחת אם היו משולשין יכתבו כהן ומה מועיל כיון שעדים חותמין אע"פ שאין מכירים בו אם הוא כהן והרי הוא יכול להעבירים ולכתוב שטר אחר בשם חבירו כהן ויוציא ממון מחבירו כהן וי"ל דהיכא דהוחזקו שני יוסף בן שמעון ודאי אכולה מילתא קא מסהדי כי אז הן צריכין לידע אם בן כהן הוא והתם ודאי מעלין משטרות ליוחסין והכא מיבעיא לן היכא דלא הוחזקו: **חד** אמר מעלין. ואם תאמר ואמאי לא חשיב ליה בהדי הנך דתנן בעשרה יוחסין (קדושין דף עו. ושם) אין בודקין מן המזבח ולמעלה ולא מדוכן כו' וי"ל דהך דשטרות מלתא דפשיטא היא דכיון דאכולה מלתא קמסהדי א"כ הוי עדות גמור ולכך לא קא חשיב עדים ומ"ת ואמאי לא חשיב תרומה ונשיאות כפים למ"ד מעלין ואור"ת דתרומה בכלל מזבח ונשיאות כפים בכלל דוכן אע"ג דההוא דוכן היינו שיר כדמשמע התם בגמרא מ"ד מעלין הוה מוקי לה נמי בדוכן כהנים שבגבולים ומיהו קשה אמאי לא חשיב ס"ת שקרא בחזקת כהן כדלקמן ויש לומר דאיכא למימר דתנא ושייר כולהו ובספר הישר פירש ר"ת דלאו בעבודת מזבח ממש איירי אלא כגון הפשט וניתוח דברים הכשרים בזרים דלא היו מניחין לעשות אותם אלא למיוחסין מן המשיאין לכהונה אבל מילי דכהונה כגון תרומה ונשיאות כפים וס"ת לא איצטריך למתני:

שאני הכא דריע חזקייהו. פי' בקונטרס שהכל רואים שאר כהנים אוכלין שאר קדשי מזבח ואלו אין אוכלין וק"ק דמ"מ תיקשי למ"ד מעלין אמאי לא אסקינהו לקדשי מזבח וליוחסין ונראה לר"ת דריע חזקייהו היינו שהיו מיחסים אותם אחר בני ברזילי שהיה ישראל ועוד שלא מצאו כתבם והיכא דאיתרע חזקה אין מעלין לכ"ע אבל קשה דפריך מעיקרא אתי לאסוקינהו הוה ליה למיפרך אמאי נגאלו כלל מן הכהונה ויש לומר דשפיר הוה ידע דריע חזקייהו ומשום הכי לא אסקינהו אלא דהוה ס"ד דאע"ג דריע חזקייהו איכא למיחש דלמא אתי לאסוקינהו לבסוף שלא ידעו שלא מצאו כתבם:

ואלא

עין משפט נר מצוה

פד א ב ג ד מי' פי"ג מהל' משכב ומושב הלכה כג:
פה ה מיי' פ"כ מהל' איסורי ביאה הלכ' ט טוש"ע אה"ע סי' ג סעיף ג:
פו ו מיי' שם הלכה ד והלכה יא:

תוספות רי"ד

לן דחלל הוא. אמאי לא ישא אשה כשרה ואפי' בתו של כ"ג. ודא קי"ל דלא הזהרו כשרות להנשא לפסולים. וני"ל לפרש דהאי דאמר להשיאו אשה לאו להשיאו לו אשה. אלא להשיא מנשיו לכהונה. כגון אלמנתו ובתו דמספקינן ליה בחלל. ובת חלל ואלמנות חלל הן פסולות לכהונה: **איבעיא להו** מהו להעלות משטרות ליוחסין. פי' אילימא דכתיב בי' אני פלוני כהן חתמתי עד מאן קמסהיד עלויה. לא צריכא דכתיב בי' אני פ' כהן לויתי מנה מפלוני וחתימי סהדי אמנה שבשטר קא מסהדי א"ד אכולה מילתא מסהדי. **ר"ה ור"ח** ח"א מעלין וח"א אין מעלין. והלכתא כדברי המיקל. ואילו כתבו שני עדים פ' כהן לוה מפלוני דליכא מאן דפליג דודאי מעלין. דהא עדים מעידים כי הוא כהן א). **איבעי'** להו מהו להעלות מכהונה ליוחסין.

חשק שלמה על הוס' רי"ד

א) וכ"כ הר"ן כאן בשם הרא"ה ז"ל ע"ש ובזה מיושב קושית תוס' ד"ה אמנה מה שהקשו מפ' גט פשוט ודו"ק ועי' בש"ך חו"מ סי' מ"ט ס"ק ט"ו.

תורה אור השלם

א) וּמִבְּנֵי הַכֹּהֲנִים בְּנֵי חֲבַיָּה בְּנֵי הַקּוֹץ בְּנֵי בַרְזִלַּי אֲשֶׁר לָקַח מִבְּנוֹת בַּרְזִלַּי הַגִּלְעָדִי אִשָּׁה וַיִּקָּרֵא עַל שְׁמָם: אֵלֶּה בִּקְשׁוּ כְתָבָם הַמִּתְיַחְשִׂים וְלֹא נִמְצָאוּ וַיְגֹאֲלוּ מִן הַכְּהֻנָּה: וַיֹּאמֶר הַתִּרְשָׁתָא לָהֶם אֲשֶׁר לֹא יֹאכְלוּ מִקֹּדֶשׁ הַקֳּדָשִׁים עַד עֲמֹד כֹּהֵן לְאוּרִים וּלְתֻמִּים: [עזרא ב, סא - סג]

מסורת הש"ס

א) טהרות פרק ז משנה א, ב) [במשנה ליתא], ג) קדושין סט:, ד) [נ"א ולתומים], ה) נ"י כ"י.

תוספות ישנים

א) [ועוד רצה ר"י לפרש טעמא דמ"ד מעלין כדי שיהו עדים מצויין ליוחסין וחזר בו משום דלא משמע הכי בסמוך דקאמר ה"מ בתרומה דעון מיתה. ת"י עה"ג]:

הגהות הב"ח

(א) רש"י ד"ה עד עמוד כו' כאדם שאומר. נ"ב הוא בפ' עגלה ערופה דף מח ע"ב:

ליקוטי רש"י

במעלין מתרומה ליוחסין. הרואה כהן אוכל בתרומה במקומו אין צריך לבדוק אחריו ביוחסין ונושא כהן בתו. **גדולה חזקה.** יש לסמוך עליה יפה. **בקשו כתבם המתיחשים.** כתב יוחסם. **התרשתא.** נחמיה בן חכליה קרוי כן בספר עזרא ובגמרת ירושלמי נמצא שעל שם שהיה משקה למלך היה צריך לשתות קודם שלא יחשדוהו שמא הטיל סם המות במשקה המלך התירו לו יין של עובדי כוכבים לשתות לכך נקרא התרשתא. **מקדש הקדשים.** מדכתיב מקדש הקדשים שמעינן דלא אסירי בתרומה אלא מקדשי המקדש. **אמר להם.** תרומה איני יכול לאסור עליכם מפני חזקתכם שהוחזקתם בבבל לאכלה. **בקדשי הגבול.** תרומה הנאכלת בכל מקום. **כיון דאכלי בתרומה אתי לאסוקינהו.** ואמאי לא חש לה נחמיה דלא לאסוקינהו. **דריע חזקייהו.** לא איצטריך למיחש להאי דכיון דשאר כהנים אוכלים בקדשי המקדש והם נגואלו מהם הורע חזקתם ויש בהם היכר ולא אתי לאסוקינהו [קידושין שם].

[מכאן שייך לדף כה.]

ואלא. כיון דליכא למגזר מידי. **מאי גדולה חזקה.** דאמר רבי יוסי מאי רבותא לא היה לו לומר אלא מנין לחזקה כו' מדקאמר גדולה רבותא אשמועינן דאע"ג דאיכא צד איסור השתא טפי מעיקרא סמכינן עלה. **בתרומה דרבנן.** תרומת חוץ לארץ. **בתרומה דאורייתא.** משבאו לארץ. **השתא נמי בתרומה דרבנן.** היא דאכול כדמעיקרא ומאי ניהו תרומת פירות וירק. **בתרומה דאורייתא.** דגן ותירוש ויצהר לא אכול. **וכל זר לא יאכל קדש.** כל אותו הענין מדבר בתרומה ולא בקדשים דכתיב ובא השמש וטהר ואחר יאכל מן הקדשים וליכא לאוקמי אלא בתרומה שמחוסר כפורים מותר בה.

הָכָא נַמִּי בְּשֶׁכְּלֵי אוּמָּנוּתוֹ בְּיָדוֹ – So **here too,** the Rabbis' ruling (viz. that the donkey driver's testimony is not accepted) should be understood as referring **to a case in which the tools of his trade are in his hand;** i.e. he is carrying tools which demonstrate that his produce is for sale. Hence, his praise of his fellow's merchandise and the denigration of his own must be the result of collusion.[1]

The Gemara provides the original context of R' Chama bar Ukva's statement:

וְהֵיכָא אִתְּמַר דְּרַבִּי חָמָא בַּר עוּקְבָא – **And where was the statement of R' Chama bar Ukva** originally **made?** אַהָא דִּתְנַן – It was made **in reference to that which we learned in a Mishnah:**[2] הַקַּדָּר שֶׁהִנִּיחַ קְדֵירוֹתָיו – IF A POTTER[3] PUT DOWN HIS POTS וְיָרַד לִשְׁתּוֹת (מַיִם מִן הַיְאוֹר) – AND WENT DOWN TO DRINK WATER (FROM THE RIVER),[4] הַפְּנִימִיּוֹת טְהוֹרוֹת וְהַחִיצוֹנוֹת טְמֵאוֹת – THE INNER ONES ARE *TAHOR* WHILE THE OUTER ONES ARE *TAMEI*.[5] And the following difficulty was raised: וְהָתַנְיָא – **But it was taught in a Baraisa:** אֵלּוּ וָאֵלּוּ טְמֵאוֹת – Both THESE [the inner ones] AND THOSE [the outer ones] ARE *TAMEI*. אָמַר רַבִּי חָמָא בַּר עוּקְבָא – To solve this contradiction, **R' Chama bar Ukva said:** בְּשֶׁכְּלֵי אוּמָּנוּתוֹ בְּיָדוֹ – The Baraisa refers **to a case where the tools of his trade are in [the potter's] hand** to indicate that his pots are for sale. Hence, they are all *tamei,* מִפְּנֵי שֶׁיַּד הַכֹּל מְמַשְׁמֶשֶׁת בָּהֶן – **because the hand of every person** (i.e. prospective customers) **feels them** to check their quality.[6]

The discussion continued:[7]

וְהָתַנְיָא – **But it was taught in** another **Baraisa:** אֵלּוּ וָאֵלּוּ טְהוֹרוֹת – Both THESE [the inner pots] AND THOSE [the outer ones] ARE *TAHOR*!

This difficulty is solved:

אָמַר רַבִּי חָמָא בַּר עוּקְבָא – **R' Chama bar Ukva said:** בְּשֶׁאֵין כְּלֵי אוּמָּנוּתוֹ בְּיָדוֹ – That Baraisa refers **to a case where the tools of his trade are *not* in his hand.** Since, in that case, it is evident that his pots are not for sale, we do not suspect that people touched them.

A final difficulty:

וְאֶלָּא הָא דִּתְנַן – **But** now there is a problem with **that which we learned in the** original **Mishnah:** הַפְּנִימִיּוֹת טְהוֹרוֹת וְהַחִיצוֹנוֹת טְמֵאוֹת – THE INNER ONES ARE *TAHOR* WHILE THE OUTER ONES ARE *TAMEI*. הֵיכִי מַשְׁכַּחַת לָהּ – **How can you find [such a case]?** If he was carrying his tools (thereby indicating that the pots are for sale), they should all be *tamei.* And if he was not carrying his tools, they should all be *tahor*!

This difficulty is resolved:

דִּסְמִיכָא לִרְשׁוּת הָרַבִּים – That Mishnah refers to a case **where** he left the pots **close to a public thoroughfare,** וּמִשּׁוּם חִיפּוּפֵי רְשׁוּת הָרַבִּים – **and** thus some of the pots became *tamei* **because** they were alongside the **buffers** at the side **of the public thoroughfare.**[8]

The Gemara gives another explanation of the dispute between R' Yehudah and the Rabbis concerning the evidence needed to establish that someone is a Kohen:[9]

וְאִיבָּעֵית אֵימָא – **Or, if you wish, say** that רַבִּי יְהוּדָה וְרַבָּנַן בְּמַעֲלִין מִתְּרוּמָה לְיוּחֲסִין קָמִיפְּלְגֵי – **R' Yehudah and the Rabbis disagree** as to **whether we elevate** a Kohen who eats ***terumah*** **to** the status of **the genealogically fit.** That is, does the mere fact that *terumah* is distributed to someone provide evidence of his genealogical purity? R' Yehudah holds that this *is* sufficient evidence.[10] Hence, if someone is given *terumah,* that could lead to him being declared genealogically fit. For this reason, R' Yehudah rules that just as genealogical purity requires two witnesses, so does permission to eat *terumah.*[11] The Rabbis, though, hold that the fact that a person was given *terumah* cannot be used to prove

NOTES

1. One who transports produce with intent to sell it carries with him tools that are used in the selling process (e.g. an instrument that levels off grain in a measure) to advertise that his merchandise is for sale. If he were merely taking his produce to a place of storage, he would not display such tools. The Gemara proposes that the donkey driver in our case is carrying these tools, thereby demonstrating that he intends to sell his grain. Consequently, it makes no sense for him to denigrate his own produce and praise his fellow's unless he were doing so as a favor to his fellow, who will return the favor at their next stop (*Rashi;* cf. *Rabbeinu Chananel* cited by *Tosafos*).

R' Yehudah, however, rules that even in this case we accept his testimony about his fellow's grain, because, as stated above, *demai* is treated leniently (*Rashba*).

2. *Tohoros* 7:1.

3. This refers to one who is a *chaver* (*Rashi*). [A *chaver* is one who undertakes to eat all his food (even if it is not sacred) in a state of *taharah,* and, to this end, he observes the laws of *tumah* and *taharah* at all times (see *Tosefta, Demai* 2:2, and *Rambam, Hil. Mishkav U'Moshav* 10:1; see also *Chazon Ish, Demai* 5:7).]

4. The parenthesized words do not appear in the Mishnah in *Tohoros.*

5. The Gemara will explain this (*Rashi*).

6. It is therefore possible that every pot was touched by someone who is *tamei.*

7. Although it has already cited the statement of R' Chama bar Ukva that it was seeking, the Gemara quotes the rest of the discussion in which that statement was made.

8. Posts or large boulders were placed [at intervals] along the sides of a public thoroughfare to prevent wagons from getting too close to the walls on the side and damaging them. The potter had left his pots next to these buffers. Therefore, the pots closest to the thoroughfare ["the inner ones"] could have been rendered *tamei* by passersby who brush against them. If the clothes of an *am haaretz,* which are *tamei* (see *Chagigah* 18b), pass over open pots, they transmit *tumah* to the pots (*Rashi;* see, however, *Tos. Yom Tov* to *Tohoros* ibid.).

This Mishnah refers to a case in which the potter did *not* display his tools to indicate that he intended to sell the pots. Otherwise, they would *all* be *tamei,* even if they were not placed next to a public thoroughfare (*Meiri*).

9. This explanation stands in contrast to the Gemara's previous assumption that their point of contention was whether a suspicion of collusion disqualifies testimony.

The Gemara above (24a) noted that the opinions of R' Yehudah and the Rabbis regarding testimony about a Kohen were contradicted by their opinions with respect to testimony about tithing. Two solutions of these contradictions have already been offered. The explanation given here provides a third solution of the contradiction between *R' Yehudah's* rulings (*Ritva;* see also note 12).

10. R' Yehudah presumes that a person would not be given *terumah* to eat (in the capacity of a Kohen) unless he were definitely a Kohen. Hence, in R' Yehudah's view, if witnesses testify that they saw someone being given *terumah,* that would suffice for the court to declare him a Kohen even with respect to genealogical fitness (see *Rashi*).

However, it is not enough for witnesses to see him merely *eating terumah,* because he might be a Kohen's slave, who is allowed to partake of *terumah.* Rather, the witnesses must testify that they saw owners of produce distribute *terumah* to him as they would to a Kohen. In that case, he is certainly not a slave, for (according to R' Yehudah) *terumah* is not given to a Kohen's slave unless he is accompanied by his master (see *Rashi* here; *Tosafos,* printed on 25a ד"ה או, based on Gemara below, 29b; *Rashi* to *Yevamos* 99b ד"ה היו מעלין; cf. *Tos. Yeshanim* on 25a; see *Pnei Yehoshua* on *Tosafos* ibid.; see also note 20).

11. If we allow a person to eat [and thus receive] *terumah,* witnesses might later testify before a court that they saw him being given *terumah,* and, on the basis of their testimony, the court would deem him genealogically fit. Genealogical fitness, however, must always have the testimony of *two* witnesses as its source (Baraisa, 24a). Therefore, we cannot allow a person whose genealogical status is unknown even to

פד א ב ג ד מיי' פ"ב מהל' משכב ומושב הלכה יג:

פה ה מיי' פ"כ מהל' איסורי ביאה הל' ב טוש"ע אה"ע סי' ג סעיף ב:

פו ו מיי' שם הלכה ד והלכה יא:

תוספות רי"ד

לן דחלל הוא. אמאי לא ישא אשה כשרה ואפי' בתו של כ"ג. והא קיי"ל דלא הוזהרו כשרות להנשא לפסולים. וי"ל לפרש דהכי דאמר להשיאו אשה לאו להשיאו לו אשה אלא להשיא מגושר לכהונה. כגון אלמנתו ובתו דמספקינן ליה בחלל. ובת חלל ואלמנת חלל הן פסולות לכהונה: איבעיא להו מהו להעלות משטרות ליוחסין. פי' אילימא דכתיב בי' אני פלוני כהן חתמתי עד מאן קמסהיד עלויה. לא צריכא דכתיב בי' אני פ' כהן לויתי מנה מפלוני וחתימו סהדי אמנה שבשטר קא מסהדי או אכולה מילתא מסהדי. ר"ה ור"ח חד אמר מעלין וח"א אין מעלין. והלכתא כדברי המיקל. ואילו כתבו שני עדים פ' כהן לוה מפלוני לדליכא מאן דפליג דוודאי מעלין. דהא עדים מעידים כי הוא כהן א). איבעי' להו מהו להעלות מכהונה ליוחסין.

חשק שלמה על תוס' רי"ד

א) וכ"כ הרי"ט ז"ל בשם הרא"ה ז"ל ע"ש ולה מיושב קושית תוס' ד"ה אמנה מה שהקשו מגט פשוט ודו"ק ועי' בש"מ פו"ח סי' מט ס"ק ט"ו:

תורה אור השלם

א) וּמִבְּנֵי הַכֹּהֲנִים בְּנֵי חֳבַיָּה בְּנֵי הַקּוֹץ בְּנֵי בַרְזִלַּי אֲשֶׁר לָקַח מִבְּנוֹת בַּרְזִלַּי הַגִּלְעָדִי אִשָּׁה וַיִּקָּרֵא עַל שְׁמָם: אֵלֶּה בִּקְשׁוּ כְתָבָם הַמִּתְיַחְשִׂים וְלֹא נִמְצָאוּ וַיְגֹאֲלוּ מִן הַכְּהֻנָּה: וַיֹּאמֶר הַתִּרְשָׁתָא לָהֶם אֲשֶׁר לֹא יֹאכְלוּ מִקֹּדֶשׁ הַקֳּדָשִׁים עַד עֲמֹד כֹּהֵן לְאוּרִים וּלְתֻמִּים: [עזרא ב, סא - סג]

הכא נמי בשכלי אומנותו בידו והיכא אתמר דרבי חמא בר עוקבא אהא דתנן [א] הקדר שהניח קדירותיו וירד לשתות [ג] (מים מן היאור) הפנימיות טהורות והחיצונות טמאות והתניא אלו ואלו טמאות אמר רבי חמא בר עוקבא [ב] בשכלי אומנותו בידו מפני שיד הכל ממשמשת בהן והתניא אלו ואלו טהורות א"ר חמא בר עוקבא [ג] בשאין כלי אומנותו בידו ואלא הא דתנן הפנימיות טהורות והחיצונות טמאות היכי משכחת לה [ד] דסמיכא לרשות הרבים ומשום חיפופי רשות הרבים ואיבעית אימא ר' יהודה ורבנן במעלין מתרומה ליוחסין קמיפלגי איבעיא להו מהו להעלות משטרות ליוחסין היכי דמי אילימא דכתיב ביה אני פלוני כהן חתמתי עד מאן קא מסהיד עילויה לא צריכא דכתיב ביה אני פלוני כהן לויתי מנה מפלוני וחתימו סהדי מאי אמנה שבשטר קא מסהדי או דלמא אכולה מילתא קא מסהדי רב הונא ורב חסדא חד אמר מעלין וחד אמר [ה] אין מעלין איבעיא להו מהו להעלות מנשיאות כפים ליוחסין תיבעי למ"ד מעלין מתרומה ליוחסין ותיבעי למ"ד אין מעלין תיבעי למ"ד מעלין הני מילי תרומה דעון מיתה היא אבל נשיאות כפים דאיסור עשה לא או דלמא לא שנא תיבעי למ"ד אין מעלין הני מילי תרומה דמיתאכלא בצנעא אבל נשיאות כפים דבפרהסיא אי לאו כהן הוא כולי האי לא מחציף איניש נפשיה או דלמא לא שנא רב חסדא ורבי אבינא חד אמר מעלין וחד אמר [ו] אין מעלין א"ל רב נחמן בר יצחק לרבא מהו להעלות מנשיאות כפים ליוחסין א"ל פלוגתא דרב חסדא ורבי אבינא הלכתא מאי א"ל אנא מתניתא ידענא דתניא ר' יוסי אומר [ז] גדולה חזקה שנאמר [א] ומבני הכהנים בני חביה בני הקוץ בני ברזילי אשר לקח מבנות ברזילי הגלעדי אשה ויקרא על שמם אלה בקשו כתבם המתיחשים ולא נמצאו ויגאלו מן הכהונה ויאמר התרשתא להם אשר לא יאכלו מקדש הקדשים עד עמוד כהן לאורים [ח] ותומים אמר להם הרי אתם בחזקתכם במה הייתם אוכלים בגולה בקדשי הגבול אף כאן בקדשי הגבול ואי סלקא דעתך מעלין מנשיאות כפים ליוחסין הני כיון דפרסי ידייהו אתי לאסוקינהו שאני הכא דריע חזקייהו דאי לא תימא הכי למאן דאמר מעלין מתרומה ליוחסין כיון דאכלי בתרומה אתי לאסוקינהו אלא לאו משום דריע חזקיהו ואלא

רש"י

בשכלי אומנותו בידו. חמר המביא תבואה למכור היה נושא בידו כלי היכר של מכירה כגון מחק שמוחקין בה המדה והמביאה להצניע אינו נושא בידו כלי אומנות מכר והכא כגון שכלי אומנותו בידו של זה המזלזל את שלו דאנן סהדי שלמוכרה הביאה הלכך אין זה אלא גומל וזה יעיד עליו בכרך שלפניהם: הקדר. שהוא חבר: הפנימיות טהורות. כולה מתרלא ואזלא לקמיה: בשכלי אומנותו בידו. להיכר שהוא נושאן למוכרן: ממשמשת בהן. לבדוק וליקח: ומשום חיפופי רשות הרבים. שנותנים בני אדם אבנים גדולות או יתדות לצידי רה"ר להרחיק העגלות מלהזיק את הכתלים ומתוך שהן דוחקות את רה"ר וזה הניח קדירותיו אצלם דחק גם הוא את הדרך והעוברין שם מתחככין בהן ובגדיהן עוברין על פני אורכן ובגדי עם הארץ טמאים הם ומטמאים את החיצוניות: במעלין מתרומה ליוחסין. רבי יהודה סבר הרואה שמאכילין תרומה לאדם בחזקת כהן מעיד עליו בכל מקום שהוא כהן ומעלין אותו ליוחסין הלכך אם תאכילהו תרומה הרי אתה מביאו להשיאו אשה וטעמיה לאו משום גומלין הוא ורבנן סברי אין מעלין מתרומה ליוחסין: דאיסור מיתה. אם זר הוא לא היה אוכל תרומה שהוא עון מיתה: דאיסור עשה. כה תברכו (במדבר ו) אתם ולא זרים ולאו הבא מכלל עשה עשה: גדולה חזקה. שאין ב"ד יכולין להוציא דבר מחזקתו: בקשו כתבם המתיחשים. שיהו כהנים כשרים לפי שהתחתנו כהנים בגולה בגויי הארץ וילדו להם בנים כדכתיב בספר עזרא והם חללים הוצרכו הנולדים בגולה להתייחס כשעלו מן הגולה לשרת בבנין שני: ויגאלו. נפסלו מלשון לחם מגואל (מלאכי א): התרשתא. הוא נחמיה בן חכליה וכן כתוב בספר עזרא (נחמיה ח): עד עמוד כהן לאורים וגו'. כאדם (א) שאומר לחבירו עד שיבא המשיח דאורים ותומים לא הוו במקדש שני שנחסרו חמשה דברים כדאמרינן בסדר יומא (דף כא:): מקדשי הקדשים. דוקא מקדשי המקדש פסלינהו אבל תרומה שהיו רגילין בה בגולה לא אסר עלייהו משום דהוחזקו בה: קדשי הגבול. תרומה שהיא נוהגת בגבולין חוץ למקדש ולירושלים: אף כאן בקדשי הגבול. ומדאמר רבי יוסי גדולה חזקה ש"מ נשיאות כפים נמי לא אסר עלייהו שהרי הוחזקו בה בגבולין: ואי סלקא דעתך כו' אתו לאסוקינהו. ומה הועילו בתקנתם: שאני הכא. דליכא למיחש לאסוקינהו דהא ריע חזקייהו שהרי הכל רואין שאר כהנים אוכלין קדשי המקדש והם אינן אוכלין יש כאן היכר גדול שיש בהן צד פסול אבל שאר בני אדם כגון בזמן הזה לעולם מעלין מנשיאות כפים ליוחסין: [ה] [דאי לא תימא הכי. דעל לא סמיך שיש בהן היכר תרומה נמי תקשי למ"ד מעלין מתרומה ליוחסין]:

ואלא

תוספות

בשכלי אומנותו בידו. פירש רבינו חננאל זה שאומר עליו שהוא כהן יש בידו כלים שמשמשין בהן בטהרה כגון כלי גללים כלי אבנים כלי אדמה שאין מקבלין טומאה שכל הרואה כלים הללו בידו מתרחק ממנו מלטמאותו ודומה שהוא כהן ולכך האמינוהו חכמים:

ואיבעית אימא רבי יהודה ורבנן במעלין מתרומה ליוחסין קמיפלגי. ולא אתא לשנויי אלא קשיא דרבי יהודה אדרבי יהודה אבל לרבנן אדרבנן לעולם צריך לתרץ בשכלי אומנותו בידו והקשה הר"ר שמואל מוורדון ומעיקרא היכי בעי למימר דטעמא דר"י משום גומלין והא בלא גומלים ע"כ סבר רבי יהודה בשילהי פרקין (לקמן דף כח:) דמעלין מתרומה ליוחסין ותירץ ר"י דמעיקרא ס"ד דלאו טעמא משום גומלים לא היינו מפקידים את הכהן מן התרומה כדי לומר מעלין כיון דמן הדין ראוי לחלוק ע"פ חבירו ולדרבנן קודם היינו אומרים אין מעלין אע"ג דגבי עבד אמר לקמן לרבי יהודה דאין חולקין לו תרומה משום דמעלין התם אין כל כך חששא בהפסד של עבד זה אם אין חולקין לו תרומה בלא רבו וא"ת ובלאו סברא פליגי לימרו תרוייהו דמעלין ולצטרך שני עדים בתרומה או לימרו תרוייהו דלא מעלין ולא יצטרך אלא עד אחד בתרומה וי"ל דבהא פליגי דמר סבר חיישינן שמא יעלו מתרומה ליוחסין לפיכך הצריכו שני עדים ומר סבר דלא חיישינן א):

אמנה שבשטר קמסהדי. וא"ת ואי לאו אכולה מילתא קמסהדי א"כ עדים חתמי אע"ג דלא ידעי אי כהן הוא אי לאו ואם כן הא דתנן בגט פשוט (ב"ב דף קסז.) שני יוסף בן שמעון הדרין בעיר אחת אם היו מסולקין יכתבו כהן ומה מועיל כיון שעדים חותמין אע"פ שאין מכירים בו אם הוא כהן והרי הוא יכול להטעים ולכתוב שטר אחר בשם חבירו כהן ויוציא ממון מחבירו כהן וי"ל דהיכא דהוחזקו שני יוסף בן שמעון ודאי אכולה מילתא קא מסהדי כי אז הן צריכין לידע אם כהן הוא והתם ודאי מעלין משטרות ליוחסין והכא מיבעיא לן היכא דלא הוחזקו: חד אמר מעלין. ואם תאמר ואמאי לא חשיב ליה בהדי הנך דתנן בעשרה יוחסין (קדושין דף עו. ושם) אין בודקין מן המזבח ולמעלה ולא מדוכן כו' וי"ל דהך דשטרות מלתא דפשיטא היא דכיון דאכולא מלתא קמסהדי א"כ הוי עדות גמור ולכך לא קא חשיב עדים וא"ת ואמאי לא חשיב תרומה ונשיאות כפים למ"ד מעלין ואור"ת דתרומה בכלל מזבח ונשיאות כפים בכלל דוכן אע"ג דההוא דוכן היינו שיר כדמשמע התם בגמרא מ"ד מעלין הוה מוקי לה נמי בדוכן כהנים שבגבולים ומיהו קשה אמאי לא חשיב ס"ת שקרא בחזקת כהן כדלקמן ויש לומר דליכא למימר דתנא ושייר כולהו ובספר הישר פירש ר"ת דלאו בעבודת מזבח ממש איירי אלא כגון הפשט וניתוח דברים הכשרים בזרים דלא היו מניחין לעשות אותם אלא למיוחסין מן המשיאין לכהונה אבל מילי דכהונה כגון תרומה ונשיאות כפים וס"ת לא איצטריך למתני: **שאני** הכא דריע חזקייהו. פי' בקונטרס שהכל רואים שאר כהנים אוכלין שאר קדשי מזבח ואלו אין אוכלין וק"ק דמ"מ תיקשי למ"ד מעלין אמאי לא אסקינהו לקדשי מזבח וליוחסין ונראה לר"ת דריע חזקייהו היינו שהיו מיחסים אותם אחר בני ברזילי שהיה ישראל ועוד שלא מצאו כתבם והיכא דאיתרע חזקה אין מעלין לכ"ע אבל קשה דפריך מעיקרא אתי לאסוקינהו הוה ליה למיפרך אמאי נגאלו כלל מן הכהונה ויש לומר דשפיר הוה ידע דריע חזקייהו ומשום הכי לא אסקינהו אלא דהוה ס"ד דאע"ג דריע חזקייהו איכא למיחש דלמא אתי לאסוקינהו לבסוף שלא ידעו שלא מצאו כתבם:

ואלא

מסורת הש"ס

א) טהרות פרק ז משנה א, ב) [במשנה ליתא], ג) קדושין סט:, ד) [צ"ל ולתומים], ה) נ"י כ"י.

תוספות ישנים

א) [ועוד רצה ר"י לפרש טעמא דמ"ד מעלין כדי שיהו עדים מצויין ליוחסין וחזר בו משום דלא משמע הכי בסמוך דקאמר ה"מ בתרומה דעון מיתה. ת"י עה"ג]:

הגהות הב"ח

(א) רש"י ד"ה עד עמוד כו' כאדם שאומר. נ"ב הוא בפ' עגלה ערופה דף מח ע"ב:

ליקוטי רש"י

במעלין מתרומה ליוחסין. הרואה כהן אוכל בתרומה במקומו אין צריך לבדוק אחריו ביוחסין ונושא כהן כמו. גדולה חזקה. יש לסמוך עליה יפה. בקשו כתבם המתיחשים. כתב יחוסם. התרשתא. נחמיה בן חכליה קרוי כן בספר עזרא ובגמרת ירושלמי נמצא שעל שם שהיה משקה למלך והיה צריך לשתות קודם שלא יחשדוהו שמא הטיל סם המות במשקה המלך התירו לו יין של עובדי כוכבים לשתות לכך נקרא התרשתא. מקדש הקדשים. מדכתיב מקדש הקדשים שמעינן דלא אסירי בתרומה אלא מקדשי המקדש. אמר להם. תרומה איני יכול לאסור עליכם מפני חזקתכם שהוחזקתם בגבול לאכלה. בקדשי הגבול. תרומה הנאכלת בכל מקום. כיון דאכלי בתרומה אתי לאסוקינהו. ואמאי לא חש לה נחמיה דלא לאסוקינהו. דריע חזקייהו. לא איצטריך למיחש להאי דכיון דשאר כהנים אוכלים בקדשי המקדש והם נגואלו מהם הורע חזקתם ויש בהם היכר ולא אתי לאסוקינהו [קידושין שם].

[מכאן שייך לדף כה.]

ואלא. כיון דליכא למגזר מידי. מאי גדולה חזקה. דקאמר רבי יוסי מאי רבותא לא היה לו לומר אלא מנין לחזקה כו' מדקאמר גדולה רבותא אשמועינן דאע"ג דליכא צד איסור השתא טפי מעיקרא סמכינן עלה. בתרומה דרבנן. תרומת חוץ לארץ. בתרומה דאורייתא. מצוה לאכלן. השתא נמי בתרומה דרבנן. היא דאכלי בה כדמעיקרא ולאו ניתנו תרומת פירות וירק. בתרומה דאורייתא. דגן ותירוש ויצהר לא אכול. וכל זר לא יאכל קדש. כל אותו הענין מדבר בתרומה ולא בקדשים דכתיב ובא השמש וטהר ואחר יאכל מן הקדשים וליכא לאוקמי אלא בתרומה שמותר כפורים מותר בה.

אימא לא ואי אשמעינן הני תרתי משום דממונא אבל אשת איש דאיסורא אימא לא נשביתי וטהורה אני למה לי משום דקא בעי למיתני ואם משנשאת באו עדים הרי זו לא תצא הניחא למאן א) דמתני לה אסיפא אלא למאן דמתני לה ארישא מאי איכא למימר משום דקא בעי למיתני שתי נשים שנשבו ושתי נשים שנשבו למה לי מהו דתימא ניחוש ב) לגומלין קמשמע לן וכן שני אנשים למה לי משום דקא בעי למיתני פלוגתא דרבי יהודה ורבנן ת״ר אני כהן וחברי כהן נאמן להאכילו בתרומה ואינו נאמן להשיאו אשה עד שיהו ג׳ שנים מעידין על זה ושנים מעידין על זה רבי יהודה אומר אף אינו נאמן להאכילו בתרומה עד שיהו שלשה שנים מעידין על זה ושנים מעידין על זה למימרא דרבי יהודה חייש לגומלין ורבנן לא חיישי לגומלין והא איפכא שמעינן להו דתנן ג) החמרין שנכנסו לעיר ואמר אחד מהן שלי חדש ושל חברי ישן שלי אינו מתוקן ושל חברי מתוקן אינו נאמן רבי יהודה אומר נאמן אמר רב אדא בר אהבה אמר רב מוחלפת השיטה אביי אמר לעולם לא תיפוך ד) בדמאי הקילו רוב עמי הארץ מעשרין הן אמר רבא דרבי יהודה אדרבי יהודה קשיא דרבנן אדרבנן לא קשיא אלא דרבי יהודה אדרבי יהודה לא קשיא כדשנינן דרבנן אדרבנן לא קשיא כדאמר רבי חמא בר עוקבא בשכלי אומנותו בידו הכא

רש״י

משום דבעי למיתני שתי נשים שנשבו. לאשמועינן דבזמן שמעידות זו את זו נאמנות: נאמן להאכילו בתרומה ואינו נאמן להשיאו אשה. מיוחסת מעלה היא ביוחסין: למימרא כו׳. קא ס״ד דטעמא דרבי יהודה משום גומלין: החמרים. סוחרי תבואה ומוליכין ממקום הזול לכרכין: שלי חדש ושל חברי ישן שלי אינו מתוקן ושל חבירי מתוקן. משבח את של חבירו ומזלזל את שלו שלי אינו מעושר של חבירי מעושר שלי חדש ואינו יבש עדיין כל צורכו ו) [ושל חבירי ישן ויבש כל צורכו] דפסח ישן טוב מן החדש בעת הגורן כדאמרי׳ באיהו נשך (ב״מ עב:) היו חדשות מארבע וישנות משלש: אינו נאמן. הואיל ועם הארץ הוא ואינו נאמן על המעשר אע״פ שמעיד על שלו שאינו מתוקן ועוד שמוסיף עם זו דברים אחרים לשבח את של חבירו אינו נאמן להחזיק את של חבירו בחזקת מתוקן שאינן אלא מערימין אמור אתה כאן ואני במקום אחר:

תוספות

נשביתי וטהורה אני למה לי. וקשה לרשב״א אמאי לא משני משום דבעי למיתני סיפא אם יש עדים שנשבית ואמרה טהורה אני אינה נאמנת וי״ל דמשום הא לא אצטריך דמסיפא דמתני׳ שמעינן לה דקתני סיפא עיר שכבשוה כרכום כל כהנות שנמצאו בתוכה פסולות ואינה נאמנת לומר טהורה אני:

שתי נשים שנשבו למה לי. דלאי לאשמעינן דאחת נאמנת על חברתה הא בהדיא תנן (לקמן כז:) דאפי׳ עבד ושפחה נאמנים: וכן שני אנשים למה לי משום דבעי למיתני פלוגתא דרבי יהודה ורבנן. אבל בשתי נשים משמע דלא פליג רבי יהודה משום דבשבויה הקילו וקשה דלקמן (דף כז.) אשכחן איפכא דמסיח לפי תומו נאמן בתרומה אפי׳ על פי עצמו כדאמר גבי יוחנן אוכל חלות דהעלהו רבי לכהונה על פיו וגבי שבויה תני לקמן (דף כז:) הכל נאמנים להעידה חוץ מבעלה ומוקי לה במסיח לפי תומו ומיהו למאי דמוקמינן פלוגתייהו במעלין מתרומה ליוחסין ניחא דטעמא דמחמיר רבי יהודה טפי בתרומה מבשבויה משום דמעלין מתרומה ליוחסין אבל רבי מיקל טפי בתרומה במסיח לפי תומו היינו משום דקסבר דאין מעלין מתרומה ליוחסין כדאמר לקמן אבל למאי דמוקי פלוגתייהו משום גומלים קשה וי״ל דבתרומה דרבנן דוקא הוא דמתכשר במסיח לפי תומו כדמשמע בהגוזל בתרא (ב״ק קיד:) אבל בתרומה דאורייתא לא:

אבל אינו נאמן להשיאו אשה. (א) פי׳ בקונטרס משום חשש ממזרות ונתינות וקשה דלהכי ליכא למיחש כדאמרינן בהחולץ (יבמות מה. ושם) גבי עובד כוכבים ועבד הבא על בת ישראל דאמרינן ליה זיל גלי או נסיב בת מינך משמע דאם ילך למקום שאין מכירים אותו ישיאוהו בת ישראל אע״פ שאין מכירים ולא יסתפקו בו בנתין וממזר וכן גבי ההוא דאתא לקמיה דרבי יהודה וא״ל נאמן אתה לפסול עצמך ואי אתה נאמן לפסול בניך משמע שהוא ובניו היו בחזקת כשרים אע״פ שלא היו מכירים בהם ונראה לר״ת דלהשיאו אשה דקאמר היינו להשיאו בדוקה מד׳ אמהות כדתנן בעשרה יוחסין (קדושין דף עו. ושם) הנושא אשה כהנת צריך שיבדוק אחריה ד׳ אמהות ואין נאמן אם ישא אשה בדוקה להכשיר בתו לכהן בלא בדיקה אלא יצטרך לבדוק אחריו וה״ה דמצי למימר ואינו נאמן להכשירו לעבודה ואותה בדיקה היא משום חללות דאין מכירין ישראל חללים שביניהם ולא משום ספק ממזרות ונתינות דלהא לא חיישינן כדפי׳ וכן משמע התם דקאמר דהיא אינה בודקת בדידיה דלא הוזהרו כשרות לינשא לפסולים ואי משום ממזרות ונתינות הא ודאי הוזהרו דהשוה הכתוב אשה לאיש לכל עונשין שבתורה ואם תאמר אי משום חללות בודקין לא יבדקו אלא יחוס אביה לבד דאפילו היתה אמה חללה כשרה היא ע״י אביה דלכ״ע בני ישראל מקוה טהרה לחללות ויש לומר מאחר שהצריכו לבדוק את יחוס האב משום חללות אגב חללות הוצרכו לבדוק כל פסול שבה גם של ממזרות ונתינות וכולה הך שמעתין דמצרכי בדיקה להשיא בתו לכהן אתיא כרבי מאיר דרבנן פליגי עליה התם ולא מצרכי בדיקה ואמרי כל משפחות בחזקת כשרות הן עומדות וא״ל אפילו עד אחד כדי להכשיר בתו לכהונה ומיהו להכשיר בנו או עצמו לעבודה צריך דלאו בחזקת כהונה עומד אי נמי אפילו כרבנן ובילא עליו ערער כדקאמר התם במילתייהו דרבנן בד״א שלא יצא עליו ערער כו׳:

שלי חדש ושל חבירי ישן. בפרק אע״פ פי׳ בקונטרס די״מ משום עומר ולאו מילתא היא דאם כן מאי מתרץ בדמאי הקילו התינח דמאי חדש ישן מאי איכא למימר ועוד דלא מצינו בשום מקום שנחשדו עמי הארץ על החדש ורשב״א פירש דקאי אשביעית וקאמר שלי חדש וגדל בשביעית ושל חבירי ישן וגדל בשנה שעברה ואשכחן דקרי לשביעית חדש דתנן במסכת שביעית (פ״ז מ״ז) ורד חדש שכבשו בשמן ישן ילקט את הורד וכי משני בדמאי הקילו בשביעית לא חש לתרץ דפשיטא ליה להש״ס דרבי יהודה מיקל בשביעית משום דבאתריה דרבי יהודה חמירא להו שביעית כדאמר בהניזקין (גיטין נד.) ואין נראה לר״ת דסתם עמי הארץ לא נחשדו אשביעית דתנן בפרק עד כמה (בכורות ל. ושם) החשוד על המעשר אינו חשוד על השביעית החשוד על השביעית אינו חשוד על המעשר אלמא דסתמא אינן חשודין בשביעית ומעשר דקתני היינו מעשר שני דאמעשר ראשון חשודין הם והא דתנן במסכת דמאי (פ״ג מ״ד) ומייתי לה בהניזקין (גיטין סא:) המוליך חיטין לטוחן כותי או לטוחן עם הארץ אינו חושש לא משום מעשר ולא משום שביעית דמשמע דחשודים על השביעית איכא למימר דמשום כותי נקט שביעית אי נמי בודאי חשוד איירי וכן ההיא דמייתי בפרק קמא דחולין (דף ו. ושם) הנותן לשכנתו עיסה לאפות וקדירה לבשל אינו חושש לשאור ותבלין שבה לא משום מעשר ולא משום שביעית ועוד קשה לר״ת דאי באיסור חדש או שביעית מיירי הוה ליה למימר של חברי אינו חדש כדקאמר אינו מתוקן ועוד הקשה ר״ת דלעיל דההיא משנה דחמרין תנן במס׳ דמאי (פ״ג) הנכנס לעיר ואינו מכיר אדם שם ואמר מי כאן נאמן מי כאן מעשר ואמר לו אחד אני איני נאמן איש פלוני נאמן הלך ולקח הימנו אמר ליה מי כאן מוכר ישן אמר ליה מי ששלחך אצלי אע״פ שהן כגומלין זה את זה הרי אלו נאמנים ואי ישן היינו דלית ביה איסור חדש או שביעית היאך קונה ממי ששלחו אצלו והלא הוא בעצמו אומר שאינו נאמן ועוד מדקא שאיל להיאך מי מוכר ישן מכלל שמה שקנה ממנו כבר היה חדש או שביעית והלא לא הלך אצלו אלא לפי שהוא נאמן ופי׳ הקונטרס נראה לר״ת עיקר להשביח קאמר ולרבותא דרבי יהודה נקטיה דאע״פ שמגרע את שלו ומשביח את של חבירו ומיחזי טפי כגומלין אפילו הכי נאמנין ואם תאמר א״כ מאי קשה ליה דרבנן אדרבנן דלמא הכא הוא דחיישינן לגומלין דדומה שהן גומלין כדפי׳ ויש לומר דאי לאו דחיישינן לגומלים בעלמא משום הכי לא הוו חיישינן טפי ו):

אביי אמר לעולם לא תיפוך בדמאי כו׳. והא דאמר אביי בפרק במה מדליקין (שבת דף כג.) ספק דבריהם לא בעי ברכה רבא אמר רוב עמי הארץ מעשרין הן וכן בפרק אע״פ (לקמן נו:) משני אביי ודאי דבריהם עשו חיזוק ספק דבריהם לא עשו חיזוק רבא אמר בדמאי הקילו לא משום דלית ליה לאביי דרבא דהא הכא אית ליה ועוד דבשילהי המביא (ביצה לה:) דייק ממתני׳ דרוב עמי הארץ מעשרין הן אלא דאית ליה לאביי דכל ספק דבריהם אע״ג דליכא רוב לא בעי ברכה וגם לא עשו חיזוק ומיהו בפרק קמא דשבת (דף יג. ושם) אההיא דלא יאכל זב פרוש עם זב עם הארץ מפרש אביי שמא יאכילנו דברים שאינם מתוקנים ולא סמיך ארוב עמי הארץ מעשרין כדקאמר רבא התם סבירא ליה דלההיא מלתא מחמירין ולא סמכינן ארובא וכן רבא בסוף הניזקין (גיטין סא. ושם) גבי משאלת אשה נפה כו׳ ולא בעי למיסמך ארוב עמי הארצות דמעשרין לענין לסייע ידי עוברי עבירה דנראה לו לענין זה להחמיר:

בשכלי

מסורת הש״ס

א) [לעיל כג.], ב) [ע״ז סא:], ג) לקמן ע: דמאי פ״ד מ״ז, ד) שבת יג. כג. גיטין סא. לקמן נו: [ביצה לה:], ה) יבמות קיד. מנחות לא.], ה) ב״מ כ״ו, ו) [ועיין היטב תוס׳ בכורות יא: ד״ה הרי ועוד שם ל. ד״ה מתני׳ ותוס׳ סוכה לט: ד״ה במה].

עין משפט נר מצוה

פג א מיי׳ פי״ב מהל׳ מעשר הלכה י:

הגהות הב״ח

(א) תום׳ ד״ה אבל כו׳ פי׳ בקונטרס. נ״ב ע״ל בפירושו סוף דף כ״ה:

ליקוטי רש״י

לגומלין. העד אתה עלי ואני עליך [לעיל כג:]. אגמול לך כיוצא בזו [ע״ז סא:]. שלי חדש. והישן טוב ממנו שהחדש עדיין אינו יבש כל צרכו והכי נמי אמרינן באיהו נשך [ב״מ עב:] היו חדשות מארבע וישנות משלש כו׳ ויש מפרשים משום עומר ולאו מילתא היא דא״כ דמתרץ בדמאי הקילו התינח דמאי חדש מאי איכא למימר ועוד לא מצינו שנחשדו עמי הארץ על איסור חדש ולא נקט לה אלא משום אין נאמנים דדמאי ורבותא אשמועינן דאע״ג דמשבח לה לחבריה נמי במילי אחרנייתא אינו נאמן על הדמאי דחיישינן לגומלין. בדמאי הקילו. משאר ספק דדבריהם ואפילו ספק ליתיה דרוב עמי הארץ מעשרין הן [לקמן נו:]. דמאי אפי׳ ספק לא הוי אלא חומרא בעלמא דרוב עמי הארץ מעשרין הן. מאי טעמא משום דרוב עמי הארץ מעשרין הן וכבר נתעשר [ב״ק קטו:].

תוספות רי״ד

נטמאת אינה נאמנת דדוקא [להתיר] נאמן ע״א [משום] דבשבוי׳ הקילו ולא לאיסור כדרבא דאמר אין דבר שבערוה פחות מב׳. אלא אעצמה אמאי לא מהימנא. אלא פשיטא דאיכא עדים פי׳ שנשבו ומ״ה אעצמה אינה נאמנת לומר נשביתי וטהורה אני וחברתה נמי אסורה בלא עדותה והא דקאמר אינה נאמנת כלומר בלא עדותה היא אסורה. אימא מציעתא אני וחברתי טמאות נאמנת ע״ע ואין נאמנת על חברתה. ואי דאיכא עידי שבויה אחברתה אמאי לא מהימנא והלא גם בלא עדותה אסורה והמורה פי׳ ואינה נאמנת על חברתה ע״כ משמע דחברתה בחזקת טהורה קיימא. דבשלמא אינה נאמנת דרישא אע״ג דאכולה מילתא משמע שייך למתני [אינה נאמנת] משום היתר. אלא הכא דבהדי׳ תניא אינה נאמנת על חברתה קשה. אלא פשיטא דליכא עדים פי׳ מ״ה על עצמה נאמנת דשויתי׳ אנפשה חתיכה דאיסורא. אבל על חברתה אינה נאמנת דכיון דליכא עדי שבוי׳ חברתה משתריא באומר׳ נשביתי וטהורה אני וזו שמעידה עלי׳ כי נטמאת אינה נאמנת כדרבא. שאין דבר שבערוה פחות מב׳. אימא סיפא אני וחברתי טהורות נאמנת על חברתה ואינה נאמנת ע״ע. ואי דליכא עדים אעצמה אמאי לא מהימנא. אלא פשיטא דאיכא עדים. פי׳ ומ״ה אעצמה אינה נאמנת ואחברתה מהימנא שע״א נאמן בשבוי׳ רישא וסיפא דאיכא עדים ומציעתא דליכא עדים. אמר ר״פ כולה דאיכא עדים ואיכא ע״א דקמפיך פי׳ [דאיכא עדים] שמעידים שנשבו וע״א בא ומהפך כל הדברים. אני טמאה וחברתי טהורה וא״ל ע״א את טהורה וחברתיך טמאה. איהי שויתה נפשה חתיכה דאיסורא וחברתה משתריא אפומא. פי׳ המורה. דבשבוי׳ האמינו חכמים ע״א להקל ואפי׳ עבד או שפחה. וכדקתני מתני׳ אם יש להן עדים אפילו עבד וכו׳ וכ״מ שנאמן ע״א הרי הוא כשנים ואין דברי א׳ שכנגדו לטמא עומד במקום שנים. ומשמע מפירושו. דאע״ג דלא נשאת וגם לא התירוה לינשא. ואינו נ״ל דכיון דאיכא עדות מכחשת לה היכי שריא לה לחברתה אפומא דידה. והתנן בפ׳ האשה רבה עד אומר מת ועד אומר לא מת ה״ז לא תנשא דכי מהימנינן ליה לע״א דאמר מת ולא מצי אידך למכחשי׳ ה״מ כשבאו בזה אח״ז וכבר התירוה ע״פ אותו העד (אמרת) [אמרינן] לא תצא מהיתירא הראשון. אבל היכא דקיימי תרווייהו ומכחשי להדדי אמרינן לא תנשא. והכא היכי אמרי׳ דהיא נאמנת אע״פ שהעד מכחישה. ובתוספתא דכתובות [בפ״ב] ברישא דהא מתני׳ תני הכי. עד אומר נשבית וטמאה היא. וע״א אומר נשבית וטהורה היא. אשה אומרת נשבית וטמאה היא ואשה אומרת נשבית וטהורה היא אין משיאין אותה. ואם נשאת ל״ת. וא״כ בע״כ מאי דתני הכא נאמנת הכי בעי׳ לפרושי כגון שהתירוה לינשא על פיה. ובתר הכי אתא ע״א ואמר נטמאת. אי נמי כגון שהלכה ונשאת דאמרינן ל״ת. אני טהורה וחברתי טמאה וא״ל עד אחד את טמאה וחברתיך טהורה. איהי כיון דאיכא עדים לאו כל כמינה. פי׳ המורה ה״ג עדים וקאי אעידי שבוי׳ דע״א בטומאה אינו כלום אלא בסוטה בלבד שרגלים לדבר שהרי קינא לה ונסתרה חברתה משתריא אפומא דעד. פי׳ ה״נ כגון שנשאת. אני וחברתי טמאה. וא״ל עד את וחברתך טהורות איהי שויתי׳ נפשה חתיכה דאיסורא. פי׳ לפיכך אין העד נאמן לטהרה חברתה משתריא אפומא דעד כגון שנשאת. אני וחברתי טהורות ואמר לה עד את וחברתיך טמאות. איהי כיון דאיכא עדים לאו כל כמינה. חברתה משתריא אפומה דידה פי׳ כגון שנשאת או התירוה לינשא כדפרי׳: מתני׳ וכן שני אנשים זה אומר כהן אני וז״א כהן אני אין נאמנים ובזמן שהן מעידים זע״ז הרי אלו נאמנים. ר״י אומר אין מעלין לכהונה ע״פ ע״א. אר״א אימתי בזמן שיש עוררים. אבל במקום שאין עוררים מעלין לכהונה ע״פ ע״א. רשב״ג אומר משום ר״ש בן הסגן מעלין לכהונה ע״פ ע״א. פי׳ ב׳ אנשים שבאו ממדה״י ולא ידענו מי הם ז״א כהן אני וז״א כהן אני. אין נאמנים ליתן להם תרומה ובזמן שמעידים זע״ז שז״א אני וחברי כהנים וכמו כן זה הרי אלו נאמנים שמעלין לכהונה ע״פ ע״א. ואפילו היכא דאיכא למיחש לגומלין. ר״י אומר אין וכו׳ ואפילו היכא דליכא גומלין וכ״ש היכא דאיכא גומלין. פי׳ העד אתה עלי ואני עליך. אר״א אימתי אין מעלין במקום שיש עוררים הבאים לפוסלו. אבל במקום שאין עוררין מעלין והוא דליכא גומלין רשב״ג אומר וכו׳. לקמן מפרש מאי בינייהו: ת״ר זה אומר אני כהן וחבירי כהן א) וז״א אני כהן וחבירי כהן נאמן להאכילו בתרומה ואינו נאמן להשיאו אשה עד שיהיה שלשה ב׳ מעידים ע״ז. וב׳ מעידים ע״ז. פי׳ המורה אינו נאמן להשיאו אשה מיוחסת ומעלה הוא בכהונה. (ולכך) [וכן] פי׳ גם ר״ח דאינו נאמן להשיאו אשה הראויה לכהונה. דחיישינן שמא חלל הוא. וק׳ לי א״כ איזה אשה יקח. דכשירה הראויה לכהונה אסרת לו ישא פסולה לכהונה אסור לו ליקח. דשויא אנפשיה חתיכה דאיסורא באומרו כהן אני. ותו אפילו אי ברירא לן

חשק שלמה על תוס׳ רי״ד א) גירסת רבינו ח״א אני כהן וחבירי כהן וכ״ה בתוספתא דמכילתין פ׳ ב׳ ע״ש.

contradiction between the statements of R' Yehudah, while the contradiction between the statements of the Rabbis (who suspect collusion in the case of tithing but not in the case of the Kohen) remains problematic.[24]

Rava therefore answers:

אֶלָּא דְרַבִּי יְהוּדָה אַדְּרַבִּי יְהוּדָה לֹא קַשְׁיָא כִּדְשַׁנִּינָן – **Rather, there is no contradiction between** one ruling of **R' Yehudah and** the other ruling of **R' Yehudah, as we answered** above (i.e. the laws of *demai* are lenient). דְּרַבָּנָן אַדְּרַבָּנָן לֹא קַשְׁיָא – And **there is no contradiction between** one ruling of **the Rabbis and** the other ruling of **the Rabbis** כִּדְאָמַר רַבִּי חָמָא בַּר עוּקְבָא – **because R' Chama bar Ukva said** in a different context: בְּשֶׁכְּלֵי אוּמָּנוּתוֹ בְּיָדוֹ – "We refer to a case **in which the tools of his trade are in his hand.**"[25]

NOTES

whereas the Tanna Kamma's (i.e. the Rabbis') statements do not. But this is clearly not true!]

24. The commentators ask why the Gemara did not resolve this problem simply by stating that the donkey driver is not believed because he is an *am haaretz,* who is not trusted with respect to *maaser.* [Although there are mitigating circumstances in this case (see note 19), perhaps the Rabbis do not take them into account.] Therefore, even if the Rabbis do not suspect collusion (as implied by their ruling in the case of the Kohen), they would still reject the donkey driver's testimony. For discussion of this issue, see *Pnei Yehoshua, Chidushei R' Akiva Eiger, Chasam Sofer, Beis Yaakov* and *Beis Aharon.*

25. This is explained below.

אימא לא ואי אשמעינן הני תרתי משום דממונא אבל אשת איש דאיסורא אימא לא נשביתי וטהורה אני למה לי משום דקא בעי למיתני ואם משנשאת באו עדים הרי זו לא תצא הניחא למאן א) דמתני לה אסיפא אלא למאן דמתני לה ארישא מאי איכא למימר משום דקא בעי למיתני שתי נשים שנשבו ושתי נשים שנשבו למה לי מהו דתימא ניחוש ג) לגומלין קמשמע לן וכן שני אנשים למה לי משום דקא בעי למיתני פלוגתא דרבי יהודה ורבנן ת"ר אני כהן וחברי כהן נאמן להאכילו בתרומה ואינו נאמן להשיאו אשה עד שיהו ג' שנים מעידין על זה ושנים מעידין על זה רבי יהודה אומר אף אינו נאמן להאכילו בתרומה עד שיהו שלשה שנים מעידין על זה ושנים מעידין על זה למימרא דרבי יהודה חייש לגומלין ורבנן לא חיישי לגומלין והא איפכא שמעינן להו דתנן ג) החמרין שנכנסו לעיר ואמר אחד מהן שלי חדש ושל חברי ישן שלי אינו מתוקן ושל חברי מתוקן אינו נאמן רבי יהודה אומר נאמן אמר רב אדא בר אהבה אמר רב מוחלפת השיטה אביי אמר לעולם לא תיפוך ד) בדמאי הקילו רוב עמי הארץ מעשרין הן אמר רבא דרבי יהודה אדרבי יהודה קשיא דרבנן אדרבנן לא קשיא אלא דרבי יהודה אדרבי יהודה לא קשיא כדשנינן דרבנן אדרבנן לא קשיא כדאמר רבי חמא בר עוקבא בשכלי אומנותו בידו הכא

רש"י

משום דבעי למיתני שתי נשים שנשבו. לאשמועינן דבזמן שמעידות זו את זו נאמנות: **נאמן להאכילו בתרומה ואינו נאמן להשיאו אשה.** מיוחסת מעלה היא ביוחסין: **למימרא כו'.** קא ס"ד דטעמא דרבי יהודה משום גומלין: **החמרים.** סוחרי תבואה ומוליכין ממקום הזול לכרכין: **שלי חדש ושל חבירי ישן שלי אינו מתוקן ושל חבירי מתוקן.** משבח את של חבירו ומזלזל את שלו שלי אינו מעושר של חבירי מעושר שלי חדש ואינו יבש עדיין כל צורכו ה) [ושל חבירי ישן ויבש כל צורכו] דסתם ישן טוב מן החדש בעת הגורן כדאמרי' באיזהו נשך (ב"מ עג:) היו חדשות מארבע וישנות משלש: **אינו נאמן.** הואיל ועם הארץ הוא ואינו נאמן על המעשר אע"פ שמעיד על שלו שאינו מתוקן ועוד שמוסיף עם זו דברים אחרים לשבח את של חבירו אינו נאמן להחזיק את של חבירו בחזקת מתוקן שאינן אלא מערימין אמור אתה כאן ואני במקום אחר:

תוספות

נשביתי וטהורה אני למה לי. וקשה לרשב"א אמאי לא משני משום דבעי למיתני סיפא אם יש עדים שנשבית ואמרה טהורה אני אינה נאמנת וי"ל דמשום הא לא אצטריך דמסיפא דמתני' שמעינן לה דקתני סיפא עיר שכבשה כרכום כל כהנות שנמצאו בתוכה פסולות ואינה נאמנת לומר טהורה אני:

שתי נשים שנשבו למה לי. דאי לאשמעינן דאחת נאמנת על חברתה הא בהדיא תנן (לקמן כז:) דאפי' עבד ושפחה נאמנים: **וכן** שני אנשים למה לי משום דבעי למיתני פלוגתא דרבי יהודה ורבנן. אבל בשני נשים משמע דלא פליג רבי יהודה משום דבשבויה הקילו וקשה דלקמן (דף כז.) אשכחן איפכא דמסיק לפי תומו נאמן בתרומה אפי' על פי עצמו כדאמר גבי יוחנן אוכל חלות דהעלהו רבי לכהונה על פיו וגבי שבויה תני לקמן (דף כז:) הכל נאמנים להעידה חוץ מבעלה ומוקי לה במסיח לפי תומו ומיהו למאי דמוקמינן פלוגתייהו במעלין מתרומה ליוחסין ניחא דטעמא דמחמיר רבי יהודה טפי בתרומה מבשבויה משום דמעלין מתרומה ליוחסין אבל רבי דמיקל טפי בתרומה במסיח לפי תומו היינו משום דקסבר דאין מעלין מתרומה ליוחסין כדאמר לקמן אבל למאי דמוקי פלוגתייהו משום גומלים קשה וי"ל דבתרומה דרבנן דוקא הוא דמתכשר במסיח לפי תומו כדמשמע בהגוזל בתרא (ב"ק קיד:) אבל בתרומה דאורייתא לא:

אבל אינו נאמן להשיאו אשה. (א) פי' בקונטרס משום חשש ממזרות ונתינות וקשה דלהכי ליכא למיחש כדאמרינן בהחולץ (יבמות מה. ושם) גבי עובד כוכבים ועבד הבא על בת ישראל דאמרינן ליה זיל גלי או נסיב בת מינך משמע דאם ילך למקום שאין מכירים אותו ישיאוהו בת ישראל אע"פ שאין מכירים ולא יסתפקו בו בנתין וממזר וכן גבי ההוא דאתא לקמיה דרבי יהודה וא"ל נאמן אתה לפסול עצמך ואי אתה נאמן לפסול בניך משמע שהוא ובניו היו בחזקת כשרים אע"פ שלא היו מכירים בהם ונראה לר"ת דלהשיאו אשה דקאמר היינו להשיאו בדוקה מד' אמהות כדתנן בעשרה יוחסין (קדושין דף עו. ושם) הנושא אשה כהנת צריך שיבדוק אחריה ד' אמהות ואין נאמן אם ישא אשה בדוקה להכשיר בתו לכהן בלא בדיקה אלא יצטרך לבדוק אחריו וה"ה דמצי למימר ואינו נאמן להכשירו לעבודה ואותה בדיקה היא משום חללות דאין מכירין ישראל חללים שביניהם ולא משום ספק ממזרות ונתינות דלהא לא חיישינן כדפי' וכן משמע התם דקאמר דהיא אינה בודקת בדידיה דלא הוזהרו כשרות לינשא לפסולים ואי משום ממזרות ונתינות הא ודאי הוזהרו דהשוה הכתוב אשה לאיש לכל עונשין שבתורה ואם תאמר אי משום חללות בודקין לא יבדקו אלא יחוס אביה לבד דאפילו היתה אמה חללה כשרה היא ע"י אביה דלכ"ע בני ישראל מקוה טהרה לחללות ויש לומר מאחר שהצריכו לבדוק את יחוס האב משום חללות אגב חללות הוצרכו לבדוק כל פסול שבה גם של ממזרות ונתינות וכולה הך שמעתין דמצרכי בדיקה להשיא בתו לכהן אתיא כרבי מאיר דרבנן פליגי עליה התם ולא מצרכי בדיקה ואמרי כל משפחות בחזקת כשרות הן עומדות וא"ל אפילו עד אחד כדי להכשיר בתו לכהונה ומיהו להכשיר בנו או עצמו לעבודה צריך דלאו בחזקת כהונה עומד אי נמי אפילו כרבנן ובילא עליו ערער כדקאמר התם במילתייהו דרבנן בד"א שלא יצא עליו ערער כו':

שלי חדש ושל חבירי ישן. בפרק אע"פ פי' בקונטרס די"מ משום עומר ולאו מילתא היא דאם כן מאי מתרץ בדמאי הקילו התינח דמאי חדש ישן מאי איכא למימר ועוד דלא מצינו בשום מקום שנחשדו עמי הארץ על החדש ורשב"א פירש דקאי אשביעית וקאמר שלי חדש וגדל בשביעית ושל חבירי ישן וגדל בשנה שעברה ואשכחן דקרי לשביעית חדש דתנן במסכת שביעית (פ"ז מ"ז) ורד חדש שכבשו בשמן ישן ילקט את הורד וכי משני בדמאי הקילו בשביעית לא הוה לתרץ דפשיטא ליה להש"ס דרבי יהודה מיקל בשביעית משום דבאתריה דרבי יהודה חמירא להו שביעית כדאמר בהניזקין (גיטין נד.) ואין נראה לר"ת דסתם עמי הארץ לא נחשדו אשביעית דתנן בפרק עד כמה (בכורות ל. ושם) החשוד על המעשר אינו חשוד על השביעית החשוד על השביעית אינו חשוד על המעשר אלמא דסתמא אינן חשודין בשביעית ומעשר דקתני היינו מעשר שני דאמעשר ראשון חשודין הם והא דתנן במסכת דמאי (פ"ג מ"ד) ומייתי לה בהניזקין (גיטין סא:) המוליך חיטין לטוחן כותי או לטוחן עם הארץ אינו חושש לא משום מעשר ולא משום שביעית דמשמע דחשודים על השביעית איכא למימר דמשום כותי נקט שביעית אי נמי בודאי חשוד איירי וכן ההיא דמייתי בפרק קמא דחולין (דף ו. ושם) הנותן לשכנתו עיסה לאפות וקדירה לבשל אינו חושש לשאור ותבלין שבה לא משום מעשר ולא משום שביעית ועוד קשה לר"ת דאי באיסור חדש או שביעית מיירי הוה ליה למימר של חברי אינו חדש כדקאמר אינו מתוקן ועוד הקשה ר"ת דלעיל דההיא משנה דחמרין תנן במס' דמאי (פ"ג) הנכנס לעיר ואינו מכיר אדם שם ואמר מי כאן נאמן מי כאן מעשר ואמר לו אחד אני איני נאמן איש פלוני נאמן הלך ולקח הימנו אמר ליה מי כאן מוכר ישן אמר ליה מי ששלחך אצלי אע"פ שהן כגומלין זה את זה הרי אלו נאמנים ואי ישן היינו דלית ביה איסור חדש או שביעית היאך קונה ממי ששלחו אצלו והלא הוא בעצמו אומר שאינו נאמן ועוד מדקא שאיל להיאך מי מוכר ישן מכלל שמה שקנה ממנו כבר היה חדש או שביעית והלא לא הלך אצלו אלא לפי שהוא נאמן ופי' הקונטרס נראה לר"ת עיקר דלהשביח קאמר ולרבותא דרבי יהודה נקטיה דאע"פ שמגרע את שלו ומשביח את של חבירו ומיחזי טפי כגומלין אפילו הכי נאמנין ואם תאמר א"כ מאי קשה ליה דרבנן אדרבנן דלמא הכא הוא דחיישינן לגומלין דדומה שהן גומלין כדפי' ויש לומר דאי לאו דחיישינן לגומלים בעלמא משום הכי לא הוו חיישינן טפי ו):

אביי אמר לעולם לא תיפוך בדמאי כו'. והא דאמר אביי בפרק במה מדליקין (שבת דף כג.) ספק דבריהם לא בעי ברכה רבא אמר רוב עמי הארץ מעשרין הן וכן בפרק אע"פ (לקמן נו:) משני אביי ודאי דבריהם עשו חיזוק ספק דבריהם לא עשו חיזוק רבא אמר בדמאי הקילו לא משום דלית ליה לאביי דרבא דהא הכא אית ליה ועוד דבשילהי המביא (ביצה לה:) דייק ממתני' דרוב עמי הארץ מעשרין הן אלא דאית ליה לאביי דכל ספק דבריהם אע"ג דליכא רוב לא בעי ברכה וגם לא עשו חיזוק ומיהו בפרק קמא דשבת (דף יג. ושם) אההיא דלא יאכל זב פרוש עם זב עם הארץ מפרש אביי שמא יאכילנו דברים שאינם מתוקנים ולא סמיך ארוב עמי הארץ מעשרין כדקאמר רבא התם סבירא ליה דלההיא מלתא מחמירין ולא סמכינן ארובא וכן רבא בסוף הניזקין (גיטין סא. ושם) גבי משאלת אשה נפה כו' ולא בעי למיסמך ארוב עמי הארצות דמעשרין לענין לסייע ידי עוברי עבירה דנראה לו לענין זה להחמיר:

בשכלי

מסורת הש"ס

א) [לעיל כג.], ב) [ע"ז סא.], ג) [לקמן ט: דמאי פ"ד מ"ו], ד) שבת יג. כג. גיטין סא. לקמן נו: [ביצה לה: יבמות קיד. מנחות לא.], ה) נ"י כ"י, ו) [ועיין תוס' סוכה לט: בכורות יא: ד"ה הרי ועוד שם ל. ד"ה מתני' ותוס' סוכה לט: ד"ה במה].

עין משפט נר מצוה

פג א מיי' פי"ב מהל' מעשר הלכה י:

הגהות הב"ח

(א) תוס' ד"ה אבל כו' פי' בקונטרס. נ"ב ע"ל בפירושו סוף דף כ"ה:

ליקוטי רש"י

לגומלין. העד אתה עלי ואני עליך [לעיל כג:]. לגמול לך כיוצא בזו [ע"ז סא.]. שלי חדש. והישן טוב ממנו שהחדש עדיין אינו יבש כל צרכו והכי נמי אמרינן באיזהו נשך (ב"מ עג:) היו חדשות מארבע וישנות משלש כו' ויש מפרשים משום עומר ולאו מילתא היא [illegible] בדמאי הקילו. [illegible] רוב עמי הארץ מעשרין הן [לקמן נו:]. [illegible] [ב"ק [illegible]].

תוספות רי"ד

נטמאת אינה נאמנת דדוקא [להתיר] נאמן ע"א [משום] דבשבוי' הקילו ולא לאיסור כדרבא דאמר אין דבר שבערוה פחות מב'. אלא אעצמה אמאי לא מהימנא. אלא פשיטא דאיכא עדים פי' שנשבו ומ"ה אעצמה אינה נאמנת לומר נשביתי וטהורה אני וחברתה נמי אסורה בלא עדותה והא דקאמר אינה נאמנת כלומר בלא עדותה היא אסורה. אימא מציעתא אני וחברתי טמאות נאמנת ע"ע ואין נאמנת על חברתה. ואי דאיכא עידי שבויה אחברתה אמאי לא מהימנא והלא גם בלא עדותה אסורה והמורה פי' ואינה נאמנת על חברתה ע"כ משמע דחברתה בחזקת טהורה קיימא. דבשלמא אינה נאמנת דרישא אע"ג דאכולה מילתא משמע שייך למתני [אינה נאמנת] משום היתר. אלא הכא דבהדי' תניא אינה נאמנת על חברתה קשה. אלא פשיטא דליכא עדים פי' מ"ה על עצמה נאמנת דשויתי' אנפשה חתיכה דאיסורא. אבל על חברתה אינה נאמנת דכיון דליכא עדי שבוי' חברתה משתריא באומר' נשביתי וטהורה אני וזו שמעידה עלי' כי נטמאת אינה נאמנת כדרבא. שאין דבר שבערוה פחות מב'. אימא סיפא אני וחברתי טהורות נאמנת על חברתה ואינה נאמנת ע"ע. ואי דליכא עדים אעצמה אמאי לא מהימנא. אלא פשיטא דאיכא עדים. פי' ומ"ה אעצמה אינה נאמנת ואחברתה מהימנא שע"א נאמן בשבוי' רישא וסיפא דאיכא עדים ומציעתא דליכא עדים. **אמר ר"פ** כולה דאיכא עדים ואיכא ע"א דקמפיך פי' [דאיכא עדים] שמעידים שנשבו וע"א בא ומהפך כל הדברים. **אני** טמאה וחברתי טהורה וא"ל ע"א את טהורה וחברתיך טמאה. איהי שויתה נפשה חתיכה דאיסורא וחברתה משתריא אפומא. פי' המורה. דבשבוי' האמינו חכמים ע"א להקל ואפי' עבד או שפחה. וכדקתני מתני' אם יש להן עדים אפילו עבד וכו' וכ"מ שנאמן ע"א הרי הוא כשנים ואין דברי א' שכנגדו לטמא עומד במקום שנים. **ומשמע** מפירושו. דאע"ג דלא נשאת וגם לא התירוה לינשא. ואינו נ"ל דכיון דאיכא עדות מכחשת לה היכי שריא לה לחברתה אפומא דידה. והתנן בפ' האשה רבה עד אומר מת ועד אומר לא מת ה"ז לא תנשא דכי מהימנינן ליה לע"א דאמר מת ולא מצי אידך למכחשי' ה"מ כשבאו בזה אח"ז וכבר התירוה ע"פ אותו העד (אמרת) [אמרינן] לא תצא מהיתירא הראשון. אבל היכא דקיימי תרווייהו ומכחשי להדדי אמרינן לא תנשא. והכא היכי אמרי' דהיא נאמנת אע"פ שהעד מכחישה. **ובתוספתא** דכתובות [בפ"ב] ברישא דהא מתני' תני הכי. עד אומר נשבית וטמאה היא. וע"א אומר נשבית וטהורה היא. אשה אומרת נשבית וטמאה היא ואשה אומרת נשבית וטהורה היא אין משיאין אותה. ואם נשאת ל"ת. וא"כ בע"כ מאי דתני הכא נאמנת הכי בעי' לפרושי כגון שהתירוה לינשא על פיה. ובתר הכי אתא ע"א ואמר [illegible] אינו כלום אלא בסוטה בלבד [illegible] **פי'** ב' אנשים שבאו [illegible] חייש לגומלין. ר"י אומר אין וכו' [illegible] וכו'. לקמן מפרש מאי בינייהו: [illegible] הוא בכהונה. (ולכך) [וכן] פי' גם [illegible] כהן אני. ותו אפילו אי ברירא לן

שְׁנַיִם מְעִידִין עַל עַד שֶׁיְּהוּ שְׁלֹשָׁה – UNLESS THERE ARE THREE men, וּשְׁנַיִם מְעִידִין עַל זֶה – TWO of whom TESTIFY ABOUT THIS ONE, זֶה – AND TWO of whom TESTIFY ABOUT THIS ONE, and so on.[13] רַבִּי יְהוּדָה אוֹמֵר – R' YEHUDAH SAYS: אַף אֵינוֹ נֶאֱמָן לְהַאֲכִילוֹ בִּתְרוּמָה – HE IS NOT BELIEVED EVEN to the extent of LETTING HIM EAT *TERUMAH* עַד שֶׁיְּהוּ שְׁלֹשָׁה – UNLESS THERE ARE THREE men, שְׁנַיִם מְעִידִין עַל זֶה – TWO of whom TESTIFY ABOUT THIS one, וּשְׁנַיִם מְעִידִין עַל זֶה – AND TWO of whom TESTIFY ABOUT THIS one, and so on.[14]

The Gemara assumes that this Tannaic dispute can be explained as follows: The Tanna Kamma holds that where two people testify about each other, they are not suspected of reciprocating favors (i.e. one testifies for the other as a favor in return for the other's testimony about him). R' Yehudah, on the other hand, does suspect collusion.[15] However, this understanding of the dispute is contradicted by a Mishnah:

לְמֵימְרָא דְּרַבִּי יְהוּדָה חָיֵישׁ לְגוֹמְלִין – Do you mean **to say that R' Yehudah is concerned for** the possibility that they are **reciprocating favors,** וְרַבָּנָן לֹא חָיְישֵׁי לְגוֹמְלִין – **whereas the Rabbis are not concerned that they are reciprocating favors?** וְהָא אִיפְּכָא שְׁמְעִינַן לְהוּ – **But we have heard them** rule **to the contrary,** דִּתְנַן – **for we learned in a Mishnah:**[16] הַחַמָּרִין שֶׁנִּכְנְסוּ לָעִיר – If two DONKEY DRIVERS who are transporting grain ENTERED A TOWN[17] וְאָמַר אֶחָד מֵהֶן – AND ONE OF THEM SAID, שֶׁלִּי חָדָשׁ וְשֶׁל חֲבֵרִי יָשָׁן – "MY [GRAIN] IS NEW BUT MY FELLOW'S IS OLD,[18] שֶׁלִּי אֵינוֹ מְתוּקָּן וְשֶׁל חֲבֵרִי מְתוּקָּן – MINE HAS NOT BEEN FIXED [i.e. it has not been tithed] BUT MY FELLOW'S HAS BEEN FIXED [i.e. tithed]," אֵינוֹ נֶאֱמָן – HE IS NOT BELIEVED to establish that his companion's grain has been tithed.[19] רַבִּי יְהוּדָה אוֹמֵר – But R' YEHUDAH SAYS: נֶאֱמָן – HE IS BELIEVED. Presumably, the reason for this dispute is as follows: The Rabbis (i.e. the Tanna Kamma) rule that the donkey driver is not believed about his fellow's grain, because they might have conspired to testify on each other's behalf. But R' Yehudah, who rules that he *is* believed, does not suspect collusion.[20] This is the opposite of their opinions recorded above!

The Gemara answers:

אָמַר רַב אַדָּא בַּר אַהֲבָה אָמַר רַב – **Rav Adda bar Ahavah said in the name of Rav:** מוּחְלֶפֶת הַשִּׁיטָה – **The opinions** of the Rabbis and R' Yehudah **have been** erroneously **reversed.**[21]

The Gemara presents an alternative answer:

אַבַּיֵּי אָמַר – **Abaye said:** לְעוֹלָם לֹא תֵּיפוֹךְ – **Actually,** you **do not** need to **reverse** the rulings, בִּדְמַאי הֵקִילוּ – because **[the Sages] ruled leniently with respect to *demai*** (i.e. the produce of an *am haaretz*) רוֹב עַמֵּי הָאָרֶץ מְעַשְּׂרִין הֵן – because **most *amei haaretz* do tithe** their produce.[22] Therefore, even though R' Yehudah usually suspects collusion (as in the case of testimony about a Kohen), he ignores this possibility with respect to *demai.*

The Gemara objects that this answer is incomplete:

אָמַר רָבָא – **Rava said:** דְּרַבִּי יְהוּדָה אַדְּרַבִּי יְהוּדָה קַשְׁיָא – **Between** one ruling of **R' Yehudah and** the other ruling of **R' Yehudah there is a contradiction,** דְּרַבָּנָן אַדְּרַבָּנָן לֹא קַשְׁיָא – and **between** one ruling of **the Rabbis and** the other ruling of **the Rabbis there is no contradiction!?**[23] You have solved only the

NOTES

pected of being a *mamzer* or *nasin.* They understand the Gemara to mean that due to the high standard of genealogical purity demanded of Kohanim (see 13a note 35), the court must suspect him of being a *chalal,* who is disqualified from the Kehunah. [A *chalal* is a child born of a union between a Kohen and a woman forbidden specifically to Kohanim, such as a divorcee. Although his father is a Kohen, a *chalal* has the status of a non-Kohen. The sons of a *chalal* are also *chalalim,* and so on down through the generations. The widow and daughters of a *chalal* are forbidden in marriage to Kohanim (see Mishnah *Kiddushin* 77a).] Although the court allows this person to eat *terumah* based on the testimony of only one witness, it requires two witnesses to accord him the full genealogical status of a Kohen who serves in the Temple. According to this approach, the Gemara's expression "but not to let him marry a woman" does not literally mean that he is forbidden to marry a woman of untainted lineage, for a *chalal* is unrestricted in terms of whom he may marry. Rather, it means that he may not marry a woman of untainted lineage and have her continue to enjoy that status. This is because, as a suspected *chalal,* he transmits his questionable status to his wife and progeny (see *Tosafos, Ramban, Rashba, Ritva, Re'ah, Tos. Rosh, Ran;* see also *Tur, Even HaEzer* 2; *Maggid Mishneh, Hil. Isurei Biah* 20:5; *Beis Shmuel* 2:2). [Elsewhere, *Rashi* (*Kiddushin* 69b ד״ה מתרומה ליוחסין) adopts this approach in explaining a parallel passage. Some commentators suggest that this is also the intent of *Rashi* here (see *Shitah Mekubetzes* to 25b סד״ה תו and *Pnei Yehoshua;* see also *Tos. Rid*). For other explanations of *Rashi,* see *Haflaah* and *Chasam Sofer.*]

13. The Baraisa's point is that *two* witnesses are required to let this person marry a woman of untainted lineage. Therefore, if a group of men testify about each other, a minimum of three would be required: The first and second testify about the third; the first and third testify about the second; the second and third testify about the first. Where two witnesses testify about a third party, there is no suspicion of collusion (see *Hagahos Radal* and *Rashash*).

14. As he stated in our Mishnah, R' Yehudah requires *two* witnesses even with respect to *terumah.*

15. [In elucidating the Mishnah, *Rashi* explained R' Yehudah's opinion to be that a single witness can *never* establish someone as a Kohen, even where collusion is not suspected at all. This is indeed the Gemara's conclusion below, 24b. At this point, however, the Gemara assumes that R' Yehudah deems a single witness insufficient only because he might have engaged in collusion (*Maharsha* to 23b).]

16. *Demai* 4:7.

17. They transported grain from places where it was cheap to cities where it commanded a higher price (*Rashi*).

18. In the season following the harvest, older grain is superior to newly cut produce because it has already dried out (*Rashi;* see also *Rashi* below, 56b ד״ה שלי חדש; cf. Rishonim cited by *Tosafos* et al.). Thus, he was saying that his fellow's produce is better than his own.

19. These donkey drivers were *amei haaretz* – Jews whose observance of certain laws cannot be relied upon. One who obtains produce from an *am haaretz* must tithe it [i.e. separate *maaser* from it (see *Demai* 1:1 with *Rav* and *Tos. Yom Tov*)], because an *am haaretz* cannot be assumed to have done so himself. [Such produce is known as דְּמַאי, *demai.*] Furthermore, an *am haaretz* is ineligible to testify that the produce of another person was tithed (see *Demai* 4:1). This Mishnah's case, however, is unusual in that the speaker – who is claiming that his fellow's produce was tithed – concedes that his own produce is untithed. In addition, he denigrates the quality of his own produce while praising his fellow's. These extra remarks lend credence to his statement that his fellow's grain is tithed. Nevertheless, the Baraisa teaches, he is still not believed, because he might have agreed to praise his companion's merchandise in this city so that his companion will do the same for him at their next destination (*Rashi;* see *Maharsha*).

20. Hence, although he is an *am haaretz,* his word is accepted in these circumstances (see previous note).

21. A Baraisa is more likely to require emendation than a Mishnah (*Tosafos* to 78b ד״ה תני, cited by *Imrei Yitzchak*). Therefore, the Gemara presumably means that the opinions of R' Yehudah and the Tanna Kamma in the Baraisa should be switched, as follows: The Tanna Kamma maintains that the two men (who each say that the other is a Kohen) are not believed, whereas R' Yehudah holds that they are believed.

22. Since most *amei haaretz* do tithe their produce, any produce obtained from an *am haaretz* can be assumed to have been tithed. Thus, although the Sages required such produce to be treated as *untithed,* this enactment was not based on a significant doubt; it was merely a Rabbinic stringency (see *Rashi* to 56b ד״ה בדמאי הקילו and to *Shabbos* 23a ד״ה רבא אמר). Since the grounds for the enactment are relatively weak, several leniencies were introduced with respect to its application.

23. [By solving only the contradiction between R' Yehudah's statements, you imply that only R' Yehudah's statements contradict each other,

עין משפט נר מצוה

פג א מיי' פי"ב מהל' מעשר הלכה י:

מסורת הש"ס

א) [לעיל כג.] ב) [ע"ז סא:] ג) לקמן טו: דמאי פ"ד מ"ו, ד) שבת יג. כג. גיטין סא. לקמן טו: [בילה לה:] יבמות קיד. מנחות לא. ה) ג"י כ"י, ו) [ועיין היטב תוס' בכורות ל: ד"ה הרי ועוד שם ג. ד"ה מתני' ותוס' סוכה לט: ד"ה במה]

גמרא

אימא לא ואי אשמעינן הני תרתי משום דממונא אבל אשת איש דאיסורא אימא לא נשביתי וטהורה אני למה לי משום דקא בעי למיתני ואם משנשאת באו עדים הרי זו לא תצא הניחא למאן א) דמתני לה אסיפא אלא למאן דמתני לה ארישא מאי איכא למימר משום דקא בעי למיתני שתי נשים שנשבו ושתי נשים שנשבו למה לי מהו דתימא ניחוש ב) לגומלין קמשמע לן וכן שני אנשים למה לי משום דקא בעי למיתני פלוגתא דרבי יהודה ורבנן ת"ר אני כהן וחברי כהן נאמן להאכילו בתרומה ואינו נאמן להשיאו אשה עד שיהו ג' שנים מעידין על זה ושנים מעידין על זה רבי יהודה אומר אף אינו נאמן להאכילו בתרומה עד שיהו שלשה שנים מעידין על זה ושנים מעידין על זה למימרא דרבי יהודה חייש לגומלין ורבנן לא חיישי לגומלין והא איפכא שמעינן להו דתנן ג) החמרין שנכנסו לעיר ואמר אחד מהן שלי חדש ושל חברי ישן שלי אינו מתוקן ושל חברי מתוקן אינו נאמן רבי יהודה אומר נאמן אמר רב נחמן אמר רב אדא בר אהבה אמר רב מוחלפת השיטה אביי אמר לעולם לא תיפוך ד) בדמאי הקילו רוב עמי הארץ מעשרין הן אמר רבא דרבי יהודה אדרבי יהודה קשיא דרבנן אדרבנן לא קשיא אלא דרבי יהודה אדרבי יהודה לא קשיא כדשנינן דרבנן אדרבנן לא קשיא כדאמר רבי חמא בר עוקבא בשכלי אומנותו בידו הכא

רש"י

נשביתי משום דבעי למיתני שתי נשים שנשבו. לאשמועינן דזמן שמעידות זו את זו נאמנות: נאמן להאכילו בתרומה ואינו נאמן להשיאו אשה. מיוחסת מעלה היא ביוחסין: למימרא כו'. קא ס"ד דטעמא דרבי יהודה משום גומלין: החמרים. סוחרי תבואה ומוליכין ממקום הזול לכרכין: שלי חדש ושל חברי ישן שלי אינו מתוקן ושל חבירי מתוקן. משבח את של חבירו ומזלזל את שלו שלי אינו מעושר של חבירי מעושר שלי חדש ואינו יבש עדיין כל צורכו [ושל חבירי ישן ויבש כל צורכו] דסתם ישן טוב מן החדש בעת הגורן כדאמרי' באיזהו נשך (ב"מ עב:) היו חדשות מארבע וישנות משלש: אינו נאמן. הואיל ועם הארץ הוא ואינו נאמן על המעשר אע"פ שמעיד על שלו שאינו מתוקן ועוד שמוסיף עם זו דברים אחרים לשבח את של חבירו אינו נאמן להחזיק את של חבירו בחזקת מתוקן שאינן אלא מערימין אמור אתה כאן ואני במקום אחר:

תוספות

נשביתי וטהורה אני למה לי. וקשה לרשב"א אמאי לא משני משום דבעי למיתני סיפא אם יש עדים שנשבית ואמרה טהורה אני אינה נאמנת וי"ל דמשום הא לא אצטריך דמסיפא דמתני' שמעינן לה דקתני סיפא עיר שכבשוה כרכום כל כהנות שנמצאו בתוכה פסולות ואינה נאמנת לומר טהורה אני:

שתי נשים שנשבו למה לי. דאי לאשמעינן דאחת נאמנת על חברתה הא בהדיא תנן (לקמן כז.) דאפי' עבד ושפחה נאמנים: וכן שני אנשים למה לי משום דבעי למיתני פלוגתא דרבי יהודה ורבנן. אבל בשתי נשים משמע דלא פליג רבי יהודה משום דבשבויה הקילו וקשה דלקמן (דף כו.) אשכחן איפכא דמסיח לפי תומו נאמן בתרומה אפי' על פי עצמו כדאמר גבי יוחנן אוכל חלות דהעלהו רבי לכהונה על פיו וגבי שבויה תני לקמן (דף כז:) הכל נאמנים להעידה חוץ מבעלה ומוקי ב במסיח לפי תומו ומיהו למאי מוקמינן פלוגתייהו במעלין מתרומה ליוחסין ניחא דטעמא דמחמיר רבי יהודה טפי בתרומה מבשבויה משום מעלין מתרומה ליוחסין אבל רבי מיקל טפי בתרומה במסיח לפי תומו היינו משום דקסבר דאין מעלין מתרומה ליוחסין כדאמר לקמן אבל למאי דמוקי פלוגתייהו משום גומלים קשה וי"ל דבתרומה דרבנן דוקא הוא דמתכשר במסיח לפי תומו כדמשמע בהגוזל בתרא (ב"ק קד:) אבל בתרומה דאורייתא לא:

אבל אינו נאמן להשיאו אשה. א) פי' בקונטרס משום חשש ממזרות ונתינות וקשה דלהכי ליכא למיחש דהא אמרינן בהחולץ (יבמות מה. ושם) גבי עובד כוכבים ועבד הבא על בת ישראל דאמרינן ליה זיל גלי או נסיב בת מינך משמע דאם ילך למקום שאין מכירים אותו ישיאוהו בת ישראל אע"פ שאין מכירים ולא יסתפקו בו בנתין וממזר וכן גבי ההוא דאתא לקמיה דרבי יהודה וא"ל נאמן אתה לפסול עצמך ואי אתה נאמן לפסול בניך משמע שהוא ובניו היו בחזקת כשרים אע"פ שלא היו מכירים בהם ונראה לר"ת להשיאו אשה דקאמר היינו להשיאו בדוקה מד' אמהות כדתנן בעשרה יוחסין (קדושין דף עו. ושם) הנושא אשה כהנת צריך שיבדוק אחריה ד' אמהות ואין נאמן אם ישא אשה בדוקה להכשיר בתו לכהן בלא בדיקה אלא יצטרך לבדוק אחריו וה"ה דמצי למימר ואינו נאמן להכשירו לעבודה ואותה בדיקה היא משום חללות דאין מכירין ישראל חללים שביניהם ולא משום ספק ממזרות ונתינות דלהא לא חיישינן כדפי' וכן משמע התם דקאמר דהיא אינה בודקת בדידיה דלא הוחזרו כשרות לינשא לפסולים ואי משום ממזרות ונתינות הא ודאי הוחזרו דהשוה הכתוב אשה לאיש לכל עונשין שבתורה ואם תאמר אי משום חללות בודקין לא יבדקו אלא יחוס אביה לבד דאפילו היתה אמה חללה כשרה היא ע"י אביה דלב"ע בני ישראל מקוה טהרה לחללות ויש לומר מאחר שהצריכו לבדוק את יחוס האב משום חללות אגב חללות הוצרכו לבדוק כל פסול שבה גם של ממזרות ונתינות וכולה הך שמעתין דבעי בדיקה להשיא בתו לכהן אתיא כרבי מאיר דרבנן פליגי עליה התם ולא מצרכי בדיקה ואמרי כל משפחות בחזקת כשרות הן עומדות ומ"מ אפילו לרבנן נמי להשיאה לא לחזקת כהונה עומד או לאחד כדי להכשיר בתו לכהונה ומיהו להכשיר בנו או עצמו לעבודה צריך לרבנן ובילא עליו ערער דקאמר התם כדמילתייהו דרבנן בד"ה שלא ילא עליו ערער כו':

שלי חדש ושל חבירי ישן. פרק אע"פ פי' בקונטרס די"מ משום עמי הארץ ואלו מילתא היא דהא כן מאי מתרך בדמאי הקילו התינח למימר דמאי חדש ושל ישן מאי איכא למימר ועוד דלא מלינו בשום מקום שנחשדו עמי הארץ על החדש ורשב"א פירש דקאי בשביעית וקאמר שלי חדש וגדל בשביעית ואסור להשהותו אחר הביעור ושל חבירי ישן וגדל בשנה שעברה ואשכחן דקרי לשביעית חדש דתנן במסכת שביעית (פ"ט מ"ז) ורב חדש שכבשו בשמן ישן ילקט את הוורד וכי משני בדמאי הקילו לא קאי אשביעית דפשיטא ליה להש"ס דרבי יהודה מיקל בשביעית משום דבאתריה דרבי יהודה חמירא להו שביעית כדאמר (גיטין נד.) ואין נראה לר"ת דסתם עמי הארץ לא נחשדו אשביעית דתנן בפרק עד כמה (בכורות ל. ושם) החשוד על השביעית אינו חשוד על המעשר החשוד על המעשר אינו חשוד על השביעית אלמא דסתמא אינן חשודין בשביעית ומעשר דקתני היינו מעשר שני דלמעשר ראשון חשודין הם והא דתנן במסכת דמאי (פ"ג מ"ד) ומייתי לה בהניזקין (גיטין סא.) המוליך חיטין לטוחן כותי או לטוחן עם הארץ אינו חושש לא משום מעשר ולא משום שביעית דמשמע דחשודים על השביעית איכא למימר משום כותי נקט שביעית אי נמי בודאי חשוד איירי וכן ההיא דמייתי בפרק קמא דחולין (דף ו. ושם) הנותן לחמותו עיסה לאפות וקדירה לבשל אינו חושש לשאור ולא משום שביעית ועוד קשה לר"ת דלאי לאיסור חדש או שביעית מיירי הוה ליה למימר של חברי אינו חדש כדקאמר אינו מתוקן ועוד הקשה ר"ת דלעיל דהכא משנה דהחמרין תנן במס' דמאי (פ"ד) הנכנס לעיר ואינו מכיר אדם שם ואמר מי כאן נאמן מי כאן מעשר ואמר לו אחד אני איני נאמן איש פלוני נאמן הלך ולקח הימנו ולקח היימנו אמר ליה מי כאן מוכר ישן אמר ליה מי ששלחך אצלי אע"פ שהן כגומלין זה את זה הרי אלו נאמנים ואי ישן היינו דלית ביה איסור חדש או שביעית היכי קונה ממי ששלחו אצלו הא ודאי הוא דחדש הוא מדקא שאיל היאך מי מוכר ישן מכלל שמה שקנה ממנו כבר היה חדש או שביעית והלא לא הלך אצלו אלא לפי שהוא נאמן ופי' הקונטרס נראה לר"ת עיקר להשביח קאמר ולרבותא דרבי יהודה נקטיה דאע"פ שמגרע את שלו ומשבח את של חבירו ומיחזי טפי דגומלין אפילו הכי נאמנין ואם תאמר א"כ קשה ליה לרבנן דלמאי הכא הוא דחיישינן לגומלין דדומה שהן גומלין כדפי' ויש לומר דלא לאו דחיישינן לגומלים בעלמא משום הכי לא הוו חיישינן טפי:

אביי אמר לעולם לא תיפוך בדמאי כו'. והא דאמר אביי בפרק במה מדליקין (שבת דף כג.) ספק דבריהם לא בעי ברכה רבא אמר רוב עמי הארץ מעשרין הן וכן בפרק קמא (לקמן טו:) משני אביי ודאי דבריהם עשו חיזוק ספק דבריהם לא עשו חיזוק רבא אמר בדמאי הקילו לא משום דלית ליה לאביי רוב עמי הארץ מעשרין הן דהא בשילהי המביא (ביצה לה:) דייק ממתני' דרוב עמי הארץ מעשרין הן אלא דלאביי לכל ספק דבריהם אע"ג דליכא רוב לא בעי ברכה ולא עשו חיזוק ומיהו בפרק קמא דשבת (דף יג. ושם) אההיא דלא יאכל זב פרוש עם זב עם הארץ מפרש אביי שמא יאכילנו דברים שאינם מתוקנים ולא סמיך ארוב עמי הארץ מעשרין כדקאמר רבא התם סבירא ליה דלההיא מלתא מחמירין ולא סמכינן ארובא וכן רבא בסוף הניזקין (גיטין סא. ושם) גבי משאלת אשה נפה כו' ולא בעי למיסמך ארוב עמי הארצות דמעשרין לענין לסייע ידי עוברי עבירה דנראה לו לענין זה להחמיר:

תוספות רי"ד

נטמאת אינה נאמנת דדוקא [להתיר] נאמן ע"א [משום] דבשבוי' הקילו ולא לאיסור כדרבא דאמר אין דבר שבערוה פחות מב'. אלא אעצמה אמאי לא מהימנא. אלא פשיטא דאיכא עדים פי' שנשבו ומ"ה אעצמה אינה נאמנת לומר נשביתי וטהורה אני וחברתה נמי אסורה בלא עדותה והא דקאמר אינה נאמנת כלומר בלא עדותה היא אסורה. אימא מציעתא אני וחברתי טמאות נאמנת ע"ע ואין נאמנת על חברתה. ואי דאיכא עידי שבויה אחברתה אמאי לא מהימנא והלא גם בלא עדותה אסורה והמורה פי' ואינה נאמנת על חברתה ע"כ משמע דחברתה בחזקת טהורה קיימא. דבשלמא אינה נאמנת דרישא אע"ג דאכולה מילתא משמע שייך למתני [אינה נאמנת] משום היתר. אלא הכא דבהדי' תניא אינה נאמנת על חברתה קשה. אלא פשיטא דליכא עדים פי' מ"ה על עצמה נאמנת דשויתי' אנפשה חתיכה דאיסורא. אבל על חברתה אינה נאמנת דכיון דליכא עדי שבוי' חברתה משתריא באומר' נשביתי וטהורה אני וזו שמעידה עלי' כי נטמאת אינה נאמנת כדרבא. שאין דבר שבערוה פחות מב'. אימא סיפא אני וחברתי טהורות נאמנת על חברתה ואינה נאמנת ע"ע. ואי דליכא עדים אעצמה אמאי לא מהימנא. אלא פשיטא דאיכא עדים. פי' ומ"ה אעצמה אינה נאמנת ואחברתה מהימנא שע"א נאמן בשבויי' רישא וסיפא דאיכא עדים ומציעתא דליכא עדים. אמר ר"פ כולה דאיכא עדים ואיכא ע"א דקמפקיף פי' [דאיכא עדים] שמעידים שנשבו וע"א בא ומהפך כל הדברים. אני טמאה וחברתי טהורה וא"ל ע"א את טהורה וחברתיך טמאה. איהי שויתה נפשה חתיכה דאיסורא וחברתה משתריא אפומא. פי' המורה. דבשבוי' האמינו חכמים ע"א להקל ואפי' עבד או שפחה. וכדקתני מתני' אם יש להן עדים אפילו עבד וכו'. וה"מ שנאמן ע"א הרי הוא כשנים ואין דברי א' שכנגדו לטמא עומד במקום שנים. ומשמע מפירושו. דאע"ג דלא נשאת וגם לא התירוה לינשא. ואינו נ"ל דכיון דאיכא עדות מכחשת לה היכי שריא לה לחברתה אפומא דידה. והתנן בפ' האשה רבה עד אומר מת ועד אומר לא מת ה"ז לא תנשא דכי מהימנינן ליה לע"א דאמר מת ולא מצי אידך למכחשי' ה"מ כשבאו בזה אח"ז וכבר התירוה ע"פ אותו העד (אמרת) [אמרינן] לא תצא מהתירה הראשון. אבל היכא דקימי תרווייהו ומכחשי להדדי אמרינן לא תנשא. והכא היכי אמרי' דהיא נאמנת אע"פ שהעד מכחישה. ובתוספתא דכתובות [בפ"ב] ברישא דהא מתני' תני הכי. עד אומר נשבית וטמאה היא. וע"א אומר נשבית וטהורה היא. אשה אומרת נשבית וטמאה היא ואשה אומרת נשבית וטהורה היא אין משיאין אותה. ואם נשאת ל"ת. וא"כ בע"כ מאי דתני הכא נאמנת הכי בעי' לפרושי כגון שהתירוה לינשא על פיה. ובתר הכי אתא ע"א ואמר שהלכה ונשאת דאמרינן ל"ת. אני טהורה וחברתי טמאה וא"ל עד אחד את טמאה וחברתיך טהורה. איהי כיון דאיכא עדים לאו כל כמינה. פי' המורה ה"ג עדים וקאי אעידי שבוי' דע"א בטומאה אינו כלום אלא בסוטה בלבד קינא לה ונסתרה חברתה משתריא אפומא דעד. פי' ה"נ כגון שנשאת. ואל"ל עד את וחברתך טהורות איהי שויתי' נפשה חתיכה דאיסורא. פי' לפיכך אין העד נאמן לטהרה חברתה משתריא אפומא דעד כגון טהורות ואמר לה עד את וחברתיך טמאות. איהי כיון דאיכא עדים לאו כל כמינה. חברתה משתריא אפומה דידה פי' כגון שנשאת או התירוה לינשא כדפרי': **מתני' וכן שני** אנשים זה אומר כהן אני וזה אומר כהן אני אין נאמנים וע"ז הרי אלו נאמנים. ר"י אומר אין מעלין לכהונה ע"פ ע"א. אר"א אימתי בזמן שיש עוררים. אבל במקום שאין עוררים מעלין לכהונה ע"פ ע"א. רשב"ג אומר משום ר"ש בן הסגן מעלין לכהונה ע"פ ע"א. **פי'** ב' אנשים שבאו מי הם ז"א כהן אני וז"א כהן אני. אין נאמנים ליתן להם תרומה ובזמן שמעידים זע"ז שז"א אני וחברי כהנים וכמו כן זה הרי אלו נאמנים שמעלין לכהונה ע"פ ע"א. ואפילו היכא דאיכא למיחש לגומלין. ר"י אומר אין וכו' גומלין וכ"ש היכא דאיכא גומלין. פי' העד אתה עלי ואני עליך. אר"א אימתי אין מעלין במקום שיש עוררים הבאים לפוסלו. אבל במקום שאין עוררין מעלין והוא דליכא גומלין רשב"ג אומר וכו'. לקמן מפרש מאי בינייהו: כהן וחבירי כהן א). וז"א אני כהן וחבירי כהן נאמן להאכילו בתרומה ואינו נאמן להשיאו אשה עד שיהיה שלשה ב' מעידים ע"ז. וב' מעידים ע"ז. פי' המורה אינו נאמן להשיאו אשה מיוחסת ומעלה הוא בכהונה. (ולכך) [וכן] פי' גם להשיאו אשה הראויה לכהונה. דכשירה הראויה לכהונה אסרת לו ישא פסולה לכהונה אסור לו ליקח. דשויא אנפשיה חתיכה דאיסורא באומרו כהן אני. ותו אפילו אי ברירא לן

הגהות הב"ח

(א) תוס' ד"ה אבל כו' פי' בקונטרס. נ"ב ע"ל בפירושו סוף דף כ"ה:

ליקוטי רש"י

לגומלין. העד אתה עלי ואני עליך [לעיל כג:]. אגמול לך כיוצא בזו [ע"ז סא:]. שלי חדש. והישן טוב ממנו שהחדש עדיין אינו יבש כל צרכו ובנכי נמי אמרינן באיזהו נשך (ב"מ עב:) היו חדשות מארבע וישנות משלש [שם]. וכו' והוא מפרשים משום עומר ולאו מילתא היא דא"כ דמתרך בדמאי הקילו הניחא בדמאי חדש מאי איכא למימר ועוד דלא מלינו שנחשדו עמי הארץ על החדש ולא עוד אלא מאי משום אין נאמנים דדמאי וכרבותא דאשמועינן דאע"ג דמשבח לה לחבריה נמי כמילי אתכרישתא אינו נאמן על דדמאי דחיישינן לגומלין. בדמאי הקילו. משאר ספק דדבריהם ואפילו ספק לא ימיה דרוב עמי הארץ מעשרין הן [לקמן טו:]. דמאי אפי' ספק לא הוי אלא חומרא בעלמא דרוב עמי הארץ מעשרין הן [שבת כג.]. משום דרוב עמי הארץ מעשרין הן וכבר מעשר [ב"ק קטו:].

אֵימָא לֹא – one could **argue** that the final part of his statement ("but I bought it from him") is **not** believed.

Having explained why the first two cases are necessary, the Gemara clarifies the purpose of the third case:

וְאִי אַשְׁמְעִינַן הָנֵי תַּרְתֵּי – **And if [the Tanna] had taught us** only **those two** cases, it could have been thought that the entire statement is believed in those cases מִשּׁוּם דְּמָמוֹנָא – **because** they involve **money.** אֲבָל אֵשֶׁת אִישׁ דְּאִיסּוּרָא – **But** in the case of **a married woman** (where she says, "I was married but I am divorced"),[1] which is a matter **of** ritual **prohibition,** אֵימָא לֹא – one could **argue** that the final part of her statement ("but I am divorced") is **not** believed.[2]

The Gemara asks:

נִשְׁבֵּיתִי וּטְהוֹרָה אֲנִי לָמָּה לִי – And **why do I need** the case in which a woman says, **"I was captured but I am pure"?**[3]

The Gemara answers that the Tanna included this case for the following reason:

מִשּׁוּם דְּקָא בָּעֵי לְמִיתְנֵי – **Because he wanted to teach** the following clause: וְאִם מִשֶּׁנִּשֵּׂאת בָּאוּ עֵדִים – HOWEVER, IF AFTER SHE MARRIED WITNESSES CAME forward and testified, הֲרֵי זוֹ לֹא תֵצֵא – THIS woman DOES NOT LEAVE.[4]

The Gemara challenges this answer:

הָנִיחָא לְמַאן דְּמַתְנֵי לָהּ אַסֵּיפָא – **This** explanation **is satisfactory according to the one** [Rabbah bar Avin] **who taught [this clause] as referring to the last** case of the Mishnah ("I was captured but I am pure"). We can then understand why that case was added. אֶלָּא לְמַאן דְּמַתְנֵי לָהּ אַרֵישָׁא מַאי אִיכָּא לְמֵימַר – **But according to the one** [R' Oshaya] **who taught it as referring to the first** case of the Mishnah ("I was married but I am divorced"), **what is there to say?**[5]

Conceding this point, the Gemara gives a different explanation for including the case of the captured woman:

מִשּׁוּם דְּקָא בָּעֵי לְמִיתְנֵי שְׁתֵּי נָשִׁים שֶׁנִּשְׁבּוּ – The Tanna included it **because he wanted to teach** the case of **two women who were captured.**[6]

The Gemara asks:

וּשְׁתֵּי נָשִׁים שֶׁנִּשְׁבּוּ לָמָּה לִי – **But why do I need** the case of **two women who were captured?**[7]

The Gemara answers:

מַהוּ דְּתֵימָא נֵיחוּשׁ לְגוֹמְלִין – **You might have thought that we should be concerned for** the possibility that they are **reciprocating favors.**[8] קָמַשְׁמַע לָן – **[The Tanna]** therefore **informs us** that this is not a concern.

The Gemara now questions the need for our Mishnah:

וְכֵן שְׁנֵי אֲנָשִׁים לָמָּה לִי – **Why do I need** our Mishnah, which begins **"And likewise** in the case of **two men"?**

The Gemara answers:

מִשּׁוּם דְּקָא בָּעֵי לְמִיתְנֵי פְּלוּגְתָּא דְּרַבִּי יְהוּדָה וְרַבָּנָן – The Tanna included this case **because he wanted to teach the** related **dispute between R' Yehudah and the Rabbis.**[9]

A Baraisa elaborates on this dispute:

תָּנוּ רַבָּנָן – **The Rabbis taught in a Baraisa:** אֲנִי כֹּהֵן וַחֲבֵרִי כֹּהֵן – If two men say about each other:[10] "I AM A KOHEN AND MY FELLOW IS A KOHEN," נֶאֱמָן לְהַאֲכִילוֹ בִּתְרוּמָה – [EACH] IS BELIEVED TO the extent of LETTING [THE OTHER] EAT *TERUMAH.*[11] וְאֵינוֹ נֶאֱמָן לְהַשִּׂיאוֹ אִשָּׁה – HOWEVER, HE IS NOT BELIEVED TO the extent of LETTING HIM MARRY A WOMAN of untainted lineage[12]

NOTES

1. Above, 22a.

2. A prohibition is treated with greater stringency than a purely monetary matter. Therefore, one could have thought that although the principle of *happeh she'assar* applies in monetary litigation, it does not suffice to permit a married woman to remarry. The third case ("I was married, etc.") is consequently needed to teach that *happeh she'assar* is effective even in the case of the married woman.

[On the other hand, the law in the first two cases, which involve monetary matters, could not be derived from the third case, which concerns the prohibitions related to a married woman. This is because the defendant in a monetary case enjoys the legal advantage of having the money or property in his possession (*chezkas mamon*). Hence, even if the principle of *happeh she'assar* is effective in determining matters of ritual prohibition, it might not be strong enough to decide against the defendant in a monetary case (*Ritva*).]

3. Ibid. [This case is apparently redundant, for the Tanna has already taught that the principle of *happeh she'assar* is effective in matters of ritual prohibition.]

4. The meaning of this clause was discussed above (see 23a with notes 17, 18 and 27).

[It emerges that the reason why the Tanna introduced this case ("I was captured but I am pure") was not to teach that the principle of *happeh she'assar* applies regarding a captured woman. Rather, his purpose was to teach that in this case the woman remains permitted even after witnesses have testified and the *happeh she'assar* principle is no longer applicable.]

5. This dispute was presented above, 23a. According to R' Oshaya, the leniency stated in this clause – namely, that a woman remains permitted even after witnesses have deprived her of the credibility afforded by *happeh she'assar* – applies even in the Mishnah's first case, where a woman says, "I was married but I am divorced" (see note 18 ibid.). Hence, the Tanna could have mentioned this leniency in the context of the Mishnah's first case, leaving us to infer that it certainly applies in the relatively lenient case of a captured woman. The Gemara's question has thus been reinstated: Why did the Tanna have to mention the case of the captured woman?

6. The Gemara accepts that (according to R' Oshaya) this Mishnah does not teach any novel point regarding a captured woman. The Tanna included this case only for the sake of introducing the next Mishnah (23b) which teaches that two captured women are believed to testify on each other's behalf (*Rashi*).

7. This Mishnah's purpose cannot be simply to teach that a single female witness suffices to establish a captive's purity, because this point is taught elsewhere, in the Mishnah on 27a (*Tosafos*).

8. Their testimony should be rejected in light of the possibility that they conspired to testify on each other's behalf.

9. I.e. the dispute in our Mishnah between R' Yehudah and the Tanna Kamma, which the Gemara now proceeds to discuss. [Based on that dispute, the Tanna also records the related opinions of R' Elazar and R' Shimon.]

10. *Tos. Rid.* (See also *Tosefta* 2:7.)

11. This Tanna (i.e. R' Yehudah's anonymous disputant both here and in our Mishnah) holds that a single witness has the authority to establish someone as a Kohen with regard to *terumah,* even where that man also testifies about him (see 23b note 28).

12. That is, we do not allow him to marry a woman who is known to be free of genealogical disqualifications (see below). At the level of Biblical law, there is no such restriction. The Rabbis, however, set a high standard in matters of genealogical purity and required the testimony of two witnesses to establish his marital eligibility (*Rashi*).

Rashi below (end of 25b ד״ה להשיאו אשה) implies that the concern here is that this person might be a *mamzer* or *nasin* (see *Tosafos* and *Hagahos HaBach*). A *mamzer* or *nasin* is prohibited in marriage to anyone except a woman of his own category (*mamzeress, nesinah*), a convert or a freed Canaanite slave. Thus, if a man comes before us whose halachic eligibility as regards marriage is unknown, we do not let him marry a woman who certainly does not belong to any of these categories, unless we can ascertain that he too is of untainted lineage. By establishing that he is a Kohen, all doubts about his status would be removed. [It is impossible for a Kohen to be a *mamzer* or a *nasin* – a *mamzer* is disqualified from the Kehunah even if his father is a Kohen, and a *nasin* is not of Kohanic origin at all.] The same result could also be obtained by establishing that he is a Yisrael of untainted lineage. This Baraisa, though, speaks of testimony regarding the Kehunah.

Most Rishonim disagree with this explanation of the Gemara, because, in their opinion, a person of unknown background is *not* sus-

Gemara Before elaborating on our Mishnah, the Gemara raises a question that concerns the preceding Mishnahs:

כָּל הָנֵי לָמָּה לִי – Why do I need all these rulings?[34]

The Gemara answers:

צְרִיכִי – They are all **needed. דְּאִי תָּנָא מוֹדֶה רַבִּי יְהוֹשֻׁעַ – For if [the Tanna] had taught** only the case introduced by the words **"R' Yehoshua agrees"** (i.e. the case in which a person says, "This field was your father's but I bought it from him"),[35] it could have been thought that the entire statement is believed **מִשּׁוּם דְּאִיכָּא דְּרָרָא דְּמָמוֹנָא – because there is a** potential **loss of money** on the speaker's part.[36] **אֲבָל עֵדִים – But** in the case where **witnesses** testify "This is our handwriting but we were coerced,"[37] **דְּלֵיכָּא דְּרָרָא דְּמָמוֹנָא – where there is no** potential **loss of money** on their part, **אֵימָא לֹא – one could argue** that the final part of their statement ("but we were coerced") is **not** believed.[38] The second Mishnah is therefore required to correct this misconception.

The Gemara now explains why the first Mishnah is required in addition to the second:

וְאִי תָּנָא עֵדִים – And if [the Tanna] had taught only the case of the **witnesses,** it could have been thought that their entire statement is believed **מִשּׁוּם דִּלְעָלְמָא – because** they are testifying **for others,** as opposed to themselves.[39] **אֲבָל אִיהוּ דִּלְנַפְשֵׁיהּ – But** in the first case ("This field was your father's, etc."), where **he** is testifying **for himself,**[40]

NOTES

34. Why did the Tanna mention all these instances of *happeh she'assar*? (*Rashi*). [The first three Mishnahs of this chapter (15b-16a, 18b, 22a) record a total of four cases in which the principle of *happeh she'assar* applies: "This field was your father's but I bought it from him" (Mishnah 15b); "this is our handwriting but we were coerced" (Mishnah 18b); "I was married but I am divorced" (Mishnah 22a); "I was captured but I am pure" (ibid.). The Gemara will clarify the need for each of these cases. This discussion will lead into explanations of why the two Mishnahs on this *amud* (which do not record cases of *happeh she'assar*) are also necessary (based on *Rashi;* see, however, *Pnei Yehoshua*).]

35. Above, 15b.

36. By admitting that the field once belonged to his opponent's father, this person risks losing it. Hence, were he not certain that he had bought the field, he would not have conceded that it ever belonged to the father. We can therefore assume that when he made the first part of his statement, "This field was your father's," he already had in mind to conclude: "but I bought it from him" (*Rashi*). [In such circumstances, where the very words that cause liability were spoken with intent to add that the liability does not apply, the principle of *happeh she'assar* is obviously effective.]

37. Above, 18b.

38. The witnesses would not have lost any money had they stopped after saying, "This is our handwriting." It is therefore possible that when they uttered these words, they had no intent to qualify their testimony by adding "but we were coerced." Their purpose at first was only to confirm the signatures on the document; they then changed their minds and added the qualification (*Rashi*). [In a case of this nature, the Gemara suggests that the principle of *happeh she'assar* does not apply and the qualification of the orginal testimony is rejected.]

39. As stated above, the witnesses gain no financial benefit by adding "but we were coerced." Since this qualification benefits only other people, and not themselves, they would not have gone to the trouble of adding it – thereby altering their original testimony – unless that was their intent from the outset (*Rashi*). [Here the Gemara argues to the contrary of what it proposed above; see the previous note.]

40. This person gains financially by adding the words "but I bought it from him" (*Rashi*). Perhaps, then, his original intent was merely to testify that the land belonged to the other person's father. It was only later, upon noticing a potential benefit for himself, that he decided to add that he had bought the land.

עין משפט נר מצוה

עט א מיי' פי"ח מהל' איסורי ביאה הלכ' יח סמג לאוין קכא טוש"ע אה"ע סימן ז סעיף א:
פ ב מיי' פ"כ שם הלכ' יג סמג לאוין קכב קמ טוש"ע שם סימן ג סעיף ו:
פא ג מיי' שם הלכה יא טוש"ע שם סעיף ד:
פב ד מיי' שם הלכה ג:

תוספות רי"ד

הזמה גמורה. כיון שאומרי' להם והלא עמנו הייתם יחד במקום פ' כל היום כולו ואנו לא ראינו. ואתם דאיך ראיתם ובהזמה דאמינה התורה האחרונים ובטלי עדות הראשונים והלכך טעמא דאמרי לא ראינוה דאינה ראיה דהצא ול"א אי איתא דקדש קלא אית לה ואכתי הזמה הוא. אבל אם העיד עדות ברורה כיון דמזימים את הראשונים א) תנשא לכתחלה: **סיפא** ב' אומרים ראינוה שנתגרשה וב' אומרים לא ראינוה שנתגרשה ה"ז ל"ת. ואם נשאת לא תצא מאי קמ"ל אע"ג דדיירו בחצר א' היינו הך מ"ד גבי קידושין הוא דעבידי אינשי דמקדשי בצנעא אבל גירושין אי איתא דאיגרשא קלא אית לי' למילתא קמ"ל דעבידי אינשי דמגרשי בצנעא פירוש אפ"ה לכתחלה לא תנשא משום ולזות שפתים הרחק ממך: **מתני' האשה שאמרה** נשביתי וטהורה אני נאמנת שהפה שאסר הוא הפה שהתיר. ואם יש עדים שנשבית והיא אומרת טהורה אני אינה נאמנת ואם משנשאת באו עדים ה"ז ל"ת. **פי'** נשביתי לבין העובדי כוכבים וטהורה אני שלא נבעלתי לעובד כוכבים **ואם משנשאת וכו'**. בגמ' מפרשי' אהיא קאי. ר"א מתני לה ארישא פי' האי ואם משנשאת באו עדים ארישא. האשה שאמרה א"א הייתי וגרושה אני. והכי קתני ואם משנשאת באו עדים שהיתה א"א. והיא נשאת ע"פ עצמה שאמרה גרושה אני ה"ז לא תצא. **ורבא** מתני לה אסיפא פי' אנשבית וטהורה אני והתירוה לינשא. ואח"כ באו עדים שנשבית. מאן דמתני לה ארישא כ"ש אסיפא דבשבויה הקילו. פי' דחששא בעלמא הוא דאיכא שמא נבעלה לעובד כוכבים ונפסלה לכהונה. ומאן דמתני לה אסיפא אבל ארישא לא. **לימא** בדר"ה קמיפלגי דאמר ר"ה האשה שאמרה לבעלה גרשתני נאמנת חזקה אין אשה מעיזה בפני בעלה. פי' דמאן דמתני לה ארישא אית ליה דר"ה ומאן דמתני לה אסיפא ל"ל דר"ה. לא דכ"ע א"ל דר"ה פי' ואע"ג דבחזקת (טומאה) [נשואה] קיימא דהלכתא כוותה. מר סבר כי אתמר דר"ד בפניו אבל שלא בפניו מעיזה ב). פי' דוקא כשנשאת ואח"כ באו עדים סמכי' אהך חזקה אפילו שלא בפניו. אבל אם לא נשאת לא סמכי' אהך חזקה כי היכי דסמכי' עלה בפניו דלא דמי שלא בפניו כבפניו:

שתי נשים שנשבו. אומר ר"י דלא גרסינן זאת אומרת נשביתי וטהורה אני כו' אלא זאת אומרת טהורה אני דהא בדליכא עדים שנשבו איירי ומיהו יש לקיים הגירסא דאיירי דאינהו לא ידעי דליכא עדים ואשמועינן דאפילו הכי לא מהימני:

אין רישא וסיפא דאיכא עדים ומציעתא דליכא עדים. השתא לא פריך הא תו למה לי כדפריך אשנויא דרב פפא דהשתא אצטריך כולהו אני טהורה וחברתי טמאה אשמעינן כיון דאיכא עדים לא מהימנא אנפשה ואני וחברתי טמאה אשמעינן דלא מהימנא אחברתה היכא דליכא עדים ומשתריא חברתה אפומא דנפשה ואני וחברתי טהורה אשמעינן אע"ג דאיכא עדים מהימנא אחברתה דרישא דרישא איכא לאוקמי בדליכא עדים ואין נראה דאי בדליכא עדים היינו מציעתא אלא בדאיכא עדים איירי ומ"מ איצטריך האי סיפא לאשמועינן דנאמנת אחברתה ואע"ג דלא פסלה נפשה והיה לנו לחוש לגומלים אפילו הכי מהימנא א): **הא** תו למה לי היינו רישא. וא"ת ואמאי לא קאמר הכא מרישא דרישא כדקאמר בסמוך דהא שמעינן מרישא דרישא דאיהי שויתה לנפשה חתיכה דאיסורא וחברתה משתריא אפומא דידה וכ"ש דמשתריא אפומא דעד אחד ב) וי"ל דהכא ניחא ליה למנקט סתמא דהיינו רישא משום דמרישא נמי שמעינן דחברתה משתריא אפומא דעד אחד אבל בסמוך לא מצי פריך אלא מרישא דרישא: **דאיכא** דררא דממונא. פירש ר"ח שהאומר הוא מוחזק בשדה אבל העדים אין בידם כלום: **אבל** הכא דליכא דררא דממונא לא. קשה לרשב"א הא אילטריך גבי עדים לאשמועינן דמהימני במגו לפסול השטר דהא אע"ג דר' מאיר פליג אסיפא מודה ברישא:

מתני' שתי נשים שנשבו. שיש עדים שנשבו: שמעידות זו את זו. כל אחת אומרת חברתי טהורה: הרי אלו נאמנות. דבשבויה הקילו להאמין עד אחד ואפילו אשה: גמ' נאמנת. על הכל: אינה נאמנת. על כלום ולקמיה מפרש לה לכולה: אי דליכא עדים. שנשבו: אלא פשיטא דאיכא עדים. הלכך לעצמה אינה נאמנת לטהרה וחברתה נמי אע"ג דלקמן אמרינן בחזקת טמאה קיימא הכא לאו משום הימנותא דהך הוא דהא אסהדותא דידה נמי בחזקת טומאה היא: ואינה נאמנת על חברתה. על כרחך משמע דמחברתה בחזקת טהורה קיימא דבשלמא אינה נאמנת דרישא אע"ג דלכולא מילתא משמע שייך למיתנייה משום דידה דבהדיא תנא אינה נאמנת על חברתה קשה: אלא פשיטא דליכא עדים. ולדידה מהימנא דשויתא לנפשה חתיכה דאיסורא: דאפיך. מיפך את כל דבריה: חברתה משתריא אפומא דידה. דבשבויה האמינו חכמים עד אחד להקל ואפילו עבד או שפחה דקתני מתני' (לקמן דף כז:) אם יש להן עדים אפילו עבד כו' וכל מקום שנאמן בו עד אחד הרי הוא כשנים ואין דברי אחד במקום שנים: הכי גרסינן איהי כיון דאיכא עדים לאו כל כמינה. ולעדי שבויה קאי דעד אחד בטומאה אינו כלום אלא בסוטה בלבד שרגלים לדבר שסתרה: שויתה לנפשה חתיכה דאיסורא. לפיכך אין העד נאמן לטהרה: היינו רישא. הני מילי תרוייהו שמעינן ברישא חתיכה דאיסורא מרישא ושמעינן שריותא דחברתה אפומא דעד מסיפא דרישא שמעינן תרתי בבי קמייתא רישא קרי להו דדמיין להדדי ותרתי בבי בתרייתא חדא מילתא היא דבכל חדא תנן מילתא וחילופה בין ברישא בין בסיפא: מהו דתימא כו'. ומשום נאמנת על עצמה תנא ליה: איהי כיון דליכא עדים גרסינן: היינו רישא דרישא. דהא ודאי משום דאינה נאמנת על עצמה לא אצטריך למיתנייה דהא טובא אשמעינן דבמקום עדי שבויה לא מהימנא למימר טהורה אני ומשום נאמנת על חברתה הוא דאצטריך דאע"ג דעד דקא מכחיש לה מהימנא והא ברישא דרישא אשמעינן: במקום דפסלה לנפשה. התם הוא דמהימנא אחברתה משום דקאמרה טמאה אני: אבל היכא דמכשרא נמי לנפשה. אימא משום דידה הוא דקאמרה ולא אחברתה: קמ"ל גרסינן: ל"א גרסינן מהו דתימא כי מהימנא במקום עד פסול כגון דעד דקא מפיך הוי אשה אבל במקום עד כשר לא תנא משנה יתירה דלאפי' במקום עד כשר: מתני' וכן שני אנשים. לא גרסינן שנשבו: אין נאמנים. ליתן להן תרומה: ובזמן שמעידין זה את זה. שכל אחד אומר אני וחברי כהן: רבי יהודה אומר אין מעלין לכהונה על פי עד אחד. ואפילו היכא דליכא גומלין וכל שכן הכא דאיכא למיחש לגומלין העד אתה עלי ואני עליך: עוררין. שקורין עליו שם פסול: מעלין. היכא דליכא גומלין והיינו דאיכא בין ר' אלעזר לתנא קמא דר' יהודה: רבן שמעון כו'. בגמ' מפרש מאי בינייהו: גמ' כל הני. דתנא מתניתין לאשמועינן הפה שאסר הוא הפה שהתיר ל"ל: משום דאיכא דררא דממונא. הלכך אי לאו דפשיטא מלתא שלקחה מאביו לא היה אומר של אביך היתה וגורם לעצמו הפסד ממון וכשאומר תחלת דבריו על שם סופו אמרו לגמור בהן ולקחתיה הימנו: אבל עדים. שאמרו כתב ידינו הוא: דליכא דררא דממונא. לגבייהו דלימטינהו פסידא בהאי עדות: אימא לא. ליתהמנו למימר אנוסין היינו דמעיקרא כי אמרו כתב ידינו הוא אדעתא דסהדותא אמרו ולאו למיגמר בה אנוסים היינו והדר אימליכו למיגמר בה הכי קמשמע לן: דלעלמא. אין הדבור האחרון מהני לעצמו אלא לאחרים ומשום אחרים לא הוו הדרי במלתייהו אבל איהו גופיה דלנפשיה מהני כי הדר ואמר לקחתיה: משום

מתני' שתי נשים שנשבו זאת אומרת נשביתי וטהורה אני וזאת אומרת נשביתי וטהורה אני אינן נאמנות [א] ובזמן שהן מעידות זו את זו הרי אלו נאמנות: גמ' ת"ר [א] אני טמאה וחברתי טהורה נאמנת אני טהורה וחברתי טמאה אינה נאמנת אני וחברתי טמאה נאמנת על עצמה ואינה נאמנת על חברתה אני וחברתי טהורה נאמנת על חברתה ואינה נאמנת על עצמה אמר מר אני טהורה וחברתי טמאה אינה נאמנת היכי דמי אי דליכא עדים על עצמה אמאי לא מהימנא נשביתי וטהורה אני קאמרה אלא פשיטא דאיכא עדים אימא מציעתא אני וחברתי טמאה נאמנת על עצמה ואינה נאמנת על חברתה ואי דאיכא עדים אמאי לא מהימנא אלא פשיטא דליכא עדים אימא סיפא אני וחברתי טהורה נאמנת על חברתה ואינה נאמנת על עצמה ואי דליכא עדים אעצמה אמאי לא מהימנא אלא פשיטא דאיכא עדים רישא וסיפא דאיכא עדים מציעתא דליכא עדים אמר אביי אין רישא וסיפא דאיכא עדים מציעתא דליכא עדים רב פפא אמר כולה דאיכא עדים ואיכא עד אחד דקא אפיך אמרה אני טמאה וחברתי טהורה ואמר לה עד אחד את טהורה וחברתך טמאה איהי שויתא לנפשה חתיכה דאיסורא חברתה משתריא אפומא דידה אני טהורה וחברתי טמאה ואמר לה עד אחד את טמאה וחברתך טהורה איהי כיון דאיכא עדים לאו כל כמינה חברתה משתריא אפומא דעד אני וחברתי טמאה ואמר לה עד אחד את וחברתך טהורה איהי שויתא לנפשה חתיכה דאיסורא חברתה משתריא אפומא דעד הא תו למה לי היינו רישא מהו דתימא הני תרוייהו טהורות נינהו והאי דקאמרה הכי [א] תמות נפשי עם פלשתים היא דקא עבדה קמ"ל אני וחברתי טהורה ואמר לה עד אחד את וחברתך טמאה איהי כיון דאיכא עדים לאו כל כמינה חברתה משתריא אפומא דידה הא תו למה לי היינו רישא דרישא מהו דתימא כי מהימנא במקום דפסלה נפשה אבל במקום דמכשרא נפשה אימא לא מהימנא קא משמע לן: מתני' [ב] וכן שני אנשים ° זה אומר כהן אני וזה אומר כהן אני אינן נאמנין [ג] ובזמן שהן מעידין זה את זה הרי אלו נאמנין [ד] רבי יהודה אומר [ג] אין מעלין לכהונה על פי עד אחד אמר רבי אלעזר אימתי במקום שיש עוררין אבל במקום שאין עוררין מעלין לכהונה על פי עד אחד רשב"ג אומר משום רבי שמעון בן הסגן מעלין לכהונה על פי עד אחד: גמ' כל הני למה לי צריכי דאי תנא מודה רבי יהושע משום דאיכא דררא דממונא אבל עדים דליכא דררא דממונא אימא לא ואי תנא עדים משום דלעלמא אבל איהו דלנפשיה אימא

מסורת הש"ס

א) [תוספתא פרק ב], ב) כ"ל לא ע"ב.

תוספות ישנים

א) [והיינו שינויא דלקמן דלא פסלה נפשה והוה מלי למיפרך השתא ולשנויי. ת"י], ב) [וי"ל דס"ד דהיא מהימנא טפי מעד אחד לפי שנשבית עמה יודעת יותר. ת"י].

גליון הש"ס

מתני' זה אומר כהן אני. עיין בהר"ן פ"ה דגיטין סי' ח באות י:

תורה אור השלם

א) וַיֹּאמֶר שִׁמְשׁוֹן תָּמוֹת נַפְשִׁי עִם פְּלִשְׁתִּים וַיֵּט בְּכֹחַ וַיִּפֹּל הַבַּיִת עַל הַסְּרָנִים וְעַל כָּל הָעָם אֲשֶׁר בּוֹ וַיִּהְיוּ הַמֵּתִים אֲשֶׁר הֵמִית בְּמוֹתוֹ רַבִּים מֵאֲשֶׁר הֵמִית בְּחַיָּיו: (שופטים טז, ל)

ליקוטי רש"י

אין מעלין לכהונה. להחזיק אדם ככהן לאכול בתרומה ולעבוד עבודה ולישא את כפיו. על פי עד אחד. המעיד שהוא כהן כדמפרש ר' אלעזר לקמיה [כשמעתין]. אמר רבי אלעזר אימתי. אין מעלין ע"פ עד אחד בזמן שיש על הכהן עוררין עדים הפוסלים אותו כדמפרש בסמוך ולפרש דברי ר' יהודה בא ולא לחלוק עליו. אבל במקום שאין עוררין. אלא קול פסול בעלמא כדמפרש לקמיה מעלין ע"פ עד אחד שמכחיש את הקול [ב"ב לא:]. דררא דממונא. הפסד ממון [ב"מ ב:].

ואב משנשאת באו עדים ה"ז ל"ת. אמר שמואל. לא נשאת ממש אלא כיון שהתירוה לינשא אע"פ שלא נשאת. והא ל"ת קתני. ל"ת מהתירא הראשון: **ת"ר** אמרה נשביתי וטהורה אני ויש לי עדים שטהורה אני פי' שהיו עמי תמיד שלא נתיחדתי עם עובד כוכבים אין אומרים נמתין עד שיבאו עדים אלא מתירין אותה מיד. **התירוה** לינשא ואח"כ באו עדים ואמרו לא ידענו ה"ז ל"ת. ואם באו עדים שאמרה האשה ושאלנו אותן ואמרו לא ידענו אין אומרים כיון שמצאנו דבריה שקר תצא. אלא ל"ת ואם באו עדי טומאה אפילו יש לה כמה בנים תצא. פי' דבעלה לעובד כוכבים הויא לה זונה ובניה הם חללים: **בנתי'** דמר שמואל אשתביין. אסקינהו לארעא דישראל. אוקמינהו לשבויינהו אבראי. [illegible]

דְּרֵישָׁא – **It is** the same as **the first part of the beginning** of the Baraisa![22]

The Gemara answers that this clause is needed to correct the following misconception:

מַהוּ דְּתֵימָא כִּי מְהֵימְנָא – **You might have said: When is she believed** to say that her companion is pure? בְּמָקוֹם דְּפַסְלָה נַפְשָׁהּ – **Where she renders herself forbidden.**[23] אֲבָל בְּמָקוֹם דְּמַכְשְׁרָא נַפְשָׁהּ – **But where she renders herself permitted,** אֵימָא לֹא מְהֵימְנָא – one could **argue** that **she is not believed** about her companion.[24] קָא מַשְׁמַע לָן – **[The Baraisa]** therefore **informs us** that she is believed about her companion even in the latter case.[25]

Mishnah Having discussed the case of two captured women who testify about each other, the Mishnah presents a parallel situation:

וְכֵן שְׁנֵי אֲנָשִׁים – **And likewise** in the case of **two men,** זֶה אוֹמֵר כֹּהֵן אֲנִי – where **this one says, "I am a Kohen,"** וְזֶה אוֹמֵר כֹּהֵן אֲנִי – **and the other one says, "I am a Kohen,"** אֵינָן נֶאֱמָנִין – **they are not believed.**[26] וּבִזְמַן שֶׁהֵן מְעִידִין זֶה אֶת זֶה – **However, when they testify about one another,**[27] הֲרֵי אֵלּוּ נֶאֱמָנִין – **they are believed.**[28]

The Mishnah records three other opinions:

רַבִּי יְהוּדָה אוֹמֵר – **R' Yehudah says:** אֵין מַעֲלִין לִכְהוּנָּה עַל פִּי עֵד אֶחָד – **We do not elevate** a person **to** the **Kehunah** based **on the word of one witness.**[29] אָמַר רַבִּי אֶלְעָזָר – **R' Elazar said:** אֵימָתַי – **When** does a single witness not suffice to establish someone as a Kohen? בְּמָקוֹם שֶׁיֵּשׁ עוֹרְרִין – **In a situation where there are challengers** who assert that this person is *not* a Kohen.[30] אֲבָל בְּמָקוֹם שֶׁאֵין עוֹרְרִין – **But in a situation where there are no challengers,** מַעֲלִין לִכְהוּנָּה עַל פִּי עֵד אֶחָד – **we do elevate** a person **to** the **Kehunah** based **on the word of one witness.**[31] רַבָּן שִׁמְעוֹן בֶּן גַּמְלִיאֵל אוֹמֵר מִשּׁוּם רַבִּי שִׁמְעוֹן בֶּן הַסְּגָן – **Rabban Shimon ben Gamliel says in the name of R' Shimon the son of the deputy** to the High Priest:[32] מַעֲלִין לִכְהוּנָּה עַל פִּי עֵד אֶחָד – **We elevate** a person **to** the **Kehunah** based **on the word of one witness.**[33]

NOTES

22. I.e. the Baraisa's very first clause (see note 17). There is no question that the Baraisa's ruling about the speaker herself is redundant. We have already learned several times that if there are witnesses to a woman's capture, she is not believed to claim that she was not violated. Hence, this clause is needed only for its ruling that the speaker can establish her companion's purity, although she is contradicted by a witness. However, the Gemara asks, there is no need for that ruling either, since this very point was already taught in the Baraisa's first clause (*Rashi*).

23. That is, as in the first case of the Baraisa, the speaker states that she herself was violated but her companion was not (*Rashi*).

24. Perhaps she said that her companion was not violated only to reinforce her claim that she herself was not violated (*Rashi*). [See *Rashi* for an alternative version of the Gemara's answer.]

25. **Summary:**

A. *A captured woman testifying about herself:*

(i) If a captured woman says, "I am defiled," she is always forbidden to a Kohen [שַׁוִּיתָא לְנַפְשָׁהּ חֲתִיכָה דְּאִיסוּרָא, *she rendered herself a forbidden object*]. This is so regardless of whether witnesses testify to her captivity, and even if a single witness asserts that she was *not* violated.

(ii) If she says, "I am pure," she is permitted to a Kohen provided that witnesses do not testify to her captivity [הַפֶּה שֶׁאָסַר הוּא הַפֶּה שֶׁהִתִּיר, *the very mouth that has forbidden is the mouth that has permitted*]. If there *are* witnesses to her captivity, she is forbidden, unless a single witness testifies that she was not violated.

B. *A captured woman testifying about a fellow captive:*

(i) If she says, "My companion is defiled," her words carry no weight. The companion is permitted to a Kohen unless witnesses testify to the captivity *and* no witness asserts that she was not violated.

(ii) If she says, "My companion is pure," the companion is always permitted to a Kohen – regardless of whether witnesses testify to the captivity, and even if a single witness asserts that the companion *was* violated. (See, however, end of note 14.)

26. Each of these men, whose Kohanic status was previously unknown, cannot be established as a Kohen on the basis of his own testimony (*Tos. Rid*). They may not be given *terumah* (*Rashi*) or enjoy any other of a Kohen's privileges, such as reading first from the Torah. They are also forbidden to recite the Priestly Blessing (*Birkas Kohanim*) or perform those Temple services that are restricted to Kohanim (see *Meiri* here and *Rashbam* to *Bava Basra* 31b ד"ה אין מעלין לכהונה; see also *Shulchan Aruch, Even HaEzer* 3:1). However, each man must abide by the *prohibitions* applicable to Kohanim, for, by claiming to be a Kohen, he automatically imposes those prohibitions on himself (*Meiri;* see note 10).

A single witness is generally believed in matters of (nonmarital) prohibition even where he testifies in his own favor. Here, however, each man's testimony about himself is not accepted, since it has ramifications for him and all his future generations with respect to monetary issues (i.e. rights to ownership of Kohanic gifts) and marital eligibility (*Rosh* to *Gittin* 54b [ch. 5 §12], as understood by *Achiezer, Chelek Aleph* 14:4; cf. *Kovetz Shiurim* below, 24a §66).

27. That is, each one says, "He and I are both Kohanim" (*Rashi*). [In explaining the parallel clause in the previous Mishnah, *Rashi* (ד"ה שמעידות) said only that each captured woman testifies about her companion. But here *Rashi* writes that in addition to testifying about his fellow, each man also testifies about himself. For explanations of this difference, see *Tos. Yom Tov, Haflaah, Rashash, Beis Aharon* and *Yefei Einayim.*]

28. According to this Tanna, a single witness suffices to establish another man (but not himself) as a Kohen. Hence, these two men may be given *terumah* on the strength of each other's testimony.

In this particular case, where two men testify on behalf of each other, there are grounds for suspecting that one (or both) agreed to lie in return for the other's testimony. This Tanna, however, is not concerned for such a possibility (see *Rashi* ד"ה רבי יהודה אומר).

29. R' Yehudah holds that one witness is never sufficient to establish a person as a Kohen. He applies this ruling even where one person testifies for another without the other testifying for him in return. And he certainly applies it in our case, where two men testify on each other's behalf, giving rise to suspicions of collusion (*Rashi;* see, however, 24a note 15). [The Gemara (24a-b) will discuss the reason for R' Yehudah's opinion.]

30. The Gemara below, 26a-b, elaborates on the circumstances of this case.

31. Thus, R' Elazar agrees with the Tanna Kamma's view that one witness has the authority to establish someone as a Kohen. The difference between their opinions is that R' Elazar accepts the testimony of a single witness only where one man testifies for another without the other testifying for him. The Tanna Kamma, however, deems a single witness sufficient even where two men testify on each other's behalf (*Rashi;* see *Pnei Yehoshua*). But in every other respect, the Tanna Kamma agrees with R' Elazar's opinion as it is explained below, 26a-b (see *Ramah,* cited by *Shitah Mekubetzes* to 26b ד"ה כבר הארכתי).

32. He was the son of R' Chanina S'gan HaKohanim (the Deputy of the Kohanim), mentioned in several places in the Six Orders of the Mishnah (*Rambam's Introduction to Commentary on the Mishnah* ד"ה הפרק השלישי).

33. The Gemara (below, 26a) will explain how this opinion differs from that of R' Elazar [and the Tanna Kamma] (*Rashi*).

עין משפט
נר מצוה

עט א מיי' פי"ח מהל' איסו"ר הלכה הלכ' יח סמג לאוין קכא טוש"ע אה"ע סימן ו סעיף א:
פ ב מיי' פ"כ שם הלכ' יג סמג לאוי' קכב קכו טוש"ע שם סימן ג סעיף א:
פא ג מיי' שם הלכה יא טוש"ע שם סעיף ד:
פב ד מיי' שם הלכה ב:

מסורת הש"ס

א) [תוספתא פרק ב], ב) ב"ב לא ע"ב.

מתני' שתי נשים שנשבו זאת אומרת נשביתי וטהורה אני וזאת אומרת נשביתי וטהורה אני אינן נאמנות ובזמן שהן מעידות זו את זו הרי אלו נאמנות: **גמ'** ת"ר אני טמאה וחברתי טהורה נאמנת אני טהורה וחברתי טמאה אינה נאמנת אני וחברתי טמאה נאמנת על עצמה ואינה נאמנת על חברתה אני וחברתי טהורה נאמנת על חברתה ואינה נאמנת על עצמה אמר מר אני טהורה וחברתי טמאה אינה נאמנת היכי דמי אי דליכא עדים על עצמה אמאי לא מהימנא נשביתי וטהורה אני קאמרה אלא פשיטא דאיכא עדים אימא מציעתא אני וחברתי טמאה נאמנת על עצמה ואינה נאמנת על חברתה ואי דאיכא עדים אמאי לא מהימנא אלא פשיטא דליכא עדים אימא סיפא אני וחברתי טהורה נאמנת על חברתה ואינה נאמנת על עצמה ואי דליכא עדים אעצמה אמאי לא מהימנא אלא פשיטא דאיכא עדים רישא וסיפא דאיכא עדים מציעתא דליכא עדים אמר אביי אין רישא וסיפא דאיכא עדים מציעתא דליכא עדים רב פפא אמר כולה דאיכא עדים ואיכא עד אחד דקא אפיך אמרה אני טמאה וחברתי טהורה ואמר לה עד אחד את טהורה וחברתך טמאה איהי שויתא לנפשה חתיכה דאיסורא חברתה משתריא אפומא דידה אני טהורה וחברתי טמאה ואמר לה עד אחד את טמאה וחברתך טהורה איהי כיון דאיכא עדים לאו כל כמינה חברתה משתריא אפומא דעד אני וחברתי טמאה ואמר לה עד אחד את וחברתך טהורה איהי שויתא לנפשה חתיכה דאיסורא חברתה משתריא אפומא דעד הא תו למה לי היינו רישא מהו דתימא הני תרוייהו טהורות נינהו והאי דקאמרה הכי תמות נפשי עם פלשתים היא דקא עבדה קמ"ל אני וחברתי טהורה ואמר לה עד אחד את וחברתך טמאה איהי כיון דאיכא עדים לאו כל כמינה חברתה משתריא אפומא דידה הא תו למה לי היינו רישא דרישא מהו דתימא כי מהימנא במקום דפסלה נפשה אבל במקום דמכשרא נפשה אימא לא מהימנא קא משמע לן: **מתני'** וכן שני אנשים זה אומר כהן אני וזה אומר כהן אני אינן נאמנין ובזמן שהן מעידין זה את זה הרי אלו נאמנין רבי יהודה אומר אין מעלין לכהונה על פי עד אחד אמר רבי אלעזר אימתי במקום שיש עוררין אבל במקום שאין עוררין מעלין לכהונה על פי עד אחד רשב"ג אומר משום רבי שמעון בן הסגן מעלין לכהונה על פי עד אחד: **גמ'** כל הני למה לי צריכי דאי תנא מודה רבי יהושע משום דאיכא דררא דממונא אבל עדים דליכא דררא דממונא אימא לא ואי תנא עדים משום דלעלמא לא אבל איהו דלנפשיה אימא

שתי נשים שנשבו. אומר ר"י דלא גרסינן זאת אומרת נשביתי וטהורה אני כו' אלא זאת אומרת טהורה אני דהא בדליכא עדים שנשבו איירי ומיהו יש לקיים הגירסא דאיירי דאינהו לא ידעי דאיכא עדים ואשמועינן דאפילו הכי לא מהימני:

אין רישא וסיפא דאיכא עדים ומציעתא דליכא עדים. השתא לא פריך הא תו למה לי כדפריך אליבא דרב פפא דהשתא אצטריך כולהו אני טהורה וחברתי טמאה אשמועינן כיון דליכא עדים לא מהימנא לנפשה ואני וחברתי טמאה אשמועינן דלא מהימנא אחברתה היכא דליכא עדים ומשתריא חברתה אפומא דנפשה ואני וחברתי טהורה אשמועינן אע"ג דליכא עדים מהימנא אחברתה דרישא דרישא איכא לאוקמי בדליכא עדים ואין נראה דאי בדליכא עדים היינו מציעתא אלא בדאיכא עדים איירי ומ"מ אצטריך האי סיפא לאשמועינן דנאמנת אחברתה ואע"ג דלא פסלה נפשה והיה לנו לחוש לגומלים אפילו הכי מהימנא א): **הא** תו למה לי היינו רישא. וא"ת ואמאי לא קאמר הכא מרישא דרישא כדקאמר בסמוך דהא שמעינן מרישא דרישא דאיהי שויתה לנפשה חתיכה דאיסורא וחברתה משתריא אפומא דידה וכ"ש דמשתריא אפומא דעד אחד ב) וי"ל דהכא ניחא ליה למנקט סתמא דהיינו רישא משום דמרישא נמי שמעינן דחברתה משתריא אפומא דעד אחד אבל בסמוך לא מצי פריך אלא מרישא דרישא: **דאיכא** דררא דממונא. פירש ר"ח שהאומר הוא מוחזק בשדה אבל העדים אין בידם כלום: **אבל** הכא דליכא דררא דממונא לא. קשה לרשב"א הא אצטריך גבי עדים לאשמועינן דמהימני כמגנו לפסול השטר דהא אע"ג דר' מאיר פליג אסיפא מודה ברישא:
נשביתי

מתני' שתי נשים שנשבו. שיש עדים שנשבו: שמעידות זו את זו. כל אחת אומרת חברתי טהורה: הרי אלו נאמנות. דבשבויה הקילו להאמין עד אחד ואפילו אשה: גמ' נאמנת. על הכל: אינה נאמנת. על כלום ולקמיה מפרש לה לכולה: אי דליכא עדים. שנשבו: אלא פשיטא דאיכא עדים. הלכך אעצמה אינה נאמנת לטהרה וחברתה נמי אע"ג דלגן אמרינן בחזקת טמאה קיימא הואיל ולאו משום הימנותא דהך הוא דלגלאי שהודאת דידה נמי בחזקת טומאה היא: ואינה נאמנת על חברתה. על כרחך משמע דחברתה בחזקת טהרה קיימא דבשלמא אינה נאמנת דרישא אע"ג דאכולה מילתא משמע שייך למיתנייה משום דידה אלא הכא דבהדיא תנא אינה נאמנת על חברתה קשה: אלא פשיטא דליכא עדים. ולדידה מהימנא דשויתה לנפשה חתיכה דאיסורא: דאפיך. מיפך את כל דבריה: חברתה משתריא אפומא דידה. דבשבויה האמינו חכמים עד אחד להקל ואפילו עבד או שפחה כדקתני מתני' (לקמן דף כז.) אם יש להן עדים אפילו עבד כו' וכל מקום שנאמן בו עד אחד הרי הוא כשנים ואין דברי אחד במקום שנים: הכי גרסינן איהי כיון דאיכא עדים לאו כל כמינה. ולעדי שבויה קאי דעד אחד בטומאה אינו כלום אלא בסוטה בלבד שרגלים לדבר שהרי קינא לה ונסתרה: שויתה לנפשה חתיכה דאיסורא. לפיכך אין העד נאמן לטהרה: היינו רישא. הני מילי תרוייהו אשמועינן ברישא חתיכה דאיסורא מרישא שמעינן שריותא דחברתה אפומא דעד מסיפא דרישא שמעינן תרתי בבי קמייתא רישא קרי להו דדמיין להדדי ותרתי בבי בתרייתא חדא מילתא היא דבכל חדא תנן מילתא וחילופה בין ברישא בין בסיפא: מהו דתימא כו'. ומשום נאמנת על עצמה תנא ליה: איהי כיון דליכא עדים לא גרסינן: היינו רישא דרישא. דהא ודאי משום דאינה נאמנת לא אצטריך למיתנייה דהא טובא אשמועינן דבמקום עדי שבויה לא מהימנא למימר טהורה אני ומשום נאמנת על חברתה הוא דאצטריך דלא"ג דעד קא מכחיש לה מהימנא והא ברישא דרישא אשמועינן: במקום דפסלה לנפשה. הכא הוא דמהימנא אחברתה משום דקאמרה טמאה אני: אבל דאיכא דמכשרא נמי לנפשה. אימא משום דידה הוא דקאמרה ולא אחברתה: קמ"ל גרסינן: ל"א גרסינן מהו דתימא כי מהימנא במקום עד פסול כגון דעד דקא מפיך הוי אשה אבל במקום עד כשר לא תנא משנה יתירה לאפי' במקום עד כשר: מתני' וכן שני אנשים. לא גרסינן שנשבו: אין נאמנים. ליתן להן תרומה: ובזמן שמעידין זה את זה. שכל אחד אומר אני וחברי כהן: רבי יהודה אומר אין מעלין לכהונה על פי עד אחד. ואפילו היכא דליכא גומלין וכל שכן הכא דאיכא למיחש לגומלין העד אתה עלי ואני עליך: עוררין. שקורין עליו שם פסול: מעלין. היכא דליכא גומלין והיינו דאיכא בין ר' אלעזר לתנא קמא דר' יהודה: רבן שמעון כו'. בגמ' מפרש מאי בינייהו: גמ' כל הני. דתנא מתניתין לאשמועינן הפה שאסר הוא הפה שהתיר ל"ל: משום דאיכא דררא דממונא. הלכך אי לאו דפשיטא מלתא שלקחה מאביו לא היה אומר של אביך היתה וגורם לעצמו הפסד ממון וכשאומר תחלת דבריו על שם סופו אמרו לגמור בהן ולקתחיה הימנו: אבל עדים. שאמרו כתב ידינו הוא: דליכא דררא דממונא. לגבייהו דלימטינהו פסידא בהאי עדות: אימא לא. ליתהמנו למימר אנוסין היינו דמעיקרא כי אמרו כתב ידינו הוא אדעתא דסהדותא אמרו ולאו למיגמר בה אנוסים היינו והדר אימליכו למיגמר בה הכי קמשמע לן: דלעלמא. אין הדבור האחרון מהני לעצמו אלא לאחרים ומשום אחרים לא הוו הדרי במלתייהו אבל איהו גופיה דלנפשיה מהני כי הדר ואמר לקתחיה:
משום

תוספות ישנים

א) [והיינו שינויא דלקמן דלא פסלה נפשה והוה מצי למיפרך השתא ולשנויי. מ"י]. ב) [וי"ל דס"ד דהיא מהימנא טפי מעד אחד לפי שנשבית עמה יודעת יותר. מ"י].

גליון הש"ס

מתני' זה אומר כהן אני. עיין בהרא"ש פ"ה דגיטין סי' ח בלוית י:

תורה אור השלם

א) וַיֹּאמֶר שִׁמְשׁוֹן תָּמוֹת נַפְשִׁי עִם פְּלִשְׁתִּים וַיֵּט בְּכֹחַ וַיִּפֹּל הַבַּיִת עַל הַסְּרָנִים וְעַל כָּל הָעָם אֲשֶׁר בּוֹ וַיִּהְיוּ הַמֵּתִים אֲשֶׁר הֵמִית בְּמוֹתוֹ רַבִּים מֵאֲשֶׁר הֵמִית בְּחַיָּיו: [שופטים טז, ל]

ליקוטי רש"י

אין מעלין לכהונה. להחזיק אדם ככהן לאכול בתרומה ולעבוד עבודה ולישא את כפיו. על פי עד אחד. המעידו שהוא כהן כדמפרש ר' אלעזר לקמיה [בסמוך]. אמר רבי אלעזר אימתי. אין מעלין ע"פ עד אחד בזמן שיש על הכהן עוררין עדים הפוסלים אותו כדמפרש בסמוך ולפרש דברי ר' יהודה בא ולא לחלוק עליו. אבל במקום שאין עוררין. אלא קול פסול בעלמא כדמפרש לקמיה מעלין ע"פ עד אחד שמכחיש את הקול [רשב"ם ב"ב לא:]. דררא דממונא. חסרון ממון [ב"מ ב:].

תוספות רי"ד

הזמה גמורה. כיון שאומרי' להם והלא עמנו הייתם יחד במקום פ' כל היום כולו ושנו לא ראינו. ואתם האיך ראיתם ובהזמה האמינה התורה האחרונים ובטלי עדות הראשונים הלכך טעמא דאמרי לא "אינה דאינה ראיה דתצא ול"א אי איתא "קדיש קלא אית לה ואכתי הזמה הוא. אבל אם העידו עדות ברורה כיון דכזימים את הראשונים א) תנשא לכתחלה: **סיפא** ב' אומרים ראינוה שנתגרשה וב' אומרים לא ראינוה שנתגרשה ה"ז ל"ת. ואם נשאת לא תצא מאי קמ"ל אע"ג דדירו בחצר א' היינו הך מ"ד גבי קידושין הוא דעבידי אינשי דמקדשי בצנעא אבל גירושין אי איתא דאיגרשא קלא אית לי' למילתא קמ"ל דעבידי אינשי דמגרשי בצנעא פירוש ואפ"ה לכתחלה לא תנשא משום ולזות שפתים הרחק ממך: **מתני'** האשה שאמרה נשביתי וטהורה אני נאמנת שהפה שאסר הוא הפה שהתיר. ואם יש עדים שנשבית והיא אומרת טהורה אני אינה נאמנת ואם משנשאת באו עדים ה"ז ל"ת. **פי'** נשביתי לבין העובדי כוכבים וטהורה אני שלא נבעלתי לעובד כוכבים **ואם** משנשאת וכו'. בגמ' מפרשי' אהיא קאי. ר"א מתני לה ארישא פי' האי ואם משנשאת באו עדים ארישא. האשה שאמרה א"א הייתי וגרושה אני. והכי קתני ואם משנשאת באו עדים שהיתה א"א. והיא נשאת ע"פ עצמה שאמרה גרושה אני ה"ז לא תצא. **ורבא** מתני לה אסיפא פי' אנשבית וטהורה אני והתירוה לינשא. ואח"כ באו עדים שנשבית. מאן דמתני' לה ארישא כ"ש אסיפא דבשבויה הקילו. פי' דחששא בעלמא הוא דאיכא שמא נבעלה לעובד כוכבים ונפסלה לכהונה ומאן דמתני לה אסיפא אבל ארישא לא. **לימא** בדר"ה קמיפלגי דאמר ר"ה האשה שאמרה לבעלה גרשתני נאמנת ח"קה אין אשה מעיזה בפני בעלה. פי' דמאן דמתני לה ארישא אית ליה דר"ה ומאן דמתני לה אסיפא ל"ל דר"ה. לא דכ"ע א"ל דר"ה פי' ובע"ג דבחזקת (טומאה) [ושואר] קיימא דהלכתא כוותיה מר סבר כי אתמר דר"ה בפניו אבל שלא בפניו מעיזה ב). פי' דוקא כשנשאת ואח"כ באו עדים סמכי' אהך חזקה אפילו שלא בפניו. אבל אם לא נשאת לא סמכי' אהך חזקה כי היכי דסמכי' עלה בפניו דלא דמי שלא בפניו כבפניו:

ואם משנשאת באו עדים ה"ז ל"ת. אמר שמואל. לא נשאת ממש אלא כיון שהתירוה לינשא אע"פ שלא נשאת. והא ל"ת קתני. ל"ת מהתירא הראשון: **ת"ר** אמרה נשביתי וטהורה אני ויש לי עדים שטהורה אני פי' שהיו עמי תמיד שלא נתיחדו עם עובד כוכבים אין אומרים נמתין לה עד שיבואו עדים אלא מתירין אותה מיד. **התירוה** לינשא ואח"כ באו עדים ואמרו לא ידענו ה"ז ל"ת. פי' אע"פ שבאו אותם העדים שאמרה האשה ושאלנו אותן ואמרו לא ידענו. אין אומרים כיון שנמצאו דבריה שקר תצא. אלא ל"ת ואם באו עדי טומאה אפילו יש לה כמה בנים תצא. פי' דנבעלה לעכו"ם הוי' לה זונה ובניה הם חללים: **בנתי'** דמר שמואל אשתביין. אסקינהו לארעא דישראל. אוקמינהו לשבוינהו אבראי. פי' שלא יבאו לפני ב"ד ולא ידעו ב"ד שהן שבויין אלא ע"פ עצמן ויתירום עיילו אינהו לבי מדרשא דר"ח. זו אומרת נשביתי וטהורה אני וזו אומרת נשביתי וטהורה אני. לסוף עול אתו שבוייהו. א"ר חנינא בנת מורין אינון. פי' בנות אדם גדול ובעל הוראה הן שידעו לעשות כך. ואיגלאי מילתא דבנתיה דמר שמואל אינון. א"ל ר"ח לרשב"א כהנא פוק איטפל בקרובותיך. פי' [קח] א' מהן שהן קרובותיך. א"ל לר"ח והא איכא עדי טומאה שראוה כשנטמאה עם העובדי כוכבים. ודילמא אתו לקמן למחר לאחר שתנשא. א"ל השתא מיהו ליתנהו פי' קודם נשואין. ומשום דלמא אתו לא (אהדרינן) [אסרינן] להו השתא עדים בצד אסתן ותאסר. פי' אסתן. צפון. כמו יומא דאיסתנא. מצפון תפתח הרעה. פי' העדים המכירים הן בבבל אנחב כאן וניחוש שמא יבואו ויעידו על הטומאה ולכולי האי לא חיישינן. ומותרות הן לכהונה אח"כ ודאי אם יבואו תצא ובניה חללים. אבל מסתמא לא חיישינן דאחזוקי איסורא לא מחזקינן ואלו הי' קרובים (לא) [לנו] היינו חוקרים אותם טרם שנתירם לינשא. עכשיו שהן רחוקים ממנו. לכולי האי לא חיישינן: **מתני' שתי נשים** שנשבו ז"א נשביתי וטהורה אני וז"א נשביתי וטהורה אני אינן נאמנות. ובזמן שמעידות זו ע"ז הרי אלו נאמנות פי' שנשבו בידוע כגון שיש עדים שנשבו הלכך אין נאמנות להעיד כל א' וא' בפ"ע. ובזמן שמעידות זו ע"ז שכל א' אומרת אני וחברתי טהורה הרי אלו נאמנות דבשבויה הקילו והאמינו בה אפילו ע"א ואפי' אשה ולא חיישינן לגומלין. **ת"ר** אני טמאה וחברתי טהורה נאמנת. אני טהורה וחברתי טמאה אינה נאמנת. פי' אינה נאמנת על כלום. אני וחברתי טמאות נאמנת על עצמה. ואינה נאמנת לפסול חברתה. אני וחברתי טהורה נאמנת על חברתה. ואינה נאמנת ע"ע: **אמר מר** אני טהורה וחברתי טמאה אינה נאמנת. ה"ד אי דליכא עדים שנשבו אעצמה אמאי לא מהימנא נשביתי וטהורה אני קאמרה. פי' בשלמא אחברתה אינה נאמנת שכיון שאין עדים שנשבית הותרה חברתה וכאומרת נשביתי וטהורה אני. וזו שאומרת עליה כי

חשק שלמה על תוס' רי"ד א) הדבר ל"ע דלאכתי איכא לאוקמי דהעידו עדות ברורה ומ"מ לא הוה הזמה כגון דאמרו דהמקדש היה עמנו במקום פלוני או דראינו דרך הקידושין קרוב לו ולא היה קידושין כלל. ב) ל"ל ומר סבר דאפי' שלא בפניו נמי אינה מעיזה פי' דוקא.

The Gemara answers:

אָמַר אַבַּיֵי – **Abaye said:** אִין – **Yes!** This is indeed so. רֵישָׁא וְסֵיפָא דְּאִיכָּא עֵדִים – **The beginning and end** of the Baraisa refer to a case **where there are witnesses,** מְצִיעֲתָא דְּלֵיכָּא עֵדִים – and **the middle** refers to a case **where there are no witnesses.**

The Gemara presents an alternative explanation of the Baraisa: רַב פָּפָּא אָמַר – **Rav Pappa said:** כּוּלָּהּ דְּאִיכָּא עֵדִים – The Baraisa **in its entirety** refers to a case **where there are witnesses** to the captivity, וְאִיכָּא עֵד אֶחָד דְּקָא אַפֵּיךְ – **but there is one witness who reverses** everything the woman reports.

Rav Pappa explains each of the Baraisa's rulings in this light, beginning with the first:

אָמְרָה – If **she said,** אֲנִי טְמֵאָה וַחֲבֶרְתִּי טְהוֹרָה – **"I am defiled but my companion is pure,"** וְאָמַר לָהּ עֵד אֶחָד – **and a single witness said to her,** אַתְּ טְהוֹרָה וַחֲבֶרְתֵּךְ טְמֵאָה – **"You are pure but your companion is defiled,"** she is believed about both for the following reasons: אִיהִי שַׁוִּיתָא לְנַפְשָׁהּ חֲתִיכָה דְּאִיסּוּרָא – **She rendered herself a forbidden object** by saying that she was defiled.[13] חֲבֶרְתָּהּ מִשְׁתַּרְיָא אַפּוּמָא דִידָהּ – **Her companion,** on the other hand, **is permitted through her word,** although it is contradicted by a witness.[14]

The second clause:

אֲנִי טְהוֹרָה וַחֲבֶרְתִּי טְמֵאָה – If she says, **"I am pure but my companion is defiled,"** וְאָמַר לָהּ עֵד אֶחָד – **and a single witness said to her,** אַתְּ טְמֵאָה וַחֲבֶרְתֵּךְ טְהוֹרָה – **"You are defiled but your companion is pure,"** she is not believed about either for the following reasons: אִיהִי כֵּיוָן דְּאִיכָּא עֵדִים לָאו כָּל כְּמִינָהּ – **She, since there are witnesses** testifying to her capture, **lacks the authority** to claim that she is pure.[15] חֲבֶרְתָּהּ מִשְׁתַּרְיָא אַפּוּמָא דְעֵד – **Her companion,** on the other hand, **is permitted through the word of the witness** even though she contradicts it.[16]

The third clause:

אֲנִי וַחֲבֶרְתִּי טְמֵאָה – If she says, **"My companion and I are defiled,"** וְאָמַר לָהּ עֵד אֶחָד – **and a single witness said to her,** אַתְּ וַחֲבֶרְתֵּךְ טְהוֹרָה – **"You and your companion are pure,"** she is believed only about herself and not about her companion. The reasoning is as follows: אִיהִי שַׁוִּיתָא לְנַפְשָׁהּ חֲתִיכָה דְּאִיסּוּרָא – **She rendered herself a forbidden object** by saying that she is defiled. חֲבֶרְתָּא מִשְׁתַּרְיָא אַפּוּמָא דְעֵד – Her **companion,** on the other hand, **is permitted through the word of the witness** even though she contradicts it.

The Gemara asks why this clause is needed:

הָא תּוּ לָמָּה לִי – **But why do I need** a **further** case? הַיְינוּ רֵישָׁא – **It is** the same as **the beginning** of the Baraisa![17]

The Gemara answers that this clause is needed to correct the following misconception:

מַהוּ דְּתֵימָא הָנֵי תַּרְוַיְיהוּ טְהוֹרוֹת נִינְהוּ – **You might have said** that actually **both of these [women] are pure.**[18] וְהַאי דְּקָאָמְרָה הָכִי – **And the reason why she said this** (viz. "My companion and I are defiled") was not that she believed it to be true, "תָּמוֹת נַפְשִׁי עִם־פְּלִשְׁתִּים" הִיא דְּקָא עָבְדָה – but rather that **she was fulfilling** the idea expressed in the verse: ***Let me perish along with the Philistines.***[19] That is, she sought to render her companion forbidden, and in order to lend credence to her negative testimony about her companion, she was prepared to become forbidden as well.[20] קָא מַשְׁמַע לָן – **[The Baraisa]** therefore **informs us** that we do accept her testimony about herself.[21]

Rav Pappa now explains the final clause of the Baraisa:

אֲנִי וַחֲבֶרְתִּי טְהוֹרָה – If she says, **"My companion and I are pure,"** וְאָמַר לָהּ עֵד אֶחָד – **and a single witness said to her,** אַתְּ וַחֲבֶרְתֵּךְ טְמֵאָה – **"You and your companion are defiled,"** she is not believed about herself but she is believed about her companion. The reasoning is as follows: אִיהִי כֵּיוָן דְּאִיכָּא עֵדִים לָאו כָּל כְּמִינָהּ – **She, since there are witnesses** to her capture, **lacks the authority** to claim that she is pure. חֲבֶרְתָּהּ מִשְׁתַּרְיָא אַפּוּמָא דִידָהּ – **Her companion,** on the other hand, **is permitted through her word,** although it is contradicted by a witness.

The Gemara questions the need for this clause as well:

הָא תּוּ לָמָּה לִי – **But why do I need** a **further** case? הַיְינוּ רֵישָׁא

NOTES

13. She has the capacity to render herself "a forbidden object" regardless of the witness' testimony to the contrary.

14. There are some specific instances in which the testimony of a single witness is sufficient. One of those instances is testimony to the effect that a captured woman was not violated (as stated in note 4). As a rule, wherever the testimony of a single witness is sufficient, the court follows it even if it is contradicted by another single witness (see 22b note 13). Hence, this woman (who says that her companion is pure) is believed despite the opposing witness (*Rashi*).

It should be noted, though, that even in those instances where a single witness is believed against another witness, that is so only where he testified (and the court ruled on the basis of his testimony) *before* the opposing witness contradicted him (*Rashba, Ritva* et al.; cf. *Rambam, Hil. Isurei Biah* 18:21; see *Ran*).

15. The primary factor in negating her word is the testimony of the two witnesses, who say that she was captured [thus making it impossible for her to benefit from the principle of *happeh she'assar*]. The single witness' testimony that she was violated is insignificant, because a single witness can establish only that a captured woman was *not* violated (see *Rashi;* see also *Tos. Rid* and *Ritva;* cf. *Mordechai* §147).

16. A single witness who attests to the purity of a captured woman is believed even where he is contradicted by another witness, as explained in note 14.

In fact, we already know from the Baraisa's first case that a single witness suffices to establish a captive's purity. Nevertheless, it might have been thought that the only type of witness eligible for this purpose is a fellow captive, whose awareness of the situation is the most reliable. But if someone else testifies that a captured woman was not violated (*and* he is contradicted by another captive), perhaps his testimony is not accepted. The Baraisa must therefore add the second case to correct this misconception (see *Tos. HaRosh* and *Ritva;* see also *Tosafos* ד״ה הא with *Tos. Yeshanim*).

[From the Gemara's wording ("a single witness said to her") it seems that the witness gave his testimony *after* the captured woman had already testified. If so, however, it is difficult to understand why he is believed. As stated in note 14, one witness overrides another only where he testifies first. For discussion of this problem, see the sources listed there.]

17. In this context the "beginning" of the Baraisa refers to both of its first two clauses. The first clause already taught that the speaker can render herself forbidden [even where she is contradicted by another witness]. And the second clause already taught that the opposing witness suffices to testify that the companion is permitted. The third clause merely seems to be reiterating these two points.

The first two clauses can together be termed the "beginning" of the Baraisa, because they form a pair in which one clause is the opposite of the other. For the same reason, the last two clauses also form a pair (*Rashi;* cf. *Rashba* and *Ritva;* see also *Tosafos*).

18. As the opposing witness testifies.

19. *Judges* 16:30. The blinded Samson prayed for a return of his superhuman strength in order to avenge his torment at the hands of the Philistines, and was willing to perish along with them as long as he would succeed (see ibid. vs. 25-30).

20. The concept of שַׁוִּיתָא לְנַפְשָׁהּ חֲתִיכָה דְּאִיסּוּרָא, *she rendered herself a forbidden object,* does not apply where the court believes that she has a reason to lie. Hence, in this case, the court should accept the testimony of the opposing witness, who says that she is permitted.

21. [This clause of the Baraisa actually stated two rulings: She is believed about herself; she is not believed about her companion. Although the Gemara's question was based on both rulings (see note 17), it emerges that only the first one was strictly necessary, and the second was included on account of the first.]

מתני' שתי נשים שנשבו זאת אומרת נשביתי וטהורה אני וזאת אומרת נשביתי וטהורה אני א) אינן נאמנות ובזמן שהן מעידות זו את זו הרי אלו נאמנות: **גמ'** ת"ר א) אני טמאה וחברתי טהורה נאמנת אני טהורה וחברתי טמאה אינה נאמנת אני וחברתי טמאה נאמנת על עצמה ואינה נאמנת על חברתה אני וחברתי טהורה נאמנת על חברתה ואינה נאמנת על עצמה אמר מר אני טהורה וחברתי טמאה אינה נאמנת היכי דמי אי דליכא עדים על עצמה אמאי לא מהימנא נשביתי וטהורה אני קאמרה אלא פשיטא דאיכא עדים אימא מציעתא אני וחברתי טמאה נאמנת על עצמה ואינה נאמנת על חברתה ואי דאיכא עדים אמאי לא מהימנא אלא פשיטא דליכא עדים אימא סיפא אני וחברתי טהורה נאמנת על חברתה ואינה נאמנת על עצמה ואי דליכא עדים אעצמה אמאי לא מהימנא אלא פשיטא דאיכא עדים רישא וסיפא דאיכא עדים מציעתא דליכא עדים אמר אביי אין רישא וסיפא דאיכא עדים מציעתא דליכא עדים רב פפא אמר כולה דאיכא עדים ואיכא עד אחד דקא אפיך אמרה אני טמאה וחברתי טהורה ואמר לה עד אחד את טהורה וחברתך טמאה איהי שויתא לנפשה חתיכה דאיסורא חברתה משתריא אפומא דידה אני טהורה וחברתי טמאה ואמר לה עד אחד את טמאה וחברתך טהורה איהי כיון דאיכא עדים לאו כל כמינה חברתה משתריא אפומא דעד אני וחברתי טמאה ואמר לה עד אחד את וחברתך טהורה איהי שויתא לנפשה חתיכה דאיסורא חברתה משתריא אפומא דעד הא תו למה לי היינו רישא מהו דתימא הני תרוייהו טהורות נינהו והאי דקאמרה הכי א) תמות נפשי עם פלשתים היא דקא עבדה קמ"ל אני וחברתי טהורה ואמר לה עד אחד את וחברתך טמאה איהי כיון דאיכא עדים לאו כל כמינה חברתה משתריא אפומא דידה הא תו למה לי היינו רישא דרישא מהו דתימא כי מהימנא במקום דפסלה נפשה אבל במקום דמכשרא נפשה אימא לא מהימנא קא משמע לן: **מתני'** ב) וכן שני אנשים ° זה אומר כהן אני וזה אומר כהן אני אינן נאמנין ג) ובזמן שהן מעידין זה את זה הרי אלו נאמנין ד) רבי יהודה אומר ה) אין מעלין לכהונה על פי עד אחד אמר רבי אלעזר אימתי במקום שיש עוררין אבל במקום שאין עוררין מעלין לכהונה על פי עד אחד רשב"ג אומר משום רבי שמעון בן הסגן מעלין לכהונה על פי עד אחד: **גמ'** כל הני למה לי צריכי דאי תנא מודה רבי יהושע משום דאיכא דררא דממונא אבל עדים דליכא דררא דממונא אימא לא ואי תנא עדים משום דלעלמא אבל איהו דלנפשיה אימא

רש"י

מתני' שתי נשים שנשבו. שיש עדים שנשבו: **שמעידות זו את זו.** כל אחת אומרת חברתי טהורה: **הרי אלו נאמנות.** דבשבויה הקילו להאמין עד אחד ואפילו אשה: **גמ' נאמנת.** על כלום ולקמיה מפרש לה לכולה: **אינה נאמנת.** על כלום: **אי דליכא עדים.** שנשבו: **אלא פשיטא דאיכא עדים.** הלכך עלמא אינה נאמנת לטהרה וחברתה נמי אע"ג דלגן אמרינן בחזקת טמאה קיימא הוא דלאו משום הימנותא דהך הוא דבלאו סהדותא דידה נמי בחזקת טומאה היא: **ואינה נאמנת על חברתה.** על כרחך משמע דחברתה בחזקת טהורה קיימא דבשלמא אינה נאמנת דרישא אע"ג דאכולה מילתא משמע שייך למיתנייה משום דידה הכא דבהדיא תנא אינה נאמנת על חברתה קשה: **אלא פשיטא דליכא עדים.** ולדידה מהימנא דשויתא לנפשה חתיכה דאיסורא: **דאפיך.** מיפך את כל דבריה: **חברתה משתריא אפומא דידה.** דבשבויה האמינו חכמים עד אחד להקל ואפילו עבד או שפחה דקתני מתני' (לקמן דף כז.) אם יש להן עדים אפילו עבד כו' וכל מקום שנאמן בו עד אחד הרי הוא כשנים ואין דברי אחד במקום שנים: **הכי גרסינן איהי כיון דאיכא עדים לאו כל כמינה.** ולעדי שבויה קלי דעד אחד בטומאה אינו כלום אלא בסוטה בלבד שרגלים לדבר שהרי קינא לה ונסתרה: **שויתא לנפשה חתיכה דאיסורא.** לפיכך אין העד נאמן לטהרה: **היינו רישא.** הני מילי תרוייהו אשמעינן ברישא חתיכה דאיסורא מרישא שמעינן שריותא דחברתה אפומא דעד מסיפא דרישא שמעינן תרתי בבי קמייתא רישא קרי להו דדמיין להדדי ותרתי בבי בתרייתא חדא מילתא היא דבכל חדא תנן מילתא וחילופה בין ברישא בין בסיפא: **מהו דתימא כו'.** ומשום נאמנת על עצמה תנא ליה: **איהי כיון דאיכא עדים גרסינן: היינו רישא דרישא.** דהא ודאי משום דאינה נאמנת על עצמה לא אצטריך למיתנייה דהא טובא אשמועינן דבמקום עדי שבויה לא מהימנא למימר טהורה אני ומשום נאמנת על חברתה הוא דאצטריך דאע"ג דעד קא מכחיש לה מהימנא והא ברישא דרישא אשמעינן: **במקום דפסלה לנפשה.** התם הוא דמהימנא אחברתה משום דקאמרה טמאה אני: **אבל היכא דמכשרא נמי לנפשה.** אימא משום דידה הוא דקאמרה ולא אחברתה: קמ"ל גרסינן: **ל"א** גרסינן מהו דתימא כי מהימנא במקום עד פסול כגון דעד דקא מפיך הוי אשה אבל במקום עד כשר לא תנא משנה יתירה לאפי' במקום עד כשר: **מתני' וכן שני אנשים.** לא גרסינן שנשבו: **אין נאמנים.** ליתן להן תרומה: **ובזמן שמעידין זה את זה.** שכל אחד אומר אני וחברי כהן: **רבי יהודה אומר אין מעלין לכהונה על פי עד אחד.** ואפילו היכא דליכא גומלין וכל שכן הכא דאיכא למיחש לגומלין העד אתה עלי ואני עליך: **עוררין.** שקורין עליו שם פסול: **מעלין.** היכא דליכא גומלין והיינו דאיכא בין ר' אלעזר לתנא קמא דר' יהודה: **רבן שמעון כו'.** בגמ' מפרש מאי ביניהו: **גמ' כל הני.** דתנא מתניתין לאשמועינן הפה שאסר הוא הפה שהתיר ל"ל: **משום דאיכא דררא דממונא.** הלכך אי לאו דפשיטא מלתא שלקחה מאביו לא היה אומר של אביך היתה וגורם לעצמו הפסד ממון וכשאומר תחלת דבריו על שם סופו אמרו לגמור בהן ולקחתיה הימנו: **אבל עדים.** שאמרו כתב ידינו הוא: **דליכא דררא דממונא.** לגבייהו דלימטינהו פסידא בהאי עדות: **אימא לא.** ליתהמנו למימר אנוסין היינו דמעיקרא כי אמרו כתב ידינו הוא אדעתא דסהדותא אמרו ולאו למיגמר בה אנוסים היינו והדר אימליכו למיגמר בה הכי קמשמע לן: **דלעלמא.** אין הדבור האחרון מהני לעצמו אלא לאחרים ומשום אחרים לא הוו הדרי במלתייהו אבל איהו גופיה דלנפשיה מהני כי הדר ואמר לקחתיה:

משום

תוספות

שתי נשים שנשבו. אומר ר"י דלא גרסינן זאת אומרת נשביתי וטהורה אני כו' אלא זאת אומרת טהורה אני דהא בדליכא עדים שנשבו איירי ומיהו יש לקיים הגירסא דאיירי דאינהו לא ידעי דליכא עדים ואשמועינן דאפילו הכי לא מהימני:

אין רישא וסיפא דאיכא עדים ומציעתא דליכא עדים. השתא לא פריך הא תו למה לי כדפריך אשנויא דרב פפא דהשתא אצטריך כולהו אני טהורה וחברתי טמאה אשמועינן כיון דאיכא עדים לא מהימנא אנפשה ואני וחברתי טמאה אשמועינן דלא מהימנא אחברתה היכא דליכא עדים ומשתריא חברתה אפומא דנפשה ואני וחברתי טהורה אשמועינן אע"ג דאיכא עדים מהימנא אחברתה דרישא דרישא איכא לאוקמי בדליכא עדים ואין נראה לאוקמי בדליכא עדים היינו מציעתא אלא בדאיכא עדים איירי ומ"מ איצטריך האי סיפא לאשמועינן דנאמנת אחברתה ואע"ג דלא פסלה נפשה והיה לנו לחוש לגומלים אפילו הכי מהימנא א):

הא תו למה לי היינו רישא. וא"ת ואמאי לא קאמר הכא מרישא דרישא כדקאמר בסמוך דהא שמעינן מרישא דרישא דאיהי שויתה לנפשה חתיכה דאיסורא וחברתה משתריא אפומא דידה וכ"ש דמשתריא אפומא דעד אחד ב) וי"ל דהכא ניחא ליה למנקט סתמא דהיינו רישא משום דמרישא נמי שמעינן דחברתה משתריא אפומא דעד אחד אבל בסמוך לא מצי פריך אלא מרישא דרישא:

דאיכא דררא דממונא. פירש ר"ח שהאומר הוא מוחזק בשדה אבל העדים אין בידם כלום:

אבל הכא דליכא דררא דממונא לא. קשה לרשב"א הא איצטריך גבי עדים לאשמועינן דמהימני במגו לפסול השטר דהא אע"ג דר' מאיר פליג אסיפא מודה ברישא:

עין משפט נר מצוה

עט א מיי' פי"ח מהל' איסורי ביאה הלכ' יז סמג לאוין קכא טוש"ע אה"ע סימן ז סעיף א:

פ ב מיי' פ"כ שם הלכ' יג סמג לאוין קכב קמ טוש"ע שם סימן ג סעיף א:

פא ג מיי' שם הלכה יא טוש"ע שם סעיף ד:

פב ד מיי' שם הלכה ג:

תוספות רי"ד

הזמה גמורה. כיון שאומרי' להם והלא עמנו הייתם יחד במקום פ' כל היום כולו ואנו לא ראינו. ואתם האיך ראיתם ובהזמה האמינה התורה האחרונים ובטלי עדות הראשונים הלכך טעמא דאמרי' לא אינה דאינה ראיה דתצא ול"א אי איתא דקדיש קלא אית לה ואכתי הזמה הוא. אבל אם העידו עדות ברורה כיון דכזימים את הראשונים א) תנשא לכתחלה: **סיפא** ב' אומרים ראינוה שנתגרשה וב' אומרים לא ראינוה שנתגרשה ה"ז ל"ת. ואם נשאר לא מצא מאי קמ"ל אע"ג דדירו בחצר א' היינו הך מ"ד גבי קידושין הוא דעבידי אינשי דמקדשי בצנעא אבל גירושין אי איתא דאיגרשא קלא אית לי' למילתא קמ"ל דעבידי אינשי דמגרשי בצנעא פירוש ופ"ה לכתחלה לא תנשא משום ולזות שפתים הרחק ממך: **מתני' האשה שאמרה** נשביתי וטהורה אני נאמנת שהפה שאסר הוא הפה שהתיר. ואם יש עדים שנשבית והיא אומרת טהורה אני אינה נאמנת ואם משנשאת באו עדים ה"ז ל"ת. **פי'** נשביתי לבין העובדי כוכבים וטהורה אני שלא נבעלתי לעובד כוכבים **ואם משנשאת וכו'.** בגמ' מפרשי' אהיא קאי. ר"ז מתני לה ארישא פי' הא' ואם משנשאת באו עדים ארישא. האשה שאמרה א"א הייתי וגרושה אני. והכי קתני ואם משנשאת באו עדים שהיתה א"א. והיא נשאת ע"פ עצמה שאמרה גרשה אני ה"ז לא תצא. **ורבא** מתני לה אסיפא פי' אנשבית וטהורה אני והתירוה לינשא. ואח"כ באו עדים שנשבית. מאן דמתני' לה ארישא כ"ש אסיפא דבשבויה הקילו. פי' דחששא בעלמא הוא דאיכא שמא נבעלה לעובד כוכבים ונפסלה לכהונה. ומאן דמתני לה אסיפא אבל ארישא לא. **לימא** בדר"ה קמיפלגי דאמר ר"ה האשה שאמרה לבעלה גרשתני נאמנת דחזקה אין אשה מעיזה בפני בעלה. פי' דמאן דמתני לה ארישא אית ליה דר"ה ומאן דמתני לה אסיפא ל"ל דר"ה. לא דכ"ע א"ל דר"ה פי' האע"ג דבחזקת (טומאה) [נשואה] קיימא דהלכתא כוותיה. מר סבר כי אתמר דר"ה בפניו אבל שלא בפניו מעיזה ב). פי' דוקא כשנשאת ואח"כ באו עדים סמכי' אהך חזקה אפילו שלא בפניו. אבל אם לא נשאת לא סמכי' אהך חזקה כי היכי דסמכי' עלה בפניו דלא דמי שלא בפניו כבפניו:

ואם משנשאת באו עדים ה"ז ל"ת. אמר שמואל. לא נשאת ממש אלא כיון שהתירה לינשא אע"פ שלא נשאת. והא ל"ת קתני. ל"ת מהתירא הראשון: **ת"ר** אמרה נשביתי וטהורה אני ויש לי עדים שטהורה אני פי' שהיו עמי תמיד שלא נתיחדתי עם עובד כוכבים אין אומרים נמתין לה עד שיבואו עדים אלא מתירין אותה מיד. **התירוה** לינשא ואח"כ באו עדים ואמרו לא ידענו ה"ז ל"ת. פי' אע"פ שבאו אותם העדים שאמרה האשה ושאלנו אותן ואמרו לא ידענו. אין אומרים כיון שנמצאו דבריה שקר תצא. אלא ל"ת ואם באו עדי טומאה אפילו יש לה כמה בנים תצא. פי' דנבעלה לעכו"ם הוי' לה זונה ובניה הם חללים: **בנתי'** דמר שמואל אשתביין. אסקינהו לארעא דישראל. אוקמינהו לשבוינהו אבראי. פי' שלא יבאו לפני ב"ד ולא ידעו ב"ד שהן שבויין אלא ע"פ עצמן ויתירום עיילו אינהו לבי מדרשא דר"ח. זו אומרת נשביתי וטהורה אני וזו אומרת נשביתי וטהורה אני. לסוף עול אתו שבוייהו. א"ר חנינא בנת מוריין אינון. פי' בנות אדם גדול ובעל הוראה הן שידעו לעשות כך. ואיגלאי מילתא דבנתיה דמר שמואל אינון. א"ל ר"ח לרשב"א כהנא פוק איטפל בקרובותיך. פי' [קח] א' מהן שהן קרובותיך. א"ל לר"ח והא איכא עדי טומאה שראוה כשנטמאה עם העובדי כוכבים. ודילמא אתו לקמן למחר לאחר שתנשא. א"ל השתא מיהו ליתנהו פי' קודם נשואין. ומשום דלמא אתו לא (אהדרינן) [אסרינן] להו השתא עדים בצד אסתן ותאסר. פי' אסתן. צפון. כמו יומא דאיסתנא. מצפון תפתח הרעה. פי' העדים המכירים הן בבבל ואנו כאן וניחוש שמא יבואו ויעידו על הטומאה ולכולי האי לא חיישינן. ומותרות הן לכהונה אח"כ ודאי אם יבואו תצא ובניה חללים. אבל מסתמא לא חיישינן דאחזוקי איסורא לא מחזקינן ואלו הי' קרובים (לא) [לנו] היינו חוקרים אותם טרם שנתירם לינשא. עכשיו שהן רחוקים ממנו. לכולי האי לא חיישינן: **מתני' שתי נשים** שנשבו ז"א נשביתי וטהורה אני וז"א נשביתי וטהורה אני אינן נאמנות. ובזמן שמעידות זו ע"ז הרי אלו נאמנות פי' שנשבו בידוע כגון שיש עדים שנשבו הלכך אין נאמנות להעיד כל א' וא' בפ"ע. ובזמן שמעידות זו ע"ז שכל א' אומרת אני וחברתי טהורה הרי אלו נאמנות דבשבויה הקילו והאמינו בה אפילו ע"א ואפי' אשה ולא חיישינן לגומלין. **ת"ר** אני טמאה וחברתי טהורה נאמנת. אני טהורה וחברתי טמאה אינה נאמנת. פי' אינה נאמנת על כלום. אני וחברתי טמאות נאמנת לפסול א"ע. ואינה נאמנת לפסול חברתה. אני וחברתי טהורה נאמנת על חברתה. ואינה נאמנת ע"ע. **אמר מר** אני טהורה וחברתי טמאה אינה נאמנת. ה"ד אי דליכא עדים שנשבו אעצמה אמאי לא מהימנא נשביתי וטהורה אני קאמרה. פי' בשלמא אחברתה אינה נאמנת שכיון שאין עדים שנשבית הותרה חברתה וכאומרת נשביתי וטהורה אני. הו שאומרת עליה כי

חשק שלמה על תוס' רי"ד א) הדבר צ"ע דלכאורה איכא לאוקמי דהעידו עדות ברורה ומ"מ לא הוה הזמה כגון דאמרו דהמקדש היה עמנו במקום פלוני או דראינו דרך הקידושין קרוב לו ולא היה קידושין כלל. ב) נ"ל ומר סבר דאפי' שלא בפניו נמי אינה מעיזה פי' דוקא.

מסורת הש"ס

א) [תוספתא פרק ב], ב) ב"ב לא ע"ב.

תוספות ישנים

א) [והיינו שינויא דלקמן דלא פסלה נפשה והוה מצי למיפרך השתא ולשנויי. מ"ין],
ב) [וי"ל דס"ד דהיא מהימנא טפי מעד אחד לפי שנשבית עמה יודעת יותר. מ"ין].

גליון הש"ס

מתני' זה אומר כהן אני. עיין בהרא"ש פ"ה דגיטין סי' ח באות י:

תורה אור השלם

א) וַיֹּאמֶר שִׁמְשׁוֹן תָּמוֹת נַפְשִׁי עִם פְּלִשְׁתִּים וַיֵּט בְּכֹחַ וַיִּפֹּל הַבַּיִת עַל הַסְּרָנִים וְעַל כָּל הָעָם אֲשֶׁר בּוֹ וַיִּהְיוּ הַמֵּתִים אֲשֶׁר הֵמִית בְּמוֹתוֹ רַבִּים מֵאֲשֶׁר הֵמִית בְּחַיָּיו: [שופטים טז, ל]

ליקוטי רש"י

אין מעלין לכהונה. להחזיק אדם בכהן לאכול בתרומה ולעבוד עבודה ולישא את כפיו. **על פי עד אחד.** המעידו שהוא כהן כדמפרש ר' אלעזר לקמיה [בשמעתין]. **אמר רבי אלעזר אימתי.** אין מעלין ע"פ עד אחד בזמן שיש על הכהן עוררין עדים הפוסלים אותו כדמפרש בסמוך ולפרש דברי ר' יהודה בא ולא לחלוק עליו. **אבל במקום שאין עוררין.** אלא קול פסול בעלמא כדמפרש לקמיה מעלין ע"פ עד אחד שמכחיש את הקול [רשב"ם ב"ב לא:]. **דררא דממונא.** חסרון ממון [ב"מ ב:].

Mishnah שְׁתֵּי נָשִׁים שֶׁנִּשְׁבּוּ – If **two women were captured** by idolaters,[1] זֹאת אוֹמֶרֶת נִשְׁבֵּיתִי וּטְהוֹרָה אֲנִי – and now **this one says, "I was captured but I am pure,"** וְזֹאת אוֹמֶרֶת נִשְׁבֵּיתִי וּטְהוֹרָה אֲנִי – **and the other one** also **says, "I was captured but I am pure,"** אֵינָן נֶאֱמָנוֹת – **they are not believed.**[2] וּבִזְמַן שֶׁהֵן מְעִידוֹת זוֹ אֶת זוֹ – **However, if they testify for one another,**[3] הֲרֵי אֵלוּ נֶאֱמָנוֹת – **they are believed.**[4]

Gemara A Baraisa elaborates on the case of one captured woman testifying about another:

תָּנוּ רַבָּנָן – **The Rabbis taught in a Baraisa:** אֲנִי טְמֵאָה וַחֲבֶרְתִּי טְהוֹרָה – If one of two captured women says, "I AM DEFILED BUT MY COMPANION IS PURE," נֶאֱמֶנֶת – SHE IS BELIEVED about both. אֲנִי טְהוֹרָה וַחֲבֶרְתִּי טְמֵאָה – If she says, "I AM PURE BUT MY COMPANION IS DEFILED," אֵינָהּ נֶאֱמֶנֶת – SHE IS NOT BELIEVED about either. אֲנִי וַחֲבֶרְתִּי טְמֵאָה – If she says: "MY COMPANION AND I ARE DEFILED," נֶאֱמֶנֶת עַל עַצְמָהּ וְאֵינָהּ נֶאֱמֶנֶת עַל חֲבֶרְתָּהּ – SHE IS BELIEVED ABOUT HERSELF BUT SHE IS NOT BELIEVED ABOUT HER COMPANION. אֲנִי וַחֲבֶרְתִּי טְהוֹרָה – If she says: "MY COMPANION AND I ARE PURE," נֶאֱמֶנֶת עַל חֲבֶרְתָּהּ וְאֵינָהּ נֶאֱמֶנֶת עַל עַצְמָהּ – SHE IS BELIEVED ABOUT HER COMPANION BUT SHE IS NOT BELIEVED ABOUT HERSELF.[5]

The Gemara begins its analysis of the Baraisa by examining the second clause:

אָמַר מַר – **The master said** in the Baraisa: אֲנִי טְהוֹרָה וַחֲבֶרְתִּי טְמֵאָה אֵינָהּ נֶאֱמֶנֶת – If she said, "I AM PURE BUT MY COMPANION IS DEFILED," SHE IS NOT BELIEVED about either. הֵיכִי דָּמֵי – **What are the circumstances** of this case? אִי דְּלֵיכָּא עֵדִים – **If there are no witnesses** to their captivity, עַל עַצְמָהּ אַמַּאי לֹא מְהֵימְנָא – **why is she not believed about herself?** נִשְׁבֵּיתִי וּטְהוֹרָה אֲנִי קָאָמְרָה – After all, **she said, "I was captured but I am pure."**[6] אֶלָּא פְּשִׁיטָא דְּאִיכָּא עֵדִים – **Rather, it is obvious that there** ***are*** **witnesses** to their captivity.[7]

The Gemara challenges this conclusion:

אֵימָא מְצִיעֲתָא – But then **consider the middle** (i.e. the third) clause: אֲנִי וַחֲבֶרְתִּי טְמֵאָה – If she says, "MY COMPANION AND I ARE DEFILED," נֶאֱמֶנֶת עַל עַצְמָהּ וְאֵינָהּ נֶאֱמֶנֶת עַל חֲבֶרְתָּהּ – SHE IS BELIEVED ABOUT HERSELF BUT SHE IS NOT BELIEVED ABOUT HER COMPANION.[8] וְאִי דְּאִיכָּא עֵדִים – **Now, if there are witnesses** to their captivity, אַמַּאי לֹא מְהֵימְנָא – **why is she not believed** to say that her companion is defiled?[9] אֶלָּא פְּשִׁיטָא דְּלֵיכָּא עֵדִים – **Rather, it is obvious that there are no witnesses** to their captivity.[10]

The Gemara questions this conclusion as well:

אֵימָא סֵיפָא – But then **consider the last** clause: אֲנִי וַחֲבֶרְתִּי טְהוֹרָה – If she says, "MY COMPANION AND I ARE PURE," נֶאֱמֶנֶת עַל חֲבֶרְתָּהּ וְאֵינָהּ נֶאֱמֶנֶת עַל עַצְמָהּ – SHE IS BELIEVED ABOUT HER COMPANION BUT SHE IS NOT BELIEVED ABOUT HERSELF. וְאִי דְּלֵיכָּא עֵדִים – **Now, if there are no witnesses** to their captivity, אַעַצְמָהּ אַמַּאי לֹא מְהֵימְנָא – **why is she not believed about herself?**[11] אֶלָּא פְּשִׁיטָא דְּאִיכָּא עֵדִים – **Rather, it is obvious that there are witnesses** to their captivity.[12]

The Gemara summarizes the inconsistencies in the Baraisa:

רֵישָׁא וְסֵיפָא דְּאִיכָּא עֵדִים – It emerges that **the beginning** of the Baraisa [the second clause] **and the end** [the fourth clause] refer to a case **where there are witnesses** to the captivity, מְצִיעֲתָא דְּלֵיכָּא עֵדִים – whereas **the middle** [the third clause] refers to a case **where there are no witnesses** to the captivity!

NOTES

1. Witnesses testified that these women were captured (*Rashi*). [Regarding a case in which *one* witness testifies to the capture, see *Pnei Yehoshua, Haflaah* and *Melo HaRo'im* to *Tosafos* ד״ה הא תו; see also the sources listed in note 10.]

2. Since there are witnesses to the capture, the women are not believed (see *Tosafos*). Hence, they are forbidden to Kohanim, as is the case with any captured woman who cannot prove that she was not violated.

3. I.e. each one says that the other woman was not violated by the kidnapers (*Rashi*).

4. The Rabbis introduced several leniencies with respect to the prohibition of a captured woman (see 23a note 20). One of those leniencies was that a single witness – even a woman – suffices to establish that a captured woman was not violated (*Rashi; see Rambam, Hil. Isurei Biah* 18:17, *Ayeles HaShachar, Birkas Avraham* and *Kovetz Shiurim* §23,24).

In the Mishnah's case, where the women testify about each other, there are grounds for suspecting that each one agreed to lie on the other's behalf so that her companion would do the same for her. The Mishnah teaches that this is not considered a serious possibility (*Ran; Tos. Rid*).

5. The Gemara will explain the rulings of the Baraisa (see *Rashi*).

In each of these cases, the other captive does not contradict the speaker. She is silent, absent or deranged (see *Ritva*).

6. The previous Mishnah (22a) taught that if a woman says, "I was captured but I am pure," and there are no witnesses to her capture, she is believed through the principle of *happeh she'assar*.

7. Therefore, she is not believed to say that she is pure [because this is not a case of *happeh she'assar*]. Regarding her claim that her companion was violated, the court does in fact rule in accordance with her words, since a captured woman is assumed to have been violated. How, then, can the Baraisa say "she is not believed" [which implies that the court rules to the contrary of what she said (see *Rashba*)]? The answer is that here the Baraisa uses the phrase "she is not believed" in the sense that her testimony (about her fellow captive) has no bearing on the court's verdict. The court prohibits the other captive to Kohanim in any event regardless of her testimony (see *Rashi* and *Ritva;* cf. *Maharsha*).

The Gemara does not discuss the Baraisa's first ruling, because that ruling applies regardless of whether or not witnesses testified to the captivity. Either way, the speaker can render herself forbidden [see note 10], and she is believed to testify that her fellow captive is permitted [see note 4] (*Ritva*).

8. This must mean that she is not believed at all – i.e. the court rules, contrary to her testimony, that the companion was *not* violated. Although the term "she is not believed" could be used imprecisely (see previous note), that interpretation is valid only in the preceding case. Since, in that case, the Baraisa uses this phrase in a precise manner regarding the speaker herself, it is justified in using the same phrase, albeit imprecisely, to include the companion as well. Here, though, the Baraisa says "she is not believed" *only* with respect to the companion. Hence, in this context, it must mean that she is not believed at all and the court rules that the companion is permitted (*Rashi*).

9. The Baraisa implies that the companion is permitted to Kohanim (see previous note). But why should this be so? Since there are witnesses to her captivity and no one testifies on her behalf, the companion ought to be prohibited.

10. Hence, although the speaker testifies that the companion was violated, the companion is still permitted, because the testimony of a single witness does not suffice in this regard (see *Rashi* ד״ה ה״ג; see also *Rambam, Hil. Sanhedrin* 16:6 with *Ayeles HaShachar, Birkas Avraham* et al.).

The speaker, however, is believed to say that she herself was violated, even without the support of any witnesses. This is because a person has the authority to establish that he or she is personally subject to a prohibition [שַׁוְּיתָא לְנַפְשָׁהּ חֲתִיכָה דְּאִיסּוּרָא] (*Rashi;* see 9a note 2).

11. In the absence of witnesses to the captivity, her claim that she was not violated should be believed through the principle of *happeh she'assar*.

12. Without the benefit of *happeh she'assar,* the speaker is not believed to say that she is pure. However, she does have the authority to establish her companion's purity, because the testimony of one female witness suffices in this respect.

מתני׳ שתי נשים שנשבו זאת אומרת נשביתי וטהורה אני וזאת אומרת נשביתי וטהורה אני אינן נאמנות [א] ובזמן שהן מעידות זו את זו הרי אלו נאמנות: גמ׳ ת״ר [א] אני טמאה וחברתי טהורה נאמנת אני טהורה וחברתי טמאה אינה נאמנת אני וחברתי טמאה נאמנת על עצמה ואינה נאמנת על חברתה אני וחברתי טהורה נאמנת על חברתה ואינה נאמנת על עצמה אמר מר אני טהורה וחברתי טמאה אינה נאמנת היכי דמי אי דליכא עדים על עצמה אמאי לא מהימנא נשביתי וטהורה אני קאמרה אלא פשיטא דאיכא עדים אימא מציעתא אני וחברתי טמאה נאמנת על עצמה ואינה נאמנת על חברתה ואי דאיכא עדים אמאי לא מהימנא אלא פשיטא דליכא עדים אימא סיפא אני וחברתי טהורה נאמנת על חברתה ואינה נאמנת על עצמה ואי דליכא עדים אעצמה אמאי לא מהימנא אלא פשיטא דאיכא עדים רישא וסיפא דאיכא עדים מציעתא דליכא עדים אמר אביי אין רישא וסיפא דאיכא עדים מציעתא דליכא עדים רב פפא אמר כולה דאיכא עדים ואיכא עד אחד דקא אפיך אמרה אני טמאה וחברתי טהורה ואמר לה עד אחד את טהורה וחברתך טמאה איהי שויתא לנפשה חתיכה דאיסורא חברתה משתריא אפומא דידה אני טהורה וחברתי טמאה ואמר לה עד אחד את טמאה וחברתך טהורה איהי כיון דאיכא עדים לאו כל כמינה חברתה משתריא אפומא דעד אני וחברתי טמאה ואמר לה עד אחד את וחברתך טהורה איהי שויתא לנפשה חתיכה דאיסורא חברתה משתריא אפומא דעד הא תו למה לי היינו רישא מהו דתימא הני תרוייהו טהורות נינהו והאי דקאמרה הכי [א] תמות נפשי עם פלשתים היא דקא עבדה קמ״ל אני וחברתי טהורה ואמר לה עד אחד את וחברתך טמאה איהי כיון דאיכא עדים לאו כל כמינה חברתה משתריא אפומא דידה הא תו למה לי היינו רישא דרישא מהו דתימא כי מהימנא במקום דפסלה נפשה אבל במקום דמכשרא נפשה אימא לא מהימנא קא משמע לן: מתני׳ [ב] וכן שני אנשים זה אומר כהן אני וזה אומר כהן אני אינן נאמנין [ג] ובזמן שהן מעידין זה את זה הרי אלו נאמנין [ד] רבי יהודה אומר אין מעלין לכהונה על פי עד אחד אמר רבי אלעזר אימתי במקום שיש עוררין אבל במקום שאין עוררין מעלין לכהונה על פי עד אחד רשב״ג אומר משום רבי שמעון בן הסגן מעלין לכהונה על פי עד אחד: גמ׳ כל הני למה לי צריכי דאי תנא מודה רבי יהושע משום דאיכא דררא דממונא אבל עדים דליכא דררא דממונא אימא לא ואי תנא עדים משום דלעלמא אבל איהו דלנפשיה אימא

רש״י

מתני׳ שתי נשים שנשבו. שיש עדים שנשבו: שמעידות זו את זו. כל אחת אומרת חברתי טהורה: הרי אלו נאמנות. דבשבויה הקילו להאמין עד אחד ואפילו אשה: גמ׳ אינה נאמנת. על כלום ולקמיה מפרש לה לכולה: אי דליכא עדים. שנשבו: אלא פשיטא דאיכא עדים. הלכך אעצמה אינה נאמנת לטהרה וחברתה נמי אע״ג דלקמן אמרינן בחזקת טמאה קיימא הוא ולאו משום הימנותא דהך הוא דבלאו סהדותא דידה נמי בחזקת טומאה היא: ואינה נאמנת על חברתה. על כרחך משמע דחברתה בחזקת טהורה קיימא דבשלמא אינה נאמנת לרישא אע״ג דאכולה מילתא משמע שייך למיתנייה משום דידה אלא הכא דכדאיל תנא אינה נאמנת על חברתה קשה: אלא פשיטא דליכא עדים. ולדידה מהימנא דשויתה לנפשה חתיכה דאיסורא: דאפיך. מיפך את כל דבריה: חברתה משתריא אפומא דידה. דבשבויה האמינו חכמים עד אחד להקל ואפילו עבד או שפחה כדקתני מתני׳ (לקמן דף כז.) אם יש להן עדים אפילו עבד כו׳ וכל מקום שנאמן בו עד אחד הרי הוא כשנים ואין דברי אחד שכנגדו לטמא עומד במקום שנים: הכי גרסינן איהי כיון דאיכא עדים לאו כל כמינה. ולעדי שבויה קאי לעד אחד בטומאה אינו כלום אלא בסוטה בלבד שרגלים לדבר שהרי קינא לה ונסתרה: שויתה לנפשה חתיכה דאיסורא. לפיכך אין העד נאמן לטהרה: היינו רישא. הני מילי תרוייהו אשמועינן ברישא חתיכה דאיסורא מרישא שמעינן שריותא לחברתה אפומא דעד מסיפא דרישא שמעינן תרתי בבי קמייתא רישא קרי להו דדמיין להדדי ותרתי בבי בתרייתא חדא מילתא היא דבכלל חדא תנן מילתא וחילופה בין ברישא בין בסיפא: מהו דתימא כו׳. ומשום דנאמנת על עצמה תנא ליה: איהי כיון דליכא עדים גרסינן: היינו רישא דרישא. דהא ודאי משום דאינה נאמנת על עצמה לא אצטריך למיתנייה דהא טובא אשמועינן דבמקום עדי שבויה לא מהימנא למימר טהורה אני ומשום נאמנת על חברתה הוא דאצטריך דאע״ג דעד קא מכחיש לה מהימנא והא ברישא דרישא אשמועינן: במקום דפסלה לנפשה. התם הוא דמהימנא אחברתה משום דקאמרה טמאה אני: אבל היכא דמכשרא נמי לנפשה. אימא משום דידה הוא דקאמרה ולא אחברתה: קמ״ל גרסינן: ל״א גרסינן מהו דתימא כי מהימנא במקום עד פסול כגון דעד דקא מפיך הוי אשה אבל במקום עד כשר לא תנא משנה יתירה דאפי׳ במקום עד כשר: מתני׳ וכן שני אנשים. לא גרסינן שנשבו: אין נאמנים. ליתן להן תרומה: ובזמן שמעידין זה את זה. שכל אחד אומר אני וחברי כהן: רבי יהודה אומר אין מעלין לכהונה על פי עד אחד. ואפילו היכא דליכא גומלין וכל שכן הכא דאיכא למיחש לגומלין העד אתה עלי ואני עליך: עוררין. שקורין עליו שם פסול: מעלין. היכא דליכא גומלין והיינו דאיכא בין ר׳ אלעזר לתנא קמא דר׳ יהודה: רבן שמעון כו׳. בגמ׳ מפרש מאי בינייהו: גמ׳ כל הני. דתנא מתניתין לאשמועינן הפה שאסר הוא הפה שהתיר צ״ל: משום דאיכא דררא דממונא. הלכך אי לאו דפשיטא מלתא שלקחה מאביו לא היה אומר של אביך היתה וגורם לעצמו הפסד ממון וכשאומר תחלת דבריו על שם סופו אמרו לגמור בהן ולקחתיה הימנו: אבל עדים. שאמרו כתב ידינו הוא: דליכא דררא דממונא. לגבייהו דלימטיינהו פסידא בהאי עדות: אימא לא. ליתהמנו למימר אנוסין היינו דמעיקרא כי אמרו כתב ידינו הוא אדעתא דסהדותא אמרו ולאו למיגמר בה אנוסים היינו והדר אימליכו למיגמר בה הכי קמשמע לן: דלעלמא. אין הדבור האחרון מהני לעצמו אלא לאחרים ומשום אחרים לא הוו הדרי במלתייהו אבל איהו גופיה דלנפשיה מהני כי הדר ואמר לקחתיה:

משום

תוספות

שתי נשים שנשבו. אומר ר״י דלא גרסינן זאת אומרת נשביתי וטהורה אני כו׳ אלא זאת אומרת טהורה אני דהא דליכא עדים שנשבו איירי ומיהו יש לקיים הגירסא דאיירי דאינהו לא ידעי דליכא עדים ואשמועינן דאפילו הכי לא מהימני:

אין רישא וסיפא דאיכא עדים ומציעתא דליכא עדים. השתא לא פריך הא תו למה לי כדפריך אשינויא דרב פפא דהשתא אצטריך כולהו אני טהורה וחברתי טמאה אשמועינן כיון דאיכא עדים לא מהימנא אנפשה ואני וחברתי טמאה אשמועינן דלא מהימנא אחברתה היכא דליכא עדים ומשתריא חברתה אפומא דנפשה ואני וחברתי טהורה אשמועינן אע״ג דאיכא עדים מהימנא אחברתה דרישא היכא דאיכא לאוקמי דליכא עדים ואין נראה לאו דליכא עדים היינו מציעתא אלא דאיכא עדים איירי ומ״מ איצטריך האי סיפא לאשמועינן דנאמנת אחברתה ואע״ג דלא פסלה נפשה והיה לנו לחוש לגומלים אפילו הכי מהימנא א):

הא תו למה לי היינו רישא. וא״ת ואמאי לא קאמר הכא מרישא דרישא כדקאמר בסמוך דהא שמעינן מרישא דרישא דאיהי שויתה לנפשה חתיכה דאיסורא וחברתה משתריא אפומא דידה וכ״ש דמשתריא אפומא דעד אחד ב) וי״ל דהכא ניחא ליה למנקט סתמא דהיינו רישא משום דמרישא נמי שמעינן דחברתה משתריא אפומא דעד אחד אבל בסמוך לא מצי פריך אלא מרישא דרישא:

דאיכא דררא דממונא. פירש ר״ח שהאומר הוא מוחזק בשדה אבל העדים אין בידם כלום:

אבל הכא דליכא דררא דממונא לא. קשה לרשב״א הא איצטריך גבי עדים לאשמועינן דמהימני במגו לפסול השטר דהא אע״ג דר׳ מאיר פליג אסיפא מודה ברישא:

נשביתי

עין משפט נר מצוה

עט א מיי׳ פי״ח מהל׳ איסורי ביאה הלכ׳ יז סמג לאוין קכא טוש״ע אה״ע סימן ז סעיף א:

פ ב מיי׳ פי״ג שם הלכ׳ יג סמג לאוין קכב קמ טוש״ע שם סימן ג סעיף א:

פא ג מיי׳ שם הלכה יא טוש״ע שם סעיף ד:

פב ד מיי׳ שם הלכה ב:

תוספות רי״ד

הזמה גמורה. כיון שאומרי׳ להם והלא עמנו הייתם יחד במקום פ׳ כל היום כולו וגנו לא ראינו. ואתם האיך ראיתם ובהזמה האמינה התורה האחרונים בטלי עדות הראשונים הלכך טעמא דאמרי לא ראינוה דאינה ראיה דתצא ול״א אי איתא דקדיש קלא אית לה ואכתי הזמה הוא. אבל אם העידו עדות ברורה כיון דמזימים את הראשונים א) תנשא לכתחלה: סיפא ב׳ אומרים ראינוה שנתגרשה וב׳ אומרים לא ראינוה שנתגרשה ה״ז ל״ת. ואם נשאת לא תצא מאי קמ״ל אע״ג דדיירו בחצר א׳ היינו הך מ״ד גבי קידושין הוא דעבידי אינשי דמקדשי בצנעא אבל גירושין אי איתא דאיגרשא קלא אית לי׳ למילתא קמ״ל דעבידי אינשי דמגרשי בצנעא פירוש ואפ״ה לכתחלה לא תנשא משום ולזות שפתים ברחק ממך: מתני׳ האשה שאמרה נשביתי וטהורה אני נאמנת שהפה שאסר הוא הפה שהתיר. ואם יש עדים שנשבית והיא אומרת טהורה אני אינה נאמנת ואם משנשאת באו עדים ה״ז ל״ת. פי׳ נשביתי בין העובדי כוכבים וטהורה אני שלא נבעלתי לעובד כוכבים ואם משנשאת וכו׳. בגמ׳ מפרשי׳ אהיא קאי. ר״א מתני לה ארישא פי׳ האי ואם משנשאת באו עדים ארישא. האשה שאמרה א״א הייתי וגרושה אני. והכי קתני ואם משנשאת באו עדים שהיתה א״א. והיא נשאת ע״פ עצמה שאמרה גרושה אני ה״ז לא תצא. ורבא מתני לה אסיפא פי׳ אנשבית וטהורה אני והתירוה לינשא. ואח״כ באו עדים שנשבית. מאן דמתני׳ לה ארישא כ״ש אסיפא דבשבויה הקילו. פי׳ דחששא בעלמא הוא דאיכא שמא נבעלה לעובד כוכבים ונפסלה לכהונה. ומאן דמתני לה אסיפא אבל ארישא לא. לימא בדר״ה קמיפלגי דאמר ר״ה האשה שאמרה לבעלה גרשתני נאמנת חזקה אין אשה מעיזה בפני בעלה. פי׳ דמאן דמתני לה ארישא אית ליה דר״ה ומאן דמתני לה אסיפא לית ליה דר״ה. לא דכ״ע אית ליה דר״ה פי׳ ואע״ג דבחזקת (טומאה) [נשואה] קיימא דהלכתא כוותיה. מר סבר כי אתמר דר״ה בפניו אבל שלא בפניו מעיזה ב). פי׳ דוקא כשנשאת ואח״כ באו עדים סמכי׳ אהך חזקה אפילו שלא בפניו. אבל אם לא נשאת לא סמכי׳ אהך חזקה כי היכי דסמכי׳ עלה בפניו דלא דמי שלא בפניו כבפניו:

ואם משנשאת באו עדים ה״ז ל״ת. אמר שמואל. לא נשאת ממש אלא כיון שהתירוה לינשא אע״פ שלא נשאת. והא ל״ת קתני. ל״ת מהתירא הראשון: ת״ר אמרה נשביתי וטהורה אני ויש לי עדים שטהורה אני פי׳ שהיו עמי תמיד שלא נתיחדתי עם עובד כוכבים אין אומרים נמתין לה עד שיבואו עדים אלא מתירין אותה מיד. התירוה לינשא ואח״כ באו עדים ואמרו לא ידענו ה״ז ל״ת. פי׳ אע״פ שבאו אותם העדים שאמרה האשה ושאלנו אותן ואמרו לא ידענו. אין אומרים כיון שנמצאו דבריה שקר תצא. אלא ל״ת ואם באו עדי טומאה אפילו יש לה כמה בנים תצא. פי׳ דנבעלה לעכו״ם הוי׳ לה זונה ובניה הם חללים: בנתי׳ דמר שמואל אשתביין. אסקינהו לארעא דישראל. אוקמינהו לשבוינהו אבראי. פי׳ שלא יבאו לפני ב״ד ולא ידעו ב״ד שהן שבויין אלא ע״פ עצמן ויתירום עיילו אינהו לבי מדרשא דר״ח. זו אומרת נשביתי וטהורה אני וזו אומרת נשביתי וטהורה אני. לסוף עול אתו שבוייהו. א״ר חנינא בנת מוריין אינון. פי׳ בנות אדם גדול ובעל הוראה הן שידעו לעשות כך. ואיגלאי מילתא דבנתיה דמר שמואל אינון. א״ל ר״י לרשב״א כהנא פוק איטפל בקרובותיך. פי׳ [קח] א׳ מהן שהן קרובותיך. א״ל לר״ח והא איכא עדי טומאה שראוה כשנטמאה עם העובדי כוכבים. ודילמא אתו לקבן לכהר לאחר שתנשא. א״ל השתא מיהו ליתנהו פי׳ קודם נשואין. ומשום דלמא אתו לא (אהדרינן) [אסרינן] להו השתא עדים בצד אסתן ותאסר. פי׳ אסתן. צפון. כמו יומא דאיסתנא. מצפון תפתח הרעה. פי׳ העדים המכירים הן בבבל ואנחנו כאן וניחוש שמא יבואו ויעידו על הטומאה ולכולי האי לא חיישינן. ומותרות הן לכהונה אח״כ ודאי אם יבואו תצא ובניה חללים. אבל מסתמא לא חיישינן דאחזוקי איסורא לא מחזקינן ואלו הי׳ קרובים (לא) [לנו] היינו חוקרים אותם טרם שנתירם לינשא. עכשיו שהן רחוקים ממנו. לכולי האי לא חיישינן: מתני׳ שתי נשים שנשבו ז״א נשביתי וטהורה אני וז״א נשביתי וטהורה אני אינן נאמנות. ובזמן שמעידות זו ע״ז הרי אלו נאמנות פי׳ שנשבו בידוע כגון שיש עדים שנשבו בלכך אין נאמנות להעיד כל א׳ וא׳ בפ״ע. ובזמן שמעידות זו ע״ז שכל א׳ אומרת אני וחברתי טהורה הרי אלו נאמנות דבשבויה הקילו והאמינו בה אפילו ע״א ואפי׳ אשה ולא חיישינן לגומלין. ת״ר אני טמאה וחברתי טהורה נאמנת. אני טהורה וחברתי טמאה אינה נאמנת. פי׳ אינה נאמנת על כלום. אני וחברתי טמאות נאמנת לפסול א״ע. ואינה נאמנת לפסול חברתה. אני וחברתי טהורה נאמנת על חברתה. ואינה נאמנת ע״ע: אמר מר אני טהורה וחברתי טמאה אינה נאמנת. ה״ד אי דליכא עדים שנשבו אעצמה אמאי לא מהימנא נשביתי וטהורה אני קאמרה. פי׳ בשלמא אחברתה אינה נאמנת שכיון שאין עדים שנשבית הותרה חברתה וכאומרת נשביתי וטהורה אני. וזו שאומרת עליה כי

חשק שלמה על תוס׳ רי״ד

א) הדבר צ״ע דלכתי איכא לאוקמי דהעידו עדות ברורה ומ״מ לא הויא הזמה כגון דאמרו דהמקדש היה עמנו במקום פלוני או דלאיתו דזרק הקידושין קרוב לו ולא היה קידושין כלל. ב) נ״ל ומר סבר דאפי׳ שלא בפניו נמי אינה מעיזה פי׳ דוקא.

מסורת הש״ס

א) [תוספתא פרק ב], ב) ב״ב לא ע״ב.

תוספות ישנים

א) והיינו סוגיא דלקמן דלא פסלה נפשה והוה אני למיפרך השתא ולשנויי. ת״י, ב) וי״ל דס״ד דהיא מהימנא טפי מעד אחד לפי שנשבית עמה ויודעת יותר. ת״י.

גליון הש״ס

מתני׳ זה אומר כהן אני. עיין בהרא״ש פ״ה דגיטין סי׳ ח בהגהות י:

תורה אור השלם

א) וַיֹּאמֶר שִׁמְשׁוֹן תָּמוֹת נַפְשִׁי עִם פְּלִשְׁתִּים וַיֵּט בְּכֹחַ וַיִּפֹּל הַבַּיִת עַל הַסְּרָנִים וְעַל כָּל הָעָם אֲשֶׁר בּוֹ וַיִּהְיוּ הַמֵּתִים אֲשֶׁר הֵמִית בְּמוֹתוֹ רַבִּים מֵאֲשֶׁר הֵמִית בְּחַיָּיו: [שופטים טז, ל]

ליקוטי רש״י

אין מעלין לכהונה. להחזיק אדם בכהן לאכול בתרומה ולעבוד עבודה ולישא את כפיו. על פי עד אחד. המעידו שהוא כהן כדמפרש ר׳ אלעזר לקמיה [בשמעתין]. אמר רבי אלעזר אימתי. אין מעלין ע״פ עד אחד בזמן שיש על הכהן עוררין עדים הפוסלים אותו כדמפרש בסמוך ולפרש דברי ר׳ יהודה בא ולא לחלוק עליו. אבל במקום שאין עוררין. אלא קול פסול בעלמא כדמפרש לקמיה מעלין ע״פ עד אחד שמכחיש את הקול [רשב״ם ב״ב לא:]. דררא דממונא. חסרון ממון [ב״מ ב:].

מאי שנא רישא ומאי שנא סיפא אמר אביי תרגמה בעד אחד [א] עד אחד אומר נתקדשה ועד אחד אומר לא נתקדשה תרווייהו בפנויה קמסהדי והאי דקאמר נתקדשה הוה ליה חד ואין דבריו של אחד במקום שנים סיפא עד אחד אומר נתגרשה ועד אחד אומר לא נתגרשה תרווייהו באשת איש קמסהדי והאי דקאמר נתגרשה הוה ליה חד ואין דבריו של אחד במקום שנים [ה] רב אשי אמר לעולם תרי ותרי ואיפוך [ב] שנים אומרים ראינוה שנתקדשה ושנים אומרים לא ראינוה שנתקדשה הרי זו לא תנשא ואם נשאת תצא פשיטא [ג] לא ראינוה אינה ראיה לא צריכא דדיירי בחצר אחד מהו דתימא אם איתא דנתקדשה קלא אית לה למילתא קא משמע לן דעבדי אינשי דמקדשי בצנעא סיפא [ד] שנים אומרים ראינוה שנתגרשה ושנים אומרים לא ראינוה שנתגרשה הרי זו לא תנשא ואם נשאת לא תצא מאי קמ"ל אע"ג דדיירי בחצר אחד היינו הך מהו דתימא גבי קדושין הוא דעבדי אינשי דמקדשי בצנעא אבל גבי גירושין אם איתא דאיגרשה קלא אית לה למילתא קמ"ל דעבידי אינשי דמקדשי ודמגרשי בצנעא: ואם משנשאת באו עדים לא תצא כו': רבי אושעיא [ג] מתני לה ארישא רבה בר אבין מתני לה אסיפא מאן דמתני לה ארישא כ"ש אסיפא [ד] דבשבויה הקילו ומאן דמתני לה אסיפא [ד] אבל ארישא לא לימא בדרב המנונא קמיפלגי דמאן דמתני לה ארישא אית ליה דרב המנונא ומאן דמתני לה אסיפא לית ליה דרב המנונא והכא בהא קמיפלגי דמר סבר כי איתמר דרב המנונא בפניו [ה] אבל שלא בפניו מעיזה ומר סבר שלא בפניו נמי אינה מעיזה: ואם משנשאת באו עדים וכו': אמר אבוה דשמואל לא נשאת נשאת ממש אלא [ו] כיון שהתירוה לינשא אע"פ שלא נשאת והא לא תצא קתני לא תצא מהתירה הראשון [ח] ת"ר אמרה [ז] נשביתי וטהורה אני ויש לי עדים שטהורה אני אין אומרים נמתין עד שיבאו עדים אלא מתירין אותה מיד התירוה לינשא ואחר כך באו עדים ואמרו לא ידענו הרי זו לא תצא [ח] ואם באו עדי טומאה אפי' יש לה כמה בנים תצא הני שבוייתא דאתיין לנהרדעא אותיב אבוה דשמואל נטורי בהדייהו א"ל שמואל ועד האידנא מאן נטרינהו א"ל אילו בנתך הווין מי הוית מזלזל בהו כולי האי הואי [א] כשגגה שיוצא מלפני השליט ואישתביין בנתיה דמר שמואל ואסקינהו לארעא דישראל אוקמן לשבויינהו מאבראי ועיילי לבי מדרשא דר' חנינא הא אמרה נשביתי וטהורה אני והא אמרה נשביתי וטהורה אני [ט] שרינהו סוף עול אתו שבויינהו אמר רבי חנינא [ט] בנן דמוריין אינון איגלאי מילתא דבנתיה דמר שמואל הווין אמר ליה רבי חנינא לרב שמן בר אבא פוק איטפל בקרובותיך אמר ליה לרבי חנינא והאיכא עדים במדינת הים השתא מיהת ליתנהו קמן עדים בצד [י] אסתן ותאסר טעמא דלא אתו עדים הא אתו עדים מיתסרא והאמר אבוה דשמואל כיון שהתירוה לינשא אף על פי שלא נשאת אמר רב אשי עדי טומאה איתמר:

מתני'

רש"י

תרווייהו בפנויה קמסהדי. לדברי שניהם עד עכשיו בחזקת פנויה היתה [קודם שנתקדשה]: איפוך. ברישא תני אם ניסת תצא וסיפא אם ניסת לא תצא: דמגרשי בצנעא. ואפילו הכי לכתחלה לא תנשא משום לזות שפתים: ארישא. אם משניסת באו עדים שהיתה אשת איש והיא ניסת על פי עצמה שאמרה גרושה אני: אסיפא. אמרה נשביתי וטהורה אני והתירוה לינשא ואח"כ באו עדים שנשבית: בשבויה הקילו. דמעשה בעלמא הוא דאיכא שמא נבעלה לעובד כוכבים ונפסלה לכהונה: דרב המנונא. דאמר האשה שאמרה לבעלה גירשתני נאמנת הלכך הא דאמרה גרושה אני מהימנא: ויש לי עדים. שהיו עמי תמיד שלא נתייחדתי עם עובד כוכבים: ואח"כ באו עדים. שנשבית דהשתא לאו הפה שאסר הוא אפי' הכי לא תצא: אפי' יש לה כמה בנים. מן הכהן הזה שנשאה: דאתיין לנהרדעא. להפדותן: אוקמינהו לשבויינהו אבראי. שלא יבואו לפני ב"ד ולא ידעו ב"ד שהן שבויות אלא ע"פ עצמן ויתירום: בנן דמוריין אינון. בנות אדם גדול ובעל הוראה הוא שידעו לעשות כן: לרב שמן. כהן היה: איטפל בקרובותיך. שלא אחת מהן שהן קרובותיך: והא איכא סהדי במדינת הים. שהלא שנשבו ודלמא אתו לקמן למחר וליימא אותן לאחר שתנשא: השתא מיהא לא איתנהו. קודם נישואין ומשום דלמא אתו לא אסרינן לה השתא: עדים בצד אסתן. בצד לפון [מלפון זהב יאתה (איוב לז) מתרגם מלאיסתנא]: ותאסר. בתמיה הא [לא] אתו קודם נשואין:

תוספות

מאי שנא רישא ומאי שנא סיפא. ואם תאמר שנא ושנא דרישא איכא לאוקמה בחזקת פנויה וסיפא בחזקת אשת איש ויש לומר דברישא אע"ג דאית לן לאוקמה בחזקת פנויה מ"מ תרי ותרי ספיקא דרבנן היא כדמוכח בפרק ד' אחין (יבמות דף לא. ושם) והוה לן למימר תצא מדרבנן וי"מ כיון דלא מפליג בין באו עדים עד שלא ניסת לבאו עדים משניסת ש"מ דלאו רבי מנחם בר יוסי היא אלא רבנן א"כ סיפא נמי אמאי תצא הא שמעינן להו דאמרי לא תצא:

תרווייהו בפנויה קמסהדי. לא הוה צריך להא דאפי' ליכא אלא ההוא דאמר נתקדשה לא תצא דאין דבר שבערוה פחות משנים אבל תימה אמאי לא תנשא לכתחלה דהוה לן לאוקמה אחזקה וי"ל כגון שאנו יודעים שזרק לה קדושין ומספקא לן אי קרוב לו או קרוב לה והני ב' סהדי חד אמר קרוב לו וחד אמר קרוב לה דכיון דודאי זרק לה הקדושין לית לן למימר אוקמה אחזקה להתירה לכתחילה אי נמי כגון שהיו נרות דולקות ומטות מוצעות שהיה עומד לקדש כדאמר בסוף המגרש (גיטין פט.) ועד אחד אומר נתקדשה ועד אחד אומר לא נתקדשה באותה שעה:

מאן דמתני לה ארישא כל שכן אסיפא. וא"ת מנא ליה דלמא אסיפא לא מצי קאי דאפי' באו עדים ואחר כך נשאת לא תצא ולמאי דמפרש בסמוך לא ניסת ניסת ממש אתי שפיר: אית ליה דרב המנונא. אע"ג [ה] דרב המנונא איירי בפניו מ"מ לענין ניסת ואח"כ באו עדים מהני שלא בפניו: לא תצא מהיתרה הראשון. פירוש ותנשא [לכתחלה] דלא שייך לזות שפתים כלל אבל אין לפרש כי ההיא דיבמות דלא תצא מהיתרה הראשון לענין דאם נשאת לא תצא אבל לכתחלה לא תינשא כדמשמע גבי בנתיה דמר שמואל בסמוך שהתירן [א] לכתחילה:

באו עדים לא תצא. פירוש לא תצא מהיתרה הראשון:

עד האידנא מאן נטרינהו. פי' דכבר נאסרו: והא איכא עדים במדינת הים. אין לפרש דלמא איכא עדים במדינת הים דאם כן תיקשי ליה נמי אמתניתין דקתני נשביתי וטהורה אני נאמנת ואמאי דלמא איכא עדים אלא הכי פירושה הא יצא קול דאיכא עדים במדינת הים שיודעים שנשבית ומיהו קשה לרשב"א דהיכי סלקא דעתיה השתא דעדים היינו עדי שבויה דא"כ מה הוה צריך למימר הא איכא עדים במדינת הים הוה ליה למימר הא איכא עדים קמן דהא איכא שבוינהו [ב]: עדי טומאה איתמר. והא איכא עדים במדינת הים דפריך לעיל פירוש והא יצא קול דאיכא התם עדי טומאה כדפירשתי הקשה ר"ת בפרק קמא דקידושין (דף יב.) גבי ההוא גברא דקדיש באבנא דכוחלא ויתיב רב חסדא וקא משער אי אית בה שוה פרוטה אי לא ומסיק לאו היינו דר' חנינא דאמר עדים בצד אסתן ותאסר וקאמר אביי ורבא לא סבירא להו הא דרב חסדא אם הקילו בשבויה נקל באשת איש והשתא למאי דמסיק דעדי טומאה איתמר מה לי עדי שבויה מה לי עדי אשת איש ורש"י [ז] פירש שם אם הקילו בשבויה דלאיסור לאו וקשה לרבינו תם דבשבויה נמי איכא איסור סקילה אם נשאת לכהן שישמש בנה על גבי מזבח בשבת ומיהו אית ספרים דגרסי התם אם הקילו בשבויה דמנוולה נפשה באפי שבויה כו' פירוש ולא שכיח כולי האי שנטמאה נקל באשת איש דשכיח דידעי אם אית בה שוה פרוטה ובלאו הך גירסא איכא למימר דלא שכיח שיהו עדי טומאה אבל עדים שידעו ששוה פרוטה שכיח [ג]:

שתי

גליון הש"ס

גמ' שרינהו סוף עול אתו שבוינהו. עיין ב"ק קמט ע"א תד"ה רב מרי. שם קנד ע"ב תד"ה ואמרי לה: תוס' ד"ה אית ליה. אע"ג דרב המנונא איירי בפניו. עיין יבמות קטו ע"ב תד"ה בלותה שעה:

תורה אור השלם

א) יֵשׁ רָעָה רָאִיתִי תַּחַת הַשָּׁמֶשׁ כִּשְׁגָגָה שֶׁיֹּצָא מִלִּפְנֵי הַשַּׁלִּיט: [קהלת י, ה]

ליקוטי רש"י

[נדפס בדף כב:]

Kohen **is that the** alleged **witnesses have not** yet **come** before the court to testify that she was captured. הָא אָתוּ עֵדִים מִיתַּסְרָא – **But** once the **witnesses come,** R' Chanina would agree that **she is forbidden.** וְהָאָמַר אֲבוּהַּ דִשְׁמוּאֵל – **However, the father of Shmuel has said:** כֵּיוָן שֶׁהִתִּירוּהָ לִינָּשֵׂא – **Once they permit her to marry,** אַף עַל פִּי שֶׁלֹּא נִשֵּׂאת – **even though she did not** yet **marry,** she remains permitted to do so, even after witnesses testify to her capture.[41] – ? –

The Gemara answers:

אָמַר רַב אַשִׁי – **Rav Ashi said:** עֲדֵי טוּמְאָה אִיתְּמַר – **It was stated** that Rav Shemen bar Abba was concerned about **witnesses to her defilement.**[42]

NOTES

41. Thus, it would appear that R' Chanina disagrees with the father of Shmuel. This cannot be treated simply as a dispute betweeen Amoraim, because the opinion of the father of Shmuel is accepted as authoritive halachah and it is supported by the Baraisa quoted earlier (*Ritva;* see note 30).

[In point of fact, other parts of the narrative demonstrate that R' Chanina *agrees* with the father of Shmuel. By praising the women ("children of a halachic master"), he indicated that their scheme was effective in allowing them to remain permitted to marry Kohanim even after the court saw their captors. Furthermore, it is evident that he considered them to still be permitted from the fact that he told Rav Shemen bar Abba, who was a Kohen, to marry one of them (see the sources listed at the end of note 38; see also *Ritva*).]

42. If witnesses testify to her *defilement* after she had already married a Kohen, she would certainly have to leave him. Therefore, the rumor about such witnesses should be sufficient grounds to prohibit her to marry a Kohen in the first place. R' Chanina nevertheless replied that since the witnesses are not currently before us, their existence can be disregarded.

The Gemara elsewhere (*Kiddushin* 12b, *Bava Basra* 135a) concludes that this is a leniency applicable only to a captured woman (see note 20). In other areas of law, the rumored existence of witnesses must be taken into consideration even if they have not yet appeared before the court (*Rashba, Ritva*).

[For the continuation of this incident, see *Yerushalmi* (cited by *Yefei Einayim*); see also *Rashi* to *Berachos* 16a ד״ה ברה דבת שמואל, *Tosefos* to *Shabbos* 154a ד״ה ואמרי and to *Bava Basra* 149a.]

מאי שנא רישא ומאי שנא סיפא אמר אביי תרגמה בעד אחד [א] עד אחד אומר נתקדשה ועד אחד אומר לא נתקדשה תרוייהו בפנויה קמסהדי והאי דקאמר נתקדשה הוה ליה חד ואין דבריו של אחד במקום שנים סיפא עד אחד אומר נתגרשה ועד אחד אומר לא נתגרשה תרוייהו באשת איש קמסהדי והאי דקאמר נתגרשה הוה ליה חד ואין דבריו של אחד במקום שנים (א) רב אשי אמר לעולם תרי ותרי ואיפוך [ב] שנים אומרים ראינוה שנתקדשה ושנים אומרים לא ראינוה שנתקדשה הרי זו לא תנשא ואם נשאת תצא פשיטא (ג) לא ראינוה אינה ראיה לא צריכא דדיירי בחצר אחד מהו דתימא אם איתא דנתקדשה קלא אית לה למילתא קא משמע לן דעבדי אינשי דמקדשי בצנעא סיפא [ג] שנים אומרים ראינוה שנתגרשה ושנים אומרים לא ראינוה שנתגרשה הרי זו לא תנשא ואם נשאת לא תצא מאי קמ"ל אע"ג דדיירי בחצר אחד היינו הך מהו דתימא גבי קדושין הוא דעבדי אינשי דמקדשי בצנעא אבל גבי גירושין אם איתא דאיגרשה קלא אית לה למילתא קמ"ל דעבדי אינשי דמקדשי ודמגרשי בצנעא: ואם משנשאת באו עדים לא תצא כו': רבי אושעיא (ג) מתני לה ארישא רבה בר אבין מתני לה אסיפא מאן דמתני לה ארישא כ"ש אסיפא (ד) דבשבויה הקילו ומאן דמתני לה אסיפא [ד] אבל ארישא לא לימא בדרב המנונא קמיפלגי דמאן דמתני לה ארישא אית ליה דרב המנונא ומאן דמתני לה אסיפא לית ליה דרב המנונא לא דכולי עלמא אית להו דרב המנונא והכא בהא קמיפלגי דמר סבר כי איתמר דרב המנונא בפניו [ה] אבל שלא בפניו מעיזה ומר סבר שלא בפניו נמי אינה מעיזה: ואם משנשאת באו עדים וכו': אמר אבוה דשמואל לא נשאת נשאת ממש אלא [ו] כיון שהתירוה לינשא אע"פ שלא נשאת והא לא תצא קתני לא תצא מהתירה הראשון (ה) ת"ר אמרה [ז] נשביתי וטהורה אני ויש לי עדים שטהורה אני אין אומרים נמתין עד שיבאו עדים אלא מתירין אותה מיד התירוה לינשא ואחר כך באו עדים ואמרו לא ידענו הרי זו לא תצא [ח] ואם באו עדי טומאה אפי' יש לה כמה בנים תצא הני שבוייתא דאתיין לנהרדעא אותיב אבוה דשמואל נטורי בהדייהו א"ל שמואל ועד האידנא מאן נטרינהו א"ל אילו בנתך הוין מי הוית מזלזל בהו כולי האי הואי (א) כשגגה שיוצא מלפני השליט ואישתביין בנתיה דמר שמואל ואסקינהו לארעא דישראל אוקמן לשבוינהו מאבראי ועיילי לבי מדרשא דר' חנינא הא אמרה נשביתי וטהורה אני והא אמרה נשביתי וטהורה אני [ט] שרינהו סוף אתו שבוינהו [ט] אמר רבי חנינא בנן דמוריין אינון אגלאי מילתא דבנתיה דמר שמואל הוין אמר ליה רבי חנינא לרב שמן בר אבא פוק איטפל בקרובותיך אמר ליה לרבי חנינא והאיכא עדים במדינת הים השתא מיהת ליתנהו קמן עדים בצד [י] אסתן ותאסר טעמא דלא אתו עדים הא אתו עדים מיתסרא והאמר אבוה דשמואל כיון שהתירוה לינשא אף על פי שלא נשאת אמר רב אשי עדי טומאה איתמר: מתני'

רש"י

תרוייהו בפנויה קמסהדי. לדברי שניהם עד עכשיו בחזקת פנויה היתה [קודם שנתקדשה]: **איפוך.** ברישא תני אם ניסת תצא וסיפא אם ניסת לא תצא: **דמגרשי בצנעא.** ואפילו הכי לכתחלה לא תנשא משום לזות שפתים: **ארישא.** אם משניסת באו עדים שהיתה אשת איש והיא ניסת על פי עצמה שאמרה גרושה אני: **אסיפא.** אנשביתי וטהורה אני והתירוה לינשא ואח"כ באו עדים שנשבית: **בשבויה הקילו.** דחששא בעלמא הוא דאיכא שמא נבעלה לעובד כוכבים ונפסלה לכהונה: **דרב המנונא.** דאמר האשה שאמרה לבעלה גירשתני נאמנת הלכך הא דאמרה גרושה אני מהימנא: **ויש לי עדים.** שהיו עמי תמיד שלא נתייחדתי עם עובד כוכבים: **ואח"כ באו עדים.** שנשבית דהשתא לאו הפה שאסר הוא אפי' הכי לא תצא: **אפי' יש לה כמה בנים.** מן הכהן הזה שנשאה: **דאתיין לנהרדעא.** להפדותן: **אוקמינהו לשבויינהו אבראי.** שלא יבואו לפני ב"ד ולא ידעו ב"ד שהן שבויות אלא ע"פ עצמן ויתירום: **בנן דמוריין אינון.** בנות אדם גדול ובעל הוראה הוא שידעו לעשות כן: **לרב שמן.** כהן היה: **איטפל בקרובותיך.** שא אחת מהן שהן קרובותיך: **והא איכא סהדי במדינת הים.** שראו שנשבו ודלמא אתו לקמן למחר וליומא אוחרן לאחר שתנשא: **השתא מיהא לא איתנהו.** קודם נישואין ומשום דלמא אתו לא אסרינן לה השתא: **עדים בצד אסתן.** בצד צפון [מצפון זהב יאתה (איוב לז) מתרגם מדאיסתנא]: **ותאסר.** בתמיה הא [לא] אתו קודם נשואין: מתני'

תוספות

מאי שנא רישא ומאי שנא סיפא. ואם תאמר שנא ושנא דרישא אית לן לאוקמה בחזקת פנויה וסיפא בחזקת אשת איש ויש לומר דברישא אע"ג דאית לן לאוקמה בחזקת פנויה מ"מ תרי ותרי ספיקא דרבנן היא כדמוכח בפרק ד' אחין (יבמות דף לא. ושם) והוה לן למימר תצא מדרבנן וי"מ כיון דלא מפליג בין באו עדים עד שלא ניסת לבאו עדים משניסת ש"מ דלאו רבי מנחם בר יוסי היא אלא רבנן א"כ סיפא נמי אמאי תצא הא שמעינן להו דאמרי לא תצא:

תרוייהו בפנויה קמסהדי. לא הוה צריך להא דאפי' ליכא אלא ההוא דאמר נתקדשה לא תצא דאין דבר שבערוה פחות משנים אבל תימה אמאי לא תנשא לכתחלה דהוה לן לאוקמה אחזקה וי"ל כגון שאנו יודעים שזרק לה קדושין ומספקא לן אי קרוב לו או קרוב לה והני ב' סהדי חד אמר קרוב לו וחד אמר קרוב לה דכיון דודאי זרק לה הקדושין לית לן למימר אוקמה אחזקה להתירה לכתחילה אי נמי כגון שהיו נרות דולקות ומטות מוצעות שהיה עומד לקדש כדאמר בסוף המגרש (גיטין פט.) ועד אחד אומר נתקדשה ועד אחד אומר לא נתקדשה באותה שעה:

מאן דמתני לה ארישא כל שכן אסיפא. וא"ת מנא ליה דלמא אסיפא לא מצי קאי דאפי' באו עדים ואחר כך נשאת לא תצא ולמאי דמפרש בסמוך לא ניסת ממש אתי שפיר: **אית** ליה דרב המנונא. אע"ג ה) דרב המנונא איירי בפניו מ"מ לענין ניסת ואח"כ באו עדים מהני שלא בפניו: **לא** תצא מהיתרה הראשון. פירוש ותנשא [לכתחלה] דלא שייך לזות שפתים כלל אבל אין לפרש כי ההיא דיבמות דלא תצא מהיתרה הראשון לענין דאם נשאת לא תצא אבל לכתחלה לא תינשא כדמשמע גבי בנתיה דמר שמואל בסמוך שהתירן אף לכתחילה:

באו עדים לא תצא. פירוש לא תצא מהיתרה הראשון:

עד האידנא מאן נטרינהו. פי' דכבר נאסרו:

והא איכא עדים במדינת הים. אין לפרש דלמא איכא עדים במדינת הים דאם כן מיקשי ליה נמי אמתניתין דקתני נשביתי וטהורה אני נאמנת ומאי דלמא איכא אלא הכי פירושו הא יצא קול דאיכא עדים במדינת הים שיודעים שנשבית ומיהו קשה לרשב"א דהיכי סלקא דעתיה השתא דעדים היינו עדי שבויה דא"כ מה הוה צריך למימר הא איכא עדים במדינת הים הוה ליה למימר הא איכא עדים קמן דהא איכא שבוינהו ב):

עדי טומאה איתמר. והא איכא עדים במדינת הים דפריך לעיל פירוש והא יצא קול דאיכא התם עדי טומאה כדפירשתי הקשה ר"ת בפרק קמא דקידושין (דף יב.) גבי ההוא גברא דקדיש באבנא דכוחלא ויתיב רב חסדא וקא משער אי אית בה שוה פרוטה אי לא ומסיק לאו היינו דר' חנינא דאמר עדים בצד אסתן ותאסר וקאמר אביי ורבא לא סבירא להו הא דרב חסדא אם הקילו בשבויה נקל באשת איש והשתא למאי דמסיק דעדי טומאה איתמר מה לי עדי שבויה מה לי עדי אשת איש ורש"י ז) פירש שם אם הקילו בשבויה דאיסור לאו וקשה לרבינו תם דבשבויה נמי איכא איסור סקילה אם נשאת לכהן שישמש בנה על גבי מזבח בשבת ומיהו אית ספרים דגרסי התם אם הקילו בשבויה דמנוולה נפשה באפי שבויה כו' פירוש ולא שכיח כולי האי שנטמאה נקל באשת איש דשכיח דידעי אם אית בה שוה פרוטה ובלאו הך גירסא איכא למימר דלא שכיח שיהו עדי טומאה אבל עדים שידעו ששוה פרוטה שכיח ג):

שתי

מסורת הש"ס

א) פ"א רב אפי, ב) [זבחים קג:], ג) [לקמן כד.], ד) [לקמן מו: נא: קדושין יב: ב"ק קיד.], ה) [תוס' פ"ב], ו) קדושין יב: ב"ב קלה., ז) [לפנינו שם ברש"י לא נמצא ועי' תוס' שם ד"ה אם הקלנו וכו' כתבו דבר זה בשם יש מפרשים].

תוספות ישנים

א) [לכתחלה דפריך טעמא דליכא עדים הא איכא עדים מתסרא ומאי פריך אי מתסרא לכתחלה. ת"י עה"ג]. ב) [וי"ל דמתמת השבאים לא אימסרו דהא לאו אתו בתר דשרינהו אבל הכא מתמת שבא הקול מקמי שריותא דידהו איכא למסרינהו וה"פ טעמא דלא אתו עדים הא אתו עדים מיתסרא כיון שנתגלה הקול שיש עדים מלפני ההיתר. ת"י עה"ג]. ג) [ולמאי דס"ד מעיקרא דעדי שבויה ניחא דהוי ספק ספיקא ספק אם נשבית אם לאו ואת"ל נשבית ספק לא נטמאת ובאשת איש ליכא אלא חדא ספיקא. ת"י עה"ג]:

גליון הש"ס

גמ' שרינהו סוף עול' אתו שבוינהו. עיין ב"ב קמט ע"א תד"ה כל מרי. שבת קנד ע"ב תד"ה ואמרי לה: תוס' ד"ה אית ליה. אע"ג דרב המנונא איירי בפניו. עיין יבמות קטז ע"ב תד"ה באותה שעה:

תורה אור השלם

א) יֵשׁ רָעָה רָאִיתִי תַּחַת הַשָּׁמֶשׁ כִּשְׁגָגָה שֶׁיֹּצָא מִלִּפְנֵי הַשַּׁלִּיט: [קהלת י, ה]

ליקוטי רש"י

[נדפס בדף כב:]

עין משפט נר מצוה

עא א מיי' פ"ע מהל' אישות הלכה לא טוש"ע אה"ע סימן מז סעיף ג:
עב ב מיי' שם הלכה ל טוש"ע שם סעיף א:
עג ג מיי' פי"ב מהל' גירושין הלכה ח טוש"ע שם סימן קנב סעיף ד:
עד ד מיי' שם הלכה א טור שו"ע שם סעיף ז:
עה ה מיי' שם הלכה ד טוש"ע שם סימן יח סעיף ג:
עו ו מיי' פי"ח מהל' איסורי ביאה הלכ' כב טוש"ע שם סי' ז סעיף ו:
עז ז מיי' שם הלכה כג טור שו"ע שם סעי':
עח ח ט מיי' שם טור שו"ע שם סעיף ו:

תוספות רי"ד

מ"ש רישא ומ"ש סיפא פי' שאין לומר טעמא דרישא משום דאמרינן אוקי תרי לבהדי תרי ואוקי איתתא (אחזקה) [בחזקת פנויה] דהוו תרי ותרי הן ספיקא דאורייתא ובספיקא דאורייתא לא אזלינן בתר חזקה אלא הבא עליה באשם תלוי קאי אמר (ר"פ) [אביי] תרגמה בע"א. ע"א אומר נתקדשה וע"א אומר לא נתקדשה תרוייהו בפנויה קמסהדי והאי דאמר נתקדשה הו"ל חד ואין דבריו של א' במקום ב'. ע"א אומר נתגרשה וע"א אומר לא נתגרשה תרוייהו באשת איש קמסהדי והאי דאמר נתגרשה הו"ל חד ואין דבריו של א' במקום שנים. ופי' לאו במוחזקת לפנינו שהיא א"א איירי. דא"כ מה צורך להכחשת העד שאומר לא נתגרשה בלא הכחשתו נמי אינו נאמן ע"א בגירושין ואפי' לאביי דאמר ע"א נאמן באיסורין ואפילו באשה ה"מ לאסור כגון אשתו דינתה בע"א בפ' האומר [קדושין סו ע"ש] דאביי אמר ע"א נאמן בכל איסורין שבתורה ורבא אמר אין דבר שבערוה פחות משנים. ודוקא לאיסור היה אומר אביי דע"א נאמן אבל אשה שהוחזקה בא"א אין מי שיאמר שיהא ע"א נאמן לומר נתגרשה ולהוציאה מחזקת א"א דדוקא במת בעלך האמינו חכמים ע"א משום דמילתא דעבידי לגלויי לא משקרא והיא גופא דייקא ומנסבא. ומתוך חומר שהחמרת עליה בסופה הקלת עליה מתחלתה אבל בגירושין לא מהימן. עיין בהאשה רבה. ולא מתוקמא אלא באשה הבאה ממדה"י שלא ידענו מי היא ובאים אלה השנים ומעידים עליה כי א"א היתה אלא שא' אומר נתגרשה ואחד אומר לא נתגרשה. והלשון מוכיח כן שאומר תרוייהו בא"א קמסהדי. דמשמע שלא החזקה א"א אלא על פיהם. ואע"ג דאיהי נמי אמרה א"א הייתי וגרושה אני [מ"מ] כיון שיש עדים (שהיתה) [שאומרים] שא"א היתה אינה נאמנת. ועוד שהעד מכחישה ואומר לא נתגרשה. והלכך אם נשאת תצא אבל בודאי אם נשאת תחלה על פיה כשאמרה א"א הייתי וגרושה אני ואח"כ בא העד שאוסרה שאומר לא נתגרשה לא תצא. שאין מוציאין אשה מבעלה בע"א כדרבא דאמר אין דבר שבערוה פחות מב'. וכי היכי דבגירושין לא מתוקמא אלא באשה הבאה ממדה"י שאין לה חזקה מה היא ה"נ עדות דקידושין לא מתוקם אלא בבאה ממדה"י שלא הוחזקה מה היא. והלשון מוכיח דקאמר תרוייהו בפנויה מסהדי. דמשמע שלא הוחזקה פנויה אלא על פיהן. אבל אשה העומדת לפנינו בחזקת פנויה. ובא ע"א ואמר נתקדשה בפני פ' ופ' והלכו להן למדינת הים. אע"פ שאין עד אחר שיכחישנו. אינו נאמן לאוסרה עד שיבואו שנים כדרבא דאמר אין דבר שבערוה פחות מב'. ולכתחלה לא תנשא. ר"א אמר לעולם תרי ותרי ואיפוך פי' המורה ברישא תני תצא. ובסיפא תני לא תצא. **ב' אומרים** ראינוה שנתקדשה וב' אומרים לא ראינוה שנתקדשה ה"ז לא תנשא. פשיטא לא ראינו אינו ראיה. ל"צ דדיירו בחצר א'. מ"ד אי איתא דקדיש קלא אית ליה למילתא קמ"ל דעבידי אינשי דמקדשי בצנעא. **ואי קשה** טעמא דאמר' לא ראינוה שנתקדשה דלא ראינוה אינה ראיה אבל אי אמרי (בעיקר) [בבירור] דלא נתקדשה כגון דאמרו האשה או המקדש הי' עמנו במקום פ' שמעידים עדות ברורה. ה"נ דאם נשאת לא תצא א) ואמאי לא תצא. תרי ותרי נינהו והבא עלי' באשם תלוי קאי. ואי אמרת דר"א קסבר דאפילו בתרי ותרי אמרי' אוקי אתתא אחזקתה. א"כ מה צורך לאפוכי במאי דתניא מפרשא שפיר גבי נתקדשה לא תצא דאוקמי' לה אחזקה קמייתא ופנויה הות וגבי נתגרשה תצא דמוקמינן לה אחזקתה דא"א הות. ומדלא אוקמוה הכי ש"מ דלא אמרינן תרי ותרי אוקמה אחזקתה. משום דהוי ספק תורה והבא עליה באשם תלוי קאי. תשובה. אילו העידו עדות ברורה. כגון שאמרו אנו היינו כל היום עמכם באותו חצר ולא נתפרדנו מהם כלל ולא יתכן שנתקדשה באותו היום שאילו כך גם אנחנו היינו רואים המעשה. אלא שקר אתם מעידים. אין לומר בכאן תרי ותרי נינהו. שזאת היא הזמה

חשק שלמה על תוס' רי"ד א) ולפי מש"כ הר"ן כאן דמיירי שנשאת לאחד מעדיה שאמרו לא ראינו שנתקדשה לק"מ ועי' לעיל (דף כב ע"ב) כגון שנשאת וכו' ודו"ק.

A related Baraisa:
תָּנוּ רַבָּנָן – **The Rabbis taught in a Baraisa:** אָמְרָה נִשְׁבֵּיתִי וּטְהוֹרָה אֲנִי – **IF [A WOMAN] SAID], "I WAS CAPTURED BUT I AM PURE,** וְיֵשׁ לִי עֵדִים שֶׁטְּהוֹרָה אֲנִי – **AND I HAVE WITNESSES** who can testify **THAT I AM PURE,"**[28] אֵין אוֹמְרִים – **WE DO NOT SAY:** נַמְתִּין עַד שֶׁיָּבֹאוּ עֵדִים – **LET US WAIT UNTIL THE WITNESSES COME;** אֶלָּא מַתִּירִין אוֹתָהּ מִיָּד – **RATHER, WE PERMIT HER IMMEDIATELY** to marry a Kohen. הִתִּירוּהָ לִינָּשֵׂא – **IF THEY** [the court] **HAD ALREADY PERMITTED HER TO MARRY** a Kohen, וְאַחַר כָּךְ בָּאוּ עֵדִים וְאָמְרוּ לֹא יָדַעְנוּ – **AND THEN WITNESSES CAME AND SAID, "WE DO NOT KNOW** [whether she is pure],"[29] הֲרֵי זוֹ לֹא תֵּצֵא – **THIS** woman **DOES NOT LEAVE.**[30] וְאִם בָּאוּ עֵדֵי טוּמְאָה – **BUT IF WITNESSES TO** her **DEFILEMENT CAME,** אֲפִילוּ יֵשׁ לָהּ כַּמָּה בָּנִים תֵּצֵא – **EVEN IF SHE** had married a Kohen in the meantime and **HAS MANY CHILDREN** from him, **SHE** must **LEAVE** him.[31]

The Gemara narrates two incidents involving women who were captured by idolaters:
הָנֵי שְׁבוּיָיתָא דְּאַתְיָין לִנְהַרְדְּעָא – There were **these captured women who were brought to Nehardea** to be ransomed. אוֹתֵיב אֲבוּהַ דִּשְׁמוּאֵל נָטוֹרֵי בַּהֲדַיְיהוּ – **The father of Shmuel placed guards over them** so that they would not be violated by their captors. אֲמַר לֵיהּ שְׁמוּאֵל – **Shmuel asked [his father]:** וְעַד הָאִידָּנָא מַאן נַטְרִינְהוּ – **"And until now who was guarding them?"** What is the point of guarding them now?[32] אֲמַר לֵיהּ – **He answered [Shmuel]:** אִילּוּ בְּנָתָךְ הֲוְיָין מִי הֲוֵית מְזַלְזֵל בְּהוּ כּוּלֵּי הַאי – **"If they were your daughters, would you treat them so lightly?"**[33] הֲוַאי ,,כִּשְׁגָגָה שֶׁיֹּצָא מִלִּפְנֵי הַשַּׁלִּיט" – **It** [the preceding remark] **was** *like an error proceeding from a ruler,*[34] וְאִישְׁתַּבְיָין בְּנָתֵיהּ דְּמָר שְׁמוּאֵל – **and the daughters of the master Shmuel were captured.** וְאַסְּקִינְהוּ לְאַרְעָא דְּיִשְׂרָאֵל – **They were taken up** from Babylonia **to Eretz Yisrael.** אוֹקְמָן לִשְׁבוּיַיְנְהוּ וְעַיְילֵי לְבֵי מַאַבְרַאי – **They left their captors standing outside** מִדְרְשָׁא דְּרַבִּי חֲנִינָא – **and entered the study hall of R' Chanina.**[35] הָא אָמְרָה נִשְׁבֵּיתִי וּטְהוֹרָה אֲנִי – **This one said, "I was captured but I am pure,"** וְהָא אָמְרָה נִשְׁבֵּיתִי וּטְהוֹרָה אֲנִי – **and this one said, "I was captured but I am pure."** שָׁרְינְהוּ – **[R' Chanina] permitted them** to marry Kohanim. סוֹף עוּל אַתּוּ שְׁבוּיַיְנְהוּ – **Afterwards, their captors entered** the study hall. אָמַר רַבִּי חֲנִינָא – **R' Chanina said:** בְּנָן דְּמוֹרְיָין אִינּוּן – **"[These women] are** evidently **children of a halachic master!"**[36] אִיגַּלְאֵי מִילְּתָא דִּבְנָתֵיהּ דְּמָר שְׁמוּאֵל הֲוְיָין – **It became known that they were the daughters of the master Shmuel.** אָמַר לֵיהּ רַבִּי חֲנִינָא לְרַב שֶׁמֶן בַּר אַבָּא – **R' Chanina said to Rav Shemen bar Abba,** פּוּק אִיטַּפַּל בִּקְרוֹבוֹתֶיךָ – **"Go out, take care of your relatives."** That is, marry one of them![37] אָמַר לֵיהּ לְרַבִּי חֲנִינָא – **[Rav Shemen bar Abba] replied to R' Chanina:** וְהָאִיכָּא עֵדִים בִּמְדִינַת הַיָּם – **"But there are witnesses abroad!"**[38] הַשְׁתָּא מִיהַת לֵיתְנְהוּ קַמָּן – R' Chanina replied: **"Now, at least, they are not before us.** עֵדִים בְּצַד אִסְתָּן – **Witnesses are in the North,**[39] וְתֵאָסֵר – **and she should be prohibited** now on account of them?!"[40]

The Gemara finds difficulty with this last exchange:
טַעְמָא דְּלֹא אַתּוּ עֵדִים – **The reason** she is permitted to marry a

NOTES

it retains its literal meaning — namely, that should witnesses testify to her previous marriage *after* she has remarried, she does not have to leave her new husband. But if they testify *before* she remarries, she would be forbidden to marry in the first place, and if she nevertheless married, she would have to leave (*Ramban* et al. as explained by *Re'ah;* see *Rashi* ד״ה ארישא וד״ה אסיפא). Other Rishonim, though, hold that the Gemara's present interpretation of the final clause is valid even in the context of the Mishnah's first case (see *Re'ah; Ran; Tosafos* ד״ה מאן with *Pnei Yehoshua*). [Of course, this dispute is relevant only according to R' Oshaya, who maintains that the Mishnah's last clause does refer to the first case. Rabbah bar Avin, however, applies it *only* to the second case (see Gemara above). Thus, in *his* opinion, if a woman says, "I was married but I am divorced," and later witnesses testify that she was married, she would *always* have to leave her second husband, regardless of whether they testified before or after she remarried. The halachah accords with this opinion (see *Ran* and *Meiri*).]

28. She claims to have witnesses who can testify that they were with her constantly and [thus] she was never alone with an idolater (*Rashi*).

29. These witnesses, however, do know that she was captured. Thus, they provide the court with independent knowledge of her prohibited state, in which case the principle of *happeh she'assar* no longer applies (*Rashi*).

30. That is, she does not leave the state of permission already granted her by the court [as the father of Shmuel interpreted our Mishnah] (*Tosafos*). [This is evidently what the Baraisa means, for it specifies that the witnesses testified after the woman was *permitted* to marry (rather than after she *married*). See *Ran,* who explains why the Gemara did not say that this Baraisa corroborates the interpretation of our Mishnah given by the father of Shmuel.]

31. [Although the woman was previously believed (by virtue of the *happeh she'assar* principle) to say that she was not violated, and she has already married a Kohen, her word does not carry any weight at all where it is contradicted by two witnesses.]

32. They are already prohibited to Kohanim (*Tosafos*), for the very fact that they were captured suffices to render them forbidden.

Shmuel certainly recognized the need to appoint guards to protect the women from being violated by their kidnapers. His point was purely a theoretical one; namely, that the guards would not affect the women's status with respect to marrying Kohanim, since they are already forbidden (*Maharsha*).

33. Although Shmuel was speaking from a theoretical point of view, he should not have even *implied* that it was acceptable to leave the women without protection (*Maharsha;* see *Ritva* for another approach).

34. *Ecclesiastes* 10:5. I.e. like a royal decree made in error which is irreversible (*Rashi* ad loc.).

A man's words may inadvertently contain some prophecy of the future (see *Maharsha* to *Moed Katan* 18a). [One should therefore avoid the mention of anything undesirable that could happen in the future, lest his words carry a prophetic message, which once expressed is less likely to be reversed.]

35. By leaving their captors outside, the women ensured that R' Chanina's court would know of their captivity only through their own word. The court would consequently permit them to marry Kohanim [in accordance with the principle of *happeh she'assar*] (*Rashi*).

36. For they knew to do such a thing [i.e. to speak to the court before their captors entered] (*Rashi*).

37. R' Chanina told Rav Shemen (who was a Kohen) to marry one of the captives, because Rav Shemen was related to them (*Rashi*).

38. The Gemara initially assumes this to mean that there are witnesses who can testify that the women were *captured.* The existence of such witnesses was the subject of a rumor circulating among the local people (*Tosafos* et al.). Alternatively, there was definite knowledge that such witnesses existed (see *Tos. HaRosh*).

Rav Shemen was concerned that these witnesses might arrive and testify to the capture of these women after one had already married a Kohen (*Rashi*). He argued, therefore, that they should be prohibited to marry Kohanim in the first place.

[The Gemara's assumption that Rav Shemen refers to witnesses to the *capture* is problematic, because, if that were the case, Rav Shemen had no need to mention the existence of witnesses in a foreign land. After all, the court already knew of the capture by seeing the captors themselves, as is evident from the narrative. For solutions of this problem, see *Tos. Yeshanim, Ramban, Rashash, Mayim Chaim* and *Hagahos Yavetz.*]

39. An expression indicating that they are not currently before us (see *Rashi* to *Kiddushin* 12b ד״ה עידיה).

40. If these witnesses do not testify prior to the woman's marriage, we do not forbid her to marry a Kohen on the chance that they will testify after she is married (*Rashi;* see *Ritva*).

מאי שנא רישא ומאי שנא סיפא אמר אביי תרגמה בעד אחד [א]עד אחד אומר נתקדשה ועד אחד אומר לא נתקדשה תרוייהו בפנויה קמסהדי והאי דקאמר נתקדשה הוה ליה חד ואין דבריו של אחד במקום שנים סיפא עד אחד אומר נתגרשה ועד אחד אומר לא נתגרשה תרוייהו באשת איש קמסהדי והאי דקאמר נתגרשה הוה ליה חד ואין דבריו של אחד במקום שנים [ה]רב אשי אמר לעולם תרי ותרי ואיפוך [ב]שנים אומרים ראינוה שנתקדשה ושנים אומרים לא ראינוה שנתקדשה הרי זו לא תנשא ואם נשאת תצא פשיטא [ג]לא ראינוה אינה ראיה לא צריכא דדיירי בחצר אחד מהו דתימא אם איתא דנתקדשה קלא אית לה למילתא קא משמע לן דעבידי אינשי דמקדשי בצנעא סיפא [ד]שנים אומרים ראינוה שנתגרשה ושנים אומרים לא ראינוה שנתגרשה הרי זו לא תנשא ואם נשאת לא תצא מאי קמ"ל אע"ג דדיירי בחצר אחד היינו הך מהו דתימא גבי קדושין הוא דעבידי אינשי דמקדשי בצנעא אבל גבי גירושין אם איתא דאיגרשא קלא אית לה למילתא קמ"ל דעבידי אינשי דמקדשי ודמגרשי בצנעא: ואם משנשאת באו עדים לא תצא כו': רבי אושעיא [ג]מתני לה ארישא רבה בר אבין מתני לה אסיפא מאן דמתני לה ארישא כ"ש אסיפא [ד]דבשבויה הקילו ומאן דמתני לה אסיפא [ד]אבל ארישא לא לימא בדרב המנונא קמיפלגי דמאן דמתני לה ארישא אית ליה דרב המנונא ומאן דמתני לה אסיפא לית ליה דרב המנונא והכא בהא קמיפלגי דמר סבר כי איתמר דרב המנונא בפניו [ה]אבל שלא בפניו נמי אינה מעיזה: ואם משנשאת באו עדים וכו': אמר אבוה דשמואל לא נשאת נשאת ממש אלא [ו]כיון שהתירוה לינשא אע"פ שלא נשאת והא לא תצא קתני לא תצא מהתירה הראשון [ח]ת"ר אמרה [ז]נשביתי וטהורה אני ויש לי עדים שטהורה אני אין אומרים נמתין עד שיבאו עדים אלא מתירין אותה מיד התירוה לינשא ואחר כך באו עדים ואמרו לא ידענו הרי זו לא תצא [ח]ואם באו עדי טומאה אפי' יש לה כמה בנים תצא הני שבוייתא דאתיין לנהרדעא אותיב אבוה דשמואל נטורי בהדייהו א"ל שמואל ועד האידנא מאן נטרינהו א"ל אילו בנתך הוין מי הוית מזלזל בהו כולי האי הואי [א]כשגגה שיוצא מלפני השליט ואישתביין בנתיה דמר שמואל ואסקינהו לארעא דישראל אוקמן לשבויינהו מאבראי ועיילי לבי מדרשא דר' חנינא הא אמרה נשביתי וטהורה אני והא אמרה נשביתי וטהורה אני [ס]שרינהו סוף עול אתו שבויינהו אמר רבי חנינא [ט]בנן דמוריין אינון איגלאי מילתא דבנתיה דמר שמואל הוין אמר ליה רבי חנינא לרב שמן בר אבא פוק איטפל בקרובותיך אמר ליה לרבי חנינא והאיכא עדים במדינת הים השתא מיהת ליתנהו קמן עדים בצד [י]אסתן ותאסר טעמא דלא אתו עדים הא אתו עדים מיתסרא והאמר אבוה דשמואל כיון שהתירוה לינשא אף על פי שלא נשאת אמר רב אשי עדי טומאה איתמר:

מתני'

מאי שנא רישא ומאי שנא סיפא. ואם תאמר שנא ושנא דרישא לית לן לאוקמה בחזקת פנויה וסיפא בחזקת אשת איש ויש לומר דברישא אע"ג דאית לן לאוקמה בחזקת פנויה מ"מ תרי ותרי ספיקא דרבנן היא כדמוכח בפרק ד' אחין (יבמות דף לא. ושם) והוה לן למימר תלא מדרבנן וי"מ כיון דלא מפליג בין באו עדים עד שלא ניסת לבאו עדים משניסת ש"מ דלאו רבי מנחם בר יוסי היא אלא רבנן א"כ סיפא נמי אמאי תלא הא שמעינן להו דאמרי לא תלא:

תרוייהו בפנויה קמסהדי. לא הוה צריך להא דאפי' ליכא אלא ההוא דאמר נתקדשה לא תלא דאין דבר שבערוה פחות משנים אבל קיימא אמאי לא תנשא לכתחלה דהוה לן לאוקמה אחזקה וי"ל כגון שאנו יודעים שזרק לה קדושין ומספקא לן אי קרוב לו או קרוב לה והני ב' סהדי חד אמר קרוב לו וחד אמר קרוב לה דכיון דודאי זרק לה הקדושין לית לן למימר אוקמה אחזקה להתירה לכתחלה אי נמי כגון שהיו נרות דולקות ומטות מוצעות שהיה עומד לקדש כדאמר בסוף המגרש (גיטין פט.) ועד אחד אומר נתקדשה ועד אחד אומר לא נתקדשה באותה שעה:

מאן דמתני לה ארישא כ"ש אסיפא. וא"ת מנא ליה דלמא אסיפא לא מלי קאי דאפי' באו עדים ואחר כך נשאת לא תצא ולמאי דמפרש בסמוך לא ניסת ממש אתי שפיר:

אית ליה דרב המנונא. אע"ג [ס]דרב המנונא איירי בפניו מ"מ לענין ניסת ואח"כ באו עדים מהני שלא בפניו: **לא** תצא מהתירה הראשון. פירוש ותנשא [לכתחלה] דלא שייך לומר שפסים כלל אבל אין לפרש כי ההיא דיבמות דלא תלא מהיתרה הראשון לענין דאם נשאת לא תלא אבל לכתחלה לא תינשא כדמשמע גבי בנתיה דמר שמואל בסמוך שהתירן א) לכתחילה:

באו עדים לא תצא. פירוש לא תלא מהיתרה הראשון:

עד האידנא מאן נטרינהו. פי' לכבר נאסרו: **והא** איכא עדים במדינת הים. אין לפרש דלמא איכא עדים במדינת הים דאם כן תיקשי ליה נמי ממתניתין דקתני נשביתי וטהורה אני נאמנת ולמאי דלמא איכא עדים אלא הכי פירושה הא יצא קול דאיכא עדים במדינת הים שיודעים שנשבית ומיהו קשה לרשב"א דהיכי סלקא דעתיה השתא דעדים היינו עדי שבויה דא"כ מה הוה צריך למימר הא איכא עדים במדינת הים הוה ליה למימר הא איכא עדים קמן דהא איכא שבויינהו ב): **עדי** טומאה איתמר. והא איכא עדים במדינת הים דפריך לעיל פירוש והא יצא קול דאיכא התם עדי טומאה כדפירשתי הקשה ר"ת בפרק קמא דקידושין (דף יב.) גבי ההוא גברא דקדיש במאבא דכותלא ויתיב רב חסדא וקא מעיין אי אית בה שוה פרוטה אי לא ומסיק דלאו היינו דר' חנינא דאמר עדים בצד אסתן ותאסר וקאמר אביי ורבא לא סבירא להו הא דרב חסדא אם הקילו בשבויה נקל באשת איש והשתא למאי דמסיק דעדי טומאה איתמר מה לי עדי שבויה מה לי עדי אשת איש ורש"י [ז]פירש שם אם הקילו בשבויה דלאיסור לאו וקשה לרבינו תם דבשבויה נמי איכא איסור סקילה אם נשאת לכהן שישמש בנה על גבי מזבח בשבת ומיהו אית ספרים דגרסי התם אם הקילו בשבויה דמנוולה נפשה באפי שבויה כו' פירוש ולא שכיח כולי האי שנטמאה נקל באשת איש דשכיח דידעי אם אית בה שוה פרוטה ובלאו הך גירסא איכא למימר דלא שכיח שיהו עדי טומאה אבל עדים שידעו ששוה פרוטה שכיח ג):

שתי

שנא רישא. שנאמנה: **בפנויה קמסהדי.** דהא ודאי תלא לכתחלה דלאו בחזקת פנויה... [Rashi:]

תרוייהו בפנויה קמסהדי. לדברי שניהם עד עכשיו בחזקת פנויה היתה [קודם שנתקדשה]: איפוך. ברישא תני אם ניסת תלא וסיפא אם ניסת לא תלא: דמגרשי בצנעא. ואפילו הכי לכתחלה לא תנשא משום לזות שפתים: ארישא. אם משניסת באו עדים שהיתה אשת איש והיא ניסת על פי עצמה שאמרה גרושה אני: אסיפא. נשביתי וטהורה אני והתירוה לינשא ואח"כ באו עדים שנשבית: בשבויה הקילו. דמספקא בעלמא הוא דליכא שמא נבעלה לעובד כוכבים ונפסלה לכהונה: דרב המנונא. דאמר האשה שאמרה לבעלה גירשתני נאמנת הלכך הא דאמרה גרושה אני מהימנא: ויש לי עדים. שהיו עמי תמיד שלא נתייחדתי עם עובד כוכבים: ואח"כ באו עדים. שנשבית דהשתא לאו הפה שאסר הוא אפי' הכי לא תלא: אפי' יש לה כמה בנים. מן הכהן הזה שנשאה: דאתיין לנהרדעא. להפדות: אוקמינהו לשבוייהו אבראי. שלא יבואו לפני ב"ד ולא ידעו ב"ד שהן שבויות אלא ע"פ עצמן ויתירום: בנן דמוריין אינון. בנות אדם גדול ובעל הוראה הוא שידעו לעשות כן: לרב שמן. כהן היה: איטפל בקרובותיך. שא אחת מהן שהן קרובותיך: והא איכא סהדי במדינת הים. שראו שנשבו ולמאי אתו לקמן למחר וליתמה אוסרן לאחר שתנשא: השתא מיהא לא איתנהו. קודם נישואין ומשום דלמא אתו לא אסרינן לה השתא: עדים בצד אסתן. בלד לפון [מלפון זהב יאתה (איוב לז) מתרגם מלאיסתנא]: ותאסר. בתמיה הא [לא] אתו קודם נשואין. מתני'

תוספות רי"ד

מ"ש רישא ומ"ש סיפא פי' שאין לומר טעמא דרישא משום דאמרינן אוקי תרי לבהדי תרי ואוקי איתתא (אחזקה) [בחזקת פנויה] דתרי ותרי הן ספיקא דאורייתא ובספיקא דאורייתא לא אזלינן בתר חזקה אלא הבא עליה באשם תלוי קאי אמר (ר"פ) [אביי] תרגמה בע"א. ע"א אומר נתקדשה וע"א אומר לא נתקדשה תרווייהו בפנויה קמסהדי והאי דאמר נתקדשה הו"ל חד ואין דבריו של א' במקום ב'. ע"א אומר נתגרשה וע"א אומר לא נתגרשה תרווייהו באשת איש קמסהדי והאי דאמר נתגרשה הו"ל חד ואין דבריו של א' במקום שנים. ופי' לאו במוחזקת לפנינו שהיא א"א מיירי. דא"כ מה צורך להכחשת העד שאומר לא נתגרשה בלא הכחשתו נמי אינו נאמן ע"א בגירושין ואפי' לאביי דאמר ע"א נאמן באיסורין ואפילו באשה ה"מ לאסור כגון אשתו זינתה בע"א בפ' האומר [קדושין סו ע"ש] דאביי אמר ע"א נאמן בכל איסורין שבתורה ורבא אמר אין דבר שבערוה פחות משנים. ודוקא לאיסור היה אומר אביי דע"א נאמן אבל אשה שהוחזקה בא"א אין מי שיאמר שיהא ע"א נאמן לומר נתגרשה ולהוציאה מחזקת א"א דודקא בתלה בעלך דאמינו חכמים ע"א משום דמילתא דעבידי לגלויי לא משקרא והיא גופא דייקא ומנסבא. ומתוך חומר שהחמרת עליה בסופה הקלת עליה מתחלתה אבל בגירושין לא מהימן. עיין בהאשה רבה. ולא מתוקמא באשה הבאה ממדה"י שלא ידענו מי היא ובאים אלה השנים ומעידים עליה כי א"א היתה אלא שא' אומר נתגרשה ואחד אומר לא נתגרשה. והלשון מוכיח כן שאומר תרווייהו בא"א קמסהדי. דמשמע שלא החזקה א"א אלא על פיהם. ואע"ג דאיהי נמי אמרה א"א הייתי וגרושה אני [מ"מ] כיון שיש עדים (שהיתה) [שאומרים] שא"א היתה אינה נאמנת. ועוד שהעד מכחישה ואומר לא נתגרשה. והלכך אם נשאת תצא אבל בודאי אם נשאת תחלה על פיה כשאמרה א"א הייתי וגרושה אני ואח"כ בא העד שאוסרה שאומר לא נתגרשה לא תצא. שאין מוציאין אשה מבעלה בע"א כדרבא דאמר אין דבר שבערוה פחות מב'. וכי היכי דבגירושין לא מתוקמא אלא באשה הבאה ממדה"י שאין לה חזקה מה היא ה"נ עדות דקידושין לא מתוקם אלא בבאה ממדה"י שלא הוחזקה מה היא. והלשון מוכיח דקאמר תרוייהו בפנויה מסהדי. דמשמע שלא הוחזקה פנויה אלא על פיהן. אבל אשה העומדת לפנינו בחזקת פנויה. ובא ע"א ואמר נתקדשה בפני פ' ופ' והלכו להן למדינת הים. אע"פ שאין עד אחר שיכחישנו. אינו נאמן לאוסרה עד שיבואו שנים כדרבא דאמר אין דבר שבערוה פחות מב'. ולכתחלה לא תנשא. ר"א אמר לעולם תרי ותרי ואיפוך פי' המורה ברישא תני תצא. ובסיפא תני לא תצא. **ב' אומרים** ראינוה שנתקדשה וב' אומרים לא ראינוה שנתקדשה ה"ז לא תנשא. פשיטא לא ראינו אינו ראיה. ל"צ דדיירו בחצר א'. מ"ד אי איתא דקדיש קלא אית ליה למילתא קמ"ל דעבידי אינשי דמקדשי בצנעא. **ואי קשה** טעמא דאמר' לא ראינוה שנתקדשה דלא ראינוה אינה ראיה אבל אי אמרי (בעיקר) [בבירור] דלא נתקדשה כגון דאמרו האשה או המקדש הי' עמנו במקום פ' שמעידים עדות ברורה. ה"נ דאם נשאת לא תצא א) ואמאי לא תצא. תרי ותרי נינהו והבא עלי' באשם תלוי קאי. ואי אמרת דר"א קסבר דאפילו בתרי ותרי אמרי' אוקי אתתא אחזקתה. א"כ מה צורך לאפוכי במאי דתניא מפרשא שפיר גבי נתקדשה לא תצא דאוקמי' לה אחזקה קמייתא ופנויה הות וגבי נתגרשה תצא דמוקמינן לה אחזקתה דא"א הות. ומדלא אוקמוה הכי ש"מ דלא אמרינן תרי ותרי אוקמה אחזקתה. משום דהוי ספק תורה והבא עליה באשם תלוי קאי. תשובה. אילו העידו עדות ברורה. כגון שאמרו אנו היינו כל היום עמכם באותו חצר ולא נתפרדנו מהם כלל ולא יתכן שנתקדשה באותו היום שאילו כך גם אנחנו היינו רואים המעשה. אלא שקר אתם מעידים. אין לומר בכאן תרי ותרי נינהו. שזאת היא הזמה

חשק שלמה על תוס' רי"ד א) ולפי מש"כ הר"ן כאן דמיירי שנשאת לאחד מעדיה שאמרו לא ראינו שנתקדשה לק"מ ועי' לעיל (דף כב ע"ב) כגון שניסאת וכו' ודו"ק.

עין משפט נר מצוה

עא א מיי' פ"ט מהל' אישות הלכה לא טוש"ע אה"ע סימן מז סעיף ג:
עב ב מיי' שם הלכה ל טוש"ע שם סעיף א:
עג ג מיי' פי"ב מהל' גירושין הלכה ח טוש"ע שם סימן קנב סעיף ד:
עד ד מיי' שם הלכה א טור שו"ע שם סעיף ז:
עה ה מיי' שם הלכה ד טוש"ע שם סימן יז סעיף ג:
עו ו מיי' פי"ח מהל' איסורי ביאה הלכ' כב טוש"ע שם סי' ז סעיף ו:
עז ז מיי' שם הלכה כג טור שו"ע שם סעי' ז:
עח ח ט מיי' שם טור שו"ע שם סעיף ו:

מסורת הש"ס

א) ס"א רב אסי, ב) [זבחים קג:], ג) [לקמן כד.], ד) [לקמן מ: נא: קדושין יב: ב"ק קיד:], ה) [תוס' פ"ב], ו) קדושין יב: ב"ב קלה., ז) [לפנינו שם ברש"י לא נמלא ועי' תוס' שם ד"ה אם הקלנו וכו' כתבו דבר זה בשם יש מפרשים].

תוספות ישנים

א) [לכתחלה דפריך טעמא דליכא עדים הא איכא עדים מתסרא ומאי פריך אי מתסרא לכתחלה. ת"י עה"ג]:
ב) [וי"ל דמחמת השבאים לא איתסרו דהא איתו אתו בתר דשרינהו אבל הכא מחמת שבא הקול מקמי שריותא דידהו איכא למסרינהו וה"פ טעמא דלא אתו עדים הא אתו עדים מיתסרו כיון שנתגלה הקול שיש עדים מלפני ההיתר. ת"י עה"ג]:
ג) [ולמאי דס"ד מעיקרא דעדי שבויה ניחא דהוי ספק ספיקא ספק אם נשבית אם לאו ואת"ל נשבית ספק לא נטמאת ובאשת איש ליכא אלא חדא ספיקא. ת"י עה"ג]:

גליון הש"ס

גמ' שרינהו סוף עול אתו שבויינהו. עיין ב"ב קמט ע"א תד"ה רב מרי. שבת קנד ע"א תד"ה ואמרי לה: תוס' ד"ה אית ליה. אע"ג דרב המנונא איירי בפניו. עיין יבמות קטו ע"ב תד"ה באותה שעה:

תורה אור השלם

א) יֵשׁ רָעָה רָאִיתִי תַּחַת הַשָּׁמֶשׁ כִּשְׁגָגָה שֶׁיֹּצָא מִלִּפְנֵי הַשַּׁלִּיט: [קהלת י, ה]

ליקוטי רש"י

[נדפס בדף כב:]

bar Avin] **who taught it as referring to the last part** of the Mishnah would hold: אֲבָל אַרֵישָׁא לֹא – **But** it does **not** refer **to the first part.**[21]

It emerges that these Amoraim disagree regarding the first case of the Mishnah, where a woman says, "I was married but I am divorced." If she remarried and later witnesses testified that she was married previously, R' Oshaya holds that she does not have to leave her new husband, whereas Rabbah bar Avin maintains that she does. The Gemara attempts to explain the two sides of this dispute:

לֵימָא בִּדְרַב הַמְנוּנָא קָמִיפַּלְגֵי – **Let us say that they disagree about** the ruling **of Rav Hamnuna,** who said that if a woman declares before her husband, "You divorced me," she is believed.[22] דְּמַאן דְּמַתְנֵי לָהּ אַרֵישָׁא – **For the one** [R' Oshaya] **who taught it** [the Mishnah's concluding section] **as referring to the first part** of the Mishnah אִית לֵיהּ דְּרַב הַמְנוּנָא – **accepts** the ruling **of Rav Hamnuna.** Therefore, in our case, this woman's claim that she was divorced is always believed, even if witnesses testify (after she remarried) that she was previously married.[23] וּמַאן דְּמַתְנֵי לָהּ אַסֵּיפָא – **And the one** [Rabbah bar Avin] **who taught it as referring** only **to the last part** of the Mishnah לֵית לֵיהּ דְּרַב הַמְנוּנָא – **does not accept** the ruling of **Rav Hamnuna.**[24]

The Gemara responds:

לֹא – **No!** This is not necessarily the correct explanation of the dispute. דְּכוּלֵּי עָלְמָא אִית לְהוּ דְּרַב הַמְנוּנָא – It is possible **that everyone accepts** the ruling of **Rav Hamnuna.** וְהָכָא בְּהָא קָמִיפַּלְגֵי – **And here** it is **in the following** point that **they disagree:** דְּמַר סָבַר – **For one master** [Rabbah bar Avin] **holds:** כִּי אִיתְּמַר דְּרַב הַמְנוּנָא – **In reference to which case was Rav Hamnuna's** ruling **stated?** בְּפָנָיו – It refers to a case **where** the wife spoke **in front of [her husband].** Only when she is confronting her husband can we be sure that she would not be so brazen as to falsely declare that she is divorced. אֲבָל שֶׁלֹּא בְּפָנָיו – **But when** she is **not in front of him,** מְעִיזָּה – **she** might indeed **be** so **brazen.** Hence, in our case, where her husband is not present, even Rav Hamnuna would agree that she is not believed to say she is divorced.[25] וּמַר סָבַר – **And** the other **master** [R' Oshaya] **holds** שֶׁלֹּא בְּפָנָיו נַמִּי אֵינָהּ מְעִיזָּה – **that even** when she is **not in front of him, she would not be** so **brazen** as to falsely declare that she is divorced.[26]

The Gemara again quotes the Mishnah's final ruling:

וְאִם מִשֶּׁנִּשֵּׂאת בָּאוּ עֵדִים וכו׳ – HOWEVER, IF AFTER SHE MARRIED WITNESSES CAME etc. [she does not have to leave her present husband].

The Gemara interprets the Mishnah's statement:

אָמַר אֲבוּהַ דִּשְׁמוּאֵל – **The father of Shmuel said:** לֹא נִשֵּׂאת נִשֵּׂאת מַמָּשׁ – The term **"married"** in our Mishnah does **not literally mean married.** אֶלָּא כֵּיוָן שֶׁהִתִּירוּהָ לִינָּשֵׂא – **Rather,** it means that **once they** [the court] **have** ***permitted*** **her to marry,** אַף עַל פִּי שֶׁלֹּא נִשֵּׂאת – **even though she did not** yet **marry,** she is still permitted to do so.

The Gemara objects:

וְהָא לֹא תֵצֵא קָתָנֵי – **But [the Mishnah] stated:** SHE DOES NOT have to LEAVE, which indicates that she is already married!

The Gemara answers:

לֹא תֵצֵא מֵהֶתֵּירָהּ הָרִאשׁוֹן – This means that **she does not leave her original** state of **permission** to marry.[27]

NOTES

marrying a Kohen. This is merely a possibility for which we must be concerned (*Rashi*). [Since the grounds for prohibiting a captured woman to a Kohen are relatively weak, the Sages allowed several leniencies with respect to this prohibition. This is in contrast to the Mishnah's first case, which concerns the severe prohibitions related to a married woman.]

Rashi's comment here seems to contradict his assertion above (13b; see note 13 there) that a captured woman is *assumed* to have been violated. This contradiction can be resolved by explaining that since the woman's captors are of low moral character, Rabbinic law regards her *as though* she was certainly violated unless it is proven otherwise. However, this is only a Rabbinic enactment. In truth, the possibility of her having been violated is relatively small, because a captured woman typically deters the advances of her captors by making herself appear repulsive to them (*Pnei Yehoshua,* based on *Kiddushin* 12b; see also *Birkas Avraham* at length).

Tosafos (ד״ה עדי טומאה) quote *Rashi* as giving a different reason for treating a captured woman with relative leniency: At worst, even if she was violated by an idolater, a Kohen who cohabits with her is not liable to the death penalty. This is unlike the sin of cohabitation with a married woman, which is a capital crime. *Tosafos,* however, reject this explanation and offer an alternative. See also *Ritva*.

21. For according to Rabbah bar Avin this is a leniency that applies only in the case of a captured woman. In the Mishnah's first case, however, where a woman said, "I was married but I am divorced," even if the witnesses to her first marriage testified *after* she had remarried, she would have to leave her second husband (*Meiri;* see note 27).

22. Because there is a presumption that a woman will not be so brazen as to tell her husband that he has divorced her unless that were the truth (Gemara above, 22b).

23. Although once the witnesses have testified she loses the credibility afforded her by the principle of *happeh she'assar,* her claim that she was divorced is still accepted by virtue of Rav Hamnuna's ruling. Therefore, she is allowed to stay with her second husband.

The Rishonim ask: According to Rav Hamnuna, a woman who says she was divorced is allowed to remarry even in the first place. Hence, if our Mishnah follows Rav Hamnuna's ruling, why does it permit her to remain in her second marriage only if the witnesses testified *after* she remarried? The Mishnah implies that had they testified earlier, she would have been forbidden to remarry in the first place, and if she did, she would have had to leave her new husband.

They answer that Rav Hamnuna refers specifically to a case in which the woman's claim to be divorced was made in the husband's presence ("before her husband"). Only then does Rav Hamnuna grant her complete credibility and allow her to remarry even in the first place. But if, as in our Mishnah's case, the claim was not made in the husband's presence, her credibility is more limited; it allows her only to remain married to her new husband, but not to remarry in the first place. And if she did remarry despite being forbidden to do so, she would have to leave her second husband as a penalty for disobeying the directives of the Sages (see *Tosafos, Ramban, Rashba, Ritva, Ran* et al.).

24. Since Rabbah bar Avin does not accept Rav Hamnuna's ruling, the woman's claim that she was divorced is believed *only* on account of the *happeh she'assar* principle. Therefore, once the witnesses have testified and the *happeh she'assar* principle ceases to apply, she is not believed at all. Even if they testify after she has already remarried, she must leave her new husband.

25. According to this approach, Rabbah bar Avin *does* accept Rav Hamnuna's ruling, but only where the woman's claim of divorce was made before her husband. If it was made in his absence, she is not believed at all (see *Rashba*). [Rabbah bar Avin maintains that either the woman is believed completely, or she is not believed at all. He disagrees with the middle ground presented in note 23, third paragraph.]

26. R' Oshaya holds that even where the woman's claim was made in her husband's absence, it is still sufficiently credible to allow her to stay with her second husband [as explained in note 23] (see *Rashba*).

27. According to this interpretation, once the court has permitted the woman to marry (by virtue of the *happeh she'assar* principle), it does not retract that permission even after witnesses testify and the principle of *happeh she'assar* ceases to apply. Thus, even if the witnesses testify before the woman marries, she is still permitted to marry in the first place (*Tosafos*).

Some Rishonim maintain that this interpretation of the Mishnah's last clause is valid only if it refers to the second case ("I was captured but I am pure"), which is treated with relative leniency (see note 20). If, however, it refers to the first case ("I was married but I am divorced"),

מאי שנא רישא ומאי שנא סיפא אמר אביי תרגמה בעד אחד עד אחד אומר נתקדשה ועד אחד אומר לא נתקדשה תרוייהו בפנויה קמסהדי והאי דקאמר נתקדשה הוה ליה חד ואין דבריו של אחד במקום שנים סיפא עד אחד אומר נתגרשה ועד אחד אומר לא נתגרשה תרוייהו באשת איש קמסהדי והאי דקאמר נתגרשה הוה ליה חד ואין דבריו של אחד במקום שנים רב אשי אמר לעולם תרי ותרי ואיפוך שנים אומרים ראינוה שנתקדשה ושנים אומרים לא ראינוה שנתקדשה הרי זו לא תנשא ואם נשאת תצא פשיטא לא ראינוה אינה ראיה לא צריכא דדיירי בחצר אחד מהו דתימא אם איתא דנתקדשה קלא אית לה למילתא קא משמע לן דעבדי אינשי דמקדשי בצנעא סיפא שנים אומרים ראינוה שנתגרשה ושנים אומרים לא ראינוה שנתגרשה הרי זו לא תנשא ואם נשאת לא תצא מאי קמ"ל אע"ג דדיירי בחצר אחד היינו הך מהו דתימא גבי קדושין הוא דעבידי אינשי דמקדשי בצנעא אבל גבי גירושין אם איתא דאיגרשא קלא אית לה למילתא קמ"ל דעבידי אינשי דמקדשי ודמגרשי בצנעא: ואם משנשאת באו עדים לא תצא כו': רבי אושעיא מתני לה ארישא רבה בר אבין מתני לה אסיפא מאן דמתני לה ארישא כ"ש אסיפא דבשבויה הקילו ומאן דמתני לה אסיפא אבל ארישא לא לימא בדרב המנונא קמיפלגי דמאן דמתני לה ארישא אית ליה דרב המנונא ומאן דמתני לה אסיפא לית ליה דרב המנונא והכא בהא קמיפלגי דמר סבר כי איתמר דרב המנונא בפניו אבל שלא בפניו מעיזה ומר סבר שלא בפניו נמי אינה מעיזה: ואם משנשאת באו עדים וכו': אמר אבוה דשמואל לא נשאת נשאת ממש אלא כיון שהתירוה לינשא אע"פ שלא נשאת והא לא תצא קתני לא תצא מהתירה הראשון ת"ר אמרה נשביתי וטהורה אני ויש לי עדים שטהורה אני אין אומרים נמתין עד שיבאו עדים אלא מתירין אותה מיד התירוה לינשא ואחר כך באו עדים ואמרו לא ידענו הרי זו לא תצא ואם באו עדי טומאה אפי' יש לה כמה בנים תצא הני שבוייתא דאתיין לנהרדעא אותיב אבוה דשמואל נטורי בהדייהו א"ל שמואל ועד האידנא מאן נטרינהו א"ל אילו בנתך הוין מי הוית מזלזל בהו כולי האי הואי כשגגה שיוצא מלפני השליט ואישתביין בנתיה דמר שמואל ואסקינהו לארעא דישראל אוקמן לשבויינהו מאבראי ועיילי לבי מדרשא דר' חנינא הא אמרה נשביתי וטהורה אני והא אמרה נשביתי וטהורה אני שרינהו סוף עול אתו שבויינהו אמר רבי חנינא בנן דמוריין אינון איגלאי מילתא דבנתיה דמר שמואל הווין אמר ליה רבי חנינא לרב שמן בר אבא פוק איטפל בקרובותיך אמר ליה לרבי חנינא והאיכא עדים במדינת הים השתא מיהת ליתנהו קמן עדים בצד אסתן ותאסר טעמא דלא אתו עדים הא אתו עדים מיתסרא והאמר אבוה דשמואל כיון שהתירוה לינשא אף על פי שלא נשאת אמר רב אשי עדי טומאה איתמר:

מתני'

רש"י

תרוייהו בפנויה קמסהדי. לדברי שניהם פנויה היתה [קודם שנתקדשה]: איפוך. ברישא תני אם ניסת תצא וסיפא אם ניסת לא תצא: דמגרשי בצנעא. ואפילו הכי לכתחלה לא תנשא משום לזות שפתים: ארישא. אם משניסת באו עדים שהיתה אשת איש והיא ניסת על פי עצמה שאמרה גרושה אני: אסיפא. אנשביתי וטהורה אני והתירוה לינשא ואח"כ באו עדים שנשבית: בשבויה הקילו. דחששא בעלמא הוא דאיכא שמא נבעלה לעובד כוכבים ונפסלה לכהונה: דרב המנונא. דאמר האשה שאמרה לבעלה גירשתני נאמנת הלכך הא דאמרה גרושה אני מהימנא: ויש לי עדים. שהיו עמי תמיד שלא נתייחדתי עם עובד כוכבים: ואח"כ באו עדים. שנשבית דהשתא לאו הפה שאסר הוא אפי' הכי לא תצא: אפי' יש לה כמה בנים. מן הכהן הזה שנשאה: דאתיין לנהרדעא. להפדותן: אוקמינהו לשבויינהו אבראי. שלא יבואו לפני ב"ד ולא ידעו ב"ד שהן שבויות אלא ע"פ עצמן ויתירום: בנן דמוריין אינון. בנות אדם גדול ובעל הוראה הוא שידעו לעשות כן: לרב שמן. כהן היה: איטפל בקרובותיך. שא אחת מהן שהן קרובותיך: והא איכא סהדי במדינת הים. שראו שנשבו ודלמא אתו לקמן למחר וליומא אוחרן לאחר שתנשא: השתא מיהא לא איתנהו. קודם נישואין ומשום דלמא אתו לא אסרינן לה השתא: עדים בצד אסתן. בצד צפון [מצפון זהב יאתה (איוב לז) מתרגם מדאיסתנא]: ותאסר. בתמיה הא [לא] אתו קודם נשואין:

תוספות

מאי שנא רישא ומאי שנא סיפא. ואם תאמר מאי קושיא דרישא איירי בחזקת פנויה וסיפא בחזקת אשת איש ויש לומר דברישא נמי לא הוי חזקת פנויה ואע"ג דליכא לאוקמה בחזקת פנויה מ"מ תרי ותרי ספיקא דרבנן היא כדמוכח בפרק ד' אחין (יבמות דף לא. ושם) והוה לן למימר תלא מדרבנן וי"מ כיון דלא מפליג בין באו עדים עד שלא ניסת לבאו עדים משניסת ש"מ דלאו רבי מנחם בר יוסי היא אלא רבנן וא"כ סיפא נמי אמאי תלא הא שמעינן להו דאמרי לא תלא:

תרוייהו בפנויה קמסהדי. לא הוה צריך להא דאפי' ליכא אלא האי דאמר דקדשה לא תלא דאין דבר שבערוה פחות משנים אבל תימה אמאי לא תנשא לכתחלה דהוה לן לאוקמה אחזקה וי"ל כגון שאנו יודעים שזרק לה קדושין ומספקא לן אי קרוב לו או קרוב לה והני ב' סהדי חד אמר קרוב לו וחד אמר קרוב לה דכיון דודאי זרק לה קדושין לית לן למימר אוקמה אחזקה להתירה לכתחלה אי נמי כגון שהיו נרות דולקות ומטות מוצעות והיה עומד לקדש כדאמר בסוף המגרש (גיטין פט.) ועד אחד אומר נתקדשה ועד אחד אומר לא נתקדשה באותה שעה:

מאן דמתני לה ארישא כל שכן אסיפא. וא"ת מנא לן דלמאן דמתני לה אסיפא לא קאי דאפי' באו עדים ואחר כך נשאת לא תלא ולמאי דמפרש בסמוך לא ניסת ממש אתי שפיר: אית ליה דרב המנונא. אע"ג דרב המנונא איירי בפניו מ"מ לענין ניסת ואח"כ באו עדים מהני שלא בפניו: לא תצא מהיתרה הראשון. פירוש ותנשא [לכתחלה] דלא שייך לזות שפתים כל כך אבל אין לפרש כי ההיא דיבמות דלא תלא מהיתרה הראשון לענין דאם נשאת לא תלא אבל לכתחלה לא תינשא כדמשמע גבי בנתיה דמר שמואל בסמוך שהתירן א) לכתחילה:

באו עדים לא תצא. פירוש לא תלא מהיתרה הראשון:

עד האידנא מאן נטרנהו. פי' דכבר נאסרו: והא איכא עדים במדינת הים. אין לפרש דלמא איכא עדים במדינת הים דאם כן תיקשי ליה נמי אמתניתין דקתני נשביתי וטהורה אני נאמנת ואמאי דלמא איכא עדים אלא הכי פירושה הא יצא קול דאיכא עדים במדינת הים שיודעים שנשבית ומיהו קשה לרשב"א דהיכי סלקא דעתיה השתא דעדים היינו עדי שבויה דא"כ מה הוה צריך למימר הא איכא עדים במדינת הים הוה ליה למימר הא איכא עדים קמן דהא איכא שבויינהו ב): עדי טומאה איתמר. והא איכא עדים במדינת הים דפריך לעיל פירוש והא יצא קול דאיכא התם עדי טומאה כדפירשתי הקשה ר"ת בפרק קמא דקידושין (דף יב.) גבי ההוא גברא דקדיש באבנא דכוחלא ויתיב רב חסדא וקא מעער אי אית בה שוה פרוטה אי לא ומסיק לאו היינו דר' חנינא דאמר עדים בצד אסתן ותאסר וקאמר אביי ורבא לא סבירא להו הא דרב חסדא אם הקילו בשבויה נקל באשת איש והשתא למאי דמסיק דעדי טומאה איתמר מה לי עדי שבויה מה לי עדי אשת איש ורש"י ז) פירש שם אם הקילו בשבויה דאיסור לאו וקשה לרבינו תם דבשבויה נמי איכא איסור סקילה אם נשאת לכהן שישמש בנה על גבי מזבח בשבת ומיהו אית ספרים דגרסי התם אם הקילו בשבויה דמנוולה נפשה באפי שבויה כו' פירוש ולא שכיח כולי האי שנטמאה נקל באשת איש דשכיח דידעי אם אית בה שוה פרוטה ובלאו הך גירסא איכא למימר דלא שכיח שיהו עדי טומאה אבל עדים שידעו ששוה פרוטה שכיח ג):

שתי

מסורת הש"ס

א) ס"א רב אסי, ב) [זבחים קג:], ג) [לקמן כז.], ד) [לקמן מ: נא.] קדושין יב: ב"ק קיז:, ה) [תוס' פ"ג], ו) קדושין יב: ב"ב קלה, ז) [לפנינו שם ברש"י לא נמצא ועי' תוס' שם ד"ה אם הקלנו וכו' כתבו דבר זה בשם יש מפרשים].

עין משפט נר מצוה

עא א מיי' פ"ט מהל' אישות הלכה לא טוש"ע אה"ע סימן מז סעיף ג:
עב ב מיי' שם הלכה כ טוש"ע שם סעיף א:
עג ג מיי' פי"ב מהל' גירושין הלכה ח טוש"ע שם סימן קנב סעיף ד:
עד ד מיי' שם הלכה ט טור שו"ע שם סעיף ז:
עה ה מיי' שם הלכה ד טוש"ע שם סימן קנב סעיף ג:
עו ו מיי' פי"ח מהל' איסורי ביאה הלכ' כב טוש"ע שם סי' ז סעיף ו:
עז ז מיי' שם הלכה כג טור שו"ע שם סעי' ז:
עח ח ט מיי' שם טור שו"ע שם סעיף ו:

תוספות ישנים

א) [לכתחלה דפריך טעמא דליכא עדים הא איכא עדים מתסרא ומאי פריך אי מתסרא לכתחלה. מ"י עה"ג] ב) [וי"ל דמתמת השבאים לא איתסרו דהא אינהו אתו בתר דשרינהו אבל הכא מתמת שבא הקול מקמי שריותא דידהו איכא למסרינהו וה"פ טעמא דלא אתו עדים הא אתו עדים מיתסרו כיון שנתגלה הקול שיש עדים מלפני היתרה. מ"י עה"ג] ג) [ולמאי דס"ד מעיקרא דעדי שבויה ניחא דהוי ספק ספיקא ספק נשבית אם לאו ואת"ל נשבית ספק לא נטמאת ובאשת איש ליכא אלא חדא ספיקא. מ"י עה"ג]

גליון הש"ס

גמ' שרינהו סוף עול אתו שבוינהו. עיין ב"ב קמט ע"א תד"ה כי מרי. שבת קנד ע"א תד"ה ואמרי לה: תוס' ד"ה אית ליה. אע"ג דרב המנונא איירי בפניו. עיין יבמות קטז ע"ב תד"ה באותה שעה:

תורה אור השלם

א) יֵשׁ רָעָה רָאִיתִי תַּחַת הַשָּׁמֶשׁ כִּשְׁגָגָה שֶׁיֹּצָא מִלִּפְנֵי הַשַּׁלִּיט: [קהלת י, ה]

ליקוטי רש"י

[נדפס בדף כב:]

תוספות רי"ד

מ"ש רישא ומ"ש סיפא פי' שאין לומר טעמא דרישא משום דאמרינן אוקי תרי לבהדי תרי ואוקי איתתא (אחזקה) [בחזקת פנויה] דתרי ותרי הן ספיקא דאורייתא ובספיקא דאורייתא לא אזלינן בתר חזקה אלא הבא עליה באשם תלוי קאי אמר (ר"פ) [אביי] תרגמה בע"א. ע"א אומר נתקדשה וע"א אומר לא נתקדשה תרוייהו בפנויה קמסהדי והאי דאמר נתקדשה הו"ל חד ואין דבריו של א' במקום ב'. ע"א אומר נתגרשה וע"א אומר לא נתגרשה תרוייהו באשת איש קמסהדי והאי דאמר נתגרשה הו"ל חד ואין דבריו של א' במקום שנים. ופי' לאו במוחזקת לפנינו שהיא א"א איירי. דא"כ מה צורך להכחשת העד שאומר לא נתגרשה בלא הכחשתו נמי אינו נאמן ע"א בגירושין ואפי' לאביי דאמר ע"א נאמן באיסורין ואפילו באשה דה"מ לאסור כגון אשתו זינתה בע"א כבפ' האומר [קדושין סו ע"ש] דאביי אמר ע"א נאמן בכל איסורין שבתורה ורבא אמר אין דבר שבערוה פחות משנים. ודוקא לאיסור היה אומר אביי דע"א נאמן אבל אשה שהוחזקה בא"א אין מן שיאמר שהיא ע"א נאמן לומר נתגרשה ולהוציאה מחזקת א"א דודקא במת בעלך דאמינו חכמים ע"א משום דמילתא דעבידי לגלויי לא משקרא והיא גופא דייקא ומנסבא. ומתוך חומר שהחמרת עליה בסופה הקלת עליה מתחלתה אבל בגירושין לא מהימן. עיין בהאשה רבה. ולא מתוקמא אלא באשה הבאה ממדה"י שלא ידענו מי היא ובאים אלה השנים ומעידים עליה כי א"א היתה אלא שא' אומר נתגרשה ואחד אומר לא נתגרשה. והלשון מוכיח כן שאומר תרוייהו בא"א קמסהדי. דמשמע שלא הוחזקה א"א אלא על פיהם. ואע"ג דאיהי נמי אמרה א"א הייתי וגרושה אני (מ"מ) כיון שיש עדים (שהיתה) [שאומרים] שא"א היתה אינה נאמנת. ועוד שהעד מכחישה ואומר לא נתגרשה. והלכך אם נשאת תצא אבל בודאי אם נשאת תחלה על פיה כשאמרה א"א הייתי וגרושה אני ואח"כ בא העד שאוסרה שאומר לא נתגרשה לא תצא. שאין מוציאין אשה מבעלה בע"א כדרבא דאמר אין דבר שבערוה פחות מב'. וכי היכי דבגירושין לא מתוקמא אלא באשה הבאה ממדה"י כאין לה חזקה מה היא ה"נ עדות דקידושין לא מתוקמא אלא בבאה ממדה"י שלא הוחזקה מה היא. והלשון מוכיח דקאמר תרוייהו בפנויה מסהדי. דמשמע שלא הוחזקה פנויה אלא על פיהן. אבל אשה העומדת לפנינו בחזקת פנויה. ובא ע"א ואמר נתקדשה בפני ב' ופ' והלכו להן למדינת הים. אע"פ שאין עד אחר שיכחישנו. אינו נאמן לאוסרה עד שיבואו שנים כדרבא דאמר אין דבר שבערוה פחות מב'. ולכתחלה לא תנשא. ר"א אמר לעולם תרי ותרי ואיפוך פי' המורה ברישא תני תצא. ובסיפא תני לא תצא. ב' אומרים ראינוה שנתקדשה וב' אומרים לא ראינוה שנתקדשה ה"ז לא תנשא. פשיטא לא ראינו אינו ראיה. ל"צ דדיירו בחצר א'. מ"ד אי איתא דקדיש קלא אית ליה למילתא קמ"ל דעבידי אינשי דמקדשי בצנעא. ואי קשה טעמא דאמר' לא ראינוה שנתקדשה דלא ראינוה אינה ראיה אבל אי אמרי (בעיקר) כגון דאמרו האשה או המקדש הי' עמנו במקום פ' שמעידים עדות ברורה. ה"נ דאם נשאת לא תצא א) ואמאי לא תצא. תרי ותרי נינהו והבא עלי' באשם תלוי קאי. ואי אמרת דר"א קסבר דאפילו בתרי ותרי אמרי' אוקי אתתא אחזקתה. א"כ מה צורך לאפוכי במאי דתניא מפרשא שפיר גבי נתקדשה לא תצא דאוקמי' לה אחזקה קמייתא ופנויה הות וגבי נתגרשה תצא דמוקמינן לה אחזקתה דא"א הות. ומדלא אוקמוה הכי ש"מ דלא אמרינן תרי ותרי אוקמה אחזקתה. משום דהוי ספק תורה והבא עליה באשם תלוי קאי. תשובה. אילו העידו עדות ברורה. כגון שאמרו אנו היינו כל היום עמכם באותו חצר ולא נתפרדנו מהם כלל ולא יתכן שנתקדשה באותו היום שאילו כך גם אנחנו היינו רואים המעשה. אלא שקר אתם מעידים. אין לומר בכאן תרי ותרי נינהו. שזאת היא הזמה

חשק שלמה על תוס' רי"ד א) ולפי מש"כ הר"ן כאן דמיירי שנשאת לאחד מעדיה שאמרו לא ראינו שנתקדשה לק"מ ועי' לעיל (דף כב ע"ב) כגון שניסאת וכו' ודו"ק.

betrothal, their testimony proves that it did not take place.[10] קָא מַשְׁמַע לָן דְּעָבְדֵי אִינְשֵׁי דִּמְקַדְּשֵׁי בְּצִנְעָא – To correct this notion, **[the Baraisa] informs us that people do** sometimes **betroth privately,** without the matter becoming known to the neighbors. Thus, the testimony of the witnesses who say "we did not *see* that she was betrothed" carries no weight.[11]

Rav Ashi explains the Baraisa's clause concerning divorce:

סֵיפָא – The **last part** of the Baraisa is understood as follows: שְׁנַיִם אוֹמְרִים רְאִינוּהָ שֶׁנִּתְגָּרְשָׁה – If **two** witnesses **say, "We saw her become divorced,"** וּשְׁנַיִם אוֹמְרִים לֹא רְאִינוּהָ שֶׁנִּתְגָּרְשָׁה – **and two** witnesses **say, "We did not see her become divorced,"**[12] הֲרֵי זוֹ לֹא תִנָּשֵׂא – **this** woman **may not marry,** וְאִם נִשֵּׂאת לֹא תֵצֵא – **but if she did marry, she does not** have to **leave** her second husband.

The Gemara asks:

מַאי קָא מַשְׁמַע לָן – **What is [the Baraisa] teaching us** here? אַף עַל גַּב דְּדָיְירֵי בְּחָצֵר אֶחָד – Is it teaching us that **although they** [the woman and the witnesses who say they did not see the divorce] **live in the same courtyard,** their testimony is nevertheless rejected?[13] הַיְינוּ הַךְ – But **that is** the same point as **that** taught by the first part of the Baraisa![14] – ? –

The Gemara answers:

מַהוּ דְּתֵימָא גַּבֵּי קִדּוּשִׁין הוּא דַּעֲבִידֵי אִינְשֵׁי דִּמְקַדְּשֵׁי בְּצִנְעָא – **You might have said** that **it is** only **in the case of betrothal that people** sometimes **betroth privately.** אֲבָל גַּבֵּי גֵּירוּשִׁין – **But in the case of divorce,** אִם אִיתָא דְּאִיגָּרְשָׁא – **if she were indeed divorced,** קָלָא אִית לָהּ לְמִילְּתָא – **it is a matter that would have been publicized** among the neighbors.[15] קָא מַשְׁמַע לָן דַּעֲבִידֵי אִינְשֵׁי דִּמְקַדְּשֵׁי וּדְמְגָרְשֵׁי בְּצִנְעָא – **[The Baraisa]** therefore **teaches us that people** not only **betroth** privately **but** also **divorce privately.**[16]

The Gemara resumes its elaboration of our Mishnah, which concluded:

וְאִם מִשֶּׁנִּשֵּׂאת בָּאוּ עֵדִים – HOWEVER, IF AFTER SHE MARRIED WITNESSES CAME forward and testified, לֹא תֵצֵא כו׳ – SHE DOES NOT have to LEAVE her present husband, **etc.**

The Gemara cites a dispute as to whether this clause refers to the first or second of the Mishnah's two cases:[17]

רַבִּי אוֹשַׁעְיָא מַתְנֵי לָהּ אַרֵישָׁא – **R' Oshaya taught it as referring to the first part** of the Mishnah, where a woman says, "I was married but I am divorced."[18] רַבָּה בַּר אָבִין מַתְנֵי לָהּ אַסֵּיפָא – **Rabbah bar Avin taught it as referring to the last part,** where a woman says, "I was captured but I am pure."[19]

The Gemara elaborates:

מַאן דְּמַתְנֵי לָהּ אַרֵישָׁא – **The one** [R' Oshaya] **who taught it as referring to the first part** of the Mishnah כָּל שֶׁכֵּן אַסֵּיפָא – would **certainly** apply it **to the last part,** דִּבְשְׁבוּיָה הֵקִילוּ – **because [the Sages] rule leniently regarding a captured woman.**[20] וּמַאן דְּמַתְנֵי לָהּ אַסֵּיפָא – **However, the one** [Rabbah

NOTES

10. The court is thus faced with two conflicting testimonies, one attesting to the betrothal and one denying that it happened. In accordance with the Tanna Kamma of the Baraisa (top of 22b), the law then ought to be that the woman may not marry another man in the first place, but if she does marry another man, she is not required to leave him. [This is so provided that she married one of the witnesses who testified that there was no betrothal and she herself is certain that she was not betrothed in a valid manner. Otherwise, she would indeed have to leave her new husband (based on *Ritva;* see also *Rashba, Ran, Tos. HaRosh* and *Maharam Schif;* cf. *Tos. Rid*).]

11. It emerges that the only witnesses whose testimony is effective are those who testify that she was betrothed. Consequently, the Baraisa rules (according to Rav Ashi's emendation) that even after she has married another man, she must leave him. This ruling applies even if he is one of the witnesses who testified against the betrothal [and she herself is sure that it did not take effect] (*Ritva*).

12. See note 7.

13. That is, one might have thought that since these witnesses live in the same courtyard as the woman, they would surely know whether she was divorced. Hence, their claim to be unaware of a divorce should carry sufficient weight to offset the witnesses who testify that a divorce did take place. In a case such as this, where two groups of witnesses provide conflicting testimonies, the law is that even after the woman has remarried she must leave her husband [unless he is one of the witnesses to the divorce and she herself is sure that the divorce took effect]. It was therefore necessary for the Baraisa to teach that in fact we disregard the witnesses who say they did not see the divorce, because a woman's divorce is not necessarily known even to her neighbors. The court is thus left only with the testimony of the witnesses who assert that this woman was divorced. Consequently, the law is that if she marries a second husband, she does not have to leave him [even if he was not one of the witnesses to the divorce or she is not certain that the divorce took effect] (*Ritva;* cf. *Ramban* and *Re'ah*). However, she may not remarry in the first place lest her behavior provide grist for disparaging gossip (*Rashi, Ran;* see *Meiri*).

14. Both parts of the Baraisa teach the same principle: If witnesses testify that they are not aware that a certain event (betrothal or divorce) took place, their testimony is discounted, even if they live in the same courtyard as the event's principals. Why did the Baraisa find it necessary to repeat this point, albeit in a different context?

15. A man might betroth a woman in secret because she is not [socially] eligible for him, or because he wants to prevent another man from betrothing her first (see *Ritva;* see, however, *Melo HaRo'im*). These reasons obviously do not apply in the case of divorce. Hence, there are grounds for presuming that, unlike betrothal, every divorce is known to the public.

16. So that the woman would not be disgraced before the court (*Ritva*).

On the other hand, if the Baraisa had mentioned only divorce, it still would have had to mention betrothal as well. This is because it might have been thought that only divorce, which is a source of embarrassment to the woman, might be performed privately, whereas betrothal, which accords her honor and praise, is always done publicly (*Ritva*).

17. The Mishnah had earlier presented two cases: (a) If a woman said, "I was married but I am divorced," we believe that she was divorced and permit her to marry another man. (b) If a woman said, "I was captured but I am pure," we believe that she was not violated by her captors and allow her to marry a Kohen. In both cases, her credibility is based on the principle of *happeh she'assar,* which dictates that where a prohibited state is established solely through the word of a particular person, that person has the authority to report that the prohibition does not apply (see Chapter Introduction). Hence, this woman's credibility is limited to a circumstance in which she is the only one to report her marriage or capture. Should witnesses also testify to this effect, she is not believed under the *happeh she'assar* principle. The Mishnah ended, however, by stating that if witnesses testified *after* she was already married, she does not have to leave her husband. The Gemara discusses whether this last point was made in reference to the Mishnah's first or second case.

18. Thus the end of the Mishnah describes the following scenario: A woman claimed, "I was married but I am divorced," and then she remarried, which she was permitted to do in light of the *happeh she'assar* principle. After she remarried, witnesses came forward and testified that she had indeed been married to another man (*Rashi*). The Mishnah teaches that in those particular circumstances she may remain with her second husband.

[The commentators ask why, according to this view, the final clause of the Mishnah was not placed immediately after the first case (see *Yefei Einayim* and *Mayim Chaim*).]

19. According to this view, the end of the Mishnah means that if a woman said, "I was captured but I am pure," and then married a Kohen, she may remain with him even if witnesses subsequently testify to her capture. [For explanation of *Rashi's* wording הִתִּירוּהָ לִינָּשֵׂא, *they permitted her to marry,* see note 27.]

20. If a woman is captured by idolaters, it is not a foregone conclusion that she was violated by them and thereby became disqualified from

מאי שנא רישא ומאי שנא סיפא אמר אביי תרגמה בעד אחד [א]עד אחד אומר נתקדשה ועד אחד אומר לא נתקדשה תרוייהו בפנויה קמסהדי והאי דקאמר נתקדשה הוה ליה חד ואין דבריו של אחד במקום שנים סיפא עד אחד אומר נתגרשה ועד אחד אומר לא נתגרשה תרוייהו באשת איש קמסהדי והאי דקאמר נתגרשה הוה ליה חד ואין דבריו של אחד במקום שנים [א] רב אשי אמר לעולם תרי ותרי ואיפוך [ב]שנים אומרים ראינוה שנתקדשה ושנים אומרים לא ראינוה שנתקדשה הרי זו לא תנשא ואם נשאת תצא פשיטא [ג]לא ראינוה אינה ראיה לא צריכא דדיירי בחצר אחד מהו דתימא אם איתא דנתקדשה קלא אית לה למילתא קא משמע לן דעבדי אינשי דמקדשי בצנעא סיפא [ג]שנים אומרים ראינוה שנתגרשה ושנים אומרים לא ראינוה שנתגרשה הרי זו לא תנשא ואם נשאת לא תצא מאי קמ"ל אע"ג דדיירי בחצר אחד היינו הך מהו דתימא גבי קדושין הוא דעבדי אינשי דמקדשי בצנעא אבל גבי גירושין אם איתא דאיגרשא קלא אית לה למילתא קמ"ל דעבדי אינשי דמקדשי ודמגרשי בצנעא: ואם משנשאת באו עדים לא תצא כו': רבי אושעיא מתני לה ארישא רבה בר אבין מתני לה אסיפא מאן דמתני לה ארישא כ"ש אסיפא [ד]דבשבויה הקילו ומאן דמתני לה אסיפא [ד]אבל ארישא לא לימא בדרב המנונא קמיפלגי דמאן דמתני לה ארישא אית ליה דרב המנונא ומאן דמתני לה אסיפא לית ליה דרב המנונא לא דכולי עלמא אית להו דרב המנונא והכא בהא קמיפלגי דמר סבר כי איתמר דרב המנונא בפניו [ה]אבל שלא בפניו מעיזה ומר סבר שלא בפניו נמי אינה מעיזה: ואם משנשאת באו עדים וכו': אמר אבוה דשמואל לא נשאת נשאת ממש אלא [ו]כיון שהתירוה לינשא אע"פ שלא נשאת והא לא תצא קתני לא תצא מהתירה הראשון [ז]ת"ר אמרה [ז]נשביתי וטהורה אני ויש לי עדים שטהורה אני אין אומרים נמתין עד שיבאו עדים אלא מתירין אותה מיד התירוה לינשא ואחר כך באו עדים ואמרו לא ידענו הרי זו לא תצא [ח]ואם באו עדי טומאה אפי' יש לה כמה בנים תצא הני שבוייתא דאתיין לנהרדעא אותיב אבוה דשמואל נטורי בהדייהו א"ל שמואל ועד האידנא מאן נטרינהו א"ל אילו בנתך הוין מי הוית מזלזל בהו כולי האי הואי [א]כשגגה שיוצא מלפני השליט ואישתביין בנתיה דמר שמואל ואסקינהו לארעא דישראל אוקמן לשבוינהו מאבראי ועיילי לבי מדרשא דר' חנינא הא אמרה נשביתי וטהורה אני והא אמרה נשביתי וטהורה אני שרינהו סוף עול אתו שבוינהו אמר רבי חנינא בנן דמוריין אינון איגלאי מילתא דבנתיה דמר שמואל הוין אמר ליה רבי חנינא לרב שמן בר אבא פוק איטפל בקרובותיך אמר ליה לרבי חנינא והאיכא עדים במדינת הים השתא מיהת ליתנהו קמן עדים בצד אסתן ותאסר טעמא דלא אתו עדים הא אתו עדים מיתסרא והאמר אבוה דשמואל כיון שהתירוה לינשא אף על פי שלא נשאת אמר רב אשי עדי טומאה איתמר:

מתני'

רש"י

תרוייהו בפנויה קמסהדי. לדברי שניהם עד עכשיו בחזקת פנויה היתה [קודם שנתקדשה]: איפוך. ברישא תני אם ניסת תצא וסיפא אם ניסת לא תצא: דמגרשי בצנעא. ואפילו הכי לכתחלה לא תנשא משום לזות שפתים: ארישא. אם משניסת באו עדים שהיתה אשת איש והיא ניסת על פי עצמה שאמרה גרושה אני: אסיפא. אנשביתי וטהורה אני והתירוה לינשא ואח"כ באו עדים שנשבית: בשבויה הקילו. דחששא בעלמא הוא דאיכא שמא נבעלה לעובד כוכבים ונפסלה לכהונה: דרב המנונא. דאמר האשה שאמרה לבעלה גירשתני נאמנת דלא חציפא הלכך הא דאמרה גרושה אני מהימנא: ויש לי עדים. שהיו עמי תמיד שלא נתייחדתי עם עובד כוכבים: ואח"כ באו עדים. שנשבית דהשתא לאו הפה שאסר הוא אפי' הכי לא תצא: אפי' יש לה כמה בנים. מן הכהן הזה שנשאה: דאתיין לנהרדעא. להפדותן: אוקמינהו לשבויינהו אבראי. שלא יבואו לפני ב"ד ולא ידעו ב"ד שהן שבויות אלא ע"פ עצמן ומירוס: בנן דמוריין אינון. בנות אדם גדול ובעל הוראה הוא שידעו לעשות כן: לרב שמן. כהן היה: איטפל בקרובותיך. שא אתה מהן שהן קרובותיך: והא איכא סהדי במדינת הים. שראו שנשבו ודלמא אתו לקמן למחר וליומא אוחרן לאחר שתנשא: השתא מיהא לא איתנהו. קודם נישואין ומשום דלמא אתו לא אסרינן לה השתא: עדים בצד אסתן. בלד לפון [מלפון זהב יאתה (איוב לז) מתרגם מדלצפונא]: ותאסר. בתמיה הא [לא] אתו קודם נשואין:

תוספות

מאי שנא רישא ומאי שנא סיפא. ואם תאמר שנא ושנא דרישא אית לן לאוקמה בחזקת פנויה וסיפא בחזקת אשת איש ויש לומר דברישא אע"ג דאית לן לאוקמה בחזקת פנויה מ"מ תרי ותרי ספיקא דרבנן היא כדמוכח בפרק ד' אחין (יבמות דף לא. ושם) והוה לן למימר תצא מדרבנן וי"מ כיון דלא מפליג בין באו עדים עד שלא ניסת לבאו עדים משניסת ש"מ דלאו רבי מנחם בר יוסי היא אלא רבנן א"כ סיפא נמי אמאי תצא הא שמעינן להו דאמרי לא תצא:

תרוייהו בפנויה קמסהדי. לא הוה צריך להא דאפי' ליכא אלא ההוא דאמר נתקדשה לא תצא דאין דבר שבערוה פחות משנים אבל תימה אמאי לא תנשא לכתחלה דהוה לן לאוקמה אחזקה וי"ל כגון שאנו יודעים שזרק לה קדושין ומספקא לן אי קרוב לו או קרוב לה והני ב' סהדי חד אמר קרוב לו וחד אמר קרוב לה דכיון דודאי זרק לה הקדושין לית לן למימר אוקמה אחזקה להתירה לכתחילה אי נמי כגון שהיו נרות דולקות ומטות מוצעות שהיה עומד לקדש כדאמר בסוף המגרש (גיטין פט.) ועד אחד אומר נתקדשה ועד אחד אומר לא נתקדשה באותה שעה:

מאן דמתני לה ארישא כל שכן אסיפא. וא"ת מנא ליה דלמא אסיפא לא מני קאי דאפי' באו עדים ואחר כך נשאת לא תצא ולמאי דמפרש בסמוך לא ניסת ניסת ממש אתי שפיר:

אית ליה דרב המנונא. אע"ג ° דרב המנונא איירי בפניו מ"מ לענין ניסת ואח"כ באו עדים מהני שלא בפניו:

לא תצא מהיתרה הראשון. פירוש ותנשא [לכתחלה] דלא שייך לזות שפתים כלל אבל אין לפרש כי ההיא דיבמות דלא תצא מהיתרה הראשון לענין דאם נשאת לא תצא אבל לכתחלה לא תינשא כדמשמע גבי בנתיה דמר שמואל בסמוך שהתירן א) לכתחילה:

באו עדים לא תצא. פירוש לא תצא מהיתרה הראשון:

עד האידנא מאן נטרינהו. פי' דכבר נאסרו:

והא איכא עדים במדינת הים. אין לפרש דלמא איכא עדים במדינת הים דאם כן תיקשי ליה נמי אמתניתין דקתני נשביתי וטהורה אני נאמנת ואמאי דלמא איכא עדים אלא הכי פירושה הא יצא קול דאיכא עדים במדינת הים שיודעים שנשבית ומיהו קשה לרשב"א היכי סלקא דעתיה השתא דעדים היינו עדי שבויה דא"כ מה הוה צריך למימר הא איכא עדים במדינת הים הוה ליה למימר הא איכא עדים קמן דהא איכא שבוינהו ב):

עדי טומאה איתמר. והא איכא עדים במדינת הים דפריך לעיל פירוש והא יצא קול דאיכא התם עדי טומאה כדפירשתי הקשה ר"ת בפרק קמא דקידושין (דף יב.) גבי ההוא גברא דקדיש באבנא דכוחלא ויתיב רב חסדא וקא משער אי אית בה שוה פרוטה אי לא ומסיק לאו היינו דר' חנינא דאמר עדים בלד אסתן ותאסר וקאמר אביי ורבא לא סבירא להו הא דרב חסדא אם הקילו בשבויה נקל באשת איש והשתא למאי דמסיק דעדי טומאה איתמר מה לי עדי שבויה מה לי עדי אשת איש ורש"י ז) פירש שם אם הקילו בשבויה דאיסור לאו וקשה לרבינו תם דבשבויה נמי איכא איסור סקילה אם נשאת לכהן שישמש בנה על גבי מזבח בשבת ומיהו אית ספרים דגרסי התם אם הקילו בשבויה דמנוולה נפשה באפי שבויה כו' פירוש ולא שכיח כולי האי שנטמאה נקל באשת איש דשכיח דידעי אם אית בה שוה פרוטה ובלאו הך גירסא איכא למימר דלא שכיח שיהו עדי טומאה אבל עדים שידעו ששוה פרוטה שכיח ג):

שתי

עין משפט נר מצוה

עא א מיי' פ"ט מהל' אישות הלכה לא טוש"ע אה"ע סימן מז סעיף ג:
עב ב מיי' שם הלכה ל טוש"ע שם סעיף א:
עג ג מיי' פי"ב מהל' גירושין הלכה ח טוש"ע שם סימן קנב סעיף ד:
עד ד מיי' שם הלכה א טור שו"ע שם סעיף ז:
עה ה מיי' שם הלכה ב טוש"ע שם סימן ז סעיף ג:
עו ו מיי' פי"ח מהל' איסורי ביאה הלכ' כב טוש"ע שם סי' ז סעיף ו:
עז ז מיי' שם הלכה כג טור שו"ע שם סעי' :
עח ח ט מיי' שם טור שו"ע שם סעיף ו:

מסורת הש"ס

א) פ"ח רב אשי, ב) [זבחים קג:], ג) [לקמן כז.], ד) [לקמן סו: נה. קדושין יג: ב"ק קיד:], ה) [תוס' פ"ב], ו) קדושין יב: ב"ב קלה., ז) [לפניו שם ברש"י לא נמצא ועי' תוס' שם ד"ה אם הקלנו וכו' כתבו דבר זה בשם יש מפרשים].

תוספות ישנים

א) לכתחלה. דפריך טעמא דליכא עדים הא איכא עדים מתסרא ומאי פריך לא מתסרא לכתחלה. מ"י עס"ג:
ב) וי"ל דמתמת השבאים לא איתסרו דהא לאינהו אתו בתר דשרינהו הקול מקמי שריותא דידהו איכא למסרינהו עדים הא אתו עדים מיתסרו כיון שנתגלה הקול שיש עדים מלפני הסיפור. מ"י עס"ג:
ג) ולמאי דס"ד מעיקרא דעדי שבויה ניחא לדר ספק ספיקא ספק אם נשבית אם לאו ואת"ל נשבית ספק אם לא נבעלה ובאשת איש ליכא אלא חדא ספיקא. מ"י עס"ג:

תוספות רי"ד

מ"ש רישא ומ"ש סיפא פי' שאין לומר טעמא דרישא משום דאמרינן אוקי תרי לבהדי תרי ואוקי איתתא (אחזקה) [בחזקת פנויה] דהוי ותרי הן ספיקא דאורייתא ובספיקא דאורייתא לא אזלינן בתר חזקה אלא הבא עליה באשם תלוי קאי אמר (ר"פ) [אביי] תרגמה בע"א. ע"א אומר נתקדשה וע"א אומר לא נתקדשה תרוייהו בפנויה קמסהדי והאי דאמר נתקדשה הו"ל חד ואין דבריו של א' במקום ב'. ע"א אומר נתגרשה וע"א אומר לא נתגרשה תרוייהו באשת איש קמסהדי והאי דאמר נתגרשה הו"ל חד ואין דבריו של א' במקום שנים. ופי' לאו במוחזקת לפנינו שהיא א"א מיירי. דא"כ מה צורך להכחשת העד שאומר לא נתגרשה בלא הכחשתו נמי אינו נאמן ע"א בגירושין ואפי' לאביי דאמר ע"א נאמן באיסורין ואפילו באשה ה"מ לאסור כגון אשתו זינתה בע"א בפ' האומר (קדושין סו ע"ש) דאביי אמר ע"א נאמן בכל איסורין שבתורה ורבא אמר אין דבר שבערוה פחות משנים. ודוקא לאיסור היה אומר אביי דע"א נאמן אבל אשה שהוחזקה בא"א אין מי שיאמר שיהא ע"א נאמן לומר נתגרשה ולהוציאה מחזקת א"א דדוקא במת בעלך האמינו חכמים ע"א משום דמילתא דעבידי לגלויי לא משקרא והיא גופא דייקא ומנסבא. ומתוך חומר שהחמרת עליה בסופה הקלת עליה מתחלתה אבל בגירושין לא מהימן. עיין בהאשה רבה. ולא מתוקמא אלא באשה הבאה ממדה"י שלא ידענו מי היא ובאים אלה השנים ומעידים עליה כי א"א היתה אלא שא' אומר נתגרשה ואחד אומר לא נתגרשה. והלשון מוכיח כן שאומר תרוייהו בא"א קמסהדי. דמשמע שלא הוחזקה א"א אלא על פיהם. ואע"ג דאיהי נמי אמרה א"א הייתי וגרושה אני [מ"מ] כיון שיש עדים (שהיתה) [שאומרים] שא"א היתה אינה נאמנת. ועוד שהעד מכחישה ואומר לא נתגרשה. והלכך אם נשאת תצא אבל בודאי אם נשאת תחלה על פיה כשאמרה א"א הייתי ונגרשה אני ואח"כ בא העד שאוסרה שאומר לא נתגרשה לא תצא. שאין מוציאין אשה מבעלה בע"א כדרבא דאמר אין דבר שבערוה פחות מב'. וכי היכי דבגירושין לא מתוקמא אלא באשה הבאה ממדה"י שאין לה חזקה מה היא ה"נ עדות דקידושין לא מתוקם אלא בבאה ממדה"י שלא הוחזקה מה היא. והלשון מוכיח דקאמר תרוייהו בפנויה מסהדי. דמשמע שלא הוחזקה לפנינו בחזקת פנויה. אבל אשה העומדת לפנינו בחזקת פנויה. ובא ע"א ואמר נתקדשה בפני פ' ופ' והלכו להן למדינת הים. אע"פ שאין עד אחר שיכחישנו. אינו נאמן לאוסרה עד שיבואו שנים כדרבא דאמר אין דבר שבערוה פחות מב'. ולכתחלה לא תנשא. ר"א אמר לעולם תרי ותרי ואיפוך פי' המורה ברישא תני תצא. ובסיפא תני לא תצא. ב' אומרים ראינוה שנתקדשה וב' אומרים לא ראינוה שנתקדשה ה"ז לא תנשא. פשיטא לא ראינו אינו ראיה. ל"צ דדיירו בחצר א'. מ"ד אי איתא דקדיש קלא אית ליה למילתא קמ"ל דעבידי אינשי דמקדשי בצנעא. ואי קשה טעמא דאמר' לא ראינוה שנתקדשה דלא ראינוה אינה ראיה [בבירור] דלא נתקדשה כגון דאמרו האשה או המקדש הי' עמנו במקום פ' שמעידים עדות ברורה. ה"נ דאם נשאת לא תצא (א) ואמאי לא תצא. תרי ותרי נינהו והבא עלי' באשם תלוי קאי. ואי אמרת דר"א קסבר דאפילו בתרי ותרי אמרי' אוקי מה דתניא מפרשא שפיר גבי נתקדשה לא תצא דאוקמי' לה אחזקה קמייתא ופנויה הות וגבי נתגרשה תצא דמוקמינן לה אחזקתה דא"א הות. ומדלא אוקמוה הכי ש"מ דלא אמרינן תרי ותרי אוקמה אחזקתה. משום דהוי ספק תורה והבא עליה באשם תלוי קאי תשובה. אילו העידו עדות ברורה. כגון שאמרו אנו היינו כל היום עמכם באותו חצר ולא נתפרדנו מהם כלל ולא יתכן שנתקדשה באותו היום שאילו כך גם אנחנו היינו רואים המעשה. אלא שקר אתם מעידים. אין לומר בכאן תרי ותרי נינהו. שזאת היא הזמה

גליון הש"ס

גמ' שרינהו סוף עול אתו שבוינהו. עיין ב"ב קמנו ע"א תד"ה רב מרי. שבת קנד ע"ב תוס' ד"ה ואמרי לה: תוס' ד"ה אית ליה. אע"ג דרב המנונא איירי בפניו. עיין יבמות קטז ע"ב תד"ה באותה שעה:

תורה אור השלם

א) יֵשׁ רָעָה רָאִיתִי תַּחַת הַשָּׁמֶשׁ כִּשְׁגָגָה שֶׁיֹּצָא מִלִּפְנֵי הַשַּׁלִּיט: [קהלת י, ה]

ליקוטי רש"י

[נדפס בדף כב:]

חשק שלמה על תוס' רי"ד א) ולפי מש"כ הר"ן כאן דמיירי שנשאת לאחד מעדיה שאמרו לא ראינו שנתקדשה לק"מ ועי' לעיל (דף כב ע"ב) כגון שנישאת וכו' ודו"ק.

The Gemara questions the Baraisa:

מַאי שְׁנָא רֵישָׁא וּמַאי שְׁנָא סֵיפָא – **What is the difference between the first** case **and the last** case? Why does the Baraisa allow the woman to remain married where the issue is betrothal, but requires her to leave where the issue is divorce?[1]

The Gemara answers:

אָמַר אַבַּיֵי – **Abaye**[2] **said:** תַּרְגְּמָהּ בְּעֵד אֶחָד – **Render it** [the Baraisa] as referring **to one witness.**[3] Thus, the Baraisa's first clause can be explained as follows: עֵד אֶחָד אוֹמֵר נִתְקַדְּשָׁה – If **one witness says** that [**a woman**] **was betrothed**[4] וְעֵד אֶחָד אוֹמֵר לֹא נִתְקַדְּשָׁה – **and one witness says** that **she was not betrothed,** תַּרְוַיְיהוּ בִּפְנוּיָה קָמַסְהֲדֵי – **they are both testifying about an unmarried woman** (i.e. both agree that she was previously unmarried). וְהַאי דְּקָאָמַר נִתְקַדְּשָׁה הֲוָה לֵיהּ חַד – **Now, this** witness **who says** that **she was betrothed is** only **one witness,** וְאֵין דְּבָרָיו שֶׁל אֶחָד בִּמְקוֹם שְׁנַיִם – **and the words of one** witness **are not** significant **next to** the words of **two** witnesses.[5] סֵיפָא – As for **the last part** of the Baraisa, it is understood as follows: עֵד אֶחָד אוֹמֵר נִתְגָּרְשָׁה – If **one witness says** that **she was divorced** וְעֵד אֶחָד אוֹמֵר לֹא נִתְגָּרְשָׁה – **and one witness says** that **she was not divorced,** תַּרְוַיְיהוּ בְּאֵשֶׁת אִישׁ קָמַסְהֲדֵי – **they are both testifying about a married woman** (i.e. both agree that she was previously married). וְהַאי דְּקָאָמַר נִתְגָּרְשָׁה הֲוָה לֵיהּ חַד – **Now, this** witness **who says that she was divorced is** only **one witness,** וְאֵין דְּבָרָיו שֶׁל אֶחָד בִּמְקוֹם שְׁנַיִם – **and the words of one** witness **are not** significant **next to** the words of **two** witnesses.[6]

The Gemara offers a different explanation of the Baraisa:

רַב אַשִׁי אָמַר – **Rav Ashi said:** לְעוֹלָם תְּרֵי וּתְרֵי – **Actually,** the Baraisa does refer to **two** witnesses testifying that the woman was betrothed or divorced **and two** witnesses testifying to the contrary. וְאֵיפוּךְ – **But** one must **reverse** the rulings in the two cases. That is, where the witnesses disagree regarding betrothal, the law is that the woman must leave her new husband; but where the issue is divorce, she may stay with him.

Rav Ashi proceeds to explain the Baraisa's first clause:

שְׁנַיִם אוֹמְרִים רְאִינוּהָ שֶׁנִּתְקַדְּשָׁה – If **two** witnesses **say, "We saw her become betrothed,"** וּשְׁנַיִם אוֹמְרִים לֹא רְאִינוּהָ שֶׁנִּתְקַדְּשָׁה – **and two** witnesses **say, "We did not see her become betrothed,"**[7] הֲרֵי זוֹ לֹא תִנָּשֵׂא – **this** woman **may not marry** another man, וְאִם נִשֵּׂאת תֵּצֵא – **and if she did marry** another man, **she** must **leave** him.

The Gemara questions why this ruling is needed:

פְּשִׁיטָא – **It is obvious!** לֹא רְאִינוּהָ אֵינָהּ רְאָיָה – After all, **"we have not seen" is not a proof.**[8]

The Gemara isolates the circumstance in which this ruling is necessary:

לֹא צְרִיכָא דְּדָיְירֵי בְּחָצֵר אֶחָד – **It is needed only where they** [the woman and the witnesses who did not see the betrothal][9] **live in the same courtyard.** מַהוּ דְּתֵימָא אִם אִיתָא דְּנִתְקַדְּשָׁה – **You might have said that if she was indeed betrothed,** קָלָא אִית לָהּ לְמִילְּתָא – **the matter would have been publicized** among the neighbors. Accordingly, since these witnesses, who are also residents of the courtyard, claim to have no knowledge of the

NOTES

1. The Rishonim find difficulty with the Gemara's question. There would appear to be a simple explanation for this difference: Where the witnesses dispute whether this woman was betrothed, she was previously in the permitted state of being single. Hence, even after her marital status is cast into doubt, the rule of *chazakah* should dictate that she remain permitted. [She should therefore be allowed to remain with her new husband. Since, however, there is some disagreement about her status, she may not marry in the first place, lest she become the subject of disparaging gossip (*Maharam Schif*).] But where the issue is divorce, she was previously in the prohibited state of a married woman. She should therefore remain prohibited and be required to leave her present husband. Why did the Gemara not understand the Baraisa in this manner? (*Tosafos* et al.).

Some Rishonim answer that this approach fails to explain why in the case of betrothal the woman may stay in her subsequent marriage. Even where a woman is Biblically permitted according to the rule of *chazakah,* Rabbinic law still regards her as possibly married (see 22b note 7). This Rabbinic injunction would suffice to render her forbidden to her new husband (*Tosafos'* first answer; *Ritva;* cf. *Rashba, Tos. Rid* and *Shitah Mekubetzes* ד״ה וז״ל שיטה ישנה; see also *Tosafos* to 26b ד״ה אנן). [It should be noted that if her new husband is one of the witnesses who testified that she is permitted and she herself is sure that she is permitted, she may remain with him in both cases, betrothal and divorce. This follows the halachically accepted view of the Tanna Kamma of the Baraisa (top of 22b), as explained by the Gemara there.]

2. The text of *Rif* and the other Rishonim reads רַב פָּפָּא, *Rav Pappa.* (See *Ramban* cited by *Ran* et al.)

3. The Baraisa should be emended to read that *one* witness said that she was betrothed (or divorced) and *one* witness denied it (*Ran* ד״ה עד).

4. That is, one witness reports that she was betrothed before *two* witnesses (who are not available to testify). A betrothal is not valid unless it is performed before two witnesses (see *Ran* et al.).

5. Once it has been established (through the testimony of two witnesses) that this woman was previously single, one witness does not suffice to testify that she was subsequently betrothed.

The Rishonim question the role served by the witness who says that the woman was not betrothed. Even without him, the witness to the betrothal would be rejected in light of the rule: אֵין דָּבָר שֶׁבְּעֶרְוָה פָּחוֹת מִשְּׁנַיִם, *no matter that concerns ervah* (i.e. marital relationship or status) *can be [resolved] by less than two [witnesses].* Now, by saying "they are both testifying about an unmarried woman, etc.," the Gemara implies that this witness (who denies that the betrothal took place) is required to help establish that the woman was previously unmarried. However, he is not needed for this either, because this woman was not assumed to be previously married in any event. For various solutions of these and other related issues, see *Tosafos, Tos. HaRosh, Rashba, Ritva, Ran* et al.

[From the preceding it is evident that if a single witness testifies that a woman was betrothed (before two witnesses), even if he is not contradicted by anyone, his testimony would not suffice to require her to leave a different husband. According to some authorities, though, she may not marry in the first place (even if the witness *is* contradicted), lest her behavior invoke disparaging gossip (*Meiri; Rashba; Raavad, Hil. Ishus* 9:31; cf. *Tosafos* and *Tos. HaRosh;* see *Maggid Mishneh* ibid. and *Shulchan Aruch, Even HaEzer* 47:3, with *Beis Shmuel;* see also *Shaar HaMelech, Hil. Ishus* 9:31).]

6. That is, a single witness does not suffice to effect a change in a woman's marital status. This being so, the woman is viewed as still married to her first husband, and thus if she marries another man, she would have to leave him. [In this case, we *do* need the witness who denies that the divorce took effect, because the woman was assumed to be single until now (see 22b note 17). Hence, without this witness, the woman would still be assumed to be single, and she would be permitted to remarry.]

Regarding the question of why the witness claiming to have seen the divorce is not believed by virtue of *happeh she'assar,* see the sources cited in 22b note 18.

7. Instead of saying, "We saw that she was *not betrothed,*" they said, "We did *not see* that she was betrothed." Until now, the Gemara discussed cases in which one set of witnesses testify that a certain event (betrothal, divorce) happened at a particular time, and an opposing set of witnesses are certain that the event in question did not happen then (e.g. they were with the woman at that time and saw that she was not betrothed or divorced). Rav Ashi, however, interprets this Baraisa as referring to a case in which the second witnesses say only that they failed to observe the event; they do not claim to have seen that the event did *not* occur (*Tos. HaRosh*). The Gemara will ask why this type of testimony is of any value.

8. Just because these witnesses did not see the betrothal does not indicate that it did not occur. Hence, the testimony of the other witnesses, who did see the betrothal, is in effect unopposed.

9. *Shitah Mekubetzes* ד״ה לא ראינוה.

אִם אִיתָא דְּהָכִי הֲוָה – **"If this is indeed what happened** [viz. that you were recently divorced], אַחֲוֵי לָן גִּיטִּיךְ – **show us your *get*!"**[25]

Another Baraisa that discusses the law where two sets of witnesses contradict each other about a woman's marital status: תָּנוּ רַבָּנָן – **The Rabbis taught in a Baraisa:** שְׁנַיִם אוֹמְרִים נִתְקַדְּשָׁה – If TWO witnesses SAY that [A WOMAN] WAS BETROTHED, וּשְׁנַיִם אוֹמְרִים לֹא נִתְקַדְּשָׁה – AND TWO witnesses SAY THAT SHE WAS NOT BETROTHED, הֲרֵי זוֹ לֹא תִּנָּשֵׂא – THIS woman MAY NOT MARRY another man. וְאִם נִשֵּׂאת לֹא תֵּצֵא – BUT IF SHE DID MARRY another man, SHE DOES NOT have to LEAVE him.

A second case:

שְׁנַיִם אוֹמְרִים נִתְגָּרְשָׁה – If TWO witnesses SAY that [A WOMAN] WAS DIVORCED, וּשְׁנַיִם אוֹמְרִים לֹא נִתְגָּרְשָׁה – AND TWO witnesses SAY THAT SHE WAS NOT DIVORCED, הֲרֵי זוֹ לֹא תִּנָּשֵׂא – THIS woman MAY NOT MARRY another man. וְאִם נִשֵּׂאת תֵּצֵא – AND IF SHE DID MARRY another man, SHE must LEAVE him.

NOTES

25. If she was recently divorced, she would still have the *get* (divorce document) in her possession. A woman cannot claim that she lost her *get* in such a short time (*Rashi*). Hence, this woman's failure to produce a *get* indicates that the truth lies with the witnesses who say that she was not divorced. She must consequently leave her second husband, even if he is one of the witnesses who testified that she was divorced [and she too is sure that the divorce was valid] (*Ritva, Meiri*).

The Rishonim note that her lack of a *get* is not an absolute proof; it is significant only in a case such as ours, where witnesses disagree as to whether there was a divorce. Should the witnesses to the divorce be unopposed, her failure to produce the *get* would be immaterial (*Rashba, Ran;* see also *Meiri* סד״ה זה שכתבנו). [It should also be noted that according to this explanation of his rulings, R' Yochanan does *not* speak of an instance in which the doubt is whether the *get* ever reached close enough to her to effect her divorce (see note 17). In that case, her current lack of a *get* would not be a factor.]

אמתלא לדבריה נאמנת תנא מיניה ארבעים זימנין ואפ"ה לא עבד שמואל עובדא בנפשיה ת"ר שנים אומרים מת ושנים אומרים לא מת שנים אומרים נתגרשה ושנים אומרים לא נתגרשה הרי זו לא תנשא ואם נשאת לא תצא רבי מנחם בר יוסי אומר תצא אמר רבי מנחם בר יוסי אימתי אני אומר תצא בזמן שבאו עדים ואח"כ נשאת אבל נשאת ואח"כ באו עדים לא תצא מכדי תרי ותרי נינהו הבא עליה באשם תלוי קאי א"ר ששת כגון שנשאת לאחד מעדיה היא גופה באשם תלוי קיימא באומרת ברי לי אמר רבי יוחנן שנים אומרים מת ושנים אומרים לא מת הרי זו לא תנשא ואם נשאת לא תצא שנים אומרים נתגרשה ושנים אומרים לא נתגרשה הרי זו לא תנשא ואם נשאת תצא מאי שנא רישא ומאי שנא סיפא אמר אביי תרגמה בעד אחד עד אחד אומר מת הימנוהו רבנן כבי תרי וכדעולא דאמר עולא כל מקום שהאמינה תורה עד אחד הרי כאן שנים והאי דקאמר לא מת הוה ליה חד ואין דבריו של אחד במקום שנים אי הכי אפי' לכתחלה נמי משום דרב אסי דא"ר אסי הסר ממך עקשות פה ולזות שפתים הרחק ממך סיפא עד אחד אומר נתגרשה ועד אחד אומר לא נתגרשה תרוייהו באשת איש קמסהדי והאי דקאמר נתגרשה הוה ליה חד ואין דבריו של אחד במקום שנים רבא אמר לעולם תרי ותרי נינהו וראה ר' יוחנן דבריו של ר' מנחם בר יוסי בגרושין ולא ראה במיתה מ"ט מיתה אינה יכולה מכחשתו ומי חציפה כולי האי והאמר רב המנונא האשה שאמרה לבעלה גרשתני נאמנת חזקה אין אשה מעיזה פניה בפני בעלה הני מילי היכא דליכא עדים דקא מסייעי לה אבל היכא דאיכא עדים דקא מסייעי לה מעיזה ומעיזה רב אסי אמר כגון דאמרי עדים עכשיו מת עכשיו גירשה מיתה ליכא לברורה גירושין איכא לברורה דאמרינן לה אם איתא דהכי הוה אחוי לן גיטיך תנו רבנן שנים אומרים נתקדשה ושנים אומרים לא נתקדשה הרי זו לא תנשא ואם נשאת לא תצא שנים אומרים נתגרשה ושנים אומרים לא נתגרשה הרי זו לא תנשא ואם נשאת תצא

מאי

רש"י

אמתלא. משל וטעם למה אמרה תחלה מקודשת אני: אם נתנה אמתלא לדבריה נאמנת. הואיל ונתנה אמתלא נאמנת: אמרה טמאה אני. אמרה לבעלה נדה אני: טהורה אני. לא הייתי נדה: לא עבד שמואל עובדא בנפשיה. פעם אחת אמרה לו אשתו כן ונתנה אמתלא לדבריה ופירש הימנה עד שטבלה: לא תצא. ולקמיה פריך תרי ותרי נינהו: שבאו עדים. שאמרו לא מת: באשם תלוי. בא על ספק כרת: לאחד מעדיה. שאמרו מת דאין אשם תלוי אלא למי שלבו נוקפו וזה אומר ברי לי: באומרת ברי לי. אין לבי נוקפי שברי לי שאילו היה קיים היה בא: תרגמה. להא דר' יוחנן: בעד אחד. ולאו שנים איתמר אלא עד אומר כו' ועד אומר כו': הימנוהו רבנן כבתרי. לומר מת כדאמרינן ביבמות בהאשה מתוך חומר שהחמרת עליה בסופה הקלת עליה בתחלתה: אפי' לכתחלה נמי. תינשא: דרב אסי. ביבמות בפ' שני: תרוויהו באשת איש קא מסהדי. שניהן מעידין שאשת איש היתה: מיתה אינה יכולה מכחשתו. אם יבא בעלה אינה יכולה לומר מת אתה הלכך אי לאו דברי לה שמת מירתתא ולא מינסבא: גירושין יכולה מכחשתו. אם יבא ויאמר לא גירשתיך היא תאמר גירשתני הלכך אי שרית לה סמכה אהכחשה ומינסבא על פי עדים הללו מספק ולא מירתתא למידק שפיר: עכשיו מת. היום: ליכא לברורה. אם אמרו טבע במים או אכלו ארי אין אנו יכולין לברר הדברים הלכך לכתחלה לא תינשא ואם ניסת לא תצא כרבנן וכשניסת לאחד מעדיה: אחוי גיטך. דבשעתא פורתא לא מהימנא למימר אירכס לי: הרי זו לא תנשא. לאחר:

תוספות

חזרה ואמרה טהורה אני מהו. פירוש מועיל אמתלא או לא אלא אין לפרש מהו אם צריכה אמתלא או לא דמדקאמר אף בזו אם נתנה כו': ואפילו הכי לא עבד שמואל עובדא בנפשיה. ר"ח הביא ירושלמי שמואל בעא לאזדקוקי לאתתיה אמרה ליה טמאה אני ולמחר אמרה טהורה אני אמר לה אתמול טמאה יומא דין טהורה אמרה ליה אתמול לא הוות בי חילא כי ההיא שעתא אתא שאיל לרב אמר ליה אם נתנה אמתלא לדבריה נאמנת.

הבא עליה באשם תלוי קאי. תימה דלמסקנא קאי דהא מסקינן בפרק ד' אחים (יבמות דף לא. ושם) דתרי ותרי ספיקא דרבנן ומדאורייתא אוקמה אחזקה ומאי משני נמי כשניסת לאחד מעדיה הא עד נמי בתנק קאי דלוקמה אחזקה ואומר ר"ת דחזקה דאשה דייקא ומנסבא מרעה לה להך חזקה דמהאי טעמא נמי שרינן לה כי ליכא עדים כלל א) אע"פ שהיא בחזקת אשת איש: באשם תלוי. אפי' למאן דבעי חתיכה אחת משתי חתיכות הכא לא בעינן שתי חתיכות דמאן דמפרש בפרק ספק אכל (כריתות דף יז: ושם) טעמא דבעינן חתיכה משתי חתיכות משום דאפשר לברר איסורו פי' אפשר לברר על ידי בקי שיכיר חתיכה הנשארת אם חלב היא אם שומן היא הכא נמי אפשר לברר ע"י הזמה ולמאן דמפרש משום דבעינן חתיכות אחת של חלב ואחת של שומן איקבע איסורא ה"נ איקבע איסורא שהיתה בחזקת אשת איש אי נמי לאו אשם תלוי ממש קאמר אלא כלומר באיסור אשם תלוי: כגון שניסת לאחד מעדיה. והא דתנן בפ' שני דיבמות (דף כה. ושם) הרגנוהו לא ישא את אשתו לאו ששנים מעידין כן דבשום מקום אין שנים חשודין כדמוכח לקמן דאפילו למאן דחייש לגומלין אם שנים מעידין על זה ושנים על זה נאמנין וכן מוכח נמי בפ"ב דיבמות (ג"ז שם) דתנן התם מיאנה או שחלצה בפניו ישאנה מפני שהוא ב"ד ודייק בגמרא טעמא דב"ד הא בתרי לא מאי שנא מהא דתנן עדים החתומים על שדה מקח או על גט אשה לא חשו חכמים לדבר זה היא גופה קמשמע לן לאפוקי ממ"ד מילון בשנים אלא כלומר שהרגו עם אנשים הרבה: אי הכי לכתחלה נמי.

ומהא דתנן בהאשה שלום (יבמות דף קיז: ושם) עד אחד אומר מת ועד אחד אומר לא מת הרי זו לא תנשא ליכא לאקשויי לעולא דהתם איירי בבת אחת ואפילו אם ניסת תצא ועולא איירי בזה אחר זה כשבא עד אחד ואמר מת התירוה ואח"כ בא אחר ואמר לא מת אם נשאת לא תצא אבל לכתחלה לא תנשא משום דרב אסי כדמסיק ומרישא דהתם יש להוכיח שיש חילוק בין בבת אחת בין בזה אחר זה דקתני עד אחד אומר מת וניסת ובא אחר ואמר לא מת לא תצא ומפרש בגמרא דלא ניסת ממש אלא התירוה לינשא אע"פ שלא ניסת ולא תצא היינו מהתירה הראשון משמע דווקא התירוה קודם שבא העד ואמר לא מת הא בא קודם שהתירוה לא וכ"ע בפ' מי שקינא (סוטה דף לא:) דמשמע דאיירי עולא בכל ענין בין בב"א בין בזה אחר זה דתנן התם עד אחד אומר נטמאת ועד אחד אומר לא נטמאת היתה שותה ודייק בגמ' טעמא דהאי מכחיש אבל לא מכחיש עד אחד נאמן מנא ה"מ כו' ופריך כיון דמדאורייתא עד אחד נאמן אידך היכי מצי מכחיש ליה והאמר עולא כל מקום שהאמינה כו' אלא אמר עולא תני לא היתה שותה ור' חייא אומר היתה שותה לר' חייא קשיא דעולא לא קשיא כאן בבת אחת כאן בזה אחר זה משמע דעולא נמי איירי בבת אחת ולכך צריך להגיה ולא משני כדמשני ר' חייא ומיהו איכא למימר דעולא לא מיירי אלא בזה אחר זה אלא שנראה לו דוחק להעמיד המשנה בבת אחת משום דמשמע ליה דמיירי בזה אחר זה ועוד אומר ר"י דאפילו איירי לעולא בכל ענין הני מילי התם דמדאורייתא עד אחד מהימן בסוטה כדנפקא ליה התם מועד אין בה אבל הכא גבי אשה דלא מהימן אלא מדרבנן לא חשיב כשנים אלא בזה אחר זה ואע"ג דיש חילוק בין דאורייתא לרבנן מייתי מדעולא דנראה לו דחשיב כשנים בזה אחר זה בדרבנן כמו בבת אחת בדאורייתא:

משום דרב אסי הסר ממך עקשות פה. פסוק הוא אלא דרב אסי רגיל להביאו וא"ת והא דתנן בהאשה שלום (יבמות דף קיז: ושם) עד אחד אומר מת וניסת ובא עד אחד ואמר לא מת לא תצא ופריך בגמרא טעמא דניסת הא לא ניסת לא תנשא והאמר עולא כל מקום כו' ומאי פריך והא עולא לא קאמר אלא בדיעבד אבל לכתחלה מודה דלא תנשא משום דרב אסי ואומר ר"י דהתם דייק טעמא דניסת הא אם לא נשאת לא תנשא ואם נשאת תצא דהכי משמע מתניתין דוקא נשאת ואחר כך בא העד לא תצא הא בא העד קודם שנשאת ואחר כך ניסת תצא משום הכי פריך מדעולא ואם תאמר והיכי משני התם דה"ק עד אחד אומר מת והתירוה לינשא ובא אחר ואמר לא מת לא תצא מהתירה הראשון משמע ותנשא לכתחלה וי"ל דודאי לכתחלה לא תנשא ולא תצא מהתירה הראשון לענין דאם ניסת לא תצא:

תרוייהו באשת איש קמסהדי. תימה דמה לנו לאותו עד שאומר לא נתגרשה בלא איהו נמי תצא דאין דבר שבערוה פחות משנים דהא ליכא למימר שלא היינו יודעים שהיא א"א כי אם על פיהם דא"כ להימניה להאי דאמר מגורשת במיגו דאי בעי שתק וי"ל דאין זה מיגו דשמא רוצה להעיד כדי לפוסלה מן הכהונה. ת"י:

עין משפט נר מצוה

סה א ב ג מיי' פ"ב מהל' גירושין הל' יג טוש"ע אה"ע סימן יז סעיף מב:
סו ד מיי' שם הלכה ח טוש"ע אה"ע סימן קנב סעיף ג:
סז ה מיי' שם הלכה יח טוש"ע אה"ע סימן יז סעיף נב:
סח ו מיי' שם הלכה ט טוש"ע אה"ע סימן קנב סעיף ה:
סט ז מיי' שם הלכה ד ופ"ד מהל' אישות הלכה יג סמג עשין מח טוש"ע אה"ע סימן מז סעיף ב:
ע ח ט מיי' פי"ב מהל' גירושין הל' ו ז טוש"ע אה"ע סי' קנב סעיף ג:

תוספות רי"ד

גדולה בנוי' קפצו עליה בני אדם לקדשה וא"ל מקודשת אני לימים עמדה וקדש' ע"א אמרו לה חכמים מה ראית א"ל בתחלה שבאו עלי בני אדם שאינם מהוגנים אמרתי מקודשת אני עכשיו שבאו עלי בני אדם שהן הגונים לי עמדתי וקדשתי את עצמי וזו הלכה העלה ר"א שר הבירה לפני חכמים ואמרו אם נתנה אמתלא לדבריה נאמנת בעא מיניה שמואל מרב אמרה טמאה אני פי' נדה וחזרה ואמרה טהורה אני מהו א"ל אף בזו אם נתנה אמתלא לדבריה נאמנת: תנא מיניה מ' זמנין ואפ"ה לא עביד שמואל עובדא בנפשיה כדאיתא בירושלמי פעם אחת אמרה ל' אשתו כן ונתנה אמתלא לדבריה ופירש ממנ' עד שטבלה: ת"ר שנים אומרים מת ושנים אומרים לא מת שנים אומרים נתגרשה ושנים אומרים לא נתגרשה ה"ז ל"ת ואם נשאת לא תצא מכדי תרי ותרי נינהו הבא עלי' באשם תלוי קאי פי' בא על ספק כרת אר"ש כגון שנשאת לאחד מעדיה פי' שאומר מת שאין אשם תלוי אלא למי שלבו נוקפו אבל זה אומר ברי לי לאינש דעלמא תצא ואע"ג דתנן בפ"ב דיבמות מת לא ישא את אשתו דוקא בחד אבל בתרי ליכא למיחש כדאוקימנא התם דתרי לא חשידי. היא גופה באשם תלוי קיימא באומרת ברי לי פי' שאבאת גם היא אומרת משם שהיא אומרת מת בעלי ואם על העדים סמכה תצא ור"מ בר"י מפליג ואמר שאם באו עדי האוסרים תחלה ואח"כ נשאת ואפילו לאחד מעדיה ואע"ג דאמרה ברי לי תצא ניין בהאשה רבה. אר"י ב' אומרים מת וב' אומרים לא מת ה"ז ל' תנשא ואם נשאת ל"ת ב' אומרים נתגרשה וב' אומרים לא נתגרשה ה"ז לא תנשא ואם נשאת תצא מ"ש רישא ומ"ש סיפא ואוקמי' רבא ראה ר"י דברי ר' מנחם בר"י בגירושין ולא ראה דבריו במיתה מ"ש מיתה אינה יכולה להכחישו פי' אם יבא בעלה א"י לומר לו מת אתה הלכך אי לאו דברי לה שמת מירתתא ולא מינסבא עד דדייקא שפיר דחיישי לקלקולא ולא גירושין יכולה להכחישו פי' אם יבא ויאמר לא גרשתיך היא תאמר גרשתני הלכך אי שרית לה סמכא אדעתא ומינסבא ע"פ עדות הללו מספק ולא מירתתא למידק שפיר ומי מחצפי בי' והאמר ר"ה האשה שאמרה לבעלה גרשתני נאמנת דחזקתו אין אשה מעיזה פניה בפני בעלה ה"מ היכא דליכא עדים דמסייע לה אבל היכא דאיכא עדים דמסייע לה מעיזה ומעיזה ומדמקשינן ממילתא דר"ה ש"מ דהכי הל' שאין התלמוד מקשה אלא מהל' פסוקה כך העמדנו בגיטין בריש פ' התקבל: ר"א אמר דאמרו עדים עכשיו מת פי' היום מת עכשיו גירשה מיתה ליכא לברורי פי' אם אמרו טבע בים או אכלו ארי אין אנו יכולים לברר הדברים הלכך לכתחלה לא תנשא מיד דהא צריכה להמתין שלשה חדשים ואם נשאת לא תצא כרבנן וכשנשאת לאחד מעדיה. גירושין איכא לברורינהו דאמרי לה אי איתא דהכי הוא אחוי גיטך פי' ולא תנשא מיד דהא צריכה להמתין ג' חדשים אלא כגון שהמתינה ג' חדשים ונשאת ואפ"ה כיון שעדים העידו שעכשיו גירשה אמרינן לה אי איתא כדאמרת הוה לך לאחזי גיטא דבשעתא פורתא לא מהימנא למימר אירכס לי א"נ שקרא מסהדי דמשקרי אבל אם מעידים שגירשה זה כמה ימים

מסורת הש"ס

א) [לקמן דף כ. וש"נ], ב) יבמות פח: ב"ב לא., ג) [שם ביבמות], ד) יבמות פח: קח: סוטה לא: מז., ה) יבמות כד:, ו) שם קטז. נדרים לא. גיטין סד: סט:, ז) [שייך לע"ל עד ד"ה לא עבד שמואל כו'], ח) [שייך לע"ל], ט) [יבמות פח: כתבו תוס' דבר זה בשם ר"י וע"ע תוס' ב"ב לב. ד"ה אלו], י) [וע"ע תוס' לקמן כו: ד"ה אלו].

תוספות ישנים

א) ובשנים אומרים נתגרשה נמי דייקא כי ירא שלא יוחזו עדיה אבל חזקה דאין אשה מעיזה ליכא כיון דליכא עדים דקא מסייעי לה. ת"י עה"ג.

תורה אור השלם

א) הָסֵר מִמְּךָ עִקְּשׁוּת פֶּה וּלְזוּת שְׂפָתַיִם הַרְחֵק מִמֶּךָּ: [משלי ד, כד]

ליקוטי רש"י

שנים אומרים מת. אשה שהלך בעלה למדינת הים ובאו שנים ואמרו לה מת בעליך ושנים אומרים לא מת וא"נ שנים אומרים נתגרשה בחיי בעלה ואינה זקוקה ליבם ושנים אומרים לא נתגרשה וזקוקה ליבם א"נ כגון שעדיין בעלה קיים ובאין להתירה לאחר. הרי זו לא תנשא. דלאוקי תרי לתרי ואוקמה בחזקת איסור אשת איש קיימא. ואם נשאת לא תצא. דיעבד אין מוציאין לה. בזמן שבאו עדים. המכחישים שאמרו לא מת ולא נשאת. אבל נשאת. על פי עדי מיתה שהתירוה בית דין לינשא ואחר כך באו עדים שהוא קיים לא תצא דמחזקינן לזילותא דבי דינא. עד אחד אומר מת. בעלה שמתה ואחד אומר מת וכו' דמי לאומרת ברי לי. כגון ע"י סימנים וכו' אלא על מי שלבו נוקפו. תרגמה. פרש אותה [סוטה ח:]. הרי כאן שנים. הרי הוא חשוב כשנים כגון בעדות אשה לומר שמת בעלה ובעדות סוטה לומר נטמאה. ואין דבריו של אחד. דאמר לא מת במקום שנים [יבמות שם]. הסר ממך עקשות פה. לא תעשה דבר שילעיזו בו הבריות ויעקימו עליך פיהם. עקשות פה. לשון עקוס כמו תם אני ויעקשני (איוב ט) ובמשנה שיהו עקומות ועקושות. ולזות שפתים. עקמימות שפתים שלא ירחיבו הבריות פה עליך [משלי ד, כד].

[מכאן שייך לדף כג.]

תרגמה. פרש אותה [סוטה ח:]. דבשבויה הקילו. דספיקא בעלמא היא [ב"ק קיד:]. שלא ראינוה שנבעלה [לקמן נא:]. דהרבה הקילו בה חכמים במסכת כתובות דאפי' אשה ועד אחד נאמנין לומר טהורה וטעמא דבשביל שנתייחדה בין השבאין אין לנו לאסרה שהרי סתם אשה משמרת עצמה מזונות ואוקמה אחזקתה ואיסור קל הוא אם ניסאת לכהן [רשב"ם ב"ב קלה.]. אבוה דשמואל. אבא בר אבא אבוה דשמואל הוה, וחסיד גדול היה [חולין קיא:]. שרינהו. רבי חנינא להנשא לכהנים [רשב"ם שם]. כשגגה שיוצא מלפני השליט. דומה הוא לשליט שהוציא דבר שגגה מפיו שוגג ואי אפשר לחזור כך אומר הקב"ה ואין להשיב [קהלת ז, ה]. השתא מיהת ליתנהו. ואינן מעידין על שבייתן ונתירם. עדים בצד אפתן. רוח צפונית ואינן באים ומעידים ותאסר בתמיה [קידושין יב:].

witnesses attest that she was previously married),[17] וְהַאי דְּקָאָמַר נִתְגָּרְשָׁה הָוֵה לֵיהּ חַד – **and this** witness **who says that she was divorced is** only **one** witness, וְאֵין דְּבָרָיו שֶׁל אֶחָד בִּמְקוֹם שְׁנַיִם – **and the words of one** witness **are not** significant **next to** the words of **two** witnesses.[18]

The Gemara offers a second explanation of R' Yochanan's rulings:

רָבָא אָמַר – **Rava said:** לְעוֹלָם תְּרֵי וּתְרֵי נִינְהוּ – **Actually,** R' Yochanan does refer to a case in which **they** [the witnesses] **are two** testifying that the husband died or divorced his wife **and two** witnesses testifying to the contrary. וְרָאָה רַבִּי יוֹחָנָן דְּבָרָיו שֶׁל רַבִּי מְנַחֵם בַּר יוֹסֵי בְּגֵרוּשִׁין – **However, R' Yochanan accepted the opinion of R' Menachem bar Yose in the case of divorce,** וְלֹא רָאָה בְּמִיתָה – **and he did not accept** the opinion of R' Menachem bar Yose **in the case of death.**[19] מַאי טַעְמָא – **What is the reason** for this difference? מִיתָה אֵינָהּ יְכוֹלָה מַכְחַשְׁתּוֹ – In the case of **death,** if the husband returns, **[the woman] cannot contradict him** and claim that he is dead! גֵּרוּשִׁין יְכוֹלָה מַכְחַשְׁתּוֹ – But in the case of **divorce,** if the husband claims that he did not divorce her, **she can contradict him.**[20]

The Gemara challenges the last point:

וּמִי חֲצִיפָה כּוּלֵּי הַאי – **But would she be so impudent** as to lie about having been divorced? וְהָאָמַר רַב הַמְנוּנָא – **Why, Rav Hamnuna has said:** הָאִשָּׁה שֶׁאָמְרָה לְבַעְלָהּ גֵּרַשְׁתַּנִי – **If a woman said to her husband, "You have divorced me,"** נֶאֱמֶנֶת – **she is believed,** חֲזָקָה אֵין אִשָּׁה מְעִיזָּה פָּנֶיהָ בִּפְנֵי בַּעְלָהּ – because there is **a presumption** that **a woman would not be** so **brazen** as to declare **before her husband** that he divorced her unless that were the truth.[21] – ? –

The Gemara answers:

הָנֵי מִילֵּי – **This ruling** by Rav Hamnuna applies only הֵיכָא דְּלֵיכָּא עֵדִים דְּקָא מְסַיְּיעֵי לָהּ – **where there are no witnesses who support her** claim that she was divorced; אֲבָל הֵיכָא דְּאִיכָּא עֵדִים דְּקָא מְסַיְּיעֵי לָהּ – **but where there are witnesses who support her** claim, מְעִיזָּה וּמְעִיזָּה – **she would indeed be brazen** and lie to her husband's face.[22]

The third explanation of R' Yochanan's rulings:

רַב אַסִּי אָמַר – **Rav Assi**[23] **said:** כְּגוֹן דְּאָמְרֵי עֵדִים – R' Yochanan refers to **a case where the witnesses said,** עַכְשָׁיו מֵת – **"He died now"** [i.e. today], עַכְשָׁיו גֵּירְשָׁהּ – or **"He divorced her now."** מִיתָה לֵיכָּא לְבְרוּרָה – In the case of **death, there is no** way **to determine** whether **it** occurred.[24] גֵּירוּשִׁין אִיכָּא לְבְרוּרָה – But in the case of **divorce, there is** a way **to determine** whether **it** occurred, דְּאָמְרִינַן לָהּ – **because we say to her,**

NOTES

17. Until these witnesses testified, this woman was assumed to be single. Accordingly, their testimony is required to establish that in fact she was married (see *Tos. Yeshanim, Rashba, Ritva* et al.).

The Rishonim ask: A witness who deliberately lies is ineligible to give any testimony. Hence, in this case, where one of the witnesses must be lying (for they contradict each other), how can the Gemara say that both witnesses can be used to establish that this woman was married? One answer given is that the Gemara refers to a case where the husband attempted to divorce his wife, but it is not clear whether he succeeded. For example, he threw the *get* (divorce document) to her; one witness testified that it landed close enough to her to effect her divorce and the other witness testified that it did not (see Mishnah *Gittin* 78a). This is something about which a person can make an honest mistake. Hence, neither of the witnesses can be regarded a deliberate liar whose testimony must be completely rejected (*Rashba, Ritva, Ran* [folio 10a ד״ה עד] et al.; see also *Shach, Choshen Mishpat* 31:1 and *Nesivos* there).

18. Since two witnesses are required to effect a change in a woman's marital status, one witness does not suffice to testify that this woman was divorced.

The novel point of this part of R' Yochanan's teaching (according to Abaye's explanation) is that the witness to the divorce is not believed although the following argument could be made in his favor: Since he is required to establish that this woman was married, he should also have the authority to assert that her marriage has ended, in accordance with the rule of *happeh she'assar.* See *Tos. Yeshanim, Rashba, Re'ah, Ran* (ibid.) and *Maharam Schif,* who explain why indeed the rule of *happeh she'assar* is not effective here.

19. The Baraisa recorded previously on this *amud* considered the law in this very case, where two sets of witnesses disagree whether or not a husband died or divorced his wife. In both cases – death and divorce – the Tanna Kamma ruled that if the wife remarries, she does not have to leave her new husband, whereas R' Menachem bar Yose ruled that she does have to leave (unless she remarried before the opposing witnesses testified). [As the Gemara explained above, the Baraisa refers to an instance in which her new husband is one of the witnesses to the death or divorce and she herself is sure that the event occurred (*Ritva*).]

Rava asserts that R' Yochanan's position lies between these two. That is, R' Yochanan adopts the Tanna Kamma's lenient ruling where the issue is the husband's death, but he agrees with R' Menachem bar Yose where the issue is divorce.

20. The premise of this explanation is that the woman may not remain with her new husband unless the court has reason to assume that she fully investigated the matter and concluded that her first husband did in fact die or divorce her. [The Gemara stated above that she must say that she is certain of the death or divorce. Here Rava adds that the court must have grounds for believing that she is truly certain (see *Kovetz Shiurim* §61).] Where the issue is her husband's death, the court can indeed be sure that she made such an investigation. The reason is that if her husband returns, she obviously cannot claim that he is dead! Hence, unless she thoroughly examined the matter and determined that he died, she would not remarry for fear that he might subsequently return. But in the case of divorce, she might think that if her husband comes forward and declares that he did not divorce her, she can simply contradict him. She might therefore remarry relying solely on the witnesses who testify that she is divorced, without investigating the matter properly (*Rashi*). [There are scenarios in which the wife herself would require an investigation to determine whether she has been divorced (see, for example, note 17).]

[It was explained earlier (note 4) that the reason R' Menachem bar Yose requires her to leave her second husband is that she disobeyed the court's directive forbidding her to get married in the first place. According to R' Yochanan (as explained by Rava) this Rabbinic penalty is applied only in the case of divorce, where there are other grounds as well for prohibiting her to remarry (see *Chidushei R' Akiva Eiger* to 23a ד״ה ואולם; cf. *Pnei Yehoshua*).]

21. According to this ruling [which is accepted as authoritative halachah (*Tos. Rid;* see *Meiri* to 23a)], even where the issue is divorce, the woman in R' Yochanan's case would not remarry without first determining for herself the truth of the matter. Otherwise, she would be afraid that her husband will come forward and declare that he had not divorced her, and then, lacking definite knowledge to the contrary, she would not have the gall to contradict him. (See *R' Akiva Eiger* for elaboration on the Gemara's question.)

22. Thus, in the present case – where one of the two groups of witnesses testify that she was divorced – even if her husband comes forward and declares that he did not divorce her, she would not be afraid to falsely claim to the contrary. She would, therefore, lack a compelling motivation to make her own investigation of the divorce before remarrying. In the absence of such an investigation, R' Yochanan rules that even after she has remarried, she must leave her new husband.

23. The texts of *Rif* and *Rosh* read: רַב אַשִׁי, *Rav Ashi.* See also *Maharsha* to 23a ד״ה גמ׳ רב אשי (*Rashash*).

24. If, for example, the witnesses testify that the husband drowned at sea or was devoured by a lion, it is impossible to confirm their words [e.g. by finding the body]. Thus, we do not know which set of witnesses is telling the truth. The law, therefore, is that she may not remarry in the first place; but if she does remarry she is permitted to stay with her new husband, as the Tanna Kamma ruled in the Baraisa – provided, of course, that he is one of the witnesses to the death [and she herself is sure that the death occurred, as the Gemara explained above] (*Rashi*).

עין משפט נר מצוה

סה א ב ג מיי' פי"ט מהל' גירושין הל' יג טוש"ע אה"ע סימן יז סעיף מג:
סו ד מיי' שם הלכה ח טוש"ע אה"ע סימן קנב סעיף ג:
סז ה מיי' שם הלכה יח טוש"ע אה"ע סימן יז סעיף מ:
סח ו מיי' שב הלכה ט טוש"ע אה"ע סימן קנב סעיף ה:
סט ז מיי' שם הלכה ד ופ"ג מהל' אישות הלכה יג סמג עשין מח טוש"ע אה"ע סימן יז סעיף
ע ח ט מיי' פי"ג מהל' גירושין הל' י ז טוש"ע אה"ע סי' קמ סעיף ג:

אמתלא לדבריה נאמנת תנא [א] מיניה ארבעים זימנין ואפ"ה לא עבד שמואל עובדא בנפשיה [ב] ת"ר שנים אומרים מת ושנים אומרים לא מת שנים אומרים נתגרשה ושנים אומרים לא נתגרשה הרי זו לא תנשא ואם נשאת לא תצא רבי מנחם בר יוסי אומר תצא אמר רבי מנחם בר יוסי אימתי אני אומר תצא בזמן שבאו עדים ואח"כ נשאת אבל נשאת ואח"כ באו עדים לא תצא [ג] מכדי תרי ותרי נינהו הבא עליה באשם תלוי קאי א"ר ששת כגון [א] שנשאת לאחד מעדיה היא גופה באשם תלוי קיימא [ב] באומרת ברי לי אמר רבי יוחנן [ג] שנים אומרים מת ושנים אומרים לא מת הרי זו לא תנשא ואם נשאת לא תצא [ד] שנים אומרים נתגרשה ושנים אומרים לא נתגרשה הרי זו לא תנשא ואם נשאת תצא מאי שנא רישא ומאי שנא סיפא אמר אביי תרגמה בעד אחד [ה] עד אחד אומר מת הימנוהו רבנן כבי תרי וכדעולא דאמר עולא כל מקום [ד] שהאמינה תורה עד אחד הרי כאן שנים והאי דקאמר לא מת הוה ליה חד ואין דבריו של אחד במקום שנים אי הכי אפי' לכתחלה נמי משום דרב אסי דא"ר אסי [ה] הסר ממך עקשות פה ולזות שפתים הרחק ממך סיפא [ו] עד אחד אומר נתגרשה ועד אחד אומר לא נתגרשה תרוייהו באשת איש קמסהדי והאי דקאמר נתגרשה הוה ליה חד ואין דבריו של אחד במקום שנים רבא אמר לעולם תרי ותרי נינהו וראה ר' יוחנן דבריו של ר' מנחם בר יוסי בגרושין ולא ראה במיתה מ"ט מיתה אינה יכולה מכחשתו גרושין יכולה מכחשתו ומי חציפה כולי האי והאמר רב המנונא [ז] האשה שאמרה לבעלה גרשתני נאמנת חזקה אין אשה מעיזה פניה בפני בעלה הני מילי היכא דליכא עדים דקא מסייעי לה [ח] אבל היכא דאיכא עדים דקא מסייעי לה מעיזה ומעיזה רב אסי אמר כגון דאמרי עדים עכשיו מת עכשיו גירשה מיתה ליכא לברורה [ט] גירושין איכא לברורה דאמרינן לה אם איתא דהכי הוה אחזי לן גיטיך תנו רבנן שנים אומרים נתקדשה ושנים אומרים לא נתקדשה הרי זו לא תנשא ואם נשאת לא תצא שנים אומרים נתגרשה ושנים אומרים לא נתגרשה הרי זו לא תנשא ואם נשאת תצא מאי

[י] **אמתלא.** משל וטעם למה אמרה תחלה מקודשת אני: **אם נתנה אמתלא לדבריה נאמנת.** הואיל ונתנה אמתלא נאמנת: **אמרה טמאה אני.** אמרה לבעלה נדה אני: **טהורה אני.** לא הייתי נדה: **לא עבד שמואל עובדא בנפשיה.** פעם אחת אמרה לו אשתו כן ונתנה אמתלא לדבריה ופירש הימנה עד שטבלה: **לא תצא.** ולקמיה פריך תרי ותרי נינהו: **שבאו עדים.** שאמרו לא מת: **באשם תלוי.** בא על ספק כרת: **לאחד מעדיה.** שאמרו מת דאין אשם תלוי אלא למי שלבו נוקפו וזה אומר ברי לי: **באומרת ברי לי.** אין לבי נוקפי שברי לי שאילו היה קיים היה בא: **תרגמה.** להא דר' יוחנן: **בעד אחד.** ולאו שנים קאמר אלא עד אחד אומר כו' ועד אחד אומר כו': **הימנוהו רבנן כבתרי.** לומר מת דאמרינן ביבמות דהאשה מתוך חומר שהחמרת עליה בסופה הקלת עליה בתחלתה: **אפי' לכתחלה נמי.** תינשא: **דרב אסי.** ביבמות בפ' שני: **תרוויהו באשת איש קא מסהדי.** שניהן מעידין שאשת איש היתה: **מיתה אינה יכולה מכחשתו.** אם יבא בעלה אינה יכולה לומר מת אתה הלכך אי לאו דברי לה שמת מירתתא ולא מינסבא: **גירושין יכולה מכחשתו.** אם יבא ויאמר לא גירשתיך היא תאמר גירשתני הלכך אי שריא לה סמכה אהכחשה ומינסבא על פי עדים הללו מספק ולא מירתתא למידק שפיר: **עכשיו מת.** היום: **ליכא לברורה.** אם אמרו טבע במים או אכלו ארי אין אנו יכולין לברר הדברים הלכך לכתחלה לא תינשא ואם נשאת לא תצא כרבנן וכשנשאת לאחד מעדיה: **אחזי גיטיך.** דבשעתא פורתא לא מהימנא למימר אירכס לי: **הרי זו לא תנשא.** לאחר: תרויהו

[ח] **חזרה** ואמרה טהורה אני מהו. פירוש מועיל אמתלא או לא אבל אין לפרש מהו אם צריכה אמתלא או לא מדקאמר אף בזו אם נתנה כו': **ואפילו** הכי לא עבד שמואל עובדא בנפשיה. ר"ח הביא ירושלמי שמואל בעא לאזדקוקי לאתתיה אמרה ליה טמאה אני ולמחר אמרה טהורה אני אמר לה אתמול טמאה יומא דין טהורה אמרה ליה אתמול לא הוות בי חילא כי ההיא עובדא אתא שאיל לרב אמר ליה אם נתנה אמתלא לדבריה נאמנת: **הבא** עליה באשם תלוי קאי. תימה דבמעלת קאי דהא מסקינן בפרק ד' אחים (יבמות דף לא. ושם) דתרי ותרי ספיקא דרבנן ומדאורייתא אוקמה אחזקה ומאי משני נמי כשניסת לאחד מעדיה הא עד נמי בחנק קאי דאוקמה אחזקה ואומר [ט] ר"ת דחזקה דאשה דייקא ומנסבא מרעה לה להך חזקה דמהאי טעמא נמי שרינן לה כי ליכא עדים כלל [י] אע"ג שהיא בחזקת אשת איש: **באשם** תלוי. אפי' למאן דבעי חתיכה אחת משתי חתיכות הכא לא בעינן שתי חתיכות דמאן דמפרש בפרק ספק אכל (כריתות דף יז: ושם) טעמא דבעינן חתיכה משתי חתיכות משום דאפשר לברר איסורו פי' אפשר לברר על ידי בקי שיכיר חתיכה הנשארת אם חלב היא אם שומן היא הכא נמי אפשר לברר ע"י הזמה ולמאן דמפרש משום דבעינן חתיכות אחת של חלב ואחת של שומן איקבע איסורא ה"נ איקבע איסורא שהיתה בחזקת אשת איש אי נמי לאו אשם תלוי ממש קאמר אלא כלומר באיסור אשם תלוי: **כגון** שניסת לאחד מעדיה. והא דתנן בפ' שני דיבמות (דף כה. ושם) הרגוהו לא ישא את אשתו לא משום שמעידין כן דבשום מקום אין שנים חשודין כדמוכח לקמן דאפילו למאן דחייש לגומלין אם שנים מעידין על זה ושנים על זה נאמנין וכן מוכח נמי בפ"ב דיבמות (ג"ז שם) דתנן התם מיאנה או שחלצה בפניו ישאנה מפני שהוא ב"ד ודייק בגמרא טעמא דב"ד הא בתרי לא מאי שנא מהא דתנן עדים החתומים על שדה מקח או על גט אשה לא חשו חכמים לדבר זה היא גופה קמשמע לן לאפוקי ממ"ד מיאון בשנים אלא כלומר שהרגו עם אנשים הרבה: **אי** הכי לכתחלה נמי.

ומהא דתנן בהאשה שלום (יבמות דף קיז: ושם) עד אחד אומר מת ועד אחד אומר לא מת הרי זו לא תנשא ליכא לאקשויי לעולא דהתם איירי בבת אחת ואפילו אם ניסת תצא ועולא איירי בזה אחר זה כשבא עד אחד ואמר מת התירוה ואח"כ בא אחר ואמר לא מת אם נשאת לא תצא אבל לכתחלה לא תנשא משום דרב אסי כדמסיק ומרישא דהתם יש להוכיח שיש חילוק בין בבת אחת בין בזה אחר זה דקתני עד אחד אומר מת וניסת ובא אחר ואמר לא מת לא תצא ומפרש בגמרא דלא ניסת ממש אלא התירוה לינשא אע"פ שלא ניסת ולא תצא היינו מהתירה הראשון משמע דווקא התירוה קודס שבא העד ואמר לא מת הא בא קודם שהתירוה לא וכ"ע בפ' מי שקינא (סוטה דף לא:) דמשמע דאיירי עולא בכל ענין בין בב"א בין בזה אחר זה דתנן התם עד אחד אומר נטמאת ועד אחד אומר לא נטמאת היתה שותה ודייק בגמ' טעמא דהאי מכחיש אבל לא מכחיש עד אחד נאמן מנא ה"מ כו' ופריך כיון דמדאורייתא עד אחד נאמן אידך היכי מצי מכחיש ליה והאמר עולא כל מקום שהאמינה כו' אלא אמר עולא תני לא היתה שותה ור' חייא אומר היתה שותה לר' חייא קשיא דעולא לא קשיא כאן בבת אחת כאן בזה אחר זה משמע דעולא נמי איירי בבת אחת ולכך צריך להגיה ולא משני כדמשני ר' חייא ומיהו איכא למימר דעולא לא מיירי אלא בזה אחר זה אלא שנראה לו דוחק להעמיד המשנה בבת אחת משום דמשמע ליה דמיירי בזה אחר זה ועוד אומר ר"י דאפילו איירי לעולא בכל ענין הני מילי התם דמדאורייתא עד אחד מהימן בסוטה כדנפקא ליה התם מועד אין בה אבל הכא גבי אשה דלא מהימן אלא מדרבנן לא חשיב כשנים אלא בזה אחר זה ואע"ג דיש חילוק בין דאורייתא לדרבנן מייתי מדעולא דנראה לו דחשיב כשנים בזה אחר זה בדרבנן כמו בבת אחת בדאורייתא: **משום** דרב אסי הסר ממך עקשות פה. פסוק הוא אלא דרב אסי רגיל להביאו וא"ת והא דתנן בהאשה שלום (יבמות דף קיז: ושם) עד אחד אומר מת וניסת ובא עד אחד ואמר לא מת לא תצא ופריך בגמרא טעמא דניסת הא לא ניסת לא תנשא והאמר עולא כל מקום כו' ומאי פריך והא עולא לא קאמר אלא בדיעבד אבל לכתחלה מודה דלא תנשא משום דרב אסי ואומר ר"י דהתם דייק טעמא דניסת הא אם לא נשאת לא תנשא ואם נשאת תצא דהכי משמע מתניתין דוקא נשאת ואחר כך בא העד לא תצא הא בא העד קודם שנשאת ואחר כך ניסת תצא משום הכי פריך מדעולא ואם תאמר והיכי משני התם דה"ק עד אחד אומר מת והתירוה לינשא ובא אחר ואמר לא מת לא תצא מהתירה הראשון משמע ותנשא לכתחלה וי"ל דודאי לכתחלה לא תנשא ולא תצא מהתירה הראשון לענין דאם ניסת לא תצא: **תרוייהו** באשת איש קמסהדי. תימה דמה לנו לאותו עד שאומר לא נתגרשה בלא איהו נמי תצא דאין דבר שבערוה פחות משנים דהא ליכא למימר שלא היינו יודעים שהיא א"א כי אם על פיהם דא"כ להימניה להאי דאמר מגורשת במיגו דאי בעי שתק וי"ל דאין זה מיגו דשמא רוצה להעיד כדי לפוסלה מן הכהונה. ת"י:

מאי

לא גירושין יכולה להכחישתו פי' אם יבא ויאמר לא גרשתיך היא תאמר גרשתני הלכך אי שרית לה סמכא אהכחשה ומינסבא ע"פ עדות הללו מספק ולא מירתתא למידק שפיר **ומי** מחצפי בי' והאמר ר"ה האשה שאמרה לבעלה גרשתני נאמנת דחזקתה אין אשה מעיזה פניה בפני בעלה ה"מ היכא דליכא עדים דמסייע לה אבל היכא דאיכא עדים דמסייע לה מעיזה ומעיזה ומדמקשינן ממילתא דר"ה ש"מ דהכי הל' שאין התלמוד מקשה אלא מהל' פסוקה כך בריש פ' התקבל: **ר"א אמר** דאמרו עדים עכשיו מת פי' היום מת עכשיו גירשה מיתה ליכא טבע בים או אכלו ארי אין אנו יכולים לברר הדברים הלכך לכתחלה לא תנשא מיד דהא צריכה ים ואם נשאת לא תצא כרבנן וכשנשאת לאחד מעידיה. גירושין איכא לברורינהו דאמרי לה אי איתא דהכי הוא אחוי גיטך פי' ולא תנשא מיד דהא צריכה להמתין ג' חדשים אלא כגון שהמתינה ג' חדשים ונשאת ואפ"ה עכשיו גירשה אמרינן לה אי איתא כדאמרת הוה לך לאחזי גיטא דבשעתא פורתא לא מהימנא למימר אירכס לי א"נ שקרא מסהדי והני דאמרו לא גירשך הם נאמנים והלכך תצא ודוקא כשאמרו עכשיו גירשך דמוכחא מילתא מעידים שגירשה זה כמה ימים לא תצא כרבנן וליתא לר' מנחם בר"י לא במיתה ולא בגירושין והלכה כר"א דהוא בתרא: **ת"ר** ב' אומרים נתקדשה וב' אומרים לא נתקדשה ה"ז ל"ת ואם נשאת ל"ת

נאמנין לומר טהורה וטעמא דבשביל שנתייחדה בין השבאין אין לנו לאסרה שהרי סתם אשה משמרת עצמה מזונות ואוקמה אחזקתה ואיסור קל הוא אם נישאת לכהן [רשב"ם ב"ב קלה.]. **אבוה דשמואל.** אלא בר אבא אבוה דשמואל הוא, וחסיד גדול היה [חולין קיא:]. **שרינהו.** רבי תנינא להנשא לכהנים [רשב"ם שם]. **כשגגה שיוצא מלפני השליט.** דומה הוא לשליט שהוציא דבר שגגה מפיו שוגג ואי אפשר לחזור כך אומר הקב"ה ואין להשיב [קהלת ז, ה]. **השתא מיהת ליתנהו.** ואינן מעידין על שבייתן ונתירם. **עדים בצד אסתן.** רוח לפונית ואינן באים ומעידים ותאסר בתמיה [קידושין יב:].

מסורת הש"ס

א) [לקמן דף כ: וש"נ], ב) יבמות פח: ב"ב לא. ג) [שם ביבמות], ד) יבמות פח: קיז: סוטה לא: מז, ה) יבמות כד: ו) שם קטו. נדרים לא. גיטין סד: סט: ז) [שייך לע"א על ד"ה עבד שמואל כו'], ח) [שייך לע"א], ט) [כתובות פח: כתבו תוס' דבר זה בשם ר"י וע"ע תוס' ב"ב לב. ד"ה אלא], י) [וע"ע תוס' לקמן כו: ד"ה אלן].

תוספות ישנים

א) ובשנים אומרים נתגרשה לא מצי דייק כי ירא שלא יחזרו עדיה אבל חזקה דאין אשה מעיזה ליכא כיון דאיכא עדים דקא מסייעי לה. ת"י עס"ג.

תורה אור השלם

א) הָסֵר מִמְּךָ עִקְּשׁוּת פֶּה וּלְזוּת שְׂפָתַיִם הַרְחֵק מִמֶּךָּ: [משלי ד, כד]

ליקוטי רש"י

שנים אומרים מת. אשה שהלך בעלה למדינת הים ובאו שנים ואמרו לה מת בעליך ושנים אומרים לא מת וא"נ שנים אומרים נתגרשה בחיי בעלה ואינה זקוקה ליבם ושנים אומרים לא נתגרשה וזקוקה ליבם א"נ כגון [שעדיין] בעלה קיים ובאין להתירה לאחר. **הרי זו לא תנשא.** דאוקי תרי להדי תרי ואוקמא בחזקת איסור אשת איש קיימא. **ואם נשאת לא תצא.** דיעבד אין לכתחלה לא. **בזמן שבאו עדים.** האחרונים שאמרו לא מת ואח"כ ניסת לפיכך תצא שהרי באיסור נשאת שאלו שאלה מב"ד היו אוסרין לה לינשא. **אבל נשאת.** על פי עדי מיתה שהתירוה בית דין לינשא ואחר כך באו עדים שהוא קיים לא תצא. **באומרת ברי לי.** **תרגמה.** פרש אותה [סוטה ח:]. **הרי כאן שנים.** **הסר ממך עקשות פה.** **ולזות שפתים.** עקימות שפתים שלא ירמיזו הבריות פה עליך [משלי ד, כד].

[מכאן שייך לדף כג.]

תרגמה. פרש אותה [סוטה ח:]. **דבשבויה הקילו.** דספיקא בעלמא היא [ב"ק קיד:]. שלא ראינוה שנבעלה [לקמן נא:]. דהרבה הקילו בה חכמים במסכת כתובות דלפי' אשה ועד אחד

תוספות רי"ד

גדולה בנוי וקפצו עליה בני אדם לקדשה וא"ל מקודשת אני לימים עמדה וקדשה ע"א א"ל חכמים מה ראית א"ל בתחלה שבאו עלי בני אדם שאינם מהוגנים אמרתי מקודשת אני עכשיו שבאו עלי בני אדם שהן הגונים לי עמדתי וקדשתי את עצמי וזו הלכה העלה ר"א שר הבירה לפני חכמים ואמרו אם נתנה אמתלא לדבריה נאמנת בעא מיניה שמואל מרב אמרה טמאה אני פי' נדה וחזרה ואמרה טהורה אני מהו א"ל אף בזו אם נתנה אמתלא לדבריה נאמנת: תנא מיניה מ' זמנין ואפ"ה לא עביד שמואל עובדא בנפשיה פי' פעם אחת אמרה לו אשתו כן ונתנה אמתלא לדבריה ופירש ממנה עד שטבלה: ת"ר שנים אומרים מת ושנים אומרים לא מת שנים אומרים נתגרשה ושנים אומרים לא נתגרשה ה"ז לא תנשא ואם נשאת לא תצא מכדי תרי ותרי נינהו הבא עליה באשם תלוי קאי פי' בא על ספק כרת א"ר ששת כגון שנשאת לאחד מעידיה פי' שאמרו מת היא גופה באשם תלוי קיימא באומרת ברי לי

The Gemara answers:

בְּאוֹמֶרֶת בָּרִי לִי – The Baraisa refers to a case where **where she says, "I am certain."**[10]

The Gemara presents another set of rulings on this matter:

אָמַר רַבִּי יוֹחָנָן – **R' Yochanan said:** שְׁנַיִם אוֹמְרִים מֵת – If **two** witnesses **say** that [**a man**] **died,** וּשְׁנַיִם אוֹמְרִים לֹא מֵת – **and two** other witnesses **say** that **he did not die,** הֲרֵי זוֹ לֹא תִנָּשֵׂא – **this** woman (i.e. his wife) **may not marry** another man. וְאִם נִשֵּׂאת לֹא תֵצֵא – **But if she did marry** another man, **she does not** have to **leave** him. שְׁנַיִם אוֹמְרִים נִתְגָּרְשָׁה – If **two** witnesses **say** that [**a woman**] **is divorced,** וּשְׁנַיִם אוֹמְרִים לֹא נִתְגָּרְשָׁה – **and two** witnesses **say** that **she is not divorced,** הֲרֵי זוֹ לֹא תִנָּשֵׂא – **this** woman **may not marry** another man, וְאִם נִשֵּׂאת תֵּצֵא – **and if she did marry** another man, **she** must **leave** him.

The Gemara asks:

מַאי שְׁנָא רֵישָׁא וּמַאי שְׁנָא סֵיפָא – **What is the difference between the former** case **and the latter** case? Why does R' Yochanan allow her to stay married where the issue is her husband's death, yet requires her to leave where the issue is divorce?

The Gemara presents three explanations of R' Yochanan's rulings, beginning with one proposed by Abaye:

אָמַר אַבַּיֵי – **Abaye said:** תַּרְגְּמָה בְּעֵד אֶחָד – **Render it** [R' Yochanan's statement] **as** referring to **one witness,** i.e. only one witness said that the husband died (or gave a divorce) and only one witness contradicted him.[11] עֵד אֶחָד אוֹמֵר מֵת – Now, the law is that where **one witness says** that [**a husband**] **died,** הֵימְנוּהוּ רַבָּנָן כְּבֵי תְרֵי – **the Rabbis believe him as** though he were **two** witnesses.[12] וְכִדְעוּלָּא – **And** this **accords with Ulla's** teaching, דְּאָמַר עוּלָּא – **for Ulla said:** כָּל מָקוֹם שֶׁהֶאֱמִינָה תּוֹרָה עֵד אֶחָד – **Wherever the Torah believes one witness** הֲרֵי כָּאן שְׁנַיִם – it is as though **there are two** witnesses.[13] Thus, the testimony of the single witness who said that the husband died is treated like the testimony of two witnesses. וְהַאי דְּקָאָמַר לֹא מֵת הָוֵה לֵיהּ חַד – **And this** other witness, **who said that** [**the husband**] **did** ***not*** **die, is** only **one,** וְאֵין דְּבָרָיו שֶׁל אֶחָד בִּמְקוֹם שְׁנַיִם – **and the words of one** witness **are not** significant **next to** the words of **two** witnesses.[14]

The Gemara interrupts Abaye's answer to ask:

אִי הָכִי – **If so,** that R' Yochanan refers to a case of one witness, אֲפִילּוּ לְכַתְּחִלָּה נַמִּי – then this woman should be allowed to remarry **even in the first place!**[15] Why does R' Yochanan allow her only to stay with her new husband, but not to marry him in the first place?

The Gemara answers:

מִשּׁוּם דְּרַב אַסִּי – R' Yochanan prohibits her to remarry **because of** that which **Rav Assi** said, דְּאָמַר רַב אַסִּי – **for Rav Assi recited** the following verse in reference to a similar situation: "הָסֵר מִמְּךָ עִקְּשׁוּת פֶּה וּלְזוּת שְׂפָתַיִם הַרְחֵק מִמֶּךָּ" – ***Remove from yourself distortion of the mouth, and distance perversity of lips from yourself.***[16]

Abaye continues his answer:

סֵיפָא – As for **the last part** of R' Yochanan's ruling (concerning divorce), it should also be rendered as referring to one witness, as follows: עֵד אֶחָד אוֹמֵר נִתְגָּרְשָׁה – **One witness says** that **she was divorced** וְעֵד אֶחָד אוֹמֵר לֹא נִתְגָּרְשָׁה – **and one witness says** that **she was not divorced.** תַּרְוַיְיהוּ בְּאֵשֶׁת אִישׁ קָמַסְהֲדֵי – Now, **both of them are testifying about a married woman** (i.e. both

NOTES

10. The woman is sure that her husband has died, because she believes that if he were alive, he would have returned (*Rashi*). [Since she is confident that she is not committing adultery by cohabiting with her second husband, the law of the *asham talui* does not apply to her (see note 8). Even in this case, however, she is not allowed to remarry in the first place.]

Other Rishonim, however, object that this argument — "if he were alive, he would have returned" — is too weak to allow this woman to stay in her second marriage. Although it suffices to exclude her from the *asham talui* obligation (*Ritva;* cf. *Ran*), there would nevertheless be a Biblical or Rabbinic ban on her second marriage based on the possibility that she is still married to her original husband. Furthermore, this argument would certainly not be effective in counteracting her *chazakah* as a married woman, which requires us to view her as *definitely* married (see note 7). Hence, they explain the Gemara as meaning that the woman claims to have absolute knowledge of her husband's death, e.g. she saw him die or identified his corpse. Only a claim of such a definite nature would allow her to remain married to her second husband (*Re'ah, Ritva, Ran, Tos. Rid;* see also *Tos. Yeshanim* to *Yevamos* 88b ד״ה באומרת ברי לי). [For explanations of *Rashi,* see *Pnei Yehoshua* and *Tumim, Kelalei Migo* 82:16; see also *Beis Yaakov* ד״ה אמנם התוס׳, *Maharam Schif, Hagahos Radal* and *Birkas Avraham.*]

11. According to Abaye, R' Yochanan did not actually say "two [witnesses]"; rather, he said "one [witness]" (*Rashi;* see also *Rashba* סד״ה סיפא [א]; cf. *Ritva, Pnei Yehoshua*).

12. The Gemara in *Yevamos* (88a) states that if one witness testifies that a man has died, his wife is allowed to remarry. Although two witnesses are usually required to effect a change in a woman's marital status [אֵין דָּבָר שֶׁבְּעֶרְוָה פָּחוֹת מִשְּׁנַיִם], in this case one witness is enough. The reason is that if his testimony is found to be false and the husband returns after his wife has remarried, she would suffer severe consequences [e.g. she would have to leave both men, she would not receive a *kesubah* payment from either, etc. (see Mishnah ibid.)]. A woman would not risk such dire consequences unless she had thoroughly investigated the matter and was sure that her husband had in fact died. Hence, her very preparedness to remarry, together with the testimony of the single witness, provides sufficient grounds for the court to permit her to proceed (see *Rashi*).

[According to most Poskim, this is a Rabbinic enactment, which was legislated in order to make it easier for women whose husbands have died to remarry (see, for example, *Tosafos* to *Yevamos* ibid. ד״ה מתוך; *Tosafos* here ד״ה אי; *Rashi* to *Shabbos* 145b ד״ה לעדות אשה and to *Yevamos* 92a ד״ה תדע; see also *Rambam, Hil. Gerushin* 13:29). A minority view, though, holds that this law is valid even on the Biblical level (*Ritva* citing *Re'ah*). See *Noda BiYehudah, Mahadura Kamma, Even HaEzer* §27 ד״ה ועדיין.]

13. One witness is enough to testify that a woman's husband has died or that a *sotah* has committed adultery (*Rashi* to *Yevamos* 88b ד״ה הרי כאן שנים). Ulla teaches that in these cases the testimony of a single witness is viewed as though it were given by two witnessses. The primary consequence of Ulla's teaching is that this single witness is believed even if another single witness contradicts him. It should be noted, however, that he is not believed where he is contradicted by two (actual) witnesses. Furthermore, he is not believed even against another single witness unless the court had already ruled on the basis of his testimony before the opposing witness testified (see *Tosafos* et al.).

There is a question whether Ulla's teaching also applies to ritual prohibitions where the rule is that one witness normally suffices (עֵד אֶחָד נֶאֱמָן בְּאִסּוּרִין). See *Ritva* here; *Re'ah* to 23a ד״ה אמר רב פפא; *Shach, Yoreh Deah* 127:14; *Shev Shmaatsa* 6:20-21.

14. As taught by Ulla, where the testimony of a single witness is sufficient, another single witness has no authority to contradict it (see previous note).

15. For the testimony of the single witness is worthless in this case, as explained above (*Ritva*).

16. *Proverbs* 4:24. The verse exhorts a person to avoid behavior that would provide grounds for others to speak disparagingly of him (*Maharatz Chayes* to *Yevamos* 24b). R' Yose quoted this verse to explain a Mishnah in *Yevamos* (ibid.). Our Gemara borrows his statement from there (*Rashi;* cf. *Tosafos* and *Ritva*).

People generally do not know that a single witness who testifies that a husband died is equivalent to two witnesses. Hence, if such a witness is contradicted by another single witness, people will think that this man's wife has no right to remarry, and they will disparage her for doing so. This consideration, however, is strong enough only to forbid her to marry in the first place; it does not suffice to make her leave her second husband after she has already married him (*Rashba*).

אמתלא לדבריה נאמנת תנא א) מיניה ארבעים זימנין ואפ"ה לא עבד שמואל עובדא בנפשיה ב) ת"ר שנים אומרים מת ושנים אומרים לא מת שנים אומרים נתגרשה ושנים אומרים לא נתגרשה הרי זו לא תנשא ואם נשאת לא תצא רבי מנחם בר יוסי אומר תצא אמר רבי מנחם בר יוסי אימתי אני אומר תצא בזמן שבאו עדים ואח"כ נשאת אבל נשאת ואח"כ באו עדים לא תצא ג) מכדי תרי ותרי נינהו הבא עליה באשם תלוי קאי א"ר ששת כגון א שנשאת לאחד מעדיה היא גופה באשם תלוי קיימא ב באומרת ברי לי אמר רבי יוחנן ג שנים אומרים מת ושנים אומרים לא מת הרי זו לא תנשא ואם נשאת לא תצא ד שנים אומרים נתגרשה ושנים אומרים לא נתגרשה הרי זו לא תנשא ואם נשאת תצא מאי שנא רישא ומאי שנא סיפא אמר אביי תרגמה בעד אחד ה עד אחד אומר מת הימנוהו רבנן כבי תרי וכדעולא דאמר עולא כל מקום ו שהאמינה תורה עד אחד הרי כאן שנים והאי דקאמר לא מת הוה ליה חד ואין דבריו של אחד במקום שנים אי הכי אפי' לכתחלה נמי משום דרב אסי דא"ר אסי ז) א) הסר ממך עקשות פה ולזות שפתים הרחק ממך סיפא י עד אחד אומר נתגרשה ועד אחד אומר לא נתגרשה תרוייהו באשת איש קמסהדי והאי דקאמר נתגרשה הוה ליה חד ואין דבריו של אחד במקום שנים רבא אמר לעולם תרי ותרי נינהו וראה ר' יוחנן דבריו של ר' מנחם בר יוסי בגרושין ולא ראה במיתה מ"ט מיתה אינה יכולה מכחשתו גרושין יכולה מכחשתו ומי חציפה כולי האי והאמר רב המנונא ח) י האשה שאמרה לבעלה גרשתני נאמנת חזקה אין אשה מעיזה פניה בפני בעלה הני מילי היכא דליכא עדים דקא מסייעי לה ח אבל היכא דאיכא עדים דקא מסייעי לה מעיזה ומעיזה רב אסי אמר כגון דאמרי עדים עכשיו מת עכשיו גירשה מיתה ליכא לברורה ט גירושין איכא לברורה דאמרינן לה אם איתא דהכי הוה אחזי לן גיטיך תנו רבנן שנים אומרים נתקדשה ושנים אומרים לא נתקדשה הרי זו לא תנשא ואם נשאת לא תצא שנים אומרים נתגרשה ושנים אומרים לא נתגרשה הרי זו לא תנשא ואם נשאת תצא

מאי

ז) **אמתלא.** משל וטעם למה אמרה תחלה מקודשת אני: **אם נתנה אמתלא לדבריה נאמנת.** הואיל ונתנה אמתלא נאמנת: **אמרה טמאה אני.** אמרה לבעלה נדה אני: **טהורה אני.** לא הייתי נדה: **לא עבד שמואל עובדא בנפשיה.** פעם אחת אמרה לו אשתו כן ונתנה אמתלא לדבריה ופירש הימנה עד שטבלה: **לא תצא.** ולקמיה פריך תרי ותרי נינהו: **שבאו עדים.** שאמרו לא מת: **באשם תלוי.** בא על ספק כרת: **לאחד מעדיה.** שאמרו מת דאין אשם תלוי אלא למי שלבו נוקפו וזה אומר ברי לי: **באומרת ברי לי.** אין לבי נוקפי שברי לי אילו היה קיים היה בא: **תרגמה.** להא דר' יוחנן: **בעד אחד.** ולאו שנים איתמר אלא עד אומר כו' ועד אומר כו': **הימנוהו רבנן כבתרי.** לומר מת דאמרינן ביבמות דהאשה מתוך חומר שהחמרת עליה בסופה הקלת עליה בתחלתה: **אפי' לכתחלה** נמי. תינשא: **דרב אסי.** ביבמות בפ' שני: **תרוייהו באשת איש קא מסהדי.** שניהן מעידין שאשת איש היתה: **מיתה אינה יכולה מכחשתו.** אם יבא בעלה אינה יכולה לומר מת אתה הלכך אי לאו דברי לה שמת מירתתא ולא מינסבא: **גירושין יכולה מכחשתו.** אם יבא ויאמר לא גירשתיך היא תאמר גירשתני הלכך אי שרית לה סמכא אהכחשה ומינסבא על פי עדים הללו מספק ולא מירתתא למידק שפיר: **עכשיו מת. היום: ליכא לברורה.** אם אמרו טבע במים או אכלו ארי אין אנו יכולין לברר הדברים הלכך לכתחלה לא תינשא ואם ניסת לא תצא כרבנן וכשניסת לאחד מעדיה: **אחזי גיטיך.** דבשעתא פורתא לא מהימנא למימר אירכס לי: **הרי זו לא תנשא.** לאחר:

תרוייהו

ח) **חזרה** ואמרה טהורה אני מהו. פירוש מועיל אמתלא או לא אבל אין לפרש מהו אם צריכה אמתלא או לא מדקאמר אף בזו אם נתנה כו': **ואפילו** הכי לא עבד שמואל עובדא בנפשיה. ר"ח הביא ירושלמי שמואל בעא לאזדקוקי לאתתיה אמרה ליה טמאה אני ולמחר אמרה טהורה אני אמר לה אתמול טמאה יומא דין טהורה אמרה ליה אתמול לא הוות בי חילא כי ההיא שעתא אתא שאיל לרב אמר ליה אם נתנה אמתלא לדבריה נאמנת:

הבא עליה באשם תלוי קאי. תימה דבהתחלת קאי דהא מסקינן בפרק ד' אחים (יבמות דף ל. ושם) דתרי ותרי ספיקא דרבנן ומדאורייתא אוקמה אחזקה ומאי משני נמי כשניסת לאחד מעדיה הא על נמי בתנק קאי דאוקמה אחזקה ואומר ט) ר"ת מחזקה דאשה דייקא ומנסבא מרעה לה להך חזקה דמהאי טעמא נמי שרינן לה כי ליכא עדים כלל א) אע"פ שהיא בחזקת אשת איש י): **באשם** תלוי. אפי' למאן דבעי חתיכה אחת משתי חתיכות הכא לא בעינן שתי חתיכות דלמאן דמפרש בפרק ספק אכל (כריתות דף יז: ושם) טעמא דבעינן חתיכה משתי חתיכות משום דאפשר לברר איסורו פי' אפשר לברר על ידי בקי שיכיר חתיכה הנשארת אם חלב היא אם שומן היא הכא נמי אפשר לברר ע"י זומה ולמאן דמפרש משום דבעינן שתי חתיכות אחת של חלב ואחת של שומן איקבע איסורא ה"נ איקבע איסורא שהיתה בחזקת אשת איש אי נמי לאו אשם תלוי ממש קאמר אלא כלומר באיסור אשם תלוי: **כגון** שניסת לאחד מעדיה. והא דתנן בפ' שני דיבמות (דף כה. ושם) הרגנוהו לא ישא את אשתו לא ששנים מעידין כן דבשום מקום אין שנים חשודין כדמוכח לקמן דאפילו למאן דחייש לגומלין אם שנים מעידין על זה ושנים על זה נאמנין וכן מוכח נמי בפ"ב דיבמות (ג"ז שם:) דתנן התם מיאנה או שחלצה בפניו ישאנה מפני שהוא ב"ד ודייק בגמרא טעמא דב"ד הא בתרי לא מאי שנא מהא דתנן עדים החתומים על שדה מקח או על גט אשה לא חשו חכמים לדבר זה היא גופה קמשמע לן לאפוקי ממ"ד מיאון בשנים אלא כלומר שהרגו עם אנשים הרבה: **אי** הכי לכתחלה נמי.

ומהא דתנן בהאשה שלום (יבמות דף קיז: ושם) עד אחד אומר מת ועד אחד אומר לא מת הרי זו לא תנשא ליכא לאקשויי לעולא דהתם איירי בבת אחת ואפילו אם ניסת תצא ועולא איירי בזה אחר זה כשבא עד אחד ואמר מת התירוה ואח"כ בא אחר ואמר לא מת אם נשאת לא תצא אבל לכתחלה לא תנשא משום דרב אסי כדמסיק ומרישא דהתם יש להוכיח שיש חילוק בין בבת אחת בין בזה אחר זה דקתני עד אחד אומר מת וניסת ובא אחר ואמר לא מת לא תצא ומפרש בגמרא דלא ניסת ממש אלא התירוה לינשא אע"פ שלא ניסת ולא תצא היינו מהתירה הראשון משמע דווקא התירוה קודם שבא העד ואמר לא מת הא בא קודם שהתירוה לא ול"ע בפ' מי שקינא (סוטה דף לא:) דמשמע דאיירי עולא בכל ענין בין בבת אחת בין בזה אחר זה דתנן התם עד אחד אומר נטמאת ועד אחד אומר לא נטמאת היתה שותה ודייק בגמ' טעמא דהאי מכחיש אבל לא מכחיש עד אחד נאמן מנא ה"מ כו' ופריך כיון דמדאורייתא עד אחד נאמן אידך היכי מצי מכחיש ליה והאמר עולא כל מקום שהאמינה כו' אלא אמר עולא תני לא היתה שותה ור' חייא אומר היתה שותה לר' חייא קשיא דעולא לא קשיא כאן בבת אחת כאן בזה אחר זה משמע דעולא נמי איירי בבת אחת ולכך צריך להגיה ולא משני כדמשני ר' חייא ומיהו איכא למימר דעולא לא מיירי אלא בזה אחר זה אלא שנראה לו דוחק להעמיד המשנה בבת אחת משום דמשמע ליה דמיירי בזה אחר זה ועוד אומר ר"י דאפילו איירי לעולא בכל ענין הני מילי התם דמדאורייתא עד אחד מהימן בסוטה כדנפקא ליה התם מועד אין בה אבל הכא גבי אשה דלא מהימן אלא מדרבנן לא חשיב כשנים אלא בזה אחר זה ואע"ג דיש חילוק בין דאורייתא לרבנן מייתי מדעולא דנראה לו דחשיב כשנים בזה אחר זה בדרבנן כמו בבת אחת בדאורייתא:

משום דרב אסי הסר ממך עקשות פה. פסוק הוא אלא דרב אסי רגיל להביאו וא"ת והא דתנן בהאשה שלום (יבמות דף קיז: ושם) עד אחד אומר מת וניסת ובא עד אחד ואמר לא מת לא תצא ופריך בגמרא טעמא דניסת הא לא ניסת לא תנשא והאמר עולא כל מקום כו' ומאי פריך והא עולא לא קאמר אלא בדיעבד אבל לכתחלה מודה דלא תנשא משום דרב אסי ואומר ר"י דהתם דייק טעמא דניסת הא אם לא נשאת לא תנשא ואם נשאת תצא דהכי משמע מתניתין דוקא נשאת ואחר כך בא העד לא תצא הא בא העד קודם שנשאת ואחר כך ניסת תצא משום הכי פריך מדעולא ואם תאמר והיכי משני התם דה"ק עד אחד אומר מת והתירוה לינשא ובא אחר ואמר לא מת לא תצא מהתירה הראשון משמע ותנשא לכתחלה וי"ל דודאי לכתחלה לא תנשא ולא תצא מהתירה הראשון לענין דאם ניסת לא תצא:

[תרוייהו באשת איש קמסהדי. תימה דמה לנו לאותו עד שאומר לא נתגרשה בלא איהו נמי תצא דאין דבר שבערוה פחות משנים דהא ליכא למימר שלא היינו יודעים שהיא א"א כי אם על פיהם דא"כ להימניה להאי דאמר מגורשת במיגו דאי בעי שתק וי"ל דאין זה מיגו דשמא רוצה להעיד כדי לפוסלה מן הכהונה. ת"י]:

מאי

עין משפט
נר מצוה

פה א ב מיי' פ"ג מהל' גירושין הל' ... סמג עשין ... טוש"ע אה"ע סימן יז סעיף מב:
פו ג מיי' שם הלכה יח טוש"ע אה"ע סימן קנב סעיף ג:
פז ד מיי' שם הלכה יח טוש"ע אה"ע סימן יז סעיף לז:
פח ו מיי' שם הלכה ט טוש"ע אה"ע סימן קנב סעיף ה:
פט ז מיי' פ"ח מהל' אישות הלכה ... טוש"ע אה"ע סימן ... סעיף ... :
ע ח ט מיי' פי"ג מהל' גירושין הל' ו ז טוש"ע אה"ע סי' קנב סעיף ב:

מסורת הש"ס

א) [לקמן דף כ. וש"נ], ב) יבמות פח: כ"ב לו., ג) [שם ביבמות], ד) יבמות פח: קיז: סוטה לא: מ., ה) יבמות כד: ו) שם קטו. נדרים לא. גיטין סד: פט:, ז) [שייך לע"א של ד"ה לא עבד שמואל כו'], ח) [שייך לע"א], ט) [ביבמות פח: כתבו תוס' דבר זה בשם ר"י וע"ע תוס' ב"ב לב. ד"ה אקן], י) [וע"ע תוס' לקמן כו: ד"ה אקן].

תוספות ישנים

א) ובשנים אומרים נתגרשה נמי דייקא כי יראה שלא יותו עדיה אבל חזקה דאין אשה מעיזה ליכא כיון דאיכא עדים דקא מסייעי לה. ת"י עס"ג.

תורה אור השלם

א) הָסֵר מִמְּךָ עִקְּשׁוּת פֶּה וּלְזוּת שְׂפָתַיִם הַרְחֵק מִמֶּךָּ: [משלי ד, כד]

ליקוטי רש"י

שנים אומרים מת. אשה שהלך בעלה למדינת הים ובאו שנים ואמרו לה מת בעליך ושנים אומרים לא מת א"נ שנים אומרים נתגרשה בפנינו ושנים אומרים לא נתגרשה **הרי זו לא תנשא.** דלוקי תרי להדי תרי ואוקמה בחזקת איסור אשת איש קיימא. **ואם נשאת לא תצא.** דיעבד אין לכתחלה לא. **בזמן שבאו עדים.** האחרונים שאמרו לא מת ולאח"כ ניסת לפיכך תצא שהרי באיסור נשאת שאלה מב"ד היו אוסרין לה לינשא. **אבל נשאת.** על פי עדי מיתה שהתירוה בית דין לינשא ואחר כך באו הללו שאומרים קיים לא תצא לפי שלא חיישינן לזילותא דבי דינא שמא ילגלגו הבריות על ב"ד שהיו סומכין על עדים ... **באומרת ברי לי.** [רשב"ם ב"ב לא.]. כגון ע"י קיימים ואשם תלוי אינו בא אלא על מי שלבו נוקפו [יבמות פח:]. **תרגמה.** פרש אותה [סוטה ח:]. **הרי כאן שנים.** הרי הוא חשוב כשנים כגון בעדות אשה לומר שמת בעלה ובעדות סוטה לומר שנטמאה, ואין דבריו של אחד. לאחר לא מת במקום שנים [יבמות שם]. **הסר ממך עקשות פה.** לא תעשה דבר שילעיגו בו הבריות ויעקמו עליך פיהם. **עקשות פה.** לשון עקום כמו ... ויעקשו ... ט) ועקומות פה. **ולזות שפתים.** עקימות שפתים שלא ירחיבו הבריות פה עליך [משלי ד, כד].

[מכאן שייך לדף כג.]

תרגמה. פרש אותה [סוטה ח:]. **דבשבויה הקילו.** דספיקא בעלמא היא [ב"ק קיד:]. שלא ראינוה שנבעלה [לקמן נא:]. דהרבה הקילו בה חכמים במסכת כתובות דאפי' אשה ועד אחד נאמנין לומר טהורה וטעמא דבשביל שנתייחדה בין השבאין אין לנו לאסרה שהרי סתם אשה משמרת עצמה מזנות ואוקמה אחזקתה ואיסור קל הוא אם נישאת לכהן [רשב"ם ב"ב קלה.]. **אבוה דשמואל.** אבא בר אבא אבוה דשמואל הוה, וחסיד גדול היה [חולין קיא:]. **שרינהו.** רבי חנינא להנשא לכהנים [רשב"ם שם]. **כשגגה שיוצא מלפני השליט.** דומה הוא לשליט שהוציא דבר שגגה מפיו שוגג ואי אפשר לחזור כך אומר הקב"ה ואין להשיב [קהלת ז, ה]. **השתא מיהת ליתנהו.** ואינן מעידין על שביין ונמירס. **עדים בצד אפתן.** רוח לפונית ואינן באים ומעידים ותאסר בתמיה [קידושין יב:].

תוספות רי"ד

גדולה בנוי דקפצו עליה בני אדם לקדשה וא"ל מקודשת אני לימים עמדה וקדשה א"ע א"ל חכמים מה ראית א"ל בתחלה שבאו עלי בני אדם שאינם מהוגנים אמרתי מקודשת אני עכשיו שבאו עלי בני אדם שהן הגונים לי עמדתי וקדשתי את עצמי וזו הלכה העלה ר"א שר הבירה לפני חכמים ואמרו אם נתנה אמתלא לדבריה נאמנת בעא מיניה שמואל מרב אמרה טמאה אני ואח"כ אמרה טהורה אני מהו א"ל אף בזו אם נתנה אמתלא לדבריה נאמנת. תנא מיניה מ' זמנין ואפ"ה לא עביד שמואל עובדא בנפשיה פי' פעם אחת אמרה לו אשתו כן ונתנה אמתלא לדבריה ופירש ממנה עד שטבלה: ת"ר שנים אומרים מת שנים אומרים לא מת ושנים אומרים נתגרשה ושנים אומרים לא נתגרשה ה"ז לא תנשא ואם נשאת לא תצא מכדי תרי ותרי נינהו הבא עליה באשם תלוי קאי פי' בא על ספק כרת כגון שנשאת לאחד מעדיה שאמרו מת שאין אשם תלוי אלא למי שלבו נוקפו אבל זה אומר ברי לי ואיבע"א היא גופה באשם תלוי קיימא באומרת ברי לי פי' שבאתה גם היא משם ואמרה מת בעלי ואם ... ור"מ בר"י פליג ואמר שאם באו עדי האוסרים תחלה ואח"כ נשאת ואפילו לאחד מעדיה תצא [illegible] וכיון שהאשה רבה. אר"י ב' אומרים מת וב' אומרים לא מת ה"ז לא תנשא ואם נשאת לא תצא ב' אומרים נתגרשה וב' אומרים לא נתגרשה ה"ז לא תנשא ואם נשאת תצא מ"ש רישא ומ"ש סיפא ואוקמי' רבא דראה ר"י דברי ר' מנחם בר"י בגירושין ולא ראה דבריו במיתה מ"ש מיתה אינה יכולה להכחישתו פי' אם יבא בעלה א"י לומר לו מת אתה הלכך אי לא דברי לה שמת מירתתא ולא מינסבא עד דדייקא שפיר דחיישי לקלקולא גירושין יכולה להכחישתו פי' אם יבא ויאמר לא גרשתיך היא תאמר גרשתני הלכך אי שרית לה סמכא אדעתא ומינסבא ע"פ עדות הללו מספק ולא מירתתא למידק שפיר ומי מחצפי בי' והאמר ר"ה האשה שאמרה לבע"ה גרשתני נאמנת דחזקתה אין אשה מעיזה פניה בפני בעלה ה"מ היכא דליכא עדים דמסייע לה אבל היכא דאיכא עדים דמסייע לה מעיזה ומעיזה ומדמקשינן ממילתא דר"ה ש"מ דהכי הל' שאין התלמוד מקשה אלא מהל' פסוקה כך העמדנו נמי בגיטין בריש פ' התקבל: ר"א אמר דאמרו עדים עכשיו מת פי' היום מת עכשיו גירשה מיתה ליכא לברורי פי' אם אמרו טבע בים או אכלו ארי אין אנו יכולים לברר הדברים הלכך לכתחלה לא תנשא מיד דהא צריכה להמתין שלשה חדשים ואם נשאת לא תצא כרבנן וכשנשאת לאחד מעידיה. גירושין איכא לברורינהו דאמרי לה אי איתא דהכי הוא אחוי גיטך פי' ולא תנשא מיד דהא צריכה להמתין ג' חדשים אלא כגון שהמתינה ג' חדשים ונשאת ואפ"ה כיון שעדים העידו שעכשיו גירשה אמרינן לה אי איתא כדאמרת הוה לך לאחזי גיטא דבשעתא פורתא לא מהימנא למימר אירכס לי א' שקרא מסהדי והני דאמרו לא גירשך הם נאמנים והלכך תצא ודוקא כשאמרו עכשיו גירשך דמוכחא מילתא דמשקרי אבל אם מעידים שגירשה זה כמה ימים לא תצא כרבנן וליתא לר' מנחם בר"י לא במיתה ולא בגירושין והלכה כר"א דהוא בתרא: ת"ר ב' אומרים נתקדשה וב' אומרים לא נתקדשה ה"ז ל"ת ואם נשאת ל"ת

אַמְתְּלָא לִדְבָרֶיהָ – a plausible **reason for her** original **words,** נֶאֱמֶנֶת – **she is believed** to say that she was not a *niddah.*

The narrative continues:

תָּנָא מִינֵּיהּ אַרְבָּעִים זִימְנִין – [Shmuel] **reviewed** this ruling **from** [Rav] **forty times** in order not to forget it. וַאֲפִילוּ הָכִי לֹא עָבַד שְׁמוּאֵל עוּבְדָא בְּנַפְשֵׁיהּ – **But even so, Shmuel did not rule** accordingly **in an incident involving himself.**[1]

The Gemara introduces further cases in which a woman's marital status is subject to conflicting reports:

תָּנוּ רַבָּנָן – **The Rabbis taught in a Baraisa:** שְׁנַיִם אוֹמְרִים מֵת – If TWO witnesses SAY that [A MAN] DIED,[2] thereby permitting his wife to remarry, וּשְׁנַיִם אוֹמְרִים לֹא מֵת – AND TWO other witnesses SAY that HE DID NOT DIE; שְׁנַיִם אוֹמְרִים נִתְגָּרְשָׁה – or if TWO witnesses SAY that [A WOMAN] WAS DIVORCED, וּשְׁנַיִם אוֹמְרִים לֹא נִתְגָּרְשָׁה – AND TWO witnesses SAY THAT SHE WAS NOT DIVORCED, הֲרֵי זוֹ לֹא תִנָּשֵׂא – THIS woman MAY NOT MARRY another man; וְאִם נִשֵּׂאת לֹא תֵצֵא – BUT IF SHE DID MARRY another man, SHE DOES NOT have to LEAVE him.[3]

The Baraisa presents a dissenting view:

רַבִּי מְנַחֵם בַּר יוֹסֵי אוֹמֵר – But R' MENACHEM BAR YOSE SAYS that תֵּצֵא – SHE DOES have to LEAVE her new husband. אָמַר רַבִּי מְנַחֵם בַּר יוֹסֵי – R' MENACHEM BAR YOSE SAID in explanation of his own ruling: אֵימָתַי אֲנִי אוֹמֵר תֵּצֵא – WHEN DO I SAY that SHE has to LEAVE her new husband? בִּזְמַן שֶׁבָּאוּ עֵדִים וְאַחַר כָּךְ נִשֵּׂאת – IN AN INSTANCE WHERE THE WITNESSES (who testified that she was forbidden to remarry) CAME first AND SHE MARRIED AFTERWARDS.[4] אֲבָל נִשֵּׂאת וְאַחַר כָּךְ בָּאוּ עֵדִים – BUT IF SHE MARRIED first, after the testimony of the supporting witnesses, AND THE opposing WITNESSES CAME AFTERWARDS, לֹא תֵצֵא – SHE DOES NOT have to LEAVE her new husband.[5]

The Gemara asks how the Baraisa could permit the second marriage to continue:[6]

מִכְּדִי – **Now,** let us see. תְּרֵי וּתְרֵי נִינְהוּ – **There are two** witnesses testifying that she is still married to her original husband **and two** witnesses testifying that he died or divorced her. הַבָּא עָלֶיהָ בְּאָשָׁם תָּלוּי קָאֵי – Therefore, **one who cohabits with her would be subject to** the obligation to offer **an *asham talui*!**[7] How can the second husband be permitted to remain married to her in such circumstances?

The Gemara answers:

אָמַר רַב שֵׁשֶׁת – **Rav Sheishess said:** כְּגוֹן שֶׁנִּשֵּׂאת לְאֶחָד מֵעֵדֶיהָ – The Baraisa refers to **a case where she married one of her witnesses** who testified that her first marriage ended.[8]

The Gemara persists:

הִיא גּוּפָהּ בְּאָשָׁם תָּלוּי קַיְימָא – **But she herself is subject to** the obligation to offer **an *asham talui*!**[9]

NOTES

1. This very situation once occurred to Shmuel himself. His wife told him that she was a *niddah,* but later said that she was not a *niddah* and explained why she originally asserted to the contrary (see *Yerushalmi,* cited by *Tosafos* et al., where her explanation is recorded; see *Shitah Mekubetzes* ד״ה והכין for another version; see also *Beis Yosef, Yoreh Deah* 185:3 ד״ה ומ״ש רבינו דאמתלא). Shmuel, however, refused to accept her explanation. He abstained from marital intimacy until she immersed herself in a *mikveh* (*Rashi*).

The reason why Shmuel did not rely on her explanation was that he acted beyond the letter of the law (see *Korban Nesanel* 22:20 and *Beis Yosef* ibid. ד״ה ומ״ש ואם נותנת). Alternatively, Shmuel did not find her explanation convincing. He felt that if it were true, she would have told it to him in the first place and not engaged in deception (*Meiri*).

2. He had traveled to a distant land and did not return. Now, two witnesses testify that he has died (*Rashbam* to *Bava Basra* 31b ד״ה שנים אומרים מת).

3. The Gemara will ask why she is permitted to stay with her new husband when two sets of witnesses disagree whether her previous marriage has ended [and thus it is possible that she is still married to her first husband] (*Rashi*).

4. Because she remarried despite being forbidden to do so (*Rashbam* ibid. ד״ה בזמן). Since she transgressed the law, the Sages penalized her by requiring her to leave her new husband (*Meiri, Chacham Zvi* §2; cf. *Rashba* to *Kiddushin* 66a, *R' Akiva Eiger* vol. II §111 and *Pnei Yehoshua*).

5. In this instance, where she was allowed to remarry, there are no grounds for a Rabbinic penalty.

6. The following difficulty apparently pertains both to the Tanna Kamma and to R' Menachem bar Yose. (See *Shitah Mekubetzes* ד״ה וז״ל הרא״ה.)

7. An *asham talui* is a sacrifice brought by one who suspects that he inadvertently committed a transgression whose intentional violation carries the penalty of *kares* (*Leviticus* 5:17-19; *Rambam, Hil. Shegagos* 8:1). [For example, two pieces of fat were on his plate, and, thinking that both were שׁוּמָן, *permissible fat,* he ate one of them. Later, it is discovered that one of them was חֵלֶב, *forbidden fat,* but he does not know whether that piece was the one he ate (see *Tosafos* here ד״ה באשם and to *Yevamos* 88b ד״ה והבא).]

The penalty for cohabitation with a married woman is *kares.* Hence, in our case, where this woman might still be married to her first husband, one who sins with her inadvertently (i.e. without being aware of her possibly forbidden status) would be obligated to bring an *asham talui.* And if he sins deliberately (i.e. with knowledge of her status), his transgression would be even more severe. In a situation of this nature, they should certainly be forbidden to remain married (see *Shitah Mekubetzes* ד״ה וז״ל שיטה ישנה; cf. *Shitah Mekubetzes* ד״ה וז״ל תלמידי ה״ר רבינו יונה ז״ל).

The Rishonim ask: Before the witnesses testified, this woman was assumed to be married; thus, her *chazakah* is that of a married woman. The Gemara in *Yevamos* (31a) presents two different ways of treating a *chazakah* in a case such as ours, where it is contradicted by one of two sets of conflicting witnesses: (a) The *chazakah* is disregarded and the matter is treated as being in doubt [תְּרֵי וּתְרֵי סְפֵיקָא דְאוֹרַיְיתָא]. (b) Under Biblical law the matter is decided by the *chazakah;* but Rabbinic law does not follow the *chazakah* where it would result in a leniency [תְּרֵי וּתְרֵי סְפֵיקָא דְרַבָּנָן]. According to the first position, this woman's marital status would be in doubt under Biblical law; hence, a man who sins with her inadvertently would indeed be Biblically obligated to offer an *asham talui.* The Gemara (ibid.), however, concludes that the second position is correct (*Tosafos, Re'ah, Ran;* see also *Rashi* to 26b ד״ה ואנן מסקינן ליה and *Tosafos* there). Therefore, we should follow this woman's *chazakah,* which would mean that she is viewed as *definitely* still married to her first husband. If so, one who sins with her inadvertently is obligated to offer not an *asham talui,* which is brought only in cases of doubt, but a *chatas,* which is the sacrifice brought for *definite* transgressions. [And if he knew that she was definitely married, he would incur the death penalty or *kares*! (see *Maharsha*).] Why, then, does our Gemara say that he only has to bring an *asham talui*?

Some Rishonim answer that our Gemara did not want to get involved in the preceding controversy. It therefore mentioned an *asham talui* to show that *even* according to the lenient opinion in this case, there would still be consequences under Biblical law. But indeed, according to the opposing view, the penalty would be a *chatas* [or even execution] (*Ran, Re'ah;* see *Rashba* and *Ritva;* cf. *Tosafos*).

8. I.e. he is one of the two witnesses who testified that she was widowed or divorced (see *Chemdas Shlomo* on *Tosafos* ד״ה הבא). Since he is sure that this woman is no longer married, he would not be required to bring an *asham talui* for cohabiting with her. The *asham talui* is brought only by someone who suspects that he sinned (*Rashi;* see *Kereisos* 23b).

Moreover, even according to the position that this woman is treated as definitely married under Biblical law on the basis of her *chazakah* (see previous note), she is permitted to remain with someone who is certain that in fact she is not married (see *Rashba* to *Kiddushin* 66a ד״ה מאי; *Maharsha* to *Yevamos* 88b on *Tosafos* ד״ה והבא; *Pnei Yehoshua* here ד״ה עדיין on *Tosafos* ד״ה הבא; *Kuntres HaS'feikos* 2:5; *Terumas HaKri* §31; cf. *Tosafos* cited in the previous note).

9. Although her second husband is certain that she is widowed or divorced, as he testified, the woman herself does not know which set of witnesses is telling the truth.

עין משפט נר מצוה

פה א ב ג מיי' פי"ח מהל' גירושין הל' כג. טוש"ע אה"ע סימן יז סעיף מג:

פו ד מיי' שם הלכה כ טוש"ע אה"ע סימן קנב סעיף ב:

פז ה מיי' שם הלכה יח טוש"ע אה"ע סימן יז סעיף לז:

פח ו מיי' שם הלכה ט טוש"ע אה"ע סימן קנב סעיף ה:

פט ז מיי' שם הלכה ד ופ"ד מהל' אישות הלכה יג סמג עשין סח טוש"ע אה"ע סימן יז סעיף ב:

צ ח ט מיי' פי"ב מהל' גירושין הל' ז טוש"ע אה"ע סי' קנב סעיף ב:

גמרא

אמתלא לדבריה נאמנת תנא מיניה ארבעים זימנין ואפ"ה לא עבד שמואל עובדא בנפשיה ת"ר שנים אומרים מת ושנים אומרים לא מת שנים אומרים נתגרשה ושנים אומרים לא נתגרשה הרי זו לא תנשא ואם נשאת לא תצא רבי מנחם בר יוסי אומר תצא אמר רבי מנחם בר יוסי אימתי אני אומר תצא בזמן שבאו עדים ואח"כ נשאת אבל נשאת ואח"כ באו עדים לא תצא מכדי תרי ותרי נינהו הבא עליה באשם תלוי קאי א"ר ששת כגון שנשאת לאחד מעדיה היא גופה באשם תלוי קיימא באומרת ברי לי אמר רבי יוחנן שנים אומרים מת ושנים אומרים לא מת הרי זו לא תנשא ואם נשאת לא תצא שנים אומרים נתגרשה ושנים אומרים לא נתגרשה הרי זו לא תנשא ואם נשאת תצא מאי שנא רישא ומאי שנא סיפא אמר אביי תרגמה בעד אחד עד אחד אומר מת הימנוהו רבנן כבי תרי וכדעולא דאמר עולא כל מקום שהאמינה תורה עד אחד הרי כאן שנים והאי דקאמר לא מת הוה ליה חד ואין דבריו של אחד במקום שנים אי הכי אפי' לכתחלה נמי משום דרב אסי דא"ר אסי הסר ממך עקשות פה ולזות שפתים הרחק ממך סיפא עד אחד אומר נתגרשה ועד אחד אומר לא נתגרשה תרווייהו באשת איש קמסהדי והאי דקאמר נתגרשה הוה ליה חד ואין דבריו של אחד במקום שנים רבא אמר לעולם תרי ותרי נינהו וראה ר' יוחנן דבריו של ר' מנחם בר יוסי בגרושין ולא ראה במיתה מ"ט מיתה אינה יכולה מכחשתו גרושין יכולה מכחשתו ומי חציפה כולי האי והאמר רב המנונא האשה שאמרה לבעלה גרשתני נאמנת חזקה אין אשה מעיזה פניה בפני בעלה הני מילי היכא דליכא עדים דקא מסייעי לה אבל היכא דאיכא עדים דקא מסייעי לה מעיזה ומעיזה רב אסי אמר כגון דאמרי עדים עכשיו מת עכשיו גירשה מיתה ליכא לברורה גירושין איכא לברורה גירושין דאמרינן לה אם איתא דהכי הוה אחזי לן גיטיך תנו רבנן שנים אומרים נתקדשה ושנים אומרים לא נתקדשה הרי זו לא תנשא ואם נשאת לא תצא שנים אומרים נתגרשה ושנים אומרים לא נתגרשה הרי זו לא תנשא ואם נשאת תצא מאי

רש"י

אמתלא. משל וטעם למה אמרה תחלה מקודשת אני: אם נתנה אמתלא לדבריה נאמנת. הואיל ונתנה אמתלא נאמנת: אמרה טמאה אני. אמרה לבעלה נדה אני: טהורה אני. לא הייתי נדה: לא עבד שמואל עובדא בנפשיה. פעם אחת אמרה לו אשתו כן ונתנה אמתלא לדבריה ופירש הימנה עד שטבלה: לא תצא. ולקמיה פריך תרי ותרי נינהו: שבאו עדים. שאמרו לא מת: באשם תלוי. בא על ספק כרת: לאחד מעדיה. שאמרו מת דלאין אשם תלוי אלא למי שלבו נוקפו וזה אומר ברי לי: באומרת ברי לי. אין לבי נוקפי שברי לי שאלו היה קיים היה בא: תרגמה. להא דר' יוחנן: בעד אחד. ולאו שנים קאמר אלא עד אומר כו' ועד אומר כו': הימנוהו רבנן כבתרי. לומר מת כדאמרינן ביבמות בהאשה שהלכה מתוך חומר שהחמרת עליה בסופה הקלת עליה בתחלתה: אפי' לכתחלה נמי. תינשא: דרב אסי. ביבמות בפ' שני: תרווייהו באשת איש קא מסהדי. שניהן מעידין באשת איש היתה: מיתה אינה יכולה מכחשתו. אם יבא בעלה אינה יכולה לומר מת אתה הלכך אי לאו דברי לה שמת מירתתא ולא מינסבא: גירושין יכולה מכחשתו. אם יבא ויאמר לא גירשתיך היא תאמר גירשתני הלכך אי שרית לה סמכה אהכחשה ומינסבא על פי עדים הללו מספק ולא מירתתא למידק שפיר: עכשיו מת. היום: ליכא לברורה. אם אמרו טבע במים או אכלו ארי אין אנו יכולין לברר הדברים הלכך לכתחלה לא תינשא ואם ניסת לא תצא כרבנן וכשניסת לאחד מעדיה: אחזי גיטיך. דבשעתא פורתא לא מהימנא לה למימר אירכס לי: הרי זו לא תנשא. לאחר:

תוספות

חזרה ואמרה טהורה אני מהו. פירוש מועיל אמתלא או לא אבל אין לפרש מהו אם צריכה אמתלא או לא מדקאמר אף בזו אם נתנה כו': ואפילו הכי לא עבד שמואל עובדא בנפשיה. ר"ח הביא ירושלמי שמואל בעא לאזדקוקי לאתתיה אמרה ליה טמאה אני ולמחר אמרה טהורה אני אמר לה אתמול טמאה יומא דין טהורה אמרה ליה אתמול לא הוות בי חילא כי הויא שעתא חדא שאיל לרב אמר ליה אם נתנה אמתלא לדבריה נאמנת:

הבא עליה באשם תלוי קאי. תימה דבשמעתא קמי דהא מסקינן בפרק ד' אחים (יבמות דף לא. ושם) דתרי ותרי ספיקא דרבנן ומדאורייתא אוקמה אחזקה ומאי משני נמי כשניסת לאחד מעדיה הא עד נמי בחנק קאי לאוקמה אחזקה ואומר ר"ח דחזקה דאשה דייקא ומנסבא מרעה לה להך חזקה דמהאי טעמא נמי שרינן לה כי ליכא עדים כלל א) אע"פ שהיא בחזקת אשת איש:

באשם תלוי. אפי' למאן דבעי חתיכה אחת משתי חתיכות הכא לא בעינן שתי חתיכות דמאן דמפרש בפרק ספק אכל (כריתות דף יז. ושם) טעמא דבעינן חתיכה משתי חתיכות משום דאפשר לברר איסורו פי' אפשר לברר על ידי בקי שיכיר חתיכה הנשארת אם חלב היא אם שומן היא הכא נמי אפשר לברר ע"י עדים ולמאן דמפרש משום דבעינן שתי חתיכות אחת של חלב ואחת של שומן אכל חדא מינייהו לקבוע איסורא ה"נ איקבע איסורא שהיתה בחזקת אשת איש אי נמי לאו אשם תלוי ממש קאמר אלא כלומר באיסור אשם תלוי:

כגון שניסת לאחד מעדיה. והא דתנן בפ' שני דיבמות (דף כה. ושם) הרגוהו לא ישא את אשתו לא שאנו מעידין כן דבשום מקום אין אנו חוששין דמוכח לקמן דאפילו למאן דחייש לגומלין אם שנים מעידין על זה ושנים על זה נאמנין וכן מוכח נמי בפ"ב דיבמות (ג"ז שם:) דתנן התם מיאונה או שחלצה בפניו ישאנה מפני שהוא ב"ד ודייק בגמרא טעמא דב"ד הא בתרי לא מאי שנא מהא דתנן עדים החתומים על שדה מקח או על גט אשה לא חשו חכמים לדבר זה היא גופה קמשמע לן לאפוקי ממ"ד מילתא בשנים אלא כלומר שהרגו עם אנשים הרבה: אי הכי לכתחלה נמי. ומהא דתנן בהאשה שלום (יבמות דף קיז: ושם) עד אחד אומר מת ועד אחד אומר לא מת הרי זו לא תנשא ליכא לאקשויי לעולא דהתם איירי בבת אחת ואפילו אם ניסת תצא ועולא איירי בזה אחר זה כשבא עד אחד ואמר מת התירוה ואח"כ בא אחר ואמר לא מת אם נשאת לא תצא אבל לכתחלה לא תנשא משום דרב אסי כדמסיק ומרישא דהתם יש להוכיח שיש חילוק בין בבת אחת בין בזה אחר זה דקתני עד אחד אומר מת וניסת ובא אחר ואמר לא מת לא תצא ומפרש בגמרא דלא ניסת ממש אלא התירוה לינשא אע"פ שלא ניסת ולא תצא היינו מהתירה הראשון משמע דווקא התירוה קודם שבא העד ואמר לא מת הא בא קודם שהתירוה לא ונ"ע בפ' מי שקינא (סוטה דף לא:) דמשמע דאיירי עולא בכל ענין בין בב"א בין בזה אחר זה דתנן התם עד אחד אומר נטמאת ועד אחד אומר לא נטמאת היתה שותה ודייק בגמ' טעמא דהאי מכחיש אבל לא מכחיש עד אחד נאמן מנא ה"מ כו' ופריך כיון דמדאורייתא עד אחד נאמן אידך היכי מצי מכחיש ליה והאמר עולא כל מקום שהאמינה כו' אלא אמר עולא תני לא היתה שותה ור' חייא אומר היתה שותה לר' חייא קשיא דעולא לא קשיא כאן בבת אחת כאן בזה אחר זה משמע דעולא נמי איירי בבת אחת ולכך צריך להגיה ולא משני כדמשני ר' חייא ומיהו איכא למימר דעולא לא מיירי אלא בזה אחר זה אלא שנראה לו דוחק להעמיד המשנה בבת אחת משום דמשמע ליה דמיירי בזה אחר זה ועוד אומר ר"י דאפילו איירי לעולא בכל ענין הני מילי התם דמדאורייתא עד אחד מהימן בסוטה כדנפקא ליה התם מועד אין בה אבל הכא גבי אשה דלא מהימן אלא מדרבנן לא חשיב כשנים אלא בזה אחר זה ואע"ג דיש חילוק בין דאורייתא לרבנן מייתי מדעולא דנראה לו דחשיב כשנים בזה אחר זה בדרבנן כמו בבת אחת בדאורייתא:

משום דרב אסי הסר ממך עקשות פה. פסוק הוא אלא דרב אסי רגיל להביאו וא"ת והא דתנן בהאשה שלום (יבמות דף קיז: ושם) עד אחד אומר מת וניסת ובא עד אחד ואמר לא מת לא תצא ופריך בגמרא טעמא דניסת הא לא ניסת לא תנשא והאמר עולא כל מקום כו' ומאי פריך והא עולא לא קאמר אלא בדיעבד אבל לכתחלה מודה דלא תנשא משום דרב אסי ואומר ר"י דהתם דייק טעמא דניסת הא אם לא נשאת לא תנשא ואם נשאת תצא דהכי משמע מתניתין דוקא נשאת ואחר כך בא העד לא תצא הא בא העד קודם שנשאת ואחר כך ניסת תצא משום הכי פריך מדעולא ואם תאמר והיכי משני התם דה"ק עד אחד אומר מת והתירוה לינשא ובא אחר ואמר לא מת לא תצא מהתירה הראשון משמע ותנשא לכתחלה וי"ל דודאי לכתחלה לא תנשא ולא תצא מהתירה הראשון לענין דאם ניסת לא תצא:

תרווייהו באשת איש קמסהדי. תימה דמה לנו לאותו עד שאומר לא נתגרשה בלא איהו נמי תצא דאין דבר שבערוה פחות משנים דהא ליכא למימר שלא היינו יודעים שהיא א"א כי אם על פיהם דא"כ להימניה להאי דאמר מגורשת במיגו דאי בעי שתק וי"ל דאין זה מיגו דשמא רוצה להעיד כדי לפוסלה מן הכהונה. ת"י:

מסורת הש"ס

א) [לקמן דף כ: וש"נ], ב) יבמות פח. ב"ב לא., ג) [עס כיבמות], ד) יבמות פח: קיח: סוטה לא: מז., ה) יבמות כד. ו) שם קטו. נדרים לא. גיטין סד: פטו: ז) [שייך לע"ב עד ד"ה לא עבד שמואל כו'], ח) [שייך לע"א], ט) [ביבמות פח: בתוס' דבר זה בשם ר"י וע"ע תוס' ב"ב לב. ד"ה לאו], י) [וע"ע תוס' לקמן כו: ד"ה לאו].

תוספות ישנים

א) ובשנים אומרים נתגרשה נמי דייקא כי ירא שלא יוחזו עדיה אבל חזקה דלאין אשה מעיזה ליכא כיון דליכא עדים דקא מסייעי לה. ת"י עה"ג.

תורה אור השלם

א) הָסֵר מִמְּךָ עִקְּשׁוּת פֶּה וּלְזוּת שְׂפָתַיִם הַרְחֵק מִמֶּךָּ: [משלי ד, כד]

ליקוטי רש"י

שנים אומרים מת. אשה שהלך בעלה למדינת הים ובאו שנים ואמרו לה מת בעליך ושנים אומרים לא מת ... [ברשב"ם ב"ב לא:]. כגון ע"י סימנים וכגון ... תרגמה. פרש אותה. [סוטה ח:]. הרי כאן שנים. ... דבריו של אחד. ... [יבמות שם]. הסר ממך עקשות פה. ... [משלי ד, כד]. ... תרגמה. פרש אותה [סוטה ח:]. דבשבויה הקילו. דספיקא בעלמא היא [ב"ק קיד:].

תוספות רי"ד

גדולה בנורי הקצוו עליה בני אדם לקדשה ... תנא מיניה מ' זמנין ואפ"ה לא עביד שמואל עובדא בנפשיה ...

מסורת הש"ס

א) סנהדרין ג. ה: ל. פז:, ב) [בכורות לו.], ג) קדושין סד. [ע"ש], ד) לקמן מו., ה) [ה: ועי' תוס' שם ג. ד"ה לרבא].

תוספות ישנים

א) [וה"ה דהוה מלי למימר בערער דפגם משפחה וכגון דקאמרי ידענו שנשתחרר. ת"י עה"ג].

גליון הש"ס

גמ' למה לי קרא סברא. ב"ק מו ע"ב נדה כה ע"א:

תורה אור השלם

א) וְאָמַר אֲבִי הַנַּעֲרָ אֶל הַזְּקֵנִים אֶת בִּתִּי נָתַתִּי לָאִישׁ הַזֶּה לְאִשָּׁה וַיִּשְׂנָאֶהָ: [דברים כב, טז]

ליקוטי רש"י

בי דינא. הכול יודעין שאין שנים קרוים ב"ד [סנהדרין ל.]. בית דין חצוף. שעברו על תקנת חכמים [שם ג.]. בי דינא דרבנא אשי. דאינהו ודאי ידעי שאין ב"ד קרויין בשנים. ואמר לנא רבנא אשי. לכתוב כך דכיון דהוא היה שם מסתמא לא נזה לפחות משלשה לכתוב והאי דנקט רב אשי לפי שבית דינו היה ראש בימי רבינא ושניהם סידרו גמרא של תלמוד בבלי כדאמרינן התם (בהשוכר את הפועלים דף פו.) רב אשי ורבינא סוף הוראה ובימיו נאמרו דברים הללו והוקבעו בגמרא [שם ל.]. אשת איש הייתי. ולא היינו מוחזקין בה שהיא אשת איש מעולם. נאמנת. ומותרת להנשא. שהפה שאסר וכו'. דאי בעיא לא אמרה, כלומר אי הוה משקרא להיתרא הוה שתקה ולא הוה אמרה אשת איש הייתי [...] מחזקינן לה [בכורות לו.]. לאיש אסרה. על הכל שאין אנו יודעים למי וכי אמר הזה התירה לזה [קידושין סד.]. ולא ליבם. אין יבם שהוציא שם רע על נישואי אחיו בכלל פרשה זו לטעון טענת בתולים [לקמן מו.]. שר הבירה. כך כינויו [לקמן פח.].

רש"י

תרי ותרי נינהו. כי אמרי לא גזל הוו להו תרי ותרי ולא מתכשר בהכי דקי"ל לקמן בפרקין (דף כו.) אין ערער פחות משנים: דפגם משפחה. שהעידו עליו שהוא עבד ועבד פסול לדין ולעדות ק"ו מאשה כדאמר בפ' החובל (ב"ק פח.): גלוי מילתא בעלמא הוא. משמתמו אמאי אין מעידין עליו מאי חשד נוגע בעדות איכא הכא דבר זה צריכין הן לברר ודבר העשוי לגלות הוא שיבדקו אחריו עד שיבורר הדבר ואין עדותן של אלו תלוי בהגדתן ואינן אלא מגלי דבר בעלמא: דעבד תשובה. והשיב את הגזלה: ואי לאו רבי אבא דמן עכו. שהזכירה לי לאחר זמן: שכחתה. שכחתיה: ומת אחד מהן. על שלא חתמו: צריכין למיכתב כו'. דקיום השטר בשלשה והרואה שנים חתומין בו יאמר שבשנים קיימוהו: ואי כתב ביה שטרא דנן נפק קדמנא בי דינא תו לא צריך. דלא מקרי בי דינא בציר מתלתא: בי דינא דרבנא אשי. אורחא דמילתא נקט שהוא היה ראש ישיבה במתא מחסיא בימי רב נחמן בר יצחק להוה מרא דשמעתא דודאי בי דינא דרב אשי לא עבדין בתרין: ואמר לנא רבנא אשי. לאחזוקי ליה ולקיומי דכיון דרב אשי גופיה הזקיקן איהו ודאי לתלתא אמר ויש מפרשין ואמר לנא רבנא אשי תלתא ניהו כי אמירה לי דאי רב אשי חד מנהון מאי ואמר לנא דכתבי ביה: מתני' נשביתי. לבין העובדי כוכבים: וטהורה אני. שלא נבעלתי לעובד כוכבים: נאמנת. ומותרת לכהן: ואם משנשאת באו עדים. בגמרא מפרש להיא קאי: גמ' נתתי לאיש אסרה. לכל העולם דלא ידעינן למאן וכי אמר הזה התירה לו: שנאמן לאסור את בתו. כשהיא קטנה או נערה שבידו לקדשה כדאמרי' בפ' נערה שנתפתתה מנין שאם אמר קדשתיה לפלוני שהוא נאמן לאוסרה על הכל: את בתי נתתי. אלמא בדידיה תליא נתינה והימניה קרא למימר הכי: הזה למה לי. כיון דלאו להפה שאסר מיבעי ליה: ולא ליבם. אם הוליה שם רע על נישואי אחיו אין היבם נידון כמוציא שם רע ליענש במאה כסף והכי מוכח לקמן בפרק נערה: אמתלא

גמרא

תרי ותרי נינהו א אי ערער דפגם משפחה גלוי מלתא בעלמא הוא לעולם אימא לך ערער דגזלנותא וקאמרי ב הני ידעינן ביה דעבד תשובה א"ר זירא הא מלתא מרבי אבא שמיע לי ואי לאו רבי אבא דמן עכו שכחתיה ג ג' שישבו לקיים את השטר ומת אחד מהם צריכין למיכתב במותב תלתא הוינא וחד ליתוהי אמר רב נחמן בר יצחק ואי כתב ביה שטרא דנן נפק לקדמנא בי דינא תו לא צריך ודלמא בית דין חצוף הוא וכדשמואל דאמר שמואל ד שנים שדנו דיניהם דין אלא שנקרא ב"ד חצוף דכתיב ביה בי דינא דרבנא אשי ודלמא רבנן דבי רב אשי כדשמואל סבירא להו דכתיב ביה ואמר לנא רבנא אשי:

מתני' ה האשה שאמרה אשת איש הייתי וגרושה אני נאמנת שהפה שאסר הוא הפה שהתיר ו ואם יש עדים שהיתה אשת איש והיא אומרת גרושה אני אינה נאמנת ז אמרה נשביתי וטהורה אני נאמנת שהפה שאסר הוא הפה שהתיר ח ואם יש עדים שנשבית והיא אומרת טהורה אני אינה נאמנת ט ואם משנשאת באו עדים הרי זו לא תצא:

גמ' א"ר אסי מנין להפה שאסר הוא הפה שהתיר מן התורה שנאמר א) את בתי נתתי לאיש הזה לאשה לאיש אסרה הזה התירה ל"ל קרא סברא היא הוא אסרה והוא שרי לה אלא כי איצטריך קרא לכדרב הונא אמר רב דא"ר הונא אמר רב י מנין לאב שנאמן לאסור את בתו מן התורה שנאמר את בתי נתתי לאיש הזה הזה למה לי מיבעי ליה לכדתני ר' יונה דתני ר' יונה את בתי נתתי לאיש הזה ולא ליבם ת"ר כ האשה שאמרה אשת איש אני וחזרה ואמרה פנויה אני נאמנת והא שוויה לנפשה חתיכה דאיסורא אמר רבא בר רב הונא כגון ל שנתנה אמתלא לדבריה תניא נמי הכי אמרה אשת איש אני וחזרה ואמרה פנויה אני אינה נאמנת ואם נתנה אמתלא לדבריה נאמנת ומעשה נמי באשה אחת שהיתה גדולה בנוי וקפצו עליה בני אדם לקדשה ואמרה להם מקודשת אני לימים עמדה וקידשה את עצמה אמרו לה חכמים מה ראית לעשות כן אמרה להם בתחלה שבאו עלי אנשים שאינם מהוגנים אמרתי מקודשת אני עכשיו שבאו עלי אנשים מהוגנים עמדתי וקדשתי את עצמי וזו הלכה העלה רב אחא שר הבירה לפני חכמי' באושא ואמרו אם נתנה אמתל' לדבריה נאמנת בעא מיניה שמואל מרב אמרה טמאה אני וחזרה ואמרה טהורה אני מהו אמר ליה נ אף בזו אם נתנה אמתלא

תוספות

תרי ותרי נינהו. פירש בקונטרס וכי אמרי לא גזל הוו להו תרי ותרי ולא מתכשר בהכי וקשה דהכא אליבא דרב הונא קיימינן דלית ליה (שבועות דף מז:) דזו באה בפני עצמה ומעידה דלית לן למימר אוקי גברא אחזקתיה ועוד דלרב חסדא דאמר (שם) בהדי שהדי שקרי למה לי מודה הכא דהאי גברא ממילא מתכשר שהרי אם כת אחת אמרו מאלו מעידה על אדם אחד שהוא פסול לרב חסדא דחשיב להו סהדי שקרי לא היתה נאמנת אע"ג דאין אדם מכחישה וכ"ש היכא דאיכא סהדי דמכחשי דלא מהימני וע"ק לר"י דקאמר אי ערער דפגם משפחה גלוי מילתא בעלמא הוא ופי' הקונט' דדבר העשוי ליגלות הוא שיבדקו עד שיתברר הדבר וזהו תימה איך יתברר הדבר לעולם כיון שאלו ב' אומרים שהוא עבד אין כל העולם יכולים להכחישן דתרי כמאה על כן נראה כפר"ח דלא איירי בעדות דיינין אלא בעדות אחרים וה"פ אם עד שלא חתמו קרא ערער על אחד מהם מעידים שנים מן השוק עליו וחותם דהוי כאילו ישבו בית דין אחר שהכשירוהו ולא בטל ועוד המושב וחותמין משחתמו השנים ולא הספיק השלישי לחתום עד שקרא עליו ערער בא ערער וביטל ועוד המושב של אותו ב"ד אע"פ שאחרי שהעידו אחרים שהוא כשר כיון שביטל הוא מושב בטל וצריך לחזור ולהושיב ב"ד על כך ערער דמאי אי ערער דגזלנותא תרי ותרי נינהו ולא מיפסיל דאוקי תרי בהדי תרי ואוקי גברא אחזקתיה וכיון דאיגלאי מלתא למפרע שלא היה פסול הרי לא היה בטל וועד המושב של אותו ב"ד אי ערער דפגם משפחה שאמרו עליו שהוא עבד ואלו מזימים אותם דאי אומרים שאינו עבד א"כ היה נפסל דליכא למימר אוקי גברא אחזקה דאם הוא עבד לא היה לו חזקת כשרות מעולם א) א"כ גלוי מילתא בעלמא הוא דכיון דאיגלאי מלתא דכשר היה מה איכפת לן בההוא ערעור ולא בטל ועוד המושב לעולם ערער דגזלנותא ודקאמרי הנך סהדי ידעינן ביה דעבד תשובה וכיון דמודו לקמאי דגזלן הוה הוה ערער דידהו ערער ובטל ועוד המושב דהואיל ואמת הוא שנפסל הוי בחזקת פסלות עד שנודע לנו כשרותו:

במותב תלתא כחדא הוינא וחד ליתוהי. פירוש לריך לכתוב וחד ליתוהי כיון דכתב בהדיא במותב תלתא הוינא ואין חותמין בו כי אם שנים אבל ודאי אם לא כתב וחד ליתוהי כשר תדע מדקאמר ואי כתב ביה בי דינא תו לא צריך ומיירי דלא כתב וחד ליתוהי מדפריך ודלמא ב"ד חצוף הוה:

ודלמא רבנן דבי רב אשי כשמואל סבירא להו. פי' כמו שסובר שמואל בעלמא כן סבירא להו בקיום שטרות אבל שמואל מלי סבר שפיר דבקיום שטרות בעי ג' דהא רב נחמן סבר לה כשמואל בפ"ק דסנהדרין ה) (דף ג. ושם) דשנים שדנו דיניהם דין ורב נחמן גופיה סבר דקיום שטרות בשלשה בפ' חזקת הבתים (ב"ב מ.) גבי ג' ארצות לחזקה:

מנין להפה שאסר הוא הפה שהתיר מן התורה שנאמר את בתי נתתי לאיש וגו'. משמע דאין האב נאמן להתיר את בתו כשאסרה אלא מחמת מגו ותימה דאם בא אחד ואמר קדשתי את בתי ולאחר שעה או למחר אמר לפלוני קדשתיה לא יהא נאמן כיון דהשתא ליכא מגו ואומר ר"י דבענין זה שאינו סותר דבריו הראשונים מהימן אע"ג דליכא מגו והכא דריש מאת בתי הפה שאסר הוא הפה שהתיר כגון דקאי האיש שקידש לו קמיה וקאמר את בתי נתתי לאיש ושתיק דמשמע ודאי שאינו מכיר שזה חתנו מדלא אמר את בתי נתתי לזה או לאיש הזה ביחד בלא הפסק מרווה הלכך לא יהא נאמן אחר כך אלא תוך כדי דבור דאיכא מגו ועוד אומר ר"י דאיכא למימר אפילו בכה"ג מהימן בלא מגו וקרא יתירא קדריש ואם אינו ענין כאן דאפילו לאחר זמן נאמן דסברא הוא שיהא נאמן לפרש למי נתנה אע"פ שלא פירש מתחלה שלא היה חושש לפרש תנהו ענין להיכא דאינו נאמן לאחר זמן שיהא נאמן בתוך כדי דבור במגו:

[מנין לאב שנאמן לאסור וכו'. תימה מה לריך קרא תיפוק ליה דנאמן הואיל ובידו לקדשה כדאמר ביש נוחלין (ב"ב קלד:) בעל שאמר גרשתי את אשתי נאמן הואיל ובידו לגרשה וי"ל דהכא אין בידו כל כך דשמא לא ימצא אדם שיקדשנה (כדאיתא קדושין סד.) להכי איצטריך קרא ומיהו אם אמר על בתו בוגרת קדשתיה כשהיתה נערה או קטנה נראה דאינו נאמן דהשתא אין בידו כלל דאף על גב דלקמן בפ' נערה שנתפתתה (דף מו:) פריך ואימא הנ"מ קטנה אבל נערה איהי מיקדש נפשה לפי זה היה נ"ל דנאמן לאסור אפילו בשעה שאין בידו לקדשה דקרא בנערה כתיב ובעי למימר דאין בידו לקדשה ואת בתי נתתי כשהיתה קטנה וגזרת הכתוב הוא דנאמן אע"פ שאין בידו אבל לפי המסקנא לא נאמר כן]:

חזרה

עין משפט נר מצוה

נד א מיי' פ"ו מהלכות עדות הלכה ז טוש"ע ח"מ סי' מו סעיף מ:
נה ב מיי' שם טוש"ע שם סעיף כו:
נו ג ד מיי' שם הלכה ו טוש"ע שם סעיף כט:
נז ה מיי' פי"ב מהלכות גירושין הלכה א סמג עשין מח טוש"ע אה"ע סימן קנב סעיף ו:
נח ו מיי' שם טוש"ע שם סעיף ז:
נט ז ח מיי' פי"ח מהל' איסורי ביאה הלכה כא סמג לאוין קלא טוש"ע אה"ע סימן ז סעיף ד:
ס ט מיי' שם הלכה כב טוש"ע שם סעיף ו:
סא י מיי' פ"ט מהלכות אישות הל' ג ופי"ח מהלכות איסורי ביאה הלכה כד סמג עשין מ טוש"ע אה"ע סימן לז סעיף כא:
סב כ מיי' פ"ג מהל' נערה בתולה הלכה ט סמג עשין כה:
סג ל מ מיי' פ"ט מהל' אישות הלכה לא סמג עשין מח טוש"ע אה"ע סימן מו סעיף ד:
סד נ מיי' פ"ד מהלכות איסורי ביאה הל' י סמג לאוין קיא טוש"ע י"ד סימן קפה סעיף ג:

תוספות רי"ד

תרי ותרי נינהו פי' ועד שלא חתמו אמאי מעידין והא אין ערער פחות מב' שאין משגיחים בדברי היחיד וכיון שב' אומרים גזלן הוא ואלו אומרים שלא גזל הו"ל תרי ותרי וכל תו"ת הו"ל ספיקא דאורייתא ובספיקא דאורייתא לא אמרינן אוקי גברא אחזקתיה כדאמרינן לקמן בפירקין וכיון דהאידנא איתוקם בספק גזלן היכי מחתמינן ליה ומפקינן ממונא אפומיה הלכך אע"פ שלא חתמו לא יכלו להכשירו ואי ערעור דפגם משפחה גלוי מילתא בעלמא הוא ואפי' משחתמו מעידים פי' ערעור דפגם משפחה שאלו השנים שבאו לפוסלו לא העידו עליו עדות ברורה אלא העידו שבמשפחתו נטמע שם עבד שהוא פסול לעדות וכל המשפחה הן בחזקת שהוא ספק פסול שמא מזרע אותו עבד נולד ואלה מעידים שזה אינו מן המסופקין דברי לן שמייחוס כשרות הוא בא ואינן מכחישין את העדים אלא מוציאים את זה מספק פסול שלא יהיה מסופק כשאר כל בני המשפחה וזהו גילוי מילתא שיכול להתברר ע"פ אחרים שנבדוק אחריו ויתברר אם נולד מן הכשרים או מן הפסולין ובמילתא דעביד לגלויי לא משקרי אינשי והלכך אע"פ שחתמו והן נוגעים בעדות נאמנים דבאיזה עדות אינן נאמנין בדבר שלא נוכל להתברר על ידי אחרים כ"א על פיהם כדלקמן שמעידין שעשה תשובה שאין מכירין תשובתו אלא הם אבל ייחוס האדם דהוא מילתא דעביד לגלויי ע"פ אחרים אע"פ שהן נוגעים בעדותן נאמנים הם. לעולם ערער דגזלנותא ודקאמרי הני ידעי' ביה דעשה תשובה שהחזיר את הגזילה ואין כאן משום הכחשה הלכך עד שלא חתמו מעידין עליו וחותם ומשחתמו שהן נוגעים בעדות אין מעידין עליו וחותם עי' בס"ה בערך מ"ר:

רבינו חננאל

א"ר זירא האי מילתא מר' אבא שמיעא לי שלשה שישבו לקיים את השטר ומת אחד מהן צריכים למיכתב במותב תלתא כחדא הוינא וחד ליתוהי פי' צריכים להודיע למה לא חתם הג' שיש לך לומר הא' היה קרוב או פסול ומפני זה לא חתם ובעבור זה האשרתא היא פסולה והמורה פי' צריכים לכתוב קודם שיחתמוהו דקיום שטרות בשלשה והרואה ב' חתומים יאמר שבשנים קיימוהו ואי כתיב [ביה] הא שטרא דנן נפק קדמנא בב"ד תו לא צריך דלא מקרי ב"ד בציר מתלתא. והגאון פי' אם כתבו בפנינו בב"ד הנפק שטרא דנן ואע"ג דלא כתבו במותב תלתא תו לא צריך למכתב וחד ליתוהי דסתם ב"ד כשרי' משמע ולא פסולים ולא קרובים ומקשינן דלמא ב"ד חצוף הוא דאמר שמואל שנים שדנו דיניהם דין אלא שנקרא ב"ד חצוף פי' והאשרתא בטילה דלית הלכתא כשמואל אלא כר' אבהו דאמר אין דיניהם דין ומהדר דכתיב ביה בי דינא דרבנא אשי פי' ב"ד מומחה שבדור והמורה פי' אורחא דמילתא נקט שהוא היה ראש ישיבה במתא מחסי' בימי רנב"י דהוא מרה שמעתתא ובודאי בי דינא דר' אשי לא עביד בתרין ומקשי' ודלמא ב"ד דר' אשי כשמואל ס"ל ואין הלכה כמותן ומהדר דכתיב ביה ואמר לנא רבנא אשי פי' רב אשי צוה לנו להזקק לו וכיון שע"פ ר"א עשו בודאי בי ג' היו דר"א לא טעה בדשמואל דלית הל' כוותיה וכ"ש אם כתבו בבי ב"ד במותב תלתא כחדא הוינא דתו ליכא למיחש לא לדשמואל ולא לקרוב ופסול שחותמים בו שנים ואין צריכין לומר וחד ליתוהי ודוקא אם מ. . אבל אם חי צריך לחתום שלא יאמרו השנים שהעידו בפניהם חתמו והשלישי לא העידו בפניו ומש"ה לא חתם והאשרתא בטלה: מתני' האשה שאמרה אשת איש הייתי וגרושה אני נאמנת שהפה שאסר הוא הפה שהתיר ואם יש עדים שהיא אשת איש והיא אומרת גרושה אני אינה נאמנת. ת"ר אמרה אשת איש אני וחזרה ואמרה פנויה אני אינה נאמנת ואם נתנה אמתלא לדבריה נאמנת ומעשה באשה אחת שהיתה

— AND THEY SAID: אִם נָתְנָה אֲמַתְלָא לִדְבָרֶיהָ נֶאֱמֶנֶת — IF SHE GAVE A plausible REASON FOR HER WORDS, SHE IS BELIEVED.[30]

A parallel case:

בְּעָא מִינֵּיהּ שְׁמוּאֵל מֵרַב — Shmuel asked Rav: אָמְרָה טְמֵאָה אֲנִי — If [a woman] told her husband, "I am *tamei*" (i.e. I am a *niddah*), וְחָזְרָה וְאָמְרָה טְהוֹרָה אֲנִי — and then she went back and said, "I am *tahor*" (i.e. I was not a *niddah*),[31] מַהוּ — what is [the law]?[32]

Rav answers:

אָמַר לֵיהּ — He said to [Shmuel]: אַף בְּזוֹ אִם נָתְנָה — Even in this case, if she gave

NOTES

30. This decision was made in reference to the incident recorded above. Therefore, the meaning is "*since* she gave a reason" (*Rashi,* printed on 22b).

The Gemara records the circumstances of the case to teach that the explanation must be convincing. The fact that she was beautiful lends credence to her claim that she had many suitors; and the fact that she hailed from a prestigious family supports her assertion that she sought to avoid anyone not similarly eligible (*Chasam Sofer;* see note 26).

31. The second statement was not made immediately after the first one [תּוֹךְ כְּדֵי דִבּוּר] (*Rosh; Rabbeinu Yerucham,* cited by *Beis Yosef, Yoreh Deah* 185:3; see note 26).

32. That is, if she can explain why she (falsely) claimed to be a *niddah,* do we accept her explanation and rule that she is permitted to her husband? (*Tosafos* printed on 22b, *Tos. HaRosh* et al.; see *Shitah Mekubetzes* ד״ה וחזרה ואמרה).

A *niddah* can purify herself simply by counting the requisite number of days and immersing herself in a *mikveh.* Since it is a relatively simple matter for her to exit her prohibited state, perhaps we should require her to do so and not rely on her explanation. [This is in contrast to the previous case of a possibly betrothed woman, where she cannot readily extricate herself from the prohibited state] (*Tos. HaRosh;* see also *Ran, Ritva* and *Chasam Sofer*). For other approaches, see *Rashba, Maharsha, Chidushei Anshei Shem, Maharam Schif* and *Cheshek Shlomo.*

תרי ותרי נינהו א) אי ערער דפגם משפחה גלוי מלתא בעלמא הוא לעולם אימא לך ערער דגזלנותא וקאמרי ב) הני ידעינן ביה דעבד תשובה א"ר זירא הא מלתא מרבי אבא שמיע לי ואי לאו רבי אבא דמן עכו שכחתה ג' שישבו לקיים את השטר ומת אחד מהם צריכין למיכתב במותב תלתא הוינא וחד ליתוהי אמר רב נחמן בר יצחק ואי כתב ביה שטרא דנן נפק לקדמנא בי דינא תו לא צריך ודלמא בית דין חצוף הוא וכדשמואל דאמר שמואל שנים שדנו דיניהם דין אלא שנקרא ב"ד חצוף דכתיב ביה בי דינא דרבנא אשי ודלמא רבנן דבי רב אשי כדשמואל סבירא להו דכתיב ביה ואמר לנא רבנא אשי:

מתני' ג) האשה שאמרה אשת איש הייתי וגרושה אני נאמנת שהפה שאסר הוא הפה שהתיר ואם יש עדים שהיתה אשת איש והיא אומרת גרושה אני אינה נאמנת אמרה נשביתי וטהורה אני נאמנת שהפה שאסר הוא הפה שהתיר ואם יש עדים שנשבית והיא אומרת טהורה אני אינה נאמנת ואם משנשאת באו עדים הרי זו לא תצא:

גמ' א"ר אסי מנין להפה שאסר הוא הפה שהתיר מן התורה שנאמר א) את בתי נתתי לאיש הזה לאשה לאיש אסרה הזה התירה ל"ל קרא סברא היא הוא אסרה והוא שרי לה אלא כי איצטריך קרא לכדרב הונא אמר רב דא"ר הונא אמר רב מנין לאב שנאמן לאסור את בתו מן התורה שנאמר את בתי נתתי לאיש הזה למה לי מיבעי ליה לכדתני ר' יונה דתני ר' יונה את בתי נתתי לאיש הזה ולא ליבם ת"ר האשה שאמרה אשת איש אני וחזרה ואמרה פנויה אני נאמנת והא שויה לנפשה חתיכה דאיסורא אמר רבא בר רב הונא כגון שנתנה אמתלא לדבריה תניא נמי הכי אמרה אשת איש אני וחזרה ואמרה פנויה אני אינה נאמנת ואם נתנה אמתלא לדבריה נאמנת ומעשה נמי באשה אחת גדולה שהיתה גדולה בנוי וקפצו עליה בני אדם לקדשה ואמרה להם מקודשת אני לימים עמדה וקידשה את עצמה אמרו לה חכמים מה ראית לעשות כן אמרה להם בתחלה שבאו עלי אנשים שאינם מהוגנים אמרתי מקודשת אני עכשיו שבאו עלי אנשים מהוגנים עמדתי וקדשתי את עצמי וזו הלכה העלה רב אחא שר הבירה לפני חכמי' באושא ואמרו אם נתנה אמתל' לדבריה נאמנת בעא מיניה שמואל מרב אמרה טמאה אני וחזרה ואמרה טהורה אני מהו אמר ליה אף בזו אם נתנה אמתלא

רש"י

תרי ותרי נינהו. כי אמרי לא גזל הוו להו תרי ותרי ולא מתכשר בהכי דקי"ל לקמן בפרקין (דף כו.) אין ערער פחות משנים: דפגם משפחה. שהעידו עליו שהוא עבד ועבד פסול לדין ולעדות ק"ו מאשה כדאמר בפ' החובל (ב"ק פח.): גלוי מילתא בעלמא הוא. משחתמו אמאי אין מעידין עליו מאי חשד נוגע בעדות איכא הכא דבר זה צריכין הן לברר ודבר העשוי לגלות הוא שיבדקו אחריו עד שיבורר הדבר ואין עדותן של אלו תלוי בהגדתן ואינן אלא מגלי דבר בעלמא: דעבד תשובה. והשיב את הגזלה: ואי לאו רבי אבא דמן עכו. שהזכירה לי לאחר זמן: שכחתה. שכחתיה: ומת אחד מהן. עד שלא חתמו: צריכין למיכתב כו'. דקיום השטר בשלשה והרואה שנים חתומין בו יאמר שבשנים קיימוהו: ואי כתב ביה שטרא דנן נפק קדמנא בי דינא תו לא צריך. דלא מקרי בי דינא בציר מתלתא: בי דינא דרבנא אשי. אורחא דמילתא נקט שהוא היה ראש ישיבה במתא מחסיא בימי רב נחמן בר יצחק דהוא מרא דשמעתא דודאי בי דינא דרב אשי לא עבדין בתרין: ואמר לנא רבנא אשי. לאזדקוקי ליה ולקיומי דכיון דרב אשי גופיה הזקיקן איהו ודאי לתלתא אמר ויש מפרשין ואמר לנא רבנא אשי חד מנהון מאי ואמר לנא דכתבי ביה: מתני' נשביתי. לבין העובדי כוכבים: וטהורה אני. שלא נבעלתי לעובד כוכבים: נאמנת. ומותרת לכהן: ואם משנישאת באו עדים. בגמרא מפרש אהייא קאי: גמ' נתתי לאיש אסרה. לכל העולם דלא ידעינן למאן וכי אמר הזה התירה לו: שנאמן לאסור את בתו. כשהיא קטנה או נערה שבידו לקדשה כדאמרי' בפ' נערה שנתפתתה מנין שאם אמר קדשתיה לפלוני שהוא נאמן לאוסרה על הכל: את בתי נתתי. אלמא בדידיה תליא נתינה והימניה קרא למימר הכי: הזה למה לי. כיון דלאו להפה שאסר מיבעי ליה: ולא ליבם. אם הוציא שם רע על נישואי אחיו שאין היבם נידון כמוציא שם רע ליענש במאה כסף והכי מוכח לקמן בפרק נערה: אמתלא

תוספות

תרי ותרי נינהו. פירש בקונטרס וכי אמרי לא גזל הוו להו תרי ותרי ולא מתכשר בהכי וקשה דהכא אליבא דרב הונא קיימינן דאית ליה (שבועות דף מב.) דזה בא בפני עצמה ומעידה דאית לן למימר אוקי גברא אחזקתיה ועוד דלרב חסדא דאמר (שם) בההי סהדי שקרי למה לי מודה הכא דהכא גברא ממילא מתכשר שהרי אם כל אחת מאלו מעידה על אדם אחד שהוא פסול לרב חסדא דחשיב להו סהדי שקרי לא היתה נאמנת אע"ג דלאין אדם מכחישה וכ"ש היכא דאיכא סהדי דמכחשי דלא מהימני ונ"ק לר"י דקאמר אי ערער דפגם משפחה גלוי מילתא בעלמא הוא ופי' הקונט' דדבר העשוי ליגלות הוא שיבדקו עד שיתברר הדבר וזהו תימה איך יתברר הדבר לעולם כיון שאלו ג' אומרים שהוא עבד שאין כל העולם יכולים להכחישן דתרי כמאה על כן נראה כפר"ח דלא איירי בעדות דיינין אלא בעדות אחרים וה"פ אם עד שלא חתמו קרא ערער על אחד מהם מעידים שנים מן השוק עליו וחותם דהוי כאילו ישבו בית דין אחר שהכשירוהו ולא בטל וועד המושב וחותמין משחתמו השנים ולא הספיק השלישי לחתום עד שקרא עליו ערער בא ערער וביטל וועד המושב של אותו ב"ד אע"פ שאחרי כן העידו אחרים שהוא כשר כיון שביטל ההוא מושב בטל וצריך לחזור ולהושיב ב"ד על כן ערער דמאי אי ערער דגזלנותא תרי ותרי נינהו ולא מיפסיל דאוקי תרי בהדי תרי ואוקי גברא אחזקתיה וכיון דאיגלאי מלתא דמעולם לא היה פסול הרי לא היה בטל וועד המושב של אותו ב"ד אי ערער דפגם משפחה שאמרו עליו שהוא עבד ואלו מזימים אותם דאי אומרים שאינו עבד א"כ היה נפסל דליכא למימר אוקי גברא אחזקה דאם הוא עבד לא היה לו חזקת כשרות מעולם א) א"כ גלוי מילתא בעלמא הוא דכיון דאיגלאי מלתא דכשר היה מה איכפת לן בההוא ערעור ולא בטל וועד המושב לעולם ערער דגזלנותא ודקאמרי הנך סהדי ידעינן ביה דעבד תשובה וכיון דמודו לקמאי דגזלן הוא הוה ערער דידהו ערער ובטל וועד המושב דהואיל ואמת הוא שנפסל הוי בחזקת פסלות עד שנודע לנו כשרותו:

במותב תלתא כחדא הוינא וחד ליתוהי. פירוש צריך לכתוב וחד ליתוהי כיון דכתב בהדיא במותב תלתא הוינא ואין חותמין בו כי אם שנים אבל ודאי אם לא כתב וחד ליתוהי כשר תדע מדקאמר ואי כתב ביה בי דינא תו לא צריך ומיירי דלא כתב וחד ליתוהי מדפריך ודלמא ב"ד חצוף הוה:

ודלמא רבנן דבי רב אשי כשמואל סבירא להו. פי' כמו שסובר שמואל בעלמא כן סבירא להו בקיום שטרות אבל שמואל מצי סבר שפיר דבקיום שטרות בעי ג' דהא רב נחמן סבר לה כשמואל בפ"ק דסנהדרין ה) (דף ג. ושם) דשנים שדנו דיניהם דין ורב נחמן גופיה סבר דקיום שטרות בשלשה בפ' חזקת הבתים (ב"ב מ.) גבי ג' ארצות לחזקה:

מנין להפה שאסר הוא הפה שהתיר מן התורה שנאמר את בתי נתתי לאיש וגו'. משמע דאין האב נאמן להתיר את בתו כשאסרה אלא מחמת מגו ותימה דאם בא אחד ואמר קדשתי את בתי ולאחר שעה או למחר אמר לפלוני קדשתיה לא יהא נאמן כיון דהשתא ליכא מגו ואומר ר"י דבענין זה שאינו סותר דבריו הראשונים מהימן אע"ג דליכא מגו והכא דריש מאת בתי הפה שאסר הוא הפה שהתיר כגון דקאי האיש שקידש לו קמיה וקאמר את בתי נתתי לאיש ושתיק דמשמע ודאי שאינו מכיר שזה חתנו מדלא אמר את בתי נתתי לזה או לאיש הזה ביחד בלא הפסק מרובה הלכך לא יהא נאמן אחר כך אלא תוך כדי דבור דאיכא מגו ועוד אומר ר"י דאיכא למימר אפילו בכה"ג מהימן בלא מגו וקרא יתירא קדריש ואם אינו ענין כאן דאפילו לאחר זמן נאמן דסברא הוא שיהא נאמן לפרש למי נתנה אע"פ שלא פירש מתחלה שלא היה חושש לפרש תנהו ענין להיכא דאינו נאמן לאחר זמן שיהא נאמן בתוך כדי דבור במגו:

[**מנין** לאב שנאמן לאסור וכו'. תימה מה צריך קרא תיפוק ליה דנאמן הואיל ובידו לקדשה כדאמר ביש נוחלין (ב"ב קלד:) בעל שאמר גרשתי את אשתי נאמן הואיל ובידו לגרשה וי"ל דהכא אין בידו כל כך דשמא לא ימצא אדם שיקדשנה (כדאיתא קדושין סד.) להכי איצטריך קרא ומיהו אם אמר על בתו בוגרת קדשתיה כשהיתה נערה או קטנה נראה דאינו נאמן דהשתא אין בידו כלל דאף על גב דלקמן בפ' נערה שנתפתתה (דף מו:) פריך ואימא הנ"מ קטנה אבל נערה איהי תיקדש נפשה לפי זה היה נ"ל דנאמן לאסור אפילו בשעה שאין בידו לקדשה דקרא בנערה כתיב ובעי למימר דאין בידו לקדשה ואת בתי נתתי כשהיתה קטנה וגזרת הכתוב הוא דנאמן אע"פ שאין בידו אבל לפי המסקנא לא נאמר כן]:

חזרה

עין משפט נר מצוה

נד א מיי' פ"י מהלכות עדות הלכה ז טוש"ע ח"מ סי' מו סעיף כז:
נה ב מיי' שם טוש"ע שם סעיף כו:
נו ג ד מיי' שם הלכה ו טוש"ע שם סעיף כט:
נז ה מיי' פ"י מהלכות גירושין הלכה ד סמג עשין נ טוש"ע אה"ע סימן קנב סעיף ו:
נח ו מיי' שם טוש"ע שם סעיף ז:
נט ז ח מיי' פי"ח מהל' איסורי ביאה הלכה כא סמג לאוין קכח טוש"ע אה"ע סימן ז סעיף ד:
ס ט מיי' שם הלכה כב טוש"ע שם סעיף ו:
סא י מיי' פ"ג מהלכות אישות הל' יג ופי"ח מהלכות איסורי ביאה הלכה כד סמג עשין מח טוש"ע אה"ע סימן לז סעיף כח:
סב כ מיי' פ"ג מהל' נערה בתולה הלכה ט סמג עשין כה:
סג ל מ מיי' פ"ט מהל' אישות הלכה לא סמג עשין מח טוש"ע אה"ע סימן מו סעיף ד:
סד נ מיי' פי"ד מהלכות איסורי ביאה הל' יט סמג לאוין קיא טוש"ע יו"ד סימן קפה סעיף ג:

תוספות רי"ד

תרי ותרי נינהו פי' ועד שלא חתמו אמאי מעידין והא אין ערער פחות מב' שאין משגיחים בדברי היחיד וכיון שב' אומרים גזלן הוא ואלו אומרים שלא גזל הוא הו"ל תרי ותרי וכל תו"ת הו"ל ספיקא דאורייתא ובספיקא דאורייתא לא אמרינן אוקי גברא אחזקתיה כדאמרינן לקמן בפירקין וכיון דהדאידנא איתותב בספק גזלן היכי מחתמינן ליה ומפקינן ממונא אפומיה הלכך אע"פ שלא חתמו לא יכולו להכשיר ואי ערער דפגם משפחה גלוי מילתא בעלמא הוא ואפי' משחתמו מעידים פי' ערער דפגם משפחה שאלו השנים שבאו לפוסלו לא העידו עליו עדות ברורה אלא העידו שבמשפחתו נטמע שם עבד שהוא פסול לעדות וכל המשפחה בחזקת שהוא ספק פסול שמא מזרע אותו עבד הוא נולד ואלה מעידים שזה אינו מן המסופקין דברי לן שמיחוס כשרות הוא בא ואינן מכחישין את העדים אלא מוציאים את זה מספק פסול שלא יהיה מסופק כשאר כל בני המשפחה והוו גילוי מילתא שיכול להתברר ע"פ אחרים שנבדוק אחריו ויתברר אם נולד מן הכשרים או מן הפסולין ובמילתא דעביד לגלויי לא משקרי אינשי והלכך אע"פ שחתמו והן נוגעים בעדות נאמנים דבאיזה עדות אינן נאמנין בדבר שלא נוכל להתברר על ידי אחרים כ"א על פיהם כדלקמן שמעידין שעשה תשובה שאין מכירין תשובתו אלא הם אבל ייחוס האדם דהוא מילתא דעביד לגלויי אחרים אע"פ שהן נוגעים בעדותן נאמנים הם. לעולם ערער דגזלנותא ודקאמרי הני ידעי' ביה דעשה תשובה שהחזיר את הגזילה הלכך אין כאן משום הכחשה והלכך אע"פ שלא חתמו מעידין עליו וחותם ומשחתמו שהן נוגעים בעדות אין מעידין עליו

מסורת הש"ס

א) סנהדרין ג. ה: ל. פז, ב) [בכורות לו.], ג) קדושין סג: [ע"ש], ד) לקמן מו, ה) [ועי' תוס' שם ג. ד"ה לרבה].

תוספות ישנים

א) [וה"ה דהוה מצי למימר בערער דפגם משפחה וכגון דקאמרי ידעינן שנשתחרר. תו"ח עפ"ג].

גליון הש"ס

גמ' למה לי קרא סברא. ב"ק מו ע"ב נדה כה ע"א:

תורה אור השלם

א) וְאָמַר אֲבִי הַנַּעֲרָ אֶל הַזְּקֵנִים אֶת בִּתִּי נָתַתִּי לָאִישׁ הַזֶּה לְאִשָּׁה וַיִּשְׂנָאֶהָ: [דברים כב, טז]

ליקוטי רש"י

בי דינא. הכל יודעין שאין שנים קרויים ב"ד [סנהדרין ל.]. בית דין חצוף. שעברו על תקנת חכמים [שם ג.]. בי דינא דרבנא אשי. דאיהו ודאי ידעי שאין ב"ד קרויין בשנים. ואמר לנא רבנא אשי. לכתוב כך דכיון דהוא היה ראש מסתמא לא זזה לפסות משלשה [illegible]. אשת איש הייתי. ולא היינו מוחזקין בה שהיתה אשת איש מעולם. נאמנת. ומותרת להנשא. שהפה שאסר וכו'. דאי בעיא לא אמרה, כלומר אי לאו היא מי הוה ידעינן דאסורה [illegible]. לאיש אסרה. לכל העולם שלא נודע למי היא אסורה. הזה התירה לו [קידושין סג.]. ולא ליבם. אין יבם שהוציא שם רע על נישואי אחיו בכלל פרשה זו לטעון טענת בתולים [לקמן מו.]. שר הבירה. כך כינוי [לקמן פח.].

והותם עי' בס"ה בערך מ"ר: א"ר זירא האי מילתא מר' אבא שמיע לי שלשה שישבו לקיים את השטר ומת אחד מהן צריכים למיכתב במותב תלתא הוינא וחד ליתוהי צריכים להודיע למה לא חתם האי' היה קרובו או פסול ומפני
זה לא חתם ובעבור זה האשרתא היא פסולה [illegible]
[illegible]

Conceding that the verse is not needed to teach the aforementioned principle, the Gemara asserts that it serves a different purpose:

אֶלָּא כִּי אִיצְטְרִיךְ קְרָא לְכִדְרַב הוּנָא אָמַר רַב – **Rather, the verse is needed for** the law taught **by Rav Huna in the name of Rav,** דְּאָמַר רַב הוּנָא אָמַר רַב – **for Rav Huna said in the name of Rav:** מִנַּיִן לָאָב שֶׁנֶּאֱמָן לֶאֱסוֹר אֶת־בִּתּוֹ מִן הַתּוֹרָה – **From where** in the Torah is it known **that a father is believed to render his daughter forbidden** to all men by according her the status of a married woman? שֶׁנֶּאֱמַר ,,אֶת־בִּתִּי נָתַתִּי לָאִישׁ'' – **For it is stated:** ***My daughter I have given to this man as a wife.***[21]

The Gemara asks:

,,הַזֶּה'' לָמָּה לִי – But, still, **why do I need** the word ***this?***[22]

The Gemara answers:

מִיבָּעֵי לֵיהּ לְכִדְתָנֵי רַבִּי יוֹנָה – **It is needed for** the law **that R' Yonah taught in a Baraisa,** דְּתָנֵי רַבִּי יוֹנָה – **for R' Yonah taught** the following **Baraisa:** ,,אֶת־בִּתִּי נָתַתִּי לָאִישׁ הַזֶּה'' – When the Torah states, ***MY DAUGHTER I HAVE GIVEN TO THIS MAN AS A WIFE,*** ,,הַזֶּה'' וְלֹא לְיָבָם – it adds the word ***THIS*** to teach that the laws of the defamer apply only to a regular husband **AND NOT TO A *YAVAM.***[23]

The Gemara introduces a case related to our Mishnah:

תָּנוּ רַבָּנָן – **The Rabbis taught in a Baraisa:** הָאִשָּׁה שֶׁאָמְרָה אֵשֶׁת אִישׁ אֲנִי – If **A WOMAN SAID, "I AM MARRIED,"** וְחָזְרָה וְאָמְרָה פְּנוּיָה אֲנִי – **AND THEN WENT BACK AND SAID, "I AM UNMARRIED,"** נֶאֱמֶנֶת – **SHE IS BELIEVED** to say that she is unmarried.

The Gemara asks:

וְהָא שַׁוְּיָה לְנַפְשָׁהּ חֲתִיכָה דְּאִיסּוּרָא – **But** when she says that she is married, **she renders herself a forbidden object!**[24] How can she then permit herself by saying that she is not married?[25]

The Gemara answers:

אָמַר רָבָא בַּר רַב הוּנָא – **Rava bar Rav Huna said:** כְּגוֹן שֶׁנָּתְנָה אֲמַתְלָא לִדְבָרֶיהָ – The Baraisa refers to **a case where she gave a** plausible **reason for her** first **words.**[26]

The Gemara presents support for this explanation:

תַּנְיָא נַמִּי הָכִי – **This was also taught in** another **Baraisa:** אָמְרָה אֵשֶׁת אִישׁ אֲנִי – If **[A WOMAN] SAID, "I AM MARRIED,"** וְחָזְרָה וְאָמְרָה פְּנוּיָה אֲנִי – **AND THEN WENT BACK AND SAID, "I AM UNMARRIED,"** אֵינָהּ נֶאֱמֶנֶת – **SHE IS NOT BELIEVED** to say that she is unmarried. וְאִם נָתְנָה אֲמַתְלָא לִדְבָרֶיהָ נֶאֱמֶנֶת – **BUT IF SHE GAVE A** plausible **REASON FOR HER** first **WORDS, SHE IS BELIEVED.**

The Baraisa records an incident that illustrates this law:

וּמַעֲשֶׂה נַמִּי בְּאִשָּׁה אַחַת גְּדוֹלָה שֶׁהָיְתָה גְּדוֹלָה בְּנוֹי – **AND THERE WAS ALSO AN INCIDENT WITH ONE PRESTIGIOUS WOMAN WHO WAS VERY BEAUTIFUL,** וְקָפְצוּ עָלֶיהָ בְּנֵי אָדָם לְקַדְּשָׁהּ – **AND PEOPLE WERE PURSUING HER**[27] **TO BETROTH HER,** וְאָמְרָה לָהֶם מְקוּדֶּשֶׁת אֲנִי – **AND SHE WOULD SAY TO THEM, "I AM BETROTHED."** לְיָמִים עָמְדָה וְקִידְּשָׁה אֶת עַצְמָהּ – **SOME TIME LATER SHE AROSE AND BETROTHED HERSELF.** אָמְרוּ לָהּ חֲכָמִים – **THE SAGES ASKED HER,** מָה רָאִית לַעֲשׂוֹת כֵּן – **"WHAT DID YOU SEE** that permitted you **TO DO THIS?"**[28] אָמְרָה לָהֶם – **SHE ANSWERED THEM,** בַּתְּחִלָּה שֶׁבָּאוּ עָלַי אֲנָשִׁים שֶׁאֵינָם מְהוּגָּנִים – **"IN THE BEGINNING, WHEN MEN WHO WERE NOT ELIGIBLE CAME TO ME** for marriage, אָמַרְתִּי מְקוּדֶּשֶׁת אֲנִי – **I TOLD** them **THAT I WAS BETROTHED** so that they would not bother me. עַכְשָׁיו שֶׁבָּאוּ עָלַי אֲנָשִׁים מְהוּגָּנִים – **NOW THAT ELIGIBLE MEN CAME TO ME,** עָמַדְתִּי וְקִדַּשְׁתִּי אֶת עַצְמִי – **I AROSE AND BETROTHED MYSELF** to one of them." וְזוֹ הֲלָכָה הֶעֱלָה רַב אַחָא שַׂר הַבִּירָה לִפְנֵי חֲכָמִים בְּאוּשָׁא – **AND THIS** question of **LAW WAS RAISED BY RAV ACHA LORD OF THE BIRAH**[29] **BEFORE THE SAGES IN USHA,** וְאָמְרוּ

NOTES

21. By specifying the father as the one who effected the marriage ("*I have given, etc.*"), the verse teaches that a father has the legal capacity to marry off his daughter (under the age of twelve and a half) to a man of his choosing (see below, 46b). Thus, the verse also teaches that if a father claims to have married off his daughter, he is believed, because a person is generally believed to say he has done something that is within his power to do [for example, a husband is believed to say that he has divorced his wife (*Bava Basra* 134b)] (see *Rashi* and *Ritva*). [For discussion of why a verse is needed to teach that the father is believed, see *Tos. Yeshanim, Pnei Yehoshua, R' Akiva Eiger, Haflaah* and *Shev Shmaatsa* 6:8,12.]

22. As the Gemara concluded above, it is not needed to teach the principle of *happeh she'assar* (*Rashi*).

23. A מוֹצִיא שֵׁם רַע, *defamer,* is a husband who declares in court that his wife was not a virgin when their marriage was consummated (*nisuin*). He claims that she had committed adultery after they were legally married (*erusin*), and he produces witnesses to that effect. If the witnesses are found to be false, he must pay a fine of one hundred *shekels* to her father and is liable to lashes. He may never divorce his wife against her will (*Deuteronomy* 22:13-19; *Rambam, Hil. Naarah Besulah* 3:6).

R' Yonah's Baraisa derives from our verse that the law of the "defamer" does not extend to a *yavam.* [The Torah provides for the brother of a man who died childless to marry his widow. The surviving brother in such a case is known as a *yavam.*] The Baraisa refers to a case where a married man died before his marriage was consummated. His brother (*yavam*) then married the widow and claimed that she was not a virgin because she had committed adultery before her husband died. The verse teaches that the *yavam* is not liable to the special penalties of a "defamer" (see *Rashi; Rambam* ibid. §9).

24. See 9a note 2.

25. The principle of *happeh she'assar* is not applicable in this case, because the second statement directly contradicts the first one. This is unlike the cases of our Mishnah (e.g. "I was married but I am divorced"), where the second clause merely *qualifies* the first. See *Shitah Mekubetzes* to 18b ד״ה הרי אלו נאמנין and *Maggid Mishneh* to *Hil. Gerushin* 12:1.

26. She explained why initially she said, "I am betrothed" (*Rashi,* printed on 22b). Her explanation must ring true (*Ritva* to 22b סד״ה ואפילו; *Rambam, Hil. Ishus* 9:31; see also note 30).

In most areas of law if a person issues two contradictory statements, one immediately after the other [תּוֹךְ כְּדֵי דִבּוּר], the first statement is treated as having been retracted and only the second statement carries weight. Hence, in our case, if the woman would have said, "I am not betrothed," immediately after saying, "I am betrothed," her last statement would be accepted even if she does not explain why she changed her story. A plausible explanation is required only where the second statement was issued after some time had lapsed. [In our Mishnah's cases, though, where the second statement merely qualifies the first, it is not a retraction of the first statement even if it was issued immediately afterwards. Thus, our Mishnah requires the principle of *happeh she'assar* for the second statement to negate the effect of the first one (see note 13)] (*Rashba, Rosh, Meiri; Tur* and *Shulchan Aruch, Even HaEzer* 47:4; cf. *Maharsha*).

[Thus, the Gemara could alternatively have answered that this woman's second statement is believed because it was made immediately after the first one. The Gemara, however, chose not to give this answer because the wording of the Baraisa (וְחָזְרָה וְאָמְרָה וכו׳, *and then went back and said,* etc.) indicates that there was a significant time lapse between the two statements (*Shitah Mekubetzes* ד״ה והא שויא).]

[The commentators discuss the use of an אֲמַתְלָא, *reason,* in other contexts. *Rambam* rules that witnesses who testify in court cannot change their testimony even if they give a plausible reason for the change (*Hil. Eidus* 3:5; see *Shulchan Aruch, Choshen Mishpat* 29:1; see also *Chavos Daas* 185:5 and *Shev Shmaatsa* 6:8; cf. *Responsa* of *Chasam Sofer, Even HaEzer* I:75). Regarding the admission of a litigant in a monetary case (as opposed to ritual prohibition), see *Ketzos HaChoshen* 80:1.]

27. Literally: jumped on her.

28. Since, according to your own words, you are already betrothed, how could you betroth yourself to another man?

29. This was his nickname (*Rashi* below, 88a ד״ה שר הבירה). [The word בִּירָה, *birah,* might refer to a capital city, fortress or manor.]

תרי ותרי נינהו [א]אי ערער דפגם משפחה גלוי מלתא בעלמא הוא לעולם אימא לך ערער דגזלנותא וקאמרי [ב]הני ידעינן ביה דעבד תשובה א"ר זירא הא מלתא מרבי אבא שמיע לי ואי לאו רבי אבא דמן עכו שכחתה [ג]ג' שישבו לקיים את השטר ומת אחד מהם צריכין למיכתב במותב תלתא הוינא וחד ליתוהי אמר רב נחמן בר יצחק ואי כתב ביה שטרא דנן נפק לקדמנא בי דינא תו לא צריך ודלמא בית דין חצוף הוא וכדשמואל דאמר שמואל (א) שנים שדנו דיניהם דין אלא שנקרא ב"ד חצוף דכתיב ביה בי דינא דרבנא אשי ודלמא רבנן דבי רב אשי כדשמואל סבירא להו [ד]דכתיב ביה ואמר לנא רבנא אשי:

מתני' (ב) [ה]האשה שאמרה אשת איש הייתי וגרושה אני נאמנת שהפה שאסר הוא הפה שהתיר [ו]ואם יש עדים שהיתה אשת איש והיא אומרת גרושה אני אינה נאמנת [ז]אמרה נשביתי וטהורה אני נאמנת שהפה שאסר הוא הפה שהתיר [ח]ואם יש עדים שנשבית והיא אומרת טהורה אני אינה נאמנת [ט]ואם משנשאת באו עדים הרי זו לא תצא:

גמ' א"ר אסי מנין להפה שאסר הוא הפה שהתיר מן התורה שנאמר (א) את בתי נתתי לאיש הזה לאשה לאיש אסרה הזה התירה ל"ל קרא סברא היא הוא אסרה והוא שרי לה אלא כי איצטריך קרא לכדרב הונא אמר רב דא"ר הונא אמר רב (ג) מנין [י]לאב שנאמן לאסור את בתו מן התורה שנאמר את בתי נתתי לאיש הזה הזה למה לי מיבעי ליה לכדתני ר' יונה דתני ר' יונה את בתי נתתי לאיש הזה (ד) [כ]ולא ליבם ת"ר [ל]האשה שאמרה אשת איש אני וחזרה ואמרה פנויה אני נאמנת והא שוויה לנפשה חתיכה דאיסורא אמר רבא בר רב הונא כגון [מ]שנתנה אמתלא לדבריה תניא נמי הכי אמרה אשת איש אני וחזרה ואמרה פנויה אני אינה נאמנת ואם נתנה אמתלא לדבריה נאמנת ומעשה נמי באשה אחת גדולה שהיתה גדולה בנוי וקפצו עליה בני אדם לקדשה ואמרה להם מקודשת אני לימים עמדה וקידשה את עצמה אמרו לה חכמים מה ראית לעשות כן אמרה להם בתחלה שבאו עלי אנשים שאינם מהוגנים אמרתי מקודשת אני עכשיו שבאו עלי אנשים מהוגנים עמדתי וקדשתי את עצמי וזו הלכה העלה רב אחא שר הבירה לפני חכמי' באושא ואמרו אם נתנה אמתל' לדבריה נאמנת בעא מיניה שמואל מרב אמרה טמאה אני וחזרה ואמרה טהורה אני מהו אמר ליה [נ]אף בזו אם נתנה אמתלא

רש"י

תרי ותרי נינהו. כי אמרי לא גזל הוו להו תרי ותרי ולא מתכשר בהכי דקי"ל לקמן בפרקין (דף כו.) אין ערער פחות משנים: דפגם משפחה. שהעידו עליו שהוא עבד ועבד פסול לדין ולעדות ק"ו מאשה כדאמר בפ' החובל (ב"ק פח.): גלוי מילתא בעלמא הוא. משחתמו אמאי אין מעידין עליו מאי חשד נוגע בעדות איכא הכא דבר זה צריכין הן לברר ודבר העשוי לגלות הוא שיבדקו אחריו עד שיבורר הדבר ואין עדותן של אלו תלוי בהגדתן ואינן אלא מגלי דבר בעלמא: דעבד תשובה. והשיב את הגזלה: ואי לאו רבי אבא דמן עכו. שהזכירה לי לאחר זמן: שכחתה. שכחתיה: ומת אחד מהן. עד שלא חתמו: צריכין למיכתב כו'. דקיום השטר בשלשה והרואה שנים חתומין בו יאמר שבשנים קיימוהו: ואי כתב ביה שטרא דנן נפק קדמנא בי דינא תו לא צריך. דלא מקרי בי דינא בליר מתלתא: בי דינא דרבנא אשי. אורחא דמילתא נקט שהוא היה ראש ישיבה במתא מחסיא בימי רב נחמן בר יצחק דהוא מרא דשמעתא דודאי בי דינא דרב אשי לא עבדין בתרין: ואמר לנא רבנא אשי. לאזדקוקי ליה ולקיומי דכיון דרב אשי גופיה הזקיקן איהו ודאי לתלתא אמר ויש מפרשין ואמר לנא רבנא אשי תלתא נינהו ולא נהירא לי דאי רב אשי חד מנהון מאי ואמר לנא דכתבי ביה: מתני' נשביתי. לבין העובדי כוכבים: וטהורה אני. שלא נבעלתי לעובד כוכבים: נאמנת. ומותרת לכהן: ואם משניסת באו עדים. בגמרא מפרש אהייא קאי: גמ' נתתי לאיש אסרה. לכל העולם דלא ידעינן למאן וכי אמר הזה התירה לו: שנאמן לאסור את בתו. כשהיא קטנה או נערה שבידו לקדשה כדאמרי' בפ' נערה שנתפתתה מנין שאם אמר קדשתיה לפלוני שהוא נאמן לאוסרה על הכל: את בתי נתתי. אלמא בדידיה תליא נתינה והימניה קרא למימר הכי: הזה למה לי. כיון דלאו להפה שאסר מיבעי ליה: ולא ליבם. אם הוציא שם רע על יבמתו אחיו של מוציא שם רע נידון כמוציא שם רע ליענש במאה כסף והכי מוכח לקמן בפרק נערה:

תוספות

תרי ותרי נינהו. פירש בקונטרס וכי אמרי לא גזל הוו להו תרי ותרי ולא מתכשר בהכי וקשה דהכא אליבא דרב הונא קיימינן דאית ליה (שבועות דף מז:) דזו באה בפני עצמה ומעידה דאית לן למימר אוקי גברא אחזקתיה ועוד דלרב חסדא דאמר (שם) בהדי סהדי שקרי למה לי מודה הכא דהאי גברא ממילא מתכשר שהרי אם כת אחת מאלו מעידה על אדם אחד שהוא פסול לרב חסדא דחשיב להו סהדי שקרי לא היתה נאמנת אע"ג דאין אדם מכחישה וכ"ש היכא דאיכא סהדי דמכחשי דלא מהימני וע"ק לר"י דקאמר אי ערער דפגם משפחה גלוי מילתא בעלמא הוא ופי' הקונט' לדבר העשוי ליגלות הוא שיבדקו עד שיתברר הדבר וזהו תימה איך יתברר הדבר לעולם כיון שאלו ב' אומרים שהוא עבד אין כל העולם יכולים להכחישן דתרי כמאה על כן נראה כפר"ח דלא איירי בעדות דיינין אלא בעדות אחרים וה"פ אם עד שלא חתמו קרא ערער על אחד מהם מעידים שנים מן השוק עליו וחותם דהוי כאילו ישבו בית דין אחר שהכשירוהו ולא בטל וועד המושב וחותמין משחתמו השנים ולא הספיק השלישי לחתום עד שקרא עליו ערער בא ערער וביטל וועד המושב של אותו ב"ד אע"פ שאחרי כן העידו אחרים שהוא כשר כיון שביטל ההוא מושב בטל וצריך לחזור ולהושיב ב"ד על כן ערער דמאי אי ערער דגזלנותא תרי ותרי נינהו ולא מיפסיל דאוקי תרי בהדי תרי ואוקי גברא אחזקתיה וכיון דאיגלאי מלתא דמעולם לא היה פסול הרי לא היה בטל וועד המושב של אותו ב"ד אי ערער דפגם משפחה שאמרו עליו שהוא עבד ואלו מזימים אותם דאי אומרים שאינו עבד א"כ היה נפסל דליכא למימר אוקי גברא אחזקה דאם הוא עבד לא היה לו חזקת כשרות מעולם א) א"כ גלוי מילתא בעלמא הוא דכיון דאיגלאי מלתא דכשר היה מה איכפת לן בההוא ערעור ולא בטל וועד המושב לעולם ערער דגזלנותא ודקאמרי הנך סהדי ידעינן ביה דעבד תשובה וכיון דמודו לקמאי דגזלן הוה הוה ערער דידהו ערער ובטל וועד המושב דהואיל ואמת הוא שנפסל הוי בחזקת פסלות עד שנודע לנו כשרותו:

במותב תלתא כחדא הוינא וחד ליתוהי. פירוש צריך לכתוב וחד ליתוהי כיון דכתב בהדיא במותב תלתא הוינא ואין חותמין בו כי אם שנים אבל ודאי אם לא כתב וחד ליתוהי כשר תדע מדקאמר ואי כתב ביה בי דינא תו לא צריך ומיירי דלא כתב וחד ליתוהי מדפריך ודלמא ב"ד חצוף הוה:

ודלמא רבנן דבי רב אשי כשמואל סבירא להו. פי' כמו שסובר שמואל בעלמא כן סבירא להו בקיום שטרות אבל שמואל מלי סבר שפיר דבקיום שטרות בעי ג' דהא רב נחמן סבר לה כשמואל בפ"ק דסנהדרין (ה) (דף ג. ושם) דשנים שדנו דיניהם דין ורב נחמן גופיה סבר דקיום שטרות בשלשה בפ' חזקת הבתים (ב"ב מ.) גבי ג' ארצות לחזקה:

מנין להפה שאסר הוא הפה שהתיר מן התורה שנאמר את בתי נתתי לאיש וגו'. משמע דאין האב נאמן להתיר את בתו כשאסרה אלא מחמת מגו ותימה דאם בא אחד ואמר קדשתי את בתי ולאחר שעה או למחר אמר לפלוני קדשתיה לא יהא נאמן כיון דהשתא ליכא מגו ואומר ר"י דבענין זה שאינו סותר דבריו הראשונים ולא בא אלא לפרש דבריו הראשונים מהימן אע"ג דליכא מגו והכא דריש מאת בתי הפה שאסר הוא הפה שהתיר כגון דקאי האיש שקידש לו קמיה וקאמר את בתי נתתי לאיש ושתיק דמשמע ודאי שאינו מכיר שזה חתנו מדלא אמר את בתי נתתי לזה או לאיש הזה ביחד בלא הפסק מרובה הלכך לא יהא נאמן אחר כך אלא תוך כדי דבור דאיכא מגו ועוד אומר ר"י דאיכא למימר אפילו בכה"ג מהימן בלא מגו וקרא יתירא קדריש ואם אינו ענין כאן דאפילו לאחר זמן נאמן דסברא הוא שיהא נאמן לפרש למי נתנה אע"פ שלא פירש מתחלה שלא היה חושש לפרש תנהו ענין להיכא דאינו נאמן לאחר זמן שיהא נאמן בתוך כדי דבור במגו:

מנין לאב שנאמן לאסור וכו'. תימה מה צריך קרא תיפוק ליה דנאמן הואיל ובידו לקדשה כדאמר ביש נוחלין (ב"ב קלד:) בעל שאמר גרשתי את אשתי נאמן הואיל ובידו לגרשה וי"ל דהכא אין בידו כל כך דשמא לא ימצא אדם שיקדשנה (כדאיתא קדושין סד.) להכי איצטריך קרא ומיהו אם אמר על בתו בוגרת קדשתיה כשהיתה נערה או קטנה נראה דאינו נאמן דהשתא אין בידו כלל דאף על גב דלקמן בפ' נערה שנתפתתה (דף מו:) פריך ואימא הני...

א) סנהדרין ג. ה: ל: ב) [בכורות לו.], ג) קדושין סד. [ע"ש], ד) לקמן מו., ה) [ש: ועי' תוס' שם ג. ד"ה לרבות].

תוספות ישנים

א) [וה"ה דהוה מלי למימר בערער דפגם משפחה וכגון דקאמרי ידענו שנשתחרר. ת"י עה"ג].

גליון הש"ס

גמ' למה לי קרא סברא. ב"ק מו ע"ב נדה כה ע"א.

תורה אור השלם

א) וְאָמַר אֲבִי הַנַּעֲרָ אֶל הַזְּקֵנִים אֶת בִּתִּי נָתַתִּי לָאִישׁ הַזֶּה לְאִשָּׁה וַיִּשְׂנָאֶהָ: [דברים כב, טז]

ליקוטי רש"י

בי דינא. הכל יודעין שאין שנים קרוים ב"ד [סנהדרין ל.]. בית דין חצוף. שעברו על תקנת חכמים [שם ה.]. בי דינא דרבנא אשי. דאיהו ודאי ידעי שאין ב"ד קרוים בשנים. ואמר לנא רבנא אשי.

עין משפט נר מצוה

נד א מיי' פ"ו מהלכות עדות הלכה ז טוש"ע ח"מ סי' מו סעיף כז:
נה ב מיי' שם טוש"ע שם סעיף כו:
נו ג ד מיי' שם הלכה ו טוש"ע שם סעיף כט:
נז ה מיי' פי"ב מהלכות גירושין הלכה א סמג עשין מח טוש"ע אה"ע סימן קנב סעיף ו:
נח ו מיי' שם טוש"ע שם סעיף ז:
נט ז ח מיי' פי"ח מהל' איסורי ביאה הלכה יז סמג לאוין קכח טוש"ע אה"ע סימן ז סעיף ד:
ס ט מיי' שם הלכה כ טוש"ע שם סעיף ו:
סא י מיי' פ"ג מהלכות אישות הל' ג ופי"ח מהלכות איסורי ביאה הלכה כד סמג עשין מ טוש"ע אה"ע סימן לז סעיף כא:
סב כ מיי' פ"ג מהל' נערה בתולה הלכה ט סמג עשין כה:
סג ל מ מיי' פ"ט מהל' אישות הלכה לא סמג עשין מח טוש"ע אה"ע סימן מו סעיף ד:
סד נ מיי' פי"ד מהלכות איסורי ביאה הל' י סמג לאוין קיא טוש"ע י"ד סימן קפה סעיף ג:

תוספות רי"ד

The Gemara answers:

דִּכְתִיב בֵּיהּ וְאָמַר לָנָא רַבָּנָא אַשִׁי – Rav Nachman bar Yitzchak refers to a case **where there was** also **written in [the certification], "And Rav Ashi instructed us** to engage in this certification." Since Rav Ashi himself was involved, we need not be concerned that the certification was done by only two judges.[11]

Mishnah The following Mishnah presents another application of the principle "the very mouth that has forbidden is the mouth that has permitted":

הָאִשָּׁה שֶׁאָמְרָה אֵשֶׁת אִישׁ הָיִיתִי וּגְרוּשָׁה אָנִי – **If a woman said, "I was married but I am divorced,"**[12] נֶאֱמֶנֶת – **she is believed** and may remarry, שֶׁהַפֶּה שֶׁאָסַר הוּא הַפֶּה שֶׁהִתִּיר – **because the very mouth that has forbidden is the mouth that has permitted.**[13] וְאִם יֵשׁ עֵדִים שֶׁהָיְתָה אֵשֶׁת אִישׁ – **However, if there are witnesses** who testify **that she was married,** וְהִיא אוֹמֶרֶת גְּרוּשָׁה אָנִי – **and she says, "I am divorced,"** אֵינָהּ נֶאֱמֶנֶת – **she is not believed.**[14]

A parallel case:

אָמְרָה נִשְׁבֵּיתִי וּטְהוֹרָה אָנִי – **If [a woman] said, "I was captured but I am pure,"**[15] נֶאֱמֶנֶת – **she is believed** and may marry a Kohen, שֶׁהַפֶּה שֶׁאָסַר הוּא הַפֶּה שֶׁהִתִּיר – **because the very mouth that has forbidden is the mouth that has permitted.** וְאִם יֵשׁ עֵדִים שֶׁנִּשְׁבֵּית – **But if there are witnesses** who testify **that she was captured,** וְהִיא אוֹמֶרֶת טְהוֹרָה אָנִי – **and she says, "I am pure,"** אֵינָהּ נֶאֱמֶנֶת – **she is not believed.**[16] וְאִם מִשֶּׁנִּשֵּׂאת בָּאוּ עֵדִים – **However, if after she married,** the **witnesses came** forward and testified, הֲרֵי זוֹ לֹא תֵצֵא – **she does not** have to **leave** her husband.[17]

Gemara The Gemara offers a Biblical source for the principle presented in our Mishnah:

אָמַר רַב אַסִּי – **Rav Assi said:** מִנַּיִן לְהַפֶּה שֶׁאָסַר הוּא הַפֶּה שֶׁהִתִּיר מִן הַתּוֹרָה – **From where in the Torah** do we derive the principle **that "the very mouth that has forbidden is the mouth that has permitted"?** שֶׁנֶּאֱמַר ,,אֶת־בִּתִּי נָתַתִּי לָאִישׁ הַזֶּה לְאִשָּׁה'' – **For it is stated:** ***My daughter I have given to this man as a wife.***[18] ,,לָאִישׁ'' אֲסָרָהּ – As soon as the father says that he married his daughter ***to the man*** (i.e. before identifying the husband) **he forbids her** to all men. ,,הַזֶּה'' הִתִּירָהּ – But then, upon adding the word ***this*** (i.e. he identifies the husband), **he permits her** to him.[19]

The Gemara questions the need for this source:

לָמָּה לִי קְרָא – **Why do I need a verse?** סְבָרָא הִיא – **It is a logical argument!** הוּא אֲסָרָהּ וְהוּא שָׁרֵי לָהּ – **He prohibited her and** hence **he permits her.**[20] – ? –

NOTES

similar court — are above reproach? Perhaps the judges who made this certification acted without Rav Ashi's knowledge and erred!]

11. Rav Ashi himself [or a comparable sage] would certainly not err in so basic a matter (*Rashi's* preferred explanation, *Ritva*).

12. The speaker is a woman who is assumed to be single, either because the people in her town never heard anything about her getting married, or because she had moved there without a husband. She claims that she was married and is now divorced, but does not present a divorce document (*get*) as proof (*Meiri*).

13. Had this woman remained silent, we would have had no knowledge of her marriage. Thus, it is her word that establishes the fact that she was married. Since we accept her word that she was married, we should also believe her claim that she was divorced (see the Introduction to this chapter).

The plain meaning of the Mishnah is that she said, "I am divorced," immediately after saying, "I was married"; i.e. the time between the two statements was less than the time it takes to make an utterance [תּוֹךְ כְּדֵי דִבּוּר]. Some authorities maintain that otherwise she would not be believed to say that she is divorced (*R' Moshe HaKohen* and other commentators cited by *Maggid Mishneh* to *Hil. Gerushin* 12:1; *R' Yonah* cited by *Tur Even HaEzer* 152:6; see also *Rama* ibid.). This opinion, however, is disputed by *Meiri, Maggid Mishneh* and *Tur* (see *Bach* there for an explanation of the latter view; cf. *Chasam Sofer*). See also *Sefer HaShlamah* (cited by *Shitah Mekubetzes* to 23a ד"ה כתוב בהשלמה) and *Machaneh Efraim, Hil. Isurei Biah* 18:15. [See Chapter Introduction.]

14. Since her word is not needed to establish that she was married, the principle of *happeh she'assar* cannot be used to lend credence to her claim that she was divorced.

[Regarding the law where the witnesses testify *after* the court has already permitted the woman to marry by virtue of *happeh she'assar,* see end of the Mishnah and 23a note 27; see also *Tos. R' Akiva Eiger* and *Rashash*).]

15. If a woman cohabits with an idolater, she becomes forbidden to wed a Kohen (see *Yevamos* 68a-69a). Because of this, the Sages decreed that a Kohen may not marry a woman who was once abducted by idolaters, for there is a presumption that they violated her.

In our Mishnah's case, a woman declares that she was captured by idolaters, but adds that they did not defile her. The question is whether her word suffices for her to be permitted to marry a Kohen.

16. Since we have independent knowledge of her prohibited state, this is not a case of *happeh she'assar.*

17. The Gemara (23a) explains exactly what this means and to which part of the Mishnah it refers.

18. *Deuteronomy* 22:16. In this verse, a father declares that he had effected a marriage between his underage daughter and a certain man. [The verse appears in the passage of the מוֹצִיא שֵׁם רַע, *defamer* (see note 23).]

19. The father's words can be divided into two parts: The first part is אֶת־בִּתִּי נָתַתִּי לָאִישׁ, *My daughter I have given to the man,* in which the father testifies to her status as a married woman; the second part is הַזֶּה, *this [man],* where the father identifies the husband. [In the Hebrew, the adjective ("this") follows the noun ("man").] Had the father stopped after the first part, before identifying the husband, the daughter would have been forbidden to all men, because at that point she would have the status of a married woman whose husband is not known. When the father identifies the husband by adding the word הַזֶּה, *this,* he renders her permitted to him (*Rashi*).

Thus, the father began by establishing a prohibition that would not otherwise have existed, and then he testified that the prohibition is not applicable. By granting him the power to lift the prohibition, the Torah demonstrates the principle that one who created a prohibition has the authority to remove it.

[*Tosafos* note, however, that there is a significant difference between this case and a regular case of *happeh she'assar.* The first part of the father's statement is incomplete insofar as it states that there is a husband but fails to identify him. The second part thus merely clarifies what was left vague by the first part. To clarify one's original words should be possible even without recourse to the principle of *happeh she'assar* (see *Responsa of R' Akiva Eiger* §125 and *Gra* to *Choshen Mishpat* §82 *Kelalei Migo* 5:3). How, then, does this Scriptural source teach anything about the standard cases of *happeh she'assar,* where the two statements are independent? See *Tosafos* for two solutions of this problem. (See also *Beis Yosef, Even HaEzer* 152 ד"ה ומ"ש רבינו ונ"ל שא"צ לא זה ולא לזה and *Bach* ibid.)]

[See *Beis Yaakov,* who discusses why a Scriptural source is required for the principle of *happeh she'assar* when the rule of *migo* is already known.]

20. If the prohibition applies only on account of his words, his words should also suffice to lift the prohibition. [See *Beis Yaakov.*]

מסורת הש"ס

א) סנהדרין ג. ה: ל. מו: ב) [בכורות לו.] ג) קדושין סד. [ע"ש] ד) לקמן מו. ה) [ה: ועי' תוס' שם ד"ה לרבנן].

עין משפט נר מצוה

נד א מיי' פ"ו מהלכות עדות הלכה ז טוש"ע ח"מ סי' מו סעיף מ:
נה ב מיי' שם טוש"ע שם סעיף כו:
נו ג ד מיי' שם הלכה ו טוש"ע שם סעיף כט:
נז ה מיי' פי"ב מהלכות גירושין הלכה א סמג עשין מח טוש"ע אה"ע סימן קנב סעיף ו:
נח ו מיי' שם טוש"ע שם סעיף ז:
נט ז ח מיי' פי"ט מהל' איסורי ביאה הלכה כא סמג לאוין קיא טוש"ע אה"ע סימן ז סעיף ד:
ס ט מיי' שם הלכה כב טוש"ע שם סעיף ו:
סא י מיי' פ"ט מהלכות אישות הל' ג ופי"ח מהלכות איסורי ביאה הלכה כד סמג עשין מח טוש"ע אה"ע סימן לו סעיף כט:
סב כ מיי' פ"ג מהל' נערה בתולה הלכה ט סמג עשין כה:
סג ל מ מיי' פ"ט מהל' אישות הלכה לא סמג עשין מח טוש"ע אה"ע סימן מו סעיף ד:
סד נ מיי' פ"ד מהלכות איסורי ביאה הל' י סמג לאוין קיא טוש"ע יו"ד סימן קפה סעיף ג:

תרי ותרי נינהו אי ערער דפגם משפחה גלוי מילתא בעלמא הוא לעולם אימא לך ערער דגזלנותא וקאמרי הני ידעינן ביה דעבד תשובה א"ר זירא הא מילתא מרבי אבא שמיע לי ואי לאו רבי אבא דמן עכו שכחתה ג' שישבו לקיים את השטר ומת אחד מהם צריכין למיכתב במותב תלתא הוינא וחד ליתוהי אמר רב נחמן בר יצחק ואי כתב ביה שטרא דנן נפק לקדמנא בי דינא תו לא צריך ודלמא בית דין חצוף הוא וכדשמואל דאמר שמואל שנים שדנו דיניהם דין אלא שנקרא ב"ד חצוף דכתיב ביה בי דינא דרבנא אשי ודלמא רבנן דבי רב אשי כדשמואל סבירא להו דכתיב ביה ואמר לנא רבנא אשי:

מתני' האשה שאמרה אשת איש הייתי וגרושה אני נאמנת שהפה שאסר הוא הפה שהתיר ואם יש עדים שהיתה אשת איש והיא אומרת גרושה אני אינה נאמנת אמרה נשביתי וטהורה אני נאמנת שהפה שאסר הוא הפה שהתיר ואם יש עדים שנשבית והיא אומרת טהורה אני אינה נאמנת ואם משנשאת באו עדים הרי זו לא תצא:

גמ' א"ר אסי מנין להפה שאסר הוא הפה שהתיר מן התורה שנאמר את בתי נתתי לאיש הזה לאשה לאיש אסרה הזה התירה ל"ל קרא סברא היא הוא אסרה והוא שרי לה אלא כי איצטריך קרא לכדרב הונא אמר רב דא"ר הונא אמר רב מנין לאב שנאמן לאסור את בתו מן התורה שנאמר את בתי נתתי לאיש הזה הזה למה לי מיבעי ליה לכדתני ר' יונה דתני ר' יונה את בתי נתתי לאיש הזה ולא ליבם ת"ר האשה שאמרה אשת איש אני וחזרה ואמרה פנויה אני נאמנת והא שוויה לנפשה חתיכה דאיסורא אמר רבא בר רב הונא כגון שנתנה אמתלא לדבריה תניא נמי הכי אמרה אשת איש אני וחזרה ואמרה פנויה אני אינה נאמנת ואם נתנה אמתלא לדבריה נאמנת ומעשה נמי באשה אחת גדולה שהיתה גדולה בנוי וקפצו עליה בני אדם לקדשה ואמרה להם מקודשת אני לימים עמדה וקידשה את עצמה אמרו לה חכמים מה ראית לעשות כן אמרה להם בתחלה שבאו עלי אנשים שאינם מהוגנים אמרתי מקודשת אני עכשיו שבאו עלי אנשים מהוגנים עמדתי וקדשתי את עצמי וזו הלכה העלה רב אחא שר הבירה לפני חכמי' באושא ואמרו אם נתנה אמתל' לדבריה נאמנת בעא מיניה שמואל מרב אמרה טמאה אני וחזרה ואמרה טהורה אני מהו אמר ליה אף בזו אם נתנה אמתלא

רש"י

תרי ותרי נינהו. כי אמרי לא גזל הוו להו תרי ותרי ולא מתכשר בהכי דקי"ל לקמן בפרקין (דף כו.) אין ערער פחות משנים: דפגם משפחה. שהעידו עליו שהוא עבד ועבד פסול לדין ולעדות ק"ו מאשה כדאמר בפ' החובל (ב"ק פח.): גלוי מילתא בעלמא הוא. משחתמו אמאי אין מעידין עליו מאי חשד נוגע בעדות איכא הכא דבר זה צריכין הן לברר ודבר העשוי לגלות הוא שידקו אחריו עד שיתברר הדבר ואין עדותן של אלו תלוי בהגדתן ואינן אלא מגלי דבר בעלמא: דעבד תשובה. והשיב את הגזלה: ואי לאו רבי אבא דמן עכו. שהזכירה לי לאחר זמן: שכחתה. שכחתיה: ומת אחד מהן. עד שלא חתמו: צריכין למיכתב כו'. דקיום השטר בשלשה והרואה שנים חתומין בו יאמר שבשנים קיימוהו: ואי כתב ביה שטרא דנן נפק קדמנא בי דינא תו לא צריך. דלא מקרי בי דינא בציר מתלתא: בי דינא דרבנא אשי. אורחא למילתא נקט שהוא היה ראש ישיבה במתא מחסיא בימי רב נחמן בר יצחק הוא מרא דשמעתא דודאי בי דינא דרב אשי לא עבדין בתרין: ואמר לנא רבנא אשי. לאחזוקי ליה ולקיומי דכיון דרב אשי גופיה הזקיקן איהו ודאי לתלתא אמר ויש מפרשים ואמר לנא רבנא אשי לא סגי דלאו רבנא אשי ולא נהירא לי דאי רב אשי חד מינהון מאי ואמר לנא דכתבי ביה: מתני' נשביתי. לבין העובדי כוכבים: וטהורה אני. שלא נבעלתי לעובד כוכבים: נאמנת. ומותרת לכהן: ואם משנשאת באו עדים. בגמרא מפרש אהייא קאי: גמ' נתתי לאיש אסרה. לכל העולם דלא ידעינן למאן וכי אמר הזה התירה לו: שנאמן לאסור את בתו. כשהיא קטנה או נערה שבידו לקדשה כדאמרי' בפ' נערה שנתפתתה מנין שאם אמר קדשתיה לפלוני שהוא נאמן לאוסרה על הכל: את בתי נתתי. אלמא בדידיה תליא נתינה והימנה קרא למימר הכי: הזה למה לי. כיון דלאו להפה שאסר מיבעי ליה: ולא ליבם. אם הוציא שם רע על נישואי אחיו אין היבם נידון כמוציא שם רע ליענש במאה כסף והכי מוכח לקמן בפרק נערה: אמתלא

תוספות

תרי ותרי נינהו. פירש בקונטרס וכי אמרי לא גזל הוו להו תרי ותרי ולא מתכשר בהכי וקשה דהכא אליבא דרב הונא קיימינן דאית ליה (שבועות דף מז:) דזו באה בפני עצמה ומעידה דאית לן למימר אוקי גברא אחזקתיה ועוד דלרב חסדא דאמר (שם) בהדי סהדי שקרי למה לי מודה הכא דהאי גברא כשר ומילתא מתכשר שהרי אם כת אחת מאלו מעידה על אדם אחד שהוא פסול לרב חסדא דמחשיב להו סהדי שקרי לא היתה נאמנת אע"ג דלאין אדם מכחישם וכ"ש היכא דליכא סהדי דמכחשי דלא מהימני וע"ק לר"י דקאמר אי ערער דפגם משפחה גלוי מילתא בעלמא הוא ופי' הקונט' לדבר העשוי ליגלות הוא שידקו עד שיתברר הדבר וזהו תימה אין יתברר הדבר לעולם כיון שאלו ב' אומרים שהוא עבד ואין כל העולם יכולים להכחישן דתרי כמאה על כן נראה כפר"ח דלא איירי בעדות דיינין אלא בעדות אחרים וה"פ אם עד שלא חתמו קרא ערער על אחד מהם מעידים שנים מן השוק עליו ומותם דהוי כאילו ישבו בית דין אחר שהכשירוהו ולא בטל וועד המושב ומותמין משחתמו השנים ולא הספיק השלישי לחתום עד שקרא עליו ערער לא ערער וביטל וועד המושב אותו ב"ד אע"פ שאחרי כן העידו אחרים שהוא כשר כיון שביטל ההוא מושב בטל וצריך לחזור ולהושיב ב"ד על כן ערער דמאי אי ערער דגזלנותא תרי ותרי נינהו ולא מיפסיל דאוקי בהדי תרי ואוקי גברא אחזקתיה וכיון דאיגלאי מלתא דמעולם לא היה פסול הרי לא היה בטל וועד המושב של אותו ב"ד אי ערער דפגם משפחה שאמרו עליו שהוא עבד ואלו מזימים אותם דלאו אומרים שאינו עבד אע"כ היה נפסל דליכא למימר אוקי גברא אחזקה דאם הוא עבד לא היה לו חזקת כשרות מעולם א) א"כ גלוי מילתא בעלמא הוא דכיון דאיגלאי מלתא דכשר היה מה איכפת לן בההוא ערעור ולא בטל וועד המושב לעולם ערער דגזלנותא ודקאמרי הנך סהדי ידעינן ביה דעבד תשובה וכיון דמודו לקמאי דגזלן הוה ערער וביטל וועד המושב דהואיל ואמת הוא שנפסל הוי בחזקת פסלות עד שנודע לנו כשרותו:

במותב תלתא כחדא הוינא וחד ליתוהי. פירוש צריך לכתוב וחד ליתוהי כיון דכתב בהדיא במותב תלתא הוינא ואין חותמין בו כי אם שנים אבל ודאי אם לא כתב וחד ליתוהי כשר תדע מדקאמר ואי כתב ביה בי דינא תו לא צריך ומיירי דלא כתב וחד ליתוהי מדפריך ודלמא ב"ד חצוף הוה: ודלמא רבנן דבי רב אשי כשמואל סבירא להו. פי' כמו שסובר שמואל בעלמא כן סבירא להו בקיום שטרות אבל שמואל מצי סבר שפיר דבקיום שטרות בעי ג' דהא רב נחמן סבר לה כשמואל בפ"ק דסנהדרין ה) (דף ג. ושם) דשנים שדנו דיניהם דין ורב נחמן גופיה סבר דקיום שטרות בשלשה בפ' חזקת הבתים (ב"ב מ.) גבי ג' ארצות לחזקה:

מנין להפה שאסר הוא הפה שהתיר מן התורה שנאמר את בתי נתתי לאיש וגו'. משמע דאין האב נאמן להתיר את בתו כשאסרה אלא מחמת מגו ותימה דאם בא אחד ואמר קדשתי את בתי ולאחר שעה או למחר אמר לפלוני קדשתיה לא יהא נאמן כיון דהשתא ליכא מגו ואומר ר"י דבענין זה שאינו סותר דבריו הראשונים מהימן אע"ג דליכא מגו והכא דריש מאת בתי הפה שאסר הוא הפה שהתיר כגון דקאי האיש שקידש לו קמיה וקאמר את בתי נתתי לאיש ושתיק דמשמע ודאי שאינו מכיר שזה חתנו מדלא אמר את בתי נתתי לזה או לאיש הזה ביחד בלא הפסק מרווח הלכך לא יהא נאמן אחר כך אלא תוך כדי דבור דאיכא מגו ועוד אומר ר"י דאיכא למימר אפילו בכה"ג מהימן בלא מגו וקרא יתירא קדריש ואם אינו ענין כאן דאפילו לאחר זמן נאמן דסברא הוא שיהא נאמן לפרש למי נתנה אע"פ שלא פירש מתחלה שלא היה חושש לפרש תנהו ענין להיכא דאינו נאמן לאחר זמן שיהא נאמן בתוך כדי דבור במגו:

מנין לאב שנאמן לאסור וכו'. תימה מה צריך קרא תיפוק ליה דנאמן הואיל ובידו לקדשה כדאמר ביש נוחלין (ב"ב קלד:) בעל שאמר גרשתי את אשתי נאמן הואיל ובידו לגרשה וי"ל דהכא אין בידו כל כך דשמא לא ימצא אדם שיקדשנה (כדאיתא קדושין סד.) להכי איצטריך קרא ומיהו אם אמר על בתו בוגרת קדשתיה כשהיתה נערה או קטנה נראה דאינו נאמן דהשתא אין בידו כלל דאף על גב דלקמן בפ' נערה שנתפתתה (דף מו:) פריך ואימא הנ"מ קטנה אבל נערה איהי תיקדש נפשה לפי זה היה צ"ל דנאמן לאסור אפילו בשעה שאין בידו לקדשה דקרא בנערה כתיב ובעי למימר דאין בידו לקדשה ולא בתי נתתי בתו שכיחה קטנה וגזרת הכתוב הוא דנאמן אע"פ שאין בידו אבל לא במקדשה לא נאמר כן:

תוספות ישנים

א) [וע"ש דהוה מצי למימר בערער דפגם משפחה וכגון דקאמרי ידענו שנתכשר. תו"י עה"ג].

גליון הש"ס

גמ' למה לי קרא סברא. ב"ק מו ע"ב נדה כה ע"א.

תורה אור השלם

א) וְאָמַר אֲבִי הַנַּעֲרָ אֶל הַזְּקֵנִים אֶת בִּתִּי נָתַתִּי לָאִישׁ הַזֶּה לְאִשָּׁה וַיִּשְׂנָאֶהָ: [דברים כב, טז]

ליקוטי רש"י

בי דינא. הכול יודעין שאין שנים קרוים ב"ד [סנהדרין ל.]. בית דין חצוף. שעברו על תקנת חכמים [שם ג.]. בי דינא דרבנא אשי. לאותו ולאו ידעי שאין ב"ד קרויין בשנים. ואמר לנא רבנא אשי. לכתוב כך דכיון דהוא היה שם מסתמא לא גזה לפחות משלשה. אשת איש הייתי. ולא היינו מוחזקין בה שהיא אשת איש מעולם. נאמנת. ומותרת להנשא. שהפה שאסר וכו'. לאו בעיא לא אמרה, כלומר אי הוה מסיחה להינשא בחזקת פנויה היתה. ולא הייתי [הוה] מחזקין [בכורות לו.]. לאיש אסרה. על כל שאין אנו יודעים למי וכי אמר הזה התירה לו [קדושין סד.]. ולא ליבם. אם יוציא שם רע על נישואי אחיו בכלל פרשה זו לטעון טענת בתולים [לקמן מו.].

תוספות רי"ד

תרי ותרי נינהו פי' ועד שלא חתמו אמאי מעידין והא אין ערער פחות מב' שאין משגיחים בדברי היחיד וכיון שב' אומרים גזלן הוא ואלו אומרים שלא גזל הו"ל תרי ותרי וכל תו"ת הו"ל ספיקא דאורייתא ובספיקא דאורייתא לא אמרינן אוקי גברא אחזקתיה כדאמרינן לקמן בפירקין וכיון דהאידנא איתוקם בספק גזלן היכי מחתמינן ליה ומפקינן ממונא אפומיה הלכך אע"פ שלא חתמו לא יכלו להכשירו ואי ערעור דפגם משפחה גלוי מילתא בעלמא הוא ואפי' משחתמו מעידים פי' ערעור דפגם משפחה שאלו השנים שבאו לפוסלו לא העידו עדות ברורה אלא העידו שבמשפחתו נטמע שם עבד שהוא פסול לעדות וכל המשפחה הן בחזקת שהוא ספק פסול שמא מזרע אותו עבד נולד ואלה מעידים שזה אינו מן המסופקין דברי לן שמייחוס כשרות הוא בא ואינן מכחישים את העדים אלא מוציאים את זה מספק פסול שלא יהיה מסופק כשאר כל בני המשפחה וזהו גילוי מילתא שיכול להתברר ע"פ אחרים שנבדוק אחריו ויתברר אם נולד מן הכשרים או מן הפסולין ובמילתא דעביד לגלויי לא משקרי אינשי והלכך אע"פ שחתמו והן נוגעים בעדות נאמנים דבאיזה עדות אינן נאמנין בדבר שלא נוכל להתברר על ידי אחרים כ"א על פיהם כדלקמן שמעידין שעשה תשובה שאין מכירין תשובתו אלא הם אבל ייחוס האדם דהוא מילתא דעביד לגלויי אע"פ שהן נוגעים בעדותן נאמנים הם. לעולם ערער דגזלנותא ודקאמרי הני ידעי' ביה דעשה תשובה שהחזיר את הגזילה ואין כאן משום הכחשה הלכך עד שלא חתמו מעידין עליו וחותם ומשחתמו שהן נוגעים בעדות אין מעידין עליו

חזרה

תְּרֵי וּתְרֵי נִינְהוּ – **These are** merely **two** witnesses in his favor pitted **against** the **two** witnesses accusing him of thievery. Their testimony is not sufficient to eradicate the protest![1] אִי עַרְעָר דִּפְגַם מִשְׁפָּחָה – And **if** it is **a challenge involving** an accusation of **tainted lineage,**[2] then even if the first two judges have already signed, why can they not testify in his favor? גִּלּוּי מִלְתָא בְּעָלְמָא הוּא – **[Their testimony] is a mere clarification of the matter.**[3] – ? –

The Gemara answers:

לְעוֹלָם אֵימָא לָךְ עַרְעָר דְּגַזְלָנוּתָא – **Actually, I can tell you** that Rav is dealing with **a challenge involving** an accusation of **thievery,** וְקָאָמְרִי הָנֵי יַדְעִינַן בֵּיהּ דְּעָבַד תְּשׁוּבָה – **but** he refers specifically to a case **where these** two judges **say,** "Although our colleague did commit theft, **we know that he repented** afterwards."[4] Since they do not contradict the testimony of the first two witnesses, but declare their colleague fit because of repentance, their testimony is believed. Rav teaches, however, that it is acceptable only if they offer it before signing the certification, for once they have signed, they are considered biased.[5]

The Gemara turns to a related law:

אָמַר רַבִּי זֵירָא – **R' Zeira said:** הָא מִלְתָא מֵרַבִּי אַבָּא שְׁמִיעַ לִי – **This** following **matter, I** originally **learned from R' Abba,** וְאִי לָאו רַבִּי אַבָּא דְמִן עַכּוֹ שְׁכַחְתָּהּ – **and if not for R' Abba of Acco,** who reminded me of it at a later time, **I would have forgotten it:** שְׁלֹשָׁה שֶׁיָּשְׁבוּ לְקַיֵּים אֶת הַשְּׁטָר – **If three** judges **sat down to certify a document** וּמֵת אֶחָד מֵהֶם – **and one of them died** before they signed, צְרִיכִין לְמִיכְתַּב – **they must write** the certification as follows: בְּמוֹתַב תְּלָתָא הֲוֵינָא וְחַד לֵיתוֹהִי – **"We were seated as three, and one** of us **is no longer** alive."[6]

An alternative option is presented:

אָמַר רַב נַחְמָן בַּר יִצְחָק – **Rav Nachman bar Yitzchak said:** וְאִי כָּתַב בֵּיהּ – **But if there was written in [the certification],** שְׁטָרָא דְּנַן נְפַק לְקֳדָמָנָא בֵּי דִינָא – **"This document emerged before us, the** ***court*** **. . .,"** תּוּ לֹא צָרִיךְ – **further** elaboration **is not needed,** because everyone realizes that a "court" consists of at least three judges and one of them must have died before signing the certification.

The Gemara objects to Rav Nachman bar Yitzchak's option:

וְדִלְמָא בֵּית דִּין חָצוּף הוּא – **But perhaps it was an insolent court** comprised of only two judges, וּכִדְשְׁמוּאֵל – **in accordance with** a dictum **of Shmuel!** דְּאָמַר שְׁמוּאֵל – **For Shmuel said:** שְׁנַיִם שֶׁדָּנוּ דִּינֵיהֶם דִּין – **If two** judges **adjudicated** a case, **their adjudication is valid,** אֶלָּא שֶׁנִּקְרָא בֵּית דִּין חָצוּף – **but they are considered an insolent court.**[7] Since according to Shmuel a panel of two judges can be considered a "court," if Rav Nachman bar Yitzchak's version is used, how will it prove that there were originally three judges?[8]

The Gemara answers:

דִּכְתִיב בֵּיהּ בֵּי דִינָא דְּרַבָּנָא אַשִׁי – Rav Nachman bar Yitzchak refers to a case **where there was** also **written in [the certification], "The court of Rav Ashi."**[9]

The Gemara asks:

וְדִלְמָא רַבָּנַן דְּבֵי רַב אַשִׁי כִּדְשְׁמוּאֵל סְבִירָא לְהוּ – **But perhaps the Rabbis of Rav Ashi's academy hold like Shmuel,** that a panel of two judges can be called a "court."[10] – ? –

NOTES

1. Since two witnesses claim the judge is a thief, while two others refute the accusation and declare him qualified, [his status remains in doubt and] he cannot sit on a court (*Rashi*). Clearly, then, Rav did not refer to a case in which the challenge against the judge involved an accusation such as thievery.

Tosafos object to *Rashi's* explanation, arguing that since it is impossible to determine whether the person stooped to thievery and was disqualified, we should apply the principle of *chazakah* and regard him as remaining in his original state of fitness to be a judge! *Tosafos* therefore cite a completely different explanation of the Gemara, in the name of *Rabbeinu Chananel*. However, *Rif* agrees with *Rashi* and explains that although the judge has a *chazakah* of fitness he cannot issue a judicial ruling that would extract money from a litigant, because the litigant has a *chazakah* of ownership of that money! The litigant's *chazakah* of ownership outweighs the judge's *chazakah* of fitness, for several reasons. Firstly, the possession of property is a superior form of *chazakah*. Secondly, even if the *chazakos* would be equal, it would behoove us to leave matters as is and refrain from extracting the litigant's money under questionable terms (*Rif,* as elucidated by *Ramban* in *Chidushim* and *Milchamos Hashem*).

Ramban states further that whenever we are left in doubt by a contradiction between two sets of witnesses, we cannot resolve the doubt on the basis of *chazakah*. For the testimony of a pair of witnesses is considered the ultimate verification of facts, and when two pairs are in contradiction all options for verification have been exhausted – the *chazakah* cannot outweigh the testimony of either set of witnesses. For further discussion, see *Milchamos Hashem, Ran* and *Rosh; Beur HaGra, Choshen Mishpat* 34:60; and especially *Teshuvos R' Akiva Eiger,* vol. I §136. [See further, 22b note 7.]

2. I.e. two witnesses appeared and testified that the judge is a Canaanite slave, and therefore unfit to render judgment or give testimony, as derived in *Bava Kamma* 88a (*Rashi;* see *Chasam Sofer*).

3. Since it is possible to investigate the matter and determine unequivocally whether the person is a slave, the favorable testimony of the two judges cannot be discarded because of bias. For in any event, we do not rely upon their word alone against the word of the protesting witnesses; rather, their testimony spurs us to investigate until we clarify the matter beyond any doubt. If we ultimately determine that the person is not a slave, we obviously declare him fit to be a judge. [The testimony of the protesting witnesses cannot stand up against facts that are known to all] (*Rashi,* as explained by *Shach, Choshen Mishpat* 46:66 and *Pnei Yehoshua;* see also *Ramban;* cf. *Tosafos*). Thus, Rav could not have referred to a case in which the protest involved an accusation of tainted lineage.

4. And he returned the stolen property (*Rashi;* see *Choshen Mishpat* 34:29 for elaboration of what additional penitence is required).

5. *Rashi, Ritva;* see *Tosafos* ד״ה תרי ותרי for a completely different interpretation of the entire passage.

6. [Even though all three judges concluded that the document was valid,] their decision will not be enforceable on the basis of the two survivors' signatures unless they insert this clause. Without it, one who sees only two signatures on the certification will mistakenly conclude that the note was [illegally] certified by a panel of two judges (*Rashi;* see *Tosafos* ד״ה במותב).

7. Shmuel maintains that under Biblical law monetary matters may be adjudicated by a single judge or a panel of two, but the Rabbis decreed that adjudication be done by no less than three judges. A ruling by one or two judges is valid after the fact, but even a court of two is considered insolent for having disregarded the Sages' enactment (see *Rashi* to *Sanhedrin* 3a ד״ה בית דין חצוף; for further discussion of Shmuel's opinion, see *Sanhedrin* 5b). The halachah does not follow Shmuel; rather, generally speaking, a decision rendered by less than three judges is void (see *Sanhedrin* 2b and *Choshen Mishpat* 3:2).

8. One who sees it might think that only two people certified the note but they called themselves a "court" because they hold like Shmuel. And since the halachah does not follow Shmuel, their certification will be considered void (*Ritva;* cf. *Tosafos* ד״ה ודלמא).

9. Rav Ashi's court was the most prominent one in existence in the times of Rav Nachman bar Yitzchak, for Rav Ashi headed the yeshivah in the town of Mechasya [which was that generation's leading Torah institution]. The Gemara therefore uses "Rav Ashi's court" as an example of one that is above reproach with respect to [blatant] errors. If the note includes the clause, "This document came before us, the *court* of Rav Ashi," then even if it contains only two signatures we may rest assured that the certification was performed by a panel of three and one of them died (*Rashi*).

10. [Although Rav Ashi was the greatest sage of his generation, who is to say that all the members of the court under his jurisdiction – or a

do I need to go **so far** as to add members to the court? לֵיתְבוּ בְּדוּכְתַּיְיהוּ וְלִיקַדְּשֵׁי – Let two of the judges testify before the third one and then **let them sit down in their places and sanctify** the month along with him.[20] – ? –

R' Abba responds:

אָמַר לֵיהּ – **He said to [Rav Safra]:** אַף לְדִידִי קַשְׁיָא לִי – **I also had this difficulty,** וּשְׁאִילְתֵּיהּ לְרַב יִצְחָק בַּר שְׁמוּאֵל בַּר מָרְתָא – **and I asked it of Rav Yitzchak bar Shmuel bar Marta,** וְרַב יִצְחָק לְרַב הוּנָא וְרַב הוּנָא לְחִיָּיא בַּר רַב – **and Rav Yitzchak** asked it **of Rav Huna, and Rav Huna of Chiya bar Rav,** וְחִיָּיא בַּר רַב לְרַב – **and Chiya bar Rav** asked it **of Rav,** וְאָמַר לְהוּ – **and [Rav] told them:** הַנַּח לְעֵדוּת הַחֹדֶשׁ דְּאוֹרַיְיתָא – **Leave aside** the matter of **testimony regarding the** new **month,** which is a **Biblical** requirement, וְקִיּוּם שְׁטָרוֹת דְּרַבָּנָן – **whereas the certification of documents is** merely a **Rabbinic** requirement.[21]

The Gemara turns to another ruling regarding the court that performs certification:

אָמַר רַבִּי אַבָּא אָמַר רַב הוּנָא אָמַר רַב – **R' Abba said in the name of Rav Huna** who said **in the name of Rav:** שְׁלֹשָׁה שֶׁיָּשְׁבוּ לְקַיֵּים אֶת הַשְּׁטָר – **If three** judges **sat down to certify a document** וְקָרָא עַרְעָר עַל אֶחָד מֵהֶן – **and someone raised a challenge about** the fitness of **one of them** to serve as a judge, the law is as follows: עַד שֶׁלֹּא חָתְמוּ – **Before [the other two judges] have signed** the certification, מְעִידִין עָלָיו וְחוֹתֵם – **they may testify** before another court **about** the fitness of **[the third judge] and he may** then **sign** the certification along with them. מִשֶּׁחָתְמוּ – But **once they have signed,** אֵין מְעִידִין עָלָיו וְחוֹתֵם – **they may not testify about** the fitness of **[the third judge]** and have **him sign** with them.[22]

The Gemara analyzes this ruling:

אִי עַרְעָר דְּמַאי – **What** type **of challenge** does this refer to? אִי עַרְעָר דְּגַזְלָנוּתָא – **If** it is **a challenge involving** an accusation of **thievery** against the judge by two witnesses,[23] then even if the two other judges have not yet signed, how can their testimony render him fit?

NOTES

20. *Rashi.* When these two are testifying, they simultaneously serve as judges, so that there is a court of three judges accepting their testimony as they relate it (*Chasam Sofer,* 5573 ed.; see also *Ritva* cited in note 4; cf. *Ran, Rashash*). [See *Ritva* for an alternative explanation of the Gemara's question.]

21. Under Biblical law, when a document signed by witnesses is presented, it is automatically considered as though their testimony has been examined by the court, because people generally lack the audacity to forge the signatures of witnesses. The Rabbis imposed the requirement that a document be authenticated (*Rashi* below, 28a ד״ה קיום שטרות דרבנן and *Gittin* 3a ד״ה נעשה; see *Tosafos* to 28a ד״ה קיום; cf. *Rambam, Hil. Eidus* 3:4, 6:1, and *Shitah Mekubetzes*). Since the certification is merely required Rabbinically, the Rabbis were lenient and allowed a witness who authenticates the signatures to also serve as a judge. But in cases where the action of a court is required Biblically, a testifying witness cannot also serve as a judge (see *Tosafos* ד״ה הנח, who cite several possible reasons; these are analyzed by *Ketzos HaChoshen* 7:4). [See *Shach, Choshen Mishpat* 46:9, who discusses a case in which certification might be required even on the Biblical level.]

Even in Biblical cases, only a witness who actually testifies is precluded from becoming a judge in the case. A person who witnessed the incident in question is allowed to be a judge if his testimony is not required. This occurs in the cited case of sanctification of the month, where only the two who testify are disqualified from being judges, whereas the third one — who also saw the new moon but is not needed to testify — does serve as a judge. However, in capital cases, a person who witnessed the crime may not be a judge, because the Torah dictates that judges in capital cases give strong consideration to the possibility of innocence, and one who witnessed the crime will be unable to do so (*Tosafos;* see *Rosh Hashanah* 25b-26a; cf. *Ramban*).

22. Once they signed [and acted in the capacity of a court], their testimony that their colleague is fit is considered biased, since it would be embarrassing for them to have sat in judgment with an unqualified person (*Rashi;* see *Kovetz Shiurim* §57; cf. *Rif, Tosafos* to 22a ד״ה תרי ותרי).

23. [I.e. two witnesses appear before us and claim that one of the judges is a thief and therefore disqualified from sitting on a court.] Whatever the details of the challenge are, it must have been lodged by two witnesses. We will learn below (26a) that a challenge registered by less than two witnesses is disregarded, since the accused enjoys a *chazakah* (presumption) of validity [חֶזְקַת כַּשְׁרוּת], since he was originally deemed qualified to judge (*Rashi,* top of 22a).

איקלע רבנאי אחוה דר' חייא בר אבא למזבן שומשמי ואמר הכי אמר שמואל עד ודיין מצטרפין אמר אמימר כמה מעליא הא שמעתא אמר ליה רב אשי לאמימר משום דקלסה אבוה דאמך את נמי מקלסת לה כבר פרכה רבא: אמר רב ספרא אמר רבי אבא אמר רב יצחק בר שמואל בר מרתא אמר רב הונא ואמרי ליה אמר רב הונא אמר רב [א] שלשה שישבו לקיים את השטר שנים מכירין חתימות ידי עדים ואחד אינו מכיר עד שלא חתמו מעידין בפניו וחותם משחתמו אין מעידין בפניו וחותם ומי כתבינן והאמר רב פפי משמיה דרבא [ה] האי אשרתא דדייני דניכתב מקמיה דניחוו סהדי אחתימת ידייהו פסולה דמתחזי כשקרא הכא נמי מתחזי כשקרא אלא אימא עד שלא כתבו מעידין בפניו וחותם משכתבו אין מעידין בפניו וחותם ש"מ תלת ש"מ [ג] עד נעשה דיין וש"מ [ב] דיינין המכירין חתימות ידי עדים אינן צריכין להעיד בפניהם וש"מ דיינין שאין מכירין חתימות ידי עדים צריכין להעיד בפני כל אחד ואחד מתקיף לה רב אשי בשלמא עד נעשה דיין שמעינן מינה אלא דיינין המכירין חתימות ידי עדים אין צריכין להעיד בפניהם דלמא לעולם אימא לך צריכין ושאני הכא דקא מקיימא הגדה בחד ודיינין שאין מכירין חתימות ידי עדים צריכין להעיד בפני כל אחד ואחד דלמא לעולם אימא לך אין צריכין ושאני הכא דלא קא מקיימא הגדה כלל יתיב ר' אבא וקאמר לה להא שמעתא דעד נעשה דיין איתיביה רב ספרא לרבי אבא [ג] ראוהו שלשה והן בית דין יעמדו שנים ויושיבו מחבריהם אצל היחיד ויעידו בפניהם ויאמרו מקודש החדש מקודש שאין היחיד נאמן על ידי עצמו ואי סלקא דעתך דעד נעשה דיין למה לי כולי האי ליתבו בדוכתייהו וליקדשי אמר ליה אף לדידי קשיא לי ושאילתיה לרב יצחק בר שמואל בר מרתא ורב יצחק לרב הונא ורב הונא לחייא בר רב וחייא בר רב לרב ואמר להו [ד] הנח [ד] לעדות החדש דאוריית' [ה] וקיום שטרות דרבנן אמר רבי אבא אמר רב הונא אמר רב [ו] שלשה שישבו לקיים את השטר וקרא ערער על אחד מהן עד שלא חתמו מעידין עליו וחותם משחתמו אין מעידין עליו וחותם ערער דמאי אי ערער דגזלנותא תרי

רש"י

איקלע רבנאי למיזבן שומשמי גרסי' ולא גרסי' דאיקלע ולא גרסינן לגבן ולאו רמי אמרה דא"א לומר כן שאמר רמי עדות זו על אמימר ורב אשי שהרי רב אשי כמה דורות היה אחריו דאמרינן בקדושין (דף עב:) יום שמת רב יהודה נולד רבא יום שמת רבא נולד רב אשי: אבוה דאמך. רמי בר חמא: שלשה שישבו. בב"ד: לקיים השטר. ובלא העדאת עדים שיעידו על כתב ידן לפי שהדיינין עצמן מכירין אותה השנים מכירין אותה ואחד אינו מכיר: עד שלא חתמו. השנים על ההנפק: מעידין. לפני השלישי שזהו כתב ידן של חתומים: וחותם. עמהם על מה שכותבין אשרנוהי וקיימנוהי לשטרא דנן במותב תלתא דאשתמודענא דחתימת ידא דסהדי היא: משחתמו אין מעידין. דחתימה קמייתא בשקרא הוה דלאו תלתא הוו דידעי: ומי כתבינן. לאשרתא דידיה בתמיה וכי קודם שנתקיים לפני שלשתן יכתבו במותב תלתא הוינא ואשתמודענא כו': אשרתא. לשון חוזק שמחזקים [את השטר] וכותבין אשרנוהי: דנתכתבא מקמי דניחוו סהדי כו'. עד שלא העידו העדים על כתב ידם כתבו הדיינין במותב תלתא הוינא ונפיק שטרא דנן קדמנא ואסהידו פלוני ופלוני אחתימת ידייהו ואשרנוהי וקיימנוהי: עד נעשה דיין. שהרי השנים העידו על החתימות: צריכין להעיד בפני כל אחד ואחד. שאם העידו בפני השנים אין הג' יכול לחתום דהא הכא הוצרכו השנים להעיד בפני הג': דלמא לעולם צריכין. להעיד שאין עדות אלא ע"י הגדת עדות: ושאני הכא דקא מקיימא הגדה. בפני היחיד שאינו מכיר: דלא מקיימא הגדה כלל. אי לא הוו מסהדי באפיה: ראוהו ג'. בעדות החדש קאי: והן בית דין. מסנהדרין המקדשין את החדש: יעמדו השנים. להיות עדים והתם פרכינן לא תהא שמיעה גדולה מראיה ומוקמינן לה כשראוהו בלילה לפיכך אם לא יעידו לבקר על מה יאמרו מקודש: שאין היחיד נאמן. לקדש החדש ביחידי: ליתבו בדוכתייהו. אחר שהעידו בפניו: וקרא ערער על האי. שהוא פסול: עד שלא חתמו. השני דיינים על האשרתא: מעידין. על זה שהוא כשר: משחתמו. הוו להו נוגעין בעדות שגנאי להם שישבו עם פסול לדין:

תוספות

האמר רב פפי האי אשרתא. תימה דפריך מדרב פפי ובפרק הכותב (לקמן דף פה. ושם) מסיק דליתא לדרב פפי מדרב נחמן כו' ועוד דבפ' כל הגט (גיטין כו: ושם) מסיק דרב לית ליה דרב פפי והיכי פריך הכא מדרב פפי אמילתיה דרב מיהו הא איכא לתרץ דאלישנא דאמרי לה משמיה דרב הונא פריך ואין לומר דהכי פריך כיון דאמר משחתמו אין מעידין לפניו וחותם אלמא חיישינן למיחזי כשקרא אם כן משכתבו עד שלא חתמו נמי דכתיבה נמי מיחזי כשקרא דא"כ הוה קשיא דרב אדרב דהכא חייש למיחזי כשקרא ובפרק כל הגט (שם) לא חייש אלא טעמא דמשחתמו דמי לנוגעים בעדות כעין שפירש בקונט' גבי ההוא שקרא ערער על אחד מהן ותירץ ר"ת [ו] דדרך הש"ס להקשות אפילו מדבר דלא הוי הלכתא הכי ופוסק ר"ת דכתבינן [ז] אורכתא אפילו אמטלטלי דכפריה דלא קיי"ל כרב פפי דחייש למיחזי כשקרא אע"ג דפריך מינה ופריך נמי מנהרדעי בכמה מקומות בפרק שבועת העדות (שבועות דף לג: ושם) ובפרק יש בכור (בכורות דף מט.) והאמרי נהרדעי לא כתבינן אורכתא כו' וי"מ וליתא דקאמר בהכותב ובפ' כל הגט (גיטין דף כו: ושם) דלא בעי למימר דליתא לדרב פפי אלא דליתא לקושיא שאין לדמות אשרתא שהוא מעשה ב"ד לשאר שטרות דבמעשה ב"ד לכ"ע חיישינן למיחזי [א] כשקרא ור"י מדנפי"ר תירץ לכתחלה ודאי חיישינן למיחזי כשקרא כדאמר להו רב לספרי כי יתביתו בהיני כו' (ב"ב דף קעב.) אבל בדיעבד לא חיישינן ולהכי פריך הכא דהוי לכתחלה והא דקאמר דליתא לדרב פפי היינו דיעבד דההיא איתתא דהכותב (לקמן דף פה. ושם) כיון שהיתה צריכה לחזור לב"ד כדיעבד דמי והרשאה נמי דכתבינן אמטלטלי דכפריה היינו משום כיון דאינו יכול לילך שם כדיעבד דמי[ז]: **וש"מ** דיינין המכירין חתימת עדים א"צ להעיד בפניהם. דקס"ד דצריך להעיד בפניהם אע"ג דלא תהא שמיעה גדולה מראייה לפי שהיו נראין יותר בית דין דכשאין מעידין בפניהם אין נראה אלא כעד מפי עד ומטעם זה הצריכו ג' בקיום שטרות דהוה סגי בב' אלא משום דבעינן שיהא ב"ד כדפרישית ועוד אומר ר"י דס"ד דצרי' להעיד בפניהם משום דפעמים אין מכירין אלא על ידי שראו בלילה דליכא למימר לא תהא שמיעה גדולה מראייה דשמיעה אינה יכולה להיות בלילה כדאמר בר"ה (דף כה: ושם) דחקירת עדים כתחלת דין דמי ותחלת דין אינו אלא ביום כדאמרינן בסנהדרין (דף לב.): **בפני** כל אחד ואחד. דס"ד כיון שהעידו בפני שנים יכול השלישי לכתוב על סמך השנים אע"פ שלא העידו בפניו: **הנח** לעדות החדש דאורייתא. ובדאורייתא אין עד נעשה דיין וטעמא דאין עד נעשה דיין משום דבעינן שיעידו לפני הדיינין כמו שמפרש רשב"ם דכתיב ועמדו שני האנשים אלו העדים לפני ה' אלו הדיינין וי"מ משום דבעינן עדות שאתה יכול להזימה ואם העדים נעשו דיינין עדות שאין אתה יכול להזימה היא שלא יקבלו הזמה על עצמן ומיהו לפי טעם זה אם העדים קרובים לדיינין אינם יכולים להעיד דלא יקבלו הזמה עליהם אלא כיון דבני הזמה נינהו בב"ד אחר עדות שאתה יכול להזימה קרינא בהו ה"נ יהיה הדיין נעשה עד [ח] ודוקא בעד המעיד אמרינן דאין עד נעשה דיין אבל עד שאינו צריך להעיד כגון שיש אחרים שיעידו או כגון שראוהו ביום שאינו צריך להעיד דלא תהא שמיעה גדולה מראייה נעשה דיין ודווקא בדיני ממונות אבל בדיני נפשות אפילו עד שאין צריך להעיד אין נעשה דיין לר"ע דאמר במסכת מכות (דף ו. ושם) אפילו הן מאה כולן עדים וטעמא מפרש בפרק ראוהו ב"ד (ר"ה דף כו. ושם) משום דכתיב והצילו העדה והכא כיון דחזו דקטל תו לא חזי ליה זכותא ודווקא בדאורייתא אבל בדרבנן אפילו עד המעיד נעשה דיין:

עין משפט נר מצוה

מח א מיי' פ"ז מהל' עדות הלכה ז סמג עשין קט טוש"ע ח"מ סימן מו סעיף כד:

מט ב מיי' פ"ו שם הל' ג סמג שם טוש"ע שם סעיף ז:

נ ג מיי' פ"ב מהלכות קידוש החדש הלכה ט:

נא ד מיי' פ"ה מהלכות עדות הלכה ו סמג עשין קט טוש"ע ח"מ סי' ז סעיף ה:

נב ה מיי' שם הל' א ופ"ו הלכה ו סמג עשין קט טוש"ע ח"מ סימן מו סעיף ד בהג"ה:

נג ו מיי' שם טוש"ע שם סעיף כו:

תוספות רי"ד

דאיקלע רבנאי אחוה דר' חייא בר אבא לקמן למיזבן שומשמי ואמר הכי אמר שמואל עד ודיין אין מצטרפים הכי הלכה: אר"ה א"ר ג' שישבו לקיים את השטר פי' בלא העדאת עדים שיעידו על כת"י לפי שהדיינים עצמם מכירין אותה ב' מהן מכירין חתימת ידי העדים וא' אינו מכיר עד שלא חתמו ב' בהנפק מעידים בפניו לפני השלישי שזה כת"י החתומים משחתמו אין מעידין בפניו וחותם פירוש [אחר] עד שלא חתמו דין בההיא אשרתא עמהן כותבין כך נפק שטרא ד"ן קדמנא ואתברר שהוא חתימות העדים ואשרנוהו וקיימנוהו כדחזי אבל אחר שחתמו אין מעידין בפניו מפני שהן נוגעים בעדותן שנראה שמה שעשו שלא כדין לקיים חתימתן שלא תבטל: ש"מ תלת ש"מ עד שהעיד ונעשה עד חוזר עוד ונעשה דיין וש"מ דיינין המכירין חתימת ידי העדים א"צ להעיד בפניהם וש"מ דיינים שאין מכירין חתימות העדים צריכים להעיד בפני כא"א פי' שאם העידו בפני ב' אין הג' יכול לחתום שהרי כאן הצרכו להעיד בפני הג' ולא יועיל הנה שיעידו בפני ב' והב' יעידו לג' כדאמרינן בשנים מכירין משום דהוי להו עד מפי עד אבל כשמכירין מעצמן אינו עד מפ"ע: איתבי' רב ספרא לר"א וגו' עד מי נעשה דיין והתנן ראוהו ג' והם ב"ד פי' מסנהדרין שמקדשים את החדש יעמדו ב' ויושיבו מחבריהם אצל היחיד ויעידו בפניהם ויאמרו מקודש מקודש שאין היחיד נאמן ע"י עצמו והתם פרכינן ולא תהא שמיעה גדולה מראייה ומתוקמ' לה כשראוהו בלילה לפיכך אם לא יעידו בבקר על מה יאמרו מקודש אין היחיד ראוי לקדש את החדש דקידוש החדש צריך שלשה הלכך יושיבו ב' דיינים אחרים מחבריהם מיושבי סנהדרין ואלה הב' שראו יעמדו בפניהם והם יקדשוהו ואי איתא ליתבו בדוכתייהו ולקדשו פי' אי איתא דעד נעשה דיין היה צריך להושיב מחבריהם אצל היחיד והם שהעידו יצטרפו עמו לקדש ומסקנא הנח לעדות החדש דאורייתא ובדאורייתא אין עד נעשה דיין אבל קיום שטרות דרבנן ובדרבנן עד נעשה דיין: אמר ר"א אר"ה א"ר ג' שישבו לקיים את השטר וקרא ערער על א' מהן עד שלא חתמו מעידין עליו וחותם פי' כיון שחתמו הן נוגעים בעדות שהם מתכוונים שלא תבטל חתימתן וגם גנאי הוא להם שישבו עם הפסול וחתמו. וערעור דמאי אי ערעור דגזלנותא

מסורת הש"ס

א) גיטין כו: לקמן פה. [ועי' בטוש"ע ח"מ סימן מו סעיף כד ובש"ך ובסמ"ע שם], ב) סנהדרין לד: ר"ה כו. גיטין ה: ב"ק ל: ב"ב קיד., ג) ר"ה כה:, ד) [לקמן כח. ע"ש בתוס'], ה) [וע"ע תוס' ב"מ קיג. ד"ה מחזיר], ו) [פי' הרשאה], ז) [וע"ע תוס' גיטין כו. ד"ה ליתא וב"מ יג: ד"ה כותבין], ח) [וע"ע תוס' ב"ק ל: ד"ה כגון שראוהו בלילה כו' עוד טעם אחר בשם ר"י דנפקא לן מכיום הנחלו כו'].

תוספות ישנים

א) [והיא הכותב לא חשיב מעשה ב"ד דבעדים סגי שיעידו שנשבעה. ת"י].

ליקוטי רש"י

ורבנן לחומרא. דצריך שנים מן השוק להעיד על חתימות יד המת והחי יעיד הוא לבדו על חתימות ידו אבל העד החי לא יצטרף עם אחר מן השוק להעיד על חתימת המת [רשב"ם שם]. שנים החתומין. וכו' ושדי ליה בבי דינא. אמר אביי לא לזוי איניש חתימת ידיה כו', אדם שצריך לכתוב חתימת ידו על קלף ולהשליך לבית דין כדי שיכירו בית דין חתימתו כי היכא דאמרינן בכתובות בפרק האשה שנתארמלה (דף כא.), כגון ראובן ושמעון שהיו חתומין בשטר ומת שמעון ואין מי שיכיר חתימת שמעון אלא ראובן ואחד מן השוק ואמרינן התם שיכתוב ראובן כתב ידו וישליכו לבית דין ובית דין מקיימין חתימת ידי ראובן הכתוב בשטר מכתב ידו שהשליך בב"ד ואין צריך לראובן להעיד על כתב ידו ובאין ראובן ואחד מן השוק ומעידין על חתימת שמעון ואמר אביי כשיחתום ראובן להשליך לב"ד לא יחתום בסוף הקלף אלא בראשיתו שלא יהא חלק מלמעלה שמא ימלאנו אדם רע ויכתוב בחלק שלמעלה מחתימתו אני החתום לויתי מפלוני כך וכך ממון ונמצא הוציא עליו כתב ידו כו' והיינו חתימת ידו דלקמן (גיטין דף עא) כתב סופר ועד כשר ואמר ר' ירמיה מתם סופר שנינו [שם קטו.]. חספא. חרס [חולין קה:]. הוציא עליו. מלוה. כתב ידו. שלו שהוא חייב לו ממון ואין כאן עדות אחרת. גובה מנכסים בני חורין. שלא גובה משעבדים שלא מלוה הכתוב בשטר שיש בו עדים דצריך שלא תרמי שטר ועדים שם מפקי ליה לקלא ולקוחות הוא דאפסידו אנפשייהו שלא חקרו בדבר ויניחו בני תרי למוכר לגבות מהם [רשב"ם ב"ב קעה.]. ודאע"ג דהלכה כרבי מחבירו. קא משמע לן במקום יחיד בין היכא כמותו מחבירו ולומר

במקום רבים [פסחים כז.] [ע"כ שייך לע"א] אשרתא. לשון חוזק כמו ישר כחך (יבמות סב.) קיום השטר שכותבין דייני במותב תלתא הוינא ואתו פלוני ופלוני ואסהידו אחתימות ידייהו ואשרנוהו וקיימנוהו [לקמן פה.]. קיום השטר שכותבים הדיינים כשהעדים מעידים על כתב ידיהם בב"ד וב"ד כותבין במותב תלתא הוינא ואתו פלוני ופלוני ואסהידו אחתימת ידייהו ואשרנוהי וקיימנוהי כדחזי [גיטין כו:]. דניחוו. שיעידו זה כתב ידנו [לקמן שם]. עד נעשה דיין. מי שראה להיות עד נעשה דיין. ויעידו בפניהם. השנים. ויאמרו. הג' מקודש. שאין היחיד נאמן. לומר מקודש בפני עצמו [רשב"ם ב"ב קיד.]. וקיום שטרות דרבנן. דמדאורייתא לא בעינן קיום דאמר לקמן (דף יט:) עדים החתומים כמי שנחקרה עדותן בב"ד [לקמן כח.].

Having clarified Rav Huna's ruling, the Gemara notes several lessons that may be derived from it:

שְׁמַע מִינָּהּ תְּלָת – **Learn from this three** laws: שְׁמַע מִינָּהּ עֵד נַעֲשֶׂה דַּיָּין – **Learn from it that a witness may become a judge** in the very case concerning which he testified.[11] וּשְׁמַע מִינָּהּ דַּיָּינִין הַמַּכִּירִין חֲתִימוֹת יְדֵי עֵדִים – **And learn from it** concerning **judges who recognize the signatures of the witnesses,** אֵינָן צְרִיכִין לְהָעִיד בִּפְנֵיהֶם – that **it is not necessary** for others **to testify before them** concerning the signatures' authenticity.[12] וּשְׁמַע מִינָּהּ דַּיָּינִין שֶׁאֵין מַכִּירִין חֲתִימוֹת יְדֵי עֵדִים – **And learn from it** concerning **judges who do not recognize the signatures of the witnesses,** צְרִיכִין לְהָעִיד בִּפְנֵי כָל אֶחָד וְאֶחָד – that **it is necessary** for witnesses **to testify before each and every one** of them concerning the signatures' authenticity.[13]

The Gemara rejects the latter two inferences:

מַתְקִיף לָהּ רַב אַשִׁי – **Rav Ashi objected to this:** בִּשְׁלָמָא עֵד נַעֲשֶׂה דַּיָּין שָׁמְעִינַן מִינָּהּ – **All is well** concerning your inference that **a witness** who testified **may become a judge** in that very case – **we** truly **learn it from this** ruling of Rav Huna. אֶלָּא דַּיָּינִין הַמַּכִּירִין חֲתִימוֹת יְדֵי עֵדִים אֵין צְרִיכִין לְהָעִיד בִּפְנֵיהֶם – **But** as for your inference that concerning **judges who recognize the signatures of the witnesses, it is not necessary** for others **to testify before them** about the signatures' authenticity, this is questionable: דִּלְמָא לְעוֹלָם אֵימָא לָךְ צְרִיכִין – **Perhaps, in fact, I can tell you that it is necessary** for others to testify before the judges about the signatures' authenticity, וְשָׁאנֵי הָכָא דְּקָא מִקַּיְּימָא הַגָּדָה בְּחַד – **but here it is different, because** the requirement of **testimony is fulfilled through** the presentation of testimony to the **one** judge who does not recognize the signatures by the two who do recognize them.[14] וְדַיָּינִין שֶׁאֵין מַכִּירִין חֲתִימוֹת יְדֵי עֵדִים צְרִיכִין לְהָעִיד בִּפְנֵי כָל אֶחָד וְאֶחָד – **Furthermore,** as for your inference that concerning **judges who do not recognize the signatures of the witnesses, it is necessary** for witnesses **to testify before each and every one** of them, this too is questionable: דִּלְמָא לְעוֹלָם אֵימָא לָךְ אֵין צְרִיכִין – **Perhaps, in fact, I can tell you that it is not necessary** for witnesses to testify before each and every judge, וְשָׁאנֵי הָכָא דְּלֹא קָא מִקַּיְּימָא הַגָּדָה כְּלָל – **but here it is different, because** the requirement of **testimony would not be fulfilled at all** if the two judges would not testify before the third one.[15] Thus, Rav Huna's ruling does not provide a firm basis for your two latter conclusions![16]

Having rejected the latter two inferences, the Gemara elaborates on the first inference, which it accepted:

יָתִיב רַבִּי אַבָּא וְקָאָמַר לָהּ לְהָא שְׁמַעְתָּא דְּעֵד נַעֲשֶׂה דַּיָּין – **R' Abba was sitting and stating this teaching, that a witness may become a judge** in the very case concerning which he testified. אֵיתִיבֵיהּ רַב סָפְרָא לְרַבִּי אַבָּא – **Rav Safra challenged R' Abba** on the basis of the following Mishnah:[17] רָאוּהוּ שְׁלֹשָׁה – If only **THREE** people **SAW [THE NEW MOON]** וְהֵן בֵּית דִּין – **AND THEY ARE** members of the **COURT,**[18] יַעַמְדוּ שְׁנַיִם – **TWO** of them **SHOULD STAND** ready to testify וְיוֹשִׁיבוּ מֵחַבְרֵיהֶם אֵצֶל הַיָּחִיד – **AND SHOULD SEAT** two other sages **FROM** among **THEIR COLLEAGUES BESIDE THE SINGLE** remaining judge, וְיָעִידוּ בִּפְנֵיהֶם – **AND** then **[THE TWO DESIGNATED WITNESSES] SHOULD TESTIFY BEFORE [THE THREE JUDGES]** regarding the appearance of the new moon, וְיֹאמְרוּ מְקוּדָּשׁ הַחֹדֶשׁ מְקוּדָּשׁ – **AND THEY SHOULD** then **PROCLAIM: "THE MONTH IS SANCTIFIED, IT IS SANCTIFIED,"** שֶׁאֵין הַיָּחִיד נֶאֱמָן עַל יְדֵי עַצְמוֹ – **FOR THE INDIVIDUAL** judge **IS NOT TRUSTED** to proclaim Rosh Chodesh **BY HIMSELF.**[19] וְאִי סָלְקָא דַּעְתָּךְ דְּעֵד נַעֲשֶׂה דַּיָּין – **Now, if you should think that a witness may become a judge** in the very case concerning which he testified, לָמָּה לִי כּוּלֵּי הַאי – **why**

NOTES

11. For in our case the two men who recognize the signatures first testify as witnesses before the third one, and then sign the certification themselves as judges (*Rashi*). [One might have thought that it is contradictory to serve as a witness and judge in the same case (see note 20).]

12. [I.e. if all three judges recognize the signatures, there is no need for them to go through the formality of hearing testimony. This is derived from the fact that in our case the two judges who recognize the signatures do not have to hear testimony about that fact.] See note 14 for explanation of why we might have thought that the court must hear testimony.

13. I.e. if two of the judges heard testimony about the signatures, the third judge may not sign the certification on that basis; he needs to hear the testimony himself. This is derived from the fact that in our case the two judges who recognize the signatures must present their knowledge to the third one in the capacity of witnesses testi- fying before him (*Rashi*). Since certification is merely a Rabbinic requirement, one might have thought that the Rabbis were lenient and allowed the third judge to rely upon his colleagues (*Re'ah;* cf. *Ritva*).

14. I.e. perhaps the court cannot rule a document valid unless it formally accepts testimony concerning its authenticity. Even if the judges all recognize the signatures they must fulfill the formality of hearing testimony, because Scripture (*Leviticus* 5:1) implies that monetary matters can be decided only on the basis of *spoken* testimony. However, it is not necessary for all three judges to perform this formality; the presentation of testimony to one of the judges suffices (*Rashi,* as elucidated by *Ramban;* see also *Ritva;* cf. *Tosafos* ד״ה ושמ״מ).

15. I.e. perhaps when two of the judges have heard testimony concerning the authenticity of a note the third one may rely upon them. However, if none of the judges has heard testimony, they may not certify the note even though they know the signatures are authentic, because Scripture stipulates that there be *spoken* testimony. Perhaps when Rav Huna ruled that the two judges who recognize the signatures must testify before the third one, it was because of this stipulation and not because he is forbidden to rely upon them (see *Rashi*).

16. Although Rav Ashi has deflected the *proof* to these conclusions, they are in fact halachically valid. The law is that if all the judges recognize the signatures as authentic they do not have to hear testimony to this effect, and if they do not recognize the signatures, each and every one of them must hear the testimony (*Ramban;* see also *Choshen Mishpat* 46:7; for a thorough discussion of this passage, see *Baal HaMaor* and *Milchamos Hashem*).

17. *Rosh Hashanah* 25b.

18. I.e. they are members of the Great Sanhedrin, and thereby authorized to sanctify the months (*Rashi*).

In former times, the day on which Rosh Chodesh fell was not predetermined by the calendar but was decided on a month-to-month basis by the central Sanhedrin. The court would hear testimony from witnesses as to their sighting of the new moon. Upon cross-examining the witnesses and determining their testimony to be correct, the court would declare that day to be Rosh Chodesh by publicly sanctifying it, i.e. announcing מְקוּדָּשׁ הַחֹדֶשׁ, *the month is sanctified.*

19. I.e. a single judge is not qualified to sanctify the new month. Hence, two other colleagues are required to join the single judge (who is not testifying), so as to constitute a proper court (*Rashi;* see *Ritva*).

The Gemara in *Rosh Hashanah* (ibid.) wonders why the original three judges cannot sanctify the month on the basis of their having seen the new moon. Can a judgment based on the hearing of testimony be greater than one based on their own sighting of the moon? [The Gemara's question is based on the fact that in regard to sanctifying the month Scripture does not mention *testimony,* but rather, implies that all depends upon the sighting of the new moon – by either the court or witnesses (*Rashi* ad loc.; cf. *Ramban* and *Ritva* ד״ה ודיינים here).] The Gemara answers that we are dealing with a case where the judges saw the new moon at night, when they are not authorized to act as a court and sanctify the new month. On the morrow, if there are no witnesses to report the new moon's appearance the previous night, the court cannot perform the sanctification on the basis of their prior sighting – see Schottenstein edition of *Rosh Hashanah,* 25b note 30. Therefore, two judges must detach themselves from the court and serve as witnesses (*Rashi;* see *Ran*).

מח א מיי' פ"ו מהל' עדות הלכה ה סמג עשין קט טוש"ע ח"מ סימן מו סעיף כד:
מט ב מיי' פ"ו שם הל' ג סמג שם טוש"ע שם סעיף ה:
נ ג מיי' פ"ב מהלכות קידוש החדש הלכה ט:
נא ד מיי' פ"ה מהלכות עדות הלכה ט סמג עשין קט טוש"ע ח"מ סי' ז סעיף ה:
נב ה מיי' פ"ו שם הל' א ופי"ו הלכה ו סמג עשין פב טוש"ע שם סימן מו סעיף ד בהג"ה:
נג ו מיי' שם טוש"ע שם סעיף כו:

איקלע רבנאי אחוה דר' חייא בר אבא למזבן שומשמי ואמר הכי אמר שמואל עד ודיין מצטרפין אמר אמימר כמה מעליא הא שמעתא אמר ליה רב אשי לאמימר משום דקלסה אבוה דאמך את נמי מקלסת לה כבר פרכה רבא: אמר רב ספרא אמר רבי אבא אמר רב יצחק בר שמואל בר מרתא אמר רב הונא ואמרי ליה אמר רב הונא אמר רב א שלשה שישבו לקיים את השטר ואחד אינו מכיר עד שלא חתמו מעידין בפניו וחותם משחתמו אין מעידין בפניו וחותם ומי כתבינן והאמר רב פפי משמיה דרבא ב האי אשרתא דדייני דניכתב מקמיה דניחוו סהדי אחתימת ידייהו פסולה דמתחזי כשקרא הכא נמי מתחזי כשקרא אלא אימא עד שלא כתבו מעידין בפניו וחותם משכתבו אין מעידין בפניו וחותם ש"מ תלת ש"מ ג עד נעשה דיין וש"מ ד דיינין המכירין חתימות ידי עדים אינן צריכין להעיד בפניהם וש"מ דיינין שאין מכירין חתימות ידי עדים צריכין להעיד בפני כל אחד ואחד מתקיף לה רב אשי בשלמא עד נעשה דיין שמעינן מינה אלא דיינין המכירין חתימות ידי עדים אין צריכין להעיד בפניהם דלמא לעולם אימא לך צריכין ושאני הכא דקא מקיימא הגדה בחד ודיינין שאין מכירין חתימות ידי עדים צריכין להעיד בפני כל אחד ואחד דלמא לעולם אימא לך אין צריכין ושאני הכא דלא קא מקיימא הגדה כלל יתיב ר' אבא וקאמר לה להא שמעתא דעד נעשה דיין איתיביה רב ספרא לרבי אבא ג ראוהו שלשה והן בית דין יעמדו שנים ויושיבו מחבריהם אצל היחיד ויעידו בפניהם ויאמרו מקודש החדש מקודש שאין היחיד נאמן על ידי עצמו ואי סלקא דעתך דעד נעשה דיין למה לי כולי האי ליתבו בדוכתייהו וליקדשי אמר ליה אף לדידי קשיא לי ושאילתיה לרב יצחק בר שמואל בר מרתא ורב יצחק לרב הונא ורב הונא לחייא בר רב וחייא בר רב לרב ואמר להו הנח ד לעדות החדש דאוריית' ה וקיום שטרות דרבנן אמר רבי אבא אמר רב הונא אמר רב ו שלשה שישבו לקיים את השטר וקרא ערער על אחד מהן עד שלא חתמו מעידין עליו וחותם משחתמו אין מעידין עליו וחותם ערער דמאי אי ערער דגזלנותא תרי

רש"י

איקלע רבנאי למיזבן שומשמי גרסי' ולא גרסי' דאיקלע ולא גרסינן לגבן ולאו רמי אמרה דא"ל לומר כן שאמר רמי עדות זו על אמימר ורב אשי שהרי רב אשי כמה דורות היה אחריו דאמרינן בקדושין (דף עב:) יום שמת רבא נולד רב אשי: אבוה דאמך. רמי בר חמא: שלשה שישבו. בב"ד: לקיים השטר. ובלא העדאת עדים שיעידו על כתב ידן לפי שהדיינין עצמן מכירין אותה השנים מכירין אותה ואחד אינו מכיר: עד שלא חתמו. השנים על הנפקק: מעידין. לפני השלישי שזהו כתב ידן של חתומים: וחותם. עמהם על מה שכותבין אשרנוהי וקיימנוהי לשטרא דנן במותב תלתא דאשתמודענא לחתימת ידא דסהדי היא: משחתמו אין מעידין. דחתימה קמייתא בשקרא הוה דלאו תלתא הוו דידעי: ומי כתבינן. לאשרתא דידיה בחתימה וכי קודם שנתקיים לפני שלשתן יכתבו במותב תלתא הוינא ואשתמודענא כו': אשרתא. לשון חוזק שמחזקים [את השטר] וכותבין אשרנוהי: דניכתבא מקמי דניחוו סהדי כו'. עד שלא העידו העדים על כתב ידם כתבו הדיינין במותב תלתא הוינא ונפיק שטרא דנן קדמנא ואסהידו פלוני ופלוני אחתימת ידייהו ואשרנוהי וקיימנוהי: עד נעשה דיין. שהרי השנים העידו על החתימות: צריכין להעיד בפני כל אחד ואחד. שאם העידו בפני השנים אין הג' יכול לחתום דהא הכא הוצרכו השנים להעיד בפני הג': דלמא לעולם צריכין. להעיד שאין עדות אלא ע"י הגדת עדות: ושאני הכא דקא מקיימא הגדה. בפני היחיד שאינו מכיר: דלא מקיימא הגדה כלל. אי לא הוו מסהדי בפניה: ראוהו ג'. בעדות החדש קאי: והן בית דין. מסנהדרין המקדשין את החדש: יעמדו השנים. להיות עדים והתם פרכינן לא תהא שמיעה גדולה מראיה ומוקמינן לה כשראוהו בלילה לפיכך אם לא יעידו לבקר על מה יאמרו מקודש: שאין היחיד נאמן. לקדש החדש ביחידי: ליתבו בדוכתייהו. אחר שהעידו בפניו: וקרא ערער על הא'. שהוא פסול: עד שלא חתמו. השני דיינים על האשרתא: מעידין. על זה שהוא כשר: משחתמו. הוו להו נוגעין בעדות שגנאי להם שישבו עם פסול בדין:

תוספות

האמר רב פפי האי אשרתא. תימה דפריך מדרב פפי ובפרק הכותב (לקמן דף פה. ושם) מסיק ליתא לדרב פפי מדרב נחמן כו' ועוד דבפ' כל הגט (גיטין כו: ושם) מסיק דרב לית ליה דרב פפי והיכי פריך הכא מדרב פפי אמילתיה דרב מיהו הא ליכא לתרץ דאליבא דאמרי לה משמיה דרב הונא פריך ואין לומר דהכי פריך כיון דאמר משחתמו אין מעידין לפניו וחותם אלמא חיישינן למיחזי כשקרא אם כן משכתבו עד שלא חתמו נמי דכתיבה נמי מיחזי כשקרא דא"כ הוה קשיא דרב אדרב דהכא חייש למיחזי כשקרא ובפרק כל הגט (שם) לא חייש אלא טעמא דמשחתמו דמי לנוגעים בעדות כעין שפירש בקונט' גבי ההוא שקרא ערער על אחד מהן ותירץ ר"ת ה) דדרך הש"ס להקשות אפילו מדבר דלא הוי הלכתא הכי ופוסק ר"ת דכתבינן ו) אורכתא אפילו אמטלטלי דכפריה דלא קיי"ל כרב פפי דחייש למיחזי כשקרא אע"ג דפריך מינה ופריך נמי מנהרדעי בכמה מקומות בפרק שבועת העדות (שבועות דף לג: ושם) ובפרק יש בכור (בכורות דף מט.) והאמרי נהרדעי לא כתבינן אורכתא כו' וי"מ וליתא דקאמר בהכותב ובפ' כל הגט (גיטין דף כו: ושם) דלא בעי למימר דליתא לדרב פפי אלא דליתא לקושיא שאין לדמות אשרתא שהוא מעשה ב"ד לשאר שטרות דבמעשה ב"ד לכ"ע חיישינן למיחזי א) כשקרא ור"י מדנפי"ר תירץ דלכתחלה ודאי חיישינן למיחזי כשקרא כדאמר להו רב לספרי כי יתביתו בהיני כו' (ב"ב דף קעב.) אבל בדיעבד לא חיישינן ולהכי פריך הכא דהוי לכתחלה והא דקאמר דליתא לדרב פפי היינו דיעבד דההיא איתתא דהכותב (לקמן דף פה. ושם) כיון שהיתה צריכה לחזור לב"ד כדיעבד דמי והרשאה נמי דכתבינן אמטלטלי דכפריה היינו משום כיון דאינו יכול לילך שם כדיעבד דמי ז): **וש"מ** דיינין המכירין חתימת עדים א"צ להעיד בפניהם. דקס"ד דצריך להעיד בפניהם אע"ג דלא תהא שמיעה גדולה מראייה לפי שהיו נראין יותר בית דין דכשאין מעידין בפניהם אין נראה אלא כעד מפי עד ומטעם זה הצריכו ג' בקיום שטרות דהוה סגי בב' אלא משום דבעינן שיהא ב"ד כדפרישית ועוד אומר ר"י דס"ד דצרי' להעיד בפניהם משום דפעמים אין מכירין אלא על ידי שראו בלילה דליכא למימר לא תהא שמיעה גדולה מראייה דשמיעה אינה יכולה להיות בלילה כדאמר בר"ה (דף כה: ושם) דמקבלת עדים כתחלת דין דמי ותחלת דין אינו אלא ביום כדאמרינן בסנהדרין (דף לג.): **בפני** כל אחד ואחד. דס"ד כיון שהעידו בפני שנים יכול השלישי לכתוב על סמך השנים אע"פ שלא העידו בפניו: **הנח** לעדות החדש דאורייתא. ובדאורייתא אין עד נעשה דיין וטעמא דאין עד נעשה דיין משום דבעינן שיעידו לפני הדיינין כמו שמפרש רשב"ם דכתיב ועמדו שני האנשים אלו העדים לפני ה' אלו הדיינין וי"מ משום דבעינן עדות שאתה יכול להזימה ואם העדים נעשו דיינין עדות שאין אתה יכול להזימה היא שלא יקבלו הזמה על עצמן ומיהו לפי טעם זה אם העדים קרובים לדיינין אינם יכולים להעיד דלא יקבלו הזמה עליהם אלא כיון דבני הזמה נינהו בב"ד אחר עדות שאתה יכול להזימה קרינא בהו וה"נ יהיה הדיין נעשה עד ח) ודוקא בעד המעיד אמרינן דאין עד נעשה דיין דשייכי הני טעמי אבל עד שאינו צריך להעיד כגון שיש אחרים שיעידו או כגון שראוהו ביום שאינו צריך להעיד דלא תהא שמיעה גדולה מראיה נעשה דיין ודוקא בדיני ממונות אבל בדיני נפשות אפילו עד שאין צריך להעיד אין נעשה דיין כר"ע דאמר במסכת מכות (דף ו. ושם) אפילו הן מאה כולן עדים וטעמא מפרש בפרק ראוהו ב"ד (ר"ה דף כו. ושם) משום דכתיב והצילו העדה והכא כיון דחזו דקטל לא חזי ליה זכותא ודוקא בדאורייתא אבל בדרבנן אפילו עד המעיד נעשה דיין:

תוספות ישנים

א) [והסיא דהכותב לא חשיב מעשה ב"ד דבפני שני שיעידו שנשבעה. מ"י].

A related discussion is cited:

אִיקְלַע רַבְנַאי אֲחוּהַ דְּרַבִּי חִיָּיא בַּר אַבָּא לְמִזְבַּן שׁוּמְשְׁמֵי – **Ravnai the brother of R' Chiya bar Abba visited** a certain place **to buy sesame seeds,** וְאָמַר הָכִי אָמַר שְׁמוּאֵל – **and** while there, **he said: Shmuel stated the following:** עֵד וְדַיָּין מִצְטָרְפִין – **A witness** who signed a document **and a judge** who signed its certification **can combine** to authenticate it. אָמַר אַמֵימָר – **Ameimar said:** כַּמָּה מְעַלְּיָא הָא שְׁמַעְתָּא – **How excellent this teaching** is! אָמַר לֵיהּ רַב אַשִׁי לְאַמֵימָר – **Rav Ashi said to Ameimar:** מִשּׁוּם דְּקַלְּסָהּ אֲבוּהָ דְּאִמָּךְ אַתְּ נַמִּי מְקַלְּסַתְּ לָהּ – Is it **because your mother's father,** Rami bar Chama, **praised [this ruling]** when he heard it from Rav Yehudah, that **you also praise it?** כְּבָר פִּרְכָהּ רָבָא – **Rava has already refuted it!**[1]

The Gemara turns to another aspect of document certification. The discussion focuses on a case in which a document is brought before the court for certification and some of the judges themselves recognize the witnesses' signatures:[2]

אָמַר רַב סַפְרָא אָמַר רַבִּי אַבָּא אָמַר רַב יִצְחָק בַּר שְׁמוּאֵל בַּר מָרְתָא אָמַר רַב הוּנָא – **Rav Safra said in the name of R' Abba,** who **said in the name of Rav Yitzchak bar Shmuel bar Marta,** who **said in the name of Rav Huna,** וְאָמְרִי לֵיהּ אָמַר רַב הוּנָא אָמַר רַב – **and some say, Rav Huna said in the name of Rav:** שְׁלֹשָׁה שֶׁיָּשְׁבוּ לְקַיֵּים אֶת הַשְּׁטָר – **If three** judges **sat down** as a court **to certify a document,** שְׁנַיִם מַכִּירִין חֲתִימוֹת יְדֵי עֵדִים וְאֶחָד אֵינוֹ מַכִּיר – and **two** of them **recognize the signatures of the witnesses while** only the third **one does not recognize** them, the law is as follows:[3] עַד שֶׁלֹּא חָתְמוּ – **Before [those two judges] sign** the certification, מְעִידִין בְּפָנָיו וְחוֹתֵם – **they may testify before [the remaining judge]** about the authenticity of the witnesses' signatures **and he may** then **sign** the certification along with them. מִשֶּׁחָתְמוּ – But **once [those two judges] have signed** the certification, אֵין מְעִידִין בְּפָנָיו וְחוֹתֵם – **they may not testify before [the remaining judge] and** have **him sign** it.[4]

The Gemara objects to the notion that the judges must testify only before *signing* the certification:

וּמִי כָּתְבִינַן – **But may we** even ***write*** a certification before all three judges have determined that the signatures are authentic?[5] וְהָאָמַר רַב פַּפִּי מִשְּׁמֵיהּ דְּרָבָא – **Why, Rav Pappi said in the name of Rava:** הַאי אַשְׁרָתָא דְּדַיָּינֵי – **A judicial certification**[6] דְּנִיכְתַּב מִקַּמֵּיהּ דְּנִיחֲווּ סַהֲדֵי אַחֲתִימַת יְדַיְיהוּ – **that was written before the witnesses testify**[7] **about** the authenticity of **their signatures** פְּסוּלָה – **is invalid.**[8] דְּמִתְחֲזֵי כְּשִׁקְרָא – The reason is **because [the certification]** ***appears*** **like a falsehood.**[9] הָכָא נַמִּי מִתְחֲזֵי כְּשִׁקְרָא – **Here too,** in the case where the certification was written while only two of the judges knew that the signatures are authentic, **it appears like a falsehood** and should be invalid.[10] – ? –

The Gemara therefore revises its citation of Rav Huna's ruling:

אֶלָּא אֵימָא – **Rather, state** it as follows: If two of the three judges recognize the signatures on a document, the law is that עַד שֶׁלֹּא כָּתְבוּ מְעִידִין בְּפָנָיו וְחוֹתֵם – **before they** ***write*** the certification, **they may testify before [the remaining judge]** about the authenticity of the signatures, **and he may** then **sign** with them the certification that they write afterwards. מִשֶּׁכָּתְבוּ אֵין מְעִידִין בְּפָנָיו וְחוֹתֵם – But **once they have** ***written*** the certification, **they may not testify before [the remaining judge] and** have **him sign** it with them, because it appears like a falsehood.

NOTES

1. The text follows *Rashi's* reading, according to which this discussion is cited by the Gemara as a parallel to the previous one. According to an alternative version, cited by *Tos. Rid,* this incident was cited by Rami bar Yechezkel in support of his rejection of Rav Yehudah's ruling. However, *Rashi* discards that reading, arguing that Rami bar Yechezkel could not have quoted Rav Ashi. The Gemara states in *Kiddushin* (72b) that Rav Ashi was born several decades after the death of Rami's brother, Rav Yehudah. [See *Doros Rishonim,* v. 5 p. 569, and *Toldos Tannaim VeAmoraim,* p. 1095, for a defense of *Tos. Rid's* reading.]

2. Ordinarily, when the court certifies a document, it writes a text such as the following below the witnesses' signatures: "We were seated as three [judges] together when this document was brought before us, and So-and-so and So-and so testified (or: and we ascertained) that these are the [authentic] signatures of the witnesses, so we reinforced it and certified it as fit." Each of the judges then signs the certification (see *Rashi* below). The Gemara discusses the procedure that is followed when some — but not all — of the judges recognize the signatures themselves.

3. It is unnecessary to seek witnesses who will authenticate the signatures, since two of the judges can authenticate them (*Rashi*). However, a specific procedure must be followed.

4. The judges initially write the text of the certification on the note, but before any of them signs it, the two who recognize the signatures must present their testimony before the third one. If the first two sign the certification before presenting their testimony to the third one, they will have signed to a falsehood, since the certification states that all *three* of them ascertained that the witnesses' signatures are authentic (*Rashi*). The falsely signed certification would be invalid (*Ramban, Rashba, Ritva, Ran;* see *Hagahos Radal;* cf. *Tosafos* ד״ה האמר).

The Rishonim wonder how the two judges can stand up as witnesses and state their testimony before only one sitting judge, when a court that hears testimony must ordinarily be comprised of three men! Because of this question, *Rosh* concludes that, with respect to the certification of documents, the three judges do not have to hear testimony about the signatures together. Even when two strangers come to authenticate the signatures, they may present their testimony to each of the judges individually, and the judges may then seat themselves together to certify the note. [This dispensation is allowed because certification is merely a Rabbinic requirement, as the Gemara states below (*Ramah,* cited by *Shitah Mekubetzes* below ד״ה וכתב הרמ״ה ז״ל; cf. *Shach* 46:63; see *Rashash*).]

Others explain that even in the case of certification all three judges must normally hear the testimony together. In our case, however, the two men who testify before the third judge act as witnesses and judges simultaneously (see Gemara below). Thus, three judges are technically hearing the testimony together (*Ritva, Ran;* see note 19). For further discussion of this matter, see *Choshen Mishpat* 46:25 with *Shach* §63; see also *Ramban* and *Re'ah*.

5. Is it legal for the judges to *write* on the note "We were seated as three [judges] together . . . and we ascertained that these are the [authentic] signatures of the witnesses . . ." before all three of them have made this determination? (*Rashi*).

6. Literally: reinforcement. By certifying the document, the judges reinforce it [so that it may be used for collection]. They also include in the text of their certification ". . . we reinforced it . . ." (*Rashi;* see note 2).

7. Literally: indicate. Our translation follows *Rashi* here and below, 85a.

8. The reference is to a case where the witnesses who signed the document planned to testify that the signatures were indeed their own. In anticipation of hearing the testimony, the judges wrote the certification: "We were seated as three [judges] together when this document was brought before us, and So-and-so and So-and so testified that these are their signatures, so we reinforced it and certified it." Although they did not sign the certification until they heard the testimony, it is invalid (*Rashi*).

9. Although the judges signed truthfully, the mere fact that they wrote the certification in advance of hearing the testimony suffices to void it, because of the appearance of falsehood.

10. Interestingly, the Gemara below (85a) rules against Rav Pappi, concluding that a document written in advance of the event it describes is valid, as long as it is signed after the event. See *Tosafos, Rosh, Ran* and *Ritva* for various explanations of why our Gemara raises a question on the basis of Rav Pappi's rejected ruling, and for the halachah followed in practice.

עין משפט נר מצוה

מח א מיי' פ"ו מהל' עדות הלכה ו סמג עשין קט טוש"ע ח"מ סימן מו סעיף כח:

מט ב מיי' פ"ו שם הל' ב סמג שם טוש"ע שם סעיף ז:

נ ג מיי' פ"ב מהלכות קידוש החדש הלכה ט:

נא ד מיי' פ"ה מהלכות עדות הלכה ט סמג עשין קט טוש"ע ח"מ סי' ז סעיף ה:

נב ה מיי' פ"ו שם הל' א ופ"ו הלכה ו סמג עשין פב טוש"ע שם סימן מו סעיף ד ובה"ה:

נג ו מיי' שם טוש"ע שם סעיף כ:

תוספות רי"ד

דאיקלע רבנאי אחוה דר' חייא בר אבין לקמן למיזבן שומשמי ואמר הכי אמר שמואל עד ודיין אין מצטרפים וכך הלכה: **אר"ה א"ר** ג' שישבו לקיים את השטר פי' בלא העדאת עדים שיעידו על כת"י לפי שהדיינים עצמם מכירין אותה ב' מהן מכירין חתימת ידי העדים וא' אינו מכיר עד שלא חתמו פי' בהנפק מעידים בפניו וחותם פי' לפני השלישי שזה כת"י החתומים משחתמו אין מעידין בפניו וחותם פירוש (אחד) עד שלא חתמו הן בההיא אשרתא מעידים בפני זה וחותם עמהן וכותבין כך נפק שטרא דנן קדמנא ונתבררנו שהוא חתימות העדים ואשרנוהו וקיימנוהו כדחזי אבל אחר שחתמו אין מעידין בפניו מפני שהן נוגעים בעדותן שנראה שמה שמעידים כך כדי לקיים חתימתן שלא תבטל: **ש"מ תלת** ש"מ עד נעשה דיין פי' אחר שהעיד העשה עד חוזר עוד ונעשה דיין וש"מ דדיינים המכירים חתימת ידי העדים א"צ להעיד בפניהם וש"מ דיינים שאין מכירין חתימות העדים צריכים להעיד בפני כ"א פי' שאם העידו בפני הב' אין הג' יכול לחתום שהרי כאן הצריכו להעיד בפני הג' ולא יועיל הנה שיעידו בפני ב והב' יעידו לג' כדאמרינן בשנים מכירין משום דהוי להו עד מפי עד אבל כשמכירין מעצמן אינו עד מפ"ע: **איתבי'** רב ספרא לר"א ועד מי נעשה דיין והתנן ראוהו ג' והם ב"ד פי' מסנהדרין שמקדשים את החדש יעמדו ב' ויושיבו מחבריהם אצל היחיד ויעידו בפניהם ויאמרו מקודש מקודש שאין היחיד נאמן ע"י עצמו והתם פרכינן ולא תהא שמיעה גדולה מראייה ומתוקמ' לה כשראוהו בליל' לפיכך אם לא יעידו בבקר על מה יאמרו מקודש אין היחיד ראוי לקדש את החדש דקידוש החדש צריך שלשה והלכך יושיבו ב' דיינים אחרים מחבריהם מיושבי סנהדרין ואלה הב' שראו יעמ"ו בפניהם והם יקדשוהו ואי איתא ליתבו בדוכתייהו ולקדשו פי' אי איתא דעד שהעיד נעשה דיין מה צריך להושיב מחבריהם אצל היחיד הם שהעידו יצטרפו עמו לקדש אלא לאו ש"מ אין עד שהגיד עדותו כשר להיות דיין והכא היכי אמרינן דמעידים ומס"ק הנח לעדות החדש דאורייתא ובדאורייתא אין עד נעשה דיין אבל קיום שטרות דרבנן ובדרבנן עד נעשה דיין פי' מה"ת ליכא למיחש לזיופא אלא אפי' בלי קיום יגבה ולכי מתבורר דזייף מהדר ליה ורבנן הוא דאצרכי' לקיומי' ועד דלא מק"ים לא גבי. **עי'** דיני עד נעשה דיין בס"פ ששם ביארתי שאם יש עדים רבים שיגמר הדין ע"פ שנים עדים ושלשה דיי"ם עד שהגיד עדותו נעשה דיין: **אמר ר"פ** משמיה דרבא האי אשרתא דדייני דנכתבא מקמי דנחזו סהדי אחתימות ידייהו פסולה פי' דכיון דליכא בפ' הכותב ובגיטין בפ' כל הגט מתיב' ליה ואמרינן וליתא לר"פ: **אמר ר' אבא אר"ה א"ר** ג' שישבו לקיים את השטר וקרא ערער על א' מהן עד שלא חתמו מעידים עליו פי' על זה שהוא כשר וחותם פי' כיון שחתמו הן נוגעים בעדות שהם מתכוונים שלא תבטל חתימתן וגם גנאי הוא להם שיאמרו עם הפסול חתמו. **וערעור** דמאי אי ערעור דגזלנותא

האמר רב פפי האי אשרתא. תימה דפריך מדרב פפי ובפרק הכותב (לקמן דף פה. ושם) מסיק דליתא לדרב פפי מדרב נחמן כו' ועוד דבפ' כל הגט (גיטין כו: ושם) מסיק דרב לית ליה דרב פפי והיכי פריך הכא מדרב פפי אמילתיה דרב מיהו הא איכא לתרץ דאלישנא דאמרי לה משמיה דרב הונא פריך ואין לומר דהכי פריך כיון דאמר משחתמו אין מעידין לפניו וחותם אלמא חיישינן למיחזי כשקרא אם כן משכתבו עד שלא חתמו נמי דכתיבה נמי מיחזי כשקרא דא"כ הוה קשיא דרב אדרב דהכא חייש למיחזי כשקרא ובפרק כל הגט (שם) לא חייש אלא טעמא דמשחתמו דמי לנוגעים בעדות כעין שפירש בקונט' גבי ההוא שקרא ערער על אחד מהן ותירץ ר"ת [ט] דדרך הש"ס להקשות אפילו מדבר דלא הוי הלכתא הכי ופוסק ר"ת דכתבינן [י] אורכתא אפילו אמטלטלי דכפריה דלא קי"ל כרב פפי דחייש למיחזי כשקרא אע"ג דפריך מינה ופריך נמי מנהרדעי בכמה מקומות בפרק שבועת העדות (שבועות דף לג: ושם) ובפרק יש בכור (בכורות דף מט.) והאמרי נהרדעי לא כתבינן אורכתא כו' וי"מ וליתא דקאמר בהכותב ובפ' כל הגט (גיטין דף כו: ושם) דלא בעי למימר דליתא לדרב פפי אלא דליתא לקושיא שאין לדמות אשרתא שהוא מעשה ב"ד לשאר שטרות דבמעשה ב"ד לכ"ע חיישינן למיחזי [א] כשקרא ור"י מדנפי"ר מירך לכתחלה ולאו חיישינן למיחזי כשקרא כדאמר להו רב לספרי כי יתביתו בהיני כו' (ב"ב דף קעב.) אבל בדיעבד לא חיישינן ולהכי פריך הכא דהוי לכתחלה והא דקאמר ליתא לדרב פפי היינו דיעבד דההיא דהכותב (לקמן דף פה. ושם) כיון שהיתה צריכה לחזור לב"ד כדיעבד דמי והרשאה נמי דכתבינן אמטלטלי דכפריה היינו משום כיון דאינו יכול לילך שם כדיעבד דמי [ב]: **וש"מ** דיינין המכירין חתימת עדים א"צ להעיד בפניהם. דקס"ד דצריך להעיד בפניהם אע"ג דלא תהא שמיעה גדולה מראייה לפי שהיו נראין יותר בית דין דכשאין מעידין בפניהם אין נראה אלא כעד מפי עד ומטעם זה הצריכו ג' בקיום שטרות דהוה סגי בב' אלא משום דבעינן שיהא ב"ד כדפרישית ועוד אומר ר"י דס"ד דלרי' להעיד בפניהם משום דפעמים אין מכירין אלא על ידי שראו בלילה דליכא למימר לא תהא שמיעה גדולה מראייה דשמיעה אינה יכולה להיות בלילה כדאמר בר"ה (דף כה: ושם) דמקדשת עדים כתחלת דין דמי ותחלת דין אינו אלא ביום כדאמרינן בסנהדרין (דף לב.): **בפני** כל אחד ואחד. דס"ד כיון שהעידו בפני שנים יכול השלישי לכתוב על סמך השנים אע"פ שלא העידו בפניו: **הנח** לעדות החדש דאורייתא. ודאורייתא אין עד נעשה דיין וטעמא דאין עד נעשה דיין משום דבעינן שיעידו לפני הדיינין כמו שמפרש רשב"ם דכתיב ועמדו שני האנשים אלו העדים לפני ה' אלו הדיינין וי"מ משום דבעינן עדות שאתה יכול להזימה ואם העדים נעשו דיינין עדות שאין אתה יכול להזימה היא שלא יקבלו הזמה על עצמן ומיהו לפי טעם זה אם העדים קרובים לדיינין אינם יכולים להעיד דלא יקבלו הזמה עליהם אלא כיון דבני הזמה נינהו בב"ד אחר עדות שאתה יכול להזימה קרינא בהו וה"נ יהיה הדיין נעשה עד [ח] ודוקא בעד המעיד אמרינן דאין עד נעשה דיין דשייכי הני טעמי אבל עד שאינו צריך להעיד כגון שיש אחרים שיעידו או כגון שראוהו ביום שאינו צריך להעיד דלא תהא שמיעה גדולה מראייה נעשה דיין ודווקא בדיני ממונות אבל בדיני נפשות אפילו עד שאין צריך להעיד אין נעשה דיין לר"ע דאמר במסכת מכות (דף ו. ושם) אפילו הן מאה כולן עדים וטעמא מפרש בפרק ראוהו ב"ד (ר"ה דף כו. ושם) משום דכתיב והצילו העדה והכא כיון דחזו דקטל תו לא חזי ליה זכותא ודווקא בדאורייתא אבל בדרבנן אפילו עד המעיד נעשה דיין:

תרי

איקלע רבנאי אחוה דר' חייא בר אבא למזבן שומשמי ואמר הכי אמר שמואל עד ודיין מצטרפין אמר אמימר כמה מעליא הא שמעתא אמר ליה רב אשי לאמימר משום דקלסה אבוה דאמך את נמי מקלסת לה כבר פרכה רבא: אמר רב ספרא אמר רבי אבא אמר רב הונא ואמרי ליה אמר רב יצחק בר שמואל בר מרתא אמר רב הונא ואמרי ליה אמר רב הונא אמר רב [א] שלשה שישבו לקיים את השטר שנים מכירין חתימות ידי עדים ואחד אינו מכיר עד שלא חתמו מעידין בפניו וחותם משחתמו אין מעידין בפניו וחותם ומי כתבינן והאמר רב פפי משמיה דרבא [ב] האי אשרתא דדייני דניכתב מקמיה דניחזו סהדי אחתימת ידייהו פסולה דמתחזי כשקרא הכא נמי מתחזי כשקרא אלא אימא עד שלא כתבו מעידין בפניו וחותם משכתבו אין מעידין בפניו וחותם ש"מ תלת ש"מ [ג] עד נעשה דיין וש"מ [ד] דיינין המכירין חתימות ידי עדים אינן צריכין להעיד בפניהם וש"מ דיינין שאין מכירין חתימות ידי עדים צריכין להעיד בפני כל אחד ואחד מתקיף לה רב אשי בשלמא עד נעשה דיין שמעינן מינה אלא דיינין המכירין חתימות ידי עדים אין צריכין להעיד בפניהם דלמא לעולם אימא לך צריכין ושאני הכא דקא מקיימא הגדה בחד ודיינין שאין מכירין חתימות ידי עדים צריכין להעיד בפני כל אחד ואחד דלמא לעולם אימא לך אין צריכין ושאני הכא דלא קא מקיימא הגדה כלל יתיב ר' אבא וקאמר לה להא שמעתא דעד נעשה דיין איתיביה רב ספרא לרבי אבא [ה] ראוהו שלשה והן בית דין יעמדו שנים ויושיבו מחבריהם אצל היחיד ויעידו בפניהם ויאמרו מקודש החדש מקודש שאין היחיד נאמן על ידי עצמו ואי סלקא דעתך דעד נעשה דיין למה לי כולי האי ליתבו בדוכתייהו וליקדשי אמר ליה אף לדידי קשיא לי ושאילתיה לרב יצחק בר שמואל בר מרתא ורב יצחק לרב הונא ורב הונא לחייא בר רב וחייא בר רב לרב ואמר להו הנח [ד] לעדות החדש דאורייתא [ז] וקיום שטרות דרבנן אמר רבי אבא אמר רב הונא אמר רב [ו] שלשה שישבו לקיים את השטר וקרא ערער על אחד מהן עד שלא חתמו מעידין עליו וחותם משחתמו אין מעידין עליו וחותם ערער דמאי אי ערער דגזלנותא

תרי

איקלע רבנאי למיזבן שומשמי גרסי' ולא גרסי' דאיקלע ולא גרסינן לגבן ולאו רמי אמרה דא"א לומר כן שאמר רמי עדות זו על אמימר ורב אשי שהרי רב אשי כמה דורות היה אחריו דאמרינן בקדושין (דף עב:) יום שמת רב יהודה נולד רבא יום שמת רבא נולד רב אשי: **אבוה דאמך.** רמי בר חמא: **שלשה שישבו.** בב"ד: **לקיים השטר.** ובלא העדאת עדים שיעידו על כתב ידן לפי שהדיינין עצמן מכירין אותה השנים מכירין אותה והאחד אינו מכיר: **עד שלא חתמו.** השנים על ההנפק: **מעידין.** לפני השלישי שזהו כתב ידן של חתומים: **וחותם.** עמהם על מה שכותבין אשרנוהי וקיימנוהי לשטרא דנן במותב תלתא הוינא דאשתמודענא דחתימת ידא דסהדי היא: **משחתמו אין מעידין.** דחתימה קמייתא כשקרא הוה דלאו תלתא הוו דידעי: **ומי כתבינן.** לאשרתא דידיה בחתימה וכי קודם שנתקיים לפני שלשתן יכתבו במותב תלתא הוינא ואשתמודענא כו': **אשרתא.** לשון חוזק שמחזקים [את השטר] וכותבין אשרנוהי: **דנכתבא** מקמי דניחזו סהדי כו'. עד שלא העידו העדים על כתב ידם כתבו הדיינין במותב תלתא הוינא ונפיק שטרא דנן קדמנא ואסהידו פלוני ופלוני אחתימת ידייהו ואשרנוהי וקיימנוהי: **עד נעשה דיין.** שהרי השנים העידו על החתימות: **צריכין להעיד בפני כל אחד ואחד.** שאם העידו בפני השנים אין הג' יכול לחתום דהא הכא הוצרכו השנים להעיד בפני הג': **דלמא לעולם צריכין.** להעיד שאין עדות אלא ע"י הגדת עדות: **ושאני הכא דקא מקיימא הגדה.** בפני היחיד שאינו מכיר: **דלא מקיימא הגדה כלל.** אי לא הוו מסהדי בהפיה: **ראוהו ג'.** בעדות החדש קאי: **והן בית דין.** מסנהדרין המקדשין את החדש: **יעמדו השנים.** להיות עדים שהרי פרכינן לא תהא שמיעה גדולה מראיה ומוקמינן לה כשראוהו בלילה לפיכך אם לא יעידו לבקר על מה יאמרו מקודש: **שאין היחיד נאמן.** לקדש ביחידי: **ליתבו בדוכתייהו.** אחר שהעידו בפניו: **וקרא ערער על הא'.** שהוא פסול: **עד שלא חתמו.** השני דיינים על האשרתא: **מעידין.** על זה שהוא כשר: **משחתמו.** הוו להו נוגעין בעדות שמגנאי להם שישבו עם פסול בדין:

מסורת הש"ס

א) גיטין כו: לקמן פה. [ועי' בטוש"ע ח"מ סימן מו סעיף כד ובש"ך ובסמ"ע שם], ב) סנהדרין לד: ר"ה כו. גיטין ה: ב"ק ל: ב"ב קיד., ג) ר"ה כה:, ד) [לקמן כח. ע"ש בתוס'], ה) [וע"ע בתוס' ב"מ קיג. ד"ה מחזיר], ו) [פי' הרשאה], ז) [וע"ע תוס' גיטין כו. ד"ה ליתא וב"מ יב: ד"ה כותבין], ח) [וע"ע מ"ש תוס' ב"ק ל: ד"ה כגון שראוהו בלילה כו' טעם אחר בשם ר"י דנפקא לן מביום הנחילו כו'].

תוספות ישנים

א) [והיא דהכותב לא חשיב מעשה ב"ד דבעדים סגי שיעידו שנשבעה. ת"י].

ליקוטי רש"י

ורבנן לחומרא. דצריך שנים מן השוק להעיד על חתימת יד המת והאי יעיד הוא לבדו על חתימת ידו אבל העד החי לא יצטרף עם אחר מן השוק להעיד על חתימת המת [רשב"ם שם]. **שנים החתומין** וכו' **ושדי ליה בבי דינא.** אמר אביי לא לחוי איניש חתימת ידיה כו', אדם שצריך לכתוב חתימת ידו על קלף ולהשליך לבית דין כדי שיכירו בית דין חתימתו כי ההיא דאמרינן בכתובות בפרק האשה שנתארמלה (דף כא.) כגון ראובן ושמעון שהיו חתומין בשטר ומת שמעון ואין מי שיכיר חתימת שמעון אלא ראובן ואחד מן השוק ואמרינן התם שיכתוב ראובן כתב ידו וישליכהו לבית דין ובית דין מקיימין חתימת ידי ראובן הכתוב בשטר מכתב ידו שהשליך בב"ד ואין צריך ראובן להעיד על כתב ידו שבשטר זה כתב ידי ובאין ראובן ואחד מן השוק ומעידין על חתימת שמעון ואמר אביי כשיחתום ראובן להשליך לב"ד לא יחתום בסוף הקלף אלא בתחלתו שלא יהא חלק מלמעלה שמא ימצאנו אדם רע ויכתוב בחלק שלמעלה מחתימתו אני החתום לויתי מפלוני כך וכך ממון ותנן הוציא עליו כתב ידו כו' והיינו חתימת ידו כדתנן (גיטין דף עא) כתב סופר ועד כשר ואמר ר' ירמיה חתם סופר שנינו [שם קסז.]. **חספא.** חרס [חולין קה:]. **הוציא עליו.** מלוה. **כתב ידו.** של לוה שהוא חייב לו ממון ואין כאן עדות אחרת. **גובה מנכסים בני חורין.** דלא גובה ממשועבדים אלא מלוה הכתוב בשטר שיש בו עדים דכיון דאיכא תרתי שטר ועדים מפקי ליה לקלא ולקוחות הוא דאפסידו אנפשייהו שלא חקרו בדבר ויניחו בני חרי למוכר לגבות מהם [רשב"ם ב"ב קעה:]. **דאע"ג דהלכה כרבי מחבירו.** קא משמע לן במקום יחיד אין הלכה כמותו מחביריו כלומר במקום רבים [פסחים כז.]. [ע"כ שייך לע"א] **אשרתא.** לשון חוזק כמו יישר כחך (יבמות סב.) קיום השטר שכותבין דיינין במותב תלתא הוינא ואתא פלוני ופלוני ואסהידו אחתימות ידייהו ואשרנוהו וקיימנוהו [לקמן פה.]. קיום השטר שהעדים מעידין על כתב ידיהם בב"ד וב"ד כותבין בו במותב תלתא הוינא ואתו פלוני ופלוני ואסהידו אחתימות ידייהו ואשרנוהי וקיימנוהי כדחזי ומותמן [גיטין כו:]. **דניחזו.** שיעידו זה כתב ידי [לקמן שם]. **עד נעשה דיין.** מי שראוי להיות עד בדבר נעשה דיין. **ויעידו בפניהם.** השנים. **ויאמרו.** השלשה [רשב"ם ב"ב קיד.]. **שאין היחיד נאמן.** לומר מקודש דאין יחיד דן לבד [ר"ה כה:]. **וקיום שטרות דרבנן.** אלו המחתימים על השטר נעשה כמי שנתקרה עדותן בב"ד [לקמן כח.]

על כתב ידן הם מעידים לדברי חכמים על מנה שבשטר הם מעידים פשיטא מהו דתימא לרבי ספוקי מספקא ליה אי על כתב ידם הם מעידים או על מנה שבשטר הם מעידים ונפקא מינה היכא דמית חד מינייהו לבעי שנים מן השוק להעיד עליו דאם כן קנפיק נכי ריבעא דממונא אפומא דחד סהדא והכא לחומרא והכא לחומרא קמ"ל דרבי מיפשט פשיטא ליה בין לקולא בין לחומרא דאמר רב יהודה אמר רב שנים החתומין על השטר ומת אחד מהן צריכין שנים מן השוק להעיד עליו בזו רבי לקולא ורבנן לחומרא ואי ליכא תרי אלא חד מאי אמר אביי לכתוב חתימת ידיה אחספא ושדיו ליה בבי דינא (א) ומחזקי ליה בי דינא (וחזו ליה) ולא צריך איהו לאסהודי אחתימת ידיה ואזיל איהו והאי ומסהדי אאידך ודוקא אחספא אבל אמגלתא לא דלמא משכח לה איניש דלא מעלי וכתב עילויה מאי דבעי ותנן הוציא עליו כתב ידו שהוא חייב לו גובה מנכסים בני חורין א"ר יהודה אמר שמואל הלכה כדברי חכמים פשיטא יחיד ורבים הלכה כרבים מהו דתימא הלכה כרבי מחבירו ואפילו מחביריו קא משמע לן: סימן נח נד חד: אמר ליה רב חננא בר חייא לרב יהודה ואמרי לה רב הונא בר יהודה לרב יהודה ואמרי לה רב חייא בר יהודה לרב יהודה ומי אמר שמואל הכי והא ההוא שטרא דנפיק מבי דינא דמר שמואל והוה כתיב ביה מדאתא רב חייא ואסהיד אחתימות ידיה ואדחד דעמיה ומנו רב חנן בר רבה ומדאתא רב חנן בר רבה ואסהיד אחתימות ידיה ואדחד דעמיה ומנו רב ענן בר חייא אשרנוהי וקימנוהי כדחזי א"ל ההוא שטרא דיתמי הוה וחש שמואל לב"ד טוען וסבר שמואל דלמא איכא דסבירא ליה הלכה כרבי מחבירו ולא מחביריו ובהא אפילו מחביריו סבר אעביד רווחא כי היכי דלא מפסדי יתמי אמר רב יהודה אמר שמואל עד ודיין מצטרפין אמר רמי בר חמא כמה מעליא הא שמעתא אמר רבא מאי מעליותא מאי דקא מסהיד סהדא לא קא מסהיד דיינא ומאי דקא מסהיד דיינא לא קא מסהיד סהדא אלא כי אתא רמי בר יחזקאל אמר לא תציתינהו להני כללי דכייל יהודה אחי משמיה דשמואל איקלע

על כתב ידן הן מעידין. להעיד כשמקיימין השטר בב"ד לפיכך צריך שנים על כל כתב וכתב: לדברי חכמים על מנה שבשטר הם מעידים. אנחנו ראינו המלוה ומתחנו הלכך בתרי סגי ולא צריך חד מינייהו לאסהודי אחבריה: מהו דתימא לרבי ספוקי מספקא ליה אי על כתב ידן. אנו זוקקין שיעידו: או על מנה שבשטר. ומשום שמא על כתב ידן הן מעידין מצריך תרי לכל כתב וכתב ומיפשט מיהא לא פשיטא ליה: ונפקא מינה. בין ספק לודאי לשנים החתומים על השטר ומת אחד מהן צריך שנים מן השוק להעיד עליו ואין זה כשר להעיד על כתב ידו ועל של חבירו ולצרף אחד עמו שיעיד על שתיהן דדלמא על מנה שבשטר הן מעידין וכי אומר זה כתב ידי נפיק פלגא דממונא אפומיה וזה שמעיד עמו על חתימתו לא מעלה ולא מוריד דלאו צריך לו וכי הדר מצטרף עם ההוא מן השוק להעיד על חתימת המת הדר נפיק ריבעא דממונא אפומיה אשתכח דכולא ממונא נכי ריבעא נפיק אפומיה ואנן ע"פ שנים עדים בעינן אלי דבר על פיו של זה ואלי דבר על פיו של זה הלכך ניבעי תרי דכיון דספיקא היא ניזיל הכא לחומרא והכא לחומרא היכא דשניהם קיימים אזלינן לחומרא ואמרינן על כתב ידן הן מעידין ובעינן תרין על כל כתב וכתב והיכא דמית חד מינייהו בעינן תרין מן השוק שיעיד האחד על כתב יד המת ואחד מהן יעיד על כתב יד המת והאי דלאי הוה פשיטא לן דעל כתב ידן הן מעידין הוי סגי בחד מן השוק שיעיד על שתי החתימות והאי יעיד גם הוא על שתיהם ולא נפיק כולא ממונא נכי ריבעא אפומא דחד דלאו נמי צריך לאותו מן השוק שיעיד על חתימתו אבל השתא דמספקא לן דלמא על מנה שבשטר הן מעידין ועל כתב ידו הוא נאמן ואין צריך לצירוף ועוד אנו צריכים לו שיעיד על חותם המת נפקי תלתא ריבעי אפומיה אי ליכא תרין מן השוק שלא יהא זה צריך להעיד על המת קמ"ל דפשיטא ליה וסגי בחד מן השוק ושניהם יעידו על שתיהן: בין לקולא. כי הכא דאלו לרבנן בעי שנים מן השוק שיעידו על של מת וזה לבדו יעיד על חתימתו: נכי ריבעא. חסר ריבעא: צריך שנים. לדברי חכמים: ואי ליכא שנים. שיכירו כתב המת: אלא חד. וזה השני נמי מכירה מאי ניעביד: לכתוב. זה שנשאר בחיים: חתימת ידיה אחספא ונשדייה בבי דינא. ויטלוה הדיינים ויקיפוה אצל חתימתו שבשטר: ומחזקי. ההיא דשטרא מהך דאחספא דלא צריך לאסהודי אחתימת ידיה: וכתב עליה מאי דבעי. למעלה מן החתימה יכתוב שזה החתום לוה ממנו מנה וכותב כך אני פלוני החתום למטה לויתי מנה מפלוני: מנכסים בני חורין. וממשעבדי לא דלית ליה קלא לדבר שאינו עשוי בעדים: מהו דתימא. כי היכי דהלכה כרבי מחבירו ה"נ אפילו מחביריו: דנפיק מבי דינא דמר שמואל. שקיימוהו בבית דינו וכך נמצא כתוב בהנפק שכתבו הדיינים בו: מדאתא רב ענן כו'. אלמא כרבי ס"ל שצריך לומר זה כתב ידי וזה כתב ידו של חבירי: שטרא דיתמי הוה. שהולך לעיין בתקנתם: וחש שמואל. שאם לא כתב בו אלא פלוני העיד על כתב ידו ופלוני על כתב ידו שמא כשיוציאו היתומים שטר זה בב"ד לגבות יהא אותו ב"ד טועה לומר שהלכה כרבי ויאמרו שאין זה קיום: איכא דס"ל. בעלמא ולא מחביריו ובהא אפי' מחביריו: עד ודיין. שטר שכתוב בו הנפק וחתמו הדיינין על הנפק שלו ולאחר זמן כשהוציאו המלוה לגבות ערער הלוה לומר מזויף הוא ובא אחד מעדי השטר והעיד על כתב ידו ואחד מן הדיינים העיד על כתב ידו מצטרפין להכשירו: מאי דקא מסהיד סהדא כו'. עדי השטר מעידין על מנה שבשטר כרבנן והדיינין מעידין בפנינו נתקיים: רב יהודה אחוה דרמי בר יחזקאל הוה: איקלע

על כתב ידן הן מעידין. נראה לרבי דאפילו אומרים בפירוש דמעידין על מנה שבשטר חשיב כאילו מעידין על כתב ידן וכן לרבנן אפי' אומרי' בהדיא דעל כתב ידן הן מעידין מדאמרי' בסמוך ואי ליכא תרי אלא חד היכי נעביד משמע דלא יועיל לרבנן אם יעידו בהדיא על כתב ידן: **ודוקא** אחספא. וה"ה ארישא דמגלתא כדאמר בגט פשוט (ב"ב דף קסז. ושם) דליכא למיחש למידי והא דתניא בפ"ק דקדושין (דף ט. ושם) כתב על הנייר או על החרס בתך מקודשת לי כו' וכן גבי שדה (שם ט.) כתב על הנייר או על החרס כו' הרי זה מכורה נראה דאתיא כר"מ דאמר ז) עדי מסירה כרתי דלר"מ כיון דעדי חתימה כרתי לא מהני על דבר שיכול לזייף כדאמר בפרק ב' דגיטין (דף כב: ושם) אין כותבין לא על הנייר כו' וחכמים מכשירין ומפרש בגמרא ח) מאן חכמים ר"א ואע"ג דאמר התם שלא הכשיר ר"א אלא בגיטין אבל בשאר שטרות לא ה"פ אלא בגיטין ודכוותייהו דהיינו שטרות שאין עומדין לראיה כגון אותו שאינו עשוי אלא לקנות בו אשה ושדה כעין גיטין שעשוין לפי שעה לגרש בו אע"פ שיכול השטר של קנין להועיל לראיה גם הגט יכול להועיל כדאמר בהכותב (לקמן דף פה:) ובפ"ק דב"מ (דף יח. ושם) וכ"ש נקרעיה בעינא לאיטנוסי ביה אלא שעיקרן לא לכך נעשו ולא ממעט אלא שטרות שעיקרן לראיה ועשוין לעמוד ימים רבים כדמייתי התם קרא ונתתם בכלי חרש וגו': **הוציא** עליו כתב ידו שהוא חייב לו גובה מנכסים בני חורין. פסק ר"ח אלפס דווקא כשאומר לא היו דברים מעולם אבל נאמן הוא לומר פרעתי ולא מצי א"ל שטרך בידי מאי בעי אלא בשטר שיש בו עדים דגובה בו מנכסים משועבדים ואין נראה לרבינו יצחק כי מנין לו זה החילוק כי סבר דבכל שטר אינו רגיל לפרוע עד שיחזיר לו שטרו: **עד** ודיין מצטרפין. משמע דאפילו בשטר מקויים חיישינן שמא זייף לחתימת הדיינין וכן משמע בירושלמי דגיטין ובפרק בן סורר והא דתניא בתוספתא דשביעית פרוזבול המקושר ר' יהודה אומר עדים חותמין מבחוץ והדיינים מבפנים אמרו לו אין מעשה בית דין צריך קיום היינו דווקא בפרוזבול משום דנאמן אדם לומר פרוזבול היה לי ואבד ואפי' למ"ד אינו נאמן מודה הוא דלא בעי קיום: האמר

מסורת הש"ס

א) רש"ל מ"ז, ב) ב"ב קעה:, ג) [ברכות ע. וש"נ], ד) [לקמן נא. עירובין מו: פסחים מ. ב"ב קכד:], ה) [יבמות קו. ב"ב קלט: קסד. סנהדרין ל.], ו) גי' רש"ל אמר ליה רבא, ז) [גיטין פו.], ח) [שם כב.].

הגהות הב"ח

(א) גמ' ושדי ליה בבי דינא וחזו ליה ומחזקי ליה בי דינא ולא צריך כצ"ל:

גליון הש"ס

גמ' אבל אמגלתא לא. עיין ב"ב דף קס ע"א תוס' ד"ה מקושר עדיו מאחוריו: שם כמה מעליא. כעין זה שבועות דף מו ע"ב: שם לא תציתינהו. לקמן דף ס ע"א ודף עו ע"ב חולין דף מד ע"א:

ליקוטי רש"י

היכא דמית וכו' קנפיק וכו'. דקי"ל נאמן אדם לומר זה כתב ידי הרי אלי עדות ואם בא להצטרף להעיד על חותם חבירו עם אחר הרי ג' רביעית העדות על פיו ורחמנא אמר (דברים יז) על פי שנים דמשמע פלגא אפומא דהאי ופלגא אפומא דהאי [גיטין טו:]. דכיון דעל מנה שבשטר הן מעידין וכי אמר זה כתב ידי נפקא פלגא דממונא אפומיה שהרי הוא לבדו מעיד על חתימתו ואין צריך אחר להעיד עמו וכי הדר מצטרף עם ההוא מן השוק להעיד על חתימת המת הדר נפיק ריבעא דממונא על פומיה אשתכח דכוליה ממונא נכי ריבעא נפק אפומיה ואנן על פי שנים עדים בעינן אלי דבר על פיו של זה ואלי דבר על פיו של זה והלכך הכא דשכיב חד מינייהו אין עד החי יכול להצטרף עם אחר מן השוק להעיד על חתימת יד המת אלא צריך שנים מן השוק להעיד עליו [רשב"ם ב"ב נז.]. נכי ריבעא דממונא. כל הממון יוצא על פיו חסר רביע [גיטין שם].

[המשך בע"ב]

עין משפט נר מצוה

מג א ב מיי' פ"ז מהל' עדות הלכה ג סמג עשין קט טוש"ע ח"מ סימן מו סעיף י יא:

מד ג ד מיי' שם הל' ה טוש"ע שם סעיף יג:

מה ה טוש"ע שם סי' סט סעיף ב:

מו ו מיי' פי"א מהל' מלוה ולוה הלכה ג ופכ"ז הלכה ב סמג עשין לד טוש"ע שם סימן לט סעיף א וסימן סט סעיף א:

מז ז מיי' פ"ד מהלכות עדות הלכה ו סמג עשין קט טוש"ע ח"מ סימן ל סעיף יב וסימן מו סעיף יד:

תוספות רי"ד

ת"ר כותב אדם עדותו על השטר ומעיד עליה אפילו לאחר כמה שנים פי' אם עשהו עד בדבר ויירא לשכחו כותבו על חתיכת קלף ומצניעה ומעיד ע"פ אותו כתב אפילו לאחר כמה שנים א"ר הונא והוא שזוכרה מעצמו פי' בלא ראיית השטר זוכר קצת מעדיותו מאליו ואין זה מדבר משטר שיצא מת"י ומסרו למלוה או ללוקח דהתם אע"ג דלא דכירי לסהדותייהו כלל כיון שמעיד שזה כת"י ומקיים חתימתו או אחרים מעידין על חתימתו השטר קיים ואף על פי שאינו זוכר עדותו ואע"פ שמת חתימתו קיימת שעדים המעידים על השטר נעשה כמי שנחקרה עדותן בב"ד ולא מיירי הכא אלא בעודו תחת ידו כגון ספר זכרונות שאדם כותב בו עסקיו שלא ישכחם גם העדות זו שנאמרה לו בפה כתבה שם שלא ישכחנה ומ"ה א"ר הונא והוא שזוכרה מעצמו אבל אם שכחה בטל כתבו ואל יראה ויעיד מתוך כתבו ואהני ליה כתבא שיעיין שם לפרקים ולא (יטרחנה) [ישכחנה] ור"י אמר אף על פי שאינו זוכרה מעצמו פי' אלא לאחר שראה השטר נותן בלבו ויזכיר שלא נשתכחה ממנו כל כך רק כשמזכירים אותו נזכר אבל אם אינו נזכר כלל לא דהכי אמרינן בפרק ד' אחין לינחוהו גבי עדים אם מדכירי ליתי ולסהודי ואי לא זמנין דחזי מכתבא ומסהדי ורחמנא אמר מפיהם ולא מפי כתבם: (ארב"א) [אמר רבא] שמע מיניה מר' יוחנן הני תרי דידעי בסהדותא ומינשי חד מינייהו מדכיר ליה חברי' ומדכר איבעיא להו מלוה בעצמו מאי פי' אם בעל דין מזכירו עד שנזכר מאי ר"ח אמר אפילו מלוה בעצמו מר בר אשי אמר (אפי') מלוה בעצמו לא והלכתא מלוה בעצמו לא ואי צורבא מרבנן אפילו מלוה בעצמו פי' דאי לאו רמי אנפשי' ומדכיר שפיר לא הוי סמיך אספיקא למיקם לאסהודי כי הא דרב אשי הו"ל סהדותא לרב כהנא א"ל מדכיר מר ההוא סהדותא א"ל לא א"ל ולאו הכי והכי הוה א"ל לא ידענא לסוף אדכיר ר"א ואזיל אסהיד ליה חזי' לרב כהנא דהוה קא

מהסם פי' מגמגם פי' לתמוה על ר"א שהעיד בדבר א"ל מי סברת עלך קסמכנא אנא רמאי אנפשאי ואידכרי עיין בפסקי בפרק ד' אחין: **מתני' זה אומר** זה כתב ידי וזה כתב ידו של חבירי וזה אומר זה כת"י וזה כת"י של חבירי הרי אלו נאמנים זה אומר זה כתב ידי וזה אומר זה כת"י צריכים שיצטרף אחר עמהן דברי רבי וחכ"א אין צריכין לצרף עמהן אחר אלא נאמן אדם לומר זה כתב ידי. רבי סבר תרי סהדי בעי' אכל חתימה וחתימה הלכך אם כל אחד העיד על שלו ועל של חבירו יש שני עדים אכל חתימה וחתימה ואם כל אחד ואחד מעיד על שלו ולא על של חבירו צריכים לצרף עמהן אחר שיכיר שתי החתימות שיבואו על כל חתימה שני עדים. וחכמים סברי כל אחד נאמן על חתימתו שבוודאי כשבאו העדים לקיים חתימת עדים אחרים צריכים להיות שנים על כל חתימה וחתימה אבל כשעדי השטר הן בעצמן מקיימין חתימתן אין צריכין צירוף אלא כל אחד נאמן לומר זה כתב ידי ופריש תלמודא טעמייהו **כשתמצא** לומר לדברי רבי על כת"י הן מעידין ולפיכך צריך שיצטרף עמהן אחר ולדברי חכמים על מנה שבשטר הן מעידין והרי הם שנים ופי' המורה שהם זקוקין לומר אנחנו ראינו המלוה והחתמנו ואינו נ"ל שבין שזוכרין אותה ומעידין עליה בין אין זוכרין אותה שכבר שכחו העדות אלא שמכירין חתימתן ומעידין עליה. פליגי רבי ורבנן רבי סבר אע"פ שזוכרים הלואה ומעידים עליה אפ"ה על כת"י מעידין שאם לא יקיימו החתימה הוה לה מלוה ע"פ ולא טרפא ממשעבדי א"נ מצי אידך למיטען פרעתי הלכך זקוקים אנו לעדותן לומר מכירים אנו חתימתינו ולשויי שטרא מעליא למיטרף מן הלקוחות ושלא לטעון פרעתי ורבנן סברי לא מיבעי אם זוכרים המלוה ומעידים עליה אלא אע"פ שאין זוכרים אותה כי אם מכירין חתימתן על מנה שבשטר מעידין שמתחלה כשחתמו העידו כל אחד על המנה גם עתה שבאים לקיים חתימתן כל עדותן אינה באה אלא על המנה א) ואע"פ שעכשיו אינן זוכרין אותו שכיון שבאים לקיים החתימה שנעשית על המנה נמצא שכל עדותן על זו הוא: **אר"י אמר שמואל** הל' כחכמים פשיטא יחיד ורבים הלכה כרבים מ"ד הל' כרבי מחבירו ב) ובהא אפי' מחביריו קמ"ל: **אר"י א"ר** שנים החתומים על השטר ומת אחד מהן צריכים שנים מן השוק להעיד עליו ואל יצטרף הוא עם א' כי היכי דלא ליפוק נכי רבעא דממונא אפומא דחד סהדא פי' הוא שהעיד על חתימתו נאמן וא"צ לצירוף מן השוק להעיד על חתימתו עכשיו ואם יצטרף הוא עם אחר נמצא שיצאו שלשת חלקי המנה שבשטר ע"פ זה והתורה אמרה על פי שנים עדים יקום דבר חצי דבר ע"פ זה וחצי דבר ע"פ זה ופי' נכי חסר: **ואי** ליכא אלא חד מהו פי' שמכירה מאי לעבד אמר אביי כותב האיך פי' שנשאר בחיים חתימות ידו אחספא ושדי ליה בב"ד וחזי ליה ב"ד פי' ויטלוה הדיינים ויקיפוה אצל חתימות שבשטר ומחזקי ליה פי' ההיא דשטרא מהך דחספא ולא יצטריך איהו לאסהודי אחתימות ידיה ואזיל איהו והאי ומסהיד אאידך ודוקא אחספא אבל אמגילתא לא דלמא משכח ליה איניש דלא מעלי וכתב עלויה מה דבעי ותנן הוציא עליו כת"י שהוא חייב לו גובה מנכסים בנ"ח פי' ממשעבדי לא דל"ל קלא שאינו עשוי בעדים וכן נמי יכול לכתוב אריש מגילתא כדאמרי' בפ' ג"פ האי מאן דמחזי חתימות ידיה בב"ד לא לחזי בסוף מגילתא אלא ברישא דלמא משכח ליה אחר וכתב אגבי' דמסיק בי' פי' יכתוב מלמעלה אני החתום לויתי מפלוני מנה עיין בפ"ק דקדושין בהלכה ובשטר (דף כ"ו): **אר"י א"ש** עד ודיין מצטרפים פי' ראובן שהוציא על שמעון שטר חתום ואשרתא דדייני מלמטה שחתמו הדיינים שם שקיימו החתימה וטען שמעון איני מכיר לא חתימת העדים ולא חתימת הדיינים ושמא הוא זייף הכל ובא ע"א מעדי השטר והעיד על חתימתו ואחד מן הדיינים בא והעיד על חתימתו מצטרפים זה עם זה דכולהו לקיומא שטרא אתי. **אמר רמב"ח** כמה מעליא האי שמעתא א"ל מאי מעליותא מאי דמסהיד סהדא לא מסהיד דיינא ומאי דמסהיד דיינא לא מסהיד סהדא. אלא כי אתא רמי בר יחזקאל אמר לא תציתו להו להני כללי דכייל יהודה אחי משמי' דשמואל

חשק שלמה על תוס' רי"ד א) והיינו כדעת הראב"ד בהשגות פ"ח מהלכות עדות הלכה ד' ע"ש. ב) נראה דרבינו היה גורס כאן ובהא אפילו מחביריו וכ"ה הגירסא באמת בפסחים מ.

the following **was written on it** as the court's text of certification: מִדְּאָתָא רַב עָנָן בַּר חִיָּיא וְאַסְהֵיד אַחֲתִימוּת יְדֵיהּ – **"Since Rav Anan bar Chiya came and testified about** the authenticity of **his signature** וְאַדְּחַד דְּעִמֵּיהּ וּמַנּוּ רַב חָנָן בַּר רַבָּה – **and about** the authenticity of the signature **of the one** who signed **with him** – **and who is he** – it is **Rav Chanan bar Rabbah;** וּמִדְּאָתָא רַב חָנָן בַּר רַבָּה וְאַסְהֵיד אַחֲתִימוּת יְדֵיהּ – **and since Rav Chanan bar Rabbah came and testified about** the authenticity of **his signature** וְאַדְּחַד דְּעִמֵּיהּ וּמַנּוּ רַב עָנָן בַּר חִיָּיא – **and about** the authenticity of the signature **of the one** who signed **with him** – **and who is he** – it is **Rav Anan bar Chiya;** אִשַּׁרְנוּהִי וְקַיְּמְנוּהִי כִּדְחָזֵי – **we reinforced it and certified it as fit."** Thus, we see that Shmuel required each of the signed witnesses to testify about his fellow's signature as well as his own, in accordance with Rebbi's view. – ? –

Rav Yehudah defends his quote:

אֲמַר לֵיהּ – **He replied:** הַהוּא שְׁטָרָא דְּיַתְמֵי הֲוָה – **That** certified document to which you refer **was a document of orphans,** וְחָשׁ שְׁמוּאֵל לְבֵית דִּין טוֹעִין – **and Shmuel was concerned about an erring court.**[16] וְסָבַר שְׁמוּאֵל דִּלְמָא אִיכָּא דִּסְבִירָא לֵיהּ הֲלָכָה כְּרַבִּי מֵחֲבֵירוֹ וְלֹא מֵחֲבֵירָיו – **For Shmuel thought** that **perhaps there is** a court **that holds that** although **the halachah** normally **follows Rebbi over his colleague but not over his colleagues,** וּבְהָא אֲפִילּוּ מֵחֲבֵירָיו – **in this** case the halachah follows Rebbi **even over his colleagues.**[17] סָבַר אַעֲבִיד רַוְוחָא כִּי הֵיכִי דְּלָא מַפְסְדֵי יַתְמֵי – **[Shmuel]** therefore **thought, "I will leave a margin** for error **in order that the orphans should not suffer a loss."**[18]

The Gemara cites another ruling of Rav Yehudah in the name of Shmuel concerning the certification of documents:

אָמַר רַב יְהוּדָה אָמַר שְׁמוּאֵל – **Rav Yehudah said in the name of Shmuel:** עֵד וְדַיָּין מִצְטָרְפִין – **A witness** who signed a document **and a judge** who signed its certification **can combine** to authenticate it.[19]

The Gemara records a reaction to this ruling:

אָמַר רָמִי בַּר חָמָא – **Rami bar Chama said:** כַּמָּה מְעַלְיָא הָא שְׁמַעְתָּא – **How excellent this teaching** is!

An objection is cited:

אָמַר רָבָא – **Rava said:** מַאי מְעַלְיוּתָא – **What is** its **excellence?** To the contrary, it is difficult, מַאי דְּקָא מַסְהִיד סַהֲדָא לָא קָא מַסְהִיד דַּיָּינָא – for **that which the witness testifies** about **the judge does not testify** about, וּמַאי דְּקָא מַסְהִיד דַּיָּינָא לָא קָא מַסְהִיד סַהֲדָא – **and that which the judge testifies** about **the witness does not testify** about.[20] How can their testimonies be combined?

The Gemara therefore rejects Rav Yehudah's ruling:

אֶלָּא כִּי אֲתָא רָמִי בַּר יְחֶזְקֵאל אָמַר – **Rather, when Rami bar Yechezkel came** to Babylonia, **he said:** לָא תְּצִיתוּ נְהוּ לְהָנֵי כְּלָלֵי דִּכְיֵיל יְהוּדָה אָחִי מִשְּׁמֵיהּ דִּשְׁמוּאֵל – **Do not listen to those rules that my brother Yehudah compiled in the name of Shmuel!**[21] Rather, the law is that the testimonies of a witness who signed a note and a judge who certified it cannot be combined.[22]

NOTES

16. Shmuel was concerned for the possibility that when the orphans would eventually produce the document for collection, they might come before a court that erroneously follows Rebbi's view. If the certification would state that each witness authenticated only his own signature, the court might refuse to honor it! Since it is incumbent upon us to look after the welfare of orphans, Shmuel took pains to certify the orphans' note in a manner that is valid even according to Rebbi's opinion – i.e. by having each witness attest to the validity of both signatures (*Rashi*).

17. I.e. Shmuel was not concerned that a court might erroneously think the halachah *always* follows Rebbi's opinion even in opposition to a majority view (see *Beis Yaakov* and *Rashash* for reasons). However, he was afraid that a court might favor Rebbi's minority opinion in this exceptional case, because it seems more logical than the Sages' opinion. As explained in note 3, there is a difficulty inherent in the Rabbis' opinion (*Rashba*).

18. Accordingly, Shmuel authenticated the signatures in a manner that was valid even according to Rebbi, and he clarified this in his certification. Apparently, Shmuel also spelled out the names of the certifying witnesses as an extra measure of scrupulousness, as this is normally not required (see *Ritva;* but see *Rashi* to 21b ד״ה דנכתבא).

19. Rav Yehudah refers to a case where a note presented for collection already bears the signed certification of a court, but the borrower claims that both the original signatures and the certification are forged! Rav Yehudah cites Shmuel's ruling that if one of the original signers and one of the judges who certified the note each authenticates his own signature, the note is deemed valid (*Rashi;* see *Tosafos* ד״ה עד ודיין). In accordance with the Sages' opinion above, the witness, by authenticating his signature, attests to the initial transaction and the making of the note, and the judge, by authenticating his signature, attests to the certification of the note [i.e. he asserts that he was a member of the certifying court and witnessed its certification]. We combine these testimonies to validate the note (*Rabbeinu Yonah,* cited by *Rosh* §18, as explained by *Shach* 46:39; cf. *Rosh;* see also *Maharam Schif* and *Haflaah*).

The Rishonim wonder: In reality, there is only one confirmed signature attesting to the loan – that of the original witness! The judge has no knowledge concerning the loan; he simply informs us that the original signatures were certified before him. Practically speaking, he is merely a single witness authenticating the signature of the second original witness. How can we collect the loan on the basis of one witness' confirmed signature and the second one's partially confirmed signature? *Ritva* answers that the method of authentication mentioned here actually represents a special leniency. As has been mentioned (see note 3), the requirement to certify documents is a Rabbinic institution. Since realistically it is quite unlikely that the signatures of the witnesses *and* judges were forged, the Rabbis were lenient in the case of a previously "certified" note, and relied upon the authentication of one witness' signature and one judge's signature (*Ritva,* based on *Rashi*). Since each of these signatures in its own way attests to the validity of the note – i.e. the witness attests that it was made legally, and the judge attests that the signatures are authentic – we may combine the testimonies and collect on its basis (*Ran;* cf. *Rashba, Shitah Mekubetzes*).

The Rishonim raise yet another question: Since it is obvious from our Gemara that a claim of forgery can be advanced even against a certified note, of what use is certification? *Ran* answers that the certification makes it easier to deflect a claim of forgery, since there may be witnesses who recognize the signatures of the judges but not those of the original signers. See *Ritva* for another answer; see also *Rashba.*

20. The original witness testifies about the transaction recorded in the document – in accordance with the Sages' opinion above – whereas the judge testifies that the signatures were certified in his presence (*Rashi*). Although we may be lenient regarding certification in this case, as explained in the previous note, it is illogical to validate the note by combining two diverse testimonies [since they do not add up to one *set* of witnesses testifying about any specific point] (*Ritva,* in explanation of *Rashi;* see *Maharam Schif* and *Rashash*).

21. Rami bar Yechezkel was Rav Yehudah's brother (*Rashi;* see *Kiddushin* 32a). He was apparently born and raised in Babylonia, where he studied under Rav and Shmuel, but he traveled to Eretz Yisrael (see below, end of 111b), and ultimately, returned to Babylonia. Upon returning, he disputed Rav Yehudah's version of various teachings of Rav and Shmuel (see below, 60a and 76b, and *Chullin* 44a).

22. And in order for the note to be considered valid, the signatures of either the two original witnesses or two of the judges must be authenticated. Thus, we will have either a set of two witnesses to the original transaction or a set of two witnesses to the certification (*Ran;* see also *Shach* 46:43).

על כתב ידן הם מעידים לדברי חכמים [א] על מנה שבשטר הם מעידים פשיטא מהו דתימא לרבי ספוקי מספקא ליה אי על כתב ידם הם מעידים או על מנה שבשטר הם מעידים ונפקא מינה [ב] היכא דמית חד מינייהו לבעי שנים מן השוק להעיד עליו דאם כן קנפיק נכי ריבעא דממונא אפומא דחד סהדא והכא לחומרא והכא לחומרא קמ"ל דרבי מיפשט פשיטא ליה בין לקולא בין לחומרא דאמר רב יהודה אמר רב [ג] שנים החתומין על השטר ומת אחד מהן צריכין שנים מן השוק להעיד עליו בזו רבי לקולא ורבנן לחומרא ואי ליכא תרי אלא חד מאי אמר אביי [ד] לכתוב חתימת ידיה אחספא ושדי ליה בבי דינא (א) ומחזקי ליה בי דינא (א) (וחזו ליה) ולא צריך איהו לאסהודי אחתימת ידיה ואזיל איהו והאי ומסהדי אאידך ודוקא אחספא אבל [ה] אמגלתא לא דלמא משכח לה איניש דלא מעלי וכתב עילויה מאי דבעי ותנן [ו] הוציא עליו כתב ידו שהוא חייב לו גובה מנכסים בני חורין אמר רב יהודה אמר שמואל הלכה כדברי חכמים [ג] פשיטא יחיד ורבים הלכה כרבים מהו דתימא [ד] הלכה כרבי מחבירו ואפילו מחביריו קא משמע לן: סימן נח נד חד: אמר ליה רב חננא בר חייא לרב יהודה ואמרי לה רב הונא בר יהודה לרב יהודה ואמרי לה רב חייא בר יהודה לרב יהודה ומי אמר שמואל הכי והא ההוא שטרא דנפיק מבי דינא דמר שמואל והוה כתיב ביה מדאתא רב ענן בר חייא ואסהיד אחתימות ידיה ואדחד דעמיה ומנו רב חנן בר רבה ומדאתא רב חנן בר רבה ואסהיד אחתימות ידיה ואדחד דעמיה ומנו רב ענן בר חייא אשרנוהי וקימנוהי כדחזי א"ל ההוא שטרא דיתמי הוה וחש שמואל [ה] לב"ד טועין וסבר שמואל דלמא איכא דסבירא ליה הלכה כרבי מחבירו ולא מחביריו ובהא אפילו מחביריו סבר אעביד רווחא כי היכי דלא מפסדי יתמי אמר רב יהודה אמר שמואל עד ודיין מצטרפין אמר רמי בר חמא כמה מעליא הא שמעתא [ו] אמר רבא מאי מעליותא מאי דקא מסהיד סהדא לא קא מסהיד דיינא ומאי דקא מסהיד דיינא לא קא מסהיד סהדא אלא כי אתא רמי בר יחזקאל אמר [ז] לא תציתינהו להני כללי דכייל יהודה אחי משמיה דשמואל

איקלע

רש"י

על כתב ידן הן באין להעיד כשמקיימין השטר בב"ד לפיכך צריך שנים על כל כתב וכתב: לדברי חכמים על מנה שבשטר הם מעידים. אנחנו ראינו המלוה וחתמנו הלכך בתרי סגי ולא צריך חד מינייהו לאסהודי אחבריה: מהו דתימא לרבי ספוקי מספקא ליה אי על כתב ידן. אנו נזקקין שיעידו: או על מנה שבשטר. ומשום שמא על כתב ידן הן מעידין מצריך תרי לכל כתב וכתב ומיפשט מיהא לא פשיטא ליה: ונפקא מינה. בין ספק לודאי לשנים החתומים על השטר ומת אחד מהן צריך שנים מן השוק להעיד עליו ואין זה כשר להעיד על כתב ידו ועל של חבירו ולצרף אחד עמו שיעיד על שתיהן דדלמא על מנה שבשטר הן מעידין וכי אומר זה כתב ידי נפיק פלגא דממונא אפומיה וזה שמעיד עמו על חתימתו לא מעלה ולא מוריד דאינו צריך לו וכי הדר מצטרף עם ההוא מן השוק להעיד על חתימת המת הדר נפיק ריבעא דממונא אפומיה אשתכח דכולא ממונא נכי ריבעא נפיק אפומיה ואנן ע"פ שנים עדים בעינן חצי דבר על פיו של זה וחצי דבר על פיו של זה הלכך ניבעי תרי דכיון דספיקא היא ניזיל הכא לחומרא והכא לחומרא היכא דשניהם קיימים אזלינן לחומרא ואמרינן על כתב ידן הן מעידין ובעינן תרין על כל כתב וכתב והיכא דמית חד מנייהו בעינן תרין מן השוק שיעיד האחד על כתב יד המת ואחד מהן יעיד על כתב יד המת והאי דלאי הוה פשיטא לן דעל כתב ידן מעידין הוי סגי באחד מן השוק שיעיד על שתי החתימות והאי יעיד גם הוא על שתיהם ולא נפיק כולא ממונא נכי ריבעא אפומא דחד דאיהו נמי צריך לאותו מן השוק שיעיד על חתימתו אבל השתא דמספקא לן דלמא על מנה שבשטר הן מעידין ועל כתב ידו הוא נאמן ואין צריך לצירוף ועוד אנו צריכים לו שיעיד על חותם המת נפקי תלתא ריבעי אפומיה אי ליכא תרין מן השוק שלא יהא זה צריך להעיד על המת קמ"ל דפשיטא ליה וסגי באחד מן השוק ושניהם יעידו על שתיהן: בין לקולא. כי הכא דאילו לרבנן בעי שנים מן השוק שיעידו על של מת וזה לבדו יעיד על חתימתו: נכי ריבעא. חסר ריבעא: צריך שנים. לדברי חכמים: ואי ליכא שנים. שיכירו כתב המת: אלא חד. וזה האי נמי מכירה מאי ניעביד: לכתוב. זה שנשאר בחיים: חתימת ידיה אחספא ונשדייה בבי דינא. ויטלוה הדיינים ויקיפוה אצל חתימתו שבשטר: ומחזקי. ההיא דשטרא מהך דאחספא דלא צריך לאסהודי אחתימת ידיה: וכתב עליה מאי דבעי. למעלה מן החתימה יכתוב שזה החתום לוה ממנו מנה וכותב כך אני פלוני החתום למטה לויתי מנה מפלוני: מנכסים בני חורין. וממשעבדי לא דלית ליה קלא לדבר שאינו עשוי בעדים: מהו דתימא. כי היכי דהלכה כרבי מחבירו ה"נ אפילו מחביריו: דנפיק מבי דינא דמר שמואל. שקיימוהו בבית דינו וכך נמצא כתוב בהנפק שכתבו הדיינים בו: מדאתא רב ענן כו'. אלמא כרבי ס"ל שצריך לומר זה כתב ידי וזה כתב ידו של חבירי: שטרא דיתמי הוה. שהולך לעיין בתקנתם: וחש שמואל. שאם לא כתב בו אלא פלוני העיד על כתב ידו ופלוני על כתב ידו שמא כשיוציאו היתומים שטר זה בב"ד לגבות יהא אותו ב"ד טועה לומר שהלכה כרבי ויאמרו שאין זה קיום: איכא דס"ל. בעלמא ולא מחביריו והא אפי' מחביריו: עד ודיין. שטר שכתוב בו הנפק וחתמו הדיינין על הנפק שלו ולאחר זמן כשהוציאו המלוה לגבות ערער הלוה לומר מזוייף הוא ובא אחד מעדי השטר והעיד על כתב ידו ואחד מן הדיינים העיד על כתב ידו מצטרפין להכשירו: מאי דקא מסהיד סהדא כו'. עדי השטר מעידין על מנה שבשטר כרבנן והדיינין מעידין בפנינו נתקיים: רב יהודה אחוה דרמי בר יחזקאל הוה:

איקלע

תוספות

על כתב ידן הן מעידין. נראה דלרבי אפילו אומרים בפירוש דמעידין על מנה שבשטר חשיב כאילו מעידין על כתב ידן וכן לרבנן אפי' אומרי' בהדיא דעל כתב ידן הן מעידין מדאמרי' בסמוך ואי ליכא תרי אלא חד היכי נעביד משמע דלא יועיל לרבנן אם יעידו בהדיא על כתב ידן:

ודוקא אחספא. וה"ה אריסא דמגלתא כדאמר בגט פשוט (ב"ב דף קס: ושם) דליכא למיחש למידי והא דתניא בפ"ק דקדושין (דף ט. ושם) כתב על הנייר או על החרס בתך מקודשת לי כו' וכן גבי שדה (שם כו.) כתב על הנייר או על החרס כו' הרי זה מכורה נראה דאתיא כר"א דאמר ז) עדי מסירה כרתי דלר"מ כיון דעדי חתימה כרתי לא מהני על דבר שיכול לזייף כדאמר בפרק ב' דגיטין (דף כא: ושם) אין כותבין לא על הנייר כו' וחכמים מכשירין ומפרש בגמרא ח) מאן חכמים ר"א ואע"ג דאמר התם לא הכשיר ר"א אלא בגיטין אבל בשאר שטרות לא ה"פ אלא בגיטין ודכוותייהו דהיינו שטרות שאין עומדין לראיה כגון אותו שאינו עשוי אלא לקנות בו אשה ושדה כעין גיטין שעשוין לפי שעה לגרש בו אע"פ שיכול השטר של קנין להועיל לראיה גם הגט יכול להועיל כדאמר בהכותב (לקמן דף פט:) ובפ"ק דב"מ (דף יח. ושם) וכ"ת נקרעיה בעינא לאינסובי ביה אלא שעיקרן לא לכך נעשו ולא ממעט אלא שטרות שעיקרן לראיה ועשוין לעמוד ימים רבים כדמייתי התם קרא ונתתם בכלי חרש וגו':

הוציא עליו כתב ידו שהוא חייב לו גובה מנכסים בני חורין. פסק רב אלפס דווקא כשאומר לא היו דברים מעולם אבל נאמן הוא לומר פרעתי ולא מצי א"ל שטרך בידי מאי בעי אלא בשטר שיש בו עדים דגובה בו מנכסים משועבדים ואין נראה לרבינו יצחק כי מנין לו זה החילוק כי סבר דבכל שטר אינו רגיל לפרוע עד שיחזיר לו שטרו:

עד ודיין מצטרפין. משמע דאפילו בשטר מקויים חיישינן שמא זייף לחתימת הדיינין וכן משמע בירושלמי דגיטין ובפרק בן סורר והא דתניא בתוספתא דשביעית פרוזבול המקושר ר' יהודה אומר עדים חותמין מבחוץ והדיינים מבפנים אמרו לו אין מעשה בית דין צריך קיום היינו דווקא בפרוזבול משום דנאמן אדם לומר פרוזבול היה לי ואבד ואפי' למ"ד אינו נאמן מודה הוא דלא בעי קיום:

האמר

מסורת הש"ס

א) רש"ל מ"ז, ב) ב"ב קעה:, ג) [ברכות ט. וש"נ], ד) [לקמן נא. עירובין מו: פסחים כז. ב"ב קכד:], ה) [יבמות קו. ב"ב קלט. קסה. סנהדרין ל.], ו) גי' רש"ל אמר ליה רבא, ז) [גיטין פו.], ח) [שם כב.].

הגהות הב"ח

(א) גמ' ושדי ליה בבי דינא וחזו ליה ומחזקי ליה בי דינא ולא צריך כצ"ל:

גליון הש"ס

גמ' אבל אמגלתא לא. עיין ב"ב דף קס ע"א תוס' ד"ה מקושר עדיו מאחוריו: שם כמה מעליא. כעין זה שבועות דף מז ע"ב: שם לא תציתינהו. לקמן דף ס ע"א ודף עו ע"ב חולין דף מד ע"א:

ליקוטי רש"י

היכא דמית וכו' קנפיק וכו'. דקי"ל נאמן אדם לומר זה כתב ידי הרי אלו עדות ואם בא להצטרף להעיד על חותם חבירו עם אחר הרי ג' רביעית העדות על פיו והתורה אמר (דברים יז) על פי שנים שמשמע פלגא אפומא דהאי ופלגא אפומא דהאי [גיטין טו:]. דכיון דעל מנה שבשטר הן מעידין וכי אמר זה כתב ידי נפקא פלגא דממונא אפומיה שהרי הוא לבדו מעיד על חתימתו ואין צריך אחר להעיד עמו וכי הדר מצטרף עם ההוא מן השוק להעיד על חתימת המת הדר נפיק ריבעא דממונא על פומיה אשתכח דכולא ממונא נכי ריבעא נפק אפומיה ואנן על פי שנים עדים בעינן חצי דבר על פיו של זה וחצי דבר על פיו של זה והכא דמוכח חד מינייהו אין עד השני יכול להצטרף עם אחר מן השוק להעיד על חתימת יד המת אלא צריך שנים מן השוק להעיד עליו [רשב"ם ב"ב נז.]. נכי ריבעא דממונא. כל הממון יוצא על פיו חסר רביע [גיטין שם]. [המשך בע"ב]

עין משפט נר מצוה

מג א ב מיי' פ"ז מהל' עדות הלכה ג סמג עשין קט טוש"ע ח"מ סימן מו סעיף יא:
מד ג ד מיי' שם הל' ה טוש"ע שם סעיף יג:
מה ה טוש"ע שם סי' סט סעיף ב:
מו ו מיי' פי"א מהל' מלוה ולוה הלכה ג ופכ"ז הלכה ב סמג עשין לד טוש"ע שם סימן לט סעיף א וסימן סט סעיף א:
מז ז מיי' פ"ד מהלכות עדות הלכה ו סמג עשין קט טוש"ע ח"מ סימן ל סעיף יב וסימן מו סעיף יד:

תוספות רי"ד

ת"ר כותב אדם עדותו על השטר ומעיד עליה אפילו לאחר כמה שנים פי' אם עשהו עד בדבר וירא לשכחו כותבו על חתיכת קלף ומצניעה ומעיד ע"פ אותו כתב אפילו לאחר כמה שנים א"ר הונא והוא שזוכרה מעצמו פי' בלא ראיית השטר זוכר קצת מעדיותו מאליו ואין זה מדבר משטר שיצא מת"י ומסרו למלוה או ללוקח דהתם אע"ג דלא דכירי לסהדותייהו כלל כיון שמעיד שזה כת"י ומקיים חתימתו או אחרים מעידין על חתימתו השטר קיים ואף על פי שאינו זוכר עדותו ואע"פ שמת חתימתו קיימת שעדים המעידים על השטר נעשה כמי שנחקרה עדותן בב"ד ולא מיירי הכא אלא בעדו תחת ידו כגון ספר זכרונות שאדם כותב בו עסקיו שלא ישכחם גם העדות זו שנאמרה לו בפה כתבה כדי שלא ישכחנה ומה א"ר הונא והוא שזוכרה מעצמו אבל אם שכחה בטל כתבו ואל יראה ויעיד מתוך כתבו ואהני ליה כתבא שיעיין שם לפרקים ולא (יטרחנה) [ישכחנה] ור' אמר אף על פי שאינו זוכרה מעצמו פי' אלא לאחר שראה השטר נותן בלבו ויזכיר שלא נשתכחה ממנו כל כך רק כשמזכירים אותו נזכר אבל אם אינו נזכר כלל לא דהכי אמרינן בפרק ד' אחין לינהוו גבי עדים אם מדכירי ליתי ולסהדו ואי לא דמכין דחזו מכתבא ומסהדי ורחמנא אמר מפיהם ולא מפי כתבם: (ארב"א) [אמר רבא] שמע מיניה מר' יוחנן הני תרי דידעי בסהדותא ומינשי חד מינייהו מדכיר ליה חבריה ומדכר איבעיא להו מלוה בעצמו מאי פי' אם בא דין מזכירו עד שנזכר מאי ר"ח אומר אפילו מלוה בעצמו מר בר אשי אמר (אפי') מלוה בעצמו לא והלכתא מלוה בעצמו לא ואי צורבא מרבנן אפילו מלוה בעצמו פי' דאי לאו רמי אנפשי' ומדכיר שפיר לא הוי סמיך אספיקא למיקם לאסהודי כי הא דרב אשי הו"ל סהדותא לרב כהנא א"ל מדכיר מר ההוא סהדותא א"ל לא א"ל ולאו הכי והכי הוה א"ל לא ידענא לסוף אדכיר ר"א ואזיל אסהיד ליה חזי' לרב כהנא דהוה קא

מהסם פי' מגמגם פי' לתמוה על ר"א שהעיד בדבר א"ל מי סברת עלך קסמכנא אנא רמאי אנפשאי ואידכרי עיין בפסקי בפרק ד' אחין: מתני' זה אומר זה כתב ידי וזה כתב ידו של חבירי וזה כת"י של חבירי אלו נאמנים

חשק שלמה על תוס' רי"ד א) והיינו מעת הרלב"ג בתשובות פ"ח מהלכות עדות הלכה ד' ע"ש. ב) נראה דרבינו היה גורס כאן וכהא אפילו מחביריו וכ"ה הגירסא בלחת בפסחים ס.

Support is adduced for this explanation:

דְּאָמַר רַב יְהוּדָה אָמַר רַב – **For Rav Yehudah said in the name of Rav:** שְׁנַיִם הַחֲתוּמִין עַל הַשְּׁטָר וּמֵת אֶחָד מֵהֶן – **If two** people **were signed on a document and one of them died,** צְרִיכִין שְׁנַיִם מִן הַשּׁוּק לְהָעִיד עָלָיו – **we need two** people **from the market to testify about [his signature],** in accordance with the opinion of the Rabbis. בְּזוֹ רַבִּי לְקוּלָּא וְרַבָּנַן לְחוּמְרָא – **In this** case **Rebbi** rules **leniently and the Rabbis** rule **stringently,** for according to Rebbi only one person from the market is needed to join the surviving witness and testify about both signatures.

Having cited the ruling of Rav Yehudah that when one of the witnesses has died two new people must authenticate his signature and the surviving witness cannot be one of them, the Gemara explores this case further:

וְאִי לֵיכָּא תְּרֵי אֶלָּא חַד מַאי – **And if there are not two** new witnesses who recognize the signature of the deceased, **but** there is **one** new witness – and the surviving witness also recognizes the signature – **what** can be done to certify the document?

The Gemara answers:

אָמַר אַבַּיֵי – **Abaye said:** לִכְתּוֹב חֲתִימַת יְדֵיהּ אַחַסְפָּא – **Let [the surviving witness] write his signature on a shard** וְשָׁדֵי לֵיהּ וּמַחְזְקֵי לֵיהּ בֵּי דִינָא (וחזו ליה) בְּבֵי דִינָא – **and throw it into the court, and the court will verify [his signature on the document]** by comparing it to that on the shard, וְלָא צָרִיךְ אִיהוּ לְאַסְהוּדֵי אַחֲתִימַת יְדֵיהּ – **so that he will not have to testify about** the authenticity of **his own signature** on the document. וְאָזִיל אִיהוּ וְהָאִי וּמְסַהֲדֵי אַאִידָךְ – **Then, he can go with this [person]** from the market **and testify about the other** signature on the document, for he will be providing only one half of the testimony needed.[9]

The Gemara comments:

וְדַוְקָא אַחַסְפָּא – **However,** the surviving witness should write his signature **specifically on a shard,** אֲבָל אַמְּגִלְּתָא לָא – **but not on a scroll.** דִּלְמָא מַשְׁכַּח לַהּ אִינִישׁ דְּלָא מְעַלֵּי – For if he affixes his signature to a scroll, **perhaps a dishonest person will find it** וְכָתַב עִילָּוֵיהּ מַאי דְּבָעֵי – **and write on it whatever he wants** above the signature – for example, that the undersigned owes him a sum of money. וּתְנַן – **And we learned in a Mishnah:**[10] הוֹצִיא עָלָיו כְּתַב יָדוֹ שֶׁהוּא חַיָּיב לוֹ – **If [THE LENDER] PRODUCES AGAINST [THE BORROWER]** a note **WRITTEN IN [THE BORROWER'S] OWN HAND** which states **THAT HE IS INDEBTED TO HIM,**[11] גּוֹבֶה מִנְּכָסִים בְּנֵי חוֹרִין – **HE COLLECTS FROM UNENCUMBERED PROPERTIES.**[12]

The Gemara cites a ruling concerning the dispute in our Mishnah:

אָמַר רַב יְהוּדָה אָמַר שְׁמוּאֵל – **Rav Yehudah said in the name of Shmuel:** הֲלָכָה כְּדִבְרֵי חֲכָמִים – **The halachah follows the Sages.**[13]

The Gemara questions the necessity of this ruling:

פְּשִׁיטָא – This is **obvious,** יָחִיד וְרַבִּים הֲלָכָה כְּרַבִּים – for we have a rule that in disputes between **an individual and a majority, the halachah follows the majority!** Why was it necessary, then, to state that the halachah follows the Sages?

The Gemara answers:

מַהוּ דְּתֵימָא – **You might have said** that הֲלָכָה כְּרַבִּי מֵחֲבֵירוֹ וַאֲפִילּוּ מֵחֲבֵירָיו – **the halachah follows Rebbi over his colleague and even over his colleagues.**[14] קָא מַשְׁמַע לָן – **[Rav Yehudah]** therefore **informs us** that the halachah follows the Sages.

The Gemara presents an objection to this ruling, but prefaces it with a mnemonic:

סִימָן נח נד חד – **The mnemonic** for the name of the objecting sage **is *NaCh, NaD, ChaD.***[15]

The objection to the ruling of Rav Yehudah in the name of Shmuel:

אָמַר לֵיהּ רַב חֲנַנָא בַּר חִיָּיא לְרַב יְהוּדָה – **Rav Chinana bar Chiya said to Rav Yehudah,** וְאָמְרֵי לָהּ רַב הוּנָא בַּר יְהוּדָה לְרַב יְהוּדָה – **and some say Rav Huna bar Yehudah** said **to Rav Yehudah,** וְאָמְרֵי לָהּ רַב חִיָּיא בַּר יְהוּדָה לְרַב יְהוּדָה – **and some say Rav Chiya bar Yehudah** said **to Rav Yehudah:** וּמִי אָמַר שְׁמוּאֵל הָכִי – **Now, did Shmuel actually say this** – that the halachah follows the Rabbis? וְהָא הַהוּא שְׁטָרָא דִּנְפִיק מִבֵּי דִינָא דְּמָר שְׁמוּאֵל – **But** there was **a certain document that emerged** with certification **from the court of the master Shmuel,** וַהֲוָה כְּתִיב בֵּיהּ – **and**

NOTES

be accomplishing nothing more than half the authentication of each signature. According to the Rabbis, though, the surviving witness may verify only his own signature and two other people must attest to the authenticity of the second signature (*Rashi*). [In the Mishnah's case, Rebbi rules stringently and requires each witness to verify *both* signatures, whereas the Rabbis deem it sufficient for each to merely confirm his own signature.]

9. The surviving witness is not considered to have offered any testimony regarding his own signature; rather, the court on its own verifies it through comparison to the sample he provides (*Rashi, Ritva;* see *Ritva* for another instance in which this method of verification is advised). [Although we learned above (20a) that when a document is certified through comparison it must be compared to *two* other documents, in this case one sample suffices because the court *knows* that the sample is authentic (see *Shach* 46:26).]

10. *Bava Basra* 175b.

11. That is, the note, written in the borrower's own hand states: "I, So-and-so, owe So-and-so X amount of money," and there are no witnesses are signed on the bottom. Alternatively, the text of the note is not written in the borrower's own hand, but it is signed by him at the bottom (see *Meiri,* and *Baal HaTerumos* cited by *Beis Yosef, Choshen Mishpat* 69:1 ד״ה מי שלוה; see also *Ran* to *Gittin* 86a [fol. 46a in *Rif*], and *Rashi* below, 101b ד״ה ה״ג).

12. The holder of the note can collect on its basis, because since it is written in the borrower's own hand [or signed by him], it provides evidence of the debt. [For discussion of the extent of its efficacy, see *Tosafos* ד״ה הוציא, *Rosh, Ritva* and *Choshen Mishpat* 69:1 with commentators.] However, since the note is not signed by witnesses, it does not afford the lender a lien on the borrower's property as does a loan document signed by witnesses. A lien is created only when the loan is public knowledge; otherwise, those who buy the borrower's property might not be aware of its existence. And what makes a loan public knowledge is the combination of the recording of the loan in a document *and* the presence of witnesses. One of these factors alone is insufficient (*Rashi;* see also *Rashbam* to *Bava Basra* 175b).

In order to preclude the possibility of anyone making improper use of his sample signature, the witness should affix it to a shard rather than a scroll. Earthenware shards are disqualified from use as documents, because erasures and alterations in the text would not be discernible. [The witness could also affix his sample signature to the very *top* of a scroll, leaving no room for anything to be written above it] (see *Tosafos* ד״ה ודוקא; cf. *R' Yechiel* cited by *Ritva;* see also *Shach* 42:2 with *Ketzos HaChoshen* §1).

13. Who stated that it is sufficient for each witness to verify his own signature and not that of his colleague.

14. [The Gemara states in Tractate *Eruvin* (46b) that as a general rule, the halachah follows Rebbi's view when he is in dispute with one of his colleagues.] One might have thought that this applies even when Rebbi maintains a minority view in opposition to the opinion of a group of his colleagues (*Rashi*). [See *Bava Basra* 124b, where such a position is in fact espoused, and see Gemara below; however, see *Hagahos Cheshek Shlomo.*]

15. The Gemara will cite three versions of the name of the sage who objected to Rav Yehudah's ruling. In the mnemonic, *NaCh* stands for Rav Chi***na***na bar ***Ch***iya, *NaD* for Rav Hu***na*** bar Yehu***d***ah, and *ChaD* for Rav ***Ch***iya bar Yehu***d***ah.

על כתב ידן הם מעידים לדברי חכמים על מנה שבשטר הם מעידים פשיטא מהו דתימא לרבי ספוקי מספקא ליה אי על כתב ידם הם מעידים או על מנה שבשטר הם מעידים ונפקא מינה היכא דמית חד מינייהו לבעי שנים מן השוק להעיד עליו דאם כן קנפיק נכי ריבעא דממונא אפומא דחד סהדא והכא לחומרא והכא לחומרא קמ"ל דרבי מיפשט פשיטא ליה בין לקולא בין לחומרא דאמר רב יהודה אמר רב שנים החתומין על השטר ומת אחד מהן צריכין שנים מן השוק להעיד עליו בזו רבי לקולא ורבנן לחומרא ואי ליכא תרי אלא חד מאי אמר אביי לכתוב חתימת ידיה אחספא ושדי ליה בבי דינא (א) ומחזקי ליה בי דינא (וחזו ליה) ולא צריך איהו לאסהודי אחתימת ידיה ואזיל איהו והאי ומסהדי אאידך ודוקא אחספא אבל אמגלתא לא דלמא משכח לה איניש דלא מעלי וכתב עילויה מאי דבעי ותנן הוציא עליו כתב ידו שהוא חייב לו גובה מנכסים בני חורין אמר רב יהודה אמר שמואל הלכה כדברי חכמים פשיטא יחיד ורבים הלכה כרבים מהו דתימא הלכה כרבי מחבירו ואפילו מחביריו קא משמע לן: סימן נח נד חד: אמר ליה רב חנא בר חייא לרב יהודה ואמרי לה רב הונא בר יהודה לרב יהודה ואמרי לה רב חייא בר יהודה לרב יהודה ומי אמר שמואל הכי והא ההוא שטרא דנפיק מבי דינא דמר שמואל והוה כתיב ביה מדאתא רב ענן בר חייא ואסהיד אחתימות ידיה ואדחד דעמיה ומנו רב חנן בר רבה ומדאתא רב חנן בר רבה ואסהיד אחתימות ידיה ואדחד דעמיה ומנו רב ענן בר חייא אשרנוהי וקיימנוהי כדחזי א"ל ההוא שטרא דיתמי הוה וחש שמואל לב"ד טועין וסבר שמואל דלמא איכא דסבירא ליה הלכה כרבי מחבירו ולא מחביריו ובהא אפילו מחביריו סבר אעביד רווחא כי היכי דלא מפסדי יתמי אמר רב יהודה אמר שמואל עד ודיין מצטרפין אמר רמי בר חמא כמה מעליא הא שמעתא אמר רבא מאי מעליותא מאי דקא מסהיד סהדא לא קא מסהיד דיינא ומאי דקא מסהיד דיינא לא קא מסהיד סהדא אלא כי אתא רמי בר יחזקאל אמר לא תציתינהו להני כללי דכייל יהודה אחי משמיה דשמואל איקלע

רש"י

על כתב ידן הן באין להעיד כשמקיימין השטר בב"ד לפיכך צריך שנים על כל כתב וכתב: **לדברי חכמים על מנה שבשטר הם מעידים.** אנחנו ראינו המלוה ותתמנו הלכך בתרי סגי ולא צריך חד מינייהו לאסהודי אלחבריה: **מהו דתימא לרבי ספוקי מספקא ליה אי על כתב ידן.** אנו מזקקין שיעידו: **או על מנה שבשטר.** ומשום שמא על כתב ידן הן מעידין מצריך תרי לכל כתב וכתב ומיפשט מיהא לא פשיטא ליה: **ונפקא מינה.** בין ספק לודאי לשנים החתומים על השטר ומת אחד מהן צריך שנים מן השוק להעיד עליו ואין זה כשר להעיד על כתב ידו ועל של חבירו ולצרף אחד עמו שיעיד על שתיהן דדלמא על מנה שבשטר הן מעידין וכי אומר זה כתב ידי נפיק פלגא דממונא אפומיה וזה שמעיד עמו על חתימתו לא מעלה ולא מוריד דלאו צריך לו וכי הדר מצטרף עם ההוא מן השוק להעיד על חתימת המת הדר נפיק ריבעא דממונא אפומיה אשתכח דכולה ממונא נכי ריבעא נפיק אפומיה ואנן ע"פ שנים עדים בעינן תלי דבר על פיו של זה ותלי דבר על פיו של זה הלכך ניבעי תרי דכיון דספיקא היא ניזיל לחומרא והכא לחומרא היכא דליכא שניהם קיימים אזלינן לחומרא ואמרינן על כתב ידן הן מעידין ובעינן תרין על כל כתב וכתב והיכא דמית חד מינייהו בעינן תרין מן השוק שיעיד האחד על כתב יד המת ואחד מהן יעיד על כתב יד המת והשני דאי הוה פשיטא לן דעל כתב ידן מעידין הוי סגי בחד מן השוק שיעיד על שתי החתימות והשני יעיד גם הוא על שתיהם ולא נפיק כולא ממונא נכי ריבעא אפומא דחד דלאיהו נמי צריך לאותו מן השוק שיעיד על חתימתו אבל השתא דמספקא לן דלמא על מנה שבשטר הן מעידין ועל כתב ידו הוא נאמן ואין צריך לצירוף ועוד אנו צריכים לו שיעיד על המת נפקי תלתא ריבעי אפומיה אי ליכא תרין מן השוק שלא יהא זה צריך להעיד על המת קמ"ל דפשיטא ליה וסגי בחד מן השוק ושניהם יעידו על שתיהן: **בין לקולא.** כי הכא דאילו לרבנן בעי שנים מן השוק שיעידו על של מת וזה לבדו יעיד על חתימתו: **נכי ריבעא.** חסר ריבעא: **צריך שנים.** שיכירו כתב המת: **ואי ליכא שנים.** לדברי חכמים: **אלא חד.** וזה השני נמי מכירה מאי ניעביד: **לכתוב.** זה שנשאר בחיים: **חתימת ידיה אחספא ונשדייה בבי דינא.** ויטלוה הדיינים ויקיימוה אצל חתימתו שבשטר: **ומחזקי.** הויא לשטרא מהך דאחספא דלא צריך לאסהודי אחתימת ידיה: **וכתב עליה מאי דבעי.** למעלה מן החתימה יכתוב שזה החתום לזה ממנו מנה וכותב כך אני פלוני החתום למטה לויתי מנה מפלוני: **מנכסים בני חורין.** וממשעבדי לא דלית ליה קלא לדבר שאינו עשוי בעדים: **מהו דתימא.** כי היכי דהלכה כרבי מחבירו ה"נ אפילו מחביריו: **דנפיק מבי דינא דמר שמואל.** שקיימוהו בבית דינו וכך נמצא כתוב בהנפק שכתבו הדיינים בו: **מדאתא רב ענן כו'.** אלמא כרבי ס"ל שצריך לומר זה כתב ידי וזה כתב ידו של חבירי: **שטרא דיתמי הוה.** שהולך לעיין בתקנתם: **וחש שמואל.** שאם לא כתב בו אלא פלוני העיד על כתב ידו ופלוני על כתב ידו שמא כשיוציאו היתומים שטר זה בב"ד לגבות יהא אותו ב"ד טועה לומר שהלכה כרבי ויאמרו שאין זה קיום: **איכא דס"ל.** בעלמא ולא מחביריו ובהא אפי' מחביריו: **עד ודיין.** שטר שכתוב בו הנפק וחתמו הדיינין על הנפק שלו ולאחר זמן כשהוציאו המלוה לגבות ערער הלוה לומר מזויף הוא ובא אחד מעדי השטר והעיד על כתב ידו ואחד מן הדיינים העיד על כתב ידו מצטרפין להכשירו: **מאי דקא מסהיד סהדא כו'.** עדי השטר מעידין על מנה שבשטר כרבנן והדיינין מעידין בפנינו נתקיים: רב יהודה אחוה דרמי בר יחזקאל הוה:

תוספות

על כתב ידן הן מעידין. נראה דלרבי אפילו אומרים בפירוש למעידין על מנה שבשטר חשיב כאילו מעידין על כתב ידן וכן לרבנן אפי' אומרי' בהדיא דעל כתב ידן הן מעידין מדאמרי' בסמוך ואי ליכא תרי אלא חד היכי נעביד משמע דלא יועיל לרבנן אם יעידו בהדיא על כתב ידן: **ודוקא** אחספא. וה"ה אריסא דמגלתא כדאמר בגט פשוט (ב"ב דף קס: ושם) דליכא למיחש למידי והא דתניא בפ"ק דקדושין (דף ט. ושם) כתב על הנייר או על החרס בתך מקודשת לי כו' וכן גבי שדה (שם כו.) כתב על הנייר או על החרס כו' הרי זה מכורה נראה דאתיא כר"א דאמר עדי מסירה כרתי דלר"מ כיון דעדי חתימה כרתי לא מהני על דבר שיכול לזייף כדאמר בפרק ב' דגיטין (דף כא: ושם) אין כותבין לא על הנייר כו' וחכמים מכשירין ומפרש בגמרא מאן חכמים ר"א ואע"ג דאמר התם לא הכשיר ר"א אלא בגיטין אבל בשאר שטרות לא ה"פ אלא בגיטין ודכוותייהו דהיינו שטרות שאין עומדין לראיה כגון אותו שאינו עשוי אלא לקנות בו אשה ושדה כעין גיטין שעשוין לפי שעה לגרש בו אע"פ שיכול השטר של קנין להועיל לראיה גם הגט יכול להועיל כדאמר בהכותב (לקמן דף פט:) ובפ"ק דב"מ (דף יח. ושם) וכ"ת נקרעיה בעינא לאינסובי ביה אלא שעיקרן לא לכך נעשו ולא ממעט אלא שטרות שעיקרן לראיה ועשוין לעמוד ימים רבים כדמייתי התם קרא ונתתם בכלי חרש וגו': **הוציא** עליו כתב ידו שהוא חייב לו גובה מנכסים בני חורין. פסק רב אלפס דווקא כשאומר לא היו דברים מעולם אבל נאמן הוא לומר פרעתי ולא מצי א"ל שטרך בידי מאי בעי אלא בשטר שיש בו עדים דגובה בו מנכסים משועבדים ואין נראה לרבינו יצחק כי מנין לו זה החילוק כי סבר דבכל שטר אינו רגיל לפרוע עד שיחזיר לו שטרו: **עד** ודיין מצטרפין. משמע דאפילו בשטר מקויים חיישינן שמא זייף לחתימת הדיינין וכן משמע בירושלמי דגיטין ובפרק בן סורר והא דתניא בתוספתא דשביעית פרוזבול המקושר ר' יהודה אומר עדים חותמין מבחוץ והדיינים מבפנים אמרו לו אין מעשה בית דין צריך קיום היינו דווקא בפרוזבול משום דנאמן אדם לומר פרוזבול היה לי ואבד ואפי' למ"ד אינו נאמן מודה הוא דלא בעי קיום:

האמר

עין משפט נר מצוה

מג א ב מיי' פ"ז מהל' עדות הלכה ג סמג עשין קט טוש"ע ח"מ סימן מו סעיף יא: מד ג ד מיי' שם הל' ה טוש"ע שם סעיף יג: מה ה טוש"ע שם סי' סט סעיף ב: מו ו מיי' פי"א מהל' מלוה ולוה הלכה ג ופכ"ו הלכה ב סמג עשין צד טוש"ע שם סימן נו סעיף א וסימן סט סעיף א: מז ז מיי' פ"ד מהלכות עדות הלכה ו סמג עשין קט טוש"ע ח"מ סימן ל סעיף יג וסימן מו סעיף יד:

מסורת הש"ס

א) רש"ל מ"ז, ב) ב"ב קעה:, ג) [ברכות ט. וש"נ], ד) [לקמן נא. ערכין כו: פסחים מ. ב"ב קכד:], ה) [יבמות קו. ב"ב קלט. קכד. סנהדרין ל.], ו) [גי' רש"ל אמר ליה רבא], ז) [גיטין פו.], ח) [שם כב.]

הגהות הב"ח

(א) גמ' ושדי ליה בבי דינא וחזו ליה ומחזקי ליה בי דינא ולא צריך כו"ל:

גליון הש"ס

גמ' אבל אמגלתא לא. עיין ב"ב דף קסז ע"א תוס' ד"ה מקושר עדיו מאחוריו: שם כמה מעליא. כעין זה שבועות דף מז ע"ב: שם לא תציתינהו. לקמן דף עה ע"ב חולין דף מד ע"א:

עַל כְּתַב יָדָן הֵם מְעִידִים – **[the witnesses] are testifying about** the authenticity of **their signatures.** Therefore, the testimony of two witnesses is required concerning each signature.[1] לְדִבְרֵי חֲכָמִים – But **according to the Sages,** עַל מָנֶה שֶׁבַּשְּׁטָר הֵם מְעִידִים – **they are testifying about the** loan of a ***maneh*** (i.e. one hundred *zuz*) described **in the document.**[2] It is therefore sufficient for each witness to authenticate his own signature.[3]

The Gemara wonders:

פְּשִׁיטָא – This is **obvious!** What else could be the basis of the dispute?

The Gemara answers:

מַהוּ דְּתֵימָא לְרַבִּי סְפוּקֵי מְסַפְּקָא לֵיהּ – **You might have said** that **Rebbi is actually uncertain** אִי עַל כְּתַב יָדָם הֵם מְעִידִים – **whether [the witnesses] are testifying about** the authenticity of **their signatures** אוֹ עַל מָנֶה שֶׁבַּשְּׁטָר הֵם מְעִידִים – **or they are testifying about the** loan of a ***maneh*** described **in the document.**[4] וְנַפְקָא מִינָּהּ – **And the practical difference** that would emerge from this explanation is that הֵיכָא דְּמֵית חַד מִינַּיְיהוּ – in a case **where one of [the witnesses]** who signed the note **has died,** לִבְעֵי שְׁנַיִם מִן הַשּׁוּק לְהָעִיד עָלָיו – **we would require two** people **from the market to testify about [his signature],** and the surviving witness would be ineligible to testify about it. דְּאִם כֵּן – **For if** it would be **so** – that the surviving witness could join with one other witness to authenticate both signatures – קָנָפִיק נְכֵי רִיבְעָא דְּמָמוֹנָא אַפּוּמָא דְּחַד סָהֲדָא – then **three-quarters**[5] **of the money would be exacted through the testimony of** this **one** surviving **witness.**[6] וְהָכָא לְחוּמְרָא – **Thus,** due to his uncertainty regarding the matter, Rebbi rules **stringently here,** in the Mishnah's case where both witnesses who signed are still living, and he requires each of them to verify both signatures, וְהָכָא לְחוּמְרָא – **and** he would also rule **stringently here,** in the case where one witness has died, and would require two new witnesses to verify that signature.[7] קָא מַשְׁמַע לָן דְּרַבִּי מִיפְשַׁט פְּשִׁיטָא לֵיהּ – **[The Gemara]** therefore **informs us that Rebbi is actually certain** that the witnesses testify only about their signatures, and he therefore follows this view בֵּין לְקוּלָּא בֵּין לְחוּמְרָא – **both** where it leads **to a leniency and** where it leads **to a stringency.**[8]

NOTES

1. According to Rebbi [when the witnesses who signed authenticate their own signatures, it is the same as when other witnesses authenticate them. In either event,] the witnesses are testifying to nothing more than the validity of these signatures. Once authenticated, the signatures testify about the loan (or other transaction) recorded in the note. Therefore, the authentication of each signature must be accomplished by two witnesses – like any other testimony (*Rashi,* as elucidated by *Talmidei Rabbeinu Yonah*).

2. [The Gemara focuses by way of example on a case where the document was a note of indebtedness for a *maneh.*] According to the Sages, when the witnesses who signed authenticate their own signatures, they are not deemed to be merely telling us that these are their signatures; rather, it is as if they are saying, "We *witnessed* this loan and signed the note" (*Rashi;* see following note).

3. Since the witnesses are not merely informing us that the signatures are authentic, but are in effect reiterating their signed testimony, even if each witness merely authenticates his own signature we have before us two witnesses stating that the defendant owes the plaintiff a *maneh.* It is therefore unnecessary for an additional witness to authenticate each signature (*Rashi,* as elucidated by *Talmidei Rabbeinu Yonah;* cf. elucidation of *Tos. Rid*). [This applies even if the witnesses concede explicitly that they have no recollection of the loan. The self-confirmation of their signatures is automatically judged as a reiteration of their signed testimony (*Tosafos* ד״ה על כתב ידן, *Rav Hai Gaon, Talmidei Rabbeinu Yonah*). Similarly, according to Rebbi, even if the witnesses state explicitly that they remember the transaction recorded in the note, they must each authenticate both signatures, for their current testimony is merely an authentication of the signatures (*Tosafos* ibid.; cf. *Rav Hai Gaon, Talmidei Rabbeinu Yonah*).]

The position of the Sages is somewhat problematic. Even if we regard the witnesses as testifying that the loan took place, this should be considered no better than an *undocumented* loan, since the document has not been authenticated by two witnesses who recognize both signatures! [A lender has less authority to collect an undocumented loan than a documented one. For example, if the borrower sold mortgaged properties, the lender cannot confiscate them unless his loan is backed by a document.] Why is the *document* considered certified in our case? *Nesivos HaMishpat* (46:11) and *Chasam Sofer* (5573 version) answer that since the requirement to certify a document is merely Rabbinic (see below, 21b note 20), the Rabbis were lenient and considered the document valid with this form of authentication. See *Rashba* (ד״ה ובהא) and *Beis Yaakov* for alternative explanations.

[*Rambam* (*Hil. Eidus* 8:1,4) has an entirely different understanding of the dispute between the Sages and Rebbi. According to his approach, the Sages maintain that witnesses who signed a note *must* remember the testimony in order to authenticate their signatures. *Yerushalmi,* cited by *Tosafos* to 20b end of ד״ה ורבי יוחנן, provides the basis for this interpretation. See also *Rosh,* and see *Choshen Mishpat* 46:10, where both views are cited and discussed by the commentators.]

4. I.e. one could argue that Rebbi does not hold with certainty that the witnesses are testifying specifically about the authenticity of their signatures. Rather, Rebbi is in doubt about the matter, and he requires two witnesses for each signature because of the *possibility* that they are testifying about the signatures and not the *maneh* (*Rashi*).

5. Literally: [all] minus one quarter (*Rashi*).

6. According to the view that a self-authentication is considered a reiteration of the initial testimony, when the surviving witness confirms his own signature he automatically provides half of the testimony needed. Even if someone from the market joins him in authenticating his own signature, that person's testimony is irrelevant. If the surviving witness and someone from the market now authenticate the signature of the deceased one, the surviving witness will have provided another quarter of the total testimony needed [since he will have accomplished half of the authentication of the second signature]. In sum, therefore, the suviving witness will have provided three-quarters of the needed testimony! [The Gemara refers to this figuratively as "exacting three-quarters of the money."] This is improper, because the Torah states (*Deuteronomy* 19:15) that matters should be confirmed by *two* witnesses, implying that each witness should provide no more than half the testimony needed. To avoid this problem, after the surviving witness confirms his own signature, two *other* people must authenticate the second signature. Thus, the surviving witness will have provided half the testimony, and the two strangers will have combined to provide the second half.

Now, if Rebbi was certain that the witnesses who signed testify only about their signatures and not about the loan recorded in the document, he would allow the surviving witness to join with one person from the market and testify together about the authenicity of both signatures. For the surviving witness would merely be accomplishing half the authentication of his own signature and half the authentication of the other one – totaling half the testimony needed. However, since [as is now being argued] Rebbi considers the possibility that one who confirms his own signature is deemed to be testifying about the loan itself, he cannot allow the surviving witness to authenticate the note in conjunction with only one other person. This would result in the surviving witness providing three-quarters of the needed testimony (*Rashi*).

7. Due to his uncertainty, Rebbi would be forced to adopt the stringency that arises from each of the possibilities. In the case where both witnesses are living, the possibility that they testify only about their signatures forces each of them to confirm both signatures – so that there are two witnesses authenticating each signature. And in the case where one of the witnesses has died, the possibility that the one who confirms his own signature is testifying about the loan forces us to require two *other* people to authenticate the signature of the deceased witness – so that the surviving witness should not be providing three-quarters of the testimony needed (*Rashi*).

8. Thus, in the case where one witness has died, Rebbi rules leniently and allows the surviving witness to authenticate the two signatures in conjunction with *one* other person – because the survivor is deemed to

Mishnah The Mishnah continues its discussion concerning the certification of documents: זֶה אוֹמֵר כְּתַב יָדִי וְזֶה כְּתַב יָדוֹ שֶׁל חֲבֵירִי – If **this** witness **says,** "This is **my handwriting, and this is my fellow's handwriting,"** וְזֶה אוֹמֵר זֶה כְּתַב יָדִי וְזֶה כְּתַב יָדוֹ שֶׁל חֲבֵירִי – **and that** witness **says, "This is my handwriting, and this is my fellow's handwriting,"** הֲרֵי אֵלוּ נֶאֱמָנִין – **these** witnesses **are believed** and the document is deemed authentic.[21] זֶה אוֹמֵר זֶה כְּתַב יָדִי – However, if **this** one **says** only, **"This is my handwriting,"** וְזֶה אוֹמֵר זֶה כְּתַב יָדִי – **and that** one **says** only, **"This is my handwriting,"** צְרִיכִין לְצָרֵף עִמָּהֶם אַחֵר – **they must join to themselves another** person who can authenticate each signature.[22] דִּבְרֵי רַבִּי – These are **the words of Rebbi.** וַחֲכָמִים אוֹמְרִים – **But the Sages say:** אֵינָם צְרִיכִין לְצָרֵף עִמָּהֶן אַחֵר – **They do not need to join another** person **to themselves;** אֶלָּא נֶאֱמָן אָדָם לוֹמַר זֶה כְּתַב יָדִי – **rather, a person is believed to say, "This is my handwriting,"** and thereby authenticate it.

Gemara The Gemara analyzes the dispute cited in the Mishnah:

כְּשֶׁתִּימְצֵי לוֹמַר – **When you thoroughly analyze** this dispute, you will conclude that לְדִבְרֵי רַבִּי – **according to Rebbi's opinion,**

NOTES

Tur (*Choshen Mishpat* 28:13) omit this distinction, implying that the testimony is deemed reliable even if the person was not designated as a witness. Apparently, they interpret the Gemara's expression כֵּיוָן דְּרָמֵי עֲלֵיהּ as *since he concentrates upon it.* Thus, the Gemara means that in the case of a mound – where we are dealing with the *lack* of definite knowledge of *tumah* – we consider the lack of information significant for only sixty years; afterwards we assume that the *tumah* may once have existed but was simply forgotten. However, in the case of testimony – where the witness claims that he concentrated and *does* have the information we need – we may rely upon him indefinitely (*Bach, Choshen Mishpat* loc. cit.; cf. *Beis Yosef* ad loc.; see *Haflaah* and *Chasam Sofer,* 5573 ed.).]

21. Because each of the signatures has been authenticated by two witnesses (*Rashi*). [This ruling is rather obvious; see *Shitah Mekubetzes* and *Haflaah* for explanations of its necessity.]

22. For each signature requires authentication by two witnesses. The Gemara will explain why authentication by the witness who signed is not sufficient (*Rashi*).

לט א מיי' פ"ח מהל' עדות הלכה ג סמג עשין קט טוש"ע ח"מ סימן מו סעיף יד:
מ ב ג ד ה ו מיי' פ"ט מהלכות טומאת מת הלכה ג:
מא ו טוש"ע ח"מ סימן מו סעיף ג:
מב ז ח טוש"ע ח"מ סימן מו סעיף י:

ואי צורבא מרבנן הוא אפילו עצמו כי הא דרב אשי הוה ידיע ליה בסהדותא לרב כהנא אמר ליה מי דכיר מר האי סהדותא אמר ליה לא ולאו הכי והכי הוה א"ל לא ידענא לסוף אידכר רב אשי אסהיד ליה חזייה לרב כהנא דהוה מחסם א"ל מי סברת עלך קא סמיכנא אנא הוא דרמאי אנפשאי ואדכרי א) תנן התם ב התלוליות הקרובות בין לעיר ובין לדרך אחד חדשות ואחד ישנות טמאות הרחוקות חדשות טהורות ישנות טמאות איזוהי קרובה חמשים אמה ואיזו היא ישנה ששים שנה דברי ר"מ רבי יהודה אומר ג קרובה שאין קרובה הימנה ישנה ד שאין אדם זוכרה מאי עיר ומאי דרך אילימא עיר ממש דרך דרך ממש מספיקא מי מחזקינן טומאה והאמר ריש לקיש ג) עילה מצאו וטהרו ארץ ישראל א"ר זירא ה עיר הסמוכה לבית הקברות ודרך דרך בית הקברות בשלמא דרך בית הקברות דזמנין דמתרמי בין השמשות ומקרו קברו בתל אלא עיר הסמוכה לבית הקברות כולהי לבית הקברות אזלי אמר רבי חנינא ו מתוך שהנשים קוברות שם נפליהן ומוכי שחין זרועותיהם עד חמשים אמה אזלא איהי לחודה טפי דברא איניש בהדה ולבית הקברות אזלא הלכך טומאה בארץ ישראל לא מחזקינן אמר רב חסדא ש"מ מרבי מאיר האי סהדותא עד שיתין שנין מידכר טפי לא מידכר ולא היא התם הוא דלא רמיא עליה אבל הכא ז כיון דרמי עליה אפילו טובא נמי:

מתני' ח זה אומר כתב ידי וזה כתב ידו של חבירי וזה אומר זה כתב ידי וזה כתב ידו של חבירי הרי אלו נאמנין זה אומר זה כתב ידי וזה אומר זה כתב ידי צריכין לצרף עמהם אחר דברי רבי וחכמים אומרים אינם צריכין לצרף עמהן אחר ט אלא נאמן אדם לומר זה כתב ידי: גמ' כשתימצי לומר לדברי רבי על

ואי צורבא מרבנן הוא. העד: אפי' לעצמו. של בעל דין דצורבא דרבנן אי לאו דכי רמי אנפשיה מדכר שפיר לא הוה סמיך אספיקא למיקם ולאסהודי: מחסם. מגמגם תמה על רב אשי שהעיד בדבר: התלוליות. תילי קרקע ודרך בני אדם לקבור בתל משום דאין בני אדם מטין מן הדרך לעבור עליו ועיר ודרך לקמן מפרש להו: אחד חדשות. שאין זמן רחוק שלא היה כאן תל דאיכא למימר כיון דחדשה היא אם איתא שנקבר שם מת מדכר דכיר ליה אפ"ה טמאות מספק דכיון דסמוכה לעיר איכא למימר אשה יחידה הלכה וקברה שם נפל שלה: הרחוקות. דאין אשה יחידה הולכת שם: חדשות טהורות. דאם איתא דנקבר ביה הוו ידעי ליה: ישנות טמאות. שכבר נשתכח הדבר מן היודעים: ואיזו היא קרובה. לעיר שאנו אומרים עליה שאף החדשה טמאה חמשים אמה: ואיזו היא ישנה. שאנו אומרים עליה שאפי' היא רחוקה טמאה ששים שנה: שאין קרובה הימנה. אבל אם יש קרובה הימנה אפי' היא בתוך חמשים אמה הויא כרחוקה וחדשה טהורה דאם איתא דהלכה אשה יחידה לקבור לא שבקה קרובה הימנה ואזלה לגבי דהך: שאין אדם זוכרה. שאין אדם אומר זכור אני שלא היה כאן תל ובימי נעשה תל זה הו כאן: עילה מצאו. עלילה בעלמא מצאו חכמים והחזיקו בה לתלות עליה ולטהר את ארץ ישראל במסכת נזיר בפרק בתרא אלמא מספיקא לא מחזקינן טומאה בקרקעה של ארץ ישראל: וטיהרו את א"י גרסי' ולא גרסינן כל: דמתרמי בין השמשות. של ערב שבת ואין שהות לילך עד בית הקברות: ומוכי שחין. שאבריהן נופלין או שמחתכין אותן ואבר מן החי מטמא כאבר מן המת כדאמרינן בהעור והרוטב (חולין קכט.): ש"מ. מדקתני לעיל איזו היא ישנה ששים שנה וטעמא משום דלא דכירי לה הוא האי סהדות' כו': אבל הכא. שעשאוהו עד בדבר אפילו טובא נמי סמכינן אסהדותיה אי מסהיד: מתני' הרי אלו נאמנין. דאיכא תרי סהדי דמסהדי אכל כתב וכתב: צריכים לצרף עמהן אחר. שיכיר כתב ידי שניהם דתרי סהדי בעינן אכל כתב וכתב וטעמא מפרש בגמרא: גמ' כשתימצי לומר לדברי רבי. כשתעמוד לסוף דבריו קסבר על

שטרו בב"ד ויש לומר דע"א בשטר לא חשיב שטר אלא אותו שיש בו שני עדים דומיא דספר מקנה והא דאמר בגט פשוט (ב"ב דף קסה.) עד אחד בכתב ועד אחד בעל פה אין מצטרפין דמשמע הא שנים בשטר אפילו בשתי אגרות מצטרפין התם מיירי כגון שהאחד בשטר והאחד בעל פה לא שאומר שראה הוא המלוה אלא שראה מסירת השטר מלוה למלוה דהוי כשנים החתומים בשטר לר"א דאמר עדי מסירה כרתי ועוד דבירושלמי מפרש עד א' בשטר היינו שנים חתומים בשטר וקיימו כתב ידו של אחד ולא מצאו לקיים כתב ידו של שני ומ"מ נהי דעד אחד לא חשיב שטר לענין שאם יבואו עדים ויאמרו כך ראינו בשטר דחשבינן להו כעד מפי עד עדות מיהא הוי ויכול לשלוח כתב ידו לב"ד ולא חשיב מפיהם ולא מפי כתבם כיון שהוא כותב העדות ורש"י פי' בפירוש החומש ג) מפיהם ולא מפי כתבם שלא ישלח בכתב עדותו לב"ד א"נ אומר ר"י דע"א מועיל בשטר אם יש שני שטרות בכל אחד חתום עד א' חשוב כשטר שלם וכו"מ א"כ כשמעתין יבא כתבו לב"ד אפילו אינו זוכר כלל ויש לומר דלא חשיב שטר אלא כשעשוי מדעת שניהם מדעת הלוה שהוא חייב או חשיב שטר אבל הכא שכותב עדותו שלא מדעת הלוה לא חשיב שטרא והקשה ה"ר שמואל מוורדון"ן דאמר בחזקת הבתים (ב"ב דף לט.) מחאה בפני שנים וא"צ לומר כתובו ומה מועיל כתובו כיון דאין עשוי מדעת המחזיק ולפי מה שפירשנו לעדות מיהא הוי כל זמן שזוכר אתי שפיר מיהו בלאו הכי מתרץ ר"י דגבי מחאה הקילו שאינה אלא מדרבנן דהכי נמי הקילו לומר דמחאה שלא בפניו הויא מחאה אע"פ שלפעמים לא ישמע וסמכו על זה דחברך חברא אית ליה וכן במודעא בפני שנים הקילו לכתוב להציל אנוס מאונסו ועוד אומר ר"י דלא בעינן דעת שניהם והכא היה יכול להביא שטרו אם היה כתוב כתיקון שטרות אבל הכא מיירי שאינו כתוב כסדר השטר אלא זכרון דברים בעלמא ומתוך הירושלמי נראה לפ' בענין אחר סוגיא זו דקאמר התם רב הונא כרבי ור' יוחנן כרבנן פירוש כשהעדים באים לקיים חתימתן אם זוכרין המלוה בלא שטר אפי' לרבי א"צ לצרף עמהן אחר מן השוק דעל מנה שבשטר הן מעידין וכשאין זוכרים המלוה אפילו ע"י השטר אפי' רבנן מודו דצריכין לצרף עמהן דעל כרחין אין מעידין אלא על כתב ידן וכי פליגי היינו כשזוכרין המלוה ע"י השטר דלרבנן חשיב זכירה ועל מנה הן מעידין ולרבי לא חשיב זכירה ולשון כותב אדם לא משמע הכי:

אחד חדשות ואחד ישנות. תימה דהכא מזכיר שאינו פשוט קודם וכן בהחולץ (יבמות דף מא.) לא יתארסו ולא ינשאו עד שיהו להן ג' חדשים אחד בתולות ואחד בעולות מזכיר אירוסין קודם נישואין ובתולות קודם בעולות דהיינו שאינו פשוט קודם ובר"ה (דף כט:) תנן אחד יבנה ואחד כל מקום שיש בו ב"ד התם נקט דבר פשוט ברישא וכן בב"ק (דף ג:) אחד החופר בור שיח ומערה ובמס' סוטה (דף מג.) אחד הבונה ואחד הלוקח כו' גבי מערכי מלחמה ורש"י נמי גרים בפ"ק דסוכה (דף ב. ושם) גבי מחללת גדולה שעשאה לשכיבה טמאה ואין מסככין בה רבי אליעזר אומר אחת קטנה ואחת גדולה וא' קטנה מבעי ליה והיה כתוב בספרים להפך ורש"י מהפך הגירסא משום דדרך התנאים להזכיר הפשוט קודם ואומר ר"י א) דהיכא דקאי אפלוגתא או אקרא מזכיר הפשוט קודם כי ההיא דפליג ר' אליעזר את"ק בסוכה והוה ליה למימר אחת גדולה שאתה מודה לי כך תודה בקטנה וכן אחד יבנה פליג אדר' אליעזר דאמר לא התקין רבן יוחנן בן זכאי שיהו תוקעין אלא ביבנה בלבד ובב"ק (דף ג:) ובסוטה (דף מג.) קאי אקרא אבל הכא ובהחולץ לא קאי אמידי אין להקפיד איזה נשנה תחלה: [ועי' תוס' שבת כ: ד"ה אחד מבושל פסחים פה. קח: סוכה כ. זבחים לב: ד"ה אי הכי ומנחות סג: ד"ה אחד שבת ועי' תוס' קדושין יג. ד"ה כשם]:

טמאות. פירש בקונטרס דבקרובות אפילו חדשות טמאות משום דאזלא איהי לחודה ואין ידוע אם קברה שם אבל רחוקה דדברא איניש בהדה ואלמלי קברה איניש דאזיל בהדה היה מגלה ולפיכך ישנות טמאות דאע"פ דדברא איניש בהדה נשתכח הדבר וקשה [לר"י] דאם כן אמאי ב) נ"ל בסמוך דדברא איניש בהדה ולבית הקברות אזלא לא הוה ליה למימר אלא דברא איניש בהדה ותו לא ולכך טפי חדשות טהורות דאם איתא דקברה שם היה הדבר ידוע ועוד אי לבית הקברות אזלא ישנות אמאי טמאות ונראה לר"י כר"ח דפירש דישנות טמאות אפילו רחוקות דחיישינן שמא קרובות היו שהיה העיר אצלה וחרב ולפי זה לא נאמר משום דדברא איניש בהדה היה ידוע יותר ולהכי איצטריך לומר ולבית הקברות אזלא: **עילה** מצאו. פירש רבינו חננאל נגע ותלו הטומאה באותה נגע והשאר טהרו:

מסורת הש"ס
א) אהלות פרק ט"ז מ"ב, ב) נזיר סה. ג) [דברים יט פט"ו].

תוספות ישנים

גליון הש"ס
גמ' שאין אדם זוכרה. עיין תוס' יו"ט פ"ב (מ"ג) (מ"ד) דכ"ב ד"ה לא ימנוך:

ליקוטי רש"י
צורבא מרבנן. תלמיד חכם. מחסם. לשון לא תחסום (דברים כה). עילה מצאו. דברא. אלדברא. הנהיגו (ביצה כה:).

תוספות רי"ד

תוספות רי"ד

חשק שלמה על תוס' רי"ד

near **the graveyard path** should be *tamei;* **דִּזְמְנִין דְּמִתְרַמֵּי בֵּין הַשְּׁמָשׁוֹת** – it is **because sometimes twilight** of the eve of the Sabbath **occurs** while a funeral is in progress, **וּמִקְּרוּ קָבְרוּ בְּתֵל** – **and they happen to bury** the corpse **in a mound** in the vicinity of the path because they cannot reach the graveyard in time.[15] **אֶלָּא עִיר הַסְּמוּכָה לְבֵית הַקְּבָרוֹת** – **But** regarding **a town that is close to a graveyard, כּוּלְּהִי לְבֵית הַקְּבָרוֹת אָזְלֵי** – **everyone goes to the graveyard** for burials. Why would a mound in the vicinity of the town and not on the graveyard path contain a corpse?

The Gemara answers:

אָמַר רַבִּי חֲנִינָא – **R' Chanina said: מִתּוֹךְ שֶׁהַנָּשִׁים קוֹבְרוֹת שָׁם נִפְלֵיהֶן** – It is **because women** who miscarry **bury their fetuses there, וּמוּכֵּי שְׁחִין זְרוֹעוֹתֵיהֶם** – **and people with skin afflictions** who lose arms bury **their** amputated **arms** there.[16]

The Gemara explains why the Mishnah differentiates between mounds within fifty *amos* and those further away:

עַד חֲמִשִּׁים אַמָּה אָזְלָא אִיהִי לְחוּדָהּ – **Up to fifty *amos*** from the town limits, **[a woman] would go by herself** and bury her fetus in a mound. **טְפֵי** – But if the mound is **further** than fifty *amos* from the town, **דְּבָרָא אִינִישׁ בַּהֲדָהּ וּלְבֵית הַקְּבָרוֹת אָזְלָא** – **she would take a man with her and go to the graveyard.**[17] **הִלְכָּךְ טוּמְאָה בְּאֶרֶץ יִשְׂרָאֵל לֹא מַחְזְקִינַן** – **Therefore, we do not make a presumption of *tumah* in Eretz Yisrael** with regard to mounds more than fifty *amos* from the town.[18]

The Gemara connects the preceding discussion to the matter of testimony:

אָמַר רַב חִסְדָּא – **Rav Chisda said: שְׁמַע מִינָּהּ מִדְּרַבִּי מֵאִיר** – **Learn from** the words of **R' Meir הַאי סַהֲדוּתָא** – that **concerning testimony, עַד שִׁיתִּין שְׁנִין מִידְכַּר** – **it is remembered for** up to **sixty years, טְפֵי לֹא מִידְכַּר** – but **it is not remembered for longer** than that. Thus, a witness may testify concerning a fact that he saw up to sixty years earlier.[19]

The Gemara rejects this analogy:

וְלֹא הִיא – **But this is not** so. **הָתָם הוּא דְּלָא רְמִיָא עֲלֵיהּ** – **It is** only **there,** in the case of the mound, **where it is not incumbent upon [any particular person]** to remember a burial, that we suspect people may forget after sixty years. **אֲבָל הָכָא** – **But here,** in the case of testimony, **כֵּיוָן דִּרְמֵי עֲלֵיהּ אֲפִילּוּ טוּבָא נַמֵּי** – **since it is incumbent upon [the witness]** to remember it, **even if more** than sixty years have passed he **also** retains the memory.[20]

NOTES

15. I.e. the procession sets out on the road early, but underestimates how long it would take to reach the distant graveyard (*Radvaz,* cited by *Shitah Mekubetzes*). When the mourners realize that the Sabbath is approaching, they hurriedly make the burial in a nearby mound (*Rashi*).

Since there is a very real possibility that over the years funeral processions had to be aborted on Sabbath eves, we must be concerned for *tumah* even though people do not seem to remember such an occurrence. Accordingly, any mound that is "near" the path (as defined above) is *tamei* even if it is a new mound and nobody recalls a burial in it. However, with regard to mounds that are "far" from the path [where burials are less likely to have been made], we rely upon people's memories. Therefore, "new" mounds that are distant are *tahor* when nobody is aware of a burial having occurred there. Nevertheless, "old" mounds are *tamei* even if they are distant from the path, since a burial may have been done there long ago and since been forgotten (*Ramban,* in explanation of *Rashi;* see also *Maharam Schif*).

16. People with certain severe skin afflictions (such as leprosy) sometimes lose limbs through decay or amputation. A limb detached from a live person is *tamei* just like the limb of a corpse (*Rashi*). [It is therefore common to bury such a limb. Regarding whether the burial is obligatory, see *Shevus Yaakov* vol. II §101 and *Or HaYashar.*]

Although all complete corpses would certainly be buried in the town cemetery, that is not true of fetuses and limbs. Since a woman is embarrassed about her miscarriage and afflicted people are embarrassed about their lost limbs, they make their burials privately and do so in any convenient mound. We must therefore be concerned for the existence of *tumah* even though nobody is aware of it (*Radvaz,* cited by *Shitah Mekubetzes*).

17. Men with skin afflictions also go no further than fifty *amos* from the town alone to bury their limbs (*Maharam Schif;* cf. *Shitah Mekubetzes*). Therefore, "new" mounds within fifty *amos* of the town must be deemed *tamei* out of doubt, but the more distant ones are deemed *tahor.* As for "old" mounds, they are deemed *tamei* even beyond fifty *amos,* since a corpse might have been in them in decades past and since been forgotten (*Ramban,* in explanation of *Rashi;* see also *Maharam Schif;* cf. *Maharsha*).

Tosafos ask: Why must the Gemara state that when the nearest mound is beyond fifty *amos* the woman takes a man with her *and goes to the graveyard*? Even if it is possible that she went to the nearest mound with the man, we have no concern for *tumah,* since the man would have publicized the fact! *Maharam Schif* explains according to *Rashi* that the Gemara means to remove the *basis* for any concern of *tumah.* When a mound is more than fifty *amos* from the town the woman will not go alone, and once she takes a man with her she most likely goes all the way to the graveyard for the burial. Thus, the distant mounds are *tahor* not merely because nobody is aware of *tumah,* but because there is no basis for any such concern. As the Gemara said originally, we do not declare any area in Eretz Yisrael *tamei* without a firm basis. [See *Ramban* and *Shitah Mekubetzes* (ד״ה ועוד הקשה) for alternative resolutions of *Rashi's* approach.]

Another point needs to be addressed: According to R' Chanina's answer, the concern for *tumah* would seem to be even greater in a town that has no graveyard. Yet R' Chanina seems to concur with R' Zeira that it applies only in a town that is near a graveyard! How can these opinions be reconciled? The answer is that when the town is not near a graveyard and there is no known *tumah* in the vicinity at all, women avoid burying their fetuses in the local mounds because they do not wish to create *tumah* where none existed previously. However, when the town is near a graveyard, so that many burials are done in its environs and *tumah* is prevalent, women freely bury their fetuses in local mounds and afflicted people bury their limbs as well. Thus, the mounds must be considered *tamei* (*Shitah Mekubetzes;* cf. *Pnei Yehoshua*).

18. I.e. since there is no firm basis for suspecting *tumah* in "new" mounds that are beyond fifty *amos* from the town, we consider them *tahor* (*Maharam Schif*).

In conclusion, the concern for *tumah* in the vicinity of graveyard paths, and the vicinity of towns that are near graveyards, is based on two different factors. With respect to paths, the concern is that funeral processions had to be aborted on Sabbath eves and ordinary burials were done in mounds at the side of the path. With respect to towns that have graveyards, the concern is that women who miscarry bury their fetuses privately in surrounding mounds, and afflicted people bury their detached limbs there (*Ramban,* in explanation of *Rashi*).

[In explaining the preceding Gemara, we have followed *Ramban's* understanding of *Rashi,* with the elaborations of *Shitah Mekubetzes* and *Maharam Schif.* However, *Maharsha, Pnei Yehoshua* and *Haflaah* have a different understanding of *Rashi.* See *Tosafos,* who cite *Rabbeinu Chananel's* alternative approach to the Gemara, and see *Shitah Mekubetzes* for a lengthy discussion of the entire passage.]

19. Since R' Meir defines an "old" mound as one that has existed for sixty years – and the reason it is considered *tamei* is that people cannot be relied upon to remember whether a burial occurred there sixty years ago – we learn that people's memories are considered reliable for up to sixty years (*Rashi*). Although R' Yehudah disputes R' Meir's definition of "old," that is because he maintains that since those who remember the burial always beware of the *tumah* in that location, they retain the memory for longer than sixty years. He concedes, however, that the memory is ordinarily reliable for only sixty years (*Shitah Mekubetzes* ד״ה שאין אדם זוכרה; see there for an alternative explanation; cf. *Beis Yosef, Choshen Mishpat* 28:13, who states that Rav Chisda means to infer his ruling only from R' Meir's opinion).

20. When a person was designated as a witness to a particular transaction or event, he makes sure to remember it, and we may rely upon his testimony whenever he presents it (*Rashi*). [*Rashi* implies that if the person was not designated as a witness we cannot rely upon his recollection of events after sixty years have passed. However, *Rosh* and

לט א מיי' פ"ח מהל' עדות הלכה ג סמג עשין קט טוש"ע ח"מ סימן מו סעיף יד:
מ ב ג ד ה מיי' פ"ט מהלכות טומאת מת הלכה ג:
מא ו טוש"ע ח"מ סימן כח סעיף ג:
מב ז ח טוש"ע ח"מ סימן מו סעיף י:

א) אהלות פרק ט"ו מ"ב, ב) נזיר סה:, ג) [דברים יט פט"ו].

ואי צורבא מרבנן הוא אפילו עצמו כי הא דרב אשי הוה ידיע ליה בסהדותא לרב כהנא אמר ליה מי דכיר מר האי סהדותא אמר ליה לא ולאו הכי והכי הוה א"ל לא ידענא לסוף אידכר רב אשי אסהיד ליה חזייה לרב כהנא דהוה מחסם א"ל מי סברת עלך קא סמיכנא אנא הוא דרמאי אנפשאי ואדכרי תנן התם התלוליות הקרובות בין לעיר ובין לדרך אחד חדשות ואחד ישנות טמאות הרחוקות חדשות טהורות ישנות טמאות איזוהי קרובה חמשים אמה ואיזו היא ישנה ששים שנה דברי ר"מ רבי יהודה אומר קרובה שאין קרובה הימנה ישנה שאין אדם זוכרה מאי עיר ומאי דרך אילימא עיר עיר ממש דרך דרך ממש מספיקא מי מחזקינן טומאה והאמר ריש לקיש עילה מצאו וטהרו ארץ ישראל א"ר זירא עיר עיר הסמוכה לבית הקברות ודרך דרך בית הקברות בשלמא דרך בית הקברות דזמנין דמתרמי בין השמשות ומקרו קברו בתל אלא עיר הסמוכה לבית הקברות כולהי לבית הקברות אזלי אמר רבי חנינא מתוך שהנשים קוברות שם נפליהן ומוכי שחין זרועותיהם עד חמשים אמה אזלא איהי לחודה טפי דברא איניש בהדה ולבית הקברות אזלא הלכך טומאה בארץ ישראל לא מחזקינן אמר רב חסדא ש"מ מרבי מאיר האי סהדותא עד שיתין שנין מידכר טפי לא מידכר ולא היא התם הוא דלא רמיא עליה אבל הכא כיון דרמי עליה אפילו טובא נמי:

מתני' זה אומר זה כתב ידי וזה כתב ידו של חבירי וזה אומר זה כתב ידי וזה כתב ידו של חבירי הרי אלו נאמנין זה אומר זה כתב ידי וזה אומר זה כתב ידי צריכין לצרף עמהם אחר דברי רבי וחכמים אומרים אינם צריכין לצרף עמהן אחר אלא נאמן אדם לומר זה כתב ידי:

גמ' כשתימצי לומר לדברי רבי על

רש"י

ואי צורבא מרבנן הוא. העד: אפי' לעצמו. של בעל דין לצורבא דרבנן לא נהו כי רמי אנפשיה מדכר שפיר לא הוה סמיך אספיקא למיקם ואסהודי: מחסם. מגמגם מתה על רב אשי שהעיד בדבר: התלוליות. תילי קרקע והדרך בני אדם לקבור בתל משום דאין בני אדם מנין מן הדרך לעבור עליו ועיר ודרך לקמן מפרש להו: אחד חדשות. שאין זמן רחוק שלא היה כאן תל דליכא למימר כיון דחדשה היא אם איתא שנקבר שם מת מדכר דכיר ליה אפ"ה טמאות מספק דכיון דסמוכה לעיר איכא למימר אשה יחידה הלכה וקברה שם נפל שלה: הרחוקות. דאין אשה יחידה הולכת שם: חדשות טהורות. דאם איתא דנקבר ביה הוו ידעי ליה: ישנות טמאות. שכבר נשכחה הדבר מן היודעים: ואיזו היא קרובה. לעיר שאנו אומרים עליה שאף החדשה טמאה חמשים אמה: ואיזו היא ישנה. שאנו אומרים עליה שאפי' היא רחוקה טמאה ששים שנה: שאין קרובה הימנה. אבל אם יש קרובה הימנה אפי' היא בתוך חמשים אמה הויא כרחוקה וחדשה טהורה דאם איתא דהלכה אשה יחידה לקבור לא שבקה קרובה הימנה ואזלא לגבי דהך: שאין אדם זוכרה. שאין אדם אומר זכור אני שלא היה כאן תל ובימי נעשה תל זה היה כאן: עילה מצאו. עילה בעלמא מצאו חכמים והחזיקו בה לתלות עליה ולטהר את ארץ ישראל במסכת נזיר בפרק בתרא אלמא מספיקא לא מחזקינן טומאה בקרקעה של ארץ ישראל: וטיהרו את א"י גרסי' ולא גרסינן: דמתרמי בין השמשות. של ערב השבת ואין שהות לילך עד בית הקברות: ומוכי שחין. שאבריהן נופלין או שחותכין אותן ואבר מן החי מטמא כאבר מן המת כדאמרינן בהעור והרוטב (חולין קכח:): ש"מ. מדקתני לעיל איזו היא ישנה ששים שנה וטעמא משום דלא דכירי לה הוא הדין לסהדות' כו': אבל הכא. שעשאוהו עד בדבר אפילו טובא נמי סמכינן אסהדותיה אי מסהיד: מתני' הרי אלו נאמנין. דאיכא תרי סהדי דמסהדי אכל כתב וכתב: צריכים לצרף עמהן אחר. שיכיר כתב ידי שניהם דתרי סהדי בעינן אכל כתב וכתב וטעמא מפרש בגמרא: גמ' כשתמצי לומר לדברי רבי. כשתעמוד לסוף דבריו קסבר על

תוספות

שטרו בב"ד ויש לומר דע"א בשטר לא חשיב שטר אלא אותו שיש בו שני עדים דומיא דספר מקנה והא דאמר בגט פשוט (ב"ב דף קסה.) עד אחד בכתב ועד אחד בעל פה אין מצטרפין דמשמע הא שנים בשטר אפילו בשתי אגרות מצטרפין התם מיירי כגון שהאחד בשטר והאחד בעל פה לא שאומר שראה הוא המלוה אלא שראה מסירת השטר מלוה למלוה דהוי כשנים החתומים בשטר לר"ח דאמר עדי מסירה כרתי ועוד דבירושלמי מפרש עד א' בשטר היינו שנים חתומים בשטר וקיימו כתב ידו של אחד ולא מצאו לקיים כתב ידו של שני ומ"מ נהי דעד אחד לא חשיב שטר לענין שאם יבואו עדים ויאמרו כך ראינו בשטר דחשבינן להו כעד מפי עד עדות מיהא הוי ויכול לשלוח כתב ידו לב"ד ולא חשיב מפיהם ולא מפי כתבם כיון שהוא זוכר העדות ורש"י פי' בפירוש החומש ג) מפיהם ולא מפי כתבם שלא ישלח בכתב עדותו לב"ד א"נ אומר ר"י דע"א מועיל בשטר אם יש שני שטרות בכל אחד חתום עד א' חשוב כשטר שלם וכ"ת א"כ בשמעתין יביא כתבו לב"ד אפילו אינו זוכר כלל ויש לומר דלא חשיב שטר אלא כשעשוי מדעת שניהם מדעת הלוה שהוא חייב או חשיב שטר אבל הכא שכותב עדותו שלא מדעת הלוה לא חשיב שטרא והקשה ה"ר שמואל מוורדו"ן דאמר בחזקת הבתים (ב"ב דף מ. ושם) מחאה בפני שנים וא"צ לומר כתובו ומה מועיל כתובו כיון דאין עשוי מדעת המחזיק ולפי מה שפירשנו דעדות מיהא הוי כל זמן שזוכר אתי שפיר מיהו בלאו הכי מתרץ ר"י דגבי מחאה הקילו שאינה אלא מדרבנן דהכי נמי הקילו לומר דמחאה שלא בפניו הויא מחאה אע"פ שלפעמים לא ישמע וסמכו על זה דחברך חברא אית ליה וכן במודעא בפני שנים הקילו לכתוב להציל אנוס מאונסו ועוד אומר ר"י דלא בעינן דעת שניהם והכא היה יכול להביא שטרו אם היה כתוב כתיקון שטרות אבל הכא מיירי שאינו כתוב כסדר השטר אלא זכרון דברים בעלמא ומתוך הירושלמי נראה לפ' בענין אחר סוגיא זו דקאמר התם רב הונא כרבי ור' יוחנן כרבנן פירוש כשהעדים באים לקיים חתימתן אם זוכרין המלוה בלא שטר אפי' לרבי א"צ לצרף עמהן אחר מן השוק דעל מנה שבשטר הן מעידין וכשאין זוכרים המלוה אפילו ע"י השטר אפי' רבנן מודו דצריכין לצרף עמהן דעל כרחין אין מעידין אלא על כתב ידן וכי פליגי היינו כשזוכרין המלוה ע"י השטר דלרבנן חשיב זכירה ועל מנה הן מעידין ולרבי לא חשיב זכירה ולשון כותב אדם לא משמע הכי:

אחד חדשות ואחד ישנות. תימה דהכא מזכיר שאינו פשוט קודם וכן בהחולץ (יבמות דף מא.) לא יתארסו ולא ינשאו עד שיהו להן ג' חדשים אחד בתולות ואחד בעולות מזכיר אירוסין קודם נישואין ובתולות קודם בעולות דהיינו שאינו פשוט קודם ובר"ה (דף כט:) תנן אחד יבנה ואחד כל מקום שיש בו ב"ד התם נקט דבר פשוט ברישא וכן בב"ק (דף נ:) אחד החופר בור שיח ומערה ובמ' סוטה (דף מג.) אחד הבונה ואחד הלוקח כו' גבי מערכי מלחמה ורש"י נמי גרים בפ"ק דסוכה (דף כ. ושם) גבי מחצלת גדולה שעשאה לשכיבה טמאה ואין מסככין בה רבי אליעזר אומר אחת קטנה ואחת גדולה ופריך א' גדולה וא' קטנה מבעי ליה והיה כתוב בספרים להפך ורש"י מהפך הגירסא משום דדרך התנאים להזכיר הפשוט קודם ואומר ר"י א) דהיכא דקאי אפלוגתא או אקרא מזכיר הפשוט קודם כי ההיא דפליג ר' אליעזר את"ק בסוכה והוה ליה למימר אחת גדולה שאתה מודה לי כך תודה בקטנה וכן אחד יבנה פליג אדר' אליעזר דאמר לא התקין רבן יוחנן בן זכאי שיהו תוקעין אלא ביבנה בלבד ובב"ק (דף נ:) ובסוטה (דף מג.) קאי אקרא אבל הכא ובהחולץ לא קאי אמידי אין להקפיד איזה נשנה תחלה: [ועי' תוס' שבת כ: ד"ה אחד מבושל פסחים פה. קח: סוכה כ. זבחים לג: ד"ה אי הכי ומנחות סג: ד"ה אחד שבת ועי' תוס' קדושין יג. ד"ה כשם]:

טמאות. פירש בקונטרס דבקרובות אפילו חדשות טמאות משום דאזלא איהי לחודה ואין ידוע אם קברה שם אבל רחוקה דדברא איניש בהדה ואלמלי קברה איניש דאזיל בהדה היה מגלה ולפיכך ישנות טמאות דאע"פ דדברא איניש בהדה נשתכח הדבר וקשה [לר"י] דאם כן אמאי ב) נ"ל בסמוך דדברא איניש בהדה ולבית הקברות אזלא לא הוה ליה למימר אלא דברא איניש בהדה ותו לא ולכך טפי חדשות טהורות דאם איתא דקברה שם היה הדבר ידוע ועוד אי לבית הקברות אזלא ישנות אמאי טמאות ונראה לר"י כר"ח דפירש דישנות טמאות אפילו רחוקות דחיישינן שמא קרובות היו שהיה העיר אצלה וחרב ולפי זה לא נאמר משום דדברא איניש בהדה היה ידוע יותר ולהכי איצטריך לומר ולבית הקברות אזלא: **עילה** מצאו. פירש רבינו חננאל צלע ותלו הטומאה באותה צלע והשאר טהרו:

תוספות ישנים

א) [וי"מ הכא דנקט אחד חדשות לפי שכל דבר חדש הוא תחלה ואח"כ ישן וכמו כן באירוסין קודם נישואין ובתולות שהם קודם בעולות. ומ"מ קשה דבפרק כיצד צולין (דף פה.) קאמר אחד עצם שיש בו מוח ואחד עצם שאין בו מוח ועצם שאין בו מוח פשוט יותר שיש בו משום ועצם לא מצבירי בו והתם לא שייך האי טעמא ולריך לפרש כדפרש"י. ת"י עי"ג]. ב) [ומלי למימר דהרי טעמי לטיבותא נקט. ת"י].

גליון הש"ס

גמ' שאין אדם זוכרה. עיין תוס' יו"ט פ"ב (מ"ג) [מ"ד] דכ"ב ד"ה לא יסמון:

ליקוטי רש"י

צורבא מרבנן. תלמיד חכם [ע"פ שבת קיד.]. דהוה מחסם. לשון לא תחסום (דברים כה) מגמגם בדבר ולא נוקפו [ב"מ כג.]. עילה מצאו וכו'. צלע של ממיס דמתרגמינן (בראשית ב) צלע עילה [כן הגירסא שם נזיר סה:]. דברא. לדברא, הנהיגו [ביצה כט.].

תוספות רי"ד

אומרים שהיו קטנים או אנוסים או פסולי עדות והשטר חתום מסתמא בכשרות וכאילו קיימו סהדי ששטרא קדמאה ואמרו גדולים היינו ורחוקין ולא היינו אנוסים דמי וה"י להו תרי ותרי ולמה אתה מאמין אלה החתומים בשטר יותר מאלה האחרונים ואתה מגבה בו כתב רבינו יוסף הלוי ז"ל וגאון הדברים שזו הקושיא לא אכולהו היא א"א אנוסים בלחוד היא שאומרים מעידים שהעדות לא היתה אמת ולפיכך הקשינו והא תרי ותרי נינהו אבל קטנים היו פסולי עדות היו אין בהן דרך לקושיא זו שהרי עדותן על גוף העדים הוא ולא על העדות הלכך לא מציה לאוקמי לקושיא זו אלא על אנוסים היו בלחוד ונראין עתה דבריו שכ"ז שהיו מעידין על גוף העדים ואומרים שהיו קטנים או פסולים שהן נאמנין ולא אמרינן תרי ותרי נינהו אלא דחינן לסהדותא דקמאי ופסלינן להו לגמרי משום סהדותא דהני בתראי דמסהדי על קמאי ופסלו להו [...]

להו מתורת עדות לגמרי אבל כשאומרים קטנים הייתם או קרובים הייתם כיון דמודו דהשתא בני עדות נינהו ומסהדי על ההיא זימנא בלחוד הוו להו תרי ותרי דהא השתא הם כשרי' לעדות ואמרי לא היינו קטנים לא היינו קרובים ומש"ה לא מהימנינן לבתראי. ומקשינן אמאי קאמר ת"ק שאין נאמנים ומגבינן ביה תרי ותרי נינהו ועל כולן מקשינן בין על קטנים היו בין על אנוסים היו בין על קרובים היו אלא א"ר נחמן אוקי תרי לבהדי תרי ואוקי ממונא בחזקת מריה [...]

[...] אתם אלא נאמנים הם לפוסלן כדאמרינן בפרק דיני ממונות בתרא גבי עד זומם דאמר רבא [...]

חזקה דנפשיה פירוש שקנאם הוא והוחזקו בידו אמרינן כשהוא שוטה זבן וכשהוא שוטה זבין פי' כקנ[...] חזקתו חזקה לבטל מכירתו עי' בפ"ג דיבמות: א"ר אבהו אין מזימין את העדים אלא בפניהם ומכחי[...] בפניהם והזמה שלא בפניהם נהי דהזמה לא הוי הכחשה מיהא הוי פירוש בהזמה דמענש בכאשר זמ[...]

חשק שלמה על תוס' רי"ד א) נ"ל והזמה שלא בפניהם הכחשה מיהו הוי פי' הסורה וכו'.

וְאִי צוּרְבָא מֵרַבָּנָן הוּא – **But if [the witness]**[1] **is a young Rabbinical scholar,** אֲפִילּוּ עַצְמוֹ – his testimony is accepted **even** if he was prodded by the litigant **himself.**[2]

The Gemara cites an example of this exception:

כִּי הָא דְּרַב אַשִׁי הֲוָה יְדִיעַ לֵיהּ בְּסַהֲדוּתָא לְרַב כַּהֲנָא – **As in that** incident **in which Rav Ashi had knowledge of testimony** pertaining **to Rav Kahana.** אֲמַר לֵיהּ מִי דְּכִיר מַר הַאי סַהֲדוּתָא – **[Rav Kahana] said to [Rav Ashi], "Does the master remember this testimony?"** אֲמַר לֵיהּ לֹא – **[Rav Ashi] replied, "No!"** וְלָאו הָכִי וְהָכִי הֲוָה – Rav Kahana attempted to remind Rav Ashi, **"Was it not thus and thus?"** אֲמַר לֵיהּ לֹא יָדַעְנָא – **[Rav Ashi] replied, "I do not know."** לְסוֹף אִידְּכַר רַב אַשִׁי – **Eventually, Rav Ashi remembered** the incident. אַסְהִיד לֵיהּ – **He** then **testified on behalf of [Rav Kahana].** חַזְיֵיהּ לְרַב כַּהֲנָא דַּהֲוָה מְחַסֵּם – **He saw that Rav Kahana was stammering** in amazement.[3] אֲמַר לֵיהּ – **[Rav Ashi]** therefore **said to [Rav Kahana],** מִי סָבְרַתְּ אֲנָא עֲלָךְ קָא סָמִיכְנָא – **"Do you think I am relying upon you?** הוּא דִּרְמַאי אַנַּפְשַׁאי וְאִדְּכַרִי – **It was I who concentrated, and I** finally **remembered** the incident."[4]

In connection with its discussion of the remembering of testimony, the Gemara introduces another subject concerning which memory is a factor. This is the matter of an unidentified mound in the vicinity of a town, that might contain an old grave:

תְּנַן הָתָם – **We learned in a Mishnah there:**[5] הַתְּלוּלִיּוֹת הַקְּרוֹבוֹת בֵּין לָעִיר וּבֵין לַדֶּרֶךְ – Concerning MOUNDS THAT ARE NEAR EITHER THE TOWN OR THE PATH,[6] אֶחָד חֲדָשׁוֹת וְאֶחָד יְשָׁנוֹת טְמֵאוֹת – BOTH NEW ONES AND OLD ONES ARE *TAMEI*.[7] הָרְחוֹקוֹת – But concerning THOSE THAT ARE FAR from the town or path, חֲדָשׁוֹת טְהוֹרוֹת – THE NEW ONES ARE *TAHOR*, whereas THE OLD ONES יְשָׁנוֹת טְמֵאוֹת – ARE *TAMEI*.[8]

The Mishnah defines the above-mentioned terms:

אֵיזוֹהִי קְרוֹבָה – WHICH IS called "NEAR" the town or path – and deemed *tamei* even if new? חֲמִשִּׁים אַמָּה – Any that is within FIFTY *AMOS*. וְאֵיזוֹ הִיא יְשָׁנָה – AND WHICH IS called "OLD" – and deemed *tamei* even if far? שִׁשִּׁים שָׁנָה – Any that is SIXTY YEARS old.[9] דִּבְרֵי רַבִּי מֵאִיר – These are THE WORDS OF R' MEIR. רַבִּי יְהוּדָה אוֹמֵר – R' YEHUDAH SAYS: קְרוֹבָה שֶׁאֵין קְרוֹבָה הֵימֶנָּה – "NEAR" means THAT THERE IS NONE CLOSER THAN IT;[10] יְשָׁנָה שֶׁאֵין אָדָם זוֹכְרָהּ – "OLD" means THAT NO ONE REMEMBERS the origin of IT.[11]

The Gemara seeks clarification of the Mishnah:

מַאי עִיר וּמַאי דֶּרֶךְ – **What is** the **"town" and what is** the **"path"** to which the Mishnah refers? אִילֵימָא עִיר עִיר מַמָּשׁ דֶּרֶךְ דֶּרֶךְ מַמָּשׁ – **If you say** that **"town"** means **literally** *any* **town** and **"path"** means **literally** *any* **path,** I will ask: מִסְפֵּיקָא מִי מַחְזְקִינַן טוּמְאָה – **Do we make a presumption of *tumah* out of doubt** without a firm basis?[12] וְהָאָמַר רֵישׁ לָקִישׁ – **Why Reish Lakish said:** עִילָּה מָצְאוּ וְטִהֲרוּ אֶרֶץ יִשְׂרָאֵל – **They found a pretext and declared Eretz Yisrael *tahor*!**[13] Thus, we see that without a compelling reason we do not declare any area in Eretz Yisrael *tamei* out of doubt. – ? –

The Gemara therefore narrows the definition of "town" and "path":

אָמַר רַבִּי זֵירָא – **R' Zeira said:** עִיר עִיר הַסְּמוּכָה לְבֵית הַקְּבָרוֹת – The **"town"** to which the Mishnah refers is **a town that is close to a graveyard,** וְדֶרֶךְ דֶּרֶךְ בֵּית הַקְּבָרוֹת – **and** the **"path"** to which it refers is **a path** leading **to a graveyard.**[14] There is a real basis to be concerned for *tumah* in mounds in those areas.

The Gemara seeks a clarification:

בִּשְׁלָמָא דֶּרֶךְ בֵּית הַקְּבָרוֹת – **It is understandable** why a mound

---

NOTES

1. *Rashi;* cf. *Rambam, Hil. Eidus* 8:3.

2. [A Torah scholar is very meticulous in all of his actions.] We may safely assume that if he were not now certain about the details of the incident himself he would not testify on the basis of the litigant's words (*Rashi;* see also *Ritva;* cf. *Rambam* ibid.; see *Urim VeTumim* 28:17).

3. Rav Kahana wondered how Rav Ashi could have testified after stating that he did not remember the incident (*Rashi*). [*Rosh* has a variant reading, according to which Rav Kahana expressed his amazement when Rav Ashi was *preparing* to testify.]

4. We learn from this incident that a witness who initially says he does not remember is allowed to later retract and say that he remembered. In this regard, we do not say that כֵּיוָן שֶׁהִגִּיד שׁוּב אֵינוֹ חוֹזֵר וּמַגִּיד – once the witness has stated something he cannot retract it (*Mordechai* to *Shevuos* §763; see also *Ran* to *Shevuos* 31b, end of folio 14b in Vilna ed. of *Rif; Beis Yosef, Choshen Mishpat* 29:1; cf. *Hagahos Asheri* here).

5. *Oholos* 16:2.

6. The Gemara will explain what type of "town" and "path" this refers to (*Rashi*). The Mishnah itself will discuss the definition of "near."

7. Mounds were commonly used as burial sites, since passersby were unlikely to leave the road and walk over them. [The reference is to mounds that have a degree of elevation which discourages traffic (*Radvaz,* cited by *Shitah Mekubetzes*).] The Mishnah teaches that any mound "near" the town or path is deemed *tamei,* because of the possibility that it contains a corpse. Even if the mound is a relatively "new" one, in which case one could argue that if a corpse had been buried there people would remember, it is deemed *tamei* out of doubt. [As the Gemara will explain below,] since the mound is near the town, there is a possibility that a woman who miscarried went there alone and buried her fetus – and the matter never became known publicly (*Rashi;* see *Shitah Mekubetzes*).

8. The "new" mounds are *tahor* because if anyone had been buried there it would be common knowledge. The concern that a woman buried her fetus there privately does not apply, since the mounds are too distant from the town for a woman to have gone there alone. However, the "old" mounds are *tamei* because it is possible that a burial was done there long ago and was common knowledge at that time, but people have since forgotten (*Rashi*). The Mishnah will presently define the terms "new" and "old."

9. Thus, any mound within fifty *amos* of the town or path is *tamei* even if it is new, and any mound more than sixty years old is *tamei* even if it is more distant that fifty *amos* (*Rashi*). [However, even the "old" mounds are *tamei* only if they are located between the town or path and the nearest graveyard. Those beyond the graveyard are *tahor,* since there is no reason to suspect that anyone would have traveled there to bury someone (*Ramban;* see *Pnei Yehoshua*).]

10. Only then must we be concerned for *tumah* in a new mound. If there is a mound closer than this one, the further one is *tahor* even though it is within fifty *amos* of the town or path – because if a woman went out alone to bury her fetus she would not have passed over the nearby mound and gone to the more distant one (*Rashi*). R' Yehudah concedes that any new mound more than fifty *amos* from the town or path is *tahor.* He simply adds that even within fifty *amos* only the very first mound is *tamei* (*Shitah Mekubetzes*).

11. That is, no one can say, "I remember when there was no mound here and when it came into being" (*Rashi;* see note 20 for clarification of R' Yehudah's dispute with R' Meir). Since the mound has existed longer than anyone can remember, we need to be concerned for the possibility that a corpse was once buried here and has been forgotten (*Ramban;* cf. *Maharsha, Shitah Mekubetzes*).

12. [I.e. would we indiscriminately render mounds all over Eretz Yisrael *tamei,* without a compelling basis?]

13. Reish Lakish stated this in Tractate *Nazir* (65b), concerning a certain leniency that the Rabbis relied upon with respect to a specific possibility of *tumah* in Eretz Yisrael (*Rashi*). He meant that in order to minimize the areas in the Holy Land that are off limits to Kohanim and others for whom *taharah* is important, the Rabbis used even a weak justification to avoid declaring land *tamei* out of doubt (*Rosh, Nazir* 65b; cf. *Tosafos* ד"ה עילה).

14. I.e. the path leading from a town that has no graveyard towards the graveyard of another town (*Radvaz,* cited by *Shitah Mekubetzes;* see *Shitah Mekubetzes* and *Chazon Ish, Oholos* 22:5, for clarification of the term "town that is close to a graveyard").

ואי צורבא מרבנן הוא אפילו עצמו כי הא דרב אשי הוה ידיע ליה בסהדותא לרב כהנא אמר ליה מי דכיר מר האי סהדותא אמר ליה לא ולאו הכי והכי הוה א"ל לא ידענא לסוף אידכר רב אשי אסהיד ליה חזייה לרב כהנא דהוה מחסם א"ל מי סברת עלך קא סמיכנא אנא הוא דרמאי אנפשאי ואדכרי א) תנן התם ב התלוליות הקרובות בין לעיר ובין לדרך אחד חדשות ואחד ישנות טמאות הרחוקות חדשות טהורות ישנות טמאות איזוהי קרובה חמשים אמה ואיזו היא ישנה ששים שנה דברי ר"מ רבי יהודה אומר ג קרובה שאין קרובה הימנה ישנה ד שאין אדם זוכרה מאי עיר ומאי דרך אילימא עיר ממש דרך דרך ממש מספיקא מי מחזקינן טומאה והאמר ריש לקיש ב) עילה מצאו וטהרו ארץ ישראל א"ר זירא ה עיר עיר הסמוכה לבית הקברות ודרך דרך בית הקברות בשלמא דרך בית הקברות זימנין דמתרמי בין השמשות ומקרו קברו בתל אלא עיר הסמוכה לבית הקברות כולהי לבית הקברות אזלי אמר רבי חנינא ו מתוך שהנשים קוברות שם נפליהן ומוכי שחין זרועותיהם עד חמשים אמה אזלא איהי לחודה טפי דברא איניש בהדה ולבית הקברות אזלא הלכך טומאה בארץ ישראל לא מחזקינן אמר רב חסדא ש"מ מרבי מאיר האי סהדותא עד שיתין שנין מידכר טפי לא מידכר ולא היא התם הוא דלא רמיא עליה אבל הכא ז כיון דרמי עליה אפילו טובא נמי: **מתני'** ז זה אומר כתב ידי וזה כתב ידו של חבירי וזה אומר זה כתב ידי וזה כתב ידו של חבירי הרי אלו נאמנין זה אומר זה כתב ידי וזה אומר זה כתב ידי צריכין לצרף עמהם אחר דברי רבי וחכמים אומרים אינם צריכין לצרף עמהן אחר ח אלא נאמן אדם לומר זה כתב ידי: **גמ'** כשתימצי לומר לדברי רבי על

רש"י

ואי צורבא מרבנן הוא. הכי גרסי': אפי' לעצמו. של בעל דין לצורבא דרבנן אי לאו דכי רמי אנפשיה מדכר שפיר לא הוה סמיך אספיקא למיקם ולאסהודי: מחסם. מגמגם ממה על רב אשי שהעיד לדבר: התלוליות. תילי קרקע ודרך בני אדם לקבור בתל משום דאין בני אדם מטין מן הדרך לעבור עליו ועיר ודרך לקמן מפרש להו: אחד חדשות. שאין זמן רחוק שלא היה כאן תל דליכא למימר כיון דחדשה היא אם איתא שנקבר שם מת מדכר דכיר ליה אפ"ה טמאות משום מספק דכיון דסמוכה לעיר איכא למימר אשה יחידה הלכה וקברה שם נפל שלה: הרחוקות. דאין אשה יחידה הולכת שם: חדשות טהורות. דאם איתא דנקבר ביה הוו ידעי ליה: ישנות טמאות. שכבר נשתכח הדבר מן היודעים: ואיזו היא קרובה. לעיר שאנו אומרים עליה שאף החדשה טמאה חמשים אמה: ואיזו היא ישנה. שאנו אומרים עליה שאפי' היא רחוקה טמאה ששים שנה: שאין קרובה הימנה. אבל אם יש קרובה הימנה אפי' היא בתוך חמשים אמה הויא כרחוקה וחדשה טהורה דאם איתא דהלכה אשה יחידה לקבור לא שבקה קרובה הימנה ואזלה לגבי דהך: שאין אדם זוכרה. שאין אדם אומר זכור אני שלא היה כאן תל ובימי נעשה תל זה כאן: עילה מצאו. עלילה בעלמא מצאו חכמים והחזיקו בה לתלות עליה ולטהר את ארץ ישראל במסכת נזיר בפרק בתרא אלמא מספיקא לא מחזקינן טומאה בקרקעה של ארץ ישראל: וטיהרו את א"י גרסי' ולא גרסינן כל: דמתרמי בין השמשות. של ערב שבת ואין שהות לילך עד בית הקברות: ומוכי שחין. שאבריהן נופלין או שחותכין אותן ואבר מן החי מטמא כאבר מן המת כדאמרינן בהעור והרוטב (חולין קכט.): ש"מ. מדקתני לעיל איזו היא ישנה ששים שנה וטעמא משום דלא דכירי לה הוא הדין להאי סהדות' כו': אבל הכא. שעשאוהו עד בדבר אפילו טובא נמי סמכינן אאדכרותיה אי מסהיד: מתני' הרי אלו נאמנין. דאיכא תרי סהדי למסהדי אכל כתב וכתב: צריכים לצרף עמהן אחר. שיכיר כתב ידי שניהם דתרי סהדי בעינן אכל כתב וכתב וטעמא מפרש בגמרא: גמ' כשתימצי לומר לדברי רבי. כשתעמוד לסוף דבריו קסבר על

תוספות

שטרו בב"ד ויש לומר דע"א בשטר לא חשיב שטר אלא אותו שיש בו שני עדים דומיא דספר מקנה והא דאמר בגט פשוט (ב"ב דף קסה.) עד אחד בכתב ועד אחד בעל פה אין מצטרפין משמע דאם שניהם בשטר אפילו בשתי אגרות מצטרפין התם מיירי כגון שהאחד בשטר והאחד בעל פה שאומר שראה מסירת השטר למלוה דהוי כשנים החתומים בשטר לר"א דאמר עדי מסירה כרתי ועוד דבירושלמי מפרש עד א' בשטר היינו שנים חתומים בשטר וקיימו כתב ידו של אחד ולא מצאו לקיים כתב ידו של שני ומ"מ נהי דעד אחד לא חשיב שטר לענין שאם יבואו עדים ויאמרו כך ראינו בשטר דתחשבינן להו כעד מפי עד עדות מיהא הוי ויכול לשלוח כתב ידו לב"ד ולא חשיב מפיהם ולא מפי כתבם כיון שהוא זוכר העדות ורש"י פי' בפירוש החומש ג) מפיהם ולא מפי כתבם שלא ישלח בכתב עדותו לב"ד א"נ אומר ר"י דע"א מועיל בשטר אם יש שני שטרות בכל אחד חתום עד א' חשוב כשטר שלם וכו' א"כ בשמעתין יביא כתבו לב"ד אפילו אינו זוכר כלל ויש לומר דלא חשיב שטר אלא כשעשוי מדעת שניהם מדעת הלוה שהוא חייב אז חשיב שטר אבל הכא שכותב עדותו שלא מדעת הלוה לא חשיב שטרא והקשה ה"ר שמואל מוורדון דאמר בחזקת הבתים (ב"ב דף מ. ושם) מחאה בפני שנים וא"צ לומר כתובו ומה מועיל כתובו כיון דאין עשוי מדעת המחזיק ולפי מה שפירשנו לעדות מיהא הוי כל זמן שזוכר אתי שפיר מיהו בלאו הכי מתרץ ר"י דגבי מחאה הקילו שאינה אלא מדרבנן דהכי נמי הקילו לומר דמחאה שלא בפניו הויא מחאה אע"פ שלפעמים לא ישמע וסמכו על דחברך חברא אית ליה וכן במודעא בפני שנים הקילו לכתוב להציל אנוס מאונסו ועוד אומר ר"י דלא בעינן דעת שניהם והכא היה יכול להביא שטרו אם היה כתוב כתיקון שטרות אבל הכא מיירי שאינו כתוב כסדר השטר אלא זכרון דברים בעלמא ומתוך הירושלמי נראה לפ' בענין אחר סוגיא זו דקאמר התם רב הונא כרבי ור' יוחנן כרבנן פירוש כשהעדים באים לקיים חתימתן אם זוכרין המלוה בלא שטר אפי' לרבי א"צ לצרף עמהן אחר מן השוק דעל מנה שבשטר הן מעידין וכשאין זוכרים המלוה אפילו ע"י השטר אפי' רבנן מודו דצריכין לצרף עמהן דעל כרחין אין מעידין אלא על כתב ידן וכי פליגי היינו כשזוכרין המלוה ע"י השטר דלרבנן חשיב זכירה ועל מנה הן מעידין ולרבי לא חשיב זכירה ולשון כותב אדם לא משמע הכי: **אחד** חדשות ואחד ישנות. תימה דהכא מזכיר שאינו פשוט קודם וכן בהחולץ (יבמות דף מא.) לא יתארסו ולא ינשאו עד שיהו להן ג' חדשים אחד בתולות ואחד בעולות מזכיר אירוסין קודם נישואין ובתולות קודם בעולות דהיינו שאינו פשוט קודם ובר"ה (דף כט:) תנן אחד יבנה ואחד כל מקום שיש בו ב"ד התם נקט דבר פשוט ברישא וכן בב"ק (דף נ:) אחד החופר בור שיח ומערה ובמס' סוטה (דף מג.) אחד הבונה ואחד הלוקח כו' גבי מערכי מלחמה ורש"י נמי גריס בפ"ק דסוכה (דף כ. ושם) גבי מחצלת גדולה שעשאה לשכיבה טמאה ואין מסככין בה רבי אליעזר אומר אחת קטנה ואחת גדולה ופריך א' גדולה וא' קטנה מבעי ליה והיה כתוב בספרים להפך ורש"י מהפך הגירסא משום דדרך התנאים להזכיר הפשוט קודם ואומר ר"י א) דהיכא דקאי אפלוגתא או אקרא מזכיר הפשוט קודם כי ההיא דפליג ר' אליעזר את"ק בסוכה והוה ליה למימר אחת גדולה שאתה מודה לי כך תודה בקטנה וכן אחד יבנה פליג אדר' אליעזר דאמר לא התקין רבן יוחנן בן זכאי שיהו תוקעין אלא ביבנה בלבד ובב"ק (דף נ:) ובסוטה (דף מג.) קאי אקרא אבל הכא ובהחולץ לא קאי אמידי אין להקפיד איזה נשנה תחלה: [ועי' תוס' שבת כ: ד"ה אחד מבושל פסחים פה. קח: סוכה כ. זבחים לב: ד"ה אי הכי ומנחות סג: ד"ה אחד שבת ועי' תוס' קדושין יג. ד"ה כשם]:

טמאות. פירש בקונטרס דבקרובות אפילו חדשות טמאות משום דאזלא איהי לחודה ואין ידוע אם קברה שם אבל רחוקה דדברא איניש בהדה ואלמלי קברה איניש דאזיל בהדה היה מגלה ולפיכך ישנות טמאות דאע"פ דדברא איניש בהדה נשתכח הדבר וקשה [לר"י] דאם כן אמאי ב) נ"ל בסמוך דדברא איניש בהדה ולבית הקברות אזלא לא הוה ליה למימר אלא דברא איניש בהדה ותו לא ולכך טפי חדשות טהורות דאם איתא דקברה שם היה הדבר ידוע ועוד אי לבית הקברות אזלא ישנות אמאי טמאות ונראה לר"י כר"ח דפירש דישנות טמאות אפילו רחוקות דחיישינן שמא קרובות היו שהיה העיר אצלה וחרב ולפי זה לא נאמר משום דדברא איניש בהדה היה ידוע יותר ולהכי איצטריך לומר ולבית הקברות אזלא: **עילה** מצאו. פירש רבינו חננאל צלע ותלו הטומאה באותה צלע והשאר טהרו:

עין משפט נר מצוה

לט א מיי' פ"ט מהל' עדות הלכה ג סמג עשין קט טוש"ע ח"מ סימן כח סעיף יד:
מ ב ג ד ה מיי' פ"ט מהלכות טומאת מת הלכה ג:
מא ו טוש"ע ח"מ סימן כח סעיף ג:
מב ז ח טוש"ע ח"מ סימן מו סעיף י:

מסורת הש"ס

א) אהלות פרק ט"ז מ"ב, ב) נזיר סה:, ג) [דברים יט טו].

תוספות ישנים

א) [וי"מ הכא דנקט אחד חדשות לפי שכל דבר חדש הוא תחלה ואח"כ ישן וכמו כן באירוסין קודם נישואין ובתולות שהם קודם בעולות. ומ"מ קשה דבפרק כיצד צולין (דף פה.) קאמר אחד עצם שיש בו מוח ואחד עצם שאין בו מוח וע"כ שאין בו מוח פשוט יותר שיש בו משום ועצם לא תשברו בו והתם לא שייך האי טעמא. וצריך לפרש כדפרש"י. ת"י עס"ג]. ב) ומצי למימר דתרי טעמי אצטריכותא נקט. [ת"י].

גליון הש"ס

גמ' שאין אדם זוכרה. עיין תוס' יו"ט פ"ב (מ"ג) [מ"ד] דב"ב ד"ה לא ימנון:

ליקוטי רש"י

צורבא מרבנן. תלמיד חכם [ע"פ שבת קיד.]. דהוה מחסם. לשון לא תחסום (דברים כה) מגמגם בדבר ולבו נוקפו [ב"מ כג:]. עילה מצאו וכו'. צלע של מתים דמתרגמינן (בראשית ב) צלע עילע [בן הגירסא שם, נזיר סה:]. דברא. לדבריה, הנהיגו [ביצה כט.].

תוספות רי"ד

[illegible]

תוספות רי"ד

[illegible]

מסורת הש"ס

א) יבמות לא. ב) [נ"ל ארעא וכן איתא ביבמות לא: וכן העתיק הרשב"ם בב"ב מג: ד"ה ואי בעית אימא], ג) [תוספתא פ"ב], ד) [נ"ל רבא וכן איתא בשאלתות פ' יתרו סימן נה וכ"א ברי"ף והרא"ש], ה) [וע"ע תוס' ב"ב קה. ד"ה אבל].

עין משפט נר מצוה

לב א מיי' פ"ו מהלכות עדות הלכה ז סמג עשין קט טוש"ע ח"מ סימן מו סעיף לז:
לג ב מיי' פכ"ט מהל' מכירה הלכה ה סמג עשין פב טוש"ע ח"מ סי' רלה סעיף כא בהגה"ה:
לד ג ב"י ח"מ שם:
לה ד מיי' פי"ח מהל' עדות הלכה ה סמג עשין קו טור ח"מ סימן לח:
לו ה ו ז מיי' פ"ו שם הלכה ג סמג שם טוש"ע ח"מ סימן מו סעיף ז:
לז ח ט מיי' פ"ח מהל' עדות הלכה א סמג עשין קט טוש"ע ח"מ סימן כח סעיף יג:
לח י כ מיי' שם הלכה ג טוש"ע ח"מ שם סעיף יד:

גמרא

וכשם שאין מזימין את העדים אלא בפניהם כך אין מכחישין את העדים אלא בפניהם אמר ליה רב נחמן אילו הוו קמן ומכחישין להו הוה הכחשה ולא הוה משגיחין בהו דהוי לה עדות מוכחשת השתא דליתנהו דאילו הוו לקמן דלמא הוו מודו להו מהימני אלא אמר רב נחמן א אוקי תרי להדי תרי ואוקי ממונא בחזקת מריה (א) מידי דהוה אנכסי דבר שטיא דבר שטיא זבין ונכסי אתו בי תרי אמרי כשהוא שוטה זבין ואתו בי תרי ואמרי כשהוא חלים זבין אמר רב אשי ב אוקי תרי להדי תרי ואוקי ב ממונא בחזקת בר שטיא ולא אמרן ג אלא דאית ליה חזקה דאבהתיה אבל לית ליה חזקה דאבהתיה אמרינן כשהוא שוטה זבן • וכשהוא שוטה זבין א"ר אבהו ד אין מזימין את העדים אלא בפניהן ומכחישין את העדים שלא בפניהן והזמה שלא בפניהן נהי דהזמה לא הוי הכחשה מיהא הויא אמר מר אם יש עדים שכתב ידם הוא זה או שהיה כתב ידם יוצא ממקום אחר משטר שקרא עליו ערער והוחזק בב"ד אין נאמנין (א) קרא עליו ערער אין לא קרא עליו ערער לא מסייע ליה לרבי אסי דאמר רבי אסי ה אין מקיימין את השטר אלא משטר שקרא עליו ערער והוחזק בב"ד אמרי נהרדעי ו אין מקיימין את השטר אלא משתי כתובות [או] משתי שדות והוא שאכלום בעליהן ג' שנים ובשופי א"ר שימי בר אשי ז וביוצא מתחת יד אחר אבל מיד עצמו לא מאי שנא תחת יד עצמו דלא דלמא זיופי מזייף מתחת ידי אחר נמי דלמא אזל והזא אתא וזייף כולי האי לא מצי מכוין ת"ר ח כותב אדם עדותו על השטר ומעיד עליה אפילו לאחר כמה שנים אמר רב הונא והוא שזוכרה מעצמו רבי יוחנן אמר ט אע"פ שאין זוכרה מעצמו אמר ד רבה ש"מ מדרבי יוחנן י הני בי תרי דידעי סהדותא ומנשי חד מנייהו מדכר חד לחבריה איבעיא להו עצמו מאי רב חביבא אמר אפילו עצמו מר בריה דרב אשי אמר עצמו לא והלכתא כ עצמו לא

רש"י

וכשם שאין מזימין העדים אלא בפניהם. שהרי הם באין לחייבן כדי לעונשן או נפש או ממון והתורה אמרה והועד בבעליו יבא בעל השור ויעמוד על שורו (ב"ק דף קיב:): **כך אין מכחישין.** אפילו לבטל עדותן: **לא הוו משגיחין בהו.** בעדי השטר לגבות על פיהם: **השתא.** דליכא למימר אילו הוו קמן הוו מודו להני אמרת מהימני: **ואוקי ממונא בחזקת מריה.** בחזקת הלוה ואם קרקע היא תעמוד בחזקת המוכר ודקתני בברייתא אין נאמנים לא ליהוי שטרא מעליא למיגבי ביה אלא דלא קרעינן ליה ואי תפיס מידי והדר אתי האי ותבע מיניה לא מפקינן מיניה דאמרינן אוקי תרי לגבהי תרי וממונא בחזקת היכא דקאי: **זבין נכסיה.** מכר קרקעותיו: **חלים.** בריא: **ולא אמרן.** דאוקי נכסי בחזקת בר שטיא: **אלא דאית ליה.** בנכסים הללו חזקה דאבהתא שהיו של אבותיו לחזקה מעלייתא היא: **אבל לית ליה בהו חזקה דאבהתא.** אלא חזקה דנפשיה שקנאן הוא והוחזקו בידו כקנייתו כך מכירתו ואין חזקתו חזקה לבטל מכירתו: **נהי דהזמה לא הויא.** לעונשם לא נפש ולא ממון הכחשה הויא לבטל עדותן: **אין מקיימין את השטר.** מתוך שטר אחר: **אא"כ קרא ערער.** על אותו שטר האחר והוחזק בב"ד על ידי עדיו דאי לא קרא עליו ערער חיישינן דלמא הוא הוא גופיה מזויף הוא: **משתי שדות.** מעדים האלה אם חתומים על שני שטרות אחרים שהן מכר שתי שדות ואכלום הלקוחות ע"י שטרות הללו שלש שנים מקיימין שטר שלישי מהן אם החתימות דומות: **בשופי.** בלא ערעור: **וביוצא מתחת ידי אחר.** שהשטרות הללו שמקיימין את השלישי מהם יוצא מתחת ידי אחר ולא מתחת ידיו של זה המוציא את השלישי: **זיופי זייף.** הסתכל בכתב של אותן שטרות וכוון ותפס הוא עצמו את השלישי דוגמת אותה חתימה: **מכוין.** מתכוין לכתוב הואיל ואינו לפניו: **כותב אדם.** אם עשאוהו עד בדבר וירא לשכוח כותבו על חתיכת קלף ומניחה: **ומעיד.** על פי אותו כתב אפי' לאחר כמה שנים: **שזוכרה מעצמו.** בלא ראיית השטר מכר קצת מעדותו מאליו: **אע"פ שאין זוכרה מעצמו.** אלא לאחר שרואה בשטר נתן בלבו ונזכר שלא נשכחת ממנו כל כך שכשמזכירים לו נזכר אבל אינו נזכר לגמרי לא דרחמנא אמר מפיהם ולא מפי כתבם: **עצמו מאי.** אם בעל דין עצמו מזכירו עד שנזכר מאי:

תוספות

ואוקי ממונא בחזקת מריה. פירש בקונט' ולאו נאמנין דקתני לאו דמגבינא בשטרא אלא דלא קרעינן ליה ונפקא מינה דאי תפס לא מפקינן מיניה וקשה דאמר בפ"ק דב"מ (דף ו: ושם) גבי ספק בכור תקפו כהן מוציאין אותו מידו דלמא תפיסה דלאחר ספיקא לאו כלום היא ומיהו אההוא דסוף השואל (שם דף קב: ושם) לא קשה מידי דאמרי' גבי משכיר בית לחבירו בי"ב זהובים לשנה מדינר זהב לחדש בא בתחלת החדש כולו למשכיר אלמא דבחזקת משכיר הוא ואפ"ה קאמר בא בסוף החדש כולו לשוכר דשאני התם דכיון דלא בא בתחלת החדש איכא למימר לשוכר דאשתעבד הדר ביה ויש לומר דשאני גבי בכור שכהן תופס מספק דאין יודע אם בכור הוא אבל הכא שטוען ברי מהני תפיסה וה"נ בחזקת הבתים (ב"ב דף לד:) גבי זה אומר של אבותי כו' אמר ר"נ כל דאלים גבר ופריך מהמחליף פרה בחמור זה אומר ברשותו ילדה וזה אומר כו' יחלוקו ומאי קושיא הא התם אתיא כסומכוס ור"נ כרבנן דלרבנן דאמרי המע"ה היינו דינא דכל דאלים גבר כיון דמהניא תפיסה דשוטען ברי ויש לומר דהכי פריך דלפי' דרבנן לא פליגי אסומכוס אלא משום דחד מינייהו מוחזק ואיכא למימר המע"ה אבל הכא דלאו אחד מוחזק יותר מחבירו מודו לסומכוס דיחלוקו וי"ל דהכא מיירי כשתפס קודם שנולד הספק ורשב"א נראה לו להעמיד הברייתא בשוכר והכי אין נאמנין דאוקי ממונא בחזקת מריה ומחזקין להו שקרא אוי שוכר בכספים ולא יפרע: **אלא אמר ר"נ אוקי תרי להדי תרי כו'.** וא"ת ולר"נ אמאי לא מגבינן ביה בשטרא הא סבר ר"נ כרב הונא (שבועות מז) [ב"ב דף לא:] בשני כתי עדים המכחישות זו את זו דכל אחת באה בפ"ע ומעידה אע"ג דלפי עדות כל אחת חבירתה פסולה לכל עדות הכא נמי כיון דאין מכחישין אותן לומר שלא לוה כלום אלא אומרים אינכם נאמנים בדבר זה דפסולין הייתם ליהכתבו ואמאי לא מגבינן ביה בשטר ויש לומר דהתם באה כל אחת בפ"ע ומעידה משום דמוקמינן כל אחת בחזקת כשרות אבל הכא שאומרים קטנים היו או קרובים משנולדו עד עתה שנתרחקו ליכא למימר אוקמינהו אחזקתייהו דפסלינן אותן משנולדו ואנוסים היו נמי מחמת נפשות לא שייך לאוקמי אחזקה דהא לא פסלי להו כלל ורשב"א אומר דהכא לא מוקמינן להו אחזקה כדאמר לעיל משום דאילו הוו קמן דלמא הוו מודו:

ואוקי ארעא בחזקת בר שטיא. דוקא בקרקע הוא דאמרינן הכי אבל במטלטלים אמרינן דהוו בחזקת המוחזק כדאמר בפרק השואל (ב"מ דף ק.) גבי המחליף פרה בחמור דפריך וליחזי פרה ברשותא דמאן קיימא ולהוי איהו המע"ה ומשני דקיימא באגם אומר ר"י דהכא לא שייך למימר כדאמרי' בסוף קדושין (דף עט:) ובמי שמת (ב"ב דף קנג: ושם) אם שכיב מרע הוא עליהם להביא ראיה שבריא היה ואם בריא הוא כו' דבר שטיא דהכא כיון דעתים חלים ועתים שוטה אין ראיה ממה שהוא עכשיו: **דלמא זיופי זייף.** אור"ת ° דדוקא היכא שאין אנו מכירין החתימה להחתימה אלא ע"י דמיון החתימה אבל היכא דמכירין חתימת העדים בטביעת עין אע"פ שיש לו חתימה אחרת תחת ידו ליכא למיחש דלמא זייף דכיון דמכירין החתימה אם זייף היה ניכר היטב: **ורבי יוחנן אומר אע"פ שאין זוכרה מעצמו.** פי' אבל ע"י השטר זוכרה אבל אם אין זוכרה כלל לא דמפיהם ולא מפי כתבם כדאמרינן פ' ד' אחין (יבמות דף לא: ושם) גבי מפני מה לא תקנו זמן בקדושין דקאמר לינחי גבי עדים אי דכירי ליתו ולסהדו ואי לא זמנין דחזו בכתבא ואתו ומסהדי ואמר רחמנא מפיהם ולא מפי כתבם וא"ת הכא נמי אמאי לא אסרינן לכתוב עדות על השטר שמא ישכח לגמרי ואתו ומסהדי מכתבא כדחיישינן התם ויש לומר דודאי התם חשו חכמים לפי שב"ד מוסרין לו השטר ויסבור שלכך מסרוהו לו שיעיד אפי' לא יזכור אבל הכא שמעצמו כותב עדותו על השטר לא חשו חכמים לכך וא"ת ואמאי לא מצו חזו בכתבא ולאסהודי הא תנן בגט פשוט (ב"ב דף קסח.) מי שנמחק שטר חובו מעמיד עליו עדים ובא לב"ד ועושין לו קיומו ומפרש בגמ' מהו קיומו וכן בהגוזל קמא (ב"ק דף צח.) דאמרינן גבי שורף שטרותיו של חבירו פטור מדיני אדם כו' ה"ד אי דאיכא סהדי דידעי מה הוה כתוב ביה בשטרא נכתוב ליה שטרא אחרינא אלמא לא חשבינן ליה מפיהם ולא מפי כתבם וי"ל דבפ' ד' אחין (יבמות לא: ושם) חיישינן דלמא אתו ומסהדי בסתם כאילו זוכרין העדות אבל ודאי אם היו מעידין שכך ראו בחתימתן הא לא חשיב מפיהם ולא מפי כתבם דעדים החתומין על השטר נעשה כמי שנחקרה עדותן בבית דין והוי כאילו מעידין ראינו עדות שנחקרה בבית דין ואם תאמר והכא אפילו אין זה זוכרה כלל מה בכך יביא שטרו

תוספות רי"ד

לכתב מש"ה אין נאמנים אפילו ע"י מיגו משום דעולה היא וכי אמרו חתמנו משוי נפשייהו רשיעא ואין אדם משים עצמו רשע אבל מודעא ניתן לכתוב כדי לפצות המוכר מאונסו מאי אמרת הוו להו למיכתב מודעא ברישא מירתת מוכר דלמא מרגיש לוקח ואניס ליה טפי ואי אמרת ומשום אונסיה היכי חתמו שקרא מימר אמר להו סוף סוף על פומייכו בעי לאיתקיימא שטרא אתון דמיתקיימתון ליה אתון אמריתו דאנוס הייתי ותהימנו ע"י מיגו מש"ה סבר מר בר ר"א דניתן לכתוב ונאמנים ור"נ סבר דלמא לא מקיים שטרא מפומייהו אלא אפומי דסהדי אחרינא או מכת"י יוצא ממקום אחר דתו ל"ל מיגו נמצא שחתמו על שקר הלכך לא ניתן לכתוב והל' כר"נ דמסתבר טעמי' ותו דבחזקת הבתים מקשי תלמודא ממילתי' לר"ה דאמר התם מאן דחתם אאשקלתא שפיר חתם איני והא א"ר נחמן מודעא היה דברינו אין נאמנים וקי"ל שאין התלמוד מקשה אלא מהל' פסוקה ואדמקשה מר"נ לסייע ממר בר ר"א אלא לאו ש"מ קים ליה לתלמודא דהלכה כר"נ ע"י בחז"ה שטאבא תלה לפפי בבנרא וזבין ליה ארעא חתם רבב"ח אמודעא ואאשקלתא. **אמר ר"ה** מאן דחתם אמודעא שפיר חתם ומאן דחתם אאשקלתא שפיר חתם ומק' אי מודעא לא אשקלתא ואי אשקלתא לא מודעא א"ל ה"ק אי לאו מודעא מאן דחתם אאשקלתא שפיר חתם ר"ה לטעמיה דאמר ר"ה תלויה וזבין זביניה זביני איני והא אמר ר"נ מודעא היה דברינו אין נאמנים ה"מ ע"פ דלא אתי ע"פ ומרע לשטרא אבל בשטר אתי שטר ומרע שטרי פי' טבי גברא אלמא הוה תלה לפפי באילן ששמו בינרא למכור לו שדהו ולא תלהו כדי שימכור לו האילן וזבין כלומר וכן עשה שמכר לו וחתם רבה בב"ח ועד אחר עמו אמודעא שמסר פפי קודם שנכתב שטר מכירה ואאשקלתא פי' גם על שטר מכירה חתם מאן דחתם אמודעי וכו' דאע"ג דתלויה וזבין זביניה זביני ה"מ היכא דלא מסר מודעא אבל המודעא שנכתב תבטל שטר המכירה ומאן דחתם אאשקלתא וכו' דתלויה וזבין זביניה זביני כדאסיקנא ר"ה לטעמיה וכו' ור' יצחק אלפסי פסיק הל' כמר בר רב אשי: **בעא מיניה** רבא מר"נ

הגהות הב"ח

(א) גמ' תיבות קרא עליו וכו' עד ערער לא. באשר"י מבואר דלא הוה גרס להו:

גליון הש"ס

גמ' וכשהוא שוטה זבין. עי' סוכה דף מו ע"ב תוס' ד"ה דינוקא: תוס' ד"ה דלמא כו' אור"ת דדוקא כו'. עיין לקמן דף כח ע"א תוס' ד"ה קיום שטרות:

ליקוטי רש"י

ובשופי. וילך שפי, וכו' לשון שופי ושקט שאין עמו אלא שתיקה [במדבר כג, ג]. ומנשי. ושכח [ע"פ סנהדרין פב.].

רבא מר"נ תנאי היה דברינו מהו מודעא ואמנה טעמא מאי דעקר לי' לשטרא והאי נמי עקר לה לשטריה או דלמא תנאי מילתא אחריתי (והרב מוליך השיטה בשכת"י יוצא ממקום אחר ובעי' דרבא כשת"י ימ"א) פירוש
מודעא ואמנה מ"ט אמרת דאין נאמנים אע"פ שאין כת"י יוצא ממקום אחר משום דעקרי לה לשטרא השתא בעדותן והלכך אמרינן להו א"כ דאמנה היה ולא הלוה לו או מודעא היה ולא מכר לו מרצונו למה חתמתם אעולה ו

[illegible]

The Gemara questions this statement:

מַאי שְׁנָא תַּחַת יַד עַצְמוֹ דְּלֹא – **What is different** about the case where the source documents are produced **by the person himself, that** you say they are **not** reliable? דִּלְמָא זַיּוּפֵי מְזַיֵּיף – Apparently, it is because there is a concern that **perhaps he accurately forged** the signatures on the document under question after closely examining those on the authentic documents in his possession. מִתַּחַת יְדֵי אַחֵר נַמִּי – If so, even when the source documents are produced **by another person** we should **also** be concerned דִּלְמָא אָזַל וַחֲזָא אָתָא וְזַיֵּיף – that **perhaps he went** to the other person **and saw** the documents, then **came** home **and forged** this third one. – **?** –

The Gemara answers:

כּוּלֵּי הַאי לֹא מָצֵי מְכַוֵּין – **One cannot match** signatures **that well** when the originals are not before him.[16]

Having discussed the certification of documents, the Gemara turns to matters concerning other types of written testimony:

תָּנוּ רַבָּנָן – **The Rabbis taught in a Baraisa:** כּוֹתֵב אָדָם עֵדוּתוֹ עַל הַשְּׁטָר – A PERSON MAY WRITE HIS TESTIMONY ON A DOCUMENT וּמֵעִיד עָלֶיהָ אֲפִילּוּ לְאַחַר כַּמָּה שָׁנִים – AND TESTIFY orally ON ITS BASIS EVEN MANY YEARS LATER.[17]

The Baraisa's ruling is qualified:

אָמַר רַב הוּנָא – **Rav Huna said:** וְהוּא שֶׁזּוֹכְרָהּ מֵעַצְמוֹ – **And this** applies only in a case **where he remembers [the testimony] on his own.**[18]

A dissenting view is cited:

רַבִּי יוֹחָנָן אָמַר – **R' Yochanan said:** אַף עַל פִּי שֶׁאֵין זוֹכְרָהּ מֵעַצְמוֹ – He may testify **even though he does not remember [the testimony] on his own.**[19]

The Gemara analyzes the latter opinion:

אָמַר רַבָּה – **Rabbah**[20] **said:** שְׁמַע מִינָּהּ מִדְּרַבִּי יוֹחָנָן – **Learn from this** ruling **of R' Yochanan** הָנֵי בֵּי תְּרֵי דְּיָדְעֵי סַהֲדוּתָא – that if there are **these two** people **who have knowledge of testimony** regarding a certain matter וּמִנְּשֵׁי חַד מִנַּיְיהוּ – **and one of them forgot** it, מַדְכַּר חַד לְחַבְרֵיהּ – **the** other **one may remind his fellow.**[21]

A related inquiry is cited:

אִיבַּעְיָא לְהוּ – **They inquired:** עַצְמוֹ מַאי – If the litigant **himself** reminded the witness, **what is [the law]?**[22]

The Gemara presents opposing views:

רַב חֲבִיבָא אָמַר – **Rav Chaviva said:** אֲפִילּוּ עַצְמוֹ – **Even** if the litigant **himself** reminded the witness, it is valid testimony.[23]

מַר בְּרֵיהּ דְּרַב אַשִׁי אָמַר – **Mar the son of Rav Ashi said:** עַצְמוֹ לֹא – If the litigant **himself** reminded the witness it is **not** valid testimony.[24]

The Gemara rules on this dispute:

וְהִלְכְתָא עַצְמוֹ לֹא – **And the halachah is** that if the litigant **himself** reminded the witness, it is **not** valid testimony.

NOTES

16. It is highly unlikely that he was able to produce an accurate forgery without having the authentic signatures available for constant comparison (see *Rashi*).

17. That is, if a person was designated as a witness to a certain matter and he is concerned that he might forget what he witnessed, he may record it on a scrap of paper and file it for later use (*Rashi;* cf. *Rav Hai Gaon,* cited by *Rif* and *Rosh; Rambam, Hil. Eidus* 8:1 and *Ritva*).

There is a rule that the court is allowed to accept only the oral testimony of witnesses. If a witness sends the court a written record of something that he saw, it is not admissible as testimony. This is derived from the verse (*Deuteronomy* 19:15): *Through the* ***mouths*** *of two witnesses or three witnesses shall a matter be confirmed* (*Rashi* ad loc.; see *Yevamos* 31b and *Gittin* 71a, and *Choshen Mishpat* 28:11; cf. *Tosafos* ד״ה ורבי יוחנן; see further, note 18). The Baraisa teaches that if a witness recorded that which he observed, he is allowed to come to court even many years later and testify orally to the facts that he finds in his written notes.

18. That is, even before looking at his notes he remembers the facts somewhat [and he looks at the notes merely to fill in the missing details] (*Rashi,* as explained by *Ran* and *Beis Yaakov;* cf. *Ritva, Meiri*). According to Rav Huna, if the witness did not remember the incident at all without looking at his notes, it constitutes written testimony and is unacceptable (*Ran*).

19. Even if he is reminded of the incident entirely through reading his notes, as long as he retained the memory subconsciously so that the notes jar his memory into recalling the incident, R' Yochanan considers it his own oral testimony. However, if he forgot it completely and is relying solely on his notes, his testimony is not valid because it is considered written testimony (*Rashi*). Thus, both Rav Huna and R' Yochanan agree that we cannot accept the witness' written testimony. They disagree only regarding the degree to which the witness must remember the incident to be able to testify. According to Rav Huna, he must remember the basic facts on his own and may rely upon the notes for missing details. According to R' Yochanan, he may rely entirely upon the notes to jog his memory, but after reading the notes must remember *all* the details himself (*Beis Yaakov*).

The Rishonim ask: We know that a signed document is admissible as evidence, and is not subject to the restriction against written testimony. As we learned above (18b), witnesses who are signed on a document are considered as though their testimony has been examined in court. Furthermore, if a witness testifies that he saw a document containing the record of a loan, his testimony based on the document is acceptable (see *Bava Basra* 168a-b). In our case, why are the notes of the witness not regarded as a "document"?

Several fundamental answers are given to this question. *Rashi* to *Gittin* (71a) answers that to be a valid document the instrument must be signed on the day that the transaction took place. This is the usual manner of making a "document"; anything else constitutes a mere writing, which is unacceptable in court. *Tosafos* (ד״ה ורבי יוחנן) suggest three other answers: (a) A document is valid only when *two* witnesses are signed on it; a note signed by a single witness is not considered a "document." (b) A note does not become a legal document unless it is drawn up with the consent of the person that it obligates (e.g. the borrower or seller). (c) A "document" contains formal language, whereas our Gemara deals with notes written in an informal style.

[We have presented *Rashi's* understanding that written testimony is never acceptable in court. Others maintain that written testimony is excluded only if the witness is unable to testify orally, i.e. he is mute or does not recall the incident, but a witness who can speak and recalls that which he wrote down is allowed to send his testimony to court in writing (*Tosafos* ד״ה ורבי יוחנן et al.). For further discussion, see *Rama, Choshen Mishpat* 28:11 with *Sma* §42, *Shach* 39:9 and *Ketzos HaChoshen* 46:19.]

[*Rambam* has an entirely different opinion concerning this matter. He writes (*Hil. Eidus* 3:4) that even written "documents" are in fact not valid under Biblical law. However, since people would be unwilling to lend money if they had to rely upon living witnesses, the Sages instituted that documents be accepted. This view is subject to considerable discussion among the commentators. See especially *Shach* 28:14, *Urim VeTumim* 28:16, *Nesivos HaMishpat* 28:7, and *Chasam Sofer* here; see also *Ketzos HaChoshen* 28:6 and 46:5. For *Rambam's* explanation of our Gemara, see *Hil. Eidus* 8:1-4.]

20. See *Mesoras HaShas* that a variant reading – Rava – is found in some Rishonim.

21. [Just as R' Yochanan permits a person to testify when he is reminded of the incident through his written notes, so too, he will permit him to testify when reminded by his fellow witness. In either case, since he eventually recalls the incident, the testimony is considered his own.]

22. I.e. the litigant prodded the witness until he recalled the facts himself (*Rashi*). Need we be concerned that the litigant will exaggerate the facts in his favor and the witness will rely upon him? This concern does not exist when one witness reminds the other, since there is no reason to suspect that the first witness might twist the facts (*Meiri*).

23. [That is, we can trust that after being prodded by the litigant the witness will testify only to the facts that he remembers on his own.]

24. [Since it might be tainted.]

וכשם שאין מזימין את העדים אלא בפניהם כך אין מכחישין את העדים אלא בפניהם אמר ליה רב נחמן אילו הוו קמן ומכחישין להו הוה הכחשה ולא הוה משגיחין בהו דהוי לה עדות מוכחשת השתא דליתנהו דאילו הוו לקמן דלמא הוו מודו להו מהימני אלא אמר רב נחמן אוקי תרי להדי תרי ואוקי ממונא בחזקת מריה מידי דהוה אנכסי דבר שטיא דבר שטיא זבין נכסי אתו בי תרי אמרי כשהוא שוטה זבין ואתו בי תרי ואמרי כשהוא חלים זבין אמר רב אשי אוקי תרי להדי תרי ואוקי ממונא בחזקת בר שטיא ולא אמרן אלא דאית ליה חזקה דאבהתיה אבל לית ליה חזקה דאבהתיה אמרינן כשהוא שוטה זבין וכשהוא שוטה זבין א"ר אבהו אין מזימין את העדים אלא בפניהן ומכחישין את העדים שלא בפניהן והזמה שלא בפניהן נהי דהזמה לא הוי הכחשה מיהא הויא אמר מר אם יש עדים שכתב ידם הוא זה או שהיה כתב ידם יוצא ממקום אחר משטר שקרא עליו ערער והוחזק בב"ד אין נאמנין קרא עליו ערער אין לא קרא עליו ערער לא מסייע ליה לרבי אסי דאמר רבי אסי אין מקיימין את השטר אלא משטר שקרא עליו ערער והוחזק בב"ד אמרי נהרדעי אין מקיימין את השטר אלא משתי כתובות [או] משתי שדות והוא שאכלום בעליהן ג' שנים ובשופי א"ר שימי בר אשי וביוצא מתחת יד אחר אבל מיד עצמו לא מאי שנא תחת יד עצמו דלא דלמא זיופי מזייף מתחת ידי אחר נמי דלמא אזל וחזא אתא וזייף כולי האי לא מצי מכוין ת"ר כותב אדם עדותו על השטר ומעיד עליה אפילו לאחר כמה שנים אמר רב הונא והוא שזוכרה מעצמו ורבי יוחנן אמר אע"פ שאין זוכרה מעצמו אמר רבה ש"מ מדרבי יוחנן הני בי תרי דידעי סהדותא ומנשי חד מנייהו מדכר חד לחבריה איבעיא להו עצמו מאי רב חביבא אמר אפילו עצמו מר בריה דרב אשי אמר עצמו לא והלכתא עצמו לא

רש"י

וכשם שאין מזימין העדים אלא בפניהם. שהרי הם באין לחייבן כדי לעונשן או נפש או ממון והתורה אמרה והועד בבעליו יבא בעל השור ויעמוד על שורו (ב"ק דף קיב:): **כך אין מכחישין.** אפילו לבטל עדותן: **לא הוו משגיחין בהו.** בעלי השטר לגבות על פיהם: **השתא.** דאיכא למימר אילו הוו קמן הוו מודו להני אמרת מהימני: **ואוקי ממונא בחזקת מריה.** בחזקת הלוה ואם קרקע היא תעמוד בחזקת המוכר ודקתני בברייתא אין נאמנים לא ליהוי שטרא מעליא למיגבי ביה אלא דלא קרעינן ליה ואי תפיס מידי והדר אתי האי ותבע מיניה לא מפקינן מיניה דאמרינן אוקי תרי להדי תרי וממונא בחזקה היכא דקאי: **זבין נכסיה.** מכר קרקעותיו: **חלים.** בריא: **ולא אמרן.** דאוקי נכסי בחזקת בר שטיא: **אלא דאית ליה.** בנכסים הללו חזקה דאבהתיה שהיו של אבותיו דחזקה מעלייתא היא: **אבל לית ליה בהו חזקה דאבהתא.** אלא חזקה דנפשיה שקנאן הוא והוחזקו בידו כקנייתו כך מכירתו ואין חזקתו חזקה לבטל מכירתו: **נהי דהזמה לא הויא.** לעונשם לא נפש ולא ממון הכחשה הויא לבטל עדותן: **אין מקיימין את השטר.** מתוך שטר אחר: **אא"כ קרא ערער.** על אותו שטר האחר והוחזק בב"ד על ידי עדיו דאי לא קרא עליו ערער חיישינן דלמא הוא גופיה מזייף הוא: **משתי שדות.** מעדים הללו אם חתומים על שני שטרות אחרים שהן מכר שתי שדות ואכלום הלקוחות ע"י שטרות הללו שלש שנים מקיימין שטר שלישי מהן אם החתימות דומות: **בשופי.** בלא ערעור: **וביוצא מתחת ידי אחר.** שהשטרות הללו שמקיימין את השלישי מהם יוצא מתחת ידי אחר ולא מתחת ידיו של זה המוציא את השלישי: **זיופי זייף.** הסתכל בכתב של אותן שטרות וכוון והתם הוא עצמו את השלישי דוגמת אותה חתימה: **מכוין.** מלמכס כתב בכתב הוא ואינו לפניו: **כותב אדם.** אם עשאוהו עד בדבר וירא לשוכחו כותבו על חתיכת קלף ומלגיעה: **ומעיד.** ע"פ אותו כתב אפי' לאחר כמה שנים: **שזוכרה מעצמו.** בלא ראיית השטר מכר קצת מעדותו מאליו: **אע"פ שאין זוכרה מעצמו.** אלא לאחר שרואה בשטר נתן בלבו ומזכר שלא נשתכח ממנו כל כך שכשמזכירים לו נזכר אבל אינו נזכר לגמרי לא דרחמנא אמר מפיהם ולא מפי כתבם: **עצמו מאי.** אם בעל דין עצמו מזכירו עד שנזכר מאי:

תוספות

ואוקי ממונא בחזקת מריה. פירש בקונט' ואין נאמנין דקתני לאו דמגבינן בשטרא אלא דלא קרעינן ליה ונפקא מינה דאי תפס לא מפקינן מיניה וקשה דאמר בפ"ק דב"מ (דף ז: ושם) גבי ספק בכור תקפו כהן מוציאין אותו מידו אלמא תפיסה דלאחר ספיקא לאו כלום היא ומיהו אההיא דסוף השואל (ב"מ דף קב: ושם) לא קשה מידי דאמרי' גבי משכיר בית לחבירו בי"ב זהובים לשנה מדינר זהב לחדש בא בתחלת החדש כולו למשכיר אלמא דבחזקת משכיר הוא ואפ"ה קאמר בא בסוף החדש כולו לשוכר דשאני התם דכיון דלא בא בתחלת החדש איכא למימר דאודויי אודי ליה ויש לומר דשאני גבי בכור שכבר תופס מספק דאין יודע אם בכור הוא אבל הכא שטוען ברי מהניא תפיסה ול"ע בחזקת הבתים (ב"ב דף לד:) גבי זה אומר של אבותי כו' אמר ר"נ כל דאלים גבר ופריך מהמחליף פרה בחמור דזה אומר ברשותו ילדה וזה אומר כו' יחלוקו ומאי קושיא הא התם היא אליבא דסומכוס ורב נחמן כרבנן דלרבנן דאמרי המע"ה היינו דינא דכל דאלים גבר כיון דמהניא תפיסה כשטוען ברי ויש לומר דהכי פריך דאפי' רבנן לא פליגי אסומכוס אלא משום דחד מינייהו מוחזק ואיכא למימר המע"ה אבל הכא דאין אחד מוחזק יותר מחבירו מודו לסומכוס דיחלוקו ועי"ל דהכא איירי כשתפס קודם שנולד הספק ורשב"א נראה לו להעמיד הברייתא בשובר ולהכי אין נאמנין דאוקי ממונא בחזקת מריה ומחזקינן עדי שובר בכשרים ולא יפרע: **אלא** אמר ר"נ אוקי תרי להדי כו'. וא"ת ולר"נ אמאי לא מגבינן ביה בשטרא הא סבר ר"נ כרב הונא (שבועות מז) [ב"ב דף לא:] בשני כתי עדים המכחישות זו את זו דכל אחת באה בפ"ע ומעידה אע"ג דלפי עדות כל אחת חבירתה פסולה לכל עדיות הכא נמי כיון דאין מכחישין אותן לומר שלא לוה כלום אלא אומרים אינכם נאמנים בדבר זה דפסולין הייתם ליתכשרו ואמאי לא מגבינן ביה בשטר ויש לומר דהתם באה כל אחת בפ"ע ומעידה משום דמוקמינן כל אחת בחזקת כשרות אבל הכא שאומרים קטנים היו או קרובים משנולדו עד עתה שנתרחקו ליכא למימר אוקמינהו אחזקתייהו דפסלינן אותן משנולדו ואנוסים היו נמי מחמת נפשות לא שייך לאוקמי אחזקה דהא לא פסלי להו כלל ורשב"א אומר דהכא לא מוקמינן להו אחזקה כדאמר לעיל משום דאילו הוו קמן דלמא הוו מודו:

ואוקי ארעא בחזקת בר שטיא. דוקא בקרקע הוא דאמרינן הכי אבל במטלטלים אמרינן דהוו בחזקת המוחזק כדאמר בפרק השואל (ב"מ דף ק.) גבי המחליף פרה בחמור דפריך וליחזי פרה ברשותא דמאן קיימא ולהוי אידך המע"ה ומשני דקיימא באגם אומר ר"י דהכא לא שייך למימר כדאמרי' בסוף קדושין (דף עט:) ובמי שמת (ב"ב דף קנג: ושם) אם שכיב מרע הוא עליהם להביא ראיה שבריא היה ואם בריא הוא כו' דבר שטיא דהכא כיון דעתים חלים ועתים שוטה אין ראיה ממה שהוא עכשיו: **דלמא** זיופי זייף. אור"ת דדוקא היכא שאין אנו מכירין החתימה אלא ע"י דמיון החתימה להחתימה אבל היכא דמכירין חתימת העדים בטביעת עין אע"פ שיש לו חתימה אחרת תחת ידו ליכא למיחש דלמא זייף דכיון דמכירין החתימה אם זייף היה ניכר היטב: **ורבי** יוחנן אומר אע"פ שאין זוכרה מעצמו. פי' אבל ע"י השטר זוכרה אבל אם אין זוכרה כלל לא דמפיהם ולא מפי כתבם כדאמרינן פ' ד' אחין (יבמות דף לא: ושם) גבי מפני מה לא תקנו זמן בקדושין דקאמר לינחי גבי עדים אי דכירי ליתו ולסהדו ואי לא זימנין דחזו בכתבא ואתו ומסהדי ואמר רחמנא מפיהם ולא מפי כתבם וא"ת הכא נמי אמאי לא אסרינן לכתוב עדות על השטר שמא ישכח לגמרי ואתו ומסהדי מכתבא כדחיישינן התם ויש לומר דודאי התם חשו חכמים לפי שב"ד מוסרין לו השטר ויסבור שלכך מסרוהו לו שיעיד אפי' לא יזכור אבל הכא שמעצמו כותב עדותו על השטר לא חשו חכמים לכך וא"ת ואמאי לא מצו חזו בכתבא ולאסהודי הא תנן בגט פשוט (ב"ב דף קסח.) מי שנמחק שטר חובו מעמיד עליו עדים ובא לב"ד ועושין לו קיומו ומפרש בגמ' מהו קיומו וכן בהגוזל קמא (ב"ק דף צח.) דאמרינן גבי שורף שטרותיו של חבירו פטור מדיני אדם כו' ה"ד אי דאיכא סהדי דידעי מה הוה כתוב ביה בשטרא נכתוב ליה שטרא אחרינא אלמא לא חשבינן ליה מפיהם ולא מפי כתבם וי"ל דבפ' ד' אחין (יבמות לא: ושם) חיישינן דלמא אתו ומסהדי בסתם כאילו זוכרין העדות אבל ודאי אם היו מעידין שכך ראו בחתימתן הא לא חשיב מפיהם ולא מפי כתבם דעדים החתומין על השטר נעשה כמי שנחקרה עדותן בבית דין והוי כאילו מעידין ראינו עדות שנחקרה בבית דין ואם תאמר והכא אפילו אין זה זוכרה כלל מה בכך יביא שטרו

מסורת הש"ס

א) יבמות לא. ב) [נ"ל ארעא וכן איתא ביבמות לא. וכן העתיק הרשב"א בב"ב מג: ד"ה ולי' בעית איתמא], ג) [תוספתא פ"ב], ד) [נ"ל רבא וכן איתא בשאלתות פ' יתרו סימן נה וכ"א בר"ף והרא"ש], ה) [וע"ע תוס' ב"ב קה. ד"ה אלא].

תוספות רי"ד

לכתב מש"ה אין נאמנים אפילו ע"י מיגו משום דעולה היא וכי אמרו חתמנו משוי נפשייהו רשיעא ואין אדם משים עצמו רשע אבל מודעא ניתן לכתב כדי לפצות המוכר מאונסו מאי אמרת הוו להו למיכתב מודעא בריש מירחת מוכר דלמא מרגיש לוקח ואניס ליה טפי ואי אמרת ומשום אנוסיה היכי חתמו שקרא מימר אמר להו סוף סוף על פומייהו בעי' לאיתקיימא שטרא אתון דמיתקיימתון ליה אתון אמריתו דאנוס הייתי והימנוהו ע"י מיגו מש"ה סבר מר בר ר"א דניתן לכתוב ונאמנים ור"נ סבר דלמא לא מקיים שטרא מפומייהו אלא אפומי דסהדי אחריני או מכת"י יוצא ממקום אחר דהו ל"ל מיגו נמצא שחתמו על שקר הלכך לא ניתן לכתב והל' כר"נ דמסתבר טעמי' ותו דבחזקת הבתים מקשי תלמודא ממילתי' לר"ה דאמר התם מאן דחתם אאשקלתא שפיר חתם איני והא א"ר נחמן מודעא היה דברינו אין נאמנים וקי"ל שאין התלמוד מקשה אלא מהל' פסוקה והא דמקשה מר"נ לסייע מר בר ר"א אלא לאו ש"מ קם ליה לתלמודא דהלכה כר"נ עי' בחז"ה שטבא תלה לפפי בבנרא וזבין ליה ארעא חתם רבב"ח אמודעא ואאשקלתא. אמר ר"ה מאן דחתם אמודעא שפיר חתם ומאן דחתם אאשקלתא שפיר חתם ומק' אי מודעא לא אשקלתא ואי אשקלתא לא מודעא א"ל ה"ק לאו מודעא ואשקלתא שפיר חתם ר"ה לטעמיה דאמר תלויה וזבין זביניה זביני איני והא אמר ר"נ מודעא היה דברינו אין נאמנים ה"מ ע"פ דלא אתי ע"פ ומרע לשטרא אבל בשטר אתי שטר ומרע שטר פי' סבי גברא אלמא הוה תלה לפפי באילן שישמו בינרא למכור לו שדהו ולא תלהו כדי שיסבור לו האילן הזבין כלומר וכן עשה שמכר לו וחתם רבה בב"ח ועד אחר עמו אמודעא שמסר מפני קודם שנכתב שטר מכירה ואאשקלתא פי' גם על שטר מכירה חתם מאן דחתם אמודעי וכו' דאע"ג דתלויה וזבין זביניה זביני ה"מ היכא דלא מסר מודעא אבל המודעא שנכתב תבטל שטר המכירה ומאן דחתם אאשקלתא וכו' דתלויה וזבין זביניה זביני כדאסיקנא ר"ה לטעמיה וכו' ור' יצחק אלפסי פסיק הל' כמר בר רב אשי: **בעא מיניה** רבא מר"נ תנאי היה דברינו מהו מודעא ואמנה טעמא מאי דעקר לי' לשטרא והאי נמי עקר לה לשטריה או דלמא תנאי מילתא אחריתי (והרב מוליך השיטה בשכת"י יוצא ממקום אחר ובעי' דרבא כשת"י ימ"א) פירוש מודעא ואמנה מ"ט אמרת דאין נאמנים אע"פ שאין כת"י יוצא ממקום אחר משום דעקרי לה לשטרא השתא בעדותן והלכך אמרינן להו א"כ דאמנה היה ולא הלוה לו או מודעא היה ולא מכר לו מרצונו למה חתמתם אעולה ורשע עשיתים לפי דבריכם וכיון דמשוי נפשייהו רשיעי אין נאמנים וה"נ קעקרי לה לשטרא באומרם תנאי היה דברינו אם יבא פלוני ממקום פלוני ויסכים בדבר זה יהא מכר ואם לא לא יהא מכר למה חתמתם בשטר המכר שבלא שום תנאי מכר לו לא היה לכם לעשות דבר זה והלכך גם זה עולה הוא ודומיא דשטר אמנה אע"פ שהאמינו המוכר שאם לא יקיים תנאו שיהא המכר בטל לא היה להם לחתום כדאמרינן בשטר אמנה שאע"פ שהאמינו שלוהו ויקרא עולה ואין לחתום בו או דלמא תנאי מלתא אחריתי הוא פי' שכיון שמכר לו מכר מקוים אע"פ שהתלה המכר על תנאי שאמר אם יבא אותו פלוני ויסכים יהא קיים ואם לאו יהא בטל רשאים העדים לחתום בו כיון שהמוכר מאמינו ולא רצה שיכתבו התנאי בתוך השטר א"ל כי אתי לקמן פי' לקוחות שעדיהם מעידים שתנאי היה דבריהם אמרינן להו זילו קיימו תנאייכו פי' לבעל וחותו לדינא פי' אם יעכב שוב הקרקע שנאמנים לומר תנאי היה דברינו וכיון שאין כת"י יוצא ממקום אחר ולא דמי לא למודעא ולא לאמנה דמודעא הא קא חזי דאנוס הוה ולא היה להם לחתום עד שלא יכתבו לו שטר מודעא ואמנה נמי לא אע"ג דאמרינן שאע"פ שהלוה מאמינו למלוה שילוהו אפ"ה אין לחתום בו דהתם לאו משום פסידא דלוה שכיון שהוא מתרצה בכך אין אנו חוששים בדבר אלא משום פסידא דלקוחות הוא כדאמרינן הכי שכיון שכתב ללוות ולא לוה אתי למיטרף לקוחות שלא כדין תדע דהכי הוא דהא בשטרא דלאו אקנייתא אין כותבין שטר ללוה עד שיהא מלוה עמו משום פסידא דלקוחות אבל בשטרא אקנייתא כותבין דאי טריף כדין טריף ועא"ג דאיכא למיחש דלמא ממטי ליה לוה למלוה ומאמינו עד שילוהו ולבסוף לא ילוהו אפ"ה לא חיישינן כיון שהוא מאמינו ה"נ כיון דהוא מאמינו שאם לא יתקיים התנאי יבטל לו המכר אין לנו לחוש להפסדו והלכך רשאים לחתום בו ולא הוי עולה כיון דלא מפסיד לאחריני אבל אם היה כת"י יוצא ממקום אחר אין נאמנים שכיון שהגיד שוב אין חוזר ומגיד (א"כ) [א"נ] י"ל כיון דפשיט ליה דתנאי מילתא אחריתי הוא ואינה עולה מהימני אף על פי שכת"י יוצא ממקום אחר נאמנים דמה לי אחרים מה לי הם כמו שאם מעידים אחרים על התנאי נאמנים כמו כן כשהעידו הן בעצמן נאמנים והרבה בני אדם עושים דבר זה שאינם רוצים להזכיר שום תנאי בשטר שהוא עתיד להתקיים ימים רבים ואומר התנאי לפני עדי השטר שלא יכפור איש לחבירו הלכך אע"ג דליכא מיגו מהימן: **עד אומר** תנאי ועד אומר אינו תנאי א"ר פפא תרווייהו בשטר מעליא קמסהדי והאי דאמר תנאי הו"ל חד ואין דבריו של אחד במקום שנים **מתקיף** ליה ר"ה בריה דר"י א"ה אפילו תרווייהו נמי אלא אמרי' הני למיעקר סהדותיהו קאתי חד נמי למיעקר סהדותיה קאתי פי' א"ה כיון שהעיד על כת"י עשיתם לזה א' ממקיימי השטר כמו שהוא כתוב בלא תנאי והוי ליה עידיו שנים ועדות אחרונה דברי אחד במקום שנים אפי' תרווייהו נמי אמרו תנאי היה דברינו לא להימנו כיון שהעידו על כת"י קיימו השטר שהוא כמו שהוא כתוב וכי אמרו תנאי היה דברינו הו"ל מגידים וחוזרים ומגידים ואמאי הם נאמנים אלא ע"כ לא חתימה מקויימת הוא דכיון דבתוך כ"ד מסקי דבוריהו ואמרו אבל תנאי היה ביניהן אמרי' הני למיעקר סהדותייהו קאתי שאמרו כת"י הוא ועכשיו אומרים לא חתמנו אלא על מנת שיתקיים התנאי וכיון דתנאי מילתא אחריתא היא שאינה עוקרתו אלא לאחר זמן לא דמיא למודעא ואמנה ומהימני דלאו עולה היא שהרי היא עדות בפ"ע האי חד נמי כי סיים ואמר תנאי הוה עקר לחתימת ידיה לומר לא חתמתי אלא על מנת כן וכיון דלאו עולה הוא מהימן ואשתכח דאין בשטר חתום אלא ע"א ומסיק תלמודא והל' כר"ה [בריה] דר"י: **ת"ר** שנים החתומים על השטר ומתו ובאו שנים ואמרו ידענו שכת"י הוא זה אבל אנוסים היו קטנים היו פסולי עדות היו הרי אלו נאמנים ואם יש עדים שהוא כת"י או שכת"י יוצא ממקום אחר משטר שקרא עליו ערעור פי' שרצה הנתבע לפוסלו והוחזק בב"ד אין נאמנים פי' היכא דאיכא מיגו נאמנים ולא מגבינן ביה והיכא דליכא מיגו אין נאמנים ומגבינן ביה **ומקשה** תרי ותרי נינהו פי' אלו

עין משפט נר מצוה

לב א מיי' פ"ג מהלכות עדות הלכה ז סמג עשין קט טוש"ע ח"מ סימן מו סעיף לג:
לג ב מיי' פכ"ט מהל' מכירה הלכה ה סמג עשין פב טוש"ע ח"מ סי' רלה סעיף לא בהגה"ה:
לד ג ב"מ שם:
לה ד מיי' פ"ו מהל' עדות הלכה ה סמג עשין קט טור ח"מ סימן מו:
לו ה ו ז מיי' פ"ח שם הלכה ג סמג שם טוש"ע ח"מ סימן מו סעיף ז:
לז ח ט מיי' פ"ח מהל' עדות הלכה א סמג עשין קט טוש"ע ח"מ סימן כח סעיף יג:
לח י כ מיי' פ"ח שם הלכה ב טוש"ע ח"מ שם סעיף יד:

הגהות הב"ח

(א) גמ' קרא עליו ערער וכו' עד ערער לא. נ"ב באשר"י מבואר דלא הוה גרס להו:

גליון הש"ס

גמ' וכשהוא שוטה זבין. עי' סוטה דף מו ע"ב תוס' ד"ה דינוקא: תוס' ד"ה דלמא כו' אור"ת דדוקא כו'. עיין לקמן דף כח ע"א תוס' ד"ה קיום שטרות:

ליקוטי רש"י

ובשופי. וילך שפי, וכו' לשון שופי ושקט שאין עמו אלא שתיקה [במדבר כג, ג]. ומנשי. ושכח [ע"פ סנהדרין סב.].

The Gemara rules on an issue that was raised above:

אָמַר רַבִּי אַבָּהוּ – **R' Abahu said:** אֵין מְזִימִין אֶת הָעֵדִים אֶלָּא בִּפְנֵיהֶן – **We cannot render witnesses *zomemin* except in their presence,** וּמַכְחִישִׁין אֶת הָעֵדִים שֶׁלֹּא בִּפְנֵיהֶן – **but we can contradict** the testimony of **witnesses** even **not in their presence.**[10] וַהֲזָמָה שֶׁלֹּא בִּפְנֵיהֶן – **Furthermore,** regarding ***hazamah*** made **not in their presence,** נְהִי דַּהֲזָמָה לֹא הָוֵי – **although it is not a** valid ***hazamah,*** הַכְחָשָׁה מִיהָא הָוְיָא – **it is at least a** valid **contradiction** of their testimony.[11]

The Gemara quotes a section of the Baraisa cited above:

אָמַר מַר – **The master said:** אִם יֵשׁ עֵדִים שֶׁכְּתַב יָדָם הוּא זֶה – IF THERE ARE other WITNESSES who testify THAT THIS IS THEIR HANDWRITING, אוֹ שֶׁהָיָה כְּתַב יָדָם יוֹצֵא מִמָּקוֹם אַחֵר – OR THEIR HANDWRITING IS VERIFIED FROM ANOTHER SOURCE, מִשְּׁטָר שֶׁקָּרָא עָלָיו עַרְעָר וְהוּחְזַק בְּבֵית דִּין – namely, FROM A different DOCUMENT AGAINST WHICH A CHALLENGE HAD BEEN RAISED AND WHICH WAS then UPHELD IN COURT, אֵין נֶאֱמָנִין – THESE new witnesses ARE NOT BELIEVED.

The Gemara infers from the Baraisa:

קָרָא עָלָיו עַרְעָר אִין – If **a challenge was raised against [the other document]** and it was then certified in court, it can **indeed** be used for authenticating the signatures on this document; קָרָא עָלָיו עַרְעָר לֹא – but if **no challenge was raised against [the other document],** it may **not** be used for authenticating this document. מְסַיֵּיע לֵיהּ לְרַבִּי אַסִּי – **This is a support to R' Assi.** דְּאָמַר רַבִּי אַסִּי – **For R' Assi said:** אֵין מְקַיְּימִין אֶת הַשְּׁטָר אֶלָּא מִשְּׁטָר שֶׁקָּרָא עָלָיו עַרְעָר וְהוּחְזַק בְּבֵית דִּין – **We may certify a document only from a document against which a challenge had been raised and which was** then **upheld in court.**[12]

The Gemara mentions another method of authenticating the signatures on a document:

אָמְרֵי נְהַרְדָּעֵי – **The Nehardeans said:** אֵין מְקַיְּימִין אֶת הַשְּׁטָר אֶלָּא מִשְּׁתֵּי כְתוּבּוֹת – **We may certify a document only from two *kesubah* documents,**[13] [אוֹ] מִשְּׁתֵּי שָׂדוֹת – **or from** the bills of sale of **two fields,** וְהוּא שֶׁאֲכָלוּם בַּעֲלֵיהֶן שָׁלֹשׁ שָׁנִים וּבְשׁוֹפִי – **provided that their owners harvested them for three years peacefully,** without any protest.[14]

The Nehardeans' ruling is qualified:

אָמַר רַב שִׁימִי בַּר אַשִׁי – **Rav Shimi bar Ashi said:** וּבְיוֹצֵא מִתַּחַת יַד אַחֵר – **And** this applies only **when [the two source documents] are produced by another person,** אֲבָל מִיַּד עַצְמוֹ לֹא – **but** if they are produced **by the person** who is holding the document under question **himself,** they are **not** reliable proof of its authenticity.[15]

NOTES

claim that Bar Shatya subsequently sold it. Therefore, we would not void the sale and give the property to Bar Shatya on the basis of his prior ownership (see *Rashi*). [I.e. if we assume he was deranged when he sold the property, we ought to also assume he was deranged when he bought it, and if we take the position that he was normal when he bought it, we ought to concede that he was normal when he sold it as well. Thus, his prior ownership cannot be a factor in voiding the sale (*Yam Shel Shlomo;* see also *Ritva*).]

If the original owners of the property would come and claim that Bar Shatya purchased it from them while he was deranged, we would accept their claim and return the property to them on the basis of their known previous possession. However, as long as they do not present this argument, we need not return the property to them. Nevertheless, since it is not clear that Bar Shatya acquired it properly, and the original owners *could* argue that he did not, we have no basis for awarding it to him (*Rashba, Re'ah, Ran;* cf. *Yam Shel Shlomo*).

One might wonder: Since witnesses signed Bar Shatya's bill of acquisition, it should be presumable that they determined that he was normal at the time and the sale was valid! Since no witnesses contradict them concerning this matter, why do we doubt it? The answer is that the witnesses concern themselves only with the status of the maker of the document – in this case, the seller. Their signatures attest that he willingly and legally made the note that obligates him. They need not concern themselves with the status of the beneficiary (i.e. the buyer), since they are allowed to sign even when he is not present. Thus, their signatures on the bill of sale do not prove that Bar Shatya was normal when he acquired it (*Ritva;* cf. *Ran;* see *Yam Shel Shlomo*).

10. This follows Rav Nachman's previously cited opinion.

11. That is, the original witnesses cannot be punished as *zomemin,* but their testimony stands contradicted (*Rashi*). Insofar as contradiction is concerned, the only criterion is that the disputant who stands to lose money be present for the testimony; as long as we do not seek to punish the witnesses, there is no need for them to be present even when the latter testimony takes the form of *hazamah* (*Ritva*). This is an extension of the principle mentioned in note 4 (see *Re'ah* above).

[For further discussion of the ramifications of **hazamah** not in the presence of the original witnesses, see *Rivash* §266, *Shach* and *Nesivos HaMishpat* 38:2, and *Noda BiYehudah* vol. I, *Even HaEzer* §72.]

12. I.e. when we seek to authenticate a document by comparing its signatures to those on another document, the source document must be one that had been challenged and was then authenticated by the witnesses who signed it [or other witnesses]. If the source document was never challenged, we need to be concerned for the possibility that that one is also a forgery (*Rashi*).

It is unclear why the source document must be one that was *challenged* and then certified. Seemingly, we should be able to rely upon a document that bears the certification of a court, whether the certification came in response to a challenge or not! Some say that when there was no challenge we must be concerned that the certifying court did not investigate thoroughly before issuing its certification (*Rashi,* as explained by *Ran; Ramah,* cited by *Tur Choshen Mishpat* 46:7). Others argue that there is no basis for questioning the procedure of a court, and we must rely upon the certification in all circumstances. Rather, they explain that the critical point is that the source document was certified, not that it was challenged. The reason the Gemara mentions that the source document must have had a challenge raised against it is that it was unusual to certify documents unless their authenticity was challenged. Saying that the document was challenged is simply another way of saying that it was certified (*Rosh* §13, as explained by *Tur* ibid.; according to *Pnei Yehoshua,* this is *Rashi's* intent as well). See *Shach* 46:25 and *Haflaah* for alternative explanations. See also *Rif, Ramban, Rashba* and *Ritva,* who have a variant version of the text.

13. The Nehardeans do not mean to dispute R' Assi's previous ruling. Rather, they mean that even when we have no previously certified document to which to compare the signatures in question, there is a method of authenticating them – but this method requires comparing the signatures to those on *two* other documents. If the witnesses had previously signed two *kesubos* and the signatures in question match those on both *kesubos,* they are authenticated (*Ritva; Shulchan Aruch, Choshen Mishpat* 46:7; see following note; cf. *Raavad* cited by *Ramban, Ritva* and *Ran*).

14. I.e. the signatures in question are comparable to those on two separate documents attesting to the sale of two fields, and the buyers of those fields harvested the land for three years without anyone disputing their ownership. Since [there is evidence that both documents are valid and] the signatures on the document in question match both previous sets, we can authenticate it (*Rashi*).

[According to *Rama* (cited by *Tur Choshen Mishpat* ibid.), two *kesubos* are similarly valid as source documents only when the women holding them were married for at least three years. Others maintain that even one day of marriage suffices to prove that the *kesubos* are authentic (see *Shach* 46:20).]

A document cannot be authenticated through comparison to two uncertified notes of indebtedness, since there is no way of proving that those notes themselves are authentic (*Ran, Tur* ibid.).

15. Although we know that those documents are authentic – because they allowed the owner to harvest the fields uncontested for three years – comparing the signatures does not prove anything. Since the person himself is holding the authentic documents, he might have studied their signatures and copied them onto a bogus document (*Rashi;* cf. *Rambam, Hil. Eidus* 6:3 with *Lechem Mishneh; Rashba, Ritva, Ran*). The Gemara will elaborate further.

וכשם שאין מזימין את העדים אלא בפניהם כך אין מכחישין את העדים אלא בפניהם אמר ליה רב נחמן אילו הוו קמן ומכחשין להו הוה הכחשה ולא הוה משגיחין בהו דהוי לה עדות מוכחשת השתא דליתנהו דאילו הוו לקמן דלמא הוו מודו להו מהימני אלא אמר רב נחמן אוקי תרי להדי תרי ואוקי ממונא בחזקת מריה מידי דהוה אנכסי דבר שטיא דבר שטיא זבין נכסי אתו בי תרי אמרי כשהוא שוטה זבין ואתו בי תרי ואמרי כשהוא חלים זבין אמר רב אשי אוקי תרי להדי תרי ואוקי ממונא בחזקת בר שטיא ולא אמרן אלא דאית ליה חזקה דאבהתיה אבל לית ליה חזקה דאבהתיה אמרינן כשהוא שוטה זבין וכשהוא שוטה זבין א"ר אבהו אין מזימין את העדים אלא בפניהן ומכחישין את העדים שלא בפניהן והזמה שלא בפניהן נהי דהזמה לא הוי הכחשה מיהא הויא אמר מר אם יש עדים שכתב ידם הוא זה או שהיה כתב ידם יוצא ממקום אחר משטר שקרא עליו ערער והוחזק בב"ד אין נאמנין (א) קרא עליו ערער אין לא קרא עליו ערער לא מסייע ליה לרבי אסי דאמר רבי אסי אין מקיימין את השטר אלא משטר שקרא עליו ערער והוחזק בב"ד אמרי נהרדעי אין מקיימין את השטר אלא משתי כתובות [או] משתי שדות והוא שאכלום בעליהן ג' שנים ובשופי א"ר שימי בר אשי וביוצא מתחת יד אחר אבל מיד עצמו לא מאי שנא תחת יד עצמו דלא דלמא זויפי מזייף מתחת ידי אחר נמי דלמא אזל וחזא אתא וזייף כולי האי לא מצי מכוין ת"ר כותב אדם עדותו על השטר ומעיד עליה אפילו לאחר כמה שנים אמר רב הונא והוא שזוכרה מעצמו ורבי יוחנן אמר אע"פ שאין זוכרה מעצמו אמר רבה ש"מ מדרבי יוחנן הני בי תרי דידעי סהדותא ומנשי חד מנייהו מדכר חד לחבריה איבעיא להו עצמו מאי רב חביבא אמר אפילו עצמו מר בריה דרב אשי אמר עצמו לא והלכתא עצמו לא

רש"י

וכשם שאין מזימין העדים אלא בפניהם. שהרי הם באין לחייבן כדי לעונשן או נפש או ממון והתורה אמרה והועד בבעליו יבא בעל השור ויעמוד על שורו (ב"ק דף קיב:): **כך אין מכחישין.** אפילו לבטל עדותן: **לא הוו משגיחין בהו.** בעדי השטר לגבות על פיהם: **השתא.** דליכא למימר אילו הוו קמן הוו מודו להני אמרת מהימני: **ואוקי ממונא בחזקת מריה.** בחזקת הלוה ואם קרקע היא תעמוד בחזקת המוכר ודקתני בברייתא אין נאמנים לא ליהוי שטרא מעליא למיגבי ביה אלא דלא קרעינן ליה ואי תפיס מידי והדר אתי האי ותבע מיניה לא מפקינן מיניה דאמרינן אוקי תרי להדי תרי וממונא בחזקה היכא דקאי: **זבין נכסיה.** מכר קרקעותיו: **חלים.** בריא: **ולא אמרן.** דאוקי נכסי בחזקת בר שטיא: **אלא דאית ליה.** בנכסים הללו חזקה דאבהתא שהיו של אבותיו דחזקה מעלייתא היא: **אבל לית ליה בהו חזקה דאבהתא.** אלא חזקה דנפשיה שקנאן הוא והוחזקו בידו כקיימינו כך מכרתו ואין חזקתו חזקה לבטל מכירתו: **נהי דהזמה לא הויא.** לעונשם לא נפש ולא ממון הכחשה הויא לבטל עדותן: **אין מקיימין את השטר.** מתוך שטר אחר: **אא"כ קרא ערער.** על אותו שטר האחר והוחזק בב"ד על ידי עדיו דאי לא קרא עליו ערער חיישינן דלמא השטר גופיה מזויף הוא: **משתי שדות.** מעדים הללו אם חתומים על שני שטרות אחרים שהן מכר שתי שדות ואכלום הלקוחות ע"י שטרות הללו שלש שנים מקיימין שטר שלישי מהן אם החתימות דומות: **בשופי.** בלא ערעור: **וביוצא מתחת ידי אחר.** שהשטרות הללו שמקיימין את השלישי מהם יוצא מתחת ידי אחר ולא מתחת ידיו של זה המוציא את השלישי: **זויפי זייף.** הסתכל בכתב של אותן שטרות וכוון ותפס הוא עצמו את השלישי דוגמת אותה חתימה: **מכוין.** מלמלם כתב בכתב הוא ולא לפניו: **כותב אדם.** עד שיש עדות בדבר וירא שלא ישכח כותבו על חתיכת קלף ומצניעה: **ומעיד.** ע"פ אותו כתב אפי' לאחר כמה שנים: **שזוכרה מעצמו.** בלא ראיית השטר מכר קצת עדותו מאליו: **אע"פ שאין זוכרה מעצמו.** אלא לאחר שרואה בשטר נתן בלבו ומזכר שלא נשתכח ממנו כל כך שכשמזכירים לו נזכר אבל אינו נזכר לגמרי לא דרחמנא אמר מפיהם ולא מפי כתבם: **עצמו מאי.** אם בעל דין עצמו מזכירו עד שנזכר מאי:

תוספות

ואוקי ממונא בחזקת מריה. פירש בקונט' ואין נאמנין דקתני לאו דמגבינא בשטרא אלא דלא קרעינן ליה ונפקא מינה דאי תפס לא מפקינן מיניה וקשה דאמר בפ"ק דב"ק (דף יו: וסס) גבי ספק בכור תקפו כהן מוציאין אותו מידו אלמא תפיסה דאמר ספיקא לא כלום היא ומיהו אההוא דסוף השואל (דף קב: וסס) לא קשה מידי דאמרי' גבי משכיר בית לחבירו בי"ב זהובים לשנה מדינר זהב לחדש בא בתחלת החדש כולו למשכיר אלמא בחזקת משכיר הוא ואפ"ה קאמר בא בסוף החדש כולו לשוכר דשאני התם דכיון דלא בא בתחלת החדש איכא למימר לאודויי אודי ליה ויש לומר דשאני גבי בכור שכהן תופס מספק דאין יודע אם בכור הוא אבל הכא שטוען ברי מהניא תפיסה וא"ת בחזקת הבתים (ב"ב דף לד.) גבי זה אומר של אבותי כו' אמר ר"נ כל דאלים גבר ופריך מהמחליף פרה בחמור זה אומר כו' יחלוקו ומאי קושיא הא התם אתיא כסומכוס ורב נחמן כרבנן דלרבנן דאמרי המע"ה היינו דינא דכל דאלים גבר כיון דמהניא תפיסה דטוען ברי ויש לומר דהכי פריך דאפי' רבנן לא פליגי אסומכוס אלא משום דחד מינייהו מוחזק ואיכא למימר המע"ה אבל הכא דאין אחד מוחזק יותר מחבירו מודו לסומכוס דיחלוקו ועי"ל דהכא מיירי כשתפס קודם שנולד הספק ורשב"א נראה לו להעמיד הברייתא בשוכר והכי אין נאמנין דאוקי ממונא בחזקת מריה ומחזקינן עדי שוכר בכשרים ולא יפרע: **אלא** אמר ר"נ אוקי תרי להדי תרי כו'. וא"ת ולר"נ ומאי לא מגבינן ביה בשטרא הא סבר ר"נ כרב הונא בשבועות (ב"ב דף לא:) בשני כתי עדים המכחישות זו את זו דכל אחת באה בפ"ע ומעידה אע"ג דלפי עדות כל אחת חבירתה פסולה לכל עדות הכא נמי כיון דאין מכחישין אותן לומר שלא היו כלום אלא אומרים אינכם נאמנים בדבר זה דפסולין הייתם ליתכשרו ואמאי לא מגבינן ביה בשטר ויש לומר דהתם באה כל אחת בפ"ע ומעידה משום דמוקמינן כל אחת בחזקת כשרות אבל הכא שאומרים קטנים היו או קרובים משנולדו עד עתה שנתרחקו ליכא למימר אוקמינהו אחזקתייהו דפסלינן אותן משנולדו ואנוסים היו נמי מחמת נפשות לא שייך לאוקמי אחזקה דהא לא פסלי להו כלל ורשב"א אומר דהכא לא מוקמינן להו אחזקה כדאמר לעיל משום דאילו הוו קמן דלמא הוו מודו:

ואוקי ארעא בחזקת בר שטיא. דוקא בקרקע הוא דאמרינן הכי אבל במטלטלים אמרינן דהוו בחזקת המוחזק כדאמר בפרק השואל (ב"מ דף ק.) גבי המחליף פרה בחמור דפריך וליחזי פרה ברשותא דמאן קיימא ולהוי אידך המע"ה ומשני דקיימא באגם אומר ר"י דהכא לא שייך למימר כדאמרי' בסוף קדושין (דף עט:) ובמי שמת (ב"ב דף קנג: וסס) אם שכיב מרע הוא עליהם להביא ראיה שבריא היה ואם בריא הוא כו' דבר שטיא דהכא כיון דלעתים חלים ולעתים שוטה אין ראיה ממה שהוא עכשיו: **דלמא** זויפי זייף. אור"ת ° דדוקא היכא שאין אנו מכירין החתימה אלא ע"י דמיון החתימה להחתימה אבל היכא דמכירין חתימת העדים בטביעת עין אע"פ שיש לו חתימה אחרת תחת ידו ליכא למיחש דלמא זייף דכיון דמכירין החתימה אם זייף היה ניכר היטב: **ורבי** יוחנן אומר אע"פ שאין זוכרה מעצמו. פי' אבל ע"י השטר זוכרה אבל אם אין זוכרה כלל לא דמפיהם ולא מפי כתבם כדאמרינן פ' ד' אחין (יבמות דף לא: וסס) גבי מפני מה לא תקנו זמן בקדושין דקאמר ליתני גבי עדים אי דכירי ליתו ולסהדו ואי לא זימנין דחזו בכתבא ואתו ומסהדי ואמר רחמנא מפיהם ולא מפי כתבם וא"ת הכא נמי אמאי לא אסרינן לכתוב עדות על השטר שמא ישכח לגמרי ואתו ומסהדי מכתבא כדחיישינן התם ויש לומר דודאי התם חשו חכמים לפי שב"ד מוסרין לו השטר ויסבור שלכך מסרוהו לו שיעיד אפי' לא יזכור אבל הכא שמעצמו כותב עדותו על השטר לא חשו חכמים לכך וא"ת ואמאי לא מצו חזו בכתבא ולאסהודי הא תנן בגט פשוט (ב"ב דף קסח.) מי שנמחק שטר חובו מעמיד עליו עדים ובא לב"ד ועושין לו קיומו ומפרש בגמ' מהו קיומו וכן בהגוזל קמא (ב"ק דף לח.) דאמרינן גבי שורף שטרותיו של חבירו פטור מדיני אדם כו' ה"ד אי דאיכא סהדי דידעי מה הוה כתוב ביה בשטרא נכתוב ליה שטרא אחרינא אלמא לא חשבינן ליה מפיהם ולא מפי כתבם וי"ל דבפ' ד' אחין (יבמות לא: וסס) חיישינן דלמא אתו ומסהדי בסתם כאילו זוכרין העדות אבל ודאי אם היו מעידין שכך ראו בחתימתן הא לא חשיב מפיהם ולא מפי כתבם דעדים החתומין על השטר נעשה כמי שנחקרה עדותן בבית דין והוי כאילו מעידין ראינו עדות שנחקרה בבית דין ואם תאמר והכא אפילו אין זה זוכרה כלל מה בכך יביא שטרו

עין משפט נר מצוה

לב א מיי' פי"ז מהלכות עדות הלכה ז סמג עשין קט טוש"ע ח"מ סימן מו סעיף לו:
לג ב מיי' פכ"ט מהל' מכירה הלכה ה סמג עשין פב טוש"ע ח"מ סי' רלה סעיף לג בהגה"ה:
לד ג ב"י ח"מ שם:
לה ד מיי' פ"ח מהל' עדות הלכה ה סמג עשין קט טור ח"מ סימן מו:
לו ה ו ז מיי' פ"ו שם הלכה ג סמג שם טוש"ע ח"מ סימן מו סעיף ז:
לז ח ט מיי' פ"ח מהל' עדות הלכה א סמג עשין קט טוש"ע ח"מ סי' כח סעיף יג:
לח י כ מיי' שם הלכה ב טוש"ע ח"מ שם סעיף יד:

הגהות הב"ח

(א) גמ' מיתות קרא עליו וכו' עד ערער לא. באשר"י מבואר דלא הוה גרס להו:

גליון הש"ס

גמ' וכשהוא שוטה זבין. עי' סוכה דף מו ע"ב תוס' ד"ה דיניקא: תוס' ד"ה דלמא כו'. אור"ת דדוקא כו'. עיין לקמן דף כח ע"א תוס' ד"ה קיום שטרות:

ליקוטי רש"י

ובשופי. ולך שפי, וכו' לשון שופי ושקט שאין עמו אלא שתיקה [במדבר כג, ג]. ומנשי. ושכח [ע"פ סנהדרין פב.].

מסורת הש"ס

א) יבמות לא., ב) [נ"ל ארעא וכן איתא בירושלמי וכן העתיק הרא"ש], ג) ב"ב מג: ד"ה ואי בעית איתא], ג) [תוספתא פ"ב], ד) [נ"ל רבא וכן איתא בשאלתות פ' יתרו סימן נה וכ"ה ברי"ף והרא"ש], ה) [וע"ע תוס' ב"ב קט. ד"ה אלא].

תוספות רי"ד

לכתב מש"ה אין נאמנים אפילו ע"י מיגו משום דעולה היא וכי אמרו חתמנו משוי נפשייהו רשיעא ואין אדם משים עצמו רשע אבל מודעא ניתן לכתב כדי לפצות המוכר מאונסו מאי אמרת אית להו למיכתב מודעא ברישא מירתת מוכר דלמא מרגיש לוקח ואניס ליה טפי ואי אמרת ומשום אונסיה היכי חתמו שטרא מימר אמר להו סוף סוף על פומיכו בעי לאיתקיימא שטרא אתון דמיתקיימתון ליה אתון אמריתו דאנוס הייתי ותהימנו ע"י מיגו מש"ה סבר מר בר"א דינהו לכתוב ונאמנים ור"נ סבר דלמא לא מקיים שטרא מפומייהו דסהדי אחריניא או דאמרו מכת"י יוצא ממקום אחר דהו ל"ל מיגו נמצא שחתמו על שקר הלכך לא ניתן לכתוב והל' כר"נ דמסתבר טעמי' ותו דבחזקת הבתים מקשי התלמוד ממילתי' דר"ה דאמר החם מאן דחתם אאשקלתא חתם שפיר חתם איני והא א"ר נחמן מודעא היה דברינו אין נאמנים וקי"ל שאין התלמוד מקשה אלא מהל' פסוקה ודאמקשה מר"נ לסייע ממר בר"א אלא לאו ש"מ קים ליה לתלמודא דהלכה כר"נ עי' בחי"ב שטבאה תלה לפני בבברא וזבין ליה ארעא חתם רבה בב"ח מודעא ואשקלתא. אמר ר"ה מאן דחתם אמודעא שפיר חתם דחתם אשקלתא שפיר חתם ומק' אי מודעא לא אשקלתא ואי אשקלתא לא מודעא א"ל ר"ק אי לאו מודעא לא אשקלתא אשקלתא שפיר חתם ר"ה לטעמיה דאמר ר"ה תלויה וזבין זביניה זביני איני והא אמר ר"נ מודעא היה דברינו אין נאמנים ה"מ ע"פ דלא אתי ע"פ ומרע לשטרא אבל בשטר אתי שטר ומרע שטרי פי' טבי גברא אלמא הוה תלה לפני באילן שמש בינרא למכור לו שדהו ולא תלהו כדי שימכור לו האילן וזבין כלומר וכן עשה שמכר לו וחתם רבה בב"ח ועד אחר עמו מודעא שמסר פפי קודם שנכתב שטר מכירה ואאשקלתא פי' גם על שטר מכירה מאן דחתם אמודעי וכו' דאע"ג דתלויה וזבין זביניה זביני ה"מ היכא דלא מסר מודעא אבל המודעא שנכתב תבטל שטר המכירה ומאן דחתם אאשקלתא וכו' דתלויה וזבין זביניה וזביני כדאסיקנא ר"ה לטעמיה וכו' ור' יצחק אלפסי פסיק הל' כמר בר רב אשי: **בעא מיניה** רבא מר"נ תנאי היה דברינו מהו מודעא ואמנה טעמא מאי דעקר לי' לשטריה והאי נמי עקר לה לשטרא או דלמא תנאי מילתא אחריתי (והרב מוליך השיטה בשכת"י יוצא ממקום אחר ובעי' דרבא כשת"י ימ"א) פירוש מודעא ואמנה מ"ט אמרת דאין נאמנים אע"פ שאין כת"י יוצא ממקום אחר משום דעקרי לה לשטרא השתא בעדותן והלכך אמרינן להו א"כ דאמנה היה ולא הלוה לו או מודעא היה ולא מכר לו מרצונו למה חתמתם עולה ורשע עשיתים לפי דבריכם וכיון דמשוי נפשייהו רשיעי אין נאמנים וה"נ קעקרי לה לשטרא באמרו להו כיון שעל תנאי היה דברינו באומרים תנאי היה דברינו באמרו להו כיון שעל תנאי היה המכר כגון אם יבא פלוני ממקום פלוני ויסכים בדבר זה יהא מכר ואם לא לא יהא מכר למה חתמתם בשטר המכר שבלא שום תנאי מכר לו לא היה לכם לעשות דבר זה והלכך גם זה עולה הוא דומיא דשטר אמנה אע"פ שהאמינו המוכר שאם לא יקיים תנאו שיהא המכר בטל לא היה להם לחתום כדאמרינן בשטר אמנה שאע"פ שהאמינו שילוהו ויקרא עולה ואין לחתום בו או דלמא תנאי מלתא אחריתי הוא פי' שכיון שמכר לו מכר מקוים אע"פ שהתלה המכר על תנאי שאמר אם יבא אותו פלוני ויסכים יהא קיים ואם לאו יהא בטל רשאים העדים לחתום בו כיון שהמוכר מאמינו ולא רצה שיכתבו התנאי בתוך השטר א"ל כי אתי לקמן פי' לקוחות שעדיהם מעידים שתנאי היה דבריהם אמרינן להו זילו קיימו תנאייכו פי' לבעל וחותו לדינא פי' אם יעכב שוב הקרקע שנאמנים לומר תנאי היה דברינו וכיון שאין כת"י יוצא ממקום אחר ולא דמי לא למודעא ולא לאמנה דמודעא הא קא חזי דאנוס הוה ולא היה להם לחתום עד שלא יכתבו לו שטר מודעא אאמנה נמי לא אע"ג דאמרינן שאע"פ שהלוה מאמינו למלוה שילוהו אפ"ה אין לחתום בו דהתם לאו משום פסידא דלוה שכיון שהוא מתרצה בכך אין אנו חוששים בדבר אלא משום פסידא דלקוחות הוא כדאמרינן הכי שכיון שכתב ללוות ולא לוה אתי למיטרף לקוחות שלא כדין תדע דהכי הוא דהא בשטרא דלאו אקנייתא אין כותבין שטר ללוה עד שיהא מלוה עמו משום פסידא דלקוחות אבל בשטרא אקנייתא כותבין דאי טריף כדין טריף ואע"ג דאיכא למיחש דלמא ממטי ליה לוה למלוה ומאמינו עד שילוהו ולבסוף לא ילוהו אפ"ה לא חיישינן כיון שהוא מאמינו ה"נ כיון דהוא מאמינו שאם לא יתקיים התנאי יבטל לו המכר אין לנו לחוש להפסדו והלכך רשאים לחתום בו ולא הוי עולה כיון דלא מפסיד לאחריני אבל אם היה כת"י יוצא ממקום אחר אין נאמנים שכיון שהגיד שוב אין חוזר ומגיד (א"כ) [א"נ] י"ל כיון דפשיט ליה דהתנאי מילתא אחריתי הוא ואינה עולה מהימני אף על פי שכת"י יוצא ממקום אחר נאמנים דמה לי אחרים מה לי הם כמו שאם מעידים אחרים על התנאי נאמנים כמו כן כשהעידו הן בעצמן נאמנים והרבה בני אדם עושים כן דבר זה שאינם רוצים להזכיר שום תנאי בשטר שהוא עתיד להתקיים ימים רבים ואומר התנאי לפני עדי השטר שלא יכפור איש לחבירו הלכך אע"ג דליכא מיגו מהימן: **עד אומר** תנאי ועד אומר אינו תנאי א"ר פפא תרווייהו בשטר מעליא קמסהדי והאי דאמר תנאי הו"ל חד ואין דבריו של אחד במקום שנים **מתקיף** ליה ר"ה בריה דר"י א"ה אפילו תרוייהו נמי אלא אמרי' הני למיעקר סהדותיה קאתי חד למיעקר סהדותיה קאתי פי' א"ה כיון שהעיד על כת"י עשיתם לזה א' ממקיימי השטר כמו שהוא כתוב בלא תנאי והוי ליה עידיו שנים ועדות אחרונה דברי אחד במקום שנים אפי' תרוייהו נמי אמרו תנאי היה דברינו לא להימנו כיון שהעידו על כת"י קיימו השטר שהוא כמו שהוא כתוב וכי אמרו תנאי היה דברינו הו"ל מגידים וחוזרים ומגידים ואמאי הם נאמנים אלא ע"כ לא חתימה מקויימת הוא דכיון דבתוך כ"ד מסקי דבורייהו ואמרו אבל תנאי היה ביניהן אמרי' הני למיעקר סהדותייהו קאתי שאמרו כת"י הוא ועכשיו אומרים לא חתמנו אלא על מנת שיתקיים התנאי וכיון דהתנאי מילתא אחריתא היא שאינה עוקרתו אלא לאחר זמן לא דמיא למודעא ואמנה ומהימני דלאו עולה היא שהרי עדות היא בפ"ע האי חד נמי כי סיים ואמר תנאי הוה עקר לחתימת ידיה לומר לא חתמתי אלא על מנת כן וכיון דלאו עולה הוא מהימן ואשתכח דאין בשטר חתום אלא ע"א ומסיק תלמודא והל' כר"ה [בריה] דר"י: **ת"ר** שנים החתומים ע"ש השטר ומתו ובאו שנים ואמרו ידענו שכת"י הוא זה אבל אנוסים היו קטנים היו פסולי עדות היו הרי אלו נאמנים ואם יש עדים שהוא כת"י או שכת"י יוצא ממקום אחר משטר שקרא עליו ערעור פי' שרצה הנתבע לפוסלו והוחזק בב"ד אין נאמנים פי' היכא דאיכא מיגו נאמנים ולא מגבינן ביה והיכא דליכא מיגו אין נאמנים ומגבינן ביה **ומקשה** אין נאמנים ומגבינן ביה תרי ותרי נינהו פי' אלו

וּכְשֵׁם שֶׁאֵין מְזִימִין אֶת הָעֵדִים אֶלָּא בִּפְנֵיהֶם – **and just as we cannot render witnesses *zomemin* except in their presence,**[1] כָּךְ אֵין מַכְחִישִׁין אֶת הָעֵדִים אֶלָּא בִּפְנֵיהֶם – **so too, we cannot contradict witnesses except in their presence.**[2] In our Baraisa's case, since the witnesses who signed the document have died, their testimony can no longer be contradicted. Therefore the document is deemed valid.

Rav Sheishess' explanation is rejected:

אָמַר לֵיהּ רַב נַחְמָן – **Rav Nachman said to [Rav Sheishess]:** אִילּוּ הֲווּ קַמָּן וּמַכְחִישִׁין לְהוּ – **If [the signers]** of the note **were in our presence when [the latter witnesses] contradicted them,** then even if the signers would stand by their original testimony הָוֵה הַכְחָשָׁה וְלָא הָוֵה מַשְׁגִּיחִין בְּהוּ – **[the latter testimony] would be a** valid **contradiction** of it **and we would disregard** the testimony of **[the signers]** insofar as collecting the debt to which they attested, דְּהָוֵי לָהּ עֵדוּת מוּכְחֶשֶׁת – **because it would be a contradicted testimony.**[3] הַשְׁתָּא דְּלֵיתְנְהוּ – **Now that [the signers] are *not* here** in our presence, דְּאִילּוּ הֲווּ לְקַמָּן דִּלְמָא הֲווּ מוֹדוּ לְהוּ – so we can posit **that if they were in our presence perhaps they would admit to those** who contradict their signed testimony, מְהֵימְנֵי – can we possibly say that **they are believed** in their signed testimony and we collect the debt on its basis?[4]

Rav Nachman therefore explains the Baraisa differently:

אֶלָּא אָמַר רַב נַחְמָן – **Rather, Rav Nachman said:** When the Baraisa states that the latter witnesses are not believed, it means that אוֹקֵי תְּרֵי לְהֲדֵי תְּרֵי – we **pit** the **two** witnesses who void the note **against** the **two** witnesses who signed it, וְאוֹקֵי מָמוֹנָא בְּחֶזְקַת מָרֵיהּ – **and leave the money in the possession of its** current **owner.** That is, we neither destroy the note nor enforce it, but maintain the status quo.[5]

The Gemara adduces support for Rav Nachman's opinion:

מִידֵי דַּהֲוָה אַנִּכְסֵי דְּבַר שַׁטְיָא – **This is analogous to** the incident involving **the property of Bar Shatya.** דְּבַר שַׁטְיָא זַבִּין נִכְסֵי – **For Bar Shatya sold** his real **property.** אָתוּ בֵּי תְּרֵי אָמְרֵי כְּשֶׁהוּא שׁוֹטֶה זַבִּין – **Two** witnesses later **came and said** that **he sold it while he was deranged** and the sale is therefore void. וַאֲתוּ בֵּי תְּרֵי וְאָמְרֵי כְּשֶׁהוּא חָלִים זַבִּין – **But two** other witnesses **came and said** that **he sold it while he was normal** and the sale is therefore valid.[6] אָמַר רַב אַשִׁי – **Rav Ashi stated:** אוֹקֵי תְּרֵי לְהֲדֵי תְּרֵי – **Pit** the **two** witnesses who say he was deranged **against** the **two** who say he was normal, וְאוֹקֵי מָמוֹנָא בְּחֶזְקַת בַּר שַׁטְיָא – **and leave the property in the possession of Bar Shatya,** who owned it before the questionable transaction was performed.[7]

The Gemara qualifies Rav Ashi's ruling:

וְלָא אֲמָרַן אֶלָּא דְּאִית לֵיהּ חֲזָקָה דַּאֲבָהָתֵיהּ – **This was stated only** concerning a case **where [Bar Shatya] had a *chazakah*** for ownership of this property **from his father,** i.e. his father originally owned the property and he inherited it.[8] אֲבָל לֵית לֵיהּ חֲזָקָה דַּאֲבָהָתֵיהּ – **But if [Bar Shatya] did not have a *chazakah*** for ownership **from his father,** but rather, he had purchased it from another person and then sold it, אָמְרִינַן כְּשֶׁהוּא שׁוֹטֶה זְבַן וּכְשֶׁהוּא שׁוֹטֶה זַבִּין – **we would say** that **he bought it while he was deranged and sold it while he was deranged,** and we would let the sale stand.[9]

NOTES

1. There is a rule that all testimony affecting a person must be made in his presence (see *Bava Kamma* 112b). Since if proven to be *zomemin,* the witnesses will be liable to either monetary or corporal punishment, the *hazamah* testimony must take place in their presence (*Rashi*).

2. That is, although their testimony is merely being contradicted — without any threat of the *hazamah* penalty — it must be done in their presence (*Rashi*). Despite its failure to bring on punishment, the testimony of the latter witnesses is deemed to affect the former ones, since they state that the former ones signed falsely. Even in the case where they testify that the former ones were minors or invalid when they signed, their unstated claim is that the signing was dishonest, since the signatures attest that the document is perfectly valid (as explained in 19b note 32). This contradiction of the signed testimony must take place in the presence of those who signed (*Ritva; cf. Chidushei R' Akiva Eiger;* see also *Kovetz Shiurim*).

3. [When two sets of witnesses deliver contradictory testimony, we cannot rely fully upon the word of either set.] Thus, the testimony of the witnesses signed on the document would not enable us to collect the debt recorded in it (*Rashi*).

4. [How can their signatures carry more weight in their absence than in their presence, when they might have reacted to the contradiction with an admission of perjury?] Although such an admission would be worthless — since the signers are unable to retract their established testimony — Rav Nachman argues that it is illogical to consider the contradiction ineffective when they are absent, since it is effective when they are present and arguing against it (*Maharam Schif;* cf. *Shaar Mishpat* 29:2).

Rav Nachman dismisses the argument that any testimony affecting the witnesses must be presented in their presence. In his opinion, this applies only where the objective of the testimony is that the witnesses be punished, viz. in the case of *hazamah.* Here, however, where the latter testimony is focused on the validity of the note, it is important only that the holder of the note be present, not that the original witnesses be present (*Ritva* below ד״ה והזמה; see also *Talmidei Rabbeinu Yonah* below ד״ה אין מזימין and *Birkas Shmuel* 29:1; see further, note 11).

5. If the document in question is a note of indebtedness we let the alleged borrower keep his money, and if it is a bill of sale of real property, the alleged seller retains his property (see note 7). When the Baraisa states that we do not believe the latter witnesses, it does not mean that we regard the document as fully valid. Rather, it means that we do not destroy it on the basis of their testimony (*Rashi*).

Rashi adds that if the one holding the document seizes the other party's property — i.e. the "lender" seizes the money supposedly owed to him, or the "buyer" seizes the property supposedly sold to him — we cannot force him to relinquish it. Since the note in his possession has not been positively refuted, we pit the two witnesses who signed against the other two witnesses and leave the disputed property where it presently is. See *Tosafos* ד״ה ואוקי ממונא, *Rosh* and other Rishonim, who discuss whether one who seizes disputed property is allowed to keep it in all circumstances. [The principle of pitting *two against two* will be discussed in greater detail below, 22a,b.]

According to Rav Nachman's interpretation, the contrast between the Baraisa's two clauses is as follows: When the signatures cannot be authenticated except by these latter witnesses, *happeh she'assar* causes us to believe them that the note is void and we destroy it (see 19b note 28). But when the signatures are authenticated independently, the latter witnesses are not fully believed and we leave the note intact. However, since we have a contradiction between the witnesses who signed the note and those who declare it void, we do not honor the note. It is useful only in the event that its holder seizes the disputed property (*Ritva,* based on *Rashi*).

6. Bar Shatya was a man who suffered from bouts of temporary insanity. The law concerning such a person is that when he is well, he is considered a normal person and his transactions are valid, and while insane he is considered a deranged person and his transactions are void (*Ritva,* from *Rosh Hashanah* 28a). In this case, there was a contradiction between two sets of witnesses concerning his condition at the time of the sale.

7. Even if the buyer had taken possession, we would return the property to Bar Shatya, because real property is always considered to be in the possession of the last person who is *known* to have owned it. With regard to movable property, we leave it in the possession of the person currently holding it (*Tosafos* ד״ה ואוקי ארעא, *Rosh;* cf. *Ritva*). [Indeed, *Tosafos'* reading is ... וְאוֹקֵי אַרְעָא, leave the *land* ...; see also *Mesoras HaShas* and *Dikdukei Soferim HaShalem.*]

8. That is, no one disputes the fact that Bar Shatya inherited the property from his father. The dispute centers on whether Bar Shatya's subsequent sale was valid. Since his ownership was definite and the sale is questionable, we leave the property in his possession (see *Rashi; Ri Migash*).

9. Since Bar Shatya's claim of ownership stems from his acquisition of this property, his claim of possession is no stronger than the buyer's

The Gemara explains why the latter witnesses are not believed: אָמַר רַב שֵׁשֶׁת – **Rav Sheishess said:** זאת אוֹמֶרֶת הַכְחָשָׁה תְּחִלַּת הֲזָמָה הִיא – **This tells** us that the **contradiction** of witnesses **is the beginning of** their ***hazamah,***[33]

NOTES

33. There are two ways in which the testimony of one set of witnesses can be contradicted by another set:

(a) הַכְחָשָׁה, *contradiction*: One set of witnesses testifies that a certain event occurred, and another set testifies that the event in question did not occur. In such a case, the testimony of each set of witnesses carries equal weight.

(b) הֲזָמָה, *hazamah*: One set of witnesses testifies that a certain event occurred at a particular time and place. Then another set of witnesses testifies that at that time the first witnesses were in a different place (and therefore could not have seen the event in question). The latter witnesses make no statement concerning the incident which is the subject of the testimony; they merely discredit the witnesses who previously gave testimony. Regarding such a case, the Torah decrees that the second set of witnesses is believed and the first set is treated as *zomemin,* i.e. conspirators. The *zomemin* receive whatever punishment they had conspired to inflict upon their intended victim [כַּאֲשֶׁר זָמַם], whether monetary or corporal.

The Baraisa deals with a case in which the second set of witnesses contradicts the set that signed the note, and states that it is void (e.g. because the signers were coerced). Nevertheless, Rav Sheishess posits that the contradiction of witnesses is analogous to *hazamah* – and therefore, certain laws pertaining to *hazamah* apply to contradiction as well. As Rav Sheishess will proceed to explain, in our case a certain clause in the law of *hazamah* causes the testimony of the latter witnesses to be rejected, leaving the testimony of the signers intact.

[It should be noted that the Gemara in *Bava Kamma* (73b) uses the phrase "Contradiction is the beginning of *hazamah*" in a different context. Our Gemara does not mean literally that it is the first step in the *hazamah* process (as it does in the aforementioned case), but, merely, that the two issues are analogous and have common laws (*Ritva;* cf. *Chidushei R' Akiva Eiger*).]

עין משפט
נר מצוה

כז א מיי' פ"ג מהלכות עדות הלכה ז סמג עשין קט טוש"ע ח"מ סי' מו סעיף לז:
כח ב טוש"ע ח"מ סימן נז סעיף א:
כט ג מיי' פ"ז מהלכות ס"ת הלכה יב סמג עשין כה טוש"ע י"ד סי' רעט סעיף א [וברב אלפס עוד ברים הלכות ספר תורה דף סה:]:
ל ד ה ו ז ח מיי' פ"ג מהל' עדות הל' ז ח ט ופ"ז הל' ז סמג עשין קט טוש"ע ח"מ סי' מו סעי' לז (וסי' כט סעיף א):
לא ט מיי' פי"ח מהל' עדות הלכה ד סמג עשין ק טור ח"מ סי' לח:

מסורת הש"ס

א) שבת עח:, ב) פי' שפייסו להלוות לו שטר, ג) [ב"ב מח: מט.], ד) [ב"ק עג:], ה) נ"י כ"י, ו) ובאין כתב ידן יוצא ממקום אחר נאמנין שפיר במגו דאי בעי שתקי אי נמי מגו במקום עדים הוא אי נמי הא דבתרא מהימני חידוש הוא דמאי חזית דסמכת אהני כו' הלכך אין נאמנין במגו שיכולים לפוסלן בגזלנותא אלא כשאומרים כן בפירוש.

ואמר רב ששת בריה דרב אידי ש"מ מדרב כהנא עדים שאמרו אמנה היו דברינו אין נאמנין מאי טעמא כיון דעולה הוא אעולה לא חתמי א) אמר רבי יהושע בן לוי אסור לו לאדם שישהה שטר פרוע בתוך ביתו משום שנאמר א) אל תשכן באהליך עולה במערבא משמיה דרב אמרי א) אם און בידך הרחיקהו זה שטר אמנה ושטר פסים ואל תשכן באהלך עולה זה שטר פרוע מאן דאמר שטר פרוע כל שכן שטר אמנה ומאן דאמר שטר אמנה אבל שטר פרוע לא דזימנין דמשהי ליה אפשיטי דספרא אתמר ספר שאינו מוגה אמר רבי אמי עד ל' יום מותר לשהותו מכאן ואילך אסור לשהותו משום שנא' אל תשכן באהליך עולה ג) אר"נ עדים שאמרו אמנה היו דברינו אין נאמנין מודעא היו דברינו אין נאמנין מר בר רב אשי אמר אמנה היו דברינו אין נאמנין מודעא היו דברינו נאמנין מ"ט האי ניתן ליכתב והאי לא ניתן ליכתב בעא מיניה רבא מרב נחמן תנאי היו דברינו מהו מודעא ואמנה היינו טעמא דקא עקרי ליה לשטרא והאי נמי קא עקר לשטרא או דלמא תנאי מילתא אחריתי היא א"ל כי אתו לקמן לדינא אמרינן להו זילו קיימו תנאייכו וחותו לדינא עד אומר תנאי ועד אומר אינו תנאי א"ר פפא תרוייהו בשטרא מעליא קא מסהדי והאי דקאמר תנאי הוה ליה חד ואין דבריו של אחד במקום שנים מתקיף לה רב הונא בריה דרב יהושע אי הכי אפי' תרוייהו נמי אלא אמרינן הני למיעקר סהדותייהו קאתו האי נמי למיעקר סהדותיה קאתי והלכתא כרב הונא בריה דרב יהושע ת"ר שנים חתומין על השטר ומתו ובאו שנים מן השוק ואמרו ידענו שכתב ידם הוא אבל אנוסים היו קטנים היו פסולי עדות היו הרי אלו נאמנים ואם יש עדים שכתב ידם הוא זה או שהיה כתב ידם יוצא ממקום אחר משטר שקרא עליו ערער והוחזק בב"ד אין אלו נאמנין ומגבינן ביה כבשטרא מעליא ואמאי תרי ותרי נינהו אמר רב ששת זאת אומרת ד) הכחשה תחלת הזמה היא

ואמר רב ששת גרסי'. אעולה לא חתמי. וכי אמרי חתמנו אין נאמנים להרשיע את עצמן: על פשיטי דספרא. שעל הלוה ליתן שכר הסופר ופעמים שאין לו ונותנו המלוה וחוזר וגובהו ממנו בשעת פרעון ומעכב השטר עליו: ספר שאינו מוגה. תורה נביאים וכתובים: מוגה. מן טעיות שבו: עדים. החתומים בשטר ואמרו אמנה היו דברינו לא הלוהו כלום אלא כתבנו לו לכשיצטרך ילוה לו וזה שיעבד לו נכסיו מעכשיו אם ילוה אפילו לאחר זמן דלאו מוקדם ליהוי לטרוף שלא כדין: מודעא היו דברינו. אם שטר מכר הוא ואמרו עדים החתומים בו המוכר מסר מודעא בפנינו והראנו אונסו והכרנו בו: אין נאמנין. דלא אתי על פה ומרע ליה לשטרא: מודעא ניתן לעדים לכתוב את השטר כדי להציל האנוס מאונסו אמנה לא ניתן להכתב דעולה הוא וכי אמרו חתמנו משוו לנפשייהו רשעים ואין אדם נאמן לשום עצמו רשע: תנאי היו דברינו. על תנאי מכרה לו שיעשה לו כך וכך ולא ראינו שקיים לו תנאו וזה אומר לא קיים לי ואינו מכר: מודעא ואמנה. טעמא מאי קאמר מר אין נאמנין: דקא עקרי ליה לשטרא. בעדותן זה ולא אתי על פה ומרע לשטרא הכא נמי כו': או דלמא. הא לא עקרתא דשטרא הוא דמודים הם שהשטר אמת אלא שתנאי היה ביניהם וזו עדות אחרת היא ושטרא ממילא מיעקר לאחר זמן ביום שלא קיים תנאו בזמנו: כי אתו לקמן. לקוחות שעידיהם מעידים שתנאי היו דבריהם: אמרי' להו זילו קיימו תנאייכו. לבעלים: וחותו לדינא. אם יעכב שוב הקרקע: תרווייהו בשטרא מעליא קא מסהדי. שניהם מעידים שהשטר אמת וכמות שהוא כתוב בלא תנאי חתמוהו: והאי דקאמר תנאי חד הוא. ואינו נאמן לעקור שטר ששניהם חתומים בו: אי הכי אפילו תרווייהו נמי אלא אמרינן כו'. אי הכי דכיון שהעיד על כתב ידו עשית לזה אחד ממקיימי השטר כמות שהוא כתוב בלא תנאי והוי להו עדיו שנים ועדות אחרונה דברי אחד במקום שנים: אפי' תרווייהו נמי. אמרי תנאי היו דברינו לא ליתהימנו דכיון שהעידו על כתב ידן קיימו השטר כמות שהוא כתוב וכי אמרי תנאי היו דברינו הוו להו מגידים וחוזרים ומגידים ואמאי אמר רב נחמן קיימו תנאייכו כו': אלא. על כרחך לאו חתימה מקויימת הוא דכיון דתוך כדי דבור מסקי דבורייהו ואמרי אבל תנאי היה ביניהן אמרינן הני למיעקר סהדותייהו שאמרו כתב ידינו הוא קאתו ולומר לא חתמנו אלא ע"מ שיקיים את התנאי וכיון דתנאי מלתא אחריתי היא שאינה עוקרתו אלא לאחר זמן לא דמיא למודעא ואמנה ומהימני לעדות בפני עצמה היא: האי נמי. כי סיים ואמר תנאי הוה עקר לחתימת ידיה לומר לא חתמתי אלא על מנת כן וכיון דאית לן דמלתא אחריתי היא ושטרא ממילא מיעקר אישתכח דאין בשטר חתום אלא ע"א: שקרא עליו ערער. שרצה הנתבע לפוסלו: ומגבינן ביה. בתמיה: תרי ותרי נינהו. עדי השטר ב' ואלו ב' מעידים עליהם שפסולים היו באותה שעה:

וכסס

אם און בידך הרחיקהו זה שטר פסים ושטר אמנה. הכי משמע לשון און דמעיקרא הוי שקר ואל תשכן באהליך עולה זה שטר פרוע שעתה הוא עולה אבל מעיקרא הוה אמת: זמנין דמשהי ליה אפשיטי דספרא. וע"י אותה שהייה אישתלי ליה שהותו פעם אחרת הלכך לא קרי ליה עולה ומ"ד שטר פרוע היה לו ליזהר אבל אין לפרש דמשום שהייתו אפשיטי דספרא קרי ליה עולה דמה פשע: אמר רב נחמן עדים שאמרו אמנה היו דברינו אין נאמנים. ע"כ באין כתב ידן יוצא ממקום אחר איירי דאי כתב ידן יוצא ממקום אחר פשיטא דהכי פריך לעיל ועוד דמר בר רב אשי קאמר דאין נאמנים משום דלא ניתן לכתב ואי בכתב ידן יוצא ממקום אחר אפילו ניתן לכתב פשיטא דאין נאמנים וקשה דאמאי לא מהימני במיגו דהא רב נחמן גופיה אית ליה לעיל מגו לפסול השטר דקאמר כי אתו לקמן לדינא אמרינן להו זילו קיימו שטרייכו וחותו לדינא דמהימן לומר פרוע במגו דמזויף וכ"ש עדים דאלימי לאורועי שטרא כדאמר במי שמת (ב"ב דף קנד.) ותירץ ר"י דהיינו טעמא דמודעא הואיל ומודים שהשטר נכתב ונמסר כהלכתו שוב לא אתי על פה ומרע לשטרא אפילו במגו ולא דמי לאנוסים וקטנים דמתניתין שאין מודים שהיה שטר כשר כלל אלא סותרין אותו הלכך מהימני במגו דלא שייך כאן לומר דלא אתי על פה ומרע לשטרא שהרי אינם מודים שהיה שטר ואמנה נמי נראה דהיינו טעמא דלא מהימני לרב נחמן דלא מרעי לשטרא הואיל ומודים שהשטר נכתב כדין מדעת הלוה דלא מפרש טעמא דאמנה משום דלא ניתן לכתב אלא מר בר רב אשי אבל לרב נחמן טעם אמנה ומודעא שניהם שוה והא דאית ליה לרב נחמן דנאמן לומר פרוע הוא במגו דמזויף התם נמי לא מרע לשטרא כלל הלכך מהימן במגו ואתי שפיר רב נחמן כרבנן דר"מ והא ברייתא דמי שמת (ג"ז שם:) דשטר אמנה הוא זה דאינו נאמן דבעי לאוקמי כר"מ רב נחמן מוקי לה לדברי הכל: או דלמא תנאי מילתא אחריתי היא. פי' לדבר אחר הן באין ולא לעקירת השטר אלא תוספת בעלמא שמפרשים עדותן היאך ועד השתא קיים השטר ואינו נעקר אם יתקיים התנאי הלכך אין כאן הורעת השטר אבל אין לפרש מילתא אחריתי היא לגמרי ולא שייך לעדותן ראשונה כמו שאם היו מעידין שהוא פרוע שהן נאמנים דא"כ מאי פריך בסמוך א"ה אפי' תרי נמי דכיון דתנאי מילתא אחריתי הוא לגמרי תרי נאמנים אפילו בכתב ידן יוצא ממקום אחר אבל חד לעולם אימא לך דלא מהימן כי היכי דלא מהימן לומר פרוע הוא לכך נראה כדפירשנו: ואם כתב ידן יוצא ממקום אחר אין נאמנים. ופסולי עדות דקתני לא שאומרים שעדיין פסולים דאם כן אמאי אין נאמנים אלא פסולי עדות הוו אז ועתה מודים שהם כשרים וא"ת ומכל מקום אמאי אין נאמנים להימנו במגו דאי בעו אומרים עדיין הם פסולים ה) [וכן בכלן] שתי כתי עדים המכחישות זו את זו אמאי לא מהימני בתרא' במגו דאי בעו פסלי לקמאי בגזלנותא ואור"י דבשני עדים לא שייך מגו דאין אחד יודע מה בלב חבירו ו): אמר רב ששת זאת אומרת הכחשה תחלת הזמה היא. וא"ת תקשי לרב ששת ברייתא דמי שמת (ג"ז שם) דקתני אם אמר שטר אמנה הוא אם יש עדים פירוש לשטר אמנה הולך אחר עדים ואם לאו הלך אחר השטר אלמא אע"ג דאין השטר צריך קיום כדאמר הלך אחר השטר שמודה הלוה שכתבו כדאיתא התם [ואפילו הכי] אם יש עדים הלך אחר עדים ולא אמרינן הכחשה תחלת הזמה וי"ל דזאת אומרת קאמר אבל ההיא פליג:

ואוקי

תוספות רי"ד

מכרה היא כתובתה באייר דהייב שטר חוב וחזרתה ומחלתה לבעלה בתשרי שפיר טרף בעלה וכיון א) שיכולה למחול אותה לבעלה אי לקנוניא בעי' להפסיד הלקוחות כלל למחול לבעלה ומדלא מחלה ש"מ קושטא קאמרה וה"נ הכא נהמניה על ידי ההיא מגו ונ"ל לתרץ דדוקא גבי מוכר לחבירו יכול למחול מפני שאינו יכול להקנות לחבירו גוף המנה שאינו בעין אבל ב) מלוה שלא יכול לומר הלוה ללוקח לאו בע"ד דידי את לא יהא אלא שהרשהו לגבות ממנו ומפני כך יכול המלוה למחול אבל כשחב לאחרים שהוא ד"ת אינו יכול למחול משעה שחב לאחרים לאותו ושוב אינו המלוה יכול למחול ומ"ה אוקימנא כשחב לאחרים ולא כשמכרו לאחרים דהתם ודאי מצי מחיל הנה נאמן ע"י מיגו אבל הכא לא מצי מחיל ומ"ה לא מהימן: ר"א אמר לעולם דקאמרו עדים ודאין כת"י יוצא ממקום אחר ודקאמרת אמאי לא מהימנו כדר"כ דאר"כ אסור לאדם שישהה שטר אמנה בתוך ביתו שנאמר אל תשכן באהליך עולה: א"ר [ששת] (אשישא) בריה דר"א ש"מ מדר"כ העדים שאמרו אמנה היה דברינו אין נאמנים מ"ט כיון דעולה היא אעולה לא חתמו ואע"פ שיש להן מיגו אין נאמנים: אריב"ל אסור לאדם שישהא שטר פרוע בתוך ביתו שנא' אל תשכן באהליך עולה מ"ד שטר פרוע כ"ש שטר אמנה ומ"ד שטר אמנה אבל שטר פרוע לא דזימנין משהי ליה על פשיטי דספרא פי' שיהיה לו לפרוע ללוה כדתנן והלוה נותן שכר הסופר ויפרעם המלוה ודוקא אפשיטי דספרא פליגי אבל אם חייב לו קצת מן החוב ליכא מאן דפליג שיכול להשהותו אצלו עד שיפרענו וא"צ לכתוב לו שובר כדי שלא יהא לו כפוף שיפרענו: במערבא אמרי משמיה דר"א אם און בידך הרחיקהו זה שטר פסים שטר אמנה ואל תשכן באהליך עולה זו שטר פרוע: איתמר ס"ת שאינו מוגה א"ר אמי

[illegible]

גליון הש"ס

גמ' זאת אומרת הכחשה. עיין שיטה מקובלת בב"מ דף קב ע"א ד"ה אר"א זאת אומרת בשם רבי סעדי' גאון:

תורה אור השלם

א) אִם אָוֶן בְּיָדְךָ הַרְחִיקֵהוּ וְאַל תַּשְׁכֵּן בְּאֹהָלֶיךָ עַוְלָה: [איוב יא, יד]

ליקוטי רש"י

אמנה היו דברינו. לא הלוהו כלום אלא כתבנו לו ולכשיצטרך ילוה בו והאמינו לוה למלוה שלא יוציא עליו שטר מלוה זו לגבות הימנו אא"כ ילוה לו וזה שעבד לו נכסיו מעכשיו אם ילוה אפי' לאחר זמן דלאו מוקדם הוה לטרוף שלא כדין [רשב"ם ב"ב מח:]. אין נאמנין. לא מבעיא אם כתב ידן יוצא ממקום אחר דלא מהימני לעקרו דלאו הפה שאסר הוא הפה שהתיר איכא אלא אפילו [אם] הן עצמם מקיימים אותו ואומרים חתמנו אבל אמנה היו דברינו אין נאמנים. אעולה לא חתמי. וכי אמר חתמנו אינו נאמן דאין אדם משים עצמו רשע בעדות [שם מט.]. במערבא. בארץ ישראל [שבת סה.]. אר"נ עדים שאמרו כו'. דמאחר שהודו שבכתבות כתבם הרי חתימת השטר אמת ואשר העידו בב"ד כל מה שכתוב בשטר שלוהו מלוה ללוה וכיון שהגיד שוב אינו חוזר ומגיד כדאמרינן בכתובות בפרק האשה שנתארמלה (דף יח) א"ל רבא כיון שהגיד שוב אינו חוזר ומגיד ואי תימא מה"מ הא לא אמר ר"ל בשטר לא לא אמר ר"ל עדים החתומים על השטר נעשו כמי שנחקרה עדותן בב"ד וכו' מפרש התם דטעמא דר"נ משום דעקר ליה לשטרא דבעא מיניה רבא מר"נ תנאי היו דברינו מהו מודעא ואמנה טעמא מאי אין נאמנים דקמעקר ליה לשטרא וכו'. ועוד יש אחר גבי אמנה היו דברינו דאמאי אין נאמנים כדאמרינן נמי התם וכו' דאמר רב כהנא אסור לאדם שישהה שטר אמנה בתוך ביתו משום שנאמר אל תשכן באהלך עולה וכיון דעולה היא אעולה לא חתמי ואי אמר חתמנו אינו נאמן דאין אדם משים עצמו רשע בעדות וכשעדים שאמרו כו' משום חוזר ומגיד [שם מט.].

חשק שלמה על תוס' רי"ד

[illegible]

deserves to be accepted.[24]

The Gemara concludes:

וְהִלְכְתָא כְּרַב הוּנָא בְּרֵיהּ דְּרַב יְהוֹשֻׁעַ – And the halachah follows Rav Huna the son of Rav Yehoshua, that the one who says there was a stipulation is believed. Since his certification of the note is qualified, and only the other witness made an unqualified certification, the holder of the note cannot enforce it until he fulfills the stipulation.[25]

Having discussed various cases in which the witnesses signed on a document state that it is void, the Gemara turns to a case in which two other witnesses present such testimony:

תָּנוּ רַבָּנָן – The Rabbis taught in a Baraisa: שְׁנַיִם חֲתוּמִין עַל הַשְּׁטָר וּמֵתוּ – If TWO witnesses WERE SIGNED ON A DOCUMENT AND THEY DIED,[26] וּבָאוּ שְׁנַיִם מִן הַשּׁוּק וְאָמְרוּ – AND TWO people CAME FROM THE MARKET AND SAID, יָדַעְנוּ שֶׁכְּתַב יָדָם הוּא – "WE KNOW THAT IT IS THEIR HANDWRITING, אֲבָל אֲנוּסִים הָיוּ – BUT THEY WERE COERCED to sign," קְטַנִּים הָיוּ – or "THEY WERE MINORS when they signed," פְּסוּלֵי עֵדוּת הָיוּ – or "THEY WERE INVALID WITNESSES at that time,"[27] הֲרֵי אֵלּוּ נֶאֱמָנִים – THESE witnesses ARE BELIEVED.[28] וְאִם יֵשׁ עֵדִים שֶׁכְּתַב יָדָם הוּא זֶה – BUT IF THERE ARE other WITNESSES who testify THAT THIS IS THEIR HANDWRITING, אוֹ שֶׁהָיָה כְּתַב יָדָם יוֹצֵא מִמָּקוֹם אַחֵר – OR THEIR HANDWRITING IS VERIFIED FROM ANOTHER SOURCE, מִשְּׁטָר שֶׁקָּרָא עָלָיו עַרְעָר וְהוּחְזַק בְּבֵית דִּין – namely, FROM A different DOCUMENT AGAINST WHICH A CHALLENGE HAD BEEN RAISED AND WHICH WAS then UPHELD IN COURT,[29] אֵין אֵלּוּ נֶאֱמָנִין – THESE new witnesses ARE NOT BELIEVED.[30]

The Gemara questions the Baraisa's latter ruling:

וּמַגְבִּינַן בֵּיהּ כְּבִשְׁטָרָא מְעַלְּיָא – And we collect on the basis of [this note] as we do with a proper document!?[31] **וְאַמַּאי – But why? תְּרֵי וּתְרֵי נִינְהוּ – These** witnesses who testified concerning it **are two against two,** leaving its validity in doubt.[32] – ? –

NOTES

24. I.e. his current testimony is that his signature is authentic but subject to stipulation. This qualification is acceptable, since it consists of an addition to the written testimony and not an illegal retraction. Thus, we are left with only one witness who certified his signature as is, and another who made a qualified certification. It is as though the note contains only one signature attesting to the obligation recorded in it (*Rashi*). In order to enforce his claim, the holder of the note must fulfill the stipulation, so that the claim will be supported by both witnesses (*Ritva*).

25. Note that if instead of stating there was a stipulation one of the witnesses would claim the debt was repaid, he would certainly not be believed. For this statement would not qualify his certification of the note; rather, it would be a new testimony attempting to release the borrower from obligation. The testimony of a single witness is insufficient for this. Only when the witness claims there was a stipulation do we deem him to have qualified his certification of the note (*Ritva;* see also *Tosafos* ד״ה או דלמא).

Summary

We have concluded the discussion concerning witnesses who authenticate their signatures on a document and at the same time present information to invalidate it. To summarize, there are two factors that can prevent us from accepting the testimony of witnesses who negate a document that they signed: (1) They may neither contradict nor alter their own established testimony; (2) they cannot incriminate themselves. This leads to the following rules.

(a) If the signatures are authenticated independently, the written testimony has been firmly established and the witnesses cannot say anything to negate it. [They can, however, testify that the loan recorded in the note was repaid, since that is an entirely new testimony (*Tosafos* ד״ה או דלמא).]

(b) If the signatures are authenticated only through the witnesses themselves, *happeh she'assar* allows them to qualify their authentication – provided they do not incriminate themselves. Thus, if they say they were forced to sign to avoid financial harm, they are not believed, but if they say they were forced by mortal danger, they are believed. Similarly, if they say they signed while minors, or that they were related to one of the litigants, their testimony is accepted and the document is voided. In these cases, they are in effect not certifying the note at all.

(c) If they say the note was written on trust, or that it was preceded by notification of non-intent, they are not believed. Since they concede that the note is inherently valid, they are attempting to orally *revoke* the written testimony – after having certified it. This is impossible even though they have the power of *happeh she'assar.* Additionally, in the case where they say they signed on trust, they have incriminated themselves.

(d) If they say there was an unwritten stipulation, they are believed. This is not deemed a direct contradiction of the written testimony, but an addition to it. Since they have the power of *happeh she'assar,* they are able to add this qualification of their authentication.

(e) In all cases where the witnesses are believed, they must state the qualification immediately after the authentication of their signatures – within the time it takes to make an utterance.

26. Or they are for some other reason unavailable to authenticate their own signatures (*Ritva;* see there and *Ramban* for alternative explanations, according to which the Baraisa means specifically that they died).

27. I.e. the latter witnesses do not state that the signatories are gamblers or criminals who are completely disqualified from testifying, but that they were invalid at the time that they signed, because of a family relation that no longer exists (see *Rashi* below ד״ה תרי ותרי נינהו; for further discussion of this point and its significance, see note 32; see also *Tosafos* ד״ה ואם and *Rashba;* cf. *Rosh;* see *Choshen Mishpat* 46:37).

28. Since they have the power of *happeh she'assar,* the court accepts their word and destroys the document (*Ritva* to 20a, based on *Rashi; Rashba; Shitah Yeshanah;* cf. second opinion cited by *Ritva*; see *Shach, Choshen Mishpat* 46:99).

29. That is, the same witnesses had signed another document which, when previously presented in court, had had its authenticity challenged by the obligated party, and which was then authenticated by witnesses. The court authenticates the document currently in question by comparing its signatures to those on the previously certified one (*Rashi* here and to 20a ד״ה אא״כ קרא ערער; see 20a note 12).

30. [Since they do not have the power of *happeh she'assar.*]

31. The ruling that the new witnesses are not believed implies that the document is deemed completely valid.

32. The two witnesses signed on the note [attest that it is valid], and the two witnesses now before the court testify orally that those who signed were invalid at that time [and the note is therefore void] (*Rashi*). Now, if the latter witnesses would testify that the signatories are *still* invalid witnesses, e.g. they are gamblers, the latter ones would be believed. This is because any two witnesses have the ability to disqualify two other people on account of dishonesty, and the subjects are unable to contradict them and testify on their own behalf. But since the latter witnesses state only that the former ones were invalid *when they signed,* their testimony is essentially that the note is invalid, and in this regard the former ones contradict them – making this a case of two against two (*Tosafos* ד״ה ואם; cf. *Rosh*).

It is noteworthy that the witnesses signed on the note are deemed to contradict those who say they were invalid when they signed. This is because their signatures do not merely attest that the recorded transaction took place – they implicitly declare that the document is valid in all respects, including that it was made with valid witnesses (see *Ritva* ד״ה הכחשה, *Pnei Yehoshua* on 18b to *Tosafos* ד״ה הרי אלו נאמנים and *Chidushei R' Chaim HaLevi, Hil. Eidus* 5:6 ד״ה ובעיקר).

[Others explain that it is not the witnesses who declare themselves valid. Rather, since we learned above (18b-19a) that there is a presumption (*chazakah*) that the maker of a document would not have invalid witnesses sign, it is as though *we* can attest that the witnesses were valid at that time [אֲנַן סָהֲדֵי]. Thus, we who observe the document are like two witnesses declaring it valid, and the two witnesses who came before the court declare it invalid (*Rosh;* see also *Ramban* and *Meiri*).]

At any rate, since there are two witnesses against the two who signed the note, how can we consider it definitely valid?

כז א מיי' פ"ג מהלכות עדות הלכה ז סמג עשין קט טוש"ע ח"מ סי' מו סעיף לז:

כח ב טוש"ע ח"מ סימן מו סעיף לח:

כט ג מיי' פ"י מהלכות ס"ת הלכה יא סמג עשין כה טוש"ע י"ד סי' רעט סעיף א [וברב אלפס עוד ברכ"ה הלכות ספר תורה דף סה:]:

ל ד ה ו ז ח מיי' פ"ג מהל' עדות הל' ז ח ט ופ"י הל' ו סמג עשין קט טוש"ע ח"מ סי' מו סעי' לז (וסי' כב סעיף א):

לא ט מיי' פי"ח מהל' עדות הלכה ד סמג עשין קי טור ח"מ סי' לח:

ואמר רב ששת בריה דרב אידי ש"מ מדרב כהנא עדים שאמרו א) אמנה היו דברינו אין נאמנין מאי טעמא כיון דעולה הוא אעולה לא חתמי א) אמר רבי יהושע בן לוי ב) אסור לו לאדם שישהה שטר פרוע בתוך ביתו משום שנאמר א) אל תשכן באהליך עולה במערבא משמיה דרב אמרי א) אם און בידך הרחיקהו זה שטר אמנה ושטר ג) פסים ואל תשכן באהלך עולה זה שטר פרוע מאן דאמר שטר פרוע כל שכן שטר אמנה ומאן דאמר שטר אמנה אבל שטר פרוע לא זימנין דמשהי ליה אפשיטי דספרא איתמר ג) ספר שאינו מוגה אמר רבי אמי עד ל' יום מותר לשהותו מכאן ואילך אסור לשהותו משום שנא' אל תשכן באהליך עולה ד) אר"נ עדים שאמרו אמנה היו דברינו אין נאמנין מודעא היו דברינו נאמנין מר בר רב אשי אמר ד) אמנה היו דברינו אין נאמנין ה) מודעא היו דברינו נאמנין מ"ט האי ניתן ליכתב והאי לא ניתן ליכתב בעא מיניה רבא מרב נחמן תנאי היו דברינו מהו מודעא ואמנה היינו טעמא דקא עקרי ליה לשטרא והאי נמי קא עקר לשטרא או דלמא תנאי מילתא אחריתי היא א"ל כי אתו לקמן לדינא אמרינן להו ו) זילו קיימו תנאייכו וחותו לדינא עד אומר תנאי ועד אומר אינו תנאי א"ר פפא תרווייהו בשטרא מעליא קא מסהדי והאי דקאמר תנאי הוה ליה חד ואין דבריו של אחד במקום שנים מתקיף לה רב הונא בריה דרב יהושע אי הכי אפי' תרווייהו נמי אלא אמרינן הני למיעקר סהדותיהו קאתו האי נמי למיעקר סהדותיה קאתי ז) והלכתא כרב הונא בריה דרב יהושע ת"ר ח) שנים חתומין על השטר ומתו ובאו שנים מן השוק ואמרו ידענו שכתב ידם הוא אבל אנוסים היו קטנים היו פסולי עדות היו הרי אלו נאמנים ואם יש עדים שכתב ידם הוא או שהיה כתב ידם יוצא ממקום אחר משטר שקרא עליו ערער והוחזק בב"ד אין אלו נאמנין ומגבינן ביה כבשטרא מעליא ואמאי תרי ותרי נינהו אמר רב ששת ° זאת אומרת ד) ט) הכחשה תחלת הזמה היא

רש"י

ואמר רב ששת גרסי': **אעולה לא חתמי**. וכי אמרי חתמנו אין נאמנים להרשיע את עצמן: **על פשיטי דספרא**. שבעל הלוה ליתן שכר הסופר ופעמים שאין לו ונותנו המלוה וחוזר וגובהו ממנו בשעת פרעון ומעכב השטר עליו: **ספר שאינו מוגה**. תורה נביאים וכתובים: **מוגה**. מן טעיות שבו: **עדים**. החתומים בשטר ואמרו אמנה היו דברינו לא הלוהו כלום אלא כתבנו לו לכשיצטרך ילוה לו וזה שיעבד לו נכסיו מעכשיו אם ילוה אפילו לאחר זמן דלאו מוקדם ליהוי לטרוף שלא כדין: **מודעא היו דברינו**. אם שטר מכר הוא ואמרו עדים החתומים בו המוכר מסר מודעא בפנינו והראנו אונסו והכרנו בו: **אין נאמנין**. דלא אתי על פה ומרע ליה לשטרא: מודעא ניתן לעדים לכתוב את השטר כדי להציל האנוס מאונסו אמנה לא ניתן להכתב דעולה הוא וכי אמרי חתמנו משוי לנפשייהו רשעים ואין אדם נאמן לשום עצמו רשע: **תנאי היו דברינו**. על תנאי מכרה לו שיעשה לו כך וכך ולא ראינו שקיים לו תנאו וזה אומר לא קיים לי ואינו מכר: **מודעא ואמנה**. טעמא מאי קאמר מר אין נאמנין: **דקא עקרי ליה לשטרא**. בעדותן זה ולא אתי על פה ומרע לשטרא הכא נמי כו': **או דלמא**. הא לא עקרתא לשטרא הוא דמודים הם שהשטר אמת אלא שתנאי היה ביניהם וזו עדות אחרת היא ושטרא ממילא מיעקר לאחר זמן ביום שלא קיים תנאו בזמנו: **כי אתו לקמן**. לקוחות שעדיהם מעידים שתנאי היו דבריהם: **אמרי' להו זילו קיימו תנאייכו**. לבעלים: **וחותו לדינא**. אם יעכב שוב הקרקע: **תרוייהו בשטרא מעליא קא מסהדי**. שניהם מעידים שהשטר אמת וכמות שהוא כתוב בלא תנאי חתמוהו: **והאי דקאמר תנאי חד הוא**. ואינו נאמן לעקור שטר ששניהם חתומים בו: **אי הכי אפילו תרווייהו נמי אלא אמרינן כו'**. אי הכי דכיון שהעיד על כתב ידו עשית לזה אחד ממקיימי השטר כמות שהוא כתוב בלא תנאי והוי להו עדיו שנים ועדות אחרונה דברי אחד במקום שנים: **אפי' תרוייהו נמי**. אמרי תנאי היו דברינו לא ליתהימנו דכיון שהעידו על כתב ידן קיימו השטר כמות שהוא כתוב וכי אמרי תנאי היו דברינו הוו להו מגידים וחוזרים ומגידים ואמאי אמר רב נחמן קיימו תנאייכו כו': **אלא**. על כרחך לאו חתימה מקויימת הוא דכיון דתוך כדי דבור מסקי דבורייהו ואמרי אבל תנאי היה ביניהן אמרינן הני למיעקר סהדותייהו שאמרו כתב ידינו הוא קאתו ולומר לא חתמנו אלא ע"מ שיקיים את התנאי וכיון דתנאי מלתא אחריתי היא שאינה עוקרתו אלא לאחר זמן לא דמיא למודעא ואמנה ומהימני לעדות בפני עצמה היא: **האי נמי**. כי סיים ואמר תנאי הוה עקר לחתימת ידיה לומר לא חתמתי אלא על מנת כן וכיון דלאית לן דמלתא אחריתי היא ושטרא ממילא מיעקר אישתכח דליכא בשטר חתום אלא ע"א: **שקרא עליו ערער**. שערער הנכתב לפסולו: **ומגבינן ביה**. בתמיה: **תרי ותרי נינהו**. עדי השטר ב' ואלו ב' מעידים עליהם שפסולים היו באותה שעה:

תוספות

אם און בידך הרחיקהו זה שטר פסים ושטר אמנה. דהכי משמע לשון און למעיקרא הוי שקר ואל תשכן באהליך עולה זה שטר פרוע שעתה הוא עולה אבל מעיקרא הוה אמת: **זמנין** דמשהי ליה אפשיטי דספרא. וע"י אותה שהייה אישתלי ליה שהוציא פעם אחרת הלכך לא קרי ליה עולה ומ"ד שטר פרוע היה לו ליזהר אבל אין לפרש משום שהיינו אפשיטי דספרא קרי ליה עולה דמה פשע: **אמר** רב נחמן עדים שאמרו אמנה היו דברינו אין נאמנים. ע"כ באין כתב ידן יוצא ממקום אחר איירי דאי כתב ידן יוצא ממקום אחר פשיטא דהכי פריך לעיל ועוד דמר בר רב אשי קאמר דאין נאמנים משום דלא ניתן לכתב ואי בכתב ידן יוצא ממקום אחר אפילו ניתן לכתב פשיטא דאין נאמנים וקשה דאמאי לא מהימני במיגו דהא רב נחמן גופיה אית ליה לעיל מגו לפסול השטר דקאמר לא זכו לקמן לדינא אמרינן להו זילו קיימו שטרייכו וחותו לדינא למהימן לומר פרוע במגו דמזויף וכ"ש עדים דאלימי לאורועי שטרא כדאמר במי שמת (ב"ב דף קסז.) ותירץ ר"י דהיינו טעמא דמודעא הואיל ומודים שהשטר נכתב ונמסר כהלכתו שוב לא אתי על פה ומרע לשטרא אפילו במגו ולא דמי לאנוסים וקטנים דמתניתין שאין מודים שהיה שטר כשר כלל אלא סותרין אותו הלכך מהימני במגו דלא שייך כאן לומר דלא אתי על פה ומרע לשטרא שהרי אינם מודים שהיה שטר ואמנה נמי נראה דהיינו טעמא דלא מהימני לרב נחמן דלא מרעי לשטרא הואיל ומודים שהשטר נכתב כדין מדעת הלוה לא מפרש טעמא דאמנה משום דלא ניתן לכתב אלא מר בר רב אשי אבל לרב נחמן טעם אמנה ומודעא שניהם שוה והא דאית ליה לרב נחמן דנאמן לומר פרוע הוא במגו דמזויף התם נמי לא מרע לשטרא כלל הלכך מהימן במגו ואתי שפיר רב נחמן כרבנן דר"מ והיא ברייתא דמי שמת (ג"ז שם:) לשטר אמנה הוא זה דאינו נאמן דבעי לאוקמי כר"מ רב נחמן מוקי לה לדברי הכל: **או** דלמא תנאי מילתא אחריתי היא. פי' לדבר אחר הן באין ולא לעקירת השטר אלא תוספת בעלמא שמפרשים עדותן היאך ועד השתא קיים השטר ואינו נעקר אם יתקיים התנאי הלכך אין כאן הורעת השטר אבל אין לפרש מילתא אחריתי היא לגמרי ולא שייך לעדותן ראשונה כמו שאם היו מעידין שהוא פרוע שהן נאמנים דא"כ מאי פריך בסמוך א"ה אפי' תרי נמי דכיון דתנאי מילתא אחריתי הוא לגמרי תרי נאמנים אפילו בכתב ידן יוצא ממקום אחר אבל חד לעולם אימא לך דלא מהימן כי היכי דלא מהימן לומר פרוע הוא לכך נראה כדפירשנו: **ואם** כתב ידן יוצא ממקום אחר אין נאמנים. ופסולי עדות דקתני לא שאומרים שעדיין פסולים דאם כן אמאי אין נאמנים אלא פסולי עדות הוו אז ועתה מודים שהם כשרים וא"ת ומכל מקום אמאי אין נאמנים להימנו במגו דאי בעו אומרים עדיין הם פסולים ז) [וכן בכל] שתי כתי עדים המכחישות זו את זו אמאי לא מהימני בתראי במגו דאי בעו פסלי לקמאי בגזלנותא ואור"י דבשני עדים לא שייך מגו דאין אחד יודע מה בלב חבירו ח): **אמר** רב ששת זאת אומרת הכחשה תחלת הזמה היא. וא"ת תקשי לרב ששת ברייתא דמי שמת (ג"ז שם) דקתני אם אמר שטר אמנה הוא אם יש עדים הלך אחר עדים ואם לאו הלך אחר השטר אלמא אע"ג דאין השטר צריך קיום כדאמר הלך אחר השטר שמודה לוה שכתבו כדאמרת התם [ואפילו הכי] אם יש עדים הלך אחר עדים ולא אמרינן הכחשה תחלת הזמה היא וי"ל דזאת אומרת קאמר אבל ההיא פליג:

מסורת הש"ס

א) שבת עה:, ב) פי' שפיישו להלוות לו שטר, ג) [ב"ב מח: מנו.], ד) [ב"ק עג.], ה) נ"י כ"י, ו) ובאין כתב ידן יוצא ממקום אחר נאמנין שפיר במגו דאי בעי שתקי או נמי מגו דבמקום עדים הוא או נמי הא דהמתלי מהימני מידום הוא דמאי חזית דסמכת אהני סמוך אהלך אין נאמנין במגו שיוסלים לפוסלן בגזלנותא אלא כשאומרים כן בפירוש.

גליון הש"ס

גמ' זאת אומרת הכחשה. עיין שיטה מקובצת בב"מ דף קד ע"א ד"ה אר"ל זאת אומרת בשם רבי סעדי' גאון:

תורה אור השלם

א) אִם אָוֶן בְּיָדְךָ הַרְחִיקֵהוּ וְאַל תַּשְׁכֵּן בְּאֹהָלֶיךָ עַוְלָה: [איוב יא, יד]

ליקוטי רש"י

אמנה היו דברינו. לא הלוהו כלום אלא כתבנו לו ולכשיצטרך ילוה בו והאמינו ליה למלוה שלא יוציא עליו שטר מלוה זו לגבות הימנו אא"כ ילוה לו וזה שעבד לו נכסיו מעכשיו אם ילוה אפי' לאחר זמן דלאו מוקדם הוה לטרוף שלא כדין [רשב"ם ב"ב מח:]. **אין נאמנין**. לא מבעיא אם כתב ידן יוצא ממקום אחר דלא מהימני לעקרו דלאו הפה שאסר הוא הפה שהתיר איכא אלא אפילו [אם] הן עצמם מקיימים אותו ואומרים חתמנו אלו אמנה היו דברינו אין נאמנים. **אעולה לא חתמי**. וכי אמרי חתמנו אינו נאמן דאין אדם נאמן בעדותו לעשות עצמו רשע [שם מט.]. **במערבא**. בארץ ישראל [שבת סה.]. **אר"נ עדים שאמרו כו'**.

תוספות רי"ד

מכרה היא כתובתה באייר והיינו שטר חוב וחזרה ומחלתה לבעלה בתשרי שפיר טרף בעלה וכיון שכולה לבעלה למחול אותה לבעה אי לקנוניא בעי להפסיד הלקוחות כלל למחול לבעלה ומדלא מחלה ש"מ קושטא קאמרה וה"נ הכא מגו ת"ל להתיר דדוקא גבי מוכר לחבירו יכול למחול מפני שאינו יכול להקנות לחבירו גוף המנה שאינו בעין אבל ב) מלוה שלא יכול לומר הלוה ללוקח לאו בע"ד דידי את דלא יהא אלא שהרשהו לגבות ממנו ומפני כך יכול המלוה למחול אבל כשחב לאחרים שהוא ד"ת אינו יכול למחול משעשה שחב לאחרים נשתעבד המנה הזה לעותו ושוב אינו המלוה יכול למוחלו ומ"ה עקימנא כשחב לאחרים ר"ל כשמכרו לאחרים דהתם ודאי דמצי מחיל דנה נאמן כי מצי מחיל הכא לא מצי מחיל ומ"ה יא מהימן: ר"ל אמר לעולם כשאמרו עדים דאין כת"י יוצא ממקום אחר ודקאמרת אמאי לא אהימנו כדר"כ דאר"כ אסור לאדם שישהה שטר אמנה בתוך ביתו שנאמר אל תשכן באהליך עולה: א"ר [ששת] (אשישא) בריה דר"א ש"מ מדר"כ העדים שאמרו אמנה היה דברינו אין נאמנים מ"ט כיון דעולה היא אעולה לא חתמו ואע"פ שיש להן מיגו אין נאמנים: אריב"ל אסור לאדם שישהא שטר פרוע בתוך ביתו שנא' ואל תשכן באהליך עולה מ"ד שטר פרוע כ"ש שטר אמנה ומ"ד שטר אמנה אבל שטר פרוע לא זימנין דמשהי ליה על פשיטי פי' שהיה לפרוע ללוה כדתנן נותן שכר הסופר והלוה ופרעם הוא ודוקא אפשיטי דספרא פליגי אבל אם חייב לו קצת מן החוב ליכא מאן דפליג שיכול להשהותו אצלו עד שיפרענו וא"צ לכתוב לו שובר כדי שיהא לו כפוף שיפרענו: במערבא אמרי משמיה דר"א אם און בידך הרחיקהו זה שטר פסים ושטר אמנה ואל תשכן באהליך עולה זו שטר פרוע: איתמר ס"ת שאינו מוגה א"ר אמי עד ל' יום מותר להשהותו מכאן ואילך אסור להשהותו משום אל תשכן באהליך עולה:

they are revoking the document with their testimony,[15] וְהַאי נַמִּי קָא עָקַר לִשְׁטָרָא – and in this case, too, their statement that it is subject to a stipulation is a revocation of the document – and therefore is not believed?[16] אוֹ דִּלְמָא תְּנַאי מִילְּתָא אַחֲרִיתִי הִיא – Or, perhaps, a stipulation is a different matter, i.e. it is merely an added clause and not a revocation of the document, since there is a possibility that the stipulation will be fulfilled. Thus, they should be believed.[17] – ? –

Rav Nachman replies:

אָמַר לֵיהּ – He said to [Rava]: כִּי אָתוּ לְקַמָּן לְדִינָא – When [buyers] come to us for judgment holding a document and the witnesses state that it was subject to a stipulation, אַמְרִינַן לְהוּ זִילוּ קַיְּימוּ תְּנָאַיְיכוּ וְחוּתוּ לְדִינָא – we tell [the buyers]: "Go fulfill your stipulations, and then come down for judgment if the seller still refuses to give you the property."[18]

A related ruling is cited:

עֵד אוֹמֵר תְּנַאי וְעֵד אוֹמֵר אֵינוֹ תְּנַאי – If one witness states that the document was written on stipulation and the other witness states that it was not written on stipulation,[19] אָמַר רַב פָּפָּא – Rav Pappa said: תַּרְוַיְיהוּ בִּשְׁטָרָא מְעַלְּיָא קָא מַסְהֲדֵי – Both of them are testifying about a valid document that contains no written stipulation,[20] וְהַאי דְּקָאָמַר תְּנַאי הָוָה לֵיהּ חַד – and this one who states that it was written on stipulation is only one witness, וְאֵין דְּבָרָיו שֶׁל אֶחָד בִּמְקוֹם שְׁנַיִם – and the words of one witness are not significant in the place of two witnesses.[21] The document is therefore ruled valid without qualification.

The Gemara asks:

מַתְקִיף לָהּ רַב הוּנָא בְּרֵיהּ דְּרַב יְהוֹשֻׁעַ – Rav Huna the son of Rav Yehoshua objected to this: אִי הָכִי – If it is so, that once the witness concedes he signed the note he has in effect certified it as is, without stipulation, so that his claim of stipulation goes against *both* witnesses signed on the note, including himself, אֲפִילוּ תַּרְוַיְיהוּ נַמִּי – then even if both of them state that they signed on stipulation they should also not be believed! For once they concede that they signed, the note is certified without stipulation, and their current claim that there was a stipulation is an unacceptable retraction of their earlier testimony![22] Why did Rav Nachman rule that when both witnesses say there was a stipulation they are believed? אֶלָּא אַמְרִינַן הָנֵי לְמִיעְקַר סַהֲדוּתַיְיהוּ קָאָתוּ – Perforce, we say that when they state there was a stipulation these witnesses are coming to rescind their authenticating testimony and make a *qualified* certification of the note.[23] Their statement regarding the stipulation is therefore accepted. הַאי נַמִּי לְמִיעְקַר סַהֲדוּתֵיהּ קָאָתֵי – It follows that this one witness, too, when he states that there was a stipulation, is coming to rescind his authenticating testimony and make a qualified certification of his signature. His statement therefore

NOTES

15. [I.e. their testimony undermines the document and contradicts it,] and oral testimony is unacceptable against one's established written testimony [as explained in note 12] (*Rashi*).

16. The written testimony in the document indicates that the buyer made his acquisition without any strings attached, whereas they now testify orally that he had to first fulfill a stipulation, which if left unfulfilled would nullify the sale. Since their statement that the signatures are authentic establishes the note as a valid one, their claim that there was a stipulation should constitute an unacceptable revocation of the document – as in the previous cases (*Ritva*).

17. The witnesses' claim that there was a stipulation does not invalidate the document; it merely obligates the beneficiary to fulfill an unwritten stipulation. Thus, [rather than contradicting their previous testimony] they are *adding* testimony concerning a previously undiscussed matter [and attaching this addition to their authentication of the note]. In the event the beneficiary does not fulfill the stipulation in time, the document is undermined by his inaction, not by their testimony. [Since they have the power of *happeh she'assar* and the oral testimony can be seen as conforming with the written testimony, perhaps we should believe this addition that they attached to their authentication] (*Rashi;* see *Tosafos* ד״ה או דלמא and following note).

18. That is, the witnesses are believed.

This pertains only when the signatures are authenticated through the witnesses themselves, so that they have the power of *happeh she'assar.* Since the written testimony becomes established right now, through their own authentication of the signatures, they are entitled to add that there was an unwritten stipulation. If the signatures would be authenticated independently so that their written testimony would already be established, they would not even be able to add the fact of a stipulation to it. As we have learned, once witnesses have testified, they can neither retract their testimony nor alter it in any way.

Now, if the witnesses say the note was subject to prior notification, they are not believed even if they have the power of *happeh she'assar* – because their oral testimony is a *revocation* of the written testimony that they have just established. However, when they add a stipulation – and they have the power of *happeh she'assar* – they are believed, since they are not revoking but *adding* to the written testimony (*Rashba;* see also *Rashi* below ד״ה אלא *Ritva, Chidushei Anshei Shem* to *Ran,* and *Shach* 29:2; cf. *Tur Choshen Mishpat,* end of §46 and §82).

It emerges according to Rav Nachman that *happeh she'assar* enables witnesses to make two types of statements. They may state that they signed under duress or as minors, in which case they are believed because they are not certifying the document at all. Or they may state that there was an unwritten stipulation, in which case they are believed because they are not revoking the written testimony but are adding to it. However, they may not state that the note was written with notification of non-intent or on trust, because in these cases they actually certify and validate the document yet attempt to revoke it – and a witness may not rescind his established written testimony.

If the witnesses would testify that the loan recorded in a note has been repaid, they would be believed even without *happeh she'assar,* because this would be considered a completely new testimony that is unrelated to their written record of the loan. *Hapeh she'assar* is needed where the witnesses either retract or add a clause to their original testimony (see *Tosafos* ד״ה או דלמא).

19. I.e. each of them authenticates his own signature, but one of them adds that there was an unwritten stipulation whereas the other one disclaims knowledge of any stipulation. He does not contradict the other witness, but states that *he* signed without having been notified of a stipulation (*Ritva;* see also *Shach* 46:108).

20. That is, they both agree that the document is authentic and was signed as is, without any written stipulation (*Rashi*).

21. By their own words, they certified the note as is, so that their signatures testify to an unqualified transaction. The one witness who now states there was a stipulation cannot undermine the valid document containing both of their signatures (*Rashi*).

22. We should say that once they authenticate their signatures they have established the document as valid in its written form, without stipulation, and this precludes them from stating that it was written on stipulation – for they cannot alter their established testimony (*Rashi*).

23. Since in the same utterance in which they authenticate their signatures, the witnesses state that there was an unwritten stipulation, they have qualified their certification of the document. Their testimony is that the note is authentic but subject to stipulation. And since, as explained above, they are not entirely revoking the document, but are *adding* to their previous testimony, they are believed (*Rashi;* see *Ritva*). [Thus, we do not say that they made a full certification and then stated a new testimony concerning the stipulation; such testimony would be an unacceptable alteration of the established testimony. Rather, we say that they made a qualified certification of the note – and the qualification is consistent with the initial testimony.]

ואמר רב ששת בריה דרב אידי ש"מ מדרב כהנא עדים שאמרו אמנה היו דברינו אין נאמנין מאי טעמא כיון דעולה הוא אעולה לא חתמי אמר רבי יהושע בן לוי אסור לו לאדם שישהה שטר פרוע בתוך ביתו משום שנאמר אל תשכן באהליך עולה במערבא משמיה דרב אמרי אם און בידך הרחיקהו זה שטר אמנה ושטר פסים ואל תשכן באהלך עולה זה שטר פרוע מאן דאמר שטר פרוע כל שכן שטר אמנה ומאן דאמר שטר אמנה אבל שטר פרוע לא דזמנין דמשהי ליה אפשיטי דספרא אתמר ספר שאינו מוגה אמר רבי אמי עד ל' יום מותר לשהותו מכאן ואילך אסור לשהותו משום שנא' אל תשכן באהליך עולה אר"נ עדים שאמרו אמנה היו דברינו אין נאמנין מודעא היו דברינו אין נאמנין מר בר רב אשי אמר אמנה היו דברינו אין נאמנין מודעא היו דברינו נאמנין מ"ט האי ניתן ליכתב והאי לא ניתן ליכתב בעא מיניה רבא מרב נחמן תנאי היו דברינו מהו מודעא ואמנה היינו טעמא דקא עקרי ליה לשטרא והאי נמי קא עקר לשטרא או דלמא תנאי מילתא אחריתי היא א"ל כי אתו לקמן לדינא אמרינן להו זילו קיימו תנאייכו וחותו לדינא א"ר פפא תרווייהו בשטרא מעליא קא מסהדי והאי דקאמר תנאי הוה ליה חד ואין דבריו של אחד במקום שנים מתקיף לה רב הונא בריה דרב יהושע אי הכי אפי' תרווייהו נמי אלא אמרינן הני למיעקר סהדותיהו קאתו האי נמי למיעקר סהדותיה קאתי והלכתא כרב הונא בריה דרב יהושע ת"ר שנים חתומין על השטר ומתו ובאו שנים מן השוק ואמרו ידענו שכתב ידם הוא אבל אנוסים היו קטנים היו פסולי עדות היו הרי אלו נאמנים ואם יש עדים שכתב ידם הוא זה או שהיה כתב ידם יוצא ממקום אחר משטר שקרא עליו ערער והוחזק בב"ד אין אלו נאמנין ומגבינן ביה כבשטרא מעליא ואמאי תרי ותרי נינהו אמר רב ששת זאת אומרת הכחשה תחלת הזמה היא

רש"י

ואמר רב ששת גרסי': **אעולה לא חתמי.** וכי אמרי חתמנו אין נאמנים להרשיע את עצמן: **על פשיטי דספרא.** שעל הלוה ליתן שכר הסופר ופעמים שאין לו ונותנו המלוה וחוזר וגובהו ממנו בשעת פרעון ומעכב השטר עליו: **ספר שאינו מוגה.** תורה נביאים וכתובים: **מוגה.** מן טעיות שבו: **עדים.** החתומים בשטר ואמרו אמנה היו דברינו לא הלוהו כלום אלא כתבנו לו לכשיצטרך ילוה לו וזה שיעבד לו נכסיו מעכשיו אם ילוה אפילו לאחר זמן דלאו מוקדם ליהוי לטרוף שלא כדין: **מודעא היו דברינו.** אם שטר מכר הוא ואמרו עדים החתומים בו המוכר מסר מודעא בפנינו והראנו אונסו והכרנו בו: **אין נאמנין.** דלא אתי על פה ומרע ליה לשטרא: **מודעא** ניתן לעדים לכתוב את השטר כדי להציל האנוס מאונסו אמנה לא ניתן להכתב דעולה הוא וכי אמרו חתמנו משוו לנפשייהו רשעים ואין אדם נאמן לשום עצמו רשע: **תנאי היו דברינו.** על תנאי מכרה לו שיעשה לו כך וכך ולא ראינו שקיים לו תנאו וזה אומר לא קיים לי ואינו מכר: **מודעא ואמנה.** טעמא מאי קאמר מר אין נאמנין: **דקא עקרי ליה לשטרא.** בעדותן זה ולא אתי על פה ומרע לשטרא הכא נמי כו': **או דלמא.** הא לא עקרתא לשטרא הוא דמודים הם שהשטר אמת אלא שתנאי היה ביניהם וזו עדות אחרת היא ושטרא ממילא מיעקר לאחר זמן ביום שלא קיים תנאו זמנו: **כי אתו לקמן.** לקוחות שעדיהם מעידים שתנאי היה ביניהם: **אמרי' להו זילו קיימו תנאייכו.** לבעלים: **וחותו לדינא.** אם יעכב שוב הקרקע: **תרווייהו בשטרא מעליא קא מסהדי.** שניהם מעידים שהשטר אמת וכמות שהוא כתוב בלא תנאי חתמוהו: **והאי דקאמר תנאי חד הוא.** ואינו נאמן לעקור שטר ששניהם חתומים בו: **אי הכי אפילו תרווייהו נמי אלא אמרינן כו'.** אי הכי דכיון שהעיד על כתב ידו עשית לזה אחד ממקיימי השטר כמות שהוא כתוב בלא תנאי והוי להו עדיו שנים ועדות אחרונה דברי אחד במקום שנים: **אפי' תרווייהו נמי.** אמרי תנאי היו דברינו לא ליתהימנו דכיון שהעידו על כתב ידן קיימו השטר כמות שהוא כתוב וכי אמרי תנאי היו דברינו הוו להו מגידים וחוזרים ומגידים ואמאי אמר רב נחמן קיימו תנאייכו כו': **אלא.** על כרחך לאו חתימה מקויימת הוא דכיון דתוך כדי דבור מסקי דבורייהו ואמרי אבל תנאי היה ביניהן אמרינן הני למיעקר סהדותייהו שאמרו כתב ידינו הוא קאתו ולומר לא חתמנו אלא ע"מ שיקיים את התנאי וכיון דתנאי מלתא אחריתי היא שאינה עוקרתו אלא לאחר זמן לא דמיא למודעא ואמנה ומהימני דעדות בפני עצמה היא: **האי נמי.** כי סיים ואמר תנאי הוה עקר לחתימת ידיה לומר לא חתמתי אלא על מנת כן וכיון דאית לן דמלתא אחריתי היא ושטרא ממילא מיעקר אישתכח דאין בשטר חתום אלא ע"א: **שקרא עליו ערער.** שהלה הנתבע לפוסלו: **ומגבינן ביה.** בתמיה: **תרי ותרי נינהו.** עדי השטר ב' ואלו ב' מעידים עליהם שפסולים היו באותה שעה:

תוספות

אם און בידך הרחיקהו זה שטר פסים ושטר אמנה. דהכי משמע לשון און דמעיקרא הוי שקר ואל תשכן באהליך עולה זה שטר פרוע שעתה הוא עולה אבל מעיקרא הוה אמת: **זמנין** דמשהי ליה אפשיטי דספרא. וע"י אותה שהייה אישתלי ליה שהוא פרוע הלכך לא קרי ליה עולה ומ"ד שטר פרוע היה לו ליזהר אבל אין לפרש דמשום שהייתו אפשיטי דספרא קרי ליה עולה דמה פשע: **אמר** רב נחמן עדים שאמרו אמנה היו דברינו אין נאמנים. ע"כ באין כתב ידן יוצא ממקום אחר איירי דאי כתב ידן יוצא ממקום אחר פשיטא דהכי פריך לעיל ועוד דמר בר רב אשי קאמר דאין נאמנים משום דלא ניתן לכתב ואי בכתב ידן יוצא ממקום אחר אפילו ניתן לכתב פשיטא דאין נאמנים וקשה דאמאי לא מהימני במיגו דהא רב נחמן גופיה אית ליה לעיל מגו לפסול השטר דקאמר כי אתו לקמן לדינא אמרינן להו זילו קיימו שטרייכו וחותו לדינא דמהימן לומר פרוע במגו דמזויף וכ"ש עדים דאלימי לאורועי שטרא כדאמר במי שמת (ב"ב דף קנד.) ותירץ ר"י דהיינו טעמא דמודעא הואיל ומודים שהשטר נכתב ונמסר כהלכתו שוב לא אתי על פה ומרע לשטרא אפילו במגו ולא דמי לאנוסים וקטנים דמתניתין שאין מודים שהיה שטר כשר כלל אלא סותרין אותו הלכך מהימני במגו דלא שייך כאן לומר דלא אתי על פה ומרע לשטרא שהרי אינם מודים שהיה שטר ואמנה נמי נראה דהיינו טעמא דלא מהימני לרב נחמן דלא מרעי לשטרא הואיל ומודים שהשטר נכתב כדין מדעת הלוה דלא מפרש טעמא דאמנה משום דלא ניתן לכתב אלא מר בר רב אשי אבל לרב נחמן טעם אמנה ומודעא שניהם שוה והא דאית ליה לרב נחמן דנאמן לומר פרוע הוא במגו דמזויף התם נמי לא מרע לשטרא כלל הלכך מהימן במגו ואתי שפיר רב נחמן כרבנן דר"מ והאיא ברייתא דמי שמת (ג"ז שם:) דשטר אמנה הוא זה דאינו נאמן דבעי לאוקמי כר"מ רב נחמן מוקי לה לדברי הכל: **או** דלמא תנאי מילתא אחריתי היא. פי' לדבר אחר הן באין ולא לעקירת השטר אלא תוספת בעלמא שמפרשים עדותן היאך ועד השתא קיים השטר ואינו נעקר אם יתקיים התנאי הלכך אין כאן הורעת השטר אבל אין לפרש מילתא אחריתי היא לגמרי ולא שייך לעדותן ראשונה כמו שאם היו מעידין שהוא פרוע שהן נאמנים דא"כ מאי פריך בסמוך א"ה אפי' תרי נמי דכיון דתנאי מילתא אחריתי הוא לגמרי תרי נאמנים אפילו בכתב ידן יוצא ממקום אחר אבל חד לעולם אימא לך דלא מהימן כי היכי דלא מהימן לומר פרוע הוא לכך נראה כדפירשנו: **ואם** כתב ידן יוצא ממקום אחר אין נאמנים. ופסולי עדות דקתני לא שאומרים שעדיין פסולים דאם כן אמאי אין נאמנים אלא פסולי עדות הוו אז ועתה מודים שהם כשרים וא"ת ומכל מקום אמאי אין נאמנים להימנו במגו דלא בעו אומרים עדיין הם פסולים [וכן בכלן] שתי כתי עדים המכחישות זו את זו אמאי לא מהימני בתראי במגו דלא בעו פסלי לקמאי בגזלנותא ואור"י דבשני עדים לא שייך מגו דאין אחד יודע מה בלב חבירו: **אמר** רב ששת זאת אומרת הכחשה תחלת הזמה היא. וא"ת תקשי לרב ששת ברייתא דמי שמת (ג"ז שם) דקתני אם אמר שטר אמנה הוא אם יש עדים פירוש לשטר אמנה הוא הלך אחר עדים ואם לאו הלך אחר השטר אלמא אע"ג דאין השטר צריך קיום כדאמר הלך אחר השטר שמודה הלוה שכתבו כדאיתא התם ואפילו הכי [פי'] אם יש עדים הלך אחר עדים ולא אמרינן הכחשה תחלת הזמה היא וי"ל דזאת אומרת קאמר אבל ההיא פליג:

תורה אור השלם

א) אם און בידך הרחיקהו ואל תשכן באהליך עולה: [איוב יא, יד]

מסורת הש"ס

א) שבת עה., ב) פי' שפירשו להלוות לו שטר

אֵין נֶאֱמָנִין – **are not believed.**[10] מוֹדָעָא הָיוּ דְּבָרֵינוּ – Similarly, witnesses who signed on a bill of sale and who later said, **"Our words** of testimony **were** preceded by **a notification** of non-intent by the owner,"[11] אֵין נֶאֱמָנִין – **are not believed.**[12]

A dissenting opinion is presented:

מַר בַּר רַב אַשִׁי אָמַר – **Mar bar Rav Ashi said:** אֲמָנָה הָיוּ דְּבָרֵינוּ אֵין נֶאֱמָנִין – **Witnesses** who signed on a note of indebtedness and **who** later **said, "Our words** of testimony **were** written **on trust,"** are **not believed.** מוֹדָעָא הָיוּ דְּבָרֵינוּ נֶאֱמָנִין – But witnesses who signed on a bill of sale and who later said, **"Our words** of testimony **were** preceded by **a notification** of non-intent by the owner," **are believed** and the sale is nullified. מַאי טַעְמָא – **What is the reason** to distinguish between the two cases? הַאי נִיתָן לִיכָּתֵב – **This one,** i.e. the bill of sale that was preceded by a notification of non-intent, **was allowed to be written,** וְהַאי לֹא נִיתָן לִיכָּתֵב – **whereas that one,** i.e. the note of indebtedness written on trust, **was not allowed to be written.**[13]

A related inquiry is cited:

בְּעָא מִינֵּיהּ רָבָא מֵרַב נַחְמָן – **Rava inquired of Rav Nachman:** תְּנַאי הָיוּ דְּבָרֵינוּ מַהוּ – If witnesses say, **"Our words** of testimony **were** written on **stipulation," what is [the law]?**[14]

The inquiry is clarified in light of Rav Nachman's previous ruling that when they testify a note was written with notification of non-intent or on trust they are not believed:

מוֹדָעָא וַאֲמָנָה הַיְינוּ טַעְמָא דְּקָא עָקְרֵי לֵיהּ לִשְׁטָרָא – Do we say that in the cases where they say the document was written with **notification or on trust, the reason** they are not believed **is that**

NOTES

the creditor a predated lien on the debtor's properties. In the event of default, this would enable him to illegally confiscate the properties from people who purchased them between the drafting of the note and the actual loan (see *Bava Metzia* 13a). However,] the debtor circumvented this problem by agreeing to create the lien on his properties from the date the document was drafted even though the loan would occur later (*Rashi*). [Thus, the witnesses are not incriminating themselves with an admission that they signed a predated note. The problem is purely that the note was written on trust (*Ran;* see *Shach, Choshen Mishpat* 39:40 and *Beis Yaakov*).]

10. This pertains even if the signatures cannot be authenticated independently (*Tosafos*). One reason is that, as explained above, it is illegal to sign a document on trust, so the testimony is self-incriminating (*Maharsha;* cf. *Rashba* ד״ה מודעה ואמנה). Another reason will be explained shortly.

11. I.e. the witnesses signed on the document now testify that, before they signed, the owner demonstrated to them clearly that he was being coerced to sell and made the disclaimer that he did not want the sale to be effective (*Rashi;* see *Haflaah*).

12. This, too, pertains even when the signatures cannot be authenticated independently (*Tosafos*). In this case, the witnesses committed no crime by signing, since they needed to extricate the seller from his predicament (Gemara below). [Nevertheless,] they are not believed, because their oral testimony undermining the sale cannot invalidate the signed document held by the buyer (*Rashi*). I.e. since they concede that they signed the document testifying to the sale, their current oral testimony is disqualified because it is a retraction of a standing written testimony [כֵּיוָן שֶׁהִגִּיד שׁוּב אֵינוֹ חוֹזֵר וּמַגִּיד] (*Shitah Mekubetzes;* see also *Rashbam* and *Ramban* to *Bava Basra* 49a and *Rashi* below ד״ה אפילו תרוייהו).

One might ask: Why is this different than the case of our Mishnah, in which witnesses testify that they signed a document under threat of death, or as minors or relatives? The Mishnah teaches that when the signatures cannot be authenticated independently the witnesses are believed – even though they concede that they signed the note – because they have the power of *happeh she'assar*. In our case, too, when the signatures cannot be authenticated independently, let the witnesses be believed when they say they signed after the seller gave notification of non-intent!?

The answer is that in the Mishnah's case the witnesses grant no validity whatsoever to the document; their claim that they signed under duress or as minors or relatives renders it null and void. Since they have the power of *happeh she'assar,* it emerges that they never really authenticated the note – rather, their testimony was that though the signatures are authentic it is void. Being that the oral testimony voiding the note does not contradict an *established* written testimony – for the authentication never took effect – it is accepted and the document is voided. In our case, however, the witnesses concede more than the fact that they physically signed the note. They also admit that they signed as *valid* witnesses with the *consent* of the one who becomes obligated through the document (i.e. the borrower or seller), who then willingly handed it over to the beneficiary (i.e. the lender or buyer). Thus, the note is inherently valid. Their contention is that although it is valid in every technical detail, the note should be disregarded because it was written on trust or because the seller had given prior notification of non-intent. Since even according to their words the signatures constitute a testimony that is inherently valid, the contradictory oral testimony is an unacceptable retraction. The principle of *happeh she'assar* is of no consequence, because their retraction does not undo their previous authentication of the note. This reason applies to both cases – i.e. whether the witnesses say the note was written on trust or they say the seller had given notification of non-intent (*Tosafos* ד״ה אמר רב נחמן, *Rashba*).

Thus, in the case where they say it was written on trust, there are two reasons their testimony is rejected. Firstly, it is self-incriminating, and secondly, it contradicts their own written testimony (*Maharsha; Rashbam, Bava Basra* 49a; cf. *Rashba* ibid.).

[It is noteworthy that *Rashi* states that *oral* testimony cannot invalidate a written document. When a seller gives the witnesses advance notification of non-intent to sell, they are allowed to draw up a document of notification, and when presented in court it nullifies the bill of sale (see *Bava Basra* 40a and 48b). In our case, however, since they did not draw up such a document but merely came before the court when the bill of sale was presented and stated orally that there was notification of non-intent, they are not believed. The bill of sale is the established record of their testimony in this case, and they cannot now present contradictory oral testimony (*Rashba;* see further, *Bava Basra* 49a with *Rashbam,* and *Ri Migash* there, 48b).]

13. When the seller gives the witnesses notification of non-intent, they are allowed to sign the bill of sale that he draws up, in order to rescue him from the buyer's threats. Hence, their testimony that they signed on this basis is not self-incriminating and is acceptable. However, when a person draws up a note of indebtedness on trust, the witnesses are not allowed to sign it. Hence, their testimony that they signed on trust is self-incriminating and is unacceptable (*Rashi*).

Mar bar Rav Ashi maintains that our case is similar to the Mishnah's case of *happeh she'assar,* and rejects the distinction presented in the previous note. In his opinion, just as when witnesses say they signed under duress or as minors they are believed (when they have the power of *happeh she'assar* and the testimony is not self-incriminating), so too, when they say the note was based on a notification of non-intent they are believed – as long as they have the power of *happeh she'assar* and their testimony is non-incriminating. Thus, the non-incriminating testimony that the note was based on a notification is accepted, and the incriminating testimony that it was based on trust is rejected (*Rashi,* as explained by *Ran;* see also *Ramban;* cf. *Ran's* alternative explanation, *Rashba, Ritva; Rashbam* to *Bava Basra* 49a; see further, *Choshen Mishpat* 46:37 with *Shach* §117).

14. That is, they authenticate their own signatures, but say that the seller agreed to the sale only on condition that the buyer fulfill a certain stipulation – and they have no knowledge of whether he fulfilled it. The seller claims that the stipulation was not fulfilled and the sale should be nullified [and the buyer is unable to prove that he fulfilled it] (*Rashi;* see *Ritva* ד״ה א״ל כי אתו לקמן and *Shach* 46:107).

As shall become apparent, the inquiry is based on Rav Nachman's opinion – that witnesses who state a document was written on trust or on the basis of prior notification are *not* believed, because this is considered an illegal retraction of their written testimony. The question is whether the case in which they say the note was written on stipulation is similar to those cases (*Ritva* ד״ה מ״ט).

ואמר רב ששת בריה דרב אידי ש"מ מדרב כהנא עדים שאמרו אמנה היו דברינו אין נאמנין מאי טעמא כיון דעולה הוא אעולה לא חתמי אמר רבי יהושע בן לוי אסור לו לאדם שישהה שטר פרוע בתוך ביתו משום שנאמר אל תשכן באהליך עולה במערבא משמיה דרב אמרי אם און בידך הרחיקהו זה שטר אמנה ושטר פסים ואל תשכן באהלך עולה זה שטר פרוע מאן דאמר שטר פרוע כל שכן שטר אמנה ומאן דאמר שטר אמנה אבל שטר פרוע לא דזמנין דמשהי ליה אפשיטי דספרא אתמר ספר שאינו מוגה אמר רבי אמי עד ל' יום מותר לשהותו מכאן ואילך אסור לשהותו משום שנא' אל תשכן באהליך עולה אר"נ עדים שאמרו אמנה היו דברינו אין נאמנין מודעא היו דברינו אין נאמנין מר בר רב אשי אמר אמנה היו דברינו אין נאמנין מודעא היו דברינו נאמנין מ"ט האי ניתן ליכתב והאי לא ניתן ליכתב בעא מיניה רבא מרב נחמן תנאי היו דברינו מהו מודעא ואמנה היינו טעמא דקא עקרי ליה לשטרא והאי נמי קא עקר לשטרא או דלמא תנאי מילתא אחריתי היא א"ל כי אתו לקמן לדינא אמרינן להו זילו קיימו תנאייכו והותו לדינא עד אומר תנאי ועד אומר אינו תנאי א"ר פפא תרוייהו בשטרא מעליא קא מסהדי והאי דקאמר תנאי הוה ליה חד ואין דבריו של אחד במקום שנים מתקיף לה רב הונא בריה דרב יהושע אי הכי אפי' תרוייהו נמי אלא אמרינן הני למיעקר סהדותייהו קאתו האי נמי למיעקר סהדותיה קאתי והלכתא כרב הונא בריה דרב יהושע ת"ר שנים חתומין על השטר ומתו ובאו שנים מן השוק ואמרו ידענו שכתב ידם הוא אבל אנוסים היו קטנים היו פסולי עדות היו הרי אלו נאמנים ואם יש עדים שכתב ידם הוא זה או שהיה כתב ידם יוצא ממקום אחר משטר שקרא עליו ערער והוחזק בב"ד אין אלו נאמנין ומגבינן ביה כבשטרא מעליא ואמאי תרי ותרי נינהו אמר רב ששת זאת אומרת הכחשה תחלת הזמה היא

ואמר רב ששת גרסי': אעולה לא חתמי. וכי אמרי חתמנו אין נאמנים להרשיע את עצמן: על פשיטי דספרא. שעל הלוה ליתן שכר הסופר ופעמים שאין לו ונותנו המלוה וחוזר וגובהו ממנו בשעת פרעון ומעכב השטר עליו: ספר שאינו מוגה. תורה נביאים וכתובים: מוגה. מן טעיות שבו: עדים. החתומים בשטר ואמרו אמנה היו דברינו לא הלוהו כלום אלא כתבנו לו לכשיצטרך ילוה לו וזה שיעבד לו נכסיו מעכשיו אם ילוה אפילו לאחר זמן דלאו מוקדם ליהוי לטרוף שלא כדין: מודעא היו דברינו. אם שטר מכר הוא ואמרו עדים החתומים בו המוכר מסר מודעא בפנינו והראנו אונסו והכרנו בו: אין נאמנין. דלא אתי על פה ומרע ליה לשטרא: מודעא ניתן לעדים לכתוב את השטר כדי להציל האנוס מאונסו אמנה לא ניתן להכתב דעולה הואי וכי אמרו חתמנו משוו לנפשייהו רשעים ואין אדם נאמן לשום עצמו רשע: תנאי היו דברינו. על תנאי מכרה לו שיעשה לו כך וכך ולא ראינו שקיים לו תנאו וזה אומר לא קיים לי ואינו מכר: מודעא ואמנה. טעמא מאי קאמר מר אין נאמנין: דקא עקרי ליה לשטרא. בעדותן זה ולא אתי על פה ומרע לשטרא הכא נמי כו': או דלמא. הא לא עקרתא דשטרא הוא דמודים הם שהשטר אמת אלא שתנאי היה ביניהם וזו עדות אחרת היא ושטרא ממילא מיעקר לאחר זמן ביום שלא קיים תנאו בזמנו: כי אתו לקמן. לקוחות שעדיהם מעידים שתנאי היו דבריהם: אמרי' להו זילו קיימו תנאייכו. לבעלים: וחותו לדינא. אם יעכב שוב הקרקע: תרוייהו בשטרא מעליא קא מסהדי. שניהם מעידים שהשטר אמת וכמות שהוא כתוב בלא תנאי חתמוהו: והאי דקאמר תנאי חד הוא. ואינו נאמן לעקור שטר ששניהם חתומים בו: אי הכי אפילו תרוייהו נמי אלא אמרינן כו'. אי הכי דכיון שהעיד על כתב ידו עשית לזה אחד ממקיימי השטר כמות שהוא כתוב בלא תנאי והוי להו עדיו שנים ועדות אחרונה דברי אחד במקום שנים: אפי' תרוייהו נמי. אמרי תנאי היו דברינו לא ליתהימנו דכיון שהעידו על כתב ידן קיימו השטר כמות שהוא כתוב וכי אמרי תנאי היו דברינו הוו להו מגידים וחוזרים ומגידים ואמאי אמר רב נחמן קיימו תנאייכו כו': אלא. על כרחך לאו חתימה מקויימת הוא דכיון דתוך כדי דבור מסקי דבורייהו ואמרי אבל תנאי היה ביניהן אמרינן הני למיעקר סהדותייהו שאמרו כתב ידינו הוא קאתו ולומר לא חתמנו אלא ע"מ שיקיים את התנאי וכיון דתנאי מלתא אחריתי היא שאינה עוקרתו אלא לאחר זמן לא דמיא למודעא ואמנה ומהימני דעדות בפני עצמה היא: האי נמי. כי סיים ואמר תנאי הוה עקר לחתימת ידיה לומר לא חתמתי אלא על מנת כן וכיון דאית לן דמלתא אחריתי היא ושטרא ממילא מיעקר אישתכח דאין בשטר חתום אלא ע"א: שקרא עליו ערער. שרלה הנתבע לפוסלו: ומגבינן ביה. בתמיה: תרי ותרי נינהו. עדי השטר ב' ואלו ב' מעידים עליהם שפסולים היו באותה שעה:

וכשם

אם און בידך הרחיקהו זה שטר פסים ושטר אמנה. דהכי משמע לשון און דמעיקרא הוי שקר ואל תשכן באהליך עולה זה שטר פרוע שעתה הוא עולה אבל מעיקרא הוה אמת: זמנין דמשהי ליה אפשיטי דספרא. וע"י אותה שהייה אישתלי ליה שהוצאה פעם אחרת הלכך לא קרי ליה עולה ומ"ד שטר פרוע היה לו ליזהר אבל אין לפרש דמשום שהייתו אפשיטי דספרא קרי ליה עולה דמה פשע: אמר רב נחמן עדים שאמרו אמנה היו דברינו אין נאמנים. ע"כ באין כתב ידן יוצא ממקום אחר איירי דאי כתב ידן יוצא ממקום אחר פשיטא דהכי פריך לעיל ועוד דמר בר רב אשי קאמר דאין נאמנים משום דלא ניתן לכתב ואי בכתב ידן יוצא ממקום אחר אפילו ניתן לכתב פשיטא דאין נאמנים וקשה דאמאי לא מהימני במיגו דהא רב נחמן גופיה אית ליה לעיל מגו לפסול השטר דקאמר כי אתו לקמן לדינא אמרינן להו זילו קיימו שטרייכו ותותו לדינא דמהימן לומר פרוע במגו דמזויף וכ"ש עדים דאלימי לאורועי שטרא כדאמר במי שמת (ב"ב דף קנד.) ותירץ ר"י דהיינו טעמא דמודעא הואיל ומודים שהשטר נכתב ונמסר כהלכתו שוב לא אתי על פה ומרע לשטרא אפילו במגו ולא דמי לאנוסים וקטנים דמתניתין שאין מודים שהיה שטר כשר כלל אלא סותרין אותו הלכך מהימני במגו דלא שייך כאן לומר דלא אתי על פה ומרע לשטרא שהרי אינם מודים שהיה שטר ואמנה נמי נראה דהיינו טעמא דלא מהימני לרב נחמן דלא מרעי לשטרא הואיל ומודים שהשטר נכתב כדין מדעת הלוה דלא מפרש טעמא דאמנה משום דלא ניתן לכתב אלא מר בר רב אשי אבל לרב נחמן טעם אמנה ומודעא שניהם שוה והא דאית ליה לרב נחמן דנאמן לומר פרוע הוא במגו דמזויף התם נמי לא מרע לשטרא כלל הלכך מהימן במגו ואתי שפיר רב נחמן כרבנן דר"מ וההיא ברייתא דמי שמת (ג"ז שם:) דשטר אמנה הוא זה דאינו נאמן דבעי לאוקמי כר"מ רב נחמן מוקי לה לדברי הכל: או דלמא תנאי מילתא אחריתי היא. פי' לדבר אחר הן באין ולא לעקירת השטר אלא תוספת בעלמא שמפרשים עדותן היאך ועד השתא קיים השטר ואינו נעקר אם יתקיים התנאי הלכך אין כאן הורעת השטר אבל אין לפרש מילתא אחריתי היא לגמרי ולא שייך לעדותן ראשונה כמו שאם היו מעידין שהוא פרוע שהן נאמנים דא"כ מאי פריך בסמוך א"ה אפי' תרי נמי דכיון דתנאי מילתא אחריתי הוא לגמרי תרי נאמנים אפילו בכתב ידן יוצא ממקום אחר אבל חד לעולם אימא לך דלא מהימן כי היכי דלא מהימן לומר פרוע הוא לכך נראה כדפירשנו: ואם כתב ידן יוצא ממקום אחר אין נאמנים. ופסולי עדות דקתני לא שאומרים שעדיין פסולים דאם כן אמאי אין נאמנים אלא פסולי עדות הוו אז ועתה מודים שהם כשרים וא"ת ומכל מקום אמאי אין נאמנים להימנו במגו דאי בעו אומרים עדיין הם פסולים [וכן בכלן] שתי כתי עדים המכחישות זו את זו אמאי לא מהימני בתראי במגו דאי בעו פסלי לקמאי בגזלנותא ואור"י דבשני עדים לא שייך מגו דאין אחד יודע מה בלב חבירו: אמר רב ששת זאת אומרת הכחשה תחלת הזמה היא. וא"ת תקשי לרב ששת ברייתא דמי שמת (ג"ז שם) דקתני אם אמר שטר אמנה הוא אם יש עדים פירוש דשטר אמנה הוא הלך אחר עדים ואם לאו הלך אחר השטר אלמא אע"ג דאין השטר צריך קיום כדאמר הלך אחר השטר שמודה הלוה שכתבו כדאיתא התם [ואפילו הכי] אם יש עדים הלך אחר עדים ולא אמרינן הכחשה תחלת הזמה וי"ל דזאת אומרת קאמר אבל ההיא פליג:

ואוקי

מסורת הש"ס

א) שבת עח., ב) פי' שפייסו להלוות לו שטר, ג) [ב"ב מח: מט.], ד) [ב"ק עג:], ה) נ"י כ"י, י) ובאין כתב ידן יוצא ממקום אחר נאמנין שפיר במגו דאי בעי שתקי אי נמי מגו במקום עדים הוא אי נמי הא דבתראי מהימני חידוש הוא דמאי חזית דסמכת אהני כו' הלכך אין נאמנין במגו שיכולים לפוסלן בגזלנותא אלא כשאומרים כן בפירוש.

גליון הש"ס

גמ' זאת אומרת הכחשה. עיין שיטה מקובצת בב"מ דף קב ע"א ד"ה אר"א זאת אומרת בשם רבי סעדי' גאון:

תורה אור השלם

א) אִם אָוֶן בְּיָדְךָ הַרְחִיקֵהוּ וְאַל תַּשְׁכֵּן בְּאֹהָלֶיךָ עַוְלָה: [איוב יא, יד]

ליקוטי רש"י

אמנה היו דברינו. לא הלוהו כלום אלא כתבנו לו ולכשיצטרך ילוה בו והאמינו לוה למלוה שלא יוציא עליו שטר מלוה זו לגבות הימנו אא"כ ילוה לו וזה שעבד לו נכסיו מעכשיו אם ילוה אפי' לאחר זמן דלאו מוקדם הוה לטרוף שלא כדין [רשב"ם ב"ב מח:]. אין נאמנין. לא מבעיא אם כתב ידן יוצא ממקום אחר דלא מהימני לעקרו דלאו הפה שאסר הוא הפה שהתיר איכא אלא אפילו [אם] הן עצמם מקיימים אותו ואומרים אמנה היו דברינו אין נאמנים. אעולה לא חתמי. וכי אמר חתמתי אינו נאמן דאין אדם נאמן בעדות כשמשים עצמו רשע בעדות זו [שם מט.]. במערבא. בארץ ישראל [שבת סה:]. אר"נ עדים שאמרו כו'. דמאחר שהודו שבכשרות נכתב הרי חתימת השטר כאילו העידו בב"ד כל מה שכתוב בשטר שהלוהו מלוה ללוה וכיון שהגיד שוב אינו חוזר ומגיד כדאמרינן בכתובות בפרק האשה שנתארמלה (דף יח) א"ל רבא כיון שהגיד שוב אינו חוזר ומגיד וכי תימא ה"מ על פה אבל בשטר לא הא אמר ר"ל עדים החתומים על השטר נעשו כמי שנחקרה עדותן בב"ד וה"ט מפרש התם דטעמא דר"נ משום דעקר ליה לשטרא דבעא מיניה רבא מר"נ תנאי היו דברינו מהו מודעא ואמנה טעמא מאי אין נאמנים דקמעקר ליה לשטרא וכו, ועוד יש טעם אחר גבי אמנה היו דברינו אמאי אין נאמנים כדאמר נמי התם וכו' דאמר רב כהנא אסור לאדם שישהה שטר אמנה בתוך ביתו משום שנאמר אל תשכן באהלך עולה וכיון דעולה היא עדים אעולה לא חתמי וכי אמר חתמתי אינו נאמן דאין אדם נאמן בעדות כשמשים עצמו רשע בעדות זו כדאמר התם. מודעא היו דברינו. אם שטר מכר הוא ואמרו עדים החתומים בו המוכר מסר מודעא בפנינו והראנו אנסו והכרנו בו אין נאמנין דתרוייהו מודו דשטרא מעליא הוא ועכשיו באין לבטלו ע"י עדות מודעא וקרוי זה חוזר ומגיד וכיון שהגיד עדות שבשטר אינו חוזר ומגיד לבטלו. מר בר רב אשי אמר אמנה היו דברינו אין נאמנין. כדמפרש לקמיה שלא ניתן ליכתב כדפרישית לעיל משום דכתיב אל תשכן באהלך עולה ועדים אעולה לא חתמי וכשמעיד חתמתי אינו נאמן דאין אדם משים עצמו רשע והלכך אפי' אין כתב ידן יוצא ממקום אחר אין נאמנין דאין נאמן לעשות עצמו רשע אבל לעקירת שטר לא חייש מר בר רב אשי דא"כ גבי מודעא אמאי נאמנים. מודעא היו דברינו נאמנין. שהרי ניתן ליכתב למלוה קעבדי כדי להציל האנוס מאונסו ואפי' כתב ידן יוצא ממקום אחר נאמנים דאין זה חוזר ומגיד אלא מילתא אחריתי קמסהדי כדאמרינן נמי התם חתמנו אבל תנאי היו דברינו ולא נתקיים התנאי דמילתא אחריתי היא ונאמנים שעל השטר מעידין שכשר וגם מעידים שאין חייב לו כלום והיכי דמי חוזר ומגיד כדתנן התם פסולים היינו אנוסין היינו קטנים היינו אם כתב ידן יוצא ממקום אחר אין נאמנים שהרי פוסלין את השטר לגמרי דקאמרי בפסלות נחתם הוא דפסלינן לעדותם משום חוזר ומגיד [שם מט.].

עין משפט נר מצוה

כז א מיי' פ"ג מהלכות עדות הלכה ז סמג עשין קט טוש"ע ח"מ סי' מו סעיף לג:
כח ב טוש"ע ח"מ סימן מז סעיף א:
כט ג מיי' פ"ז מהלכות ס"ת הלכה יב סמג עשין כה טוש"ע י"ד סי' רעט סעיף א [וברב אלפס עוד בפ"ב הלכות ספר תורה דף סה:]:
ל ד ה ו ז ח מיי' פ"ג מהל' עדות הל' ז ח ט ופ"ז הל' י סמג עשין קט טוש"ע ח"מ סי' מו סעי' לו (וסי' כו סעיף א):
לא ט מיי' פי"ח מהל' עדות הלכה ד סמג עשין קי טור ח"מ סי' לח:

תוספות רי"ד

מכרה היא כתובתה באייר דהיינו שטר חוב וחזרתה ומחלתה לבעלה בתשרי שפר ט"ף בעלה וכיון א) שיכולה למחול אותה לבעלה בי לקנוניא בע"י להפסיד הלקוחות כלל למחול לבעלה ומדלא מחלה ש"מ קושטא קאמרה וה"נ הכא נהימניה על ידי ההיא מיגו ונ"ל לתרץ דדוקא גבי מוכר לחבירו יכול למחול מפני שאינו יכול להקנות לחבירו גוף המנה שאינו בעין אבל ב) מלוה שכא יכול לומר הלוה לל"קח כאו בע"ד דידי את דלא יהא אלא שהרשהו לגבות ממנו ומפני כך יכול הכלוה למחול אבל כשחב לאחרים שהוא ד"ת אינו יכול למחול שמשעה שחב לאחרים נשתעבד המנה הזה לאותו שוב אינו המלוה יכול למוחלו ומ"ה אוקימנא כשחב לאחרים ולא כשמכרו לאחרים דהתם ודאי דמצי מחיל הוה נאמן ע"י מיגו אבל הכא לא מצי מחיל ומ"ה לא מרדינן: ר"א אמר לעולם דקאמרו עדים ודאין בת"י יוצא ממקום אחר ודקאמרת אמאי לא מהימנו כדר"כ דאר"כ אסור לאדם שישהה שטר אמנה בתוך ביתו שנאמר אל תשכן באהליך עולה: א"ר [ששת] (אשישא) בריה דר"א ש"מ מדר"כ דעדים שאמרו אמנה היה דברינו אין נאמנים מ"ט כיון דעולה היא אעולה לא חתמו ואע"פ שיש להן מיגו אין נאמנים: אריב"ל אסור לאדם שישהה שטר פרוע בתוך ביתו שנא' אל תשכן באהליך עולה מ"ד שטר פרוע כ"ש שטר אמנה ומ"ד שטר אמנה אבל שטר פרוע לא דזמנין דמשהי ליה על פשיטי דספרא פי' שהיה לו לפרוע ללוה כדתנן והלוה נותן שכר הסופר ויפרעם המלוה ודוקא אפשיטי דספרא פליגי אבל אם חייב לו קצת מן החוב ליכא מאן דפליג שיכול להשהותו אצלו עד שיפרענו וא"צ לכתוב לו שובר כדי שיהא לו כפוף שיפרענו: במערבא אמרי משמיה דר"א אם און בידך הרחיקהו זה שטר פסים ושטר אמנה ואל תשכן באהליך עולה זו שטר פרוע: איתמר ס"ת שאינו מוגה א"ר אמי עד ל' יום מותר להשהותו מכאן ואילך אסור להשהותו משום אל תשכן באהליך עולה: א"ר נחמן עדים שאמרו אמנה היה דברינו מודעא היה דברינו אין נאמנים פי' עדים החתומים בשטר ואמרו אמנה היה לא הלוה לו פלוני אלא כתבנוהו לו ולכשיצטרך ילוה בו וזה שיעבד לו נכסיו מעכשיו אם ילוה לו לאחר זמן דלא להוי כדין ולא מיבעיא אם כת"י יוצא ממ"א דלא מהימנו לעוקרו דלא הפה שאסר הפה שהתיר איכא אלא אפילו אם הן עצמם מקיימים אותו ואומרים כת"י הוא אבל אמנה היה דברינו אין נאמנים שמאחר שמודים שנכתב בכשרות הרי חתימתן שבשטר כאילו העידו בב"ד שכל מה [שכתוב] בשטר הלוהו מלוה ללוה וכיון שהגיד שוב אין חוזר ומגיד ותו דלא אתי ע"פ ומרע לשטרא אבל שטרא מרע לשטרא מודעא היה דברינו אין נאמנים פי' אם שטר מכר הוא ואמרו עדים החתומים בו המוכר מסר מודעא והראה אונסו והכרנו בו אין נאמנים דלא אתי ע"פ ומרע לשטרא: מר בר ר"א אמר אמנה היה דברינו אין נאמנים אבל מודעא היה דברינו נאמנים מ"ט האי ניתן לכתב והאי לא ניתן לכתב פירוש מודעא היה דברינו שאומר אם היה שטר מכר לא ברצונו מכר לו אלא אנוס היה ומסר מודעא לפנינו וקסבר ר"נ כיון שהיה אנוס ודאי ג) אונסו א"כ לא היה להם לחתום השטר מכירה וא"ת בשביל זה חתמו בו כדי להציל את המוכר מיד הלוקח שהיה אונס אותו והוא פייס שיכתבו לו ויחתמהו היה להם לכתוב שטר מודעא ברישא דמר"י ניתן לכתב והדר ליכתבו ליה להאי שטרא מכר והוי אתיא מודעא ומבטלא לשטרא והשתא דלא כתבו מודעא ברישא לא הוה להו לחתום אשטר זביני והלכך כיון שלא היה להם לחתום בו וחתמו עולה הוא כמו שטר אמנה ואע"פ שאין כת"י ימ"א דמהימני ע"י מיגו דאמרו לא חתמנו כדלעיל ואתי ע"פ דידהו ומרע לשטרא ה"מ בקטנים היינו קרובים היינו אנוסים היינו מחמת נפשות דלא הוי עולה ולא משוי נפשייהו רשיעא אבל במודעא היה דברינו שהוא עולה כמו אמנה היה דברינו אפילו על ידי מיגו אין נאמנים שאין אדם משים עצמו רשע פירוש תרוייהו מודי דשטרא מעליא הוא ועכשיו באים לבטלו ע"י עדות מודעא וזה נקרא חוזר ומגיד וכיון שהגיד עדותו בשטר שוב אינו חוזר ומגיד ע"פ פעם שני. ומר בר ר"א סבר אמנה לא ניתן

חשק שלמה על תוס' רי"ד א) אולי צ"ל וכיון שיכולה למחול אותה לבעלה יכולה נמי לעשות קנוניא כדי להפסיד הלקוחות ואף שאין כוונתה כלל למחול לבעלה וכו'. ב) נראה דצ"ל ולא מהני המכירה רק שלא יכול לומר וכו'. ג) נראה דצ"ל וודאי אינה מכירה וא"כ.

וְאָמַר רַב שֵׁשֶׁת בְּרֵיהּ דְּרַב אִידִי – And Rav Sheishess the son of Rav Idi said: שְׁמַע מִינָּהּ מִדְּרַב כַּהֲנָא – Learn from this dictum **of Rav Kahana that עֵדִים שֶׁאָמְרוּ אֲמָנָה הָיוּ דְּבָרֵינוּ – witnesses** who signed on a note of indebtedness and **who** later **said, "Our words** of testimony **were** written **on trust," אֵין נֶאֱמָנִין – are not believed. מַאי טַעְמָא – What is the reason? כֵּיוָן דְּעַוְלָה הוּא – Since [such a document] is** considered **an "injustice," אַעַוְלָה לֹא חָתְמֵי –** it is presumable that **they would not sign to an injustice.** Their statement that they did sign such a note is self-incriminating, and therefore not acceptable. Rav Yehudah, too, teaches that when witnesses say the note they signed was written on trust, they are not believed even though their signatures cannot be verified from another source.[1]

The Gemara presents another exposition of the verse cited by Rav Kahana:

אָמַר רַבִּי יְהוֹשֻׁעַ בֶּן לֵוִי – R' Yehoshua ben Levi said: אָסוּר לוֹ לְאָדָם שֶׁיַּשְׁהֶה שְׁטָר פָּרוּעַ בְּתוֹךְ בֵּיתוֹ – It is forbidden for a person (i.e. a lender) **to retain a paid-up note** of indebtedness **in his house, מִשּׁוּם שֶׁנֶּאֱמַר ,,אַל־תַּשְׁכֵּן בְּאֹהָלֶיךָ עַוְלָה'' – because it is stated:** ***let not injustice dwell in your tent.***

The Gemara cites an expanded exposition of this verse:

בְּמַעֲרָבָא מִשְּׁמֵיהּ דְּרַב אָמְרֵי – In the West [i.e. Eretz Yisrael] **they said in the name of Rav: ,,אִם־אָוֶן בְּיָדְךָ הַרְחִיקֵהוּ'' –** When the verse begins: ***If there is perversion in your hand, put it far away,***[2] **זֶה שְׁטָר אֲמָנָה וּשְׁטָר פַּסִּים – this is** a reference to **a document** written **on trust and a document** written **on persuasion.**[3] **,,וְאַל תַּשְׁכֵּן בְּאֹהָלֶיךָ עַוְלָה'' –** When that verse concludes: ***and let not injustice dwell in your tent,*** **זֶה שְׁטָר פָּרוּעַ – this is** a reference to **a paid-up document.**[4]

According to the latter exposition, the verse forbids keeping both a document written on trust and a paid-up document, whereas according to the previous expositions it forbids keeping only one of them. Rav Kahana understood it as referring to a document written on trust, whereas R' Yehoshua ben Levi understood it as referring to one that was paid up. The Gemara elaborates on these earlier opinions:

מַאן דְּאָמַר שְׁטָר פָּרוּעַ – The one [R' Yehoshua ben Levi] **who stated** that the verse calls **a paid-up document** an "injustice" **כָּל שֶׁכֵּן שְׁטָר אֲמָנָה –** maintains that **certainly a document** written **on trust** is in this category.[5] **וּמַאן דְּאָמַר שְׁטָר אֲמָנָה – However, the one** [Rav Kahana] **who stated** that the verse calls **a document** written **on trust** an "injustice" maintains that only this document is included, **אֲבָל שְׁטָר פָּרוּעַ לֹא – but a paid-up document** is **not** considered an "injustice," **דְּזִמְנִין דְּמַשְׁהֵי לֵיהּ אַפְּשִׁיטֵי דְּסַפְרָא – because sometimes [a lender] keeps it** as collateral **for** his **payment to the scribe** who wrote the note.[6]

The Gemara cites another law derived from the aforementioned verse:

אִתְּמַר – It was stated: סֵפֶר שֶׁאֵינוֹ מוּגָּה – Regarding **a book** of Scripture **that has not been corrected** of writing errors,[7] **אָמַר רַבִּי אַמִי – R' Ami said: עַד שְׁלֹשִׁים יוֹם מוּתָּר לְשַׁהוֹתוֹ – Up to thirty days, it is permitted to keep it, מִכָּאן וְאֵילָךְ אָסוּר לְשַׁהוֹתוֹ –** but **from then on it is prohibited to keep it, מִשּׁוּם שֶׁנֶּאֱמַר ,,אַל־תַּשְׁכֵּן בְּאֹהָלֶיךָ עַוְלָה'' – because it is stated:** ***let not injustice dwell in your tent.***[8]

In connection with the Mishnah's ruling, the Gemara discusses further cases in which witnesses attempt to uproot their written testimony:

אָמַר רַב נַחְמָן – Rav Nachman said: עֵדִים שֶׁאָמְרוּ אֲמָנָה הָיוּ דְּבָרֵינוּ – Witnesses who signed on a note of indebtedness and **who** later **said, "Our words** of testimony **were** written **on trust,"**[9]

NOTES

1. *Rashi.* As we learned above (18b, according to the final version of Rami bar Chama's opinion), self-incriminating testimony is rejected even when the witnesses have the power of *happeh she'assar.* [See note 9 for further discussion of the case in which the witnesses say they signed on trust.]

Rav Ashi certainly agrees with Abaye's explanation that if the holder of the note says it was written on trust, and his admission is detrimental to others, he is not believed. Rav Ashi merely means to inform us that Rav Yehudah's ruling can be applied to the witnesses as well (*Ritva*). [However, Abaye and Rav Ashi do not necessarily accept Rava's explanation of Rav Yehudah's ruling as applying to the borrower named in the note, since that explanation is debatable, as explained above, 19a note 10.]

2. *Job* 11:14. This is the beginning of the verse cited above.

3. I.e. a sham promissory note, produced because the bearer *persuaded* a dear and trusting friend to write a promissory note in his favor so that he (the bearer) would appear wealthy in the eyes of others (*Rashi* to *Gittin* 19b). Both the document of trust and the document of persuasion are not intended to be used for collection.

4. The "trust" and "persuasion" documents are classified as "perversion" because they were void from the outset, whereas the paid-up note is merely called an "injustice" because it was initially valid but is now being held unjustly (*Tosafos*).

5. [For as shall shortly be explained, there is some justification for holding a paid-up note, whereas there is no justification for holding a note written on trust.]

6. [Literally: for the scribe's coins.] It is the debtor's obligation to pay the fee of the scribe who draws up a note of indebtedness (*Bava Basra* 167b). Sometimes, however, the debtor does not have the money available at the time of the loan and the creditor makes the payment, relying upon the debtor to reimburse him later. If the creditor was not reimbursed by the time the debt is paid, he might withhold the note from the debtor until he is reimbursed for the scribe's fee (*Rashi*). Rav Kahana maintains that since the creditor keeps the note as collateral until he is reimbursed, if this leads him to erroneously keep it after he has been reimbursed he is not deemed to have committed an "injustice" — since there was a reasonable basis for his error. R' Yehoshua ben Levi, however, maintains that it is the creditor's duty to beware of holding the note longer than permitted, and thus, keeping it after the scribe's fee has been paid is considered an "injustice." All agree, however, that it is not an "injustice" to hold the note as collateral for the scribe's fee (even though this leaves open the possibility of collecting the entire amount again), since the creditor cannot be faulted for needing the collateral (*Tosafos* ד״ה וזמנין, *Rosh;* see *Beis Yaakov*).

[Others explain that R' Yehoshua ben Levi forbids the creditor to hold the note of indebtedness as collateral for the scribe's fee, since the note contains a record of a much greater debt. Accordingly, when R' Yehoshua ben Levi calls the holding of the note an "injustice," he refers even to the case where the scribe's fee was not paid (*Ran; Shulchan Aruch, Choshen Mishpat* 57:1; see *Shach* §4; for further discussion, see *Korban Nesanel* §4 to *Rosh*).]

7. I.e. one that is missing letters or words, or that contains extra ones (*Ri Migash*).

8. The term "dwell" connotes a stay of more than thirty days (*Ritva;* see *Shitah Mekubetzes* for an alternative explanation). *Rashi* states that this pertains to all Books of Scripture — Torah [Pentateuch], *Neviim* [Prophets] and *Kesuvim* [Writings] (cf. *Ri Migash*). According to *Rashi's* explanation, R' Ami's ruling applies even to books other than Scriptural works. *Rashi* interprets it specifically in reference to Scripture simply because in R' Ami's times there were no other written books of Torah knowledge. Nowadays, when the Talmud and other Halachic works have been committed to writing, the same rule applies to any of these books. Keeping a flawed volume in one's possession for more than thirty days is considered an "injustice," because this might lead to the commission of halachic errors (*Rosh, Ritva;* see also *Rama, Yoreh Deah* 279:1 with *Beur HaGra*).

9. I.e. the prospective borrower handed the note to the prospective lender in advance of any loan, so that it would be available when needed. [Now, even if a loan would eventually take place, the predated note of indebtedness would presumably be illegal, because it would give

כז א מיי' פ"ג מהלכות עדות הלכה ז סמג עשין קט טוש"ע ח"מ סי' מו סעיף לו:
כח ב טוש"ע ח"מ סימן נז סעיף א:
כט ג מיי' פ"ז מהלכות ס"ת הלכה יב סמג עשין כה טוש"ע י"ד סי' רעט סעיף א [וברב אלפס עוד בהלכות ספר תורה דף קה:]:
ל ד ה ו ז ח מיי' פ"ג מהל' עדות הל' ז ח ט סמג עשין קט טוש"ע ח"מ סי' מו סעי' לו:
לא ט מיי' פי"ח מהל' עדות הלכה ב סמג עשין קי טור ח"מ סי' לח:

ואמר רב ששת בריה דרב אידי ש"מ מדרב כהנא עדים שאמרו אמנה היו דברינו אין נאמנין מאי טעמא כיון דעולה הוא אעולה לא חתמי אמר רבי יהושע בן לוי אסור לו לאדם שישהה שטר פרוע בתוך ביתו משום שנאמר אל תשכן באהליך עולה במערבא משמיה דרב אמרי אם און בידך הרחיקהו זה שטר אמנה ושטר פסים ואל תשכן באהלך עולה זה שטר פרוע מאן דאמר שטר פרוע כל שכן שטר אמנה ומאן דאמר שטר אמנה אבל שטר פרוע לא דזמנין דמשהי ליה אפשיטי דספרא אתמר ספר שאינו מוגה אמר רבי אמי עד ל' יום מותר לשהותו מכאן ואילך אסור לשהותו משום שנא' אל תשכן באהליך עולה אר"נ עדים שאמרו אמנה היו דברינו אין נאמנין מודעא היו דברינו אין נאמנין מר בר רב אשי אמר אמנה היו דברינו אין נאמנין מודעא היו דברינו נאמנין מ"ט האי ניתן ליכתב והאי לא ניתן ליכתב בעא מיניה רבא מרב נחמן תנאי היו דברינו מהו מודעא ואמנה היינו טעמא דקא עקרי ליה לשטרא והאי נמי קא עקר לשטרא או דלמא תנאי מילתא אחריתי היא א"ל כי אתו לקמן לדינא אמרינן להו זילו קיימו תנאייכו וחותו לדינא עד אומר תנאי ועד אומר אינו תנאי א"ר פפא תרוייהו בשטרא מעליא קא מסהדי והאי דקאמר תנאי הוה ליה חד ואין דבריו של אחד במקום שנים מתקיף לה רב הונא בריה דרב יהושע אי הכי אפי' תרוייהו נמי אלא אמרינן הני למיעקר סהדותייהו קאתו האי נמי למיעקר סהדותיה קאתי והלכתא כרב הונא בריה דרב יהושע ת"ר שנים חתומין על השטר ומתו ובאו שנים מן השוק ואמרו ידענו שכתב ידם הוא אבל אנוסים היו קטנים היו פסולי עדות היו הרי אלו נאמנים ואם יש עדים שכתב ידם הוא זה או שהיה כתב ידם יוצא ממקום אחר משטר שקרא עליו ערער והוחזק בב"ד אין אלו נאמנין ומגבינן ביה כבשטרא מעליא ואמאי תרי ותרי נינהו אמר רב ששת זאת אומרת הכחשה תחלת הזמה היא

רש"י

ואמר רב ששת גרס': **אעולה לא חתמי.** וכי אמרי חתמנו אין נאמנים להרשיע את עצמן: **על פשיטי דספרא.** שעל הלוה ליתן שכר הסופר ופעמים שאין לו ונותנו המלוה וחוזר וגובהו ממנו בשעת פרעון ומעכב השטר עליו: **ספר שאינו מוגה.** תורה נביאים וכתובים: **מוגה.** מן טעיות שבו: **עדים.** החתומים בשטר ואמרו אמנה היו דברינו לא הלוהו כלום אלא כתבנו לו לכשיצטרך ילוה לו וזה שיעבד לו נכסיו מעכשיו אם ילוה אפילו לאחר זמן דלאו מוקדם ליהוי לטרוף שלא כדין: **מודעא היו דברינו.** אם שטר מכר הוא ואמרו עדים החתומים בו המוכר מסר מודעא בפנינו והראנו אונסו והכרנו בו: **אין נאמנין.** דלא אתי על פה ומרע ליה לשטרא: מודעא ניתן לעדים לכתוב את השטר כדי להציל הנאנס מאונסו אמנה לא ניתן להכתב דעולה הוא וכי אמרו חתמנו משוי לנפשייהו רשעים ואין אדם נאמן לשום עצמו רשע: **תנאי היו דברינו.** על תנאי מכרה לו שיעשה לו כך וכך ולא ראינו שקיים לו תנאו וזה אומר לא קיים לי ואינו מכר: **מודעא ואמנה.** טעמא מאי קאמר מר אין נאמנין: **דקא עקרי ליה לשטרא.** בעדותן זה ולא אתי על פה ומרע לשטרא הכא נמי כו': **או דלמא.** הא לא עקרתא דשטרא הוא דמודים הם שהשטר אמת אלא שתנאי היה ביניהם וזו עדות אחרת היא ושטרא ממילא מיעקר לאחר זמן ביום שלא קיים תנאו בזמנו: **כי אתו לקמן.** לקוחות שעדיהם מעידים שתנאי היו דבריהם: **אמרי' להו זילו קיימו תנאייכו.** לבעלים: **וחותו לדינא.** אם יעכב שוב הקרקע: **תרוייהו בשטרא מעליא קא מסהדי.** שניהם מעידים שהשטר אמת וכמות שהוא כתוב בלא תנאי חתמוהו: **והאי דקאמר תנאי חד הוא.** ואינו נאמן לעקור שטר ששניהם חתומים בו: **אי הכי אפילו תרוייהו נמי אלא אמרינן** כו'. אי הכי דכיון שהעיד על כתב ידו עשית לזה אחד ממקיימי השטר כמות שהוא כתוב בלא תנאי והוי להו עדיו שנים ועדות אחרונה דברי אחד במקום שנים: **אפי' תרוייהו נמי.** אמרי תנאי היו דברינו לא ליתהימנו דכיון שהעידו על כתב ידן קיימו השטר כמות שהוא כתוב וכי אמרי תנאי היו דברינו הוו להו מגידים וחוזרים ומגידים ואמאי אמר רב נחמן קיימו תנאייכו כו': **אלא.** על כרחך לאו חתימה מקויימת הוא דכיון דתוך כדי דבור מסקי דבורייהו ואמרי אבל תנאי היה ביניהן אמרינן הני למיעקר סהדותייהו שאמרו כתב ידינו הוא קאתו ולומר לא חתמנו אלא ע"מ שיקיים את התנאי וכיון דתנאי מלתא אחריתי היא שאינה עוקרתו אלא לאחר זמן לא דמיא למודעא ואמנה ומהימני לעדות בפני עצמה היא: **האי נמי.** כי קיים ואמר תנאי הוה עקר לחתימת ידיה לומר לא חתמתי אלא על מנת כן וכיון דאית לן דמלתא אחריתי היא ושטרא ממילא מיעקר איסתכת דאין בשטר חתום אלא ע"א: **שקרא עליו ערער.** שרצה הנתבע לפוסלו: **ומגבינן ביה.** בתמיה: **תרי ותרי נינהו.** עדי השטר ב' ואלו ב' מעידים עליהם שפסולים היו באותה שעה:

תוספות

אם און בידך הרחיקהו זה שטר פסים ושטר אמנה. דהכי משמע לשון און דמעיקרא הוי שקר ואל תשכן באהליך עולה זה שטר פרוע שעתה הוא עולה אבל מעיקרא הוה אמת: **זמנין** דמשהי ליה אפשיטי דספרא. וע"י אותה שהייה אישתלי ליה שהוציאה פעם אחרת הלכך לא קרי ליה עולה ומ"ד שטר פרוע היה לו ליזהר אבל אין לפרש למשום שהיינו אפשיטי דספרא קרי ליה עולה דמה פשע: **אמר** רב נחמן עדים שאמרו אמנה היו דברינו אין נאמנים. ע"כ באין כתב ידן יוצא ממקום אחר איירי דאי כתב ידן יוצא ממקום אחר פשיטא דהכי פריך לעיל ועוד דמר בר רב אשי קאמר דאין נאמנים משום דלא ניתן לכתוב ואי בכתב ידן יוצא ממקום אחר אפילו ניתן לכתב פשיטא דאין נאמנים וקשה דאמאי לא מהימני במיגו דהא רב נחמן גופיה אית ליה לעיל מגו לפסול השטר דקאמר כי אתו לקמן לדינא אמרינן להו זילו קיימו תנאייכו וחותו לדינא דמהימן לומר פרוע במגו דמזויף וכ"ש עדים דאלימי לאורועי שטרא כדאמר במי שמת (ב"ב דף קנד.) ותירץ ר"י דהיינו טעמא דמודעא הואיל ומודים שהשטר נכתב ונמסר כהלכתו שוב לא אתי על פה ומרע לשטרא אפילו במגו ולא דמי לאנוסים וקטנים דמתניתין שאין מודים שהיה שטר כשר כלל אלא סותרין אותו הלכך מהימני במגו דלא שייך כאן לומר דלא אתי על פה ומרע לשטרא שהרי אינם מודים שהיה שטר ואמנה נמי נראה דהיינו טעמא דלא מהימני לרב נחמן דלא מרעי לשטרא הואיל ומודים שהשטר נכתב כדין מדעת הלוה דלא מפרש טעמא דאמנה משום דלא ניתן לכתוב אלא מר בר רב אשי אבל לרב נחמן טעם אמנה ומודעא שניהם שוה והא דלית ליה לרב נחמן דנאמן לומר פרוע במגו דמזויף התם נמי לא מרע לשטרא כלל הלכך מהימן במגו ואתי שפיר רב נחמן כרבנן דר"מ והאיך בריש מי שמת (ג"ז שם:) לשטר אמנה הוא זה דאינו נאמן דבעי לאוקמי כר"מ רב נחמן מוקי לה לדברי הכל: **או** דלמא תנאי מילתא אחריתי היא. פי' לדבר אחר הן באין ולא לעקירת השטר אלא תוספת בעלמא שמפרשים עדותן היאך ועד השתא קיים השטר ואינו נעקר אם יתקיים התנאי הלכך אין כאן הורעת השטר אבל אין לפרש מילתא אחריתי היא לגמרי ולא שייך לעדותן ראשונה כמו שאם היו מעידין שהוא פרוע שהן נאמנים דא"כ מאי פריך בסמוך א"ה אפי' תרי נמי דכיון דתנאי מילתא אחריתי הוא לגמרי תרי נאמנים אפילו בכתב ידן יוצא ממקום אחר אבל חד לעולם אימא לך דלא מהימן כי היכי דלא מהימן לומר פרוע הוא לכך נראה כדפירשנו: **ואם** כתב ידן יוצא ממקום אחר אין נאמנים. ופסולי עדות דקתני לא שאומרים שעדיין פסולים דאם כן אמאי אין נאמנים אלא פסולי עדות הוו אז ועתה מודים שהם כשרים וא"ת ומכל מקום אמאי אין נאמנים להימנו במגו דאי בעו אומרים עדיין הם פסולים [וכן בכלן] שתי כתי עדים המכחישות זו את זו אמאי לא מהימני בתראי במגו דאי בעו פסלי לקמאי בגזלנותא ואור"י דבשני עדים לא שייך מגו דאין אחד יודע מה בלב חבירו: **אמר** רב ששת זאת אומרת הכחשה תחלת הזמה היא. וא"ת תקשי לרב ששת בריש מי שמת (ג"ז שם) דקתני אם אמר שטר אמנה הוא זה הלך אחר עדים ואם לאו הלך אחר השטר אלמא אע"ג דאין שטר צריך קיום [ואפילו הכי] אם יש עדים הלך אחר עדים

ואוקי

תורה אור השלם

א) אִם אָוֶן בְּיָדְךָ הַרְחִיקֵהוּ וְאַל תַּשְׁכֵּן בְּאֹהָלֶיךָ עַוְלָה: [איוב יא, יד]

גליון הש"ס

גמ' זאת אומרת הכחשה. עיין שיטה מקובצת בב"מ דף קב ע"ב ד"ה ואי זאת אומרת בשם רבי סעדי' גאון:

תוספות רי"ד

ליקוטי רש"י

עין משפט נר מצוה

כב א מיי' פכ"ד מהל' מלוה ולוה הלכה ה טוש"ע ח"מ סימן מו סעיף לח:
כג ב מיי' פ"ה מהלכות יסודי התורה הלכה א ג טוש"ע י"ד סימן קנז סעיף א:
כד ג מיי' פ"ד מהלכות מלוה ולוה הל' ה יא סמג עשין נד טוש"ע ח"מ סימן מו סעיף לח וסימן פב סעיף א:
כה ד מיי' פ"ב שם הל' ה סמג שם טוש"ע ח"מ סימן מז סעיף א:
כו ה מיי' שם הלכה ו וסמג שם טוש"ע ח"מ סימן פו סעיף א:

גמרא

חזקה אין העדים חותמין על השטר אא"כ נעשה בגדול אלא אנוסין מ"ט אמר רב חסדא קסבר ר"מ עדים שאמרו להם חתמו שקר ואל תהרגו יהרגו ואל יחתמו שקר אמר ליה רבא השתא אילו אתו לקמן לאמלוכי אמרינן להו זילו חתומו ולא תתקטלון דאמר מר אין לך דבר שעומד בפני פיקוח נפש אלא עבודת כוכבים וגלוי עריות ושפיכות דמים בלבד השתא דחתמו אמרינן להו אמאי חתמיתו אלא טעמא דר"מ כדרב הונא אמר רב דא"ר הונא אמר רב מודה בשטר שכתבו אין צריך לקיימו גופא אמר רב הונא אמר רב מודה בשטר שכתבו אין צריך לקיימו א"ל רב נחמן גנובא גנובי למה לך אי סבירא לך כר"מ אימא הלכה כר"מ ומר היכי סבירא ליה אמר ליה כי אתו לקמן לדינא אמרינן להו זילו קיימו שטרייכו וחותו לדינא א"ר יהודה אמר רב האומר שטר אמנה הוא זה אינו נאמן דקאמר מאן אילימא דקאמר לוה פשיטא כל כמיניה ואלא דקאמר מלוה תבוא עליו ברכה אלא דקאמרי עדים אי דכתב ידם יוצא ממקום אחר פשיטא דלא מהימני ואי דאין כתב ידם יוצא ממקום אחר אמאי לא מהימני (סימן בא"ש) אמר רבא לעולם דקאמר לוה וכדרב הונא דא"ר הונא אמר רב מודה בשטר שכתבו אין צריך לקיימו אביי אמר לעולם דאמר מלוה וכגון שחב לאחרים וכדרבי נתן דתניא רבי נתן אומר מנין לנושה בחבירו מנה וחבירו בחבירו מנין שמוציאין מזה ונותנין לזה תלמוד לומר ונתן לאשר אשם לו רב אשי אמר לעולם דקאמרי עדים ודאין כתב ידם יוצא ממקום אחר ודקאמרת אמאי לא מהימני כדרב כהנא דא"ר כהנא אסור לו לאדם שישהה שטר אמנה בתוך ביתו משום שנאמר אל תשכן באהליך עולה ואמר

רש"י

אלא אנוסים מ"ט לא. נימא הפה שאסר הוא שהתיר: **אא"כ נעשה בגדול.** כל מעשה השטר בגדולים הלוקח והמוכר וגבי עדים נמי אמרי' חזקה אין הלוקח מתמים בו קטנים: **יהרגו ואל יחתמו שקר.** הלכך כי אמרי נמי אנוסים היינו ממש שמשימין נפשייהו רשעים: **מודה בשטר שכתבו.** לוה שהודה בשטר שכתבו ועל פיו נחתמו העדים: **אין המלוה צריך לקיימו.** בעדים החתומים בו שאין הלוה שוב נאמן לומר פרעתיו ולא אמרינן בהאי הפה שאסר הוא שהתיר דמכיון שאמר כשר היה הרי הוחזק השטר וכי אמר פרעתיו לא מהימן שהרי ביד המלוה הוא ור"מ נמי דאמר אין נאמנים לפוסלו במודה לוה שכתבו קאמר וקסבר לא צריכינן תו לעדים ולאו אפומייהו מקיים שטרא: **גנבא.** מתגנב אתה לומר דבריך בלשון שלא נחלקו בו היחיד והמרובים כדי שלא יבטלו את דבריך לאמרת כיחידאה: **אי סבירא לך כר"מ אימא הלכה כר"מ.** ולא תנקוט לה כמילתא באנפי נפשה: **ומר היכי סבירא ליה.** במודה בשטר שכתבו: **כי אתו לקמן.** מלוין מבזין שטרות: **קיימו שטרייכו.** כך אני רגיל לומר למלוים המביאים שטרותיהם לפני ואין עדיהם עמהם אני אומר להם לכו ובקשו עדיכם וקיימוהו דאי לאו הכי אע"ג דמודה לוה שכתבו מצי למימר פרעתיו: **שטר אמנה.** לא לוה כלום אלא כתבו ומסרו למלוה שאם יצטרך ללוות ילוה והאמינו שלא יתבענו אא"כ מלוהו: **כל כמיניה.** והלא עדים חתומים בו ופשיטא דיתקיים בחותמיו: **כדרב הונא.** ואשמעינן רב יהודה נמי הכי דלוה שאמר כתבתיו ומסרתיו לו אבל שטר אמנה הוא אין צריך המלוה לחזור ולהביא להעיד על החתימה דאין נאמן לוה לפוסלו דלא עביד איניש דכתב ומסר בלא הלואה: **שחב לאחרים.** בהודאה זו שהוא מודה שהוא שטר אמנה חב ומפסיד את אחרים הנושים בו ואין לו מה להגבותם והיו רוצים לגבות חוב זה: **ונתן לאשר אשם לו.** ולא כתב לאשר הלוהו אלא לאשר האשם שלו ואשם הוא קרן כדאמרי' בהגוזל (ב"ק דף קי.) למי שהקרן שלו:

תוספות

חזקה אין כו'. הכא משמע דלא אמרינן מגו במקום חזקה ולרבנן אמרינן ול"ע דבעיא היא בפרק קמא דב"ב (דף ה: ושם) ולא אפשיטא גבי תבע אחר זמנו ואמר ליה פרעתיך תוך זמני: **דאמר מר אין לך דבר כו'.** פירוש אפי' מאן דמחמיר לא מחמיר אלא בהנך דרבא גופיה קסבר דאפילו בהני אינו חייב למסור עצמו בצינעא במס' ע"ז בפרק ר' ישמעאל (דף נד. ושם) ואין חילוק בין הנך ושאר ובפרהסיא בכולהו יהרג ואל יעבור: **טעמא דר"מ כדרב הונא כו'.** פירש בקונטרס דמיירי פלוגתייהו במודה לוה שכתבו והיינו טעמא דר"מ דאין נאמנין דהואיל ולוה קיימו לא צריכי תו עדים ולאו אפומייהו מקיים שטרא ורבנן סברי צריך לקיימו וקשה לר"י דא"כ ליפלגו בלא עדים בלוה גופי' הואיל וטעמייהו תלי בלוה ועוד דבפרק מי שמת (ב"ב דף קנד: ושם) משמע דלא פליגי בלוה דקאמר רבי יוחנן שאני אומר מודה בשטר שכתבו א"צ לקיימו דברי הכל היא ופריך והא מפלג פליגי אין נאמנים לפוסלו כו' אמר ליה אי אלימי עדים לאורועי שטרא איהו לא כמיניה ועוד דהוה ליה למימר בדרב הונא קמיפלגי ונראה לר"ת ולר"י דה"פ טעמא דר"מ כדרב הונא דכמו שאומר רב הונא דלא אמרינן מגו לפסול השטר בלוה ה"נ אומר ר"מ בעדים דאע"ג דאלימי לא פסלי שטרא במגו: **מודה בשטר שכתבו א"צ לקיימו.** וא"ת ומ"ט לא מהימן במגו דאי בעי אמר מזויף וי"ל דשמא ירא לומר מזויף פן יכחישוהו וליכא מגו ופירש הקונט' במקום אחר דטעמא משום דדבר תורה א"צ קיום דעדים החתומים על השטר נעשה כמי שנחקרה עדותן בב"ד ורבנן הוא דאצרכוהו קיום כי טוען מזויף הוא אבל בשאר טענות כגון פרוע הוא לא הצריכוהו קיום וכן נראה לר"י (ח) אבל אין לפרש דלא מהימן במגו לומר פרוע הוא משום דאי פרעיה שטרא בידיה מאי בעי דהא כי טוען נמי אמנה הוא מסקינן בסמוך אמילתיה דרב דלא מהימן והתם לא שייך האי טעמא:

אי סבירא לך כר"מ כו'. וא"ת ולימא משום הכי לא קאמר הלכה כר"מ משום דאיכא בפ' מי שמת (ב"ב קנד: ושם) דמפיך דר"מ לרבנן ויש לומר דהוה מצי למימר דהלכה כרשב"ג דאית ליה בהדיא בפ"ק דב"מ (דף ז.) דמודה בשטר שכתבו אין צריך לקיימו:

אימא הלכה כרבי מאיר. תימה דאפילו כרבנן נמי מצי סבר ושאני עדים דאלימי לאורועי שטרא דהכי אית ליה לרבי יוחנן ויש לומר דרב נחמן אין נראה לו לחלק ואם תאמר ולימא דאפילו רב נחמן מודה לקמן ויש לומר דרב הונא סתם קאמר ולא מפליג: **לעולם** דקאמר לוה וכדרב הונא כו'. ואם תאמר ואמאי לא קאמר נמי לעולם דקאמרי עדים וכדרב הונא ויש לומר דלא ניחא ליה לאוקמי דלא כרבנן דאמרי אלימי עדים לאורועי שטרא: **וכדרב** הונא אמר רב. וא"ת תרתי מילי דרב למה לי וי"ל דחדא מכלל חבירתה אתמר: **וכגון** שחב לאחרים. וא"ת ולהימניה במגו דאי בעי מחיל ליה דהא המוכר שטר חוב לחבירו וחזר ומחלו מחול (לקמן דף פה:) ויש לומר דלאו מגו הוא דשמא אין דעתו למחול ולהפסיד חובו דעכשיו שאומר אמנה הוא לא מפסיד מידי כיון שאין הלוה גזלן אע"ג דבספ"ק דב"מ (דף כ. ושם) אמרינן מגו כה"ג גבי מצא שובר בזמן שהאשה מודה יחזיר לבעל דקאמר ש"מ איתא לדשמואל שמא התם סמכינן אמגו כל דהו משום דאיכא שובר דמוכח ואם נאמר דמכירת שטר חוב אינו אלא מדרבנן הוה אתי שפיר דמצינן למימר דווקא מוכר שטר חוב דהוי מדרבנן יכול למחול אבל בנושה בחבירו כו' דחייב לו מן התורה אינו יכול למחול וכן משמע בפרק מי שמת (ב"ב דף קמז: ושם) דקאמר ומודה שמואל דאם נתנו במתנת ש"מ שאינו יכול למחול ומסיק מתנת ש"מ דאורייתא ואינו יכול למחול דאי ס"ד מדרבנן אמאי אינו יכול למחול משמע דבמידי דאורייתא אינו יכול למחול ויש לדחות דהתם ודאי אי מתנת שכיב מרע דאורייתא אין היורש יכול למחול דמאי אולמיה האי יורש מהאי יורש ועוד יש להביא ראיה דנושה בחבירו וחבירו בחבירו אינו יכול למחול דאמרי' בסוף האשה שנפלו (לקמן פא:) הרי שהיה נושה באחיו מנה ומת והניח שומרת יבם לא יאמר הואיל ואני יורש החזקתי אלא מוציאין מידו ולוקח בהן קרקעות והוא אוכל פירות ומוקמי' לה כר' נתן דהא הוי כמו נושה בחבירו מנה וחבירו בחבירו דכל אשר לבעלה משועבד לה לכתובתה ואי יכול למחול אמאי ילקח בהן קרקע ימחול לעצמו שהוא יורש ויכול למחול ויש לדחות דשאני התם דאין יורש אלא מכחה ואינו יכול להפקיע זכותה [וי"מ דדוקא במוכר שט"ח יכול למחול שקדם חובו לחוב של חבירו אינו יכול למחול ושומרת יבם נמי קדם שטר חובה לחוב בעלה] וא"ת אכתי נהימניה במגו דאי בעי קלתיה כדאמרינן בסוף זה בורר (סנהדרין דף לא:) ויש לומר דהכא אתחזק בבי דינא דאמרינן התם כיון דאתחזק בבי דינא אי בעי קלתיה לא אמרינן אי נמי הכא מיירי כשהשטר הוא ביד שליש: **מנין** לנושה בחבירו כו'. משמע דהלכה כר' נתן וכגיטין (דף לז.) פירשנוה: (ט) **אעולה** לא חתמי. והא דכותבין שטר ללוה אע"פ שאין מלוה עמו היינו למוסרו ללוה ולא למלוה: אם

מסורת הש"ס

א) ב"ב קנד. סנהדרין כט:, ב) סנהדרין עד., ג) שבת עט. ב"מ ז, עב:, ד) ב"ב קנד. קע., ה) [יבמות לא. ב"ב קנג.], ו) פסחים לא. לקמן פו. גיטין לו., ז) ב"מ ז: [קדושין טו.], ח) [דבור זה שייך לעיל קודם לדבור אלא אנוסים וכו'], ט) [וע"ע תוס' ע"ז מ: ד"ה יסוק], י) [ועיין תוס' לקמן כח. ד"ה קיים], ט) שייך לע"ב.

גליון הש"ס

גמ' אין לך דבר שעומד בפני פיקוח נפש. עיין סוטה דף י ע"ב תוס' ד"ה תוס' לו: תוס' ד"ה וכדרב הונא אמר רב וכו' וי"ל דחדא מכלל חבירתה. עיין ברמב"ן במלחמות פ"ב דשבת ד"ה ועוד כתב בס"פ דלעיל א"ר: באד דחדא מכלל חבירתה. כה"ג מגילה דף כט ע"ב כתובות דף לו ע"א:

תורה אור השלם

א) וְהִתְוַדּוּ אֶת חַטָּאתָם אֲשֶׁר עָשׂוּ וְהֵשִׁיב אֶת אֲשָׁמוֹ בְּרֹאשׁוֹ וַחֲמִישִׁתוֹ יֹסֵף עָלָיו וְנָתַן לַאֲשֶׁר אָשַׁם לוֹ: [במדבר ה, ז]

ב) אִם אָוֶן בְּיָדְךָ הַרְחִיקֵהוּ וְאַל תַּשְׁכֵּן בְּאֹהָלֶיךָ עַוְלָה: [איוב יא, יד]

ליקוטי רש"י

אא"כ נעשה בגדול. המוכר קרקע לן (ב"ב דף קנו.) ולמכור נכסי אביו עד שיהא בן עשרים [סנהדרין כט.]. נותן ומקבל ועדים כולם גדולים וכשרים [רשב"ם ב"ב קנד.]. **אין צריך לקיימו.** דכיון דמודה שכתבו ולוה בו הרי הוא כאלו קיימוהו חותמיו ונוגה בו כל זמן שמוציאו [שבת עט.]. מאחר שכתבו מודה ששטר אמת הוא אין המלוה צריך לחזור אחר העדים החתומין בו ולהעיד על חתימתן ולקיימו [ב"מ עב.]. **גנובא גנובי למה לך.** לפתות דבריך [רשב"ם ב"ב קנ.]. **אמאי לא מהימני.** והא איכא למימר הפה שאסר הוא הפה שהתיר דאי בעי אמרו לא חתמנו [רשב"ם שם קנ.]. **לאשר אשם לו.** למי שנתחייב לו [במדבר ה, ז]. לאשר הלוהו לו לא נאמר אלא לאשר אשם לו לאשר הקרן שלו [פסחים לא.]. לאשר הקרן שלו ולא כתיב לאשר נושה בו [לקמן פב.].

תוספות רי"ד

אמר ר"ה א"ר מודה בשטר שכתבו א"צ לקיימו. פי' לוה שהודה שכתבו ועל פיו נחתמו העדים אין המלוה צריך לקיימו בעדים החתומים בו שכבר קיימו הלוה שהודה לו כי הוא כתבו והחתימו ואם טוען הלוה פרעתיך אינו נאמן שכבר השטר מקוים דכל שטר מקוים אין הלוה יכול לומר פרעתי דא"ל מלוה שטרך בידי מאי בעי ול"א בזה הפה שאסר הוא הפה שהתיר: **א"ל ר"נ** גנובא גנובא למה לך פי' המורה מתגנב אתה לומר דבריך בלשון שלא נחלקו היחיד והרבים כדי שלא יבטלו את דבריך דאמרת כיחידאה אי ס"ל כרבי מאיר אימא הלכה כר"מ פי' דפלוגתא דר"מ ורבנן הוא דר"מ אומר אצ"ל ורבנן אמרו צריך לקיימו ולא תנקוט לה למילתא באנפי נפשי' א"ל ומר היכי ס"ל פי' במודה בשטר שכתבו א"ל כי אתו לקמן פי' מלוים [המביאין] שטרות אמרינן להו זילו קיימו שטרייכו וחותו לדינא פי' כך אני רגיל לומר למלוים המביאים שטרותיהם לפני ואין עדיהם עמהן לכו ובקשו עדיכם וקיימוהו שאם לא תקיימוהו קיומו של לוה שמודה שכתבו אינו מועיל לך שהרי חוזר ואומר פרעתיך ויש להאמינו ע"י מיגו ומש"ה טרח לקיים ושוב לא יהא נאמן לומר פרעתי והל' כר"נ בדיני שאינו נאמן עיין בפסקי בפ' מי שמת עיין לקמן: **אמר ר"י א"ר** האומר שטר אמנה הוא זה אינו נאמן. פי' המורה שטר אמנה שלא לוה כלום אלא כתבו ומסרו למלוה שאם יצטרך ללוות ילוהו והאמינו שלא יתבענו אא"כ מלוהו ואינו נ"ל דמשמע מפירושו שהעדים נתנוהו ללוה והוא נתנו למלוה וא"כ אמאי קרי לי' לקמן עולה ולא מהימני עדים בזה והתנן כותבין שטר ללוה אע"פ שאין מלוה עמו וכ"ת הא אוקימנא לההוא בשטרא אקנייתא פי' שמקנהו לו נכסיו מהיום בין ילוה בין לא ילוה יגבה מהן לאותו זמן מהיום הרי אביי מעמידה בשטרי דלאו אקנייתא דאמר אביי הא דתנן כותבין שטר ללוה בלא מלוה אפילו בשטרא דלאו אקנייתא נמי וא"נ אתי למיטרף לקוחות מההיא זמנא והוא לא

לוה עד תשרי לאו שלא כדין טריף דעדיו בחתומין זכין לו פי' מיום שחתמוהו יחול השעבוד ואפילו לא לוה המעות עד תשרי וכל ההיא חששא אינה שמא כתב ללוות בניסן ולא לוה עד תשרי ואתי למטרף לקוחות שלא כדין אבל לשמא לא הלוהו כלל לא חיישינן דאיהו דאפסיד אנפשי' דהימני' ומאי עולה איכא גביה סהדי אי איהו מהימן ליה וגם שטר אמנה מנין שלא יהיה אפילו בשטרא אקנייתא ואם העדים נתנוהו למלוה ברצון הלוה שצוה להם ליתנו לו אע"פ שלא ראו ההלואה בעיני' כשר וכשר הוא שאם הלוה רוצה להאמין למלוה שילוהו מה יש לעדים לומר לא ניתן לו השטר עד שנראה ההלואה בעינינו (דשמא לא ילוך הוא בושת עלי ומאמין בו ואומר להם תנו לו השטר והעדים יעברו ע"י שלא ליתן) ובמתני' הכי תנן ואין כותבין למלוה עד שיהא לוה עמו ולא קתני עד שיראו מתן מעות אלא עד שיהא הלוה עמו דכיון דלוה עמו אם רוצה שיתנוהו למלוה יתנו ואם לאו לא יתנו והאיך קרי לה עולה דלמא יהיב ליה בינו לבינו ואי לא יהיב ליה לעולם איהו הוא דאפסיד אנפשיה ושטר כשר הוא וגובה בו ממשעבדי אלא ודאי שטר אמנה הוא שלא נעשה מתחלה ללוות בו אלא הלוה עשאו כדי להראות עצמו לעולם שאינו עשיר שהרי לוה מאחרים ומוסרו למלוה ומאמין בו שלא יתבענו כלום אלא שיראה לעולם כי הוא חייב לו ומחפה עליו שלא יראה עשיר מפני שהוא אוהבו ודומה הוא לשטר פסים שלא נעשה בתחלה בעבור הלואה אלא המלוה פייס את הלוה עשה לי שטר שאתה חייב לי כך וכך כדי שאראה עשיר ויתנו לי אשה והאמן באהבתי שלעולם לא אתבעך בו ולשניהם פתרון א' אלא זה שעושה המלוה כדי שיראה עשיר קורא שטר פסים שצריך לפייס את הלוה שיעשה עליו שט"ח כי הוא חייב לו ויאמין בו שלא יתבענו ומה שהלוה כותב על עצמו כדי שיראה עני קורא אמנה שא"צ לפייס את המלוה בזה ושטר אמנה כזה ודאי הוא עולה שלא נעשה בשביל הלואה ואין העדים רשאים לחתום בו אבל שטר הלואה שנעשה כדי ללוות אין בו שום עולה כדפרי': **ואמרינן** דקאמר מאן אי לימא דקאמר לוה פשיטא פי' והלא עדים חתומים בו ופשיטא דיתקיים בחותמיו כל כמיניה ואלא דקאמר מלוה תבא עליו ברכה ואלא דקאמרו עדים אי כת"י יוצא ממקום אחר פשיטא דלא מהימני ואי אין כת"י יוצא ממ"א אמאי לא מהימני פי' והאיכא הפה שאסר הוא הפה שהתיר ומיגו דאי בעי אמרי לא חתמנו והשתא דאמרו חתמנו וכך היה ליהמנו א"ר לעולם דקאמר לוה וכדר"ה א"ר פי' כלומר ור"י נמי אשמעינן הכי דלוה שאומר כתבתיו ומסרתיו לו אבל שטר אמנה הוא א"צ המלוה לחזור ולהביא עדים להעיד על החתימה שאין נאמן לוה לפוסלו דלא עביד איניש דכתב ומסר בלא הלואה דאר"ה א"ר מודה בשטר שכתבו אצ"ל פי' וליתא לדרבא דאיהו מתרץ מילתא דרב אליבא דידיה דר"ה משמיה דרב קאמר ליה וכבר ר"נ פליג עלויה ואוקי מילתא כר"מ ולא כרבנן למימר דלית הל' כוותיה: **אביי אמר** לעולם דקאמר מלוה וכגון שחב לאחרים וכדר"נ דתניא ר"נ אומר מנין לנושה בחבירו מנה וחבירו בחבירו מנין שמוציאים מזה ונותנים לזה שנאמר ונתן לאשר אשם לו וקי"ל כיון דאמרי' המוכר שט"ח לחבירו וחזר ומחלו מחול יהיה נאמן לומר שטר אמנה ע"י מיגו דמה לו לשקר אי בעי למיפטרי' הלוה מיד הנושים בו הוה מחיל ליה השתא דאמר שטר אמנה הוא יהיה נאמן דהכי אמרי' בשנים אוחזין ת"ר מצא שובר פי' שכתבה אשה לבעלה התקבלתי כתובתי ועודה תחתיו בזמן שהאשה מודה יחזיר לבעל אין האשה מודה לא יחזיר לא לזה ולא לזה ודייקינן עלה בזמן שהאשה מודה מיהת יחזיר לבעלה ואמאי ניחוש דלמא כתבה ליה בניסן ולא נתנה עד תשרי והוא לא פרע עד תשרי ואזלא היא בעודה תחתיו בין ניסן לתשרי וזבנה לכתובתה לאחר בטובת הנאה מניסן ועד תשרי פי' בזול לפי שנותן מעותיו בספק שאם תמות היא ירשנה בעלה ואם ימות הבעל או יגרשנה יהיה הלוקח במקומה לגבות כתובתה ושוב אין לבעלה לפרוע כתובתה אלא ללוקח ושובר שנכתב בשמה אינה כלום ומפיק ליה לשובר דכתב בניסן ואתי למיטרף לקוחות שלא כדין פי' שהשובר קודם לשטרו של לוקח ויחזיק הבעל בקרקע המיוחד לכתובתה ומהדרי' א"ר ש"מ איתא לדשמואל דאמר המוכר שט"ח לחבירו וחזר ומחלו מחול פי' ש"מ מדלא חיישינן להכי דא"נ הוה הכי שפיר זכה בעל השובר שנכתב בשמה הלכך אם

detrimental to these creditors, he is not believed.

The third answer:

רַב אַשִׁי אָמַר – Rav Ashi said: לְעוֹלָם דְּקָאָמְרֵי עֵדִים – Actually, Rav Yehudah refers to a case **where the witnesses say** that the note was written on trust, **וּדְאֵין כְּתַב יָדָם יוֹצֵא מִמָּקוֹם אַחֵר – and** he refers to an instance **in which their handwriting cannot be verified from another source. וּדְקָאָמְרַתְּ אַמַּאי לֹא מְהֵימְנֵי – And** concerning **that which you asked: Why,** then, **are they not believed? כִּדְרַב כַּהֲנָא** – The answer is **in accordance with** a dictum **of Rav Kahana. דְּאָמַר רַב כַּהֲנָא – For Rav Kahana said: אָסוּר לוֹ לְאָדָם שֶׁיַּשְׁהֶה שְׁטַר אֲמָנָה בְּתוֹךְ בֵּיתוֹ – It is prohibited for a person to keep a document** written **on trust in his house, מִשּׁוּם שֶׁנֶּאֱמַר ,,[וְ]אַל־תַּשְׁכֵּן בְּאֹהָלֶיךָ עַוְלָה'' – because it is stated:** ***and let not injustice dwell in your tent.***[18]

NOTES

of these words is that the robber pays the person from whom he stole (see *Rashi* ad loc.). However, since the Torah could have stated that he shall pay *the one to whom he owes,* and instead employs the unusual expression לַאֲשֶׁר אָשַׁם לוֹ (literally: the one to whom he is guilty), R' Nassan expounds the root אשם to connote "the principal sum of money" (which is a secondary meaning of the word, as evident from *Numbers* 5:8; see *Bava Kamma* 110a). Thus, the expression לַאֲשֶׁר אָשַׁם לוֹ means "the one who owns the principal sum of money," indicating that if the person who was robbed in turn owes money to a creditor, the robber must pay this creditor – who is the true "owner of the principal" (see *Rashi*). This is known as שִׁעְבּוּדָא דְרַ' נָתָן, *R' Nassan's lien.*

18. *Job* 11:14. It is improper to keep a document of trust, because even someone with the best intentions may die, raising the possibility of his heirs wrongly thinking it is a bona fide document and proceeding to enforce it (*Nesivos HaMishpat* 46:26; see *Bava Metzia* 68a; see also *Meiri* ד"ה אמר מלוה and ד"ה כל שטר).

א חזקה אין העדים חותמין על השטר אא"כ נעשה בגדול אלא אנוסין מ"ט אמר רב חסדא קסבר ר"מ עדים שאמרו להם חתמו שקר ואל תהרגו יהרגו ואל יחתמו שקר אמר ליה רבא השתא אילו אתו לקמן לאמלוכי אמרינן להו זילו חתומו ולא תתקטלון ג) דאמר מר ב אין לך דבר שעומד בפני פיקוח נפש אלא עבודת כוכבים וגלוי עריות ושפיכות דמים בלבד השתא דחתמו אמרינן להו אמאי חתמיתו אלא טעמא דר"מ כדרב הונא אמר רב דא"ר הונא אמר רב ג מודה בשטר שכתבו אין צריך לקיימו גופא אמר רב הונא אמר רב מודה בשטר שכתבו אין צריך לקיימו א"ל רב נחמן ד) גנובא גנובי למה לך אי סבירא לך כר"מ אימא הלכה כר"מ אמר ליה ומר היכי סבירא ליה אמר ליה כי אתו לקמן לדינא אמרינן להו ג זילו קיימו שטרייכו וחותו לדינא א"ר יהודה אמר רב האומר שטר אמנה הוא זה אינו נאמן דקאמר מאן אילימא דקאמר לוה פשיטא כל כמיניה ואלא דקאמר מלוה תבוא עליו ברכה אלא דקאמרי עדים אי דכתב ידם יוצא ממקום אחר פשיטא דלא מהימני ואי דאין כתב ידם יוצא ממקום אחר אמאי לא מהימני (סימן בא"ש) אמר רבא לעולם דקאמר לוה וכדרב הונא דא"ר הונא אמר רב מודה בשטר שכתבו אין צריך לקיימו אביי אמר לעולם דאמר מלוה ד וכגון שחב לאחרים וכדרבי נתן ה) דתניא רבי נתן אומר ה מנין לנושה בחבירו מנה וחבירו בחבירו מנין שמוציאין מזה ונותנין לזה תלמוד לומר א) ונתן לאשר אשם לו רב אשי אמר לעולם דקאמרי עדים ודאין כתב ידם יוצא ממקום אחר ודקאמרת אמאי לא מהימני כדרב כהנא דא"ר כהנא אסור לו לאדם שישהה שטר אמנה בתוך ביתו משום שנאמר ב) אל תשכן באהליך עולה ואמר

רש"י

אלא אנוסים מ"ט לא. נימא הפה שאסר הוא שהתיר: ו) **אא"כ נעשה בגדול.** כל מעשה השטר בגדולים הלוקח והמוכר וגבי עדים נמי אמרי' חזקה אין הלוקח מחתים בו קטנים: **יהרגו ואל יחתמו שקר.** הלכך כי אמרי נמי אנוסים היינו מחמת נפשות משום נפשייהו רשעים: **מודה בשטר שכתבו.** לוה שהודה בשטר שכתבו ועל פיו נחתמו העדים: **אין המלוה צריך לקיימו.** בעדים החתומים בו שאין הלוה שוב נאמן לומר פרעתיו ולא אמרינן בהאי הפה שאסר הוא שהתיר דמכיון שאמר כשר היה הרי הוחזק השטר וכי אמר פרעתיו לא מהימן שהרי ביד המלוה הוא ור"מ נמי דאמר אין נאמנים לפוסלו במודה לוה שכתבו קאמר וקסבר לא צריכין תו לעדים ולאו אפומייהו מקיים שטרא: **גנבא.** מתגנב אתה לומר דבריך בלשון שלא נחלקו בו היחיד והמרובים כדי שלא יבטלו את דבריך דאמרת כיחידאה: **אי סבירא לך כר"מ אימא הלכה כר"מ.** ולא תנקוט לה כמילתא באנפי נפשה: **ומר היכי סבירא ליה.** במודה בשטר שכתבו: **כי אתו לקמן.** מלוין מביאין שטרות: **קיימו שטרייכו.** כך אני רגיל לומר למלוים המביאים שטרותיהם לפני ואין עדיהם עמהם אני אומר להם לכו ובקשו עדיכם וקיימוהו דלאו הכי אע"ג דמודה לוה שכתבו מצי למימר פרעתיו: **שטר אמנה.** לא לוה כלום אלא כתבו ומסרו למלוה שאם יצטרך ללות ילוה והאמינו שלא יתבענו אא"כ מלוהו: **כל כמיניה.** והלא עדים חתומים בו ופשיטא דיתקיים בחותמיו: **כדרב הונא.** ואשמעינן רב יהודה נמי הכי דלוה שאמר כתבתיו ומסרתיו לו אבל שטר אמנה הוא אין צריך המלוה לחזור ולהביא עדים להעיד על החתימה דאין נאמן לוה לפוסלו דלא עביד איניש דכתב ומסר בלא הלואה: **שחב לאחרים.** בהודאה זו שהוא מודה שהוא שטר אמנה חב ומפסיד את אחרים הנושים בו ואין לו מה להגבותם והיו רוצים לגבות חוב זה: **ונתן לאשר אשם לו.** ולא כתב לאשר הלוהו אלא לאשר האשם שלו ואשם הוא קרן כדאמרי' בהגוזל (ב"ק דף קי.) למי שהקרן שלו:

תוספות

חזקה אין כו'. הכא משמע דלא אמרינן מגו במקום חזקה ולרבנן אמרינן וצ"ע דבעיא היא בפרק קמא דב"ב (דף ה: ושם) ולא אפשיטא גבי תבע אחר זמנו ואמר ליה פרעתיך תוך זמני: **דאמר** מר אין לך דבר כו'. פירוש אפי' מאן דמחמיר לא מחמיר אלא בהנך דרבא גופיה קסבר דאפילו בהני אינו חייב למסור עצמו בצינעא במס' ע"ז בפרק ר' ישמעאל (דף נד. ושם) ואין חילוק בין הנך לשאר ובפרהסיא בכולהו יהרג ולא יעבור ז):

טעמא דר"מ כדרב הונא כו'. פירש בקונטרס דמיירי פלוגתייהו במודה לוה שכתבו והיינו טעמא דר"מ דאין נאמנין דהואיל ולוה קיימו לא צריכי תו לעדים ולאו אפומייהו מקיים שטרא ורבנן סברי צריך לקיימו וקשה לר"י דא"כ ליפלגו בלא עדים בלוה גופי' הואיל וטעמייהו תלי בלוה ועוד דבפרק מי שמת (ב"ב דף קנד: ושם) משמע דלא פליגי בלוה דקאמר רבי יוחנן שאני אומר מודה בשטר שכתבו א"צ לקיימו דברי הכל היא ופריך והא מפלג פליגי אין נאמנים לפוסלו כו' אמר ליה אי אלימי עדים לאורועי שטרא איהו כל כמיניה ועוד דהוה ליה למימר בדרב הונא קמיפלגי ונראה לר"ת ולר"י דה"פ טעמא דר"מ כדרב הונא דכמו שאומר רב הונא דלא אמרינן מגו לפסול השטר בלוה ה"נ אומר ר"מ בעדים דאע"ג דאלימי לא פסלי שטרא במגו:

מודה בשטר שכתבו א"צ לקיימו. וא"ת ומ"ט לא מהימן במגו דאי בעי אמר מזויף וי"ל דשמא ירא לומר מזויף פן יכחישוהו וליכא מגו ופירש הקונט' במקום אחר דטעמא משום דדבר תורה א"צ קיום דעדים החתומים על השטר נעשה כמי שנחקרה עדותן בב"ד ורבנן הוא דאצרכוהו קיום כי טעין מזויף הוא אבל בשאר טענות כגון פרוע הוא לא הצריכוהו קיום וכן נראה לר"י ח) אבל אין לפרש דלא מהימן במגו לומר פרוע הוא משום דאי פרעיה שטרא בידיה מאי בעי דהא כי טעין נמי אמנה הוא מסקינן בסמוך אמילתיה דרב דלא מהימן והתם לא שייך האי טעמא:

אי סבירא לך כר"מ כו'. וא"ת ולמא משום הכי לא קאמר הלכה כר"מ משום דאיכא בפ' מי שמת (ב"ב קנד: ושם) דמפיך דר"מ לרבנן ויש לומר דהוה מצי למימר דהלכה כרשב"ג דאית ליה בהדיא בפ"ק דב"מ (דף ז.) דמודה בשטר שכתבו אין צריך לקיימו:

אימא הלכה כרבי מאיר. תימה דאפילו כרבנן נמי מצי סבר ושאני עדים דאלימי לאורועי שטרא דהכי אית ליה לרבי יוחנן ויש לומר דרב נחמן אין נראה לו לחלק ואם תאמר ולמא רב הונא מיירי במודעא ואמנה דאפילו רב נחמן מודה לקמן ויש לומר דרב הונא סתם קאמר ולא מפליג: **לעולם** דקאמר לוה וכדרב הונא כו'. ואם תאמר ואמאי לא קאמר נמי לעולם דקאמרי עדים וכדרב הונא ויש לומר דלא ניחא ליה לאוקמי דלא כרבנן דאמרי אלימי עדים לאורועי שטרא: **וכדרב** הונא אמר רב. וא"ת תרתי מילי דרב למה לי ° וי"ל דהדא מכלל חבירתה אתמר: **וכגון** שחב לאחרים. וא"ת ולהימניה במגו דאי בעי מחיל ליה דהא המוכר שטר חוב לחבירו וחזר ומחלו מחול (לקמן דף פה:) ויש לומר דלאו מגו הוא דשמא אין דעתו למחול ולהפסיד חובו דעכשיו שאומר אמנה הוא לא מפסיד מידי כיון שאין הלוה גזלן אע"ג דבספ"ק דב"מ (דף כ. ושם) אמרינן מגו כה"ג גבי מצא שובר בזמן שהאשה מודה יחזיר לבעל דקאמר ש"מ איתא לדשמואל שמא התם סמכינן אמגו כל דהו משום דאיכא שובר דמוכח ואם נאמר דמכירת שטר חוב אינו אלא מדרבנן הוה אתי שפיר דמצינן למימר דווקא מוכר שטר חוב דהוי מדרבנן יכול למחול אבל בנושה בחבירו כו' דחייב לו מן התורה אינו יכול למחול וכן משמע בפרק מי שמת (ב"ב דף קמז: ושם) דקאמר ומודה שמואל דאם נתנו במתנת ש"מ שאינו יכול למחול ומסיק מתנת ש"מ דאורייתא ואינו יכול למחול דאי ס"ד מדרבנן אמאי אינו יכול למחול משמע דבמידי דאורייתא אינו יכול למחול ויש לדחות דהתם ודאי אי מתנת שכיב מרע דאורייתא אין היורש יכול למחול דמאי אולמיה האי יורש מהאי יורש ועוד יש להביא ראיה דנושה בחבירו וחבירו בחבירו אינו יכול למחול דאמרי' בסוף האשה שנפלו (לקמן פא:) הרי שהיה נושה באחיו מנה ומת והניח שומרת יבם לא יאמר הואיל ואני יורש החזקתי אלא מוציאין מידו ולוקח בהן קרקעות והוא אוכל פירות ומוקמי' לה כר' נתן דהא הוי כמו נושה בחבירו מנה וחבירו בחבירו דכל אשר לבעלה משועבד לה לכתובתה ואי יכול למחול אמאי ילקח בהן קרקע ימחול לעצמו שהוא יורש ויכול למחול ויש לדחות דשאני התם דלאין יורש אלא מכחה ואינו יכול להפקיע זכותה [וי"מ דדוקא במוכר שט"ח יכול למחול שקדם חובו של מוכר אבל הנושה בחבירו שקדם חובו לחוב של חבירו אינו יכול למחול ושומרת יבם נמי קדם שטר חובה לחוב בעלה] וא"ת אכתי נהימניה במגו דאי בעי קלתיה כדאמרינן בסוף זה בורר (סנהדרין דף לא:) ויש לומר דהכא אתחזק בבי דינא דאמרינן התם כיון דאתחזק בבי דינא אי בעי קלתיה לא אמרינן אי נמי הכא מיירי כשהשטר הוא ביד שליש: **מנין** לנושה בחבירו כו'. משמע דהלכה כר' נתן ובגיטין (דף לז.) פירשנוה: ט) **אעולה** לא חתמי. והא דכותבין שטר ללוה אע"פ שאין מלוה עמו היינו למוסרו ללוה ולא למלוה: אם

עין משפט נר מצוה

כב א מיי' פכ"ד מהל' מלוה ולוה הלכה ה טוש"ע ח"מ סימן מו סעיף לח:
כג ב מיי' פ"ה מהלכות יסודי התורה הלכה א ב טוש"ע י"ד סימן קנז סעיף א:
כד ג מיי' פי"ד מהלכות מלוה ולוה הל' ה יג סמג עשין נד טוש"ע ח"מ סימן מו סעיף א וסימן פב סעיף א:
כה ד מיי' פ"ב שם הל' ה סמג שם טוש"ע ח"מ סימן מז סעיף א:
כו ה מיי' שם הלכה ו וסמג שם טוש"ע ח"מ סימן פו סעיף א:

מסורת הש"ס

א) ב"ב קנה. סנהדרין כט:, ב) סנהדרין עד., ג) שבת עט. ב"מ ז. עג. ב"ב קנד. קנה., ד) [יבמות לא. ב"ב קנג.], ה) פסחים לא. לקמן פב. גיטין לז. ב"ק מ: [קדושין טו.], ו) [דבור זה שייך לעיל קודם לדבור אלא אנוסים וכו'], ז) [וע"ע תוס' ע"ז נד. ד"ה יכול], ח) [ועיין תוס' לקמן כב. ד"ה קיום], ט) שייך לע"ב.

גליון הש"ס

גמ' אין לך דבר שעומד בפני פיקוח נפש. עיין סוטה דף ע"ב תוס' ד"ה נוח לו: תוס' ד"ה וכדרב הונא אמר רב וכו' וי"ל דהדא מכלל חבירתה. עיין כתובות במלחמות פ"ב דשבת ד"ה ועוד כתב הרי"ף הא דאמר"ג א"ר: באד דהדא מכלל חבירתה. כה"ג מגילה דף כט ע"ב בכורות דף לו ע"א:

תורה אור השלם

א) וְהִתְוַדּוּ אֶת חַטָּאתָם אֲשֶׁר עָשׂוּ וְהֵשִׁיב אֶת אֲשָׁמוֹ בְּרֹאשׁוֹ וַחֲמִישִׁתוֹ יֹסֵף עָלָיו וְנָתַן לַאֲשֶׁר אָשַׁם לוֹ: [במדבר ה, ז]

ב) אִם אָוֶן בְּיָדְךָ הַרְחִיקֵהוּ וְאַל תַּשְׁכֵּן בְּאֹהָלֶיךָ עַוְלָה: [איוב יא, יד]

ליקוטי רש"י

אא"כ נעשה בגדול. המוכר דקיימא לן (ב"ב דף קנו.) ולמכור נכסי אביו עד שיהא בן עשרים [סנהדרין כט:]. נותן ומקבל ועדים כולם גדולים ובקיאים [רשב"ם ב"ב דף קנה.]. **אין צריך לקיימו.** דכיון דמודה שכתבו ולוה בו הרי הוא כאלו קיימוהו חותמיו וגובה בו כל זמן שמוציאו [שבת עט.]. מאחר שלוה מודה שטר זה שכתבו הוא עליו שטר אמת הוא ואין המלוה צריך לקיימו שהרי לא הכחישו ולא אמר מזוייף הוא [ב"מ עג:]. **גנובא גנובי למה לך.** למה לך לשנות דבריך בלשון גניבה [רשב"ם ב"ב קנג.]. **אמאי לא מהימני.** והא איכא הפה שאסר הוא הפה שהתיר דאי בעו אמרו לא חתמנו [רשב"ם שם]. **לאשר אשם לו.** למי שנתחייב לו [במדבר ה, ז]. לאשר הלוהו לא נאמר אלא לאשר אשם לו לאשר הקרן שלו בבבא קמא אמרינן אשם זה קרן [פסחים לא.]. לאשר הקרן שלו ולא כתיב לאשר נושה בו [לקמן פב.].

תוספות רי"ד

אמר ר"ה א"ר מודה בשטר שכתבו א"צ לקיימו. פי' לוה שהודה שכתבו ועל פיו נחתמו העדים אין המלוה צריך לקיימו בעדים החתומים בו שכבר קיימו הלוה שהודה לו כי הוא כתבו והחתימו ואם טוען הלוה פרעתיך אינו נאמן שכבר השטר מקוים דכל שטר מקוים אין הלוה יכול לומר פרעתי דא"ל מלוה שטרך בידי מאי בעי ול"א בזה הפה שאסר הוא הפה שהתיר: **א"ל ר"נ** גנובא גנובא למה לך פי' המורה מתגנב אתה לומר דבריך בלשון שלא נחלקו היחיד והרבים כדי שלא יבטלו את דבריך דאמרת כיחידאה אי ס"ל כרבי מאיר אימא הלכה כר"מ פי' דפלוגתא דר"מ ורבנן הוא דר"מ אומר אצ"ל ורבנן אמרו צריך לקיימו ולא תנקוט לה למילתא באנפי נפשי' א"ל ומר היכי ס"ל פי' במודה בשטר שכתבו א"ל כי אתו לקמן פי' מלוים [המביאין] שטרות אמרינן להו זילו קיימו שטרייכו וחותו לדינא פי' כך אני רגיל לומר למלוים המביאים שטרותיהם לפני ואין עדיהם עמהן לכו ובקשו עדיכם וקיימוהו שאם לא תקיימוהו קיומו של לוה שמודה שכתבו אינו מועיל לך שהרי חוזר ואומ' פרעתיך וריש להאמינו ע"י מיגו ומש"ה טרח לקיים ושוב לא יהא נאמן לומר פרעתי והל' כר"נ בדיני שאינו נאמן עיין בפסקי בפ' מי שמת עיין לקמן: **אמר ר"י א"ר** האומר שטר אמנה הוא זה אינו נאמן. פי' המורה שטר אמנה שלא לוה כלום אלא כתבו ומסרו למלוה שאם יצטרך ללות ילוהו והאמינו שלא יתבענו אא"כ מלוהו ואינו נ"ל דמשמע מפירושו שהעדים נתנוהו ללוה והוא נתנו למלוה וא"כ אמאי קרי לי' לקמן עולה ולא מהימני עדים בזה והתנן כותבין שטר ללוה אע"פ שאין מלוה עמו וכ"ת הא אוקימנא לההוא בשטרא אקנייתא פי' שמקנהו לו נכסיו מהיום בין ילוה בין לא ילוה יגבה מהן לאותו זמן מהיום הרי אביי מעמידה בשטרי דלאו אקנייתא דאמר אביי הא דתנן כותבין שטר ללוה בלא מלוה אפילו בשטרא דלאו אקנייתא נמי וא"נ אתי למיטרף לקוחות מההיא זמנא והוא לא לוה עד תשרי לאו שלא כדין טריף דעדיו בחתומין זכין לו פי' מיום שחתמוהו יחול השעבוד ואפילו לא לוה המעות עד תשרי וכל ההיא חששא אינה שמא כתב ללוות בניסן ולא לוה עד תשרי ואתי למטרף לקוחות שלא כדין אבל לשמא לא הלוהו כלל לא חיישינן דאיהו דאפסיד אנפשי' דהימני' ומאי עולה איכא גביה סהדי אי איהו מהימן ליה וגם שטר אמנה מנין שלא יהיה אפילו בשטרא אקנייתא ואם העדים נתנוהו למלוה ברצון הלוה שצוה להם ליתנו לו אע"פ שלא ראו ההלואה בעיני' כשר וכשר הוא שאם הלוה רוצה להאמין למלוה שילוהו מה יש לעדים לומר לא ניתן לו השטר עד שנראה ההלואה בעינינו (דשמא לא ילוך הוא ברשת עלי ומאמין בו ואומר להם תנו לו השטר והעדים יעברו ע"י שלא ליתן) ובמתני' הכי תנן ואין כותבין למלוה עד שיהא לוה עמו ולא קתני עד שיראו מתן מעות אלא עד שיהא הלוה עמו דכיון דלוה עמו אם רוצה שיתנוהו למלוה יתנו ואם לאו לא יתנו והאיך קרי לה עולה דלמא יהיב ליה בינו לבינו ואי לא יהיב ליה לעולם איהו הוא דאפסיד אנפשיה ושטר כשר הוא וגובה בו ממשעבדי אלא ודאי שטר אמנה הוא שלא נעשה מתחלה ללוות בו אלא הלוה עשאו כדי להראות עצמו לעולם שאינו עשיר שהרי לוה מאחרים ומסרו למלוה ומאמין בו שלא יתבענו כלום אלא שיראה לעולם כי הוא חייב לו ומחפה עליו שלא יראה עשיר מפני שהוא אוהבו ודומה הוא לשטר פסים שלא נעשה בתחלה בעבור הלואה אלא המלוה פייס את הלוה עשה לי שטר שאתה חייב לי כך וכך כדי שאראה עשיר ויתנו לי אשה והאמן באהבתי שלעולם לא אתבעך בו ולשניהם פתרון א' אלא זה שעושה המלוה כדי שיראה עשיר קורא שטר פסים שצריך לפייס את הלוה שיעשה עליו שט"ח כי הוא חייב לו ויאמין בו שלא יתבענו ומה שהלוה כותב על עצמו כדי שיראה עני קורא אמנה שא"צ לפייס את המלוה בזה ושטר אמנה כזה ודאי הוא עולה שלא נעשה בשביל הלואה ואין העדים רשאים לחתום בו אבל שטר הלואה שנעשה כדי ללוות אין בו שום עולה כדפרי': **ואמרינן** דקאמר מאן אי לימא דקאמר לוה פשיטא פי' והלא עדים חתומים בו ופשיטא דיתקיים בחותמיו כל כמיניה ואלא דקאמר מלוה תבא עליו ברכה ואלא דקאמרו עדים אי כת"י יוצא ממקום אחר פשיטא דלא מהימני ואי אין כת"י יוצא ממ"א אמאי לא מהימני פי' והאיכא הפה שאסר הוא הפה שהתיר ומיגו דאי בעי אמרי לא חתמנו והשתא דאמרו חתמנו וכך היה ליהמנו א"ר לעולם דקאמר לוה וכדר"ה א"ר פי' כלומר ור"י נמי אשמעינן הכי דלוה שאומר כתבתיו ומסרתיו לו אבל שטר אמנה הוא א"צ המלוה לחזור ולהביא עדים להעיד על החתימה שאין נאמן לוה לפוסלו דלא עביד איניש דכתב ומסר בלא הלואה דאר"ה א"ר מודה בשטר שכתבו אצ"ל פי' וליתא לדרבא דאיהו מתרץ מילתא דרב אליבא דידיה דר"ה משמיה דרב קאמר ליה וכבר ר"נ פליג עלויה ואוקי מילתא כר"מ ולא כרבנן למימר דלית הל' כוותיה: **אביי אמר** לעולם דקאמר מלוה וכגון שחב לאחרים וכדר"נ דתניא ר"נ אומר מנין לנושה בחבירו מנה וחבירו לחבירו מנין שמוציאים מזה ונותנים לזה שנאמר ונתן לאשר אשם לו וק"ל כיון דאמרי' המוכר שט"ח לחבירו וחזר ומחלו מחול יהיה נאמן לומר שטר אמנה ע"י מיגו דמה לו לשקר אי בעי למיפטרי' הלוה מיד הנושים בו הוה מחיל ליה השתא דאמר שטר אמנה הוא יהיה נאמן דהכי אמרי' בשנים אוחזין ת"ר מצא שובר פי' שכתבה אשה לבעלה התקבלתי כתובתי ועודה תחתיו בזמן שהאשה מודה יחזיר לבעל אין האשה מודה לא יחזיר לא לזה ולא לזה ודייקינן עלה בזמן שהאשה מודה מיהת יחזיר לבעלה ואמאי ניחוש דלמא כתבה ליה בניסן ולא נתנה עד תשרי והוא לא פרע עד תשרי ואזלא היא בעודה תחתיו בין ניסן לתשרי זבנה לכתובתה לאחר בטובת הנאה מניסן ועד תשרי פי' בזול לפי שנותן מעותיו בספק שאם תמות היא ירשנה בעלה ומפסיד לוקח שלקחה ואם ימות הבעל או יגרשנה יהיה הלוקח במקומה לגבות כתובתה ושוב אין לבעלה לפרוע כתובתה אלא ללוקח ושובר שנכתב בשמה אינה כלום ומפיק ליה לשובר דכתב בניסן ואתי למיטרף לקוחות שלא כדין פי' שהשובר קודם לשטרו של לוקח ויחזיק הבעל בקרקע המיוחד לכתובתה ומהדרי' א"ר ש"מ איתא לדשמואל דאמר המוכר שט"ח לחבירו וחזר ומחלו מחול פי' ש"מ מדלא חיישינן להכי דא"נ הוה הכי שפיר זכה בעל השובר שנכתב בשמה הלכך אם

אָמַר לֵיהּ – **He said to [Rav Huna]:** כִּי אָתוּ לְקַמָּן לְדִינָא – **When [creditors] come to us for judgment** bringing uncertified documents, אָמְרִינַן לְהוּ זִילוּ קַיְּימוּ שְׁטָרַייכוּ וְחוּתוּ לְדִינָא – **we tell them, "Go certify your documents and** then **come down for judgment."**[8]

A related ruling is cited:

אָמַר רַב יְהוּדָה אָמַר רַב – **Rav Yehudah said in the name of Rav:** הָאוֹמֵר שְׁטָר אֲמָנָה הוּא זֶה – **If one says** concerning a note of indebtedness, **"This is a document** written **on trust,"**[9] אֵינוֹ נֶאֱמָן – **he is not believed.**

The Gemara wonders to whom this ruling applies:

דְּקָאָמַר מַאן – In Rav Yehudah's case, **who said** that the document was written on trust? אִילֵימָא דְּקָאָמַר לֹוֶה – **If you say** it is a case **where the borrower said** it, פְּשִׁיטָא – **it is obvious** that he is not believed! כָּל כְּמִינֵיהּ – **Is it in his power** to make such a claim against a valid document?[10] וְאֶלָּא דְּקָאָמַר מַלְוֶה – **And** if you say **rather** that Rav Yehudah refers to a case **where the lender said** that the note was written on trust, תָּבוֹא עָלָיו בְּרָכָה – **let a blessing come upon him** for admitting that his note is void! Why should he not be believed? אֶלָּא דְּקָאָמְרֵי עֵדִים – **Rather,** you might say that Rav Yehudah refers to a case **where the witnesses say** that the note they signed was written on trust. If so, I ask: אִי דִּכְתַב יָדָם יוֹצֵא מִמָּקוֹם אַחֵר – **If their handwriting can be verified from another source,** פְּשִׁיטָא דְּלֹא מְהֵימְנֵי – **it is obvious that they are not believed.**[11] וְאִי דְּאֵין כְּתַב יָדָם יוֹצֵא מִמָּקוֹם אַחֵר – **And if their handwriting cannot be verified from another source,** אַמַּאי לֹא מְהֵימְנֵי – **why are they not believed?**[12] What, then, is the case to which Rav Yehudah refers?

The Gemara presents a mnemonic for the names of the Amoraim whose answers will be cited:

(סִימָן בא״ש – **The mnemonic is** ***v'a'sh.***)[13]

The first answer:

אָמַר רָבָא – **Rava said:** לְעוֹלָם דְּקָאָמַר לֹוֶה – **Actually,** Rav Yehudah refers to a case **where the borrower said** that the document was written on trust, וּכְדְרַב הוּנָא – **and** his ruling is **in accordance with** the previously cited dictum of **Rav Huna.** דְּאָמַר רַב הוּנָא אָמַר רַב – **For Rav Huna said in the name of Rav:** מוֹדֶה בִּשְׁטָר שֶׁכְּתָבוֹ אֵין צָרִיךְ לְקַיְּימוֹ – **If one concedes that he drafted a document, [the holder] need not have it certified.**[14] Here too, the lender may collect on the basis of this note without further authentication of the signatures.

The second answer:

אַבַּיֵּי אָמַר – **Abaye said:** לְעוֹלָם דְּאָמַר מַלְוֶה – **Actually,** Rav Yehudah refers to a case **where the lender said** that the document was written on trust, וּכְגוֹן שֶׁחָב לַאֲחֵרִים – **and** the reason he is not believed is that this is **a case where [his admission] is detrimental to others.** For example, he has his own creditors, who wish to use this note to collect *his* debt to them,[15] וְכִדְרַבִּי נָתָן – **in accordance with** a ruling **of R' Nassan.** דְּתַנְיָא – **For it was taught in a Baraisa:** רַבִּי נָתָן אוֹמֵר – R' NASSAN SAYS: מִנַּיִן לְנוֹשֶׁה בַּחֲבֵירוֹ מָנֶה – FROM WHERE in Scripture can we derive THAT if ONE HAS A CLAIM OF A *MANEH* (i.e. one hundred *zuz*) AGAINST HIS FELLOW וַחֲבֵירוֹ בַּחֲבֵירוֹ – AND HIS FELLOW in turn has a claim of a *maneh* AGAINST HIS FELLOW – מִנַּיִן שֶׁמּוֹצִיאִין מִזֶּה וְנוֹתְנִין לָזֶה – FROM WHERE can we derive THAT WE TAKE the *maneh* FROM THIS last ONE [the debtor's debtor] AND GIVE IT directly TO THIS first ONE [the original creditor]?[16] תַּלְמוּד לוֹמַר ,,וְנָתַן לַאֲשֶׁר אָשַׁם לוֹ" – FOR [SCRIPTURE] STATES: *AND HE SHALL GIVE IT TO THE ONE TO WHOM HE IS GUILTY.*[17] In our case, if the lender himself owes money to other parties, they may collect directly from the one who borrowed from him. Since his admission that the note was written on trust is

NOTES

or he meant that the ruling is wrong because it represents a minority opinion? (*Shitah Mekubetzes;* see there for an alternative explanation).

8. For unless the creditor has the note certified, even if the debtor concedes it is authentic he can claim that he repaid the debt (*Rashi*) – in accordance with the Sages' opinion.

The halachah follows this view. If the debtor claims that he paid, or he enters any similar plea to dispute liability (e.g. the debt was contingent on a certain stipulation that the creditor did not fulfill), the creditor cannot collect on the basis of the note unless he has it certified (*Choshen Mishpat* 46:1, 82:1).

9. The person claims that the loan recorded in the note never took place. Rather, he states, the borrower wrote it in anticipation of taking the loan and handed it to the prospective lender, *trusting* that the latter would not present it for payment unless the transaction actually took place – but the latter broke his trust (*Rashi*).

10. Why, witnesses signed the document [indicating that the loan did take place]! Obviously, the lender should have it certified [and he may then use it for collection] (*Rashi*).

[Although Rav himself was cited above as stating that when a debtor concedes he drafted a document the creditor does not need to have it certified, that applies in the case where the debtor claims he repaid the debt. According to Rav, his claim is rejected despite his having the power of *happeh she'assar,* because it is disproven by the fact that the creditor has possession of the note. Here, however, where the creditor's possession of the note does not contradict the claim that it was written on trust, even Rav concedes that if the debtor has the power of *happeh she'assar* he is believed. Therefore, the creditor needs to have the note certified independently. Once he deprives the debtor of the power of *happeh she'assar,* he may collect on the basis of the note, for the claim that it was written on trust is too weak to be believed on its own merit (based on *Rashi* and *Shitah Mekubetzes* ד״ה לעולם דקאמר לוה; cf. *Rashba*).]

11. As we learned above (18b), once the signatures on a document are authenticated independently, the witnesses who signed cannot retract their testimony [כֵּיוָן שֶׁהִגִּיד שׁוּב אֵינוֹ חוֹזֵר וּמַגִּיד].

12. [Since they state in a single testimony that the signatures are theirs but the note was written on trust, they have the power of *happeh she'assar* and are able to void it!]

13. ב is for Rava; א is for Abaye; ש is for Rav Ashi.

14. Rav Yehudah, too, means to inform us that when the defendant admits to writing the document and handing it to the lender but claims that it was written on trust, the plaintiff does *not* need to have it certified. [Although the defendant is supported by the power of *happeh she'assar,*] his plea is rejected because it is highly unusual for a person to trust someone with a note when he has not borrowed the money (*Rashi*). I.e. Rav Yehudah informs us that since the plea is not credible, Rav rejects it despite the *happeh she'assar,* just as Rav Huna taught that Rav rejects a claim of payment even when it is supported by *happeh she'assar* (*Haflaah;* see *Shitah Mekubetzes*).

15. Shimon has a document stating that Reuven owes him money, but Shimon himself owes money to Levi. Furthermore, Shimon has no funds of his own with which to pay Levi, so Levi expected to collect his debt by going directly to Reuven and demanding the money that is due Shimon. (We shall learn shortly that Levi is entitled to do so.) Thus, Shimon's admission that Reuven's note was written on trust deprives Levi of the ability to collect his debt. Since the admission is detrimental to another party, it is not believed [in the face of the evidence presented by the note that the loan did take place] (*Rashi;* see *Tosafos* ד״ה וכגון; see further, *Kovetz Shiurim* vol. II §3).

16. That is, although Reuven did not borrow from Levi, if Levi demands payment from him he must recognize Levi as his creditor and litigate with him (*Shitah Yeshanah*). *Rashba* states that this applies only if Shimon does not have the means to pay Levi on his own. See also *Rashi* cited in the previous note. Cf. *Shach, Choshen Mishpat* 86:5.

17. The verse (*Numbers* 5:7) deals with a robber who denies under oath that he stole, but later confesses his guilt. Concerning such a case, the verse declares that the robber must pay the amount he stole plus a penalty of a fifth לַאֲשֶׁר אָשַׁם לוֹ, *to the one to whom he is guilty.* The plain meaning

חזקה אין העדים [א] חותמין על השטר אא"כ נעשה בגדול אלא אנוסין מ"ט אמר רב חסדא קסבר ר"מ עדים שאמרו להם חתמו שקר ואל תהרגו יהרגו ואל יחתמו שקר אמר ליה רבא השתא אילו אתו לקמן לאמלוכי אמרינן להו זילו חתומו ולא תתקטלון [ג] דאמר מר [ב] אין לך דבר שעומד בפני פיקוח נפש אלא עבודת כוכבים וגלוי עריות ושפיכות דמים בלבד השתא דחתמו אמרינן להו אמאי חתמיתו אלא טעמא דר"מ כדרב הונא אמר רב דא"ר הונא אמר רב [ד] מודה בשטר שכתבו אין צריך לקיימו גופא אמר רב הונא אמר רב מודה בשטר שכתבו אין צריך לקיימו א"ל רב נחמן [ז] גנובא גנובי למה לך אי סבירא לך כר"מ אימא הלכה כר"מ אמר ליה ומר היכי סבירא ליה אמר ליה כי אתו לקמן לדינא אמרינן להו [ג] זילו קיימו שטריכו וחותו לדינא א"ר יהודה אמר רב האומר שטר אמנה הוא זה אינו נאמן דקאמר מאן אילימא דקאמר לוה פשיטא כל כמיניה ואלא דקאמר מלוה תבוא עליו ברכה אלא דקאמרי עדים אי דכתב ידם יוצא ממקום אחר פשיטא דלא מהימני ואי דאין כתב ידם יוצא ממקום אחר אמאי לא מהימני (סימן בא"ש) אמר רבא לעולם דקאמר לוה וכדרב הונא דא"ר הונא אמר רב מודה בשטר שכתבו אין צריך לקיימו אביי אמר לעולם דאמר מלוה [ד] וכגון שחב לאחרים וכדרבי נתן [ט] דתניא רבי נתן אומר [ה] מנין לנושה בחבירו מנה וחבירו בחבירו מנין שמוציאין מזה ונותנין לזה תלמוד לומר [א] ונתן לאשר אשם לו רב אשי אמר לעולם דקאמרי עדים ודאין כתב ידם יוצא ממקום אחר ודקאמרת אמאי לא מהימני כדרב כהנא דא"ר כהנא אסור לו לאדם שישהה שטר אמנה בתוך ביתו משום שנאמר [ב] אל תשכן באהליך עולה ואמר

רש"י

אלא אנוסים מ"ט לא. נימא הפה שאסר הוא שהתיר: [י] **אא"כ נעשה בגדול.** כל מעשה השטר בגדולים הלוקח והמוכר וגבי עדים נמי אמרי' חזקה אין הלוקח מחתים בו קטנים: **יהרגו ואל יחתמו שקר.** הלכך כי אמרי נמי אנוסים היינו מחמת נפשות משוו נפשייהו רשעים: **מודה בשטר שכתבו.** לוה שהודה בשטר שכתבו ועל פיו נחתמו העדים: **אין המלוה צריך לקיימו.** בעדים החתומים בו שאין הלוה שוב נאמן לומר פרעתיו ולא אמרינן בהאי הפה שאסר הוא שהתיר דמכיון שאמר כשר היה הרי הוחזק השטר וכי אמר פרעתיו לא מהימן שהרי ביד המלוה הוא ור"מ נמי דאמר אין נאמנים לפוסלו במודה לוה שכתבו קאמר וקסבר לא צריכין תו לעדים ולאו אפומייהו מיקיים שטרא: **גנבא.** מתגנב אתה לומר דבריך בלשון שלא נחלקו בו היחיד והמרובים כדי שלא יבטלו את דבריך דאמרת כיחידאה: **אי סבירא לך כר"מ אימא הלכה כר"מ.** ולא תנקוט לה כמילתא באנפי נפשה: **ומר היכי סבירא ליה.** במודה בשטר שכתבו: **כי אתו לקמן.** מלוין מגבלין שטרות: **קיימו שטריכו.** כך אני רגיל לומר למלוים המביאים שטרותיהם לפני ואין עדיהם עמהם אני אומר להם לכו ובקשו עדיכם וקיימוהו דלאו הכי אע"ג דמודה לוה שכתבו מצי למימר פרעתיו: **שטר אמנה.** לא לוה כלום אלא כתבו ומסרו למלוה שאם יצטרך ללוות ילוה והאמינו שלא יתבענו אא"כ מלוהו: **כל כמיניה.** והלא עדים חתומים בו פשיטא דיתקיים בחותמיו: **כדרב הונא.** ולשמעינן רב יהודה נמי הכי דלוה שאמר כתבתיו ומסרתיו לו אבל שטר אמנה הוא אין צריך המלוה לחזור ולהביא להעיד על החתימה דלאו נאמן לוה לפוסלו דלא עביד איניש דכתב ומסר בלא הלואה: **שחב לאחרים.** בהודאה זו שהוא מודה שהוא שטר אמנה חב ומפסיד את אחרים הנושים בו ואין לו מה להגבותם והיו רוצים לגבות חוב זה: **ונתן לאשר אשם לו.** ולא כתב לאשר הלוהו אלא לאשר האשם שלו והאשם הוא קרן כדאמרי' בהגזל (ב"ק דף קי.) למי שהקרן שלו:

תוספות

חזקה אין כו'. הכא משמע דלא אמרינן מגו במקום חזקה ולרבנן אמרינן ול"ע דבעיא היא בפרק קמא דב"ב (דף ה: ושם) ולא אפשיטא גבי תבע אחר זמנו ואמר ליה פרעתיך תוך זמני: **דאמר** מר אין לך דבר כו'. פירוש אפי' מאן דמחמיר לא מחמיר אלא בהנך דרבה גופיה קסבר דאפילו בהני אינו חייב למסור עצמו בצינעא כמס' ע"ז בפרק ר' ישמעאל (דף נד. ושם) ואין חילוק בין הנך לשאר ובפרהסיא כולהו יהרג ואל יעבור [י]: **טעמא** דר"מ כדרב הונא כו'. פירש בקונטרס דמיירי פלוגתייהו במודה לוה שכתבו והיינו טעמא דר"מ דלאו נאמנין דהואיל ולוה קיימו לא צריכי תו לעדים ולאו אפומייהו מקיים שטרא ורבנן סברי צריך לקיימו וקשה לר"י ליפלגו בלא עדים בלוה גופי' הואיל וטעמייהו תלי בלוה ועוד דבפרק מי שמת (ב"ב דף קנד: ושם) משמע דלא פליגי בלוה דקאמר רבי יוחנן שאני אומר מודה בשטר שכתבו א"צ לקיימו דברי הכל היא ופריך והא מפלג פליגי אין נאמנים לפוסלו כו' אמר ליה אי אלימי עדים לאורועי שטרא איהו כל כמיניה ועוד דהוה ליה למימר כדרב הונא קמיפלגי ונראה לר"ת ולר"י דה"פ טעמא דר"מ כדרב הונא דכמו שאומר רב הונא דלא אמרינן מגו לפסול השטר בלוה ה"נ אומר ר"מ בעדים דאע"ג דאלימי לא פסלי שטרא במגו: **מודה** בשטר שכתבו א"צ לקיימו. וא"ת ומ"ט לא מהימן במגו דאי בעי אמר מזויף וי"ל דשמא ירא לומר מזויף פן יכחישוהו וליכא מגו ופירש הקונט' במקום אחר דטעמא משום דלדבר תורה א"צ קיום דעדים החתומים על השטר נעשה כמי שנחקרה עדותן בב"ד ורבנן הוא דאצריכוהו קיום וכן נראה לר"י [ח] אבל אין לפרש דלא מהימן במגו לומר פרוע הוא משום דאי פרעיה שטרא בידיה מאי בעי דהא כי טוען נמי אמנה הוא מסקינן בסמוך אמילתיה דרב דלא מהימן והתם לא שייך האי טעמא: **אי** סבירא לך כר"מ כו'. וא"ת ולמה משום הכי לא קאמר הלכה כר"מ משום דאיכא בפ' מי שמת (ב"ב קנד: ושם) דמפיך דר"מ לרבנן ויש לומר דהוה מצי למימר דהלכה כרשב"ג דאית ליה בהדיא בפ"ק דב"מ (דף ז.) דמודה בשטר שכתבו אין צריך לקיימו: **אימא** הלכה כרבי מאיר. תימה דאפילו כרבנן נמי מצי סבר ושאני עדים דאלימי לאורועי שטרא דהכי אית ליה לרבי יוחנן ויש לומר דרב נחמן אין נראה לו לחלק ואם תאמר ולמאי רב הונא מיירי במודעא ואמנה דאפילו רב נחמן מודה לקמן ויש לומר דרב הונא סתם קאמר ולא מפליג: **לעולם** דקאמר לוה וכדרב הונא כו'. ואם תאמר ואמאי לא קאמר נמי לעולם דקאמרי עדים וכדרב הונא ויש לומר דלא ניחא ליה לאוקמי דלא כרבנן דאמרי אלימי עדים לאורועי שטרא: **וכדרב** הונא אמר רב. וא"ת תרתי מילי דרב למה לי * וי"ל דחדא מכלל חבירתה אתמר: **וכגון** שחב לאחרים. וא"ת ולהימניה במגו דאי בעי מחיל ליה דהא המוכר שטר חוב לחבירו וחזר ומחלו מחול (לקמן דף פה:) ויש לומר דלאו מגו הוא דשמא אין דעתו למחול ולהפסיד חובו דעכשיו שאומר אמנה הוא לא מפסיד מידי כיון שאין הלוה גזלן אע"ג דבספ"ק דב"מ (דף כ. ושם) אמרינן מגו כה"ג גבי מצא שובר בזמן שהאשה מודה יחזיר לבעל דקאמר ש"מ איתא לדשמואל שמא התם סמכינן אמגו כל דהו משום דאיכא שובר דמוכח ואם נאמר דמכירת שטר חוב אינו אלא מדרבנן הוה אתי שפיר דמלינן למימר דווקא מוכר שטר חוב דהוי מדרבנן יכול למחול אבל בנושה בחבירו כו' דחייב לו מן התורה אינו יכול למחול וכן משמע בפרק מי שמת (ב"ב דף קמז: ושם) דקאמר ומודה שמואל דאם נתנו במתנת ש"מ שאינו יכול למחול ומסיק מתנת ש"מ דאורייתא ואינו יכול למחול דאי ס"ד מדרבנן אמאי אינו יכול למחול משמע דבמידי דאורייתא אינו יכול למחול ויש לדחות דהתם ודאי אי מתנת שכיב מרע דאורייתא אין היורש יכול למחול דמאי אולמיה האי יורש מהאי יורש ועוד יש להביא ראיה דנושה בחבירו וחבירו בחבירו אינו יכול למחול דאמרי' בסוף האשה שנפלו (לקמן פא:) הרי שהיה נושה באחיו מנה ומת והניח שומרת יבם לא יאמר הואיל ואני יורש החזקתי אלא מוציאין מידו ולוקח בהן קרקעות והוא אוכל פירות ומוקמי' לה כר' נתן דהא הוי כמו נושה בחבירו מנה וחבירו בחבירו דכל אשר לבעלה משועבד לה לכתובתה ואי יכול למחול אמאי ילקח בהן קרקע ימחול לעצמו שהוא יורש ויכול למחול ויש לדחות דשאני התם דאין יורש אלא מכחה ואינו יכול להפקיע זכותה [וי"מ דדוקא במוכר שט"ח יכול למחול שקדם חובו של מוכר אבל הנושה בחבירו שקדם חובו לחוב של חבירו אינו יכול למחול ושומרת יבם נמי קדם שטר חובה לחוב בעלה] וא"ת אכתי נהימניה במגו דאי בעי קלתיה כדאמרינן בסוף זה בורר (סנהדרין דף לא:) ויש לומר דהכא אתחזק בבי דינא דאמרינן התם כיון דאתחזק בבי דינא אי בעי קלתיה לא אמרינן אי נמי הכא מיירי כשהשטר הוא ביד שליש: **מנין** לנושה בחבירו כו'. משמע דהלכה כר' נתן וכגיטין (דף לז.) פירשנוה: [ט] **אעולה** לא חתמי. והא דכותבין שטר ללוה אע"פ שאין מלוה עמו היינו למוסרו ללוה ולא למלוה: אם

תוספות רי"ד

אמר ר"ה א"ר מודה בשטר שכתבו א"צ לקיימו. פי' לוה שהודה שכתבו ועל פיו נחתמו העדים אין המלוה צריך לקיימו בעדים החתומים בו שכבר קיימו הלוה שהודה לו כי הוא כתבו והחתימו ואם טוען הלוה פרעתיך אינו נאמן שכבר השטר מקוים דכל שטר מקוים אין הלוה יכול לומר פרעתי דא"ל מלוה שטרך בידי מאי בעי ול"א בזה הפה שאסר הוא הפה שהתיר: א"ל ר"נ גנובא גנובי למה לך. פי' המורה מתגנב אתה לומר דבריך בלשון שלא נחלקו היחיד והרבים כדי שלא יבטלו את דבריך דאמרת כיחידאה אי ס"ל כרבי מאיר אימא הלכה כר"מ פי' דפלוגתא דר"מ ורבנן הוא דר"מ אומר אצ"ל ורבנן אמרי צריך לקיימו ולא תנקוט לה למילתא באנפי נפשי' א"ל ומר היכי ס"ל פי' במודה בשטר שכתבו א"ל כי אתו לקמן פי' מלוים [המביאין] שטרות אמרינן להו זילו קיימו שטריכו וחותו לדינא פי' כך אני רגיל לומר למלוים המביאים שטרותיהם לפני ואין עדיהם עמהן לכו ובקשו עדיכם וקיימוהו שאם לא תקיימוהו קיומו של שמודה שכתבו אינו מועיל לך שהרי חוזר ואומר פרעתיך ויש להאמינו ע"י מיגו ומש"ה טרח לקיים שטרו ושוב לא יהא נאמן לומר פרעתי והל' כר"נ בדיני שאינו נאמן עיין בפסקי בפ' מי שמת עיין לקמן: אמר ר"י א"ר האומר שטר אמנה הוא זה אינו נאמן. פי' המורה שטר אמנה שלא לוה כלום אלא כתבו ומסרו למלוה שאם יצטרך ללוות ילוהו והאמינו שלא יתבענו א"כ מלוהו ואינו נ"ל דמשמע מפירושו שהעדים נתנוהו ללוה והוא נתנו למלוה וא"כ אמאי קרי לי' לקמן עולה ולא מהימני עדים בזה והתנן כותבין שטר ללוה אע"פ שאין מלוה עמו וכ"ת הא אוקימנא להוא בשטרא אקנייתא פי' שמקנהו לו נכסיו מהיום בין ילוה בין לא ילוה יגבה מהן לאותו זמן מהיום הרי אביי מעמידה בשטרי דלאו אקנייתא דאמר אביי הא דתנן כותבין שטר ללוה בלא מלוה אפילו בשטרא דלאו אקנייתא נמי וא"נ אתי למיטרף לקוחות מההיא זמנא והוא לא לוה עד תשרי לאו שלא כדין טריף דעדיו בחתומין זכין לו פי' מיום שחתמוהו יחול השעבוד ואפילו לא לוה המעות עד תשרי וכל ההיא חששא אינה שמא כתב ללוות בניסן ולא לוה עד תשרי ואתי למטרף לקוחות שלא כדין אבל לשמא לא הלוהו כלל לא חיישינן דאיהו דאפסיד אנפשי' דהימני' ומאי עולה איכא גביה סהדי אי איהו מהימן ליה וגם שטר אמנה מנין שלא יהיה אפילו בשטרא אקנייתא ואם העדים נתנוהו למלוה ברצון הלוה שצוה להם ליתנו לו אע"פ שלא ראו ההלואה בעיני' כשר וכשר הוא שאם הלוה רוצה להאמין למלוה שילוהו מה יש לעדים לומר לא ניתן לו השטר עד שנראה ההלואה בעינינו (דשמא לא ילוך הוא בושת עלי ומאמין בו ואומר להם תנו לו השטר והעדים יעברו ע"י שלא ליתן) ובמתני' הכי תנן ואין כותבין למלוה עד שיהא לוה עמו ולא קתני עד שיראו מתן מעות אלא עד שיהא הלוה עמו דכיון דלוה עמו אם רוצה שיתנוהו למלוה יתנו ואם לאו לא יתנו והאיך קרי לה עולה דלמא יהיב ליה בינו לבינו ואי לא יהיב ליה לעולם איהו הוא דאפסיד אנפשיה ושטר כשר הוא וגובה בו ממשעבדי אלא ודאי שטר אמנה הוא שלא נעשה מתחלה ללוות בו אלא הלוה עשאו כדי להראות עצמו לעולם שאינו עשיר שהרי לוה מאחרים ומוסרו למלוה ומאמין בו שלא יתבענו כלום אלא שיראה לעולם כי הוא חייב לו ומחפה עליו שלא יראה עשיר מפני שהוא אוהבו ודומה הוא לשטר פסים שלא נעשה בתחלה בעבור הלואה אלא המלוה פייס את הלוה עשה לי שטר שאתה חייב לי כך וכך כדי שאראה עשיר ויתנו לי אשה והאמן באהבתי שלעולם לא אתבעך בו ולשניהם פתרון א' אלא זה שעושה המלוה כדי שיראה עשיר קורא שטר פסים שצריך לפייס את הלוה שיעשה עליו שט"ח כי הוא חייב לו ויאמין בו שלא יתבענו ומה שהלוה כותב על עצמו כדי שיראה עני קורא אמנה שא"צ לפייס את המלוה בזה ושטר אמנה כזה ודאי הוא עולה שלא נעשה בשביל הלואה ואין העדים רשאים לחתום בו אבל שטר הלואה שנעשה כדי ללוות אין בו שום עולה כדפרי': **ואמרינן** דקאמר מאן אי לימא דקאמר לוה פשיטא פי' והלא עדים חתומים בו ופשיטא דיתקיים בחותמיו כל כמיניה ואלא דקאמר מלוה תבא עליו ברכה ואלא דקאמרו עדים אי כת"י יוצא ממקום אחר פשיטא דלא מהימני ואי אין כת"י יוצא ממ"א אמאי לא מהימני פי' והאיכא הפה שאסר הוא הפה שהתיר ומיגו דאי בעי אמרי לא חתמנו והשתא דאמרו חתמנו וכך היה ליהמנו א"ר לעולם דקאמר לוה וכדר"ה א"ר פי' כלומר ור"י נמי אשמעינן הכי דלוה שאומר כתבתיו ומסרתיו לו אבל שטר אמנה הוא א"צ המלוה לחזור ולהביא עדים להעיד על החתימה שאין נאמן לוה לפוסלו דלא עביד איניש דכתב ומסר בלא הלואה דאר"ה א"ר מודה בשטר שכתבו אצ"ל פי' וליתא לדרבא דאיהו מתרץ מילתא דרב אליבא דידיה דר"ה משמיה דרב קאמר ליה וכבר ר"נ פליג עלויה ואוקי מילתא כר"מ ולא כרבנן למימר דלית הל' כוותיה: **אביי אמר** לעולם דקאמר מלוה וכגון שחב לאחרים וכדר"נ דתניא ר"נ אומר מנין לנושה בחבירו מנה וחבירו לחבירו מנין שמוציאים מזה ונותנים לזה שנאמר ונתן לאשר אשם לו וק"ל כיון דאמרי' המוכר שט"ח לחבירו וחזר ומחלו מחול יהיה נאמן לומר שטר אמנה ע"י מיגו דמה לו לשקר אי בעי למיפטרי הלוה מיד הנושים בו הוה מחיל ליה השתא דאמר שטר אמנה הוא יהיה נאמן דהכי אמרי' בשנים אוחזין ת"ר מצא שובר פי' שכתבה אשה לבעלה התקבלתי כתובתי ועודה תחתיו בזמן שהאשה מודה יחזיר לבעל אין האשה מודה לא יחזיר לא לזה ולא לזה ודייקינן עלה בזמן שהאשה מודה מיהת יחזיר לבעלה ואמאי ניחוש דלמא כתבה ליה בניסן ולא נתנה עד תשרי והוא לא פרע עד תשרי ואזלא היא בעודה תחתיו בין ניסן לתשרי חבנה לכתובתה לאחר בטובת הנאה מניסן ועד תשרי בזול לפי שנותן מעותיו בספק שאם תמות היא ירשנה בעלה ומפסיד לוקח שלקחה ואם ימות הבעל או יגרשנה יהיה הלוקח במקומה לגבות כתובתה ושוב אין לבעלה לפרוע כתובתה אלא ללוקח ושובר שנכתב בניסן ומפיק ליה לשובר דכתב בניסן ואתי למיטרף לקוחות שלא כדין פי' שהשובר קודם לשטרו של לוקח ויחזיק הבעל בקרקע המיוחד לכתובתה ומהדרי' א"ר ש"מ איתא לדשמואל דאמר המוכר שט"ח לחבירו וחזר ומחלו מחול פי' ש"מ מדלא חיישינן להכי דא"נ הוה הכי שפיר זכה בעל השובר שנכתב בשמה הלכך אם

עין משפט נר מצוה

כב א מיי' פכ"ד מהל' מלוה ולוה הלכה ה טוש"ע ח"מ סימן סט סעיף לח:

כג ב מיי' פ"ה מהלכות יסודי התורה הלכה א ג טוש"ע י"ד סימן קנז סעיף א:

כד ג מיי' פ"ד מהלכות מלוה ולוה הל' ה יג סמג עשין נד טוש"ע ח"מ סימן סט סעיף א וסימן פב סעיף א:

כה ד מיי' פ"ב שם הל' ה סמג שם טוש"ע ח"מ סימן סט סעיף ה:

כו ה מיי' שם הלכה ו וסמג שם טוש"ע ח"מ סימן סו סעיף ה:

מסורת הש"ס

א) ב"ב קנה. סנהדרין כט:, ב) סנהדרין עד., ג) שבת עח: ב"מ ז. עב:, ד) [יבמות לא. ב"ב קנב.], ה) פסחים לא. לקמן פט. גיטין לז. ב"ק מ: [קדושין טו:], ו) [לדבור זה שייך לעיל קודם לדבור אלא אנוסים וכו'], ז) [וע"ע תוס' ע"ז מ: ד"ה יכול], ח) [ועיין תוס' לקמן כח. ד"ה קיום], ט) שייך לע"ב.

גליון הש"ס

גמ' אין לך דבר שעומד בפני פיקוח נפש. עיין סוטה דף י ע"ב תוס' ד"ה נוח לו: תוס' ד"ה וכדרב הונא אמר רב וכו' וי"ל דחדא מכלל חבירתה. עיין ברמב"ן במלחמות פ"ב דשבת ד"ה ועוד כתב הרי"ף הא דאמר ר"ה א"ר: באו"ד דחדא מכלל חבירתה. כה"ג מגילה דף כט ע"ב בכורות דף לו ע"א:

תורה אור השלם

א) וְהִתְוַדּוּ אֶת חַטָּאתָם אֲשֶׁר עָשׂוּ וְהֵשִׁיב אֶת אֲשָׁמוֹ בְּרֹאשׁוֹ וַחֲמִישִׁתוֹ יֹסֵף עָלָיו וְנָתַן לַאֲשֶׁר אָשַׁם לוֹ: [במדבר ה, ז]

ב) אִם אָוֶן בְּיָדְךָ הַרְחִיקֵהוּ וְאַל תַּשְׁכֵּן בְּאֹהָלֶיךָ עַוְלָה: [איוב יא, יד]

ליקוטי רש"י

אא"כ נעשה בגדול. המוכר דקיימא לן [ב"ב דף קנה.] ולמכור נכסי אביו עד שיהא בן עשרים [סנהדרין כט:]. נותן ומקבל ועדים כולם גדולים [רשב"ם ב"ב קנה.]. **אין צריך לקיימו.** דכיון שהודה שכתבו ולוה בו הרי זה כאלו קיימוהו חותמיו וגובה בו כל זמן שמוציאו [שבת עח:]. מאחר שהודה שטר חוב שהוציא עליו שטר אמת הוא אין המלוה צריך לחזור אחר העדים החתומים בו ולהעיד על חתימתו ולקיימו [ב"מ עב:]. **גנובא גנובי למה לך.** למסתם דבריך [רשב"ם ב"ב קנב.]. **אמאי לא מהימני.** והא אמרינן הפה שאסר הוא הפה שהתיר דלאי בעי שתקי [רשב"ם שם מט.]. **לאשר אשם לו.** למי שהחייב לו [במדבר ה, ז]. לאשר הלוהו לו לא נאמר אלא לאשר אשם לו לאשר הקרן שלו בבבא קמא אמרינן אשם זה קרן [פסחים לא.]. לאשר הקרן שלו ולא כתיב לאשר נושה בו [לקמן פב.].

חֲזָקָה אֵין הָעֵדִים חוֹתְמִין עַל הַשְּׁטָר – **There is a** legal **presumption that witnesses do not sign on a note** אֶלָּא אִם כֵּן נַעֲשָׂה בְּגָדוֹל – **unless it is made in adulthood.**[1] אֶלָּא אֲנוּסִין מַאי טַעְמָא – **But** in the case where the witnesses say, "We were **coerced," what is the reason** that they are not believed, according to R' Meir? Why, they have the power of *happeh she'assar.* – ? –

The Gemara answers:

אָמַר רַב חִסְדָּא – **Rav Chisda said:** קָסָבַר רַבִּי מֵאִיר – **R' Meir holds** that עֵדִים שֶׁאָמְרוּ לָהֶם חִתְמוּ שֶׁקֶר וְאַל תֵּהָרְגוּ – **if witnesses were told, "Sign falsely and you will not be killed,** but if you refuse to sign you will be killed," יֵהָרְגוּ וְאַל יַחְתְּמוּ שֶׁקֶר – **they should** allow themselves to **be killed rather than sign falsely.** Therefore, when they say that they signed under mortal duress they incriminate themselves.[2]

The answer is rejected:

אָמַר לֵיהּ רָבָא – **Rava said to [Rav Chisda]:** הַשְׁתָּא אִילּוּ אָתוּ לְקַמָּן לְאִמְּלוּכֵי – **Now, if they had come before us** (the court) while under duress **to consult** with us, אָמְרִינַן לְהוּ זִילוּ חֲתוֹמוּ וְלָא תִּתְקַטְלוּן – **we would** certainly **have told them, "Go sign** the false note **and do not be killed"** – דְּאָמַר מַר – **for the master has said:** אֵין לְךָ דָּבָר שֶׁעוֹמֵד בִּפְנֵי פִּיקּוּחַ נֶפֶשׁ – **You have nothing that stands in the way of mortal danger** אֶלָּא עֲבוֹדַת כּוֹכָבִים וְגִלּוּי עֲרָיוֹת וּשְׁפִיכוּת דָּמִים בִּלְבַד – **except for idol worship, illicit relations, and murder**[3] – הַשְׁתָּא דְּחָתְמוּ אָמְרִינַן לְהוּ אַמַּאי חֲתַמִיתוּ – **now that they signed,** can it be that **we tell them,** "**Why did you sign?**"[4]

The Gemara therefore presents another explanation of R' Meir's ruling:

אֶלָּא טַעְמָא דְּרַבִּי מֵאִיר כִּדְרַב הוּנָא אָמַר רַב – **Rather, R' Meir's reasoning is in accordance with** a dictum of **Rav Huna in the name of Rav.** דְּאָמַר רַב הוּנָא אָמַר רַב – **For Rav Huna said in the name of Rav:** מוֹדֶה בִּשְׁטָר שֶׁכְּתָבוֹ אֵין צָרִיךְ לְקַיְּימוֹ – **If one concedes that he drafted a document, [the holder] need not have it certified.**[5] Since the document is valid without the witnesses' certification, they cannot testify that it is void.

The Gemara elaborates on the ruling just cited:

גּוּפָא – **The text itself** stated: אָמַר רַב הוּנָא אָמַר רַב – **Rav Huna said in the name of Rav:** מוֹדֶה בִּשְׁטָר שֶׁכְּתָבוֹ אֵין צָרִיךְ לְקַיְּימוֹ – **If one concedes that he drafted a document, [the holder] need not have it certified.** אָמַר לֵיהּ רַב נַחְמָן – **Rav Nachman said to [Rav Huna]:** גְּנוּבָא גְּנוּבֵי לָמָּה לָךְ – **Why do you act deceitfully** and present this as an independent ruling?[6] אִי סְבִירָא לָךְ כְּרַבִּי מֵאִיר – **If you hold in accordance with R' Meir,** אֵימָא הֲלָכָה כְּרַבִּי מֵאִיר – **state** directly that **the halachah follows R' Meir.** – ? –

Rav Huna responds:

אָמַר לֵיהּ – **He said to [Rav Nachman]:** וּמַר הֵיכִי סְבִירָא לֵיהּ – **And how does master hold** regarding this matter?[7]

Rav Nachman answers:

NOTES

1. That is, witnesses would not sign a document of sale unless all the involved parties (e.g. the buyer and the seller) were adults. It follows that there is a similar presumption that the buyer [or lender] would not let witnesses sign on his note unless they were adults (*Rashi;* cf. *Rashi* to *Sanhedrin* 29b). [This is basically the same as the previous presumption that the lender would not rely upon invalid witnesses (*Tosafos* to 18b ד״ה קטנים; see *Beis Yaakov*). As above, the Sages maintain that this presumption of validity is outweighed by the power of *happeh she'assar* (*Tosafos* ד״ה חזקה).]

2. *Rashi.* Thus, R' Meir rejects their statement that they were coerced, because this testimony is self-incriminating.

The Rishonim state that Rav Chisda does not mean literally that according to R' Meir one must surrender his life to avoid testifying falsely. Martyrdom is required only in the face of three cardinal sins – idolatry, illicit relations and murder. What Rav Chisda means is that most people consider false testimony so loathsome that they would sooner die than testify falsely. When the witnesses say that they succumbed to mortal pressure and signed falsely, they are denigrating themselves. And according to R' Meir, just as self-incriminating testimony is unacceptable, so too, self-demeaning testimony is unacceptable (*Re'ah, Ritva;* according to *Shitah Mekubetzes,* this is *Rashi's* intent as well; cf. *Ramban, Rashba;* for further discussion, see *Shev Shmaatsa* 7:5, *Or Gadol* §1 p. 20b-21a, *Or Same'ach, Hil Eidus* 7:7, *Afikei Yam* vol. II §32).

3. One is not required to give up his life for any commandment of the Torah, other than these three (see *Sanhedrin* 74a). [See *Ritva,* and *Shulchan Aruch Yoreh Deah* 157:1 with *Shach* §1 for a discussion of whether one is *allowed* to sacrifice his life for the sake of another commandment.]

4. I.e. since the court would have advised them in the first place to sign the false note, if they claim that this is what they did, how can we reject their testimony as "self-incriminating" – even if the general population considers it reprehensible (*Re'ah;* see *Ramban* and *Ritva*).

5. I.e. if a man produces a note stating that his fellow owes him money, and the borrower concedes that he drafted the note and told the witnesses to sign but claims that he has paid off the debt, the lender does not need to have the note certified independently; the borrower is presumed to still be indebted. Although the borrower himself is the one who authenticated the note through his admission, and he would seem to have the power of *happeh she'assar,* his argument that he paid is not believable. Once he admits that he drafted the document, it is deemed a valid note of indebtedness, and his claim of payment is disproven by the fact that the lender still has the note. We do not rely upon *happeh she'assar* in the face of this evidence.

R' Meir refers to such a case – the borrower admitted that the note is authentic but claimed that he repaid the debt. Then, the witnesses came and testified that they signed the note but did so under duress. Since we do not need the witnesses to authenticate the note – as it was certified on the basis of the borrower's admission – they do not have the power of *happeh she'assar.* [Their testimony that the note is void is thus unacceptable, since it constitutes a retraction of an established testimony] (*Rashi,* as explained by *Maginei Shlomo, Haflaah, Chasam Sofer* [5573 ed.]; cf. *Tosafos* ד״ה טעמא and ד״ה מודה). The Sages, on the other hand, maintain that even though the borrower admitted that the note is authentic, his claim of payment is accepted unless the note is independently certified – for he has the power of *happeh she'assar* (*Rashi* to *Shabbos* 78b ד״ה במודה). Since the note is not considered fully certified on the basis of the borrower's admission – for the holder is unable to collect on its basis – when the witnesses say they signed under duress they, too, have the power of *happeh she'assar.* Therefore, their testimony is accepted (see below).

[Others explain the opinion that the borrower's claim of payment is not accepted as follows: Under Biblical law, any signed document is considered valid even without certification – because people generally did not have the audacity to forge documents. The Rabbis are the ones who required certification of documents (see below, 21b). According to Rav Huna, the Rabbis imposed this requirement only if the defendant claims specifically that the document is forged. Thus, the Rabbis did not revoke the validity of all uncertified documents; rather, they gave a claimant the right to challenge a document's authenticity. If the defendant does not claim that it is forged, Biblical law remains in force – and the validity of the document is not in doubt. Thus, in a case where the defendant admits that he drafted the note but claims he repaid the debt, he does not have the power of *happeh she'assar;* he did not validate the note, for in absence of his claiming forgery it is inherently valid! Since the note is inherently valid and is in the hands of the lender, the borrower cannot enter a claim of payment (*Tosafos* ד״ה מודה, citing *Kuntres* – i.e. *Rashbam* to *Bava Basra* 154a and 170a; *Rashba;* for further discussion, see *Even HaAzel, Hil. Malveh VeLoveh* 14:14 and *Hil. To'ein VeNitan* 14:8; *Kovetz Shiurim, Bava Basra* §426 and vol. II, 3:2-5; see also *Beis HaLevi* vol. III §42:3).]

6. Your ruling is actually a matter of Tannaic dispute, and it accords with the minority view of R' Meir (see previous note). Why do you state it as if it were undisputed and hide the fact that you are following a minority opinion? (*Rashi;* see *Shitah Mekubetzes*).

7. Rav Huna was uncertain whether Rav Nachman merely meant to chide him for failing to ascribe the ruling to R' Meir, its true originator,

A related Baraisa is cited:

תָּנוּ רַבָּנָן – **The Rabbis taught in a Baraisa:** אֵין נֶאֱמָנִים לְפוֹסְלוֹ – [WITNESSES] who authenticate their signatures on a document ARE NOT BELIEVED TO INVALIDATE IT. דִּבְרֵי רַבִּי מֵאִיר – These are THE WORDS OF R' MEIR.[24] וַחֲכָמִים אוֹמְרִים – BUT THE SAGES SAY: נֶאֱמָנִים – THEY ARE BELIEVED.[25]

The dispute is analyzed:

בִּשְׁלָמָא לְרַבָּנָן כִּי טַעֲמַיְיהוּ – The ruling of **the Rabbis is understandable in accordance with their own reasoning** – שֶׁהַפֶּה שֶׁאָסַר הוּא הַפֶּה שֶׁהִתִּיר – the witnesses are believed **because the very mouth that has forbidden is the one that has permitted.**[26] אֶלָּא לְרַבִּי מֵאִיר מַאי טַעְמָא – **But as for R' Meir, what is the reason** for his ruling? Let us apply the principle of *happeh she'assar.* – ? –

The question is qualified:

בִּשְׁלָמָא פְּסוּלֵי עֵדוּת – **All is well** concerning the case in which the witnesses say, "We were **unfit for testimony** when we signed," מַלְוֶה גּוּפֵיהּ מֵעִיקָּרָא מֵידַק דָּיֵיק וּמַחְתֵּם – because it is presumable that **the lender himself investigated** the witnesses **and had** them **sign** his document only after determining that they were fit.[27] קְטַנִּים נַמִּי – Concerning the case in which witnesses say, "We were **minors,**" R' Meir's ruling is **also** understandable, כְּדְרַבִּי שִׁמְעוֹן בֶּן לָקִישׁ – **in accordance with** a dictum **of R' Shimon ben Lakish.** דְּאָמַר רֵישׁ לָקִישׁ – **For Reish Lakish said:**

NOTES

that their initial concession is not deemed to have granted the note any validity whatsoever. Since the testimony of invalidation does not contradict an *established* written testimony, it is accepted and the document is deemed void (*Shitah Yeshanah* to 19b ד״ה הרי אלו נאמנין, *Kehillos Yaakov* 15:4). Thus, *happeh she'assar* erases the effect of their initial concession, leaving them in the position to void the note despite the authenticity of the signatures, but they must do this within the same utterance in order to abide by the rules governing the retraction of testimony.

In summation: This version of Rami bar Chama's explanation disagrees with the first version in two ways: (a) The original version held that even when a document is independently authenticated the witnesses can retract by saying that they signed falsely under mortal duress; the final version rejects this because the original testimony is considered as though it was examined in court and accepted; thus, like oral testimony, it cannot be retracted. (b) The original version held that when witnesses have the power of *happeh she'assar* they are allowed to say that they signed under financial duress, even though this testimony is self-incriminating; the final version holds that self-incriminating testimony is rejected even when supported by *happeh she'assar.* For discussion of how these two issues are related, see *Haflaah, R' Shlomo Eiger* cited in *Chidushei R' Akiva Eiger, Shaarei Yosher* 7:11 and *Kehillos Yaakov* §15.

24. R' Meir disagrees with the opening ruling of our Mishnah. He rules that even when the witnesses themselves authenticate the signatures, they cannot then say, "We were coerced" etc. (*Rashi*).

25. The Sages' opinion is that of our Mishnah.

26. [I.e. the Rabbis apply the principle of *happeh she'assar,* which was set forth in the previous Mishnah, on 16a.] As long as the witnesses do not incriminate themselves they are believed, as explained in note 23 (*Rashi*).

27. Since the witnesses concede that the loan or other transaction took place as recorded in the document, but merely claim that they were not fit for testimony at the time, R' Meir does not consider their claim believable. He deems it inconceivable that the lender would throw his money away and let invalid witnesses sign his document. Before letting them sign, the lender must have ascertained that they were fit to sign (*Rashi*). [The Sages nevertheless accept the witnesses' claim because they have the power of *happeh she'assar* (see *Tosafos* to 19a ד״ה חזקה).]

ובכולה בעי דלודי ליה והאי דלא אודי ליה כי היכי דלישתמיט ליה וסבר עד דהוה לי זוזי ופרענא ליה ורחמנא אמר רמי שבועה עליה כי היכי דלודי ליה בכוליה רבי אליעזר בן יעקב סבר לא שנא בו ולא שנא בבנו אינו מעיז והלכך לאו משיב אבידה הוי ורבנן סברי בו הוא דאינו מעיז אבל בבנו מעיז ומדלא העיז משיב אבידה הוי: **מתני'** א העדים שאמרו כתב ידינו הוא זה אבל אנוסים היינו קטנים היינו פסולי עדות היינו הרי אלו נאמנים ואם יש עדים שהוא כתב ידם או שהיה כתב ידם יוצא ממקום אחר אינן נאמנין: **גמ'** אמר רמי בר חמא לא שנו אלא שאמרו אנוסים היינו מחמת ממון אבל אנוסים היינו מחמת נפשות הרי אלו נאמנין אמר ליה רבא ב כל כמיניה ו) כיון שהגיד שוב אינו חוזר ומגיד וכי תימא הני מילי על פה אבל בשטר לא והא אמר ריש לקיש ג) עדים החתומים על השטר ג נעשה כמי שנחקרה עדותן בב"ד אלא כי אתמר ארישא אתמר הרי אלו נאמנין אמר רמי בר חמא לא שנו אלא ג שאמרו אנוסין היינו מחמת נפשות אבל אמרו אנוסין היינו מחמת ממון אין נאמנין ד) מאי טעמא אין אדם משים עצמו רשע תנו רבנן ה) אין נאמנים לפוסלו דברי רבי מאיר וחכמים אומרים נאמנים בשלמא לרבנן כי טעמייהו שהפה שאסר הוא הפה שהתיר אלא לר' מאיר מ"ט בשלמא פסולי עדות מלוה גופיה מעיקרא מידק דייק ומחתם קטנים נמי כדרשב"ל דאמר ריש לקיש חזקה

רש"י

לא שנא בו ולא שנא בבנו. ואפילו הוא קטן: **אינו מעיז.** ולהכי קרי ליה טוענת עצמו משום דטענת קטן בעלמא לית בה ממשא: **אבל בבנו מעיז.** ואפילו הוא גדול: **מתני' העדים שאמרו כו'.** שהיו מעידים על חתימתם לקיים את השטר: **פסולי עדות היינו.** קרובים או משחקים בקוביא: **הרי אלו נאמנים.** כיון דאין כתב ידם ניכר אלא על פיהם הפה שאסר הוא הפה שהתיר כי היכי דמהימנת להו אהא הימנינהו אהא: **יוצא ממקום אחר.** חתומים בשטר אחר שהוחזק בב"ד וכתוב בו הנפק וזה אותו שטר לפנינו עם זה וכתב חותמן דומין של זה לשל זה אין כאן הפה שאסר ואין נאמנים לומר פסולים היינו: **גמ' לא שנו.** דאם כתב ידן יוצא ממקום אחר אין נאמנין: **אלא שאמרו אנוסים היינו מחמת ממון.** דלאו כל כמינייהו לשווי נפשייהו רשעים בעדות פיהם ולפסול את השטר דאדם קרוב אצל עצמו ואינו נאמן על עצמו לא לזכות ולא לחובה בדיני נפשות ובפסולי עדות להעשות רשע ופסול על פיו ואלו פוסלים עצמן באומרים חתמנו שקר בשביל אונס ממון וריבוי טעמא משום הפה שאסר הוא הפה שהתיר: **מחמת נפשות.** שאמר בעל השטר הזה להרגנו ואדם חזק הוא: **כיון שהגיד שוב אינו חוזר ומגיד.** דגבי עדות תלה הגדה כתיבה אם לא יגיד וגו' (ויקרא ה) והכא נמי כיון דחתימי בשטרא היינו הגדה דידהו והיכי מהימני תו למיעקר הואיל וכתב ידן יוצא ממקום אחר בשלמא רישא כשאין כתב ידן יוצא ממקום אחר ועלייהו סמכינן כולה חדא הגדה היא דהא באותו דבור [בכדי] שאילת שלום קאמרי אבל אנוסים היינו אבל הכא לאו אפומייהו סמכינן: **הני מילי על פה.** כגון המעיד בב"ד ולאחר כדי דבור בא לשנות בו: **אבל בשטר לא.** דהגדה כתיב: **לא שנו.** דאמרינן הפה שאסר כו': **אלא דאמרי מחמת נפשות.** נאנסנו דלא משוו נפשייהו רשעים וכיון דעלייהו סמכינן הא בתוך כדי דבור עקרוה לסהדותייהו והפה שאסר התיר: **אין אדם משים עצמו רשע.** אינו נאמן לפסול את עצמו מחזקתו דקרוב הוא אצל עצמו וקרוב פסול לעדות: **אין נאמנין לפוסלו.** ארישא דמתניתין פליג העדים שאמרו כתב ידינו הוא אבל אנוסים היינו כו': **הפה שהתיר.** וכיון דמחמת נפשות קאמרי נאנסנו לא משוו נפשייהו רשעים ופסולי עדות דקאמרי היינו טעמא דלאו בעדותן משוו נפשייהו רשעים אלא דאמרי קרובים או עבדים היינו ועכשיו אנו משוחררים: **בשלמא פסולי עדות.** או קטנים כיון דמודים הם שהשטר כדין נכתב שההלואה או המקח אמת אבל אנחנו לא היינו רואים והויא לה כמלוה על פה או אי מכירה היא לא נקנה הקרקע בשטר זה אמר ר"מ דלא מהימני דא"כ מלוה לא שדי זוזי בכדי וכי מחתים עדים על שטרו מידק דייק שיהו כשרים:

אלא

תוספות

ובכולי בעי דלודי. פירש בקונטרס בב"מ (דף ג: ושם) דאתא לפרש דלא תימא אמאי נשבע נימא מגו דחשיד אממונא חשיד נמי אשבועתא ולהכי קאמר ובכולי בעי דלודי ליה ולא חשיד אממונא וקשה לר"י דהא אמר בפ"ק דב"מ (דף ה:) דלא אמרינן מגו דחשיד אממונא חשיד נמי אשבועתא ואין לומר דמן התורה חשיד נמי אשבועתא ומדרבנן הוא דאמרינן דלא חשיד לפי שראו שהיו מקילין בממון יותר משבועה ותקנו שבועה על החשודים כל זמן שלא נודע שהוא גזלן שכבר מן התורה עדיין אבל גזלן ידוע שפסול מן התורה לא תקנו ולפי זה שבועה שלא שלחתי בו יד היא מדרבנן ז) [ולא הויא דאורייתא אלא שבועה שלא פשעתי בה] והא דכתיב אם לא שלח לא שנשבע שלא שלח אלא ה"ק קרא נשבע שלא פשע אימתי בזמן שלא שלח בו יד דאם שלח בו יד חייב אפילו שלא פשע דנתחייב באונסים דהא גבי נסכא דרבי אבא (שבועות דף לג:) משמע דלאי אמר לא תפסי היה נשבע להכחיש את העד אע"ג דחשיד אממונא והתם הויא שבועה דאורייתא' דבשבועה דרבנן לא אמרינן מתוך שאינו יכול לישבע משלם כדמשמע בפ"ק דב"מ (שם) גבי ההוא רעיא ונראה דאתא לפרש דלא תקשי כיון דאין אדם מעיז יהא נאמן במה שכפר מקצת וכיון דמחייבינן שבועה אם כן מחשבו עזות פנים א"כ יהא נאמן במגו דאי בעי כפר הכל וקאמר דאין זו עזות מה שכופר קצת וא"ת כיון דלא חשיד אשבועתא למה גזלן פסול לשבועה ותירץ הר' יהודה חסיד דדוקא כשהוא חשוד על אותו ממון שבא לישבע אמרינן דלא חשיד אשבועתא דעל ידי השבועה יפרוש אבל אותו ממון שכבר גזל לא יפרוש ע"י השבועה וגבי ההוא רעיא דחשיב ליה גזלן משום דאכל תרי מינייהו אע"פ שצריך לפרוע הני תרי דאכל מ"מ לא יפרוש מן השאר משום שבועה דמה שמשלם בע"כ אין זה השבה מעליא וי"מ דגזלן כשר לשבועה מן התורה דלא חשיד אשבועתא אלא דמדרבנן פסלוהו כשהוא גזלן ואם תאמר ומאי שנא דלעדות פסול דכתיב אל תשת ידך עם רשע וגו' ולשבועה כשר וי"ל דבשבועת שקר יש בה עונש גדול דכתיב בה לא ינקה וכדאמר בשבועת הדיינין (שבועות דף לט.) שכל העולם כולו נזדעזע כשאמר הקב"ה (לא תשבעו ו)לא תשא ועוד דבעדות שקר ליכא אלא לא תענה ובשבועת שקר איכא לא תגזול ולא תשבעו ז) לשקר: **הרי אלו נאמנים.** וא"ת ולמה נאמנים והא מגו במקום עדים הוא דאנן סהדי שלא היו אנוסים ולא פסולי עדות דהא לקמן אמרינן תרי ותרי נינהו וי"ל כיון דהצריכו חכמים קיום הכא לא חשיב כלל קיום מה שאומרים כתב ידינו הוא זה כיון דאינהו גופייהו אמרי תוך כדי דבור קטנים או אנוסים היינו אבל לקמן חשבינן להו כשני עדים כיון דכבר מקויים הוא שכתב ידן יוצא ממקום אחר: **אין נאמנים.** הכא ליכא לאקשויי להימנו במגו דאי בעו אמרי פרוע הוא דכיון דמקויים הוא הוי מגו במקום עדים כדפירשנו ועוד דחוזרים ומגידים הם וכיון שהגיד שוב אינו חוזר ומגיד כדאמרי' בגמרא ועוד דבשני עדים לא אמרינן מגו וברישא נאמנים משום דאי בעו שתקי: **לא שנו אלא שאמרו אנוסים** היינו מחמת ממון. דלא מהימני משום דלא משוו נפשייהו רשעים וקטנים כדרשב"ל ופסולי עדות משום דמלוה גופיה מידק דייק כדאמרינן בסמוך: **מחמת נפשות הרי אלו נאמנים.** וא"ת וכי אמרו קטנים היינו או אנוסים מחמת ממון היינו להימנו במגו דאמרי אנוסים היינו מחמת נפשות דהא ברישא דאיכא מגו נאמנים לומר אנוסים היינו מחמת ממון וי"ל דאונס מחמת נפשות לא שכיח א] ועוד דבשני עדים לא אמרינן מגו כדפרישית: **ואין אדם משים עצמו רשע.** וא"ת והא קסבר רבא דפלגינן דיבורא בפ"ק דסנהדרין (דף ט: ושם) גבי פלוני רבעני לרצוני ופלוני בא על אשתי אם כן הכא נהימנו דאנוסים היו אבל לא מחמת ממון אלא מחמת נפשות דאליבא דרבא קיימא וי"ל כיון דקיום שטרות דרבנן לא פלגינן דיבורא כדי לפסול השטר ועוד דאין לנו לומר מעצמינו דאנוסים היו מחמת נפשות דאונס מחמת נפשות לא שכיח כדפרישית אבל התם שכיח שבא על אשת איש אחרת כמו על אשתו או שרבעו אדם אחר וכן בהרגתיו בספ"ב דיבמות (דף כה: ושם) יכול להיות דאדם אחר הרגו אי נמי שאני הכא דמחמת ממון או מחמת נפשות הוי פירושא דאנוסים היינו הלכך לא פלגינן דיבורא אבל לרצונו ובא על אשתו הוי דיבור בפ"ע א"נ הכא עיקר עדות הוא במה שאומרים אנוסים היינו שבאו לומר שלא ראו המלוה א"כ מיד עושין עצמן רשעים כיון שחתמו אם לא יעשו פירוש לדבריהם הלכך לא שייך הכא פלגינן דיבורא אבל ההיא דהרגתיו עיקר עדות הוא לומר שנהרג להשיא את אשתו וכן פלוני רבעו או בא על אשתו עיקר עדות להרוג פלוני הלכך פלגינן דיבורא ולגבי להשים עצמו רשע או לגבי אשתו לא יהא נאמן: **מלוה** גופיה מידק דייק. ולרבנן אפי' מלוה על פה לא הויא דבעינן שיהא תחלתו וסופו בכשרות כדאמרי' ביש נוחלין (ב"ב דף קכח. ושם): **קטנים** נמי כדרשב"ל. ה"מ למימר וקטנים נמי משום דמלוה גופיה מידק דייק אלא דניחא ליה למינקט בכל חד טעמא אחרינא א"נ טעמא דריש לקיש גופיה נמי משום דמלוה מידק דייק והא דלא מייתי דרשב"ל אפסולי עדות משום דר"ל לא הזכיר אלא קטנים בדבריו:

חזקה

עין משפט נר מצוה

כא א ב ג מיי' פ"ג מהלכות עדות הל' ו ז סמג עשין קט טוש"ע ח"מ סימן מו סעיף ם [וברב אלפס עוד בסנהדרין פ"ג דף רטו]:

תוספות רי"ד

מתני' העדים שאמרו כתב ידינו הוא זה אבל אנוסים היינו קטנים היינו פסולי עדות היינו הרי אלו נאמנים ואם יש עדים שהוא כתב ידם או שהיה כתב ידן יוצא ממקום אחר אין נאמנים. פי' ראובן הוציא שט"ח על שמעון ושמעון טען איני מכיר חתימת העדים ושמא מזייף הוא אינו יכול ראובן לגבות בו עד שלא יקיים שטרו או באו העדים הם עצמן לפני ב"ד ואמרו כתב ידינו הוא זה וקיימוהו וחזרו ואמרו אנוסים היינו מחמת נפשות כדאמר לקמן ובשקר חתמנו אלא כדי להציל את נפשנו עשינו וחתמנו שאין לך דבר שעומד בפני פקוח נפש או שאמרו קטנים היינו בשעה שחתמנו או בעת שראינו ההלואה בעינינו וראיית הקטן אינה ראייה ואע"פ שבשעת הגדה הוא גדול דתניא ראה או ידע עד שלא יגיד נשא עונו בעינן שתהא הראייה והגדה בכשרות או שאמרו פסולים היינו מחמת קורבה שהיינו בשעת הכתיבה או בעת המלוה קרובים ללוה או למלוה או העדים זה לזה ונתרחקנו עכשיו ועדותנו הוא בטלה הרי אלו נאמנים משום מגו. דאי בעי אמרי אין זה כתב ידינו הוא אבל התימתנו בטלה מחמת הטענות האלו הם נאמנים אבל אם יש עדים אחרים שמכירים חתימתן ואומרים לב"ד שזו היא חתימתן ומקיימים השטר על פיהם או שכתב ידן יוצא ממקום אחר שכבר חתמו בשטר אחר שהוחזק ונתקיים בב"ד וב"ד רואים זה וזה ומשוין אותן ונתחברין שזו היא חתימתן אומרים אלו הטענות לבטל השטר אין נאמנים שכיון שחתמו השטר בחזקת כשרות הוא דסתמא דמילתא החותם השטר בכשרות חותם וכיון שחתמו והגיד שוב אינן חוזרין ומגידים דבריהא דאית להו מגו מהימנו אבל השתא דליכא להו מגו לא מהימנו אלא השטר מקוים ע"פ אחרים ופי' המורה פסולים היינו קרובים או משחקין בקוביא ואינו נ"ל שיהיו נאמנין לומר משחקי בקוביא דאמרינן לקמן שאין אדם נאמן לשום עצמו רשע ואפילו ע"י מגו הלכך אין לפרש פסולים היינו אלא מחמת קורבה: א"ר ב"ח לא שנו פי' שאם כתב ידם יוצא ממקום אחר אינן נאמנים אלא שאמרו אנוסים היינו מחמת ממון פי' שהיה אונס את ממוננו אם לא היינו חתמנו לו שקר בזה ודאי אין נאמנים כשהשטר מתקיים ע"פ אחרים שאין אדם רשאי להחתם שקר כדי להציל את ממונו והמפרש פי' דלאו כל כמינייהו לשווי נפשייהו רשעי בעדות פיהם ולפסול השטר דאדם קרוב אצל עצמו ואין אדם נאמן על עצמו לא לזכות ולא לחובה אבל אנוסים היינו מחמת נפשות נאמנים פי' שאין לך דבר שעומד בפני פיקוח נפש. **א"ל רבא** כיון שהגיד שוב אינו חוזר ומגיד וכ"ת ה"מ ע"פ פי' כגון המעיד בב"ד ולאחר כדי דיבור בא לשנות בו אבל בשטר לא והאמר ר"ל עדים החתומים בשטר נעשה כמי שנחקרה עדותן בב"ד פי' מ"ה אמר כמו שנחקרה עדותן ולא אמר כמו שהגידו עדותן בב"ד שאם הגידו ועדיין לא נחקרה עדותן יכולין לחזור בהם ולומר שקר העדנו דתניא בתוספתא דפ"ב דכתובות העדים שאמרו מעידים אנו בפלוני שהוא בן גרושה בן חלוצה נתין וממזר עד שלא נחקרה עדותן אמרו בדאים אנו נאמנים ואם משנחקרה עדותן אמרו בדאים אנו אין נאמנים כללו של דבר העדים שהעידו לטמא ולטהר לקרב ולרחק עד שלא נחקרה עדותן נאמנים ואם משנחקרה עדותן אין נאמנים. **אלא** אי איתמר אהא איתמר הרי אלו נאמנים אמר רמי בר חמא לא שנו אלא שאמרו אנוסים היינו מחמת נפשות אבל אמרו אנוסים היינו מחמת ממון אין נאמנים מ"ט אין אדם משים עצמו רשע ואפילו ע"י מגו פי' שאין נאמנים לפסול עצמו מחזקתו דקרוב הוא אצל עצמו וקרוב פסול לעדות:

מסורת הש"ס

א) [ב"ב קסח. סנהדרין מד. מכות ג:], ב) [גיטין ג.], ג) [עי' תוספות לקמן כח. ד"ה קיום], ד) סנהדרין ט: כה. יבמות כה:, ה) ב"ב קנד., ו) נ"י כ"י, ז) נ"ל בשמו. יעב"ץ.

הגהות מהר"ב רנשבורג

א] תד"ה מחמת כו' ועוד דבשני עדים לא אמרינן כו'. עי' קדושין מג ע"ב תד"ה והשתא וכו':

ליקוטי רש"י

[תחילת לקוטי רש"י ששייך לכאן נדפס בעמוד א']

אין אדם משים עצמו רשע. אינו נאמן לפסול עצמו מחזקתו דקרוב הוא אצל עצמו וקרוב פסול לעדות והעדים שאמרו כתב ידינו הוא אבל אנוסין היינו וכו' כיון דמחמת נפשות קאמרי דנאנסו לא משוו נפשייהו רשעים, ופסולי עדות דקאמרי לאו בעדותן שוו נפשייהו רשעים אלא דאמרי קרובים או עבדים היינו ועכשיו אנו משוחררין [רש"י כת"י בשיטמ"ק]. אין אדם משים את עצמו עדות אלא עצמו לגיעת רשע והא דקי"ל (ב"מ דף ג:) הודאת פיו כמאה עדים דמי ה"מ לממונא אבל לקנסא ולעונש מלקות ולפסול לא [יבמות כה:]. אין אדם נפסל בעדות בהודאת פיו דאדם קרוב אצל עצמו הלכך אין אדם יכול לשום עצמו רשע כלומר על עדות עצמו אינו נעשה רשע שהרי תורה פסלה קרוב לעדות [סנהדרין ט:]. אינו יכול לפסול עצמו על פיו דהא אין קרוב מעיד לא לזכות ולא לחובה ואדם קרוב אצל עצמו [שם כה.]. אין נאמנין כו'. דתנן התם העדים שאמרו כתב ידינו הוא זה אבל אנוסים היינו קטנים היינו פסולי עדות היינו הרי אלו נאמנים דהפה שאסר הוא הפה שהתיר ואמר בגמרא אין נאמנין לפסלו דברי ר"מ ופליג אמתני' דלא חיש לפה שאסר גבי שטרות דלא מחתמי ישראל על כך ומפרש התם במתקנה טעמא דקסבר ר"מ מודה בשטר שכתבו לוה שלא [דכיון] שמלוה לקיימו [דשמר לו] אם כתבו לו לא מהימני עדים למפסליה שהרי אין לך קיום גדול מזה שלוה מודה שכתבו ומשמצא הלוה שכתבו ומה שכתבו נעשה כבפסלות וכמו שכתב ידן יוצא ממקום אחר דהיא דתנן התם אין נאמנין דלאו כאן הפה שאסר. וחכמים אומרים נאמנים. דאע"ג דמודה לוה שכתבו צריך לקיימו וכיון שאינו מתקיים כי אם ע"פ עדים הללו שאומרים כתב ידינו הוא זה והא קאמרי נמי קטנים היינו ונאמנים דהפה שאסר הוא הפה שהתיר [רשב"ם ב"ב קנד.].

Is it in [a witness'] power to testify that he was coerced because of mortal danger? כֵּיוָן שֶׁהִגִּיד שׁוּב אֵינוֹ חוֹזֵר וּמַגִּיד – But there is a rule that **once [a witness] has testified** and completed his testimony **he cannot testify again** and retract his words.[17] Since by signing the document the witnesses testified that it is valid, once their signatures are authenticated independently how can they testify that it is void?[18]

Rava suggests a possible solution and immediately rejects it: וְכִי תֵּימָא הָנֵי מִילֵּי עַל פֶּה – **And if you will say** that **this** (the rule that a witness cannot retract his previous testimony) **applies** only **regarding** testimony that is offered **orally** in court,[19] אֲבָל בִּשְׁטָר לֹא – **but** regarding testimony recorded **in a document** it does **not** apply,[20] I will respond: וְהָא אָמַר רֵישׁ לָקִישׁ – **But Reish Lakish said:** עֵדִים הַחֲתוּמִים עַל הַשְּׁטָר – **Witnesses who are signed on a document** נַעֲשָׂה כְּמִי שֶׁנֶּחְקְרָה עֵדוּתָן בְּבֵית דִּין – **are considered as if their testimony has been examined in court** and accepted.[21] – ? –

The Gemara therefore revises Rami bar Chama's statement: אֶלָּא כִּי אִתְּמַר – **Rather, when was** Rami bar Chama's **statement made?** אַרֵישָׁא אִתְּמַר – **It was made in reference to the first clause** of the Mishnah, which states that if the witnesses themselves are our only source for authenticating the signatures and they say they were coerced, הֲרֵי אֵלּוּ נֶאֱמָנִין – THEY ARE BELIEVED. אָמַר רָמִי בַּר חָמָא – Regarding this ruling, **Rami bar Chama said:** לֹא שָׁנוּ אֶלָּא שֶׁאָמְרוּ אֲנוּסִין הָיִינוּ מֵחֲמַת נְפָשׁוֹת – **They taught** this **only** concerning a case **where [the witnesses] said, "We were coerced because of** a threat to our **lives."**[22] אֲבָל אָמְרוּ אֲנוּסִין הָיִינוּ מֵחֲמַת מָמוֹן – **But if they said, "We were coerced because of** a threat to our **finances,"** אֵין נֶאֱמָנִין – **they are not believed.** מַאי טַעְמָא – **What is the reason?** אֵין אָדָם מֵשִׂים עַצְמוֹ רָשָׁע – **A person cannot establish himself as a criminal.**[23]

NOTES

17. The Torah states concerning a witness who is asked by a litigant to testify (*Leviticus* 5:1): אִם־לוֹא יַגִּיד וְנָשָׂא עֲוֹנוֹ, *If he does not testify he shall bear his iniquity.* This implies that a witness has only one opportunity to relate his testimony. [I.e. the implication is that a witness who has information is liable only if he does not testify at all. But if he does testify he is free of sin even if he later retracts and denies any knowledge of the facts in question. The reason must be that once he has testified he cannot retract, so his denial is irrelevant] (*Rashi,* as explained by *Shitah Mekubetzes; cf. Rabbeinu Yonah, Ritva*).

18. It is understandable that in the Mishnah's first case – where the witnesses themselves authenticate their signatures – they are able to add that the document is invalid. Since after saying, "These are our signatures," the witnesses continue in the same utterance [תוך כְּדֵי דיבור] with "but we were coerced," the authentication and invalidation are a single testimony. But in the case where we have independent authentication of the signatures, their statement of invalidation is in effect a retraction of an established testimony (*Rashi*).

One might ask: Even in the case where we rely upon the witnesses themselves for authentication, once they concede that they signed the note it emerges that they testified about the transaction at the moment of signing. How can they now testify that the signatures are invalid? The answer is that since the document is worthless until it is certified, the testimony of the signatories is deemed to be concluded only through the certification. As long as the invalidating testimony comes in the same utterance as the certifying testimony, it is acceptable (*Kehillos Yaakov* 15:4, based on *Shitah Mekubetzes* to 19b ד״ה הרי אלו נאמנין; see note 23 for further elaboration).

However, this applies only in the case where they authenticate the signatures themselves. In the case where there is independent authentication, they cannot retract even by saying that they were under a mortal threat – since their written testimony has already been established (*Rashi*).

19. That is, when a witness has finished testifying in court, he may not add to his testimony after "the time it takes to make an utterance" [כְּדֵי דבור] has passed (*Rashi;* see *Sma* 29:1 and *Beur HaGra* ad loc.).

20. Because the verse from which we derive the rule against double testimony (see note 17) uses the term יַגִּיד, which implies a *spoken* testimony (*Rashi;* see *Chasam Sofer,* 5562 version, at length). Thus, perhaps the signatories on a note are allowed to retract their written testimony.

21. I.e. just as witnesses who testified in court cannot recant their testimony, so too, witnesses who signed a document cannot retract (*Yerushalmi* 2:3, cited by *Ramban, Re'ah* and *Ritva;* see *Sma* and *Beur HaGra* ibid.; see also *Rashash*). Since documents require certification, this applies only after the note has been certified (see *Shitah Yeshanah* to the Mishnah). At any rate, how can you say concerning the case where the signatures have been authenticated independently that if the witnesses claim they signed falsely because of mortal danger they are believed?

22. In this case, they are not incriminating themselves. Since we rely on them to authenticate their signatures – and they stated the retraction within the same utterance as the authentication – we must accept it, for they have the power of *happeh she'assar* (*Rashi;* see following note for elaboration).

23. A person who was considered a reliable witness cannot disqualify himself from fitness with a self-incriminating statement, because a person is unfit to testify about his relative, and everyone is related to himself (*Rashi*). Therefore, we accept the statement that these are their signatures and discard the statement that they signed under financial duress (see note 15).

According to this version of Rami bar Chama's statement, self-incriminating testimony is not accepted even when the witnesses have the power of *happeh she'assar.* [For various explanations of the reason, see *Haflaah, R' Shlomo Eiger* (cited in *Chidushei R' Akiva Eiger*) and *Kehillos Yaakov* 15:1-2.] Thus, the witnesses are believed only if they say that they were coerced by a mortal threat. Concerning the case in which they say, "We were unfit for testimony," the meaning must be that at the time they signed they were related to one of the parties [through marriage], or they were Canaanite slaves who were later emancipated. Thus, their words are not self-incriminating (for they are not testifying that they are unfit *now*). If they were to say that they had been gamblers, they would be incriminating themselves and would not be believed (*Rashi* ד״ה הפה שהתיר; see *Shitah Mekubetzes*). [*Rashi's* earlier explanation (see note 11) that they mean they were gamblers followed the first version of Rami bar Chama's opinion, which considers self-incriminating testimony acceptable when the power of *happeh she'assar* exists. According to the latter version, however, this testimony is void (*Shitah Mekubetzes; cf. Pnei Yehoshua* and *Chasam Sofer* to the Mishnah).]

Testimony that is nonincriminating (i.e. "We were coerced by a mortal threat") is accepted when the witnesses have the power of *happeh she'assar.* However, *Rashi* adds (see previous note) that the witnesses must also state the retraction within the same utterance as the authentication. *Rashi* does not mean that *happeh she'assar* is subject to a time limit. Rather, he means that since these people are speaking in the capacity of *witnesses* they must state the retraction immediately, for witnesses cannot retract testimony after it is accepted [כֵּיוָן שֶׁהִגִּיד שוב אינו חוזר ומגיד]. Any retraction of testimony – even one that is based on *happeh she'assar* – must occur within the same utterance as the authentication (*Hashlamah,* cited by *Shitah Mekubetzes* to 23a; see also *Shitah Yeshanah* to the Mishnah; cf. *Bach, Kuntres Acharon* to *Even HaEzer* 47:2; see Chapter Introduction for further discussion).

One might ask: Since witnesses are allowed to retract testimony within the time of an utterance, why are they believed here only on the basis of *happeh she'assar*? The answer is that if after saying, "These are our signatures," they would immediately make a complete retraction and state, "No, these are not our signatures," they would indeed be believed without *happeh she'assar.* However, since they stand by the statement that the signatures are theirs and merely claim that the signatures are *invalid,* they require the power of *happeh she'assar.* For according to their concession of authenticity, it emerges that *at the moment of signing the note* they attested to the transaction recorded in it; the statement "We were coerced" comes too late to be acceptable on its own merit! It is because they have the power of *happeh she'assar* that their authentication of the note – and by extension, the original testimony itself – is tentative even after their concession that the signatures are theirs. By concluding that they signed under duress or as minors or relatives, they nullify their authentication, with the effect

ובכולה בעי דלודי ליה והאי דלא אודי ליה כי היכי דלישתמיט ליה וסבר עד דהוה לי זוזי ופרענא ליה ורחמנא אמר רמי שבועה עליה כי היכי דלודי ליה בכוליה רבי אליעזר בן יעקב סבר לא שנא בו ולא שנא בבנו אינו מעיז והלכך לאו משיב אבידה הוי ורבנן סברי בו הוא דאינו מעיז אבל בבנו מעיז ומדלא העיז משיב אבידה הוי: **מתני׳** [א] העדים שאמרו כתב ידינו הוא זה אבל אנוסים היינו קטנים היינו פסולי עדות היינו הרי אלו נאמנים ואם יש עדים שהוא כתב ידם או שהיה כתב ידם יוצא ממקום אחר אינן נאמנין: **גמ׳** אמר רמי בר חמא לא שנו אלא שאמרו אנוסים היינו מחמת ממון אבל אנוסים היינו מחמת נפשות הרי אלו נאמנין אמר ליה רבא [ב] כל כמיניה כיון שהגיד שוב אינו חוזר ומגיד וכי תימא הני מילי על פה אבל בשטר לא והא אמר ריש לקיש עדים החתומים על השטר [ג] נעשה כמי שנחקרה עדותן בב״ד אלא כי אתמר ארישא אתמר הרי אלו נאמנין אמר רמי בר חמא לא שנו אלא [ג] שאמרו אנוסין היינו מחמת נפשות אבל אמרו אנוסין היינו מחמת ממון אין נאמנין [ד] מאי טעמא אין אדם משים עצמו רשע תנו רבנן [ה] אין נאמנים לפוסלו דברי רבי מאיר וחכמים אומרים נאמנים בשלמא לרבנן כי טעמייהו שהפה שאסר הוא הפה שהתיר אלא לר׳ מאיר מ״ט בשלמא פסולי עדות מלוה גופיה מעיקרא מידק דייק ומחתם קטנים נמי כדרשב״ל דאמר ריש לקיש

חזקה

רש״י

לא שנא בו ולא שנא בבנו. ואפילו הוא קטן: **אינו מעיז.** ולהכי קרי ליה טוענת עצמו משום דטענת קטן בעלמא לית בה מששא: **אבל בבנו מעיז.** ואפילו הוא גדול: **מתני׳ העדים שאמרו כו׳.** שהיו מעידים על חתימתם לקיים את השטר: **פסולי עדות היינו.** קרובים או משחקים בקוביא: **הרי אלו נאמנים.** כיון דאין כתב ידם ניכר אלא על פיהם הפה שאסר הוא הפה שהתיר כי היכי דמהימנת להו אהא הימנינהו אהא: **יוצא ממקום אחר.** חתומים בשטר אחר שהוחזק בב״ד וכתוב בו הנפק ובא אותו שטר לפנינו עם זה וכתב חותמן דומין של זה לשל זה אין כאן הפה שאסר ואין נאמנים לומר פסולים היינו: **גמ׳ לא שנו.** דאם כתב ידן יוצא ממקום אחר אין נאמנין: **אלא שאמרו אנוסים היינו מחמת ממון.** דלאו כל כמינייהו לשווי נפשייהו רשעים בעדות פיהם ולפסול את השטר דאדם קרוב אצל עצמו ואינו נאמן על עצמו לא לזכות ולא לחובה בדיני נפשות ובפסולי עדות להעשות רשע ופסול על פיו ואלו פוסלים עצמן באומרם חתמנו שקר בשביל אונס ממון ורישא טעמא משום הפה שאסר הוא הפה שהתיר: **מחמת נפשות.** שאמר בעל השטר הזה להרגנו ואדם חזק הוא: **כיון שהגיד שוב אינו חוזר ומגיד.** דגבי עדות חדא הגדה כתיבא אם לא יגיד וגו׳ (ויקרא ה) והכא נמי כיון דחתימי בשטרא היינו הגדה דידהו והיכי מהימני תו למיעקר הואיל וכתב ידן יוצא ממקום אחר בשלמא רישא כשאין כתב ידן יוצא ממקום אחר ועלייהו סמכינן כולה חדא הגדה היא דהא באותו דבור [בכדי] שאילת שלום קאמרי אבל אנוסים היינו אבל הכא לאו אפומייהו סמכינן: **הני מילי על פה.** כגון המעיד בב״ד ולאחר כדי דבור בא לשנות בו: **אבל בשטר לא.** דהגדה כתיב: **לא שנו.** דאמרינן הפה שאסר כו׳: **אלא דאמרי מחמת נפשות.** דאנסנו דלא משוו נפשייהו רשעים וכיון דעלייהו סמכינן הא בתוך כדי דבור עקרוה לסהדותייהו והפה שאסר התיר: **אין אדם משים עצמו רשע.** אינו נאמן לפסול את עצמו מחזקתו דקרוב הוא אצל עצמו וקרוב פסול לעדות: **אין נאמנין לפוסלו.** ארישא דמתניתין פליג העדים שאמרו כתב ידינו הוא אבל אנוסים היינו כו׳: **הפה שהתיר.** וכיון דמחמת נפשות קאמרי דאנסנו לא משוו נפשייהו רשעים ופסולי עדות דקאמרי היינו טעמא דלאו בעדותן משוו נפשייהו רשעים אלא דאמרי קרובים או עבדים היינו ועכשיו אנו משוחררים: **בשלמא פסולי עדות.** או קטנים כיון דמודים הם שהשטר כדין נכתב שההלואה או המקח אמת אבל אנחנו לא היינו ראוים והויא לה כמלוה על פה או אי מכירה היא לא נקנה הקרקע בשטר זה אמר ר״מ דלא מהימני דא״כ מלוה לא שדי זוזי בכדי וכי מחתים עדים על שטרו מידק דייק שיהו כשרים:

אלא

תוספות

ובכולי בעי דלודי. פירש בקונטרס בב״מ (דף ג: ושם) דאתא לפרש דלא תימא אמאי נשבע נימא מגו דחשיד אממונא חשיד נמי אשבועתא ולהכי קאמר ובכולי בעי דלודי ליה ולא חשיד אממונא וקשה לר״י דהא אמר בפ״ק דב״מ (דף ה:) דלא אמרינן מגו דחשיד אממונא חשיד נמי אשבועתא ואין לומר דמן התורה חשיד נמי אשבועתא ומדרבנן הוא דאמרינן דלא חשיד לפי שראו שהיו מקילין בממון יותר מבשבועה ותקנו שבועה על החשודים כל זמן שלא נודע שהוא גזלן שכשר מן התורה עדיין אבל גזלן ידוע שפסול מן התורה לא תקנו ולפי זה שבועה שלא שלחתי בו יד היא מדרבנן [ו] [ולא הויא דאורייתא אלא שבועה שלא פשעתי בה] והא דכתיב אם לא שלח לא שנשבע שלא שלח אלא ה״ק קרא נשבע שלא פשע אימתי בזמן שלא שלח בו יד דאם שלח בו יד חייב אפילו שלא פשע דנתחייב באונסים דהא גבי נסכא דרבי אבא (שבועות דף לב:) משמע דאי אמר לא חטפי היה נשבע להכחיש את העד אע״ג דחשיד אממונא והתם הויא שבועה דאוריית׳ דבשבועה דרבנן לא אמרינן מתוך שאינו יכול לישבע משלם כדמשמע בפ״ק דב״מ (שם) גבי ההוא רעיא ונראה דאתא לפרש דלא תקשי כיון דאין אדם מעיז יהא נאמן במה שכפר מקצת וכיון דמחייבינן שבועה אם כן מחשבו עזות פנים א״כ יהא נאמן במגו דאי בעי כפר הכל וקאמר דאין זה עזות מה שכופר קצת וא״ת כיון דלא חשיד אשבועתא למה גזלן פסול לשבועה ותירץ הר׳ יהודה חשיד דדוקא כשהוא חשוד על אותו ממון שבא לישבע אמרינן דלא חשיד אשבועתא דעל ידי השבועה יפרוש אבל אותו ממון שכבר גזל לא יפרוש ע״י השבועה וגבי ההוא רעיא דחשיב ליה גזלן משום דאכל תרי מינייהו אע״פ שצריך לפרוע הני תרי דאכל מ״מ לא יפרוש מן השאר משום שבועה דמה שמשלם בע״כ אין זה השבה מעליא וי״מ דגזלן כשר לשבועה מן התורה דלא חשיד אשבועתא אלא דמדרבנן פסלוהו כשהוא גזלן ואם תאמר ומאי שנא דלעדות פסול כדכתיב אל תשת ידך עם רשע וגו׳ ולשבועה כשר וי״ל דבשבועת שקר יש בה עונש גדול דכתיב בה לא ינקה וכדאמר בשבועת הדיינין (שבועות דף לט.) שכל העולם כולו נזדעזע כשאמר הקב״ה (לא תשבעו ו)לא תשא ועוד דבעדות שקר ליכא אלא לא תענה ובשבועת שקר איכא לא תגזול ולא תשבעו [ז] לשקר: **הרי אלו נאמנים.** וא״ת ולמה נאמנים והא מגו במקום עדים הוא דאין סהדי שלא היו אנוסים ולא פסולי עדות דהא לקמן אמרינן תרי ותרי נינהו וי״ל כיון דהצריכו חכמים קיום הכא לא חשיב כלל קיום מה שאומרים כתב ידינו הוא זה כיון דאינהו גופייהו אמרי תוך כדי דבור קטנים או אנוסים היינו אבל לקמן חשבינן להו כשני עדים כיון דכבר מקויים הוא שכתב ידן יוצא ממקום אחר: **אין נאמנים.** הכא ליכא לאקשויי להימנו במגו דאי בעו אמרי פרוע הוא דכיון דמקויים הוא הוי מגו במקום עדים כדפירשנו ועוד דחוזרים ומגידים הם וכיון שהגיד שוב אינו חוזר ומגיד כדאמרי׳ בגמרא ועוד דבשני עדים לא אמרינן מגו וברישא נאמנים משום דאי בעו שתקי: **לא שנו אלא שאמרו אנוסים** היינו מחמת ממון. דלא מהימני משום דלא משוו נפשייהו רשעים וקטנים כדרשב״ל ופסולי עדות משום דמלוה גופיה מידק דייק כדאמרינן בסמוך: **מחמת נפשות הרי אלו נאמנים.** וא״ת וכי אמרו קטנים היינו או אנוסים מחמת ממון היינו להימנו במגו דאמרי אנוסים היינו מחמת נפשות דהא ברישא דליכא מגו נאמנים לומר אנוסים היינו מחמת ממון וי״ל דאונס מחמת נפשות לא שכיח [א] ועוד דבשני עדים לא אמרינן מגו כדפרישית: **ואין אדם משים עצמו רשע.** וא״ת והא קסבר רבא דפלגינן דיבורא בפ״ק דסנהדרין (דף ט: ושם) גבי פלוני רבעני לרצוני ופלוני בא על אשתי אם כן הכא נהימנו דאנוסים היו אבל לא מחמת ממון אלא מחמת נפשות דאליבא דרבא קיימא וי״ל כיון דקיום שטרות דרבנן לא פלגינן דיבורא כדי לפסול השטר ועוד דאין לנו לומר מעצמינו דאנוסים היו מחמת נפשות דאונס מחמת נפשות לא שכיח כדפרישית אבל התם שכיח שבא על אשת איש אחרת כמו על אשתו או שרבעו אדם אחר וכן בהרגתיו בספ״ב דיבמות (דף כה: ושם) יכול להיות דאדם אחר הרגו אי נמי שאני הכא דמחמת ממון או מחמת נפשות הוי פירושא דאנוסים היינו הלכך לא פלגינן דיבורא אבל לרצונו ובא על אשתו הוי דיבור בפ״ע א״נ הכא עיקר עדות הוא במה שאומרים אנוסים היינו שבאו לומר שלא ראו המלוה א״כ מיד עושין עצמן רשעים כיון שחתמו אם לא יעשו פירוש לדבריהם הלכך לא שייך הכא פלגינן דיבורא אבל ההיא דהרגתיו עיקר עדות הוא לומר שנהרג להשיא את אשתו וכן פלוני רבעו או בא על אשתו עיקר עדות להרוג פלוני הלכך פלגינן דיבורא ולגבי להשים עצמו רשע או לגבי אשתו לא יהא נאמן: **מלוה** גופיה מידק דייק. ולרבנן אפי׳ מלוה על פה לא הויא דבעינן שיהא תחלתו וסופו בכשרות כדאמרי׳ ביש נוחלין (ב״ב דף קכח. ושם): **קטנים** נמי כדרשב״ל. ה״מ למימר וקטנים נמי משום דמלוה גופיה מידק דייק אלא דניחא ליה למינקט בכל חד טעמא אחרינא א״נ טעמא דריש לקיש גופיה נמי משום דמלוה מידק דייק והא דלא מייתי דרשב״ל אפסולי עדות משום דר״ל לא הזכיר אלא קטנים בדבריו:

חזקה

עין משפט נר מצוה

כא א ב ג מיי׳ פ״ג מהלכות עדות הל׳ ו ז סמג עשין קט טוש״ע ח״מ סימן מו סעיף לו [וברב אלפס עוד בסנהדרין פ״ג דף רסג]:

תוספות רי״ד

מתני׳ העדים שאמרו כתב ידינו הוא זה אבל אנוסים היינו קטנים היינו פסולי עדות היינו הרי אלו נאמנים ואם יש עדים שהוא כתב ידם או שהיה כתב ידם יוצא ממקום אחר אין נאמנים. פי׳ ראובן הוציא שט״ח על שמעון ושמעון טען איני מכיר חתימת העדים ושמא מזרף הוא אינו יכול ראובן לגבות בו עד שלא יקיים שטרו ואם באו העדים החתומים בו לפני ב״ד ואמר׳ כתב ידינו הוא זה וקיימוהו וחזרו ואמרו אנוסים היינו מחמת נפשות כדאמר לקמן ובשקר חתמנו אלא כדי להציל את נפשינו עשינו ותחמנו שאין לך דבר שעומד בפני פקוח נפש או שאמרו קטנים היינו בשעה שחתמנו או בעת שראינו ההלוואה בעינינו וראיית הקטן אינה ראייה ואע״פ שבשעת הגדה הוא גדול דכתיב או ראה או ידע אם לא יגיד ונשא עונו שתהא הראייה וההגדה בכשרות או שאמרו פסולים היינו מחמת קורבה בשעת הכתיבה או בעת המלוה קרובים ללוה או למלוה או לזה לזה ונתרחקנו עכשיו ועדותנו הוא בטלה הרי אלו נאמנים מ״ג. מגו דאי בעי אמרי אין זה כתב ידינו ועכשיו אומרים כתב ידינו הוא אבל דחתימתנו בטלה מחמת הטענות האלו הם נאמנים אבל אם יש אחרים שמכירים חתימתן ואומרים לב״ד שזו היא חתימתן ומתקיים השטר על פיהם א״נ שכתב ידן יוצא ממקום אחר שכבר חתמו בשטר אחר שהוחזק ונתקיים בב״ד וב״ד רואים דזה וזה ומשוין אותן ומתבררין שזו היא חתימתן ואומרים אלו הטענות לבטל השטר אין נאמנים שכיון שחתמו השטר בחזקת כשרות הוא דסתמא דמילתא החותם השטר בכשרות חותם וכיון שהעידו שוב אינן חוזרין ומגידים דבריש׳ דאית להו מגו מהימנו אבל השתא דליכא להו מ״ג לא מהימנו אלא השטר מקוים ע״פ אחרים ופי׳ המורה פסולים היינו קרובים או משחקים בקוביא ואינו נ״ל שיהיו נאמנים לומר משחקי בקוביא דאמרינן לקמן שאין אדם נאמן לשום עצמו רשע ואפילו ע״י מגו הלכך אין לפרש פסולים היינו אלא מחמת קורבה: א״ר ב״ח לא שנו שאם כתב ידם יוצא ממקום אחר אינן נאמנים אלא שאמרו אנוסים היינו מחמת ממון פי׳ שהיה אנס את ממוננו או לא היינו חתמנו לו שקר בזה ודאי אין נאמנים כששטר מתקיים ע״פ אחרים שאין אדם ראשי לחתום שקר כדי להציל ממונו והמודה פי׳ דלאו כל כמיניה לשויי נפשיה רשעי בעדות פיהם ולפסול השטר דאדם קרוב אצל עצמו ואין נאמן על עצמו לא

לזכות ולא לחובה אבל אמרו אנוסים היינו מחמת נפשות נאמנים פי׳ שאין לך דבר שעומד בפני פיקוח נפש. א״ל רבא כיון שהגיד שוב אינו חוזר ומגיד וכ״ת ה״מ ע״פ פי׳ כגון המעיד בב״ד ולאחר כדי דיבור בא לשנות בו אבל בשטר לא והאמר ר״ל עדים החתומים על השטר נעשה כמי שנחקרה עדותן בב״ד פי׳ ה״ה כאלו העידו בב״ד ואח״כ באו לחזור בהם [illegible] בתוספתא פ״ב דכתובות העדים שאמרו מעידים היינו אבל בלפלוני שהוא בן גרושה בן חלוצה נתין וממזר עד שלא נחקרה עדותן אמרו בדאים אנו נאמנים ואם משנחקרה עדותן אין נאמנים כללו של דבר העדים שהעידו לטמא ולטהר לקרב ולרחק עד שלא נחקרה עדותן אמרו בדאים אנו נאמנים ואם משנחקרה עדותן אין נאמנים. אלא אי אתמר ארישא אתמר הרי אלו נאמנים אמר רמב״ח לא שנו שהוא הפה שאסר הוא הפה שהתיר אלא שאמרו אנוסים היינו מחמת נפשות אבל אמרו אנוסים היינו מחמת ממון אין נאמנים שאין אדם נאמן לשום עצמו רשע ואפילו ע״י מגו פי׳ אינו נאמן לפסול עצמו מחזקתו דקרוב הוא אצל עצמו וקרוב פסול לעדות:

מסורת הש״ס

א) [ב״ב קסט. סנהדרין מד. מכות ג.], ב) גיטין ג., ג) [עי׳ תוספות לקמן כח. ד״ה קיים], ד) סנהדרין ט: כה. יבמות כה:, ה) ב״ב קנד., ו) נ״י כ׳, ז) ל״ל בשמי. יעב״ץ.

הגהות מהר״ב רנשבורג

א] תד״ה מחמת כו׳ ועוד דבשני עדים לא אמרינן כו׳. עי׳ קדושין סג ע״ב תד״ה והשתא וכו׳:

ליקוטי רש״י

[תחילת לקוטי רש״י ששייך לכאן נדפס בעמוד א׳] **אין אדם משים עצמו רשע.** אינו נאמן לפסול עצמו מחזקתו דקרוב הוא אצל עצמו וקרוב פסול לעדות והעדים שאמרו כתב ידינו הוא אבל אנוסין היינו וכו׳ כיון דמחמת נפשות קאמרי דאנסום לא משוו נפשייהו רשעים, ופסולי עדות דקאמרי לאו בעדותן שוו נפשייהו רשעים אלא דאמרי קרובים או עבדים היינו ועכשיו אנו משוחררין [רש״י כת״י בשיטמ״ק]. אין אדם משים את עדותו עדות אבל עצמו נאמן לעשות רשע הוא דקי״ל (ב״מ דף ג:) הודאת פיו כמאה עדים דמי הנ״מ לממונא אבל לקנסא ולעונש מלקות וליפסל לא (יבמות כה:). אין אדם נפסל לעדות בהודאת פיו לאדם קרוב אצל עצמו הלכך אין אדם יכול לשום עצמו רשע כלומר על עדות עצמו אינו נעשה רשע שהרי תורה פסלה קרוב לעדות [סנהדרין ט:]. אינו יכול לפסול עצמו על פיו דהא אין קרוב מעיד לא לזכות ולא לחובה ואדם קרוב אצל עצמו [שם כה.]. **אין נאמנים כו׳.** דתנן התם העדים שאמרו כתב ידינו הוא זה אבל אנוסים היינו קטנים היינו פסולי עדות היינו הרי אלו נאמנים לפי שהפה שאסר הוא הפה שהתיר ותניא בגמרא אין נאמנים לפסלו דברי ר״מ ופליג אמתני׳ דלא חייש להפה שאסר. גבי שטרות דלא נחשדו ישראל על כך ומפרש התם במסקנא טעמא דקסבר ר״מ מודה בשטר שכתבו צריך לקיימו [דכיון] שאמר לוה לאו כתבתיו או למפסליה שהרי אין לך קיום גדול מזה שהלוה מודה שכתבו ומשמעות נעשה כפלסתר וכמו שכתב [ידן] יוצא ממקום אחר דמי דתנן התם אם יש עדים שכתב ידן יוצא ממקום אחר אין נאמנים דאין כאן הפה שאסר. **וחכמים אומרים נאמנים.** דלא״ע מודה לוה שכתבו צריך לקיימו וכיון שאינו מתקיים כי אם ע״פ עדים הללו שאומרים כתב ידינו הוא זה הוא דאמרינן נמי קטנים היינו ונאמנים דהפה שאסר הוא הפה שהתיר [רשב״ם ב״ב קנד.].

recognize the signatures as authentic; (c) the court compares the signatures to those on another document that these witnesses are *known* to have signed. The Mishnah focuses on the case in which the witnesses themselves come before the court to authenticate their signatures:

הָעֵדִים שֶׁאָמְרוּ – If witnesses coming to certify a document **said,** כְּתַב יָדֵינוּ הוּא זֶה – **"This is our handwriting,** אֲבָל אֲנוּסִים הָיִינוּ – **but we were coerced** to sign,"[9] קְטַנִּים הָיִינוּ – or **"We were minors** when we signed,"[10] פְּסוּלֵי עֵדוּת הָיִינוּ – or **"We were unfit for testimony,"**[11] הֲרֵי אֵלוּ נֶאֱמָנִים – **they are believed.**[12] וְאִם יֵשׁ עֵדִים שֶׁהוּא כְּתַב יָדָם – **But if there are** other **witnesses** who verify **that it is their handwriting,** אוֹ שֶׁהָיָה כְּתַב יָדָם יוֹצֵא מִמָּקוֹם אַחֵר – or if **their handwriting was verified from another source,**[13] אֵינָן נֶאֱמָנִין – **they are not believed.**[14]

Gemara The Gemara begins by citing a qualification of the Mishnah's ruling. Initially, the Gemara understands this qualification as applying to the Mishnah's latter clause: אָמַר רָמִי בַּר חָמָא – **Rami bar Chama said:** לֹא שָׁנוּ – **They taught** this – that when the signatures can be authenticated independently the witnesses are not believed – אֶלָּא שֶׁאָמְרוּ אֲנוּסִים הָיִינוּ מֵחֲמַת מָמוֹן – **only** concerning a case **where they said, "We were coerced because of** a threat to our **finances."**[15] אֲבָל אֲנוּסִים הָיִינוּ מֵחֲמַת נְפָשׁוֹת – **But** if they said, **"We were coerced because of** a threat to our **lives,"** הֲרֵי אֵלוּ נֶאֱמָנִין – **they are believed** even though their signatures have been authenticated independently.[16]

This interpretation of the Mishnah is rejected:

אָמַר לֵיהּ רָבָא – **Rava said to [Rami bar Chama]:** כָּל כְּמִינֵיהּ –

NOTES

9. I.e. we did not witness the transaction mentioned in the document, but signed falsely under duress.

10. I.e. we witnessed the transaction as minors, who are not acceptable witnesses.

11. I.e. at the time of the transaction we were disqualified from testifying about it because we were related to one of the parties (*Rashi*). [The past tense of "We *were* related" might mean that they were related through a marriage that was later terminated (see *Ramban,* cited by *Shitah Mekubetzes*).] Alternatively, they say that at the time of the transaction they were disqualified from testifying about anything because they were gamblers (*Rashi;* cf. *Ramban, Rashba;* see note 23).

In all three cases cited by the Mishnah, the witnesses confirm that they signed the document but state that it is nevertheless void.

12. [Ordinarily, witnesses do not have the power to testify that they were coerced or were disqualified when they signed, for reasons that will be explained in the Gemara. In our case, however,] since their signatures have not been authenticated except by their own testimony, we apply the principle of *happeh she'assar:* Just as we believe their authentication of the note, we must also believe their disqualification of it (*Rashi*). The court therefore destroys the document (*Shitah Mekubetzes, Maharsha;* see *Choshen Mishpat* 46:37 with *Shach* §99).

13. I.e. their signatures appear on another note that was previously certified by a court, and by comparing the two documents the court determines that these signatures are authentic (*Rashi;* see Gemara, 20a).

14. Since we have evidence other than their testimony that the signatures are theirs, they do not have the power of *happeh she'assar.* Consequently, their testimony that the note is void is not accepted (*Rashi*).

The Rishonim ask: It is granted that the witnesses do not have the power of *happeh she'assar* (i.e. they are not our sole source of information), and that they cannot enter an unsupported claim that they were coerced or disqualified (as shall be explained in the Gemara). Nevertheless, let them be believed on the basis of *migo* (the option of a superior claim; see Chapter Introduction). That is, since they could have testified that the note is valid but the borrower repaid the debt in their presence, and they would have been believed, their testimony that it is void should also be believed! *Ramban* and *Re'ah* (to 19b) answer that the principle of *migo* can be used to bolster the plea of a *litigant* (because his forsaking of the superior plea proves that he is telling the truth); however, the testimony of *witnesses* must stand on its own feet. A statement that relies upon *migo* for corroboration is not in the category of "testimony." By contrast, when witnesses are our sole source of information and have the power of *happeh she'assar,* their entire statement is deemed inherently sound and qualifies as "testimony"; *happeh she'assar* dictates that we cannot accept part of their testimony without accepting its entirety. In our case, then, our only consideration is whether the witnesses have the power of *happeh she'assar;* the fact that they have a *migo* is irrelevant (see *Birchas Shmuel* 28:1 and *Kehillos Yaakov* 15:2 at length). [*Tosafos* ד״ה אין נאמנים have a different approach to this issue. Their view was presented in the Chapter Introduction; see note 2 there.]

15. I.e. they say that the "lender" threatened to harm them financially unless they signed this false document. With this statement, the witnesses incriminate themselves – for they were forbidden to save their own property at their fellow's expense. Certainly, if they say they were "coerced" to sign by a large bribe, they incriminate themselves (*Rambam, Commentary;* see *Rama, Yoreh Deah* 157:1; see also *Chemdas Shlomo*).

Self-incriminating testimony is not acceptable in court, the reason being that every person is deemed "related" to himself, and one cannot offer testimony regarding his relative. [This disqualifies a person from testifying to his benefit *or* his detriment in criminal matters.] Since self-incriminating testimony is unacceptable, we do not believe them that they signed under financial duress (*Rashi*). Rather, we accept the statement that these are their signatures and discard the statement that they were coerced. When part of a witness' statement is unacceptable, the court has the right to accept the remainder, based on the principle of פַּלְגִינַן דִּבּוּרָא, *we divide a statement* (*Ritva;* see *Sanhedrin* 9b; see also *Ramban* and *Tosafos* ד״ה ואין אדם משים עצמו רשע).

Nonetheless, in the Mishnah's first case – where we have no outside verification of the witnesses' signatures – we do accept their testimony regarding the document, because of *happeh she'assar*: Since the very testimony that authenticated the document stated that it is void, we have no choice but to consider it void (*Rashi*). [Presumably, this does not mean that we henceforth consider the witnesses unfit; their self-incriminating testimony is not inherently valid. Rather, it means that *happeh she'assar* forces us to consider the *document* void despite the fact that our information stems from self-incriminating testimony.]

16. That is, if they say that the "lender" threatened to kill them unless they signed, and he is capable of carrying out his threat, their testimony is accepted (*Rashi*). In this case, their testimony is not self-incriminating since they were justified in signing, for one is not required to sacrifice his life in order to avoid testifying falsely (see *Yoreh Deah* ibid.).

As the Gemara currently understands Rami bar Chama, a person is allowed to retract his signed testimony – as opposed to testimony that he offers orally in court (*Ramban;* see below). Thus, even when the signatures were authenticated independently, if the witnesses assert that they were coerced to sign – and they do not incriminate themselves – we accept their retraction of the signatures and destroy the note (*Maharam Schif;* cf. *Beis Yaakov*).

The Mishnah, however, refers to a case in which the witnesses do incriminate themselves, and thus, we cannot accept their testimony unless they have the power of *happeh she'assar.* This applies to the situation in which they say, "We were coerced." Concerning the cases in which they say, "We were minors," or "We were invalid," there is no self-incrimination (see *Sma* 46:100 and *Taz* ad loc.). The reason the witnesses are not believed unless supported by *happeh she'assar* is that there is a presumption [חֲזָקָה] that the lender would not let invalid witnesses sign his document. Therefore, once we have confirmed that the signatures are not forged, we automatically presume that the witnesses were fit to testify. There is no qualification of the Mishnah's rule regarding these cases (*Tosafos* ד״ה לא שנו, based on Gemara below; cf. *Ramban, Ritva;* see also *Chidushei R' Shimon Shkop* §18 and *Divrei Yechezkel* §19).

ובכולה בעי דלודי ליה והאי דלא אודי ליה כי היכי דלישתמיט ליה וסבר עד דהוה לי זוזי ופרענא ליה ורחמנא אמר רמי שבועה עליה כי היכי דלודי ליה בכוליה רבי אליעזר בן יעקב סבר לא שנא בו ולא שנא בבנו אינו מעיז והלכך לאו משיב אבידה הוי ורבנן סברי בו הוא דאינו מעיז אבל בבנו מעיז ומדלא העיז משיב אבידה הוי: **מתני'** העדים שאמרו כתב ידינו הוא זה אבל אנוסים היינו קטנים היינו פסולי עדות היינו הרי אלו נאמנים ואם יש עדים שהוא כתב ידם או שהיה כתב ידם יוצא ממקום אחר אינן נאמנין: **גמ'** אמר רמי בר חמא לא שנו אלא שאמרו אנוסים היינו מחמת ממון אבל אנוסים היינו מחמת נפשות הרי אלו נאמנין אמר ליה רבא כל כמיניה כיון שהגיד שוב אינו חוזר ומגיד וכי תימא הני מילי על פה אבל בשטר לא והא אמר ריש לקיש עדים החתומים על השטר נעשה כמי שנחקרה עדותן בב"ד אלא כי אתמר ארישא אתמר הרי אלו נאמנין אמר רמי בר חמא לא שנו אלא שאמרו אנוסין היינו מחמת ממון אבל אמרו אנוסין היינו מחמת נפשות אין נאמנין מאי טעמא אין אדם משים עצמו רשע תנו רבנן אין נאמנים לפוסלו דברי רבי מאיר וחכמים אומרים נאמנים בשלמא לרבנן כי טעמייהו שהפה שאסר הוא הפה שהתיר אלא לר' מאיר מ"ט בשלמא פסולי עדות מלוה גופיה מעיקרא מידק דייק ומחתם קטנים נמי כדרשב"ל דאמר ריש לקיש

חזקה

רש"י

לא שנא בו ולא שנא בבנו. ואפילו הוא קטן: **אינו מעיז.** ולהכי קרי ליה טוענת עצמו משום דטענת קטן בעלמא לית בה משמא: **אבל בבנו מעיז.** ואפילו הוא גדול: **מתני' העדים שאמרו כו'.** שהיו מעידים על חתימתם לקיים את השטר: **פסולי עדות היינו.** קרובים או משחקים בקוביא: **הרי אלו נאמנים.** כיון דאין כתב ידם ניכר אלא על פיהם הפה שאסר הוא הפה שהתיר כי היכי דמהימנת להו אהא הימנינהו אהא: **יוצא ממקום אחר.** חתומים בשטר אחר שהוחזק בב"ד וכתוב בו הנפק ובא אותו שטר לפנינו עם זה וכתב חותמן דומין של זה לשל זה אין כאן הפה שאסר ואין נאמנים לומר פסולים היינו: **גמ' לא שנו.** דאם כתב ידן יוצא ממקום אחר אין נאמנין: **אלא שאמרו אנוסים היינו מחמת ממון.** דלאו כל כמינייהו לשווי נפשייהו רשעים בעדות פיהם ולפסול את השטר דאדם קרוב אצל עצמו ואין נאמן על עצמו לא לזכות ולא לחובה בדיני נפשות ובפסולי עדות להעשות רשע ופסול על פיו ואלו פוסלים עצמן באומרם חתמנו שקר בשביל אונס ממון וריש' טעמא משום הפה שאסר הוא הפה שהתיר: **מחמת נפשות.** שאמר בעל השטר הזה להרגנו ואדם מוזק הוא: **כיון שהגיד שוב אינו חוזר ומגיד.** דגבי עדות תלא הגדה כתיבה אם לא יגיד וגו' (ויקרא ה) והכא נמי כיון דחתמי בשטרא היינו הגדה דידהו והיכי מהימני תו למיעקר הואיל וכתב ידן יוצא ממקום אחר בשלמא רישא כשאין כתב ידן יוצא ממקום אחר ועלייהו סמכינן כולה חדא הגדה היא דהא באותו דבור [בכדי] שאילת שלום קאמרי אבל אנוסים היינו אבל הכא לאו אפומייהו סמכינן: **הני מילי על פה.** כגון המעיד בב"ד ולאחר כדי דבור בא לשנות בו: **אבל בשטר לא.** דהגדה כתיב: **לא שנו.** דאמרינן הפה שאסר כו': **אלא דאמרי מחמת נפשות.** דאנסנו דלא משוו נפשייהו רשעים וכיון דעלייהו סמכינן הא בתוך כדי דבור עקרוה לסהדותייהו והפה שאסר התיר: **אין אדם משים עצמו רשע.** אינו נאמן לפסול את עצמו מחזקתו דקרוב הוא אצל עצמו וקרוב פסול לעדות: **אין נאמנין לפוסלו.** ארישא דמתניתין פליג העדים שאמרו כתב ידינו הוא אבל אנוסים היינו כו': **הפה שהתיר.** וכיון דמחמת נפשות קאמרי אנסנו לא משוו נפשייהו רשעים ופסולי עדות דקאמרי היינו טעמא דלאו בעדותן משוו נפשייהו רשעים אלא דאמרי קרובים או עבדים היינו ועכשיו אנו משוחררים: **בשלמא פסולי עדות.** או קטנים כיון דמודים הם שהשטר כדין נכתב שהלוהו או המקח אמת אבל אנחנו לא היינו ראויים והויא לה כמלוה על פה או אי מכירה היא לא נקנה הקרקע בשטר זה אמר ר"מ דלא מהימני דא"כ מלוה לא שדי זוזי בכדי וכי מחתים עדים על שטרו מידק דייק שיהו כשרים:

אלא

תוספות

ובכולה בעי דלודי. פירש בקונטרס בב"מ (דף ג. ושם) דאתא לפרש דלא תימא אמאי נשבע נימא מגו דחשיד אממונא חשיד נמי אשבועתא והכי קאמר ובכולה בעי דלודי ליה ולא חשיד אממונא וקשה לר"י דהא אמר בפ"ק דב"מ (דף ה:) דלא אמרינן מגו דחשיד אממונא חשיד נמי אשבועתא ואין לומר דמן התורה חשיד נמי אשבועתא ומדרבנן הוא דאמרינן דלא חשיד לפי שראו שהיו מקילין בממון יותר משבועה ותקנו שבועה על החשודים כל זמן שלא נודע שהוא גזלן שכבר מן התורה עדיין אבל גזלן ידוע שפסול מן התורה לא תקנו ולפי זה שבועה שלא שלחתי בו יד היא מדרבנן [ו]לא הוי לאורייתא אלא שבועה שלא פשעתי בה) והא דכתיב אם לא שלח לא שנשבע שלא שלח אלא ה"ק קרא נשבע שלא פשע אימתי בזמן שלא שלח בו יד דאם שלח בו יד חייב אפילו שלא פשע דנתחייב באונסים דהא גבי נסכא דרבי אבא (שבועות דף מז:) משמע דלאי אמר לא מהימני היה נשבע להכחיש את העד אע"ג דחשיד אממונא והתם הויא שבועה דאורייתא דבשבועה דרבנן לא אמרינן מתוך שאינו יכול לישבע משלם כדמשמע בפ"ק דב"מ (שם) גבי ההוא רעיא ונראה דאתא לפרש דלא תקשי כיון דאין אדם מעיז יהא נאמן במה שכפר מקצת וכיון דמחייבינן שבועה אם כן מחשבו עזות פנים א"כ יהא נאמן במגו דאי בעי כפר הכל וקאמר דאין זה עזות מה שכופר קצת וא"ת כיון דלא חשיד אשבועתא למה גזלן פסול לשבועה ותירץ הר"ר יהודה חסיד דדוקא כשהוא חשוד על אותו ממון שלא לישבע אמרינן דלא חשיד אשבועתא דעל ידי השבועה יפרוש אבל אותו ממון שכבר גזל לא יפרוש ע"י השבועה וגבי ההוא רעיא לא חשיב ליה גזלן משום דהכל תרי מינייהו אע"פ שצריך לפרוע הני תרי דהכל מ"מ לא יפרוש מן השאר משום שבועה דמה שמשלם בע"כ אין זה השבה מעליא וי"מ דגזלן כשר לשבועה מן התורה דלא חשיד אשבועתא אלא דמדרבנן פסלוהו כשהוא גזלן ואם תאמר ומאי שנא לעדות פסול כדכתיב אל תשת ידך עם רשע וגו' ולשבועה כשר וי"ל דבשבועת שקר יש בה עונש גדול דכתיב בה לא ינקה וכדאמר בשבועת הדיינין (שבועות דף לט.) שכל העולם כולו נזדעזע כשאמר הקב"ה (לא תשבעו ו)לא תשא ועוד דבעדות שקר ליכא אלא לא תענה ובשבועת שקר איכא לא תגזול ולא תשבעו ז) לשקר: **הרי אלו נאמנים.** וא"ת ולמה נאמנים והא מגו במקום עדים הוא דאין סהדי שלא היו אנוסים ולא פסולי עדות דהא לקמן אמרינן תרי ותרי נינהו וי"ל כיון דהצריכו חכמים קיום הכא לא חשיב כלל קיום מה שאומרים כתב ידינו הוא זה כיון דאינהו גופייהו אמרי תוך כדי דבור קטנים או אנוסים היינו אבל לקמן חשבינן להו כשני עדים כיון דכבר מקויים הוא שכתב ידן יוצא ממקום אחר: **אין נאמנים.** הכא ליכא לאקשויי להימנו במגו דאי בעו אמרי פרוע הוא דכיון דמקויים הוא הוי מגו במקום עדים כדפירשנו ועוד דחוזרים ומגידים הם וכיון שהגיד שוב אינו חוזר ומגיד כדאמרי' בגמרא ועוד דבשני עדים לא אמרינן מגו וברישא נאמנים משום דאי בעו שתקי: **לא שנו אלא שאמרו אנוסים היינו מחמת ממון.** דלא מהימני משום דלא משוו נפשייהו רשעים וקטנים כדרשב"ל ופסולי עדות משום דמלוה גופיה מידק דייק כדאמרינן בסמוך: **מחמת נפשות הרי אלו נאמנים.** וא"ת וכי אמרו קטנים היינו או אנוסים מחמת ממון היינו להימנו במגו דאמרי אנוסים היינו מחמת נפשות דהא ברישא דאיכא מגו נאמנים לומר אנוסים היינו מחמת ממון וי"ל דאונס מחמת נפשות לא שכיח א] ועוד דבשני עדים לא אמרינן מגו כדפרישית: **ואין אדם משים עצמו רשע.** וא"ת והא קסבר רבא דפלגינן דיבורא בפ"ק דסנהדרין (דף ט: ושם) גבי פלוני רבעני לרצוני ופלוני בא על אשתי אם כן הכא נהימנו דאנוסים היו אבל לא מחמת ממון אלא מחמת נפשות דאליבא דרבא קיימא וי"ל כיון דקיום שטרות דרבנן לא פלגינן דיבורא כדי לפסול השטר ועוד דאין לנו לומר מעצמינו דאנוסים היו מחמת נפשות דאונס מחמת נפשות לא שכיח כדפרישית אבל התם שכיח שבא על אשת איש אחרת כמו על אשתו או שרבעו אדם אחר וכן בהרגתיו בספ"ב דיבמות (דף כה: ושם) יכול להיות דאדם אחר הרגו אי נמי שאני הכא דמחמת ממון או מחמת נפשות הוי פירושא דאנוסים היינו הלכך לא פלגינן דיבורא אבל לרצונו ולא על אשתו הוי דיבור בפ"ע א"נ הכא עיקר עדות הוא במה שאומרים אנוסים היינו שבאו לומר שלא ראו המלוה א"כ מיד עושין עצמן רשעים כיון שחתמו אם לא יעשו פירוש לדבריהם הלכך לא שייך הכא פלגינן דיבורא אבל ההיא דהרגתיו עיקר עדות הוא לומר שנהרג להשיא את אשתו וכן פלוני רבעו או בא על אשתו עיקר עדות להרוג פלוני הלכך פלגינן דיבורא ולגבי להשים עצמו רשע או לגבי אשתו לא יהא נאמן: **מלוה גופיה מידק דייק.** ולרבנן אפי' מלוה על פה לא הויא דבעינן שיהא תחלתו וסופו בכשרות כדאמרי' ביש נוחלין (ב"ב דף קכח. ושם): **קטנים נמי כדרשב"ל.** ה"מ למימר וקטנים נמי משום דמלוה גופיה מידק דייק אלא דניחא ליה למינקט בכל חד טעמא אחרינא א"נ טעמא דריש לקיש גופיה נמי משום דמלוה מידק דייק והא דלא מייתי דרשב"ל אפסולי עדות משום דר"ל לא הזכיר אלא קטנים בדבריו:

חזקה

עין משפט נר מצוה

כא א ב ג מיי' פ"ג מהלכות עדות הל' ו ז סמג עשין קט טוש"ע ח"מ סימן מו סעיף לז [וברב אלפס עוד בסנהדרין פ"ג דף רסג.]:

תוספות רי"ד

מתני' העדים שאמרו כתב ידינו הוא זה אבל אנוסים היינו קטנים היינו פסולי עדות היינו הרי אלו נאמנים ואם יש עדים שהוא כתב ידן או שהיה כתבן יוצא ממקום אחר אין נאמנים. פי' דראובן הוציא שט"ח על שמעון ושמעון טען איני מכיר חתימת העדים ושמא בזיוף הוא אינו יכול ראובן לגבות בו עד שלא יקיים שטרו ואם באו העדים החתומים בו לפני ב"ד ואמרו כתב ידינו הוא זה וקיימוהו וחזרו ואמרו אנוסים היינו מחמת נפשות כדאמר לקמן ובשקר חתמנו אלא כדי להציל את נפשנו עשינו וחתמנו שאין לך דבר שעומד בפני פקוח נפש או שאמרו קטנים היינו בשעה שחתמנו או בעת שראינו ההלואה בעינינו וראית הקטן אינה ראייה ואע"פ שבשעת הגדה הוא גדול כתיב או ראה או ידע אם לא יגיד ונשא עונו בעינן שתהא הראייה והגדה בכשרות או שאמרו פסולים היינו מחמת קורבה שהיינו בשעת הכתיבה או בעת המלוה קרובים או למלוה או ללוה או העדים זה לזה ונתרחקו עכשיו ועדותנו בטלה הרי אלו נאמנים משום מגו. מגו דאי בעי אמרי אין זה כתב ידינו הוא אבל חתימתנו בטלה מחמת הטענות האלו הם נאמנים אבל אם יש עדים אחרים שמכירים חתימתן ואומרים לב"ד שזו היא חתימתן ומקיימים השטר על פיהם או שכתב ידן יוצא ממקום אחר שכבר חתמו בשטר אחר שהוחזק ונתקיים בב"ד וב"ד רואים זה וזה שזו היא חתימתן ומתברדין אלו הטענות לבטל השטר אין נאמנים שכיון שחתמו השטר בחזקת כשרות הוא דסתמא דמילתא החותם השטר בכשרות חותם וכיון שחתמו והדרו שוב אינן חוזרין ומגידים דבריהם ואית להו מגו מהימנו אבל השתא דליכא להו מגו לא מהימנו אלא השטר מקוים ע"פ אחרים ופי' המורה פסולים היינו קרובים או משחקים בקוביא ואינו נ"ל שיהיו נאמנים לומר משחקי קוביא דאמרי' לקמן שאין אדם נאמן לשום עצמו רשע ואפי' ע"י מגו הלכך אין לפרש פסולים היינו אלא מחמת קורבה: א"ר ב"ח לא שנו פי' שאם כתב ידם יוצא ממקום אחר אינן נאמנים אלא שאמרו אנוסים היינו מחמת ממון פי' שהיה אנס מגזמנו לו אם לא היינו חותמין לו שקר בזה ודאי אין נאמנים כשהשטר מתקיים ע"פ אחרים שאין אדם רשאי לחתום שקר כדי להציל ממונו והמורה פי' דלאו כל כמינייהו לשוויי נפשייהו רשיעי בעדות פיהם ולפסול השטר דאדם קרוב אצל עצמו ואין נאמן על עצמו לא לזכות ולא לחובה אבל אנוסים היינו מחמת נפשות נאמנים פי' שאין לך דבר שעומד בפני פיקוח נפש. **א"ל רבא** כיון שהגיד שוב אינו חוזר ומגיד וכ"ת ה"מ ע"פ פי' כגון המעיד בב"ד ולאחר כדי דיבור בא לשנות בו אבל בשטר לא והאמר ר"ל עדים החתומים בשטר נעשה כמי שנחקרה עדותן בב"ד פי' מ"ה אמר כמו שנחקרה עדותן ולא אמר כמו שהגידו עדותן בב"ד שאם הגידו ועדיין לא נחקרה עדותן יכולין לחזור בהם ולומר שקר העדנו דתניא בתוספתא דפ"ב דכתובות העדים שאמרו מעידים אנו בפלוני שהוא בן גרושה בן חלוצה נתין וממזר עד שלא נחקרה עדותן אמרו בדאים אנו נאמנים ואם משנחקרה עדותן אמרו בדאים אנו אין נאמנים כללו של דבר העדים שהעידו לטמא ולטהר לקרב ולרחק עד שלא נחקרה עדותן אמרו בדאים אנו נאמנים ואם משנחקרה עדותן אין נאמנים. **אלא** אי אתמר ארישא אתמר הרי אלו נאמנים ארמב"ח לא שנו פירוש דאמרינן הפה שאסר הוא הפה שהתיר אלא שאמרו אנוסים היינו מחמת נפשות אבל אמרו אנוסים היינו מחמת ממון אין נאמנים שאין אדם משים עצמו רשע ואפילו ע"י מיגו פי' אינו נאמן לפסול עצמו מחזקתו דקרוב הוא אצל עצמו וקרוב פסול לעדות:

מסורת הש"ס

א) [ב"ב קמח. סנהדרין מד. מכות ג:], ב) גיטין ג, ג) [ע' תוספות לקמן כח. ד"ה קיים], ד) סנהדרין ט: כה. יבמות כה:, ה) ב"ב קנד., ו) ב"ק כ"ו, ז) נ"ל בשמי. יעב"ץ.

הגהות מהר"ב רנשבורג

א] תד"ה מחמת כו' ועוד דבשני עדים לא אמרינן כו'. ע' קדושין סג ע"ב תד"ה והשתא וכו':

ליקוטי רש"י

[תחילת לקוטי רש"י ששייך לכאן נדפס בעמוד א']

אין אדם משים עצמו רשע. אינו נאמן לפסול עצמו מחזקתו דקרוב הוא אצל עצמו וקרוב פסול לעדות והעדים שאמרו כתב ידינו הוא אבל אנוסים היינו וכו' כיון דמחמת נפשות קאמרי דנאנסו לא משוו נפשייהו רשעים, ופסולי עדות דקאמרי לאו בעדותן שוו נפשייהו רשעים אלא דאמרי קרובים או עבדים היינו ועכשיו אנו משוחררים [רש"י כת"י בשיטמ"ק]. אין אדם משים את עדותו עדות אלא עלמו ולא רשע והא דקי"ל (ב"מ דף ג:) הודאת פיו כמאה עדים דמי הנ"מ לממונא אבל לקנסא ולעונש מלקות וליפסל לא [יבמות כה.]. אין אדם נפסל לעדות בהודאת פיו לאדם קרוב אצל עצמו ולא הלכך אין אדם יכול לשום עצמו רשע כלומר על עדות עצמו אינו נעשה רשע שהרי תורה פסלה קרוב לעדות [סנהדרין ט:]. אינו יכול לפסול עצמו על פיו דהא אין קרוב מעיד לא לזכות ולא לחובה ואדם קרוב אצל עצמו [שם כה.]. **אין נאמנין כו'.** דתנן התם העדים שאמרו כתב ידינו הוא זה אבל אנוסים היינו קטנים היינו פסולי עדות היינו הרי אלו נאמנין שהפה שאסר הוא הפה שהתיר ותניא בגמרא אין נאמנין לפוסלו דברי ר"מ ופליג אמתני' דלא חייש להפה שאסר גבי שטרות שלא נתקיימו ומפרש התם טעמא דקסבר ר"מ מודה בשטר שכתבו אין צריך לקיימו וכיון שאמר לוה לא כתבתיו לא מהימני עדים למפסליה שהרי אין לך קיום גדול מזה שהלוה מודה שכתבו דמשתמש נעשה כנפסלות וכמו שכתב [ידן] יוצא ממקום אחר דמי דתנן התם אין נאמנין דאין כאן הפה שאסר. **וחכמים אומרים נאמנים.** דלא סבירא להו מודה בשטר שכתבו אין צריך לקיימו וכיון שלא מקיים כי אם ע"פ עדים הללו שאומרים כתב ידינו הוא זה הן הן קאמרי נמי קטנים היינו וקאמרי הכא הפה שאסר הוא הפה שהתיר [רשב"ם ב"ב קנד.].

Rabbah continues:[1] וּבְכוּלָּהּ בָּעֵי דְלוֹדֵי לֵיהּ – Now, in reality, [the debtor] may have wanted to admit the entire [claim] to [the creditor], וְהַאי דְּלָא אוֹדֵי לֵיהּ – and the reason he did not admit the entire claim to him כִּי הֵיכִי דְּלִישְׁתַּמִּיט לֵיהּ – is in order to evade [the creditor], וְסָבַר עַד דְּהָוְיָא לִי זוּזֵי וּפָרַעְנָא לֵיהּ – thinking, "I will put him off until I have money, and then I will repay him."[2] וְרַחֲמָנָא אָמַר – And so the Merciful One said: רְמֵי שְׁבוּעָה עֲלֵיהּ – Impose an oath upon [the debtor], כִּי הֵיכִי דְּלוֹדֵי לֵיהּ בְּכוּלֵּיהּ – so that he will admit the entire [claim] to [the creditor].[3]

The Gemara now explains the disagreement between R' Eliezer ben Yaakov and the Sages in light of Rabbah's teaching:[4] רַבִּי אֱלִיעֶזֶר בֶּן יַעֲקֹב סָבַר – R' Eliezer ben Yaakov holds לָא שְׁנָא בּוֹ וְלָא שְׁנָא בִּבְנוֹ – that there is no difference whether the creditor himself or his son is the plaintiff; אֵינוֹ מֵעִיז – in either case, [a debtor] is not brazen enough to deny the entire claim. וְהִלְכָּךְ לָאו מֵשִׁיב אֲבֵידָה הָוֵי – Therefore, even when the son presents the claim [the debtor] is not like one who returns lost property, and he must swear.[5] וְרַבָּנָן סָבְרֵי – But the Rabbis hold בּוֹ הוּא דְּאֵינוֹ מֵעִיז – that it is only to the creditor himself that [a debtor] is not brazen enough to deny the entire debt; אֲבָל בִּבְנוֹ מֵעִיז – however, he would be brazen enough to deny the entire debt to [the creditor's] son, even if he is an adult.[6] וּמִדְּלָא הֵעִיז – Therefore, since he admitted part of the orphan's claim and was not brazen, מֵשִׁיב אֲבֵידָה הָוֵי – he is regarded as one who returns lost property, and is therefore exempt from an oath.[7]

Mishnah The Mishnah discusses another case to which we apply the principle of *happeh she'assar* – "The very mouth that has forbidden is the mouth that has permitted."

When a man produces a loan document against his fellow and the fellow denies having borrowed the money, the holder of the note cannot collect on its basis unless he has it authenticated through the process of קִיּוּם שְׁטָרוֹת, *document certification.*[8] This can be accomplished by any one of three basic methods: (a) The witnesses who signed the note come to court and attest to the authenticity of their own signatures; (b) any two witnesses testify that they

NOTES

1. *Rashi* (to *Gittin* 51b and *Bava Metzia* 3b) explains that Rabbah now addresses the following problem: If the reason for requiring an oath is our suspicion that the debtor is lying and attempting to escape paying the remainder of the debt, how can we resolve the matter by having him swear? Just as we suspect him of stealing, we should also suspect him of swearing falsely! (cf. *Tosafos*).

2. Since the debtor admits part of the claim, it is quite possible that he does not really mean to steal any of the money, but wishes only to delay having to pay [because he does not now have the full amount]. Thus, his partial denial [even if untrue] does not demonstrate that he is an untrustworthy person (*Rashi* to *Gittin* and *Bava Metzia* ibid.; see *R' Akiva Eiger* to *Gittin* ibid.).

3. Thus, the oath is not directed at an outright thief, but at a debtor who would really like to admit the entire debt but is seeking to buy time with his partial denial in order to obtain the money to repay it. Such a person will stop short of swearing falsely.

One might ask: If the debtor plans on eventually paying back, why should the Torah require him to take an oath? The answer is that were the debtor to leave the court completely cleared, he might be tempted to keep pushing off the payment and never pay. The oath prevents this from happening (*Ritva, Tos. HaRosh;* cf. *Ketzos HaChoshen* 73:2).

4. R' Eliezer ben Yaakov and the Sages agree that someone who admits part of a debt that would not otherwise have been claimed, or that could easily have been denied, is exempt from swearing the oath of partial admission as a *meishiv aveidah*. The purpose of this exemption is to encourage people to confess their debts (see 18a notes 9 and 14). In the case of the Baraisa, however, the son *does* claim the full amount. Thus, the debtor should be subject to the oath of partial admission. The Gemara now explains why this matter is disputed.

5. Since the debtor is not brazen enough to deny the debt entirely even to the lender's son, he is not voluntarily "returning" anything by admitting part of it. He is forced to respond to the son's definite claim as in every case of partial admission (see *Rashi* to *Gittin* 51b), and has no alternative but to admit part of it. Requiring him to swear the oath will not dissuade him from admitting part of the claim, and so there is no reason to exempt him from swearing.

6. [Since the son is not the one who did him the favor of lending him the money, or alternatively, the son is not fully aware of his father's affairs and cannot know for sure that he is lying (see 18a note 23), the debtor is not mbarrassed to make an outright denial of his obligation.]

7. Since the debtor would not feel inhibited to deny the son's claim entirely and yet he condescended to admit to part of it, we must consider him to be "returning" something that would otherwise have been lost to the son. The debtor is therefore exempt from swearing.

According to the Sages, the debtor would not be inhibited to deny the claim of even an adult son. Thus, the debtor is considered a *meishiv aveidah* and is exempt from swearing regardless of whether the claim was put forward by an adult son or a minor. The reverse is true according to R' Eliezer ben Yaakov – the debtor would be embarrassed to deny completely even the claim of a son who is a minor, and certainly of one who is an adult. Thus, he is not a *meishiv aveidah* and he must swear regardless of whether he is being sued by a minor or an adult (*Beis Yaakov;* see *Rashi* above, 18a ד״ה אלא). Nevertheless, R' Eliezer ben Yaakov speaks of the case of a minor, which is why he characterizes the debtor in this case as "one who swears in response to his own claim" (*Rashi* here).

There is a significant difficulty that remains to be resolved: The Gemara originally asked why the Tanna of our Mishnah did not cite R' Yehoshua's opinion (that a defendant is believed "when there is no slaughtered ox") in regard to the case where one volunteers to his fellow, "A *maneh* of your father's was in my possession but I repaid him half of it." In response, the Gemara stated that this would not accord with either the opinion of R' Eliezer ben Yaakov or that of the Sages. For R' Eliezer ben Yaakov obligates the debtor to swear the oath of partial admission even though no claim was advanced against him, and the Sages would exempt him from the oath even if a claim would have been advanced (and there was a "slaughtered ox"). However, the Gemara has now revised its understanding of R' Eliezer ben Yaakov's opinion, and has concluded that even R' Eliezer ben Yaakov obligates the debtor to swear only if the orphan initiated the litigation by making a claim for his father's debt. Accordingly, the original question returns: Let the Tanna of our Mishnah cite R' Yehoshua's opinion in regard to the case of partial admission to an orphan concerning his father's loan! R' Yehoshua's ruling – that the debtor is fully believed "when there is no slaughtered ox" – would fit precisely with the opinion of R' Eliezer ben Yaakov, who maintains that the debtor must swear when a claim was initiated against him but not when his admission was volunteered!

Numerous commentators answer as follows: In reversing its understanding of R' Eliezer ben Yaakov's opinion, the Gemara brought to light the explanation that the reason R' Eliezer frees the debtor from swearing when his admission was volunteered is that he is a *meishiv aveidah,* whom the Rabbis exempted by special ordinance from the oath of partial admission. The crux of R' Yehoshua's opinion, however, is that a litigant is always believed "when there is no slaughtered ox" (i.e. when he had the option of remaining silent), because he has the power of *happeh she'assar*! This is unrelated to the law of *meishiv aveidah* (and accordingly, applies even when the litigant does not admit to *any* liability). Thus, if the Tanna had chosen the case discussed by R' Eliezer ben Yaakov, he would have failed to properly illustrate R' Yehoshua's opinion. Therefore, the Tanna was forced to choose the case in which a person said to his fellow, "This field was originally your father's, but I purchased [all of] it from him" (*Maharam Schif, Pnei Yehoshua, Haflaah*). [For alternative resolutions of this question, see *Maharshal, Maharsha, Beis Yaakov* and *Haflaah.*]

8. See *Choshen Mishpat* 46:1, 82:1.

ובבולה בעי דלודי ליה והאי דלא אודי ליה כי היכי דלישתמיט ליה וסבר עד דהוה לי זוזי ופרענא ליה ורחמנא אמר רמי שבועה עליה כי היכי דלודי ליה בכוליה רבי אליעזר בן יעקב סבר לא שנא בו ולא שנא בבנו אינו מעיז והלכך לאו משיב אבידה הוי ורבנן סברי בו הוא דאינו מעיז אבל בבנו מעיז ומדלא העיז משיב אבידה הוי: **מתני׳** א העדים שאמרו כתב ידינו הוא זה אבל אנוסים היינו קטנים היינו פסולי עדות היינו הרי אלו נאמנים ואם יש עדים שהוא כתב ידם או שהיה כתב ידם יוצא ממקום אחר אינן נאמנין: **גמ׳** אמר רמי בר חמא לא שנו אלא שאמרו אנוסים היינו מחמת ממון אבל אנוסים היינו מחמת נפשות הרי אלו נאמנין אמר ליה רבא כל כמיניה כיון שהגיד שוב אינו חוזר ומגיד וכי תימא הני מילי על פה אבל בשטר לא והא אמר ריש לקיש עדים החתומים על השטר נעשה כמי שנחקרה עדותן בב"ד אלא כי אתמר ארישא אתמר הרי אלו נאמנין אמר רמי בר חמא לא שנו אלא שאמרו אנוסין היינו מחמת נפשות אבל אמרו אנוסין היינו מחמת ממון אין נאמנין מאי טעמא אין אדם משים עצמו רשע תנו רבנן אין נאמנים לפוסלו דברי רבי מאיר וחכמים אומרים נאמנים בשלמא לרבנן כי טעמייהו שהפה שאסר הוא הפה שהתיר אלא לר׳ מאיר מ"ט בשלמא פסולי עדות מלוה גופיה מעיקרא מידק דייק ומחתם קטנים נמי כדרשב"ל דאמר ריש לקיש חזקה

רש"י

לא שנא בו ולא שנא בבנו. ואפילו הוא קטן: **אינו מעיז.** ולהכי קרי ליה טוענת עצמו משום דטענת קטן בעלמא לית בה מששא: **אבל בבנו מעיז.** ואפילו הוא גדול: **מתני׳ העדים שאמרו כו׳.** שהיו מעידים על חתימתם לקיים את השטר: **פסולי עדות היינו.** קרובים או משחקים בקוביא: **הרי אלו נאמנים.** כיון דאין כתב ידם ניכר אלא על פיהם הפה שאסר הוא הפה שהתיר כי היכי דמהימנת להו אהא הימנינהו אהא: **יוצא ממקום אחר.** חתומים בשטר אחר שהוחזק בב"ד וכתוב בו הנפק ובא אותו שטר לפניו עם זה וכתב חותמן דומין דומין של זה לשל זה אין כאן הפה שאסר ואין נאמנים לומר פסולים היינו: **גמ׳ לא שנו.** דאם כתב ידן יוצא ממקום אחר אין נאמנין **אלא שאמרו אנוסים היינו מחמת ממון.** דלאו כל כמינייהו לשווי נפשייהו רשעים בעדות פיהם ולפסול את השטר דאדם קרוב אצל עצמו ואינו נאמן על עצמו לא לזכות ולא לחובה בדיני נפשות ובפסולי עדות להעשות רשע ופסול על פיו ואלו פוסלים עצמן באומרם חתמנו שקר בשביל אונס ממון וקישא טעמא משום הפה שאסר הוא הפה שהתיר: **מחמת נפשות.** שאמר בעל השטר הזה להרגנו ואדם חזק הוא: **כיון שהגיד שוב אינו חוזר ומגיד.** דגבי עדות אלא הגדה כתיבה אם לא יגיד וגו׳ (ויקרא ה) והכא נמי כיון דחתימי בשטרא היינו הגדה דידהו והיכי מהימני תו למיעקר הוא"ל וכתב ידן יוצא ממקום אחר בשלמא רישא דליכא כתב ידן יוצא ממקום אחר ועלייהו סמכינן כולה חדא הגדה היא דהא באותו דבור [בכדי] שאלת שלום קאמרי אבל אנוסים היינו אבל הכא לאו אפומייהו סמכינן: **הני מילי על פה.** כגון המעיד בב"ד ולאחר כדי דבור בא לשנות בו: **אבל בשטר לא.** דהגדה כתיב: **לא שנו.** דאמרינן הפה שאסר כו׳: **אלא דאמרי מחמת נפשות.** נאנסנו דלא משוו נפשייהו רשעים וכיון דעלייהו סמכינן הא בתוך כדי דבור עקרוה לסהדותייהו והפה שאסר התיר: **אין אדם משים עצמו רשע.** אינו נאמן לפסול את עצמו מחזקתו דקרוב הוא אצל עצמו וקרוב פסול לעדות: **אין נאמנין לפוסלו.** ארישא דמתניתין פליג העדים שאמרו כתב ידינו הוא אבל אנוסים היינו כו׳: **הפה שהתיר.** וכיון דמחמת נפשות קאמרי נאנסנו לא משוו נפשייהו רשעים ופסולי עדות דקאמרי היינו טעמא דלאו בעדותן משוו נפשייהו רשעים אלא דאמרי קרובים או עבדים היינו ועכשיו אנו משוחררים: **בשלמא פסולי עדות.** או קטנים כיון דמודים הם שהשטר כדין נכתב שהלואה או המקח אמת אבל אנחנו לא היינו ראוים והויא לה כמלוה על פה או אי מכירה היא לא נקנה הקרקע בשטר זה אמר ר"מ דלא מהימני דא"כ מלוה לא שדי זוזי בכדי וכי מחתים עדים על שטרו מידק דייק שיהו כשרים:

אלא

תוספות

ובכולי בעי דלודי. פירש בקונטרס בב"מ (דף ג: ושם) דאתא לפרש דלא תימא אמאי נשבע נימא מגו דחשיד אממונא חשיד נמי אשבועתא ולהכי קאמר ובכולי בעי דלודי ליה ולא חשיד אממונא וקשה לר"י דהא אמר בפ"ק דב"מ (דף ה:) דלא אמרינן מגו דחשיד אממונא חשיד נמי אשבועתא ואין לומר דמן התורה חשיד נמי אשבועתא ומדרבנן הוא דאמרינן דלא חשיד לפי שראו שהיו מקילין בממון יותר מבשבועה ותקנו שבועה על החשודים כל זמן שלא נודע שהוא גזלן שבשר מן התורה עדיין אבל גזלן ידוע שפסול מן התורה לא תקנו ולפי זה שבועה שלא שלחתי בו יד היא מדרבנן ז) [ולא הויא דאורייתא אלא שבועה שלא פשעתי בה] והא דכתיב אם לא שלח לא שנשבע שלא שלח אלא ה"ק קרא נשבע שלא פשע אימתי בזמן שלא שלח בו יד דאם שלח בו יד חייב אפילו שלא פשע דנתחייב באונסים דהא גבי נסכא דרבי אבא (שבועות דף לג:) משמע דאי אמר לא חטפי היה נשבע להכחיש את העד אע"ג דחשיד אממונא והתם הויא שבועה דאורייית׳ דבשבועה דרבנן לא אמרינן מתוך שאינו יכול לישבע משלם כדמשמע בפ"ק דב"מ (שם) גבי ההוא רעיא ונראה דאתא לפרש דלא תקשי כיון דאין אדם מעיז יהא נאמן במה שכפר מקצת וכיון דמחייבינן שבועה אם כן מחשבו עזות פנים א"כ יהא נאמן במגו דאי בעי כפר הכל וקאמר דאין זה עזות מה שכופר קצת וא"ת כיון דלא חשיד אשבועתא למה גזלן פסול לשבועה ותירץ הר׳ יהודה חשיד דדוקא כשהוא חשוד על אותו ממון שבא לישבע אמרינן דלא חשיד אשבועתא דעל ידי השבועה יפרוש אבל אותו ממון שכבר גזל לא יפרוש ע"י השבועה וגבי ההוא רעיא דחשיב ליה גזלן משום דאכל תרי מינייהו אע"פ שצריך לפרוע הני תרי דאכל מ"מ לא יפרוש מן השאר משום שבועה דמה שמשלם בע"כ אין זה השבה מעליא וי"מ דגזלן כשר לשבועה מן התורה דלא חשיד אשבועתא אלא דמדרבנן פסלוהו כשהוא גזלן ואם תאמר ומאי שנא דלעדות פסול כדכתיב אל תשת ידך עם רשע וגו׳ ולשבועה כשר וי"ל דבשבועת שקר יש בה עונש גדול דכתיב בה לא ינקה וכדאמר בשבועת הדיינין (שבועות דף לט.) שכל העולם כולו נזדעזע כשאמר הקב"ה (לא תשבעו ו)לא תשא ועוד דבעדות שקר ליכא אלא לא תענה ובשבועת שקר איכא לא תגזול ולא תשבעו ז) לשקר: **הרי אלו נאמנים.** וא"ת ולמה נאמנים והא מגו במקום עדים הוא דאנן סהדי שלא היו אנוסים ולא פסולי עדות דהא לקמן אמרינן תרי ותרי נינהו וי"ל כיון דהצריכו חכמים קיום הכא לא חשיב כלל קיום מה שאומרים כתב ידינו הוא זה כיון דאינהו גופייהו אמרי תוך כדי דבור קטנים או אנוסים היינו אבל לקמן חשבינן להו כשני עדים כיון דכבר מקויים הוא שכתב ידן יוצא ממקום אחר: **אין נאמנים.** הכא ליכא לאקשויי להימנו במגו דאי בעו אמרי פרוע הוא דכיון דמקויים הוא הוי מגו במקום עדים כדפירשנו ועוד דחוזרים ומגידים הם וכיון שהגיד שוב אינו חוזר ומגיד כדאמרי׳ בגמרא ועוד דבשני עדים לא אמרינן מגו וברישא נאמנים משום דאי בעו שתקי: **לא שנו אלא שאמרו אנוסים היינו מחמת ממון.** דלא מהימני משום דלא משוו נפשייהו רשעים וקטנים כדרשב"ל ופסולי עדות משום דמלוה גופיה מידק דייק כדאמרינן בסמוך: **מחמת נפשות הרי אלו נאמנים.** וא"ת וכי אמרו קטנים היינו או אנוסים מחמת ממון היינו להימנו במגו דאמרי אנוסים היינו מחמת נפשות דהא ברישא דליכא מגו נאמנים לומר אנוסים היינו מחמת ממון וי"ל דאונס מחמת נפשות לא שכיח א] ועוד דבשני עדים לא אמרינן מגו כדפרישית: **ואין אדם משים עצמו רשע.** וא"ת והא קסבר רבא דפלגינן דיבורא בפ"ק דסנהדרין (דף ט: ושם) גבי פלוני רבעני לרצוני ופלוני בא על אשתי אם כן הכא נהימנו דאנוסים היו אבל לא מחמת ממון אלא מחמת נפשות דאליבא דרבא קיימא וי"ל כיון דקיום שטרות דרבנן לא פלגינן דיבורא כדי לפסול השטר ועוד דאין לנו לומר מעצמינו דאנוסים היו מחמת נפשות דאונס מחמת נפשות לא שכיח כדפרישית אבל התם שכיח שבא על אשת איש אחרת כמו על אשתו או שרבעו אדם אחר וכן בהרגתיו בספ"ב דיבמות (דף כה: ושם) יכול להיות דאדם אחר הרגו אי נמי שאני הכא דמחמת ממון או מחמת נפשות הוי פירושא דאנוסים היינו הלכך לא פלגינן דיבורא אבל לרצונו ובא על אשתו הוי דיבור בפ"ע א"נ הכא עיקר עדות הוא במה שאומרים אנוסים היינו שבאו לומר שלא ראו המלוה א"כ מיד עושין עצמן רשעים כיון שחתמו אם לא יעשו פירוש לדבריהם הלכך לא שייך הכא פלגינן דיבורא אבל ההיא דהרגתיו עיקר עדות הוא לומר שנהרג להשיא את אשתו וכן פלוני רבעו או בא על אשתו עיקר עדות להרוג פלוני הלכך פלגינן דיבורא ולגבי להשים עצמו רשע או לגבי אשתו לא יהא נאמן: **מלוה** גופיה מידק דייק. ולרבנן אפי׳ מלוה על פה לא הויא דבעינן שיהא תחלתו וסופו בכשרות כדאמרי׳ ביש נוחלין (ב"ב דף קכח. ושם): **קטנים** נמי כדרשב"ל. ה"מ למימר וקטנים נמי משום דמלוה גופיה מידק דייק אלא דניחא ליה למינקט בכל חד טעמא אחרינא א"נ טעמא דריש לקיש גופיה נמי משום דמלוה מידק דייק והא דלא מייתי דרשב"ל אפסולי עדות משום דר"ל לא הזכיר אלא קטנים בדבריו:

חזקה

עין משפט נר מצוה

כא א ב ג מיי׳ פ"ג מהלכות עדות הל׳ ז סמג עשין קט טוש"ע ח"מ סימן מו סעיף ט [וברב אלפס עוד בסנהדרין פ"ג דף רסב]:

תוספות ר"י"ד

מתני׳ העדים שאמרו כתב ידינו הוא זה אבל אנוסים היינו קטנים היינו פסולי עדות היינו הרי אלו נאמנים ואם יש עדים שהוא כתב ידם או שהיה כתב ידן יוצא ממקום אחר אין נאמנים. פי׳ ראובן הוציא שט"ח על שמעון ושמעון טען איני מכיר חתימת העדים ושמא מזויף הוא אינו יכול ראובן לבוא לגבות בו עד שלא יקיים שטרו באו העדים החתומים בו לפני ב"ד ואמרו כתב ידינו הוא וזה הקימוהו וחזרו ואמרו אנוסים היינו מחמת נפשות כדאמר לקמן ובשקר חתמנו אלא כדי להציל את נפשנו עשינו וחתמנו שאין לך דבר שעומד בפני פקוח נפש או שאמרו קטנים היינו בשעה שחתמנו או בעת שראינו ההלואה בעינינו וראיית הקטן אינה ראייה ואע"פ שבשעת הגדה הוא גדול אינה ראייה כדאמר כל שתחלתו ראה או ידע לא יגיד ונשא עונו בעינן שתהא הראייה וההגדה בכשרות או שאמרו פסולים היינו מחמת קורבה שהיינו בשעת החתימה קרובים או בעת המלוה קרובים ללוה או למלוה או העדים זה לזה ונתרחקנו עכשיו עדותן הוא בטלה הרי אלו נאמנים משום מגו. דאי בעי אמר אין זה כתב ידינו ועכשיו אומרים כתב ידינו הוא אבל חתימתנו בטלה מחמת טענות האלו הם נאמנים אבל אם יש עדים אחרים שמכירים חתימתן ואומרים לב"ד שזו היא חתימתם ונתקיים השטר על פיהם או שכתב ידן יוצא ממקום אחר שכבר חתמו בשטר אחר שהוחזק ונתקיים בב"ד וב"ד רואים זה וזה ומשוין אותן וכשנמצא שזו היא חתימתן הם אומרים אלו הטענות לבטל השטר אין נאמנים שכיון שחתמו השטר בחזקת כשרות הוא וסתמא דמילתא החותם השטר בכשרות חותם וכיון שחתמו והגידו שוב אינן חוזרין ומגידים דבדאיכא מגו להו מהימני אבל השתא דליכא להו מגו לא מהימני אלא השטר קיים ע"פ אחרים ופי׳ המורה פסולים היינו קרובים או משחקים בקוביא ואינו נ"ל שיהיו נאמנים לומר משחקי בקוביא דאמרינן לקמן שאין אדם משים עצמו רשע ואפילו ע"י מגו הלכך אין פי׳ פסולים היינו אלא מחמת קורבה: א"ר ב"ח לא שנו פי׳ שאם כתב ידן יוצא ממקום אחר אינן נאמנים אלא שאמרו אנוסים היינו מחמת ממון פי׳ שהיה אנוס את ממונו אם לא היינו חתמנו לו שקר בזה ודאי אין נאמנים שהשטר מתקיים ע"פ אחרים שאין אדם לאחר שאין חותם שקר כדי להציל ממונו ומורה פי׳ דלאו כל כמיניה לשווי נפשייהו רשעי בעדות פיהם ולפסול השטר דאדם קרוב אצל עצמו ואין נאמן על עצמו לא לזכות ולא לחובה אבל

מסורת הש"ס

א) [ב"ב קסח. סנהדרין מד. מכות ג:], ב) [עי׳ גיטין ג.], ג) [עי׳ תוספות לקמן כח. ד"ה קיים], ד) סנהדרין ט: כה. יבמות כה:, ה) ב"ב קנד., ו) נ"י כ"י, ז) צ"ל בשמי. יעב"ץ.

הגהות מהר"ב רנשבורג

א] תד"ה מחמת כו׳ ועוד דבשני עדים לא אמרינן כו׳. עי׳ קדושין סג ע"ב תד"ה ושמא וכו׳.

ליקוטי רש"י

[תחילת לקוטי רש"י שייך לכאן נדפס בעמוד א׳]

אין אדם משים עצמו רשע. אינו נאמן לפסול עצמו מחזקתו דקרוב הוא אצל עצמו וקרוב פסול לעדות והעדים שאמרו כתב ידינו הוא אבל אנוסין היינו וכו׳ כיון דמחמת נפשות קאמרי דנאנסנו לא משוו נפשייהו רשעים, ופסולי עדות דקאמרי לאו בעדותן שוו נפשייהו רשעים אלא דאמרי קרובים או עבדים היינו ועכשיו אנו משוחררין [רש"י כת"י בשיטמ"ק]. אין אדם משים את עצמו עדות אלא עצמו לא ליעשות רשע והא דקי"ל (ב"ב דף ג:) הודאת פיו כמאה עדים דמי הנ"מ לממונא אבל לקנסא ולעונש ולמלקות וליפסל לא [יבמות כה:]. אין אדם נפסל לעדות בהודאת פיו דאדם קרוב אצל עצמו הלכך אין אדם יכול לשום עצמו רשע כלומר על עדות עצמו אינו נעשה רשע שהרי תורה פסלה קרוב לעדות [סנהדרין ט:]. אינו יכול לפסול עצמו על פיו דהא אין קרוב מעיד לא לזכות ולא לחובה ואדם קרוב אצל עצמו [שם כה.]. **אין נאמנין כו׳.** דתנן התם העדים שאמרו כתב ידינו הוא זה אבל אנוסים היינו קטנים היינו פסולים היינו נאמנים שהפה שאסר הוא הפה שהתיר ותניא בגמרא אין נאמנין לפסלו דברי ר"מ ופליג אמתני׳ דלא חייש להפה שאסר גבי שטרות דלא נחשדו ישראל על כך ומפרש התם בגמרא טעמא דקסבר ר"מ מודה לשטר שכתבו לוה שלא לקיימו [דיכון] שאמר לוה אל תכתבו תו לא מהימני עדים למפסליה שהרי אין לך קיום גדול מזה שהלוה מודה שכתבו ומסתמא בכשרות נעשה וכמו שכתב [ידן] יוצא ממקום אחר דמי דתנן התם אין נאמנין דאין כאן הפה שאסר. **וחכמים אומרים נאמנים.** דלא"ג מודה לוה שכתבו צריך לקיימו וכיון שאינו מתקיים כי אם ע"פ עדים הללו אומרים כתב ידינו הוא זה אלא קאמרי נמי קטנים היינו ונאמנים דהפה שאסר הוא הפה שהתיר [רשב"ם ב"ב קנד.].

אנוסים היינו מחמת נפשות נאמנים פי׳ שאין לך דבר שעומד בפני פיקוח נפש. **א"ל רבא** כיון שהגיד שוב אינו חוזר ומגיד וכ"ת ה"מ ע"פ פי׳ כגון המעיד בב"ד ולאחר כדי דיבור בא לשנות בו אבל בשטר לא והאמר ר"ל עדים החתומים בשטר נעשה כמי שנחקרה עדותן בב"ד פי׳ מ"ה אמר כמו שנחקרה עדותן ולא אמר כמו שהגידו עדותן בב"ד שאם הגידו ועדיין לא נחקרה עדותן יכולין לחזור בהם ולומר שקר העדנו דתניא בתוספתא דפ"ב דכתובות העדים שאמרו מעידים אנו בפלוני שהוא בן גרושה בן חלוצה נתין וממזר עד שלא נחקרה עדותן אמרו בדאים אנו נאמנים ואם משנחקרה עדותן אמרו בדאים אנו אין נאמנים כללו של דבר העדים שהעידו לטמא ולטהר לקרב ולרחק עד שלא נחקרה עדותן אמרו בדאים אנו נאמנים ואם משנחקרה עדותן אין נאמנים. **אלא** אי אתמר ארישא אתמר הרי אלו נאמנין לא שנו אלא שאמרו אנוסים היינו מחמת נפשות אבל אמרו אנוסים היינו מחמת ממון אין נאמנים פי׳ שאין אדם משים עצמו רשע ואפילו ע"י מגו מפני שאין נאמנים לפסול עצמו מחזקתו דקרוב הוא אצל עצמו וקרוב פסול לעדות:

דסתם יהודה וגליל כשעת חירום דמו ^א וליתני מודה רבי יהושע באומר לחבירו מנה לויתי ממך ופרעתיו לך שהוא נאמן משום דקא בעי למיתני סיפא אם יש עדים שהוא לוה ממנו והוא אומר פרעתיו אינו נאמן והא קיימא לן ^א המלוה את חבירו בעדים אינו צריך לפרעו בעדים וליתני מודה ר' יהושע באומר לחבירו מנה לאביך בידי והאכלתיו פרס שהוא נאמן אליבא דמאן אי אליבא דרבנן הא אמרי משיב אבידה הוי אי אליבא דרבי אליעזר בן יעקב הא אמר שבועה בעי דתניא ^ג רבי אליעזר בן יעקב אומר פעמים שאדם נשבע על טענת עצמו כיצד מנה לאביך בידי והאכלתיו פרס הרי זה נשבע וזהו שנשבע על טענת עצמו וחכמים אומרים ^ב אינו אלא כמשיב אבידה ופטור ור' אליעזר בן יעקב לית ליה משיב אבידה פטור אמר רב בטוענו קטן ^ג והאמר מר ^ד אין נשבעין על טענת חרש שוטה וקטן מאי קטן גדול ואמאי קרי ליה קטן דלגבי מילי דאביו קטן הוא אי הכי טענת עצמו טענת אחרים היא טענת אחרים והודאת עצמו כולהי טענתא טענת אחרים והודאת עצמו נינהו אלא הכא בדרבה קמיפלגי דאמר רבה ^ד מפני מה אמרה תורה מודה מקצת הטענה ישבע חזקה אין אדם מעיז פניו בפני בעל חובו והאי בכולה בעי דלכפריה והאי דלא כפר ליה משום דאין אדם מעיז פניו הוא

וליתני מנה לויתי ממך. מלתיה דר' יהושע לאשמועינן דמודה היכא דאין שור שחוט לפניך מאי שנא לאשמועינן בקרקע ולא איצטריך למתנייה באביו משום סיפא לנקוט מלתיה במטלטלין ולאשמועינן בדידיה גופיה: נאמן. מדאורייתא בלא שבועה: וניתני מודה ר' יהושע כו' והאכלתיו פרס. פרעתיו חציו שהוא נאמן בלא שבועה הואיל ואין שור שחוט לפניו לאשמועינן רבותא דלא"ג דמודה במקצת פטור הואיל ואינו תובעו: אליבא דמאן. תנאי פליגי בהא מילתא בשבועות (דף מב.) ולא אמר רבי יהושע הכי לא כחד מינייהו הוא דאי כרבנן הא אמרי אפי' תובעו וזה מודה במקצת משיב אבידה הוא דתנן בשבועות מנה לאבא בידך אין לך בידי אלא חמשים דינר פטור משום שהוא כמשיב אבידה ומאי אשמועינן רבי יהושע באין שור שחוט אפי' שור שחוט לפניו נמי נאמן ואי אליבא דר' אליעזר בן יעקב כי לא תבע ליה נמי האמר שבועה בעי: ורבי אליעזר לית ליה משיב אבידה פטור. מן השבועה בתמיה הא תקנתא דרבנן היא במס' גיטין (דף מח:) המוצא מציאה לא ישבע מפני תיקון העולם וכיון דכי אינו תובעו נמי מחייב ליה שבועה הרי אין לך משיב אבידה גדולה מזה וחייב: אין נשבעין על טענת חרש שוטה וקטן. משנה היא בשבועות: טענת אחרים הוא. ומאי פעמים דקאמר ומאי טענת עצמו: אלא הכא בדרבה קא מיפלגי. אלא לעולם בטוענו קטן ודקשיא לך אין נשבעין על טענת קטן הני מילי בשטוענו קטן אני נתתיו לך וקרא כתיב כי יתן איש אל רעהו ולא קטן ומהכא יליף לה בשבועות אבל הכא שבא בטענת אביו אית ליה לרבי אליעזר בן יעקב נשבעין ורבנן פליגי עליה אפילו בטוענו גדול וקרו ליה משיב אבידה ובדרבה קא מיפלגי:

דסתם יהודה וגליל כשעת חירום דמי. תימה דבריש גיטין (דף ז: ושם) תנן דבארץ ישראל א"צ לומר בפני נכתב ובפני נחתם אפי' מיהודה לגליל משום דאיכא עולי רגלים ומי דינין ועדים מצוין לקיימו ויש לומר דהתם האשה מחזרת אחר עדי קיום אע"ג דיהודה וגליל כשעת חירום דמי תמצא עדי קיום כיון דאיכא עולי רגלים אבל המחזיק אין רגיל לחזור אחר עדי מחאה ואם תאמר התם ^ה דאמר שאני בני מחוזא דניידי וצריך לומר אפי' באותה שכונה בפני נכתב (א) דאין עדים מצוין לקיימו אטו במחזה לא תועיל מחאה שלא בפניו וי"ל דהתם דרך הליכתן מן העיר כששמעו מחאה רגילות הוא לומר פלוני מיחה ושומעין אחרים עד שנשמע הקול למחזיק אבל גבי גט אין רגיל שיאמרו בהליכתן אנו חתמנו על הגט ^ו [או מכירין אנו חתימת עדים החתומים]: אין צריך לפרעו בעדים. ואם תאמר למאן דאמר צריך לפרעו בעדים מאי איכא למימר וי"ל דהכא מקשי ליה מתניתין הכא לליתני מנה לך בידי ויש לומר דפלוגתא דתנאי היא בפרק שבועת הדיינין (שבועות דף מא:) אי נמי דלא חשיב לה מירכא דניחא ליה לאשמועינן דאין מחזיקין בנכסי קטן ואם תאמר מאי משני אכתי ליתני ואם יש עדים ואמר לו לא תפרעני אלא בפני פלוני ופלוני אינו נאמן וי"ל דלא היה רוצה להאריך בלשונו או שמא מילתא דפשיטא הוא: אי אליבא דרבנן הא אמרי משיב אבידה הוי. כדמסיק דבנו מעיז וא"כ לא מלי למיתני ואם יש עדים אינו נאמן דלעולם נאמן במגו דאי בעי אמר פרעתי הכל דבנו מעיז ומעיז: ורבי אליעזר בן יעקב לית ליה משיב אבידה פטור. פי' בקונטרס התנן המוצא מציאה לא ישבע מפני תיקון העולם ואית ספרים דגרסי הכי בהדיא ואין נראה לרבינו יצחק דמשיב אבידה פטור מדאורייתא מטעם מגו ולא מכח ההיא משנה פריך אלא פריך וכי לית ליה מגו וכן משמע בהניזקין (גיטין דף נא. ושם) דפריך ולית ליה לרבי יצחק המוצא מציאה כו' ומשני הוא דאמר כר"א בן יעקב דאמר פעמים שאדם נשבע וכו' ופריך ור"א בן יעקב לית ליה משיב אבידה פטור והשתא אי מכח מתני' פריך הוה ליה למימר ולית ליה לר"א בן יעקב המוצא מציאה כדקאמר ארבי יצחק ועוד כיון דמשני הוא דאמר כר"א בן יעקב א"כ רוצה לומר דר"א פליג אמתניתין א"כ מאי פריך ור"א בן יעקב לית ליה משיב אבידה פטור אין הכי נמי דלית ליה אלא מכח מגו פריך כדפרישית: אלא הכא בדרבה קא מיפלגי. פירש בקונטרס לעולם בטוענו קטן ודקא קשיא לך הא אין נשבעין על טענת קטן ה"מ בבא בטענת עצמו אבל בבא בטענת אביו טענה חשובה היא וכי תימא מ"ט דרבנן דאין סברא לומר דסברי דאף בבא בטענת אביו לית ביה ממשא אלא בדרבה קמיפלגי ונראה דמשום דקרי ליה טענת עצמו דחקו להעמיד בטוענו קטן אבל קשה דעיקר התירוץ חסר מן הספר ועוד דבהגוזל קמא (ב"ק דף קו: ושם) ממעטינן נתנו כשהוא קטן ותבעו כשהוא גדול עד שתהא תביעה ונתינה שוין בגדלות וה"ה דמהאי קרא ממעט נתנו כשהוא גדול ותבעו כשהוא קטן דהיינו כגון שנתן לו אביו ותבעו בקטנות ונראה דה"פ לעולם בגדול מיירי אלא לא תימא דקרי ליה טענת עצמו משום דהודאת עצמו היא אלא בדרבה קמיפלגי ולרבנן דסברי דבנו מעיז טענת עצמו היא וה"ק ראב"י פעמים שאדם נשבע על מה שאתם מחשיבים טענת עצמו אבל לדידי דאינו מעיז טענת אחרים היא ובסוף שבועת הדיינין (שבועות דף מב. ושם) דתנן אבל נשבעין לקטן ומפרש בבא בטענת אביו וראב"י היא ההוא קטן נמי לאו דווקא אלא גדול וקרי ליה קטן משום דלגבי מילי דאבוה קטן הוא כדמפרש הכא וקשה קצת דהוה ליה לאקשויי ולשנויי אמתניתין דהתם כמו שמקשה על רב דההיא שמעתא גופה לא מקשה על המשנה אלא על רב: מפני מה אמרה תורה מודה מקצת הטענה ישבע. אפילו לרבנן דר"ש דלא דרשי טעמא דקרא קא בעי רבה שפיר מפני מה אמרה תורה כו' דלמאי לא מהימן בלא שבועה במגו דאי בעי כפר הכל או נילף מהכא דלא אמרינן מגו ומשני דאין זה מגו דאין אדם מעיז לכפור ואף על גב דבפרק שבועת הדיינין (שם דף מ:) אמרינן בכופר הכל משביעין אותו שבועת היסת משום דחזקה אין אדם תובע אלא אם כן יש לו ופריך אדרבה חזקה דאין אדם מעיז פניו בפני בעל חובו ומשני דאשתמוטי קמשתמיט אלמא בכופר בכל נמי אדם מעיז לכפור דאשתמוטי קא משתמיט כמו במודה מקצת מ"מ קאמר הכא שפיר חזקה דאין אדם מעיז לכפור הכל כל כך ולא הוי מגו דיותר ברצון הוא מודה במקצת הטענה דאינו מעיז כל כך אבל אין לפרש דרבה אתא לפרושי מפני מה אמרה תורה מודה מקצת ולא כופר הכל וקאמר חזקה דאין אדם מעיז לכך נאמן כשכופר הכל דאם כן במקום שיכול להעיז אפילו כופר הכל חייב ובסמוך אמרינן איפכא לרבנן דבנו מעיז ופטור אף מודה מקצת הטענה משום דמשיב אבידה הוא מגו דאי בעי כפר הכל ואם תאמר ומנלן דכופר הכל פטור וליכא למימר מדאצטריך קרא לחייב שבועה בעד אחד מכלל דכופר הכל פטור דהא איצטריך להיכא שמעידים שגנב לו והוא אינו יודע אלא י"ל דגזירת הכתוב היא דכי הוא זה משמע דבעינן כפירה והודאה ועוד מודה מקצת יש להשביעו שחייב לו ממון שהודה ועל ידי כך מגלגל עליו שבועה כעין גלגול אבל כופר הכל נסתלק לגמרי ממנו: חזקה אין אדם מעיז פניו. לא כמו שפי' בקונטרס בהגוזל (ב"ק דף קז.) דאין אדם מעיז לפי שעשה לו טובה שהלוהו אבל בפקדון מעיז דאם כן בפקדון מודה מקצת נמי יהא פטור במגו דאי בעי כופר הכל ובכל דוכתא משמע דמודה מקצת חייב בפקדון גבי עשר גפנים טעונות מסרתי לך כו' (שבועות דף מג:) דמשמע דאיירי בפקדון וגבי סלע הלויתני עליו ושתים היה שוה (שם מג.) וגבי מציאה נמי אמרי' בהניזקין (גיטין נא. ושם) דמודה מקצת חייב ולא מהימן במגו אלא אור"ת דהיינו כגון חזקה שאין האשה מעיזה פניה בפני בעלה שאין לאדם פנים לכפור הכל וריב"א פי' אין אדם מעיז היכא שחבירו מכיר בשקרו ואין להאריך ^ז:

וכולי

מסורת הש"ס

א) ב"ב דף קע. שבועות מא: [ועיין קדושין מג:], ב) גיטין נא: שבועות מב., ג) שם, ד) גיטין נא. ב"ק קז. שבועות מב: ב"מ ג., ה) [שם דף ו.], ו) נ"י כ"י, ז) [ונתוס' ב"ק קז. ד"ה עירוב וכו' האריכו טובא].

תוספות ישנים

א) [השתא קס"ד דהמלוה את חבירו בעדים ואין צריך לפרעו בעדים ואין נאמן לומר פרעתי כיון דליה ליה מגו ומסיק דקי"ל דא"צ לפרעו בעדים ונאמן לומר פרעתי אפילו בלא מגו. ת"י].

הגהות הב"ח

(א) תוס' ד"ה דסתם וכו' בפני נכתב ובפני נחתם דאין עדים:

עין משפט נר מצוה

יח א מיי' פ"א מהל' מלוה ולוה הלכה א סמג עשין צד טוש"ע ח"מ סימן ע סעיף א:

יט ב מיי' פ"ד מהלכות טוען ונטען הלכה ה סמג שם טוש"ע שם סי' עה סעיף ג:

כ ג מיי' פ"ה שם הל' ט סמג שם טוש"ע שם סימן לו סעיף א:

ליקוטי רש"י

דסתם יהודה וגליל. אפי' בשעת שלום. כשעת חירום דמו. שאין שיירות מצויות מזו לזו אבל בשאר מלכיות אי איכא חירום לא הויא חזקה אבל בשעת שלום הויא חזקה דהא שיירות מצויות והאי דקאמר רבי אבא בשעת חירום שנו הכי קאמר יהודה וגליל הרי הן כשעת חירום של שאר מלכיות [רשב"ם ב"ב לח:]. והאכלתיו פרס. והחזרתי לו חצי והחציו בידי חייב לישבע על השאר [שבועות מב.]. על טענת עצמו. השתא משמע שאין אדם תובעו ולקמן מפרש לה בטוענו זה בן המת. ורבי אליעזר בן יעקב לית ליה כו'. כמו והוינן בה ור"א לית ליה חששא דתיקון העולם דמשיב אבידה פטור משבועה דא"כ שביק לה ואזיל והאי נמי כיון דלא תבעו כמשיב אבידה הוא [גיטין נא:]. בטוענו קטן. יתום קטן תובע. אין נשבעין על טענת חרש שוטה וקטן. כגון שטענו ברמיזה דחרש שדיברו חכמים בכל מקום לא מדבר ולא שומע [שבועות שם]. אי הכי. דטוענו גדול טענת עצמו קרי לה טענת אחרים היא. והודאת עצמו. על שהודה לו שאמת כדבריו ומודה שעדיין חייב לו פרס הוא נשבע. כולהי טענתא טענת אחרים והודאת עצמו נינהו. ולכך נשבעין עליה וכי האי גוונא מי פליגי רבנן עליה ומי הוה קאמר פעמים שאדם נשבע כל שעתא כי האי גוונא משתבע. אלא הכא בדרבה קמיפלגי. לא תימא בטוענו גדול אלא כי טוענו קטן ודקשיא לך אין נשבעין על טענת קטן הני מילי בשטוענו הפקדתי לך דגבי שבועה כתיב (שמות כב) כי יתן איש ולא קטן אבל הכא בטענת אביו נשבעין אפילו לקטן ולרבנן אפילו לגדול אין נשבעין דתנן בשבועות מנה לאבא בידך אין לך בידי אלא חמשים דינר פטור ובדרבה פליגי [גיטין שם]. ולעולם בטוענו קטן ומשום דאין טענתו חשובה במקום אחר דכתיב כי יתן איש קרי ליה הכא טענת עצמו מיהו הכא טענה היא והיינו דקאמר פעמים ומאי פליגי עליה בדרבה קמיפלגי [שבועות שם]. מפני מה אמרה תורה כו'. ולא חשבו כמשיב אבידה לפוטרו שלא כפר בכולו [ב"מ ג.]. חזקה אין אדם מעיז פניו וכו'. לכפור את הכל הלכך בשבועה הודאת המקצת אינו נאמן על השאר דהאי בכוליה בעי דלכפריה כו' [גיטין שם]. אין אדם מעיז פניו בפני זה שעושה לו טובה הלכך היכא דכפר הכל פטור משבועה דאי לאו קושטא בהדיא לא הוה והיכא דמודה מקצת בכולה בעי למכפריה והא דלא כפריה משום דאין אדם מעיז [ב"ק קז.]. [מכאן שייך לע"ב] ובכולה בעי דלודי ליה. וכי תימא לא נשבעיה אשארא דמיגו דחשוד לממונא חשוד נמי אשבועתא מדלא כפריה בכוליה דהאי כי אודי בפלגא בכוליה נמי בעי דלודי והאי דלא אודי ליה לאו דעתו למיגזליה אלא אישתמוטי אישתמיט לדחויי השתא [גיטין נא:]. וכ"ת מגו דחשיד אממונא חשיד אשבועתא לא חשיד אממונא לפי שברצונו היה מודה בכולו אלא שאין בידו לפרוע וסבר עד דהוי לי [זוזי] ופרענא ליה [ב"מ ג:]. כיון שהגיד שוב אינו חוזר ומגיד. דבר המכחיש את הראשון דכתיב (ויקרא ה) אם לא יגיד קפיד קרא [סנהדרין מד:]. דמאחר שהודו שבכשרות נכתב הרי חתימת השטר כאילו העידו בב"ד כל מה שכתוב בשטר שהלוהו מלוה ללוה וכיון שהגיד שוב אינו חוזר ומגיד [רשב"ם ב"ב מט.]. נעשה כמי שנחקרה עדותן בב"ד. משעה שנכתב ונחתם ואין עדות אחרון מבטל את הראשון דכיון שהגיד שוב אינו חוזר ומגיד לא אתא על פה דהשתא ומרע לשטרא דקדים [רשב"ם ב"ב מט.].

there is a legal **presumption** אֵין אָדָם מֵעִיז פָּנָיו בִּפְנֵי בַּעַל חוֹבוֹ – **that a person is not brazen** enough to deny his obligation **to the face of his creditor.**[24] וְהַאי בְּכוּלָּהּ בָּעֵי דְּלִכְפְּרֵיהּ – **Thus,** it is possible that **this** debtor really **wished to deny the entire [claim] to [the creditor],** וְהַאי דְּלֹא כָּפַר לֵיהּ – **and the reason he did not deny it** entirely מִשּׁוּם דְּאֵין אָדָם מֵעִיז פָּנָיו הוּא – **is** only **because [a person] is not brazen** enough to deny the entire obligation **to the face of his creditor.**[25] Therefore, the Torah required him to swear about the part he denies.

NOTES

plaintiff (by putting pressure on the defendant to admit). But not requiring an oath would seem to benefit him more, since it would make it more likely for debtors to admit at least part of the claim. Why, then, did the Torah decree that the defendant swear for partial admission? (*Chidushei HaRim* to *Bava Metzia* 3a, in explanation of *Rashi;* see also *Chasam Sofer* here, and *Pnei Yehoshua* and *Nachalas David* to *Bava Metzia* 3a; cf. *Tosafos* ד״ה מפני מה et al.).

24. Because the creditor has done him a favor by lending him money (*Rashi* to *Bava Kamma* 107a), or because the creditor knows full well that he is lying (*Tosafos* ד״ה חוקה). See *Beis Yaakov, Chasam Sofer* and *Kovetz Shiurim* §50.

25. Thus, it cannot be argued that the defendant is a *meishiv aveidah* with his partial admission. That would be true only if it were clear that he could deny everything; his admission would then be a favor to the claimant. But, in fact, it is possible that he cannot bring himself to lie so brazenly to his creditor by denying the entire obligation. Thus, his admission is not equivalent to returning lost property to the claimant (*Rashi* to *Gittin* 51b, as explained by *Chidushei HaRim* loc. cit.).

דסתם יהודה וגליל כשעת חירום דמו [א] וליתני מודה רבי יהושע באומר לחבירו מנה לויתי ממך ופרעתיו לך שהוא נאמן משום דקא בעי למיתני סיפא אם יש עדים שהוא לוה ממנו והוא אומר פרעתיו אינו נאמן והא [א] קיימא לן המלוה את חבירו בעדים אינו צריך לפרעו בעדים וליתני מודה ר' יהושע באומר לחבירו מנה לאביך בידי והאכלתיו פרס שהוא נאמן אליבא דמאן אי אליבא דרבנן הא אמרי משיב אבידה הוי אי אליבא דרבי אליעזר בן יעקב הא אמר שבועה בעי דתניא [ג] רבי אליעזר בן יעקב אומר פעמים שאדם נשבע על טענת עצמו כיצד מנה לאביך בידי והאכלתיו פרס הרי זה נשבע וזהו שנשבע על טענת עצמו וחכמים אומרים [ב] אינו אלא כמשיב אבידה ופטור ור' אליעזר בן יעקב לית ליה משיב אבידה פטור אמר רב בטוענו קטן [ג] והאמר מר [ג] אין נשבעין על טענת חרש שוטה וקטן מאי קטן גדול ואמאי קרי ליה קטן דלגבי מילי דאביו קטן הוא אי הכי טענת עצמו טענת אחרים היא טענת אחרים והודאת עצמו כולהי טענתא טענת אחרים והודאת עצמו נינהו אלא הכא בדרבה קמיפלגי דאמר רבה [ד] מפני מה אמרה תורה מודה מקצת הטענה ישבע חזקה אין אדם מעיז פניו בפני בעל חובו והאי בכולה בעי דלכפריה והאי דלא כפר ליה משום דאין אדם מעיז פניו הוא

רש"י

וליתני מנה לויתי ממך. מלתיה דר' יהושע דאשמועינן דמודה היכא דאין שור שחוט לפניך מאי שנא דאשמעינן בקרקע ואיצטריך למתנייה באביו משום סיפא לנקוט מלתיה במטלטלין ולישמעינן בדידיה גופיה: נאמן. מדאורייתא בלא שבועה: וניתני מודה ר' יהושע כו' והאכלתיו פרם. פרעתיו חציו שהוא נאמן בלא שבועה הואיל ואין שור שחוט לפניו דאשמועינן רבותא דאע"ג דמודה במקצת פטור הואיל ואינו תובעו: אליבא דמאן. תנאי פליגי בהא מילתא בשבועות (דף מב.) ואי אמר רבי יהושע הכי לא כחד מנייהו הוא דאי כרבנן הא אמרי אפי' תובעו וזה מודה במקצת משיב אבידה הוא דתנן בשבועות מנה לאבא בידך אין לך בידי אלא חמשים דינר פטור משום שהוא כמשיב אבידה ומאי אשמעינן רבי יהושע דאין שור שחוט אפי' שור שחוט לפניו נמי נאמן ואי אליבא דר' אליעזר בן יעקב כי לא תבע ליה נמי האמר שבועה בעי: ורבי אליעזר לית ליה משיב אבידה פטור. מן השבועה בתמיה הא תקנתא דרבנן היא במס' גיטין (דף מח:) המוצא מציאה לא ישבע מפני תיקון העולם וכיון דכי אינו תובעו נמי מחייב ליה שבועה הרי אין לך משיב אבידה גדולה מזה וחייב: אין נשבעין על טענת חרש שוטה וקטן. משנה היא בשבועות: טענת אחרים הוא. ומאי פעמים דקאמר ומאי טענת עצמו: אלא הכא בדרבה קא מיפלגי. אלא לעולם בטוענו קטן ודקשיא לך אין נשבעין על טענת קטן הני מילי בשטוענו קטן אני נתתיו לך וקרא כתיב כי יתן איש אל רעהו ולא קטן ומהכא יליף לה בשבועות אבל הכא שבא בטענת אביו אית ליה לרבי אליעזר בן יעקב נשבעין ורבנן פליגי עליה אפילו בטוענו גדול וקרו ליה משיב אבידה ובדרבה קא מיפלגי:

תוספות

דסתם יהודה וגליל כשעת חירום דמי. תימה דבריש גיטין (דף ד:) (ושם) תנן דבארץ ישראל א"צ לומר בפני נכתב ובפני נחתם אפי' מיהודה לגליל משום דאיכא עולי רגלים ובתי דינין ועדים מצויין לקיימו ויש לומר דהתם האשה מחזרת אחר עדי קיום אע"ג דיהודה וגליל כשעת חירום דמי תמצא עדי קיום כיון דאיכא עולי רגלים אבל המחזיק אין רגיל לחזר אחר עדי מחאה ואם תאמר התם [ה] דאמר שאני בני מחוזא דניידי וצריך לומר אפי' באותה שכונה בפני נכתב (א) דאין עדים מצויין לקיימו אטו במחוזא לא תועיל מחאה שלא בפניו וי"ל דהתם דרך הליכתן מן העיר כששמעו מחאה רגילות הוא לומר פלוני מיחה ושומעין אחרים עד שנשמע הקול למחזיק אבל גבי גט אין רגיל שיאמרו בהליכתן אנו חתמנו על הגט [ו] [או מכירין אנו חתימת עדים החתומים]: אין צריך לפרעו בעדים. ואם תאמר למאן דאמר צריך לפרעו בעדים תקשי ליה מתניתין דהכא דליתני מנה לך בידי ויש לומר דפלוגתא דתנאי היא בפרק שבועת הדיינין (שבועות דף מא:) אי נמי דלא חשיב לה פירכא דניחא ליה לאשמועינן דאין מחזיקין בנכסי קטן ואם תאמר מאי משני אכתי ליתני ואם יש עדים ואמר לו אל תפרעני אלא בפני פלוני ופלוני אינו נאמן וי"ל דלא היה רוצה להאריך בלשונו או שמא מילתא דפשיטא הוא: אי אליבא דרבנן הא אמרי משיב אבידה הוי. כדמסיק דבכנו מעיז וא"כ לא מצי למיתני ואם יש עדים אינו נאמן דלעולם נאמן במגו דאי בעי אמר פרעתי הכל דבכנו מעיז ומעיז: ורבי אליעזר בן יעקב לית ליה משיב אבידה פטור. פי' בקונטרס התנן המוצא מציאה לא ישבע מפני תיקון העולם ואית ספרים דגרסי הכי בהדיא ואין נראה לרבינו יצחק דמשיב אבידה פטור מדאורייתא מטעם מגו ולא מכח ההיא משנה פריך אלא פריך וכי לית ליה מגו וכן משמע בהניזקין (גיטין דף נא. ושם) דפריך ולית ליה לרבי יצחק המוצא מציאה כו' ומשני הוא דאמר כר"א בן יעקב דאמר פעמים שאדם נשבע וכו' ופריך ור"א בן יעקב לית ליה משיב אבידה פטור והשתא אי מכח מתני' פריך הוה ליה למימר ולית ליה לר"א בן יעקב המוצא מציאה כדקאמר ארבי יצחק ועוד כיון דמשני הוא דאמר כר"א בן יעקב א"כ רוצה לומר דר"א פליג אמתניתין א"כ מאי פריך ור"א בן יעקב לית ליה משיב אבידה פטור אין הכי נמי דלית ליה אלא מכח מגו פריך כדפרישית: אלא הכא בדרבה קא מיפלגי. פירש בקונטרס לעולם בטוענו קטן ודקא קשיא לך הא אין נשבעין על טענת קטן ה"מ בבא בטענת עצמו אבל בבא בטענת אביו טענה חשובה היא וכי תימא מ"ט דרבנן דאין סברא לומר דסברי דאף בבא בטענת אביו לית ביה ממשא אלא בדרבה קמיפלגי ונראה דמשום דקרי ליה טענת עצמו דחקו להעמיד בטוענו קטן אבל קשה דעיקר התירוץ חסר מן הספר ועוד דבהגוזל קמא (ב"ק דף קו: ושם) ממעטינן נתנו כשהוא קטן ותבעו כשהוא גדול עד שתהא תביעה ונתינה שוין בגדלות וה"ה דמהאי קרא ממעט נתנו כשהוא גדול ותבעו כשהוא קטן דהיינו כגון שנתן לו אביו ותבעו בקטנות ונראה דה"פ לעולם בגדול מיירי אלא לא תימא דקרי ליה טענת עצמו משום דהודאת עצמו היא אלא בדרבה קמיפלגי ורבנן דסברי דבכנו מעיז טענת עצמו היא וה"ק ראב"י פעמים שאדם נשבע על מה שאתם מחשיבים טענת עצמו אבל לדידי דאינו מעיז טענת אחרים היא ובסוף שבועת הדיינין (שבועות דף מג. ושם) דתנן אבל נשבעין לקטן ומפרש בבא בטענת אביו וראב"י היא ההוא קטן נמי לאו דווקא אלא גדול וקרי ליה קטן משום דלגבי מילי דאבוה קטן הוא כדמפרש הכא וקשה קצת דהוה ליה לאקשויי ולשנויי אמתניתין דהתם כמו שמקשה על רב דבההיא שמעתא גופה לא מקשה על המשנה אלא על רב: מפני מה אמרה תורה מודה מקצת הטענה ישבע. אפילו לרבנן דר"ש דלא דרשי טעמא דקרא קא בעי רבה שפיר מפני מה אמרה תורה כו' דאמאי לא מהימן בלא שבועה במגו דאי בעי כפר הכל או נילף מהכא דלא אמרינן מגו ומשני דאין זה מגו דאין אדם מעיז לכפור ואף על גב דבפרק שבועת הדיינין (שם דף מ:) אמרינן בכופר הכל משביעין אותו שבועת היסת משום דחזקה אין אדם תובע אלא אם כן יש לו ופריך אדרבה חזקה דאין אדם מעיז פניו בפני בעל חובו ומשני דאשתמוטי קמשתמיט אלמא בכופר בכל נמי אדם מעיז לכפור דאשתמוטי קא משתמיט כמו במודה מקצת מ"מ קאמר הכא שפיר חזקה דאין אדם מעיז לכפור הכל כל כך ולא הוי מגו דיותר ברצון הוא מודה במקצת הטענה דאינו מעיז כל כך אבל אין לפרש דרבה אתא לפרושי מפני מה אמרה תורה מודה מקצת ולא כופר הכל וקאמר חזקה דאין אדם מעיז לכך נאמן כשכופר הכל דאם כן במקום שיכול להעיז אפילו כופר הכל חייב ובסמוך אמרינן איפכא לרבנן דבכנו מעיז ופטור אף מודה מקצת הטענה משום דמשיב אבידה הוא מגו דאי בעי כפר הכל ואם תאמר ומנלן דכופר הכל פטור וליכא למימר מדאצטריך קרא לחייב שבועה בעד אחד מכלל דכופר הכל פטור דהא איצטריך להיכא שמעידים שגנב לו והוא אינו יודע אלא י"ל דגזירת הכתוב היא דכי הוא זה משמע דבעינן כפירה והודאה ועוד מודה מקצת יש להשביעו שחייב לו ממון שהודה ועל ידי כך מגלגל עליו שבועה כעין גלגול אבל כופר הכל נסתלק לגמרי ממנו: חזקה אין אדם מעיז פניו. לא כמו שפי' בקונטרס בהגוזל (ב"ק דף קז.) דאין אדם מעיז לפי שעשה לו טובה שהלוהו אבל בפקדון מעיז דאם כן בפקדון מודה מקצת נמי יהא פטור במגו דאי בעי כופר הכל ובכל דוכתא משמע דמודה מקצת חייב בפקדון גבי עשר גפנים טעונות מסרתי לך כו' (שבועות דף מג:) דמשמע דאיירי בפקדון וגבי סלע הלויתני עליו ושתים היה שוה (שם מג.) וגבי מציאה נמי אמרי' בהניזקין (גיטין נא. ושם) דמודה מקצת חייב ולא מהימן במגו אלא אור"ת דהיינו כגון חזקה שאין האשה מעיזה פניה בפני בעלה שאין לאדם פנים לכפור הכל וריב"א פי' אין אדם מעיז היכא שחבירו מכיר בשקרו ואין להאריך [ז]:

ובכולי

עין משפט נר מצוה

יח א מיי' פ"א מהל' מלוה ולוה הלכה א סמג עשין צד טוש"ע ח"מ סימן ע סעיף א:

יט ב מיי' פ"ד מהלכות טוען ונטען הלכה ה סמג שם טוש"ע ח"מ סי' עה סעיף ג:

כ ג מיי' פ"ה שם הל' ט סמג שם טוש"ע שם סימן צו סעיף א:

מסורת הש"ס

א) ב"ב דף קע. שבועות מא: [ועיין קדושין מג:], ב) גיטין נא. שבועות מב., ג) שם, ד) גיטין נא. ב"ק קז. שבועות מב: ב"מ ג., ה) [שם דף ו.], ו) כ"י כ', ז) [ונמוק' ב"ק קז. ד"ה עירוב וכו' האריכו טובא].

תוספות ישנים

א) [השתא קס"ד דהמלוה את חבירו בעדים צריך לפרעו בעדים ואין נאמן לומר פרעתי כיון דלית ליה מגו ומסיק דקי"ל דא"צ לפרעו בעדים ונאמן לומר פרעתי אפילו בלא מגו. מ"י].

הגהות הב"ח

(א) תוס' ד"ה דסתם וכו' בפני נכתב ובפני נחתם דאין עדים:

ליקוטי רש"י

דסתם יהודה וגליל. אפי' בשעת שלום. כשעת חירום דמו. שאין שיירות מצויות מזו לזו אבל בשאר מלכיות אי איכא חירום לא הויא חזקה אבל בשעת שלום הויא חזקה דהא שיירות מצויות והאי דקאמר רבי אבא בשעת חירום שנו הכי קאמר יהודה וגליל הרי הן כשעת חירום של שאר מלכיות [רשב"ם ב"ב לח:]. והאכלתיו פרס. והחזרתי לו חצי והחציו בידי חייב לישבע על השאר [שבועות מב.]. על טענת עצמו. השתא משמע שאין אדם תובעו ולקמן מפרש לה בטוענו זה בן המת. ורבי אליעזר בן יעקב לית ליה כו'. כמו והוינן בה ור"א לית ליה תקנתא דתיקון העולם דמשיב אבידה פטור משבועה דא"כ שביק לה ואזיל והאי נמי כיון דלא תבעו כמשיב אבידה הוא [גיטין נא.]. בטוענו קטן. יתום קטן תובעו. אין נשבעין על טענת חרש שוטה וקטן. כגון שטענו ברמאות חרש שדיברו חכמים בכל מקום לא מדבר ולא שומע [שבועות שם]. אי הכי. דטוענו גדול טענת עצמו קרי לה טענת אחרים היא. והודאת עצמו. על שהודה לו שאמת מדבריו ומודה שעדיין חייב לו פרס הוא נשבע. כולהי טענתא טענת אחרים והודאת עצמו נינהו. ולכך נשבעין עליה וכי האי גוונא מי פליגי רבנן עליה ומי הוה קאמר פעמים שאדם נשבע כל שעתא כי האי גוונא משתבע. אלא הכא בדרבה קמיפלגי. לא תימא בטוענו גדול אלא בטוענו קטן ודקשיא לך אין נשבעין על טענת קטן הני מילי בטוענו קטן הפקדתי לך דגבי קטן כתיב (שמות כב) כי יתן איש ולא קטן אבל בבא בטענת אביו נשבעין אפילו לקטן ולרבנן אפילו לגדול אין נשבעין כדתנן בשבועות מנה לאבא בידך אין לך בידי אלא חמשים דינר פטור ובדרבה פליגי [גיטין שם]. ולעולם בטוענו קטן ומשום דאין טענתו חשובה במקום אחר דכתיב כי יתן איש קרי ליה הכא טענת עצמו מיהו הכא טענה היא דהא איכא נתינת איש והיינו דקאמר פעמים וכי תימא רבנן אמאי פליגי עליה בדרבה קמיפלגי [שבועות שם]. מפני מה אמרה תורה כו'. לא חשבו כמשיב אבידה לפטור אלא כפר בכולו [ב"מ ג.]. חזקה אין אדם מעיז פניו וכו'. לכפור את הכל הלכך בשביל הודאת המקצת...

נאמן על השאר דהאי בכוליה בעי לכפריה כו' [גיטין שם]. אין אדם מעיז פניו בפני זה שעושה לו טובה הלכך היכא דכפר הכל פטור משבועה דאי לאו קושטא בהדיה לא הוה והיכא דמודה מקצת בכולה בעי למכפריה והא דלא כפריה משום דאין אדם מעיז [ב"ק קז.]. [מכאן שייך לע"ב] ובכולה בעי דלודי ליה. וכי תימא לא נשבעיה אשארא דמיגו דחשוד אממונא חשוד נמי אשבועתא מדלא כפריה בכוליה דהאי כי אודי בפלגא בכוליה נמי בעי לאודי והאי דלא אודי ליה לאו לדעתו למיגזליה אלא אישתמוטי אישתמיט לדחויי השתא [גיטין נא:]. וכ"ת מגו דחשיד אממונא חשיד אשבועתא ולא חשיד אממונא לפי שברצונו היה מודה בכולו אלא שאין בידו לפרוע וסבר עד דהוי לי [זוזי] ופרענא ליה [ב"מ ג:]. כיון שהגיד שוב אינו חוזר ומגיד. דבר המכחיש את הראשון דכתיב (ויקרא ה) אם לא יגיד קפיד קרא [סנהדרין מד:]. דמאחר שהודו שבכשרות נכתב הרי חתימת השטר כאילו העידו בב"ד כל מה שכתוב בשטר שהלוהו מלוה ללוה וכיון שהגיד שוב אינו חוזר ומגיד [רשב"ם ב"ב מט.]. נעשה כמי שנחקרה עדותן בב"ד. משעה שנכתב ונחתם ואין עדות אחרון מבטל את הראשון דכיון שהגיד שוב אינו חוזר ומגיד לא אתא על פה להשתא ומרע לשטרא דקדים [רשב"ם ב"ב מט.].

The Gemara rejects this explanation:

וְהָאָמַר מַר – **But the master said** in a Mishnah:[17] אֵין נִשְׁבָּעִין עַל טַעֲנַת חֵרֵשׁ שׁוֹטֶה וְקָטָן – WE DO NOT SWEAR IN RESPONSE TO THE CLAIM OF A DEAF-MUTE, A DERANGED PERSON OR A MINOR.[18] Hence, the defendant should not be required to swear because of his response to the minor's claim. – ? –

The Gemara reinterprets Rav's answer:

מַאי קָטָן – **What is** the intent of Rav's explanation that the case involves a claim by a **minor?** גָּדוֹל – It means that **an adult** orphan made the claim. וְאַמַּאי קָרֵי לֵיהּ קָטָן – **And why did [Rav] call [the orphan] a minor** if he is actually an adult? דִּלְגַבֵּי מִילֵּי דְאָבִיו קָטָן הוּא – **Because concerning his father's affairs** even **[an adult]** orphan **is** like **a minor,** since he is not fully aware of his father's dealings.[19] However, his claim is valid, and since the debtor's admission of partial liability came in response to a valid claim by an adult, R' Eliezer ben Yaakov obligates him to swear.

The Gemara asks:

אִי הָכִי – **If** it is **so** that the orphan is an adult, טַעֲנַת עַצְמוֹ – why does R' Eliezer ben Yaakov say that the debtor must swear in response to **"his own claim"?** טַעֲנַת אֲחֵרִים הִיא – **It is the claim of others** (i.e. the orphan) that causes him to swear![20] – ? –

The Gemara answers:

טַעֲנַת אֲחֵרִים – Indeed, it is **the claim of others** to which he must respond, וְהוֹדָאַת עַצְמוֹ – **but** it is **[the debtor's] own** partial **admission** that obligates him to swear. Therefore, it is appropriate for R' Eliezer ben Yaakov to refer to the defendant's obligation to swear as a consequence of his own claim.

The Gemara rejects this explanation as well:

כּוּלְּהִי טַעֲנְתָּא – **All [claims]** that cause one to swear the oath of partial admission **are** also cases of טַעֲנַת אֲחֵרִים וְהוֹדָאַת עַצְמוֹ נִינְהוּ – **the claim of others and [the debtor's] own admission.** Why, then, does R' Eliezer ben Yaakov say, "There are times" when a person swears in response to this type of claim, and why does he call it the defendant's "own claim"? This is no different that any other case of a plaintiff's claim and a defendant's partial admission![21] – ? –

Because of this question, the Gemara returns to its original understanding of Rav's answer – that the Baraisa speaks of a case in which the orphan claiming the debt was actually a minor. Although the Gemara had previously argued that a minor's claim cannot obligate a person to swear, the Gemara now assumes that a minor's claim may indeed obligate an oath as long as it concerns an action (e.g. a loan) entered into by an adult (his father).[22] Based on this understanding, the Gemara now explains the dispute between R' Eliezer ben Yaakov and the Sages:

אֶלָּא הָכָא בִּדְרַבָּה קָמִיפַּלְגֵי – **Rather, here [R' Eliezer ben Yaakov and the Sages] disagree concerning** the implication of **Rabbah's** teaching. דְּאָמַר רַבָּה – **For Rabbah said:** מִפְּנֵי מָה אָמְרָה תּוֹרָה – **For what** reason **did the Torah say** מוֹדֶה מִקְצָת הַטַּעֲנָה יִשָּׁבַע – that **one who admits part of a claim must swear** that his denial of the other part is true?[23] חֲזָקָה – **Because**

NOTES

the debtor's "own claim." The claim of a minor has no validity and the debtor was not *required* by law to respond to it; his conscience impelled him to do so. Hence, according to R' Eliezer ben Yaakov, his admission is legally deemed voluntary, yet he is not in the category of *meishiv aveidah* (*Ritva* to *Gittin* ibid.).

17. *Shevuos* 38b.

18. [The reason for this, as the Gemara now understands it, is that since these three are all legally incompetent, their claims have no legal standing. Since no oath is imposed without the plaintiff's presentation of a valid claim, their claims cannot obligate one to swear.]

Although a deaf-mute is incapable of speaking, it is possible for him to convey his claim by motioning (*Rashi* to *Shevuos* 42a ד״ה אין).

19. [I.e. he is as unaware of his father's affairs as a minor is of his own affairs.]

20. If the orphan is an adult whose claim is legally valid and requires a response, the debtor's admission cannot be considered "voluntary" (*Ritva* to *Gittin* ibid.).

21. *Rashi.* Furthermore, if the debtor's admission came in response to an adult's claim, why do the Rabbis exempt him from the oath? (*Rashi* to *Gittin* 51b and *Shevuos* 42b).

22. *Rashi.* The Gemara now reverses its previous assumption that one never swears in response to a minor's claim. Indeed, it is possible that one must swear in response to a minor's claim. The rule of the Mishnah cited above means only that one does not swear for a monetary obligation *incurred* to a minor [or deaf-mute, or deranged person]. Thus, for example, one would not swear where a minor claims, "I entrusted my property to you for safekeeping." But where a minor claims that the debtor owed money to his father, the debtor must swear if he acknowledges part of the claim.

This is learned from the verse in regard to the oath of a *shomer* (custodian of an object left in his care). That passage begins with the words: כִּי־יִתֵּן אִישׁ אֶל־רֵעֵהוּ, *If a man should give to his fellow* [an article to keep for him] (*Exodus* 22:6). The word אִישׁ, *man,* implies that the passage speaks of an article entrusted to the *shomer* by a *man,* not a minor. Now, the oath for partial admission is derived from verse 8 of this passage, as stated in *Bava Kamma* (107a). Thus, we learn that the oath for partial admission applies only where the money in dispute was *given* to the debtor by an adult, not a minor. The verse, however, does not indicate that the money must also be *claimed* by an adult. Therefore, in a case where the father lent the money, the debtor is required to swear for his admission of part of the debt even if the money is being claimed only by a son who is a minor (*Rashi;* see *Shevuos* 42a).

Accordingly, the Gemara returns to its original understanding of Rav's explanation: The dispute between R' Eliezer ben Yaakov and the Sages concerns a case where a minor claims that the debtor never paid any part of the debt to his father. Since the money was lent by an adult (the father), R' Eliezer ben Yaakov holds that the minor can, in this case, force the debtor to swear about the part of the debt he claims to have paid. Nevertheless, since a minor cannot *ordinarily* obligate someone to swear in regard to his money, R' Eliezer ben Yaakov characterizes the debtor in this case as "one who swears in response to his own claim" (*Rashi* to 18b). The Sages, however, hold that the defendant is exempt from an oath even if an *adult* orphan lodges the complaint (*Rashi*). The Gemara proceeds to explain the basis of their disagreement with R' Eliezer ben Yaakov.

[According to *Rashi,* the Gemara's change of mind about why one does not swear in response to a minor's claim is never stated explicitly, but is understood to be implicit in the Gemara's new explanation of the dispute between R' Eliezer ben Yaakov and the Sages. *Tosafos* object to *Rashi's* explanation for this very reason; such a reversal, in their opinion, should certainly have been stated explicitly. Therefore, *Tosafos* explain the Gemara differently; see there. See also *Rashba* and *Ritva.* For analysis of *Rashi's* opinion, see *Beis Yaakov, Chasam Sofer* et al.]

23. This obligation is derived from Scripture (*Exodus* 22:8; see previous note). [Rabbah questions why the Torah obligated one who admits part of a claim to swear, when logic dictates that he should be exempted. The plaintiff in such a case does not put forth any evidence to support his full claim (since if he did, there would be nothing about which to swear). The defendant's admission of part of the claim is thus a virtual windfall to the claimant, who could not have recovered anything had the defendant been disinclined to give it to him.] Thus, it seems to make no sense to require the defendant to swear about the part he denies. In a sense, he is a classic *meishiv aveidah* (one who returns otherwise lost property), and the Torah should exempt him from having to swear for that very reason – so as not to discourage honest people from admitting their debts (*Rashi* to *Bava Metzia* 3a ד״ה מפני מ״ה אמרה תורה).

Now, it is true that the rule that a *meishiv aveidah* need not swear is a Rabbinic innovation (see note 10). However, the logic of it seems to be compelling and should be meaningful even on the Biblical level (see *Chidushei HaRan* to *Bava Metzia* 3a). In fact, the very function of the oath imposed by the Torah for partial admission is to benefit the

דסתם יהודה וגליל בשעת חירום דמו [א] וליתני מודה רבי יהושע באומר לחבירו מנה לויתי ממך ופרעתיו לך שהוא נאמן משום דקא בעי למיתני סיפא אם יש עדים שהוא לוה ממנו והוא אומר פרעתיו אינו נאמן והא קיימא לן [א] המלוה את חבירו בעדים אינו צריך לפרעו בעדים וליתני מודה ר' יהושע באומר לחבירו מנה לאביך בידי והאכלתיו פרס שהוא נאמן אליבא דמאן אי אליבא דרבנן הא אמרי משיב אבידה הוי אי אליבא דרבי אליעזר בן יעקב הא אמר שבועה בעי דתניא [ג] רבי אליעזר בן יעקב אומר פעמים שאדם נשבע על טענת עצמו כיצד מנה לאביך בידי והאכלתיו פרס הרי זה נשבע וזהו שנשבע על טענת עצמו וחכמים אומרים [ב] אינו אלא כמשיב אבידה ופטור ור' אליעזר בן יעקב לית ליה משיב אבידה פטור אמר רב בטוענו קטן [ג] והאמר מר [ג] אין נשבעין על טענת חרש שוטה וקטן מאי קטן גדול ואמאי קרי ליה קטן דלגבי מילי דאביו קטן הוא אי הכי טענת עצמו טענת אחרים היא טענת אחרים והודאת עצמו כולהי טענתא טענת אחרים והודאת עצמו נינהו אלא הכא בדרבה קמיפלגי דאמר רבה [ד] מפני מה אמרה תורה מודה מקצת הטענה ישבע חזקה אין אדם מעיז פניו בפני בעל חובו והאי בכולה בעי דלכפריה והאי דלא כפר ליה משום דאין אדם מעיז פניו הוא

רש"י

וליתני מנה לויתי ממך. מלתיה דר' יהושע לאשמועינן דמודה היכא דאין שור שחוט לפניך מאי שנא דאשמועינן בקרקע וליצטריך למתנייה בהדיא משום סיפא לנקוט מלתיה במטלטלין ולישמעינן בדידיה גופיה: נאמן. מדאורייתא בלא שבועה: וניתני מודה ר' יהושע כו' והאכלתיו פרס. פרעתיו חציו שהוא נאמן בלא שבועה הואיל ואין שור שחוט לפניו דלאשמועינן רבותא דלא"ג דמודה במקצת פטור הואיל ואינו תובעו: אליבא דמאן. תנאי פליגי בהא מילתא בשבועות (דף מב.) ואי אמר רבי יהושע הכי לא כחד מינייהו הוא דאי כרבנן הא אמרי אפי' תובעו ומודה במקצת משיב אבידה הוא דתנן בשבועות מנה לאבא בידך אין לך בידי אלא חמשים דינר פטור משום שהוא כמשיב אבידה ומאי אשמועינן רבי יהושע דאין שור שחוט אפי' שור שחוט לפניו נמי נאמן ואי אליבא דר' אליעזר בן יעקב כי לא תבע ליה נמי האמר שבועה בעי: ורבי אליעזר לית ליה משיב אבידה פטור. מן השבועה בתמיה הא תקנתא דרבנן היא במס' גיטין (דף מח.) המוצא מציאה לא ישבע מפני תיקון העולם וכיון דכי אינו תובעו נמי מחייב ליה שבועה הרי אין לך משיב אבידה גדולה מזה ומחייב: אין נשבעין על טענת חרש שוטה וקטן. משנה היא בשבועות: טענת אחרים הוא. ומאי פעמים דקאמר ומאי טענת עצמו: אלא הכא בדרבה קא מיפלגי. אלא לעולם בטוענו קטן ודקשיא לך אין נשבעין על טענת קטן הני מילי בשטוענו קטן אני נתתיו לך וקרא כתיב כי יתן איש אל רעהו ולא קטן ומהכא יליף לה בשבועות אבל הכא שבא בטענת אביו אית ליה לרבי אליעזר בן יעקב נשבעין ורבנן פליגי עליה אפילו בטוענו גדול וקרו ליה משיב אבידה ובדרבה קא מיפלגי:

תוספות

דסתם יהודה וגליל בשעת חירום דמי. תימה דבריש גיטין (דף ד: ושם) תנן דבארץ ישראל א"צ לומר בפני נכתב ובפני נחתם אפי' מיהודה לגליל משום דאיכא עולי רגלים ובתי דינין ועדים מצויין לקיימו ויש לומר דהתם האשה מחזרת אחר עדי קיום אע"ג דיהודה וגליל בשעת חירום דמי תמצא עדי קיום כיון דאיכא עולי רגלים אבל המחזיק אין רגיל לחזור אחר עדי מחאה ואם תאמר התם (א) דאמר שאני בני מחוזא דניידי וצריך לומר אפי' באותה שכונה בפני נכתב (א) דאין עדים מצוין לקיימו אטו במחוזא לא מועיל מחאה שלא בפניו וי"ל דהתם דרך הליכתן מן העיר כשמעו מחאה רגילות הוא לומר פלוני מיחה ושומעין אחרים עד שנשמע הקול למחזיק אבל גבי גט אין רגיל שיאמרו בהליכתן אנו חתמנו על הגט [ו] [או מכירין אנו חתימת עדים החתומים]: **אין** צריך לפרעו בעדים. ואם תאמר למאן דאמר צריך לפרעו בעדים תקשי ליה מתניתין הכל הכא דליתני מנה לך בידי ויש לומר לפלוגתא דתנאי היא בפרק שבועת הדיינין (שבועות דף מא:) אי נמי דלא חשיב לה פירכא דניחא ליה לאשמועינן דאין מחזיקין בנכסי קטן ואם תאמר מאי משני אכתי ליתני ואם יש עדים ואמר לו אל תפרעני אלא בפני פלוני ופלוני אינו נאמן וי"ל דלא היה רוצה להאריך בלשונו או שמא מילתא דפשיטא הוא: **אי** אליבא דרבנן הא אמרי משיב אבידה הוי. כדמסיק דבבנו מעיז וא"כ לא מצי למיתני ואם יש עדים אינו נאמן דלעולם נאמן במגו דאי בעי אמר פרעתי הכל דבבנו מעיז ומעיז: **ורבי** אליעזר בן יעקב לית ליה משיב אבידה פטור. פי' בקונטרס התקן המוצא מציאה לא ישבע מפני תיקון העולם ואית ספרים דגרסי הכי בהדיא ואין נראה לא לרבינו יצחק דמשיב אבידה פטור מדאורייתא מטעם מגו ולא מכח ההיא משנה פריך אלא פריך וכי לית ליה מגו וכן משמע בהניזקין (גיטין דף נא. ושם) דפריך ולית ליה לרבי יצחק המוצא מציאה כו' ומשני הוא דאמר כר"א בן יעקב דאמר פעמים שאדם נשבע וכו' ופריך ור"א בן יעקב לית ליה משיב אבידה פטור והשתא אי מכח מתני' פריך הוה ליה למימר ולית ליה לר"א בן יעקב המוצא מציאה כדקאמר ארבי יצחק ועוד כיון דמשני הוא דאמר כר"א בן יעקב א"כ רוצה לומר דר"א פליג אמתניתין א"כ מאי פריך ור"א בן יעקב לית ליה משיב אבידה פטור אין הכי נמי דלית ליה אלא מכח מגו פריך כדפרישית: **אלא** הכא בדרבה קא מיפלגי. פירש בקונטרס לעולם בטוענו קטן ודקא קשיא לך הא אין נשבעין על טענת קטן ה"מ בבא בטענת עצמו אבל בבא בטענת אביו טענה חשובה היא וכי תימה מ"ט דרבנן דאין סברא לומר דסברי דאף בבא בטענת אביו לית ביה ממשא אלא בדרבה קמיפלגי ונראה דמשום דקרי ליה טענת עצמו דחקו להעמיד בטוענו קטן אבל קשה דעיקר התירוץ חסר מן הספר ועוד דבהגוזל קמא (ב"ק דף קו: ושם) ממעטינן נתנו כשהוא קטן ותבעו כשהוא גדול עד שתהא תביעה ונתינה שוין בגדלות וה"ה דמהאי קרא ממעט נתנו כשהוא גדול ותבעו כשהוא קטן דהיינו כגון שנתן לו אביו ותבעו בקטנות ונראה דה"פ לעולם בגדול מיירי אלא לא תימא דקרי ליה טענת עצמו משום דהודאת עצמו היא אלא בדרבה קמיפלגי ולרבנן דסברי דבבנו מעיז טענת עצמו היא וה"ק ראב"י פעמים שאדם נשבע על מה שאתם מחשיבים טענת עצמו אבל לדידי דאינו מעיז טענת אחרים היא ובסוף שבועת הדיינין (שבועות דף מב. ושם) דתנן אבל נשבעין לקטן ומפרש בבא בטענת אביו וראב"י היא ההוא קטן נמי לאו דווקא אלא גדול וקרי ליה קטן משום דלגבי מילי דאבוה קטן הוא כדמפרש הכא וקשה קצת דהוה ליה לאקשויי ולשנויי אמתניתין דהתם כמו שמקשה על רב דבההיא שמעתא גופה לא מקשה על המשנה אלא על רב: **מפני** מה אמרה תורה מודה מקצת הטענה ישבע. אפילו לרבנן דר"ש דלא דרשי טעמא דקרא קא בעי רבה שפיר מפני מה אמרה תורה כו' דלמאי לא מהימן בלא שבועה במגו דאי בעי כפר הכל או נילף מהכא דלא אמרינן מגו ומשני דאין זה מגו דאין אדם מעיז לכפור ואף על גב דבפרק שבועת הדיינין (שם דף מ:) אמרינן בכופר הכל משביעין אותו שבועת היסת משום דחזקה אין אדם תובע אלא אם כן יש לו ופריך אדרבה חזקה דאין אדם מעיז פניו בפני בעל חובו ומשני דאשתמוטי קמשתמיט אלמא בכופר בכל נמי אדם מעיז לכפור דאשתמוטי קא משתמיט כמו במודה מקצת מ"מ קאמר הכא שפיר חזקה דאין אדם מעיז לכפור הכל כל כך ולא הוי מגו דיותר ברצון הוא מודה במקצת הטענה דאינו מעיז כל כך אבל אין לפרש דרבה אתא לפרושי מפני מה אמרה תורה מודה מקצת ולא כופר הכל וקאמר חזקה דאין אדם מעיז לכך נאמן כשכופר הכל דאם כן במקום שיכול להעיז אפילו כופר הכל חייב ובסמוך אמרינן איפכא לרבנן דבבנו מעיז ופטור אף מודה מקצת הטענה משום דמשיב אבידה הוא מגו דאי בעי כפר הכל ואם תאמר ומנלן דכופר הכל פטור וליכא למימר מדאצטריך קרא לחייב שבועה בעד אחד מכלל דכופר הכל פטור דהא איצטריך להיכא שמעידים שגנב לו והוא אינו יודע אלא י"ל דגזירת הכתוב היא דכי הוא זה משמע דבעינן כפירה והודאה ועוד מודה מקצת יש להשביעו שחייב לו ממון שהודה ועל ידי כך מגלגל עליו שבועה כעין גלגול אבל כופר הכל נסתלק לגמרי ממנו: **חזקה** אין אדם מעיז פניו. לא כמו שפי' בקונטרס בהגוזל (ב"ק דף קז.) דאין אדם מעיז לפי שעשה לו טובה שהלוהו אבל בפקדון מעיז דאם כן בפקדון מודה מקצת נמי יהא פטור במגו דאי בעי כופר הכל ובכל דוכתא משמע דמודה מקצת חייב בפקדון גבי עשר גפנים טעונות מסרתי לך כו' (שבועות דף מג:) דמשמע דאיירי בפקדון וגבי סלע הלויתני עליו ושתים היה שוה (שם מג.) וגבי מציאה נמי אמרי' בהניזקין (גיטין נא. ושם) דמודה מקצת חייב ולא מהימן במגו אלא אור"ת דהיינו כגון חזקה שאין האשה מעיזה פניה בפני בעלה שאין לאדם פנים לכפור הכל וריב"א פי' אין אדם מעיז היכא שחבירו מכיר בשקרו ואין להאריך [ז]: ובכולי

[illegible]

מסורת הש"ס

א) ב"ב דף קע. שבועות מא: [ועיין קדושין מג:], ב) גיטין נא. שבועות מב., ג) שם, ד) גיטין נא. ב"ק קז. שבועות מב: ב"מ ג., ה) [שם דף ו.], ו) ג"י כ"י, ז) [ובתוס' ב"ק קז. ד"ה עירוב וכו' האריכו טובא].

תוספות ישנים

א) [השתא קס"ד דהמלוה את חבירו בעדים צריך לפרעו בעדים ואין נאמן לומר פרעתי כיון דקי"ל דלא"צ לפרעו בעדים ונאמן לומר פרעתי אפילו בלא מגו. ת"י].

הגהות הב"ח

(א) תוס' ד"ה דסתם וכו' בפני נכתב ובפני נחתם דאין עדים:

עין משפט נר מצוה

יח א מיי' פי"א מהל' מלוה ולוה הלכה א סמג עשין צד טוש"ע ח"מ סימן ע סעיף א:

יט ב מיי' פ"ד מהלכות טוען ונטען הלכה ה סמג שם טוש"ע שם סי' עה סעיף ג:

כ ג מיי' פ"ה שם הל' ט סמג שם טוש"ע שם סימן לו סעיף א:

ליקוטי רש"י

דסתם יהודה וגליל. אפי' בשעת שלום. כשעת חירום דמו. שאין שיירות מצויות מזו לזו אבל בשאר מלכיות אי איכא חירום לא הויא חזקה אבל בשעת שלום הויא חזקה דהא שיירות מצויות והאי דקאמר רבי אבא בשעת חירום שנו הכי קאמר יהודה וגליל הרי הן כשעת חירום של שאר מלכיות [רשב"ם ב"ב לח:]. והאכלתיו פרס. והחזרתי לו חצי והחציו בידי חייב לישבע על השאר [שבועות מב.]. על טענת עצמו. השתא משמע שאין אדם תובעו ולקמן מפרש לה בטוענו זה בן המת. ורבי אליעזר בן יעקב לית ליה כו'. כמו והוינן בה ור"א לית ליה חששא דתיקון העולם דמשיב אבידה פטור משבועה דא"כ שביק לה ואזיל והאי נמי כיון דלא תבעו כמשיב אבידה הוא [גיטין נא:]. בטוענו קטן. יתום קטן תובע. אין נשבעין על טענת חרש שוטה וקטן. כגון שטענו ברמיזה דחרש שדיברו חכמים בכל מקום לא מדבר ולא שומע [שבועות שם]. אי הכי. דטוענו גדול טענת עצמו קרי לה טענת אחרים היא. והודאת עצמו. על שהודה לו שאמת כדבריו ומודה שעדיין חייב לו פרס הוא נשבע. כולהי טענתא טענת אחרים והודאת עצמו נינהו. ולכך נשבעין עליה וכי האי גוונא מי פליגי רבנן עליה ומי הוה קאמר פעמים שאדם נשבע כל שעתא כי האי גוונא משתבע. אלא הכא בדרבה קמיפלגי. לא תימא בטוענו גדול אלא בטוענו קטן ודקשיא לך אין נשבעין על טענת קטן הני מילי בשטוענו הפקדתי לך דגבי שבועה כתיב (שמות כב) כי יתן איש ולא קטן אבל בא בטענת אביו נשבעין אפילו לקטן ולרבנן אפילו לגדול אין נשבעין כדתנן בשבועות מנה לאבא בידך אין לו בידי אלא חמשים דינר פטור ובדרבה פליגי [גיטין שם]. ולעולם בטוענו קטן ומשום דאין טענתו חשובה במקום אחר דכתיב כי יתן איש קרי ליה הכא טענת עצמו מיהו הכא טענה היא דהא איכא נתינת איש דמכח נתינת האב היא באה והיינו דקאמר פעמים וכי תימא רבנן אמאי פליגי עליה בדרבה קמיפלגי [שבועות שם:]. מפני מה אמרה תורה כו'. ולא חשבו כמשיב אבידה לפטרו שלא כפר בכולו [ב"מ ג.]. חזקה אין אדם מעיז פניו וכו'. לכפור את הכל הלכך בשביל הודאת המקצת אינו

The Gemara responds:

אַלִּיבָּא דְּמַאן – **With whom** would this ruling **accord?** I.e. this precise case is actually the subject of a Tannaic dispute between the Rabbis and R' Eliezer ben Yaakov, as we shall see shortly, and the opinion that you propose to attribute to R' Yehoshua does not accord with either of these known Tannaic views:[9] אִי אַלִּיבָּא דְּרַבָּנָן – **If** you say it **accords with** the opinion of **the Rabbis,** I will respond: הָא אָמְרֵי מֵשִׁיב אֲבֵידָה הָוֵי – **Why, [the Rabbis] say** that **[one who admits liability based on a debt to his fellow's *father*] is** like **one who returns a lost object** and is exempt from an oath even if his partial admission came in response to his fellow's claim![10] How could the Mishnah teach that R' Yehoshua agrees specifically in the instance in which the admission was unprompted?[11] אִי אַלִּיבָּא דְּרַבִּי אֱלִיעֶזֶר בֶּן יַעֲקֹב – And **if** you say it **accords with** the opinion of **R' Eliezer ben Yaakov,** I will respond: הָא אָמַר שְׁבוּעָה בָּעֵי – **Why, [R' Eliezer ben Yaakov] says** that **an oath is required** of the one who admits partial liability based on a debt to his fellow's father, even when he made the admission without having a claim lodged against him (as we shall see shortly). Thus, the ruling you proposed to attribute to R' Yehoshua contradicts R' Eliezer ben Yaakov's opinion!

The source of the dispute between the Rabbis and R' Eliezer ben Yaakov is the following:

דְּתַנְיָא – **For it was taught in a Baraisa:** רַבִּי אֱלִיעֶזֶר בֶּן יַעֲקֹב אוֹמֵר – R' ELIEZER BEN YAAKOV SAYS: פְּעָמִים שֶׁאָדָם נִשְׁבָּע עַל טַעֲנַת עַצְמוֹ – THERE ARE TIMES WHEN A PERSON SWEARS IN RESPONSE TO HIS OWN CLAIM. כֵּיצַד – HOW SO? מָנֶה לְאָבִיךְ בְּיָדִי וְהֶאֱכַלְתִּיו פְּרַס – If one said to an orphan: "A *MANEH* OF YOUR FATHER'S WAS IN MY POSSESSION BUT I REPAID HIM HALF of it," הֲרֵי זֶה נִשְׁבָּע – THIS person MUST SWEAR that he repaid half. וְזֶהוּ שֶׁנִּשְׁבָּע עַל טַעֲנַת עַצְמוֹ – AND THIS IS THE ONE WHO SWEARS IN RESPONSE TO HIS OWN CLAIM.[12] וַחֲכָמִים אוֹמְרִים – BUT THE SAGES SAY: אֵינוֹ אֶלָּא כְּמֵשִׁיב אֲבֵידָה וּפָטוּר – [THE DEBTOR] IS ONLY LIKE ONE WHO RETURNS A LOST ARTICLE, AND IS therefore EXEMPT from swearing. Elsewhere, the Sages rule that for this reason he is exempt from swearing even if the orphan initiated the litigation with a claim against him.[13] Thus, the ruling that you proposed for our Mishnah would not accord with either of the Tannaic opinions concerning this matter. That is why our Tanna was unable to cite it.

The Gemara now digresses to discuss the Baraisa, and asks:

וְרַבִּי אֱלִיעֶזֶר בֶּן יַעֲקֹב לֵית לֵיהּ מֵשִׁיב אֲבֵידָה פָּטוּר – **But does R' Eliezer ben Yaakov,** who rules that the debtor must swear, **not accept** the necessary rule that **one who returns a lost article is exempt** from swearing? Of course he does![14] Why, then, does he not extend the exemption to the parallel case of a debtor who agrees to pay something that was not claimed of him?[15]

The Gemara answers:

אָמַר רַב – **Rav said:** בְּטוֹעֲנוֹ קָטָן – R' Eliezer ben Yaakov speaks of a case **where a minor makes a claim against [the debtor].** That is, the minor, who is an orphan, initiates the litigation by claiming that he knows of the debt to his father, and that it is completely unpaid, and the defendant claims that he repaid half of it. Since the orphan initiated the claim, R' Eliezer ben Yaakov does not liken the debtor to one who returns lost property. Hence, he requires the debtor to swear.[16]

NOTES

the entire amount." In this situation, there is a basis for imposing the Biblical oath of partial admission, for the fellow disputes the defendant's claim. However, since his knowledge of the loan itself is based on the defendant's initial admission – and thus, "there was no slaughtered ox" and the defendant had the power of *happeh she'assar* – he should be free from taking the oath (*Baal HaMaor* to *Gittin* 51a, *Maharshal, Haflaah, Beis Yaakov, Chasam Sofer;* see *Shach, Choshen Mishpat* 88:55 and *Nesivos HaMishpat* ad loc.).

[It seems curious that the Gemara does not suggest that the Tanna should have addressed the case where someone says to his fellow, "A *maneh* of *yours* was in my possession and I repaid half of it." For possible reasons, see *Maharam Schif, Beis Yaakov, Chasam Sofer* and *Beis HaLevi* 3:20.]

9. The Gemara will shortly cite a Baraisa containing the Tannaic dispute. R' Eliezer ben Yaakov rules that when one says, "I owed your father a *maneh* but I repaid half" [and the fellow claims that nothing was paid,] the debtor is subject to the oath of partial admission. The Rabbis, on the other hand, exempt him from the oath. Their respective opinions will be clarified below.

10. The Mishnah teaches in *Shevuos* 38b: If someone tells his fellow, "You owed my father a *maneh* (one hundred *zuz*)," and the fellow responds, "I owed him only fifty *zuz,*" he is exempt from the oath of partial admission, because he is like one who returned a lost article. I.e. since the child does not claim that he lent the money himself, but merely states that his *father* supposedly made the loan, the defendant could easily have denied the charge completely. And since he did not make the complete denial, but condescended to admit partial liability, he is regarded as one who returns what would otherwise be a lost article [מֵשִׁיב אֲבֵידָה, *meishiv aveidah*]. In such a case, even where the owner claims that the return is incomplete, the returner is exempt from swearing (*Rashi* there; see below for further clarification).

This Mishnah follows the Rabbis' opinion, and teaches that they exempt the partial admitter – for they consider him a *meishiv aveidah* – even when the son of the deceased initiated the litigation by presenting a claim against him (*Rashi*).

11. The point of our Mishnah is that R' Yehoshua agrees that a defendant is believed on the basis of *happeh she'assar* "when there is no slaughtered ox," i.e. when he himself initiates the claim against him. But according to the Rabbis' opinion, in this case the defendant is believed even if the plaintiff initiated matters by lodging a claim against him [since he is regarded as one who returns a lost article] (*Rashi;* cf. *Tosafos* ד״ה אי אליבא דרבנן).

12. Since he admits to still owing half, he must take the Biblical oath of partial admission. As explained previously, this pertains only when the orphan responds, "You definitely did not repay my father anything, and therefore, you still owe the full amount that you admit to having borrowed." The defendant is described as "swearing in response to his own claim" because the orphan would not have known about the loan at all if not for the defendant's voluntary confession (*Maharshal;* see note 8). [This reflects the Gemara's current understanding of R' Eliezer ben Yaakov's opinion. However, the Gemara will revise its understanding below.]

13. See note 10.

14. The Mishnah in *Gittin* (48b) teaches that, for the betterment of society, a *meishiv aveidah* (one who returns lost property) need not swear. I.e. the Sages enacted that if the owner claims the return is incomplete, the returner is exempt from the oath of partial admission, so that people should not be deterred from returning lost property out of concern that they might be required to swear about it (*Rashi* here and to *Gittin* 51b).

15. There is no better example of *meishiv aveidah* than a person who voluntarily steps forward and admits to an unknowing orphan that he owed the orphan's father a sum of money! Surely, when the Sages exempted a *meishiv aveidah* from the oath of partial admission, they included this person as well [so that people would be unafraid to step forward and pay unclaimed debts] (*Rashi;* cf. *Tosafos* ד״ה ורבי אליעזר בן יעקב; see *Pnei Yehoshua*). Thus, even though the orphan subsequently claims that his father was not paid at all and the entire sum must still be owed, the debtor ought to be exempt from the oath, since he initiated the matter by "returning a lost article" to the orphan (*Haflaah, Beis Yaakov*).

16. Since the orphan claims with certainty (בָּרִי) that the debtor still owes the full amount, R' Eliezer ben Yaakov does not consider the debtor to be returning something that would otherwise be lost (*Rashi* to *Gittin* 51b ד״ה הוא דאמר כר״א בן יעקב; *Ritva* here). Nevertheless, R' Eliezer ben Yaakov characterizes the oath as being taken in response to

דסתם יהודה וגליל כשעת חירום דמו א) וליתני מודה רבי יהושע באומר לחבירו מנה לויתי ממך ופרעתיו לך שהוא נאמן משום דקא בעי למיתני סיפא אם יש עדים שהוא לוה ממנו והוא אומר פרעתיו אינו נאמן והא ב) קיימא לן א המלוה את חבירו בעדים אינו צריך לפרעו בעדים וליתני מודה ר' יהושע באומר לחבירו מנה לאביך בידי והאכלתיו פרס שהוא נאמן אליבא דמאן אי אליבא דרבנן הא אמרי משיב אבידה הוי אי אליבא דרבי אליעזר בן יעקב הא אמר שבועה בעי דתניא ג) רבי אליעזר בן יעקב אומר פעמים שאדם נשבע על טענת עצמו כיצד מנה לאביך בידי והאכלתיו פרס הרי זה נשבע וזהו שנשבע על טענת עצמו וחכמים אומרים ב אינו אלא כמשיב אבידה ופטור ור' אליעזר בן יעקב לית ליה משיב אבידה פטור אמר רב בטוענו קטן ג) והאמר מר ג אין נשבעין על טענת חרש שוטה וקטן מאי קטן גדול ואמאי קרי ליה קטן דלגבי מילי דאביו קטן הוא אי הכי טענת עצמו טענת אחרים היא טענת אחרים והודאת עצמו כולהי טענתא טענת אחרים והודאת עצמו נינהו אלא הכא בדרבה קמיפלגי דאמר רבה ד) מפני מה אמרה תורה מודה מקצת הטענה ישבע חזקה אין אדם מעיז פניו בפני בעל חובו והאי בכולה בעי דלכפריה והאי דלא כפר ליה משום דאין אדם מעיז פניו הוא

רש"י

וליתני מנה לויתי ממך. מלתיה דר' יהושע למודה היכא דליכא שום שטות לפניך מאי שנא דלאשמועינן בקרקע ואיצטריך למתנייה באביו משום סיפא לנקוט מלתיה במטלטלין ולאשמועינן בדידיה גופיה: נאמן. מדאורייתא בלא שבועה: וניתני מודה ר' יהושע כו' והאכלתיו פרס. פרעתי חציו שהוא נאמן בלא שבועה הואיל ואין שור שחוט לפניו לאשמועינן רבותא דלע"ג דמודה במקצת פטור הואיל ואינו תובעו: אליבא דמאן. תנאי פליגי בהא מילתא בשבועות (דף מב.) ולאי אמר רבי יהושע הכי לא כחד מנייהו הוא דאי כרבנן הא אמרי אפי' תובעו וזה מודה במקצת משיב אבידה הוא דתנן בשבועות מנה לאבא בידך אין לך בידי אלא חמשים דינר פטור משום שהוא כמשיב אבידה ומאי אשמועינן רבי יהושע בלאין שור שחוט אפי' שור שחוט לפניו נמי נאמן ואי אליבא דר' אליעזר בן יעקב כי לא תבע ליה נמי האמר שבועה בעי: ורבי אליעזר לית ליה משיב אבידה פטור. מן השבועה בתמיה הא תקנתא דרבנן היא במס' גיטין (דף מח.) המוצא מציאה לא ישבע מפני תיקון העולם וכיון דכי אינו תובעו נמי מחייב ליה שבועה הרי אין לך משיב אבידה גדולה מזו וחייב: אין נשבעין על טענת חרש שוטה וקטן. משנה היא בשבועות: טענת אחרים הוא. ומאי פעמים דקאמר ומאי טענת עצמו: אלא הכא בדרבה קא מיפלגי. אלא לעולם בטוענו קטן ודקשיא לך אין נשבעין על טענת קטן הני מילי בשטוענו קטן אני נתתיו לך וקרא כתיב כי יתן איש אל רעהו ולא קטן ומהכא יליף לה בשבועות אבל הכא שבא בטענת אביו אית ליה לרבי אליעזר בן יעקב נשבעין ורבנן פליגי עליה אפילו בטוענו גדול וקרו ליה משיב אבידה ובדרבה קא מיפלגי:

תוספות

דסתם יהודה וגליל כשעת חירום דמי. תימה דבריש גיטין (דף ז: ושם) תנן דבארץ ישראל א"צ לומר בפני נכתב ובפני נחתם אפי' מיהודה לגליל משום דאיכא עולי רגלים ובתי דינין ועדים מצויין לקיימו ויש לומר דהתם האשה מחזרת אחר עדי קיום אע"ג דיהודה וגליל כשעת חירום דמי תמצא עדי קיום כיון דאיכא עולי רגלים אבל המחזיק אין רגיל לחזור אחר עדי מחאה ואם תאמר התם ה) דאמר שאני בני מחוזא דניידי וא"צ לומר אפי' בלותה שכונה בפני נכתב (א) דאין עדים מצויין לקיימו אטו במחוזא לא תועיל מחאה אלא בפניו וי"ל דהתם דרך הליכתן מן העיר כששמעו מחאה רגילות הוא לומר פלוני מיחה ושומעין אחרים עד שנשמע הקול למחזיק אבל גבי גט אין רגיל שיאמרו בהליכתן אנו חתמנו על הגט ו) [או מכירין אנו חתימת עדים החתומים]: אין צריך לפרעו בעדים. ואם תאמר למאן דאמר צריך לפרעו בעדים ולא מקשי ליה מתניתין דהכא לליתני מנה לך בידי ויש לומר דפלוגתא דתנאי היא בפרק שבועת הדיינין (שבועות דף מא:) אי נמי דלא חשיב לה פירכא דניחא ליה לאשמועינן דאין מחזיקין בנכסי קטן ואם תאמר מאי משני אכתי ליתני ואם יש עדים ואמר לו אל תפרעני אלא בפני פלוני ופלוני אינו נאמן וי"ל דלא היה רוצה להאריך בלשונו או שמא מילתא דפשיטא הוא: אי אליבא דרבנן הא אמרי משיב אבידה הוי. כדמסיק דבבנו מעיז וא"כ לא מצי למיתני ואם יש עדים אינו נאמן דלעולם נאמן במגו דאי בעי אמר פרעתי הכל דבבנו מעיז ומעיז: ורבי אליעזר בן יעקב לית ליה משיב אבידה פטור. פי' בקונטרס התנן המוצא מציאה לא ישבע מפני תיקון העולם ואית ספרים דגרסי הכי בהדיא ואין נראה לרבינו יצחק דמשיב אבידה פטור מדאורייתא מטעם מגו ולא מכח ההיא משנה פריך אלא פריך וכי לית ליה מגו וכן משמע בהניזקין (גיטין דף נא. ושם) דפריך ולית ליה לרבי יצחק המוצא מציאה כו' ומשני הוא דאמר כר"א בן יעקב דאמר פעמים שאדם נשבע וכו' ופריך ור"א בן יעקב לית ליה משיב אבידה פטור והשתא אי מכח מתני' פריך הוה ליה למימר ולית ליה לר"א בן יעקב המוצא מציאה כדקאמר ארבי יצחק ועוד כיון דמשני הוא דאמר כר"א בן יעקב א"כ רוצה לומר דר"א פליג אמתניתין א"כ מאי פריך ור"א בן יעקב לית ליה משיב אבידה פטור אין הכי נמי דלית ליה אלא מכח מגו פריך כדפרישית: **אלא** הכא בדרבה קא מיפלגי. פירש בקונטרס לעולם בטוענו קטן ודקא קשיא לך הא אין נשבעין על טענת קטן ה"מ בבא בטענת עצמו אבל בבא בטענת אביו טענה חשובה היא וכי תימא מ"ט דרבנן דאין סברא לומר דסברי דאף בבא בטענת אביו לית ביה ממשא אלא בדרבה קמיפלגי ונראה דמשום דקרי ליה טענת עצמו דחקו להעמיד בטוענו קטן אבל קשה דעיקר התירוץ חסר מן הספר ועוד דבהגוזל קמא (ב"ק דף קו: ושם) ממעטינן נתנו כשהוא קטן ותבעו כשהוא גדול עד שתהא תביעה ונתינה שוין בגדלות וה"ה דמהאי קרא ממעט נתנו כשהוא גדול ותבעו כשהוא קטן דהיינו כגון שנתן לו אביו ותבעו בקטנות ונראה דה"פ לעולם בגדול מיירי אלא לא תימא דקרי ליה טענת עצמו משום דהודאת עצמו היא אלא בדרבה קמיפלגי ורבנן דסברי דבבנו מעיז טענת עצמו היא וה"ק ראב"י פעמים שאדם נשבע על מה שאתם מחשיבים טענת עצמו אבל לדידי דאינו מעיז טענת אחרים היא ובסוף שבועת הדיינין (שבועות דף מב. ושם) דתנן אבל נשבעין לקטן ומפרש בבא בטענת אביו וראב"י היא ההוא קטן נמי לאו דווקא אלא גדול וקרי ליה קטן משום דלגבי מילי דאבוה קטן הוא כדמפרש הכא וקשה קצת דהוה ליה לאקשויי ולשנויי אמתניתין דהתם כמו שמקשה על רב דההיא שמעתא גופה לא מקשה על המשנה אלא על רב: **מפני** מה אמרה תורה מודה מקצת הטענה ישבע. אפילו לרבנן דר"ש דלא דרשי טעמא דקרא קא בעי רבה שפיר מפני מה אמרה תורה כו' דלמאי לא מהימן בלא שבועה במגו דאי בעי כפר הכל או נילף מהכא דלא אמרינן מגו ומשני דאין זה מגו דאין אדם מעיז לכפור ואף על גב דבפרק שבועת הדיינין (שם דף מ:) אמרינן בכופר הכל משביעין אותו שבועת היסת משום דחזקה אין אדם תובע אלא אם כן יש לו ופריך אדרבה חזקה דאין אדם מעיז פניו בפני בעל חובו ומשני דלאשתמוטי קמשתמיט אלמא בכופר בכל נמי אדם מעיז לכפור דלאשתמוטי קא משתמיט כמו במודה מקצת מ"מ קאמר הכא שפיר חזקה דאין אדם מעיז לכפור הכל כל כך ולא הוי מגו דיותר ברצון הוא מודה במקצת הטענה דאינו מעיז כל כך אבל אין לפרש דרבה אתא לפרושי מפני מה אמרה תורה מודה מקצת ולא כופר הכל וקאמר חזקה דאין אדם מעיז לכך נאמן כשכופר הכל דאם כן במקום שיכול להעיז אפילו כופר הכל חייב ובסמוך אמרינן איפכא לרבנן דבבנו מעיז ופטור אף מודה מקצת הטענה משום דמשיב אבידה הוא מגו דאי בעי כפר הכל ואם תאמר ומנלן דכופר הכל פטור וליכא למימר מדאצטריך קרא לחייב שבועה בעד אחד מכלל דכופר הכל פטור דהא איצטריך להיכא שמעידים שגנב לו והוא אינו יודע אלא י"ל דגזירת הכתוב היא דכי הוא זה משמע דבעינן כפירה והודאה ועוד מודה מקצת יש להשביעו שחייב לו ממון שהודה ועל ידי כך מגלגל עליו שבועה כעין גלגול אבל כופר הכל נסתלק לגמרי ממנו: **חזקה** אין אדם מעיז פניו. לא כמו שפי' בקונטרס בהגוזל (ב"ק דף קז.) דאין אדם מעיז לפי שעשה לו טובה שהלוהו אבל בפקדון מודה מקצת נמי יהא פטור במגו דאי בעי כופר הכל ובכל דוכתא משמע דמודה מקצת חייב בפקדון גבי עשר גפנים טעונות מסרתי לך כו' (שבועות דף מג:) דמשמע דאיירי בפקדון וגבי סלע הלויתני עליו ושתים היה שוה (שם מג.) וגבי מציאה נמי אמרי' בהניזקין (גיטין נא. ושם) דמודה מקצת חייב ולא מהימן במגו אלא אור"ת דהיינו כגון חזקה שאין האשה מעיזה פניה בפני בעלה שאין לאדם פנים לכפור הכל וריב"א פי' אין אדם מעיז היכא שחבירו מכיר בשקרו ואין להאריך ז):

ובכולי

מסורת הש"ס

א) כ"ב דף קע. שבועות מא: [ועיין קדושין מג:], ב) גיטין נא: שבועות מב., ג) שם, ד) גיטין נא. ב"ק קז. שבועות מב: ב"מ ג., ה) [שם דף ו:], ו) נ"י כ"י, ז) [ובתוס' ב"ק קז. ד"ה עירוב וכו' האריכו טובא].

תוספות ישנים

א) [השתא] קס"ד דהמלוה את חבירו בעדים צריך לפרעו בעדים ואין נאמן לומר פרעתי כיון דלית ליה מגו ומסיק דקי"ל דא"צ לפרעו בעדים ונאמן לומר פרעתי אפילו בלא מגו. מ"י.

הגהות הב"ח

(א) תוס' ד"ה דסתם וכו' בפני נכתב ובפני נחתם דאין עדים:

עין משפט נר מצוה

יח א מיי' פי"א מהל' מלוה ולוה הלכה א סמג עשין לה טוש"ע ח"מ סימן ע סעיף א:

יט ב מיי' פ"ד מהלכות טוען ונטען הלכה ה סמג שם טוש"ע שם סי' עה סעיף ג:

כ ג מיי' פ"ה שם הל' ט סמג שם טוש"ע שם סימן לו סעיף א:

ליקוטי רש"י

דסתם יהודה וגליל. אפי' בשעת שלום. כשעת חירום דמו. שאין שיירות מלויות מזו לזו אבל בשאר מלכיות אי איכא חירום לא הויא חזקה אבל בשעת שלום הויא חזקה דהא שיירות מלויות והאי דקאמר רבי אבא בשעת חירום שנו הכי קאמר יהודה וגליל הרי הן כשעת חירום של שאר מלכיות [רשב"ם ב"ב לח:]. והאכלתיו פרס. והחזרתי לו חלי והחליו בידי חייב לישבע על השאר [שבועות מב.]. על טענת עצמו. השתא משמע שאין אדם תובעו ולקמן מפרש לה בטוענו זה בן המת. ורבי אליעזר בן יעקב לית ליה כו'. כמו והוינן בה ור"א לית ליה תקנתא דתיקון העולם דמשיב אבידה פטור משבועה דא"כ שביק לה ואזיל והאי נמי כיון דלא תבעו כמשיב אבידה הוא [גיטין נא:]. בטוענו קטן. יתום קטן תובעו. אין נשבעין על טענת חרש שוטה וקטן. כגון שטענו ברמיזה דחרש שדיברו חכמים בכל מקום לא מדבר ולא שומע [שבועות שם]. אי הכי. דטוענו גדול טענת עצמו קרי לה טענת אחרים היא. והודאת עצמו. על שהודה לו שאמת כדבריו ומודה שעדיין חייב לו פרס הוא נשבע. כולהי טענתא טענת אחרים והודאת עצמו נינהו. ולכך נשבעין עליה ובכי האי גוונא מי פליגי רבנן עליה ומי הוה קאמר פעמים שאדם נשבע כל שעתא כי האי גוונא משתבע. אלא הכא בדרבה קמיפלגי. לא תימא בטוענו גדול אלא בטוענו קטן ודקשיא לך אין נשבעין על טענת קטן הני מילי בשטוענו הפקדתי לך דגבי שבועה כתיב (שמות כב) כי יתן איש ולא קטן אבל בא בטענת אביו נשבעין אפילו לקטן ולרבנן אפילו לגדול אין נשבעין כדתנן בשבועות מנה לאבא בידך אין לך בידי אלא חמשים דינר פטור ובדרבה פליגי [גיטין שם]. ולעולם בטוענו קטן ומשום דאין טענתו חשובה במקום אחר דכתיב כי יתן איש קרי ליה הכא טענת עצמו מיהו הכא טענה היא דהא איכא נתינת איש דמכח נתינת האב היא באה והיינו דקאמר פעמים וכי תימא רבנן אמאי פליגי עליה בדרבה קמיפלגי [שבועות שם:]. מפני מה אמרה תורה כו'. ולא חשבו כמשיב אבידה לפטרו שלא כפר בכולו [ב"מ ג.]. חזקה אין אדם מעיז פניו וכו'. לכפור את הכל הלכך בשביל הודאת המקצת אינו נאמן על השאר דהאי בכוליה בעי דלכפריה כו' [גיטין שם]. אין אדם מעיז פניו בפני זה שעושה לו טובה הלכך היכא דכפר הכל פטור משבועה דאי לאו קושטא בהדיה לא הוה מצי למכפר ביה והיכא דמודה מקצת בכולה בעי למכפריה והא דלא כפריה משום דאין אדם מעיז [ב"ק קז.]. [מכאן שייך לע"ב] ובכולה בעי דלודי ליה. וכי תימא לא נשבעיה אשארא דמיגו דחשוד אממונא חשוד נמי אשבועה מדלא כפריה בכוליה דהאי כי אודי בפלגא בכוליה נמי בעי דלודי והאי דלא אודי ליה לאו דלעתו למיגזליה אלא אישתמוטי אישתמיט לדחויי השתא [גיטין נא:]. וכ"ת מגו דחשיד אממונא חשיד אשבועתא ולא נרמי עליה שבועתא לא חשיד אממונא לפי שברצונו היה מודה בכולו אלא שאין בידו לפרוע וסבר עד דהוי לי [זוזי] ופרענא ליה [ב"מ ג:]. כיון שהגיד שוב אינו חוזר ומגיד. דבר המכחיש את הראשון דכתיב (ויקרא ה) אם לא יגיד והגדה קמייתא קפיד קרא [סנהדרין מד:]. דאמר שהודו שבשטרות נכתב הרי חתימת השטר כאלו העידו בב"ד כל מה שכתוב בשטר שהלוהו מלוה לזה וכיון שהגיד שוב אינו חוזר ומגיד [רשב"ם ב"ב מט.]. נעשה כמי שנחקרה עדותן בב"ד. משעה שנכתב ונחתם ואין עדות אחרון מבטל את הראשון דכיון שהגיד שוב אינו חוזר ומגיד לא אתא על פה השתא ומרע לשטרא דקדים [רשב"ם ב"ב מט.].

דִּסְתָם יְהוּדָה וְגָלִיל כִּשְׁעַת חֵירוּם דָּמוּ – It is that as a **general** rule, **Judea and Galilee** always **have the same status** concerning *chazakah* **as** that of other lands during **times of hostility.** That is, if the original owner and occupant are in different provinces, one in Judea and the other in Galilee, the owner cannot lodge an effective protest even during peacetime (and thus the occupant has not established a valid *chazakah*).[1] At any rate, we learn from the cited Mishnah that a protest lodged not in the presence of the occupant is generally considered an effective protest.

The Gemara accepts that the Mishnah could not have discussed the case proposed above, but suggests yet another case that it might have chosen:[2]

וְלִיתְנֵי – **But [the Tanna] should have taught:** מוֹדֶה רַבִּי יְהוֹשֻׁעַ – **"R' Yehoshua agrees** concerning a case בְּאוֹמֵר לַחֲבֵירוֹ מָנֶה לָוִיתִי מִמְּךָ וּפְרַעְתִּיו לְךָ – **where [someone] says to his fellow, 'I borrowed a *maneh*** (i.e. one hundred *zuz*) **from you and** subsequently **repaid you,'** שֶׁהוּא נֶאֱמָן – **that he is believed."**[3] – ? –

In response, the Gemara explains why it was impossible for the Tanna to discuss this case:

מִשּׁוּם דְּקָא בָּעֵי לְמִיתְנֵי סֵיפָא – **Because he would** then **have to teach** the Mishnah's **final clause** as follows: אִם יֵשׁ עֵדִים שֶׁהוּא לָוָה מִמֶּנּוּ – "But **if there are witnesses that he borrowed from him** וְהוּא אוֹמֵר פְּרַעְתִּיו אֵינוֹ נֶאֱמָן – **and [the borrower] claims, 'I repaid him,' he is not believed."** וְהָא קַיְימָא לָן – **But** the Mishnah could not conclude that way because **we have established**[4] that the halachah is הַמַּלְוֶה אֶת חֲבֵירוֹ בְּעֵדִים – that if **one lends his fellow** money **in [the presence of] witnesses,** אֵינוֹ צָרִיךְ לְפָרְעוֹ בְּעֵדִים – **[the borrower] is not required to repay him in [the presence of] witnesses.**[5] The defendant would therefore be believed to say that he repaid the loan even if there are witnesses who testify that he borrowed the money. Since the Tanna would be unable to teach this final clause, he could not discuss the case of an admission concerning a loan.[6]

The Gemara suggests yet another case that the Mishnah could have discussed:

וְלִיתְנֵי – **But [the Tanna] should have taught:** מוֹדֶה רַבִּי יְהוֹשֻׁעַ – **"R' Yehoshua agrees** concerning a case בְּאוֹמֵר לַחֲבֵירוֹ מָנֶה לְאָבִיךְ בְּיָדִי וְהֶאֱכַלְתִּיו פְּרָס – **where [someone] says to his fellow, 'A *maneh* of your father's was in my possession but I repaid him**[7] **half** of it,' שֶׁהוּא נֶאֱמָן – **that he is believed** without having to take an oath."[8] – ? –

NOTES

1. I.e. travel between Judea and the Galilee is so rare, even during peacetime, that these are considered like countries with hostilities between them. We can never assume that word of a protest lodged in one of these provinces will reach an occupant in the other province. With regard to provinces in other countries, or cities within the same province in Eretz Yisrael, it is generally presumed that travelers do carry word of a protest from one to the other, unless traffic has been disrupted as a result of hostilities (*Rashbam* to *Bava Basra* 38b).

2. The Tanna's objective in the latter part of the Mishnah is to teach that R' Yehoshua agrees that a litigant is believed on the basis of *happeh she'assar* "when there is no slaughtered ox before us," i.e. when no claim was advanced against him. Thus, when a litigant of his own accord admits to a past liability but contends that the liability no longer exists, and there is no independent evidence of the liability at all, his denial is believed (see 16a note 1). The Tanna contrasts this with the case in which there are witnesses to the past liability; in that instance, the defendant's denial of current liability is not accepted.

Now, it was explained above that the reason the Tanna needed to describe the litigant's admission as being that the property once belonged to his fellow's *father* – as opposed to the fellow himself – is that regarding the fellow himself he would be unable to conclude with the clause, "But if there are witnesses . . . he is not believed." Even if there were witnesses that the property once belonged to the fellow himself, the current occupant could be believed that he bought it, on the basis of his three-year *chazakah*. However, this explanation is valid only in regard to a claim involving land, since three years of uncontested occupancy creates a presumption of ownership only for real property. One does not gain a *chazakah* on movable objects by holding them for three years (see below, 84b). The Gemara will now ask why the Tanna chose to discuss a claim concerning real property, and thus allowed himself to be forced into describing the admission as pertaining to the fellow's father. He should have discussed a claim involving money and focused on an admission of liability to the fellow himself (*Rashi*).

3. [The man would be believed that he repaid the loan, because since he need not have admitted to the previous liability at all, his claim of payment is backed by the power of *happeh she'assar.*]

Rashi states that the defendant would be believed under *Biblical* law without taking an oath. The intent is that he would, however, have to take the Rabbinic *hesseis* oath (see *Shevuos* 40b) imposed upon defendants who completely deny claims against them (*Chasam Sofer*). I.e. if after the defendant opens the subject and says, "I borrowed a *maneh* from you but I repaid it," the plaintiff responds, "You have reminded me about the loan and I say you definitely did not repay it," the defendant must take the *hesseis* oath in denial of the claim. But if the plaintiff never contradicts the defendant, there is no basis for the *hesseis* oath, since the oath is not imposed in absence of a claim (see *Shach, Choshen Mishpat* 88:56; cf. *Shulchan Aruch Choshen Mishpat* 88:32; see also *Rashash*).

At any rate, since under Biblical law one who tells his fellow, "I borrowed a *maneh* from *you* and repaid you," is believed completely, the Mishnah could have chosen this case to illustrate the principle of *happeh she'assar*!

4. *Shevuos* 41b.

5. The lender's arranging for witnesses to observe the giving of the loan is not considered an implicit stipulation that he wishes to be repaid in the presence of witnesses as well – and thus the borrower will not be believed that he paid unless he can produce the witnesses. Rather, the borrower may repay the loan privately, and his claim to that effect is believed (see *Rashba* to *Shevuos* 41b; cf. *Ran* there).

6. The commentators wonder why the Gemara needed to resort to the explanation that the Tanna was unable to teach the *final* clause in regard to a loan. The initial clause would also not fit in regard to a loan. For since the halachah is that the borrower does not have to repay his loan in the presence of witnesses, even if he took it in the presence of witnesses, his claim of repayment would be believed *without* the benefit of *happeh she'assar*. Thus, the Mishnah could not even have stated the initial clause of "But R' Yehoshua agrees etc." – which introduces the principle of *happeh she'assar* – in regard to an admission concerning a loan!? For resolutions of this difficulty, see *Maharsha* with *Karnei Re'eim, Maharam Schif,* and *Urim VeTumim* 90:10 ד״ה אבל; see also *Haflaah* and *Beis HaLevi* 3:19.

7. Literally: I fed him.

8. Ordinarily, when a person admits to part of a claim but denies the remainder, he is Biblically required to take an oath in support of his denial. This is known as the oath of partial admission [מוֹדֶה בְּמִקְצָת]. However, it would seem that in a case where the plaintiff did not present a claim, but rather, the defendant initiated the matter and stated that there was once a large liability but only part of it still exists, the defendant is believed without taking the oath [because he has the power of *happeh she'assar*]. Presumably, even R' Yehoshua concedes concerning this case, since "there is no slaughtered ox," i.e. the defendant himself initiated the matter. Let the Tanna teach us R' Yehoshua's opinion in regard to this case. [Why must he cite R' Yehoshua's opinion in regard to an admission concerning real property?] (*Rashi*).

Note that if the other fellow did not dispute the defendant's claim, there would be no basis at all for imposing the Biblical oath upon the defendant, and he would certainly be believed that he repaid part of the loan. An oath is never imposed in absence of a firm claim by a plaintiff. The Gemara refers, however, to a case in which the defendant initiated matters by stating, "I owed your father a *maneh,* but I repaid him half of it on a certain date," and the other fellow responded, "Though I was unaware that you borrowed anything from my father, I know that you did not pay him anything on that date, and therefore, you must still owe

And if he holds that a protest lodged **not in [the occupant's] presence is not an** effective **protest,**[38] **אֲפִילוּ יְהוּדָה וִיהוּדָה נַמִּי לֹא – then even** if the original owner was in one city located in **Judea and** the occupied field in another city in **Judea, too,** the protest should **not** be effective – and it should thus be impossible for the occupant to establish a *chazakah.*[39] Why does the Mishnah differentiate between the case in which the original owner and the occupant were in different provinces and the case in which they were in different cities within the same province? And we answered this question as follows: **אָמַר רַבִּי אַבָּא בַּר מַמָּל – R' Abba bar Mammal said: לְעוֹלָם קָסָבַר מְחָאָה שֶׁלֹּא בְּפָנָיו הַוְיָא מְחָאָה – Actually, [the Tanna] holds that a protest** lodged **not in [the occupant's] presence is an** effective **protest.**[40] **וּמַתְנִיתִין בִּשְׁעַת חֵירוּם שָׁנוּ – And** as to the ruling of **our Mishnah,** it **was taught regarding a time** of **hostility** during which travel between provinces was severely curtailed. During such times, if the owner lodges a protest while he and the occupant are in different provinces, it is indeed meaningless, because the hostilities prevent word of the protest from reaching the occupant.[41] **וּמַאי שְׁנָא יְהוּדָה וְגָלִיל דְּנָקַט – And what is different about Judea and Galilee that** explains why the Tanna Kamma **chose** to discuss them specifically?[42]

NOTES

38. I.e. even if the original owner presents his protest to two witnesses, if he is not in the same city as the occupant it cannot be assumed that his protest will reach the occupant (*Rashi*).

39. Since the original owner was not in the city where his property was occupied, he had no way of lodging an effective protest, and consequently, his failure to protest does not legitimize the other person's occupancy. The occupant should thus be unable to establish a *chazakah* (*Rashi*).

40. Because the people who hear his protest will spread the word until the occupant finds out, and he will know that he must preserve his deed (*Rashi*).

41. The occupant can therefore claim that he did not hear any protest that would cause him to guard his deed after three years (*Rashi*). And since the protest would be ineffective, the owner's failure to protest does not prove anything, so that the *chazakah* itself is not valid (*Maharam Schif*).

42. The same law would be true regarding two cities in the same province, if there were hostilities between them! Why did the Tanna choose the case of hostilities between Judah and the Galilee to inform us of this law? (*Rashi*).

גמרא

אבל למאן דמתני לית ליה שיעורא: ואם יש עדים שיצתה בהינומא וכו': מאי הינומא סורחב בר פפא משמיה דזעירי אמר תנורא דאסא רבי יוחנן אמר קריתא דמנמנה בה כלתא: רבי יוחנן בן ברוקא אומר וכו': תנא ביהודה ראיה בבבל מאי אמר רב דרדוגי דמשחא ארישא דרבנן אמר ליה רב פפא לאביי משחא דחפיפותא קאמר מר אמר ליה יתמא לא עבדא לך אמך דרדוגי משחא ארישא דרבנן בשעת מעשה כי הא דההוא מרבנן דאיעסק ליה לבריה בי רבה בר עולא ואמרי לה רבה בר עולא איעסק ליה לבריה בי ההוא מרבנן ודרדיג משחא ארישא דרבנן בשעת מעשה ארמלתא מאי תאני רב יוסף ארמלתא לית לה כיסני: ומודה רבי יהושע באומר לחבירו כו': וליתני מודה ר' יהושע באומר לחבירו שדה זו שלך היתה ולקחתיה ממך משום דקא בעי למיתני סיפא [א] אם יש עדים שהיא שלו והוא אומר לקחתיה ממנו אינו נאמן היכי דמי אי דאכלה שני חזקה אמאי לא מהימן ואי דלא אכלה שני חזקה פשיטא דלא מהימן אי הכי גבי אביו נמי אי דאכלה שני חזקה אמאי לא מהימן ואי דלא אכלה שני חזקה פשיטא דלא מהימן בשלמא גבי אביו משכחת לה [ח] כגון [ב] שאכלה שתים בחיי האב ואחת בחיי בנו וכדרב הונא [ט] דאמר רב הונא [ג] אין מחזיקין בנכסי קטן אפילו הגדיל ורב הונא [ט] מתניתין אתא לאשמועינן איבעית אימא רב הונא [י] דיוקא דמתני' קאמר ואיבעית אימא אפילו הגדיל קמ"ל וליתנייה בדידיה ולוקמה כגון שאכלה שתים בפניו ואחת שלא בפניו וכגון שברח ברח מחמת מאי אי [ד] דברח מחמת נפשות פשיטא דלא מהימן דלא מצי מחי ואי דברח מחמת ממון איבעי ליה למחויי [ה] דקי"ל מחאה שלא בפניו הויא מחאה דתנן [ו] שלש ארצות לחזקה יהודה ועבר הירדן והגליל היה ביהודה והחזיק בגליל בגליל והחזיק ביהודה אינה חזקה עד שיהא עמו במדינה והוינן בה [ז] מאי קסבר אי קסבר מחאה שלא בפניו הויא מחאה אפילו ביהודה וגליל נמי ואי קסבר מחאה שלא בפניו לא הויא מחאה אפילו יהודה ויהודה נמי לא אמר רבי אבא בר ממל לעולם קסבר מחאה שלא בפניו הויא מחאה ומתניתין בשעת [י] חירום שנו ומאי שנא יהודה וגליל דנקט דסתם

רש"י

אבל למאן דמתני. לאחרים: לית ליה שיעורא. וממילא שמעינן למאן דלא קרי ולא תני אין מבטלין אם יש לו מתעסקין כדי קבורה בשלמא בשאלתות דרב אחאי [ז] מצאתי כן: תנורא דאסא. כמין חופה של הדס עגולה: קריתא. לנעיף על ראשה משורבב על עיניה כמו שעושין במקומינו ופעמים שמנמנמת בתוכו מתוך שאין עיניה מגולין ולכך נקרא הינומא על שם תנומה: ביהודה ראיה. כל הני דמתני' שאם היו רגילין בסימנין הללו לבתולה: דרדוגי משחא. הכוס נותנים שמן בראש התלמידים ושפות: משחא דחפיפותא. [ח] [שמן של בשמים שמתוקן [ט] לחופות] קאמר מר וכי בעלי חפיפות הן לסוכן שמן: יתמא. יתום ממנהג הנוהג: איעסק לבריה. לישא לו אשה: ודרדיג משחא. שפך שמן בראש התלמידים: ארמלתא מאי. מה סימנין עושים לאלמנה להודיע שאלמנה נישאת: לית לה כיסני. אין לה קליות וזה סימנה: וליתני מודה ר' יהושע כו' שדה זו שלך היתה. כיון דטעמא משום דלאין שור שחוט לפניו הוא שלא היה אדם תובעו מה לי של אביו ומה לי שלו ומאי שנא של אביך דנקט: שני חזקה. שלש שנים שתיקנו חכמים לכל מחזיקים בקרקע דמשאכלה שלש שנים בלא עירעור נאמן לומר לקחתיה ולאבד שטרי דכולי האי לא מזדהר איניש בשטרא: בשלמא גבי אביו משכחת לה. דאיצטריך למיתנייה כגון דאכלה שני חזקה ואפילו הכי לא מהימן וכגון שאכלה שתי שנים לאשוטות בחיי אביו ומת ואכלה השלישית לפני הבן הזה והוא היה קטן ולא עירער ואיצטריך לאשמועינן דכיון דקטן היה אין השנה הזאת עולה מן המנין: וכדרב הונא דאמר אין מחזיקין בנכסי קטן. המחזיק בנכסי קטן שלש שנים אינה חזקה דהאי דלא מיחה משום דקטן הוא ואפילו הגדיל לאחר מיכן והחזיק זה בפניו כמה שנים אינה חזקה הואיל ותחלתו כשהוא קטן ראהו מוחזק בה לא ידע כשהגדיל שהיתה של אביו עד ששומע מפי אחרים: ורב הונא מתניתין אתא לאשמועינן. בתמיה כיון דמתניתין בהכי עסקינן ולא מיתוקמא אלא בהכי מאי אתא רב הונא לאשמועינן הרי כבר שנויה ועומדת ודבר השנוי במשנתינו שגור בפי הכל: דיוקא דמתניתין אתא לאשמועינן. משום דמתני' לא מיפרשא בהדיא דבהכי עסקינן ואתא רב הונא לאשמועינן בהדיא ומדיוקא דמתני' קא יליף לה: וליתנייה בדידיה. שדה זו שלך היתה אם יש עדים כו' אינו נאמן ואע"ג שאכלה שני חזקה וכגון שהיו שתים בפניו ואחת שלא בפניו: כגון שברח. ואשמעינן דההיא שתא לא סלקא ליה: אי ברח מחמת ממון. שאינו ירא מן המלכות אלא מצעקת הנועקים בעיר: איבעי ליה למחויי. במקום שהוא שם וכיון דלא מיחה חזקה מעלייתא היא: שלש ארצות לחזקה. שלש ארצות של א"י חשובות חלוקות זו מזו לענין חזקה כאילו הן ארצות נכריות ואם היה בזו והחזיק אחר בקרקע שיש לו בחברתה אינה חזקה: במדינה. או שניהם בגליל או שניהם ביהודה ואפי' הן בשתי עיירות: אפי' יהודה וגליל נמי. הוה ליה למחויי היכא דהוי ומדלא מחי תיהוי חזקה: ואי קסבר מחאה שלא בפניו לא הויא מחאה. כגון אם היה בעיר אחת ומיחה שלא בפניו בפני שנים בעיר אחרת: אפילו יהודה ויהודה. בשתי עיירות נמי לא תיהוי חזקה דלא הוה ליה למחויי שלא בפניו: הויא מחאה. דסבירא אית ליה דהני דמחי באנפייהו מגלו לאחריני ובא הדבר לאזני המחזיק וה"ל לאזדהורי בשטריה: ומתני'. דקתני יהודה וגליל לא: בשעת חירום שנו. דיכול לומר לא נגלית לי מחאתו שאשמור את שטרי: ומאי שנא יהודה וגליל דנקט. אם יש חירום נמי מעיר לעיר אפי' שתי עיירות באותה מדינה נמי לא:

וליתני

תוספות

אבל מאן דמתני לית ליה שיעורא. בשאלתות דרב אחאי כתוב וממילא שמעינן למאן דלא קרי ולא תני אין מבטלין אם יש לו מתעסקין כדי קבורה ונראה לר"י דלענין מלאכה מבטלין כל בני העיר ואסור אפילו למאן דלא קרי ולא תני דלא מפליג מידי באלו מגלחין (מו"ק דף כז:) גבי: אלמנה מאי. ביהודה בעי שלא היה אלא חילוק קליות לכך בעי אלמנה מאי והלא פעמים אפילו בלא חופה היו רגילין לחלוק ויש לחוש שמא חילקו בחופת אלמנה ומשני לית לה כיסני פירוש היו נזהרין הרבה שלא יחלקו קליות בחופת אלמנה: וליתני מודה רבי יהושע שדה זו שלך היתה. דהוי רבותא טפי דהוי ברי וברי: ואחת בחיי הבן. ודווקא שהוא קטן כפי' הקונט' אבל אם הוא גדול הוי חזקה כדאמרי' בחזקת הבתים (ב"ב דף מב. ושם) אכלה בפני האב שנה ובפני הבן שנה ובפני לוקח שנה הרי זו חזקה ורבינו שמואל פי' אהא דאמר בסמוך ואפילו הגדיל אפילו הגדיל בחיי האב דגדול לגבי מילי דאבוה קטן הוא ואור"ת דלפירושו הא דאמר בחזקת הבתים (ג"ז שם) דהויא חזקה בפני הבן היינו כשהיה גדול בתחילת חזקה: ורב הונא מתני' אתא לאשמועינן. לאו דווקא נקט רב הונא דהא לא איירי רב הונא התם [ז] אלא במורידין קרוב לנכסי קטן והא לא שמעינן ממתני' אלא כלומר רבא דדייק התם [ט] ש"מ מדרב הונא דאין מחזיקין בנכסי קטן מאי אתא לאשמועינן: מחאה שלא בפניו כו'. תימה אמאי נקט בכל דוכתא מחאה שלא בפניו הוה ליה למינקט חזקה שלא בפניו כו' וי"ל דעיקר הטעם תלוי במחאה דחזקה ודאי יש לה קול אפי' שלא בפניו ואפ"ה אי מחאה אין לה קול לא הוי חזקה והכי נקט מחא' דסתם

עין משפט נר מצוה

יג א מיי' פי"ד מהלכות טוען ונטען הלכה ג סמג עשין לה טוש"ע ח"מ סימן קמ סעיף א:
יד ב מיי' פי"ג שם הל' ח סמג שם טוש"ע שם סימן קמד סעיף ד:
טו ג מיי' פי"ד שם הל' ז טוש"ע שם סימן קמט סעיף יט:
טז ד מיי' שם הלכה י סמג שם טור ש"ע שם סימן קמג סעיף ג:
יז ה מיי' שם פי"א הלכה ה טוש"ע שם סימן קמו סעיף א:

תוספות רי"ד

דלא קרי ולא תני אין מבטלין ת"ת אב יש לו מתעסקים כדי קבורה בעלמא בשאלתות דרב אחא מצאתי כן: אם יש עדים שיצתה בהינומא מאי הינומא סורחב בר פפא אמר משמיה דזעירי תנורא דאסא פי' כמין כיפה של הדס עגולה ר"י אמר קריתא ומנמנמא בה כלה פי' צניף על ראשה משורבב על עיניה כמו שעושים בהרבה מקומות ופעמים שמנמנמת בתוכו מתוך שאין עיניה מגולות ולכך נקרא הינומא ע"ש תנומה: מתני' ומודה ר"י באומר לחבירו שדה זו של אביך היתה ולקחתיה ממנו נאמן שהפה שאסר הוא הפה שהתיר ואם יש עדים שהוא של אביו והוא אומר לקחתיה ממנו אינו נאמן ואסיקנא ר' יהושע אפרק קמא קאי והא קאי דתנן הנושא את האשה ולא מצא לה בתולים היא אומרת משארסתני נאנסתי ונסתחפה שדך והוא אומר לא כי אלא עד שלא ארסתיך והיה מקחי מקח טעות ר"ג ור"א [אומרים] נאמנת ור"י אומר לא מפיה אנו חיין והתם מאי מיגו איכא מיגו דאי בעי אמרה מוכת עץ אני ולא פסלה נפשה מכהונה וקאמרה נאנסתי דפסלה נפשה מכהונה מהימנא וא"ל ר"י לר"ג בההיא מיגו דהכא מודנא לך בההיא מיגו דהתם פליגנא עלך. מ"ש הכא ומ"ש התם הכא אין שור שחוט לפניך. פי' ואם רוצה לומר אינו של אביך ולהכחישו יכול אם עתה כשהודה שהיתה של אביו ולקחה ממנו נאמן אבל התם גבי אשה אם תרצה להכחישו ולומר בתולה הייתי אינה יכולה שהרי [שור] שחוט לפניך השושבינים המעידים שלא נמצאו לה בתולים הלכך כל טענה דאמרה בין מוכת עץ אני בין נאנסתי תחתיך לא מהימנא:

מתני'

מסורת הש"ס

א) ב"ב מב., ב) ב"מ לט., ג) [פסחים קא: ר"ה ח.], ד) ב"ב לח., ה) [שם ע"ש], ו) [פי' בערוך ערך חרס א' סיכסוך איש באחיו ועיר בעיר], ז) [פרשת ויחי סימן לב], ח) נ"י כ"י, ט) נ"ל לחפיפות. יעב"ץ, י) [ב"מ לט.], כ) [שם].

גליון הש"ס

גמ' דיוקא דמתניתין קאמר. שבת דף לו ע"ב שבועות דף כט ע"ב:

ליקוטי רש"י

תנורא דאסא. נערה המאורסה היו רגילין לעשות לה חופה של הדס בכניסתה לחופה וקורין לה הינומא כדאמרינן בכתובות (דף טו:) שיצאתה בהינומא וראשה פרוע [ברכות נו:]. ההוא מרבנן. תלמיד חכם זקן לא קרי צורבא אלא ההוא מרבנן קרי ליה [תענית ד.]. אין מחזיקין בנכסי קטן. אם לא אכל בפני האב שלש שנים אין שלש שנים שאכלן בפני הקטן חזקה [ב"מ לט.]. ואפילו הגדיל. הקטן משירד לתוכו ואכלו שלש שנים בפניו משהגדיל לא הויא חזקה דהואיל ותחלת ירידתו לתוכו הוה קטן לא ידע כשהגדיל שהן של אביו ולפיכך לא מיחה [שם:]. מחמת נפשות. מחמת רציחת נפשות ירא למחות פן יודע מקום מחבואו וירדוף גואל הדם אחריו כי יחם לבבו והשיגו והרגו. איבעי ליה למחויי. דמצי למחויי וכל מקום שזה יכול למחות חזקתו של חבירו בנכסיו הויא חזקה הואיל ולא מיחה דכיון דמחמת חוב ממון הוא בורח אין זה בורח אלא לאיטמוטי בעלמא עד דהוה ליה ופרע ואינו ירא למחות דכיון דאנוס הוא ואין לו מה לפרוע אין רודפין אחריו ואם נודע מקומו שברח שם אינו חושש [רשב"ם ב"ב לח:]. שלש ארצות. בארץ ישראל. לחזקה. חלוקות זו מזו לענין חזקת שלש שנים כדמפרש ואזיל. היה. בעל הקרקע. ביהודה והחזיק בגליל. שהיה הקרקע בגליל והחזיק בה אדם שלש שנים בלא מחאה. אינה חזקה. כדמפרש טעמא בגמרא דסתם יהודה וגליל כשעת חירום דמי שאין שיירות מצויות מזו לזו ולא הויא מחאת בעל הקרקע מחאה שהרי אין מי שיגיד לו למחזיק שמיחה זה ויזהר בשטרו דהא אין שיירות מצויות הלכך כיון דאינו יכול למחות אע"ג דלא מיחה לא הפסיד בשתיקתו והיה לו לזה המחזיק ליזהר בשטרו שהרי יודע שאין בעל הקרקע יכול למחות. עד שיהא עמו במדינה. כגון שהיה ביהודה בעיר אחת והחזיק ביהודה בעיר אחרת דכיון דשיירות מצויות הוה ליה למחויי ומדלא מיחה הפסיד. אי קסבר מחאה וכו'. שמוחה בעל הקרקע במחזיק אפי' שלא בפניו כגון שניהם דרין בעיר אחת ומיחה בפני שנים מן השוק שלא בפניו של מחזיק אפי' הכי הוי' מחאה דהכך חברא אית ליה ושמע המחזיק בדבר זה והיה לו להזהר בשטרו ומדלא נזהר הפסיד והלכך קתני עד שיהא עמו במדינה אחת דכיון ששניהם במדינה אחת הויא מחאה אע"פ שאינם בעיר אחת. אפילו ביהודה וגליל נמי. היה ביהודה והחזיק בגליל תיהוי מחאה. ואי קסבר וכו' לא הויא מחאה. דקתני היה ביהודה והחזיק ביהודה בעיר אחרת נמי לא תיהוי חזקה. [illegible]
[illegible]
[illegible]

clause **in reference to** a claim that the field was purchased from the fellow **himself,** rather than his father,[23] וְלוֹקְמָהּ כְּגוֹן שֶׁאֲכָלָהּ שְׁתַּיִם בְּפָנָיו וְאַחַת שֶׁלֹּא בְּפָנָיו – **and** we could **interpret it** as applying **to a case where [the occupant] used it** for **two** years **in [the original owner's] presence and** for **one** year **not in his presence,** וּכְגוֹן שֶׁבָּרַח – that is, **a case where [the original owner] fled** the area during the third year of occupancy. The Mishnah would inform us that the third year does not count towards a *chazakah,* since the previous owner was not present in the area.[24] Why is it necessary to introduce a case involving a claim of purchase from the father?

The Gemara answers that it would be impossible to teach the rule concerning this case:

בָּרַח מֵחֲמַת מַאי – In the case that you proposed, **why would [the original owner] have fled** the area? אִי דְּבָרַח מֵחֲמַת נְפָשׁוֹת – **If he fled because of** a threat to his **life,**[25] פְּשִׁיטָא דְּלֹא מְהֵימָן – **it is obvious that** when there are witnesses regarding his previous ownership **[the occupant] is not believed** on the basis of his occupancy to say that he purchased it, דְּלֹא מָצֵי מַחֵי – **since [the original owner] was unable to protest** his occupancy.[26] The Mishnah would not need to inform us of this. וְאִי דְּבָרַח מֵחֲמַת מָמוֹן – **And if [the original owner] fled because of** difficulties involving his **finances,**[27] אִיבָּעֵי לֵיהּ לְמַחוּיֵי – then **he should have protested** from wherever he was, דְּקַיְימָא לָן – **for we have established**[28] that the halachah is מְחָאָה שֶׁלֹּא בְּפָנָיו הַוְיָא מְחָאָה – that **a protest** lodged **not in [the occupant's] presence is an** effective **protest.**[29] Since he did not bother to protest from his new location, the occupant's *chazakah* would be valid and his claim that he purchased the field would be believed! Thus, the Tanna could not have taught this clause of the Mishnah in reference to the case where the original owner fled the area.[30]

The Gemara cites the proof that a protest lodged not in the occupant's presence is effective:

דִּתְנַן – **For we learned in a Mishnah:**[31] שָׁלֹשׁ אֲרָצוֹת לַחֲזָקָה – There are THREE LANDS in Eretz Yisrael WITH REGARD TO *CHAZAKAH*: יְהוּדָה וְעֵבֶר הַיַּרְדֵּן וְהַגָּלִיל – JUDEA, TRANSJORDAN AND THE GALILEE.[32] הָיָה בִּיהוּדָה וְהֶחֱזִיק בַּגָּלִיל – If [THE ORIGINAL OWNER] WAS IN JUDEA AND SOMEONE ASSUMED OCCUPANCY of his land IN THE GALILEE, בַּגָּלִיל וְהֶחֱזִיק בִּיהוּדָה – or the original owner was IN THE GALILEE AND [SOMEONE] ASSUMED OCCUPANCY of his land IN JUDEA, אֵינָהּ חֲזָקָה – THIS IS NOT A valid *CHAZAKAH,*[33] עַד שֶׁיְּהֵא עִמּוֹ בַּמְּדִינָה – UNLESS [THE ORIGINAL OWNER] IS WITH [THE OCCUPANT] IN THE SAME PROVINCE. The Mishnah implies that if the owner and occupant are in the same province, the *chazakah* is valid even if they are in different cities.[34] וְהָוִינַן בָּהּ – **And we analyzed [the Mishnah]** as follows:[35] מַאי קָסָבַר – **What does [the Tanna] hold** regarding a protest lodged not in the occupant's presence?[36] אִי קָסָבַר מְחָאָה שֶׁלֹּא בְּפָנָיו הַוְיָא מְחָאָה – **If he holds** that **a protest** lodged **not in [the occupant's] presence is an** effective **protest,** אֲפִילוּ בִּיהוּדָה וְגָלִיל נַמִּי – **then even** if the original owner protested in **Judea and** the occupied field was in **Galilee, too,** the protest should be effective.[37] וְאִי קָסָבַר מְחָאָה שֶׁלֹּא בְּפָנָיו לֹא הַוְיָא מְחָאָה –

NOTES

23. I.e. he should have stated: R' Yehoshua agrees concerning a case where someone says to his fellow, "This field was *yours* but I purchased it from you," that he is believed. But if there are witnesses that it was once *his,* and the occupant says, "I purchased it from him," he is not believed. This ruling could apply to a case in which the occupant used the field for three years while the previous owner was an adult, and nevertheless, he would not have a valid *chazakah,* as the Gemara proceeds to explain (*Rashi*).

24. This would be the lesson of the concluding clause, "But if there are witnesses that it was once *his,* and the occupant says, 'I purchased it from him,' he is not believed" (see *Rashi*).

[The basis of a *chazakah* is the fact that the previous owner *neglected* to protest another person's occupancy of his property. Presumably, no true owner would tolerate someone's squatting on his property for three full years; he would surely protest the unauthorized use of his land and demand that the occupant vacate it. His failure to protest indicates that the occupant is the rightful owner, and frees the occupant of the burden of preserving his deed. If the original owner was *unable* to protest, the three years of occupancy do not prove anything, and the occupant is obliged to retain his deed. Thus, the occupant cannot establish a *chazakah* in a case where the owner was forced to flee the country.]

25. For example, he ran afoul of the government and is in fear of execution (see *Rashi*).

26. He could not even publicize his protest from his new location, since he is in hiding from the government.

27. That is, he is not concerned with any danger from the government, but he has creditors in this town who are badgering him (*Rashi*). [Thus, it suffices for him to merely leave the immediate area.]

28. *Bava Basra* 38a, cited below.

29. Because the people who hear the protest relate it to their friends, who in turn relate it to their friends etc., until the occupant eventually hears about it. Thus, the occupant is deemed to have been alerted to preserve his deed (*Rashi* below).

30. For if he fled out of fear for his life, it is obvious that the *chazakah* is void, and if he fled to escape creditors the *chazakah* is in fact valid.

31. *Bava Basra* 38a.

32. The three provinces of Eretz Yisrael are considered like separate countries in regard to the laws of *chazakah.* If a man was in one land and someone occupied his property in a second land, that occupancy cannot lead to a valid *chazakah* (*Rashi*). [As shall be explained, the owner is unable to lodge an effective protest from the "foreign country."]

33. If the owner of a field located in the Galilee was living in Judea and someone occupied that field for three years, the occupant has not established a *chazakah.* Since the owner was in a different province, it could not be assumed that word of his protest would reach the occupant. Accordingly, there was no point for the owner of the field to protest its occupation even if he knew about it. The latter, knowing that this is the situation, is clearly expected to preserve his deed. Therefore, if he cannot produce it when the case comes to court, he loses the property (*Rashbam* to *Bava Basra* ibid.).

34. *Rashi.* If the owner of the field is in the same province as the field (e.g. both are in the Galilee), the absence of a protest establishes a *chazakah* even if they are in different towns, because it is assumed that word of his protest would reach the occupant. Since there is no plausible rationale for the owner's failure to protest, the occupant is awarded presumptive title to the field (*Rashbam* ibid.).

35. The discussion is quoted from *Bava Basra* 38a.

36. Can it be assumed that the occupant will undoubtedly hear about it by word of mouth so that the protest is effective, or not? (*Rashbam* ibid.).

It would seem that the question should more accurately be whether a *chazakah* in the owner's absence is a valid *chazakah,* or not. However, the root of the question lies in the matter of his protest. For it is obvious that news of a stranger occupying someone's property travels even to distant places, so that the original owner certainly receives this information. What is unclear, however, is whether news of the owner's protest also travels. If it does travel, then he is considered able to lodge an effective protest, and it follows that if he fails to protest, the occupant's *chazakah* is valid. If news of the protest does not travel, so that the owner is unable to lodge an effective protest, the lack of any protest is meaningless, and thus, the occupant's *chazakah* is not valid. Accordingly, the validity of a *chazakah* not in the owner's presence hinges upon the effectiveness of his protest (*Tosafos* ד״ה מחאה).

37. That is, he ought to have protested wherever he was, and his failure to protest should allow the *chazakah* to take effect (*Rashi*). [The Gemara assumes that travel between the various provinces in Eretz Yisrael was very common. Thus, since the Tanna presumes that word of the owner's protest reaches a different city within the same province, he should make this presumption regarding a different province as well.]

עין משפט נר מצוה

יג א מיי' פי"ד מהלכות טוען ונטען הלכה ג סמג עשין לה טוש"ע ח"מ סימן קמ סעיף א:
יד ב מיי' פי"ג שם הל' ח סמג שם טוש"ע שם סימן קמב סעיף ד:
טו ג מיי' פי"ג שם הל' ז טוש"ע שם סימן קמט סעיף יט:
טז ד מיי' שם הלכה ב סמג שם טור ש"ע שם סימן קמג סעיף ג:
יז ה מיי' שם פי"א הלכה ה טוש"ע שם סימן קמו סעיף א:

אבל למאן דמתני לית ליה שיעורא: ואם יש עדים שיצתה בהינומא וכו': מאי הינומא סורחב בר פפא משמיה דזעירי אמר תנורא דאסא רבי יוחנן אמר קריתא דמנמנה בה כלתא: רבי יוחנן בן ברוקא אומר וכו': תנא ביהודה ראיה בבבל מאי אמר רב דרדוגי דמשחא ארישא דרבנן אמר ליה רב פפא לאביי משחא דחפיפותא קאמר מר אמר ליה יתמא לא עבדא לך אמך דרדוגי משחא ארישא דרבנן בשעת מעשה כי הא דההוא מרבנן דאיעסק ליה לבריה בי רבה בר עולא ואמרי לה רבה בר עולא איעסק ליה לבריה בי ההוא מרבנן ודרדיג משחא ארישא דרבנן בשעת מעשה ארמלתא מאי תאני רב יוסף ארמלתא לית לה כיסני: ומודה רבי יהושע באומר לחבירו כו': וליתני מודה ר' יהושע באומר לחבירו שדה זו שלך היתה ולקחתיה ממך משום דקא בעי למיתני סיפא אם יש עדים שהיא שלו והוא אומר לקחתיה ממנו אינו נאמן היכי דמי אי דאכלה שני חזקה אמאי לא מהימן ואי דלא אכלה שני חזקה פשיטא דלא מהימן אי הכי גבי אביו נמי אי דאכלה שני חזקה אמאי לא מהימן ואי דלא אכלה שני חזקה פשיטא דלא מהימן בשלמא גבי אביו משכחת לה כגון שאכלה שתים בחיי האב ואחת בחיי בנו וכדרב הונא דאמר רב הונא אין מחזיקין בנכסי קטן אפילו הגדיל ורב הונא מתניתין אתא לאשמועינן איבעית אימא רב הונא דיוקא דמתני' קאמר ואיבעית אימא אפילו הגדיל קמ"ל וליתנייה בדידיה ולוקמה כגון שאכלה שתים בפניו ואחת שלא בפניו וכגון שברח ברח מחמת מאי אי דברח מחמת נפשות פשיטא דלא מהימן דלא מצי מחי ואי דברח מחמת ממון איבעי ליה למחויי דקי"ל מחאה שלא בפניו הויא מחאה דתנן שלש ארצות לחזקה יהודה ועבר הירדן והגליל היה ביהודה והחזיק בגליל בגליל והחזיק ביהודה אינה חזקה עד שיהא עמו במדינה והוינן בה מאי קסבר אי קסבר מחאה שלא בפניו הויא מחאה אפילו ביהודה וגליל נמי ואי קסבר מחאה שלא בפניו לא הויא מחאה אפילו יהודה ויהודה נמי לא אמר רבי אבא בר ממל לעולם קסבר מחאה שלא בפניו הויא מחאה ומתניתין בשעת חירום שנו ומאי שנא יהודה וגליל דנקט

דסתם

רש"י

אבל למאן דמתני. לאחרים: לית ליה שיעורא. וממילא שמעינן למאן דלא קרי ולא תני אין מבטלין אם יש לו מתעסקין כדי קבורה בעלמא בשאלתות דרב אחאי מצאתי כן: תנורא דאסא. כמין חופה של הדס עגולה: קריתא. לציף על ראשה מורכב על עיניה כמו שעושין במקומינו ופעמים שמנמנמת בתוכו מתוך שאין עיניה מגולין ולכך נקרא היינומא על שם תנומה: ביהודה ראיה. כל הני דמתני' שהם היו רגילין בסימנין הללו לבתולה: דרדוגי משחא. הנסים נותנים שמן בראש התלמידים ושפות: משחא דחפיפותא. [שמן של בשמים שממוקן לחופות] קאמר מר וכי בעלי חפיפות הן לסוכן שמן: יתמא. יתום ממנהג הנוהג: איעסק לבריה. לישא לו אשה: ודרדיג משחא. שף שמן בראש התלמידים: ארמלתא מאי. מה סימנין עושים לאלמנה להודיע שאלמנה נישאת: לית לה כיסני. אין לה קליות זהו סימנה: וליתני מודה ר' יהושע כו' שדה זו שלך היתה. כיון דטעמא משום דאין שור שחוט לפניו הוא שלא היה אדם תובעו מה לי של אביו ומה לי שלו ומאי שנא של אביך דנקט: שני חזקה. שלש שנים שתיקנו חכמים לכל מחזיקים בקרקע דמשאכלה שלש שנים בלא עירעור נאמן לומר לקחתיה ואבד שטרי דכולי האי לא מזדהר איניש בשטרא: בשלמא גבי אביו משכחת לה. דאיצטריך למיתנייה כגון דאכלה שני חזקה ואפילו הכי לא מהימן וכגון שאכלה שתי שנים ראשונות בחיי אביו ומת ואכלה השלישית לפני הבן הזה והוא היה קטן ולא עירער ואיצטריך לאשמועינן דכיון דקטן היה אין השנה הזאת עולה מן המנין: וכדרב הונא דאמר אין מחזיקין בנכסי קטן. המחזיק בנכסי קטן שלש שנים אינה חזקה דהאי דלא מיחה משום דקטן הוא ואפילו הגדיל לאחר מיכן והחזיק זה בפניו כמה שנים אינה חזקה הואיל ותחלתו כשהוא קטן ראהו מוחזק בה לא ידע כשהגדיל שהיתה של אביו עד ששומע מפי אחרים: ורב הונא מתניתין אתא לאשמועינן. בתמיה כיון דמתניתין בהכי עסקינן ולא מיתוקמא אלא בהכי מאי אתא רב הונא לאשמועינן הרי כבר שנויה ועומדת ודבר השנוי במשנתינו שגור בפי הכל: דיוקא דמתניתין אתא לאשמועינן. משום דמתני' לא מיפרשא בהדיא דבהכי עסקינן ואתא רב הונא לאשמועינן בהדיא ומדיוקא דמתני' קא יליף לה: וליתנייה בדידיה. שדה זו שלך היתה אם יש עדים כו' אינו נאמן ואע"ג שאכלה שני חזקה וכגון שהיו שתים בפניו ואחת שלא בפניו: כגון שברח. ולאשמועינן דההיא שתא לא סלקא ליה: אי ברח מחמת ממון. שאינו ירא מן המלכות אלא מצעקת הצועקים בעיר: איבעי ליה למחויי. במקום שהוא שם וכיון דלא מיחה חזקה מעלייתא היא: שלש ארצות לחזקה. שלש ארצות של א"י חשובות חלוקות זו מזו לענין חזקה כאילו הן ארצות נכריות ואם היה בזו והחזיק אחר בקרקע שיש לו בחברתה אינה חזקה: במדינה. או שניהם בגליל או שניהם ביהודה ואפי' הן בשתי עיירות: אפי' יהודה וגליל נמי. הוה ליה למחויי היכא דהוי ומדלא מחי תיהוי חזקה: ואי קסבר מחאה שלא בפניו לא הויא מחאה. כגון אם היה בעיר אחת ומיחה שלא בפניו בפני שנים בעיר אחרת: אפילו יהודה ויהודה. בשתי עיירות נמי לא תיהוי חזקה דלא הוה ליה למחויי שלא בפניו: הויא מחאה. דחברך חברא אית ליה דהני דמחי באנפייהו מגלו לאחריני ובא הדבר לאזני המחזיק וה"ל לאזדהורי בשטריה: ומתני'. דקתני יהודה וגליל לא: בשעת חירום שנו. דיכול לומר לא נגלית לי מחאתו שאשמור את שטרי: ומאי שנא יהודה וגליל דנקט. אם יש חירום נמי מעיר לעיר אפי' שתי עיירות באותה מדינה נמי לא:

וליתני

תוספות

אבל מאן דמתני לית ליה שיעורא. בשאלתות דרב אחאי כתוב וממילא שמעינן למאן דלא קרי ולא תני אין מבטלין אם יש לו מתעסקין כדי קבורה ונראה לר"י דלענין מלאכה מבטלין כל בני העיר ואסור אפילו למאן דלא קרי ולא תני מפליג מידי דאלו מגלחין (מו"ק דף ח:) דהכי: אלמנה מאי. ביהודה בעי שלא היה אלא חילוק קליות לכך בעי אלמנה מאי והלא פעמים אפילו בלא חופה היו רגילין לחלוק ויש לחוש שמא חילקו בחופת אלמנה ומשני לית לה כיסוי פירוש היו מוסרין הרבה שלא יחלקו קליות בחופת אלמנה: וליתני מודה רבי יהושע שדה זו שלך היתה. דהוי רבותא טפי דהוי ברי וברי: ואחת בחיי הבן. ודווקא שהוא קטן כפי' הקונט' אבל אם הוא גדול הוי חזקה כדאמרי' בחזקת הבתים (ב"ב מב. ושם) אכלה בפני האב שנה ובפני הבן שנה ובפני לוקח שנה הרי זו חזקה ורבינו שמואל פי' אהא דאמר בסמוך ואפילו הגדיל אפילו הגדיל בחיי האב דגדול לגבי מילי דאבוה קטן הוא ואור"ת דלפירושו הא דאמר בחזקת הבתים (ג"ז שם) דהויא חזקה בפני הבן היינו כשהיה גדול בתחילת חזקה: ורב הונא מתני' אתא לאשמועינן. לאו דווקא נקט רב הונא דהא לא איירי רב הונא התם אלא במורידין קרוב לנכסי קטן והא לא שמעינן ממתני' אלא כלומר רבא דדייק התם ש"מ מדרב הונא דאין מחזיקין בנכסי קטן מאי אתא לאשמועינן: מחאה שלא בפניו כו'. תימה אמאי נקט בכל דוכתא מחאה שלא בפניו הוה ליה למינקט חזקה שלא בפניו כו' וי"ל דעיקר הטע' תלוי במחאה דחזקה ודאי יש לה קול אפי' שלא בפניו ואפ"ה אי מחאה אין לה קול לא הוי חזקה ולהכי נקט מחא':

תוספות רי"ד

דלא קרי ולא תני אין מבטלין ת"ת אם יש לו מתעסקים כדי קבורה בעלמא בשאלתות דרב אחא מצאתי כן: אם יש עדים שיצאת בהינומא מאי הינומא סורחב בר פפא אמר משמיה דזעירי תנורא דאסא פי' כמין כיפה של הדס שגולה ר"י אמר קריתא דמנמנא בה כלה פי' צניף על ראשה משורבב על עיניה כמו שעושים בהרבה מקומות ופעמים שמנמנמת בתוכה מתוך שאין עיניה מגולות ולכך נקרא הינומא ע"ש תנומה: מתני' ומודה ר"י באומר לחבירו שדה זו של אביך היתה ולקחתיה ממנו נאמן שהפה שאסר הוא הפה שהתיר ואם יש עדים שהוא של אביו והוא אומר לקחתיה הימנו אינו נאמן ואסיקנא ר' יהושע אפרק קמא קאי דהא קאי התם דתנן הנושא את האשה ולא מצא לה בתולים היא אומרת משארסתני נתאנסתי ונסתחפה שדך והוא אומר לא כי אלא עד שלא ארסתיך והיה מקחי מקח טעות ר"ג ור"א [אומרים] נאמנת ור"י אומר לא מפיה אנו חיין התם מאי מיגו איכא מיגו דאי בעי אמרה מוכת עץ אני ולא פסלה נפשה מכהונה וקאמרה נאנסתי דפסלה נפשה מכהונה מהימנא וא"ל ר"י לר"ג בההיא מיגו דהכא מודינא לך בההיא מיגו דהתם פליגנא עלך. מ"ש הכא ומ"ש התם הכא אין שור שחוט לפניך. פי' ואם רוצה לומר לא שלך היא ולהכחישו יכול גם עתה כשהודה שהיתה של אביו ולקחה ממנו נאמן אבל התם גבי אשה אם תרצה להכחישו ולומר בתולה הייתי אינה יכולה שהרי [שור] שחוט לפניך השושבינים המעידים שלא נמצאו לה בתולים הלכך כל טענה דאמרה בין מוכת עץ בין נאנסתי תתחזק לא מהימנא מתני'

מסורת הש"ס

א) ב"ב מב. ב) ב"ב לט: ג) [פסחים קח: ר"ה ח.] ד) ב"ב לח. ה) [שם ע"ש] ו) [פי' בערוך ערך חרס א'] ז) [פרשת ויחי סימן לג] ח) ג"י כ"י, ט) נ"ל לחפיפות. עב"ג י) [ב"מ לט.] כ) [שם].

גליון הש"ס

גמ' דיוקא דמתניתין קאמר. עכה דף ע"ב שבועות דף כט ע"ב:

ליקוטי רש"י

תנורא דאסא. נערה המאורסה היו רגילין לעשות לה חופה של הדס בכניסתה לחופה וקורין לה הינומא כדאמרינן בכתובות (דף טו:) שיצאתה בהינומא וראשה פרוע [ברכות נו:]. ההוא מרבנן. תלמיד חכם זקן לא קרי ליה צורבא אלא ההוא מרבנן קרי ליה [תענית ד.]. אין מחזיקין בנכסי קטן. אם לא אכל בפני האב שלש שנים אין שלש שנים שאכלן בפני קטן חזקה [ב"מ לט.]. ואפילו הגדיל. הקטן משירד לתוכו ואכל שלש שנים בפניו משהגדיל לא הויא חזקה הואיל ותחלת ירידתו לתוכו היה קטן לא ידע כשהגדיל שהן של אביו ולפיכך לא מיחה [שם]. מחמת נפשות. מחמת רציחת נפשות ירא למחות פן יודע מקום מחבואו וירדפו גואלי הדם אחריו כי יחם לבבו והשיגו והרגו. איבעי ליה למחויי. דמצי למחוי בכל מקום שהוא ומדלא מיחה חזקתו של חבירו בנכסיו הויא חזקה הואיל ולא מיחה דכיון דמחמת ממון הוא בורח אין צריך לאשתמוטי בעלמא אלא עד דהוה ליה מחאה ואינו ירא למחות דכיון דממון הוא ואין לו מה לפחד ואין רודפין אחריו ואם נודע מקומו שברח שם אינו חושש [רשב"ם ב"ב לח.]. שלש ארצות. בארץ ישראל. לחזקה. חלוקות זו מזו לענין חזקה שאם שלש שנים כמפורש ואותו בעל הקרקע. היה ביהודה והחזיק בגליל. שהיה הקרקע בגליל והחזיק בו אדם שלש שנים אינה חזקה. דמפרש טעמא בגמרא דשאני יהודה וגליל בשעת חירום שאין שיירות מצויות מזו לזו ולא יגיע לו למחזיק מחאתו של זה ויזהר בשטרו והיה לו לזה המחזיק ליזהר בשטרו שהרי יודע שאין בעל הקרקע יכול למחות. עד שיהא עמו במדינה. כגון שהיה ביהודה בעיר אחת והחזיק ביהודה בעיר אחרת דכיון דשיירות מצויות הוה ליה למחויי ומדלא מיחה הפסיד. אי קסבר מחאה וכו'. שמוחה בעל הקרקע במחזיק אפי' שלא בפניו כגון שניהם דרין בעיר אחת ומיחה בפני שנים מן השוק שלא בפניו של מחזיק אפי' הכי הויא מחאה דחברך חברא אית ליה ושמע המחזיק בדבר זה והיה לו להזהר בשטרו ומדלא נזהר הפסיד והלכך קתני עד שיהא עמו במדינה אחת דכיון ששניהם במדינה אחת הויא מחאה אע"פ שאינם בעיר אחת. אפילו ביהודה וגליל נמי. היה ביהודה והחזיק בגליל תיהוי מחאה. ואי קסבר וכו' לא הויא מחאה. כדקתני דהיה ביהודה והחזיק בגליל אינה חזקה. אפילו יהודה. אפי' היה ביהודה והחזיק ביהודה בעיר אחרת נמי לא תיהוי מחאה ואמאי קתני עד שיהא עמו במדינה. לעולם קסבר מחאה שלא בפניו הויא מחאה. ומשום הכי קתני עד שיהא עמו במדינה ודקשיא לך אפילו יהודה וגליל נמי תיהוי מחאה מתני' בשעת חירום תיגרות יש בין יהודה וגליל ואין שיירות מצויות מזו לזו ואם ימחה לא יצא הדבר לאזניו של מחזיק שיזהר בשטרו והלכך לא הויא מחאה וכיון דלא הויא מחאתו של מערער מחאה חזקתו של זה נמי לא הוי חזקה דטעמא דחזקה ג' שנים קונה משום דמצי טעין ליה מחזיק אמאי לא מחית בתוך שלש ואילו הכא לא מצי למטען הכי דהא לא יכול למחות דהא אינה מחאה. ומאי שנא יהודה וגליל דנקט. דכיון דבשעת חירום מיירי הוא הדין לכל המלכיות שיש חירום בין זו לזו והכי הוה ליה למיתני כל הארצות חלוקות לחזקה בשעת חירום ואית דמפרשי מ"ש יהודה וגליל דנקט כיון דבשעת חירום מוקמת לה מ"ש יהודה וגליל דלא הויא חזקה אפילו יהודה ויהודה לא תיהוי חזקה ואין נראה בעיני דאם כן הוה ליה למימר כדלעיל אי הכי אפילו יהודה ויהודה נמי לא ועוד דהכי מתרץ ר' אבא בשעת חירום שנו שיש תגרה בין המלכיות אבל עיירות של מדינה ומדינה אין בינותם תגרה [רשב"ם ב"ב לח.].

says, 'I purchased it from him,' he is not believed."[13] The Tanna could not teach the clause in this fashion, for the following reason: הֵיכִי דָּמֵי – **What would be the case** to which the Tanna would refer? I.e. for how long would the current occupant need to have held the property in question, in order for the Tanna's ruling to be applicable. אִי דְּאַכְלָהּ שְׁנֵי חֲזָקָה – **If he used it** for **the** three **years** needed to establish a ***chazakah,***[14] אַמַּאי לֹא מְהֵימַן – **why would he not be believed?**[15] וְאִי דְּלֹא אַכְלָהּ שְׁנֵי חֲזָקָה – **And if he did not use it** for **the** three **years** needed to establish a ***chazakah,*** פְּשִׁיטָא דְּלֹא מְהֵימַן – **it is obvious that he would not be believed!**[16] Since there is no case concerning which the Tanna could teach this clause, he focused initially on the case in which the occupant told his fellow that he purchased the field from his father.[17]

The Gemara counters:

אִי הָכִי גַּבֵּי אָבִיו נַמֵּי – **If so,** then **regarding** the case involving a claim of purchase from **[the fellow's] father, too,** the same argument can be made: To what case does the Mishnah's concluding clause refer? אִי דְּאַכְלָהּ שְׁנֵי חֲזָקָה – **If [the occupant] used [the field]** for **the** three **years** needed to establish a ***chazakah,*** אַמַּאי לֹא מְהֵימַן – **why is he not believed** when there are witnesses that it once belonged to his fellow's father? וְאִי דְּלֹא אַכְלָהּ שְׁנֵי חֲזָקָה – **And if he did not use it** for **the** three **years** needed to establish a ***chazakah,*** פְּשִׁיטָא דְּלֹא מְהֵימַן – **it is obvious that he is not believed. – ? –**

The Gemara answers:

בִּשְׁלָמָא גַּבֵּי אָבִיו – **All is well** now that the Mishnah was taught **in reference to** a claim of purchase from **[the fellow's] father,** מַשְׁכַּחַת לָהּ – because **you can find [the final clause]** to apply כְּגוֹן שֶׁאֲכָלָהּ שְׁתַּיִם בְּחַיֵּי הָאָב וְאַחַת בְּחַיֵּי בְנוֹ – to **a case where [the occupant] used it** for **two** years **during the life of the father and** for **one** additional year **during the life of his son,** who was a minor.[18] The Mishnah teaches that although the occupant enjoyed three consecutive years of uncontested occupancy, he has not established a valid *chazakah* and his claim that he purchased the field is not believed, because the third year of occupancy occurred only when the claimant was a minor. וּכְדְרַב הוּנָא – **And** this ruling is **in accordance with** a dictum **of Rav Huna.** דְּאָמַר רַב הוּנָא – **For Rav Huna said:** אֵין מַחֲזִיקִין בְּנִכְסֵי קָטָן – **One cannot establish a *chazakah* in a minor's property** on the basis of uncontested occupancy, אֲפִילּוּ הִגְדִּיל – **even** if **[the minor] became an adult** after his property was occupied.[19] However, if the Mishnah had discussed a claim of purchase from the son himself, the latter clause would be irreconcilable.

The Gemara questions Rav Huna's ruling:

וְרַב הוּנָא מַתְנִיתִין אֲתָא לְאַשְׁמוּעִינָן – **Now, did Rav Huna** merely **come to inform us** that which was taught in **our Mishnah?**[20]

Two resolutions are presented:

אִיבָּעֵית אֵימָא – **If you prefer, say** that רַב הוּנָא דִּיוּקָא דְּמַתְנִיתִין קָאָמַר – **Rav Huna spelled out** for us **the inference** that is contained **in the Mishnah.**[21] וְאִיבָּעֵית אֵימָא – **And if you prefer, say** that אֲפִילּוּ הִגְדִּיל קָא מַשְׁמַע לָן – **[Rav Huna] informs us** the added novelty that the *chazakah* is ineffective **even** if **[the minor] became an adult** and the occupant continued to use the land.[22]

The Gemara accepts the explanation of why the Mishnah could not have discussed the precise case proposed above, but insists that the Mishnah could have chosen a similar case:

וְלִיתְנְיֵיהּ בִּדְידֵיהּ – **But [the Tanna] should** still **have taught** this

NOTES

13. The Mishnah actually concludes: "But if there are witnesses that it was once *his father's,* and [the occupant] says, 'I purchased it from him,' he is not believed." As explained on 15b, since there are witnesses, the current occupant does not have the power of *happeh she'assar,* and therefore, his claim that he purchased the land is not believed unless he can prove it. Now, if the Mishnah's previous clause would refer to a claim that the land was purchased from the son himself, the concluding clause would have to be constructed similarly – and would perforce refer to a case where there are witnesses that it was previously the *son's.*

14. The Sages instituted that if someone occupies land for three consecutive years, during which his occupancy is unchallenged, he establishes a presumption of title known as חֲזָקָה, *chazakah.* The occupant can then claim that he purchased the field and he need not even produce a deed to that effect, because a person is not expected to keep deeds for longer than three years [if his occupancy has gone uncontested]. After a three-year period of unchallenged occupancy, the burden of proof lies with the contestant (*Rashi;* see *Bava Basra* 28a-29a and *Ketzos HaChoshen* 140:2).

15. The three years of *chazakah* are effective against the claim of a disputant even when he was known to be the original owner of the property. Our Mishnah would not be able to conclude that when there are witnesses regarding the original ownership the occupant loses the property!

16. If the current occupant had actually purchased the field, he should still have the deed. No occupant of a property is believed to say that he purchased it and lost the deed within three years. The Mishnah's latter ruling would be utterly superfluous if it were referring to this case!

17. This enabled him to conclude with the clause, "But if there are witnesses that it was once *his father's,* and [the occupant] says, 'I purchased it from him,' he is not believed." The Gemara goes on to explain why the objections just raised do not apply to this version.

18. I.e. after two years of his uncontested occupancy, the father died leaving this son, who was a minor, and the occupant used the field for another year without any protest by the son (*Rashi*).

19. A minor's failure to protest a stranger's occupancy of his land does not prove that the stranger has the right to occupy it. Therefore, the uncontested occupancy does not contribute towards a *chazakah.* Even if the stranger continues to occupy the property for many years after the child comes of age, this is not considered a valid *chazakah.* Since he first occupied the property while the child was a minor, the child takes the occupant's possession for granted and does not realize – even after attaining adulthood – that the property once belonged to his father. Years may pass before the child is informed by others that he has a claim on the land. [Thus, if he remained silent during his first three years of adulthood and protested afterwards, his protest is considered valid and the burden of proof lies with the occupant. If the occupant truly purchased the land, he must preserve his deed indefinitely in order to deflect any possible claim against him] (*Rashi*).

[Others explain that if the occupant used the property for three years after the son became an adult, his *chazakah* is valid – even if his occupancy began while the child was a minor. Once the child attains adulthood, he presumably inquires after his father's affairs. He must therefore present any claims within the usual three-year period, beginning from the day he comes of age. Rav Huna refers to a case where the occupant's total occupancy of three years began while the child was a minor and less than the full term occurred after he reached adulthood (*Ri Migash,* cited by *Ramban; Rambam, Hil. To'ein VeNitan* 14:7 with *Lechem Mishneh; Meiri*). See *Tosafos* ד״ה ואחת for yet another opinion.]

20. Since our Mishnah *must* be interpreted as dealing with the case where the occupant settled in the field while the son was a minor, it clearly teaches that one cannot establish a *chazakah* in a minor's properties. Why did Rav Huna need to state this ruling, when anything found in a Mishnah is common knowledge? (*Rashi;* see *Tosafos* ד״ה ורב הונא).

21. The Mishnah does not state explicitly that it deals with the case of a *chazakah* in a minor's property and that this is why the *chazakah* is ineffective. Rav Huna derived this by analyzing the Mishnah, and he sought to inform us of this law explicitly (*Rashi*).

22. The Mishnah could have been interpreted as referring to a case where the occupancy took place while the son was yet a minor. It is Rav Huna's original ruling that the *chazakah* is ineffective even if the person continued to occupy the property after the son became an adult. [This holds true according to either interpretation cited in note 19.]

עין משפט נר מצוה

יג א מיי' פי"ד מהלכות טוען ונטען הלכה ג סמג עשין לה טוש"ע ח"מ סימן קמ סעיף ז:
יד ב מיי' פי"ג שם הל' ח סמג שם טוש"ע שם סימן קמט סעיף יז:
טו ג מיי' פי"ד שם הל' ז טוש"ע שם סימן קמט סעיף יט:
טז ד מיי' שם הלכה י סמג שם טור ש"ע שם סימן קמג סעיף ד:
יז ה מיי' שם פי"א הלכה ה טוש"ע שם סימן קמו סעיף א:

אבל למאן דמתני לית ליה שיעורא: ואם יש עדים שיצתה בהינומא וכו': מאי הינומא סורחב בר פפא משמיה דזעירי אמר תנורא דאסא רבי יוחנן אמר קריתא דמנמנה בה כלתא: רבי יוחנן בן ברוקא אומר וכו': תנא ביהודה ראיה בבבל מאי אמר רב דרדוגי דמשחא ארישא דרבנן אמר ליה רב פפא לאביי משחא דחפיפותא קאמר מר אמר ליה יתמא לא עבדא לך אמך דרדוגי משחא ארישא דרבנן בשעת מעשה כי הא דההוא מרבנן דאיעסק ליה לבריה בי רבה בר עולא ואמרי לה רבה בר עולא איעסק ליה לבריה בי ההוא מרבנן ודרדיג משחא ארישא דרבנן בשעת מעשה ארמלתא מאי תאני רב יוסף ארמלתא לית לה כיסני: ומודה רבי יהושע באומר לחבירו כו': וליתני מודה ר' יהושע באומר לחבירו שדה זו שלך היתה ולקחתיה ממך משום דקא בעי למיתני סיפא [א] אם יש עדים שהיא שלו והוא אומר לקחתיה ממנו אינו נאמן היכי דמי אי דאכלה שני חזקה אמאי לא מהימן ואי דלא אכלה שני חזקה פשיטא דלא מהימן אי הכי גבי אביו נמי אי דאכלה שני חזקה אמאי לא מהימן ואי דלא אכלה שני חזקה פשיטא דלא מהימן בשלמא גבי אביו משכחת לה [ה] כגון [ב] שאכלה שתים בחיי האב ואחת בחיי בנו וכדרב הונא [ג] דאמר רב הונא [ג] אין מחזיקין בנכסי קטן אפילו הגדיל [ג] מתניתין אתא לאשמועינן איבעית אימא רב הונא [ד] דיוקא דמתני' קאמר ואיבעית אימא אפילו הגדיל קמ"ל וליתנייה בדידיה ולוקמה כגון שאכלה שתים בפניו ואחת שלא בפניו וכגון שברח ברח מחמת מאי אי [ד] דברח מחמת נפשות פשיטא דלא מהימן דלא מצי מחי ואי דברח מחמת ממון איבעי ליה למחויי [ה] דקי"ל מחאה שלא בפניו הויא מחאה דתנן [ז] שלש ארצות לחזקה יהודה ועבר הירדן והגליל היה ביהודה והחזיק בגליל בגליל והחזיק ביהודה אינה חזקה עד שיהא עמו במדינה והוינן בה [ח] מאי קסבר אי קסבר מחאה שלא בפניו הויא מחאה אפילו ביהודה וגליל נמי ואי קסבר מחאה שלא בפניו לא הויא מחאה אפילו יהודה ויהודה נמי לא אמר רבי אבא בר ממל לעולם קסבר מחאה שלא בפניו הויא מחאה ומתניתין בשעת [י] חירום שנו ומאי שנא יהודה וגליל דנקט דסתם

רש"י

אבל למאן דמתני. לאחרים: לית ליה שיעורא. וממילא שמעינן דלמאן דלא קרי ולא תני אין מבטלין אם יש לו מתעסקין כדי קבורה בעלמא בשאלתות דרב אחאי [ו] מצאתי כן: תנורא דאסא. כמין חופה של הדס עגולה: קריתא. לעיף על ראשה מסורבב על עיניה כמו שעושין במקומינו ופעמים שמנמנמת בתוכו מתוך שאין עיניה מגולין ולכך נקרא הינומא על שם תנומה: ביהודה ראיה. כל הני דמתני' ששם היו רגילין בסימנין הללו לבתולה: דרדוגי מישחא. הנשים נותנים שמן בראש התלמידים ושפות: מישחא דחפיפותא. [שמן של בשמים שממוקין [ט] לחופות] קאמר מר וכי בעלי חפיפות הן לסוך שמן: יתמא. יתום ממנהג הנוהג: איעסק לבריה. לישא לו אשה: ודרדיג מישחא. שפך שמן בראש התלמידים: ארמלתא מאי. מה סימנין עושים לאלמנה להודיע שאלמנה נישאת: לית לה כיסני. אין לה קליות וזה סימנה: וליתני מודה ר' יהושע כו' שדה זו שלך היתה. כיון דטעמא משום דאין שור שחוט לפניו הוא שלא היה אדם תובעו מה לי של אביו ומה לי שלו ומאי שנא של אביך דנקט: שני חזקה. שלש שנים שתיקנו חכמים לכל מחזיקים בקרקע דמשאכלה שלש שנים בלא עירעור נאמן לומר לקחתיה ואבד שטרי דכולי האי לא מזהר איניש בשטרא: בשלמא גבי אביו משכחת לה. דאיצטריך למיתנייה כגון דאכלה שני חזקה ואפילו הכי לא מהימן וכגון שאכלה שתי שנים ראשונות בחיי אביו ומת ואכלה השלישית לפני הבן הזה והוא היה קטן ולא עירער ואיצטריך לאשמועינן דכיון דקטן היה אין השנה הזאת עולה מן המנין: וכדרב הונא דאמר אין מחזיקין בנכסי קטן. המחזיק בנכסי קטן שלש שנים אינה חזקה דהאי דלא מיחה משום דקטן הוא ואפילו הגדיל לאחר מיכן והחזיק זה בפניו כמה שנים אינה חזקה הואיל ותחלתו כשהוא קטן ראהו מוחזק בה לא ידע כשהגדיל שהיתה של אביו עד ששומע מפי אחרים: ורב הונא מתניתין אתא לאשמועינן. בתמיה כיון דמתניתין בהכי עסקינן ולא מיתוקמא אלא בהכי מאי אתא רב הונא לאשמועינן הרי כבר שנויה ועומדת ודבר השנוי במשנתינו שגור בפי הכל: דיוקא דמתניתין אתא לאשמועינן. משום דמתני' לא מיפרשא בהדיא דבהכי עסקינן ואתא רב הונא לאשמועינן בהדיא ומדיוקא דמתני' קא יליף לה: וליתנייה בדידיה. שדה זו שלך היתה אם יש עדים כו' אינו נאמן ואע"ג שאכלה שני חזקה וכגון שהיו שתים בפניו ואחת שלא בפניו: כגון שברח. ואשמעינן דההיא שתא לא סלקא ליה: אי ברח מחמת ממון. שאינו ירא מן המלכות אלא מלעקת הנועקים בעיר: איבעי ליה למחויי. במקום שהוא שם וכיון דלא מיחה חזקה מעלייתא היא: שלש ארצות לחזקה. שלש ארצות של א"י חשובות חלוקות זו מזו לענין חזקה כאילו הן ארצות נכריות ואם היה בזו והחזיק אחר בקרקע שיש לו בחברתה אינה חזקה: במדינה. או שניהם בגליל או שניהם ביהודה ואפי' הן בשתי עיירות: אפי' יהודה וגליל נמי. הוה ליה למחויי היכא דהוי ומדלא מחי תיהוי חזקה: ואי קסבר מחאה שלא בפניו לא הויא מחאה. כגון אם היה בעיר אחת ומיחה שלא בפניו בפני שנים בעיר אחרת: אפילו יהודה ויהודה. בשתי עיירות נמי לא תיהוי חזקה דלא הוה ליה למחויי שלא בפניו: הויא מחאה. דחברך חברא אית ליה דהני דמחי באנפייהו מגלו לאחריני ובא הדבר לאזני המחזיק וה"ל לאזדהורי בשטריה: ומתני'. דקתני יהודה וגליל לא: בשעת חירום שנו. דיכול לומר לא נגלית לי מחאתו שאשמור את שטרי: ומאי שנא יהודה וגליל דנקט. אם יש חירום נמי מעיר לעיר אפי' שתי עיירות באותה מדינה נמי לא: וליתני

תוספות

אבל מאן דמתני לית ליה שיעורא. בשאלתות דרב אחאי כתוב וממילא שמעינן למאן דלא קרי ולא תני אין מבטלין אם יש לו מתעסקין כדי קבורה ונראה לר"י דלענין מלאכה מבטלין כל בני העיר ואסור אפילו למאן דלא קרי ולא תני דלא מפליג מידי באלו מגלחין (מו"ק דף כח:) בהכי: **אלמנה** מאי. ביהודה בעי שלא היה אלא חילוק קליות לכך בעי אלמנה מאי והלא פעמים אפילו בלא חופה היו רגילין לחלוק ויש לחוש שמא חילקו בחופת אלמנה ומשני לית לה כיסני פירוש היו נזהרין הרבה שלא יחלקו קליות בחופת אלמנה: **וליתני** מודה רבי יהושע שדה זו שלך היתה. דהוי רבותא טפי דהוי ברי וברי: **ואחת** בחיי הבן. ודווקא שהוא קטן כפי' הקונט' אבל אם הוא גדול הוי חזקה כדאמרי' בחזקת הבתים (ב"ב דף מב. ושם) אכלה בפני האב שנה ובפני הבן שנה ובפני לוקח שנה הרי זו חזקה ורבינו שמואל פי' אהא דאמר בסמוך ואפילו הגדיל אפילו הגדיל בחיי האב דגדול לגבי מילי דאבוה קטן הוא ואור"ת דלפירושו הא דאמר בחזקת הבתים (ג"ז שם) דהויא חזקה בפני הבן היינו כשהיה גדול בתחילת חזקה: **ורב** הונא מתני' אתא לאשמועינן. לאו דווקא נקט רב הונא דהא לא איירי רב הונא התם [י] אלא במורידין קרוב לנכסי קטן והא לא שמעינן ממתני' אלא כלומר רבא דדייק התם [כ] ש"מ מדרב הונא דאין מחזיקין בנכסי קטן מאי אתא לאשמועינן: **מחאה** שלא בפניו כו'. תימה אמאי נקט בכל דוכתא מחאה שלא בפניו הוה ליה למינקט חזקה שלא בפניו כו' וי"ל דעיקר הטעם תלוי במחאה לחזקה ולאי יש לה קול אפי' שלא בפניו ואפ"ה אי מחאה אין לה קול לא הוי חזקה והכי נקט בכל דסתם

בהדיא דבהכי עסקינן ואתא רב הונא לאשמועינן בהדיא ומדיוקא דמתני' קא יליף לה: וליתנייה בדידיה.

ביהודה בעיר אחת והחזיק ביהודה בעיר אחרת דכיון דשיירות מצויות הוה ליה למחויי ומדלא מיחה הפסיד. **אי קסבר מחאה וכו'.** שמוחה בעל הקרקע במחזיק אפי' שלא בפניו כגון ששניהם דרין בעיר אחת ומיחה בפני שנים מן השוק שלא בפניו של מחזיק אפי' הכי ה"א מחאה דחברך חברא אית ליה ושמע המחזיק בדבר זה והיה לו להזהר בשטרו ומדלא נזהר הפסיד והלכך קתני עד שיהא עמו במדינה אחת דכיון ששניהם במדינה אחת הויא מחאה אע"פ שאינם בעיר אחת. **אפילו ביהודה וגליל נמי.** היה ביהודה והחזיק בגליל תיהוי מחאה. **ואי קסבר וכו' לא הויא מחאה.** אפי' היה ביהודה והחזיק ביהודה בעיר אחרת נמי לא תיהוי מחאה ואמאי קתני עד שיהא עמו במדינה. **לעולם קסבר מחאה שלא בפניו הויא מחאה.** ומשום הכי קתני עד שיהא עמו במדינה ודקשיא לך אפילו יהודה וגליל נמי תיהוי מחאה מתני' בשעת חירום מיגרים יש בין יהודה וגליל ואין שיירות מצויות מזו לזו ואם ימחה לא יבא הדבר לאזניו של מחזיק שיזהר בשטרו והלכך לא ה"א מחאה וכיון דלא הויא מחאתו של מערער מחאה חזקתו של זה נמי לא הוי חזקה דטעמא דחזקה ג' שנים קונה משום דמצי טעין ליה מחזיק אמאי לא מחית בתוך שלש ואילו הכא לא מצי למטען הכי דהא לא יכול למחות דהא אינה מחאה. **ומאי שנא יהודה וגליל דנקט.** דכיון דבשעת חירום מיירי הוא הדין לכל המלכות שיש חירום בין זו לזו והכי הוה ליה למיתני כל הארצות חלוקות לחזקה בשעת חירום ואית דמפרשי מ"ש יהודה וגליל דנקט כיון דבשעת חירום מוקמת לה מ"ש יהודה וגליל דלא הויא חזקה אפילו יהודה ויהודה לא תיהוי חזקה ואין נראה בעיני דאם כן הוה ליה למימר כדלעיל אי הכי אפילו יהודה ויהודה נמי לא ועוד דהכי מתרץ ר' אבא בשעת חירום שנו שיש מגרה בין המלכות אבל עיירות של מדינה ומדינה אין ביניהם מגרה [רשב"ם ב"ב לח.].

תוספות רי"ד

דלא קרי ולא תני אין מבטלין ת"ת אם יש לו מתעסקים כדי קבורה בעלמא בשאלתות דרב אחא מצאתי כן: **אם יש** עדים שיצאת בהינומא מאי הינומא סרחב בר פפא אמר משמיה דזעירי תנורא דאסא כו' כמין כיפה של הדס עגולה ר"י אמר קריתא ומנמנמא בה כלה פי' צניף על ראשה משורבב על עיניה כמו שעושים בהרבה מקומות ופעמים שמנמנמת בתוכו מתוך שאין עיניה מגולות ולכך נקרא הינומא ע"ש תנומה: **מתני' ומודה** ר"י באומר לחברו שדה זו של אביך היתה ולקחתיה ממנו נאמן שהפה שאסר הוא הפה שהתיר ואם יש עדים שהוא של אביו והוא אומר לקחתיה ממנו אינו נאמן ואסיקנא ר' יהושע אפרק קמא קאי והא קאי דתנן הנושא את האשה ולא מצא לה בתולים היא אומרת משארסתני נאנסתי ונסתחפה שדך והוא אומר לא כי אלא עד שלא ארסתיך והיה מקחי מקח טעות ר"ג ור"א [אומרים] נאמנת ור"י אומר לא מפיה אנו חיין והתם מאי מיגו איכא מיגו דאי בעי אמרה מוכת עץ אני ולא פסלה נפשה מכהונה וקאמרה נאנסתי דפסלה נפשה מכהונה מהימנא וא"ל ר"י לר"ג בההיא מיגו דהכא מרינא לך בההיא מיגו דהתם פליגנא עלך. **מ"ש הכא** ומ"ש התם הכא אין שור שחוט לפניך. פי' ואם רוצה לומר אינו של אביך ולהכחישו יכול גם עתה כשהודה שהיתה של אביו ולקחה ממנו נאמן אבל התם גבי אשה אם תרצה להכחישו לומר בתולה הייתי אינה יכולה שהרי [שור] שחוט לפניך השושבינים המעידים שלא נמצאו לה בתולים הלכך כל טענה דאמרה בין מוכת עץ אני בין נאנסתי תחתך לא מהימנא
מתני'

מסורת הש"ס

א) ב"ב מב., ב) ב"מ לט., ג) [פסחים קא: ר"ה ח.], ד) ב"ב לח., ה) [שם ע"ש], ו) [פי' בערוך ערך תרס א' סיכסוך איש באחיו ועיר בעיר], ז) [פרשת וחזי סימן לב], ח) ב"ב כח., ט) נ"ל לחפיפות. יעב"ץ, י) [ב"מ לט.], כ) [שם].

גליון הש"ס

גמ' דיוקא דמתניתין קאמר. שבת דף לט ע"ב שבועות דף כט ע"ב:

ליקוטי רש"י

תנורא דאסא. נערה המאורסה היו רגילין לעשות לה חופה של הדס בכניסתה לחופה וקורין לה הינומא כדאמרינן בכתובות (דף יז:) שיצאתה בהינומא וראשה פרוע [ברכות נו:]. ההוא מרבנן. תלמיד חכם וזקן לא קרי אורבא אלא ההוא מרבנן קרי ליה [תענית ד.]. אין מחזיקין בנכסי קטן. אם לא בפני האב שלש שנים שאכלן בפני הקטן חזקה [ב"ב לט.]. ואפילו הגדיל. הקטן משהגדיל לתוכו ואכלו שלש שנים בפניו משהגדיל לא הוי חזקה הואיל ותחלה ירידתו לתוכו היה קטן לא ידע כשהגדיל שהיא של אביו ולפיכך לא מיחה [שם:]. מחמת נפשות. מחמת לגיסות ירא למות ... אחריו כי יחם לבבו והשיגו והרגו. איבעי ליה למחויי. דמצי למחויי ולא מחה ולא קבע מקום שהוא יושב הוא חזקה: ... שלש ארצות. בארץ ישראל לחזקה. חלוקות זו מזו לענין חזקה דבעל הקרקע ... בעל הקרקע ... עד שיהא עמו במדינה. כגון שהיה ... ואינו יכול למחות ... ולא ... בשטרו שהרי יודע שאין בעל הקרקע יכול למחות. עד שיהא עמו במדינה. כגון שהיה

אֲבָל לְמַאן דְּמַתְנֵי – **but for one who has** studied and **taught Mishnah** to others,[1] לֵית לֵיהּ שִׁיעוּרָא – **there is no limit.**[2]

The Gemara returns to its analysis of our Mishnah:

וְאִם יֵשׁ עֵדִים שֶׁיָּצְתָה בְּהִינוּמָא וכו׳ – IF THERE ARE WITNESSES THAT SHE WENT OUT WITH A *HINUMA* **etc.** her *kesubah* is two hundred *zuz.*

The Gemara inquires:

מַאי הִינוּמָא – **What is a** ***hinuma*****?**

The Gemara presents two explanations:

סוּרְחַב בַּר פָּפָּא מִשְּׁמֵיהּ דִּזְעֵירִי אָמַר – **Surchav bar Pappa said in the name of Zeiri:** תַּנּוּרָא דְּאָסָא – It is **a round myrtle canopy.**[3] רַבִּי יוֹחָנָן אָמַר – **R' Yochanan said:** קְרִיתָא דִּמְנַמְנָה בָּהּ כַּלְּתָא – It is **a veil in which the bride dozes.**[4]

The Mishnah continued listing evidence that a woman may bring to prove that she was a virgin:

רַבִּי יוֹחָנָן בֶּן בְּרוֹקָא אוֹמֵר וכו׳ – R' YOCHANAN BEN BEROKA SAYS: **etc.** [The distribution of parched grain is also proof].

The Gemara inquires:

תְּנָא בִּיהוּדָה רְאָיָה – **[The Mishnah] taught** what a **proof** is **in Judea;**[5] בְּבָבֶל מַאי – **what** proof is there **in Babylonia** that the bride is a virgin?

The Gemara answers:

אָמַר רַב – **Rav said:** דַּרְדּוּגֵי דִּמְשְׁחָא אַרֵישָׁא דְּרַבָּנָן – **Rubbing oil on the heads of the Rabbis.**[6]

The Gemara seeks a clarification:

אָמַר לֵיהּ רַב פָּפָּא לְאַבָּיֵי – **Rav Pappa said to Abaye:** מִשְׁחָא דַּחֲפִיפוּתָא קָאָמַר מַר – **Is the master talking** about **oil for shampooing?**[7]

Abaye answers:

אָמַר לֵיהּ – **He said to [Rav Pappa]:** יַתְמָא – **Bereft one!**[8] לֹא עָבְדָא לָךְ אִמָּךְ דַּרְדּוּגֵי מִשְׁחָא אַרֵישָׁא דְּרַבָּנָן בִּשְׁעַת מַעֲשֶׂה – **Did your mother not rub oil on the heads of the Rabbis during [your wedding]?**[9] כִּי הָא דְּהַהוּא מֵרַבָּנָן – **Like this case of a certain Rabbi** דְּאִיעֲסַק לֵיהּ לִבְרֵיהּ בֵּי רַבָּה בַּר עוּלָּא – **who arranged a match for his son with** a member of **the house of Rabbah bar Ulla** – וְאָמְרֵי לָהּ רַבָּה בַּר עוּלָּא אִיעֲסַק לֵיהּ לִבְרֵיהּ בֵּי הַהוּא מֵרַבָּנָן – **and some say it: Rabbah bar Ulla arranged a match for his son with** a member of **the house of a certain one of the Rabbis** – וְדַרְדִּיג מִשְׁחָא אַרֵישָׁא דְּרַבָּנָן בִּשְׁעַת מַעֲשֶׂה – **and oil was rubbed on the heads of the Rabbinic students during the wedding.**

The Gemara asks:

אַרְמַלְתָּא מַאי – **What** do they do to show that the bride is a **widow?**[10]

The Gemara answers:

תָּאנֵי רַב יוֹסֵף – **Rav Yosef taught** the following **Baraisa:** אַרְמַלְתָּא לֵית לָהּ כִּיסָנֵי – A WIDOW DOES NOT HAVE PARCHED GRAIN. That is a sign that the bride is a widow.[11]

The Mishnah stated:

וּמוֹדֶה רַבִּי יְהוֹשֻׁעַ בְּאוֹמֵר לַחֲבֵירוֹ כו׳ – AND R' YEHOSHUA AGREES concerning a case WHERE [SOMEONE] SAYS TO HIS FELLOW, **etc.** ["This field was your father's but I purchased it from him," that he is believed].

The Gemara wonders why the Tanna did not cite a simpler case:

וְלִיתְנֵי – **[The Tanna] should have taught:** מוֹדֶה רַבִּי יְהוֹשֻׁעַ – **"R' Yehoshua agrees** concerning a case בְּאוֹמֵר לַחֲבֵירוֹ שָׂדֶה זוֹ שֶׁלְּךָ הָיְתָה וּלְקַחְתִּיהָ מִמְּךָ – **where [someone] says to his fellow, 'This field was** ***yours*** **but I purchased it from you,'** that he is believed." Why does the Tanna focus on a claim of purchase from the person's father?[12]

The Gemara responds by explaining why it was impossible for the Tanna to discuss a claim involving the son himself:

מִשּׁוּם דְּקָא בָּעֵי לְמִיתְנֵי סֵיפָא – **Because he would** then **have to teach** the Mishnah's **final clause** as follows: אִם יֵשׁ עֵדִים שֶׁהִיא שֶׁלּוֹ – "But **if there are witnesses that it was** once ***his*** (i.e. the son's), וְהוּא אוֹמֵר לְקַחְתִּיהָ מִמֶּנּוּ אֵינוֹ נֶאֱמָן – **and [the occupant]**

NOTES

1. *Rashi;* cf. *Tur Yoreh Deah* 361:1 with *Bach.*

2. I.e. everyone is required to attend the funeral of such a person.

Our Gemara implies that we do not suspend Torah study to attend the funeral of someone who did not study Torah at all, provided there are enough people there to perform the actual burial (*Rashi* and *Tosafos,* from *She'iltos*). However, *Tosafos* and *Rosh* add that this leniency applies only to Torah scholars; regular workers must stop their work to attend the funeral of any Jew. This view is accepted by *Shulchan Aruch* (*Yoreh Deah* 361:2).

Ritva (citing *Smag*) writes that nowadays the assumption is that every Jew is replete with mitzvos and probably studied either Scripture or Mishnah. *Rama* (ibid. 361:1) mentions this opinion. See *Ran* and *Shitah Mekubetzes* regarding the status of a woman.

It should emerge from the above that in a city with a large Jewish population it would be difficult to maintain a steady schedule of Torah study or work, since it would be necessary to attend every funeral that one hears of. However, some rule that the requirement to suspend Torah study and work applies only when one sees the deceased being taken to burial (*Haamek She'eilah* 34:2; cf. *Beis Shmuel, Even HaEzer* 65:3). On this basis, the current practice is not to cancel Torah study or work unless one actually sees the burial taking place or unless the deceased was a major Torah scholar.

3. *Rashi.* It is called a תַּנּוּרָא [literally: oven] because it is shaped like a *tanur,* oven – wide at the bottom and narrow at the top (*Ri Migash*).

4. Since the bride's eyes are covered by the veil (*Rashi* adds: like those of our times), she sometimes dozes behind it. The term *hinuma* is related to *tenumah,* which is Hebrew for *slumber* (*Rashi*).

5. The actions listed in the Mishnah to indicate that the bride was a virgin were done in Judea [where the Mishnah was redacted] (*Rashi*).

6. The women would pour oil on the heads of the Rabbinic students and rub it in (*Rashi*). There were thus two unusual actions taken: (a) Oil is usually applied to other parts of the body, but not to one's hair. (b) It was done by women (see *Rama, Even HaEzer* 21:5). Such an occurrence would certainly be remembered (*Chasam Sofer,* cited in *Yalkut Peirushim* to *Maseches Kesubos*).

7. I.e. Do they need their heads shampooed? (*Rashi*; see *Chasam Sofer*).

8. Literally: orphan. Abaye did not mean that Rav Pappa was an orphan. Rather, he had been left out of the common practice (*Rashi*).

9. Literally: at the time of the action.

10. That is, in Judea, where there are many customs to show that the bride is a virgin, the absence of *all* of them proves that she is a widow. But in Babylonia, where the only custom is oil rubbing, certainly if there are no witnesses that this was performed, there is no proof that the bride was not a virgin (as evident from Rav Pappa's case). Hence, what proof is there in Babylonia that the bride is a widow?

11. That is, they were very careful not to distribute parched grain at the wedding of a widow [which otherwise was a common serving at a feast]; this was the special practice that symbolized a widow's wedding (*Shitah Mekubetzes,* explaining *Rashi;* cf. *Tosafos* with *Maharsha;* see also *Ritva*). For other explanations of this *sugya,* see *Haflaah* and *Beis Aharon.*

12. Since R' Yehoshua's ruling – that the occupant of the field is believed – is based on the fact that there was no "slaughtered ox," i.e. no one had lodged a complaint against the person [as explained on 15a], the law should be the same whether he claims that he bought the field from the fellow's father or he claims he bought it from the fellow himself. Why does the Mishnah discuss the [more complicated] case involving the father? (*Rashi;* see *Beis Yaakov,* and *Beis HaLevi* 3:19, for an analysis of *Rashi's* words; cf. *Tosafos* ד״ה וליתני and *Tosafos* to 15b ד״ה ומודה; see also *Maharsha, Maharam Schif* and *Pnei Yehoshua*).

עין משפט נר מצוה

יג א מיי' פי"ד מהלכות טוען ונטען הלכה ג סמג עשין לה טוש"ע ח"מ סימן קמ סעיף א:

יד ב מיי' פי"ב שם הל' ח סמג שם טוש"ע שם סימן קמד סעיף ד:

טו ג מיי' פי"ד שם הל' ז טוש"ע שם סימן קמט סעיף יט:

טז ד מיי' שם הלכה י סמג שם טור ש"ע שם סימן קמג סעיף ג:

יז ה מיי' שם פי"א הלכה ה טוש"ע שם סימן קמו סעיף א:

גמרא

אבל למאן דמתני לית ליה שיעורא: ואם יש עדים שיצתה בהינומא וכו': מאי הינומא סורחב בר פפא משמיה דזעירי אמר תנורא דאסא רבי יוחנן אמר קריתא דמנמנה בה כלתא: רבי יוחנן בן ברוקא אומר וכו': תנא ביהודה ראיה בבבל מאי אמר רב דרדוגי דמשחא ארישא דרבנן אמר ליה רב פפא לאביי משחא דחפיפותא קאמר מר אמר ליה יתמא לא עבדא לך אמך דרדוגי משחא ארישא דרבנן בשעת מעשה כי הא דההוא מרבנן דאיעסק ליה לבריה בי רבה בר עולא ואמרי לה רבה בר עולא איעסק ליה לבריה בי ההוא מרבנן ודרדיג משחא ארישא דרבנן בשעת מעשה ארמלתא מאי תאני רב יוסף ארמלתא לית לה כיסני: ומודה רבי יהושע באומר לחבירו כו': וליתני מודה ר' יהושע באומר לחבירו שדה זו שלך היתה ולקחתיה ממך משום דקא בעי למיתני סיפא [א] אם יש עדים שהיא שלו והוא אומר לקחתיה ממנו אינו נאמן היכי דמי אי דאכלה שני חזקה אמאי לא מהימן ואי דלא אכלה שני חזקה פשיטא דלא מהימן אי הכי גבי אביו נמי אי דאכלה שני חזקה אמאי לא מהימן ואי דלא אכלה שני חזקה פשיטא דלא מהימן בשלמא גבי אביו משכחת לה כגון [ב] שאכלה שתים בחיי האב ואחת בחיי בנו וכדרב הונא דאמר רב הונא [ג] אין מחזיקין בנכסי קטן אפילו הגדיל ורב הונא מתניתין אתא לאשמועינן איבעית אימא רב הונא דיוקא דמתני' קאמר ואיבעית אימא אפילו הגדיל קמ"ל וליתנייה בדידיה ולוקמה כגון שאכלה שתים בפניו ואחת שלא בפניו וכגון שברח ברח מחמת מאי אי [ד] דברח מחמת נפשות פשיטא דלא מהימן דלא מצי מחי ואי דברח מחמת ממון איבעי ליה למחויי [ה] דקי"ל מחאה שלא בפניו הויא מחאה דתנן [ו] שלש ארצות לחזקה יהודה ועבר הירדן והגליל היה ביהודה והחזיק בגליל בגליל והחזיק ביהודה אינה חזקה עד שיהא עמו במדינה והוינן בה [ז] מאי קסבר אי קסבר מחאה שלא בפניו הויא מחאה אפילו ביהודה וגליל נמי ואי קסבר מחאה שלא בפניו לא הויא מחאה אפילו יהודה ויהודה נמי לא אמר רבי אבא בר ממל לעולם קסבר מחאה שלא בפניו הויא מחאה ומתניתין בשעת [י] חירום שנו ומאי שנא יהודה וגליל דנקט

דסתם

רש"י

אבל למאן דמתני. לאחרים: לית ליה שיעורא. וממילא שמעינן דלמאן דלא קרי ולא תני אין מבטלין אם יש לו מתעסקין כדי קבורה בעלמא בשאלתות דרב אחאי [ז] מצאתי כן: תנורא דאסא. כמין חופה של הדס עגולה: קריתא. לעיף על ראשה מסורבב על עיניה כמו שעושין במקומינו ופעמים שמנמנמת בתוכו מתוך שאין עיניה מגולין ולכך נקרא הינומא על שם תנומה: ביהודה ראיה. כל הני דמתני' שהם היו רגילין בסימנין הללו לבתולה: דרדוגי מישחא. הנשים נותנים שמן בראש התלמידים ושפות: מישחא דחפיפותא. [ח] [שמן של בשמים שמתוקן [ט] לחופות] קאמר מר וכי בעלי חפיפות הן לסוכן שמן: יתמא. יתום ממנהג הנוהג: איעסק לבריה. לישא לו אשה: ודרדיג מישחא. שפך שמן בראש התלמידים: ארמלתא מאי. מה סימנין עושים לאלמנה להודיע שאלמנה נישאת: לית לה כיסני. אין לה קליות וזה סימנה: וליתני מודה ר' יהושע כו' שדה זו שלך היתה. כיון דטעמא משום דאין שור שחוט לפניו הוא שלא היה אדם תובעו מה לי של אביו ומה לי שלו ומאי שנא של אביך דנקט: שני חזקה. שלש שנים שתיקנו חכמים לכל מחזיקים בקרקע דמשאכלה שלש שנים בלא עירעור נאמן לומר לקחתיה ואבד שטרי דכולי האי לא מזדהר איניש בשטרא: בשלמא גבי אביו משכחת לה. דאיצטריך למיתנייה כגון דאכלה שני חזקה ואפילו הכי לא מהימן וכגון שאכלה שתי שנים ראשונות בחיי אביו ומת ואכלה השלישית לפני הבן הזה והוא היה קטן ולא עירער ואיצטריך לאשמועינן דכיון דקטן היה אין השנה הזאת עולה מן המנין: וכדרב הונא דאמר אין מחזיקין בנכסי קטן. המחזיק בנכסי קטן שלש שנים אינה חזקה דהאי דלא מיחה משום דקטן הוא ואפילו הגדיל לאחר מיכן והחזיק זה בפניו כמה שנים אינה חזקה הואיל ותחלתו כשהוא קטן ראהו מוחזק בה לא ידע כשהגדיל שהיתה של אביו עד ששומע מפי אחרים: ורב הונא מתניתין אתא לאשמועינן. בתמיה כיון דמתניתין בהכי עסקינן ולא מיתוקמא אלא בהכי מאי אתא רב הונא לאשמועינן הרי כבר שנויה ועומדת ודבר השנוי במשנתינו שגור בפי הכל: דיוקא דמתניתין אתא לאשמועינן. משום דמתני' לא מיפרשא בהדיא דבהכי עסקינן ואתא רב הונא לאשמועינן בהדיא ומדיוקא דמתני' קא יליף לה: וליתנייה בדידיה. שדה זו שלך היתה אם יש עדים כו' אינו נאמן ואע"ג שאכלה שני חזקה וכגון שהיו שתים בפניו ואחת שלא בפניו: כגון שברח. ואשמעינן דההיא שתא לא סלקא ליה: אי ברח מחמת ממון. שאינו ירא מן המלכות אלא מנושת הנושים בעיר: איבעי ליה למחויי. במקום שהוא שם וכיון דלא מיחה חזקה מעלייתא היא: שלש ארצות לחזקה. שלש ארצות של א"י חשובות חלוקות זו מזו לענין חזקה כאילו הן ארצות נכריות ואם היה בזו והחזיק אחר בקרקע שיש לו בחברתה אינה חזקה: במדינה. או שניהם בגליל או שניהם ביהודה ואפי' הן בשתי עירות: אפי' יהודה וגליל נמי. הוה ליה למחויי היכא דהוי ומדלא מחי תיהוי חזקה: ואי קסבר מחאה שלא בפניו לא הויא מחאה. כגון אם היה בעיר אחת ומיחה שלא בפניו בפני שנים בעיר אחרת: אפילו יהודה ויהודה. בשתי עיירות נמי לא תיהוי חזקה דלא הוה ליה למחויי שלא בפניו: הויא מחאה. דחברך חברא אית ליה דהני דמחי באנפייהו מגלו לאחריני ובא הדבר לאזני המחזיק וה"ל לאזדהורי בשטריה: ומתני'. דקתני יהודה וגליל לא: בשעת חירום שנו. דיכול לומר לא נגלית לי מחאתו שאשמור את שטרי: ומאי שנא יהודה וגליל דנקט. אם יש חירום נמי מעיר לעיר אפי' שתי עיירות באותה מדינה נמי לא:

וליתני

תוספות

אבל מאן דמתני לית ליה שיעורא. בשאלתות דרב אחאי כתוב וממילא שמעינן למאן דלא קרי ולא תני אין מבטלין אם יש לו מתעסקין כדי קבורה ונראה לר"י דלענין מלאכה מבטלין כל בני העיר ולאסור אפילו למאן דלא קרי ולא תני דלא מפליג מידי באלו מגלחין (מו"ק דף כח:) בהכי:

אלמנה מאי. ביהודה בעי שלא היה אלא חילוק קליות לכך בעי אלמנה מאי והלא פעמים אפילו בלא חופה היו רגילין לחלוק ויש לחוש שמא חילקו בחופת אלמנה ומשני לית לה כיסני פירוש היו נזהרין הרבה שלא יחלקו קליות בחופת אלמנה:

וליתני מודה רבי יהושע שדה זו שלך היתה. דהוי רבותא טפי דהוי בריו וברי:

ואחת בחיי הבן. ודווקא שהוא קטן כפי' הקונט' אבל אם הוא גדול הוי חזקה כדאמרי' בחזקת הבתים (ב"ב דף מב. ושם) אכלה בפני האב שנה ובפני הבן שנה ובפני לוקח שנה הרי זו חזקה ורבינו שמואל פי' הא דאמר בסמוך ואפילו הגדיל אפילו הגדיל בחיי האב דגדול לגבי מילי דאבוה קטן הוא ואור"ת דלפירושו הא דאמר בחזקת הבתים (ג"ז שם) דהויא חזקה בפני הבן היינו כשהיה גדול בתחילת חזקה:

ורב הונא מתני' אתא לאשמועינן. לאו דווקא נקט רב הונא דהא לא איירי רב הונא התם [י] אלא במורידין קרוב לנכסי קטן והא לא שמעינן ממתני' אלא כלומר רבא דדייק התם [כ] ש"מ מדרב הונא דאין מחזיקין בנכסי קטן מאי אתא לאשמועינן:

מחאה שלא בפניו כו'. תימה אמאי נקט בכל דוכתא מחאה שלא בפניו הוה ליה למינקט חזקה שלא בפניו כו' וי"ל דעיקר הטע' תלוי במחאה דחזקה ודאי יש לה קול אפי' שלא בפניו ואפ"ה אי מחאה אין לה קול לא הוי חזקה ולהכי נקט מחא':

תוספות רי"ד

דלא קרי ולא תני אין מבטלין ת"ת אב יש לו מתעסקים כדי קבורה בעלמא בשאלתות דרב אחאי מצאתי כן: אם יש עדים שיצאת בהינומא מאי הינומא סרחב בר פפא אמר משמיה דזעירי תנורא דאסא פי' כמין כיפה של הדס עגולה ר"י אמר קריתא ומנמנמא בה כלה פי' צניף על ראשה משורבב על עיניה כמו שעושים בהרבה מקומות ופעמים שמנמנמת בתוכו מתוך שאין עיניה מגולות ולכך נקרא הינומא ע"ש תנומה: מתני' ומודה ר"י באומר לחבירו שדה זו של אביך היתה ולקחתיה ממנו נאמן שהפה שאסר הוא הפה שהתיר ואם יש עדים שהוא של אביו והוא אומר לקחתיה הימנו אינו נאמן ואסיקנא ר' יהושע אפרק קמא קאי דתנן הנושא את האשה ולא מצא לה בתולים היא אומרת משארסתני נאנסתי ונסתחפה שדהו והוא אומר לא כי אלא עד שלא ארסתיך והיה מקחי מקח טעות ר"ג ור"א [אומרים] נאמנת ור"י אומר לא מפיה אנו חיין והתם מאי מיגו איכא מיגו דאי בעי אמרה מוכת עץ אני ולא פסלה נפשה מכהונה ואמרה נאנסתי ופסלה נפשה מכהונה מהימנא ואמר ר"י לר"ג בההיא מיגו דהכא מודינא לך בההיא מיגו דהתם פליגינא עלך. מ"ש הכא ומ"ש התם הכא אין שור שחוט לפניך. פי' ואם רוצה לומר אינו של אביך ולהכחישו יכול הוא עתה כשהודה שהיתה של אביו ולקחה ממנו נאמן אבל התם גבי אם תרצה להכחישו ולומר בתולה הייתי אינה יכולה שהרי [שור] שחוט לפניך השישבים המעידים שלא נמצא לה בתולים הלכך כל טענה דאמרה בין מוכת עץ אני בין נאנסתי תחתיו לא מהימנא: מתני'

מסורת הש"ס

א) ב"ב מב., ב) ב"מ לט., ג) [פסחים קא: ר"ה ח.], ד) ב"ב לח., ה) [שם ע"ש], ו) [פי' בערוך ערך חרס א סיכסוך איש באחיו ועיר בעיר], ז) [פרשת ויחי סימן לב], ח) נ"י כ"י, ט) נ"ל לחפיפות. יעב"ץ, י) [ב"מ לט.], כ) [שם].

גליון הש"ס

גמ' דיוקא דמתניתין קאמר. שבת דף לו ע"ב שבועות דף כט ע"ב:

ליקוטי רש"י

תנורא דאסא. נערה המאורסה היו רגילין לעשות לה חופה של הדס בכניסתה לחופה וקורין לה הינומא כדאמרינן בכתובות (דף טו:) שיוצאה בהינומא וראשה פרוע [ברכות נז.]. ההוא מרבנן. תלמיד חכם וזקן לא קרי ליה מרבנן קרי ליה [תענית ד.]. אין מחזיקין בנכסי קטן. אם לא אכל בפני שלש שנים שאכלן בפני הקטן אין חזקה [ב"מ לט.]. ואפילו הגדיל. הקטן ומשהגדיל לתוכו ואכלו שלש שנים בפניו משהגדיל לא הויא חזקה הואיל ותחלת ירידתו לתוכו היה קטן לא ידע כשהגדיל שהן של אביו ולפיכך לא מיחה [שם]. מחמת נפשות. מחמת רציחת נפשות ירא למחות כי יודע מקום מחזיק ויראו גואל הדם אחריו כי יחם לבבו והשיגו והרגו. איבעי ליה למחויי. דמצי למחויי וכל מקום שהוא יכול למחות חזקתו של חבירו בנכסיו הויא חזקה הואיל ולא מיחה דכיון דמחמת ממון הוא בורח אין זה בורח אלא לאשמועינן בעלמא עד דהוה ליה ופרע ולקח ויליף אין לו לכחם לא מחה מה לפרוע אין רודפין אחריו ושם נודע מקומו שברח אל שם והיו מושט [רשב"ם ב"ב לח.]. שלש ארצות. בארץ ישראל לחזקה. חלוקות זו מזו לענין חזקת שלש שנים כדמפרש ואזיל. היה. בעל הקרקע. ביהודה והחזיק בגליל. שהיה הקרקע בגליל והחזיק בה אדם שלש שנים לא מחאה. אינה חזקה. כדמפרש טעמא בגמרא דסתם יהודה וגליל בשעת חירום דמי שאין שיירות מצויות מזו לזו ולא הוה מחאת בעל הקרקע מחאה שהרי אין מי שיגיד למחזיק שמיחה זה ויזהר בשטרו דהא אין שיירות מצויות הלכך כיון דאינו יכול למחות אע"ג דלא מיחה לא הוה מחזיק צריך להביא ראיה והיה לו לזה המחזיק ליזהר בשטרו שהרי יודע שאין בעל הקרקע יכול למחות. עד שיהא עמו במדינה. כגון שהיה ביהודה בעיר אחת והחזיק ביהודה בעיר אחרת דכיון דשיירות מצויות הוה ליה למחויי ומדלא מיחה הפסיד. אי קסבר מחאה וכו'. שמוחה בעל הקרקע במחזיק אפי' שלא בפניו כגון שניהם דרין בעיר אחת ומיחה בפני שנים מן השוק שלא בפני מחזיק אפי' הכי הויא מחאה דחברך חברא אית ליה ושמע המחזיק בדבר זה והיה לו להזהר בשטרו ומדלא נזהר הפסיד והלכך קתני עד שיהא עמו במדינה דכיון ששניהם במדינה אחת הויא מחאה אע"פ שאינם בעיר אחת. אפילו ביהודה וגליל נמי. תיהוי מחאה. ואי קסבר וכו' לא הויא מחאה. כדקתני דהיה ביהודה והחזיק בגליל אינה חזקה. אפילו יהודה. אפי' היה ביהודה והחזיק ביהודה בעיר אחרת נמי לא תיהוי מחאה ואמאי קתני עד שיהא עמו במדינה הא לא הויא מחאה. ומשום הכי קתני עד שיהא עמו במדינה ודקשיא לך אפילו יהודה וגליל נמי תיהוי מחאה מתני' בשעת חירום תיגרות יש בין יהודה וגליל ואין שיירות מצויות מזו לזו ואם ימחה לא יצא הדבר לאזניו של מחזיק וכיון דלא הויא מחאתו של מערער מחאה חזקתו של זה נמי לא הוי חזקה דטעמא דחזקה ג' שנים קונה משום דמצי טעין ליה מחזיק אמאי לא מחית בתוך שלש ואילו הכא לא מצי למטען הכי דהא לא יכול למחות. דנקט. דכיון דבשעת חירום מיירי הוא הדין לכל המלכיות שיש חירום בין זו לזו והכי הוה ליה למיתני כל הארצות חלוקות לחזקה בשעת חירום ואית דמפרשי מ"ש יהודה וגליל דנקט כיון דבשעת חירום מוקמת לה מ"ש יהודה ויהודה לא תיהוי חזקה ואין נראה בעיני דאם כן הוה ליה למימר כדלעיל אי הכי אפילו יהודה ויהודה נמי לא ועוד דהכי מתרץ ר' אבא בשעת חירום שנו שיש תגרה בין המלכיות אבל עיירות של מדינה ומדינה אין בינותם תגרה [רשב"ם ב"ב לח.].

כלה כמות שהיא ובית הלל אומרים [א]כלה נאה וחסודה אמרו להן ב"ש לב"ה הרי שהיתה חיגרת או סומא אומרי' לה כלה נאה וחסודה והתורה אמרה [א)]מדבר שקר תרחק אמרו להם ב"ה לב"ש לדבריכם מי שלקח מקח רע מן השוק ישבחנו בעיניו או יגננו בעיניו הוי אומר ישבחנו בעיניו מכאן אמרו חכמים [ב]לעולם תהא דעתו של אדם מעורבת עם הבריות כי אתא רב דימי אמר הכי משרו קמי כלתא במערבא לא כחל ולא שרק ולא פירכום ויעלת חן [ח] כי סמכו רבנן לרבי זירא שרו ליה הכי לא כחל ולא שרק ולא פירכום ויעלת חן כי סמכו רבנן לרבי אמי ולרבי אסי שרו להו הכי כל מן דין וכל מן דין סמוכו לנא לא תסמכו לנא לא מן סרמיסין ולא מן סרמיטין ואמרי לה לא מן חמיסין ולא מן [ט]טורמיסין ר' אבהו כי הוה אתי ממתיבתא לבי קיסר נפקן אמהתא דבי קיסר לאפיה ומשרין ליה הכי רבא דעמיה ומדברנא דאומתיה בוצינא דנהורא בריך מתייך לשלם אמרו עליו על רבי יהודה בר אילעאי שהיה נוטל בד של הדס ומרקד לפני הכלה ואומר כלה נאה וחסודה רב שמואל בר רב יצחק [ד]מרקד אתלת א"ר זירא קא מכסיף לן סבא כי נח נפשיה [ג]איפסיק עמודא דנורא בין דידיה לכולי עלמא וגמירי דלא אפסיק עמודא דנורא אלא אי לחד בדרא אי לתרי בדרא א"ר זירא אהנייה ליה שוטיתיה לסבא ואמרי לה שטותיה לסבא ואמרי לה שיטתיה לסבא רב אחא מרכיב לה אכתפיה ומרקד אמרי ליה רבנן אנן מהו למיעבד הכי אמר להו אי דמיין עלייכו ככשורא לחיי ואי לא לא א"ר שמואל בר נחמני א"ר יונתן מותר להסתכל בפני כלה כל שבעה כדי לחבבה על בעלה [ו]ולית הלכתא כוותיה ת"ר [ז]מעבירין את המת מלפני כלה [ה]וזה וזה מלפני מלך ישראל אמרו עליו על אגריפס המלך שעבר מלפני כלה ושבחוהו חכמים שבחוהו מכלל דשפיר עבד [ט]והא א"ר אשי אפילו למ"ד [י]נשיא שמחל על כבודו כבודו מחול [י]מלך שמחל על כבודו אין כבודו מחול דאמר מר [ב)]שום תשים עליך מלך שתהא אימתו עליך פרשת דרכים הואי תנו רבנן [ח]מבטלין תלמוד תורה להוצאת המת ולהכנסת כלה אמרו עליו על רבי יהודה ברבי אלעאי שהיה מבטל תלמוד תורה להוצאת המת ולהכנסת כלה במה דברים אמורים [ט]כשאין עמו כל צרכו אבל יש עמו כל צרכו אין מבטלין וכמה כל צרכו אמר רב שמואל בר איני משמיה דרב תריסר אלפי גברי ושיתא אלפי שיפורי ואמרי לה [ח)]תליסר אלפי גברי ומינייהו שיתא אלפי שיפורי עולא אמר כגון דחייצי גברי מאבולא ועד סיכרא רב ששת ואיתימא רבי יוחנן אמר [י]נטילתה כנתינתה מה נתינתה בששים רבוא אף נטילתה בששים רבוא [כ]וה"מ למאן דקרי ותני אבל

רש"י

כמות שהיא. לפי יופיה וחשיבותה מקלסין אותה: חסודה. חוט של חסד משוך עליה: מכאן אמרו. מדברי ב"ה שאמרו ישבחנה: תהא דעתו של אדם מעורבת עם הבריות. לעשות לאיש ולאיש כרצונו: משרו. משוררים: לא כחל. אינה צריכה כחל: ולא שרק. לבע המאדים את הפנים: פירכום. קליעת שיער זו לא כחלה ולא שרקה ולא פירכסה והרי היא יעלת חן: כל מן דין. כל כמות אלו הוו סומכין לנו לקרותן רבי ולמנותם דיינין: סרמיסין. מסרסין הלכות ההיפך טעמיהן: סרמיטין. לשון סמרטוטין: חמיסין. אומרים חמישית הטעם: טורמיסין. לא איתפרש: (טורמיסין כי ההיא דאמר בב"ר (פ' מ"א) על טורמיסין למיקרב למסאבא למטרוניתא אנשים ריקנים): ממתיבתא. מבית המדרש: רבא דעמיה. גשיא בעמו: מדברנא. מנהיג: בריך מתייך לשלם. ברוך בואך לשלום: בוצינא דנהורא. על שהיה קלסתר פניו מבהיק כדאמרינן בב"ב (דף נח.) שופריה דרבי אבהו מעין שופריה דרבי יוחנן דנפקי זהרורית מיניה כדמפרש התם: אתלת. שלש בדין זורק אחת ומקבל אחת: מכסיף לן סבא. שמזלזל בכבוד תלמידי חכמים ונוהג קלות ראש בעצמו: שוטיתיה. שוט של הדס שהיה מרקד בו: שיטתיה. שיטתו ומנהגו: שטותיה. שהיה מתנהג כשוטה: מרכיב לה אכתפיה. את הכלה: כי כשורא. כקורה בעלמא שאין אתם מהרהרין עליה: לחבבה. כשרואה הכל מסתכלים בה נכנס יופיה בלבו: מעבירין. כשכלה יוצאה מבית אביה לבית חתונתה ונושאי את המת יוצאים וזו וזו אוכלוסים הרבה ואין רוצין להתערב מעבירין את המת (אפילו) דרך אחרת: אפילו למ"ד. פלוגתא בפרק קמא דקדושין: שום תשים עליך מלך. ישראל הוזהרו שישימו עליהם שימות הרבה כלומר שתהא אימתו עליהם הלכך אין כבודו מחול שלפיכך ריבה הכתוב שימות הרבה: פרשת דרכים הוה. ולא ניכר שעבר מלפניה אלא כאילו הוא צריך לפנות לאותו הדרך: שיפורי. מכריזין עליו שיבואו לכבודו: דחייצי גברי מאבולא לסיכרא. משער העיר שהיא עד הקבר: נטילתה. של תורה ממנו כנתינתה בסיני נטילתה היינו כשמת ותלמודו בטל: למאן דקרי. מקרא: ותני. משנה אבל עדיין לא שנה לתלמידים:

תוספות

כלה כמות שהיא. ואם יש בה מום ישתקו ולא ישבחוה אי נמי ישבחוה בדבר נאה שיש בה כגון בעיניה או בידיה אם הם יפות וב"ה אומרים ישבחוה לגמרי דכשמזכירין מה שיש בה לשבח מכלל דשאר לגנאי: ישבחנו בעיניו או יגננו בעיניו. וב"ש סברי אע"ג דישבחנו בעיניו אין להם לחכמים לתקן להזקיק לומר שקר דהתורה אמרה מדבר שקר תרחק: שיטתיה לסבא. פר"ח לשון שיטה והדס (ישעיה מ"א) אע"ג דלא הוי ממש מין אחד מיני שניהם מין ארז ואר"ח ומגלה ליה דבשביל כן זכה וי"ל דעמוד דנורא היה כעין שיבשא דהדס כדאמרינן בבראשית רבה (פ' פא) נחת שיבשא דנורא ולאיתעבידא כעין שיבשא דהדס ולהפסקת בין דידיה לחברוהי אמרי חמית הדין סבא דקאי שיבשא דנורא קומיה משום דעביד קמוהי דכלתא: מלך שמחל על כבודו אין כבודו מחול. אע"ג דלא היה מלך גמור כדמשמע באלו נאמרין (סוטה דף מא.) מ"מ היו נוהגין בו כבוד כמלך גמור: פרשת דרכים הואי. הכא לא מצי לשנויי מצוה שאני כדמשני באלו נאמרין (ג"ז שם) גבי מקרא מעומד דהתם מצוה הוא שיש למלך לחלוק כבוד לתורה החשובה ממנו אבל הכא ליכא מצוה דכבודו עדיף מכבוד הכלה:

[ת"ר מעבירין את המת מלפני הכלה. מכאן משמע כשיש אבל וחתן בבית הכנסת החתן יוצא תחלה ושושביניו ושוב יוצא האבל ומנחמיו וגם הקרובים לחתן ולאבל יאכלו בבית החתן אם ירצו דהא כבודו קודם וכן בבקר כשמוליכים הכלה לבית החתן מוליכין הכלה תחלה אם יש מת בעיר או יקברוהו קודם שיגיע הזמן דהכנסת כלה. להראב"י"ה]:

מבטלין תלמוד תורה להוצאת המת. וקשה [מ] דבהלכות דרך ארץ אמר ר"ע תחלת תשמישי לפני חכמים פעם אחת הייתי מהלך בדרך ומצאתי מת מצוה ונטפלתי בו ד' מילין עד שהבאתיו לבית הקברות וקברתיו וכשבאתי והרציתי דברי לפני ר"א ור' יהושע אמרו לי על כל פסיעה ופסיעה כאילו שפכת דם נקי וי"ל דהתם לאו משום ביטול תורה אלא משום דמת מצוה קנה מקומו והיה לו לקוברו במקום שמצאו וכן משמע במס' שמחות (פ"ד) דקאמר מת מצוה קנה מקומו [נ] והעובר על דברי חכמים חייב מיתה [ס] וכן אמר ר' עקיבא תחלת תשמישי כו' והר"ר יהודה מקורביי"ל תירץ דהתם משום דביטל עצמו משימוש ת"ח קאמר [ע] דגדול שימושה יותר מלימודה: להוצאת המת. לא במת מצוה איירי אלא בכל המתים ואע"ג דבפ"ק דמגילה (דף ג: ושם) אומר פשיטא דמת מצוה ותלמוד תורה מת מצוה עדיף דתניא מבטלין ת"ת להוצאת המת נקט מת מצוה אגב מילי אחריני דהתם דהוו דווקא מת מצוה והא דאמר באלו מגלחין (מו"ק דף כז:) מת בעיר כל בני העיר אסורים בעשיית מלאכה ומוקי לה בדליכא חבורתא אבל אי איכא חבורתא מותרין השאר פירוש חבורתא שנחלקו בני העיר לחבורות שתעסוק כל אחת במת שלה בפני עצמה היינו שלא בשעת הוצאה אבל בשעת הוצאה כולם צריכין לצאת: אבל

מסורת הש"ס

א) [סנהדרין דף יד.], ב) [בערוך ערך חמם האריך לפרש כל המלות אלו בכמה אופנים קח לא משם], ג) לקמן עז:, ד) [שמחות פי"א ע"ש], ה) קדושין לב: סוטה מא: סנהדרין יט:, ו) [שם ובסנהדרין כב.], ז) מגילה ג: כט., ח) [נ"ל תריסר וכן איתא במגילה], ט) [ח"ל הערוך בערך חמם חמישין שבחון חומשה של מסכת ועיין רש"י בסנהדרין מפרש מלשון חמשתן שמונין מלומר טעמי תורה], י) הגה"ה היא זו. רש"ל, כ) שם הגירסא טולמוסין ופרש"י כפירושו שם טולמוסין אנשי חמס מרגום אדם בליעל (משלי ו) בר נש טולמוס וע"ש במ"ל ערך טרמס, ל) [ליתא הכי לא בב"ב גם בב"מ פד. קאמר להדיא דר' יוחנן והנה ברש"י דסנהדרין יד. ד"ה בוצינא וכו' שופר לתקן להגיה דל"ל מעין שופריה דיעקב אבל ברש"י הכא דנפקי זהרורית מיניה ולתקן בגופן], מ) [נ"ל דבמסכת דרך ארץ זוטא פ"ח], נ) ברכות ד: עירובין כא:.

גליון הש"ס

גמ' מרקד אתלת. ירושלמי פ"א דפאה על מתני' א' ובשינוי קצת ועיד בב"ר פרשה נט: תוס' ד"ה מבטלין וכו' דגדול שימושה. ברכות דף ז ע"ב.

תורה אור השלם

א) מִדְּבַר שֶׁקֶר תִּרְחָק וְנָקִי וְצַדִּיק אַל תַּהֲרֹג כִּי לֹא אַצְדִּיק רָשָׁע: [שמות כג, ז]

ב) שׂוֹם תָּשִׂים עָלֶיךָ מֶלֶךְ אֲשֶׁר יִבְחַר יְיָ אֱלֹהֶיךָ בּוֹ מִקֶּרֶב אַחֶיךָ תָּשִׂים עָלֶיךָ מֶלֶךְ לֹא תוּכַל לָתֵת עָלֶיךָ אִישׁ נָכְרִי אֲשֶׁר לֹא אָחִיךָ הוּא: [דברים יז, טו]

ליקוטי רש"י

וחסודה. חוט של חסד, שהיא מקובל לכל רואיו לשון כלה נאה וחסודה שבמשנה (כתובות דף ז.) [בראשית לט, כא]. כחל. לעינים. שרק. לפנים. פירכום. לשער שיר הוא לכלה נאה שלא יצאת מן הכלל קישוט. כל מן דין. כל כמו אלו וכיוצא בהן היו סומכין לנו שראויים אנו לסמיכה. סרמיסין. לשון הפכים כמו סרס את המקרא ודרשהו מקומו לראשו (ב"ב דף קיט:) שמהפכין את טעמי תורה. סרמיטין. לשון סמרטוט כלומר שאין נותנים טעם הגון לדבריהם. חמיסין. ממשכין שמונין טעמי תורה. רבא דעמיה. נשיא בעמו. מדברנא. מנהיג על שם שהיה פרנס וקרוב למלכות [סנהדרין יד.]. רבי אבהו הוה קרוב למלכות כדאמרינן בסנהדרין ובכתובות דנפקי אמהתא דבי קיסר ומשרו ליה ומלעזר למיני בקראי [ע"ז כח. וכע"ז יבמות סה:]. בוצינא דנהורא. על שם שהיה גדול בנוי כדאמרינן בהשוכר את הפועלים (ב"מ דף פד:) שופריה דר' אבהו מעין שופריה (דר' יוחנן) [דיעקב אבינו]. בריך מתייך. ברוך בואך [סנהדרין שם]. לחיי. כלומר שפיר [גיטין ו:]. פרשת דרכים הואי. דרך מתחלפת ומתפרשת לכמה דרכים ושם פגע בכלה והוא נטה לדרך האחרת לימין או לשמאל ולא נראה כמסתלק מלפני הכלה [רש"י מה"ק בשיטמ"ק]. ולהכנסת כלה. ללוותה מבית אביה לבית חופתה. דחייצי גברי מאבולא ועד סיכרא. מחיצת אנשים משער העיר עד בית הקברות מקום שסופדין אותו שם [מגילה כט.].

עין משפט נר מצוה

ה א טוש"ע אה"ע סימן סה סעיף א:
ו ב מיי' פ"ו מהלכות דעות הלכה א:
ז ג טוש"ע שם סימן סה סעיף ג:
ח ד מיי' פי"ד מהל' אבל הלכה ח סמג עשין דרבנן ג טוש"ע י"ד סימן שס וטוש"ע אה"ע סי' סה סעיף ד:
ט ה מיי' שם הלכה ט:
י ו מיי' פ"ו מהלכות ת"ת הלכה יג סמג עשין יג טוש"ע י"ד סי' רמב סעיף יד:
יא ז מיי' פ"ג מהלכות מלכים הלכה ג סמג עשין ה:
יב ח ט י כ מיי' פי"ד מהלכות אבל הלכה ט והלכה יא טוש"ע י"ד סימן שסא סעיף א:

תוספות רי"ד

כלה כמות שהיא פי' לפי יפיה וחשיבותה מקלסין אותה ולא במה שאין בה ובה"א כלה נאה וחסודה חוט של חסד משוך עליה ומראיתה נאה פי' נאה בעיני הבריות **אמרי ב"ש** לב"ה לדבריך הרי שהיתה חגרת או סומא אומרים לה כלה נאה וחסודה והתורה אמרה מדבר שקר תרחק א"ל ב"ה לדבריכם מי שלקח מקח רע מן השוק ישבחנו בעיניו או יגננו בעיניו הוי אומר ישבחנו בעיניו מכאן אמרו חכמים תהא דעתו של אדם מעורבת עם הבריות פי' לומר דבר המתקבל ואע"פ שאומר שקר: **ת"ר** מעבירין את המת מלפני הכלה וזה וזה מלפני מלך ישראל. **ת"ר** מבטלין ת"ת להוצאת המת ולהכנסת כלה אמרו עליו על ר"י בר אלעאי שהיה מבטל ת"ת להוצאת המת ולהכנסת כלה בד"א כשאין עמו כל צרכו אבל יש עמו כל צרכו אין מבטלין וכמה כל צרכו אמר ר"ש בר (איקא) [איני] משמיה דרב תליסר אלפי גברי ושיתא אלפי שיפורי ואמרי לה תריסר אלפי גברא ומנייהו שיתא אלפי שיפורי פי' מכריזין עליו שיבואו לכבודו וגם מקוננים ומספידים אותו בחלילים עולא אמר כגון דחייצי גברא מאבולא ועד סכרא פי' מפתח העיר עד הקבר **ר"ש** ואיתימא ר' אמי ואיתימא רבי יוחנן נטילתה כנתינתה מה נתינתה בס' רבוא אף נטילתה בס' רבוא וה"מ למאן דקרי ותני אבל למאן דמתני לית ליה שיעורא פי' דקרי מקרא ותני משנה אבל עדיין לא שנה לתלמידים אבל למתני לתלמידים לית ליה שיעורא וכתב המורה וממילא שמעינן דלמאן דלא

The Gemara answers:

פָּרָשַׁת דְּרָכִים הֲוָאי – **It was at a crossroads** that this incident occurred, so it was not apparent that he was waiving his honor.[33]

The Gemara cites another Baraisa about the obligation to participate in weddings and burials:

תָּנוּ רַבָּנָן – **The Rabbis taught in a Baraisa:** מְבַטְּלִין תַּלְמוּד תּוֹרָה לְהוֹצָאַת הַמֵּת – THE STUDY OF TORAH SHOULD BE INTERRUPTED TO CARRY THE DEAD OUT to burial[34] וּלְהַכְנָסַת כַּלָּה – AND TO ACCOMPANY A BRIDE to her wedding.[35] אָמְרוּ עָלָיו עַל רַבִּי יְהוּדָה בְּרַבִּי אִלְעַאי – IT WAS SAID ABOUT R' YEHUDAH SON OF R' IL'AI שֶׁהָיָה מְבַטֵּל תַּלְמוּד תּוֹרָה לְהוֹצָאַת הַמֵּת וּלְהַכְנָסַת כַּלָּה – THAT HE WOULD INTERRUPT his LEARNING OF TORAH TO CARRY THE DEAD OUT to burial AND TO ACCOMPANY A BRIDE to her wedding. בַּמֶּה דְּבָרִים אֲמוּרִים – REGARDING WHAT case WAS this RULING that one may interrupt his Torah study SAID? כְּשֶׁאֵין עִמּוֹ כָּל צָרְכּוֹ – WHEN the number of people THERE IS NOT SUFFICIENT without him. אֲבָל יֵשׁ עִמּוֹ כָּל צָרְכּוֹ – BUT WHEN the number of people IS SUFFICIENT, אֵין מְבַטְּלִין – ONE MAY NOT INTERRUPT his Torah study.

The Gemara clarifies an ambiguity in the Baraisa:

וְכַמָּה כָּל צָרְכּוֹ – **And how many** people are considered **sufficient** to honor the deceased? אָמַר רַב שְׁמוּאֵל בַּר אִינִי מִשְּׁמֵיהּ דְּרַב – **Rav Shmuel bar Ini said in the name of Rav:** תְּרֵיסַר אַלְפֵי גַּבְרֵי – **Twelve thousand men** וְשִׁיתָּא אַלְפֵי שִׁיפּוּרֵי – **and six thousand** men with **shofars.**[36]

The Gemara presents another version of Rav's statement:

וְאָמְרֵי לַהּ – **And some say:** תְּלֵיסַר אַלְפֵי גַּבְרֵי וּמִינַּיְיהוּ שִׁיתָּא אַלְפֵי שִׁיפּוּרֵי – **Thirteen**[37] **thousand men, among whom** there are **six thousand** with **shofars.**

The Gemara defines *sufficient* in other ways:

עוּלָּא אָמַר – **Ulla said:** כְּגוֹן דְּחַיְיצֵי גַּבְרֵי מֵאַבּוּלָּא וְעַד סִיכְרָא – **For example, if men form a line from the** town **gate to the cemetery.** רַב שֵׁשֶׁת וְאִיתֵּימָא רַבִּי יוֹחָנָן אָמַר – **Rav Sheishess,** and some say it was **R' Yochanan, said:** נְטִילָתָהּ כִּנְתִינָתָהּ – **[The Torah's] removal should be as its giving:**[38] מַה נְּתִינָתָהּ בְּשִׁשִּׁים רִבּוֹא – **Just as its giving** took place **before six hundred thousand** men,[39] אַף נְטִילָתָהּ בְּשִׁשִּׁים רִבּוֹא – **so too** should **its removal** take place **before six hundred thousand** men.[40]

Ulla adds:

וְהָנֵי מִילֵּי לְמַאן דְּקָרֵי וְתָנֵי – **This ruling** applies **to one who has** only **studied Scripture and Mishnah,**[41] but did not teach it to others;

NOTES

is wrong with Agrippas *himself,* diverging and going on a different path? Why does the Gemara imply that he deserved to be castigated for doing so? *Kovetz Shiurim* (§47) answers that implicit in this command is a duty to honor the position of the king, and the king himself is obligated in this duty as well! See also *Talmidei Rabbeinu Yonah,* cited in *Shitah Mekubetzes.*]

33. To all appearances, it seemed as if he just wanted to turn onto the other road (*Rashi*). Thus it entailed no slighting of the royal honor.

34. This rule applies in the case of any deceased person (see further).

35. This means that one is *obligated* to suspend his Torah study for these activities. And as the Baraisa demonstrates next, this applies even to someone whose entire day is spent in Torah study (*Ritva, Rosh,* as explained by *Beis Shmuel* 65:3; see also *Pnei Yehoshua*). See below, note 40.

36. It was customary to sound the shofar at funeral processions to publicize the proceedings (see *Rashi*). Thus, according to this view a crowd of less than eighteen thousand people is not considered sufficient.

37. Or, twelve (emendation of *Mesoras HaShas,* based on *Megillah* 29a).

38. A Torah scholar's death and the resultant cessation of his study constitutes the removal of his Torah (*Rashi*).

39. The Torah (*Exodus* 12:37) relates that the Israelite host that left Egypt numbered six hundred thousand men. It also notes (ibid. 20:15) that the entire nation witnessed the giving of the Torah (i.e. the Ten Commandments) seven weeks after the Exodus.

40. The Gemara does not define the term *sufficient* with regard to a bride; hence, there is no limit to the bride's needs and Torah study is always interrupted for her sake (*Likkutei HaGeonim,* cited by *Shitah Mekubetzes;* see also *Meiri*). Alternatively, the Gemara does not state any specific amount because it depends on the particular bride and her stature (*Talmidei Rabbeinu Yonah,* cited there).

As noted above (note 35) even a Torah scholar is obligated to suspend his Torah study for this mitzvah. However, various authorities write that this applies only to someone on his way to the study hall who meets a wedding ceremony; in that case he must join the ceremony rather than continue to the study hall. But if he is already in the study hall, he is not required to leave to attend a wedding taking place elsewhere in the city (*Chelkas Mechokeik* 65:2; cf. *Beis Shmuel* 65:3; see *Otzar HaPoskim* 65:6:4,5,8).

It has been argued that even someone who is not engaged in Torah study is not required to attend every wedding ceremony in town. A person can generally assume that the families of the groom and bride invited enough people to satisfy the requirements of this particular couple. Hence, even if one passes by a wedding ceremony, he is not obligated to join it (see *Otzar HaPoskim* 65:6:7). [This apparently follows the view of *Talmidei Rabbeinu Yonah* cited in the beginning of this note.]

41. *Shach* (*Yoreh Deah* 361:2) infers from *Ritva* [cited below 17b note 1] that this means the person studied Scripture *or* Mishnah.

כלה כמות שהיא ובית הלל אומרים [א]כלה נאה וחסודה אמרו להן ב"ש לב"ה הרי שהיתה חיגרת או סומא אומרי' לה כלה נאה וחסודה והתורה אמרה (א) מדבר שקר תרחק אמרו להם ב"ה לב"ש לדבריכם מי שלקח מקח רע מן השוק ישבחנו בעיניו או יגננו בעיניו הוי אומר ישבחנו בעיניו מכאן אמרו חכמים [ב]לעולם תהא דעתו של אדם מעורבת עם הבריות כי אתא רב דימי אמר הכי משרו קמי כלתא במערבא לא כחל ולא שרק ולא פירכום ויעלת חן (א)כי סמכו רבנן לרבי זירא שרו ליה הכי לא כחל ולא שרק ולא פירכום ויעלת חן כי סמכו רבנן לרבי אמי ולרבי אסי שרו להו הכי כל מן דין וכל מן דין סמוכו לנא לא תסמכו לנא לא מן סרמיסין ולא מן סרמיטין ואמרי לה לא מן חמיסין ולא מן (ג)טורמיסין ר' אבהו כי הוה אתי ממתיבתא לבי קיסר נפקן אמהתא דבי קיסר לאפיה ומשרין ליה הכי רבא דעמיה ומדברנא דאומתיה בוצינא דנהורא בריך מתייך לשלם אמרו עליו על רבי יהודה בר אילעאי שהיה נוטל בד של הדס ומרקד לפני הכלה ואומר כלה נאה וחסודה רב שמואל בר רב יצחק (ס)מרקד אתלת א"ר זירא קא מכסיף לן סבא כי נח נפשיה (ג)איפסיק עמודא דנורא בין דידיה לכולי עלמא וגמירי דלא אפסיק עמודא דנורא אלא אי לחד בדרא אי לתרי בדרא א"ר זירא אהנייה ליה שוטיתיה לסבא ואמרי לה שטותיה לסבא ואמרי לה שיטתיה לסבא רב אחא מרכיב לה אכתפיה ומרקד אמרי ליה רבנן אנן מהו למיעבד הכי אמר להו אי דמיין עלייכו ככשורא לחיי ואי לא לא א"ר שמואל בר נחמני א"ר יונתן מותר להסתכל בפני כלה כל שבעה כדי לחבבה על בעלה [ג]ולית הלכתא כוותיה ת"ר [ד]מעבירין את המת מלפני כלה [ה]וזה וזה מלפני מלך ישראל אמרו עליו על אגריפס המלך שעבר מלפני כלה ושבחוהו חכמים שבחוהו מכלל דשפיר עבד (ה)והא א"ר אשי אפילו למ"ד נשיא שמחל על כבודו כבודו מחול [ו]מלך שמחל על כבודו אין כבודו מחול דאמר מר (ב)שום תשים עליך מלך שתהא אימתו עליך פרשת דרכים הואי תנו רבנן [ח]מבטלין תלמוד תורה להוצאת המת ולהכנסת כלה אמרו עליו על רבי יהודה ברבי אלעאי שהיה מבטל תלמוד תורה להוצאת המת ולהכנסת כלה במה דברים אמורים [ט]כשאין עמו כל צרכו אבל יש עמו כל צרכו אין מבטלין וכמה כל צרכו אמר רב שמואל בר איני משמיה דרב תריסר אלפי גברי ושיתא אלפי שיפורי ואמרי לה (י)תליסר אלפי גברי ומיניהו שיתא אלפי שיפורי עולא אמר כגון דחייצי גברי מאבולא ועד סיכרא רב ששת ואיתימא רבי יוחנן אמר [י]נטילתה כנתינתה מה נתינתה בששים רבוא אף נטילתה בששים רבוא [כ]וה"מ למאן דקרי ותני אבל

רש"י

כמות שהיא. לפי יופיה וחשיבותה מקלסין אותה: חסודה. חוט של חסד משוך עליה: מכאן אמרו. מדברי ב"ה שאמרו ישבחנה: תהא דעתו של אדם מעורבת עם הבריות. לעשות לאיש ואיש כרצונו: משרו. משוררים: לא כחל. אינה צריכה כחל: ולא שרק. צבע המאדים את הפנים: פירכום. קליעת שיער זו לא כחלה ולא שרקה ולא פירכסה והרי היא יעלת חן: כל מן דין. כל כמות אלו הוו סומכין לנו לקרותן רבי ולמנותם דיינין: סרמיסין. מסרסין הלכות בהיפך טעמיהן: סרמיטין. לשון סמרטוטין: חמיסין. אומרים חמישית הטעם(ט): טורמיסין. לא איתפרש: (י)טורמיסין כי ההיא דאמר בב"ר (פ' מ"א) על טורמיסין למיקרב למסאנא דמטרוניתא אנשים ריקנים(כ): ממתיבתא. מבית המדרש: רבא דעמיה. נשיא בעמו: מדברנא. מנהיג: בריך מתייך לשלם. ברוך בואך לשלום: בוצינא דנהורא. על שהיה קלסתר פניו מבהיק כדאמרינן בב"ב (דף נח.) שופריה דרבי אבהו מעין שופריה (ל)דרבי יוחנן דנפקי זהרורית מיניה כדמפרש התם: אתלת. שלש בדין זורק אחת ומקבל אחת: מכסיף לן סבא. שמזלזל בכבוד תלמידי חכמים ונוהג קלות ראש בעצמו: שוטיתיה. שוט של הדס שהיה מרקד בו: שיטתיה. שיטתו ומנהגו: שטותיה. שהיה מתנהג כשוטה: מרכיב לה אכתפיה. את הכלה: כי כשורא. כקורה בעלמא שאין אתם מהרהרין עליה: לחבבה. כשרואה הכל מסתכלים בה נכנס יופיה בלבו: מעבירין. כשכלה יוצאה מבית אביה לבית חתונתה ונושאי את יוצאים ובזו ובזו אוכלוסים הרבה ואין רוצין להתערב מעבירין את המת (אפילו) דרך אחרת: אפילו למ"ד. פלוגתא בפרק קמא דקדושין: שום תשים עליך מלך. ישראל הוזהרו שישימו עליהם שימות הרבה כלומר שתהא אימתו עליהם הלכך אין כבודו מחול שלפיכך ריבה הכתוב שימות הרבה: פרשת דרכים הוה. ולא ניכר שעבר מלפניה אלא כאילו הוא צריך לפנות לאותו הדרך: שיפורי. מכריזין עליו שיבואו לכבדו: דחייצי גברי מאבולא לסיכרא. משער העיר ההיא עד הקבר: נטילתה. של תורה ממנו כנתינתה בסיני נטילתה היינו כשמת ותלמודו בטל: למאן דקרי. מקרא: ותני. משנה אבל עדיין לא שנה לתלמידים:

תוספות

כלה כמות שהיא. ואם יש בה מום ישתקו ולא ישבחוה אי נמי ישבחוה בדבר נאה שיש בה כגון בעיניה או בידיה אם הם יפות וב"ה אומרים ישבחוה לגמרי דכשמזכירין מה שיש בה לשבח מכלל דשאר לגנאי: ישבחנו בעיניו או יגננו בעיניו. וב"ש סברי אע"ג דישבחנו בעיניו אין להם לחכמים לתקן להזקיק לומר שקר דהתורה אמרה מדבר שקר תרחק: שיטתיה לסבא. פר"ח לשון שיטה והדס (ישעיה מ"א) אע"ג דלא הוי ממש מין אחד מ"מ שניהם מין ארז וא"ת ומנא ליה דבשביל כן זכה וי"ל דעמוד דנורא היה כעין שיבשא דהדס כדאמרינן בבראשית רבה (פ' סא) נחת שיבשא דנורא ואיתעבידא כעין שיבשא דהדס ואפסקת בין דידיה לחברוהי אמרי חמית הדין סבא דקאי שיבשא דנורא קומיה משום דעביד קמוהי דכלתא: מלך שמחל על כבודו אין כבודו מחול. אע"ג דלא היה מלך גמור כדמשמע באלו נאמרין (סוטה דף מא.) מ"מ היו נוהגין בו כבוד כמלך גמור: פרשת דרכים הואי. הכא לא מצי לשנויי מצוה שאני כדמשני באלו נאמרין (ג"ז שם) גבי שקרא מעומד דהתם מצוה הוא שיש למלך לחלוק כבוד לתורה החשובה ממנו אבל הכא ליכא מצוה דכבודו עדיף מכבוד הכלה: [ת"ר מעבירין את המת מלפני הכלה. מכאן משמע כשיש אבל וחתן בבית הכנסת החתן יוצא תחלה ושושביניו ושוב יוצא האבל ומנחמיו וגם הקרובים לחתן ולאבל יאכלו בבית החתן אם ירצו דהא כבודו קודם וכן בבקר כשמוליכים הכלה לבית החתן מוליכין הכלה תחלה אם יש מת בעיר או יקברוהו קודם שיגיע הזמן דהכנסת כלה. להרא"ש"ה]: מבטלין תלמוד תורה להוצאת המת. וקשה (מ) דבהלכות דרך ארץ אמר ר"ע תחלת תשמישי לפני חכמים פעם אחת הייתי מהלך בדרך ומצאתי מת מצוה ונטפלתי בו ד' מילין עד שהבאתיו לבית הקברות וקברתיו וכשבאתי והרציתי דברי לפני ר"א ור' יהושע אמרו לי על כל פסיעה ופסיעה כאילו שפכת דם נקי וי"ל דהתם לאו משום ביטול תורה אלא משום דמת מצוה קנה מקומו והיה לו לקוברו במקום שמצאו וכן משמע במס' שמחות (פ"ד) דקאמר מת מצוה קנה מקומו (י) והעובר על דברי חכמים חייב מיתה (פ) וכן אמר ר' עקיבא תחלת תשמישי כו' והר"ר יהודה מקורבי"ל תירץ דהתם משום דביטל עצמו משימוש ת"ח קאמר (ס) דגדול שימושה יותר מלימודה: להוצאת המת. לא במת מצוה איירי אלא בכל המתים ואע"ג דפ"ק דמגילה (דף ג: ושם) אומר פשיטא דמת מצוה ותלמוד תורה מת מצוה עדיף דתניא מבטלין ת"ת להוצאת המת נקט מת מצוה אגב מילי אחריני דהתם דהוו דווקא מת מצוה והא דאמר באלו מגלחין (מו"ק דף כז:) אבל מת בעיר כל בני העיר אסורים בעשיית מלאכה ומוקי לה בדליכא חברותא אבל אי איכא חברותא מותרין השאר פירוש חברותא שנחלקו בני העיר לחבורות שתעסוק כל אחת במת שלה בפני עצמה היינו שלא בשעת הוצאה אבל בשעת הוצאה כולם צריכין לצאת: אבל

מסורת הש"ס

א) [סנהדרין דף יד.], ב) [בערוך ערך חמס העתיק לפרש כל המלות אלו בכמה אופנים קח נא משם], ג) לקמן עז:, ד) [שמות פי"א ע"ש], ה) קדושין לג: סוטה מא: סנהדרין יד., ו) [שם ושם], ז) [מגילה ג: כט.], ח) [צ"ל תריסר וכן איתא במגילה], ט) [ח"ל הערוך בערך חמס חמשין חומשה של מסכת ועיין רש"י בסנהדרין מפרש שמועין מלומר טעמי תורה], י) [ח"ל הערוך בערך טורמס טולמוסין ופרש"י בפירושו שם טולמוסין אנשי חמס תרגום אדם בליעל (משלי ו יב) בר נש טולמוס ועי' במ"ל ערך טורמס], ל) [ליתא הכי לא בב"ר גם בב"מ פד. קאמר להדיא טעם דלא שבח שופריה דר' יוחנן והנה בסנהדרין שם ד"ה בוצינא וכו' אפשר לתקן ולומר דצ"ל מעין שופריה דיעקב אבל ברש"י דהכא שהזכיר זהרורית מיניה דמפרש התם מיירי ע"כ בשופריה לשנויי ולתקנו בטופן אחר], מ) [צ"ל דבמסכת דרך ארץ זוטא פ"ח], נ) [ברכות ד: עירובין כא:].

גליון הש"ס

גמ' מרקד אתלת. ירושלמי פ"א דפאה על מתני' א' ובשינוי קלת. ע"ע בגמ"ר בראשית פ' נט: תוס' ד"ה מבטלין וכו' דגדול שימושה. ברכות דף ז ע"ב.

תורה אור השלם

א) מִדְּבַר שֶׁקֶר תִּרְחָק וְנָקִי וְצַדִּיק אַל תַּהֲרֹג כִּי לֹא אַצְדִּיק רָשָׁע: [שמות כג, ז]

ב) שׂוֹם תָּשִׂים עָלֶיךָ מֶלֶךְ אֲשֶׁר יִבְחַר יְיָ אֱלֹהֶיךָ בּוֹ מִקֶּרֶב אַחֶיךָ תָּשִׂים עָלֶיךָ מֶלֶךְ לֹא תוּכַל לָתֵת עָלֶיךָ אִישׁ נָכְרִי אֲשֶׁר לֹא אָחִיךָ הוּא: [דברים יז, טו]

ליקוטי רש"י

וחסודה. ויש אלו חסד, שהיה מקובל בה רוצו לשון כלה נאה וחסודה שבמשנה (כתובות דף יז.) [בראשית לט, כא]. כחל. לעינים. שרק. לפנים. פירכום. לשער שיר הוא לכלה לא כמתאלת לה קישוט. כל מן דין. כמו אלו ויוצא בהן היו סומכין לנו שרמיסין לסמיכה. סרמיטין. לשון הפסיק כמו פרס את מקופו (ב"ב דף קיט:) שמפסקין את טעמי תורה. סרמיטין. לשון סמרטוט כלומר שאין נותנים טעם הגון לדבריהם. חמיסין. חמסנין שמונעין מלומר טעמי תורה. רבא דעמיה. נשיא בעמיו. מדברנא. מנהיג על שם שהיה פרנס וקרוב למלכות [סנהדרין יד.]. רבי אבהו הוה קרוב למלכות כדאמרינן בסנהדרין ובכתובות דנפקי אמהתא דבי קיסר ומשרו ליה ומגער למיני בקראי [ע"ז כח. וכע"ז יבמות סה:]. בוצינא דנהורא. על שם שהיה גדול בנוי כדאמרינן בהשוכר את הפועלים (ב"מ דף פד:) שופריה דר' אבהו מעין שופריה (דר' יוחנן) [דיעקב אבינו]. בריך מתייך. ברוך בואך [סנהדרין שם]. לחיי. כלומר שפיר [גיטין ו:]. פרשת דרכים הואי. דרך מתפלגת ומתפרשת לכמה דרכים ושם פגע בכלה והוא נטה לדרך האחרת לימין או לשמאל ולא נראה כמסתלק מלפני הכלה [רש"י מה"ק בשיטמ"ק]. ולהכנסת כלה. ללוותה מבית אביה לבית חופתה. דחייצי גברי מאבולא ועד סיכרא. מחילת אנשים משער העיר עד בית הקברות מקום שסופדין אותו שם [מגילה כט.].

עין משפט נר מצוה

ה א טוש"ע אה"ע סימן סה סעיף א:

ו ב מיי' פ"ו מהלכות דעות הלכה א:

ז ג טוש"ע שם סימן סה סעיף ב:

ח ד מיי' פי"ד מהל' אבל הלכה ח סמג עשין דרבנן ב טוש"ע יו"ד סימן שס וטוש"ע אה"ע סי' סה סעיף ד:

ט ה מיי' שם הלכה ט:

י ו מיי' פ"ג מהלכות מ"ת הלכה יג סמג עשין יג טוש"ע יו"ד סי' רמב סעיף יד:

יא ז מיי' פ"ב מהלכות מלכים הלכה ג סמג עשין ה:

יב ח ט י כ מיי' פי"ד מהלכות אבל הלכה ט והלכה יא טוש"ע יו"ד סימן שסא סעיף א:

תוספות רי"ד

כלה כמות שהיא פי' לפי יפיה וחשיבותה מקלסין אותה ולא במה שאין בה ובה"א כלה נאה וחסודה חוט של חסד משוך עליה ומראיתה נאה פי' נאה בעיני הבריות אמרו ב"ש לב"ה לדבריך הרי שהיתה חגרת או סומא אומרים לה כלה נאה וחסודה והתורה אמרה מדבר שקר תרחק א"ל ב"ה לדבריכם מי שלקח מקח רע מן השוק ישבחנו בעיניו או יגננו בעיניו הוי אומר ישבחנו בעיניו מכאן אמרו חכמים תהא דעתו של אדם מעורבת עם הבריות פי' לומר דבר המתקבל ואע"פ שאומר שקר: ת"ר מעבירין את המת מלפני הכלה וזה וזה מלפני מלך ישראל. ת"ר מבטלין ת"ת להוצאת המת ולהכנסת כלה אמרו עליו על ר"י בר אלעאי שהיה מבטל ת"ת להוצאת המת ולהכנסת כלה בד"א כשאין עמו כל צרכו אבל יש עמו כל צרכו אין מבטלין וכמה כל צרכו אמר ר"ש בר (איקא) [איני] משמיה דרב תליסר אלפי גברי ושיתא אלפי שיפורי ואמרי לה תריסר אלפי גברא ומניהון שיתא אלפי שיפורי פי' מכריזין עליו שיבואו לכבודו וגם מקוננים ומספידים אותו בחלילים עולא אמר כגון דחייצי גברא מאבולא ועד סכרא פי' מפתח העיר עד הקבר ר"ש ואיתימא ר' אמי ואיתימא רבי יוחנן נטילתה כנתינתה מה נתינתה בס' רבוא אף נטילתה בס' רבוא וה"מ למאן דקרי ותני אבל למאן דמתני לית ליה שיעורא פי' דקרי מקרא ותני משנה אבל עדיין לא שנה לתלמידים אבל למתני לתלמידים לית ליה שיעורא וכתב המורה וממילא שמעינן דלמאן דלא

Yitzchak would dance, juggling **three** myrtle branches. אָמַר רַבִּי זֵירָא – **R' Zeira said,** קָא מַכְסִיף לַן סָבָא – **"The elder is embarrassing us."**[21] כִּי נָח נַפְשֵׁיהּ אִיפְסִיק עַמּוּדָא דְנוּרָא בֵּין דִּידֵיהּ לְכוּלֵּי עָלְמָא – **When [Rav Shmuel bar Rav Yitzchak] passed away, a pillar of fire separated him from everyone else,** according him great honor. וּגְמִירֵי דְּלָא אַפְסִיק עַמּוּדָא דְנוּרָא אֶלָּא אִי לְחַד בְּדָרָא אִי לְתְרֵי בְּדָרָא – **And we have a tradition that a pillar of fire separates only either one in a generation or two in a generation.**

The Gemara records three versions of R' Zeira's reaction to that honor:

אָמַר רַבִּי זֵירָא – **R' Zeira said,** אַהֲנְיָיה לֵיהּ שׁוּטִיתֵיהּ לְסָבָא – **"The elder's branch** of myrtle (*shutisei*) **helped him** achieve this honor." וְאָמְרֵי לַהּ שְׁטוּתֵיהּ לְסָבָא – **Some say** that R' Zeira said, **"The elder's foolishness** (*shetusei*) helped him." וְאָמְרֵי לַהּ שִׁיטָתֵיהּ לְסָבָא – **And some say** that R' Zeira said, **"The elder's opinion** (*sheetasei*) and practice helped him."[22]

Another description of dancing at a wedding:

רַב אַחָא מַרְכִּיב לַהּ אַכַּתְפֵיהּ וּמְרַקֵּד – **Rav Acha put [the bride] on his shoulder and danced.** אָמְרֵי לֵיהּ רַבָּנַן – **The Rabbis said to him,** אֲנַן מַהוּ לְמֵיעֲבַד הָכִי – **"Are we too allowed to do so?"** אָמַר לְהוּ – **He replied to them,** אִי דָּמְיָין עֲלַיְיכוּ כִּכְשׁוּרָא לְחַיֵּי – **"If they resemble a beam to you,**[23] **it is fine;** וְאִי לָא לָא – **but if not,** you may **not** do so."[24]

Another aspect of wedding celebrations:

אָמַר רַבִּי שְׁמוּאֵל בַּר נַחְמָנִי אָמַר רַבִּי יוֹנָתָן – **R' Shmuel bar Nachmani said in the name of R' Yonasan:** מוּתָּר לְהִסְתַּכֵּל בִּפְנֵי כַּלָּה כָּל שִׁבְעָה – **It is permitted to gaze at the face of a bride all seven** days of feasting כְּדֵי לְחַבְּבָהּ עַל בַּעְלָהּ – **in order to make her beloved to her husband.**[25]

The Gemara concludes:

וְלֵית הִלְכְתָא כְּוָותֵיהּ – **But the law is not in accordance with him.**[26]

The Gemara cites another law about a wedding:

תָּנוּ רַבָּנַן – **The Rabbis taught in a Baraisa:** מַעֲבִירִין אֶת הַמֵּת מִלִּפְנֵי כַלָּה – WE DIVERT THE DEAD FROM BEFORE A BRIDE.[27] וְזֶה וְזֶה מִלִּפְנֵי מֶלֶךְ יִשְׂרָאֵל – AND we divert both THIS ONE [the bride] AND THAT ONE [the corpse] FROM BEFORE A JEWISH KING. אָמְרוּ עָלָיו עַל אַגְרִיפַּס הַמֶּלֶךְ שֶׁעָבַר מִלִּפְנֵי כַלָּה – Nevertheless, THEY SAID ABOUT KING AGRIPPAS THAT HE once DIVERGED FROM a path that led BEFORE A BRIDE so that she could continue on her way unimpeded וְשִׁבְּחוּהוּ חֲכָמִים – AND THE SAGES PRAISED HIM.

The Gemara questions the Baraisa's conclusion:

שִׁבְּחוּהוּ – **They praised him?** מִכְּלָל דְּשַׁפִּיר עֲבַד – **This implies that** what **he did** was **proper!** וְהָא אָמַר רַב אַשִׁי – **But Rav Ashi said:** אֲפִילוּ לְמַאן דְּאָמַר נָשִׂיא שֶׁמָּחַל עַל כְּבוֹדוֹ כְּבוֹדוֹ מָחוּל – **Even according to the one who says that if a *Nasi***[28] **renounced his honor, his honor is renounced,**[29] מֶלֶךְ שֶׁמָּחַל עַל כְּבוֹדוֹ – **if a king renounced his honor,** אֵין כְּבוֹדוֹ מָחוּל – **his honor is not renounced;** דְּאָמַר מַר – **for the master said:** "שׂוֹם תָּשִׂים עָלֶיךָ מֶלֶךְ" – The verse states: ***Surely you shall appoint*** (*som tasim*) ***a king over you.***[30] The double expression (*som tasim*) serves to teach שֶׁתְּהֵא אֵימָתוֹ עָלֶיךָ – **that the awe [of the king] is to be upon you** [the people] at all times.[31] How, then, did the Sages praise King Agrippas for waiving his honor and deferring to the bride?[32]

NOTES

21. He is belittling the status of Torah scholars by treating himself so lightly (*Rashi*).

Although a Torah scholar is permitted to waive the honor due him, he may not act in a way that denigrates him (see *Rivash* §220). R' Zeira thus held that Rav Shmuel bar Rav Yitzchak's actions were prohibited. Rav Shmuel bar Rav Yitzchak, though, held that since he was clearly acting to perform the mitzvah of rejoicing at a wedding it was permitted (see *Kovetz Shiurim* §47. See also *Beur Halachah,* end of §250).

22. R' Zeira knew that this honor was due to Rav Shmuel bar Rav Yitzchak's practice at weddings because the pillar was in the shape of a myrtle (*Tosafos, Rashba, Ritva* et al.). See *Maharam Schif,* who explains that each of the three phrases corresponds to a different part of Rav Shmuel's practice. [See *Anaf Yosef* who explains why such a pillar did not appear at R' Yehuda bar Il'ai's funeral.]

23. That is, if carrying the bride is like carrying a beam in that you are not thinking about her (*Rashi*).

24. And since nowadays there is no one who could say that holding the bride affects him just like holding a beam, one should refrain from this form of dancing with the bride (*Pischei Teshuvah* to *Shulchan Aruch Even HaEzer* 65:1, citing *Toras Chaim* to *Avodah Zarah* 17a).

[*Toras Chaim* adds that dancing hand in hand with the bride – even when separated by a kerchief, as was the custom of some scholars – is also not appropriate. From the conclusion of the Gemara below, that one is prohibited to gaze at a bride, it is evident that there is no leniency for a bride in regard to these issues; the law governing interaction with her is similar to the one that governs any other married woman (ibid.). Nevertheless, the custom is still practiced in some Chassidic communities. See also *Bach* to *Even HaEzer* §21 ד״ה והמחבק; *Chelkas Mechokeik* 21:5; *Beis Shmuel* 21:11.

25. When he sees everyone gazing at his bride, he will feel that she is beautiful (*Rashi*).

26. That is, it is prohibited to gaze at the bride (see *Shulchan Aruch, Even HaEzer* 65:2).

The Rishonim ask: If it is prohibited to look at the bride, how can anyone testify that she was wearing a veil at the wedding? (see Mishnah above, 15b). *Rosh* answers that the witnesses see the veil and everyone says that it belongs to a certain bride (see *Rosh* and *Shitah Mekubetzes;* see also *Rosh* for a second answer). *Shitah Mekubetzes* cites another answer from *Rabbeinu Meir HaLevi:* Only *gazing* is prohibited, but it is permitted to glance at the bride enough to know that she is wearing a veil (see also *Magen Avraham* 128:35, *Sefer HaMiknah* to 65:2). However, this last answer is subject to dispute (see *Pesach Einayim* to *Avodah Zarah* 20b, *Beur Halachah* §225 ד״ה אפילו; see also *Mishnah Berurah* 75:7).

27. That is, when the bride is leaving her father's house to the place of her wedding and her entourage meets a group of people carrying a corpse to burial, the people carrying the corpse have to find a new route – if they do not want to intermingle (*Rashi*). [For the different customs of escorting the bride and groom to the *chuppah* where the law of "diverting the dead" is applicable, see *Tosafos* ד״ה ת״ר מעבירין, *Derishah* 65:1; *Beis Shmuel* 65:3 and *Taz* 65:2.]

Ramban (*Toras HaAdam* p. 108, cited by *Ritva*) writes that this indicates a principle that applies to other situations as well: All of a bride's needs are given priority over those of a corpse. However, *Rambam* (*Hil. Aveil* 14:8) implies that in other matters, the corpse takes precedence (see *Lechem Mishneh* there; cf. *Sefer HaMiknah* to 65:4). See also *Yoreh Deah* 360:1 with commentators.

28. נָשִׂיא, *Nasi* [literally: prince], refers to the spiritual leader of the people. In the Second Temple era, the title of *Nasi* was automatically conferred upon the head of the Sanhedrin.

29. This matter is debated in *Kiddushin* 32b (*Rashi*).

30. *Deuteronomy* 17:15.

31. The repetitive phrase, *som tasim* (implying many times), indicates that the Jewish people must enthrone a king over them continually. A practical outcome of this exposition is that his honor cannot be renounced (*Rashi*). That is, even if the king chooses to waive his honor, symbolically "resigning" from royalty, we are required to "reinstate" him – with the attendant obligation to give him honor (*Shitah Mekubetzes,* in explanation of *Rashi;* cf. *Maharam Schif* who interprets the exposition of this verse differently).

32. Even though Agrippas was not entitled to the throne (see *Sotah* 41a,b), since he was at any rate the king, he received the honors due a king (*Tosafos, Ritva;* see also *Haflaah*).

[There is an apparent difficulty with the Gemara's question: Our verse teaches merely that it is incumbent upon *us* to honor the king under all circumstances, even when he has waived his honor. But what

כלה כמות שהיא ובית הלל אומרים א כלה נאה וחסודה אמרו להן ב"ש לב"ה הרי שהיתה חיגרת או סומא אומרי' לה כלה נאה וחסודה והתורה אמרה א) מדבר שקר תרחק אמרו להם ב"ה לב"ש לדבריכם מי שלקח מקח רע מן השוק ישבחנו בעיניו או יגננו בעיניו הוי אומר ישבחנו בעיניו מכאן אמרו חכמים ב לעולם תהא דעתו של אדם מעורבת עם הבריות כי אתא רב דימי אמר הכי משרו קמי כלתא במערבא לא כחל ולא שרק ולא פירכום ויעלת חן א) כי סמכו רבנן לרבי זירא שרו ליה הכי לא כחל ולא שרק ולא פירכום ויעלת חן כי סמכו רבנן לרבי אמי ולרבי אסי שרו להו הכי כל מן דין וכל מן דין סמוכו לנא לא תסמכו לנא לא מן סרמיסין ולא מן סרמיטין ואמרי לה לא מן חמיסין ולא מן ג) טורמיסין ר' אבהו כי הוה אתי ממתיבתא לבי קיסר נפקן אמהתא דבי קיסר לאפיה ומשרין ליה רבא דעמיה ומדברנא דאומתיה בוצינא דנהורא בריך מתיך לשלם אמרו עליו על רבי יהודה בר אילעאי שהיה נוטל בד של הדס ומרקד לפני הכלה ואומר כלה נאה וחסודה רב שמואל בר רב יצחק ד מרקד אתלת א"ר זירא קא מכסיף לן סבא כי נח נפשיה ג) איפסיק עמודא דנורא בין דידיה לכולי עלמא וגמירי דלא אפסיק עמודא דנורא אלא אי לחד בדרא אי לתרי בדרא א"ר זירא אהנייה ליה שוטיתיה לסבא ואמרי לה שטותיה לסבא ואמרי לה שיטתיה לסבא רב אחא מרכיב לה אכתפיה ומרקד אמרי ליה רבנן אנן מהו למיעבד הכי אמר להו אי דמיין עלייכו כשורא לחייו ואי לא לא א"ר שמואל בר נחמני א"ר יונתן מותר להסתכל בפני כלה כל שבעה כדי לחבבה על בעלה ו ולית הלכתא כוותיה ת"ר ד) מעבירין את המת מלפני כלה ה וזה וזה מלפני מלך ישראל אמרו עליו על אגריפס המלך שעבר מלפני כלה ושבחוהו חכמים שבחוהו מכלל דשפיר עבד ה) והא א"ר אשי אפילו למ"ד ו נשיא שמחל על כבודו כבודו מחול ז מלך שמחל על כבודו אין כבודו מחול דאמר מר ו) ב) שום תשים עליך מלך שתהא אימתו עליך פרשת דרכים הואי תנו רבנן ז) ח מבטלין תלמוד תורה להוצאת המת ולהכנסת כלה אמרו עליו על רבי יהודה ברבי אלעאי שהיה מבטל תלמוד תורה להוצאת המת ולהכנסת כלה במה דברים אמורים ט כשאין עמו כל צרכו אבל יש עמו כל צרכו אין מבטלין וכמה כל צרכו אמר רב שמואל בר איני משמיה דרב תריסר אלפי גברי ושיתא אלפי שיפורי ואמרי לה ח) תליסר אלפי גברי ומינייהו שיתא אלפי שיפורי עולא אמר כגון דחייצי גברי מאבולא ועד סיכרא רב ששת ואיתימא רבי יוחנן אמר י נטילתה כנתינתה מה נתינתה בששים רבוא אף נטילתה בששים רבוא כ והני מילי למאן דקרי ותני אבל

רש"י

כמות שהיא. לפי יופיה וחשיבותה מקלסין אותה: חסודה. חוט של חסד משוך עליה: מכאן אמרו. מדברי ב"ה שאמרו ישבחנה: תהא דעתו של אדם מעורבת עם הבריות. לעשות לאיש ואיש כרצונו: משרו. משוררים: לא כחל. אינה צריכה כחל. לצבע המכחלים את העינים: פירכוס. קליעת שיער זו לא כחלה ולא סרקה ולא פירכסה והרי היא יעלת חן: כל מן דין. כל כמות אלו הוו סומכין לנו לקרותן רבי ולמנותא דיינין: סרמיסין. מסרסין הלכות בהיפך טעמיהן: סרמיטין. לשון סמרטוטין: חמיסין. אומרים חמישית הטעם: טורמיסין. לא איתפרש: (טורמיסין כי ההיא דאמר בב"ר (פ' מ"א) על טורמיסין למיקרב למסאבא למטרוניתא אנשים ריקנים): ממתיבתא. מבית המדרש: רבא דעמיה. נשיא בעמו: מדברנא. מנהיג: בריך מתיך לשלם. ברוך בואך לשלום: בוצינא דנהורא. על שהיה קלסתר פניו מבהיק כדאמרינן בב"ב (דף נח.) שופריה דרבי אבהו מעין שופריה דרבי יוחנן דנפקי זיהרורית מיניה כדמפרש התם: אתלת. שלש בדין זורק אחת ומקבל אחת: מכסיף לן סבא. שמזלזל בכבוד תלמידי חכמים ונוהג קלות ראש בעצמו: שוטיתיה. שוט של הדס שהיה מרקד בו: שיטתיה. שהיה מתנהג ומנהגו: שטותיה. שהיה מתנהג כשוטה: מרכיב לה אכתפיה. את הכלה: כי כשורא. כקורה בעלמא שאין אתם מהרהרים עליה: לחבבה. כשרואה הכל מסתכלים בה נכנס יופיה בלבו: מעבירין. כשכלה יוצאה מבית אביה לבית חתונתה ונושאי את המת יוצאים וזו וזו אוכלוסים הרבה ואין רוצין להתערב מעבירין את המת (אפילו) לדרך אחרת: אפילו למ"ד. פלוגתא בפרק קמא דקדושין: שום תשים עליך מלך. ישראל הוזהרו שישימו עליהם שימות הרבה כלומר שתהא אימתו עליהם הלכך אין כבודו מחול שלפיכך ריבה הכתוב שימות הרבה: פרשת דרכים הוה. ולא ניכר שעבר מלפניה אלא כאילו הוא צריך לפנות לאותו הדרך: שיפורי. מכריזין עליו שיבואו לכבודו: דחייצי גברי מאבולא לסיכרא. משער העיר ההיא עד הקבר: נטילתה. של תורה ממנו כנתינתה בסיני נטילתה היינו כשמת ותלמודו בטל: למאן דקרי. מקרא: ותני. משנה אבל עדיין לא שנה לתלמידים:

תוספות

כלה כמות שהיא. ואם יש בה מום ישתקו ולא ישבחוה אי נמי ישבחוה בדבר נאה שיש בה כגון בעיניה או בידיה אם הם יפות וב"ה אומרים ישבחוה לגמרי דכשמזכירין מה שיש בה לשבח מכלל דשאר לגנאי: **ישבחנו** בעיניו או יגננו בעיניו. וב"ש סברי אע"ג דישבחנו בעיניו אין להם לחכמים לתקן להזקיק לומר שקר דהתורה אמרה מדבר שקר תרחק: **שיטתיה** לסבא. פר"ח לשון שיטה והדס (ישעיה מ"א) אע"ג דלא הוי ממש מין אחד מ"מ שניהם מין ארז וא"ת ומנא ליה דבשביל כן זכה וי"ל דעמוד דנורא היה כעין שיבשא דהדס כדאמרינן בבראשית רבה (פ' סא) נחת שיבשא דנורא ואיתעבידא כעין שיבשא דהדס ואפסקת בין דידיה לחברוהי אמרי חמית הדין סבא דקאי שיבשא דנורא קומיה משום דעביד קמוהי דכלתא: **מלך** שמחל על כבודו אין כבודו מחול. אע"ג דלא היה מלך גמור כדמשמע באלו נאמרין (סוטה דף מא.) מ"מ היו נוהגין בו כבוד כמלך גמור: **פרשת** דרכים הואי. הכא לא מצי לשנויי מצוה שאני כדמשני באלו נאמרין (ג"ז שם) גבי מקרא מעומד דהתם מצוה הוא שיש למלך לחלוק כבוד לתורה החשובה ממנו אבל הכא ליכא מצוה דכבודו עדיף מכבוד הכלה:

[**ת"ר** מעבירין את המת מלפני הכלה. מכאן משמע כשיש אבל וחתן בבית הכנסת החתן יוצא תחלה ושושביניו ושוב יוצא האבל ומנחמיו וגם הקרובים לחתן ולאבל יאכלו בבית החתן אם ירצו דהא כבודו קודם וכן בבקר כשמוליכים הכלה לבית החתן מוליכין הכלה תחלה אם יש מת בעיר או יקברוהו קודם שיגיע הזמן דהכנסת כלה. להראבי"ה]:

מבטלין תלמוד תורה להוצאת המת. וקשה מ) דבהלכות דרך ארץ אמר ר"ע תחלת תשמישי לפני חכמים פעם אחת הייתי מהלך בדרך ומצאתי מת מצוה ונטפלתי בו ד' מילין עד שהבאתיו לבית הקברות וקברתיו וכשבאתי והרציתי דברי לפני ר"א ור' יהושע אמרו לי על כל פסיעה ופסיעה כאילו שפכת דם נקי וי"ל דהתם לאו משום ביטול תורה אלא משום דמת מצוה קנה מקומו והיה לו לקוברו במקום שמצאו וכן משמע במס' שמחות (פ"ד) דקאמר מת מצוה קנה מקומו ס) והעובר על דברי חכמים חייב מיתה ע) וכן אמר ר' עקיבא תחלת תשמישי כו' והר"ר יהודה מקורבי"ל תירץ דהתם משום דביטל עצמו משימוש ת"ח קאמר פ דגדול שימושה יותר מלימודה: **להוצאת** המת. לא במת מצוה איירי אלא בכל המתים ואע"ג דבפ"ק דמגילה (דף ג: ושם) אומר פשיטא דמת מצוה ותלמוד תורה מת מצוה עדיף דתניא מבטלין ת"ת להוצאת המת נקט מת מצוה אגב מילי אחריני דהתם דהוו דווקא מת מצוה והא דאמר באלו מגלחין (מו"ק דף כז:) מת בעיר כל בני העיר אסורים בעשיית מלאכה ומוקי לה בדליכא חבורתא אבל אי איכא חבורתא מותרין השאר פירוש חבורתא שנחלקו בני העיר לחבורות שתעסוק כל אחת במת שלה בפני עצמה היינו שלא בשעת הוצאה אבל בשעת הוצאה כולם צריכין לצאת: אבל

מסורת הש"ס

א) [סנהדרין דף יד.], ב) [ערכין ערך חמם הצריך לפרש כל המלות אלו בכמה אופנים קח לא מסם], ג) לקמן עו:, ד) [שמחות פי"א], ה) קדושין לב: סוטה מא: סנהדרין יט., ו) [שם וסנהדרין כב.], ז) מגילה ג: כט., ח) [נ"ל תריסר וכן איתא במגילה], ט) [ח"ל הערוך בערך חמם חמישין שמין מומשם של מסכת ועיין רש"י בסנהדרין מפרש מלשון חמסן ממסין מלומר טעמי תורה], י) הגה"ה היא ז. כש"ל, כ) שם בב"ר הגירסא טולמוסין ופרש"י בפירושו שם טולמוסין אנשי חמס תרגום אדם בליעל (משלי ו) בר נש טולמוס וע' מ"ל ערך טרמס, ל) [ליתא הכי לא בב"ר גם בב"מ פד. קאמר להדיא דר' יוחנן והנה ברש"י דסנהדרין יד. ד"ה בוצינא וכו' אפשר לתקן ולומר ד"ל מעין שופריה דיעקב אבל ברש"י דהכא שפיר דנפקי זיהרורית מיניה כדמפרש התם מוכח דלא גרס לה ולקתו באופן אחר], מ) [נ"ל דמסכת דרך ארץ זוטא פ"ח], נ) [ערכין ח. ס. ברכות ו: עירובין כח:].

גליון הש"ס

גמ' מרקד אתלת. ירושלמי פ"א דפאה על מתני' א' ובשינוי קצת ועוד במ"ר בראשית פ' וכו'. תוס' ד"ה מבטלין וכו' דגדול שימושה. ברכות דף ז ע"ב:

תורה אור השלם

א) מִדְּבַר שֶׁקֶר תִּרְחָק וְנָקִי וְצַדִּיק אַל תַּהֲרֹג כִּי לֹא אַצְדִּיק רָשָׁע: [שמות כג, ז]

ב) שׂוֹם תָּשִׂים עָלֶיךָ מֶלֶךְ אֲשֶׁר יִבְחַר יְיָ אֱלֹהֶיךָ בּוֹ מִקֶּרֶב אַחֶיךָ תָּשִׂים עָלֶיךָ מֶלֶךְ לֹא תוּכַל לָתֵת עָלֶיךָ אִישׁ נָכְרִי אֲשֶׁר לֹא אָחִיךָ הוּא: [דברים יז, טו]

ליקוטי רש"י

וחסודה. ויש אליו חסד, שהיא מקובל לכל רואיו לשון כלה נאה וחסודה שבמשנה [כתובות דף יז.]. כחל. לעינים. שרק. לפנים. פירכוס. לשער שיר הוא לכלה נאה שמעלת חן בלא קישוט. כל מן דין. כל כמו אלו ונולה כהן היו סומכין לנו שראויים הם לסמיכה. סרמיסין. לשון הפכסם כמו פרק את המקרא מקופו להשו (ב"ב דף קיט:) שמהפכין את טעמי תורה. סרמיטין. לשון סמרטוט כלומר שאין נותנים טעם הגון לדבריהם. חמיסין. ממסין שנותנים מלומר טעמי תורה. רבא דעמיה. נשיא בעמו.

עין משפט נר מצוה

ה א טוש"ע אה"ע סימן סה סעיף א:
ו ב מיי' פ"ו מהלכות דעות הלכה א:
ז ג טוש"ע שם סימן סה סעיף ג:
ח ד מיי' פי"ד מהל' אבל הלכה ח סמג עשין דרבנן ב טוש"ע י"ד סימן שס וטוש"ע אה"ע סי' סה סעיף ד:
ט ה מיי' שם הלכה ח:
י ו מיי' פ"ז מהלכות ת"ת הלכה יג סמג עשין יג טוש"ע י"ד סי' רמד סעיף יד:
יא ז מיי' פ"ב מהלכות מלכים הלכה ג סמג עשין ה:
יב ח ט י כ מיי' פי"ד מהלכות אבל הלכה ט והלכה יא טוש"ע י"ד סימן שסא סעיף א:

תוספות רי"ד

כלה כמות שהיא פי' לפי יפיה וחשיבותה מקלסין אותה ולא במה שאין בה ובה"א כלה נאה וחסודה חוט של חסד משוך עליה ומראיתה נאה פי' נאה בעיני הבריות **אמרי ב"ש** לב"ה לדבריך הרי שהיתה חגרת או סומא אומרים לה כלה נאה וחסודה והתורה אמרה מדבר שקר תרחק א"ל ב"ה לדבריכם מי שלקח מקח רע מן השוק ישבחנו בעיניו או יגננו בעיניו הוי אומר ישבחנו בעיניו מכאן אמרו חכמים תהא דעתו של אדם מעורבת עם הבריות פי' לומר דבר המתקבל ואע"פ שאומר שקר: **ת"ר** מעבירין את המת מלפני הכלה וזה וזה מלפני מלך ישראל. **ת"ר** מבטלין ת"ת להוצאת המת ולהכנסת כלה אמרו עליו על ר"י בר אלעאי שהיה מבטל ת"ת להוצאת המת ולהכנסת כלה בד"א כשאין עמו כל צרכו אבל יש עמו כל צרכו אין מבטלין וכמה כל צרכו אמר ר"ש בר (איקא) [איני] משמיה דרב תליסר אלפי גברי ושיתא אלפי שיפורי ואמרי לה תריסר אלפי גברא ומנייהו שיתא אלפי שיפורי פי' מכריזין עליו שיבואו לכבודו וגם מקוננים ומספידים אותו בחלילים עולא אמר כגון דחייצי גברא מאבולא ועד סכרא פי' מפתח העיר עד הקבר **ר"ש** ואיתימא ר' אמי ואיתימא רבי יוחנן נטילתה כנתינתה מה נתינתה בס' רבוא אף נטילתה בס' רבוא וה"מ למאן דקרי ותני אבל למאן דמתני לית ליה שיעורא פי' דקרי מקרא ותני משנה אבל עדיין לא שנה לתלמידים אבל למתני לתלמידים לית ליה שיעורא וכתב המורה וממילא שמעינן דלמאן דלא

דעמיה. נשיא בעמו. מדברנא. מנהיג על שם שהיה פרנס וקרוב למלכות כדאמרינן בסנהדרין ובכתובות דנפקי אמהתא דבי קיסר ומשרו ליה ומלער למיני בקרא' [ע"ז כח. וכע"ז יבמות סה:]. רבי אבהו הוה קרוב למלכות [סנהדרין יד.]. בוצינא דנהורא. על שם שהיה גדול בנוי כדאמרינן בהשוכר את הפועלים (ב"מ דף פד:) שופריה דר' אבהו מעין שופריה (דר' יוחנן) [דיעקב אבינו]. בריך מתיך. ברוך בואך [סנהדרין שם]. לחיי. כלומר שפיר [גיטין ו:]. פרשת דרכים הואי. דרך מתפצלת ומתפרשת לכמה דרכים ושם פגע בכלה והוא נטה לדרך האחרת לימין או לשמאל ולא נראה כמסתלק מלפני הכלה [רש"י מה"ק בשיטמ"ק]. ולהכנסת כלה. ללוותה מבית אביה לבית חופתה. דחייצי גברי מאבולא ועד סיכרא. מחילת אנשים משער העיר עד בית הקברות מקום שסופדין אותו שם [מגילה כט.].

וּבֵית הִלֵּל כַּלָּה כְּמוֹת שֶׁהִיא – We praise THE BRIDE AS SHE IS.[1] אוֹמְרִים – BUT BEIS HILLEL SAY: כַּלָּה נָאָה וַחֲסוּדָה – In all cases we say that she is A BEAUTIFUL AND CHARMING BRIDE.[2] אָמְרוּ לָהֶן בֵּית שַׁמַּאי לְבֵית הִלֵּל – BEIS SHAMMAI SAID TO BEIS HILLEL: הֲרֵי שֶׁהָיְתָה חִיגֶּרֶת אוֹ סוּמָא – NOW, IF SHE WAS LAME OR BLIND, אוֹמְרִים לָהּ כַּלָּה נָאָה וַחֲסוּדָה – DO WE SAY ABOUT HER that she is A BEAUTIFUL AND CHARMING BRIDE? וְהַתּוֹרָה אָמְרָה ,,מִדְּבַר־שֶׁקֶר תִּרְחָק'' – BUT THE TORAH HAS SAID:[3] *DISTANCE YOURSELF FROM FALSEHOOD.* אָמְרוּ לָהֶם בֵּית הִלֵּל לְבֵית שַׁמַּאי – BEIS HILLEL SAID TO BEIS SHAMMAI: לְדִבְרֵיכֶם מִי שֶׁלָּקַח מִקָּח רַע מִן הַשּׁוּק – ACCORDING TO YOUR VIEW, if SOMEONE MADE A BAD PURCHASE IN THE MARKET, יְשַׁבְּחֶנּוּ בְּעֵינָיו אוֹ יְגַנֶּנּוּ בְּעֵינָיו – SHOULD ONE PRAISE IT IN [THE PURCHASER'S] EYES OR DENIGRATE IT IN HIS EYES? הֱוֵי אוֹמֵר יְשַׁבְּחֶנּוּ בְּעֵינָיו – Of course YOU WOULD SAY THAT ONE SHOULD PRAISE IT IN HIS EYES.[4] We should therefore praise even a homely bride.[5] מִכָּאן אָמְרוּ חֲכָמִים – FROM HERE [i.e. this statement of Beis Hillel] THE SAGES SAID: לְעוֹלָם תְּהֵא דַּעְתּוֹ שֶׁל אָדָם מְעוֹרֶבֶת עִם הַבְּרִיּוֹת – A PERSON'S MIND SHOULD ALWAYS BE MINGLED (i.e. compatible) WITH PEOPLE.[6]

The Gemara presents another song for brides:

כִּי אֲתָא רַב דִּימִי אֲמַר – **When Rav Dimi came** to Babylonia from the Land of Israel, **he said:** הָכִי מְשָׁרוּ קַמֵּי כַּלְּתָא בְּמַעֲרָבָא – **This is how they sing before a bride in the West** [i.e. Eretz Yisrael]: לֹא כְּחָל וְלֹא שְׂרָק וְלֹא פִּירְכּוּס וְיַעֲלַת חֵן – **With neither eye makeup nor blush nor hair braids,**[7] **she radiates grace.**[8]

The Gemara relates how this song was used in a different context:

כִּי סָמְכוּ רַבָּנָן לְרַבִּי זֵירָא שָׁרוּ לֵיהּ הָכִי – **When the Rabbis ordained R' Zeira, this is how they sang about him:** לֹא כְּחָל וְלֹא שְׂרָק וְלֹא פִּירְכּוּס וְיַעֲלַת חֵן – **With neither eye makeup nor blush nor hair braids, she radiates grace.**[9]

The Gemara notes another song recited at ordinations:

כִּי סָמְכוּ רַבָּנָן לְרַבִּי אַמִי וּלְרַבִּי אַסִי שָׁרוּ לְהוּ הָכִי – **When the Rabbis ordained R' Ami and R' Assi, this is how they sang about them:** כָּל מִן דֵּין וְכָל מִן דֵּין סְמוֹכוּ לָנָא – **Anyone like these and anyone like these, ordain for us;** such people deserve to be ordained.[10] לֹא תִסְמְכוּ לָנָא לֹא מִן סַרְמִיסִין וְלֹא מִן סַרְמִיטִין – **Do not ordain for us neither distorters**[11] **nor "rags."**[12] וְאָמְרֵי לָהּ – **And some relate [the following version]:** לֹא מִן חֲמִיסִין וְלֹא מִן טוּרְמִיסִין – **Neither the withholders**[13] **nor the lupines.**[14]

Another example of praise sung for a leader:

רַבִּי אַבָּהוּ כִּי הֲוָה אָתֵי מִמְּתִיבְתָּא לְבֵי קֵיסָר – **When R' Abahu would go from** his **academy to the house of** the **Caesar,**[15] נָפְקָן אַמְהָתָא דְּבֵי קֵיסָר לְאַפֵּיהּ וּמְשָׁרְין לֵיהּ הָכִי – **the matrons of the Caesar's household would go out towards him and sing to him** as follows: רַבָּא דְעַמֵּיהּ – **Prince of his people!**[16] וּמַדְבְּרָנָא דְאוּמְּתֵיהּ – **Leader of his nation!**[17] בּוּצִינָא דִנְהוֹרָא – He is as radiant as **a lit candle.**[18] בְּרִיךְ מֵתָיָיךְ לִשְׁלָם – **May your arrival be blessed in peace.**[19]

The Gemara returns to the topic of dancing before the bride:

אָמְרוּ עָלָיו עַל רַבִּי יְהוּדָה בַּר אִילְעַאי – **They said about R' Yehudah bar Il'ai** שֶׁהָיָה נוֹטֵל בַּד שֶׁל הֲדַס וּמְרַקֵּד לִפְנֵי הַכַּלָּה – **that he would take a branch of myrtle and dance before the bride,** וְאוֹמֵר כַּלָּה נָאָה וַחֲסוּדָה – **saying, "A beautiful and charming bride."**[20]

Another example:

רַב שְׁמוּאֵל בַּר רַב יִצְחָק מְרַקֵּד אַתְּלָת – **Rav Shmuel bar Rav**

NOTES

1. That is, we praise her based on her actual beauty and stature (*Rashi;* see *Ritva* for an alternative). If she has a blemish, we say nothing at all. Alternatively, we praise whatever fine quality she does have (*Tosafos*), for it is not possible that she will possess absolutely no virtue (*Ritva*).

2. That is, there is a thread of grace (חוּט שֶׁל חֶסֶד) drawn over her (*Rashi*). A similar expression is used concerning Queen Esther: Even though she had a greenish complexion (according to one opinion) she was endowed with an aura of charm (*Shitah Mekubetzes* from *Megillah* 13a). See below, note 5.

3. *Exodus* 23:7. See *Birkas Avraham.*

4. It is a general principle that the maintenance of harmony and peaceful relations overrides the problems of speaking a falsehood (*Ritva;* see *Tos. Rid;* see also *Rashi* to *Genesis* 18:13).

This rule refers to a case in which nothing will be gained by pointing out a problem with the purchase – e.g. it is an obvious defect that the buyer must not have minded when he bought it. However, if the flaw is concealed and the buyer was cheated, then one is obligated to advise him of the defect, if it is possible for him to recover his money (*Beis Aharon*).

5. And being silent or offering very limited praise is an implied insult (*Tosafos*). Although it is a lie to say she is beautiful, the importance of harmony overrides this concern (based on *Ritva* cited in previous note). Alternatively, we are not praising the homely bride for her physical beauty, but rather for her beautiful deeds (*Perishah* 65:1, *Beis Shmuel* 65:2; cf. *Taz* there). See *Haflaah* and *Chasam Sofer* for other interpretations of this formulation.

6. One should always act towards a person in the manner in which the particular person prefers (*Rashi*). [And since the bride evidently found favor in the groom's eyes, we also praise her to him.]

7. See above, 4b *Tosafos* ד״ה פוקסת and *Ritva* ibid. ד״ה פוקסת.

8. That is, this bride needs none of these things to enhance her beauty (*Rashi*).

9. When they said this about R' Zeira, they meant that although he dressed modestly and never adorned himself with fine clothing, nevertheless, his fine character adorned him (*Yad Ramah* to *Sanhedrin* 14a; see also *Pesach Einayim* and *Iyun Yaakov* for other meanings).

10. To be called "Rabbi" and to be appointed as judges (*Rashi*). See *Rambam, Hil. Sanhedrin* ch. 4 for a detailed explanation of the nature of ordination and its procedures.

11. People who distort the law through inverted logic (from the root word סרס, *to invert*) (*Rashi*).

12. This refers to people who do not properly explain the reasons for their opinions. [Just as a rag does not properly cover a person, the views of these people are not properly "covered" by ample reasoning] (*Rashi* to *Sanhedrin* 14a).

13. The term חמיסין is related to חֲמִישִׁין, *one fifth.* That is, they state only one fifth of their reasoning (*Rashi*). Alternatively, they study only one fifth of the tractate (*Aruch,* cited in margin; see also *Maharsha*). *Rashi* to *Sanhedrin* (ibid.) interprets חֲמִיסִין as plunderers [from חָמָס] – i.e. those that plunder others by withholding Torah interpretations from them (*Rashi*).

14. *Rashi* writes that the meaning of lupines in this context remains unexplained. However, *Yad Ramah* (to *Sanhedrin* ibid.) writes that it refers to embittered people, who are as bitter as lupines (a certain kind of legume). Alternatively, an explanation inserted in our editions of *Rashi* translates טוּרְמִיסִין as empty people, based on *Bereishis Rabbah* 41:2.

15. To speak to the Caesar about communal matters (*Yad Ramah* ibid.).

16. They referred to R' Abahu as a prince, because he was the Torah leader of his people (*Maharsha* to *Sanhedrin* loc. cit.).

17. I.e. he was a confidant of the Caesar and was thus able to look after Jewish interests (*Maharsha* to *Sanhedrin* loc. cit.; see *Rashi* there).

18. I.e. exceedingly radiant and beautiful (*Rashi;* see *Rashi* to *Sanhedrin* 14a ד״ה בוצינא דנהורא; cf. *Yad Ramah*).

19. *Rashi. Ritva* disagrees with this interpretation because we never find that someone's coming is an object of blessing. Rather, the statement should be translated, "Blessed is the One Who brought you in peace." [See *Pesach Einayim* and *Haflaah* for further explanations of R' Abahu's praises.]

20. He took a myrtle branch in an allusion to Queen Esther: Even though she had a complexion that was greenish like a myrtle (and was therefore called הֲדַסָּה, *Myrtle*), she was endowed with charm (*Pesach Einayim;* see above, note 2; cf. *Haflaah*).

The Gemara digresses to discuss other customs practiced at weddings:

תָּנוּ רַבָּנָן – **The Rabbis taught in a Baraisa:** כֵּיצַד מְרַקְּדִין לִפְנֵי הַכַּלָּה – HOW DO WE DANCE BEFORE THE BRIDE? What do we say in her presence?[25] בֵּית שַׁמַּאי אוֹמְרִים – BEIS SHAMMAI SAY:

NOTES

that she is entitled to only one hundred *zuz* because no barrel was passed before her and thus she was evidently not a virgin, she can counter that she was really a virgin and the barrel ceremony was omitted for another reason: The members of the wedding party had become intoxicated from the wine at the wedding feast [and had neglected to perform that ceremony]. In order to eliminate all doubt regarding her virgin status, the Sages instituted that an open barrel be passed before a nonvirgin. Witnesses can later testify to this and refute any false claims (*Rashi*). [*Tosafos* add that she must seize the money when no witnesses are present. Only then would she be believed since she could also deny that she had ever seized the money at all. However, *Chasam Sofer* writes that *Rashi* disagrees. See there, and see *Ramban, Rashba* et al. for a comprehensive discussion of the matter.]

25. *Rashi*. That is, what praise do we say about the bride when we dance before her? (*Shitah Mekubetzes*). [The praises were sung at the dance (*Maharsha*). See *Chochmas Manoach* for various homiletic interpretations.] The expressions of praise for the bride recorded in the Gemara below were recited in order to enhance the groom's joy in his fulfillment of the mitzvah to procreate (*Kovetz Shiurim* §46; see, however, *Shulchan Aruch Even HaEzer* 65:1; see also *Birkas Avraham*).

וזו הואיל ואין לה קול איתרע לה רובא * אי כל הנשאת בתולה יש לה קול כי אתו עדים מאי הוי הנך סהדי שקרי נינהו אלא אמר רבינא רוב הנשאת בתולה יש לה קול וזו הואיל ואין לה קול איתרע לה רובא: אם יש עדים שיצתה בהינומא וכו': וליחוש דלמא מפקא עדים בהאי בי דינא וגביא והדר מפקא לה לכתובה בהאי ב"ד וגביא בה א"ר אבהו זאת אומרת [א] כותבין שובר רב פפא אמר א במקום שאין כותבין כתובה עסקינן ואיכא דמתני לה אברייתא איבדה כתובתה הטמינה כתובתה נשרפה כתובתה רקדו לפניה שחקו לפניה העבירו לפניה כוס של בשורה או מפה של בתולים אם יש לה עדים באחד מכל אלו כתובתה מאתים וליחוש דלמא מפקא עדים בהאי ב"ד וגביא והדר מפקא לכתובתה בהאי ב"ד וגביא בה א"ר אבהו זאת אומרת [ב] כותבין שובר רב פפא אמר במקום שאין כותבין כתובה עסקינן והא איבדה כתובתה קתני דכתב לה איהו סוף סוף מפקא לה וגביא בה מאי איבדה איבדה באור א"ה היינו נשרפה ועוד הטמינה מאי איכא למימר ותו איבדה למה לי אלא כל איבדה כי הטמינה בפנינו דמי ולא יהבינן לה עד דאמרי עדים נשרפה כתובתה מאן דמתני לה אברייתא כל שכן אמתני' ומאן דמתני לה אמתני' אבל אברייתא לא כי קושיא: אם יש עדים כו': וליחוש דלמא מפקא עדי הינומא בהאי ב"ד וגביא והדר מפקא עדי הינומא בבי דינא אחרינא וגביא במקום דלא אפשר ודאי כתבינן שובר: העבירו לפניה כוס של בשורה: מאי כוס של בשורה אמר רב אדא בר אהבה כוס יין של תרומה מעבירין לפניה כלומר ראויה היתה זו לאכול בתרומה מתקיף לה רב פפא אטו אלמנה מי לא אכלה בתרומה אלא אמר רב פפא זו ראשית כתרומה ראשית תניא רבי יהודה אומר חבית של יין מעבירין לפניה אמר רב אדא בר אהבה בתולה מעבירין לפניה סתומה בעולה מעבירין לפניה פתוחה אמאי ניעבר קמי בתולה וקמי בעולה לא ניעבר כלל זימנין דתפסה מאתים ואמרה אנא בתולה הואי והאי דלא עברו קמאי אתנוסי הוא דאתניסו [ג] תנו רבנן כיצד מרקדין לפני הכלה בית שמאי אומרים כלה

רש"י

וזו הואיל ואין לה קול. שאין מעיד עליה שילאה בהינומא: כי אתו עדים מאי הוי. כיון דחזקה דיש לה קול הרבה היו יודעין: דלמא מפקא עדים. עדי הינומא: כותבין שובר. שכשיפרע לה כתובתה תכתוב לו שקבלה כתובתה ויהיה בידו לזכות: זאת אומרת. ודלא כמאן דאמר אין כותבין בבבא בתרא: רב פפא אמר. לעולם אין כותבין דנמצא זה לריך לשמור שוברו מן העכברים ומי שיש לו שטר על חברו או יביא השטר ויחזירנו או לא יטול כלום ומתני' במקום שאין כותבין כתובה אלא סומכין על תנאי בית דין שתקנו לבתולה מאתים ולאלמנה מנה דליכא למיחש לדלמא הדרא ומפקא לה: דמתני לה. לדרבי אבהו ולדרב פפא: הטמינה כתובתה. והיא תובעת מאתים והוא אומר אלמנה נשאתיך: רקדו לפניה. אם יש עדים שרקדו לפניה ביום נשואיה: כוס של בשורה. המבשר עליה סימני בתולות ולקמן מפרש מאי היא: אלא. הכי קאמר כל איבדה כמי שהטמינה בפנינו דמי ולא גביא והכי קתני איבדה כתובתה הטמינה כתובתה נשרפה כתובתה אם רקדו לפניה וכו' והכי פירושה אמרה אבד שטר כתובתה הרי היא כמו שהטמינה כתובתה בפנינו כדי להוליא ולגבות פעם שניה ואינה גובה כלום אא"כ תביא השטר ואם אמרה נשרפה ויש עדים שנשרפה השתא ליכא למיחש למידי תביא עדים שרקדו לפניה שזהו סימן לבתולה ותגבה מאתים: מאן דמתני לה. לדרבי אבהו ורב פפא אברייתא: כל שכן אמתניתין. דכיון דאברייתא דקתני בהדיא איבדה כתובתה גביא ועלה קאמר רב פפא דלא גביא ומתרץ לה דהכא קתני איבדה כתובת' הרי היא כמו שהטמינה וכשנשרפה הוא דקא גביא ולעולם אין כותבין שובר כל שכן דאמתני' איכא למיתני פלוגתא דרב פפא אדר' אבהו למימר דבמקום שאין כותבין כתובה עסקי': ומאן דמתני. פלוגתא דרב פפא ודר' אבהו אמתני': אבל אברייתא לא. מתני ליה דודאי שמעינן מינה דכותבין שובר דהא במקום שכותבין כתובה עסקינן: כי קושיין. דקתני איבדה כתובתה ולא ניחא לשנויי שינויא דחיקא למימר איבדה כתובת' כהטמינה כתובתה קאמר: כיון דלא אפשר. כגון במקום שאין כותבין כתובה וגובות על פי עדים ויש לחוש לשמא תלך לב"ד אחר ותביא עדים אחרים ותגבה פעם שניה ודאי כתבינן שובר: ראויה היתה זו לאכול בתרומה. אי נישאת לכהן דבתולה שלמה נמלאת ולא בעולה שתפסל לכהן מחמת זנות: מתקיף לה רב פפא. ומה זו עדות ללא נישאת אלמנה: אטו. אי נישאת כשהיא אלמנה לכהן הדיוט מי לא אכלה בתרומה: זו ראשית. בעילתה ראשית: זימנין דתפסה מאתים. בלא בית דין וכי בעינן לאפוקי מינה משום דאין עדים שהעבירו לפניה אמרה איתנוסי הוא דאיתניסו שיכורים היו מאונס יין המשתה הלכך השתא אתו עדים שהעבירו לפניה פתוחה ותו ליכא מידי: כיצד מרקדים. מה אומרים לפניה:

כמות

תוספות

וזו הואיל ואין לה קול איתרע לה רובא. תימה דתנן בפירקין (לקמן כח.) אלו נאמנים להעיד בגודלן מה שראו בקטנותן זכורני בפלונית שילאה בהינומא וראשה פרוע וקאמר בגמ' מ"ט כיון דרוב נשים בתולות נישאות גילוי מילתא בעלמא הוא והשתא היכי מיירי אם יש לה קול למה לריך שום עדות לרב ניזיל בתר רובא כדפריך הכא ואי אין לה קול א"כ איתרע לה רובא ולטרך שני עדים כשרים וכי תימא דכשמעיד הוא שראה בקטנו ואחר עמו חשבינן קול הא פריך הכא סהדי שקרי נינהו וי"ל דרוב נשים בתולות נישאות עדיף מרוב נשים הנישאות בתולות יש לה קול וכי אין לה קול לא יתרע כל כך רוב דבתולות נישאות שלא יועיל עדות דראה בקוטנו ואחר עמו:

וליחוש דלמא מפקא כו'. ואפי' ע"י עדי הינומא לא היה לה לגבות עד שתחזיר לו הכתובה כיון שיכול לבא לידי הפסד במה שנשארה כתובה תחת ידה דלא מיבעיא למ"ד דיכול לטעון אחר מעשה ב"ד דמפסיד דאם לא יהיה לה כתובה יהי' נאמן לומר פרעתי אלא אפילו למ"ד דלא מצי טעין אחר מעשה בית דין מפסיד במה שהכתובה תחת ידה שאם תתבענו פעם אחרת ולא יהיו לה עדי הינומא יהא נאמן לומר פרעתי מנה במגו דאי בעי אמר אלמנה נשאתיך או אם יהא במקום שאין מכירין אם היא אשתו יהיה נאמן לומר פרעתי הכל במגו דאי בעי אמר אין את אשתי והשתא שהכתובה בידה תוליא מאתים וכיון שיכול לבא לידי הפסד אין לו לפרוע: זאת אומרת כותבין שובר. אע"ג דהכא לא אפשר דאיכא למיחש דלמא תטרוף כתובתה בעדים והדרא וגביא בעדי הינומא כדאמרינן בסמוך ודלמא הדרא ומפקא בעדי הינומא וגביא למ"ד הטוען אחר מעשה בית דין לא אמר כלום וע"כ זקוק הוא לשובר מ"מ דייק שפיר דבעלמא נמי כותבין שובר דאי אין כותבין בעלמא למה יפרע כאן כיון שיכול לבא לידי הפסד במה שהכתובה בידה כדפירשנו:

כותבין שובר. אע"ג דבפרק גט פשוט (ב"ב קעא: ושם) מפרש טעמא דמאן דאמר כותבין שובר משום דעבד לוה לאיש מלוה לאו דוקא לוה אלא הוא הדין בכל חוב כמו כתובה דהכא ושטרי מקח דאמר התם דכותבין שובר: מאי איבדה איבדה באור. וא"ת א"כ אפי' במקום שכותבין הוה ליה לאוקמי ומאי דוחקא לאוקמי במקום שאין כותבין וכתב לה איהו ואור"ת דבמקום שכותבין ונשרפה איכא למיחש שכתב לה כתובה אחרת דאסור להשהותה בלא כתובה מיהו הוה מצי לאוקומה במקום שכותבין ונשרפה אחר הגירושין דליכא למיחש שמא כתב לה אחרת אלא שנראה לו דוחק: ותו איבדה למה לי. אף על גב דלכאורה היינו פירכא קמייתא דפריך היינו נשרפה יש ליישב דהכי קאמר ותו אפילו אם נאמר דנשרפה הוי פירושא דנאבדה מכל מקום תקשי איבדה למה לי: איתנוסי הוא דאיתניסו. נראה דמיירי כגון דאיכא מגו דאי בעיא אמרה אין בידי כלום דאי לאו הכי אמאי מהימנא ואם תאמר בחילוק קליות דאמר לקמן ארמלתא לית לה כסני אמאי לא חיישינן דלמא תפסה כו' כדאמר הכא ואומר רבינו תם דדוקא בדבר שיש טורח כגון חבית דהכא יכולה לומר דאיתניסו אבל קליות ושאר דברים שהן קלים לעשות לא:

כלה

עין משפט נר מצוה

ג א מיי' פט"ו מהלכות אישות הלכה כב סמג עשין מח טוש"ע אה"ע סימן נו סעיף טו:

ד ב מיי' פכ"ג מהלכות מלוה הלכה טו טז סמג עשין לד טוש"ע ח"מ סימן נד סעיף ג:

תוספות רי"ד

וליחוש דלמא מפקא עדי הינומא בהאי בי דינא וגביא ומפקא כתובתה או עדי הינומא בב"ד אחרינא וגביא א"ר אבהו זאת אומרת כותבין שובר פי' ולא מצי אידך למימר א"א לשמור שוברי מפני העכברים אלא או תקרע לי שטרא או לא אית לך כלום אלא פורעו בע"כ והוא כותב לו שובר ודלא כמ"ד בב"ב דאין כותבין שובר והכי אסיקנא שם בב"פ [דף קעא ע"ב] דכותבין שובר: ת"ר כיצד מרקדין לפני הכלה. ב"ש אומרים

מסורת הש"ס

א) [שבת עט. לקמן ע. פט. סוטה ז: ב"ב קעב. קעא:], ב) שבת עט. ב"ב קעא:, ג) מסכת דרך ארץ פ"ה.

גליון הש"ס

גמ' אי כל הנישאת. עיין זה נדה דף כט ע"א:

ליקוטי רש"י

כי אתו עדים. שילאה בהינומא. מאי הוי. מאחר שכן עלמן אין יודעין אם נישאת בתולה או אלמנה נמלא דאין כאן קול כלל. סהדי שקרי נינהו. ולא ראוה יולאת בהינומא. בתולה יש לה קול. מתוך שיש שמחה בנישואי בתולה מזכרים בה בני אדם. איתרע לה רובא. דבתולות נישאות דרובן יש להן קול מכחיש כמו של אותו רוב וכיון דאיכא למימר הכי איכא למימר הכי המוליא מחבירו עליו הראיה [רשב"ם ב"ב צב:].

teach it **with regard to the Mishnah.**[15] וּמַאן דְּמַתְנֵי לַהּ אַמַּתְנִיתִין – **But the one who taught [the exchange] with regard to the Mishnah** – אֲבָל אַבָּרַיְיתָא לֹא – **with regard to the Baraisa, however,** he will **not** teach it, כִּי קוּשְׁיָא – **as per the question** that was raised above.[16]

The Mishnah stated:

אִם יֵשׁ עֵדִים כו׳ – IF THERE ARE WITNESSES [that she went out with a *hinuma* . . . her *kesubah* payment is two hundred] **etc.**

The previous Gemara wondered why the Mishnah is not concerned that the woman will first collect with these witnesses, and then collect a second time using the *kesubah.* R' Abahu answered that it is because the husband possesses a receipt. Rav Pappa answered that it is because no *kesubah* exists, for the Mishnah is dealing with a place where they do not write a *kesubah.* The Gemara now questions Rav Pappa further:

וְלֵיחוּשׁ – **But let us be concerned** דִּלְמָא מַפְּקָא עֵדֵי הִינוּמָא בְּהַאי בֵּי דִינָא וְגָבְיָא – **that she will perhaps produce witnesses to** the wearing of **the** ***hinuma*** **in this** one **court and collect** her *kesubah* there, וְהָדַר מַפְּקָא עֵדֵי הִינוּמָא בְּבֵי דִינָא אַחֲרִינָא וְגָבְיָא – **and afterwards produce** other **witnesses to** the wearing of **the** ***hinuma*** **in this other court and collect** another payment **with it** there.[17] Even if no *kesubah* exists, there is still room for foul play. How, then, can the Mishnah obligate the husband to pay on account of these witnesses?

The Gemara explains:

בְּמָקוֹם דְּלֹא אֶפְשָׁר – **In a case where there is no other choice,** וַדַּאי כָּתְבִינַן שׁוֹבֵר – **we certainly write a receipt** for the *kesubah* payment. In a place where they do not write *kesubah* documents, but collect their *kesubah* payments with witnesses, the only way to protect the husband is with a receipt. For if no receipt is written, there is a danger that she will produce other witnesses and collect a second time in another court.[18]

The Gemara analyzes the Baraisa it cited above:

הֶעֱבִירוּ לְפָנֶיהָ כּוֹס שֶׁל בְּשׂוֹרָה – IF THEY PASSED BEFORE HER AN ANNOUNCEMENT CUP, this is proof that she was a virgin.

The Gemara inquires:

מַאי כּוֹס שֶׁל בְּשׂוֹרָה – **What is "an announcement cup"?**

The Gemara answers:

אָמַר רַב אַדָּא בַּר אַהֲבָה – **Rav Adda bar Ahavah said:** כּוֹס יַיִן שֶׁל תְּרוּמָה מַעֲבִירִין לְפָנֶיהָ – **They pass before her a cup of wine of** ***terumah,*** כְּלוֹמַר רְאוּיָה הָיְתָה זוֹ לֶאֱכוֹל בִּתְרוּמָה – **as if to say that [this bride] would have been fit to partake of** ***terumah.***[19]

The Gemara assails this explanation:

מַתְקִיף לַהּ רַב פַּפָּא – **Rav Pappa objected:** אַטּוּ אַלְמָנָה מִי לֹא אָכְלָה בִּתְרוּמָה – **But can a widow** who marries a Kohen **not partake of** ***terumah?*** How does such a cup indicate that the bride is a virgin?[20]

Rav Pappa therefore offers a different explanation:

אֶלָּא אָמַר רַב פַּפָּא – **Rather, Rav Pappa said:** זוֹ רֵאשִׁית כִּתְרוּמָה רֵאשִׁית – **This** bride's cohabitation with her groom **is the first** for her, just **like** ***terumah*** **is the first** portion separated from one's produce.[21]

The Gemara cites a Baraisa describing a variant custom:

תַּנְיָא – **It was taught in a Baraisa:** רַבִּי יְהוּדָה אוֹמֵר – R' YEHUDAH SAYS: חָבִית שֶׁל יַיִן מַעֲבִירִין לְפָנֶיהָ – THEY PASS BEFORE [THE VIRGIN BRIDE] A BARREL OF WINE.

The Gemara explains:

אָמַר רַב אַדָּא בַּר אַהֲבָה – **Rav Adda bar Ahavah said:** בְּתוּלָה – In the case of **a virgin,** מַעֲבִירִין לְפָנֶיהָ סְתוּמָה – **they pass before her a sealed** barrel; בְּעוּלָה – and in the case of **a nonvirgin,** מַעֲבִירִין לְפָנֶיהָ פְּתוּחָה – **they pass before her an open** barrel.[22]

The Gemara asks:

אַמַּאי – **Why** do we need to actively indicate her status in both cases? נִיעֲבַר קַמֵּי בְּתוּלָה – **They should pass** a sealed barrel **before a virgin,** וְקַמֵּי בְּעוּלָה לֹא נִיעֲבַר כְּלָל – **and before a nonvirgin they should not pass** any barrel **at all.** The lack of the positive indication that usually accompanies a virgin's wedding would be evidence in itself that the bride was not a virgin! – ? –

The Gemara answers:

זִימְנִין דְּתָפְסָה מָאתַיִם – **Sometimes [a woman who had been a nonvirgin] might seize two hundred** *zuz*[23] וְאָמְרָה אֲנָא בְּתוּלָה הֲוַאי – **claiming, "I was really a virgin** at my wedding וְהַאי דְּלֹא עָבְרוּ קַמַּאי – **and that which they did not pass** a barrel **before me** אִתְּנוּסֵי הוּא דְּאִתְּנִיסוּ – **was because of uncontrollable circumstances."** We therefore pass an open barrel before nonvirgins to prevent this from happening.[24]

NOTES

15. If in the case of the Baraisa, which seems to state clearly that she can collect even though a *kesubah* exists, Rav Pappa will not concede that a receipt is written, but instead reinterprets the Baraisa (in a strained manner) to say that she *cannot* collect, then in the case of the Mishnah, which does not say whether a *kesubah* ever existed, he certainly will not concede that a receipt is written, but will interpret the Mishnah as discussing a place where they do not write *kesubos* (*Rashi*).

16. The question raised above is that since the Baraisa discusses a *kesubah* that is lost, a *kesubah* evidently exists; clearly then, the Baraisa is discussing a place where they write *kesubos.* Yet, the Baraisa allows the woman to collect; perforce, it is in consonance with those who allow a creditor (i.e. the woman) to write a receipt instead of returning the original document. This stands in opposition to Rav Pappa, who states that the reason she may collect is because we are dealing with a place where they do not write *kesubos.* Now, it is true that if the Baraisa is interpreted as saying that a woman who claims she lost her *kesubah* is like one who hid her *kesubah,* Rav Pappa's comment *can* be applied to it (see note 14); however, this is a strained interpretation, and the one who applies the exchange to the Mishnah would certainly prefer not to use it (*Rashi*).

17. Although the Gemara addresses this question to Rav Pappa's comment regarding the Mishnah, it applies also according to the one who applies Rav Pappa's comment to the Baraisa (see *Ramban* and *Re'ah,* cited in *Shitah Mekubetzes;* but see *Chidushei R' Akiva Eiger; Pnei Yehoshua*). According to Rav Pappa, the Baraisa states that she collects with these witnesses only if the *kesubah* has been destroyed. The Gemara therefore asks that even if no *kesubah* exists, we should still be concerned that she will collect a second time using other witnesses.

18. *Rashi.*

19. That is, if she were to marry a Kohen, she would be permitted to eat *terumah* because she was a virgin; had she previously cohabited with someone, this act would disqualify her from marrying a Kohen and having the benefit of eating *terumah* (*Rashi*; see *Rashash*).

20. If an ordinary Kohen [not the Kohen Gadol] marries a widow [who had been married to someone fit for her], she is permitted to eat *terumah,* even though she is no longer a virgin. How then does a cup of *terumah* wine provide testimony that the woman is a virgin? She could just as well be a widow (*Rashi*).

21. That is, a cup of *terumah* wine is used because *terumah* is the first offering of one's crop (not because it is permitted to certain wives of Kohanim). [See *Deuteronomy* 18:4, where *terumah* is referred to as רֵאשִׁית, *the first.*]

22. The sealed barrel indicates that the bride's hymen was not ruptured and the open barrel indicates that it was (*Shitah LeRan*).

23. [Even though she is entitled to a *kesubah* of only one hundred *zuz.*]

24. The fear is that she would seize the two hundred *zuz* (in lieu of her *kesubah*) instead of extracting it through the offices of a Rabbinical court from her husband's estate. When the other side attempts to prove

ג א מיי' פט"ז מהלכות אישות הלכה כה סמג עשין מח טוש"ע אה"ע סימן לו סעיף טו:
ד ב מיי' פכ"ג מהלכות מלוה הלכה טו טז סמג עשין צד טוש"ע ח"מ סימן נד סעיף ג:

תוספות רי"ד

וליחוש דלמא מפקא עדי הינומא בהאי בי דינא וגביא ומפקא כתובתה או עדי הינומא בב"ד אחרינא וגביא **א"ר אבהו** זאת אומרת כותבין שובר פי' ולא מצי אידך למימר א"א לשמור שוברי מפני העכברים אלא או תקרע לי שטרא או לא אית לך כלום אלא פורעו בע"כ והוא כותב לו שובר ודלא כמ"ד בב"ב דאין כותבין שובר והכי אסיקנא שם בג"פ [דף קעא ע"ב] דכותבין שובר: **ת"ר** כיצד מרקדין לפני הכלה. ב"ש אומרים

וזו הואיל ואין לה קול איתרע לה רובא ◦ אי כל הנשאת בתולה יש לה קול כי אתו עדים מאי הוי הנך סהדי שקרי נינהו אלא אמר רבינא רוב הנשאת בתולה יש לה קול וזו הואיל ואין לה קול איתרע לה רובא: אם יש עדים שיצתה בהינומא וכו': וליחוש דלמא מפקא עדים בהאי בי דינא וגביא והדר מפקא לה לכתובה בהאי ב"ד וגביא בה א"ר אבהו זאת אומרת א) כותבין שובר רב פפא אמר א במקום שאין כותבין כתובה עסקינן ואיכא דמתני לה אברייתא איבדה כתובתה הטמינה כתובתה נשרפה כתובתה רקדו לפניה שחקו לפניה העבירו לפניה כוס של בשורה או מפה של בתולים אם יש לה עדים באחד מכל אלו כתובתה מאתים וליחוש דלמא מפקא עדים בהאי ב"ד וגביא והדר מפקא לכתובתה בהאי ב"ד וגביא בה א"ר אבהו זאת אומרת ב) כותבין שובר רב פפא אמר במקום שאין כותבין כתובה עסקינן והא איבדה כתובתה קתני דכתב לה איהו סוף סוף מפקא לה וגביא בה מאי איבדה איבדה באור א"ה היינו נשרפה ועוד הטמינה מאי איכא למימר ותו איבדה למה לי אלא כל איבדה כי הטמינה בפנינו דמי ולא יהבינן לה עד דאמרי עדים נשרפה כתובתה מאן דמתני לה אברייתא כל שכן אמתני' ומאן דמתני לה אמתני' אבל אברייתא לא כי קושיא: אם יש עדים כו': וליחוש דלמא מפקא עדי הינומא בהאי ב"ד וגביא והדר מפקא עדי הינומא בבי דינא אחרינא וגביא במקום דלא אפשר ודאי כתבינן שובר: העבירו לפניה כוס של בשורה: מאי כוס של בשורה אמר רב אדא בר אהבה כוס יין של תרומה מעבירין לפניה כלומר ראויה היתה זו לאכול בתרומה מתקיף לה רב פפא אטו אלמנה מי לא אכלה בתרומה אלא אמר רב פפא זו ראשית כתרומה ראשית תניא רבי יהודה אומר חבית של יין מעבירין לפניה אמר רב אדא בר אהבה בתולה מעבירין לפניה סתומה בעולה מעבירין לפניה פתוחה אמאי ניעבר קמי בתולה וקמי בעולה לא ניעבר כלל זימנין דתפסה מאתים ואמרה אנא בתולה הואי והאי דלא עברו קמאי אתנוסי הוא דאתניסו ג) תנו רבנן כיצד מרקדין לפני הכלה בית שמאי אומרים

כלה

תוספות

וזו הואיל ואין לה קול איתרע לה רובא. תימה דתנן בפירקין (לקמן כח.) אלו נאמנים להעיד בגודלן מה שראו בקטנותן זכורני בפלונית שיצאה בהינומא וראשה פרוע וקאמר בגמ' מ"ט כיון דרוב נשים בתולות נישאות גילוי מילתא בעלמא הוא והשתא היכי מיירי אם יש לה קול למה צריך שום עדות לרב ניזיל בתר רובא כדפריך הכא ואי אין לה קול א"כ איתרע לה רובא ויצטרך שני עדים כשרים וכי תימא דכשמעיד הוא שראה בקוטנו ואחר עמו חשבינן קול הא פריך הכא סהדי שקרי נינהו ויש לומר דרוב נשים בתולות נישאות עדיף מרוב נשים הנישאות בתולות יש לה קול וכי אין לה קול לא יתרע כל כך רוב דבתולות נישאות שלא יועיל עדות דראה בקוטנו ואחר עמו:

וליחוש דלמא מפקא כו'. ואפי' ע"י עדי הינומא לא היה לה לגבות עד שתחזיר לו הכתובה כיון שיכול לבא לידי הפסד במה שנשארה כתובה תחת ידה דלא מיבעיא למ"ד דיכול לטעון אחר מעשה ב"ד דמפסיד דאם לא יהיה לה כתובה יהי' נאמן לומר פרעתי אלא אפילו למ"ד דלא מצי טעין אחר מעשה בית דין מפסיד במה שהכתובה תחת ידה שאם תתבענו פעם אחרת ולא יהיו לה עדי הינומא יהא נאמן לומר פרעתי מנה במגו דאי בעי אמר אלמנה נשאתיך או אם יהא במקום שאין מכירין אם היא אשתו יהיה נאמן לומר פרעתי הכל במגו דאי בעי אמר אין את אשתי והשתא שהכתובה בידה תוליא מאתים וכיון שיכול לבא לידי הפסד אין לו לפרוע: **זאת** אומרת כותבין שובר. אע"ג דהכא לא אפשר דאיכא למיחש דלמא תשרוף כתובתה בעדים והדרא וגביא בעדי הינומא כדאמרינן בסמוך ודלמא הדרא ומפקא בעדי הינומא וגביא למ"ד הטוען אחר מעשה בית דין לא אמר כלום וע"כ זקוק הוא לשובר מ"מ דייק שפיר דבעלמא נמי כותבין שובר דאי אין כותבין בעלמא למה יפרע כאן כיון שיכול לבא לידי הפסד במה שהכתובה בידה כדפירשנו:

כותבין שובר. אע"ג דבפרק גט פשוט (ב"ב קעא: ושם) מפרש טעמא דמאן דאמר כותבין שובר משום דעבד לוה לאיש מלוה לאו דוקא לוה אלא הוא הדין בכל חוב כמו כתובה דהכא ושטרי מקח דאמר התם דכותבין שובר: **מאי** איבדה איבדה באור. וא"ת א"כ אפי' במקום שכותבין הוה ליה לאוקמי ומאי דוחקא לאוקמי במקום שאין כותבין וכתב לה איהו ואור"ת דבמקום שכותבין ונשרפה איכא למיחש שכתב לה כתובה אחרת דאסור להשהותה בלא כתובה מיהו הוה מצי לאוקומה במקום שכותבין ונשרפה אחר הגירושין דליכא למיחש שמא כתב לה אחרת אלא שנראה לו דוחק: **ותו** איבדה למה לי. אף על גב דלכאורה היינו פירכא קמייתא דפריך היינו נשרפה יש ליישב דהכי קאמר ותו אפילו אם נאמר דנשרפה הוי פירושא דנאבדה מכל מקום תקשי איבדה למה לי: **איתנוסי** הוא דאיתניסו. נראה דמיירי כגון דאיכא מגו דאי בעיא אמרה אין בידי כלום דאי לאו הכי אמאי מהימנא ואם תאמר בחילוק קליות דאמר לקמן ארמלתא לית לה כסני אמאי לא חיישינן דלמא תפסה כו' כדאמר הכא ואומר רבינו תם דדוקא בדבר שיש טורח כגון חבית דהכא יכולה לומר דאיתניסו אבל קליות ושאר דברים שהן קלים לעשות לה:

רש"י

וזו הואיל ואין לה קול. שאין מעיד עליה שיצתה בהינומא: כי אתו עדים מאי הוי. כיון דחזקה דיש לה קול הרבה היו יודעין: דלמא מפקא עדים. עדי הינומא: כותבין שובר. שכשיפרע לה כתובתה תכתוב לו שקבלה כתובתה ויהיה בידו לזכות: זאת אומרת. ודלא כמאן דאמר אין כותבין בבבא בתרא: רב פפא אמר. לעולם אין כותבין דנמצא זה צריך לשמור שוברו מן העכברים ומי שיש לו שטר על חברו או יביא השטר ויחזירנו או לא יטול כלום ומתני' במקום שאין כותבין כתובה אלא סומכין על תנאי בית דין שתקנו לבתולה מאתים ולאלמנה מנה דליכא למיחש לדלמא הדרה ומפקא לה: דמתני לה. לדרבי אבהו ולדרב פפא: הטמינה כתובתה. והיא תובעת מאתים והוא אומר אלמנה נשאתיך: רקדו לפניה. אם יש עדים שרקדו לפניה ביום נישואיה: כוס של בשורה. המבשר עליה סימני בתולות ולקמן מפרש מאי היא: אלא. הכי קאמר כל איבדה כמי שהטמינה בפנינו דמי ולא גביא והכי קתני איבדה כתובתה הטמינה כתובתה נשרפה כתובתה אם רקדו לפניה וכו' והכי פירושה אמרה אבד שטר כתובתה הרי היא כמו שהטמינה כתובתה בפנינו כדי להוציא ולגבות פעם שניה ואינה גובה כלום אא"כ תביא השטר ואם אמרה נשרפה ויש עדים שנשרפה דהשתא ליכא למיחש למידי תביא עדים שרקדו לפניה שזהו סימן לבתולה ותגבה מאתים: מאן דמתני לה. לדרבי אבהו ורב פפא אברייתא: כל שכן אמתניתין. דכיון דאברייתא דקתני בהדיא איבדה כתובתה גביא ועלה קאמר רב פפא דלא גביא ומתרץ לה דהדא קתני איבדה כתובת' הרי היא כמו שהטמינה וכשנשרפה הוא דקא גביא ולעולם אין כותבין שובר כל שכן דאמתני' איכא למיתני פלוגתא דרב פפא אדר' אבהו למימר דבמקום שאין כותבין כתובה עסקי': ומאן דמתני. פלוגתא דרב פפא ודר' אבהו אמתני': אבל אברייתא לא. מתני ליה דודאי שמעינן מינה דכותבין שובר דהא במקום שכותבין כתובה עסקינן: כי קושיין. דקתני איבדה כתובתה ולא ניחא לשנויי שינויא דחיקא למימר איבדה כתובת' כהטמינה כתובתה קאמר: כיון דלא אפשר. כגון במקום שאין כותבין כתובה וגובות על פי עדים ויש לחוש שמא תלך לב"ד אחר ותביא עדים אחרים ותגבה פעם שניה ודאי כתבינן שובר: ראויה היתה זו לאכול בתרומה. אי נישאת לכהן דבתולה שלמה נמצאת ולא בעולה שתפסל לכהן מחמת זנות: מתקיף לה רב פפא. ומה זו עדות ללא נישאת אלמנה: אטו. אי נישאת כשהיא אלמנה לכהן הדיוט מי לא אכלה בתרומה: זו ראשית. בעילתה ראשית: זימנין דתפסה מאתים. בלא בית דין וכי בעינן לאפוקי מינה משום דאין עדים שהעבירו לפניה אמרה איתנוסי הוא דאיתניסו שיכורים היו מאונס יין המשתה הלכך השתא אתו עדים שהעבירו לפניה פתוחה ותו ליכא מידי: כיצד מרקדים. מה אומרים לפניה:

כמות

א) [שבת עט. לקמן ט. פט. סוטה ז: ב"ב קע: קעא:], ב) שבת עט. ב"ב קעא:, ג) מסכת דרך ארץ פ"ה.

גליון הש"ס

גמ' אי כל הנישאת. כעין זה נדה דף כט ע"א:

ליקוטי רש"י

כי אתו עדים. שיצאה בהינומא. מאי הוי. מאחר שהן עצמן אין יודעין אם ניסת בתולה או אלמנה נמצא דאין כאן קול כלל. סהדי שקרי נינהו. ולא ראוה יוצאת בהינומא. בתולה יש לה קול. מתוך שיש שמחה בנישואי בתולה מזכרים בה בני אדם. איתרע לה רובא. דבתולות נישאות דרובן יש להן קול מכחיש כמו של אותו רוב וכיון דאיכא למימר הכי ואיכא למימר הכי המוציא מחבירו עליו הראיה [רשב"ם ב"ב צב:].

A CLOTH OF proof of her **VIRGINITY**[12] – אִם יֵשׁ לָהּ עֵדִים בְּאֶחָד מִכָּל אֵלוּ – **IF SHE HAS WITNESSES** who will testify **TO** the performance of **ANY ONE OF THESE** acts, כְּתוּבָּתָהּ מָאתַיִם – **HER *KESUBAH*** payment **IS TWO HUNDRED** *zuz,* for all these are acts customarily performed on the occasion of a virgin marriage.

The Gemara questions this ruling:

וְלֵיחוּשׁ – **But let us be concerned** דִּלְמָא מַפְּקָא עֵדִים בְּהַאי בֵּי דִינָא וְגַבְיָא – **that she will perhaps produce** these **witnesses in this** one **court and collect** her *kesubah* payment there, וַהֲדַר מַפְּקָא לִכְתוּבָּתָהּ בְּהַאי בֵּי דִינָא וְגַבְיָא בָּהּ – **and afterwards produce her *kesubah*** document **in this** other **court and collect** another payment **with it** there. By requiring payment on account of this testimony, we leave the husband open to foul play. Why does the Baraisa obligate him to pay on this basis?

The Gemara explains:

אָמַר רַבִּי אַבָּהוּ – **R' Abahu said:** זאת אוֹמֶרֶת כּוֹתְבִין שׁוֹבֵר – **This** ruling **is** in effect **saying that we** allow a creditor (in this case, the wife) to **write a receipt** instead of returning the original debt document, for were it not so, these witnesses could not obligate the husband to pay while the *kesubah* is extant. Once the husband possesses a receipt, there is no danger that he will be made to pay a second time.

Rav Pappa holds that we do not allow the writing of a receipt. He therefore explains the Baraisa differently:

רַב פָּפָּא אָמַר – **Rav Pappa said:** In fact, we do not allow a creditor to write a receipt instead of returning the original document. The reason the Baraisa is not concerned with the possibility of foul play is because בְּמָקוֹם שֶׁאֵין כּוֹתְבִין כְּתוּבָּה עָסְקִינַן – **we are dealing with a place where they do not write a *kesubah*.** Since there is no *kesubah* extant, there is no danger that the husband will be made to pay a second time.

The Gemara questions Rav Pappa's explanation:

וְהָא אִיבְּדָה כְּתוּבָּתָהּ קָתָנֵי – **But the Baraisa taught:** If **SHE LOST HER *KESUBAH*.** This implies that she originally had a *kesubah*. How then can Rav Pappa say that the Baraisa is dealing with a place where they do not write a *kesubah*?

Rav Pappa answers:

דְּכָתַב לָהּ אִיהוּ – The Baraisa is speaking of a case **where [the husband] did** happen to **write** a ***kesubah* for her.** However, it was a place where it was not the custom to do so.

The Gemara retorts:

סוֹף סוֹף מַפְּקָא לָהּ וְגַבְיָא בָּהּ – But **in the final analysis, she can produce [the *kesubah*]** he wrote for her **and collect with it!** The fact that they do not usually write *kesubos* in this place is entirely irrelevant. The question thus returns: How can the Baraisa require the husband to pay in the face of an extant *kesubah*?

Rav Pappa explains:

אִיבְּדָה מַאי אִיבְּדָה – **What** is meant by **SHE LOST** her *kesubah*? בְּאוּר – That **she lost** it **in a fire,** i.e. it was burned up. Since the *kesubah* no longer exists, there is no danger that she will use it to collect a second time.

The Gemara objects:

אִי הָכִי – **If it is so,** that "she lost it" refers to losing it in a fire, הַיְינוּ נִשְׂרְפָה – then **this** case **is** identical to the Baraisa's next case, which discusses a *kesubah* that **WAS BURNED!** It is unlikely that the Baraisa would repeat itself in this manner. וְעוֹד – **And furthermore,** even if you will say that in the case of "she lost it" the *kesubah* was destroyed, הִטְמִינָה מַאי אִיכָּא לְמֵימַר – when it comes to the case of **SHE HID [THE *KESUBAH*], what is there to say?** In that case, the *kesubah* is certainly intact. Why, then, is the Baraisa not concerned that it will be used to make the husband pay twice? וְתוּ אִיבְּדָה לָמָּה לִי – **And furthermore, why do I need** the case of **SHE LOST IT?**[13]

It is clear that with the words "she lost it," the Baraisa is *not* discussing a case in which the *kesubah* was destroyed. The original question then returns: If the *kesubah* exists, why is the Baraisa not concerned that it will be used to collect twice?

Rav Pappa's explanation having been disproven, he is compelled to reinterpret the Baraisa:

אֶלָּא – **Rather,** this is what the Baraisa is saying: כָּל אִיבְּדָה כִּי הִטְמִינָה בְּפָנֵינוּ דָּמֵי – **Any** case in which she claims that **she lost** the *kesubah* **is comparable to** a case in which **she hid** it **in front of us.** For if the *kesubah* is extant, we fear that she will use it to collect a second time. וְלָא יַהֲבִינַן לָהּ – **Therefore, we do not give her** any money עַד דְּאָמְרֵי עֵדִים נִשְׂרְפָה כְּתוּבָּתָהּ – **until witnesses testify that her *kesubah* was burned.** Once we are sure that the *kesubah* no longer exists, we will award her the two hundred *zuz,* provided she brings witnesses that the customs performed at virgin weddings were performed at hers.[14]

According to Rav Pappa, then, the Baraisa is actually saying that if the *kesubah* document exists, the testimony of these witnesses does not obligate the husband to pay. Their testimony is accepted only if the *kesubah* no longer exists. Thus, the reason we are not concerned for foul play is not because a receipt is written, but because there is no *kesubah*.

The Gemara has now cited one tradition that applies R' Abahu's and Rav Pappa's exchange to our Mishnah, and another that applies it to the Baraisa. The Gemara concludes:

מַאן דְּמַתְנֵי לָהּ אַבָּרַיְיתָא – **The one who taught [the exchange] with regard to the Baraisa** כָּל שֶׁכֵּן אַמַּתְנִיתִין – will **certainly**

NOTES

12. [I.e. the sheet of the marriage bed, bearing the proof of her virginity.]

13. This third question bears some explaining. At first glance, it appears to be the same as the first question asked – that if "she lost it" refers to the burning of the *kesubah,* then it is identical to the case of "it was burned." Obviously, though, the Gemara would not ask the same question twice. *Tosafos* therefore explain this question differently: The Gemara is assuming that one might answer the first question by saying that the case of "it was burned" is intended not as a separate case, but as an *explanation* of "she lost it," in which case there is no repetition. To this the Gemara responds that the difficulty is still not resolved! For the Baraisa could simply have written "it was burned." "She lost it" adds nothing. However, other Rishonim (e.g. *Ritva*) hold that this third question is merely a repetition of the first. They maintain that this question was mistakenly inserted into the text and should be omitted.

14. According to Rav Pappa's re-interpretation, the Baraisa is translated as follows: אִיבְּדָה כְּתוּבָּתָהּ – If *she lost her kesubah,* הִטְמִינָה כְּתוּבָּתָהּ – it is as if *she hid her kesubah* in order to use it to collect a second time. Therefore, she receives nothing. נִשְׂרְפָה כְּתוּבָּתָהּ – She collects only if there are witnesses who testify that *her kesubah was burned.* רָקְדוּ לְפָנֶיהָ – Thereupon, if *they danced before her* at the wedding, שִׂחֲקוּ לְפָנֶיהָ – or if *they sported before her,* הֶעֱבִירוּ לְפָנֶיהָ כּוֹס שֶׁל בְּשׂוֹרָה – or if *they passed before her an announcement cup,* אוֹ מַפָּה שֶׁל בְּתוּלִים – *or a cloth of* proof of her *virginity* – אִם יֵשׁ לָהּ עֵדִים בְּאֶחָד מִכָּל אֵלוּ – *if she has witnesses* who will testify *to* the performance of *any one of these* acts, כְּתוּבָּתָהּ מָאתַיִם – *her kesubah* payment *is two hundred zuz* (*Rashi*).

[According to this explanation of the Baraisa, the witnesses are effective *only* if we are certain that the *kesubah* was destroyed. Accordingly, *Tosafos* ask: If the *kesubah* was destroyed, it should make no difference whether or not this is a place where they write *kesubos* – either way, she should be permitted to collect on the strength of these witnesses, since there is no danger that the *kesubah* will be used to collect a second time. Why, then, does Rav Pappa interpret the Baraisa as discussing a place where they do not write *kesubos*? For different approaches to this problem, see *Tosafos; Rashba.*]

עין משפט נר מצוה

ג א מיי' פט"ז מהלכות אישות הלכה כה סמג עשין מח טוש"ע אה"ע סימן צו סעיף יו:

ד ב מיי' פכ"ג מהלכות מלוה הלכה טו סמג עשין צד טוש"ע ח"מ סימן נד סעיף ב:

מסורת הש"ס

א) [שבת עט. לקמן ט. פט. סוטה ז: ב"ב קע: קעא:], ב) שבת עט. ב"ב קעא:, ג) מסכת דרך ארץ פ"ה.

וזו הואיל ואין לה קול איתרע לה רובא ° אי כל הנשאת בתולה יש לה קול כי אתו עדים מאי הוי הנך סהדי שקרי נינהו אלא אמר רבינא רוב הנשאת בתולה יש לה קול וזו הואיל ואין לה קול איתרע לה רובא: אם יש עדים שיצתה בהינומא וכו': וליחוש דלמא מפקא עדים בהאי בי דינא וגביא והדר מפקא לה לכתובה בהאי ב"ד וגביא בה א"ר אבהו זאת אומרת [א] כותבין שובר רב פפא אמר [א] במקום שאין כותבין כתובה עסקינן ואיכא דמתני לה אברייתא איבדה כתובתה הטמינה כתובתה נשרפה כתובתה רקדו לפניה שחקו לפניה העבירו לפניה כוס של בשורה או מפה של בתולים אם יש לה עדים באחד מכל אלו כתובתה מאתים וליחוש דלמא מפקא עדים בהאי ב"ד וגביא והדר מפקא לכתובתה בהאי ב"ד וגביא בה א"ר אבהו זאת אומרת [ג] [ב] כותבין שובר רב פפא אמר במקום שאין כותבין כתובה עסקינן והא איבדה כתובתה קתני דכתב לה איהו סוף סוף מפקא לה וגביא בה מאי איבדה איבדה באור א"ה היינו נשרפה ועוד הטמינה מאי איכא למימר ותו איבדה למה לי אלא כל איבדה כי הטמינה בפנינו דמי ולא יהבינן לה עד דאמרי עדים נשרפה כתובתה מאן דמתני לה אברייתא כל שכן אמתני' ומאן דמתני לה אמתני' אבל אברייתא לא כי קושיא: אם יש עדים כו': וליחוש דלמא מפקא עדי הינומא בהאי ב"ד וגביא והדר מפקא עדי הינומא בבי דינא אחרינא וגביא במקום דלא אפשר ודאי כתבינן שובר: העבירו לפניה כוס של בשורה: מאי כוס של בשורה אמר רב אדא בר אהבה כוס יין של תרומה מעבירין לפניה כלומר ראויה היתה זו לאכול בתרומה מתקיף לה רב פפא אטו אלמנה מי לא אכלה בתרומה אלא אמר רב פפא זו ראשית כתרומה ראשית תניא רבי יהודה אומר חבית של יין מעבירין לפניה אמר רב אדא בר אהבה בתולה מעבירין לפניה סתומה בעולה מעבירין לפניה פתוחה אמאי ניעבר קמי בתולה וקמי בעולה לא ניעבר כלל זימנין דתפסה מאתים ואמרה אנא בתולה הואי והאי דלא עברו קמאי אתנוסי הוא דאתניסו [ג] תנו רבנן כיצד מרקדין לפני הכלה בית שמאי אומרים כלה

רש"י

וזו הואיל ואין לה קול. שאין מעיד עליה שילתה בהינומא: כי אתו עדים מאי הוי. כיון דחזקה דיש לה קול הרבה היו יודעין: דלמא מפקא עדים. עדי הינומא: כותבין שובר. שכשיפרע לה כתובתה תכתוב לו שקבלה כתובתה ויהיה בידו לזכות: זאת אומרת. ודלא כמאן דאמר אין כותבין בבבא בתרא: רב פפא אמר. לעולם אין כותבין דנמלא זה לריך לשמור שוברו מן העכברים ומי שיש לו שטר על חברו או יביא השטר ויחזירנו או לא יטול כלום ומתני' במקום שאין כותבין כתובה אלא סומכין על תנאי בית דין שתקנו לבתולה מאתים ולאלמנה מנה דליכא למיחש לדלמא הדרא ומפקא לה: דמתני לה. לדרבי אבהו ולדרב פפא: הטמינה כתובתה. והיא תובעת מאתים והוא אומר אלמנה נשאתיך: רקדו לפניה. אם יש עדים שרקדו לפניה ביום נישואיה: כוס של בשורה. המבשר עליה סימני בתולות ולקמן מפרש מאי היא: אלא. הכי קאמר כל איבדה כמי שהטמינה בפנינו דמי ולא גביא והכי קתני איבדה כתובתה הטמינה כתובתה נשרפה כתובתה אם רקדו לפניה וכו' והכי פירושה אמרה אבד שטר כתובתה הרי היא כמו שהטמינה כתובתה בפנינו כדי להוליא ולגבות פעם שניה ואינה גובה כלום אא"כ תביא השטר ואם אמרה נשרפה ויש עדים שנשרפה דהשתא ליכא למיחש למידי תביא עדים שרקדו לפניה שזהו סימן לבתולה ותגבה מאתים: מאן דמתני לה. לדרבי אבהו ורב פפא אברייתא: כל שכן אמתניתין. דכיון דאברייתא דקתני בהדיא איבדה כתובתה גביא ועלה קאמר רב פפא דלא גביא ומתרץ לה דהכא קתני איבדה כתובת' הרי היא כמו שהטמינה וכשנשרפה הוא דקא גביא ולעולם אין כותבין שובר כל שכן דאמתני' איכא למיתני פלוגתא דרב פפא אדר' אבהו למימר דבמקום שאין כותבין כתובה עסקי': ומאן דמתני. פלוגתא דרב פפא ודר' אבהו אמתני': אבל אברייתא לא. מתני ליה דודאי שמעינן מינה דכותבין שובר דהא במקום שכותבין כתובה עסקינן: כי קושיין. דקתני איבדה כתובתה ולא ניחא לשנויי שינויא דחיקא למימר איבדה כתובת' כהטמינה כתובתה קאמר: כיון דלא אפשר. כגון במקום שאין כותבין כתובה וגובות על פי עדים ויש לחוש לשמא תלך לב"ד אחר ותביא עדים אחרים ותגבה פעם שניה ודאי כתבינן שובר: ראויה היתה זו לאכול בתרומה. אי נישאת לכהן דבתולה שלמה נמלאת ולא בעולה שתפסל לכהן מחמת זנות: מתקיף לה רב פפא. ומה זו עדות ללא נישאת אלמנה: אטו. אי נישאת כשהיא אלמנה לכהן הדיוט מי לא אכלה בתרומה: זו ראשית. בעילתה ראשית: זימנין דתפסה מאתים. בלא בית דין וכי בעינן לאפוקי מינה משום דאין עדים שהעבירו לפניה אמרה איתנוסי הוא דאיתניסו שיכורים היו מאונס יין המשתה הלכך השתא אתו עדים שהעבירו לפניה פתוחה ותו ליכא מידי: כיצד מרקדים. מה אומרים לפניה:

תוספות

וזו הואיל ואין לה קול איתרע לה רובא. תימה דתנן בפירקין (לקמן כח.) אלו נאמנים להעיד בגודלן מה שראו בקטנותן זכורני בפלונית שיצאה בהינומא וראשה פרוע וקאמר בגמ' מ"ט כיון דרוב נשים בתולות נישאות גילוי מילתא בעלמא הוא והשתא היכי מיירי אם יש לה קול למה צריך שום עדות לרב ניזיל בתר רובא כדפריך הכא ואי אין לה קול א"כ איתרע לה רובא ולצריך שני עדים כשרים וכי תימא דכשמעיד הוא שראה בקטנותו ואחר עמו מסייעין קול הא פריך הכא סהדי שקרי נינהו ויש לומר דרוב נשים בתולות נישאות עדיף מרוב נשים הנישאות בתולות יש להן קול וכי אין לה קול לא יתרע כל כך רוב דבתולות נישאות שלא יועיל עדות דראה בקטנותו ואחר עמו:

וליחוש דלמא מפקא כו'. ואפי' ע"י עדי הינומא לא היה לה לגבות עד שתחזיר לו הכתובה כיון שיכול לבא לידי הפסד במה שנשארה כתובה תחת ידה דלא מיבעיא למ"ד דיכול לטעון אחר מעשה ב"ד דמפסיד דאם לא יהיה לה כתובה יהי' נאמן לומר פרעתי אלא אפילו למ"ד דלא מצי טעין אחר מעשה בית דין מפסיד במה שהכתובה תחת ידה שאם תתבענו פעם אחרת ולא יהיו לה עדי הינומא יהא נאמן לומר פרעתי מנה במגו דאי בעי אמר אלמנה נשאתיך או אם יהא במקום שאין מכירין אם היא אשתו יהיה נאמן לומר פרעתי הכל במגו דאי בעי אמר אין את אשתי והשתא שהכתובה בידה תוציא מאתים וכיון שיכול לבא לידי הפסד אין לו לפרוע: זאת אומרת כותבין שובר. אע"ג דהכא לא אפשר דאיכא למיחש דלמא תטרוף כתובתה בעדים והדרא וגביא בעדי הינומא כדאמרינן בסמוך ודלמא הדרא ומפקא בעדי הינומא וגביא למ"ד הטוען אחר מעשה בית דין לא אמר כלום וע"כ זקוק הוא לשובר מ"מ דייק שפיר דבעלמא נמי כותבין שובר דאי אין כותבין בעלמא למה יפרע כאן כיון שיכול לבא לידי הפסד במה שהכתובה בידה כדפירשנו:

כותבין שובר. אע"ג דבפרק גט פשוט (ב"ב קעא: ושם) מפרש טעמא דמאן דאמר כותבין שובר משום דעבד לוה לאיש מלוה לאו דוקא לוה אלא הוא הדין בכל חוב כמו כתובה דהכא ושטרי מקח דאמר התם דכותבין שובר: מאי איבדה איבדה באור. וא"ת א"כ אפי' במקום שכותבין הוה ליה לאוקמי ומאי דוחקא לאוקמי במקום שאין כותבין וכתב לה איהו ואור"ת דבמקום שכותבין ונשרפה איכא למיחש שכתב לה כתובה אחרת דאסור להשהותה בלא כתובה מיהו הוה מצי לאוקומה במקום שכותבין ונשרפה אחר הגירושין דליכא למיחש שמא כתב לה אחרת אלא שנראה לו דוחק: ותו איבדה למה לי. אף על גב דלכאורה היינו פירכא קמייתא דפריך היינו נשרפה יש ליישב דהכי קאמר ותו אפילו אם נאמר דנשרפה הוי פירושא דנאבדה מכל מקום תקשי איבדה למה לי: איתנוסי הוא דאיתניסו. נראה דמיירי כגון דאיכא מגו דאי בעיא אמרה אין בידי כלום דאי לאו הכי אמאי מהימנא ואם תאמר בחילוק קליות דאמר לקמן ארמלתא לית לה כסני אמאי לא חיישינן דלמא תפסה כו' כדאמר הכא ואומר רבינו תם דדוקא בדבר שיש טורח כגון חבית דהכא יכולה לומר דאיתניסו אבל קליות ושאר דברים שהן קלים לעשות לא:

תוספות רי"ד

וליחוש דלמא מפקא עדי הינומא בהאי בי דינא וגביא ומפקא כתובתה בב"ד אחרינא וגביא א"ר אבהו זאת אומרת כותבין שובר פי' ולא מצי איך לומר א"א לשמור שוברי מפני העכברים אלא אי תקרע לי שטרא או לא אית לך כלום אלא פורע בע"כ והוא כותב לו שובר דלא כמ"ד בב"ב דאין כותבין שובר והכי אסיקנא שם בב"ב [דף קעא ע"ב] דכותבין שובר: ת"ר כיצד מרקדין לפני הכלה. ב"ש אומרים

גליון הש"ס

גמ' אי כל הנישאת. כעין זה נדה דף כט ע"א:

ליקוטי רש"י

כי אתו עדים. שילאה בהינומא. מאי הוי. מאחר שהן עלמן אין יודעין אם ניסת בתולה או אלמנה נמלא דאין כאן קול כלל. סהדי שקרי נינהו. ולא ראוה יולאת בהינומא. בתולה יש לה קול. מתוך שיש שמחה בנישואי בתולה נוכרים בה בני אדם. איתרע לה רובא. דבתולות נישאות דרובן יש להן קול מכחיש כחו של אותו רוב וכיון דאיכא למימר הכי ואיכא למימר הכי המוליא מחבירו עליו הראיה [רשב"ם ב"ב צב:].

כמות

כלה

וְזוֹ הוֹאִיל וְאֵין לָהּ קוֹל – **Therefore,** as for **this** woman, **since it is not** a matter of **public knowledge** that she was a virgin,[1] אִיתְרַע לָהּ רוּבָּא – **the** capacity of the **majority** to determine **is weakened regarding her.**[2]

The Gemara asks:

אִי כָּל הַנִּשֵּׂאת בְּתוּלָה יֵשׁ לָהּ קוֹל – But **if** it is true that **when any woman marries as a virgin it is** a matter of **public knowledge,** כִּי אָתוּ עֵדִים מַאי הָוֵי – then even **when witnesses come, what of it?** הָנָךְ סַהֲדֵי שַׁקְרֵי נִינְהוּ – We should assume that **they are false witnesses!**[3] **–?–**

The Gemara therefore modifies its answer:

אֶלָּא אָמַר רָבִינָא – **Rather, Ravina said:** רוֹב הַנִּשֵּׂאת בְּתוּלָה יֵשׁ לָהּ קוֹל – **In *most* cases when a woman marries as a virgin it is** a matter of **public knowledge.**[4] וְזוֹ הוֹאִיל וְאֵין לָהּ קוֹל – **Regarding this** woman, **therefore, since it is not** a matter of **public knowledge** that she was a virgin, אִיתְרַע לָהּ רוּבָּא – **the** capacity of the **majority** to determine **is weakened regarding her.**[5]

The Mishnah stated:

אִם יֵשׁ עֵדִים שֶׁיָּצְתָה בְּהִינוּמָא וכו׳ – IF THERE ARE WITNESSES THAT SHE WENT OUT WITH A *HINUMA* **etc.,** her *kesubah* payment is two hundred *zuz.*

The Mishnah is discussing a woman who lost her *kesubah* document.[6] It rules that if witnesses testify that the customs reserved for virgin marriages were performed at her marriage, she receives the higher payment. The Gemara questions this ruling:

וְלֵיחוּשׁ – **But let us be concerned** דִּלְמָא מַפְּקָא עֵדִים בְּהַאי בֵּי דִינָא וְגָבְיָא – that **she will perhaps produce witnesses**[7] **in this** one **court and collect** her *kesubah* payment there, וַהֲדַר מַפְּקָא לָהּ לִכְתוּבָּה בְּהַאי בֵּי דִינָא וְגָבְיָא בָּהּ – **and afterwards produce the** lost ***kesubah*** document **in this** other **court and collect** another payment **with it** there. By requiring payment on the strength of testimony that she wore a *hinuma,* we leave the husband open to foul play. Why does the Mishnah obligate him to pay on this basis?

The Gemara explains:

אָמַר רַבִּי אַבָּהוּ – **R' Abahu said:** זֹאת אוֹמֶרֶת כּוֹתְבִין שׁוֹבֵר – **This** ruling **is** in effect **saying that we** allow a creditor (in this case, the wife) to **write a receipt** instead of returning the original debt document, for were it not so, these witnesses could not obligate the husband to pay while the *kesubah* is extant.[8] Once the husband is in possession of a receipt, there is no danger that he will be made to pay a second time.

Rav Pappa holds that we generally do *not* compel a borrower to accept a receipt in place of the debt document. He therefore explains the Mishnah's ruling differently:

רַב פָּפָּא אָמַר – **Rav Pappa said:** In fact, we do not allow a creditor to write a receipt instead of returning the original document. The reason the Mishnah is not concerned with the possiblity of foul play is because בְּמָקוֹם שֶׁאֵין כּוֹתְבִין כְּתוּבָּה עָסְקִינַן – **we are dealing with a place where they do not write a *kesubah.***[9] Since no *kesubah* exists, there is no danger that the husband will be made to pay a second time.

The Gemara cites another version of the foregoing exchange, in which the subject is not our Mishnah, but a Baraisa:

וְאִיכָּא דְּמַתְנֵי לָהּ אַבָּרַיְיתָא – **There are those who taught [this exchange] with regard to** the ruling of **a** certain **Baraisa,** as follows. It has been taught in a Baraisa: אִיבְּדָה כְּתוּבָּתָהּ – IF SHE LOST HER *KESUBAH,* הִטְמִינָה כְּתוּבָּתָהּ – or if SHE HID HER *KESUBAH,*[10] נִשְׂרְפָה כְּתוּבָּתָהּ – or if HER *KESUBAH* WAS BURNED, and she and her husband disagree as to whether she was a virgin when she married, this is the law: רָקְדוּ לְפָנֶיהָ – If THEY DANCED BEFORE HER at the wedding, שִׂחֲקוּ לְפָנֶיהָ – or if THEY SPORTED BEFORE HER, הֶעֱבִירוּ לְפָנֶיהָ כּוֹס שֶׁל בְּשׂוֹרָה – or if THEY PASSED BEFORE HER AN ANNOUNCEMENT CUP,[11] אוֹ מַפָּה שֶׁל בְּתוּלִים – OR

NOTES

1. As evidenced by the fact that she cannot produce witnesses that she was wearing a *hinuma* like a virgin bride (*Rashi*).

2. The principle of majority can be used to determine the law only where there is no reason to assume that the case in question is different from a standard case. In this case, however, the fact that no one remembers her having been a virgin bride indicates that she was *not* one of the majority of women who marry as virgins.

3. If it is true that every virgin marriage is a matter of public knowledge, then many people should know that she was a virgin (*Rashi*). Since this is not the case, it is evident that she was not a virgin, and these "witnesses" must not have seen her wearing a *hinuma* as they claim (*Rashba*; cf. *Rashbam* to *Bava Basra* 92b ד״ה כי איכא עדים).

[Generally, two valid witnesses serve as stronger proof than what the public says (see *Gittin* 89b). This is true, however, only because what the public says can have an untrue source; for example, enemies of the subject may have spread a rumor about him. Here, however, it is what the public is *not* saying that contradicts the witnesses. The lack of public knowledge when such knowledge is expected is stronger proof than witnesses (*Ritva*).]

4. That is, not *all* cases of brides who marry as virgins become public knowledge; rather, *most* do.

5. Thus if she finds witnesses, we say that she happened to be one of the minority whose marriage as a virgin did not become public knowledge (*Ritva*).

6. See *Rashi* to the Mishnah ד״ה והוא אומר; see end of note 9.

7. Who testify that she wore a *hinuma* at her wedding (*Rashi*).

8. Normally, when a borrower repays a debt that was recorded in a document, the lender returns the document to the borrower. If the lender cannot produce the document, there is a dispute as to how to proceed. According to one opinion, we permit the lender to substitute a receipt for the loan document. Although this imposes upon the borrower the burden of guarding the receipt (so that he will not be dunned a second time), he must accept this responsibility (for reasons explained in *Bava Basra* 171b) and repay the debt. Others maintain that the borrower may demand the actual document, and refuse to accept a receipt in its place. He cannot be compelled to pay until the document is returned to him (see *Bava Basra* 170b-171b). R' Abahu maintains that the fact that our Mishnah requires the husband to pay even though the *kesubah* has not been returned demonstrates that it is in consonance with those who hold that we allow a creditor (in this case the wife) to substitute a receipt for the original document (*Rashi;* see *Tosafos* ד״ה זאת אומרת). Hence, the case in which the wife collects on the strength of witnesses to the *hinuma* is when she writes a receipt stating that she received her *kesubah* payment. The husband keeps the receipt as proof; thus, there is no danger that he will be made to pay a second time (*Rashi; see Tosafos; Ritva* et al.).

9. Even if one did not give his wife a document guaranteeing fulfillment of the *kesubah* obligations, he is still obligated to fulfill them, for the Rabbis made these obligations a stipulation of every marriage. In fact, there are places where *kesubos* are not written at all; in these areas, people rely upon the Rabbis' stipulation, and pay the appropriate *kesubah* amount (100 or 200 *zuz*) on that basis. There is no *kesubah* document to present, so a woman simply presents her *get* or brings witnesses that her husband died, and collects her *kesubah* (*Rashi* here and to *Sotah* 7b ד״ה במקום שאין כותבין). Rav Pappa maintains that our Mishnah is discussing such a place. Since no *kesubah* exists, there is no danger that the woman will present the *kesubah* in another court and collect a second time (*Rashi*).

[When *Rashi* to the Mishnah states that the Mishnah is discussing a *kesubah* that was lost (see note 6), he is following R' Abahu. According to Rav Pappa, however, there is no *kesubah* to begin with.]

10. I.e. for safekeeping, and now she cannot remember where she hid it (see *Ritva* below ד״ה ועוד הטמינה).

11. This cup was passed before her to announce that she was found a virgin. The Gemara below will discuss this further (*Rashi*).

וזו הואיל ואין לה קול איתרע לה רובא [a] אי כל הנשאת בתולה יש לה קול כי אתו עדים מאי הוי הנך סהדי שקרי נינהו אלא אמר רבינא רוב הנשאת בתולה יש לה קול וזו הואיל ואין לה קול איתרע לה רובא: אם יש עדים שיצתה בהינומא וכו': וליחוש דלמא מפקא עדים בהאי בי דינא וגביא והדר מפקא לה לכתובה בהאי ב"ד וגביא בה א"ר אבהו זאת אומרת [א] כותבין שובר רב פפא אמר [א]במקום שאין כותבין כתובה עסקינן ואיכא דמתני לה אברייתא איבדה כתובתה הטמינה כתובתה נשרפה כתובתה רקדו לפניה שחקו לפניה העבירו לפניה כוס של בשורה או מפה של בתולים אם יש לה עדים באחד מכל אלו כתובתה מאתים וליחוש דלמא מפקא עדים בהאי ב"ד וגביא והדר מפקא לכתובתה בהאי ב"ד וגביא בה א"ר אבהו זאת אומרת [ג]כותבין שובר רב פפא אמר במקום שאין כותבין כתובה עסקינן והא איבדה כתובתה קתני דכתב לה איהו סוף סוף מפקא לה וגביא בה מאי איבדה איבדה באור א"ה היינו נשרפה ועוד הטמינה מאי איכא למימר ותו איבדה למה לי אלא כל איבדה כי הטמינה בפנינו דמי ולא יהבינן לה עד דאמרי עדים נשרפה כתובתה מאן דמתני לה אברייתא כל שכן אמתני' ומאן דמתני לה אמתני' אבל אברייתא לא כי קושיא: אם יש עדים כו': וליחוש דלמא מפקא עדי הינומא בהאי ב"ד וגביא והדר מפקא עדי הינומא בבי דינא אחרינא וגביא במקום דלא אפשר ודאי כתבינן שובר: העבירו לפניה כוס של בשורה: מאי כוס של בשורה אמר רב אדא בר אהבה כוס יין של תרומה מעבירין לפניה כלומר ראויה היתה זו לאכול בתרומה מתקיף לה רב פפא אטו אלמנה מי לא אכלה בתרומה אלא אמר רב פפא זו ראשית כתרומה ראשית תניא רבי יהודה אומר חבית של יין מעבירין לפניה אמר רב אדא בר אהבה בתולה מעבירין לפניה סתומה בעולה מעבירין לפניה פתוחה אמאי ניעבר קמי בתולה וקמי בעולה לא ניעבר כלל זימנין דתפסה מאתים ואמרה אנא בתולה הואי והאי דלא עברו קמאי אתנוסי הוא דאתניסו [ג] תנו רבנן כיצד מרקדין לפני הכלה בית שמאי אומרים כלה

רש"י

וזו הואיל ואין לה קול. שאין מעיד עליה שילתה בהינומא: כי אתו עדים מאי הוי. כיון דחזקה דיש לה קול הרבה היו יודעין: דלמא מפקא עדים. עדי הינומא: כותבין שובר. שכשיפרע לה כתובתה תכתוב לו שקבלה כתובתה ויהיה בידו לזכות: זאת אומרת. ודלא כמאן דאמר אין כותבין בבבא בתרא: רב פפא אמר. לעולם אין כותבין דמגלגל זה צריך לשמור שוברו מן העכברים ומי שיש לו שטר על חברו או יביא השטר ויחזירנו או לא יטול כלום ומתני' במקום שאין כותבין כתובה אלא סומכין על תנאי בית דין שתקנו לבתולה מאתים ולאלמנה מנה דליכא למיחש לדלמא הדרה ומפקא לה: דמתני לה. לדרבי אבהו ולדרב פפא: הטמינה כתובתה. והיא תובעת מאתים והוא אומר אלמנה נשאתיך: רקדו לפניה. אם יש עדים שרקדו לפניה ביום נישואיה: כוס של בשורה. המבשר עליה סימני בתולות ולקמן מפרש מאי היא: אלא. הכי קאמר כל איבדה כמי שהטמינה בפנינו דמי ולא גביא והכי קתני איבדה כתובתה הטמינה כתובתה נשרפה כתובתה אם רקדו לפניה וכו' והכי פירושה אמרה אבד שטר כתובתה הרי היא כמו שהטמינה כתובתה בפנינו כדי להוציא ולגבות פעם שניה ואינה גובה כלום אא"כ תביא השטר ואם אמרה נשרפה ויש עדים שנשרפה השתא ליכא למיחש למידי תביא עדים שרקדו לפניה שזהו סימן לבתולה ותגבה מאתים: מאן דמתני לה. לדרבי אבהו ורב פפא אברייתא: כל שכן אמתניתין. דכיון דאברייתא דקתני בהדיא איבדה כתובתה גביא ועלה קאמר רב פפא דלא גביא ומתרץ לה דהכא קתני איבדה כתובת' הרי היא כמו שהטמינה וכשנשרפה הוא דקא גביא ולעולם אין כותבין שובר כל שכן דאמתני' איכא למיתני פלוגתא דרב פפא ודר' אבהו למימר דבמקום שאין כותבין כתובה עסקי': ומאן דמתני. פלוגתא דרב פפא ודר' אבהו אמתני': אבל אברייתא לא. מתני ליה דודאי שמעינן מינה דכותבין שובר דהא במקום שכותבין כתובה עסקינן: כי קושיין. דקתני איבדה כתובתה ולא ניחא לשנויי שינויא דחיקא למימר איבדה כתובת' כהטמינה כתובתה קאמר: כיון דלא אפשר. כגון במקום שאין כותבין כתובה וגובות על פי עדים ויש לאו לשמא תלך לב"ד אחר ותביא עדים אחרים ותגבה פעם שניה ודאי כתבינן שובר: ראויה היתה זו לאכול בתרומה. אי נישאת לכהן דבתולה שלמה נמצאת ולא בעולה שתפסל לכהן מחמת זנות: מתקיף לה רב פפא. ומה זו עדות ללא נישאת אלמנה: אטו. אי נישאת כשהיא אלמנה לכהן הדיוט מי לא אכלה בתרומה: זו ראשית. בעילתה ראשית: זימנין דתפסה מאתים. בלא בית דין וכי בעינן לאפוקי מינה משום דאין עדים שהעבירו לפניה אמרה איתנוסי הוא דאיתניסו שיכורים היו מאונס יין המשתה הלכך השתא אתו עדים שהעבירו לפניה פתוחה ותו ליכא מידי: כיצד מרקדים. מה אומרים לפניה: כמות כלה

תוספות

וזו הואיל ואין לה קול איתרע לה רובא. תימה דתנן בפירקין (לקמן כח.) אלו נאמנים להעיד בגודלן מה שראו בקטנותן וזכורני בפלונית שיצאה בהינומא וראשה פרוע וקאמר בגמ' מ"ט כיון דרוב נשים בתולות נישאות גילוי מילתא בעלמא הוא והשתא היכי מיירי אם יש לה קול למה צריך שום עדות לרב ניזיל בתר רובא כדפריך הכא ואי אין לה קול א"כ איתרע לה רובא וילטרך שני עדים כשרים וכי תימא דכשמעיד הוא שראה בקטנו ואחר עמו חשבינן קול הא פריך הכא סהדי שקרי נינהו ויש לומר דרוב נשים בתולות נישאות עדיף מרוב נשים הנישאות בתולות יש לה קול וכי אין לה קול לא יתרע כל כך רוב דבתולות נישאות שלא יועיל עדות דראה בקטנו ואחר עמו:

וליחוש דלמא מפקא כו'. ואפי' ע"י עדי הינומא לא היה לה לגבות עד שתחזיר לו הכתובה כיון שיכול לבא לידי הפסד במה שנשארה כתובה תחת ידה דלא מיבעיא למ"ד דיכול לטעון אחר מעשה ב"ד דמפסיד דאם לא יהיה לה כתובה יהי' נאמן לומר פרעתי אלא אפילו למ"ד דלא מצי טעין אחר מעשה בית דין מפסיד במה שהכתובה תחת ידה שאם תתבענו פעם אחרת ולא יהיו לה עדי הינומא יהא נאמן לומר פרעתי מנה במגו דאי בעי אמר אלמנה נשאתיך או אם יהא במקום שאין מכירין אם היא אשתו יהיה נאמן לומר פרעתי הכל במגו דאי בעי אמר אין את אשתי והשתא שהכתובה בידה תוציא מאתים וכיון שיכול לבא לידי הפסד אין לו לפרוע: זאת אומרת כותבין שובר. אע"ג דהכא לא אפשר דאיכא למיחש דלמא תשרוף כתובתה בעדים והדרא וגביא בעדי הינומא כדאמרינן בסמוך ודלמא הדרא ומפקא בעדי הינומא וגביא למ"ד הטוען אחר מעשה בית דין לא אמר כלום וע"כ זקוק הוא לשובר מ"מ דייק שפיר דבעלמא נמי כותבין שובר דאי אין כותבין בעלמא למה יפרע כאן כיון שיכול לבא לידי הפסד במה שהכתובה בידה כדפירשנו:

כותבין שובר. אע"ג דבפרק גט פשוט (ב"ב קעא: ושם) מפרש טעמא דמאן דאמר כותבין שובר משום דעבד לוה לאיש מלוה לאו דוקא לוה אלא הוא הדין בכל חוב כמו כתובה דהכא ושטרי מקח דאמר התם דכותבין שובר: מאי איבדה איבדה באור. וא"ת א"כ אפי' במקום שכותבין הוה ליה לאוקמי ומאי דוחקא לאוקמי במקום שאין כותבין וכתב לה איהו ואור"ת דבמקום שכותבין ונשרפה איכא למיחש שכתב לה כתובה אחרת לאסור להשהותה בלא כתובה מיהו הוה מצי לאוקומה במקום שכותבין ונשרפה אחר הגירושין דליכא למיחש שמא כתב לה אחרת אלא שנראה לו דוחק: ותו איבדה למה לי. אף על גב דלכאורה היינו פירכא קמייתא דפריך היינו נשרפה יש ליישב דהכי קאמר ותו אפילו אם נאמר דנשרפה הוי פירושא דנאבדה מכל מקום תקשי איבדה למה לי: איתנוסי הוא דאיתניסו. נראה דמיירי כגון דאיכא מגו דאי בעיא אמרה אין בידי כלום דאי לאו הכי אמאי מהימנא ואם תאמר בחילוק קליות דאמר לקמן ארמלתא לית לה כסני אמאי לא חיישינן דלמא תפסה כו' כדאמר הכא ואומר רבינו תם דדוקא בדבר שיש טורח כגון חבית דהכא יכולה לומר דאיתניסו אבל קליות ושאר דברים שהן קלים לעשות לא:

עין משפט נר מצוה

ג א מיי' פט"ז מהלכות אישות הלכה כה סמג עשין מח טוש"ע אה"ע סימן נו סעיף טו:

ד ב מיי' פכ"ג מהלכות מלוה הלכה טו טז סמג עשין לד טוש"ע ח"מ סימן נד סעיף ב:

תוספות רי"ד

וליחוש דלמא מפקא עדי הינומא בהאי בי דינא וגביא ומפקא כתובתה או עדי הינומא בב"ד אחרינא וגביא א"ר אבהו זאת אומרת כותבין שובר פי' ולא מצי אידך למימר א"א לשמור שוברי מפני העכברים אלא או תקרע לי שטרא או לא אית לך כלום אלא פורעו בע"כ והוא כותב לו שובר ודלא כמ"ד בב"ב דאין כותבין שובר והכי אסקנא שם בג"פ [דף קעא ע"ב] דכותבין שובר: ת"ר כיצד מרקדין לפני הכלה. ב"ש אומרים

מסורת הש"ס

א) [שבת עט. לקמן נו. פט. סוטה ז: ב"ב קע: קעא:], ב) שבת עט. ב"ב קעא:, ג) מסכת דרך ארץ פ"ה.

גליון הש"ס

גמ' אי כל הנישאת. כעין זה נדה דף כט ע"א:

ליקוטי רש"י

כי אתו עדים. שיצאה בהינומא. מאי הוי. מאחר שהן עצמן אין יודעין אם ניסת בתולה או אלמנה נמצא דאין כאן קול כלל. סהדי שקרי נינהו. ולא ראוה יוצאת בהינומא. בתולה יש לה קול. מתוך שיש שמחה בנישואי בתולה מכריס בה בני אדם. איתרע לה רובא. דבתולות נישאות דרובן יש להן קול מכחיש כמו של אותו רוב וכיון דאיכא למימר הכי ואיכא למימר הכי המוציא מחבירו עליו הראיה [רשב"ם ב"ב צב:].

שהפה שאסר הוא הפה שהתיר ואם יש עדים שהיא של אביו והוא אומר לקחתיה הימנו אינו נאמן: **גמ'** טעמא [א]דאיכא עדים הא ליכא עדים בעל מהימן לימא תנן סתמא דלא כרבן גמליאל דאי ר"ג הא אמר איהי מהימנא אפילו תימא רבן גמליאל עד כאן לא קאמר ר"ג התם אלא בברי ושמא אבל הכא בברי וברי לא אמר [א] ודקארי לה מאי קארי לה הא ברי וברי הוא [ב] כיון דרוב נשים בתולות נישאות כי ברי ושמא דמי והכי נמי מסתברא מדקתני ומודה רבי יהושע אי אמרת בשלמא איירי ר"ג במודה שפיר אלא אי אמרת לא איירי ר"ג במודה רבי יהושע למאן מודה מי סברת ר' יהושע אהאי פירקין קאי אמגו קאי ואפירקין קמא קאי אהייא אילימא אהא [ג] היתה מעוברת ואמרו לה מה טיבו של עובר זה מאיש פלוני וכהן הוא ר"ג ור"א אומרים נאמנת רבי יהושע אומר לא מפיה אנו חיין התם מאי מגו איכא הרי כריסה בין שיניה אלא אהא [ד] ראוה מדברת עם אחד ואמרו לה מה טיבו של איש זה איש פלוני וכהן הוא ר"ג ור"א אומרים נאמנת רבי יהושע אומר לא מפיה אנו חיין התם מאי מגו איכא הניחא [ה] לזעירי דאמר מאי מדברת נסתרה מגו דאי בעיא אמרה לא נבעלתי וקאמרה נבעלתי מהימנא אלא לרב אסי דאמר מאי מדברת [א] נבעלת מאי מגו איכא ואלא אהא [ו] היא אומרת מוכת עץ אני והוא אומר לא כי אלא דרוסת איש את ר"ג ור"א אומרים נאמנת ורבי יהושע אומר לא מפיה אנו חיין התם מאי מגו איכא בשלמא לרבי אלעזר דאמר במנה ולא כלום מגו דאי בעיא אמרה מוכת עץ אני תחתיך ואית לה מאתים וקאמרה מעיקרא דלית לה אלא מנה מהימנא אלא לר' יוחנן דאמר במאתים ומנה מאי מגו איכא אלא אהא [ז] הנושא את האשה ולא מצא לה בתולים היא אומרת משארסתני נאנסתי ונסתחפה שדהו והוא אומר לא כי אלא עד שלא אירסתיך ר"ג ור"א אומרים נאמנת ור' יהושע אומר לא מפיה אנו חיין דמגו דאי בעיא אמרה מוכת עץ אני תחתיך דלא קא פסלה נפשה מכהונה וקאמרה נאנסתי דקא פסלה נפשה מכהונה משום הכי קאמר ר"ג דמהימנא וקאמר רבי יהושע לר"ג בהאי מגו דהכא מודינא לך בההוא מגו דהתם פליגנא עילוך מכדי האי מגו והאי מגו מאי שנא האי מגו מהאי מגו הכא אין שור שחוט לפניך התם הרי שור שחוט לפניך וכיון דרוב נשים בתולות נישאות כי לא אתו עדים מאי הוי [ח] אמר רבינא משום דאיכא למימר רוב נשים בתולות נישאות ומיעוט אלמנות וכל הנשאת בתולה יש לה קול וזו

רש"י

שהפה שאסר. זה אינו יודע שהיתה של אביו אלא על פיו של זה ומה שאסר הרי התיר: **גמ' טעמא דאיכא עדים.** דילאה בהינומא: **הבעל מהימן.** ולא אמרינן הואיל ומספקא לן על יום נישואיה אם בתולה היתה אם בעולה העמד אותה על חזקתה של קודם לכן ומתחלה בתולה היתה: **היא נאמנת.** דאזיל בתר חזקה דגופא: **בברי ושמא.** גבי משארסתני נאנסתי היא טוענת ברי לי הוא והוא אינו טוען אלא שמא עד שלא ארסתיך דהא אינו יודע מתי נאנסה: **ודקארי לה.** למימר סתמא דלא כרבן גמליאל: **מאי קארי לה.** ומאי עלה בדעתו לאפוקי מדר"ג הא לא דמיא לה: **כיון דרוב נשים בתולות נישאות.** קרובה טענתה להיות אמת יותר משלו וכברי ושמא דמיא: **והכי נמי מסתברא.** דר"ג מודה בה דבעל מהימן: **אי אמרת בשלמא איירי ר"ג במודה.** דהך רישא הודאה הוא דקא מודה ר"ג לרבי יהושע ואמר אע"ג דפליגנא עלך בברי ושמא מודינא לך בברי וברי היינו דשייך למיתני בתריה ור' יהושע מודה לר"ג בהאומר לחברו שדה זו כו' דאע"ג דפליגנא בפ"ק במשארסתני נאנסתי דאע"ג דאיכא למימר מגו לא מהימנא מודינא בהאי מגו דאי בעי שתיק ולא א"ל של אביך היתה כי אמר ליה נמי לקחתיה הימנו מהימן כדלקמן: **אלא אי אמרת לא איירי.** רישא במודה ר"ג מאי מודה רבי יהושע מאי שייך למיתנייה הכא והיכא קאי: **אמגו קאי.** אפלוגתא דאיכא למימר בה מגו בפ' קמא קאי וקאמר אע"ג דפליגנא במגו דהתם במגו דהכא מודינא כדלקמן: **אהייא.** איכא מגו: **הרי כריסה בין שיניה.** ואינה יכולה לומר לא נבעלתי: **וקאמרה נבעלתי.** ולכשר נבעלתי מהימנא: **בשלמא לר' אלעזר דאמר.** בפרק קמא טענתייהו במנה ולא כלום מוכת עץ שלא הכיר בה אינה יכולה לתובעו אלא מנה והוא אומר דרוסת איש את ואין ליך כלום איכא מגו דאי בעיא אמרה מוכת עץ אני תחתיך: [ט] **משארסתני.** אירע לי ונסתחפה שדהו ואית לי מאתים: **וקאמרה.** מוכת עץ אני מעיקרא ולא תבעה אלא מנה מהימנא: **אלא לר' יוחנן.** דאמר טענתייהו במאתי' ומנה שהיא תובעתו מאתים ליכא מידי בין תחתיו למעיקרא מאי מגו איכא: **הכא.** גבי שדה אין שור שחוט לפניך שיעלה על לב בעליו לתבוע מי שחטו כלומר אם שתק זה לא היו לו עוררים הלכך אי לאו דדבר פשוט הוא שלקחה הימנו לא היה אומר לו של אביך היתה הלכך אמרי' מגו אבל גבי לא מצא לה בתולים שור שחוט לפניך בתולים שלא מצא לה הם הסיתוהו לבא לב"ד ואע"פ שיש לה להשיב טענה טובה מזו לא אמרינן מגו דלמא לא אסקה אדעתה א"נ איערומי קא מערמא: **וכיון שרוב נשים.** קושיא היא: **יש לה קול.** והרבה יודעים שילאה בהינומא: וזו

תוספות

דאי רבן גמליאל הא אמר איהי מהימנא. נראה דלמ"ד [י] הטוען אחר מעשה ב"ד לא אמר כלום פריך דלמ"ד דמלי טוען פרעתי הכא נאמן הבעל אפילו לר"ג לומר אלמנה נשאתיך במגו דאי בעי אמר פרעתי: **הכי** נמי מסתברא. פי' בקונטרס הכי נמי מסתברא דמתני' אתיא כרבן גמליאל כדמשנינן דבברי וברי מודה מדקתני ומודה ר' יהושע כו' וקשה לפי' דכי לא איירי נמי ר"ג במודה אתי שפיר ומודה רבי יהושע כלומר אע"ג דברישא פליגנא עלך בסיפא מודינא לך אע"ג דרישא וסיפא אין מענין אחד כי היכי דאתיא ליה שפיר ומודה רבי יהושע אי איירי ר"ג במודה אע"ג דמודה דר' גמליאל אינו מענין ומודה דרבי יהושע ויש ליישב דודאי כי איירי ר"ג במודה שייך למיתני שפיר ומודה רבי יהושע אע"ג דלא הוי מענין אחד כלומר דאגב דתנא מילתא דמודה ר"ג תני נמי מילתא דמודה בה רבי יהושע אבל אי לא איירי רבן גמליאל במודה לא שייך למיתני ומודה רבי יהושע לאשמועינן אע"ג דפליג ברישא מודה בסיפא כיון דרישא וסיפא אינם מענין אחד אבל קשה דלא הוה ליה למימר אמגו קאי דעד השתא נמי לפ"ה אמגו הוי קאי ונראה לר"י דה"פ הכי נמי מסתברא דכברי ושמא דמי ולא בא לומר דפליג רבן גמליאל ברישא אלא אע"ג דכברי ושמא דמי מודה ר"ג משום דלאו שמא ממש הוא מדקאמר ומודה רבי יהושע אי אמרת בשלמא איירי ר"ג במודה כלומר אע"ג דכברי ושמא דמי מודה ר"ג דבעל נאמן היינו דקתני ומודה רבי יהושע דבהאי ברי נאמן דס"ד דטעמא דרבי יהושע משום ברי ושמא דזה אינו תובעו כדפי' בקונט' והשתא הוה מודה דר"ג ומודה דר"י מענין אחד אלא אי אמרת דרישא בברי וברי גמור הוא ולא איירי רבן גמליאל במודה דפשיטא דכיון דברי וברי הוא דלא פליג ר"ג מאי ומודה וקאמר מי סברת דארישא קאי וטעמא דר"י משום ברי ושמא אמגו קאי דטעמא דר' יהושע משום מגו ונאמן אפי' הלה תובעו ואפירקין קמא קאי: **התם** שור שחוט לפניך. פירש בקונטרס שהוא טוען עד שלא אירסתיך נאנסת והכא אין שור שחוט לפניך דאין הלה תובעו ור"י מפרש דהכא נמי איירי בהלה תובעו כדפי' וה"פ התם שור שחוט לפניך דהרי אין לה בתולים ואינה יכולה לומר בתולה אני כמו בשור שחוט שאין יכול לומר חי הוא ולהכי בין אומרת משארסתני נאנסתי בין אומרת מוכת עץ אני תחתיך לא מהימנא הכא אין שור שחוט לפניך ונאמן במגו דאי בעי אמר לא היתה של אביך מעולם: **כיון** דרוב נשים בתולות נישאות כי ליכא עדים מאי הוי. לרב פריך דאית ליה [ט] הולכין בממון אחר הרוב [ב]: וזו

מסורת הש"ס

א) כ"ב לג: [ע' פרש"י לקמן לו. ד"ה ודקארי], ב) לקמן כח., ג) לעיל יג., ד) שם, ה) [שם], ו) שם [ודף יא:], ז) לעיל יב:, ח) [כ"ב לג.], ט) [ד"ז שייך לקמן אחר ד"ה אלא לר' יוחנן ויותר טפי יש לדיבור זה שייכות לעיל יב: במשנה הנושא וכו'], י) [כ"מ יז:, כ) [ב"ק מו: כ"ב לג.].

גליון הש"ס

גמ' ודקארי לה מאי קארי לה. לקמן לו ע"א [יומא ל ע"ב] יבמות יא ע"א יד ע"א [עב ע"א] גיטין פא ע"ב קט ע"ב [שבת מז ע"ב] ב"ב ב ע"ב [יז ע"ב] קמו ע"א [בכורות ד ע"ב] נדה סד ע"א:

ליקוטי רש"י

דרוב נשים. שנשואות שנישאות לבעל בתולות הן [רשב"ם ב"ב צב:]. **ודקארי לה מאי קארי לה.** מי שהשיב תשובה זו בבית המדרש מה עלתה על רוחו בעל מהימן. בתולתה מנה, דהמשיב ששאלו מחבירו עליו הכלים [לקמן לו.]. **ראוה מדברת.** בפנויה ומשום חששא דספולין לנתין ולממזר וכיון שנבעלה לפסול פסלה מן הכהונה]. **נאמנת.** וכשרה לכהונה ולא מספקינן לה בנבעלה לפסול לה [לעיל יג.]. **וכהן הוא.** כלומר מיוחס הוא [קידושין עד.]. **נסתרה.** ולפ"ש שלא ראוה שנבעלה נפסלה לכהונה לרבי יהושע דלקמן דמעלה עשו ביוחסין [לעיל יד:]. **היא אומרת מוכת עץ אני.** הנשא את האשה בחזקת בתולה ולא מצא לה בתולים היא אומרת מוכת עץ אני כו' [לעיל יא:]. **מוכת עץ.** שתקע לה עץ במקום ההוא מקום [לעיל יא.]. **דרוסת איש.** קודם שארסתיך [לעיל יב.]. **ונסתחפה שדהו.** לשון מטר סוחף (משלי כח) נשטפה שדך כלומר מזלך גרם [לעיל ב.]. **נסחף.** נשטפו והחליקו גבוליך כמו מטר סוחף (משלי כח) נסתחפה שדהו בלשון משנה ומנסח חברו לשון כליון וכן תבר מטר סוחף ודוגמ פתר מטר סוחף כמו מטר סוחף כמו מטפף פלה במערלה (ישעיה י) [ירמיה מו, טו]. **סוחף.** שוטף ובמשנה נסחפה שדהו וכן נסחף אביריך (ירמיה מו) נשטפו ומעדו וכשלו [משלי כח, ג]. מזלך גרס כאדם שמטר בא וסוחף את זריעתו ועוקרה [לעיל יא:]. **ומיעוט אלמנות.** חז איכא למימר דמן המיעוט היא הואיל ואין לה קול כדמפרש ואזיל [רשב"ם ב"ב שם].

עין משפט נר מצוה

ב א מיי' פט"ז מהלכות אישות הלכה כה סמג עשין מח טוש"ע אה"ע סימן לו סעיף טו:

תוספות רי"ד

מיתמי גובה בלא כתובה **ודייקינן** טעמא דאיכא עדים פי' שיצאת בהינומא וראשה פרוע הא ליכא עדים בעל מהימן פי' ולא אמרינן הואיל ומספקא לן על יום נשואיה אם היתה בעולה או בתולה העמד אותה על חזקתה של קודם לכן ובתולה היתה לימא תנן סתמא דלא כר"ג דאי ר"ג האמר איהי מהימנא פי' דאזיל בתר חזקה דגופה וה"נ נימא העמד אשה על חזקתה ובתולה היתה ומהדר אפילו תימא ר"ג ע"כ לא קאמר ר"ג אלא ברי ושמא אבל ברי וברי לא אמר עיין בפ"ק. **ודקארי לה מאי קארי לה.** כיון דרוב נשים בתולות נשאות כברי ושמא דמי. וכיון דרוב נשים בתולות נשאות כי לא אתי עדי הינומא מאי הוה ניזיל בתר רובא. פי' ואע"ג דיש פלוגתא בהא מילתא רב ושמואל בפרק המוכר פירות דרב אמר הולכין בממון אחר הרוב ושמואל אמר אין הולכין בממון אחר הרוב וקי"ל הלכה כשמואל הכא משום דאיכא תרתי רובא וחזקה העמד אשה על חזקתה ובתולה היתה אפי' שמואל מודה. **אמר רבינא** משום דא"ל דרוב נשים בתולות נשאות ומיעוט אלמנות ורוב הנשאת בתולה יש לה קול וזו הואיל ואין לה קול איתרע לה רובא:

תוספות ישנים

א) אע"ג דאיתותב כו' מ"מ בעי נמי לשנויי מתני' אליביה. מ"י.

ב) אפשר דאפילו לשמואל הוי לן למיזל בתר רובא ולא אחר חזקת ממון כיון דחזקת הגוף מסייע לרוב ופריך שפיר אפילו אליביה דשמואל קאי אמאי דאמרינן לעיל כיון דרוב נשים בתולות נישאות הוי ליה ברי דידיה כי שמא וכברי ושמא פסק שמואל כר"ג הכא דמהני לה חזקת הגוף למד לישנא דפ"ק דהכי פריך וניזיל בתר רובא דס"ד דהוי רוב גמור. מ"י.

עֵץ אֲנִי תַּחְתֶּיךָ וְאִית לָהּ מָאתַיִם – Accordingly, we can say that **since had she wanted** to lie **she could have said, "I became a wood-injury victim while under you"** [i.e. after you betrothed me], **by which** claim **she would** be entitled to **receive** a *kesubah* of **two hundred** *zuz*,[20] וְקָאָמְרָה מֵעִיקָּרָא דְּלֵית לָהּ אֶלָּא מָנֶה מְהֵימְנָא – **when she says** it happened **before** the betrothal, **by which** claim **she receives only a *maneh*, she should be believed.** אֶלָּא לְרַבִּי יוֹחָנָן דְּאָמַר בְּמָאתַיִם וּמָנֶה – **But according to R' Yochanan, who says** that the Mishnah is dealing **with** a bride who claims a *kesubah* of **two hundred** *zuz* **and** a groom who agrees to pay only **a *maneh*,** מַאי מִגּוֹ אִיכָּא – **what *migo* is there?**[21]

The Gemara identifies the case to which R' Yehoshua refers: אֶלָּא אַהָא – **Rather,** he refers **to the following** Mishnah:[22] הַנּוֹשֵׂא אֶת הָאִשָּׁה וְלֹא מָצָא לָהּ בְּתוּלִים – Consider the case of ONE WHO MARRIES A WOMAN AND DOES NOT FIND HER TO POSSESS signs of VIRGINITY. הִיא אוֹמֶרֶת מִשֶּׁאֵרַסְתַּנִי נֶאֱנַסְתִּי וְנִסְתַּחְפָה שָׂדֵהוּ – SHE SAYS, "AFTER YOU BETROTHED ME I WAS VIOLATED, AND this is a case of '[THE BUYER'S] FIELD WAS INUNDATED,' " וְהוּא אוֹמֵר לֹא כִּי אֶלָּא עַד שֶׁלֹּא אֵירַסְתִּיךְ – WHILE HE SAYS, "NOT SO, RATHER it happened BEFORE I BETROTHED YOU." רַבָּן גַּמְלִיאֵל וְרַבִּי אֱלִיעֶזֶר אוֹמְרִים נֶאֱמֶנֶת – RABBAN GAMLIEL AND R' ELIEZER SAY: SHE IS BELIEVED. וְרַבִּי יְהוֹשֻׁעַ אוֹמֵר לֹא מִפִּיהָ אָנוּ חַיִּין – R' YEHOSHUA, HOWEVER, SAYS: NOT BY HER MOUTH DO WE LIVE. דְּמִגּוֹ דְּאִי בָּעְיָא אָמְרָה מוּכַּת עֵץ אֲנִי תַּחְתֶּיךָ – In that case a *migo* argument bolsters the woman's claim, **for since had she wanted** to lie **she could have said, "I became a wood-injury victim while under you,"** דְּלָא קָא פָּסְלָה נַפְשָׁהּ מִכְּהוּנָּה – **by which** claim **she would not have disqualified herself from Kehunah;** וְקָאָמְרָה נֶאֱנַסְתִּי דְּקָא פָּסְלָה נַפְשָׁהּ מִכְּהוּנָּה – **when she** instead **says, "I was violated," by which** claim **she disqualifies herself from Kehunah,**[23] מִשּׁוּם הָכִי קָאָמַר רַבָּן גַּמְלִיאֵל דִּמְהֵימְנָא – **she is believed according to Rabban Gamliel.** וְקָאָמַר רַבִּי יְהוֹשֻׁעַ לְרַבָּן גַּמְלִיאֵל – **And R' Yehoshua said to Rabban Gamliel:** בְּהַאי מִגּוֹ דְּהָכָא מוֹדִינָא לָךְ – **Concerning this *migo* here** [i.e. in our Mishnah, regarding the field] **I admit to you,** בְּהַהוּא מִגּוֹ דְּהָתָם פְּלִיגְנָא עִילָוָיךְ – but **concerning that *migo* there I dispute you.**

Having discovered the Mishnah in which R' Yehoshua does not accept a *migo* argument, the Gemara now asks why R' Yehoshua in fact accepts the *migo* in our Mishnah:

מִכְּדִי – **Now,** let us see. הַאי מִגּוֹ וְהַאי מִגּוֹ – **This is a *migo* and that is a *migo*.** מַאי שְׁנָא הַאי מִגּוֹ מֵהַאי מִגּוֹ – **How is this *migo* different from that *migo*?**

The Gemara answers:

הָכָא אֵין שׁוֹר שָׁחוּט לְפָנֶיךָ – **Here,** in the case of the field, **there is no slaughtered ox before you,** הָתָם הֲרֵי שׁוֹר שָׁחוּט לְפָנֶיךָ – whereas **there,** in the case of the wife, **there is a slaughtered ox before you.**[24]

The Gemara questions the ruling of our Mishnah:

וְכֵיוָן דְּרוֹב נָשִׁים בְּתוּלוֹת נִישָּׂאוֹת – **But since the majority of women marry as virgins,** כִּי לֹא אָתוּ עֵדִים מַאי הָוֵי – then **even if no witnesses come, what of it?** We should still assume that she was a virgin.[25] – ? –

The Gemara answers:

אָמַר רָבִינָא – **Ravina said:** מִשּׁוּם דְּאִיכָּא לְמֵימַר רוֹב נָשִׁים בְּתוּלוֹת נִישָּׂאוֹת – **For it is possible to say** that while it is true that **a majority of women marry as virgins,** וּמִיעוּט אַלְמָנוֹת – **and** only **a minority as widows,** וְכָל הַנִּשֵּׂאת בְּתוּלָה יֵשׁ לָהּ קוֹל – **but** it is also true that **when any woman marries as a virgin, it is a** matter of **public knowledge.**[26]

NOTES

discovers that she is a wood-injury victim is required to give her only a *maneh*. Hence, the woman in that Mishnah must be claiming that she is entitled to a *maneh*, while the husband counters that she cohabited with a man and is entitled to no *kesubah* at all (*Rashi*).

20. [For having married her before the injury occurred, the husband would have to bear the loss (*Rashi;* see *Rashash*).]

21. According to R' Yochanan a wood injury is not considered a significant enough blemish to reduce a woman's *kesubah*. Hence, since there is no difference if she claims that she was injured before or after *erusin*, her claim is not bolstered by a *migo* (*Rashi*).

22. Above, 12b.

23. As stated numerous times in Chapter One, a woman who cohabits with anyone not fit for her becomes disqualified from marrying a Kohen. Thus, if she was violated when she was married, she would become prohibited to a Kohen.

24. "A slaughtered ox before you" is a metaphor for a situation in which there are grounds for a claim. When a man discovers his ox slaughtered, he is moved to investigate who slaughtered it. On the other hand, if he makes no such discovery, he has no reason to initiate a claim against anyone.

Thus, in the case of the field, if the present occupant had kept quiet, no one would have lodged a complaint against him ("there is no slaughtered ox before you"). We can therefore assume that if it was not true beyond a shadow of a doubt that he purchased the field, he would not have told the son that it had belonged to his father. Such a *migo* — called *happeh she'assar* in the Mishnah — is valid even according to R' Yehoshua. This is as opposed to the case of the Mishnah on 12b, where it was not the bride who raised the issue. Rather, it was the husband's failure to find evidence of his bride's virginity that motivated him to come to court and initiate the proceeding ("there is a slaughtered ox before you"). Accordingly, even though she could have defended her position better than she actually did, she is not believed, for perhaps she simply did not think of the better claim, or perhaps she purposely made the weaker claim so as to make her claim seem more believable (*Rashi*).

[The above is *Rashi's* understanding of the Gemara's answer, in line with his understanding of *happeh she'assar* as elaborated in note 1. As explained there, however, *Tosafos* maintain that R' Yehoshua accords the defendant believability even where the plaintiff initiated the case. *Tosafos,* therefore, explain the Gemara's answer differently, as follows.

In the case of the field, the claimant has no basis for his claim against the defendant ("there is no slaughtered ox before you"), because he does not have proof that the field was ever his father's. Thus although the defendant admits that the field indeed belonged to the claimant's father, he is believed with a *migo* that he could have denied this fact. To such a *migo* R' Yehoshua subscribes, since the other claim that the defendant could have made would have *won* the case for him. This is in contrast to the case of the Mishnah on 12b, where the husband has solid grounds for his claim — the fact that he found the wife not to possess signs of virginity. She, in turn, has no claim by which she could have won the case, for she cannot deny the fact that she did not possess signs of virginity, just as one before whom an ox lies slaughtered cannot claim that the ox is alive. Her entire "*migo*" when claiming that she was violated after *erusin* is the fact that she could have made *the more advantageous claim* that she had been injured by a piece of wood (since that claim would not render her forbidden to a Kohen as does her present one). R' Yehoshua does not subscribe to a *migo* of a mere more advantageous claim. See also 13a note 24.

25. Therefore, why does the Mishnah require her to find witnesses who can attest to her having come out with a *hinuma*?

This question is asked according to the opinion of Rav, who holds (*Bava Basra* 92b) that we follow the majority even regarding monetary matters [הוֹלְכִין בְּמָמוֹן אַחַר הָרוֹב]. However according to Shmuel, who holds (there) that we do not exact money from its current owner based on a majority [אֵין הוֹלְכִין בְּמָמוֹן אַחַר הָרוֹב] (which is the opinion accepted as law — see *Choshen Mishpat* 232:23), the Gemara has no question (*Tosafos,* from *Bava Basra* ibid.; see *Tos. Yeshanim* and *Baal HaMaor* for an alternative explanation, and see also *Milchamos Hashem*).

26. Literally: she has a voice. Many people know that she went out with a *hinuma* (*Rashi*).

Because the marriage of a virgin is an exceptionally joyous event [in contrast to a widow's wedding, which is generally lowkeyed], the fact of her virgin marriage is remembered by people for a long time (*Rashbam* to *Bava Basra* 92b ד״ה יש לה קול).

שהפה שאסר הוא הפה שהתיר ואם יש עדים שהיא של אביו והוא אומר לקחתיה הימנו אינו נאמן: גמ' טעמא דאיכא עדים הא ליכא עדים בעל מהימן לימא תנן סתמא דלא כרבן גמליאל דאי ר"ג הא אמר איהי מהימנא אפילו תימא רבן גמליאל עד כאן לא קאמר ר"ג התם אלא בברי ושמא אבל הכא בברי וברי לא אמר ודקארי לה מאי קארי לה הא ברי וברי הוא כיון דרוב נשים בתולות נישאות כי ברי ושמא דמי והכי נמי מסתברא מדקתני ומודה רבי יהושע אי אמרת בשלמא איירי ר"ג במודה שפיר אלא אי אמרת לא איירי ר"ג במודה רבי יהושע למאן מודה מי סברת ר' יהושע אהאי פירקין קאי אמגו קאי ואפירקין קמא קאי אהייא אילימא אהא היתה מעוברת ואמרו לה מה טיבו של עובר זה מאיש פלוני וכהן הוא ר"ג ור"א אומרים נאמנת רבי יהושע אומר לא מפיה אנו חיין התם מאי מגו איכא הרי כריסה בין שיניה אלא אהא ראוה מדברת עם אחד ואמרו לה מה טיבו של איש זה איש פלוני וכהן הוא ר"ג ור"א אומרים נאמנת רבי יהושע אומר לא מפיה אנו חיין התם מאי מגו איכא הניחא לזעירי דאמר מאי מדברת נסתרה מגו דאי בעיא אמרה לא נבעלתי וקאמרה נבעלתי מהימנא אלא לרב אסי דאמר מאי מדברת נבעלת מאי מגו איכא ואלא אהא היא אומרת מוכת עץ אני והוא אומר לא כי אלא דרוסת איש את ר"ג ור"א אומרים נאמנת ורבי יהושע אומר לא מפיה אנו חיין התם מאי מגו איכא בשלמא לרבי אלעזר דאמר במנה ולא כלום מגו דאי בעיא אמרה מוכת עץ אני תחתיך ואית לה מאתים וקאמרה מעיקרא דלית לה אלא מנה מהימנא אלא לר' יוחנן דאמר במאתים ומנה מאי מגו איכא אלא אהא הנושא את האשה ולא מצא לה בתולים היא אומרת משארסתני נאנסתי ונסתחפה שדהו והוא אומר לא כי אלא עד שלא אירסתיך ר"ג ור"א אומרים נאמנת ור' יהושע אומר לא מפיה אנו חיין דמגו דאי בעיא אמרה מוכת עץ אני תחתיך דלא קא פסלה נפשה מכהונה וקאמרה נאנסתי דקא פסלה נפשה מכהונה משום הכי קאמר ר"ג דמהימנא וקאמר רבי יהושע לר"ג בהאי מגו דהכא מודינא לך בההוא מגו דהתם פליגנא עילוך מכדי האי מגו והאי מגו מאי שנא האי מגו מהאי מגו הכא אין שור שחוט לפניך התם הרי שור שחוט לפניך וכיון דרוב נשים בתולות נישאות כי לא אתו עדים מאי הוי אמר רבינא משום דאיכא למימר רוב נשים בתולות נישאות ומיעוט אלמנות וכל הנשאת בתולה יש לה קול וזו

רש"י

שהפה שאסר. זה אינו יודע שהיתה של אביו אלא על פיו של זה ומה שאסר הרי התיר: גמ' טעמא דאיכא עדים. דילתה בהינומא: הבעל מהימן. ולא אמרינן הואיל ומספקא לן על יום נישואיה אם בעולה היתה אם בתולה העמד אותה על חזקתה של קודם לכן ומתחלה בתולה היתה: היא נאמנת. דאזיל בתר חזקה דגופה: בברי ושמא. גבי משארסתני נאנסתי היא טוענת ברי לי הוא והוא אינו טוען אלא שמא עד שלא ארסתיך דהא אינו יודע מתי נאנסה: ודקארי לה. למימר סתמא דלא כרבן גמליאל: מאי קארי לה. ומאי עלה בדעתו לאפוקי מדר"ג הא לא דמיא לה: כיון דרוב נשים בתולות נישאות. קרובה טענתה להיות אמת יותר משלו וכברי ושמא דמיא: והכי נמי מסתברא. דר"ג מודה בה דבעל מהימן: אי אמרת בשלמא איירי ר"ג במודה. הכך רישא הודאה הוא דקא מודה ר"ג לרבי יהושע ואמר אע"ג דפליגנא עלך בברי ושמא מודינא לך בברי וברי היינו דשייך למיתני בתריה ור' יהושע מודה לר"ג בהאומר לחברו שדה זו כו' דאע"ג דפליגנא בפ"ק במשארסתני נאנסתי דאע"ג דליכא למימר מגו לא מהימנא מודינא בהאי מגו דהכא דלא בעי שתיק ולא א"ל של אביך היתה כי אמר ליה נמי לקחתיה הימנו מהימן כדלקמן: אלא אי אמרת לא איירי. ר"ג במודה ר"ג מאי מודה רבי יהושע מאי שייך למיתנייה הכא והיכא קאי: אמגו קאי. אפלוגתא דליכא למימר בה מגו בפ' קמא קאי וקאמר אע"ג דפליגנא במגו דהתם במגו דהכא מודינא כדלקמן: אהייא. איכא מגו: הרי כריסה בין שיניה. ואינה יכולה לומר לא נבעלתי: נסתרה. ולא נבעלתי: וקאמרה נבעלתי. ולכשר נבעלתי מהימנא: בשלמא לר' אלעזר דאמר. בפרק קמא טענתייהו במנה ולא כלום מוכת עץ שלא הכיר בה אינה יכולה לתובעו אלא מנה והוא אומר דרוסת איש את ואין ליך כלום איכא מגו דאי בעיא אמרה מוכת עץ אני תחתיך: משארסתני. אירע לי ונסתחפה שדהו ואית לי מאתים: וקאמרה. מוכת עץ אני מעיקרא ולא תבעה אלא מנה מהימנא: אלא לר' יוחנן. דאמר טענתייהו במאתי' ומנה שהיא תובעתו מאתים ליכא מידי בין תחתיו למעיקרא מאי מגו איכא: הכא. גבי שדה אין שור שחוט לפניך שיעלה על לב בעליו לתבוע מי שחטו כלומר אם שתק זה לא היו לו עוררים הלכך אי לאו דדבר פשוט הוא שלקחה הימנו לא היה אומר לו של אביך היתה הלכך אמרי' מגו אבל גבי לא מצא לה בתולים שור שחוט לפניך בתולים שלא מצא לה הם הסיתוהו לבא לב"ד ואע"פ שיש לה להשיב טענה טובה מזו לא אמרינן מגו דדלמא לא אסקה אדעתה א"נ איערומי קא מערמא: וכיון שרוב נשים. קושיא היא: יש לה קול. והרבה יודעים שילאה בהינומא: וזו

תוספות

דאי רבן גמליאל הא אמר איהי מהימנא. נראה דלמ"ד הטוען אחר מעשה ב"ד לא אמר כלום פריך דלמ"ד דמצי טוען פרעתי הכא נאמן הבעל אפילו לר"ג לומר אלמנה נשאתיך במגו דאי בעי אמר פרעתי: הכי נמי מסתברא. פי' בקונטרס הכי נמי מסתברא דמתני' אתיא כרבן גמליאל כדמשנינן דבברי וברי מודה מדקתני ומודה ר' יהושע כו' וקשה לפי' דכי לא איירי נמי ר"ג במודה אתי שפיר ומודה רבי יהושע כלומר אע"ג דברישא פליגנא עלך בסיפא מודינא לך אע"ג דרישא וסיפא אינן מענין אחד כי היכי דאתיא ליה שפיר ומודה רבי יהושע אי איירי ר"ג במודה אע"ג דמודה דר' גמליאל אינו מענין ומודה דרבי יהושע ויש ליישב דודאי כי איירי ר"ג במודה שייך למיתני שפיר ומודה רבי יהושע אע"ג דלא הוי מענין אחד כלומר דאגב דתנא מילתא דמודה ר"ג תני נמי מילתא דמודה בה רבי יהושע אבל אי לא איירי רבן גמליאל במודה לא שייך למיתני ומודה רבי יהושע לאשמועינן אע"ג דפליג ברישא מודה בסיפא כיון דרישא וסיפא אינם מענין אחד אבל קשה דלא הוה ליה למימר אמגו קאי דעד השתא נמי לפ"ה אמגו הוי קאי ונראה לר"י דה"פ הכי נמי מסתברא דכברי ושמא דמי ולא בא לומר דפליג רבן גמליאל ברישא אלא אע"ג דכברי ושמא דמי מודה ר"ג משום דלאו שמא ממש הוא מדקאמר ומודה רבי יהושע אי אמרת בשלמא איירי ר"ג במודה כלומר אע"ג דכברי ושמא דמי מודה ר"ג דבעל נאמן היינו דקתני ומודה רבי יהושע דבהאי ברי נאמן דס"ד דטעמא דרבי יהושע משום ברי ושמא דזה אינו תובעו כדפי' בקונט' והשתא הוה מודה דר"ג ומודה דר"י מענין אחד אלא אי אמרת דרישא בברי וברי גמור הוא ולא איירי רבן גמליאל במודה דפשיטא דכיון דברי וברי הוא דלא פליג ר"ג מאי ומודה וקאמר מי סברת דארישא קאי וטעמא דר"י משום ברי ושמא אמגו קאי דטעמא דר' יהושע משום מגו ונאמן אפי' הלה תובעו ואפירקין קמא קאי:

התם שור שחוט לפניך. פירש בקונטרס שהוא טוען עד שלא אירסתיך נאנסת והכא אין שור שחוט לפניך דאין הלה תובעו ור"י מפרש דהכא נמי איירי בהלה תובעו כדפי' וה"פ התם שור שחוט לפניך דהרי אין לה בתולים ואינה יכולה לומר בתולה אני כמו בשור שחוט שאין יכול לומר חי הוא ולהכי בין אומרת משארסתני נאנסתי בין אומרת מוכת עץ אני תחתיך לא מהימנא הכא אין שור שחוט לפניך ונאמן במגו דאי בעי אמר לא היתה של אביך מעולם:

כיון דרוב נשים בתולות נישאות כי ליכא עדים מאי הוי. לרב פריך דאית ליה הולכין בממון אחר הרוב ב):

וזו

ב א מיי' פט"ז מהלכות אישות הלכה כה סמג עשין מח טוש"ע אה"ע סימן נו סעיף טו:

תוספות רי"ד

מיתמי גובה בלא כתובה ודייקינן טעמא דאיכא עדים פי' שיצאת בהינומא וראשה פרוע הא ליכא עדים בעל מהימן פי' ולא אמרינן הואיל ומספקא לן על יום נשואיה אם היתה בעולה או בתולה העמד אותה על חזקתה של קודם לכן ובתולה היתה לימא תנן סתמא דלא כר"ג דאי ר"ג האמר איהי מהימנא פי' דאזיל בתר חזקה דגופה וה"נ נימא העמד אשה על חזקתה ובתולה היתה ומהדר אפילו תימא ר"ג ע"כ לא קאמר ר"ג אלא ברי ושמא אבל ברי וברי לא אמר עיין בפ"ק. ודקארי לה מאי קארי לה. כיון דרוב נשים בתולות נשאות כברי ושמא דמי. וכיון דרוב נשים בתולות נשאות כי לא אתי עדי הינומא מאי הוה ניזיל בתר רובא. פי' ואע"ג דיש פלוגתא בהא מילתא רב ושמואל בפרק המוכר פירות דרב אמר הולכין בממון אחר הרוב ושמואל אמר אין הולכין בממון אחר הרוב וקי"ל הלכה כשמואל הכא משום דאיכא תרתי רובא וחזקה העמד אשה על חזקתה ובתולה היתה אפי' שמואל מודה. אמר רבינא משום דא"ל דרוב נשים בתולות נשאות ומיעוט אלמנות ורוב הנשאת בתולה יש לה קול וזו הואיל ואין לה קול איתרע לה רובא:

תוספות ישנים

א) אע"ג דאיתותב כו' מ"מ בעי נמי לשנויי מתני' אליביה. ת"י.

ב) אפשר דאפילו לשמואל הוה לן למיזל בתר רובא ולא אחר חזקת ממון כיון דחזקת הגוף מסייע לרוב ופריך שפיר אפילו אליביה דשמואל קאי אמאי דאמרינן לעיל כיון דרוב נשים בתולות נישאות הוי ליה ברי דידיה כי שמא ובברי ושמא פסק שמואל כר"ג הכא דמהני לה חזקת הגוף לחד לישנא דפ"ק להכי פריך וניזיל בתר רובא דס"ד דהוי רוב גמור. ת"י.

א) ב"ב לב: [עי' פרש"י לקמן לו. ד"ה ודקארי], ב) לקמן כח., ג) לעיל יג., ד) שם, ה) [שם], ו) שם [ודף יא:], ז) לעיל יב:, ח) [ב"ב לב:], ט) [ד"ז שייך לקמן אחר ד"ה אלא לר' יוחנן ויותר טפי יש לדיבור זה שייכות לעיל יב: במשנה הנושא וכו'], י) [ב"מ יז.], כ) [ב"ק מו: ב"ב לב:].

גליון הש"ס

גמ' ודקארי לה מאי קארי לה. לקמן לו ע"א [יומא ל ע"ב] יבמות יא ע"א יד ע"א [עב ע"א] גיטין סא ע"ב ב"ק מז ע"ב] ב"ב ב ע"ב [יז ע"ב] קמז ע"א [בכורות ד ע"ב] נדה סד ע"א:

ליקוטי רש"י

דרוב נשים. שבעולם שנישאות לבעל בתולות הן [רשב"ם ב"ב צב:]. ודקארי לה מאי קארי לה. מי שהשיב תשובה זו בבית המדרש מה עלתה על רוחו בעל מהימן. כתובתה מנה, דהמוציא מחבירו עליו הראיה. [לקמן לו.]. ראוה מדברת. [בפנויה ומשום חששא דפסולין לנתין ולממזר וכיון שנבעלה לפסול פסלה מן הכהונה]. נאמנת. וכשרה לכהונה ולא מספקינן לה בנבעלה לפסול לה [לעיל יג.]. וכהן הוא. כלומר מיוחס הוא [קידושין עד.]. נסתרה. ואע"פ שלא ראוה שנבעלה נפסלה לכהונה לרבי יהושע כדלקמן דמעלה עשו ביוחסין [לעיל שם]. היא אומרת מוכת עץ אני. הנושא את האשה בחזקת בתולה ולא מצא לה בתולים היא אומרת מוכת עץ אני כו' [לעיל יא:]. מוכת עץ. שנתקע לה עץ באותו מקום [לעיל יא.]. דרוסת איש. קודם שארסתיך [לעיל יג.]. ונסתחפה שדהו. לשון מטר סוחף (משלי כח) נשטפה שדך כלומר מזלך גרם [לעיל ב.]. נסחף, נשטפו והחליקו גבוריך כמו מטר סוחף (משלי כח) נסתחפה שדהו בלשון משנה ומנחם חברו לשון כליון וכן חבר מטר סוחף ודונש פתר מטר סוחף כמו מטר סועף כמו מסעף פארה במערצה (ישעיה י) [ירמיה מו, טו]. סוחף, שוטף ובמשנה נסתחפה שדהו וכן נסחף אביריך (ירמיה מו) נשטפו ומעדו וכשלו [משלי כח, ג]. מזלך גרם כאדם שהמטר בא וסוחף את זריעתו ועוקרה [לעיל יא:]. ומיעוט אלמנות. וזו איכא למימר דמן המיעוט היא הואיל ואין לה קול כדמפרש ואזיל [רשב"ם ב"ב שם].

admits to R' Yehoshua, שַׁפִּיר – for it is then **fitting** that the Mishnah afterwards states a case wherein R' Yehoshua admits to Rabban Gamliel.[9] אֶלָּא אִי אָמְרַתְּ לֹא אַיְירֵי רַבָּן גַּמְלִיאֵל בְּמוֹדֶה – **But if you say** that in the first section of the Mishnah **Rabban Gamliel was not discussing** a case **where he admits** to R' Yehoshua, רַבִּי יְהוֹשֻׁעַ לְמַאן מוֹדֶה – **to whom is R' Yehoshua admitting** in the last half of the Mishnah?[10]

The Gemara rejects this proof:

מִי סָבְרַתְּ רַבִּי יְהוֹשֻׁעַ אַהָאי פִּירְקִין קָאֵי – **Do you think that R' Yehoshua is referring to** a statement of Rabban Gamliel in **this chapter?** אַמִּגּוֹ קָאֵי – No, **he is referring to a** *migo* argument, וְאַפִּירְקִין קַמָּא קָאֵי – **and is referring to the first chapter.**[11]

Before explaining why R' Yehoshua accepts the *migo* in the case of our Mishnah, the Gemara first seeks to find where in the first chapter R' Yehoshua rejects a *migo* argument:

אַהֵייָא – **To which** case of the previous chapter is R' Yehoshua referring?

The Gemara suggests and rejects one possibility:

אִילֵימָא אַהָא – **Perhaps you will say** he refers **to the following** Mishnah:[12] הָיְתָה מְעוּבֶּרֶת – [AN UNMARRIED WOMAN] WAS PREGNANT, וְאָמְרוּ לָהּ מַה טִּיבוֹ שֶׁל עוּבָּר זֶה – AND [THE COURT] SAID TO HER, "WHAT IS THE NATURE OF THIS FETUS?" מֵאִישׁ פְּלוֹנִי וְכֹהֵן הוּא – and she replied, "It was fathered BY SO-AND-SO, AND HE IS A KOHEN [i.e. one of untainted lineage]." רַבָּן גַּמְלִיאֵל וְרַבִּי אֱלִיעֶזֶר אוֹמְרִים נֶאֱמֶנֶת – RABBAN GAMLIEL AND R' ELIEZER SAY: SHE IS BELIEVED. רַבִּי יְהוֹשֻׁעַ אוֹמֵר לֹא מִפִּיהָ אָנוּ חַיִּין – R' YEHOSHUA, however, SAYS: NOT BY HER MOUTH DO WE LIVE [i.e. she is not believed]. הָתָם מַאי מִגּוֹ אִיכָּא – But this cannot be the Mishnah to which R' Yehoshua refers, for **what** *migo* **is there in that** case? הֲרֵי כְּרֵיסָהּ בֵּין שִׁינֶּיהָ – **Why, her stomach is between her teeth!**[13] – ? –

The Gemara suggests and rejects another case from the previous chapter:

אֶלָּא אַהָא – **Rather,** perhaps R' Yehoshua refers **to the following** Mishnah:[14] רָאוּהָ מְדַבֶּרֶת עִם אֶחָד – THEY [the court] SAW [AN UNMARRIED WOMAN] SPEAKING WITH SOMEONE, וְאָמְרוּ לָהּ מַה טִּיבוֹ שֶׁל אִישׁ זֶה – AND SAID TO HER, "WHAT IS THE NATURE OF THIS MAN?" אִישׁ פְּלוֹנִי וְכֹהֵן הוּא – and she replied, "HE IS SO-AND-SO, AND HE IS A KOHEN." רַבָּן גַּמְלִיאֵל וְרַבִּי אֱלִיעֶזֶר אוֹמְרִים נֶאֱמֶנֶת – RABBAN GAMLIEL AND R' ELIEZER SAY: SHE IS BELIEVED. רַבִּי יְהוֹשֻׁעַ אוֹמֵר לֹא מִפִּיהָ אָנוּ חַיִּין – R' YEHOSHUA, however, SAYS: NOT BY HER MOUTH DO WE LIVE [i.e. she is not believed]. הָתָם מַאי מִגּוֹ אִיכָּא – But that too cannot be the case, for **what** *migo* **is there in that** case as well? הָנִיחָא לִזְעִירִי דְּאָמַר מַאי מְדַבֶּרֶת נִסְתְּרָה – **It is understandable according to Zeiri who says** that **"she was speaking" means** that **she was secluded.**[15] מִגּוֹ דְּאִי בָּעֲיָא אָמְרָה לֹא נִבְעַלְתִּי – Accordingly, we can say that **since had she wished** to lie **she could have said, "I did not cohabit,"** וְקָאָמְרָה נִבְעַלְתִּי מְהֵימְנָא – **when she says** instead, **"I cohabited** with a Kohen," **she should be believed.**[16] אֶלָּא לְרַב אַסִּי דְּאָמַר מַאי מְדַבֶּרֶת נִבְעֶלֶת – **But according to Rav Assi who says** that **"she was speaking" means** that **she cohabited,** מַאי מִגּוֹ אִיכָּא – **what** *migo* **is there?**[17]

The Gemara attempts and rejects a third suggestion:

וְאֶלָּא אַהָא – **Rather,** perhaps R' Yehoshua refers **to the following** Mishnah:[18] הִיא אוֹמֶרֶת מוּכַּת עֵץ אֲנִי – SHE SAYS, "I AM A WOOD-INJURY VICTIM," וְהוּא אוֹמֵר לֹא כִּי אֶלָּא דְּרוּסַת אִישׁ אַתְּ – AND HE SAYS, "Perhaps it is NOT SO, RATHER YOU WERE DEFLOWERED BY A MAN." רַבָּן גַּמְלִיאֵל וְרַבִּי אֱלִיעֶזֶר אוֹמְרִים נֶאֱמֶנֶת – RABBAN GAMLIEL AND R' ELIEZER SAY: SHE IS BELIEVED. וְרַבִּי יְהוֹשֻׁעַ אוֹמֵר לֹא מִפִּיהָ אָנוּ חַיִּין – R' YEHOSHUA, HOWEVER, SAYS: NOT BY HER MOUTH DO WE LIVE. הָתָם מַאי מִגּוֹ אִיכָּא – But that also cannot be the sought-after case, for **what** *migo* **is there in that** case as well? בִּשְׁלָמָא לְרַבִּי אֶלְעָזָר דְּאָמַר בְּמָנֶה וְלֹא כְּלוּם – **It is understandable according to R' Elazar, who says** that that Mishnah deals **with** a bride who claims **a** *maneh* **and** a groom who does **not** want to pay anything **at all.**[19] מִגּוֹ דְּאִי בָּעֲיָא אָמְרָה מוּכַּת

NOTES

9. In the first part of the Mishnah Rabban Gamliel tells R' Yehoshua, "Even though I disagree with you in a case in which the plaintiff is certain of his claim and the defendant can claim only 'perhaps,' I agree with you that if both parties are certain of their claims the defendant wins." Then the second part of the Mishnah describes a case in which R' Yehoshua, in turn, agrees with Rabban Gamliel. R' Yehoshua states, "Though I disagree with you in the first chapter and maintain that the woman is not believed even though her claim is bolstered by a *migo* (the Gemara will identify shortly the *migo* to which R' Yehoshua refers), I agree with you in the case of our Mishnah – where the plaintiff has a *migo* that he could have remained silent and not admitted that the field had belonged to the defendant's father – that the plaintiff's claim that he purchased the field is believed" (*Rashi*).

10. If Rabban Gamliel does not agree to the first ruling of our Mishnah, how can the Mishnah continue that R' Yehoshua agrees with Rabban Gamliel? How does such a statement belong in our Mishnah, and to what does it refer? (*Rashi*).

11. R' Yehoshua is thus saying that even though he disagrees with Rabban Gamliel about a *migo* argument in the previous chapter, he accepts the *migo* in this Mishnah.

[Although the Gemara was originally also willing to accept that R' Yehoshua referred to a *migo* argument in the first chapter, that was provided that the first part of the Mishnah was understood to be stating that Rabban Gamliel admits to R' Yehoshua also in regard to a point discussed in the first chapter. In that case we can say that our chapter is simply a continuation of the discussion of the dispute between Rabban Gamliel and R' Yehoshua mentioned in the first chapter. But if we say that the first part of our Mishnah is not Rabban Gamliel admitting to R' Yehoshua, but is rather an anonymous Mishnah formulated in accordance with R' Yehoshua, then the discussion of the dispute of Rabban Gamliel and R' Yehoshua was already concluded in the first chapter. It then seemed to the Gemara to be out of place for our Mishnah to suddenly record, in its second half, an admission of R' Yehoshua in regard to that dispute. The Gemara answers that, nevertheless, this may be the Tanna's intention (see *Maginei Shlomo*).]

12. Bottom of 13a. [There are four cases of dispute between Rabban Gamliel and R' Yehoshua recorded in the Mishnah in Chapter One. The first appears in the Mishnah on 12b, the second in the Mishnah on the top of 13a, and the last two in the Mishnah on the bottom of 13a. The Gemara assumes that if we must say that R' Yehoshua in our chapter is referring to one of those disputes, it would be the most recent one, i.e. the fourth dispute. Once the Gemara rejects this assumption, it moves on to suggest that he refers to the third dispute, etc., until all the disputes are considered.]

13. I.e. she is very obviously pregnant. Accordingly, she had no better claim available to her than to say that the person with whom she cohabited was fit for her (*Rashi*).

14. Ibid.

15. On 13a, the Gemara recorded a dispute as to the meaning of the expression "she was speaking" used in that Mishnah. Zeiri says it means that she was secluded with the man (see note 25 there).

16. [Although according to most Rishonim even had she in fact claimed that she did not cohabit with the man she would not have been believed according to R' Yehoshua (see 13a note 23), such a claim would have been more advantageous to her, since she would thereby not have been admitting to any wrongdoing. The fact that she used a less advantageous claim when she had available to her a more advantageous one constitutes a *migo* (*Ramban, Rashba;* see above, 12b note 22; cf. *Tosafos* to 13a ד"ה ואין אוסרין).]

17. [Rav Assi maintains that "speaking" is a euphemism for cohabiting (see Gemara above, 13a).] Since we know that she cohabited, she could not have made any claim other than that the man was fit for her.

18. Top of 13a.

19. R' Elazar maintains on 13a that that Mishnah follows the opinion of the Rabbis, who hold that a man who marries a woman and then

עין משפט נר מצוה

ב א מיי' פט"ז מהלכות אישות הלכה כה סמג עשין מח טוש"ע אה"ע סימן נו סעיף טו:

גמרא

שהפה שאסר הוא הפה שהתיר ואם יש עדים שהיא של אביו והוא אומר לקחתיה הימנו אינו נאמן: **גמ'** טעמא [א]דאיכא עדים הא ליכא עדים בעל מהימן לימא תנן סתמא דלא כרבן גמליאל דאי ר"ג הא אמר איהי מהימנא אפילו תימא רבן גמליאל עד כאן לא קאמר ר"ג התם אלא בברי ושמא אבל הכא בברי וברי לא אמר [ב] ודקארי לה מאי קארי לה הא ברי וברי הוא [ג] כיון דרוב נשים בתולות נישאות כי ברי ושמא דמי והכי נמי מסתברא מדקתני ומודה רבי יהושע אי אמרת בשלמא איירי ר"ג במודה שפיר אלא אי אמרת לא איירי ר"ג במודה רבי יהושע למאן מודה מי סברת ר' יהושע אהאי פירקין קאי אמגו קאי ואפירקין קמא קאי אהייא אילימא אהא [ד] היתה מעוברת ואמרו לה מה טיבו של עובר זה מאיש פלוני וכהן הוא ר"ג ור"א אומרים נאמנת ורבי יהושע אומר לא מפיה אנו חיין התם מאי מגו איכא הרי כריסה בין שיניה אלא אהא [ה] ראוה מדברת עם אחד ואמרו לה מה טיבו של איש זה איש פלוני וכהן הוא ר"ג ור"א אומרים נאמנת רבי יהושע אומר לא מפיה אנו חיין התם מאי מגו איכא הניחא [ו] לזעירי דאמר מאי מדברת נסתרה מגו דאי בעיא אמרה לא נבעלתי וקאמרה נבעלתי מהימנא אלא לרב אסי דאמר מאי מדברת [א] נבעלת מאי מגו איכא ולא אהא [ז] היא אומרת מוכת עץ אני והוא אומר לא כי אלא דרוסת איש את ר"ג ור"א אומרים נאמנת ורבי יהושע אומר לא מפיה אנו חיין התם מאי מגו איכא בשלמא לרבי אלעזר דאמר במנה ולא כלום מגו דאי בעיא אמרה מוכת עץ אני תחתיך ואית לה מאתים וקאמרה מעיקרא דלית לה אלא מנה מהימנא אלא לר' יוחנן דאמר במאתים ומנה מאי מגו איכא אלא אהא [ח] הנושא את האשה ולא מצא לה בתולים היא אומרת משארסתני נאנסתי ונסתחפה שדהו והוא אומר לא כי אלא עד שלא אירסתיך ר"ג ור"א אומרים נאמנת ור' יהושע אומר לא מפיה אנו חיין דמגו דאי בעיא אמרה מוכת עץ אני תחתיך דלא קא פסלה נפשה מכהונה וקאמרה נאנסתי דקא פסלה נפשה מכהונה משום הכי קאמר ר"ג דמהימנא וקאמר רבי יהושע לר"ג בהאי מגו דהכא מודינא לך בההוא מגו דהתם פליגנא עילוך מכדי האי מגו והאי מגו מאי שנא האי מגו מהאי מגו הכא אין שור שחוט לפניך התם הרי שור שחוט לפניך וכיון דרוב נשים בתולות נישאות כי לא אתו עדים מאי הוי [ט] אמר רבינא משום דאיכא למימר רוב נשים בתולות נישאות ומיעוט אלמנות וכל הנשאת בתולה יש לה קול וזו

רש"י

שהפה שאסר. זה אינו יודע שהיתה של אביו אלא על פיו של זה ומה שאסר הרי התיר: **גמ' טעמא דאיכא עדים.** דילתה בהינומא: **הבעל מהימן.** ולא אמרינן הואיל ומספקא לן על יום נשואיה אם בתולה היתה אם בעולה העמד אותה על חזקתה של קודם לכן ומתחלה בתולה היתה: **היא נאמנת.** דאזיל בתר חזקה דגופה: **בברי ושמא.** גבי משארסתני נאנסתי היא טוענת ברי לי הוא והוא אינו טוען אלא שמא עד שלא ארסתיך דהא אינו יודע מתי נאנסה: **ודקארי לה.** למימר סתמא דלא כרבן גמליאל: **מאי קארי לה.** ומאי עלה בדעתו לאפוקי מדר"ג הא לא דמיא לה: **כיון דרוב נשים בתולות נישאות.** קרובה טענתה להיות אמת יותר משלו וכברי ושמא דמיא: **והכי נמי מסתברא.** דר"ג מודה בה דבעל מהימן: **אי אמרת בשלמא איירי ר"ג במודה.** דהך רישא הודאה הוא דקא מודה ר"ג לרבי יהושע ואמר אע"ג דפליגנא עלך בברי ושמא מודינא לך בברי וברי היינו דשייך למיתני בתריה ור' יהושע מודה לר"ג בהאומר לחברו שדה זו כו' דאע"ג דפליגנא בפ"ק במשארסתני נאנסתי דאע"ג דליכא למימר מגו לא מהימנא מודינא בהאי מגו דאי בעי שתיק ולא א"ל של אביך היתה כי אמר ליה נמי לקחתיה הימנו מהימן כדלקמן: **אלא אי אמרת לא איירי.** רישא במודה ר"ג מאי מודה רבי יהושע מאי שייך למיתנייה הכא והיכא קאי: **אמגו קאי.** אפלוגתא דליכא למימר בה מגו בפ' קמא קאי וקאמר אע"ג דפליגנא במגו דהכא מודינא לך: **אהייא.** איכא מגו: **הרי כריסה בין שיניה.** ואינה יכולה לומר לא נבעלתי: **וקאמרה נבעלתי.** ולכשר נבעלתי מהימנא: **בשלמא לר' אלעזר דאמר.** בפרק קמא טענתייהו במנה ולא כלום מוכת עץ שלא הכיר בה אינה יכולה לתובעו אלא מנה והוא אומר דרוסת איש את ואין ליך כלום איכא מגו דאי בעיא אמרה מוכת עץ אני תחתיך: [ט] **משארסתני.** אירע לי ונסתחפה שדהו ואית לי מאתים: **וקאמרה.** מוכת עץ אני מעיקרא ולא תבעה אלא מנה מהימנא: **אלא לר' יוחנן.** דאמר טענתייהו במאתי' ומנה שהיא תובעתו מאתים ליכא מידי בין תחתיו למעיקרא מאי מגו איכא: **הכא.** גבי שדה אין שור שחוט לפניך שיעלה על לב בעליו לתבוע מי שחטו כלומר אם שתק זה לא היו לו עוררים הלכך אי לאו לדבר פשוט הוא שלקחה הימנו לא היה אומר לו של אביך היתה הלכך אמרי' מגו אבל גבי לא מצא לה בתולים שור שחוט לפניך בתולים שלא מצא לה הם הסיתוהו לבא לב"ד ואע"פ שיש לה להשיב טענה טובה מזו לא אמרינן מגו דדלמא לא אסקה אדעתה א"נ איערומי קא מערמא: **וכיון שרוב נשים.** קושיא היא: **יש לה קול.** והרבה יודעים שילאה בהינומא:

וזו

תוספות

דאי רבן גמליאל הא אמר איהי מהימנא. נראה דלמ"ד [י] הטוען אחר מעשה ב"ד לא אמר כלום פריך דלמ"ד דמצי טעין בתריה הכא נאמן הבעל אפילו לר"ג לומר אלמנה נשאתיך במגו דאי בעי אמר פרעתי: **הכי** נמי מסתברא. פי' בקונטרס הכי נמי מסתברא דמתני' אתיא כרבן גמליאל כדמשנינן דבברי וברי מודה דקתני ומודה ר' יהושע כו' וקשה לפי' דמי לא איירי נמי ר"ג במודה אתי שפיר ומודה רבי יהושע כלומר אע"ג דברישא פליגנא עלך בספיקא מודינא לך אע"ג דרישא וסיפא אינן מענין אחד כי היכי דאתיא ליה שפיר ומודה רבי יהושע אי איירי ר"ג במודה אע"ג דמודה דר' גמליאל אינו מענין ומודה דרבי יהושע ויש לישב דודאי כי איירי ר"ג במודה שייך למיתני שפיר ומודה רבי יהושע אע"ג דלא הוי מענין אחד כלומר דלאגב דתנא מילתא דמודה ר"ג תני נמי מילתא דמודה בה רבי יהושע אבל אי לא איירי רבן גמליאל במודה לא שייך למיתני ומודה רבי יהושע לאשמועינן אע"ג דפליג ברישא מודה בסיפא כיון דרישא וסיפא אינם מענין אחד אבל קשה דלא הוה ליה למימר אמגו קאי דעד השתא נמי לפ"ה אמגו הוי קאי ונראה לר"י דה"פ הכי נמי מסתברא דכברי ושמא דמי ולא בא לומר דפליג רבן גמליאל ברישא אלא אע"ג דבברי ושמא דמי מודה ר"ג משום דלאו שמא ממש הוא מדקאמר ומודה רבי יהושע אי אמרת בשלמא איירי ר"ג במודה כלומר אע"ג דכברי ושמא דמי מודה ר"ג דבעל נאמן היינו דקתני ומודה רבי יהושע דבהאי ברי נאמן דס"ד דטעמא דרבי יהושע משום ברי ושמא דזה אינו תובעו כדפי' בקונט' והשתא הוה מודה דר"ג ומודה דר"י מענין אחד אלא אי אמרת דרישא בברי ובברי גמור הוא ולא איירי רבן גמליאל במודה דפשיטא דכיון דברי וברי הוא דלא פליג ר"ג מאי ומודה וקאמר מי סברת דארישא קאי וטעמא דר"י משום ברי ושמא אמגו קאי דטעמא דר' יהושע משום מגו ונאמן אפי' הלה תובעו ואפירקין קמא קאי:

התם שור שחוט לפניך. פירש בקונטרס שהוא טוען עד שלא אירסתיך נאנסת והכא אין שור שחוט לפניך דאין הלה תובעו ור"י מפרש דהכא נמי איירי בהלה תובעו כדפי' וה"פ התם שור שחוט לפניך דהרי אין לה בתולים ואינה יכולה לומר בתולה אני כמו בשור שחוט שאין יכול לומר חי הוא ולהכי בין אומרת משארסתני נאנסתי בין אומרת מוכת עץ אני תחתיך לא מהימנא הכא אין שור שחוט לפניך ונאמן במגו דאי בעי אמר לא היתה של אביך מעולם: **כיון** דרוב נשים בתולות נישאות כי ליכא עדים מאי הוי. לרב פריך דאית ליה [כ] הולכין בממון אחר הרוב [ב]:

וזו

תוספות רי"ד

מיתמי גובה בלא כתובה **ודייקינן** טעמא דאיכא עדים פי' שיצאת בהינומא וראשה פרוע הא ליכא עדים בעל מהימן פי' ולא אמרינן הואיל ומספקא לן על יום נשואיה אם היתה בעולה או בתולה העמד אותה על חזקתה של קודם לכן ובתולה היתה לימא תנן סתמא דלא כר"ג דאי ר"ג האמר איהי מהימנא פי' דאזיל בתר חזקה דגופה וה"נ נימא העמד אשה על חזקתה ובתולה היתה ומהדר אפילו תימא ר"ג ע"כ לא קאמר ר"ג אלא ברי ושמא אבל ברי וברי לא אמר עיין בפ"ק. **ודקארי לה מאי קארי לה.** כיון דרוב נשים בתולות נשאות כברי ושמא דמי. וכיון דרוב נשים בתולות נשאות כי לא אתי עדי הינומא מאי הוה ניזיל בתר רובא. פי' ואע"ג דיש פלוגתא בהא מילתא רב ושמואל בפרק המוכר פירות דרב אמר הולכין בממון אחר הרוב ושמואל אמר אין הולכין בממון אחר הרוב וקי"ל הלכה כשמואל הכא משום דאיכא תרתי רובא וחזקה העמד אשה על חזקתה ובתולה היתה אפי' שמואל מודה. **אמר רבינא** משום דא"ל דרוב נשים בתולות נשאות ומיעוט אלמנות ורוב הנשאת בתולה יש לה קול וזו הואיל ואין לה קול איתרע לה רובא:

תוספות ישנים

א) אע"ג דאימותב כו' מ"מ בעי נמי לשנויי מתני' אליביה. ת"י.

ב) אפשר דאפילו לשמואל הוה לן למיזל בתר רובא ולא אחר חזקת ממון כיון דחזקת הגוף מסייע לרוב ופריך שפיר אפילו אליביה דשמואל קאי אמאי דאמרינן לעיל כיון דרוב נשים בתולות נישאות הוי ליה ברי דידיה כי שמא ובברי ושמא פסק שמואל כר"ג הכא דמהני לה חזקת הגוף לחד לישנא דפ"ק להכי פריך וניזיל בתר רובא דס"ד דהוי רוב גמור. ת"י.

מסורת הש"ס

א) ב"ב לג: [עי' פרש"י לקמן לו. ד"ה ודקארי], ב) לקמן כח., ג) לעיל יג., ד) שם, ה) [שם], ו) שם [ודף יא:], ז) לעיל יב:, ח) [ב"ב לג:], ט) [ד"ז שייך לקמן אחר ד"ה אלא לר' יוחנן ויותר טפי יש לדיבור זה שייכות לעיל יב: במשנה הנושא וכו'], י) [ב"מ יז.], כ) [ב"ק מו: ב"ב לב:].

גליון הש"ס

גמ' ודקארי לה מאי קארי לה. לקמן לו ע"א [יומא ל ע"ב] יבמות יא ע"א יד ע"א [עב ע"א גיטין סא ע"ב ב"ק מז ע"ב] ב"ב ב ע"ב [יז ע"ב] קמו ע"א [בכורות ד ע"ב] נדה סד ע"א:

ליקוטי רש"י

דרוב נשים. שבעולם שניסאות לבעל בתולות הן [רשב"ם ב"ב צב:]. **ודקארי לה מאי קארי לה.** מי שהשיב תשובה זו בבית המדרש מה עלתה על רוחו בעל מהימן. כתובתה מנה, דהמוליא מחבירו עליו הראיה [לקמן לו.]. **ראוה מדברת.** [בפנויה ומשום חששא דפסולין לנתין ולממזר וכיון שנבעלה לפסול פסלה מן הכהונה]. **נאמנת.** וכשרה לכהונה ולא מספקינן לה בנבעלה לפסול לה [לעיל יג.]. **וכהן הוא.** כלומר מיוחס הוא [קידושין עד.]. **נסתרה.** ואע"פ שלא ראוה שנבעלה נפסלה לכהונה לרבי יהושע כדלקמן דמעלה עשו ביוחסין [לעיל שם]. **היא אומרת מוכת עץ אני.** הנושא את האשה בחזקת בתולה ולא מצא לה בתולים היא אומרת מוכת עץ אני כו' [לעיל יא:]. **מוכת עץ.** שנתקע לה עץ באותו מקום [לעיל יא.]. **דרוסת איש.** קודם שארסתיך [לעיל יג.]. **ונסתחפה שדהו.** לשון מטר סוחף (משלי כח) נשטפה שדך כלומר מזלך גרם [לעיל ב.]. נסחף, נשטפו והחליקו גבוריך כמו מטר סוחף (משלי כח) נסתחפה שדהו בלשון משנה ומנחם חברו לשון כליון וכן חבר מטר סוחף ודונש פתר מטר סוחף כמו מטר סועף כמו מסעף פארה במערצה (ישעיה י) [ירמיה מו, טו]. סוחף, שוטף ומשנה נסתחפה שדהו וכן נסחף אביריך (ירמיה מו) נשטפו ועמדו וכשלו [משלי כח, ג]. מזלך גרס כלומר שהמזל גרם וסופו את זריעתו ועוקרה [לעיל יא.]. **ומיעוט אלמנות.** הוי איכא למימר דמן המיעוט היא הואיל ואין לה קול כדמפרש ואזיל [רשב"ם ב"ב שם].

שֶׁהַפֶּה שֶׁאָסַר הוּא הַפֶּה שֶׁהִתִּיר – **for the very mouth that has forbidden is the mouth that has permitted.**[1] וְאִם יֵשׁ עֵדִים שֶׁהִיא שֶׁל אָבִיו – **But if there are witnesses that it was his father's,** וְהוּא אוֹמֵר לְקַחְתִּיהָ הֵימֶנּוּ – **and [the claimant] says, "I purchased it from him,"** אֵינוֹ נֶאֱמָן – **he is not believed.**[2]

Gemara The Mishnah ruled that where the husband and wife disagree as to whether she was a virgin or a widow at the time of their marriage, if witnesses testify that she left her father's house with a *hinuma* and her hair down, her *kesubah* is two hundred *zuz*. The Gemara draws an inference from this ruling:

טַעְמָא דְּאִיכָּא עֵדִים – **The reason** she is believed **is that there are witnesses.** הָא לֵיכָּא עֵדִים – **This implies that if there are no witnesses** בַּעַל מְהֵימָן – **the husband is believed.**[3] לֵימָא תְּנַן סְתָמָא דְּלָא כְּרַבָּן גַּמְלִיאֵל – **Shall we say that we have** here **an anonymous Mishnah not in accordance with Rabban Gamliel?** דְּאִי רַבָּן גַּמְלִיאֵל – **For if** it is in accordance with **Rabban Gamliel,** הָא אָמַר אִיהִי מְהֵימְנָא – **why, he says** in the Mishnah on 12b that **[the wife] is believed.**[4] – ? –

The Gemara answers:

אֲפִילוּ תֵּימָא רַבָּן גַּמְלִיאֵל – **You may even say** that the Mishnah follows **Rabban Gamliel.** עַד כָּאן לֹא קָאָמַר רַבָּן גַּמְלִיאֵל הָתָם אֶלָּא בְּבָרִי וְשֶׁמָּא – For **Rabban Gamliel went so far** as to say that the wife is believed **only there,** in the Mishnah on 12b, **where [the case] is** one of **"certainly and perhaps"** [i.e. the wife claims she *certainly* was a virgin at the time of the betrothal while the husband argues that *perhaps* she was not].[5] אֲבָל הָכָא בְּבָרִי וּבָרִי לֹא אָמַר – **But here,** in our Mishnah, **where [the case] is** one of **"certainly and certainly"** [i.e. the husband is certain about his claim that she was not a virgin], **[Rabban Gamliel] did not say** it.[6]

The Gemara asks:

וּדְקָאָרֵי לָהּ – **And the one who asked [this question],** מַאי קָאָרֵי לָהּ – **why** indeed **did he ask it?** הָא בָּרִי וּבָרִי הוּא – **Why, [our Mishnah]** is a case of **"certainly and certainly,"** making the difference between the two Mishnahs obvious! – ? –

The Gemara answers:

כֵּיוָן דְּרוֹב נָשִׁים בְּתוּלוֹת נִישָּׂאוֹת – The questioner reasoned that **since most women marry as virgins,** כִּי בָּרִי וְשֶׁמָּא דָּמֵי – **it** [our Mishnah's case] **is similar to** a case of **"certainly and perhaps."**[7]

The Gemara supports its contention that Rabban Gamliel agrees with the ruling of our Mishnah:[8]

וְהָכִי נַמִּי מִסְתַּבְּרָא – **This is also reasonable.** מִדְּקָתָנֵי וּמוֹדֶה רַבִּי יְהוֹשֻׁעַ – **For the Mishnah taught** in its next section: AND R' YEHOSHUA ADMITS etc. אִי אָמְרַתְּ בִּשְׁלָמָא אַיְירֵי רַבָּן גַּמְלִיאֵל בְּמוֹדֶה – Now, **it is understandable if you say** that in the first part of the Mishnah **Rabban Gamliel was discussing** a case **where he**

NOTES

1. Since the other person has no knowledge of his father's having owned the field except through the occupant's admission, the occupant's additional claim that he purchased it is believed (*Rashi*).

This is an application of the principle known as *happeh she'assar,* which was explained at length in the Chapter Introduction. According to *Rashi's* explanation, the occupant has the right of *happeh she'assar* only because his fellow had no knowledge of any rights to the field. If he had come to court with a claim that the field was his father's, the defendant's response that he purchased it would not be believed unless he could produce evidence, since he would not have the power of *happeh she'assar* (see *Rashi* below ד״ה הכא).

[*Tosafos* (15b ד״ה ומודה), however, have a different understanding of this matter. In their opinion, even if the litigant had lodged a complaint, the defendant's claim that he purchased the property would be believed, based on the principle of *migo* (see Chapter Introduction). I.e. since the defendant could have flatly denied that the field ever belonged to the plaintiff's father and he would have been believed (for the plaintiff has no *proof* of this fact), his weaker claim that he purchased it from the father is also believed – despite his lack of evidence.]

2. Since there are witnesses that the field belonged to the plaintiff's father, the occupant is not the sole source of that information, and consequently his claim does not have the power of *happeh she'assar.*

[According to *Rashi's* explanation, R' Yehoshua would state the same ruling if there were no witnesses and the plaintiff had lodged the claim. The reason the Mishnah discusses a case in which there were witnesses is that this last half of the ruling (i.e. "But if there were witnesses . . .") is being stated even according to Rabban Gamliel, who maintains in the first chapter that a defendant is believed even in cases in which the plaintiff lodged a claim (such as in the Mishnah on 12b, where the woman is believed with a *migo* even though the husband lodged a complaint that he did not find signs of virginity). The Mishnah therefore teaches that even according to Rabban Gamliel, if there are witnesses who state that the field belonged to the plaintiff's father, the defendant is not believed, because he has no *migo* (*She'eilos U'Teshuvos Beis HaLevi,* vol. 3 *siman* 20; cf. *Shitah Mekubetzes* ד״ה ולי דברי רש״י).]

3. We do not say that since we are in doubt as to whether she was a virgin or a widow at the time of her marriage, we preserve her *chazakah* [previous status], which is that of a virgin [since every girl is born a virgin] (*Rashi;* cf. *Milchamos Hashem*).

4. The Mishnah on 12b discusses a case in which a woman was found by her husband not to possess signs of virginity at the time of their first cohabitation after the *nisuin.* She claims that she was violated after the *erusin,* and should therefore be entitled to a full *kesubah,* while he counters that perhaps she cohabited before *erusin,* thereby forfeiting her rights to a full *kesubah.* Rabban Gamliel rules that the woman is believed, because her claim is bolstered by a *chazakah* that she was a virgin, since every woman starts out at birth as a virgin. Thus, our Mishnah, which accepts the husband's claim that his wife was a widow when they married, is in dispute with Rabban Gamliel, because it does not utilize her *chazakah* of virginity.

[The commentators ask why the Gemara on 12b gave an alternative explanation of Rabban Gamliel's ruling there, namely, that she is believed to say she was violated after the *erusin* because her claim is bolstered by a *migo*: She could have made the better claim that her hymen was ruptured by a piece of wood. That claim would have been more advantageous to her in that she would thereby not have been rendered forbidden to a Kohen as she is with the present claim that she was violated after *erusin.* According to this alternative explanation, our Mishnah would have no bearing on Rabban Gamliel's ruling, because in our Mishnah the woman has no *migo.*

The commentators answer that from another Mishnah in the previous chapter it is evident, according to one Amora at least, that the woman is believed according to Rabban Gamliel even where she has no *migo.* That is the Mishnah on 13a, which discusses a case wherein the woman claims that she was injured by a piece of wood prior to the *erusin* while the husband counters that perhaps she was deflowered by a man. On 13a R' Yochanan interpreted that Mishnah (for reasons explained there) as following the opinion of R' Meir that a wood-injury victim receives a *kesubah* of two hundred *zuz.* Accordingly, even had the woman claimed that she had been injured by a piece of wood *after* the *erusin* (the only conceivable more advantageous claim she could have made), her position would not have been any better, because even with her present claim she is entitled to this amount. Since Rabban Gamliel nevertheless rules there that the woman is believed, it is evident that he relies solely on her *chazakah* (*Maharam Schif, Pnei Yehoshua, Haflaah;* see also *Ritva*).]

5. The husband cannot possibly know with certainty when she was deflowered (*Rashi*). Accordingly, Rabban Gamliel maintains that together with her *chazakah* of virginity, her claim of "certainly" is stronger than his claim of "perhaps"(*Ritva*).

6. Rather, even though she has a *chazakah* of virginity, his *chezkas mamon* [i.e. the fact that he is currently holding the money – see 12b note 14] is stronger (*Ritva*).

7. The statistical fact that the majority of women marry as virgins makes her claim more likely to be true than his (*Rashi*). Thus, vis-a-vis her claim, his claim has the force of only a claim of "perhaps" (*Ritva*).

8. *Rashi;* cf. *Tosafos.*

Chapter Two

Mishnah As explained in the Mishnah on 10b, the *kesubah* of a virgin is two hundred *zuz,* while that of a widow or divorcee is a *maneh* (one hundred *zuz*). This sum is written by the groom into a document, known as the *kesubah* document, which is given to the bride at the time of the wedding. Our Mishnah discusses a case in which the *kesubah* document was lost, and the amount of the *kesubah* is therefore in doubt:

הָאִשָּׁה שֶׁנִּתְאַרְמְלָה אוֹ שֶׁנִּתְגָּרְשָׁה – **A woman who was widowed or divorced** is claiming her *kesubah.* הִיא אוֹמֶרֶת בְּתוּלָה נְשָׂאתַנִי – **She says, "You married me as a virgin,** and my *kesubah* is therefore two hundred *zuz,"* וְהוּא אוֹמֵר לֹא כִּי אֶלָּא אַלְמָנָה נְשָׂאתִיךְ – **and he says, "Not so, rather I married you as a widow,** and thus owe you only a *maneh."*[1] אִם יֵשׁ עֵדִים שֶׁיָּצְאת בְּהִינוּמָא וְרֹאשָׁהּ פָּרוּעַ – **If there are witnesses that she went out with a *hinuma*** [2] **and her hair down,**[3] כְּתוּבָּתָהּ מָאתַיִם – **her *kesubah* is two hundred** *zuz.*[4] רַבִּי יוֹחָנָן בֶּן בְּרוֹקָה אוֹמֵר – **R' Yochanan ben Berokah says:** אַף חִילּוּק קְלָיוֹת רְאָיָה – **The distribution of parched grain is also proof.**[5]

The Mishnah continues:[6]

וּמוֹדֶה רַבִּי יְהוֹשֻׁעַ – **And R' Yehoshua admits** בְּאוֹמֵר לַחֲבֵירוֹ שָׂדֶה זוֹ שֶׁל אָבִיךְ הָיְתָה וּלְקַחְתִּיהָ הֵימֶנּוּ – concerning a case **where someone says to his fellow, "This field was your father's, but I bought it from him,"** שֶׁהוּא נֶאֱמָן – **that he is believed,**

NOTES

1. [Obviously this wording ("*You* married me . . .," "*I* married you . . .") refers to a case in which the woman was divorced and is speaking to her ex-husband. If she was widowed, the exchange takes place between the woman and her husband's heirs ("*Your father* married me . . .," "*Our father* married you . . .") (*Rashi* and *Rashash*).]

2. The Gemara (17b) will define this term.

3. I.e. with her hair on her shoulders. Such was the custom when they led the virgin brides from their fathers' houses to the wedding place (*Rashi*).

[Some cite this Mishnah as proof that the obligation of a married woman to cover her hair begins only with *nisuin* (*Shitah Mekubetzes* ד״ה וראשה פרוע in the name of *Likkutei HaGeonim;* see also at length *She'eilos U'Teshuvos Yeshuos Yaakov, Even HaEzer* 21:1; *Sdei Chemed, Maareches Das Yehudis* אות א). Others (see *Teshuvos R' Akiva Eiger* vol. II §79) maintain that the obligation applies to an *arusah* as well, and that the custom was merely to allow *some* of the *arusah's* hair to protrude from its covering, and even then only while she was being led from her father's house to the wedding hall.]

4. [In the beginning of the last chapter we learned that a virgin gets married on Wednesday, so that if there should be any question regarding her virginity, it can be settled the next day in court. If so, why did our Mishnah not state that a Wednesday wedding is also proof that the woman was a virgin? *Hagahos Asheri* answers that some women who are entitled to a two hundred-*zuz kesubah* do not need to get married on Wednesday. For example, a *bogeress* receives a full *kesubah,* but still does not have to get married on a Wednesday, since she is not expected to possess signs of virginity (see above, 11b note 9). The Mishnah therefore lists proofs that are more definite (cf. *Rashba*). In addition, women who are not virgins can also marry on Wednesday; thus, a Wednesday wedding is not definite proof of virginity (*Shitah Mekubetzes*).]

5. The fresh ears of grain were dried in an oven, and remained sweet permanently. It was customary to distribute such grain to the children at the weddings of virgin brides (*Rashi;* see *Tiferes Yisrael* §7).

6. The following part of the Mishnah seems out of place at this point. The Gemara (16a) will discuss this issue (*Rashi*).

עין משפט
נר מצוה

צד א מיי' פט"ו מהל' איסורי ביאה הלכה כה טוש"ע אה"ע סימן ד סעיף לג:

צה ב ג ד ה מיי' שם הל' כו וטו"ר וש"ע שם סעיף לד:

א ו מיי' פט"ז מהלכות אישות הלכה כה טור ש"ע שם סי' צו סעיף טו:

תוספות ישנים

א) נראה לר"י דמשום דדרשינן וחי בהם ולא שימות בהם ומשמע שלא יבוא לידי מיתה משום ענין לכך יש לחוש לכל מיעוט ישראל. מ"י.

הגהות הב"ח

(א) רש"י ד"ה אבל כו' ולמ"ד גיורת. נ"ב בפרק הבא על יבמתו דף ס ע"ב:

לעזי רש"י

איצטיינ"דיר"א. פירוש פרוש, מגהץ שבר (רש"י ויקרא יג, מה):

תוספות רי"ד

האשה שנתארמלה או שנתגרשה היא אומרת בתולה נשאתני והוא אומר לא כי אלא אלמנה נשאתיך אם יש עדים שיצאת בהינומא וראשה פרוע כתובתה מאתים. פי' הוא אומר אנתגרשה קאי ולאלמנה אומרים לה היורשים אבינו אלמנה נשאך ואין לך אלא מנה ושטר כתובה אבד אם יש עדים שיצאת בהינומא וראשה פרוע כתובתה מאתים.

מצא בה תינוק מושלך. משנה היא בסדר טהרות גבי עיר שישראלים ועובדי כוכבים דרים בה: מחצה על מחצה ישראל. לקמיה מפרש מאי איכא בין רוב ישראל למחצה על מחצה דפליג להו בתרי: לא שנו. דאם רוב ישראל ישראל: אלא להחיותו. ב"ד מצווין לפרנסו משום וחי אחיך עמך (ויקרא כה): אבל ליוחסין לא. דאם בת היא אסורה לכהן ואפי' ליכא למיחש משום אסופי כגון הנך דאמרינן בעשרה יוחסין (קדושין עג:) ג) משלטי הדמיה תלי פיתקא תלי קמיעא מיהו חיישינן שמא בת עובד כוכבים היא (א) ולמ"ד גיורת פסולה לכהונה אפילו קטנה וזו אסורה לכהן דתרי רובי בעינן ליוחסין: ושמואל אמר אף לפקח עליו את הגל. בשבת חשבינן ליה לישראל: אשתמיטתיה. לרבי ירמיה: הא דאמר רב יהודה. דהכא נמי תרי רובי הוו: ולרב חנן בר רבא דאמר. משמיה דרב: הוראת שעה היתה. והתם תרי רובי הוו וקאמר הוראת שעה היתה אבל לדורות לא בעינן תרי רובי: קשיא הא. דרב דאמר אבל ליוחסין לא אלמא רב תרי רובי בעי: לא מתני הא. דאמר רב יהודה אמר רב בקרונות של צפורי הוה מעשה וחד רובא הוה הלכך הוראת שעה היתה: מי אמר שמואל הכי. דלענין פיקוח נפש בעינן רובא: אין הולכין כו'. דאפילו בספק עובד כוכבים ספק ישראל ברוב עובדי כוכבים מפקחין: ולענין פיקוח נפש אינו כן. דאפילו ברוב עובדי כוכבים מפקחין דאין הולכין בה אחר הרוב: למאי הלכתא. כיון דאמר שמואל מפקחין עליו את הגל אלמא לאו עובד כוכבים הוא לכל מילי ולמאי הלכתא חשיב ליה עובד כוכבים: להאכילו נבלות. בידים וכ"ש שלא יחזירו לו אבידה ולנזקין: להחזיר לו אבידה. רבותא היא דמוציאין מיד ישראל הזוכה בה ועוד דאמור רבנן (סנהדרין דף עו:) המחזיר אבידה לכנעני עליו הכתוב אומר למען ספות הרוה את הצמאה שהשוה מגרים לחשיבתן של ישראל ונאמר לא יאבה ה' סלוח לו: מחצה על מחצה ישראל למאי הלכתא. להחזיר לו אבידה לא מצית אמרת דא"כ למאי הלכתא פלגינהו מהדדי: לנזקין. דתנן ב"ק (דף לז:) שור של ישראל שנגח לשור של כנעני פטור ושור של כנעני שנגח לשור של ישראל בין תם בין מועד משלם נזק שלם וישראל לישראל תם משלם חצי נזק ומועד משלם נזק שלם: אילימא כו'. וקאמרת דדיינינן ליה כישראל ומחייבת ליה לשלם לו חצי נזקו: לימא ליה. ישראל אייתי ראיה דהא מחצה על מחצה הוא וספיקא הוא: לא צריכא כו'. וקא תבע ליה ישראל נזק שלם לתם כדין כנעני ואשמעינן תנא דכישראל דיינינן ליה ולא משלם אלא חצי נזק דא"ל אייתי ראיה:

הדרן עלך בתולה נשאת

האשה שנתארמלה או נתגרשה. ותובעת כתובתה: והוא אומר. אנתגרשה קאי ולאלמנה היורשין אומרים לה אלמנה נשאך אבינו ואין לך אלא מנה ושטר הכתובה אבד: אם יש עדים. על נשואיה שיצאת מבית אביה לבית בעלה: בהינומא. בגמ' מפרש: וראשה פרוע. שערה על כתיפיה כך היו נוהגין להוציא את הבתולות מבית אביהן לבית החתונה: אף חילוק קליות. רגילים היו לחלק קליות לתינוקות בנישואי הבתולות: קליות. כששבולין לחין מייבשין אותן בתנור והן קליות וממתקין לעולם: ומודה ר' יהושע. מפרש בגמ' אהיכא קאי ומאי מודה: שהפה

א) מצא בה תינוק מושלך אם רוב עובדי כוכבים עובד כוכבי' אם רוב ישראל ישראל מחצה על מחצה ישראל ואמר רב לא שנו אלא להחיותו א אבל ליוחסין לא ושמואל אמר לפקח עליו את הגל אשתמיטתיה הא דא"ר יהודה אמר רב בקרונות של צפורי הוה מעשה ולרב חנן בר רבא דאמר הוראת שעה היתה קשיא הא מאן דמתני הא לא מתני הא גופא מצא בה תינוק מושלך אם רוב עובדי כוכבים עובד כוכבים אם רוב ישראל ישראל מחצה על מחצה ישראל אמר רב לא שנו אלא להחיותו אבל ליוחסין לא ושמואל אמר לפקח עליו את הגל ומי אמר שמואל הכי והאמר רב יוסף אמר רב יהודה אמר שמואל אין הולכין בפיקוח נפש אחר הרוב אלא כי איתמר דשמואל ארישא אתמר אם רוב עובדי כוכבים עובד כוכבים אמר שמואל א) ב ולפקח עליו את הגל אינו כן אם רוב עובדי כוכבים עובד כוכבים למאי הלכתא אמר רב פפא ג להאכילו נבילות אם רוב ישראל ישראל למאי הלכתא אמר רב פפא ד להחזיר לו אבידה מחצה על מחצה ישראל למאי הלכתא אמר ריש לקיש ה לנזקין ה"ד אי נימא דנגחיה תורא דידן לתורא דידיה לימא ליה אייתי ראיה דישראל את ושקול לא צריכא דנגחיה תורא דידיה לתורא דידן פלגא משלם ואידך פלגא אמר להו אייתי ראיה דלאו ישראל אנא ואתן לכון:

הדרן עלך בתולה נשאת

האשה ג) שנתארמלה או שנתגרשה היא אומרת בתולה נשאתני והוא אומר לא כי אלא אלמנה נשאתיך ו אם יש עדים שיצאת בהינומא וראשה פרוע כתובתה מאתים רבי יוחנן בן ברוקה אומר אף חילוק קליות ראיה ומודה רבי יהושע באומר לחבירו שדה זו של אביך היתה ולקחתיה הימנו שהוא נאמן שהפה

ולרב חנן דאמר הוראת שעה היתה. ולדורות סגי בחד רובא קשיא הך ולא מיסתברא ליה למימר דהוראת שעה היתה שהתיר בתרי רובי אבל לדורות לא סגי אפילו בתרי רובי: **מאן** דמתני הא לא מתני הא. פי' בקונטרס דרב חנן לא מתני דקרונות של צפורי היה מעשה ולא הוה אלא חד רובא ולפירושו לא פליגי דלדורות לכ"ע בעינן תרי רובי ולא פליגי אלא במעשה היכי הוה ור"ת פי' דרב חנן לא מתני אבל ליוחסין לא וסגי לדידיה לדורות בחד רובא אבל קשה לפירושו לרב חנן תקשי ר' יוחנן בן נורי דאמר כמאן דסגי בחד רובא כדפריך לעיל ועוד דלא מיסתבר דשום אמורא יחלוק אההיא דאבל ליוחסין לא דרב גופיה קאמר לה בלא אמורא ולהכי אפירכא דרבי ירמיה לא משני מאן דמתני הא לא מתני הא: **אם** רוב עובדי כוכבים עובד כוכבים למאי הלכתא. לא מצי למימר לענין שלא להחיותו דמאי איריא רוב עובדי כוכבים אפילו מחצה נמי דדוקא ברוב ישראל קאמר רב דהוי ישראל להחיותו: **להחזיר** לו אבדה. הוה מצי למימר להחיותו כדאמר רב אלא נקט להחזיר לו אבדה דהוי רבותא טפי דאיסור גדול הוא ד) משום למען ספות הרוה וגו' אבל להחיותו לא הוי רבותא כל כך דהא ה) מפרנסין עניי עובדי כוכבים עם עניי ישראל ואפי' לשמואל דאמר ו) אין הולכין בממון אחר הרוב היינו ז) במוכר שור לחבירו ונמצא נגחן שהיתר בא המעות לידו ומדעתו נתנם לו הלוקח אבל הכא מודי דאזלינן בתר רובא: **לא** צריכא דנגחיה תורא דידיה כו'. תימה דהכי נמי הוה מצי למימר מחצה על מחצה עובד כוכבים ומנגח תורא דידן לתורא דידיה [כולה מילתא הוי מצי למימר לענין נגיחה אלא ניחא בכל חד למנוח דבר חדש. מהר"ס]:

הדרן עלך בתולה נשאת

האשה. אם יש עדים שיצאת בהינומא כו'. בדלא נקיטא כתובה איירי דאי איכא כתובה ניחזי כתובתה אם היא בתולה או אלמנה ואפילו למ"ד ח) הטוען אחר מעשה ב"ד ואמר פרעתי נאמן מ"מ אין נאמן לומר כאן אלמנה נשאתיך מגו דאי בעי אמר פרעתי דמגו במקום עדים הוא:

ומודה רבי יהושע באומר שדה כו' דנאמן. מתוך פירוש הקונט' משמע דדוקא כשאין הלה תובעו ונאמן במגו דאי בעי שתיק אבל אם תובעו אינו נאמן ואינו נראה דהא קתני סיפא ואם יש עדים כו' משמע דדוקא אם יש עדים שהיתה של אביו אינו נאמן אבל אם אין עדים אע"ג דהלה תובעו נאמן מגו דאי בעי אמר לא היתה של אביך מעולם מדלא נקט אם תובעו אינו נאמן ובגמרא נמי פריך וליתני שדה זו של אביך היתה משמע דבהלה תובעו איירי ולכך משיב ודאי שלך היתה ולקחתיה ממך אבל אם לא תובעו אין צריך לומר שלך היתה כי מסתמא הוא יודע בעצמו דבר זה: דאי

מסורת הש"ס

א) מכשירין פ"ב מ"ז יומא פד., ב) ב"ב כג: [וש"ג], ג) הגה"ה פי' משלטי הדמיה. מתוקנין אבריו. פיתקא. קמיע של כתב. קמיעא. קמיע של עיקרין דהא פסק על מיו והוציא חתלתו שאוהבת אותו ולא השליכתו למות, ד) כדאיתא סנהדרין עו:, ה) [ב"ק מז: וב"ב לב:], ו) [עי' תוס' ב"ק מו: ותוס' ב"מ כ: ד"ה איסורא ותוס' סנהדרין ג: ד"ה דיני ותוס' יומא פה.], ח) [עי' תוס' לקמן פח: ופט: בד"ה הוציאה וכו' א"כ אי שמואל לית ליה דר' יוחנן וכו'].

ליקוטי רש"י

ואמר רב לא שנו. דאם רוב ישראל מחזקינן ליה לישראל. אלא להחיותו אבל ליוחסין לא. כגון אם נקבה היא שיהא כהן מותר בה לא ואפילו ליכא למיחש לאסופי כגון הנך דאמרינן במסכת קידושין (דף עג:) תלי דביקולא תלי פיתקא רמי מוהלא משלטי הדמיה חיישינן שמא כותית היא וגיורת אסורה לכהונה ואע"ג דרוב ישראל מעלה עשו ביוחסין דבעינן תרי רובי כדאמרי' בכתובות בפרק קמא (דף טו.) [יומא פד:]. ושמואל אמר לפקח עליו את הגל. קאמר דאם רוב ישראל [ישראל] אבל במחצה על מחצה לא וכ"ש ברוב כותים [שם פה.]. בקרונות של צפורי. ביום השוק שעוברות ושיירות ממקום אחר באות שם [לעיל ע"א]. ולפקח וכו' אינו כן. דאמר אפילו ברוב כותים מפקחין. למאי הילכתא. הוי כותי אליבא דשמואל כיון דאמר מפקחין עליו ולא שכן דמצוה להחיותו ולמאי הילכתא הוי כותי. להאכילו נבילות. עד שיגדל ויקבל עליו גירות. מחצה על מחצה ישראל. אם רוב ישראל למאי הילכתא. הוי ישראל ברוב ישראל טפי ממחצה על מחצה [דא'] שלא להאכילו נבילות במחצה על מחצה [נמי] לא ספינן ליה. לנזקין. שור של כותי שנגח של ישראל פטור ושור של ישראל שנגח של כותי תם משלם חצי נזק בין תם בין מועד ושל ישראל שנגח של ישראל תם משלם חצי נזק ומועד משלם נזק שלם. אי נימא דנגחיה תורא דידן לתורא דידיה. וקאמרינן דמחייבינן ליה לשלומי. אייתי ראיה דישראל את ושקול. וכל זמן שלא גדל בבית דין לשם גירות לא מצינן [לחיוביה לישראל] לשלומי. פלגא משלם. דישראל הוא ואידך פלגא ספק הוא הא תובעו נזק שלם כדין כותי אמר ליה אייתי ראיה דלאו ישראל אנא ונשקול [יומא פה.]. האשה שנתארמלה. וטוענת כתובתי מ"ב

במקום שאין כותבין כתובה כדמפרש בכתובות. בתולה נשאתני. ויש לי מאתים. אלמנה נשאתיך. ואין לך אלא מנה. שיצאת. מבית אביה לבית בעלה כשנכנסה לחופה. בהינומא. קלתא דמנמנמא ביה כלתא או ראשה פרוע בשעת כניסה לחופה שכן דרך הנישאות בתולות [רשב"ם ב"ב צב:]. נערה המאורסה היו רגילין לעשות לה חופה של הדס כשמכניסה לחופה וקורין לה הינומא כדאמרינן בכתובות (דף טו:) שיצאתה בהינומא וראשה פרוע [ברכות נ:]. כתובתה מאתים. ואע"פ שאין לה עדים מעידים על בתוליה ואין יודעין אם נישאת בתולה או בעולה [רשב"ם שם].

person could have refrained from making his admission at all, we believe him when he qualifies the admission. However, *Rashi* often seems to explain *happeh she'assar* as a new principle: Since this person is our sole source of information regarding the matter, just as we believe him concerning the prohibition or liability we must also believe him regarding the qualification.[2]

☙ Time Constraint of *Happeh She'assar* Rights

There is disagreement among the Rishonim as to the latitude that *happeh she'assar* provides. Some state that *happeh she'assar* merely gives a person the right to qualify his statement *immediately*. That is, after stating the prohibition or liability, he must qualify it תּוֹךְ כְּדֵי דִּיבּוּר, *within the time it takes to make an utterance* [i.e. within the time it takes to say the words שָׁלוֹם עָלֶיךָ רַבִּי, *Peace unto you, master*]. Others maintain that there is no such time limit.[3] The dispute pertains to a litigant in a monetary case, as well as to one who makes a statement concerning prohibitory law. It is clear, however, that *witnesses* who wish to qualify their testimony must do so within the time of an utterance. This is because of the special law that once a witness has completed his testimony he may not add to or detract from it [כֵּיוָן שֶׁהִגִּיד שׁוּב אֵינוֹ חוֹזֵר וּמַגִּיד].[4]

NOTES

2. See *Rashi* to 16a ד״ה שהפה שאסר, 18b ד״ה הרי אלו נאמנים, 109b ד״ה נאמן. One ramification of *Rashi's* explanation is that *happeh she'assar* is deemed effective even in certain situations where *migo* would be ineffective. Thus, whereas *migo* is effective only at the moment when the admission of liability is made, *happeh she'assar* gives a person the right to modify his admission even at a later time (*Machaneh Ephraim, Hil. Isurei Biah* 18:15 ד״ה ולכאורה נראה; see *Hashlamah,* cited by *Shitah Mekubetzes* to 23a; see also below). For another ramification, see *Ramban* cited below, 18b note 14. See also *Tosafos, Bava Kamma* ibid.; *Shach, Choshen Mishpat* 108:7; *Kehillos Yaakov* 15:2. On the other hand, *Rashi* has stricter guidelines than *Tosafos* for defining *happeh she'assar*. These shall come to light in the first Mishnah and Gemara of the chapter.

Even according to *Tosafos,* a *migo* that is based on the fact that one could have remained silent (i.e. *happeh she'assar*) is effective in some instances where an ordinary *migo* is not. However, that is simply because the position of one who has the option to remain silent is superior to that of one who merely has the option of presenting a stronger claim. For example, witnesses whose testimony is faulty are not believed on the basis of *migo,* because perhaps it might not have occurred to both of them to present the identical alternative and superior testimony. Nevertheless, if they could have attained the desired result by remaining silent, they are believed, since this argument does not apply (see *Tosafos* to 18b ד״ה אין נאמנים, and to 19b ד״ה ואם כתב ידן).

Our interpretation of *Rashi's* view is based on *Hashlamah* and *Machaneh Ephraim* ibid. Cf. *Urim VeTumim, Kelalei Migo* §109; *Kovetz Shiurim* §43; *Achiezer* vol. III §74. See further, *Beis Yaakov* to 22a and 23a.

3. Both opinions are cited by *Maggid Mishneh, Hil. Gerushin* 12:1 (see *Tur Even HaEzer* 152:6 for yet another opinion; see also 22a note 13). According to *Machaneh Ephraim* (ibid.), this dispute hinges on the previous issue of whether *happeh she'assar* is a form of *migo* or not. If it is related to *migo,* it is effective only within the time of an utterance, because *migo* itself is ineffective *after* a liability has been established (see *Bava Basra* 34a with *Tosafos* ד״ה הוי מחוייב שבועה). But if *happeh she'assar* is an independent principle, it is not bound by a time limit. Rather, the person who is our sole source of information concerning a certain liability can add a qualification at any time. See also *Kovetz Shiurim* ibid; cf. *Chidushei R' Shimon Shkop, Bava Basra* §21.

4. See *Rashi* to 18b ד״ה כיון שהגיד שוב אינו חוזר ומגיד, and *Hashlamah* cited by *Shitah Mekubetzes* to 23a. Cf. *Bach, Kuntres Acharon* to *Even HaEzer* 47:2.

Chapter Two

Introduction

The following chapter continues the discussion concerning cases in which the amount of the *kesubah* obligation is in question, and digresses to discuss related issues. A major focus of this chapter is the principle called הַפֶּה שֶׁאָסַר הוּא הַפֶּה שֶׁהִתִּיר, literally: *The very mouth that has forbidden is the mouth that has permitted.*

◆§ הַפֶּה שֶׁאָסַר – The *Happeh She'assar* Principle

The basic idea behind the principle of הַפֶּה שֶׁאָסַר הוּא הַפֶּה שֶׁהִתִּיר [which we will henceforth refer to simply as *happeh she'assar*], is that when a claimant or witness states a previously unknown fact, he has the right to qualify it. For example, if a woman not known to have ever been married states that she was in fact once married (and thus *forbidden* to marry another man) but is now divorced (and thus *permitted* to marry), she is allowed to remarry without producing proof of the divorce. Now, if we had independent knowledge of her marriage, she would not be allowed to marry another man without proof of divorce. However, since we have no independent knowledge, we say that "The very mouth that has forbidden is the one that has permitted" – i.e. just as we accept her word that she was married, we must also accept her word that she was divorced (Mishnah 22a).

The above case is an example of how the *happeh she'assar* principle applies to אִיסוּרִים, *prohibitory law*: The principle precludes us from establishing a forbidden status based on part of a claimant's statement when the rest of the statement indicates that such status does not exist. The same principle also applies to monetary law. In monetary cases, the principle states that where the first part of a claimant's statement cedes some of his monetary rights but the next part of the statement restores them, we may not deprive him of those rights. In this context, the phrase *happeh* ***she'assar****, the mouth that has* ***forbidden,*** refers in a borrowed sense to the claimant's concession of monetary rights. An example appears in the first Mishnah of this chapter: A man tells his fellow, "This field [which everyone presumes to be mine] originally belonged to your father, but I purchased it from him." Since we have no independent knowledge of the field having belonged to the other man's father, we apply the *happeh she'assar* principle: The current occupant keeps the field even though he has no proof of ownership, because if we accept his admission that it was previously not his we must also accept his claim that he purchased it. However, if there are witnesses that it once belonged to the other man's father, the occupant loses the field unless he can produce proof of purchase.

◆§ *Happeh She'assar* and *Migo*

There is another principle similar to that of *happeh she'assar* – the principle of *migo* (literally: since). *Migo* states that when a litigant had the opportunity to win his case with a strong plea and instead advanced a weaker one, the weaker plea is believed – since if he had wanted to lie he could have advanced the stronger plea. There is considerable discussion whether *happeh she'assar* is merely an extension of the *migo* principle or it is a new concept. *Tosafos* throughout our chapter[1] seem to understand *happeh she'assar* as a form of *migo*. I.e. since the

NOTES

1. See *Tosafos* to 15b ד״ה ומודה, 16a ד״ה התם, 18b ד״ה הרי and ד״ה אין נאמנים, 19b ד״ה אמר רב נחמן, 22a ד״ה מנין. Cf. *Tosafos, Bava Kamma* 72b ד״ה אין לך בו.

The Gemara asks:

מֶחֱצָה עַל מֶחֱצָה יִשְׂרָאֵל – When the Mishnah states: If HALF are Jews AND HALF are idolaters, HE IS treated as A JEW, לְמַאי הִילְכְתָא – to what law does it refer?[15]

The Gemara answers:

אָמַר רֵישׁ לָקִישׁ – **Reish Lakish said:** לִנְזָקִין – It refers **to** the law of **damages.**[16]

The Gemara analyzes this answer:

הֵיכִי דָמֵי – **What is the case?** אִי נֵימָא דְנַגְחֵיהּ תּוֹרָא דִידַן לְתוֹרָא דִידֵיהּ – **If we say that** it refers to a case in which **an ox of ours** (one belonging to a definite Jew) **gored [the child's] ox,**[17] לֵימָא לֵיהּ – **let [the owner]** of the ox that did the damage **say to [the child]** whose ox was damaged: אַיְיתֵי רְאָיָה דְּיִשְׂרָאֵל אַתְּ וּשְׁקוֹל – **"Produce proof that you are a Jew and** then **collect!"**[18]

The Gemara concludes:

לֹא צְרִיכָא דְנַגְחֵיהּ תּוֹרָא דִידֵיהּ לְתוֹרָא דִידַן – **It** (the Mishnah's ruling that where half the inhabitants are Jews the child is considered a Jew) **must** therefore **be needed only where [the child's] ox gored an ox of ours.**[19] פַּלְגָא מְשַׁלֵּם – If the ox is a *tam,* **[the child] pays half** the damages **to [the claimant],**[20] וְאִידָךְ פַּלְגָא – **and** with regard to **the other half,** אָמַר לְהוּ – **he can say to [the claimants]:** אַיְיתוּ רְאָיָה דְּלָאו יִשְׂרָאֵל אֲנָא וְאֶתֵּן לְכוֹן – **"Produce proof that I am not a Jew, and** then **I will give** it **to you!"**[21]

הדרן עלך בתולה נשאת

WE SHALL RETURN TO YOU, BESULAH NISEIS

NOTES

indicates that the claimant is entitled to the money. For Shmuel holds (*Bava Kamma* 46b) that we do not follow the rule of majority regarding monetary matters [אֵין הוֹלְכִין בְּמָמוֹן אַחַר הָרוֹב]. Thus, compelling the finder to return the lost object to this child is a more novel ruling than placing an obligation on the courts to support the child if he is needy (*Rashba*).

[Why then must the finder return the lost object? *Rashba* answers that since from the very moment he took it, the finder was subject to a possible Biblical requirement to return it, he never became established as the rightful holder of this object. In such a case, even Shmuel agrees that the law of the majority can dictate that it be returned to the child when the majority indicates that he is a Jew (see *Tosafos* for a similar answer).

For another aspect of the novelty of Rav Pappa's example over Rav's, see *Rashi* and *Tosafos*. For a completely different answer to the question of why Rav Pappa did not give Rav's answer, see *Ramban* and *Rosh* (cited by *Shitah Mekubetzes*).]

15. The purpose of this clause cannot be to teach that we must return his lost property even in a place in which just half the inhabitants are Jews, because if that were so, the Mishnah would have combined this case with the case of a majority of Jews, since their laws would then be identical (*Rashi;* see *Tosafos* to *Yoma* 85a [ד״ה להחזיר [ב for why, in fact, there is no obligation to return it where only half are Jews).

16. A Mishnah (*Bava Kamma* 37b) rules that if the ox of a Jew gores the ox of an idolater, the Jew is exempt; but if the ox of an idolater gores the ox of a Jew, the idolater must pay full damages, even if his ox was a *tam* [an ox that had not gored three times]. This is in contrast to the case in which a Jew's ox gores another Jew's ox, where the law calls for the owner to pay half-damages in the case of a *tam* and full damages in the case of a *muad* [an animal that has gored three times] (*Rashi*). This section of the Mishnah in *Machshirin* thus rules that when half of the city is Jewish, the child is considered a Jew with respect to these laws – as the Gemara proceeds to explain.

Rambam (*Nizkei Mamon* 8:5) explains the reason for the distinction between the law for Jews and idolaters to be that we treat the idolaters according to their own laws. Since idolaters among themselves do not consider an owner liable for the damage done by his animal, there is no reason for them to collect when a Jew's animal damages their property. Really, the same should hold true in the reverse – they should not be held liable for damage done by their animals to a Jew's property. The Torah, however, penalized them in this regard for their failure to live up to its standards [among themselves], and to spur them to guard their animals by requiring them to pay for such damage.

17. The Mishnah would thus be saying that the child is considered a Jew insofar as collecting payment of half the damages from the owner of the goring ox [if it was a *tam*] (*Rashi*).

18. Since the child is the claimant, the burden of proof lies on him [הַמּוֹצִיא מֵחֲבֵרוֹ עָלָיו הָרְאָיָה]. Therefore, since there is doubt whether he is a Jew, he cannot obligate the defendant to pay him until he proves that he is a Jew (*Rashi*).

19. The damaged party now puts in a claim for full damages, claiming that the child is really an idolater, who pays full damages even for a *tam* (*Rashi*).

20. This is the amount a Jew pays for damage by his *tam.*

21. Since the claimant is trying to exact money from the child, the burden of proof is on the claimant to prove his claim. Since he cannot, the Mishnah teaches that the child is treated as a Jew – and thus need pay only half damages (*Rashi*).

[This answer leaves an obvious question. If he is treated as a Jew only because his claimant cannot prove otherwise, then the Mishnah could just as well have ruled that the child is treated as an idolater, and refer to the opposite case – where the ox of a definite Jew gored the child's ox. Since the child would then have to prove his claim and could not, he would be unable to collect – just like an idolater! *Tos. HaRosh* answers that the Mishnah's ruling is the bigger novelty because it teaches that we deprive a definite Jew (the owner of the gored ox) of half his damages because of this doubt.]

[The Gemara has concluded that if the ox of a definite Jew gored the child's ox, the child cannot collect because he cannot prove that he is a Jew. There is a dispute among the Rishonim whether this is true only where the child was found in a city that was half Jews and half idolaters (the case discussed by the Gemara) or even where most of the city was Jewish. See *Yom Shel Shlomo* §45 for a lengthy discussion of this point. See also *Haflaah* and *Chidushei R' Akiva Eiger.*]

צד א מיי' פט"ו מהל' איסורי ביאה הלכה כה טוש"ע אה"ע סימן ד סעיף יג:

צה ב ג ד ה מיי' שם הל' כו וטור וש"ע שם סעיף לד:

א ו מיי' פט"ז מהלכות אישות הלכה כה טור ש"ע שם סי' לו סעיף טו:

א) מצא בה תינוק מושלך אם רוב עובדי כוכבים עובד כוכבי' אם רוב ישראל ישראל מחצה על מחצה ישראל ואמר רב לא שנו אלא להחיותו א אבל ליוחסין לא ושמואל אמר לפקח עליו את הגל אשתמיטתיה הא דא"ר יהודה אמר רב בקרונות של צפורי הוה מעשה ולרב חנן בר רבא דאמר הוראת שעה היתה קשיא הא מאן דמתני הא לא מתני הא גופא מצא בה תינוק מושלך אם רוב עובדי כוכבים עובד כוכבים אם רוב ישראל ישראל מחצה על מחצה ישראל אמר רב לא שנו אלא להחיותו אבל ליוחסין לא ושמואל אמר לפקח עליו את הגל ומי אמר שמואל הכי והאמר רב יוסף אמר רב יהודה אמר שמואל אין הולכין בפיקוח נפש אחר הרוב אלא כי איתמר דשמואל ארישא איתמר אם רוב עובדי כוכבים עובד כוכבים אמר שמואל א) ולפקח עליו את הגל אינו כן אם רוב עובדי כוכבים עובד כוכבים למאי הלכתא אמר רב פפא ג להאכילו נבילות אם רוב ישראל ישראל למאי הלכתא אמר רב פפא ד להחזיר לו אבידה מחצה על מחצה ישראל למאי הלכתא אמר ריש לקיש ה לנזקין ה"ד אי נימא דנגחיה תורא דידן לתורא דידיה לימא ליה אייתי ראיה דישראל את ושקול לא צריכא דנגחיה תורא דידיה לתורא דידן פלגא משלם ואידך פלגא אמר להו אייתי ראיה דלאו ישראל אנא ואתן לכון:

הדרן עלך בתולה נשאת

האשה ג) שנתארמלה או שנתגרשה היא אומרת בתולה נשאתני והוא אומר לא כי אלא אלמנה נשאתיך ו אם יש עדים שיצאת בהינומא וראשה פרוע כתובתה מאתים רבי יוחנן בן ברוקה אומר אף חילוק קליות ראיה ומודה רבי יהושע באומר לחבירו שדה זו של אביך היתה ולקחתיה הימנו שהוא נאמן שהפה

מצא בה תינוק מושלך. משנה היא בסדר טהרות גבי עיר שישראלים ועובדי כוכבים דרים בה: **מחצה על מחצה ישראל.** לקמיה מפרש מאי איכא בין רוב ישראל למחצה על מחצה דפליג להו בתרי: **לא שנו.** דאם רוב ישראל: **אלא להחיותו.** ב"ד מצווין לפרנסו משום וחי אחיך עמך (ויקרא כה): **אבל ליוחסין לא.** דאם בת היא אסורה לכהן ואפי' ליכא למיחש משום אסופי כגון הנך דאמרינן בעשרה יוחסין (קדושין עג:) ג) משלטי הדמיה תלי פיתקא תלי קמיעא מיהו חיישינן שמא בת עובד כוכבים היא (א) ולמ"ד גיורת פסולה לכהונה אפילו קטנה זו אסורה לכהן דתרי רובי בעינן ליוחסין: **ושמואל אמר אף לפקח עליו את הגל.** בשבת חשבינן ליה לישראל: **אשתמיטתיה.** לרבי ירמיה: **הא דאמר רב יהודה.** דהכא נמי תרי רובי הוו: **ולרב חנן בר רבא דאמר.** משמיה דרב: **הוראת שעה היתה.** והתם תרי רובי הוו וקאמר הוראת שעה היתה אבל לדורות לא בעינן תרי רובי: **קשיא הא.** דרב דאמר אבל ליוחסין לא אלמא רב תרי רובי בעי: **לא מתני הא.** דאמר רב יהודה אמר רב בקרונות של צפורי הוה מעשה וחד רובא הוה הלכך הוראת שעה היתה: **מי אמר שמואל הכי.** דלענין פיקוח נפש בעינן רובא: **אין הולכין כו'.** דאפילו בספק עובד כוכבים ספק ישראל ברוב עובדי כוכבים מפקחין: **ולענין פיקוח נפש אינו כן.** דאפילו ברוב עובדי כוכבים מפקחין דאין הולכין בה אחר הרוב: **למאי הלכתא.** כיון דאמר שמואל מפקחין עליו את הגל אלמא לאו עובד כוכבים הוא לכל מילי ולמאי הלכתא חשיב ליה עובד כוכבים: **להאכילו נבלות.** בידים וכ"ש שלא יחזירו לו אבידה ולמזקין: **להחזיר לו אבידה.** רבותא היא דמוציאין מיד ישראל הזוכה בה ועוד דאמור רבנן (סנהדרין דף עו:) המחזיר אבידה לכנעני עליו הכתוב אומר למען ספות הרוה את הצמאה שהשוה מגרים לחשיבתן של ישראל ונאמר לא יאבה ה' סלוח לו: **מחצה על מחצה ישראל למאי הלכתא.** להחזיר לו אבידה לא מצית אמרת דא"כ למאי הלכתא פלגינהו מהדדי: **לנזקין.** דתנן ב"ק (דף לז:) שור של ישראל שנגח לשור של כנעני פטור ושור של כנעני שנגח לשור של ישראל בין תם בין מועד משלם נזק שלם וישראל לישראל תם משלם חצי נזק ומועד משלם נזק שלם: **אילימא כו'.** וקאמרת דדיינין ליה כישראל ומחייבת ליה לשלם לו חצי נזקו: **לימא ליה.** ישראל אייתי ראיה דהא מחצה על מחצה הוא וספיקא הוא: **לא צריכא כו'.** וקא תבע ליה ישראל נזק שלם לתם כדין כנעני ואשמעינן תנא דכישראל דיינין ליה ולא משלם אלא חצי נזק דא"ל אייתי ראיה:

הדרן עלך בתולה נשאת

האשה שנתארמלה **או נתגרשה.** ותובעת כתובתה: **והוא אומר.** אנתגרשה קאי ולאלמנה היורשין אומרים לה אלמנה נשאך אבינו ואין לך אלא מנה וסטר הכתובה אבד: **אם יש עדים.** על נשואיה שיצאת מבית אביה לבית בעלה: **בהינומא.** בגמ' מפרש: **וראשה פרוע.** אלטייבליד"ה שערה על כתיפיה כך היו נוהגין להוציא את הבתולות מבית אביהן לבית החתונה: **אף חילוק קליות.** רגילים היו לחלק קליות להתינוקות בנישואי הבתולות: **קליות.** כשהשבולין לחין מייבשין אותן בתנור והן קליות ומתוקין לעולם: **ומודה ר' יהושע.** מפרש בגמ' אהיכא קאי ומאי מודה:
שהפה

ולרב חנן דאמר הוראת שעה היתה. ולדורות סגי בחד רובא קשיא הך ולא מיסתברא ליה למימר דהוראת שעה היתה שהתיר בתרי רובי אבל לדורות לא סגי אפילו בתרי רובי: **מאן דמתני הא לא מתני הא.** פי' בקונטרס דרב חנן לא מתני דקרונות של צפורי היה מעשה ולא הוה אלא חד רובא ולפירושו לא פליגי דלדורות לכ"ע בעינן תרי רובי ולא פליגי אלא במעשה היכי הוה ור"ח פי' דרב חנן לא מתני אבל ליוחסין לא וסגי לדידיה לדורות בחד רובא אבל קשה לפירושו לרב חנן תקשי ר' יוחנן בן נורי דאמר כמאן דסגי בחד רובא כדפריך לעיל ועוד דלא מיסתבר דשום אמורא יחלוק אההיא דאבל ליוחסין לא דרב גופיה קאמר לה בלא אמורא ולהכי אפירכא דרבי ירמיה לא משני מאן דמתני הא לא מתני הא: **אם רוב עובדי כוכבים עובד כוכבים למאי הלכתא.** לא מצי למימר לענין שלא להחיותו דמאי איריא רוב עובדי כוכבים אפילו מחצה נמי דדוקא ברוב ישראל קאמר רב דהוי ישראל להחיותו: **להחזיר לו אבדה.** הוה מצי למימר להחיותו כדאמר רב אלא נקט להחזיר לו אבדה דהוי רבותא טפי דאיסור גדול הוא ד) משום למען ספות הרוה וגו' אבל להחיותו לא הוי רבותא כל כך דהא ה) מפרנסין עניי עובדי כוכבים עם עניי ישראל ואפי' לשמואל דאמר ו) אין הולכין בממון אחר הרוב היינו ז) במוכר שור לחבירו ונמצא נגחן שבהיתר באו המעות לידו ומדעתו נתנם לו הלוקח אבל הכא מודי דאזלינן בתר רובא: **לא צריכא דנגחיה תורא דידיה כו'.** תימה דהכי נמי הוה מצי למימר מחצה על מחצה עובד כוכבים ומנגח תורא דידן לתורא דידיה [כולה מילתא הוי מצי למימר לענין נגיחה אלא ניחא בכל חד למנקט דבר חדש. מהר"ס]:

הדרן עלך בתולה נשאת

האשה. אם יש עדים שיצאת בהינומא כו'. בדלא נקיטא כתובה איירי דאי איכא כתובה ניחזי כתובתה אם היא בתולה או אלמנה ואפילו למ"ד ח) הטוען אחר מעשה ב"ד ואמר פרעתי נאמן מ"מ אין נאמן לומר כאן אלמנה נשאתיך מגו דאי בעי אמר פרעתי דמגו במקום עדים הוא:

ומודה רבי יהושע באומר שדה כו' דנאמן. מתוך פירוש הקונט' משמע דדוקא כשאין הלה תובעו ונאמן במגו דאי בעי שתיק אבל אם תובעו אינו נאמן ואינו נראה דהא קתני סיפא ואם יש עדים כו' משמע דדוקא אם יש עדים שהיתה של אביו אינו נאמן אבל אם אין עדים אע"ג דהלה תובעו נאמן מגו דאי בעי אמר לא היתה של אביך מעולם מדלא נקט אם תובעו אינו נאמן ובגמרא נמי פריך וליתני שדה זו שלך היתה משמע דהלה תובעו איירי ולכך משיב ודאי שלך היתה ולקחתיה ממך אבל אם לא תובעו אין צריך לומר שלך היתה כי מסתמא הוא יודע בעצמו דבר זה:
דאי

תוספות ישנים

א) [נראה לר"י דמשום דדרשינן וחי עמך ולא שימות בהכ ומשמע שלא יבוא לידי מיתה בשום ענין לכך יש לחוש למיעוט ישראל. ת"י].

הגהות הב"ח

(א) רש"י ד"ה אבל כו' ולמ"ד גיורת. נ"ב בפרק הבא על יבמתו דף ס כ"ב:

לעזי רש"י

איצטיבליד"ה. פירוש פרוע, מגודל שער (רש"י ויקרא יג, מה):

תוספות רי"ד

האשה שנתאלמנה או שנתגרשה היא אומרת בתולה נשאתני והוא

א) מכשירין פ"ב מ"ז יומא פד:, ב) כ"ב לב: [ושם איתא שנתאלמנה], ג) הגה"ה פי' משלטי הדמיה. מתוקנין אבריו. פיתקא. קמיע של כתב. קמיעא. קמיע של עיקרין דהא חסה על חייו והניחה תחלתו שאוהבתו אותו ולא השליכתו למות, ד) כדאיתא סנהדרין עו:, ה) כדאיתא גיטין סא., ו) [ב"ק מו: וב"ב לב:], ז) [עי' תוס' ב"ק מו: ותוס' ב"מ ל: ד"ה איסורא ותוס' סנהדרין עו: ד"ה דיה ותוס' יומא פה.], ח) [עי' תוס' לקמן פח: ופט. בד"ה הולכה וכו' א"כ לא שמואל לית ליה דר' יוחנן וכו'].

ליקוטי רש"י

ואמר רב לא שנו. דאם רוב ישראל מחזקין ליה לישראל. **אלא להחיותו. אבל ליוחסין לא.** כגון אם נקבה היא שיהא כהן מותר בה ואפי' ליכא למיחש לאסופי כגון הנך דאמרינן במסכת קידושין (דף עג:) תלי דכיקולא תלי פיתקא משלטי הדמיה חיישינן שמא כותית היא וגיורת אסורה לכהונה ואע"ג דרוב ישראל מעלה עשו ליוחסין דבעינן תרי רובי כדאמרי' בכתובות בפרק קמא (דף טו.) [יומא פד:]. **ושמואל אמר לפקח עליו את הגל.** קאמר דאם רוב ישראל [ישראל] אבל במחצה לא וכ"ש ברוב כותים [שם פה.]. **בקרונות של צפורי.** ביום השוק שסיעות ושיירות ממקום אחר באות שם [לעיל ע"א]. **ולפקח וכו' אינו כן.** דאמר אפילו ברוב כותים מפקחין. **למאי הילכתא.** הוי כותי אליבא דשמואל כיון דאמר מפקחין עליו כל שכן דמצוה להחיותו ולמאי הילכתא הוי כותי. **להאכילו נבילות.** עד שיגדל ויקבל עליו גירות. **מחצה על מחצה ישראל למאי הילכתא.** הוי ישראל ברוב ישראל טפי ממחצה על מחצה [דאי] שלא להאכילו נבילות במחצה על מחצה [נמי] לא ספיקי ליה. **לנזקין.** שור של ישראל שנגח של כותי פטור ושור של כותי שנגח של ישראל בין תם בין מועד משלם נזק שלם ושל ישראל שנגח של ישראל תם משלם חצי נזק מועד משלם נזק שלם. **אי נימא דנגחיה תורא דידן לתורא דידיה.** וקאמרינן דמחייבינן ליה לשלומי. **אייתי ראיה דישראל את ושקול.** וכל זמן שלא טבל בבית דין לשם גירות לא מצינן [לחיובי לישראל] לשלומי. **פלגא משלם.** כישראל ואידך פלגא ספק הוא וזה תובעו נזק שלם כדין כותי אמר ליה אייתי ראיה דלאו ישראל אנא ושקול [יומא פה.]. **האשה שנתארמלה.** וטוענת אבדתי כתובתי א"נ

במקום שאין כותבין כתובה כדמפרש בכתובות. **בתולה נשאתני.** ויש לי מאתים. **אלמנה נשאתיך.** ואין לך אלא מנה. **שיצאת.** מבית אביה לבית בעלה כשנכנסה לחופה. **בהינומא.** קלתא דמנמנמא ביה כלתא או ראשה פרוע בשוק בשעת כניסה לחופה שכן דרך הנישאות בתולות [רשב"ם ב"ב צב:]. נערה המאורסה היו רגילין לעשות לה חופה של הדס בכניסתה לחופה וקורין לה הינומא כדאמרינן בכתובות (דף טו:) שיצאתה בהינומא וראשה פרוע [ברכות נז:]. **כתובתה מאתים.** ואע"פ שאין לה עדים מעידים על בתוליה ואין יודעין אם נישאת בתולה או בעולה [רשב"ם שם].

The Gemara returns to the dispute of Rav and Shmuel just cited and elaborates Shmuel's view:

גּוּפָא – The text itself read: מָצָא בָּהּ תִּינוֹק מוּשְׁלָךְ – IF ONE FOUND AN ABANDONED CHILD IN [A CITY], and we do not know whether he is a Jew or an idolater, his identity is determined as follows: אִם רוֹב עוֹבְדֵי כּוֹכָבִים עוֹבֵד כּוֹכָבִים – IF A MAJORITY of the city's inhabitants ARE IDOLATERS, HE IS treated as AN IDOLATER; אִם רוֹב יִשְׂרָאֵל יִשְׂרָאֵל – and IF A MAJORITY of the inhabitants ARE JEWS, HE IS treated as A JEW. מֶחֱצָה עַל מֶחֱצָה יִשְׂרָאֵל – IF HALF are Jews AND HALF are idolaters, HE IS treated as A JEW. אָמַר רַב – **Rav said** in reference to this Mishnah: לֹא שָׁנוּ אֶלָּא לְהַחֲיוֹתוֹ – **They taught that** if most of the city's inhabitants are Jews the child is treated as a Jew **only with respect to sustaining him,** אֲבָל לְיוּחֲסִין לֹא – **but not with respect to** ascribing pure **lineage** to him. וּשְׁמוּאֵל אָמַר – **But Shmuel says:** לְפַקֵּחַ עָלָיו אֶת הַגַּל – The child is treated as a Jew even **with respect to clearing a heap** of rubble **from upon him** on the Sabbath.

The Gemara asks:

וּמִי אָמַר שְׁמוּאֵל הָכִי – **Now did Shmuel** actually **say this** (that we desecrate the Sabbath to save this child only if the law of majority dictates that we may)?[8] וְהָאָמַר רַב יוֹסֵף אָמַר רַב יְהוּדָה אָמַר שְׁמוּאֵל – **But Rav Yosef said in the name of Rav Yehudah who said** it **in the name of Shmuel:** אֵין הוֹלְכִין בְּפִיקּוּחַ נֶפֶשׁ אַחַר הָרוֹב – **We do not follow the majority where saving a life** is concerned; rather, we favor the saving of a life even in situations where this runs counter to the majority.[9] – ? –

The Gemara accepts this refutation and therefore reinterprets the focus of Shmuel's earlier ruling:[10]

אֶלָּא כִּי אִיתְּמַר דִּשְׁמוּאֵל אַרֵישָׁא אִתְּמַר – Rather, **when Shmuel's statement** regarding the unidentified child **was made, it was made in reference to the beginning** of the Mishnah, which states: אִם רוֹב עוֹבְדֵי כּוֹכָבִים עוֹבֵד כּוֹכָבִים – IF A MAJORITY of the city's inhabitants ARE IDOLATERS, HE IS treated as AN IDOLATER. אָמַר שְׁמוּאֵל – Concerning this ruling **Shmuel said:** וּלְפַקֵּחַ עָלָיו אֶת הַגַּל אֵינוֹ כֵּן – **But with regard to clearing** a heap **of rubble from upon him** on the Sabbath, **it is not so.** Although most of the inhabitants are idolaters, we treat the child as a Jew insofar as desecrating the Sabbath for him.[11]

In light of this answer, the Gemara asks:

אִם רוֹב עוֹבְדֵי כּוֹכָבִים עוֹבֵד כּוֹכָבִים – When the Mishnah states: IF A MAJORITY of the city's inhabitants ARE IDOLATERS, HE IS treated as AN IDOLATER, לְמַאי הִלְכְתָא – **to what law** does it refer?[12]

The Gemara answers:

אָמַר רַב פַּפָּא – **Rav Pappa said:** לְהַאֲכִילוֹ נְבֵילוֹת – It means that we are permitted **to feed him *neveilos.***[13]

The Gemara asks further:

אִם רוֹב יִשְׂרָאֵל יִשְׂרָאֵל – When the Mishnah states: IF A MAJORITY of the city's inhabitants ARE JEWS HE IS treated as A JEW, לְמַאי הִילְכְתָא – **to what law** does it refer?

The Gemara answers:

אָמַר רַב פַּפָּא – **Rav Pappa said:** לְהַחֲזִיר לוֹ אֲבֵידָה – **To return** his **lost property to him.**[14]

NOTES

explicitly in explanation of the Mishnah concerning a child found in the city. The disagreement as to whether Rav considered our Mishnah authoritative, or he dismissed it as a special ruling for the moment, centers on whether the Mishnah's case involved two favorable majorities or only a simple majority (*Tosafos* ד"ה מאן). [This represents *Rashi's* understanding of the passage. See *Tosafos* for *Rabbeinu Chananel's* alternative approach.]

[It is noteworthy that *Rashi* on 15a explained R' Yochanan ben Nuri's ruling as concurring with the opinion of R' Yehoshua, as opposed to Rabban Gamliel (see 15a note 3). Thus, Rav's ruling that the halachah follows R' Yochanan ben Nuri seems at odds with the ruling of Shmuel (on 12b and the top of 14a) that the halachah follows Rabban Gamliel in his dispute with R' Yehoshua (*Baal HaMaor*). However, as we explained on 15a (note 3), many Rishonim understand R' Yochanan ben Nuri's opinion as unrelated to the dispute between Rabban Gamliel and R' Yehoshua, so that the halachic rulings of Rav and Shmuel are compatible (see *Milchamos Hashem* et al.). For a reconciliation of the two rulings even according to *Rashi's* approach, see *Rashba* to 15a. See also *Pnei Yehoshua* to 15a.]

8. [Shmuel's statement was apparently said in response to Rav's ruling. Now Rav clearly refers to the case where most of the inhabitants of the city are Jews, since this is the only case in which he needs to teach that he is not considered a Jew in regard to lineage (*Maharam Schif*). It follows from this that Shmuel also made his statement with regard to this case, making it evident that Shmuel allows the Sabbath to be desecrated only because the majority of the inhabitants are Jews.]

9. That is, even if there is only a small possibility that the person in danger is a Jew and the principle of following the majority should dictate that he is an idolater (for whom we may not desecrate the Sabbath), the matter is still regarded to be in doubt, and we follow the rule that in cases of doubt involving danger to life the lenient position must be taken (*Rashi,* as explained by *Shitah Mekubetzes* ד"ה ומי).

[The basis for this rule of Shmuel is the verse from which Shmuel derives the law that we may desecrate the Sabbath to save a Jew's life (*Yoma* 85b): וָחַי בָּהֶם, *by which he shall live* (*Leviticus* 18:5). This implies that we must act to make *certain* that the observance of mitzvos does not lead to the death of the observer under *any* circumstances (*Tos. Yeshanim* here; *Tosafos, Yoma* 85a ד"ה ולפקח).]

10. [The Gemara has to this point assumed that Shmuel's ruling was directed at the case of a majority of Jews, as explained in note 8. The Gemara will now revise this understanding.]

11. According to this version of Shmuel's statement, Rav and Shmuel refer to different parts of the Mishnah. For as stated above (note 8), Rav refers to the Mishnah's ruling that when the majority are Jews the child is considered a Jew, whereas Shmuel refers to the ruling that when the majority are idolaters he is treated as an idolater.

[Accordingly, there is no longer a necessity to assume that Rav and Shmuel disagree. Rather, Rav may well agree with Shmuel's ruling that we desecrate the Sabbath for the child even where the majority were idolaters, and Shmuel may agree with Rav that we are obligated to support him only if the majority were Jews (see *Ramban,* cited by *Shitah Mekubetzes* ד"ה ומי and *Ritva;* cf. *Shitah Mekubetzes* ד"ה אלא כי איתמר, and see *Kereisi U'Peleisi* 63:1).]

12. That is, now that we have explained Shmuel to be saying that even where most of the city's inhabitants are idolaters, he is not treated as an idolater in regard to all matters (for we desecrate the Sabbath to save the child), in regard to what laws is he treated as an idolater? (*Rashi*).

[*Ritva,* following his view in the previous note that Rav agrees with Shmuel's ruling, explains that this question is relevant even according to Rav.]

13. [A *neveilah* is any animal that died without being rendered permissible for consumption through *shechitah* – i.e. non-kosher meat.] Since we have a principle of following the majority, if a majority of the city's inhabitants are idolaters, we may even *feed* the child *neveilos* and other non-kosher foods. It goes without saying that we also treat him as an idolater in regard to the obligations of returning a lost object and paying for damages (see notes 14 and 16) [where treating him as an idolater does not involve any direct action on our part, merely refraining from paying him or returning his object to him] (*Rashi;* see also *Rashi* to *Yoma* 85a).

14. [The Torah (*Deuteronomy* 22:1-3) commands one who finds a lost item to return it to its owner. This obligation does not apply where the owner is an idolater. (See note 16 for a possible rationale.)] The Mishnah in *Machshirin* thus teaches that if a majority of the city's inhabitants are Jews, if the lost object can be identified as the property of the child, the one who found it must return it to the child (*Rashi*).

Actually, the Gemara could have answered that this clause teaches that we support the child from charity, as Rav said above. Rav Pappa prefers this example because he considers it a greater novelty. Ordinarily, in cases of doubt we do not force a person holding money to give it up (*Rashi*). [Rather, we demand of the person claiming the money to prove that it is his. Thus, we should demand that the child prove absolutely that he is Jewish before requiring the finder to return the lost object to him.] This is true, according to Shmuel, even where a majority

ⁱ⁾ מצא בה תינוק מושלך אם רוב עובדי כוכבים עובד כוכבי' אם רוב ישראל ישראל מחצה על מחצה ישראל ואמר רב לא שנו אלא להחיותו ᵃאבל ליוחסין לא ושמואל אמר לפקח עליו את הגל אשתמיטתיה הא דא"ר יהודה אמר רב בקרונות של צפורי הוה מעשה ולרב חנן בר רבא דאמר הוראת שעה היתה קשיא הא מאן דמתני הא לא מתני הא גופא מצא בה תינוק מושלך אם רוב עובדי כוכבים עובד כוכבים אם רוב ישראל ישראל מחצה על מחצה ישראל אמר רב לא שנו אלא להחיותו אבל ליוחסין לא ושמואל אמר לפקח עליו את הגל ומי אמר שמואל הכי והאמר רב יוסף אמר רב יהודה אמר שמואל אין הולכין בפיקוח נפש אחר הרוב אלא כי איתמר דשמואל ארישא איתמר אם רוב עובדי כוכבים עובד כוכבים אמר שמואל ᵃ⁾ ᵇולפקח עליו את הגל אינו כן אם רוב עובדי כוכבים עובד כוכבים למאי הלכתא אמר רב פפא ᶜלהאכילו נבילות אם רוב ישראל ישראל למאי הלכתא אמר רב פפא ᵈלהחזיר לו אבידה מחצה על מחצה ישראל למאי הלכתא אמר ריש לקיש ᵉלנזקין ה"ד אי נימא דנגחיה תורא דידן לתורא דידיה לימא ליה אייתי ראיה דישראל את ושקול לא צריכא דנגחיה תורא דידיה לתורא דידן פלגא משלם ואידך פלגא אמר להו אייתי ראיה דלאו ישראל אנא ואתן לכון:

הדרן עלך בתולה נשאת

האשה ᵍ⁾ שנתארמלה או שנתגרשה היא אומרת בתולה נשאתני והוא אומר לא כי אלא אלמנה נשאתיך ᶦאם יש עדים שיצאת בהינומא וראשה פרוע כתובתה מאתים רבי יוחנן בן ברוקה אומר אף חילוק קליות ראיה ומודה רבי יהושע באומר לחבירו שדה זו של אביך היתה ולקחתיה הימנו שהוא נאמן שהפה

רש"י

ולרב חנן דאמר הוראת שעה היתה. ולדורות סגי בחד רובא קשיא הך ולא מיסתברא ליה למימר דהוראת שעה היתה שהתיר בתרי רובי אבל לדורות לא סגי אפילו בתרי רובי: **מאן** דמתני הא לא מתני הא. פי' בקונטרס דרב חנן לא מתני דקרונות של צפורי היה מעשה ולא הוה אלא חד רובא ולפירושו לא פליגי לדורות לכ"ע בעינן תרי רובי ולא פליגי אלא במעשה היכי הוה ור"ת פי' דרב חנן לא מתני אבל ליוחסין לא וסגי לדידיה לדורות בחד רובא אבל קשה לפירושו לרב חנן תקשי ר' יוחנן בן נורי דאמר כמאן דסגי בחד רובא דכדפריך לעיל ועוד דלא מיסתבר דשום אמורא יחלוק אהאי דאבל ליוחסין לא דרב גופיה קאמר לה בלא אמורא ולהכי אפירכא דרבי ירמיה לא משני מאן דמתני הא לא מתני הא: **אם** רוב עובדי כוכבים עובד כוכבים למאי הלכתא. לא מצי למימר לענין שלא להחיותו דמאי איריא רוב עובדי כוכבים אפילו מחצה נמי דדוקא ברוב ישראל קאמר רב דהוי ישראל להחיותו: **להחזיר** לו אבדה. הוה מצי למימר להחיותו כדאמר רב אלא נקט להחזיר לו אבדה דהוי רבותא טפי דלאיסור גדול הוא ⁷⁾ משום למען ספות הרוה וגו' אבל להחיותו לא הוי רבותא כל כך דהא ⁸⁾ מפרנסין עניי עובדי כוכבים עם עניי ישראל ואפי' לשמואל דאמר ⁹⁾ אין הולכין בממון אחר הרוב היינו ¹⁾ במוכר שור לחבירו ונמצא נגחן שבהיתר בא המעות לידו ומדעתו נתנם לו הלוקח אבל הכא מודי דאזלינן בתר רובא: **לא** צריכא דנגחיה תורא דידיה כו'. תימה דהכי נמי הוה מצי למימר מחצה על מחצה עובד כוכבים ומנגח תורא דידן לתורא דידיה [כולה מילתא הוי מצי למימר לענין נגיחה אלא ניחא בכל חד למאות דבר חדש. מהר"ס]:

הדרן עלך בתולה נשאת

האשה. אם יש עדים שיצאת בהינומא כו'. בדלא נקיטא כתובה איירי דאי איכא כתובה ניחזי כתובתה אם היא בתולה או אלמנה ואפילו למ"ד ⁸⁾ הטוען אחר מעשה ב"ד ואמר פרעתי נאמן מ"מ אין נאמן לומר כאן אלמנה נשאתיך מגו דאי בעי אמר פרעתי דמגו במקום עדים הוא:

ומודה רבי יהושע באומר שדה כו' דנאמן. מתוך פירוש הקונט' משמע דלדוקא כשאין הלה תובעו ונאמן במגו דאי בעי שתיק אבל אם תובעו אינו נאמן ואינו נראה דהא קתני סיפא ואם יש עדים כו' משמע דלדוקא אם יש עדים שהיתה של אביו אינו נאמן אבל אם אין עדים אע"ג דהלה תובעו נאמן מגו דאי בעי אמר לא היתה של אביך מעולם מדלא נקט אם תובעו אינו נאמן ובגמרא נמי פריך וליתני שדה זו שלך היתה משמע דבהלה תובעו איירי ולכך משיב ודאי שלך היתה ולקחתיה ממך אבל אם לא תובעו אין שייך לומר שלך היתה כי מסתמא הוא יודע בעצמו דבר זה: דאי

רש"י

מצא בה תינוק מושלך. משנה היא בסדר טהרות גבי עיר שישראלים ועובדי כוכבים דרים בה: מחצה על מחצה ישראל. לקמיה מפרש מאי איכא בין רוב ישראל למחצה על מחצה דפליג להו בתרי: **לא** שנו. דאם רוב ישראל ישראל: **אלא** להחיותו. ב"ד מצווין לפרנסו משום וחי אחיך עמך (ויקרא כה): **אבל** ליוחסין לא. דאם בת היא אסורה לכהן ואפי' ליכא למיחש משום אסופי כגון הנך דאמרינן בעשרה יוחסין (קדושין עג:) ᵍ⁾ משלטי הדמיה תלי פיתקא תלי קמיעא מיהו חיישינן שמא בת עובד כוכבים היא ᵈ⁾ ולמ"ד גיורת פסולה לכהונה אפילו קטנה זו אסורה לכהן דתרי רובי בעינן ליוחסין: **ושמואל** אמר אף לפקח עליו את הגל. בשבת חשבינן ליה לישראל: **אשתמיטתיה.** לרבי ירמיה: **הא דאמר** רב יהודה. דהכא נמי תרי רובי הוו: **ולרב חנן בר רבא דאמר.** משמיה דרב: הוראת שעה היתה. והתם תרי רובי הוו וקאמר הוראת שעה היתה אבל לדורות לא בעינן תרי רובי: **קשיא הא.** דרב דאמר אבל ליוחסין לא אלמא רב תרי רובי בעי: **לא מתני הא.** דאמר רב יהודה אמר רב בקרונות של צפורי הוה מעשה וחד רובא הוה הוראת שעה היתה: **מי אמר שמואל הכי.** דלענין פיקוח נפש בעינן רובא: **אין הולכין כו'.** דאפילו בספק עובד כוכבים ספק ישראל ברוב עובדי כוכבים מפקחין: **ולענין פיקוח נפש אינו כן.** דאפילו ברוב עובדי כוכבים מפקחין דאין הולכין בה אחר הרוב: **למאי הלכתא.** כיון דאמר שמואל מפקחין עליו את הגל אלמא לאו עובד כוכבים הוא לכל מילי ולמאי הלכתא חשיב ליה עובד כוכבים: **להאכילו נבלות.** בידים וכ"ש שלא יחזירו לו אבידה ולמקין: **להחזיר לו אבידה.** רבותא היא דמוליאין מיד ישראל הזוכה בה ועוד דאמור רבנן (סנהדרין עו:) המחזיר אבידה לכנעני עליו הכתוב אומר למען ספות הרוה את הצמאה שהשוה מלריס להשיבהן של ישראל ואמר לא יאבה ה' סלוח לו: **מחצה על מחצה ישראל למאי הלכתא.** להחזיר לו אבידה לא אבידה לא מלית אמרת דה"ל למאי הלכתא פלגינהו מהדדי: **לנזקין.** דתנן בב"ק (דף לז:) שור של ישראל שנגח לשור של כנעני פטור ושור של כנעני שנגח לשור של ישראל בין תם בין מועד משלם נזק שלם וישראל לישראל תם משלם חצי נזק ומועד משלם נזק שלם: **אילימא כו'.** וקאמרת דדיינין ליה כישראל ומחייבת ליה לשלם לו חצי נזקו: **לימא ליה.** ישראל אייתי ראיה דהא מחצה על מחצה הוא וספיקא הוא: **לא צריכא כו'.** וקא תבע ליה ישראל נזק שלם לאם כדין כנעני ואשמעינן תנא דכישראל דיינינן ליה ולא משלם אלא חצי נזק דה"ל אייתי ראיה:

הדרן עלך בתולה נשאת

האשה שנתארמלה או נתגרשה. ותובעת כתובתה: **והוא אומר.** אנתגרשה קאי ולאלמנה היורשין אומרים לה אלמנה נשאך אבינו ואין לך אלא מנה ושטר הכתובה אבד: **אם יש עדים.** על נשואיה שילאת מבית אביה לבית בעלה: **בהינומא.** בגמ' מפרש: **וראשה פרוע.** שערה על כתיפיה כך היו נוהגין להוליא את הבתולות מבית אביהן לבית החתונה: **אף חילוק קליות.** רגילים היו לחלק קליות להתינוקות בנישואי הבתולות: **קליות.** כשהשבולין לחין מייבשין אותן בתנור והן קליות ומתוקין לעולם: **ומודה ר' יהושע.** מפרש בגמ' אהיכא קאי ומאי מודה: שהפה

עין משפט נר מצוה

צד א מיי' פט"ו מהל' איסורי ביאה הלכה כה טוש"ע אה"ע סימן ד סעיף לג:

צה ב ג ד ה מיי' שם הל' כו ועור שו"ע שם סעיף לד:

א ו מיי' פט"ו מהלכות אישות הלכה כה טור ש"ע שם סי' צו סעיף טו:

תוספות ישנים

א) [נראה לר"י דמשום דדרשינן ומי כסף ולא שימות כסף ומשמע שלא יבא לידי מתה בשום ענין לכך יש לפוש למיעוט ישראל. ת"י].

הגהות הב"ח

(א) רש"י ד"ה אבל וכו' ולמ"ד גיורת. נ"ב בפרק הבא על יבמתו דף ם ע"ב:

לעזי רש"י

איצטייבלי"ה. פירוש פרוע, מגודל שער (רש"י ויקרא י, מה).

תוספות רי"ד

האשה שנתארמלה או שנתגרשה היא אומרת בתולה נשאתני והוא אומר לא כי אלא אלמנה נשאתיך אם יש עדים שיצאה בהינומא וראשה פרוע כתובתה מאתים ר"י אומר אף חילוק קליות ראיה. פי' הוא אומר אנתגרשה קאי ולאלמנה אומרים לה היורשים אבינו לא אלמ"ה ואין לך אלא מנה ושטר כתובה אבד אם יש עדים על נשואיה שיצאת מבית אביה בעלה בהינומא שהיא סימן הבתולות כדמפרש לקמן וראשה פרוע שערה על כתפה וכך היו מוציאים הבתולות מבית אביהן לבית החתונה. **אף חילוק וכו'** רגילין היו לחלק מיני פירות וקליות שהיו מייבשין השבלים כשהם לחים בתנור והם מתוקין ובשואי הבתולות נותנים ומחלקין מהם לתינוקות ואי איכא עדי הינומא אע"ג שהיא אלמנה בגביא דאיכא בעדי הינומא ואע"ג דאיכא למיחש לפרעון הכל טענו דהוה מצי למיטען איהו ב"ד טוענין בעבור היתומים גביא כתובתה דהכי אמרינן בשנים אוחזין הטוען אחר מעשה ב"ד לא אמר כלום דכל מעשה ב"ד כמאן דנקט שטרא בידיה דמי ותנן נמי בפרק הכותב בוציאה גט ואין עמה כתובה גובה כתובתה ולא מצי למטען פרעתי עד שיראה שטר כתובתה קרוע או שובר והתם מכח דלא מבעי' במנה משתים שהיא תנאי ב"ד דגביא אלא אפילו תוספת בלא כתובה נמי גביא ולא מהימן לומר פרעתיך הלכך ה"נ מיתמי

מסורת הש"ס

א) מכשירין פ"ב מ"ז יומא פד., ב) ב"ב לב: [וסם איתא שנתארמנה], ג) הגה"ה פי' משלטי הדמיה. מתוקנין אבריו. פיתקא. קמיע של כתב. קמיעא. קמיע של עיקרין דהא תלה על פיו והוכיח מתלתו שאוהבת אותו ולא השליכתו למות, ד) כדאיתא סנהדרין עו:, ה) כדאיתא גיטין סא., ו) [ב"ק מו: וב"ב לב:], ז) [עי' תוס' ב"ק מו. ותוס' ב"מ כ: ד"ה איסורא ותוס' סנהדרין ג: ד"ה דיני ותוס' יומא פה.], ח) [עי' תוס' לקמן פח: וסט. בד"ה הולאה וכו' ה"א אי שמואל לית ליה דר' יוחנן וכו'].

ליקוטי רש"י

ואמר רב לא שנו. דאם רוב ישראל מחזקין ליה לישראל. **אלא להחיותו אבל ליוחסין לא.** כגון אם נקבה היא שיאה כהן מותר בה לא ואפילו ליכא למיחש לאסופי כגון הנך דאמרינן במסכת קידושין (דף עג:) תלי דבידולא תלי פיתקא רמי מוזרלא משלטי הדמיה חיישינן שמא כותית היא וגיורת אסורה לכהונה ואע"ג דרוב ישראל מעלה עשו ליוחסין דבעינן תרי רובי כדאמרי' בכתובות בפרק קמא (דף טו.) [יומא פד:]. **ושמואל אמר לפקח עליו את הגל.** קאמר דאם רוב ישראל [ישראל] אבל במחצה על מחצה לא וכ"ש ברוב עובד כוכבים [שם פה.]. **בקרונות של צפורי.** ביום השוק סחורות ומטמון מחד באחת שם [לעיל ע"א]. **ולפקח וכו' אינו כן.** דאמר אפילו רוב כותים מפקחין. **למאי הילכתא.** הוי כותי אליבא דשמואל כיון דאמר מפקחין עליו את הגל ואמאי כותי בהחיותו ולמאי הילכתא הוי כותי. **להאכילו נבילות.** עד שיגדל ויקבל עליו גירות. **אם רוב ישראל ישראל למאי הילכתא.** הוי ישראל ברוב ישראל טפי ממחצה על מחצה. **להחזיר לו אבידה.** שלא להחזיר נבילות מחצה על מחצה [ואין] [נמין] [ישראל] הוא פסיק ליה. **לנזקין.** שור של ישראל שנגח שור של כותי פטור ושור של כותי שנגח שור של ישראל בין תם בין מועד משלם נזק שלם ושל ישראל שנגח של ישראל תם משלם חצי נזק מועד משלם נזק שלם. **אי נימא דנגחיה תורא דידיה.** וקאמרינן דמחייבינן ליה לשלומי. **אייתי ראיה דישראל את ושקול.** וכל זמן שלא טבל בבית דין לשם גירות לא מצינן [לחיובי לישראל] לשלומי. **פלגא משלם.** כישראל ואידך פלגא ספק הוא וזה תובעו נזק שלם כדין כותי אמר ליה אייתי ראיה דלאו ישראל אנא ושקול [יומא פה.]. **האשה שנתארמלה.** ותובעת אבדתי כתובתי א"נ

במקום שאין כותבין כתובה כדמפרש בכתובות. **בתולה נשאתני.** ויש לי מאתים. **אלמנה נשאתיך.** ואין לך אלא מנה. **שיצאת.** מבית אביה לבית בעלה כשנכנסה לחופה. **בהינומא.** קלתא דמנמנמא ביה כלתא או ראשה פרוע בשוק בשעת כניסה לחופה שכן דרך הנישאות בתולות [רשב"ם ב"ב צב:]. נערה המאורסה היו רגילין לעשות לה חופה של הדס בכניסתה לחופה וקורין לה הינומא כדאמרינן בכתובות (דף טו:) שילאתה בהינומא וראשה פרוע [ברכות נו.]. **כתובתה מאתים.** ואע"פ שאין לה עדים מעידים על בתוליה ואין יודעין אם נישאת בתולה או בעולה [רשב"ם שם].

מָצָא בָּהּ תִּינוֹק מוּשְׁלָךְ — IF ONE FOUND AN ABANDONED CHILD IN [A CITY], and we do not know whether he is a Jew or an idolater, his identity is decided as follows: אִם רוֹב עוֹבְדֵי כוֹכָבִים עוֹבֵד כּוֹכָבִים — IF A MAJORITY of the city's inhabitants ARE IDOLATERS, HE IS treated as AN IDOLATER; אִם רוֹב יִשְׂרָאֵל יִשְׂרָאֵל — and IF A MAJORITY of the inhabitants ARE JEWS, HE IS treated as A JEW. מֶחֱצָה עַל מֶחֱצָה יִשְׂרָאֵל — If HALF of the inhabitants are Jews AND HALF are idolaters, HE IS treated as A JEW.[1] וְאָמַר רַב — And Rav said in reference to this Mishnah: לֹא שָׁנוּ אֶלָּא לְהַחֲיוֹתוֹ — They taught that if most of the city's inhabitants are Jews the child is treated as a Jew only with respect to sustaining him,[2] אֲבָל לְיוֹחֲסִין לֹא — but not with respect to ascribing pure lineage to him.[3] וּשְׁמוּאֵל אָמַר — But Shmuel said: לְפַקֵּחַ עָלָיו אֶת הַגַּל — The child is treated as a Jew even with respect to clearing a heap of rubble from upon him on the Sabbath.[4] At any rate, we see from Rav's explanation of this Mishnah that a simple majority is not a sufficient basis for ruling someone to be of fit lineage. How, then, could Rav have ruled in accordance with R' Yochanan ben Nuri of our Mishnah, who permitted the young girl to the Kehunah on the basis of a simple majority?

The Gemara rejects the question:

אִשְׁתְּמִיטְתֵּיהּ הָא דְּאָמַר רַב יְהוּדָה אָמַר רַב — [R' Yirmiyah], who presented this challenge, forgot that which Rav Yehudah said in the name of Rav: בְּקְרוֹנוֹת שֶׁל צִפּוֹרִי הָיָה מַעֲשֶׂה — The incident recorded in our Mishnah occurred among the wagons of Tzippori, during the market day when the city was visited by traveling caravans. Since it was unclear whether her assailant was a resident of the city or one of the visitors, R' Yochanan ben Nuri ruled that if a majority of each group was of fit lineage she would be permitted to the Kehunah on the basis of the two favorable majorities. Thus, Rav Chiya bar Ashi's quotation of Rav, as ruling in accordance with R' Yochanan ben Nuri, actually accords with Rav's explanation of the cited Mishnah — that a simple majority is insufficient regarding matters of lineage.

Having established that Rav explained our Mishnah's case as one in which there were two favorable majorities, the Gemara examines the second version of Rav's opinion concerning the Mishnah's ruling:

וּלְרַב חָנָן בַּר רָבָא דְּאָמַר הוֹרָאַת שָׁעָה הָיְתָה — And according to Rav Chanan bar Rava, who said in the name of Rav that it was a special ruling for the moment, קַשְׁיָא הָא — this, i.e. Rav's explanation of the Mishnah about the abandoned child, is difficult. For the statement that our Mishnah represents an exceptional ruling implies that, ordinarily, a woman can be ruled permitted to the Kehunah on the basis of a *single* majority.[5] Why, then, did Rav state that a single majority is effective only in regard to sustaining the child who is found, but not in regard to ascribing pure lineage to him?

The Gemara answers:

מַאן דְּמַתְנֵי הָא — The one [Rav Chanan bar Rava] who taught this statement of Rav, that our Mishnah's ruling represents an exception to the general rule, לֹא מַתְנֵי הָא — did not teach this other statement of Rav, that the incident recorded in the Mishnah occurred among the wagons of Tzippori when there were visiting caravans. Rather, he maintains that the girl was definitely assaulted by a resident of the town, so that the only consideration was the existence of a majority of fit people within the town.[6] R' Yochanan ben Nuri thus ruled her fit for the Kehunah on the basis of a simple majority. For this reason, Rav stated that it was a special ruling for the moment. As taught by Rav in regard to the case of a child who was found in a city, a simple majority is normally insufficient for matters of lineage.[7]

NOTES

1. [Thus, if either the majority of the city's inhabitants, or half of them, are Jews, we treat the child as a Jew.] Since the Mishnah rules separately on both the cases, it is apparent that there are legal differences between them. The Gemara will explain what they are (*Rashi*).

2. That is, in regard to the court's obligation to support him [if he is in need, as they do for any Jew in need]. This obligation is based on the verse (*Leviticus* 25:36, see *Bava Metzia* 88b): וְחֵי אָחִיךָ עִמָּךְ, *and your brother shall live with you* (*Rashi*) [which is why it is referred to as לְהַחֲיוֹת]. By the same token, he is treated as a Jew in regard to all other matters, except for the one mentioned below (*Yam Shel Shlomo* §45; *Beis Shmuel* 4:54, in explanation of *Rashi;* cf. *Rambam, Isurei Biah* 16:25; see commentators to *Tur* and *Shulchan Aruch, Even HaEzer* 4:33). [The reason Rav refers specifically to supporting him, is because it involves the expenditure of money, which the rule of majority does not always suffice to require (see note 14 below, and *Haflaah* to *Tosafos* ד"ה להחזיר).]

Rav's statement implies that if only half the city's residents were Jews, the court would not be obligated to give support to this unidentified child unless, of course, he was in danger of dying (*Ritva,* in explanation of *Rashi;* see also *Tosafos* ד"ה אם). See *Kovetz Shiurim* §42 for a discussion about why in fact the courts would not be required to support someone who has a fifty percent chance of being a Jew.

[*Ramban* cited in *Shitah Mekubetzes* (ד"ה הא דאמרינן) has a variant reading of *Rashi* here, as noted by *Rashba,* which he struggles to explain. Indeed, *Rashi's* commentary to *Yoma* 84b seems to follow *Ramban's* explanation, as we explained there. Our explanation of the Gemara here, however, follows the version of *Rashi* found here.]

3. That is, in relation to lineage we must be concerned that the child is an idolater even if the majority of the city's inhabitants are Jews. Therefore, if the child is a female, she is prohibited to a Kohen even if she converts to Judaism, since a Kohen may not marry a convert [see *Yevamos* 60b]. Although the principle of majority should dictate that this child is a Jew, we require two majorities for matters of lineage (*Rashi;* see *Noda BiYehudah* I, *Even HaEzer* §7 and *Shev Shmaatsa* 4:20; see also *Haflaah*).

The Mishnah refers to a child who appears to have been well looked after, and hence is unlikely to be a *mamzer.* If there were a possibility of the child being a *mamzer,* he or she would be forbidden to both Kohanim and non-Kohanim, even if found in a city inhabited only by Jews (*Rashi,* based on *Kiddushin* 73a-b).

4. *Rashi.* [The Gemara in *Yoma* (85a-85b) cites several derivations for the principle that we are allowed to desecrate the Sabbath in order to save a life. This dispensation was not granted by the Torah for idolaters.]

Shmuel apparently means that we desecrate the Sabbath to save the unidentified child's life only where the majority of the city's inhabitants are Jews. This implies that where half are Jews and half are idolaters, and certainly where most of the inhabitants are idolaters, we do not desecrate the Sabbath to save the child (*Rashi* below ד"ה מי אמר). The Gemara below will, however, challenge and reject this interpretation of Shmuel's statement.

[Shmuel's statement should not be understood to imply that Rav, who seems to dispute Shmuel's ruling, forbids desecrating the Sabbath even if most of the inhabitants are Jews. This certainly cannot be. Rather, Rav (according to the Gemara's current understanding) permits desecrating the Sabbath for the child even if only half the inhabitants are Jews, whereas Shmuel does not permit this unless most are Jews (see *Ritva*).]

5. Since R' Yochanan ben Nuri's ruling in our Mishnah was a stringent one — for he imposed the requirement for two favorable majorities — the statement that this was an exceptional case implies that in general a more lenient rule applies, viz. a simple majority is sufficient even concerning matters of lineage (*Rashi, Ritva*).

6. *Rashi.* The incident was not so well known, and there was thus disagreement as to the exact circumstances surrounding it (*Ritva*).

7. *Rashi.* Thus, Rav meant that R' Yochanan ben Nuri's *lenient* ruling was a special ruling for the moment (as explained above, 15a note 43).

On the other hand, Rav Yehudah, who stated in the name of Rav that the incident occurred among the wagons of Tzippori — and who thus understands R' Yochanan ben Nuri as having ruled the girl permitted on the basis of *two* majorities — holds like Rav Chiya bar Ashi, who quoted Rav as saying that the halachah follows our Mishnah.

In summary, all of Rav's disciples agree that Rav considers a simple majority insufficient for deciding matters of lineage, as Rav stated

מצא בה תינוק מושלך אם רוב עובדי כוכבים עובד כוכבי' אם רוב ישראל ישראל מחצה על מחצה ישראל ואמר רב לא שנו אלא להחיותו [א] אבל ליוחסין לא ושמואל אמר לפקח עליו את הגל אשתמיטתיה הא דא"ר יהודה אמר רב בקרונות של צפורי הוה מעשה ולרב חנן בר רבא דאמר הוראת שעה היתה קשיא הא מאן דמתני הא לא מתני הא גופא מצא בה תינוק מושלך אם רוב עובדי כוכבים עובד כוכבים אם רוב ישראל ישראל מחצה על מחצה ישראל אמר רב לא שנו אלא להחיותו אבל ליוחסין לא ושמואל אמר לפקח עליו את הגל ומי אמר שמואל הכי והאמר רב יוסף אמר רב יהודה אמר שמואל אין הולכין בפיקוח נפש אחר הרוב אלא כי איתמר דשמואל ארישא אתמר אם רוב עובדי כוכבים עובד כוכבים אמר שמואל [ב] ולפקח עליו את הגל אינו כן אם רוב עובדי כוכבים עובד כוכבים למאי הלכתא אמר רב פפא [ג] להאכילו נבילות אם רוב ישראל ישראל למאי הלכתא אמר רב פפא [ד] להחזיר לו אבידה מחצה על מחצה ישראל למאי הלכתא אמר ריש לקיש [ה] לנזקין ה"ד אי נימא דנגחיה תורא דידן לתורא דידיה לימא ליה אייתי ראיה דישראל את ושקול לא צריכא דנגחיה תורא דידיה לתורא דידן פלגא משלם ואידך פלגא אמר להו אייתי ראיה דלאו ישראל אנא ואתן לכון:

הדרן עלך בתולה נשאת

האשה [ג] שנתארמלה או שנתגרשה היא אומרת בתולה נשאתני והוא אומר לא כי אלא אלמנה נשאתיך [ו] אם יש עדים שיצאת בהינומא וראשה פרוע כתובתה מאתים רבי יוחנן בן ברוקה אומר אף חילוק קליות ראיה ומודה רבי יהושע באומר לחבירו שדה זו של אביך היתה ולקחתיה הימנו שהוא נאמן שהפה

רש"י

מצא בה תינוק מושלך. משנה היא בסדר טהרות גבי עיר שישראלים ועובדי כוכבים דרים בה: **מחצה על מחצה ישראל.** לקמיה מפרש מאי איכא בין רוב ישראל למחצה על מחצה דפליג להו בתרי: **לא שנו.** דאם רוב ישראל ישראל: **אלא להחיותו.** ב"ד מצווין לפרנסו משום וחי אחיך עמך (ויקרא כה): **אבל ליוחסין לא.** דאם בת היא אסורה לכהן ואפי' ליכא למיחש משום אסופי כגון הנך דאמרינן בעשרה יוחסין (קדושין עג:) [ג] משלטי הדמיה תלי פיתקא תלי קמיעא מיהו חיישינן שמא בת עובד כוכבים היא (א) ולמ"ד גיורת פסולה לכהונה אפילו קטנה זו אסורה לכהן דתרי רובי בעינן ליוחסין: **ושמואל אמר אף לפקח עליו את הגל.** בשבת חשבינן ליה לישראל: **אשתמיטתיה.** לרבי ירמיה: **הא דאמר רב יהודה.** דהכא נמי תרי רובי הוו: **ולרב חנן בר רבא דאמר.** משמיה דרב: **הוראת שעה היתה.** והתם תרי רובי הוו וקאמר הוראת שעה היתה אבל לדורות לא בעינן תרי רובי: **קשיא הא.** דרב דאמר אבל ליוחסין לא אלמא רב תרי רובי בעי: **לא מתני הא.** דאמר רב יהודה אמר רב בקרונות של צפורי הוה מעשה וחד רובא הוה הלכך הוראת שעה היתה: **מי אמר שמואל הכי.** לענין פיקוח נפש בעינן רובא: **אין הולכין כו'.** דאפילו בספק עובד כוכבים ספק ישראל ברוב עובדי כוכבים מפקחין: **ולענין פיקוח נפש אינו כן.** דאפילו ברוב עובדי כוכבים מפקחין דאין הולכין בה אחר הרוב: **למאי הלכתא.** כיון דאמר שמואל מפקחין עליו את הגל אלמא לאו עובד כוכבים הוא לכל מילי ולמאי הלכתא חשיב ליה עובד כוכבים: **להאכילו נבלות.** בידים וכ"ש שלא יחזירו לו אבידה ולמקין: **להחזיר לו אבידה.** רבותא היא דמוציאין מיד ישראל הזוכה בה ועוד דאמור רבנן (סנהדרין דף עו:) המחזיר אבידה לכנעני עליו הכתוב אומר למען ספות הרוה את הצמאה שהשוה מלכים לחשיבון אבידת ישראל ונאמר לא יאבה ה' סלוח לו: **מחצה על מחצה ישראל למאי הלכתא.** להחזיר לו אבידה לא מצית אמרת דא"כ למאי הלכתא פלגינהו מהדדי: **לנזקין.** דתנן ב"ק (דף לז:) שור של ישראל שנגח לשור של כנעני פטור ושור של כנעני שנגח לשור של ישראל בין תם בין מועד משלם נזק שלם וישראל לישראל תם משלם חצי נזק ומועד משלם נזק שלם: **אילימא כו'.** וקאמרת דדיינין ליה כישראל ומחייבת ליה לשלם לו חצי נזקו: **לימא ליה.** ישראל אייתי ראיה דהא מחצה על מחצה הוא וספיקא הוא: **לא צריכא כו'.** וקא תבע ליה ישראל נזק שלם לאם כדין כנעני ואשמעינן תנא דכישראל דיינינן ליה ולא משלם אלא חצי נזק דא"ל אייתי ראיה:

הדרן עלך בתולה נשאת

האשה שנתארמלה או נתגרשה. ותובעת כתובתה: **והוא אומר.** אנתגרשה קאי ולאלמנה היורשין אומרים לה אלמנה נשאך אבינו ואין לך אלא מנה ושטר הכתובה אבד: **אם יש עדים.** על נשואיה שיצאת מבית אביה לבית בעלה: **בהינומא.** בגמ' מפרש: **וראשה פרוע.** אילטיי"לד"ה שערה על כתיפיה כך היו נוהגין להוציא את הבתולות מבית אביהן לבית החתונה: **אף חילוק קליות.** רגילים היו לחלק קליות להתינוקות בנישואי הבתולות: **קליות.** כשהשבולין לחין מייבשין אותן בתנור והן קליות ומתוקין לעולם: **ומודה ר' יהושע.** מפרש בגמ' אהיכא קאי ומאי מודה:

תוספות

ולרב חנן דאמר הוראת שעה היתה. ולדורות סגי בחד רובא קשיא הך ולא מיסתברא ליה למימר דהוראת שעה היתה שהתיר בתרי רובי אבל לדורות לא סגי אפילו בתרי רובי: **מאן** דמתני הא לא מתני הא. פי' בקונטרס דרב חנן לא מתני דבקרונות של צפורי היה מעשה ולא הוה אלא חד רובא ופירושו לא פליגי לדורות לכ"ע בעינן תרי רובי ולא פליגי אלא במעשה היכי הוה ור"ת פי' דרב חנן לא מתני אבל ליוחסין לא וסגי לדידיה לדורות בחד רובא אבל קשה לפירושו לרב חנן תקשי ר' יוחנן בן נורי דאמר כמאן דסגי בחד רובא כדפריך לעיל ועוד דלא מיסתבר דשום אמורא יחלוק אההיא דאבל ליוחסין לא דרב גופיה קאמר לה בלא אמורא ולהכי אפירכא דרבי ירמיה לא משני מאן דמתני הא לא מתני הא: **אם** רוב עובדי כוכבים עובד כוכבים למאי הלכתא. לא מצי למימר לענין שלא להחיותו דמאי איריא רוב עובדי כוכבים אפילו מחצה נמי דדוקא ברוב ישראל קאמר רב דהוי ישראל להחיותו: **להחזיר** לו אבדה. הוה מצי למימר להחיותו כדאמר רב אלא נקט להחזיר לו אבדה דהוי רבותא טפי דלאיסור גדול הוא [ד] משום למען ספות הרוה וגו' אבל להחיותו לא הוי רבותא כל כך דהא [ה] מפרנסין עניי עובדי כוכבים עם עניי ישראל ואפי' לשמואל דאמר [ו] אין הולכין בממון אחר הרוב היינו [ז] במוכר שור לחבירו ונמצא נגחן שבהיתר באו המעות לידו ומדעתו נתנם לו הלוקח אבל הכא מודי דאזלינן בתר רובא: **לא** צריכא דנגחיה תורא דידיה כו'. תימה דהכי נמי הוה מצי למימר מחצה על מחצה עובד כוכבים ומנגח תורא דידן לתורא דידיה [כולה מילתא הוי מצי למימר לענין נגיחה אלא ניחא בכל חד למנקט דבר חדש. מהר"ס]:

הדרן עלך בתולה נשאת

האשה. אם יש עדים שיצאת בהינומא כו'. בדלא נקיטא כתובה איירי דאי איכא כתובה ניחזי כתובתה אם היא בתולה או אלמנה ואפילו למ"ד [ח] הטוען אחר מעשה ב"ד ואמר פרעתי נאמן מ"מ אין נאמן לומר כאן אלמנה נשאתיך מגו דאי בעי אמר פרעתי דמגו במקום עדים הוא:

ומודה רבי יהושע באומר שדה כו' דנאמן. מתוך פירוש הקונט' משמע דדוקא כשאין הלה תובעו ונאמן במגו דאי בעי שתיק אבל אם תובעו אינו נאמן ואינו נראה דהא קתני סיפא ואם יש עדים כו' משמע דדוקא אם יש עדים שהיתה של אביו אינו נאמן אבל אם אין עדים אע"ג דהלה תובעו נאמן מגו דאי בעי אמר לא היתה של אביך מעולם מדלא נקט אם תובעו אינו נאמן ובגמרא נמי פריך וליתני שדה זו שלך היתה משמע דבהלה תובעו איירי ולכך משיב ודאי שלך היתה ולקחתיה ממך אבל אם לא תובעו אין שייך לומר שלך היתה כי מסתמא הוא יודע בעצמו דבר זה: דאי

עין משפט נר מצוה

צד א מיי' פט"ו מהל' איסורי ביאה הלכה כה טוש"ע אה"ע סימן ד סעיף לג:

צה ב ג ד ה מיי' שם הל' כו וטור וש"ע שם סעיף לד:

א ו מיי' פט"ז מהלכות אישות הלכה כה טור ש"ע שם סי' ל סעיף טו:

תוספות ישנים

א) [נראה לר"י דמשום דדרשינן וחי אחיך ולא שימות בהם ומשמע שלא יבוא לידי מיתה בשום ענין לכך יש לחוש למיעוט ישראל. ת"י].

הגהות הב"ח

(א) רש"י ד"ה אבל כו' ולמ"ד גיורת. נ"ב בפרק הבא על יבמתו דף ס ע"ב:

לעזי רש"י

אישטייליד"ה. פירוש פרוע, מגודל שער (רש"י ויקרא יג, מה):

תוספות רי"ד

האשה שנתאלמנה או שנתגרשה היא אומרת בתולה נשאתני והוא אומר לא כי אלא אלמנה נשאתיך אם יש עדים שיצאת בהינומא וראשה פרוע כתובתה מאתים ר"י אומר אף חילוק קליות ראיה. פי' הוא אומר אנתגרשה קאי ולאלמנה אומרים לה היורשים אבינו אלמנה נשאך ואין לך אלא מנה ושטר כתובה אבד אם יש עדים על נשואיה שיצאת מבית אביה לבית בעלה בהינומא שהיא סימן הבתולות כדמפרש לקמן וראשה פרוע שערה על כתפה וכך היו מוציאים הבתולות מבית אביהן לבית החתנה. **אף חילוק וכו'** רגילין היו לחלק מיני פירות וקליות שהיו מייבשין השבלים כשהם לחים בתנור והם מתוקין ובנשואי הבתולות נותנים ומחלקין מהם לתינוקות ואי איכא עדי הינומא אע"ג שהיא אלמנה גביא בעדי הינומא ואע"ג דאיכא למיחש לפרעון וכל טענה דהוה מצי למיטען איהו ב"ד טוענין בעבור היתומים גביא כתובתה דהכי אמרינן בשנים אוחזין הטוען אחר מעשה ב"ד לא אמר כלום דכל מעשה ב"ד כמאן דנקט שטרא בידיה דמי ותנן נמי בפרק הכותב הוציאה גט ואין עמה כתובה גובה כתובתה ולא מצי למטען פרעתי כד שיראה שטר כתובתה קרוע או שובר והתם מוכח דלא מבעי' במנה מאתים שהיא תנאי ב"ד דגביא אלא אפילו תוספת בלא כתובה נמי גביא ולא מהימן לומר פרעתיך הלכך ה"נ מיתמי

מסורת הש"ס

א) מכשירין פ"ב מ"ז יומא פד:, ב) ב"ב לג: [ושם איתא שנתאלמנה], ג) הגה"ה פי' משלטי הדמיה. מתוקנין אבריו. פיתקא. קמיע של כתב. קמיעא. קמיע של עיקרין דהא חסה על חייו והוכיח תחלתו שאוהבת אותו ולא השליכתו למות, ד) כדאיתא סנהדרין עו:, ה) כדאיתא גיטין סא., ו) [ב"ק מו: וב"ב לג:], ז) [עי' תוס' ב"ק מו: ותוס' ב"מ כ: ד"ה איסורא ותוס' סנהדרין ג: ד"ה דיני ותוס' יומא פה.], ח) [עי' תוס' לקמן פח: ופט. בד"ה הוציאה וכו' א"נ אי שמואל לית ליה דר' יוחנן וכו'].

ליקוטי רש"י

ואמר רב לא שנו. דאם רוב ישראל מחזקינן ליה לישראל. **אלא להחיותו אבל ליוחסין לא.** כגון אם נקבה היא שיהא כהן מותר בה לא ואפילו ליכא למיחש לאסופי כגון הנך דאמרינן במסכת קידושין (דף עג.) תלי בדיקולא תלי פיתקא רמי חומרא משלטי הדמיה חיישינן שמא כותית היא וגיורת אסורה לכהונה ואע"ג דרוב ישראל מעלה עשו ביוחסין דבעינן תרי רובי כדאמרי' בכתובות בפרק קמא (דף טו.) [יומא פד:]. **ושמואל אמר לפקח עליו את הגל.** קאמר דאם רוב ישראל [ישראל] אבל במחצה על מחצה לא וכ"ש ברוב כותים [שם פה.]. **בקרונות של צפורי.** ביום השוק שסיעות ושיירות ממקום אחר באות שם [לעיל ע"א]. **ולפקח וכו' אינו כן.** דאמר אפילו ברוב כותים מפקחין. **למאי הילכתא.** הוי כותי אליבא דשמואל כיון דאמר מפקחין עליו כל שכן דמצוה להחיותו ולמאי הילכתא הוי כותי. **להאכילו נבילות.** עד שיגדל ויקבל עליו גירות. **אם רוב ישראל ישראל למאי הילכתא.** הוי ישראל ברוב ישראל טפי ממחצה על מחצה [דאי] שלא להאכילו נבילות במחצה על מחצה [נמי] לא ספינן ליה. **לנזקין.** שור של ישראל שנגח של כותי פטור ושור של כותי שנגח של ישראל בין תם בין מועד משלם נזק שלם ושל ישראל שנגח של ישראל תם משלם חצי נזק מועד משלם נזק שלם. **אי נימא דנגחיה תורא דידן לתורא דידיה.** וקאמרינן דמחייבינן ליה לשלומי. **אייתי ראיה דישראל את ושקול.** וכל זמן שלא טבל בבית דין לשם גירות לא מצינן [לחיובי לישראל] לשלומי. **פלגא משלם.** כישראל אידך פלגא ספק הוא וזה תובעו נזק שלם כדין כותי אמר ליה אייתי ראיה דלאו ישראל אנא ושקול [יומא פה.]. **האשה שנתארמלה.** וטוענת אבדתי כתובתי א"נ במקום שאין כותבין כתובה כדמפרש בכתובות. **בתולה נשאתני.** ויש לי מאתים. **אלמנה נשאתיך.** ואין לך אלא מנה. **שיצאת.** מבית אביה לבית בעלה כשנכנסה לחופה. **בהינומא.** קלתא דמנמנמא ביה כלתא או ראשה פרוע בשוק בשעת כניסה לחופה שכן דרך הניכאות בתולות [רשב"ם ב"ב צב:]. נערה המאורסה היו רגילין לעשות לה חופה של הדס בכניסתה לחופה וקורין לה הינומא כדאמרינן בכתובות (דף טו:) שיצאתה בהינומא וראשה פרוע [ברכות נו:]. **כתובתה מאתים.** ואע"פ שאין לה עדים מעידים על בתוליה ואין יודעין אם נישאת בתולה או בעולה [רשב"ם שם].

בקרונות של ציפורי היה מעשה וכדרבי אמי דאמר רבי אמי והוא שהיתה סיעה של בני אדם כשרין עוברת לשם וכדר' ינאי דאמר ר' ינאי נבעלת בקרונות כשרה לכהונה בקרונות סלקא דעתך אלא נבעלת בשעת קרונות כשרה לכהונה אבל פירש אחד מציפורי ובעל הולד שתוקי כי הא דכי אתא רב דימי אמר זעירי א"ר חנינא ואמרי לה אמר זעירי אמר ר' חנינא הולכין אחר רוב העיר ואין הולכין אחר רוב סיעה כלפי לייא הני ניידי והני קביעי וקיימי אלא א הולכין אחר רוב העיר והוא דאיכא רוב סיעה בהדה ואין הולכין אחר רוב העיר גרידתא ולא אחר רוב סיעה גרידתא מ"ט גזרה רוב סיעה אטו רוב העיר ורוב העיר נמי א) אי דקא אזלי אינהו לגבה כל דפריש ב) מרובא פריש ג) ב לא צריכא דקא אזלא איהי לגבייהו דהוה ליה קבוע וא"ר זירא כל קבוע כמחצה על מחצה דמי ומי בעינן תרי רובי והתניא ד) ג תשע חנויות כולן מוכרות בשר שחוטה ואחת מוכרת בשר נבלה ולקח מאחת מהן ואינו יודע מאי זה מהן לקח ספיקו אסור ד ובנמצא הלך אחר הרוב וכי תימא בשאין דלתות מדינה נעולות דקא אתי לה רובא מעלמא והא א"ר זירא ה) אע"פ שדלתות מדינה נעולות ו) מעלה עשו ביוחסין גופא א"ר זירא כל קבוע כמחצה על מחצה דמי בין לקולא בין לחומרא מנא ליה לר' זירא הא אילימא מתשע חנויות כולן מוכרות בשר שחוטה ואחת מוכרת בשר נבלה ולקח מאחת מהן ואינו יודע מאיזה מהן לקח ספיקו אסור ובנמצא הלך אחר הרוב התם לחומרא אלא ה מתשעה צפרדעים ושרץ אחד ביניהם ונגע באחד מהן ואינו יודע באיזה מהן נגע ספיקו טמא התם נמי לחומרא אלא ו מתשעה שרצים וצפרדע אחד ביניהם ונגע באחד מהן ואינו יודע באיזה מהן נגע ברה"י ספיקו טמא ברשות הרבי' ספיקו טהור ומדאורייתא מנא לן ח) אמר קרא א) וארב לו וקם עליו עד שיתכוין לו ורבנן אמרי דבי ר' ינאי פרט לזורק אבן לגו ט) היכי דמי אילימא דאיכא תשעה כנענים ואחד ישראל ביניהם ותיפוק ליה דרובא כנענים נינהו אי נמי פלגא ופלגא י) ספק נפשות להקל לא צריכא דאיכא תשעה ישראלים וכנעני אחד ביניהם דהוה ליה כנעני קבוע וכל קבוע כמחצה על מחצה דמי איתמר רב חייא בר אשי אמר רב הלכה כרבי יוסי ורב חנן בר רבא אמר רב הוראת שעה היתה מתיב רבי ירמיה וליוחסין לא בעינן תרי רובי והתנן מצא

רש"י

בקרונות של ציפורי. ביום השוק שסיעות ושיירות ממקום אחר באות שם: **וכדרבי אמי.** דהשתא איכא רוב סיעה ורוב העיר: **נבעלת בקרונות.** משמע על הקרון: **בשעת קרונות.** שהשיירות באות לעיר: **כשרה לכהונה.** דקאמר והוא שהיתה סיעה של בני אדם כשרים עוברת שם דאיכא למימר שמהם היה: **אבל פירש אחד מציפורי.** דידעינן ודאי דמן העיר היה אע"פ שציפורי עיר שרובה משיאין לכהונה: **הולד שתוקי.** דבתר רובא לא מכשר: **וכי הא דכי אתא רב דימי אמר זעירי אמר רבי חנינא ואמרי לה.** שלא הזכיר רב דימי כאן אלא זעירי אמר רבי חנינא דבעינן תרי רובי וכדמפרש טעמא: **הולכין אחר רוב העיר.** להכשיר: **ואין הולכין אחר רוב סיעה.** כגון במקום רחוק מן העיר דבודאי מאנשי הסיעה הוה אין מכשירין אותה ואפילו רובן כשרין: **וקשיא לן כלפי לייא.** כנגד איפוך הדבר הזה סובב: **הני ניידי.** רוב סיעה ניידי ויש להלך בהן אחר הרוב: **והני.** של עיר: **קביעי.** ואמרינן לקמן כל קבוע כמחצה על מחצה דמי ואפילו אין שם אלא אחד פסולה: **ולא אחר רוב סיעה גרידתא.** והכי קאמר אין הולכין אחר רוב סיעה לבדה וכל שכן אחר רוב העיר לבדה: **מ"ט.** אחר רוב סיעה לא: **גזרה אטו רוב העיר.** דקביעי: ופרכינן רוב העיר נמי. אי עקר הבועל מביתו ואזל לגבה הוה נייד וקי"ל כל דפריש מרובא פריש: ומשני **איכא דקאזלא איהי לגבייהו כו'.** ולא גרסינן כ) מאי איכא יש שהולכת היא אצלו והוה ליה קבוע הלכך אפילו ברוב כשרים או רוב העיר או רוב סיעה פסול כרבי יהושע ומשום תרי רובי ליכא למיגזר מידי: **ולקח בשר מאחת מהן.** במקום קביעות: **ספיקו אסור.** דכל קבוע כמחצה על מחצה דמי: **ובנמצא.** בשר הנמצא בשוק ולא ידעינן מאיזה פירש: **הלך אחר הרוב.** הואיל והבא לפנינו לא במקום קביעות לקחה וכבר פירשה על ידי אחר וכל דפריש מרובא פריש: **דקאתי לה רובא מעלמא.** וכגון שרוב סיעת עכו"ם ישראל כשרים באו לכאן דאיכא תרי רובי רוב העיר ורוב המדינה דנייד: **אלא מתשעה צפרדעים כו'.** תוספתא היא במס' טהרות תשעה צפרדעים מתים ברשות היחיד ושרץ אחד כגון זה שהוא דומה לצפרדע ביניהם ונגע באחד מהן ספיקו טמא: **אלא מתשעה שרצים כו'.** אף היא תוספתא במס' טהרות וקתני ברה"י ספיקו טמא ברה"ר ספיקו טהור אלמא כמחצה דמי ולקולא דאי לאו כמחצה דמי אין כאן ספק טומאה אלא ודאי טומאה דהא רובא שרצים: **אמר קרא וארב לו עד שיהא מתכוין לו.** פרט למתכוין להרוג את זה והרג את זה הכי דריש ליה ר"ש בסנהדרין ואמרינן התם ורבנן היכי דרשי ליה: **אמרי דבי ר' ינאי פרט לזורק אבן לגו.** לתוך חבורת בני אדם כנענים וישראלים אבל שני ישראלים עומדין ונתכוין להרוג (א) זה (והרג זה) והתרו בו וקבל התראה ונפלה הכאה על חבירו חייב והיינו טעמא דקאמר הכא ורבנן משום דבסנהדרין הכי איתא: **תיפוק ליה דרובא כנענים נינהו.** ולמה לי קרא ואי נמי פלגא ופלגא אכתי לא איצטריך קרא דמהיכא תיתי דניקטליה: **ספק נפשות.** דיני נפשות להקל דהא והצילו העדה כתיב (במדבר לה): **דהוה ליה כנעני קבוע ביניהם.** ואשמועינן האי קרא דכל קבוע כמחצה על מחצה דמי: **הוראת שעה היתה.** הך דריב"נ לורך שעה היתה או ראו שם שאר לידי היכר דברים להתיר אבל לדורות תרי רובי בעינן: **מתיב רבי ירמיה כו'.** קס"ד דמשום רוב העיר גרידתא אכשרוה ואמר רב הלכה כרבי יוסי:

תוספות

אמר רב בקרונות של ציפורי היה מעשה כו' פי' לעולם דלא טוענה ברי ור' יוחנן בן נורי בתרוייהו היכא דלא טוענה ברי לכ"ע בעינן תרי רובי והא דלא קאמר בשינויא לעולם דלא טוענה ברי משום דאתקפתא לא קאמר אי בטוענת ברי כו' אי נמי נוכל לפרש דבשינויא נמי איירי בברי ודאיכא מגו ולא תקשי הלכתא אהלכתא דדוקא דיעבד פסיק שמואל כר"ג כדאמר לעיל ואת לא תעביד עובדא עד דאיכא רוב כשרין אף על גב דלעיל משמע דברוב אחד שרי לכתחלה רב חייא בר אשי סבר דלכתחלה בעינן תרי רובי ומתני' קתני הרי זו תנשא דמשמע לכתחלה:

דלמא אזלא איהי לגבייהו. פי' לתוך ביתם דאפילו בתוך העיר לא חשיב קבוע דדמי לנמלא בין החנויות דלא חשיב קבוע וכן גבי תינוק מושלך בעיר לא חשיב קבוע הואיל ולא נמלא בבית ולכך פירש בקונטרס שפירש בועל מביתו וא"ת דבנזיר פ"ב (דף יב. ושם) פריך אהא דאמר האומר לשלוחו לא וקדש לי אשה סתם אסור בכל הנשים שבעולם מקן סתומה ומסיק אמינא לך אנא אשה דלא ניידא ואת אמרת לי איסורא דנייד וכי תימא ה"נ בשוקא אשכחה וקדיש התם הדרא לניחותא משמע לגבי אדם לא שייך כל דפריש מרובא פריש משום דהדר לניחותיה ולאו פירכא היא דהתם בשעת האיסור כשזה בא על שום אשה הדרא לניחותא האשה שקידש השליח אבל הכא כי אזלי אינהו לגבה בשעה שאוסרה הרי הוא נייד: **פרט** לזורק אבן לגו. תימה דלר' שמעון קבוע מנא ליה ואין לומר דמסקינן בפ' הנשרפין (סנהדרין דף עט. ושם) דר"ש סבר כרבי דיליף נתינה נתינה ואייתר ליה וארב לו לקבוע דאכתי לתנא דבי חזקיה מנא ליה קבוע דלית ליה דרבי דהא באין מתכוין פטור ממון ל):

וספק נפשות להקל. תימה למ"ד התראת ספק לא שמה התראה אפילו ספק נפשות להחמיר פטור משום דהתראת ספק היא ואי למ"ד שמה התראה היכי פטרינן ליה כשנמלא שישראל הרג הא מיחייב בהכה את זה וחזר והכה את זה מ) ובנותר כשאמרו לו אל תותיר אע"ג דספק הוא וי"ל דשאני התם שיודע בודאי שיבא לידי איסור אם יותיר או יכה שניהם מש"ה שמה התראה אבל הכא אינו יודע שודאי יבוא לידי איסור שאינו יודע את מי יכה:

וליוחסין לא בעינן תרי רובי ורמינהי כו'. הוה מצי לשנויי שאני תינוק דלית לי' חזק' דכשרו': ולרב מלא

עין משפט נר מצוה

פט א ב מיי' פי"ח מהלכות איסורי ביאה הל' יד סמג לאוין קכא טוש"ע אה"ע סימן ו סעיף יח יט:

צ ג מיי' פ"ח מהלכות מאכלות אסורות הל' יא סמג לאוין קמא טור ש"ע י"ד סימן קי סע"ג:

צא ד מיי' שם וטוש"ע שם וכסי' סג ס"א:

צב ה ו מיי' פי"ח מהלכות אבות הטומאות הלכה ג:

צג ז מיי' פ"ד מהל' רוצח הלכה א סמג לאוין קמג:

תוספות רי"ד

בקרונות של צפורי היה מעשה וכדר' ינאי דאמר נבעלה בשעת קרונות כשירה לכהונה פי' קרוניות הבאים ממקום אחר ומתקבצים שם ליום השוק והוא שהיתה סיעה של בני אדם כשרים עוברים שם דהוה תרי רובא לכשרות רוב העיר ורוב סיעה. פי' כל זה מפני שלא ידעה למי נבעלה אבל אי ידעה ואמרה לכשר נבעלתי הלכה כר"ג ונאמנת אפילו ברוב פסולים: ומקשי' ומי בעי תרי רובי והתניא ט' חנויות כולן מוכרות בשר שחוטה ואחת מוכרת בשר נבילה ולקח מאחת מהן ואינו יודע מאיזה מהן לקח ספיקו אסור שכל קבוע כמחצה על מחצה דמי ובנמצא הלך אחר הרוב דכל דפריש מרובא פריש. ומהדר מעלה עשו ביוחסין: איתמר אר"ח אמר רב הלכה כר' יוסי פי' דבעי' תרי רובי: א"ר זירא כל קבוע כמחצה על מחצה דמי בין לקולא בין לחומרא כגון ט' חנויות דאמרן. א"נ ט' צפרדעים ושרץ א' ביניהם ברה"י ונגע באח' מהן ואינו יודע באיזה מהן נגע ספיקו טמא. לקולא כגון ט' שרצים וצפרדע א' ביניהן ברה"ר ונגע באח' מהן וא"י באיזה מהן נגע ספיקו טהור אלא כמחצה על מחצה דמי ולקולא. דאי לאו כמחצה על מחצה דמי אין כאן ספק טומאה אלא ודאי טומאה דהא רובא שרצים: האשה

מסורת הש"ס

א) [קדושין דף עג.], ב) [ברכות כח. וש"נ], ג) [רש"ל מוחק וכ"ז גורס רש"י איכא דקאזלא לגבייהו וכו' גירסת בה"ג א"ה סימן ו], ד) פסחים ט: חולין לה. נדה יח., ה) ב"ק כד., ו) [לעיל יג. וש"נ], ז) נדה יח. ע"ש תוספתא טהרות פ"ו, ח) ב"ק מד: סנהדרין עט., ט) [שבת קכג. וש"נ], כ) צ"ל מאי רוב העיר איכא כו'. רש"ל, ל) [וכסנהדרין עט. ד"ה וכל כתבו תוס' תירוץ זה וכ"כ בב"ק מד: ד"ה ולפי תוס' נדה יח. ד"ה ספיקא], מ) יבמות קא ע"ש.

הגהות הב"ח

(א) רש"י ד"ה אמרי וכו' להרוג את זה והרג את זה:

תורה אור השלם

א) וְכִי יִהְיֶה אִישׁ שֹׂנֵא לְרֵעֵהוּ וְאָרַב לוֹ וְקָם עָלָיו וְהִכָּהוּ נֶפֶשׁ וָמֵת וְנָס אֶל אַחַת הֶעָרִים הָאֵל: [דברים יט, יא]

ליקוטי רש"י

כלפי לייא. שמי מלות כלפי היכן נוטה דבר זה הא איפכא מסתברא. לייא, היכן ובירו בברכות בפרק הרואה (דף נח.) אלוי לנהרא כגוי לייא מרכיס כלפי היכן הולכים [פסחים ה:]. כנגד איפוך הסכת דבריך לייא איפוך כדאמרינן בברכות כגוי לייא כדים שבורים להיכן הולכים [סוטה מד.]. כנגד מה וכו' ולאן לשון כדאמרינן בברכות מאלי לנהרא כגוי לייא הקדירות שלמות להיכן הולכין לשאוב בהן מים אבל השבורין להיכן הולכין [רשב"ם ב"ב קד:]. **אי דקא אזלי אינהו וכו' מרובא פריש.** ואם בבעילה זו הלך הבועל אצלה דהשתא נד ליה ממקום קביעתו ואין לדון כתורת קבוע לדון כמחצה על מחצה יש לנו לומר כל דפריש מרובא פריש והולד כשר [קידושין עג.]. **ולקח מאחת מהן.** בתוך החנות. **ספיקו אסור.** דקבוע כמחצה על מחצה נידון דנפקא לן מוארב לו וקם עליו [כפ"ק] דכתובות [טו.] [פסחים ט:]. דכל קבוע כמחצה על מחצה דמיא וכיון שלקחה ממקום הקביעות מחזקין לה כמחצה על מחצה [נדה יח.]. **ובנמצא הלך אחר הרוב.** בשר הנמצא בקרקע בין החנויות הלך אחר הרוב דכל דפריש מרובא פריש דכיון דפירש אין כאן תורת קבוע ולא כמחצה על מחצה הלכך הלך אחר הרוב דהשתא לאו קבוע הוא [חולין צה.]. **בשאין דלתות מדינה נעולות.** כגון דלתות מדינות פתוחות ורוב ישראל דאיכא למיזל בתר תרי רובי להכשיר רוב העיר ורוב הבאין מחוצה לה. **אע"פ שדלתות מדינה נעולות.** דליכא אלא חד רובא להכשירה רוב העיר שתשע חנויות שבה מוכרות בשר שחוטה והאחת מוכרת נבילה [ב"ב כד.]. **מתשעה צפרדעים** ... הוה ליה ספק ואע"ג דרובא צפרדעים ואין להם טומאה כיון דשרץ קבוע ביניהם הוה ליה מחצה על מחצה [נדה שם]. **וארב לו.** קרא יתירא הוא נכתוב כי יהיה איש שונא לרעהו וקם עליו. **ורבנן.** דפליגי ... דרשי ביה. **אמרי דבי ר' ינאי פרט לזורק אבן לגו.** לתוך חבורה של בני אדם כותים וישראלים אבל נתכוין לישראל זה והרג את חבירו לא אתא קרא למעוטי [סנהדרין עט.]. לתוך חבורת אנשים ויש שם ... לא למימר לכנענים נתכוין. ותיפוק ליה דרובא כנענים נינהו. ולא איצטריך קרא למפטריה. **אי נמי.** מחצה כנענים ומחצה ישראלים לא איצטריך קרא למפטריה דרחמנא אמר (במדבר לה) ושפטו העדה ... ספק נפשות להקל [ב"ק מד:]. למה לי קרא למיפטריה הא כיון דמאי למימר לכותים קא מתכוונא אית לך למפטריה משום דספק נפשות להקל מוהצילו העדה (יומא דף פד:) [סנהדרין שם]. **לא צריכא דאיכא** ... דאי לאו קרא הוה אמינא זיל בתר רובא ולישראל איכוון ואע"ג דדלמא לאו להאי איכוון נתכוון להרוג את זה והרג את זה חייב קא משמע לן קרא דהואיל והוה ליה כנעני קבוע ביניהן כמחצה על מחצה דמי ... כל מילי דקיימא לן קבוע כמחצה על מחצה מהאי קרא נפקא לן [ב"ק שם]. ואשמעינן קרא דפטור משום דהוה ליה כותי קבוע ביניהם וילפינן מהאי קרא דכל קבוע לא פחות מלהיות נדון כמחצה על מחצה ... ומהכא נפקא לן בכל דוכתי דכל קבוע כמחצה על מחצה דמי דהא מהיכא תיתי לן דילמא האי דפטר ליה להאי משום דספק נפשות להקל ולא משום דחשבינן ליה כרובא אבל ... על מחצה ילפינן מיניה דאי לאו כמחצה על מחצה דמי לא הוה ליה ספק נפשות להקל ומאי פטור הא רובא דישראל נינהו ורבנן אית להו נתכוון לזה והרג את זה חייב [סנהדרין שם].

majority of the people in the group **are Canaanites!** There is no need for a special verse to teach that he is not executed.[38] **אִי נַמִּי פַּלְגָּא וּפַלְגָּא** – **And even** if the group consists **half** of Jews **and half** of Canaanites, we still do not require this verse to teach that the perpetrator is not executed, for it is a case of doubt, **סְפֵק נְפָשׁוֹת לְהָקֵל** – and wherever there is **a doubt** in a case **involving capital punishment,** the law is that the court is **to rule leniently.**[39] – ? –

The Gemara finally explains the view of the Rabbis and thereby demonstrates the Biblical source for R' Zeira's principle concerning items stationed in place:

לֹא צְרִיכָא דְּאִיכָּא תִּשְׁעָה יִשְׂרְאֵלִים וּכְנַעֲנִי אֶחָד בֵּינֵיהֶם – Perforce, **[the verse] is needed only for** a situation **where there are nine Jews** in the group **and** there is **one Canaanite among them.** The verse teaches that the perpetrator is not executed, **דַּהֲוָה לֵיהּ כְּנַעֲנִי קָבוּעַ** – **because the Canaanite is "stationed** in place,"[40] **וְכָל קָבוּעַ כְּמֶחֱצָה עַל מֶחֱצָה דָּמֵי** – **and any** doubt relating to something **stationed** in place **is** treated **as** having a probability of **fifty-fifty.**[41]

The Gemara cites a ruling concerning our Mishnah:

אִיתְּמַר – **It was stated:** **רַב חִיָּיא בַּר אַשִׁי אָמַר רַב** – **Rav Chiya bar Ashi said in the name of Rav:** **הֲלָכָה כְּרַבִּי יוֹסֵי** – **The halachah follows R' Yose,** who in our Mishnah conveyed the ruling of R' Yochanan ben Nuri that a violated girl is fit for the Kehunah when the majority of the townspeople are of fit lineage.[42]

Another version of Rav's opinion:

וְרַב חָנָן בַּר רָבָא אָמַר רַב – **But Rav Chanan bar Rava said in the name of Rav:** **הוֹרָאַת שָׁעָה הָיְתָה** – **That** action **was a** special **ruling for the moment.**[43]

The Gemara objects to the first version:

מָתִיב רַבִּי יִרְמְיָה – **R' Yirmiyah challenged** Rav Chiya bar Ashi's version of Rav's opinion: **וּלְיוּחֲסִין לֹא בְּעִינַן תְּרֵי רוּבֵּי** – **Now,** is it possible that **for** questions of **lineage we do not need two majorities?**[44] **וְהָתְנַן** – **But we learned in a Mishnah** regarding a city inhabited by both Jews and idolaters:[45]

NOTES

38. The principle of following the majority would tell us that since the stone was (based on the rule of majority) more likely to hit a Canaanite than a Jew, throwing it cannot be deemed an act of murdering a Jew. Hence, there is no need for a special Scriptural source to teach that the thrower is not liable to execution in this case.

39. Since there was an equal number of Jews and Canaanites in the group, there was a fifty-fifty chance that the stone would kill a Canaanite. Thus, it is a matter of doubt whether to define this act as one of killing a Jew. From *Numbers* 35:25: וְהִצִּילוּ הָעֵדָה, *And the assembly* (i.e. the court) *shall rescue,* it is derived that in cases of doubt, such as this, the court must lean towards the side of leniency and avoid imposing the death penalty (*Rashi;* see *Pesachim* 12a; cf. *Tosafos* to *Bava Basra* 50b ד״ה וספק).

Therefore, we do not need the words וְאָרַב לוֹ, *and ambushes him,* to teach that one is not liable for throwing a stone into a group consisting of an equal number of Jews and Canaanites. Thus, the difficulty remains: How do the Rabbis interpret these words?

40. I.e. he is among a group assembled in a fixed place, and clearly identifiable within the group (see *Tosafos* to *Zevachim* 73b ד״ה אלא and *Shaarei Yosher* ibid. at length). [Even if the people are moving about within the group, they are considered *kavua,* since they *assembled* in this particular spot and the stone was thrown into their midst. For this reason, too, it is apparently irrelevant whether they reside here. By contrast, the travelers to Tzippori (in the previous Gemara) did not assemble as a group; they merely arrived in town together for the market day (see *Binas Adam* ibid. §8).]

41. Since most of the people in the group are Jews, the rule of majority would yield that the perpetrator should be executed. The Torah teaches, however, that he is not executed. The reason is that the Canaanite is viewed as half of the group, and the group is thus deemed to consist half of Jews and half of Canaanites, in which case the law is that the perpetrator is given the benefit of the doubt (as explained previously). Thus, the verse teaches that when uncertainty arises regarding something that is *kavua,* we treat it as having a probability of fifty-fifty (*Rashi*). [By contrast, if one man would emerge from the group, he would be presumed to have come from the majority (see note 16).]

It is clear that the Torah regards the Canaanite as comprising *half* of the group, for if he were regarded as only a *minority,* there would be no reason for acquittal. (The fact that several Jews were present and the thrower did not have specific intent for one of them is immaterial according to the Rabbis.) On the other hand, since, in order to acquit the defendant, it suffices for the Canaanite to be treated as half of the group, we cannot assume that the Torah regards him as a *majority.* We therefore say that the Torah views him as *half* of the group (*Rashi* to *Sanhedrin* 79a).

[This proof is valid only according to the Rabbis' interpretation of this verse. The Gemara does not state how R' Shimon derives the principle of *kavua.* See *Tosafos* ד״ה פרט, *Ritva* and *Shitah Mekubetzes* for discussion of this issue.]

42. As was explained above, this ruling was based on the unspoken fact that there was also a second majority applicable, for there was a caravan in the area containing a majority of fit men. However, the Gemara here at first understands the Mishnah literally – as meaning that the decisive factor was simply the existence of a majority among the townspeople. It thus takes Rav's ruling as meaning that a single majority is sufficient to rule a woman fit for a Kohen (see note 44).

43. R' Yochanan ben Nuri's lenient ruling [as recorded by R' Yose] cannot serve as a precedent. He declared the violated girl fit for a Kohen [and disregarded the Rabbinic decree against relying upon a single majority] because circumstances at that time demanded that the matter be treated with leniency [and that Biblical law be followed in that exceptional case]. Alternatively, R' Yochanan ben Nuri had other, unstated, reasons which indicated that the girl was permitted to a Kohen. Generally, however, a woman cannot be ruled fit for a Kohen unless there are two favorable majorities dictating that she is fit (*Rashi*).

44. R' Yirmiyah understood Rav as meaning that a single majority suffices (*Rashi*).

45. *Machshirin* 2:7.

בקרונות של ציפורי היה מעשה וכדרבי אמי דאמר רבי אמי והוא שהיתה סיעה של בני אדם כשרין עוברת לשם וכדר' ינאי דאמר ר' ינאי נבעלת בקרונות כשרה לכהונה בקרונות סלקא דעתך אלא נבעלת בשעת קרונות כשרה לכהונה אבל פירש אחד מציפורי ובעל הולד שתוקי כי הא דכי אתא רב דימי אמר זעירי א"ר חנינא ואמרי לה אמר זעירי אמר ר' חנינא הולכין אחר רוב העיר ואין הולכין אחר רוב סיעה כלפי לייא הני ניידי והני קבעי וקיימי אלא א) הולכין אחר רוב העיר והוא דאיכא רוב סיעה בהדה ואין הולכין אחר רוב העיר גרידתא ולא אחר רוב סיעה גרידתא מ"ט גזרה רוב סיעה אטו רוב העיר ורוב העיר נמי ב) אי דקא אזלי אינהו לגבה כל דפריש ג) מרובא פריש ג) לא צריכא דקא אזלא איהי לגבייהו דהוה ליה קבוע וא"ר זירא כל קבוע כמחצה על מחצה דמי ומי בעינן תרי רובי והתניא ד) תשע חנויות כולן מוכרות בשר שחוטה ואחת מוכרת בשר נבלה ולקח מאחת מהן ואינו יודע מאי זה מהן לקח ספיקו אסור ה) ובנמצא הלך אחר הרוב וכי תימא בשאין דלתות מדינה נעולות דקא אתי לה רובא מעלמא והא א"ר זירא ו) אע"פ שדלתות מדינה נעולות ז) מעלה עשו ביוחסין גופא א"ר זירא כל קבוע כמחצה על מחצה דמי בין לקולא בין לחומרא מנא ליה לר' זירא הא אילימא מתשע חנויות כולן מוכרות בשר שחוטה ואחת מוכרת בשר נבלה ולקח מאחת מהן ואינו יודע מאיזה מהן לקח ספיקו אסור ובנמצא הלך אחר הרוב התם לחומרא אלא ח) מתשעה צפרדעים ושרץ אחד ביניהם ונגע באחד מהן ואינו יודע באיזה מהן נגע ספיקו טמא התם נמי לחומרא אלא ט) מתשעה שרצים וצפרדע אחד ביניהם ונגע באחד מהן ואינו יודע באיזה מהן נגע ברה"י ספיקו טמא ברשות הרבים ספיקו טהור ומדאורייתא מנא לן י) אמר קרא א) וארב לו וקם עליו כ) עד שיתכוין לו ורבנן אמרי דבי ר' ינאי פרט לזורק אבן לגו ל) היכי דמי אילימא דאיכא תשעה כנענים ואחד ישראל ביניהם ותיפוק ליה דרובא כנענים נינהו אי נמי פלגא ופלגא מ) ספק נפשות להקל לא צריכא דאיכא תשעה ישראלים וכנעני אחד ביניהם דהוה ליה כנעני קבוע וכל קבוע כמחצה על מחצה דמי איתמר רב חייא בר אשי אמר רב הלכה כרבי יוסי ורב חנן בר רבא אמר רב הוראת שעה היתה מתיב רבי ירמיה וליוחסין לא בעינן תרי רובי והתנן מצא

בקרונות של ציפורי. ביום השוק שסיעות ושיירות ממקום אחר באות שם: וכדרבי אמי. דהשתא איכא רוב סיעה ורוב העיר: נבעלת בקרונות. משמע על הקרון: בשעת קרונות. שהשיירות באות לעיר: כשרה לכהונה. כדקאמר והוא שהיתה סיעה של בני אדם כשרים עוברת שם דאיכא למימר שמהם היה: אבל פירש אחד מציפורי. דידעינן ודאי דמן העיר היה אע"פ שציפורי עיר שרובה משיאין לכהונה: הולד שתוקי. דבחד רובא לא מכשר: וכי הא דכי אתא רב דימי אמר זעירי אמר רבי חנינא ואמרי לה. שלא הזכיר רב דימי כאן אלא זעירי אמר רבי חנינא דבעינן תרי רובי ולמפרש טעמא: הולכין אחר רוב העיר. להכשיר: ואין הולכין אחר רוב סיעה. כגון במקום רחוק מן העיר דודאי מאנשי הסיעה הוה אין מכשירין אותה ואפילו רובן כשרין: וקשיא לן כלפי לייא. כנגד איפוא הדבר הזה סובב: הני ניידי. רוב סיעה ניידי ויש להלך בהן אחר הרוב: והני. של עיר: קביעי. ואמרינן לקמן כל קבוע כמחצה על מחצה דמי ואפילו אין שם אלא אחד פסולה: ולא אחר רוב סיעה גרידתא. והכי קאמר אין הולכין אחר רוב סיעה לבדה וכל שכן אחר רוב העיר לבדה: מ"ט. אחר רוב סיעה לא: גזרה אטו רוב העיר. דקביעי ופרכינן רוב העיר נמי. אי עקר הבועל מביתו ואזל לגבה הוה נייד וקי"ל כל דפריש מרובא פריש: ומשני איכא דקאזלא לגבייהו כו'. ולא גרסינן ג) מאי איכא יש שהולכת היא אצלו והוה ליה קבוע הלכך אפילו ברוב כשרים או רוב העיר או רוב סיעה פסול כרבי יהושע ומשום תרי רובי אכשרה דליכא למיגזר מידי: ולקח בשר מאחת מהן. במקום קביעות: ספיקו אסור. דכל קבוע כמחצה על מחצה דמי: ובנמצא. בשר הנמצא בשוק ולא ידעינן מאיזה פירש: הלך אחר הרוב. הואיל והבא לפנינו לא במקום קביעות לקחה וכבר פירשה על ידי אחר וכל דפריש מרובא פריש: דקאתי לה רובא מעלמא. וכגון שרוב סיעת טבחי ישראל כשרים באו לכאן דאיכא תרי רובי או שרוב טבחי כל המדינה ישראל דאיכא תרי רובי רוב העיר ורוב המדינה דניידי: אלא מתשעה צפרדעים כו'. תוספתא היא במס' טהרות תשעה צפרדעים מתים ברשות היחיד ושרץ אחד כגון צב שהוא דומה לצפרדע ביניהם ונגע באחד מהן ספיקו טמא: אלא מתשעה שרצים כו'. אף היא תוספתא במס' טהרות וקתני ברה"י ספיקו טמא ברה"ר ספיקו טהור אלמא כמחצה דמי ולקולא דאי לאו כמחצה דמי אין כאן ספק טומאה אלא ודאי טומאה דהא רובא שרצים: אמר קרא וארב לו עד שיהא מתכוין לו. פרט למתכוין להרוג את זה והרג את זה הכי דריש ליה ר"ש בסנהדרין ואמרינן התם ורבנן היכי דרשי ליה: אמרי דבי ר' ינאי פרט לזורק אבן לגו. לתוך חבורת בני אדם כנענים וישראלים אבל שני ישראלים עומדין ונתכוין להרוג (א) זה (והרג זה) והתרו בו וקבל התראה ונפלה הכאה על חבירו חייב והיינו טעמא דקאמר הכא ורבנן משום דבסנהדרין הכי איתא: תיפוק ליה דרובא כנענים נינהו. ולמה לי קרא ואי נמי פלגא ופלגא אכתי לא איצטריך קרא דמהיכא תיתי דניקטליה: ספק נפשות. דיני נפשות להקל דהא והצילו העדה כתיב (במדבר לה): דהוה ליה כנעני קבוע ביניהם. ואשמועינן האי קרא דכל קבוע כמחצה על מחצה דמי: הוראת שעה היתה. הך דריב"נ לורך שעה היתה או ראו שם שאר ליד היכר דברים להתיר אבל לדורות תרי רובי בעינן: מתיב רבי ירמיה כו'. קס"ד דמשום רוב העיר גרידתא אכשרוה ואמר רב הלכה כרבי יוסי:

אמר רב בקרונות של צפורי היה מעשה כו' פי' לעולם דלא טוענה ברי ור' יוחנן בן נורי במתניתין היכא דלא טוענה ברי לכ"ע בעינן תרי רובי והא דלא קאמר בשניה לעולם דלא טוענה ברי משום דבתקפתא לא קאמר אי בטוענת ברי כו' אי נמי ניחא לפרש דבשניה נמי איירי בברי ודאיכא מגו ולא תקשי הלכתא אהלכתא דדוקא דיעבד פסיק שמואל כר"ג כדאמר לעיל ואת לא תעביד עתידא עד דאיכא רוב כשרין אף על גב דלעיל משמע דברוב אחד סגי לכתחלה רב חייא בר אשי סבר דלכתחלה בעינן תרי רובי ומתני' קתני הרי זו תנשא דמשמע לכתחלה:

דלמא אזלא איהי לגבייהו. פי' לתוך ביתם דאפילו בתוך העיר לא חשיב קבוע דדמי במאה בין החנויות דלא חשיב קבוע וכן גבי תינוק מושלך בעיר לא חשיב קבוע הואיל ולא נמצא בבית ולכך פירש בקונטרס שפירש בועל מביתו ואע"ג דבנזיר פ"ב (דף יב. ושם) פריך אהא דאמר האומר לשלוחו צא וקדש לי אשה סתם אסור בכל הנשים שבעולם מקן ספק חזקה ומשני אמינא לך לא אשה דלא ניידא ולא אמרת לי איסורא דנייד וכי תימא ה"נ בשוקא אשכחה וקידש התם הדרא לניחותא משמע דאי אזל אדם לא שייך כל דפריש מרובא פריש משום הדהר לניחותא ולאו פירכא היא דהתם בשעת האיסור כשזה בא על שום אשה הדרא לניחותא האשה שקידש השליח אבל הכא כי אזלי אינהו לגבה בשעה שאוכרה הרי הוא נייד: פרט לזורק אבן לגו. תימה דלר' שמעון קבוע מנא ליה ואין לומר דמסקינן בפ' הנשרפין (סנהדרין דף עט. ושם) דר"ש סבר כרבי דיליף נתינה נתינה ואייתר ליה וארב לו לקבוע דאכתי לתנא ליה לדרבי דהא חוקה מנא ליה קבוע דלית ליה דרבי דהא לאין מתכוין פטור ממוון ט):

וספק נפשות להקל. תימה למ"ד התראת ספק לא שמה התראה אפילו ספק נפשות להחמיר פטור משום דהתראת ספק היא ואי למ"ד שמה התראה היכי פטרינן ליה כשנמצא שישראל הרג הא מיחייב בהכאה את זה וחזר והכה את זה ט) ובנותר כשאמרו לו אל תותיר אע"ג דספק הוא וי"ל דשאני התם שיודע בודאי שיבא לידי איסור אם יהרוג או יכה שניהם מש"ה שמה התראה אבל הכא אינו יודע שודאי יבוא לידי איסור שאינו יודע את מי יכה:

וליוחסין לא בעינן תרי רובי ורמינהו כו'. הוה מצי לשנויי שאני תינוק דלית ליה חזק' הכשרו': ורב

זה והרג את זה הכי דריש ליה ר"ש בסנהדרין ואמרינן התם ורבנן היכי דרשי ליה: אמרי דבי ר' ינאי פרט לזורק אבן לגו. לתוך חבורת בני אדם כנענים וישראלים אבל שני ישראלים עומדין ונתכוין להרוג (א) זה (והרג זה) והתרו בו וקבל התראה ונפלה הכאה על חבירו חייב והיינו טעמא דקאמר הכא ורבנן משום דבסנהדרין הכי איתא: תיפוק ליה דרובא כנענים נינהו. ולמה לי קרא ואי נמי פלגא ופלגא אכתי לא איצטריך קרא דמהיכא תיתי דניקטליה: ספק נפשות. דיני נפשות להקל דהא והצילו העדה כתיב (במדבר לה): דהוה ליה כנעני קבוע ביניהם. ואשמועינן האי קרא דכל קבוע כמחצה על מחצה דמי: הוראת שעה היתה. הך דריב"נ לורך שעה היתה או ראו שם שאר ליד היכר דברים להתיר אבל לדורות תרי רובי בעינן: מתיב רבי ירמיה כו'. קס"ד דמשום רוב העיר גרידתא אכשרוה ואמר רב הלכה כרבי יוסי:

עין משפט
נר מצוה

פט א ב מיי' פי"ח מהלכות איסורי ביאה הל' יד סמג לאוין קכא טוש"ע אה"ע סימן ו סעיף יז יח:
צ ג מיי' פ"ח מהלכות מאכלות אסורות הל' יא סמג לאוין קמא טור ש"ע י"ד סימן קי סע"ג:
צא ד מיי' שם וטוש"ע שם ובסי' סג ס"א:
צב ה ו מיי' פי"ח מהלכות אבות הטומאות הלכה ב:
צג ז מיי' פ"ד מהל' רוצח הלכה א סמג לאוין קמג:

תוספות רי"ד

בקרונות של צפורי היה מעשה וכדר' ינאי דאמר נבעלה בשעת קרונות כשירה לכהונה פי' קרוניות הבאים ממקום אחר ומתקבצים שם ליום השוק והוא שהיתה סיעה של בני אדם כשרים עוברים שם דהוה תרי רובא לכשרות רוב העיר ורוב סיעה. פי' כל זה מפני שלא ידעה למי נבעלה אבל אי ידעה ואמרה לכשר נבעלתי הלכה כר"ג ונאמנת אפילו ברוב פסולים: ומקשי' ומי בעי תרי רובי והתניא ט' חנויות כולן מוכרות בשר שחוטה ואחת מוכרת בשר נבילה ולקח מאחת מהן ואינו יודע מאיזה מהן לקח ספיקו אסור שכל קבוע כמחצה על מחצה דמי ובנמצא הלך אחר הרוב דכל דפריש מרובא פריש. ומהדר מעלה עשו ביוחסין: איתמר אר"ח אמר רב הלכה כר' יוסי פי' דבעי' תרי רובי: א"ר זירא כל קבוע כמחצה על מחצה דמי בין לקולא בין לחומרא כגון ט' חנויות דאמרן. א"נ ט' צפרדעים ושרץ א' ביניהם ברה"י ונגע באח' מהן ואינו יודע באיזה מהן נגע ספיקו טמא. לקולא כגון ט' שרצים וצפרדע א' ביניהם ברה"י ונגע באח' מהן ואי"י באיזה מהן נגע ספיקו טהור אלא כמחצה על מחצה דמי ולקולא. דאי לאו כמחצה על מחצה דמי אין כאן ספק טומאה אלא ודאי טומאה דהא רובא שרצים: האשה

מסורת הש"ס

א) [קדושין דף עג.], ב) [ברכות כח. וש"נ], ג) [רש"ל מוחק ונ"ב גירסת רש"י איכא דקאזלא לגבייהו ועי' ב' גירסות בב"ש אה"ע סימן ו], ד) פסחים ט: חולין לה. נדה יח., ה) ב"ב כד., ו) [לעיל יג. וש"נ], ז) נדה יח. ע"ש תוספתא טהרות פ"ו, ח) ב"ק מד: סנהדרין עט., ט) [יומא פד:], י) [שבת קנה. וש"נ], כ) נ"ל מאי רוב העיר איכא כו'. רש"ל, ל) [וסנהדרין עט. ד"ה וכל כתבו תוס' תירוץ לזה וכ"כ בב"ק מד: ד"ה כל ועי' תוספות נדה יח. ד"ה ספיקא], מ) יבמות קא ע"א.

הגהות הב"ח

(א) רש"י ד"ה אמרי וכו' להרוג את זה והרג את זה:

תורה אור השלם

א) וְכִי יִהְיֶה אִישׁ שֹׂנֵא לְרֵעֵהוּ וְאָרַב לוֹ וְקָם עָלָיו וְהִכָּהוּ נֶפֶשׁ וָמֵת וְנָס אֶל אַחַת הֶעָרִים הָאֵל: [דברים יט, יא]

ליקוטי רש"י

כלפי לייא. שתי מלות כלפי היכן נוטה דבר זה הא איפכא מסתברא. לייא, היכן ותמירו בברכות בפרק הרואה (דף נח.) אלכי לנהרא כגבי לייא תרסים שבורים להיכן הולכים [פסחים ה:]. כנגד איפוא הפכת דבריך לייא איפוא כדאמר בברכות כגבי לייא כדים שבורים להיכן הולכים [סוטה מד.]. כנגד מה וכו' ולאן הדבר נוטה כדאמרינן בברכות אלכי לנהרא כגבי לייא הקדירות שלמות הולכין לנהר לשאוב בהן מים אבל השבורין להיכן הולכין [רשב"ם ב"ב קד:]. אי דקא אזלי אינהו וכו' מרובא פריש. ואם בבעילה זו הלך הבועל אצלה דהשתא נד ליה ממקום קביעתו ואין לדונו בתורת קבוע שלא נדון כמחצה על מחצה יש לנו לומר כל דפריש מרובא פריש והולד כשר [קידושין עג.]. ולקח מאחת מהן. בתוך החנות. ספיקו אסור. דכל קבוע כמחצה על מחצה ונידון דנפקא לן מן וארב לו וקם עליו [בפ"ט דסנהדרין עט: ובפ"ק דכתובות (טו.) (פסחים ט:). דכל קבוע כמחצה על מחצה דמיא וכיון שלקחה ממקום הקביעות מחזקינן לה כמחצה על מחצה [נדה יח.]. ובנמצא הלך אחר הרוב. בשר הנמצא בקרקע בין החנויות הלך אחר הרוב דכל דפריש מרובא פריש דכיון דפריש אין כאן תורת קבוע [פסחים שם]. נמצא דנייד הלך אחר הרוב דהשתא לאו קבוע הוא [חולין צה.]. בשאין דלתות מדינה נעולות. כגון דלתות מדינות פתוחות ורוב טבחים סביבות המדינה ישראל דאיכא למיזל בתר

תרי רובי להכשירה רוב העיר ורוב הבאין מחוצה לה. אע"פ שדלתות מדינה נעולות. דליכא אלא חד רובא להכשירה רוב העיר שתשע חנויות שבה מוכרות בשר שחוטה והאחת מוכרת נבילה [ב"ב כד.]. מתשעה צפרדעים וכו' ספיקו טמא. דהוה ליה ספק ואע"ג דרובא צפרדעים ואין להם טומאה כיון דשרץ קבוע ביניהם הוה ליה מחצה על מחצה [נדה שם]. וארב לו. קרא יתירא הוא נכתוב כי יהיה איש שונא לרעהו וקם עליו. ורבנן. דפליגי עליה דר' שמעון מאי דרשי ביה. אמרי דבי ר' ינאי פרט לזורק אבן לגו. לתוך חבורה של בני אדם כותים וישראלים אבל נתכוין לישראל זה והרג את חבירו לא אתא קרא למעוטי [סנהדרין עט.]. לתוך חבורת אנשים ויש שם כנענים וישראלים ואיכא למימר לכנענים נתכוון. ותיפוק ליה דרובא כנענים נינהו. ולא איצטריך קרא למפטריה. אי נמי. מחצה כנענים ומחצה ישראלים לא איצטריך קרא למפטריה דרחמנא אמר (במדבר לה) ושפטו העדה והצילו העדה דהא ספק נפשות להקל [ב"ק מד:]. למה לי קרא למיפטריה הא כיון דמצי למימר לכותים קא מתכווינא אית לן למפטריה משום דספק נפשות להקל מוהצילו העדה (יומא דף פד:) [סנהדרין שם]. לא צריכא דאיכא תשעה ישראלים. דאי לאו קרא הוה אמינא זיל בתר רובא ולישראל איכוין ואע"ג דדלמא לאו להאי איכוין נתכוין להרוג את זה והרג את זה חייב קא משמע לן קרא דהואיל והוה ליה כנעני קבוע ביניהן כמחצה על מחצה דמי וספק נפשות להקל ולכל מילי דקיימא לן קבוע כמחצה על מחצה דמי מהאי קרא נפקא לן [ב"ק שם]. ואשמעינן קרא דפטור משום דהוה ליה כותי קבוע ביניהם וילפינן מהאי קרא דכל קבוע לא פחות מלהיות נדון כמחצה על מחצה והוי ספק נפשות להקל, ומהכא נפקא לן בכל דוכתי דכל קבוע כמחצה על מחצה דמי והא ליכא למילף מיניה כרובא דמי דהא מהיכא תיתי לן דילמא האי דפטר ליה להאי לאו משום דספק נפשות להקל ולא משום דחשבינן ליה כרובא אבל מחצה על מחצה ילפינן מיניה דאי לאו כמחצה על מחצה דמי לא הוה ליה ספק נפשות להקל ואמאי פטור הא רובא דישראל נינהו ורבנן אית להו נתכוון לזה והרג את זה חייב [סנהדרין שם].

determined from which store it came, הֲלֵךְ אַחַר הָרוֹב – FOLLOW THE MAJORITY; I will respond: הָתָם לְחוּמְרָא – There, the principle leads **to a stringency,** whereas R' Zeira said that this principle can be applied even as a leniency.[29] – ? –

The Gemara suggests another source, but rejects this one as well:

אֶלָּא מִתִּשְׁעָה צְפַרְדְּעִים וְשֶׁרֶץ אֶחָד בֵּינֵיהֶם – **Rather,** perhaps it can be derived **from** the Baraisa that states: If there are NINE dead FROGS in a group, AND ONE dead *SHERETZ* AMONG THEM[30] וְנָגַע בְּאֶחָד מֵהֶן – AND [SOMEONE] TOUCHED ONE OF THESE carcasses וְאֵינוֹ יוֹדֵעַ בְּאֵיזֶה מֵהֶן נָגַע – BUT HE DOES NOT KNOW WHICH OF THEM HE TOUCHED, that of a frog or that of the *sheretz,* סְפֵיקוֹ טָמֵא – THIS DOUBT IS ruled *TAMEI* even though the majority of the carcasses in the group do not transmit *tumah;*[31] I will respond: הָתָם נַמִּי לְחוּמְרָא – **There too,** the principle leads **to a stringency!**[32] From where did R' Zeira learn that it can be applied even as a leniency?

The Gemara finally finds a Tannaic source for R' Zeira's ruling:

אֶלָּא מִתִּשְׁעָה שְׁרָצִים וּצְפַרְדֵּעַ אֶחָד בֵּינֵיהֶם – **Rather** it can be derived **from** the beginning of that Baraisa, which states: If there are NINE dead *SHERATZIM* in a group, AND ONE dead FROG AMONG THEM, וְנָגַע בְּאֶחָד מֵהֶן – AND [SOMEONE] TOUCHED ONE OF THESE carcasses, וְאֵינוֹ יוֹדֵעַ בְּאֵיזֶה מֵהֶן נָגַע – BUT HE DOES NOT KNOW WHICH OF THEM HE TOUCHED, that of a *sheretz* or that of the frog, the following law applies: בִּרְשׁוּת הַיָּחִיד סְפֵיקוֹ טָמֵא – If it occurred IN A PRIVATE DOMAIN, THIS DOUBT IS ruled *TAMEI;* בִּרְשׁוּת הָרַבִּים סְפֵיקוֹ טָהוֹר – but if it occurred IN A PUBLIC DOMAIN, THIS DOUBT IS ruled *TAHOR.*[33] This Baraisa teaches that we do not follow the majority when the minority item was stationed in place even though this leads to a leniency.

Having found a Tannaic precedent for R' Zeira's teaching, the Gemara seeks its Biblical source:[34]

וּמִדְּאוֹרַיְיתָא מְנָא לָן – **And from where in the Torah do we derive** this?

The Gemara answers:

אָמַר קְרָא ,,וְאָרַב לוֹ וְקָם עָלָיו" – **Scripture states:**[35] *But if there will be a man who hates his fellow* ***and ambushes him and rises up against him,*** *and strikes him mortally and he dies* etc. The words *and ambushes him* are superfluous, and thus are available to teach that עַד שֶׁיִּתְכַּוֵּין לוֹ – a murderer is not liable to execution **unless he intends to** kill **[a specific person].** If he intended to kill one person but killed another instead, he is not liable. This is the opinion of only one Tanna – R' Shimon – in Tractate *Sanhedrin* (79a).[36] וְרַבָּנָן – **And the Rabbis,** who disagree with R' Shimon, how do they interpret this verse? אָמְרֵי דְּבֵי רַבִּי יַנַּאי – **It was stated in the academy of R' Yannai:** פְּרָט לְזוֹרֵק אֶבֶן לְגוֹ – This verse serves to **exclude** from capital punishment **one who throws a stone into a group** of people consisting of Jews and Canaanites and he kills a Jew. The verse teaches that throwing the stone is not deemed an act of murdering a Jew because there was a significant chance that it would hit a Canaanite instead.[37]

The Gemara seeks to define the circumstances in which the phrase *"and ambushes him"* is needed to exempt the perpetrator. This will lead us to find in it the source for R' Zeira's principle concerning items stationed in place:

הֵיכִי דָמֵי – **What is the case** in which this teaching applies? אִילֵימָא דְּאִיכָּא תִּשְׁעָה כְּנַעֲנִים וְאֶחָד יִשְׂרָאֵל בֵּינֵיהֶם – **If you say** that it applies where there are **nine Canaanites** in the group **and** there is **one Jew among them,** the following difficulty arises: וְתֵיפּוּק לֵיהּ דְּרוּבָּא כְּנַעֲנִים נִינְהוּ – **Let [the perpetrator's exemption] emerge** from the fact **that the**

NOTES

29. The Baraisa rules stringently that when the meat was *kavua* it may not be eaten because it may have come from the one store selling *neveilah* meat. We still do not know that the principle of *kavua* can be used to rule leniently.

30. [A *sheretz* is any one of the eight creeping creatures listed in *Leviticus* (11:29-30) whose carcasses convey *tumah* upon contact. The frog is not one of them, and so, does not contaminate a person who touches it.] However, the צָב, *toad,* which resembles a frog, is one of the creaures that conveys *tumah* when dead (v. 29). The Baraisa (which is found in *Tosefta* of Tractate *Tohoros,* 6:2), presumably refers to a case where a dead toad was lying among nine dead frogs (*Rashi*).

31. In this case, the person touched one of the carcasses while the *sheretz* was set in place (*kavua*) within the group. Thus, the minority object [the *sheretz*] is regarded as equal in number to the majority [the frogs], and the effect of the majority is lost (*Rashi* to *Niddah* 18a). This proves that we do not follow the majority in cases of *kavua.* Although the person who touched the carcass is unable to tell the difference between the frogs and the toad, each of them is considered identifiable in its place (and hence, *kavua*), since more knowledgeable people can easily discern among them (*Shaarei Yosher* 4:11, based on *Tosafos* to *Zevachim* 73b ד״ה אלא; cf. *Binas Adam, Shaar HaKavua* §3).

[As quoted here, the Baraisa is abbreviated, but at its source in *Tosefta* it states that the carcasses were found in a private domain; it is in that case that the person is deemed *tamei* out of doubt, as shall be taught below (see *Rashi* and see note 33.]

32. For we rule the person *tamei* out of doubt even though the majority of the carcasses in the group do not convey *tumah.*

33. [Unresolved questions as to whether a person is *tahor* or *tamei* are unique in that they are judged according to the place in which the uncertainty arose. Uncertainties arising in a public domain are judged to be *tahor,* and those arising in a private domain are judged to be *tamei* (see *Niddah* 3a, and *Chullin* 9b with *Rashi* and *Tosafos* at length; see also *Rambam, Hil. Avos HaTumos* 16:1).]

Since the Baraisa differentiates between a case where the doubt arose in a public domain and one where it arose in a private domain, it obviously considers the matter unresolved – despite the presence of a majority of *sheratzim.* Clearly, we do not apply the rule of 'majority'' here; if we would, it would be presumed that the person touched a *sheretz* and he would be judged *tamei* even if this occurred in a public domain. The reason we ignore the majority is that since we are dealing with *kavua* the case is regarded as having a probability of fifty-fifty. Thus, we see that we apply the principle of *kavua* even when it results in a leniency, such as judging the person who touched the unidentified creature *tahor* out of doubt (*Rashi*).

[See *Shitah Mekubetzes* for an explanation of why the Gemara cites this first section of the Baraisa only after having cited the latter section.]

34. Since R' Zeira stated his ruling without providing the Scriptural source, the Gemara assumed that it was not his own innovation, but was based upon a Tannaic teaching. Now that this has been confirmed, the Gemara wonders from where the Tannaim learned this principle (*Shitah Mekubetzes* ד״ה מנא ליה).

35. *Deuteronomy* 19:11.

36. R' Shimon's interpretation of the verse is not relevant to our discussion here; it is the following interpretation of R' Shimon's disputants that contains the source for the law of *kavua.* See *Shitah Mekubetzes* for an explanation of why our Gemara quotes R' Shimon's view. Cf. *Ritva.*

37. [The Canaanites were the pagan people who lived in Eretz Yisrael before the Israelites entered the land. One who killed a Canaanite could not be executed by a Jewish court. The verse teaches that when there was a distinct possibility that one's stone would kill a Canaanite, he is exempt from punishment even if it actually killed a Jew.] However, if there were two Jews standing together and someone intended to kill one of them – and he was duly warned by witnesses that he would incur the death penalty, and he accepted their warning but delivered the blow anyway – he is liable to death even if his blow killed the Jew for whom he did not intend.

The Gemara could simply have cited this exposition of R' Yannai, without mentioning the Rabbis at all. [As shall be explained, this exposition is the source of the rule of *kavua.*] However, since the Gemara in *Sanhedrin* cites R' Yannai in the context of explaining the position of the Rabbis, our Gemara quotes him that way as well (*Rashi*).

בקרונות של ציפורי היה מעשה וכדרבי אמי דאמר רבי אמי והוא שהיתה סיעה של בני אדם כשרין עוברת לשם וכדר' ינאי דאמר ר' ינאי נבעלת בקרונות כשרה לכהונה בקרונות סלקא דעתך אלא נבעלת בשעת קרונות כשרה לכהונה אבל פירש אחד מציפורי ובעל הולד שתוקי כי הא דכי אתא רב דימי אמר זעירי א"ר חנינא ואמרי לה אמר זעירי אמר ר' חנינא הולכין אחר רוב העיר ואין הולכין אחר רוב סיעה כלפי לייא הני ניידי והני קביעי וקיימי אלא הולכין אחר רוב העיר והוא דאיכא רוב סיעה בהדה ואין הולכין אחר רוב העיר גרידתא ולא אחר רוב סיעה גרידתא מ"ט גזרה רוב סיעה אטו רוב העיר ורוב העיר נמי אי דקא אזלי אינהו לגבה כל דפריש מרובא פריש לא צריכא דקא אזלא איהי לגבייהו דהוה ליה קבוע וא"ר זירא כל קבוע כמחצה על מחצה דמי ומי בעינן תרי רובי והתניא תשע חנויות כולן מוכרות בשר שחוטה ואחת מוכרת בשר נבלה ולקח מאחת מהן ואינו יודע מאי זה מהן לקח ספיקו אסור ובנמצא הלך אחר הרוב התם וכי תימא בשאין דלתות מדינה נעולות דקא אתי לה רובא מעלמא והא א"ר זירא אע"פ שדלתות מדינה נעולות מעלה עשו ביוחסין גופא א"ר זירא כל קבוע כמחצה על מחצה דמי בין לקולא בין לחומרא מנא ליה לר' זירא הא אילימא מתשע חנויות כולן מוכרות בשר שחוטה ואחת מוכרת בשר נבלה ולקח מאחת מהן ואינו יודע מאיזה מהן לקח ספיקו אסור ובנמצא הלך אחר הרוב התם לחומרא אלא מתשעה צפרדעים ושרץ אחד ביניהם ונגע באחד מהן ואינו יודע באיזה מהן נגע ספיקו טמא התם נמי לחומרא אלא מתשעה שרצים וצפרדע אחד ביניהם ונגע באחד מהן ואינו יודע באיזה מהן נגע ברה"י ספיקו טמא ברשות הרבי' ספיקו טהור ומדאורייתא מנא לן אמר קרא א) וארב לו וקם עליו עד שיתכוין לו ורבנן אמרי דבי ר' ינאי פרט לזורק אבן לגו היכי דמי אילימא דאיכא תשעה כנענים ואחד ישראל ביניהם ותיפוק ליה דרובא כנענים נינהו אי נמי פלגא ופלגא ספק נפשות להקל לא צריכא דאיכא תשעה ישראלים וכנעני אחד ביניהם דהוה ליה כנעני קבוע וכל קבוע כמחצה על מחצה דמי איתמר רב חייא בר אשי אמר רב הלכה כרבי יוסי ורב חנן בר רבא אמר רב הוראת שעה היתה מתיב רבי ירמיה וליוחסין לא בעינן תרי רובי והתנן

מצא

רש"י

בקרונות של ציפורי. ביום השוק שסיעות ושיירות ממקום אחר באות שם: וכדרבי אמי. דהשתא איכא רוב סיעה ורוב העיר: נבעלת בקרונות. משמע על הקרון: בשעת קרונות. שהשיירות באות לעיר: כשרה לכהונה. כדקאמר והוא שהיתה סיעה של בני אדם כשרים עוברת שם דאיכא למימר שמהם היה: אבל פירש אחד מציפורי. דידעינן ודאי דמן העיר היה אע"פ שציפורי עיר שרובה משיאין לכהונה: הולד שתוקי. דבחד רובא לא מכשר: וכי הא דכי אתא רב דימי אמר זעירי אמר רבי חנינא ואמרי לה. שלא הוזכר רב דימי כאן אלא זעירי אמר רבי חנינא דבעינן תרי רובי וכדמפרש טעמא: הולכין אחר רוב העיר. להכשיר: ואין הולכין אחר רוב סיעה. כגון במקום רחוק מן העיר דבודאי מאנשי הסיעה הוה אין מכשירין אותה ואפילו רובן כשרין: וקשיא לן כלפי לייא. כנגד איפוא הדבר הזה סובב: הני ניידי. רוב סיעה ניידי ויש להלך בהן אחר הרוב: והני. של עיר: קביעי. ואמרינן לקמן כל קבוע כמחצה על מחצה דמי ואפילו אין שם אלא אחד פסולה: ולא אחר רוב סיעה גרידתא. והכי קאמר אין הולכין אחר רוב סיעה לבדה וכל שכן אחר רוב העיר לבדה: מ"ט. אחר רוב סיעה לא: גזרה אטו רוב העיר. דקביעי: ופרכינן רוב העיר נמי. אי עקר הבועל מביתו ואזל לגבה הוה נייד וקי"ל כל דפריש מרובא פריש: ומשני איכא דקאזלא לגבייהו כו'. ולא גרסינן ב) מאי איכא יש שהולכת היא אצלו והוה ליה קבוע הלכך אפילו ברוב כשרים או רוב העיר או רוב סיעה פסול כרבי יהושע ומשום תרי רובי אכשרה דליכא למיגזר מידי: ולקח בשר מאחת מהן. במקום קביעות: ספיקו אסור. דכל קבוע כמחצה על מחצה דמי: ובנמצא. בשר הנמצא בשוק ולא ידעינן מאיזה פירש: הלך אחר הרוב. הואיל והבא לפנינו לא במקום קביעות לקחה וכבר פירשה על ידי אחר וכל דפריש מרובא פריש: דקאתי לה רובא מעלמא. וכגון שרוב סיעת טבחי ישראל כשרים באו לכאן דאיכא תרי רובי או שרוב טבחי כל המדינה ישראל דאיכא תרי רובי רוב העיר ורוב המדינה דניידי: אלא מתשעה צפרדעים כו'. תוספתא היא במס' טהרות תשעה צפרדעים מתים ברשות היחיד ושרץ אחד כגון צב שהוא דומה לצפרדע ביניהם ונגע באחד מהן ספיקו טמא: אלא מתשעה שרצים כו'. אף היא תוספתא במס' טהרות וקתני ברה"י ספיקו טמא ברה"ר ספיקו טהור אלמא כמחצה דמי ולקולא דאי לאו כמחצה דמי אין כאן ספק טומאה אלא ודאי טומאה דהא רובא שרצים: אמר קרא וארב לו עד שיהא מתכוין לו. פרט למתכוין להרוג את זה והרג את זה הכי דריש ליה ר"ש בסנהדרין ואמרינן התם ורבנן היכי דרשי ליה: אמרי דבי ר' ינאי פרט לזורק אבן לגו. לתוך חבורת בני אדם כנענים וישראלים אבל שני ישראלים עומדין ונתכוין להרוג (א) זה (והרג זה) והתרו בו וקבל התראה ונפלה הכאה על חבירו חייב והיינו טעמא דקאמר הכא ורבנן משום דבסנהדרין הכי איתא: תיפוק ליה דרובא כנענים נינהו. ולמה לי קרא ואי נמי פלגא ופלגא אכתי לא איצטריך קרא דמהיכא תיתי דניקטליה: ספק נפשות. דיני נפשות להקל דהא והצילו העדה כתיב (במדבר לה): דהוה ליה כנעני קבוע ביניהם. ואשמועינן האי קרא דכל קבוע כמחצה על מחצה דמי: הוראת שעה היתה. הך דריב"ג צורך שעה היתה או ראו שם שאר לידי היכר דברים להתיר אבל לדורות תרי רובי בעינן: מתיב רבי ירמיה כו'. קס"ד דמשום רוב העיר גרידתא אכשרוה ואמר רב הלכה כרבי יוסי:

מלא

תוספות

אמר רב בקרונות של צפורי היה מעשה כו' פי' לעולם דלא טוענה ברי ור' יוחנן בן נורי בתרוייהו היכא דלא טוענה ברי לכ"ע בעינן תרי רובי והא דלא קאמר בשניה לעולם דלא טוענה ברי משום דבאתקפתא לא קאמר אי בטוענת ברי כו' אי נמי נוכל לפרש דבשניה נמי איירי בברי ודאיכא מגו ולא תקשי הלכתא אהלכתא דדוקא דיעבד פסיק שמואל כר"ג כדאמר לעיל ואת לא תעביד עובדא עד דאיכא רוב כשרין אף על גב דלעיל משמע דברוב אחד שרי לכתחלה רב חייא בר אשי סבר דלכתחלה בעינן תרי רובי ומתני' קתני הרי זו תנשא דמשמע לכתחלה:

דלמא אזלא איהי לגבייהו. פי' לתוך ביתם דאפילו בתוך העיר לא חשיב קבוע דדמי לנמצא בין החנויות דלא חשיב קבוע וכן גבי תינוק מושלך בעיר לא חשיב קבוע הואיל ולא נמצא בבית ולכך פירש בקונטרס שפירש בועל מביתו וא"ת דבנזיר פ"ב (דף יב. ושם) פריך אהא דאמר האומר לשלוחו צא וקדש לי אשה סתם אסור בכל הנשים שבעולם מקן סתומה ומסיק אמינא לך אנא אשה דלא נידא ואת אמרת לי איסורא דנייד וכי תימא ה"נ בשוקא אשכחה וקידש התם הדרא לניחותא משמע לגבי אדם לא שייך כל דפריש מרובא פריש משום דהדר לניחותיה ולאו פירכא היא דהתם בשעת האיסור כשזה בא על שום אשה הדרא לניחותא האשה שקידש השליח אבל הכא כי אזלי אינהו לגבה בשעה שאוסרה הרי הוא נייד:

פרט לזורק אבן לגו. תימה דלר' שמעון קבוע מנא ליה ואין לומר דמסקינן בפ' הנשרפין (סנהדרין דף עט. ושם) דר"ש סבר כרבי דיליף נתינה נתינה ואייתר ליה וארב לו לקבוע דאכתי לתנא דבי חזקיה מנא ליה קבוע דלית ליה דרבי דהא באין מתכוין פטור ממון ל):

וספק נפשות להקל. תימה למ"ד התראת ספק לא שמה התראה אפילו ספק נפשות להחמיר פטור משום דהתראת ספק היא ואי למ"ד שמה התראה היכי פטרינן ליה כשנמצא שישראל הרג הא מיחייב בהכה את זה וחזר והכה את זה מ) ובנותר כשאמרו לו אל תותיר אע"ג דספק הוא וי"ל דשאני התם שיודע בודאי שיבא לידי איסור אם יותיר או יכה שניהם מש"ה שמה התראה אבל הכא אינו יודע שודאי יבוא לידי איסור שאינו יודע את מי יכה:

וליוחסין לא בעינן תרי רובי ורמינהי כו'. הוה מצי לשנויי שאני תינוק דלית לי' חזק' דכשרו':

ולרב

עין משפט נר מצוה

פט א ב מיי' פי"ח מהלכות איסורי ביאה הל' יד סמג לאוין קכא טוש"ע אה"ע סימן ו סעיף יז יח:

צ ג מיי' פ"ח מהלכות מאכלות אסורות הל' יא סמג לאוין קמא טור ש"ע י"ד סימן קי סע"ג:

צא ד מיי' שם ומוש"ע שם וכסף' סג ס"ח:

צב ה ו מיי' פי"ח מהלכות אבות הטומאות הלכה ב:

צג ז מיי' פ"ד מהל' רוצח הלכה א סמג לאוין קמג:

תוספות רי"ד

בקרונות של צפורי היה מעשה וכדר' ינאי דאמר נבעלה בשעת קרונות כשירה לכהונה פי' קרוניות הבאים ממקום אחר ומתקבצים שם ליום השוק והוא שהיתה סיעה של בני אדם כשרים עוברים שם דהוו תרי רובא לכשרות רוב העיר ורוב סיעה. פי' כל זה מפני שלא ידעה למי נבעלה אבל אי ידעה ואמרה לכשר נבעלתי הלכה כר"ג ונאמנת אפילו ברוב פסולים: ומקשי' ומי בעי' תרי רובי והתניא ט' חנויות כולן מוכרות בשר שחוטה ואחת מוכרת בשר נבילה ולקח מאחת מהן ואינו יודע מאיזה מהן לקח ספיקו אסור שכל קבוע כמחצה על מחצה דמי ובנמצא הלך אחר הרוב דכל דפריש מרובא פריש. ומהדר מעלה עשו ביוחסין: איתמר א"ר חייא בר אשי אמר רב הלכה כר' יוסי פי' דבעי' תרי רובי: א"ר זירא כל קבוע כמחצה על מחצה דמי בין לקולא בין לחומרא כגון ט' חנויות דאמרן. א"נ ט' צפרדעים ושרץ א' ביניהם ברה"י ונגע באחד מהן ואינו יודע באיזה מהן נגע ספיקו טמא. לקולא כגון ט' שרצים וצפרדע א' ביניהן ברה"ר ונגע באח' מהן וא"י באיזה מהן נגע ספיקו טהור אלא כמחצה על מחצה דמי ולקולא. דאי לאו כמחצה על מחצה דמי אין כאן ספק טומאה אלא ודאי טומאה דהא רובא שרצים:

האשה

מסורת הש"ס

א) [קדושין דף עג.], ב) [ברכות כח. וש"נ], ג) [רש"ל מוחק וכ"ב גירסת רש"י איכא דקאזלא לגבייהו ועי' ב' גירסות בב"י אה"ע סימן ו], ד) פסחים ט: חולין לה. נדה יח., ה) ב"ב כד., ו) [לעיל יג. וש"נ], ז) נדה יח. ע"ש תוספתא טהרות פ"ו, ח) ב"ק מד: סנהדרין עט., ט) [יומא פד:], י) [שבת קכט. וש"נ], כ) נ"ל מאי רוב העיר איכא כו'. רש"ל, ל) [וסנהדרין עט. ד"ה וכל כתבו תוס' מירוץ לזה וכ"כ בב"ק מד: ד"ה כל ועי' תוספות נדה יח. ד"ה ספיקא], מ) יבמות קא ע"א.

הגהות הב"ח

(א) רש"י ד"ה אמרי וכו' להרוג את זה והרג את זה:

תורה אור השלם

א) וְכִי יִהְיֶה אִישׁ שֹׂנֵא לְרֵעֵהוּ וְאָרַב לוֹ וְקָם עָלָיו וְהִכָּהוּ נֶפֶשׁ וָמֵת וְנָס אֶל אַחַת הֶעָרִים הָאֵל: [דברים יט, יא]

ליקוטי רש"י

כלפי לייא. שתי מלות כלפי היכן נוטה דבר זה הא איפכא מסתברא. לייא, היכן וחבירו בברכות בפרק הרואה (דף נח.) אמצי לנהרא כגני לייא מרכסים שבורים להיכן הולכים [פסחים ה:]. כנגד איפוא הפכת דבריך לייא איפוא כדאמר בברכות כגני לייא כדים שבורים להיכן הולכים [סוטה מד.]. כנגד מה וכו' ולאן הדבר נוטה כדאמרינן בברכות אמצי לנהרא כגני לייא הקדירות שלמות הולכין לנהר לשאוב בהן מים אבל השבורין להיכן הולכין [רשב"ם ב"ב קד.]. אי דקא אזלי אינהו וכו' מרובא פריש. ואם בבעילה זו הלך הבועל אצלה דהשתא נד ליה ממקום קביעתו ואין לדונו בתורת קבוע שהוא נדון כמחצה על מחצה יש לנו לומר כל דפריש מרובא פריש והולד כשר [קידושין עג.]. ולקח מאחת מהן. בתוך החנות. ספיקו אסור. דכל קבוע כמחצה על מחצה נידון דנפקא לן מן וארב לו וקם עליו [בפ"ט דסנהדרין עט:] ובפ"ק דכתובות (טו.) [פסחים ט:]. דכל קבוע כמחצה על מחצה דמיא וכיון שלקחה ממקום הקביעות מחזקינן לה כמחצה על מחצה [נדה יח.]. ובנמצא הלך אחר הרוב. בשר הנמצא בקרקע בין החנויות הלך אחר הרוב דכל דפריש מרובה פריש דכיון דפריש אין כאן תורת קבוע [פסחים שם]. נמצא דנייד הלך אחר הרוב דהשתא לאו קבוע הוא [חולין צה.]. בשאין דלתות מדינה נעולות. כגון דלתות מדינות פתוחות ורוב טבחים סביבות המדינה ישראל דאיכא למיזל בתר תרי רובי להכשירה רוב העיר ורוב הבאין מחוצה לה. אע"פ שדלתות מדינה נעולות. דליכא אלא חד רובא להכשירה רוב העיר שתשע חנויות שבה מוכרות בשר שחוטה והאחת מוכרת נבילה [ב"ב כד.]. מתשעה צפרדעים וכו' ספיקו טמא. דהוה ליה ספק ואע"ג דרובא צפרדעים ואין להם טומאה כיון דשרץ קבוע ביניהם הוה ליה מחצה על מחצה [נדה שם]. וארב לו. קרא יתירא הוא נכתוב כי יהיה איש שונא לרעהו וקם עליו. ורבנן. דפליגי עליה דרבי שמעון מאי דרשי ביה. אמרי דבי ר' ינאי פרט לזורק אבן לגו. לתוך חבורה של בני אדם כותים וישראלים אבל נתכוון לישראל זה והרג את חבירו לא אתא קרא למעוטי [סנהדרין עט.]. לתוך חבורת אנשים ויש שם כנענים וישראלים ואיכא למימר לכנענים נתכוון. ותיפוק ליה דרובא כנענים נינהו. ולא איצטריך קרא למפטריה. אי נמי. חמשה כנענים וחמשה ישראלים לא איצטריך קרא למפטריה דרחמנא אמר (במדבר לה) ושפטו העדה והצילו העדה ספק נפשות להקל [ב"ק מד:]. למה לי קרא למיפטריה הא כיון דמצי למימר לכותים קא מתכוונא אית לך למפטריה משום דספק נפשות להקל מוהצילו העדה (יומא דף פד:) [סנהדרין שם]. לא צריכא דאיכא תשעה ישראלים. דאי לאו קרא הוה אמינא זיל בתר רובא ולישראל איכוין ואע"ג דדלמא לאו להאי איכוין נתכוון להרוג את זה והרג את זה חייב קא משמע לן קרא דהואיל והוה ליה כנעני קבוע ביניהן כמחצה על מחצה דמי וספק נפשות להקל ולכל מילי דקיימא לן קבוע כמחצה על מחצה דמי מהאי קרא נפקא לן [ב"ק שם]. ואשמעינן קרא דפטור משום דהוה ליה כותי קבוע ביניהם וילפינן מהאי קרא דכל קבוע לא פחות מלהיות נדון כמחצה על מחצה והוי ספק נפשות להקל, ומהכא נפקא לן בכל דוכתי דכל קבוע כמחצה על מחצה דמי דהא מהיכא תיתי לן דילמא האי דפטר ליה להאי משום דספק נפשות להקל ולא משום דחשבינן ליה כרובא אבל מחצה על מחצה ילפינן מיניה דאי לאו כמחצה על מחצה דמי לא הוה ליה ספק נפשות להקל ואמאי פטור הא רובא דישראל נינהו ורבנן אית להו נתכוון לזה והרג את זה חייב [סנהדרין שם].

The Gemara objects to the notion that the Sages decreed not to follow a single majority:[20]

וּמִי בְּעֵינַן תְּרֵי רוּבֵּי – But do we actually **need two majorities?** **וְהָתַנְיָא – Why, it was taught in a Baraisa:** תֵּשַׁע חֲנוּיוֹת כּוּלָּן מוֹכְרוֹת בְּשַׂר שְׁחוּטָה – If there are NINE STORES in town, ALL SELLING MEAT OF A properly SLAUGHTERED [ANIMAL], וְאַחַת מוֹכֶרֶת בְּשַׂר נְבֵלָה – AND ONE other store that SELLS MEAT OF A *NEVEILAH* [an animal not properly slaughtered], וְלָקַח מֵאַחַת מֵהֶן – AND SOMEONE PURCHASED meat FROM ONE OF THESE stores, וְאֵינוֹ יוֹדֵעַ מֵאֵי זֶה מֵהֶן לָקַח – BUT HE DOES NOT KNOW FROM WHICH OF THEM HE PURCHASED it, סְפֵיקוֹ אָסוּר – THIS DOUBT IS ruled FORBIDDEN and the meat may not be eaten.[21] וּבְנִמְצָא – HOWEVER, in a situation WHERE [THE MEAT] WAS FOUND in the street outside the stores and it cannot be determined from which store it came, הַלֵּךְ אַחַר הָרוֹב – FOLLOW THE MAJORITY; since the majority of stores sell kosher meat, the found meat is permitted.[22] Thus, we see that we do rely upon a single majority. — ? —

The Gemara suggests and immediately rejects a possible solution:

וְכִי תֵּימָא בְּשֶׁאֵין דַּלְתוֹת מְדִינָה נְעוּלוֹת – **And if you will say** that the Baraisa refers to a case **where the gates of the country are not locked,** דְּקָא אָתֵי לָהּ רוּבָּא מֵעָלְמָא – **so that a majority** of kosher meat **comes in from the** outside **world,** resulting in two majorities of kosher meat,[23] I will respond: וְהָא אָמַר רַבִּי זֵירָא – **But R' Zeira said:** אַף עַל פִּי שֶׁדַּלְתוֹת מְדִינָה נְעוּלוֹת – The Baraisa's ruling applies **even where the gates of the city are locked** (i.e. there are no visiting merchants, so that there is only one "majority").[24] — ? —

The Gemara answers:

מַעֲלָה עָשׂוּ בְּיוּחֲסִין – Our Mishnah's case is different, because **they set a high standard in genealogical matters** regarding a Kohen.[25] Only in the case of uncertainty whether someone is fit for the Kehunah are two majorities required.

The Gemara cites an expanded version of R' Zeira's earlier ruling concerning items "stationed in place":[26]

גּוּפָא – The text itself stated: אָמַר רַבִּי זֵירָא – **Rav Zeira said:** כָּל קָבוּעַ כְּמֶחֱצָה עַל מֶחֱצָה דָּמֵי – **Any** doubt relating to something **stationed** in its place **is treated as** having a probability of **fifty-fifty,** בֵּין לְקוּלָּא בֵּין לְחוּמְרָא – **whether** this leads **to a leniency or** it leads **to a stringency.**[27]

The Gemara seeks a Tannaic precedent for the assertion that this principle is true even when it leads to a leniency:

מְנָא לֵיהּ לְרַבִּי זֵירָא הָא – **From where did R' Zeira derive this?**

The Gemara suggests and rejects one source:

אִילֵימָא מִתֵּשַׁע חֲנוּיוֹת – **If you say** it is **from** the Baraisa that stated: If there are NINE STORES in town, כּוּלָּן מוֹכְרוֹת בְּשַׂר שְׁחוּטָה – ALL SELLING MEAT OF a properly SLAUGHTERED [ANIMAL], וְאַחַת בְּשַׂר נְבֵלָה – AND ONE other store that SELLS MEAT OF A *NEVEILAH,* וְלָקַח מֵאַחַת מֵהֶן – AND SOMEONE PURCHASED meat FROM ONE OF THESE stores, וְאֵינוֹ יוֹדֵעַ מֵאֵיזֶה מֵהֶן לָקַח – BUT HE DOES NOT KNOW FROM WHICH OF THEM HE PURCHASED it, סְפֵיקוֹ אָסוּר – THIS DOUBT IS ruled FORBIDDEN and the meat may not be eaten, because when it was purchased it was stationed in its place;[28] וּבְנִמְצָא – HOWEVER, in a situation WHERE [THE MEAT] WAS FOUND on the street outside the stores and it cannot be

NOTES

men who are not *kavua*).] See the end of note 3 for discussion of *Rashi's* comment.

20. The Gemara currently assumes that this decree applies in regard to all areas of Torah law: Whenever a matter is in doubt, we do not rule leniently based on a single majority if possible confusion could arise involving a case where the items in question are *kavua* (see *Ritva* and *Maharam Schif*).

21. Since the meat was purchased in the store where it had been stationed [and the uncertainty thus *arose* when the item was *kavua* (*Ritva; Tosafos* to *Pesachim* 9b ד״ה היינו and *Chidushei HaRan* there ד״ה ולקח)], the case must be treated as one having a probability of fifty-fifty (as though there were an equal number of kosher and non-kosher stores). And being that the uncertainty concerning the origin of the meat cannot be resolved, it it forbidden out of doubt (*Rashi*).

22. Since the uncertainty concerning the origin of the meat arose after it had been *removed* from its station in the group of which it was a part, the law allows us to assume that it came from the majority — i.e. the kosher stores in the group (*Rashi;* see note 16). We learn from the Mishnah that the meat found outside the store was not decreed prohibited on account of possible confusion with cases where the uncertainty arose inside a store (*Ritva*).

23. I.e. perhaps the Baraisa's ruling applies only in a town that has local butchers *as well as* visiting meat merchants, and the majority of the itinerant merchants also sell kosher meat. If we do not know whether the meat that was found came from a local butcher or an itinerant, there would be two "majorities" dictating that the meat is kosher: (a) The majority of stores in the town sell kosher; (b) the majority of butchers visiting the town sell kosher (*Rashi;* see there for an alternative explanation). And since the second majority (i.e. that of itinerant butchers) by definition consists of items that are not *kavua* (like the visitors to a town in the Mishnah's case), there is no concern for confusion with the case in which the majority is *kavua.* Perhaps it is only in this case that the meat is permitted.

24. That is, even where the gates of the city are locked and no one brings in meat from outside, the found meat is presumed to be kosher — based on the simple majority of kosher meat in the city. Thus, we see that the rule of majority is applied to an item "removed" from its station, and we are not concerned that this might lead to confusion in the case where the item was *kavua.*

25. I.e. the Rabbis treated cases of uncertainty concerning a woman's fitness to marry into the Kehunah with utmost gravity, and imposed this decree here even though it was not imposed in other areas of Torah law (see *Rashi* to 15b ד״ה אבל ליוחסין לא; *Noda BiYehudah, Even HaEzer I* §7; *Shev Shmaatsa* 4:20).

26. At this point we should note that the law governing an item stationed in place (*kavua*) does not seem to apply universally. There is a rule that when an item becomes intermingled with a larger number of similar items — e.g. a piece of non-kosher meat is mixed in a pot with several pieces of kosher meat — the minority item is nullified [בָּטֵל] and every individual piece of meat in the pot is deemed kosher. Why do we not say that since the non-kosher piece is in its place it is considered as though there were an equal number of kosher and non-kosher pieces, so that all must be forbidden out of doubt?

The answer is that the rule of *kavua* applies only when the stationed item is clearly identifiable in its place, and thus, not subject to nullification. The classic example is the cited case of a town in which nine stores sell kosher meat and one sells non-kosher meat. Since the non-kosher meat was at the time of the purchase clearly defined in its place, the law dictates that a person who does not recall in which of the stores he purchased meat cannot assume that it came from the majority. However, when the item is not identifiable in its place, such as the instance in which pieces of meat became mixed in a pot, the minority item is nullified (*Ritva; Tosafos* to *Zevachim* 73b ד״ה אלא; *Tur, Yoreh De'ah* 110:3; see also *Tosafos* to *Nazir* 12a ד״ה אסור; cf. *Haflaah* to *Tosafos* ד״ה פרט and to 14b ד״ה בגמרא רמי ליהא אביי). [For an alternative type of case that is subject to the law of *kavua,* see *Rashba* in *Toras HaBayis* 4:1 and *Ran* to *Chullin* 95a ד״ה ובנמצא, but see *Tosafos* to *Chullin* 95a ד״ה ספיקו and *Chidushei HaRan* to *Pesachim* 9b ד״ה ולקח. This issue is discussed in depth by *Binas Adam, Shaar HaKavua* §1-3 and *Shaarei Yosher* 4:10-11.]

27. This means that the principle of *kavua* is rooted in Biblical law, so that we may rely upon it even if ignoring the majority results in a leniency. If it was a Rabbinic enactment, it would apply only in instances where this results in a stringency. The Gemara will later find a Scriptural source for the *kavua* principle. First, however, it seeks Tannaic support for R' Zeira's assertion.

28. Thus, we see that we do not follow the majority where the state of *kavua* exists.

בקרונות של ציפורי היה מעשה וכדרבי אמי דאמר רבי אמי והוא שהיתה סיעה של בני אדם כשרין עוברת לשם וכדר' ינאי דאמר ר' ינאי נבעלת בקרונות כשרה לכהונה בקרונות סלקא דעתך אלא נבעלת בשעת קרונות כשרה לכהונה אבל פירש אחד מציפורי ובעל הולד שתוקי כי הא דכי אתא רב דימי אמר זעירי א"ר חנינא ואמרי לה אמר זעירי אמר ר' חנינא הולכין אחר רוב העיר ואין הולכין אחר רוב סיעה כלפי לייא הני ניידי והני קביעי וקיימי אלא א הולכין אחר רוב העיר והוא דאיכא רוב סיעה בהדה ואין הולכין אחר רוב העיר גרידתא ולא אחר רוב סיעה גרידתא מ"ט גזרה רוב סיעה אטו רוב העיר ורוב העיר נמי ו) אי דקא אזלי אינהו לגבה כל דפריש י) מרובא פריש ב לא צריכא דקא אזלא איהי לגבייהו דהוה ליה קבוע וא"ר זירא כל קבוע כמחצה על מחצה דמי ומי בעינן תרי רובי והתניא ז) ג תשע חנויות כולן מוכרות בשר שחוטה ואחת מוכרת בשר נבלה ולקח מאחת מהן ואינו יודע מאי זה מהן לקח ספיקו אסור ד ובנמצא הלך אחר הרוב וכי תימא בשאין דלתות מדינה נעולות דקא אתי לה רובא מעלמא והא א"ר זירא ח) אע"פ שדלתות מדינה נעולות ט) מעלה עשו ביוחסין גופא א"ר זירא כל קבוע כמחצה על מחצה דמי בין לקולא בין לחומרא מנא ליה לר' זירא הא אילימא מתשע חנויות כולן מוכרות בשר שחוטה ואחת בשר נבלה ולקח מאחת מהן ואינו יודע מאיזה מהן לקח ספיקו אסור ובנמצא הלך אחר הרוב התם לחומרא אלא ה מתשעה צפרדעים ושרץ אחד ביניהם ונגע באחד מהן ואינו יודע באיזה מהן נגע ספיקו טמא התם נמי לחומרא אלא ו מתשעה שרצים וצפרדע אחד ביניהם ונגע באחד מהן ואינו יודע באיזה מהן נגע ברה"י ספיקו טמא ברשות הרבים ספיקו טהור ומדאורייתא מנא לן ל) אמר קרא א) וארב לו וקם עליו ז עד שיתכוין לו ורבנן אמרי דבי ר' ינאי פרט לזורק אבן לגו מ) היכי דמי אילימא דאיכא תשעה כנענים ואחד ישראל ביניהם ותיפוק ליה דרובא כנענים נינהו אי נמי פלגא ופלגא ספק נפשות להקל לא צריכא דאיכא תשעה ישראלים וכנעני אחד ביניהם דהוה ליה כנעני קבוע וכל קבוע כמחצה על מחצה דמי איתמר רב חייא בר אשי אמר רב הלכה כרבי יוסי ורב חנן בר רבא אמר רב הוראת שעה היתה מתיב רבי ירמיה וליוחסין לא בעינן תרי רובי והתנן
מצא

רש"י

בקרונות של ציפורי. ביום השוק שסיעות ושיירות ממקום אחר באות שם: **וכדרבי אמי.** דהשתא איכא רוב סיעה ורוב העיר: **נבעלת בקרונות.** משמע על הקרון: **בשעת קרונות.** שהשיירות באות לעיר: **כשרה לכהונה.** כדקאמר והוא שהיתה סיעה של בני אדם כשרים עוברת שם דאיכא למימר שמהם היה: **אבל פירש אחד מציפורי.** דידעינן ודאי דמן העיר היה אע"פ שציפורי עיר שרובה משיאין לכהונה: **הולד שתוקי.** דבחד רובא לא מכשר: **וכי הא דכי אתא רב דימי אמר זעירי אמר רבי חנינא ואמרי לה.** שלא הוזכר רב דימי כאן אלא זעירי אמר רבי חנינא דבעינן תרי רובי וכדמפרש טעמא: **הולכין אחר רוב העיר.** להכשיר: **ואין הולכין אחר רוב סיעה.** כגון במקום רחוק מן העיר דבודאי מאנשי הסיעה הוה אין מכשירין אותה ואפילו רובן כשרין: **וקשיא** לן **כלפי לייא.** כנגד איפוא הדבר הזה סובב: **הני ניידי.** רוב סיעה ניידי ויש להלך בהן אחר הרוב: **והני.** של עיר: **קביעי.** ואמרינן לקמן כל קבוע כמחצה על מחצה דמי ואפילו אין שם אלא אחד פסולה: **ולא אחר רוב סיעה גרידתא.** והכי קאמר אין הולכין אחר רוב סיעה לבדה וכל שכן אחר רוב העיר לבדה: **מ"ט.** אחר רוב סיעה לא: **גזרה אטו רוב העיר.** דקביעי: **ופרכינן רוב העיר נמי.** אי עקר הבועל מביתו ואזל לגבה הוה נייד וקי"ל כל דפריש מרובא פריש: **ומשני איכא דקאזלא לגבייהו כו'.** ולא גרסינן נ) מאי איכא יש שהולכת היא אצלו והוה ליה קבוע הלכך אפילו ברוב כשרים או רוב העיר או רוב סיעה פסול כרבי יהושע ומשום תרי רובי אכשרה דליכא למיגזר מידי: **ולקח בשר מאחת מהן.** במקום קביעות: **ספיקו אסור.** דכל קבוע כמחצה על מחצה דמי: **ובנמצא.** בשר הנמצא בשוק ולא ידעינן מאיזה פירש: **הלך אחר הרוב.** הואיל והבא לפנינו לא במקום קביעות לקחה וכבר פירשה על ידי אחר וכל דפריש מרובא פריש: **דקאתי לה רובא מעלמא.** וכגון שרוב סיעת טבחי ישראל כשרים באו לכאן דאיכא תרי רובי או שרוב טבחי כל המדינה ישראל דאיכא תרי רובי רוב העיר ורוב המדינה דניידי: **אלא מתשעה צפרדעים כו'.** תוספתא היא במס' טהרות תשעה צפרדעים מתים ברשות היחיד ושרץ אחד כגון צב שהוא דומה לצפרדע ביניהם ונגע באחד מהן ספיקו טמא: **אלא מתשעה שרצים כו'.** אף היא תוספתא במס' טהרות וקתני ברה"י ספיקו טמא ברה"ר ספיקו טהור אלמא כמחצה דמי ולקולא דאי לאו כמחצה דמי אין כאן ספק טומאה אלא ודאי טומאה דהא רובא שרצים: **אמר קרא וארב לו** עד שיהא מתכוין לו. פרט למתכוין להרוג את זה והרג את זה הכי דריש ליה ר"ש בסנהדרין ואמרינן התם ורבנן היכי דרשי ליה: **אמרי דבי ר' ינאי פרט לזורק אבן לגו.** לתוך חבורת בני אדם כנענים וישראלים אבל שני ישראלים עומדין ונתכוין להרוג (א) זה (והרג זה) והתרו בו וקבל התראה ונפלה הכאה על חבירו חייב והיינו טעמא דקאמר הכא ורבנן משום דבסנהדרין הכי איתא: **תיפוק ליה דרובא כנענים נינהו.** ולמה לי קרא ואי נמי פלגא ופלגא אכתי לא איצטריך קרא דמהיכא תיתי דניקטליה: **ספק נפשות.** דיני נפשות להקל דהא והצילו העדה כתיב (במדבר לה): **דהוה ליה כנעני קבוע** ביניהם. ואשמועינן האי קרא דכל קבוע כמחצה על מחצה דמי: **הוראת שעה היתה.** הך דריב"נ לורך שעה היתה או ראו שם שאר לידי היכר דברים להתיר אבל לדורות תרי רובי בעינן: **מתיב רבי ירמיה כו'.** קס"ד דמשום רוב העיר גרידתא אכשרוה ואמר רב הלכה כרבי יוסי:
מלא

תוספות

אמר רב בקרונות של צפורי היה מעשה כו' פי' לעולם דלא טענה ברי ור' יוחנן בן נורי בתרוייהו היכא דלא טענה ברי לכ"ע בעינן תרי רובי והא דלא קאמר בשניה לעולם דלא טענה ברי משום דלתקפתא לא קאמר אי בטוענת ברי כו' אי נמי נוכל לפרש דבשניה נמי איירי בברי ודאיכא מגו ולא תקשי הלכתא אהלכתא דדוקא דיעבד פסיק שמואל כר"ג כדאמר לעיל ואת לא תעביד עובדא עד דאיכא רוב כשרין אף על גב דלעיל משמע דברוב אחד שרי לכתחלה רב חייא בר אשי סבר דלכתחלה בעינן תרי רובי ומתני' קתני הרי זו תנשא דמשמע לכתחלה:

דלמא אזלא איהי לגבייהו. פי' לתוך ביתם דאפילו בתוך העיר לא חשיב קבוע דדמי לנמלא בין החנויות דלא חשיב קבוע וכן גבי תינוק מושלך בעיר לא חשיב קבוע הואיל ולא נמלא בבית ולכך פירש בקונטרס שפירש בועל מביתו וא"ת דבנזיר פ"ב (דף יב. ושם) פריך אהא דאמר האומר לשלוחו צא וקדש לי אשה סתם אסור בכל הנשים שבעולם מקן סתומה ומסיק אמינא לך הנא אשה דלא ניידא ואת אמרת לי איסורא דנייד וכי תימא ה"נ בשוקא אשכחה וקדיש התם הדרא לניחותא משמע לגבי אדם לא שייך כל דפריש מרובא פריש משום דהדר לניחותיה ולאו פירכא היא דהתם בשעת האיסור כשזה בא על שום אשה הדרא לניחותא האשה שקידש השליח אבל הכא כי אזלי אינהו לגבה בשעה שאוסרה הרי הוא נייד:

פרט לזורק אבן לגו. תימה דלר' שמעון קבוע מנא ליה ואין לומר דמסקינן בפ' הנשרפין (סנהדרין דף עט. ושם) דר"ש סבר כרבי דיליף נתינה נתינה ואייתר ליה וארב לו לקבוע דאכתי לתנא דבי חזקיה מנא ליה קבוע דלית ליה דרבי דהא באין מתכוין פטור ממון ל):

וספק נפשות להקל. תימה למ"ד התראת ספק לא שמה התראה אפילו ספק נפשות להחמיר פטור משום דהתראת ספק היא ואי למ"ד שמה התראה היכי פטרינן ליה כשנמצא שישראל הרג הא מיחייב בהכה את זה וחזר והכה את זה מ) ובנותר כשאמרו לו אל תותיר אע"ג דספק הוא וי"ל דשאני התם שיודע בודאי שיבא לידי איסור אם יותיר או יכה שניהם מש"ה שמה התראה אבל הכא אינו יודע שודאי יבוא לידי איסור שאינו יודע את מי יכה:

וליוחסין לא בעינן תרי רובי ורמינהי כו'. הוה מצי לשנויי שאני תינוק דלית לי' חזק' דכשרו':
ולרב

מסורת הש"ס

א) [קדושין דף עג.], ב) [כתובות כח. וש"נ], ג) [רש"ל מוחק ונ"ב גירסת רש"י איכא דקאזלא לגבייהו וע' ב' גירסות בב"י אה"ע סימן ו], ד) פסחים ט: חולין צה. נדה יח., ה) ב"ב כד., ו) [לעיל יא. וש"נ], ז) נדה יח. ע"ש תוספתא טהרות פ"ו, ח) ב"ק מד: סנהדרין עט., ט) [יומא פד:], י) [שבת קכט. וש"נ], כ) נ"ל מאי רוב העיר אלא כו'. רש"ל, ל) [וסנהדרין עט. ד"ה וכל ועי' תוס' מירוך לזה וכ"כ בב"ק מד: ד"ה כו' ועי' תוספות נדה יח. ד"ה ספיקא], מ) יבמות קא ע"א.

הגהות הב"ח

(א) רש"י ד"ה אמרי וכו' להרוג את זה והרג את זה:

תורה אור השלם

א) וְכִי יִהְיֶה אִישׁ שֹׂנֵא לְרֵעֵהוּ וְאָרַב לוֹ וְקָם עָלָיו וְהִכָּהוּ נֶפֶשׁ וָמֵת וְנָס אֶל אַחַת הֶעָרִים הָאֵל: [דברים יט, יא]

ליקוטי רש"י

כלפי לייא. שתי מלות כלפי היכן נוטה דבר זה הא מילתא מתהפכתא. לייא, היכן ומצינו בברכות בפרק הרואה [דף נח.] אבני נהגה כגוי לייא תרסים שורים להיכן הולכים [פסחים ה:]. כנגד איפוא הפכת דבריך לייא איפוא כלפי תרסים כגוי לייא שורים להיכן הולכים [סוטה מד:]. כנגד מה וכו' ולאן הדבר נוטה דאמרינן בברכות אבני נהגה כגוי לייא הקדירות שלמות הולכות לנהר לשבור בהן מים אבל השבורין להיכן הולכין [רשב"ם ב"ב קד:]. **אי דקא אזלי אינהו וכו' מרובא פריש.** ואם בעבעלה זו הלך הבועל אללה דהשתא נד ליה ממקום קביעתו ואין לדונו כמחצה שהוא נדון כמחצה על מחצה יש לנו לומר כל דפריש מרובא פריש [קידושין עג.]. **ולקח מאחת מהן.** מתוך החנות. **ספיקו אסור.** דכל קבוע כמחצה על מחצה נידון דנפקא לן מן וארב לו וקם עליו [בפ"ק דסנהדרין עט:] [ועי' תוס' כתובות (טו.)] [פסחים ט:]. דכל קבוע כמחצה על מחצה דמיא וכיון שלקחה ממקום הקביעות מחזקינן לה כמחצה על מחצה [נדה יח.]. **ובנמצא הלך אחר הרוב.** בשר הנמצא בקרקע בין החנויות הלך אחר הרוב דכל דפריש מרובה פריש דכיון דפריש אין כאן תורת קבוע [פסחים שם]. מלא דנייד הלך אחר הרוב דהשתא לאו קבוע הוא [חולין צה.]. **בשאין דלתות מדינה נעולות.** כגון דלתות מדינות פתוחות ורוב מדינות סביבות המדינה ישראל דאיכא למיזל בתר תרי רובי לקמן להכשירה רוב העיר ורוב הבאין מחוצה לה. **אע"פ שדלתות מדינה נעולות.** דליתא אלא חד רובא להכשירה רוב העיר שתשע חנויות שבה מוכרות בשר שחוטה והאחת מוכרת נבילה [ב"ב כד.]. **מתשעה צפרדעים** ובכי ספיקו טמא. דהוה ליה ספק ואע"ג דרובא צפרדעים ואין להם טומאה כיון דשרץ קבוע ביניהם הוה ליה מחצה על מחצה [נדה שם]. **וארב לו.** קרא יתירא הוא נכתוב כי יהיה איש שונא לרעהו וקם עליו. **ורבנן.** דפליגי עליה דרבי שמעון מאי דרשי ביה. **אמרי דבי ר' ינאי פרט לזורק אבן לגו.** לתוך חבורה של בני אדם כותים וישראלים אבל נתכוין לישראל זה והרג את חבירו לא אתא קרא למעוטי [סנהדרין עט.]. לתוך חבורת אנשים ויש שם כנענים וישראלים ואיכא למימר לכנענים נתכוין. **ותיפוק ליה דרובא כנענים נינהו.** ולא איצטריך קרא למפטריה. **אי נמי.** חמשה כנענים וחמשה ישראלים לא איצטריך קרא למפטריה דרחמנא אמר (במדבר לה) ושפטו העדה והצילו העדה ודא ספק נפשות להקל [ב"ק מד:]. למה לי קרא למיפטריה הא כיון דמצי למימר לכותים קא מתכווינא אית לן למפטריה משום דספק נפשות להקל מוהצילו העדה (יומא דף פד:) [סנהדרין שם]. **לא צריכא דאיכא תשעה ישראלים.** דאי לאו קרא הוה אמינא זיל בתר רובא ולישראל איכוין ואע"ג דדלמא לאו להאי איכוין נתכוין להרוג את זה והרג את זה חייב קא משמע לן קרא דהואיל והוה ליה כנעני קבוע ביניהן כמחצה על מחצה דמי וספק נפשות להקל ולכל מילי דקיימא לן קבוע כמחצה על מחצה דמי מהאי קרא נפקא לן [ב"ק שם]. ואשמעינן קרא דפטור משום דהוה ליה כותי קבוע ביניהם וילפינן מהאי קרא דכל קבוע לא פחות מלהיות נדון כמחצה על מחצה והוי ספק נפשות להקל, ומהכא נפקא לן בכל דוכתי דכל קבוע כמחצה על מחצה דמי והא ליכא למילף מיניה כרובא דמי דהא מהיכא תיתי לן דילמא האי דפטר ליה להאי משום דספק נפשות להקל ולא משום דחשבינן ליה כרובא אבל ממחצה על מחצה ילפינן מיניה דאי לאו כמחצה על מחצה דמי לא הוה ליה ספק נפשות להקל ואמאי פטור הא רובא דישראל נינהו ורבנן אית להו נתכוון לזה והרג את זה חייב [סנהדרין שם].

עין משפט נר מצוה

פט א ב מיי' פי"ח מהלכות איסורי ביאה הל' יד סמג לאוין קכה טוש"ע אה"ע סימן ו סעיף יח יט:
צ ג מיי' פ"ח מהלכות מאכלות אסורות הלכ' יא סמג לאוין קמא טור ש"ע י"ד סימן קי סע' ג:
צא ד מיי' שם וטוש"ע שם וסי' סג ס"ח:
צב ה ו מיי' פ"ו מהלכות אבות הטומאות הלכה ב:
צג ז מיי' פ"ד מהל' רוצח הלכה א סמג לאוין קמב:

תוספות רי"ד

בקרונות של צפורי היה מעשה וכדר' ינאי דאמר נבעלה בשעת קרונות כשירה לכהונה פי' קרוניות הבאים ממקום אחר ומתקבצים שם ליום השוק והוא שהיתה סיעה של בני אדם כשרים עוברים שם דהוה תרי רובא לכשרות רוב העיר ורוב סיעה. פי' כל זה מפני שלא ידעה למי נבעלה אבל אי ידעה ואמרה לכשר נבעלתי הלכה כר"ג ונאמנת אפילו ברוב פסולים: ומקשי' ומי בעי תרי רובי והתניא ט' חנויות כולן מוכרות בשר שחוטה ואחת מוכרת בשר נבילה ולקח מאחת מהן ואינו יודע מאיזה מהן לקח ספיקו אסור שכל קבוע כמחצה על מחצה דמי ובנמצא הלך אחר הרוב דכל דפריש מרובא פריש. ומהדר מעלה עשו ביוחסין: איתמר אר"ח אמר רב הלכה כר' יוסי פי' דבעי' תרי רובי: א"ר זירא כל קבוע כמחצה על מחצה דמי בין לקולא בין לחומרא לחומרא כגון ט' חנויות דאמרן. א"נ ט' צפרדעים ושרץ א' ביניהם ברה"י ונגע באחד מהן ואינו יודע באיזה מהן נגע ספיקו טמא. לקולא כגון ט' שרצים וצפרדע א' ביניהם ברה"ר ונגע באח' מהן ואי"ו באיזה מהן נגע ספיקו טהור אלא כמחצה על מחצה דמי ולקולא. דאי לאו כמחצה על מחצה דמי אין כאן ספק טומאה אלא ודאי טומאה דהא רובא שרצים:
האשה

following: הוֹלְכִין אַחַר רוֹב הָעִיר – **We follow the majority of the city,** וְהוּא דְּאִיכָּא רוֹב סִיעָה בַּהֲדֵהּ – **but that is** only **when there is a majority of a** visiting **group** to go **along with it,** so that there are two favorable majorities.[10] וְאֵין הוֹלְכִין אַחַר רוֹב הָעִיר גְּרֵידְתָּא – **However, we do not follow a mere majority of the city,** וְלֹא אַחַר רוֹב סִיעָה גְּרֵידְתָּא – **nor a mere majority of a** visiting **group.**[11]

The Gemara explains:

מַאי טַעְמָא – **What is the reason** that we do not follow a simple majority if we know that she cohabited with one of the visitors?[12] גְּזֵרָה רוֹב סִיעָה אַטּוּ רוֹב הָעִיר – There was **a decree** enacted by the Rabbis that we should not rely upon **the majority of a** visiting **group, because** this might lead to reliance upon **the majority of a city.**[13] Thus, when there is only one favorable majority, we may not rely upon it. If our only consideration is that a majority of the local residents is fit, the "majority" is inherently unreliable because the residents are in their place. And if our only consideration is that a majority of the visitors is fit, the "majority" may not be relied upon because of the Rabbinic decree. However, when we are able to consider both of these majorities together, we rule the woman fit for the Kehunah, because in that case there is no basis for any decree.[14]

The Gemara asks:

וְרוֹב הָעִיר נַמִּי – **But even** in a case where our only consideration is that **a majority of the city** is fit, i.e. when we know that she cohabited with a local resident but cannot identify him, אִי דְּקָא אַזְלֵי אִינְהוּ לְגַבָּהּ – **if he**[15] left his home and **went to her** for the cohabitation, כָּל דְּפָרִישׁ מֵרוּבָּא פָּרִישׁ – then we can apply the rule that **"whatever departs,** is assumed to have **departed from the majority."** Thus, the unidentified man is presumed to be a member of the majority of men who are of fit lineage, and the woman can be ruled fit for the Kehunah![16] Why do we rule her fit only when there are two favorable majorities in consideration?

The Gemara answers:

לֹא צְרִיכָא דְּקָא אַזְלָא אִיהִי לְגַבַּיְיהוּ – **[This ruling] is needed only** because there are cases **where she goes to** one of **them** for cohabitation,[17] דַּהֲוָה לֵיהּ קָבוּעַ – so **that he** [the unidentified man] **was stationed** in his place when she cohabited with him; וְאָמַר רַבִּי זֵירָא – **and R' Zeira said:** כָּל קָבוּעַ כְּמֶחֱצָה עַל מֶחֱצָה דָּמֵי – **Any** doubt relating to something **stationed** in its place **is treated as** having a probability of **fifty-fifty.**[18] Since in *some* cases we cannot rely upon the majority consisting of city residents, the Rabbis decreed that we may *never* consider the woman fit for the Kehunah unless there is also a favorable majority consisting of visitors, who are certainly not stationed in their place.[19]

NOTES

applies only in the case where the unknown entity is removed from its place — but not when it is stationed in its place [קָבוּעַ, *kavua*]. If at the critical moment of uncertainty the item in question is standing in its place, clearly defined within the group (see note 26), then the case is treated like one having a probability of "fifty-fifty" and no presumption based on the majority can be made.

Hence, if we know that the woman cohabited with one of the city residents (and so the man was stationed in his place at the moment of cohabitation), there can be no determination on the basis of majority. Even if only one person in the city is of tainted lineage, the case is considered like one of "fifty-fifty," and the woman ought to be ruled tainted out of doubt. By contrast, there is a basis for following the majority if we know that she cohabited with one of the visitors, since they are not in their place. How could R' Chanina have said that we follow the majority of a city but not the majority of a visiting group? (see *Rashi*).

10. I.e. if both the majority of the local residents and the majority of the visitors are of pure lineage — and we do not know which group the man with whom she cohabited came from, so that both majorities enter into consideration — we rule the woman fit for the Kehunah.

11. I.e. if we know either that the woman cohabited with a resident of the town, or that she cohabited with a visitor, so that there is only one majority in her favor, she is deemed unfit for the Kehunah. It is only where she could have cohabited with a man from either of two distinct groups, each containing a majority of men who are of fit lineage, that she remains fit for the Kehunah.

When R' Chanina said in the second part of his statement that we do not follow the [single] majority of the group of visitors, he meant that *certainly* we do not follow the single majority of the city residents. In the latter case, since the residents are in their place, the rule of "majority" does not apply at all (*Rashi*). The Gemara proceeds to explain why — being that the visitors are not stationed in their place — we do not follow the rule of "majority" when we know that she cohabited with a visitor.

12. Since the visitors are not *kavua* (i.e. not in their place), we should certainly assume that the man with whom she cohabited is a member of the majority, and thus, of pure lineage!

13. I.e. if we would allow the rule of "majority" to be applied in the case where she is known to have cohabited with a visitor, then people might also apply it in a case where she is known to have cohabited with a resident — and in that case the rule is not applicable, since the residents are *kavua*. The Rabbis therefore decreed that whenever there is only one majority the woman is deemed unfit out of doubt (*Rashi, Ran*).

14. *Rashi* ד״ה ומשני, *Ran*. See further, note 19.

15. Literally: they.

16. When an unidentified person or object emerges from a group containing different elements, the law assumes the unidentified entity to have been one of the majority element of the group even though the rest of the group is in place (see *Chullin* 11a). Thus, even if we know that she cohabited with a city resident, we should apply the principle of "majority," for once the man left his home to cohabit with her, he is no longer *kavua* (*Rashi;* see *Tosafos* ד״ה דלמא).

[Not all of the men have to leave their homes to break the status of being in place. Rather, even if just the one who cohabited with her left his house, we would apply the principle of *whatever departs, departs from the majority* and rule her permitted (*Ritva;* see *Shitah Mekubetzes* ד״ה הולכין and *Kovetz Shiurim* §37).]

17. I.e. since the man does not always leave his residence for cohabitation, but sometimes the woman goes to him, we treat every case of doubt stringently — as if we know that she went to him (*Rashi;* see following note). [Our translation of the Gemara follows *Rashi's* explanation (see also *Meiri*), but actually, *Rashi* had a slightly different reading here. His text read: אִיכָּא דְּקָאָזְלָא לְגַבַּיְיהוּ, *There are [cases] in which she goes to them.* For an alternative interpretation of our version, see *Beis Yosef, Even HaEzer* 6:18. *Rashi* cites yet another reading but rejects it. For an explanation of that version, see *Shev Shmaatsa* 4:19; see also *Haflaah* for a lengthy discussion of the various opinions here.]

18. [Literally: is like half and half.] Thus, if the man remained in his residence and the woman came to him to cohabit, the probability of his being a person who would disqualify her to a Kohen must be considered fifty-fifty even if most of the men in the city are of fit lineage (see note 8).

19. Even if we know that the woman cohabited with a city resident who came to her, we do not rely upon the rule of "majority," because this might lead people to apply the rule of "majority" in a case in which she went to the man's house. Furthermore, even if we know that she cohabited with a member of the visiting group — who was obviously not *kavua* — we do not rely upon the rule of "majority," because this might lead people to apply the rule of "majority" in a case in which we know that she cohabited with a local resident. The only time we apply the rule of "majority" is the case in which we do not know which group the man was from and each of the groups has a majority of fit men [and one of the groups — the visitors — is clearly not *kavua*]. In that instance, there is no possibility of confusion, so that there is no basis for decreeing against the application of the "majority" principle (*Rashi, Ran;* see also *Rashba, Ritva* and *Shitah Mekubetzes;* cf. *Meiri* and *Tur Even HaEzer,* end of §6).

Rashi states that this follows the opinion of R' Yehoshua, and although he does not rely upon the basic rule of "majority" to render a woman fit for the Kehunah, he does rely upon it when there are two majorities in her favor. [In essence, he would agree that a single majority is sufficient, but to preclude any possible error he rules her permitted only when there are two majorities present (one of them consisting of

אמר רב בקרונות של צפורי היה מעשה כו' פי' לעולם דלא טענה ברי ור' יוחנן בן נורי בתרוייהו היכא דלא טענה ברי לכ"ע בעינן תרי רובי והא דלא קאמר בשניה לעולם דלא טענה ברי משום דבתקפתא לא קאמר אי בטוענת ברי כו' אי נמי נוכל לפרש דבשניה נמי איירי בברי ודאיכא מגו ולא תקשי הלכתא אהלכתא דדוקא דיעבד פסיק שמואל כר"ג כדאמר לעיל ואת לא תעביד עובדא עד דאיכא רוב כשרין אף על גב דלעיל משמע דברוב אחד שרי לכתחלה רב חייא בר אשי סבר דלכתחלה בעינן תרי רובי ומתני' קתני הרי זו תנשא דמשמע לכתחלה:

בקרונות של ציפורי היה מעשה וכדרבי אמי דאמר רבי אמי והוא שהיתה סיעה של בני אדם כשרין עוברת לשם וכדר' ינאי דאמר ר' ינאי נבעלת בקרונות כשרה לכהונה בקרונות סלקא דעתך אלא נבעלת בשעת קרונות כשרה לכהונה אבל פירש אחד מציפורי ובעל הולד שתוקי כי הא דכי אתא רב דימי אמר זעירי א"ר חנינא ואמרי לה אמר זעירי אמר ר' חנינא הולכין אחר רוב העיר ואין הולכין אחר רוב סיעה כלפי לייא הני ניידי והני קביעי וקיימי אלא א הולכין אחר רוב העיר והוא דאיכא רוב סיעה בהדה ואין הולכין אחר רוב העיר גרידתא ולא אחר רוב סיעה גרידתא מ"ט גזרה רוב סיעה אטו רוב העיר ורוב העיר נמי ב אי דקא אזלי אינהו לגבה כל דפריש ג מרובא פריש ג לא צריכא דקא אזלא איהי לגבייהו דהוה ליה קבוע וא"ר זירא כל קבוע כמחצה על מחצה דמי ומי בעינן תרי רובי והתניא ד תשע חנויות כולן מוכרות בשר שחוטה ואחת מוכרת בשר נבלה ולקח מאחת מהן ואינו יודע מאי זה מהן לקח ספיקו אסור ה ובנמצא הלך אחר הרוב וכי תימא בשאין דלתות מדינה נעולות דקא אתי לה רובא מעלמא והא א"ר זירא ו אע"פ שדלתות מדינה נעולות ז מעלה עשו ביוחסין גופא א"ר זירא כל קבוע כמחצה על מחצה דמי בין לקולא בין לחומרא מנא ליה לר' זירא הא אילימא מתשע חנויות כולן מוכרות בשר שחוטה ואחת בשר נבלה ולקח מאחת מהן ואינו יודע מאיזה מהן לקח ספיקו אסור ובנמצא הלך אחר הרוב התם לחומרא אלא ח מתשעה צפרדעים ושרץ אחד ביניהם ונגע באחד מהן ואינו יודע באיזה מהן נגע ספיקו טמא התם נמי לחומרא אלא ט מתשעה שרצים וצפרדע אחד ביניהם ונגע באחד מהן ואינו יודע באיזה מהן נגע ברה"י ספיקו טמא ברשות הרבים ספיקו טהור ומדאורייתא מנא לן י אמר קרא א וארב לו וקם עליו עד שיתכוין לו ורבנן אמרי דבי ר' ינאי פרט לזורק אבן לגו כ היכי דמי אילימא דאיכא תשעה כנענים ואחד ישראל ביניהם ותיפוק ליה דרובא כנענים נינהו אי נמי פלגא ופלגא ל ספק נפשות להקל לא צריכא דאיכא תשעה ישראלים וכנעני אחד ביניהם דהוה ליה כנעני קבוע וכל קבוע כמחצה על מחצה דמי איתמר רב חייא בר אשי אמר רב הלכה כרבי יוסי ורב חנן בר רבא אמר רב הוראת שעה היתה מתיב רבי ירמיה וליוחסין לא בעינן תרי רובי והתנן

מצא

רש"י

בקרונות של ציפורי. ביום השוק שסיעות ושיירות ממקום אחר באות שם: **וכדרבי אמי.** דהשתא איכא רוב סיעה ורוב העיר: **נבעלת בקרונות.** משמע על הקרון: **בשעת קרונות.** שהשיירות באות לעיר: **כשרה לכהונה.** כדקאמר והוא שהיתה סיעה של בני אדם כשרים עוברת שם דאיכא למימר שמהם היה: **אבל פירש אחד מציפורי.** דידעינן ודאי דמן העיר היה אע"פ שציפורי עיר שרובה משיאין לכהונה: **הולד שתוקי.** דבחד רובא לא מכשר: **וכי הא דכי אתא רב דימי אמר זעירי אמר רבי חנינא ואמרי לה.** שלא הוזכר רב דימי כאן אלא זעירי אמר רבי חנינא דבעינן תרי רובי וכדמפרש טעמא: **הולכין אחר רוב העיר.** להכשיר: **ואין הולכין אחר רוב סיעה.** כגון במקום רחוק מן העיר דבודאי מאנשי הסיעה הוה אין מכשירין אותה ואפילו רובן כשרין: **וקשיא לן כלפי לייא.** כנגד איפוא הדבר הזה סובב: **הני ניידי.** רוב סיעה ניידי ויש להלך בהן אחר הרוב: **והני.** של עיר: **קביעי.** ואמרינן לקמן כל קבוע כמחצה על מחצה דמי ואפילו אין שם אלא אחד פסולה: **ולא אחר רוב סיעה גרידתא.** והכי קאמר אין הולכין אחר רוב סיעה לבדה וכל שכן אחר רוב העיר לבדה: **מ"ט.** אחר רוב סיעה לא: **גזרה אטו רוב העיר.** דקביעי: **ופרכינן רוב העיר נמי.** אי עקר הבועל מביתו ואזל לגבה הוה נייד וקי"ל כל דפריש מרובא פריש: **ומשני איכא דקאזלא לגבייהו כו'.** ולא גרסינן נ מאי איכא יש שהולכת היא אצלו והוה ליה קבוע הלכך אפילו ברוב כשרים או רוב העיר או רוב סיעה פסול כרבי יהושע ומשום תרי רובי אכשרה דליכא למיגזר מידי: **ולקח בשר מאחת מהן.** במקום קביעות: **ספיקו אסור.** דכל קבוע כמחצה על מחצה דמי: **ובנמצא.** בשר הנמצא בשוק ולא ידעינן מאיזה פירש: **הלך אחר הרוב.** הואיל והבא לפנינו לא במקום קביעות לקחה וכבר פירשה על ידי אחר וכל דפריש מרובא פריש: **דקאתי לה רובא מעלמא.** וכגון שרוב סיעת טבחי ישראל כשרים באו לכאן דאיכא תרי רובי או שרוב טבחי כל המדינה ישראל דאיכא תרי רובי רוב העיר ורוב המדינה דניידי: **אלא מתשעה צפרדעים כו'.** תוספתא היא במס' טהרות תשעה צפרדעים מתים ברשות היחיד ושרץ אחד כגון צב שהוא דומה לצפרדע ביניהם ונגע באחד מהן ספיקו טמא: **אלא מתשעה שרצים כו'.** אף היא תוספתא במס' טהרות וקתני ברה"י ספיקו טמא ברה"ר ספיקו טהור אלמא כמחצה דמי ולקולא דאי לאו כמחצה דמי אין כאן ספק טומאה אלא ודאי טומאה דהא רובא שרצים: **אמר קרא וארב לו עד שיהא מתכוין לו.** פרט למתכוין להרוג את זה והרג את זה הכי דריש ליה ר"ש בסנהדרין ואמרינן התם ורבנן היכי דרשי ליה: **אמרי דבי ר' ינאי פרט לזורק אבן לגו.** לתוך חבורת בני אדם כנענים וישראלים אבל שני ישראלים עומדין ונתכוון להרוג (א) זה (והרג זה) והתרו בו וקבל התראה ונפלה הכאה על חבירו חייב והיינו טעמא דקאמר הכא ורבנן משום דבסנהדרין הכי איתא: **תיפוק ליה דרובא כנענים נינהו.** ולמה לי קרא ואי נמי פלגא ופלגא אכתי לא איצטריך קרא דמהיכא תיתי דניקטליה: **ספק נפשות.** דיני נפשות להקל דהא והצילו העדה כתיב (במדבר לה): **דהוה ליה כנעני קבוע ביניהם.** ואשמועינן האי קרא דכל קבוע כמחצה על מחצה דמי: **הוראת שעה היתה.** הן דריב"נ לורך שעה היתה או ראו שם שאר לידי היכר דברים להתיר אבל לדורות תרי רובי בעינן: **מתיב רבי ירמיה כו'.** קס"ד דמשום רוב העיר גרידתא אכשרוה ואמר רב הלכה כרבי יוסי:

מלא

תוספות

דלמא אזלא איהי לגבייהו. פי' לתוך ביתם דאפילו בתוך העיר לא חשיב קבוע דדמי לנמצא בין החנויות דלא חשיב קבוע וכן גבי תינוק מושלך בעיר לא חשיב קבוע הואיל ולא נמצא בבית ולכך פירש בקונטרס שפירש בועל מביתו וא"ת דבנזיר פ"ב (דף יב. ושם) פריך אהא דאמר האומר לשלוחו צא וקדש לי אשה סתם אסור בכל הנשים שבעולם מקן סתומה ומסיק אמינא לך הנא אשה דלא ניידא ואת אמרת לי איסורא דנייד וכי תימא ה"נ בשוקא אשכחה וקדיש התם הדרא לניחותא משמע לגבי אדם לא שייך כל דפריש מרובא פריש משום דהדר לניחותיה ולאו פירכא היא דהתם בשעת האיסור כשזה בא על שום אשה הדרא לניחותא האשה שקידש השליח אבל הכא כי אזלי אינהו לגבה בשעה שאוסרה הרי הוא נייד:

פרט לזורק אבן לגו. תימה דלר' שמעון קבוע מנא ליה ואין לומר דמסקינן בפ' הנשרפין (סנהדרין דף עט. ושם) דר"ש סבר כרבי דיליף נתינה נתינה ואייתר ליה וארב לו לקבוע דאכתי לתנא דבי חזקיה מנא ליה קבוע דלית ליה דרבי דהא באין מתכוין פטור ממִמון ל:

וספק נפשות להקל. תימה למ"ד התראת ספק לא שמה התראה אפילו ספק נפשות להחמיר פטור משום דהתראת ספק היא ואי למ"ד שמה התראה היכי פטרינן ליה כשנמצא שישראל הרג הא מיחייב בהכה את זה וחזר והכה את זה מ ובנותר כשאמרו לו אל תותיר אע"ג דספק הוא וי"ל דשאני התם שיודע בודאי שיבא לידי איסור אם יותיר או יכה שניהם מש"ה שמה התראה אבל הכא אינו יודע שודאי יבוא לידי איסור שאינו יודע את מי יכה:

וליוחסין לא בעינן תרי רובי ורמינהו כו'. הוה מצי לשנויי שאני תינוק דלית לי' חזק' דכשרו':

ולרב

עין משפט נר מצוה

פט א ב מיי' פ"ח מהלכות איסורי ביאה הל' יד סמג לאוין קכח טוש"ע אה"ע סימן ד סעיף יח יט:

צ ג מיי' פ"ח מהלכות מאכלות אסורות הל' יא סמג לאוין קמא טור ש"ע י"ד סימן קי סע' ג:

צא ד מיי' שם וטוש"ע שם וכסף סע' ה:

צב ה ו מיי' פ"ה מהלכות אבות הטומאות הלכה ג:

צג ז מיי' פ"ד מהל' רוצח הלכה א סמג לאוין קמג:

תוספות רי"ד

בקרונות של צפורי היה מעשה וכדר' ינאי דאמר נבעלה בשעת קרונות כשירה לכהונה פי' קרוניות הבאים ממקום אחר ומתקבצים שם ליום השוק והוא שהיתה סיעה של בני אדם כשרים עוברים שם דהוה תרי רובא לכשרות רוב העיר ורוב סיעה. פי' כל זה מפני שלא ידעה למי נבעלה אבל אי ידעה ואמרה לכשר נבעלתי הלכה כר"ג ונאמנת אפילו ברוב פסולים: ומקשי' ומי בעי תרי רובי והתניא ט' חנויות כולן מוכרות בשר שחוטה ואחת מוכרת בשר נבלה ולקח מאחת מהן ואינו יודע מאיזה מהן לקח ספיקו אסור שכל קבוע כמחצה על מחצה דמי ובנמצא הלך אחר הרוב דכל דפריש מרובא פריש. ומהדר מעלה עשו ביוחסין: איתמר א"ר חייא אמר רב הלכה כר' יוסי פי' דבעי' תרי רובי: א"ר זירא כל קבוע כמחצה על מחצה דמי בין לקולא בין לחומרא כגון ט' חנויות דאמרן. א"נ ט' צפרדעים ושרץ א' ביניהם ברה"י ונגע באחד מהן ואינו יודע באיזה מהן נגע ספיקו טמא. לקולא כגון ט' שרצים וצפרדע א' ביניהם ברה"ר ונגע באחד מהן וא"י באיזה מהן נגע ספיקו טהור אלא כמחצה על מחצה. דאי לאו כמחצה על מחצה דמי אין כאן ספק טומאה אלא ודאי טומאה דהא רובא שרצים:

האשה

הגהות הב"ח

(א) רש"י ד"ה אמרי וכו' להרוג את זה והרג את זה:

תורה אור השלם

א) וְכִי יִהְיֶה אִישׁ שֹׂנֵא לְרֵעֵהוּ וְאָרַב לוֹ וְקָם עָלָיו וְהִכָּהוּ נֶפֶשׁ וָמֵת וְנָס אֶל אַחַת הֶעָרִים הָאֵל: [דברים יט, יא]

בְּקְרוֹנוֹת שֶׁל צִיפּוֹרִי הָיָה מַעֲשֶׂה – **The incident** mentioned in the Mishnah **occurred among the wagons of Tzippori,** during the market day when caravans from outside the city visited.[1] There was thus a possibility that one of the visitors from those wagons violated the girl – along with the possibility that it was a local man. R' Yochanan ben Nuri meant that if the majority of the men of the city *and* the majority of the visitors are of fit lineage, she remains permitted for the Kehunah.[2] This accords with the opinion of R' Yehoshua, for when there are *two* distinct majorities of fit men among those with whom she might have cohabited, R' Yehoshua does rule her fit for the Kehunah.[3]

This explanation is supported:

וּכְדְרַבִּי אַמִּי – **And** this is **in accordance with** a teaching of **R' Ami.** דְּאָמַר רַבִּי אַמִּי – **For R' Ami said** in explanation of our Mishnah: וְהוּא שֶׁהָיְתָה סִיעָה שֶׁל בְּנֵי אָדָם כְּשֵׁרִין עוֹבֶרֶת לְשָׁם – **This is** applicable concerning the case **where there was a group of people** of **fit** lineage **passing by there.**[4]

Another support for this explanation:

וּכְדְרַבִּי יַנַּאי – **And** this is also **in accordance with** a teaching of **R' Yannai.** דְּאָמַר רַבִּי יַנַּאי – **For R' Yannai said:** נִבְעֶלֶת בְּקְרוֹנוֹת כְּשֵׁרָה לִכְהוּנָּה – **If she cohabited among the wagons she is fit to** marry into **the Kehunah.**

Understanding this literally, the Gemara wonders:

בְּקְרוֹנוֹת סַלְקָא דַעְתָּךְ – **Do you think** her fitness depends upon whether she cohabited **on the wagons** or elsewhere?

The Gemara therefore explains R' Yannai's words:

אֶלָּא נִבְעֶלֶת בִּשְׁעַת קְרוֹנוֹת כְּשֵׁרָה לִכְהוּנָּה – **Rather,** R' Yannai means: If **she cohabited at the time of wagons,** i.e. when a caravan was in the area, **she is fit to** marry into **the Kehunah,** because there are then two majorities in her favor.[5]

Having explained that the incident recorded in our Mishnah occurred during the market time in Tzippori, the Gemara states a further qualification of its rule:

אֲבָל פֵּירַשׁ אֶחָד מִצִּיפּוֹרִי וּבָעַל – **However, if** we would know that **one of** those living in **Tzippori came out** of his home **and cohabited** with the woman, and her assailant was not a visitor, הַוָּלָד שְׁתוּקִי – **the child** born from that union **is a *shetuki,*** even though the majority of Tzippori is of fit lineage, and even though there was also a visiting caravan containing a majority of fit men.[6]

The Gemara cites a concurrent ruling, which leads into the explanation of why the combination of two favorable majorities serves to render a woman permitted to the Kehunah, whereas a simple majority is insufficient:

כִּי הָא דְּכִי אָתָא רַב דִּימִי אָמַר זְעִירִי אָמַר רַבִּי חֲנִינָא – This **is like that which Rav Dimi, when he came** to Babylonia, **said in the name of Zeiri who** had **said in the name of R' Chanina;** וְאָמְרֵי לָהּ אָמַר זְעִירִי אָמַר רַבִּי חֲנִינָא – **and some say** only that **Zeiri said in the name of R' Chanina:**[7] הוֹלְכִין אַחַר רוֹב הָעִיר וְאֵין הוֹלְכִין אַחַר רוֹב סִיעָה – **We follow the majority of the city, but we do not follow the majority of a** visiting **group.**[8] Now, this requires analysis: כְּלַפֵּי לַיָּיא – **To which way** does the logic of the matter point? It seems quite contrary! הָנֵי נַיְידֵי וְהָנֵי קְבִיעֵי וְקַיְימֵי – **These** people of the group **are moving, while these** people of the city **are stationary.** If anything, then, we should follow a majority composed of visitors and not a majority composed of city residents!?[9] אֶלָּא – **Rather,** R' Chanina must have meant the

NOTES

1. *Rashi* (see *Eruvin* 54b; cf. *Aruch,* cited by *Mesoras HaShas* to *Megillah* 5b). [The Gemara states that it occurred in Tzippori because R' Yose, who related the incident in our Mishnah, resided there (*Rashash,* based on *Succah* 16b and *Sanhedrin* 32b).]

2. The reason he said only "If the majority of the men of the city are fit" is that it was known that the majority of the visitors were fit, and the only uncertainty concerned the status of the townspeople (*Ritva* to the Mishnah on 14b).

3. R' Yehoshua rules the woman unfit only when the possibility of fitness is supported by a simple majority, but when it is supported by two distinct majorities he rules her fit. The Gemara will explain below why two majorities are better than one (*Rashi*). Thus, if no group of fit men was visiting in the area when the assault occurred, so that the presumption would be that a townsperson assaulted the girl, she would be forbidden for the Kehunah even though the majority of the town was fit. It is because of the added consideration involving the visitors that she can be ruled fit (see *Pnei Yehoshua*). [Our explanation of the "two majorities" follows *Rashi. Rambam* (*Hil. Isurei Biah* 18:14), however, presents a different view. See *Tos. Yom Tov* to the Mishnah for discussion of this matter.]

It is unclear, according to Rav's interpretation of the Mishnah, whether the girl must also claim with certainty that her assailant was fit. Most Rishonim maintain that since there are two majorities in her favor, the claim of certainty is superfluous. In fact, they point out that the Mishnah refers to a "young girl" who was violated, and it is unlikely that the young girl could have known with certainty the status of her assailant. Although the Gemara initially assumed that she must have claimed with certainty that he was fit (see 14b note 20), that was simply because we had no explanation for the Mishnah's ruling other than that it accords with Rabban Gamliel, who attaches importance to a claim of "certainly." But now that we are no longer forced into this explanation, we ought to take the Mishnah at face value and assume that the young girl was unfamiliar with her assailant. Thus, even if she admits ignorance, she is deemed fit on the basis of the double majority in her favor. Accordingly, this case is not subject to the dispute between Rabban Gamliel and R' Yehoshua. All agree with the ruling of R' Yochanan ben Nuri that the girl is considered fit (*Ramban, Rashba, Ritva;* cf. *Tosafos* ד"ה כמאן; *Rambam, Hil. Isurei Biah* 18:15 with *Kesef Mishneh*).

However, *Rashi* states (on 14b) that according to the current interpretation the Mishnah accords with R' Yehoshua, implying that it does not accord with Rabban Gamliel. Apparently, *Rashi* maintains that even according to Rav's interpretation the girl is claiming to know with certainty that her assailant was fit. Thus, the Mishnah cannot accord with Rabban Gamliel, because, as the Gemara stated earlier, he would rule her fit even where the majority of men was unfit. The Mishnah which rules her fit on the basis of two favorable majorities accords only with R' Yehoshua (*Ramban* and *Tos. HaRosh* in explanation of *Rashi;* cf. other explanations of *Rashi* by *Baal HaMaor, Rashba, Ritva, Pnei Yehoshua*). [See the abovementioned Rishonim for their discussion of various difficulties arising from *Rashi's* approach.]

4. I.e. the majority of the visiting group was of fit lineage (*Rashash*). Thus, there are two majorities working in her favor – that of the visitors and that of the townspeople (*Rashi*).

5. That is [as R' Ami explained above], the Mishnah refers to the case where a caravan was passing through the area, creating the possibility that she cohabited with one of the visitors, on top of the standard possibility that she cohabited with a townsperson (*Rashi*).

6. Since we know with certainty that her assailant was a townsperson, the fact that the majority of visitors to the town are fit is irrelevant (*Rashba, Ritva;* cf. *Meiri*). And when there is only one favorable majority, R' Yochanan ben Nuri does not assume that the girl cohabited with a man of pure lineage. The child from this union would therefore be ruled a *shetuki,* i.e. of questionable lineage (*Rashi*). [See *Maharam Schif* with *Beur* for discussion of why the Gemara focuses on the child, rather than simply stating that the woman herself would be considered tainted.]

7. According to the latter version, Rav Dimi was not involved in conveying this teaching (*Rashi*).

8. Taken at face value, this means that we permit the woman to marry a Kohen only if she cohabited within the city limits (so that the man was presumably a citizen), and the majority of the city's residents are of fit lineage. But if she cohabited far from the city, in which case the man was certainly a member of the traveling group, she would become invalid for Kehunah, even if the majority of the group was of fit lineage (*Rashi*).

9. We know that the principle of "majority" entitles us to presume that an unidentified person [or object] came from the majority of people [or similar objects] in the area. However, as we shall learn below, this

Mishnah The Mishnah continues its discussion concerning a woman who has cohabited with an unidentified man:

אָמַר רַבִּי יוֹסֵי – **R' Yose said:** מַעֲשֶׂה בְּתִינוֹקֶת שֶׁיָּרְדָה לְמַלְּאוֹת מַיִם מִן הָעַיִן וְנֶאֶנְסָה – There was **an incident involving a young girl who went down to draw water from a spring and was violated** by an unknown man. אָמַר רַבִּי יוֹחָנָן בֶּן נוּרִי – Ruling on that case, **R' Yochanan ben Nuri said:** אִם רוֹב אַנְשֵׁי הָעִיר מַשִּׂיאִין לִכְהוּנָּה – **If the majority of the townspeople** are fit to have their daughters and widows **marry into the Kehunah,**[17] הֲרֵי זוֹ תִּינָּשֵׂא לִכְהוּנָּה – then **this [girl] may be married into the Kehunah.**[18]

Gemara The Gemara analyzes the Mishnah:

אָמַר לֵיהּ רָבָא לְרַב נַחְמָן – **Rava said to Rav Nachman:** רַבִּי יוֹחָנָן בֶּן נוּרִי דְּאָמַר כְּמַאן – **In accordance with whose** opinion **did R' Yochanan ben Nuri state** that when the majority of the city is of fit lineage the girl may marry into the Kehunah?[19] אִי כְּרַבָּן גַּמְלִיאֵל – **If** you say he stated this **in accordance with** the opinion of **Rabban Gamliel** in the previous Mishnah, I will respond: אֲפִילּוּ בְּרוֹב פְּסוּלִין נַמִּי מַכְשֵׁר – Why, **[Rabban Gamliel] rules** the woman **fit even where the majority** of the men were **not** of **fit** lineage.[20] אִי כְּרַבִּי יְהוֹשֻׁעַ – And **if** you say he stated it **in accordance with** the opinion of **R' Yehoshua** in the previous Mishnah, I will respond: אֲפִילּוּ בְּרוֹב כְּשֵׁרִים נַמִּי פָּסִיל – Why, **[R' Yehoshua] rules** the woman **not fit even where the majority** of the men were of **fit** lineage.[21] – ? –

Rav Nachman replies:

אָמַר לֵיהּ – **He said to [Rava]:** הָכִי אָמַר רַב יְהוּדָה אָמַר רַב – **This is what Rav Yehudah said in the name of Rav:** The Mishnah actually follows the view of R' Yehoshua, and he rules leniently here for the following reason:[22]

NOTES

factor that causes him to be considered unfit (*Ritva,* in explanation of *Rashi*).

[We have based our elucidation on *Rashi. Rabbeinu Tam* (cited by *Tosafos* 14a ד״ה תנו רבנן and *Ritva* here), however, has an entirely different explanation, with many halachic ramifications (see *Chelkas Mechokeik* 2:6, *Taz* 2:3, *Avnei Miluim* 2:3; *Beis Shmuel* 2:11).]

17. I.e. most men in the city are of pure lineage, so that by having relations with a woman they do not disqualify her from marrying a Kohen [and a daughter born from their union is also fit for the Kehunah] (*Rashi;* see *Chasam Sofer* and *Rashash*).

18. Because we assume that the assailant was a member of the majority, and his cohabitation did not disqualify her from marrying a Kohen.

[*R' Akiva Eiger* makes an interesting point. If the number of fit men in the city totals only one more than the number of unfit men, then a fit Kohen of the city cannot marry her. Since he himself knows that he was not the one who violated her, to him the possibilities of the assailant having been fit and unfit are equal; there is no majority of fit men with respect to his personal uncertainty. The Mishnah must therefore mean that a majority is needed besides the Kohen who now wants to marry her. Cf. *Rashash.*]

19. He must accord with the opinion of either Rabban Gamliel or R' Yehoshua in the previous Mishnah, for if his opinion was a third one it would have been cited above (*Rashba;* cf. *Ritva*).

20. [The Gemara stated above (13b) that according to Rabban Gamliel a woman is fit for the Kehunah even in a case where the majority of the men with whom she might have cohabited are unfit.] This is so because he holds that a woman keeps her *chazakah* (presumptive status) of being fit for a Kohen until it is proven otherwise (*Rashi*).

Rabban Gamliel actually holds this opinion only if the girl claims with certainty [בָּרִי] that the man who cohabited with her was fit (see 14a). It is in that case that we rely upon her *chazakah* of fitness. What Rava means is that if you wish to explain R' Yochanan ben Nuri's ruling in accordance with Rabban Gamliel – and to therefore interpret the Mishnah as dealing with a case in which she claims with certainty that her assailant was fit – you will be wrong, since Rabban Gamliel rules the woman fit on the basis of her claim and *chazakah* even when there is no majority of fit men (*Tosafos* et al.). [Although *Rashi* mentions only the *chazakah,* he too must mean that the girl also claims with certainty that she is fit (*Pnei Yehoshua;* cf. *Baal HaMaor*).]

21. The Gemara stated above (13b) that R' Yehoshua rules a woman unfit even in a case where the majority of the men with whom she might have cohabited are fit and she claims with certainty that she cohabited with such a man.

22. *Rashi;* see 15a note 3.

שמעתי כל שאין בה אחד מכל אלו משיאין לכהונה ר"ש בן אלעזר אומר משום ר"מ וכן היה ר"ש בן מנסיא אומר כדבריו איזוהי אלמנת עיסה כל שנטמע בה ספק חלל מכירין ישראל ממזרים שביניהם ואין מכירין חללין שביניהם אמר מר איזוהי אלמנת עיסה כל שאין בה לא משום ממזרות ולא משום נתינות ולא משום עבדי מלכים הא חלל כשר מאי שנא הנך דאורייתא חלל נמי דאורייתא ותו אמר רבי מאיר שמעתי כל שאין בה אחד מכל אלו משיאין לכהונה היינו תנא קמא ותו ר"ש בן אלעזר אומר משום ר' מאיר וכן היה ר"ש בן מנסיא אומר כדבריו איזוהי אלמנת עיסה כל שנטמע בה ספק חלל מכירין ישראל ממזרים שביניהן ואין מכירין חללין שביניהן והא אמרת רישא חלל כשר א"ר יוחנן ממזר צווח וחלל שותק איכא בינייהו תנא קמא סבר [א]כל פסול דקרו ליה ושתיק פסול והכי קאמר ת"ק איזוהי אלמנת עיסה כל שאין בה לא שתוק ממזרות ולא שתוק נתינות ולא שתוק עבדי מלכים ולא שתוק חלל וקאמר ליה ר"מ הנך הוא דקא פסיל ליה בקהל אבל שתוק חלל כשר והא דשתיק משום דלא איכפת ליה וקאמר ליה ר"ש בן אלעזר לתנא קמא דר' מאיר אי שמיע לך דמכשר ר"מ בשתיקה לא דקרו ליה חלל ושתיק אלא דקרו ליה ממזר ושתיק והאי דשתיק סבר ממזר קלא אית ליה אבל ממזר וצווח חלל ושותק פסול והאי דאשתיק סבר מיסתייה דלא מפקי ליה מקהל תני חדא ר' יוסי אומר שתוק ממזר כשר שתוק חלל פסול ותניא אידך שתוק חלל כשר שתוק ממזר פסול לא קשיא הא ת"ק אליבא דר"מ הא דר"ש בן אלעזר אליבא דר"מ: **מתני'** ° א"ר יוסי מעשה בתינוקת שירדה למלאות מים מן העין ונאנסה אמר רבי יוחנן בן נורי אם רוב אנשי העיר משיאין לכהונה הרי זו תינשא לכהונה: **גמ'** אמר ליה רבא לרב נחמן ר' יוחנן בן נורי דאמר כמאן אי כרבן גמליאל אפילו ברוב פסולין נמי מכשר אי כרבי יהושע אפילו ברוב כשרים נמי פסיל אמר ליה הכי אמר רב יהודה אמר רב

בקרונות

רש"י

שמעתי כו'. לקמיה פריך היינו תנא קמא דתנא קמא נמי הכי אמר דמשום דאין בה אחד מכל אלו העידו עליה להכשיר: **מכירין ישראל** ממזרין שביניהן. וספק ממזר יש לך להכשיר דאי ממזר הוה מידע הוו ידעי ביה: **ואין מכירין חללין שביניהן.** וספק חלל יש לך לפסול ולקמיה פריך הא אמרת רישא איזוהי אלמנת עיסה כל שנטמע בה ספק חלל אלמא ספק חלל כשר: **הא חלל** כשר. משום ספק חלל לא פסיל לה: **מאי שנא הנך.** דפסיל לה ספק דידהו: **דאורייתא.** משום דוודאן פוסלין מן התורה בביאה דנפקא לן ביבמות (דף סח.) מכי תהיה לאיש זר כיון שנבעלה לפסול לה פסלה: **חלל נמי.** ודאי פסול מדאורית' דילפינן לה התם מלא יחלל זרעו מקיש זרעו לו מה הוא פוסל בביאתו אף זרעו פוסל והוא גופיה נפקא לן מלא יחלל שני חילולין במשמע אחד לזרעו ואחד לאשתו: **ר"ש בן אלעזר כו'.** סיפא דמילתיה ארישא דמילתיה פריך דקתני סיפא אין מכירין חללין שביניהן משמע אפשר שהיה חלל אבל לא היו מכירין בו אלמא אית ליה דפסיל ורישא אמר איזוהי אלמנת עיסה והכשיר כל שנטמע בה ספק חלל: **אמר ר' יוחנן ממזר צווח וחלל שותק איכא בינייהו.** אדם שכשקורין אותו ממזר הוא צווח וכשקורין אותו חלל שותק איכא בין ר"מ לת"ק ובין תנא קמא דברייתא אליבא דר"מ ור"ש בן אלעזר אליבא דר"מ: **תנא קמא סבר כל פסול דקרו ליה ושתיק פסול.** דהודאה היא וכל שאין בה לא משום ממזרות כו' דקאמר אשתיקות קאי: **והכי קאמר איזוהי אלמנת עיסה. להכשיר: כל שאין בה לא שתוק ממזרות ולא שתוק נתינות.** וכיון דתלה טעמא בשתיקה הוא הדין לכל שתוקי פסול ולא הוצרך למנות את כולם ובאיזו הכשירו באשת ספק חלל שאנו מכירין את ספיקו שנתגרשה אמו ספק אבל מי שאין מכירין בו ושמענו שפוסלין אותו ושותק פסול: **וקאמר ליה ר"מ.** דוקא הני אבל שתוק חלל לא פסול: **והא דשתיק.** לאו משום דאודי אלא משום דלא איכפת ליה הואיל ולאו פסול קהל הוא והיינו דקאמר כל שאין בה אחד מכל אלו שתיקות משיאין בנותיהן לכהונה ואפי' יש בו שתוק חלל: **וקאמר ליה ר"ש לתנא קמא.** לאו לתנא קמא דברייתא קאמר דההיא רבנן היא אלא לתנא ששנה דברי ר"מ בבית המדרש ואמר בשם ר"מ שמעתי כל שאין בה כו': **אי שמיע לך כו'.** והכי קאמר איזו היא אלמנת עיסה כל שנטמע בה ספק חלל שאנו מכירין את פסולו שהיתה אמו ספק גרושה אבל שתוק חלל ואין אנו מכירין בו פסול כתנא קמא ומיהו בהא פליג רבי מאיר אתנא קמא דאיהו כל פסול דשתיק ביה פסיל ולרבי מאיר חלל שתוק הוא דפסול דסבר מסתייה דלא מפקי ליה מקהל ואם אני צווח יכריזו עלי ויודע פסולי בברור ועכשיו אין מכירין ישראל חללין שביניהם אבל שתוק ממזר כשר דהאי דשתיק סבר הכל יודעין שאיני ממזר דמכירין ישראל ממזרין שבייניהן: **מתני'** מן העין. מן המעיין: אם רוב העיר. כשרין להשיא בנותיהן ואלמנותיהן לכהונה שאין רוב בני העיר מן הפוסלין אשה לכהונה בביאתן אף זו תינשא לכהונה: **גמ'** דאמר כמאן. דבעי רוב כשרין: **אפילו ברוב פסולין נמי מכשר.** דאית ליה העמד אשה על חזקתה: **אמר ליה הכי אמר כו'.** לעולם כרבי יהושע והכא משום דאיכא תרי רובי לכשרות אכשרה וכדרב יהודה ולקמן מפרש טעמא ואזיל מאי שנא תרי רובי מחד רובא:

בקרונות

תוספות

לא משום ממזרות כו'. הא דלא חשיב עמוני ומואבי משום דלא פסיקא דזכרים אסורין ונקבות מותרות ומצרי ואדומי לא חשיב דאינן אסורין אלא עד דור שלישי: **ותו** ר"ש בן אלעזר אומר איזוהי עיסה כל שנטמע בה ספק חלל והאמרת רישא חלל כשר. ה"ג בכל הספרים ובפירוש ר"ח ומפרש כל שנטמע בה ספק חלל הא ודאי חלל פסול והא אמרת רישא חלל כשר והיינו ודאי חלל ואין נראה דמאי פריך מתנא קמא דלמא ת"ק פליג עליה ופירוש הקונטרס וגרסתו עיקר: **ממזר** צווח וחלל שותק איכא בינייהו. תימה דהוה ליה למימר ממזר צווח ושותק וחלל שותק איכא בינייהו דבממזר שותק נמי פליגי דהא מכשר ליה ר"ש בן אלעזר [א]: **אבל** ממזר צווח וחלל שותק פסול. וא"ת ממזר צווח מנא ליה דפסל ר"ש בן אלעזר ואומר ר"י מדקתני במילתיה איזוהי עיסה כל שנטמע בה ספק חלל דלא הוה ליה למימר אלא מכירין ישראל ממזרים שביניהם ואין מכירין חללין שביניהם דמינה שמעינן בחלל צווח דכשר כי היכי דלא הוצרך להשמיענו כל שנטמע בה ספק ממזר אלא ודאי אתא למידק דחלל צווח דוקא כשר הא ממזר צווח פסול: **מסתייה** דלא מפקינן ליה מקהל. וא"ת מה צריך להאי טעמא לימא הא דשתיק משום דאודויי קא מודי דהא ממזר שותק פסול לת"ק משום דשתיקה כהודאה וה"ה דחלל שותק לר"ש דפסול מהאי טעמא ואע"ג דגבי ממזר שותק לדידיה לא הוי שתיקה כהודאה היינו משום דסבר דממזר קלא אית ליה וי"ל דהכי פירושא סבר מסתייה דלא מפקינן ליה מקהל (כהונה) פי' אפי' מקהל כהונה אע"פ שזה מחרפו וקוראו חלל סבור דאין מוציאין אותו מקהל כהונה וסבור אם יצווח יחזרו לברר הדבר ויפסלוהו וטעם זה שייך גם בממזר שותק לת"ק ולא נאמר דשתיקה כהודאה וכן פירש בקונטרס: **כמאן** אי כר"ג אפילו ברוב פסולין נמי מכשר. וא"ת והא לא מכשר ברוב פסולין אלא כשטוענת ברי ואית לה מיגו דאי בעיא אמרה לא נבעלתי או בלא מגו היכא דאיכא למימר בודקת ומזנה אבל הכא אפילו טוענת ברי הא לית לה מגו וליכא למימר בודקת ומזנה דהא נאנסה ואפי' אם נאמר דהכא לא ראוה שנאנסה אלא היא אמרה כן דאית לה מגו א"כ תקשי הלכתא אהלכתא דלקמן פסיק רב הלכה כר' יוסי ולעיל פסיק רב יהודה אמר שמואל הלכה כר"ג ואין נראה לומר דפליגי דא"כ מאי מייתי אעובדא דארום וארוסתו מרב יהודה אמר שמואל וכן לעיל (דף יג.) פריך הלכתא אהלכתא קי"ל כרב נחמן בדיני כו' ולדרבה הא רב פסיק כר' יהושע וקי"ל כרב באיסורי ויש לומר דהכי פירושו כמאן אי כר"ג ובטוענת ברי ובלא ראוה שנאנסה דאיכא מגו אפילו ברוב פסולים נמי מכשר ואיירי נמי כשראוה מדברת דאי לא ראוה מדברת מאי פריך אי כרבי יהושע אפילו ברוב כשרים נמי פסול ומשני אמר

עין משפט נר מצוה

פח א מיי' פי"ח מהל' איסורי ביאה הלכה כב טוש"ע אה"ע סימן ג סעיף ד:

תוספות רי"ד

נאמנת: **מתני'** א"ר יוסי מעשה בתינוקת שירדה למלאות מים מן המעיין ונאנסה אר"י בן נורי אם רוב העיר משיאים לכהונה ה"ז תנשא [לכהונה] אר"י אמר רב

תוספות ישנים

א) [ושמא לא נקיט אלא מאי דאכשר ר"מ ור"ש בן אלעזר פוסל. ת"י].

גליון הש"ס

מתני' א"ר יוסי מעשה בתינוקת. עיין יבמות דף סז ע"ב תוס' ד"ה אין חוששין:

ליקוטי רש"י

מיסתייה. דיו [ברכות נה.].

person making the accusation] thereby **invalidates [the accused] from** entering into **the** general **congregation** of Jews.[11] אֲבָל שְׁתוּק חָלָל כָּשֵׁר – **But** if he exhibits **silence** in response to an accusation **of** being **a *chalal,* he is fit,** וְהָא דְשָׁתִיק מִשּׁוּם דְּלָא אִיכְפַּת לֵיהּ – **for the reason he is silent is that [the accusation] does not matter to him,** since even if he is a *chalal* he can still marry freely.[12] וְקָאָמַר לֵיהּ רַבִּי שִׁמְעוֹן בֶּן אֶלְעָזָר לְתַנָּא קַמָּא דְּרַבִּי מֵאִיר – **And R' Shimon ben Elazar said to the first Tanna** who quoted the ruling **of R' Meir:** אִי שְׁמִיעַ לָךְ דְּמַכְשַׁר רַבִּי מֵאִיר בִּשְׁתִיקָה – **If you have heard that R' Meir rules** the widow **fit in** a case of **silence,** לָא דְּקָרוּ לֵיהּ חָלָל וְשָׁתִיק – **it is not where,** when her husband is still alive, **he is called a *chalal* and is silent,** אֶלָּא דְּקָרוּ לֵיהּ מַמְזֵר וְשָׁתִיק – **but rather where he is called a *mamzer* and is silent.**[13] וְהַאי דְּשָׁתִיק סָבַר מַמְזֵר קָלָא אִית לֵיהּ – **For the reason he is silent is that he thinks:** Everyone knows that I am not really a *mamzer,* **for a *mamzer* is** a matter of **public knowledge.**[14] אֲבָל מַמְזֵר וְצוֹוֵחַ חָלָל וְשׁוֹתֵק פָּסוּל – **But** if he is accused of being **a *mamzer* and he protests** and then he is accused of being **a *chalal* and he is silent, he is disqualified.** וְהַאי דְּאִשְׁתִּיק סָבַר מִיסְתַּיֵּיהּ דְּלָא מַפְּקֵי לֵיהּ מִקָּהָל – Because we say that **the reason he is silent is that he reasons: It is sufficient that they are not excluding him** [i.e. me] **from the congregation** with their accusation.[15]

The Gemara poses a contradiction:

תָּנֵי חֲדָא – **It was taught in one Baraisa:** רַבִּי יוֹסֵי אוֹמֵר שְׁתוּק מַמְזֵר כָּשֵׁר – **R' YOSE SAYS:** One who reacts with **SILENCE** to an accusation **OF** being **A *MAMZER* IS FIT;** שְׁתוּק חָלָל פָּסוּל – one who reacts with **SILENCE** to an accusation **OF** being **A *CHALAL* IS UNFIT.** וְתַנְיָא אִידָךְ – **And it was taught in another Baraisa:** שְׁתוּק חָלָל כָּשֵׁר – One who reacts with **SILENCE** to an accusation **OF** being **A *CHALAL* IS FIT;** שְׁתוּק מַמְזֵר פָּסוּל – one who reacts with **SILENCE** to an accusation **OF** being **A *MAMZER* IS UNFIT.** –?–

The Gemara resolves the contradiction:

לָא קַשְׁיָא – **This is not a difficulty:** הָא תַּנָּא קַמָּא אַלִּיבָּא דְּרַבִּי מֵאִיר – **This** [the second Baraisa] follows the **first Tanna according to R' Meir,** הָא דְּרַבִּי שִׁמְעוֹן בֶּן אֶלְעָזָר אַלִּיבָּא דְּרַבִּי מֵאִיר – whereas **this** [the first Baraisa] follows **R' Shimon ben Elazar according to R' Meir.**[16]

NOTES

11. Since the stakes are so high (both a *mamzer* and a *nasin* are prohibited from marrying genealogically fit Jewesses), the accused can be expected to respond to any untrue accusation regarding them. Failure to respond is considered acquiescence to the charge.

12. [A *chalal* is not in any way restricted as to whom he may marry.]

The sense of R' Meir's statement, "Anyone who does not have any of these we allow to marry a Kohen," is therefore this: Only silence in response to one of "these," i.e. the three disqualifications specifically mentioned by the Tanna Kamma, is tantamount to admission. However, silence in response to an accusation of *chalalus* does *not* indicate admission, and the accused's widow is therefore permitted to marry a Kohen (*Rashi*).

[Apparently, the Sages mentioned in this Baraisa were in possession of a tradition from earier generations as to this matter. As received, the tradition mentioned only *mamzerus, nesinus* and the slaves of kings (exactly as the Tanna Kamma quoted it). The dispute between the Tanna Kamma and R' Meir is whether that list was intended as specific (R' Meir), or whether the three items were meant only as examples (the Tanna Kamma).]

13. I.e. R' Shimon ben Elazar is saying in the name of R' Meir: "Who is the widow of a man of uncertain status? Anyone who became mixed up with a doubtful *chalal.*" Only then do we disregard the possibility that he is a *chalal.* But if he is silent in the face of an accusation that he is a *chalal,* then he *is* considered a *chalal* — as the Tanna Kamma indeed ruled. But it is *only* in that case that I agree with the Tanna Kamma. However, in the case of one who is silent when called a *mamzer,* I disagree with the Tanna Kamma (who holds that silence in the face of *any* accusation is construed as admission), and I hold that the one who is silent is *not* deemed to be a *mamzer* (*Rashi*). [The significance of R' Shimon ben Elazar's concluding statement, "Israel recognizes the *mamzerim* among them, but they do not recognize the *chalalim* among them," will be explained below.]

14. And since there is no public knowledge to this effect, everyone realizes that there is no substance to this accusation. Therefore, there is no need for me to protest it (see *Rashi,* end of ד״ה אי שמיע לך).

15. That is, he reasons: "If I protest, they will begin an investigation and discover and then publicize that I really am a *chalal.* If I remain silent, 'Israel does not recognize the *chalalim* among them'; thus, the charge of being a *chalal* will not be widely known. It is thus better for me to remain silent, since they are not, after all, disqualifying me from marrying into the congregation." Accordingly, his silence is construed as an attempt to forestall further investigation and thus supports the accusation.

Where the accusation is that he is a *mamzer,* however, his silence is not suspicious, because he might very well feel no need to protest, as "Israel recognizes the *mamzerim* among them" [and thus everyone will realize that there is no substance to the accusation] (see *Rashi*).

[The following question, though, arises: Why did the Gemara have to introduce a new reason that his silence in face of being accused of being a *chalal* lends credence to the accusation (namely, because we construe that silence as an attempt to forestall further investigation)? Why not say simply (as we said until now) that silence is construed as admission unless there is good reason to remain silent? Thus, the Gemara could have said simply that silence in the face of an accusation of being a *mamzer* is not deemed an admission, since he sees no need to protest so obviously false a charge (as "Israel recognizes the *mamzerim* among them"). Silence in the face of being accused of being a *chalal,* on the other hand, *is* deemed an admission, because "Israel does *not* recognize the *chalalim* among them" and there would thus be a clear need for him to protest! [See *Tosafos,* who raise this question. *Tosafos'* answer, however, does not seem to fit with our versions of *Rashi. Shitah Yeshanah* (cited in *Shitah Mekubetzes*) suggests that the new reason is not really necessary, and is presented only as an additional reason for why he is silent (see there). See also *Shitah Mekubetzes* for an extensive elaboration on *Rashi's* commentary to this *sugya.*]

In conclusion:

The Baraisa thus lists three distinct opinions about when we must be concerned about the widow of a man with questionable lineage: (a) According to the Tanna Kamma, a man who does not respond to any charge against his lineage is considered to have admitted to its truth — provided that he once before had denied another charge against him. (b) The first version of R' Meir holds that to be true only in cases where the charge would disqualify him from marrying a Jewess, such as where he is accused of being a *mamzer* (or anything else disqualifying him from marrying into the congregation), but not if he is silent to a charge of being a *chalal*. (c) R' Shimon ben Elazar's version of R' Meir does not consider silence a problem in the case of a *mamzer*, but does consider it a problem in the case of a *chalal*.

The view of the Tanna Kamma is accepted as halachah. Therefore, if someone is silent to any charge leveled against him, we suspect him of having tainted lineage until our investigation proves that there is no problem (*Ran*). As stated throughout according to *Rashi*, however, this is true only if he once before reacted to another claim against him; then we construe his current silence as acquiescence. In addition, *Raavad* (cited by *Ran*) holds that this entire discussion held true only in former times, when the courts would prosecute a person who falsely accused another of tainted lineage, either by flogging or excommunicating him. Thus, someone who when accused was silent and did not come to court was assumed to be acquiescing to the charge. Nowadays, however, it is praiseworthy to be silent to such accusations. However, this is true only of accusations made in the heat of an argument. But if someone calmly accuses another of having tainted lineage, that charge must be answered. Other Rishonim (see *Ran*) understand this *sugya* as referring only to a family known to contain [unidentified] members of tainted lineage — in such an instance, silence in the face of an accusation is deemed acquiescence to the charge. See *Rama, Even HaEzer* 2:4, who cites this and various other views.

16. Both Baraisos refer to silence following the man's protest to another charge against him. They mention only the silence because that is the

שמעתי כל שאין בה אחד מכל אלו משיאין לכהונה ר"ש בן אלעזר אומר משום ר"מ וכן היה ר"ש בן מנסיא אומר כדבריו איזוהי אלמנת עיסה כל שנטמע בה ספק חלל מכירין ישראל ממזרים שביניהם ואין מכירין חללין שביניהם אמר מר איזוהי אלמנת עיסה כל שאין בה לא משום ממזרות ולא משום נתינות ולא משום עבדי מלכים הא חלל כשר מאי שנא הנך דאורייתא חלל נמי דאורייתא ותו אמר רבי מאיר שמעתי כל שאין בה אחד מכל אלו משיאין לכהונה היינו תנא קמא ותו ר"ש בן אלעזר אומר משום ר' מאיר וכן היה ר"ש בן מנסיא אומר כדבריו איזוהי אלמנת עיסה כל שנטמע בה ספק חלל מכירין ישראל ממזרים שביניהן ואין מכירין חללין שביניהן והא אמרת רישא חלל כשר א"ר יוחנן ממזר צווח וחלל שותק איכא בינייהו תנא קמא סבר *כל פסול דקרו ליה ושתיק פסול והכי קאמר ת"ק איזוהי אלמנת עיסה כל שאין בה לא שתוק ממזרות ולא שתוק נתינות ולא שתוק עבדי מלכים ולא שתוק חלל וקאמר ליה ר"מ הנך הוא דקא פסיל ליה בקהל אבל שתוק חלל כשר והא דשתיק משום דלא איכפת ליה וקאמר ליה ר"ש בן אלעזר לתנא קמא דר' מאיר אי שמיע לך דמכשר ר"מ בשתיקה לא דקרו ליה חלל ושתיק אלא דקרו ליה ממזר ושתיק והאי דשתיק סבר ממזר קלא אית ליה אבל ממזר וצווח חלל ושותק פסול והאי דאשתיק סבר מיסתייה דלא מפקי ליה מקהל תני חדא ר' יוסי אומר שתוק ממזר כשר שתוק חלל פסול ותניא אידך שתוק חלל כשר שתוק ממזר פסול לא קשיא הא ת"ק אליבא דר"מ הא דר"ש בן אלעזר אליבא דר"מ: **מתני'** *א"ר יוסי מעשה בתינוקת שירדה למלאות מים מן העין ונאנסה אמר רבי יוחנן בן נורי אם רוב אנשי העיר משיאין לכהונה הרי זו תינשא לכהונה: **גמ'** אמר ליה רבא לרב נחמן ר' יוחנן בן נורי דאמר כמאן אי כרבן גמליאל אפילו ברוב פסולין נמי מכשר אי כרבי יהושע אפילו ברוב כשרים נמי פסיל אמר ליה הכי אמר רב יהודה אמר רב

בקרונות

רש"י

שמעתי כו'. לקמיה פריך היינו תנא קמא דתנא קמא נמי הכי אמר דמשום דאין בה אחד מכל אלו העידו עליה להכשיר: מכירין ישראל ממזרין שביניהן. וספק ממזר יש לך להכשיר דאי ממזר הוה מידע הוו ידעי ביה: ואין מכירין חללין שביניהן. וספק חלל יש לך לפסול ולקמיה פריך הא אמרת רישא איזוהי אלמנת עיסה כל שנטמע בה ספק חלל אלמא ספק חלל כשר: הא חלל כשר. משום ספק חלל לא פסיל לה: מאי שנא הנך. דפסיל לה ספק דידהו: דאורייתא. משום דודאן פוסלין מן התורה בביאה דנפקא לן ביבמות (דף סח.) מכי תהיה לאיש זר כיון שנבעלה לפסול לה פסלה: חלל נמי. ודאי פסול מדאורייתא' דילפינן לה התם מלא יחלל זרעו מקיש זרעו לו מה הוא פוסל בביאתו אף זרעו פוסל והוא גופיה נפקא לן מלא יחלל שני חילולין במשמע אחד לזרעו ואחד לאשתו: ר"ש בן אלעזר כו'. סיפא דמילתיה ארישא דמילתיה פריך דקתני סיפא אין מכירין חללין שביניהן משמע אפשר שהיה חלל אבל לא היו מכירין בו אלמא אית ליה דפסיל ורישא אמר איזוהי אלמנת עיסה והכשיר כל שנטמע בה ספק חלל: אמר ר' יוחנן ממזר צווח וחלל שותק איכא בינייהו. אדם שכשקורין אותו ממזר הוא צווח וכשקורין אותו חלל שותק איכא בין ר"מ לת"ק ובין תנא קמא דברייתא אליבא דר"מ ור"ש בן אלעזר אליבא דר"מ: תנא קמא סבר כל פסול דקרו ליה ושתיק פסול. דהודאה היא וכל שאין בה לא משום ממזרות כו' דקאמר אשתיקות קאי: והכי קאמר איזוהי אלמנת עיסה. להכשיר: כל שאין בה לא שתוק ממזרות ולא שתוק נתינות. וכיון דתלה טעמא בשתיקה הוא הדין לכל שתוקי פסול ולא הוצרך למנות את כולם ובאיזו הכשירו באשת ספק חלל שאנו מכירין את ספיקו שנתגרשה אמו ספק אבל מי שאין מכירין בו ושמענו שפוסלין אותו ושותק פסול: וקאמר ליה ר"מ. דוקא הני אבל שתוק חלל לא פסול: והא דשתיק. לאו משום דאודי אלא משום דלא איכפת ליה הואיל ולאו פסול קהל הוא והיינו דקאמר כל שאין בה אחד מכל אלו שתיקות משיאין בנותיהן לכהונה ואפי' יש בו שתוק חלל: וקאמר ליה ר"ש לתנא קמא. לאו לתנא קמא דברייתא קאמר דההיא רבנן היא אלא לתנא ששנה דברי ר"מ בבית המדרש ואמר בשם ר"מ שמעתי כל שאין בה כו': אי שמיע לך כו'. והכי קאמר איזו היא אלמנת עיסה כל שנטמע בה ספק חלל שאנו מכירין את פסולו שהיתה אמו ספק גרושה אבל שתוק חלל ואין אנו מכירין בו פסול כתנא קמא ומיהו בהא פליג רבי מאיר אתנא קמא דאיהו כל פסול דשתיק ביה פסיל ולרבי מאיר חלל שתוק הוא דפסול דסבר מסתייה דלא מפקי ליה מקהל ואם אני צווח יכריזו עלי ויודע פסולי בברור ועכשיו אין מכירין ישראל חללין שביניהם אבל שתוק ממזר כשר דהאי דשתיק סבר הכל יודעין שאיני ממזר דמכירין ישראל ממזרין שביניהן: **מתני'** מן העין. מן המעיין: אם רוב העיר. כשרין להשיא בנותיהן ואלמנותיהן לכהונה שאין רוב בני העיר מן הפוסלין אשה לכהונה בביאתן אף זו תינשא לכהונה: **גמ'** דאמר כמאן. דבעי רוב כשרין: אפילו ברוב פסולין נמי מכשר. דאית ליה העמד אשה על חזקתה: אמר ליה הכי אמר כו'. לעולם כרבי יהושע והכא משום דאיכא תרי רובי לכשרות אכשרה וכדרב יהודה ולקמן מפרש טעמא ואזיל מאי שנא תרי רובי מחד רובא:

בקרונות

תוספות

לא משום ממזרות כו'. הא דלא חשיב עמוני ומואבי משום דלא פסיקא דזכרים אסורין ונקבות מותרות ומצרי ואדומי לא חשיב דאינן אסורין אלא עד דור שלישי: **ותו** ר"ש בן אלעזר אומר איזוהי עיסה כל שנטמע בה ספק חלל והאמרת רישא חלל כשר. ה"ג בכל הספרים ובפירוש ר"ח ומפרש כל שנטמע בה ספק חלל הא ודאי חלל פסול והא אמרת רישא חלל כשר והיינו ודאי חלל ואין נראה דמאי פריך מתנא קמא דלמא ת"ק פליג עליה ופירוש הקונטרס וגרסתו עיקר: **ממזר** צווח וחלל שותק איכא בינייהו. תימה דהוה ליה למימר ממזר צווח ושותק וחלל שותק איכא בינייהו דבממזר שותק נמי פליגי דהא מכשר ליה ר"ש בן אלעזר א): **אבל** ממזר צווח וחלל שותק פסול. וא"ת ממזר צווח מנא ליה דפסל ר"ש בן אלעזר ואומר ר"י מדקתני במילתיה איזוהי עיסה כל שנטמע בה ספק חלל דלא הוה ליה למימר אלא מכירין ישראל ממזרים שביניהם ואין מכירין חללין שביניהם דמינה שמעינן בחלל צווח דכשר כי היכי דלא הוצרך להשמיענו כל שנטמע בה ספק ממזר אלא ודאי אתא למידק דחלל צווח דוקא כשר הא ממזר צווח פסול: **מסתייה** דלא מפקינן ליה מקהל. וא"ת מה צריך להאי טעמא לימא הא דשתיק משום דאודויי קא מודי דהא ממזר שותק פסול לת"ק משום דשתיקה כהודאה וה"ה דחלל שותק לר"ש דפסול מהאי טעמא ואע"ג דגבי ממזר שותק לדידיה לא הוי שתיקה כהודאה היינו משום דסבר דממזר קלא אית ליה וי"ל דהכי פירושא סבר מסתייה דלא מפקינן ליה מקהל (כהונה) פי' אפי' מקהל כהונה אע"פ שזה מחרפו וקוראו חלל סבור דאין מוציאין אותו מקהל כהונה וסבור אם יצווח יחזרו לברר הדבר ויפסלוהו וטעם זה שייך גם בממזר שותק לת"ק ולא נאמר דשתיקה כהודאה וכן פירש בקונטרס: **כמאן** אי כר"ג אפילו ברוב פסולין נמי מכשר. וא"ת והא לא מכשר ברוב פסולין אלא כשטוענת ברי ואית לה מיגו דאי בעיא אמרה לא נבעלתי או בלא מגו היכא דאיכא למימר בודקת ומזנה אבל הכא אפילו טוענת ברי הא לית לה מגו וליכא למימר בודקת ומזנה דהא נאנסה ואפי' אם נאמר דהכא לא ראוה שנאנסה אלא היא אמרה כן דאית לה מגו א"כ תקשי הלכתא אהלכתא דלקמן פסיק רב הלכה כר' יוסי ולעיל פסיק רב יהודה אמר שמואל הלכה כר"ג ואין נראה לומר דפליגי דא"כ מאי מייתי אעובדא דארוס וארוסתו מרב יהודה אמר שמואל וכן לעיל (דף יג.) פריך הלכתא אהלכתא קי"ל כרב נחמן בדיני כו' ואדרבה הא רב פסיק כר' יהושע וקי"ל כרב באיסורי ויש לומר דהכי פירושו כמאן אי כר"ג ובטוענת ברי ובלא ראוה שנאנסה דאיכא מגו אפילו ברוב פסולים נמי מכשר ואיירי נמי כשראוה מדברת דאי לא ראוה מדברת מאי פריך אי כרבי יהושע אפילו ברוב כשרים נמי פסול ומשני

אמר

עין משפט נר מצוה

פח א מיי' פי"ט מהל' איסורי ביאה הלכה כב טוש"ע אה"ע סימן ב סעיף ד:

תוספות רי"ד

נאמנת: מתני' א"ר יוסי מעשה בתינוקת שירדה למלאות מים מן המעיין ונאנסה *אר"י בן נורי אם רוב העיר משיאים לכהונה ה"ז תנשא [לכהונה] אר"י אמר רב

תוספות ישנים

א) [ושמא לא נקיט אלא מאי דאכשר ר"מ ור"ש בן אלעזר פוסל. ת"י].

גליון הש"ס

מתני' א"ר יוסי מעשה בתינוקת. עיין יבמות דף סז ע"ב תוס' ד"ה אין חוששין:

ליקוטי רש"י

מיסתייה. דיו [ברכות נה.].

שָׁמַעְתִּי כָּל שֶׁאֵין בָּהּ אֶחָד מִכָּל אֵלּוּ – I HAVE HEARD THAT ANYONE WHO on account of her marriage DOES NOT HAVE ANY OF THESE possible disqualifications מַשִּׂיאִין לִכְהוּנָּה – WE ALLOW TO MARRY A KOHEN.[1] רַבִּי שִׁמְעוֹן בֶּן אֶלְעָזָר אוֹמֵר מִשּׁוּם רַבִּי מֵאִיר – R' SHIMON BEN ELAZAR SAYS IN THE NAME OF R' MEIR,[2] וְכֵן הָיָה רַבִּי שִׁמְעוֹן בֶּן מְנַסְיָא אוֹמֵר כִּדְבָרָיו – AND SO WOULD R' SHIMON BEN MENASYA SAY LIKEWISE: אֵיזוֹהִי אַלְמְנַת עִיסָּה – WHO IS THE WIDOW OF A person of UNCERTAIN STATUS? כָּל שֶׁנִּטְמַע בָּהּ סָפֵק חָלָל – ANYONE WHO through her marriage BECAME MIXED UP WITH A DOUBTFUL *CHALAL.* מַכִּירִין יִשְׂרָאֵל מַמְזֵרִים שֶׁבֵּינֵיהֶם – ISRAEL RECOGNIZES THE *MAMZERIM* AMONG THEM וְאֵין מַכִּירִין חֲלָלִין שֶׁבֵּינֵיהֶם – BUT THEY DO NOT RECOGNIZE THE *CHALALIM* AMONG THEM.[3]

The Gemara analyzes the Baraisa:

אָמַר מַר – **The master said:** אֵיזוֹהִי אַלְמְנַת עִיסָּה – WHO IS THE WIDOW OF A person of UNCERTAIN STATUS? כָּל שֶׁאֵין בָּהּ לֹא מִשּׁוּם מַמְזֵרוּת וְלֹא מִשּׁוּם נְתִינוּת וְלֹא מִשּׁוּם עַבְדֵי מְלָכִים – ANYONE WHO DOES NOT HAVE concerning her EITHER an uncertainty ON ACCOUNT OF *MAMZERUS,* OR an uncertainty ON ACCOUNT OF *NESINUS,* OR an uncertainty ON ACCOUNT OF THE SLAVES OF KINGS. הָא חָלָל כָּשֵׁר – **This implies** that if her deceased husband was **an** uncertain ***chalal,*** she would be ruled **fit** for a Kohen. מַאי שְׁנָא הָנָךְ דְּאוֹרַיְיתָא – Now **what is unique about those** other men (i.e. the *mamzer* etc.) that uncertainties regarding them are sufficient to render her unfit? Presumably that their cohabitation disqualifies a woman **according to Biblical law.**[4] חָלָל נַמִּי דְּאוֹרַיְיתָא – But the cohabitation of **a** ***chalal*** **also** disqualifies a woman **according to Biblical law.**[5] Why, then, is the Baraisa strict regarding the possibility of *mamzerus* or *nesinus* and lenient regarding the possibility of *chalalus*?

The Gemara raises a second objection to the Baraisa:

וְתוּ – **And furthermore,** the Baraisa stated: אָמַר רַבִּי מֵאִיר – R' MEIR SAID: שָׁמַעְתִּי כָּל שֶׁאֵין בָּהּ אֶחָד מִכָּל אֵלּוּ מַשִּׂיאִין לִכְהוּנָּה – I HAVE HEARD THAT ANYONE WHO DOES NOT HAVE ANY OF THESE possible disqualifications WE ALLOW TO MARRY A KOHEN. הַיְינוּ תַּנָּא קַמָּא – But **that is** exactly what **the Tanna Kamma** said![6] —?—

A third question:

וְתוּ – **And furthermore,** the Baraisa stated: רַבִּי שִׁמְעוֹן בֶּן אֶלְעָזָר אוֹמֵר מִשּׁוּם רַבִּי מֵאִיר – R' SHIMON BEN ELAZAR SAYS IN THE NAME OF R' MEIR, וְכֵן הָיָה רַבִּי שִׁמְעוֹן בֶּן מְנַסְיָא אוֹמֵר כִּדְבָרָיו – AND SO WOULD R' SHIMON BEN MENASYA SAY LIKEWISE: אֵיזוֹהִי אַלְמְנַת עִיסָּה – WHO IS THE WIDOW OF A person of UNCERTAIN STATUS? כָּל שֶׁנִּטְמַע בָּהּ סָפֵק חָלָל – ANYONE WHO BECAME MIXED UP WITH A DOUBTFUL *CHALAL.* מַכִּירִין יִשְׂרָאֵל מַמְזֵרִים שֶׁבֵּינֵיהֶן – ISRAEL RECOGNIZES THE *MAMZERIM* AMONG THEM וְאֵין מַכִּירִין חֲלָלִין שֶׁבֵּינֵיהֶן – BUT THEY DO NOT RECOGNIZE THE *CHALALIM* AMONG THEM. וְהָא אָמַרְתְּ רֵישָׁא חָלָל כָּשֵׁר – **But you said in the beginning** that if her husband was a possible ***chalal*** she is ***fit*** for a Kohen![7] —?—

The Gemara answers all three questions:

אָמַר רַבִּי יוֹחָנָן – **R' Yochanan said:** מַמְזֵר צוֹוֵחַ וְחָלָל שׁוֹתֵק אִיכָּא בֵּינַיְיהוּ – At issue **between [the Tannaim of the Baraisa]** is the case of someone who when called **a *mamzer* protests and** when called **a *chalal* remains silent.**[8] תַּנָּא קַמָּא סָבַר כָּל פְּסוּל דְּקָרוּ לֵיהּ וְשָׁתֵיק פָּסוּל – **The Tanna Kamma holds that any time [a person] is called a disqualification and he is silent,** it indicates that **he is** in fact **unfit.**[9] וְהָכִי קָאָמַר תַּנָּא קַמָּא – **And this is what the Tanna Kamma is saying:** אֵיזוֹהִי אַלְמְנַת עִיסָּה – **Who is the widow of** a person of **uncertain status** who is permitted to marry a Kohen? כָּל שֶׁאֵין בָּהּ לֹא שְׁתוּק מַמְזֵרוּת וְלֹא שְׁתוּק נְתִינוּת וְלֹא שְׁתוּק עַבְדֵי מְלָכִים וְלֹא שְׁתוּק חָלָל – **Anyone who does not have** on account of her marriage a problem stemming from **silence of *mamzerus*** [i.e. her husband was called a *mamzer* and remained silent] **or silence of *nesinus*** [he was called a *nasin* and remained silent] **or silence of slaves of kings or silence of a *chalal.***[10] וְקָאָמַר לֵיהּ רַבִּי מֵאִיר – **And R' Meir said to [the Tanna Kamma]:** הָנָךְ הוּא דְּקָא פָּסִיל לֵיהּ בְּקָהָל – **It is only regarding those,** i.e. the three accusations specifically mentioned, that silence is construed as an admission, **because [the**

NOTES

1. The Gemara will ask that this view is identical to that of the Tanna Kamma, since the Tanna Kamma also said that R' Yehoshua testified that a woman is fit when her deceased husband did not have any of these possible problems (*Rashi*).

2. R' Shimon ben Elazar has a different version than the previous Tanna about what R' Meir said.

3. Therefore, if there is a question of the deceased husband being a *mamzer*, we should rule her fit, because if he was in fact a *mamzer* we would know about it. But if he was a possible *chalal,* we must rule her disqualified, because he might actually have been a *chalal* without our knowing it. The Gemara will ask that this seems to contradict the beginning of R' Shimon ben Elazar's statement [''Who is the widow of someone of uncertain status? Anyone who became mixed up with a doubtful *chalal*''], which indicates that the possibility of the man being a *chalal* does *not* invalidate his widow (*Rashi*).

4. If we know with certainty that a woman has cohabited with a *mamzer* or a *nasin* she is prohibited to a Kohen according to Biblical law, as the Gemara in *Yevamos* (68a) derives from a verse (*Rashi*).

5. The Gemara in *Yevamos* (69a) derives from another verse that cohabitation with a definite *chalal* also causes a woman to become prohibited to a Kohen (*Rashi*).

6. See above, note 1.

7. The end of R' Shimon ben Elazar's statement implies that there is a problem if the man was a possible *chalal* (because that taint is not as well publicized as the taint of *mamzerus*). But he began by stating that the widow of a possible *chalal* is *permitted* to a Kohen! (*Rashi*).

8. That is, the case regarding which R' Yehoshua testified was one in which the uncertainty over the widow's fitness was due to a specific doubt regarding her husband, e.g. a *get* was given to his mother in a questionably valid way (as explained above, on 14a). But what if the husband was not the subject of an actual doubt, but rather had his fitness called into question due to a totally different set of circumstances: viz. he was silent when a charge about his lineage was leveled against him — when we know that he generally reacts to charges about his lineage. For example, when the husband was accused of being a *mamzer* he protested that accusation, but when he was accused of being a *chalal* he remained silent (*Rashi,* as explained by *Ritva, Shitah Mekubetzes* ד״ה ולי איברא; see also *Ran; Maharam Schif* ד״ה ראוי לעיין and *Beur HaGra, Even HaEzer* 2:22). The Tannaim of this Baraisa debate whether that silence can be viewed as an admission to the charge leveled against him.

9. Because his silence is tantamount to an admission that the accusation is true. When the Tanna Kamma states that the widow is fit if there is no uncertainty on account of *mamzerus, nesinus,* etc., he is referring to the husband's *silence in the face of accusations regarding these matters* [after his having protested an earlier accusation regarding a different disqualification] (*Rashi*).

10. The Tanna Kamma maintains that the only case regarding which R' Yehoshua testified is one in which we are aware of a specific doubt concerning her deceased husband's genealogy, e.g. we are unsure if the *get* thrown to his mother by her first husband was valid. But if the doubt arose as a result of the husband's silence in response to an accusation of unfitness hurled at him, then he is in fact assumed to be unfit, because his silence is taken as an admission to that accusation. And since the reason for his unfitness is his silence, it makes no difference what the accusation was. Although the Tanna lists only three possible accusations (*mamzerus, nesinus* and the slaves of kings), the logic of his ruling makes it clear that the ruling would hold true for any accusation. Accordingly, even if he were accused of being a *chalal* and he remained silent, his widow is disqualified from the Kehunah (*Rashi*; see *Ran;* cf. *Ritva*).

עין משפט
נר מצוה

פח א מיי' פי"ט מהל' איסורי ביאה הלכה כב טוש"ע אה"ע סימן ג סעיף ד:

תוספות רי"ד

נאמנת: מתני' א"ר יוסי מעשה בתינוקת שירדה למלאות מים מן המעיין ונאנסה אר"י בן נורי אם רוב העיר משיאים לכהונה ה"ז תנשא [לכהונה] אר"י אמר רב.

תוספות ישנים

א) [ושמא לא נקיט אלא מאי דאכשר ר"מ ור"ש בן אלעזר פוסל. ת"י].

גליון הש"ס

מתני' א"ר יוסי מעשה בתינוקת. עיין יבמות דף סז ע"ב תוס' ד"ה אין חוששין:

ליקוטי רש"י

מיסתייה. דיו [ברכות נה.].

לא משום ממזרות כו'. הא דלא חשיב עמוני ומואבי משום דלא פסיקא דזכרים אסורין ונקבות מותרות ומצרי ואדומי לא חשיב דאינן אסורין אלא עד דור שלישי: ותו ר"ש בן אלעזר אומר איזוהי עיסה כל שנטמע בה ספק חלל והאמרת רישא חלל כשר. ה"ג בכל הספרים ובפירוש ר"ח ומפרש כל שנטמע בה ספק חלל הא ודאי חלל פסול והא אמרת רישא חלל כשר והיינו ודאי חלל ואין נראה דמאי פריך מתנא קמא דלמא ת"ק פליג עליה ופירוש הקונטרס וגרסתו עיקר: ממזר צווח וחלל שותק איכא בינייהו. תימה דהוה ליה למימר ממזר צווח ושותק וחלל שותק איכא בינייהו דבממזר שותק נמי פליגי דהא מכשר ליה ר"ש בן אלעזר[א]: אבל ממזר צווח וחלל שותק פסול. וא"ת ממזר צווח מנא ליה דפסל ר"ש בן אלעזר ואומר ר"י מדקתני במילתיה איזוהי עיסה כל שנטמע בה ספק חלל דלא הוה ליה למימר אלא מכירין ישראל ממזרים שביניהם ואין מכירין חללין שביניהם למינה שמעינן בחלל צווח דכשר כי היכי דלא הוצרך להשמיענו כל שנטמע בה ספק ממזר אלא ודאי אתא למידק דחלל צווח דוקא כשר הא ממזר צווח פסול: מסתייה דלא מפקינן ליה מקהל. וא"ת מה צריך להאי טעמא לימא הא דשתיק משום דאודויי קא מודי דהא ממזר שותק פסול לת"ק משום דשתיקה כהודאה וה"ה דחלל שותק לר"ש דפסול מהאי טעמא ואע"ג דגבי ממזר שותק לדידיה לא הוי שתיקה כהודאה היינו משום דסבר דממזר קלא אית ליה וי"ל דהכי פירושא סבר מסתייה דלא מפקינן ליה מקהל (כהונה) פי' אפי' מקהל כהונה אע"פ שזה מחרפו וקורהו חלל סבור דאין מוציאין אותו מקהל כהונה וסבור אם יצווח יחזרו לברר הדבר ויפסלוהו וטעם זה שייך גם בממזר שותק לת"ק ולא נאמר דשתיקה כהודאה וכן פירש בקונטרס: כמאן אי כר"ג אפילו ברוב פסולין נמי מכשר. וא"ת והא לא מכשר ברוב פסולין אלא כשטוענת ברי ואית לה מיגו דאי בעיא אמרה לא נבעלתי או בלא מגו היכא דאיכא למימר בודקת ומזנה אבל הכא אפילו טוענת ברי הא לית לה מגו וליכא למימר בודקת ומזנה דהא נאנסה ואפי' אם נאמר דהכא לא ראוה שנאנסה אלא היא אמרה כן דאית לה מגו א"כ תקשי הלכתא אהלכתא דלקמן פסיק רב הלכה כר' יוסי ולעיל פסיק רב יהודה אמר שמואל הלכה כר"ג ואין נראה לומר דפליגי דא"כ מאי מייתי מעובדא דארוס וארוסתו מרב יהודה אמר שמואל וכן לעיל (דף יג.) פריך הלכתא אהלכתא קי"ל כרב נחמן בדיני כו' ואדרבה הא רב פסיק כר' יהושע וקי"ל כרב באיסורי ויש לומר דהכי פירושו כמאן אי כר"ג ובטוענת ברי ובלא ראוה שנאנסה דאיכא מגו אפילו ברוב פסולים נמי מכשר ואיירי נמי כשראוה מדברת דאי לא ראוה מ"ברת מאי פריך אי כרבי יהושע אפילו ברוב כשרים נמי פסול ומשני אמר

שמעתי כל שאין בה אחד מכל אלו משיאין לכהונה ר"ש בן אלעזר אומר משום ר"מ וכן היה ר"ש בן מנסיא אומר כדבריו איזוהי אלמנת עיסה כל שנטמע בה ספק חלל מכירין ישראל ממזרים שביניהם ואין מכירין חללין שביניהם אמר מר איזוהי אלמנת עיסה כל שאין בה לא משום ממזרות ולא משום נתינות ולא משום עבדי מלכים הא חלל כשר מאי שנא הנך דאורייתא חלל נמי דאורייתא ותו אמר רבי מאיר שמעתי כל שאין בה אחד מכל אלו משיאין לכהונה היינו תנא קמא ותו ר"ש בן אלעזר אומר משום ר' מאיר וכן היה ר"ש בן מנסיא אומר כדבריו איזוהי אלמנת עיסה כל שנטמע בה ספק חלל מכירין ישראל ממזרים שביניהן ואין מכירין חללין שביניהן והא אמרת רישא חלל כשר א"ר יוחנן ממזר צווח וחלל שותק איכא בינייהו תנא קמא סבר *כל פסול דקרו ליה ושתיק פסול והכי קאמר ת"ק איזוהי אלמנת עיסה כל שאין בה לא שתוק ממזרות ולא שתוק נתינות ולא שתוק עבדי מלכים ולא שתוק חלל וקאמר ליה ר"מ הנך הוא דקא פסיל ליה בקהל אבל שתוק חלל כשר והא דשתיק משום דלא איכפת ליה וקאמר ליה ר"ש בן אלעזר לתנא קמא דר' מאיר אי שמיע לך דמכשר ר"מ בשתיקה לא דקרו ליה חלל ושתיק אלא דקרו ליה ממזר ושתיק והאי דשתיק סבר ממזר קלא אית ליה אבל ממזר וצווח חלל ושותק פסול והאי דאשתיק סבר מיסתייה דלא מפקי ליה מקהל תני חדא ר' יוסי אומר שתוק ממזר כשר שתוק חלל פסול ותניא אידך שתוק חלל כשר שתוק ממזר פסול לא קשיא הא ת"ק אליבא דר"מ הא דר"ש בן אלעזר אליבא דר"מ: מתני' *א"ר יוסי מעשה בתינוקת שירדה למלאות מים מן העין ונאנסה אמר רבי יוחנן בן נורי אם רוב אנשי העיר משיאין לכהונה הרי זו תינשא לכהונה: גמ' אמר ליה רבא לרב נחמן ר' יוחנן בן נורי דאמר כמאן אי כרבן גמליאל אפילו ברוב פסולין נמי מכשר אי כרבי יהושע אפילו ברוב כשרים נמי פסיל אמר ליה הכי אמר רב יהודה אמר רב

בקרונות

שמעתי כו'. לקמיה פריך היינו תנא קמא דתנא קמא נמי הכי אמר דמשום דאין בה אחד מכל אלו העידו עליה להכשיר: מכירין ישראל ממזרין שביניהן. וספק ממזר יש לך להכשיר דאי ממזר הוה מידע הוו ידעי ביה: ואין מכירין חללין שביניהן. וספק חלל יש לך לפסול ולקמיה פריך הא אמרת רישא איזוהי אלמנת עיסה כל שנטמע בה ספק חלל אלמא ספק חלל כשר: הא חלל כשר. משום ספק חלל לא פסיל לה: מאי שנא הנך. דפסיל לה ספק דידהו: דאורייתא. משום דודאן פוסלין מן התורה בביאה דנפקא לן ביבמות (דף סח.) מכי תהיה לאיש זר כיון שנבעלה לפסול לה פסלה: חלל נמי. ודאי פסול מדאוריית' דילפינן לה התם מלא יחלל זרעו מקיש זרעו לו מה הוא פוסל בביאתו אף זרעו פוסל והוא גופיה נפקא לן מלא יחלל שני חילולין במשמע אחד לזרעו ואחד לאשתו: ר"ש בן אלעזר כו'. סיפא דמילתיה ארישא דמילתיה פריך דקתני סיפא אין מכירין חללין שביניהן משמע אפשר שהיה חלל אבל לא היו מכירין בו אלמא אית ליה דפסיל ורישא אמר איזוהי אלמנת עיסה והכשיר כל שנטמע בה ספק חלל: אמר ר' יוחנן ממזר צווח וחלל שותק איכא בינייהו. אדם שכשקורין אותו ממזר הוא צווח וכשקורין אותו חלל שותק איכא בין ר"מ לת"ק ובין תנא קמא דברייתא אליבא דר"מ ור"ש בן אלעזר אליבא דר"מ: תנא קמא סבר כל פסול דקרו ליה ושתיק פסול. דהודאה היא וכל שאין בה לא משום ממזרות כו' דקאמר אשתיקות קאי: והכי קאמר איזוהי אלמנת עיסה. להכשיר: כל שאין בה לא שתוק ממזרות ולא שתוק נתינות. וכיון דתלה טעמא בשתיקה הוא הדין לכל שתוקי פסול ולא הוצרך למנות את כולם ובאיזו הכשירו באשת ספק חלל שאנו מכירין את ספיקו שנתגרשה אמו ספק אבל מי שאין מכירין בו ושמענו שפוסלין אותו ושותק פסול: וקאמר ליה ר"מ. דוקא הני אבל שתוק חלל לא פסול: והא דשתיק. לאו משום דאודי אלא משום דלא איכפת ליה הואיל ולאו פסול קהל הוא והיינו דקאמר כל שאין בה אחד מכל אלו שתיקות משיאין בנותיהן לכהונה ואפי' יש בו שתוק חלל: וקאמר ליה ר"ש לתנא קמא. לאו לתנא קמא דברייתא קאמר דההיא רבנן היא אלא לתנא ששנה דברי ר"מ בבית המדרש ואמר בשם ר"מ שמעתי כל שאין בה כו': אי שמיע לך כו'. והכי קאמר איזו היא אלמנת עיסה כל שנטמע בה ספק חלל שאנו מכירין את פסולו שהיתה אמו ספק גרושה אבל שתוק חלל ואין אנו מכירין בו פסול כתנא קמא ומיהו בהא פליג רבי מאיר אתנא קמא דאיהו כל פסול דשתיק ביה פסיל ולרבי מאיר חלל שתוק הוא דפסול דסבר מסתייה דלא מפקי ליה מקהל ואם אני צווח יכריזו עלי ויודע פסולי בברור ועכשיו אין מכירין ישראל חללין שביניהם אבל שתוק ממזר כשר דהאי דשתיק סבר הכל יודעין שאיני ממזר דמכירין ישראל ממזרין שביניהן: מתני' מן העין. מן המעיין: אם רוב העיר. כשרין להשיא בנותיהן ואלמנותיהן לכהונה שאין רוב בני העיר מן הפוסלין אשה לכהונה בביאתן אף זו תינשא לכהונה: גמ' דאמר כמאן. דבעי רוב כשרין: אפילו ברוב פסולין נמי מכשר. דאית ליה העמד אשה על חזקתה: אמר ליה הכי אמר כו'. לעולם כרבי יהושע והכא משום דאיכא תרי רובי לכשרות אכשרה וכדרב יהודה ולקמן מפרש טעמא ואזיל מאי שנא תרי רובי מחד רובא:

בקרונות

אין מינאי אמר רב יוסף למאי ניחוש לה חדא דהא קא מודה ועוד הא א) אמר רב יהודה אמר שמואל הלכה כרבן גמליאל אן אמר ליה אביי ב) ובהא כי לא מודה מכשר רבן גמליאל והאמר ליה שמואל לרב יהודה שיננא א הלכה כר"ג ואת לא תעביד עובדא עד דאיכא רוב כשרין אצלה והכא רוב פסולין אצלה וליטעמיך תקשי לך היא גופא הלכה ואת לא תעביד עובדא אלא מאי אית לך למימר ב הא לכתחלה הא דיעבד והא נמי כדיעבד דמי רמי ליה אביי ג) לרבא ומי אמר רבי יהושע אינה נאמנת ורמינהו ד) העיד ר' יהושע ורבי יהודה בן בתירא ג על אלמנת עיסה שהיא כשרה לכהונה א"ל הכי השתא התם אשה נישאת בודקת ונישאת הכא אשה מזנה בודקת ומזנה אמר רבא דרבי יהושע אדרבי יהושע קשיא דרבן גמליאל אדרבן גמליאל לא קשיא והא קתני סיפא אמר להן רבן גמליאל קבלנו עדותכם ד אבל מה נעשה שהרי גזר רבן יוחנן בן זכאי שלא להושיב בית דין על כך שהכהנים שומעין לכם לרחק אבל לא לקרב אלא אמר רבא דרבן גמליאל אדרבן גמליאל לא קשיא התם ברי הכא שמא דר' יהושע אדר' יהושע נמי לא קשיא התם חד ספיקא הכא תרי ספיקי הלכך לרבן גמליאל אלים ליה ברי דאפילו בחד ספיקא נמי מכשיר וקיל ליה שמא דאפילו בספק ספיקא נמי פסיל לרבי יהושע אלים ליה חד ספיקא דאפילו בברי נמי פסיל וקיל ליה ספק ספיקא דאפילו בשמא נמי מכשיר תנו רבנן ה) איזוהי אלמנת עיסה ה כל שאין בה לא משום ממזרות ולא משום נתינות ולא משום עבדי מלכים רבי מאיר אומר שמעתי

רש"י

אין מינאי. אמת ממני הוא: ובהא כי לא מודי כו'. דקא אמרת ועוד: ארוסה הכל פסולין אצלה חוץ מן הארוס: הא לכתחלה. אם בא כהן לימלך לבית דין לא שרינן ליה לכונסה אא"כ היו רוב כשרים אצלה: דיעבד. אם נשאה כהן ולא נמלך לא מפקינן לה מיניה: והא נמי כדיעבד דמי. שנתעברה ואתה בא לפסול העובר ולאוסרה על הארוס דאם אין אתה מאמינה הרי אתה מוציאה מבעלה: מי אמר רבי יהושע אינה נאמנת. אלמא לא מוקמינן לה אחזקה: עיסה. לשון ספק: על אלמנת עיסה. שהיא באה מכח ספק חלל דלקמן שנטמע בה ספק חלל כגון זרק בעל אמו הראשון לה גט ספק קרוב לו ספק קרוב לה ומת ונמצאת זו ספק גרושה ספק אלמנה ונשאה כהן והוליד ממנה בן זהו ספק חלל והעיד ר"י על אלמנתו של זה שהיא כשרה אלמא מוקמינן לה אחזקה ואמרינן אל תפסילנה לזו מספק כלומ' שמא בעלה חלל היה: בודקת וניסת. וי"ל שבדקה אחר אותן גירושין והוגד לה שקרוב לו היו ולא נתגרשה כלל ואלמנה היתה וכשרה לכהן: בודקת ומזנה. בתמיה: דרבן גמליאל אדרבן גמליאל לא קשיא. בתמיה דלא חיישת לתרווייהו: הא קתני סיפא. דההיא אמר להן כו': קבלנו עדותכם. נאמנים אתם לנו שכך שמעתם: על כך. להתירה לכהונה דודאי אסורה: שהכהנים שומעין לכם. אם תאמרו אסורה: אבל לא לקרב. אם תאמרו מותרת: התם ברי. מתניתין היא אומרת ברי לי שלכשר נבעלתי: הכא. גבי אלמנת עיסה כי היכי דלדידן מספקא לן לדידה נמי מספקא לה וליכא למימר בה ברי ושמא ברי עדיף: חד ספיקא. מתניתין חד ספיקא היא ספק נבעלה לכשר ספק נבעלה לפסול שהרי לא בא זה לפנינו ואילו בא שמא היינו מכירים בו שהוא פסול: הכא. גבי אלמנת עיסה: תרי ספיקי. אמו של ספק חלל זה בה נולד הספק והיא עצמה לא נאסרה אלא מספק וזו שבאה מחמת בנה קרי לה ספק ספיקא ומדברי רבי יוסף טוב עלם מצאתי [אלמנת עיסה] אשה שהיה בעלה ספק ספיקא כגון שנתגרשה אמו מבעלה הראשון ספק קרוב לו ספק קרוב לה ומת בתוך שלשה חדשים ונשאת לכהן תוך שלשה חדשים וילדה את זה ספק שהוא בן תשעה לראשון וכשר ואפילו היתה מגורשת שהרי קודם לגט נתעברה או אפילו אחר הגט והוא ישראל ולא כהן וספק בן שבעה לאחרון ובנו של כהן הוא והרי הוא ספק חלל הרי ספק ספיקא שמא אינו בנו של כהן ואת"ל בנו שמא לא היתה אמו גרושה אלא אלמנה ולהכי קרי לה עיסה שיש בה עירובי ספיקות הרבה כעיסה זו שהיא בלוסה והא דאמרינן לקמן שנטמע בה ספק חלל היינו פירושה כל שנטמעו בה ספק עירובי חלל: נטמע. נתערב: איזוהי אלמנת עיסה. שהעידו עליה שהיא כשרה: כל שאין. בעירובי ספקותיה לא ספק ממזרות ולא ספק נתינות ולא ספק עבדי מלכים אלא ספק חלל לבדו מש"ה נקט עבדי מלכים משום עבדי שלמה ו) שהיו עשירים ובעלי זרוע ונשאו להם בנות ישראל וכגון זרעו של הורדוס שהי' עבד לבית חשמונאי וגברה ידו ומלך:

תוספות

דמי דהא מודה דהכא ליכא אלא שהיא אומר שבא עליה דפשיטא שלא היה מזנב אחריה לאורבה שלא תזנה ובין לרב ובין לשמואל אסור הוא בבת ישראל דשתוקי דקאמר לשמואל היינו דאסור בבת ישראל כולהו לישני דבפרק בתרא דקדושין ולישנא דבדוקי נמי קשה טפי דמשמע דאפילו ע"י בדיקת האם לא מיתכשר אלא לר"ג אבל לרבי יהושע לא והכא אמר דהא קא מודה וכשר לכ"ע ושמא יש לחלק דבא דהתם היינו שפעם אחת בא עליה אבל מודה דהכא דקאמר מיניה היינו שבא עליה ביום הרבה והיה רגיל אצלה תמיד וכדאמרינן רוב בעילות הלך אחר הבעל: **חדא** דקא מודה. וללישנא קמא דיבמות דלא דיימא מעלמא וליכא דאמרי דאפילו דיימא מעלמא כיון דקא מודה מבתריה דידיה שדינן ליה: **חדא** דקא מודה. מלינן לפרש דאיירי לענין לאוסרה על הארוס וה"ה אלא דקא מודה הלכך אינה נאסרת עליו ועוד הא אמר רב יהודה כו' לא קאמר ועוד אפילו לא מודה דאם אינו מודה פשיטא דנאסרת עליו אלא כלומר אפילו כי ליכא טעמא דמודה כגון לאביי דס"פ אלמנה מדלפקרה נפשה לגבי ארוס מפקרה נפשה נמי לגבי עלמא אפ"ה אינה נאסרת עליו משום דנאמנת כר"ג. כן פי' לנו ר"י ואי אפשר להעמידה דלפי דבריו אם כן הא דאמר אביי מדלפקרה נפשה היינו בשלא בדקו את אמו וזה אינו דהא פלוגתא דרב ושמואל קאי דמוקמי בקדושין מאי שתוקי בדוקי ולמאי דגרסינן בקדושין ארוסה שעיברה לא קשה מידי על כן צריך לפרש דהכא לא איירי לאוסרה עליו אלא לענין להכשיר את הולד והשתא הוי ועוד כפשוטו ועוד דאפילו לא יודה ולאו דוקא דקאמר דלאו מיניה דהא לא מכשיר ר"ג כיון דהוי ברי וברי כדאמר ברפ"ב אלא כגון שמת או דליתיה קמן דלישייליה והא דחשיב ליה בסמוך דיעבד לפי שלא היה יכול הולד להינשא לבת ישראל ואפילו לממזרת אסור דמדאורייתא כשר הוא דהאי הוי כדיעבד הלכה כר"ג]: (מן ד"ה ההוא ארוס ע"כ היה חסר מהתוספות):

אלמנת עיסה. פירש בקונטרס שני פירושין ושניהם דחוקים דהא אמרינן לקמן איזו היא אלמנת עיסה כל שנטמע בה ספק חלל ז) ומה טימוע שייך במה שנישאת לספק חלל ועוד דאין לשון עיסה נופל על אדם אחד אלא על משפחה שייך לשון עיסה כדאמרינן (קדושין דף סט:) כל הארצות עיסה לארץ ישראל וא"י עיסה לבבל ובתוספתא תניא מפני מה אמרו עיסה פסולה מפני ספיקי חללין ומה ספיקי חללין שייך לאלו הפירושין ונראה לר"י ולריב"א דעיסה קורא המשפחה שנטמע בהם ספק חלל אחד או הרבה ספיקי חללים ולהכי חשיב ליה לקמן ספק ספיקא דכל אחד מבני המשפחה ספק אם הוא אותו ספק שנתערב בהן אם לאו ולקמן גרסינן איזהו עיסה כל שנטמע בה כו' ולא גרסינן אלמנת והכי איתא בירושלמי ואפילו גרסינן אלמנת כל שנטמע בה קאי אעיסה ואם תאמר דבפרק עשרה יוחסין (שם דף עה.) משמע דאפילו מאן דמכשר אלמנת עיסה מודה בבת דפסולה גבי הא דאמר רב חסדא הכל מודים באלמנת עיסה שפסולה לכהונה כו' ולאפוקי מהני תנאי דתנן העיד רבי יהושע כו' ומה לי אלמנה מה לי בת דבת נמי הוי ספק ספיקא כמו באלמנה וי"ל דבת העיסה אין לה חזקה דכשרות ואע"ג דבעלמא מקילין בספק ספיקא הכא מעלה עשו ביוחסין כי היכי דמצריך לקמן תרי רובי להכשיר אף על גב דבעלמא סגי בחד רובא: **דרבי** יהושע אדר"י לא קשיא. והשתא לא מצי לשנויי דבודקת ונישאת כדמשני לעיל כיון דהשתא אוקימנא באומרת שמא: **תנו** רבנן איזו היא אלמנת עיסה. קשה לרבינו תם על גרסת הספרים דגרסי אלמנת עיסה דאם כן אית ליה לרבי יוסי דאלמנת עיסה כשרה דהא מכשר לקמן שתוק ממזר וכל שכן דמכשר באלמנת עיסה כדמוכח הסוגיא ובפרק עשרה יוחסין (ג"ז שם) אמר בהדיא דלרבי יוסי אלמנת עיסה פסולה לכך מוחק רבינו תם אלמנת וגריס איזוהי עיסה ולענין בת קתני וקאי אהאי דתנא בשילהי עדיות העיסה נאמנת לטהר ולטמא לרחק ולקרב לאסור ולהתיר וה"פ נאמנת לטהר עצמה בנויחה או בשתיקה למר כדאית ליה ולמר כדאית ליה לטמא ולטהר שייך לענין ממזרות ונתינות כדתנן (קדושין דף עב:) ממזרים ונתינים עתידין ליטהר לרחק ולקרב שייך אחללות כדתנן הכהנים שומעים לכם לרחק ולא לקרב וכן לקמן (דף מ.) וריחקום בני משפחה ולאסור ולהתיר שייך אעבדים והא דפריך בפ"ב (לקמן דף כח:) טמאה וטהורה ס"ד התם דכייל כל פסולי בחד לישנא הוה ליה למיתני משפחה זו כשרה וזו פסולה אבל אממזרות ונתינות לחודא שייך שפיר לשון טומאה וטהרה ונאמנת נקט משום לטהר לקרב ולהתיר אף על גב דלטמא ולרחק ולאסור בנויחה או בשתיקה לא שייך נאמנות ועלה קתני בברייתא דהכא איזו היא עיסה שנאמנת בנויחה או בשתיקה לטהר את הבת כל שאין בה כו' והכי משמע בתוספתא דקתני נאמנת עיסה לטהר ולטמא לאסור ולהתיר לרחק ולקרב ובאלמנת עיסה לא נגעו והשתא לא קשה דרבי יוסי אדרבי יוסי דהא דאכשר רבי יוסי בשתוק ממזר אגוף העיסה קאי להכשיר את הבת אבל במקום שמזכיר אלמנת עיסה להכשיר דוקא אלמנה ולא הבת כדמוכח בקדושין (דף עה.) ושם ודאי פוסל רבי יוסי אפילו את האלמנה כדמוכח נמי בקדושין ולדברי ר"ת משמע בירושלמי דקתני איזהו עיסה כל שאין בה לא ממזר ולא נתין ולא עבדי מלכים רבי מאיר אומר כל שאין בה אחד מכל אלו בתה כשרה אלמא דבכשרות דבת מיירי ולא באלמנה ומיהו קשה לרשב"א כיון דהך ברייתא קיימא לפרושי ההיא דסוף עדיות אם כן רבי מאיר דסבר דחלל בין נוח בין שתק כשר א"כ היכי מפרש הא דקתני לרחק ואור"י הא דמכשר ר"מ חלל שותק הני מילי כשאחרי כן שואלין ממנו אם הוא חלל אם לאו ונוח אבל אם לעולם שותק פשיטא דפסול והא דקתני דנאמנת לרחק אם לעולם שותק:

לא

מסורת הש"ס

א) [לעיל יג:], ב) [ע' תוס' יבמות קטו: ד"ה וכן הוין ותוס' ב"מ ע. ד"ה אתא ותוס' לקמן פה: ד"ה ועוד], ג) [נ"ל לרבה], ד) קדושין עה. עדיות פרק ח מ"ג, ה) [תוספתא קדושין פ"ה], ו) [יבמות כח:], ז) [וגם על חלל עצמו אין שייך לשון טימוע].

הגהות מהר"ב רנשבורג

אן גמ' א"ל אביי ובהא כי לא מודה מי מכשיר ר"ג. עיין ב"מ ע ע"א תד"ה אתא מריה וכו':

ליקוטי רש"י

אלמנת עיסה. בכתובות (דף יד.) מפרש אלמנת ספק חלל שהיא מעורבת בספקות בעלה היה ספק והיא באה מכחו דהויא לה ספק ספיקא [קידושין עה.].

עין משפט נר מצוה

פו א ב מיי' פט"ו מהל' איסורי ביאה הלכה יא ופי"ח הלכה יג יד סמג לאוין קטז טוש"ע אה"ע סימן ו סעיף יז [וברב אלפס עוד ביבמות פ"ז דף כ"ז]:
פז ג ד ה מיי' פי"ט שם הלכה ט טור אה"ע סימן ו וש"ע אה"ע סימן ג סעיף ה:

תוספות רי"ד

אין מינאי הוא אר"י למאי ניחוש לה חדא דהא קא מודי ותו הא אר"י אמר שמואל הל' כר"ג פי' דכי אומרת מאיש פלוני וכהן הוא נאמנת ואע"ג דאתי ההוא פלוני ומכחיש לה ואמר לא באתי עלי' מעולם היא נאמנת דאי איתא דהיכא דקא מכחיש לה לא מהימנא א"כ אמאי מהימן לה ר"ג מסתמא יבוא אותו פלוני ויאמר אם בא עליה אם לאו אלא ודאי דאע"ג דהוה אתי ומכחיש לה היא נאמנת בין להכשיר בה בין להכשיר בתה והכא נמי אע"ג דאתי ארוס ואמר מעולם לא באתי עליה היא נאמנת להכשיר העובר ולהכשיר עצמה אם תתאלמן אבל לארוס ודאי אסורה דשויא אנפשיה חתיכה דאיסור׳ א"ל אביי ובהא כי לא מודה מי מכשיר ר"ג והא"ל שמואל לר"י שיננא הלכתא כר"ג ואת לא תעביד עובדא [עד] דאיכא רוב כשרים אצלה והכא רוב פסולים אצלה פי' ארוסה הכל פסולין אצלה חוץ מן הארוס וליטעמך תיקשי לך היא גופא הלכה ואת לא תעביד עובדא. אלא הא לכתחלה הא דיעבד והכא נמי כדיעבד דמי פי' אם בא כהן לימלך לב"ד לא שרינן ליה לכתחלה אלא א"כ הוי רוב כשרים אצלה והא דיעבד פי' המורה אם נשאה כהן ולא נמלך לא מפקינן לה מיניה והא נמי כדיעבד דמי שנתעברה ואתה בא לפסול העובר ולאסרה על הארוס אם אין אתה מאמינה הרי אתה מוציאה מבעלה. ואינו נ"ל דאפי' אם מהימנינן לה ה"מ להכשיר גופה ובתה לכהונה אבל על בעלה לא ומשום דשויתה אנפשיה חתיכה דאיסורא אלא נ"ל כך [פירושו] אי לא מהימנינן לה משוינן לבתה ממזרת ואסורה לבא בקהל ולא דמיא לפנויה שנתעברה דאע"ג דפסיל לה לכהונה לא פסיל לה לקהל דאימר לחלל נבעלה ואסורה לכהן ומותרת לישראל אבל הכא אי מספקת לה דנתעברה מאחר הריא לה ממזרת ומה לי לאפוקי מקהל ומה לי לאפקה מבעלה כל היכי דדיעבד דהתם אמרת נאמנת הכא נמי נאמנת ומותרת בתה לכהן כדי שלא תוציאנה מקהל והא דר"י אתיא כשמואל דבפרק אלמנה לכ"ג פליגי רב ושמואל בארוסה שעיברה דרב אמר הולד ממזר ושמואל אמר הולד שתוקי ובפרק עשרה יוחסין מפרשי' אמילתא דשמואל מאי שתוקי בדוקי כאבא שאול דבדקי' לי' לאימי' ואי אמרה מארוסה נתעברה

Accepting the explanation of Rava as authoritative, the Gemara summarizes the views of Rabban Gamliel and R' Yehoshua:[22] הִלְכָּךְ לְרַבָּן גַּמְלִיאֵל – **Therefore, as regards Rabban Gamliel,** אַלִּים לֵיהּ בָּרִי דַּאֲפִילּוּ בְּחַד סְפֵיקָא נַמִּי מַכְשִׁיר – **he considers** a claim of **"certainly" so strong that even with one doubt he rules** her **fit;**[23] וְקִיל לֵיהּ שֶׁמָּא דַּאֲפִילּוּ בִּסְפֵק סְפֵיקָא נַמִּי פָּסִיל – **but he considers** a claim of **"perhaps" so weak that even in** a case of **a double doubt he also rules** her **unfit.** לְרַבִּי יְהוֹשֻׁעַ – **As regards R' Yehoshua,** אַלִּים לֵיהּ חַד סְפֵיקָא דַּאֲפִילּוּ בְּבָרִי נַמִּי פָּסִיל – **he considers** a case of only **one doubt so strong that even** where she claims **"certainly" he rules** her **unfit;** וְקִיל לֵיהּ סְפֵק סְפֵיקָא דַּאֲפִילּוּ בְּשֶׁמָּא נַמִּי מַכְשִׁיר – **but he considers** a case of **a double doubt so weak that even** where she claims **"perhaps" he rules** her **fit.**[24]

The Gemara cites a teaching that elaborates on the Mishnah in *Eduyos* cited above:

תָּנוּ רַבָּנָן – **The Rabbis taught in a Baraisa:** אֵיזוֹהִי אַלְמְנַת עִיסָּה – WHO IS THE WIDOW OF A person of UNCERTAIN STATUS whom R' Yehoshua and R' Yehudah ben Beseira testified may marry a Kohen? כָּל שֶׁאֵין בָּהּ לֹא מִשּׁוּם מַמְזֵרוּת וְלֹא מִשּׁוּם נְתִינוּת וְלֹא מִשּׁוּם עַבְדֵי מְלָכִים – ANYONE WHO, due to her marriage to the man of uncertain status, DOES NOT HAVE concerning her EITHER an uncertainty ON ACCOUNT OF *MAMZERUS,* OR an uncertainty ON ACCOUNT OF *NESINUS,* OR an uncertainty ON ACCOUNT OF THE SLAVES OF KINGS.[25] אָמַר רַבִּי מֵאִיר – SAID R' MEIR:

NOTES

אַלְמְנַת עִיסָּה. *Tosafos* and most other Rishonim, however, take issue with it and explain instead that עִיסָּה refers to a family into which a possible *chalal* had married. (The family is like a dough, being a mixture of different elements.) The case of the widow is as follows: It is known that one of the males in the family is a possible *chalal,* but it is not known which one. Thus, this widow, who was married to one of those males, remains with a compound doubt: She does not know whether her husband was the doubtful *chalal* or not, and even if he was, she does not know whether he was truly a *chalal* or not. According to this interpretation, the term *sefeik sefeika* is understood in its usual sense. The first doubt affecting the widow's status is whether her husband was in fact the possible *chalal.* Beyond this, there is yet another doubt that even if he was the possible *chalal,* he was perhaps not truly a *chalal* after all. *Rashi* too quotes an alternative explanation of אַלְמְנַת עִיסָּה in the name of *R' Yosef Tov Elam,* which, although different from the explanation of *Tosafos* and the Rishonim, also allows for the standard explanation of the term *sefeik sefeika.* See *Pnei Yehoshua* to *Kiddushin* 75a for a suggestion as to why *Rashi* opted for his explanation over the seemingly more straightforward one of the Rishonim.]

22. *Ritva.*

23. That is, her *chazakah* is effective because it supports a claim of "certainly" (*Ritva*).

24. **To summarize** the laws of an unmarried woman who has possibly cohabited with someone who would render her unfit for the Kehunah: There are three cases: that of a woman who went into seclusion with a man unknown to us; that of a woman who is pregnant by a man unknown to us; and that of a captive woman. [The case of a woman who was *violated* by an unidentified assailant will be discussed below, 14b-15a.]:

(a) If she was merely secluded with a man and she claims with certainty that he was fit for her, she is believed according to Rabban Gamliel, because her claim is bolstered by a *chazakah* that she was born fit for a Kohen (*chezkas kashrus*) and by a *migo* that she could have claimed that she did not cohabit. R' Yehoshua essentially agrees with Rabban Gamliel's argument, except that he holds that the Rabbis set a higher standard for genealogical matters [מַעֲלָה עָשׂוּ בְּיוּחֲסִין] and she may therefore not marry a Kohen.

(b) In the case of a pregnant woman, who certainly cohabited and the issue is only with whom, Rabban Gamliel accepts her claim that the man was fit, because it is at least bolstered by her *chezkas kashrus* (there is no *migo* here). [According to some Rishonim there is an additional presumption that she was discriminating about whom she would cohabit with – see above, 13b note 20.] R' Yehoshua, however, holds that her claim is not accepted. Although the Gemara accepts the view of Rabban Gamliel in both of these cases, according to Shmuel if most of the men available to her were unfit, we cannot accept her claim initially; but if she did marry a Kohen, we would not mandate a divorce.

(c) If she was held captive by idolaters, everyone agrees that in all cases we must assume that she was violated by one of them and is therefore disqualified from marrying a Kohen.

25. I.e. the descendants of the slaves of kings (see next paragraph). Each of these men – a *mamzer,* a *nasin* and a descendant of the slaves of kings – with his cohabitation renders a woman unfit to marry a Kohen. The Baraisa teaches that in their testimony permitting "a widow of a person of uncertain status," R' Yehoshua and R' Yehudah ben Beseira were not referring to widows of uncertain *mamzerim, nesinim* or descendants of slaves of kings. Rather, they referred *only* to the widow of an uncertain *chalal.*

The Baraisa mentions "slaves of kings" (rather than simply "slaves") because due to their wealth and power, the slaves of King Solomon were able to intermarry with Jewish families. ["The children of the slaves of Solomon" are mentioned several times in Scripture (*Ezra* 2:58, *Nechemiah* 7:60 and 11:3) grouped together with the unfit *nesinim.*] Alternatively, "slaves of kings" refers to the descendants of King Herod, who was originally a slave to the Hashmonean dynasty before seizing the throne from them [as recounted in *Bava Basra* 3b] (see *Rashi* and *Shitah LaRan*). [The Baraisa apparently follows the opinion that a child born from the union of a Jewish woman and a slave is a *mamzer* (see *Rashi* to *Yevamos* 16b ד״ה מתרמוד).] Cf. *Meiri.*

אין מינאי אמר רב יוסף למאי ניחוש לה חדא דהא קא מודה ועוד הא [ה] אמר רב יהודה אמר שמואל הלכה כרבן גמליאל [א] אמר ליה אביי [ג] ובהא כי לא מודה מכשר רבן גמליאל והאמר ליה שמואל לרב יהודה שיננא [א] הלכה כר"ג ואת לא תעביד עובדא עד דאיכא רוב כשרין אצלה והכא רוב פסולין אצלה וליטעמיך תקשי לך היא גופא הלכה ואת לא תעביד עובדא אלא מאי אית לך למימר [ב] הא לכתחלה הא דיעבד והא נמי כדיעבד דמי רמי ליה אביי [ג] לרבא ומי אמר רבי יהושע אינה נאמנת ורמינהו [ד] העיד ר' יהושע ורבי יהודה בן בתירא [ג] על אלמנת עיסה שהיא כשרה לכהונה א"ל הכי השתא התם אשה נישאת בודקת ונישאת הכא אשה מזנה בודקת ומזנה אמר רבא אדרבי יהושע אדרבי יהושע קשיא דרבן גמליאל אדרבן גמליאל לא קשיא והא קתני סיפא אמר להן רבן גמליאל קבלנו עדותכם [ד] אבל מה נעשה שהרי גזר רבן יוחנן בן זכאי שלא להושיב בית דין על כך שהכהנים שומעין לכם לרחק אבל לא לקרב אלא אמר רבא דרבן גמליאל אדרבן גמליאל לא קשיא התם ברי הכא שמא דר' יהושע אדר' יהושע נמי לא קשיא התם חד ספיקא הכא תרי ספיקי הלכך לרבן גמליאל אלים ליה ברי דאפילו בחד ספיקא נמי מכשיר וקיל ליה שמא דאפילו בספק ספיקא נמי פסיל לרבי יהושע אלים ליה חד ספיקא דאפילו בברי נמי פסיל וקיל ליה ספק ספיקא דאפילו בשמא נמי מכשיר תנו רבנן [ו] איזוהי אלמנת עיסה [ה] כל שאין בה לא משום ממזרות ולא משום נתינות ולא משום עבדי מלכים אמר רבי מאיר שמעתי

רש"י

אין מינאי. אמת ממני הוא: **ובהא כי לא מודי כו'.** דקא אמרת ועוד: ארוסה הכל פסולין אצלה חוץ מן הארוס: **הא לכתחלה.** אם בא כהן לימלך לבית דין לא שרינן ליה לכונסה אא"כ היו רוב כשרים אצלה: **דיעבד.** אם נשאה כהן ולא נמלך לא מפקינן לה מיניה: **והא נמי כדיעבד דמי.** שנתעברה ואתה בא לפסול העובר ולאוסרה על הארוס דאם אין אתה מאמינה הרי אתה מוציאה מבעלה: **מי אמר רבי יהושע אינה נאמנת.** אלמא לא מוקמינן לה אחזקה: **עיסה.** לשון ספק: **על אלמנת עיסה.** שהיא בלא מכה ספק חלל כדלקמן שנטמע בה ספק חלל כגון שזרק בעל אמו הראשון לה גט ספק קרוב לו ספק קרוב לה ומת ונמצאת זו ספק גרושה ספק אלמנה ונשאה כהן והוליד ממנה בן וזהו ספק חלל והעיד ר"י על אלמנתו של זה שהיא כשרה אלמא מוקמינן לה אחזקה ואמרינן אל תפסילנה לזו מספק כלומ' שמא בעלה חלל היה: **בודקת ונישאת.** וי"ל שבדקה אחר אותן גירושין והוגד לה שקרוב לו היו ולא נתגרשה כלל ואלמנה היתה וכשרה לכהן: **בודקת ומזנה.** בתמיה: **דרבן גמליאל אדרבן גמליאל לא קשיא.** בתמיה דלא חיישת לתרוייהו: **הא קתני סיפא.** דהסיא אמר להן כו': **קבלנו עדותכם.** אלמנה אתם לנו שכך שמעתם: **על כך.** להתירה לכהונה דודאי אסורה: **שהכהנים שומעין לכם.** אם תאמרו אסורה: **אבל לא לקרב.** אם תאמרו מותרת: **התם ברי.** מתניתין היא אומרת ברי לי שלכשר נבעלתי: **הכא.** גבי אלמנת עיסה כי היכי דלדידן מספקא לן לדידה נמי מספקא לה וליכא למימר בה ברי ושמא ברי עדיף: **חד ספיקא.** מתניתין חד ספיקא היא ספק נבעלה לכשר ספק נבעלה לפסול שהרי לא בא זה לפנינו ואילו בא שמא היינו מכירים בו שהוא פסול: **הכא.** גבי אלמנת עיסה: **תרי ספיקי.** אמו של ספק חלל זה בה נולד הספק והיא עצמה לא נאסרה אלא מספק וזו שבאה מחמת בנה קרי לה ספק ספיקא ומדברי רבי יוסף טוב עלם מלאתי [אלמנת עיסה] אשה שהיה בעלה ספק ספיקא כגון שנתגרשה אמו מבעלה הראשון ספק קרוב לו ספק קרוב לה ומת בתוך שלשה חדשים ונשאת לכהן תוך שלשה חדשים וילדה את זה ספק שהוא בן תשעה לראשון וכשר ואפילו היתה מגורשת שהרי קודם לגט נתעברה או אפילו אחר הגט והוא ישראל ולא כהן וספק בן שבעה לאחרון ובנו של כהן הוא והרי הוא ספק חלל הרי ספק ספיקא שמא אינו בנו של כהן ואת"ל בנו שמא לא היתה אמו גרושה אלא אלמנה ולהכי קרי לה עיסה שיש בה עירובי ספיקות הרבה כעיסה זו שהיא בלוסה והא דאמרינן לקמן כל שנטמע בה ספק חלל היינו פירושה כל שנטמעו בה ספק עירובי חלל: **נטמע.** נתערב: **איזוהי אלמנת עיסה.** שהעידו עליה שהיא כשרה: **כל שאין.** בעירובי ספקותיה לא ספק ממזרות ולא ספק נתינות ולא ספק עבדי מלכים אלא ספק חלל לבדו מש"ה נקט עבדי מלכים משום עבדי שלמה [י] שהיו עשירים ובעלי זרוע ונשאו להם בנות ישראל וכגון זרעו של הורדוס שהי' עבד לבית חשמונאי וגברה ידו ומלך:

תוספות

דמי להא מודה דהכא אינו אלא שהיה אומר שבא עליה דפשיטא שלא היה מזנה אחריה לאורסה שלא מזנה ובין לרב ובין לשמואל אסור הוא בבת ישראל דשתוקי דקאמר לשמואל היינו לאסור בבת ישראל לכולהו לישני דבפרק בתרא דקדושין ולישנא דדוקי נמי קשה טפי דמשמע דאפילו ע"י בדיקת האם לא מיתכשר אלא לר"ג אבל לרבי יהושע לא והכא אמר דהא קא מודה וכשר לכ"ע ושמא יש לחלק דבא דהתם היינו שפעם אחת בא עליה אבל מודה דהכא דקאמר מיניה היינו שבא עליה ביאות הרבה והיה רגיל אצלה תמיד וכדאמרינן רוב בעילות הלך אחר הבעל: **חדא דקא מודה.** ולישנא קמא דיבמות לא דייק מעלמא ולישנא דלאחרי דאפילו דייתה מעלמא כיון דקא מודה בתריה לדידיה שדינן ליה: **חדא דקא מודה.** מצינן לפרש דאיירי לענין לאוסרה על הארוס וה"פ חדא דקא מודה הלכך אינה נאסרת עליו ועוד הא הלכה כר"ג כו' לא קאמר ועוד אפילו לא מודה דאם אינו מודה פשיטא דנאסרת עליו אלא כלומר אפילו כי ליכא טעמא דמודה כגון לאביי דס"פ אלמנה מדאפקרה נפשה לגבי ארוס מפקרה נפשה נמי לגבי עלמא אפ"ה אינה נאסרת עליו משום דנאמנת כר"ג. כן פי' לנו ר"י ואי אפשר להעמידה לפי דבריו אם כן הא דאמר אביי מדאפקרה נפשה היינו בשלא בדקו את אמו וזה אינו דהא אפלוגתא דרב ושמואל קאי דמוקמי בקדושין מאי שתוקי בדוקי ולמאי דגרסינן בקדושין ארוסה שעיברה לא קשה מידי על כן צריך לפרש דהכא לא איירי לאוסרה עליו אלא לענין להכשיר את הולד והשתא הוי ועוד כפשוטו ועוד דאפילו לא יודה ולא דקאמר דלאו מיניה דהא לא מכשיר ר"ג כיון דהוי ברי וברי דלאמר ברפ"ב אלא כגון שמת או דליתיה קמן לשיילה והא דחשיב ליה בסמוך דיעבד לפי שלא היה יכול הולד להינשא לבת ישראל ואפילו לממזרת אסור דמדאורייתא כשר הוא דהאי הוי כדיעבד הלכה כר"ג]: (מן ד"ה ההוא ארוס ע"כ היה חסר מהתוספות):

אלמנת עיסה. פירש בקונטרס שני פירושין ושניהם דחוקים דהא אמרינן לקמן איזו היא אלמנת עיסה כל שנטמע בה ספק חלל [ז] ומה טימוע שייך במה שנישאת לספק חלל ועוד דאין לשון עיסה נופל על אדם אחד אלא על משפחה שייך לשון עיסה כדאמרינן (קדושין דף סט:) כל הארצות עיסה לארץ ישראל וא"י עיסה לבבל ובתוספתא תניא מפני מה אמרו עיסה פסולה מפני ספיקי חללין ומה ספיקי חללין שייך לאלו הפירושין ונראה לר"י ולריב"א דעיסה קורא המשפחה שנטמע בהם ספק חלל אחד או הרבה ספיקי חללים ולהכי חשיב ליה לקמן ספק ספיקא דכל אחד מבני המשפחה ספק אם הוא אותו ספק שנתערב בהן אם לאו ולקמן גרסינן איזהו עיסה כל שנטמע בה כו' ולא גרסינן אלמנת והכי איתא בירושלמי ואפילו גרסינן אלמנת כל שנטמע בה קאי אעיסה ואם תאמר דבפרק עשרה יוחסין (שם דף עה.) משמע דאפילו מאן דמכשר אלמנת עיסה מודה בבת דפסולה גבי הא דאמר רב חסדא הכל מודים באלמנת עיסה שפסולה לכהונה כו' ולאפוקי מהני תנאי דתנן העיד רבי יהושע כו' ומה לי אלמנה מה לי בת דבת נמי הוי ספק ספיקא כמו באלמנה וי"ל דבת העיסה אין לה חזקה דכשרות ואע"ג דבעלמא מקילין בספק ספיקא הכא מעלה עשו ביוחסין כי היכי דמצריך לקמן תרי רובי להכשיר אף על גב דבעלמא סגי בחד רובא: **דרבי** יהושע אדר"י **לא קשיא.** והשתא לא מצי לשנויי דבודקת ונישאת כדמשני לעיל כיון דהשתא אוקימנא באומרת שמא: **תנו** רבנן **איזו היא אלמנת עיסה.** קשה לרבינו תם על גרסת הספרים דגרסי אלמנת עיסה דאם כן אית ליה לרבי יוסי דאלמנת עיסה כשרה דהא מכשר לקמן שתוק ממזר וכל שכן דמכשר באלמנת עיסה כדמוכח הסוגיא ובפרק עשרה יוחסין (ג"ז שם) אמר בהדיא דלרבי יוסי אלמנת עיסה פסולה לכך מוחק רבינו תם אלמנת וגרים איזוהי עיסה ולענין בת קתני וקאי אהאי דתנא בשילהי עדיות העיסה נאמנת לטהר ולטמא לרחק ולקרב לאסור ולהתיר וה"פ נאמנת לטהר עצמה בגויה או בשתיקה למר כדאית ליה ולמר כדאית ליה לטמא ולטהר שייך לענין ממזרות ונתינות כדתנן (קדושין דף עב:) ממזרים ונתינים עתידין ליטהר לרחק ולקרב שייך אחללות כדתנן הכהנים שומעים לכם לרחק ולא לקרב וכן לקמן (דף כ.) וריחקום בני משפחה ולאסור ולהתיר שייך אעבדים והא דפריך בפ"ב (לקמן דף כח:) טמאה וטהורה ס"ד התם דכייל כל פסולי בחד לישנא הוה ליה למיתני משפחה זו כשרה וזו פסולה אבל אממזרות ונתינות לחודא שייך שפיר לשון טומאה וטהרה ונאמנת נקט משום לטהר לקרב ולהתיר אף על גב דלטמא ולרחק ולאסור בגויה או בשתיקה לא שייך נאמנות ועלה קתני בברייתא דהכא איזו היא עיסה שנאמנת בגויה או בשתיקה לטהר את הבת כל שאין בה כו' והכי משמע בתוספתא דקתני נאמנת עיסה לטהר ולטמא לאסור ולהתיר לרחק ולקרב ובאלמנת עיסה לא נגעו והשתא לא קשה דרבי יוסי אדרבי יוסי דהא דאכשר רבי יוסי בשתוק ממזר אגוף העיסה קאי להכשיר את הבת אבל במקום שמזכיר אלמנת עיסה להכשיר דוקא אלמנה ולא הבת כדמוכח בקדושין (דף עה.) ושם ודאי פוסל רבי יוסי אפילו את האלמנה כדמוכח נמי בקדושין וכדברי ר"ת משמע בירושלמי דקתני איזהו עיסה כל שאין בה לא ממזר ולא נתין ולא עבדי מלכים רבי מאיר אומר כל שאין בה אחד מכל אלו בתה כשרה אלמא דבכשרות דבת מיירי ולא באלמנה ומיהו קשה לרשב"א כיון דהך ברייתא קיימא לפרושי הסיא דסוף עדיות אם כן רבי מאיר דסבר דחלל בין צווח בין שתק כשר א"כ היכי מפרש הא דקתני לרחק ואור"י הא דמכשר ר"מ חלל שותק הני מילי כשאחרי כן שואלין ממנו אם הוא חלל אם לאו וצווח אבל אם לעולם שותק פשיטא דפסול והא דקתני דנאמנת לרחק אם לעולם שותק:

לא

מסורת הש"ס

א) [לעיל יג.], ב) [ע' תוס' יבמות קטו: ד"ה וכן הורו ותוס' ב"מ ע. סד"ה אתא ותוס' לקמן פה: ד"ה ועתי], ג) [צ"ל לרבה], ד) קדושין עה. עדיות פרק ח מ"ג, ה) [תוספתא קדושין פ"ה], ו) [יבמות סח:], ז) [וגם על חלל עצמו אין שייך לשון טימוע].

הגהות מהר"ב רנשבורג

א] גמ' א"ל אביי ובהא כי לא מודה מי מכשיר ר"ג. עיין ב"מ ע ע"א תד"ה אתא מריש וכו'.

ליקוטי רש"י

אלמנת עיסה. בכתובות (דף יד.) מפרש אלמנת ספק חלל שהיתה מעורבת בספקות בעלה היה ספק והיא באה מכחו הוויא לה ספק ספיקא [קידושין עה.].

עין משפט נר מצוה

פו א ב מיי' פט"ו מהל' איסורי ביאה הלכה יא ופי"ח הלכה יג יד סמג לאוין קכא טוש"ע אה"ע סימן ו סעיף יז [וברב אלפס עוד ביבמות פ"ז דף כ"ז]:
פז ג ד ה מיי' פי"ט שם הלכה ט טור אה"ע סימן ו וש"ע אה"ע סימן ג סעיף ה:

תוספות רי"ד

אין מינאי הוא אר"י למאי ניחוש לה חדא דהא קא מודי ותו הא ר"י אמר שמואל הל' כר"ג פי' דכי אומרת מאיש פלוני וכהן הוא נאמנת ואע"ג דאתי ההוא פלוני ומכחיש לה ואמר לא באתי עלי' מעולם היא נאמנת דאי איתא דהיכא דקא מכחיש לה לא מהימנא א"כ אמאי מהימן לה ר"ג מסתמא יבוא אותו פלוני ויאמר אם בא עליה אם לאו אלא ודאי דאע"ג דהוה אתי ומכחיש לה היא נאמנת בין להכשיר בה בין להכשיר בתה והכא נמי אע"ג דאתי ארוס ואמר מעולם לא באתי עליה היא נאמנת להכשיר העובר ולהכשיר עצמה אם תתאלמן אבל לארוס ודאי אסורה דשויא אנפשיה חתיכה דאיסור' **א"ל אביי** ובהא כי לא מודה מי מכשיר ר"ג והא"ל שמואל לר"י שיננא הלכתא כר"ג ואת לא תעביד עובדא [עד] דאיכא רוב כשרים אצלה והכא רוב פסולים אצלה פי' ארוסה הכל פסולין אצלה חוץ מן הארוס וליטעמך תיקשי לך היא גופא הלכה ואת לא תעביד עובדא. אלא הא לכתחלה הא דיעבד והכא נמי כדיעבד דמי פי' אם בא כהן לימלך לב"ד לא שרינן ליה לכתחלה אלא א"כ הוי רוב כשרים אצלה והא דיעבד פי' המורה אם נשאה כהן ולא נמלך לא מפקינן לה מיניה והא נמי כדיעבד דמי שנתעברה ואתה בא לפסול העובר ולאסרה על הארוס אם אין אתה מאמינה הרי אתה מוציאה מבעלה. ואינו נ"ל דאפי' אם מהימנינן לה ה"מ להכשיר גופה ובתה לכהונה אבל על בעלה לא ומשום דשויתה אנפשיה חתיכה דאיסורא אלא נ"ל כך [פירושו] אי לא מהימנינן לה משוינן לבתה ממזרת ואסורה לבא בקהל ולא דמיא לפניה שנתעברה דאע"ג דפסיל לה לכהונה לא פסיל לה לקהל דיאמר לחלל נבעלה ואסורה לכהן ומותרת לישראל אבל הכא אי מספקת לה דנתעברה מאחר הויא לה ממזרת ומה לי לאפוקי מקהל ומה לי לאפקה מבעלה וכי היכי דדיעבד דהתם אמרת שהיא נאמנת הכא נמי נאמנת ומותרת בתה לכהן כדי שלא תוציאנה מקהל והא דר"י אתיא כשמואל דבפרק אלמנה לכ"ג פליגי רב ושמואל בארוסה שעיברה דרב אמר הולד ממזר ושמואל אמר הולד שתוקי ובפרק עשרה יוחסין מפרש' אמילתא דשמואל מאי שתוקי בדוקי כאבא שאול דבדקי' לי' לאימי' ואי אמרה ארוסה נתעברה

in fact follows a woman's *chazakah* to permit her to the Kehunah.[15] — ? —

Rabbah responds:

אָמַר לֵיהּ – He said to [Abaye]: הָכִי הַשְׁתָּא – Now, is this a valid comparison? **הָתָם אִשָּׁה נִישֵּׂאת בּוֹדֶקֶת וְנִישֵּׂאת – There,** we can say that **a woman who marries investigates** her proposed husband's genealogical fitness **and** only then **marries** him.[16] **הָכָא אִשָּׁה מְזַנָּה בּוֹדֶקֶת וּמְזַנָּה** – But **here,** are we to say that **a woman who acts immorally investigates** her partner's fitness **and** only then **acts immorally** with him?

The Gemara analyzes Abaye's question further:

אָמַר רָבָא – Rava said: דְּרַבִּי יְהוֹשֻׁעַ אַדְּרַבִּי יְהוֹשֻׁעַ קַשְׁיָא – Is there a contradiction between [one statement] of R' Yehoshua and [the other statement] of R' Yehoshua דְּרַבָּן גַּמְלִיאֵל אַדְּרַבָּן גַּמְלִיאֵל לֹא קַשְׁיָא – but no contradiction between [one statement] of Rabban Gamliel and [the other statement] of Rabban Gamliel?[17] **וְהָא קָתָנֵי סֵיפָא – For the end** of that very same Mishnah **teaches: אָמַר לָהֶן רַבָּן גַּמְלִיאֵל – RABBAN GAMLIEL SAID TO THEM** [R' Yehoshua and R' Yehudah ben Beseira]: **קִבַּלְנוּ עֵדוּתְכֶם – WE ACCEPT YOUR TESTIMONY,** i.e. you are trustworthy to testify that this is what you heard, **אֲבָל מָה נַּעֲשֶׂה – BUT WHAT CAN WE DO, שֶׁהֲרֵי גָּזַר רַבָּן יוֹחָנָן בֶּן זַכַּאי שֶׁלֹּא לְהוֹשִׁיב בֵּית דִּין עַל כָּךְ – SINCE RABBAN YOCHANAN BEN ZAKKAI HAS DECREED NOT TO CONVENE A COURT FOR THIS PURPOSE** [i.e. to declare such a doubtful case legitimate], **שֶׁהַכֹּהֲנִים שׁוֹמְעִין לָכֶם לְרַחֵק – BECAUSE THE KOHANIM OBEY [THE COURT] TO DISTANCE** women whom it rules prohibited **אֲבָל לֹא לְקָרֵב – BUT NOT TO BRING CLOSE** those it rules permitted?[18] We thus see that Rabban Gamliel rules a woman of uncertain status to be prohibited to marry a Kohen, whereas in our Mishnah he permits such a union.[19] — ? —

Rava therefore presents a different reconciliation between our Mishnah and the Mishnah in *Eduyos*:

אֶלָּא אָמַר רָבָא – Rather, Rava said: דְּרַבָּן גַּמְלִיאֵל אַדְּרַבָּן גַּמְלִיאֵל לֹא קַשְׁיָא – [The one ruling] of Rabban Gamliel and [the other ruling] of Rabban Gamliel do not contradict each other, **הָתָם בָּרִי הָכָא שֶׁמָּא** – because **there,** in the case of our Mishnah, the woman claims **"certainly,"** whereas **here,** in the Mishnah in *Eduyos,* her claim is only **"perhaps."**[20] **דְּרַבִּי יְהוֹשֻׁעַ אַדְּרַבִּי יְהוֹשֻׁעַ נַמִּי לֹא קַשְׁיָא** – And **[the one ruling] of R' Yehoshua and [the other ruling] of R' Yehoshua also do not contradict** each other, **הָתָם חַד סְפֵיקָא הָכָא תְּרֵי סְפֵיקֵי** – because **there,** in the case of our Mishnah, there is only **one doubt,** whereas **here,** in the Mishnah in *Eduyos,* there are **two doubts.**[21]

NOTES

closer to him or closer to her. If it was closer to him, she is not divorced; if it was closer to her she is divorced (see Mishnah, *Gittin* 78a). The man then died, leaving it uncertain whether his wife was a divorcee or a widow. The woman subsequently married a Kohen and bore a child from him; the child's status is therefore also unclear, for if his mother was a divorcee he is a *chalal.* That child grew up, married and died, leaving us in doubt whether his wife is the widow of a *chalal* and forbidden to a Kohen, or the widow of a legitimate Kohen and thus permitted to a Kohen. R' Yehoshua and R' Yehudah ben Beseira testified that the widow is permitted.

15. Presumably R' Yehoshua's reasoning is that since the woman was fit for a Kohen before her marriage to the possible *chalal,* and it is uncertain whether the marriage caused her to lose that fitness, we maintain her *chezkas kashrus* and continue to rule her fit. This stands in contradiction to R' Yehoshua's ruling in our Mishnah, where he does not rely on a woman's *chezkas kashrus* to permit her to a Kohen (*Rashi*).

16. We can therefore assume that this woman investigated the circumstances of her mother-in-law's divorce and discovered that the *get* had landed closer to her mother-in-law's husband. Her mother-in-law was therefore not a divorcee but rather a widow, and was fit to marry a Kohen (see *Rashi*).

[We have explained that when the Gemara says, "A woman who marries investigates and marries," it is referring to the widow of the uncertain *chalal.* That this is the Gemara's intention is implied by *Tosafos* ד"ה דרבי יהושע and stated openly by *Ritva* and *Tos. HaRosh.* (The woman is afraid that if he is a *chalal* and she marries him and he dies, she would be forbidden to a Kohen – *Ayeles HaShachar.*) *Rashash,* however, apparently understood the Gemara to be referring to the woman to whom the *get* was thrown, i.e. the mother-in-law, and *Chazon Ish* (*Even HaEzer* 1:4) maintains that this is in fact *Rashi's* understanding.]

17. I.e. why do you concern yourself only with the contradiction in R' Yehoshua's rulings but not with a similar contradiction in the rulings of Rabban Gamliel? (*Rashi*).

18. [Presumably Rabban Yochanan ben Zakkai was concerned that if the Sanhedrin were to issue a ruling only to have it ignored by the Kohanim, the Sanhedrin's reputation would be damaged.]

19. In the Mishnah in *Eduyos* [he does not rely on the *chezkas kashrus* of the woman (albeit because of Rabban Yochanan ben Zakkai's decree), and] the woman is forbidden to a Kohen (see *Rashi* ד"ה על כך). If so, in the case of our Mishnah Rabban Gamliel should likewise not rely on the woman's *chezkas kashrus.*

20. In our Mishnah the woman claims with certainty that the man with whom she cohabited was fit for her. [Together with her *chazakah* she is therefore believed.] But the widow of the doubtful *chalal* is as uncertain as to her late husband's status as is the court (see *Rashi*). Without a claim of "certainly," even Rabban Gamliel does not follow her *chazakah.*

[Although we said above that the widow investigated the circumstances of her mother-in-law's divorce before marrying, this was Rabbah's opinion. Rava, however, maintains that the widow does not perform such an investigation, and her claim is therefore one of "perhaps" (see *Tosafos* ד"ה דרבי יהושע and *Ritva;* cf. *Chazon Ish* cited in note 16).]

21. In our Mishnah's case the sole doubt is whether the woman cohabited with someone fit or unfit. In the case in *Eduyos,* however, the mother of the deceased Kohen was herself only possibly prohibited. And this widow of the son is a second doubt (*Rashi*).

The Gemara below will call this situation a סָפֵק סְפֵיקָא, *sefeik sefeika* (doubt of a doubt), a term usually used when the situation under consideration is subject to two separate uncertainties (such as the double doubt on 9a, see note 5 there). However, according to *Rashi's* explanation of אַלְמְנַת עִיסָה, "the widow of a possible *chalal,*" only one doubt exists, namely, whether her husband was a *chalal* or not. *Rashi* therefore explains that the term double doubt in our context means a secondary doubt (rather than a double doubt); i.e. the doubt about the widow's fitness for the Kehunah derives from the doubt about the status of her husband (as explained in note 14).

[Since this is not a classical *sefeik sefeika,* the question arises as to why it should be treated leniently. The reason apparently is that the doubt concerning her fitness should actually be treated leniently in any event because she has a *chezkas kashrus;* i.e. since she was fit for a Kohen before her marriage to the possible *chalal,* and it is uncertain whether she has lost that fitness, the law of *chazakah* should dictate that she is still fit. The reason *chazakah* is not applied in such situations (e.g. where a woman cohabited with someone and it is not known whether the man was genealogically fit or unfit) is only because the Rabbis set a higher standard for genealogical matters [מַעֲלָה עָשׂוּ בְּיוּחֲסִין]. Accordingly, the Rabbis were strict only where the uncertainty was initiated in the woman under question herself, such as in our Mishnah, where the uncertainty is with whom *she* cohabited. (We cannot say that the uncertainty was born in the *man* with whom she had relations, because that man never came before us, and if he had, we might have recognized his status.) In such a case her *chazakah* is viewed as "weakened" (at least with respect to the higher standard demanded in genealogical matters). This is in contrast to the case of the widow of the possible *chalal,* where the doubt was born outside of her, i.e. in her mother-in-law, and was merely transferred to her through her husband. The widow's *chazakah* is therefore considered strong, and we rely on it to permit her to a Kohen (see *Shitah Mekubetzes* ד"ה אלמנת עיסה).]

[The above explanation follows *Rashi's* understanding of the case of

אין מינאי אמר רב יוסף למאי ניחוש לה חדא דהא קא מודה ועוד הא ח) אמר רב יהודה אמר שמואל הלכה כרבן גמליאל אמר ליה אביי ט) ובהא כי לא מודה מכשר רבן גמליאל והאמר ליה שמואל לרב יהודה שיננא א הלכה כר"ג ואת לא תעביד עובדא עד דאיכא רוב כשרין אצלה והכא רוב פסולין אצלה וליטעמיך תקשי לך היא גופא הלכה ואת לא תעביד עובדא אלא מאי אית לך למימר ב הא לכתחלה הא דיעבד והא נמי כדיעבד דמי רמי ליה אביי ג לרבא ומי אמר רבי יהושע אינה נאמנת ורמינהו ד) העיד ר' יהושע ורבי יהודה בן בתירא ג על אלמנת עיסה שהיא כשרה לכהונה א"ל הכי השתא התם אשה נישאת בודקת ונישאת הכא אשה מזנה בודקת ומזנה אמר רבא אדרבי יהושע אדרבי יהושע קשיא דרבן גמליאל אדרבן גמליאל לא קשיא והא קתני סיפא אמר להן רבן גמליאל קבלנו עדותכם ד אבל מה נעשה שהרי גזר רבן יוחנן בן זכאי שלא להושיב בית דין על כך שהכהנים שומעין לכם לרחק אבל לא לקרב אלא אמר רבא דרבן גמליאל אדרבן גמליאל לא קשיא התם ברי הכא שמא דר' יהושע אדר' יהושע נמי לא קשיא התם חד ספיקא הכא תרי ספיקי הלכך לרבן גמליאל אלים ליה ברי דאפילו בחד ספיקא נמי מכשיר וקיל ליה שמא דאפילו בספק ספיקא נמי פסיל לרבי יהושע אלים ליה חד ספיקא דאפילו בברי נמי פסיל וקיל ליה ספק ספיקא דאפילו בשמא נמי מכשיר תנו רבנן ט) איזוהי אלמנת עיסה ה כל שאין בה לא משום ממזרות ולא משום נתינות ולא משום עבדי מלכים אמר רבי מאיר שמעתי

רש"י

אין מינאי. אלמא ממני הוא: **ובהא כי לא מודי כו'.** דקא אמרת ועוד: ארוסה הכל פסולין אצלה חוץ מן הארוס: **הא לכתחלה.** אם בא כהן לימלך לבית דין לא שרינן ליה לכונסה אא"כ היו רוב כשרים אצלה: **דיעבד.** אם נשאה כהן ולא נמלך לא מפקינן לה מיניה: **והא נמי כדיעבד דמי.** שנתעברה ואתה בא לפסול העובר ולאוסרה על הארוס דאם אין אתה מאמינה הרי אתה מוציאה מבעלה: **מי אמר רבי יהושע אינה נאמנת.** אלמא לא מוקמינן לה אחזקה: **עיסה.** לשון ספק: **על אלמנת עיסה.** שהיא באה מכח ספק חלל כדלקמן שנטמע בה ספק חלל כגון שזרק בעל אמו הראשון לה גט ספק קרוב לו ספק קרוב לה ומת ונמצאת זו ספק גרושה ספק אלמנה ונשאת לכהן והוליד ממנה בן וזהו ספק חלל והעיד ר"י על אלמנתו של זה שהיא כשרה אלמא מוקמינן לה אחזקה ואמרינן אל תפסילנה לזו מספק כלומר שמא בעלה חלל היה: **בודקת ונישאת.** וי"ל שבדקה אחר אותן גירושין והוגד לה שקרוב לו היו ולא נתגרשה כלל ואלמנה היתה וכשרה לכהן: **בודקת ומזנה.** בתמיה: **דרבן גמליאל אדרבן גמליאל לא קשיא.** בתמיה דלא חיישת לתרוייהו: **הא קתני סיפא.** דהסיפא אמר להן כו': **קבלנו עדותכם.** נאמנים אתם לנו שכך שמעתם: **על כך.** להתירה לכהונה דודאי אסורה: **שהכהנים שומעין לכם.** אם תאמרו אסורה: **אבל לא לקרב.** אם תאמרו מותרת: **התם ברי.** מתניתין היא אומרת ברי לי שלכשר נבעלתי: **הכא.** גבי אלמנת עיסה כי היכי דלדידן מספקא לן לדידה נמי מספקא לה וליכא למימר בה ברי ושמא ברי עדיף: **חד ספיקא.** מתניתין חד ספיקא היא ספק נבעלה לכשר ספק נבעלה לפסול שהרי לא בא זה לפנינו ואילו בא שמא היינו מכירים בו שהוא פסול: **הכא.** גבי אלמנת עיסה: **תרי ספיקי.** אמו של ספק חלל זה בה נולד הספק והיא עצמה לא נאסרה אלא מספק וזו שבאה מחמת בנה קרי לה ספק ספיקא ומדברי רבי יוסף טוב עלם מלאתי [אלמנת עיסה] אשה שהיה בעלה ספק ספיקא כגון שנתגרשה אמו מבעלה הראשון ספק קרוב לו ספק קרוב לה ומת ונשאת בתוך שלשה חדשים ונשאת לכהן תוך שלשה חדשים וילדה את זה ספק שהוא בן תשעה לראשון וכשר ואפילו היתה מגורשת שהרי קודם לגט נתעברה או אפילו אחר הגט והוא ישראל ולא כהן וספק בן שבעה לאחרון ובנו של כהן הוא והרי הוא ספק חלל הרי ספק ספיקא שמא אינו בנו של כהן ואת"ל בנו הוא שמא לא היתה אמו גרושה אלא אלמנה ולהכי קרי לה עיסה שיש בה עירובי ספיקות הרבה כעיסה זו שהיא בלוסה והא דאמרינן לקמן כל שנטמע בה ספק חלל היינו פירושה כל שנטמעו בה ספק עירובי חלל: **נטמע.** נתערב: **איזוהי אלמנת עיסה.** שהעידו עליה שהיא כשרה: **כל שאין.** בעירובי ספקותיה לא ספק ממזרות ולא ספק נתינות ולא ספק עבדי מלכים אלא ספק חלל לבדו מש"ה נקט עבדי מלכים משום עבדי שלמה י) שהיו עשירים ובעלי זרוע ונשאו להם בנות ישראל וכגון זרעו של הורדוס שהי' עבד לבית חשמונאי וגברה ידו ומלך: שמעתי

תוספות

דמי דהא מודה דהכא אינו אלא שהיא אומר שבא עליה דפשיטא שלא היה מזנה אחריה לאורחה שלא מזנה ובין לרב ובין לשמואל שבא עליה אומר הוא בבת ישראל דשתוקי דקאמר לשמואל היינו דאסור בבת ישראל לכהונה לישני דבפרק בתרא דקדושין ולישנא דדוקי נמי קשה טפי דמשמע דאפילו ע"י בדיקת האם לא מיתכשר אלא לר"ג אבל לרבי יהושע לא והכא אמר דהא קא מודה וכשר לר"ג ושמא יש לחלק דהא דהתם היינו שפעם אחת בא עליה אבל מודה דהכא דקאמר מיניה היינו שבא עליה בילות הרבה והיה רגיל אצלה תמיד וכדאמרינן רוב בעילות הלך אחר הבעל: **חדא** דקא מודה. ולישנא קמא דיבמות דלא דייקא מעלמא ולאיכא דאמרי דאפילו דייקא מעלמא כיון דקא מודה בתריה דידיה שדינן ליה: **חדא** דקא מודה. מצינן לפרש דאיירי לענין לאוסרה על הארוס וה"פ חדא דקא מודה הלכך אינה נאסרת עליו ועוד הא רב יהודה כו' לא קאמר ועוד אפילו לא מודה דאם אינו מודה פשיטא דנאסרת עליו אלא כלומר אפילו כי ליכא טעמא דמודה כגון לאביי דס"פ אלמנה מדאפקרה נפשה לגבי ארוס מפקרה נפשה נמי לגבי עלמא אפ"ה אינה נאסרת עליו משום דנאמנת כר"ג. כן פי' לנו ר"י ואי אפשר להעמידה לפי דבריו אם כן הא דאמר אביי מדאפקרה נפשה היינו בשלא בדקו את אמו וזה אינו דהא אפלוגתא דרב ושמואל קאי דמוקמי בקדושין מאי שתוקי בדוקי ולמאי דגרסינן בקדושין ארוסה שעיברה לא קשה מידי על כן צריך לפרש דהכא לא איירי לאוסרה עליו אלא לענין להכשיר את הולד והשתא הוי ועוד כפשוטו ועוד דאפילו לא יודה ולאו דקאמר דלאו מיניה דבהא לא מכשיר ר"ג כיון דהוי ברי וברי כדאמר ברפ"ב אלא כגון שמת או דליתיה קמן דלישייליה והא דחשיב ליה בסמוך דיעבד לפי שלא היה יכול הולד להינשא לבת ישראל ואפילו לממזרת אסור דמדאורייתא כשר הוא דהאי הוי כדיעבד הלכה כר"ג]: (מן ד"ה ההוא ארוס ע"כ היה חסר מהתוספות): **אלמנת** עיסה. פירש בקונטרס שני פירושין ושניהם דחוקים דהא אמרינן לקמן איזו היא אלמנת עיסה כל שנטמע בה ספק חלל ז) ומה טימוע שייך במה שנישאת לספק חלל ועוד דאין לשון עיסה נופל על אדם אחד אלא על משפחה שייך לשון עיסה כדאמרינן (קדושין דף סט:) כל הארצות עיסה לארץ ישראל וא"י עיסה לבבל ובתוספתא תניא מפני מה אמרו עיסה פסולה מפני ספיקי חללין ומה ספיקי חללין שייך לאלו הפירושין ונראה לר"י ולריב"א דעיסה קורא המשפחה שנטמע בהם ספק חלל אחד או הרבה ספיקי חללים ולהכי חשיב ליה לקמן ספק ספיקא דכל אחד מבני המשפחה ספק אם הוא אותו ספק שנתערב בהן אם לאו ולקמן גרסינן איזהו עיסה כל שנטמע בה כו' ולא גרסינן אלמנת והכי איתא בירושלמי ואפילו גרסינן אלמנת כל שנטמע בה קאי אעיסה ואם תאמר דבפרק עשרה יוחסין (שם דף עה.) משמע דאפילו מאן דמכשר אלמנת עיסה מודה בבת דפסולה גבי הא דאמר רב חסדא הכל מודים באלמנת עיסה שפסולה לכהונה כו' ולאפוקי מהני תנאי דתנן העיד רבי יהושע כו' ומה לי אלמנה מה לי בת דבת נמי הוי ספק ספיקא כמו באלמנה וי"ל דבת העיסה אין לה חזקה דכשרות ואע"ג דבעלמא מקילין בספק ספיקא הכא מעלה עשו ביוחסין כי היכי דמצריך לקמן תרי רובי להכשיר אף על גב דבעלמא סגי בחד רובא: **דרבי** יהושע אדר"י לא קשיא. והשתא לא מצי לשנויי דבודקת ונישאת כדמשני לעיל כיון דהשתא אוקימנא באומרת שמא: **תנו** רבנן איזו היא אלמנת עיסה. קשה לרבינו תם על גרסת הספרים דגרסי אלמנת עיסה דאם כן אית ליה לרבי יוסי דאלמנת עיסה כשרה דהא מכשר לקמן שתוק ממזר וכל שכן דמכשר באלמנת עיסה כדמוכח הסוגיא ובפרק עשרה יוחסין (ג"ז שם) אמר בהדיא דלרבי יוסי אלמנת עיסה פסולה לכך מוחק רבינו תם אלמנת וגרים איזוהי עיסה ולענין בת קתני וקאי אהאי דתנא בשילהי עדיות העיסה נאמנת לטהר ולטמא לרחק ולקרב לאסור ולהתיר וה"פ נאמנת לטהר עצמה בנויחה או בשתיקה למר כדאית ליה ולמר כדאית ליה לטמא ולטהר שייך לענין ממזרות ונתינות כדתנן (קדושין דף עב:) ממזרים ונתינים עתידין ליטהר לרחק ולקרב שייך אחללות כדתנן הכהנים שומעים לכם לרחק ולא לקרב וכן לקמן (דף ס.) וריחקום בני משפחה ולאסור ולהתיר שייך אעבדים והא דפריך בפ"ב (לקמן דף כח:) טמאה וטהורה ס"ד התם דכייל כל פסולי בחד לישנא הוה ליה למיתני משפחה זו כשרה וזו פסולה אבל אממזרות ונתינות לחודא שייך שפיר לשון טומאה וטהרה ונאמנת נקט משום לטהר לקרב ולהתיר אף על גב דלטמא ולרחק ולאסור בנויחה או בשתיקה לא שייך נאמנות ועלה קתני בברייתא דהכא איזו היא עיסה שנאמנת בנויחה או בשתיקה לטהר את הבת כל שאין בה כו' והכי משמע בתוספתא דקתני נאמנת עיסה לטהר ולטמא לאסור ולהתיר לרחק ולקרב ובאלמנת עיסה לא נגעו והשתא לא קשה דרבי יוסי אדרבי יוסי דהא דאכשר רבי יוסי בשתוק ממזר אגוף העיסה קאי להכשיר את הבת אבל במקום שמזכיר אלמנת עיסה להכשיר דוקא אלמנה ולא הבת כדמוכח בקדושין (דף עה.) ושם ודאי פוסל רבי יוסי אפילו את האלמנה כדמוכח נמי בקדושין וכדברי ר"ת משמע בירושלמי דקתני איזהו עיסה כל שאין בה לא ממזר ולא נתין ולא עבדי מלכים רבי מאיר אומר כל שאין בה אחד מכל אלו בתה כשרה אלמא דבכשרות דבת מיירי ולא באלמנה ומיהו קשה לרשב"א כיון דהך ברייתא קיימא לפרושי ההיא דסוף עדיות אם כן רבי מאיר דסבר דחלל בין נושא בין שתק כשר א"כ היכי מפרש הא דקתני לרחק ולאור"י הא דמכשר ר"מ חלל שותק הני מילי כשאמרי כן שואלין ממנו אם הוא חלל אם לאו ולעולם אבל אם לעולם שותק פשיטא דפסול והא דקתני דנאמנת לרחק אם לעולם שותק:

לא

מסורת הש"ס

א) [לעיל יב:], ב) [ע' תוס' יבמות קטו: ד"ה וכן הדין ותוס' ב"מ ע. סד"ה אתא ותוס' לקמן פה: ד"ה ועוד], ג) [נ"ל לרבה], ד) קדושין עה. עדיות פרק ח מ"ג, ה) [תוספתא קדושין פ"ה], ו) [יבמות טז.], ז) [וגם על חלל עצמו אין שייך לשון טימוע].

הגהות מהר"ב רנשבורג

אן גמ' א"ל אביי ובהא כי לא מודה מי מכשיר ר"ג. עיין ב"מ ע ע"א תד"ה אתא מריה וכו'.

ליקוטי רש"י

אלמנת עיסה. בכתובות (דף יד.) מפרש אלמנת ספק חלל שהיתה מעורבת בספקות בעלה היה ספק והיא באה מכחו דהויא לה ספק ספיקא [קידושין עה.].

עין משפט נר מצוה

פו א ב מיי' פט"ו מהל' איסורי ביאה הלכה יא ופי"ח הלכה יג יד סמג לאוין קכח טוש"ע אה"ע סימן ו סעיף יז [וכרב אלפס עוד ביבמות פ"ז דף כ"ו]:

פז ג ד ה מיי' פי"ט שם הלכה טו טור אה"ע סימן ו וש"ע אה"ע סימן ג סעיף ה:

תוספות רי"ד

אין מינאי הוא אר"י למאי ניחוש לה חדא דהא קא מודי ותו הא אר"י אמר שמואל הל' כר"ג פי' דכי אומרת מאיש פלוני והכהן הוא נאמנת ואע"ג דאתי ההוא פלוני ומכחיש לה ואמר לא באתי עלי' מעולם היא נאמנת דאי איתא דהיכא דקא מכחיש לה לא מהימנא א"כ אמאי מהימן לה ר"ג מסתמא יבוא אותו פלוני ויאמר אם בא עליה אם לאו אלא ודאי אע"ג דההוא אתי ומכחיש לה היא נאמנת בין להכשיר בה בין להכשיר בתה והכא נמי אע"ג דאתי ארוס ואמר מעולם לא באתי עליה היא נאמנת להכשיר העובר ולהכשיר עצמה אם תאלמן אבל לארוס ודאי אסורה דשויא אנפשיה חתיכה דאיסורא: א"ל אביי ובהא כי לא מודה מי מכשיר ר"ג והא"ל שמואל לר"י שיננא הלכתא כר"ג ואת לא תעביד עובדא [עד] דאיכא רוב כשרים אצלה והכא רוב פסולים אצלה פי' ארוסה הכל פסולין אצלה חוץ מן הארוס וליטעמיך תיקשי לך היא גופא הלכה ואת לא תעביד עובדא. אלא הא לכתחלה הא דיעבד והכא נמי כדיעבד דמי פי' אם בא כהן לימלך לב"ד לא שרינן ליה לכתחלה אלא א"כ הוי רוב כשרים אצלה והא דיעבד פי' המורה אם נשאה כהן ולא נמלך לא מפקינן לה מיניה והא נמי כדיעבד דמי שנתעברה ואתה בא לפסול העובר ולאסרה על הארוס אם אין אתה מאמינה הרי אתה מוציאה מבעלה. ואינו נ"ל דאפי' אם מהימנינן לה ה"מ להכשיר גופה ובתה לכהונה אבל על בעלה לא ומשום דשויתה אנפשיה חתיכה דאיסורא אלא נ"ל כך [פירושו] אי לא מהימנינן לה משוינן לבתה ממזרת ואסורה לבא בקהל ולא דמיא לפנויה שנתעברה דאע"ג דפסיל לה לכהונה לא פסיל לה לקהל דאימר לחלל נבעלה ואסורה לכהן ומותרת לישראל אבל הכא אי מספקת לה דנתעברה מאחר הויא לה ממזרת ומה לי לאפוקי מקהל ומה לי לאפקה מבעלה וכי היכי דדיעבד דהתם אמרת נאמנת הכא נמי נאמנת ומותרת בתה לכהן כדי שלא תרציאנה מקהל והא דר"י אתיא כשמואל דבפרק אלמנה לכ"ג פליגי רב ושמואל בארוסה שעיברה דרב אמר הולד ממזר ושמואל אמר הולד שתוקי ובפרק עשרה יוחסין מפרשי' אמילתא דשמואל מאי שתוקי בדוקי כבא שאול (קדושין דף עה.) דבדקי' לי' לאימ' ואי אמרה מארוסה נתעברה

אִין מִינַּאי – "True, she is pregnant **from me.**"[1]

Rav Yosef issues a ruling:

אָמַר רַב יוֹסֵף – **Rav Yosef said:** לְמַאי נֵיחוּשׁ לָהּ – **For what should we be concerned,** i.e. why should she or the child be forbidden? חֲדָא דְּהָא קָא מוֹדֶה – **First of all, he admits** to the act. וְעוֹד הָא אָמַר רַב יְהוּדָה אָמַר שְׁמוּאֵל הֲלָכָה כְּרַבָּן גַּמְלִיאֵל – **And furthermore,** even had he not admitted anything, **Rav Yehudah has said in the name of Shmuel that the law is in accordance with Rabban Gamliel.**[2]

Another Amora questions Rav Yosef's second reason:

אָמַר לֵיהּ אַבַּיֵי – **Abaye said to him:** וּבְהָא כִּי לֹא מוֹדֶה מַכְשַׁר רַבָּן גַּמְלִיאֵל – **And in this** case **had [the husband] not admitted would Rabban Gamliel indeed rule** her **fit?**[3] וְהָאָמַר לֵיהּ שְׁמוּאֵל לְרַב יְהוּדָה – **Why, Shmuel said to Rav Yehudah:** שִׁינָּנָא – **Sharp one!**[4] הֲלָכָה כְּרַבָּן גַּמְלִיאֵל – **The law is in accordance with Rabban Gamliel,** וְאַתְּ לֹא תַעֲבִיד עוּבְדָא עַד דְּאִיכָּא רוֹב כְּשֵׁרִין אֶצְלָהּ – **but you should not act upon it**[5] **except where most** men **are fit for her.**[6] וְהָכָא רוֹב פְּסוּלִין אֶצְלָהּ – **But here, most** men **are unfit for her.**[7] Therefore, had the husband not admitted that he was the father, we could not render her or the child fit for a Kohen based on Rabban Gamliel's ruling.[8] – ? –

Rav Yosef counters:

וְלִיטַעֲמֵיךְ תִּקְשֵׁי לָךְ הִיא גוּפָא – **And according to your reasoning, you should find difficult [that statement]** of Shmuel **itself:** הֲלָכָה וְאַתְּ לֹא תַעֲבִיד עוּבְדָא – First he states, **"The law is** in accordance with Rabban Gamliel," and then he concludes, **"but you should not act upon it"!**[9] אֶלָּא מַאי אִית לָךְ לְמֵימַר – **Rather, what must you say?** הָא לְכַתְּחִלָּה – That **this** second statement of Shmuel applies **initially;** i.e. if a Kohen comes to inquire if he may marry such a woman [or the daughter], we do not permit him to do so unless most of the available men were fit for her, הָא דִיעֲבַד – whereas **this** first statement of Shmuel refers to **after the fact;** i.e. if a Kohen already married her [or her daughter], without having first inquired as to the law, we do not force him to divorce her.[10] וְהָא נַמִּי כְּדִיעֲבַד דָּמֵי – **Accordingly,** we can say that **this** case of the betrothed woman **is also like** an **after-the-fact** situation.[11]

The Gemara analyzes R' Yehoshua's view in our Mishnah:

רָמֵי לֵיהּ אַבַּיֵי (לרבא) [לְרַבָּה] – **Abaye posed a contradiction to Rabbah:**[12] וּמִי אָמַר רַבִּי יְהוֹשֻׁעַ אֵינָהּ נֶאֱמֶנֶת – **Did R' Yehoshua** really **say that [the woman] is not believed,** meaning that her *chazakah* of fitness to the Kehunah is not followed? וּרְמִינְהוּ – **But contrast [our Mishnah with the following one]:**[13] הֵעִיד רַבִּי יְהוֹשֻׁעַ וְרַבִּי יְהוּדָה בֶּן בְּתֵירָא – **R' YEHOSHUA AND R' YEHUDAH BEN BESEIRA TESTIFIED** עַל אַלְמְנַת עִיסָּה שֶׁהִיא כְּשֵׁרָה לִכְהוּנָּה – **REGARDING THE WIDOW OF A** person of **UNCERTAIN STATUS,** i.e. the widow of an uncertain *chalal,* **THAT SHE IS PERMITTED TO MARRY INTO THE KEHUNAH.**[14] Thus, we see that R' Yehoshua

---

NOTES

1. I.e. I was intimate with her and therefore presume that she is pregnant from me (*Ramban, Rashba;* see also *Tosafos* ד״ה ההוא; cf. *Ri Migash,* cited by *Shitah Mekubetzes; Ritva*).

At issue was both the woman's status and that of her child (see *Rashi* ד״ה והא). Do we assume that she is indeed pregnant from him, in which case although she sinned by cohabiting during *erusin* she would be permitted to remain with her husband and the child permitted to marry into the congregation, or do we worry that she committed adultery, in which case she would be forbidden to her husband and the child would be a possible *mamzer*? [A definite *mamzer* is forbidden to marry into the congregation by Biblical law. One who is only possibly a *mamzer* is prohibited by Rabbinic enactment.]

2. Rabban Gamliel in our Mishnah rules that we believe a pregnant unmarried woman to say that the man with whom she cohabited was not one who would render her ineligible to marry a Kohen. By extension, it follows that in the present case Rabban Gamliel would believe the betrothed bride to say that the man with whom she had relations was the groom (since he is the only man whose cohabitation would not cause her to become forbidden).

[In saying, "And furthermore . . .," Rav Yosef meant that even had the groom been silent about whether he had lived with her (*Ritva*), or had admitted to having lived with her but expressed doubt as to whether he had completed the marital act enough to have impregnated her (*Maharsha,* in explanation of *Rashi;* cf. *Rashash*), she would still be believed. However, had the groom *contradicted* her claim, asserting that he had *not* lived with her, she would *not* be believed, because the Gemara states on 16a that Rabban Gamliel rules the woman to be believed only where her claim is not contradicted by the husband (*Tosafos* [ד״ה חדא [ב׳, *Ramban* et al., *Rosh* §29; cf. *Tos. Rid; Beur HaGra, Even HaEzer* 4:67). See also 12b note 20.]

3. Rav Yosef indicated that even had the husband not admitted we would still rule her and the child fit, based on Rabban Gamliel's ruling in our Mishnah that a woman is believed to say with whom she cohabited. Abaye challenges this assumption.

4. See above, 12b note 17.

5. Literally: do a deed.

6. Such as in the case of a single woman who was secluded or became pregnant in a mostly Jewish city, where most men are permitted to her.

7. Since she is betrothed, every man in the world is prohibited to her except for her husband (*Rashi*).

8. Abaye was under the impression that Shmuel's statement meant that although the law is in accordance with Rabban Gamliel, one should not act upon it except in a case in which most men are fit for her, because *Rabban Gamliel himself* ruled that she is believed only in such a case. Rav Yosef proceeds to prove to Abaye that this understanding of Shmuel's statement is incorrect (*Ramban, Rashba*).

9. According to your understanding, Shmuel should have said, "The law is in accordance with Rabban Gamliel, *but even he ruled so* only where most men are fit for her." From the fact that he said, "but *you should not act upon it* except where most men are fit for her," it is implied that Rabban Gamliel himself issued his ruling even where most men are unfit for her. Why, then, did Shmuel instruct Rav Yehudah, after telling him that the halachah follows Rabban Gamliel, not to rule leniently unless the majority was fit for her? (*Ramban, Rashba*).

10. Thus, according to Rav Yosef, Shmuel holds that Rabban Gamliel stated his law in all cases — even if most of the men around were not fit for her. Initially [לְכַתְּחִלָּה], however, one should not rely on this ruling and allow a Kohen to marry unless most of the men with whom she could have cohabited were fit for her (*Ramban; Rashba*).

11. Since she is a married woman, if we do not believe her claim that her husband is the father of the child, the child will become disqualified to marry even a non-Kohen, because it will be suspected of being a *mamzer;* moreover, it will not even be permitted to marry another *mamzer,* since it might actually not be a *mamzer.* This condition of not being able to marry anyone is equivalent to the after-the-fact [*bedi'avad*] situation of forcing someone who is already married to get divorced. This is in addition to the fact that the mother will be prohibited to stay with her husband [because she will be a suspected adulteress], which is a true *bedi'avad* situation (*Rashi,* as explained by *Ritva;* cf. explanation of *Rashi* suggested by *Ramban*).

12. [Emendation of "Rava" to "Rabbah" based on *Mesoras HaShas.*]

13. *Eduyos* 8:3.

14. A *chalal* is a man born from a union between a Kohen and a woman forbidden specifically to a Kohen, e.g. a divorcee. Although there are no marriage restrictions on the *chalal,* the law is that any woman with whom he cohabits is rendered forbidden to marry a Kohen (see *Yevamos* 69a, cited by *Rashi* below, 14b ד״ה חלל נמי). Therefore, should a *chalal* marry and then die, his widow would be forbidden to a Kohen.

The Mishnah in *Eduyos* cited here discusses the widow of a man whose status as a *chalal* is in doubt. [The word עִיסָּה literally means *dough,* but it is translated by *Rashi* in this context as a *doubt;* i.e. she is mixed up in a situation involving uncertainties, like ingredients in a dough (*Shitah Mekubetzes* ד״ה אלמנת עיסה).] For example, a man threw a bill of divorce to his wife and it was unclear whether the bill landed

written:[33] ***It shall be for him and for his offspring after him a covenant of eternal priesthood,*** from which we derive: מִי שֶׁזַּרְעוֹ מְיוּחָס אַחֲרָיו – **One whose offspring is pedigreed after him,** such a man's offspring can take part in the priesthood; יָצָא זֶה שֶׁאֵין זַרְעוֹ מְיוּחָס אַחֲרָיו – **excluded is this** child **who is not pedigreed after [his father]** – i.e. we do not know who his father is.[34]

The Gemara cites a related incident:

הַהוּא אָרוּס וַאֲרוּסָתוֹ דְּאָתוּ לְקַמֵּיה דְּרַב יוֹסֵף – **There was this** betrothed **groom and his** pregnant **bride who came before Rav Yosef.**[35] הִיא אָמְרָה מִינֵּיה – **She said,** "I am pregnant **from him,"** וְהוּא אָמַר – **and he** agreed and **said,**

NOTES

33. *Numbers* 25:13.

34. Thus R' Yochanan maintains that when the Baraisa states that the mother's testimony in regard to her child is not accepted and the child is a *shetuki,* it is not referring to the case discussed previously in the Baraisa, where a woman was discovered to be pregnant and the court is inquiring as to the child's status as far as marrying a Kohen. In such a case the mother is indeed believed to declare the child fit. Rather, the Baraisa refers to a case such as Shmuel's, where ten Kohanim were standing and one of them separated and cohabited with a woman. The Baraisa rules that we do not believe the woman to say which Kohen it was, and the child is therefore silenced from the law of the Kehunah (*Shitah Mekubetzes* ד״ה לא שתוקי וכשר, in explanation of *Rashi* ד״ה לא; cf. *Rashba*).

The restriction against eating *terumah* applies regardless of the child's gender; thus we can say that when the Baraisa states that "in regard to the woman's testimony as it regards her *daughter,* the child is a *shetuki,*" it means that we silence the girl from eating *terumah* (*Rivash* §229 ד״ה הראשונה; *Rashash*).

[The Rishonim (*Tosafos, Rashba*) note, based on *Yevamos* 100b, that this law – requiring a Kohen to know who his father is – is only of Rabbinic origin (and the verse is thus only a Scriptural allusion [אַסְמַכְתָּא]). At the Biblical level there is no such requirement.]

35. As we have already learned, the Rabbis prohibited a husband and wife to cohabit if they have only been betrothed through *erusin;* rather, they are required to wait until after *chuppah* (i.e. *nisuin*). In this case, however, a betrothed woman [*arusah*] showed up in court pregnant.

או לחורבה ואמרו לה מה טיבו של איש זה כהן הוא ובן אחי אבא הוא רבן גמליאל ור"א אומרים נאמנת רבי יהושע אומר לא מפיה אנו חיין אלא הרי זו בחזקת בעולה לנתין ולממזר עד שתביא ראיה לדבריה בשלמא לזעירי היינו דקתני תרתי לסתר או לחורבה אלא לרב אסי דאמר נבעלה תרתי למה לי חדא קתני לסתר דחורבה והא לסתר או לחורבה קתני חדא לחורבה דמתא וחדא לחורבה דדברא וצריכי דאי אשמעינן חורבה דמתא בהא קמכשר רבן גמליאל משום דרוב כשרים אצלה אבל לחורבה דדברא דרוב פסולין אצלה אימא מודה ליה לרבי יהושע ואי אשמעינן בההיא בההיא קאמר רבי יהושע אבל בהא אימא מודה לר"ג צריכא מיתיבי א) זו עדות שהאשה כשרה לה ורבי יהושע אומר אינה נאמנת אמר להם ר' יהושע אי אתם מודים א בשבויה שנשבית ויש לה עדים שנשבית והיא אומרת טהורה אני שאינה נאמנת אמרו לו אבל ומה הפרש יש בין זו לזו לזו יש עדים ולזו אין לה עדים אמר להם אף לזו יש עדים שהרי כריסה בין שיניה אמרו לו רוב עובדי כוכבים פרוצים בעריות הם אמר להן ג) אין אפוטרופוס לעריות בד"א בעדות אשה בגופה אבל עדות אשה בבתה דברי הכל הולד שתוקי מאי קאמר להו ומאי קמהדרי ליה הכי קאמרי ליה השבתנו על המעוברת מה תשיבנו על המדברת אמר להם מדברת היינו שבויה אמרו לו שאני שבויה דרוב עובדי כוכבים פרוצים בעריות הם אמר להם הא נמי כיון דאיסתתר אין אפוטרופוס לעריות קתני מיהת תרתי מדברת ומעוברת תיובתא דרב אסי תיובתא ותיפוק ליה דהתם רוב פסולין אצלה והכא רוב כשרין אצלה מסייע ליה לרבי יהושע בן לוי דאמר רבי יהושע בן לוי לדברי המכשיר מכשיר אפילו ברוב פסולין לדברי הפוסל פוסל אפילו ברוב כשרים א"ר יוחנן ב לדברי המכשיר בה מכשיר בבתה לדברי הפוסל בה פוסל בבתה ורבי אלעזר אומר לדברי המכשיר בה פוסל בבתה אמר רבה מ"ט דר"א בשלמא איהי אית לה חזקה דכשרות בתה לית לה חזקה דכשרות איתיביה ר"א לרבי יוחנן בד"א בעדות אשה בגופה אבל עדות אשה בבתה דברי הכל הולד שתוקי מאי לאו שתוקי ופסול לא שתוקי וכשר ומי איכא שתוקי כשר אין כדשמואל דאמר שמואל ד) עשרה כהנים עומדים ופירש אחד מהם ובעל הולד שתוקי מאי שתוקי אילימא שמשתיקין אותו מנכסי אביו פשיטא ומי ידעינן אבוה מנו אלא שמשתיקין אותו מדין כהונה דכתיב א) והיתה לו ולזרעו אחריו ברית כהונת עולם מי שזרעו מיוחס אחריו יצא זה שאין זרעו מיוחס אחריו ה ההוא ארוס וארוסתו דאתו לקמיה דרב יוסף היא אמרה מיניה והוא אמר אין

רש"י

לחורבה. סתמא לבעולה שהוא מקום לזנות: חורבה דמתא. סתם בעילתה מאחד מבני העיר ואיכא למימר בעיר שרובה ישראל כשרים קאמר: דדברא. ספק אחד מסוף העולם בא לכאן ורוב העולם עובדי כוכבים הם ופסולים אשה בביאתם לכהונה כדאמר ביבמות (דף מה.) ובקדושין (דף עה:) יאלו עובד כוכבים ועבד שאין לו אלמנות וגירושין בה: זו עדות שהאשה. עלמה כשרה לומר לכשר נבעלתי: אינה נאמנת. לינשא לכהן: אמרו לו אבל. הן כמו אבל שרה אשתך (בראשית יז) דמתרגמינן בקושטא: ומה הפרש בין זו לזו. ר' יהושע קאמר לה: לזו יש עדים. שנבעלה דכיון דנשבית לבין העובדי כוכבים והם פרוצים בעריות כולנו עדים שנבעלה: ולזו אין עדים. שנבעלה שלא ראוה אלא מדברת ומיגו דאי בעיא אמרה לא נבעלתי כי אמרה נמי לכשר נבעלתי מהימנא: אף לזו. כלומר אף כאן יש אחת שיש לה עדים ואתם חולקים עלי בהיותה מעוברת: אמרו ליה כו'. לקמיה מפרש מאי קא מהדרי ליה על מאי דקאמר להו: אין אפוטרופוס כו'. לקמן מפרש: בד"א. דנאמנת לר"ג: בעדות אשה בגופה. כלומר להכשיר את עלמה לכהונה דלא מחזקינן לה בנבעלה לפסול: מאי קאמר להו כו'. כלומר מאי קאמר להו איהו דקא מהדרי ליה איהו רוב עובדי כוכבים פרוצים בעריות כלום תשובה היא זו על מה שאמר להם אף לזו יש לה עדים אין לך פרוץ גדול מזה דקחזינן דנתעברה ממנו: השבתנו על המעוברת. תשובה גמורה ונלחת: מדברת היינו שבויה. מה מדברת אין לה עדים אף שבויה אין לה עדים בבעילה ואתם מחזיקים אותה כנבעלה: פרוצים בעריות. והא ודאי נבעלה: אין אפוטרופוס לעריות. אין אתם יכולים להיות לה אפוטרופוס לומר לא נבעלה: ותיפוק ליה וכו'. לרבי יהושע פריך נהי נמי דאין אפוטרופוס לעריות תיפוק ליה דלא דמי לשבויה דהתם רוב פסולין כו': מכשיר אפי' ברוב פסולים. דאמרינן אוקמה אחזקה ועל רוב פסולים שהיו מכשירים אותה הביא הוא להם ראיה מן השבויה: אית לה חזקה דכשרות. וי"ל אשה זו בחזקת כשרות עומדת ומספק אתה בא לפסולה אל תפסילנה מספק: לא שתוקי וכשר. כלומר שתוקי הוא במקצת שאם כהן היה הבועל והעובר יהיה זכר משתקין אותו מדין כהונה כדלקמן אבל כשר הוא ליוחסין שאם נקבה היא תינשא לכהונה ואם זכר הוא בנו ולאמנתו כשרות לכהונה: ופירש אחד מהן. ואין ידוע איזה הוא: הולד שתוקי. ואע"פ שברור לנו שמכהן כשר בא והאי שתוקי על כרחך כשר ליוחסין ואם נקבה היא ראויה לכהן וקרי ליה שתוקי: מדין כהונה. שלא יעבוד עבודה ולא יאכל תרומה: מיוחס אחריו. שאנו יודעין מי אביו:

תוספות

השבתנו על המעוברת. פי' לדידן ומזנה ולא דמיא לשבויה סברא תינח מעוברת אבל מדברת אפילו לפי דבריך יש הפרש דלזו יש עדים ולזו אין עדים ואיכא מיגו אמר להם מדברת היינו שבויה וכמו ששבויה אין נאמנת לומר לא נבעלתי ה"נ מדברת כדמסיק לפי שאין אפוטרופוס לעריות ומיהו פי' זה לא יתכן למאי דפרישית לעיל דלר' יהושע נאמנת לומר לא נבעלתי ופר"י בדוחק מדברת היינו שבויה דכמו א) ששבויה בחזקת בעולה כך מדברת בחזקת בעולה לענין שאם אמרה לכשר נבעלתי שאינה נאמנת במיגו לפי שיראה לומר לא נבעלתי ולהכי אהני דאין אפוטרופוס לעריות דלא חשבינן ליה מיגו: מסייע ליה לר' יהושע בן לוי. הקשה ר"ת אכתי תיפוק ליה דהתם בשבויה כל פסולים והכא בחורבה דדברא רוב ותירץ דרוב ככל וליכא למימר במדברת דליכא אלא רוב איכא למימר סמוך מיעוטא לחזקה ואיתרע לה רובא דאפילו אית להו סמוך מיעוטא לחזקה לר"ג ור' יהושע מ"מ לא הוי אלא פלגא ופלגא ודין הוא שתאסר מספק דספק איסורא לחומרא ולא דמי לתינוק שנמצא בצד העיסה בפרק עשרה יוחסין (קדושין דף פ. ושם) דמטהרין מטעם סמוך מיעוטא לחזקה דאם אמרו ספק טומאה לטהר יאמרו ספק איסור להתיר כדאמרינן פרק כיסוי הדם (חולין דף פו:): מכשיר אפילו ברוב פסולים. והא דקאמרינן בפ' עשרה יוחסין (קדושין עד. ושם) גבי אבא שאול היה קורא לשתוקי בדוקי ומפרש בגמרא שבודקין אמו ואומרת לכשר נבעלתי ופריך כמאן כר"ג תנינא חדא זימנא היתה מעוברת כו' פי' והוה ליה למתני וכן אמר אבא שאול וכן פי' שם בקונטרס ומשני דאבא שאול עדיפא מר"ג דאי מהתם הוה אמינא ברוב כשרים אלא כו' אע"ג דאמרי' הכא דר"ג מכשיר אפילו ברוב פסולין אבא שאול קאי אמתני' וממתני' לא משמע מידי דאיירי ברוב פסולים והא דפריך התם לעיל למאי דהוה בעי למימר דאבא שאול אתא להכשיר בבתה ניחא למ"ד לדברי המכשיר בה פוסל בבתה אבל למ"ד מכשיר בבתה מאי איכא למימר התם פריך שפיר דאפי' לזעירי לשון המשנה דקתני מה טיבו של עובר זה משמע דאתא להכשיר בבתה: פשיטא מי ידעינן אבוה מנו. הכא לא בעי לשנויי לא צריכא דאי תפס כדמשני בפרק עשרה יוחסין (שם דף עה. ושם) גבי ארוסה שעיברה דהתם רגלים לדבר דמארוס נתעברה ואיכא למיתלי ביה טפי מבאינש דעלמא: בעינן זרעו מיוחס אחריו. והא דאמר בהחולץ (יבמות דף לז.) ראשון ראוי להיות כ"ג גבי ספק בן תשע לראשון בפרק נושאין על האנוסה (שם דף ק:) פריך לה ומשני זרעו מיוחס אחריו דרבנן וקרא אסמכתא בעלמא הוא וכי גזור רבנן בזנות בנישואין לא גזור:

ההוא ארוס וארוסתו. והא דאמר בעשרה יוחסין (קדושין דף עה.) איתמר הבא על ארוסתו בבית חמיו רב אמר הולד ממזר ושמואל אמר הולד שתוקי כשלא בדקו את אמו דאי בשבדקו קשיא דשמואל אדשמואל דהכא אמר שמואל דנאמנת דהלכה כרבן גמליאל דנאמנת והתם קאמר איפוך שמואל אמר הולד ממזר וכן משמע דבמסקנא משני התם לעולם לא תיפוך כו' ומפרש מאי שתוקי שבודקין את אמו ואומרת לכשר נבעלתי ואם תאמר אכתי לשמואל דהתם משמע דוקא בבא על ארוסתו בבית חמיו מהני בדיקה והכא משמע אפילו כי לא מודה אמר שמואל דנאמנת כרבן גמליאל ויש לומר דהא דנקט בא היינו משום רבותא דרב נקטיה דאפילו הכי אמר הולד ממזר אי נמי התם הוא דבעינן בא משום דאיירי בדדיימא מעלמא כדאמר רבא ביבמות בשלהי אלמנה לכהן גדול מסתברא מילתא דרב בדדיימא מעלמא והכא בדלא דיימא מעלמא מיירי ועוד דבכל הספרים גרס בקדושין ארוסה שעיברה וההיא דוקא קאמר שבודקין אבל בבא א"צ בדיקה ומיהו קשה ללישנא קמא ביבמות בסוף פ' אלמנה דפליגי רב ושמואל בבא ומסיק התם אביי דאע"ג דלא דיימא מעלמא פליגי דדלמא מדאפקרה נפשה לגבי ארוס מפקרה נפשה לגבי עלמא הא אמר הכא חדא דקא מודה ומשמע דכשר אפילו לר' יהושע ובא כמודה דמי

עין משפט נר מצוה

פב א מיי' פי"ח מהל' איסורי ביאה הלכה כא סמג לאוין קכא טור ש"ע אה"ע סימן ז ס"ד:

פג ב מיי' פט"ו שם הלכה יא סמג שם טוש"ע שם סי' ד סעיף יח:

פד ג מיי' פ"כ שם הל' ב סמג לאוין קכב טוש"ע שם סימן ג סעיף ט:

פה ד מיי' פט"ו שם הלכה ח טוש"ע שם סימן ד סעיף כו [וברב אלפס עוד ביבמות פ"ו דף כ ע"א]:

תוספות רי"ד

היחיד וה"ק אוסרים על היחיד לימא דלא כר"י פי' דמשים יחיד מחזיק לה כנבעלה פי' מלקין מכות מרדות לאשת איש שנתייחד עם א' אבל אין אוסרין אותה על בעלה בעידי יחוד אלא היכא דקיימא לך מעיקרא בפני שנים ואמר לה אל תסתרי עם איש פלוני אם נסתרה עמו היא סוטה האמורה בתורה והא אסורה לו עד שתתברר במים המאררים אבל בלא קינוי מעיקרא אינה נאסרת לו בסתירה בלבד. מהדר מעלה עשר בירושלמי פי' דלא אסרה ר"י אלא אם היתה פנויה ש"א תנשא לכהן דאמרינן דלמא נבעלה לפסול לו אבל לבעלה לא אסרה ואפי' אם היה בעלה כהן. אר"א ש"ה הלכה בר"ג אריב"ל לדב"י המכשיר מכשיר אפילו ברוב פסולים לדב"י הפוסל פוסל אפי' ברוב כשרים: ההוא ארוס וארוסתו דאתו לקמיה דר"י היא אומרת מיני והוא אומר

מסורת הש"ס

א) תוספתא סוף פרק א, ב) [חולין יא: נדה לג.], ג) [קדושין עב.], ד) יבמות ק.:

תוספות ישנים

א) ולא"ג דמיעוט עובדי כוכבים אין פרוצים מ"מ חשבינן לה ודאי בעולה מן הרוב הפרוצים. ת"י.

תורה אור השלם

א) וְהָיְתָה לּוֹ וּלְזַרְעוֹ אַחֲרָיו בְּרִית כְּהֻנַּת עוֹלָם תַּחַת אֲשֶׁר קִנֵּא לֵאלֹהָיו וַיְכַפֵּר עַל בְּנֵי יִשְׂרָאֵל: [במדבר כה, יג]

ליקוטי רש"י

דברא. שדה [ברכות ג.]. שתוקי. שקורא פלוני אבא ואמו משתקתו [קידושין סט.]. שהרי כריסה בין שיניה. ואינה יכולה לומר לא נבעלתי [לקמן טז.]. הולד שתוקי. וכשר הוא דהא פשיטא לן דבן כהן הבא על הפנויה הוא. מדין כהונה. מלעבוד עבודה ואף על גב דלענין יוחסין ליכא אשה כשר הוא פסול לעבודה. אחריו. שיכיר זרעו שהוא שלו [יבמות ק.].

her; לְדִבְרֵי הַפּוֹסֵל פּוֹסֵל אֲפִילוּ בְּרוֹב כְּשֵׁרִים – **the one who rules her unfit** for the Kehunah [i.e. R' Yehoshua] **rules her unfit even where most** of the available men **are fit** for her.[26]

The Gemara elaborates on our Mishnah:

אָמַר רַבִּי יוֹחָנָן – **R' Yochanan said:** לְדִבְרֵי הַמַּכְשִׁיר בָּהּ מַכְשִׁיר בְּבִתָּהּ – **The one who rules her fit** [Rabban Gamliel and R' Eliezer] **rules her daughter fit** as well; לְדִבְרֵי הַפּוֹסֵל בָּהּ פּוֹסֵל בְּבִתָּהּ – **the one who rules her unfit** [R' Yehoshua] **rules her daughter unfit** as well. וְרַבִּי אֶלְעָזָר אוֹמֵר – **But R' Elazar says:** לְדִבְרֵי הַמַּכְשִׁיר בָּהּ פּוֹסֵל בְּבִתָּהּ – Even **the one who rules her fit rules her daughter unfit.**

The Gemara explains the logic of the latter opinion:

אָמַר רַבָּה – **Rabbah said:** מַאי טַעְמָא דְּרַבִּי אֶלְעָזָר – **What is R' Elazar's reason?** Why is the mother permitted to a Kohen while her daughter is forbidden?[27] בִּשְׁלָמָא אִיהִי אִית לָהּ חֲזָקָה דְּכַשְׁרוּת – Because he reasons: **It is well** that **[the mother]** is fit, for **she has a *chazakah* of fitness;** בִּתָּהּ לֵית לָהּ חֲזָקָה דְּכַשְׁרוּת – **her daughter,** however, **has no *chazakah* of fitness.**[28]

The disputants debate the question:

אֵיתִיבֵיהּ רַבִּי אֶלְעָזָר לְרַבִּי יוֹחָנָן – **R' Elazar challenged R' Yochanan** from the previously cited Baraisa: בַּמֶּה דְּבָרִים אֲמוּרִים – WHEN ARE THESE WORDS STATED? בְּעֵדוּת אִשָּׁה בְּגוּפָהּ – IN REGARD TO THE WOMAN'S TESTIMONY AS IT REGARDS HERSELF; אֲבָל עֵדוּת אִשָּׁה בְּבִתָּהּ דִּבְרֵי הַכֹּל הַוָּלָד שְׁתוּקִי – BUT in regard to THE WOMAN'S TESTIMONY AS IT REGARDS HER DAUGHTER, ALL AGREE THAT THE CHILD IS A *SHETUKI*. מַאי לָאו שְׁתוּקִי וּפָסוּל – Now, **does this not mean** that the child is **a *shetuki* and disqualified** for the Kehunah?

R' Yochanan replies:

לֹא – **No!** שְׁתוּקִי וְכָשֵׁר – It means that the child is **a *shetuki* but is fit** for the Kehunah.[29]

R' Elazar counters:

וּמִי אִיכָּא שְׁתוּקִי כָּשֵׁר – **And is there** such a thing as **a *shetuki* who is fit** for the Kehunah?

R' Yochanan replies:

אִין כִּדְשְׁמוּאֵל – **Yes, as Shmuel** ruled. דְּאָמַר שְׁמוּאֵל – **For Shmuel stated** the following ruling: עֲשָׂרָה כֹּהֲנִים עוֹמְדִים – If **ten** fit **Kohanim are standing** together וּפֵירַשׁ אֶחָד מֵהֶם וּבָעַל – **and one of them separated** from the group **and cohabited** with a woman, and we do not know which Kohen it was, הַוָּלָד שְׁתוּקִי – **the child is a *shetuki*.** מַאי שְׁתוּקִי – Now, **what** does ***shetuki*** mean in this context?[30] אִילֵימָא שֶׁמְּשַׁתְּקִין אוֹתוֹ מִנִּכְסֵי אָבִיו – **If you say** it means **we silence him from the property of his father,** i.e. we prevent him from taking possession of his father's inheritance when his father dies, פְּשִׁיטָא – why, **that is quite obvious,** וּמִי יָדְעִינַן אֲבוּהּ מַנּוּ – **for do we know who his father is?**[31] אֶלָּא שֶׁמְּשַׁתְּקִין אוֹתוֹ מִדִּין כְּהוּנָּה – **Rather,** it means **that we silence him from** taking part in **the law of the Kehunah.**[32] דִּכְתִיב ,,וְהָיְתָה לּוֹ וּלְזַרְעוֹ אַחֲרָיו בְּרִית כְּהֻנַּת עוֹלָם" – **For it is**

NOTES

26. Rabban Gamliel and R' Eliezer rule the woman fit even where most of the men with whom she could have cohabited disqualify her for the Kehunah with their cohabitation [such as where the seclusion occurred in a ruin located in the field], because we preserve her *chazakah* of fitness to the Kehunah. It was regarding this case in which most of the men are unfit that R' Yehoshua brought his proof from the captive woman (*Rashi*).

[Even though there is still a difference between the cases – in that regarding the captive woman *all* of the men with whom she could have cohabited are unfit while in the case of the secluded woman only *most* are – R' Yehoshua's comparison is still valid, because from a halachic standpoint, "most" is like "all" (*Tosafos*).]

[The question arises: How does R' Yehoshua ben Levi know this? Granted that the fact that Rabban Gamliel rules the woman fit for the Kehunah even where most of the men available are unfit can be proven from the Baraisa, from the fact that R' Yehoshua challenged Rabban Gamliel from the case of the captive woman, but how does he know that R' Yehoshua rules her unfit even where most of the men are fit?

Pnei Yehoshua suggests that his source is our Mishnah. R' Yehoshua states there that the woman is presumed to have cohabited with "a *nasin* or a *mamzer.*" Now, *nesinim* and *mamzerim* form the minority of the population (only a Jew can be a *mamzer*) while gentiles form the majority. Why, then, does R' Yehoshua state that we are worried that she cohabited with a *nasin* or a *mamzer,* rather than assuming it was with a gentile? Apparently R' Yehoshua means to indicate that even where the seclusion took place in a Jewish city, where most of the population is fit to marry her, she is still disqualified. Cf. *Beis Yaakov.*]

27. R' Yochanan's logic is easily understood, because if the mother is qualified the daughter is perforce qualified as well (*Ritva;* see next note). But what is R' Elazar's logic?

28. Before the woman was secluded or pregnant she had a *chazakah* of fitness to a Kohen. Now that an uncertainty has arisen, we do not, out of doubt, remove her from that *chazakah* (*Rashi*). But the daughter never had a *chazakah* of fitness, since we were uncertain as to her status from the very moment of her birth. We must therefore consider her unfit out of doubt. R' Yochanan, however, maintains that the *chazakah* of the mother is effective for the daughter [חֶזְקַת הָאֵם מְהַנֵּי לַבַּת] (*Ritva,* see also *Tosafos* to 26b ד״ה אנן; cf. *Maggid Mishneh, Hil. Isurei Biah* 15:12 and *Ran* to *Kiddushin* folio 30b in the pages of *Rif* ד״ה מתני׳ אי זהו שתוקי for a completely different approach to R' Yochanan's view, and see *Beis Shmuel* 4:39, *Shev Shmaatsa* 2:15, and *Kehillos Yaakov* §11).

It should be pointed out that the unfitness of the daughter (if indeed she is unfit) does not stem from the unfitness of the mother, such that if we rule the mother fit the daughter must perforce be ruled fit as well. Rather, the status of the mother and that of the daughter are two independent issues. If the mother is unfit, it is because she had relations with someone forbidden to her. The daughter's invalidity, by contrast, stems from the father: If he was a *nasin* or a *mamzer,* she will be a *nesinah* or a *mamzeress* as well (*Shev Shmaatsa* 4:4). Thus R' Elazar's position that the *chazakah* of the mother is ineffective for the daughter is understandable. R' Yochanan, however, maintains that the mechanics of *chazakah* are such that it *decides,* in a legal sense, the doubt (rather than simply telling us to maintain the status quo). We assume, based on the mother's *chezkas kashrus,* that the mother cohabited with someone fit for her. Once this assumption is made, it follows that the daughter too should be ruled fit, even though she herself does not possess a *chazakah* of her own. See *Chidushei R' Shlomo* §8, end of ד״ה אבל.

[Note that when R' Elazar states that the one who rules her fit rules her daughter unfit, he refers to the child born from *this* union. However should the mother later marry a Kohen, the child born from *that* union *would* be fit, since we already ruled the mother permitted to the Kehunah (*She'eilos U'Teshuvos R' Akiva Eiger, Tinyana,* 111 ד״ה ולכאורה; *Afikei Yam, siman* 27 ד״ה וע״ב; *Chazon Ish, Even HaEzer* 1:12).]

29. That is, it is only a partial *shetuki,* as follows: If the father was a Kohen (see below, note 34, for how this fact could be known) and the child from this union is a boy, we silence him from certain privileges of the Kehunah, for the reason that will be stated below. [Similarly if the child is a girl, she loses the privileges enjoyed by the daughter of a Kohen – see below, note 34.] But regarding the child's marital status, there is no disqualification: If the child is a girl, she may marry a Kohen, and if it is a boy, his daughter or widow may marry a Kohen as well (*Rashi*). [The daughter or widow of a man born from a union of a Kohen and a woman forbidden to a Kohen is likewise forbidden to marry a Kohen (Mishnah, *Kiddushin* 77a and Gemara *Yevamos* 68a).]

30. It certainly cannot mean that the child is disqualified from marrying a Kohen, because we know that the father – whichever one of the ten men he may have been – was a fit Kohen. Yet the child is called a *shetuki.* What then does the term *shetuki* mean?

31. Even if the child seizes the property of one of the ten men upon that man's death, claiming that he is that man's son, he may not keep it, because one may not collect an inheritance unless he can prove unequivocally that he is entitled to it (*Ritva*).

32. I.e. he cannot serve in the Temple or eat *terumah* (*Rashi;* cf. *Ritva*).

או לחורבה ואמרו לה מה טיבו של איש זה כהן הוא ובן אחי אבא הוא רבן גמליאל ור"א אומרים נאמנת רבי יהושע אומר לא מפיה אנו חיין אלא הרי זו בחזקת בעולה לנתין ולממזר עד שתביא ראיה לדבריה בשלמא לזעירי היינו דקתני תרתי לסתר או לחורבה אלא לרב אסי דאמר נבעלה תרתי למה לי חדא קתני לסתר דחורבה והא לסתר או לחורבה קתני חדא לחורבה דמתא וחדא לחורבה דדברא וצריכי דאי אשמעינן חורבה דמתא בהא קמכשר רבן גמליאל משום דרוב כשרים אצלה אבל לחורבה דדברא דרוב פסולין אצלה אימא מודה ליה לרבי יהושע ואי אשמעינן בההיא בההיא קאמר רבי יהושע אבל בהא אימא מודה לר"ג צריכא מיתיבי [א] זו עדות שהאשה כשרה לה ורבי יהושע אומר אינה נאמנת אמר להם ר"י אי אתם מודים [א] בשבויה שנשבית ויש לה עדים שנשבית והיא אומרת טהורה אני שאינה נאמנת אמרו לו אבל ומה הפרש יש בין זו לזו לזו יש עדים ולזו אין לה עדים אמר להם אף לזו יש עדים שהרי כריסה בין שיניה אמרו לו רוב עובדי כוכבים פרוצים בעריות הם אמר להן [ג] אין אפוטרופוס לעריות בד"א בעדות אשה בגופה אבל עדות אשה בבתה דברי הכל הולד שתוקי מאי קאמר להו ומאי קמהדרי ליה הכי קאמרי ליה השבתנו על המעוברת מה תשיבנו על המדברת אמר להם מדברת היינו שבויה אמרו לו שאני שבויה דרוב עובדי כוכבים פרוצים בעריות הם אמר להם הא נמי כיון דאיסתתר אין אפוטרופוס לעריות קתני מיהת תרתי מדברת ומעוברת תיובתא דרב אסי תיובתא ותיפוק ליה דהתם רוב פסולין אצלה והכא רוב כשרין אצלה מסייע ליה לרבי יהושע בן לוי דאמר רבי יהושע בן לוי לדברי המכשיר מכשיר אפילו ברוב פסולין לדברי הפוסל פוסל אפילו ברוב כשרים א"ר יוחנן [ב] לדברי המכשיר בה מכשיר בבתה לדברי הפוסל בה פוסל בבתה ורבי אלעזר אומר לדברי המכשיר בה פוסל בבתה אמר רבה מ"ט דר"א בשלמא איהי אית לה חזקה דכשרות בתה לית לה חזקה דכשרות איתיביה ר"א לרבי יוחנן בד"א בעדות אשה בגופה אבל עדות אשה בבתה דברי הכל הולד שתוקי מאי לאו שתוקי ופסול לא שתוקי וכשר ומי איכא שתוקי כשר אין כדשמואל דאמר שמואל [ד] עשרה כהנים עומדים ופירש אחד מהם ובעל הולד שתוקי מאי שתוקי אילימא שמשתיקין אותו מנכסי אביו פשיטא ומי ידעינן אבוה מנו [ג] אלא שמשתיקין אותו מדין כהונה דכתיב [א] והיתה לו ולזרעו אחריו ברית כהונת עולם מי שזרעו מיוחס אחריו יצא זה שאין זרעו מיוחס אחריו

[ד] ההוא ארוס וארוסתו דאתו לקמיה דרב יוסף היא אמרה מיניה והוא אמר אין

לחורבה. סתמא לבעילה שהוא מקום לזנות: חורבה דמתא. סתם בעילתה מאחד מבני העיר ואיכא למימר בעיר שרובה ישראל כשרים קאמר: דברא. ספק אחד מסוף העולם בא לכאן ורוב העולם עובדי כוכבים הם ופסולים אשה בביאתם לכהונה כדאמר ביבמות (דף מה.) ובקדושין (דף עה:) עובד כוכבים ועבד שאין לו אלמנות וגירושין בה: זו עדות שהאשה. עצמה כשרה לומר לכשר נבעלתי: אינה נאמנת. לינשא לכהן: אמרו לו אבל. הן כמו אבל שרה אשתך (בראשית יז) דמתרגמינן בקושטא: ומה הפרש בין זו לזו. ר' יהושע קאמר לה: לזו יש עדים. שנבעלה דכיון דנשבית לבין העובדי כוכבים והם פרוצים בעריות כולנו עדים שנבעלה: ולזו אין עדים. שנבעלה שלא ראוה אלא מדברת ומיגו דאי בעיא אמרה לא נבעלתי כי אמרה נמי לכשר נבעלתי מהימנא: אף לזו. כלומר אף כאן יש לך אחת שיש לה עדים ואתם חולקים עלי בהיותה מעוברת: אמרו ליה כו'. לקמיה מפרש מאי קא מהדרי ליה על מאי דקאמר להו: אין אפוטרופוס כו'. לקמן מפרש: בד"א. דנאמנת לר"ג: בעדות אשה בגופה. כלומר להכשיר את עצמה לכהונה דלא מחזקינן לה בנבעלה לפסול: מאי קאמר להו כו'. כלומר מאי קאמר להו איהו דקא מהדרי ליה איהו רוב עובדי כוכבים פרוצים בעריות כלום תשובה היא זו על מה שאמר להם אף לזו יש לה עדים אין לך פרוץ גדול מזה דקחזינן דנתעברה ממנו: השבתנו על המעוברת. תשובה גמורה ונלחת: מדברת היינו שבויה. מה מדברת אין לה עדים אף שבויה אין לה עדים בבעילה ואתם מחזיקים אותה כנבעלה: פרוצים בעריות. והא ודאי נבעלה: אין אפוטרופוס לעריות. אין אתם יכולים להיות לה לאפוטרופוס לומר לא נבעלה: ותיפוק ליה כו'. לרבי יהושע פריך נהי נמי דאין אפוטרופוס לעריות תיפוק ליה דלא דמי לשבויה דהתם רוב פסולין כו': מכשיר אפי' ברוב פסולים. דאמרינן אוקמה אחזקה ועל רוב פסולים שהיו מכשירים אותה הביא הוא להם ראיה מן השבויה: אית לה חזקה דכשרות. וי"ל אשה זו בחזקת כשרות עומדת ומספק אתה בא לפוסלה אל תפסילנה מספק: לא שתוקי וכשר. כלומר שתוקי הוא במקצת שאם כהן היה הבועל והעובר יהיה זכר משתקין אותו מדין כהונה כדלקמן אבל כשר הוא ליוחסין שאם נקבה היא תינשא לכהונה ואם זכר הוא בתו ואלמנתו כשרות לכהונה: ופירש אחד מהן. ואין ידוע איזה הוא: הולד שתוקי. ואע"פ שברור לנו שמכהן כשר בא והאי שתוקי על כרחך כשר ליוחסין ואם נקבה היא ראויה לכהן וקרי ליה שתוקי: מדין כהונה. שלא יעבוד עבודה ולא יאכל תרומה: מיוחס אחריו. שאנו יודעין מי אביו:

השבתנו על המעוברת. פי' לדידן ניחא דלאשה מזנה בודקת ומזנה ולא דמיא לשבויה אלא לדידך דלית לך הך סברא תינח מעוברת אבל מדברת אפילו לפי דבריך יש עדים ולזו אין עדים ואיכא מיגו אמר להם מדברת היינו שבויה וכמו ששבויה אין נאמנת לומר לא נבעלתי ה"נ מדברת כדמסיק לפי שאין אפוטרופוס לעריות ומיהו פי' זה לא יתכן למאי דפרישית לעיל דלר' יהושע נאמנת לומר לא נבעלתי ופר"י בדוחק מדברת היינו שבויה דכמו [א] ששבויה בחזקת בעולה כך מדברת בחזקת בעולה לענין שאם אמרה לכשר נבעלתי שאינה נאמנת במיגו לפי שיראה לומר לא נבעלתי ולהכי אהני דאין אפוטרופוס לעריות דלא חשבינן ליה מיגו: מסייע ליה לר' יהושע בן לוי. הקשה ר"ת אכתי תיפוק ליה דהתם בשבויה כל פסולים והכא בחורבה דדברא רוב ותירץ דרוב ככל וליכא למימר במדברת דליכא אלא רוב איכא למימר סמוך מיעוטא לחזקה ואיתרע לה רובא דאפילו אית להו סמוך מיעוטא לחזקה לר"ג ור' יהושע מ"מ לא הוי אלא פלגא ופלגא ודין הוא שתאסר מספק דספק איסורא לחומרא ולא דמי לתינוק שנמצא בצד העיסה בפרק עשרה יוחסין (קדושין דף פ. ושם) דמטהרין מטעם סמוך מיעוטא לחזקה דלא אמרו ספק טומאה לטהר יאמרו ספק איסור להתיר כדאמרינן פרק כיסוי הדם (חולין דף פו:): מכשיר אפילו ברוב פסולים. והא דקאמרינן בפ' עשרה יוחסין (קדושין עד. ושם) גבי אבא שאול היה קורא לשתוקי בדוקי ומפרש בגמרא שבודקין אמו ואומרת לכשר נבעלתי ופריך כמאן כר"ג תנינא חדא זימנא היתה מעוברת כו' פי' והוה ליה למתני וכן אמר אבא שאול וכן פי' שם בקונטרס ומשני דאבא שאול עדיפא מר"ג דאי מהתם הוה אמינא ברוב כשרים אבל כו' קמ"ל אע"ג דאמרי' הכא דר"ג מכשיר אפילו ברוב פסולין אבא שאול קאי אמתני' וממתני' לא משמע מידי דאיירי ברוב פסולים והא דפריך התם לעיל למאי דהוה בעי למימר דאבא שאול אתא להכשיר בבתה ניחא למ"ד לדברי המכשיר בה פוסל בבתה אבל למ"ד מכשיר בבתה מאי איכא למימר התם פריך שפיר דאפי' לזעירי לשון המשנה דקתני מה טיבו של עובר זה משמע דאתא להכשיר בבתה: פשיטא מי ידעינן אבוה מנו. הכא לא בעי לשנויי לא צריכא דאי תפס כדמשני בפרק עשרה יוחסין (שם דף עה. ושם) גבי ארוסה שעיברה דהתם רגילים לדבר דמארוס נתעברה ואיכא למיתלי ביה טפי מבאינש דעלמא: בעינן זרעו מיוחס אחריו. והא דאמר בהחולץ (יבמות דף לז.) ראשון ראוי להיות כ"ג גבי ספק בן תשע לראשון בפרק נושאין על האנוסה (שם דף ק:) פריך לה ומשני זרעו מיוחס אחריו דרבנן וקרא אסמכתא בעלמא הוא וכי גזור רבנן בזנות בנישואין לא גזור:

[ההוא ארוס וארוסתו. והא דאמר בעשרה יוחסין (קדושין דף עה.) איתמר הבא על ארוסתו בבית חמיו רב אמר הולד שתוקי כשלא בדקו את אמו דאי בשבדקו קשיא דשמואל אדשמואל דהכא אמר שמואל דנאמנת דהלכה כרבן גמליאל דנאמנת והתם קאמר איפוך שמואל אמר הולד ממזר וכן משמע דבמסקנא משני התם לעולם לא תיפוך כו' ומפרש מאי שתוקי שבודקין את אמו ואומרת לכשר נבעלתי ואם תאמר אכתי לשמואל דהתם משמע דוקא בבא על ארוסתו בבית חמיו מהני בדיקה והכא משמע אפילו כי לא מודה אמר שמואל דנאמנת כרבן גמליאל ויש לומר דהא דנקט בא היינו משום רבותא דרב נקטיה דאפילו הכי אמר הולד ממזר אי נמי התם הוא דבעינן בא משום דאיירי בדליכא מעלמא כדאמר רבא ביבמות בשלהי אלמנה לכהן גדול מסתברא מילתא דרב בדליכא מעלמא והכא בדלא דייקא מעלמא מיירי ועוד דבכל הספרים גרס בקדושין ארוסה שעיברה והיא דוקא קאמר שבודקין אבל בבא א"צ בדיקה ומיהו קשה ללישנא קמא ביבמות בסוף פ' אלמנה דפליגי רב ושמואל בבא ומסיק התם אביי דאע"ג דלא דייקא מעלמא פליגי דדלמא מדאפקרה נפשה לגבי ארוס מפקרה נפשה לגבי עלמא הא אמר הכא חדא דקא מודה ומשמע דכשר אפילו לר' יהושע ובא כמודה דמי

פב א מיי' פי"ח מהל' איסורי ביאה הלכה כא סמג לאוין קכא טוש"ע אה"ע סימן ו ס"ד:
פג ב מיי' פט"ו שם הלכה יא סמג שם טוש"ע שם סי' ו סעיף יז:
פד ג מיי' פ"כ שם הל' כ סמג לאוין קכב טוש"ע שם סימן ג סעיף טו:
פה ד מיי' פט"ו שם הלכה יח טוש"ע שם סימן ד סעיף כו [וכרב אלפס עוד ביבמות פ"ו דף מ ע"א]:

א) [תוספתא סוף פרק א], ב) [חולין יא: נדה ל:], ג) [קדושין עד.], ד) יבמות ק.

תוספות ישנים

א) ולא"ג דמיעוט עובדי כוכבים אין פרוצים מ"מ חשבינן לה ודאי בעולה מן הרוב הפרוצים. מ"י.

תורה אור השלם

א) וְהָיְתָה לּוֹ וּלְזַרְעוֹ אַחֲרָיו בְּרִית כְּהֻנַּת עוֹלָם תַּחַת אֲשֶׁר קִנֵּא לֵאלֹהָיו וַיְכַפֵּר עַל בְּנֵי יִשְׂרָאֵל: [במדבר כה, יג]

ליקוטי רש"י

דברא. שדה [ברכות ג:]. שתוקי. שקורא פלוני אבא ואמו משתקתו [קידושין סט.]. שהרי כריסה בין שיניה. ואינה יכולה לומר לא נבעלתי [לקמן טז.]. הולד שתוקי. וכשר הוא דהא פשיטא לן דכן כהן בא על הפנויה הוא. מדין כהונה. מלעבוד עבודה ואף על גב דלענין יוחסין לישא אשה כשר הוא פסול לעבודה. אחריו. שיכר זרעו שהוא שלו [יבמות ק:].

תוספות רי"ד

היחוד ואף אוסרים על היחוד ליבא דלא כר"י פי' דמשום יחוד מחזיק לה בנבעלה פי' מלקין מכות מרדות לאשת איש שנתייחדה עמם א' אבל אין אוסרין אותה על בעלה בעידי יחוד אלא היכא דקינא לה מעיקרא בפני שנים ואמר לה אל תסתרי עם איש פ' ונתי אם נסתרה עמו היא סוטה האמורה בתורה והיא אסורה לו עד שתשבדק במים המאררים אבל בלא קינוי מעיקרא אינה נאסרת לו בסתירה בלחוד. ההדר מעלה עשו ביוחסין פי' דלא אסרו ר"י אלא אם היתה פנויה שלא תנשא לכהן דאמרינן דלמא נבעלה לפסול לו אבל לבעלה לא אסרה ואפי' אם היה בעלה כהן. אר"א א"ש הלכה כר"ג אריב"ל לדברי המכשיר מכשיר אפילו ברוב פסולים לדברי הפוסל פוסל אפי' ברוב כשרים. ההוא ארוס וארוסתו דאתו לקמיה דר"י היא אומרת מיני' והוא אומר

REGARD TO FORBIDDEN RELATIONS.[16] אָמַר לָהֶן – HE SAID TO THEM: אֵין אַפּוֹטְרוֹפּוֹס לַעֲרָיוֹת – THERE IS NO GUARANTOR AGAINST FORBIDDEN RELATIONS.[17]

The Baraisa concludes with a qualification of Rabban Gamliel and R' Eliezer's ruling:

בַּמֶּה דְּבָרִים אֲמוּרִים – WHEN ARE THESE WORDS [i.e. that the woman is believed] STATED? בְּעֵדוּת אִשָּׁה בְּגוּפָהּ – IN REGARD TO THE WOMAN'S TESTIMONY AS IT REGARDS HERSELF, i.e. her own status of eligibility for the Kehunah. אֲבָל עֵדוּת אִשָּׁה בְּבִתָּהּ – BUT in regard to THE WOMAN'S TESTIMONY AS IT REGARDS HER DAUGHTER, i.e. the status of a girl born from this union, דִּבְרֵי הַכֹּל הַוָּלָד שְׁתוּקִי – ALL AGREE THAT THE CHILD IS A *SHETUKI*.[18]

Before posing its challenge to Rav Assi, the Gemara seeks a clarification of part of the exchange between R' Yehoshua and Rabban Gamliel and R' Eliezer cited in the Baraisa:

מַאי קָאָמַר לְהוּ וּמַאי קָמְהַדְרֵי לֵיהּ – **What did he say to them and what did they respond to him?**[19]

The Gemara answers that a part of the exchange is missing from the Baraisa's account:

הָכִי קָאָמְרֵי לֵיהּ – **They said to him thus:** הֲשֵׁבְתָּנוּ עַל הַמְעוּבֶּרֶת – **You have answered us** convincingly **with regard to the pregnant woman,** מַה תְּשִׁיבֵנוּ עַל הַמְדַבֶּרֶת – but **what will you answer us with regard to the woman who was speaking?**[20]

אָמַר לָהֶם מְדַבֶּרֶת הַיְינוּ שְׁבוּיָה – **He said to them:** The case of **the woman speaking is equivalent to** the case of **the captive woman.**[21] אָמְרוּ לוֹ שָׁאנֵי שְׁבוּיָה דְּרוֹב עוֹבְדֵי כוֹכָבִים פְּרוּצִים בַּעֲרָיוֹת הֵם – **They said to him: A captive woman is different, because most idolaters are unrestrained with regard to forbidden relations.**[22] אָמַר לָהֶם הָא נַמִּי כֵּיוָן דְּאִיסְתַּתַּר אֵין אַפּוֹטְרוֹפּוֹס לַעֲרָיוֹת – **He said to them: This** woman who was speaking **also** is no different, because **once she was secluded, there is no guarantor against forbidden relations.**[23]

Having elucidated the Baraisa, the Gemara returns to its objection to Rav Assi's interpretation of our Mishnah:

קָתָנֵי מִיהַת תַּרְתֵּי – **At any rate, the Baraisa taught two** cases: מְדַבֶּרֶת וּמְעוּבֶּרֶת – one of **a woman who was "speaking" and** one of **a woman who was pregnant.** תְּיוּבְתָּא דְּרַב אַסִּי – This is **a refutation of Rav Assi.**[24] – ? –

The Gemara concedes:

תְּיוּבְתָּא – Indeed it is **a refutation.**

The Gemara continues to analyze the Baraisa:

וְתִיפּוֹק לֵיהּ – **But let [R' Yehoshua] derive** a difference between the captive woman and the one who was speaking דְּהָתָם רוֹב פְּסוּלִין אֶצְלָהּ – in **that there,** in the case of the captive woman, **most** of the men who could have cohabited with her **are unfit for her** (i.e. their cohabitation would have rendered her forbidden to a Kohen), וְהָכָא רוֹב כְּשֵׁרִין אֶצְלָהּ – **whereas here,** in the case of the woman who was speaking, **most** men **are fit for her.**[25] – ? –

The Gemara answers:

מְסַיֵּיעַ לֵיהּ לְרַבִּי יְהוֹשֻׁעַ בֶּן לֵוִי – **This is a support to R' Yehoshua ben Levi,** דְּאָמַר רַבִּי יְהוֹשֻׁעַ בֶּן לֵוִי – **for R' Yehoshua ben Levi said:** לְדִבְרֵי הַמַּכְשִׁיר מַכְשִׁיר אֲפִילּוּ בְּרוֹב פְּסוּלִין – **The one who rules her fit** for the Kehunah [i.e. Rabban Gamliel and R' Eliezer] **rules her fit even where most** of the available men **are unfit** for

NOTES

pregnant ("her stomach is between her teeth"). Yet even in regard to the pregnant woman you maintain that she is believed (*Rashi*). How do you distinguish between *that* case and the case of the captive woman?

16. The Gemara below will explain how this response addresses R' Yehoshua's challenge (*Rashi*).

17. This rejoinder too will be explained by the Gemara (*Rashi*).

18. *Shetuki* literally means "the quieted one" (from the root שתק, *quiet*). [A child who does not know the identity of his father is liable to address any adult male as "Father." When he does so, his mother silences him (*Rashi* to *Kiddushin* 69a ד״ה ואינו).] The Gemara will explain what the term means in this context.

19. [Obviously, he must have said something to them which the Baraisa omits, for] what kind of response is the fact that most idolaters are unrestrained in matters of forbidden relations to R' Yehoshua's argument that we have "witnesses" to her cohabitation from the fact that she is pregnant? Why, the very fact that she is pregnant is the *ultimate proof* that the man with whom she was secluded was unrestrained! (*Rashi*).

20. That is, we admit that we have no answer to your argument about the pregnant woman. [The fact that she is pregnant proves that she cohabited, and, as such, she should be as prohibited to a Kohen as the captive woman. But why should the woman who was merely secluded be prohibited? What proof do you have that *she* is not believed?] (*Rashi*).

Shitah Mekubetzes (ד״ה מאי) elaborates on *Rashi's* explanation: Rabban Gamliel and R' Eliezer did not mean to say that they conceded the law to R' Yehoshua regarding the pregnant woman. This is evident from the Gemara on the top of 14a where Rav Yosef is cited as ruling in accordance with Rabban Gamliel in an actual case of a pregnant woman. Rather, they meant that in the battle of logical arguments R' Yehoshua had bested them. Nevertheless, they still stick by their ruling that the pregnant woman is believed, because they received it as a tradition from their teachers [who, presumably, would have been able to defend it].

Other Rishonim interpret Rabban Gamliel and R' Eliezer's response to mean that R' Yehoshua had bested them *according to his line of thinking,* which is, as stated on 14a, that a woman who is prepared to engage in out-of-wedlock relations is not particular as to the genealogical fitness of her partner. For their part, however, Rabban Gamliel and R' Eliezer maintain that even a loose woman is presumed to be careful not to cohabit with anyone who would render her unfit to marry a Kohen. She is thus unlike the captive woman, who is at the total mercy of her captors (see *Tosafos, Rashba, Ritva* et al.).

21. In both cases there are no witnesses that cohabitation occurred, yet in the case of the captured woman we assume as much. We should thus assume the same in the case of a woman who was secluded (*Rashi*).

22. Thus, in the case of a captive woman we assume with certainty that she was violated (*Rashi*). See below, 23a note 20.

23. No one can guarantee that she did not in fact cohabit (*Rashi*). She thus loses her *chazakah* of fitness (*Ritva*), and, as in the case of a captive woman, we must assume that she was rendered prohibited to a Kohen through forbidden cohabitation until she proves otherwise.

24. From Rabban Gamliel and R' Eliezer's reply to R' Yehoshua [as elaborated by the Gemara], "You have answered us with regard to the pregnant woman, what will you answer us with regard to the woman who was speaking?" it is apparent that "she was speaking" means that she was secluded. For if it means that she was seen cohabiting, what difference is there between the case of the woman speaking and the case of the pregnant woman, such that Rabban Gamliel and R' Yehoshua could debate whether they are comparable? (*Shitah Mekubetzes* ד״ה קתני מיהת).

25. That is, how can R' Yehoshua compare even the case of the pregnant woman to the case of the captive woman? Naturally in the case of the captive woman we forbid her, because most of the people who could have cohabited with her were idolaters, who render her forbidden to a Kohen with their cohabitation. But in the case of the pregnant woman most of the men who could have impregnated her were genealogically fit Jews, whose cohabitation would not disqualify her for the Kehunah (see *Rashi*).

[Alternatively, some commentators explain the Gemara's question as being directed at Rabban Gamliel and R' Eliezer, as follows: Why, in the case of the pregnant woman, did they concede that R' Yehoshua's logic was correct (*Mahari ben Lev, Maharam Schif*), and why, in the case of the woman who was secluded, were they forced to resort to the answer that most idolaters are unrestrained in the matter of illicit relations? (*Ritva, Tos. HaRosh*). They should have answered more simply, that in the case of the captive woman most of the men are unfit for her, while in the case at hand most are fit (see *Shitah Mekubetzes* ד״ה ותיפוק ליה and *Maharam Schif* for suggestions as to why *Rashi* deviated from this seemingly more straightforward explanation).]

או לחורבה ואמרו לה מה טיבו של איש זה כהן הוא ובן אחי אבא הוא רבן גמליאל ור"א אומרים נאמנת ורבי יהושע אומר לא מפיה אנו חיין אלא הרי זו בחזקת בעולה לנתין ולממזר עד שתביא ראיה לדבריה בשלמא לזעירי היינו דקתני תרתי לסתר או לחורבה אלא לרב אסי דאמר נבעלה תרתי למה לי חדא קתני לסתר דחורבה והא לסתר או לחורבה קתני חדא לחורבה דמתא וחדא לחורבה דדברא וצריכי דאי אשמעינן חורבה דמתא בהא קמכשר רבן גמליאל משום דרוב כשרים אצלה אבל לחורבה דדברא דרוב פסולין אצלה אימא מודה ליה לרבי יהושע ואי אשמעינן בההיא בההיא קאמר רבי יהושע אבל בהא אימא מודה לר"ג צריכא מיתיבי א) זו עדות שהאשה כשרה לה ורבי יהושע אומר אינה נאמנת אמר להם ר"י אי אתם מודים א בשבויה שנשבית ויש לה עדים שנשבית והיא אומרת טהורה אני שאינה נאמנת אמרו לו אבל ומה הפרש יש בין זו לזו לזו יש עדים ולזו אין לה עדים אמר להם אף לזו יש עדים שהרי כריסה בין שיניה אמרו לו רוב עובדי כוכבים פרוצים בעריות הם אמר להן ב) אין אפוטרופוס לעריות בד"א בעדות אשה בגופה אבל עדות אשה בבתה דברי הכל הולד שתוקי מאי קאמר להו ומאי קמהדרי ליה הכי קאמרי ליה השבתנו על המעוברת מה תשיבנו על המדברת אמר להם מדברת היינו שבויה אמרו לו שאני שבויה דרוב עובדי כוכבים פרוצים בעריות הם אמר להם הא נמי כיון דאיסתתר אין אפוטרופוס לעריות קתני מיהת תרתי מדברת ומעוברת תיובתא דרב אסי תיובתא ותיפוק ליה דהתם רוב פסולין אצלה והכא רוב כשרין אצלה מסייע ליה לרבי יהושע בן לוי דאמר רבי יהושע בן לוי לדברי המכשיר מכשיר אפילו ברוב פסולין לדברי הפוסל פוסל אפילו ברוב כשרים א"ר יוחנן ג) ב לדברי המכשיר בה מכשיר בבתה לדברי הפוסל בה פוסל בבתה ורבי אלעזר אומר לדברי המכשיר בה פוסל בבתה אמר רבה מ"ט דר"א בשלמא איהי אית לה חזקה דכשרות בתה לית לה חזקה דכשרות איתיביה ר"א לרבי יוחנן בד"א בעדות אשה בגופה אבל עדות אשה בבתה דברי הכל הולד שתוקי מאי לאו שתוקי ופסול לא שתוקי וכשר ומי איכא שתוקי כשר אין כדשמואל דאמר שמואל ד) עשרה כהנים עומדים ופירש אחד מהם ובעל הולד שתוקי מאי שתוקי אילימא שמשתיקין אותו מנכסי אביו פשיטא ומי ידעינן אבוה מנו ג אלא שמשתיקין אותו מדין כהונה דכתיב א) והיתה לו ולזרעו אחריו ברית כהונת עולם מי שזרעו מיוחס אחריו יצא זה שאין זרעו מיוחס אחריו ד ההוא ארוס וארוסתו דאתו לקמיה דרב יוסף היא אמרה מיניה והוא אמר אין

רש"י

לחורבה. סתמא לנבעלה שהוא מקום לזנות: **חורבה דמתא.** סתם בעילתה מאחד מבני העיר ואיכא למימר בעיר שרובה ישראל כשרים קאמר: **דדברא.** ספק אחד מסוף העולם בא לכאן ורוב העולם עובדי כוכבים הם ופסולים אשה בביאתם לכהונה כדאמר ביבמות (דף מה.) ובקדושין (דף עה:) ילאו עובד כוכבים ועבד שבאו על אלמנות וגרושות בה: **זו עדות שהאשה.** עלמה כשרה לומר לכשר נבעלתי: **אינה נאמנת.** לינשא לכהן: **אמרו לו אבל.** הן כמו אבל שרה אשתך (בראשית יז) דמתרגמינן בקושטא: **ומה הפרש בין זו לזו.** ר' יהושע קאמר להו: **לזו יש עדים.** שנבעלה דכיון דנשבית לבין העובדי כוכבים והם פרוצים בעריות כולהו עדים שנבעלה: **ולזו אין עדים.** שנבעלה שלא ראוה אלא מדברת ומיגו דאי בעיא אמרה לא נבעלתי כי אמרה נמי לכשר נבעלתי מהימנא: **אף לזו.** כלומר אף כאן יש אחת שיש לה עדים ואתם מכשירים אותה בהיותה מעוברת: **אמרו ליה כו'.** לקמיה מפרש מאי קא מהדרי ליה על מאי דקאמר להו: **אין אפוטרופוס כו'.** לקמן מפרש: **בד"א.** דנאמנת לר"ג: **בעדות אשה בגופה.** כלומר להכשיר את עלמה לכהונה דלא מחזקינן לה בנבעלה לפסול: **מאי קאמר להו כו'.** כלומר מאי קאמר להו איהו דקא מהדרי ליה איהו רוב עובדי כוכבים פרוצים בעריות כלום תשובה היא זו זה מה שאמר להם אף לזו יש לה עדים אין לך פרוץ גדול מזה דקחזינן דנתעברה ממנו: **השבתנו על המעוברת.** תשובה גמורה ונלחת: **מדברת היינו שבויה.** מה מדברת אין לה עדים אף שבויה אין לה עדים בנבעלה ואתם מחזיקים אותה כנבעלה: **פרוצים בעריות.** והא ודאי נבעלה: **אין אפוטרופוס לעריות.** אין אתם יכולים להיות לה אפוטרופוס לומר לא נבעלה: **ותיפוק ליה וכו'.** לרבי יהושע פריך נהי נמי דאין אפוטרופוס לעריות תיפוק ליה דלא דמי לשבויה דהתם רוב פסולין כו': **מכשיר אפי' ברוב פסולים.** דאמרינן אוקמה אחזקה ועל רוב פסולים שהיו מכשירים אותה הביא הוא להם ראיה מן השבויה: **אית לה חזקה דכשרות.** וי"ל אשה זו בחזקת כשרות עומדת ומספק אתה בא לפוסלה אל תפסילנה מספק: **לא שתוקי וכשר.** כלומר שתוקי הוא במקלת שאם כהן היה הבועל והעובר יהיה זכר משתקין אותו מדין כהונה כדלקמן אבל כשר הוא ליוחסין שאם נקבה היא תינשא לכהונה ואם זכר הוא בתו ואלמנתו כשרות לכהונה: **ופירש אחד מהן.** ואין ידוע איזה הוא: **הולד שתוקי.** ואע"פ שברור לנו שמכהן כשר בא והאי שתוקי על כרחך כשר ליוחסין ואם נקבה היא ראויה לכהן וקרי ליה שתוקי: **מדין כהונה.** שלא יעבוד עבודה ולא יאכל תרומה: **מיוחס אחריו.** שאנו יודעין מי אביו:

תוספות

השבתנו על המעוברת. פי' לדידן ניחא דאשה מזנה בודקת ומזנה ולא דמיא לשבויה אלא לדידך לית לך הך סברא תינח מעוברת אבל מדברת אפילו לפי דבריך יש הפרש דלזו יש עדים ולזו אין עדים ואיכא מיגו אמר להם מדברת היינו שבויה וכמו ששבויה אין נאמנת לומר לא נבעלתי ה"נ מדברת כדמסיק לפי שאין אפוטרופוס לעריות ומיהו פי' זה לא יתכן למאי דפרישית לעיל דלר' יהושע נאמנת לומר לא נבעלתי ופר"י בדוחק מדברת היינו שבויה דכמו א) ששבויה בחזקת בעולה קך מדברת בחזקת בעולה לענין שאם אמרה לכשר נבעלתי שאינה נאמנת במיגו לפי שיכלה לומר לא נבעלתי ולהכי אהני דאין אפוטרופוס לעריות דלא חשבינן ליה מיגו: **מסייע ליה לר' יהושע בן לוי.** הקשה ר"ת אמאי תיפוק ליה דהתם בשבויה כל פסולים והכא בחורבה דדברא רוב ותירץ דרוב ככל ואיכא למימר במדברת דליכא אלא רוב איכא למימר סמוך מיעוטא לחזקה ואיתרע לה רובא דאפילו אית להו סמוך מיעוטא לחזקה לר"ג ור' יהושע מ"מ לא הוי אלא פלגא ופלגא ודין הוא שתאסר מספק דספק איסורא לחומרא ולא דמי לתינוק שנמצא בצד העיסה בפרק עשרה יוחסין (קדושין דף פ. ושם) דמטהרין מטעם סמוך מיעוטא לחזקה דהם אמרו ספק טומאה לטהר יאמרו ספק איסור להתיר כדאמרינן פרק גיד הנשה (חולין דף פו:): **מכשיר אפילו ברוב פסולים.** והא דקאמרינן בפ' עשרה יוחסין (קדושין עד. ושם) גבי אבא שאול היה קורא לשתוקי בדוקי ומפרש בגמרא שבודקין אמו ואומרת לכשר נבעלתי ופריך כמאן כר"ג תנינא חדא זימנא היתה מעוברת כו' פי' והוה ליה למתני וכן אמר אבא שאול וכן פי' שם בקונטרס ומשני דאבא שאול עדיפא מר"ג דאי מהתם הוה אמינא ברוב כשרים אלא כו' אע"ג דאמרי' הכא דר"ג מכשיר אפילו ברוב פסולין אבא שאול קאי אמתני' וממתני' לא משמע מידי דאיירי ברוב פסולים והא דפריך התם לעיל למאי דהוה בעי למימר דאבא שאול אתא להכשיר בבתה ניחא למ"ד לדברי המכשיר בה פוסל בבתה אבל למ"ד מכשיר בבתה מאי איכא למימר התם פריך שפיר דאפי' לזעירי לשון המשנה דקתני מה טיבו של עובר זה משמע דאתא להכשיר בבתה: **פשיטא** מי ידעינן אבוה מנו. הכא לא בעי לשנויי לא צריכא דאי תפס כדמשני בפרק עשרה יוחסין (שם דף עה. ושם) גבי ארוסה שעיברה דהתם רגלים לדבר דמארוס נתעברה ואיכא למיתלי ביה טפי מבאינך דעלמא: **בעינן** זרעו מיוחס אחריו. והא דאמר בהחולץ (יבמות דף לז.) ראשון ראוי להיות כ"ג גבי ספק בן תשעה לראשון בפרק נושאין על האנוסה (שם דף ק:) פריך לה ומשני זרעו מיוחס אחריו דרבנן וקרא אסמכתא בעלמא הוא וכי גזור רבנן בזנות בנישואין לא גזור: **ההוא** ארוס וארוסתו. והא דאמר בעשרה יוחסין (קדושין דף עה.) איתמר הבא על ארוסתו בבית חמיו רב אמר הולד ממזר ושמואל אמר הולד שתוקי כשלא בדקו את אמו דאי בשבדקו קשיא דשמואל אדשמואל דהכא אמר שמואל דנאמנת דהלכה כרבן גמליאל דנאמנת והתם קאמר איפוך שמואל אמר הולד ממזר וכן משמע דבמסקנא משני התם לעולם לא תיפוך כו' ומפרש מאי שתוקי שבודקין את אמו ואומרת לכשר נבעלתי ואם תאמר אכתי לשמואל דהתם משמע דוקא בבא על ארוסתו בבית חמיו מהני בדיקה והכא משמע אפילו כי לא מודה אמר שמואל דנאמנת כרבן גמליאל ויש לומר דהא דנקט בא היינו משום רבותא דרב נקטיה דאפילו הכי אמר הולד ממזר אי נמי התם הוא דבעינן בא משום דאיירי בדליתא מעלמא כדאמר רבא ביבמות בשלהי אלמנה לכהן גדול מסתברא מילתא דרב בדליתא מעלמא והכא בדלא ליתא מעלמא איירי ועוד דבכל הספרים גרס בקדושין ארוסה שעיברה והיא דוקא קאמר שבודקין אבל בבא א"נ בדיקה ומיהו קשה ללישנא קמא ביבמות בסוף פ' אלמנה דפליגי רב ושמואל בבא ומסיק התם אביי דאע"ג דלא ליתא מעלמא פליגי דלמא מדאפקרה נפשה לגבי ארוס מפקרה נפשה לגבי עלמא הא אמר הכא חדא דקא מודה ומשמע דכשר אפילו לר' יהושע ובא כמודה דמי

עין משפט נר מצוה

פב א מיי' פי"ח מהל' איסורי ביאה הלכה כא סמג לאוין קכא טור ש"ע אה"ע סימן ז ס"ד:

פג ב מיי' שם[?] הלכה יא סמג שם טוש"ע שם סי' ו סעיף יז:

פד ג מיי' פ"כ שם הל' כ סמג לאוין קכב טוש"ע שם סימן ג סעיף ט:

פה ד מיי' פט"ו שם הלכה יז טוש"ע שם סימן ד סעיף כו [וברב אלפס עוד ביבמות פ"ז דף כו ע"א]:

תוספות רי"ד

היחוד ואנן אוסרים על היחוד ליתא דלא כר"י פי' דמש"ם יחוד מחזיק לה כנבעלה פי' מלקין מכות מרדות לאשת איש שנתייחדה עם א' אבל אין אוסרין אותה על בעלה בעידי יחוד אלא היכא דקינא לה מעיקרא בפני שנים ואמר לה אל תסתרי עם איש פלוני אם נסתרה עמו היא סוטה האמורה בתורה והיא אסורה לו עד שתבורר במים המאררים אבל בלא קינוי מעיקרא אינה נאסרת לו בסתירה בלחוד. ימהדר מעלה עשו ביוחסין פי' דלא אסרה ר"י אלא אם היתה פנויה שלא תנשא לכהן דאמרינן דלמא נבעלה לפסול לה אבל לבעלה לא אסרה ואפי' אם היה בעלה כהן. **אר"י א"ש** הלכה כר"ג אריב"ל לדברי המכשיר מכשיר אפילו ברוב פסולים לדברי הפוסל פוסל אפי' ברוב כשרים: **ההוא** ארוס וארוסתו דאתו לקמיה דר"י היא אומרת מיני' והוא אומר

מסורת הש"ס

א) [תוספתא סוף פרק א], ב) [חולין יא: נדה ל:], ג) [קדושין עד.], ד) יבמות ק.:

תוספות ישנים

א) ואע"ג דמיעוט עובדי כוכבים אין פרוצים מ"מ חשבינן לה ודאי בעולה מן הרוב הפרוצים. ת"י.

תורה אור השלם

א) וְהָיְתָה לּוֹ וּלְזַרְעוֹ אַחֲרָיו בְּרִית כְּהֻנַּת עוֹלָם תַּחַת אֲשֶׁר קִנֵּא לֵאלֹהָיו וַיְכַפֵּר עַל בְּנֵי יִשְׂרָאֵל: [במדבר כה, יג]

ליקוטי רש"י

דברא. שדה [ברכות ג:]. **שתוקי.** שקורא פלוני אבא אמו משתקתו [קידושין סט.]. **שהרי כריסה בין שיניה.** ואינה יכולה לומר לא נבעלתי [לקמן טז.]. **הולד שתוקי.** וכשר הוא דהא פשיטא לן דכן כהן הבא על הפנויה הוא. **מדין כהונה.** מלעבוד עבודה ואף על גב דלענין יוחסין לישא אשה כשר הוא פסול לעבודה. **אחריו.** שניכר זרעו שהוא שלו [יבמות ק:].

או לְחוּרְבָּה – OR INTO A RUIN,[1] וְאָמְרוּ לָהּ מַה טִּיבוֹ שֶׁל אִישׁ זֶה – AND THEY SAID TO HER, "WHAT IS THE NATURE OF THIS MAN?" כֹּהֵן הוּא וּבֶן אֲחִי אַבָּא הוּא – and she replied: "HE IS A KOHEN, THE SON OF MY FATHER'S BROTHER." רַבָּן גַּמְלִיאֵל וְרַבִּי אֱלִיעֶזֶר אוֹמְרִים – RABBAN GAMLIEL AND R' ELIEZER SAY: נֶאֱמֶנֶת – SHE IS BELIEVED and is permitted to marry a Kohen. רַבִּי יְהוֹשֻׁעַ אוֹמֵר – R' YEHOSHUA, however, SAYS: לֹא מִפִּיהָ אָנוּ חַיִּין – NOT FROM HER MOUTH DO WE LIVE. אֶלָּא הֲרֵי זוֹ בְּחֶזְקַת בְּעוּלָה לְנָתִין וּלְמַמְזֵר – RATHER, SHE IS PRESUMED TO HAVE COHABITED WITH A *NASIN* OR A *MAMZER* עַד שֶׁתָּבִיא רְאָיָה לִדְבָרֶיהָ – UNTIL SHE BRINGS PROOF TO HER CLAIM.

The Gemara formulates its question:

בִּשְׁלָמָא לִזְעִירִי – Now, **it is understandable according to Zeiri** that "speaking" means secluded, הַיְינוּ דְּקָתָנֵי תַּרְתֵּי לְסֵתֶר אוֹ לְחוּרְבָּה – **for that is why [the Baraisa] teaches two cases: into a secluded place or into a ruin.**[2] אֶלָּא לְרַב אַסִּי דְּאָמַר נִבְעֲלָה – **But according to Rav Assi who says** that "speaking" means **she cohabited,** תַּרְתֵּי לָמָּה לִי – **why do I need two** cases?[3]

The Gemara answers:

חֲדָא קָתָנֵי – **[The Baraisa]** actually **teaches** only **one** case: לְסֵתֶר דְּחוּרְבָּה – They went **into the seclusion of a ruin.**[4]

The Gemara rejects this answer:

וְהָא לְסֵתֶר אוֹ לְחוּרְבָּה קָתָנֵי – **But [the Baraisa] taught: "into a secluded place *or* into a ruin,"** indicating that it speaks of two separate cases![5] – ? –

The Gemara answers that the Baraisa indeed speaks of two cases, but each is a type of ruin:

חֲדָא לְחוּרְבָּה דְּמָתָא – In **one** case they went **into a ruin in a city** וַחֲדָא לְחוּרְבָּה דְּדַבְרָא – **and in one** case they went **into a ruin in a field.**[6] וּצְרִיכֵי – **And [both cases] are needed.** דְּאִי אַשְׁמְעִינַן חוּרְבָּה דְּמָתָא – **For had [the Baraisa] informed us** only of the case **of a ruin in a city,** בְּהָא קָמַכְשַׁר רַבָּן גַּמְלִיאֵל מִשּׁוּם דְּרוֹב כְּשֵׁרִים אֶצְלָהּ – I might have thought that only **in that** case **Rabban Gamliel rules** her **permitted** to the Kehunah, **because most** men found there **are fit for her.**[7] אֲבָל לְחוּרְבָּה דְּדַבְרָא – **But in** the case of **a ruin in a field,** דְּרוֹב פְּסוּלִין אֶצְלָהּ – **where most** men **are unfit for her,**[8] אֵימָא מוֹדֶה לֵיהּ לְרַבִּי יְהוֹשֻׁעַ – **I would say** that **[Rabban Gamliel] agrees with R' Yehoshua** that she may not marry a Kohen. וְאִי אַשְׁמְעִינַן בְּהַהִיא – **And had [the Baraisa] informed us** only **of that** case of the ruin in the field, בְּהַהִיא קָאָמַר רַבִּי יְהוֹשֻׁעַ – I might have thought it is only **in that** case that **R' Yehoshua says** she is disqualified, אֲבָל בְּהָא – **but in this** case of a ruin in a city אֵימָא מוֹדֶה לְרַבָּן גַּמְלִיאֵל – **I would say he agrees with Rabban Gamliel.** צְרִיכָא – Both cases are therefore **needed.**

The Gemara raises another objection to Rav Assi's interpretation of our Mishnah:

מֵיתִיבֵי – **They challenged** him from a Baraisa:[9] זוֹ עֵדוּת שֶׁהָאִשָּׁה כְּשֵׁרָה לָהּ – . . . THIS IS TESTIMONY FOR WHICH THE WOMAN herself IS FIT.[10] וְרַבִּי יְהוֹשֻׁעַ אוֹמֵר – BUT R' YEHOSHUA SAYS: אֵינָהּ נֶאֱמֶנֶת – SHE IS NOT BELIEVED.

R' Yehoshua attempts to disprove Rabban Gamliel and R' Eliezer:

אָמַר לָהֶם רַבִּי יְהוֹשֻׁעַ – R' YEHOSHUA SAID TO THEM: אִי אַתֶּם מוֹדִים בִּשְׁבוּיָה שֶׁנִּשְׁבֵּית – DO YOU NOT AGREE REGARDING A WOMAN WHO WAS CAPTURED, וְיֵשׁ לָהּ עֵדִים שֶׁנִּשְׁבֵּית – AND SHE HAS WITNESSES THAT SHE WAS CAPTURED, וְהִיא אוֹמֶרֶת טְהוֹרָה אֲנִי – AND SHE SAYS, "I AM PURE" [i.e. no man had relations with me during my captivity], שֶׁאֵינָהּ נֶאֱמֶנֶת – THAT SHE IS NOT BELIEVED, and she may not marry a Kohen?[11] אָמְרוּ לוֹ אֲבָל – THEY SAID TO HIM: INDEED we do.[12] וּמַה הֶפְרֵשׁ יֵשׁ בֵּין זוֹ לְזוֹ – THEN WHAT, R' Yehoshua responded, IS THE DIFFERENCE BETWEEN THIS woman AND THAT one, i.e. why is the woman who was secluded believed according to you while the captive woman is not? לְזוֹ יֵשׁ עֵדִים – They replied: Because there is a difference between the two women. REGARDING THIS ONE [the captive woman] THERE ARE "WITNESSES" that she had relations,[13] וְלְזוֹ אֵין לָהּ עֵדִים – WHILE REGARDING THAT ONE [the woman who was secluded] THERE ARE NO WITNESSES.[14] אָמַר לָהֶם – [R' YEHOSHUA] SAID TO THEM: אַף לְזוֹ יֵשׁ עֵדִים שֶׁהֲרֵי כְרֵיסָהּ בֵּין שִׁינֶּיהָ – REGARDING THIS ONE AS WELL THERE ARE WITNESSES, FOR HER STOMACH IS BETWEEN HER TEETH![15] אָמְרוּ לוֹ – THEY REPLIED TO HIM: רוֹב עוֹבְדֵי כוֹכָבִים פְּרוּצִים בַּעֲרָיוֹת הֵם – MOST IDOLATERS ARE UNRESTRAINED WITH

NOTES

1. This is tantamount to seeing them cohabit, because a ruin is a location notorious for sinning (*Rashi;* see *Berachos* 3a).

2. This conforms with Zeiri's understanding of our Mishnah, which first teaches a case of seclusion ["speaking"] and then of cohabitation ["pregnant"]. Similarly, the Baraisa states two cases: seclusion ["entering a secluded place"] and cohabitation ["entering a ruin"].

3. I.e. even if we say that "a secluded place" means a ruin, why would the Baraisa need to state *two* cases? (*Rashba*).

4. At present the Gemara takes this to mean that the term לְסֵתֶר, *into seclusion,* is not an independent case, but is rather connected to לְחוּרְבָּה, *into a ruin.* They entered into the seclusion *of* a ruin (presumably to cohabit).

5. The term אוֹ, *or,* clearly divides the Baraisa into *two* cases (*Rashba*).

6. When we said that the Baraisa "teaches one case," we did not mean that only one case is *spoken of* in the Baraisa, for the word "or" proves that two cases are being discussed. Rather, we meant that the two cases are *similar* in that each refers to a type of ruin [in which the couple is presumed to have cohabited] (*Shitah Mekubetzes* ד״ה חדא). The first case, "a place of seclusion," refers to a ruin located in a city, and is called "a place of seclusion" by the Baraisa in comparison to a ruin in a field. The second case refers to a ruin in a field, and is called by the Baraisa simply "a ruin" (*Maharam Schif*).

7. We can assume that she cohabited with one of the city-dwellers; therefore if most of the city is Jewish, she would be permitted to marry a Kohen (*Rashi*).

8. If she cohabited with someone outside of the city, the man could have come from anywhere in the world, and most of the world consists of gentiles, whose cohabitation disqualifies a woman from marrying a Kohen – see *Yevamos* 45a and *Kiddushin* 75b (*Rashi*).

9. The Baraisa that follows is actually an excerpt from *Tosefta* 1:9. Previously, in a section not cited by the Gemara, the *Tosefta* had quoted Rabban Gamliel and R' Eliezer as saying (as they do in our Mishnah) that we believe a pregnant unmarried woman to say that the man with whom she cohabited was fit for her and was not someone whose cohabitation would disqualify her from the Kehunah. The section of the *Tosefta* quoted here, which goes on to cite an attempted rebuttal by R' Yehoshua of Rabban Gamliel and R' Eliezer's ruling, opens with Rabban Gamliel and R' Eliezer finishing their ruling in which they declare the woman to be believed.

10. I.e. she is believed regarding herself to say she cohabited with someone who would not disqualify her (*Rashi*).

11. For we assume that she was violated by her captors. (This ruling is stated in a Mishnah on 22a without any dissenting opinion, indicating that it is undisputed.)

12. [The term אֲבָל connotes "truth," as, for example, in *Genesis* 17:19: אֲבָל שָׂרָה אִשְׁתְּךָ, which *Targum Onkelos* renders: *Truly, Sarah your wife* (*Rashi*).]

13. Since we saw that she was captured by idolaters, whose lack of restraint in matters of forbidden relations is well known, we are all "witnesses" that she was violated (*Rashi*).

14. The witnesses saw only seclusion. And even if she admits that she cohabited but claims that the man was someone who was fit for her, she is believed with a *migo,* for had she wanted to lie, she could have said that she did not cohabit (see *Rashi*).

15. That is, in regard to one of the cases in which you dispute me, there are also "witnesses" that she cohabited, for the woman is very obviously

עין משפט נר מצוה

פב א מיי' פי"ח מהל' איסורי ביאה הלכה כא סמג לאוין קכא טור ש"ע אה"ע סימן ו ס"ד:

פג ב מיי' פט"ו שם הלכה יא סמג שם טוש"ע שם סי' ו סעיף יז:

פד ג מיי' פי"ט שם הל' כ סמג לאוין קכב טוש"ע שם סימן ג סעיף ט:

פה ד מיי' פט"ו שם הלכה יא טוש"ע שם סימן ד סעיף כו [וברב אלפס עוד ביבמות פ"ז דף כו ע"א]:

תוספות רי"ד

היחוד ואין אוסרים על היחוד לימא דלא כר"י פי' דמשום יחוד מחזיק לה כבבעלה פי' מלקין מכות מרדות לאשת איש שנתייחד עם א' אבל אין אוסרין אותה על בעלה בעידי יחוד אלא היכא דקינא לה מעיקרא בפני שנים ואמר לה אל תסתרי עם איש פלוני אם נסתרה עמו היא סוטה האמורה בתורה וזהו נאסרת לו עד שתתברר במים המאררים אבל בלא קינוי מעיקרא אינה נאסרת לו בסתירה בלבד. ומהדר מעלה עשו ביוחסין דלא אסרה רי"א אלא אם היתה פנויה שלא תנשא לכהן דאמרינן דלמא נבעלה לפסול שה אבל לבעלה לא אסרה ואפי' אם היה בעלה כהן. אר"י א"ש הלכה כר"ג אריב"ל לדברי מכשיר מכשיר אפילו ברוב פסולים לדברי הפוסל פוסל אפי' ברוב כשרים: ההוא ארוס וארוסתו דאתו לקמיה דר"י היא אומרת מיני' והוא אומר

תוספות

השבתנו על המעוברת. פי' לדידן ניחא דלאשה מזנה בודקת ומזנה ולא דמיא לשבויה אלא לדידך דלית לך הך סברא תינח מעוברת אבל מדברת אפילו לפי דבריך יש הפרש דלזו יש עדים ולזו אין עדים ואיכא מיגו אמר להם מדברת היינו שבויה וכמו ששבויה אין נאמנת לומר לא נבעלתי ה"נ מדברת כדמסיק לפי שאין אפוטרופוס לעריות ומיהו פי' זה לא יתכן למאי דפרישית לעיל דלר' יהושע נאמנת לומר לא נבעלתי ופר"י בדוחק מדברת היינו שבויה דכמו א) ששבויה בחזקת בעולה כך מדברת בחזקת בעולה לענין שאם אמרה לכשר נבעלתי שאינה נאמנת במיגו לפי שיראה לומר לא נבעלתי ולהכי אהני דאין אפוטרופוס לעריות דלא חשבינן ליה מיגו: **מסייע** ליה לר' יהושע בן לוי. הקשה ר"ת אכתי תיפוק ליה דהתם בשבויה כל פסולים והכא בחורבה דדברא רוב ותירץ דרוב ככל וליכא למימר במדברת דליכא אלא רוב איכא למימר סמוך מיעוטא לחזקה ואיתרע לה רובא דאפילו אית להו סמוך מיעוטא לחזקה לר"ג ור' יהושע מ"מ לא הוי אלא פלגא ופלגא ודין הוא שתאסר מספק דספק איסורא לחומרא ולא דמי לתינוק שנמצא בצד העיסה בפרק עשרה יוחסין (קדושין דף פ. ושם) דמטהרין מטעם סמוך מיעוטא לחזקה דלא אמרו ספק טומאה לטהר יאמרו ספק איסור להתיר כדאמרינן פרק כיסוי הדם (חולין דף פו:): **מכשיר** אפילו ברוב פסולים. והא דקאמרינן בפ' עשרה יוחסין (קדושין עד. ושם) גבי אבא שאול היה קורא לשתוקי בדוקי ומפרש בגמרא שבודקין אמו ואומרת לכשר נבעלתי ופריך כמאן כר"ג תנינא חדא זימנא היתה מעוברת כו' פי' והוה ליה למתני וכן אמר אבא שאול וכן פי' שם בקונטרס ומשני דאבא שאול עדיפא מר"ג דאי מהתם הוה אמינא ברוב כשרים אבל כו' אע"ג דאמרי' הכא דר"ג מכשיר אפילו ברוב פסולין אבא שאול קאי אמתני' וממתני' לא משמע מידי דאיירי ברוב פסולים והא דפריך התם לעיל למאי דהוה בעי למימר דאבא שאול אתא להכשיר בבתה ניחא למ"ד לדברי המכשיר בה פוסל בבתה אבל למ"ד מכשיר בבתה מאי איכא למימר התם פריך שפיר דאפי' לזעירי לשון המשנה דקתני מה טיבו של עובר זה משמע דאתא להכשיר בבתה: **פשיטא** מי ידעינן אבוה מנו. הכא לא בעי לשנויי לא צריכא דאי תפס כדמשני בפרק עשרה יוחסין (שם דף עה. ושם) גבי ארוסה שעיברה דהתם רגילים לדבר דמארוס נתעברה ואיכא למיתלי ביה טפי מבאינש דעלמא: **בעינן** זרעו מיוחס אחריו. והא דאמר בהחולץ (יבמות דף לז.) ראשון ראוי להיות כ"ג גבי ספק בן תשעה לראשון בפרק נושאין על האנוסה (שם דף ק:) פריך לה ומשני זרעו מיוחס אחריו דרבנן וקרא אסמכתא בעלמא הוא וכי גזור רבנן בזנות בנישואין לא גזור:

[ההוא ארוס וארוסתו. והא דאמר בעשרה יוחסין (קדושין דף עה.) איתמר הבא על ארוסתו בבית חמיו רב אמר הולד ממזר ושמואל אמר הולד שתוקי כשלא בדקו את אמו דאי בשבדקו קשיא דשמואל אדשמואל דהכא אמר שמואל דנאמנת דהלכה כרבן גמליאל דנאמנת והתם קאמר איפוך שמואל אמר הולד ממזר וכן משמע דבמסקנא משני התם לעולם לא תיפוך כו' ומפרש מאי שתוקי שבודקין את אמו ואומרת לכשר נבעלתי ואם תאמר אכתי לשמואל דהתם משמע דוקא בבא על ארוסתו בבית חמיו מהני בדיקה והכא משמע אפילו כי לא מודה אמר שמואל דנאמנת כרבן גמליאל ויש לומר דהא דנקט בא היינו משום רבותא דרב נקטיה דאפילו הכי אמר הולד ממזר אי נמי התם הוא דבעינן בא משום דאיירי בדדיימא מעלמא כדאמר רבא ביבמות בשלהי אלמנה לכהן גדול מסתברא מילתא דרב בדדיימא מעלמא והכא בדלא דיימא מעלמא מיירי ועוד דבכל הספרים גרס בקדושין ארוסה שעיברה והיא דוקא קאמר שבודקין אבל בבא א"צ בדיקה ומיהו קשה ללישנא קמא ביבמות בסוף פ' אלמנה דפליגי רב ושמואל בבא ומסיק התם אביי דאע"ג דלא דיימא מעלמא פליגי דדלמא מדאפקרה נפשה לגבי ארוס מפקרה נפשה לגבי עלמא הא אמר הכא חדא דקא מודה ומשמע דכשר אפילו לר' יהושע ובא כמודה דמי

גמרא

או לחורבה ואמרו לה מה טיבו של איש זה כהן הוא ובן אחי אבא הוא רבן גמליאל ור"א אומרים נאמנת ורבי יהושע אומר לא מפיה אנו חיין אלא הרי זו בחזקת בעולה לנתין ולממזר עד שתביא ראיה לדבריה בשלמא לזעירי היינו דקתני תרתי לסתר או לחורבה אלא לרב אסי דאמר נבעלה תרתי למה לי חדא קתני לסתר דחורבה והא לסתר או לחורבה קתני חדא לחורבה דמתא וחדא לחורבה דדברא וצריכי דאי אשמעינן חורבה דמתא בהא קמכשר רבן גמליאל משום דרוב כשרים אצלה אבל לחורבה דדברא דרוב פסולין אצלה אימא מודה ליה לרבי יהושע ואי אשמעינן בההיא בההיא קאמר רבי יהושע אבל בהא אימא מודה לר"ג צריכא מיתיבי [א] זו עדות שהאשה כשרה לה ורבי יהושע אומר אינה נאמנת אמר להם ר"י אי אתם מודים [א]בשבויה שנשבית ויש לה עדים שנשבית והיא אומרת טהורה אני שאינה נאמנת אמרו לו אבל ומה הפרש יש בין זו לזו לזו יש עדים ולזו אין לה עדים אמר להם אף לזו יש עדים שהרי כריסה בין שיניה אמרו לו רוב עובדי כוכבים פרוצים בעריות הם אמר להן [ב] אין אפוטרופוס לעריות בד"א בעדות אשה בגופה אבל עדות אשה בבתה דברי הכל הולד שתוקי מאי קאמר להו ומאי קמהדרי ליה הכי קאמרי ליה השבתנו על המעוברת מה תשיבנו על המדברת אמר להם מדברת היינו שבויה אמרו לו שאני שבויה דרוב עובדי כוכבים פרוצים בעריות הם אמר להם הא נמי כיון דאיסתתר אין אפוטרופוס לעריות קתני מיהת תרתי מדברת ומעוברת תיובתא דרב אסי תיובתא ותיפוק ליה דהתם רוב פסולין אצלה והכא רוב כשרין אצלה מסייע ליה לרבי יהושע בן לוי דאמר רבי יהושע בן לוי לדברי המכשיר מכשיר אפילו ברוב פסולין לדברי הפוסל פוסל אפילו ברוב כשרים א"ר יוחנן [ג] [ב]לדברי המכשיר בה מכשיר בבתה לדברי הפוסל בה פוסל בבתה ורבי אלעזר אומר לדברי המכשיר בה פוסל בבתה אמר רבה מ"ט דר"א בשלמא איהי אית לה חזקה דכשרות בתה לית לה חזקה דכשרות איתיביה ר"א לרבי יוחנן בד"א בעדות אשה בגופה אבל עדות אשה בבתה דברי הכל הולד שתוקי מאי לאו שתוקי ופסול לא שתוקי וכשר ומי איכא שתוקי כשר אין כדשמואל דאמר שמואל [ד] עשרה כהנים עומדים ופירש אחד מהם ובעל הולד שתוקי מאי שתוקי אילימא שמשתיקין אותו מנכסי אביו ומי ידעינן אבוה מנו [ג]אלא שמשתיקין אותו מדין כהונה דכתיב [א] והיתה לו ולזרעו אחריו ברית כהונת עולם מי שזרעו מיוחס אחריו יצא זה שאין זרעו מיוחס אחריו [ד]ההוא ארוס וארוסתו דאתו לקמיה דרב יוסף היא אמרה מיניה והוא אמר אין

רש"י

לחורבה. סתמא לבעילה שהוא מקום לזנות: חורבה דמתא. סתם בעילתה מאחד מבני העיר ואיכא למימר בעיר שרובה ישראל כשרים קאמר: דדברא. ספק אחד מסוף העולם בא לכאן ורוב העולם עובדי כוכבים הם ופסולים אשה בביאתם לכהונה כדאמר ביבמות (דף מה.) ובקדושין (דף עה:) ילאו עובד כוכבים ועבד שאין לו אלמנות וגירושין בה: זו עדות שהאשה. עלמה כשרה לומר לכשר נבעלתי: אינה נאמנת. לינשא לכהן: אמרו לו אבל. הן כמו אבל שרה אשתך (בראשית יז) דמתרגמינן בקושטא: ומה הפרש בין זו לזו. ר' יהושע קאמר לה: לזו יש עדים. שנבעלה דכיון דנשבית לבין העובדי כוכבים והם פרוצים בעריות כולנו עדים שנבעלה: ולזו אין עדים. שנבעלה שלא ראוה אלא מדברת ומיגו דאי בעיא אמרה לא נבעלתי כי אמרה נמי לכשר נבעלתי מהימנא: אף לזו. כלומר אף כאן יש אחת שיש לה עדים ואתם חולקים עלי בהיותה מעוברת: אמרו ליה כו'. לקמיה מפרש מאי קא מהדרי ליה על מאי דקאמר להו: אין אפוטרופוס כו'. לקמן מפרש: בד"א. דנאמנת לר"ג: בעדות אשה בגופה. כלומר להכשיר את עלמה לכהונה דלא מחזקינן לה בנבעלה לפסול: מאי קאמר להו כו'. כלומר מאי קאמר להו איהו דקא מהדרי ליה איהו רוב עובדי כוכבים פרוצים בעריות כלום תשובה היא זו על מה שאמר להם אף לזו יש לה עדים אין לך פרוץ גדול מזה דקחזין דנתעברה ממנו: השבתנו על המעוברת. תשובה גמורה ונלחת: מדברת היינו שבויה. מה מדברת אין לה עדים אף שבויה אין לה עדים בבעילה ואתם מחזיקים אותה כנבעלה: פרוצים בעריות. והא ודאי נבעלה: אין אפוטרופוס לעריות. אין אתם יכולים להיות לה אפוטרופוס לומר לא נבעלה: ותיפוק ליה וכו'. לרבי יהושע פריך נהי נמי דאין אפוטרופוס לעריות תיפוק ליה דלא דמי לשבויה דהתם רוב פסולין כו': מכשיר אפי' ברוב פסולים. דאמרינן אוקמה אחזקה ועל רוב פסולים שהיו מכשירים אותה הביא הוא להם ראיה מן השבויה: אית לה חזקה דכשרות. וי"ל אשה זו בחזקת כשרות עומדת ומספק אתה בא לפוסלה אל תפסילנה מספק: לא שתוקי וכשר. כלומר שתוקי הוא במקלת שאם כהן היה הבועל והעובר יהיה זכר משתקין אותו מדין כהונה כדלקמן אבל כשר הוא ליוחסין שאם נקבה היא תינשא לכהונה ואם זכר הוא בתו ואלמנתו כשרות לכהונה: ופירש אחד מהן. ואין ידוע איזה הוא: הולד שתוקי. ואע"פ שברור לנו שמכהן כשר בא והאי שתוקי על כרחך כשר ליוחסין ואם נקבה היא ראויה לכהן וקרי ליה שתוקי: מדין כהונה. שלא יעבוד עבודה ולא יאכל תרומה: מיוחס אחריו. שאנו יודעין מי אביו:

מסורת הש"ס

א) [תוספתא סוף פרק א], ב) [חולין יא: נדה לג:], ג) [קדושין עד.], ד) יבמות ק.

תוספות ישנים

א) ולפע"ג למיעוט עובדי כוכבים אין פרולים מ"מ חשבינן לה ודאי בעולה מן הרוב הפרולים. מ"י.

תורה אור השלם

א) וְהָיְתָה לּוֹ וּלְזַרְעוֹ אַחֲרָיו בְּרִית כְּהֻנַּת עוֹלָם תַּחַת אֲשֶׁר קִנֵּא לֵאלֹהָיו וַיְכַפֵּר עַל בְּנֵי יִשְׂרָאֵל: [במדבר כה, יג]

ליקוטי רש"י

דברא. שדה [ברכות ג:]. שתוקי. שקורא פלוני אבא ואמו משתקתו [קידושין סט.]. שהרי כריסה בין שיניה. ואינה יכולה לומר לא נבעלתי [לקמן טז.]. הולד שתוקי. וכשר הוא דהא פשיטא לן דבן כהן הבא על הפנויה הוא. מדין כהונה. מלעבוד עבודה ואף על גב דלענין יוחסין לישא אשה כשר הוא פסול לעבודה. אחריו. שיכיר זרעו שהוא שלו [יבמות ק:].

מסורת הש"ס

א) [קדושין עו: ב"מ קי.], ב) [לעיל יא: לקמן טז.], ג) [לקמן טז.], ד) [לעיל יא.], ה) [לקמן טז.], ו) [קדושין עד. ?], ז) [לקמן טו. יבמות יא:], ח) [פסחים ג. וש"נ], ט) [קדושין עד.], י) [סס פא.], כ) [קדושין עג. לקמן טו.], ל) נ"י כ"י.

רש"י

דא"כ. דרב נחמן לא מיתוקס כרבן גמליאל אלא כרבי יהושע קשיא הלכתא אהלכתא: מתני' דרוסת איש את. קודם שארסתיך: גמ' טענתייהו במאי. מה היא תובעתו ומה הוא רוצה ליתן: במאתים ומנה. היא אומרת מוכת עץ אני ויש לי מאתים ועכשיו שלא הכרת בי והוא אומר דרוסת איש את ואין לך אלא מנה וקסבר כנסה בחזקת בתולה ונמצאת בעולה יש לה כתובה מנה: במנה ולא כלום. היא תובעת מנה והוא אומר אין ליך כלום: סבר לה. תנא דמתני' דאילו רבי יוחנן לא שביק רבנן ועביד כר"מ: קסבר. ר' יוחנן כנסה בחזקת בתולה ונמצאת בעולה יש לה מנה הלכך על כרחך מוכת עץ דמתני' ר"מ היא דאמר מאתים והוא אומר דרוסת איש את ויש ליך מנה דאי רבנן היא לא תבעה אלא מנה והוא אומר דרוסת איש את ויש לך מנה מאי איכא בין טענתא דידיה לטענתא דידה: בשלמא לרבי אלעזר. דאמר דרוסת איש אין לה כלום: היינו דקתני תרתי. גבי במתני' גבי פלוגתא דממונא היא אומרת משארסתני נאנסתי והיא אומרת מוכת עץ אני: חדא לאפוקי מדרמי בר חמא וחדא לאפוקי כו'. היא אומרת משארסתני נאנסתי תנא למיתני בה והיה מקחי מקח טעות לגמרי משמע ואין לה כלום לאפוקי מדרב חייא בר אבין דאמר לעיל (דף יא:) כנסה בחזקת בתולה ונמצאת בעולה יש לה כתובה מנה ותנא היא אומרת מוכת עץ אני לאפוקי מדרמי בר חמא דאמר לעיל גבי מוכת עץ אבל לא הכיר בה דברי הכל ולא כלום: אלא לרבי יוחנן. דאמר כנסה בחזקת בתולה ונמצאת בעולה יש לה כתובה מנה אם כן מאי מקח טעות דקתני אמאתים אבל מנה יש לה למה לי למיתני כלל להאי אי לאשמועינן פלוגתא דרבן גמליאל ור' יהושע בברי ושמא ואוקי ממונא בחזקת מריה ליתני חדא לאפוקי מדרמי בר חמא ולאשמעינן פלוגתייהו: דאיכא למימר מגו. מגו דאי בעיא אמרה מוכת עץ אני: בתרייתא. ליכא למימר מגו לר' יוחנן דמוקי מתני' כרבי מאיר דאמר מוכת עץ שלא הכיר בה כתובתה מאתים ליכא שום מגו דמה לי אומרת מוכת עץ אני תחתיך מה לי אמרה מעיקרא: מתני' [ראוה מדברת. בפנויה ומשום חששא דפסולין לנתין ולממזר וכיון שנבעלה לפסול פסלה מן הכהונה]: נאמנת. וכשרה לכהונה ולא מספקינן לה בנבעלה לפסול לה: היתה מעוברת כו'. בגמ' מפרש תרתי למה לי: גמ' נסתרה. ואע"פ שלא ראוה שנבעלה נפסלה לכהונה לרבי יהושע כדלקמן דמעלה עשו ביוחסין: אכלה ומחתה פיה. אלמא נקט תשמיש בלשון אכילה: בשלמא לזעירי היינו דקתני תרתי. מדברת להודיעך כחו דר' יהושע דאע"ג דלא ראוה שנבעלה פסולה ומעוברת להודיעך כחו דרבן גמליאל: בבתה. אם העובר הזה נקבה תנשא לכהונה לר"ג דאי אשמועינן בדידה הוה אמינא איהי הוא דהוה לה חזקה דכשרות מעיקרא אמרי' אוקמה אחזקה ואל תפסילנה מספק אבל עובר דלא הוה ליה חזקה דכשרות אימא לא: הניחא למ"ד כו'. לקמן בשמעתין: מאי איכא למימר. תרתי להכשיר בה למה לי כיון דמדברת בראוה שנבעלה: מלקין על היחוד. מכת מרדות: ואין אוסרין. אשה על בעלה בשביל יחוד בעלמא: לימא דלא כרבי יהושע. דמשום יחוד מחזיק לה בנבעלת: ביוחסין. בכהונה: לסתר. משמע יחוד בעלמא: לחורבה

גמרא

דאם כן קשיא הלכתא אהלכתא דקיימא לן א) הלכתא כרב נחמן בדיני ובהא אמר רב יהודה אמר שמואל הלכה כרבן גמליאל אלא לאו ש"מ כדמשנינן ש"מ: **מתני'** ג) היא אומרת מוכת עץ אני והוא אומר לא כי אלא דרוסת איש את ד)רבן גמליאל ורבי אליעזר אומרים נאמנת ורבי יהושע אומר לא מפיה אנו חיין אלא הרי זו בחזקת דרוסת איש עד שתביא ראיה לדבריה: **גמ'** טענתייהו במאי ג) רבי יוחנן אמר במאתים ומנה רבי אלעזר אמר במנה ולא כלום רבי יוחנן אמר במאתים ומנה סבר לה ד) כר"מ דאמר בין הכיר בה ובין לא הכיר בה מאתים ורבי אלעזר אומר במנה ולא כלום סבר לה כרבנן דאמרי בין הכיר בה בין לא הכיר בה מנה בשלמא ר' אלעזר לא קאמר כר' יוחנן דקא מוקי לה כרבנן אלא רבי יוחנן מ"ט לא אמר כר' אלעזר קסבר כנסה בחזקת בתולה ונמצאת בעולה יש לה כתובה מנה הכא הוא קאמר מנה והיא קאמרה מנה מאי איכא בין טענה דידיה לטענה דידה בשלמא לר' אלעזר היינו דקתני תרתי חדא לאפוקי מדרמי בר חמא וחדא לאפוקי מדרב חייא בר אבין א"ר ששת אלא לר' יוחנן תרתי למה לי חדא להודיעך כחו דרבן גמליאל וחדא להודיעך כחו דרבי יהושע קמייתא להודיעך כחו דרבי יהושע דאף על גב דאיכא למימר מיגו לא מהימנא בתרייתא להודיעך כחו דרבן גמליאל דאע"ג דליכא למימר מיגו מהימנא: **מתני'** ה) ראוה מדברת עם אחד ואמרו לה מה טיבו של איש זה איש פלוני וכהן הוא ו)רבן גמליאל ורבי אליעזר אומרים נאמנת ור' יהושע אומר לא מפיה אנו חיין אלא הרי זו בחזקת בעולה ° לנתין ולממזר עד שתביא ראיה לדבריה ז) היתה מעוברת ואמרו לה מה טיבו של עובר זה מאיש פלוני וכהן הוא ג)רבן גמליאל ורבי אליעזר אומרים נאמנת ור' יהושע אומר לא מפיה אנו חיין אלא הרי זו בחזקת מעוברת לנתין ולממזר עד שתביא ראיה לדבריה: **גמ'** מאי מדברת ז) זעירי אמר נסתרה רב אסי אמר ד) נבעלה בשלמא לזעירי היינו דקתני מדברת אלא לרב אסי מאי מדברת ה) לישנא מעליא כדכתיב א) אכלה ומחתה פיה ואמרה לא פעלתי און בשלמא לזעירי היינו דקתני תרתי מדברת ומעוברת אלא לרב אסי תרתי למה לי ח) חדא להכשיר בה וחדא להכשיר בבתה ט) הניחא למאן דאמר לדברי המכשיר בה מכשיר בבתה אלא למ"ד לדברי המכשיר בה פוסל בבתה מאי איכא למימר רב אסי סבר כמ"ד לדברי המכשיר בה מכשיר בבתה א"ל רב פפא לאביי לזעירי דאמר מאי מדברת נסתרה וא"ר יהושע לא מהימנא האמר רב י) מלקין על היחוד ואין אוסרין על היחוד לימא דלא כר"י אפי' תימא ר' יהושע כ) מעלה עשו ביוחסין מיתיבי ראוה שנכנסה עם אחד לסתר או

תוספות

רב אסי אמר נבעלה. אבל נסתרה מודה ר' יהושע דנאמנת לומר לכשר נבעלתי במגו דאי בעיא אמרה לא נבעלתי וא"ת והא רבי יהושע לית ליה מגו גבי משארסתני נאנסתי ויש לומר דהתם לא הוי מגו גמור דהא אפילו אמרה מוכת עץ אני אינה נאמנת לרבי יהושע כדתנן במתני' ולא קרי ליה מגו אלא לפי שהיא ° טענה מעולה ביותר: **חדא** להכשיר בה וחדא להכשיר בבתה. וצריכי תרוייהו חדא להודיעך כחו דרבן גמליאל וחדא להודיעך כחו דרבי יהושע: **לדברי** המכשיר בה פוסל בבתה. ומעוברת דנקט משום לישנא מעליא: **ואין** אוסרין על היחוד לימא דלא כרבי יהושע. תימה לרשב"א דלזעירי (נמי) דאמר נסתרה איירי כגון דמודה היא שנבעלה דאי אמרה לא נבעלתי אם כן הוי ספק ספיקא דמכשיר רבי יהושע כדאמר לקמן התם ספק ספיקא ויש לומר דלעולם איירי דקאמרה לא נבעלה וחשיב ליה חדא ספיקא משום דאין אפוטרופוס לעריות אבל קשה דבהדי' משמע בריש פרק שני (לקמן טז.) דאיירי בנבעלת דקאמר הניחא לזעירי דאמר מאי מדברת נסתרה דמגו דאי בעיא אמרה לא נבעלתי מהימנא כו' לכך נראה דפריך לזעירי דבספיקא חדא אסרינן לה והא יחוד דאשת איש דספיקא חדא היא ואין אוסרים על היחוד וק"ק דלכאורה נראה דיחוד איחוד פריך מדפריך לזעירי ולא לרב אסי: **מעלה** עשו ביוחסין. תימה דמשמע דאין אוסרין על היחוד איירי באשת איש ולא בפנויה ובסוף קדושין (דף פא. וסס) מוקי מלקין על היחוד דוקא בפנויה אבל באשת איש לא דאתה מוציא לעז על בניה ואפי' למר זוטרא דמלקין ומכריז באשת איש מודה דבפנויה נמי איירי ואור"ת דאף על גב דמלקין על היחוד איירי בפנויה אין אוסרין על היחוד לא איירי אלא באשת איש א) וא"ת והא אמרינן בפ' בתרא דנדרים (דף צא:) גבי ההוא נואף דעייל לגבה דההיא איתתא אמר ליה נואף לא תיכול מינהון דטעמינהו חויא אמר רבא איתתא שריא אם איתא דעבד איסורא ניחא ליה דלימות משמע דאי לאו האי טעמא היתה נאסרת על ידי יחוד ויש לומר דנואף שאני וה"ר יוסף דשליטן תירץ דאין אוסרים על היחוד איירי בפנויה כמו מלקין על היחוד ולא איירי לכהונה אלא אין אוסרין אותה לבנו כשתתייחד עם אביו לרבי יהודה דאסר באנוסת אביו (יבמות דף צז.): השבתנו

עין משפט נר מצוה

עט א מיי' פי"א מהל' אישות הלכה י טוש"ע אה"ע סימן סח סעיף ט: פ ב ג ד ה מיי' פט"ו מהלכות איסורי ביאה הלכה יא ופי"ח הלכה יג יד סמג לאוין קכח טור שו"ע שם סי' ו סעיף יז: פא ו מיי' פכ"ב שם הל' ג סמג לאוין רכו טוש"ע שם סימן כב סעיף ג:

תוספות רי"ד

כר' יהושע. פי' דהכא נמי אשה אומרת ברי ובעל אומר שמא אמר לך ר"נ אנא דאמרי אפילו לר"ג ע"כ לא קאמר ר"ג התם אלא משום דא"ל אוקי איתתא אחזקתה פי' מספקא לן אשעת אירוסין אי בתולה הוה ואי בעולה הוה העמד אשה על חזקתה ובתולה היתה והשתא היא דאיתנס לאחר אירוסין אבל הכא מאי חזקה אית לי' להאי תובע דנוקמי' אחזקתה לגבות הלכך זיל בתר חזקת דממונא דאל"כ [אלא] דרב נחמן לא מתוקם כר"ג אלא כר' יהושע וק' הילכתא אהלכתא. והמורה גריס ע"כ לא קאמר ר"ג התם אלא משום דאיכא למימר מיגו. פי' מיגו דאי בעי' טענה טענה מעלייתא מהך כגון גבי משארסתני נאנסתי מיגו דאי בעיא אמרה מוכת עץ אני ולא פסלה נפשה מכהונה וקאמרה נאנסתי דקא פסלה נפשה מכהונה ש"מ קושטא קאמרה וגבי היא אומרת מוכת עץ אני מיגו דאי בעי' אמ' מוכ"ע אני תחתיך ואית לה מאתים וקאמרה מוכת עץ אני מקודם לכן ואין לה אלא מנה נאמנת אלא הכא גבי האי תובע מאי מיגו איכא וה"ה נמי דהוה מצי ר"נ למימר ע"כ לא קאמר ר"ג התם אלא משום דבעל הוה מחויב לה כתובה מעיקרא ועכשיו הוא בא לפטור עצמו אבל במנה לי בידך שלא ידענו שנתחייב לו מקודם לכן אלא עכשיו אנו רוצים לחייבו לא אמר וכו' וכדכתיבנא לעיל אלא חד מתרי טעמא נקט. **ה"נ** מסתברא כדשנינן דא"כ קשה הלכתא אהלכתא דקיי"ל הלכה כר"נ בדיני. ובהא אמר ר"י אמר שמואל הלכה כר"ג ש"מ: **מתני' היא** אומרת מוכת עץ אני והוא אומר לא כי אלא דרוסת איש את ר"ג ור"א אומרים נאמנת ור"י אומר לא מפיה אנו חיין אלא ה"ז בחזקת דרוסת איש עד שתביא ראיה לדבריה: **טענתייהו במאי.** פי' מה היא תובעתו ומה הוא רוצה ליתן **ר' יוחנן אמר** במאתים ומנה פי' היא אומרת מוכת עץ אני ויש לי מאתים ואע"פ שלא הכרת בי והוא אומר דרוסת איש את ואין לך אלא מנה וכנסה בחזקת בתולה ונמצאת בעולה יש לה כתובה מנה וסבר לה כר"מ דאמר מוכת עץ בין הכיר בה בין לא הכיר בה כתובתה מאתים וכנסה בחזקת בתולה ונמצאת בעולה כתובתה מנה הלכך ע"כ מוכת עץ דמתני' ר"מ היא דאמר מאתים והוא אומר דרוסת איש את ואין לך אלא מנה

תוספות ישנים

א) [מיהו קשה לאדפריך מרב דאמר אין אוסרין על היחוד הוה ליה למיפרך מהא דקי"ל כולי תלמודא וכתב משניות דאין אשה נאסרת על בעלה אלא על ידי קינוי וסתירה לכך נ"ל דרב איירי בפנויה דוקא ואפ"ה מעלה עשו ביוחסין לאסור היכא דאמרה לכשר נבעלתי דמודה מיהא ולא מהימנינן לה במגו אבל אי אמרה לא נבעלתי בהא לא עשו מעלה והכא איירי רב. מ"י].

גליון הש"ס

מתניתין לנתין ולממזר. עי' גיטין פט ע"א תוס' ד"ה בעולה ובמהרש"א שם: תוס' ד"ה רב אסי וכו' טענה מעולה ביותר. וכ"כ הרשב"א קדושין דף ג ע"א ד"ה הא.

תורה אור השלם

א) כֵּן דֶּרֶךְ אִשָּׁה מְנָאָפֶת אָכְלָה וּמָחֲתָה פִיהָ וְאָמְרָה לֹא פָעַלְתִּי אָוֶן: [משלי ל, כ]

ליקוטי רש"י

היא אומרת מוכת עץ אני. הנושא את האשה בחזקת בתולה ולא מצא לה בתולים והיא אומרת מוכת עץ אני כו' [לעיל יא.]. מוכת עץ. שנפגעה בעץ או באבן ונשברו בתוליה [שם]. במנה ולא כלום. מוכת עץ שלא הכיר בה אינה יכולה לתובעו אלא מנה והוא אומר דרוסת איש את ואין ליך כלום [לקמן טז.]. הכיר בה. כשכנסה וכתב לה כתובה היה יודע שהיא מוכת עץ [שם.]. וכהן הוא. כלומר מיוחס הוא [לעיל יב:]. לישנא מעליא. לשון מכסים לומר לשון אחר שמלוה ודרך נקיי הדעת בלשון נקיה [פסחים ג.]. אכלה. לשון נקיה דבר הכתוב. ומחתה. כופה פיה למטה כמו כדכתיב כאשר ימחה את הצלחת מחה והפך על פניה [משלי ל, כ]. פוסל בבתה. [דר"ג לא] האמינה אלא לעצמה שלא נתחללה מן התרומה אבל לא להכשיר אותו עובר שאם בת היא לא תינשא לכהן [קדושין עד.]. מלקין על היחוד. מרדות. ואין אוסרין. אשה לאיש על בעלה מחמת יחוד [שם פא.].

דאי רבנן היא לא טענה אלא מנה מאי איכא בין טענה דידיה לטענה דידה במנה טענה לו ומנה מודה לה ופי' [המורה] סבר לה דלעיל סבר לה תנא דמתני' דאילו ר' יוחנן לא שביק רבנן ועביד כר"מ **ור"א** סבר במנה ולא כלום סבר לה כרבנן דאמרי בין הכיר בה בין לא הכיר בה כתובתה מנה וכנסה בחזקת בתולה ונמצאת בעולה אין לה כלום **בשלמא** ר"א לא אמר כר"י דקא מוקי לה כרבנן פי' במנה ולא כלום: היינו דקתני תרי בבא במתני' גבי פלוגתא דממונא היא אומרת משארסתני נאנסתי וכו' והוא אומר לא כי והיה מקחי מקח טעות לגמרי משמע ואין לה כלום **אלא ר"י** מ"ט לא אמר כר"א קסבר כנסה בחזקת בתולה ונמצאת בעולה יש לה כתובה מנה הכא הוא אומר מנה והיא אומרת מנה מאי איכא בין טענתה לטענתיה והלכתא כר"א דקיימי רבא ורב אשי כוותיה דכנסה בחזקת בתולה ונמצאת בעולה אין לה כלום כדכתיבנא לעיל ובמוכת עץ נמי הלכתא כרבנן דאמרי מנה: **מתני' ראוה** מדברת עם א' מה טיבו של זה איש פלוני וכהן הוא ר"ג ור"א אומרים נאמנת ור"י אומר לא מפיה אנו חיין אלא ה"ז בחזקת בעולה לנתין ולממזר עד שתביא ראיה לדבריה היתה מעוברת מה טיבו של עובר זה מאיש פלוני וכהן הוא ר"ג ור"א אומרים נאמנת ור"י אומר לא מפיה אנו חיין אלא ה"ז בחזקת מעוברת מנתין וממזר עד שתביא ראיה לדבריה: **וכהן הוא** פי' מיוחס ולא כהן ממש שאינה נאמנת להחזיק העובר בחזקת כהן אלא בחזקת כשר שאם הוא בת תנשא לכהונה: **מאי מדברת** זעירא אמר נסתרה ואע"פ שלא ראוה שנבעלה פסולה לכהונה לר"י כדלקמן שמעלה עשו ביוחסין ור"א אמר נבעלה בשלמא לזעירא היינו דקתני מדברת אלא לר"א מאי מדברת לישנא מעליא כדכתיב אכלה ומחתה פיה וגו' פי' נקט תשמיש בלשון אכילה בשלמא לזעירא היינו דקתני תרתי מדברת ומעוברת פי' מדברת להודיעך כחו דר"י דאפילו בעדי יחוד בלבד אסורה היא לכהן משום דמעלה עשו ביוחסין ומעוברת להודיעך כחו דר"ג אלא לר"א תרתי למה לי פי' לתני מדברת וכ"ש מעוברת. חדא להכשיר בה וחדא להכשיר בבתה **דאתמר** ר"י אמר לדברי המכשיר בה מכשיר בבתה לדברי הפוסל בה פוסל בבתה ור"א אומר אף לדברי המכשיר בה פוסל בבתה דבשלמא איהי אית לה חזקה דכשרות פי' מעיקרא ואוקמה אחזקה ולא תפסלנה מספק אבל בתה לית לה חזקה דכשרות והלכתא כר' יוחנן דהוא רביה דר"א שאין הלכה כתלמיד במקום הרב ותו דקאי כאבא שאול דתנן בעשרה יוחסין אבא שאול היה קורא לשתוקי בדוקי ואמרי בגמ' מאי בדוקי שבודקין את אמו ואי אמרה לכשר נבעלתי נאמנת ואע"ג דאיכא רוב פסולים אצלה וא"ר הל' כאבא שאול: **א"ל** ר"פ לאביי לזעירי דאמר נסתרה ואר"י דלא מהימנא הא דאמר רב מלקין על

the case of "speaking" [i.e. cohabiting] is equivalent to the case in which she is pregnant![28] – ? –

The Gemara answers:

חֲדָא לְהַכְשִׁיר בָּהּ – One case is needed **to rule *her* fit** to a Kohen, **וַחֲדָא לְהַכְשִׁיר בְּבִתָּהּ – and the other to rule her *daughter* fit.**[29]

The Gemara questions this answer:

הָנִיחָא לְמַאן דְּאָמַר לְדִבְרֵי הַמַּכְשִׁיר בָּהּ מַכְשִׁיר בְּבִתָּהּ – This is satisfactory according to the one who says that **the one who rules her fit** [i.e. Rabban Gamliel and R' Eliezer] **rules her daughter fit** as well.[30] **אֶלָּא לְמַאן דְּאָמַר לְדִבְרֵי הַמַּכְשִׁיר בָּהּ פּוֹסֵל בְּבִתָּהּ – But according to the one who says** that **the one who rules her fit rules her daughter *unfit,***[31] **מַאי אִיכָּא לְמֵימַר – what is there to say?**

The Gemara answers:

רַב אַסִי סָבַר כְּמַאן דְּאָמַר לְדִבְרֵי הַמַּכְשִׁיר בָּהּ מַכְשִׁיר בְּבִתָּהּ – Rav Assi holds in accordance with the one who says that **the one who rules her fit rules her daughter fit** as well.

The Gemara raises an objection to Zeiri's view:

אָמַר לֵיהּ רַב פָּפָּא לְאַבַּיֵי – Rav Pappa said to Abaye: **לִזְעִירִי דְּאָמַר מַאי מְדַבֶּרֶת נִסְתְּרָה – According to Zeiri who says "she was speaking" means she was secluded,** **וְאָמַר רַבִּי יְהוֹשֻׁעַ לֹא מְהֵימְנָא – and R' Yehoshua says** that **she is not believed,** which shows that R' Yehoshua considers seclusion evidence of cohabitation, **הָאָמַר רַב – why, Rav has said: מַלְקִין עַל הַיִּחוּד – "We administer lashes for seclusion,**[32] **וְאֵין אוֹסְרִין עַל הַיִּחוּד – but we do not rule** a woman **prohibited** to her husband **for seclusion."**[33] **לֵימָא דְּלָא כְּרַבִּי יְהוֹשֻׁעַ – Shall we say that [Rav]'s** ruling **is not in accordance with R' Yehoshua?**[34]

The Gemara answers:

אֲפִילוּ תֵּימָא רַבִּי יְהוֹשֻׁעַ – You can even say that he follows the view of **R' Yehoshua.** **מַעֲלָה עָשׂוּ בְּיוּחֲסִין – They set a higher standard in genealogical matters** regarding a Kohen.[35]

The Gemara raises an objection to Rav Assi's interpretation:

מֵיתִיבֵי – They challenged him **from a Baraisa:** **רָאוּהָ שֶׁנִּכְנְסָה עִם אֶחָד לְסֵתֶר – THEY SAW HER ENTER WITH [A MAN] INTO A SECLUDED PLACE**[36]

NOTES

28. [In both cases she clearly cohabited, the question being only with whom.]

29. I.e. the second case adds that according to Rabban Gamliel if the unborn child is a girl, she too is permitted to marry a Kohen. It is necessary for the Mishnah to teach us this fact because otherwise we might think that only the woman herself is permitted to a Kohen, since she has a *chazakah* of fitness (i.e. she was fit for a Kohen until now). Thus we do not, out of doubt, remove her from this *chazakah*. But the daughter, who was *born* into a state of doubt, has no such *chazakah*. We might therefore think that she should be disqualified (*Rashi*). [And had the Mishnah stated only the second case, I might have thought that it meant to permit only the woman herself, and it used the term "pregnant" only as a euphemism (*Maharsha,* in explanation of *Rashi, Ritva;* cf. *Tosafos*).]

30. The Gemara below (13b) will describe an Amoraic debate as to how far Rabban Gamliel's lenient ruling extends. According to one opinion, Rabban Gamliel rules even her daughter fit. Accordingly, we can say that this is what the second case of the Mishnah adds.

31. [And the Mishnah uses the expression "pregnant" merely as a euphemism (*Tosafos*).]

32. I.e. Rabbinically imposed lashes (*Rashi;* see *Tosafos,* who explain that this refers to seclusion with an unmarried woman).

33. If a married woman was secluded with a strange man, she does not become prohibited to her husband (*Rashi*), because we do not take the seclusion as evidence of cohabitation. [If we did, she would become forbidden to her husband, as we learned above, 9a.]

34. According to Zeiri, R' Yehoshua disqualifies from the Kehunah a woman who was secluded with a man because he assumes that they cohabited (*Rashi*). This seems to contradict Rav's ruling.

35. Although ordinarily we do not assume that a man and woman who were secluded cohabited, with regard to the Kehunah we are more stringent and fear for the worst.

36. This implies that the witnesses saw only seclusion [but not an act of cohabitation] (*Rashi*).

דאם כן קשיא הלכתא אהלכתא דקיימא לן הלכתא כרב נחמן בדיני ובהא אמר רב יהודה אמר שמואל הלכה כרבן גמליאל אלא לאו ש"מ כדמשנינן ש"מ: **מתני'** היא אומרת מוכת עץ אני והוא אומר לא כי אלא דרוסת איש את רבן גמליאל ורבי אליעזר אומרים נאמנת ורבי יהושע אומר לא מפיה אנו חיין אלא הרי זו בחזקת דרוסת איש עד שתביא ראיה לדבריה: **גמ'** טענתיהו במאי רבי יוחנן אמר במאתים ומנה רבי אלעזר אמר במנה ולא כלום רבי יוחנן אמר במאתים ומנה סבר לה כר"מ דאמר בין הכיר בה ובין לא הכיר בה מאתים ורבי אלעזר אומר במנה ולא כלום סבר לה כרבנן דאמרי בין הכיר בה בין לא הכיר בה מנה בשלמא ר' אלעזר לא קאמר כר' יוחנן דקא מוקי לה כרבנן אלא רבי יוחנן מ"ט לא אמר כר' אלעזר קסבר כנסה בחזקת בתולה ונמצאת בעולה יש לה כתובה מנה הכא הוא קאמר מנה והיא קאמרה מנה מאי איכא בין טענה דידיה לטענה דידה בשלמא לר' אלעזר היינו דקתני תרתי חדא לאפוקי מדרמי בר חמא וחדא לאפוקי מדרב חייא בר אבין א"ר ששת אלא לר' יוחנן תרתי למה לי חדא להודיעך כחו דרבן גמליאל וחדא להודיעך כחו דרבי יהושע קמייתא להודיעך כחו דרבי יהושע דאף על גב דאיכא למימר מיגו לא מהימנא בתרייתא להודיעך כחו דרבן גמליאל דאע"ג דליכא למימר מיגו מהימנא: **מתני'** ראוה מדברת עם אחד ואמרו לה מה טיבו של איש זה איש פלוני וכהן הוא רבן גמליאל ורבי אליעזר אומרים נאמנת ור' יהושע אומר לא מפיה אנו חיין אלא הרי זו בחזקת בעולה לנתין ולממזר עד שתביא ראיה לדבריה היתה מעוברת ואמרו לה מה טיבו של עובר זה מאיש פלוני וכהן הוא רבן גמליאל ורבי אליעזר אומרים נאמנת ור' יהושע אומר לא מפיה אנו חיין אלא הרי זו בחזקת מעוברת לנתין ולממזר עד שתביא ראיה לדבריה: **גמ'** מאי מדברת זעירי אמר נסתרה רב אסי אמר נבעלה בשלמא לזעירי היינו דקתני מדברת אלא לרב אסי מאי מדברת לישנא מעליא כדכתיב אכלה ומחתה פיה ואמרה לא פעלתי און בשלמא לזעירי היינו דקתני תרתי מדברת ומעוברת אלא לרב אסי תרתי למה לי חדא להכשיר בה וחדא להכשיר בבתה הניחא למאן דאמר לדברי המכשיר בה מכשיר בבתה אלא למ"ד לדברי המכשיר בה פוסל בבתה מאי איכא למימר רב אסי סבר כמ"ד לדברי המכשיר בה מכשיר בבתה א"ל רב פפא לאביי לזעירי דאמר מאי מדברת נסתרה וא"ר יהושע לא מהימנא האמר רב מלקין על היחוד ואין אוסרין על היחוד לימא דלא כר"י אפי' תימא ר' יהושע מעלה עשו ביוחסין מיתיבי ראוה שנכנסה עם אחד לסתר או

רש"י

דא"כ. דרב נחמן לא מיתוקם כרבן גמליאל אלא כרבי יהושע קשיא הלכתא אהלכתא: **מתני'** דרוסת איש את. קודם שארסתיך: **גמ'** טענתיהו במאי. מה היא תובעתו ומה הוא רוצה ליתן: **במאתים ומנה.** היא אומרת מוכת עץ אני ויש לי מאתים ואע"פ שלא הכרת בי והוא אומר לדרוסת איש את ואין לך אלא מנה וקסבר כנסה בחזקת בתולה ונמצאת בעולה יש לה כתובה מנה: **במנה ולא כלום.** היא תובעת מנה והוא אומר אין ליך כלום: **סבר לה.** תנא דמתני' דאילו רבי יוחנן לא שביק רבנן ועביד כר"מ: **קסבר.** ר' יוחנן כנסה בחזקת בתולה ונמצאת בעולה יש לה מנה הלכך על כרחך מוכת עץ דמתני' ר"מ היא דאמר מאתים והוא אומר לדרוסת איש את ויש ליך מנה דאי רבנן היא לא תבעה אלא מנה והוא אומר לדרוסת איש את ויש לך מנה מאי איכא בין טענתא דידיה לטענתא דידה: **בשלמא לרבי אלעזר.** דאמר לדרוסת איש אין לה כלום: **היינו דקתני תרתי.** בבי מתני' גבי פלוגתא דממונא היא אומרת משארסתני נאנסתי והיא אומרת מוכת עץ אני: **חדא לאפוקי מדרמי בר חמא וחדא לאפוקי כו'.** היא אומרת משארסתני נאנסתי תנא למיתני בה והיה מקחי מקח טעות לגמרי משמע ואין לה כלום לאפוקי מדרב חייא בר אבין דאמר לעיל (דף יא:) כנסה בחזקת בתולה ונמצאת בעולה יש לה כתובה מנה ותנא היא אומרת מוכת עץ אני לאפוקי מדרמי בר חמא דאמר לעיל גבי מוכת עץ אבל לא הכיר בה דברי הכל ולא כלום: **אלא לרבי יוחנן.** דאמר כנסה בחזקת בתולה ונמצאת בעולה יש לה כתובה מנה אם כן מאי מקח טעות דקתני במאתים אבל מנה יש לה למה לי למיתני כלל להכי אי לאשמועינן פלוגתא דרבן גמליאל ור' יהושע בבבי וסמא ואוקי ממונא בחזקת מריה ליתני חדא לאפוקי מדרמי בר חמא ולאשמעינן פלוגתייהו: **דאיכא למימר מיגו.** מגו דאי בעיא אמרה מוכת עץ אני: **בתרייתא.** ליכא למימר מגו לר' יוחנן דמוקי מתני' כרבי מאיר דאמר מוכת עץ שלא הכיר בה כתובתה מאתים ליכא שום מגו דמה לי אומרת מוכת עץ אני מה לי אמרה מעיקרא: **מתני'** **ראוה מדברת.** בפנויה ומשום חששא דפסולין לנתין ולממזר וכיון שנבעלה לפסול פסלה מן הכהונה: **נאמנת.** וכשרה לכהונה ולא מספקינן לה בנבעלה לפסול לה: **היתה מעוברת כו'.** בגמ' מפרש תרתי למה לי: **גמ'** **נסתרה.** ואע"פ שלא ראוה שנבעלה נפסלה לכהונה לרבי יהושע כדלקמן למעלה עשו ביוחסין: **אכלה ומחתה פיה.** אלמא נקט תשמיש בלשון אכילה: **בשלמא לזעירי היינו דקתני תרתי.** מדברת להודיעך כחו דר' יהושע דאע"ג דלא ראוה שנבעלה פסולה ומעוברת להודיעך כחו דרבן גמליאל: **בבתה.** אם העובר הזה נקבה תנשא לכהונה לר"ג דאי אשמועינן בדידה הוה אמינא איהי הואיל דהוה לה חזקה דכשרות מעיקרא אמרי' אוקמה אחזקה ולא תפסילנה מספק אבל עובר דלא הוה ליה חזקה דכשרות אימא לא: **הניחא למ"ד כו'.** לקמן בשמעתין: **מאי איכא למימר.** תרתי להכשיר בה למה לי כיון דמדברת ברואה שנבעלה: **מלקין על היחוד.** מכת מרדות: **ואין אוסרין.** אשה על בעלה בשביל יחוד בעלמא: **לימא דלא כרבי יהושע.** דמשום יחוד מחזיק לה בנבעלת: **ביוחסין.** בכהונה: **לסתר.** משמע יחוד בעלמא: לחורבה

תוספות

רב אסי אמר נבעלה. אבל נסתרה מודה ר' יהושע דנאמנת לומר לכשר נבעלתי במגו דאי בעיא אמרה לא נבעלתי וא"ת והא רבי יהושע לית ליה מגו גבי משארסתני נאנסתי ויש לומר דהתם לא הוי מגו גמור דהא אפילו אמרה מוכת עץ אני אינה נאמנת לרבי יהושע כדתנן במתני' ולא קרי ליה מגו אלא לפי שהיא [ט] טענה מעולה ביותר: **חדא** להכשיר בה וחדא להכשיר בבתה. ולריכי תרוייהו חדא להודיעך כחו דרבן גמליאל וחדא להודיעך כחו דרבי יהושע: **לדברי** המכשיר בה פוסל בבתה. ומעוברת דנקט משום לישנא מעליא: **ואין** אוסרין על היחוד לימא דלא כרבי יהושע. תימה לרשב"א דלזעירי (נמי) דאמר נסתרה איירי כגון דמודה היא שנבעלה דאי אמרה לא נבעלתי אם כן הוי ספק ספיקא דמכשיר רבי יהושע כדאמר לקמן התם ספק ספיקא ויש לומר דלעולם איירי דקאמרה לא נבעלה וחשיב ליה חדא ספיקא משום דאין אפוטרופוס לעריות אבל קשה דבהדי' משמע בריש פרק שני (לקמן טו.) דאיירי בנבעלת דקאמר הניחא לזעירי דאמר מאי מדברת נסתרה דמגו דאי בעיא אמרה לא נבעלתי מהימנא כו' לכך נראה דפריך לזעירי דבספיקא חדא אסרינן לה והא יחוד דאשת איש דספיקא חדא היא ואין אוסרים על היחוד וק"ק דלכאורה נראה דיחוד איחוד פריך מדפריך לזעירי ולא לרב אסי: **מעלה** עשו ביוחסין. תימה דמשמע דאין אוסרין על היחוד איירי באשת איש ולא בפנויה ובסוף קדושין (דף פא. ושם) מוקי מלקין על היחוד דוקא בפנויה אבל באשת איש לא דאתה מוציא לעז על בניה ואפי' למר זוטרא דמלקין ומכריז באשת איש מודה דבפנויה נמי איירי ואור"ת דאף על גב דמלקין על היחוד איירי בפנויה אין אוסרין על היחוד לא איירי אלא באשת איש א) וא"ת והא אמרינן בפ' בתרא דנדרים (דף צא:) גבי ההוא נואף דעייל לגבה דההיא איתתא אמר ליה נואף לא תיכול מינהון דטעמינהו חויא אמר רבא איתתא שריא אם איתא דעבד איסורא ניחא ליה דלימות משמע דאי לאו האי טעמא היתה נאסרת על ידי יחוד ויש לומר דנואף שאני וה"ר יוסף דשליטן תירץ דאין אוסרים על היחוד איירי בפנויה כמו מלקין על היחוד ולא איירי לכהונה אלא אין אוסרין אותה לבנו כשמתייחד עם אביו לרבי יהודה דאסר באנוסת אביו (יבמות דף צז.):

השבתנו

מסורת הש"ס

א) [קדושין עג: ב"מ קי.], ב) [לעיל יא: לקמן טו.], ג) [לקמן טו.], ד) [לעיל יא.], ה) [לקמן טו.], ו) שם קדושין עד. [עיי"ש], ז) [לקמן טו. יבמות לז:], ח) [פסחים ג. וש"נ], ט) [קדושין פא.], י) שם פא., כ) [קדושין עג. לקמן טו.], ל) ג"י כי'.

תוספות ישנים

א) [מיהו קשה לדפריך מרב דאמר אין אוסרין על היחוד הוה ליה למיפרך מהא דקי"ל בכולי תלמודא וכמה משניות דאין אשה נאסרת על בעלה אלא על ידי קינוי וסתירה לכך נ"ל דרב איירי בפנויה דוקא וה"פ למעלה עשו ביוחסין לכשר נבעלתי דמודה מיהא ולא מהימנינן לה במגו אבל אי אמרה לא נבעלתי בהא לא עשו מעלה והא איירי רב. ת"י].

גליון הש"ס

מתניתין לנתין ולממזר. עי' גיטין פט ע"א תוס' ד"ה בעולה ובמהרש"א שם: תוס' ד"ה רב אסי וכו' טענה מעולה ביותר. וכ"כ הרשב"א קדושין דף ג ע"א ד"ה הא:

תורה אור השלם

א) כֵּן דֶּרֶךְ אִשָּׁה מְנָאָפֶת אָכְלָה וּמָחֲתָה פִיהָ וְאָמְרָה לֹא פָעַלְתִּי אָוֶן: [משלי ל, כ]

ליקוטי רש"י

היא אומרת מוכת עץ אני. הנושא את האשה בחזקת בתולה ולא מלא לה בתולים היא אומרת מוכת עץ אני כו' [לעיל יא.]. **מוכת עץ.** שנתקע לה עץ באותו מקום [שם]. **במנה ולא כלום.** מוכת עץ שלא הכיר בה אינה יכולה לתובעו אלא מנה והוא אומר דרוסת איש את ואין ליך כלום [לקמן טז.]. **הכיר בה.** כשכנסה וכתב לה כתובה היה יודע שהיא מוכת עץ [שם]. **וכהן הוא.** כלומר מיוחס הוא [לעיל יב:]. **לישנא מעליא.** לשון מכובס לחזר לשון תם ונקי שמצוה לאדם לספר בלשון נקיה [פסחים ג.]. **אכלה.** לשון נקיה דבר הכתוב. **ומחתה.** [illegible] **פוסל בבתה.** [illegible] **מלקין על היחוד.** מרדות. **ואין אוסרין.** אשה על בעלה משום יחוד [שם פא.].

עין משפט נר מצוה

עט א מיי' פי"ח מהל' איסורי ביאה הלכה י טוש"ע אה"ע סימן סח סעיף ט:
פ ב ג ד ה מיי' פט"ו מהלכות איסורי ביאה הלכה יא ופכ"א הלכה יג יד סמג לאוין קכו טור שו"ע שם סי' ו סעיף יז:
פא ו מיי' פכ"א שם הל' ג סמג לאוין רכו טוש"ע שם סימן כב סעיף ג:

תוספות רי"ד

כר' יהושע. פי' דהכא נמי אשה אומרת ברי ובעל אומר שמא אמר לך ר"ג אנא דאמרי אפילו לר"ג ע"כ לא קאמר ר"ג התם אלא משום דא"ל אוקי איתתא אחזקתה פי' מספקא לן אשעת אירוסין אי בתולה הוה ואי בעולה הוה העמד אשה על חזקתה ובתולה היתה והשתא היא דאיתנס לאחר אירוסין אבל הכא מאי חזקה אית לי' להאי תובע דנוקמי' אחזקתא [illegible] [אלא] דרב נחמן לא מתוקם כר"ג אלא כר' יהושע וק' הילכתא אהלכתא. [illegible]

דאי רבנן היא לא טענה אלא מנה מאי איכא בין טענה דידיה לטענה דידה [illegible] סבר לה דלעיל סבר לה תנא דמתני' דאילו ר' יוחנן לא שביק רבנן ועביד כר"מ ור"א סבר לה כרבנן דאמרי בין הכיר בה בין לא הכיר בה מנה וכנסה בחזקת בתולה ונמצאת בעולה אין לה כלום בשלמא [illegible] והלכתא כר"א [illegible] **מתני'** ראוה מדברת עם אחד [illegible] **גמ'** מאי מדברת [illegible]

נֶאֱמֶנֶת – She is believed.[19] **וְרַבִּי יְהוֹשֻׁעַ אוֹמֵר – R' Yehoshua, however, says:** **לֹא מִפִּיהָ אָנוּ חַיִּין – Not by her mouth do we live.** **אֶלָּא הֲרֵי זוֹ בְּחֶזְקַת בְּעוּלָה לְנָתִין וּלְמַמְזֵר – Rather, she is presumed to have cohabited with a *nasin* or a *mamzer*** **עַד שֶׁתָּבִיא רְאָיָה לִדְבָרֶיהָ – until she brings proof to her claim.**[20]

The second case:

הָיְתָה מְעוּבֶּרֶת – [An unmarried woman] was pregnant, **וְאָמְרוּ לָהּ מַה טִּיבוֹ שֶׁל עוּבָּר זֶה – and [the court] said to her, "What is the nature of this fetus?"** **מֵאִישׁ פְּלוֹנִי וְכֹהֵן הוּא** – and she replied, "It was fathered **by So-and-so, and he is a Kohen."** **רַבָּן גַּמְלִיאֵל וְרַבִּי אֱלִיעֶזֶר אוֹמְרִים – Rabban Gamliel and R' Eliezer say:** **נֶאֱמֶנֶת – She is believed.** **וְרַבִּי יְהוֹשֻׁעַ אוֹמֵר – R' Yehoshua, however, says:** **לֹא מִפִּיהָ אָנוּ חַיִּין – Not by her mouth do we live.** **אֶלָּא הֲרֵי זוֹ בְּחֶזְקַת מְעוּבֶּרֶת לְנָתִין וּלְמַמְזֵר – Rather, she is presumed to be pregnant from a *nasin* or a *mamzer*** **עַד שֶׁתָּבִיא רְאָיָה לִדְבָרֶיהָ – until she brings proof to her claim.**[21]

Gemara The Gemara seeks an explanation of the Mishnah's first case:

מַאי מְדַבֶּרֶת – What is meant by **"speaking"?**[22]

The Gemara presents two views:

זְעֵירִי אָמַר – Zeiri says: **נִסְתְּרָה** – It means that **she was secluded** with him.[23] **רַב אַסִּי אָמַר – Rav Assi**, however, **says:** **נִבְעֲלָה** – It means that **she cohabited** with him.[24]

The Gemara questions one of the views:

בִּשְׁלָמָא לִזְעֵירִי – It is understandable according to Zeiri that she was merely secluded, **הַיְינוּ דְּקָתָנֵי מְדַבֶּרֶת – for that is why [the Mishnah] taught "she was speaking."**[25] **אֶלָּא לְרַב אַסִּי – But according to Rav Assi,** **מַאי מְדַבֶּרֶת – what** implication of cohabitation is contained in the word **"speaking"?**

The Gemara answers:

לִישָּׁנָא מְעַלְיָא – The Mishnah uses a euphemism, **כִּדְכְתִיב – as it is written:** **,,אָכְלָה וּמָחֲתָה פִיהָ וְאָמְרָה לֹא פָעַלְתִּי אָוֶן״** – *Such is the way of the adulterous woman:* ***She eats and wipes her mouth and says, "I have done no wrong."***[26]

The Gemara persists:

בִּשְׁלָמָא לִזְעֵירִי – It is understandable according to Zeiri, **הַיְינוּ דְּקָתָנֵי תַּרְתֵּי מְדַבֶּרֶת וּמְעוּבֶּרֶת** – for **that is why [the Mishnah] taught two** cases: one where **she was "speaking"** [i.e. secluded] **and** one where **she was pregnant.**[27] **אֶלָּא לְרַב אַסִּי תַּרְתֵּי לָמָּה לִי – But according to Rav Assi, why do I need two** cases? Why,

NOTES

19. We maintain her *chazakah* [previous status] of fitness (see *Ritva*) and allow her to marry a Kohen. We do not suspect her of having cohabited with someone forbidden to her (*Rashi*).

20. R' Yehoshua maintains that having compromised herself by speaking to a strange man (see the Gemara below for exactly what "speaking" means), the woman has lost her *chazakah* of fitness (*Ritva*). Accordingly, she is under suspicion of having cohabited with someone whose cohabitaion would disqualify her from marrying a Kohen, such as a *nasin* or a *mamzer,* until she proves otherwise.

A *nasin* is a descendant of the Gibeonites, whom Joshua designated as woodcutters and water-drawers for the Tabernacle (see *Joshua* 9:27). A *mamzer* is a person born from a forbidden union punishable by either *kares* or death. Marriage with either of these men is forbidden (the prohibition to marry a *mamzer* is stated in *Deuteronomy* 23:3; the prohibition against marrying a *nasin* is discussed on 29a note 5). Accordingly, a woman who cohabits with either of them becomes forbidden to marry a Kohen (see note 17).

21. The Gemara will explain what this case adds to the previous one (*Rashi*).

From the fact that R' Yehoshua states that she is suspected of being pregnant by a *nasin* or *mamzer* rather than by a gentile – which would seem to be a much more likely possibility, since gentiles comprise the majority of the population – it is evident that he holds that the child is prohibited to marry any Jew, not just a Kohen (*Pnei Yehoshua;* see also *Chasam Sofer*). (A child of a *nasin* or *mamzer* is likewise a *nasin* or *mamzer* and is prohibited to marry any Jew. A child fathered by a gentile, on the other hand, is permitted to marry an ordinary Jew, and is forbidden only to a Kohen.) See further 13b note 26.

[The Rishonim (*Shitah Mekubetzes* ד״ה ר״ג ור״א, in explanation of *Rashi* ד״ה נאמנת; *Rambam, Commentary to Mishnah*; *Ritva*) point out that although the Mishnah describes the woman as naming the man in question ("He is So-and-so"), and Rabban Gamliel states that she is believed, this does not mean that she is believed to identify the man to the extent that, for example, if she is pregnant, the child inherits the man, or, if he is a Kohen, the child assumes the privileges of the Kehunah, for, as explained in note 19, Rabban Gamliel's ruling is based on *chazakah,* and in regard to the man's identity no *chazakah* exists. Rather, her believability extends only to being declared fit to marry a Kohen. Indeed, in order for Rabban Gamliel's ruling to apply it is altogether unnecessary for her to identify the man; she is permitted to marry a Kohen even if she does not name him but states simply that he was fit for her (see *Rambam, Hil. Isurei Biah* 18:13). The Mishnah portrays her as identifying him only because it is common for a woman who is defending herself against an accusation such as the present one to name the man in question [in order to lend more credence to her claim] (*Rivash* §231, cited by *Shitah Mekubetzes* loc. cit., first explanation; see *Chemdas Shlomo* at length).]

22. Surely it cannot be understood literally, because her having spoken with a stranger is not, in and of itself, reason to suspect her of having cohabited with him (*Shitah Mekubetzes* ד״ה מאי).

23. Witnesses saw her enter a secluded place with him. Although they did not witness any cohabitation, she is still prohibited to a Kohen according to R' Yehoshua, because in regard to the Kehunah the Rabbis set a higher-than-usual standard, as the Gemara will explain below (*Rashi*).

[By stating that the man was "a Kohen," the woman is apparently admitting that she cohabited with him, but is claiming that she should nevertheless be permitted to a Kohen, because the man was fit for her. Nevertheless most Rishonim (with the notable exception of *Tosafos*) maintain that R' Yehoshua's ruling applies even if she asserts that no cohabitation occurred (see *Ritva* here and *Ramban* and *Rashba* to 14a and 16a). Our commentary will follow this opinion.]

24. The witnesses saw her engage in an actual act of cohabitation with the man. But if they merely saw them go into seclusion, the woman would, according to Rav Assi, be permitted to a Kohen, because R' Yehoshua does not consider seclusion proof of cohabitation. Moreover, even if she admits that cohabitation took place but asserts that the man was fit for her, she is believed (*Ritva*), because her claim is supported by a *migo* that she could have said she did not cohabit (*Tosafos*).

[Although we learned on 12b that according to R' Yehoshua a woman found by her husband not to possess signs of virginity at the time of the first cohabitation is not believed to say she was violated after *erusin* with a *migo* that she could have claimed she was injured by a piece of wood, R' Yehoshua would still believe her with a *migo* in this case. In the case on 12b the woman's *migo* is weak, since she would not have been *believed* with the other claim she could have made; the advantage of the other claim is only that it would have been *more advantageous* (see 12b note 22 paragraph 4 for elaboration). Here, however, where she would have been *believed* had she claimed that she did not cohabit, the *migo* is strong, and R' Yehoshua relies on it (*Tosafos*).]

25. "Speaking" can mean that she was whispering to him in private (*Shitah Mekubetzes* ד״ה בשלמא, in the name of the Geonim; cf. *Rashash*).

26. *Proverbs* 30:20. Here "eats" is a euphemism for cohabitation (*Rashi*) [and "wipes her mouth" for wiping the genitals (*Rashi* to *Yoma* 75a ד״ה ומחתה)]. Similarly, "speaking" is also used as a euphemism for cohabitation (*Hagahos Yavetz*).

27. The case where she was secluded teaches that R' Yehoshua rules her prohibited even though the witnesses did not see her cohabit. And the case where she was pregnant teaches that Rabban Gamliel and R' Eliezer rule her permitted even though she obviously cohabited (*Rashi*).

דאם כן קשיא הלכתא אהלכתא דקיימא לן הלכתא כרב נחמן בדיני ובהא אמר רב יהודה אמר שמואל הלכה כרבן גמליאל אלא לאו ש"מ כדמשנינן ש"מ: **מתני'** היא אומרת מוכת עץ אני והוא אומר לא כי אלא דרוסת איש את רבן גמליאל ורבי אליעזר אומרים נאמנת ורבי יהושע אומר לא מפיה אנו חיין אלא הרי זו בחזקת דרוסת איש עד שתביא ראיה לדבריה: **גמ'** טענתייהו במאי רבי יוחנן אמר במאתים ומנה רבי אלעזר אמר במנה ולא כלום רבי יוחנן אמר במאתים ומנה סבר לה כר"מ דאמר בין הכיר בה ובין לא הכיר בה מאתים ורבי אלעזר אומר במנה ולא כלום סבר לה כרבנן דאמרי בין הכיר בה בין לא הכיר בה מנה בשלמא ר' אלעזר לא קאמר כר' יוחנן דקא מוקי לה כרבנן אלא רבי יוחנן מ"ט לא אמר כר' אלעזר קסבר כנסה בחזקת בתולה ונמצאת בעולה יש לה כתובה מנה הכא הוא קאמר מנה והיא קאמרה מנה מאי איכא בין טענה דידיה לטענה דידה בשלמא לר' אלעזר היינו דקתני תרתי חדא לאפוקי מדרמי בר חמא וחדא לאפוקי מדרב חייא בר אבין א"ר ששת אלא לר' יוחנן תרתי למה לי חדא להודיעך כחו דרבן גמליאל וחדא להודיעך כחו דרבי יהושע דאף על גב דאיכא למימר מיגו לא מהימנא בתרייתא להודיעך כחו דרבן גמליאל דאע"ג דליכא למימר מיגו מהימנא: **מתני'** ראוה מדברת עם אחד ואמרו לה מה טיבו של איש זה איש פלוני וכהן הוא רבן גמליאל ורבי אליעזר אומרים נאמנת ור' יהושע אומר לא מפיה אנו חיין אלא הרי זו בחזקת בעולה לנתין ולממזר עד שתביא ראיה לדבריה היתה מעוברת ואמרו לה מה טיבו של עובר זה מאיש פלוני וכהן הוא רבן גמליאל ורבי אליעזר אומרים נאמנת ור' יהושע אומר לא מפיה אנו חיין אלא הרי זו בחזקת מעוברת לנתין ולממזר עד שתביא ראיה לדבריה: **גמ'** מאי מדברת זעירי אמר נסתרה רב אסי אמר נבעלה בשלמא לזעירי היינו דקתני מדברת אלא לרב אסי מאי מדברת לישנא מעליא כדכתיב אכלה ומחתה פיה ואמרה לא פעלתי און בשלמא לזעירי היינו דקתני תרתי מדברת ומעוברת אלא לרב אסי תרתי למה לי חדא להכשיר בה וחדא להכשיר בבתה הניחא למאן דאמר לדברי המכשיר בה מכשיר בבתה אלא למ"ד לדברי המכשיר בה פוסל בבתה מאי איכא למימר רב אסי סבר כמ"ד לדברי המכשיר בה מכשיר בבתה א"ל רב פפא לאביי לזעירי דאמר מאי מדברת נסתרה וא"ר יהושע לא מהימנא האמר רב מלקין על היחוד ואין אוסרין על היחוד לימא דלא כר"י אפי' תימא ר' יהושע מעלה עשו ביוחסין מיתיבי ראוה שנכנסה עם אחד לסתר או

לחורבה

רש"י

דא"כ. דרב נחמן לא מיתוקם כרבן גמליאל אלא כרבי יהושע קשיא הלכתא אהלכתא: **מתני'** דרוסת איש את. קודם שארסתיך: **גמ'** טענתייהו במאי. מה היא תובעתו ומה הוא רוצה ליתן: במאתים ומנה. היא אומרת מוכת עץ אני ויש לי מאתים ואע"פ שלא הכרת בי והוא אומר לא דרוסת איש את ואין לך אלא מנה וקסבר כנסה בחזקת בתולה ונמצאת בעולה יש לה כתובה מנה: במנה ולא כלום. היא תובעת מנה והוא אומר אין ליך כלום: סבר לה. תנא דמתני' דאילו רבי יוחנן לא שביק רבנן ועביד כר"מ: קסבר. ר' יוחנן כנסה בחזקת בתולה ונמצאת בעולה יש לה מנה הלכך על כרחך מוכת עץ דמתני' ר"מ היא דאמר מאתים והוא אומר דרוסת איש את ויש ליך מנה דאי רבנן היא לא תבעה אלא מנה והוא אומר דרוסת איש את ויש לך מנה מאי איכא בין טענתא דידיה לטענתא דידה: בשלמא לרבי אלעזר. דאמר דרוסת איש אין לה כלום: היינו דקתני תרתי. בבי במתני' גבי פלוגתא דממונא היא אומרת משארסתני נאנסתי והיא אומרת מוכת עץ אני: חדא לאפוקי מדרמי בר חמא וחדא לאפוקי כו'. היא אומרת משארסתני נאנסתי תנא למיתני בה והיה מקחי מקח טעות לגמרי משמע ואין לה כלום לאפוקי מדרב חייא בר אבין דאמר לעיל (דף יא:) כנסה בחזקת בתולה ונמצאת בעולה יש לה כתובה מנה ותנא היא אומרת מוכת עץ אני לאפוקי מדרמי בר חמא דאמר לעיל גבי מוכת עץ אבל לא הכיר בה דברי הכל לא כלום: אלא לרבי יוחנן. דאמר כנסה בחזקת בתולה ונמצאת בעולה יש לה כתובה מנה אם כן מאי מקח טעות דקתני מאתים אבל מנה יש לה למה לי למיתני כלל להכי אי לאשמועינן פלוגתא דרבן גמליאל ור' יהושע בברי ושמא ואוקי ממונא בחזקת מריה ליתני חדא ולאפוקי מדרמי בר חמא ולאשמועינן פלוגתייהו: דאיכא למימר מגו. מגו דאי בעיא אמרה מוכת עץ אני: בתרייתא. ליכא למימר מגו לר' יוחנן דמוקי מתני' כרבי מאיר דאמר מוכת עץ שלא הכיר בה כתובתה מאתים ליכא שום מגו דמה לי אומרת מוכת עץ אני תחתיך מה לי אמרה מעיקרא: **מתני'** ראוה מדברת. בפנויה ונגוס חששא דפסולין לנתין ולממזר וכיון שנבעלה לפסול פסלה מן הכהונה]: נאמנת. וכשרה לכהונה ולא מספקינן לה בנבעלה לפסול לה: היתה מעוברת כו'. בגמ' מפרש תרתי למה לי: **גמ'** נסתרה. ואע"פ שלא ראוה שנבעלה נפסלה לכהונה לרבי יהושע כדלקמן דמעלה עשו ביוחסין: אכלה ומחתה פיה. אלמא נקט תשמיש בלשון אכילה: בשלמא לזעירי היינו דקתני תרתי. מדברת להודיעך כחו דר' יהושע דלאע"ג דלא ראוה שנבעלה פסולה ומעוברת להודיעך כחו דרבן גמליאל: בבתה. אם העובר הזה נקבה תנשא לכהונה לר"ג דלא אשמועינן בדידה הוה אמינא איהי הואיל דהוה לה חזקה דכשרות מעיקרא אמרי' אוקמה אחזקה ואל תפסילנה מספק אבל עובר דלא הוה ליה חזקה דכשרות אימא לא: הניחא למ"ד כו'. לקמן בשמעתין: מאי איכא למימר. תרתי להכשיר בה למה לי כיון דמדברת בראוה שנבעלה: מלקין על היחוד. מכת מרדות: ואין אוסרין. אשה על בעלה בשביל יחוד בעלמא: לימא דלא כרבי יהושע. דמשום יחוד מחזיק לה בנבעלת: ביוחסין. בכהונה: לסתר. משמע יחוד בעלמא:

תוספות

רב אסי אמר נבעלה. אבל נסתרה מודה ר' יהושע דנאמנת לומר לכשר נבעלתי במגו דאי בעיא אמרה לא נבעלתי וא"ת והא רבי יהושע לית ליה מגו גבי משארסתני נאנסתי ויש לומר דהתם לא הוי מגו גמור דהא אפילו אמרה מוכת עץ אני אינה נאמנת לרבי יהושע כדתנן במתני' ולא קרי ליה מגו אלא לפי שהיא טענה מעולה ביותר: **חדא** להכשיר בה וחדא להכשיר בבתה. וצריכי תרוייהו חדא להודיעך כחו דרבן גמליאל וחדא להודיעך כחו דרבי יהושע: **לדברי** המכשיר בה פוסל בבתה. ומעוברת דנקט משום לישנא מעליא: **ואין** אוסרין על היחוד לימא דלא כרבי יהושע. תימה לרשב"א דלזעירי (נמי) דאמר נסתרה איירי כגון דמודה היא שנבעלה דאי אמרה לא נבעלתי אם כן הוי ספק ספיקא דמכשיר רבי יהושע כדאמר לקמן התם ספק ספיקא ויש לומר דלעולם איירי דקאמרה לא נבעלה וחשיב ליה חדא ספיקא משום דאין אפוטרופוס לעריות אבל קשה דבהדי' משמע בריש פרק שני (לקמן טז.) דאיירי בנבעלת דקאמר הניחא לזעירי דאמר מאי מדברת נסתרה דמגו דאי בעיא אמרה לא נבעלתי מהימנא כו' לכך נראה דפריך לזעירי דבספיקא חדא אסרינן לה והא יחוד דאשת איש דספיקא חדא היא ואין אוסרים על היחוד וק"ק דלכאורה נראה דיחוד איחוד פריך מדפריך לזעירי ולא לרב אסי: **מעלה** עשו ביוחסין. תימה דמשמע דאין אוסרין על היחוד איירי באשת איש ולא בפנויה ובסוף קדושין (דף פא. ושם) מוקי מלקין על היחוד דוקא בפנויה אבל באשת איש לא דאתה מוציא לעז על בניה ואפי' למר זוטרא דמלקין ומכריז באשת איש מודה דבפנויה נמי איירי ואור"ת דאף על גב דמלקין על היחוד איירי בפנויה אין אוסרין על היחוד לא איירי אלא באשת איש א) וא"ת והא אמרינן בפ' בתרא דנדרים (דף צא:) גבי ההוא נואף דעייל לגבה דההיא איתתא אמר ליה נואף לא תיכול מינהון דטעמינהו חויא אמר רבא איתתא שריא אם איתא דעבד איסורא ניחא ליה דלימות משמע דאי לאו האי טעמא היתה נאסרת על ידי יחוד ויש לומר דנואף שאני וה"ר יוסף דשליטן תירץ דאין אוסרים על היחוד איירי בפנויה כמו מלקין על היחוד ולא איירי לכהונה אלא אין אוסרין אותה לבנו כשמתייחד עם אביו לרבי יהודה דאסר באנוסת אביו (יבמות דף צז.):

השבתנו

תורה אור השלם

א) כֵּן דֶּרֶךְ אִשָּׁה מְנָאָפֶת אָכְלָה וּמָחֲתָה פִיהָ וְאָמְרָה לֹא פָעַלְתִּי אָוֶן: [משלי ל, כ]

The Gemara analyzes the dispute:

בִּשְׁלָמָא רַבִּי אֶלְעָזָר לֹא קָאָמַר כְּרַבִּי יוֹחָנָן – **It is understandable that R' Elazar did not say as R' Yochanan,** דְּקָא מוֹקֵי לָהּ כְּרַבָּנָן – **for he establishes [the Mishnah] in accordance with** the majority view of **the Rabbis.**[8] אֶלָּא רַבִּי יוֹחָנָן מַאי טַעְמָא לֹא אָמַר כְּרַבִּי אֶלְעָזָר – **But R' Yochanan, why did he not say as R' Elazar,** i.e. why did he choose to explain the Mishnah in accordance with R' Meir's minority opinion?

The Gemara answers:

קָסָבַר כְּנָסָהּ בְּחֶזְקַת בְּתוּלָה וְנִמְצֵאת בְּעוּלָה – **He maintains that** if **one married [a woman] on the presumption she was a virgin and she was found to be a nonvirgin,** יֵשׁ לָהּ כְּתוּבָּה מָנֶה – **she has a *kesubah* of a *maneh.*** הָכָא הוּא קָאָמַר מָנֶה וְהִיא קָאָמְרָה מָנֶה – Thus the Mishnah **here** cannot follow the opinion of the Rabbis that a wood-injury victim receives a *maneh,* for if **[the husband] is saying** that she is due **a *maneh* and [the wife] is saying** that she is due **a *maneh,*** מַאי אִיכָּא בֵּין טַעֲנָה דִּידֵיהּ לְטַעֲנָה דִּידָהּ – **what** difference **is there between his claim and her claim?** Perforce, therefore, our Mishnah follows the minority view of R' Meir that a wood-injury victim receives a *kesubah* of two hundred *zuz*.[9]

The Gemara again challenges R' Yochanan's opinion:

בִּשְׁלָמָא לְרַבִּי אֶלְעָזָר – **It is understandable according to R' Elazar** who holds that if she really was not a virgin she receives no *kesubah* at all, הַיְינוּ דְּקָתָנֵי תַּרְתֵּי – **for that is why [the Mishnah] taught** the dispute of Rabban Gamliel and R' Yehoshua in regard to **two** different monetary **cases:**[10] חֲדָא לְאַפּוּקֵי מִדְּרָמִי בַּר חָמָא – **one to exclude** the opinion **of Rami bar Chama**[11] חֲדָא לְאַפּוּקֵי מִדְּרַב חִיָּיא בַּר אָבִין אָמַר רַב שֵׁשֶׁת – **and one to exclude** the opinion **of Rav Chiya bar Avin in the name of Rav Sheishess.**[12] אֶלָּא לְרַבִּי יוֹחָנָן תַּרְתֵּי לָמָּה לִי – **But according to R' Yochanan, why do I need two cases?**[13]

The Gemara answers:

חֲדָא לְהוֹדִיעֲךָ כֹּחוֹ דְּרַבָּן גַּמְלִיאֵל – **One** is necessary **to inform you of the extent of** the view of **Rabban Gamliel,** וַחֲדָא לְהוֹדִיעֲךָ כֹּחוֹ דְּרַבִּי יְהוֹשֻׁעַ – **and the other to inform you of the extent of** the view of **R' Yehoshua,** as follows: קַמַּיְיתָא לְהוֹדִיעֲךָ כֹּחוֹ דְּרַבִּי יְהוֹשֻׁעַ – **The first** Mishnah serves **to inform you of the extent of** the view of **R' Yehoshua,** דְּאַף עַל גַּב דְּאִיכָּא לְמֵימַר מִיגּוֹ – **that even though it is** possible **to say** that her claim is bolstered by a ***migo,*** לֹא מְהֵימְנָא – **she is not believed.**[14] בָּתְרַיְיתָא לְהוֹדִיעֲךָ כֹּחוֹ דְּרַבָּן גַּמְלִיאֵל – And **the latter** Mishnah serves **to inform you of the extent of** the view of **Rabban Gamliel,** דְּאַף עַל גַּב דְּלֵיכָּא לְמֵימַר מִיגּוֹ – **that even though it is not** possible **to say** that her claim is bolstered by a *migo*, מְהֵימְנָא – **she is believed.**[15]

Mishnah The Mishnah presents two more cases in which Rabban Gamliel and R' Eliezer dispute R' Yehoshua.[16] The first case:

רָאוּהָ מְדַבֶּרֶת עִם אֶחָד – **They** [the court] **saw [an unmarried woman] speaking with someone,** וְאָמְרוּ לָהּ מַה טִּיבוֹ שֶׁל אִישׁ זֶה – **and said to her, "What is the nature of this man?"**[17] אִישׁ פְּלוֹנִי וְכֹהֵן הוּא – and she replied, **"He is So-and-so, and he is a Kohen."**[18] רַבָּן גַּמְלִיאֵל וְרַבִּי אֱלִיעֶזֶר אוֹמְרִים – **Rabban Gamliel and R' Eliezer say:**

NOTES

only a *maneh*, her husband must be claiming that she deserves nothing at all.

8. [It is always preferable to expain a Mishnah in accordance with the majority opinion, since this is the view that the halachah generally follows.]

9. R' Elazar, however, maintains that a woman married on the presumption of being a virgin but found to be a nonvirgin receives no *kesubah* at all. He is therefore free to say that our Mishnah follows the majority view of the Rabbis that a wood-injury victim receives only a *maneh*.

10. I.e. the case of the previous Mishnah (12b), where the groom and bride disagree about whether she cohabited before or after the *erusin,* and the case of our Mishnah, where they disagree as to whether she cohabited or was merely injured by a piece of wood (*Rashi*).

11. Our Mishnah — which quotes the woman as explaining that she was a wood-injury victim and demanding a *kesubah,* even though her husband did not know of her injury before the *erusin* — is necessary to exclude the opinion of Rami bar Chama, cited above on 11b, that if the husband did not realize she was wood injured she receives no *kesubah* at all.

12. The Mishnah on 12b, in which the groom claims that she cohabited before the *erusin* and his marriage was "an acquisiton in error" [מִקַּח טָעוּת] — which implies that the bride should not receive any *kesubah* at all — is needed to exclude the view of Rav Chiya bar Avin, also cited on 11b, that a woman wed on the presumption of being a virgin but found to be a nonvirgin is entitled to a *kesubah* of a *maneh* (*Rashi*). See the Gemara on 11b.

13. If our Mishnah holds that a woman who was married under the presumption of being a virgin but was found to be a non-virgin can still collect a *kesubah* of a *maneh,* then we must interpret the groom's claim "and my acquisition was made in error" in the previous Mishnah to mean that he should not have to pay the complete two hundred-*zuz kesubah* but rather a *maneh* (as Rav Chiya bar Avin indeed explained on 12b). If that is the case, what does the previous Mishnah add to what we would know from our Mishnah alone? If the Tanna wished to teach us the dispute between Rabban Gamliel and R' Yehoshua, he could have done so by writing only our Mishnah (*Rashi*).

[The commentators ask that even according to R' Elazar it should have sufficed to write only our Mishnah. For according to R' Elazar the woman in our Mishnah claims a *maneh,* which means that the husband, who charges that perhaps she cohabited before *erusin,* is arguing that she should receive nothing at all. Thus from our Mishnah alone it is clear that R' Chiya bar Avin is incorrect!

Tos. HaRosh answers that if not for the Mishnah on 12b, R' Elazar could not have been certain that in our Mishnah the claims are a *maneh* versus nothing. Perhaps the claims are two hundred versus a *maneh* [and the Mishnah follows R' Meir, as R' Yochanan in fact explained]. It is only from the Mishnah on 12b, where the expression "my acquisition was made in error" is used, which implies that the husband claims that he is not liable to pay anything, that R' Elazar knows with certainty that this is the husband's claim in our Mishnah as well. See also *Rashash.*

(It is, however, still difficult to understand why the Tanna did not phrase the husband's claim in our Mishnah as, "You were deflowered by a man *and my acquisition was made in error.*" This would have obviated the need for the previous Mishnah. See *Maharam Schif* and *Rashash*, and see *Shitah Mekubetzes* for a possible answer.)]

14. In the previous Mishnah, where the bride claimed her *kesubah* because she was violated after *erusin*, had she wanted to lie she could have used a better claim — that she was a wood-injury victim. Nevertheless, R' Yehoshua holds that she is not believed.

15. Since R' Yochanan explained that in our Mishnah the bride is claiming her full two hundred-*zuz kesubah* even though her husband did not realize that she had been injured by a piece of wood before the *erusin,* she is already making the best claim possible; a claim that she was injured after the *erusin* would not serve her interests any better. Nevertheless, Rabban Gamliel rules even in this case that she is believed (*Rashi*; cf. *Ritva*).

16. The previous cases discussed claims initiated by a husband against his wife due to his failure to find in her evidence of virginity, and pertained to the amount of the *kesubah* payment he was required to give her. The coming two cases involve accusations of impropriety leveled by the court against a single woman.

17. Is he someone whose cohabitation would render you unfit to marry a Kohen? [A man whom a woman is forbidden to marry renders her, with his cohabitation, a *zonah* [harlot], and she may not marry a Kohen (see *Rashi;* see *Leviticus* 21:7 and *Yevamos* 61b, 68a; cf. *Rashi* to *Kiddushin* 74a ד״ה חדא and *Chasam Sofer* here).]

[The Gemara will explain the meaning of "speaking" in this context.]

18. I.e. one of untainted lineage [with whom cohabitation would not damage my marriage eligibility] (see above, 12b note 17).

דאם כן קשיא הלכתא אהלכתא דקיימא לן א) הלכתא כרב נחמן בדיני ובהא אמר רב יהודה אמר שמואל הלכה כרבן גמליאל אלא לאו ש"מ כדמשנינן ש"מ: **מתני'** ב) היא אומרת מוכת עץ אני והוא אומר לא כי אלא דרוסת איש את רבן גמליאל ורבי אליעזר אומרים נאמנת ורבי יהושע אומר לא מפיה אנו חיין אלא הרי זו בחזקת דרוסת איש עד שתביא ראיה לדבריה: **גמ'** טענתייהו במאי ג) רבי יוחנן אמר במאתים ומנה רבי אלעזר אמר במנה ולא כלום רבי יוחנן אמר במאתים ומנה סבר לה ד) כר"מ דאמר בין הכיר בה ובין לא הכיר בה מאתים ורבי אלעזר אומר במנה ולא כלום סבר לה כרבנן דאמרי בין הכיר בה בין לא הכיר בה מנה בשלמא ר' אלעזר לא קאמר כר' יוחנן דקא מוקי לה כרבנן אלא רבי יוחנן מ"ט לא אמר כר' אלעזר קסבר כנסה בחזקת בתולה ונמצאת בעולה יש לה כתובה מנה הכא הוא קאמר מנה והיא קאמרה מנה מאי איכא בין טענה דידיה לטענה דידה בשלמא לר' אלעזר היינו דקתני תרתי חדא לאפוקי מדרמי בר חמא וחדא לאפוקי מדרב חייא בר אבין א"ר ששת אלא לר' יוחנן תרתי למה לי חדא להודיעך כחו דרבן גמליאל וחדא להודיעך כחו דרבי יהושע דאף על גב דאיכא למימר מיגו לא מהימנא בתרייתא להודיעך כחו דרבן גמליאל דאע"ג דליכא למימר מיגו מהימנא: **מתני'** ה) ראוה מדברת עם אחד ואמרו לה מה טיבו של איש זה איש פלוני וכהן הוא רבן גמליאל ורבי אליעזר אומרים נאמנת ור' יהושע אומר לא מפיה אנו חיין אלא הרי זו בחזקת בעולה לנתין ולממזר עד שתביא ראיה לדבריה: היתה מעוברת ואמרו לה מה טיבו של עובר זה מאיש פלוני וכהן הוא רבן גמליאל ורבי אליעזר אומרים נאמנת ור' יהושע אומר לא מפיה אנו חיין אלא הרי זו בחזקת מעוברת לנתין ולממזר עד שתביא ראיה לדבריה: **גמ'** מאי מדברת ז) זעירי אמר נסתרה רב אסי אמר נבעלה בשלמא לזעירי היינו דקתני מדברת אלא לרב אסי מאי מדברת ח) לישנא מעליא כדכתיב א) אכלה ומחתה פיה ואמרה לא פעלתי און בשלמא לזעירי היינו דקתני תרתי מדברת ומעוברת אלא לרב אסי תרתי למה לי חדא להכשיר בה וחדא להכשיר בבתה ט) הניחא למאן דאמר לדברי המכשיר בה מכשיר בבתה אלא למ"ד לדברי המכשיר בה פוסל בבתה מאי איכא למימר רב אסי סבר כמ"ד לדברי המכשיר בה מכשיר בבתה א"ל רב פפא לאביי לזעירי דאמר מאי מדברת נסתרה וא"ר יהושע לא מהימנא האמר רב י) מלקין על היחוד ואין אוסרין על היחוד לימא דלא כר"י אפי' תימא ר' יהושע כ) מעלה עשו ביוחסין מיתיבי ראוה שנכנסה עם אחד לסתר או

רש"י

דא"כ. דרב נחמן לא מיתוקם כרבן גמליאל אלא כרבי יהושע קשיא הלכתא אהלכתא: **מתני'** דרוסת איש את. קודם שארסתיך: **גמ'** טענתייהו במאי. מה היא תובעתו ומה הוא רוצה ליתן: במאתים ומנה. היא אומרת מוכת עץ אני ויש לי מאתים ואע"פ שלא הכרת בי והוא אומר דרוסת איש את ואין לך אלא מנה וקסבר כנסה בחזקת בתולה ונמצאת בעולה יש לה כתובה מנה: במנה ולא כלום. היא תובעת מנה והוא אומר אין ליך כלום: סבר לה. תנא דמתני' דאילו רבי יוחנן לא שביק רבנן ועביד כר"מ: קסבר. ר' יוחנן כנסה בחזקת בתולה ונמצאת בעולה יש לה מנה הלכך על כרחך מוכת עץ דמתני' ר"מ היא דאמר מאתים והוא אומר דרוסת איש את ויש ליך מנה דאי רבנן היא לא תבעה אלא מנה והוא אומר דרוסת איש את ויש לך מנה מאי איכא בין טענתא דידיה לטענתא דידה: בשלמא לרבי אלעזר. דאמר דרוסת איש אין לה כלום: היינו דקתני תרתי. בבי במתני' גבי פלוגתא דממונא היא אומרת משארסתני נאנסתי והיא אומרת מוכת עץ אני: חדא לאפוקי מדרמי בר חמא וחדא לאפוקי כו'. היא אומרת משארסתני נאנסתי תנא למיתני בה והיה מקחי מקח טעות לגמרי משמע ואין לה כלום לאפוקי מדרב חייא בר אבין דאמר לעיל (דף יא:) כנסה בחזקת בתולה ונמצאת בעולה יש לה כתובה מנה ותנא היא אומרת מוכת עץ אני לאפוקי מדרמי בר חמא דאמר לעיל גבי מוכת עץ אבל לא הכיר בה דברי הכל ולא כלום: אלא לרבי יוחנן. דאמר כנסה בחזקת בתולה ונמצאת בעולה יש לה כתובה מנה אם כן מאי מקח טעות דקתני אמאתים אבל מנה יש לה למה לי למיתני כלל להניא אי לאשמועינן פלוגתא דרבן גמליאל ור' יהושע בברי ושמא ואוקי ממונא בחזקת מריה ליתני חדא לאפוקי מדרמי בר חמא ולאשמועינן פלוגתייהו: דאיכא למימר מגו. מגו דאי בעיא אמרה מוכת עץ אני: בתרייתא. ליכא למימר מגו לר' יוחנן דמוקי מתני' כרבי מאיר דאמר מוכת עץ שלא הכיר בה כתובתה מאתים ליכא שום מגו דמה לי אומרת מוכת עץ אני תחתיך מה לי אמרה מעיקרא: **מתני'** [ראוה מדברת. בפנויה ומשום חששא דפסולין לנתין ולממזר וכיון שנבעלה לפסול פסלה מן הכהונה]: נאמנת. וכשרה לכהונה ולא מספקינן לה בנבעלה לפסול לה: היתה מעוברת כו'. בגמ' מפרש תרתי למה לי: **גמ'** נסתרה. ואע"פ שלא ראוה שנבעלה נפסלה לכהונה לרבי יהושע כדלקמן דמעלה עשו ביוחסין: אכלה ומחתה פיה. אלמא נקט תשמיש בלשון אכילה: בשלמא לזעירי היינו דקתני תרתי. מדברת להודיעך כחו דר' יהושע דאע"ג דלא ראוה שנבעלה פסולה ומעוברת להודיעך כחו דרבן גמליאל: בבתה. אם העובר הזה נקבה תנשא לכהונה לר"ג דלאי אשמועינן בדידה הוה אמינא איהי הואיל דהוה לה חזקה דכשרות מעיקרא אמרי' אוקמה אחזקה ואל תפסילנה מספק אבל עובר דלא הוה ליה חזקה דכשרות אימא לא: הניחא למ"ד כו'. לקמן בשמעתין: מאי איכא למימר. תרתי להכשיר בה למה לי כיון דמדברת בראוה שנבעלה: מלקין על היחוד. מכת מרדות: ואין אוסרין. אשה על בעלה בשביל יחוד בעלמא: לימא דלא כרבי יהושע. דמשום יחוד מחזיק לה בנבעלת: ביוחסין. בכהונה: לסתר. משמע יחוד בעלמא: לחורבה

תוספות

רב אסי אמר נבעלה. אבל נסתרה מודה ר' יהושע דנאמנת לומר לכשר נבעלתי במגו דאי בעיא אמרה לא נבעלתי וא"ת והא רבי יהושע לית ליה מגו גבי משארסתני נאנסתי וי"ל דהתם לא הוי מגו גמור דהא אפילו אמרה מוכת עץ אני אינה נאמנת לרבי יהושע כדתנן במתני' ולא קרי ליה מגו אלא לפי שהיא ° טענה מעולה ביותר: **חדא** להכשיר בה וחדא להכשיר בבתה. ולריכי תרוייהו חדא להודיעך כחו דרבן גמליאל וחדא להודיעך כחו דרבי יהושע: **לדברי** המכשיר בה פוסל בבתה. ומעוברת דנקט משום לישנא מעליא: **ואין** אוסרין על היחוד לימא דלא כרבי יהושע. תימה לרשב"א דלזעירי (נמי) דאמר נסתרה איירי כגון דמודה היא שנבעלה דאי אמרה לא נבעלתי אם כן הוי ספק ספיקא דמכשיר רבי יהושע כדאמר לקמן התם ספק ספיקא ויש לומר דלעולם איירי דקאמרה לא נבעלה וחשיב ליה חדא ספיקא משום דאין אפוטרופוס לעריות אבל קשה דבהדי' משמע בריש פרק שני (לקמן טו.) דאיירי בנבעלת דקאמר הניחא לזעירי דאמר מאי מדברת נסתרה דמגו דאי בעיא אמרה לא נבעלתי מהימנא כו' לכך נראה דפריך לזעירי דבספיקא חדא אסרינן לה והא יחוד דאשת איש דספיקא חדא היא ואין אוסרים על היחוד וק"ק דלכאורה נראה דיחוד איחוד פריך מדפריך לזעירי ולא לרב אסי: **מעלה** עשו ביוחסין. תימה דמשמע דאין אוסרין על היחוד איירי באשת איש ולא בפנויה ובסוף קדושין (דף פא. ושם) מוקי מלקין על היחוד דוקא בפנויה אבל באשת איש לא דאתה מוציא לעז על בניה ואפי' למר זוטרא דמלקין ומכריז באשת איש מודה דבפנויה נמי איירי ואור"ת דאף על גב דמלקין על היחוד איירי בפנויה אין אוסרין על היחוד לא איירי אלא באשת איש א) וא"ת והא אמרינן בפ' בתרא דנדרים (דף צא:) גבי ההוא נוקף דעייל לגבה דההיא איתתא אמר ליה נוקף לא תיכול מינהון טעמינהו חויא אמר רבא איתתא שריא אם איתא דעבד איסורא ניחא ליה לימות משמע דלאו הכי הוה טעמא היתה נאסרת על ידי יחוד ויש לומר דנוקף שאני והר"י יוסף דשליטן מיהך דאין אוסרים על היחוד איירי בפנויה כמו מלקין על היחוד ולא איירי לכהונה אלא אין אוסרין אותה לבעלה לכנו כשתתייחד עם אביו לרבי יהודה לאסר באשת אביו (יבמות דף נז.):

מסורת הש"ם

א) [קדושין נט: ב"מ קי.], ב) [לעיל יא: לקמן טז.], ג) [לקמן טז.], ד) [לעיל יא.], ה) [לקמן טז.], ו) שם קדושין עד. [עה.], ז) [לקמן טז. יבמות יא:], ח) [פסחים ג. וש"נ], ט) [קדושין עד.], י) שם פא., כ) [קדושין עג. לקמן טו.], ל) נ"י כ"י.

תוספות ישנים

א) [מיהו קשה לאדפריך מרב דאמר אין אוסרין על היחוד הוה ליה למיפרך מהא דקי"ל בכולי תלמודא וסתם משניות דאין אשה נאסרת על בעלה אלא על ידי קינוי וסתירה לכך נ"ל דרב איירי בפנויה דוקא וה"פ דמעלה עשו ביוחסין לאסור היכא דאמרה לכשר נבעלתי דמודה מיהא ולא מהימנינן לה במגו אבל אי אמרה לא נבעלתי בהא לא עשו מעלה ובהא איירי רב. ת"י].

גליון הש"ס

מתניתין לנתין ולממזר. עי' גיטין פט ע"א תוס' ד"ה בעולה ובמהרש"א שם: תוס' ד"ה רב אסי וכו' טענה מעולה ביותר. וכ"כ הרשב"א קדושין דף נ ע"א ד"ה הא:

תורה אור השלם

א) כֵּן דֶּרֶךְ אִשָּׁה מְנָאָפֶת אָכְלָה וּמָחֲתָה פִיהָ וְאָמְרָה לֹא פָעַלְתִּי אָוֶן: [משלי ל, כ]

ליקוטי רש"י

היא אומרת מוכת עץ אני. הנושא את האשה בחזקת בתולה ולא מצא לה בתולים היא אומרת מוכת עץ אני כו' [לעיל יא:]. **מוכת עץ.** שנתקע לה עץ באותו מקום [שם]. **במנה ולא כלום.** מוכת עץ שלא הכיר אינה יכולה לתובעו אלא מנה והוא אומר דרוסת איש את ואין ליך כלום [לקמן טז.]. **הכיר בה.** כשכנסה וכתב לה כתובה היה יודע שהיא מוכת עץ [שם:]. **וכהן הוא.** כלומר מיוחס הוא [לעיל יב:]. **לישנא מעליא.** לשון חכמים לחזר אחר לשון נא ונקי. שמלוה ולכך נקיי הדעת לספר בלשון נקיה [פסחים ג.]. **אכלה.** לשון נקיה דבר הכתוב. **ומחתה.** כופה פיה למטה כדכתיב כאשר ימחה הצלחת מחה והפך על פניה [משלי ל, כ]. **פוסל בבתה.** [דר"ג לא] האמינה אלא לעצמה שלא נתחללה מן התרומה אבל לא להכשיר אותו עובר שאם בת היא לא תינשא לכהן [קידושין עד.]. **מלקין על היחוד.** מרדות. **ואין אוסרין.** אשת איש על בעלה מחמת ייחוד [שם פא.].

עין משפט נר מצוה

עט א מיי' פי"א מהל' אישות הלכה י טוש"ע אה"ע סימן סח סעיף ט:
פ ב ג ד ה מיי' פט"ו מהלכות איסורי ביאה הלכה יא ופי"ח הלכה יג יד סמג לאוין קכא טור שו"ע שם סי' ו סעיף יז:
פא ו מיי' פכ"ב שם הל' ג סמג לאוין רכו טוש"ע שם סימן כב סעיף ג:

תוספות רי"ד

כר' יהושע. פי' דהכא נמי אשה אומרת ברי ובעל אומר שמא אמר לך ר"ג אנא דאמרי אפילו לר"ג ע"כ לא קאמר ר"ג התם אלא משום דא"ל אוקי איתתא אחזקתה פי' מספקא לן אשעת אירוסין אי בתולה הוה ואי בעולה הוה העמד אשה על חזקתה ובתולה היתה והשתא היא דאיתנס לאחר אירוסין אבל הכא מאי חזקה אית לי' להאי תובע דנוקמי' אחזקתה לגבות הלכך זיל בתר חזקת דממונא דאל"כ [אלא] דרב נחמן לא מתוקם כר"ג אלא כר' יהושע וק' הילכתא אהלכתא. והמורה גריס ע"כ לא קאמר ר"ג התם אלא משום דאיכא למימר מיגו. פי' מיגו דאי בעי' טענה טענה מעלייתא מהך כגון גבי משארסתני נאנסתי מיגו דאי בעיא אמרה מוכת עץ אני ולא פסלה נפשה מכהונה וקאמרה נאנסתי דקא פסלה נפשה מכהונה ש"מ קושטא קאמרה וגבי היא אומרת מוכת עץ אני מיגו דאי בעי' אמ' מוכ"ע אני תחתיך ואית לה מאתים וקאמרה מוכת עץ אני מקודם לכן ואין לה אלא מנה נאמנת אלא הכא גבי האי תובע מאי מיגו איכא וה"ה נמי דהוה מצי ר"נ למימר ע"כ לא קאמר ר"ג התם אלא משום דבעל הוה מחויב לה כתובה מעיקרא ועכשיו הוא בא לפטור עצמו אבל במנה לי בידך שלא ידענו שנתחייב לו מקודם לכן אלא עכשיו אנו רוצים לחייבו לא אמר וכו' וכדכתיבנא לעיל אלא חד מתרי טעמא נקט. **ה"נ** מסתברא כדשנינן דא"כ קשה הלכתא אהלכתא דקיי"ל הלכה כר"נ בדיני. ובהא אמר ר"י אמר שמואל הלכה כר"ג ש"מ: **מתני' היא** אומרת מוכת עץ אני והוא אומר לא כי אלא דרוסת איש את ר"ג ור"א אומרים נאמנת ור"י אומר לא מפיה אנו חיין אלא ה"ז בחזקת דרוסת איש עד שתביא ראיה לדבריה: **טענתייהו במאי.** פי' מה היא תובעתו ומה הוא רוצה ליתן ר' **יוחנן אמר** במאתים ומנה פי' היא אומרת מוכת עץ אני ויש לי מאתים ואע"פ שלא הכרת בי והוא אומר דרוסת איש את ואין לך אלא מנה וכנסה בחזקת בתולה ונמצאת בעולה יש לה כתובה מנה וסבר לה כר"מ דאמר מוכת עץ בין הכיר בה בין לא הכיר בה כתובתה מאתים וכנסה בחזקת בתולה ונמצאת בעולה כתובתה מנה הלכך ע"כ מוכת עץ דמתני' ר"מ היא דאמר מאתים והוא אומר דרוסת איש את ואין לך אלא מנה

דאי רבנן היא לא טענה אלא מנה מאי איכא בין טענה דידיה לטענה דידה במנה טענה לו ומנה מודה לה ופי' [המורה] סבר לה דלעיל סבר לה תנא דמתני' דאילו ר' יוחנן לא שביק רבנן ועביד כר"מ **ור"א** סבר במנה ולא כלום סבר לה כרבנן דאמרי בין הכיר בה בין לא הכיר בה כתובתה מנה וכנסה בחזקת בתולה ונמצאת בעולה אין לה כלום **בשלמא** ר"א לא אמר כר"י דקא מוקי לה כרבנן פי' במנה ולא כלום: היינו דקתני תרי בבא במתני' גבי פלוגתא דממונא היא אומרת משארסתני נאנסתי וכו' והוא אומר לא כי והיה מקחי מקח טעות לגמרי משמע ואין לה כלום **אלא ר"י** מ"ט לא אמר כר"א קסבר כנסה בחזקת בתולה ונמצאת בעולה יש לה כתובה מנה הכא הוא אומר מנה והיא אומרת מנה מאי איכא בין טענתה לטענתיה והלכתא כר"א דקיימי רבא ורב אשי כוותיה דכנסה בחזקת בתולה ונמצאת בעולה אין לה כלום כדכתיבנא לעיל ובמוכת עץ נמי הלכתא כרבנן דאמרי מנה: **מתני' ראוה** מדברת עם א' מה טיבו של זה איש פלוני וכהן הוא ר"ג ור"א אומרים נאמנת ור"י אומר לא מפיה אנו חיין אלא ה"ז בחזקת בעולה לנתין ולממזר עד שתביא ראיה לדבריה היתה מעוברת מה טיבו של עובר זה מאיש פלוני וכהן הוא ר"ג ור"א אומרים נאמנת ור"י אומר לא מפיה אנו חיין אלא ה"ז בחזקת מעוברת מנתין וממזר עד שתביא ראיה לדבריה: **וכהן הוא** פי' מיוחס ולא כהן ממש שאינה נאמנת להחזיק העובר בחזקת כהן אלא בחזקת כשר שאם הוא בת תנשא לכהונה: **מאי מדברת** זעירא אמר נסתרה ואע"פ שלא ראוה שנבעלה פסולה לכהונה לר"י כדלקמן שמעלה עשו ביוחסין ור"א אמר נבעלה בשלמא לזעירא היינו דקתני מדברת אלא לר"א מאי מדברת לישנא מעליא כדכתיב אכלה ומחתה פיה וגו' פי' נקט תשמיש בלשון אכילה בשלמא לזעירא היינו דקתני תרתי מדברת ומעוברת פי' מדברת להודיעך כחו דר"י דאפילו בעדי יחוד בלבד אסורה היא לכהן משום דמעלה עשו ביוחסין ומעוברת להודיעך כחו דר"ג אלא לר"א תרתי למה לי פי' לתני מדברת וכ"ש מעוברת. חדא להכשיר בה וחדא להכשיר בבתה **דאתמר** ר"י אמר לדברי המכשיר בה מכשיר בבתה ור"א אומר אף לדברי המכשיר בה פוסל בבתה דבשלמא איהי אית לה חזקה דכשרות פי' מעיקרא ואוקמה אחזקה ולא תפסלנה מספק אבל בתה לית לה חזקה דכשרות והלכתא כר' יוחנן דהוא רביה דר"א שאין הלכה כתלמיד במקום הרב ותו דקאי כאבא שאול דתנן בעשרה יוחסין אבא שאול היה קורא לשתוקי בדוקי ואמרי' בגמ' מאי בדוקי שבודקין את אמו ואי אמרה לכשר נבעלתי נאמנת ואע"ג דאיכא רוב פסולים אצלה וא"ר הל' כאבא שאול: **א"ל** ר"פ לאביי לזעירי דאמר נסתרה ואר"י דלא מהימנא הא דאמר רב מלקין על

דְּאִם כֵּן – **For if** it is **so** that Rav Nachman's ruling does not accord with Rabban Gamliel, but only with R' Yehoshua, קַשְׁיָא הִלְכְתָא אַהִלְכְתָא – there would be **a contradiction between** one **law and** another **law.** דְּקַיְימָא לָן הִלְכְתָא כְּרַב נַחְמָן בְּדִינֵי – **For we have** an **established** rule **that the law is** always **in accordance with Rav Nachman regarding monetary matters;** we should therefore rule that in a case of "certainly and perhaps" the certain claim *cannot* exact money from the current owner. וּבְהָא אָמַר רַב יְהוּדָה אָמַר שְׁמוּאֵל הֲלָכָה כְּרַבָּן גַּמְלִיאֵל – **Yet in this** Tannaic dispute **Rav Yehudah said** above **in the name of Shmuel: The law is in accordance with Rabban Gamliel** that we believe the wife's claim, allowing her to collect her *kesubah.* אֶלָּא לָאו שְׁמַע מִינָּהּ כִּדְמְשַׁנֵּינַן – **Rather, should we not conclude from this, as we answered,** that Rav Nachman accords with the view of Rabban Gamliel?

The Gemara concludes:

שְׁמַע מִינָּהּ – Indeed, **conclude** it **from this.**[1]

Mishnah The Mishnah discusses a second claim and counterclaim between the groom and bride over her lack of signs of virginity:

הִיא אוֹמֶרֶת מוּכַּת עֵץ אָנִי – **She says, "I am a wood-injury victim,"**[2] וְהוּא אוֹמֵר לֹא כִּי אֶלָּא דְּרוּסַת אִישׁ אַתְּ – **and he says,** "Perhaps it is **not so, rather you were deflowered by a man."**[3] רַבָּן גַּמְלִיאֵל וְרַבִּי אֱלִיעֶזֶר אוֹמְרִים – **Rabban Gamliel and R' Eliezer say:** נֶאֱמֶנֶת – **She is believed.** וְרַבִּי יְהוֹשֻׁעַ אוֹמֵר – **R' Yehoshua, however, says:** לֹא מִפִּיהָ אָנוּ חַיִּין – **Not by her mouth do we live** [i.e. she is not believed]. אֶלָּא הֲרֵי זוֹ בְּחֶזְקַת דְּרוּסַת אִישׁ – **Rather, she is presumed to have been deflowered by a man** עַד שֶׁתָּבִיא רְאָיָה לִדְבָרֶיהָ – **until she brings proof to her claim.**[4]

Gemara The Gemara seeks an explanation of our Mishnah:

טַעֲנָתַיְיהוּ בְּמַאי – **What are their claims?** How much money is the bride demanding, and what is the groom agreeing to pay?

The Gemara presents two interpretations:

רַבִּי יוֹחָנָן אָמַר – **R' Yochanan says:** בְּמָאתַיִם וּמָנֶה – The Mishnah is dealing **with** a bride who claims a *kesubah* of **two hundred and** a groom who agrees to pay only **a *maneh.***[5] רַבִּי אֶלְעָזָר אָמַר – **R' Elazar says:** בְּמָנֶה וְלֹא כְלוּם – The Mishnah is dealing **with** a bride who claims a *kesubah* of **a *maneh* and** the groom who does **not** want to pay anything **at all.**

The Gemara elaborates:

רַבִּי יוֹחָנָן אָמַר בְּמָאתַיִם וּמָנֶה – **R' Yochanan says** that the dispute is **concerning two hundred versus a *maneh,*** סָבַר לָהּ כְּרַבִּי מֵאִיר – because he maintains that **[the Tanna of our Mishnah] holds in accordance with R' Meir,** דְּאָמַר בֵּין הִכִּיר בָּהּ וּבֵין לֹא הִכִּיר בָּהּ – **who says** that **whether [the groom] recognized [the bride]** to be a wood-injury victim at the time of the marriage **or whether he did not recognize** this fact about **her,** מָאתַיִם – she receives a *kesubah* of **two hundred.**[6] וְרַבִּי אֶלְעָזָר אוֹמֵר בְּמָנֶה וְלֹא כְלוּם – **But R' Elazar says** that the dispute is **concerning a *maneh* versus nothing at all,** סָבַר לָהּ כְּרַבָּנָן – **because he holds** that the Mishnah is **in accordance with the Rabbis,** דְּאָמְרֵי בֵּין הִכִּיר בָּהּ בֵּין לֹא הִכִּיר בָּהּ – **who say** that **whether he recognized her** condition **or whether he did not recognize her** condition, מָנֶה – she receives **a *maneh.***[7]

NOTES

1. To sum up, therefore: The halachah follows Rav Nachman that a claim of "certainly" does not win out over a claim of "perhaps," and thus a defendant who, when confronted with a claim that he owes money, responds that he is unsure of the obligation, is not required to pay. (He must, however, swear a *hesseis* oath that he is unsure, as explained in note 14 to 12b. Additionally, though he cannot be forced by the court to pay, if he wishes to avoid the possibility of Heavenly retribution for wrongly withholding someone else's money [לָצֵאת יְדֵי שָׁמַיִם, *to discharge his Heavenly obligation*], he should pay voluntarily – *Ran,* from *Bava Kamma* 118a; see *Choshen Mishpat* 75:9.) Nevertheless the law accords with Rabban Gamliel that the woman in our Mishnah is believed with her claim of "certainly" over the husband's claim of "perhaps," because in that case a *migo* or a *chazakah* bolsters her claim.

[This credence accorded the wife's claim applies to exacting the *kesubah* from the husband. However, how does this affect permitting her to live with him? We learned on 9a that where the husband claims to have found his wife to be a nonvirgin, and he is a Kohen or she was betrothed younger than age three, she becomes forbidden to him (since there is only one doubtful issue in each case – in the case of the wife of a Kohen, did the cohabitation occur before or after *erusin,* and in the case of the woman betrothed younger than three, was she violated or did she cohabit willingly). However, as explained in 12b note 21, that case referred to where the woman disputed the husband's charge and claimed that she had been a virgin, so that the case involved a situation of "certainly and certainly." What, however, would be the law in a scenario such as the present one, where she agrees that she did not possess signs of virginity, but explains it by saying that she had been violated before the *erusin*, or, in the case of the next Mishnah, by saying that she had been injured by a piece of wood? Is her claim of "certainly" believed against his claim of "perhaps" to permit her to remain married to him, or not?

Some Rishonim (see *Maggid Mishneh, Hil. Isurei Biah* 18:10 and *Rav* to the following Mishnah) maintain that she remains forbidden to him. Apparently they feel that a claim of "certainly" has an advantage over a claim of "perhaps" only in regard to monetary litigation, but not in regard to prohibitory law. Most Rishonim (*Ramban* to 9b, *Rashba, Ritva, Ran, Meiri* to 9a, *Rosh* §18 in the name of *Rabbeinu Yonah*), however, are of the opinion that in this case she is permitted to him, either because a claim of "certainly" (when accompanied by a *migo* or a *chazakah*) is stronger than a claim of "perhaps" even in regard to prohibitory law (*Ritva, Rosh* in the name of *Rabbeinu Yonah* ibid.), or because the woman is considered a single witness, and a single witness is believed in matters of prohibitory law [עֵד אֶחָד נֶאֱמָן בְּאִסּוּרִין] (see *Rashba; Meiri*). For analysis and discussion of this issue see, in the *poskim, Noda BiYehudah, Tinyana, Even HaEzer* 14 and *She'eilos U'Teshuvos Chasam Sofer, Even HaEzer* 131 (2), and, in the commentaries, *Kovetz Shiurim* 21-4, *Shaarei Yosher* 6:18, *Kehillos Yaakov* 6.] See also above, 9a note 2.

2. I was injured by a piece of wood before the *erusin* (see *Rashi* to 12b ד״ה אלא).

3. Before the *erusin* (*Rashi*). The dispute is in regard to the disposition of her *kesubah*. The Gemara will discuss how much money she is claiming and how much, if any, he is willing to give.

4. The reasons given for the opinions in the previous Mishnah apply here as well: Rabban Gamliel and R' Eliezer believe the woman because her claim is "certainly" while her husband's is "perhaps," coupled with the fact that her words are supported by a *migo* or a *chazakah*. R' Yehoshua, however, maintains that this is insufficient reason to exact the *kesubah* money from the possession of the husband, who is holding it.

5. She claims she was injured by a piece of wood before the *erusin* and should receive the full two hundred-*zuz kesubah* of a virgin – even though she had not told him about her injury beforehand. He, however, argues that perhaps she cohabited with another man before the *erusin,* and deserves a *kesubah* of only a *maneh*. R' Yochanan is of the opinion that a woman wed on the presumption of being a virgin but found to be a nonvirgin receives a *kesubah* of a *maneh* (*Rashi*).

6. R' Yochanan can therefore say that the groom agrees to pay a *maneh* and that his disagreement with the bride is over his obligation to pay the second hundred.

7. Therefore, if even according to the wife's own claim she should receive

וְרַב נַחְמָן וְרַבִּי יוֹחָנָן דְּאָמְרֵי כְּרַבִּי יְהוֹשֻׁעַ – **while Rav Nachman and R' Yochanan state** their view **in accordance with R' Yehoshua,** who rules that the groom can keep his money until the bride proves that she was a virgin at the time of betrothal?

The Gemara responds that this is not necessarily the case:

אָמַר לָךְ רַב נַחְמָן – **Rav Nachman can tell you:** אֲנָא דְּאָמְרֵי אֲפִילּוּ כְּרַבָּן גַּמְלִיאֵל – **I state** my ruling even in accordance with Rabban Gamliel. עַד כָּאן לֹא קָאָמַר רַבָּן גַּמְלִיאֵל הָתָם – **For Rabban Gamliel went so far there** to believe the wife's claim אֶלָּא דְּאִיכָּא מִגּוֹ – **only because there is a *migo*** to bolster it.[22] אֲבָל הָכָא מַאי מִגּוֹ אִיכָּא – **But here,** in the case of the loan dispute, **what *migo* is there** to bolster the claim of the plaintiff?[23] אִי נַמִּי עַד כָּאן לֹא קָאָמַר רַבָּן גַּמְלִיאֵל הָתָם – **Alternatively, Rabban Gamliel went so far there** אֶלָּא דְּאָמְרִינַן אוֹקְמָהּ אַחֲזָקָהּ – **only because we say: Keep [the woman] in her *chazakah*** (previous state) of virginity.[24] אֲבָל הָכָא מַאי חֲזָקָה אִית לֵיהּ לְהַאי – **But here** in the case of the loan dispute, **what *chazakah* does [the plaintiff] have** to enable him to collect the money?[25]

The Gemara notes:

הָכִי נַמִּי מִסְתַּבְּרָא כִּדְקָא מְשַׁנֵּינַן – **It is also reasonable** to say **as we answered,** דְּרַב נַחְמָן הוּא דְּאָמַר כְּרַבָּן גַּמְלִיאֵל – **that Rav Nachman stated** his ruling **in accordance with Rabban Gamliel.**

NOTES

22. The principle of *migo* (literally: since) as used here is explained as follows: A dishonest litigant would prefer to enter a more advantageous plea rather than a less advantageous one. Therefore, if a litigant enters a less advantageous plea, the court assumes that he is telling the truth. Thus, in our case, the bride is assumed to be telling the truth about being violated after *erusin, since* if she wanted to gain her *kesubah* illegally she could have advanced a claim that would be of greater benefit to her – that she had been injured by a stick of wood. This claim would have the advantage that she would not become forbidden to a Kohen as she is based on her present claim that she was violated after being married (*Rashi;* see also *Meiri*).

This same explanation applies to the identical ruling of Rabban Gamliel in the very next Mishnah (top of 13a). The Mishnah there discusses a case in which the bride explains her lack of signs of virginity on the wedding night by saying that she had been injured by a piece of wood prior to *erusin.* The groom counters that perhaps she had cohabited with a man. Again, Rabban Gamliel and R' Eliezer rule that her claim of "certainly" is believed against his claim of "perhaps" and she may collect the *kesubah,* while R' Yehoshua maintains that the money is left with the husband until she can prove her claim. Here too we can say that the reason for Rabban Gamliel's ruling is that the bride's claim is bolstered by a *migo*: Rather than say that she was injured by a stick of wood *before* the *erusin,* which allows her to collect only one hundred *zuz* [according to the view of the Sages in the Mishnah on 11a], she could have said, if she were lying, that she had been injured *after* the *erusin.* That claim would have had the advantage of allowing her to collect the full two hundred *zuz* (*Rashi*).

[The Rishonim point out that this is a most unusual *migo,* not at all similar to the numerous *migos* found throughout the Talmud. In the standard type of *migo* the claim that the litigant could have used, but did not, would have won the case for him. Thus, we believe him with his present claim *since* if he were lying he would presumably have used the other, winning claim. (For example, someone is presented with a document stating that he owes money, but the holder of the document cannot verify the authenticity of the signatures of the witnesses on the document. The defendant replies that he already repaid the loan. Normally such a claim would be rejected out of hand by the court, since if it were true, the defendant should have asked for the document back upon payment. Nevertheless, he is believed with a *migo* that he could have declared the document to be a forgery, since he would have won with that claim.) In the present case, however, the claim that the woman could have used, namely, that she was injured by a piece of wood, would have had no more believability than the claim she in fact uses, i.e. that she was violated after *erusin.* What, then, is the strength of this *migo*?

The Rishonim answer that, indeed, such a *migo* is ordinarily ineffective. Here, however, the main reason for believing the woman is the fact that her husband's claim is "perhaps" while hers is "certainly." As a buttress for such a claim, even a weak *migo* is effective (*Rashba* here and to *Kiddushin* 50a ד״ה הא; *Ritva;* see also *Tosafos* to 13a ד״ה רב אסי; see further *Kovetz Shiurim* vol. 2, 3:24; cf. *Pnei Yehoshua*).]

(This also explains another point. According to many Rishonim a claim bolstered by a *migo* is effective only to permit someone to retain money, but not to allow him to exact money from someone else [מִגּוֹ לְהוֹצִיא לֹא אָמְרִינַן] [see *Tosafos* to 9b ד״ה לא, end, and *Choshen Mishpat* 82:12]. Why, then, is the *migo* effective here? Again, the answer is that the main reason the wife wins is because her claim of "certainly" is stronger than the husband's claim of "perhaps." The *migo* serves merely to *bolster* her claim. In this capacity a *migo* may be used even to exact money. See *Shach* to *Choshen Mishpat* §82, *Principles of Migo* §1 and 15.)

23. The claimant does not have any alternative claim that would have been better than the one he is presently advancing. He therefore does not have the strength of a *migo* to exact money from the defendant. The money therefore remains in the possession of the defendant (*Rashi*).

24. Throughout the Talmud, we find the principle of חֲזָקָה, *chazakah,* which says that we rely on a certain state of a person or thing until there is evidence to the contrary. This general term "*chazakah*" covers a variety of presumptions, ranging from presumptions based on the nature of things (such as the *chazakah* mentioned on 10a that a man would not trouble himself to prepare a wedding feast only to waste it) to the presumption that what used to be still is. This forward extension of the last previously known status is called חֲזָקָה דְּמֵעִיקָּרָא, *the chazakah that what existed previously [exists now].*

Here, the Gemara uses *chazakah* in the sense of חֲזָקָה דְּמֵעִיקָּרָא. Since the woman was known to be a virgin at birth and at the time of the first cohabitation with her husband after the *chuppah* she was no longer a virgin, her status during the intervening period of doubt is legally resolved by preserving her last-known state until the point at which it is known to have changed. Thus, she is presumed to be a virgin until now, when she was violated after the *erusin* (see *Rashi*).

25. The claimant does not have any *chazakah* to bolster his claim to the money. We therefore leave the money with its current owner (*Rashi*), even though his claim is only one of "perhaps."

[The Gemara has explained that the woman is believed because her claim is backed by a *chazakah.* This is very understandable in the case of our Mishnah, because the question is when she lost her virginity, before *erusin* or afterwards. The *chazakah* therefore tells us to presume that it happened at the latest possible time, i.e. after *erusin.* But what of the next Mishnah? There the woman admits that her hymen was ruptured before *erusin.* The question is only whether this happened through a piece of wood (as she claims) or via cohabitation (as the husband suggests). Since the issue is *what* happened rather than *when* it happened, how is *chazakah* relevant?

Ramban (to 16a) suggests that since a woman who has lost her hymen through a piece of wood is still "cohabitation-free," the principle of *chazakah* tells us to extend this status forward and say that she remained "cohabitation-free" until marriage. *Ran* (to *Rif* folio 4b ד״ה אלא דאמרינן), however, explains that in this case the *chazakah* is not that what existed previously exists now [i.e. חֲזָקָה דְּמֵעִיקָּרָא]. Rather, it is a *chazakah* based on the nature of things, that Jewish daughters do not engage in illicit relations. Cf. *Rashash* to *Rashi* ד״ה אלא and *She'eilos U'Teshuvos Beis HaLevi* vol. 3, 17:4.]

עג א טוש"ע אה"ע סי' סו סעיף ז:
עד ב מיי' פי"א מהל' אישות הל' יא סמג עשין מח טוש"ע שם סי' סח סעיף ט:
עה ג מיי' פ"א מהל' טוען ונטען הל' ח סמג עשין צה טוש"ע ח"מ סימן עה סעיף ט:

כיון דחזו דמזלזלי בהו תקינו להו מאתן כיון דחזו דקא פרשין מינייהו דאמרי עד דנסבינן אלמנת כהנים ניזיל ניסיב בתולה בת ישראל אהדרינהו למלתייהו: בית דין של כהנים כו': אמר רב יהודה אמר שמואל לא ב"ד של כהנים בלבד אמרו אלא אפי' משפחות המיוחסות בישראל אם רצו לעשות כדרך שהכהנים עושין עושין מיתיבי הרוצה לעשות כדרך שהכהנים עושין כגון בת ישראל לכהן ובת כהן לישראל עושין בת ישראל לכהן ובת כהן לישראל הוא דאיכא צד כהונה אבל בת ישראל לישראל לא מבעיא קאמר לא מבעיא בת ישראל לישראל דלא מצי אמר לה עלויי קא מעלינן ליך אבל בת ישראל לכהן דמצי אמר לה עלויי קא מעלינן ליך אימא לא קמ"ל: **מתני'** הנושא את האשה ולא מצא לה בתולים היא אומרת משארסתני נאנסתי ונסתחפה שדהו והוא אומר לא כי אלא עד שלא ארסתיך והיה מקחי מקח טעות רבן גמליאל ורבי אליעזר אומרים נאמנת רבי יהושע אומר לא מפיה אנו חיין אלא הרי זו בחזקת בעולה עד שלא תתארס והטעתו עד שתביא ראיה לדבריה: **גמ'** איתמר מנה לי בידך והלה אומר איני יודע רב הונא ורב יהודה אמרי חייב ורב נחמן ורבי יוחנן אמרי פטור רב הונא ורב יהודה אמרי חייב ברי ושמא ברי עדיף רב נחמן ורבי יוחנן אמרי פטור אוקי ממונא בחזקת מריה א"ל אביי לרב יוסף הא דרב הונא ורב יהודה דשמואל היא דתנן היתה מעוברת ואמרו לה מה טיבו של עובר זה מאיש פלוני וכהן הוא רבן גמליאל ורבי אליעזר אומרים נאמנת ואמר רב יהודה אמר שמואל הלכה כרבן גמליאל ואמר ליה רב שמואל בר יהודה לרב יהודה שיננא אמרת לן משמיה דשמואל הלכה כרבן גמליאל אף בראשונה מאי אף בראשונה אע"ג דאיכא למימר אוקי ממונא בחזקת מריה אמר רבן גמליאל ברי עדיף לימא רב יהודה ורב הונא דאמרי כר"ג ורב נחמן ורבי יוחנן דאמרי כרבי יהושע אמר לך רב נחמן אנא דאמרי אפילו כרבן גמליאל עד כאן לא קאמר ר"ג התם אלא דאיכא מגו אבל הכא מאי מגו איכא אי נמי עד כאן לא קאמר רבן גמליאל התם אלא דאמרינן אוקמה אחזקה אבל הכא מאי חזקה אית ליה להאי הכי נמי מסתברא כדקא משנינן דרב נחמן הוא דאמר כר"ג דאם

רש"י

דמזלזלי בהו. באלמנות קלות בעיניהם להוציאן מפני שכתובתן מועטת תקינו להו מאתן דגנאי היה להן ואע"פ שאלמנות ישראל נמי כתובתן מנה מיהו כהנים חשיבי טפי וגנאי להם גירושי בנותיהן יותר מישראל: **מתני' נאמנת.** קא סלקא דעתך משום דברי ושמא ברי עדיף: **הרי זו בחזקת.** שנבעלה עד שלא תתארס והטעתו: **גמ' חייב.** לשלם: **פטור.** מלשלם ומכל מקום משביעין ליה שבועת היסת שכן הוא כדבריו שאינו יודע שהוא חייב לו: **וכהן הוא.** כלומר מיוחס הוא: **אף בראשונה.** גבי תביעת כתובה: [אוקי כתובה אחזקתה אחזקת הבעל ה"נ גבי מנה לי בידך איכא למימר נמי אוקי ממונא בחזקת מריה ופטור: **אלא דאיכא מגו**]. כגון משארסתני נאנסתי וכגון היא אומרת מוכת עץ אני דאמרינן מגו דאי בעיא טענה טענה מעלייתא מהך כגון גבי משארסתני נאנסתי הוה טוענה מוכת עץ אני [טענה מעלייתא] דלא פסלה נפשה מכהונה וקאמרה נאנסתי [משארסתני] וקא מיפסלה נפשה דאשת ישראל שנאנסה אסורה לכהן ש"מ קושטא קאמרה וגבי היא אומרת מוכת עץ אני אי בעיא אמרה מוכת עץ אני תחתיך ואית לה מאתן וקא אמרה מוכת עץ אני קודם לכן ואין לי אלא מנה: **אבל הכא.** גבי האי תובע מאי מגו איכא דלהמניה הלכך אוקי ממונא בחזקת מריה: **אוקמה אחזקה.** מספקא לן אשעת ארוסין אי בתולה הואי ונשתעבד לה למאתים אי בעולה הואי העמד אשה על חזקתה ובתולה נולדה והן השתא הוא דאיתניסה אחר אירוסין: **מאי חזקה אית ליה להאי.** תובע דנוקמיה אחזקיה לגבות הלכך זיל בתר חזקה דממונא: דא"כ

תוספות

כיון דחזו דמזלזלי בהו. פירש בקונטרס שהיו קלות בעיניהן להוציאן לפי שהיתה כתובתן מועטת וקשה דמעיקרא נמי הוו ידעי שקלות בעיניהן להוציאן כיון דמנה חשיב דבר מועט ונראה לר"י לפרש דמזלזלי בהו כמו שמקצת בני אדם היו נמנעים מלנושאם לפי שהיו קלות בעיניהן שאין לה כתובה אלא רביע ממה שיש לה לבתולה ותקינו לה מאתן כיון דחזו דפרשי מינייהו לגמרי והיו קופצים קודם על בתולות ישראל ולא היה שום אדם קופץ עליהם אהדרינהו למילתייהו היינו דנקט מעיקרא מזלזלי שהיו נמנעים ולא לגמרי פורשים ובתר הכי נקט ופרשי: **בית** דין של כהנים היו גובין כו' ולא מיחו בידם חכמים. אע"פ שלא כתב בלשון תוספת אלא ארבע מאות דחזו ליכי וקא ס"ד דלא תגבה דלא הוי בלשון תוספת לא כתב קא משמע לן דמנהג טוב הוא ולאו להיות בכהונה ובמשפחות המיוחסות ושייך בהו למימר דחזו ליכי ואפי' לא כתב לה כתובה גובה ארבע מאות דתנאי ב"ד כמו בבנות ישראל מאתים דתקנה גמורה היא: **והוא** אומר לא כי כו'. אע"ג דבסוף המניח (ב"ק דף לה: ושם) דייק מדקתני לא כי דמיירי בברי הכל לאפוקי מלמיטעי קתני לא כי אע"ג דאיירי בשמא: **מנה** לי בידך והלה אומר איני יודע. פי' איני יודע אם הלויתני אבל לויתי ואיני יודע אם פרעתיך תנן בהדיא בהגוזל בתרא (שם קיח.) דחייב: **רב** הונא ורב יהודה אמרי חייב. לכאורה נראה דלית להו דרבי אבא דאמר מתוך שאינו יכול לישבע משלם דטעמייהו דר' אבא משום דלדריש (שבועות ד' מז.) שבועת ה' תהיה בין שניהם ולא בין היורשין כגון אמר מנה לאבא ביד אביך ואמר מקצת ידענא ומקצת לא ידענא ואבוה כה"ג מתוך שאין יכול לישבע משלם ואי מנה לי בידך והלה אומר איני יודע חייב בכל ענין אין כאן שבועה דלפי' הוא אומר אין יודע חייב ותימה דבפרק יש נוחלין (ב"ב דף קלה. ושם) גבי האומר זה אחי משמע דלאבי אית ליה מנה לי בידך והלה אומר איני יודע חייב ובפ' חזקת הבתים (שם לג. ושם) משמע דלית ליה לדר' אבא וי"ל דלפי' לרמ"ד חייב איכא למידרש שבועת ה' תהיה בין שניהם ולא בין היורשין דשניהם לא ידעי אלא שעד אחד מעיד שאחד חייב לחבירו מנה דבאבוה מתוך שאינו יכול לישבע משלם תימה דרב יהודה גופיה אית ליה ברים הפרה (ב"ק מו. ושם) אפילו ניזק אומר ברי ומזיק אומר שמא המע"ה ואין לומר דרב יהודה כסומכוס דאמר ממון המוטל בספק חולקין ולא אזיל בתר חזקת ממון ולהכי כי איכא ברי ושמא נוטל הכל והתם דקאמר אמר רב יהודה אמר שמואל זו דברי סומכוס אומרים אבל חכמים אומרים זה כלל ג"ול בדין כו' אליבא דרבנן קאמר וליה לא סבירא ליה דהתם (בכ"ב דף לג:) משמע דסבר כרבנן גבי מוכר שור לחבירו ונמצא נגחן ועוד דתנן בפרק השואל (ב"מ לז. ושם) המשאיל אומר שאולה מתה והלה אומר איני יודע חייב וקאמר בגמרא לימא תיהוי תיובתא דרב נחמן ור' יוחנן ומאי קושיא הא ע"כ מתני' כסומכוס אפי' לרב יהודה דלרבנן מודה רב יהודה דפטור ורב נחמן ורבי יוחנן ע"כ כרבנן דלסומכוס לכל הפחות חולקין אבל אי פליגי אליבא דרבנן ולסומכוס לעולם חולקין אפי' בברי ושמא פריך שפיר ממתני' דכרבנן אתיא דלסומכוס חולקין וי"ל דהתם ברי גרוע ושמא טוב דלפי שהמזיק לא היה שם טוען זה ברי ושמא דמזיק טוב דלא הוה ליה למידע אבל מנה לי בידך הברי טוב והשמא גרוע דהוה ליה לידע אם חייב אם לאו אבל קשה דבעי למימר הכא הא דרב יהודה דשמואל היא דפסק כרבן גמליאל והתם ברי גרוע ושמא טוב שהבעל אינו יודע מתי נבעלה ואם כן תיקשי דשמואל אדשמואל דפ' הפרה (ב"ק מו. ושם) ויש לומר דה"מ למימר וליטעמיך ועוד יש לומר דסוגיא דהכא סברה דזה כלל גדול בדין לא לניזק אומר ברי ומזיק אומר שמא אלא כדקאמר התם אי נמי לכי הא וקשה על זה דאפילו לפי אי נמי דהתם לא אתי שפיר דהא בסוף המניח (שם דף לה: ושם) אית להו לרבנן בהדיא דאפי' ניזק אומר ברי כו' ושמואל סובר כרבנן כדמוכח בהמוכר שור לחבירו: **אלא** דאיכא מגו. האי שנויא לא אתיא אלא לרב נחמן דלר' יוחנן בהדיא דמוכת עץ ליכא מגו כדמוכח לקמן הקשה ה"ר יעקב מקורביי"ל אכתי ע"כ הא דרב יהודה דשמואל היא דאי לשמואל פטור תקשי ליה ממתניתין דהשואל (ב"מ ד' לז. ושם:) המשאיל אומר שאולה מתה והלה אומר איני יודע חייב דלשמואל ליכא לשנויי כדמשני לרב נחמן ולרבי יוחנן כגון שיש עסק שבועה ביניהן ומתוך שאינו יכול לישבע משלם דשמואל לית ליה בהדיא בפ' כל הנשבעין (שבועות ד' מז. ושם) דחזרה שבועה לסיני ולא משלם וי"ל דאיכא למימר דלעולם מנה לי בידך והלה אומר איני יודע לשמואל פטור ומוקי שמואל מתני' דהשואל כשיש עסק שבועה וכההוא תנא דאית ליה מתוך שאינו יכול לישבע משלם והוא סבר כאידך תנא דפלוגתא דתנאי היא בפרק כל הנשבעין (שם). [ועי' ביתר ביאור תוס' ב"מ לז: סד"ה רב הונא]:

תוספות רי"ד

ב"ד של כהנים וכו'. אמר רב יהודה לא ב"ד של כהנים בלבד אמרו אלא אפילו משפחות המיוחסות שבישראל אם רצו לעשות כדרך שהכהנים עושין ולא אמרי' דמחזי כעוקרים תיקון חכמים: **מתני'** הנושא את האשה ולא מצא לה בתולים היא אומרת משארסתני נאנסתי ונסתחפה שדהו והוא אומר לא כי אלא עד שלא ארסתיך והיה מקחי מקח טעות ר"ג ור"א אומרי' נאמנת ור"י אומר לא מפיה אנו חיין אלא הרי היא בחזקת בעולה עד שלא תתארס והטעתו עד שתביא ראיה לדבריה. **היא אומרת וכו'** מכאן מוכח שיש כתובה לארוסה ומשעת שאירסה נתחייב בכתובתה בתנאי ב"ד וכ"ה קאמרה ליה הכי המקודש שנבעלה הוה משועבד לה ועכשיו שנאנסתי לא הפסידה שעבודה דאי אמרת אין כתובה לארוסה עד שיכנוס וזאת כבר נבעלה קודם הנשואין אדרבה אומר הבעל לאשה נסתחפה שדך שהפסדת בתוליך ובעת הנשואין בעולה היית א"נ טעמא הוא משום דיש כתובה לארוסה ומשום אירוסין נתחייב לה: **והוא אומר לא כי וכו'.** פי' ואין לך כלום דהכי אוקימה רבא לעיל מקח טעות לגמרי משמע דכנסה בחזקת בתולה ונמצאת בעולה א"ל כלום: **ר"ג ור"א אומרים נאמנת.** פי' ואפילו לבעלה מותרת אם היה ישראל דמאי דאמרן לעיל שהבעל נאמן לאוסרה עליו דוקא בברי וברי הוא אומר פתח פתוח מצאתי והיא אומרת לא כי אלא פתח סתום היה והכחשה ליה התם בעל נאמן לאוסרה עליו דשוייה אנפשיה חתיכה דאיסורא אבל הכא דאיהי טענה ברי ובעל שמא מותרת היא לו שהיא נאמנת בכל הן ליטול כתובתה והן להיות מותרה לו: **ור"י אומר וכו'.** פי' בהא פליגי דר"ג סבר אוקי איתתא אחזקה ובחזקת בתולה הות לימא ומספיקא לא מפקינן לה מחזקתה ור"י סבר אוקי ממוניה בחזקת מריה ומן ספיקא לא מפקינן ממונא עד שתביא ראיה לדבריה מר אזיל בתר חזקה דגופא. ומר אזיל בתר חזקה דממונא. ואמרי' לקמן דהיכא אזיל ר"ג בתר חזקה דגופא דוקא בברי ושמא דאיהי טענה ברי והבעל שמא התם אזיל ר"ג בתר חזקה דגופא ומפקינן ממונא מחזקת מריה אבל בשמא ושמא מודה ר"ג דלא אזלי' בתר חזקה דגופא אלא בתר חזקה דממונא והמע"ה: **אר"י א"ש הלכה כר"ג** ואי קשיא היכי פסק שמואל הלכה כר"ג דאזיל בתר חזקה דגופא ומפיק ממונא מחזק' מרי' והתנן בב"ק שור שנגח את הפרה ונמצא עוברה בצידה ואין ידוע אם עד שלא ילדה נגחה ואם משילדה נגחה משלם חצי נזק לפרה ורביע נזק לולד ואמרי' עלה בגמרא אר"י א"ש זו דברי סומכוס דאמר ממון המוטל בספק חולקין אבל חכמים אומרים זה כלל גדול בדין המע"ה למה פי' דלמימר זה כלל גדול בדין אפילו ניזק אומר ברי ומזיק אומר שמא הוה אמינא דאיכא חזקה דממונא ולהכי ניזק לא בעי לאוקמא איכא חזקה דגופא פריה וכיון דאית לניזק חזקה דגופא פליג ר"ג דאזיל בתר חזקה דגופא ושמא זהו ... כסומכוס ...

א) [לעיל יא: לקמן טו.], ב) [לקמן לו.], ג) לקמן עה., ד) ב"ק קיח. בבא מציעא לז: ודף קטו: [עי' ב"ב קלה.], ה) [קדושין מה: וש"נ], ו) [עיין תוס' יבמות יח: ד"ה דלא דרך מאי], ז) [לקמן יג.], ח) לקמן יד. ט) [ברכות לו. וש"נ ועי' מ"ש תגיגה טו: פירוש על שיננא], י) [גי' כ"י], כ) [שייך לע"א].

גליון הש"ס

גמ' הא דרב הונא ור"י דשמואל היא. עיין יבמות יח ע"ב תד"ה דלא דרך:

ליקוטי רש"י

הנושא את האשה. בחזקת בתולה [לעיל יא:]. **משארסתני.** אירע לי ונסתחפה שדהו ואית לי מאתים [לקמן טו.]. **נסתחפה שדהו.** לשון מטר סוחף (משלי כח) נשטפה שדך כלומר מזלך גרם [לעיל ב.]. **נסחף.** נשטפו והסליקו בגורף כמו מטר סוחף (משלי כח) נסתחפה שדהו בלשון משנה ומנחם חברו לשון כליון וכן חבר מטר סוחף ודוגמא פתר מטר סוחף כמו מטר סוחף כמו מספף פאה במערלה (ישעיה י) (ירמיה מו, טו) סוחף, שוטף, ובמשנה נסתחפה שדהו וכן נסחף אביריך (ירמיה מו) נשטפו ומעדו והבליעו [משלי כח, ג]. **לא מפיה אנו חיין.** שתהא נאמנת אלא העמד ממון אבל חזקתו ולא אזלינן בתר חזקה דגופא לומר הואיל וספק בידינו על שעת אירוסין מה היא העמד הגוף על חזקתו על קודם לכן והרי נולדה בתולה [לקמן עה.]. **רב יהודה ורב הונא אמרי חייב.** לשלם. **פטור.** ומיהו ישבע כדאמר שאין יודע שחייב לו כלום דברי עדיף שמא מכרי דהלא ה"ל הוה טעין ליה אין לך בידי כלום הוי מחייבין ליה שבועת היסת [ב"ק קיח.] וקיימא לן דפטור דהלכתא כרב נחמן בדיני ממון ואלא כרב יוחנן בדיני אלא דמחייבינן ליה שבועת היסת שאינו יודע [רשב"ם ב"ב קלה.]. **בחזקת מריה.** ולא תפקינן מספיקא [ב"מ צז:].

חשק שלמה על תוס' רי"ד

א) ר"ל דאפי' אם קיבל בה קדושין פתות מג' שנים ולכן נ"ע דה"ל היכי טוען שמא על שלא ארסתיך.

נֶאֱמֶנֶת – **She is believed.**[11] רַבִּי יְהוֹשֻׁעַ אוֹמֵר – **R' Yehoshua,** however, **says:** לֹא מִפִּיהָ אָנוּ חַיִּין – **Not by her mouth do we live** [i.e. she is not believed].[12] אֶלָּא הֲרֵי זוֹ בְּחֶזְקַת בְּעוּלָה עַד שֶׁלֹּא תִּתְאָרֵס וְהִטְעַתּוּ – **Rather, she is presumed** to have been **a nonvirgin before she was betrothed, and to have misled him,** עַד שֶׁתָּבִיא רְאָיָה לִדְבָרֶיהָ – **until she brings proof to her claim.**[13]

Gemara The Gemara cites an Amoraic dispute:

אִתְּמַר – **It was stated:** מָנֶה לִי בְּיָדְךָ – If one person says to another, **"You owe me a** ***maneh,*"** וְהַלָּה אוֹמֵר אֵינִי יוֹדֵעַ – **and the other one says, "I do not know,"** רַב יְהוּדָה וְרַב הוּנָא אָמְרֵי חַיָּיב – **Rav Yehudah and Rav Huna say** that [the defendant] **is liable,** וְרַב נַחְמָן וְרַבִּי יוֹחָנָן אָמְרֵי פָּטוּר – **while Rav Nachman and R' Yochanan say he is not liable.**

The Gemara analyzes the dispute:

רַב הוּנָא וְרַב יְהוּדָה אָמְרֵי חַיָּיב – **Rav Huna and Rav Yehudah say he is liable,** בָּרִי וְשֶׁמָּא בָּרִי עָדִיף – because in a case in which one litigant claims **"certainly"** and the other claims **"perhaps,"** the claim of **"certainly" is stronger.** רַב נַחְמָן וְרַבִּי יוֹחָנָן אָמְרֵי פָּטוּר – **Rav Nachman and R' Yochanan say he is not liable,** אוֹקֵי מָמוֹנָא בְּחֶזְקַת מָרֵיהּ – because we **let the** contested **money remain in the possession of its** current **owner.** [14]

Another Amora comments about this dispute:

אָמַר לֵיהּ אַבַּיֵי לְרַב יוֹסֵף – **Abaye said to Rav Yosef:** הָא דְּרַב הוּנָא וְרַב יְהוּדָה דִּשְׁמוּאֵל הִיא – **That** opinion **of Rav Huna and Rav Yehudah is** in accordance with **Shmuel.** דִּתְנַן – **For we learned in a Mishnah:**[15] הָיְתָה מְעוּבֶּרֶת – **If [AN UNMARRIED WOMAN] WAS PREGNANT,** וְאָמְרוּ לָהּ מַה טִּיבוֹ שֶׁל עוּבָּר זֶה – **AND [THE COURT] SAID TO HER, "WHAT IS THE NATURE OF THIS FETUS?"**[16] מֵאִישׁ פְּלוֹנִי וְכֹהֵן הוּא – and she replied: "It was fathered **BY SO-AND-SO, AND HE IS A KOHEN,"**[17] רַבָּן גַּמְלִיאֵל וְרַבִּי אֱלִיעֶזֶר אוֹמְרִים נֶאֱמֶנֶת – **RABBAN GAMLIEL AND R' ELIEZER SAY: SHE IS BELIEVED,** while R' Yehoshua says that she is not believed. וְאָמַר רַב יְהוּדָה אָמַר שְׁמוּאֵל – **And Rav Yehudah said in the name of Shmuel:** הֲלָכָה כְּרַבָּן גַּמְלִיאֵל – **The law follows** the opinion of **Rabban Gamliel.** וְאָמַר לֵיהּ רַב שְׁמוּאֵל בַּר יְהוּדָה לְרַב יְהוּדָה – **And Rav Shmuel bar Yehudah said to Rav Yehudah:** שִׁינָּנָא – **Sharp one!**[18] אָמְרַתְּ לָן מִשְּׁמֵיהּ דִּשְׁמוּאֵל הֲלָכָה כְּרַבָּן גַּמְלִיאֵל אַף בָּרִאשׁוֹנָה – **You told us in the name of Shmuel that the law is in accordance with Rabban Gamliel even in the first** case, i.e. in our Mishnah, where the woman is believed to say that she was a virgin at the time of her betrothal against the husband's claim that she had previously cohabited. מַאי אַף בָּרִאשׁוֹנָה – Now, **what** does Rav Shmuel bar Yehudah mean by **"*even* in the first** case"?[19] אַף עַל גַּב דְּאִיכָּא לְמֵימַר אוֹקֵי מָמוֹנָא בְּחֶזְקַת מָרֵיהּ – That **even though it is** possible **to say: Let the** contested **money remain in the possession of its** current **owner,** אָמַר רַבָּן גַּמְלִיאֵל בָּרִי עָדִיף – still **Rabban Gamliel states that** the claim of **"certainly" is stronger.**[20] Thus we see that Shmuel agrees with Rav Huna and Rav Yehudah that a claim of "certainly" is believed against a claim of "perhaps" even to exact money.[21]

The Gemara suggests that the dispute between the Amoraim is linked to the dispute of the Tannaim in our Mishnah:

לֵימָא רַב יְהוּדָה וְרַב הוּנָא דְּאָמְרֵי כְּרַבָּן גַּמְלִיאֵל – **Shall we say that Rav Yehudah and Rav Huna state** their view **in accordance with Rabban Gamliel,** who rules that the bride's claim of "certainly" wins against the groom's claim of "perhaps,"

NOTES

11. Her explanation is accepted. Initially the Gemara presumes the reason for this to be that since the bride states her claim with certitude while the groom is unsure, her claim of "certainly" wins out over his claim of "perhaps" (*Rashi*).

12. [The expression "not by her mouth do we live" is an allusion to the Mishnah in *Avos* (1:18): *On three things the world endures: on justice, truth and peace.* R' Yehoshua asserts here that her words are not necessarily the truth, and thus do not assure the continued existence of the world (*Talmidei Rabbeinu Yonah* and *Radbaz,* quoted in *Shitah Mekubetzes; Ritva* below, 13a).]

13. This follows the principle (see *Bava Kamma* 46b): הַמּוֹצִיא מֵחֲבֵירוֹ עָלָיו הָרְאָיָה, *the [burden of] proof is on the one who seeks to exact [property] from [the possession of] another.* Since the bride seeks to exact a *kesubah* payment from her husband, she must prove that she is entitled to it (see Gemara).

14. Property or money whose ownership is in doubt is presumed to belong to the person in whose possession it is presently found until proven otherwise. (This presumption is known as חֶזְקַת מָמוֹן, *chezkas mamon.*) The fact that the plaintiff is certain of his claim while the defendant is unsure is insufficient proof that the plaintiff's claim is true.

[This ruling of nonliability applies only insofar as payment is concerned. The Rabbis in the post-Mishnaic era, however, instituted that someone who denies a claim of money against him, even if that claim is not substantiated by any evidence, must take an oath, known as שְׁבוּעַת הֶיסֵּת, *shevuas hesseis,* to substantiate his denial. The reason for this enactment is that it is presumed that a plaintiff would not make a totally frivolous claim. Thus, the claim itself creates the suspicion that the defendant might be lying. This suspicion exists at least as much where the defendant's claim is only "perhaps." Thus, in the present case the defendant would be required to swear that he indeed does not know whether he is liable (see *Rashi* here and to *Bava Kamma* 118a ד״ה פטור; see *Tosafos* to *Bava Kamma* ibid. ד״ה רב נחמן at length).]

[The dispute applies only to where the defendant claims to be unsure if he ever became obligated in the *maneh* in the first place. If, however, he admits to having become obligated but does not remember if he paid, all agree that he is liable, since there is a חֶזְקַת חִיּוּב, *presumption of liability* (*Tosafos,* from *Bava Kamma* 118a).]

15. Below, 13a.

16. I.e. is the father someone who disqualifies his offspring from marrying a Jew, or, if the fetus is a girl, from marrying a Kohen?

Offspring of certain people, such as *mamzerim,* are likewise *mamzerim,* and are forbidden to marry Jews. Additionally, if the father and mother are Biblically forbidden to marry each other, their daughter is forbidden to marry a Kohen. It is therefore important for the court to know who the father of the fetus was.

17. I.e. one of untainted lineage (*Rashi*). [The Mishnah does not mean literally that he was a Kohen, but simply that he was someone who would not, through his cohabitation, cause the child he sired to become prohibited to marry in any way.]

18. Shmuel often addressed his student Rav Yehudah this way because of the latter's sharp analytical mind (*Aruch* ע׳ שן [2], first explanation; cf. *Shitah Mekubetzes* below, 14a, in the name of *Rav Hai Gaon*). Here, the Amora Rav Shmuel bar Yehudah addresses Rav Yehudah, his colleague, in the same way.

19. In what way is Rabban Gamliel's ruling in our Mishnah more of a novelty than in the Mishnah below? In both cases he states that we believe the wife's claim of "certainly" over a claim of "perhaps."

20. In the case of the Mishnah on 13a money is not the issue; it is purely a matter of deciding someone's eligibility for marriage to a Jew. Thus, the fact that Rabban Gamliel believes the wife's claim of "certainly" over the court's charge of "perhaps" is not that great a novelty. But in our Mishnah's case believing the wife's claim means exacting money (i.e. the *kesubah*) from the husband's possession.

21. [Although Shmuel himself ruled on 9b that a husband who claims not to have found his wife a virgin is believed to deprive her of her *kesubah,* that ruling referred to where she contradicted him and claimed that she was a virgin, or at least did not respond to his accusation. Thus, his claim was just as certain as hers (i.e. it was a case of "certainly" and "certainly"). Here, however, she agrees to his claim that she was not a virgin; she asserts, however, that it was due to her having been forced after the *erusin.* In such a case, where her claim is certain while his is only "perhaps," Shmuel rules in accordance with Rabban Gamliel that she is believed (*Rashba, Ritva* to 9a; *Rosh* 1:18).]

עין משפט
נר מצוה

עו א טוש"ע אה"ע סי' סו סעיף ז:
עז ב מיי' פי"א מהל' אישות הל' יא סמג עשין מח טוש"ע שם סי' סח סעיף ט:
עח ג מיי' פ"א מהל' טוען ונטען הל' ח סמג עשין לב טוש"ע ח"מ סימן עה סעיף ט:

מסורת הש"ס

א) [לעיל יא: לקמן כח.], ב) [לקמן לו.], ג) לקמן עה., ד) ב"ק קיח. בבא מציעא לז: ודף קטז: [ע' ב"ב קלה.], ה) [קדושין מה: וש"נ], ו) [עיין תוס' יבמות יח: ד"ה דאי דרב מאי], ז) [לקמן יג.], ח) לקמן יד., ט) [ברכות לו. וש"נ וע' מ"ש חגיגה טו: פירוש על שיננא], י) [נ"י כ"י], כ) [שייך לע"א].

גמרא

כיון דחזו דמזלזלי בהו תקינו להו מאתן כיון דחזו דקא פרשין מינייהו דאמרי עד דנסבינן אלמנת כהנים ניזיל ניסיב בתולה בת ישראל אהדרינהו למלתייהו: בית דין של כהנים כו': אמר רב יהודה אמר שמואל לא ב"ד של כהנים בלבד אמרו אלא אפי' משפחות המיוחסות בישראל אם רצו לעשות כדרך שהכהנים עושין עושין מיתיבי הרוצה לעשות כדרך שהכהנים עושין כגון בת ישראל לכהן ובת כהן לישראל עושין בת ישראל לכהן ובת כהן לישראל הוא דאיכא צד כהונה אבל בת ישראל לישראל לא לא מבעיא קאמר לא מבעיא בת ישראל לישראל דלא מצי אמר לה עלויי קא מעלינן ליך אבל בת ישראל לכהן דמצי אמר לה עלויי קא מעלינן ליך אימא לא קמ"ל: מתני' הנושא את האשה ולא מצא לה בתולים היא אומרת משארסתני נאנסתי ונסתחפה שדהו והוא אומר לא כי אלא עד שלא ארסתיך והיה מקחי מקח טעות רבן גמליאל ורבי אליעזר אומרים נאמנת רבי יהושע אומר לא מפיה אנו חיין אלא הרי זו בחזקת בעולה עד שלא תתארס והטעתו עד שתביא ראיה לדבריה: גמ' איתמר מנה לי בידך והלה אומר איני יודע רב יהודה ורב הונא אמרי חייב ורב נחמן ורבי יוחנן אמרי פטור רב הונא ורב יהודה אמרי חייב ברי ושמא ברי עדיף רב נחמן ורבי יוחנן אמרי פטור אוקי ממונא בחזקת מריה א"ל אביי לרב יוסף הא דרב הונא ורב יהודה דשמואל היא דתנן היתה מעוברת ואמרו לה מה טיבו של עובר זה מאיש פלוני וכהן הוא רבן גמליאל ורבי אליעזר אומרים נאמנת ואמר רב יהודה אמר שמואל הלכה כרבן גמליאל ואמר ליה רב שמואל בר יהודה לרב יהודה שיננא אמרת לן משמיה דשמואל הלכה כרבן גמליאל אף בראשונה מאי אף בראשונה אע"ג דאיכא למימר אוקי ממונא בחזקת מריה אמר רבן גמליאל ברי עדיף לימא רב יהודה ורב הונא דאמרי כר"ג ורב נחמן ורבי יוחנן דאמרי כרבי יהושע אמר לך רב נחמן אנא דאמרי אפילו כרבן גמליאל עד כאן לא קאמר ר"ג התם אלא דאיכא מגו אבל הכא מאי מגו איכא אי נמי עד כאן לא קאמר רבן גמליאל התם אלא דאמרינן אוקמה אחזקה אבל הכא מאי חזקה אית ליה להאי הכי נמי מסתברא כדקא משנינן דרב נחמן הוא דאמר כר"ג דאם

רש"י

דמזלזלי בהו. באלמנות קלות בעיניהם להוציאן מפני שכתובתן מועטת תקינו להו מאתן דגבאי היה להן ולא כשאלמנות ישראל. גמי כתובתן מנה מיהו כהנים חשיבי טפי וגבאי להם גירושי בנותיהן יותר מישראל: מתני' נאמנת. קא סלקא דעתך משום דברי ושמא ברי עדיף: הרי זו בחזקת. שנבעלה עד שלא תתארס והטעתו: גמ' חייב. לשלם: פטור. מלשלם ומכל מקום משביעין ליה שבועת היסת שכן הוא לדבריו שאינו יודע שהוא חייב לו: וכהן הוא. כלומר מיוחס הוא: אף בראשונה. גבי תביעת כתובה: [אוקי] ממונא אחזקת הבעל ה"נ גבי מנה לי בידך איכא למימר נמי אוקי ממונא בחזקת מריה ופטור: אלא דאיכא מגו. כגון משארסתני נאנסתי וכגון היא אומרת מוכת עץ אני דאמרינן מגו דאי בעיא טענה טענה מעלייתא מהך כגון גבי משארסתני נאנסתי הוה טענה מוכת עץ אני [טענה מעלייתא] דלא פסלה נפשה מכהונה וקאמרה [משארסתני] נאנסתי וקא מיפסלה נפשה דאשת ישראל שנאנסה אסורה לכהן ש"מ קושטא קאמרה וגבי היא אומרת מוכת עץ אני בעיא אני מוכת עץ אני תחתיך ואית לה מאתן וקא אמרה מוכת עץ אני קודם לכן ואין לי אלא מנה: אבל הכא. גבי האי תובע מאי מגו איכא להחזקיה הלכך אוקי ממונא בחזקת מריה: אוקמה אחזקה. אי מספקא לן אשעת ארוסין אי בתולה הואי ונשתעבד לה למאתים אי בעולה הואי העמד אשה על חזקתה ובתולה נולדה והך השתא הוא דאיתניסא אחר ארוסין: מאי חזקה אית ליה להאי. תובע דנוקמיה אחזקיה לגבות הלכך זיל בתר חזקה דממונא:

תוספות

כיון דחזו דמזלזלי בהו. פירש בקונטרס שהיו קלות בעיניהן להוציאן לפי שהיתה כתובתן מועטת וקשה דמעיקרא נמי הוו ידעי שקלות בעיניהן להוציאן כיון דמנה חשיב דבר מועט ונראה לר"י לפרש דמזלזלי בהו שמקלת בני אדם היו נמנעים מלנושאם לפי שהיו קלות בעיניהן שאין לה כתובה אלא רביע ממה שיש לה לבתולה ותקינו לה מאתן כיון דחזו דפרשי מינייהו לגמרי והיו קופצים קודם על בתולות ישראל ולא היה שום אדם קופץ עליהם אהדרינהו למילתייהו היינו דנקט מעיקרא מזלזלי שהיו נמנעים ולא לגמרי פורשים ובתר הכי נקט ופרשי: בית דין של כהנים היו גובין כו' ולא מיחו בידם חכמים. אע"פ שלא כתב בלשון תוספת אלא ארבע מאות דחזו ליכי וקא ס"ד דלא תגבה דלא חזו ובלשון תוספת לא כתב קא משמע לן דמנהג טוב מאד הוא וראוי להיות בכהונה ובמשפחות המיוחסות ושייך בהו למימר דחזו ליכי ואפי' לא כתב לה כתובה גובה ארבע מאות בתנאי ב"ד כמו בבנות ישראל מאתים דתקנה גמורה היא: והוא אומר לא כי כו'. אע"ג דבסוף המניח (ב"ק דף לה: ושם) דייק מדקתני לא כי דמיירי בברי הכא דליכא למיטעי קתני לא כי אע"ג דאיירי בשמא: מנה לי בידך והלה אומר איני יודע. פי' איני יודע אם הלויתני מעולם אבל הלויתני ואיני יודע אם פרעתיך תנן בהדיא בהגוזל בתרא (שם קיח.) דחייב: רב הונא ורב יהודה אמרי חייב. לכאורה נראה דלית להו דרבי אבא דאמר מתוך שאינו יכול לישבע משלם דטעמיה דר' אבא משום דדריש (שבועות ד' מז.) שבועת ה' תהיה בין שניהם ולא בין שני היורשין כגון אמר מנה לאבא ביד אביך ואמר חמשין ידענא וחמשין לא ידענא ואבוה כה"ג מתוך שאין יכול לישבע משלם ואי מנה לי בידך והלה אומר איני יודע חייב אין כאן שבועה דאפי' הוא אומר אין יודע בכל חייב ותימה דבפרק יש נוחלין (ב"ב דף קלה. ושם) גבי האומר זה אחי משמע דאביי אית ליה מנה לי בידך והלה אומר איני יודע חייב ובפ' חזקת הבתים (שם לד. ושם) משמע דאית ליה לדר' אבא וי"ל דאפי' למ"ד חייב איכא למידרש שבועת ה' תהיה בין שניהם ולא בין היורשין דשניהם לא ידעי אלא שעד אחד מעיד שאחד חייב לחבירו מנה דאבוה מתוך שאינו יכול לישבע משלם תימה דרב יהודה גופיה אית ליה בריש הפרה (ב"ק מו. ושם) אפילו ניזק אומר ברי ומזיק אומר שמא המע"ה ואין לומר דרב יהודה כסומכוס דאמר ממון המוטל בספק חולקין ולא אזיל בתר חזקת ממון ולהכי כי איכא ברי ושמא נוטל הכל והתם דקאמר אמר רב יהודה אמר שמואל זו דברי סומכוס אבל חכמים אומרים זה כלל גדול בדין דרבנן קאמר וליה לא סבירא ליה דהתם (בב"ב דף לה:) משמע דסבר כרבנן גבי מוכר שור לחבירו ונמצא נגחן ועוד דתנן בפרק השואל (ב"מ צז: ושם) המשאיל אומר שאולה מתה והלה אומר איני יודע חייב וקאמר בגמרא לימא תיהוי תיובתא דרב נחמן ור' יוחנן ומאי קושיא הא ע"כ מתני' כסומכוס אפי' לרב יהודה דלרבנן מודה רב יהודה דפטור ורב נחמן ורבי יוחנן ע"כ כרבנן אתיא לסומכוס לכל הפחות חולקין אבל אי פליגי דרבנן ולסומכוס לעולם חולקין אפי' בברי ושמא פריך שפיר ממתני' דכרבנן אתיא לסומכוס חולקין וי"ל דהתם ברי גרוע ושמא טוב דלפי שהמזיק לא היה שם טוען זה ברי ושמא דמזיק טוב דלא הוה ליה למידע אבל מנה לי בידך הוה ליה ברי טוב והשמא גרוע דהוה ליה לידע אם חייב אם לאו אבל קשה דבעי למימר הכא הא דרב יהודה דשמואל היא דפסק כרבן גמליאל והתם ברי גרוע ושמא טוב שהבעל אינו יודע מתי נבעלה ואם כן תיקשי דשמואל אדשמואל דפ' הפרה (ב"ק מו. ושם) ויש לומר דה"מ למימר ולטעמיך ועוד יש לומר דסוגיא דהכא סברה דזה כלל גדול לא קאי אניזק אומר ברי ומזיק אומר שמא ולא כדקאמר התם אי נמי לכי הא וקשה על זה דאפילו לפי אי נמי דהתם לא אתי שפיר הכא בסוף המניח (שם דף לה: ושם) אית להו לרבנן בהדיא דאפי' ניזק אומר ברי כו' ושמואל סובר כרבנן כדמוכח בהמוכר שור לחבירו: אלא דאיכא מגו. הא שנויא לא אתיא אלא לרב נחמן דלר' יוחנן בהדיא דמוכח עד דליכא מגו דמוכח לקמן הקשה ה"ר יעקב מקורביל דאכתי ע"כ הא דרב יהודה דשמואל היא דאי לאו הכי ממתניתין דהשואל (ב"מ צז: ושם) המשאיל אומר שאולה מתה והלה אומר איני יודע חייב תקשי ליה לשמואל [illegible] ליכא לשנויי כדמשני לרב נחמן ולרבי יוחנן כגון שיש עסק שבועה ביניהן ומתוך שאינו יכול לישבע משלם דלית ליה (שבועות ד' מז. ושם) דחזרה שבועה לסיני ולא משלם וי"ל דאיכא למימר לעולם מנה לי בידך והלה אומר איני יודע לשמואל פטור ומוקי שמואל מתני' דהשואל כשיש עסק שבועה וכההוא תנא דאית ליה מתוך שאינו יכול לישבע משלם והוא סבר כאידך תנא דפלוגתא דתנאי היא בפרק כל הנשבעין (שם). [ועי' ביתר ביאור תוס' ב"מ לז: סד"ה רב הונא]:

רב

תוספות רי"ד

ב"ד של כהנים וכו'. אמר רב יהודה לא ב"ד של כהנים בלבד אמרו אלא אפילו משפחות המיוחסות שבישראל אם רצו לעשות כדרך שהכהנים עושין ולא אמרי' דמחזי כעוקרים תקון חכמים: מתני' הנושא את האשה ולא מצא לה בתולים היא אומרת משארסתני נאנסתי ונסתחפה ש"ך והוא אומר לא כי אלא עד שלא ארסתיך והיה מקחי מקח טעות ר"ג ור"א אומרי' נאמנת ור"י אומר לא מפיה אנו חיין אלא הרי היא בחזקת בעולה עד שלא תתארס והטעתו עד שתביא ראיה לדבריה. היא אומרת וכו' מכאן מוכח שיש כתובה לארוסה ומשעת שאירסה נתחייב בכתובתה בתנאי ב"ד ומ"ה קאמרה ליה הכי דמקודם שנבעלה הוה משועבד לה ועכשיו שנאנסה לא הפסידה שעבודה דאי אמרת אין כתובה לארוסה עד שיכנסה וזאת כבר נבעלה קודם הנשואין אדרבה אומר הבעל לאשה נסתחפה ש"ך שהפסדת בתוליך ובעת הנשואין בעולה היית א"ו טעמא הוא משום דיש כתובה לארוסה ומשום אירוסין נתחייב לה: והוא אומר לא כי וכו'. פי' ואין לך כלום דהכי אוקמיה רבא לעיל מקח טעות לגמרי משמע דכסה בחזקת בתולה ונמצאת בעולה א"ל כלום: ר"ג ור"א אומרים נאמנת. פי' ואפילו לבעלה מותרת אם היה ישראל א) דמאי דאמרן לעיל שהבעל נאמן לאוסרה עליו דוקא בברי וברי דהוא אומר פתח פתוח מצאתי והיא אומרת לא כי אלא פתח סתום היה ומכחשה ליה התם בעל נאמן לאוסרה עליו דשוייה אנפשיה חתיכה דאיסורא אבל הכא דאיהי טענה ברי ובעל שמא מותרת היא לו שהיא נאמנת בכל הן ליטול כתובתה והן להיות מותרת לו: ור"י אומר וכו'. פי' בהא פליגי דר"ג סבר אוקי איתתא אחזקתה ובחזקת בתולה הות קיימא ומספיקא לא מפקינן לה מחזקתה ור"י סבר אוקי ממוניה בחזקת מריה ומן ספיקא לא מפקינן ממונא עד שתביא ראיה לדבריה מר אזיל בתר חזקה דגופא. ומר אזיל בתר חזקה דממונא. ואמרי' לקמן דהיכא אזיל ר"ג בתר חזקה דגופא דוקא בברי ושמא דאיהי טענה ברי והבעל שמא התם אזיל ר"ג בתר חזקה דגופא ומפקינן ממונא מחזקת מריה אבל בשמא ושמא מודה ר"ג דלא אזלי' בתר חזקה דגופא אלא בתר חזקה דממונא והמע"ה: א"י א"ש הלכה כר"ג ואי קשיא היכי פסיק שמואל הלכה כר"ג דאזיל בתר חזקה דגופא ומפיק ממונא מחזקת מרי' התנן בב"ק שור שנגח את הפרה ונמצא עוברה בצידה ואין ידוע אם עד שלא ילדה נגחה ואם משילדה נגחה משלם חצי נזק לפרה ורביע נזק לולד ואמרי' עלה בגמרא אר"י א"ש זו דברי סומכוס דאמר ממון המוטל בספק חולקין אבל חכמים אומרים זה כלל גדול בדין המע"ה למה לי' למימר זה כלל גדול בדין ואפילו ניזק אומר ברי ומזיק אומר שמא והא במתני' איכא חזקה דגופא ואיכא חזקה דממונא דאוקי פרה אחזקתה ואימור מעוברת היתה בשעת נגיחה ומחמת נגיחת השור הפילה וחייב ליתן לו חצי נזק ולמזיק איכא חזקה דממונא וכיון דאית לנזק חזקה דגופא פליג ר"ג דאזיל בתר חזקה דגופא ומפיק ממונא מחזקת מריה ובשלמא אמתני' לא פליג ר"ג משום דהו"ל שמא ושמא דהכי אמרי' לקמן דבשמא ושמא לא אזיל ר"ג בתר חזקה דגופא אלא במאי דאמרי' ואפילו ניזק אומר ברי ומזיק אומר שמא אמרי' המע"ה והא בהא מילתא פליג ר"ג דהיכא דתובע אומר ברי ונתבע אומר שמא אזלי' בתר חזקה דגופא ומפקינן ממונא מחזקת מריה והיכי אר"י משמיה דשמואל דחכמים פליגי על סומכוס ואמרי המע"ה ולמימרא דהלכה כחכמים דהא כחכמים איפסקא הלכתא וא"כ קשה דשמואל אדשמואל וי"ל דלא ק' דהיכי אזיל ר"ג בתר חזקה דגופא ואפיק ממונא מחזקת מריה ה"מ גבי אשה ובעל שכבר הבעל מחויב ועומד בכתובת האשה ושטר כתובה עליו והוא בא מספק לפטור א"ע ממה שהוא מחויב ועומד בו התם ודאי אר"ג אוקי אתתי' אחזקתה ואפיק ממונא מיני' דבעל כי היכי דהוה משועבד לה מעיקרא ור"י אפ"ה פליג עלי' ולא מפיק ממונא מחזקת מריה אבל הכא שהמזיק לא נתחייב ממון לניזק מקודם לכן (ואפילו) [ולא] בא לפטור עצמו [שנאמר] שנעמיד הניזק בחזקת הגוף הוציא ממון ממנו אלא זה החיוב עכשיו יבוא עליו מספק וכיון שעכשיו רוצה לחול עליו מודה ר"ג דמספיקא לא מחייבינן לי' ואע"ג שיש לתובע חזקה דגופא אלא אמרי' המע"ה ולא ק' דשמואל אדשמואל: איתמר מנה לי בידך והלה אמר א"י ר"ה ור"י אמרי חייב ר"נ ור"י אמרי פטור מלשלם ר"ה ור"י אמרי חייב ברי ושמא ברי עדיף ר"נ ור"י אמרי פטור אוקי ממונא בחזקת מרי' פי' ומ"מ משבעי' לי' שבועת היסת שכן הוא כדבריו שא"י שחייב לו ונפטר: לימא ר"ה ור"י דאמרי כר"ג ור"נ ור"י דאמרי

גליון הש"ס

גמ' הא דרב הונא ור"י דשמואל היא. עיין יבמות יח ע"ב תד"ה דאי דרב:

ליקוטי רש"י

הנושא את האשה. בחזקת בתולה [לעיל יא:]. משארסתני. אירע לי ונסתחפה שדהו ואית לי מאתים [לקמן טז.]. נסתחפה שדהו. לשון מטר סוחף (משלי כח) נשטפה שדך כלומר מזלך גרם [לעיל ב.]. נסחף, נשטפו והליכו גבוריך כמו מטר סוחף (משלי כח) נסתחפה שדהו בלשון משנה ומנחם חברו לשון כליון וכן חבר מטר סוחף ודונש פתר מטר סוחף כמו מטר סועף כמו מסעף פארה במערצה (ישעיה י) [ירמיה מו, טו]. סוחף, שוטף ובמשנה נסתחפה שדהו וכן נסחף אביריך (ירמיה מו) נשטפו ומעדו וכשלו [משלי כח, ג]. לא מפיה אנו חיין. שתהא נאמנת אלא העמד ממון על חזקתו ולא אזלינן בתר חזקה דגופא לומר הואיל וספק בידינו על שעת אירוסין מה היא העמד הגוף על חזקתו של קודם לכן והרי נולדה בתולה [לקמן עה:]. רב יהודה ורב הונא אמרי חייב. לשלם. פטור. ומיהו ישבע כדלאמר שאין יודע שחייב לו כלום דלא עדיף שמא מברי דהא א"נ הוה טעין ליה אין לך בידי כלום הוי משביעין ליה שבועת היסת [ב"ק קיח.]. וקיימא לן דפטור דהלכתא כרבי יוחנן מחבירו וכרב נחמן בדיני אלא שישבע שבועת היסת שאינו יודע [רשב"ם ב"ב קלה.]. בחזקת מריה. ולא תפקיע מספיקא [ב"מ צז:].

חשק שלמה
על תוס' רי"ד

א) נ"ל דאפי' אם קיבל בה קדושין פתוח מב' שנים ולכן ל"ש דא"כ היאך טוען שמא אם לא ארסתיך.

כֵּיוָן דְּחָזוּ דְּמִזַּלְזְלֵי בְּהוּ – However, **when [the Kohanim] saw that [people] were treating [widows]** of their family **lightly,** תַּקִּינוּ לְהוּ מָאתָן – **they enacted** a **two hundred-***zuz kesubah* **for [widows].**[1] It is that enactment to which the Baraisa refers. כֵּיוָן דְּחָזוּ דְּקָא פָּרְשִׁין מִינַּיְיהוּ – Then, **when [the Kohanim] saw that [people] were refraining from** marrying **[the widows],** – דְּאָמְרֵי עַד דְּנַסְבִינַן אַלְמְנַת כֹּהֲנִים נֵיזִיל נִיסִיב בְּתוּלָה בַּת יִשְׂרָאֵל – **because they would say, "instead of marrying a widow who is** the daughter of **Kohanim, let us go marry a virgin who is the daughter of a non-Kohen!",**[2] אַהַדְרִינְהוּ לְמִלְּתַיְיהוּ – **they returned them** (the widows who were daughters of Kohanim) **to their** initial **status** of receiving a *kesubah* of one hundred *zuz,* like any other widow.[3]

The Mishnah stated:

בֵּית דִּין שֶׁל כֹּהֲנִים כו׳ – THE COURT OF KOHANIM etc. would collect four hundred *zuz* for a virgin who was the daughter of a Kohen.

The Gemara elaborates:

אָמַר רַב יְהוּדָה אָמַר שְׁמוּאֵל – **Rav Yehudah said in the name of Shmuel:** לֹא בֵּית דִּין שֶׁל כֹּהֲנִים בִּלְבַד אָמְרוּ – **They did not say** this **only** concerning **the court of the Kohanim.** אֶלָּא אֲפִילּוּ מִשְׁפָּחוֹת הַמְיוּחָסוֹת בְּיִשְׂרָאֵל – **Rather, even** any **eminent family in Israel,** אִם רָצוּ לַעֲשׂוֹת כְּדֶרֶךְ שֶׁהַכֹּהֲנִים עוֹשִׂין – **if they want to act the way the Kohanim act,** עוֹשִׂין – **they may do so** and institute a *kesubah* of four hundred *zuz* for their daughters.[4]

The Gemara objects:

מֵיתִיבֵי – **They challenged** this **from a Baraisa:** הָרוֹצָה לַעֲשׂוֹת כְּדֶרֶךְ שֶׁהַכֹּהֲנִים עוֹשִׂין – If [AN EMINENT FAMILY] WISHES TO ACT THE WAY THE KOHANIM ACT and institute a *kesubah* of four hundred *zuz,* כְּגוֹן בַּת יִשְׂרָאֵל לְכֹהֵן וּבַת כֹּהֵן לְיִשְׂרָאֵל – FOR EXAMPLE, in the cases of A DAUGHTER OF A NON-KOHEN who is to be married TO A KOHEN, OR A DAUGHTER OF A KOHEN who is to be married TO A NON-KOHEN, עוֹשִׂין – THEY MAY DO SO. בַּת יִשְׂרָאֵל לְכֹהֵן וּבַת כֹּהֵן לְיִשְׂרָאֵל – Now this Baraisa implies that only in the cases of **a daughter of a non-Kohen married to a Kohen, or a daughter of a Kohen** married **to a non-Kohen,** הוּא – **it is** that the *kesubah* can be increased, דְּאִיכָּא צַד כְּהוּנָּה – **for there is** at least one **Kehunah side** in the marriage. אֲבָל בַּת יִשְׂרָאֵל לְיִשְׂרָאֵל לֹא – **But** in the case of **a daughter of a non-Kohen** married **to a non-Kohen,** where no Kohanim are involved in the match at all, her standard *kesubah* is **not** increased.[5] – ? –

The Gemara answers:

לֹא מִבַּעְיָא קָאָמַר – **[The Mishnah] adopted a style of "it need not be said . . .,"** as follows: לֹא מִבַּעְיָא בַּת יִשְׂרָאֵל לְיִשְׂרָאֵל – **It need not be said** that in the case of **the daughter of a non-Kohen** married **to a non-Kohen** an increased *kesubah* can be instituted, דְּלֹא מָצֵי אָמַר לָהּ עַלּוּיֵי קָא מְעַלֵּינַן לִיךְ – **because [the husband] cannot say to her** in return, **"I elevated you** to a higher status," and therefore there is no reason to think that a higher *kesubah* cannot be instituted if the bride is from an eminent family. אֲבָל בַּת יִשְׂרָאֵל לְכֹהֵן – **But** in the case of **the daughter of a non-Kohen** married **to a Kohen** דְּמָצֵי אָמַר לָהּ עַלּוּיֵי קָא מְעַלֵּינַן לִיךְ – **where [the husband] can say to her, "I elevated you** to a higher status,"[6] אֵימָא לֹא – **I would say** that her family is **not** able to institute an increased *kesubah.* קָא מַשְׁמַע לָן – **[The Baraisa]** therefore **informs us** that even in that case, an increased *kesubah* can be instituted.[7]

Mishnah This Mishnah introduces the role that the bride's claim plays in disputes concerning her virginity:[8]

הַנּוֹשֵׂא אֶת הָאִשָּׁה וְלֹא מָצָא לָהּ בְּתוּלִים – Consider the case of **one who marries a woman and does not find her to possess** signs of **virginity.** הִיא אוֹמֶרֶת מִשֶּׁאֵרַסְתַּנִי נֶאֱנַסְתִּי וְנִסְתַּחֲפָה שָׂדֵהוּ – **She says, "After you betrothed me I was violated, and** this is a case of **'[the buyer's] field was inundated,' "**[9] וְהוּא אוֹמֵר לֹא כִּי אֶלָּא עַד שֶׁלֹּא אֵרַסְתִּיךְ וְהָיָה מִקָּחִי מִקַּח טָעוּת – **while he says, "Not so, rather** it happened **before I betrothed you, and my acquisition was an acquisition made in error."**[10] רַבָּן גַּמְלִיאֵל וְרַבִּי אֱלִיעֶזֶר אוֹמְרִים – **Rabban Gamliel and R' Eliezer say:**

NOTES

1. That is, the second husbands who married these widows did not find the one hundred *zuz* a significant enough deterrent to divorce. The court of the Kohanim therefore raised the *kesubah* of a widow in their tribe to two hundred *zuz.* Now, it is true that the *kesubah* of a widow from a non-Kohen family remained at one hundred *zuz,* but the Kohanim, who were prominent people, found it more degrading for their daughters to be divorced than non-Kohanim did [and therefore the courts increased the *kesubah* amount for widows who were from families of Kohanim] *(Rashi;* cf. *Tosafos).*

2. The elevated status associated with marrying a Kohen's daughter did not compensate for the fact that she was not a virgin. Since their *kesubah* obligations were the same, people began to prefer virgin daughters of a non-Kohen over nonvirgin daughters of a Kohen.

3. This was not a new enactment; rather, they just returned the amount of such a widow's *kesubah* back to the original *maneh* *(Rashba).*

4. Here too, this means that the standard *kesubah* amount for these women became four hundred *zuz* *(Tosafos;* see above, 12a note 20).

5. That is, any increase has to be classified as an addition to the basic *kesubah* obligation (see above).

6. [The wife of a Kohen is treated like a Kohen in certain respects (e.g. she is able to eat *terumah,* which is forbidden to other non-Kohanim). Thus, her Kohen husband, by marrying her, has raised her status.]

7. The Gemara explains only why the Baraisa stated a case of the daughter of a non-Kohen who married a Kohen; it does not explain why the Baraisa stated the second case of a Kohen's daughter marrying a non-Kohen. See *Rashba* and *Ritva* for various answers to this question.

8. Thus far the Mishnah has discussed cases in which the groom claims not to have found in his bride signs of virginity, without going into the bride's response to this claim. [As explained by the Rishonim, the Mishnah referred to where the bride disputed the groom's claim and asserted that she *had* been a virgin on the wedding night (see below, note 21 and note 1 to 13a).] The coming two Mishnahs consider situations in which the bride admits to the truth of the groom's claim that signs of virginity were absent, but provides an explanation, which, if true, would permit her to still collect her *kesubah.*

9. [The standard Mishnayos texts read here: וְנִסְתַּחֲפָה שָׂדְךָ, *and your field was inundated* (see *Rashash* and *Chidushim U'Veurim* 8:10).]

She admits to his claim that she was not a virgin when they cohabited for the first time, but claims that this was the result of her having been violated after the betrothal. Since she was already his wife at the time of the incident, it is he, she argues, who must bear the loss. It is as if he had purchased a field and afterwards torrential rains had flooded it, in which case he, rather than the seller, would have to suffer the loss. Accordingly, she demands her full *kesubah* of two hundred *zuz.*

10. He does not state this as a definite accusation, for how could he know for sure when she lost her virginity? However, he argues that *perhaps* it occurred before the *erusin* (whether through being violated, as she claims, or through voluntary cohabitation), and he was misled by not being told of her condition (see *Rashi* to 16a ד״ה בברי ושמא). Thus, he wishes to be freed of having to pay her any *kesubah.*

[This follows the Gemara's conclusion on 11b, which the halachah follows, that a woman married on the presumption of being a virgin but found to be a nonvirgin receives no *kesubah* at all. Rav Chiya bar Avin (cited there) and R' Yochanan (cited below on 13a), however, maintain that such a woman receives a *kesubah* of a *maneh.* According to them, the meaning of the husband's claim is that he should be obligated to give her only a *maneh.*]

עין משפט
נר מצוה

עו א טוש"ע אה"ע סי' סו סעיף ז:
עז ב מיי' פ"א מהל' אישות הל' יא סמג עשין מח טוש"ע שם סי' סח סעיף ט:
עח ג מיי' פ"א מהל' טוען ונטען הל' ח סמג עשין צה טוש"ע ח"מ סימן עה סעיף ט:

מסורת הש"ס

א) [לעיל יא: לקמן עח.] ב) [לקמן לו.] ג) לקמן עה. ד) ב"ק קיח. בבא מציעא לז: [ע"ש] ה) ב"ב קלה. ו) [קדושין עה: וש"נ] ז) [עיין תוס' יבמות יח: ד"ה דלי דרך מאי] ח) [לקמן יג.] ט) [לקמן יד.] [ברכות לו. וש"נ ועי' תוס' חגיגה טו: פירוש על שיננא] י) [ג"י כ"י] כ) [שייך לע"א]

כיון דחזו דמזלזלי בהו תקינו להו מאתן כיון דחזו דקא פרשין מינייהו דאמרי עד דנסבינן אלמנת כהנים ניזיל ניסיב בתולה בת ישראל אהדרינהו למלתייהו: בית דין של כהנים כו': אמר רב יהודה אמר שמואל א לא ב"ד של כהנים בלבד אמרו אלא אפי' משפחות המיוחסות בישראל אם רצו לעשות כדרך שהכהנים עושין עושין מיתיבי הרוצה לעשות כדרך שהכהנים עושין כגון בת ישראל לכהן ובת כהן לישראל ובת כהן לכהן ובת כהן לישראל עושין בת ישראל לכהן לישראל הוא דאיכא צד כהונה אבל בת ישראל לישראל לא מבעיא קאמר לא מבעיא בת ישראל לישראל דלא מצי אמר לה עלויי קא מעלינן ליך אבל בת ישראל לכהן דמצי אמר לה עלויי קא מעלינן ליך אימא לא קמ"ל: מתני' ב הנושא את האשה ולא מצא לה בתולים היא אומרת משארסתני נאנסתי ונסתחפה שדהו והוא אומר לא כי אלא עד שלא ארסתיך והיה מקחי מקח טעות ג רבן גמליאל ורבי אליעזר אומרים נאמנת ד רבי יהושע אומר לא מפיה אנו חיין אלא הרי זו בחזקת בעולה עד שלא תתארס והטעתו עד שתביא ראיה לדבריה: גמ' ה אתמר מנה לי בידך והלה אומר איני יודע רב יהודה ורב הונא אמרי חייב ורב נחמן ורבי יוחנן אמרי פטור רב הונא ורב יהודה אמרי חייב ברי ושמא ברי עדיף רב נחמן ורבי יוחנן אמרי פטור אוקי ממונא בחזקת מריה א"ל אביי לרב יוסף הא דרב הונא ורב יהודה דשמואל היא דתנן היתה מעוברת ואמרו לה מה טיבו של עובר זה מאיש פלוני וכהן הוא רבן גמליאל ורבי אליעזר אומרים נאמנת ואמר רב יהודה אמר שמואל הלכה כרבן גמליאל ואמר ליה רב שמואל בר יהודה לרב יהודה שיננא אמרת לן משמיה דשמואל הלכה כרבן גמליאל אף בראשונה מאי אף בראשונה אע"ג דאיכא למימר אוקי ממונא בחזקת מריה אמר רבן גמליאל ברי עדיף לימא רב יהודה ורב הונא דאמרי כר"ג ורב נחמן ורבי יוחנן דאמרי כרבי יהושע אמר לך רב נחמן אנא דאמרי אפילו כרבן גמליאל עד כאן לא קאמר ר"ג התם אלא דאיכא מגו אבל הכא מאי מגו איכא אי נמי עד כאן לא קאמר רבן גמליאל התם אלא דאמרינן אוקמה אחזקה אבל הכא מאי חזקה אית ליה להאי הכי נמי מסתברא כדקא משנינן דרב נחמן הוא דאמר כר"ג דאם

רש"י

דמזלזלי בהו. באלמנות קלות בעיניהם להוציאן מפני שכתובתן מועטת תקינו להו מאתן דגנאי היה להן ואע"פ שאלמנות ישראל נמי כתובתן מנה מיהו כהנים חשיבי טפי וגנאי להם גירושי בנותיהן יותר מישראל: מתני' נאמנת. קא סלקא דעתך משום דברי ושמא ברי עדיף: הרי זו בחזקת. שנבעלה עד שלא תתארס והטעתו: גמ' חייב. לשלם: פטור. מלשלם ומכל מקום משביעין ליה שבועת היסת שכן הוא כדבריו שאינו יודע שהוא חייב לו: וכהן הוא. כלומר מיוחס הוא: אף בראשונה. גבי תביעת כתובה: [אוקי כתובה אחזקתה אחזקת הבעל ה"נ גבי מנה לי בידך איכא למימר נמי אוקי ממונא בחזקת מריה ופטור: אלא דאיכא מגו]. כגון משארסתני נאנסתי וכגון היא אומרת מוכת עץ אני דאמרינן מגו דאי בעיא טענה טענה מעלייתא מהך כגון גבי משארסתני נאנסתי הוה טענה מוכת עץ אני [טענה מעלייתא] דלא פסלה נפשה מכהונה וקאמרה נאנסתי [משארסתני] וקא מיפסלה נפשה דאשת ישראל שנאנסה אסורה לכהן ש"מ קושטא קאמרה וגבי היא אומרת מוכת עץ אני אי בעיא אמרה מוכת עץ אני תחתיך ואית לה מאתן וקא אמרה מוכת עץ אני קודם לכן ואין לי אלא מנה: אבל הכא. גבי האי תובע מאי מגו איכא להמניה הלכך אוקי ממונא בחזקת מריה: אוקמה אחזקה. מספקא לן אשעת ארוסין אי בתולה הואי ונשתעבד לה למאתים אי בעולה הואי העמד אשה על חזקתה ובתולה נולדה והן השתא הוא דאיתניסה אחר אירוסין: מאי חזקה אית ליה להאי. תובע דנוקמיה אחזקיה לגבות הלכך זיל בתר חזקה דממונא:
דא"כ

תוספות

כיון דחזו דמזלזלי בהו. פירש בקונטרס שהיו קלות בעיניהן להוציאן לפי שהיתה כתובתן מועטת וקשה דמעיקרא נמי הוו ידעי שקלות בעיניהן להוציאן כיון דמנה חשיב דבר מועט ונראה לר"י לפרש דמזלזלי בהו שמקצת בני אדם היו נמנעים מלנושאם לפי שהיו קלות בעיניהן שאין לה כתובה אלא רביע ממה שיש לה לבתולה ותקינו לה מאתן כיון דחזו דפרשי מינייהו לגמרי והיו קופצים קודם על בתולות ישראל ולא היה שום אדם קופץ עליהם אהדרינהו למילתייהו היינו דנקט מעיקרא מזלזלי שהיו נמנעים ולא לגמרי פורשים ובתר הכי נקט ופרשי: בית דין של כהנים היו גובין כו' ולא מיחו בידם חכמים. אע"פ שלא כתב בלשון תוספת אלא ארבע מאות דחזו ליכי וקא ס"ד דלא תגבה דלא חזו ובלשון תוספת לא כתב קא משמע לן דמנהג טוב מאד הוא וראוי להיות בכהונה ובמשפחות המיוחסות ושייך בהו למימר דחזו ליכי ואפי' לא כתב לה כתובה גובה ארבע מאות בתנאי ב"ד כמו בבנות ישראל מאתים דתקנה גמורה היא: והוא אומר לא כי כו'. אע"ג דבסוף המניח (ב"ק דף לה: ושם) דייק מדקתני לא כי דמיירי בברי הכא דליכא למיטעי קתני לא כי אע"ג דאיירי בשמא: מנה לי בידך והלה אומר איני יודע. פי' איני יודע אם הלויתני מעולם אבל הלויתני ואיני יודע אם פרעתיך תנן בהדיא בהגוזל בתרא (שם קיח.) דחייב: רב הונא ורב יהודה אמרי חייב. לכאורה נראה דלית להו דרבי אבא דאמר מתוך שאינו יכול לישבע משלם דטעמיה דר' אבא משום דדריש (שבועות ד' מז.) שבועת ה' תהיה בין שניהם ולא בין שני היורשין כגון אמר מנה לאבא ביד אביך ואמר חמשין ידענא וחמשין לא ידענא ואבוה כה"ג מתוך שאין יכול לישבע משלם ואי מנה לי בידך והלה אומר איני יודע חייב אין כאן שבועה דאפי' הוא אומר אין יודע בכל חייב ותימה דבפרק יש נוחלין (ב"ב דף קלה. ושם) גבי האומר זה אחי משמע דאביי אית ליה מנה לי בידך והלה אומר איני יודע חייב ובפ' חזקת הבתים (שם לד. ושם) משמע דאית ליה לדר' אבא וי"ל דאפי' למ"ד חייב איכא למידרש שבועת ה' תהיה בין שניהם ולא בין היורשין דשניהם לא ידעי אלא שעד אחד מעיד שאחד חייב לחבירו מנה דאבוה מתוך שאינו יכול לישבע משלם תימה דרב יהודה גופיה אית ליה בריש הפרה (ב"ק מו. ושם) אפילו ניזק אומר ברי ומזיק אומר שמא המע"ה ואין לומר דרב יהודה כסומכוס דאמר ממון המוטל בספק חולקין ולא אזיל בתר חזקת ממון ולהכי כי איכא ברי ושמא נוטל הכל והתם דקאמר אמר רב יהודה אמר שמואל זו דברי סומכוס אבל חכמים אומרים זה כלל גדול בדין כו' אליבא דרבנן קאמר וליה לא סבירא ליה דהתם (בב"ב דף נג:) משמע דסבר כרבנן גבי מוכר שור לחבירו ונמצא נגחן ועוד דתנן בפרק השואל (ב"מ צז. ושם) המשאיל אומר שאולה מתה והלה אומר איני יודע חייב וקאמר בגמרא לימא תיהוי תיובתא דרב נחמן ור' יוחנן ומאי קושיא הא ע"כ מתני' כסומכוס אפי' לרב יהודה דלרבנן מודה רב יהודה דפטור ורב נחמן ורבי יוחנן ע"כ כרבנן דלסומכוס לכל הפחות חולקין אבל אי פליגי אליבא דרבנן ולסומכוס לעולם חולקין אפי' בברי ושמא פריך שפיר ממתני' דכרבנן אתיא דלסומכוס חולקין וי"ל דהתם ברי גרוע ושמא טוב דלפי שהמזיק לא היה שם טוען זה ברי ושמא דמזיק טוב דלא הוה ליה למידע אבל מנה לי בידך הברי טוב והשמא גרוע דהוה ליה לידע אם חייב אם לאו אבל קשה דבעי למימר הכא הא דרב יהודה דשמואל היא דפסק כרבן גמליאל והתם ברי גרוע ושמא טוב שהבעל אינו יודע מתי נבעלה ואם כן תיקשי דשמואל אדשמואל דפ' הפרה (ב"ק מו. ושם) ויש לומר דה"מ למימר וליטעמיך ועוד יש לומר דסוגיא דהכא סברה דזה כלל גדול בדין לא לניזק אומר ברי ומזיק אומר שמא אלא כדקאמר התם אי נמי לכי הא וקשה על זה דאפילו לפי אי נמי דהתם לא אתי שפיר דהא בסוף המניח (שם דף לה: ושם) אית להו לרבנן בהדיא דאפי' ניזק אומר ברי כו' ושמואל סובר כרבנן כדמוכח בהמוכר שור לחבירו: אלא דאיכא מגו. הא שניא לא אתיא אלא לרב נחמן דלר' יוחנן בההיא דמוכת עץ ליכא מגו כדמוכח לקמן הקשה ה"ר יעקב מקורביי"ל אכתי ע"כ הא דרב יהודה דשמואל היא דאי לשמואל פטור תקשי ליה ממתניתין דהשואל (ב"מ ד' צז. ושם:) המשאיל אומר שאולה מתה והלה אומר איני יודע חייב דלשמואל ליכא לשנויי כדמשני לרב נחמן ולרבי יוחנן כגון שיש עסק שבועה ביניהן ומתוך שאינו יכול לישבע משלם דשמואל לית ליה בהדיא בפ' כל הנשבעין (שבועות ד' מז. ושם) דחזרה שבועה לסיני ולא משלם וי"ל דאיכא למימר דלעולם מנה לי בידך והלה אומר איני יודע לשמואל פטור ומוקי שמואל מתני' דהשואל כשיש עסק שבועה וכההוא תנא דלית ליה מתוך שאינו יכול לישבע משלם והוא סבר כאידך תנא דפלוגתא דתנאי היא בפרק כל הנשבעין (שם). [ועי' ביתר ביאור תוס' ב"מ צז: סד"ה רב הונא]:
רב

גליון הש"ס

גמ' הא דרב הונא ור"י דשמואל היא. עיין יבמות יח ע"ב תד"ה דלי דרך:

ליקוטי רש"י

הנושא את האשה. בחזקת בתולה [לעיל יא.]. היא אומרת משארסתני. אירע לי ונסתחפה שדהו ולית לי מאתים [לקמן טז.]. נסתחפה שדהו. לשון מטר סוחף (משלי כח) נשטפה שדך כלומר מזלך גרם [לעיל ב.].

תוספות רי"ד

ב"ד של כהנים וכו'. אמר רב יהודה לא ב"ד של כהנים בלבד אמרו אלא אפי' משפחות המיוחסות שבישראל אם רצו לעשות כדרך שהכהנים עושין עושין ולא אמרי' דמחזי כעוקרים תקון חכמים: מתני' הנושא את האשה ולא מצא לה בתולים היא אומרת משארסתני נאנסתי ונסתחפה שדך והוא אומר לא כי אלא עד שלא ארסתיך והי' מקחי מקח טעות ר"ג ור"א אומרי' נאמנת ור"י אומר לא מפיה אנו חיין אלא הרי היא בחזקת בעולה עד שלא תתארס והטעתו עד שתביא ראיה לדבריה.

חשק שלמה על תוס' רי"ד

א) ר"ל אפי' אם קיבל בה קדושין מפחות מג' שנים ולכן ל"ש הכא לא כ"כ דיכול טוען שמא עד שלא ארסתיך:

אמר רבה זאת אומרת כנסה בחזקת בתולה ונמצאת בעולה יש לה כתובה מנה רב אשי אמר בעלמא אימא לך לעולם לית לה כלל ושאני הכא שהרי כנסה ראשון וניחוש שמא תחתיו זינתה אמר רב שרביא כגון שקידש ובעל לאלתר ואיכא דמתני לה אמתניתין בתולה אלמנה גרושה חלוצה מן הנישואין כתובתן מנה ואין להן טענת בתולין בתולה מן הנישואין היכי משכחת לה כגון שנכנסה לחופה ולא נבעלה אמר רבה זאת אומרת כנסה בחזקת בתולה ונמצאת בעולה כתובתה מנה רב אשי אמר לעולם אימא לך בעלמא לית לה כלל ושאני הכא שהרי נכנסה לחופה וליחוש שמא תחתיו זינתה אמר רב שרביא כגון שקידש ובעל לאלתר מאן דמתני לה אברייתא כל שכן אמתניתין ומאן דמתני לה אמתני' אבל אברייתא לא משום דמצי אמר לה אנא אעדים סמכי: מתני' האוכל אצל חמיו ביהודה שלא בעדים אינו יכול לטעון טענת בתולים מפני שמתייחד עמה: גמ' מדקתני האוכל מכלל דאיכא דוכתא ביהודה נמי דלא אכיל אמר אביי ש"מ ביהודה נמי מקומות מקומות יש כדתניא א"ר יהודה ביהודה בראשונה היו מייחדין את החתן ואת הכלה שעה אחת קודם כניסתן לחופה כדי שיהא לבו גס בה ובגליל לא היו עושין כן ביהודה בראשונה היו מעמידין להם שני שושבינין אחד לו ואחד לה כדי למשמש את החתן ואת הכלה בשעת כניסתן לחופה ובגליל לא היו עושין כן ביהודה בראשונה היו שושבינין ישנים בבית שחתן וכלה ישנים בה ובגליל לא היו עושין כן וכל שלא נהג כמנהג הזה אינו יכול לטעון טענת בתולים אהייא אילימא ארישא כל שנהג מיבעי ליה אלא אסיפא כל שלא מושמש מיבעי ליה אמר אביי לעולם ארישא ותני כל שנהג אמר ליה רבא והא כל שלא נהג קתני אלא אמר רבא הכי קאמר כל שלא נהג מנהג גליל בגליל אלא מנהג יהודה בגליל אינו יכול לטעון טענת בתולים רב אשי אמר לעולם אסיפא ותני כל שלא מושמש: מתני' אחת אלמנת ישראל ואחת אלמנת כהנים כתובתה מנה בית דין של כהנים היו גובין לבתולה ארבע מאות זוז ולא מיחו בידם חכמים: גמ' תנא ואלמנת כהנים כתובתה מאתים והאנן תנן אחת אלמנת ישראל ואחת אלמנת כהנים כתובתן מנה אמר רב אשי שתי תקנות הוו מעיקרא תקינו לבתולה ארבע מאות זוז ולאלמנה מנה כיון

זאת אומרת כו'. דהא ודאי בחזקת בתולה כנסה דסמך אעדים וקאמר אין יכול להפסידה מנה הראוי לאלמנה מן הנישואין: וניחוש שמא תחתיו זינתה. ואמתניתין פריך דקתני אין השני יכול לטעון טענת בתולים ולא מזקיקנן ליה לבא לבית דין ולא יתברר הדבר אם תחתיו זינתה אם לא ושמא אסורה היא לו בשלמא אהנך דלעיל דאמרן כנסה בחזקת בתולה ונמצאת בעולה יש לה כתובה לא מקשינן דאיכא למימר כשבא לבית דין ובאו עדים שזינתה קודם לכן אבל הכא קתני אין יכול לטעון מתוך כך לא יבא לב"ד: כשקידש ובעל לאלתר גרסינן ולא גרסינן כשקידש לאלתר ובעל לאלתר. שלא פירש ממנה בין קידושין לבעילה דודאי לא תחתיו זינתה: ואיכא דמתני לה. להא דרבה ורב אשי ורב שרביא אמתני': זאת אומרת. מדקתני מתני' אין להן טענת בתולים: וליחוש שמא תחתיו זינתה. ולמאי תני אין להן טענת בתולים: מאן דמתני לה. להא דרבה ורב אשי אברייתא. כ"ש אמתני'. דכיון דאברייתא אע"ג דאמרו עדים לא נסתרה לראשון ושני זה בחזקת בתולה כנסה ואפילו הכי אהדר ליה רב אשי לרבה לעולם לא תשמע כנסה בחזקת בתולה ונמצאת בעולה יש לה כתובה דשאני הכא שהרי כנסה ראשון כל שכן אמתניתין דלא הבטיחוהו עדים על כך איכא למתנייה לדרבה ומאי לאהדר ליה רב אשי: ומאן דתני לה. לדרבה ורב אשי אמתניתין: אבל אברייתא לא. מתני להו דמברייתא ודאי ספיר ש"מ זאת אומרת דרבה ועלה לא הוה לרב אשי לאהדורי שאני הכא שהרי כנסה ראשון דמצי אמר אנא אעדים סמכי וכיון דקתני אין השני יכול לטעון טענת בתולים שמעינן ודאי דזאת אומרת כנסה בחזקת בתולה ונמצאת בעולה יש לה כתובה: מקומות מקומות יש. שחלוקין במנהגם ונפקא מינה דהיכא דלא נהיגי לייחד יכול לטעון: כדתניא. דמקומות מקומות יש: למשמש. לפשפש ולמשמש במעשיהן באותו הלילה שלא יקלקלו זה את זה במעשיהם בתרמית שלא יראה זה דם בתולים ויאבד וזו לא תביא מפה שיש עליה טיפי דמים ובמקום שנהגו למשמש לא נהגו לייחד דאילו במקום שנהגו לייחד מאי מישמוש בעי הרי אין שם טענת בתולים אלמא ביהודה מקומות מקומות יש: אילימא ארישא. אמנהג דמייחדין: כל שנהג להתייחד מיבעי ליה. דאין יכול לטעון: אלא אסיפא. אמנהג דמשמוש שושבינין: כל שלא מושמש מיבעי ליה. דהטוען טענת בתולים הוא הבעל והוא אינו נוהג מישמוש שבו [שאינו תלוי בבעל] אלא על אבי הכלה למשמשו שלא יאבד את בתוליה ומשמוש בכלה שלא תביא דם מן החוץ תלוי בבעל והיכי תני כל בעל שלא נהג מישמוש אינו יכול לטעון טענת בתולים כ"ש דאם לא נהג למשמש והם מישמשו אותו דיכול לטעון הכי איבעי ליה למתני כל שלא מושמש אינו יכול לטעון דשמא ראה ואבד: אלא אמר רבא. האי כל שלא נהג אמנהג דגליל קאי דתנא בברייתא ובגליל לא היו עושין כן ועלה קאי כל שלא נהג כמנהג הזה בגליל אלא נתייחד כמנהג שביהודה אינו יכול לטעון: מתני' אלמנת כהנים. אלמנה בת כהן: היו גובין לבתולה. בת כהן וכ"ש כשניסאת לכהן וכ"ש כשניסאת לישראל: גמ' שתי תקנות הוו. לאלמנה בת כהן: דמזלזלי

אמר רבה זאת אומרת. נראה דהכא גרסינן רבה דהא רבה קאמר לעיל דמקח טעות לגמרי משמע ולא גרסינן הכא רבא א"כ תיקשי מתניתין רישא לסיפא דהא זאת אומרת איכא למידק נמי ממתניתין דלאמרינן בסמוך אלא ודאי נראה דהכא גרס רבה דרבא דאמר לעיל מקח טעות גמורי משמע יפרק כמו רב אשי: כנסה בחזקת בתולה ונמצאת בעולה יש לה מנה. והא דקתני שהרי כנסה ראשון פירש ריב"ם דהכי משמע ליה אין לשני טענת בתולין לחסרה מכתובתה כלום שהרי כנסה ראשון והיא כתובתה מנה ואינו יכול לחסרה כלום מאותה מנה לא מהניא טענת בתולין אלא ממנה דבתולין: שאני הכא שהרי כנסה ראשון. ולדעתה דבעולה נישאת ואע"ג דעדים מעידים שלא נבעלה אינו סומך על זה מאחר שהיו נישואין וסבר דלשבחה אומרים כן: וניחוש שמא תחתיו זינתה. אין לומר דפריך למאי אינו יכול לטעון טענת בתולים לאוסרה עליו ניחוש בלאו הכי שמא תחתיו זינתה דליכא אלא חדא ספיקא ספק תחתיו ספק אין תחתיו דהא מצי לשנויי דהא דאינו יכול לטעון היינו להפסידה מכתובתה דאיכא ספק ספיקא דאפי' תחתיו איכא למימר באונס הוה ואין זה דוחק דלעיל נמי מפרש אינו יכול לטעון טענת בתולים הכי דקאמר למאי הלכתא לאוסרה עליו ביהודה ומאי לא כו' אלא לכתובה פריך מאי אינו מפסיד לה ונראה לר"י דלרב אשי פריך כיון דבעלמא אית ליה דאין לה כלום והכא יש לה לפי שכנסה ראשון א"כ יבא לידי איסור שזה האיש סבור כיון שזו יש לה אע"ג דבעלמא לית לה אם כן מחזקינן אותה ודאי בעולה מבעל ראשון ולדעת כן רוצים לומר שנשאתי ובחנם אטרח לבית דין שודאי לא יאסרוה עלי ולכך היה לנו להפסיד כתובתה שיבא לב"ד ולא יטעה לומר שמותרת לו ואפי' באשת ישראל יש לנו להפסידה גזירה שיראה כהן שזו לא תאבד כתובתה ויסבור אף בשלו כן ולא יבא לב"ד אבל לרבה לא פריך מידי כיון דבעלמא נמי יש לה ליכא למיטעי: כגון שקידש ובעל לאלתר. וכן צריך נמי להעמיד שהראשון אחר שקידש כנסה לאלתר ומת מיד ועדים מעידים שלא זינתה תחתיו דאם נבעלה תחת הראשון הרי נבעלה לפסול לה ואסורה לכהונה: א) שתי תקנות הוו. וליכא למימר דחדא תקנה הואי ומתני' קודם תקנה וברייתא לאחר תקנה שתיקנו לאלמנה מאתים דהא חזינן השתא דלית להו מאתים וליכא למימר נמי דמעיקרא כי תקינו לבתולה ארבע מאות תקינו גם כן לאלמנה מאתים דאין סברא לתקן לאלמנה מאתים אם לא אחר שראו צורך דמזלזלי בהו [הילכך מעיקרא לא רצו לשנותה משאר אלמנה וכיון דחזו דקא מזלזלי בהו ראו שהיה צורך תקון להם מאתן וכיון דחזו דפרשי מינייהו אהדרינהו למילתייהו] ולכך הוצרך לומר שתי תקנות הוו:

עין משפט נר מצוה

עד א מיי' פי"א מהל' אישות הלכה ח סמג עשין מח טוש"ע אה"ע סימן סח סעיף א:
עה ב טוש"ע שם ס"ג:

תוספות רי"ד

אמר רבא זאת אומרת כנסה בחזקת בתולה ונמצאת בעולה יש לה כתובה מנה. פי' כיון שהעדים מבררים ומעידים שלא בא עליה כשכנסה [ראשון] א"כ בחזקת בתולה כונסה וש"מ כנסה בחזקת בתולה ונמצאת בעולה כתובתה מנה. ר"א אמר בעלמא לעולם אימא לך דלית לה מידי ושאני הכא שכבר כנסה הראשון. פי' ואע"פ שמעידים העדים שלאחר שכנסה לא בא עליה יש לומר כיון שנתרצית לו לכונסה מאותה שעה היא נשאת לו. והל' כרב אשי דכנסה בחזקת בתולה ונמצאת בעולה אין לה כלום ורבא נמי הכי אמר לעיל במאי דתנן הנושא את האשה ולא מצא לה בתולים וכו' ואמר רבא מקח טעות לגמרי משמע ולית לה כלל. והכא דקאמר זאת אומרת דיוקא בעלמא סבר לדייק מינה ולמימר דתנא דהאי מתניתא ס"ל הכי וליתא אלא כדתרצה רב אשי. ומקשה וליחוש שמא תחתיו זינתה וא"ר שרביא כגון שקידש ובעל לאלתר. פי' כל היכא דהיא טענה טענת ברי ובעל טעין טענת שמא כגון תחתיך נאנסתי או מוכת עץ אני נאמנת ושקלא כתובה ושריא לבעלה כדלקמן ואפילו ר' יהושע דאמר לקמן בראוה מדברת חיישינן שמא נבעלה לנתין ולממזר דוקא להנשא לכהונה אבל לאוסרה על בעלה בייחוד בעלמא הא אמרי' לקמן דמודה ר"י דלא אסרה לה אפי' אם הוא כהן וה"נ אילו טענה האשה ואמרה שבעלי בא עלי קודם נשואין לא הוה מקשי' וליחוש שמא תחתיו זינתה דהיא נאמנת אלא התנא לא שנה טענת האשה אלמא לא טענה הכי ואפ"ה אומר' לו ב"ד שאינך יכול לטעון טענת בתולים שמא בא עליה קודם נשואין משעה ששניהם נאותו לכנוס ואע"פ שהאשה אינה יודעת לטעון. י"ל שלמפרע היה מערה בה והוציא בתוליה ולא הרגישה שלא עלו במטה כדרך חתן וכלה אלא עד אז היה מערה בה ולא שתה לבה ולא ידעה ומ"ה פריך וליחוש שמא תחתיו זינתה דהניחא שלא להפסידה כתובתה אמרי' שמא בעלה בא עליה ולא תפסיד כתובה מספק אבל מספקא תאסר עליו כיון שעדים מעידים שלאחר שכנסה לא בא עליה והיא נמי לא טענה טענה ודאית תאסר עליו מספק שמא תחתיו זינתה ולהכי איצטריך רב שרביא לומר שקידש ובעל לאלתר שיצאנו מזה הספק ויש כאן ספק שמא בעולה היתה מקודם לכן והרי מקחו מקח טעות בזה הספק אנו תולין כי בעלה בא עליה ואין כאן מקח טעות א) פי' המורה וניחוש שמא תחתיו זינתה אמתניתין פריך דקתני אין השני יכול לטעון טענת

בתולים ולא מזקיקנן ליה לבוא לב"ד ולא מתברר אם זינתה תחתיו אם לאו ושמא אסורה לו דבשלמא אהך דלעיל דאמרת כנסה בחזקת בתולה ונמצאת בעולה יש לה כתובה מנה לא מקשי' דא"ל כשבא לב"ד באו עדים שזינתה קודם לכן אבל הכא קתני אין יכול לטעון מתוך כך לא יבא לב"ד אמר רב שרביא כשקידש ובעל לאלתר. פי' שלא פירשה ממנו בין קידושין לבעילה דודאי לא ניחוש לזינתה: מתני' האוכל אצל חמיו ביהודה שלא בעדים אינו יכול לטעון טענת בתולים מפני שמתיחד עמה. אחד אלמנת ישראל ואחד אלמנת כהנים כתובתן מנה ב"ד של כהנים היה גובין לבתולה ד' מאות זוז ולא מיחו בידם חכמים: תניא א"ר יהודה בראשונה ביהודה היה מיחדים את החתן ואת הכלה שעה אחת קודם כניסתן לחופה כדי שיהיה לבו גס בה ובגליל לא היו עושים כן. ביהודה בראשונה היה מעמידים להם שני שושבינים אחד לו ואחד לה כדי למשמש את החתן ואת הכלה בשעת כניסתן לחופה פי' למשמש ולפשפש באותו הלילה במעשיהן שלא יקלקלו זה על זה שלא יראה זה דם בתולים ויאבד וזו תביא מפה שיש עלי' טפת דם ובגליל לא היו עושין כן. פי' גם ביהודה הי' מקומות שלא היו מיחדין. ושם היו מעמידים שושבינין דאי במקום שהיו מייחדים לא יועילו שושבינין שהרי אין שם טענת בתולים. ביהודה בראשונה היו שושבינים ישינים בבית שחתן וכלה ישנים בו ובגליל לא היו עושים כן. וכל שלא נהג כמנהג זה אינו יכול לטעון טענות בתולים. שהרי נתיחד עמה. אבל נהג מנהג גליל ולא נתייחד יכול לטעון ואע"פ שלא היו שם שושבינים יכול לטעון ומהימן ורב אשי פי' כל שלא משמש ביהודה אינו יכול לטעון פי' כיון שביהודה ממשמשים והוא לא משמש אמרי' לכתחלה עשה כדי להעליל עלילה עלי' אבל בגליל שלא נהגו מצי טעין אע"פ שלא משמש. ושמואל דאמר נאמן להפסידה כתובתה בטענת פתח פתוח דליכא למיקם עלה דמלתא להתברר ע"י שושבינים. וכגון שהיתה בוגרת שכלו בתוליה או אם היתה ממשפחת דורקטי אבל בטענות דמים אם נהגו למשמש ולא משמש אינו נאמן ובמקום שלא נהגו למשמש נאמן:

מסורת הש"ס

א) [לעיל ט:], ב) [תוספתא פרק א], ג) [במשנה שבמשניות איתא כהן], ד) נ"ל אברייתא.

תוספות ישנים

א) [רב אשי אומר תני כל שלא מושמש. אומר רבינו יצחק בן רבינו מאיר דרב אשי פליג ארב נחמן דלית ליה חזקה דאין אדם טורח כו' כדפי' לעיל. ור"ת אומר דלא פליג דדוקא ביהודה שנהגו למשמש ואירע שלא משמש אינו יכול לטעון דדומה לדבר שהוא ברמאות גילגל שלא מישמשוהו וכן משמע קצת דהא קתני ביהודה אינו יכול לטעון הא בגליל מצי טעין כדדייק לעיל אע"ג דבגליל לא היו ממשמשין כדקתני בברייתא ומיהו יש לפרש הא בגליל מצי טעין היינו אם אירע שמישמשוהו וע"כ צריך לפרש כן למאי דדמי לעיל לא דקא טעין טענת דמים ולא אמרי' חזקה דאין אדם טורח כו'].

ליקוטי רש"י

האוכל אצל חמיו. בימים שבין אירוסין לנשואין. אינו יכול לטעון טענת בתולים. כשתכנס לחופה. מפני שמתייחד עמה. ביהודה היו מייחדים החתן והכלה קודם כניסתן לחופה כדי שיהא לבו גס בה [יבמות מא.]. כדי שיהא לבו גס בה. כלומר רגיל ומלחק עמה שלא יהיו בושין זה מזה בבעילת מלוה הלכך חיישינן דלמא בעיל [יבמות מא.]. רגיל בה ומכירה ומרוצה לו [עירובין מז.]. למשמש את החתן ואת הכלה. כלומר לבקר אחריהם שלא ינהגו בה רמאות בטענת בתולים [לעיל ו:].

חשק שלמה על תוס' רי"ד

א) נ"ל והמורה פירש. ור"ל דרש"י ז"ל פירש.

[the Baraisa] means: כָּל שֶׁלֹּא נָהַג מִנְהַג גָּלִיל בַּגָּלִיל – Anyone who does not practice the custom of Galilee in Galilee, אֶלָּא מִנְהַג יְהוּדָה בַּגָּלִיל – but rather, practices the custom of Judea in Galilee [i.e. allowing the groom and bride to be secluded together after betrothal], אֵינוֹ יָכוֹל לִטְעוֹן טַעֲנַת בְּתוּלִים – cannot lodge a complaint concerning her virginity.[17]

The Gemara offers an alternative interpretation:

רַב אַשִׁי אָמַר – Rav Ashi said: לְעוֹלָם אַסֵּיפָא – Actually, the concluding statement refers to the end of the Baraisa, which mentioned the custom of having attendants. וּתְנֵי כָּל שֶׁלֹּא מוּשְׁמָשׁ – And teach it as saying, "anyone [i.e. any groom] who is not examined" cannot lodge a complaint.[18]

Mishnah This Mishnah returns to the topic of the value of the *kesubah*:

אַחַת אַלְמְנַת יִשְׂרָאֵל וְאַחַת אַלְמְנַת כֹּהֲנִים – Both a widow who is the daughter of a Yisrael (i.e. a non-Kohen), and a widow who is the daughter of Kohanim כְּתוּבָּתָהּ מָנֶה – have a *kesubah* of a *maneh.*[19] בֵּית דִּין שֶׁל כֹּהֲנִים הָיוּ גוֹבִין לִבְתוּלָה אַרְבַּע מֵאוֹת זוּז – However, the court of Kohanim would collect four hundred *zuz* for a virgin who was the daughter of a Kohen,[20] וְלֹא מִיחוּ בְּיָדָם חֲכָמִים – and the Sages did not protest their action.

Gemara The Gemara cites a Baraisa related to our Mishnah:

תָּנָא – A Baraisa taught: וְאַלְמְנַת כֹּהֲנִים כְּתוּבָּתָהּ מָאתַיִם – THE *KESUBAH* OF A WIDOW who is the daughter OF KOHANIM IS TWO HUNDRED *zuz.*

The Gemara asks:

וְהָאֲנַן תְּנַן – But we learned in our Mishnah: אַחַת אַלְמְנַת יִשְׂרָאֵל וְאַחַת אַלְמְנַת כֹּהֲנִים – BOTH A WIDOW who is the daughter of A NON-KOHEN AND A WIDOW who is the daughter OF KOHANIM כְּתוּבָּתָן מָנֶה – HAVE A *KESUBAH* OF A *MANEH.* – ? –

The Gemara answers:

אָמַר רַב אַשִׁי – Rav Ashi said: שְׁתֵּי תַקָּנוֹת הֲווּ – There were two enactments concerning a widow who was the daughter of a Kohen: מֵעִיקָּרָא תַּקִּינוּ לִבְתוּלָה אַרְבַּע מֵאוֹת זוּז וּלְאַלְמָנָה מָנֶה – Originally, they enacted for a virgin a *kesubah* of four hundred *zuz* and for a widow a *maneh.*[21]

NOTES

17. Normally, a groom in Galilee may lodge a complaint if he suspects his bride of not being a virgin, because in that area couples do not seclude themselves together until after *nisuin;* thus, the bride cannot defend herself by saying that she lost her virginity to the groom. The Baraisa concludes, though, that if a certain person in Galilee adopted the custom of Judea, and secluded himself with his bride after *erusin,* then he can no longer lodge a complaint about his bride's virginity. [Although this would seem to be self-evident, perhaps it could have been thought that since the prevailing custom in Galilee is not to seclude oneself with the bride at all, such seclusion would not be likely to lead to cohabitation, and a complaint could still be lodged; the Baraisa therefore teaches us that this is not the case.]

18. As the Gemara maintained previously that the Baraisa should have stated.

[Presumably, Rav Ashi preferred his emendation of the Baraisa to Abaye's because the placing of the clause at the end of the Baraisa would seem to indicate that it refers to the custom of having attendants, rather than to the custom of allowing the bride and groom to seclude themselves after *erusin.*]

19. Even though the *kesubah* of a virgin from a Kohen's family is different than that of a virgin from a non-Kohen's family (as the Mishnah proceeds to state), all widows receive a *kesubah* valued at a *maneh* (*Meiri*).

20. When she married a Kohen, and certainly when she married a non-Kohen (*Rashi*). [Any husband may commit himself to pay an amount greater than the standard two hundred *zuz.* However, that is called the *addition to the kesubah* (תּוֹסֶפֶת כְּתוּבָּה) – see General Introduction. The court of Kohanim, though, established the standard *kesubah* of a Kohen's daughter at four hundred *zuz.* The Sages accepted this enactment and gave that obligation the same weight as the two hundred-*zuz* obligation for a non-Kohen's daughter (*Tosafos* below, 12b ד״ה בית דין).]

[These courts, in the cities of the Kohanim, were composed of twenty-three judges, as were similar courts in every Jewish city (*Shitah Mekubetzes,* quoting *Likkutei HaGeonim*).]

21. As stated in our Mishnah (see *Rashba* below, 12b).

אמר רבה זאת אומרת כנסה בחזקת בתולה ונמצאת בעולה יש לה כתובה מנה אמר רב אשי אמר בעלמא אימא לך לית לה כלל ושאני הכא שהרי כנסה ראשון וניחוש שמא תחתיו זינתה אמר רב שרביא כגון שקידש ובעל לאלתר ואיכא דמתני לה אמתניתין בתולה אלמנה גרושה חלוצה מן הנישואין כתובתן מנה ואין להן טענת בתולין בתולה מן הנישואין היכי משכחת לה כגון שנכנסה לחופה ולא נבעלה אמר רבה זאת אומרת כנסה בחזקת בתולה ונמצאת בעולה כתובתה מנה רב אשי אמר לעולם אימא לך בעלמא לית לה כלל ושאני הכא שהרי נכנסה לחופה וליחוש שמא תחתיו זינתה אמר רב שרביא כגון שקידש ובעל לאלתר מאן דמתני לה אברייתא כל שכן אמתניתין ומאן דמתני לה אמתני' אבל אברייתא לא משום דמצי אמר לה אנא אעדים סמכי: **מתני'** [א] האוכל אצל חמיו ביהודה שלא בעדים אינו יכול לטעון טענת בתולים מפני שמתייחד עמה: **גמ'** מדקתני האוכל מכלל דאיכא דוכתא ביהודה נמי דלא אכיל אמר אביי ש"מ ביהודה נמי מקומות מקומות יש כדתניא א"ר יהודה [ב] ביהודה בראשונה היו מייחדין את החתן ואת הכלה שעה אחת קודם כניסתן לחופה כדי שיהא לבו גס בה ובגליל לא היו עושין כן ביהודה בראשונה היו מעמידין להם שני שושבינין אחד לו ואחד לה כדי למשמש את החתן ואת הכלה בשעת כניסתן לחופה ובגליל לא היו עושין כן ביהודה בראשונה היו שושבינין ישנים בבית שחתן וכלה ישנים בה ובגליל לא היו עושין כן וכל שלא נהג כמנהג הזה אינו יכול לטעון טענת בתולים אהייא אילימא ארישא כל שנהג מיבעי ליה אלא אסיפא כל שלא מושמש מיבעי ליה אמר אביי לעולם ארישא ותני כל שנהג אמר ליה רבא והא כל שלא נהג קתני אלא אמר רבא הכי קאמר כל שלא נהג מנהג גליל בגליל אלא מנהג יהודה בגליל אינו יכול לטעון טענת בתולים רב אשי אמר לעולם [ד] אסיפא ותני כל שלא מושמש: **מתני'** אחת אלמנת ישראל ואחת אלמנת [ג] כהנים כתובתה מנה בית דין של כהנים היו גובין לבתולה ארבע מאות זוז ולא מיחו בידם חכמים: **גמ'** תנא ואלמנת כהנים כתובתה מאתים והאנן תנן אחת אלמנת ישראל ואחת אלמנת כהנים כתובתן מנה אמר רב אשי שתי תקנות הוו מעיקרא תקינו לבתולה ארבע מאות זוז ולאלמנה מנה כיון

רש"י

זאת אומרת כו'. דהא ודאי בחזקת בתולה כנסה דסמך אעדים וקאמר אין יכול להפסידה מנה הראוי לאלמנה מן הנישואין: **וניחוש שמא תחתיו זינתה.** [ד] אמתניתין פריך דקתני אין השני יכול לטעון טענת בתולים ולא מזקיקנן ליה לבא לבית דין ולא יתברר הדבר אם תחתיו זינתה אם לא ושמא אסורה היא לו בשלמא אהך דלעיל דאמרן כנסה בחזקת בתולה ונמצאת בעולה יש לה כתובה לא מקשינן דאיכא למימר כשבא לבית דין ובאו עדים שזינתה קודם לכן אבל הכא קתני אין יכול לטעון מתוך כך לא יבא לב"ד: **כשקידש ובעל לאלתר** גרסינן ולא גרסינן כשקידש לאלתר ובעל לאלתר. שלא פירש ממנה בין קידושין לבעילה דודאי לא תחתיו זינתה: **ואיכא דמתני לה.** להא דרבה ורב אשי ורב שרביא אמתני': **זאת אומרת.** מדקתני מתני' אין להן טענת בתולים: **וליחוש שמא תחתיו זינתה.** ולמאי תני אין להן טענת בתולים: **מאן דמתני לה.** להא דרבה ורב אשי אברייתא: **כ"ש אמתני'.** דכיון דלברייתא אע"ג דאמרו עדים לא נסתרה לראשון ושני זה בחזקת בתולה כנסה ואפילו הכי אהדר ליה רב אשי לרבה לעולם לא תשמע כנסה בחזקת בתולה ונמצאת בעולה יש לה כתובה דשאני הכא שהרי כנסה ראשון כל שכן אמתניתין דלא הבטיחוהו עדים על כך איכא למתנייה לדרבה ומאי דאהדר ליה רב אשי: **ומאן דתני לה.** לדרבה ורב אשי אמתניתין: **אבל אברייתא לא.** מתני להו למברייתא ודאי שפיר ש"מ זאת אומרת דרבה ועלה לא הוה לרב אשי לאהדורי שאני הכא שהרי כנסה ראשון דמצי אמר אנא אעדים סמכי וכיון דקתני אין השני יכול לטעון טענת בתולים שמעינן ודאי דזאת אומרת כנסה בחזקת בתולה ונמצאת בעולה יש לה כתובה: **מקומות מקומות יש.** שחלוקין במנהגם ונפקא מינה דהיכא דלא נהיגי לייחד יכול לטעון: **כדתניא.** דמקומות מקומות יש: **למשמש.** לפשפש ולמשמש במעשיהן באותו הלילה שלא יקלקלו זה את זה במעשיהם בתרמית שלא יראה זה דם בתולים ויאבד וזו לא תביא מפה שיש עליה טיפי דמים ובמקום שנהגו למשמש לא נהגו לייחד דאילו במקום שנהגו לייחד מאי משמוש בעי הרי אין שם טענת בתולים אלמא ביהודה מקומות מקומות יש: **אילימא ארישא.** אמנהג דמייחדין: **כל שנהג להתייחד מיבעי ליה.** דאין יכול לטעון: **אלא אסיפא.** אמנהג דמשמוש שושבינין: **כל שלא מושמש מיבעי ליה.** דהטוען טענת בתולים הוא הבעל והוא אינו נוהג משמוש שבו [שאינו תלוי בבעל] אלא על אבי הכלה למשמשו שלא יאבד את בתוליה ומשמוש בכלה שלא תביא דם מן החוץ תלוי בבעל והיכי תני כל בעל שלא נהג מישמוש אינו יכול לטעון טענת בתולים כ"ש דאם לא נהג למשמש והם מישמשו אותו דיכול לטעון הכי איבעי ליה למתני כל שלא מושמש אינו יכול לטעון דשמא ראה ואבד: **אלא אמר רבא.** האי כל שלא נהג אמנהג דגליל קאי דתנא בברייתא ובגליל לא היו עושין כן ועלה קאי כל שלא נהג כמנהג הזה בגליל אלא נתייחד כמנהג שביהודה אינו יכול לטעון: **מתני' אלמנת כהנים.** אלמנה בת כהן: **היו גובין לבתולה.** בת כהן כשניסאת לכהן וכ"ש כשניסאת לישראל: **גמ' שתי תקנות הוו.** לאלמנה בת כהן: דמזלזלי

תוספות

אמר רבה זאת אומרת. נראה דהכא גרסינן רבה דהא רבא קאמר לעיל דמקח טעות לגמרי משמע ואי גרסינן הכא רבא א"כ תיקשי מתניתין רישא לסיפא דהא זאת אומרת איכא למידק נמי ממתניתין דלאמרינן בסמוך אלא ודאי נראה דהכא גרס רבה דרבא דאמר לעיל מקח טעות לגמרי משמע יפרש כמו רב אשי: **כנסה** בחזקת בתולה ונמצאת בעולה יש לה מנה. והא דקתני שהרי כנסה ראשון פירש ריב"ס דהכי משמע ליה אין לשני טענת בתולין לחסרה מכתובתה כלום שהרי כנסה ראשון וגרס להיות כתובתה מנה ואינו יכול לחסרה כלום מאותה מנה דלא מהניא טענת בתולין אלא ממנה דבתולין: **שאני** הכא שהרי כנסה ראשון. ולדעתא דבעולה ניסאת ואע"ג דעדים מעידים שלא נבעלה אינו סומך על זה מאחר שהיו נישואין וסבר דלשבחה אומרים כן: **וניחוש** שמא תחתיו זינתה. אין לומר דפריך אמאי אינו יכול לטעון טענת בתולים לאוסרה עליו ניחוש באשת כהן שמא תחתיו זינתה דליכא אלא חדא ספיקא ספק תחתיו ספק אין תחתיו דהא מצי לשנויי דהא דאינו יכול לטעון היינו להפסידה מכתובתה דאיכא ספק ספיקא דאפי' תחתיו אימור באונס הוה ואין זה דוחק דלעיל נמי מפרש אינו יכול לטעון טענת בתולים הכי דקאמר למאי אי לאוסרה עליו ביהודה אמאי לא כו' אלא אכתובה פריך אמאי אינו מפסיד לה ונראה לר"י דלרב אשי פריך כיון דבעלמא אית ליה דאין לה כלום והכא יש לה לפי שכנסה ראשון א"כ יבא לידי איסור שזה האיש סבור כיון שזו יש לה אע"ג דבעלמא לית לה אם כן מחזקין אותה ודאי בעולה מבעל ראשון ולדעת כן רוצים לומר שנשאתי ובחנם אטרח לבית דין שודאי לא יאסרוה עלי ולכך היה לנו להפסיד כתובתה שיבא לב"ד ולא יטעה לומר שמותרת לו ואפי' באשת ישראל יש לנו להפסידה גזירה שיראה כהן שזו לא תאבד כתובתה ויסבור אף בשלו כן ולא יבא לב"ד אבל לרבה לא פריך מידי כיון דבעלמא נמי יש לה ליכא למיטעי: **כגון** שקידש ובעל לאלתר. וכן צריך נמי להעמיד שהראשון אחר שקידש כנסה לאלתר ומת מיד ועדים מעידים שלא זינתה תחתיו דאם נבעלה תחת הראשון הרי נבעלה לפסול לה ואסורה לכהונה:[א] **שתי** תקנות הוו. וליכא למימר דחדא תקנה הואי ומתני' קודם תקנה וברייתא לאחר תקנה שתיקנו לאלמנה מאתים דהא חזינן השתא דלית להו מאתים וליכא למימר נמי דמעיקרא כי תקינו לבתולה ארבע מאות תקינו גם כן לאלמנה מאתים דאין סברא לתקן לאלמנה מאתים אם לא אחר שראו צורך דמזלזלי בהו [הילכך מעיקרא לא רצו לשנותה משאר אלמנה וכיון דחזו דקא מזלזלי בהו ראו שהיה צורך תקון להם מאתן וכיון דחזו דפרשי מינייהו אהדרינהו למילתייהו] ולכך הוצרך לומר שתי תקנות הוו:

עין משפט נר מצוה

עד א מיי' פי"א מהל' אישות הלכה ח סמג עשין מח טוש"ע אה"ע סימן סח סעיף ח:
עה ב טוש"ע שם ס"ב:

מסורת הש"ס

א) [לעיל ט:], ב) [תוספתא פרק א], ג) [במשנה שבמשניות איתא בהן], ד) נ"ל אברייתא.

תוספות ישנים

א) **רב אשי אמר תני כל שלא מושמש.** אומר רבינו יצחק בן רבינו מאיר דרב אשי פליג ארב נחמן דלית לי' חזקה דאין אדם טורח כו' כדפי' לעיל. ור"ח אומר דלא פליג דדוקא ביהודה שנהגו למשמש ואירע שלא משמש אינו יכול לטעון דדומה לדבר שסוף ברמאות גילגל שלא משמשוהו וכן משמע קצת דהא קתני ביהודה אינו יכול לטעון בגליל מאי טעין כדדייק לעיל אע"ג דבגליל לא היו משמשין כדקתני בברייתא ומיהו יש לפרש הא דבגליל מצי טעין היינו אם אירע שמשמשוהו וע"כ צריך לפרש כן למאי דדחי לעיל לא דקא טעין טענת דמים ולא אמרי' חזקה דאין אדם טורח כו'].

ליקוטי רש"י

האוכל אצל חמיו. בימים שבין אירוסין לנשואין. **אינו יכול לטעון טענת בתולים.** כשכנסה לחופה. **מפני שמתייחד עמה.** ביהודה היו מייחדים החתן והכלה קודם כניסתן לחופה כדי שיהא לבו גס בה [יבמות מא.]. **כדי שיהא לבו גס בה.** כלומר רגיל ומלחק מזה לכלה שלא יהיו בושים זה מזה בבעילת מצוה הלכך חיישינן דלמא בעיל [יבמות מא.]. רגיל בה ומורגלת לו [עירובין מז.]. **למשמש את החתן ואת הכלה.** כלומר לבקר אחריהם שלא ירמו בה לחמוס בטענת בתולים [לעיל ו:].

חשק שלמה על תוס' רי"ד

א) נ"ל והמורה פירש. ור"ל דרש"י ז"ל פירש.

תוספות רי"ד

אמר רבא זאת אומרת כנסה בחזקת בתולה ונמצאת בעולה יש לה כתובה מנה. פי' כיון שהעדים מבררים ומעידים שלא בא עליה כשכנסה [ראשון] א"כ בחזקת בתולה כנסה וש"מ כנסה בחזקת בתולה ונמצאת בעולה כתובתה מנה. ר"א אמר בעלמא לעולם אימא לך דלית לה מידי ושאני הכא שכבר כנסה הראשון. פי' ואע"פ שמעידים העדים שלאחר שכנסה לא בא עליה יש לומר כיון שנתרצית לו לכונסה מאותה שעה היא נשאת לו. והל' כרב אשי דכנסה בחזקת בתולה ונמצאת בעולה אין לה כלום ורבא נמי הכי אמר לעיל בגמ' דתנן הנושא את האשה ולא מצא לה בתולים וכו' ואמר רבא מקח טעות לגמרי משמע ולית לה כלל. והכא דקאמר זאת אומרת דיוקא בעלמא סבר לדייק מינה ולמימר דתנא דהאי מתניתא ס"ל הכי וליתא אלא כדתרצה רב אשי. **ומקשה** וליחוש שמא תחתיו זינתה וא"ר שרביא כגון שקידש ובעל לאלתר. פי' כל היכא דהיא טענה טענת ברי ובעל טוען טענת שמא כגון תחתיך נאנסתי או מוכת עץ אני נאמנת ושקלא כתובה ושריא לבעלה כדלקמן ואפילו ר' יהושע דאמר לקמן בראוה מדברת חיישינן שמא נבעלה לנתין ולממזר דוקא להנשא לכהונה אבל לאוסרה על בעלה ביחוד בעלמא לא אמרי' לקמן דמודה ר"י דלא אסרה לה אפי' אם הוא כהן וה"נ אילו טענה האשה ואמרה שבעלי בא עלי קודם נשואין לא הוה מקשי' וליחוש שמא תחתיו זינתה דהיא נאמנת אלא התנא לא שנה טענת האשה אלמא לא טענה הכי ואפ"ה אומר לו ב"ד שאינך יכול לטעון טענת בתולים שמא בא עליה קודם נשואין משום ששניהם נאותו לכנוס ואע"פ שהאשה אינה יודעת לטעון. וי"ל שלמפרע היה מערה בה והוציא בתוליה ולא הרגישה שלא עלו בבעילה כדרך חתן וכלה אלא עד אז היה מערה בה ולא שתה לבה ולא ידעה ומ"ה פריך וליחוש שמא תחתיו זינתה דהניחא שלא להפסידה כתובתה אמרי' שמא בעלה בא עליה ולא תפסיד כתובה מספק אבל מספקא תאסר עליו כיון שעדים מעידים שלאחר שכנסה לא בא עליה והיא נמי לא טענה ודאית תאסר עליו מספק שמא תחתיו זינתה ולהכי איצטריך רב שרביא לומר שקידש ובעל לאלתר שיצאנו מזה הספק ויש כאן ספק שמא בעולה היתה מקודם לכן והרי שהיה לקחו מקח טעות בזה הספק אנו תולין כי בעלה בא עליה ואין כאן מקח טעות א) פי' המורה וניחוש שמא תחתיו זינתה אמתניתין פריך דקתני אין השני יכול לטעון טענת בתולים ולא מזקיקנן ליה לבוא לב"ד ולא מתברר אם זינתה תחתיו אם לאו ושמא אסורה לו דבשלמא אהך דלעיל דאמרת כנסה בחזקת בתולה ונמצאת בעולה יש לה כתובה מנה לא מקשי' דא"ל כשבא לב"ד באו עדים שזינתה קודם לכן אבל הכא קתני אין יכול לטעון מתוך כך לא יבא לב"ד אמר רב שרביא כשקידש ובעל לאלתר. פי' שלא פירשה ממנו בין קידושין לבעילה דודאי לא ניחוש לזינתה: **מתני' האוכל** אצל חמיו ביהודה שלא בעדים אינו יכול לטעון טענת בתולים מפני שמתיחד עמה. אחד אלמנת ישראל ואחד אלמנת כהנים כתובתן מנה ב"ד של כהנים היה גובין לבתולה ד' מאות זוז ולא מיחו בידם חכמים: **תניא** א"ר יהודה בראשונה ביהודה היה מיחדים את החתן ואת הכלה שעה אחת קודם כניסתן לחופה כדי שיהיה לבו גס בה ובגליל לא היו עושים כן. **ביהודה** בראשונה היה מעמידים להם שני שושבינים אחד לו ואחד לה כדי למשמש את החתן ואת הכלה בשעת כניסתן לחופה פי' למשמש ולפשפש באותו הלילה במעשיהן שלא יקלקלו זה על זה שלא יראה זה דם בתולים ויאבד וזו תביא מפה שיש עלי' טפת דם ובגליל לא היו עושין כן. פי' גם ביהודה הי' מקומות שלא היו מיחדין. ושם היו מעמידים שושבינין דאי במקום שהיו מייחדים לא יועילו שושבינין שהרי אין שם טענת בתולים. **ביהודה** בראשונה היו שושבינים ישנים בבית שחתן וכלה ישנים בו ובגליל לא היו עושים כן. וכל שלא נהג כמנהג זה אינו יכול לטעון טענות בתולים. שהרי נתיחד עמה. אבל נהג מנהג גליל ולא נתייחד יכול לטעון ואע"פ שלא היו שם שושבינים יכול לטעון ומהימן ורב אשי פי' כל שלא משמש ביהודה אינו יכול לטעון פי' כיון שביהודה ממשמשים והוא לא משמש אמרי' לכתחלה עשה כדי להעליל עלילה עלי' אבל בגליל שלא נהגו מצי טעין אע"פ שלא משמש. ושמואל דאמר נאמן להפסידה כתובתה בטענת פתח פתוח דליכא למיקם עלה דמלתא להתברר ע"י שושבינים. וכגון שהיתה בוגרת שכלו בתוליה או אם היתה ממשפחת דורקטי אבל בטענות דמים אם נהגו למשמש ולא משמש אינו נאמן ובמקום שלא נהגו למשמש נאמן:

Mishnah The Mishnah adds another case where the groom cannot lodge a complaint about his bride's virginity:

הָאוֹכֵל אֵצֶל חָמִיו בִּיהוּדָה שֶׁלֹּא בְעֵדִים – If ONE EATS IN HIS FATHER-IN-LAW'S HOUSE IN JUDEA during his betrothal period WITHOUT WITNESSES to testify that he did not seclude himself with his betrothed, אֵינוֹ יָכוֹל לִטְעוֹן טַעֲנַת בְּתוּלִים – HE CANNOT MAKE A CLAIM CONCERNING his bride's VIRGINITY after they marry, מִפְּנֵי שֶׁמִּתְיַיחֵד עִמָּהּ – BECAUSE it is customary in Judea that HE SECLUDES himself WITH HER during these visits.[7]

Gemara The Gemara draws an inference from the language used by the Mishnah:

מִדְּקָתָנֵי הָאוֹכֵל – Since the Mishnah states: If ONE EATS, מִכְּלָל דְּאִיכָּא דוּכְתָּא בִּיהוּדָה נַמִּי דְּלָא אָכִיל – it is implied that there is a place in Judea as well where [the groom] does not eat in his father-in-law's house after betrothal.[8] אָמַר אַבַּיֵי – Abaye therefore said: שְׁמַע מִינָּהּ בִּיהוּדָה נַמִּי מְקוֹמוֹת מְקוֹמוֹת יֵשׁ – Learn from this that even in Judea, there are various places that have different customs.[9]

Abaye supports his statement:

כִּדְתַנְיָא – This is as it was taught in a Baraisa: אָמַר רַבִּי יְהוּדָה – R' YEHUDAH SAID: בִּיהוּדָה בָּרִאשׁוֹנָה – IN JUDEA, ORIGINALLY the custom was that הָיוּ מְיַיחֲדִין אֶת הֶחָתָן וְאֶת הַכַּלָּה שָׁעָה אַחַת קוֹדֶם כְּנִיסָתָן לַחוּפָּה – THEY WOULD SECLUDE THE GROOM AND BRIDE for A short TIME BEFORE THEY ENTERED THE *CHUPPAH* כְּדֵי שֶׁיְּהֵא לִבּוֹ גַּס בָּהּ – SO THAT HE WOULD BE FAMILIAR TO HER.[10] וּבַגָּלִיל לֹא הָיוּ עוֹשִׂין כֵּן – BUT IN GALILEE THEY WOULD NOT DO SO. בִּיהוּדָה בָּרִאשׁוֹנָה – IN JUDEA, ORIGINALLY the custom was that הָיוּ מַעֲמִידִין לָהֶם שְׁנֵי שׁוֹשְׁבִינִין אֶחָד לוֹ וְאֶחָד לָהּ – THEY WOULD SET UP TWO ATTENDANTS, ONE FOR HIM AND ONE FOR HER, כְּדֵי לְמַשְׁמֵשׁ אֶת הֶחָתָן וְאֶת הַכַּלָּה בִּשְׁעַת כְּנִיסָתָן לַחוּפָּה – IN ORDER TO EXAMINE THE GROOM AND THE BRIDE WHEN THEY WERE TO ENTER THE *CHUPPAH*.[11] וּבַגָּלִיל לֹא הָיוּ עוֹשִׂין כֵּן – BUT IN GALILEE THEY WOULD NOT DO SO. בִּיהוּדָה בָּרִאשׁוֹנָה – IN JUDEA, ORIGINALLY the custom was that הָיוּ שׁוֹשְׁבִינִין יְשֵׁנִים בַּבַּיִת שֶׁחָתָן וְכַלָּה יְשֵׁנִים בָּהּ – ATTENDANTS WOULD SLEEP IN THE HOUSE THAT THE GROOM AND BRIDE WERE SLEEPING IN. וּבַגָּלִיל לֹא הָיוּ עוֹשִׂין כֵּן – BUT IN GALILEE THEY WOULD NOT DO SO.[12] וְכָל שֶׁלֹּא נָהַג כְּמִנְהָג הַזֶּה – THEREFORE, ANYONE WHO DOES NOT PRACTICE THIS CUSTOM אֵינוֹ יָכוֹל לִטְעוֹן טַעֲנַת בְּתוּלִים – IS NOT ABLE TO LODGE A COMPLAINT CONCERNING her VIRGINITY. It is thus obvious that not everyone in Judea had the custom to allow seclusion after the betrothal in Judea.[13]

Having cited this Baraisa, the Gemara analyzes its concluding statement:

אַהֵיָיא – On which case of the Baraisa does this last statement ("Therefore, anyone who does not practice . . .") elaborate? אִילֵימָא אַרֵישָׁא – If you say that it elaborates on the beginning of the Baraisa, which stated the practice of allowing the groom and bride to be secluded together in Judea, כָּל שֶׁנָּהַג מִיבָּעֵי לֵיהּ – it should have stated, "Anyone who *does* practice" this custom cannot lodge a complaint about her virginity![14] אֶלָּא אַסֵּיפָא – And if you say, rather, that it refers to the end of the Baraisa, which spoke of the practice to have attendants, כָּל שֶׁלֹּא מוּשְׁמָשׁ מִיבָּעֵי לֵיהּ – it should have stated, "Anyone [i.e. any groom] who is not examined" cannot lodge a complaint about her virginity![15]

The Gemara offers a possible resolution:

אָמַר אַבַּיֵי – Abaye said: לְעוֹלָם אַרֵישָׁא – Actually, this clause refers to the beginning of the Baraisa. וּתְנֵי כָּל שֶׁנָּהַג – And teach it as saying, "Anyone who practices," etc.

The Gemara objects to that answer:

אָמַר לֵיהּ רָבָא – Rava said to [Abaye]: וְהָא כָּל שֶׁלֹּא נָהַג קָתָנֵי – But [the Baraisa] stated: ANYONE WHO DOES *NOT* PRACTICE. How can you say that it means anyone who *does* practice the custom?[16]

Rava therefore presents another interpretation of the Baraisa:

אֶלָּא אָמַר רָבָא – Rather, Rava said: הָכִי קָאָמַר – This is what

NOTES

7. This has been explained above, 9b note 14-15.

8. If the universal custom in all of Judea was to allow grooms to seclude themselves with their betrothed brides after *erusin,* the Mishnah should have stated its rule categorically: One who marries a woman in Judea, etc. By specifying that its ruling applies to a groom who stays with his bride after *erusin,* the Mishnah indicates that this practice was not followed in all areas of Judea (*Ritva*).

9. Therefore, if someone is in an area of Judea where the groom does not seclude himself with the bride after *erusin,* he has the right to lodge a complaint following *nisuin* concerning her virginity (*Rashi;* see *Ritva*).

10. Literally: so that his heart would become familiar with her.

11. That is, to examine and investigate the deeds of the bride and groom on the night of the first cohabitation. These attendants would ensure that neither the groom nor bride would employ any underhanded stratagems: For example, the groom "losing" the cloth that showed the hymenal bleeding, and then substituting a clean cloth of his own and claiming that his bride had not been a virgin; or the bride bringing a blood-stained cloth into the house to use as "evidence" that she was a virgin when in fact she was not (*Rashi*).

12. This third statement is apparently superfluous, because the Baraisa just wrote in its second statement that there were no attendants at all in Galilee! In fact, *Maharam Schif* notes that this clause is not found at all in *Rosh's* version of the Gemara; our Gemara below also seems to ignore this clause. See, however, *Ritva* for a possible explanation of what this clause could be adding.

13. By stating Judea's custom of having attendants, the Baraisa indicates that some areas of Judea did not allow the groom and bride to be secluded together after the *erusin.* For if that custom were universally held in Judea, what purpose would attendants serve? Even if there were attendants present who could attest to the fact that the groom had not employed any improper stratagems, the groom would still not be able to lodge a complaint about the bride's virginity, because he had already secluded himself with her before bringing her under the *chuppah* (*Rashi*).

14. Since they are secluded together after *erusin,* we can assume that he cohabited with her and can no longer expect her to be a virgin.

15. As explained above, the attendants of both the groom and the bride ensured that neither party tried to trick the other. That is, it was in the groom's interest to provide an attendant for the bride to ensure that she did not smuggle in a blood-stained cloth to provide false evidence to her virginity. And the bride would want the groom to be attended, to prevent him from destroying the blood-stained cloth and substituting false evidence of her non-virginity. The Baraisa's sentence, "Anyone who does not practice this custom cannot lodge a complaint concerning virginity," conveys that any groom who did not use an attendant to watch the *bride* cannot lodge a complaint concerning her virginity – because it is the groom, not the bride, who would lodge a complaint about virginity. Now, the Baraisa cannot mean that if the groom did not provide an attendant for his bride he cannot lodge a complaint, because there is no reason why he could not lodge a complaint, as long as the bride's family watched that *he* did not destroy any evidence! Thus, if the Baraisa's conclusion refers to the practice of having attendants, it should have stated that in a case where the *groom* was not attended he may not lodge a complaint, because of the possibility that he tampered with the evidence. Thus, the Baraisa should have stated, "Any [groom] who was not examined . . ." (*Rashi*).

16. [Rava was loath to accept an interpretation based on an emendation of the Baraisa because, in his view, the Baraisa could be satisfactorily interpreted without emendation, as the Gemara proceeds to state.]

אמר רבה זאת אומרת כנסה בחזקת בתולה ונמצאת בעולה יש לה כתובה מנה רב אשי אמר בעלמא לעולם אימא לך לית לה כלל ושאני הכא שהרי כנסה ראשון וניחוש שמא תחתיו זינתה אמר רב שרביא כגון שקידש ובעל לאלתר ואיכא דמתני לה אמתניתין בתולה אלמנה גרושה חלוצה מן הנישואין כתובתן מנה ואין להן טענת בתולין בתולה מן הנישואין היכי משכחת לה כגון שנכנסה לחופה ולא נבעלה אמר רבה זאת אומרת כנסה בחזקת בתולה ונמצאת בעולה כתובתה מנה רב אשי אמר לעולם אימא לך בעלמא לית לה כלל ושאני הכא שהרי נכנסה לחופה וליחוש שמא תחתיו זינתה אמר רב שרביא כגון שקידש ובעל לאלתר מאן דמתני לה אברייתא כל שכן אמתניתין ומאן דמתני לה אמתני' אבל אברייתא לא משום דמצי אמר לה אנא אעדים סמכי: מתני' [א] האוכל אצל חמיו ביהודה שלא בעדים אינו יכול לטעון טענת בתולים מפני שמתייחד עמה: גמ' מדקתני האוכל מכלל דאיכא דוכתא ביהודה נמי דלא אכיל אמר אביי ש"מ ביהודה נמי מקומות מקומות יש כדתניא א"ר יהודה [ג] ביהודה בראשונה היו מייחדין את החתן ואת הכלה שעה אחת קודם כניסתן לחופה כדי שיהא לבו גס בה ובגליל לא היו עושין כן ביהודה בראשונה היו מעמידין להם שני שושבינין אחד לו ואחד לה כדי למשמש את החתן ואת הכלה בשעת כניסתן לחופה ובגליל לא היו עושין כן ביהודה בראשונה היו שושבינין ישנים בבית שחתן וכלה ישנים בה ובגליל לא היו עושין כן וכל שלא נהג כמנהג הזה אינו יכול לטעון טענת בתולים אהייא אילימא ארישא כל שנהג מיבעי ליה אלא אסיפא כל שלא מושמש מיבעי ליה אמר אביי לעולם ארישא ותני כל שנהג אמר ליה רבא והא כל שלא נהג קתני אלא אמר רבא הכי קאמר כל שלא נהג מנהג גליל בגליל אלא מנהג יהודה בגליל אינו יכול לטעון טענת בתולים רב אשי אמר לעולם [ב] אסיפא ותני כל שלא מושמש: מתני' אחת אלמנת ישראל ואחת אלמנת [ג] כהנים כתובתה מנה בית דין של כהנים היו גובין לבתולה ארבע מאות זוז ולא מיחו בידם חכמים: גמ' תנא ואלמנת כהנים כתובתה מאתים והאנן תנן אחת אלמנת ישראל ואחת אלמנת כהנים כתובתן מנה אמר רב אשי שתי תקנות הוו מעיקרא תקנו לבתולה ארבע מאות זוז ולאלמנה מנה כיון

רש"י

זאת אומרת כו'. דהא ודאי בחזקת בתולה כנסה דסמך אעדים וקאמר אין יכול להפסידה מנה הראוי לאלמנה מן הנישואין: וניחוש שמא תחתיו זינתה. [ד] ממתניתין פריך דקתני אין השני יכול לטעון טענת בתולים ולא מזקיקנן ליה לבא לבית דין ולא יתברר הדבר אם תחתיו זינתה אם לא ושמא אסורה היא לו בשלמא אהך דלעיל דאמרן כנסה בחזקת בתולה ונמצאת בעולה יש לה כתובה לא מקשינן דליכא למימר כשבא לבית דין ובאו עדים שזינתה קודם לכן אבל הכא קתני אין יכול לטעון מתוך כך לא יבא לב"ד: כשקידש ובעל לאלתר גרסינן ולא גרסינן כשקידש לאלתר ובעל לאלתר. שלא פירש ממנה בין קידושין לבעילה דודאי לא תחתיו זינתה: ואיכא דמתני לה. להא דרבה ורב אשי ורב שרביא אמתני': זאת אומרת. מדקתני מתני' אין להן טענת בתולים: וליחוש שמא תחתיו זינתה. ולמאי תני אין להן טענת בתולים: מאן דמתני לה. להא דרבה ורב אשי אברייתא. כ"ש אמתני'. דכיון דאברייתא אע"ג דאמרו עדים לא נסתרה לראשון ושני זה בחזקת בתולה כנסה ואפילו הכי אהדר ליה רב אשי לרבה לעולם לא תשמע כנסה בחזקת בתולה ונמצאת בעולה יש לה כתובה דשאני הכא שהרי כנסה ראשון כל שכן אמתניתין דלא הבטיחוהו עדים על כך דאיכא למתלייה לדרבה ומאי דאהדר ליה רב אשי: ומאן דתני לה. לדרבה ורב אשי אמתניתין: אבל אברייתא לא. מתני להו דאברייתא ודאי שפיר ש"מ זאת אומרת דרבה ועלה לא הוה לרב אשי לאהדורי שאני הכא שהרי כנסה ראשון דמצי אמר אנא אעדים סמכי וכיון דקתני אין השני יכול לטעון טענת בתולים שמעינן ודאי דזאת אומרת כנסה בחזקת בתולה ונמצאת בעולה יש לה כתובה: מקומות מקומות יש. שחלוקין במנהגם ונפקא מינה היכא דלא נהיגי לייחד יכול לטעון: כדתניא. דמקומות מקומות יש: למשמש. לפשפש ולמשמש במעשיהן באותו הלילה שלא יקלקלו זה את זה במעשיהם בתרמית שלא יראה זה דם בתולים ויאבדו או תביא מפה שיש עליה טיפי דמים ומקום שנהגו למשמש לא נהגו לייחד דאלו במקום שנהגו לייחד מאי מישמוש בעי הרי אין שם טענת בתולים אלמא ביהודה מקומות מקומות יש: אילימא ארישא. אמנהג דמייחדין: כל שנהג להתייחד מיבעי ליה. דאין יכול לטעון: אלא אסיפא. אמנהג דמשמוש שושבינין: כל שלא מושמש מיבעי ליה. דהטוען טענת בתולים הוא הבעל והוא אינו נוהג מישמוש שבו [שאינו תלוי בבעל] אלא על אבי הכלה למשמשו שלא יאבד את בתוליה ומשמוש בכלה שלא תביא דם מן החוץ תלוי בבעל והיכי תני כל בעל שלא נהג מישמוש אינו יכול לטעון טענת בתולים כ"ש דאם לא נהג למשמש והם מישמשו אותו דיכול לטעון הכי איבעי ליה למתני כל שלא מושמש אינו יכול לטעון דשמא רמה ואבד: אלא אמר רבא. מאי כל שלא נהג מנהג דגליל קאי דתנא בברייתא ובגליל לא היו עושין כן ועלה קאי כל שלא נהג כמנהג הזה בגליל אלא נתייחד כמנהג שביהודה אינו יכול לטעון: מתני' אלמנת כהנים. אלמנה בת כהן: היו גובין לבתולה. בת כהן כשניסאת לכהן וכ"ש כשניסאת לישראל: גמ' שתי תקנות הוו. לאלמנה בת כהן: דמזלזלי

תוספות

אמר רבה זאת אומרת. נראה דהכא גרסינן רבה דהא רבא קאמר לעיל דמקח טעות לגמרי משמע ואי גרסינן הכא רבא א"כ תיקשי מתניתין רישא לסיפא דהא זאת אומרת איכא למידק נמי ממתניתין כדאמרינן בסמוך אלא ודאי נראה דהכא גרס רבה דרבא דאמר לעיל מקח טעות לגמרי משמע יפרש כמו רב אשי:

כנסה בחזקת בתולה ונמצאת בעולה יש לה מנה. והא דקתני שהרי כנסה ראשון פירש ריב"ם דהכי משמע ליה אין לשני טענת בתולין לחסרה מכתובתה כלום שהרי כנסה ראשון וגרס להיות כתובתה מנה ואינו יכול לחסרה כלום מאותה מנה דלא מהניא טענת בתולין אלא ממנה דבתולין: שאני הכא שהרי כנסה ראשון. ולדעתא דבעולה ניסאת ואע"ג דעדים מעידים שלא נבעלה אינו סומך על זה מאחר שהיו נישואין וסבר דלשבחה אומרים כן:

וניחוש שמא תחתיו זינתה. אין לומר דפריך אמאי אינו יכול לטעון טענת בתולים לאוסרה עליו ניחוש באשת כהן שמא תחתיו זינתה דליכא אלא חדא ספיקא ספק תחתיו ספק אין תחתיו דהא מצי לשנויי דהא דאינו יכול לטעון היינו להפסידה מכתובתה דאיכא ספק ספיקא דאפי' תחתיו אימור באונס הוה ואין זה דוחק דלעיל נמי מפרש אינו יכול לטעון טענת בתולים הכי דקאמר למאי אי לאוסרה עליו ביהודה אמאי לא כו' אלא אכתובה פריך אמאי אינו מפסיד לה ונראה לר"י דלרב אשי פריך כיון דבעלמא אית ליה דאין לה כלום והכא יש לה לפי שכנסה ראשון א"כ יבא לידי איסור שזה האיש סבור כיון שזו יש לה אע"ג דבעלמא לית לה אם כן מחזיקין אותה ודאי בעולה מבעל ראשון ואדעת כן רוצים לומר שנשאתי ובחנם אטרח לבית דין שודאי לא יאסרוה עלי ולכך היה לנו להפסיד כתובתה שיבא לב"ד ולא יטעה לומר שמותרת לו ואפי' באשת ישראל יש לנו להפסידה גזירה שיראה כהן שזו לא תאבד כתובתה ויסבור אף בשלו כן ולא יבא לב"ד אבל לרבה לא פריך מידי כיון דבעלמא נמי יש לה ליכא למיטעי:

כגון שקידש ובעל לאלתר. וכן צריך נמי להעמיד שהראשון אחר שקידש כנסה לאלתר ומת מיד ועדים מעידים שלא זינתה תחתיו דאם נבעלה תחת הראשון הרי נבעלה לפסול לה ואסורה לכהונה: א)

שתי תקנות הוו. וליכא למימר דחדא תקנה הואי ומתני' קודם תקנה וברייתא לאחר תקנה שתיקנו לאלמנה מאתים דהא חזינן השתא דלית להו מאתים וליכא למימר נמי דמעיקרא כי תקינו לבתולה ארבע מאות תקינו גם כן לאלמנה מאתים דאין סברא לתקן לאלמנה מאתים אם לא אחר שראו צורך דמזלזלי בהו [הילכך מעיקרא לא רצו לשנותה משאר אלמנה וכיון דחזו דקא מזלזלי בהו ראו שהיה צורך תקון להם מאתן וכיון דחזו דפרשי מינייהו אהדרינהו למילתייהו] ולכך הוצרך לומר שתי תקנות הוו:

תוספות רי"ד

אמר רבא זאת אומרת כנסה בחזקת בתולה ונמצאת בעולה יש לה כתובה מנה. פי' כיון שהעדים מבררים ומעידים שלא בא עליה כשכנסה [ראשון] א"כ בחזקת בתולה כנסה וש"מ כנסה בחזקת בתולה ונמצאת בעולה כתובתה מנה. ר"א אמר בעלמא לעולם אימא לך דלית לה מידי ושאני הכא שכבר כנסה הראשון. פי' ואע"פ שמעידים העדים שלאחר שכנסה לא בא עליה לומר כיון שנתרצית לו לכונסה מאותה שעה היה נשאת לו. והל' כרב אשי דכנסה בחזקת בתולה ונמצאת בעולה אין לה כלום ורבא נמי הכי אמר לעיל במאי דתנן הנושא את האשה ולא מצא לה בתולים וכו' ואמר רבא מקח טעות לגמרי משמע ולית לה כלל. והכא דקאמר זאת אומרת דיוקא בעלמא סבר לדייק מינה ולמימר דתנא דהאי מתניתא ס"ל הכי וליתא אלא כדתרצה רב אשי. ומקשה וליחוש שמא תחתיו זינתה וא"ר שרביא כגון שקידש ובעל לאלתר. פי' כל היכא דהיא טוענת ברי ובעל טוען טענת שמא כגון תחתיך נאנסתי אתה מוכת עץ אני נאמנת ושקלא כתובה ושריא לבעלה כדלקמן ואפילו ר' יהושע דאמר לקמן בראוה מדברת חיישינן שמא נבעלה לנתין ולממזר דוקא להנשא לכהונה אבל לאוסרה על בעלה בייחוד בעלמא הא אמרי' לקמן דמודה ר"י דלא אסרה לה אפי' אם הוא כהן וה"נ אילו טענה האשה ואמרה שבעלי בא עלי קודם נשואין לא הוה מקשי' וליחוש שמא תחתיו זינתה דהיא נאמנת אלא התנא לא שנה טענה האשה אלמא לא טענה הכי ואפ"ה אומר' לו ב"ד שאינך יכול לטעון טענת בתולים שמא בא עליה קודם נשואין משעה ששניהם נשואין לכנוס ואע"פ שהאשה אינה יודעת לטעון. וי"ל שלמפרע היה מערה בה והוציא בתוליה ולא הרגישה שלא עלו במטה כדרך חתן וכלה אלא עד אז היה מערה בה שתה לבה ולא ידעה ומ"ה פריך וליחוש שמא תחתיו זינתה דהניחא שלא להפסידה כתובתה אמרי' שמא בעלה בא עליה ולא תפסיד כתובה מספק אבל מספקא תאסר עליו כיון שעדים מעידים שלאחר שכנסה לא בא עליה והיא נמי לא טענה טענה ודאית תאסר עליו מספק שמא תחתיו זינתה ולהכי איצטריך רב שרביא לומר שקידש ובעל לאלתר שיצאנו מזה הספק ויש כאן ספק שמא בעולה היתה מקודם לכן והרי מקחו מקח טעות בזה הספק אנו תולין כי בעלה בא עליה ואין כאן מקח טעות א) פי' המורה וניחוש שמא תחתיו זינתה אמתניתין פריך דקתני אין השני יכול לטעון טענת בתולים ולא מזקיקנן ליה לבוא לב"ד ולא מתברר אם זינתה תחתיו אם לאו ושמא אסורה לו דבשלמא אהך דלעיל דאמרת כנסה בחזקת בתולה ונמצאת בעולה יש לה כתובה מנה לא מקשי' דא"ל כשבא לב"ד באו עדים שזינתה קודם לכן אבל הכא קתני אין יכול לטעון מתוך כך לא יבא לב"ד אמר רב שרביא כשקידש ובעל לאלתר. פי' שלא פירשה ממנו בין קידושין לבעילה דודאי לא ניחוש לזינתה: מתני' האוכל אצל חמיו ביהודה שלא בעדים אינו יכול לטעון טענת בתולים מפני שמתיחד עמה. אחד אלמנת ישראל ואחד אלמנת כהנים כתובתן מנה ב"ד של כהנים היה גובין לבתולה ד' מאות זוז ולא מיחו בידם חכמים: תניא א"ר יהודה בראשונה ביהודה היה מיחדים את החתן ואת הכלה שעה אחת קודם כניסתן לחופה כדי שיהיה לבו גס בה ובגליל לא היו עושים כן. ביהודה בראשונה היה מעמידים להם שני שושבינים אחד לו ואחד לה כדי למשמש את החתן ואת הכלה בשעת כניסתן לחופה פי' למשמש ולפשפש באותו הלילה במעשיהן שלא יקלקלו זה על זה שלא יראה זה דם בתולים ויאבד וזו תביא מפה שיש עלי' טפת דם ובגליל לא היו עושים כן. פי' גם ביהודה הי' מקומות שלא היו מיחדין. ושם היו מעמידים שושבינין דאי במקום שהיו מייחדים לא יועילו שושבינין שהרי אין שם טענת בתולים. ביהודה בראשונה היו שושבינים ישנים בבית שחתן וכלה ישנים בו ובגליל לא היו עושים כן. וכל שלא נהג כמנהג זה אינו יכול לטעון טענות בתולים. שהרי נתיחד עמה. אבל נהג מנהג גליל ולא נתייחד יכול לטעון ואע"פ שלא היו שם שושבינים יכול לטעון ומהימן ורב אשי פי' כל שלא משמש ביהודה אינו יכול לטעון פי' כיון שביהודה ממשמשים והוא לא משמש אמרי' לכתחלה עשה כדי להעליל עלילה עלי' אבל בגליל שלא נהגו מצי טעין אע"פ שלא משמש. ושמואל דאמר נאמן להפסידה כתובתה בטענת פתח פתוח דליכא למיקם עלה דמלתא להתברר ע"י שושבינים. וכגון שהיתה בוגרת שכלו בתוליה או אם היתה ממשפחת דורקטי אבל בטענות דמים אם נהגו למשמש ולא משמש אינו נאמן ובמקום שלא נהגו למשמש נאמן:

עין משפט נר מצוה

עד א מיי' פ"א מהל' אישות הלכה ח סמג עשין מח טוש"ע אה"ע סימן סח סעיף א:
עה ב טוש"ע שם ס"ג:

מסורת הש"ס

א) [לעיל ט:], ב) [תוספתא פרק א], ג) [במשנה שבמשניות ליתא כהן], ד) נ"ל אברייתא.

תוספות ישנים

א) [רב אשי אומר תני כל שלא מושמש. אומר רבינו יצחק בן רבינו מאיר דרב אשי פליג ארב נחמן דלית ליה מוקי דאין אדם עושה כו' כדפי' לעיל. ור"ם אומר דלא פליג דדוקא ביהודה שנהגו למשמש ומירע שלא משמש אינו יכול לטעון דדומה לדבר ברמאות בגלגל שלא מישמשוהו ולכן משמע קצת דהא קתני ביהודה אינו יכול לטעון אבל בגליל מצי טוען כדדייק לעיל אע"ג בגליל לא היו ממשמשין בברייתא ומיהו יש לפרש הא בגליל מצי טוען היינו היכא שמישמשוהו ואע"ג צריך לפרש כן למאי דדייק לעיל לא דקא טוען טענת דמים ולא אמרי' מוקי דאין אדם עושה כו'].

ליקוטי רש"י

האוכל אצל חמיו. בימים שבין אירוסין לנשואין. אינו יכול לטעון טענת בתולים. כשתכנס לחופה. מפני שמתייחד עמה. ביהודה היו מייחדים החתן והכלה קודם כניסתן לחופה כדי שיהא לבו גס בה [יבמות מה.]. כדי שיהא לבו גס בה. כלומר רגיל ומלמח עמה שלא יהו בושין זה מזה בכניסתן מלוה הלכך חיישינן דלמא בעיל [יבמות מה.]. רגיל בה ומרוצה לה [עירובין מו:]. למשמש את החתן ואת הכלה. לבקר אחריהם שלא ינהגו בה רמאות בטענת בתולים [לעיל ז:].

חשק שלמה על תוס' רי"ד

א) נ"ל וכמורה פירש. ור"ל דרש"י ז"ל פירש.

An Amora draws an inference from this Baraisa:

אָמַר רַבָּה – **Rabbah said:** זאת אומֶרֶת כְּנָסָהּ בְּחֶזְקַת בְּתוּלָה וְנִמְצֵאת בְּעוּלָה – **This** Baraisa **teaches that if one married [a woman] on the presumption that she was a virgin but she was found to be a nonvirgin,** יֵשׁ לָהּ כְּתוּבָּה מָנֶה – **she receives a *kesubah* of a *maneh*.**[1]

The inference is refuted:

רַב אַשִׁי אָמַר – **Rav Ashi said:** בְּעָלְמָא לְעוֹלָם אֵימָא לָךְ לֵית לָהּ כְּלָל – **Actually, I could tell you that in general** [i.e. in regard to the standard case of a woman wed on the presumption of being a virgin but found to be a nonvirgin] **she receives nothing at all.** וְשָׁאנֵי הָכָא שֶׁהֲרֵי כְּנָסָהּ רִאשׁוֹן – **And here it is different, because the first [husband]** already **brought her in** to the *chuppah.* The second husband should therefore have realized that she might no longer be a virgin.[2]

The Gemara raises a question concerning the Baraisa:

וְנֵיחוּשׁ שֶׁמָּא תַּחְתָּיו זִינְּתָה – **But let us be concerned that she committed adultery while under him** [i.e. during *erusin*] and became forbidden to him. Why, then, does the Baraisa state that the groom may not lodge a complaint concerning her virginity, implying that he need not go to court? He should be *encouraged* to do so, so that the matter becomes publicized and if there are witnesses somewhere who know that she committed adultery, they will hear of the case and come forward.[3] – ? –

The Gemara answers:

אָמַר רַב שֵׁרַבְיָא – **Rav Sheravya said:** כְּגוֹן שֶׁקִּידֵּשׁ וּבָעַל לְאַלְתַּר – The Baraisa refers to **a case where he betrothed** her **and cohabited immediately** thereafter.[4]

The Gemara presents a different version of the aforementioned exchange:

וְאִיכָּא דְּמַתְנֵי לָהּ אַמַּתְנִיתִין – **Some teach [this exchange]** as having occurred **in regard to our Mishnah:** בְּתוּלָה אַלְמָנָה גְּרוּשָׁה חֲלוּצָה – A VIRGIN WIDOW, DIVORCEE OR *CHALUTZAH* מִן הַנִּישּׂוּאִין – FROM *NISUIN* – כְּתוּבָּתָן מָנֶה – THEIR *KESUBAH* IS A *MANEH,* וְאֵין לָהֶן טַעֲנַת בְּתוּלִין – AND NO CLAIM CONCERNING their VIRGINITY CAN BE MADE AGAINST THEM. בְּתוּלָה מִן הַנִּישּׂוּאִין הֵיכִי מַשְׁכַּחַתְּ לָהּ – Now **how is** the case of **a virgin from *nisuin* found?** כְּגוֹן שֶׁנִּכְנְסָה לַחוּפָּה וְלֹא נִבְעֲלָה – Obviously, **where she entered the *chuppah*** with her first husband **but did not cohabit** with him.

An inference is drawn from this Mishnah:

אָמַר רַבָּה – **Rabbah said:** זאת אומֶרֶת כְּנָסָהּ בְּחֶזְקַת בְּתוּלָה וְנִמְצֵאת בְּעוּלָה – **This teaches that if one married [a woman] on the presumption that she was a virgin but she was found to be a nonvirgin,** כְּתוּבָּתָהּ מָנֶה – **her *kesubah* is a *maneh*.**

The inference is refuted:

רַב אַשִׁי אָמַר – **Rav Ashi said:** לְעוֹלָם אֵימָא לָךְ בְּעָלְמָא לֵית לָהּ כְּלָל – **Actually I could tell you that in general** [i.e. in the standard case of a woman wed on the presumption of being a virgin but found to be a nonvirgin] **she receives nothing at all.** וְשָׁאנֵי הָכָא שֶׁהֲרֵי נִכְנְסָה לַחוּפָּה – **And here it is different, because she** already **entered into the *chuppah*.**

The Gemara raises a question about the Mishnah:

וְלֵיחוּשׁ שֶׁמָּא תַּחְתָּיו זִינְּתָה – **But let us be concerned that she committed adultery while under him** and became prohibited to him. – ? –

The Gemara answers:

אָמַר רַב שֵׁרַבְיָא – **Rav Sheravya said:** כְּגוֹן שֶׁקִּידֵּשׁ וּבָעַל לְאַלְתַּר – The Baraisa refers to **a case where he betrothed** her **and cohabited immediately** thereafter.

The Gemara compares the two versions of this exchange:

מַאן דְּמַתְנֵי לָהּ אַבָּרַיְיתָא – **The one who teaches** the exchange between Rabbah and Rav Ashi **in reference to the Baraisa** כָּל שֶׁכֵּן אַמַּתְנִיתִין – would **certainly** apply it **to the Mishnah** as well.[5] וּמַאן דְּמַתְנֵי לָהּ אַמַּתְנִיתִין – **However the one who teaches** it **in reference to the Mishnah** could say it is relevant only there, אֲבָל אַבָּרַיְיתָא לֹא – **but not to the Baraisa,** מִשּׁוּם דְּמָצֵי אָמַר לָהּ אֲנָא אַעֵדִים סָמְכִי – **because [the groom] can say to her, "I was relying on the witnesses."**[6]

NOTES

1. For the new husband certainly relied on the testimony of the witnesses that the marriage was not consummated, yet the Baraisa states that he cannot lodge a complaint against her to deprive her of the *maneh* to which a widow is entitled (*Rashi*).

[According to this inference of Rabbah, when the Baraisa gives the reason for the husband's not being able to lodge a claim of virginity as being "because the first husband already brought her in," it means that even were he to lodge a claim, his claim would be meaningless, since having been married before, the bride's *kesubah* is in any case only that of a nonvirgin. A claim concerning virginity is effective only to reduce a *kesubah* from that of a virgin to that of a nonvirgin (i.e. from two hundred *zuz* to a *maneh* [one hundred *zuz*]), not to reduce it from a *maneh* to less than a *maneh* (*Tosafos*).]

2. See 11b note 36.

3. By ruling that the second husband has no claim of virginity, the Baraisa implies that there is no requirement for him to come to court to report that he did not find her a virgin. But in truth we should *want* him to come to court, so that word of his claim will go out, and if any witnesses know that she did in fact commit adultery they will come forward, thereby saving the husband from the sin of living with a woman who is forbidden to him (*Rashi,* as understood by *Re'ah; Pnei Yehoshua* in his comments to *Rashi* and *Tosafos* ד״ה וניחוש; cf. variant explanations of *Rashi* in *Rashba, Ritva* and *Tos. HaRosh*).

[*Rashi* adds that this question poses no difficulty to those who ruled above that if someone married a woman under the presumption that she was a virgin and she was found to be a nonvirgin she still receives a *kesubah* (which would imply that we assume that the cohabitation took place before *erusin,* since if it occurred after *erusin* she would be considered an adulteress and forfeit her *kesubah*), because there they did not say that the husband "cannot raise a claim." Rather, they said that he has to pay her *kesubah,* which could mean that if the husband did come to court but the woman produced witnesses that the cohabitation took place before the *erusin,* she still receives a *maneh.* But the Baraisa under question states that the husband *is unable to make a claim,* which implies that it is not necessary for him to come to court at all.]

4. He did not leave her from the time he betrothed her until they cohabited (*Rashi*). There is therefore no concern that she committed adultery after the betrothal and became prohibited to him

5. If in the case of the Baraisa, where even though witnesses assured the groom that his bride had not been secluded with her first husband, so that he married her on the presumption that she was a virgin, Rav Ashi still told Rabbah that he had no proof that a woman married on the presumption of being a virgin but found to be a nonvirgin receives a *kesubah,* because she (the woman discussed in the Baraisa) already entered the *chuppah* [and the new groom should have realized that she may have cohabited with the first husband], then in the case of our Mishnah, where no witnesses assured the groom of his bride's virginity, surely Rav Ashi would say this, because the groom had even less basis for assuming her to be a virgin (*Rashi*).

6. Since in the case of the Baraisa the groom had strong reason to assume that his bride was a virgin, and she is nevertheless awarded her *kesubah,* Rabbah can indeed infer that in any case where someone married a woman under the false presumption that she was a virgin, she still receives the *kesubah* of a nonvirgin. Rav Ashi could not counter that here it is different because she was previously married, since the witnesses attesting to her virginity made that fact meaningless (*Rashi*).

As stated in 11b note 33, the halachah is that a woman married on the presumption that she is a virgin but who is found to be a nonvirgin receives no *kesubah* at all. Evidently, the halachah assumes that the exchange between Rabbah and Rav Ashi occurred in regard to the Baraisa as well (*Ritva*).

Having concluded its citation of the Amoraic exchange regarding the Baraisa, the Gemara returns to its original point, which is to prove that Rava retracted his earlier ruling:

וְהָא רָבָא הוּא דְּאָמַר לְרַבָּנָן – **But it was Rava** himself **who said according to the Rabbis** לֹא הִכִּיר בָּהּ וְלֹא כְלוּם – that if **[the groom] did not recognize her** to be a wood-injury victim she receives **nothing at all.**[33] אֶלָּא שְׁמַע מִינָּהּ הֲדַר בֵּיהּ רָבָא מֵהַהִיא – **Rather, conclude from this that Rava retracted that** ruling.[34]

The Gemara cites further Amoraic discussion concerning a woman who was wed on the presumption that she is a virgin but was found to be a nonvirgin:

תָּנוּ רַבָּנָן – **The Rabbis taught in a Baraisa:** כְּנָסָהּ רִאשׁוֹן לְשׁוּם נִישּׂוּאִין – IF THE FIRST [HUSBAND] BROUGHT HER IN to the *chuppah* FOR THE SAKE OF performing *NISUIN* וְיֵשׁ לָהּ עֵדִים שֶׁלֹּא נִסְתְּרָה – BUT SHE HAS WITNESSES THAT SHE WAS NOT SECLUDED with him, אִי נַמִּי נִסְתְּרָה וְלֹא שָׁהֲתָה כְּדֵי בִּיאָה – OR the witnesses say that SHE WAS SECLUDED with him BUT DID NOT STAY AS LONG AS NECESSARY FOR COHABITATION,[35] אֵין הַשֵּׁנִי יָכוֹל לִטְעוֹן טַעֲנַת בְּתוּלִים – THE SECOND [HUSBAND] CAN nevertheless NOT LODGE A CLAIM CONCERNING her VIRGINITY, שֶׁהֲרֵי כְּנָסָהּ רִאשׁוֹן – BECAUSE THE FIRST [HUSBAND] HAS already BROUGHT HER IN.[36]

NOTES

33. Whereas here he emends the Baraisa to read, "If she *is found* to be a wood-injury victim," which implies that the husband did not initially recognize her condition, "she has a *kesubah* of a *maneh.*" And Rava must be saying this according to the view of the Rabbis, because R' Meir definitely maintains that she receives two hundred *zuz,* as explained in note 17 (*Rashi*).

34. According to this conclusion, which the halachah follows, a wood-injury victim receives a *kesubah* of a *maneh* whether or not the groom recognized her condition. If, however, he married a woman on the presumption that she was a virgin and she was then discovered to be a non-virgin (i.e. she had cohabited with someone else before *erusin*), she loses her entire *kesubah* (see *Rif* and *Rosh*).

35. For the definition of the term "as long as necessary for cohabitation," see *Sotah* 4a.

[This case constitutes a novelty over the corresponding one in the Mishnah. In the case in the Mishnah someone married a widow or divorcee on the *presumption* that she had not cohabited with her first husband (because he had died or divorced her so soon after the *chuppah*). Here, however, the Baraisa refers to where *witnesses testified* that cohabitation did not take place (see *Rashi*).]

36. The second husband cannot claim that, based on the witnesses' testimony, he was fully expecting her to be a virgin and, now that she was found to be a non-virgin, his acquisition should be deemed to have been made in error, thereby absolving him from having to pay her any *kesubah.* Rather, he should have realized that she [could very well have] cohabited with her first husband *(Rashi)*, for no witnesses can guarantee that a couple who is permitted to cohabit did not in fact do so (*Shitah LeRan;* cf. *Tosafos* below, 12a ד״ה שאני; *Ramban*).

עין משפט
נר מצוה

ע א מיי' פי"א מהל' אישות הל"א טוש"ע אה"ע סי' סז סעי' ג:
עא ב מי' שם הל"ג טוש"ע שם סעי' ד:
עב ג ד מיי' שם טוש"ע שם סעי' ה:
עג ה טוש"ע שם סעי' ב:

גליון הש"ם

גמ' ואמר רבא מאן דקא מותיב שפיר. שבת קכג ע"ב ר"ה ו נ"ב:

תוספות ישנים

א) ועוד י"ל דניחא ליה טפי דלרבנן לא הכיר בה מנה דהשתא מיתוקמא מתני' ובריתא נמי כרבנן. ת"י עה"ג:

ליקוטי רש"י

משארסתני. אירע לי ואית לי מאפים [לקמן טז.]. ונסתחפה שדהו. לשון מטר סוחף (משלי כח) נשטפה שדך כלומר מזלך גרם [לעיל ב.]. נסחף, נשטף והחליקו גבוריך כמו מטר סוחף (משלי כח) נסתחפה שדהו בלשון משנה ומנחם חברו לשון כלין וכן חבר מטר סחף דונש פתר מטר סוחף כמו מטר סועף כמו מסעף פארה במערצה (ישעיה י) [ירמיה מו, טו]. סחף, סוטף ובמשנה נסתחפה שדהו וכן נסחף אביריך (ירמיה מו) נשטפו העדו וכשלו [משלי כח, ג].

ואין להן טענת בתולים [א] הגיורת והשבויה והשפחה שנפדו ושנתגיירו ושנשתחררו יתירות על בנות שלש שנים ויום אחד כתובתן מנה ואין להן טענת בתולין: **גמ'** אמר רב יהודה אמר רב קטן הבא על הגדולה עשאה מוכת עץ כי אמריתה קמיה דשמואל אמר [ב] אין מוכת עץ בבשר איכא דמתני לה להא שמעתא באפי נפשה קטן הבא על הגדולה רב אמר עשאה מוכת עץ ושמואל אמר אין מוכת עץ בבשר מתיב רב אושעיא גדול שבא על הקטנה וקטן הבא על הגדולה ומוכת עץ כתובתן מאתים דברי ר"מ וחכמים אומרים מוכת עץ כתובתה מנה אמר רבא הכי קאמר גדול הבא על הקטנה ולא כלום [ו] דפחות מכאן כנותן אצבע בעין דמי וקטן הבא על הגדולה עשאה מוכת עץ ומוכת עץ גופא פלוגתא דר"מ ורבנן אמר רמי בר חמא [ג] מחלוקת כשהכיר בה דר"מ מדמי לה לבוגרת ורבנן מדמו לה לבעולה אבל לא הכיר בה דברי הכל ולא כלום ור"מ אמאי מדמי לה לבוגרת נדמייה לבעולה בעולה איתעביד בה מעשה בידי אדם הא לא איתעביד בה מעשה בידי אדם ורבנן אדמדמו לה לבעולה נדמייה לבוגרת בוגרת לא איתעביד בה מעשה כלל הא איתעביד בה מעשה אבל לא הכיר בה לדברי הכל ולא כלום מתיב רב נחמן [ד] היא אומרת מוכת עץ אני והוא אומר לא כי אלא דרוסת איש את ר"ג ור' אליעזר אומרים נאמנת אלא אמר רבא בין הכיר בה ובין לא הכיר בה לר"מ מאתים לרבנן הכיר בה מנה לא הכיר בה ולא כלום והדר ביה רבא דתניא כיצד [ז] הוצאת שם רע בא לבית דין ואמר פלוני לא מצאתי לבתך בתולים אם יש עדים שזינתה תחתיו יש לה כתובה מנה אם יש עדים שזינתה תחתיו בת סקילה היא הכי קאמר אם יש עדים שזינתה תחתיו בסקילה זינתה מעיקרא יש לה כתובה מנה [ח] ואמר רב חייא בר אבין אמר רב ששת זאת אומרת כנסה בחזקת בתולה ונמצאת בעולה יש לה כתובה מנה ומתיב רב נחמן [ט] הנושא את האשה ולא מצא לה בתולים היא אומרת משארסתני נאנסתי ונסתחפה שדהו והוא אומר לא כי אלא עד שלא אירסתיך והיה מקחי מקח טעות ולית לה כלל ואמר להו רב חייא בר אבין אפשר רב עמרם וכל גדולי הדור יתבי כי אמר רב ששת להא שמעתא וקשיא להו ושני מאי מקח טעות נמי ממאתים אבל מנה אית לה ואת אמרת לית לה כלל [י] ואמר רבא מאן דקא מותיב שפיר קא מותיב [ג] מקח טעות לגמרי משמע ואלא קשיא הך תריץ ואימא הכי אם יש עדים שזינתה תחתיו בסקילה זינתה מעיקרא ולא כלום [ד] נמצאת מוכת עץ יש לה כתובה מנה והא רבא הוא דאמר לרבנן לא הכיר בה ולא כלום אלא ש"מ הדר ביה רבא מההיא ת"ר כנסה ראשון לשום נישואין [ה] ויש לה עדים שלא נסתרה אי נמי נסתרה ולא שהתה כדי ביאה אין השני יכול לטעון טענת בתולים שהרי כנסה ראשון אמר

ושמואל אמר אין מוכת עץ בבשר. בלא השיר בתולין איירי דאי בהשיר למה יש לה להיות פחותה ממוכת עץ: **לרבנן** הכיר בה מנה לא הכיר בה ולא כלום. ומתני' ר"מ היא ולא רבנן ואם תאמר אמאי לא קאמר לרבנן בין הכיר בה בין לא הכיר בה מנה כדקאמר במסקנא ותיתי מתניתין לדברי הכל וי"ל דלא ניחא ליה למימר הכי דכיון דרבנן מדמו לה לבעולה הויא בלא הכיר בה כמו כנסה בחזקת בתולה ונמצאת בעולה וסבירא ליה דלית לה ולא כלום ובמסקנא סבר הא דמדמו לה לבעולה היינו לענין מנה אבל מקח טעות לא הויא כמו בעולה דאינו מקפיד כ"כ במוכת עץ שיהא מקח טעות: **הדר** ביה רבא מההיא. אבל מהא לא בעי למימר דהדר ביה משום דמקח טעות לגמרי משמע וא"ת מנא לן דהדר ביה ממה שאמר לרבנן לא הכיר בה ולא כלום נאמר שחזר בו ממה שאמר לא הכיר בה לר"מ מאתים אלא נפרש לא הכיר בה מנה ונוקי ברייתא כרבי מאיר וי"ל כדפי' לעיל בקונטרס דאין זה סברא דאי חשיב מקח טעות לא יהא לה כלום ואי לא חשיב מקח טעות למה לא יהא לה מאתים כיון דמדמה לה לבוגרת דאטו לבוגרת פוחתין לה מכתובתה א):

ואין להן טענת בתולין. אין יכול להפסידה אותה מנה ולומר בחזקת בתולה נשאתיך והרי מקחי מקח טעות: **גמ' עשאה מוכת עץ.** נהי דאין ביאתו ביאה מיהו לא גרע מעץ הנתקע ולרבנן דפליגי אמוכת עץ כתובתה מנה וכן לענין כהן גדול דתנן (יבמות דף נט.) לא ישא את מוכת עץ הא נמי אסירא ליה: **אין מוכת עץ בבשר אדם.** ואי בעולה לא הויא מוכת עץ נמי ליתא: **באפי נפשה.** בלא גברי דלא אמר רב יהודה משמיה דרב ומשמיה דשמואל אלא אינהו גופייהו איפלוג בה: **וקטן שבא על הגדולה ומוכת עץ.** ומדפלגינהו תנא לתרתי ולא איפלוג רבנן אלא במוכת עץ שמעת מינה אין מוכת עץ בבשר: **הכי קאמר גדול הבא על הקטנה ולא כלום.** אינה ביאה לדברי הכל הלכך כתובתה מאתים ולא איפלוג רבנן עלה דפחות מכאן כנותן אצבע בעין דתנן במסכת נדה (דף מד:) גבי בת פחותה מג' שנים ויום אחד מה הדמעה היוצאת ע"י אצבע באה אחרת תחתיה אף בתולים של פחות מכן חוזרין אחרים תחתיהם: **וקטן שבא על הגדולה.** מוכת עץ היא זו וכתובתה מאתים דברי רבי מאיר וחכמים אומרים כל מוכת עץ כתובתה מנה והא נמי דקא משוית לה מוכת עץ כתובתה מנה: **כשהכיר בה.** כשכנסה וכתב לה כתובה היה יודע שהיא מוכת עץ: **מדמי לה לבוגרת.** דקיימא לן שכלו בתוליה במס' יבמות (דף נט.) דקתני בבתוליה פרט לבוגרת שכלו בתוליה ואפי' הכי כתובתה מאתים: **ולא כלום.** דמקח טעות הוא ואפי' מנה אין לה: **היא אומרת מוכת עץ אני.** משנתנו היא: **והוא אומר לא כי אלא דרוסת איש את.** הנושא את האשה בחזקת בתולה ולא מצא לה בתולים היא אומרת מוכת עץ אני ולא כו' ש"מ אית לה כתובה או מנה או מאתים דאי לית לה מאי נאמנת דקאמר רבן גמליאל אלמא מוכת עץ שלא הכיר בה יש לה כתובה תיובתא דרמי בר חמא דאמר לא הכיר בה דברי הכל ולא כלום: **אלא אמר רבא לר"מ בין הכיר בה בין לא הכיר בה מאתים.** ומתני' דקתני היא אומרת מוכת עץ אני וקא תבעה מאתים רבי מאיר היא: **לרבנן הכיר בה מנה.** ומתני' דהכא דקתני וחכמים אומרים מוכת עץ מנה כשהכיר בה: **לא הכיר בה ולא כלום.** והא לא מצינו למימר לר' מאיר הכיר בה מאתים לא הכיר בה מנה דאי במקח טעות מחזקינן ליה משום דלא הכיר בה לית לה מידי ואי לאו מקח טעות הוא אין חילוק בין הכיר ללא הכיר: **והדר ביה רבא** גר' ול"ג מההיא. והדר ביה רבא ממאי דאמר לרבנן לא הכיר בה ולא כלום אלא בין הכיר בין לא הכיר יש לה מנה לרבנן ומאתים לר"מ ומתני' דהתם דברי הכל: **הוצאת שם רע.** ליענש מאה כסף אם שקר וליסקל אם אמת היה: **בא לב"ד.** זקוק לבוא לב"ד ולומר כו': **ואמר רב חייא** גרסי': **ומותיב רב נחמן** גר': **נסתחפה שדהו.** מזלך גרם כאדם שהמטר בא וסוחף את זריעתו ועוקרה: **מקח טעות לגמרי משמע.** ואין לה כלום: **כי אמרה רב ששת להא שמעתתא.** להאי זאת אומרת דלעיל דיש לה כתובה מנה: **וקשיא להו.** הא דאותבינן: **ואמר רבא** גרסי': **ואלא קשיא הך.** ואקשינן לרבא אלא קשיא הך דלעיל דקתני זינתה מעיקרא יש לה כתובה מנה: **תריץ.** להדיא דלעיל דכולך הואיל וש"ר תירוצא דתרצת לה לא תתרצה הכי אלא הכי אם יש עדים כו': **נמצאת.** לא הכיר בה משמע וקא מתרץ רבא יש לה כתובה מנה אלמא הדר ביה מההיא דלעיל דהא איהו אמר לרבנן ולא כלום וכרבי מאיר נמי לא תוקמה דהא רבי מאיר מאתים קאמר: **ויש לה עדים שלא נסתרה.** רבותא אשמעינן דאפי' הכי אין השני יכול לטעון טענת בתולים להפסידה כתובתה ולימא מקח טעות הוא: **שהרי כנסה ראשון.** ועליו לדעת שנבעלה:
זאת

מסורת הש"ס

א) [נדה מד:], ב) [לקמן יג.], ג) לקמן יג. [טז.], ד) לקמן מו., ה) [לקמן יג.], ו) [לקמן יב: טז.].

תוספות רי"ד

איתמר קטן שבא על הגדולה רב אמר עשאה מוכת עץ. פי' דכיון שהוציא בתוליה אע"ג שאין ביאתו ביאה לא גרע מעץ הנתקע וכתובתה מנה לרבנן ושמואל אמר אין מוכת עץ בבשר פי' בבשר אדם. ואי בעולה לא הויא מוכת עץ נמי לא הויא והרי היא כאילו מיעכה היא באצבעה שהממעכת בתוליה באצבעה לא הפסידה מאתים דדוקא דרוסת איש ומוכת עץ לרבנן הפסידה המאתים אבל במיעוך לא הפסידה המאתים כיון שאין כוונתה אלא שלא להצטער תחת בעלה ובמוכת עץ דפליגי רבנן משום דהוי שלא לדעתה ומיסניא בהכי. אמרי' בפ' ד' אחין כל הני מיעכות של בית ר' תמר שמן וקי"ל כשמואל בדיני: **אמר רמב"ח** מחלוקת כשהכיר בה. פי' כשכנסה וכתב לה כתובה היה יודע שהיא מוכת עץ דר"מ מדמי לה לבוגרת פי' דקי"ל דכלו בתוליה ואפ"ה כתובתן מאתים ורבנן מדמו לה לבעולה ור"מ אדמדמי לה לבוגרת לדמו לה לבעולה בעולה איתעביד בה מעשה (בוגרת) [בידי אדם הא] לא איתעביד בה מעשה ורבנן אדמדמו לה לבעולה לדמו לה לבוגרת בוגרת לא איתעביד בה מעשה כלל הא איתעביד בה מעשה. אבל לא הכיר בה ד"ה ולא כלום פי' שמקח טעות הוא. ורבא אסיק דבין הכיר בה ובין לא הכיר בה לר"מ כתובתה מאתים לרבנן כתובתה מנה. וקי"ל כרבנן ולא כר"מ דיחיד ורבים הלכה כרבים: **מתני' בתולה** אלמנה גרושה וחלוצה מן הנשואין כתובתן מנה ואין להן טענת בתולים. הגיורת והשבויה והשפחה שנפדו ושנתגיירו ושנשתחררו יתירות על ג' שנים ויום א' כתובתן מנה ואין להן טענת בתולים. פי' בתולה מן הנשואין וכגון שנכנסה לחופה ומת בעלה בחזקת בעולה קיימא משעה שנכנסה תחתיו וכתובתה מנה אם נשאת לאחר מכאן ואין להם טענת בתולים להפסידה אותה מנה ולומר בחזקת בתולה נשאתיך והרי מקחי מקח טעות: **תנו רבנן** כנסה הראשון לשם נשואין ויש לה עדים שלא נסתרה או שנסתרה אלא שלא שהתה עמו כדי ביאה אין השני יכול לטעון טענת בתולים פי' להפסידה מנה הראוי לאלמנה מן הנשואין שהרי כנסה הראשון. ואע"פ שהעדים מעידין אינו יכול לטעון.
אמר

HOW does the case of DEFAMATION take place?[20] בָּא לְבֵית דִּין וְאָמַר – [THE GROOM] COMES TO COURT[21] AND SAYS to the bride's father, פְּלוֹנִי לֹא מָצָאתִי לְבִתְּךָ בְּתוּלִים – "SO AND SO, I DID NOT FIND YOUR DAUGHTER TO POSSESS signs of VIRGINITY!" אִם יֵשׁ עֵדִים שֶׁזִּינְּתָה תַּחְתָּיו יֵשׁ לָהּ כְּתוּבָּה מָנֶה – IF THERE ARE WITNESSES THAT SHE STRAYED WHILE UNDER HIM [i.e. she cohabited with another man after *erusin*], SHE RECEIVES A *KESUBAH* OF A *MANEH*.

The Gemara asks, incredulously:

אִם יֵשׁ עֵדִים שֶׁזִּינְּתָה תַּחְתָּיו בַּת סְקִילָה הִיא – **If there are witnesses that she strayed while under him,** she receives a *kesubah* of a *maneh*?! Why, **she is** an adulteress and **liable to stoning!**[22] – ? –

The Gemara emends the Baraisa:

הָכִי קָאָמַר – **This is what [the Baraisa] is saying:** אִם יֵשׁ עֵדִים שֶׁזִּינְּתָה תַּחְתָּיו בִּסְקִילָה – **If there are witnesses that she strayed while under him, she is liable to stoning.** זִינְּתָה מֵעִיקָּרָא יֵשׁ לָהּ כְּתוּבָּה מָנֶה – But if **she strayed beforehand,** i.e. prior to *erusin,* **she receives a *kesubah* of a *maneh*.**

Having explained the Baraisa, the Gemara cites an Amoraic discussion regarding it:

וְאָמַר רַב חִיָּיא בַּר אָבִין אָמַר רַב שֵׁשֶׁת – **And Rav Chiya bar Avin said in the name of Rav Sheishess:** זֹאת אוֹמֶרֶת – **This teaches** כְּנָסָהּ בְּחֶזְקַת בְּתוּלָה וְנִמְצֵאת בְּעוּלָה – that **if one married [a woman] on the presumption that she was a virgin but she was found to be a nonvirgin** [i.e. it was discovered that she had cohabited with another man before the *erusin*], יֵשׁ לָהּ כְּתוּבָּה מָנֶה – **she receives a *kesubah* of a *maneh*.**[23]

This ruling is questioned:

וּמָתִיב רַב נַחְמָן – **And Rav Nachman challenged** this **from a Mishnah:**[24] הַנּוֹשֵׂא אֶת הָאִשָּׁה וְלֹא מָצָא לָהּ בְּתוּלִים – Consider the case of ONE WHO MARRIES A WOMAN AND DOES NOT FIND HER TO POSSESS signs of VIRGINITY. הִיא אוֹמֶרֶת מִשֶּׁאֵרַסְתַּנִי נֶאֱנַסְתִּי וְנִסְתַּחֲפָה שָׂדֵהוּ – SHE SAYS, "AFTER YOU BETROTHED ME I WAS VIOLATED, AND this is a case of '[THE BUYER'S] FIELD WAS INUNDATED,' "[25] וְהוּא אוֹמֵר לֹא כִּי אֶלָּא עַד שֶׁלֹּא אֵירַסְתִּיךְ וְהָיָה מִקָּחִי מִקַּח טָעוּת – AND HE SAYS, "Perhaps it is NOT SO, RATHER the cohabitation occurred BEFORE I BETROTHED YOU, AND MY ACQUISITION WAS AN ACQUISITION MADE IN ERROR." וְלֵית לָהּ כְּלָל – **Now** the Mishnah implies that according to the groom **she does not have any** claim to a *kesubah* **at all.**[26] – ? –

The question is rejected:

וְאָמַר לְהוּ רַב חִיָּיא בַּר אָבִין – **And Rav Chiya bar Avin said to [Rav Nachman]:**[27] אֶפְשָׁר רַב עַמְרָם וְכָל גְּדוֹלֵי הַדּוֹר יָתְבֵי כִּי אָמַר רַב שֵׁשֶׁת לְהָא שְׁמַעְתָּא – **Is it possible that Rav Amram and all the greats of the generation were sitting** there **when Rav Sheishess stated that teaching,**[28] וְקַשְׁיָא לְהוּ – **and they found it difficult** for the very same reason as you (i.e. it seemingly contradicts the Mishnah on 12b), וְשַׁנִּי – **and [Rav Sheishess] answered** them: מַאי מִקַּח טָעוּת נַמִּי מִמָּאתַיִם – **"What** does the Mishnah mean by **'an acquisition made in error'? Indeed** that she is deprived **of two hundred** *zuz,* אֲבָל מָנֶה אִית לָהּ – **but she does receive a *maneh*,"** וְאַתְּ אָמְרַתְּ לֵית לָהּ כְּלָל – **and you say that** the Mishnah implies that **she receives nothing at all?**[29]

Rava defends Rav Nachman:

וְאָמַר רָבָא – **But Rava said:** מַאן דְּקָא מוֹתִיב שַׁפִּיר קָא מוֹתִיב – **The one that challenged, challenged well.** מִקַּח טָעוּת לְגַמְרֵי מַשְׁמַע – For the expression **"an acquisition made in error"** used by the husband in the Mishnah **implies** that he claims to be **completely** exempt from any payment. Obviously, then, if a nonvirgin is betrothed on the presumption that she is a virgin, she loses her entire *kesubah* – in contradiction to Rav Chiya bar Avin's ruling.

The Gemara asks:

וְאֶלָּא קַשְׁיָא הָךְ – **But then [the above-cited Baraisa]** about the defamer **is difficult,** because it states that if she strayed before the *erusin* she receives a *kesubah* of a *maneh*. – ? –

Rava resolves the problem by emending the Baraisa in a different way than that suggested above:[30]

תָּרִיץ וְאֵימָא הָכִי – **Emend** the Baraisa **and state** it **this way:** אִם יֵשׁ עֵדִים שֶׁזִּינְּתָה תַּחְתָּיו בִּסְקִילָה – **If there are witnesses that she strayed while under him, she is subject to stoning.** זִינְּתָה מֵעִיקָּרָא וְלֹא כְלוּם – If **she strayed beforehand,** i.e. before *erusin,* she receives **nothing at all.**[31] נִמְצֵאת מוּכַּת עֵץ יֵשׁ לָהּ כְּתוּבָּה מָנֶה – **If she is found to be a wood-injury victim, she receives a *kesubah* of a *maneh*.**[32]

NOTES

20. [הוֹצָאַת שֵׁם רַע, *defamation,* involves a groom who declares that he found his bride not to be a virgin when their marriage was consummated, and asserts, by producing witnesses, that she had committed adultery after they were legally married through *erusin.*] If his claim is found to be untrue [i.e. the witnesses are proven false], he must pay a fine of one hundred *shekels;* if it is substantiated, she is liable to death through stoning (*Rashi* ; see *Deuteronomy* 22:13-21).

21. [That is, the rules of a *defamer* do not apply unless he makes his claim in court (see *Rashi*).]

22. A woman who commits adultery during the *erusin* stage of marriage after being duly warned is stoned (*Deuteronomy* 22:20,21). Even if she was not warned, in which case she cannot be stoned, she certainly does not receive any *kesubah* money, for any woman who commits adultery forfeits her *kesubah* (*Ritva*).

23. The marriage is not considered an acquisition made in error, in which case she would receive no *kesubah* at all. Rather, she receives a *maneh,* just as would any other nonvirgin who marries. [This is similar to one who purchases an item and discovers that he was overcharged by a sixth, where the law is that the deal stands and the amount of the overcharge is refunded. Here too, we assume that the groom still wants the marriage, only he does not wish to be obligated to the same *kesubah* as for a virgin (see *R' Crescas* below ד״ה אלא אמר רבא).]

24. Below, 12b.

25. It is as though you purchased a field which was later flooded by torrential rains, uprooting all the crops. Here too, the calamity took place after I was your betrothed, and was a result of your bad fortune (*Rashi*).

26. The Mishnah seems to be stating that if the groom's claim is correct that he betrothed the bride under false pretenses, he should not have to pay her anything. This contradicts Rav Chiya bar Avin's ruling in the name of Rav Sheishess.

27. The translation follows *Rashash,* who emends לְהוּ to לֵיהּ.

28. I.e. the statement, "This Baraisa teaches us etc.," mentioned above (*Rashi*). [Rav Chiya bar Avin was present when Rav Sheishess made this statement, and testifies that it was made in the presence of Rav Amram and the other leading scholars of the generation.]

29. Rav Amram and all the Torah greats were willing to accept Rav Sheishess' answer that the Mishnah means that according to the husband's claim she receives one *maneh.* How, then, can you insist that it means she should not receive any *kesubah* at all?

30. As quoted originally, the Baraisa was untenable, and had to be emended by adding to it several words. It is this emended version that caused the problem, standing in contradiction to the Mishnah on 12b. Accordingly, Rava suggests that the Baraisa be emended in a different way, so as not to contradict the Mishnah.

31. As the Mishnah on 12b implies, because the marriage is an acquisition made in error.

32. The phrase "she receives a *kesubah* of a *maneh* " which appears in the Baraisa does not refer to a woman who strayed while under her husband (as the original version of the Baraisa had it), nor to a woman who strayed before the *erusin* (as the first emended version of the Baraisa would have it). Rather, it refers to a woman who was injured by a piece of wood.

ואין להן טענת בתולים [א] הגיורת והשבויה והשפחה שנפדו ושנתגיירו ושנשתחררו יתירות על בנות שלש שנים ויום אחד כתובתן מנה ואין להן טענת בתולין: **גמ׳** אמר רב יהודה אמר רב קטן הבא על הגדולה עשאה מוכת עץ כי אמריתה קמיה דשמואל אמר [ב] אין מוכת עץ בבשר איכא דמתני לה להא שמעתא באפי נפשה קטן הבא על הגדולה רב אמר עשאה מוכת עץ ושמואל אמר אין מוכת עץ בבשר מתיב רב אושעיא גדול שבא על הקטנה וקטן הבא על הגדולה ומוכת עץ כתובתן מאתים דברי ר״מ וחכמים אומרים מוכת עץ כתובתה מנה אמר רבא הכי קאמר גדול הבא על הקטנה ולא כלום [א] דפחות מכאן כנותן אצבע בעין דמי וקטן הבא על הגדולה עשאה מוכת עץ ומוכת עץ גופא פלוגתא דר״מ ורבנן אמר רמי בר חמא [ב] מחלוקת כשהכיר בה דר״מ מדמי לה לבוגרת ורבנן מדמו לה לבעולה אבל לא הכיר בה דברי הכל ולא כלום ור״מ אמאי מדמי לה לבוגרת נדמייה לבעולה בעולה איתעביד בה מעשה בידי אדם הא לא איתעביד בה מעשה בידי אדם ורבנן אדמדמו לה לבעולה נדמייה לבוגרת בוגרת לא איתעביד בה מעשה כלל הא איתעביד בה מעשה אבל לא הכיר בה לדברי הכל ולא כלום מתיב רב נחמן [ג] היא אומרת מוכת עץ אני והוא אומר לא כי אלא דרוסת איש את ר״ג ור׳ אליעזר אומרים נאמנת אלא אמר רבא בין הכיר בה ובין לא הכיר בה לר״מ מאתים לרבנן הכיר בה מנה לא הכיר בה ולא כלום והדר ביה רבא דתניא כיצד [ד] הוצאת שם רע בא לבית דין ואמר פלוני לא מצאתי לבתך בתולים אם יש עדים שזינתה תחתיו יש לה כתובה מנה אם יש עדים שזינתה תחתיו בת סקילה היא הכי קאמר אם יש עדים שזינתה תחתיו בסקילה זינתה מעיקרא יש לה כתובה מנה [ה] ואמר רב חייא בר אבין אמר רב ששת זאת אומרת כנסה בחזקת בתולה ונמצאת בעולה יש לה כתובה מנה ומתיב רב נחמן [ו] הנושא את האשה ולא מצא לה בתולים היא אומרת משארסתני נאנסתי ונסתחפה שדהו והוא אומר לא כי אלא עד שלא אירסתיך והיה מקחי מקח טעות ולית לה כלל ואמר להו רב חייא בר אבין אפשר רב עמרם וכל גדולי הדור יתבי כי אמר רב ששת להא שמעתא וקשיא להו ושני מאי מקח טעות נמי ממאתים אבל מנה אית לה ואת אמרת לית לה כלל ° ואמר רבא מאן דקא מותיב שפיר קא מותיב [ג] מקח טעות לגמרי משמע ואלא קשיא הך תריץ ואימא הכי אם יש עדים שזינתה תחתיו בסקילה זינתה מעיקרא ולא כלום [ד] נמצאת מוכת עץ יש לה כתובה מנה והא רבא הוא דאמר לרבנן לא הכיר בה ולא כלום אלא ש״מ הדר ביה רבא מההיא ת״ר כנסה ראשון לשום נישואין [ה] ויש לה עדים שלא נסתרה אי נמי נסתרה ולא שהתה כדי ביאה אין השני יכול לטעון טענת בתולים שהרי כנסה ראשון אמר

ואין להן טענת בתולין. אין יכול להפסידה אותה מנה ולומר בחזקת בתולה נשאתיך והרי מקחי מקח טעות: **גמ׳ עשאה מוכת עץ.** נהי דלאו ביאתו ביאה מיהו לא גרע מעץ הנתקע ולרבנן דפליגי אמוכת עץ כתובתה מנה וכן לענין כהן גדול דתנן (יבמות דף נט.) לא ישא את מוכת עץ הא נמי אסירא ליה: **אין מוכת עץ בבשר אדם.** ולאו בעולה לא הויא מוכת עץ נמי לא הויא: **באפי נפשה.** בלא גברי דלא אמר רב יהודה משמיה דרב ומשמיה דשמואל אלא איהו גופייהו איפלוג בה: **וקטן שבא על הגדולה ומוכת עץ.** ומדפלגינהו תנא לתרתי ולא איפלוג רבנן אלא במוכת עץ שמעת מינה אין מוכת עץ בבשר: **הכי קאמר גדול הבא על הקטנה ולא כלום.** אינה ביאה לדברי הכל הלכך כתובתה מאתים ולא איפלוג רבנן עלה דפחות מכאן כנותן אצבע בעין דתנן במסכת נדה (דף מה:) גבי בת פחותה מג׳ שנים ויום אחד מה הדמעה היוצאת ע״י אצבע בזה אחרת תחתיה אף בתולים של פחות מכן חוזרין אחרים תחתיהם: **וקטן שבא על הגדולה.** מוכת עץ היא זו וכתובתה מאתים דברי רבי מאיר וחכמים אומרים כל מוכת עץ כתובתה מנה והא נמי דקא משוית לה מוכת עץ כתובתה מנה: **כשהכיר בה.** כשכנסה וכתב לה כתובה היה יודע שהיא מוכת עץ: **מדמי לה לבוגרת.** דקיימא לן שכלו בתוליה במס׳ יבמות (דף נט.) דקתני בבתוליה פרט לבוגרת שכלו בתוליה ואפי׳ הכי כתובתה מאתים: **ולא כלום.** דמקח טעות הוא ואפי׳ מנה אין לה: **היא אומרת מוכת עץ אני.** משנתנו היא: **והוא אומר לא כי אלא דרוסת איש את.** הנושא את האשה בחזקת בתולה ולא מצא לה בתולים היא אומרת מוכת עץ אני ש״מ אית לה כתובה או מנה או מאתים דאי לית לה מאי נאמנת דקאמר רבן גמליאל אלמא מוכת עץ שלא הכיר בה יש לה כתובה תיובתא דרמי בר חמא דאמר לא הכיר בה דברי הכל ולא כלום: **אלא אמר רבא לר״מ בין הכיר בה בין לא הכיר בה מאתים.** ומתני׳ דקתני היא אומרת מוכת עץ אני וקא תבעה מאתים רבי מאיר היא: **לרבנן הכיר בה מנה.** ומתני׳ דהכא דקתני וחכמים אומרים מוכת עץ מנה כשהכיר בה: **לא הכיר בה ולא כלום.** והא לא מצינו למימר לר׳ מאיר הכיר בה מאתים לא הכיר בה מנה דלאו במקח טעות מחזקינן ליה משום דלא הכיר בה לית לה מידי ואי לאו מקח טעות הוא אין חילוק בין הכיר ללא הכיר: **והדר ביה רבא** גר׳ ול״ג מההיא. והדר ביה רבא ממאי דאמר לרבנן לא הכיר בה ולא כלום אלא בין הכיר בין לא הכיר יש לה מנה לרבנן ומאתים לר״מ ומתני׳ דהתם דברי הכל: **הוצאת שם רע.** ליענש מאה כסף אם שקר וליסקל אם אמת היה: **בא לב״ד.** זקוק לבוא לב״ד ולומר כו׳: **ואמר רב חייא** גרסי׳: **ומותיב רב נחמן** גר׳: **נסתחפה שדהו.** מזלך גרם כלשון שהמטר בא וסוחף את זרעיו ועוקרה: **מקח טעות לגמרי משמע.** ואין לה כלום: **כי אמרה רב ששת להא שמעתתא.** להאי זאת אומרת דלעיל דיש לה כתובה מנה: **וקשיא להו.** הא דאותבינן: **ואמר רבא** גרסי׳: **ואלא קשיא הך.** ואקשינן לרבא אלא קשיא הך דלעיל דקתני זינתה מעיקרא יש לה כתובה מנה: **תריץ.** להכיא דלעיל [illegible] לה לא מתרלא הכי אלא הכי אם יש עדים כו׳: **נמצאת.** לא הכיר בה משמע וקא מתרץ רבא יש לה כתובה מנה אלמא הדר ביה מההיא דלעיל דהא איהו אמר לרבנן לא הכיר בה ולא כלום וכרבי מאיר נמי לא תוקמה דהא רבי מאיר מאתים קאמר: **ויש לה עדים שלא נסתרה.** רבותא אשמעינן דאפי׳ הכי אין השני יכול לטעון טענת בתולים להפסידה כתובתה ולימא מקח טעות הוא: **שהרי כנסה ראשון.** ועליו לדעת שנבעלה:

ושמואל אמר אין מוכת עץ בבשר. בלא הטיל בתולין איירי דאי בהטיל למה יש לה להיות פחותה ממוכת עץ: **לרבנן הכיר בה מנה לא הכיר בה ולא כלום.** ומתני׳ ר״מ היא ולא רבנן ואם תאמר אמאי לא קאמר לרבנן בין הכיר בה בין לא הכיר בה מנה כדקאמר במסקנא ותירץ מתניתין לדברי הכל וי״ל דלא ניחא ליה למימר הכי דכיון דרבנן מדמו לה לבעולה הויא בלא הכיר בה כמו כנסה בחזקת בתולה ונמצאת בעולה וסבירא ליה דלית לה ולא כלום ובמסקנא סבר הא דמדמו לה לבעולה היינו לענין מנה אבל מקח טעות לא הויא כמו בעולה דלאו מקפיד כ״כ במוכת עץ שיהא מקח טעות: **הדר ביה רבא מההיא.** אבל מהא לא בעי למימר דהדר ביה משום דמקח טעות לגמרי משמע ול״ת מנא לן דהדר ביה ממה שאמר לרבנן לא הכיר בה ולא כלום ונאמר שחזר בו ממה שאמר לא הכיר בה לר״מ מאתים אלא נפרש לא הכיר בה מנה ונוקי ברייתא כרבי מאיר וי״ל כדפי׳ לעיל בקונטרס דאין זה סברא דלאי חשיב מקח טעות לא יהא לה כלום ואי לא חשיב מקח טעות למה לא יהא לה מאתים כיון דמדמה לה לבוגרת דאטו לבוגרת פוחתין לה מכתובתה א): אמר

עין משפט
נר מצוה

ע א מיי׳ פ״א מהל׳ אישות הל״א טוש״ע אה״ע סי׳ סז סעי׳ ג:
עא ב מיי׳ שם הל״ג טוש״ע שם סעי׳ ד:
עב ג ד מיי׳ שם טוש״ע שם סעי׳ ה:
עג ה טוש״ע שם סעי׳ ג:

גליון הש״ס

גמ׳ ואמר רבא מאן דקא מותיב שפיר. שבת קכ: ע״א ר״ה ו ע״ב

תוספות ישנים

א) ועוד נ״ל דניחא ליה טפי דלרבנן לא הכיר בה מנה דהשתא מיתוקמא מתני׳ וב״ייתא נמי כרבנן. ס״י ע״ג:

ליקוטי רש״י

משארסתני. אירע לי ואית לי מאתים [לקמן טז.]. ונסתחפה שדהו. לשון מטר סוחף (משלי כח) נשטפה שדך כלומר מזלך גרם [לעיל ב.]. נסחף, נשטפו והחליקו גבוריך כמו מטר סוחף (משלי כח) נסתחפה שדהו בלשון משנה ומנחם חברו לשון ליון וכן חבר מטר סוחף ודונש פתר מטר סוחף כמו מטר סועף כמו מסעף פארה במערצה (ישעיה י) [ירמיה מו, טו]. סוחף, שוטף ובמשנה נסתחפה שדהו וכן נסחף אביריך (ירמיה מו) נשטפו ומעדו וכשלו [משלי כח, ג].

מסורת הש״ס

א) [נדה מד:], ב) [לקמן יג.], ג) לקמן יג. [טו.], ד) לקמן מו., ה) [לקמן יג.], ו) [לקמן יג: טו.].

תוספות רי״ד

איתמר קטן שבא על הגדולה רב אמר עשאה מוכת עץ. פי׳ דכיון שהוציא בתוליה אע״ג שאין ביאתו ביאה לא גרע מעץ הנתקע וכתובתה מנה לרבנן ושמואל אמר אין מוכת עץ בבשר פי׳ בבשר אדם. ואי בעולה לא הויא מוכת עץ נמי לא הויא והרי היא כאילו מיעכה היא באצבעה שהממעכת בתוליה באצבעה לא הפסידה מאתים דדוקא דרוסת איש ומוכת עץ לרבנן הפסידה המאתים אבל במיעוך לא הפסידה המאתים כיון שאין כוונתה אלא שלא להצטער תחת בעלה ובמוכת עץ דפליגי רבנן משום דהוי שלא לדעתה ומיסניא בהכי. אמרי׳ בפ׳ ד׳ אחין כל הני מיעכות של בית ר׳ תמר שמן וקי״ל כשמואל בדיני: **אמר רמב״ח** מחלוקת כשהכיר בה. פי׳ כשכונסה וכתב לה כתובה היה יודע שהיא מוכת עץ דר״מ מדמי לה לבוגרת פי׳ דקי״ל דכלו בתוליה ואפ״ה כתובתן מאתים ורבנן מדמו לה לבעולה ור״מ אדמדמי לה לבוגרת לדמו לה לבעולה בעולה איתעביד בה מעשה (בוגרת) [בידי אדם הא] לא איתעביד בה מעשה ורבנן אדמדמו לה לבעולה לדמו לה לבוגרת בוגרת לא איתעביד בה מעשה כלל הא איתעביד בה מעשה. אבל לא הכיר בה ד״ה ולא כלום פי׳ שמקח טעות הוא. ורבא אסיק דבין הכיר בה ובין לא הכיר בה לר״מ כתובתה מאתים לרבנן כתובתה מנה. וקי״ל כרבנן ולא כר״מ דיחיד ורבים הלכה כרבים: **מתני׳ בתולה** אלמנה גרושה וחלוצה מן הנשואין כתובתן מנה ואין להן טענת בתולים. הגיורת והשבויה והשפחה שנפדו ושנתגיירו ושנשתחררו יתירות על ג׳ שנים ויום א׳ כתובתן מנה ואין להן טענת בתולים. פי׳ בתולה מן הנשואין וכגון שנכנסה לחופה ומת בעלה בחזקת בעולה קיימא משעה שנכנסה תחתיו וכתובתה מנה אם נשאת לאחר סתם ואין להם טענת בתולים להפסידה אותה מנה ולומר בחזקת בתולה נשאתיך והרי מקחי מקח טעות: **תנו רבנן** כנסה הראשון לשם נשואין ויש לה עדים שלא נסתרה או שנסתרה אלא שלא שהתה עמו כדי ביאה אין השני יכול לטעון טענת בתולים להפסידה מנה הראוי לאלמנה מן הנשואין שהרי כנסה הראשון. ואע״פ שהעדים מעידין אינו יכול לטעון. אמר

זאת

The Gemara elaborates on the dispute between R' Meir and the Rabbis:

אָמַר רָמִי בַּר חָמָא – **Rami bar Chama said:** מַחֲלוֹקֶת כְּשֶׁהִכִּיר בָּהּ – **The dispute refers to where [the groom] recognized** at the time of the marriage that **[the bride]** was a wood-injury victim, דְּרַבִּי מֵאִיר מְדַמֵּי לָהּ לְבוֹגֶרֶת – **for R' Meir compares her to a *bogeress,*** who receives the full *kesubah* of a virgin,[9] וְרַבָּנַן מְדַמּוּ לָהּ לִבְעוּלָה – **while the Rabbis compare her to a non-virgin,** who receives a one-*maneh kesubah.*[10] אֲבָל לֹא הִכִּיר בָּהּ – **But if he did not recognize her** condition at the time of the marriage, and discovers this fact only later, דִּבְרֵי הַכֹּל וְלֹא כְלוּם – **all agree** that she receives **nothing** [i.e. no *kesubah*] **at all.**[11]

The Gemara analyzes the two Tannaic views:

וְרַבִּי מֵאִיר – **Now R' Meir,** אַמַּאי מְדַמֵּי לָהּ לְבוֹגֶרֶת – **why does he compare her to a *bogeress*?** נְדַמְיָיהּ לִבְעוּלָה – **Let him compare her to a non-virgin.** – ? –

The Gemara answers:

בְּעוּלָה אִיתְעֲבִיד בָּהּ מַעֲשֶׂה בִּידֵי אָדָם – **A non-virgin had an act done to her by a man** הָא לֹא אִיתְעֲבִיד בָּהּ מַעֲשֶׂה בִּידֵי אָדָם – whereas **this** woman **did not have an act done to her by a man.**

The Gemara asks:

וְרַבָּנַן – **And the Rabbis,** אַדְּמְדַמּוּ לָהּ לִבְעוּלָה – **rather than compare her to a non-virgin,** נְדַמְיָיהּ לְבוֹגֶרֶת – **let them compare her to a *bogeress.*** – ? –

The Gemara answers:

בּוֹגֶרֶת לֹא אִיתְעֲבִיד בָּהּ מַעֲשֶׂה כְּלָל – **A *bogeress* had no act done to her at all** הָא אִיתְעֲבִיד בָּהּ מַעֲשֶׂה – whereas **this** woman **had an act done to her.**

The Gemara quotes the end of Rami bar Chama's statement: אֲבָל לֹא הִכִּיר בָּהּ – **But if [the groom] did not recognize her** condition at the time of the marriage, לְדִבְרֵי הַכֹּל וְלֹא כְלוּם – **all agree** that she receives **nothing at all.**

This ruling is questioned:

מָתִיב רַב נַחְמָן – **Rav Nachman challenged** this **from a Mishnah:**[12] הִיא אוֹמֶרֶת מוּכַּת עֵץ אֲנִי – SHE SAYS, "I AM A WOOD-INJURY VICTIM," וְהוּא אוֹמֵר לֹא כִּי אֶלָּא דְּרוּסַת אִישׁ אַתְּ – AND HE SAYS, "Perhaps it is NOT SO, RATHER YOU WERE DEFLOWERED[13] BY A MAN" – רַבָּן גַּמְלִיאֵל וְרַבִּי אֱלִיעֶזֶר אוֹמְרִים נֶאֱמֶנֶת – RABBAN GAMLIEL AND R' ELIEZER SAY: SHE IS BELIEVED. It is apparent from this Mishnah that a woman is entitled to at least some *kesubah* payment even if she is a wood-injury victim.[14] – ? –

Rava therefore suggests another explanation of the dispute between R' Meir and the Rabbis:

אֶלָּא אָמַר רָבָא – **Rather, Rava said:** בֵּין הִכִּיר בָּהּ וּבֵין לֹא הִכִּיר בָּהּ – **Whether he recognized her** condition **or whether he did not recognize her** condition, לְרַבִּי מֵאִיר מָאתַיִם – **according to R' Meir** she receives a *kesubah* of **two hundred.**[15] לְרַבָּנַן – **According to the Rabbis,** however, it depends: הִכִּיר בָּהּ מָנֶה – If **he recognized her** condition, she receives **a *maneh,***[16] לֹא הִכִּיר בָּהּ וְלֹא כְלוּם – but if **he did not recognize her** condition, she receives **nothing at all.**[17]

The Gemara notes:

וַהֲדַר בֵּיהּ רָבָא – **But Rava** subsequently **retracted** his statement that the Rabbis maintain that if he did not recognize her condition she receives no *kesubah* at all. Rather, whether or not he recognized her condition, she receives one hundred *zuz* according to the Rabbis.[18]

The Gemara offers proof of Rava's retraction:[19]

דְּתַנְיָא – **For it was taught in a Baraisa:** כֵּיצַד הוֹצָאַת שֵׁם רַע –

NOTES

by a piece of wood as two separate cases. Rather, they are one case.] The Mishnah thus is to be read as follows: The minor boy who cohabited with an adult female has rendered her a wood-injury victim, and the *kesubah* of a wood-injury victim is two hundred *zuz;* these are the words of R' Meir. The Sages, however, say: Any wood injury victim receives a *kesubah* of one hundred *zuz;* hence, this woman, who has been rendered a wood-injury victim, also receives only one hundred *zuz* (see *Rashi; Shitah Mekubetzes* ד״ה אמר רבא).

9. [A girl becomes a *bogeress* six months after reaching the age of twelve and sprouting two pubic hairs.] Although any young girl who has never cohabited possesses a hymen, the *bogeress'* hymen naturally disintegrates due to maturity (see *Yevamos* 59a). Despite this fact, a *bogeress* is considered a full-fledged virgin, and is entitled to a *kesubah* of two hundred *zuz* (*Rashi*). R' Meir compares a wood-injury victim, who has likewise lost her hymen, to a *bogeress.*

10. They consider her to be as blemished as a woman who has cohabited.

The dispute between R' Meir and the Rabbis is thus what type of *kesubah* a groom who is aware of his bride's condition as a wood-injured victim is required to write her, that of a virgin or that of a nonvirgin. Cf. *Rashash.*

11. Not having been told otherwise, the groom had the right to assume that his bride was not wood-injured (*Rashba*). Accordingly, his wedding her was an "acquisition made in error" [מִקַּח טָעוּת], and she cannot claim even a *maneh* (*Rashi*).

12. Below, 13a. This Mishnah is a continuation of a Mishnah on 12b which describes a case in which a man marries a woman and, upon cohabiting with her for the first time, is surprised to find no signs of virginity. What follows are the claim and counterclaim of the bride and groom (*Rashi*).

13. Literally: trodden.

14. For if she receives no *kesubah* at all, what does Rabban Gamliel mean by saying that she is believed? We may thus infer that even if the groom did not know beforehand that his bride was a wood-injury victim, she still receives a *kesubah.* This refutes Rami bar Chama's statement that in such a case everyone agrees that she collects nothing at all (*Rashi*).

[The Gemara assumes the Mishnah's case to be where the bride claims that she was a wood-injury victim *before* the *erusin,* for otherwise the Mishnah would have stated her claim as, "I became a wood-injury victim *while married to you*" (*Ritva*).]

See *Ritva* and *R' Akiva Eiger* מערכה יב ס״ק יח for suggestions as to how Rami bar Chama himself, who surely was aware of this Mishnah (since all Amoraim were familiar with all Mishnahs), might explain it. Whatever the case, our Gemara considers this Mishnah to be a refutation of Rami bar Chama.

15. And the Mishnah below in which she says that she is a wood-injury victim and claims a *kesubah* is in accordance with the view of R' Meir (*Rashi*).

16. And our Mishnah, which quotes the Rabbis as granting a wood-injury victim a *kesubah* of a *maneh,* refers to where the groom knew of her condition prior to the marriage (*Rashi*).

17. Because the marriage is considered an acquisition made in error.

Rava does not suggest that according to R' Meir where the groom recognized her condition she receives two hundred *zuz* and where he did not recognize her condition she receives one hundred. This is because if we consider her injury significant enough to render the marriage an acquisition made in error, she should receive nothing at all, and if it is not that significant, she should not lose any of her two hundred *zuz* (*Rashi*).

Rava also does not now suggest (as the Gemara will in fact conclude below) that according to the Rabbis whether or not he recognized her condition she receives one hundred *zuz* (an approach which would allow us to explain the Mishnah on 13a in accordance with all Tannaim), for since the Rabbis compare a wood-injury victim to a nonvirgin, it is as if he married her on the presumption that she was a virgin and found her to be a nonvirgin, and Rava is of the opinion that such a woman does not receive any *kesubah* at all (*Tosafos*).

18. And two hundred according to R' Meir. Thus, the Mishnah on 13a, which indicates that a wood-injury victim receives a *kesubah,* is in accordance with all Tannaim (*Rashi*).

19. [This proof will involve a Baraisa and a lengthy Amoraic exchange regarding that Baraisa. Only after the exchange is completed will the proof emerge.]

ואין להן טענת בתולים הגיורת והשבויה והשפחה שנפדו ושנתגיירו ושנשתחררו יתירות על בנות שלש שנים ויום אחד כתובתן מנה ואין להן טענת בתולין: גמ' אמר רב יהודה אמר רב קטן הבא על הגדולה עשאה מוכת עץ כי אמריתה קמיה דשמואל אמר אין מוכת עץ בבשר איכא דמתני לה להא שמעתא באפי נפשה קטן הבא על הגדולה רב אמר עשאה מוכת עץ ושמואל אמר אין מוכת עץ בבשר מתיב רב אושעיא גדול שבא על הקטנה וקטן הבא על הגדולה ומוכת עץ כתובתן מאתים דברי ר"מ וחכמים אומרים מוכת עץ כתובתה מנה אמר רבא הכי קאמר גדול הבא על הקטנה ולא כלום דפחות מכאן כנותן אצבע בעין דמי וקטן הבא על הגדולה עשאה מוכת עץ ומוכת עץ גופא פלוגתא דר"מ ורבנן אמר רמי בר חמא מחלוקת כשהכיר בה דר"מ מדמי לה לבוגרת ורבנן מדמו לה לבעולה אבל לא הכיר בה דברי הכל ולא כלום ור"מ אמאי מדמי לה לבוגרת נדמייה לבעולה בעולה איתעביד בה מעשה בידי אדם הא לא איתעביד בה מעשה בידי אדם ורבנן אדמדמו לה לבעולה נדמייה לבוגרת בוגרת לא איתעביד בה מעשה כלל הא איתעביד בה מעשה אבל לא הכיר בה לדברי הכל ולא כלום מתיב רב נחמן היא אומרת מוכת עץ אני והוא אומר לא כי אלא דרוסת איש את ר"ג ור' אליעזר אומרים נאמנת אלא אמר רבא בין הכיר בה ובין לא הכיר בה לר"מ מאתים לרבנן הכיר בה מנה לא הכיר בה ולא כלום והדר ביה רבא דתניא כיצד הוצאת שם רע בא לבית דין ואמר פלוני לא מצאתי לבתך בתולים אם יש עדים שזינתה תחתיו יש לה כתובה מנה אם יש עדים שזינתה תחתיו בת סקילה היא הכי קאמר אם יש עדים שזינתה תחתיו בסקילה זינתה מעיקרא יש לה כתובה מנה ואמר רב חייא בר אבין אמר רב ששת זאת אומרת כנסה בחזקת בתולה ונמצאת בעולה יש לה כתובה מנה ומתיב רב נחמן הנושא את האשה ולא מצא לה בתולים היא אומרת משארסתני נאנסתי ונסתחפה שדהו והוא אומר לא כי אלא עד שלא אירסתיך והיה מקחי מקח טעות ולית לה כלל ואמר להו רב חייא בר אבין עמרם וכל גדולי הדור יתבי כי אמר רב ששת להא שמעתא וקשיא להו ושני מאי מקח טעות נמי ממאתים אבל מנה אית לה ואת אמרת לית לה כלל ואמר רבא מאן דקא מותיב שפיר קא מותיב מקח טעות לגמרי משמע ואלא קשיא הך תריץ ואימא הכי אם יש עדים שזינתה תחתיו בסקילה זינתה מעיקרא ולא כלום נמצאת מוכת עץ יש לה כתובה מנה והא רבא הוא דאמר לרבנן לא הכיר בה ולא כלום אלא ש"מ הדר ביה רבא מההיא ת"ר כנסה ראשון לשום נישואין ויש לה עדים שלא נסתרה אי נמי נסתרה ולא שהתה כדי ביאה אין השני יכול לטעון טענת בתולים שהרי כנסה ראשון

אמר

רש"י

ואין להן טענת בתולין. אין יכול להפסידה אותה מנה ולומר בחזקת בתולה נשאתיך והרי מקחי מקח טעות: גמ' עשאה מוכת עץ. נהי דאין ביאתו ביאה מיהו לא גרע מעץ הנתקע ולרבנן דפליגי אמוכת עץ כתובתה מנה וכן לענין כהן גדול דתנן (יבמות דף נט.) לא ישא את מוכת עץ הא לא נמי פסילא ליה: אין מוכת עץ בבשר אדם. ואי בעולה לא הויא מוכת עץ נמי לא ליתא: באפי נפשה. בלא גברי דלא אמר רב יהודה משמיה דרב ומשמיה דשמואל אלא איניהו גופייהו איפלוג בה: וקטן שבא על הגדולה ומוכת עץ. ומדפלגינהו תנא לתרתי ולא איפלוג רבנן אלא במוכת עץ שמעת מינה אין מוכת עץ בבשר: הכי קאמר גדול הבא על הקטנה ולא כלום. אינה ביאה לדברי הכל הלכך כתובתה מאתים ולא איפלוג רבנן עלה דפחות מכאן כנותן אצבע בעין דתנן במסכת נדה (דף מד:) גבי בת פחותה מג' שנים ויום אחד מה הדמעה היוצאת ע"י אצבע באה אחרת תחתיה אף בתולים של פחות מכאן חוזרין אחרים תחתיהם: וקטן שבא על הגדולה. מוכת עץ היא וכתובתה מאתים דברי רבי מאיר וחכמים אומרים כל מוכת עץ כתובתה מנה והא נמי דקא משוית לה מוכת עץ כתובתה מנה: כשהכיר בה. כשכנסה וכתב לה כתובה היה יודע שהיא מוכת עץ: מדמי לה לבוגרת. דקיימא לן שכלו בתוליה במס' יבמות (דף נט.) דקתני בבתוליה פרט לבוגרת שכלו בתוליה ואפי' הכי כתובתה מאתים: ולא כלום. דמקח טעות הוא ואפי' מנה אין לה: היא אומרת מוכת עץ אני. משנתנו היא: והוא אומר לא כי אלא דרוסת איש את. הנושא את האשה בחזקת בתולה ולא מצא לה בתולים היא אומרת מוכת עץ אני כו' ש"מ אית לה כתובה או מנה או מאתים דאי לית לה מאי נאמנת דקאמר רבן גמליאל אלמא מוכת עץ שלא הכיר בה יש לה כתובה תיובתא דרמי בר חמא דאמר לא הכיר בה דברי הכל ולא כלום: אלא אמר רבא לר"מ בין הכיר בה בין לא הכיר בה מאתים. ומתני' דקתני היא אומרת מוכת עץ אני וקא תבעה מאתים רבי מאיר היא: לרבנן הכיר בה מנה. ומתני' דהכא דקתני וחכמים אומרים מוכת עץ מנה כשהכיר בה: לא הכיר בה ולא כלום. והא לא מצינו למימר לר' מאיר הכיר בה מאתים לא הכיר בה מנה דאי במקח טעות מחזקינן ליה משום דלא הכיר בה לית לה מידי ואי לאו מקח טעות הוא אין חילוק בין הכיר ללא הכיר: והדר ביה רבא גר' ול"ג מההיא. והדר ביה רבא ממאי דאמר לרבנן לא הכיר בה ולא כלום אלא בין הכיר בין לא הכיר יש לה מנה לרבנן ומאתים לר"מ ומתני' דהתם דברי הכל: הוצאת שם רע. ליענש מאה כסף אם שקר וליסקל אם אמת היה: בא לב"ד. זקוק לבוא לב"ד ואומר כו': ואמר רב חייא גרסי': ומותיב רב נחמן גר': נסתחפה שדהו. מזלו גרם כאדם שהמטר בא וסוחף את זריעתו ועוקרה: מקח טעות לגמרי משמע. ואין לה כלום: כי אמרה רב ששת להא שמעתתא. להאי זאת אומרת דלעיל דיש לה כתובה מנה: וקשיא להו. הא דאותבינן: ואמר רבא גרסי': ואלא קשיא הך. ואקשינן לרבא אלא קשיא הך דלעיל דקתני זינתה מעיקרא יש לה כתובה מנה: תריץ. להאי דלעיל דכיצד הוצאת ש"ר תירוצא דתרצת לה לא תתרצה הכי אלא הכי אם יש עדים כו': נמצאת. לא הכיר בה משמע וקא מתרץ רבא יש לה כתובה מנה אלמא הדר ביה מההיא דלעיל דהא איהו אמר לרבנן ולא כלום וכרבי מאיר נמי לא תוקמה דהא רבי מאיר מאתים קאמר: ויש לה עדים שלא נסתרה. רבותא אשמעינן דאפי' הכי אין השני יכול לטעון טענת בתולים להפסידה כתובתה ולימא מקח טעות הוא: שהרי כנסה ראשון. ועליו לדעת שנבעלה:

זאת

תוספות

ושמואל אמר אין מוכת עץ בבשר. בלא הכיר בתולין איירי דאי בהכיר למה יש לה להיות פחותה ממוכת עץ:

לרבנן הכיר בה מנה לא הכיר בה ולא כלום. ומתני' ר"מ היא ולא רבנן ואם תאמר אמאי לא קאמר לרבנן בין הכיר בה בין לא הכיר בה מנה כדקאמר במסקנא ותיתי מתניתין לדברי הכל וי"ל דלא ניחא ליה למימר הכי דכיון דרבנן מדמו לה לבעולה הויא בלא הכיר בה כמו כנסה בחזקת בתולה ונמצאת בעולה וסבירא ליה דלית לה ולא כלום ובמסקנא סבר הא דמדמו לה לבעולה היינו לענין מנה אבל מקח טעות לא הויא כמו בעולה דאינו מקפיד כ"כ במוכת עץ שיהא מקח טעות:

הדר ביה רבא מההיא. אבל מהא לא בעי למימר דהדר ביה משום דמקח טעות לגמרי משמע וא"ת מנא לן דהדר ביה ממה שאמר לרבנן לא הכיר בה ולא כלום נאמר שחזר בו ממה שאמר לא הכיר בה לר"מ מאתים אלא נפרש לא הכיר בה מנה ונוקי ברייתא כרבי מאיר וי"ל כדפי' לעיל בקונטרס דאין זה סברא דאי חשיב מקח טעות לא יהא לה כלום ואי לא חשיב מקח טעות למה לא יהא לה מאתים כיון דמדמה לה לבוגרת דאטו לבוגרת פוחתין לה מכתובתה א):

אמר

עין משפט נר מצוה

עא א מיי' פי"א מהל' אישות הל"ח טוש"ע אה"ע סי' סז סעי' ג:
עא ב מיי' שם הל"ג טוש"ע שם סעי' ד:
עב ג ד מיי' שם טוש"ע שם סעי' ב:
עג ה טוש"ע שם סעי' ג:

גליון הש"ס

גמ' ואמר רבא מאן דקא מותיב שפיר. שבת קכג ע"ב ר"ה ו ע"ג:

תוספות ישנים

א) ועוד נ"ל יותר ניחא ליה טפי דלרבנן לא הכיר בה מנה דהשתא מיתוקמא מתני' וברייתא נמי כרבנן. ת"י עה"ג.

ליקוטי רש"י

משארסתני. אירע לי ולית לי מאתים [לקמן טז.]. ונסתחפה שדהו. לשון מטר סוחף (משלי כח) נשטפה שדך כלומר מזלך גרם [לעיל ב.]. נסחף, נשטפו והחליקו גבוליך כמו מטר סוחף (משלי כח) נסתחפה שדהו בלשון משנה ומנחם חברו לשון כלים וכן חבר מטר סוחף ודונש פתר מטר סוחף כמו מטר סוחף כמו כסחף פארה במעצה (ישעיה י) [ירמיה מו, טו]. סחף, שוטף ובמשנה נסתחפה שדהו וכן נסחף אביריך (ירמיה מו) נשטפו מעדו וכשלו [משלי כח, ג].

מסורת הש"ס

א) נדה מד., ג) לקמן יג., ג) לקמן יג. [טז.], ד) לקמן מו., ה) [לקמן יג.], ו) לקמן יב: טז.

תוספות רי"ד

איתמר קטן שבא על הגדולה רב אמר עשאה מוכת עץ. פי' דכיון שהוציא בתולים אע"ג שאין ביאתו ביאה לא גרע מעץ הנתקע וכתובתה מנה לרבנן ושמואל אמר אין מוכת עץ בבשר פי' בבשר אדם. ואי בעולה לא הויא מוכת עץ נמי לא הויא והרי היא כאילו מיעכה היא באצבעה שהממעכת באצבעה בתולה לא הפסידה מאתים דדוקא דרוסת איש ומוכת עץ הוא הפסידה המאתים אבל במיעוך לא הפסידה המאתים כיון שאין כוונתה אלא שלא להצטער תחת בעלה ובמוכת עץ דפליגי רבנן משום דהוי שלא לדעתה ומיטניא בהכי. אמורי בפ' ד' אחין כל הני מיעכות של בית ר' תמר שמן וקי"ל כשמואל בדיני: אמר רמב"ח מחלוקת כשהכיר בה. פי' כשכנסה וכתב לה כתובה היה יודע שהיא מוכת עץ דר"מ מדמי לה לבוגרת פי' דקי"ל דכלו בתוליה ואפ"ה כתובתן מאתים ורבנן מדמו לה לבעולה ור"מ אדמדמי לה לבוגרת לדמו לה לבעולה בעולה איתעביד בה מעשה (בוגרת) [בידי אדם הא] לא איתעביד בה מעשה ורבנן אדמדמו לה לבעולה לדמו לה לבוגרת בוגרת לא איתעביד בה מעשה כלל הא איתעביד בה מעשה. אבל לא הכיר בה ד"ה ולא כלום פי' שמקח טעות הוא. ורבא אסיק דבין הכיר בה ובין לא הכיר בה לר"מ כתובתה מאתים לרבנן כתובתה מנה. וקי"ל כרבנן ולא כר"מ דיחיד ורבים הלכה כרבים: מתני' בתולה אלמנה גרושה וחלוצה מן הנשואין כתובתן מנה ואין להן טענת בתולים. הגיורת והשבויה והשפחה שנפדו ושנתגיירו ושנשתחררו יתירות על ג' שנים ויום א' כתובתן מנה ואין להן טענת בתולים. פי' בתולה מן הנשואין וכגון שנכנסה לחופה ומת בעלה בחזקת בעולה קיימא משעה שנכנסה תחתיו וכתובתה מנה אם נשאת לאחר סתם ואין להם טענת בתולים להפסידה אותה מנה ולומר בחזקת בתולה נשאתיך והרי מקחי מקח טעות: תנו רבנן כנסה הראשון לשם נשואין ויש לה עדים שלא נסתרה או שנסתרה אלא שלא שהתה עמו כדי ביאה אין השני יכול לטעון טענת בתולים פי' להפסידה מנה הראוי לאלמנה מן הנשואין שהרי כנסה הראשון. ואע"פ שהעדים מעידין אינו יכול לטעון.

אמר

וְאֵין לָהֶן טַעֲנַת בְּתוּלִים – and no claim concerning their virginity can be made against them.[1] הַגִּיוֹרֶת וְהַשְּׁבוּיָה וְהַשִּׁפְחָה – A convert, a captive or a slavewoman שֶׁנִּפְדּוּ וְשֶׁנִּתְגַּיְּירוּ וְשֶׁנִּשְׁתַּחְרְרוּ – who were ransomed, converted or emancipated יְתֵירוֹת עַל בְּנוֹת שָׁלֹשׁ שָׁנִים וְיוֹם אֶחָד – over the age of three years and one day – כְּתוּבָּתָן מָנֶה – their *kesubah* is a *maneh,*[2] וְאֵין לָהֶן טַעֲנַת בְּתוּלִין – and no claim concerning their virginity can be made against them.[3]

Gemara The Gemara presents an Amoraic ruling related to our Mishnah:

אָמַר רַב יְהוּדָה אָמַר רַב – **Rav Yehudah said in the name of Rav:** קָטָן הַבָּא עַל הַגְּדוֹלָה – **A minor boy who cohabited with an adult female** עֲשָׂאָה מוּכַּת עֵץ – **has rendered her a wood-injury victim.**[4]

Rav Yehudah continued:

כִּי אַמְרִיתָהּ קַמֵּיהּ דִּשְׁמוּאֵל אָמַר – However, **when I stated [this ruling] in the presence of Shmuel, he** dismissed it and **said:** אֵין מוּכַּת עֵץ בְּבָשָׂר – **There is no** such thing as a **wood-injury victim through** human **flesh** [i.e. cohabitation].[5]

The Gemara cites an alternative tradition regarding this dispute:

אִיכָּא דְּמַתְנֵי לָהּ לְהָא שְׁמַעְתָּא בְּאַפֵּי נַפְשָׁהּ – **There are those who teach this discussion as an independent one:**[6] קָטָן הַבָּא עַל הַגְּדוֹלָה – Concerning **a minor boy who cohabited with an adult female,** רַב אָמַר עֲשָׂאָה מוּכַּת עֵץ – **Rav says: He has rendered her a wood-injury victim,** וּשְׁמוּאֵל אָמַר אֵין מוּכַּת עֵץ בְּבָשָׂר – **while Shmuel says: There is no** such thing as a **wood-injury victim through** human **flesh.**

The Gemara discusses the dispute:

מֵתִיב רַב אוֹשַׁעְיָא – **Rav Oshaya challenged** Rav's view from our Mishnah: גָּדוֹל שֶׁבָּא עַל הַקְּטַנָּה – AN ADULT MALE WHO COHABITED WITH A MINOR GIRL, וְקָטָן הַבָּא עַל הַגְּדוֹלָה – OR A MINOR BOY WHO COHABITED WITH AN ADULT FEMALE, וּמוּכַּת עֵץ – OR [A WOMAN] INJURED BY A piece of WOOD – כְּתוּבָּתָן מָאתַיִם – THEIR *KESUBAH* IS TWO HUNDRED *zuz;* דִּבְרֵי רַבִּי מֵאִיר – these are THE WORDS OF R' MEIR. וַחֲכָמִים אוֹמְרִים – BUT THE SAGES SAY: מוּכַּת עֵץ כְּתוּבָּתָהּ מָנֶה – THE *KESUBAH* OF ONE INJURED BY A piece of WOOD IS A *MANEH.* Now, since the Mishnah enumerates the minor boy who cohabited with an adult female and the woman injured by a piece of wood as two separate cases, and the Sages disagree only in regard to the woman injured by a piece of wood, it is apparent that they agree that a minor boy who cohabits with an adult female does not render her a wood-injury victim. – ? –

The Gemara defends Rav by reinterpreting the Mishnah:

אָמַר רָבָא – **Rava said:** הָכִי קָאָמַר – **This is what [the Mishnah] is saying:** גָּדוֹל הַבָּא עַל הַקְּטַנָּה וְלֹא כְלוּם – **If an adult male cohabited with a minor girl, it is nothing,** i.e. the act has no legal significance at all, and her *kesubah* remains two hundred *zuz* even according to the Rabbis, דִּפְחוֹת מִכָּאן כְּנוֹתֵן אֶצְבַּע בָּעַיִן דָּמֵי – **for** cohabitation with a girl **less than [three years old] is like sticking one's finger in the eye.**[7] וְקָטָן הַבָּא עַל הַגְּדוֹלָה עֲשָׂאָה מוּכַּת עֵץ – **But if a minor boy cohabited with an adult female, he has rendered her a wood-injury victim,** וּמוּכַּת עֵץ גּוּפָא פְּלוּגְתָּא דְּרַבִּי מֵאִיר וְרַבָּנָן – **and a wood-injury victim itself is** the subject of **a dispute between R' Meir and the Rabbis.**[8]

NOTES

1. Since they were already married, they are presumed to be nonvirgins (see below, note 36 for the reason). Therefore, even if they did not explicitly state prior to their marriage with their new husbands that they were no longer virgins, they are nevertheless awarded a *kesubah* of one hundred *zuz.* Their silence regarding their state of virginity does not constitute a misrepresentation of the facts [with the consequent annulment of their entire *kesubah* – see Gemara below], since it was presupposed that they were nonvirgins (*Rashi* here and to 11a).

[*Rashba* points out that the case of the *chalutzah* is actually superfluous in our Mishnah, for the *chalutzah* already lost her right to a virgin's *kesubah* at the time she was widowed (after *nisuin*) from her first husband (the fact that she later became a *chalutzah* is obviously no reason for the virgin *kesubah* to be reinstated). The Mishnah nevertheless includes this case here to make the Mishnah's language parallel to that of the earlier Mishnah (10b) where the case of the *chalutzah* was in fact needed, to state that even though she is both a widow and a *chalutzah,* she still receives a *kesubah* of two hundred *zuz.*]

2. It is presumed that they had relations prior to their conversion or being ransomed from their captors, as explained in the Mishnah on 11a. Since they became Jews or were ransomed after reaching the age of three – when their hymen no longer grows back if it has been ruptured – they are regarded as nonvirgins.

3. Since we assume that they are nonvirgins when they marry, their *kesubah* is one hundred *zuz,* and no suit can be lodged to deprive them of it by claiming that their marriage was based on a misrepresentation.

4. Even though the cohabitation of a minor boy [less than nine years old] is not legally considered an act of cohabitation, it is no less intrusive than if a stick of wood had penetrated the woman [and ruptured her hymen]. Therefore, according to the Rabbis who say that a woman injured by a piece of wood receives only one hundred *zuz,* a woman who cohabited with a minor also receives only this amount. Also, just as a Kohen Gadol, who is commanded to marry only a virgin (*Leviticus* 21:13), may not marry a wood-injury victim (see Mishnah, *Yevamos* 59a), so too he may not marry a woman who has cohabited with a minor (*Rashi*).

5. Cohabitation either renders the woman a full-fledged nonvirgin [such as where the male is nine years or older, in which case the act is legally considered an act of cohabitation], or else it [has no effect on the woman at all, such as where the male is younger than nine years, and] does not even render her the equivalent of a wood-injury victim (*Rashi*). Even if the woman experienced bleeding as a result of the cohabitation, the hymenal membrane is assumed to have remained at least partially intact, for a boy this young is incapable of totally rupturing the hymen (see *Shitah Mekubetzes* ד״ה אבל בשיטה ישנה, first explanation; *Shiyarei Korban* to *Yerushalmi* 1:3 ד״ה אבל; cf. *Tos. Rid; Haflaah* to *Tosafos* ד״ה ושמואל).

[We have explained the dispute between Rav and Shmuel to be referring to where the woman bled as a result of the relations. This is how the majority of the commentators understand *Rashi* (see *Shitah Mekubetzes* ד״ה ורש״י, *Shiyarei Korban* and *Haflaah* ibid., *Chidushim U'Veurim;* cf. *Minchas Chinuch* 272:2). Many other Rishonim, however (*Tosafos, Rashba, Rosh* §24), assert that Shmuel would agree that if the woman bled she would be treated as a wood-injury victim. Rather, the dispute is where there was no bleeding, meaning that her hymen was definitely not ruptured. Shmuel maintains that her *kesubah* remains at two hundred *zuz,* while Rav holds that since she had relations after attaining the age at which *she* was legally capable of cohabitation (even though the *male* with whom she cohabited was *beneath* the age of cohabitation), she loses the charm an uncompromised virgin has in the eyes of a prospective husband [בָּטֵל חִנָּהּ], and her *kesubah* is reduced to one hundred *zuz.* According to this explanation, Rav compares the woman to a wood-injury victim only as an example. Just as a wood-injury victim, though she never cohabited with anyone, nevertheless receives a reduced *kesubah* because an action done to her has caused her to lose her charm, so too a woman who cohabited with a boy younger than nine receives a reduced *kesubah* for the same reason (*Rashba*).]

6. Rather than say that it was Rav Yehudah who related the above-cited opinions in the name of Rav and in the name of Shmuel, this version asserts that Rav and Shmuel disputed the matter themselves [face to face] (*Rashi;* see *Poras Yosef* for a possible halachic difference between these two versions; cf. *Rashash*).

7. Just as the tear shed by placing a finger in the eye is replaced by a new tear, so too the hymen of a girl less than three years old grows back after it has been removed (*Rashi*; see Mishnah, *Niddah* 44b).

8. [Rava answers that the Mishnah does not mean to enumerate the minor boy who cohabited with an adult female and the woman injured

ואין להן טענת בתולים [א]הגיורת והשבויה והשפחה שנפדו ושנתגיירו ושנשתחררו יתירות על בנות שלש שנים ויום אחד כתובתן מנה ואין להן טענת בתולין: **גמ'** אמר רב יהודה אמר רב קטן הבא על הגדולה עשאה מוכת עץ כי אמריתה קמיה דשמואל אמר [ב]אין מוכת עץ בבשר איכא דמתני לה להא שמעתא באפי נפשה קטן הבא על הגדולה רב אמר עשאה מוכת עץ ושמואל אמר אין מוכת עץ בבשר מתיב רב אושעיא גדול שבא על הקטנה וקטן הבא על הגדולה ומוכת עץ כתובתן מאתים דברי ר"מ וחכמים אומרים מוכת עץ כתובתה מנה אמר רבא הכי קאמר גדול הבא על הקטנה ולא כלום [ו]דפחות מכאן כנותן אצבע בעין דמי וקטן הבא על הגדולה עשאה מוכת עץ ומוכת עץ גופא פלוגתא דר"מ ורבנן אמר רמי בר חמא [ג]מחלוקת כשהכיר בה דר"מ מדמי לה לבוגרת ורבנן מדמו לה לבעולה אבל לא הכיר בה דברי הכל ולא כלום ור"מ אמאי מדמי לה לבוגרת נדמייה לבעולה בעולה איתעביד בה מעשה בידי אדם הא לא איתעביד בה מעשה בידי אדם ורבנן אדמדמו לה לבעולה נדמייה לבוגרת בוגרת לא איתעביד בה מעשה כלל הא איתעביד בה מעשה אבל לא הכיר בה לדברי הכל ולא כלום מתיב רב נחמן [ג]היא אומרת מוכת עץ אני והוא אומר לא כי אלא דרוסת איש את ר"ג ור' אליעזר אומרים נאמנת אלא אמר רבא בין הכיר בה ובין לא הכיר בה לר"מ מאתים לרבנן הכיר בה מנה לא הכיר בה ולא כלום והדר ביה רבא דתניא כיצד [ד]הוצאת שם רע בא לבית דין ואמר פלוני לא מצאתי לבתך בתולים אם יש עדים שזינתה תחתיו יש לה כתובה מנה אם יש עדים שזינתה תחתיו בת סקילה היא הכי קאמר אם יש עדים שזינתה תחתיו בסקילה זינתה מעיקרא יש לה כתובה מנה [ה]ואמר רב חייא בר אבין אמר רב ששת זאת אומרת כנסה בחזקת בתולה ונמצאת בעולה יש לה כתובה מנה ומתיב רב נחמן [ו]הנושא את האשה ולא מצא לה בתולים היא אומרת משארסתני נאנסתי ונסתחפה שדהו והוא אומר לא כי אלא עד שלא אירסתיך והיה מקחי מקח טעות ולית לה כלל ואמר להו רב חייא בר אבין רב עמרם וכל גדולי הדור יתבי כי אמר רב ששת להא שמעתא וקשיא להו ושני מאי מקח טעות נמי ממאתים אבל מנה אית לה ואת אמרת לית לה כלל ° ואמר רבא מאן דקא מותיב שפיר קא מותיב [ג]מקח טעות לגמרי משמע ואלא קשיא הך תריץ ואימא הכי אם יש עדים שזינתה תחתיו בסקילה זינתה מעיקרא ולא כלום [ד]נמצאת מוכת עץ יש לה כתובה מנה והא רבא הוא דאמר לרבנן לא הכיר בה ולא כלום אלא ש"מ הדר ביה רבא מההיא ת"ר כנסה ראשון לשום נישואין [ה]ויש לה עדים שלא נסתרה אי נמי נסתרה ולא שהתה כדי ביאה אין השני יכול לטעון טענת בתולים שהרי כנסה ראשון אמר

רש"י

ואין להן טענת בתולין. אין יכול להפסידה אותה מנה ולומר בחזקת בתולה נשאתיך והרי מקחי מקח טעות: **גמ' עשאה מוכת עץ.** נהי דאין ביאתו ביאה מיהו לא גרע מעץ הנתקע ולרבנן דפליגי אמוכת עץ כתובתה מנה וכן לענין כהן גדול דתנן (יבמות דף נט.) לא ישא את מוכת עץ הא נמי פסילא ליה: **אין מוכת עץ בבשר אדם.** ואי בעולה לא הויא מוכת עץ נמי ליתא: **באפי נפשה.** בלא גברי דלא אמר רב יהודה משמיה דרב ומשמיה דשמואל אלא אינהו גופייהו איפלוג בה: **וקטן שבא על הגדולה ומוכת עץ.** ומדפלגינהו תנא לתרתי ולא איפלוג רבנן אלא במוכת עץ שמעת מינה אין מוכת עץ בבשר: **הכי קאמר גדול הבא על הקטנה ולא כלום.** אינה ביאה לדברי הכל הלכך כתובתה מאתים ולא איפלוג רבנן עלה דפחות מכאן כנותן אצבע בעין דתנן במסכת נדה (דף מה:) גבי בת פחותה מג' שנים ויום אחד מה הדמעה היוצאת ע"י אצבע באה אחרת תחתיה אף בתולים של פחות מכן חוזרין אחרים תחתיהם: **וקטן שבא על הגדולה.** מוכת עץ היא זו וכתובתה מאתים דברי רבי מאיר וחכמים אומרים כל מוכת עץ כתובתה מנה והא נמי דקא משוית לה מוכת עץ כתובתה מנה: **כשהכיר בה.** כשכנסה וכתב לה כתובה היה יודע שהיא מוכת עץ: **מדמי לה לבוגרת.** דקיימא לן שכלו בתוליה במס' יבמות (דף נט.) דקתני בבתוליה פרט לבוגרת שכלו בתוליה ואפי' הכי כתובתה מאתים: **ולא כלום.** דמקח טעות הוא ואפי' מנה אין לה: **היא אומרת מוכת עץ אני.** משנתנו היא: **והוא אומר לא כי אלא דרוסת איש את.** הנושא את האשה בחזקת בתולה ולא מצא לה בתולים היא אומרת מוכת עץ אני כו' ש"מ אית לה כתובה או מנה או מאתים דאי לית לה מאי נאמנת דקאמר רבן גמליאל אלמא מוכת עץ שלא הכיר בה יש לה כתובה תיובתא דרמי בר חמא דאמר לא הכיר בה דברי הכל ולא כלום: **אלא אמר רבא לר"מ בין הכיר בה לא הכיר בה מאתים.** ומתני' דקתני היא אומרת מוכת עץ אני וקא תבעה מאתים רבי מאיר היא: **לרבנן הכיר בה מנה.** ומתני' דהכא דקתני וחכמים אומרים מוכת עץ מנה כשהכיר בה: **לא הכיר בה ולא כלום.** והא לא מצינו למימר לר' מאיר הכיר בה מאתים לא הכיר בה מנה דאי במקח טעות מחזקינן ליה משום דלא הכיר בה לית לה מידי ואי לאו מקח טעות הוא אין חילוק בין הכיר ללא הכיר: **והדר ביה רבא גר'** ול"ג מההיא. והדר ביה רבא ממאי דאמר לרבנן לא הכיר בה ולא כלום אלא בין הכיר בין לא הכיר יש לה מנה לרבנן ומאתים לר"מ ומתני' דהכא דברי הכל: **הוצאת שם רע.** ליענש מאה כסף אם שקר וליסקל אם אמת היה: **בא לב"ד.** זקוק לבוא לב"ד ואומר כו': **ואמר רב חייא גרסי':** **ומותיב רב נחמן גר':** **נסתחפה שדהו.** מזלך גרם כאדם שהמטר בא וסוחף את זריעתו ועוקרה: **מקח טעות לגמרי משמע.** ואין לה כלום: **כי אמרה רב ששת להא שמעתתא.** להאי זאת אומרת דלעיל דיש לה כתובה מנה: **וקשיא להו.** הא דאותבינן: **ואמר רבא גרסי':** **ואלא קשיא הך.** ואקשינן לרבא אלא קשיא הך דלעיל דקתני זינתה מעיקרא יש לה כתובה מנה: **תריץ.** להאי דלעיל דכיצד הוצאת ש"ר תירוצא דתרלת לה לא תתרצה הכי אלא הכי אם יש עדים כו': **נמצאת.** לא הכיר בה משמע וקא מתרץ רבא יש לה כתובה מנה אלמא הדר ביה מההיא דלעיל דהא איהו אמר לרבנן ולא כלום וכרבי מאיר נמי לא תוקמה דהא רבי מאיר מאתים קאמר: **ויש לה עדים שלא נסתרה.** רבותא אשמעינן דאפי' הכי אין השני יכול לטעון טענת בתולים להפסידה כתובתה ולימא מקח טעות הוא: **שהרי כנסה ראשון.** ועליו לדעת שנבעלה:

זאת

תוספות

ושמואל אמר אין מוכת עץ בבשר. בלא הכיר בתולין איירי דאי בהכיר למה יש לה להיות פחותה ממוכת עץ: **לרבנן** הכיר בה מנה לא הכיר בה ולא כלום. ומתני' ר"מ היא ולא רבנן ואם תאמר אמאי לא קאמר לרבנן בין הכיר בה בין לא הכיר בה מנה כדקאמר במסקנא ותיתי מתניתין לדברי הכל וי"ל דלא ניחא ליה למימר הכי דכיון דרבנן מדמו לה לבעולה הויא בלא הכיר בה כמו כנסה בחזקת בתולה ונמצאת בעולה וסבירא ליה דלית לה ולא כלום ובמסקנא סבר הא דמדמו לה לבעולה היינו לענין מנה אבל מקח טעות לא הויא כמו בעולה דאינו מקפיד כ"כ במוכת עץ שיהא מקח טעות: **הדר** ביה רבא מההיא. אבל מהא לא בעי למימר דהדר ביה משום דמקח טעות לגמרי משמע וא"ת מנא לן דהדר ביה ממה שאמר לרבנן לא הכיר בה ולא כלום נאמר שחזר בו ממה שאמר לא הכיר בה לר"מ מאתים אלא נפרש לא הכיר בה מנה ונוקי ברייתא כרבי מאיר וי"ל כדפי' לעיל בקונטרס דאין זה סברא דאי חשיב מקח טעות לא יהא לה כלום ואי לא חשיב מקח טעות למה לא יהא לה מאתים כיון דמדמה לה לבוגרת דאטו לבוגרת פוחתין לה מכתובתה א):

אמר

עין משפט נר מצוה

ע א מיי' פי"א מהל' אישות הל"א טוש"ע אה"ע סי' סז סעי' ג:
עא ב מיי' שם הל"ג טוש"ע שם סעי' ד:
עב ג ד מיי' שם טוש"ע שם סעי' ה:
עג ה טוש"ע שם סעי' ב:

גליון הש"ס

גמ' ואמר רבא מאן דקא מותיב שפיר. שבת קכג ע"א ר"ה ו ע"ב:

תוספות ישנים

א) ועוד נ"ל דניחא ליה טפי דלרבנן לא הכיר בה מנה דהשתא מיתוקמא מתני' וברייתא נמי כרבנן. ת"י עה"ג:

ליקוטי רש"י

משארסתני. אירע לי ואית לי מאתים [לקמן טז.]. **ונסתחפה שדהו.** לשון מטר סוחף (משלי כח) נשטפה שדך כלומר מזלך גרם [לעיל ב.]. נסחף, נשטפו והחליקו גבוריך כמו מטר סוחף (משלי כח) נסתחפה שדהו לשון משנה ומנחם חברו לשון סליון וכן חבר מטר סוחף ודונש פתר מטר סוחף כמו מטר סועף כמו מסעף פארה במערצה (ישעיה י) [ירמיה מו, טו]. סוחף, שוטף ובמשנה נסתחפה שדהו וכן נסחף אביריך (ירמיה מו) נשטפו ומעדו וכשלו [משלי כח, ג].

מסורת הש"ס

א) [נדה מד:], ב) [לקמן יג.], ג) לקמן יג. [טז.], ד) לקמן מו., ה) [לקמן יג.], ו) [לקמן יב: טז.].

תוספות רי"ד

איתמר קטן שבא על הגדולה רב אמר עשאה מוכת עץ. פי' דכיון שהוציא בתוליה אע"ג שאין ביאתו ביאה לא גרע מעץ הנתקע וכתובתה מנה לרבנן ושמואל אמר אין מוכת עץ בבשר פי' בבשר אדם. ואי בעולה לא הויא מוכת עץ נמי לא הויא והרי היא כאילו מיעכה היא באצבעה שהממעכת בתוליה באצבעה לא הפסידה מאתים דדוקא דרוסת איש ומוכת עץ לרבנן הפסידה המאתים אבל במיעוך לא הפסידה המאתים כיון שאין כוונתה אלא שלא להצטער תחת בעלה ובמוכת עץ דפליגי רבנן משום דהוי שלא לדעתה ומיסניא בהכי. אמרי' בפ' ד' אחין כל הני מיעכות של בית ר' תמר שמן וקי"ל כשמואל בדיני: **אמר רמב"ח** מחלוקת כשהכיר בה. פי' כשכונסה וכתב לה כתובה היה יודע שהיא מוכת עץ דר"מ מדמי לה לבוגרת פי' דקי"ל דכלו בתוליה ואפ"ה כתובתן מאתים ורבנן מדמו לה לבעולה ור"מ אדמדמי לה לבוגרת לדמו לה לבעולה בעולה איתעביד בה מעשה (בוגרת) [בידי אדם הא] לא איתעביד בה מעשה ורבנן אדמדמו לה לבעולה לדמו לה לבוגרת בוגרת לא איתעביד בה מעשה כלל הא איתעביד בה מעשה. אבל לא הכיר בה ד"ה ולא כלום פי' שמקח טעות הוא. ורבא אסיק דבין הכיר בה ובין לא הכיר בה לר"מ כתובתה מאתים לרבנן כתובתה מנה. וקי"ל כרבנן ולא כר"מ דיחיד ורבים הלכה כרבים: **מתני' בתולה** אלמנה גרושה וחלוצה מן הנשואין כתובתן מנה ואין להן טענת בתולים. הגיורת והשבויה והשפחה שנפדו ושנתגיירו ושנשתחררו יתירות על ג' שנים ויום א' כתובתן מנה ואין להן טענת בתולים. פי' בתולה מן הנשואין וכגון שנכנסה לחופה ומת בעלה בחזקת בעולה קיימא משעה שנכנסה תחתיו וכתובתה מנה אם נשאת לאחר סתם ואין להם טענת בתולים להפסידה אותה מנה ולומר בחזקת בתולה נשאתיך והרי מקחי מקח טעות: **תנו רבנן** כנסה הראשון לשם נשואין ויש לה עדים שלא נסתרה או שנסתרה אלא שלא שהתה עמו כדי ביאה אין השני יכול לטעון טענת בתולים פי' להפסידה מנה הראוי לאלמנה מן הנשואין שהרי כנסה הראשון. ואע"פ שהעדים מעידין אינו יכול לטעון.

אמר

אף אנו נאמר איילונית דוכרנית דלא ילדה: **מתני'** א הגיורת והשבויה והשפחה שנפדו ושנתגיירו ושנשתחררו פחותות מבנות שלש שנים ויום אחד כתובתן מאתים ויש להן טענת בתולין: **גמ'** אמר רב הונא ב גר קטן מטבילין אותו על דעת בית דין מאי קמ"ל דזכות הוא לו וזכין לאדם שלא בפניו תנינא ג זכין לאדם שלא בפניו ואין חבין לאדם שלא בפניו מהו דתימא עובד כוכבים בהפקירא ניחא ליה דהא קיימא לן דעבד ודאי בהפקירא ניחא ליה קמ"ל דהני מילי גדול דטעם טעם דאיסורא אבל קטן זכות הוא לו לימא מסייע ליה הגיורת והשבויה והשפחה שנפדו ושנתגיירו ושנשתחררו פחותות מבנות שלש שנים ויום אחד מאי לאו דאטבלינהו על דעת בית דין לא הכא במאי עסקינן בגר שנתגיירו בניו ובנותיו עמו ד דניחא להו במאי דעביד אבוהון אמר רב יוסף ה הגדילו יכולין למחות איתיביה אביי הגיורת והשבויה והשפחה שנפדו ושנתגיירו ושנשתחררו פחותות מבנות שלש שנים ויום אחד כתובתן מאתים ואי ס"ד הגדילו יכולין למחות יהבינן לה כתובה דאזלה ואכלה בגיותה ו לכי גדלה לכי גדלה נמי ממחייא ונפקא ז כיון שהגדילה א) שעה אחת ולא מיחתה שוב אינה יכולה למחות מתיב רבא ח אלו נערות שיש להן קנס הבא על הממזרת ועל הנתינה ועל הכותית ועל הגיורת ועל השבויה ועל השפחה שנפדו ושנתגיירו ושנשתחררו פחותות מבנות שלש שנים ויום אחד יש להן קנס ואי אמרת הגדילו יכולין למחות יהבינן לה קנס דאזלה ואכלה בגיותה לכי גדלה נמי ממחייא ונפקא כיון שהגדילה שעה אחת ולא מיחתה שוב אינה יכולה למחות אביי לא אמר כרבא התם קנסא היינו טעמא ט) שלא יהא חוטא נשכר רבא לא אמר כאביי י) ח כתובה היינו טעמא שלא תהא קלה בעיניו להוציאה: **מתני'** ט הגדול שבא על הקטנה וקטן שבא על הגדולה ומוכת עץ כתובתן מאתים דברי רבי מאיר י) וחכ"א י מוכת עץ כתובתה מנה כ בתולה אלמנה גרושה וחלוצה מן הנישואין כתובתן מנה ואין

רש"י

אף אנו נאמר. אף אנו נדרוש את השמות מה לשון איילונית שקראו חכמים לאשה שאינה ראויה לילד: **דוכרנית.** לשון איל תמים דמתרגמינן דכר שלים (ויקרא ה) הרי היא כאיל שאינו יולד: **גמ'** (ה) **על דעת ב"ד.** אם אין לו אב ואמו הביאתו להתגייר: **מטבילין.** לאין לך גר בלא מילה וטבילה: **על דעת בית דין.** שלשה יהו בטבילתו כדין כל טבילת גר שלריכים ג' והן נעשין לו אב והרי הוא גר על ידיהן ומגעו ביין כשר: **מהו דתימא עובד כוכבים בהפקירא ניחא ליה.** וחוב הוא לו ואין אדם נעשה שליח לאדם לחובתו שלא בפניו כלומר שלא מדעתו וקטן לאו בר דיעה הוא: **דהא גבי עבד קי"ל.** בפ"ק דגיטין (דף יג.) דודאי בהפקירא ניחא ליה נוח לו להיות עבד והא מותר בהפקר זימת השפחות מהיות בן חורין להיות מותר בבת ישראל דלא זילא ליה ולא שכיחא ליה להפקירא: **קמ"ל.** הכא דגבי עובד כוכבים קטן לא אמרינן הכי: **דהני מילי.** דניחא ליה בהפקירא: **גדול.** שגדל [במדות] הפקירות וטעים ליה טעמא דאיסורא: **הגדילו.** קטנים שנתגיירו ואפי' עם אביהן: **יכולין למחות.** ולומר אי אפשינו להיות גרים ומחזרין לסורן ואין לנו לענשן בב"ד ואפי' ידינו תקיפה ואם קדש אשה משמיחה אינה צריכה גט להיות כישראל מומר: **לכי גדלה.** לא יהבינן לה עד שתגדיל: **שוב אינה יכולה למחות.** ואם מיחתה הרי היא כישראלית מומרת ליענש בכל עונשי ב"ד: **שיש להן קנס.** נ' כסף אם יאנסו: **הבא על הממזרת.** ואע"ג דלא קרינן ביה ולו תהיה לאשה שהרי אינה ראויה לקיימה אפילו הכי יש לה קנס כדלקמן: **אביי לא אמר כרבא.** דמותיב מקנסא דקסבר לאו תיובתא היא דטעמא דקנסא שלא יהא חוטא נשכר להפטר: **רבא לא אמר כאביי.** דמותיב מכתובה דהתם טעמא מאי תקינו לה רבנן כתובה שלא תהא קלה בעיניו להוציאה וכל זמן שלא מיחתה גיורת היא ועבדינן לה תקנתא: **מתני' הבא על הקטנה.** פחותה מבת שלש שאין ביאתה ביאה שהרי בתוליה חוזרין: **וקטן.** פחות מבן תשע שאמרו חכמים אין ביאתו ביאה ובא על הגדולה: **ומוכת עץ.** שנתקע לה עץ באותו מקום: **כתובתן מאתים.** אם נשאו לאיש אחרי כן לא אבדו בכך את כתובתן אם נשאה סתם ולא פירש לה כלום: **בתולה.** שהיא אלמנה או גרושה או חלוצה: **מן הנישואין.** כגון שנכנסה לחופה ומת בעלה בחזקת שלא נבעלה: **כתובתה מנה.** אם ניסת לאחר סתם כתובתה מנה דבחזקת בעולה קיימא משנכנסה לחופה: ואין

תוספות

מטבילין אותו על דעת ב"ד משום דזכות הוא. ותימה דהא זכייה הוי מטעם שליחות דכיון דזכות הוא לו אנן סהדי דעביד ליה שליח כדמוכח בפ"ק דב"מ (דף יב.) גבי חצר משום יד איתרבאי ולא גרע משליחות וא"כ היאך זכין לקטן והלא אין שליחות לקטן כדאמרינן באיזהו נשך (שם עא:) ועוד דאכתי עובד כוכבים הוא ואמרי' התם דקטן דאתי לכלל שליחות אית ליה זכייה מדרבנן עובד כוכבים דלא אתי לכלל שליחות אפילו זכייה מדרבנן לית ליה ונראה לר"י דהכא נמי דזכין לו מדרבנן כדאמרינן התם דקטן אית ליה זכייה מדרבנן ואע"ג דאכתי עובד כוכבים הוא הא אתי לכלל שליחות א"נ כיון דבהך זכייה נעשה ישראל הוה ליה כישראל גמור לעניין זכייה וא"ת היכי הוי גר מדרבנן ושרינן ליה בבת ישראל וקידושיו קידושין הא מן התורה עובד כוכבים הוא וי"ל דקסבר כמ"ד בהאשה רבה (יבמות דף פט:) דיש כח ביד חכמים לעקור דבר מן התורה בקום ועשה וכי פריך מאי קמ"ל הוה מצי לשנויי קמ"ל דיש כח ביד חכמים לעקור דבר מן התורה בקום ועשה וחד מתרי טעמי נקט והא דאמרי' בריש בן סורר (סנהדרין דף סח: ושם) גבי גזל הגר אם אין לאיש גואל איש אתה צריך לחזר אחריו אם יש לו גואל אבל קטן אי אתה צריך לחזר אחריו כו' משכחת לה גר קטן מן התורה במעוברת שנתגיירה ט) כדאמרי' בפרק הערל (יבמות דף עח. ושם) עובדת כוכבים מעוברת שנתגיירה בנה אין צריך טבילה והוי גר מן התורה דישראל גמור הוא ואית ליה ממון מן התורה כגון שירש את אמו ואי אתה צריך לחזר עליו שאין לו יורשין שאינו מוליד ואחיו מן האם אין יורשין אותו ולפי ספרים דגרסינן בב"מ (דף עא:) זכייה מיהא אית ליה ולא גרס מדרבנן ניחא דמצי למימר דאית ליה זכייה מן התורה ועובד כוכבים קטן כיון דבא להתגייר חשבינן ליה כישראל קטן ואע"ג דזכייה הוי מטעם שליחות ואין לו שליחות מן התורה ה"מ בדבר שיש בו קצת חובה כגון להפריש תרומתו דשמא היה רוצה לפוטרה בחטה אחת או שמא היה רוצה להעדיף אבל הכא שזכות גמור הוא לו יש לו שליחות: **מהו** דתימא עובד כוכבים בהפקירא ניחא ליה. ואע"ג דרבנן פליגי אר' מאיר בפ' קמא דגיטין (דף יג. ושם) ולית להו טעמא דבהפקירא ניחא ליה ה"מ גבי עבד שאינו חושש בהפקירא שמפקיע עצמו מן השעבוד אבל גבי עובד כוכבים שאינו משועבד ניחא ליה בהפקירא וכן נראה דאי לא תימא הכי היכי מייתי סייעתא מההוא דגיורת דלמא רבנן היא דאפילו בגדול לית להו בהפקירא ניחא ליה: **אבל** קטן זכות הוא לו. והא דתנן בפרק קמא דגיטין (ג"ז שם) האומר תנו גט זה לאשתי ושיחרור זה לעבדי רצה לחזור בשניהם יחזור דברי רבי מאיר היינו בעבד גדול דבקטן מודה רבי מאיר דזכות הוא לו דלא ניחא ליה בהפקירא כדאמרינן הכא משום דלא טעים טעמא דאיסורא א"כ איירי בעבד קטן וכגון שהוא של כהן דחוב הוא לו שיצא לחירות לפי שמפסידו מלאכול בתרומה: **לכי** גדלה. ° וא"ת והלא כבר גדולה היא שהיא נערה כיון שהיא בת קנס ומפרש ר"י לכי גדלה ונהגה מנהג יהודית: **אביי** לא אמר כרבא שלא יהא חוטא נשכר. משמע דרבא לית ליה טעמא דשלא יהא חוטא נשכר וקשה דאמרי' בפ' שור שנגח ד' וה' (ב"ק דף לח: ושם) קסבר רבי מאיר כותים גירי אמת הן וקנס הוא דקניס ר"מ בממונם לענין שור שנגח שלא יטמעו בהן ופריך אלו נערות שיש להן קנס הבא על הכותית ואי קניס ר"מ בממונם ה"נ ניקנס ומשני דהכא לא בעי למקנס שלא יהא חוטא נשכר והשתא לרבא דלית ליה הכא טעם דחוטא נשכר היכי מצי משני התם וי"ל דהתם אית ליה שפיר האי טעמא כיון דבדין יש להן קנס דגרי אמת הן אלא דבעי' למקנס להו סברא הוא דמשום טעמא שלא יהא חוטא נשכר מוקמינן לה אדינא אבל הכא סבירא ליה לרבא דמשום טעמא שלא יהא חוטא נשכר אין ליתן לה כיון דמן הדין לית לה שהרי עובדת כוכבים גמורה היא אם תמחה ובפ' אלו נערות (לקמן דף לו:) דלית ליה לרבא שלא יהא חוטא נשכר גבי שבויה משום דמוקמינן לה בקדושתה: ושמואל

מסורת הש"ס

א) [ע' תוס' גיטין ה: ד"ה והא קי"ל], ב) [עירובין פא: יבמות קיח: וש"נ], ג) [גיטין יא: ע' תוס' שם], ד) לקמן כט. ב"ק לח., ה) [יבמות מח: וש"נ], ו) [יבמות מח.], ז) [לקמן יג.], ח) [ל"ל גר קטן], ט) [וע' תוס' ב"ק קט: ד"ה גר קטן ותוס' סנהדרין סח:].

תוספות ישנים

א) [קשה א"כ ממי תדע שעת התמאה דהא בקטנות אינה יכולה למחות כר"י ז"ל כגון שהתמאה מנהג גיות לפני גדלותה ונהגה יום או יומים לאחר גדלותה. מ"י עס"י]:

גליון הש"ס

גמ' שלא יהא חוטא נשכר. ע"ב דמלה מ"ז נדה דף ד ע"ב: תוס' ד"ה לכי גדלה. וא"ת והלא כבר גדולה. עיין נדה מד ע"ב תוס' ד"ה שלשים יום:

ליקוטי רש"י

איילונית. שאין לה סימני נערות לעולם ואינה יולדת, לשון איל זכר דוכרנית דלא ילדה [לקמן לה:]. ממעי אמה ויש לה סימנין שאין לה שערות ולא דדין ולשון איילונית דוכרנית כאיל זכר שאינו יולד [ערובין מז:]. **זכין לאדם שלא בפניו.** ושלא מדעתו דאנן סהדי דניחא ליה שתהא שלוחו [ב"מ יב:]. דכיון אנן סהדי דניחא ליה לפיכך זכין ואין חבין [חולין פג.]. **ואין חבין לאדם שלא בפניו.** אין אדם יכול ליעשות שלוחו שלא מדעתו לדבר שהוא חוב לו או הפסד [קידושין כג.]. דבר שהוא חוב לו שאינו חפץ בו [סוטה כד.]. דבר שהוא זכות לו לדעתו קרוי חובה [לעיל י:]. כלומר אין אדם נכסף על ידו אלא ע"י עשאו הוא שליח הוא וזהו כבפניו [גיטין ט:]. דאין אדם נעשה שליח לחבירו שלא מדעתו להפסידו [חולין שם]. **אלו נערות.** דוקא נערה משהגדילה שתי שערות עד שתבגר והם ששה חדשים שבין נערות לבגרות אבל קטנה ובוגרת אין להם קנס. **שיש להן קנס.** אם אנסה אדם נותן לאביה חמשים כסף כדכתיב ונתן האיש השוכב וגו' [דברים כב]. **הבא על הממזרת.** בגמרא פריך אבל כשירות לא ומשני פסולות אילטריכא ליה [שם]. **הנתינה.** מן הגבעונים והיא אסורה לקהל דדוד גזר עליהם כדאמרינן ביבמות (דף עח:) ועל שם ויתנם יהושע חוטבי עלים ושאבי מים וגו' (יהושע ט) קרי להו נתינים. **הכותית.** קסבר גירי אריות הן ויש בהן כלאו לא תתחתן בם (דברים ז). **ועל השבויה.** ישראלית שנשבית פחותה מבת שלש שנים בחזקת שלא נבעלה היא שאפילו נבעלה בתוליה חוזרין (לקמן כט.).

עין משפט נר מצוה

סב א מיי' פי"ג מהל' איסורי ביאה הל' ו' סמג עשין מח טוש"ע יו"ד סי' רסח סעי' ג:

סג ב מיי' פי"ג מהל' איסורי ביאה הל' ז סמג לאוין קח טוש"ע יו"ד סי' רסח סעי' ז:

סד ג מיי' פ"ד מהל' זכיה הל' ב סמג עשין פ"ב טוש"ע חו"מ סי' רמג סעי' א וטוש"ע יו"ד סי' רסח סעי' ז:

סה ד ה ו ז מיי' פ"ו מהל' מלכים הל' ג טוש"ע יו"ד סי' רסח סעי' ז:

סו ח מיי' פי"א מהל' אישות הל' ז טור [וטו"ע] אה"ע סי' סז [ס"א בהגה"ה]:

סז ט מיי' פי"א מהל' אישות הל"ג סמג עשין מח טוש"ע שם סי' סז סעיף ד:

סח י מיי' שם טוש"ע שם סעיף ה:

סט כ מיי' שם הל' א טוש"ע שם סעי' ב:

תוספות רי"ד

הגיורת והשבויה והשפחה שנפדו ושנתגיירו ושנשתחררו פחותות מבנות ג' שנים ויום אחד כתובתן מאתים ויש להן טענת בתולים. פי' בחזקת בתולות הן. ואם נמצאת בעולה אומר לה מקחי מקח טעות ואבדה כל כתובתה. אמר ר"ה גר קטן מטבילין אותו ע"ד ב"ד. פי' אע"פ שאין לו אב ואם כגון תינוק שנמצא מושלך או ששבו ישראל קטני פלשתים ב"ד מלין אותם והם כישראל לכל דבר. והמורה פי' מטבילין אותו. דאינו גר עד שימול ויטבול. עיין פרק החולץ [דף מו] ובפ"ח דיבמות [דף עא]. מאי קמ"ל דזכין לאדם שלא בפניו תנינא זכין לאדם שלא בפניו ואין חבין לו לאדם אלא בפניו. מ"ד בהפקירא ניחא ליה וחוב הוא לו. פי' שאין אדם נעשה שליח לחובתו שלא בפניו כלומר שלא מדעת. קמ"ל דה"מ גדול דטעים טעמא דאיסורא אבל קטן זכות הוא [לו]. **אמר ר"י ואם הגדילו.** פי' הקטנים שנתגיירו ואפי' עם אביהן יכולין למחות. פי' יכולין לומר אי אפשינו להיות גרים ואין לנו לענשן בב"ד. ואפילו ידינו תקיפה. ואפי' אם קידש אשה משמיחה אינה צריכה גט להיות כישראל מומר. ודוקא שלא הגיעו לכלל שתי שערות אבל אם הגדילו ולא מיחו אין יכולין למחות ואם מיחו הרי הן כישראל מומר וקדושיו קדושין. א) והגדילו דר"י לאו דוקא שבאו לכלל עונשין אלא שבאו לכלל דעת ועדיין לא באו לכלל עונשין: **מתני' הגדול** שבא על הקטנה וקטן שבא על הגדולה ומוכת עץ כתובתן מאתים. דברי ר"מ וחכ"א מוכת עץ כתובתה מנה. פי' קטנה פחותה מבת ג' שנים ויום אחד שאין ביאתה ביאה שהרי בתולים חוזרין. וקטן פחות מבן ט' שאמרו חכמים אין ביאתו ביאה לקנות קנין גמור. כגון אם בא על יבמתו דהתם אמרי' אין ביאתו ביאה ב) חשובה לקנות לגמרי. פי' לא גרעה אותה ביאה ממאמר בגדול. שכמו שמאמר בגדול פוסלה על שאר האחין. כך ביאת [פחות] בן ט' פסלה על האחין. עיין בס"פ האשה רבה: מוכת עץ שנתקע לה עץ באותו מקום ויצאו בתוליה כתובתה מאתים. פי' לא הפסידו כתובתן אם נישאו סתם וחכ"א מוכת עץ כיון שאיבדה בתוליה כתובתה מנה:

חשק שלמה על תוס' רי"ד א) ובדברי רבינו אלו נתיישב קושיית התוס' כאן בד"ה לכי גדלה וע"ש. ב) ע' ביבמות דף לג ע"א דמייתי שם בגמ' בן ט' לא הוי כמאמר בגדול אבל בפחות מבן ט' לא מיירי התם כלל וצ"ע.

of **wood**[29] – **כְּתוּבָּתָן מָאתַיִם** – **their *kesubah* is two hundred** *zuz*;[30] **דִּבְרֵי רַבִּי מֵאִיר** – these are **the words of R' Meir. וַחֲכָמִים אוֹמְרִים** – **But the Sages say: מוּכַּת עֵץ כְּתוּבָּתָהּ מָנֶה** – **The *kesubah* of one injured by a** piece of **wood is a *maneh*** [one hundred *zuz*].[31]

The Mishnah continues:

בְּתוּלָה אַלְמָנָה גְּרוּשָׁה וַחֲלוּצָה – **A virgin widow, divorcee or *chalutzah*** **מִן הַנִּישׂוּאִין** – **from *nisuin*** –[32] **כְּתוּבָּתָן מָנֶה** – **their *kesubah* is a *maneh*** [one hundred *zuz*],

NOTES

reaches the age of thirteen. However, with regard to cohabitation he is deemed mature at the age of nine years and a day (Mishnah, *Niddah* 45a).]

29. I.e. a piece of wood was thrust into her vagina (*Rashi*) and ruptured her hymen (*Ritva* to 11b).

30. If one of these women marries afterwards she does not forfeit her *kesubah* on account of her history, provided [in the case of the woman injured by a piece of wood] that her husband does not stipulate at the time of the betrothal [that he wishes to marry a virgin] (*Rashi*; see *Shitah Mekubetzes*).

31. The Gemara (11b) will elaborate on this dispute.

32. She entered the *chuppah* with her first husband but he died [or divorced her] immediately afterwards, such that it is assumed that the marriage was not consummated (*Rashi*).

אף אנו נאמר איילונית דוכרנית דלא ילדה: **מתני'** א הגיורת והשבויה והשפחה שנפדו ושנתגיירו ושנשתחררו פחותות מבנות שלש שנים ויום אחד כתובתן מאתים ויש להן טענת בתולין: **גמ'** אמר רב הונא ב גר קטן מטבילין אותו על דעת בית דין מאי קמ"ל א) דזכות הוא לו וזכין לאדם שלא בפניו תנינא ב) ג זכין לאדם שלא בפניו ואין חבין לאדם שלא בפניו מהו דתימא עובד כוכבים בהפקירא ניחא ליה דהא קיימא לן ג) דעבד ודאי בהפקירא ניחא ליה קמ"ל דהני מילי גדול דטעם טעם דאיסורא אבל קטן זכות הוא לו לימא מסייע ליה הגיורת והשבויה והשפחה שנפדו ושנתגיירו ושנשתחררו פחותות מבנות שלש שנים ויום אחד מאי לאו דאטבלינהו על דעת בית דין לא הכא במאי עסקינן בגר שנתגיירו בניו ובנותיו עמו ד דניחא להו במאי דעביד אבוהון אמר רב יוסף ה הגדילו יכולין למחות איתיביה אביי הגיורת והשבויה והשפחה שנפדו ושנתגיירו ושנשתחררו פחותות מבנות שלש שנים ויום אחד כתובתן מאתים ואי ס"ד הגדילו יכולין למחות יהבינן לה כתובה דאזלה ואכלה בגיותה ו לכי גדלה לכי גדלה נמי ממחייא ונפקא ז כיון שהגדילה א) שעה אחת ולא מיחתה שוב אינה יכולה למחות מתיב רבא ד) אלו נערות שיש להן קנס הבא על הממזרת ועל הנתינה ועל הכותית ועל הגיורת ועל השבויה ועל השפחה שנפדו ושנתגיירו ושנשתחררו פחותות מבנות שלש שנים ויום אחד יש להן קנס ואי אמרת הגדילו יכולין למחות יהבינן לה קנס דאזלה ואכלה בגיותה לכי גדלה נמי ממחייא ונפקא כיון שהגדילה שעה אחת ולא מיחתה שוב אינה יכולה למחות אביי לא אמר כרבא התם קנסא היינו טעמא ה) שלא יהא חוטא נשכר רבא לא אמר כאביי ו) ח כתובה היינו טעמא שלא תהא קלה בעיניו להוציאה: **מתני'** ט הגדול שבא על הקטנה וקטן שבא על הגדולה ומוכת עץ כתובתן מאתים דברי רבי מאיר ז) וחכ"א י מוכת עץ כתובתה מנה כ בתולה אלמנה גרושה וחלוצה מן הנישואין כתובתן מנה ואין

אף אנו נאמר. אף אנו נדרוש את השמות מה לשון איילונית שקראו חכמים לאשה שאינה ראויה לילד: **דוכרנית.** לשון איל תמים דמתרגמינן דכר שלים (ויקרא ה) הרי היא כאיל שאינו יולד: **גמ'** (ה) על דעת ב"ד). אם אין לו אב ואמו הביאתו להתגייר: **מטבילין.** דאין לך גר בלא מילה וטבילה: **על דעת בית דין.** שלשה יהו בטבילתו כדין כל טבילת גר שצריכים ג' והן נעשין לו אב והרי הוא גר על ידיהן ומגעו ביין כשר: **מהו דתימא עובד כוכבים בהפקירא ניחא ליה.** וחוב הוא לו ואין אדם נעשה שליח לאדם לחובתו שלא בפניו כלומר שלא מדעתו וקטן לאו בר דיעה הוא: **דהא גבי עבד קי"ל.** בפ"ק דגיטין (דף יג.) דודאי בהפקירא ניחא ליה נוח לו להיות עבד ויהא מותר בהפקר זימת השפחות מהיות בן חורין להיות מותר בבת ישראל דלא זילא ליה ולא שכיחא ליה להפקירא: **קמ"ל.** הכא דגבי עובד כוכבים קטן לא אמרינן הכי: **דהני מילי.** דניחא ליה בהפקירא: **גדול.** שגדל [במדות] הפקירות וטעים ליה טעמא דאיסורא: **הגדילו.** קטנים שנתגיירו ואפי' עם אביהן: **יכולין למחות.** ולומר אי אפשינו להיות גרים וחוזרין לסורן ואין לנו לענשן בב"ד ואפי' ידינו תקיפה ואם קדש אשה משמיחה אינה צריכה גט להיות כישראל מומר: **לכי גדלה.** לא יהבינן לה עד שתגדיל: **שוב אינה יכולה למחות.** ואם מיחתה הרי היא כישראלית מומרת ליענש בכל עונשי ב"ד: **שיש להן קנס.** נ' כסף אם יאנסו: **הבא על הממזרת.** ואע"ג דלא קרינן ביה ולו תהיה לאשה שהרי אינה ראויה לקיימה אפילו הכי יש לה קנס כדלקמן: **אביי לא אמר כרבא.** דמותיב מקנסא דקסבר לאו תיובתא היא דטעמא דקנסא שלא יהא חוטא נשכר להפטר: **רבא לא אמר כאביי.** דמותיב מכתובה דהתם טעמא מאי תקינו לה רבנן כתובה שלא תהא קלה בעיניו להוציאה וכל זמן שלא מיחתה גיורת היא ועבדינן לה תקנתא: **מתני' הבא על הקטנה.** פחותה מבת שלש שאין ביאתה ביאה שהרי בתוליה חוזרין: **וקטן.** פחות מבן תשע שאמרו חכמים אין ביאתו ביאה ובא על הגדולה: **ומוכת עץ.** שנתקע לה עץ באותו מקום: **כתובתן מאתים.** אם נשאו לאיש אחרי כן לא אבדו בכך את כתובתן אם נשאה סתם ולא פירש לה כלום: **בתולה.** שהיא אלמנה או גרושה או חלוצה: **מן הנישואין.** כגון שנכנסה לחופה ומת בעלה בחזקת שלא נבעלה: **כתובתה מנה.** אם ניסת לאחר סתם כתובתה מנה דבחזקת בעולה קיימא משנכנסה לחופה: ואין

מטבילין אותו על דעת ב"ד משום דזכות הוא. ותימה דהא זכייה הוי מטעם שליחות דכיון דזכות הוא לו אנן סהדי דעביד ליה שליח כדמוכח בפ"ק דב"מ (דף יב.) גבי חצר משום יד איתרבאי ולא גרע משליחות וא"כ היאך זכין לקטן והלא אין שליחות לקטן כדאמרינן באיזהו נשך (שם עא:) ועוד דאכתי עובד כוכבים הוא ואמרי' התם דקטן דאתי לכלל שליחות אית ליה זכייה מדרבנן עובד כוכבים דלא אתי לכלל שליחות אפילו זכייה מדרבנן לית ליה ונראה לר"י דהכא נמי דזכין לו מדרבנן כדאמרינן התם דקטן אית ליה זכייה מדרבנן ואע"ג דאכתי עובד כוכבים הוא הא אתי לכלל שליחות א"נ כיון דבהך זכייה נעשה ישראל הוה ליה כישראל גמור לענין זכייה וא"ת היכי הוי גר מדרבנן ושרינן ליה בבת ישראל וקידושיו קידושין הא מן התורה עובד כוכבים הוא וי"ל דקסבר כמ"ד בהאשה רבה (יבמות דף פט:) דיש כח ביד חכמים לעקור דבר מן התורה בקום ועשה וכי פריך מאי קמ"ל הוה מצי לשנויי קמ"ל דיש כח ביד חכמים לעקור דבר מן התורה בקום ועשה וחד מתרי טעמי נקט והא דאמרי' בריש בן סורר (סנהדרין דף סח: ושם) גבי גזל הגר אם אין לאיש גואל איש אתה צריך לחזור אחריו אם יש לו גואל אבל קטן אי אתה צריך לחזור אחריו כו' משכחת לה גר קטן מן התורה במעוברת שנתגיירה ט) כדאמרי' בפרק הערל (יבמות דף עח. ושם) עובדת כוכבים מעוברת שנתגיירה בנה אין צריך טבילה והוי גר מן התורה דישראל גמור הוא ואית ליה ממון מן התורה כגון שירש את אמו ואי אתה צריך לחזור עליו שאין לו יורשין שאינו מוליד ואחיו מן האם אין יורשין אותו ולפי ספרים דגרסינן בב"מ (דף עא:) זכייה מיהא אית ליה ולא גרס מדרבנן ניחא דמצי למימר דאית ליה זכייה מן התורה ועובד כוכבים קטן כיון דבא להתגייר חשבינן ליה כישראל קטן ואע"ג דזכייה הוי מטעם שליחות ואין לו שליחות מן התורה ה"מ בדבר שיש בו קצת חובה כגון להפריש תרומתו דשמא היה רוצה לפוטרה בחטה אחת או שמא היה רוצה להעדיף אבל הכא שזכות גמור הוא לו יש לו שליחות: **מהו** דתימא עובד כוכבים בהפקירא ניחא ליה. ואע"ג דרבנן פליגי אר' מאיר בפ' קמא דגיטין (דף יג. ושם) ולית להו טעמא דבהפקירא ניחא ליה ה"מ גבי עבד שאינו חושש בהפקירא שמפקיע עצמו מן השעבוד אבל גבי עובד כוכבים שאינו משועבד ניחא ליה בהפקירא וכן נראה דאי לא תימא הכי היכי מייתי סייעתא מההוא דגיורת דלמא רבנן היא דאפילו בגדול לית להו בהפקירא ניחא ליה: **אבל** קטן זכות הוא לו. והא דתנן בפרק קמא דגיטין (ג"ז שם) האומר תנו גט זה לאשתי ושיחרור זה לעבדי רצה לחזור בשניהם יחזור דברי רבי מאיר היינו בעבד גדול דבקטן מודה רבי מאיר דזכות הוא לו דלא ניחא ליה בהפקירא כדאמרינן הכא משום דלא טעים טעמא דאיסורא א"נ איירי אף בעבד קטן וכגון שהוא של כהן דחוב הוא לו שיצא לחירות לפי שמפסידו מלאכול בתרומה: **לכי** גדלה. ° וא"ת והלא כבר גדולה היא שהיא נערה כיון שהיא בת קנס ומפרש ר"י לכי גדלה ונהגה מנהג יהודית: **אביי** לא אמר כרבא שלא יהא חוטא נשכר. משמע דרבא לית ליה טעמא דשלא יהא חוטא נשכר וקשה דאמרי' בפ' שור שנגח ד' וה' (ב"ק דף לח: ושם) קסבר רבי מאיר כותים גירי אמת הן וקנס הוא דקניס ר"מ בממונם לענין שור שנגח שלא יטמעו בהן ופריך אלו נערות שיש להן קנס הבא על הכותית ואי קניס ר"מ בממונם ה"נ ניקנוס ומשני דהכא לא בעי למקנס שלא יהא חוטא נשכר והשתא לרבא דלית ליה הכא טעם דחוטא נשכר היכי מצי משני התם וי"ל דהתם אית ליה שפיר האי טעמא כיון דבדין יש להן קנס דגרי אמת הן אלא דבעי' למקנס להו סברא הוא דמשום טעמא שלא יהא חוטא נשכר מוקמינן לה אדינא אבל הכא סבירא ליה לרבא דמשום טעמא שלא יהא חוטא נשכר אין ליתן לה כיון דמן הדין לית לה שהרי עובדת כוכבים גמורה היא אם תמחה ובפ' אלו נערות (לקמן דף לו:) דאית ליה לרבא שלא יהא חוטא נשכר גבי שבויה משום דמוקמינן לה בקדושתה: ושמואל

עין משפט נר מצוה

סב א מיי' פי"א מהל' אישות הל' ח' סמג עשין מח טוש"ע אה"ע סי' סז סעי' ג:

סג ב מיי' פי"ג מהל' איסורי ביאה הל' ז' סמג לאוין קטו טוש"ע יו"ד סי' רסח סעי' ז:

סד ג מיי' פ"ד מהל' זכיה הל"ב סמג עשין פ"ב טוש"ע חו"מ סי' רמג סעי' א וטוש"ע יו"ד סי' רסח סעי' ז:

סה ד ה ו ז מיי' פ"י מהל' מלכים הל"ג טוש"ע יו"ד סי' רסח סעי' ז:

סו ח מיי' פי"א מהל' אישות הל"ז טור [ושו"ע] אה"ע סי' סז [ס"א בהג"ה]:

סז ט מיי' פי"א מהל' אישות הל"ג סמג עשין מח טוש"ע שם סעיף ד:

סח י מיי' שם טוש"ע שם סעיף ה:

סט כ מיי' שם הל' א טוש"ע שם סעי' ב:

תוספות רי"ד

הגיורת והשבויה והשפחה שנפדו ושנתגיירו ושנשתחררו פחותות מבנות ג' שנים ויום אחד כתובתן מאתים ויש להן טענת בתולים. פי' בחזקת בתולות הן. ואם נמצאת בעולה אומר לה מקחי מקח טעות ואבדה כל כתובתה. **אמר ר"ה** גר קטן מטבילין אותו ע"ד ב"ד. פי' אע"פ שאין לו אב ואם כגון תינוק שנמצא מושלך או ששבו ישראל קטני פלשתים ב"ד מלין אותם והם כישראל לכל דבר. והמורה פי' מטבילין אותו. דאינו גר עד שימול ויטבול. עיין פרק החולץ [דף מו] ובפ"ח דיבמות [דף עא]. מאי קמ"ל דזכין לאדם שלא בפניו תנינא זכין לאדם שלא בפניו ואין חבין לו לאדם אלא בפניו. מ"ד בהפקירא ניחא ליה וחוב הוא לו. פי' שאין אדם נעשה שליח לחובתו שלא בפניו כלומר שלא מדעת. קמ"ל דה"מ גדול דטעים טעמא דאיסורא אבל קטן זכות הוא [לו]. **אמר ר"י ואם הגדילו.** פי' הקטנים שנתגיירו ואפי' עם אביהן יכולין למחות. פי' יכולין לומר אי אפשינו להיות גרים ואין לנו לעונשם בב"ד. ואפילו ידינו תקיפה. ואם קידש אשה משמיחה אינה צריכה גט להיות כישראל מומר. ודוקא שלא הגיעו לכלל שתי שערות אבל אם הגדילו ולא מיחו אין יכולין למחות ואם מיחו הרי הן כישראל מומר וקדושי' קדושין. א) והגדילו דר"י לאו דוקא שבאו לכלל עונשין אלא שבאו לכלל דעת ועדיין לא באו לכלל עונשין: **מתני' הגדול** שבא על הקטנה וקטן שבא על הגדולה ומוכת עץ כתובתן מאתים. דברי ר"מ וחכ"א מוכת עץ כתובתן מנה. פי' קטנה פחותה מבת ג' שנים ויום אחד שאין ביאתה ביאה שהרי בתוליה חוזרין. וקטן פחות מבן ט' שאמרו חכמים אין ביאתו ביאה לקנות קנין גמור. כגון אם בא על יבמתו דהתם אמרי' אין ביאתו ביאה ב) חשובה לקנות לגמרי. פי' לא גרעה אותה ביאה ממאמר בגדול. שכמו שמאמר בגדול פוסלה על שאר האחין. כך ביאת [פחות] בן ט' פסלה על האחין. עיין בס"פ האשה רבה: **מוכת עץ** שנתקע לה עץ באותו מקום ויצאו בתוליה כתובתה מאתים. פי' לא הפסידו כתובתן אם נישאו סתם וחכ"א מוכת עץ כיון שאיבדה בתוליה כתובתה מנה:

חשק שלמה על תוס' רי"ד א) ובדברי רבינו אלו נתיישב קושית הת"י כאן בד"ה קטן ועי"ש. ב) ע"ש ביבמות דף לג לא דמיירי שם בביאת בן תשע שעשו כמאמר בגדול אבל בפחות מבן תשע לא מיירי התם כלל ול"ע.

מסורת הש"ס

א) [עי' תוס' גיטין ה: ד"ה והא קי"ל], ב) [עירובין פא: יבמות קיח: וש"נ], ג) [גיטין יג. עי' תוס' שם], ד) לקמן כט. ב"ק לח:, ה) [יבמות לג: וש"נ], ו) [יבמות פט. לקמן לט: נד.], ז) [לקמן יג.], ח) [צ"ל גר קטן], ט) [ועי' תוס' ב"ק קט: ד"ה קטן ותוס' סנהדרין סח:].

תוספות ישנים

א) [קשה א"כ מתי תדע שעת המחאה דהא בקטנות אינה יכולה למחות כר"י י"ל כגון שהתחילה מנהג גיות יום לפני גדלותה וכן נהגה יום או יומים לאחר גדלותה. ת"י עה"ג]:

גליון הש"ס

גמ' **שלא יהא חוטא נשכר.** פ"ב דחלה מ"ז נדה דף ד ע"ב: **תוס' ד"ה לכי גדלה. וא"ת והלא כבר גדולה.** עיין נדה מד ע"ב תוס' ד"ה שלשים יום:

ליקוטי רש"י

איילונית. שאין לה סימני נערות לעולם ואינה יולדת, לשון איל זכר דוכרניתא דלא ילדה [לקמן לה:]. ממעי אמה ויש לה סימנין שאין לה שערות ולא דדין ולשון איילונית דוכרניתא כאיל זה שאינו יולד [עירובין מז.]. **זכין לאדם שלא בפניו.** ושלא מדעתו דאנן סהדי דניחא ליה שתהא שלוחו [ב"מ יב.]. להרויחו אנן סהדי דניחא ליה לפיכך זכין ואין חבין [חולין פג.]. **ואין חבין לאדם שלא בפניו.** אין אדם יכול ליעשות שלוחו שלא מדעתו לדבר שאינה טובה או הפסד [קידושין כג.]. דבר שהוא טוב לו שאינו הפסד בו [סוטה כה.]. דבר שלעתו קרוי טובה [לעיל י.]. כלומר אין אדם נעשה שליח לאדם לחובתו ולא להיות נפסד על ידו אא"כ עשאו הוא שליח הוא דהיינו כבפניו [גיטין ט:]. דאין אדם נעשה שליח לחבירו שלא מדעתו להפסידו [חולין שם]. **אלו נערות.** דוקא נערה כשיצאה מקטנות שתי שערות עד שתבגר והם ששה חדשים שבין נערות לבגרות אבל קטנה ובוגרת אין להם קנס. **שיש להן קנס.** אם אנסה אדם נותן לאביה חמשים כסף בכתוב ונתן האיש השוכב וגו' [דברים כב]. **הבא על הממזרת.** בגמרא פריך אבל כשירות לא ומשני פסולות איצטריכא ליה לאשמועינן. **הנתינה.** גבעונים ויהיו לגזור לו דוד גזר עליהם כדאמרינן ביבמות [דף עח:] ועל שם ויתנם יהושע חוטבי עצים ושואבי מים [יהושע ט] קרי להו נתינים. **הכותית.** קסבר גירי אריות הן ויש בלאו לא תתחתן בם [דברים ז]. **ועל השבויה.** ישראלית שנשבית פחותה מבת שלש שנים ויום אחד דבחזקת בתולה היא שאפילו נבעלה בשביה בתוליה חוזרים [לקמן כט.].

The Gemara objects:

אִיתִיבֵיהּ אַבַּיֵי – **Abaye challenged this from** our **Mishnah:** הַגִּיוֹרֶת וְהַשְּׁבוּיָה וְהַשִּׁפְחָה – THE CONVERT, THE CAPTIVE AND THE SLAVE GIRL, שֶׁנִּפְדּוּ וְשֶׁנִּתְגַּיְּירוּ וְשֶׁנִּשְׁתַּחְרְרוּ – WHO WERE RANSOMED, CONVERTED OR EMANCIPATED פְּחוּתוֹת מִבְּנוֹת שָׁלֹשׁ שָׁנִים וְיוֹם אֶחָד – UNDER THE AGE OF THREE YEARS AND ONE DAY, כְּתוּבָּתָן מָאתַיִם – THEIR *KESUBAH* IS TWO HUNDRED *zuz,* like that of a virgin. וְאִי סָלְקָא דַּעְתָּךְ הִגְדִּילוּ יְכוֹלִין לִמְחוֹת – **Now, if you think that when they become adults they may renounce** their conversion, יַהֲבִינַן לָהּ כְּתוּבָּה דְּאָזְלָה וְאָכְלָה בְּגֵיוּתָהּ – is it right that **we should pay her a *kesubah* that she would go and spend as a gentile!?**[19]

The Gemara answers:

לִכִי גָּדְלָה – We give it to her **when she becomes an adult.**[20]

The Gemara objects:

לִכִי גָּדְלָה נַמִּי מְמַחְיָא וְנָפְקָא – But **when she becomes an adult she can also renounce** the conversion **and leave** Judaism! – ? –

The Gemara answers:

כֵּיוָן שֶׁהִגְדִּילָה שָׁעָה אַחַת וְלֹא מִיחֲתָה – **Once she becomes an adult for one moment and does not renounce** her conversion, שׁוּב אֵינָהּ יְכוֹלָה לִמְחוֹת – **she can no longer renounce** it.[21] Hence, at that time she may collect her *kesubah.*

The Gemara raises a second objection to Rav Yosef's ruling:

מָתִיב רָבָא – **Rava challenged** this from the following **Mishnah:**[22] אֵלּוּ נְעָרוֹת שֶׁיֵּשׁ לָהֶן קְנָס – THESE ARE THE *NE'AROS*[23] WHO ARE ENTITLED TO A FINE if they are violated: הַבָּא עַל הַמַּמְזֶרֶת וְעַל הַנְּתִינָה וְעַל הַכּוּתִית – If ONE VIOLATES A *MAMZERESS*, A *NESINAH* OR A CUTHEAN;[24] וְעַל הַגִּיוֹרֶת וְעַל הַשְּׁבוּיָה וְעַל הַשִּׁפְחָה – OR A CONVERT, A CAPTIVE OR SLAVE GIRL, שֶׁנִּפְדּוּ וְשֶׁנִּתְגַּיְּירוּ וְשֶׁנִּשְׁתַּחְרְרוּ – WHO WERE RANSOMED, CONVERTED, OR EMANCIPATED פְּחוּתוֹת מִבְּנוֹת שָׁלֹשׁ שָׁנִים וְיוֹם אֶחָד – UNDER THE AGE OF THREE YEARS AND ONE DAY, יֵשׁ לָהֶן קְנָס – THEY ARE ENTITLED TO A FINE.[25] The Mishnah's list includes a girl who converted before the age of three. וְאִי אָמְרַתְּ הִגְדִּילוּ יְכוֹלִין לִמְחוֹת – **Now, if you should say that when [minors who converted] become adults they may renounce** the conversion, יַהֲבִינַן לָהּ קְנָס דְּאָזְלָה וְאָכְלָה בְּגֵיוּתָהּ – is it right that **we should pay her a fine that she would go and spend as a gentile!?**

The Gemara answers:

לִכִי גָּדְלָה – We give it to her **when she becomes an adult.**

The Gemara objects:

לִכִי גָּדְלָה נַמִּי מְמַחְיָא וְנָפְקָא – But **when she becomes an adult she can also renounce** the conversion **and leave** Judaism! – ? –

The Gemara answers:

כֵּיוָן שֶׁהִגְדִּילָה שָׁעָה אַחַת וְלֹא מִיחֲתָה – **Once she becomes an adult for one moment and does not renounce** the conversion, שׁוּב אֵינָהּ יְכוֹלָה לִמְחוֹת – **she may no longer renounce** it.

Abaye and Rava both asked the identical question, but from different Mishnahs. The Gemara now explains why each preferred to ask the question from his Mishnah:

אַבַּיֵי לֹא אָמַר כְּרָבָא – **Abaye did not say** (i.e. ask) **as Rava** did from the Mishnah regarding the fine, הָתָם קְנָסָא הַיְינוּ טַעְמָא שֶׁלֹּא יְהֵא חוֹטֵא נִשְׂכָּר – because one could answer that **there** in the case of the **fine, the reason** we pay her the fine and are not concerned that she may renounce her conversion, **is so that the sinner not profit.**[26] Abaye therefore posed the question from our Mishnah of *kesubah.* רָבָא לֹא אָמַר כְּאַבַּיֵי – And **Rava did not say** (i.e. ask) **as Abaye** did from the Mishnah concerning the fine, כְּתוּבָּה הַיְינוּ טַעְמָא שֶׁלֹּא תְּהֵא קַלָּה בְּעֵינָיו לְהוֹצִיאָהּ – because one could answer that **the reason for** the institution of **a *kesubah* is so that [one's wife] should not be easy in his eyes to send away** (divorce). Therefore, as long as she did not yet renounce her conversion, the Rabbis wished to protect her and they therefore allowed her to collect the *kesubah.*

Mishnah The Mishnah lists circumstances under which a woman may be entitled only to a reduced *kesubah*: הַגָּדוֹל שֶׁבָּא עַל הַקְּטַנָּה – **An adult male who cohabited with a minor girl,**[27] וְקָטָן שֶׁבָּא עַל הַגְּדוֹלָה – **a minor boy who cohabited with an adult female,**[28] וּמוּכַּת עֵץ – **and** [**a woman**] **injured by a** piece

NOTES

19. It would not be right to allow her, once she renounces Judaism, to benefit from money to which she was entitled only under Jewish law (*Rambam, Melachim* 10:3).

20. If she was divorced or widowed while still a minor, the *kesubah* money is collected and held for her by the court until she attains her majority (*Rambam* ibid.).

21. Once the child convert becomes an adult, the conversion becomes irrevocable. And if he should renounce Jewish practices at that point, he is treated as a lapsed Jew, who is liable to full punishment for all transgressions (*Rashi*).

The Rishonim ask how it is possible for someone converted as a minor to ever renounce his conversion. For Rav Yosef said that they may renounce it when they become adults, implying that before they become adults, the renunciation is not meaningful. But we have now said that if they do not renounce it the moment they become adults it is too late to renounce it. It seems then that they have only one brief moment in which to renounce it, which is implausible. *Tos. Yeshanim* answer that they renounce it by acting as gentiles before reaching adulthood and then continuing in that manner past the day of their adulthood, so that from the moment of their adulthood on they were in a continuous state of renunciation (*Rashba, Ritva*). Others answer that the right to renounce does not lapse after the first moment of adulthood unless we see the person act in a way that is clearly Jewish. As long as he has not done anything that only Jews do, he may still renounce his conversion (*Tosafos* ד״ה לכי; *Ritva*). *Rashba* (quoting *Tosafos;* see ד״ה לכי) states that even this does not prevent him from renouncing his conversion. Rather, on reaching adulthood the convert must be informed of the rewards and punishments associated with mitzvah observance, and only if he continues to observe mitzvos after being so informed does he lose the right to renounce his conversion (see also *Rosh* and *Ran*).

22. Below, 29a. The Mishnah speaks of the fifty-*shekel* fine imposed on a man who violates or seduces a virgin *naarah* (see note 2 there).

23. Plural of *naarah.* See 29a note 1.

24. Although the *mamzeress* (a girl born of illicit relations that are punishable by *kares* or court-imposed execution [see *Yevamos* 49a]), *nesinah* (Giveonite woman; see *Joshua* 9:3-27 and 29a note 5), and Cuthean (see 29a note 6) are forbidden in marriage to ordinary Jews, and thus the Torah's requirement that the violator marry his victim (if she wishes) is not applicable in their cases, the Mishnah teaches that he must nevertheless pay them the fine – for the reason that will be taught below (*Rashi*).

25. These last three are entitled to the fine because even if someone had molested them before the age of three, they are considered virgins, as explained above (see note 5).

26. That is, even if by rights we should not give a girl converted as a minor the fine because she could always renounce her conversion, the one who violated her must nevertheless pay it so that he should not be freed from this punishment (*Rashi*).

27. I.e. one less than three years old. The cohabitation of a girl this young does not have the legal status of cohabitation, since if her hymen is ruptured it grows back (*Rashi*).

[Generally, in Biblical law a female is considered mature at the age of twelve years and a day. However, any relations in which she engages after turning three are legally considered to be an act of cohabitation (Mishnah, *Niddah* 44b).]

28. I.e. a boy less than nine years old had relations with a female three years or older. The cohabitation of a boy this young is not legally considered to be an act of cohabitation (*Rashi*).

[Generally, in Biblical law a male is considered mature when he

אף אנו נאמר איילונית דוכרנית דלא ילדה: **מתני׳** הגיורת והשבויה והשפחה שנפדו ושנתגיירו ושנשתחררו פחותות מבנות שלש שנים ויום אחד כתובתן מאתים ויש להן טענת בתולין: **גמ׳** אמר רב הונא גר קטן מטבילין אותו על דעת בית דין מאי קמ״ל דזכות הוא לו וזכין לאדם שלא בפניו תנינא זכין לאדם שלא בפניו ואין חבין לאדם שלא בפניו מהו דתימא עובד כוכבים בהפקירא ניחא ליה דהא קיימא לן דעבד ודאי בהפקירא ניחא ליה קמ״ל דהני מילי גדול דטעם טעם דאיסורא אבל קטן זכות הוא לו לימא מסייע ליה הגיורת והשבויה והשפחה שנפדו ושנתגיירו ושנשתחררו פחותות מבנות שלש שנים ויום אחד מאי לאו דאטבלינהו על דעת בית דין לא הכא במאי עסקינן בגר שנתגיירו בניו ובנותיו עמו דניחא להו במאי דעביד אבוהון אמר רב יוסף הגדילו יכולין למחות איתיביה אביי הגיורת והשבויה והשפחה שנפדו ושנתגיירו ושנשתחררו פחותות מבנות שלש שנים ויום אחד כתובתן מאתים ואי ס״ד הגדילו יכולין למחות יהבינן לה כתובה דאזלה ואכלה בגיותה לכי גדלה לכי גדלה נמי ממחייא ונפקא כיון שהגדילה שעה אחת ולא מיחתה שוב אינה יכולה למחות מתיב רבא אלו נערות שיש להן קנס הבא על הממזרת ועל הנתינה ועל הכותית ועל הגיורת ועל השבויה ועל השפחה שנפדו ושנתגיירו ושנשתחררו פחותות מבנות שלש שנים ויום אחד יש להן קנס ואי אמרת הגדילו יכולין למחות יהבינן לה קנס דאזלה ואכלה בגיותה לכי גדלה נמי ממחייא ונפקא כיון שהגדילה שעה אחת ולא מיחתה שוב אינה יכולה למחות אביי לא אמר כרבא התם קנסא היינו טעמא שלא יהא חוטא נשכר רבא לא אמר כאביי כתובה היינו טעמא שלא תהא קלה בעיניו להוציאה: **מתני׳** הגדול שבא על הקטנה וקטן שבא על הגדולה ומוכת עץ כתובתן מאתים דברי רבי מאיר וחכ״א מוכת עץ כתובתה מנה בתולה אלמנה גרושה וחלוצה מן הנישואין כתובתן מנה ואין

רש״י

אף אנו נאמר. אף אנו נדרוש את השמות מה לשון איילונית שקראו חכמים לאשה שאינה ראויה לילד: **דוכרנית.** לשון איל תמים דמתרגמינן דכר שלים (ויקרא ה) הרי היא כאיל שאינו יולד: **גמ׳ על דעת ב״ד.** אם אין לו אב ואמו הביאתו להתגייר: **מטבילין.** דאין לך גר בלא מילה וטבילה: **על דעת בית דין.** שלשה יהו בטבילתו כדין כל טבילת גר שלריכים ג׳ והן נעשין לו אב והרי הוא גר על ידיהן ומגעו ביין כשר: **מהו דתימא עובד כוכבים בהפקירא ניחא ליה.** וחוב הוא לו ואין אדם נעשה שליח לאדם לחובתו שלא בפניו כלומר שלא מדעתו וקטן לאו בר דיעה הוא: **דהא גבי עבד קי״ל.** בפ״ק דגיטין (דף יג.) דודאי בהפקירא ניחא ליה נוח לו להיות עבד ויהא מותר בהפקר זימת השפחות מהיות בן חורין להיות מותר בבת ישראל דלא זילא ליה ולא שכיחא ליה להפקירא: **קמ״ל.** הכא דגבי עובד כוכבים קטן לא אמרינן הכי: **דהני מילי.** דניחא ליה בהפקירא: **גדול.** שכבר [במדות] הפקירות וטועם ליה טעמא דאיסורא: **הגדילו.** קטנים שנתגיירו ואפי׳ עם אביהן: **יכולין למחות.** ולומר אי אפשינו להיות גרים וחוזרין לסורן ואין לנו לענשן בב״ד ואפי׳ ידינו תקיפה ואם קדש אשה משמיחה אינה לריכה גט להיות כישראל מומר: **לכי גדלה.** לא יהבינן לה עד שתגדיל: **שוב אינה יכולה למחות.** ואם מיחתה הרי היא כישראלית מומרת ליענש בכל עונשי ב״ד: **שיש להן קנס.** נ׳ כסף אם יאנסו: **הבא על הממזרת.** ואע״ג דלא קרינן ביה ולו תהיה לאשה שהרי אינה ראויה לקיימה אפילו הכי יש לה קנס כדלקמן: **אביי לא אמר כרבא.** דמותיב מקנסא דקסבר לאו מיובתא היא דטעמא דקנסא שלא יהא חוטא נשכר להפטר: **רבא לא אמר כאביי.** דמותיב מכתובה דהתם טעמא מאי תקינו לה רבנן כתובה שלא תהא קלה בעיניו להוציאה וכל זמן שלא מיחתה גיורת היא ועבדינן לה תקנתא: **מתני׳ הבא על הקטנה.** פחותה מבת שלש שאין ביאתה ביאה שהרי בתוליה חוזרין: **וקטן.** פחות מבן תשע שאמרו חכמים אין ביאתו ביאה ובא על הגדולה: **ומוכת עץ.** שנתקע לה עץ באותו מקום: **כתובתן מאתים.** אם נשאו לאיש אחרי כן לא אבדו בכך את כתובתן אם נשאה סתם ולא פירש לה כלום: **בתולה.** שהיא אלמנה או גרושה או חלוצה: **מן הנישואין.** כגון שנכנסה לחופה ומת בעלה בחזקת שלא נבעלה: **כתובתה מנה.** אם ניסת לאחר סתם כתובתה מנה דבחזקת בעולה קיימא משנכנסה לחופה: ואין

תוספות

מטבילין אותו על דעת ב״ד משום דזכות הוא. ותימה דהא זכייה הוי מטעם שליחות דכיון דזכות הוא לו אנן סהדי דעביד ליה שליח כדמוכח בפ״ק דב״מ (דף יב.) גבי חצר משום יד איתרבאי ולא גרע משליחות וא״כ היאך זכין לקטן והלא אין שליחות לקטן כדאמרינן באיזהו נשך (שם עא:) ועוד דלאכתי עובד כוכבים הוא ואמרי׳ התם דלקטן דאתי לכלל שליחות אית ליה זכייה מדרבנן עובד כוכבים דלא אתי לכלל שליחות אפילו זכייה מדרבנן לית ליה ונראה לר״י דהכא נמי דזכין לו מדרבנן כדאמרינן התם דקטן אית ליה זכייה מדרבנן ואע״ג דלאכתי עובד כוכבים הוא הא אתי לכלל שליחות א״נ כיון דהכן זכייה נעשה ישראל הוה ליה כישראל גמור לענין זכייה וא״ת היכי הוי גר מדרבנן והרינן ליה בבת ישראל וקידושיו קידושין הא מן התורה עובד כוכבים הוא וי״ל דקסבר כמ״ד בהאשה רבה (יבמות דף פט:) דיש כח ביד חכמים לעקור דבר מן התורה בקום ועשה וכי פריך מאי קמ״ל הוה מצי לשנויי קמ״ל דיש כח ביד חכמים לעקור דבר מן התורה בקום ועשה וחד מתרי טעמי נקט והא דאמרי׳ בריש בן סורר (סנהדרין דף סח: ושם) גבי גזל הגר קסבר אין לך לאיש גואל אית אתה לריך לחזור אחריו אם יש לו גואל אבל קטן אי אתה לריך לחזור אחריו כו׳ משכחת לה גר קטן מן התורה במעוברת שנתגיירה כדאמרי׳ בפרק הערל (יבמות דף עח. ושם) עובדת כוכבים מעוברת שנתגיירה בנה אין לריך טבילה והוי גר מן התורה דישראל גמור הוא ואית ליה ממון מן התורה כגון שירש את אמו ולי אתה לריך לחזור עליו שאין לו יורשין שאינו מולד ואחיו מן האם אין יורשין אותו ולפי ספרים דגרסינן בב״מ (דף עא:) זכייה מיהא אית ליה ולא גרע מדרבנן ניחא דמלי למימר דאית ליה זכייה מן התורה ועובד כוכבים קטן דבא כיון להתגייר חשבינן ליה כישראל קטן ואע״ג דזכייה הוי מטעם שליחות ואין לו שליחות מן התורה ה״מ בדבר שיש בו קלת חובה כגון להפריש תרומתו דשמא היה רוצה לפטורה בחטה אחת או שמא היה רוצה להעדיף אבל הכא שזכות גמור הוא אף על פי שאין לו שליחות: **מהו** דתימא עובד כוכבים בהפקירא ניחא ליה. ואע״ג דרבנן פליגי אר׳ מאיר בפ׳ קמא דגיטין (דף יג. ושם) ולית להו טעמא דבהפקירא ניחא ליה ה״מ גבי עבד שאינו חושש בהפקירא שמפקיע עלמו מן השעבוד אבל גבי עובד כוכבים שאינו משועבד ניחא ליה בהפקירא וכן נראה דאי לא תימא הכי היכי מייתי סייעתא מההוא דגיורת דלמא רבנן היא דאפילו בגדול לית להו בהפקירא ניחא ליה: **אבל** קטן זכות הוא לו. והא דתנן בפרק קמא דגיטין (ג״ז שם) האומר תנו גט זה לאשתי ושיחרור זה לעבדי רלה לחזור בשניהם יחזור דברי רבי מאיר היינו בעבד גדול דבקטן מודה רבי מאיר דזכות הוא לו דלא ניחא ליה בהפקירא כדאמרינן הכא משום דלא טעים טעמא דאיסורא א״נ איירי אף בעבד קטן וכגון שהוא של כהן דחוב הוא לו שילא לחירות לפי שמפסידו מלאכול בתרומה: **לכי** גדלה. וא״ת והלא כבר גדולה היא שהיא נערה כיון שהיא בת קנס ומפרש ר״י לכי גדלה ונהגה מנהג יהודית: **אביי** לא אמר כרבא שלא יהא חוטא נשכר. משמע דרבא לית ליה טעמא דשלא יהא חוטא נשכר וקשה דאמרי׳ בפ׳ שור שנגח ד׳ וה׳ (ב״ק דף לח: ושם) קסבר רבי מאיר כותים גירי אמת הן וקנס הוא דקניס ר״מ בממונם לענין שור שנגח שלא יטמעו בהן ופריך אלו נערות שיש להן קנס הבא על הכותית ואי קניס ר״מ בממונם ה״נ ניקנוס ומשני דהכא לא בעי למקנס שלא יהא חוטא נשכר והשתא לרבא דלית ליה הכא טעם דחוטא נשכר היכי מלי משני התם וי״ל דהתם אית ליה שפיר האי טעמא כיון דבדין יש להן קנס דגרי אמת הן אלא דבעי׳ למקנס להו סברא הוא דמשום טעמא שלא יהא חוטא נשכר מוקמינן לה אדינא אבל הכא סבירא ליה לרבא דמשום טעמא שלא יהא חוטא נשכר אין ליתן לה כיון דמן הדין לית לה שהרי עובדת כוכבים גמורה היא אם תמחה ובפ׳ אלו נערות (לקמן דף לו:) דאית ליה לרבא שלא יהא חוטא נשכר גבי שבויה משום דמוקמינן לה בקדושתה: ושמואל

מסורת הש״ס

א) [עי׳ תוס׳ גיטין ה: ד״ה והא קי״ל], ב) [ערובין פא: יבמות קיח: וש״נ], ג) [גיטין יג. עי׳ תוס׳ שם], ד) לקמן כט. ב״ק לח., ה) [יבמות לב: וש״נ], ו) [יבמות פט. לקמן לו: נד.], ז) לקמן יג., ח) [ל״ל גר קטן], ט) [ועי׳ תוס׳ ב״ק קטו: ד״ה קטן ותוס׳ סנהדרין סח:].

תוספות ישנים

א) [קשה א״כ מתי מדע שעת המחאה דהא בקטנות אינה יכולה למחות כר״י י״ל כגון שהתחילה מנהג גיות יום לפני גדלותה וכן נהגה יום או יומים לאחר גדלותה. מ״י עה״ג]:

גליון הש״ס

גמ׳ שלא יהא חוטא נשכר. פ״ב דחלה מ״ז נדה דף ד ע״ב: **תוס׳ ד״ה לכי גדלה. וא״ת והלא כבר גדולה.** עיין נדה מד ע״ב תוס׳ ד״ה שלשים יום:

ליקוטי רש״י

איילונית. שאין לה סימני נערות לעולם ואינה יולדת, לשון איל זכר דוכרנית דלא ילדה [לקמן לה:]. ממעי אמה ויש לה סימנין שאין לה שערות ולא דדין ולשון איילונית דוכרניתא כאיל זה שאינו יולד [עירובין מז.]. **זכין לאדם שלא בפניו.** ושלא מדעתו דאנן סהדי דניחא ליה שתהא שלוחו [ב״מ יב.] להרויחו אנן סהדי דניחא ליה לפיכך זכין ואין חבין [חולין פג.]. **ואין חבין לאדם שלא בפניו.** אין אדם יכול ליעשות שלוחו שלא מדעתו לדבר שהוא חובה או הפסד [קידושין כג.]. דבר שהוא טוב לו שאינו חסן בו [סוטה כה.]. דבר שהוא לרעתו קרוי חובה [לעיל י׳.]. כלומר אין אדם נעשה שליח לאדם להיות נפסד על ידו אא״כ עשאו הוא שליח היינו כבפניו [גיטין ט:]. דאין אדם נעשה שליח לחבירו שלא מדעתו להפסידו [חולין שם]. **אלו נערות.** דוקא נערה משהביאה שתי שערות עד שתבגר והם ששה חדשים שבין נערות לבגרות אבל קטנה ובוגרת אין להם קנס. **שיש להן קנס.** אם אנסה אדם נותן לאביה חמשים כסף כדכתיב ונתן האיש השוכב וגו׳ (דברים כב). **הבא על הממזרת.** בגמרא פריך אבל כשירות לא ומשני פסולות אילטריכא ליה לאשמועינן. **הנתינה.** מן הגבעונים והיא אסורה לקהל דדוד גזר עליהם כדאמרינן ביבמות (דף עח:) ועל שם ויתנם יהושע חוטבי עלים ושואבי מים וגו׳ (יהושע ט) קרי להו נתינים. **הכותית.** קסבר גירי אריות הן ויש בלאו לא תתחתן בם (דברים ז). **ועל השבויה.** ישראלית שנפדית פחותה מבת שלש שנים דבחזקת בתולה היא שאפי׳ נבעלה בשביה בתוליה חוזרים [לקמן כט.].

עין משפט נר מצוה

סב א מיי׳ פי״א מהל׳ אישות הל׳ ח׳ סמג עשין מח טוש״ע אה״ע סי׳ סז סעי׳ ג:

סג ב מיי׳ פי״ג מהל׳ איסורי ביאה הל׳ ז סמג לאוין קטז טוש״ע יו״ד סי׳ רסח סעי׳ ז:

סד ג מיי׳ פ״ד מהל׳ זכיה הל״ב סמג עשין פ״ב טוש״ע חו״מ סי׳ רמג סעי׳ א וטוש״ע יו״ד סי׳ רסח סעי׳ ז:

סה ד ה ו ז מיי׳ פ״י מהל׳ מלכים הל״ג טוש״ע יו״ד סי׳ רסח סעי׳ ז:

סו ח מיי׳ פי״א מהל׳ אישות הל״ו טור [וש״ע] אה״ע סי׳ סז [ס״א בהג״ה]:

סז ט מיי׳ פי״א מהל׳ אישות הל״ג סמג עשין מח טוש״ע שם סי׳ סז סעיף ד:

סח י מיי׳ שם טוש״ע שם סעיף ה:

סט כ מיי׳ שם הל׳ א טוש״ע שם סעי׳ ג:

תוספות רי״ד

הגיורת והשבויה והשפחה שנפדו ושנתגיירו ושנשתחררו פחותות מבנות ג׳ שנים ויום אחד כתובתן מאתים ויש להן טענת בתולים. פי׳ בחזקת בתולות הן. ואם נמצאת בעולה אומר לה מקחי מקח טעות ואבדה כל כתובתה. **אמר ר״ה** גר קטן מטבילין אותו ע״ד ב״ד. פי׳ אע״פ שאין לו אב ואם וכגון תינוק שנמצא מושלך או שבוי ישראל קטני פלשתים ב״ד מלין אותם והם כישראל לכל דבר. והמורה פי׳ מטבילין אותו. דאינו גר עד שימול ויטבול. עיין פרק החולץ [דף מו] ובפ״ח דיבמות [דף עא]. מאי קמ״ל דזכין לאדם שלא בפניו תנינא זכין לאדם שלא בפניו ואין חבין לו לאדם אלא בפניו. מ״ד בהפקירא ניחא ליה וחוב הוא לו. פי׳ שאין אדם נעשה שליח לחובתו שלא בפניו כלומר שלא מדעת. קמ״ל דה״מ גדול דטעים טעמא דאיסורא אבל קטן זכות הוא [לו]. **אמר ר״י ואם הגדילו.** פי׳ הקטנים שנתגיירו ואפי׳ עם אביהן יכולין למחות. פי׳ יכולין לומר אי אפשינו להיות גרים ואין לנו לעונשם בב״ד. ואפילו ידינו תקיפה. ואם קידש אשה משמיחה אינה צריכה גט להיות כישראל מומר. ודוקא שלא הגיעו לכלל שתי שערות אבל אם הגדילו ולא מיחו אין יכולין למחות ואם מיחו הרי הן כישראל מומר וקדושי׳ קידושין. א) והגדילו דר״י לאו דוקא שבאו לכלל עונשין אלא שבאו לכלל דעת ועדיין לא באו לכלל עונשין: **מתני׳ הגדול** שבא על הקטנה וקטן שבא על הגדולה ומוכת עץ כתובתן מאתים. דברי ר״מ וחכ״א מוכת עץ כתובתן מנה. פי׳ קטנה פחותה מבת ג׳ שנים ויום אחד שאין ביאתה ביאה שהרי בתוליה חוזרין. וקטן פחות מבן ט׳ שאמרו חכמים אין ביאתו ביאה לקנות קנין גמור. כגון אם בא על יבמתו דהתם אמרי׳ אין ביאתו ביאה ב) חשובה לקנות לגמרי. פי׳ לא גרעא אותה ביאה ממאמר בגדול. שכמו שמאמר בגדול פוסלה על שאר האחין. כך ביאת [פחות] בן ט׳ פסלה על האחין. עיין בס״פ האשה רבה: **מוכת עץ** שנתקע לה עץ באותו מקום ויצאו בתוליה כתובתה מאתים. פי׳ לא הפסידו כתובתן אם נישאו סתם וחכ״א מוכת עץ כיון שאיבדה בתוליה כתובתה מנה:

חשק שלמה על תוס׳ רי״ד א) ובדברי רבינו אלו נתיישב קושיית התו׳ כאן בד״ה קשה וע״ש. ב) ע״ש ביבמות דף לו דמיירי שם בביאת בן תשע דעשו כמאמר בגדול אבל בפחות מבן תשע לא מיירי התם כלל וצ״ע.

The Gemara explains why Rav Huna's ruling was needed:

מַהוּ דְּתֵימָא עוֹבֵד כּוֹכָבִים בְּהֶפְקֵירָא נִיחָא לֵיהּ – **You might have said that an idolater prefers** a life of **license,**[13] דְּהָא קַיְימָא לָן דְּעֶבֶד וַדַּאי בְּהֶפְקֵירָא נִיחָא לֵיהּ – **because we have already established that a slave certainly prefers** a life of **license.**[14] קָמַשְׁמַע לָן – **Rav Huna** therefore **informs us** דְּהָנֵי מִילֵּי גָּדוֹל – **that this is so** only for **an adult** דְּטָעַם טַעַם דְּאִיסוּרָא – **who has tasted the taste of the forbidden;**[15] אֲבָל קָטָן זְכוּת הוּא לוֹ – **but for a minor it is an advantage** to be converted.[16]

The Gemara cites our Mishnah as an apparent proof to Rav Huna's ruling:

לֵימָא מְסַיֵּיע לֵיהּ – **Let us say that [our Mishnah] supports [Rav Huna],** for it states: הַגִּיוֹרֶת וְהַשְּׁבוּיָה וְהַשִּׁפְחָה – THE CONVERT, THE CAPTIVE AND THE SLAVE GIRL, שֶׁנִּפְדּוּ וְשֶׁנִּתְגַּיְּירוּ וְשֶׁנִּשְׁתַּחְרְרוּ – WHO WERE RANSOMED, CONVERTED, OR EMANCIPATED פְּחוּתוֹת מִבְּנוֹת שָׁלֹשׁ שָׁנִים וְיוֹם אֶחָד – UNDER THE AGE OF THREE YEARS AND ONE DAY, receive the *kesubah* of a virgin. This Mishnah lists a girl who converted below the age of three — clearly a minor! מַאי לָאו דְּאַטְבְּלִינְהוּ עַל דַּעַת בֵּית דִּין – **Is it not** referring to a case **in which they immersed her** in the *mikveh* **on the understanding of the court,** as Rav Huna taught?

The Gemara rejects the proof:

לֹא – **No!** הָכָא בְּמַאי עַסְקִינַן – **With what** case **are we dealing here?** בְּגֵר שֶׁנִּתְגַּיְּירוּ בָּנָיו וּבְנוֹתָיו עִמּוֹ – **With** the case of **a convert whose sons and daughters converted along with him,** דְּנִיחָא לְהוּ בְּמַאי דְּעָבֵיד אֲבוּהוֹן – **where** it can be assumed that **they are satisfied to** go along with **what their father is doing.**[17] There is thus no proof to Rav Huna's ruling that a minor can be converted on the understanding of the court.

The Gemara elaborates further on the law of a minor who converts:

אָמַר רַב יוֹסֵף – **Rav Yosef said:** הִגְדִּילוּ יְכוֹלִין לִמְחוֹת – **When they become adults, they may renounce** their earlier conversion.[18]

NOTES

[שְׁלִיחוּת], and a minor cannot legally appoint an agent (see *Bava Metzia* 71b). Because of this question, *Tosafos* (ד״ה מטבילין) conclude that the conversion works only at the Rabbinic level, where agency is effective even for a minor (see there). *Tosafos* also cite a variant reading of the Gemara in *Bava Metzia,* according to which it is possible that a minor can have an agent for something that is *completely* beneficial to him. This would enable the conversion to be Biblically valid (see also *Chidushei R' Akiva Eiger* and *Kehillos Yaakov* §9). *Ritva,* however, disputes the premise that acting for the benefit of another person requires one to become his agent. In his view, this is effective even without resort to agency and therefore is effective for minors as well. See *Ketzos HaChoshen* 105:1 for elaboration of this dispute. See also *Gilyon Maharsha* to *Yoreh Deah* 268:4, and *Gidulei Shmuel.*

The Rishonim raise yet another problem. The Gemara in *Bava Metzia* 71b states explicitly that a Jew cannot act as an agent for an idolater even when it is to his benefit! They answer that this is so only where the idolater will remain an idolater even after the completion of the agency. However, where he becomes a Jew through that agency, the agency is effective — since the agency and his Jewishness are viewed as coming simultaneously [גֵּרוּתוֹ וּזְכוּתוֹ בָּאִין כְּאֶחָד] (*Rashba;* see *Tosafos* for another answer).]

13. I.e. a life in which he is not subject to restrictions on promiscuity, as is a Jew. Thus, it is to his disadvantage to be converted, and we may not do something to disadvantage him without his knowledge and consent. Since a minor does not legally have the ability to make his own decision, converting a minor would be tantamount to taking this action without his consent [even if he says that he agrees] (*Rashi*).

14. The Gemara in *Gittin* (13a) states that a slave prefers to remain in servitude and be permitted to continue a promiscuous life with slavewomen than to be freed and become subject to the sexual restrictions incumbent upon Jews. And though his freedom gains him the right to marry a Jewess, he prefers life with slavewomen because he cannot treat Jewish women cheaply nor are they available to him promiscuously (*Rashi*).

[Actually, this is only the opinion of R' Meir. The Sages there rule that the slave would prefer freedom. Nevertheless, the Sages agree in principle that a slave prefers a life of license to a life of marriage. It is only that they hold he prefers his freedom still more. This, of course, is not a factor in the case of a [free] idolater, and the analogy is therefore valid (*Tosafos; Rashba; Ritva*).]

15. That is, he has already experienced the life of promiscuity and has grown to like it. Accordingly, he does not want to become restricted (*Rashi*).

16. [Because he has not yet been corrupted and does not have to give up any forbidden pleasures. The benefits of conversion are therefore a pure advantage to him.]

Shitah Mekubetzes infers from *Rashi* (ד״ה קמ״ל) that this is true only in the case of an underage idolater, but not in the case of an underage slave. Since a slave has the benefit of at least partial Jewishness, he may prefer to remain in his current state and still be able to pursue the life of license permitted by the Torah to a Canaanite slave (cf. *Tosafos*).

17. Because the child wishes to continue living with his father, he is willing to adopt the religious lifestyle of his father (see *Teshuvos Chasam Sofer, Yoreh Deah* §253). [In such a case, therefore, it is clearly a benefit for them to be converted. Rav Huna teaches that even if the child is not joining his father in conversion — either because he has no father (see *Rashi* above ד״ה קטן and note 7), or because his father is not converting but merely having him converted (*Rashba, Ritva*) — it is nonetheless a benefit for the child to be converted and the courts may therefore convert him.]

Rashba and *Ritva* argue that this reason should apply just as well to a fatherless child who converts along with his mother. From *Rashi* ד״ה גר קטן (quoted in note 7), however, it seems that it is true only of a father, not a mother (*Bach, Yoreh Deah* §268; see also *Tur* and *Shulchan Aruch* 268:7).

[*Rashi* to *Yevamos* 48a (end of ד״ה עבד איש) implies that a gentile has a Biblically ordained right to convert his underage children. Our Gemara, however, implies that it is not a special authority but merely something that he can do because it is for the benefit of the child. See *Chidushei Chasam Sofer* here for a discussion of this problem.]

18. When they become of age (i.e. thirteen years old for a boy, twelve years old for a girl — and have at least two pubic hairs), they may renounce their conversion and revert to being gentiles. They are then not subject to punishment by a Jewish court [for their transgressions of Torah law], and if a man were to betroth a Jewish woman following his renunciation of his conversion, she would not need a *get* to be permitted to marry someone else, as would a woman married to a Jew who rejected Jewish practice (*Rashi*).

Rashi states that Rav Yosef's ruling applies to both a minor converted on the understanding of the court and a minor who converts along with his father. It is for this reason that Rav Yosef speaks of underage converts in the plural ("when *they* become adults"), although Rav Huna spoke in the singular ("a minor who converts") (*Rashba, Ritva*). [*Ramban,* however (cited by *Ran*), suggests that *Rif* holds that Rav Yosef speaks only of a child converted by his father, not one converted by the courts. See *Teshuvos Chasam Sofer* (*Yoreh Deah* 253) for yet another view.]

Why is renunciation effective? *Ritva,* in his discussion of whether a child's conversion is Biblically or only Rabbinically valid (see note 8), notes that its effectiveness is easier to understand if the conversion is merely a Rabbinic institution. According to the view that a child's conversion is Biblically valid, *Chasam Sofer* (*Teshuvos* ibid.) suggests that the renunciation demonstrates that the conversion was never truly a benefit for this child. [See also *Rashba* at the end of this Gemara.]

[It is evident from a number of Rishonim that the renunciation annuls the conversion retroactively. Nevertheless, as long as they have not renounced the conversion, they are treated as full Jews, because it may be assumed that since they now live a Jewish life, they will continue doing so and not renounce their conversion (*Rashba, Ritva;* see further, *Meiri* and *Teshuvos Chasam Sofer* §253). However, *Rashi's* statement that the betrothal received from this convert is invalid from the time of his renunciation forward indicates that the conversion is not retroactively annulled. Similarly, *Meiri* cites the ruling of some Geonim that wine touched by the convert before his renunciation does not become forbidden.]

עין משפט נר מצוה

סב א מיי' פי"א מהל' אישות הל' א' סמג עשין מח טוש"ע אה"ע סי' סז סעי' ג:

סג ב מיי' פי"ג מהל' איסורי ביאה הל' ז סמג לאוין קח טוש"ע יו"ד סי' רסח סעי' ז:

סד ג מיי' פ"ד מהל' זכיה הל"ב סמג עשין פ"ב טוש"ע חו"מ סי' רמג סעי' א וטוש"ע יו"ד סי' רסח סעי' ז:

סה ד ה ו ז מיי' פי' מהל' מלכים הל"ג טוש"ע יו"ד סי' רסח סעי' ז:

סו ח מיי' פי' מהל' אישות הל"ז טור [ושו"ע] אה"ע סי' סו [ס"א בהג"ה]:

סז ט מיי' פי"א מהל' אישות הל"ג סמג עשין מח טוש"ע שם סי' סז סעיף ד:

סח י מיי' שם טוש"ע שם סעיף ה:

סט כ מיי' שם הל' א טוש"ע שם סעי' ג:

תוספות רי"ד

הגיורת והשבויה והשפחה שנפדו ושנתגיירו ושנשתחררו פחותות מבנות ג' שנים ויום אחד כתובתן מאתים ויש להן טענת בתולים. פי' בחזקת בתולות הן. ואם נמצאת בעולה אומר לה מקחי מקח טעות ואבדה כל כתובתה. אמר ר"ה גר קטן מטבילין אותו ע"ד ב"ד. פי' אע"פ שאין לו אב ואם כגון תינוק שנמצא מושלך או ששבו ישראל קטני פלשתים ב"ד מלין אותם והם כישראל לכל דבר. והמורה פי' מטבילין אותו. דאינו גר עד שימול ויטבול. עיין פרק החולץ [דף מו] ובפ"ח דיבמות [דף עא]. מאי קמ"ל דזכין לאדם שלא בפניו תנינא זכין לאדם שלא בפניו ואין חבין לו לאדם אלא בפניו. מ"ד דבהפקירא ניחא ליה וחוב הוא לו. פי' שאין אדם נעשה שליח לחובתו שלא בפניו כלומר שלא מדעת. קמ"ל דה"מ גדול דטעים טעמא דאיסורא אבל קטן זכות הוא [לו]. אמר ר"י ואם הגדילו. פי' הקטנים שנתגיירו ואפי' עם אביהן יכולין למחות. פי' יכולין לומר אי אפשינו להיות גרים ואין לנו לענשם בב"ד. ואפילו ידינו תקיפה. ואם קידש אשה משמיחה אינה צריכה גט להיות כישראל מומר. ודוקא שלא הגיעו לכלל שתי שערות אבל אם הגדילו ולא מיחו אין יכולין למחות ואם מיחו הרי הן כישראל מומר וקדושי' קדושין. א) והגדילו דר"י לאו דוקא שבאו לכלל עונשין אלא שבאו לכלל דעת ועדיין לא באו לכלל עונשין: מתני' הגדול שבא על הקטנה וקטן שבא על הגדולה ומוכת עץ כתובתן מאתים. דברי ר"מ וחכ"א מוכת עץ כתובתן מנה. פי' קטנה פחותה מבת ג' שנים וקטן אחד שאין ביאתו ביאה שהרי בתוליה חוזרין. וקטן פחות מבן ט' שאמרו חכמים אין ביאתו ביאה לקנות קנין גמור. כגון אם בא על יבמתו דהתם אמרי' אין ביאתו ביאה. ב) חשובה לקנות לגמרי. פי' לא גרעה ביאה ממאמר בגדול. שכמו שמאמר בגדול פוסלה על שאר האחין. כך ביאת [פחות] בן ט' פסלה על האחין. עיין בס"פ האשה רבה: מוכת עץ שנתקע לה עץ באותו מקום ויצאו בתוליה כתובתה מאתים. פי' לא הפסידו כתובתן אם נישאו סתם וחכ"א מוכת עץ כיון שאיבדה בתוליה כתובתה מנה:

חשק שלמה על תוס' רי"ד א) ונדברי רבינו אלו נתיישב קושיית התו"י כאן בד"ה קשה וע"ש. ב) ע"ש ביבמות דף לו דמיירי שם בביאת בן תשע דעשו כמאמר בגדול אבל בפחות מבן תשע לא מיירי התם כלל וצ"ע.

גמרא

אף אנו נאמר איילונית דוכרנית דלא ילדה: מתני' [א] הגיורת והשבויה והשפחה שנפדו ושנתגיירו ושנשתחררו פחותות מבנות שלש שנים ויום אחד כתובתן מאתים ויש להן טענת בתולין: גמ' אמר רב הונא [ב] גר קטן מטבילין אותו על דעת בית דין מאי קמ"ל דזכות הוא לו וזכין לאדם שלא בפניו תנינא [ג] זכין לאדם שלא בפניו ואין חבין לאדם שלא בפניו מהו דתימא עובד כוכבים בהפקירא ניחא ליה דהא קיימא לן [ג] דעבד ודאי בהפקירא ניחא ליה קמ"ל דהני מילי גדול דטעם טעם דאיסורא אבל קטן זכות הוא לו לימא מסייע ליה הגיורת והשבויה והשפחה שנפדו ושנתגיירו ושנשתחררו פחותות מבנות שלש שנים ויום אחד מאי לאו דאטבלינהו על דעת בית דין לא הכא במאי עסקינן בגר שנתגיירו בניו ובנותיו עמו [ד] דניחא להו במאי דעביד אבוהון אמר רב יוסף [ה] הגדילו יכולין למחות איתיביה אביי הגיורת והשבויה והשפחה שנפדו ושנתגיירו ושנשתחררו פחותות מבנות שלש שנים ויום אחד כתובתן מאתים ואי ס"ד הגדילו יכולין למחות יהבינן לה כתובה דאזלה ואכלה בגיותה [ו] לכי גדלה לכי גדלה נמי ממחייא ונפקא [ז] כיון שהגדילה [א] שעה אחת ולא מיחתה שוב אינה יכולה למחות מתיב רבא [ד] אלו נערות שיש להן קנס הבא על הממזרת ועל הנתינה ועל הכותית ועל הגיורת ועל השבויה ועל השפחה שנפדו ושנתגיירו ושנשתחררו פחותות מבנות שלש שנים ויום אחד יש להן קנס ואי אמרת הגדילו יכולין למחות יהבינן לה קנס דאזלה ואכלה בגיותה לכי גדלה נמי ממחייא ונפקא כיון שהגדילה שעה אחת ולא מיחתה שוב אינה יכולה למחות אביי לא אמר כרבא התם קנסא היינו טעמא [ה] שלא יהא חוטא נשכר רבא לא אמר כאביי [ח] כתובה היינו טעמא שלא תהא קלה בעיניו להוציאה: מתני' [ט] הגדול שבא על הקטנה וקטן שבא על הגדולה ומוכת עץ כתובתן מאתים דברי רבי מאיר [י] וחכ"א מוכת עץ כתובתה מנה [כ] בתולה אלמנה גרושה וחלוצה מן הנישואין כתובתן מנה

ואין

רש"י

אף אנו נאמר. אף אנו נדרוש את השמות מה לשון איילונית שקראו חכמים לאשה שאינה ראויה לילד: דוכרנית. לשון איל תמים דמתרגמינן דכר שלים (ויקרא ה) הרי היא כאיל שאינו יולד: גמ' על דעת ב"ד. אם אין לו אב ואמו הביאתו להתגייר: מטבילין. דאין לך גר בלא מילה וטבילה: על דעת בית דין. שלשה יהו בטבילתו כדין כל טבילת גר שצריכים ג' והן נעשין לו אב והרי הוא גר על ידיהן ומגעו ביין כשר: מהו דתימא עובד כוכבים בהפקירא ניחא ליה. וחוב הוא לו ואין אדם נעשה שליח לאדם לחובתו שלא בפניו כלומר שלא מדעתו וקטן לאו בר דיעה הוא: דהא גבי עבד קי"ל. בפ"ק דגיטין (דף יג.) דודאי בהפקירא ניחא ליה נוח לו להיות עבד ויהא מותר בהפקר זימת השפחות מהיות בן חורין להיות מותר בבת ישראל דלא זילא ליה ולא שכיחא ליה להפקירא: קמ"ל. הכא דגבי עובד כוכבים קטן לא אמרינן הכי: דהני מילי. דניחא ליה בהפקירא: גדול. שגדל [בטמדות] הפקירות וטעים ליה טעמא דאיסורא: הגדילו. קטנים שנתגיירו ואפי' עם אביהן: יכולין למחות. ולומר אי אפשינו להיות גרים וחוזרין לסורן ואין לנו לענשן בב"ד ואפי' ידינו תקיפה ואם קדש אשה משמיחה אינה צריכה גט להיות כישראל מומר: לכי גדלה. לא יהבינן לה עד שתגדיל. שוב אינה יכולה למחות. ואם מיחתה הרי היא כישראלית מומרת ליענש בכל עונשי ב"ד: שיש להן קנס. נ' כסף אם יאנסן: הבא על הממזרת. ואע"ג דלא קרינן ביה ולו תהיה לאשה שהרי אינה ראויה לקיימה אפילו הכי יש לה קנס כדלקמן: אביי לא אמר כרבא. דמותיב מקנסא דקסבר לאו מיובתא היא דטעמא דקנסא שלא יהא חוטא נשכר להפטר: רבא לא אמר כאביי. דמותיב מכתובה דהתם טעמא מאי תקינו לה רבנן כתובה שלא תהא קלה בעיניו להוציאה וכל זמן שלא מיחתה גיורת היא ועבדינן לה תקנתא: מתני' הבא על הקטנה. פחותה מבת שלש שאין ביאתה ביאה שהרי בתוליה חוזרין: וקטן. פחות מבן תשע שאמרו חכמים אין ביאתו ביאה ובא על הגדולה: ומוכת עץ. שנתקע לה עץ באותו מקום: כתובתן מאתים. אם נשאו לאיש אחרי כן לא אבדו בכך את כתובתן אם נשאה סתם ולא פירש לה כלום: בתולה. שהיא אלמנה או גרושה או חלוצה: מן הנישואין. כגון שנכנסה לחופה ומת בעלה בחזקת שלא נבעלה: כתובתה מנה. אם ניסת לאחר סתם כתובתה מנה דבחזקת בעולה קיימא משנכנסה לחופה:

ואין

תוספות

מטבילין אותו על דעת ב"ד משום דזכות הוא. ותימה דהא זכייה הוי מטעם שליחות דכיון דזכות הוא לו אנן סהדי דעביד ליה שליח כדמוכח בפ"ק דב"מ (דף יב.) גבי חצר משום יד איתרבאי ולא גרע משליחות וא"כ היאך זכין לקטן והלא אין שליחות לקטן כדאמרינן באיזהו נשך (שם עא:) ועוד דאמרי' עובד כוכבים הוא ואמרי' התם דקטן דאתי לכלל שליחות אית ליה זכייה מדרבנן עובד כוכבים דלא אתי לכלל שליחות אפילו זכייה מדרבנן לית ליה ונראה לר"י דהכא נמי דזכין לו מדרבנן כדאמרינן התם דקטן אית ליה זכייה מדרבנן ואע"ג דלאכתי עובד כוכבים הוא הא אתי לכלל שליחות א"נ כיון דבהך זכייה נעשה ישראל הוה ליה כישראל גמור לענין זכייה ולא"ת היכי הוי גר מדרבנן ושרינן ליה בבת ישראל וקידושיו קידושין הא מן התורה עובד כוכבים הוא וי"ל דקסבר כמ"ד בהאשה רבה (יבמות דף פט:) דיש כח ביד חכמים לעקור דבר מן התורה בקום ועשה וכי פריך מאי קמ"ל הוה מצי לשנויי קמ"ל דיש כח ביד חכמים לעקור דבר מן התורה בקום ועשה וחד מתרי טעמי נקט והא דאמרי' בריש בן סורר (סנהדרין דף סח: ושם) גבי גזל הגר דאם אין לאיש גואל אין אתה צריך לחזור אחריו אם יש לו גואל אבל קטן אי אתה צריך לחזור אחריו כו' משכחת לה גר קטן מן התורה במעוברת שנתגיירה ט) דאמרי' בפרק הערל (יבמות דף עח. ושם) עובדת כוכבים מעוברת שנתגיירה בנה אין צריך טבילה והוי גר מן התורה דישראל גמור הוא ואית ליה ממון מן התורה כגון שירש את אמו ואי אתה צריך לחזור עליו שאין לו יורשין שאינו מוליד ואחיו מן האם אין יורשין אותו ולפי ספרים דגרסינן בב"מ (דף עא:) זכייה מיהא אית ליה ולא גרס מדרבנן ניחא דמצי למימר דמלי ליה זכייה מן התורה ועובד כוכבים קטן כיון דבא להתגייר חשבינן ליה כישראל קטן ואע"ג דזכייה הוי מטעם שליחות ואין לו שליחות מן התורה ה"מ בדבר שיש בו קצת חובה כגון להפריש תרומתו דשמא היה רוצה לפטורה במטה אחת או שמא היה רוצה להעדיף אבל הכא שזכות גמור הוא לו יש לו שליחות: מהו דתימא עובד כוכבים בהפקירא ניחא ליה. ואע"ג דרבנן פליגי אר' מאיר בפ' קמא דגיטין (דף יג. ושם) ולית להו טעמא דבהפקירא ניחא ליה ה"מ גבי עבד שאינו חושש בהפקירא שמפקיע עצמו מן השעבוד אבל גבי עובד כוכבים שאינו משועבד ניחא ליה בהפקירא וכן נראה דאי לא תימא הכי היכי מייתי סייעתא מההוא דגיורת דלמא רבנן היא דאפילו בגדול לית להו בהפקירא ניחא ליה: אבל קטן זכות הוא לו. והא דתנן בפרק קמא דגיטין (ג"ז שם) האומר תנו גט זה לאשתי ושחרור זה לעבדי רצה לחזור בשניהם יחזור דברי רבי מאיר היינו בעבד גדול דבקטן מודה רבי מאיר דזכות הוא לו דלא ניחא ליה בהפקירא כדאמרינן הכא משום דלא טעים טעמא דאיסורא א"נ איירי אף בעבד קטן וכגון שהוא של כהן דחוב הוא לו שיצא לחירות לפי שמפסידו מלאכול בתרומה: לכי גדלה. ° וא"ת והלא כבר גדולה היא שהיא נערה כיון שהיא בת קנס ומפרש ר"י לכי גדלה ונהגה מנהג יהודית: אביי לא אמר כרבא שלא יהא חוטא נשכר. משמע דרבא לית ליה טעמא דשלא יהא חוטא נשכר וקשה דאמרי' בפ' שור שנגח ד' וה' (ב"ק דף לח: ושם) קסבר רבי מאיר כותים גירי אמת הן וקנס הוא דקניס ר"מ בממונם לענין שור שנגח שלא יטמעו בהן ופריך אלו נערות שיש להן קנס הבא על הכותית ואי קניס ר"מ בממונם ה"נ ניקנוס ומשני דהכא לא בעי למקנס שלא יהא חוטא נשכר והשתא לרבא דלית ליה הכא טעם דחוטא נשכר היכי מצי משני התם וי"ל דהתם אית ליה שפיר האי טעמא כיון דבדין יש להן קנס דגרי אמת הן אלא דבעי' למקנס להו סברא הוא דמשום טעמא שלא יהא חוטא נשכר מוקמינן לה אדינא אבל הכא סבירא ליה לרבא דמשום טעמא שלא יהא חוטא נשכר אין ליתן לה כיון דמן הדין לית לה שהרי עובדת כוכבים גמורה היא אם תמחה ובפ' אלו נערות (לקמן דף לו:) דאית ליה לרבא שלא יהא חוטא נשכר גבי שבויה משום דמוקמינן לה בקדושתה:

ושמואל

מסורת הש"ס

א) [עי' תוס' גיטין ה: ד"ה והא קי"ל], ב) [עירובין פא: יבמות קיח: וש"נ], ג) [גיטין יא. עי' תוס' שם], ד) לקמן כט. ב"ק לח., ה) [יבמות לג: וש"נ], ו) [יבמות פט. לקמן לט: נד.], ז) [לקמן יג.], ח) [צ"ל גר קטן], ט) [ועי' תוס' ב"ק קט: ד"ה קטן ותוס' סנהדרין סח:].

תוספות ישנים

א) [קשה א"כ מתי תדע שעת המחאה דהא בקטנות אינה יכולה למחות כר"י י"ל כגון שהתחילה מנהג גיות יום לפני גדלותה וכן נהגה יום או יומים לאחר גדלותה. ת"י עה"ג]:

גליון הש"ס

גמ' שלא יהא חוטא נשכר. פ"ב דחלה מ"ז נדה דף ד ע"ב: תוס' ד"ה לכי גדלה. וא"ת והלא כבר גדולה. עיין נדה מד ע"ב תוס' ד"ה שלשים יום:

ליקוטי רש"י

איילונית. שאין לה סימני נערות לעולם ואינה יולדת, לשון איל זכר דוכרניתא דלא ילדה [לקמן לה:]. ממעי אמה ויש לה סימנין שאין לה שערות ולא דדין ולשון איילונית דוכרניתא כאיל זה שאינו יולד [עירובין מז.]. זכין לאדם שלא בפניו. ושלא מדעתו דאנן סהדי דניחא ליה שתהא שלוחו [ב"מ יב.]. להרויחו אנן סהדי דניחא ליה לפיכך זכין ואין חבין [חולין פג.]. ואין חבין לאדם שלא בפניו. אין אדם יכול ליעשות שלוחו של חבירו שלא מדעתו לדבר שהוא חובה לו הספד [קידושין כג.]. דבר שהוא טוב לו שאינו חפץ בו [סוטה כה.]. דבר שהוא לרעתו קרוי חובה [לעיל י.]. כלומר אין אדם נעשה שליח לאדם שלא מדעתו להפסידו [גיטין ט:]. אלו נערות. דוקא נערה משבגרה שתי שערות עד שתבגר והם ששה חדשים שבין נערות לבגרות אבל קטנה ובוגרת אין להם קנס. שיש להן קנס. אם אנסם אדם נותן לאביה חמשים כסף כדכתיב ונתן האיש השוכב עמה וגו' [דברים כב]. הבא על הממזרת. בגמרא פריך אבל כשירות לא ומשני מלות פסולות לאשמועינן. הנתינה. מן הגבעונים שהיו אסורים לבא בקהל דדוד גזר עליהם כדאמרינן ביבמות (דף עח:) ועל שם שעשו לישראל חוטבי עצים ושואבי מים וגו' (יהושע ט) קרי להו נתינים. הכותית. מן כותי גירי אריות הן וישבן בלאו לא תתחתן בם (דברים ז). ועל השבויה. ישראלית שנשבית שנפדית פחותה מבת שלש שנים דבחזקת בתולה היא שאפילו נבעלה בתוליה חוזרים [לקמן כט.].

אַף אֲנוּ נֹאמַר – **We too will state** an etymology: אַיְילוֹנִית – A woman who is unfit to give birth[1] is called an ***aylonis,*** דּוּכְרָנִית דְּלָא יָלְדָה – as if to say she is **a ram, which,** being a male, **cannot give birth.**[2]

Mishnah The Mishnah lists women of various backgrounds who are entitled to the *kesubah* of a virgin despite their previous circumstances:

הַגִּיּוֹרֶת וְהַשְּׁבוּיָה וְהַשִּׁפְחָה – **The convert, the captive and the slave girl,**[3] שֶׁנִּפְדּוּ וְשֶׁנִּתְגַּיְּירוּ וְשֶׁנִּשְׁתַּחְרְרוּ – **who were ransomed, converted or emancipated**[4] פְּחוּתוֹת מִבְּנוֹת שָׁלֹשׁ שָׁנִים וְיוֹם אֶחָד – **under the age of three years and one day,**[5] כְּתוּבָּתָן מָאתַיִם – **their *kesubah* is two hundred** *zuz* like that of a virgin; וְיֵשׁ לָהֶן טַעֲנַת בְּתוּלִין – **and a claim concerning** their **virginity can be made against them.**[6]

Gemara The Gemara presents a ruling, concerning the conversion of a minor, which will be challenged from our Mishnah:

אָמַר רַב הוּנָא – **Rav Huna said:** גֵּר קָטָן – In the case of **a minor** who **converts,**[7] מַטְבִּילִין אוֹתוֹ עַל דַּעַת בֵּית דִּין – **we immerse him** in the *mikveh* **on the understanding of the court.**[8]

The Gemara asks:

מַאי קָמַשְׁמַע לָן – **What is [Rav Huna] informing us** by this teaching? דִּזְכוּת הוּא לוֹ – Is it **that it is a benefit for [the minor]** to convert to Judaism,[9] וְזָכִין לְאָדָם שֶׁלֹּא בְּפָנָיו – **and that we may benefit a person in his absence** (i.e. without his knowledge)?[10] תְּנֵינָא – But **we have already learned** this principle **in a Baraisa,** which states: זָכִין לְאָדָם שֶׁלֹּא בְּפָנָיו – WE MAY BENEFIT A PERSON IN HIS ABSENCE,[11] וְאֵין חָבִין לְאָדָם שֶׁלֹּא בְּפָנָיו – BUT WE MAY NOT DISADVANTAGE A PERSON IN HIS ABSENCE.[12]

NOTES

1. [Because she failed to mature physically (see *Yevamos* 80a, 97a and *Niddah* 47b).]

2. דְּכַר is the *Targum* of the Hebrew word (*Leviticus* 5:15) אַיִל, *a ram* (*Rashi*).

3. [That is, a Canaanite slave girl, who is not fully Jewish until she is emancipated.]

The Tanna speaks of a "convert . . . who converted," rather than a gentile who converted, because having become Jewish, we no longer wish to refer to her as a gentile (*Ritva*).

4. These three categories of women are all suspected of having lost their virginity before converting: the convert because gentiles tend to be promiscuous; the ransomed captive because captured women were frequently violated by their captors; and the slave girl because slaves are known to have loose morals.

The order of the verbs *ransomed, converted* and *emancipated* does not correspond to the order of the people listed, the *convert, captive* and *slave girl. Ritva* explains that the people are listed according to their stature. Because of our high regard for a person who willingly enters the covenant of Hashem, the convert is listed first. The captive is next because she is fully Jewish, and the slave girl is last. The verbs, however, are listed in order of the priority of their activities. Redeeming a captive is a great mitzvah and it is therefore listed first. Converting a gentile, on the other hand, is not regarded as a mitzvah [on the contrary, we first attempt to dissuade the person from taking this step]. It is therefore listed second. And since emancipating a Canaanite slave is, under most circumstances, an infraction of a Biblical precept (see *Berachos* 47b), it is listed last. A similar idea is mentioned by *Tos. Yom Tov* in the name of *Maharal.* See *Shitah Mekubetzes* for other explanations.

5. At that age, even if they had indeed been violated, their hymen would have grown back. Hence, they are still regarded as virgins (see *Rashi* below ד״ה הבא and 9a note 7).

6. Since they are presumed to be virgins, if they are found to be otherwise, they lose their *kesubah* (see 10b note 23).

7. Conversion requires intent on the part of the person to convert to Judaism. Such intent is legally lacking in the case of a minor, who does not have mature intelligence (*Shach, Yoreh Deah* 268:16, from *Mordechai, Yevamos* ch. 4 §40; see also *Bach* ibid.). An underage gentile can be converted by his father (as the Gemara will state below). Rav Huna, however, speaks of a child without a father who was brought by his mother for conversion (*Rashi;* see *Tur, Yoreh Deah* 268; *Bach* there ד״ה נכרי קטן; *Yam Shel Shlomo;* cf. *Rashba,* whose view will be discussed in note 17, and *Ritva,* who has a different reading of *Rashi*).

[The reason *Rashi* states that the child was brought by his mother is because Jewish courts do not involve themselves in converting a person unless asked to do so (see *Rashba, Ritva*). Indeed, there are many who hold that an unsolicited conversion is not even valid (*Mordechai* ibid., quoted by *Bach, Yoreh Deah* 268 ד״ה נכרי; cf. *Ran* here, and see *Darchei Moshe* to *Yoreh Deah* 268, who cites both opinions). *Ritva* adds that the courts can also convert a child who asks on his own to be converted, if they see that he understands what he is asking (see *Shulchan Aruch, Yoreh Deah* 268:7).

8. I.e. the court of three judges required for the immersion of every convert serves in place of the child's father, enabling him to become a convert through them (*Rashi*). [Thus, Rav Huna's teaching is not that a child can be converted – that principle is well established in the law that a father can convert his children (as the Gemara will teach below). Rav Huna's point is that where the child has no father, the court may do for him what his father could have done and enter him into conversion (see *Meiri*).]

To become a convert one must undergo both circumcision and immersion in a *mikveh* (*Rashi,* from *Yevamos* 46b). Rav Huna talks about immersion specifically because circumcision alone does not suffice without immersion (*Rashba, Ritva;* see *Rashi*), and immersion is the concluding step in the conversion process (*Meiri, Tos. Rid;* see *Darchei Moshe, Yoreh Deah* 268:2 about whether immersion must *follow* the circumcision). Moreover, immersion applies to both men and women, whereas circumcision does not (*Rashba, Ritva,* who give several other answers as well; see further, *Pnei Yehoshua* and *Haflaah*).

Rashi states that the effect of this conversion is that the child does not prohibit wine by touching it, as does a gentile. Since this prohibition is merely Rabbinic, *Rashi's* words indicate that he considers the conversion valid only on the Rabbinic level (*Pnei Yehoshua*), and valid only in regard to Rabbinic laws (see *Ritva,* who cites such a view). *Tosafos* (ד״ה מטבילין) cite a similar view in the name of *Ri* but nevertheless maintain that Rav Huna holds that a Rabbinic convert would be allowed to marry a Jew for the reason given there (see *Ritva* for yet a different reason). In *Sanhedrin* (68b ד״ה קטן) *Tosafos* say that even if the conversion is only Rabbinically valid while the child is a minor, it becomes Biblically valid once he becomes an adult and decides to remain a Jew. *Rashba* and *Ritva* (here) hold that the conversion is Biblically valid [even while he is still a child], and *Tosafos* too suggest such a possibility. See further in note 12.

9. For this brings him closer to God and earns him a place in the World to Come (see *Yevamos* 47a).

10. *Rashi* ד״ה מהו דתימא. [Although the child is physically present and may even be aware of what is happening, since he is legally not considered to have understanding, it is as if the matter is being done without his knowledge and presence.]

11. Where something is a clear benefit to a person, we can assume that the person would want someone to acquire it for him [and perform for him whatever action is necessary to make that acquisition]. Therefore, even though the beneficiary did not explicitly appoint an agent [to obtain this for him], someone wishing to benefit him may act as his agent (*Rashi* to *Gittin* 9b ד״ה יחזור).

12. That is, where the action might be disadvantageous to the beneficiary, one cannot act as his agent without his knowledge [and instruction, since it is not clear that he wants him to do so] (*Rashi* below and to *Gittin* ibid.). By extension, therefore, it is evident that the court may act in place of the child's father and convert him even without the child's knowledge and consent because it is to the child's benefit. (See *Birkas Shmuel* to *Kiddushin* §15 for a discussion of what exactly the court does in their role as the child's agent.)

[The Rishonim are bothered by the question of how the court can act for the child's benefit when this is based on the principle of agency

The Gemara resumes its citation of the teachings of Rav Chana of Baghdad:

וְאָמַר רַב חָנָא בַּגְדָתָאָה – **And Rav Chana of Baghdad said:** תַּמְרֵי מְשַׁחֲנָן מַשְׂבְּעָן – **Dates warm** the body, **satiate,** מְשַׁלְשְׁלָן – **loosen the bowels,** מְאַשְׁרָן – **provide energy** וְלֹא מְפַנְקָן – **and** although sweet, **do not lead to finickiness.**[35]

Another statement about dates:

אָמַר רַב – **Rav said:** אָכַל תְּמָרִים אַל יוֹרֶה – **If one ate dates, he should not render legal decisions.**[36]

The Gemara asks:

מֵיתִיבֵי – **They challenged** this **from a Baraisa:** תְּמָרִים שַׁחֲרִית וְעַרְבִית יָפוֹת – DATES – when eaten IN THE MORNING AND EVENING, they ARE GOOD for a person;[37] בְּמִנְחָה רָעוֹת – when eaten IN THE AFTERNOON,[38] THEY ARE BAD for a person;[39] בַּצָּהֳרַיִם אֵין כְּמוֹתָן – when eaten AT NOON,[40] THERE IS NOTHING LIKE THEM,[41] וּמְבַטְּלוֹת שְׁלֹשָׁה דְּבָרִים – AND THEY NULLIFY THREE THINGS: מַחֲשָׁבָה רָעָה וְחוֹלִי מֵעַיִם וְתַחְתּוֹנִיּוֹת – BAD THOUGHTS, i.e. worry,[42] INTESTINAL SICKNESS AND HEMORRHOIDS. Since they are so healthful, how can Rav say that a person who eats them may not render a legal decision?

The Gemara answers:

מִי אַמְרִינַן דְּלָא מְעַלּוּ – **Did we say that they are not beneficial?** עַלּוּיֵי מְעַלּוּ – **They are certainly beneficial,** וּלְפִי שַׁעְתָּא טָרְדָא – **but they can temporarily disorient** one who eats them, מִידֵי דַּהֲוָה אַחַמְרָא – **just like wine.** דְּאָמַר מַר – **For the master said:** הַשּׁוֹתֶה רְבִיעִית יַיִן אַל יוֹרֶה – **If someone drank a *reviis* of wine, he may not render legal decisions.**[43]

The Gemara suggests an alternative answer:

וְאִיבָּעֵית אֵימָא לָא קַשְׁיָא – **And if you prefer, you may say that there is no difficulty** (i.e. contradiction) between the two statements concerning date consumption. הָא מִקַּמֵּי נַהֲמָא – **This** statement of Rav forbidding legal decisions after eating dates refers to dates eaten **before** eating **bread,** which have a disorienting effect; הָא לְבָתַר נַהֲמָא – while **this** Baraisa extolling the virtues of dates refers to dates eaten **after** eating **bread,** which do not adversely affect a person. דְּאָמַר אַבַּיֵי – **For Abaye said:** אָמְרָה לִי אֵם – **Mother told me:**[44] תַּמְרֵי מִקַּמֵּי נַהֲמָא – **Dates** eaten **before** eating **bread** כִּי נַרְגָּא לְדִיקוּלָא – **are like an ax to a palm tree;** בָּתַר נַהֲמָא – **after** eating **bread,** כִּי עַבְרָא לְדַשָּׁא – **they are like a bar to a door.**[45]

The Gemara digresses to discuss the etymology of other words, including the last word mentioned by Abaye:[46]

דַּשָּׁא – Why is a door called a ***dasha?*** אָמַר רָבָא דֶּרֶךְ שָׁם – **Rava said:** Because **the way** to the house **is** through **there** (*derech sham*).[47] דַּרְגָּא – Why is a ladder called a ***darga?*** אָמַר רָבָא דֶּרֶךְ גַּג – **Rava said:** Because it is **the way to the roof** (*derech gag*).[48] פּוּרְיָא – Why is a bed called a ***purya?*** אָמַר רַב פָּפָּא שֶׁפָּרִין וְרָבִין עָלֶיהָ – **Rav Pappa said: Because [people] are fruitful and multiply** (*parin v'ravin*) **upon it.**[49]

The Gemara notes one more etymology relevant to our tractate:

אָמַר רַב נַחְמָן בַּר יִצְחָק – **Rav Nachman bar Yitzchak said:**

NOTES

35. Consumption of them does not lead to a dependency on fine foods (*Rashi* to *Gittin* 70a).

36. Dates can have a disorienting affect on a person, making him feel drunk (*Rashi*).

37. Dates are good for a person when they are eaten after a meal. Thus, in the morning, when people commonly eat bread for breakfast (see *Bava Metzia* 107b), a snack of dates is beneficial. Similarly, in the evening when people eat their dinner meal, a serving of dates afterwards is beneficial (*Rashi*).

38. That is, after the midday nap [when the morning meal has been fully digested] and before the midday meal (*Rashi*).

39. [Since it is not after a meal.]

40. After one has eaten a full meal (*Rashi*).

41. They are even more beneficial than after supper, because it is not bothersome during the day to go out to the fields to use the latrines, as it is at night (*Rashi*). [Dates have a laxative effect, as taught above.]

42. Dates gladden a person, and are especially effective in the afternoon, which is generally a time of light and joy (*Rashi*).

43. [Not because wine is harmful, but because it intoxicates and clouds one's judgment.]

44. Abaye's mother died while giving birth to him. Thus, whenever Abaye quotes his "mother," he is actually referring to the nursemaid who raised him (*Kiddushin* 31b).

45. They fortify the body like a bar to a door (*Rashi*). [Bread in the stomach shields the system from the disruptive effects of the dates without blocking their positive effects.]

46. The Gemara quotes three entries from a long list of words analyzed in Tractate *Shabbos* (77b). The only obvious relationship to our Gemara is that the first of these words, דַּשָּׁא, *door,* was used by Abaye in the previous section. After explaining the meaning of that word, the Gemara explains two other related words. *Ben Yehoyada,* however, suggests a deeper connection to our Gemara; see there.

47. The word *dasha* (door) is a contraction of the words *derech sham* (the way is there); thus, the name *dasha* echoes the function of the door.

[It should be noted that the word *dasha* is Aramaic while the words *derech sham* are Hebrew. See *Maharsha* to *Shabbos* (77b), who notes that the two languages share many common words, and explains that Rava teaches that these Aramaic words are actually derived from contractions of Hebrew words.]

48. [In Talmudic times it was common to enter the upper stories (and roofs) of houses via ladders rather than built-in stairs.]

49. [I.e. the bed is used for procreation.]

גיהוץ שלנו ככיבוס שלהם ואי אמרת ניעבד גיהוץ מעברא ליה חומרתא ההוא דאתא לקמיה דרבן גמליאל ב"ר אמר ליה רבי בעלתי ולא מצאתי דם אמרה ליה רבי עדיין בתולה אני אמר להן הביאו לי שתי שפחות אחת בתולה ואחת בעולה הביאו לו והושיבן על פי חבית של יין בעולה ריחה נודף בתולה אין ריחה נודף אף זו הושיבה ולא היה ריחה נודף אמר לו לך זכה במקחך ונבדוק מעיקרא בגווה גמרא הוה שמיע ליה מעשה לא הוה חזי וסבר דלמא לא קים ליה בגווה דמלתא שפיר ולאו אורח ארעא לזלזולי בבנות ישראל ההוא דאתא לקמיה דרבן גמליאל הזקן אמר לו רבי בעלתי ולא מצאתי דם אמרה לו רבי ממשפחת דורקטי אני שאין להן לא דם נדה ולא דם בתולים בדק רבן גמליאל בקרובותיה ומצא כדבריה אמר לו לך זכה במקחך אשריך שזכית למשפחת דורקטי מאי דורקטי דור קטוע אמר רבי חנינא תנחומים של הבל ניחמו רבן גמליאל לאותו האיש דתני רבי חייא כשם שהשאור יפה לעיסה כך דמים יפים לאשה ותנא משום רבי מאיר כל אשה שדמיה מרובין בניה מרובים אתמר רבי ירמיה בר אבא אמר זכה במקחך אמר ליה ורבי יוסי בר אבין אמר נתחייב במקחך אמר ליה בשלמא למאן דאמר נתחייב היינו דרבי חנינא אלא למאן דאמר זכה מאי זכותא דלא אתי לידי ספק נדה ההוא דאתא לקמיה דרבי אמר ליה רבי בעלתי ולא מצאתי דם אמרה לו רבי עדיין בתולה הייתי ושני בצורת הוה ראה רבי שפניהם שחורים צוה עליהן והכניסום למרחץ והאכילום והשקום והכניסום לחדר בעל ומצא דם אמר לו לך זכה במקחך קרי רבי עליהם צפד עורם על עצמם יבש היה כעץ: **מתני'** בתולה כתובתה מאתים ואלמנה מנה בתולה אלמנה גרושה וחלוצה מן האירוסין כתובתן מאתים ויש להן טענת בתולים: **גמ'** מאי אלמנה אמר רב חנא בגדתאה אלמנה על שם מנה אלמנה מן האירוסין מאי איכא למימר איידי דהאי קרי לה אלמנה הא נמי קרי לה אלמנה אלמנה דכתיבא באורייתא מאי איכא למימר דעתידין רבנן דמתקני לה מנה ומי כתב קרא לעתיד אין דכתיב ושם הנהר השלישי חדקל הוא ההולך קדמת אשור ותנא רב יוסף אשור זו סליקא ומי הואי אלא דעתידה הכא נמי דעתידה ואמר רב חנא בגדתאה מטר משקה מרוה ומזבל ומעדן וממשיך אמר רבא בר רבי ישמעאל ואיתימא רב יימר בר שלמיא מאי קרא תלמיה רוה נחת גדודיה ברביבים תמוגגנה צמחה תברך אמר רבי אלעזר מזבח מזיח ומזין מחבב מכפר היינו מכפר היינו מזיח מזיח גזירות ומכפר עונות ואמר רב חנא בגדתאה תמרי משחנן משבען משלשלן מאשרן ולא מפנקן אמר רב אכל תמרים אל יורה מיתיבי תמרים שחרית וערבית יפות במנחה רעות בצהרים אין כמותן ומבטלות שלשה דברים מחשבה רעה וחולי מעים ותחתוניות מי אמרינן דלא מעלו עלויי מעלו ולפי שעתא טרדא מידי דהוה אחמרא דאמר מר השותה רביעית יין אל יורה ואיבעית אימא לא קשיא הא מקמי נהמא הא לבתר נהמא דאמר אביי אמרה לי אם תמרי מקמי נהמא כי נרגא לדיקולא בתר נהמא כי עברא לדשא דשא אמר רבא דרך שם דרגא אמר רבא דרך גג פוריא א"ר פפא שפרין ורבין עליה אמר רב נחמן בר יצחק

בתולה אלמנה גרושה חלוצה. נראה לפרש דלרבותא נקט חלוצה דסלקא דעתך אמינא כיון דשומרת יבם לא מיתסרא כניסה לחופה שהרי יבמה יבא עליה בעל כרחה וה"א דכנשואה דמיא קמ"ל: **אלמנה** דכתיבא באורייתא מאי איכא למימר. והא ליכא למימר דתפשוט מהכא דכתובת אלמנה מנה מדאורייתא דהא מנה לא היה בימי משה דלא הזכירה תורה אלא ככר והא דאמרינן בבכורות (דף ה. ושם) משה רבינו נאמן היה ובקי בחשבונות אלא שמנה של קודש כפול היה לא שהיה מנה בימי משה אלא כלומר כמו שמנה של קודש בימי יחזקאל כפול היה כך היה ככר של קודש כפול בימי משה: **ותנא** רב יוסף אשור זו סליקא ומי הואי. פי' בקונטרס ומי הואי בבריאת עולם ובלא רב יוסף מאשור וכן מכוש לא מצי למיפרך דמצינן למימר דאשור וכוש שם המחוז ולא שם העיר ומימות עולם היה שמם כך אבל קשה דמאי מייתי מאשור דאשור אע"ג דלא הוה בבריאת עולם כיון דהוה בימי משה שפיר הוה ליה למכתב אבל מנה לא היה לו לכתוב כיון שעדיין לא היה בדורו ונראה לר"י לפרש דסליקא בימי משה מי הואי דקיס ליה דסליקא לא היה בימי משה וסביב סליקא הולך חדקל ולא אבל אשור שהיה בימי משה: **אמר** רב אכל תמרים אל יורה. ואם תאמר דבפ"ג דכריתות (דף יג: ושם) (אמר רב הונא) אמר רב הלכה כר' אלעזר דאינו מחייב על שאר משכרין אלא על היין בלבד וי"ל אע"ג דלא מחייב על ביאת מקדש אסור להורות וה"נ משמע בס"פ אלו מומין (בכורות מה:) דפסול לעבודה למאן דלא מחייב אשאר משכרין אף על גב דעבודה לא אחיל הוא הדין נמי דאל יורה: מטבילין

גיהוץ. לשיקיי"ר בלע"ז בלבן הזכוכית: ככיבוס שלהן. שהיו מימיהם יפים לכבס או שמנין יפים היו להן לכבס וכיבוס שלנו אין הבגד מלובן עד שיהיה מגוהץ: **מעברא** ליה חומרתא. שפשוף האבן מעביר את הדם: חומרתא. אבן כדאמרינן בגיטין (דף סט:) ומזהר בחומרתא דנפק מיניה אבן הנמצאת בחמה מחמת חולי: ריחה נודף. מפיה מריחין ריח היין שנכנס לה דרך פתח הפתוח: **גמרא** הוה שמיע ליה. שעשו כן לבנות יבש גלעד במסכת יבמות (דף ס:): דור קטוע. שאין להם לא דם נדה ולא דם בתולים: יפין לאשה. למהר לה הריון: נתחייב במקחך. על כרחך תקבל חובה הבאה לך במקחך לשון אין חבין לאדם (לקמן דף יא.) דבר שהוא לרעתו קרוי חובה: שפניהם שחורים. מחמת רעבון: צפד עורם. דונש פירש כמו דבק עורם על עצמם ומנחם פירש שחר עורם: **מתני'** בתולה אלמנה וגרושה. בין בתולה שהיא אלמנה או גרושה או חלוצה מן האירוסין וחזרה ונשאת: כתובתה. מן השני: מאתים. שהרי בחזקת בתולה היא נשאת לו: ויש להם טענת בתולים. אם לא מצאה הב' בתולה אבדה כל כתובתה דמקח טעות היא לו: **גמ'** בגדתאה. דמן בגדת: על שם מנה. שאם נשאת משנתאלמנה אין לה כתובה אלא מנה: דכתיבא באורייתא. ועדיין לא נתקנו כתובות: ומי כתיב קרא. לקרות על שם דבר העתיד: זו סליקא. שם עיר: ומי הואי. העיר בנויה בבריאת עולם דכתיב ההולך קדמת אשור: [מטר. ולא מאותיות דריש הכי אלא לפום סברא]: מזבל. את הארץ: מעדן. נותן עדנה וזיו בפירות: תלמיה. של א"י: רוה נחת גדודיה כאשר ברביבים תמוגגנה. רוה הרי משקה ומרוה תמוגגנה הרי מזבל מעדן וממשיך את הפירות נפקא מצמחה תברך. תמוגגנה דישטנפי"ר: מזיח. קס"ד מזיח עונות: מזין. בזכות הקרבנות העולם נזון שהקרבנו' באין מן המזון וגורמין לו ברכה: מחבב. את ישראל אל אביהם: היינו מזיח היינו מכפר. הי ניהו מזיח הי ניהו מכפר: מזיח גזירות. רעות מעל ישראל: משחנן. מחממות: משלשלן. שלשול: מאשרן. מחזיקות כח כמו אשרו חמוץ (ישעיה א): ולא מפנקן. אינן מרבות אסטניסא על הלב וכלן לשבח: אל יורה. שום הוראה לפי שטורדות דעתו כשיכור: שחרית וערבית יפות. כללא דמילתא לאחר אכילה יפות שחרית דרכן של בני אדם בפת שחרית כדאמר בהמקבל (ב"מ קז:) ערבית לאחר אכילה: במנחה רעות. שהן קודם אכילה לאחר שינת הצהרים: בצהרים. לאחר הסעודה שאכל ושבע: אין כמותם. וטובות יותר מערבית לפי שאינו מעוכב ביום מלילך לשדות לבית הכסא בכל עת שירצה אבל בלילה טורח הוא לו: מבטלות מחשבה רעה. דאגה לפי שמשמחות את הלב והרהור שעת אורה ולהלה היא: כי עברא לדשא. מחזיקות את הגוף כבריח את הדלת:

אף

נז א מיי' פי"ב מהל' אישות הל' יג טוש"ע אה"ע סי' סח סעיף ד [ע' מ"מ]:
נח ב ג מיי' שם טור שו"ע שם סעיף ה:
נט ד מיי' פי"א שם הל' ט והלכה ח סמג עשין מח טוש"ע שם סי' סו סעי' ו:
ס ה מיי' פי"א שם הל' ו סמג שם טוש"ע שם סימן סו סעיף ח:
סא ו מיי' פ"א מהל' ביאת מקדש הל' ג (סמג לאוין ס) טוש"ע יו"ד סימן רמב סעיף יג בהגהה:

תורה אור השלם

א) חָשַׁךְ מִשְּׁחוֹר תָּאֳרָם לֹא נִכְּרוּ בַּחוּצוֹת צָפַד עוֹרָם עַל עַצְמָם יָבֵשׁ הָיָה כָעֵץ: [איכה ד, ח]
ב) וְשֵׁם הַנָּהָר הַשְּׁלִישִׁי חִדֶּקֶל הוּא הַהֹלֵךְ קִדְמַת אַשּׁוּר וְהַנָּהָר הָרְבִיעִי הוּא פְרָת: [בראשית ב, יד]
ג) תְּלָמֶיהָ רַוֵּה נַחֵת גְּדוּדֶיהָ בִּרְבִיבִים תְּמֹגְגֶנָּה צִמְחָהּ תְּבָרֵךְ: [תהלים סה, יא]

תוספות רי"ד

ההוא דאתא לקמיה דר"ג. א"ל בעלתי ולא מצאתי דם. אמרה לו רבי עדיין בתולה אני. אמר להן הביאו לי שתי שפחות א' בעולה וא' בתולה הביאו לו הושיבם על פי חבית של יין. בתולה אין ריחה נודף. בעולה ריחה נודף מפיה (כרימון) [כריח] בית היין. שנכנס לה דרך (הפגם הפגום) [פתח הפתוח] הושיבה ולא היה ריחה נודף. א"ל לך זכי במקחך. **ההוא דאתא** לקמיה דר"ג הזקן א"ל רבי בעלתי ולא מצאתי דם. אמרה לו רבי בתולה שלימה נבעלתי אלא ממשפחת דורקטי אני שאין להם לא דם בתולים ולא דם נדה בדק ר"ג בקרובותיה ומצא כדבריה א"ל לך זכי במקחך: **ההוא דאתא** לקמיה דרבי. א"ל רבי בעלתי ולא מצאתי דם אמרה לו בתולה שליכה אני. אלא שני בצורת היו. ראה פניה מוריקות. פי' משחרים מחמת רעבון. צוה עליהם והכניסום למרחץ והאכילום והשקום ובעל ומצא דם. א"ל לך זכי במקחך. קרא עליהם צפד עורם על עצמם יבש היה כעץ. אפי' פי' לשון דבק: **מתני' בתולה** כתובתה מאתים. ואלמנה מנה. בתולה אלמנה גרושה וחלוצה מן האירוסין כתובתן מאתים מן הנשואין כתובתן מנה. פי' בתולה שהיא אלמנה או גרושה וחלוצה מן האירוסין כתובתה מן השני מאתים שהרי בחזקת בתולה נשאת לו ויש לה טענת בתולים:

א) [תענית דף כט:], ב) [יבמות ס:], ג) [ערוך ערך דרקט מאי דורקטי תנא דור קטוע], ד) מדם. גי' רש"ל, ה) נדה סו. סד:, ו) יומא י., ז) גיטין ע., ח) [ועי' תוס' סנהדרין מב. ד"ה העוסקים], ט) עירובין סד. [נזיר לח.], י) [קדושין לא: וש"נ], כ) [שבת עז:], ל) גי' כ"י, מ) [בכורות מילרו התם מדאורייתא והכא מדרבנן הוא דאסור].

ליקוטי רש"י

גיהוץ שלנו. אינו יפה אלא ככיבוס שלהן [תענית כט:]. **דור קטוע.** [דכיון] שאין להן דמים מרובים אין בניהן מרובין [נדה סד:]. **צפד.** נקמט ונתחבר ואין לו דמיון [איכה ד, ח]. **בגדתאה.** שם עירו כנגד היא עיר החשובה שבבבל משחרבה בבל [ברכות נד:]. בעל אגדה לא"י שם מקום שהוא בבבל ששמו נגנד [יבמות סז.]. עיר שבבבל ושמה בגנדא בספק סדרו של רב שרירא גאון היא נזכרת [לעיל ז:]. דמן בגדד עיר שבולד בה ובכתבי רב שרירא גאון היא נזכרת [רשב"ם ב"ב קנב:]. **חדקל.** שמימיו חדין וקלין. **קדמת אשור.** למזרחה של אשור [בראשית ב, יד]. **תלמיה.** הן שורות המחרישה. **רוה.** כמו לרוה. **נחת גדודיה.** כמו לנחת גדודיה להניח לגדוד אתה לעשות נחת לגרוים אתה תמוגגה ברביבים של מטר. **תמוגגנה.** לשון המסה [תהלים סה, יא]. **משלשלן.** משלשלות. **מאשרן.** נותנות כח. **ולא מפנקן.** אינן מתעננגות את הלב לרות איסטנים ואע"פ שהן מתוקות [גיטין ע.]. **השותה רביעית יין אל יורה.** כדכתיב יין ושכר אל תשת וסמיך ליה ולהבדיל ולהורות (ויקרא י) דמשמע לענין הוראה נמי לא ישתה [נזיר לח.]. **אמרה לי אם.** אומנתו היתה [לקמן לט:]. **נרגא.** גרזן [סוכה יג.]. **דיקולא.** סל [שבת קי.]. **פוריא.** מטה [גיטין סט.].

לעזי רש"י

לשיקיי"ר. פירוש לגהץ, שמחליקין את הבגדים באבן זכוכית לאחר הכיבוס (סמ"ג לאוין ע"ה ועיין ערוך השלם ערך גהץ א'). **דישטנפי"ר.** פירוש להמס (עיין רש"י תהלים סה, יא), להתיך (רש"י נזיר דף נ ע"ב ד"ה מ"ש וחולין דף קכ ע"א ד"ה המחהו):

Gemara The Gemara inquires: מַאי אַלְמָנָה – **What is** the origin of the Hebrew word *almanah* (widow)?[23]

The Gemara answers: אָמַר רַב חָנָא בַּגְדְּתָאָה – **Rav Chana of Baghdad said:** אַלְמָנָה עַל שֵׁם מָנֶה – A widow is called an *almanah* **on account of the** *maneh* she receives for her *kesubah,* as stated in the Mishnah.[24]

The Gemara asks: אַלְמָנָה מִן הָאֵירוּסִין מַאי אִיכָּא לְמֵימַר – **What is there to say about a widow from** *erusin,* who receives two hundred *zuz* (two *maneh*) as her *kesubah,* as stated in our Mishnah? Why is she called an *almanah*?

The Gemara answers: אַיְּידֵי דְּהָא קָרֵי לָהּ אַלְמָנָה – **Since this one** (the widow from *nisuin*) **is called** *almanah,* הָא נַמִּי קָרֵי לָהּ אַלְמָנָה – **this one too** (the widow from *erusin*) **is called** *almanah.*

The Gemara asks: אַלְמָנָה דִּכְתִיבָא בְּאוֹרַיְיתָא מַאי אִיכָּא לְמֵימַר – **What is there to say about** the term *almanah* **that is written in the Torah?** Since her *kesubah* was not yet instituted in Biblical times,[25] why does the Torah call her an *almanah*?

The Gemara answers: דַּעֲתִידִין רַבָּנָן דְּמִתַקְּנֵי לָהּ מָנֶה – The Torah calls her an *almanah* **because the Rabbis were destined to institute a** *maneh* **for her** *kesubah.*

The Gemara asks: וּמִי כָּתַב קְרָא לֶעָתִיד – **Does a verse write** something **based on the future?**[26]

The Gemara answers: אִין – **Yes!** דִּכְתִיב ,,וְשֵׁם הַנָּהָר הַשְּׁלִישִׁי חִדֶּקֶל הוּא הַהֹלֵךְ קִדְמַת אַשּׁוּר" – **For it is written** concerning the four rivers that flowed out of Eden at the time of Creation:[27] ***And the name of the third river is Hidekel, it is the one that flows east of Ashur.*** וְתָנֵא רַב יוֹסֵף – **And Rav Yosef taught:** אַשּׁוּר זוֹ סְלִיקָא – **Ashur** mentioned in this verse **is the city of Seleucia.**[28] וּמִי הֲוַאי – **Now was [this city] in existence** at the time of Creation? Obviously not! אֶלָּא דַּעֲתִידָה – **Rather,** the verse refers to the place as Ashur because it was destined to be called by that name. הָכָא נַמִּי דַּעֲתִידָה – Here, too, the Torah called a widow an *almanah* because she was destined to be given a *kesubah* of a *maneh* by the Rabbis of a later time.

Having cited one statement of Rav Chana of Baghdad, the Gemara cites several others: וְאָמַר רַב חָנָא בַּגְדְּתָאָה – **And Rav Chana of Baghdad said:** מָטָר מַשְׁקֶה מְרַוֶּה וּמְזַבֵּל – **Rain** serves to **water, saturate** and **fertilize** the ground, וּמְעַדֵּן וּמַמְשִׁיךְ – **and it gives luster and adds growth** to the produce.[29]

The Gemara supports this: אָמַר רָבָא בַּר רַבִּי יִשְׁמָעֵאל – **Rava bar R' Yishmael said,** וְאִיתֵימָא רַב יֵימַר בַּר שֶׁלֶמְיָא – **and some say it was Rav Yeimar bar Shelemia** who said this: מַאי קְרָא – **What is the verse** that supports this statement? ,,תְּלָמֶיהָ רַוֵּה נַחֵת גְּדוּדֶהָ בִּרְבִיבִים תְּמֹגְגֶנָּה צִמְחָהּ תְּבָרֵךְ" – ***. . . To saturate its ridges, settle its furrows; with showers You soften it, its growth You bless.***[30]

The Gemara interjects a similarly styled elaboration of a word made by another Amora: אָמַר רַבִּי אֶלְעָזָר – **R' Elazar said:** מִזְבֵּחַ מֵזִיחַ וּמֵזִין מְחַבֵּב מְכַפֵּר – **The Altar** serves to **dislodge** [sins,] **provide sustenance,**[31] **endear** the Jew to God, and **atone.**[32]

The Gemara asks: הַיְינוּ מְכַפֵּר הַיְינוּ מֵזִיחַ – **Which are the [sins] for which it atones and which are the ones that it dislodges?**[33] – ? –

The Gemara answers: מֵזִיחַ גְּזֵירוֹת וּמְכַפֵּר עֲוֹנוֹת – **[The Altar] dislodges** the evil **decrees** from Israel **and atones** for their **sins.**[34]

NOTES

loss of *kesubah* (*Shitah Mekubetzes;* see *Pnei Yehoshua* for another explanation).]

23. Although the root of the word אַלְמָנָה is אלם, *mute* – because a widow sits silently after the death of her husband – the Gemara inquires what the letters נה added to the end of the word are meant to convey (*Ritva;* cf. *Maharam Schif*).

24. That is, the amount she receives in her *kesubah* should she remarry (*Rashi*). *Almanah* is thus a contraction of the words אַל מָנֶה, *no maneh,* i.e. minus a *maneh,* since her *kesubah* is a *maneh* less than a virgin's (*Geonim,* cited by *Shitah Mekubetzes*). Alternatively, it is a contraction of אֶלָּא מָנֶה, *ela maneh* [only a *maneh*], for her *kesubah,* unlike that of a virgin, is only a *maneh* *Shitah Mekubetzes;* see *Rashash* for yet another explanation). [Regarding the translation of בַּגְדְּתָאָה, see above, 7b note 16.]

25. Even Rabban Shimon ben Gamliel who holds that the *kesubah* of a virgin is of Biblical origin agrees that a widow's *kesubah* is only a Rabbinic enactment, as the Gemara stated on 10a.

26. That is, does the Torah refer to something in one historical era by a name derived from something that would not occur until a later era? (*Rashi*).

27. *Genesis* 2:14.

28. *Rashi.* We see, then, that the "Ashur" mentioned in this verse is not the country of that name (Assyria), which might have been known by that name from the time of Creation, but rather a city called Ashur [later called Seleucia] which had obviously not yet been built at the time of Creation (*Tosafos;* see there for an alternative explanation of our Gemara).

29. This statement of Rav Chana [unlike the previous one] is not intended to expound the Hebrew word, but simply to elaborate the qualities of rain (*Rashi*).

30. *Psalms* 65:11 (as explained by *Rashi* to the verse). רַוֵּה [*saturate*] indicates that the rain waters and saturates the ground; תְּמֹגְגֶנָּה [*soften*] indicates that the rain fertilizes the land (by making it muddy and dissolving various nutrients into it); צִמְחָהּ תְּבָרֵךְ [*its growth You bless*] teaches that the rain adds luster and growth to the produce (*Rashi*).

31. The world is sustained through the merit of the sacrifices. For the sacrifices are brought from foodstuffs [grain, meat, wine], whose offering therefore brings blessing upon foodstuffs (*Rashi*).

Maharsha adds that the Torah refers to the daily *talmid* offering as לַחְמִי, *My* [God's] *food* (see *Numbers* 28:2). Clearly, God does not need our food. By calling it "food," the verse teaches that the sacrifices have the quality of food – if not for God, then for us. For in the merit of these sacrifices, our food supply is blessed.

32. Although the previous exposition (regarding rain) was not based on the letters of the word מָטָר, R' Chana's current exposition may well take its impetus from the letters of the word מִזְבֵּחַ (*Maharsha*). Each of the qualities expounded contains one or more of the letters of this word מִזְבֵּחַ (*Shitah Mekubetzes*).

33. The word הַיְינוּ is used here as a contradiction of הֵי נִיהוּ, *which are they?* (*Rashi,* as explained by *Shitah Mekubetzes*).

34. The term מֵזִיחַ, *dislodges,* does not refer to the sins themselves as originally thought. Rather, it refers to the evil decrees [that result from those sins] (*Rashi*). [Protection from punishment is not the same as atonement for sin. Even when God forgives to the extent of withholding punishment, the blot of the sin remains. Hence, it is necessary for the Altar to *atone* for sin even after it *dislodges* the evil decree brought about by the sin.]

Maharsha suggests that each of these functions of the Altar is associated with a different offering. The dislodging of evil decrees is accomplished by the *ketores* (incense) offering, as we see in the case of Aaron, who used it to stop a plague that struck the Jews in the Wilderness (see *Numbers* ch. 17). The *chatas* (sin offering) and *asham* (guilt offering) atone for sins, the *tamid* and other *olah* offerings serve to provide sustenance for the nation (see note 31), and the *shelamim* (peace) offerings endear the Jews to God.

א) גיהוץ שלנו ככיבוס שלהם ואי אמרת ניעבד גיהוץ מעברא ליה חומרתא ההוא דאתא לקמיה דרבן גמליאל ב"ר אמר ליה רבי בעלתי ולא מצאתי דם אמרה ליה רבי עדיין בתולה אני ב) אמר להן הביאו לי שתי שפחות אחת בתולה ואחת בעולה הביאו לו והושיבן ג) על פי חבית של יין בעולה ריחה נודף בתולה אין ריחה נודף אף זו הושיבה ולא היה ריחה נודף אמר לו לך זכה במקחך ונבדוק מעיקרא בגווה גמרא הוה שמיע ליה מעשה לא הוה חזי וסבר דלמא לא קים ליה בגווה דמלתא שפיר ולאו אורח ארעא לזלולי בבנות ישראל ההוא דאתא לקמיה דרבן גמליאל הזקן אמר לו רבי בעלתי ולא מצאתי דם ג אמרה לו רבי ממשפחת דורקטי אני שאין להן לא דם נדה ולא דם בתולים בדק רבן גמליאל בקרובותיה ומצא כדבריה אמר לו לך זכה במקחך אשריך שזכית למשפחת דורקטי ג) מאי דורקטי דור קטוע ד) אמר רבי חנינא תנחומים של הבל ניחמו רבן גמליאל לאותו האיש דתני רבי חייא כשם ה) שהשאור יפה לעיסה כך דמים יפים לאשה ותנא משום רבי מאיר כל אשה שדמיה מרובין בניה מרובים אתמר רבי ירמיה בר אבא אמר זכה במקחך אמר ליה ורבי יוסי בר אבין אמר נתחייב במקחך אמר ליה בשלמא למאן דאמר נתחייב היינו דרבי חנינא אלא למאן דאמר זכה מאי זכותא דלא אתי לידי ספק נדה ההוא דאתא לקמיה דרבי אמר ליה רבי בעלתי ולא מצאתי דם ג אמרה לו רבי עדיין בתולה הייתי ושני בצורת הוה ראה רבי שפניהם שחורים ושני צוה עליהן והכניסום למרחץ והאכילום והשקום והכניסום לחדר בעל ומצא דם אמר לו לך זכה במקחך קרי רבי עליהם א) צפד עורם על עצמם יבש היה כעץ: מתני' ד בתולה כתובתה מאתים ואלמנה מנה ה בתולה אלמנה גרושה וחלוצה מן האירוסין כתובתן מאתים ויש להן טענת בתולים: גמ' מאי אלמנה אמר רב חנא בגדתאה אלמנה על שם מנה אלמנה מן האירוסין מאי איכא למימר איידי דהא קרי לה אלמנה הא נמי קרי לה אלמנה אלמנה דכתיבא באורייתא מאי איכא למימר דעתידין רבנן דמתקני לה מנה ומי כתב קרא לעתיד אין דכתיב ב) ושם הנהר השלישי חדקל הוא ההולך קדמת אשור ותנא רב יוסף ו) אשור זו סליקא ומי הואי אלא דעתידה הכא נמי דעתידה ואמר רב חנא בגדתאה מטר משקה מרוה ומזבל ומעדן וממשיך אמר רבא בר רבי ישמעאל ואיתימא רב יימר בר שלמיא מאי קרא ג) תלמיה רוה נחת גדודיה ברביבים תמוגגנה צמחה תברך אמר רבי אלעזר מזבח מזיח ומזין מחבב מכפר היינו מכפר היינו מזיח מזיח גזירות ומכפר עונות ואמר רב חנא בגדתאה ז) תמרי משחנן משבען משלשלן מאשרן ולא מפנקן אמר רב אכל תמרים ו אל יורה מיתיבי תמרים שחרית וערבית יפות במנחה רעות בצהרים אין כמותן ומבטלות שלשה דברים מחשבה רעה וחולי מעים ותחתוניות מי אמרינן דלא מעלו עלויי מעלו ולפי שעתא טרדא מידי דהוה אחמרא ח) דאמר מר ט) השותה רביעית יין אל יורה ואיבעית אימא לא קשיא הא מקמי נהמא הא לבתר נהמא דאמר אביי י) אמרה לי אם תמרי מקמי נהמא כי נרגא לדיקולא בתר נהמא כי עברא לדשא כ) דשא אמר רבא דרך שם דרגא אמר רבא דרך גג פוריא א"ר פפא שפרין ורבין עליה אמר רב נחמן בר יצחק

רש"י

גיהוץ. לשיקיי"ר בלעז הזכוכית: ככיבוס שלהן. שהיו מימיהם יפים לכבס או סמנין יפים היו להן לכבס וכיבוס שלנו אין הבגד מלובן עד שיהיה מגוהץ: מעברא ליה חומרתא. שפשוף האבן מעביר את הדם: חומרתא. אבן כדאמרינן בגיטין (דף סט:) ומזהר בחומרתא דנפק מיניה אבן הנמצאת באמה מחמת חולי: ריחה נודף. מפיה מריחין ריח היין שנכנס לה דרך פתח הפתוח: גמרא הוה שמיע ליה. שעשו כן לבנות יבש גלעד במסכת יבמות (דף ס:): דור קטוע. שאין להם לא דם נדה ולא דם בתולים: יפין לאשה. למהר לה הריון: נתחייב במקחך. על כרחך תקבל חובה הבאה לך במקחך לשון אין חבין לאדם (לקמן דף יא.) דבר שהוא לרעתו קרוי חובה: שפניהם שחורים. מחמת רעבון: צפד עורם. דונש פירש כמו דבק עורם על עצמם ומנחם פירש שחר עורם: מתני' בתולה אלמנה וגרושה. בין בתולה שהיא אלמנה או גרושה או חלוצה מן האירוסין וחזרה ונשאת: כתובתה. מן השני: מאתים. שהרי בחזקת בתולה היא נשאת לו: ויש להם טענת בתולים. אם לא מצאה הב' בתולה אבדה כל כתובתה דמקח טעות היא לו: גמ' בגדתאה. דמן בגדת: על שם מנה. שאם נשאת משנתאלמנה אין לה כתובה אלא מנה: דכתיבא באורייתא. ועדיין לא נתקנו כתובות: ומי כתיב קרא. לקרות על שם דבר העתיד: זו סליקא. שם עיר: ומי הואי. העיר בנויה בבריאת עולם דכתיב ההולך קדמת אשור: [ל) מטר. ולא מאותיות דריש הכי אלא לפום סברא]: מזבל. את הארץ: מעדן. נותן עדנה וזיו בפירות: תלמיה. של א"י: רוה נחת גדודיה כאשר ברביבים תמוגגנה. רוה הרי משקה ומרוה תמוגגנה הרי מזבל מעדן וממשיך את הפירות נפקא מצמחה תברך. תמוגגנה דישטנפי"ר: מזיח. קס"ד מזיח עונות: מזין. בזכות הקרבנות העולם נזון שהקרבנו' באין מן המזון וגורמין לו ברכה: מחבב. את ישראל אל אביהם: היינו מזיח היינו מכפר. הי ניהו מזיח הי ניהו מכפר: מזיח גזירות. רעות מעל ישראל: משחנן. מחממות: משלשלן. שלשול: מאשרן. מחזיקות כח כמו אשרו חמוץ (ישעיה א): ולא מפנקן. אין מרבות אסטניסא על הלב וכלן לשבח: אל יורה. שום הוראה לפי שטורדות דעתו כשיכור: שחרית וערבית יפות. כללא דמילתא לאחר אכילה יפות שחרית דרכן של בני אדם בפת שחרית כדאמר בהמקבל (ב"מ קז:) ערבית לאחר אכילה: במנחה רעות. שהן קודם אכילה לאחר שינת הצהרים: בצהרים. לאחר הסעודה שאכל ושבע: אין כמותם. וטובות יותר מערבית לפי שאינו מעוכב ביום מלילך לשדות לבית הכסא בכל עת שירצה אבל בלילה טורח הוא לו: מבטלות מחשבה רעה. דאגה לפי שמשמחות את הלב והרהור שעת אורה ותלה היא: כי עברא לדשא. מחזיקות את הגוף כבריח את הדלת:

אף

תוספות

בתולה אלמנה גרושה חלוצה. נראה לפרש דנקט חלוצה דסלקא דעתך אמינא כיון דשומרת יבם לא מיתסרא כניסה לחופה שהרי יבמה יבא עליה בעל כרחה וה"א דכנשואה דמיא קמ"ל: אלמנה דכתיבא באורייתא מאי איכא למימר. והא ליכא למימר דתפשוט מהכא דכתובת אלמנה מנה מדאורייתא דהא מנה לא היה בימי משה דלא הזכירה תורה אלא ככר והא דאמרינן בבכורות (דף ה. ושם) משה רבינו נאמן היה ובקי בחשבונות אלא שמנה של קודש כפול היה לא שהיה מנה בימי משה אלא כלומר כמו שמנה של קודש בימי יחזקאל כפול היה כך היה ככר של קודש כפול בימי משה: ותנא רב יוסף אשור זו סליקא ומי הואי. פי' בקונטרס ומי הואי בבריאת עולם ובלא רב יוסף מאשור וכן מכוש לא מצי למיפרך דמצינן למימר דאשור וכוש שם המחוז ולא שם העיר ומימות עולם היה שמם כך אבל קשה דמאי מייתי מאשור לאשור אע"ג דלא הוה בבריאת עולם כיון דהוה בימי משה שפיר הוה ליה למכתב אבל מנה לא היה לו לכתוב כיון שעדיין לא היה בדורו ונראה לר"י לפרש דסליקא בימי משה מי הואי דקים ליה דסליקא לא היה בימי משה וסביב סליקא הולך חדקל ולא אצל אשור שהיה בימי משה: אמר רב אכל תמרים אל יורה. ואם תאמר דבפ"ג דכריתות (דף יג: ושם) (אמר רב הונא) אמר רב הלכה כר' אלעזר דאינו מחייב על שאר משכרין אלא על היין בלבד וי"ל אע"ג דלא מחייב על ביאת מקדש אסור להורות מ) וה"נ משמע בפ"ק אלו מומין (בכורות מה:) דפסול לעבודה למאן דלא מחייב אשאר משכרין אף על גב דעבודה לא אחיל הוא הדין נמי דאל יורה:

מטבילין

עין משפט נר מצוה

נז א מיי' פי"א מהל' אישות הל' יג טוש"ע אה"ע סי' סח סעי' ד [עי' מ"מ]:

נח ב ג מיי' שם טור שו"ע שם סעיף ה:

נט ד מיי' פ"י שם הל' ט סמג עשין מח טוש"ע שם סי' סו סעי' ו:

ס ה מיי' פי"א שם הל' א והלכה ח סמג שם טוש"ע שם סימן סז סעיף א:

סא ו מיי' פ"א מהל' ביאת מקדש הל"ג (סמג לאוין ס) טוש"ע יו"ד סימן רמב סעיף יג בהגה:

תורה אור השלם

א) חָשַׁךְ מִשְּׁחוֹר תָּאֳרָם לֹא נִכְּרוּ בַּחוּצוֹת צָפַד עוֹרָם עַל עַצְמָם יָבֵשׁ הָיָה כָעֵץ: [איכה ד, ח]

ב) וְשֵׁם הַנָּהָר הַשְּׁלִישִׁי חִדֶּקֶל הוּא הַהֹלֵךְ קִדְמַת אַשּׁוּר וְהַנָּהָר הָרְבִיעִי הוּא פְרָת: [בראשית ב, יד]

ג) תְּלָמֶיהָ רַוֵּה נַחֵת גְּדוּדֶיהָ בִּרְבִיבִים תְּמֹגְגֶנָּה צִמְחָהּ תְּבָרֵךְ: [תהלים סה, יא]

תוספות רי"ד

ההוא דאתא לקמיה דר"ג. א"ל בעלתי ולא מצאתי דם. אמרה לו רבי עדיין בתולה אני. אמר להן הביאו לי שתי שפחות א' בעולה וא' בתולה הביאו לו הושיבם על פי חבית של יין. בתולה אין ריחה נודף. בעולה ריחה נודף מפיה (כרימון) [כריח] בית היין. שנכנס לה דרך (הפגם הפגום) [פתח הפתוח] הושיבוה ולא היה ריחה נודף. אמר לה לך זכי במקחך. ההוא דאתא לקמיה דר"ג הזקן א"ל רבי בעלתי ולא מצאתי דם. אמרה לו רבי בתולה שלימה נבעלתי אלא ממשפחת דורקטי אני שאין להם לא דם בתולות ולא דם נדה בדק ר"ג בקרובותיה ומצא כדבריה א"ל לך זכי במקחך: ההוא דאתא לקמיה דרבי. א"ל רבי בעלתי ולא מצאתי דם אמרה לו בתולה שלימה אני. אלא שני בצורת הם. ראה פניה מוריקות. פי' משחרים מחמת רעבון צוה עליהם והכניסום למרחץ והאכילום והשקום והכניסום לחופה ובעל ומצא דם. א"ל לך זכי במקחך. קרא עליהם צפד עורם על עצמם יבש היה כעץ. צפד פי' לשון דבק: מתני' בתולה כתובתה מאתים. ואלמנה מנה. בתולה אלמנה גרושה וחלוצה מן האירוסין כו' כתובתן מאתים מן הנשואין כתובתן מנה. פי' בתולה שהיא אלמנה או גרושה וחלוצה מן האירוסין ונשאת. כתובתה מן השני מאתים שהרי בחזקת בתולה נשאת לו ויש לה טענת בתולים:

מסורת הש"ס

א) [תענית דף כט:], ב) [יבמות ס:], ג) [בערוך איתא מאי דורקטי תנא דור קטוע], ד) מדם. גי' רש"ל, ה) נדה ח: סד:, ו) יומא י., ז) גיטין ע., ח) [ועי' תוס' סנהדרין מב. ד"ה העוסקים], ט) ערכין סד. [נזיר לח.], י) [קדושין לא: וש"נ], כ) [שבת עז:], ל) נ"י כ"י, מ) [בכריתות תירצו דהתם מדאורייתא והכא מדרבנן הוא דאסור].

ליקוטי רש"י

גיהוץ שלנו. אינו יפה אלא ככיבוס שלהן [תענית כט:]. דור קטוע. [דכיון] שאין להן דמים מרובים אין בניהן מרובין [נדה סד:]. צפד. נקמט ונתחבר ואין לו דמיון [איכה ד, ח]. בגדתאה. שם עירו בגדד היא עיר החשובה שבבבל משתרבה בבל [ברכות נד:]. בעל אגדה לי"א שם מקום שהוא בבבל ששמו בגדד [יבמות סז.]. עיר שבבבל ושמה בגדת בפסק סדרו של רב שרירא גאון היא נזכרת [לעיל ז:]. דמן בגדד עיר שנולד בה ובכתבי רב שרירא היא נזכרת [רשב"ם ב"ב קמב:]. חדקל. שמימיו חדין וקלין. קדמת אשור. למזרחה של אשור [בראשית ב, יד]. תלמיה. הן שורות המחרישה. רוה. כמו לרוה. נחת גדודיה. כמו לנחת גדודיה להניח לגדודיה לעשות נחת לבריות אתה תמוגגנה ברביבים של מטר. תמוגגנה. לשון המסה [תהילים סה, יא]. משלשלן. משלשלות. מאשרן. נותנות כח. ולא מפנקן. אין מתענגות את הלב להיות איסטניס ואע"פ שהן מתוקות [גיטין ע.]. השותה רביעית יין אל יורה. דכתיב יין ושכר אל תשת וסמיך ליה ולהבדיל ולהורות (ויקרא י) דמשמע דלענין הוראה נמי לא ישתה [נזיר לח.]. אמרה לי אם. אומנתו היתה [לקמן לט:]. נרגא. גרזן [סוכה יג.]. דיקולא. סל [שבת קי.]. פוריא. מיטה [גיטין סט:].

לעזי רש"י

לשיקיי"ר. פירוש לגהץ, שמחליקין את הבגדים באבן זכוכית לאחר הכיבוס (סמ"ג לאוין ע"ה ועיין ערוך השלם ערך גהץ א'). דישטנפי"ר. פירוש להמס (עיין רש"י תהלים סה, יא), להמיך (רש"י נזיר דף נ ע"א ד"ה מ"ש וחולין דף קכ ע"א ד"ה המחהו).

הַהוּא דְּאָתָא לְקַמֵּיהּ דְּרַבִּי – There was this [groom] who came before Rebbi: אָמַר לֵיהּ – He said to [Rebbi]: רַבִּי בָּעַלְתִּי וְלֹא מָצָאתִי דָּם – My teacher! I cohabited but did not find blood. אָמְרָה לוֹ – [The bride] said to [Rebbi]: רַבִּי עֲדַיִין בְּתוּלָה הָיִיתִי – My teacher! I was still a virgin at the time we first cohabited. וּשְׁנֵי בַּצּוֹרֶת הֲוָה – Now it was during the year of famine that this occurred.[15] רָאָה רַבִּי שֶׁפְּנֵיהֶם שְׁחוֹרִים – Rebbi saw that their faces were dark from malnutrition. צִוָּה עֲלֵיהֶן וְהִכְנִיסוּם לַמֶּרְחָץ – He commanded that they should be brought into the bathhouse to be bathed,[16] וְהֶאֱכִילוּם וְהִשְׁקוּם – and he gave them to eat and to drink, וְהִכְנִיסוּם לְחֶדֶר – and then brought them into a room. בָּעַל וּמָצָא דָּם – [The groom] cohabited and found blood.[17] אָמַר לוֹ לֵךְ זְכֵה בְּמִקְחָךְ – [Rebbi] said to [the groom]: Go and collect your acquisition. קָרֵי רַבִּי עֲלֵיהֶם ,,צָפַד עוֹרָם עַל־עַצְמָם יָבֵשׁ הָיָה כָעֵץ" – Thereupon, Rebbi recited the following verse about them: ***their skin cleaved to their bones, it became dry as wood.***[18]

יוֹסֵי בַּר אָבִין אָמַר נִתְחַיֵּיב בְּמִקְחָךְ אָמַר לֵיהּ – However, R' Yose bar Avin said: [Rabban Gamliel] told him, "You suffered a liability in your acquisition" – in a negative sense.[13]

The Gemara examines the dispute:

בִּשְׁלָמָא לְמַאן דְּאָמַר נִתְחַיֵּיב – Now, the view of **the one who said "you suffered a liability** in your acquisition" **is understandable,** הַיְינוּ דְּרַבִּי חֲנִינָא – for **this** is consistent with what **R' Chanina** said above, that it was a false consolation that Rabban Gamliel offered him.[14] אֶלָּא לְמַאן דְּאָמַר זְכֵה – **However, according to the one who said, "Collect** your acquisition," which implies a beneficial acquisition, מַאי זְכוּתָא – **what benefit is there** in marrying a woman who does not menstruate?

The Gemara answers:

דְּלָא אָתֵי לִידֵי סְפֵק נִדָּה – The benefit is **that he will never encounter a doubtful *niddah*** situation with his wife.

The Gemara cites one last incident:

Mishnah The Mishnah defines the basic *kesubah* obligation:

בְּתוּלָה כְּתוּבָּתָהּ מָאתַיִם – **The *kesubah* of a virgin is two hundred** ***zuz,*** וְאַלְמָנָה מָנֶה – **and** that of **a widow is a *maneh*** (one hundred *zuz*).[19] בְּתוּלָה אַלְמָנָה גְּרוּשָׁה וַחֲלוּצָה – **A virgin** who is **a widow, or a divorcee, or a *chalutzah*[20]** מִן הָאֵירוּסִין – **from *erusin,*[21]** כְּתוּבָּתָן מָאתַיִם – **her *kesubah*** when she remarries **is two hundred** *zuz* like that of a virgin, וְיֵשׁ לָהֶן טַעֲנַת בְּתוּלִים – **and a claim concerning** their **virginity can be made against them.**[22]

NOTES

13. That is, you must accept the disadvantage that came with your acquisition (*Rashi*). [See *Rashash,* who emends the text to read נִתְחַיַּיבְתָּ in place of נִתְחַיֵּיב. See also *Re'ah* and *Dikdukei Soferim HaShalem.* Our translation has followed this emendation.]

Shitah Mekubetzes suggests (in his preferred explanation) that R' Yose bar Avin does not dispute the actual words used by Rabban Gamliel. He agrees that Rabban Gamliel *said* זְכֵה בְּמִקְחָךְ, *collect your acquisition* (which implies a beneficial acquisition), but he argues that Rabban Gamliel meant this in the opposite sense – "accept the liability of your acquisition." He used this expression to avoid articulating the liability, in the manner of one who refers to a blind man as a סַגִּי נְהוֹר, *one who is full of light. Shitah Mekubetzes* also considers the explanation that R' Yose bar Avin was disputing the actual wording of Rabban Gamliel's response. This is the view of *Yam Shel Shlomo* as well. [See, however, *Yerushalmi* (end of 1:1), which explains a similar dispute (involving other disputants) in the manner explained by *Shitah Mekubetzes* in his preferred explanation.]

14. [For the lack of blood diminishes a woman's ability to have children.]

15. This clause is not part of her response but the Gemara's description of the event. See, however, *Rif,* according to whose reading this was part of her response (*Yam Shel Shlomo*).

16. To soften and moisturize their dried-out skin (see Gemara below and *Rambam, Ishus* 11:12).

17. For this test to work, it was only necessary to rejuvenate the bride for her to be able to produce blood (see *Rambam* ibid.). But he refreshed the groom too as an act of charity (*Yam Shel Shlomo*).

18. *Lamentations* 4:8. The translation follows *Donash,* cited by *Rashi,* who also cites the alternative translation of *Menachem: their skin blackened on their bones.*

19. When one marries a virgin, he must give her a marriage contract that states that he or his estate will pay her 200 *zuz* upon their divorce or his death. In the case of one who marries a widow, the contract is for 100 *zuz* rather than 200 (as it is for a divorcee or any other nonvirgin). [This is the minimum *kesubah* obligation. Additional sums can be, and often were, added to this obligation. These are known as תּוֹסֶפֶת כְּתוּבָּה, *additional kesubah.*]

According to *Rambam,* the *kesubah* amounts to two hundred *zuz* of כֶּסֶף מְדִינָה, *provincial silver,* which is a silver alloy made up of one part silver and seven parts copper. This is in contrast to כֶּסֶף צוֹרִי, *Tyrian silver,* which is pure silver. Since the provincial *zuz* was worth one-eighth of a Tyrian *zuz,* 200 *zuz* of כֶּסֶף מְדִינָה, *provincial silver,* equal 25 *zuz* of כֶּסֶף צוֹרִי, *Tyrian* (pure) *silver.* A *zuz* of pure silver equals 96 barleycorns of silver; hence, 25 *zuz* equals 2,400 barleycorns of silver (*Rambam, Hil. Ishus* 10:8). A single barleycorn weighs 0.05 grams; thus, the total *kesubah* obligation amounts to 120 grams of pure silver [3.86 troy ounces] (*Chazon Ish, Nashim* 66:21). However, many Rishonim (see, for example, *Tosafos* and *Rosh* to 10a) hold that the *kesubah* obligation is two hundred *zuz* of Tyrian (i.e. pure) silver. Accordingly, the obligation is eight times higher. This point is debated by later authorities as well (see *Shulchan Aruch, Rama, Even HaEzer* 66:6). Contemporary *kesubos* use an entirely different standard – two hundred *zekukin.* This is a much larger sum (see *Chazon Ish* ibid.). *Igros Moshe* (*Even HaEzer* vol. IV §91-92) discusses the decline in relative value of silver and the need to adjust the value of the *kesubah* to reflect this. *Igros Moshe* (ibid.) rules that the two hundred *zekukin* of the modern *kesubah* should be calculated as one hundred *pounds* of silver.

20. A *chalutzah* is a special case of widow. When a man dies childless and is survived by brothers, his widow is not free to remarry anyone she wishes. Rather, she is supposed to marry a brother of the deceased, in a marriage known as *yibum.* If the brothers refuse to marry her, the Torah provides a procedure known as *chalitzah* [literally: taking off (the shoe)] to release the widow from her restricted status (see *Deuteronomy* 25:5-10). A *chalutzah* is a widow who has been released from the *yibum* obligation through *chalitzah.*

[See *Tosafos* and *Shitah Mekubetzes* for why the Mishnah lists all these cases.]

21. I.e. she was widowed, or divorced, or had undergone *chalitzah* while in the *erusin* stage of marriage, without ever having completed her marriage with *nisuin.* Thus, she may be assumed to still be a virgin (*Rashi*).

22. If the second husband did not find her a virgin, she loses her entire *kesubah* because the marriage took place on the assumption that she was a virgin, and it was thus a mistaken transaction [מקח טעות] (*Rashi*).

Our version of *Rashi* indicates that the woman cannot even collect the one hundred *zuz* to which a nonvirgin is entitled. However, the Gemara below (11b) will cite a dispute regarding this matter. For this reason, *Shitah Mekubetzes* favors a different version of *Rashi,* which omits the term כָּל, *entire.* According to this reading, *Rashi* remains neutral as to whether she loses the entire *kesubah* or merely the extra 100 *zuz* to which a virgin is entitled (see also *Rashash*).

[Although *Rashi* explains the Mishnah's teaching in regard to the loss of *kesubah,* in fact the claim of non-virginity would sometimes also be effective in prohibiting her to him [as taught on 9a] (see *Meiri*). *Rashi* does not mention this effect because it could sometimes apply even to a woman widowed after *nisuin* (see *Shitah Mekubetzes* for the case). Thus, the Mishnah's distinction between a woman widowed during *erusin* and a woman widowed after *nisuin* is completely valid only in regard to the

עין משפט
נר מצוה

נז א מיי' פי"א מהל' אישות הל' יג טוש"ע אה"ע סי' סח סעי' ד [עי' מ"מ]:

נח ב ג מיי' שם ט ר שו"ע שם סעיף ה:

נט ד מיי' פ"י שם הל' ט סמג עשין מח טוש"ע שם סי' סו סעי' ו:

ס ה מיי' פי"א שם הל' א והלכה ח סמג שם טוש"ע שם סימן מז סעיף א:

סא ו מיי' פ"א מהל' ביאת מקדש הל' ג (סמג לאוין ס) טוש"ע יו"ד סימן רמב סעיף יג בהגהה:

תורה אור השלם

א) חָשַׁךְ מִשְּׁחוֹר תָּאֳרָם לֹא נִכְּרוּ בַּחוּצוֹת צָפַד עוֹרָם עַל עַצְמָם יָבֵשׁ הָיָה כָעֵץ: [איכה ד, ח]

ב) וְשֵׁם הַנָּהָר הַשְּׁלִישִׁי חִדֶּקֶל הוּא הַהֹלֵךְ קִדְמַת אַשּׁוּר וְהַנָּהָר הָרְבִיעִי הוּא פְרָת: [בראשית ב, יד]

ג) תְּלָמֶיהָ רַוֵּה נַחֵת גְּדוּדֶיהָ בִּרְבִיבִים תְּמֹגְגֶנָּה צִמְחָהּ תְּבָרֵךְ: [תהלים סה, יא]

תוספות רי"ד

ההוא דאתא לקמיה דר"ג. א"ל בעלתי ולא מצאתי דם. אמ"ה לו רבי עדיין בתולה אני. אמר להן הביאו לי שתי שפחות א' בעולה וא' בתולה הביאו לו הושיבם על פי חבית של יין. בתולה אין ריחה נודף. בעולה ריחה בדרך מפיה (כרימון) [בית היין]. שנכנס לה דרך (הפגם הפגום) [פתח הפתוח] הושיבוה ולא היה ריחה נודף. אמר ליה לך זכי במקחך. ההוא דאתא לקמיה דר"ג הזקן א"ל רבי בעלתי ולא מצאתי דם. אמרה לו רבי בתולה שלימה נבעלתי אלא ממשפחת דרקטי אני שאין להם לא דם בתולות ולא דם נדה בדק ר"ג בקרובותי' ומצא כדבריה א"ל לך זכי במקחך: ההוא דאתא לקמיה דרבי. א"ל רבי בעלתי ולא מצאתי דם אמרה לו בתולה שלימה אני. אלא שני בצורת הב. ראה פניה מוריקות. פי' מושחרים מחמת רעבון. צוה עליהם והכניסם למרחץ והאכילם והשקם והכניסם לחופה ובעל ומצא דם. א"ל לך זכי במקחך. קרא עליהם צפר עורם על עצמם יבש היה כעץ. צפר פי' לשון דבק: מתני' בתולה כתובתה מאתים. ואלמנה מנה. בתולה אלמנה גרושה וחלוצה מן האירוסין כתובתן מאתים מן הנשואין כתובתן מנה. פי' בתולה שהיא אלמנה או גרושה וחלוצה מן האירוסין ונשאת. כתובתה מן השני מאתים שהרי בחזקת בתולה נשאת לו ויש לה טענת בתולים:

בתולה אלמנה גרושה חלוצה. נראה לפרש דלרבותא נקט חלוצה דסלקא דעתך אמינא כיון דשומרת יבם לא מיתסרא כניסה לחופה שהרי יבמה יבא עליה בעל כרחה וה"א דכנסוה דמיא קמ"ל: אלמנה דכתיבא באורייתא מאי איכא למימר. והא ליכא למימר דתפשוט מהכא דכתובת אלמנה מנה מדאורייתא דהא מנה לא היה בימי משה דלא הזכירה תורה אלא ככר והא דאמרינן בבכורות (דף ה. ושם) משה רבינו נאמן היה ובקי בחשבונות אלא שמנה של קודש כפול היה לא שהיה מנה בימי משה אלא כלומר כמו שמנה של קודש בימי יחזקאל כפול היה כך היה ככר של קודש כפול בימי משה: ותנא רב יוסף אשור זו סליקא ומי הואי. פי' בקונטרס ומי הואי בבריאת עולם ובלא רב יוסף מאשור וכן מכוש לא מצי למיפרך דמצינן למימר דאשור וכוש שם המחוז ולא שם העיר ומימות עולם היה שמם כך אבל קשה דמאי מייתי מאשור דאשור אע"ג דלא הוה בבריאת עולם כיון דהוה בימי משה שפיר הוה ליה למכתב אבל מנה לא היה לו לכתוב כיון שעדיין לא היה בדורו ונראה לר"י לפרש דסליקא בימי משה מי הואי דקים ליה דסליקא לא היה בימי משה וסביב סליקא הולך חדקל ולא אבל אשור שהיה בימי משה:

אמר רב אכל תמרים אל יורה. ואם תאמר דפ"ג דכריתות (דף יג: ושם) (אמר רב הונא) אמר רב הלכה כר' אלעזר דאינו מחייב על שאר משכרין אלא על היין בלבד וי"ל אע"ג דלא מחייב על ביאת מקדש אסור להורות [מ] וה"נ משמע בס"פ אלו מומין (בכורות מה:) דפסול לעבודה למאן דלא מחייב אשאר משכרין אף על גב דעבודה לא אחיל הוא הדין נמי דאל יורה:

מטבילין

[א] גיהוץ שלנו ככיבוס שלהם ואי אמרת ניעבד גיהוץ מעברא ליה חומרתא ההוא דאתא לקמיה דרבן גמליאל בר"ר אמר ליה רבי בעלתי ולא מצאתי דם אמרה ליה רבי עדיין בתולה אני אמר להן הביאו לי שתי שפחות אחת בתולה ואחת בעולה הביאו לו והושיבן [ב] על פי חבית של יין בעולה ריחה נודף בתולה אין ריחה נודף אף זו הושיבה ולא היה ריחה נודף אמר לו לך זכה במקחך ונבדוק מעיקרא בגווה גמרא הוה שמיע ליה מעשה לא הוה חזי וסבר דלמא לא קים ליה בגווה דמלתא שפיר ולאו אורח ארעא לזלזולי בבנות ישראל ההוא דאתא לקמיה דרבן גמליאל הזקן אמר לו רבי בעלתי ולא מצאתי דם [ב] אמרה לו רבי ממשפחת דורקטי אני שאין להן לא דם נדה ולא דם בתולים בדק רבן גמליאל בקרובותיה ומצא כדבריה אמר לו לך זכה במקחך אשריך שזכית למשפחת דורקטי [ג] מאי דורקטי דור קטוע [ד] אמר רבי חנינא תנחומים של הבל ניחמו רבן גמליאל לאותו האיש דתני רבי חייא כשם [ה] שהשאור יפה לעיסה כך דמים יפים לאשה ותנא משום רבי מאיר כל אשה שדמיה מרובין בניה מרובים אתמר רבי ירמיה בר אבא אמר זכה במקחך אמר ליה ורבי יוסי בר אבין אמר נתחייב במקחך אמר ליה בשלמא למאן דאמר נתחייב היינו דרבי חנינא אלא למאן דאמר זכה מאי זכותא דלא אתי לידי ספק נדה ההוא דאתא לקמיה דרבי אמר ליה רבי בעלתי ולא מצאתי דם [ג] אמרה לו רבי עדיין בתולה הייתי ושני בצורת הוה ראה רבי שפניהם שחורים צוה עליהן והכניסום למרחץ והאכילום והשקום והכניסום לחדר בעל ומצא דם אמר לו לך זכה במקחך קרי רבי עליהם [א] צפר עורם על עצמם יבש היה כעץ:

מתני' [ה] בתולה כתובתה מאתים ואלמנה מנה [ה] בתולה אלמנה גרושה וחלוצה מן האירוסין כתובתן מאתים ויש להן טענת בתולים:

גמ' מאי אלמנה אמר רב חנא בגדתאה אלמנה על שם מנה אלמנה מן האירוסין מאי איכא למימר אידי דהא קרי לה אלמנה הא נמי קרי לה אלמנה אלמנה דכתיבא באורייתא מאי איכא למימר דעתידין רבנן דמתקני לה מנה ומי כתב קרא לעתיד אין דכתיב [ב] ושם הנהר השלישי חדקל הוא ההולך קדמת אשור ותנא רב יוסף [ו] אשור זו סליקא ומי הואי אלא דעתידה הכא נמי דעתידה ואמר רב חנא בגדתאה מטר משקה מרוה ומזבל ומעדן וממשיך אמר רבא בר רבי ישמעאל ואיתימא רב ייסר בר שלמיא מאי קרא [ג] תלמיה רוה נחת גדודיה ברביבים תמוגגנה צמחה תברך אמר רבי אלעזר מזבח מזיח ומזין מחבב מכפר היינו מזיח היינו מכפר מזיח גזירות ומכפר עונות ואמר רב חנא בגדתאה [ז] תמרי משחנן משבען משלשלן מאשרן ולא מפנקן אמר רב אכל תמרים [ח] אל יורה מיתיבי תמרים שחרית וערבית יפות במנחה רעות בצהרים אין כמותן ומבטלות שלשה דברים מחשבה רעה וחולי מעים ותחתוניות מי אמרינן דלא מעלו עלויי מעלו ולפי שעתא טרדא מידי דהוה אחמרא [ט] דאמר מר [ט] השותה רביעית יין אל יורה ואיבעית אימא לא קשיא הא מקמי נהמא הא לבתר נהמא דאמר אביי [י] אמרה לי אם תמרי מקמי נהמא כי נרגא לדיקולא בתר נהמא כי עברא לדשא [כ] דשא אמר רבא דרך שם דרגא אמר רבא דרך גג פוריא א"ר פפא שפרין ורבין עליה אמר רב נחמן בר יצחק

רש"י

גיהוץ. לשיקיי"ר בלע"ז הזוכית: ככיבוס שלהן. שהיו מימיהם יפים לכבס או סמנין יפים היו להן לכבס וכיבוס שלנו אין הבגד מלובן עד שיהיה מגוהץ: מעברא ליה חומרתא. שפשוף האבן מעביר את הדם: חומרתא. אבן כדאמרינן בגיטין (דף סט:) ומזהר בחומרתא דנפק מיניה אבן הנמלאת באמה מחמת חולי: ריחה נודף. מפיה מריחין ריח היין שנכנס לה דרך פתח הפתוח: גמרא הוה שמיע ליה. שעשו כן לבנות יבש גלעד במסכת יבמות (דף ס:): דור קטוע. שאין להם לא דם נדה ולא דם בתולים: יפין לאשה. למהר לה הריון: נתחייב במקחך. על כרחך תקבל חובה הבאה לך במקחך לשון אין חבין לאדם (לקמן דף יא.) דבר שהוא לרעתו קרוי חובה: שפניהם שחורים. מחמת רעבון: צפד עורם. דוגש פירש כמו דבק עורם על עצמם ומנחם פירש שחר עורם:

מתני' בתולה אלמנה וגרושה. בין בתולה שהיא אלמנה או גרושה או חלוצה מן האירוסין וחזרה ונשאת: כתובתה. מן השני: מאתים. שהרי בחזקת בתולה היא נשאת לו: ויש להם טענת בתולים. אם לא מצאה הב' בתולה אבדה כל כתובתה דמקח טעות היא לו:

גמ' בגדתאה. דמן בגדת: על שם מנה. שאם נשאת משנתאלמנה אין לה כתובה אלא מנה: דכתיבא באורייתא. ועדיין לא נתקנו כתובות: ומי כתיב קרא. לקרות על שם דבר העתיד: זו סליקא. שם עיר: ומי הואי. העיר בנויה בבריאת עולם דכתיב ההולך קדמת אשור: [ל] מטר. ולא מאותיות דריש הכי אלא לפום סברא]: מזבל. את הארץ: מעדן. נותן עדנה וזיו בפירות: תלמיה. של א"י: רוה נחת גדודיה כאשר ברביבים תמוגגנה. רוה הרי משקה ומרוה תמוגגנה הרי מזבל מעדן וממשיך את הפירות נפקא מצמחה תברך. תמוגגנה דישטנפי"ר: מזיח. קס"ד מזיח עונות: מזין. בזכות הקרבנות העולם ניזון שהקרבנו' באין מן המזון וגורמין לו ברכה: מחבב. את ישראל אל אביהם: היינו מזיח היינו מכפר. הי ניהו מזיח הי ניהו מכפר: מזיח גזירות. רעות מעל ישראל: משחנן. מחממות: משלשלן. שלשול: מאשרן. מחזיקות כח כמו אשרו חמוץ (ישעיה א): ולא מפנקן. אינן מרבות אסטניסא על הלב וכלן לשבח: אל יורה. שום הוראה לפי שטורדות דעתו כשיכור: שחרית וערבית יפות. כללא דמילתא לאחר אכילה יפות שחרית דרכן של בני אדם בפת שחרית כדאמר בהמקבל (ב"מ קז:) ערבית לאחר אכילה: במנחה רעות. שהן קודם אכילה לאחר שינת הצהרים: בצהרים. לאחר הסעודה שאכל ושבע: אין כמותם. וטובות יותר מערבית לפי שאינו מעוכב ביום מלילך לשדות לבית הכסא בכל עת שירצה אבל בלילה טורח הוא לו: מבטלות מחשבה רעה. לפי שמשמחות את הלב והרהור שעת אורה ואהרס היא: כי עברא לדשא. מחזיקות את הגוף כבריח את הדלת:

מסורת הש"ס

א) [תענית דף כט:], ב) [יבמות ס:], ג) [בערוך איתא מאי דורקטי תנא דור קטוע], ד) מדם. גי' רש"ל, ה) נדה ח: סד:, ו) יומא י., ז) גיטין ע., ח) [ועי' תוס' סנהדרין מב. ד"ה העוסקים], ט) עירובין סד. [נזיר לח.], י) [קדושין לא: וש"נ], כ) [שבת עז:], ל) נ"י כ"י, מ) [בכריתות אילו דהתם מדאורייתא והכא מדרבנן הוא דאסור].

ליקוטי רש"י

גיהוץ שלנו. אינו יפה אלא ככיבוס שלהן [תענית כט:]. דור קטוע. [דכיון] שאין להן דמים מרובים אין בניהן מרובין [נדה סד:]. צפד. נקמט ונתכבר ואין לו דמיון [איכה ד, ח]. בגדתאה. שם עירו בגדד היא עיר החשובה שבבבל משתרבה בבל [ברכות נד:]. בעל אגדה ל"א שם מקום שהוא בבבל ששמו בגדד [יבמות סז.]. עיר שבבבל ושמה בגדת בפסק סדרו של רב שרירא גאון היא נזכרת [לעיל ז:]. דמן בגדד עיר שנולד בה ובכתבי רב שרירא היא נזכרת [רשב"ם ב"ב קמב:]. חדקל. שמימיו חדין וקלין. קדמת אשור. למזרחה של אשור [בראשית ב, יד]. תלמיה. הן שורות המחרישה. רוה. כמו לרוה. נחת גדודיה. כמו לנחת גדודיה להניח לגדודיה לעשות נחת לבריות אתה תמוגגנה ברביבים של מטר. תמוגגנה. לשון המסה [תהלים סה, יא]. משלשלן. משלשלות. מאשרן. נותנות כח. ולא מפנקן. אינן מתענגות את הלב להיות איסטנים ואע"פ שהן מתוקות [גיטין ע.]. השותה רביעית יין אל יורה. כדכתיב יין ושכר אל תשת וסמיך ליה ולהבדיל ולהורות (ויקרא י) דמשמע דלענין הוראה נמי לא ישתה [נזיר לח.]. אמרה לי אם. אומנתו היתה [לקמן לט:]. נרגא. גרזן [סוכה יב.]. דיקולא. סל [שבת קי.]. פוריא. מיטה [גיטין סט.].

לעזי רש"י

לשיקיי"ר. פירוש לגהץ, שמחליקין את הבגדים באבן זכוכית אחר הכיבוס (סמ"ג לאוין ע"ה ועיין ערוך השלם ערך גהץ א'). דישטנפי"ר. פירוש להמס (עיין רש"י תהלים סה, יא), להתיך (רש"י נזיר דף ג ע"ב ד"ה וחולין דף קכ ע"א ד"ה המחהו).

אף

גִּיהוּץ שֶׁלָּנוּ כְּכִיבּוּס שֶׁלָּהֶם – Our pressing (in Babylonia) **is like their** simple **laundering** (in Eretz Yisrael).[1] Thus, in order for us to achieve the degree of cleansing attained by Rabban Gamliel bar Rebbi, we would have to press the cloth after washing it. **וְאִי אָמְרַתְּ נִיעֲבַד גִּיהוּץ – And if you will say** that **we should** go ahead and **press** it, **מְעַבְּרָא לֵיהּ חוּמַרְתָּא – the** pressing **stone** rubbing over it **would remove** the stains. We therefore have no effective method for uncovering hidden bloodstains.

Another incident:

הַהוּא דְּאָתָא לְקַמֵּיהּ דְּרַבָּן גַּמְלִיאֵל בַּר רַבִּי – There was this [groom] who came before Rabban Gamliel bar Rebbi: אָמַר לֵיהּ – He said to [Rabban Gamliel bar Rebbi]: רַבִּי בָּעַלְתִּי וְלֹא מָצָאתִי דָּם – My teacher! I cohabited but did not find blood. אָמְרָה לֵיהּ – [The bride] said to [Rabban Gamliel bar Rebbi]: רַבִּי עֲדַיִין בְּתוּלָה אֲנִי – My teacher! I am still a virgin![2] **אָמַר לָהֶן – He said to them: הָבִיאוּ לִי שְׁתֵּי שְׁפָחוֹת אַחַת בְּתוּלָה וְאַחַת בְּעוּלָה – Bring me two female slaves, one a virgin and one a nonvirgin. הֵבִיאוּ לוֹ – They brought** the slave girls **to him, וְהוֹשִׁיבָן עַל פִּי חָבִית שֶׁל יַיִן – and he seated them on the opening of a wine barrel. בְּעוּלָה רֵיחָהּ נוֹדֵף –** In the case of **the nonvirgin, her breath was fragrant** from the aroma of the wine that had permeated through her,[3] **בְּתוּלָה אֵין רֵיחָהּ נוֹדֵף –** while in the case of **the virgin, her breath was not fragrant. אַף זוֹ הוֹשִׁיבָהּ וְלֹא הָיָה רֵיחָהּ נוֹדֵף – He** then **seated this [bride]** on the wine barrel **as well, and** found that **her breath was not fragrant,** demonstrating that she was still a virgin as she claimed. **אָמַר לוֹ לֵךְ זְכֵה בְּמִקָּחֲךָ – He said to [the groom]: Go** and **collect your acquisition.**

The Gemara asks why the slaves were needed:

וְנִבְדּוֹק מֵעִיקָּרָא בְּגַוַּוהּ – Let [Rabban Gamliel bar Rebbi] have tested [the bride] in the first place! Since he knew this to be an effective test, why did he need to try it first on the slave girls?

The Gemara answers:

גְּמָרָא הֲוָה שְׁמִיעַ לֵיהּ – [Rabban Gamliel bar Rebbi] had heard the tradition that such a test is effective,[4] **מַעֲשֶׂה לָא הֲוָה חֲזֵי –** but **he had never witnessed it** being **done. וְסָבַר דִּלְמָא לָא קִים לֵיהּ בְּגַוַּוהּ דְּמִלְּתָא שַׁפִּיר – He therefore thought that he was perhaps not expert enough in the matter** to perform the test properly, **וְלָאו אוֹרַח אַרְעָא לְזַלְזוּלֵי בִּבְנוֹת יִשְׂרָאֵל – and it is not proper to demean the daughters of Israel** by testing it on Jewish girls.[5] He therefore first tried the test on slave girls to ascertain whether he could administer it correctly.[6]

Another incident:

הַהוּא דְּאָתָא לְקַמֵּיהּ דְּרַבָּן גַּמְלִיאֵל הַזָּקֵן – There was this [groom] who came before Rabban Gamliel the Elder:[7] **אָמַר לוֹ – He said to [Rabban Gamliel the Elder]: רַבִּי בָּעַלְתִּי וְלֹא מָצָאתִי דָּם – My teacher! I cohabited but did not find blood. אָמְרָה לוֹ – [The bride] said to [Rabban Gamliel the Elder]: רַבִּי מִמִּשְׁפַּחַת דּוֹרְקְטִי אֲנִי – My teacher! I am from a *dorketi* family שֶׁאֵין לָהֶן לֹא דַּם נִדָּה וְלֹא דַּם בְּתוּלִים – whose [women] have neither menstrual blood nor hymenal blood.**[8] **בָּדַק רַבָּן גַּמְלִיאֵל בִּקְרוֹבוֹתֶיהָ וּמָצָא כִּדְבָרֶיהָ – Rabban Gamliel investigated her relatives and found that it was as she had said. אָמַר לוֹ לֵךְ זְכֵה בְּמִקָּחֲךָ – He said to [the groom]: Go** and **collect your acquisition. אַשְׁרֶיךָ שֶׁזָּכִיתָ לְמִשְׁפַּחַת דּוֹרְקְטִי – Fortunate are you that you merited to** marry into **a *dorketi* family.**

The Gemara elaborates on the family name:

מַאי דּוֹרְקְטִי – What is the meaning of ***dorketi***? **דּוֹר קָטוּעַ – A generation that is cut off** [*dor katua*].[9]

The Gemara comments:

אָמַר רַבִּי חֲנִינָא – R' Chanina said: תַּנְחוּמִים שֶׁל הֶבֶל נִיחֲמוֹ רַבָּן גַּמְלִיאֵל לְאוֹתוֹ הָאִישׁ – It was with a false consolation that Rabban Gamliel consoled that man. דְּתָנֵי רַבִּי חִיָּיא – For R' Chiya taught in a Baraisa: **כְּשֵׁם שֶׁהַשְּׂאוֹר יָפֶה לָעִיסָּה – JUST AS YEAST IS BENEFICIAL TO A DOUGH, כָּךְ דָּמִים יָפִים לָאִשָּׁה – SO TOO ARE** discharges of **BLOOD BENEFICIAL TO A WOMAN.**[10] **וְתָנָא מִשּׁוּם רַבִּי מֵאִיר – And it was taught in a Baraisa in the name of R' Meir: כָּל אִשָּׁה שֶׁדָּמֶיהָ מְרוּבִּין – ANY WOMAN WHOSE** discharges of **BLOOD ARE ABUNDANT, בָּנֶיהָ מְרוּבִּים – HER CHILDREN ARE ABUNDANT.**[11]

In light of this statement, the Gemara cites two versions of Rabban Gamliel's reply to the groom:

אִתְּמַר – It has been said: רַבִּי יִרְמְיָה בַּר אַבָּא אָמַר זְכֵה בְּמִקָּחֲךָ אָמַר לֵיהּ – R' Yirmiyah bar Abba said: [Rabban Gamliel] told him, "Collect your acquisition," in a positive sense.[12] **וְרַבִּי**

NOTES

1. *Ritva* and *Ran* to *Taanis* 29b; see *Orach Chaim* 651:3. [Our definition of גיהוץ as *pressing* follows *Rashi* (as rendered by *Targum HaLaaz*). This is also the view of *Rav Hai Gaon* cited by *Ritva* to *Taanis* 29b and *Moed Katan* 23a. Laundered clothing was [placed on a table and then] rubbed with a glass stone (*Rashi;* see *Talmid R' Yechiel MiParis* to *Moed Katan* ibid.). This whitened the clothing further. Others explain גיהוץ to be a special laundering process using hot water and special detergents (see *Rabbeinu Yehonasan MiLunel* and *Meiri* to *Moed Katan* 23a and *Nimukei Yosef* there, folio 14b).]

Eretz Yisrael had either better water or better detergents. Rabban Gamliel bar Rebbi was therefore able to simply launder the cloth to uncover the hidden bloodstains. But in Babylonia it is necessary to rub clothes with a glass stone after washing them in order to achieve this level of cleansing (*Rashi*). [See *Ran* to *Taanis* 29b, who questions whether this is true of all lands outside of Eretz Yisrael or only of Babylonia, whose water was less pure.]

2. [Unlike the previous case, in which the bride said that she *had been* a virgin at the time of her cohabitation with the groom, here she said that she was *still* a virgin.] I.e. she either contradicted the groom and said that they had not cohabited [properly, i.e. he had not penetrated completely] (*Rambam, Ishus* 11:12, as explained by *Chazon Ish, Nashim* 67:18), or she claimed that he had cohabited at an angle (*Meiri; Beis Shmuel* 68:5), so that her hymen was still intact.

3. Via her open entrance (*Rashi*).

4. The Gemara in *Yevamos* (60b) states that they used such a test to determine which women of Yavesh Gilad were virgins (*Rashi*). These women were then allowed to marry the remnants of the tribe of Benjamin after the tribe had nearly been wiped out for its role in the death of the concubine in Givah (see *Judges* chs. 19-21).

5. See *Talmidei Rabbeinu Yonah* cited by *Shitah Mekubetzes.*

6. Although it is also prohibited to demean even a slave, perhaps Rabban Gamliel bar Rebbi paid them for their embarrassment, as Shmuel did in a similar situation – see *Niddah* 47a (*Hagahos Yavetz*). As to whether we rely on such a test nowadays, see *Rama,* cited by *Tur, Even HaEzer* 68; *Chelkas Mechokeik* 68:4; *Taz* 68:2; and *Chasam Sofer.*

7. Rabban Gamliel the Elder was the grandson of Hillel and a *Nasi* of the Sanhedrin. He is called "the Elder" to distinguish him from his grandson of the same name (mentioned above, 10a). The latter Rabban Gamliel was in turn the grandfather of R' Yehudah HaNasi, redactor of the Mishnah (*Rashi* to *Shabbos* 15b), whose son, Rabban Gamliel, is called (above, 10a) Rabban Gamliel bar Rebbi.

8. The Gemara will explain why such a family is called *dorketi.*

9. [From the normal female biology,] since they do not bleed like other women (*Rashi*). *Aruch* (cited by *Maharsha*) explains this to mean a generation destined to be cut off, since they do not reproduce properly, as the Gemara will explain shortly (see also *Rama, Even HaEzer* 68:5).

10. I.e. just as yeast speeds the rising of a dough, so too discharges of blood hasten a woman's ability to conceive (*Rashi*).

11. [Nevertheless, someone who marries a *dorketi* woman cannot claim that the marriage should be annulled on account of this serious defect of which he was unaware, because even a *dorketi* woman can eventually conceive. It is just not as easy for her as it is for a woman with regular menstrual bleeding (*Yam Shel Shlomo;* cf. *Beis Aharon*).]

12. According to R' Yirmiyah bar Abba, Rabban Gamliel's consolation was not false, for the reason that will be given below (*Yam Shel Shlomo*).

גיהוץ שלנו ככיבוס שלהם ואי אמרת ניעבד גיהוץ מעברא ליה חומרתא ההוא דאתא לקמיה דרבן גמליאל ב"ר אמר ליה רבי בעלתי ולא מצאתי דם אמרה ליה רבי עדיין בתולה אני אמר להן הביאו לי שתי שפחות אחת בתולה ואחת בעולה הביאו לו והושיבן על פי חבית של יין בעולה ריחה נודף בתולה אין ריחה נודף אף זו הושיבה ולא היה ריחה נודף אמר לו לך זכה במקחך ונבדוק מעיקרא בגווה גמרא הוה שמיע ליה מעשה לא הוה חזי וסבר דלמא לא קים ליה בגווה דמלתא שפיר ולאו אורח ארעא לזלזולי בבנות ישראל ההוא דאתא לקמיה דרבן גמליאל הזקן אמר לו רבי בעלתי ולא מצאתי דם אמרה לו רבי ממשפחת דורקטי אני שאין להן לא דם נדה ולא דם בתולים בדק רבן גמליאל בקרובותיה ומצא כדבריה אמר לו לך זכה במקחך אשריך שזכית למשפחת דורקטי מאי דורקטי דור קטוע אמר רבי חנינא תנחומים של הבל ניחמו רבן גמליאל לאותו האיש דתני רבי חייא כשם שהשאור יפה לעיסה כך דמים יפים לאשה ותנא משום רבי מאיר כל אשה שדמיה מרובין בניה מרובים אתמר רבי ירמיה בר אבא אמר זכה במקחך אמר ליה ורבי יוסי בר אבין אמר נתחייב במקחך אמר ליה בשלמא למאן דאמר נתחייב היינו דרבי חנינא אלא למאן דאמר זכה מאי זכותא דלא אתי לידי ספק נדה ההוא דאתא לקמיה דרבי אמר ליה רבי בעלתי ולא מצאתי דם אמרה לו רבי עדיין בתולה הייתי ושני בצורת הוה ראה רבי שפניהם שחורים צוה עליהן והכניסום למרחץ והאכילום והשקום והכניסום לחדר בעל ומצא דם אמר לו לך זכה במקחך קרי רבי עליהם צפד עורם על עצמם יבש היה כעץ:

מתני' בתולה כתובתה מאתים ואלמנה מנה בתולה אלמנה גרושה וחלוצה מן האירוסין כתובתן מאתים ויש להן טענת בתולים:

גמ' מאי אלמנה אמר רב חנא בגדתאה אלמנה על שם מנה מאי איכא למימר אידי דהאי קרי לה אלמנה הא נמי קרי לה אלמנה אלמנה דכתיבא באורייתא מאי איכא למימר דעתידין רבנן דמתקני לה מנה ומי כתב קרא לעתיד אין דכתיב ושם הנהר השלישי חדקל הוא ההולך קדמת אשור ותנא רב יוסף אשור זו סליקא ומי הואי אלא דעתידה הכא נמי דעתידה ואמר רב חנא בגדתאה מטר משקה מרוה ומזבל ומעדן וממשיך אמר רבא בר רבי ישמעאל ואיתימא רב יימר בר שלמיא מאי קרא תלמיה רוה נחת גדודיה ברביבים תמוגגנה צמחה תברך אמר רבי אלעזר מזבח מזיח ומזין מחבב מכפר היינו מכפר היינו מזיח מזיח גזירות ומכפר עונות ואמר רב חנא בגדתאה תמרי משחנן משבען משלשלן מאשרן ולא מפנקן אמר רב אכל תמרים אל יורה מיתיבי תמרים שחרית וערבית יפות במנחה רעות בצהרים אין כמותן ומבטלות שלשה דברים מחשבה רעה וחולי מעים ותחתוניות מי אמרינן דלא מעלו עלויי מעלו ולפי שעתא טרדא מידי דהוה אחמרא דאמר מר השותה רביעית יין אל יורה ואיבעית אימא לא קשיא הא מקמי נהמא הא לבתר נהמא דאמר אביי אמרה לי אם תמרי מקמי נהמא כי נרגא לדיקולא בתר נהמא כי עברא לדשא דשא אמר רבא דרך שם דרגא אמר רבא דרך גג פוריא א"ר פפא שפרין ורבין עליה אמר רב נחמן בר יצחק

רש"י

גיהוץ. לשיקיי"ר באבן הזכוכית: ככיבוס שלהן. שהיו מימיהם יפים לכבס או סמנין יפים היו להן לכבס וכיבוס שלנו אין הבגד מלובן עד שיהיה מגוהץ: מעברא ליה חומרתא. שפשוף האבן מעביר את הדם: חומרתא. אבן כדאמרינן בגיטין (דף סט:) ומזהר בחומרתא דנפק מיניה אבן הנמצאת באמה מחמת חולי: ריחה נודף. מפיה מריחין ריח היין שנכנס לה דרך פתח הפתוח: גמרא הוה שמיע ליה. שעשו כן לבנות יבש גלעד במסכת יבמות (דף ס:): דור קטוע. שאין להם לא דם נדה ולא דם בתולים: יפין לאשה. למהר לה הריון: נתחייב במקחך. על כרחך תקבל מוטב הבאה לך במקחך לשון אין חבין לאדם (לקמן דף יא.) דבר שהוא לרעתו קרוי חובה: שפניהם שחורים. מחמת רעבון: צפד עורם. דונש פירש כמו דבק עורם על עצמם ומנחם פירש שחר עורם: מתני' בתולה אלמנה וגרושה. בין בתולה שהיא אלמנה או גרושה או חלוצה מן האירוסין וחזרה ונשאת: כתובתה. מן השני: מאתים. שהרי בחזקת בתולה היא נשאת לו: ויש להם טענת בתולים. אם לא מצאה הב' בתולה אבדה כל כתובתה דמקח טעות הוא לו: גמ' בגדתאה. דמן בגדת: על שם מנה. שאם נשאת משנתאלמנה אין לה כתובה אלא מנה: דכתיבא באורייתא. ועדיין לא נתקנו כתובות: ומי כתיב קרא. לקרות על שם דבר העתיד: זו סליקא. שם עיר: ומי הואי. העיר בנויה בבריאת עולם דכתיב ההולך קדמת אשור: [י] מטר. ולא אותיות דריש הכי אלא לפום סברא: מזבל. את הארץ: מעדן. עושה עדנה וזיו בפירות: תלמיה. של א"י: רוה נחת גדודיה כאשר ברביבים תמוגגנה. רוה הרי משקה ומרוה תמוגגנה הרי מזבל מעדן וממשיך את הפירות נפקא מצמחה תברך. תמוגגנה דישטנפי"ר: מזיח. קס"ד מזיח עונות: מזין. בזכות הקרבנות העולם זון שהקרבנו' באין מן המזון וגורמין לו ברכה: מחבב. את ישראל אל אביהם: היינו מזיח היינו מכפר. הי ניהו מזיח הי ניהו מכפר: מזיח גזירות. רעות מעל ישראל: משחנן. מחממות: משלשלן. שלשול: מאשרן. מחזיקות כח כמו אשרו חמוץ (ישעיה א): ולא מפנקן. אינן מרכות אסטניסא על הלב ולכן לשבת: אל יורה. שום הוראה לפי שטורדות דעתו כשיכור: שחרית וערבית יפות. כללא דמילתא לאחר אכילה יפות שחרית דרכן של בני אדם בפת שחרית כדאמר בהמקבל (ב"מ קז:) ערבית לאחר אכילה: במנחה רעות. שהן קודם אכילה לאחר שינת הצהרים: בצהרים. לאחר הסעודה שאכל ושבע: אין כמותם. וטובות יותר מערבית לפי שאינו מעוכב ביום מלילך לשדות לבית הכסא בכל עת שירצה אבל בלילה טורח הוא לו: מבטלות מחשבה רעה. דאגה לפי שמשמחות את הלב והרים שעת אורה והלה היא: כי עברא לדשא. מחזיקות את הגוף כבריח את הדלת:

אף

תוספות

בתולה אלמנה גרושה חלוצה. נראה לפרש דלרבותא נקט חלוצה דסלקא דעתך אמינא כיון דשומרת יבם לא מיחסרא כניסה לחופה שהרי יבמה יבא עליה בעל כרחה וה"א דכנסוה דמיא קמ"ל: אלמנה דכתיבא באורייתא מאי איכא למימר. והא ליכא למימר דתפשוט מהכא דכתובת אלמנה מנה מדאורייתא דהא מנה לא היה בימי משה דלא הוזכרה תורה אלא ככר והא דאמרינן בבכורות (דף ה. ושם) משה רבינו גזבר נאמן היה ובקי בחשבונות אלא שמנה של קודש כפול היה לא שהיה מנה בימי משה אלא כלומר כמו שמנה של קודש בימי יחזקאל כפול היה כך היה ככר של קודש כפול בימי משה: ותנא רב יוסף אשור זו סליקא ומי הואי. פי' בקונטרס ומי הואי בבריאת עולם ובלא רב יוסף מאשור וכן מכוש לא מצי למיפרך דמצינן למימר דאשור וכוש שם המחוז ולא שם העיר ומימות עולם היה שמם כך אבל קשה דמאי מייתי מאשור דאשור אע"ג דלא הוה בבריאת עולם כיון דהוה בימי משה שפיר הוה ליה למכתב אבל מנה לא היה לו לכתוב כיון שעדיין לא היה בדורו ונראה לר"י לפרש דסליקא בימי משה מי הואי דקים ליה דסליקא לא היה בימי משה וסביב סליקא הולך חדקל ולא אצל אשור שהיה בימי משה:

אמר רב אכל תמרים אל יורה. ואם תאמר דבפ"ג דכריתות (דף יג: ושם) (אמר רב הונא) אמר רב הלכה כר' אלעזר דאינו מחייב על שאר משכרין אלא על היין בלבד וי"ל אע"ג דלא מחייב על ביאת מקדש אסור להורות [מ] וה"נ משמע בס"פ אלו מומין (בכורות מה:) דפסול לעבודה למאן דלא מחייב אשאר משכרין אף על גב דעבודה לא אחיל הוא הדין נמי דאל יורה:

מטבילין

עין משפט נר מצוה

נז א מיי' פ"כ מהל' אישות הל' יג טוש"ע אה"ע סי' סח סעי' ד [עי' מ"מ]:

נח ב ג מיי' שם טוש"ע שם סעיף ה:

נט ד מיי' פ"י שם הל' ט סמג עשין מח טוש"ע שם סי' סו סעי' ו:

ס ה מיי' פ"א שם הל' א והלכה ח סמג שם טוש"ע שם סימן נו סעיף א:

סא ו מיי' פ"א מהל' ביאת מקדש הל' ג (סמג לאוין ס) טוש"ע י"ד סימן רמב סעיף יג בהגהה:

תורה אור השלם

א) חָשַׁךְ מִשְּׁחוֹר תָּאֳרָם לֹא נִכְּרוּ בַּחוּצוֹת צָפַד עוֹרָם עַל עַצְמָם יָבֵשׁ הָיָה כָעֵץ: [איכה ד, ח]

ב) וְשֵׁם הַנָּהָר הַשְּׁלִישִׁי חִדֶּקֶל הוּא הַהֹלֵךְ קִדְמַת אַשּׁוּר וְהַנָּהָר הָרְבִיעִי הוּא פְרָת: [בראשית ב, יד]

ג) תְּלָמֶיהָ רַוֵּה נַחֵת גְּדוּדֶיהָ בִּרְבִיבִים תְּמֹגְגֶנָּה צִמְחָהּ תְּבָרֵךְ: [תהלים סה, יא]

תוספות רי"ד

ההוא דאתא לקמיה דר"ג. א"ל בעלתי ולא מצאתי דם. אמרה לו רבי עדיין בתולה אני. אמר להן הביאו לי שתי שפחות א' בתולה וא' בתולה הביאו ל' הושיבם על פי חבית של יין. בתולה אין ריחה נודף. בעולה ריחה נודף מפיה (כרימון) [כריח] בית היין. שנכנס לה דרך (הפגם הפגום) [פתח הפתוח] הושיבוה ולא היה ריחה נודף. אמר ליה לך זכי במקחך. ההוא דאתא לקמיה דר"ג הזקן א"ל רבי בעלתי ולא מצאתי דם. אמרה לו רבי בתולה שלימה נבעטתי אלא ממשפחת דורקטי אני שאין להם לא דם בתולות ולא דם נדה. בדק ר"ג בקרובותי' ומצא כדבריה א"ל לך זכי במקחך. ההוא דאתא לקמיה דרבי. א"ל רבי בעלתי ולא מצאתי דם. אמרה לו בתולה שלימה הייתי. אלא שני בצורת הם ראה פניה מוריקות. פי' מושחרים מחמת רעבון. צוה עליהם והכניסום למרחץ והאכילום והשקום והכניסום לחופה ובעל ומצא דם. א"ל לך זכי במקחך. קרא עליהם צפד עורם על עצמם יבש היה כעץ. צפד פי' לשון דבק: מתני' בתולה כתובתה מאתים. ואלמנה מנה. בתולה אלמנה גרושה וחלוצה מן האירוסין כתובתן מאתים מן הנשואין כתובתן מנה. פי' בתולה שבא אלמנה או גרושה וחלוצה מן האירוסין ונשאת. כתובתה מן השני מאתים שהרי בחזקת בתולה נשאת לו ויש לה טענת בתולים:

מסורת הש"ס

א) [תענית דף כט:], ב) [יבמות ס:], ג) [בערוך איתא מאי דורקטי תנא דור קטוע], ד) מדם. גי' רש"ל, ה) נדה ס: מד:, ו) יומא י., ז) גיטין ע., ח) [ועי' תוס' סנהדרין מב. ד"ה העוסקים], ט) עירובין סב. [נזיר לח.], י) [קדושין לא: וש"נ], כ) [שבת עז:], ל) נ"י כ"י, מ) [בכריתות מילתא מדאורייתא והכא מדרבנן הוא דאסור].

ליקוטי רש"י

גיהוץ שלנו. אינו יפה אלא ככיבוס שלהן [תענית כט:]. דור קטוע. [דריון] שאין להן דמים מרובים אין בניהן מרובין [נדה סד:]. צפד. נקמט ונתכווץ ואין לו דמיון [איכה ד, ח]. בגדתאה. שם עירו בגד היא עיר המשובה שבבבל משמרתה בבל [ברכות נד:]. בעל אגדה ל"א שם מקום שהוא בבבל ששמו בגד [יבמות סז.]. עיר שבבבל ושמה בגדא בפסק קדרו של רב שרירא גאון היא מוכרת [לעיל ז:]. דמן בגדד עיר שהולך בה וכבתבי רב שרירא היא מוכרת [רשבים ב"ב קמב:]. חדקל. שמימיו חדין וקלין. קדמת אשור. למזרחה של אשור [בראשית ב, יד]. תלמיה. הן שורות המחרישה. רוה. כמו לרוה. נחת גדודיה. כמו לנחת גדודיה להניח לגדודיה לעשות נחת לבריות אתה ממוגגנה ברביבים של מטר. תמוגגנה. לשון המסה [תהלים סה, יא]. משלשלן. משלשלות. מאשרן. נותנות כח. ולא מפנקן. אינן מתענגות את הלב לחיות איסטניס ועפ"ש שהן מתוקות [גיטין ע.]. השותה רביעית יין אל יורה. דכמשתי יין ושכר אל תשת וסמיך ליה ולהבדיל ולהורות (ויקרא י) דמשמע לעניין הוראה נמי לא ישתה [נזיר לח.]. אמרה לי אם. אומנתו היתה [לקמן לט:]. נרגא. גרזן [סוכה יב.]. דיקולא. סל [שבת קי:]. פוריא. מיטה [גיטין סט.].

לעזי רש"י

לשיקיי"ר. פירוש לגהץ, שמחליקין את הבגדים באבן זכוכית לאחר הכיבוס (קמ"ע לאוין ע"ה ועיין ערוך השלם ערך גהץ א'). דישטנפי"ר. פירוש להמס (עיין רש"י תהלים סה, יא), להמיך (רש"י נזיר דף נ ע"ח ע"ש וחולין דף קכ ע"א ד"ה המחהו):

איתמר אמר רב נחמן אמר שמואל משום רבי שמעון בן אלעזר חכמים תקנו להם לבנות ישראל לבתולה מאתים ולאלמנה מנה והם האמינוהו שאם אמר פתח פתוח מצאתי נאמן א"כ מה הועילו חכמים בתקנתם אמר רבא חזקה אין אדם טורח בסעודה ומפסידה תנא הואיל וקנס חכמים הוא לא תגבה אלא מן הזיבורית קנסא מאי קנסא אלא אימא הואיל ותקנת חכמים הוא לא תגבה אלא מן הזיבורית רבן שמעון בן גמליאל אומר כתובת אשה מן התורה ומי אמר רבן שמעון בן גמליאל הכי והתניא כסף ישקול כמוהר הבתולות שיהא זה כמוהר הבתולות ומוהר הבתולות כזה מכאן סמכו חכמים לכתובת אשה מן התורה רבן שמעון בן גמליאל אומר כתובת אשה אינה מדברי תורה אלא מדברי סופרים איפוך ומאי חזית דאפכת בתרייתא איפוך קמייתא הא שמעינא ליה לרבן שמעון בן גמליאל דאמר כתובת אשה מדאורייתא דתנן רבן שמעון בן גמליאל אומר נותן לה ממעות קפוטקיא ואי בעית אימא כולה רבן שמעון בן גמליאל היא וחסורי מיחסרא והכי קתני מכאן סמכו חכמים לכתובת אשה מן התורה כתובת אלמנה אינה מדברי תורה אלא מדברי סופרים שרבן שמעון בן גמליאל אומר כתובת אלמנה אינה מדברי תורה אלא מדברי סופרים ההוא דאתא לקמיה דרב נחמן אמר ליה פתח פתוח מצאתי אמר ליה רב נחמן אסבוהו כופרי מברכתא חביטא ליה והא רב נחמן הוא דאמר מהימן מהימן ומסבינן ליה כופרי רב אחאי משני כאן בבחור כאן בנשוי ההוא דאתא לקמיה דרבן גמליאל אמר ליה פתח פתוח מצאתי אמר ליה שמא הטיתה אמשול לך משל למה הדבר דומה לאדם שהיה מהלך באישון לילה ואפילה היטה מצאו פתוח לא היטה מצאו נעול איכא דאמרי הכי אמר ליה שמא במזיד הטיתה ועקרת לדשא ועברא אמשול לך משל למה הדבר דומה לאדם שהוא מהלך באישון לילה ואפילה היטה במזיד מצאו פתוח לא היטה במזיד מצאו נעול ההוא דאתא לקמיה דרבן גמליאל אמר ליה רבי בעלתי ולא מצאתי דם אמרה לו רבי בתולה הייתי אמר להם הביאו לי אותו סודר הביאו לו הסודר ושראו במים וכבסו ומצא עליו כמה טיפי דמים אמר לו לך זכה במקחך אמר ליה הונא מר בריה דרבא מפרזקיא לרב אשי אנן נמי נעביד הכי אמר ליה

גיהוץ

רש"י

חכמים תקנו לאשה כו'. כלומר אי הואי כתובתה דאורייתא לא הוי נאמן להפקיעה אלא בעדות ידועה אבל כתובתה חכמים תיקנוה הם אמרו והם אמרו הם שתיקנוה אמרו שהוא נאמן להפסידה אף בטענת פתח פתוח: **א"כ.** שבידו להפקיעה: **מה הועילו חכמים בתקנתן.** שתקנו לה כתובה: **חזקה אין אדם טורח בסעודה כו'.** אין לחוש שיטעון אדם כך אלא באמת שאם היה שונא אותה מתחילה לא היה טורח בסעודה וכונסה ומפסיד סעודתו חנם אלא היה מגרשה מתחילה: **אלא מן הזיבורית.** אם באת לגבות כתובתה ויש לו עידית וזיבורית ובינונית אינה יכולה לומר תן לי עידית או בינונית בשויה אלא אם בא ליתן לה זיבורית בשויה יתן: **מאי קנסא.** כלומר מאי פשע דקא קנסינן ליה: **מן התורה.** מכסף ישקול דלקמן: **כסף ישקול.** במפתה נאמר: **כמוהר הבתולות.** האמור במאנס את הנערה (דברים כב) קנסו הכתוב נ' כסף בשביל מוהר בתולה: **שיהא זה כמוהר הבתולות.** הקיש הכתוב קנס המפתה לקנס האונס מה להלן נ' אף כאן נ' ומה כסף האמור כאן שקלים דכתיב ישקול אף להלן שקלים דלא תימא מעות: **מכאן סמכו.** מדקרי לה מוהר: **נותן לה ממעות קפוטקיא.** בפרק בתרא תנן נשא אשה בא"י וגירשה בקפוטקיא נותן לה ממעות א"י שהן קלות נשא אשה בקפוטקיא וגירשה בא"י נותן לה ממעות א"י מנין הכתוב בכתובה דאזלינן לקולא רשב"ג אומר נותן לה ממעות קפוטקיא שנשתעבד בהן כשאר מלוה דקסבר כתובה דאורייתא: **אסבוהו כופרי.** הלקוהו מלקיות במקלות חריות של דקל שיש בהן עוקצין כמין קוצין כדאמרינן בסוכה (דף לג.) ולולא כופרא דרכיה דרכי ועוצ כתיב: **מברכתא חביטא ליה.** זונות העיר הזאת שמה מברכתא חבוטות ושוכבות תמיד לפניו לזנות מאחר שהוא בקי בפתח פתוח: **בחור** לא מהימן ומסבינן ליה כופרי על שמעיז פניו נשוי מהימן ולא מסבינן ליה כופרי: **הטה.** כשהגיע לפתח ביתו הסגור ויש בו דבר מעכבו מלפתוח וכשמטין אותו לצדדין נפתח: **איכא דאמרי.** בלא מתכוין לא שכיח הטיה ולא אמרי' שמא הטה אלא כך בדקו שמא במזיד הטית ועקרת לדשא ועברא עקרת הדלת והבריח: **הטה במזיד.** במתכוין ובכח: **וכבסו.** שהיו טיפי הדמים מכוסים בשכבת זרע:

תוספות

אמר רב נחמן אמר שמואל חכמים תיקנו כו'. משמע דכתובה דרבנן וכן בהאשה רבה (יבמות פט. ושם) גבי אין לה כתובה קאמר מאי טעמא תקינו לה רבנן כתובה שלא תהא קלה בעיניו להוציאה כו' אלמא סתמא דהש"ס סבר דכתובה דרבנן וקשה דנהגו לכתוב בכתובה כסף זוזי מאתן דחזו ליכי מדאורייתא ואור"ת דסמכינן ארשב"ג דמתני' דפרק בתרא (דף קי:) דמייתי לה נמי בסמוך דאמר נותן לה ממעות קפוטקיא דקסבר כתובה דאורייתא [ז] וקי"ל כרשב"ג במשנתנו ועוד אור"י דלא קיימא לן כר"נ דאשכחנא רב אשי דהוא בתראה דפליג עליה כדמתרץ לקמן ברייתא (דף יב.) תני כל שלא מושמש אינו יכול לטעון טענת בתולים אלמא דחייש לשמא משקר ולא אמרינן חזקה אין אדם טורח בסעודה ומפסידה וכן פי' רבינו יצחק בן רבינו מאיר דרב אשי פליג אדרב נחמן והא דאמרינן בהאשה רבה (יבמות פט. ושם) מ"ט תקינו רבנן כתובה ה"פ מ"ט תקינו רבנן כתובה היכא דתקינו כגון באלמנה שלא תהא קלה בעיניו להוציאה ה"נ תקינו שלא יהא לה כדי שתהא קלה בעיניו להוציאה:

חזקה אין אדם טורח כו'. תימה תינח באשת כהן או בפחותה מג' דמיתסרא עליה הילכך כיון דמפסידה נאמן ולמ"ד נמי לקמן כנסה בחזקת בתולה ונמצאת בעולה אין לה כתובה כלל ניחא דהשתא נמי מפסידה שהרי מקח טעות הוא אבל למ"ד יש לה כתובה מנה לא מפסיד מידי אלא שבא להפסידה מכתובתה מנה אבל הסעודה לא מפסיד ואמאי מהימן ונראה דלא מהימן:

הואיל ותקנת חכמים היא לא תגבה כו'. תימה דר"מ אית ליה לקמן בפרק אע"פ (נו: ושם) דכתובה דאורייתא ובפ' הניזקין (גיטין מח: ושם) אמרי' דקסבר ר"מ דכתובת אשה בבינונית משום חינא וכיון דהויא דאורייתא דינה בעידית כדנפקא לן בריש ב"ק (דף ה.) וכולן כאבות לשלם ממיטב דאתיא תחת תחת נתינה ישלם כסף ואמאי הפקיעו דינה ועוד דלא מישתמיט תנא בשום מקום דאית ליה כתובת אשה ממטלטלי אלא לר"מ כדאמרינן בכל דוכתין (יבמות נט.) הא מני ר"מ היא דאמר מטלטלי משתעבדי לכתובה ולמ"ד דאורייתא אמאי לא גבי ממטלטלי כמו ניזקין כיון דמהתם ילפינן וי"ל דטעמא שלא יפרשו מהן בני אדם אם יצטרכו למכור עידית או מטלטלים וחשו כדי שיקפצו עליהן בני אדם:

נותן לה ממעות קפוטקיא. תימה לר"י מה ריוח הוא לה שנותן לה מאותם המעות מ"מ אינו נותן לה אלא שוה נ' שקלים ואם היינו אומרים דלעולם צריך ליתן לה שקלים שעומדין שם בקפוטקיא נ' שקלי קפוטקיא ובארץ ישראל נ' שקלים של ארץ ישראל הוה ניחא כדאמרינן גבי ה' סלעים דפדיון בכור בפ' יש בכור (בכורות נ. ושם) לישדר מר תילתא אחרינא דאוסיפו עלייהו ושדר להו מיהו אין נראה דהתם כשהוסיפו בכל מקום הוסיפו אבל כשמוסיפין במקום אחד אין נראה שבכך תשתנה מדה דאורייתא ומיהו בירושלמי דפירקין גרסינן אמתניתין דכתובה מאתים רבי מונא בשם שמואל אמר בשקל הקדש רבי אבא בר בונא אמר מטבע יוצא וכן מסקי התם כמה אמוראי:

מברכתא חביטא ליה. פירוש הלקוהו שמוציא ש"ר על בת ישראל שהרי משקר וכי זונות חבוטות לפניו שיהיה בקי הלכך לא מהימן והא אמר רב נחמן מהימן ומשני מהימן ומסבינן ליה כופרי ורב נחמן דאמר אסבוהו לא משום שלא היה מאמינו אלא היה מאמינו ואמר להלקותו לפי שחשוד על הזנות ורב אחא משני כדסבירא לן מעיקרא דלא מהימן ואיירי בבחור ועי"ל דאתא מברכתא חביטא ליה אף על פי שהוא נאמן הלקוהו לפי שחשוד על הזנות והאמר רב נחמן נאמן ולא פירש להלקותו ומשני מהימן ומסבינן ליה ורב נחמן לא איירי במלקות רב אחא אמר לעולם נאמן דאמר רב נחמן היינו בלא מלקות ובנשוי:

בתולה

מסורת הש"ס

א) קדושין מה: [יבמות קז.], ב) [לקמן טו:], ג) לקמן לח: [כט:], ד) [ועי' תוס' סוטה ט. ד"ה אלא], ה) לקמן קי:, ו) נ"י כ"י, ז) [ועי' תוס' סוטה ט. ד"ה אלא]

גליון הש"ס

גמ' חכמים תקנו להם. עיין סנהדרין ח ע"א תד"ה מולא שם רע:

תורה אור השלם

א) אם מאן ימאן אביה לתתה לו כסף ישקל כמהר הבתולת: [שמות כב, טז]

ליקוטי רש"י

בסעודה. סעודת נישואין [יבמות קז.]. כמוהר הבתולות. חמשים כסף האמורים במאנס את הבתולה. שיהא זה. חמשים כמוהר הבתולות. ומוהר הבתולות. יהיו שקלים כזה [לקמן כט:]. כזה. שכתוב בו ישקול [לקמן לח:]. ממעות קפוטקיא. גדולות ושוקלות יותר משל א"י [לקמן קי:].

עין משפט נר מצוה

נב א מיי' פי"א מהל' אישות הל' א סמג עשין מח טוש"ע אה"ע סי' סח סעי' א וסעי' ח:
נג ב מיי' פט"ז שם הל' ג סמג שם טוש"ע שם סי' ק סעי' ג:
נד ג מיי' פ"י שם הל' ז טוש"ע שם סימן סו סעיף ו:
נה ד טוש"ע שם סי' סח סעי' ו בהגהה:
נו ה ו מיי' פי"א שם הל' יב טוש"ע שם:

תוספות רי"ד

אמר ר"נ אמר שמואל משום ר"ש ב"א חכמים תקנו להם לבנות ישראל לבתולה מאתים ולאלמנה מנה. והם הימנוהו שאם אמר פתח פתוח מצאתי נאמן א"כ מה הועילו חכמים בתקנתם. א"ר חזקה אין אדם טורח בסעודה ומפסידה. פי' המורה אין לחוש שיטעון כך אלא באמת שאם היה שונאה מתחילה לא היה טורח בסעודה לכונסה ומפסיד סעודתו חנם אלא מתחלה [היה] מגרשה והגאון פי' אימתי הבעל מהימן כששניהם טוענים ברי על הפתח הבעל אומר פתח פתוח מצאתי והיא טוענת לא כי אלא פתח נעול מצאת ותרוויהו טענו טענות ברי אז הבעל מהימן אבל אם היא מודה ליה אין פתח פתוח מצאת אבל תחתיך נאנסתי ונסתחפה שדך או מוכת עץ אני ואית לי כתובה ואיהו אמר שמא עד שלא ארסתיך והיה מקחי מקח טעות כיון דאיהי טוענת ודאי ואיהו ספק אינו נאמן כדאמר לקמן דפסק שמואל הלכתא כרבן גמליאל דאמר דאשה נאמנת ולא קשיא דשמואל אדשמואל דלא דמי תרתי טעניתא להדדי דהכא טענו ברי וברי והתם טענו ברי ושמא ואית לה מיגו וחזקה. פי' מיגו דאי בעי אמרה מוכת עץ אני תחתיך ולא פסלה נפשה מכהונה וכו' וחזקה דגופה דבתולה נולדה: **וראיתי** כתוב בה"ג דאי עביד בעל סעודה רבתי דינא הוא דשקיל אודינא מן האשה מטעם רבה ואינו נ"ל דעד כאן לא האמינוהו אלא להפסידה כתובתה שהוא מוחזק בה אבל להוציא ממון ממנה אינו נאמן בטענתו. וכתב רבינו יצחק ז"ל חזינן לגאון דקאמר ה"מ לענין מנה מאתים אבל לתוספת לא מהימן וטעמא דמסתבר הוא דלא תקינו רבנן אלא מנה מאתים אבל תוספת איהו כתב לה מנפשיה הלכך לא מהימן: **תנא** הואיל וכן דכתובתה תיקון חכמים היא לא תגבה אלא מן הזיבורית. פי' אם באת לגבות כתובתה ויש לו עידית בינונית וזיבורית אין יכולה לומר תן לי עידית או בינונית ובשוויה אלא זיבורית נותן לה ובשוויה: **רשב"ג** אומר כתובת אשה מן התורה. ומי ארשב"ג הכי והא תניא כסף ישקול כמוהר הבתולות מכאן סמכו חכמים לכתובת אשה מן התורה. רשב"ג אומר כתובת אשה אינה מה"ת אלא מדברי סופרים. איפוך ומאי חזית דאפכית בתרייתא איפוך קמייתא. דהא שמעינן ליה לרשב"ג דאמר כתובת אשה דאורייתא פי' דתנן בפ' בתרא דמכלתין נשא אשה בא"י וכו' רשב"ג אומר נותן לה ממעות קפוטקיא פי' נשתעבד בהן כשאר מלוה דקסבר כתובה דאורייתא. עי' בסו"פ: **ההוא דאתא** לקמיה דרב נחמן אמר פתח פתוח מצאתי אמר להו ר"נ אסבוהו כופרא. פי' הלקוהו בחריות של דקל שיש בהן עוקצין כמין קוצין: **מברכתא** חביטא ליה. פי' זונות מופקרות היו חבוטות לפניו שלכך היה בקי בפתח פתוח. והאר"נ האומר וכו' נאמן. נאמן ומספינן ליה כופרא. רב אחא משני כאן בבחור כאן בנשוי בחור שמעיז פניו לא מהימן נשוי מהימן ולא מספינן ליה כופרי: **ההוא דאתא** לקמיה דר"ג א"ל פ"פ מצאתי. א"ל שמא הטית אמשול לך משל למה הדבר דומה לאדם שמהלך באישון לילה ואפילה הטה מצאו פתוח לא הטה מצאו נעול. פי' כשהגיע לפתח ביתו הסגור ויש בו דבר המעכבו מלפתוח וכשמטין אותו לצדדין נפתח. ואי קשיא היכא שריא ליה. והא אמרן לעיל האומר פ"פ מצאתי מהימן לאוסרה עליו. תשובה אי הוה מהדר ליה ברי לי שלא הטיתי הוה אסורה עליו. אבל כיון דשתיק הרגיש ר"ג מתוך דבריו כמסתפק ליה ואין טענתו טענה ברורה ולפיכך שריא עליה:

[The groom] said to [Rabban Gamliel bar Rebbi]: רַבִּי, בָּעַלְתִּי וְלֹא מָצָאתִי דָּם – My teacher! I cohabited but did not find blood. אָמְרָה לוֹ – [The bride] said to [Rabban Gamliel bar Rebbi]: רַבִּי, בְּתוּלָה הָיִיתִי – My teacher! I was a virgin! אָמַר לָהֶם הָבִיאוּ לִי אוֹתוֹ סוּדָר – [Rabban Gamliel bar Rebbi] said to them: Bring me that cloth that you cleaned yourselves with after you cohabited. הֵבִיאוּ לוֹ הַסּוּדָר – They brought him the cloth, וּשְׁרָאוֹ בְּמַיִם וְכִבְּסוֹ – and he soaked it in water and washed it, וּמָצָא עָלָיו כַּמָּה טִיפֵּי דָמִים – and found several drops of blood on it.[25] אָמַר לוֹ לֵךְ זְכֵה בְּמִקָּחֲךָ – He said to [the groom]: Go and collect your acquisition.

The Gemara considers the current use of that method:

אָמַר לֵיהּ הוּנָא מַר בְּרֵיהּ דְּרָבָא מִפַּרְזַקְיָא לְרַב אַשִׁי – Huna Mar the son of Rava of Parzakya said to Rav Ashi: אֲנַן נַמִּי נַעֲבִיד הָכִי – We should also do this to determine if there is blood!

Rav Ashi replies:

אָמַר לֵיהּ – He said to [Huna Mar]:

NOTES

has the reading "Rabban Gamliel bar Rebbi" in the previous incident as well.]

25. The blood had been covered with semen from the cohabitation (*Rashi*).

איתמר אמר רב נחמן אמר שמואל משום רבי שמעון בן אלעזר [א] חכמים תקנו להם לבנות ישראל לבתולה מאתים ולאלמנה מנה והם האמינוהו שאם אמר פתח פתוח מצאתי נאמן א"כ מה הועילו חכמים בתקנתם אמר רבא [ב] חזקה אין אדם טורח בסעודה ומפסידה תנא הואיל וקנס חכמים הוא לא תגבה אלא מן הזיבורית קנסא מאי קנסא אלא אימא [ג] הואיל ותקנת חכמים הוא לא תגבה אלא מן הזיבורית רבן שמעון בן גמליאל אומר [ג] כתובת אשה מן התורה ומי אמר רבן שמעון בן גמליאל הכי [ג] והתניא [א] כסף ישקול כמוהר הבתולות שיהא זה כמוהר הבתולות ומוהר הבתולות כזה [ג] מכאן [ד] סמכו חכמים לכתובת אשה מן התורה רבן שמעון בן גמליאל אומר כתובת אשה אינה מדברי תורה אלא מדברי סופרים איפוך ומאי חזית דאפכת בתרייתא איפוך קמייתא הא שמעינא ליה לרבן שמעון בן גמליאל דאמר כתובת אשה מדאורייתא דתנן [ה] רבן שמעון בן גמליאל אומר נותן לה ממעות קפוטקיא ואי בעית אימא כולה רבן שמעון בן גמליאל היא וחסורי מיחסרא והכי קתני מכאן סמכו חכמים לכתובת אשה מן התורה כתובת אלמנה אינה מדברי תורה אלא מדברי סופרים שרבן שמעון בן גמליאל אומר כתובת אלמנה אינה מדברי תורה אלא מדברי סופרים ההוא דאתא לקמיה דרב נחמן אמר ליה פתח פתוח מצאתי אמר ליה רב נחמן אסבוהו כופרי מברכתא חביטא ליה והא רב נחמן הוא דאמר מהימן מהימן ומסבינן ליה כופרי רב אחאי משני [ו] כאן בבחור כאן בנשוי ההוא דאתא לקמיה דרבן גמליאל אמר ליה פתח פתוח מצאתי אמר ליה [ז] שמא הטיתה אמשול לך משל למה הדבר דומה לאדם שהיה מהלך באישון לילה ואפילה היתה מצאו פתוח לא היתה מצאו נעול איכא דאמרי הכי אמר ליה [ח] שמא במזיד הטיתה ועקרת לדשא ועברא אמשול לך משל למה הדבר דומה לאדם שהוא מהלך באישון לילה ואפילה היתה במזיד מצאו פתוח לא היתה במזיד מצאו נעול ההוא דאתא לקמיה דרבן גמליאל אמר ליה רבי בעלתי ולא מצאתי דם אמרה לו רבי בתולה הייתי אמר להם הביאו לי אותו סודר הביאו לו הסודר ושראו במים וכבסו ומצא עליו כמה טיפי דמים אמר לו לך זכה במקחך אמר ליה הונא מר בריה דרבא מפרזקיא לרב אשי אנן נמי נעביד הכי אמר ליה

גיהוץ

רש"י

חכמים תקנו לאשה כו'. כלומר אי הוי כתובתה דאורייתא לא הוי נאמן להפקיעה אלא בעדות ידועה אבל כתובתה חכמים תיקנוה הם אמרו והם אמרו הם שתיקנוה אמרו שהוא נאמן להפסידה אף בטענת פתח פתוח: **א"כ.** שבידו להפקיעה: **מה הועילו חכמים בתקנתן.** שתקנו לה כתובה: **חזקה אין אדם טורח בסעודה כו'.** אין לחוש שיטעון אדם שקר אלא באמת שאם היה שונא אותה מתחילה לא היה טורח בסעודה וכונסה ומפסיד סעודתו חנם אלא היה מגרשה מתחילה: **אלא מן הזיבורית.** אם באת לגבות כתובתה ויש לו עידית וזיבורית ובינונית אינה יכולה לומר תן לי עידית או בינונית בשווייה אלא אם בא ליתן לה זיבורית בשווייה יתן: [ט] **מאי קנסא.** כלומר מאי פשע דקא קנסינן ליה: **מן התורה.** מכסף ישקול דלקמן: **כסף ישקול.** במפתה נאמר: **כמוהר הבתולות.** האמור במאנס את הבתולה (דברים כב) קנסו הכתוב נ' כסף בשביל מוהר בתוליה: **שיהא זה כמוהר הבתולות.** הקיש הכתוב קנס המפתה לקנס האונס מה להלן נ' אף כאן נ' ומה כסף האמור כאן שקלים דכתיב ישקול אף להלן שקלים דלא תימא מעות: **מכאן סמכו.** מדקרי לה מוהר: **נותן לה ממעות קפוטקיא.** בפרק בתרא תנן נשא אשה בא"י וגירשה בקפוטקיא נותן לה ממעות א"י שכן קלות נשא אשה בקפוטקיא וגירשה בא"י נותן לה ממעות א"י מנין הכתוב בכתובה דאזלינן לקולא לשבג"א נותן לה ממעות קפוטקיא שנשתעבד בהן כשאר מלוה דקסבר כתובה דאורייתא: **אסבוהו כופרי.** הלקוהו מלקיות במקלות חריות של דקל שיש בהן עוקצין כמין קולין דלאמרינן בסוכה (דף לג.) ולימא כופרא דרכיה דרכי נועם כתיב: **מברכתא חביטא ליה.** זונות העיר הזאת שמה מברכתא חבוטות ושוכבות תמיד לפניו לזנות מאחר שהוא בקי בפתח פתוח: **בבחור** לא מהימן ומסבינן ליה כופרי על שמעיד פניו נשוי מהימן ולא מסבינן ליה כופרי: **הטה.** כשהגיע לפתח ביתו הסגור ויש בו דבר מעכבו מלפתוח וכשמטין אותו לצדדין נפתח: **איכא דאמרי.** בלא מתכוין לא שכיח הטיה ולא אמרי' שמא הטה אלא כך בדקו שמא במזיד הטית ועקרת לדשא ועברא עקרת הדלת והבריח: **הטה במזיד.** במתכוין: **וכבסו.** שהיו טיפי הדמים מכוסים בשכבת זרע:

תוספות

אמר רב נחמן אמר שמואל חכמים תיקנו כו'. משמע דכתובה דרבנן וכן בהאשה רבה (יבמות פט. ושם) גבי אין לה כתובה קאמר מאי טעמא תקינו לה רבנן כתובה שלא תהא קלה בעיניו להוציאה כו' אלמא סתמא דהש"ס סבר דכתובה דרבנן וקשה דנהגו לכתוב בכתובה כסף זוזי מאתן דחזו ליכי מדאורייתא ואור"ת דסמכינן ארשב"ג דמתני' דפרק בתרא (דף קי:) דמייתי לה נמי בסמוך דאמר נותן לה ממעות קפוטקיא דקסבר כתובה דאורייתא [י] וקי"ל כרשב"ג במשנתנו ועוד אור"י דלא קיימא לן כר"נ דאשכחנא רב אשי דהוא בתרא דפליג עליה כדמתרץ לקמן ברייתא (דף יב.) תני כל שלא מושמש אינו יכול לטעון טענת בתולים אלמא דחייש לשמא משקר ולא אמרינן חזקה אין אדם טורח בסעודה ומפסידה וכן פי' רבינו יצחק בן רבינו מאיר דרב אשי פליג אדרב נחמן והא דאמרינן בהאשה רבה (יבמות פט. ושם) מ"ט תקינו רבנן כתובה ה"פ מ"ט תקינו רבנן כתובה היכא דתקינו כגון באלמנה שלא תהא קלה בעיניו להוציאה ה"נ תקינו שלא יהא לה כדי שתהא קלה בעיניו להוציאה:

חזקה אין אדם טורח כו'. תימה תינח באשת כהן או בפחותה מג' דמיתסרא עליה הילכך כיון דמפסידה נאמן ולמ"ד נמי לקמן כנסה בחזקת בתולה ונמצאת בעולה אין לה כתובה כלל ניחא דהשתא נמי מפסידה שהרי מקח טעות הוא אבל למ"ד יש לה כתובה מנה לא מפסיד מידי אלא שבא להפסידה מכתובתה מנה אבל הסעודה לא מפסיד ואמאי מהימן ונראה דלא מהימן:

הואיל ותקנת חכמים היא לא תגבה כו'. תימה דר"מ אית ליה לקמן בפרק אע"פ (נו: ושם) דכתובה דאורייתא ובפ' הניזקין (גיטין מח: ושם) אמרי' דקסבר ר"מ דכתובת אשה בבינונית משום חינא וכיון דהויא דאורייתא דינה בעידית כדנפקא לן בריש ב"ק (דף ה.) וכולן כאבות לשלם ממיטב דאתיא תחת תחת נתינה ישלם כסף ואמאי הפקיעו דינה ועוד דלא מישתמיט תנא בשום מקום דאית ליה כתובת אשה ממטלטלי אלא לר"מ כדאמרינן בכל דוכתין (יבמות לט.) הא מני ר"מ היא דאמר מטלטלי משתעבדי לכתובה ולמ"ד דאורייתא אמאי לא גבי ממטלטלי כמו ניזקין כיון דמהתם ילפינן וי"ל דטעמא שלא יפרשו מהן בני אדם אם יצטרכו למכור עידית או מטלטלים ותשו כדי שיקפצו עליהן בני אדם:

נותן לה ממעות קפוטקיא. תימה לר"י מה ריוח הוא לה שנותן לה מאותם המעות מ"מ אינו נותן לה אלא שוה נ' שקלים ואם היינו אומרים דלעולם צריך ליתן לה שקלים שעומדין שם בקפוטקיא נ' שקלי קפוטקיא ובארץ ישראל נ' שקלים של ארץ ישראל הוה ניחא כדאמרינן גבי ה' סלעים דפדיון בכור בפ' יש בכור (בכורות נ. ושם) לישדר מר תילתא אחרינא דאוסיפו עלייהו ושדר להו מיהו אין נראה דהתם כשהוסיפו בכל מקום הוסיפו אבל כשמוסיפין במקום אחד אין נראה שבכך תשתנה מדה דאורייתא ומיהו בירושלמי דפירקין גרסינן אמתניתין דכתובה מאתים רבי מונא בשם שמואל אמר בשקל הקדש רבי אבא בר בונא אמר מטבע יוצא וכן מסקי התם כמה אמוראי:

מברכתא חביטא ליה. פירוש הלקוהו שמוציא ש"ר על בת ישראל שהרי משקר וכי זונות חבוטות לפניו שיהיה בקי הלכך לא מהימן והא אמר רב נחמן מהימן ומשני מהימן ומסבינן ליה כופרי ורב נחמן דאמר אסבוהו לא משום שלא היה מאמינו אלא היה מאמינו ואמר להלקותו לפי שחשוד על הזנות ורב אחא משני כדסבירא לן מעיקרא דלא מהימן ואיירי בבחור ועי"ל בניחותא מברכתא חביטא ליה אף על פי שהוא נאמן הלקוהו לפי שחשוד על הזנות והאמר רב נחמן נאמן ולא פירש להלקותו ומשני מהימן ומסבינן ליה ורב נחמן לא איירי במלקות רב אחא אמר לעולם נאמן דאמר רב נחמן היינו בלא מלקות ובנשוי:

בתולה

מסורת הש"ס

א) קדושין מה: [יבמות קי.], ב) [לקמן נו:], ג) לקמן לח: [סט:], ד) [ועי' תוס' סוטה מ. ד"ה אשו], ה) לקמן קי:, ו) נ"י כ"י, ז) [ועי' תוס' סוטה מ. ד"ה אשו].

גליון הש"ס

גמ' חכמים תקנו להם. עיין סנהדרין ח ע"א תד"ה מולין שם רע:

תורה אור השלם

א) אם מאן ימאן אביה לתתה לו כסף ישקל כמהר הבתולת: [שמות כב, טז]

ליקוטי רש"י

בסעודה. סעודת נישואין [יבמות קז.]. **כמוהר הבתולות.** חמשים כסף המפורשים במאנס את הבתולה. **שיהא זה.** חמשים כמוהר הבתולות. ומוהר הבתולות. יהיו שקלים כזה [לקמן כט:]. **כזה.** שכתוב בו ישקול [לקמן לח.]. **ממעות קפוטקיא.** גדולות ושוקלות יותר משל א"י [לקמן קי.].

עין משפט נר מצוה

נב א מיי' פי"א מהל' אישות הל' ל סמג עשין מח טוש"ע אה"ע סי' סח סעי' ה וסעי' ח:
נג ב מיי' פט"ו שם הל' ג סמג שם טוש"ע שם סי' ק סעי' ב:
נד ג מיי' פי"ז שם הל' ז טוש"ע שם סימן סו סעיף ו:
נה ד טוש"ע שם סי' סח סעי' ו בהגהה:
נו ה ו מיי' פי"א שם הל' יב טוש"ע שם:

תוספות רי"ד

אמר ר"נ אמר שמואל משום ר"ש ב"א חכמים תקנו להם לבנות ישראל לבתולה מאתים ולאלמנה מנה. והם האמינוהו שאם אמר פתח פתוח מצאתי נאמן א"כ מה הועילו חכמים בתקנתם. א"ר חזקה אין אדם טורח בסעודה ומפסידה. פי' המורה אין לחוש שיטעון כך אלא באמת שאם היה שונאה מתחילה לא היה טורח בסעודה לכונסה ומפסיד סעודתו חנם אלא מתחלה [היה] מגרשה והגאון פי' איפכא הבעל מהימן כשהן טוענים ברי על הפתח הבעל אומר פתח פתוח מצאתי והיא טוענת לא כי אלא פתח נעול מצאת ותרווייהו טענו טענת ברי אז הבעל מהימן אבל אם היא מודה ליה אין פתח פתוח מצאת אבל תחתיך נאנסתי ונסתחפה שדך נמי מוכת עץ אני ואית לי כתובה ואיהו אמר שמא עד שלא ארסתיך והיה מקחי מקח טעות כיון דאיהי טוענת ודאי ואיהו ספק אינו נאמן כדאמר לקמן דפסק שמואל הלכתא כרבן גמליאל דאמר דאשה נאמנת ולא קשיא דשמואל אדשמואל דלא דמי תרתי טענייתא להדדי דהכא טענו ברי וברי והתם טענו ברי ושמא ואית לה מיגו וחזקה. פי' מיגו דאי בעיי אמרה מוכת עץ אני תחתיך ולא פסלה נפשה מכהונה וכו' וחזקה דגופה דבתולה נולדה: וראיתי כתוב בה"ג דאי עביד בעל סעודה רבתי דינא הוא דשקיל אודינא מן האשה מטעם רבה ואינו נ"ל דעד כאן לא האמינוהו אלא להפסידה כתובתה שהוא מוחזק בה אבל להוציא ממון ממנה אינו נאמן בטענתו. וכתב רבינו יצחק ז"ל חזינן לגאון דקאמר ה"מ לענין מנה מאתים אבל לתוספת לא מהימן וטעמא דמסתבר הוא דלא תקינו רבנן אלא מנה מאתים אבל תוספת איהו כתב לה מנפשיה הלכך לא מהימן: **תנא** הואיל וכן דכתובתה תיקון חכמים היא לא תגבה אלא מן הזיבורית. פי' אם באת לגבות כתובתה ויש לו עידית ובינונית וזיבורית אינה יכולה לומר תן לי עידית או בינונית וכשווייה אלא זיבורית נותן לה בשווייה: **רשב"ג** אומר כתובת אשה מן התורה. ומי ארשב"ג הכי והא תניא כסף ישקול כמוהר הבתולות מכאן סמכו חכמים לכתובת אשה מן התורה. רשב"ג אומר כתובת אשה אינה מה"ת אלא מדברי סופרים. איפוך ומאי חזית דאפכית בתרייתא איפוך קמייתא. דהא שמעינן ליה לרשב"ג דאמר כתובת אשה

דאורייתא פי' דתנן בפ' בתרא דמכילתין נשא אשה בא"י וכו' רשב"ג אומר נותן לה ממעות קפוטקיא פי' נשתעבד בהן כשאר מלוה דקסבר כתובה דאורייתא. עי' בסו"פ: **ההוא דאתא** לקמיה דרב נחמן אמר פתח פתוח מצאתי אמר להו ר"נ אסבוהו כופרא. פי' הלקוהו בחריות של דקל שיש בהן עוקצין כמין קוצין: **מברכתא** חביטא ליה. פי' זונות מופקרות היו חבוטות לו שמכיר בפתח פתוח. והאר"נ האומר וכו' נאמן. נאמן ומספינן ליה כופרא. רב אחא משני כאן בבחור כאן בנשוי בחור לא מהימן ומספינן ליה כופרי נשוי מהימן ולא מספינן ליה כופרי: **ההוא דאתא** לקמיה דר"ג א"ל פ"פ מצאתי. א"ל שמא הטית אמשול לך משל למה הדבר דומה לאדם שמהלך באישון לילה ואפילה הטה מצאו פתוח לא הטה מצאו נעול. פי' בהגיעו לפתח ביתו הסגור ויש בו המעכבו מלפתוח. וכשמטין אותו לצדדין נפתח. ואי קשיא היכא שריא ליה. והא אמרן לעיל האומר פ"פ מצאתי מהימן לאוסרה עליו. תשובה אי הוה מהדר ליה ברי לי שלא הטיתי הוה אסורה עליו. אבל כיון דשתיק הרגיש ר"ג מתוך דבריו כמספקא ליה ואין טענתו טענה ברורה ולפיכך שריא עליה:

The Gemara questions Rav Nachman's ruling:
וְהָא רַב נַחְמָן הוּא דְּאָמַר מְהֵימַן – **But Rav Nachman** himself **is the one who said** above **that [a groom] is believed** when he lodges such a claim![16] – **?** –

The Gemara answers:
מְהֵימַן וּמַסְבִּינַן לֵיהּ כּוּפְרֵי – Rav Nachman meant that **he is** indeed **believed – but we** nevertheless **give him** lashes with **palm branches.**[17]

An alternative answer:
רַב אַחַאי מְשַׁנֵּי – **Rav Achai answered:**[18] כָּאן בְּבָחוּר – **Here** (in the incident under discussion), Rav Nachman was dealing **with a** previously **unmarried man,** which is why he gave him lashes. כָּאן בְּנָשׂוּי – Whereas **here** (in his ruling above), Rav Nachman was dealing **with a** previously **married man,** who does not receive lashes for making such a claim.[19]

A second incident concerning the claim of an open entrance:
הַהוּא דְּאָתָא לְקַמֵּיהּ דְּרַבָּן גַּמְלִיאֵל – **There was a [groom] who came before Rabban Gamliel.** אָמַר לֵיהּ פֶּתַח פָּתוּחַ מָצָאתִי – **He said to [Rabban Gamliel]: I found "an open entrance."** אָמַר לֵיהּ שֶׁמָּא הִטִּיתָה – **[Rabban Gamliel] said to him: Perhaps you angled** your entry, so that you thought you encountered an "open entrance" when in fact you did not.[20] אֶמְשׁוֹל לְךָ מָשָׁל – **I will give you an analogy.** לְמָה הַדָּבָר דּוֹמֶה – **To what is this matter comparable?** לְאָדָם שֶׁהָיָה מְהַלֵּךְ בְּאִישׁוֹן לַיְלָה וַאֲפֵילָה – **To a person who was walking in the black of night and darkness.**[21] הִיטָּה מְצָאוֹ פָּתוּחַ – If, on arriving home, **he angled** his approach, **he found [the door of his house] open;** לֹא הִיטָּה מְצָאוֹ נָעוּל – but if **he did not angle** his approach, **he found [the door] locked.**[22]

The Gemara presents another version of Rabban Gamliel's reply:
אִיכָּא דְּאָמְרֵי הָכִי אָמַר לֵיהּ – **There are those who say this is what [Rabban Gamliel] said to [the groom]:** שֶׁמָּא בְּמֵזִיד הִטִּיתָה – **Perhaps you angled** your entry **deliberately,** וְעָקַרְתָּ לְדַשָּׁא וְעִבְּרָא – **and tore out the door and the bar.**[23] אֶמְשׁוֹל לְךָ מָשָׁל – **I will give you an analogy.** לְמָה הַדָּבָר דּוֹמֶה – **To what is this comparable?** לְאָדָם שֶׁהוּא מְהַלֵּךְ בְּאִישׁוֹן לַיְלָה וַאֲפֵילָה – **To a person who was walking in the black of night and darkness.** הִיטָּה בְּמֵזִיד מְצָאוֹ פָּתוּחַ – **If,** when he arrived home, **he deliberately angled** his approach, **he found [the door of his house] open;** לֹא הִיטָּה בְּמֵזִיד מְצָאוֹ נָעוּל – but if **he did not deliberately angle** his approach, **he found it locked.**

The claims concerning virginity cited to this point have dealt with claims of an "open entrance." The Gemara now cites a series of incidents in which the claim was based on an absence of blood:
הַהוּא דְּאָתָא לְקַמֵּיהּ דְּרַבָּן גַּמְלִיאֵל בַּר רַבִּי – **There was a [groom] who came before Rabban Gamliel bar Rebbi:**[24] אָמַר לֵיהּ –

NOTES

Nachman did not believe that the groom could be sure of his claim and he therefore exclaimed, "Are the prostitutes of Mevarachta lying before him," that he is experienced enough to tell the difference between an open and closed entrance. Accordingly, he gave him lashes for falsely defaming his bride (*Tosafos, Ritva;* see there for their explanation of the Gemara's next question and answer).]

16. Rav Nachman is the one who cited (at the top of this *amud*) the statement of Shmuel that the Sages legislated that such a claim should be believed, and he did not qualify that ruling by saying that the groom is flogged for lodging such a claim (*Tosafos*).

17. That is, Rav Nachman's ruling above concerned only the validity of the groom's claim. In practice, though, Rav Nachman ruled that such a claim deserves lashes because it reveals the groom's previous promiscuity (*Tosafos*). This applies, of course, only to the claim of an "open entrance," which requires previous experience to be able to judge properly. If, however, the groom claims that he did not find blood, he does not get lashes because anyone can recognize whether or not there was blood (*Ritva*).

18. See 2b, *Tosafos* ד״ה פשיט concerning the unusual wording of this phrase.

19. According to Rav Achai, a previously unmarried man is *not* believed when he makes the claim of "an open entrance" because he is assumed to lack the experience to judge this properly. [Thus, when Rav Nachman questioned the groom's relationship with the prostitutes of Mevarachta, he did so sarcastically (see note 15); he did not actually accuse him of promiscuous behavior.] Such a person receives lashes [not for anything he did before, but] for his brazenness in making a defamatory claim regarding something he cannot know (*Rashi;* cf. *Raavad,* cited by *Rashba*). However, someone who was previously married is believed when he makes such a claim and does not receive lashes for it (*Rashi; Rashba; Rosh;* cf. *Rabbeinu Chananel* cited by *Rashba* and *Shitah Mekubetzes; Re'ah*).

Even according to Rav Achai, it is only in regard to the *kesubah* that we do not believe his claim, but we do accept it in regard to forbidding her to him. Since a person is believed in regard to himself, his assertion that he is sure renders her forbidden to him [שַׁוְיָהּ אַנַּפְשֵׁיהּ חֲתִיכָה דְאִיסּוּרָא] (*Rashba*). But since we [the courts] doubt that he really knows, we cannot deprive her of her *kesubah* (see 9a note 11).

[It emerges from this that according to Rav Achai, when Rav Nachman ruled in the name of Shmuel that the claim of an open entrance deprives a woman of her *kesubah,* he meant it only in regard to a previously married man. Accordingly, there is no longer any necessity to say that R' Elazar (on 9a) disputes Shmuel's ruling on 9b concerning the loss of her *kesubah* (see 9b note 12). For Shmuel speaks only of a previously married man, whereas R' Elazar speaks of even a previously unmarried man (see 9a note 11), which is why he only states that he is believed in regard to the prohibition – but not in regard to the *kesubah* [see 9b note 12] (*Shitah Mekubetzes* 9a ד״ה אבל הכא and 9b ד״ה נאמן להפסידה in explanation of *Rashi*).]

20. See note 22.

21. See *Proverbs* 7:9.

22. When an object behind a door prevents it from opening completely but allows it to open partially, a person entering the doorway at an angle will find himself able to enter, while one who enters it straightforward will find his way blocked (*Rashi;* see *Rashi* to *Rif;* the word מַטִּין in reference to a door means to open partially – see Mishnah *Taanis* 12b). [By analogy, therefore, one who cohabits in the normal manner will certainly experience some resistance. One who penetrates at an angle, however, may encounter no resistance at all since the hymen does not completely obstruct the opening. See *Shitah Mekubetzes* for a different explanation of Rabban Gamliel's statement and analogy.]

[Although we learned above that one who claims an "open entrance" is believed to render his wife forbidden to him, the incident here involved a case of double doubt (see 9a), so that she was permitted to him even if she had not been a virgin. Nevertheless, Rabban Gamliel wanted to calm the groom's mind by telling him that it was possible that she actually had been a virgin (*Ritva*). Alternatively, even if the case involved only a single doubt (e.g. he was a Kohen), Rabban Gamliel questioned him to see whether he was really sure of his claim. By suggesting ways in which he might have been mistaken Rabban Gamliel sought to get him to reconsider the certainty of his claim and thereby permit the bride. Had the groom maintained his certainty, Rabban Gamliel would have forbidden her to him. Since he remained silent, Rabban Gamliel understood that he was no longer certain and he therefore permitted her (*Ritva; Rosh* §20; *Rambam, Ishus* 11:12).

23. [I.e. by entering at an angle with force, it is possible to detach the hymen from the walls of the canal without tearing it. In this manner one would not necessarily feel resistance and would have the impression of an "open entrance."] This version of the Gemara holds it unlikely that a person could cohabit at an angle without intending to do so [since it requires an application of force at just the right angle to penetrate beyond the hymen without tearing it] (*Rashi;* see *Ritva* who explains in the name of *Tosafos* that the term "angle" is not being used literally according to this version but as a metaphor for penetrating with great force).

24. This Rabban Gamliel was the great-grandson of the Rabban Gamliel mentioned in the previous incident (see 10b note 7). [*Rosh,* however,

איתמר אמר רב נחמן אמר שמואל משום רבי שמעון בן אלעזר חכמים תקנו להם לבנות ישראל לבתולה מאתים ולאלמנה מנה והם האמינוהו שאם אמר פתח פתוח מצאתי נאמן א"כ מה הועילו חכמים בתקנתם אמר רבא חזקה אין אדם טורח בסעודה ומפסידה תנא הואיל וקנס חכמים הוא לא תגבה אלא מן הזיבורית קנסא מאי קנסא אלא אימא הואיל ותקנת חכמים הוא לא תגבה אלא מן הזיבורית רבן שמעון בן גמליאל אומר כתובת אשה מן התורה ומי אמר רבן שמעון בן גמליאל הכי והתניא כסף ישקול כמוהר הבתולות שיהא זה כמוהר הבתולות ומוהר הבתולות כזה מכאן סמכו חכמים לכתובת אשה מן התורה רבן שמעון בן גמליאל אומר כתובת אשה אינה מדברי תורה אלא מדברי סופרים איפוך ומאי חזית דאפכת בתרייתא איפוך קמייתא הא שמעינא ליה לרבן שמעון בן גמליאל דאמר כתובת אשה מדאורייתא דתנן רבן שמעון בן גמליאל אומר נותן לה ממעות קפוטקיא ואי בעית אימא כולה רבן שמעון בן גמליאל היא וחסורי מיחסרא והכי קתני מכאן סמכו חכמים לכתובת אשה מן התורה כתובת אלמנה אינה מדברי תורה אלא מדברי סופרים שרבן שמעון בן גמליאל אומר כתובת אלמנה אינה מדברי תורה אלא מדברי סופרים ההוא דאתא לקמיה דרב נחמן אמר ליה פתח פתוח מצאתי אמר ליה רב נחמן אסבוהו כופרי מברכתא חביטא ליה והא רב נחמן הוא דאמר מהימן מהימן ומסבינן ליה כופרי רב אחאי משני כאן בבחור כאן בנשוי ההוא דאתא לקמיה דרבן גמליאל אמר ליה פתח פתוח מצאתי אמר ליה שמא הטיתה אמשול לך משל למה הדבר דומה לאדם שהיה מהלך באישון לילה ואפילה היטה מצאו פתוח לא היטה מצאו נעול איכא דאמרי הכי אמר ליה שמא במזיד הטיתה ועקרת לדשא ועברא אמשול לך משל למה הדבר דומה לאדם שהוא מהלך באישון לילה ואפילה היטה במזיד מצאו פתוח לא היטה במזיד מצאו נעול ההוא דאתא לקמיה דרבן גמליאל בר רבי אמר ליה רבי בעלתי ולא מצאתי דם אמרה לו רבי בתולה הייתי אמר להם הביאו לי אותו סודר הביאו לו הסודר ושראו במים וכבסו ומצא עליו כמה טיפי דמים אמר לו לך זכה במקחך אמר ליה הונא מר בריה דרבא מפרזקיא לרב אשי אנן נמי נעביד הכי אמר ליה

גיהוץ

רש"י

חכמים תקנו לאשה כו'. כלומר אי הואי כתובתה דאורייתא לא הוי נאמן להפקיעה אלא בעדות ידועה אבל כתובתה חכמים תיקנוה הם אמרו והם אמרו הם שתיקנוה אמרו שהוא נאמן להפסידה אף בטענת פתח פתוח: **א"כ.** שבידו להפקיעה: **מה הועילו חכמים בתקנתן.** שתקנו לה כתובה: **חזקה אין אדם טורח בסעודה כו'.** אין לחוש שיטעון אדם כך אלא באמת שאם היה שונא אותה מתחילה לא היה טורח בסעודה וכונסה ומפסיד סעודתו חנם אלא היה מגרשה מתחילה: **אלא מן הזיבורית.** אם באת לגבות כתובתה ויש לו עידית וזיבורית ובינונית אינה יכולה לומר תן לי עידית או בינונית או זיבורית בשוויה אלא אם בא ליתן לה זיבורית בשוויה יתן: **מאי קנסא.** כלומר מאי פשע דקא קנסינן ליה: **מן התורה.** מכסף ישקול כדלקמן: **כסף ישקול.** במפתה נאמר: **כמוהר הבתולות.** האמור במאנס את הבתולה (דברים כב) קנסו הכתוב נ' כסף בשביל מוהר בתולים: **שיהא זה כמוהר הבתולות.** הקיש הכתוב קנס המפתה לקנס האונס מה להלן נ' אף כאן נ' ומה כסף האמור כאן שקלים דכתיב ישקול אף להלן שקלים דלא תימא מעות: **מכאן סמכו.** מדקרי לה מוהר: **נותן לה ממעות קפוטקיא.** בפרק בתרא תנן נשא אשה בא"י וגירשה בקפוטקיא נותן לה ממעות א"י שהן קלות נשא אשה בקפוטקיא וגירשה בא"י נותן לה ממעות א"י מנין הכתוב בכתובה דאזלינן לקולא רשב"ג אומר נותן לה ממעות קפוטקיא שנשתעבד בהן כשאר מלוה דקסבר כתובה דאורייתא: **אסבוהו כופרי.** הלקוהו מלקיות במקלות חריות של דקל שיש בהן עוקצין כמין קוצין כדאמרינן בסוכה (דף לג.) ואימא כופרא דרכיה דרכי נועם כתיב: **מברכתא חביטא ליה.** זונות העיר הזאת ששמה מברכתא חבוטות ושוכבות תמיד לפניו לזנות מאחר שהוא בקי בפתח פתוח: **בחור** לא מהימן ומסבינן ליה כופרי על שמעיז פניו נשוי מהימן ולא מסבינן ליה כופרי: **הטה.** כשהגיע לפתח ביתו הסגור ויש בו דבר מעכבו מלפתוח וכשמטין אותו לצדדין נפתח: **איכא דאמרי.** בלא מתכוין לא שכיח הטיה ולא אמרי' שמא הטה אלא כך בדקו שמא במזיד הטית ועקרת לדשא ועברא עקרת הדלת והבריח: **הטה במזיד.** במתכוין ובכח: **וכבסו.** שהיו טיפי הדמים מכוסים בשכבת זרע:

תוספות

אמר רב נחמן אמר שמואל חכמים תיקנו כו'. משמע לכתובה דרבנן וכן בהאשה רבה (יבמות פט. ושם) גבי אין לה כתובה קאמר מאי טעמא תקינו לה רבנן כתובה שלא תהא קלה בעיניו להוציאה כו' אלמא סתמא דהש"ס סבר דכתובה דרבנן וקשה דנהגו לכתוב בכתובה כסף זוזי מאתן דחזו ליכי מדאורייתא ואור"ת דסמכינן ארשב"ג דמתני' דפרק בתרא (דף קי:) דמייתי לה נמי בסמוך דאמר נותן לה ממעות קפוטקיא דקסבר כתובה דאורייתא וקי"ל כרשב"ג במשנתנו ועוד אור"י דלא קיימא לן כר"נ דהשתא רב אשי דהוה בתראה דפליג עליה דמתרץ לקמן ברייתא (דף יא.) תני כל שלא מושמש אינו יכול לטעון טענת בתולים אלמא דחייש לשמא משקר ולא אמרינן חזקה אין אדם טורח בסעודה ומפסידה וכן פי' רבינו יצחק בן רבינו מאיר דרב אשי פליג אדרב נחמן והא דאמרינן בהאשה רבה (יבמות פט. ושם) מ"ט תקינו רבנן כתובה ה"פ מ"ט תקינו רבנן כתובה היכא דתקינו כגון באלמנה שלא תהא קלה בעיניו להוציאה ה"נ תקינו שלא יהא לה כדי שתהא קלה בעיניו להוציאה:

חזקה אין אדם טורח כו'. תימה תינח באשת כהן או בפסולה מג' דמיתסרא עליה הילכך כיון דמפסידה נאמן ולמ"ד נמי לקמן כנסה בחזקת בתולה ונמצאת בעולה אין לה כתובה כלל ניחא דהשתא נמי מפסידה שהרי מקח טעות הוא אבל למ"ד יש לה כתובה מנה לא מפסיד מידי אלא שבא להפסידה מכתובתה מנה אבל הסעודה לא מפסיד ואמאי מהימן ונראה דלא מהימן:

הואיל ותקנת חכמים היא לא תגבה כו'. תימה דר"מ אית ליה לקמן בפרק אע"פ (נו: ושם) דכתובה דאורייתא ובפ' הניזקין (גיטין מח: ושם) אמרי' דקסבר ר"מ דכתובת אשה בבינונית משום חינא וכיון דהויא דאורייתא דינה בעידית כדנפקא לן בריש ב"ק (דף ה.) וכולן כאבות לשלם ממיטב דאתיא תחת נתינה ישלם כסף ואמאי הפקיעו דינה ועוד דלא מישתמיט תנא בשום מקום דאית ליה כתובת אשה ממטלטלי אלא לר"מ כדאמרינן בכל דוכתין (יבמות לט.) הא מני ר"מ היא דאמר מטלטלי משתעבדי לכתובה ולמ"ד דאורייתא אמאי לא גבי ממטלטלי כמו ניזקין כיון דמהתם ילפינן וי"ל דטעמא שלא יפרשו מהן בני אדם אם יצטרכו למכור עידית או מטלטלים וחשו כדי שיקפצו עליהן בני אדם:

נותן לה ממעות קפוטקיא. תימה לר"י מה ריוח הוא לה שנותן לה מאותם המעות מ"מ אינו נותן לה אלא שוה נ' שקלים ואם היינו אומרים דלעולם צריך ליתן לה שקלים שעומדין שם בקפוטקיא נ' שקלי קפוטקיא ובארץ ישראל נ' שקלים של ארץ ישראל הוה ניחא כדאמרינן גבי ה' סלעים דפדיון בכור בפ' יש בכור (בכורות נ. ושם) לישדר מר תילתא אחרינא דאוסיפו עלייהו ושדר להו מיהו אין נראה דהתם כשהוסיפו בכל מקום הוסיפו אבל כשמוסיפין במקום אחד אין נראה שבכך תשתנה מדה דאורייתא ומיהו בירושלמי דפירקין גרסינן אמתניתין דכתובה מאתים רבי מונא בשם שמואל אמר בשקל הקדש רבי אבא בר בונא אמר מטבע יוצא וכן מסקי התם כמה אמוראי:

מברכתא חביטא ליה. פירוש הלקוהו שמוליא ש"ר על בת ישראל שהרי משקר וכי זונות חבוטות לפניו שיהיה בקי הלכך לא מהימן והא אמר רב נחמן מהימן ומשני מהימן ומסבינן ליה כופרי ורב נחמן דאמר אסבוהו לא משום שלא היה מאמינו אלא היה מאמינו ואמר להלקותו לפי שחשוד על הזנות ורב אחא משני כדסבירא לן מעיקרא דלא מהימן ואיירי בבחור ועי"ל בניחותא מברכתא חביטא ליה אף על פי שהוא נאמן הלקוהו לפי שחשוד על הזנות והאמר רב נחמן נאמן ולא פירש להלקותו ומשני מהימן ומסבינן ליה ורב נחמן לא איירי במלקות רב אחא אמר לעולם נאמן דאמר רב נחמן היינו בלא מלקות ובנשוי:

בתולה

תוספות רי"ד

אמר ר"נ אמר שמואל משום ר"ש ב"א חכמים תקנו להם לבנות ישראל לבתולה מאתים ולאלמנה מנה. והם הימנוהו שאם אמר פתח פתוח מצאתי נאמן א"כ מה הועילו חכמים בתקנתם. א"ר חזקה אין אדם טורח בסעודה ומפסידה. פי' המורה אין לחוש שיטעון כך אלא באמת שאם היה שונאה מתחילה לא היה טורח בסעודה לכונסה ומפסיד סעודתו חנם אלא מתחלה [היה] מגרשה והגאון פי' אימתי הבעל מהימן כששניהם טוענים ברי על הפתח הבעל אומר פתח פתוח מצאתי והיא טוענת לא כי אלא פתח נעול מצאת ותרוייהו טענו טענות ברי אז הבעל מהימן אבל אם היא מודה ליה אין פתח פתוח מצאת אבל תחתיך נאנסתי ונסתחפה שדך או מוכת עץ אני ואית לי כתובה ואיהו אמר שמא עד שלא ארסתיך והיה מקחי מקח טעות כיון דאיהי טוענת ודאי ואיהו ספק אינו נאמן כדאמר לקמן דפסק שמואל הלכתא כרבן גמליאל דאמר דאשה נאמנת ולא קשיא דשמואל אדשמואל דלא דמי תרתי טעניתא להדדי דהכא טענו ברי וברי והתם טענו ברי ושמא ואית לה מיגו וחזקה. פי' מיגו דאי בעי אמרה מוכת עץ אני תחתיך ולא פסלה נפשה מכהונה וכו' וחזקה דגופה דבתולה נולדה: **וראיתי** כתוב בה"ג דאי עביד בעל סעודה רבתי דינא הוא דשקיל אודינא מן האשה מטעם רבה ואינו נ"ל דעד כאן לא האמינוהו אלא להפסידה כתובתה שהוא מוחזק בה אבל להוציא ממון ממנה אינו נאמן בטענתו. וכתב רבינו יצחק ז"ל חזינן לגאון דקאמר ה"מ לענין מנה מאתים אבל לתוספת לא מהימן וטעמא דמסתבר הוא דלא תקינו רבנן אלא מנה מאתים אבל תוספת איהו כתב לה מנפשיה הלכך לא מהימן: **תנא** הואיל וכן דכתובתה תיקון חכמים היא לא תגבה אלא מן הזיבורית. פי' אם באת לגבות כתובתה ויש לו עידית בינונית וזיבורית אין יכולה לומר תן לי עידית או בינונית ובשוויה אלא זיבורית נותן לה ובשוויה: **רשב"ג** אומר כתובת אשה מן התורה. ומי ארשב"ג הכי והא תניא כסף ישקול כמוהר הבתולות מכאן סמכו חכמים לכתובת אשה מן התורה. רשב"ג אומר כתובת אשה אינה מה"ת אלא מדברי סופרים. איפוך ומאי חזית דאפכית בתרייתא איפוך קמייתא. דהא שמעינן ליה לרשב"ג דאמר כתובת אשה דאורייתא פי' דתנן בפ' בתרא דמכילתין נשא אשה בא"י וכו' רשב"ג אומר נותן לה ממעות קפוטקיא פי' נשתעבד בהן כשאר מלוה דקסבר כתובה דאורייתא. עי' בסו"פ: **ההוא דאתא** לקמיה דרב נחמן אמר פתח פתוח מצאתי אמר להו ר"נ אסבוהו כופרא. פי' הלקוהו בחריות של דקל שיש בהן עוקצין כמין קוצין: **מברכתא** חביטא ליה. פי' זונות מופקרות היו חבוטות לו שמכיר בפתח פתוח. והאר"נ האומר וכו' נאמן. נאמן ומספינן ליה כופרא. רב אחא משני כאן בבחור כאן בנשוי בחור לא מהימן ומספינן ליה כופרי נשוי מהימן ולא מספינן ליה כופרי: **ההוא דאתא** לקמיה דר"ג א"ל פ"פ מצאתי. א"ל שמא הטית אמשול לך משל למה הדבר דומה לאדם שמהלך באישון לילה ואפילה הטה מצאו פתוח לא הטה מצאו נעול. פי' בהגיעו לפתח ביתו הסגור ויש בו המעכבו מלפתוח. וכשמטין אותו לצדדין נפתח. ואי קשיא היכא שריא ליה. והא אמרן לעיל האומר פ"פ מצאתי מהימן לאוסרה עליו. תשובה אי הוה מהדר ליה ברי לי שלא הטיתי הוה אסורה עליו. אבל כיון דשתיק הרגיש ר"ג מתוך דבריו כמספקא ליה ואין טענתו טענה ברורה ולפיכך שריא עליה:

עין משפט נר מצוה

נב א מיי' פי"א מהל' אישות הל' ח סמג עשין מח טוש"ע אה"ע סי' סח סעי' ח וסעי' ח:
נג ב מיי' פט"ו שם הל' ג סמג שם טוש"ע שם סי' ק סעי' ב:
נד ג מיי' פי"ט שם הל' ז טוש"ע שם סימן סו סעיף ו:
נה ד טוש"ע שם סי' סח סעי' ו בהגהה:
נו ה ו מיי' פי"א שם הל' יב טוש"ע שם:

מסורת הש"ס

א) קדושין מה: [יבמות קי.], ב) [לקמן ט:], ג) לקמן לח: [כט:], ד) [ועי' תוס' סוטה כו. ד"ה אשה], ה) לקמן קי:, ו) נ"י כ"ה, ז) [ועי' תוס' סוטה כו. ד"ה אשה]

גליון הש"ס

גמ' חכמים תקנו להם. עיין סנהדרין ח ע"א תד"ה מולא שם רע:

תורה אור השלם

א) אם מאן ימאן אביה לתתה לו כסף ישקל כמהר הבתולת: [שמות כב, טז]

ליקוטי רש"י

בסעודה. סעודת נישואין [יבמות קז.]. **כמוהר הבתולות.** חמשים כסף המפורשים במאנס את הבתולה. **שיהא זה.** חמשים כמוהר הבתולות. **ומוהר הבתולות.** יהיו שקלים כזה [לקמן כט.]. **כזה.** שכתוב בו ישקול [לקמן לח:]. **ממעות קפוטקיא.** גדולות ושוקלות יותר משל א"י [לקמן קי:].

[MADE] TO THE VIRGINS stated in the case of the violator should be LIKE THIS [the fine paid by the seducer] — i.e. silver *shekalim.*[8] מִכָּאן סָמְכוּ חֲכָמִים לִכְתוּבַּת אִשָּׁה מִן הַתּוֹרָה — FROM HERE THE SAGES FOUND SUPPORT FOR saying that THE *KESUBAH* OF A WOMAN IS OF TORAH (i.e. Biblical) ORIGIN.[9] רַבָּן שִׁמְעוֹן בֶּן גַּמְלִיאֵל אוֹמֵר — RABBAN SHIMON BEN GAMLIEL disagrees and SAYS: כְּתוּבַּת אִשָּׁה אֵינָהּ מִדִּבְרֵי תוֹרָה אֶלָּא מִדִּבְרֵי סוֹפְרִים — THE *KESUBAH* OF A WOMAN HAS ITS SOURCE NOT IN THE WORDS OF TORAH, BUT IN THE WORDS OF THE SCRIBES [i.e. Sages]. This Baraisa contradicts the previous Baraisa, which quoted Rabban Shimon ben Gamliel as saying that the law of *kesubah* is of Biblical origin. — ? —

The Gemara answers:

אֵיפוּךְ — **Reverse** the opinions in this latter Baraisa, so that it reads that Rabban Shimon ben Gamliel holds the first view [that the *kesubah* is a Biblical obligation], while the anonymous opinion puts forward the latter view [that the *kesubah* obligation is of Rabbinic origin]. Accordingly, Rabban Shimon ben Gamliel's opinion in this second Baraisa conforms to his opinion in the first Baraisa.

The Gemara asks:

וּמַאי חָזֵית דְּאַפַּכְתְּ בַּתְרַיְיתָא — **Now what did you see that** made **you** decide to **reverse** the opinions of **the latter** Baraisa? אֵיפוּךְ קַמַּיְיתָא — **Reverse** instead the opinions in **the first** Baraisa and make Rabban Shimon ben Gamliel the one who holds that the *kesubah* is a Rabbinic enactment.

The Gemara answers:

הָא שְׁמַעִינָא לֵיהּ לְרַבָּן שִׁמְעוֹן בֶּן גַּמְלִיאֵל דְּאָמַר — **Because we have learned** elsewhere **about Rabban Shimon ben Gamliel** כְּתוּבַּת אִשָּׁה מִדְּאוֹרַיְיתָא — **that he holds that the *kesubah* of a woman is of Torah** (i.e. Biblical) **origin.** דִּתְנַן — **For we have learned in a Mishnah:**[10] רַבָּן שִׁמְעוֹן בֶּן גַּמְלִיאֵל אוֹמֵר — RABBAN SHIMON BEN GAMLIEL SAYS: One who married a woman in Cappadocia and then divorced her in Eretz Yisrael, נוֹתֵן לָהּ מִמְּעוֹת קַפּוֹטְקִיָא — MUST GIVE HER THE COINS OF CAPPADOCIA in payment of her *kesubah,* because the *kesubah* obligation is Biblical.[11] Since we see from this Mishnah that Rabban Shimon ben Gamliel holds that the *kesubah* obligation is Biblical, we reverse the opinions of the second Baraisa to make the view of Rabban Shimon ben Gamliel there conform to his view in this Mishnah.

The Gemara offers an alternative to reversing the opinions in the second Baraisa:

וְאִי בָּעֵית אֵימָא — **Or, if you wish, say** that כּוּלָּהּ רַבָּן שִׁמְעוֹן בֶּן גַּמְלִיאֵל הִיא — **the entire** second **[Baraisa] is** following the view of **Rabban Shimon ben Gamliel,** וְחַסּוּרֵי מִיחַסְּרָא וְהָכִי קָתָנֵי — **and it is** as if the Baraisa were **missing words, and this is what it teaches:** מִכָּאן סָמְכוּ חֲכָמִים לִכְתוּבַּת אִשָּׁה מִן הַתּוֹרָה — **From here the Sages found support for** saying that **the *kesubah* of a woman is of Torah origin.** כְּתוּבַּת אַלְמָנָה אֵינָהּ מִדִּבְרֵי תוֹרָה אֶלָּא מִדִּבְרֵי סוֹפְרִים — However, **the *kesubah* of a widow** who remarries **has its source not in the words of the Torah but in the words of the Scribes** [i.e. Sages], שֶׁרַבָּן שִׁמְעוֹן בֶּן גַּמְלִיאֵל אוֹמֵר — **for Rabban Shimon ben Gamliel says:** כְּתוּבַּת אַלְמָנָה אֵינָהּ מִדִּבְרֵי תוֹרָה אֶלָּא מִדִּבְרֵי סוֹפְרִים — **The *kesubah* of a widow has its source not in the words of the Torah but in the words of the Scribes.**[12]

The Gemara returns to its discussion of the claim of an "open entrance" and cites two incidents involving such a claim:

הַהוּא דַּאֲתָא לְקַמֵּיהּ דְּרַב נַחְמָן — **There was a [groom] who came before Rav Nachman.** אָמַר לֵיהּ פֶּתַח פָּתוּחַ מָצָאתִי — **He said to [Rav Nachman]: I found an "open entrance."** אָמַר (לֵיהּ) [לְהוּ][13] רַב נַחְמָן — **Rav Nachman said to them:** אַסְבּוּהוּ כּוּפְרֵי — **Give him** lashes with **palm branches!**[14] מְבָרַכְתָּא חֲבִיטָא לֵיהּ — The prostitutes of **Mevarachta must be lying before him** for him to be expert enough to know this![15]

NOTES

8. The verse referring to the violator states that he pays חֲמִשִּׁים כֶּסֶף, *fifty silver [coins],* but does not specify the denomination of these coins. In theory it could refer to *ma'ah* coins [which are also silver but worth only a sixth of a *shekel*]. However, since the seducer is obligated to pay *shekalim,* as taught by the word יִשְׁקֹל, *he shall pay shekalim,* we derive that the violator too must pay fifty *shekel* coins (*Rashi*).

[*Rashi* here seems to explain this derivation as a *hekeish* (analogy). The Gemara on 29b, however, states that it is based on a *gezeirah shavah* expounded there; see note 18 there.]

9. From the fact that the Torah refers to the fifty-*shekel* penalty as מֹהַר, *mohar* (a settlement) [a term associated with the gifts and financial arrangements made to a woman at the time of her marriage — see *Genesis* 34:12: הַרְבּוּ עָלַי מְאֹד מֹהַר וּמַתָּן, *Inflate upon me exceedingly the "mohar"* (marriage settlement) *and gifts*], the Sages concluded that every virgin who marries is entitled to a settlement (*Rashi;* cf. *Rosh* §19 and *Tos. Yeshanim* below, 38b).

The expression סָמְכוּ חֲכָמִים, *the Sages found support,* indicates that this is not a true Scriptural source. *Rashba* explains that this is because the verse merely demonstrates that there is a certain amount that is settled upon the woman, but the exact figure — 200 *zuz* — as well as certain other aspects of the obligation, are by Rabbinic decree (seen also *Mitzpeh Eisan;* cf. *Tosafos* to *Sotah* 27a ד״ה איש).

10. Below, 110b.

11. The coins of Cappadocia [an ancient province in present-day Turkey] were larger and heavier [and thus worth more] than those of Eretz Yisrael (*Rashi* 110b). The Tanna Kamma of that Mishnah holds that if he divorces her in Eretz Yisrael, he may pay her the number of coins stipulated in the *kesubah* with the lighter [and thus less valuable] coins of Eretz Yisrael. [This is because of a leniency in the laws of *kesubah,* predicated on the fact that the *kesubah* obligation is only Rabbinic, as the Gemara explains there.] Rabban Shimon ben Gamliel, however, maintains that the husband must pay her with the more valuable coins of Cappadocia. This is based on the proposition that the *kesubah* obligation is Biblical. Accordingly, the *kesubah* obligation is treated no differently than any other debt, in which the debtor is obligated to pay in the currency in which the debt was incurred (*Rashi,* from the Gemara 110b).

12. Although Rabban Shimon ben Gamliel holds that the *kesubah* of a virgin is by Biblical law, the *kesubah* of a widow is certainly only by Rabbinic law. By emending Rabban Shimon ben Gamliel's statement to refer to the widow's *kesubah* rather than the ordinary [i.e. virgin's] *kesubah,* the contradiction is resolved.

There is a dispute among the Rishonim as to whose view we follow in the dispute about a virgin's *kesubah. Tosafos* (ד״ה אמר) note that the standard text of Ashkenazic *kesubos* reads: כֶּסֶף זוּזֵי מָאתָן דַּחֲזוּ לִיכִי מִדְּאוֹרַיְיתָא, *two hundred silver zuz that are appropriate to you under Biblical law.* This indicates that Rabban Shimon ben Gamliel's view is accepted as the halachah (*Rabbeinu Tam;* see also *Smag, Aseh* §48). However, *Rosh* (§19) cites the view of *Rabbeinu Chananel* and all the Geonim as ruling that the *kesubah* obligation is of Rabbinic origin. This is the view of most Rishonim (see *Rif* here and 110b; *Rambam, Ishus* 10:7, 12:2; *Ramban; Rashba; Ritva*). The language of the Ashkenazic *kesubos* can be explained even according to this view — see *Rashba* and *Rosh.*

13. Emendation follows *Rif* and *Rosh.* [Rav Nachman addressed the officers of the court.]

14. These are branches of the palm tree that have not fully hardened (*Rashi, Succah* 32a ד״ה ואימא כופרא). They have thornlike stubs protruding from them [making their lashes even more painful] (*Rashi*).

15. If the groom is so sure that he encountered "an open entrance," he must have had previous experience of cohabitation with many women — namely, the prostitutes of his town of Mevarachta — to be able to judge (*Rashi,* as explained by *Ritva* and *Maharshal;* cf. *Maharam Schif*). He therefore deserves to be flogged for his earlier promiscuous activities (*Tosafos*).

[Others explain Rav Nachman's comment in a sarcastic fashion. Rav

איתמר אמר רב נחמן אמר שמואל משום רבי שמעון בן אלעזר [א] חכמים תקנו להם לבנות ישראל לבתולה מאתים ולאלמנה מנה והם האמינוהו שאם אמר פתח פתוח מצאתי נאמן א"כ מה הועילו חכמים בתקנתם אמר רבא [א] חזקה אין אדם טורח בסעודה ומפסידה תנא הואיל וקנס חכמים הוא לא תגבה אלא מן הזיבורית קנסא מאי קנסא אלא אימא [ב] הואיל ותקנת חכמים הוא לא תגבה אלא מן הזיבורית רבן שמעון בן גמליאל אומר [ג] כתובת אשה מן התורה ומי אמר רבן שמעון בן גמליאל הכי [ג] והתניא [א] כסף ישקול כמוהר הבתולות שיהא זה כמוהר הבתולות ומוהר הבתולות כזה [ג] מכאן [ד] סמכו חכמים לכתובת אשה מן התורה רבן שמעון בן גמליאל אומר כתובת אשה אינה מדברי תורה אלא מדברי סופרים איפוך ומאי חזית דאפכת בתרייתא איפוך קמייתא הא שמעינא ליה לרבן שמעון בן גמליאל דאמר כתובת אשה מדאורייתא דתנן [ה] רבן שמעון בן גמליאל אומר נותן לה ממעות קפוטקיא ואי בעית אימא כולה רבן שמעון בן גמליאל היא וחסורי מיחסרא והכי קתני מכאן סמכו חכמים לכתובת אשה מן התורה כתובת אלמנה אינה מדברי תורה אלא מדברי סופרים שרבן שמעון בן גמליאל אומר כתובת אלמנה אינה מדברי תורה אלא מדברי סופרים ההוא דאתא לקמיה דרב נחמן אמר ליה פתח פתוח מצאתי אמר ליה רב נחמן אסבוהו כופרי מברכתא חביטא ליה והא רב נחמן הוא דאמר מהימן מהימן ומסבינן ליה כופרי רב אחאי משני [ד] כאן בבחור כאן בנשוי ההוא דאתא לקמיה דרבן גמליאל אמר ליה פתח פתוח מצאתי אמר ליה [ה] שמא הטיתה אמשול לך משל למה הדבר דומה לאדם שהיה מהלך באישון לילה ואפילה היטה מצאו פתוח לא היטה מצאו נעול איכא דאמרי הכי אמר ליה [ו] שמא במזיד הטיתה ועקרת לדשא ועברא אמשול לך משל למה הדבר דומה לאדם שהוא מהלך באישון לילה ואפילה היטה במזיד מצאו פתוח לא היטה במזיד מצאו נעול ההוא דאתא לקמיה דרבן גמליאל בר רבי אמר ליה רבי בעלתי ולא מצאתי דם אמרה לו רבי בתולה הייתי אמר להם הביאו לי אותו סודר הביאו לו הסודר ושראו במים וכבסו ומצא עליו כמה טיפי דמים אמר לו לך זכה במקחך אמר ליה הונא מר בריה דרבא מפרזקיא לרב אשי אנן נמי נעביד הכי אמר ליה גיהוץ

רש"י

חכמים תקנו לאשה כו'. כלומר אי הואי כתובתה דאורייתא לא הוי נאמן להפקיעה אלא בעדות ידועה אבל כתובתה חכמים תיקנוה הם אמרו והם אמרו הם שתיקנוה אמרו שהוא נאמן להפסידה אף בטענת פתח פתוח: א"כ. שכיון להפקיעה: מה הועילו חכמים בתקנתן. שתקנו לה כתובה: חזקה אין אדם טורח בסעודה כו'. אין לחוש שיטעון אדם שקר אלא באמת שאם היה שונא אותה מתחילה לא היה טורח בסעודה וכונס ומפסיד סעודתו חנם אלא היה מגרשה מתחילה: אלא מן הזיבורית. אם באת לגבות כתובתה ויש לו עידית וזיבורית ובינונית אינה יכולה לומר תן לי עידית או בינונית בשוויה אלא אם בא ליתן לה זיבורית בשוויה יתן: [[י] מאי קנסא. כלומר מאי פשע דקא קנסינן ליה]: מן התורה. מכסף ישקול דלקמן: כסף ישקול. במפתה נאמר: כמוהר הבתולות. האמור במאנס את הבתולה (דברים כב) קנסו הכתוב נ' כסף בשביל מוהר בתולים: שיהא זה כמוהר הבתולות. הקיש הכתוב קנס המפתה לקנס האונס מה להלן נ' אף כאן נ' ומה כסף האמור כאן שקלים דכתיב ישקול אף להלן שקלים דלא תימא מעות: מכאן סמכו. מדקרי לה מוהר: נותן לה ממעות קפוטקיא. בפרק בתרא תנן נשא אשה בא"י וגירשה בקפוטקיא נותן לה ממעות א"י שהן קלות נשא אשה בקפוטקיא וגירשה בא"י נותן לה ממעות א"י מנין הכתוב בכתובה דאזלינן לקולא רשבג"א נותן לה ממעות קפוטקיא שנשתעבד בהן כשאר מלוה דקסבר כתובה דאורייתא: אסבוהו כופרי. הלקוהו מלקיות במקלות חריות של דקל שיש בהן עוקלין כמין קולין כדאמרינן בסוכה (דף לג.) ואימא כופרא דרכיה דרכי נועם כתיב: מברכתא חביטא ליה. זונות העיר הזאת ששמה מברכתא חבוטות ושוכבות תמיד לפניו לזנות מאחר שהוא בקי בפתח פתוח: בחור לא מהימן ומסבינן ליה כופרי על שמעיז פניו נשוי מהימן ולא מסבינן ליה כופרי: הטה. כשהגיע לפתח ביתו הסגור ויש בו דבר מעכבו מלפתוח וכשמטין אותו לצדדין נפתח: איכא דאמרי. בלא מתכוין לא שכיח הטיה ולא אמרי' שמא הטה אלא כך בדקו שמא במזיד הטית ועקרת לדשא ועברא עקרת הדלת והבריח: הטה במזיד. במתכוין וכח: וכבסו. שהיו טיפי הדמים מכוסים בשכבת זרע:

גיהוץ

תוספות

אמר רב נחמן אמר שמואל חכמים תיקנו כו'. משמע דכתובה דרבנן וכן בהאשה רבה (יבמות פט. ושם) גבי אין לה כתובה קאמר מאי טעמא תקינו לה רבנן כתובה שלא תהא קלה בעיניו להוציאה כו' אלמא סתמא דהש"ס סבר דכתובה דרבנן וקשה דנהגו לכתוב בכתובה כסף זוזי מאתן דחזו ליכי מדאורייתא ואור"ת דסמכינן ארשב"ג דמתני' דפרק בתרא (דף קי:) דמייתי לה נמי בסמוך דאמר נותן לה ממעות קפוטקיא דקסבר כתובה דאורייתא [ז] וקי"ל כרשב"ג במשנתנו ועוד אור"י דלא קיימא לן כר"נ דאשכחנא רב אשי דהוא בתראה דפליג עליה כדמתרץ לקמן ברייתא (דף יב.) תני כל שלא מושמש אינו יכול לטעון טענת בתולים אלמא דחייש לשמא משקר ולא אמרינן חזקה אין אדם טורח בסעודה ומפסידה וכן פי' רבינו יצחק בן רבינו מאיר דרב אשי פליג אדרב נחמן והא דאמרינן בהאשה רבה (יבמות פט. ושם) מ"ט תקינו רבנן כתובה ה"פ מ"ט תקינו רבנן כתובה היכא דתקינו כגון באלמנה שלא תהא קלה בעיניו להוציאה ה"נ תקינו שלא יהא לה כדי שתהא קלה בעיניו להוציאה:

חזקה אין אדם טורח כו'. תימה תינח באשת כהן או בפחותה מג' דמיתסרא עליה הילכך כיון דמפסידה נאמן ולמ"ד נמי לקמן כנסה בחזקת בתולה ונמצאת בעולה אין לה כתובה כלל ניחא דהשתא נמי מפסידה שהרי מקח טעות הוא אבל למ"ד יש לה כתובה מנה לא מפסיד מידי אלא שבא להפסידה מכתובתה מנה אבל הסעודה לא מפסיד ואמאי מהימן ונראה דלא מהימן:

הואיל ותקנת חכמים היא לא תגבה כו'. תימה דר"מ אית ליה לקמן בפרק אע"פ (נו: ושם) דכתובה דאורייתא ובפ' הניזקין (גיטין מח: ושם) אמרי' דקסבר ר"מ דכתובת אשה בבינונית משום חינא וכיון דהויא דאורייתא דינה בעידית כדנפקא לן בריש ב"ק (דף ה.) וכולן כאבות לשלם ממיטב דאתיא תחת נתינה ישלם כסף ואמאי הפקיעו דינה ועוד דלא מישתמיט תנא בשום מקום דאית ליה כתובת אשה ממטלטלי אלא לר"מ כדאמרינן בכל דוכתין (יבמות לט.) הא מני ר"מ היא דאמר מטלטלי משתעבדי לכתובה ולמ"ד דאורייתא אמאי לא גבי ממטלטלי כמו ניזקין כיון דמהתם ילפינן וי"ל דטעמא שלא יפרשו מהן בני אדם אם יצטרכו למכור עידית או מטלטלים ותשו כדי שיקפצו עליהן בני אדם:

נותן לה ממעות קפוטקיא. תימה לר"י מה ריוח הוא לה שנותן לה מאותם המעות מ"מ אינו נותן לה אלא שוה נ' שקלים ואם היינו אומרים לעולם צריך ליתן לה שקלים שעומדין שם בקפוטקיא נ' שקלי קפוטקיא ובארץ ישראל נ' שקלים של ארץ ישראל הוה ניחא כדאמרינן גבי ה' סלעים דפדיון בכור בפ' יש בכור (בכורות נ. ושם) לישדר מר תילתא אחרינא דאוסיפו עלייהו ושדר להו מיהו אין נראה דהתם כשהוסיפו בכל מקום הוסיפו אבל כשמוסיפין במקום אחד אין נראה שבכך תשתנה מדה דאורייתא ומיהו בירושלמי דפירקין גרסינן אמתניתין דכתובה מאתים רבי מונא בשם שמואל אמר בשקל הקדש רבי אבא בר בונא אמר מטבע יוצא וכן מסקי התם כמה אמוראי:

מברכתא חביטא ליה. פירוש הלקוהו שמוציא ש"ר על בת ישראל שהרי משקר וכי זונות חבוטות לפניו שיהא בקי הלכך לא מהימן והא אמר רב נחמן מהימן ומשני מהימן ומסבינן ליה כופרי ורב נחמן דאמר אסבוהו לא משום שלא היה מאמינו אלא היה מאמינו ואמר להלקותו לפי שחשוד על הזנות ורב אחא משני כדסבירא לן מעיקרא דלא מהימן ואיירי בבחור ועי"ל בניחותא מברכתא חביטא ליה אף על פי שהוא נאמן הלקוהו לפי שחשוד על הזנות והאמר רב נחמן נאמן ולא פירש להלקותו ומשני מהימן ומסבינן ליה ורב נחמן לא איירי במלקות רב אחא אמר לעולם נאמן דאמר רב נחמן היינו בלא מלקות וקנסו:

בתולה

מסורת הש"ס

א) קדושין מה: [יבמות קז.], ב) [לקמן ט:], ג) לקמן לח: [כט:], ד) [ועי' תוס' סוטה מ. ד"ה איש], ה) לקמן קי., ו) נ"י כ"י, ז) [ועי' תוס' סוטה מ. ד"ה איש].

גליון הש"ס

גמ' חכמים תקנו להם. עיין סנהדרין מ ע"א תד"ה מוליא שם רע:

תורה אור השלם

א) אִם מָאֵן יְמָאֵן אָבִיהָ לְתִתָּהּ לוֹ כֶּסֶף יִשְׁקֹל כְּמֹהַר הַבְּתוּלֹת: [שמות כב, טז]

ליקוטי רש"י

בסעודה. סעודת נישואין [יבמות קז.]. כמוהר הבתולות. חמשים כסף המפורשים במאנס את הבתולה. שיהא זה. חמשים כמוהר הבתולות. ומוהר הבתולות. יהיו שקלים כזה [לקמן כט:]. כזה. שכתוב בו ישקול [לקמן לח:]. ממעות קפוטקיא. גדולות ושוקלות יותר משל א"י [לקמן קי:].

עין משפט נר מצוה

נב א מיי' פי"א מהל' אישות הל' א סמג עשין מח טוש"ע אה"ע סי' סח סעי' א וסעי' ח:

נג ב מיי' פט"ז שם הל' ג סמג שם טוש"ע שם סי' ק סעי' ג:

נד ג מיי' פ"י שם הל' ז טוש"ע שם סימן סו סעיף ו:

נה ד טוש"ע שם סי' סח סעי' ו בהגהה:

נו ה ו מיי' פי"א שם הל' יב טוש"ע שם:

תוספות רי"ד

אמר ר"נ אמר שמואל משום ר"ש ב"א חכמים תקנו להם לבנות ישראל לבתולה מאתים ולאלמנה מנה. והם הימנוהו שאם אמר פתח פתוח מצאתי נאמן א"כ מה הועילו חכמים בתקנתם. א"ר חזקה אין אדם טורח בסעודה ומפסידה. פי' המורה אין לחוש שיטעון כך אלא באמת שאם היה שונאה מתחילה לא היה טורח בסעודה לכונסה ומפסיד סעודתו חנם אלא מתחלה [היה] יגרשה והגאון פי' אימתי הבעל מהימן כשטניהם טוענים ברי על הפתח הבעל אומר פתח פתוח מצאתי והיא טוענת לא כי אלא פתח נעול מצאת ותרווייהו טענו טענות ברי אז הבעל מהימן אבל אם היא מודה ליה אין פתח פתוח מצאת אבל תחתיך נאנסתי ונסתחפה שדך או מוכת עץ אני ואית לי כתובה ואיהו אמר שמא עד שלא ארסתיך והיה מקחי מקח טעות כיון דאיהי טוענת ודאי ואיהו ספק אינו נאמן כדאמר לקמן דפסק שמואל הלכתא כרבן גמליאל דאמר דאשה נאמנת ולא קשיא דשמואל אדשמואל דלא דמי תרתי טעניתא להדדי דהכא טענו ברי וברי והתם טענו ברי ושמא ואית לה מיגו וחזקה. פי' מיגו דאי בעי אמרה מוכת עץ אני תחתיך ולא פסלה נפשה מכהונה וכו' וחזקה דגופה דבתולה נולדה: וראיתי כתוב בה"ג דאי עביד בעל סעודה רבתי דינא הוא דשקיל אורדינא מן האשה מטעם רבה ואינו נ"ל דעד כאן לא האמינוהו אלא להפסידה כתובתה שהוא מוחזק בה אבל להוציא ממון ממנה אינו נאמן בטענתו. וכתב רבינו יצחק ז"ל חזינן לגאון דקאמר ה"מ לענין מנה מאתים אבל לתוספת לא מהימן וטעמא דמסתבר הוא דלא תקינו רבנן אלא מנה מאתים אבל תוספת איהו כתב לה מנפשיה הלכך לא מהימן: תנא הואיל וכן דכתובתה תיקון חכמים היא לא תגבה אלא מן הזיבורית. פי' אם באת לגבות כתובתה ויש לו עידית בינונית וזיבורית אין יכולה לומר תן לי עידית או בינונית ובשוויה אלא זיבורית נותן לה ובשויה: רשב"ג אומר כתובת אשה מן התורה. ומי ארשב"ג הכי והא תניא כסף ישקול כמוהר הבתולות מכאן סמכו חכמים לכתובת אשה מן התורה. רשב"ג אומר כתובת אשה אינה מה"ת אלא מדברי סופרים. איפוך ומאי חזית דאפכת בתרייתא איפוך קמייתא. דהא שמעינן ליה לרשב"ג דאמר כתובת אשה דאורייתא פי' דתנן בפ' בתרא דמכילתין נשא אשה בא"י וכו' רשב"ג אומר נותן לה ממעות קפוטקיא פי' נשתעבד בהן כשאר מלוה דקסבר כתובה דאורייתא. עי' בסו"פ: ההוא דאתא לקמיה דרב נחמן אמר פתח פתוח מצאתי אמר להו ר"נ אסבוהו כופרא. פי' הלקוהו בחריות של דקל שיש בהן עוקצין כמין קוצין: מברכתא חביטא ליה. פי' זונות מופקרות היו חבוטות לו שמכיר בפתח פתוח. והאר"נ האומר וכו' נאמן. נאמן ומספינן ליה כופרא. רב אחא משני כאן בבחור כאן בנשוי בחור לא מהימן ומספינן ליה כופרי נשוי מהימן ולא מספינן ליה כופרי: ההוא דאתא לקמיה דר"ג א"ל פ"פ מצאתי. א"ל שמא הטית אמשול לך משל למה הדבר דומה לאדם שמהלך באישון לילה ואפילה הטה מצאו פתוח לא הטה מצאו נעול. פי' בהגיעו לפתח ביתו הסגור ויש בו המעכבו מלפתוח. וכשמטין אותו לצדדין נפתח. ואי קשיא היכא שריא ליה. והא אמרן לעיל האומר פ"פ מצאתי מהימן לאוסרה עליו. תשובה אי הוה מהדר ליה ברי לי שלא הטיתי הוה אסורה עליו. אבל כיון דשתיק הרגיש ר"ג מתוך דבריו כמספקא ליה ואין טענתו טענה ברורה ולפיכך שריא עליה:

The Gemara explains the legal basis for depriving a woman of her *kesubah* on account of a claim of "an open entrance":

אִיתְּמַר – **It was taught:** אָמַר רַב נַחְמָן אָמַר שְׁמוּאֵל מִשּׁוּם רַבִּי שִׁמְעוֹן בֶּן אֶלְעָזָר – **Rav Nachman said in the name of Shmuel** who said it **in the name of R' Shimon ben Elazar:** חֲכָמִים תִּקְנוּ לָהֶם לִבְנוֹת יִשְׂרָאֵל – **The Sages instituted for the daughters of Israel** לִבְתוּלָה מָאתַיִם וּלְאַלְמָנָה מָנֶה – a *kesubah* of **two hundred** *zuz* **for a virgin and one hundred** *zuz* **for a widow.**[1] וְהֵם הֶאֱמִינוּהוּ – **And they believed [the husband],** שֶׁאִם אָמַר פֶּתַח פָּתוּחַ מָצָאתִי נֶאֱמָן – **that if he says, "I found an open entrance," he is believed.**[2]

The Gemara asks:

אִם כֵּן – **If so,** מָה הוֹעִילוּ חֲכָמִים בְּתַקָּנָתָם – **what did the Sages accomplish with their institution** of the *kesubah*? A man who wishes to be rid of his wife will simply say that he found her not to be a virgin and thereby free himself of having to pay the *kesubah*! – ? –

The Gemara answers:

אָמַר רָבָא – **Rava said:** We are not concerned about this possibility, חֲזָקָה אֵין אָדָם טוֹרֵחַ בִּסְעוּדָה וּמַפְסִידָהּ – because there is **a legal presumption that a person would not go through the trouble of** preparing **a** wedding **feast and** then **waste it.**[3]

The Gemara elaborates on a ramification of the previous teaching that the *kesubah* obligation is of Rabbinic origin:

תָּנָא – **A Baraisa taught:** הוֹאִיל וּקְנַס חֲכָמִים הוּא – SINCE [THE *KESUBAH*] IS A FINE OF THE SAGES, לֹא תִּגְבֶּה אֶלָּא מִן הַזִּיבּוּרִית – SHE COLLECTS it ONLY FROM THE INFERIOR lands of her former husband.[4]

The Gemara interrupts to ask:

מַאי קְנָסָא – You refer to the *kesubah* payment as **a fine?** קְנָסָא – **What** is this **fine** for? What did he do wrong to deserve a fine?

The Gemara therefore emends the Baraisa:

אֶלָּא אֵימָא – **Rather, state** it as follows: הוֹאִיל וְתַקָּנַת חֲכָמִים הוּא – **Since [the *kesubah*] is an institution of the Sages,** לֹא תִּגְבֶּה אֶלָּא מִן הַזִּיבּוּרִית – **she collects it only from the inferior** lands.

The Gemara now resumes its citation of the Baraisa:

רַבָּן שִׁמְעוֹן בֶּן גַּמְלִיאֵל אוֹמֵר – RABBAN SHIMON BEN GAMLIEL disagrees and SAYS: כְּתוּבַּת אִשָּׁה מִן הַתּוֹרָה – THE *KESUBAH* OF A WOMAN IS OF TORAH ORIGIN.[5]

The Gemara asks:

וּמִי אָמַר רַבָּן שִׁמְעוֹן בֶּן גַּמְלִיאֵל הָכִי – **But did Rabban Shimon ben Gamliel** really **say this** – that the *kesubah* is a Biblical obligation? וְהָתַנְיָא – **But it was taught in** another **Baraisa:** "כֶּסֶף יִשְׁקֹל כְּמֹהַר הַבְּתוּלֹת" – When the verse states regarding one who seduces a *naarah: HE SHALL PAY SILVER SHEKALIM IN THE AMOUNT OF THE SETTLEMENT [MADE] TO THE VIRGINS,*[6] שֶׁיְּהֵא זֶה כְּמוֹהַר הַבְּתוּלוֹת – it teaches THAT THIS [the fine paid by the seducer] SHOULD BE LIKE THE SETTLEMENT [MADE] TO THE VIRGINS stated in the case of one who violates a *naarah* – i.e. fifty silver coins,[7] וּמוֹהַר הַבְּתוּלוֹת כָּזֶה – AND that THE SETTLEMENT

NOTES

1. That is, the *kesubah* obligation of two hundred *zuz* for a virgin and one hundred *zuz* for a widow is only a Rabbinic institution. It was instituted to protect a woman against arbitrary divorce by making it expensive for her husband to divorce her (Gemara below, 11a).

2. Since the *kesubah* is a Rabbinic institution, the Sages included in their enactment of it a provision that the courts should accept a groom's claim of an "open entrance" to nullify the *kesubah*. Had the *kesubah* been a Biblical obligation, it would have required the testimony of two witnesses that she committed adultery to deprive the wife of her *kesubah* (*Rashi; Rashba;* cf. *Shitah Mekubetzes*).

[See *Beis Shmuel* 68:18 for a discussion of whether this reason is needed for believing the claim of an absence of blood. See also *Succas David.*]

3. The only reason for a husband to lie about such a thing immediately after the wedding is because he had already come to dislike her before the *nisuin* and he is using this claim to be rid of her without having to pay the *kesubah*. But if that were the case, he would not have gone to the trouble of making a wedding feast with this plan in mind; he would simply have divorced her before the *nisuin* (*Rashi;* see *Rambam, Ishus* 11:14).

This logic works only if he protested immediately after the first cohabitation. But if he waited some time before lodging this complaint, we cannot accept it because we have to consider the possibility that he came to dislike her after the *nisuin* and now makes this claim to leave the marriage without paying the *kesubah* (*Ramban, Re'ah, Rashba* et al.; see *Yerushalmi* cited by *Rashba* concerning the length of time in which such a claim may be accepted).

[By the same token, the claim is valid only where he loses his wife as a result of it, for example in the case of a Kohen's wife or a girl betrothed before the age of three, where she becomes forbidden to him (see 9a), or even in the case of an ordinary woman according to the view that the marriage is annulled as a mistaken transaction [מִקַּח טָעוּת] if the bride is found not be a virgin (see Gemara below, 11b). However, according to the view that the marriage is not annulled and she remains his wife (albeit with a *kesubah* of only 100 *zuz*), his claim would not be believed, since he does not "waste" the marriage feast by making it (*Tosafos*). Others maintain that it is believed even in this case because a man who makes such a claim in court clearly has no intention of keeping his wife (*Ramban; Ritva*).]

Rava does not offer a new reason for believing the husband's claim. He too agrees that he is believed only because *kesubah* is a Rabbinic enactment. Rava's point is only that the Sages decided that the logic of this *chazakah* was sufficiently strong that they did not have to be concerned that allowing such a claim would undermine the *kesubah* enactment (*Rashi,* as explained by *Rashba*).

[*Ramban* asks why this reason is needed at all, when there is a rule that הַמּוֹצִיא מֵחֲבֵירוֹ עָלָיו הָרְאָיָה, *the [burden of] proof rests on the one who seeks to exact [payment] from his fellow.* As such, even if the *kesubah* obligation were Biblical, and even if there were no presumption that the husband would not lie, the burden of proof would fall on the woman to prove that she was a virgin before she could collect the *kesubah* money from her husband. See *Ramban, Re'ah, Rashba* and *Ran* for several answers to this question. See also *Pnei Yehoshua, Chidushei R' Akiva Eiger* and *Beis Aharon.*]

[On the basis of the Gemara's explanation here, it emerges that the claim of "an open entrance" is believed only where the groom prepared a wedding feast. Where there was no feast, or where the bride's family prepared the feast, he is not believed to make this claim (*Rashba;* see also *Ritva* 9b ד״ה אמר רב יהודה; *Yam Shel Shlomo* §26; see also *Beis Shmuel* 68:18).]

4. That is, if the husband has three grades of land – superior, average and inferior – and the woman comes to collect her *kesubah* from his property, she cannot claim superior or average lands of the value owed her. Rather, if the ex-husband wants, he may give her the most inferior of his properties, as long as it is equal in value to her claim (*Rashi*). [Generally, a person would prefer a smaller parcel of superior land than a larger parcel of inferior land – even though both are worth the same amount.] Had the *kesubah* obligation been Biblical, though, the woman would have had the right to collect from the superior or average lands of her ex-husband (see *Tosafos, Rashba* and *Ritva* for the reason).

5. The Gemara will soon cite the verse (*Exodus* 22:16): כֶּסֶף יִשְׁקֹל כְּמֹהַר הַבְּתוּלֹת, *he shall pay silver shekalim in the amount of the settlement [made] to the virgins,* as the source for this Biblical obligation (*Rashi*).

6. *Exodus* 22:16. This verse speaks of a man who seduced an unmarried *naarah* (*Rashi*). The Torah states that if the father of the girl refuses to allow the seducer to marry his daughter, the seducer must pay *silver shekalim in the amount of the settlement [made] to the virgins.* Now the verse does not specify how much this is. However, the Torah does state that one who violates a *naarah* pays fifty silver coins (*Deuteronomy* 22:29). That fine is understood to be compensation for her [lost] virginity. Thus, the verse in the case of the seducer means that *he* [the seducer] *shall pay silver shekalim in the amount of the settlement [made] to the virgins* in the case of the violator (*Rashi*).

7. *Rashi;* cf. *Shitah Mekubetzes* ד״ה כסף ישקול.

The Gemara asks:

אָמַר רַב יוֹסֵף – **Rav Yosef said:** מַאי קָא מַשְׁמַע לָן – **What is [Shmuel] informing us?** תְּנֵינָא – **We learned** this principle **in the** following **Mishnah:**[13] הָאוֹכֵל אֵצֶל חָמִיו בִּיהוּדָה שֶׁלֹּא בְעֵדִים – IF ONE EATS IN HIS FATHER-IN-LAW'S HOUSE IN JUDEA during his betrothal period WITHOUT WITNESSES,[14] אֵינוֹ יָכוֹל לִטְעוֹן טַעֲנַת בְּתוּלִים – HE CANNOT MAKE A CLAIM CONCERNING his bride's VIRGINITY after they marry, מִפְּנֵי שֶׁמִּתְיַיחֵד עִמָּהּ – BECAUSE it is customary in Judea that HE SECLUDES himself WITH HER during these visits.[15] We therefore suspect that he himself may have cohabited with her while they were still betrothed. בִּיהוּדָה הוּא דְּלָא מָצֵי טָעֵין – The Mishnah says that **it is in Judea that he cannot make** such **a claim,** הָא בַּגָּלִיל מָצֵי טָעֵין – which implies that **in** any other place, for example, **the Galilee, he can make** such **a claim.**[16] וּלְמַאי – **Now in regard to what** issue must we judge the validity of such a claim? אִי לְאוֹסְרָהּ עָלָיו – **If** you will say in regard **to rendering her prohibited to him,** בִּיהוּדָה אַמַּאי לֹא – **why** should he **not** be able to make such a claim even **in Judea?** Since he claims that he did not cohabit with her during their *erusin* period, and that she must therefore have cohabited with another man, he has rendered her forbidden to him.[17] אֶלָּא לָאו לְהַפְסִידָהּ כְּתוּבָּתָהּ – **Rather, is it not** clear that the Mishnah's ruling is **in regard to depriving her of her *kesubah*?**[18] וּדְקָא טָעֵין טַעֲנָה – **Now** the Mishnah speaks of a case where he merely makes a claim, without offering any evidence. It is thus evident that the claim alone suffices to deprive her of the *kesubah.* מַאי לָאו דְּקָא טָעֵין טַעֲנַת פֶּתַח פָּתוּחַ – **Would** you **not** say **that** we are speaking of a case where **he makes the claim of an open entrance?**[19] The Mishnah thus clearly states Shmuel's ruling that the groom's claim can deprive the bride of her *kesubah.*[20] Why then was it necessary for Shmuel to state it?

The Gemara answers:

לֹא – **No.** The Mishnah need not be speaking of a claim of "an open entrance." דְּקָא טָעֵין טַעֲנַת דָּמִים – Rather, the Mishnah may be dealing with a case **where he makes the claim** of an absence **of blood** after their first cohabitation.[21] Since this is a supportable claim, the Mishnah implies that it is accepted in Galilee (though not in Judea).[22]

NOTES

virgin, and then divorcing her] (*Rashi;* see note 20, and 10a note 3). The fact that he does make such a claim therefore tends to prove what he says.

Shmuel certainly agrees with R' Elazar (9a) that this claim renders her prohibited to him (*Ritva,* according to *Rashi*), for if we believe him in regard to her *kesubah,* we surely believe him in regard to his own prohibition (*Ramban;* cf. *Tosafos*). However, R' Elazar, who ruled only that she is forbidden to him, does not accept Shmuel's ruling. In his view, the claim is *not* accepted in regard to depriving her of her *kesubah* (see *Rashi* 9a ד״ה נאמן לאוסרה עליו). [R' Elazar may well accept the force of Shmuel's argument. Nevertheless, he does not consider this argument sufficient to deprive her of her *kesubah* (at least in the case of a man who was never previously married) because it only proves that *he* is convinced that he encountered an open entrance – but he may in fact be mistaken about this, since, never having been married before, he is inexperienced in these matters. Consequently, *we* (the court) cannot act on the basis of his claim to deprive her of her *kesubah* even though we accept that he is telling what he thinks is the truth. We can only say that she becomes forbidden to *him* because of his certainty, but we cannot deprive *her* on this account because he may be mistaken (*Shitah Mekubetzes* 9a ד״ה אבל הכא מיקם הוא דלא קים ליה in explanation of *Rashi;* see 9a note 11). Shmuel, however, clearly holds that he may be assumed to know with certainty whether he encountered an open entrance. See 10a note 19, where this point will be further elaborated and modified. See *Shitah Mekubetzes* ד״ה נאמן להפסידה.]

This is *Rashi's* view. *Tosafos* and other Rishonim (see *Rashba* and *Ritva* to 9a) maintain that R' Elazar may also agree with Shmuel's ruling regarding the *kesubah* but he speaks of prohibiting her (rather than of depriving her of her *kesubah*) because he considers that ruling to be the greater novelty (see *Tosafos* ד״ה אי למיתב for an explanation of why). *Tosafos,* however, cite a *Yerushalmi* that seems to indicate that R' Elazar indeed disputes Shmuel's ruling regarding the *kesubah,* as *Rashi* maintains. See further in *Ritva.*

[There is a dispute among the Rishonim whether Shmuel stated his ruling for all women or just for those who become prohibited through this claim (i.e. a Kohen's wife and a girl betrothed before the age of three; see above, 9a). *Rashba* and *Ritva* state that he refers to all women. *Tosafos* (ד״ה אי and on 10a ד״ה חזקה) challenge this (see 10a note 3). See further in *Shev Shmaatsa* 1:23.]

13. Below, 12a.

14. [I.e. without witnesses who can testify that the bride and groom were never alone together.]

15. As we will learn below (Mishnah 12a, cited above on 7b), it was the custom in the province of Judea to seclude the bride and groom together during their *erusin* period so that the groom should feel familiar and comfortable with his bride when they actually entered the *chuppah* and married (see also above, 7b note 21). [According to *Rambam* (*Commentary to Mishnah*) and *Rav,* this was done at the time that a special meal was made in the bride's home in honor of the betrothal. The Mishnah's expression "one who eats at his father-in-law's house" refers to his participation in this meal. From *Rashi,* however, it seems that the Mishnah refers to no specific occasion, but rather to any time during the *erusin* period when the groom might dine at his father-in-law's house.]

16. Because they do not seclude the bride and groom together before *nisuin.*

17. [Obviously, a groom who complains to the court that his bride was not a virgin is saying that he had not cohabited with her before their wedding night.] She should therefore be prohibited to him whether he made the claim in Galilee or in Judea! (*Rashi*).

18. Accordingly, in Judea his claim does not deprive her of the *kesubah* because we [the court] suspect him of having cohabited with her when they were secluded together. However, in Galilee where the custom is not to seclude the bride and groom together before the *nisuin,* we accept his claim (*Rashi*). This will be explained further in note 20.

19. See *Shitah Mekubetzes* for an explanation of why the Gemara considers this the more likely explanation.

20. [At least in Galilee, where there is no reason to suspect the groom himself.] We see from this Mishnah that even where there are no witnesses to support his claim, and the claim itself is not in any way substantiated, so that we have nothing to rely on but his unsupported word, it is nevertheless accepted. This is because we say that if it were not true, he would not lodge such a claim and thereby waste the wedding feast. Had he wished to be rid of her, he would simply have divorced her while they were still betrothed and spared himself the effort of making the wedding feast. The fact that he went through the trouble of making a wedding feast therefore demonstrates that his claim is not based on any previous dislike of her but rather on what he actually found during their cohabitation.

Nevertheless, we still do not accept such a claim in Judea. This is because their seclusion together (according to the custom of Judea) makes us suspect him of having cohabited with her. Although he now claims not to have done so, we consider it possible that he may have forgotten what he did, or that he may have begun cohabiting with her but did not complete the act and through that partial action, he ruptured the hymen without realizing it. Consequently, we do not accept his claim in Judea to deprive her of her *kesubah* (*Rashi;* see *Ramban* and *Rashba* for another answer to this last question, and *Shitah Mekubetzes* for an explanation of why *Rashi* did not give that answer).

21. See note 11.

22. For example, the Mishnah may be speaking of a case where special attendants were assigned to check them after their cohabitation to insure that nothing unscrupulous took place [such as the groom hiding the cloth that showed the blood; see Gemara below, 12a]. Their failure to find blood thus supports his claim, so that we need not rely on his word alone.

The claim of an open entrance, however, is by its very nature not subject to any type of confirmation, and the Mishnah may well hold that it does not suffice to deprive her of her *kesubah* (*Rashi*). Shmuel's ruling that it does is thus novel (cf. *Ritva*).

עין משפט
נר מצוה

נא א מי׳ פ״א מהל׳ אישות הלכה יב יג טוש״ע אה״ע סימן סח סעיף ג וסעיף ו:

ליקוטי רש״י

גט כריתות. על תנאי שאם ימות תהא מגורשת מעכשיו ופעמים שהוא טרוד באתו ושולחו מן המלחמה [שבת נו.]. ואת ערובתם תקח. ואת ערובת האלפים ושלומם תקח באחיך בלבבך ותגד לי וכן תרגם יונתן וית טיביהון תייתי. ערובתם, לשון הלכה כמו ערוב עבדך לטוב (תהילים קיט) גרנטי״ש בלע״ז ורבותינו אמרו גט כריתות יקח מאתם ויביא לנשותיהם להפריד כירוב שבינו לבינה [שמואל א יז, יח]. במלחמת שאול כתיב. דברים המעורבין בינו לבינה. היינו קדושין. בתולה נשאת ליום הרביעי. תקנת חכמים היא שתכנס ברביע׳ בשבת [כתובות ב.]. מפני שמתייחד עמה. דתנן פרק קמא דכתובות (דף יב.) ביהודה היו מייחדים החתן והכלה קודם כניסתן לחופה כדי שיהא לבו גס בה כלומר רגיל ומלפק עמה שלא יהיו בושין זה מזה בבעילת מצוה הלכך חיישינן דלמא בעיל [יבמות מא.].

א) כל היוצא למלחמת בית דוד גט כריתות כותב לאשתו דכתיב א) ואת אחיך תפקד לשלום ואת ערובתם תקח מאי ואת ערובתם תקח תני רב יוסף דברים המעורבין בינו לבינה אמר אביי אף אנן נמי תנינא ב) בתולה נשאת ליום הרביעי ליום רביעי אין ליום חמישי לא מאי טעמא משום איקרורי דעתא ולמאי אי למיתב לה כתובה ניתיב לה אלא לאוסרה עליו ודקא טעין טענה מאי לאו דקטעין טענת פתח פתוח א) לא דקטעין טענת דמים אמר רב יהודה אמר שמואל האומר פתח פתוח מצאתי נאמן להפסידה כתובתה אמר רב יוסף מאי קמ״ל תנינא ג) האוכל אצל חמיו ביהודה שלא בעדים אינו יכול לטעון טענת בתולים מפני שמתייחד עמה ביהודה הוא דלא מצי טעין הא בגליל מצי טעין ולמאי אי לאוסרה עליו ביהודה אמאי לא אלא לאו להפסידה כתובתה ודקא טעין טענה א) מאי לאו דקא טעין טענת פתח פתוח לא דקא טעין טענת דמים
אתמר

גט כריתות כותב לאשתו. שאם ימות במלחמה יהא גט מיום כתיבתו והרי מת אוריה במלחמה: דכתיב. במלחמת שאול ואת אחיך כו׳ ודוד למד מישי אביו להנהיג שאף היוצאין למלחמותיו עושין כן: דברים המעורבים בינו לבינה. אלו קדושין: תקח. תטול מביניהם על ידי גט: אף אנן נמי תנינא. דטוען פתח פתוח מצאתי מתסרא עליו ולא אמרינן לא קים ליה: איקרורי דעתא. עד שני בשבת הבאה: ולמאי. קפדי רבנן אי מקררא דעתיה: ניתיב לה. מה לנו להפסידה והרי הוא נותן מדעת: אלא לאו לאוסרה. הוא דקפדינן שלא יקרר דעתו ויקיים את האסורה לו אלמא כי אתי וטוען אסרינן לה עליה: טענת דמים. דטענה מבוררת היא וליכא למימר לא קים ליה אבל בפתח פתוח אימא לך לא קים ליה: להפסידה כתובתה. על פי עצמו ומטעמא דלקמן מפרש חזקה אין אדם טורח בסעודה ומפסידה: האוכל אצל חמיו. בימים שבין אירוסין לנשואין: אין יכול לטעון טענת בתולים. כשתכנס לחופה: מפני שמתייחד עמה. ביהודה היו מיחדין אותם כדי שיהא לבו גס בה: ביהודה אמאי לא. האומר פשיטא לי שלא באתי אליה והא ודאי מאחר זינתה שוייה עליה חתיכה דאיסורא מה לי גליל מה לי יהודה: אלא לאו להפסידה כתובתה. וביהודה לא מפסידה על פיו דאמרינן הוא בא עליה באירוסין ובגליל מצי טעין דהא לא נתייחד: מאי לאו דקטעין טענת פתח פתוח מצאתי. דאע״ג דאין עדים בדבר זה ולא טענה מוכחת אלא עליה סמכינן דאמרינן אי לאו דקושטא הוא לא היה מפסיד סעודתו ואם היה שונאה מתחלה היה מגרשה ולא טרח בסעודת נשואין ומיהו ביהודה לא מהימן שמא בעל בימי אירוסין ושכח או הערה בה מתוך תבהה ולא ידע ששיבר בתוליה: לא דקא טעין טענת דמים. לעולם אימא לך בדבר שאינו יכול לבררו אינו נאמן להפסיד כתובתה ודיוקא דמתני׳ דדייקינן הא בגליל מצי טעין דטעין טענת דמים וכגון שהיו להם שושבינים שמשמשו אותן ולא נעשית אונאה בדבר ולא ראה ואיבד וטענה ברורה היא:
חכמים

כל היוצא למלחמת בית דוד גט כריתות כותב לאשתו. פי׳ בקונטרס שאם ימות במלחמה יהא גט מעת כתיבתו וקשה לר״ת דא״כ מאי כל היוצא אם לא מהני אלא למי שאין לו בנים ויש לו יבם ועוד דתנן במי שאחזו (גיטין עג. ושם) מה היא באותן הימים רבי יהודה אומר הרי היא כאשת איש לכל דבריה וקאי אמאי דקתני לעיל מינה הרי זה גיטך מהיום אם מתי וכן משמע בתוספתא אלמא אע״ג דאמר מהיום הויא אשת איש גמורה כדמפרש בגמרא באומר מעת שאני בעולם פירוש דהאי דאמר מהיום לא שיחול מיד אלא דעתו שיחול שעה אחת קודם מיתתו דהיינו מעת שהוא בעולם ולא אמר מהיום אלא למעוטי לאחר מיתה כלומר מאותו יום שאני בעולם יהא גט ומיהו יש לחלק בין מהיום לפירש בהדיא שיחול משעת כתיבה דע״כ משעת כתיבה קאמר שיהא גט ועוד נראה דלפי׳ אמר מהיום יש ליישב פי׳ הקונטרס דלאו דוקא פירש שאם ימות במלחמה אלא היו מתנים אם לא יחזור מן המלחמה ואגב ריהטיה נקט בקונטרס אם ימות דסתם מי שאינו חוזר מן המלחמה אינו חוזר לפי שמת אלא ה״ה אם נשבה והשתא מהיום דהכא אין שייך לומר מעת שאני בעולם כההוא דמי שאחזו אלא מהיום מיום כתיבה קאמר ואם תאמר והרי חזר אוריה ונתבטל הגט ויש לומר שהיה מתנה אם לא יחזור בסוף המלחמה והרי לא חזר לבסוף ויתא לפירוש זה הא דאמרינן בפרק הזהב (ב״מ נט. ושם) נוח לו לאדם שיבעול ספק אשת איש ואל ילבין פני חבירו ברבים ומפיק ליה מהאי מעשה דבת שבע דספק אשת איש הואי דדלמא יחזור מן המלחמה ור״ת מפרש כותב גט כריתות לגמרי בלא שום תנאי ולפי׳ קשה אמאי קרי לה ספק אשת איש הא הואי גרושה גמורה ואר״ת דקרי לה ספק אשת איש לפי שהיו מגרשין בצינעא שלא יהא נודע ויקפצו עליהם בני אדם לקדשם ולפי׳ הקונטרס קשה קצת איך בא עליה למה לא היה ירא שמא יחזור: אי למיתב לה כתובה כו׳. משמע אם היה בא לב״ד היה נאמן להפסידה כתובתה אע״פ שלאוסרה עליו לא היה נאמן משום דאית לן למימר דשמא אינו בקי בפתח פתוח ואוקמה בחזקת היתר אבל מ״מ כתובתה הפסידה אע״פ שיש לנו לומר שהוא טועה בפתח פתוח דאית לן למימר אוקי ממונא בחזקת מריה וקשה דאמאי מפסידה כתובתה והא הוה ב) ספק ספיקא ספק אי הוא בקי בפתח פתוח אם לאו ואם תמצא לומר פתח פתוח הוה ספק באונס ספק ברצון דאפי׳ אשת כהן באונס לא מפסדה כתובתה ואין לומר דאפי׳ בספק ספיקא מפסדה כתובתה משום דמוקמינן ממונא בחזקתיה דהא לקמן (דף יב:) גבי משארסתני נאנסתי והוא אומר לא כי אלא עד שלא ארסתיך נאנסת והיה מקחי מקח טעות ואיכא מאן דמפרש לקמן (דף יא:) מקח טעות ממאתים אבל מנה אית לה אלמא משום דבאותו מנה הוי ספק ספיקא לא מפסדה דספק קודם שנתארסה ספק אחר שנתארסה ואם תמצא לומר אחר שנתארסה אימור באונס הוה דאי אמרת דאפי׳ בספק ספיקא מפסדה אמאי אית לה אפי׳ מנה וי״ל דלא חשיב ספק ספיקא כהאי גוונא משום דהאי ספיקא שמא באונס היה לא חשיב ספיקא גמורה למיתב לה כתובה דאימור קודם שנתארסה נאנסה והשתא אתי שפיר הא דתנן במתני׳ (לקמן דף יב.) היא אומרת מוכת עץ אני והוא אומר לא כי אלא דרוסת איש את וקאמר ר׳ יהושע שאינה נאמנת ומפסדת כתובתה אי לר׳ יוחנן מנה אי לר׳ אלעזר ולא כלום ואע״ג דהוי ספק ספיקא ספק מוכת עץ ויש לה כתובה ואפי׳ אם תמצא לומר דרוסת איש אימור תחתיו נאנסה ונסתחפה שדהו ויש לה כתובה אלא ודאי ספק באונס לא חשיב ספק ג) דאימור קודם שנתארסה נאנסה ועוד אומר רבינו יצחק דמוכת עץ לא שכיח דהא דאמרינן (לקמן לו:) כולהו נמי חבוטי מיחבטן היינו אליבא דר״ג אבל רבי יהושע שמעינן דלית ליה טעמא דמיחבטן דקאמר התם (לקמן לו.) חרשת ושוטה יש להן טענת בתולין והיינו משום דס״ל דחבטא לא שכיחא: מאי לאו דקא טעין טענת פתח פתוח. נראה לפרש דקס״ד דבטענת דמים ד) ליכא למיחש לאיקרורי דעתא דכיון דליכא דם לבו נוקפו ואין מתקרר אבל בפתח פתוח איכא למיחש שמא יתקרר: נאמן להפסידה כתובתה. אור״י דשמואל מודה שפיר דנאמן לאוסרה עליו ולהפסידה כתובתה איצטריך ליה לאשמעינן דלא תימא דלא יהא נאמן אע״ג דקים ליה בפתח פתוח דנימא במזיד משקר להפסיד כתובתה ור״א נמי מאי סבר דנאמן להפסידה ונקט לאוסרה לרבותא וכ״ש דנאמן להפסיד כתובתה כדמוכח הסוגיא דלעיל [ומיהו בירושלמי משמע דלר״א אינו נאמן להפסיד כתובתה]: אבל בגליל מצי טעין. וא״ת מנא ליה דלמא ביהודה נאמנת לומר שבא עליה באירוסין ולא בגליל אבל כשטוענת בתולה הייתי בגליל נמי מהימנא וי״ל דמשמע ליה אינו יכול לטעון טענת בתולים בכל ענין בין שאומרת שבא עליה מן האירוסין בין שאומרת פתח נעול מצא דביהודה נאמנת במגו דאי בעיא אמרה באירוסין בא עליה ולא בגליל דליכא מגו אבל קשה דמייתי מדיוקא והוה ליה לאתויי מרישא דקתני (לקמן דף י:) בתולה אלמנה מן האירוסין כו׳ ויש להן טענת בתולין וע״כ לענין כתובה איירי דלאוסרה עליו אפילו מן הנשואין נמי יש לה טענת בתולין כיון דכנסה בחזקת בתולה כדמוכח לקמן (דף יב.) דפריך וניחוש שמא תחתיו זינתה: מאי לאו דקא טעין טענת פתח פתוח. וביהודה אע״ג דאיכא חזקה לא מהימן כדפי׳ בקונטרס א״נ כיון דמתייחד עמה ודאי בא עליה דלא מוקי איניש אנפשיה ואע״ג דגבי יבמה אמרינן (יבמות דף קיא:) דעד ל׳ יום מוקי אנפשיה רוב פעמים לא מוקי אנפשיה אפי׳ שעה אחת דעל דעת כן מתייחד ד) [עמה] ואיתרע חזקה: לא דקא טעין טענת דמים. דהוא טענה ברורה מדאין סדינין מלוכלכים בדם ונראה דבטענת פתח פתוח וטענת דמים דשמעתין איירי שהיא טוענת שהוא בא עליה באירוסין או אומרת בתולה הייתי וא״ת ונהימנה לדידה במגו דאי בעיא אמרה משארסתני נאנסתי דנאמנת לר״ג דפסקינן לקמן (דף יג.) כוותיה וי״ל דאינה מודה ברצון שנבעלה מאחר ועוד דאין זה מגו דמיפסלא נפשה מכהונה אבל קשה דליהמנה במגו דאי בעיא אמרה מוכת עץ אני אפי׳ לרבנן דלקמן (דף יא:) דאמרי מוכת עץ כתובתה מנה דאין זה מגו דאינה רוצה להפסיד כלום מכתובתה מ״מ נאמנת במגו דאי בעיא אמרה מוכת עץ אני תחתיך ונסתחפה שדהו לכך נראה דהוי מגו במקום חזקה דאין אדם טורח בסעודה ומפסידה אע״ג דבעי׳ היא בפ״ק דבבא בתרא (דף ה: ושם) אי אמרינן מגו במקום חזקה או לא שמא חזקה דהכא עדיפא ואי לא אמרינן מגו להוציא אתי נמי שפיר:
אמר

מסורת הש״ס

א) שבת נו., ב) [לעיל ב.], ג) לקמן יב ע״א. ד) כ״ה בדפו״י.

תוספות ישנים

א) [דטענת דמים מסתבר כשנתייחד עמה אם היו או דמים בשעת תשמיש היתה מראה לאביה ולאמה או לבעלה כדי שלא יהא לו לב עליה כשישאנה וס״ד דטענת דמים אף ביהודה יכול לטעון אבל בפתח אינה מכרת אם פתחה נעול או לאו ואינה מגדת והשתא אתי שפיר דלא פריך מרישא דבפשיטות איכא לאוקמי בטענת דמים. ת״י עה״ג. ובתוס׳ הרשב״א מצאתי דפי׳ דבטענת דמים ביהודה נמי ס״ד דמהימן דליכא למימר שכח דאם איתא דהוה דם כשנתייחד עמה לא היה שוכח אבל בפתח פתוח איכא למימר דלא אסיק אדעתיה וא״ת מ״מ אם איתא דפתח לה פתח הוי דם וי״ל דאפשר למיפתח פתח בלא דם ולפי׳ ר״ח איכא לאוקמי בבוגרת שכלו דמיה שפתח פתחא ולאו אדעתיה כיון דליכא דם ובכל בתולה אפשר לפותחה בלא דם כדשמואל מיהו ההיא דשמואל נמי משמע דפתחה נעול מדאין ריחה נודף ושמא יש לומר דמחמת דם נמי אין ריחה נודף. ע״כ]:

ב) בת״י עה״ג וי״מ דהכא לא חשיב ספק ספיקא דאין יכולין להתהפך ולומר ברישא ספק באונס ספק ברצון ואת״ל ברצון ספק וכו׳ ולהכי לא חשיב אלא חדא ספיקא וה״נ י״ל בע״א דרוב בקיאין בפתח פתוח והוה ליה לענין כתובה רובא וחזקת ממונא ותו ליכא אלא חדא ספיקא אבל לענין לאוסרה איכא למימר סמוך מיעוטא דאין בקיאין לחזקה ואיתרע רובא והוי ליה פלגא ופלגא והוי ספק ספיקא ול״נ דה״פ אי למיתב לה כתובה ואיירי בטענת דמים דלענין כתובה איכא למיחש לאיקרורי דעתיה בטענת דמים:

ג) [ולהאי שינויא לא מיתוקמא מתני׳ בפתות מג׳ שנים. ת״י עה״ג]:

ד) [ולפי פי׳ ר״ח אתי שפיר דמיסתבר ליה לאוקמי מתני׳ בכל הנשים אפי׳ בבוגרת ומוכת עץ דאין להם דמים ועי״ל מאי לאו דקטעין אף פתח פתוח דאיירי מתני׳ בכל ענין שיטעון]:

תורה אור השלם

א) וְאֵת עֲשֶׂרֶת חֲרִצֵי הֶחָלָב הָאֵלֶּה תָּבִיא לְשַׂר הָאָלֶף וְאֶת אַחֶיךָ תִּפְקֹד לְשָׁלוֹם וְאֶת עֲרֻבָּתָם תִּקָּח: [שמואל א׳ יז, יח]

כָּל הַיּוֹצֵא לְמִלְחֶמֶת בֵּית דָּוִד – **Whoever would go out to** fight in a **war of the House of David** גֵּט כְּרִיתוּת כּוֹתֵב לְאִשְׁתּוֹ – would **write a bill of divorce for his wife,**[1] דִּכְתִיב ,,וְאֶת אַחֶיךָ תִּפְקֹד לְשָׁלוֹם וְאֶת־עֲרֻבָּתָם תִּקָּח" – **as it is written** in regard to the instructions given to David by his father: ***And look into your brothers' well-being, and take their "arubah."***[2]

The Gemara explains:

מַאי ,,וְאֶת־עֲרֻבָּתָם תִּקָּח" – **What** is meant by ***and take their "arubah"?*** תָּנֵי רַב יוֹסֵף – **Rav Yosef taught** the following Baraisa: דְּבָרִים הַמְעוֹרָבִין בֵּינוֹ לְבֵינָהּ – It refers to **matters that are commingled between him and her,** namely, the bond of marriage that unites them. Thus, David was instructed by his father "to take the marriages" of his brothers by obtaining from them bills of divorce.[3]

The Gemara offers support for R' Elazar's ruling:[4]

אָמַר אַבַּיֵּי – **Abaye said:** אַף אֲנַן נַמִּי תְּנֵינָא – **We have learned** this **in our Mishnah as well:** בְּתוּלָה נִשֵּׂאת לְיוֹם הָרְבִיעִי – A VIRGIN IS MARRIED ON WEDNESDAY. לְיוֹם רְבִיעִי אִין – That is, **on Wednesday** it is **indeed** proper for her to marry, לְיוֹם חֲמִישִׁי לֹא – but **not on Thursday.** מַאי טַעְמָא – **What is the reason?** מִשּׁוּם אִיקְרוּרֵי דַּעְתָּא – **Because** we are concerned about **the cooling** of his state **of mind,** i.e. we are afraid that if the marriage were to take place on Thursday and the groom were to discover that night that she was not a virgin, his anger might cool before the court were to convene again on the following Monday, and he would forego coming to court with his claim. וּלְמַאי – **Now in regard to what** issue were the Rabbis concerned about this? אִי לְמֵיתַב לָהּ כְּתוּבָּה – **If** you will say **in regard to giving her** the money stipulated in **the *kesubah*** if he should later divorce her or die, נֵיתִיב לָהּ – **let him give it to her.** Of what concern is this to the Rabbis?[5] אֶלָּא לְאוֹסְרָהּ עָלָיו – **Rather,** the issue for which the Rabbis were concerned must relate **to rendering her prohibited to him.**[6] וּדְקָא טָעִין טַעֲנָה – **Now** the Mishnah speaks of a case where **he** merely **makes a claim,** without offering any evidence. It is thus apparent that she becomes prohibited to him simply by virtue of his claim.[7] מַאי לָאו דְּקָטָעִין טַעֲנַת פֶּתַח פָּתוּחַ – **Would** you **not say that** we are speaking of a case where **he makes the claim of an "open entrance"?**[8] Our Mishnah then supports R' Elazar's ruling that this claim alone prohibits him to remain married to his bride.[9]

The Gemara rejects the proof:

לֹא – **No,** this is not necessarily his claim. דְּקָטָעִין טַעֲנַת דָּמִים – Rather, our Mishnah may be dealing with a case **where he makes the claim** of an absence **of blood** after their first cohabitation.[10] Since this is a more certain claim, it renders her forbidden. This does not prove that the less certain claim of "an open entrance" would also prohibit her.[11]

The Gemara presents another ruling about the claim of an "open entrance":

אָמַר רַב יְהוּדָה אָמַר שְׁמוּאֵל – **Rav Yehudah said in the name of Shmuel:** הָאוֹמֵר פֶּתַח פָּתוּחַ מָצָאתִי – If **[a man] says, "I found an open entrance,"** נֶאֱמָן לְהַפְסִידָהּ כְּתוּבָּתָהּ – **he is believed to deprive her of her *kesubah*.**[12]

NOTES

1. This *get* (bill of divorce) was given to her conditionally, to take effect (as of its writing) if the husband dies in battle (*Rashi*). [This was done to spare the wife of a childless man killed in battle from being bound to his brothers for *yibum* (see *Deuteronomy* 25:4-10). It also served to protect any soldier's wife from becoming an *agunah* (a woman who cannot remarry) in case he should be lost in battle without his body being recovered or witnesses being able to attest to his death. Accordingly, the condition had to be worded "in case I do not return at the end of the war" and not simply "in case I die" (*Tosafos* and *Ramban* in explanation of *Rashi;* see also *Tos. HaRosh*).] Since Uriah did die in battle, the *get* he had given Bathsheba was valid as of the day he had written [and given] it to her (*Rashi*). Hence, David's cohabitation with her was not adulterous and did not forbid her because she was actually divorced at the time.

[Although Uriah did return from the battlefield for a brief visit (see *II Samuel* 11:6-15), the condition attached to the divorce was understood to refer to returning with the rest of the army at the *end* of the war. Thus, his brief visit during the war did not abrogate the divorce (*Ramban, Ritva*).]

Tosafos take issue with *Rashi's* interpretation on a number of grounds and therefore cite *Rabbeinu Tam's* explanation that the divorce given by the soldiers of David's army was an unconditional divorce effective immediately. [However, since it was understood between husband and wife that she would remain faithful to him and that they would remarry when he returned safely from the war, David was criticized by the prophet for cohabiting with her in the interim.]

2. *I Samuel* 17:18. King Saul was waging war against the Philistines. David's brothers were at the battlefront, and his father, Jesse, sent David (his youngest son) to visit them and bring back a firsthand report on their welfare.

3. *Rashi* here and to *Shabbos* 56a. When David became king, he instituted the practice he had learned from his father for all who went forth to fight in his wars (*Ritva*).

4. That a husband's claim of an open entrance suffices to render his wife prohibited to him and we do not discount it by saying that he lacks the expertise to be sure of this claim (*Rashi;* see 9a note 11).

5. If he is willing to forego his chance to void her *kesubah* [by not pursuing his claim against her in court], why should the Rabbis involve themselves to cause her to lose it [by decreeing that a virgin marry on Wednesday, the day before a court session]? (*Rashi*).

[This seem to imply that his claim does suffice to deprive her of her *kesubah* (*Tosafos*). However, *Rashi* stated above (see 9a note 2) that R' Elazar is of the opinion that his claim does not deprive her of her *kesubah* (see further, note 12 below). See *Shitah Mekubetzes* ד״ה אי למיתב for several resolutions to this problem.]

6. That is, they were concerned that if his anger were to cool and cause him to refrain from going to court, he might remain married to someone who is actually prohibited to him (*Rashi*).

7. [For if his claim did not prohibit her to him, then there would be no reason to enact a decree to insure his coming to court!]

8. I.e. would you not say that our Mishnah refers *even* to such a claim (*Shitah Mekubetzes* ד״ה מאי לאו, according to *Rashi;* cf. *Tosafos*).

9. [*Rashi* to the Mishnah (2a ד״ה בשני ובחמישי) explained that the purpose of coming to court is to create a stir so that if there are any witnesses to her infidelity, they will step forward and testify. If so, what is the Gemara's proof from the Mishnah that she becomes forbidden to him simply by his claim? *Tosafos* (2a ד״ה שאם) answer that *Rashi* there meant only to explain why the Rabbis enacted that *every* virgin marry on Wednesday, even one who is not marrying a Kohen and one who had not been betrothed before she was three. Since it is only in these two cases that a bride becomes prohibited on the basis of the claim that she was not a virgin (as we learned on 9a), why should other women have to marry on Wednesday? The reason for this, *Rashi* explains, is because of the [slight] possibility that the claim might prompt witnesses to step forward. The Rabbis, however, would never have enacted the decree if not for the fact that the claim alone renders at least *some* women prohibited – namely, those for whom there is only a single doubt. It is thus clear from the Mishnah that at least in these cases the claim alone renders her forbidden. (See *Tosafos* there for another answer as well; cf. *Shitah Mekubetzes* ד״ה אמר אביי.)]

10. [Which is also a sign of a lack of virginity; see 8b note 47.]

11. Anyone can tell whether blood was found after cohabitation. Thus, a groom making this claim may safely be assumed to be certain of what he is saying. An inexperienced groom, however, may not be knowledgeable enough to be sure that he encountered an open entrance. Thus, the argument could be made that we should discount his claim of an open entrance (*Rashi*). The Mishnah's ruling therefore does not prove R' Elazar's ruling that his claim is accepted even where he claims an "open entrance."

12. Although a person's unsubstantiated claim is not generally accepted to cause a loss to someone else, in this case there is a certain credibility to his claim: For as the Gemara will explain on 10a, it may safely be assumed that a person would never go to the trouble of preparing an entire wedding feast and then deliberately waste it [by falsely claiming that his bride was not a

ה) כל היוצא למלחמת בית דוד גט כריתות כותב לאשתו דכתיב א) ואת אחיך תפקד לשלום ואת ערובתם תקח מאי ואת ערובתם תקח תני רב יוסף דברים המעורבין בינו לבינה אמר אביי אף אנן נמי תנינא ג) בתולה נשאת ליום הרביעי ליום רביעי אין ליום חמישי לא מאי טעמא משום איקרורי דעתא ולמאי אי למיתב לה כתובה ניתיב לה אלא לאוסרה עליו ודקא טעין טענה מאי לאו דקטעין טענת פתח פתוח ז) לא דקטעין טענת דמים אמר רב יהודה אמר שמואל האומר פתח פתוח מצאתי נאמן להפסידה כתובתה אמר רב יוסף מאי קמ"ל תנינא ג) האוכל אצל חמיו ביהודה שלא בעדים אינו יכול לטעון טענת בתולים מפני שמתייחד עמה ביהודה הוא דלא מצי טעין הא בגליל מצי טעין ולמאי אי לאוסרה עליו ביהודה אמאי לא אלא לאו להפסידה כתובתה ודקא טעין טענה מאי לאו דקא טעין א) טענת פתח פתוח לא דקא טעין טענת דמים אתמר

גט כריתות כותב לאשתו. שאם ימות במלחמה יהא גט מיום כתיבתו והרי מת אוריה במלחמה: דכתיב. במלחמת שאול ואת אחיך כו' ודוד למד מישי אביו להנהיג שאף היוצאין למלחמותיו עושין כן: דברים המעורבים בינו לבינה. אלו קדושין: תקח. תטול מביניהם על ידי גט: אף אנן נמי תנינא. דטוען פתח פתוח מצאתי אסרה עליו ולא אמרינן לא קים ליה: איקרורי דעתא. עד שני בשבת הבאה: ולמאי. קפדי רבנן אי מקררא דעתיה: ניתיב לה. מה לנו להפסידה והרי הוא נותן מדעת: אלא לאו לאוסרה. הוא דקפדינן שלא יקרר דעתו ויקיים את האסורה לו אלמא כי אתי וטעין אסרינן לה עליה: טענת דמים. דטענה מבוררת היא וליכא למימר לא קים ליה אבל בפתח פתוח אימא לך לא קים ליה: להפסידה כתובתה. על פי עצמו וטעמא לקמן מפרש חזקה אין אדם טורח בסעודה ומפסידה: האוכל אצל חמיו. בימים שבין אירוסין לנשואין: אין יכול לטעון טענת בתולים. כשתכנס לחופה: מפני שמתייחד עמה. ביהודה היו מיחדין אותם כדי שיהא לבו גס בה: ביהודה אמאי לא. האומר פשיטא לי שלא באתי אליה והא ודאי מאחר זינתה שויה עליה חתיכה דאיסורא מה לי גליל מה לי יהודה: אלא לאו להפסידה כתובתה. וביהודה לא מפסידה על פיו דאמרינן הוא בא עליה באירוסין ובגליל מצי טעין דהא לא נתייחד: מאי לאו דקטעין טענת פתח פתוח מצאתי. דאע"ג דאין עדים בדבר זה ולא טענה מוכחת אלא עליה סמכינן דאמרינן אי לאו דקושטא הוא לא היה מפסיד סעודתו ואם היה שונאה מתחלה היה מגרשה ולא טורח בסעודת נשואין ומיהו ביהודה לא מהימן שמא בעל בימי אירוסין ושכח או הערה בה מתוך חבתה ולא ידע ששיבר בתוליה: לא דקא טעין טענת דמים. לעולם אימא לך בדבר שאינו יכול לבררו אינו נאמן להפסיד כתובתה ודיוקא דמתני' דדייקינן הא בגליל מצי טעין דטעין טענת דמים וכגון שהיו להם שושבינים שמשמשו אותן ולא נעשית אונאה בדבר ולא ראה ואיבד וטענה ברורה היא:

חכמים

כל היוצא למלחמת בית דוד גט כריתות כותב לאשתו. פי' בקונטרס שאם ימות במלחמה יהא גט משעת כתיבתו וקשה לר"ת דא"כ מאי כל היוצא אם לא מהני אלא למי שאין לו בנים ויש לו יבם ועוד דתנן במי שאחזו (גיטין עג. ושם) מה היא באותן הימים רבי יהודה אומר הרי היא כאשת איש לכל דבריה וקאי אמאי דקתני לעיל מינה הרי זה גיטך מהיום אם מתי וכן משמע בתוספתא אלמא אע"ג דאמר מהיום הויא אשת איש גמורה כדמפרש בגמרא באומר מעת שאני בעולם פירוש דהאי דאמר מהיום לא שיחול מיד אלא דעתו שיחול שעה אחת קודם מיתתו דהיינו מעת שהוא בעולם ולא אמר מהיום אלא למעוטי לאחר מיתה כלומר מאותו יום שאני בעולם יהא גט ומיהו יש לחלק בין מהיום לפירש בהדיא שיחול משעת כתיבה דע"כ משעת כתיבה קאמר שיהא גט ועוד נראה דלפי' אמר מהיום יש ליישב פי' הקונטרס דלאו דוקא פירש שאם ימות במלחמה אלא היו מתנים אם לא יחזור מן המלחמה ואגב ריהטיה נקט בקונטרס אם ימות דסתם מי שאינו חוזר מן המלחמה אינו חוזר לפי שמת אלא ה"ה אם נשבה והשתא מהיום דהכא אין שייך לומר מעת שאני בעולם כההוא דמי שאחזו אלא מהיום מיום כתיבה קאמר ואם תאמר והרי חזר אוריה ונתבטל הגט ויש לומר שהיה מתנה אם לא יחזור בסוף המלחמה והרי לא חזר לבסוף ויכול לפירוש זה הא דאמרינן בפרק הזהב (ב"מ נט. ושם) נוח לו לאדם שיבעול ספק אשת איש ואל ילבין פני חבירו ברבים ומפיק ליה מהאי מעשה דבת שבע דספק אשת איש הואי דדלמא יחזור מן המלחמה ור"ת מפרש כותב גט כריתות לגמרי בלא שום תנאי ולפי' קשה אמאי קרי לה ספק אשת איש הא הואי גרושה גמורה ואר"ת דקרי לה ספק אשת איש לפי שהיו מגרשין בלינעא שלא יהא נודע ויקפצו עליהם בני אדם לקדשם ולפי' הקונטרס קשה קצת איך בא עליה למה לא היה ירא שמא יחזור: אי למיתב לה כתובה כו'. משמע אם היה בא לב"ד היה נאמן להפסידה כתובתה אע"פ שלאוסרה עליו לא היה נאמן משום דאית לן למימר דשמא אינו בקי בפתח פתוח ואוקמה בחזקת היתר אבל מ"מ כתובתה הפסידה אע"פ שיש לנו לומר שהוא טועה בפתח פתוח דאית לן למימר אוקי ממונא בחזקת מריה וקשה דאמאי מפסידה כתובתה והא הוה ב) ספק ספיקא ספק אי הוא בקי בפתח פתוח אם לאו ואם תמצא לומר פתח פתוח הוה ספק באונס ספק ברצון ולפי' אשת כהן באונס לא מפסדה כתובתה ואין לומר דאפי' בספק ספיקא מפסדה כתובתה משום דמוקמינן ממונא בחזקתיה דהא לקמן (דף יב:) גבי משארסתני נאנסתי והוא אומר לא כי אלא עד שלא ארסתיך נאנסת והיה מקחי מקח טעות ואיכא מאן דמפרש לקמן (דף יא:) מקח טעות ממאתים אבל מנה אית לה אלמא משום דבאותו מנה הוי ספק ספיקא לא מפסדה דספק קודם שנתארסה ספק אחר שנתארסה ואם תמצא לומר אחר שנתארסה אימור באונס הוה דאי אמרת דאפי' בספק ספיקא מפסדה אמאי אית לה אפי' מנה וי"ל דלא חשיב ספק ספיקא כהאי גוונא משום דהאי ספיקא שמא באונס היה לא חשיב ספיקא גמורה למיתב לה כתובה דאימור קודם שנתארסה נאנסה והשתא אתי שפיר הא דתנן במתני' (לקמן דף יג.) היא אומרת מוכת עץ אני והוא אומר לא כי אלא דרוסת איש את וקאמר ר' יהושע שאינה נאמנת ומפסדת כתובתה אי לר' יוחנן מנה אי לר' אלעזר ולא כלום ואע"ג דהוי ספק ספיקא ספק מוכת עץ ויש לה כתובה ואפי' אם תמצא לומר דרוסת איש אימור תחתיו נאנסה ונסתחפה שדהו ויש לה כתובה אלא ודאי ספק באונס לא חשיב ספק ג) דאימור קודם שנתארסה נאנסה ועוד אומר רבינו יצחק דמוכת עץ לא שכיח דהא דאמרינן (לקמן לו:) כולהו נמי תבועי מיחבטן היינו אליבא דר"ג אבל רבי יהושע שמעינן דלית ליה טעמא דמיחבטן דקאמר התם (לקמן לו.) חרשת ושוטה יש להן טענת בתולין והיינו משום דס"ל דחבטא לא שכיחא: מאי לאו דקא טעין טענת פתח פתוח. נראה לפרש דקס"ד דבטענת דמים ד) ליכא למיחש לאיקרורי דעתא דכיון דליכא דם לבו נוקפו ואין מתקרר אבל בפתח פתוח איכא למיחש שמא יתקרר: נאמן להפסידה כתובתה. אור"י דשמואל מודה שפיר דנאמן לאוסרה עליו ולהפסידה כתובתה איצטריך ליה לאשמעינן דלא תימא דלא יהא נאמן אע"ג דקים ליה בפתח פתוח דנימא במזיד משקר להפסידה כתובתה ור"א נמי מצי סבר דנאמן להפסידה ונקט לאוסרה לרבותא וכ"ש דנאמן להפסיד כתובתה כדמוכח הסוגיא דלעיל [ומיהו בירושלמי משמע דלר"א אינו נאמן להפסיד כתובתה]: אבל בגליל מצי טעין. וא"ת מנא ליה דלמא ביהודה נאמנת לומר שבא עליה באירוסין ולא בגליל הייתי בגליל אבל כשטוענת בתולה הייתי בגליל נמי מהימנא וי"ל דמשמע ליה אינו יכול לטעון טענת בתולים בכל ענין בין שאומרת שבא עליה מן האירוסין בין שאומרת פתח נעול מלא דביהודה נאמנת במגו דאי בעיא אמרה באירוסין בא עליה ולא בגליל דליכא מגו אבל קשה דמייתי מדיוקא והוה ליה לאתויי מרישא דקתני (לקמן דף י:) בתולה אלמנה מן האירוסין כו' ויש להן טענת בתולין וע"כ לענין כתובה איירי דלאוסרה עליו אפילו מן הנשואין נמי יש לה טענת בתולין כיון דכנסה בחזקת בתולה כדמוכח לקמן (דף יב.) דפריך וניחוש שמא תחתיו זינתה: מאי לאו דקא טעין טענת פתח פתוח. וביהודה אע"ג דאיכא חזקה לא מהימן כדפי' בקונטרס א"נ כיון דמתייחד עמה ודאי בא עליה דלא מוקי איניש אנפשיה ואע"ג דגבי יבמה אמרינן (יבמות דף קיא:) דעד ל' יום מוקי אנפשיה רוב פעמים לא מוקי אנפשיה אפי' שעה אחת דעל דעת כן מתייחד ז) [עמה] ואיתרע חזקה: לא דקא טעין טענת דמים. דהויא טענה ברורה מדאין סדינין מלוכלכים בדם ונראה דבטענת פתח פתוח וטענת דמים דשמעתין איירי שהיא טוענת שהוא בא עליה באירוסין או אומרת בתולה הייתי וא"ת ונהימנה לדידה במגו דאי בעיא אמרה משארסתני נאנסתי דנאמנת לר"ג דפסקינן לקמן (דף יג.) כוותיה וי"ל דאינה מודה ברצון שנבעלה מאחר ועוד דאין זה מגו דמיפסלא נפשה מכהונה אבל קשה דליהמנה במגו דאי בעיא אמרה מוכת עץ אני אפי' לרבנן דלקמן (דף יא:) דאמרי מוכת עץ כתובתה מנה דאין זה מגו דאינה רוצה להפסיד כלום מכתובתה מ"מ נאמנת במגו דאי בעיא אמרה מוכת עץ אני תחתיך ונסתחפה שדהו לכך נראה דהוי מגו במקום חזקה דאין אדם טורח בסעודה ומפסידה אע"ג דבעי' היא בפ"ק דבבא בתרא (דף ה: ושם) אי אמרינן מגו במקום חזקה או לא שאני חזקה דהכא עדיפא ואי לא אמרינן מגו להוציא אתי נמי שפיר:

אמר

עין משפט נר מצוה

נא א מיי' פ"א מהל' אישות הלכה יג יג טוש"ע אה"ע סימן סח סעיף ג וסעיף ו:

ליקוטי רש"י

גט כריתות. על תנאי שאם ימות יהא מגורשת מעכשיו וחכמים שהיה טריד בגלתו ושלומו מן המלחמה [שבת נו.]. ואת ערובתם תקח. ואת ערובת הגלאים ושלומים תקח מהם להוליך ולבכך ולנגד לי וכן תרגם יונתן וית טיביהון תייתי. ערובתם. לשון הלכה כמו ערוב עבדך לטוב (תהלים קיט) ורבותינו אמרו גט כריתות יקח מאתם ויכלו נשותיהם להפריד פירוד שבינו לבינה [שמואל א יז, יח]. במלחמת שאול כתיב. דברים המעורבין בינו לבינה. היינו קדושין. בתולה נשאת ליום הרביעי. תקנת חכמים היא שתנשא ברביעי [כתובות ב.]. מפני שמתייחד עמה. דתנן פרק קמא דכתובות (לקמן יב.) ביהודה היו מייחדים החתן והכלה קודם כניסתן לחופה כדי שיהא לבו גס בה כלומר רגיל ומלבק עמה שלא יהיו בושין זה מזה בבעילת מצוה הלכך חיישינן דלמא בעיל [יבמות מא.].

מסורת הש"ס

א) שבת נו., ב) [לעיל ב.], ג) לקמן יב ע"א. ד) כ"ה בדפו"י.

תוספות ישנים

א) [דטענת דמים מסתבר כשנתייחד עמה אם היו אז דמים בשעת תשמיש היתה מראה לאביה ולאמה או לבעלה כדי שלא יהא לו לב עליה כשישאנה וס"ד דטענת דמים אף ביהודה יכול לטעון אבל בפתח אינה מכרת אם פתחה נעול או לאו ואינה מגדת והשתא אתי שפיר דלא פריך מרישא דבפשיטות איכא לאוקמי בטענת דמים. ת"י עה"ג. ובתוס' הרשב"א מצאתי דפי' דבטענת דמים ביהודה נמי ס"ד דמהימן דליכא למימר שכח דאם איתא דהוה דם כשנתייחד עמה לא היה שוכח אבל בפתח פתוח איכא למימר דלא אסיק אדעתיה וא"ת מ"מ אם איתא דפתח לה פתח הוי דם וי"ל דאפשר למיפתח פתח בלא דם ולפי' ר"ח איכא לאוקמי בבוגרת שכלו דמיה שפתחה פתחה ולאו אדעתיה כיון דליכא דם וככל בתולה אפשר לפותחה בלא דם כדשמואל מיהו הסיא דשמואל נמי משמע דפתחה נעול מדאין ריחה נודף ושמא יש לומר דמחמת דם נמי אין ריחה נודף. ע"כ]:
ב) בת"י עה"ג וי"מ דהכא לא חשיב ספק ספיקא דאין יכולין להתהפך ולומר ברישא ספק באונס ספק ברצון ואת"ל ברצון ספק וכו' ולהכי לא חשיב אלא חדא ספיקא וה"נ י"ל בע"א דרוב בקיאין בפתח פתוח והוה ליה לענין כתובה רובא וחזקת ממונא ותו ליכא אלא חדא ספיקא אבל לענין לאוסרה איכא למימר סמוך מיעוטא דאין בקיאין לחזקה ואיתרע רובא והוי ליה פלגא ופלגא והוי ספק ספיקא ול"נ דה"פ אי למיתב לה כתובה ואיירי בטענת דמים דלענין כתובה איכא למיחש לאיקרורי דעתיה בטענת דמים:
ג) [ולהאי שיטה לא מיתוקמא מתני' בפתוח מג' שנים. ת"י עה"ג]:
ד) [ולפי' ר"ח אתי שפיר דמיסתבר ליה לאוקמי מתני' בכל הנשים אפי' בבוגרת ומוכת עץ דאין להם דמים וע"ז מאי לאו דקטעין אף פתח פתוח דאיירי מתני' בכל ענין שיטתו]:

תורה אור השלם

א) וְאֵת עֲשֶׂרֶת חֲרִצֵי הֶחָלָב הָאֵלֶּה תָּבִיא לְשַׂר הָאָלֶף וְאֶת אַחֶיךָ תִּפְקֹד לְשָׁלוֹם וְאֶת עֲרֻבָּתָם תִּקָּח: [שמואל א' יז, יח]

האומר פתח פתוח מצאתי נאמן לאוסרה עליו ואמאי [א] ספק ספיקא הוא ספק תחתיו ספק אין תחתיו ואם תמצא לומר תחתיו ספק באונס ספק ברצון לא צריכא [ב] באשת כהן ואיבעית אימא [ג] באשת ישראל וכגון דקביל בה אבוה קידושין פחותה מבת ג' שנים ויום אחד מאי קמ"ל תנינא [ד] האומר לאשה קדשתיך והיא אומרת לא קדשתני היא מותרת בקרוביו והוא אסור בקרובותיה מהו דתימא התם דודאי קים ליה אבל הכא מיקם הוא דלא קים ליה קמ"ל ומי אמר רבי אלעזר הכי והאמר רבי אלעזר אין האשה נאסרת על בעלה אלא על עסקי קינוי וסתירה וכמעשה שהיה ותסברא מעשה שהיה בקינוי וסתירה הוה ועוד מי אסרוה הא לא קשיא הכי קאמר אין האשה נאסרת על בעלה אלא על עסקי קינוי וסתירה ממעשה שהיה דלא הוה קינוי וסתירה ולא איתסרא מכל מקום קשיא קינוי וסתירה אין פתח פתוח לא ולטעמיך קינוי וסתירה אין עדים לא אלא הכי קאמר [ה] אין האשה נאסרת על בעלה בעד אחד אלא בשני עדים [ו] וקינוי וסתירה אפילו בעד אחד נמי ופתח פתוח כשני עדים דמי וכי תימא מעשה שהיה מפני מה לא אסרוה [ז] התם אונס הוה ואיבעית אימא כי הא דאמר רבי שמואל בר נחמני אמר רבי יונתן כל

רש"י

האומר פתח פתוח מצאתי. וטענת דמים אין לו כגון שהיא ממשפחת דורקטי שאין להם דם בתולים כדלקמן (דף י:) או שנאבדה ממנו מפה ולא ידע אם היה דם אם לאו אבל זאת ברורה לו שפתח פתוח מצא: **נאמן לאוסרה עליו.** ואע"פ שאין הדבר הזה יכול להתברר אלא על פיו לגבי נפשיה הוי מהימן לשוייה עליה חתיכה דאיסורא אבל להפסידה כתובתה לא מהימן: **ואמאי.** מיתסרא עליה אפי' אי מהימנת ליה דנבעלה: **ספק תחתיו.** משנתארסה זינתה: **ספק אין תחתיו.** אלא קודם שנתארסה זינתה: **ספק באונס.** ואנוסה שריא באשת ישראל כדלקמן (דף נא:) מוהיא לא נתפשה: **באשת כהן.** שהאונס אסור בה הלכך חד ספק הוא: **פחותה מבת ג' שנים.** ועכשיו היא גדולה ופיתוי פיתוי ואינו אונס הלכך חד ספק איכא ספק אונס ספק רצון אבל ספק תחתיו ספק אין תחתיו ליכא שאילו נבעלה קודם לכן היו בתוליה חוזרים כדתנן במסכת נדה (דף מד:) פחות מכאן כנותן אצבע בעין שהדמעה יוצאת וחוזרת: **מאי קמ"ל תנינא.** שאדם נאמן על עצמו לאסור לו את המותר על פיו: **הוא אסור בקרובותיה.** באמה ובתה ואחותה דשוינהו אנפשיה חתיכה דאיסורא: **והיא מותרת בקרוביו.** שהרי אינה מודה בקידושין ובמסכת קידושין מוקמינן לה באומר קידשתיך בפני עדים והלכו להם למדינת הים: **דודאי קים ליה.** שקידשה: **אבל הכא.** אימא מתוך שפנוי היה ואינו בקי מיקם הוא דלא קים ליה כסבור שמצא פתח פתוח ואינו כן ולא תיאסר קמשמע לן: **ומי אמר רבי אלעזר הכי.** דאשה מזנה נאסרת על פי בעלה: **קינוי.** שאמר לה אל תסתרי עם פלוני: **וסתירה.** שבאו עדים שנסתרה עמו אחר קינוי: **וכמעשה שהיה.** דבת שבע: **ותסברא.** דהכי א"ר אלעזר מעשה שהיה מי הוה ביה קינוי: **ועוד מי אסרוה.** על אוריה דאילו נאסרה על אוריה נאסרה אף על דוד דקיימא לן (סוטה דף כח.) כשם שאסורה לבעל כך אסורה לבועל: **הא לא קשיא.** כלומר משום הא קושיא לא תדחייה לרבי אלעזר: **הכי קאמר אין האשה נאסרת על בעלה אלא על עסקי קינוי וסתירה ממעשה שהיה.** ממעשה דבת שבע אנו למדין כן שלא היה שם קינוי וסתירה ולא אסרוה: **עדים לא.** בתמיה אפי' יש עדים שזינתה שמא אינה נאסרת בלא קינוי והא כתיב (דברים כד) כי מצא בה ערות דבר ועוד הא לא נתפשה אסורה: **אין האשה נאסרת על בעלה בעד אחד.** דיליף (סוטה דף ג:) דבר דבר ממנון: **וקינוי וסתירה.** אם יש עדים שקינא לה ויש עדים שנסתרה אחר קינוי: **אפי' בעד אחד.** אפי' אין בטומאה אלא עד אחד נאמן דכתיב (במדבר ה) ועד אין בה ואמר מר (סוטה ב:) כל מקום שנאמר עד הרי כאן שנים וקאמר רחמנא עד אין בה תרי אלא חד והיא לא נתפשה אסורה שרגלים לדבר שזינתה שהרי קינא לה ונסתרה ועד אחד מעידה שהיא טמאה ומהשתא לא תקשי לך דרבי אלעזר דפתח פתוח לאוסרה על עצמו כשני עדים דמי שהרי דבר ברור הוא לו שנבעלה: **מפני מה לא אסרוה.** על דוד שהרי עדים הרבה ידעו: גט

תוספות

האומר פתח פתוח מצאתי כו'. פירש בקונטרס דטענת דמים לא קאמר כגון שנאבדה המפה או שהיא ממשפחת דורקטי שאין להם דמים ור"ת מפרש דבוגרת ומוכת עץ אין להם דמים אבל אין פתחן פתוח ויכול לטעון טענת פתח פתוח וקשה לפר"ת דאמרי' באלו נערות (לקמן לו. ושם:) ובוגרת אין לה טענת בתולים והאמר רב בוגרת נותנים לה לילה ראשונה ומשני אי דקא טעין טענת דמים ה"נ הכא"ע דקטענין טענת פתח פתוח משמע דפתחה פתוח ויש לה דמים וי"ל דר"ת גריס כגירסא ראשונה שהיתה בספרים [ג] אי דקא טעין טענת פתח פתוח הכי נמי הכא"ע דקא טעין טענת דמים וה"פ והאמר רב בוגרת נותנין לה לילה הראשונה ומדתלינן כל הלילה בדם בתולים משמע דאיכא בוגרת דאית לה דם בתולים טובא אם כן אי אפשר לשום בוגרת שלא יהא פתחה סתום אפילו אין לה דמים וא"כ יש לה טענת בתולים בפתח פתוח ומשני אי דקטענין פתח פתוח ה"נ דיש לה טענת בתולים הכא"ע דלית לה טענת בתולים בטענת דמים משום דליכא בוגרת דדמיה כלין ומיהו בירושלמי משמע לא כפר"ת דקאמר התם ר' יונה בשם ר' קריספא בוגרת כחבית פתוחה של יין ויש ליישב לענין דמים קאמר משום דסתם חבית סתומה לעולם יש בה יין שאין דרך לסתום חבית ריקנית אבל חבית פתוחה פעמים יש בה יין פעמים אין בה יין כך בוגרת פעמים אין לה דמים פעמים יש לה ומשום הכי אין לה טענת דמים כדפר"ח ודאמר בפרק הבא על יבמתו (יבמות נט. ושם) פרט לבוגרת שכלו בתוליה: **לא** צריכא באשת כהן. וא"ת ונוקמה אחזקתה שהיא כשרה לכהונה ונימא דלאו תחתיו זינתה וי"ל דאדרבה אית לן למימר דהשתא נבעלה דאוקמה אחזקת הגוף שהיתה בתולה: **ואי** בעית אימא באשת ישראל דקביל בה אביה קידושין פחותה מבת ג' שנים. וא"ת אכתי איכא ספק ספיקא ספק באונס ספק ברצון וא"ת דברצון ספק כשהיא קטנה ופתוי קטנה אונס הוא כדאמרינן בהבא על יבמתו (שם סא:) וי"ל דשם אונס חד הוא וא"ת ונוקמה בחזקת היתר לבעלה וי"ל דאונסא קלא אית לה כדאמרינן בירושלמי [ג) אונסא יש לו קול] והשתא דליכא קלא הוי ליה רצון רובא ומיעוט אונס ורובא עדיף וא"ת א"כ בספק ספיקא נמי תיאסר דספק אונס כמאן דליתיה דמי ולא נשאר אלא חד ספק ספק תחתיו והכא לא שייך לאוקמה בחזקת היתר כדפי' א] ואומר ר"י דהאי רובא דברצון אינו רוב גמור אלא הוי מדרבנן והלכך במקום ספק ספיקא שרי ובמקום חד ספיקא חשבי רבנן רצון לגבי אונס רובא ואשכחן כי האי גוונא גבי תינוק שנמצא בצד העיסה (קידושין דף פ.) דלא הוי רובא אלא מדרבנן והכי קאמר ר' יוחנן התם דאין שורפין עליו את התרומה וא"ת אכתי באשת כהן ובקיבל אביה קידושין פחותה מבת שלש לישראל איכא ספק ספיקא דספק מוכת עץ ספק דרוסת איש [ד) באשת כהן אית לן למימר דנימא דאינה מוכת עץ מ"מ ספק תחתיו ספק אין תחתיו ובאשת ישראל דנימא דאינה מוכת עץ מ"מ ספק באונס ספק ברצון] ואין לומר דמוכת עץ לא שכיח דהא אמרינן באלו נערות (לקמן לו:) גבי סומא שאין לה טענת בתולים מפני שנחבטת על גבי קרקע ופריך כולהו נמי חבוטי מיחבטן א"כ שכיח ולפירוש ר"ת דמוכת עץ פתחה סתום אתי שפיר וי"ל דאם איתא דמוכת עץ היא הוה טוענת דאין גנאי בכך כמו בביאת אונס ומדלא טענה אין להסתפק בכך: **ומי** אמר ר' אלעזר הכי והאמר ר"א כו'. תימה השתא דבעי למימר דלא מהימן אפי' לשוייה עליה חתיכה דאיסורא תיקשי ליה מתני' דהאומר לאשה קידשתיך אסור בקרובותיה וי"ל דסבירא ליה למקשן דאין דבר שבערוה פחות משנים ואפי' ראה אדם שזינתה אשתו רק שלא היה שם עדים לא היתה נאסרת עליו והלכך ממתני' לא קשיא ליה מידי דקדשתיך בעדים קאמר דמקדש אפי' בעד אחד אין חוששין לקדושיו [ה) אבל אהא דאמר ר' אלעזר דנאמן בלא עדים לומר דמצא פתח פתוח פריך שפיר: **קינוי** וסתירה אין עדים לא. הכי נמי דלא אתא למעוטי על פי עצמו דכעדים דמי כיון דקים ליה:

מפני מה לא אסרוה. פירש הקונטרס והלא אותו מעשה בעדים הוה ואין נראה דנהי דידוע לרבים הוה שהביאה לביתו מ"מ לא ראו כמכחול בשפופרת שבפני בני אדם לא שמש ונראה לר"י לפרש וא"ת דפתח פתוח כשני עדים דמי אמאי לא אסרוה לדוד דדוד היה יודע בודאי שנבעלה ואע"פ שעשה תשובה מכל מקום עיכבה ואם היתה אסורה לו לא היה אותו צדיק לוקחה לו לאשה: כל

עין משפט נר מצוה

מז א ב ג מיי' פי"ח מהל' איסורי ביאה הל' י יא סמג לאוין קלא טוש"ע אה"ע סי' ו סעי' יד וסימן סח סעי' ז:

מח ד מיי' פ"ט מהל' אישות הל' טו טוש"ע שם סי' מח סעי' א:

מט ה מיי' פכ"ד מהל' אישות הל' יח סמג עשין מח טוש"ע סי' קטו וטוש"ע שם סי' יא סעי' א [וברב אלפס קידושין פ"ג ד' רלח:]:

נ ו מיי' פ"א מהל' סוטה הל' טו סמג עשין נו טוש"ע אה"ע סי' קעח סעי' יד [וברב אלפס שם]:

גליון הש"ס

גמ' התם אונס הוה. ע' יבמות נה ע"א תד"ה אע"פ:

הגהות מהר"ב רנשבורג

א] תד"ה ואב"א וכו' ואור"י דהאי רובא דברצון אינו רוב גמור. עי' פ"י ושו"ת הריב"ש סי' שע"ב וסדרי טהרה בנדה יח ע"א בתוס' ד"ה שלא וכו' ודו"ק:

ליקוטי רש"י

והוא אסור בקרובותיה. דשוינהו עליה חתיכה דאיסורא בהודאתו [קידושין סה.].

מסורת הש"ס

א) קדושין סה., ב) [ועיין היטב ערוך ערך פתח א'], ג) גי' רש"ל, ד) גי' רש"ל, ה) [כדאיתא קדושין סה.].

תוספות רי"ד

אמר ר"א האומר פתח פתוח מצאתי נאמן לאוסרה עליו. פי' שלא טען טענת דמים לומר בעלתי ולא מצאתי דמים כגון שהיתה בוגרת או שהיתה ממשפחת דורקטי נאמן לאוסרה עליו. פי' המורה ואע"פ שאין הדבר הזה יכול להתברר אלא על פיו לגבי נפשיה הוי מהימן לשוויה עליה חתיכה דאיסורא אבל להפסיד כתובה לא מהימן. **ואמאי** ספק ספיקא הוא ספק תחתיו זינתה וספק לא זינתה תחתיו ואת"ל תחתיו זינתה ספק באונס ספק ברצון. ל"צ באשת כהן פי' דאפילו באונס אסורה לו הלכך חד ספק הוא ואבע"א באשת ישראל וכגון דקיבל [בה] אבוה קידושין פחות מבת ג' שנים פי' שאין לומר קודם שאירסה זינתה שהרי בתוליה חוזרים ולא נשאר שם אלא חד ספק ומספיקא היא נאסרה לו: **מאי קמ"ל** תנינא פי' שאדם נאמן על עצמו לאסור לו את המותר עליו. האומר לאשה קדשתיך והיא אומרת לא קדשתני הוא אסור בקרובותיה פי' באמה ובתה ואחותה דשווינהו אנפשיה חתיכה דאיסורא והיא מותרת בקרוביו פי' שהרי אינה מודה בקידושיו ובמס' קידושין מוקי לה באומר לה קדשתיך בפני עדים והלכו להם למדינות הים. **מהו דתימא** התם הוא דודאי קים ליה פי' שקדשה אבל הכא מיקם הוא דלא קים ליה פי' מפני שהוא פנוי ויש לומר בחוצפא בעל ונ"ל כי פתוח היה ואינו כן א"כ לא תיתסר קמ"ל וכ"ש אם טען בעלתי ולא מצאתי דם בנערה שלא בגרה ואינה ממשפחת דורקטי שהוא נאמן לאוסרה עליו שהוא טענה ודאית יותר מפתח פתוח: **ומי א"ר אלעזר הכי** פי' דאשה מזנה נאסרת ע"פ עצמו והא א"ר אלעזר אין האשה נאסרת על בעלה אלא על ידי קינוי וסתירה. ולטעמיך קינוי וסתירה אין עדים לא פי' אם יש עדים שזינתה שמא אינה נאסרת בלא קינוי והכתיב כי מצא בה ערות דבר. אלא הכי קאמר אין האשה נאסרת על בעלה בעד א' אלא בשני עדים. וקינוי וסתירה אפילו בע"א. ופתח פתוח מצאתי כב' עדים דמי. פי' אע"פ שעד אחד נאמן באיסורין. היכא דאמר ליה ע"א אשתך זינתה אינו נאמן שאין דבר שבערוה פחות משנים ואם קינא ונסתרה ובא ע"א ואמר נטמאת נאמן וקורעת כתובתה ויוצאה ואם רוצה לשתות אין משקין אותה. גם אם אמר פתח פתוח מצאתי נאמן על עצמו כשני עדים ושוי אנפשיה חתיכה דאיסורא:

It is because **there it was** a case of **forced** cohabitation,[27] and a woman does not become forbidden to her husband under such circumstances.[28]

The Gemara offers a second answer to this question:

וְאִיבָּעִית אֵימָא – Or if you prefer, say that she did not become forbidden **כִּי הָא דְאָמַר רַבִּי שְׁמוּאֵל בַּר נַחְמָנִי אָמַר רַבִּי יוֹנָתָן – in accordance with that which R' Shmuel bar Nachmani said in the name of R' Yonasan:**

NOTES

rather the surviving fragment of a longer sentence, the rest of which was lost. The Gemara now reconstructs the full sentence, which was actually in the form of a question (*Rashba; Maharam Schif;* cf. *Maharsha* and *Shitah Mekubetzes*). [In this fragment, R' Elazar challenged his own ruling by asking why, if the mere knowledge of infidelity suffices to prohibit a woman, did Bathsheba not become prohibited to her husband and thus to David.] For there were many people who knew what had taken place between them (*Rashi;* see *Rashash*).

Tosafos object to this explanation because even though people knew that David had brought Bathsheba into his house, they did not actually witness their cohabitation. *Tosafos* therefore offer an alternative explanation of our Gemara. *Tos. HaRosh,* however, answers that since witnesses had seen David send for her and seclude himself with her, their knowledge was considered tantamount to witnessing cohabitation. [See *Ritva* and *Meiri* for entirely different approaches to this Gemara.]

27. [As the verse says (*II Samuel* 11:4): *And David sent messengers and took her,* indicating that she did not come to him of her own volition. According to Chida (*Teshuvos Chaim Shaal* 1:85), the Gemara means to suggest in this answer that David actually violated her. Others explain that though the act was consensual, David violated her in the legal sense, because Bathsheba was a minor at the time (see *Sanhedrin* 69b), and the seduction of a minor is considered violation [*Yevamos* 61b; see note 7 above] (*R' Yaakov Emden* in *Mitpachas Sefarim* §68; *Atzei Arazim, Even HaEzer* 11:12; see *Nachalas Shimon* to *II Samuel* Vol. 2 §20, for a discussion of these and other sources).]

28. As we learned above; see note 5. Thus, she did not become forbidden to David either, even though he was a willing participant in the adulterous act (*Ramban, Ritva, Meiri*). According to this answer, if someone rapes a married woman and her husband later divorces her, the rapist is then permitted to marry her (*Meiri*). Since the Gemara, however, offers a second answer to the question of why Bathsheba was later permitted to marry David, it is not clear that this novel ruling of the first answer is accepted as law. See *Beis Shmuel, Even HaEzer* 11:3, who discusses this matter at length.

האומר פתח פתוח מצאתי נאמן לאוסרה עליו ואמאי [א] ספק ספיקא הוא ספק תחתיו ספק אין תחתיו ואם תמצא לומר תחתיו ספק באונס ספק ברצון לא צריכא [ב] באשת כהן ואיבעית אימא [ג] באשת ישראל וכגון דקביל בה אבוה קידושין פחותה מבת ג' שנים ויום אחד מאי קמ"ל תנינא [א] [ד] האומר לאשה קדשתיך והיא אומרת לא קדשתני היא מותרת בקרוביו והוא אסור בקרובותיה מהו דתימא התם הוא דודאי קים ליה אבל הכא מיקם הוא דלא קים ליה קמ"ל ומי אמר רבי אלעזר הכי והאמר רבי אלעזר אין האשה נאסרת על בעלה אלא על עסקי קינוי וסתירה וכמעשה שהיה ותסברא מעשה שהיה בקינוי וסתירה הוה ועוד מי אסרוה הא לא קשיא הכי קאמר אין האשה נאסרת על בעלה אלא על עסקי קינוי וסתירה ממעשה שהיה דלא הוה קינוי וסתירה ולא איתסרא מכל מקום קשיא קינוי וסתירה אין פתח פתוח לא ולטעמיך קינוי וסתירה אין עדים לא אלא הכי קאמר [ה] אין האשה נאסרת על בעלה בעד אחד אלא בשני עדים [ו] וקינוי וסתירה אפילו בעד אחד נמי ופתח פתוח כשני עדים דמי וכי תימא מעשה שהיה מפני מה לא אסרוה [ט] התם אונס הוה ואיבעית אימא כי הא דאמר רבי שמואל בר נחמני אמר רבי יונתן כל

רש"י

האומר פתח פתוח מצאתי. וטענת דמים אין לו כגון שהיא ממשפחת דורקטי שאין להם דם בתולים כדלקמן (דף י:) או שנאבדה ממנו מפה ולא ידע אם היה דם אם לאו אבל זאת ברורה לו שפתח פתוח מצא: **נאמן לאוסרה עליו.** ואע"פ שאין הדבר הזה יכול להתברר אלא על פיו לגבי נפשיה הוי מהימן לשויה עליה חתיכה דאיסורא אבל להפסידה כתובתה לא מהימן: **ואמאי.** מיתסרא עליה אפי' אי מהימנת ליה דנבעלה: **ספק תחתיו.** משנתארסה זינתה: **ספק אין תחתיו.** אלא קודם שנתארסה זינתה: **ספק באונס.** ואנוסה שריא באשת ישראל כדלקמן (דף נא:) מוהיא לא נתפסה: **באשת כהן.** שהאונס אסור בה הלכך חד ספק הוא: **פחותה מבת ג' שנים.** ועכשיו היא גדולה ופיתוי ואינו אונס הלכך חד ספק איכא ספק אונס ספק רצון אבל ספק תחתיו ספק אין תחתיו ליכא שאילו נבעלה קודם לכן היו בתולים חוזרים כדתנן במסכת נדה (דף מד:) פחותה מכאן כנותן אצבע בעין שהדמעה יוצאה וחוזרת: **מאי קמ"ל תנינא.** שאדם נאמן על עצמו לאסור לו את המותר על פיו: **הוא אסור בקרובותיה.** באמה ובתה ואחותה דשוינהו אנפשיה חתיכה דאיסורא: **והיא מותרת בקרוביו.** שהרי אינה מודה בקידושין ובמסכת קידושין מוקמינן לה באומר קידשתיה בפני עדים והלכו להם למדינת הים: **דודאי קים ליה.** שקידשה: **אבל הכא.** אימא מתוך שפנוי היה ואינו בקי מיקם הוא דלא קים ליה כסבור שמצא פתח פתוח ואינו כן ולא תיאסר קמשמע לן: **ומי אמר רבי אלעזר הכי.** דאשה מזנה נאסרת על פי בעלה: **קינוי.** שאמר לה אל תסתרי עם פלוני: **וסתירה.** שבאו עדים שנסתרה עמו אחר קינוי: **וכמעשה שהיה.** דבת שבע: **ותסברא.** דהכי קא"ר אלעזר מעשה שהיה מי הוה ביה קינוי: **ועוד מי אסרוה.** על אוריה דאילו נאסרה על אוריה נאסרה אף על דוד דקיימא לן (סוטה דף כח.) כשם שאסורה לבעל כך אסורה לבועל: **הא לא קשיא.** כלומר משום הא קושיא לא תדחייה לרבי אלעזר: **הכי קאמר אין האשה נאסרת על בעלה אלא על עסקי קינוי וסתירה ממעשה שהיה.** ממעשה דבת שבע אנו למדין כן שלא היה שם קינוי וסתירה ולא אסרוה: **עדים לא.** בתמיה אפי' יש עדים שזינתה שמא אינה נאסרת בלא קינוי והא כתיב (דברים כד) כי מצא בה ערות דבר ועוד הא לא נתפסה אסורה: **אין האשה נאסרת על בעלה בעד אחד.** דיליף (סוטה דף ג:) דבר דבר מממון: **וקינוי וסתירה.** אם יש עדים שקינא לה ויש עדים שנסתרה אחר קינוי: **אפי' בעד אחד.** אפי' אין בטומאה אלא עד אחד נאמן דכתיב (במדבר ה) ועד אין בה ואמר מר (סוטה ב:) כל מקום שנאמר עד הרי כאן שנים וקאמר רחמנא עד אין בה תרי אלא חד והיא לא נתפשה אסורה שרגלים לדבר שזינתה שהרי קינא לה ונסתרה ועד אחד מעידה שהיא טמאה ומהשתא לא תקשי לך דרבי אלעזר דפתח פתוח לאוסרה על עצמו כשני עדים דמי שהרי דבר ברור הוא לו שנבעלה: **מפני מה לא אסרוה.** על דוד שהרי עדים הרבה ידעו:

גט

תוספות

האומר פתח פתוח מצאתי כו'. פירש בקונטרס דטענת דמים לא קאמר כגון שנאבדה המפה או שהיא ממשפחת דורקטי שאין להם דמים ור"ת מפרש דבוגרת ומוכת עץ אין להם דמים אבל אין פתחן פתוח ויכול לטעון טענת פתח וקשה לפר"ת דאמרי' באלו נערות (לקמן לו. ושם:) ובוגרת אין לה טענת בתולים והאמר רב בוגרת נותנים לה לילה הראשונה ומשני אי דקא טעין טענת דמים ה"נ הב"ע דקטעין טענת פתח פתוח משמע דבפתחה פתוח יש לה דמים וי"ל דר"ת גרים כגירסא ראשונה שהיתה בספרים [ג] אי דקא טעין טענת פתח פתוח הכי נמי הב"ע דקא טעין טענת דמים וה"פ והאמר רב בוגרת נותנין לה לילה הראשונה ומדתלינן כל הלילה בדם בתולים משמע דאית בוגרת דאית לה דם בתולים טובא אם כן אי אפשר לשום בוגרת שלא יהא פתחה סתום אפילו אין לה דמים וא"כ יש לה טענת בתולים בפתח פתוח ומשני אי דקטעין פתח פתוח ה"נ דיש לה טענת בתולים הב"ע דלית לה טענת בתולים בטענת דמים משום דאיכא בוגרת דדמיה כלין ומיהו בירושלמי משמע לא כפר"ת דקאמר התם ר' יונה בשם ר' קריספא בוגרת כחבית פתוחה של יין ויש לייתב לדעתי' דמים קאמר משום דקתם חבית סתומה אין לעולם יש בה יין שאין דרך לסתום חבית ריקנית אבל חבית פתוחה פעמים יש בה יין פעמים אין בה יין כך בוגרת פעמים אין לה דמים פעמים יש לה ומשום הכי אין לה טענת דמים כדפר"ת וכדאמר בפרק הבא על יבמתו (יבמות נט. ושם) פרט לבוגרת שכלו בתוליה: **לא צריכא באשת כהן.** וא"ת ונוקמה אחזקתה שהיא כשרה לכהונה ונימא דלאו תחתיו זינתה וי"ל דאדרבה אית לן למימר דהשתא נבעלה דאוקמה אחזקת הגוף שהיתה בתולה: **ואי בעית אימא באשת ישראל דקביל בה אביה קידושין פחותה מבת ג' שנים.** וא"ת אכתי איכא ספק ספיקא ספק באונס ספק ברצון ואת"ל ברצון ספק כשהיא קטנה ופתוי קטנה אונס הוא כדאמרינן בהבא על יבמתו (שם סא:) וי"ל דשם אונס חד הוא וא"ת ונוקמה בחזקת היתר לבעלה וי"ל דאונסא קלא אית לה כדאמרינן בירושלמי [ג] אונסא יש לו קול] והשתא דליכא קלא הוי ליה רצון רובא ומיעוט אונס ורובא וחזקה רובא עדיף וא"ת א"כ בספק ספיקא נמי תיאסר דספק אונס כמאן דליתיה דמי ולא נשאר אלא חד ספק ספק תחתיו והא לא שייך לאוקמה בחזקת היתר כדפי' [א] ואומר ר"י דהאי רובא דברצון אינו רוב גמור אלא הוי מדרבנן והלכך במקום ספק ספיקא שרי ובמקום חד ספיקא חשבי רבנן רצון לגבי אונס רובא ואשכחן כי האי גוונא גבי תינוק שנמצא בצד העיסה (קדושין דף פ.) דלא הוי רובא אלא מדרבנן ולהכי קאמר ר' יוחנן התם דאין שורפין עליו את התרומה וא"ת אכתי באשת כהן וקיבל אביה קידושין פחותה מבת שלש לישראל איכא ספק ספיקא דספק מוכת עץ ספק דרוסת איש [ד] באשת כהן אית לן למימר את"ל דאינה מוכת עץ מ"מ ספק תחתיו ספק אין תחתיו אשת ישראל את"ל דאינה מוכת עץ ספק באונס ספק ברצון] ואין לומר דמוכת עץ לא שכיח דהא אמרינן באלו נערות (לקמן לו:) גבי סומא שאין לה טענת בתולין מפני שנחבטה על גבי קרקע ופריך כולהו נמי חבוטי מיחבטן א"כ שכיח ולפירוש ר"ת דמוכת עץ פתחה סתום אתי שפיר וי"ל דאם איתא דמוכת עץ היא הוי טוענת דאין גנאי בכך כמו בביאת אונס ומדלא טענה אין להסתפק בכך: **ומי אמר ר' אלעזר הכי והאמר ר"א כו'.** תימה השתא דבעי למימר דלא מהימן אפי' לשויה עליה חתיכה דאיסורא תיקשי ליה מתני' דהאומר לאשה קידשתיך אסור בקרובותיה וי"ל דסבירא ליה למקשן דאין דבר שבערוה פחות משנים ואפי' ראה אדם שזינתה אשתו רק שלא היה שם עדים לא היתה נאסרת עליו והלכך ממתני' לא קשיא ליה מידי דקדשתיך בעדים קאמר דמקדש אפי' בעד אחד אין חוששין לקדושיו [ה] אבל אהא דאמר ר' אלעזר דנאמן בלא עדים לומר דמצא פתח פתוח פריך שפיר: **קינוי וסתירה אין עדים לא.** הכי נמי דלא אתא למעוטי על פי עצמו דכעדים דמי כיון דקים ליה: **מפני מה לא אסרוה.** פירש הקונטרס והלא אותו מעשה בעדים הוה ואין נראה דנהי דידוע לרבים הוה שהביאה לביתו מ"מ לא ראו כמכחול בשפופרת שבפני בני אדם לא שמש ונראה לר"י לפרש וא"ת דפתח פתוח כשני עדים דמי אמאי לא אסרוה לדוד דדוד היה יודע בודאי שנבעלה ואע"פ שעשה תשובה מכל מקום עיכבה ואם היתה אסורה לו לא היה אותו צדיק לוקחה לו לאשה:

כל

מסורת הש"ם

א) קדושין סה., ב) [ועיין היטב ערוך ערך פתח א'], ג) גי' רש"ל, ד) גי' רש"ל, ה) [כדאיתא קדושין סה.].

תוספות רי"ד

אמר ר"א האומר פתח פתוח מצאתי נאמן לאוסרה עליו. פי' שלא טען טענות דמים לומר בעלתי ולא מצאתי דמים כגון שהיתה בוגרת או שהיתה ממשפחת דורקטי נאמן לאוסרה עליו. פי' המורה ואע"פ שאין הדבר הזה יכול להתברר אלא על פיו לגבי נפשיה הוי מהימן לשוויה עליה חתיכה דאיסורא אבל להפסיד כתובה לא מהימן. **ואמאי** ספק ספיקא הוא ספק תחתיו זינתה וספק לא זינתה תחתיו ואת"ל תחתיו זינתה ספק באונס ספק ברצון. ל"צ באשת כהן פי' דאפילו באונס אסורה לו הלכך חד ספק הוא ואבע"א באשת ישראל וכגון דקיבל [בה] אבוה קידושין פחות מבת ג' שנים פי' שאין לומר קודם שאירסה זינתה שהרי בתוליה חוזרים ולא נשאר שם אלא חד ספק ומספיקא היא נאסרה לו: **מאי קמ"ל** תנינא פי' שאדם נאמן על עצמו לאסור לו את המותר עליו. האומר לאשה קדשתיך והיא אומרת לא קדשתני הוא אסור בקרובותיה פי' באמה ובתה ואחותה דשווינהו אנפשיה חתיכה דאיסורא והיא מותרת בקרוביו פי' שהרי אינה מודה בקידושיו ובמס' קידושין מוקי לה באומר לה קדשתיך בפני עדים והלכו להם למדינות הים. **מהו דתימא** התם הוא דודאי קים ליה פי' שקדשה אבל הכא מיקם הוא דלא קים ליה פי' מפני שהוא פנוי ויש לומר בחרוצפא בעל ונ"ל כי פתוח היה ואינו כן א"כ לא תיתסר קמ"ל וכ"ש אם טען בעלתי ולא מצאתי דם בנערה שלא בגרה ואינה ממשפחת דורקטי שהוא נאמן לאוסרה עליו שהוא טענה ודאית יותר מפתח פתוח: **ומי א"ר אלעזר הכי** פי' דאשה מזנה נאסרת ע"פ עצמו והא א"ר אלעזר אין האשה נאסרת על בעלה אלא על ידי קינוי וסתירה. ולטעמיך קינוי וסתירה אין עדים לא פי' אם יש עדים שזינתה שמא אינה נאסרת בלא קינוי והכתיב כי מצא בה ערות דבר. אלא הכי קאמר אין האשה נאסרת על בעלה בעד א' אלא בשני עדים. וקינוי וסתירה אפילו בע"א. ופתח פתוח מצאתי כב' עדים דמי. פי' אע"פ שעד אחד נאמן באיסורין. היכא דאמר ליה ע"א אשתך זינתה אינו נאמן שאין דבר שבערוה פחות משנים ואם קינא ונסתרה ובא ע"א ואמר נטמאת נאמן וקורעת כתובתה ויוצאה ואם רוצה לשתות אין משקין אותה. גם אם אמר פתח פתוח מצאתי נאמן על עצמו כשני עדים ושרי אנפשיה חתיכה דאיסורא:

עין משפט נר מצוה

מז א ב ג מיי' פי"ח מהל' איסורי ביאה הל' י' יא סמג לאוין קלה טוש"ע אה"ע סי' ו סעי' יד וסימן סח סעי' ז:

מח ד מיי' פ"ט מהל' אישות הל' טו טוש"ע שם סי' מח סעי' א:

מט ה מיי' פכ"ד מהל' אישות הל' יח סמג עשין מח טוש"ע סי' קטו וטוש"ע שם סי' יא סעי' א [וברב אלפס קידושין פ"ג ד' רלח:]:

נ ו מיי' פ"א מהל' סוטה הל' טו סמג עשין נו טוש"ע אה"ע סי' קעח סעי' יד [וברב אלפס שם]:

גליון הש"ס

גמ' התם אונס הוה. ע' יבמות לה ע"א תד"ה לא"פ:

הגהות מהר"ב רנשבורג

א] תד"ה ואב"א וכו' ואומר ר"י דהאי רובא דברצון אינו רוב גמור. עי' פ"י ושו"ת הרי"ם סי' שע"ג ובסדרי טהרה בנדה יח ע"א בתוס' ד"ה שלא וכו' ודו"ק:

ליקוטי רש"י

והוא אסור בקרובותיה. דשוינהו עליה חתיכה דאיסורא בהודאתו [קידושין סה.].

unfaithful to him.[16] Therefore, even if the husband's claim that he found no signs of virginity is correct, she should not become prohibited to him! — ? —

The Gemara challenges the accuracy of this last quotation: וְתִסְבְּרָא – **Now, do you think** that this is what R' Elazar actually said? How can it be? מַעֲשֶׂה שֶׁהָיָה בְּקִינּוּי וּסְתִירָה הֲוָה – **Was there any warning and seclusion in the incident that occurred** between King David and Bathsheba?[17] וְעוֹד מִי אֲסָרוּהָ – **And furthermore, did they** ever **prohibit [Bathsheba]** to her husband?[18] How then could R' Elazar have cited this incident as a precedent for his ruling that a woman becomes prohibited to her husband only by means of warning and seclusion?[19]

The Gemara defends the accuracy of the quotation by answering these questions:

הָא לֹא קַשְׁיָא – **This is not a difficulty,** הָכִי קָאָמַר – for we can say that **this is what [R' Elazar] meant:** אֵין הָאִשָּׁה נֶאֱסֶרֶת עַל בַּעְלָהּ אֶלָּא עַל עִסְקֵי קִינּוּי וּסְתִירָה – **A woman does not become prohibited to her husband except through acts of warning and seclusion,** מִמַּעֲשֶׂה שֶׁהָיָה – as evident **from the incident that occurred** between King David and Bathsheba, דְּלֹא הֲוָה קִינּוּי וּסְתִירָה וְלֹא אִיתַּסְרָא – **where there was no warning and seclusion, and she** therefore **did not become prohibited.**[20]

Having defended the accuracy of its quotation, the Gemara repeats its question:

מִכָּל מָקוֹם קַשְׁיָא – **It is nevertheless difficult.** קִינּוּי וּסְתִירָה אֵין – For R' Elazar's second ruling implies that through a **warning and seclusion** a woman does **indeed** become prohibited, פֶּתַח פָּתוּחַ לֹא – but through a claim of **an open entrance** she does **not** become prohibited. This contradicts the earlier statement of R' Elazar that a woman does become prohibited through this claim! — ? —

The Gemara begins its answer by demonstrating the inherent difficulty of R' Elazar's second ruling:

וּלְטַעֲמֵיךְ – **Now according to your reasoning,** we should also say that the wording of R' Elazar's statement implies קִינּוּי וּסְתִירָה אֵין – that through **a warning and seclusion** a woman does **indeed** becomes prohibited, עֵדִים לֹא – but through **witnesses** attesting to her adultery she does **not** become prohibited. But this is clearly not true![21] אֶלָּא הָכִי קָאָמַר – **Rather, this is what R' Elazar must mean:** אֵין הָאִשָּׁה נֶאֱסֶרֶת עַל בַּעְלָהּ בְּעֵד אֶחָד – **A woman does not become prohibited to her husband through** the testimony of **a single witness,**[22] אֶלָּא בִּשְׁנֵי עֵדִים – **but** only **through** the testimony of **two witnesses.** וְקִינּוּי וּסְתִירָה אֲפִילּוּ בְּעֵד אֶחָד נַמִּי – **However,** following **a warning and seclusion,** she becomes prohibited **even through** the testimony of **a single witness.**[23] וּפֶתַח פָּתוּחַ כִּשְׁנֵי עֵדִים דָּמֵי – **Now** the **claim of an open entrance is tantamount to** the testimony of **two witnesses** in regard to the husband himself, since he is certain about his claim.[24] Thus, R' Elazar's latter ruling does not contradict his earlier ruling.[25] וְכִי תֵּימָא מַעֲשֶׂה שֶׁהָיָה מִפְּנֵי מָה לֹא אֲסָרוּהָ – **And if you will ask why, in the incident that occurred** with King David, **did they not prohibit [Bathsheba]?**[26] הָתָם אוֹנֶס הֲוָה –

NOTES

16. See note 12.

17. Although Bathsheba had certainly secluded herself with David, there is no record that Uriah had ever warned her against such seclusion (*Ritva;* see also *Rashi* ד״ה ותסברא).

18. Had Bathsheba become prohibited to her husband Uriah as a result of her involvement with King David, she would have remained forbidden to David forever. The Gemara (*Sotah* 27b) teaches that whenever a woman becomes forbidden to her husband as a result of adultery, she also becomes forbidden to the man with whom she committed adultery (*Rashi;* cf. *Ritva, Re'ah*). Since Bathsheba married King David after Uriah's death, and remained married to him for the rest of his life, it is evident that she never became forbidden to Uriah.

19. Clearly, then, this last statement of R' Elazar cannot have been quoted accurately (see *Rashi* ד״ה ותסברא).

20. I.e. R' Elazar derives from the fact that Bathsheba did *not* become prohibited to Uriah, despite her involvement with David, that only a warning followed by seclusion [before witnesses] prohibits a woman to her husband, not adultery itself. Since no warning was ever given to Bathsheba, she did not become forbidden to Uriah (*Rashi*).

21. The testimony of two witnesses surely suffices to prohibit a woman to her husband, for the Torah states in regard to grounds for divorce (*Deuteronomy* 24:1): כִּי־מָצָא בָהּ עֶרְוַת דָּבָר, *for he found in her a matter of immorality* (*Rashi*). [Now the Gemara in *Sotah* 3b derives from a *gezeirah shavah* (explained in the next note) that this verse speaks of immorality discovered through the testimony of two witnesses. The verse teaches that upon hearing such testimony, a man has an obligation to divorce his wife. We see then that the testimony of two witnesses concerning her immorality is sufficient to prohibit her to her husband.] Moreover, the Torah states in regard to the adulteress (*Numbers* 5:13): וְהִוא לֹא נִתְפָּשָׂה, *and she had not been forced* [implying that a woman becomes an adulteress — and forbidden to her husband — simply by being a willing partner in the adulterous act, regardless of whether she was previously warned by her husband] (*Rashi;* see *Maharam Schif* who questions this latter source).

22. [This is derived from the following *gezeirah shavah:* The Torah says in regard to grounds for divorce (*Deuteronomy* 24:1): כִּי מָצָא בָהּ עֶרְוַת דָּבָר, *for he found in her a* ***matter*** *of immorality* (see previous note). In regard to monetary disputes the Torah says (*Deuteronomy* 19:15): עַל־פִּי שְׁנֵי עֵדִים ... יָקוּם דָּבָר, *according to two witnesses .... shall a* ***matter*** *be established.*] The word דָּבָר, *matter,* mentioned in each of these verses creates a *gezeirah shavah* which teaches that just as monetary matters are established only by two witnesses (as stated in that verse), so too matters of immorality (adultery) can be established (i.e. proven) only by two witnesses (*Rashi,* from Mishnah *Sotah* 31b).

23. That is, if there are two witnesses that she was warned and that she nevertheless secluded herself with the man against whom she was warned, even a single witness is then believed to establish that she committed an act of adultery (*Rashi*). This is derived from the verse concerning the suspected adulteress (*Numbers* 5:13): וְעֵד אֵין בָּהּ וְהִוא לֹא נִתְפָּשָׂה, *but there is no witness against her and she had not been forced.* Now wherever the Torah speaks of an עֵד, *witness,* without specifying a *single* witness, the Torah means two witnesses (as the Gemara demonstrates in *Sotah* 2b). Thus, when the verse says that "*there was no witness against her,*" it means that there were not *two* witnesses against her — but there was one. The verse then concludes that if *she had not been forced,* she is forbidden. This is because the warning and seclusion create a strong presumption of infidelity, making it possible to rely on the testimony of a single witness to establish definite adultery (*Rashi,* from *Sotah* 2a,b).

[Although warning and seclusion alone prohibit a woman to her husband, they do so only as a matter of doubt. Thus, the woman may still undergo the test of מֵים הַמָּרִים, *bitter waters,* to establish her innocence (see note 13). The testimony of a single witness at this point, however, renders her a confirmed adulteress, who may no longer undergo the test (*Tos. Rid*).]

24. *Rashi.* The Gemara has thus retracted its earlier position that a woman becomes forbidden only through witnesses (see note 12). The Gemara now returns to its original understanding that it is the act of infidelity alone that prohibits her; the testimony of witnesses is necessary only to establish that fact to the court. Consequently, the husband's certainty about the facts must be accepted in regard to him even though we have no way of confirming the accuracy of his claim; see note 11.

25. For as the Gemara has now explained it, the second ruling of R' Elazar is not a general statement about the only way a woman becomes forbidden to her husband, but a limited statement about the way a woman becomes forbidden by the testimony of a *single* witness (*Rashi,* as explained by *Maharam Schif; Rashba;* cf. *Maharshal, Maharsha, Pnei Yehoshua,* for other explanations).

26. This question is meant to elucidate the last phrase of R' Elazar's ruling, "and like the incident that occurred." As the Gemara now explains it, that phrase is not a support for the previous ruling, but

האומר פתח פתוח מצאתי נאמן לאוסרה עליו ואמאי א ספק ספיקא הוא ספק תחתיו ספק אין תחתיו ואם תמצא לומר תחתיו ספק באונס ספק ברצון לא צריכא ב באשת כהן ואיבעית אימא ג באשת ישראל וכגון דקביל בה אבוה קידושין פחותה מבת ג' שנים ויום אחד מאי קמ"ל תנינא א) ד האומר לאשה קדשתיך והיא אומרת לא קדשתני היא מותרת בקרוביו והוא אסור בקרובותיה מהו דתימא התם דודאי קים ליה אבל הכא מיקם הוא דלא קים ליה קמ"ל ומי אמר רבי אלעזר הכי והאמר רבי אלעזר אין האשה נאסרת על בעלה אלא על עסקי קינוי וסתירה וכמעשה שהיה ותסברא מעשה שהיה בקינוי וסתירה הוה ועוד מי אסרוה הא לא קשיא הכי קאמר אין האשה נאסרת על בעלה אלא על עסקי קינוי וסתירה ממעשה שהיה דלא הוה קינוי וסתירה ולא איתסרא מכל מקום קשיא קינוי וסתירה אין פתח פתוח לא ולטעמיך קינוי וסתירה אין עדים לא אלא הכי קאמר ה אין האשה נאסרת על בעלה בעד אחד אלא בשני עדים ו וקינוי וסתירה אפילו בעד אחד נמי ופתח פתוח כשני עדים דמי וכי תימא מעשה שהיה מפני מה לא אסרוה ◦ התם אונס הוה ואיבעית אימא כי הא דאמר רבי שמואל בר נחמני אמר רבי יונתן כל

רש"י

האומר פתח פתוח מצאתי. וטענת דמים אין לו כגון שהיא ממשפחת דורקטי שאין להם דם בתולים כדלקמן (דף י:) או שנאבדה ממנו מפה ולא ידע אם היה דם אם לאו אבל זאת ברורה לו שפתח פתוח מצא: נאמן לאוסרה עליו. ואע"פ שאין הדבר הזה יכול להתברר אלא על פיו לגבי נפשיה הוי מהימן לשוייה עליה חתיכה דאיסורא אבל להפסידה כתובתה לא מהימן: ואמאי. מיתסרא עליה אפי' אי מהימנת ליה דנבעלה: ספק תחתיו. משנתארסה זינתה: ספק אין תחתיו. אלא קודם שנתארסה זינתה: ספק באונס. ואנוסה שריא באשת ישראל כדלקמן (דף נא:) והיא לא נתפסה: באשת כהן. שהאונס אסור בה הלכך חד ספק הוא: פחותה מבת ג' שנים. ועכשיו היא גדולה ופיתוי ואינו אונס הלכך חד ספק איכא ספק אונס ספק רצון אבל ספק תחתיו ספק אין תחתיו ליכא שאילו נבעלה קודם לכן היו בתוליה חוזרים כדתנן במסכת נדה (דף מד:) פחות מכאן כנותן אצבע בעין שהדמעה יוצאה וחוזרת: מאי קמ"ל תנינא. שאדם נאמן על עצמו לאסור לו את המותר על פיו: הוא אסור בקרובותיה. באמה ובתה ואחותה דשוינהו אנפשיה חתיכה דאיסורא: והיא מותרת בקרוביו. שהרי אינה מודה בקידושין ובמסכת קידושין מוקמינן לה באומר קידשתיך בפני עדים והלכו להם למדינת הים: דודאי קים ליה. שקידשה: אבל הכא. אימא מתוך שפנוי היה ואינו בקי מיקם הוא דלא קים ליה כסבור שמצא פתח פתוח ואינו כן ולא תיאסר קמשמע לן: ומי אמר רבי אלעזר הכי. דאשה מזנה נאסרת על פי בעלה: קינוי. שאמר לה אל תסתרי עם פלוני: וסתירה. שבאו עדים שנסתרה עמו אחר קינוי: וכמעשה שהיה. דבת שבע: ותסברא. דהכי א"ר אלעזר מעשה שהיה מי הוה ביה קינוי: ועוד מי אסרוה. על אוריה דאילו נאסרה על אוריה נאסרה אף על דוד דקיימא לן (סוטה דף כז:) כשם שאסורה לבעל כך אסורה לבועל: הא לא קשיא. כלומר משום הא קושיא לא תדחייה לרבי אלעזר: הכי קאמר אין האשה נאסרת על בעלה אלא על עסקי קינוי וסתירה ממעשה שהיה. ממעשה דבת שבע אנו למדין כן שלא היה שם קינוי וסתירה ולא אסרוה: עדים לא. בתמיה אפי' יש עדים שזינתה שמא אינה נאסרת בלא קינוי והא כתיב (דברים כד) כי מצא בה ערות דבר ועוד הא לא נתפסה אסורה: אין האשה נאסרת על בעלה בעד אחד. דיליף (סוטה דף ג:) דבר דבר ממ ממון: וקינוי וסתירה. אם יש עדים שקינא לה ויש עדים שנסתרה אחר קינוי: אפי' בעד אחד. אפי' אין בטומאה אלא עד אחד נאמן דכתיב (במדבר ה) ועד אין בה ואמר מר (סוטה ב:) כל מקום שנאמר עד הרי כאן שנים וקאמר רחמנא עד אין בה תרי אלא חד והיא לא נתפסה אסורה שרגלים לדבר שזינתה שהרי קינא לה ונסתרה ועד אחד מעידה שהיא טמאה ומהשתא לא תקשי לך דרבי אלעזר דפתח פתוח לאוסרה על עצמו כשני עדים דמי שהרי דבר ברור הוא לו שנבעלה: מפני מה לא אסרוה. על דוד שהרי עדים הרבה ידעו: גט

תוספות

האומר פתח פתוח מצאתי כו'. פירש בקונטרס דטענת דמים לא קאמר כגון שנאבדה המפה או שהיא ממשפחת דורקטי שאין להם דמים ור"ת מפרש דבוגרת ומוכת עץ אין להם דמים אבל אין פתחן פתוח ויכול לטעון טענת פתח פתוח וקשה לפר"ת דאמרי' באלו נערות (לקמן לו. ושם:) ובוגרת אין לה טענת בתולים והאמר רב בוגרת נותנים לה לילה ראשונה ומשני אי דקא טעין טענת דמים ה"נ הב"ע דקטעין טענת פתח פתוח משמע דפתחה פתוח ויש לה דמים וי"ל דר"ת גרים כגירסא ראשונה שהיתה בספרים ג) אי דקא טעין טענת פתח פתוח הכי נמי הב"ע דקא טעין טענת דמים וה"פ והאמר רב בוגרת נותנין לה לילה הראשונה ומדתלין כל הלילה בדם בתולים משמע דאיכא בוגרת דאית לה דם בתולים טובא אם כן אי אפשר לשום בוגרת שלא יהא פתחה סתום אפילו אין לה דמים וא"כ יש לה טענת בתולים בפתח פתוח ומשני אי דקטעין פתח פתוח ה"נ דיש לה טענת בתולים הב"ע דלית לה טענת בתולים בטענת דמים משום דאיכא בוגרת דדמיה כלין ומיהו בירושלמי משמע לא כפר"ת דקאמר התם ר' יונה בשם ר' קריספא בוגרת כחבית פתוחה של יין ויש לייש' לענין דמים קאמר משום דסתם חבית סתומה לעולם יש בה יין שאין דרך לסתום חבית ריקנית אבל חבית פתוחה פעמים יש בה יין פעמים אין בה יין כך בוגרת פעמים אין לה דמים פעמים יש לה ומשום הכי אין לה טענת דמים כדפר"ח וכדאמר בפרק הבא על יבמתו (יבמות נט. ושם) פרט לבוגרת שכלו בתוליה: לא צריכא באשת כהן. וא"ת ונוקמה אחזקתה שהיא כשרה לכהונה ונימא דלאו תחתיו זינתה וי"ל דאדרבה אית לן למימר דהשתא נבעלה דאוקמה אחזקת הגוף שהיתה בתולה: ואי בעית אימא באשת ישראל דקביל בה אביה קידושין פחותה מבת ג' שנים. וא"ת אכתי איכא ספק ספיקא ספק באונס ספק ברצון ואת"ל ברצון ספק כשהיא קטנה ופתוי קטנה אונס הוא כדאמרינן בהבא על יבמתו (שם סא:) וי"ל דשם אונס חד הוא וא"ת ונוקמה בחזקת היתר לבעלה וי"ל דאונסא קלא אית לה כדאמרינן בירושלמי [ג) אונסא יש לו קול] והשתא דליכא קלא הוי ליה רצון רובא ומיעוט אונס ורובא וחזקה רובא עדיף וא"ת א"כ בספק ספיקא נמי תיאסר דספק אונס כמאן דליתיה דמי ולא נשאר אלא חד ספק ספק תחתיו ובהא לא שייך לאוקמה בחזקת היתר כדפי' א] ואומר ר"י דהאי רובא דברצון אינו רוב גמור אלא הוי מדרבנן והלכך במקום ספק ספיקא שרי ובמקום חד ספיקא חשבי רבנן רצון לגבי אונס רובא ואשכחן כי האי גוונא גבי תינוק שנמצא בצד העיסה (קדושין דף פ.) דלא הוי רובא אלא מדרבנן ולהכי קאמר ר' יוחנן התם דאין שורפין עליו את התרומה וא"ת אכתי באשת כהן ובקיבל אביה קדושין פחותה מבת שלש לישראל איכא ספק ספיקא דספק מוכת עץ ספק דרוסת איש [ד) באשת כהן אית לן למימר את"ל דאינה מוכת עץ מ"מ ספק תחתיו ספק אין תחתיו אשת ישראל את"ל דאינה מוכת עץ ספק באונס ספק ברצון] ואין לומר דמוכת עץ לא שכיח דהא אמרינן באלו נערות (לקמן לו:) גבי סומא שאין לה טענת בתולין מפני שנחבטה על גבי קרקע ופריך כולהו נמי חבוטי מיחבטן א"כ שכיח ולפירוש ר"ת דמוכת עץ פתחה סתום אתי שפיר וי"ל דאם איתא דמוכת עץ היא הויא טוענת דאין גנאי בכך כמו בביאת אונס ומדלא טענה אין להסתפק בכך: ומי אמר ר' אלעזר הכי והאמר ר"א כו'. תימה השתא דבעי למימר דלא מהימן אפי' לשויה עליה חתיכה דאיסורא תיקשי ליה מתני' דהאומר לאשה קידשתיך אסור בקרובותיה וי"ל דסבירא ליה למקשן דאין דבר שבערוה פחות משנים ואפי' ראה אדם שזינתה אשתו רק שלא היה שם עדים לא היתה נאסרת עליו והלכך ממתני' לא קשיא ליה מידי דקדשתיך בעדים קאמר דמקדש אפי' בעד אחד אין חוששין לקדושיו ה) אבל אהא דאמר ר' אלעזר דנאמן בלא עדים לומר דמצא פתח פתוח פריך שפיר: קינוי וסתירה אין עדים לא. הכי נמי דלא אתא למעוטי על פי עצמו דכעדים דמי כיון דקים ליה: מפני מה לא אסרוה. פירש הקונטרס והלא אותו מעשה בעדים הוה ואין נראה דנהי דידוע לרבים הוה שהביאה לביתו מ"מ לא ראו כמכחול בשפופרת שבפני בני אדם לא שמש ונראה לר"י לפרש וא"ת דפתח פתוח כשני עדים דמי אמאי לא אסרוה לדוד דדוד היה יודע בודאי שנבעלה ואע"פ שעשה תשובה מכל מקום עיכבה ואם היתה אסורה לו לא היה אותו צדיק לוקחה לו לאשה: כל

מסורת הש"ס

א) קדושין סה., ב) [ועיין היטב ערוך ערך פתח א'], ג) גי' רש"ל, ד) גי' רש"ל, ה) [כדאיתא קדושין סה.].

תוספות רי"ד

אמר ר"א האומר פתח פתוח מצאתי נאמן לאוסרה עליו. פי' שלא טען טענות דמים לומר בעלתי ולא מצאתי דמים כגון שהיתה בוגרת או שהיתה ממשפחת דורקטי נאמן לאוסרה עליו. פי' המורה ואע"פ שאין הדבר הזה יכול להתברר אלא על פיו לגבי נפשיה הוי מהימן לשוויה עליה חתיכה דאיסורא אבל להפסיד כתובה לא מהימן. ואמאי ספק ספיקא הוא ספק תחתיו זינתה וספק לא זינתה תחתיו ואת"ל תחתיו זינתה ספק באונס ספק ברצון. ל"צ באשת כהן פי' דאפילו באונס אסורה לו הלכך חד ספק הוא ואבע"א באשת ישראל וכגון דקיבל [בה] אבוה קידושין פחות מבת ג' שנים פי' שאין לומר קודם שאירסה זינתה שהרי בתוליה חוזרים ולא נשאר שם אלא חד ספק ומספיקא היא נאסרה לו: מאי קמ"ל תנינא פי' שאדם נאמן על עצמו לאסור לו את המותר עליו. האומר לאשה קדשתיך והיא אומרת לא קדשתני הוא אסור בקרובותיה פי' באמה ובתה ואחותה דשווינהו אנפשיה חתיכה דאיסורא והיא מותרת בקרוביו פי' שהרי אינה מודה בקידושיו ובמס' קידושין מוקי לה באומר קדשתיך בפני עדים והלכו להם למדינות הים. מהו דתימא התם הוא דודאי קים ליה פי' שקדשה אבל הכא מיקם הוא דלא קים ליה פי' מפני שהוא פנוי ויש לומר בחוצפא בעל ונ"ל כי פתוח היה ואינו כן א"כ לא תיתסר קמ"ל וכ"ש אם טען בעלתי ולא מצאתי דם בנערה שלא בגרה ואינה ממשפחת דורקטי שהוא נאמן לאוסרה עליו שהוא טענה ודאית יותר מפתח פתוח: ומי א"ר אלעזר הכי פי' דאשה מזנה נאסרת ע"פ עצמו והא א"ר אלעזר אין האשה נאסרת על בעלה אלא על ידי קינוי וסתירה. ולטעמיך קינוי וסתירה אין עדים לא פי' אם יש עדים שזינתה שמא אינה נאסרת בלא קינוי והכתיב כי מצא בה ערות דבר. אלא הכי קאמר אין האשה נאסרת על בעלה בעד א' אלא בשני עדים. וקינוי וסתירה אפילו בע"א. ופתח פתוח מצאתי כב' עדים דמי. פי' אע"פ שעד אחד נאמן באיסורין. היכא דאמר ליה ע"א אשתך זינתה אינו נאמן שאין דבר שבערוה פחות משנים ואם קינא ונסתרה ובא ע"א ואמר נטמאת נאמן וקורעת כתובתה ויוצאה ואם רוצה לשתות אין משקין אותה. גם אם אמר פתח פתוח מצאתי נאמן על עצמו כשני עדים ושוי אנפשיה חתיכה דאיסורא:

עין משפט
נר מצוה

מז א ב ג מיי' פי"ח מהל' איסורי ביאה הל' י יא סמג לאוין קלא טוש"ע אה"ע סי' ו סעי' יד וסימן סח סעי' ז:

מח ד מיי' פ"ט מהל' אישות הל' טו טוש"ע שם סי' מח סעי' א:

מט ה מיי' פכ"ד מהל' אישות הל' יח סמג עשין מח טוא"ע סי' קטו וטוש"ע שם סי' יא סעי' א [וברב אלפס קידושין פ"ג ד' רלח:]:

נ ו מיי' פ"א מהל' סוטה הל' טו סמג עשין נו טוש"ע אה"ע סי' קעח סעי' יד [וברב אלפס שם]:

גליון הש"ס

גמ' התם אונס הוה. ע' יבמות לה ע"א תד"ה אע"פ:

הגהות מהר"ב רנשבורג

א] תד"ה ואב"א וכו' ואור"י דהאי רובא דברצון אינו רוב גמור. עי' פ"י ושו"ת הריב"ש סי' שע"ב וסדרי טהרה בנדה יח ע"א בתוס' ד"ה שליא וכו' ודו"ק:

ליקוטי רש"י

והוא אסור בקרובותיה. דשוינהו עליה חתיכה דאיסורא בהודאתו [קידושין סה.].

with respect to **a Yisrael's** [i.e. non-Kohen's] **wife,** וּכְגוֹן דְּקַבִּיל בָּהּ אֲבוּהָ קִידּוּשִׁין פְּחוּתָה מִבַּת שָׁלֹשׁ שָׁנִים וְיוֹם אֶחָד – **in a case where her father accepted betrothal on her behalf** when she was **less than three years and a day old,** in which case her illicit cohabitation must have occurred after she was betrothed.[7]

Having defined the cases in which R' Elazar's ruling applies, the Gemara now questions the need for his ruling:

מַאי קָא מַשְׁמַע לָן – **What is [R' Elazar] informing us** by stating this ruling? תְּנֵינָא – **We have learned its** essential point [that a person's claim that something is forbidden to him is believed in regard to himself] **in the** following **Mishnah:**[8] הָאוֹמֵר לְאִשָּׁה קִדַּשְׁתִּיךְ – If [A MAN] SAYS TO A WOMAN, "I BETROTHED YOU," וְהִיא אוֹמֶרֶת לֹא קִדַּשְׁתַּנִי – AND SHE SAYS, "YOU DID NOT BETROTH ME," הִיא מוּתֶּרֶת בִּקְרוֹבָיו – SHE IS PERMITTED TO marry HIS close RELATIVES, וְהוּא אָסוּר בִּקְרוֹבוֹתֶיהָ – BUT HE IS FORBIDDEN TO marry HER close RELATIVES, since according to his own words they are his wife's relatives.[9]

The Gemara answers:

מַהוּ דְּתֵימָא הָתָם דְּוַדַּאי קִים לֵיהּ – Based on that Mishnah **you might have said that** one becomes forbidden by his own words only in the case **there, where he knows with certainty** whether he betrothed her, אֲבָל הָכָא מֵיקַם הוּא דְּלָא קִים לֵיהּ – **but here,** where he claims to have found "an open entrance," we say that **he does not really know** whether he found one or not, and we therefore permit her to him despite his claim.[10] קָא מַשְׁמַע לָן – **[R' Elazar]** therefore **informs us** that she in fact becomes prohibited to him.[11]

The Gemara asks:

וּמִי אָמַר רַבִּי אֶלְעָזָר הָכִי – **But did R' Elazar** really **say this?**[12] וְהָאָמַר רַבִּי אֶלְעָזָר – **But R' Elazar said** elsewhere: אֵין הָאִשָּׁה נֶאֱסֶרֶת עַל בַּעְלָהּ אֶלָּא עַל עִסְקֵי קִינּוּי וּסְתִירָה – **A woman does not become prohibited to her husband except through acts of warning and seclusion,**[13] וּכְמַעֲשֶׂה שֶׁהָיָה – **and like the incident that occurred** between King David and Bathsheba.[14] This implies that a woman becomes prohibited to her husband only through the formal procedures established by the Torah,[15] but not simply by the husband's knowledge that she has been

NOTES

7. When cohabitation takes place with a girl younger than three, the hymen eventually returns to a complete state (see *Niddah* 44b and Mishnah below, 11a). Hence, the absence of a hymen cannot be attributed to cohabitation that took place before the age of three. Now, if a girl's father betrothed her to a man when she was less than three years old [which he is permitted to do], and her husband later found her not to be a virgin, clearly she must have cohabited with someone *after* her betrothal. For if the illicit cohabitation had occurred before her betrothal, the signs of her virginity would have returned! Accordingly, only a single doubt remains — whether she cohabited with someone during her betrothal period willingly or by force. Since there is now but a single doubt, she is prohibited to her husband (*Rashi*).

Rashi adds that the *chuppah* in this case must have taken place when she was an adult [i.e. at least twelve years old]. For if it took place while she was still a minor, there would be *no* possibility of her being forbidden to her husband, because even if she consented to the adultery, the consent of a minor is not considered legally significant and is counted rather as coercion (פִּתּוּי קְטַנָּה אוֹנֶס; see *Yevamos* 61b; see, however, *Rambam, Isurei Biah* 3:2 and *Maggid Mishneh* there).

[*Tosafos* ask why there is not a סְפֵק סְפֵיקָא, *double doubt,* to permit her even where the *chuppah* took place when she was an adult. For it is possible that she was violated against her will, and even if she was a willing participant, it is possible that she did so as a minor, in which case the act is *legally* considered to have been coerced! *Tosafos* answer that since the *legal* basis for permitting her is the same in both cases — viz. that she was coerced — the various factual possibilities are all treated as a single doubt. (This rule, which is known as שֵׁם אוֹנֶס חַד הוּא, *the coercion classification is one,* has broad application to the rules of סְפֵק סְפֵיקָא, *double doubts.* See *Shach, Yoreh Deah* 110, *Dinei Sfeik Sfeika* §11,12.)

Tosafos also ask why even a single doubt about her permissibility should not be resolved in her favor on the basis of the rule of *chazakah,* which states that a matter of doubt is resolved by assuming that the previous status continues to prevail until it can be clearly shown to have changed. Since the bride was at one point certainly permitted to him, that earlier status should decide the doubt in favor of assuming that she is still permitted to him. *Tosafos* and other Rishonim and Acharonim discuss this and similar questions at great length, but their answers are beyond the scope of this work.]

8. *Kiddushin* 65a.

9. When a man betroths a woman, several of her immediate relatives [mother, sisters and daughters] become Biblically forbidden to him. Likewise, the woman becomes permanently prohibited to several of the man's relatives [father, sons, brothers and brothers' sons] (see *Leviticus* ch. 18).

In the Mishnah's case, a man claims to have betrothed a woman [in the presence of witnesses (*Rashi* ד״ה והיא)], but he cannot produce the witnesses to prove this, and indeed, the woman denies his claim. The woman is therefore free to marry any of his relatives, for it cannot be established that she was betrothed by him. As for the man, however, it makes no difference that his claim cannot be verified. Since he says that he betrothed her, he is in effect declaring that her close relatives are forbidden to him in marriage, and he is therefore prohibited to marry them (*Rashi*).

10. Since the groom was never married before, he does not really know what constitutes an "open entrance." Thus, he may mistakenly claim to have encountered one when in fact he did not (*Rashi*). [Although R' Elazar said his ruling in regard to all men, whether previously married or not, the *novelty* of his ruling is in regard to a man never previously married. *Rashi's* view in this matter will be discussed further on 10a in note 19; cf. *Ritva.*]

11. Since he claims to be sure, his claim renders her prohibited to him [שַׁוְּיָהּ אַנַּפְשֵׁיהּ חֲתִיכָה דְּאִיסּוּרָא] — even though he may be mistaken due to his inexperience (*Shitah Mekubetzes* ד״ה נאמן לאוסרה, in explanation of *Rashi;* see further, 9b note 12 and 10a note 19. See also *Rashba* and *Shitah LaRan* to 10a ד״ה רבי אחאי). Others explain the Gemara's answer to be that even a new husband can be assumed to know when the signs of virginity are missing and when they are not (*Ritva,* see also *Tosafos* 2a ד״ה שאם; see further, *Chavos Yair* §166).

12. I.e. did R' Elazar in fact say that a woman who is unfaithful to her husband becomes forbidden to him on the basis of his knowledge of that fact? (*Rashi,* as explained by *Rashba*). The Gemara will now attempt to prove from another statement of R' Elazar that the prohibition arising from infidelity is treated like other matters of marital law (e.g. *kiddushin* and divorce) in which an act does not have legal standing unless it is witnessed by two proper witnesses (אֵין דָּבָר שֶׁבְּעֶרְוָה פָּחוֹת מִשְּׁנַיִם). Accordingly, even if a man actually *saw* his wife being unfaithful, she would not be forbidden to him unless the act was seen by two witnesses. Certainly, then, she does not become forbidden merely because he found an open entrance (*Tosafos; Rashba,* in explanation of *Rashi;* cf. *Rashba, Ritva*).

[According to this view, we must say that the reason the Sages enacted that a virgin marry on Wednesday (Mishnah 2a) is so that the groom's complaint about a lack of virginity should prompt witnesses to come forward and testify about her act of infidelity, as *Rashi* explained on 2a (*Chidushei R' Akiva Eiger* 2a).]

13. Under Torah law (see *Numbers* 5:11-14), if a husband warns his wife [before witnesses] not to seclude herself with a specific man, and the wife disregards the warning and is observed by witnesses going into seclusion with that man, she becomes prohibited to her husband even though no one saw them actually cohabiting (*Rashi;* see Mishnah, *Sotah* 2a). Although it is not certain that she committed adultery, the Torah forbids her to her husband as a *sotah* unless she establishes her innocence by being tested in the Temple with the מַיִם הַמָּרִים, *bitter waters,* as described in *Numbers* ch. 5.

14. King David cohabited with Bathsheba after her husband, Uriah the Hittite, went off to battle (*II Samuel* 11:3). The Gemara below will elaborate on what actually happened.

15. [I.e. witnesses to her warning and seclusion, or witnesses to her infidelity.] See note 12.

האומר פתח פתוח מצאתי נאמן לאוסרה עליו ואמאי [א] ספק ספיקא הוא ספק תחתיו ספק אין תחתיו ואם תמצא לומר תחתיו ספק באונס ספק ברצון לא צריכא [ב] באשת כהן ואיבעית אימא [ג] באשת ישראל וכגון דקביל בה אבוה קידושין פחותה מבת ג' שנים ויום אחד מאי קמ"ל תנינא [א] [ד] האומר לאשה קדשתיך והיא אומרת לא קדשתני היא מותרת בקרוביו והוא אסור בקרובותיה מהו דתימא התם דודאי קים ליה אבל הכא מיקם הוא דלא קים ליה קמ"ל ומי אמר רבי אלעזר הכי והאמר רבי אלעזר אין האשה נאסרת על בעלה אלא על עסקי קינוי וסתירה וכמעשה שהיה ותסברא מעשה שהיה בקינוי וסתירה הוה ועוד מי אסרוה הא לא קשיא הכי קאמר אין האשה נאסרת על בעלה אלא על עסקי קינוי וסתירה ממעשה שהיה דלא הוה קינוי וסתירה ולא איתסרא מכל מקום קשיא קינוי וסתירה אין פתח פתוח לא ולטעמיך קינוי וסתירה אין עדים לא אלא הכי קאמר [ה] אין האשה נאסרת על בעלה בעד אחד אלא בשני עדים [ו] וקינוי וסתירה אפילו בעד אחד נמי ופתח פתוח כשני עדים דמי וכי תימא מעשה שהיה מפני מה לא אסרוה ◦ התם אונס הוה ואיבעית אימא כי הא דאמר רבי שמואל בר נחמני אמר רבי יונתן כל

רש"י

האומר פתח פתוח מצאתי. וטענת דמים אין לו כגון שהיא ממשפחת דורקטי שאין להם דם בתולים כדלקמן (דף י:) או שנאבדה ממנו מפה ולא ידע אם היה דם אם לאו אבל זאת ברורה לו שפתחה פתוח מצא: **נאמן לאוסרה עליו.** ואע"פ שאין הדבר הזה יכול להתברר אלא על פיו לגבי נפשיה הוי מהימן לשויה עליה חתיכה דאיסורא אבל להפסידה כתובתה לא מהימן: **ואמאי.** מיתסרא עליה אפי' אי מהימנת ליה דנבעלה: **ספק תחתיו.** משנתארסה זינתה: **ספק אין תחתיו.** אלא קודם שנתארסה זינתה: **ספק באונס.** ואנוסה שריא באשת ישראל כדלקמן (דף נא:) והיא לא נתפשה: **באשת כהן.** שהאונס אסור בה הלכך חד ספק הוא: **פחותה מבת ג' שנים.** ועכשיו היא גדולה ופיתויה פיתוי ואינו אונס הלכך חד ספק איכא ספק אונס ספק רצון אבל ספק תחתיו ספק אין תחתיו ליכא שאילו נבעלה קודם לכן היו בתוליה חוזרים כדתנן במסכת נדה (דף מד:) פחות מכאן כנותן אצבע בעין שהדמעה יוצאת וחוזרת: **מאי קמ"ל תנינא.** שאדם נאמן על עצמו לאסור לו את המותר על פיו: **הוא אסור בקרובותיה.** באמה ובתה ואחותה דשויהו אנפשיה חתיכה דאיסורא: **והיא מותרת בקרוביו.** שהרי אינה מודה בקידושין ובמסכת קידושין מוקמינן לה באומר קידשתיך בפני עדים והלכו להם למדינת הים: **דודאי קים ליה.** שקידשה: **אבל הכא.** אימא מתוך שפנוי היה ואינו בקי מיקם הוא דלא קים ליה כסבור שמצא פתח פתוח ואינו כן ולא תיאסר קמשמע לן: **ומי אמר רבי אלעזר הכי.** דאשה מזנה נאסרת על פי בעלה: **קינוי.** שאמר לה אל תסתרי עם פלוני: **וסתירה.** שבאו עדים שנסתרה עמו אחר קינוי: **וכמעשה שהיה. ותסברא.** דהכי א"ר אלעזר מעשה שהיה מי הוה ביה קינוי: **ועוד מי אסרוה.** על אוריה דאילו נאסרה על אוריה נאסרה אף על דוד דקיימא לן (סוטה דף כח.) כשם שאסורה לבעל כך אסורה לבועל: **הא לא קשיא.** כלומר משום הא קושיא לא תדחייה לרבי אלעזר: **הכי קאמר אין האשה נאסרת על בעלה אלא על עסקי קינוי וסתירה ממעשה שהיה.** ממעשה דבת שבע אנו למדין כן שלא היה שם קינוי וסתירה ולא אסרוה: **עדים לא.** בתמיה אפי' יש עדים שזינתה שמא אינה נאסרת בלא קינוי והא כתיב (דברים כד) כי מצא בה ערות דבר ועוד הא לא נתפשה אסורה: **אין האשה נאסרת על בעלה בעד אחד.** דיליף (סוטה דף ג:) דבר דבר ממונו: **וקינוי וסתירה.** אם יש עדים שקינא לה ויש עדים שנסתרה אחר קינוי: **אפי' בעד אחד.** אפי' אין בטומאה אלא עד אחד נאמן דכתיב (במדבר ה) ועד אין בה ואמר מר (סוטה ב:) כל מקום שנאמר עד הרי כאן שנים וקאמר רחמנא עד אין בה תרי אלא חד והיא לא נתפשה אסורה דרגלים לדבר שזינתה שהרי קינא לה ונסתרה ועד אחד מעידה שהיא טמאה ומהשתא לא תקשי לך לרבי אלעזר דפתח פתוח לאוסרה על עצמו כשני עדים דמי שהרי דבר ברור הוא לו שנבעלה: **מפני מה לא אסרוה.** על דוד שהרי עדים הרבה ידעו: גט

תוספות

האומר פתח פתוח מצאתי כו'. פירש בקונטרס דטענת דמים לא קאמר כגון שנאבדה המפה או שהיא ממשפחת דורקטי שאין להם דמים ור"ת מפרש דבוגרת ומוכת עץ אין להם דמים אבל אין פתחן פתוח ויכול לטעון טענת פתח פתוח וקשה לפר"ת דאמרי' באלו נערות (לקמן לו. ושם:) ובוגרת אין לה טענת בתולים והאמר רב בוגרת נותנים לה לילה הראשונה ומשני אי דקא טעין טענת דמים ה"נ הכ"ע דקטעין טענת פתח פתוח משמע דפתחה פתוח ויש לה דמים וי"ל דר"ת גרים כגירסא ראשונה שהיתה בספרים [ג] אי דקא טעין טענת פתח פתוח הכי נמי הכ"ע דקא טעין טענת דמים וה"פ והאמר רב בוגרת נותנין לה לילה הראשונה ומדתלין כל הלילה בדם בתולים משמע דאיכא בוגרת דאית לה דם בתולים טובא אם כן אי אפשר לשום בוגרת שלא יהא פתחה סתום אפילו אין לה דמים וא"כ יש לה טענת בתולים בפתח פתוח ומשני אי דקטעין פתח פתוח ה"נ דיש לה טענת בתולים הכ"ע דלית לה טענת בתולים בטענת דמים משום דאיכא בוגרת דדמיה כלין ומיהו בירושלמי משמע לא כפר"ת דקאמר התם ר' יונה בשם ר' קריספא בוגרת כחבית פתוחה של יין ויש לייחשב לענין דמים קאמר משום דסתם חבית סתומה לעולם יש בה יין שאין דרך לסתום חבית ריקנית אבל חבית פתוחה פעמים יש בה יין פעמים אין בה יין כך בוגרת פעמים אין לה דמים פעמים יש לה ומשום הכי אין לה טענת דמים כדפר"ת וכדאמר בפרק הבא על יבמתו (יבמות נט. ושם) פרט לבוגרת שכלו בתוליה: **לא** צריכא באשת כהן. וא"ת ונוקמה אחזקתה שהיא כשרה לכהונה ונימא דלאו תחתיו זינתה וי"ל דאדרבה אית לן למימר דהשתא נבעלה דאוקמה אחזקת הגוף שהיתה בתולה: **ואי** בעית אימא באשת ישראל דקביל בה אביה קידושין פחותה מבת ג' שנים. וא"ת אכתי איכא ספק ספיקא ספק באונס ספק ברצון וא"ת ברצון ספק כשהיא קטנה ופתוי קטנה אונס הוא כדאמרינן בהבא על יבמתו (שם סא:) וי"ל דשם אונס חד הוא וא"ת ונוקמה בחזקת היתר לבעלה וי"ל דאונסא קלא אית לה כדאמרינן בירושלמי [ז] אונסא יש לו קול] והשתא דליכא קלא הוי ליה רצון רובא ומיעוט אונס ורובא וחזקה רובא עדיף וא"ת א"כ בספק ספיקא נמי תיאסר דספק אונס כמאן דליתיה דמי ולא נשאר אלא חד ספק ספק תחתיו והא לא שייך לאוקמה בחזקת היתר כדפי' **או** ואומר ר"י דהאי רובא דברצון אינו רוב גמור אלא הוי מדרבנן והלכך במקום ספק ספיקא שרי ובמקום חד ספיקא חשבי רבנן רצון לגבי אונס רובא ואשכחן כי האי גוונא גבי תינוק שנמצא בצד העיסה (קדושין דף פ.) דלא הוי רובא אלא מדרבנן והכי קאמר ר' יוחנן התם דאין שורפין עליו את התרומה וא"ת אמאי באשת כהן וקיבל אביה קידושין פחותה מבת שלש לישראל איכא ספק ספיקא דספק מוכת עץ ספק דרוסה איש [ד] באשת כהן אית לן למימר את"ל דאינה מוכת עץ מ"מ ספק תחתיו ספק אין תחתיו אשת ישראל את"ל דאינה מוכת עץ ספק באונס ספק ברצון] ואין לומר דמוכת עץ לא שכיח דהא אמרינן באלו נערות (לקמן לו:) גבי סומא שאין לה טענת בתולין מפני שנחבטה על גבי קרקע ופריך כולהו נמי מחבטן מיחבטן א"כ שכיח ולפירוש ר"ת דמוכת עץ פתחה סתום אתי שפיר וי"ל דאם איתא דמוכת עץ היא הוית טוענת דאין גנאי בכך כמו בביאת אונס ומדלא טענה אין להסתפק בכך: **ומי** אמר ר' אלעזר הכי והאמר ר"א כו'. תימה השתא דבעי למימר דלא מהימן אפי' לשוויה עליה חתיכה דאיסורא תיקשי ליה מתני' דהאומר לאשה קדשתיך אסור בקרובותיה וי"ל דסבירא ליה למקשן דאין דבר שבערוה פחות משנים ואפי' ראה אדם שזינתה אשתו רק שלא היה לה עדים לא היה אוסרה עליו והלכך מתני' לא קשיא ליה מידי דקדשתיך בעדים קאמר דמקדש אפי' בעד אחד אין חוששין לקדושיו [ה] אבל אהא דאמר ר' אלעזר דנאמן בלא עדים לומר דמצא פתח פתוח פריך שפיר: **קינוי** וסתירה אין עדים לא. הכי נמי דלא אתא למעוטי על פי עצמו דכעדים דמי כיון דקים ליה:

מפני מה לא אסרוה. פירש הקונטרס והלא אותו מעשה בעדים הוה ואין נראה דנהי דידוע לרבים הוה שהביאה לביתו מ"מ לא ראו כמכחול בשפופרת שבפני בני אדם לא שמש ונראה לר"י דפתח פתוח כשני עדים דמי ואמאי לא אסרוה לדוד דדוד היה יודע בודאי שנבעלה ואע"פ שעשה תשובה מכל מקום עיכבה ואם היתה אסורה לו לא היה לוקחה לו לאשה: כל

מסורת הש"ס

א) קדושין סה., ב) [ועיין היטב ערוך ערך פתח א'], ג) גי' רש"ל, ד) גי' רש"ל, ה) [כדאיתא קדושין סה.].

תוספות רי"ד

אמר ר"א האומר פתח פתוח מצאתי נאמן לאוסרה עליו. פי' שלא טען טענות דמים לומר בעלתי ולא מצאתי דמים כגון שהיתה בוגרת או שהיתה ממשפחת דורקטי נאמן לאוסרה עליו. פי' המורה ואע"פ שאין הדבר הזה יכול להתברר אלא על פיו לגבי נפשיה הוי מהימן לשוויה עליה חתיכה דאיסורא אבל להפסיד כתובה לא מהימן. **ואמאי** ספק ספיקא הוא ספק תחתיו זינתה וספק לא זינתה תחתיו ואת"ל תחתיו זינתה ספק באונס ספק ברצון. ל"צ באשת כהן פי' דאפילו באונס אסורה לו הלכך חד ספק הוא ואבע"א באשת ישראל וכגון דקיבל [בה] אבוה קידושין פחות מבת ג' שנים פי' שאין לומר קודם שאירסה זינתה שהרי בתוליה חוזרים ולא נשאר שם אלא חד ספק ומספיקא היא נאסרה לו: **מאי קמ"ל** תנינא פי' שאדם נאמן על עצמו לאסור לו את המותר עליו. האומר לאשה קדשתיך והיא אומרת לא קדשתני הוא אסור בקרובותיה פי' באמה ובתה ואחותה דשווינהו אנפשיה חתיכה דאיסורא והיא מותרת בקרוביו פי' שהרי אינה מודה בקידושיו ובמס' קידושין מוקי לה באומר לה קדשתיך בפני עדים והלכו להם למדינות הים. **מהו דתימא** התם הוא דודאי קים ליה פי' שקדשה אבל הכא מיקם הוא דלא קים ליה פי' מפני שהוא פנוי ויש לומר בחוצפא בעל ונ"ל כי פתוח היה ואינו כן א"כ לא תיתסר קמ"ל וכ"ש אם טען בעלתי ולא מצאתי דם בנערה שלא בגרה ואינה ממשפחת דורקטי שהוא נאמן לאוסרה עליו שהוא טענה ודאית יותר מפתח פתוח: **ומי א"ר אלעזר הכי** פי' דאשה מזנה נאסרת ע"פ עצמו והא א"ר אלעזר אין האשה נאסרת על בעלה אלא על ידי קינוי וסתירה. ולטעמיך קינוי וסתירה אין עדים לא פי' אם יש עדים שזינתה שמא אינה נאסרת בלא קינוי והכתיב כי מצא בה ערות דבר. אלא הכי קאמר אין האשה נאסרת על בעלה בעד א' אלא בשני עדים. וקינוי וסתירה אפילו בע"א. ופתח פתוח מצאתי כב' עדים דמי. פי' אע"פ שעד אחד נאמן באיסורין. היכא דאמר ליה ע"א אשתך זינתה אינו נאמן שאין דבר שבערוה פחות משנים ואם קינא ונסתרה ובא ע"א ואמר נטמאת נאמן וקורעת כתובתה ויוצאה ואם רוצה לשתות אין משקין אותה. גם אם אמר פתח פתוח מצאתי נאמן על עצמו כשני עדים ושוי אנפשיה חתיכה דאיסורא:

עין משפט נר מצוה

מז א ב ג מיי' פי"ח מהל' איסורי ביאה הל' י יא סמג לאוין קלא טוש"ע אה"ע סי' ו סעי' יד וסימן סח סעי' ז:

מח ד מיי' פ"ט מהל' אישות הל' טו טוש"ע שם סי' מח סעי' א:

מט ה מיי' פכ"ד מהל' אישות הל' יח סמג עשין מח טואה"ע סי' קטו וטוש"ע שם סי' יא סעי' א [וברב אלפס קידושין פ"ג ד' רלח:]:

נ ו מיי' פ"א מהל' סוטה הל' טו סמג עשין ט טוש"ע אה"ע סי' קעח סעי' יד [וברב אלפס שם]:

גליון הש"ס

גמ' התם אונס הוה. ע' יבמות לה ע"א תד"ה אע"פ:

הגהות מהר"ב רנשבורג

א] תד"ה ואב"א וכו' ואור"י דהאי רובא דברצון אינו רוב גמור. ע' פ"י ושו"ת הריב"ש סי' שע"ב וסדרי טהרה בנדה יח ע"א בתוס' ד"ה שליא וכו' ודו"ק:

ליקוטי רש"י

והוא אסור בקרובותיה. דשוינהו עליה חתיכה דאיסורא בהודאתו [קידושין סה.].

הָאוֹמֵר פֶּתַח פָּתוּחַ מָצָאתִי – One who says, "I found in my bride **an 'open entrance,' "**[1] **נֶאֱמָן לְאוֹסְרָהּ עָלָיו – is believed to render her forbidden to him.**[2]

The Gemara asks:

וְאַמַּאי – But why should she be rendered forbidden on this basis? Even if we believe his claim that she previously cohabited with another man,[3] **סְפֵק סְפֵיקָא הוּא – it is** a case of **a double doubt** whether she is forbidden to him. **סָפֵק תַּחְתָּיו סָפֵק אֵין תַּחְתָּיו –** First, there is the **doubt** whether her previous cohabitation occurred **under [his authority],** i.e. during her betrothal to him, **or** whether it occurred when she was **not** yet **under [his authority],** i.e. before her betrothal.[4] **וְאִם תִּמְצָא לוֹמַר תַּחְתָּיו – And** even **if you will say** that it occurred **under [his authority], סָפֵק בְּאוֹנֶס סָפֵק בְּרָצוֹן –** there is still **a doubt** whether it occurred **by force or by consent.**[5] – ? –

The Gemara answers:

לֹא צְרִיכָא בְּאֵשֶׁת כֹּהֵן – [R' Elazar's ruling] is applicable only with reference to **a Kohen's wife,** who becomes forbidden to him even if she was violated by force.[6] **וְאִיבָּעֵית אֵימָא בְּאֵשֶׁת יִשְׂרָאֵל – Or, if you wish, say** that R' Elazar's ruling is applicable even

NOTES

1. I.e. he claims that he encountered no resistance during penetration (*Rambam, Ishus* 11:9), indicating that her hymen (בְּתוּלִים) had already been torn by a previous cohabitation with someone else. [Since the walls of the vaginal canal are drawn together by the hymenal membrane, thereby constricting the canal and partially closing it (see *Rashi* 5b ד״ה או חבורי מיחבר, and 36b ד״ה ה״ג), the failure to encounter resistance during cohabitation is euphemistically referred to as finding "an open entrance."]

The claim made in this case is only that there was an "open entrance," but not the [more clear-cut] claim that no blood was found following the first cohabitation [which also indicates a lack of virginity, see 8b note 47]. This is because R' Elazar speaks of a case in which the absence of blood was not a factor, either because the cloth that would have shown the blood was lost, or because the bride was a member of a family that did not have hymenal blood [see below, 10b] (*Rashi;* see *Rabbeinu Chananel,* cited by *Tosafos*). Thus, his only evidence for a lack of virginity is his impression of "an open entrance" [which is somewhat subjective], and not [the more objective] evidence of an absence of blood (see Gemara 9b).

[The Rishonim infer from *Rashi* that if blood had been found, the husband's claim of an open entrance would *not* be accepted. The presence of blood would prove that the bride was indeed a virgin, and that the husband was either mistaken or lying about having found no signs of virginity (*Ritva*). This appears to be the view of *Rabbeinu Chananel* as well; see *Ramban.* Other Rishonim, however, argue that since blood can come from outside sources as well, its presence does not disprove the claim of "an open entrance" (see *Rashba, Ran, Ritva, Meiri*).]

2. By stating that she was not a virgin, he raises the possibility that she was unfaithful to him during the period of their betrothal [*erusin,* which in Talmudic times could last as long as a year before the *nisuin* was performed to complete the marriage]. Infidelity during the *erusin* stage renders a wife a *sotah* (adulteress), and thus forbids her to her husband (*Sotah* 25a). Although it is not certain that she was unfaithful to him (as the Gemara will explain below), the possibility that she was is sufficient to forbid her to him (*Ritva*) [since the prohibition of a *sotah* to her husband is a Biblical prohibition, and doubts about Biblical prohibitions must be treated stringently].

Now, it is true that his claim is not subject to verification and we have only his word for the matter. Nevertheless, we accept his claim to the extent of forbidding her to him, because he has in effect stated that she is forbidden to him [שַׁוְיָהּ אַנַּפְשֵׁיהּ חֲתִיכָה דְּאִיסּוּרָא], and a person who asserts that something is forbidden to him becomes forbidden to partake of it (*Rashi*).

[Some explain the reason for this rule to be that such a declaration is tantamount to a *neder*-vow that it should be prohibited to him (*Shitah Mekubetzes* ד״ה נאמן לאוסרה עליו; *Mahari Bassan* and *Maharit,* cited by *Shaar HaMelech, Ishus* 9:15; and *Shav Yaakov,* cited by *Ketzos HaChoshen* 80:2). Others explain that the assertion is accepted as *testimony.* In their view, the Torah accorded a person's own words the status of testimony in regard to the prohibitions that affect *him;* it is only in regard to establishing prohibitions with respect to others that the Torah required a different standard of evidence. In this the law for prohibitions is similar to the law for monetary matters, where a person's admission is believed by the court in regard to monetary claims against him [הוֹדָאַת בַּעַל דִּין כְּמֵאָה עֵדִים דָּמֵי] (*Maharit* 2:1, cited by *Ketzos HaChoshen* 34:4 and *Shaar HaMelech, Hil. Ishus* 9:15). See *Kehillos Yaakov* §7 for how these differing explanations impact on our Gemara. As to whether the courts actually force him to divorce her on this basis, see *Ritva* here and *Pischei Teshuvah* 115:37 at length.]

Clearly, the court can accept a person's unsubstantiated claim only to adversely affect *himself,* not others. Thus, *Rashi* states that the husband's claim is accepted only insofar as rendering his wife forbidden to him, but not insofar as depriving her of her right to collect her *kesubah* (see, however, Gemara below, 9b, and note 12 there).

[The Gemara does not make any mention of the woman's response to her husband's claim. Most Rishonim write that R' Elazar's ruling refers to a case where the bride is either silent or flatly contradicts her husband, maintaining that she was a virgin at the time of *nisuin.* However, if she concedes that she was not a virgin and offers some explanation for that fact other than that she committed adultery, she would not become forbidden to him. This is because he does not claim to know with certainty that she is forbidden to him; he merely raises the *possibility* that she is. Therefore, her certain claim that her virginity was lost innocently carries greater weight than his uncertain claim of adultery [בָּרִי וְשֵׁמָא בָּרִי עָדִיף] (*Ramban* to 9b; see *Ritva, Ran;* see *Rashba* who explains the reason for this differently; cf. *Rosh* and *Maggid Mishneh, Isurei Biah* 18:10; see also *Kehillos Yaakov* §6 and 13a note 1).]

3. *Rashi.*

4. If she cohabited with another man *before* her *erusin* to her husband, she did not commit adultery and would consequently not become prohibited.

5. The Gemara below (51b) derives from a verse that if a married woman is violated against her will she remains permitted to her husband, unless he is a Kohen (*Rashi*). Thus, even if we accept that she previously cohabited with someone else, there are still two possible reasons to permit her to her husband: (a) Perhaps that cohabitation occurred before *erusin,* in which case she was not yet married to her husband and thus not guilty of adultery; and (b) even if it occurred after *erusin* it perhaps occurred against her will, which would not forbid her. Since in situations of double doubt we rule leniently even in regard to Biblical matters, the woman should remain permitted to her husband.

[Various reasons have been put forward to explain the principle of ruling leniently in cases of a double doubt. Some suggest that this principle is most readily understood according to the view that holds that even in the case of a Biblical prohibition, the requirement to act stringently in the case of single doubt is merely Rabbinic (*Rambam, Hilchos Tumas Meis* 9:12, as explained by *Kesef Mishneh; Ramban,* cited by *Ran* to *Kiddushin* 39a). It follows from this that in the case of a double doubt, the second doubt is actually a doubt regarding a Rabbinic stringency, for which the law is that we rule leniently (see *Pnei Yehoshua* to *Tosafos* ד״ה לא צריכא and *Gilyonei HaShas* who cites *Teshuvos Radach* 28:2). However, many Rishonim assume that the requirement to rule stringently in the case of a doubt regarding a Biblical law is a Biblical requirement (see *Raavad* to *Rambam* ibid.; *Rashba, Kiddushin* 73a; and *Ran* loc. cit.; see also *Rashi* and *Tosafos,* cited by *Pnei Yehoshua* here).

Rashba (*Teshuvos* 1:401), cited by *Pnei Yehoshua* ד״ה בא״ד ואומר ר״י, explains that a double doubt's effectiveness is based on the rule that we follow the majority. Since the majority of possibilities in the case of a double doubt favor leniency, we permit it. For example, in the case under discussion, two possibilities allow her to remain with her husband, whereas there is only one possibility that would render her forbidden: that she cohabited willingly after her betrothal. Since the majority of possibilities permit her to him, she is permitted. For a fuller treatment of this view, see *Shev Shmaatsa* 1:18. For yet another explanation, see *Shaarei Yosher* 1:19.]

6. [As derived by the Gemara below (51b) from a verse. This is one of the special stringencies that govern Kohanic marriages.] Thus, there is only one possibility of her being permitted – that the cohabitation occurred before her betrothal (*Rashi*). Since this is but a single doubt, she is forbidden.

The Gemara discusses another practice performed at a house of mourning:[34]

אָמַר עוּלָּא – Ulla said, **וְאָמְרֵי לָהּ בְּמַתְנִיתָא תָּנָא – and some say that it was taught in a Baraisa:** עֲשָׂרָה כוֹסוֹת תִּקְנוּ חֲכָמִים בְּבֵית הָאֵבֶל – THE SAGES INSTITUTED TEN CUPS of wine FOR A HOUSE OF MOURNING:[35] שְׁלֹשָׁה קוֹדֶם אֲכִילָה – THREE BEFORE EATING כְּדֵי לִפְתּוֹחַ אֶת בְּנֵי מֵעָיו – IN ORDER TO OPEN UP HIS INNARDS;[36] שְׁלֹשָׁה בְּתוֹךְ אֲכִילָה כְּדֵי לִשְׁרוֹת אֲכִילָה שֶׁבְּמֵעָיו – THREE DURING THE EATING IN ORDER TO SOAK THE FOOD THAT IS IN HIS INNARDS; וְאַרְבָּעָה לְאַחַר אֲכִילָה – AND FOUR more AFTER EATING – אֶחָד כְּנֶגֶד הַזָּן – ONE CORRESPONDING TO the first blessing of *Bircas HaMazon,* THE ONE WHO NOURISHES, etc.,[37] וְאֶחָד כְּנֶגֶד בִּרְכַּת הָאָרֶץ – ONE CORRESPONDING TO the second blessing, THE BLESSING OF THE LAND, וְאֶחָד כְּנֶגֶד בּוֹנֵה יְרוּשָׁלַיִם – ONE CORRESPONDING TO the third blessing, THE BUILDER OF JERUSALEM, וְאֶחָד כְּנֶגֶד הַטּוֹב וְהַמֵּטִיב – AND ONE CORRESPONDING TO the last blessing, THE GOOD ONE, WHO DOES GOOD. הוֹסִיפוּ עֲלֵיהֶם אַרְבָּעָה – Then THEY ADDED FOUR more cups TO THOSE ten: אֶחָד כְּנֶגֶד חַזָּנֵי הָעִיר – ONE FOR THE ATTENDANTS OF THE TOWN,[38] וְאֶחָד כְּנֶגֶד פַּרְנָסֵי הָעִיר – ONE FOR THE SUPPORTERS OF THE TOWN,[39] וְאֶחָד כְּנֶגֶד בֵּית הַמִּקְדָּשׁ – ONE FOR THE HOLY TEMPLE,[40] וְאֶחָד כְּנֶגֶד רַבָּן גַּמְלִיאֵל – AND ONE FOR RABBAN GAMLIEL.[41] הִתְחִילוּ הָיוּ שׁוֹתִין וּמִשְׁתַּכְּרִין – However, after the enactment of fourteen cups was in place, [SOME PEOPLE] BEGAN TO DRINK all these cups of wine AND BECOME INTOXICATED. הֶחֱזִירוּ הַדָּבָר לְיוֹשְׁנָהּ – So [THE SAGES] RESTORED THE MATTER TO ITS ANTIQUITY, i.e. the original practice.[42]

The Gemara explains the reason for one of the cups:

מַאי רַבָּן גַּמְלִיאֵל – What reason was a cup drunk in honor of **Rabban Gamliel? דְּתַנְיָא – For it was taught in a Baraisa:** בָּרִאשׁוֹנָה הָיְתָה הוֹצָאַת הַמֵּת קָשָׁה לִקְרוֹבָיו יוֹתֵר מִמִּיתָתוֹ – ORIGINALLY, the expense of TAKING OUT (i.e. burying) THE DECEASED WAS EVEN HARDER ON THE RELATIVES THAN HIS DEATH[43] עַד שֶׁהָיוּ מַנִּיחִים אוֹתוֹ וּבוֹרְחִין – TO THE POINT THAT [HIS RELATIVES] WOULD LEAVE HIM AND FLEE.[44] עַד שֶׁבָּא רַבָּן גַּמְלִיאֵל וְנָהַג קַלּוּת בְּעַצְמוֹ – This problem persisted UNTIL RABBAN GAMLIEL CAME AND TREATED HIMSELF LIGHTLY in instructing his attendants how his corpse should be treated, וְהוֹצִיאוּהוּ בִּכְלֵי פִשְׁתָּן – AND as per his instructions THEY TOOK HIM OUT (i.e. they buried him) IN plain LINEN GARMENTS.[45] וְנָהֲגוּ כָּל הָעָם אַחֲרָיו לְהוֹצִיא בִּכְלֵי פִשְׁתָּן – FOLLOWING HIS EXAMPLE, THE ENTIRE POPULACE TOOK OUT (i.e. buried their dead) IN plain LINEN GARMENTS.

The Gemara notes:

אָמַר רַב פָּפָּא – Rav Pappa said: וְהָאִידָּנָא נָהוּג עָלְמָא אֲפִילּוּ בִּצְרָדָא בַּר זוּזָא – Nowadays, the people have adopted the custom to dress the dead **even in** coarse **canvas worth** just **a *zuz*.**[46]

The Mishnah (2a) taught that a virgin should marry on Wednesday so that if her husband should claim that she is not a virgin, he should have immediate recourse to the courts, which sit on Thursday. The Gemara now begins a lengthy discussion of the various claims[47] a husband might make concerning lack of virginity and their practical consequences. In the course of this discussion, the Gemara will elaborate the case to which the Mishnah refers:

אָמַר רַבִּי אֶלְעָזָר – R' Elazar said:

NOTES

34. At the meal of condolence (*Meiri*).

35. It is appropriate to give a mourner much to drink, as the verse states (*Proverbs* 31:6): *Give strong drink to the woebegone and wine to those of embittered soul* (*Rashi*). Indeed, this is one of the main reasons for which wine was created (*Eruvin* 65a).

36. Three cups of wine were consumed together with pastries customarily offered before the meal. These appetizers served to whet a person's appetite for the bread and entree (see *Rashi* here and to *Succah* 27a ד״ה פרפראות).

37. Following each [of the four] blessings of *Bircas HaMazon,* the mourner would drink one cup of wine and another would be poured for him immediately (*Rashi*). [Typically, when *Bircas HaMazon* is recited, only one cup is drunk at the conclusion of the entire *Bircas HaMazon.*]

38. They would attend to burying the dead and the other needs of the community (*Rashi*).

39. These were rich people who expended a portion of their wealth in order to pay for paupers' burials (*Rashi*).

40. Beyond the immediate mourning in this house of mourning, there is a longstanding loss for which all the Jewish people mourn as if for a dead relative: the destruction of the Holy Temple. This cup of wine is drunk with the express hope that God should assuage our mourning through the Temple's rebuilding (see *Rashi*).

[Apparently, according to *Rashi* (in ד״ה כנגד חזני and ד״ה כנגד בהמ״ק) there were standard blessings that accompanied each of these four additional cups.]

41. The Gemara will explain this below.

42. That is, the original system of ten cups (*Rashi; Rambam, Hil. Aveil* 13:8). Other Rishonim dispute *Rashi's* explanation because ten cups can also lead to intoxication. They therefore interpret this to mean the original system of drinking only during the meal as needed (see *Ramban, Rashba* and *Ritva*). This is the custom nowadays (see *Yoreh Deah* 378:8).

[There is a popular misconception that a mourner may not drink wine during *shivah.* This is perhaps based on the widespread custom not to drink wine during the Nine Days (i.e. the first nine days of the month of Av) which is a time of profound mourning for the Temple. However, see *Tur* §552, who writes that the prohibition to drink wine is not due to *aveilus,* but has a different basis.

43. Because they would bury the dead clothed in expensive garments such as silk and royal garb (*Rashi*).

44. The wealthy would bury their dead in shrouds costing a thousand *zuz* and more. The poor, who could not afford such shrouds, felt so embarrassed at not being able to provide dignified shrouds for their relatives that they would abandon the corpses of their relatives and flee out of shame, effectively transferring the responsibility of burying the dead to the public (*Moed Katan* 27b).

45. See *Tosafos* to *Moed Katan* 27b ד״ה ונהג.

46. *Meiri* states that it is similarly fitting for every leader and public figure to treat himself lightly [and conduct his affairs] in a way that is beneath his means so that every person may follow his example and prevent the dissipation of his own financial base.

47. There are two signs of virginity evident during cohabitation. The first is a constriction of the vaginal canal and a resistance to penetration. The second is the bleeding that results from the first cohabitation [from the rupture of the hymen and the widening of the canal; see Gemara above, 5b] (*Rambam, Ishus* 11:9). The Gemara's initial discussion focuses on the failure to detect the first of these signs.

[It should be noted that these signs of virginity are *both* present in a girl only when she is a minor or a *naarah* (a girl during the first six months of her maturity). Once she is a *bogeress,* one of these signs is no longer necessarily present. There is a dispute among the Rishonim as to which sign disappears with age. See *Tosafos* 9a ד״ה האומר; *Rambam, Ishus* 11:12; *Rashba, Ritva* et al. and *Shulchan Aruch, Even HaEzer* 68:3.]

מג א מיי' פ"ד מהלכות אבל הלכה ו טוש"ע יו"ד סי' שעו סעיף ה: מד ב מיי' פי"ג שם הלכה א סמג עשין דרבנן ב: מה ג מיי' שם הל"ח סמג שם: מו ד מיי' פ"ד שם הל"ו סמג שם טוש"ע יו"ד סי' שנב סעיף ג:

כי תניא ההיא א בברכת המזון כי קאמר רבי יוחנן ב בשורה ואלא הא דאמר רבי יצחק אמר רבי יוחנן מברכים ברכת חתנים בעשרה וחתנים מן המנין וברכת אבלים בעשרה ואין אבלים מן המנין ברכה בשורה מי איכא אלא כי קאמר רבי יוחנן ברחבה ואלא הא דאמר רבי יצחק אמר רבי יוחנן מברכין ברכת חתנים בעשרה כל שבעה וחתנים מן המנין וברכת אבלים בעשרה כל שבעה ואין אבלים מן המנין ברכת רחבה כל שבעה מי איכא משכחת לה בפנים חדשות כי הא דרב חייא בר אבא מקרי בניה דריש לקיש הוה ואמרי לה מתני בריה דריש לקיש הוה שכיב ליה ינוקא יומא קמא לא אזל לגביה למחר דבריה ליהודה בר נחמני מתורגמניה אמר ליה קום אימא מלתא כל קביל ינוקא פתח ואמר א) וירא ה' וינאץ מכעס בניו ובנותיו דור שאבות מנאצים להקב"ה כועס על בניהם ועל בנותיהם ומתים כשהם קטנים ואיכא דאמרי בחור הוה והכי קאמר ליה ב) על כן על בחוריו לא ישמח ה' ואת יתומיו ואת אלמנותיו לא ירחם כי כולו חנף ומרע וכל פה דובר נבלה בכל זאת לא שב אפו ועוד ידו נטויה מאי ועוד ידו נטויה אמר רב חנן בר רב הכל יודעין כלה למה נכנסה לחופה אלא כל המנבל פיו ומוציא דבר נבלה מפיו אפילו נחתם לו גזר דינו של שבעים שנה לטובה נהפך עליו לרעה אתא לנחומי צעורי קמצער אמר ליה הכי קאמר ליה חשיב את לאתפוסי אדרא אמר ליה קום אימא מלתא כנגד שבחו של הקב"ה פתח ואמר האל הגדול ברוב גדלו אדיר וחזק ברוב נוראות מחיה מתים במאמרו עושה גדולות עד אין חקר ונפלאות עד אין מספר בא"י מחיה המתים א"ל קום אימא מלתא כנגד אבלים פתח ואמר אחינו המיוגעים המדוכאין באבל הזה תנו לבבכם לחקור את זאת זאת היא עומדת לעד נתיב הוא מששת ימי בראשית רבים שתו רבים ישתו כמשתה ראשונים כך משתה אחרונים אחינו בעל נחמות ינחם אתכם ברוך מנחם אבלים אמר אביי רבים שתו לימא רבים ישתו לא לימא משתה ראשונים לימא משתה אחרונים לא לימא דאר"ש בן לקיש וכן תנא משמיה דר' יוסי לעולם אל יפתח אדם פיו לשטן אמר רב יוסף מאי קרא ג) כסדום היינו לעמורה דמינו מאי אהדר ליה ד) שמעו דבר ה' קציני סדום וגו' א"ל קום אימא מלתא כנגד מנחמי אבלים פתח ואמר אחינו גומלי חסדים בני גומלי חסדים המחזיקים בבריתו של אברהם אבינו (שנאמר ה) כי ידעתיו למען אשר יצוה את בניו וגו') אחינו בעל הגמול ישלם לכם גמולכם ברוך אתה משלם הגמול א"ל קום אימא מלתא כנגד כל ישראל פתח ואמר רבון העולמים פדה והצל מלט הושע עמך ישראל מן הדבר ומן החרב ומן הביזה ומן השדפון ומן הירקון ומכל מיני פורעניות המתרגשות ובאות לעולם טרם נקרא ואתה תענה ברוך אתה עוצר המגפה אמר עולא ואמרי לה במתניתא תנא עשרה כוסות תקנו חכמים בבית האבל שלשה קודם אכילה כדי לפתוח את בני מעיו שלשה בתוך אכילה כדי לשרות אכילה שבמעיו וארבעה לאחר אכילה [א] אחד כנגד הזן ואחד כנגד ברכת הארץ ואחד כנגד בונה ירושלים ואחד כנגד הטוב והמטיב הוסיפו עליהם ארבעה אחד כנגד חזני העיר ואחד כנגד פרנסי העיר ואחד כנגד בית המקדש ואחד כנגד רבן גמליאל התחילו הוו שותין ומשתכרין החזירו הדבר ליושנה מאי רבן גמליאל דתניא בראשונה היתה הוצאת המת קשה לקרוביו יותר ממיתתו עד שהיו מניחים אותו ובורחין עד שבא רבן גמליאל ונהג קלות בעצמו והוציאוהו בכלי פשתן ונהגו העם אחריו להוציא בכלי פשתן אמר רב פפא והאידנא נהוג עלמא אפילו בצרדא בר זוזא: אמר רבי אלעזר

האומר

תוספות

כי תניא ההיא בברכת המזון. פי' בקונטרס להצטרף עם ג' לזימון שהרי הוא חייב בכל המצות ואין נראה לר"י דא"כ לא אתא לאשמועינן אלא דחייב במצות והוה ליה למימר בהדיא דחייב במצות ועוד דא"כ מאי פריך ליה מברכת אבלים בעשרה ואין אבלים מן המנין דקאמר ברכה בשורה מי איכא אלא ע"כ היינו ברכת המזון והדרן קושיא לדוכתין דקתני ואבלים מן המנין ומוקמינן בברכת המזון ולפירוש הקונטרס לא קשיא מידי דהכי קתני ואבלים מן המנין היינו להצטרף לזימון לומר נברך שאכלנו משלו אבל ברכת אבלים שמברכים בברכת המזון קאמר רבי יוחנן דאינו מן המנין לכך נראה לר"י לפרש כי תניא ההיא בברכת המזון היינו ברכת אבלים שבברכת המזון מכלל משמע שברכת אבלים שבברכת המזון לא הוי אלא בעשרה מדסליק אדעתיה דמקשן דאיירי בברכת אבלים שבברכת המזון וקאמר בעשרה והוה ניחא ליה בהכי אי לאו משום דקתני לעיל בברייתא ואבלים מן המנין אם כן צריך עשרה:

אלא כי קאמר ר' יוחנן ברחבה. אי גרסינן אלא משמע דההיא דלעיל נמי מעמיד ברחבה ותימה למה הוצרכו תרי מילי דר' יוחנן ההיא דלעיל והך וצריך לומר דחדא מכלל חברתה אתמר ההיא דלעיל מכללא דהך אבל אי ל"ג אלא ניחא דלעיל איירי בשורה והכא ברחבה בלא פנים חדשות ומימרא שלישית של רבי יוחנן הוצרך להשמיענו דבפנים חדשות אין אבלים מן המנין ואי נקט ההיא ה"א איפכא דוקא מיום ראשון ואילך אבל ביום ראשון שייכי טפי ומברכים לה בלא י':

האומר

רש"י

בברכת המזון. להצטרף לג' לזמון עליו שהרי הוא חייב בכל המצות: בשורה. כשהיו חוזרין מן הקבר היו עושין שורה סביב האבל לנחמו ומושיבין אותו והן עומדים סביב ואומרי' בסנהדרין (דף יט.) אין שורה פחות מי': ברחבה. כשמברכין את האבל סעודה ראשונה משל אחרים כדאמרינן במועד קטן (דף כז:) היו מברין אותו ברחבה ומברכין שם ברכת אבלים כדמפרש לקמיה ברוך מנחם אבלים: אמר ליה. למתורגמניה: כל קביל ינוקא. לנגד המאורע דברים ניחומים על מיתת הילד: וירא ה'. מה עשו אבות: וינאץ מכעס. שהכעיסוהו וגרמו לו לפקוד על בניהם ובנותיהם: ואית דאמרי. לא תינוק היה המת אלא בחור היה והכי קאמר על בחוריו וגו': של ע' שנה. ועוד דריש כמו ועד עולמו של אדם נטויה ונהפכת מטוב לרע: אתא לנחומי צעורי מצער ליה. בתמיה מוכיח על פניו שבשביל עונו מת בנו: חשיב את לאתפוסי אדרא. חשוב אתה למעלה לתופסך ולא בניך בעון הדור דקי"ל ט) בזמן שצדיקים בדור צדיקים נתפסים על הדור שנאמר וממקדשי תחלו (יחזקאל ט): האל הגדול ברוב גודלו. בברוך פתח בה ברוך אתה ה' אלהינו מלך העולם האל הגדול וכו': אחינו המיוגעים כו'. ברכה הסמוכה לחברתה היא וכן סדורות על הסדר: באבל הזה תנו לבבכם לחקור זאת שזאת עומדת לעד. שהכל מתים ולא תבכו יותר מדאי: משתה הראשונים לימא. משתה ראשונים הוא: בבריתו של אברהם. שגמל חסדים דכתיב (בראשית כא) ויטע אשל ר"ת אכילה שתיה לויה י): עשרה כוסות. להרבות לו בשתיה כדכתיב (משלי לא) תנו שכר לאובד ויין למרי נפש: קודם אכילה. שהיו רגילין להמשיך פרפראות לפני סעודה כגון כיסנין וסופגנין ואיסקריטין ובאותם פרפראות משקין לאבל ג' כוסות: אחד כנגד הזן. על כל ברכה שותה הכוס ומחזגין לו אחר: כנגד חזני העיר. תקנו להם ברכה עליו לפי שהיו שמשי העיר להתעסק במתים ובשאר צרכי ציבור: פרנסי העיר. שהיו עשירים מבזבזים ממונם לקבורת עניים: כנגד בהמ"ק. תקנו עליו ברכת ניחומים שינחמנו המקום בבניינו מאבלנו שאנו מתאבלים עליו כבעל מת: כנגד ר"ג. לקמן מפרש: ליושנה. עשרה כוסות: הוצאת המת. שהיו קוברים אותו בכלים יקרים כגון שיראין וסריקות: בצרדא בר זוזא. בגד קנבוס שאינו שוה אלא דינר:

האומר

מסורת הש"ס

א) מגילה דף כג., ב) [תוספתא מגילה פ"ג], ג) שבת דף לג., ד) ברכות יט. ס. ע"ש, ה) פ"א ליתא, ו) שמחות פי"ד [פסחים קיז.], ז) מ"ק כז: [תוספתא נדה פ"ט], ח) [גי' הערוך צדרא ועיין ב"מ נא. דאיתא צדרייתא ופרש"י בגדי קנבוס אבל בשאלתות איתא בצרדא כדאיתא לפנינו], ט) [שבת לג:], י) [וע"ע רש"י סוטה י. ד"ה פונדק].

הגהות הגר"א

[א] גמ' (אחד כנגד הזן כו' עד הטוב והמטיב) תא"מ (ואפשר דהכי כנגד ד' ברכות האמורים למעלה פתח ואמר כו' ואולי על כל כוס אומר ברכה א'):

תורה אור השלם

א) וַיַּרְא יְיָ וַיִּנְאָץ מִכַּעַס בָּנָיו וּבְנֹתָיו: [דברים לב, יט]

ב) עַל כֵּן עַל בַּחוּרָיו לֹא יִשְׂמַח אֲדֹנָי וְאֶת יְתֹמָיו וְאֶת אַלְמְנֹתָיו לֹא יְרַחֵם כִּי כֻלּוֹ חָנֵף וּמֵרַע וְכָל פֶּה דֹּבֵר נְבָלָה בְּכָל זֹאת לֹא שָׁב אַפּוֹ וְעוֹד יָדוֹ נְטוּיָה: [ישעיה ט, טז]

ג) לוּלֵי יְיָ צְבָאוֹת הוֹתִיר לָנוּ שָׂרִיד כִּמְעָט כִּסְדֹם הָיִינוּ לַעֲמֹרָה דָּמִינוּ: [ישעיה א, ט]

ד) שִׁמְעוּ דְבַר יְיָ קְצִינֵי סְדֹם הַאֲזִינוּ תּוֹרַת אֱלֹהֵינוּ עַם עֲמֹרָה: [ישעיה א, י]

ה) כִּי יְדַעְתִּיו לְמַעַן אֲשֶׁר יְצַוֶּה אֶת בָּנָיו וְאֶת בֵּיתוֹ אַחֲרָיו וְשָׁמְרוּ דֶּרֶךְ יְיָ לַעֲשׂוֹת צְדָקָה וּמִשְׁפָּט לְמַעַן הָבִיא יְיָ עַל אַבְרָהָם אֵת אֲשֶׁר דִּבֶּר עָלָיו: [בראשית יח, יט]

גליון הש"ס

גמ' כל המנבל פיו. עיין ט"ז יו"ד סי' קכד:

ליקוטי רש"י

כי קאמר רבי יוחנן בשורה. מוכח בכתובות (דף ח.) דר' יוחנן לאו תנא הוא דאמרינן התם אמר רב נחמן אמר רב חתנים מן המנין ואין אבלים מן המנין מיתיבי חתנים ואבלים מן המנין מתני' קרמית עליה דרב רב תנא הוא ופליג איתמר א"ר יצחק א"ר יוחנן חתנים מן המנין ואין אבלים מן המנין מיתיבי חתנים ואבלים מן המנין ומתרץ כי תניא ההיא בשורה ואם איתא דר' יוחנן נמי תנא הוא כי היכי דתריץ אליבא דרב רב תנא הוא ופליג היה לו לתרץ אליבא דר' יוחנן [נמי] ר' יוחנן תנא הוא ופליג אלא ודאי לאו תנא הוא [חגיגה ב:]. ואין אבלים מן המנין. שהרי הם אומר ברכה למנחמים בפני עצמן אחינו בעל הגמול ישלם לכם גמולכם הטוב ברוך אתה ה' משלם הגמול ולאבלים בפני עצמן אחינו בעל נחמות ינחם אתכם ברוך אתה ה' מנחם אבלים ואינו כוללן יחד [מגילה כג:]. מקרי. לקרות שבכתב. מתני. לשנות משניות [ע"פ סוכה כח:]. דבריה. הנהיגו [ע"פ ביצה כט.]. מתורגמניה. שעומד לפניו ומשמיע לרבים את הדרשה מפיו [ע"פ ברכות כז:]. מתורגמן, הוא אומר ואחר מפרש [פסחים קיז.]. מתורגמן, העומד לפני חכם הדרשן והחכם לוחש לו לשון עברית והוא מתרגם לרבים לשון שהן שומעין [יומא כ:]. לא ישמח. הרי צרות וגזירות ואת יתומיו ואת אלמנותיו לא ירחם הרי צועקין ואינם נענין בעון מה כי כלו חנף ומרע וכל פה דובר נבלה [שבת לג.]. ומרע. רשע כמו (לעיל א) זרע מרעים [ישעיה ט, טז]. ועוד ידו נטויה. לשון ועוד כל שנותיו של אדם שהן שבעים שנה יד הדין נטויה עליו לבטל זכויותיו בעון זה. הכל יודעי' כו'. ולא הוצרך לאדם לפרש למה הכלה נכנסת לחופה אפילו כו' [שבת שם]. כסדום היינו. כולנו כלים [ישעיה א, ט]. קציני סדום. שרים שמעשיהם כסדום מכאן אמרו לא יפתח אדם פיו לשטן [שם י]. כי ידעתיו וכו'. לשון חבה כמו מודע לאישה (רות ב) הלא בועז מודעתנו (שם ג) ואדעך בשם (שמות לג) ואמנם עיקר לשון כולם אינו אלא לשון ידיעה שהמחבב את האדם מקרבו אצלו ויודעו ומכירו ולמה ידעתיו למען אשר יצוה לפי שהוא מצוה את בניו עלי לשמור דרכי ואם תפרשהו כתרגומו יודע אני בו שיצוה את בניו וגו' אין למען נופל על הלשון [בראשית יח, יט]. מן השדפון ומן הירקון. מכות תבואה שבשדות. שדפון, רוח קדים שאליה"ב בלע"ז. ירקון, יובש ופני התבואה מכסיפין ומוריקין [דברים כח, כב]. קשה לקרוביו. כתכריכין טובים [מו"ק כז:].

בָּאֵבֶל הַזֶּה תְּנוּ לִבְבְכֶם לַחֲקוֹר אֶת זֹאת – ***troubled, who are crushed, during this mourning, pay attention to examine this;*** נָתִיב הוּא זֹאת הִיא עוֹמֶדֶת לָעַד – ***this occurs in all times;***[23] מִשֵּׁשֶׁת יְמֵי בְרֵאשִׁית – ***it is the way*** *[of the world]* ***from the six days of Creation.*** רַבִּים שָׁתוּ רַבִּים יִשְׁתּוּ – ***Many drank*** *[from the cup of death];*[24] ***many will drink.*** כְּמִשְׁתֵּה רִאשׁוֹנִים כָּךְ מִשְׁתֵּה אַחֲרוֹנִים – ***Like the drink of the earlier generations so is the drink of the later generations.***[25] אַחֵינוּ בַּעַל נֶחָמוֹת יְנַחֵם אֶתְכֶם – ***Our brothers! May the Master of consolations comfort you.*** בָּרוּךְ מְנַחֵם אֲבֵלִים – ***Blessed*** *are You, Hashem,* ***Who comforts the mourners.***

The Gemara takes issue with certain phrases in the above blessing:

אָמַר אַבַּיֵי – **Abaye said:** רַבִּים שָׁתוּ לֵימָא – **One should say** only, ***"Many drank"***; רַבִּים יִשְׁתּוּ לֹא לֵימָא – **but he should not say, *"Many will drink."*** מִשְׁתֵּה רִאשׁוֹנִים לֵימָא – **One should mention *"the drink of the earlier generations"***; מִשְׁתֵּה אַחֲרוֹנִים לֹא לֵימָא – **but he should not mention *"the drink of the later generations."***[26] דְּאָמַר רַבִּי שִׁמְעוֹן בֶּן לָקִישׁ – **For R' Shimon ben Lakish said,** וְכֵן תָּנָא מִשְּׁמֵיהּ דְּרַבִּי יוֹסֵי – **and, likewise, a Baraisa was taught in the name of R' Yose,** as follows: לְעוֹלָם אַל יִפְתַּח אָדָם פִּיו לַשָּׂטָן – ONE SHOULD NEVER GIVE SATAN AN OPENING.[27] אָמַר רַב יוֹסֵף – **And Rav Yosef said:** מַאי קְרָא – **What verse** supports this idea? "כִּסְדֹם הָיִינוּ לַעֲמֹרָה דָּמִינוּ" – *Had not Hashem left us a small remnant* ***we would have been like Sodom; we would have resembled Gomorrah!***[28] מַאי אַהְדַּר לֵיהּ – **And what does the prophet say in rejoinder** in the very next verse? "שִׁמְעוּ דְבַר־ה' קְצִינֵי סְדֹם וְגוֹ'" – ***Hear the word of Hashem, O chiefs of Sodom, etc.*** *give ear to the teaching of our God, O people of Gomorrah.*[29]

The Gemara returns to the incident:

קוּם אָמַר לֵיהּ – **[Reish Lakish] then said to [his spokesman],** אֵימָא מִלְּתָא כְּנֶגֶד מְנַחֲמֵי אֲבֵלִים – **"Arise and say something regarding those who comfort the mourners."** פָּתַח וְאָמַר אַחֵינוּ גּוֹמְלֵי חֲסָדִים בְּנֵי גּוֹמְלֵי חֲסָדִים – **He began to recite** the third blessing: ***Our brothers who bestow kindness, the children of those who bestow kindness,*** הַמַּחֲזִיקִים בִּבְרִיתוֹ שֶׁל אַבְרָהָם אָבִינוּ – ***who uphold the covenant of our forefather Abraham,***[30] שֶׁנֶּאֱמַר "כִּי יְדַעְתִּיו לְמַעַן אֲשֶׁר יְצַוֶּה אֶת־בָּנָיו" וגו') – ***about whom it is stated: For I have loved him because he commands his children, etc.*** *and his household after him to keep the way of Hashem, doing charity and justice.*[31]) אַחֵינוּ בַּעַל הַגְּמוּל יְשַׁלֵּם לָכֶם גְּמוּלְכֶם – ***Our brothers! May the Master of reward pay you your due.*** בָּרוּךְ אַתָּה מְשַׁלֵּם הַגְּמוּל – ***Blessed are You . . . Who pays the reward.***

The Gemara concludes the incident:

קוּם אָמַר לֵיהּ – **[Reish Lakish] then said to [his spokesman]:** אֵימָא מִלְּתָא כְּנֶגֶד כָּל יִשְׂרָאֵל – **"Arise and say something regarding all of Israel."** פָּתַח וְאָמַר רִבּוֹן הָעוֹלָמִים – **He began to recite** the fourth and final blessing of the Mourners' Blessings: ***Master of the worlds!*** פְּדֵה וְהַצֵּל מַלֵּט הוֹשַׁע עַמְּךָ יִשְׂרָאֵל – ***Redeem, spare, deliver and save Your nation Israel*** מִן הַדֶּבֶר וּמִן הַחֶרֶב וּמִן הַבִּיזָּה – ***from the pestilence, the sword, and the plunder,*** וּמִן הַשִּׁדָּפוֹן וּמִן הַיֵּרָקוֹן – ***from the windblast and the yellowing,***[32] וּמִכָּל מִינֵי פוּרְעָנִיּוֹת הַמִּתְרַגְּשׁוֹת וּבָאוֹת לָעוֹלָם – ***and from all types of misfortunes that assemble to come to the world.*** טֶרֶם נִקְרָא וְאַתָּה תַּעֲנֶה – ***Before we call, You answer.*** בָּרוּךְ אַתָּה עוֹצֵר הַמַּגֵּפָה – ***Blessed are You . . . Who contains the plague.***[33]

NOTES

Reish Lakish directed his speaker to recite this blessing second, it is actually the primary blessing of mourners – as indicated by *Rashi* above (but see note 33).

23. Every person dies [eventually], so do not cry to excess (*Rashi*).

24. Or, from the cups of mourning (see *Maharsha*).

25. See *Iyei HaYam* who elaborates on these ideas.

26. In other words, he should just say, *"It was the drink of the earlier generations"* (*Rashi;* see *Riaf* in *Ein Yaakov*).

27. [Literally: One should never open one's mouth to Satan.]

By such speech he gives Satan, who functions as the prosecutor in the Heavenly Tribunal, an opening to demand that he be punished as he himself admits that he deserves (*Maharsha*).

28. *Isaiah* 1:9. I.e. we would have been deserving of being utterly destroyed, as was Sodom (*Rashi* to *Isaiah* ibid.).

29. This illustrates the principle of R' Shimon ben Lakish and R' Yose: By confessing that they were deserving of punishment as the Sodomites of old, the people gave the prophet an opening to label them *chiefs of Sodom.* [Abaye makes similar changes to prayers on the same grounds elsewhere (see *Berachos* 19a and 60a).]

30. Abraham was exemplary in his kindness, as is evident from the verse (*Genesis* 21:33): *He planted an "eishel," where eishel* is explained as an acronym for the Hebrew words for food, drink and lodging (*Rashi,* from *Sotah* 10a).

31. *Genesis* 18:19. *Maharshal* reports that the words within parentheses do not appear in most texts of the Talmud and that *Rashi* too evidently did not have them in his text. However, these words do appear in most of the texts available to *Dikdukei Soferim HaShalem.*

32. Two types of plagues that can affect crops.

33. This concludes the text of the Mourners' Blessings. In a lengthy discussion of this and related blessings in *Toras HaAdam* (pp. 149-155 in the Chavel ed.), *Ramban* states that it is no longer customary to recite any of these blessings, not in the street nor in the synagogue nor in the mourner's home. Similar statements appear in the name of *Rav Paltoy Gaon* and *Rav Hai Gaon* (see *Rosh* and *Otzar HaGeonim, Teshuvos*). *Ramban* goes on to say that even when it was customary to say the Mourners' Blessings, only the second blessing (ending *Blessed are You, Hashem, Who comforts mourners*) is mandatory. The other three blessings may be said if one wishes or (based on *Tosefta, Berachos* 3:23) they may be combined within the second blessing. *Ramban* comments that we may be forced to say that even this second blessing is optional for, otherwise, why would people no longer be accustomed to say it?

[It is questionable whether *Rashi* subscribes to the view that only the second blessing is mandatory (see ד"ה ברחבה and ד"ה אחינו).]

Apart from the Mourners' Blessings that our Gemara details, the Gemara in *Berachos* 46b records a special version of the fourth blessing of *Bircas HaMazon* that should be recited in a house of mourning. Moreover, the Geonim record an addition to the third blessing. These additions are mentioned in *Shulchan Aruch* (see *Orach Chaim* §189 and *Yoreh Deah* 379:1-2) and some, but not all, communities were accustomed to say them (see *Be'er HaGolah* to *Yoreh Deah* 379:6). According to one version, these additions read (in translation): *Have mercy, Hashem . . . that we not .. be humiliated forever and ever. O comfort, Hashem, our God, the mourners of Jerusalem and those who mourn this sad event. Console them from their mourning and gladden them from their grief, as it is said, "Like a man whose mother consoles him, so I will console you, and in Jerusalem you will be consoled." Blessed are You, Hashem, Comforter of Zion, through the rebuilding of Jerusalem. Amen.*

Blessed are You, Hashem, our God, King of the universe, . . . He is the living King Who is good and Who does good for all, God of truth, Judge of truth, Who judges with righteousness, Who takes souls with justice, Who rules His universe to do with it as He wishes, for all His ways are with justice and we are His nation and His servants. For everything, we are obliged to thank Him and to bless Him. He Who repairs the breaches of Israel, may He repair this breach from us and from this sad event for life, for peace, and for all good; and of all good things may He never deprive us.

[There is yet another blessing mentioned by the Geonim that was recited at the onset of the mourning period and that begins בָּרוּךְ אַתָּה ה' . . . דַּיַּין רַחֲמִים שׁוֹפֵט אֱמוּנוֹת, *Blessed are You, Hashem . . . merciful Judge, trustworthy Justice.* Some of the Geonim themselves had never heard of this blessing (see *Otzar HaGeonim, Teshuvos*) and it seems to have fallen into disuse.]

מג א מיי' פ"ד מהלכות אבל הלכה ו טוש"ע יו"ד סי' שעט סעיף ה:
מד ב מיי' פי"ג שם הלכה א סמג עשין דרבנן ב:
מה ג מיי' שם הל"ט סמג שם:
מו ד מיי' פ"ד שם הל"ז סמג שם טוש"ע יו"ד סי' שנב סעי' ב:

כי תניא ההיא [א]בברכת המזון כי קאמר רבי יוחנן [ב]בשורה ואלא הא [א]דאמר רבי יצחק אמר רבי יוחנן [ג]מברכים ברכת חתנים בעשרה וחתנים מן המנין וברכת אבלים בעשרה ואין אבלים מן המנין ברכה בשורה מי איכא אלא כי קאמר רבי יוחנן ברחבה ואלא הא דאמר רבי יצחק אמר רבי יוחנן מברכין ברכת חתנים בעשרה כל שבעה וחתנים מן המנין וברכת אבלים בעשרה כל שבעה ואין אבלים מן המנין ברכת רחבה כל שבעה מי איכא משכחת לה בפנים חדשות כי הא דרב חייא בר אבא מקרי בניה דריש לקיש הוה ואמרי לה מתני בריה דריש לקיש הוה שכיב ליה ינוקא יומא קמא לא אזל לגביה למחר דבריה ליהודה בר נחמני מתורגמניה אמר ליה קום אימא מלתא כל קביל ינוקא פתח ואמר [א]וירא ה' וינאץ מכעס בניו ובנותיו דור שאבות מנאצים להקב"ה כועס על בניהם ועל בנותיהם ומתים כשהם קטנים ואיכא דאמרי בחור הוה והכי קאמר ליה [ב]על כן על בחוריו לא ישמח ה' ואת יתומיו ואת אלמנותיו לא ירחם כי כולו חנף ומרע וכל פה דובר נבלה בכל זאת לא שב אפו ועוד ידו נטויה [ג]מאי ועוד ידו נטויה אמר רב חנן בר רב הכל יודעין כלה למה נכנסה לחופה אלא [ה]כל המנבל פיו ומוציא דבר נבלה מפיו אפילו נחתם לו גזר דינו של שבעים שנה לטובה נהפך עליו לרעה אתא לנחומי צעורי קמצער ליה הכי קאמר ליה חשיב את לאתפוסי אדרא אמר ליה קום אימא מלתא כנגד שבחו של הקב"ה פתח ואמר האל הגדול ברוב גדלו אדיר וחזק ברוב נוראות מחיה מתים במאמרו עושה גדולות עד אין חקר ונפלאות עד אין מספר בא"י מחיה המתים א"ל קום אימא מלתא כנגד אבלים פתח ואמר אחינו המיוגעים המדוכאין באבל הזה תנו לבבכם לחקור את זאת זאת היא עומדת לעד נתיב הוא מששת ימי בראשית רבים שתו רבים ישתו כמשתה ראשונים כך משתה אחרונים אחינו בעל נחמות ינחם אתכם ברוך מנחם אבלים אמר אביי רבים שתו לא לימא משתה ראשונים לימא משתה אחרונים לא לימא דאר"ש בן לקיש וכן תנא משמיה דר' יוסי [ז]לעולם אל יפתח אדם פיו לשטן אמר רב יוסף מאי קרא [ג]כסדום היינו לעמורה דמינו מאי אהדר ליה [ד]שמעו דבר ה' קציני סדום וגו' א"ל קום אימא מלתא כנגד מנחמי אבלים פתח ואמר אחינו גומלי חסדים בני גומלי חסדים המחזיקים בבריתו של אברהם אבינו [ט](שנאמר [ה]כי ידעתיו למען אשר יצוה את בניו וגו') אחינו בעל הגמול ישלם לכם גמולכם ברוך אתה משלם הגמול א"ל קום אימא מלתא כנגד כל ישראל פתח ואמר רבון העולמים פדה והצל מלט הושע עמך ישראל מן הדבר ומן החרב ומן הביזה ומן השדפון ומן הירקון ומכל מיני פורעניות המתרגשות ובאות לעולם טרם נקרא ואתה תענה ברוך אתה עוצר המגפה אמר עולא ואמרי לה במתניתא תנא [י]עשרה כוסות תקנו חכמים בבית האבל שלשה קודם אכילה כדי לפתוח את בני מעיו שלשה בתוך אכילה כדי לשרות אכילה שבמעיו וארבעה לאחר אכילה [א] אחד כנגד הזן ואחד כנגד ברכת הארץ ואחד כנגד בונה ירושלים ואחד כנגד הטוב והמטיב הוסיפו עליהם ארבעה אחד כנגד חזני העיר ואחד כנגד פרנסי העיר ואחד כנגד בית המקדש ואחד כנגד רבן גמליאל התחילו היו שותין ומשתכרין החזירו הדבר לישנה מאי רבן גמליאל דתניא [י]בראשונה היתה הוצאת המת קשה לקרוביו יותר ממיתתו עד שהיו מניחים אותו ובורחין עד שבא רבן גמליאל ונהג קלות בעצמו והוציאוהו בכלי פשתן ונהגו [כ]העם אחריו להוציא בכלי פשתן אמר רב פפא והאידנא נהוג עלמא אפילו [ל]בצרדא בר זוזא: אמר רבי אלעזר

האומר

רש"י

בברכת המזון. להצטרף לג' לזמון עליו שהרי הוא חייב בכל המצות: בשורה. כשהיו חוזרין מן הקבר היו עושין שורה סביב האבל לנחמו ומושיבין אותו והן עומדים סביב ואמרי' בסנהדרין (דף יט.) אין שורה פחות מי': ברחבה. כשמברין את האבל סעודה ראשונה משל אחרים כדאמרינן במועד קטן (דף כז:) היו מברין אותו ברחבה ומברכין שם ברכת אבלים כדמפרש לקמיה ברוך מנחם אבלים: אמר ליה. למתורגמניה: כל קביל ינוקא. לנגד המאורע דברים ניחומים על מיתת הילד: וירא ה'. מה עשו אבות: וינאץ מכעס. שהכעיסוהו וגרמו לו לפקוד על בניהם ובנותיהם: ואית דאמרי. לא תינוק היה המת אלא בחור היה והך קרא אמר על בחוריו וגו': של ע' שנה. ועוד דריש כמו ועד עולמו של אדם נטויה נהפכת מטוב לרע: אתא לנחומי צעורי מצער ליה. בתמיה מוכיח על פניו שבשביל עונו מת בנו: חשיב את לאתפוסי אדרא. חשוב אתה למעלה לתופסך ואת בניך בעון הדור דקי"ל [ט] בזמן שצדיקים בדור צדיקים נתפסים על הדור שנאמר וממקדשי תחלו (יחזקאל ט): האל הגדול ברוב גודלו. בברוך פתח בה ברוך אתה ה' אלהינו מלך העולם האל הגדול וכו': אחינו המיוגעים כו'. ברכה הסמוכה לחברתה היא וכן סדורות על הסדר: באבל הזה תנו לבבכם לחקור זאת שזאת עומדת לעד. שהכל מתים ולא תבכו יותר מדאי: משתה הראשונים לימא. משתה ראשונים הוא: בבריתו של אברהם. שגמל חסדים דכתיב (בראשית כא) ויטע אשל ר"ת אכילה שתיה לויה[י]: עשרה כוסות. להרבות לו בשתיה כדכתיב (משלי לא) תנו שכר לאובד ויין למרי נפש: קודם אכילה. שהיו רגילין להמשיך פרפראות לפני סעודה כגון כיסנין וסופגנין ואיסקריטין ובאותם פרפראות משקין לאבל ג' כוסות: אחד כנגד הזן. על כל ברכה שותה הכוס ומוזגין לו אחר: כנגד חזני העיר. תקנו להם ברכה עליו לפי שהיו שמשי העיר להתעסק במתים ובשאר צרכי ציבור: פרנסי העיר. שהיו עשירים מבזבזים ממונם לקבורת עניים: כנגד בהמ"ק. תקנו עליו ברכת ניחומים שינחמנו המקום בבנינו מאבלנו שאנו מתאבלים עליו כעל מת: כנגד ר"ג. לקמן מפרש: לישנה. עשרה כוסות: הוצאת המת. שהיו קוברים אותו בכלים יקרים כגון שיראין וסרקות: בצרדא בר זוזא. בגד קנבוס שאינו שוה אלא דינר:

תוספות

כי תניא ההיא בברכת המזון. פי' בקונטרס להצטרף עם ג' לזימון שהרי הוא חייב בכל המצות ואין נראה לר"י דא"כ לא אתא לאשמועינן אלא דחייב במצות והוה ליה למימר בהדיא דחייב במצות ועוד דא"כ מאי פריך ליה מברכת אבלים בעשרה ואין אבלים מן המנין דקאמר ברכה בשורה מי איכא אלא ע"כ היינו ברכת המזון והדרן קושיא לדוכתין דקתני ואבלים מן המנין ואוקמינן בברכת המזון ולפירוש הקונטרס לא קשיא מידי דכי קתני ואבלים מן המנין היינו להצטרף לזימון לומר נברך שאכלנו משלו אבל ברכת אבלים שמברכים בברכת המזון קאמר רבי יוחנן דאינו מן המנין לכך צריך לפרש כי תניא ההיא בברכת המזון היינו ברכת אבלים שבברכת המזון מכאן משמע שברכת אבלים שבברכת המזון לא הוי אלא בעשרה מדסליק לדעתיה דמקשן דאיירי בברכת אבלים שבברכת המזון וקאמר בעשרה והוה ניחא ליה בהכי אי לאו משום דקתני לעיל בברייתא ואבלים מן המנין אם כן צריך עשרה:

אלא כי קאמר ר' יוחנן ברחבה. אי גרסינן אלא משמע דהשתא לעיל נמי מעמיד ברחבה ותימה למה הוצרכו תרי מילי דר' יוחנן ההיא לעיל והך וצריך לומר דחדא מכלל חברתה אתמר ההיא לעיל מכללא הכך אבל אי ל"ג אלא ניחא דלעיל איירי בשורה והכא ברחבה בלא פנים חדשות ומימרא שלישית של רבי יוחנן הולך להשמיענו דבפנים חדשות אין אבלים מן המנין ואי נקט ההיא ה"א איפכא דוקא מיום ראשון ואילך אבל ביום ראשון שייכי טפי ומברכים לה בלא י':

מסורת הש"ס

א) מגילה דף כג., ב) [תוספתא מגילה פ"ג], ג) שבת דף לג., ד) ברכות יט. ס. ע"ש, ה) פ"ל ליתו, ו) שמחות פי"ד [מסכת קי.], ז) מ"ק כז: [תוספתא נדה פ"ט], ח) [גי' הערוך צדרא ועיין ב"מ נא. דאיתא צדריתא ופרש"י בגדי קנבוס אבל בשאלתות איתא בצרדא כדאיתא לפנינו], ט) [שבת לג:], י) [ועי' רש"י סוטה י. ד"ה פונדק].

הגהות הגר"א

[א] גמ' אחד כנגד הזן כו' עד הטוב והמטיב. תא"מ (ולאפשר דהס כנגד ד' ברכות האמורים למעלה פתח ואמר כו' ואולי על כל כוס אומר ברכה א'):

תורה אור השלם

א) וַיַּרְא יְיָ וַיִּנְאָץ מִכַּעַס בָּנָיו וּבְנֹתָיו: [דברים לב, יט]

ב) עַל כֵּן עַל בַּחוּרָיו לֹא יִשְׂמַח אֲדֹנָי וְאֶת יְתֹמָיו וְאֶת אַלְמְנֹתָיו לֹא יְרַחֵם כִּי כֻלּוֹ חָנֵף וּמֵרַע וְכָל פֶּה דֹּבֵר נְבָלָה בְּכָל זֹאת לֹא שָׁב אַפּוֹ וְעוֹד יָדוֹ נְטוּיָה: [ישעיה ט, טז]

ג) לוּלֵי יְיָ צְבָאוֹת הוֹתִיר לָנוּ שָׂרִיד כִּמְעָט כִּסְדֹם הָיִינוּ לַעֲמֹרָה דָּמִינוּ: [ישעיה א, ט]

ד) שִׁמְעוּ דְבַר יְיָ קְצִינֵי סְדֹם הַאֲזִינוּ תּוֹרַת אֱלֹהֵינוּ עַם עֲמֹרָה: [ישעיה א, י]

ה) כִּי יְדַעְתִּיו לְמַעַן אֲשֶׁר יְצַוֶּה אֶת בָּנָיו וְאֶת בֵּיתוֹ אַחֲרָיו וְשָׁמְרוּ דֶּרֶךְ יְיָ לַעֲשׂוֹת צְדָקָה וּמִשְׁפָּט לְמַעַן הָבִיא יְיָ עַל אַבְרָהָם אֵת אֲשֶׁר דִּבֶּר עָלָיו: [בראשית יח, יט]

גליון הש"ס

גמ' כל המנבל פיו. עיין ט"ז יו"ד רסי' קכד:

ליקוטי רש"י

כי קאמר רבי יוחנן בשורה. סוכה בכתובות (דף ח.) דר' יוחנן לאו תנא הוא דאמרינן התם אמר רב נחמן אמר רב חתנים מן המנין ואין אבלים מן המנין מיתיבי חתנים ואבלים מן המנין מתני' קרקית כליה דרב רב תנא הוא ופליג איתמר א"ר יצחק א"ר יוחנן חתנים מן המנין ואין אבלים מן המנין מיתיבי חתנים ואבלים מן המנין ומתרץ כי תניא ההיא בשורה ולא קאמר דר' יוחנן נמי תנא הוא כי היכי דתריץ אליבא דרב רב תנא הוא ופליג היה לו לתרץ אליבא דר' יוחנן [נמי] ר' יוחנן תנא הוא ופליג אלא ודאי לאו תנא הוא [תמיד כב.]. ואין אבלים מן המנין. שהרי הוא אומר ברכה למנחמים בפני עצמן אחינו בעל הגמול ישלם לכם גמולכם הטוב ברוך אתה ה' משלם הגמול ולאבלים בפני עצמן אחינו בעל נחמות ינחם אתכם ברוך אתה ה' מנחם אבלים ואינו כוללן יחד [מגילה כג:]. מקרי. לקרות שבכתב מתני. לשנות משניות [ע"פ סוכה כח:]. דבריה. הנהיגו [ע"פ ביצה כט.]. מתורגמניה. שעומד לפניו ומשמיע לרבים את הדרשה מפיו [ע"פ ברכות כז:]. מתורגמן, הוא אומר ואחר מפרש [פסחים קיז.]. מתורגמן, העומד לפני חכם הדורש והחכם לוחש לו לשון עברית והוא מתרגם לרבים לשון שהן שומעין [יומא כ:]. לא ישמח. הרי לכות וגזירות ואת יתומיו ואת אלמנותיו לא ירחם הרי צועקין ואינם נענין מה כי כלו חנף ומרע וכל פה דובר נבלה [שבת לג.]. ומרע. רשע כמו (לעיל א) זרע מרעים [ישעיה ט, טז]. ועוד ידו נטויה. לשון ועוד כל שנותיו של אדם שהן שבעים שנה יד הדין נטויה עליו לבטל זכיותיו בעון זה. הכל יודעין כו'. ילא הולך לאדם לפרש מה נכנסה והמנבל פיו בכך אפילו כו' [שבת שם]. כסדום היינו. כלנו כלים [ישעיה א, ט]. קציני סדום. שרים שמעשיהם כסדום מכאן אמרו אל יפתח אדם פיו לשטן [שם י]. כי ידעתיו וכו'. לשון חבה כמו מודע לאישה (רות ב) הלא בועז מודעתנו (שם ג) ואדעך בשם (שמות לג) ואמנם עיקר לשון כולם אינו אלא לשון ידיעה שהמחבב את האדם מקרבו אצלו ויודעו ומכירו ולמה ידעתיו למען אשר יצוה לפי שהוא מצוה את בניו עלי לשמור דרכי ואם תפרשהו כתרגומו יודע אני בו שיצוה את בניו וגו' אין למען נופל על הלשון [בראשית יח, יט]. מן השדפון ומן הירקון. מכות תבואה שבשדות. שדפון, רוח קדים אשלי"ה בלע"ז. ירקון, יובש ופני התבואה מכסיפין ונהפכין לירקון קמ"א בלע"ז [דברים כח, כב]. קשה לקרוביו. בתכריכין טובים [מו"ק כז:].

קוּם אֵימָא מִלְּתָא כָּל קְבֵיל יְנוּקָא – **"Arise and say**[11] **something generally concerning the** tragedy of the **child."**[12] פָּתַח וְאָמַר ,,וַיַּרְא ה׳ וַיִּנְאָץ מִכַּעַס בָּנָיו וּבְנֹתָיו״ – **[The spokesman] began** his exposition **by quoting** the following verse:[13] ***Hashem saw and was provoked by the anger of His sons and His daughters.*** דּוֹר שֶׁאָבוֹת מְנָאֲצִים לְהַקָּדוֹשׁ בָּרוּךְ הוּא – **In a generation where the fathers provoke the Holy One, Blessed is He,** כּוֹעֵס עַל בְּנֵיהֶם וְעַל בְּנוֹתֵיהֶם – **He becomes angry at their sons and at their daughters** וּמֵתִים כְּשֶׁהֵם קְטַנִּים – **and they die when they are minors.**[14]

The Gemara cites another version of this part of the incident: וְאִיכָּא דְּאָמְרֵי בָּחוּר הֲוָה – **Some say that [the son]** of Rav Chiya bar Abba **was a young man,** not a child. וְהָכִי קָאָמַר לֵיהּ – **And this is** the verse that **[the spokesman] told [Rav Chiya bar Abba]:**[15] ,,עַל־כֵּן עַל־בַּחוּרָיו לֹא־יִשְׂמַח אֲדֹנָי וְאֶת־יְתֹמָיו וְאֶת־אַלְמְנֹתָיו לֹא יְרַחֵם – ***Therefore, my Lord shall not rejoice over their young men, and He shall not pity their orphans and widows,*** כִּי כֻלּוֹ חָנֵף וּמֵרַע וְכָל־פֶּה דֹּבֵר נְבָלָה – ***for they are all hypocritical and evil, and every mouth utters degeneracy.*** בְּכָל־זֹאת לֹא־שָׁב אַפּוֹ וְעוֹד יָדוֹ נְטוּיָה״ – ***Yet despite all this** [all the tribulations the people have already suffered]**, His anger has not subsided and His hand is still outstretched.*** מַאי ,,וְעוֹד יָדוֹ נְטוּיָה״ – **What** is the meaning of the verse's final pronouncement ***His hand is still outstretched?*** אָמַר רַב חָנָן בַּר רַב – **Rav Chanan bar Rav said:** הַכֹּל יוֹדְעִין כַּלָּה לָמָּה נִכְנְסָה לַחוּפָּה – **Everyone knows why a bride enters the *chuppah*,** אֶלָּא כָּל הַמְנַבֵּל פִּיו – **but anyone who debases his mouth**[16] וּמוֹצִיא דְּבַר נְבָלָה מִפִּיו – **and expresses himself through an explicit remark,**[17] אֲפִילוּ נֶחְתַּם לוֹ גְּזַר דִּינוֹ שֶׁל שִׁבְעִים שָׁנָה לְטוֹבָה – **then even if a favorable decree of seventy years had been sealed for him** נֶהְפָּךְ עָלָיו לְרָעָה – **it is reversed** and a seventy-year decree **for evil** is put in its place.[18]

In any case, the spokesman's theme was that the death of the child or young man was a consequence of the provocation of God or of degenerate speech.

The Gemara asks in amazement: צְעוּרֵי קָמְצַעֵר אָתָא לְנַחוּמֵי – **He came to comfort** the mourner, לֵיהּ – **and he upset him** instead?![19]

The Gemara explains: הָכִי קָאָמַר לֵיהּ – **This is what [the spokesman] was telling [Rav Chiya bar Abba]:** חָשִׁיב אַתְּ לְאִתְפּוּסֵי אַדָּרָא – **You are important** enough **to be seized for** the sins of **the generation.**[20]

The Gemara returns to the incident: קוּם אֲמַר לֵיהּ – **[Reish Lakish]** then **said to [his spokesman],** אֵימָא מִלְּתָא כְּנֶגֶד שִׁבְחוֹ שֶׁל הַקָּדוֹשׁ בָּרוּךְ הוּא – **"Arise and say something regarding the greatness of the Holy One, Blessed is He."** פָּתַח וְאָמַר הָאֵל הַגָּדוֹל בְּרוֹב גָּדְלוֹ – **He began to recite** the first of the Mourners' Blessings: *Blessed are You, Hashem, our God, King of the universe,*[21] ***the great Almighty in His vast greatness,*** אַדִּיר וְחָזָק בְּרוֹב נוֹרָאוֹת – ***Who is mighty and strong, amidst a multitude of awesome deeds,*** מְחַיֵּה מֵתִים בְּמַאֲמָרוֹ – ***Who resurrects the dead with His word,*** עוֹשֶׂה גְדוֹלוֹת עַד אֵין חֵקֶר – ***Who performs great acts that are beyond comprehension,*** וְנִפְלָאוֹת עַד אֵין מִסְפָּר – ***and wonders beyond number.*** בָּרוּךְ אַתָּה ה׳ מְחַיֵּה הַמֵּתִים – ***Blessed are You, Hashem, Who resurrects the dead.***

The Gemara continues: קוּם אֲמַר לֵיהּ – **[Reish Lakish]** then **said to [his spokesman],** אֵימָא מִלְּתָא כְּנֶגֶד אֲבֵלִים – **"Arise and say something regarding the mourners."** פָּתַח וְאָמַר אַחֵינוּ הַמְיוּגָּעִים הַמְדוּכָּאִין – **He began to recite** the second blessing:[22] ***Our brothers who are***

NOTES

11. [אֵימָא would normally be translated "I will say," but *Ramban* (*Toras HaAdam*) states that the ensuing remarks were spoken by Yehudah bar Nachmani. Therefore, we have translated it: Say.]

12. I.e. words of comfort pertaining to the loss (*Rashi*).

Beyond the standard blessings that were recited, anyone had the right to engage in homiletics in order to add words of solace (*Meiri*).

13. *Deuteronomy* 32:19.

14. As a general rule, God does not punish children for the sins of their parents; rather, each person is punished for his own transgressions. This, indeed, is stated explicitly in Scripture: אִישׁ בְּחֶטְאוֹ יוּמָתוּ, *a man dies for his [own] sin* (see *Deuteronomy* 24:16). *Rashi* (to *Deuteronomy* loc. cit.), however, explains that this applies only when one is, in the words of the verse, already *a man* – an independent adult. When one's children are minors, they are seen as elements of their parents' domain, and are indeed subject to harm as a result of their parents' misdeeds (see also *Rambam* to *Hil. Teshuvah* 6:1).

According to the spokesman's exposition, the verse should be rendered as follows: *Hashem saw and was provoked by the anger [with which the fathers angered Him. They thereby caused Him to mete out punishment against their] sons and daughters.*

15. *Isaiah* 9:16.

16. [I.e. he speaks coarsely or degenerately about the intimate relationship into which the bride will enter.]

17. The Gemara says both that he "debases his mouth" and "expresses himself through an explicit remark" to indicate that one is not held to account if such a remark escapes from his mouth without any evil intent. The Gemara is speaking of someone who utters such a remark with purpose and premeditation (*Taz* to *Yoreh Deah* 124:1, cited in *Gilyon HaShas* here).

18. The Gemara arrives at this by relating the word וְעוֹד, *and still* (in the phrase וְעוֹד יָדוֹ נְטוּיָה), to the similarly spelled word וָעֶד, *forever* – meaning the entire lifetime of a person (seventy years being a normal life span – see *Psalms* 90:10). Thus, the verse reads: *[God's] hand is outstretched [against one who speaks obscenely] forever* – i.e. for all seventy years of his lifetime (*Rashi, Ritva*).

The extreme gravity assigned to the use of obscene language may, on the surface, seem puzzling. It becomes understandable, though, in light of the fact that man is distinguished from other creatures primarily by his capacity for speech. He alone forms verbal utterances into language, communicating ideas to others of his own kind. If he degrades this capacity, then, he degrades the essence of his humanity (*Maharal* to *Shabbos* 33a; see also *Maharsha* here).

19. The spokesman is telling Rav Chiya bar Abba to his face that his son died on account of his sins (*Rashi*).

20. There is a principle that righteous people can be seized upon because of the transgressions of the generation (see *Shabbos* 33b). The speaker was comforting Rav Chiya bar Abba by telling him that God must esteem him and his son so much that they are fit to fill that role (*Rashi*). [Moses comforted his brother Aaron in a similar vein – see *Leviticus* 10:3 and *Zevachim* 115b.]

Maharal (to *Shabbos* loc. cit.) explains the idea this way: The Jewish people is not merely a collection of disparate individuals; it is an integral unit – much like a human body, that, although made up of many different organs and limbs, comprises an integrated and unified being. Carrying this analogy further, there are times when God causes certain parts of the "body" to suffer for the sins of the organism as a whole. When this occurs, the punishment is directed against the *essential* part of the organism, for, in effect, this is a strike against the body as a whole. In the case of the Jewish people, this would mean that suffering is sometimes directed against the most righteous of individuals, for these people are the community's support and lifeblood. [For alternative explanations of this concept, see *Iyun Yaakov, Eitz Yosef,* to *Shabbos* 33b, as well as *Or HaChaim* to *Exodus* 22:5; see also *Michtav MeEliyahu* vol. 3 p. 247 and vol. 4 p. 86.]

21. Based on *Rashi,* who considers this to be the first blessing of a series, which must therefore begin and end with the clause *Blessed are You, Hashem,* etc. (see above, 8a note 10; see also *Meiri;* cf. *Ramban, Toras HaAdam* p. 150).

22. This blessing follows the preceding one so it does not have to begin with the opening clause *Blessed are You,* etc. (see *Rashi*). Although

עין משפט נר מצוה

מג א מיי' פי"ג מהלכות אבל הלכה ו טוש"ע יו"ד סי' שעט סעיף ה:
מד ב מיי' פי"ג שם הלכה א סמג עשין דרבנן ב:
מה ג מיי' שם הל"א סמג שם:
מו ד מיי' פ"ד שם הל"א סמג שם טוש"ע יו"ד סי' שעו סעי' ב:

גליוני הש"ס

גמ' כל המנבל פיו. עיין ט"ז י"ד רסי' קכד:

ליקוטי רש"י

כי קאמר רבי יוחנן בשורה. מוכח בכתובות (דף ח.) דר' יוחנן לאו תנא הוא דאמרינן התם אמר רב נחמן אמר רב חתנים מן המנין ואין אבלים מן המנין מיתיבי חתנים ואבלים מן המנין מתני' קתנית עליה דרב רב תנא הוא ופליג איתמר א"ר יצחק א"ר יוחנן חתנים מן המנין ואין אבלים מן המנין מיתיבי חתנים ואבלים מן המנין ומתרץ כי תניא ההיא בשורה הא איתא דר' יוחנן נמי תנא הוא כי היכי דמתריץ אליבא דרב רב תנא הוא ופליג היה לו לתרץ אליבא דר' יוחנן [נמי] ר' יוחנן תנא הוא ופליג אלא ודאי לאו תנא הוא [תמיד כז.]. ואין אבלים מן המנין. שהרי הוא אומר ברכה למנחמים בפני עצמן אחינו בעל הגמול ישלם לכם גמולכם הטוב ברוך אתה ה' משלם הגמול ולאבלים בפני עצמן אחינו בעל נחמות ינחם אתכם ברוך אתה ה' מנחם אבלים ואינו כוללן יחד [מגילה כג:]. מקרי. לקרות שבכתב. מתני. לשנות משניות [ע"פ סוכה כח:]. דבריה. הנהיגו [ע"פ ביצה כט.]. מתורגמניה. שעומד לפניו ומשמיע לרבים את הדרשה מפיו [ע"פ ברכות כז:]. מתורגמן הוא אומר ואחר מכרש [פסחים קיז.]. מתורגמן העומד לפני חכם הדרשן והחכם לוחש לו לשון עברית והוא מתרגם לרבים לשון שהן שומעין [יומא כ:]. לא ישמח. הרי צרות וגזירות ואת יתומיו ואת אלמנותיו לא ירחם הרי לועקין ואינם נכנין בעון מה כי כלו חנף ומרע וכל פה דובר נבלה [שבת לג.]. ומרע. רשע כמו (לעיל א) זרע מרעים [ישעיה ט, טז]. ועוד ידו נטויה. לשון ועוד כל שנותיו של אדם שאף שבעים שנה יד הדין נטויה עליו לבטל זכיותיו בעון זה. הכל יודעין כו'. ולא הוצרך לאדם לפרש למה נכנסה והמנבל פיו בכך אפילו כו' [שבת שם]. כסדום היינו. כולנו כלים [ישעיה א, ט]. קציני סדום. שרים שמעשיהם כסדום מכאן אמרו אל יפתח אדם פיו לשטן [שם י]. כי ידעתיו וכו'. לשון חבה כמו מודע לאישה (רות ב) הלא בועז מדעתנו (שם ג) ואלעדך בשם (שמות לג) ואמנם עיקר לשון כולן אינו אלא לשון ידיעה שהמחבב את האדם מקרבו אצלו ויודעו ומכירו ולמה ידעתיו למען אשר יצוה לפי שהוא מצוה את

כי תניא ההיא א בברכת המזון כי קאמר רבי יוחנן ב בשורה ואלא הא א) דאמר רבי יצחק אמר רבי יוחנן ג) מברכים ברכת חתנים בעשרה וחתנים מן המנין וברכת אבלים בעשרה ואין אבלים מן המנין ברכה בשורה מי איכא אלא כי קאמר רבי יוחנן ברחבה ואלא הא דאמר רבי יצחק אמר רבי יוחנן מברכין ברכת חתנים בעשרה כל שבעה וחתנים מן המנין וברכת אבלים בעשרה כל שבעה ואין אבלים מן המנין ברכת רחבה כל שבעה מי איכא משכחת לה בפנים חדשות כי הא דרב חייא בר אבא מקרי בניה דריש לקיש הוה ואמרי לה מתני בריה דריש לקיש הוה שכיב ליה ינוקא יומא קמא לא אזל לגביה למחר דבריה ליהודה בר נחמני מתורגמניה אמר ליה קום אימא מלתא כל קביל ינוקא פתח ואמר א) וירא ה' וינאץ מכעס בניו ובנותיו דור שאבות מנאצים להקב"ה כועס על בניהם ועל בנותיהם ומתים כשהם קטנים ואיכא דאמרי בחור הוה והכי קאמר ליה ב) על כן על בחוריו לא ישמח ה' ואת יתומיו ואת אלמנותיו לא ירחם כי כולו חנף ומרע וכל פה דובר נבלה בכל זאת לא שב אפו ועוד ידו נטויה ג) מאי ועוד ידו נטויה אמר רב חנן בר רב הכל יודעין כלה למה נכנסה לחופה אלא ° כל המנבל פיו ומוציא דבר נבלה מפיו אפילו נחתם לו גזר דינו של שבעים שנה לטובה נהפך עליו לרעה אתא לנחומי צעורי קמצער ליה הכי קאמר ליה חשיב את לאתפוסי אדרא אמר ליה קום אימא מלתא כנגד שבחו של הקב"ה פתח ואמר האל הגדול ברוב גדלו אדיר וחזק ברוב נוראות מחיה מתים במאמרו עושה גדולות עד אין חקר ונפלאות עד אין מספר בא"י מחיה המתים א"ל קום אימא מלתא כנגד אבלים פתח ואמר אחינו המיוגעים המדוכאין באבל הזה תנו לבבכם לחקור את זאת זאת היא עומדת לעד נתיב הוא מששת ימי בראשית רבים שתו רבים ישתו כמשתה ראשונים כך משתה אחרונים אחינו בעל נחמות ינחם אתכם ברוך מנחם אבלים אמר אביי רבים שתו לימא רבים ישתו לא לימא משתה ראשונים לימא משתה אחרונים לא לימא דאר"ש בן לקיש וכן תנא משמיה דר' יוסי ד) לעולם אל יפתח אדם פיו לשטן אמר רב יוסף מאי קרא ג) כסדום היינו לעמורה דמינו מאי אהדר ליה ד) שמעו דבר ה' קציני סדום וגו' א"ל קום אימא מלתא כנגד מנחמי אבלים פתח ואמר אחינו גומלי חסדים בני גומלי חסדים המחזיקים בבריתו של אברהם אבינו ה) (שנאמר ה) כי ידעתיו למען אשר יצוה את בניו וגו') אחינו בעל הגמול ישלם לכם גמולכם ברוך אתה משלם הגמול א"ל קום אימא מלתא כנגד כל ישראל פתח ואמר רבון העולמים פדה והצל מלט הושע עמך ישראל מן הדבר ומן החרב ומן הביזה ומן השדפון ומן הירקון ומכל מיני פורעניות המתרגשות ובאות לעולם טרם נקרא ואתה תענה ברוך אתה עוצר המגפה אמר עולא ואמרי לה במתניתא תנא ו) ג עשרה כוסות תקנו חכמים בבית האבל שלשה קודם אכילה כדי לפתוח את בני מעיו שלשה בתוך אכילה כדי לשרות אכילה שבמעיו וארבעה לאחר אכילה [א] אחד כנגד הזן ואחד כנגד ברכת הארץ ואחד כנגד בונה ירושלים ואחד כנגד הטוב והמטיב הוסיפו עליהם ארבעה אחד כנגד חזני העיר ואחד כנגד פרנסי העיר ואחד כנגד בית המקדש ואחד כנגד רבן גמליאל התחילו הן שותין ומשתכרין החזירו הדבר ליושנה מאי רבן גמליאל דתניא ז) בראשונה היתה הוצאת המת קשה לקרוביו יותר ממיתתו עד שהיו מניחים אותו ובורחין עד שבא רבן גמליאל ונהג קלות בעצמו והוציאוהו בכלי פשתן ונהגו ד כל העם אחריו להוציא בכלי פשתן אמר רב פפא והאידנא נהוג עלמא אפילו ח) בצרדא בר זוזא: אמר רבי אלעזר

האומר

רש"י

בברכת המזון. להצטרף לג' לזמון עליו שהרי הוא חייב בכל המצות: בשורה. כשהיו חוזרין מן הקבר היו עושין שורה סביב האבל לנחמו ומושיבין אותו והן עומדים סביב ואמרי' בסנהדרין (דף יט.) אין שורה פחות מי': ברחבה. כשמברין את האבל סעודה ראשונה משל אחרים כדאמרינן במועד קטן (דף כז:) היו מברין אותו ברחבה ומברכין שם ברכת אבלים כדמפרש לקמיה ברוך מנחם אבלים: אמר ליה. למתורגמניה: כל קביל ינוקא. לנגד המאורע דברים ניחומים על מיתת הילד: וירא ה'. מה עשו אבות: וינאץ מכעס. שהכעיסוהו וגרמו לו לפקוד על בניהם ובנותיהם: ואית דאמרי. לא תינוק היה המת אלא בחור היה והכי קרא אמר על בחוריו וגו': של ע' שנה. ועוד דריש כמו ועד עולמו של אדם נטויה ונהפכת מטוב לרע: אתא לנחומי צעורי מצער ליה. בתמיה מוכיח על פניו שבשביל עונו מת בנו: חשיב את לאתפוסי אדרא. חשוב אתה למעלה לתופסך ולאת בניך בעון הדור דקי"ל ט) בזמן שצדיקים בדור צדיקים נתפסים על הדור שנאמר וממקדשי תחלו (יחזקאל ט): האל הגדול ברוב גודלו. בברוך פתח בה ברוך אתה ה' אלהינו מלך העולם האל הגדול וכו': אחינו המיוגעים כו'. ברכה הסמוכה לחברתה היא וכן סדורות על הסדר: באבל הזה תנו לבבכם לחקור זאת שזאת עומדת לעד. שהכל מתים ולא תבכו יותר מדאי: משתה הראשונים לימא. משתה ראשונים הוא: בבריתו של אברהם. שגמל חסדים דכתיב (בראשית כא) ויטע אשל ר"ת אכילה שתיה לויה י): עשרה כוסות. להרבות לו בשתיה כדכתיב (משלי לא) תנו שכר לאובד ויין למרי נפש: קודם אכילה. שהיו רגילין להמשיך פרפראות לפני סעודה כגון ליסנין וסופגנין ואיסקריטין ובאותם פרפראות משקין לאבל ג' כוסות: אחד כנגד הזן. על כל ברכה שותה הכוס ומוזגין לו אחר: כנגד חזני העיר. תקנו להם ברכה עליו לפי שהיו שמשי העיר להתעסק במתים ובשאר צרכי ציבור: פרנסי העיר. שהיו עשירים מבזבזים ממונם לקבורת עניים: כנגד בהמ"ק. תקנו עליו ברכת ניחומים שינחמנו המקום בבניינו מאבלנו שאנו מתאבלים עליו כעל מת: כנגד ר"ג. לקמן מפרש: ליושנה. עשרה כוסות: הוצאת המת. שהיו קוברים אותו בכלים יקרים כגון שיראין וסרקות: בצרדא בר זוזא. בגד הגדוס שאינו שוה אלא דינר:

האומר

תוספות

כי תניא ההיא בברכת המזון. פי' בקונטרס להצטרף עם ג' לזימון שהרי הוא חייב בכל המצות ואין נראה לר"י דא"כ לא אתא לאשמועינן אלא דחייב במצות והוה ליה למימר בהדיא דחייב במצות ועוד דא"כ מאי פריך ליה מברכת אבלים בעשרה ואין אבלים מן המנין דקאמר ברכה בשורה מי איכא אלא ע"כ היינו ברכת המזון והדרן קושיא לדוכתין דקתני ואבלים מן המנין ואוקמינן בברכת המזון ולפירוש הקונטרס לא קשיא מידי דכי קתני ואבלים מן המנין היינו להצטרף לזימון לומר נברך שאכלנו משלו אבל ברכת אבלים שמברכים בברכת המזון קאמר רבי יוחנן דאינו מן המנין לכך צריך לפרש כי תניא ההיא בברכת המזון היינו ברכת אבלים שבברכת המזון מכאן משמע שברכת אבלים שבברכת המזון לא הוי אלא בעשרה מדסליק אדעתיה דמקשן דאיירי בברכת אבלים שבברכת המזון וקאמר בעשרה והוה ניחא ליה בהכי אי לאו משום דקתני לעיל בברייתא ואבלים מן המנין אם כן צריך עשרה:

אלא כי קאמר ר' יוחנן ברחבה. אי גרסינן אלא משמע דההיא דלעיל נמי מעמיד ברחבה ותימה למה הוצרכו תרי מילי דר' יוחנן ההיא דלעיל והך וצריך לומר דחדא מכלל חברתה איתמר ההיא דלעיל מכללא דהך אבל אי ל"ג אלא ניחא דלעיל איירי בשורה והכא ברחבה בלא פנים חדשות ומימרא שלישית של רבי יוחנן הוצרך להשמיענו דבפנים חדשות אין אבלים מן המנין ואי נקט ההיא ה"א איפכא דוקא מיום ראשון ואילך אבל ביום ראשון שייכי טפי ומברכים לה בלא י':

מסורת הש"ס

א) מגילה דף כג., ב) [תוספתא מגילה פ"ג], ג) שבת דף לג., ד) ברכות יט. ס. ע"ש, ה) ס"א אינו, ו) שמחות פי"ד [פסחים קי.], ז) מ"ק כז: [תוספתא נדה פ"ט], ח) [גי' הערוך צדרא ועיין ב"מ נא. דאיתא צדריתא ופרש"י בגדי קנבוס אבל בשאלתות איתא בצרדא כדאיתא לפנינו], ט) [שבת לג:], י) [וע"ע רש"י סוטה י. ד"ה פונדק].

הגהות הגר"א

[א] גמ' (אחד כנגד הזן כו' עד הטוב והמטיב) תא"מ (ואפשר דהם כנגד ד' ברכות האמורים למעלה פתח ואמר כו' ואולי על כל כוס אומר ברכה א'):

תורה אור השלם

א) וַיַּרְא יְיָ וַיִּנְאָץ מִכַּעַס בָּנָיו וּבְנֹתָיו: [דברים לב, יט]

ב) עַל כֵּן עַל בַּחוּרָיו לֹא יִשְׂמַח אֲדֹנָי וְאֶת יְתֹמָיו וְאֶת אַלְמְנֹתָיו לֹא יְרַחֵם כִּי כֻלּוֹ חָנֵף וּמֵרַע וְכָל פֶּה דֹּבֵר נְבָלָה בְּכָל זֹאת לֹא שָׁב אַפּוֹ וְעוֹד יָדוֹ נְטוּיָה: [ישעיה ט, טז]

ג) לוּלֵי יְיָ צְבָאוֹת הוֹתִיר לָנוּ שָׂרִיד כִּמְעָט כִּסְדֹם הָיִינוּ לַעֲמֹרָה דָּמִינוּ: [ישעיה א, ט]

ד) שִׁמְעוּ דְבַר יְיָ קְצִינֵי סְדֹם הַאֲזִינוּ תּוֹרַת אֱלֹהֵינוּ עַם עֲמֹרָה: [ישעיה א, י]

ה) כִּי יְדַעְתִּיו לְמַעַן אֲשֶׁר יְצַוֶּה אֶת בָּנָיו וְאֶת בֵּיתוֹ אַחֲרָיו וְשָׁמְרוּ דֶּרֶךְ יְיָ לַעֲשׂוֹת צְדָקָה וּמִשְׁפָּט לְמַעַן הָבִיא יְיָ עַל אַבְרָהָם אֵת אֲשֶׁר דִּבֶּר עָלָיו: [בראשית יח, יט]

בניו עלי לשמור דרכי ואם תפרשהו בתרגומו יודע אני בו שיהא את בניו וגו' אין למען נופל על הלשון [בראשית יח, יט]. מן השדפון ומן הירקון. מכות תבואה שבשדות. שדפון, רוח קדים שמשלי"ה בלע"ז. ירקון, יובש ופני התבואה מכסיפין והכסיפן לירקון קמ"א בלע"ז [דברים כח, כב]. קשה לקרוביו. בתכריכין טובים [מו"ק כז:].

The Gemara answers:

כִּי תַּנְיָא הַהִיא – **When that Baraisa was taught,** בְּבִרְכַּת הַמָּזוֹן – it was taught **in** reference **to** ***Bircas HaMazon*****.** Then the mourner may be counted as one of the three required to recite the *zimun* blessing.[1] כִּי קָאָמַר רַבִּי יוֹחָנָן – And **when R' Yochanan said** that a mourner is not counted as part of a quorum בְּשׁוּרָה – he was speaking **in reference to the row** of comforters.[2]

The Gemara asks:

וְאֶלָּא הָא דְּאָמַר רַבִּי יִצְחָק אָמַר רַבִּי יוֹחָנָן – **But** now let us examine **that which R' Yitzchak said in the name of R' Yochanan:**[3] מְבָרְכִים בִּרְכַּת חֲתָנִים בַּעֲשָׂרָה – ***Sheva Berachos*** **are recited** only **in** the presence of at least **ten** people, וַחֲתָנִים מִן הַמִּנְיָן – **and the grooms**[4] **are** counted as part **of the quorum;** וּבִרְכַּת אֲבֵלִים בַּעֲשָׂרָה – **and** the **Mourners' Blessing** is recited only **in** the presence of at least **ten** people, וְאֵין אֲבֵלִים מִן הַמִּנְיָן – **but the mourners are not** counted as part **of the quorum.** בִּרְכָּה בְּשׁוּרָה מִי אִיכָּא – Now, if R' Yochanan is referring to the row of comforters, **what blessing is there** that is recited when the comforters stand **in a row?** There is no blessing said then![5] Therefore, R' Yochanan must not be referring to the quorum needed for a row. – ? –

The Gemara offers a different answer:

אֶלָּא כִּי קָאָמַר רַבִּי יוֹחָנָן – **Rather, when R' Yochanan stated** that a mourner is not counted as part of the quorum, בִּרְחָבָה – he was speaking **in reference to** the blessings recited in **the street** during the meal of condolence.[6]

The Gemara objects:

וְאֶלָּא הָא דְּאָמַר רַבִּי יִצְחָק אָמַר רַבִּי יוֹחָנָן – **But** now let us examine a more expanded version of the above statement **that R' Yitzchak said in the name of R' Yochanan:** מְבָרְכִין בִּרְכַּת חֲתָנִים בַּעֲשָׂרָה כָּל שִׁבְעָה – ***Sheva Berachos*** **are recited** only **in** the presence of at least **ten** people for **all seven** days, וַחֲתָנִים מִן הַמִּנְיָן – **and the grooms are** counted as part **of the quorum;** וּבִרְכַּת אֲבֵלִים בַּעֲשָׂרָה כָּל שִׁבְעָה – and the **Mourners' Blessing** is recited only **in** the presence of at least **ten** people for **all seven** days of *aveilus,* וְאֵין אֲבֵלִים מִן הַמִּנְיָן – but the mourners are not counted as part **of the quorum.** בִּרְכַּת רְחָבָה כָּל שִׁבְעָה מִי אִיכָּא – Now, if R' Yochanan is referring to the blessing in the street, **in what case** would the **blessing in** the **street** be recited **for "all seven** days" of mourning?[7]

The Gemara answers:

מַשְׁכַּחַתְּ לָהּ בְּפָנִים חֲדָשׁוֹת – **You may** indeed **find [such a case] when there are new faces** that come to comfort the mourner each day.[8] כִּי הָא דְּרַב חִיָּיא בַּר אַבָּא – **Like that** incident **involving Rav Chiya bar Abba:**[9] מַקְרֵי בְּנֵיהּ דְּרֵישׁ לָקִישׁ הֲוָה – **[Rav Chiya bar Abba] was the Scripture-teacher of Reish Lakish's sons,** וְאָמְרִי לָהּ מַתְנֵי בְּרֵיהּ דְּרֵישׁ לָקִישׁ הֲוָה – **and some say** instead **that he was the Mishnah-teacher of Reish Lakish's son.** שְׁכִיב לֵיהּ יְנוּקָא – **A child [of Rav Chiya bar Abba] died.** יוֹמָא קַמָּא לָא אֲזַל לְגַבֵּיהּ – **The first day [Reish Lakish] did not go to [Rav Chiya bar Abba]** to console him. לְמָחָר דַּבְרֵיהּ לִיהוּדָה בַּר נַחְמָנִי מְתוּרְגְּמָנֵיהּ – **The next day [Reish Lakish] took Yehudah bar Nachmani, his spokesman,**[10] along with him there. אָמַר לֵיהּ – **[Reish Lakish] said to [his spokesman],**

NOTES

1. [See above, 8a note 21 for a general definition of the *zimun* blessing. See *Berachos* chapter 7 for more details.]

The *zimun* blessing is not recited in any form unless there are at least three men participating. If there are less than ten, it is recited without the word אֱלֹהֵינוּ, *our God.* A mourner can be counted towards a *zimun* since he is still obligated in all of the commandments. [If he were not obligated to recite *Bircas HaMazon,* he could not participate in the *zimun*] (*Rashi*). The Rishonim object to this explanation because it is obvious that a mourner is obligated to fulfill all the mitzvos like any other person, or because the Baraisa should have said simply, "A mourner is duty bound to observe the mitzvos." Why would the Baraisa address itself specifically to the mitzvah of *zimun*?

Ritva suggests that, according to *Rashi,* the Baraisa alludes to the practice of reciting a special *zimun* in the house of a mourner [as is done in the house of a groom]. In this *zimun,* the leader says נְבָרֵךְ מְנַחֵם אֲבֵלִים שֶׁאָכַלְנוּ מִשֶּׁלוֹ, *Let us bless the One Who comforts mourners of Whose we have eaten.* [Since the mourner is not among the comforters but the comforted,] I would have thought that he cannot be one of the three for this *zimun.* The Baraisa therefore informs us that this is not so; this addition is a reference to mourners in general [not this particular mourner] (cf. *Tosafos, Ramban, Rashba*). *Ritva* reports that it was customary to say this special *zimun* in his time (see also *Yoreh Deah* 379:3; cf. *Tamim De'im* §176; see below, note 33).

2. After the burial, those present form a row around the mourner in order to comfort him; they seat him and stand around him (*Rashi;* cf. *Rashi* to *Moed Katan* 24b ד״ה ואין; *Meiri; Rashash*). [The custom today is for the people to form parallel rows and for the mourners to pass between them to receive condolences. See *Sanhedrin* 19a and *Yerushalmi, Berachos* 3:2.] The Gemara in *Sanhedrin* (ibid.) states that this row must consist of at least ten people. R' Yochanan's statement that a mourner cannot be part of a quorum means that ten people are needed besides the mourner (see also Gemara there).

[See *Tosafos* (above, 8a) as to why the Gemara offers this answer in explanation of R' Yochanan's position but not that of Rav.]

3. The Gemara cites a more complete version of R' Yochanan's statement than that cited above to disprove its current defense of R' Yochanan.

4. [When R' Yochanan speaks of "grooms" (in the plural), he is referring to grooms in general, not to a case in which there are two or more grooms within a single quorum (*Ritva* to 8a, end). The Rishonim discuss the permissibility (or advisability) of reciting one set of *Sheva Berachos* for two grooms simultaneously (see citations in *Ritva MHK* ed., note 68).]

5. Each of the people in the row tells the mourner, "You should be comforted" (*Rashi* to *Moed Katan* 24b ד״ה ואין), but no blessings are recited.

6. The Gemara in *Moed Katan* (27b) states that the acquaintances of the mourner are supposed to provide his first meal after the burial. He would be given that meal of condolence in the street upon his return to the city from the cemetery and they would recite the blessing for mourners, *Blessed are You, Hashem . . . Who comforts mourners,* that will be described below (*Rashi, Ritva*). Actually the Gemara will list a whole series of blessings below. However, this is the primary blessing; the other blessings are in the category of optional praises and prayers and may be omitted or combined with the primary blessing (*Ramban,* in *Toras HaAdam* p. 153 *MHK* ed.; see, however, below, note 33).

[In towns where there was no street that could be used for this purpose, the synagogue or the mourner's home was used instead (*Ramban,* loc. cit. p. 154, based on *Nedarim* 38b and *Yerushalmi Sanhedrin* 6:9).]

7. That blessing is recited only at the meal brought to the mourner after the burial. How then could R' Yochanan state that this blessing is recited all seven days?

8. Those friends and relatives of the mourner who had not been present the first day would come to the mourner's house with another meal of condolence and recite the Mourners' Blessing anew (*Meiri*).

9. The Gemara here begins to cite a lengthy incident that continues for most of this *amud.* The Gemara's proof that the Mourners' Blessings are said during the week of mourning whenever there are *panim chadashos* will be from that incident in which an Amora visited a house of mourning on the second day and recited these blessings then. [The Gemara will interrupt the narrative here and there to clarify a point.]

10. Yehudah bar Nachmani is identified as Reish Lakish's "*meturgeman*" (spokesman) in *Sotah* 37b (*Gilyonei HaShas;* see also *Chagigah* 16a).

Literally, *meturgeman* means "interpreter." A *meturgeman* assists a Sage delivering a Torah discourse to the community. Typically, the Sage sits and speaks a sentence, softly and in Hebrew, to the *meturgeman.* The *meturgeman* then amplifies his words to the assembled listeners, translating them into the vernacular (see *Rashi* to *Yoma* 20b ד״ה לא היה אמורא and to *Pesachim* 50b ד״ה מתורגמנין). Here, Reish Lakish directed his spokesman Yehudah bar Nachmani to comfort the mourner.

כי תניא ההיא ^א בברכת המזון כי קאמר רבי יוחנן ^ב בשורה ואלא הא ^א דאמר רבי יוחנן ^ג מברכים ברכת חתנים בעשרה וחתנים מן המנין וברכת אבלים בעשרה ואין אבלים מן המנין ברכה בשורה מי איכא אלא כי קאמר רבי יוחנן ברחבה ואלא הא דאמר רבי יצחק אמר רבי יוחנן מברכין ברכת חתנים בעשרה כל שבעה וחתנים מן המנין וברכת אבלים בעשרה כל שבעה ואין אבלים מן המנין ברכת רחבה כל שבעה מי איכא משכחת לה בפנים חדשות כי הא דרב חייא בר אבא מקרי בניה דריש לקיש הוה ואמרי לה מתני בריה דריש לקיש הוה שכיב ליה ינוקא יומא קמא לא אזל לגביה למחר דבריה ליהודה בר נחמני מתורגמניה אמר ליה קום אימא מלתא כל קבל ינוקא פתח ואמר ^א וירא ה' וינאץ מכעס בניו ובנותיו דור שאבות מנאצים להקב"ה כועס על בניהם ועל בנותיהם ומתים כשהם קטנים ואיכא דאמרי בחור הוה והכי קאמר ליה ^ב על כן על בחוריו לא ישמח ה' ואת יתומיו ואת אלמנותיו לא ירחם כי כולו חנף ומרע וכל פה דובר נבלה בכל זאת לא שב אפו ועוד ידו נטויה ^ג מאי ועוד ידו נטויה אמר רב חנן בר רב הכל יודעין כלה למה נכנסה לחופה אלא ^ה כל המנבל פיו ומוציא דבר נבלה מפיו אפילו נחתם לו גזר דינו של שבעים שנה לטובה נהפך עליו לרעה אתא לנחומי צעורי קמצער ליה הכי קאמר ליה חשיב את לאתפוסי אדרא אמר ליה קום אימא מלתא כנגד שבחו של הקב"ה פתח ואמר האל הגדול ברוב גדלו אדיר וחזק ברוב נוראות מחיה מתים במאמרו עושה גדולות עד אין חקר ונפלאות עד אין מספר בא"י מחיה המתים א"ל קום אימא מלתא כנגד אבלים פתח ואמר אחינו המיוגעים המדוכאין באבל הזה תנו לבבכם לחקור את זאת זאת היא עומדת לעד נתיב הוא מששת ימי בראשית רבים שתו רבים ישתו כמשתה ראשונים כך משתה אחרונים אחינו בעל נחמות ינחם אתכם ברוך מנחם אבלים אמר אביי רבים שתו לא לימא רבים ישתו לא לימא משתה ראשונים לימא משתה אחרונים לא לימא דאר"ש בן לקיש וכן תנא משמיה דר' יוסי ^ד לעולם אל יפתח אדם פיו לשטן אמר רב יוסף מאי קרא ^ג כסדום היינו לעמורה דמינו מאי אהדר ליה ^ד שמעו דבר ה' קציני סדום וגו' א"ל קום אימא מלתא כנגד מנחמי אבלים פתח ואמר אחינו גומלי חסדים בני גומלי חסדים המחזיקים בבריתו של אברהם אבינו ^ו (שנאמר ^ה כי ידעתיו למען אשר יצוה את בניו וגו') אחינו בעל הגמול ישלם לכם גמולכם ברוך אתה משלם הגמול א"ל קום אימא מלתא כנגד כל ישראל פתח ואמר רבון העולמים פדה והצל מלט הושע עמך ישראל מן הדבר ומן החרב ומן הביזה ומן השדפון ומן הירקון ומכל מיני פורעניות המתרגשות ובאות לעולם טרם נקרא ואתה תענה ברוך אתה עוצר המגפה אמר עולא ואמרי לה במתניתא תנא ^ז עשרה כוסות תקנו חכמים בבית האבל שלשה קודם אכילה כדי לפתוח את בני מעיו שלשה בתוך אכילה כדי לשרות אכילה שבמעיו וארבעה לאחר אכילה [א] אחד כנגד הזן ואחד כנגד ברכת הארץ ואחד כנגד בונה ירושלים ואחד כנגד הטוב והמטיב הוסיפו עליהם ארבעה אחד כנגד חזני העיר ואחד כנגד פרנסי העיר ואחד כנגד בית המקדש ואחד כנגד רבן גמליאל התחילו הן שותין ומשתכרין החזירו הדבר ליושנה מאי רבן גמליאל דתניא ^ח בראשונה היתה הוצאת המת קשה לקרוביו יותר ממיתתו עד שהיו מניחין אותו ובורחין עד שבא רבן גמליאל ונהג קלות בעצמו והוציאוהו בכלי פשתן ונהגו ^י כל העם אחריו להוציא בכלי פשתן אמר רב פפא והאידנא נהוג עלמא אפילו ^ט בצרדא בר זוזא: אמר רבי אלעזר

האומר

רש"י

בברכת המזון. להצטרף לג' לזמון עליו שהרי הוא חייב בכל המלות: בשורה. כשהיו חוזרין מן הקבר היו עושין שורה סביב האבל לנחמו ומושיבין אותו והן עומדים סביב ואמרי' בסנהדרין (דף יט.) אין שורה פחות מי': ברחבה. כשמברכין את האבל סעודה ראשונה משל אחרים כדאמרינן במועד קטן (דף כ:) היו מברין אותו ברחבה ומברכין שם ברכת אבלים כדמפרש לקמיה ברוך מנחם אבלים: אמר ליה. למתורגמניה: כל קביל ינוקא. לנגד המאורע דברים ניחומים על מיתת הילד: וירא ה'. מה עשו אבות: וינאץ מכעס. שהכעיסוהו וגרמו לו לפקוד על בניהם ובנותיהם: ואית דאמרי. לא תינוק היה המת אלא בחור היה והך קרא אמר על בחוריו וגו': של ע' שנה. ועוד דריש כמו ועד עולמו של אדם נטויה ונהפכת מטוב לרע: אתא לנחומי צעורי מצער ליה. בתמיה מוכיח על פניו שבשביל עונו מת בנו: חשיב את לאתפוסי אדרא. חשוב אתה למעלה לתופסך ולאת בניך בעון הדור דקי"ל ^י בזמן שצדיקים בדור צדיקים נתפסים על הדור שנאמר וממקדשי תחלו (יחזקאל ט): האל הגדול ברוב גודלו. בברוך פתח בה ברוך אתה ה' אלהינו מלך העולם האל הגדול וכו': אחינו המיוגעים כו'. ברכה הסמוכה לחברתה היא וכן סדורות על הסדר: באבל הזה תנו לבבכם לחקור זאת שזאת עומדת לעד. שהכל מתים ולא תבכו יותר מדאי: משתה הראשונים לימא. משתה ראשונים הוא: בבריתו של אברהם. שגמל חסדים דכתיב (בראשית כא) ויטע אשל ר"ת אכילה שתיה לויה^י: עשרה כוסות. להרבות לו בשתיה כדכתיב (משלי לא) תנו שכר לאובד ויין למרי נפש: קודם אכילה. שהיו רגילין להמשיך פרפראות לפני סעודה כגון ליסנין וסופגנין ואיסקריטין ובאותם פרפראות משקין לאבל ג' כוסות: אחד כנגד הזן. על כל ברכה שותה הכוס ומוזגין לו אחר: כנגד חזני העיר. תקנו להם ברכה עליו לפי שהיו שמשי העיר להתעסק במתים ובשאר צרכי ציבור: פרנסי העיר. שהיו עשירים מבזבזים ממונם לקבורת עניים: כנגד בהמ"ק. תקנו עליו ברכת ניחומים שינחמנו המקום בבניינו מאבלנו שאנו מתאבלים עליו כבעל מת: כנגד ר"ג. לקמן מפרש: ליושנה. עשרה כוסות: הוצאת המת. שהיו קוברים אותו בכלים יקרים כגון שיראין וסרקות: בצרדא בר זוזא. בגד קנבוס שאינו שוה אלא דינר:

תוספות

כי תניא ההיא בברכת המזון. פי' בקונטרס להצטרף עם ג' לזימון שהרי הוא חייב בכל המצות ואין נראה לר"י דא"כ לא אתא לאשמועינן אלא דחייב במצות והוה ליה למימר בהדיא דחייב במצות ועוד דא"כ מאי פריך ליה מברכת אבלים בעשרה ואין אבלים מן המנין דקאמר ברכה בשורה מי איכא אלא ע"כ היינו ברכת המזון והדין קושיא לדוכתין דקתני ואבלים מן המנין ואוקמינן בברכת המזון ולפירוש הקונטרס לא קשיא מידי דכי קתני ואבלים מן המנין היינו להצטרף לזימון לומר נברך שאכלנו משלו אבל ברכת אבלים שמברכים בברכת המזון קאמר רבי יוחנן דאינו מן המנין לכך צריך לפרש כי תניא ההיא בברכת המזון היינו ברכת אבלים שבברכת המזון מכאן משמע שברכת אבלים שבברכת המזון לא הוי אלא בעשרה מדמסליק אדעתיה דמקשן דאיירי בברכת אבלים שבברכת המזון וקאמר בעשרה והוה ניחא ליה בהכי אי לאו משום דקתני לעיל בברייתא ואבלים מן המנין אם כן צריך עשרה:

אלא כי קאמר ר' יוחנן ברחבה. אי גרסינן אלא משמע דההיא דלעיל נמי מעמיד ברחבה ותימה למה הוצרכו תרי מילי דר' יוחנן ההיא דלעיל והך וצריך לומר דחדא מכלל חברתה אתמר ההיא דלעיל מכלל דהך אבל אי ל"ג אלא ניחא דלעיל איירי בשורה והכא ברחבה בלא פנים חדשות ומימרא שלישית של רבי יוחנן הוצרך להשמיענו דבפנים חדשות אין אבלים מן המנין ואי נקט ההיא ה"א איפכא דוקא מיום ראשון ואילך אבל ביום ראשון שייכי טפי ומברכים לה בלא י':

עין משפט נר מצוה

מג א מיי' פ"ד מהלכות אבל הלכה ו טוש"ע יו"ד סי' שעט סעיף ה:
מד ב מיי' פי"ג שם הלכה א סמג עשין דרבנן ב:
מה ג מיי' שם הל"ח סמג שם:
מו ד מיי' פ"ד שם הל"א סמג שם טוש"ע יו"ד סי' שנג סעי' ב:

גליון הש"ס

גמ' כל המנבל פיו. עיין ט"ז יו"ד רסי' קכד:

ליקוטי רש"י

כי קאמר רבי יוחנן בשורה. מוכח בכתובות (דף ח.) דר' יוחנן לאו תנא הוא דאמרינן התם אמר רב נחמן אמר רב חתנים מן המנין ואין אבלים מן המנין מיתיבי חתנים ואבלים מן המנין מתני' קרמית עליה דרב רב תנא הוא ופליג איתמר א"ר יצחק א"ר יוחנן חתנים מן המנין ואין אבלים מן המנין מיתיבי חתנים ואבלים מן המנין ומתרץ כי תניא ההיא בשורה ואם איתא דר' יוחנן נמי תנא הוא כי היכי דתריך אליבא דרב רב תנא הוא ופליג היה לו לתרץ אליבא דר' יוחנן [נמי] ר' יוחנן תנא הוא ופליג אלא ודאי לאו תנא הוא [תכיד כו.]. ואין אבלים מן המנין. שהרי הוא אומר ברכה למנחמים בפני עצמן אחינו בעל הגמול ישלם לכם גמולכם הטוב ברוך אתה ה' משלם הגמול ולאבלים בפני עצמן אחינו בעל נחמות ינחם אתכם ברוך אתה ה' מנחם אבלים ואינו כוללן יחד [מגילה כג:]. מקרי. לקרות שבכתב. מתני. לשנות משניות [ע"פ סוכה כח:]. דבריה. הנהיגו [ע"פ ביצה כט.]. מתורגמניה. שעומד לפניו וסמיך לרבים את הדרשה מפיו [ע"פ ברכות כז:]. מתורגמן, הוא אומר ואחר מפרש [פסחים קיז.]. מתורגמן, העומד לפני חכם הדרשן והחכם לוחש לו לשון עברית והוא מתרגם לרבים לשון שהן שומעין [יומא כ:]. לא ישמח. הרי גרות וגזירות ואת יתומיו ואת אלמנותיו לא ירפא הרי צועקין ואינם כנענין בעון מה כי כלו חנף ומרע וכל פה דובר נבלה [שבת לג.]. ומרע. רשע כמו (לעיל א) זרע מרעים [ישעיה ט, טז]. ועוד ידו נטויה. לשון וכבר כל שנותיו של אדם שהן שבעים שנה יד הדין נטויה עליו לבטל זכיותיו בעון זה. הכל יודעין כו'. ולא הוצרך לאדם לפרש למה נכנסה והמנבל פיו בכך אפילו כו' [שבת שם]. כסדום היינו. כולנו כלים [ישעיה א, ט]. קציני סדום. שרים שמעשיהם כסדום מכאן אמרו אל יפתח אדם פיו לשטן [שם י]. כי ידעתיו וגו'. לשון חבה כמו מודע לאישה (רות ב) הלא בועז מודעתנו (שם ג) ואדעך בשם (שמות לג) ואמנם עיקר לשון כולם אינו אלא לשון ידיעה שהמחבב את האדם מקרבו אצלו ויודעו ומכירו ולמה ידעתיו למען אשר יצוה לפי שהוא מצוה את בניו עלי לשמור דרכי ואם תפרשהו כתרגומו יודע אני בו שיצוה את בניו וגו' אין למען נופל על הלשון [בראשית יח, יט]. מן השדפון ומן הירקון. מכות תבואה שבשדות. שדפון, רוח קדים שאליד"ה בלע"ז. ירקון, יובש ופני התבואה מכסיפים ונהפכין לירקון קמ"א בלע"ז [דברים כח, כב]. קשה לקרוביו. בתכריכין טובים [מו"ק כז:].

מסורת הש"ס

א) מגילה דף כג:, ב) [תוספתא מגילה פ"ג], ג) שבת דף לג., ד) ברכות יט. ס. ע"ש, ה) ס"א אינו, ו) שמחות פי"ד [פסחים קי.], ז) מ"ק כז: [תוספתא נדה פ"ט], ח) [גי' הערוך צדרא ועיין ב"מ נא. דאיתא צדרייתא ופרש"י בגדי קנבוס אבל בשאלתות איתא בצרדא כדאיתא לפנינו], ט) [שבת לג:], י) [וע"ע רש"י סוטה י. ד"ה פונדק].

הגהות הגר"א

[א] גמ' (אחד כנגד הזן כו' עד הטוב והמטיב) תא"מ (ואפשר דהם כנגד ד' ברכות האמורים למעלה פתח ואמר כו' ואולי על כל כוס אומר ברכה א'):

תורה אור השלם

א) וַיַּרְא יְיָ וַיִּנְאָץ מִכַּעַס בָּנָיו וּבְנֹתָיו: [דברים לב, יט]

ב) עַל כֵּן עַל בַּחוּרָיו לֹא יִשְׂמַח אֲדֹנָי וְאֶת יְתֹמָיו וְאֶת אַלְמְנֹתָיו לֹא יְרַחֵם כִּי כֻלּוֹ חָנֵף וּמֵרַע וְכָל פֶּה דֹּבֵר נְבָלָה בְּכָל זֹאת לֹא שָׁב אַפּוֹ וְעוֹד יָדוֹ נְטוּיָה: [ישעיה ט, טז]

ג) לוּלֵי יְיָ צְבָאוֹת הוֹתִיר לָנוּ שָׂרִיד כִּמְעָט כִּסְדֹם הָיִינוּ לַעֲמֹרָה דָּמִינוּ: [ישעיה א, ט]

ד) שִׁמְעוּ דְבַר יְיָ קְצִינֵי סְדֹם הַאֲזִינוּ תּוֹרַת אֱלֹהֵינוּ עַם עֲמֹרָה: [ישעיה א, י]

ה) כִּי יְדַעְתִּיו לְמַעַן אֲשֶׁר יְצַוֶּה אֶת בָּנָיו וְאֶת בֵּיתוֹ אַחֲרָיו וְשָׁמְרוּ דֶּרֶךְ יְיָ לַעֲשׂוֹת צְדָקָה וּמִשְׁפָּט לְמַעַן הָבִיא יְיָ עַל אַבְרָהָם אֵת אֲשֶׁר דִּבֶּר עָלָיו: [בראשית יח, יט]

א שהכל ברא לכבודו ויוצר האדם ואשר יצר את האדם בצלמו בצלם דמות תבניתו והתקין לו ממנו בנין עדי עד ברוך אתה ה' יוצר האדם שוש תשיש ותגל העקרה בקבוץ בניה לתוכה בשמחה ברוך אתה ה' משמח ציון בבניה שמח תשמח ריעים האהובים כשמחך יצירך בגן עדן מקדם ברוך אתה ה' משמח חתן וכלה ברוך אתה ה' אמ"ה אשר ברא ששון ושמחה חתן וכלה גילה רינה דיצה חדוה אהבה ואחוה ושלום וריעות מהרה ה' אלהינו ישמע בערי יהודה ובחוצות ירושלים קול ששון וקול שמחה קול חתן וקול כלה קול מצהלות חתנים מחופתם ונערים ממשתה נגינתם בא"י משמח חתן עם הכלה לוי איקלע לבי רבי בהלוליה דר"ש בריה בריך חמש רב אסי איקלע לבי רב אשי בהלוליה דמר בריה בריך שית לימא בהא קמיפלגי דמ"ס חדא יצירה הואי ומ"ס שתי יצירות הואי לא דכ"ע חדא יצירה הואי מ"ס בתר מחשבה אזלינן ומ"ס בתר מעשה אזלינן כי הא דרב יהודה רמי כתיב א) ויברא אלהים את האדם בצלמו וכתיב ב) זכר ונקבה בראם הא כיצד בתחלה עלה במחשבה לבראות שנים ולבסוף נברא אחד רב אשי איקלע לבי רב כהנא יומא קמא בריך כולהו מכאן ואילך ב אי איכא פנים חדשות בריך כולהו ואי לא אפושי שמחה בעלמא הוא מברך שהשמחה במעונו ואשר ברא משבעה ועד שלשים בין אמר להו מחמת הלולא ובין לא אמר להו מחמת הלולא מברך שהשמחה במעונו מכאן ואילך אי אמר להו מחמת הלולא מברך שהשמחה במעונו ואי לא לא וכי א"ל מחמת הלולא עד אימת אמר רב פפי משמיה דרבא ג עד תריסר ירחי שתא ומעיקרא מאימת אמר רב פפא מכי רמו שערי באסינתא איני והא רב פפא איעסק לאבא מר בריה ובריך משעת אירוסין שאני רב פפא דהוה טריח ליה רבינא איעסק ליה לבריה בי רב חביבא ובריך משעת אירוסין אמר קים לי בגוייהו דלא הדרי בהו לא אסתייע מילתא והדרי בהו רב תחליפא בר מערבא איקלע לבבל בריך שית אריכתא ולית הלכתא כוותיה רב חביבא איקלע לבי מהולא בריך שהשמחה במעונו ולית הלכתא כוותיה משום דטרידי דאית ליה צערא לינוקא א"ר נחמן אמר רב ד חתנים מן המנין ואין אבלים מן המנין מיתיבי חתנים ואבלים מן המנין מתניתא קא רמית עליה דרב רב תנא הוא ופליג איתמר אמר ר' יצחק א"ר יוחנן חתנים מן המנין ואין אבלים מן המנין כי

רש"י

והתקין לו ממנו בנין עדי עד. היא הנקבה: שוש תשיש. לפי שאנו צריכין להעלות זכרון ירושלים על ראש שמחתנו שנאמר (תהלים קלז) תדבק לשוני לחכי וגו': שמח תשמח. ברכה לחתן וכלה שיגליהו בשמחה וטוב לב ואשר ברא לשם כל ישראל ולפי שהסדר מתחיל מאשר יצר לפיכך פתח בה בברוך וחתם בה בברוך כדרך כל ראשי סדרי ברכות ושוש תשיש ושמח תשמח מפני שהן ברכה הסמוכה לחברתה לא פתח בה בברוך שכן תיקנו לכל הברכות שסמוכות אחר הראשונה על הסדר ואשר ברא מפני שהיא נאמרת יחידית ברוב ימי המשתה כשאין שם פנים חדשות לפיכך אינה מן הסמוכות והוצרך לפתוח בה בברוך ולסיים בה בברוך אבל שהכל ברא לכבודו אינה מן הסדר אלא לאסיפת העם הנאספים שם לגמול חסד זכר לחסדי המקום שנהג עם אדם הראשון שנעשה לו שושבין ונתעסק בו ואסיפה זו כבוד המקום היא וברכה זו לכך נתקנה ומשעת אסיפה היא ראויה לברך אלא מכיון שיש ברכה על הכוס הזקיקוה לסדרה עליו מידי דהוה אברכת בשמים וברכת על האור במוצאי שבת דאמרי' (ירושלמי דפסחים פ"י) רבי מפזרן וחוזר וסודרן על הכוס ורבי חייא מכנסן הואיל ויש שם כוס ולפי שאינה משאר סדר הברכות וכולה הודאה אחת לא חתמו בה בברוך מידי דהוה אברכת פירות ומצות וכן ברכת יוצר האדם שתיקנה ליצירה ראשונה של אדם הראשון דלקמן אי למ"ד ב' יצירות הוו אי למ"ד ב' יצירות עלו במחשבה ובתר מחשבה אזלינן מ"מ אינה מסדר ברכות הזווג דהא ביצירה הראשונה אכתי נקבה לא הואי וא"ת למה היא באה מתוך שאנו מברכין על יצירה השניה תקנו אף על הראשונה שהיא עיקר ותחלתו: והתקין לו ממנו. מגופו מצלעותיו: בנין עדי עד. בנין נוהג לדורות וחוה קרי לה בנין על שם ויבן את הצלע (בראשית ב): עקרה. ירושלים: ריעים האהובים. החתן והכלה שהן ריעים האוהבים זה את זה: כשמחך יצירך. כמו ששמחת את אדם הראשון: בגן עדן מקדם. דכתיב ויטע גן בעדן מקדם וישם שם וגו' (שם): משמח חתן וכלה. ובאחרונה משמח חתן עם הכלה לפי ששמחת ברכה הראשונה לא בשמחת חתונה אנו אומרים שהרי תפלה היא שמתפללים ומברכין שיהו שמחים בהצלחה כל ימיהם לפיכך אין לחתום בה משמחת חתן עם הכלה דמשמע איש באשתו אלא ברוך ה' משמח את שניהם לעולם בסיפוק מזונות וכל טוב ובאחרונה שבה משבח להקב"ה שברא חמדת דיבוק איש באשה על ידי שמחה וחדוה לפיכך יש לחתום משמח חתן עם הכלה שהוא לשון שמחת איש באשה: בריך חמש. שהכל ואשר יצר ושוש תשיש שמח תשמח אשר ברא: בריך שית. יוצר האדם הוסיף: חדא יצירה הואי. כמאן דאמר בעירובין (דף יח.) ויבן את הצלע פרצוף שמתחלת בריאתו נברא שני פרצופין זכר מלפניו ונקבה מאחור: שתי יצירות. כמאן דאמר זנב היה וממנו נבראת האשה והרי כאן שתי יצירות: בתר מחשבה אזלינן. שנים עלו במחשבה להבראות ונברא אחד בעירובין בפ' עושין פסין: מברך שהשמחה במעונו. בתחילת הזימון: בין אמר להן. לקרואין: מחמת הלולא. קראתי לכם הלום לסעודה: מעיקרא. קודם החופה אם הזמין קרואים ואמר להם מחמת שאני רוצה להכניס בני לחופה: מאימתי. הויא התחלת שמחת חופה לברך שהשמחה במעונו: מכי רמו שערי באסינתא. יש שורין שעורים בעריבת מים ח) להטיל שכר לצורך חופה וי"א לשם החתן והכלה זורעין שעורין בעציץ לומר פרו ורבו וצמחו כשעורים הללו: דהוה טריח ליה. מתוקנים היו לו כל צרכי חופה וסעודה: איעסק לבריה. שידך לו אשה: בריך משעת אירוסין. שהשמחה במעונו: והדרי בהו. לא נתנו לו האשה: שית אריכתא. הוסיף דברים על שהכל ועל ברכת יצירה ראשונה וחתם בהם בברוך: ולית הלכתא כוותיה. לבי מהולא. לסעודת מילה: חתנים מן המנין. כדפי' לעיל: לקמן מפרש למאי הלכתא:

תוספות

שהכל ברא לכבודו ויוצר האדם. פותחת בברוך לכ"פ שכל אחת סמוכה לחבירתה כיון דקצרות הן אם לא היה פותח בברוך היה נראה הכל ברכה אחת וכן אשר יצר אם לא היה פותח בברוך היה נראה שהיתה מתחלת מברוך יוצר האדם אשר יצר אבל שוש תשיש שהיא אחר ברכה ארוכה אין צריך לפתוח בברוך ואשר ברא פותחת בברוך לפי שמברכים אותה בפני עצמה כשאין פנים חדשות לכדפירש בקונטרס ועוד שהכל ברא לכבודו ויוצר האדם פי' בקונטרס טעם אחר ור"ת פירש דיוצר האדם פותחת בברוך לפי שיש שלא היו אומרים אותה כלומר בסמוך ואור"ת דבפרק קמא דברכות (דף יא:) גבי ברכת התורה גרסי' ר' יוחנן מסיים בה הכי והערב נא דברכה אחת היא דאי הוו שתי ברכות היה צריך לפתוח בברוך אע"ג דסמוכה לחברתה כיון שאותה שלפניה היא קצרה ובתר הכי גרסינן הלכך נימרינהו לתרוייהו ולא גרסינן לכולהו דאם כן הוה משמע דשלש ברכות הן: חדא יצירה הואי. צריך לומר דהיינו כמאן דאמר פרצוף אחד מדקאמר בתר הכי דכולי עלמא חדא יצירה הואי מר סבר בתר מחשבה אזלינן וכריש פרק ב' דעירובין (דף יח. ושם) משמע בהדיא דלמאן דאמר פרצוף אחד היה עלה במחשבה להבראות שנים אבל למאן דאמר התם שני פרצופים לא סבירא ליה הכי כך פירש רשב"ם: רב תנא הוא ופליג. לא בעי לשנויי כי תניא ההיא בברכת המזון דמשמע רבי יוחנן דנראה לו דוחק להעמיד כן ונוח לו לומר דפליג ומדלא קאמר ר' יוחנן תנא ופליג יש להוכיח דר' אמורא היה דאי הוה תנא הוה משני דמתני' לרב ואין להקשות דאמאי לא משני רבי יוחנן אלא דאמרי כרב דתנא הוא דרבי יוחנן לא היה מחזיק רב כתנא דפליג עליו בכל דוכתא ומיהו איכא נמי רבי יוחנן שהיה תנא דתניא בשילהי נזיר (דף סו. ושם) וכמה שיעור תפיסה פירש רבי יוחנן כו':

מסורת הש"ס

א) [עירובין יח. ע"ש היטב וע' גם ברכות סא. ומגלה ליישב. ושם איתא ר' אבהו וכ"ה בשאלתות], ב) [ע"ז מג:], ג) [סנהדרין לח.], ד) [עירובין ג: וש"נ], ה) [מגילה כג:], ו) פסחים נד., ז) צ"ל דברכות פ"א ה"ה, ח) [עיין תוס' ע"ז מ: ד"ה מכי וכו' השיגו על פירוש זה], ט) עי' יומא מג.:

עין משפט נר מצוה

לט א מיי' פ"ב מהל' ברכות הל' יא ופ"י מהל' אישות הל' ג סמג עשין מח טוש"ע אה"ע סי' סב סעי' א:
מ ב מיי' שם הל' י טוש"ע שם סעיף ז:
מא ג מיי' פ"י מהל' אישות ה"ו טוש"ע שם סעיף יג:
מב ד מיי' שם הל' ה ופ"ב מהל' ברכות ה"י טוש"ע שם סעיף ד:

תורה אור השלם

א) וַיִּבְרָא אֱלֹהִים אֶת הָאָדָם בְּצַלְמוֹ בְּצֶלֶם אֱלֹהִים בָּרָא אֹתוֹ זָכָר וּנְקֵבָה בָּרָא אֹתָם: [בראשית א, כז]
ב) זָכָר וּנְקֵבָה בְּרָאָם וַיְבָרֶךְ אֹתָם וַיִּקְרָא אֶת שְׁמָם אָדָם בְּיוֹם הִבָּרְאָם: [בראשית ה, ב]

ליקוטי רש"י

העקרה. ירושלים אשר היתה כלא ילדה [ישעיה נד, א]. בגן עדן מקדם. במזרחו של עדן נטע את הגן [בראשית ב, ח]. בהלוליה. במשתה [ע"פ עירובין נד.]. זכר ונקבה בראם. משמע מתחלת בריאתם תרי הוו [ברכות סא.]. משמע מתחלת בריאתו היה זכר ונקבה זכר מצד זה ונקבה מצד זה [עירובין יח.]. מכי רמו שערי באסינתא. לעשות שכר ליום המשתה [ע"ז ח:]. רמו. מטילין [פסחים כב:]. אסינתא. עריבות ששורין בהן שעורין לעשות שכר ובל"א נוטעין עפר בעריבות וזורעין בה שעורין קודם ימי החופה ומגדלין לפני החתן והכלה כשהן צמוחים ואומרים להם פרו ורבו כשעורין הללו שממהרין לצאת מכל התבואה [ע"ז שם]. קים לי בגווייהו. מכיר אני בהם [שם עו:]. חתנים מן המנין. לעשרה הצריכין להמנות לברכת חתנים כדאמרינן לעיל. ואין אבלים מן המנין. לקמן מפרש הלכתא [רש"י מכת"י בשיטמ"ק].

תוספות רי"ד

שעדיין לא שמען: מאי מברך ארי"ש שהכל ברא לכבודו. יוצר האדם. אשר יצר. שוש תשיש. שמח תשמח. אשר ברא. פי' תחלה מברך שהכל ברא לכבודו משום דברכת חתנים צריכה עשרה כדכתיב במקהלות ברכו ה' וכתיב ברוב עם הדרת מלך. וזו האסיפה היא על כבודו לברכו ברבים מ"ה מתחיל ומברך שהכל. אח"כ מברך יוצר האדם כנגד יצירה ראשונה שנברא לבדו. אח"כ מברך על יצירת שניהם האיך הפריד לו אשה מצלעותיו ומפני שמאריך דבריו חותם בה. אבל השתים הראשונות שהן קצרות אינו חותם בהן ואע"פ שהיא סמוכה לשלש ראשונות שבירך כבר פותח בה בברוך מפני שהשלש ראשונות פתיחה בברוך יש בהן. אבל חתימה אין בהם ואינו נקרא ברכה הסמוכה לחברתה שאין פותחים בה בברוך כשמתחיל לאחרי' כגון ברכות י"ח וברכות ק"ש. אבל הסמוכה לברכה קטנה פותחים בה בברוך כמו שאנו עושים בק' ברכות שאותן שהם קצרות מברכין על כ"א וא' בפתיחה ולא יותר וכשמתחיל לברך ברכות הארוכות פותח בה בברוך. ואין סמיכות ברכות הקצרות פוטרת מלפתוח בה בברוך. וג"ל שטועים הם בני אדם שמתחילים מאה ברכות מאלהי נשמה מפני שלא מצינו בשום מקום שיתחיל בברכות בלא פתיחת ברוך. וכך ראוי להתחיל ברוך אשר יצר את האדם בחכמה. ויש בה פתיחה לפניה וחתימה לאחריה. ואח"כ אומר אלהי נשמה וחותם בה בברוך ואינו פותח בה בברוך מפני שהיא סמוכה להו. אח"כ אומר כל הקצרות. ואח"כ אומר המעביר שינה. ופותח בברוך. מפני שסמיכות ברכות הקטנות אינה פוטרתה. ובברכת התורה פותח בה בברוך מפני שלא נתקנה עם סדר ק' ברכות אלא כשצריך ללמוד הילכך יש בה פתיחה. אח"כ מברך שוש תשיש קודם שיברך על שמחת החתן דכתיב אם לא אעלה את ירושלים על ראש שמחתי. ומפני שהיא סמוכה לחתימת אשר יצר אינו פותח בה בברוך. אח"כ אומר שמח תשמח שישמח החתן והכלה כל ימיהם ואין זו שמחת הזיווג ומסיים בה משמח חתן וכלה ואינו פותח בה בברוך מפני שסמוכה היא לחתימת שוש תשיש. אח"כ אומר אשר ברא שהוא שמחת הזיווג וחותם בה משמח חתן עם הכלה ששמחים כשמזדווגים זה עם זה ואע"פ שהיא סמוכה לחתימה הראשונה שלפניה ודין הוא שלא נפתח בה בברוך. אפ"ה מפני שמברכים אותה לבדה בדליכא פנים חדשות הוא פותח בה בברוך: רב אשי איקלע לבי רב כהנא יומא קמא בריך כולהו מכאן ואילך אמר אי איכא פנים חדשות נבריך כולהו. ואי לא אפושי שמחה בעלמא הוא. מברך שהשמחה במעונו ואשר ברא. פי' יומא קמא בין בשעת כניסתן לחופה בין בסעודה מברך כולהו ואין צריך פנים חדשות דהא מכאן ואילך לא הוי אלא בסעודה. א"כ יומא קמא אפילו בסעודה מברך ז' ברכות בלא פנים חדשות. ומכאן ואילך בלא פנים חדשות מברך שהשמחה במעונו בברהמ"ז ואשר ברא שהוא עיקר ברכת החתונות בסוף ברהמ"ז. מז' ועד ל' בין אמר מחמת הלולא בין לא אמר מחמת הילולא מברך שהשמח' במעונו. פי' אבל לא אשר ברא שהוא ברכת החתונות. וכיון שעברו ז' ימי חתונות אינו ראוי לברכם. מכאן ואילך אי אמר מחמת הלולא מברך שהשמחה במעונו ואי לא לא. וכי אמר מחמת הלולא עד אימת. א"ר פפי משמיה דרבא עד תריסר ירחי שתא. מעיקרא מאימת א"ר פפא מכי רמו שערי באסינתא פי' כיון שמשליך השעורים בגיגית לעשות מהן שכר לצורך הסעודה אבל לא משעת אירוסין: רבינא איעסיק ליה לבריה בי רב חביבא בריך משעת אירוסין. אמר קים לי בגווייהו דלא הדרי ביה ולא אסתעייא מילתא והדרי ביה: רב תחליפא איקלע לבבל בריך שית אריכתא. פי' הוסיף דברים על שהכל ועל יוצר האדם. והאריך בהן וחתם בהם ופסיק תלמודא ולית הלכתא (כסתם) [כוותיה]: רב חביבא איקלע לסעודת המילה בריך שהשמחה במעונו ופסיק תלמודא ולית הלכתא [כוותיה] משום דאית ליה צערא לינוקא. אר"י אמר ר"י מברכין ברכת חתנים בעשרה כל ז'. וחתנים מן המנין ברכת אבלים כל ז' ואין אבלים מן המנין. והוא שבאו פנים חדשות. מאי ברכת אבלים ברכת רחבה פי' היו מברין את האבל ברחובה של עיר ומברכין שם כנגד השם וכנגד אבלים וכנגד המנחמים וכנגד כל ישראל כדמפרש בגמרא וצריכה עשרה ובאותן יו"ד אין אבלים מן המנין כברכת המזון כגון ג' לזימון ויו"ד לאלהינו:

אָמַר רַב פַּפִּי מִשְּׁמֵיהּ דְּרָבָא – Rav Pappi said in the name of Rava: **עַד תְּרֵיסַר יַרְחֵי שַׁתָּא – Until twelve months of the year** have passed after the wedding.[23]

The Gemara inquires further:

וּמֵעִיקָּרָא מֵאֵימַת – And from when may we recite this formula **beforehand?**[24]

The Gemara answers:

אָמַר רַב פַּפָּא – Rav Pappa said: **מִכִּי רָמוּ שַׁעֲרֵי בְּאַסִּינְתָּא – From when they throw the barley into the** beer-making **vat,** i.e. when the preparations for the wedding have begun in earnest.[25]

The Gemara objects:

אִינִי – Is it so? **וְהָא רַב פַּפָּא אִיעֲסַק לְאַבָּא מַר בְּרֵיהּ – But Rav Pappa** himself **arranged a match for his son, Abba Mar,** **וּבָרֵיךְ מִשְּׁעַת אֵירוּסִין – and he** began **reciting** *in Whose abode* etc. **from the time of the** ***erusin*** – which is some time earlier than when they begin making beer. – ? –

The Gemara answers:

שָׁאנֵי רַב פַּפָּא – Rav Pappa was different, **דַּהֲוָה טְרִיחַ לֵיהּ – because [everything] was readied for him.**[26]

A related incident:

רָבִינָא אִיעֲסַק לֵיהּ לִבְרֵיהּ בֵּי רַב חֲבִיבָא – Ravina arranged a match for his son with one of **the house of Rav Chaviva,** i.e. Ravina's son became engaged to Rav Chaviva's daughter, **וּבָרֵיךְ מִשְּׁעַת אֵירוּסִין – and [Ravina] recited** *in Whose abode is the joy* **from the time of the** ***erusin***, even though the wedding preparations had not yet begun. **אָמַר – He said** in explanation, **קִים לִי בְּגַוַּיְיהוּ דְּלָא הַדְרֵי בְּהוּ – "I am confident of them that they will not renege."** **לֹא אִסְתַּיַּיע מִילְּתָא וְהַדְרֵי בְּהוּ** – However, **the matter did not meet with success and they did** in fact **renege** on their agreement to give their daughter as a bride.

Another incident:

רַב תַּחְלִיפָא בַּר מַעֲרְבָא – Rav Tachlifa of the West [i.e. Eretz Yisrael] **אִיקְּלַע לְבָבֶל – visited Babylonia.** When honored with the recitation of *Sheva Berachos,* **בָּרֵיךְ שִׁית אֲרִיכָתָא – he recited six long blessings.**[27] **וְלֵית הִלְכְתָא כְּוָותֵיהּ – But the law is not in accordance with him.**[28]

A related incident:

רַב חֲבִיבָא אִיקְּלַע לְבֵי מְהוּלָא – Rav Chaviva attended a **circumcision feast.**[29] At the end of the meal, they asked him to lead the *Bircas HaMazon.* **בָּרֵיךְ שֶׁהַשִּׂמְחָה בִּמְעוֹנוֹ – He recited the** formula, ***in Whose abode is the joy.***

The Gemara comments:

וְלֵית הִלְכְתָא כְּוָותֵיהּ – But the law is not in accordance with him. *In Whose abode* etc. is not said at a circumcision feast **מִשּׁוּם דְּטְרִידֵי – because they are distracted** from complete happiness **דְּאִית לֵיהּ צַעֲרָא לִינוּקָא – since the baby experiences pain.**[30]

The Gemara stated above (7b) that the recitation of *Sheva Berachos* requires ten men. The Gemara elaborates:

אָמַר רַב נַחְמָן אָמַר רַב – Rav Nachman said in the name of Rav: **חֲתָנִים מִן הַמִּנְיָן – The grooms are** counted as part **of the quorum;**[31] **וְאֵין אֲבֵלִים מִן הַמִּנְיָן – but the mourners are not** counted as part **of the quorum.**[32]

The Gemara objects:

מֵיתִיבֵי – They challenged this **from a Baraisa:** **חֲתָנִים וַאֲבֵלִים מִן הַמִּנְיָן** – THE GROOMS AND THE MOURNERS ARE counted as part OF their respective QUORUMS. – ? –

The Gemara responds:

מַתְנִיתָא קָא רָמֵית עֲלֵיהּ דְּרַב – Are you posing a challenge to Rav from a Baraisa? **רַב תַּנָּא הוּא וּפָלִיג – Rav is** considered **a Tanna and** can therefore **dispute** the Baraisa.[33]

A related exchange:

אִיתְּמַר – It has been stated: **אָמַר רַבִּי יִצְחָק אָמַר רַבִּי יוֹחָנָן – R' Yitzchak said in the name of R' Yochanan:** **חֲתָנִים מִן הַמִּנְיָן – The grooms** are counted as part **of the quorum;** **וְאֵין אֲבֵלִים מִן הַמִּנְיָן – but the mourners are not** counted as part **of the quorum.**

The Gemara objects:

מֵיתִיבֵי – They challenged this **from a Baraisa:** **חֲתָנִים וַאֲבֵלִים מִן הַמִּנְיָן** – THE GROOMS AND THE MOURNERS ARE counted as part OF their respective QUORUMS.[34] – ? –

NOTES

23. This is related to the commandment (*Deuteronomy* 24:4): *He should be free for his house for one year and rejoice with the woman whom he married.* The groom's joy extends until this time (*Ritva*).

See below, note 25, as to why this practice (of reciting *in Whose abode* etc. after seven days) is not followed nowadays.

24. That is, if the father invites guests to a meal before the *chuppah* takes place and tells them that the meal is in honor of his son's upcoming wedding, from what point can we say that the *chuppah* festivities have begun, and they can recite *in Whose abode is the joy*? (*Rashi*).

25. They soaked the barley in a vat of water in order to make beer for the wedding (*Rashi,* in his first explanation; cf. *Tosafos* to *Avodah Zarah* 8b ד״ה מכי). Alternatively, they filled a trough with earth and planted barley within it. The barley would soon sprout, since barley is the fastest growing grain. The trough would then be shown to the groom and bride and they would be told, "Be fruitful and multiply like these grains of barley!" (*Geonim,* cited in *Shitah Mekubetzes;* see *Rashi's* second explanation).

This refers to where the couple already entered into *erusin.* Then, if they have started these preparations for the celebrations surrounding the *chuppah,* we can rely on the assumption that the *chuppah* will take place as scheduled (*Rashba* and *Ritva*). [Before then, we are concerned that the bride's side may not be ready to assume the financial burdens (such as the dowry) and may therefore renege.] Nowadays, when all joy has been tempered by the long exile, we recite *in Whose abode is the joy* only during the seven days of rejoicing following the wedding (*Smag, Mitzvos Asei* §48, *Even HaEzer* 62:13; see also *Atzei Arazim* 62:2).

26. Rav Pappa was a wealthy man (*Pesachim* 113a) and all the needs of the *chuppah* and the wedding feast were already prepared for him (*Rashi;* see *Or HaYashar*). [I.e. he could meet his daughter's financial obligations easily and therefore there was no fear he might renege.]

27. He expanded upon the text of the first two blessings and then concluded with the clause *Blessed are You* etc. (*Rashi;* cf. *Rashba;* see *Ritva*). All six blessings were considered "long" because they now ended with *Blessed are You, Hashem.*

28. Rather, one says the first two blessings without a concluding clause (see above, note 10).

29. Literally: visited the house of a circumcision.

30. Our Gemara clearly implies that if not for the baby's pain (and the resulting distraction) the formula *in Whose abode is the joy* would be said at a *bris* meal. The Rishonim discuss whether this formula is therefore said at a *Pidyon HaBen* (Redemption of the Firstborn) meal since the baby does not experience pain on that occasion. At least one authority rules that this formula should be said at a *siyum* meal [celebrating the completion of a tractate of the Talmud or the like] (*Sefer HaMinhagim* of *R' Yitzchak Isaac Tirnau, Minhagei Kol Hashanah, hagahah* §14). However, this is not the custom (*Yam Shel Shlomo, Bava Kamma* 7:37).

31. That is, only nine men are needed in addition to the groom.

32. The Gemara below will identify the purpose for which this quorum is needed.

33. Rav, who lived during the transition from the Tannaic to Amoraic periods, and who received many traditions from the last of the Tannaim, was considered in certain respects a Tanna. Thus, his rulings could not be refuted from the text of a Baraisa as those of other Amoraim would be. [For a lengthy treatment of this and related matters, see *Doros HaRishonim* vol. 5, ch. 19 (pp. 75ff.).]

Rav Hai Gaon lists three places in which Rav is actually mentioned in a Baraisa. In each case, he is called "R' Abba," after his given name (*Otzar HaGeonim, Teshuvos*).

34. R' Yochanan is not considered a Tanna, so the Gemara cannot offer this as an answer as it did for Rav (see *Tosafos*).

מסורת הש"ס

א) [עירובין יח. ע"ש היטב וע' גם ברכות סא. ומהרש"א לישב. ושם איתא ר' אבהו וכ"ה בשאלתות], ב) [ע"ז ח:], ג) [סנהדרין יט.], ד) [עירובין מ: וש"נ], ה) [מגילה כג:], ו) [פסחים נד.], ז) ל"ל דברכות פ"א ה"ה, ח) [עיין תוס' ע"ז ח: ד"ה מכי וכו' הסיגו על פירוש זה], ט) עי' יומא מג.:

עין משפט נר מצוה

לט א מיי' פ"ב מהל' ברכות הל' יא ופ"י מהל' אישות הל' ג סמג עשין מח טוש"ע אה"ע סי' סב סעי' א:
מ ב מיי' שם הל' י טוש"ע שם סעיף ז:
מא ג מיי' פ"י מהל' אישות ה"ו טוש"ע שם סעיף יג:
מב ד מיי' שם הל' ה ופ"ב מהל' ברכות ה"י טוש"ע שם סעיף ד:

גמרא

[א] שהכל ברא לכבודו ויוצר האדם ואשר יצר את האדם בצלמו בצלם דמות תבניתו והתקין לו ממנו בנין עדי עד ברוך אתה ה' יוצר האדם שוש תשיש ותגל העקרה בקבוץ בניה לתוכה בשמחה ברוך אתה ה' משמח ציון בבניה שמח תשמח ריעים האהובים כשמחך יצירך בגן עדן מקדם ברוך אתה ה' משמח חתן וכלה ברוך אתה ה' אמ"ה אשר ברא ששון ושמחה חתן וכלה גילה רינה דיצה חדוה אהבה ואחוה ושלום וריעות מהרה ה' אלהינו ישמע בערי יהודה ובחוצות ירושלים קול ששון וקול שמחה קול חתן וקול כלה קול מצהלות חתנים מחופתם ונערים ממשתה נגינתם בא"י משמח חתן עם הכלה לוי איקלע לבי רבי בהלוליה דר"ש בריה בריך חמש רב אסי איקלע לבי רב אשי בהלוליה דמר בריה בריך שית לימא בהא קמיפלגי דמ"ס חדא יצירה הואי ומ"ס שתי יצירות הואי לא דכ"ע חדא יצירה הואי מ"ס בתר מחשבה אזלינן ומ"ס בתר מעשה אזלינן כי הא [ה] דרב יהודה רמי כתיב א) ויברא אלהים את האדם בצלמו וכתיב ב) זכר ונקבה בראם הא כיצד בתחלה עלה במחשבה לבראות שנים ולבסוף נברא אחד רב אשי איקלע לבי רב כהנא יומא קמא בריך כולהו מכאן ואילך [ב] אי איכא פנים חדשות בריך כולהו ואי לא אפושי שמחה בעלמא הוא מברך שהשמחה במעונו ואשר ברא משבעה ועד שלשים בין אמר להו מחמת הלולא ובין לא אמר להו מחמת הלולא מברך שהשמחה במעונו מכאן ואילך אי אמר להו מחמת הלולא מברך שהשמחה במעונו ואי לא לא וכי א"ל מחמת הלולא עד אימת אמר רב פפי משמיה דרבא [ג] עד תריסר ירחי שתא ומעיקרא מאימת [ג] אמר רב פפא מכי רמו שערי באסינתא איני והא רב פפא איעסק לאבא מר בריה ובריך משעת אירוסין שאני רב פפא דהוה טריח ליה רבינא איעסק ליה לבריה בי רב חביבא ובריך משעת אירוסין אמר קים לי בגוויהו דלא הדרי בהו לא אסתייע מילתא והדרי בהו רב תחליפא בר מערבא איקלע לבבל בריך שית אריכתא ולית הלכתא כוותיה רב חביבא איקלע לבי מהולא בריך שהשמחה במעונו ולית הלכתא כוותיה משום דטרידי דאית ליה צערא לינוקא א"ר נחמן אמר רב [ד] חתנים מן המנין [ה] ואין אבלים מן המנין מיתיבי חתנים ואבלים מן המנין מתניתא קא רמית עליה דרב [ז] רב תנא הוא ופליג איתמר [ח] אמר ר' יצחק א"ר יוחנן חתנים מן המנין ואין אבלים מן המנין

כי

רש"י

והתקין לו ממנו בנין עדי עד. היא הנקבה: שוש תשיש. לפי שאנו צריכין להעלות זכרון ירושלים על ראש שמחתנו שנאמר (תהלים קלז) תדבק לשוני לחכי וגו': שמח תשמח. ברכה לחתן וכלה שיצליחו בשמחה וטוב לב ואשר ברא לשם כל ישראל ולפי שהסדר מתחיל מאשר יצר לפיכך פתח בה בברוך וחתם בה בברוך כדרך כל ראשי סדרי ברכות ושוש תשיש ושמח תשמח מפני שהן ברכה הסמוכה לחברתה לא פתח בה בברוך שכן תיקנו לכל הברכות שסמוכות אחר הראשונה על הסדר ואשר ברא מפני שהיא נאמרת יחידית ברוב ימי המשתה כשאין שם פנים חדשות לפיכך אינה מן הסמוכות והוצרך לפתוח בה בברוך ולסיים בה בברוך אבל שהכל ברא לכבודו אינה מן הסדר אלא לאסיפת העם הנאספים שם לגמול חסד זכר לחסדי המקום שנהג עם אדם הראשון שנעשה לו שושבין ונתעסק בו ואסיפה זו כבוד המקום היא וברכה זו לכך נתקנה ומשעת אסיפה היא ראויה לברך אלא מכיון שיש ברכה על הכוס הזקיקוה לסדרה עליו מידי דהוה אברכת בשמים וברכת על האור במוצאי שבת דאמרי' ז) (ירושלמי ז) דפסחים פ"י) רבי מפזרן וחוזר וסודרן על הכוס ורבי חייא מכנסן הואיל ויש שם כוס ולפי שאינה משאר סדר הברכות וכולה הודאה אחת לא חתמו בה בברוך מידי דהוה אברכת פירות ומצות וכן ברכת יוצר האדם שתיקנוה ליצירה ראשונה של אדם הראשון כדלקמן אי למ"ד ב' יצירות הוו אי למ"ד ב' יצירות עלו במחשבה ובתר מחשבה אזלינן מ"מ אינה מסדר ברכות הזווג דהא ביצירה הראשונה אכתי נקבה לא הואי וא"ת למה היא באה מתוך שאנו מברכין על יצירה השניה תקנו אף על הראשונה שהיא עיקר ותחילתו: והתקין לו ממנו. מגופו מצלעותיו: בנין עדי עד. בנין נוהג לדורות והוה קרי לה בנין על שם ויבן את הצלע (בראשית ב): עקרה. ירושלים: ריעים האהובים. החתן והכלה שהן ריעים האוהבים זה את זה: כשמחך יצירך. כמו ששמחת את אדם הראשון: בגן עדן מקדם. דכתיב ויטע גן בעדן מקדם וישם שם וגו' (שם): משמח חתן וכלה. ובאחרונה משמח חתן עם הכלה לפי ששמחת ברכה הראשונה לא בשמחת חתונה אנו אומרים שהרי תפלה היא שמתפללים ומברכין שיהו שמחים בהצלחה כל ימיהם לפיכך אין לחתום בה משמח חתן עם הכלה דמשמע איש באשתו אלא ברוך ה' משמח את שניהם לעולם בסיפוק מזונות וכל טוב ובאחרונה שבח שמשבח להקב"ה שברא חתונת דיבוק איש באשה על ידי שמחה וחדוה לפיכך יש לחתום משמח חתן עם הכלה שהוא לשון שמחת איש באשה: בריך חמש. שהכל ואשר יצר ושוש תשיש שמח תשמח אשר ברא: בריך שית. יוצר האדם הוסיף: חדא יצירה הואי. כמאן דאמר בעירובין (דף יח.) ויבן את הצלע פרצוף שמתחילת ברייתו נברא שני פרצופין זכר מלפניו ונקבה מאחור: שתי יצירות. כמאן דאמר זנב היה וממנו נבראת האשה והרי כאן שתי יצירות: בתר מחשבה אזלינן. ששנים עלו במחשבה להבראות ונברא אחד בעירובין בפ' עושין פסין: מברך שהשמחה במעונו. בתחילת הזימון: בין אמר להן. לקרואין: מחמת הלולא. קראתי לכם הלום לסעודה: מעיקרא. קודם החופה אם הזמין קרואים ואמר להם מחמת שאני רוצה להכניס בני לחופה: מאימתי. הויא התחלת שמחת חופה לברך שהשמחה במעונו: מכי רמי שערי באסינתא. יש שורין שעורים בעריבת מים ח) להטיל שכר לצורך חופה וי"א לשם החתן והכלה זורעין שעורין בעציץ לומר פרו ורבו וצמחו כשעורים הללו: דהוה טריח ליה. מתוקנים היו לו כל צרכי חופה וסעודה: איעסק לבריה. שידך לו אשה: ובריך משעת אירוסין. שהשמחה במעונו: והדרי בהו. לא נתנו לו האשה: שית אריכתא. הוסיף דברים על שהכל ועל ברכת יצירה ראשונה וחתם בהם בברוך: ולית הלכתא כוותיה. כדפי' לעיל: לבי מהולא. לסעודת מילה: חתנים מן המנין. לקמן מפרש למאי הלכתא:

תוספות

שהכל ברא לכבודו ויוצר האדם. פותחת בברוך אע"פ שכל אחת סמוכה לחברתה כיון דקצרות הן אם לא היה פותח בברוך היה נראה הכל ברכה אחת וכן אשר יצר אם לא היה פותח בברוך היה נראה שהיתה מתחלת מברוך יוצר האדם אשר יצר אבל שוש תשיש שהיא אחר ברכה ארוכה אין צריך לפתוח בברוך ואשר ברא פותחת בברוך לפי שמברכים אותה בפני עצמה כשאין פנים חדשות כדפירש בקונטרס ועל שהכל ברא לכבודו ויוצר האדם פי' בקונטרס טעם אחר ור"ת פירש דיוצר האדם פותחת בברוך לפי שיש שלא היו אומרים אותה דלאמר בסמוך ואור"ת דבפרק קמא דברכות (דף יא:) גבי ברכת התורה גרסי' ר' יוחנן מסיים בה הכי והערב נא דברכה אחת היא דלאי הוו שתי ברכות היה צריך לפתוח בברוך אע"ג דסמוכה לחברתה כיון שאותה שלפניה היא קצרה ובתר הכי גרסינן הלכך נימרינהו לתרוייהו ולא גרסינן לכולהו דאם כן הוה משמע דשלש ברכות הן: **חדא** יצירה הואי. צריך לומר דהיינו כמאן דאמר פרצוף אחד מדקאמר בתר הכי דכולי עלמא חדא יצירה הואי מר סבר בתר מחשבה אזלינן ובריש פרק שני דעירובין (דף יח. ושם) משמע בהדיא דלמאן דאמר פרצוף אחד הוה עלה במחשבה להבראות שנים אבל למאן דאמר התם שני פרצופים לא סבירא ליה הכי כך פירש רשב"ם:

רב תנא הוא ופליג. לא בעי לשנויי כי תניא ההיא בברכת המזון כדמשני רבי יוחנן דנראה לו דוחק להעמיד כן ונוח לו טפי לומר דפליג ומדלא קאמר ר' יוחנן ט) תנא ופליג יש להוכיח דר"י אמורא היה דאי הוה תנא הוה משני כדמשני לרב ואין להקשות דאמאי לא משני רבי יוחנן אנא דאמרי כרב דתנא הוא דרבי יוחנן לא היה מחזיק רב כתנא דפליג עליו בכל דוכתא ומיהו איכא נמי רבי יוחנן שהיה תנא דתניא בשילהי דנזיר (דף סה. ושם) וכמה שיעור תפיסה פירש רבי יוחנן כו':

כי

תורה אור השלם

א) וַיִּבְרָא אֱלֹהִים אֶת הָאָדָם בְּצַלְמוֹ בְּצֶלֶם אֱלֹהִים בָּרָא אֹתוֹ זָכָר וּנְקֵבָה בָּרָא אֹתָם: [בראשית א, כז]

ב) זָכָר וּנְקֵבָה בְּרָאָם וַיְבָרֶךְ אֹתָם וַיִּקְרָא אֶת שְׁמָם אָדָם בְּיוֹם הִבָּרְאָם: [בראשית ה, ב]

ליקוטי רש"י

העקרה. ירושלים אשר היתה כלא ילדה [ישעיה נד, א]. בגן עדן מקדם. במזרחו של עדן נטע את הגן [בראשית ב, ח]. בהלוליה. כמשתה [ע"פ עירובין נד.]. זכר ונקבה בראם. משמע מתחלת בריאתו היה זכר ונקבה זכר מצד זה ונקבה מצד זה [עירובין יח.]. מכי רמו שערי באסינתא. לעשות שכר ליום המשתה [ע"ז ח:]. רמו. מטילין [פסחים נב.]. אסינתא. עריבות שורין בהן שעורין לעשות שכר כ"ל נותנין עפר בתוכן וזורעין שם שעורין קודם ימי החופה ומביאין לפני החתן והכלה כסימן לומר פרו ורבו כשעורין הללו שממהרין לצמוח יותר מכל התבואה [ע"ז שם]. קים לי בגוויהו. מכיר אני בהם [שם ט.]. חתנים מן המנין. לעשרה הצריכין לברכת חתנים כדאמרינן לעיל. ואין אבלים מן המנין. לקמן מפרש הלכתא [רש"י מכת"י בשיטמ"ק].

תוספות רי"ד

שעדיין לא שמענו: מאי מברך אר"י שהכל ברא לכבודו. יוצר האדם. אשר יצר. שוש תשיש. שמח תשמח. אשר ברא. פי' תחלה מברך שהכל ברא לכבודו משום דברכת חתנים צריכה עשרה כדכתיב במקהלות ברכו ה' וכתיב ברוב עם הדרת מלך. וזו האסיפה היא על כבודו לכך מתחיל ומברך שהכל. אח"כ מברך יוצר האדם כנגד יצירה הראשונה שנברא לבדו. אח"כ מברך על יצירת שניהם האיך הפריד לו אשה מצלעותיו ומפני שמאריך דבריו חותם בה. אבל השתים הראשונות שהן קצרות אינו חותם בהן ואע"פ שהיא סמוכה לשלש ראשונות שביניך כבר פותח בה בברוך מפני שהשלש ראשונות פתיחה בברוך יש בהן. אבל חתימה אין בהם ואיזו נקרא ברכה הסמוכה לחברתה שאין פותחים בה בברוך כשמתחיל לאחרי' כגון ברכות י"ח וברכות ק"ש. אבל הסמוכה לברכה קטנה פותחים בה בברוך כמו שאנו עושים בק' ברכות שאותן שהם קצרות מברכין על כ"א וא' בפתיחה ולא יותר וכשמתחיל לברך ברכות הארוכות פותח בה בברוך. ואין סמיכות ברכות הקצרות פוטרת מלפתוח בה בברוך. וג"ל שטועים הם בני אדם שמתחילים מאה ברכות מאלהי נשמה מפני שלא מצינו בשום מקום שיתחיל בברכות בלא פתיחת ברוך. וכך ראוי להתחיל ברוך אשר יצר את האדם בחכמה. ויש בה פתיחה לפניה וחתימה לאחריה. ואח"כ אומר אלהי נשמה וחותם בה בברוך ואינו פותח בה בברוך מפני שהיא סמוכה להו. אח"כ אומר כל הקצרות. ואח"כ אומר המעביר שינה. ופותח בברוך. מפני שסמיכות ברכות הקטנות אינה פוטרתה. ובברכת התורה פותח בה בברוך מפני שלא נתקנה עם סדר ק' ברכות אלא כשצריך ללמוד הילכך יש בה פתיחה. אח"כ מברך שוש תשיש קודם שיברך על שמחת החתן דכתיב אם לא אעלה את ירושלים על ראש שמחתי. ומפני שהיא סמוכה לחתימת אשר יצר אינו פותח בה בברוך. אח"כ אומר שמח תשמח שמשמח את החתן והכלה כל ימיהם ואין זו שמחת הזיווג ומסיים בה משמח חתן וכלה ואינו פותח בה בברוך מפני שסמוכה היא לחתימת שוש תשיש. אח"כ אומר אשר ברא שהוא שמחת הזיווג וחותם בה משמח

חתן עם הכלה ששמחים כשמזדווגים זה עם זה ואע"פ שהיא סמוכה לחתימה הראשונה שלפניה ודין הוא שלא נפתח בה בברוך. אפ"ה מפני שמברכים אותה לבדה בדליכא פנים חדשות הוא פותח בה בברוך: **רב אשי** איקלע לבי רב כהנא יומא קמא בריך כולהו. ואילך אמר אי איכא פנים חדשות נבריך כולהו. ואי לא אפושי שמחה בעלמא הוא. מברך שהשמחה במעונו ואשר ברא. פי' יומא קמא בין בשעת כניסתן לחופה בין בסעודה מברך כולהו ואין צריך פנים חדשות דהא מכאן ואילך לא הוי אלא בסעודה. א"כ יומא קמא אפילו בסעודה מברך ז' ברכות בלא פנים חדשות. ומכאן ואילך בלא פנים חדשות אינו מברך אלא שהשמחה במעונו בברהמ"ז ואשר ברא שהוא עיקר ברכת החתונות בסוף ברהמ"ז. **מז'** ועד ל' בין אמר מחמת הלולא בין לא אמר מחמת הילולא מברך שהשמח' במעונו. פי' אבל לא אשר ברא שהוא ברכת החתונות. וכיון שעברו ז' ימי חתונות אינו ראוי לברכם. מכאן ואילך אי אמר מחמת הילולא מברך שהשמחה במעונו ואי לא לא. וכי אמר מחמת הלולא עד אימת [...] שתא. **מעיקרא** מאימת א"ר פפא מכי רמו שערי באסותא פי' כיון שמשליך השעורים בגיגית לעשות מהן שכר לצורך הסעודה אבל לא משעת אירוסין: **רבינא** איעסיק ליה לבריה בי רב חביבא בריך משעת אירוסין. אמר קים לי בגוויהו דלא הדרי ביה ולא אסתעייא מילתא והדרי ביה: **רב תחליפא** איקלע לבבל בריך שית אריכתא. פי' הוסיף דברים על שהכל ועל יוצר האדם. והאריך בהן וחתם בהם ופסיק תלמודא ולית הלכתא (כסתם) [כוותיה]: **רב חביבא** איקלע לסעודת המילה בריך שהשמחה במעונו ופסיק תלמודא ולית הלכתא [כוותיה] משום דאית ליה צערא לינוקא. **אר"י אמר ר"י** מברכין ברכת חתנים בעשרה כל ז'. וחתנים מן המנין ברכת אבלים כל ז' ואין אבלים מן המנין. והוא שבאו פנים חדשות. מאי ברכת אבלים ברכת רחבה פי' היו מברכין את האבל ברחובה של עיר ומברכין שם כנגד השם וכנגד אבלים וכנגד המנחמים וכנגד כל ישראל כדמפרש בגמרא וצריכה עשרה ובאותן יו"ד אין אבלים מן המנין כגון ג' לזימון ויו"ד לאלהינו:

separate blessings discussing man's formation: *"Who fashions the Man"* and *"Who fashioned the Man in His image."* וּמָר סָבַר שְׁתֵּי יְצִירוֹת הֲוַאי – And the other **master** [Rav Assi] **holds that there were two fashionings** of man, and each blessing corresponds to one of those acts of creation.[16]

The Gemara rejects that suggestion:

לֹא – **No!** That is not necessarily true. דְּכוּלֵּי עָלְמָא חֲדָא יְצִירָה הֲוַאי – **For** it is possible that **everyone** agrees that **there was** only **one fashioning** of man and their dispute revolves around a different point: Initially, God planned to create a male person and a female person at the same time. When He came to the actual act of creation, however, He created only one double figure.[17] מַר סָבַר בָּתַר מַחֲשָׁבָה אָזְלִינַן – One **master** [Rav Assi] **holds that we follow the plan** of God, which was to make a separate male and female, each in a separate act of creation. There were two planned fashionings of man and hence two blessings are appropriate. וּמָר סָבַר בָּתַר מַעֲשֶׂה אָזְלִינַן – **Whereas** the other **master** [Levi] **holds that we follow** God's **action,** which created a single entity containing both male and female. Thus there was only one fashioning of man and one blessing is appropriate. כִּי הָא דְּרַב יְהוּדָה רָמֵי – This explanation of the dispute **follows [Rav Yehudah's view]** of the creation of man, **for Rav Yehudah noted a contradiction:** כְּתִיב ,,וַיִּבְרָא אֱלֹהִים אֶת־הָאָדָם בְּצַלְמוֹ" – **It is written:**[18] ***God created the man in His image,*** describing man's creation in the singular, indicating that a single male-and-female entity was created. וּכְתִיב ,,זָכָר וּנְקֵבָה בְּרָאָם" – **But it is written** elsewhere:[19] ***He created them male and female,*** describing man's creation in the plural, indicating that both a male entity and a female entity were created. הָא כֵּיצַד – **How is that** to be reconciled? בַּתְּחִלָּה עָלָה בְּמַחֲשָׁבָה לִבְרְאוֹת שְׁנַיִם – **Originally, the plan was that two** separate human beings **would be created,** a male and a female, וּלְבַסּוֹף נִבְרָא אֶחָד – **but in the end only one** being **was created,** a male-and-female combination.[20]

The Gemara elaborates further on these blessings:

רַב אַשִׁי אִיקְּלַע לְבֵי רַב כָּהֲנָא – **Rav Ashi visited the home of Rav Kahana** for a wedding. יוֹמָא קַמָּא בָּרֵיךְ כּוּלְּהוּ – **On the first day [Rav Ashi] recited all of the [*Sheva Berachos*].** מִכָּאן וְאֵילָךְ – **From then on** it depended: אִי אִיכָּא פָּנִים חֲדָשׁוֹת – **If there were new faces,** בָּרֵיךְ כּוּלְּהוּ – **he recited all of them;** וְאִי לֹא – **but if not,** אַפּוּשֵׁי שִׂמְחָה בְּעָלְמָא הוּא – **it was a mere extension of the** previous **joy,** מְבָרֵךְ שֶׁהַשִּׂמְחָה בִּמְעוֹנוֹ וַאֲשֶׁר בָּרָא – so **he recited** only the formula added at the beginning of *Bircas HaMazon, **in Whose abode is the joy,***[21] **and** the last of the *Sheva Berachos, **Who created joy** and gladness* etc.[22]

The Gemara continues:

מִשִּׁבְעָה וְעַד שְׁלֹשִׁים – **From seven until thirty** days after the wedding, if a person holds a meal for the bride and groom, then בֵּין אָמַר לְהוּ מֵחֶמַת הִלּוּלָא – **whether he told [the guests]** that the meal was being held **on account of the** wedding **festivities** וּבֵין לֹא אָמַר לְהוּ מֵחֶמַת הִלּוּלָא – **or whether he did not tell [the guests]** that the meal was **on account of the** wedding **festivities** מְבָרֵךְ שֶׁהַשִּׂמְחָה בִּמְעוֹנוֹ – **one should recite the** formula ***in Whose abode is the joy*** but not *Who created* etc. מִכָּאן וְאֵילָךְ – **From then on,** אִי אָמַר לְהוּ מֵחֶמַת הִלּוּלָא – **if he told [the guests]** that the meal was **on account of the** wedding **festivities,** מְבָרֵךְ שֶׁהַשִּׂמְחָה בִּמְעוֹנוֹ – **one should recite *in Whose abode is the joy.*** וְאִי לֹא – **But** if he did **not** tell the guests this, לֹא – he should **not** recite this formula.

The Gemara inquires:

וְכִי אָמַר לְהוּ מֵחֶמַת הִלּוּלָא – **And if he does tell** [the guests] that he is inviting them **on account of the** wedding **festivities,** עַד אֵימַת – **until when** would he still recite the formula ***in Whose abode is the joy?***

The Gemara answers:

NOTES

16. One act of creation created Adam and a second act of creation transformed his appendage into Eve. According to this view, the blessing *"Who fashions the Man"* refers to the creation of Adam, and the clause in the next blessing, *and He prepared for him – from himself – a building for eternity,* refers to the creation of Eve.

17. The Gemara presents this view in *Eruvin* 18a (*Rashi*). The Gemara below quotes the statement that is the basis of this view.

18. *Genesis* 1:27.

19. Ibid. 5:2.

20. The Gemara speaks anthropomorphically. God, to whom past and future are the same, does not "change" at all, nor do His plans ever need to be revised to accommodate unfolding events. Rather, God intended the husband-wife relationship to be unique in creation – two separate beings who are to experience a oneness on many levels of existence. In order to accomplish this, God created man on two planes. Physically, man and woman were created as one. But in thought, God planned for them to become separate. Thus, at the moment of his creation, man was both one with his wife and separate from her. This set the tone for the ongoing husband-wife relationship which human beings alone are capable of experiencing (see *Responsa, Rashba* I §60; *Rabbeinu Bachya* to *Genesis* 2:18).

[We have explained the Gemara's second explanation of the dispute between Levi and Rav Assi according to *Rashi* here. It should be noted, however, that the Gemara in *Berachos* 61a and in *Eruvin* 18a presents the view that man was created as a double figure as an *alternative* to the view that God planned to create him as two but actually created him as one. For this and other reasons, *Tosafos* and several Rishonim explain our Gemara differently than Rashi.]

21. Whenever three or more men participate in a meal, a leader is chosen to formally invite the others to join him in the recitation of *Bircas HaMazon.* This formal invitation is called the *zimun* blessing. When there are at least ten men, the leader says to the others: בִּרְשׁוּת מָרָנָן וְרַבָּנָן וְרַבּוֹתַי נְבָרֵךְ אֱלֹהֵינוּ שֶׁאָכַלְנוּ מִשֶּׁלּוֹ, *With the permission of the distinguished people present, let us bless our God, He of Whose we have eaten.* The others respond in kind (*Blessed is our God, He of Whose we have eaten and through Whose goodness we live*) and the leader repeats their response word for word before beginning *Bircas HaMazon.* When a meal is held in celebration of nuptials, a special *zimun* is said. The leader says בִּרְשׁוּת . . . נְבָרֵךְ אֱלֹהֵינוּ שֶׁהַשִּׂמְחָה בִּמְעוֹנוֹ וְשֶׁאָכַלְנוּ מִשֶּׁלּוֹ, *With permission . . . let us bless our God in Whose abode is the joy, of Whose we have eaten.* Their response and his repetition of it follow the same pattern.

[It has become customary for the leader to recite a brief poem before uttering this line during the week of wedding festivities. This addition begins דְּוַי הָסֵר וְגַם חָרוֹן, *Banish pain and also wrath,* and was composed by *Donash ben Labrat,* the tenth-century poet and pioneer Hebrew grammarian.]

The meaning of *in Whose abode is the joy* is that the true and perfect joy can be found only in God's abode; the joy found among us is the lowly and abridged sort (*Kol Bo* §75 ד״ה בחור; see *Talmidei Rabbeinu Yonah* cited in *Shitah Mekubetzes*). The word בִּמְעוֹנוֹ, *in His abode,* is a reference to the fifth of the seven heavens, מָעוֹן, *Abode.* The Gemara tells us (*Chagigah* 12b) that this heaven is populated by ministering angels who utter songs of praise to God. There is a tradition among the Geonim that these angels provided the wedding feast when Adam married Eve. (God Himself recited the [equivalent of the] *Sheva Berachos – Bereishis Rabbah* 8:13.) We therefore recall the joy that is in God's Abode whenever a wedding takes place (*Shitah Mekubetzes;* see *Meiri* and *Kol Bo* loc. cit.).

22. According to some Rishonim (see *Ramban,* cited by *Ran*) the single blessing, *Who created* etc., is recited only when ten men are present, since it is one of the *Sheva Berachos,* all of which require a quorum. However, other Rishonim (see *Ran, Ritva*) write that this blessing is recited even when only three men are present. This latter view is accepted by most later authorities (see, for example, *Chelkas Mechokeik* 62:8; *Chochmas Adam* 129:6; and *Aruch HaShulchan* 62:17). However, if the three men do not include any guests from outside the couple's household, this blessing, and the introductory *in Whose abode is the joy,* are not recited (ibid.; cf. *Ran;* see Responsa, *Yabia Omer* III *Even HaEzer* 11:8 for the custom among Sephardim).

שהכל ברא לכבודו ויוצר האדם ואשר יצר את האדם בצלמו בצלם דמות תבניתו והתקין לו ממנו בנין עדי עד ברוך אתה ה' יוצר האדם שוש תשיש ותגל העקרה בקבוץ בניה לתוכה בשמחה ברוך אתה ה' משמח ציון בבניה שמח תשמח ריעים האהובים כשמחך יצירך בגן עדן מקדם ברוך אתה ה' משמח חתן וכלה ברוך אתה ה' אמ"ה אשר ברא ששון ושמחה חתן וכלה גילה רינה דיצה חדוה אהבה ואחוה ושלום וריעות מהרה ה' אלהינו ישמע בערי יהודה ובחוצות ירושלים קול ששון וקול שמחה קול חתן וקול כלה קול מצהלות חתנים מחופתם ונערים ממשתה נגינתם בא"י משמח חתן עם הכלה לוי איקלע לבי רבי בהלוליה דר"ש בריה בריך חמש רב אסי איקלע לבי רב אשי בהלוליה דמר בריה בריך שית לימא בהא קמיפלגי דמ"ס חדא יצירה הואי ומ"ס שתי יצירות הואי לא דכ"ע חדא יצירה הואי מ"ס בתר מחשבה אזלינן ומ"ס בתר מעשה אזלינן כי הא דרב יהודה רמי כתיב ויברא אלהים את האדם בצלמו וכתיב זכר ונקבה בראם הא כיצד בתחלה עלה במחשבה לבראות שנים ולבסוף נברא אחד רב אשי איקלע לבי רב כהנא יומא קמא בריך כולהו מכאן ואילך אי איכא פנים חדשות בריך כולהו ואי לא אפושי שמחה בעלמא הוא מברך שהשמחה במעונו ואשר ברא משבעה ועד שלשים בין אמר להו מחמת הלולא ובין לא אמר להו מחמת הלולא מברך שהשמחה במעונו מכאן ואילך אי אמר להו מחמת הלולא מברך שהשמחה במעונו ואי לא לא וכי א"ל מחמת הלולא עד אימת אמר רב פפי משמיה דרבא עד תריסר ירחי שתא ומעיקרא מאימת אמר רב פפא מכי רמו שערי באסינתא איני והא רב פפא איעסק לאבא מר בריה ובריך משעת אירוסין שאני רב פפא דהוה טריח ליה רבינא איעסק ליה לבריה בי רב חביבא ובריך משעת אירוסין אמר קים לי בגוייהו דלא הדרי בהו לא אסתייע מילתא והדרי בהו רב תחליפא בר מערבא איקלע לבבל בריך שית אריכתא ולית הלכתא כוותיה רב חביבא איקלע לבי מהולא בריך שהשמחה במעונו ולית הלכתא כוותיה משום דטרידי דאית ליה צערא לינוקא א"ר נחמן אמר רב חתנים מן המנין ואין אבלים מן המנין מיתיבי חתנים ואבלים מן המנין מתניתא קא רמית עליה דרב רב תנא הוא ופליג איתמר אמר ר' יצחק א"ר יוחנן חתנים מן המנין ואין אבלים מן המנין מיתיבי חתנים ואבלים מן המנין

כי

רש"י

והתקין לו ממנו בנין עדי עד. היא הנקבה: שוש תשיש. לפי שאנו צריכין להעלות זכרון ירושלים על ראש שמחתנו שנאמר (תהלים קלז) תדבק לשוני לחכי וגו': שמח תשמח. ברכה לחתן וכלה שיצליחו בשמחה וטוב לב ואשר ברא לשם כל ישראל ולפי שהסדר מתחיל מאשר יצר לפיכך פתח בה בברוך וחתם בה בברוך כדרך כל ראשי סדרי ברכות ושוש תשיש ושמח תשמח מפני שהן ברכה הסמוכה לחברתה לא פתח בה בברוך שכן תיקנו לכל הברכות שסמוכות אחר הראשונה על הסדר ואשר ברא מפני שהיא נאמרת יחידית ברוב ימי המשתה כשאין שם פנים חדשות לפיכך אינה מן הסמוכות והוצרך לפתוח בה בברוך ולסיים בה בברוך אבל שהכל ברא לכבודו אינה מן הסדר אלא לאסיפת העם האוספים שם לגמול חסד זכר לחסדי המקום שנהג עם אדם הראשון שנעשה לו שושבין ונתעסק בו ואסיפה זו כבוד המקום היא וברכה זו לכך נתקנה ומשעת אסיפה היא ראויה לברך אלא מכיון שיש ברכה על הכוס הזקיקוה לסדרה עליו מידי דהוה אברכת בשמים וברכת על האור במוצאי שבת דאמרי' (ירושלמי) דפסחים פ"י רבי מפזרן וחוזר וקודרן על הכוס ורבי חייא מכנסן הואיל ויש שם כוס ולפי שאינה משאר סדר הברכות וכולה הודאה אחת לא חתמו בה בברוך מידי דהוה אברכת פירות ומצות וכן ברכת יוצר האדם שתיקנוה ליצירה ראשונה של אדם הראשון דלקמן אי למ"ד ב' יצירות הוו אי למ"ד ב' יצירות עלו במחשבה ובתר מחשבה אזלינן מ"מ אינה מסדר ברכות הזווג דהא ביצירה הראשונה אכתי נקבה לא הואי וא"ת למה היא באה מתוך שאנו מברכין על יצירה השניה תקנו אף על הראשונה שהיא עיקר ותחילתו: והתקין לו ממנו. מגופו מצלעותיו: בנין עדי עד. בנין נוהג לדורות וחוה קרי לה בנין על שם ויבן את הצלע (בראשית ב): עקרה. ירושלים: ריעים האהובים. החתן והכלה שהן ריעים האוהבים זה את זה: כשמחך יצירך. כמו ששמחת את אדם הראשון: בגן עדן מקדם. דכתיב ויטע גן בעדן מקדם וישם שם וגו' (שם): משמח חתן וכלה. ובאחרונה משמח חתן עם הכלה לפי ששמחת ברכה הראשונה לא בשמחת חתונה אנו אומרים שהרי תפלה היא שמתפללים ומברכין שיהו שמחים בהצלחה כל ימיהם לפיכך אין לחתום בה משמח חתן עם הכלה דמשמע איש באשתו אלא ברוך ה' משמח את שניהם לעולם בסיפוק מזונות וכל טוב ובאחרונה שבח שמשבח להקב"ה שברא חתונת דיבוק איש באשה על ידי שמחה וחדוה לפיכך יש לחתום משמח חתן עם הכלה שהוא לשון שמחת איש באשה: בריך חמש. שהכל ואשר יצר ושוש תשיש שמח תשמח אשר ברא: בריך שית. יוצר האדם הוסיף: חדא יצירה הואי. כמאן דאמר בעירובין (דף יח.) ויבן את הצלע פרצוף שמתחילת ברייתו נברא שני פרצופין זכר מלפניו ונקבה מאחור: שתי יצירות. כמאן דאמר זנב היה וממנו נבראת האשה והרי כאן שתי יצירות: בתר מחשבה אזלינן. ששניהם עלו במחשבה להבראות ונברא אחד בעירובין בפ' עושין פסין: מברך שהשמחה במעונו. בתחילת הזימון: בין אמר להן. לקרואין: מחמת הלולא. קראתי לכם הלום לסעודה: מעיקרא. קודם החופה אם הזמין קרואים ואמר להם מחמת שאני רוצה להכניס בני לחופה: מאימתי. הויא התחלת שמחת חופה לברך שהשמחה במעונו: מכי רמי שערי באסינתא. יש שורין שעורים בעריבת מים להטיל שכר לצורך חופה וי"א לשם החתן והכלה זורעין שעורין בעציץ לומר פרו ורבו ולמחו כשעורים הללו: דהוה טריח ליה. מתוקנים היו לו כל צרכי חופה וסעודה: איעסק לבריה. שידך לו אשה: ובריך משעת אירוסין. שהשמחה במעונו: והדרי בהו. לא נתנו לו האשה: שית אריכתא. הוסיף דברים על שהכל ועל ברכת יצירה ראשונה וחתם בהם בברוך: ולית הלכתא כוותיה. כדפי' לעיל: לבי מהולא. לסעודת מילה: חתנים מן המנין. לקמן מפרש למאי הלכתא:

תוספות

שהכל ברא לכבודו ויוצר האדם. פותחת בברוך אע"פ שכל אחת סמוכה לחברתה כיון דקצרות הן אם לא היה פותח בברוך היה נראה הכל ברכה אחת וכן אשר יצר אם לא היה פותח בברוך היה נראה שהיא מתחלת מברוך יוצר האדם אשר יצר אבל שוש תשיש שהיא אחר ברכה ארוכה אין צריך לפתוח בברוך ואשר ברא פותחת בברוך לפי שמברכים אותה בפני עצמה כשאין פנים חדשות כדפירש בקונטרס ועל שהכל ברא לכבודו ויוצר האדם פי' בקונטרס טעם אחר ור"ת פירש דיוצר האדם פותחת בברוך לפי שיש שלא היו אומרים אותה כדאמר בסמוך ואור"ת דבפרק קמא דברכות (דף יא:) גבי ברכת התורה גרסי' ר' יוחנן מסיים בה הכי והערב נא דברכה אחת היא דאי הוו שתי ברכות היה צריך לפתוח בברוך אע"ג דסמוכה לחברתה כיון שאותה שלפניה היא קצרה ובתר הכי גרסינן הלכך נימרינהו לתרוייהו ולא גרסינן לכולהו דאם כן הוה משמע דשלש ברכות הן: חדא יצירה הואי. צריך לומר דהיינו כמאן דאמר פרצוף אחד מדקאמר בתר הכי דכולי עלמא חדא יצירה הואי מר סבר בתר מחשבה אזלינן וכו' פרק שני דעירובין (דף יח. ושם) משמע בהדיא דלמאן דאמר פרצוף אחד הוה עלה במחשבה להבראות שנים אבל למאן דאמר [illegible] ליה הכי כך פירש רשב"ם:

רב תנא הוא ופליג. לא בעי לשנויי כי תניא ההיא בברכת המזון כדמשני רבי יוחנן דנראה לו דוחק להעמיד כן ונוח לו טפי לומר דפליג ומדלא קאמר ר' יוחנן תנא ופליג יש להוכיח דר"י אמורא היה דאי הוה תנא הוה משני כדמשני לרב ואין להקשות דלמאי לא משני רבי יוחנן תנא הוא [illegible] דרבי יוחנן לא היה מחזיק רב כתנא דפליג עליו בכל דוכתא ומיהו איכא נמי רבי יוחנן שהיה תנא דתניא בשילהי דנזיר (דף סו. ושם) וכמה שיעור תפיסה פירש רבי יוחנן כו':

עין משפט נר מצוה

לט א מיי' פ"ב מהל' ברכות הל' יא ופ"י מהל' אישות הל' ג סמג עשין מח טוש"ע אה"ע סי' סב סעי' א:

מ ב מיי' שם הל' י טוש"ע שם סעיף ז:

מא ג מיי' פ"י מהל' אישות ה"ו טוש"ע שם סעיף יג:

מב ד מיי' שם הל' ה ופ"ב מהל' ברכות ה"י טוש"ע שם סעיף ד:

תוספות רי"ד

שעדיין לא שמען: מאי מברך אר"י שהכל ברא לכבודו. יוצר האדם. אשר יצר. שוש תשיש. שמח תשמח. אשר ברא. פי' תחלה מברך שהכל ברא לכבודו משום דברכת חתנים צריכה עשרה כדכתיב במקהלות ברכו ה' וכתיב ברוב עם הדרת מלך. וזו האסיפה היא על כבודו לברכו ברבים מ"ה מתחיל ומברך שהכל. אח"כ מברך יוצר האדם כנגד יצירה ראשונה שנברא לבדו. אח"כ מברך על יצירת שניהם האיך הפריד לו אשה מצלעותיו ומפני שמאריך דבריו חותם בה. אבל השתים הראשונות שהן קצרות אינו חותם בהן ואע"פ שהיא סמוכה לשלש ראשונות שבירך כבר פותח בה בברוך מפני שהשלש ראשונות פתיחה בברוך יש בהן. אבל חתימה אין בהם ואיזו נקרא ברכה הסמוכה לחברתה שאין פותחים בה בברוך כשמתחיל לאחרי' כגון ברכות י"ח וברכות ק"ש. אבל הסמוכה לברכה קטנה פותחים בה בברוך כמו שאנו עושים בק' ברכות שאותן שהם קצרות מברכין על כ"א וא' בפתיחה ולא יותר וכשמתחיל לברך ברכות הארוכות פותח בה בברוך. ואין סמיכות ברכות הקצרות פוטרת מלפתוח בה בברוך. ונ"ל שטועים הם בני אדם שמתחילים מאה ברכות מאלהי נשמה מפני שלא מצינו בשום מקום שיתחיל בברכות בלא פתיחת ברוך. וכך ראוי להתחיל ברוך אשר יצר את האדם בחכמה. ויש בה פתיחה לפניה וחתימה לאחריה. ואח"כ אומר אלהי נשמה וחותם בה בברוך ואינו פותח בה בברוך מפני שהיא סמוכה להו. ואח"כ אומר כל הקצרות. ואח"כ אומר המעביר שינה. ופותח בברוך. מפני שסמיכות ברכות הקטנות אינה פוטרתו. ובברכת התורה פותח בה בברוך מפני שלא נתקנה עם סדר ק' ברכות אלא כשצריך ללמוד הילכך יש בה פתיחה. אח"כ מברך שוש תשיש קודם שיברך על שמחת החתן דכתיב אם לא אעלה את ירושלים על ראש שמחתי. ומפני שהיא סמוכה לחתימת אשר יצר אינו פותח בה בברוך. אח"כ אומר שמח תשמח שישמח החתן והכלה כל ימיהם ואין זו שמחת הזיווג ומסיים בה משמח חתן וכלה ואינו פותח בה בברוך מפני שסמוכה היא לחתימת שוש תשיש. אח"כ אומר אשר ברא שהוא שמחת הזיווג וחותם בה משמח חתן עם הכלה ששמחים כשמזדווגים זה עם זה ואע"פ שהיא סמוכה לחתימה הראשונה שלפניה ודין הוא שלא נפתח בה בברוך. אפ"ה מפני שמברכים אותה לבדה בדליכא פנים חדשות הוא פותח בה בברוך: **רב אשי** איקלע לבי רב כהנא יומא קמא בריך כולהו מכאן ואילך אמר אי איכא פנים חדשות בריך כולהו. ואי לא אפושי שמחה בעלמא הוא. מברך שהשמחה במעונו ואשר ברא. פי' יומא קמא בין בשעת כניסתן לחופה בין בסעודה מברך כולהו ואין צריך פנים חדשות דהא מכאן ואילך לא הוי אלא בסעודה. א"כ יומא קמא אפילו בסעודה מברך ז' ברכות בלא פנים חדשות. ומכאן ואילך בלא פנים חדשות מברך שהשמחה במעונו בברהמ"ז ואשר ברא שהוא עיקר ברכת החתונות בסוף ברהמ"ז. **מז' ועד ל'** בין אמר מחמת הלולא בין לא אמר מחמת הילולא מברך שהשמח' במעונו. פי' אבל לא אשר ברא שהוא ברכת החתונות. וכיון שעברו ד' ימי חתונות אינו ראו לברכם. מכאן ואילך אי אמר מחמת הלולא מברך שהשמחה במעונו ואי לא לא. וכי אמר מחמת הלולא עד אימת. א"ר פפי משמיה דרבא עד תריסר ירחי שתא. **מעיקרא** מאימת א"ר פפא מכי רמו שערי באסותא פי' כיון שמשליך השעורים בגיגית לעשות מהן שכר לצורך הסעודה אבל לא משעת אירוסין: **רבינא** איעסיק ליה לבריה בי רב חביבא בריך משעת אירוסין. אמר קים לי בגווייהו דלא הדרי ביה ולא אסתעייא מילתא והדרי ביה: **רב תחליפא** איקלע לבבל בריך שית אריכתא. פי' הוסיף דברים על שהכל ועל יוצר האדם. והאריך בהן וחתם בהם ופסיק תלמודא ולית הלכתא (כסתם) [כוותיה]: **רב חביבא** איקלע לסעודת המילה בריך שהשמחה במעונו ופסיק תלמודא ולית הלכתא [כוותיה] משום דאית ליה צערא לינוקא. **אר"י אמר ר"י** מברכין ברכת חתנים בעשרה כל ז'. וחתנים מן המנין ברכת אבלים כל ד' ואין אבלים מן המנין. והוא שבאו פנים חדשות. מאי ברכת אבלים ברכת רחבה פי' היו מברין את האבל ברחובה של עיר ומברכין שם כנגד השם וכנגד אבלים וכנגד המנחמים וכנגד כל ישראל כדמפרש בגמרא וצריכה עשרה ובאותן יו"ד אין אבלים מן המנין כברכת המזון כגון ג' לזימון ויו"ד לאלהינו:

מסורת הש"ס

א) [עירובין יח. ע"ש היטב וע' גם ברכות סא. ומגלה ליצב. ושם איתא ר' אבהו וכ"ה בשאלתות], ב) [ע"ז ח:], ג) [סנהדרין יט.], ד) [עירובין כ: וש"נ], ה) [מגילה כג.], ו) פסחים נד. ז) ל"ל דבכורות פ"ח ה"ה, ח) [עיין תוס' ע"ז ח: ד"ה מכי וכו' הביאו על פירוש זה], ט) עי' יומא מג:.

תורה אור השלם

א) וַיִּבְרָא אֱלֹהִים אֶת הָאָדָם בְּצַלְמוֹ בְּצֶלֶם אֱלֹהִים בָּרָא אֹתוֹ זָכָר וּנְקֵבָה בָּרָא אֹתָם: [בראשית א, כז]

ב) זָכָר וּנְקֵבָה בְּרָאָם וַיְבָרֶךְ אֹתָם וַיִּקְרָא אֶת שְׁמָם אָדָם בְּיוֹם הִבָּרְאָם: [בראשית ה, ב]

ליקוטי רש"י

העקרה. ירושלים אשר היתה כלא ילדה [ישעיה נד, א]. בגן עדן מקדם. במזרחו של עדן נטע את הגן [בראשית ב, ח]. בהלוליה. בחופתו [ע"פ עירובין נד.]. זכר ונקבה בראם. משמע מתחלת ברייתם תרי הוו [ברכות סא.]. משמע מתחילת בריאתו היה זכר ונקבה זכר מצד זה ונקבה מצד זה [עירובין יח.]. מכי רמו שערי באסינתא. לעשות שכר ליום המשתה [ע"ז ח:]. רמו. מטילין [פסחים מב:]. אסינתא. עריבות ששורין בהן שעורין לעשות שכר ל"א נותנין עפר בעריבות וזורעין שם שעורין קודם ימי החופה ומביאין לפני החתן והכלה כשהן נמוחים ואומרים להם פרו ורבו כשעורין הללו שממהרין לצאת מכל התבואה [ע"ז שם]. קים לי בגוייהו. מכיר אני בהם [שם עו:]. חתנים מן המנין. לעשרה הצריכין להמנות לברכת חתנים כדאמרינן לעיל. ואין אבלים מן המנין. לקמן מפרש הלכתא [רש"י מכת"י בשיטמ"ק].

song-filled feasts. בָּרוּךְ אַתָּה ה׳ מְשַׂמֵּחַ חָתָן עִם הַכַּלָּה – ***Blessed are You, Hashem, Who gladdens the groom with the bride.***[10] [11]

The Gemara notes a dispute in practice regarding these blessings:

לֵוִי אִיקְלַע לְבֵי רַבִּי בְּהִלּוּלֵיהּ דְּרַבִּי שִׁמְעוֹן בְּרֵיהּ – **Levi visited the home of Rebbi during the wedding of [Rebbi's] son R' Shimon.** בָּרִיךְ חָמֵשׁ – **[Levi] recited five blessings.**[12] רַב אַסִּי אִיקְלַע לְבֵי רַב אַשִׁי בְּהִלּוּלֵיהּ דְּמָר בְּרֵיהּ – **Rav Assi visited the home of Rav Ashi during the wedding of his son Mar** בָּרִיךְ שִׁית – **and recited six blessings.**[13]

The Gemara suggests an explanation of this dispute:[14]

לֵימָא בְּהָא קָמִיפְלְגֵי – **Let us say that [Levi and Rav Assi] disagree about this** following matter: דְּמָר סָבַר חֲדָא יְצִירָה הֲוַאי – **That** one **master** [Levi] **holds that there was** only **one fashioning** of man.[15] Therefore it is unnecessary to have two

NOTES

10. This conclusion differs slightly from that of the previous blessing. Above, the blessing concludes, *Who gladdens the groom **and** bride;* here, the blessing ends *Who gladdens the groom **with** the bride.* The earlier blessing wishes each one of the two individuals well, that the groom should find success and happiness in his life and the bride in hers; that each should merit a constant source of sustenance and every good thing (*Rashi*) whether together or distinct from each other (*Kol Bo* §75). The last blessing, on the other hand, addresses the union of these two individuals and praises God for creating the relationship between husband and wife in all its happy dimensions. The fitting conclusion is therefore *"Who gladdens the groom with the bride,"* referring to the joy a man has with his wife (*Rashi*).

The Structure of *Sheva Berachos*

The six blessings listed above in the Gemara differ from each other structurally. All but the fourth and fifth blessings begin with the words בָּרוּךְ אַתָּה ה׳ אֱלֹהֵינוּ מֶלֶךְ הָעוֹלָם, *Blessed are You, Hashem, our God, King of the universe.* Also, all but the first two have a short concluding blessing (e.g. *Blessed are You, Hashem, Who gladdens Zion through her children* at the end of the fourth blessing).

Rashi offers the following analysis: There are two guidelines that explain all these differences: (a) Whenever the Sages enacted a series of related blessings, they enacted that the first blessing should both begin and end with בָּרוּךְ אַתָּה ה׳, *Blessed are You, Hashem.* All subsequent blessings in that series do not begin with this clause but do end with it. [The reason that a blessing following another blessing does not require the opening clause *Blessed are You, Hashem,* is that the recitation of this clause at the beginning of the first blessing suffices for all the blessings that follow (*Rashi, Rashbam* to *Pesachim* 104b; cf. *Tosafos* there).] (b) A blessing that stands by itself always begins with *Blessed are You, Hashem,* but whether it ends that way depends on the content of the particular blessing. If a single topic is treated straightforwardly throughout the whole blessing there is no concluding clause; if, however, there is a digression from the main theme to a different idea or to a supplication, then a concluding clause is required (see above, 7b note 27).

If we now examine the six blessings listed in our Gemara, we can see that the first two blessings (*Who has created everything for His glory* and *Who fashions the Man*) each begins with *Blessed are You, Hashem,* because each is an independent blessing. These two do not end with this clause because they are simple one-topic blessings. The third blessing (*Who fashioned the Man*) begins and ends with this clause because this blessing is the first in a series. The fourth and fifth blessings (*Bring intense joy . . . Bring intense gladness*) have concluding but not opening clauses because they are subsequent blessings in a series.

The last blessing (*Who created joy and gladness*) is also the last in a series, and it too should have a closing clause but no opening clause. Why then does it in fact begin *Blessed are You, Hashem*? *Rashi* explains that this blessing is often said *not* as part of a series: During most of the week of rejoicing, if there are no *panim chadashos,* new faces, in attendance then all the other blessings are omitted and this blessing is said by itself (see below in the Gemara). Since in this situation the blessing stands alone and therefore requires an opening *Blessed are You, Hashem,* the Sages enacted that it should always begin that way, even when it is said as part of a series.

11. This is a summary of the marriage service according to contemporary Ashkenazic custom (once the groom and bride are already standing under the *chuppah*): A distinguished person is summoned to recite the blessing of *erusin.* He is known as the *mesader kiddushin,* the arranger of the *kiddushin.* He holds a cup of wine and recites a *borei pri hagafen* and then the blessing of *erusin,* as recorded above on 7b (except that the word לָנוּ is added as per *Rabbeinu Tam's* view [see note 25 there] and that the word עַמּוֹ is added to the concluding blessing [בָּרוּךְ אַתָּה ה׳ מְקַדֵּשׁ עַמּוֹ יִשְׂרָאֵל עַל יְדֵי חֻפָּה וְקִדּוּשִׁין, *Blessed are You, Hashem, Who sanctifies His people Israel through chuppah and kiddushin*]. The groom and bride each drink from the wine. The groom then holds his ring in readiness and says to the bride: הֲרֵי אַתְּ מְקֻדֶּשֶׁת לִי בְּטַבַּעַת זוּ כְּדַת מֹשֶׁה וְיִשְׂרָאֵל, *Behold you are consecrated to me by means of this ring, according to the ritual of Moses and Israel.* After the ring is placed on the bride's finger, the *kiddushin* is complete. The *kesubah* is read aloud. [This is a practice enacted by *Rashi* (see *Rabbeinu Tam, Responsa* §45, *Machzor Vitry* §470 and *Mordechai* §132) so as to avoid a halachic problem regarding the use of two separate cups of wine – one for *erusin* and one for *Sheva Berachos.*] The *kesubah* is then given to the groom who hands it to his bride. A second cup is poured and the *Sheva Berachos* are said, beginning with *borei pri hagafen.* (At the *Sheva Berachos* said at the conclusion of the festive meals, *borei pri hagafen* is said last. See *Beis Shmuel* 62:2 and *Siddur Derech Chaim* for two reasons explaining this difference.) Both the groom and the bride drink from the wine. According to custom, the groom then smashes a glass with his right foot. [In Eretz Yisrael, the custom is to break the glass *before* the *Sheva Berachos* are recited.] The groom and bride then seclude themselves in completely private quarters (unless the bride is a *niddah,* in which case they may not seclude themselves entirely). After they emerge from seclusion, the wedding feast and festivities are held. After the meal, *zimun* is said with certain additions (see below) and, after *Bircas HaMazon, Sheva Berachos* are recited again.

If the *Sheva Berachos* are recited out of order, the mitzvah has still been fulfilled (beginning of *Kallah Rabbasi; Responsa, Rambam* §8 in *Pe'er HaDor* and §288 in Blau ed.). However, if one has already said the blessing beginning אֲשֶׁר יָצַר, he may no longer say the blessing beginning יוֹצֵר הָאָדָם (*R' Moshe Feinstein,* cited in *Responsa, Rivevos Ephraim* III §156).

[There are two other blessings pertaining to marriage that are mentioned in early sources (but not in the Talmud): (a) *Bircas Besulim* is a blessing mentioned in *Halachos Gedolos* and cited by *Rosh* here and in *Tur, Shulchan Aruch Even HaEzer* §63. According to *Rosh,* it is recited after the newly married couple have had relations when there is virginal blood: *Blessed is He Who set a nut tree in the Garden of Eden, lily of the valleys; let no foreigner presume upon the sealed spring; therefore, the beloved hind maintained [herself] in purity and ignored no law. Blessed is He Who chooses the seed of Abraham.* According to *Bach, Kuntres Acharon,* ad loc., it is the custom to recite this blessing, but without mentioning God's Name. (b) There is also a special blessing that, according to some sources, was said instead of *Sheva Berachos* at the wedding of a widow and a widower (see *Kol Bo* §75 ד״ה ברכת אלמון ואלמנה). However, *Rashba* (*Responsa,* I §1175) states categorically that the halachah does not follow this view and the standard text of *Sheva Berachos* is said for this couple as well.]

12. That is, he said all the blessings listed above except for the second one, יוֹצֵר הָאָדָם, *"Who fashions the Man"* (*Rashi*).

13. That is, he included the blessing, *"Who fashions the Man"* (*Rashi*). [Presumably, both Levi and Rav Assi recited the blessing *borei pri hagafen* as well.]

14. The Gemara's upcoming explanation is based on a discussion in *Eruvin* 18a (see also *Berachos* 61a). The Gemara there records a dispute concerning the creation of Adam and Eve. One view holds that Adam was created by himself but with an appendage (see *Eitz Yosef* to *Berachos* 61a). Later, God removed this appendage and built Eve from it. The other view maintains that Adam and Eve were created at the same time as a single male-and-female entity: One side of the entity had the facial figure of Adam and the other side that of Eve. Later, God split this entity into two (*Bereishis Rabbah* 8:1).

According to the "appendage" account, the human species was brought into being through two acts of creation, the creation of Adam and the creation of Eve from his appendage. According to the double figure account, there was only one act of creation. [The later separation of this entity into a male and a female is not considered an act of creation, but merely an adjustment] (*Rashi;* cf. *Tosafos;* see *Ritva*).

15. Adam and Eve were created as a double figure in a single act of creation (*Rashi*).

[א] **שהכל ברא לכבודו ויוצר האדם ואשר יצר את האדם בצלמו בצלם דמות תבניתו והתקין לו ממנו בנין עדי עד ברוך אתה ה' יוצר האדם שוש תשיש ותגל העקרה בקבוץ בניה לתוכה בשמחה ברוך אתה ה' משמח ציון בבניה שמח תשמח ריעים האהובים כשמחך יצירך בגן עדן מקדם ברוך אתה ה' משמח חתן וכלה ברוך אתה ה' אמ"ה אשר ברא ששון ושמחה חתן וכלה גילה רינה דיצה חדוה אהבה ואחוה ושלום וריעות מהרה ה' אלהינו ישמע בערי יהודה ובחוצות ירושלים קול ששון וקול שמחה קול חתן וקול כלה קול מצהלות חתנים מחופתם ונערים ממשתה נגינתם בא"י משמח חתן עם הכלה** לוי איקלע לבי רבי בהלוליה דר"ש בריה בריך חמש רב אסי איקלע לבי רב אשי בהלוליה דמר בריה בריך שית לימא בהא קמיפלגי דמ"ס חדא יצירה הואי ומ"ס שתי יצירות הואי לא דכ"ע חדא יצירה הואי מ"ס בתר מחשבה אזלינן ומ"ס בתר מעשה אזלינן כי הא [ב] דרב יהודה רמי כתיב [א] ויברא אלהים את האדם בצלמו וכתיב [ב] זכר ונקבה בראם הא כיצד בתחלה עלה במחשבה לבראות שנים ולבסוף נברא אחד רב אשי איקלע לבי רב כהנא יומא קמא בריך כולהו מכאן ואילך [ג] אי איכא פנים חדשות בריך כולהו ואי לא אפושי שמחה בעלמא הוא מברך שהשמחה במעונו ואשר ברא משבעה ועד שלשים בין אמר להו מחמת הלולא ובין לא אמר להו מחמת הלולא מברך שהשמחה במעונו מכאן ואילך אי אמר להו מחמת הלולא מברך שהשמחה במעונו ואי לא לא וכי א"ל מחמת הלולא עד אימת אמר רב פפי משמיה דרבא [ד] עד תריסר ירחי שתא ומעיקרא מאימת [ה] אמר רב פפא מכי רמו שערי באסינתא איני והא רב פפא איעסק לאבא מר בריה ובריך משעת אירוסין שאני רב פפא דהוה טריח ליה רבינא איעסק ליה לבריה בי רב חביבא ובריך משעת אירוסין אמר קים לי בגווייהו דלא הדרי בהו לא אסתייע מילתא והדרי בהו רב תחליפא בר מערבא איקלע לבבל בריך שית אריכתא ולית הלכתא כוותיה רב חביבא איקלע לבי מהולא בריך שהשמחה במעונו ולית הלכתא כוותיה משום דטרידי דאית ליה צערא לינוקא א"ר נחמן אמר רב [ו] חתנים מן המנין [ז] ואין אבלים מן המנין מיתיבי חתנים ואבלים מן המנין מתניתא קא רמית עליה דרב [ח] רב תנא הוא ופליג איתמר [ט] אמר ר' יצחק א"ר יוחנן חתנים מן המנין ואין אבלים מן המנין מיתיבי חתנים ואבלים מן המנין

כי

רש"י

והתקין לו ממנו בנין עדי עד. היא הנקבה: שוש תשיש. לפי שאנו צריכין להעלות זכרון ירושלים על ראש שמחתנו שנאמר (תהלים קלז) תדבק לשוני לחכי וגו': שמח תשמח. ברכה לחתן וכלה שיהיו שמחין בשמחה וטוב לב ואשר ברא לשם כל ישראל ולפי שהסדר מתחיל מאשר יצר לפיכך פתח בה בברוך וחותם בה בברוך כדרך כל ראשי סדרי ברכות ושוש תשיש ושמח תשמח מפני שהן ברכה הסמוכה לחברתה לא פתח בה בברוך שכן תיקנו לכל הברכות שסמוכות אחר הראשונה על הסדר ואשר ברא מפני שהיא נאמרת יחידית ברוב ימי המשתה כשאין שם פנים חדשות לפיכך אינה מן הסמוכות והולרך לפתוח בה בברוך ולסיים בה בברוך אבל שהכל ברא לכבודו אינה מן הסדר אלא לאסיפת העם הנאספים שם לגמול חסד זכר לחסדי המקום שנהג עם אדם הראשון שנעשה לו שושבין ונתעסק בו ואסיפה זו כבוד המקום היא וברכה זו לכך נתקנה ומשעת אסיפה היא ראויה לברך אלא מכיון שיש ברכה על הכוס הזקיקוה לסדרה עליו מידי דהוה אברכת בשמים וברכת על האור במוצאי שבת דאמרי' (ירושלמי דפסחים פ"י) רבי מפזרן וחוזר וסודרן על הכוס ורבי חייא מכנסן הואיל ויש שם כוס ולפי שאינה משאר סדר הברכות וכולה הודאה אחת לא חתמו בה בברוך מידי דהוה אברכת פירות ומצות וכן ברכת יוצר האדם שתיקנוה ליצירה ראשונה של אדם הראשון כדלקמן אי למ"ד ב' יצירות הוו אי למ"ד ב' יצירות עלו במחשבה ובתר מחשבה אזלינן מ"מ אינה מסדר ברכות הזווג דהא ביצירה הראשונה אכתי נקבה לא הואי וא"ת למה היא באה מתוך שאנו מברכין על יצירה השניה תקנו אף על הראשונה שהיא עיקר ותחילתו: והתקין לו ממנו. מגופו מצלעותיו: בנין עדי עד. בנין נוהג לדורות והוה קרי לה בנין על שם ויבן את הצלע (בראשית ב): עקרה. ירושלים: ריעים האהובים. החתן והכלה שהן ריעים האוהבים זה את זה: כשמחך יצירך. כמו ששמחת את אדם הראשון: בגן עדן מקדם. דכתיב ויטע גן בעדן מקדם וישם שם וגו' (שם): משמח חתן וכלה. ובאחרונה משמח חתן עם הכלה לפי ששמחת ברכה הראשונה לא בשמחת חתונה אנו אומרים שהרי תפלה היא שמתפללים ומברכין שיהו שמחים בהצלחה כל ימיהם לפיכך אין לחתום בה משמח חתן עם הכלה דמשמע איש באשתו אלא ברוך ה' משמח את שניהם לעולם בסיפוק מזונות וכל טוב ובאחרונה שבח שמשבח להקב"ה שברא חדוות דיבוק איש באשה על ידי שמחה וחדוה לפיכך יש לחתום משמח חתן עם הכלה שהוא לשון שמחת איש באשה: בריך חמש. שהכל ואשר יצר ושוש תשיש שמח תשמח אשר ברא: בריך שית. יוצר האדם הוסיף: חדא יצירה הואי. כמאן דאמר בעירובין (דף יח.) ויבן את הצלע פרצוף שמתחילת ברייתו נברא שני פרצופין זכר מלפניו ונקבה מאחור: שתי יצירות. כמאן דאמר זנב היה וממנו נבראת האשה והרי כאן שתי יצירות: בתר מחשבה אזלינן. ששניים עלו במחשבה להבראות ונברא אחד בעירובין בפ' עושין פסין: מברך שהשמחה במעונו. בתחילת הזימון: בין אמר להן. לקרואין: מחמת הלולא. קראתי לכם הלום לסעודה: מעיקרא. קודם החופה אם הזמין קרואים ואמר להם מחמת שאני רוצה להכניס בני לחופה: מאימתי. הויא התחלת שמחת חופה לברך שהשמחה במעונו: מכי רמי שערי באסינתא. יש שורין שעורים בעריבת מים [ח] להטיל שכר לצורך חופה וי"א לשם החתן והכלה זורעין שעורין בעציץ לומר פרו ורבו וצמחו כשעורים הללו: דהוה טריח ליה. מתוקנים היו לו כל צרכי חופה וסעודה: איעסק לבריה. שידך לו אשה: ובריך משעת אירוסין. שהשמחה במעונו: והדרי בהו. לא נתנו לו האשה: שית אריכתא. הוסיף דברים על שהכל ועל ברכת יצירה ראשונה וחתם בהם בברוך: ולית הלכתא כוותיה. כדפי' לעיל: לבי מהולא. לסעודת מילה: חתנים מן המנין. לקמן מפרש למאי הלכתא:

תוספות

שהכל ברא לכבודו ויוצר האדם. פותחת בברוך לפי שהכל אחת סמוכה לחבירתה כיון דקלרות הן אם לא היה פותח בברוך היה נראה הכל ברכה אחת וכן אשר יצר אם לא היה פותח בברוך היה נראה שהיא מתחלת מברוך יוצר האדם אשר יצר אבל שוש תשיש שהיא אחר ברכה ארוכה אין צריך לפתוח בברוך ואשר ברא פותחת בברוך לפי שמברכים אותה בפני עצמה כשאין פנים חדשות כדפירש בקונטרס ועל שהכל ברא לכבודו ויוצר האדם פי' בקונטרס טעם אחר ור"ת פירש דיוצר האדם פותחת בברוך לפי שיש שלא היו אומרים אותה כדאמר בסמוך ואור"ת דבפרק קמא דברכות (דף יא:) גבי ברכת התורה גרסי' ר' יוחנן מסיים בה הכי והערב נא דברכה אחת היא דאי הוו שתי ברכות היה צריך לפתוח בברוך אע"ג דסמוכה לחברתה כיון שאותה שלפניה היא קלרה ובתר הכי גרסינן הלכך נימרינהו לתרווייהו ולא גרסינן לכולהו דאם כן הוה משמע דשלש ברכות הן: **חדא** יצירה הואי. צריך לומר דהיינו כמאן דאמר פרצוף אחד מדקאמר בתר הכי דכולי עלמא חדא יצירה הואי מר סבר בתר מחשבה אזלינן ובריש פרק שני דעירובין (דף יח. ושם) משמע בהדיא דלמאן דאמר פרצוף אחד הוה עלה במחשבה להבראות שנים אבל למאן דאמר התם שני פרצופים לא סבירא ליה הכי כך פירש רשב"ם: **רב** תנא הוא ופליג. לא בעי לשנויי כי תניא ההיא בברכת המזון כדמשני רבי יוחנן דנראה לו דוחק להעמיד כן ונוח לו טפי לומר דפליג ומדלא קאמר ר' יוחנן [ט] תנא ופליג יש להוכיח דר"י אמורא היה דאי הוה תנא הוה משני כדמשני לרב ואין להקשות דלמאי לא משני רבי יוחנן תנא הוא ופליג דרבי יוחנן לא היה מחזיק רב כתנא דפליג עליו בכל דוכתא ומיהו איכא נמי רבי יוחנן שהיה תנא דתניא בשילהי דנזיר (דף סה. ושם) וכמה שיעור תפיסה פירש רבי יוחנן כו':

עין משפט נר מצוה

לט א מיי' פ"ב מהל' ברכות הל' יא ופ"י מהל' אישות הל' ג סמג עשין מח טוש"ע אה"ע סי' סב סעי' א:
מ ב מיי' שם הל' י טוש"ע שם סעיף ז:
מא ג מיי' פ"י מהל' אישות ה"ו טוש"ע שם סעיף יג:
מב ד מיי' שם הל' ה ופ"ב מהל' ברכות ה"י טוש"ע שם סעיף ד:

מסורת הש"ס

א) [עירובין יח. ע"ש היטב ועי' גם ברכות סא. ומלוה ליישב. ושם איתא ר' אבהו וכ"ה בשאלתות], ב) [ע"ז ה:], ג) [סנהדרין יט.], ד) [עירובין נ: וש"נ], ה) [מגילה כג.], ו) פסחים קד., ז) נ"ל דברכות פ"ח ה"א, ח) [עיין תוס' ע"ז ח: ד"ה מכי וכו' הסיגו על פירוש זה], ט) עי' יומא מג.:

תורה אור השלם

א) וַיִּבְרָא אֱלֹהִים אֶת הָאָדָם בְּצַלְמוֹ בְּצֶלֶם אֱלֹהִים בָּרָא אֹתוֹ זָכָר וּנְקֵבָה בָּרָא אֹתָם: [בראשית א, כז]
ב) זָכָר וּנְקֵבָה בְּרָאָם וַיְבָרֶךְ אֹתָם וַיִּקְרָא אֶת שְׁמָם אָדָם בְּיוֹם הִבָּרְאָם: [בראשית ה, ב]

ליקוטי רש"י

העקרה. ירושלים אשר היתה כלא ילדה [ישעיה נד, א]. בגן עדן מקדם. במזרחו של עדן נטע את הגן [בראשית ב, ח]. בהלוליה. במשתה [ע"פ עירובין נד.]. זכר ונקבה בראם. משמע מתחלת ברייתם תרי הוו [ברכות סא.]. משמע מתחילת בריאתו היה זכר ונקבה זכר מלד זה ונקבה מלד זה [עירובין יח.]. מכי רמו שערי באסינתא. לעשות שכר ליום המשתה [ע"ז ח:]. רמו. מטילין [פסחים מב:]. אסינתא. עריבות שעורין כהן טוחנין לעשות שכר ל"א עפר בעריבות וזורעין שם שעורין קודם ימי החופה ומוליכין לפני החתן והכלה כשהן נלמחים ואומרים להם פרו ורבו כשעורים הללו שממהרין ללמוח מכל התבואה [ע"ז שם]. קים לי בגווייהו. מכיר אני בהם [שם ע:]. חתנים מן המנין. לעשרה הלריכין להמנות לברכת חתנים כדאמרינן לעיל. ואין אבלים מן המנין. לקמן מפרש הלכתא [רש"י מכת"י בשיטמ"ק].

תוספות רי"ד

שעדיין לא שמענו: מאי מברך אר"י שהכל ברא לכבודו. יוצר האדם. אשר יצר. שוש תשיש. שמח תשמח. אשר ברא. פי' תחלה מברך שהכל ברא לכבודו משום דברכת חתנים צריכה עשרה כדכתיב במקהלות ברכו ה' וכתיב ברוב עם הדרת מלך. והו האסיפה היא על כבודו לברכו ברבים מ"ה מתחיל ומברך שהכל. אח"כ מברך יוצר האדם כנגד יצירה ראשונה שנברא לבדו. אח"כ מברך על יצירת שניהם היאך הפריד לו אשה מצלעותיו ומפני שמאריך בדבריו חותם בה. אבל השתים הראשונות שהן קצרות אינו חותם בהן ואע"פ שהיא סמוכה לשלש ראשונות שבירך כבר פותח בה בברוך מפני שהשלש ראשונות פתיחה בברוך יש בהן. אבל חתימה אין בהם ואיזו נקרא ברכה הסמוכה לחברתה שאין פותחים בה בברוך כשמתחיל לאחרי' כגון ברכות י"ח וברכות ק"ש. אבל הסמוכה לברכה קטנה פותחים בה בברוך כמו שאנו עושים בק' ברכות שאותן שהם קצרות מברכין על כ"א וא' בפתיחה ולא יותר וכשמתחיל לברך ברכות הארוכות פותח בה בברוך. ואין סמיכות ברכות הקצרות פוטרת מלפתחה בה בברוך. ונ"ל שטועים הם בני אדם שמתחילים מאה ברכות מאלהי נשמה מפני שלא מצינו בשום מקום שיתחיל בברכות בלא פתיחת ברוך. וכך ראוי להתחיל ברוך אשר יצר את האדם בחכמה. ויש בה פתיחה לפניה וחתימה לאחריה. ואח"כ אומר אלהי נשמה וחותם בה בברוך ואינו פותח בה בברוך מפני שהיא סמוכה להו. אח"כ אומר כל הקצרות. ואח"כ אומר המעביר שינה. ופותח בברוך. מפני שסמיכות ברכות הקטנות אינה פוטרתו. ובברכת התורה פותח בה בברוך מפני שלא נתקנה עם סדר ק' ברכות אלא כשצריך ללמוד הילכך יש בה פתיחה. אח"כ מברך שוש תשיש קודם שיברך על שמחת החתן דכתיב אם לא אעלה את ירושלים על ראש שמחתי. ומפני שהיא סמוכה לחתימת אשר יצר אינו פותח בה בברוך. אח"כ אומר שמח תשמח שישמח החתן והכלה כל ימיהם ואין זו שמחת הזיווג ומסיים בה משמח חתן וכלה ואינו פותח בה בברוך מפני שסמוכה היא לחתימת שוש תשיש. אח"כ אומר אשר ברא שהוא שמחת הזיווג וחותם בה משמח חתן עם הכלה ששמחים כשמזדווגים זה עם זה ואע"פ שהיא סמוכה לחתימה הראשונה שלפניה ודין הוא שלא נפתח בה בברוך. אפ"ה מפני שמברכים אותה לבדה בדליכא פנים חדשות הוא פותח בה בברוך: **רב אשי** איקלע לבי רב כהנא יומא קמא בריך כולהו מכאן ואילך אמר אי איכא פנים חדשות בריך כולהו ואי לא אפושי שמחה בעלמא הוא. מברך שהשמחה במעונו ואשר ברא. פי' יומא קמא בין בשעת כניסתן לחופה בין בסעודה מברך כולהו ואין צריך פנים חדשות דהא מכאן ואילך לא הוי אלא בסעודה. א"כ יומא קמא אפילו בסעודה מברך ז' ברכות בלא פנים חדשות. [illegible]

שֶׁהַכֹּל בָּרָא לִכְבוֹדוֹ – ***Who has created everything for His glory.***[1]

The second blessing:

וְיוֹצֵר הָאָדָם – **Then,** *Blessed are You, Hashem, our God, King of the universe,* ***Who fashions the man.***[2]

The third blessing:[3]

וַאֲשֶׁר יָצַר אֶת הָאָדָם בְּצַלְמוֹ – **Then,** *Blessed are You, Hashem, our God, King of the universe,* ***Who fashioned the Man in His image,*** בְּצֶלֶם דְּמוּת תַּבְנִיתוֹ – ***in the image of a likeness of his structure,***[4] וְהִתְקִין לוֹ מִמֶּנּוּ בִּנְיַן עֲדֵי עַד – ***and He prepared for him – from himself – a building for eternity.***[5] בָּרוּךְ אַתָּה ה׳ יוֹצֵר הָאָדָם – ***Blessed are You, Hashem, Who fashions the Man.***

The fourth blessing:

שׂוֹשׂ תָּשִׂישׂ וְתָגֵל הָעֲקָרָה – ***The barren one should rejoice intensely and exalt*** בְּקִבּוּץ בָּנֶיהָ לְתוֹכָהּ בְּשִׂמְחָה – ***at the ingathering of her children amidst her in gladness.*** בָּרוּךְ אַתָּה ה׳ מְשַׂמֵּחַ צִיּוֹן בְּבָנֶיהָ – ***Blessed are You, Hashem, Who gladdens Zion through her children.***[6]

The fifth blessing:

שַׂמֵּחַ תְּשַׂמַּח רֵיעִים הָאֲהוּבִים – ***Intensely gladden the beloved companions***[7] כְּשַׂמֵּחֲךָ יְצִירְךָ בְּגַן עֵדֶן מִקֶּדֶם – ***as You gladdened Your creature in the Garden of Eden to the east.***[8] בָּרוּךְ אַתָּה ה׳ מְשַׂמֵּחַ חָתָן וְכַלָּה – ***Blessed are You, Hashem, Who gladdens the groom and bride.***

The last blessing:

בָּרוּךְ אַתָּה ה׳ אֱלֹהֵינוּ מֶלֶךְ הָעוֹלָם – ***Blessed are You, Hashem, our God, King of the universe,*** אֲשֶׁר בָּרָא שָׂשׂוֹן וְשִׂמְחָה – ***Who created joy and gladness,*** חָתָן וְכַלָּה – ***groom and bride,*** גִּילָה רִינָּה דִּיצָה חֶדְוָה – ***mirth, glad song, pleasure, delight*** אַהֲבָה וְאַחֲוָה וְשָׁלוֹם וְרֵיעוּת – ***love, brotherhood, peace, and companionship.***[9] מְהֵרָה ה׳ אֱלֹהֵינוּ יִשָּׁמַע בְּעָרֵי יְהוּדָה וּבְחוּצוֹת יְרוּשָׁלַיִם – ***Hashem, our God, let there speedily be heard in the cities of Judah and the streets of Jerusalem*** קוֹל שָׂשׂוֹן וְקוֹל שִׂמְחָה – ***the sound of joy and the sound of gladness,*** קוֹל חָתָן וְקוֹל כַּלָּה – ***the voice of the groom and the voice of the bride,*** קוֹל מִצְהֲלוֹת חֲתָנִים מֵחוּפָּתָם – ***the sound of the grooms' jubilance from their canopies*** וּנְעָרִים מִמִּשְׁתֵּה נְגִינָתָם – ***and of youths from their***

NOTES

1. This is the first of six blessings that the Gemara will list. The seventh blessing of *Sheva Berachos* is the blessing over wine and is not listed in our version of the text – see above, 7a note 15). The six blessings are divided into two parts: The last four relate directly to the groom and bride. The first two are introductory blessings that concern tangential topics.

The first of these introductory blessings, *Who has created everything for His glory,* was instituted with reference to the larger wedding party, the people who are gathered to assist the bride and groom in getting married. The Sages decreed that a special blessing be recited for these persons who are following in God's footsteps: When Adam and Eve wed, God showered them with kindness and acted in the capacity of a dear and selfless friend who occupies himself with the groom's needs. The gathering of people for this generous purpose furthers God's glory [as does any deed that emulates God] and occasions the blessing, *Who has created everything for His glory.*

Since this blessing is prompted by the gathering of the members of the wedding party, it could be recited as soon as they have assembled, long before the *chuppah* actually takes place. However, since there are other blessings that will be recited over a cup of wine, this blessing too is delayed until that time. In this respect, it is similar to the blessings on the spices and the fire recited after the Sabbath as part of the Havdalah service. Although these two blessings could be recited independently (see *Yerushalmi Berachos* 1:5), we delay them until Havdalah and then recite all of the blessings over a cup of wine (*Rashi;* cf. *Tos. Rid; Meiri*).

[*Shulchan Aruch* rules (*Even HaEzer* 55:3; see also *Rama* 61:1) that if for some reason the *Sheva Berachos* were not recited at the wedding they must be recited at a later date. Now, according to *Rashi's* explanation here – that this first blessing was instituted primarily for the people gathered at the wedding – there is reason to question whether this first blessing should be recited in such a case. See *Atzei Arazim* 55:7; *Otzar HaPoskim* 62:2:2.]

2. This is the second introductory blessing, and it too does not deal directly with the bride and groom. Rather, the blessing addresses the initial creation of Adam, at which time no female had yet been created. It serves as an introduction to the next blessing, which discusses the second stage of man's creation – when Eve was formed (*Rashi*).

3. This is the first of the set of four blessings dealing directly with the bride and groom.

4. This wording is based on the verse in *Genesis* (1:27) describing man's creation: וַיִּבְרָא אֱלֹהִים אֶת־הָאָדָם בְּצַלְמוֹ בְּצֶלֶם אֱלֹהִים בָּרָא אֹתוֹ, *God created the Man in His image; in the image of God He created him.* The term צֶלֶם, *image,* generally refers to something abstract and invisible to the eye. A תַּבְנִית, *structure,* connotes something physical (*Ritva;* see *Shitah Mekubetzes*). Man is the physical manifestation of a certain abstract concept. Although God Himself has no form and is beyond description, He has chosen this abstract concept to represent Himself within the context of this world (see *Rashi* to *Genesis* loc. cit.).

5. The phrase *Who fashioned the Man* refers to Adam; and the phrase *He prepared for him – from himself – a building for eternity* refers to Eve, since she was created from Adam's own body. She is called "a building" in consonance with the wording in the verse (*Genesis* 2:22): *He built the side that He had taken from the man into a woman.* This building is "for eternity" since the creation of a female is in effect for generations (*Rashi*). [I.e. from that point on females would come into being naturally, as would males. Women would give birth to infant girls and boys. They would grow up, wed and the cycle would begin again.]

6. The "barren one" refers to Jerusalem (*Rashi;* see *Isaiah* 54:1 with *Targum*), whose future joy is likened by the prophets to the joy of a bride and groom – see *Isaiah* 62:5 (*Meiri*). We recall Jerusalem's travails at this happy moment because it is written (*Psalms* 137:5-6): *If I forget you, O Jerusalem, let my right hand forget its skill. Let my tongue adhere to my palate, if I fail to recall you, if I fail to elevate Jerusalem above my foremost joy* (*Rashi*). The remembrance of Jerusalem is invoked at this juncture in the *Sheva Berachos* because the next blessing is the first that refers to the man and woman as a couple (*Meiri*).

7. *"The beloved companions"* refers to the groom and bride, companions who love one another (*Rashi*) and who are beloved of each other (*Ran*).

8. God gladdened Adam in the Garden of Eden. This phrase is taken from the verse (*Genesis* 2:8), *He planted a garden in Eden, to the east, and placed there* etc. (*Rashi;* see also *Rashi* to *Genesis* loc. cit.; cf. *Targum* ad loc.).

This blessing was formulated (along with the rest of *Sheva Berachos*) to be recited for every groom and bride in every generation. It may seem overreaching or extravagant to pray that every couple in every generation should merit the sublime joy of Adam and Eve in the blissful surroundings of the Garden of Eden, but that is the nature of prayer. When a person prays before God, he should not ask for a third or a fourth of what he desires, but rather the loftiest state of good that exists. It is for this sublime state that man was created (*R' Chaim Shmulevitz, Sichos Mussar,* 5732, §17).

9. Ten expressions of joy are mentioned in this blessing, all of them linked to the groom and bride. They allude to the ten canopies that, according to the Gemara (*Bava Basra* 75a), God erected for Adam and Eve in the garden of Eden. Each of the canopies was made of a different precious material (*Iyun Tefillah* in *Siddur Otzar HaTefillos;* for other allusions, see *Zohar Chadash, Midrash Rus, Maamar Sheva Berachos* and *Peirush HaTefillos VeHaBerachos* by *R' Yehudah ben R' Yakar*). [These ten expressions encompass a complete and perfect joy, joy in all its elements.]

Ramban states that there are *twelve* expressions of joy in this blessing, [i.e. he treats the *chasan* and *kallah,* the groom and the bride themselves, as two kinds of joy] (*Derashah LeChasunah, Kisvei Ramban,* Chavel ed. vol. I p. 138; see, however, *Zohar* II 169b, which counts only ten expressions. See there for a lengthy discussion of all the *Sheva Berachos*). *Lev Simchah* comments that these twelve expressions correspond to the twelve months of the year, in fulfillment of the verse (*Deuteronomy* 24:5): *When a man marries a new wife . . . he shall be free for his home for one year, and he shall gladden his wife whom he has married* (*Lev Simchah, Devarim, Nisuin*).

The Gemara returns to the topic of *Sheva Berachos*:

תָּנוּ רַבָּנָן – The Rabbis taught in a Baraisa: מְבָרְכִין בִּרְכַּת חֲתָנִים בַּעֲשָׂרָה – WE RECITE *SHEVA BERACHOS* IN THE PRESENCE OF TEN PEOPLE[29] כָּל שִׁבְעָה – ALL SEVEN days of rejoicing.[30]

The Gemara qualifies the Baraisa's rule:

אָמַר רַב יְהוּדָה – Rav Yehudah said: וְהוּא שֶׁבָּאוּ פָּנִים חֲדָשׁוֹת – **This is** so only **when new faces came** to the meal.[31]

The Gemara asks:

מַאי מְבָרֵךְ – What text **does one recite?**

The Gemara answers:

אָמַר רַב יְהוּדָה – Rav Yehudah said: He recites the blessings as follows: בָּרוּךְ אַתָּה ה' אֱלֹהֵינוּ מֶלֶךְ הָעוֹלָם – ***Blessed are You, Hashem, our God, King of the universe,***

NOTES

ing clause because it contains a statement that is somewhat of a digression: כִּי הוּא יוֹם תְּחִלָּה לְמִקְרָאֵי קֹדֶשׁ, *for it is the prologue to the holy convocations.* This line is a glorification of the Sabbath, a departure from the theme of its sanctification through God. [These two themes – the sanctity of the Sabbath and the glory of the Sabbath – are the two essential parts of Kiddush. See *Rambam, Hil. Shabbos* 29:1 and *Sefer HaChinuch* §31.]

Although the blessing of *erusin* is focused on a single topic and would therefore not require a concluding clause, since it is also speaks of sanctity, it should be modeled after Kiddush (*Rashi* here and to *Pesachim* 105a). *Ritva* explains that the blessing of *erusin* is akin to a Kiddush said upon the Jewish people, a recognition of the holiness with which God has imbued us in the area of procreation.

According to *Rambam* (*Hil. Ishus* 3:23), the blessing of *erusin* should be recited before the groom gives the bride the ring, as is the case with all blessings upon mitzvos, where the blessing is recited before the mitzvah is performed (see *Pesachim* 7b). Although some Rishonim disagree with *Rambam* (see *Raavad's* glosses to *Rambam* there, *Tosafos* to *Pesachim* 7a ד"ה בלבער), the prevailing custom is to recite the blessing before the act of betrothal takes place (see *Even HaEzer* 34:1 with commentators).

[*Sefer HaMiknah* (*Kuntres Acharon* §34) writes that according to our practice of performing the *erusin* and *nisuin* at the same time, it would not be possible to recite the blessing after the *erusin*: At that time *nisuin* has also taken place since the groom and bride are already standing under the *chuppah.*]

Although later generations may have accepted *Rambam's* ruling, they may not have necessarily accepted his reasoning. As indicated above, *Rambam* deems the act of *kiddushin* as a distinct mitzvah and the blessing of *erusin* as a blessing upon a mitzvah (see also *Sefer HaMitzvos Asei* §212 and §213). However, other Rishonim maintain that *kiddushin* itself is not a mitzvah and that the blessing of *erusin* is simply an expression of praise and thankfulness (see *Rosh*).

29. There is a dispute among the Geonim if the blessing of *erusin* is also recited only when ten people are present. *Rosh* presents both sides of this argument and then concludes that ten men are needed.

30. That is, the seven days following the *chuppah*. For example, if the marriage took place on Wednesday, the *Sheva Berachos* would be required for the rest of that Wednesday plus the following six days, through Tuesday. This is so even if the first meal was not served until Wednesday night (*Rama, Even HaEzer* 61:6).

Most authorities hold that this period concludes at the end of the seventh day – e.g. Tuesday in the example given above. However, some hold that the *Sheva Berachos* requirement lasts for seven twenty-four-hour periods following the wedding. Thus, if the wedding took place at noon on Wednesday, *Sheva Berachos* would be recited at the meals up until noon of the following week (see *Pischei Teshuvah* 61:12 for ramifications of this dispute).

31. That is, someone who was not there the previous day (*Rashi*). According to *Meiri* this means that the person could have been at the wedding or at a previous *Sheva Berachos* meal; as long as he was not there the previous day he is considered a "new face." Based on what appears to be a different version of the Gemara and *Rashi, Ritva* says that a new face is a person who was never there.

Rambam (*Hil. Berachos* 2:10) rules that *panim chadashos* are persons who did not hear the *Sheva Berachos* under the *chuppah. Ramban, Rosh, Rashba* et al. explain that they are persons who have not eaten at a previous *Sheva Berachos* meal, or been present at one (see *Rashba, MHK* ed., note 396). *Shulchan Aruch* cites both opinions (*Even HaEzer* 62:7) and comments that the custom follows the second opinion.

Tosafos write that the Sabbath is deemed *panim chadashos* by itself and therefore *Sheva Berachos* are recited on the Sabbath even when no new actual *panim chadashos* are present. This is based on an Aggadic teaching that refers to the Sabbath as "*panim chadashos*" and implies that it is a cause for increased joy. [This Aggadic teaching is no longer extant in its source; for references to the Sabbath as a day of joy, see *Sifrei, Bamidbar* §77 and end of *Siddur Rabbah DeBereishis,* found in *Batei Medrashos.*] The halachic authorities extend this idea to the first and second days of the festivals; *Rama* suggests that a public discourse on a Torah topic would suffice as *panim chadashos.*

Aruch HaShulchan (*Even HaEzer* 62:23-30) explains the basis for these rulings (according to *Ramban, Rosh* et al.): The function of *panim chadashos* is to enhance the joy of the *Sheva Berachos* meal. If there is one person at a meal who has not yet participated in any previous meal, then it is akin to a new celebration [for everyone] and it is appropriate to say *Sheva Berachos* anew. This function of enhanced joy is fulfilled as well when a *Sheva Berachos* meal is held on the Sabbath or on a festival. It is even fulfilled if a Torah discourse is delivered during the meal, since it is written (*Psalms* 19:9): *The precepts of Hashem are upright, gladdening the heart.*

מיתיבי מברכין לבתולה שבעה ולאלמנה יום אחד מאי לאו אפילו אלמנה שנשאת לבחור לא לאלמון אבל לבחור מאי שבעה אי הכי ליתני מברכין לבתולה שבעה ולאלמנה שנשאת לבחור שבעה ולאלמנה יום אחד מילתא פסיקתא קתני דליכא בתולה דבצרה משבעה וליכא אלמנה דבצרה מיום אחד: גופא אמר רב נחמן אמר לי הונא בר נתן תנא מנין לברכת חתנים בעשרה שנאמר א) ויקח עשרה אנשים מזקני העיר ויאמר שבו פה ורבי אבהו אמר מהכא ב) במקהלות ברכו אלהים ה' ממקור ישראל ורב נחמן בהאי קרא דרבי אבהו מאי דריש ביה מיבעי ליה לכדתניא היה ר"מ אומר א) מנין שאפילו עוברים שבמעי אמן אמרו שירה על הים שנאמר במקהלות ברכו אלהים ה' ממקור ישראל ואידך אם כן לימא קרא מבטן מאי ממקור על עסקי מקור ורבי אבהו בהאי קרא דרב נחמן מאי דריש ביה ההוא מיבעי ליה למידרש ג) עמוני ולא עמונית מואבי ולא מואבית דאי סלקא דעתך לברכה לא סגיא דלאו זקנים ואידך אי סלקא דעתך למידרש לא סגיא דלאו עשרה אין לפרסומי מילתא ג) וכדאמר ליה שמואל לרב חנא בגדתאה פוק ואייתי לי בי עשרה ואימא לך באנפייהו המזכה לעובר קנה והלכתא א המזכה לעובר לא קנה: תנו רבנן מברכין ברכת חתנים ב בבית חתנים ר' יהודה אומר אף בבית האירוסין מברכין אותה אמר אביי וביהודה שנו ג מפני שמתייחד עמה תניא אידך מברכין ברכת חתנים בבית חתנים וברכת אירוסין בבית האירוסין ברכת האירוסין מאי מברך רבין בר רב אדא ורבה בר רב אדא תרוייהו משמיה דרב יהודה אמרי ד בא"י אמ"ה אשר קדשנו במצותיו וצונו על העריות ואסר לנו את הארוסות והתיר לנו את הנשואות על ידי חופה וקדושין רב אחא בריה דרבא מסיים בה משמיה דרב יהודה ה בא"י מקדש ישראל על ידי חופה וקדושין מאן דלא חתים מידי דהוה אברכת פירות ואברכת מצות ומאן דחתים מידי דהוה אקידושא: ת"ר מברכין ברכת חתנים בעשרה כל שבעה אמר רב יהודה ו והוא שבאו פנים חדשות מאי מברך אמר רב יהודה בא"י אמ"ה שהכל

מברכין לבתולה שבעה. לקמן מפרש כשבאו פנים חדשות מברך כולן כל ימי המשתה ואי לא מברך חדא: במקהלות ברכו אלהים ה' ממקור ישראל. על ברכת מקור לריך קהל והיינו עשרה כמו הקהל את העדה (במדבר כ) ואין הקהל בפחות מעדה ועדה עשרה כדלפינן (ברכות דף כא:) מעדת מרגלים עד מתי לעדה הרעה ילאו יהושע וכלב: בגדתאה. עיר שבבבל ושמה בגדת בפסק סדרו של רב שרירא גאון היא מזכרת: המזכה. מתנה על ידי אחר: לעובר. שבמעי אמו קנה: בבית חתנים. כשנכנסה לחופה נישואין: אף בבית האירוסין. כשמקדשה מברכין כל ברכת חתנים כדמפרש: אמר אביי וביהודה שנו. (הא דר"י ביהודה שנו) שמתייחד עמה. באירוסין כדי שיהא לבו גס בה כדלקמן (דף יב.) לפיכך מברכין ברכת חתנים מתחלה דתניא במסכת כלה כלה שלא ברכה אסורה לבעלה כנדה: ואסר לנו את הארוסות. מדרבנן שגזרו על היחוד של פנויה ואף ארוסה לא התירו עד שתכנס לחופה ובברכה כדפרישית כלה בלא ברכה אסורה לבעלה כנדה ואדרבנן נמי מברכין וצונו ואסר לנו כדאשכחן בנר חנוכה (שבת דף כג.): והתיר לנו. את נשותינו הנשואות לנו על ידי חופה וקידושין: אברכת פירות. בורא פרי העץ: ברכת מצות. על השחיטה ועל המילה דכיון דכולה חדא הודאה היא ואין הפסק בקשה בינתיים לא בעיא חתימה כדאמר בערבי פסחים (פסחים דף קד.) ברכת המלות טעמא מאי משום דהודאה היא הא נמי כולה הודאה היא: מידי דהוה אקידושא. כיון דבלשון קדושה היא כקידוש היום חתמינן בה כי התם דבההיא חתמינן משום דיש בה הפסק כגון כי הוא יום תחלה למקראי קודש: והוא שבאו. אל המשתה: פנים חדשות. בכל יום שלא היו שם אתמול: מאי מברך אמר רב יהודה כו'. נראה בעיני סדר ברכות שנסדרו על עסקי הזוג אינו אלא מאשר יצר ואילך שאותה ברכה מתחלת לדבר בשניהם אשר יצר את האדם מדבר בזכר והתקין

במקהלות ברכו אלהים. אע"ג דמקהלות תרי קהלות משמע אין סברא לחלק בין עשרה לעשרים לענין שום מילתא ומקהלות דעלמא בעי למימר ומיהו בירושלמי דריש במקהלת כתיב ז) חסר וי"ו: **המזכה** לעובר קנה. אע"ג דשמואל גופיה פסיק כרבי יוחנן הסנדלר (לקמן דף נח:) דמקדיש מעשה ידי אשתו המותר חולין דאין אדם מקדיש דבר שלא בא לעולם וכל שכן לדבר שלא בא לעולם דגרע טפי כדאמרינן בסוף פרק קמא דגיטין (דף יג: ושם) דקאמר אפילו לרבי מאיר דאמר אדם מקנה דבר שלא בא לעולם הני מילי לדבר שלא בא לעולם אבל לדבר שלא בא לעולם לא אמר מ"מ שמואל חשיב עובר בא לעולם אי נמי שמואל אית ליה טפי אדם מקנה לדבר שלא בא לעולם ממה שמקנה דבר שלא בא לעולם והיא סוגיא דספרק קמא דגיטין (ג"ז שם) אתיא אליבא דרב הונא וכן מלינו רב נחמן דבההיא סברתו הפוכה מדרב הונא דרב הונא אית ליה ח) בפירות דקל משבאו לעולם אין יכול לחזור בו וגבי עובר קאמר ט) אף לכשתלד לא קנה ורב נחמן סבר לכשתלד קנה ובפירות דקל קאמר אף משבאו לעולם יכול לחזור בו: (שייך לע"א) **ההוא** הורוה בית הלל. גבי הילני המלכה אע"ג דמבית חשמונאי היתה שהרי אם מונבז המלך היתה כדאמר ביומא (דף לז. ושם) ומלכות הורדוס מאה ושלש שנה בפני הבית והלל לא נהג נשיאותו עד שלש שנים לאחר מלכות הורדוס כדאמרינן (שבת טו.) הלל ושמעון גמליאל ושמעון נהגו נשיאותן בפני הבית מאה שנה מכל מקום כבר היו לו אז תלמידים שהורו: (שייך לע"א) **והא** בועז אלמון שנשא אלמנה הוה. לאו דוקא אלמנה דכשנשאת למחלון (י) וכליון) היתה נכרית אלא כיון דבעולה היא כאלמנה חשיב לה: (שייך לע"א) **באלמנה** שנשאת לבחור. דכיון שאין שניהם אלמונים יש לברך כל שבעה: **שנאמר** ויקח בועז עשרה אנשים. ובמסכת כלה דמייתי קרא דויברכו את רבקה (בראשית כד) איכא למימר דהתם ברכת אירוסין והכא ברכת נישואין ויש ללמוד משם שיש לברך ברכת אירוסין לאשה המתקדשת על ידי שליח שהרי אליעזר שליח היה ונראה דאסמכתא בעלמא היא דעשרה לא מישתמע מהתם ולא איירי פשטיה דקרא בברכת אירוסין: **רבי** יהודה אומר אף בבית האירוסין מברכין אותה מפני שמתייחד עמה. ואמרי' כלה בלא ברכה אסורה לבעלה כנדה ולפי שפעמים בא עליה שלא לשם חופה עושין ברכה מתחלה כדי שתהא כלה בברכה: **מאן** דלא חתים מידי דהוה אברכת פירות. שאין בה אריכות והאי נמי אינה ארוכה ולא דמי לקידושא דאריך טפי ומאן דחתים מידי דהוה אקידושא דחתים ביה משום דאריך והאי נמי חשיבא ארוכה ומה שפירש בקונטרס דמשום דבלשון קדושה היא חתמי בה כמו בקידושא אינו נראה ק"ק מאן דלא חתים בה מאי שנא מברכת התורה דחתמינן בה באשר בחר בנו אע"ג דברכת אירוסין אריכא טפי מינה ושמא לא היה חותם בה: **והוא** שבאו פנים חדשות. אור"י דפנים חדשות אין קורא אלא בבני אדם שמרבים בשבילם השמחה יותר ושבת דחשבינן פנים חדשות דאמרינן באגדה מזמור שיר ליום השבת אמר הקב"ה פנים חדשות באו לכאן נאמר שירה התם נמי מרבין לכבוד השבת בשמחה ובסעודה: שהכל

לד א מיי' פ"ב מהל' זכיה ומתנה הל' ה סמג עשין פג טוש"ע חו"מ סי' רי סעי' א:
לה ב מיי' פ"ב מהל' ברכות הל' ט ופ"י מהל' אישות הל' ג סמג עשין מח טוש"ע אה"ע סימן סב סעי' א:
לו ג מיי' פ"י מהל' אישות הל"ו טוש"ע שם סי' נה סעי' א:
לז ד ה מיי' פ"ג שם הל' כד סמג שם טוש"ע שם סי' לד סעי' א:
לח ו מיי' פ"ב מהל' ברכות הל' ט סמג שם טוש"ע אה"ע סי' סב סעי' ז ח [ע' ב"מ]:

תוספות רי"ד

א"ר נחמן א"ר הונא תנא מ"ק לברכת חתנים שהוא בעשרה שנאמר ויקח בועז עשרה אנשים וכו'. ור' אבהו אמר במקהלות ברכו אלהים ה' ממקור ישראל. פי' בה"ג בשעה שאשה מברך על המקור משום פריה ורביה עשה קהילה. א"ר יוסף הלוי הני ד' ברכות דמברכים בבית חתנים בין בשעת הכניסה בין בשעת המשתה דאיכא פנים חדשות בין אשר ברא. בדליכא פנים חדשות לא מברכינן לה אלא בעשרה. דארי' א"ר מברכין ברכת חתנים בעשרה כל ז' ותחנים מן המני'. ואשר ברא כיון דמברכת חתנים הוא לא מברכינן ל"ג בדליכא פנים חדשות אלא בעשרה. ואינו נ"ל דכל היכא דאמרי ברכת חתנים לא משמע אא"כ ז' ברכות ולא אשר ברא בלחוד דהכי ז'. ואמר רב יהודה והוא שבאו פנים חדשות. אלמא אא"פ ברכת חתנים אלא ד' ברכות. דהא אשר ברא בלחוד לא בעיא פנים חדשות. והכך ני אר"י מברכין ברכת חתנים בעשרה כל ז' על ד' ברכות קאמר ובדאיכא פנים חדשות. אבל אשר ברא נ"ל כיון שהוא עיקר ברכת חתנות שחייב לברכה בכל יום אפילו אם אכל החתן יחיד חייב לאומרה. הגה"ה (ורב פוסק (כר') בשם רבינו יצחק הלוי ואפי' ברכת אשר ברא לא צריכה עשרה). ת"ר מברכין ברכת חתנים בבית חתנים ר"י אומר אף בבית האירוסין מברכין אותן. אמר אביי ביהודה שנו מפני שמתיחד עמה. פי' ביהודה הי' מיחדים אותם משעת אירוסין כדי שיהא לבו גס בה. ולפיכך מברכים אותם ברכת חתנים תחלה ותניא במס' כלה כלה בלא ברכה אסורה לבעלה כנדה. אע"ג דהוו מברכי להו משעת אירוסין דין ארוסה יש לה ולא דין נשואה. אינו זכאי לא במציאותי' ולא במעשה ידיה ולא בהפרת נדריה. ואם מתה אינו יורשה וכן הוא אינו חייב לה בשאר כסות ועונה ולא נקראת אשתו נשואה אלא כשמוסרים אותה לו לשם נשואין. דמסירה קונה שתהיה אשתו לכל דבר ולא ז' ברכות דז' ברכות לא עבדי אלא שיהא מותר להתיחד עמה. וכן דרך קהילות ממנאה שמברכים ז' ברכות משעת אירוסין ועומדים זמן הרבה. ואח"כ מוסרים אותה לו לחופה לשם נשואין. ומ"ה תנן בפירקין לקמן. חוץ מן הארוסה שביהודה. שאע"פ שהיו מברכים ברכות אירוסין אכתי ארוסה קרי לה עד שימסרנה לו לשם נשואין ונ"ל שכיון שבירך ז' ברכות משעת אירוסין אסור עוד לברכה בשעת נשואין דהוה להו ברכה לבטלה. א"נ י"ל משום אפושי שמחה. וכל מה שמברכין בתוך ז' ימי החתונה אין בם משום ברכה לבטלה והכי נמי עיקר חיתונים הנשואים הם שמה שבירך בשעת האירוסין לא בירך אלא להתיר היחוד ועיקר חתנותיה זו היא. הלכך מברכין אותם בשעת הנשואים: **תניא אידך** מברכין ברכות חתנים בבית חתנים וברכת האירוסין בבית האירוסין. ברכת האירוסין מאי מברך רבין בר אדא ורב' בר רב אדא תרווייהו משמיה דר"י אמרי. בא"י אמ"ה אקב"ו על העריות ואסר לנו את הארוסות והתיר לנו את הנשואות ע"י חופה וקידושין. רב אחא משמיה דרבא מסיים בא"י מקדש ישראל ע"י חופה וקידושין מאן דלא מסיים סבר מידי דהוי אברכת פירות ואברכת מצות. ומאן דמסיים סבר מידי דהוי אקדושא דעלמא. פי' שמאריך בה דבריו צריך חתימה וכך הלכה. והאי ואסר לנו את הארוסות היא מדרבנן שאמרו כלה בלא ברכה אסורה לבעלה כנדה ואפ"ה מברך עליה מידי דהוה אנר חנוכה. ונ"ל דאע"ג שכל המצות מברך עליהן עובר לעשייתן הכא ברישא מקדש והדר מברך. מפני שהוא תלוי בדעת אחרים ושמא יחזרו בהן והוו לבטלה: **ת"ר** מברכין ברכת חתנים כל ז'. אמר ר"י והוא שבאו פנים חדשות. פי' ברכות חתנים הוא ז' ברכות. ומ"ה צריך פנים חדשות אדם שעדיין

א) ברכות נ., ב) [יבמות סט. וש"נ], ג) יבמות סט. ב"ב קמב: [זבחים לב.], ד) [בספר תהלים שלפנינו נדפס מקהלות], ה) [יבמות עז.], ו) [ב"ב קמב.], ז) יעב"ץ מ"ז.

גליון הש"ס

גמ' ברכת חתנים בבית חתנים. ע' סוכה כה ע"ב תד"ה אין שמחה:

תורה אור השלם

א) וַיִּקַּח עֲשָׂרָה אֲנָשִׁים מִזִּקְנֵי הָעִיר וַיֹּאמֶר שְׁבוּ פֹה וַיֵּשֵׁבוּ: [רות ד, ב]

ב) בְּמַקְהֵלוֹת בָּרְכוּ אֱלֹהִים יְיָ מִמְּקוֹר יִשְׂרָאֵל: [תהלים סח, כז]

לקוטי רש"י

עמוני ולא עמונית. הלכה רווחת בישראל דכתיב (דברים כג) על דבר אשר לא קדמו אתכם ואין דרכה של אשה לקדם [חולין סב:]. **בגדתאה.** שם עירו בגדד היא עיר החשובה שבבבל משתרכה בבל [קדושין נד:]. בעל אגדה ל"א שם מקום שהוא בבבל ששמו בגדד [יבמות סו:]. דמן בגדד עיר שעולד בה ונכתבו רב שרירא היא נזכרת [רשב"ם ב"ב קמב:]. **בי עשרה.** עשרה בני אדם [ע"פ עירובין קב.] לפרסם את הדבר [יבמות שם]. **ואברכת מצות.** כגון להתעטף בציצית ועל נטילת לולב [פסחים קד:]. כגון להתעטף בציצית ועל נטילת לולב וטעמו של דבר לפי שאין בהן ריבוי דברים [רשב"ם שם ועי' רש"י קה. ד"ה הודאה היא ורשב"ם ד"ה הא נמי הודאה].

seclude himself with [his bride] after the *erusin.*[21][22]

The Gemara cites a related Baraisa, which introduces another blessing:

תַּנְיָא אִידָךְ – **It was taught in another Baraisa:** מְבָרְכִין בִּרְכַּת חֲתָנִים בְּבֵית חֲתָנִים – WE RECITE *SHEVA BERACHOS* IN THE HOUSE OF THE GROOMS, וּבִרְכַּת אֵירוּסִין בְּבֵית הָאֵירוּסִין – AND THE BLESSING OF *ERUSIN* IN THE HOUSE OF THE *ERUSIN.*[23]

The Gemara asks:

בִּרְכַּת הָאֵירוּסִין מַאי מְבָרֵךְ – **What** text **does one recite** for the **blessing of** *erusin*?

The Gemara replies:

רָבִין בַּר רַב אַדָּא וְרַבָּה בַּר רַב אַדָּא תַּרְוַיְיהוּ מִשְּׁמֵיהּ דְּרַב יְהוּדָה אָמְרֵי – **Ravin bar Rav Adda and Rabbah bar Rav Adda both said in the name of Rav Yehudah:** בָּרוּךְ אַתָּה ה׳ אֱלֹהֵינוּ מֶלֶךְ הָעוֹלָם – ***Blessed are You, Hashem, our God, King of the universe,*** אֲשֶׁר קִדְּשָׁנוּ בְּמִצְוֹתָיו – ***Who has sanctified us with His commandments,*** וְצִוָּנוּ עַל הָעֲרָיוֹת – ***and has commanded us regarding forbidden unions;*** וְאָסַר לָנוּ אֶת הָאֲרוּסוֹת – ***Who forbade arusos to us,***[24] וְהִתִּיר לָנוּ אֶת הַנְּשׂוּאוֹת עַל יְדֵי חוּפָּה וְקִדּוּשִׁין – ***and permitted to us those [women who are] nesuos through chuppah and kiddushin.***[25] The text of the blessing ends here.

The Gemara presents a different opinion:

רַב אַחָא בְּרֵיהּ דְּרָבָא מְסַיֵּים בָּהּ מִשְּׁמֵיהּ דְּרַב יְהוּדָה – **Rav Acha the son of Rava concluded it in the name of Rav Yehudah** as follows: בָּרוּךְ אַתָּה ה׳ מְקַדֵּשׁ יִשְׂרָאֵל עַל יְדֵי חוּפָּה וְקִדּוּשִׁין – ***Blessed are You, Hashem, Who sanctifies Israel through chuppah and kiddushin.***[26]

The Gemara analyzes the dispute:

מַאן דְּלָא חָתִים – **Those who did not require a conclusion** מִידִי דַּהֲוָה אַבִּרְכַּת פֵּירוֹת וְאַבִּרְכַּת מִצְוֹת – hold that the blessing of *erusin* is **similar to a blessing on fruit and a blessing on a mitzvah,** where no conclusion is recited.[27] וּמַאן דְּחָתִים – **And those who require a conclusion** מִידִי דַּהֲוָה אַקִּידּוּשָׁא – hold that this blessing is **similar to Kiddush,** which does have a conclusion.[28]

NOTES

21. The Mishnah states below (12a) that in the province of Judea a couple would go into seclusion together after the *erusin* but before the *nisuin.* The purpose of this seclusion [or seclusions] was to allow the man and woman an opportunity to become more familiar and comfortable with each other. The fear was that if they remained distant until their wedding night, each would be too embarrassed by the other to have relations. Now, a bride for whom *Sheva Berachos* have not been recited has the same legal status (Rabbinically) as a *niddah,* a menstruant woman. Just as a man may not be intimate or even seclude himself with a *niddah,* so too one may not do so with an unblessed bride (*Maseches Kallah* 1:1). Accordingly, in Judea they recited the *Sheva Berachos* at the time of *erusin* (see *Rashi* here and to *Yevamos* 41a ד״ה חוץ מארוסה). It goes without saying that the women in Judea would also purify themselves of any actual *niddah* contamination before being secluded (*Responsa, Binyamin Zeev* §306). [Also, this leniency never extended to a couple who were merely betrothed but had not undergone *erusin.*]

[*Yerushalmi* (1:5) traces the origin of this practice. When Jacob's sons went to the Cave of Machpelah to bury their father, Esau contested their rights to the site and refused to allow them to perform the burial. Thereupon, Judah arose and slew him (cf. *Pirkei DeRabbi Eliezer,* end of ch. 39). To avenge this, when the descendants of Esau (Rome) gained power over the Jews, they decreed in Judea the practice of *jus primae noctis,* that any virgin who weds must first have relations with the local Roman officer. In order to assure that she not submit to him willingly – for this would prohibit her to her husband – the Judeans ordained that the *arus* and the *arusah* seclude themselves at the time of *erusin.* Thus, the bride would become attached to her new husband and would not submit to the officer without coercion. Even after the decree was abolished, the practice of secluding the bride and groom continued to prevail.]

22. R' Yehudah does not dispute the Tanna Kamma. R' Yehudah agrees that the *Sheva Berachos* should be saved for the *chuppah* if the bride and groom are not customarily secluded beforehand. The Tanna Kamma in turn concedes that *Sheva Berachos* should be said earlier in Judea (*Shitah Mekubetzes* ד״ה בבית חתנים, in explanation of *Rashi*). Indeed, in any place where this practice is followed *Sheva Berachos* should be recited at the time of *erusin* (*Ritva;* see there as to whether the *Sheva Berachos* are repeated at the time of the *nisuin*). *Tos. Rid* states that this was indeed the custom in his time in Romania (*Responsa* §47; see his commentary here).

23. There is a lengthy discussion among the Rishonim whether the blessing of *erusin* must be said over a cup of wine, and if so, whether the same cup may be used for both the blessing of *erusin* and the *Sheva Berachos* said under the *chuppah* (see *Ramban, Rosh, Rashba, Ritva* et al.).

24. There is a Rabbinical decree that one may not allow himself to be secluded with any unmarried woman (see below, 36b). And the same decree forbids an *arus* from being secluded with his own *arusah.* Only when they undergo *chuppah* and *Sheva Berachos* did the Rabbis relax their decree and permit them to seclude themselves. This is the meaning of the phrase *"Who forbade arusos to us."* Now, although the decree against seclusion is a Rabbinical and not a Biblical law, it is nevertheless appropriate to say: *Who has commanded us* and *Who forbade us,* in the same way we say *Who has commanded us* in regard to lighting the Chanukah menorah (*Rashi;* see *Shabbos* 23a).

[According to many Rishonim, an *arus* and *arusah* are permitted Biblically to have relations. However, as noted, there is a Rabbinical decree that forbids them even to be secluded. *Raavad* (cited in *Rashba*) maintains, however, that there is a Biblical prohibition against relations between an *arus* and an *arusah.*]

25. That is, our own wives are permitted to us after we have undergone *chuppah* and *kiddushin* (*Rashi*).

As the blessing appears in our text, this line could be misread that once a woman undergoes *nisuin* she is permitted to any man, whether he is her husband or not. Since this blessing is recited before both scholars and the unschooled, precision of expression is vital (see *Ritva*). Accordingly, *Rabbeinu Tam* preferred the version of our text with this wording: *and permitted to us those [women who are] nesuos* ***to us*** *through chuppah and kiddushin.*

[One would have expected *kiddushin* to be mentioned before *chuppah* since the act of *kiddushin* precedes *chuppah.* In fact, one may well wonder why *chuppah* is mentioned in this blessing at all, since it is the blessing of *erusin. Nimukei Yosef* (ד״ה והנגיד) suggests that the Rabbis rejected the wording, *and permitted to us those [women who are] nesuos through kiddushin,* since people would think that a wife is permitted immediately after *kiddushin.* They therefore added the word *chuppah* and placed it directly after *and permitted to us . . .* to demonstrate that it is the *chuppah* that renders her permissible to her husband (see *Rashba, Ritva* et al. for other solutions).]

26. According to Rav Acha this concluding clause is *added* to the text of the blessing recorded by Ravin and Rabbah bar Rav Adda.

27. The rule is that if a blessing treats one topic, it is not necessary to conclude it with a short blessing [that sums up the whole]. If, however, a blessing treats two or more topics, it is deemed a "long" blessing and one should conclude with the clause *Blessed are You, Hashem,* etc. The length of the blessing is not measured in the number of words but in the number of topics. Examples of the blessings on fruit and on mitzvos are: *Blessed are You, Hashem, our God, King of the universe, Who creates the fruit of the tree; Blessed are You . . . Who sanctified us with His commandments and commanded us in regard to slaughtering; Blessed are You . . . Who . . . commanded us in regard to circumcision.* Each of these blessings contains a single straightforward topic (thankfulness to God for a specific item or situation) and requires no concluding clause. Similarly, the blessing for *erusin* is also a straightforward expression of thankfulness and no conclusion is needed [even though the blessing is relatively lengthy in words] (*Rashi,* as explained by *Ritva;* see *MHK* ed. note 85; see *Pesachim* 105a).

28. Kiddush begins on Friday night with *Blessed are You, Hashem, our God, King of the universe, Who has sanctified us with His commandments and desired us* and ends with בָּרוּךְ אַתָּה ה׳ מְקַדֵּשׁ הַשַּׁבָּת, *Blessed are You, Hashem, who sanctifies the Sabbath.* Kiddush requires a conclud-

מיתיבי מברכין לבתולה שבעה ולאלמנה יום אחד מאי לאו אפילו אלמנה שנשאת לבחור לא לאלמון אבל לבחור מאי שבעה אי הכי ליתני מברכין לבתולה שבעה ולאלמנה שנשאת לבחור שבעה ולאלמנה יום אחד מילתא פסיקתא קתני דליכא בתולה דבצירה משבעה וליכא אלמנה דבצרה מיום אחד: גופא אמר רב נחמן אמר לי הונא בר נתן תנא מנין לברכת חתנים בעשרה שנאמר א) ויקח עשרה אנשים מזקני העיר ויאמר שבו פה ורבי אבהו אמר מהכא ב) במקהלות ברכו אלהים ה' ממקור ישראל ורב נחמן בהאי קרא דרבי אבהו מאי דריש ביה מיבעי ליה לכדתניא היה ר"מ אומר א) מנין שאפילו עוברים שבמעי אמן אמרו שירה על הים שנאמר במקהלות ברכו אלהים ה' ממקור ישראל ואידך אם כן לימא קרא מבטן מאי ממקור על עסקי מקור ורבי אבהו בהאי קרא דרב נחמן מאי דריש ביה ההוא מיבעי ליה למידרש ג) עמוני ולא עמונית מואבי ולא מואבית דאי סלקא דעתך לברכה לא סגיא דלאו זקנים ואידך אי סלקא דעתך למידרש לא סגיא דלאו עשרה אין לפרסומי מילתא ג) וכדאמר ליה שמואל לרב חנא בגדתאה פוק ואייתי לי בי עשרה ואימא לך באנפייהו המזכה לעובר קנה והלכתא א המזכה לעובר לא קנה: תנו רבנן מברכין ° ברכת חתנים ב בבית חתנים ר' יהודה אומר אף בבית האירוסין מברכין אותה אמר אביי וביהודה שנו ג מפני שמתייחד עמה תניא אידך מברכין ברכת חתנים בבית חתנים וברכת אירוסין בבית האירוסין ברכת האירוסין מאי מברך רבין בר רב אדא ורבה בר רב אדא תרוייהו משמיה דרב יהודה אמרי ד בא"י אמ"ה אשר קדשנו במצותיו וצונו על העריות ואסר לנו את הארוסות והתיר לנו את הנשואות על ידי חופה וקדושין רב אחא בריה דרבא מסיים בה משמיה דרב יהודה ה בא"י מקדש ישראל על ידי חופה וקדושין מאן דלא חתים מידי דהוה אברכת פירות ואברכת מצות ומאן דחתים מידי דהוה אקידושא: ת"ר מברכין ברכת חתנים בעשרה כל שבעה אמר רב יהודה ו והוא שבאו פנים חדשות מאי מברך אמר רב יהודה בא"י אמ"ה שהכל

רש"י

מברכין לבתולה שבעה. לקמן מפרש כשבאו פנים חדשות מברך כולן כל ימי המשתה ואי לא מברך חדא: **במקהלות ברכו אלהים ה' ממקור ישראל.** על ברכת מקור צריך קהל והיינו עשרה כמו הקהל את העדה (במדבר כ) ואין הקהל בפחות מעדה ועדה עשרה כדילפינן (ברכות דף כא:) מעדת מרגלים עד מתי לעדה הרעה יצאו יהושע וכלב: **בגדתאה.** עיר שבבבל ושמה בגדת בפסק סדרו של רב שרירא גאון היא נזכרת: **המזכה.** מתנה על ידי אחר: **לעובר.** שבמעי אמו קנה: **בבית חתנים.** כשנכנסה לחופת נישואין: **אף בבית האירוסין.** כשמקדשה מברכין כל ברכת חתנים כדמפרש: **אמר אביי וביהודה שנו.** [הא דר"י ביהודה שנו]: **שמתייחד עמה.** באירוסין כדי שיהא לבו גס בה כדלקמן (דף יב.) לפיכך מברכין ברכת חתנים מתחלה דתניא במסכת כלה כלה בלא ברכה אסורה לבעלה כנדה: **ואסר לנו את הארוסות.** מדרבנן שגזרו על הייחוד של פנויה ואף ארוסה לא התירו עד שתיכנס לחופה ובברכה כדפרישית כלה בלא ברכה אסורה לבעלה כנדה ואדרבנן נמי מברכין וצונו ואסר לנו כדאשכחן בנר חנוכה (שבת דף כג.): **והתיר לנו.** את נשותינו הנשואות לנו על ידי חופה וקידושין: **אברכת פירות.** בורא פרי העץ: **ברכת מצות.** על השחיטה ועל המילה דכיון דכולה חדא הודאה היא ואין הפסק בקשה בינתיים לא בעיא חתימה כדאמר בערבי פסחים (פסחים דף קה.) ברכת המצות טעמא מאי משום דהודאה היא הא נמי כולה הודאה היא: **מידי דהוה אקידושא.** כיון דבלשון קדושה היא כקידוש היום חתמינן בה כי התם דבההיא חתמינן משום דיש בה הפסק כגון כי הוא יום תחלה למקראי קודש: **והוא שבאו.** אל המשתה: **פנים חדשות.** בכל יום שלא היו שם אתמול: **מאי מברך אמר רב יהודה כו'.** נראה בעיני סדר ברכות שנסדרו על עסקי הזוג אינו אלא מאשר יצר ואילך שאותה ברכה מתחלת לדבר בשניהם אשר יצר את האדם מדבר בזכר והתקין

תוספות

במקהלות ברכו אלהים. אע"ג דמקהלות תרי קהלות משמע אין סברא לחלק בין עשרה לעשרים לענין שום מילתא ומקהלות דעלמא בעי למימר ומיהו בירושלמי דריש במקהלת כתיב ז) חסר וי"ו: **המזכה** לעובר קנה. אע"ג דשמואל גופיה פסיק כרבי יוחנן הסנדלר (לקמן דף נח:) דמקדיש מעשה ידי אשתו המותר חולין דאין אדם מקדיש דבר שלא בא לעולם וכל שכן לדבר שלא בא לעולם דגרע טפי כדאמרינן בסוף פרק קמא דגיטין (דף יג: ושם) דקאמר אפילו לרבי מאיר דאמר אדם מקנה דבר שלא בא לעולם הני מילי לדבר שבא לעולם אבל לדבר שלא בא לעולם לא אמר מ"מ שמואל חשיב עובר בא לעולם אי נמי שמואל אית ליה טפי אדם מקנה לדבר שלא בא לעולם ממה שמקנה דבר שלא בא לעולם והיא סוגיא דבפרק קמא דגיטין (ג"ז שם) אתיא אליבא דרב הונא וכן מצינו רב נחמן דבהדיא סברתו הפוכה מדרב הונא דרב הונא אית ליה ה) בפירות דקל משבאו לעולם אין יכול לחזור בו וגבי עובר קאמר ו) אף לכשתלד לא קנה ורב נחמן סבר לכשתלד קנה ובפירות דקל קאמר אף משבאו לעולם יכול לחזור בו: **הורוה** בית הלל. (שייך לע"א) גבי הילני המלכה אע"ג דמבית חשמונאי היתה שהרי אם מונבז המלך היתה כדאמר ביומא (דף לז. ושם) ומלכות הורדוס מאה ושלש שנה בפני הבית והלל לא נהג נשיאותו עד שלש שנים לאחר מלכות הורדוס כדאמרינן (שבת טו.) הלל ושמעון גמליאל ושמעון נהגו נשיאותן בפני הבית מאה שנה מכל מקום כבר היו לו אז תלמידים שהורו: **והא** בועז אלמון שנשא אלמנה הוה. (שייך לע"א) לאו דוקא אלמנה דכשנשאת למחלון (ו) וכליון) היתה נכרית אלא כיון דבעולה היא כאלמנה חשיב לה: **באלמנה** שנשאת לבחור. (שייך לע"א) דכיון שאין שניהם אלמונים יש לברך כל שבעה: **שנאמר** ויקח בועז עשרה אנשים. ובמסכת כלה דמייתי קרא דויברכו את רבקה (בראשית כד) איכא למימר דהתם ברכת אירוסין והכא ברכת נישואין ויש ללמוד משם שיש לברך ברכת אירוסין לאשה המתקדשת על ידי שליח שהרי אליעזר שליח היה ונראה דאסמכתא בעלמא היא דעשרה לא מישתמע מהתם ולא איירי פשטיה דקרא בברכת אירוסין: **רבי** יהודה אומר אף בבית האירוסין מברכין אותה מפני שמתייחד עמה. ואמרי' כלה בלא ברכה אסורה לבעלה כנדה ולפי שפעמים בא עליה שלא לשם חופה עושין ברכה מתחלה כדי שתהא כלה בברכה: **מאן** דלא חתים מידי דהוה אברכת פירות. שאין בה אריכות והאי נמי אינה ארוכה ולא דמי לקידושא דאריך טפי ומאן דחתים מידי דהוה אקידושא דחתים ביה משום דאריך והאי נמי חשיבא ארוכה ומה שפירש בקונטרס דמשום דבלשון קדושה היא חתמי בה כמו בקידושא אינו נראה ק"ק מאן דלא חתים בה מאי שנא מברכת התורה דחתמינן בה דאשר בחר בנו אע"ג דברכת אירוסין אריכא טפי מינה ושמא לא היה חותם בה: **והוא** שבאו פנים חדשות. פר"י דפנים חדשות אין קורא אלא בבני אדם שמרבים בשבילם השמחה יותר ושבת לא חשבינן פנים חדשות דאמרינן במגדה מזמור שיר ליום השבת אמר הקב"ה פנים חדשות באו לכאן נאמר שירה התם נמי מרבין לכבוד השבת בשמחה ובסעודה:

שהכל

חייב לה בשאר כסות ועונה ולא נקראת אשתו נשואה אלא כשמוסרים אותה לו לשם נשואין. דמסירה קונה שתהיה אשתו לכל דבר ולא ד' ברכות דד' ברכות לא עבדי אלא שיהא מותר להתיחד עמה. וכן דרך קהילות מגיאה שמברכים ד' ברכות משעת אירוסין ועומדים זמן הרבה. ואח"כ מוסרים אותה לו לחופה לשם נשואין. ומ"ה תנן בפירקין לקמן. חוץ מן הארוסה שביהודה. שאע"פ שהיו מברכים ברכות אירוסין אכתי ארוסה קרי לה עד שימסרנה לו לשם נשואין וה"ל שכיון שבירך ד' ברכות משעת אירוסין אסור עוד לברכה בשעת נשואין דהוה להו ברכה לבטלה. א"נ י"ל משום אפושי שמחה. וכל מה שמברכין בתוך ז' ימי החתונה אין בו משום ברכה לבטלה דהכי עיקר חיתנם הנשואים הם שמה שבירך בשעת האירוסין לא בירך אלא להתיר היחוד ועיקר חתונתיה זו היא. הלכך מברכין אותם בשעת הנשואים: **תניא אידך** מברכין ברכות חתנים בבית חתנים וברכת האירוסין בבית האירוסין. ברכת האירוסין מאי מברך רבין בר רב אדא ורבה בר רב אדא תרוייהו משמיה דרב יהודה אמרי. בא"י אמ"ה אקב"ו על העריות ואסר לנו את הארוסות והתיר לנו הנשואות ע"י חופה וקידושין. רב אחא משמיה דרבא מסיים בה בא"י מקדש ישראל ע"י חופה וקידושין מאן דלא מסיים סבר מידי דהוי אברכת פירות ואברכת מצות. ומאן דמסיים סבר מידי דהוי אקדושא דעלמא. פי' שמארך בה דבריו צריך לחתימה. וכן הלכה. והא דאמרינן שאסר לנו את הארוסות היא מדרבנן שאמרו כלה בלא ברכה אסורה לבעלה כנדה ואפ"ה מדרבנן מברך עליהן וצונו כמו שמברך בנר חנוכה. וצ"ל דאע"ג שכל המצות מברך עליהן עובר לעשייתן הכא ברישא מקדש והדר מברך. מפני שהוא תלוי בדעת אחרים ושמא יחזרו בהן והוו ברכה לבטלה: **ת"ר** מברכין ברכת חתנים כל ז'. אמר ר"י והוא שבאו פנים חדשות. פי' ברכות חתנים הוא ד' ברכות. ומ"ה צריך פנים חדשות אדם

שעדיין

עין משפט נר מצוה

לד א מיי' פ"ג מהל' זכיה הל' ה סמג עשין פג טוש"ע חו"מ סי' רי סעי' א:

לה ב מיי' פ"ב מהל' ברכות הל' ט ופ"י מהל' אישות הל' ג סמג עשין מח טוש"ע אה"ע סימן סב סעי' א:

לו ג מיי' פ"י מהל' אישות הל' ה טוש"ע שם סי' לד סעי' א:

לז ד ה מיי' פ"ג מהל' אישות הל' כד סמג שם טוש"ע שם סי' לד סעי' א:

לח ו מיי' פ"ב מהל' ברכות הל' י סמג שם טוש"ע שם סימן סב סעי' ז [ועי' כ"מ]:

תוספות רי"ד

א"ר נחמן א"ר הונא תנא מנין לברכת חתנים שהוא בעשרה שנאמר ויקח בועז עשרה אנשים וכו'. ור' אבהו אמר במקהלות ברכו אלהים ה' ממקור ישראל. פי' בה"ג בשעה שיתחה מברך על המק"ר משום פריה ורביה צריך קהילה. א"ר יוסף הלך רבי ז' ברכות דמברכים בבית חתנים בין בשעת הכניסה בין בשעת המשתה בדאיכא פנים חדשות בין אשר ברא. בדליכא פנים חדשות לא מברכינן לה אלא בעשרה. דאר"י אר"י מברכין ברכת חתנים בעשרה כל ז' וחתנים מן המנין. אשר ברא כיון דמברכה הוא לא מברכינן לה בדליכא פנים חדשות אלא בעשרה. ואנו י"ל דכל היכא דאמרי ברכת חתנים לא משמע אלא ז' ברכות ולא אשר ברא בלחוד דהכי אמרינן ברכת חתנים כל ז' ואמר רב יהודה והוא שבאו פנים חדשות. אלמא לא מיקרייא ברכת חתנים אלא ז' ברכות. ולא אשר ברא בלחוד לא בעיא פנים חדשות. הלכך כי אר"י מברכין ברכת חתנים בעשרה כל ז' על ז' ברכות קאמר ובדאיכא פנים חדשות. אבל אשר ברא נ"ל כיון שהוא עיקר ברכת חתנות שחייב לברכה בכל יום אפי' אם אכל החתן יחיד חייב לאומרה. הגה"ה (הרב פוסק (כר') [בשם רבינו] יצחק הלוי ואפי' ברכה. אשר ברא לבדו צריכה עשרה.) ת"ר מברכין ברכת חתנים בבית חתנים ר"י אומר אף בבית האירוסין מברכין אותה. אמר אביי ביהודה שנו מפני שמתיחד עמה. פי' ביהודה הי' מיחדים אותם משעת אירוסין כדי שידא לבו גס בה. ולפיכך מברכים אותם ברכת חת"ם תחלה ותניא במס' כלה כלה בלא ברכה אסורה לבעלה כנדה. ואע"ג דהוו מברכי להו משעת אירוסין דין ארוסה יש לה ולא דין נשואה ואינו זכאי לא במציאותי' ולא במעשה ידיה ולא בהפרת נדריה. ואם מתה אינו יורשה וכן מתה אינו

מסורת הש"ס

א) ברכות נ., ב) [יבמות סט. וש"נ], ג) יבמות עז. ב"ב קמב: [זבחים לב.], ד) [בספר תהלים שלפנינו נדפס מלא], ה) [יבמות לג.], ו) [ב"ב קמב.], ז) יעב"ץ מ"ז.

גליון הש"ס

גמ' ברכת חתנים בבית חתנים. ע' סוכה כה ע"ב תד"ה אין שמחה:

תורה אור השלם

א) וַיִּקַּח עֲשָׂרָה אֲנָשִׁים מִזִּקְנֵי הָעִיר וַיֹּאמֶר שְׁבוּ פֹה וַיֵּשֵׁבוּ: [רות ד, ב]

ב) בְּמַקְהֵלוֹת בָּרְכוּ אֱלֹהִים יְיָ מִמְּקוֹר יִשְׂרָאֵל: [תהלים סח, כז]

לקוטי רש"י

עמוני ולא עמונית. הלכה רווחת בישראל דכתיב (דברים כג) על דבר אשר לא קדמו אתכם ואין דרכה של אשה לקדם [חולין סב:]. **בגדתאה.** שם עירו בגדד היא עיר החשובה שבבבל מסחרה בבל. אגדה לי"ם שם מקום שהוא בבבל ששמו בגדד [יבמות סז.]. דמן בגדד עיר שנולד בה וכבכתבי רב שרירא היא נזכרת [רשב"ם ב"ב קמב:]. **בי עשרה.** עשרה בני אדם [ע"ש עירובין קב.] לפרסם את הדבר [יבמות שם]. **ואברכת מצות.** כגון להתעטף בציצית ועל נטילת לולב [פסחים קד:] כגון להתעטף בציצית ועל נטילת לולב וטעמו של דבר לפי שאין בהן ריבוי דברים [רשב"ם שם ועי' רש"י קה. ד"ה הודאה היא ורשב"ם ד"ה הא נמי הודאה].

The Gemara explains why the second Amora did not interpret the verse that way:

וְאִידָךְ – **But the other** Amora, R' Abahu, rejects this explanation: אִם כֵּן לֵימָא קְרָא מִבֶּטֶן – **If** it is **so** that the verse refers to fetuses in the womb, **the verse should say** instead **"from the stomach."**[11] מַאי ,,מִמְּקוֹר״ – **Why** does it say, ***"from the womb"***? עַל עִסְקֵי מָקוֹר – It must be because it **refers to the matters of the womb.**[12]

The Gemara now asks what the second Amora derives from the verse cited by the first Amora:

וְרַבִּי אַבָּהוּ – **And** as for **R' Abahu,** בְּהַאי קְרָא דְרַב נַחְמָן מַאי דָרִישׁ בֵּיהּ – **how does he expound the verse cited by Rav Nachman,** *He [Boaz] took ten men from the elders of the city*?

The Gemara answers:

הַהוּא מִיבָּעֵי לֵיהּ לְמִידְרַשׁ – R' Abahu explains that **it was necessary for [Boaz]** to gather ten men in order **to proclaim** to them the following law: ,,עַמּוֹנִי״ וְלֹא עַמּוֹנִית – When the Torah prohibits a Jew from marrying ***an Ammonite,***[13] it refers to a male Ammonite, **not an Ammonitess;** ,,מוֹאָבִי״ וְלֹא מוֹאָבִית – and when the Torah prohibits ***a Moabite,*** it refers to a male Moabite, **not a Moabitess.** This law permitted Ruth to marry into the Jewish people.[14] דְּאִי סַלְקָא דַעְתָּךְ לִבְרָכָה – **For if it should enter your mind** that they were gathered together **to** recite **the blessing,** i.e. *Sheva Berachos,* לֹא סַגְיָא דְלָאו זְקֵנִים – **would it not have sufficed** to gather men **who were not elders?!**[15]

The Gemara explains why the first Amora did not interpret the verse along these lines:

וְאִידָךְ – **But the other** Amora, Rav Nachman, rejects that interpretation for this reason: אִי סַלְקָא דַעְתָּךְ לְמִידְרַשׁ – **If it should enter your mind** that Boaz gathered these elders together **to proclaim** that a Moabitess is permitted, לֹא סַגְיָא דְלָאו עֲשָׂרָה – **would it not have sufficed** to summon **less than ten** people? Certainly Boaz could have gotten the point across with fewer men!

The Gemara defends R' Abahu against this criticism:

אִין – **Yes,** ten people were, in fact, necessary לְפַרְסוּמֵי מִילְּתָא – **in order to publicize the matter.** וְכִדְאָמַר לֵיהּ שְׁמוּאֵל לְרַב חָנָא בַּגְדָּתָאָה – **And** this is **similar to** the incident in which **Shmuel told Rav Chana of Baghdad:**[16] פּוּק וְאַיְיתֵי לִי בֵּי עֲשָׂרָה – **Go out and bring me ten people,** וְאֵימָא לָךְ בְּאַנְפַּיְיהוּ – **and I will say to you in their presence:** הַמְזַכֶּה לְעוּבָּר קָנָה – **If one grants possession** of an object **to a fetus** in its mother's womb, **[the fetus] acquires** it.[17] We therefore see that if one wishes to publicize a certain ruling, one should announce it in the presence of at least ten people.

The Gemara remarks parenthetically:

וְהִלְכְתָא הַמְזַכֶּה לְעוּבָּר לֹא קָנָה – **However, the law is that** if **one grants possession** of an object **to a fetus, [the fetus] does *not* acquire** it.[18]

The Gemara cites a Baraisa that discusses when *Sheva Berachos* are said:

תָּנוּ רַבָּנָן – **The Rabbis taught in a Baraisa:** מְבָרְכִין בִּרְכַּת חֲתָנִים בְּבֵית חֲתָנִים – WE RECITE SHEVA BERACHOS IN THE HOUSE OF THE GROOMS.[19] רַבִּי יְהוּדָה אוֹמֵר – R' YEHUDAH SAYS: אַף בְּבֵית הָאֵירוּסִין מְבָרְכִין אוֹתָהּ – WE RECITE IT EVEN IN THE HOUSE OF THE *ERUSIN*.[20]

The Gemara qualifies and explains R' Yehudah's statement:

אָמַר אַבַּיֵי – **Abaye said:** וּבִיהוּדָה שָׁנוּ – **[R' Yehudah's statement] was taught in,** i.e. limited to, the province of **Judea,** מִפְּנֵי שֶׁמִּתְיַיחֵד עִמָּהּ – **because** in Judea it is customary for **[a groom]** to

NOTES

11. בֶּטֶן, *stomach,* is a standard term for the part of the body where a baby is carried; מָקוֹר, which means literally "source," is not a standard term for that usage.

12. See end of note 8 above.

13. *Deuteronomy* 23:4: לֹא־יָבֹא עַמּוֹנִי וּמוֹאָבִי בִּקְהַל ה׳, *An Ammonite or Moabite shall not enter into the congregation of Hashem.* That is, even if an Ammonite or Moabite converts to Judaism, a Jew of Israelite descent may not marry that convert.

14. Ruth was a Moabitess. If the law excluding descendants of Moab applied to females it would have been forbidden for any Jew of Israelite descent to marry Ruth. Accordingly, before Boaz offered her hand in marriage to the person who was next in line (see *Ruth* 4:1-8) and before Boaz himself took her as a wife, he had to clarify the halachah publicly.

[It may be presumed that the legal distinction between a Moabite and a Moabitess was not well known even among scholars. The nations of Moab and Israel had been enemies for centuries and the practical applications of this law may have been rare or nonexistent. We also find that the Scriptural source for this distinction – and the distinction itself – were challenged several generations later in regard to David, who was a descendant of Ruth. According to one view, the distinction was upheld solely because of an oral tradition authenticated by the court of Samuel the Prophet (see *Yevamos* 76b-77a).]

15. For there is no reason to require elders; it is sufficient to have any ten men in order to recite the blessings (see *Ritva*). [Presumably, Scripture would not have mentioned that these men were elders if this detail was irrelevant to the point at hand.]

16. *Rashi* here cites a written work of Rav Sherira Gaon that בַּגְדַּת, Bagdat, is a city in Babylonia. In two of Rav Sherira Gaon's works (cited in *Otzar HaGeonim* here, *Peirushim,* note 7) and in *Rashi* to *Berachos* 54b (ד״ה בגרתאה) the name of the city is בַּגְדָּד, Baghdad. *Rashi* there comments that after Babylon was destroyed, Baghdad emerged as Babylonia's most prominent city. *Rashbam* (to *Bava Basra* 142b) adds that Rav Chana was born there.

[It is questionable, however, whether this "Baghdad" is to be identified with the modern city of Baghdad in Iraq.]

Alternatively, בַּגְדָּתָאָה does not refer to Rav Chana's place of origin, but rather to his expertise in the area of אַגָּדְתָא, *Aggadic exposition* (*Rashi* to *Yevamos* 67a; see also *Rashi* to *Succah* 52b ד״ה אמר רב ששת).

17. That is, he gives the gift to another person to acquire it on behalf of the fetus (*Rashi*).

18. This is in accordance with the view of R' Yochanan in *Bava Basra* (142b) that a gift to a fetus is ineffective.

19. I.e. *Sheva Berachos* are said when the bride enters the *chuppah* and the couple enters into the state of *nisuin* (*Rashi*). In other words, the Baraisa need not be taken literally to mean the groom's house. Rather, it means wherever the *chuppah* happens to be (*Ritva*). According to *Rashi,* the Baraisa is teaching us *when* the *Sheva Berachos* should be said, not *where* (*Shitah Mekubetzes* ד״ה בבית חתנים).

Some Rishonim learn from this passage that during the seven days of feasting, when *Sheva Berachos* are also said, they are recited only if the meal is held where the *chuppah* took place (see *Tosafos* to *Succah* 25b ד״ה אין). Other Rishonim, though, contend that wherever the groom makes his meal, that is called "the house of the groom" (see *Rosh* there). *Meiri* adds that even if the groom and bride are invited out to someone else's house for a meal in honor of the wedding, *Sheva Berachos* are recited there. This is the prevailing custom (see *Taz, Even HaEzer* 62:7).

20. That is, when the *erusin* takes place, they recite all the *Sheva Berachos* as the Gemara proceeds to explain (*Rashi*).

[These Tannaim speak in reference to the practice common in their days to perform *erusin* when the match was agreed upon and then to wait a certain amount of time until the *nisuin* (see above, 2a). In this context, the Tanna Kamma says that the *Sheva Berachos* are recited at the time of the *nisuin;* but at the *erusin* only the single blessing of *erusin* (recorded below) is recited along with the blessing for wine (*Meiri*). Nowadays, however, it is the universal custom to perform the *erusin* and the *nisuin* together and so the distinction between the time of *erusin* and the time of *nisuin* would be moot (see Gemara below).]

מיתיבי מברכין לבתולה שבעה ולאלמנה יום אחד מאי לאו אפילו אלמנה שנשאת לבחור לא לאלמון אבל לבחור מאי שבעה אי הכי ליתני מברכין לבתולה שבעה ולאלמנה שנשאת לבחור שבעה ולאלמנה יום אחד מילתא פסיקתא קתני דליכא בתולה דבצרה משבעה וליכא אלמנה דבצרה מיום אחד: גופא אמר רב נחמן אמר לי הונא בר נתן תנא מנין לברכת חתנים בעשרה שנאמר א) ויקח עשרה אנשים מזקני העיר ויאמר שבו פה ורבי אבהו אמר מהכא ב) במקהלות ברכו אלהים ה' ממקור ישראל ורב נחמן בהאי קרא דרבי אבהו מאי דריש ביה מיבעי ליה לכדתניא היה ר"מ אומר ה) מנין שאפילו עוברים שבמעי אמן אמרו שירה על הים שנאמר במקהלות ברכו אלהים ה' ממקור ישראל ואידך אם כן לימא קרא מבטן מאי ממקור על עסקי מקור ורבי אבהו בהאי קרא דרב נחמן מאי דריש ביה ההוא מיבעי ליה למידרש ו) עמוני ולא עמונית מואבי ולא מואבית דאי סלקא דעתך לברכה לא סגיא דלאו זקנים ואידך אי סלקא דעתך למידרש לא סגיא דלאו עשרה אין לפרסומי מילתא ז) וכדאמר ליה שמואל לרב חנא בגדתאה פוק ואייתי לי בי עשרה ואימא לך באנפייהו המזכה לעובר קנה והלכתא א המזכה לעובר לא קנה: תנו רבנן מברכין ב ברכת חתנים בבית חתנים ר' יהודה אומר אף בבית האירוסין מברכין אותה אמר אביי וביהודה שנו ג מפני שמתייחד עמה תניא אידך מברכין ברכת חתנים בבית חתנים וברכת אירוסין בבית האירוסין ברכת האירוסין מאי מברך רבין בר רב אדא ורבה בר רב אדא תרוייהו משמיה דרב יהודה אמרי ד בא"י אמ"ה אשר קדשנו במצותיו וצונו על העריות ואסר לנו את הארוסות והתיר לנו את הנשואות על ידי חופה וקדושין רב אחא בריה דרבא מסיים בה משמיה דרב יהודה ה בא"י מקדש ישראל על ידי חופה וקדושין מאן דלא חתים מידי דהוה אברכת פירות ואברכת מצות ומאן דחתים מידי דהוה אקידושא: ת"ר מברכין ברכת חתנים בעשרה כל שבעה אמר רב יהודה ו והוא שבאו פנים חדשות מאי מברך אמר רב יהודה בא"י אמ"ה שהכל

רש"י

מברכין לבתולה שבעה. לקמן מפרש כשבאו פנים חדשות מברך כולן כל ימי המשתה ואי לא מברך אלא: במקהלות ברכו אלהים ה' ממקור ישראל. על ברכת מקור צריך קהל והיינו עשרה כמו הקהל את העדה (במדבר כ) ואין הקהל בפחות מעדה ועדה עשרה כדילפינן (ברכות דף כא:) מעדת מרגלים עד מתי לעדה הרעה יצאו יהושע וכלב: בגדתאה. עיר שבבבל ושמה בגדת בפסק סדרו של רב שרירא גאון היא נזכרת: המזכה. מתנה על ידי אחר: לעובר. שבמעי אמו קנה: בבית חתנים. כשנכנסה לחופת נישואין: אף בבית האירוסין. כשמקדשה מברכין כל ברכת חתנים כדמפרש: אמר אביי וביהודה שנו. [הא דר"י ביהודה שנו]: שמתייחד עמה. באירוסין כדי שיהא לבו גס בה כדלקמן (דף יב.) לפיכך מברכין ברכת חתנים מתחלה דתניא במסכת כלה כלה בלא ברכה אסורה לבעלה כנדה: ואסר לנו את הארוסות. מדרבנן שגזרו על הייחוד של פנויה ואף ארוסה לא התירו עד שתיכנס לחופה ובברכה כדפרישית כלה בלא ברכה אסורה לבעלה כנדה ואדרבנן נמי מברכין וצונו ואסר לנו כדאשכחן בנר חנוכה (שבת דף כג.): והתיר לנו. את נשותינו הנשואות לנו על ידי חופה וקידושין: אברכת פירות. בורא פרי העץ: ברכת מצות. על השחיטה ועל המילה דכיון דכולה חדא הודאה היא ואין הפסק בקשה בינתיים לא בעיא חתימה כדאמר בערבי פסחים (פסחים דף קה.) ברכת המזות טעמא מאי משום דהודאה היא הא נמי כולה הודאה היא: מידי דהוה אקידושא. כיון דבלשון קדושה היא כקידוש היום חתמינן בה כי התם דבההיא חתמינן משום דיש בה הפסק כגון כי הוא יום תחלה למקראי קודש: והוא שבאו. אל המשתה: פנים חדשות. בכל יום שלא היו שם אתמול: מאי מברך אמר רב יהודה כו'. נראה בעיני סדר ברכות שנסדרו על עסקי הזוג אינו אלא מאשר יצר ואילך שאותה ברכה מתחלת לדבר בשניהם אשר יצר את האדם מדבר בזכר

והתקין

תוספות

במקהלות ברכו אלהים. אע"ג דמקהלות תרי קהלות משמע אין סברא לחלק בין עשרה לעשרים לענין שום מילתא ומקהלות דעלמא בעי למימר ומיהו בירושלמי דריש במקהלת כתיב ד) חסר וי"ו: המזכה לעובר קנה. אע"ג דשמואל גופיה פסיק כרבי יוחנן הסנדלר (לקמן דף נח:) דמקדיש מעשה ידי אשתו המותר חולין דאין אדם מקדיש דבר שלא בא לעולם וכל שכן לדבר שלא בא לעולם דגרע טפי כדאמרינן בסוף פרק קמא דגיטין (דף יג: ושם) דקאמר אפילו לרבי מאיר דאמר אדם מקנה דבר שלא בא לעולם הני מילי לדבר שבא לעולם אבל לדבר שלא בא לעולם לא אמר ר"מ שמואל חשיב עובר בא לעולם אי נמי שמואל אית ליה טפי אדם מקנה לדבר שלא בא לעולם ממה שמקנה דבר שלא בא לעולם והיא סוגיא דפרק קמא דגיטין (ג"ז שם) אתיא אליבא דרב הונא וכן מצינו רב נחמן דהדיא סברנו הפוכה מדרב הונא דרב הונא אית ליה ה) בפירות דקל משבאו לעולם אין יכול לחזור בו וגבי עובר קאמר ו) אף לכשתלד לא קנה ורב נחמן סבר לכשתלד קנה ובפירות דקל קאמר אף משבאו לעולם יכול לחזור בו: הורוה (סייך לע"א) בית הלל. גבי הילני המלכה אע"ג דמבית חשמונאי היתה שהרי אם מונבז המלך היתה כדאמר ביומא (דף לז. ושם) ומלכות הורדוס מאה ושלש שנה בפני הבית והלל לא נהג נשיאותו עד שלש שנים לאחר מלכות הורדוס כדאמרינן (שבת טו.) הלל ושמעון גמליאל ושמעון נהגו נשיאותן בפני הבית מאה שנה מכל מקום כבר היו לו אז תלמידים שהורו: והא (סייך לע"א) בועז אלמון שנשא אלמנה הוה. לאו דוקא אלמנה דכשנשאת למחלון (ז) וכליון) היתה נכרית אלא כיון דבעולה היא כאלמנה חשיב לה: באלמנה (סייך לע"א) שנשאת לבחור. דכיון שאין שניהם אלמונים יש לברך כל שבעה: שנאמר ויקח בועז עשרה אנשים. ובמסכת כלה דמייתי קרא דויברכו את רבקה (בראשית כד) איכא למימר דהתם ברכת אירוסין והכא ברכת נישואין ויש ללמוד משם שיש לברך ברכת אירוסין לאשה המתקדשת על ידי שליח שהרי אליעזר שליח היה ונראה דאסמכתא בעלמא היא דעשרה לא משתמע מהתם ולא איירי פשטיה דקרא בברכת אירוסין: רבי יהודה אומר אף בבית האירוסין מברכין אותה מפני שמתייחד עמה. ואמרי' כלה בלא ברכה אסורה לבעלה כנדה ולפי שפעמים בא עליה שלא לשם חופה עושין ברכה מתחלה כדי שתהא כלה בברכה: מאן דלא חתים מידי דהוה אברכת פירות. שאין בה אריכות והאי נמי אינה ארוכה ולא דמי לקידושא דאריך טפי ומאן דחתים מידי דהוה אקידושא דחתים ביה משום דאריך והאי נמי חשיבא ארוכה ומה שפירש בקונטרס משום דבלשון קדושה היא חתמי בה כמו בקידושא אינו נראה ק"ק מאן דלא חתים בה מאי שנא מברכת התורה דחתמינן בה באשר בחר בנו אע"ג דברכת אירוסין אריכא טפי מינה ושמא לא היה חותם בה: והוא שבאו פנים חדשות. אור"י דפנים חדשות אין קורא אלא בני אדם שמרבים בשבילם השמחה יותר ושבת חשבינן פנים חדשות דאמרינן באגדה מזמור שיר ליום השבת אמר הקב"ה פנים חדשות באו לכאן נאמר שירה התם נמי מרבין לכבוד השבת בשמחה ובסעודה:

שהכל

עין משפט נר מצוה

לד א מיי' פ"ב מהל' זכיה הל' ב סמג עשין פג טוש"ע ח"מ סי' רי סעי' א:

לה ב מיי' פ"ב מהל' ברכות הל' ט ופ"י מהל' אישות הל' ג סמג עשין מח טוש"ע אה"ע סימן סב סעי' א:

לו ג מיי' פ"י מהל' אישות הל' ד טוש"ע שם סי' נה סעי' א:

לז ד ה מיי' פ"ג שם הל' כד סמג שם טוש"ע שם סי' לד סעי' א:

לח ו מיי' פ"ב מהל' ברכות הל' י סמג שם טוש"ע שם סימן סב סעי' ז ח [עי' כ"מ]:

תוספות רי"ד

א"ר נחמן א"ר הונא תנא מנין לברכת חתנים שהוא בעשרה שנאמר ויקח בועז עשרה אנשים וכו'. ור' אבהו אמר במקהלות ברכו אלהים ה' ממקור ישראל. פי' בה"ג בשעה שאתה מברך על המקור כשום פריה ורביה עשה קהילה. א"ר יוסף הלוי הני ד' ברכות דמברכים בבית חתנים בין בשעת הכניסה בין בשעת המשתה בדאיכא פנים חדשות בין אשר ברא. בדליכא פנים חדשות לא מברכין לה אלא בעשרה. דאר"י אר"י מברכי' ברכת חתנים בעשרה כל ז' וחתנים מן דמנין. ואשר ברא כיון דמברכת חתנים הוא לא מברכין לה בדליכא פנים חדשות אלא בעשרה. ואינו נ"ל דכל היכא דאמר ברכת חתנים לא משמע אלא ד' ברכות ולא אשר ברא בלחוד דהכי אמרינן ברכת חתנים כל ז'. ואמר רב יהודה והוא שבאו פנים חדשות. אלמא לא מיקרייא ברכת חתנים אלא ד' ברכות. דהא אשר ברא בלחוד לא בעיא פנים חדשות. והלכך כי אר"י מברכין ברכת חתנים בעשרה כל ז' על ד' ברכות קאמר ובדאיכא פנים חדשות. אבל אשר ברא נ"ל כיון שהוא עיקר ברכת חתנות שחייב לברכה בכל יום אפילו אם אכל החתן יחיד חייב לאומרה. הגה"ה (הרב פוסק (כו') [בשם רבינו] יצחק הלוי ואפי' ברכת אשר ברא לבדו צריכה עשרה.) ת"ר מברכין ברכת חתנים בבית חתנים ר"י אומר אף בבית האירוסין מברכין אותן. אמר אביי ביהודה שנו מפני שמתייחד עמה. פי' ביהודה הי' מיחדים אותם משעת אירוסין כדי שיהא לבו גס בה. ולפיכך מברכים אותם ברכת חתנים תחלה ותניא במס' כלה כלה בלא ברכה אסורה לבעלה כנדה. ואע"ג דהוו מברכי' להו משעת אירוסין דין ארוסה יש לה ולא דין נשואה ואינו זכאי לא במציאותי' ולא במעשה ידיה ולא בהפרת נדריה. ואם מתה אינו יורשה וכן הוא אינו חייב לה בשאר כסות ועונה ולא נקראת אשתו נשואה אלא כשמוסרים אותה לו לשם נשואין. דמסירה קונה שתהיה אשתו לכל דבר ולא ד' ברכות דד' ברכות לא עבדי אלא שיהא מותר להתיחד עמה. וכן דרך קהילות ממניאה שמברכים ד' ברכות משעת אירוסין ועומדים זמן הרבה. ואח"כ מוסרים אותה לו לחופה לשם נשואין. ומ"ה תנן בפירקין לקמן. חוץ מן הארוסה שביהודה. שאע"פ שהיו מברכים ברכות אירוסין אכתי ארוסה קרי לה עד שימסרנה לו לשם נשואין ונ"ל שכיון שבירך ד' ברכות משעת אירוסין אסור עוד לברכה בשעת נשואין דהוה להו ברכה לבטלה. א"נ י"ל משום אפושי שמחה. וכל מה שמברכין בתוך ד' ימי החתונה אין בם משום ברכה לבטלה והכי נמי עיקר חיתונים הנשואים הם שמה שבירך בשעת האירוסין לא בירך אלא להתיר היחוד ועיקר חתנותיה זו היא. הלכך מברכין אותם בשעת הנשואים: תניא אידך מברכין ברכות חתנים בבית חתנים וברכת האירוסין בבית האירוסין. ברכת האירוסין מאי מברך רבין בר אדא ורב' בר רב אדא תרווייהו משמיה דר"י אמרי. בא"י אמ"ה אקב"ו על העריות ואסר לנו את הארוסות והתיר לנו את הנשואות ע"י חופה וקידושין. רב אחא משמיה דרבא מסיים בא"י מקדש ישראל ע"י חופה וקידושין מאן דלא מסיים סבר מידי דהוי אברכת פירות ואברכת מצות. ומאן דמסיים סבר מידי דהוי אקדושא דעלמא. פי' שמאריך בה דבריו צריך חתימה וכך הלכה. והאי ואסר לנו את הארוסות היא מדרבנן שאמרו כלה בלא ברכה אסורה לבעלה כנדה ואפ"ה מברך עליה מידי דהוה אנר חנוכה. ונ"ל דאע"ג שכל המצות מברך עליהן עובר לעשייתן הכא ברישא מקדש והדר מברך. מפני שהוא תלוי בדעת אחרים ושמא יחזרו בהן והוו להו לבטלה: ת"ר מברכין ברכת חתנים כל ז'. אמר ר"י והוא שבאו פנים חדשות. פי' ברכות חתנים הוא ז' ברכות. ומ"ה צריך פנים חדשות אדם

שעדיין

מסורת הש"ס

א) ברכות נ., ב) יבמות סט. וש"נ, ג) יבמות מט. ב"ב קמב:, ד) [בספר תהלים שלפנינו נדפס מלאו], ה) [יבמות עו.], ו) [ב"ב קמב.], ז) יעב"ץ מ"ז.

גליון הש"ס

גמ' ברכת חתנים בבית חתנים. ע' סוכה כה ע"ב תד"ה אין שמחה:

תורה אור השלם

א) וַיִּקַּח עֲשָׂרָה אֲנָשִׁים מִזִּקְנֵי הָעִיר וַיֹּאמֶר שְׁבוּ פֹה וַיֵּשֵׁבוּ: [רות ד, ב]

ב) בְּמַקְהֵלוֹת בָּרְכוּ אֱלֹהִים יְיָ מִמְּקוֹר יִשְׂרָאֵל: [תהלים סח, כז]

לקוטי רש"י

עמוני ולא עמונית. הלכה רווחת בישראל דכתיב (דברים כג) על דבר אשר לא קדמו אתכם ואין דרכה של אשה לקדם [חולין סב:]. בגדתאה. שם עירו בגדד היא עיר החשובה שבבבל משתרבה בבל [ברכות נד:]. בעל אגדה לי שם מקום שהוא בבבל ששמו בגדד [יבמות סז.]. דמן בגדד עיר שנולד בה ובכתבי רב שרירא היא נזכרת [רשב"ם ב"ב קמב:]. בי עשרה. עשרה בני אדם [ע"פ עירובין קב.]. לפרסם את הדבר [יבמות שם]. ואברכת מצות. כגון להתעטף בציצית ועל נטילת לולב [פסחים קב:]. כגון להתעטף בציצית ועל נטילת לולב וטעמו של דבר לפי שאין בהן ריבוי דברים [רשב"ם שם ועי' רש"י קה. ד"ה הודאה היא ורשב"ם ד"ה הא נמי הודאה].

The Gemara cites a Baraisa in an attempt to reject this answer:[1]

מֵיתִיבֵי – **They challenged** this **from a Baraisa:** מְבָרְכִין לִבְתוּלָה שִׁבְעָה – WE RECITE THE BLESSINGS ON BEHALF OF A VIRGIN FOR SEVEN days,[2] וּלְאַלְמָנָה יוֹם אֶחָד – AND ON BEHALF OF A WIDOW FOR ONE DAY. מַאי לָאו – **Is this not** saying that every widow has only one day of *Sheva Berachos,* אֲפִילּוּ אַלְמָנָה שֶׁנִּשֵּׂאת לְבָחוּר – **even a widow who weds a never-married man?**

The Gemara replies:

לֹא – **No!** The Baraisa means only that a widow who is getting married לְאַלְמוֹן – **to a widower** has one day.

The Gemara objects:

אֲבָל לְבָחוּר מַאי – **But** if a widow is getting married **to a never-married man, what** would the law be? שִׁבְעָה – That she has **seven** days of *Sheva Berachos*? אִי הָכִי לִיתְנֵי – **If so, [the Baraisa] should have taught** as follows: מְבָרְכִין לִבְתוּלָה שִׁבְעָה – **We recite the blessings on behalf of a virgin for seven days;** וּלְאַלְמָנָה שֶׁנִּשֵּׂאת לְבָחוּר שִׁבְעָה – **and on behalf of a widow who weds a never-married man** we recite the blessings for **seven** days as well; וּלְאַלְמָנָה יוֹם אֶחָד – **but on behalf of a widow** who weds a widower, we recite the blessings for only **one day.**

The Gemara deflects the objection:

מִילְתָא פְּסִיקְתָא קָתָנֵי – The Baraisa is phrased the way it is because **it teaches** us **something absolute:** דְּלֵיכָּא בְּתוּלָה דְּבָצְרָה מִשִּׁבְעָה – **That there is never a virgin who has less than seven** days, וְלֵיכָּא אַלְמָנָה דְּבָצְרָה מִיּוֹם אֶחָד – **and there is never a widow who has less than one day.**[3]

The Gemara elaborates on the statement of Rav Nachman cited above:

גּוּפָא – **The text itself** stated: אָמַר רַב נַחְמָן – **Rav Nachman said:** אָמַר לִי הוּנָא בַּר נָתָן – **Huna bar Nassan told me** תָּנָא – **that a Baraisa taught** as follows: מִנַּיִן לְבִרְכַּת חֲתָנִים בַּעֲשָׂרָה – FROM WHERE DO WE KNOW THAT *SHEVA BERACHOS* ARE recited only WHEN at least TEN men are present?[4] שֶׁנֶּאֱמַר ,,וַיִּקַּח עֲשָׂרָה אֲנָשִׁים מִזִּקְנֵי הָעִיר וַיֹּאמֶר שְׁבוּ־פֹה'' – FOR IT SAYS in the verse describing the marriage of Boaz and Ruth:[5] *HE TOOK TEN MEN FROM THE ELDERS OF THE CITY, AND HE SAID, "SIT HERE," AND THEY SAT.*[6] וְרַבִּי אַבָּהוּ אָמַר – **However, R' Abahu said:** מֵהָכָא – The Baraisa derives this requirement **from here** instead:[7] ,,בְּמַקְהֵלוֹת בָּרְכוּ אֱלֹהִים ה׳ מִמְּקוֹר יִשְׂרָאֵל'' – *IN ASSEMBLAGES BLESS GOD, HASHEM, FROM THE WOMB OF ISRAEL.* This is expounded as follows: If one wishes to utter a blessing concerning matters of the womb, one must do so in an "assemblage" (*kahal*): An assemblage is no less than ten men.[8]

The Gemara asks what the first Amora derives from the verse cited by the second Amora:

וְרַב נַחְמָן – **Now** as for **Rav Nachman,** בְּהַאי קְרָא דְּרַבִּי אַבָּהוּ מַאי דָּרִישׁ בֵּיהּ – **how does he expound the verse cited by R' Abahu?**

The Gemara answers:

מִיבָּעֵי לֵיהּ לִכְדְתַנְיָא – **He needs it for that which has been taught in a Baraisa:** הָיָה רַבִּי מֵאִיר אוֹמֵר – R' MEIR USED TO SAY: מִנַּיִן שֶׁאֲפִילּוּ עוּבָּרִים שֶׁבִּמְעֵי אִמָּן אָמְרוּ שִׁירָה עַל הַיָּם – FROM WHERE do we know THAT EVEN FETUSES IN THEIR MOTHER'S WOMB CHANTED SONG ON the banks of THE SEA, after God split it?[9] שֶׁנֶּאֱמַר – FOR IT SAYS: ,,בְּמַקְהֵלוֹת בָּרְכוּ אֱלֹהִים ה׳ מִמְּקוֹר יִשְׂרָאֵל'' – *IN ASSEMBLAGES BLESS GOD, HASHEM, FROM THE WOMB OF ISRAEL.* This teaches us that a blessing went forth to God from those who were still in the wombs of the mothers of Israel.[10]

NOTES

1. The Gemara above concluded that a widow who marries a previously unmarried man requires seven days of *Sheva Berachos.* The Gemara now attempts to show that she does not.

2. [The Gemara below will explain that the full complement of *Sheva Berachos* is said for seven days only when there are פָּנִים חֲדָשׁוֹת, *new faces,* in attendance. If there are no new faces, then only one of the blessings is said (*Rashi;* see *Shitah Mekubetzes* who offers an explanation as to why *Rashi* makes this point here).]

3. Thus, the Baraisa means that we recite the blessings on behalf of a virgin for *at least* seven days and on behalf of a widow for *at least* one day; however, the Baraisa agrees that there is a widow (one who wed a never-married man) who has seven days of *Sheva Berachos.* [The difference in the number of days of *Sheva Berachos* is accounted for above, on 7a note 24; cf. *Ritva.*]

[It would seem that the Baraisa could have stated its teaching in the same absolute terms with regard to the grooms, i.e.: We recite the blessings on behalf of a never-married man for seven days and on behalf of a widower for one. See *Shitah Mekubetzes* ד״ה אבל לבחור מאי for a discussion of this point.]

The Gemara's conclusion is that a widow who marries a widower recites *Sheva Berachos* on only the first day; however, according to some views, this "first day" means only the first meal (see similar usage in *Pesachim* 36a). If other meals are held that day in honor of the bride and groom, these views maintain that *Sheva Berachos* are not said. Other authorities maintain that the "first day" is meant literally and *Sheva Berachos* would be said at the later meals (see *Rosh* below, 8a; *Beis Yosef* and *Bedek HaBayis* in *Even HaEzer* §62 ד״ה ומ״ש רבינו ואינו נקרא, *Chelkas Mechokeik* 62:6 and *Beis Shmuel* 62:5). There is also a disagreement in the case in which a couple wed during the day, but held the wedding meal at night [which is a different day] or on an even later day (see ibid.; see also *Aruch HaShulchan, Even HaEzer* 62:33 and *Igros Moshe, Even HaEzer* IV §88).

4. If one cannot assemble at least ten men, *Beis Yosef* cites *Rashba* that one should not get married (*Even HaEzer* 62 ד״ה ומ״ש גדולים). However, many authorities dispute this (see *Terumas HaDeshen* §140 and *Aruch HaShulchan, Even HaEzer* 62:12). According to these authorities, one could marry without reciting any of the *Sheva Berachos* and when one has assembled a quorum later, one may recite them then.

5. *Ruth* 4:2.

6. See above, 7a note 18.

7. *Psalms* 68:27.

8. That an assemblage (*kahal*) is ten men may be demonstrated as follows: The Gemara in *Megillah* 23b states that an עֵדָה, *eidah,* congregation, comprises at least ten men. (The Gemara there derives this from the Torah's use of the word *eidah* in reference to the wicked members of the twelve Spies [see *Numbers* 13:1-14:38]. Only two of the twelve, Joshua and Caleb, were righteous. *Eidah* thus refers to ten men in that context.) Elsewhere (*Numbers* 20:8), a verb form of *kahal* is used together with *eidah*: וְהַקְהֵל אֶת־הָעֵדָה, *Assemble the congregation.* [Since an *eidah* (congregation) is essentially ten, their assembly must involve at least ten as well. Hence *kahal,* assemblage, denotes a minimum of ten men] (*Rashi;* cf. *Tosafos* cited by *Ritva*).

The simple meaning of the phrase מִמְּקוֹר יִשְׂרָאֵל, *from the womb of Israel,* is akin to *the seed of Israel* and refers to the descendants of Israel. Accordingly, the verse should be rendered: *In massive crowds, bless God, Hashem, [you who are] the descendants of Israel* (see *Metzudas David* ad loc.). However, our Gemara expounds the verse as if it should be rendered: *In an assembly of ten, bless God, Hashem, [when the blessing] pertains to a Jewish womb.*

Sheva Berachos concern matters of the womb since these blessings attend *nisuin,* which leads to procreation (*Tos. Rid* citing *Halachos Gedolos*). According to *Rav Achai Gaon* (*She'iltos* §16), the blessing recited for *kiddushin* also pertains to the womb and should be recited in the presence of ten men. *R' Shmuel HaNagid* disputes this (see *Rosh, Ritva*).

9. That is, even the fetuses took part in the recitation of אָז יָשִׁיר after the Jews escaped the Egyptians when the sea split (*Exodus* 15:1 ff.).

10. R' Meir interprets the verse as referring to fetuses in the womb: Even they blessed God after the miracle of the Splitting of the Sea. Rav Nachman interprets this verse in this way as well.

[Although this verse makes no direct reference to the Splitting of the Sea, this psalm discusses the events surrounding the Exodus and the Giving of the Torah generally.]

מיתיבי מברכין לבתולה שבעה ולאלמנה יום אחד מאי לאו אפילו אלמנה שנשאת לבחור לא לאלמון אבל לבחור מאי שבעה אי הכי ליתני מברכין לבתולה שבעה ולאלמנה שנשאת לבחור שבעה ולאלמנה יום אחד מילתא פסיקתא קתני דליכא בתולה דבצרה משבעה וליכא אלמנה דבצרה מיום אחד: גופא אמר רב נחמן אמר לי הונא בר נתן תנא מנין לברכת חתנים בעשרה שנאמר (א) ויקח עשרה אנשים מזקני העיר ויאמר שבו פה ורבי אבהו אמר מהכא (ב) במקהלות ברכו אלהים ה' ממקור ישראל ורב נחמן בהאי קרא דרבי אבהו מאי דריש ביה מיבעי ליה לכדתניא היה ר"מ אומר [א] מנין שאפילו עוברים שבמעי אמן אמרו שירה על הים שנאמר במקהלות ברכו אלהים ה' ממקור ישראל ואידך אם כן לימא קרא מבטן מאי ממקור על עסקי מקור ורבי אבהו בהאי קרא דרב נחמן מאי דריש ביה ההוא מיבעי ליה למידרש [ב] עמוני ולא עמונית מואבי ולא מואבית דאי סלקא דעתך לברכה לא סגיא דלאו זקנים ואידך אי סלקא דעתך למידרש לא סגיא דלאו עשרה אין לפרסומי מילתא [ג] וכדאמר ליה שמואל לרב חנא בגדתאה פוק ואייתי לי בי עשרה ואימא לך באנפייהו המזכה לעובר קנה והלכתא [א] המזכה לעובר לא קנה: תנו רבנן מברכין ° ברכת חתנים [ב] בבית חתנים ר' יהודה אומר אף בבית האירוסין מברכין אותה אמר אביי וביהודה שנו [ג] מפני שמתייחד עמה תניא אידך מברכין ברכת חתנים בבית חתנים וברכת אירוסין בבית האירוסין ברכת האירוסין מאי מברך רבין בר רב אדא ורבה בר רב אדא תרוייהו משמיה דרב יהודה אמרי [ד] בא"י אמ"ה אשר קדשנו במצותיו וצונו על העריות ואסר לנו את הארוסות והתיר לנו את הנשואות על ידי חופה וקידושין רב אחא בריה דרבא מסיים בה משמיה דרב יהודה [ה] בא"י מקדש ישראל על ידי חופה וקידושין מאן דלא חתים מידי דהוה אברכת פירות ואברכת מצות ומאן דחתים מידי דהוה אקידושא: ת"ר מברכין ברכת חתנים בעשרה כל שבעה אמר רב יהודה [ו] והוא שבאו פנים חדשות מאי מברך אמר רב יהודה בא"י אמ"ה שהכל

רש"י

מברכין לבתולה שבעה. לקמן מפרש כשבאו פנים חדשות מברך כולן כל ימי המשתה ואי לא מברך חדא: **במקהלות ברכו אלהים ה' ממקור ישראל.** על ברכת מקור צריך קהל והיינו עשרה כמו הקהל את העדה (במדבר כ) ואין הקהל בפחות מעדה ועדה עשרה כדילפינן (ברכות דף כא:) מעדת מרגלים עד מתי לעדה הרעה יצאו יהושע וכלב: **בגדתאה.** עיר שבבבל ושמה בגדת בפסק סדרו של רב שרירא גאון היא נזכרת: **המזכה.** מתנה על ידי אחר: **לעובר.** שבמעי אמו קנה: **בבית חתנים.** כשנכנסה לחופת נישואין: **אף בבית האירוסין.** כשמקדשה מברכין כל ברכת חתנים כדמפרש: **אמר אביי וביהודה שנו.** [הא דר"י ביהודה שנו]: **שמתייחד עמה.** באירוסין כדי שיהא לבו גס בה כדלקמן (דף יב.) לפיכך מברכין ברכת חתנים מתחלה דתניא במסכת כלה כלה בלא ברכה אסורה לבעלה כנדה: **ואסר לנו את הארוסות.** מדרבנן שגזרו על הייחוד של פנויה ואף ארוסה לא התירו עד שתיכנס לחופה ובברכה כדפרישית כלה בלא ברכה אסורה לבעלה כנדה ואדרבנן נמי מברכין וצונו ואסר לנו כדאשכחן בנר חנוכה (שבת דף כג.): **והתיר לנו.** את נשותינו הנשואות לנו על ידי חופה וקידושין: **אברכת פירות.** בורא פרי העץ: **ברכת מצות.** על השחיטה ועל המילה דכיון דכולה חדא הודאה היא ואין הפסק בקשה בינתיים לא בעיא חתימה כדאמר בערבי פסחים (פסחים דף קה.) ברכת המצות טעמא מאי משום דהודאה היא הא נמי כולה הודאה היא: **מידי דהוה אקידושא.** כיון דבלשון קדושה היא כקידוש היום חתמינן בה כי התם דבההיא חתמינן משום דיש בה הפסק כגון כי הוא יום תחלה למקראי קודש: **והוא שבאו.** אל המשתה: **פנים חדשות.** בכל יום שלא היו שם אתמול: **מאי מברך אמר רב יהודה כו'.** נראה בעיני סדר ברכות שנסדרו על עסקי הזוג אינו אלא מאשר יצר ואילך שאותה ברכה מתחלת לדבר בשניהם אשר יצר את האדם מדבר בזכר והתקין

תוספות

במקהלות ברכו אלהים. אע"ג דמקהלות תרי קהלות משמע אין סברא לחלק בין עשרה לעשרים לענין שום מילתא ומקהלות דעלמא בעי למימר ומיהו בירושלמי דריש במקהלת כתיב [ד] חסר וי"ו: **המזכה** לעובר קנה. אע"ג דשמואל גופיה פסיק כרבי יוחנן הסנדלר (לקמן דף נח:) דמקדיש מעשה ידי אשתו המותר חולין דאין אדם מקדיש דבר שלא בא לעולם וכל שכן לדבר שלא בא לעולם דגרע טפי כדאמרינן בסוף פרק קמא דגיטין (דף יג: ושם) דקאמר אפילו לרבי מאיר דאמר אדם מקנה דבר שלא בא לעולם הני מילי לדבר שבא לעולם אבל לדבר שלא בא לעולם לא אמר מ"מ שמואל חשיב עובר בא לעולם אי נמי שמואל אית ליה טפי אדם מקנה לדבר שלא בא לעולם ממה שמקנה דבר שלא בא לעולם וההיא סוגיא דבפרק קמא דגיטין (ג"ז שם) אתיא אליבא דרב הונא וכן מצינו רב נחמן דבההיא סברתו הפוכה מדרב הונא דרב הונא אית ליה [ה] בפירות דקל משבאו לעולם אין יכול לחזור בו וגבי עובר קאמר [ו] אף לכשתלד לא קנה ורב נחמן סבר לכשתלד קנה ובפירות דקל קאמר אף משבאו לעולם יכול לחזור בו: (שייך לע"א) **הורוה** בית הלל. גבי הילני המלכה אע"ג דמבית חשמונאי היתה שהרי אם מונבז המלך היתה כדאמר ביומא (דף לז. ושם) ומלכות הורדוס מאה ושלש שנה בפני הבית והלל לא נהג נשיאותו עד שלש שנים לאחר מלכות הורדוס כדאמרינן (שבת טו.) הלל ושמעון גמליאל ושמעון נהגו נשיאותן בפני הבית מאה שנה מכל מקום כבר היו לו אז תלמידים שהורו: (שייך לע"א) **והא** בועז אלמון שנשא אלמנה הוה. לאו דוקא אלמנה דכשנשאת למחלון ([ז] וכליון) היתה נכרית אלא כיון דבעולה היא כאלמנה חשיב לה: (שייך לע"א) **באלמנה** שנשאת לבחור. דכיון שאין שניהם אלמונים יש לברך כל שבעה: **שנאמר** ויקח בועז עשרה אנשים. ובמסכת כלה דמייתי קרא דויברכו את רבקה (בראשית כד) איכא למימר דהתם ברכת אירוסין והכא ברכת נישואין ויש ללמוד משם שיש לברך ברכת אירוסין לאשה המתקדשת על ידי שליח שהרי אליעזר שליח היה ונראה דלאסמכתא בעלמא היא דעשרה לא מיסתמא מהתם ולא איירי פשטיה דקרא בברכת אירוסין: **רבי** יהודה אומר אף בבית האירוסין מברכין אותה מפני שמתייחד עמה. ולמאי כלה בלא ברכה אסורה לבעלה כנדה ולפי שפעמים בא עליה שלא לשם חופה עושין ברכה מתחלה כדי שתהא כלה בברכה: **מאן** דלא חתים מידי דהוה אברכת פירות. שאין בה אריכות והאי נמי אינה ארוכה ולא דמי לקידושא דצריך טפי ומאן דחתים מידי דהוה אקידושא דחתים ביה משום דצריך והאי נמי חשיבא ארוכה ומה שפירש בקונטרס משום דבלשון קדושה היא חתמי בה כמו בקידוש אינו נראה ק"ק מאן דלא חתים בה מאי שנא מברכת התורה דחתמינן בה כדאשר בחר בנו ואע"ג דברכת אירוסין ארוכה טפי מינה ושמא לא היה חותם בה: **והוא** שבאו פנים חדשות. אור"י דפנים חדשות אין קורא אלא בבני אדם שמרבים בשבילם השמחה יותר ושבת חשבינן פנים חדשות דאמרינן באגדה מזמור שיר ליום השבת אמר הקב"ה פנים חדשות באו לכאן נאמר שירה התם נמי מרבין לכבוד השבת בשמחה ובסעודה: שהכל

עין משפט נר מצוה

לד א מיי' פ"ט מהל' זכיה הל' ס סמג עשין פג טוש"ע ח"מ סי' רי סעי' א:

לה ב מיי' פ"ב מהל' ברכות הל' ט ופ"י מהל' אישות הל' ג סמג עשין מח טוש"ע אה"ע סימן סב סעי' א:

לו ג מיי' פ"י מהל' אישות הל' ו טוש"ע שם סי' נה סעי' א:

לז ד ה מיי' פ"ג שם הל' כד סמג שם טוש"ע שם סי' לד סעי' א:

לח ו מיי' פ"ב מהל' ברכות הל' י סמג שם טוש"ע שם סימן סב סעי' ז ח [מי' כ"מ]:

תוספות רי"ד

א"ר נחמן א"ר הונא תנא מני' לברכת חתנים שה"א בעשרה שנאמר ויקח בועז עשרה אנשים וכו'. ר' אבהו אמר במקהלות ברכו אלהים ה' ממקור ישראל. פי' בה"ג בשעה שאתה מברך על המקור משום פריה ורביה עשה קיהלא. א"ר יוסף הלוי הני ד' ברכות דמברכים בבית חתנים בין בשעת הכניסה בין בשעת המשתה בדאיכא פנים חדשות בין אשר ברא. בדליכא פנים חדשות לא מברכינן לה אלא בעשרה. [illegible]

מסורת הש"ס

א) ברכות נ., ב) [יבמות סט. וש"נ], ג) יבמות עו. ב"ב קמב: [זבחים לב.], ד) [בספר תהלים שלפנינו נדפס מלא], ה) [יבמות לג.], ו) [ב"ב קמב.], ז) יעב"ץ מ"ז.

גליון הש"ס

גמ' ברכת חתנים בבית חתנים. ע' סוכה כה ע"ב תד"ה אין שמחה:

תורה אור השלם

א) וַיִּקַּח עֲשָׂרָה אֲנָשִׁים מִזִּקְנֵי הָעִיר וַיֹּאמֶר שְׁבוּ פֹה וַיֵּשֵׁבוּ: [רות ד, ב]

ב) בְּמַקְהֵלוֹת בָּרְכוּ אֱלֹהִים יְיָ מִמְּקוֹר יִשְׂרָאֵל: [תהלים סח, כז]

ליקוטי רש"י

עמוני ולא עמונית. הלכה רווחת בישראל דכתיב (דברים כג) על דבר אשר לא קדמו אתכם ואין דרכה של אשה לקדם [חולין סב:]. בגדתאה. שם עירו בגדד היא עיר החשובה שבבבל משחרבה בבל [ברכות נד:]. בעל אגדה ל"א שם מקום שהוא בבבל ששמו בגדד [יבמות סז.]. דמן בגדד עיר שנולד בה ובכתבי רב שרירא היא נזכרת [רשב"ם ב"ב קמב.]. בי עשרה. עשרה בני אדם [ע"פ עירובין קב.]. לפרסם את הדבר [יבמות שם]. ואברכת מצות. כגון להתעטף בציצית ועל נטילת לולב [פסחים קד:]. כגון להתעטף בציצית ועל נטילת לולב וטעמו של דבר לפי שאין בהן ריבוי דברים [רשב"ם שם ועי' רש"י קה. ד"ה הודאה היא ורשב"ם ד"ה הא נמי הודאה].

חייב לה בשאר כסות ועונה ולא נקראת אשתו נשואה אלא כשמוסרים אותה לו לשם נשואין. דמסירה קונה שתהיה אשתו לכל דבר ולא ד' ברכות לא עבדי אלא שיהא מותר להתיחד עמה. וכן דרך קהלות ממגנצא שמברכים ד' ברכות משעת אירוסין ועומדים זמן הרבה. [illegible] מקדש והדר מברך. מפני שהוא תלוי בדעת אחרים ושמא יחזרו בהן והוו לבטלה: ת"ר מברכין ברכת חתנים כל ז'. אמר ר"י והוא שבאו פנים חדשות. פי' ברכות חתנים הוא ז' ברכות. ומ"ה צריך פנים חדשות אדם שעדיין

פטור התם פקיד ועקיר הכא פקיד ולא עקיר
רבי אמי שרא למיבעל בתחלה בשבת
אמרי ליה רבנן והא לא כתיבא כתובתה
אמר להו אתפסוה מטלטלין רב זביד
שרא למיבעל בתחלה בשבת איכא דאמרי
רב זביד גופיה בעל בתחלה בשבת רב
יהודה שרא למיבעל בתחלה ביו"ט אמר רב
פפי משמיה דרבא לא תימא ביו"ט דשרי
הא בשבת אסור דהוא הדין דאפילו בשבת
נמי שרי ומעשה שהיה כך היה רב פפא
משמיה דרבא אמר ביו"ט שרי בשבת אסור
א"ל רב פפי לרב פפא מאי דעתיך מתוך
שהותרה חבורה לצורך הותרה נמי שלא
לצורך אלא מעתה מותר לעשות מוגמר
ביו"ט דמתוך שהותרה הבערה לצורך
הותרה נמי שלא לצורך אמר ליה עליך
אמר קרא אך אשר יאכל לכל נפש דבר
השוה לכל נפש אמר ליה רב אחא בריה
דרבא לרב אשי אלא מעתה נזדמן לו צבי
ביו"ט הואיל ואינו שוה לכל נפש ה"נ דאסור
למשחטיה אמר ליה אנא דבר הצורך לכל
נפש קאמינא צבי צריך לכל נפש הוא אמר
רבי יעקב בר אידי הורה רבי יוחנן בציידן
אסור לבעול בתחלה בשבת ומי איכא
הוראה לאיסור אין והתנן הורה בית
הלל שתהא נזירה עוד שבע שנים אחרות
ואי נמי כי הא דתניא חוט השדרה שנפסק
ברובו דברי רבי ר' יעקב אומר אפי' ניקב
הורה רבי כר' יעקב אמר רב הונא אין
הלכה כר' יעקב רב נחמן בר יצחק מתני
הכי אמר ר' אבהו שאל ר' ישמעאל בן יעקב דמן צור את רבי יוחנן בציידן
ואנא שמעי מהו לבעול בתחלה בשבת ואמר ליה אסור והלכתא מותר
לבעול בתחלה בשבת: אמר רבי חלבו אמר רב הונא א"ר אבא בר זבדא
אמר רב אחת בתולה ואחת אלמנה טעונה ברכה ומי אמר רב הונא
הכי והאמר רב הונא אלמנה אינה טעונה ברכה לא קשיא כאן בבחור
שנשא אלמנה כאן באלמון שנשא אלמנה ואלמון שנשא אלמנה לא
והאמר רב נחמן אמר לי הונא בר נתן תנא מנין לברכת חתנים בעשרה
שנאמר ויקח עשרה אנשים מזקני העיר ויאמר שבו פה וישבו ובועז
אלמון שנשא אלמנה הוה מאי אינה טעונה ברכה דאמר רב הונא אינה טעונה
ברכה כל ז' אבל יום אחד טעונה ברכה אלא הא דתניא שקדו חכמים
על תקנת בנות ישראל שיהא שמח עמה ג' ימים במאי אי בבחור האמרת
שבעה אי באלמון האמרת יום אחד איבעית אימא באלמון יום אחד לברכה
ושלשה לשמחה ואיבעית אימא בבחור שבעה לברכה ושלשה לשמחה
מיתיבי

רש"י

פטור. וקיימא לן פטור ומותר לכתחלה ביציאות שבת (דף ג.) קשיא למאן דאסר דהאי נמי להוציא דם הוא: התם. גבי ליחה: פקיד. כנוס ביחד: ועקיר. כולו מן הבשר ועומד לצאת: הכא. דם בתולים: פקיד הוא ולא עקיר. לגמרי אלא נבלע קצת בכתלים אע"פ שאינו מחובר כשאר דם האברים אלא כנוס מיהו דומה למחובר הוא שאינו מוכן לצאת כליחה: אתפסוה מטלטלי. תנו לה מטלטלין תחת ידה במשכון לשיעבוד כתובתה עד שיכתבו שטר כתובתה בשעבוד קרקעות: מאי דעתיך. למישרי יו"ט יותר מבשבת: לצורך. אוכל נפש כגון שחיטה: מוגמר. בשמים על האש לגמר את הכלים ואת הבגדים: עליך אמר קרא לכל נפש דבר השוה לכל נפש. מותר ובעילה שוה לכל אבל מוגמר אינו אלא למפונקים: ומי איכא הוראה לאיסור. ומי קרי איסור הוראה משום דכל אדם רשאי להחמיר והאוסר אין זה סמיכת דברים שאפי' מן הספק שאין ההלכה ברורה לו הוא בא ואוסר אבל המתיר סומך על שמועתו או על סברת חכמתו והיא הוראה: הורוה ב"ה. משנה היא במסכת נזיר בהילני המלכה שיצא בנה למלחמה ונדרה שבע שנים בנזיר בחוצה לארץ ועלתה לארץ הורוה ב"ה שתהא נזירה עוד ז' שנים אחרות: חוט השדרה שנפסק ברובו. טריפה: טעונה ברכה. ברכת חתנים: בועז אלמון הוה. דאמר מר אבצן זה בועז וכבר היו לו ל' בנים ושלשים בנות בבבא בתרא (דף צא.): האמרת שבעה. דמדאינה טעונה דקאמר רב הונא אוקימנא דאינה טעונה שבעה מכלל דטעונה דקאמר רבי אבא שבעה:
מברכין

תוספות

גבי בעילה אית לן למשרי אע"ג דליכא צערא כיון דלא הוי פסיק רישיה לענין פתח כיון דאפשר להוציאת דם בלא עשיית פתח כדמוכח לעיל (דף ה:) ומשני הכא פקיד ולא עקיר דקסבר דם חבורי מיחבר והוא הדין דהוי מצי לשנויי דלפתח הוא צריך אלא לפי מאי דקים ליה דלדם הוא צריך משני ליה ותימה דהא שמואל במלאכה שאינה צריכה לגופה סבר לה כר' יהודה כדאמרי' בפ' הנחנקין (ד' פה. ושם) ובפ' כל התדיר (זבחים ד' צא.) ועוד דמדבר שאין מתכוין דשרי ר"ש ה"ל לאקשויי ולא ממלאכה שאינה צריכה לגופה כיון דרוב בקיאין ולא הוי פסיק רישיה:

מתוך שהותרה לצורך. פירוש לצורך אוכל נפש הותרה נמי שלא לצורך אוכל נפש ובלבד שיהא צורך הנאת היום או צורך קיום מצוה ביו"ט כההיא דהוצאת קטן למולו וספר תורה לקרות בו ולולב לצאת בו (ביצה דף יב.) אבל שלא לצורך היום כלל לא כמו הוצאת אבנים דמחייב והאופה מיו"ט לחול לרב חסדא דאמר לוקה (שם דף כא.) משום דלית ליה הואיל ושחיטת עולת נדבה דשרי לב"ה (שם דף כ:) היינו משום שלא יהא שלחנך מלא ושלחן רבך חסר ומוצא חמץ בתוך ביתו דאמרינן בפ"ק דפסחים (דף ו. ושם) דכופה עליו כלי ולא שרינן לשורפו משום מתוך היינו משום דאסור לשורפו מדרבנן משום מוקצה דאסור לטלטלו אבל אין לומר דאיירי כשביטלו דמכל מקום מדרבנן מצוה לשורפו והוי צורך היום דבמצוה דרבנן נמי שרינן היכא דאיכא למימר מתוך והא דפליגי ב"ש וב"ה (ביצה דף יב:) במבשל גיד הנשה ביו"ט ואכלו דלב"ש דלית להו מתוך לוקה ולב"ה דאית להו מתוך אינו לוקה צריך לומר אע"ג דלא חשיב אוכל נפש משום איסור דרביץ עליה מכל מקום צורך היום הוא כיון דאכיל ליה ונראה לר"י דהוצאת תינוק לטייל הוי צורך היום ומיהו הוצאה לצורך נכרי נראה דאסור ומה שנהגו עתה להוציא לצורך נכרי היה נראה לרשב"א משום דרשות הרבים דידן לא הוי אלא כרמלית דאין רחבין ט"ז אמה וגבי יו"ט לא גזור רבנן כי היכי דלא תקון רבנן עירובי חצירות ביו"ט כדמשמע בריש פרק שני דביצה (דף טז:) דאמר יו"ט שחל להיות ערב שבת כו' רבי אומר מערבין עירובי חצירות אבל לא עירובי תחומין לפי שאתה אוסרו בדבר האסור לו ואי אתה אוסרו בדבר המותר לו אלמא לא תקון עירובי חצירות ביו"ט והוא הדין דלא גזרו בכרמלית והא דקיימא לן בפרק אמרו לו (כריתות דף יד. ושם) ובפרק קמא דביצה (דף יב. ושם) דיש עירוב והוצאה ליו"ט נראה דאיירי בעירובי תחומין ושוב חזר בו דמאחר שאינה מעורבת אין ללמוד ממנה לכרמלית דחמיר טפי כמו שפירשתי במסכת שבת (דף קל.) ועוד נראה דהא דקיימא לן דיש עירוב והוצאה ליו"ט בעירובי חצירות מיירי מדבעי למימר בפרק אמרו לו (כריתות דף יד. ושם) דאין עירוב והוצאה ליוה"כ מדתנן התם אם היתה שבת והוציאו בפיו חייב וכן בביצה (דף יב. ושם) בעי למידק דאין עירוב והוצאה ליו"ט מדשרו בית הלל להוציא קטן ולולב והיינו עירובי חצרות דהשתא מוכח לה שפיר מדשרו הוצאה דלא גזרו רבנן אעירובי חצירות אלא משום הוצאה אבל עירובי תחומין אין עניינה להוצאה והא דקאמר ואי אתה אוסרו בדבר המותר לו היינו משום דמותר להוציא לצורך: **אלא** מעתה יהא מותר לעשות מוגמר ביו"ט. ואם תאמר לדידיה נמי תקשי וכי לא סבר דאמרינן מתוך הא טעמא דב"ה הכי הוא ויש לומר שהיה סובר דטעמא דבית הלל משום דאין עירוב והוצאה כדקא ס"ד מעיקרא בביצה אע"ג דהתם פריך עלה דלמא לרב פפי לא שמיע לה ועוי"ל שהיה סובר הותרה שלא לצורך ובלבד שיהא דבר הרגיל ולהכי פריך דזה אינו רגיל טפי ממוגמר: **אמר** ליה אנא דבר הצריך לכל נפש קאמינא וצבי צריך לכל נפש. וכן ביצה וקשה לר"י דאמר בסוף פ"ב דביצה (דף כב.) מהו לכבות הנר מפני דבר אחר ומסיק דאסור הא הכא שרי משום דצריך לכל נפש וי"ל דהכא דוקא בבעילה ראשונה דמצוה היא דהוי צורך מצות היום אבל שאר בעילות אין כל כך צורך היום ועי"ל דכיבוי הנר מפני דבר אחר הוי כמו מכשירין דאפילו באוכל נפש אסור וכן מוכח התם דפריך עלה מהא דתניא דמכבין את הבקעת כדי שלא יתעשן הבית ומשני ההיא רבי יהודה היא דשרי מכשירי אוכל נפש כי קאמינא לרבנן: **והלכתא** מותר לבעול בתחלה בשבת. ולא חיישינן שמא ישחוט בן עוף והא סמכינן למיעבד סעודה בשבת:
במקהלות

מסורת הש"ס

א) [עי' תוס' לקמן ט: ד"ה אין], ב) [עירובין סה: וש"נ], ג) [פסחים ס: ביצה יב:], ד) נזיר יט:, ה) חולין מה., ו) [לעיל ה.], ז) ומנחה בח"ל ועלתה לארץ כצ"ל. רש"ל, ח) [צ"ל בפ' כירה שבת מג.].

ליקוטי רש"י

פטור. ומותר דאין כאן תיקון ורבנן נמי לא גזור בה שבות משום צערא [שבת קז.]. מלאכה שאינה צריכה לגופה היא שהפתח היא המלאכה וזה אין צריך [לו] להיות כאן פתח מעכשיו [שם:]. מוגמר. לגמר בגדים ע"ג גחלים [ביצה כב.]. דמתוך שהותרה וכו'. הותרו נמי שלא לצורך מן התורה [שם יב.]. דבר השוה לכל נפש. וזה אינו אלא למפונקים או למי שריחו רע. צבי צריך לכל נפש הוא. דאוכל נפש הוא וראוי אף לעניים אלא שאינו מצוי להם [שם כב:]. הורה רבי. שבא מעשה לידו והורה להחמיר ולא סמך על דבריו [חולין מה.].

עין משפט נר מצוה

כו א מיי' פ"י מהל' אישות הל' ט סמג עשין מח טוש"ע אה"ע סי' סו סעי' ג:
כז ב מיי' פ"ג מהל' נזירות הל' כא:
כח ג מיי' פ"ט מהל' שחיטה הל' א סמג עשין סג טוש"ע יו"ד סי' לג סעי' א:
כט ד מיי' פ"ל מהל' שבת הל' יד סמג לאוין סה ועשין מח טוש"ע אה"ע סימן סג סעיף א וטוש"ע א"ח סי' רפ סעי' ג:
ל ה מיי' פ"ב מהל' ברכות הל' ט ומיי' פ"י מהל' אישות הל' ה סמג עשין מח טוש"ע אה"ע סי' סא סעי' ד:
לא ו ז מיי' פ"ב מהלכות ברכות הל' ט סמג שם טוש"ע שם סעי' ו:
לב ח מיי' פ"י מהלכ' אישות הל' י"ב סמג שם טוש"ע שם סי' סד סעי' ב [ועי' מ"מ]:
לג ט מיי' פ"ב מהל' ברכות ה"ט סמג שם טוש"ע שם סעי' ו:

תורה אור השלם

א) וּבַיּוֹם הָרִאשׁוֹן מִקְרָא קֹדֶשׁ וּבַיּוֹם הַשְּׁבִיעִי מִקְרָא קֹדֶשׁ יִהְיֶה לָכֶם כָּל מְלָאכָה לֹא יֵעָשֶׂה בָהֶם אַךְ אֲשֶׁר יֵאָכֵל לְכָל נֶפֶשׁ הוּא לְבַדּוֹ יֵעָשֶׂה לָכֶם: [שמות יב, טז]
ב) וַיִּקַּח עֲשָׂרָה אֲנָשִׁים מִזִּקְנֵי הָעִיר וַיֹּאמֶר שְׁבוּ פֹה וַיֵּשֵׁבוּ: [רות ד, ב]

תוספות רי"ד

א"ל והא לא כתיבא כתובה ואסרו חכמים לשהות אדם את אשתו שעה אחת בלא כתובה א"ל אתפסוה מטלטלי שיעור כתובתה. פי' שיהיה משכון בידה עד שיכתבו לה שטר כתובתה: **א"ר חלבו א"ר אדא בר זבדא אמר רב** א' בתולה וא' אלמנה טעונה ברכה [כל] שבעה. פי' טעונה ברכות כל ז' ימים ולקמן מוקי לה בדאיכא פנים חדשות: **ומי אמר רב הכי** והא"ר הונא אלמנה אינה טעונה ברכה כל ז' אלא יום א'. ל"ק כאן בבחור שנשא אלמנה כאן באלמון שנשא אלמנה. **מיתיבי** מברכים לבתולה ז' ולאלמנה יום א' מאי לאו לאלמנה שנשאת לבחור. לא לאלמון. אבל לבחור מאי ז'. א"ה ליתני מברכין לבתולה ז' ולאלמנה שנשאת לבחור ז' ולאלמנה שנשאת לאלמון יום א'. מילתא פסיקא קתני ליכא בתולה דבצירא מז' פי' ואפילו נשאת לאלמון. וליכא אלמנה דבצירא מיום א': **אלא** הא דתניא שקדו חכמים על תקנת בנות ישראל שיהא שמח עמה ג' ימים במאי אי בבחור הא אמרת ז' אם באלמון הא אמרת יום א'. איבעית אימא בבחור ז' לברכה וג' לשמחה איבע"א באלמון יום א' לברכה וג' לשמחה:

אִימָּא בְּבָחוּר – **Or if you prefer, say** that the Baraisa is dealing **with a never-married groom,** שִׁבְעָה לִבְרָכָה – in which case there are **seven** days **for** the **blessing,** וּשְׁלֹשָׁה לְשִׂמְחָה – **but** only **three** days **for rejoicing.**[24]

NOTES

24. That is, although *Sheva Berachos* are recited for seven days, there is no requirement of rejoicing after three days.

According to these conclusions, the following rules emerge regarding the requirements of *Sheva Berachos* and rejoicing. If either one of the couple was never married before, *Sheva Berachos* are recited for seven days; if both were previously married, the *Sheva Berachos* are recited for only one day. As for rejoicing, if the bride is a virgin, the obligation of rejoicing applies for seven days, regardless of the groom's previous marital history. Similarly, if the bride was previously married, the rejoicing requirement lasts for only three days, no matter what the status of the groom.

The rationale is as follows: The period of "rejoicing" was enacted for the benefit of the bride. The Sages recognized that a woman had to be gladdened by her husband at the beginning of their married life. However, not all brides are equal. A bride who has never been married before requires a full seven days of gladdening whereas a previously married woman requires only three days. [Since the requirement of rejoicing was instituted for the bride's benefit, some authorities rule she may waive it, if she wishes (*Rabbeinu Yerucham, Nesiv* 22 §2; see *Rama, Even HaEzer* 64:2; see *Beis Shmuel* 64:2).] The period of *Sheva Berachos,* on the other hand, was enacted in accordance with the groom's gladness of heart. If either he or his bride had never been married, his joy is such that seven days of *Sheva Berachos* are appropriate. If, however, both he and his wife have been married, his joy is not quite as great, and *Sheva Berachos* are said for only one day (*Tos. Rosh, Rashba, Ran*).

[Regarding a couple who divorced and are now remarrying, the prescribed times for *Sheva Berachos* and rejoicing are in dispute. *Radvaz* (Responsa §997) cites a view in the name of *Rav Hai Gaon* (and *Rabbeinu Ephraim*) that a divorced couple who remarries requires no *Sheva Berachos* (see also *Orchos Chaim, Hil. Kiddushin* §21 ד״ה תשובה לגאון). However, *Rif* (Responsa §35) and *Radvaz* himself both reject this view out of hand, and indeed question if someone of *Rav Hai Gaon's* stature could ever have said such a thing (cf. *Radvaz* VII §64). In regard to the rejoicing at the wedding of a divorced couple, *Radvaz* states (ibid.) that there is no requirement of rejoicing (based on *Moed Katan* 8b and *Sotah* 44a). Others rule that there are three days of rejoicing, similar to any other previously married bride and groom (see opinion cited in Responsa, *Maharit I* §64; *Ben Ish Chai I, Shoftim* §16; see *Pri Megadim, Mishbetzos Zahav* 135:2).]

We have explained the Gemara according to those Rishonim who maintain that the two answers presented in the text are not in conflict (*Rambam, Ramban, Re'ah, Ritva*). However, other Rishonim maintain that the two answers dispute each other and that the halachah follows only one of the answers (see *Rashba* for an explanation of this view). The practical difference of this approach is that the days allotted for rejoicing would never be less than the days allotted for *Sheva Berachos.*

See chart for a presentation of the different rules.

BRIDE/GROOM	*SHEVA BERACHOS*	REJOICING
VIRGIN/NEVER-MARRIED MAN	SEVEN DAYS	SEVEN DAYS
VIRGIN/WIDOWER	SEVEN DAYS	SEVEN DAYS
WIDOW/NEVER-MARRIED MAN	SEVEN DAYS	THREE DAYS*
WIDOW/WIDOWER	ONE DAY	THREE DAYS

* Some Rishonim say that the rejoicing is seven days in this case.

פטור התם פקיד ועקיר הכא פקיד ולא עקיר
רבי אמי שרא למיבעל בתחלה בשבת
אמרי ליה רבנן והא לא כתיבא כתובתה
אמר להו א) אתפסוה מטלטלין רב זביד
שרא למיבעל בתחלה בשבת איכא דאמרי
רב זביד גופיה בעל בתחלה בשבת רב
יהודה שרא למיבעל בתחלה ביו"ט אמר רב
פפי משמיה דרבא לא תימא ביו"ט דשרי
הא בשבת אסור דהוא הדין דאפילו בשבת
נמי שרי ב) ומעשה שהיה כך היה רב פפא
משמיה דרבא אמר ביו"ט שרי בשבת אסור
א"ל רב פפי לרב פפא מאי דעתיך מתוך
שהותרה חבורה לצורך הותרה נמי שלא
לצורך אלא מעתה מותר לעשות מוגמר
ביו"ט ג) דמתוך שהותרה הבערה לצורך
הותרה נמי שלא לצורך אמר ליה עליך
אמר קרא א) אך אשר יאכל לכל נפש דבר
השוה לכל נפש אמר ליה רב אחא בריה
דרבא לרב אשי אלא מעתה נזדמן לו צבי
ביו"ט הואיל ואינו שוה לכל נפש ה"נ דאסור
למשחטיה אמר ליה אנא דבר הצורך לכל
נפש קאמינא צבי צריך לכל נפש הוא אמר
רבי יעקב בר אידי הורה רבי יוחנן בציידן
אסור לבעול בתחלה בשבת ומי איכא
הוראה לאיסור אין והתנן ד) הורוה בית
הלל ב שתהא נזירה עוד שבע שנים אחרות
ואי נמי כי הא דתניא ה) ג חוט השדרה שנפסק
ברובו דברי רבי ר' יעקב אומר אפי' ניקב
הורה רבי כר' יעקב אמר רב הונא אין
הלכה כר' יעקב רב נחמן בר יצחק מתני
הכי אמר ר' אבהו שאל ר' ישמעאל בן יעקב דמן צור את רבי יוחנן בציידן
ואנא שמעי מהו לבעול בתחלה בשבת ואמר ליה אסור והלכתא ד מותר
לבעול בתחלה בשבת: אמר רבי חלבו אמר רב הונא א"ר אבא בר זבדא
אמר רב אחת בתולה ואחת אלמנה טעונה ברכה ומי אמר רב הונא
הכי והאמר רב הונא אלמנה אינה טעונה ברכה לא קשיא כאן בבחור
שנשא אלמנה כאן באלמון שנשא אלמנה ואלמון שנשא אלמנה לא
והאמר רב נחמן אמר לי הונא בר נתן תנא מנין ה לברכת חתנים בעשרה
שנאמר ב) ויקח עשרה אנשים מזקני העיר ויאמר שבו פה וישבו ובועז
אלמון שנשא אלמנה הוה מאי אינה טעונה ברכה דאמר רב הונא אינה טעונה
ברכה כל ז' ו אבל יום אחד טעונה ברכה אלא הא דתניא ו) שקדו חכמים
על תקנת בנות ישראל שיהא שמח עמה ג' ימים במאי אי בבחור האמרת
שבעה אי באלמון האמרת יום אחד איבעית אימא ז באלמון יום אחד לברכה
ח ושלשה לשמחה ואיבעית אימא ט בבחור שבעה לברכה ושלשה לשמחה
מיתיבי

פטור. וקיימא לן פטור ומותר לכתחלה ביציאות שבת (דף ג.) קשיא למאן דאסר דהאי נמי להוציא דם הוא: התם. גבי ליחה: פקיד. כנוס ביחד: ועקיר. כולו מן הבשר ועומד לצאת: הכא. דם בתולים: פקיד הוא ולא עקיר. לגמרי אלא נבלע קצת בכתלים אע"פ שאינו מחובר כשאר דם האברים אלא כנוס מיהו דומה למחובר הוא שאינו מוכן לצאת כליחה: אתפסוה מטלטלי. תנו לה מטלטלין תחת ידה במשכון לשיעבוד כתובתה עד שיכתבו שטר כתובתה בשעבוד קרקעות: מאי דעתיך. למישרי יו"ט יותר משבת: לצורך. אוכל נפש כגון שחיטה: מוגמר. בשמים על האש לגמר את הכלים ואת הבגדים: עליך אמר קרא לכל נפש דבר השוה לכל נפש. מותר ובעילה שוה לכל אבל מוגמר אינו אלא למפונקים: ומי איכא הוראה לאיסור. ומי קרי איסור הוראה משום דכל אדם רשאי להחמיר והאוסר אין זה סמיכת דברים שאפי' מן הספק שאין ההלכה ברורה לו הוא בא ואוסר אבל המתיר סומך על שמועתו או על סברת חכמתו והיא הוראה: הורוה ב"ה. משנה היא במסכת נזיר בהילני המלכה שילא בנה למלחמה ונדרה שבע שנים בנזיר ז) בחוצה לארץ ועלתה לארץ הורוה ב"ה שתהא נזירה עוד ז' שנים אחרות: חוט השדרה שנפסק ברובו. טריפה: טעונה ברכה. ברכת חתנים: בועז אלמון הוה. דאמר מר אבצן זה בועז וכבר היו לו ל' בנים ושלשים בנות בבבא בתרא (דף צא.): האמרת שבעה. דמדאינה טעונה דקאמר רב הונא אוקימנא דאינה טעונה שבעה מכלל דטעונה דקאמר רבי אבא שבעה:
מברכין

גבי בעילה אית לן למשרי אע"ג דליכא צערא כיון דלא הוי פסיק רישיה לענין פתח כיון דאפשר להוציא דם בלא עשיית פתח כדמוכח לעיל (דף ה:) ומשני הכא פקיד ולא עקיר דקסבר דם חבורי מיחבר והוא הדין דהוי מצי לשנויי דלפתח הוא צריך אלא לפי מאי דקים ליה דלדם הוא צריך משני ליה ותימה דהא שמואל במלאכה שאינה צריכה לגופה סבר לה כר' יהודה כדאמרי' בפ' ח) הנחנקין (ד' פה. ושם) ובפ' כל התדיר (זבחים ד' צא.) ועוד דמדבר שאין מתכוין דשרי ר"ש ה"ל לאקשויי ולא ממלאכה שאינה צריכה לגופה כיון דרוב בקיאין ולא הוי פסיק רישיה: **מתוך** שהותרה לצורך. פירוש לצורך אוכל נפש הותרה נמי שלא לצורך אוכל נפש ובלבד שיהא צורך הנאת היום או צורך קיום מצוה ביו"ט כההיא דהוצאת קטן למולו וספר תורה לקרות בו ולולב לצאת בו (ביצה דף יב.) אבל שלא לצורך היום כלל לא כמו הוצאת אבנים דמיחייב והאופה מיו"ט לחול לרב חסדא דאמר לוקה (שם דף כא.) משום דלית ליה הואיל ושחיטת עולת נדבה דשרי לב"ה (שם דף כ:) היינו משום שלא יהא שלחנך מלא ושלחן רבך חסר ומוצא חמץ בתוך ביתו דאמרינן בפ"ק דפסחים (דף ו. ושם) דכופה עליו כלי ולא שרינן לשורפו משום מתוך היינו משום דאסור לשורפו מדרבנן משום מוקצה דאסור לטלטלו אבל אין לומר דאיירי כשביטלו דמכל מקום מדרבנן מצוה לשורפו והוי צורך היום דבמצוה דרבנן נמי שרינן היכא דאיכא למימר מתוך והא דפליגי ב"ש וב"ה (ביצה דף יב:) במבשל גיד הנשה ביו"ט ואכלו דלב"ש דלית להו מתוך לוקה ולב"ה דאית להו מתוך אינו לוקה צריך לומר אע"ג דלא חשיב אוכל נפש משום איסור דרביע עליה מכל מקום צורך היום הוא כיון דאכיל ליה ונראה לר"י דהוצאת תינוק לטייל הוי צורך היום ומיהו הוצאה לצורך נכרי נראה דאסור ומה שנהגו עתה להוציא לצורך נכרי היה נראה לרשב"א משום דרשות הרבים דידן לא הוי אלא כרמלית דלאו רחבין ט"ז אמה וגבי יו"ט לא גזור רבנן כי היכי דלא תקון רבנן עירובי חצירות ביו"ט כדמשמע בריש פרק שני דביצה (דף טז:) דאמר יו"ט שחל להיות ערב שבת כו' רבי אומר מערבין עירובי חצירות אבל לא עירובי תחומין לפי שאתה אוסרו בדבר האסור לו ואי אתה אוסרו בדבר המותר לו אלמא לא תקון עירובי חצירות ביו"ט והוא הדין דלא גזרו בכרמלית והא דקיימא לן בפרק אמרו לו (כריתות דף יד. ושם) ובפרק קמא דביצה (דף יב. ושם) דיש עירוב והוצאה ליו"ט נראה דאיירי בעירובי תחומין ושוב חזר בו דמחצר שאינה מעורבת אין ללמוד ממנה לכרמלית דחמיר טפי כמו שפירשתי במסכת שבת (דף קז.) ועוד נראה דהא דקיימא לן דיש עירוב והוצאה ליו"ט בעירובי חצירות איירי מדבעי למימר בפרק אמרו לו (כריתות דף יד. ושם) דאין עירוב והוצאה ליוה"כ מדתנן התם אם היתה שבת והוציאו בפיו חייב וכן בביצה (דף יב. ושם) בעי למידק דאין עירוב והוצאה ליו"ט מדשרו בית הלל להוציא קטן ולולב והיינו עירובי חצרות דהשתא מוכח לה שפיר מדשרו הוצאה דלא גזרו רבנן אעירובי חצירות אלא משום הוצאה אבל עירובי תחומין אין ענייניה להוצאה והא דקאמר ואי אתה אוסרו בדבר המותר לו היינו משום דמותר להוציא לצורך: **אלא** מעתה יהא מותר לעשות מוגמר ביו"ט. ואם תאמר לדידיה נמי תקשי וכי לא סבר דאמרינן מתוך הא טעמא דב"ה הכי הוא ויש לומר שהיה סובר דטעמא דבית הלל משום דאין עירוב והוצאה כדקא ס"ד מעיקרא בביצה אע"ג דהתם פריך עלה דלמא לרב פפי לא שמיע לה ועוי"ל שהיה סובר הותרה שלא לצורך ובלבד שיהא דבר הרגיל ולהכי פריך דזה אינו רגיל טפי ממוגמר: **אמר** ליה אנא דבר הצריך לכל נפש קאמינא וצבי צריך לכל נפש. וכן ביאה וקשה לר"י דאמר בסוף פ"ב דביצה (דף כב.) מהו לכבות הנר מפני דבר אחר ומסיק דאסור הא הכא שרי משום דצריך לכל נפש וי"ל דהכא דוקא בבעילה ראשונה דמצוה היא דהוי צורך מצוה היום אבל שאר בעילות אין כל כך צורך היום ועי"ל דכיבוי הנר מפני דבר אחר הוי כמו מכשירין דאפילו באוכל נפש אסור וכן מוכח התם דפריך עלה מהא דמניחין את הקערה כדי שלא יתעשן הבית ומשני ההיא רבי יהודה היא דשרי מכשירי אוכל נפש כי קאמינא לרבנן: **והלכתא** מותר לבעול בתחלה בשבת. ולא חיישינן שמא ישחוט בן עוף והא סמכינן למיעבד סעודה בשבת:
במקהלות

א) [עי' תוס' לקמן ט: ד"ה אין], ב) [עירובין סה: וש"נ], ג) [פסחים ה: ביצה יב:], ד) נזיר יט:, ה) חולין מה:, ו) [לעיל ה.], ז) ומנתה בח"ל ועלתה לארץ כצ"ל רש"ל, ח) [צ"ל בפ' כירה שבת מב.].

ליקוטי רש"י

פטור. ומותר דלאין כאן תיקון ורבנן נמי לא גזור בה שבות משום צערא [שבת קז.]. מלאכה שאינה צריכה לגופה היא שהמלאכה הוא שמתעסק בה אין צריך [לו] להיות כאן פתח [שם.]. מוגמר. לבונה ע"ג גחלים [ביצה כב:]. דמתוך שהותרה וכו'. הותרו נמי שלא לצורך מן התורה [שם יב.]. דבר השוה לכל נפש. וזה אינו אלא למפונקים או למי שריחו רע. צבי צריך לכל נפש הוא. דאוכל אף לעניים אלא שאינו מצוי להם [שם כב:]. הורה רבי. שבא מעשה לידו והורה להחמיר ולא סמך על דבריו [חולין מה:].

כו א מיי' פ"י מהל' אישות הל' ט סמג עשין מח טוש"ע אה"ע סי' סו סעי' ב:
כז ב מיי' פ"ג מהל' נזירות הל' כא:
כח ג מיי' פ"ט מהל' שחיטה הל' ט סמג עשין סג טוש"ע יו"ד סי' לג סעי' א:
כט ד מיי' פ"ל מהל' שבת הל' יד סמג לאוין סה ועשין מח טוש"ע או"ח סימן רפ סעיף א וטוש"ע אה"ע סי' רפ סעי' ג:
ל ה מיי' פ"ב מהל' ברכות הל' ט ומיי' פ"י מהל' אישות הל' ה סמג עשין מח טוש"ע אה"ע סי' סב סעי' ד:
לא ו ז מיי' פ"ב מהלכות ברכות הל' ט סמג שם טוש"ע שם סעי' ו:
לב ח מיי' פ"י מהל' אישות הל' יב סמג שם טוש"ע אה"ע סי' סד סעי' ב [ועי' מ"מ]:
לג ט מיי' פ"ב מהל' ברכות הל' ט סמג שם טוש"ע שם סעי' ו:

תורה אור השלם

א) וּבַיּוֹם הָרִאשׁוֹן מִקְרָא קֹדֶשׁ וּבַיּוֹם הַשְּׁבִיעִי מִקְרָא קֹדֶשׁ יִהְיֶה לָכֶם כָּל מְלָאכָה לֹא יֵעָשֶׂה בָהֶם אַךְ אֲשֶׁר יֵאָכֵל לְכָל נֶפֶשׁ הוּא לְבַדּוֹ יֵעָשֶׂה לָכֶם: [שמות יב, טז]

ב) וַיִּקַּח עֲשָׂרָה אֲנָשִׁים מִזִּקְנֵי הָעִיר וַיֹּאמֶר שְׁבוּ פֹה וַיֵּשֵׁבוּ: [רות ד, ב]

תוספות רי"ד

א"ל והא לא כתיבא כתובה ואסרו חכמים לשהות אדם את אשתו שעה אחת בלא כתובה א"ל אתפסוה מטלטלי שיעור כתובתה. פי' שיהיה משכון בידה עד שיכתבו לה שטר כתובתה: א"ר חלבו א"ר אדא בר זבדא אמר רב א' בתולה וא' אלמנה טעונה ברכה [כל] שבעה. פי' טעונה ברכות כל ז' ימים ולקמן מוקי לה בדאיכא פנים חדשות: ומי אמר רב הכי והא"ר הונא אלמנה אינה טעונה ברכה כל ז' אלא יום א'. ל"ק כאן בבחור שנשא אלמנה כאן באלמון שנשא אלמנה. מיתיבי מברכים לבתולה ז' ולאלמנה יום א' מאי לאו לאלמנה שנשאת לבחור. לא לאלמון. אבל לבחור מאי ז'. א"ה ליתני מברכין לבתולה ז' ולאלמנה שנשאת לבחור ז' ולאלמנה שנשאת לאלמון יום א'. מילתא פסיקא קתני ליכא בתולה דבצירא מז' פי' ואפילו נשאת לאלמון. וליכא אלמנה דבצירא מיום א': אלא הא דתניא שקדו חכמים על תקנת בנות ישראל שיהא שמח עמה ג' ימים במאי אי בבחור הא אמרת ז' אם באלמון הא אמרת יום א'. איבעית אימא בבחור ז' לברכה וג' לשמחה איבע"א באלמון יום א' לברכה וג' לשמחה:

Rav Abba bar Zavda who said in the name of Rav: אַחַת בְּתוּלָה וְאַחַת אַלְמָנָה טְעוּנָה בְּרָכָה – **Both a virgin and a widow require** the recitation of the **blessing,** i.e. *Sheva Berachos,* when each gets married.[16]

The Gemara objects:

וּמִי אָמַר רַב הוּנָא הָכִי – **Did Rav Huna** really **say this,** that *Sheva Berachos* must be said at the wedding of a widow? וְהָאָמַר רַב הוּנָא – **But Rav Huna said** elsewhere: אַלְמָנָה אֵינָהּ טְעוּנָה בְּרָכָה – **A widow does not require** the recitation of the **blessing.** – ? –

The Gemara answers:

לָא קַשְׁיָא – **There is no difficulty.** כָּאן בְּבָחוּר שֶׁנָּשָׂא אַלְמָנָה – **Here,** where Rav Huna says a widow requires a blessing, he **refers to** the case of **a previously unmarried man who married a widow.** כָּאן בְּאַלְמוֹן שֶׁנָּשָׂא אַלְמָנָה – And **here,** where he ruled that a widow does not require a blessing, he **refers to** the case of **a widower who married a widow.**

The Gemara objects to that answer:

וְאַלְמוֹן שֶׁנָּשָׂא אַלְמָנָה לָא – **And** in the case of **a widower who marries a widow,** are *Sheva Berachos* **not** required? וְהָאָמַר רַב נַחְמָן – **But Rav Nachman said:** אָמַר לִי הוּנָא בַּר נָתָן – **Huna bar Nassan told me** תָּנָא – that **a Baraisa taught** as follows: מִנַּיִן לְבִרְכַּת חֲתָנִים בַּעֲשָׂרָה – FROM WHERE DO WE KNOW THAT *SHEVA BERACHOS* ARE recited only WHEN at least TEN men are present? שֶׁנֶּאֱמַר ,,וַיִּקַּח עֲשָׂרָה אֲנָשִׁים מִזִּקְנֵי הָעִיר וַיֹּאמֶר שְׁבוּ־פֹה וַיֵּשֵׁבוּ'' – FOR IT SAYS in the verse describing the marriage of Boaz and Ruth:[17] *HE TOOK TEN MEN FROM THE ELDERS OF THE CITY, AND HE SAID, "SIT HERE," AND THEY SAT.*[18] וּבוֹעַז אַלְמוֹן שֶׁנָּשָׂא אַלְמָנָה הֲוָה – **Now, Boaz was a widower who married a widow.**[19] Thus, the Baraisa assumes that *Sheva Berachos* are recited at the wedding of a widower and widow as well – ? –

The Gemara concedes the point and offers a different answer:

מַאי אֵינָהּ טְעוּנָה בְּרָכָה דְּאָמַר רַב הוּנָא – **What did Rav Huna** mean when he **said that [a widow]** who marries a widower does not require the **blessing?** אֵינָהּ טְעוּנָה בְּרָכָה כָּל שִׁבְעָה יָמִים – **She does not require** the **blessing for all seven days** after the wedding, אֲבָל יוֹם אֶחָד טְעוּנָה בְּרָכָה – **but she does require** the **blessing for one day.**[20]

The Gemara objects:

אֶלָּא הָא דְּתַנְיָא – **But** now concerning **that which was taught in a Baraisa** concerning widows: שֶׁקְּדוּ חֲכָמִים עַל תַּקָּנַת בְּנוֹת יִשְׂרָאֵל – THE SAGES WERE DILIGENT IN PROMOTING THE WELFARE OF JEWISH DAUGHTERS שֶׁיְּהֵא שָׂמֵחַ עִמָּהּ שְׁלֹשָׁה יָמִים – THAT [THE GROOM] SHOULD REJOICE WITH [THE BRIDE] FOR THREE DAYS;[21] בְּמַאי – **with what** type of marriage are we dealing? אִי בְּבָחוּר – **If** the Baraisa is discussing the marriage of a widow and **a previously unmarried man,** הָאָמַרְתְּ שִׁבְעָה – **you have said** that there are **seven** days of *Sheva Berachos* in that case, not three.[22] אִי בְּאַלְמוֹן – And **if** it is discussing the marriage of a widow and **a widower,** הָאָמַרְתְּ יוֹם אֶחָד – **you have said** that there is only **one day** of *Sheva Berachos* in that case. – ? –

The Gemara presents two answers:

אִיבָּעֵית אֵימָא בְּאַלְמוֹן – **If you wish, say** that the Baraisa is dealing **with** the marriage of a widow and **a widower,** יוֹם אֶחָד לִבְרָכָה – and there is only **one day for** the **blessing,** וּשְׁלֹשָׁה לְשִׂמְחָה – **but** there are **three** days **for rejoicing.**[23] וְאִיבָּעֵית

NOTES

HaEzer 62:1). Together with the blessing over the wine there are seven blessings, or *Sheva Berachos* in Hebrew. [One version of our Gemara's text and many early authorities list בּוֹרֵא פְּרִי הַגָּפֶן, *Who creates the fruit of the vine,* explicitly as the first of the blessings of *Bircas Chasanim* (see *Dikdukei Soferim HaShalem* to 8a, note 1).] *Bircas Chasanim* was popularly known as "*Sheva Berachos*" in earlier times (*Talmidei Rabbeinu Yonah,* cited in *Shitah Mekubetzes,* beginning of 8a). These blessings are called by this name today. We will therefore render בִּרְכַּת חֲתָנִים as *Sheva Berachos.*

16. As is clear from the Gemara's ensuing discussion, these Amoraim are speaking of the blessing recited in connection with the *chuppah* (i.e. *Sheva Berachos*). The blessing recited at the time of *kiddushin* (which is also required for both a virgin and a widow) is discussed on 7b.

[In the context of our Gemara, the term "widow" refers to any woman who is not a virgin. Thus, the laws our Gemara will apply to a "widow" apply to a divorcee as well (see *Tosafos* below, 7b ד״ה והא בועז; *Even HaEzer* 64:2 with *Beur HaGra; Responsa, Noda BiYehudah, Mahadura Tinyana, Even HaEzer* §82; *Responsa, Chikekei Lev* §31; *Aruch HaShulchan, Even HaEzer* 64:5).]

17. *Ruth* 4:2.

18. Boaz assembled the ten men, as described in this verse. Later that day, he asked the elders to be witnesses to his marriage to Ruth [and to a related acquisition of property]. The elders said to him (*Ruth* 4:11-12): *["We are] witnesses. May Hashem make the woman who is coming into your house like Rachel and like Leah, both of whom built up the House of Israel. May you prosper in Ephrath and be famous in Beth-lehem; and may your house be like the house of Perez whom Tamar bore to Judah, through the offspring which Hashem will give you by this young woman."* [Their blessings were the equivalent of the *Sheva Berachos* recited under the *chuppah.*]

19. We know Boaz had been previously married because the Gemara in *Bava Basra* (91a) identifies Boaz as the judge Ivtzan who had previously fathered thirty sons and thirty daughters (*Rashi*). Ruth had been previously married to Machlon (*Ruth* 1:4 and 4:10).

[It appears from *Rashi's* comments that "widower" in this context refers to any man who has engaged in intimate relations, just as "widow" here refers to any woman who is not a virgin (see above, note 16 and *Responsa Noda BiYehudah* cited there). Notwithstanding the meaning of "widower" in our context, Boaz was also a widower in the literal sense when he married Ruth: Boaz's wife had died the day Ruth had arrived in Eretz Yisrael from the fields of Moab (*Bava Basra* ibid.). Ruth herself was not a widow technically: Although she had been married to Machlon in Moab and he had died, her marriage was not valid since she was not a Jewess at the time. Ruth converted after Machlon's death (*Tosafos* to 7b ד״ה והא בועז, see *Rus Rabbah* 2:9). See also *Moadim U'Zmanim* 5:316 who discusses this at length.]

20. In addition to the obligation to recite *Sheva Berachos* at the wedding, there is a further obligation to recite these blessings after meals held in honor of the married couple during the seven days of rejoicing (see below, 7b). Our Gemara explains Rav Huna to hold that *Sheva Berachos* for a widow and widower are recited only during the first day.

21. [See above, 5a.] The Gemara assumes that this Baraisa requires three days of *Sheva Berachos* for a widow.

22. Rav Huna did not say explicitly that a widow who weds a previously unmarried man requires seven days. Rather, this may be deduced from his two statements if they are taken together. Rav Huna said (in the name of R' Abba) that a [certain kind of] widow requires *Sheva Berachos* and he said that a [certain kind of] widow does not require *Sheva Berachos.* The Gemara established that when he said a widow "does not require" *Sheva Berachos,* this means that she does not require them for seven days (but she does require them for one). Hence, when Rav Huna said a [different kind of] widow *does* require *Sheva Berachos,* this must mean that she requires them for the full seven days (*Rashi;* see *Shitah Mekubetzes* ד״ה ורש״י ז״ל כתב).

23. In other words, the Baraisa and Rav Huna are discussing two distinct requirements: rejoicing and the recitation of *Sheva Berachos.* "Rejoicing" (mentioned in the Baraisa) means that the groom should desist from work so as to spend the time with his new wife (*Rashba, Re'ah;* see *Tosefta* 1:1). He should also feast with her, refrain from dealing in the marketplace and be of good cheer with her (*Meiri;* see *Even HaEzer* 64:1; see *Pirkei DeRabbi Eliezer* end of ch. 16). The recitation of *Sheva Berachos* (mentioned by Rav Huna) is the utterance of the text recorded on 7b-8a.

These two requirements do not always run the same length. Occasionally they differ in their prescribed times, such as in our case: A widow who marries a widower is allotted one day of *Sheva Berachos* but three days of rejoicing.

פטור התם פקיד ועקיר הכא פקיד ולא עקיר רבי אמי שרא למיבעל בתחלה בשבת אמרי ליה רבנן והא לא כתיבא כתובתה אמר להו א) אתפסוה מטלטלין רב זביד שרא למיבעל בתחלה בשבת איכא דאמרי רב זביד גופיה בעל בתחלה בשבת רב יהודה שרא למיבעל בתחלה ביו"ט אמר רב פפי משמיה דרבא לא תימא ביו"ט דשרי הא בשבת אסור דהוא הדין דאפילו בשבת נמי שרי ב) ומעשה שהיה כך היה רב פפא משמיה דרבא אמר ביו"ט שרי בשבת אסור א"ל רב פפי לרב פפא מאי דעתיך מתוך שהותרה חבורה לצורך הותרה נמי שלא לצורך אלא מעתה מותר לעשות מוגמר ביו"ט ג) דמתוך שהותרה הבערה לצורך הותרה נמי שלא לצורך אמר ליה עליך אמר קרא א) אך אשר יאכל לכל נפש דבר השוה לכל נפש אמר ליה רב אחא בריה דרבא לרב אשי אלא מעתה נזדמן לו צבי ביו"ט הואיל ואינו שוה לכל נפש ה"נ דאסור למשחטיה אמר ליה אנא דבר הצורך לכל נפש קאמינא צבי צריך לכל נפש הוא אמר רבי יעקב בר אידי הורה רבי יוחנן בציידן אסור לבעול בתחלה בשבת ומי איכא הוראה לאיסור אין והתנן ד) הורוה בית הלל ה) שתהא נזירה עוד שבע שנים אחרות ואי נמי כי הא דתניא ו) חוט השדרה שנפסק ברובו דברי רבי ר' יעקב אומר אפי' ניקב הורה רבי כר' יעקב אמר רב הונא אין הלכה כר' יעקב רב נחמן בר יצחק מתני הכי אמר ר' אבהו שאל ר' ישמעאל בן יעקב דמן צור את רבי יוחנן בציידן ואנא שמעי מהו לבעול בתחלה בשבת ואמר ליה אסור והלכתא ז) מותר לבעול בתחלה בשבת: אמר רבי חלבו אמר רב הונא א"ר אבא בר זבדא אמר רב אחת בתולה ואחת אלמנה טעונה ברכה ומי אמר רב הונא הכי והאמר רב הונא אלמנה אינה טעונה ברכה לא קשיא כאן בבחור שנשא אלמנה כאן באלמון שנשא אלמנה ולאלמון שנשא אלמנה לא והאמר רב נחמן אמר לי הונא בר נתן תנא מנין ה) לברכת חתנים בעשרה שנאמר ב) ויקח עשרה אנשים מזקני העיר ויאמר שבו פה וישבו ובועז אלמון שנשא אלמנה הוה מאי אינה טעונה ברכה דאמר רב הונא אינה טעונה ברכה כל ז' ו) אבל יום אחד טעונה ברכה אלא הא דתניא י) שקדו חכמים על תקנת בנות ישראל שיהא שמח עמה ג' ימים במאי אי בבחור האמרת שבעה אי באלמון האמרת יום אחד איבעית אימא ז) באלמון יום אחד לברכה ח) ושלשה לשמחה ואיבעית אימא ט) בבחור שבעה לברכה ושלשה לשמחה

מיתיבי

רש"י

פטור. וקיימא לן פטור ומותר לכתחלה ביציאות שבת (דף ג.) קשיא למאן דאסר דהאי נמי הוציא דם הוא: התם. גבי ליחה: פקיד. כנוס ביחד: ועקיר. כולו מן הבשר ועומד לצאת: הכא. דם בתולים: פקיד הוא ולא עקיר. לגמרי אלא נבלע קצת בכתלים אע"פ שאינו מחובר כשאר דם האברים אלא כנוס מיהו דומה למחובר הוא שאינו מוכן לצאת כליחה: אתפסוה מטלטלי. תפסו לה מטלטלין תחת ידה במשכון לשיעבוד כתובתה עד שיכתבו שטר כתובתה בשעבוד קרקעות: מאי דעתיך. למישרי יו"ט יותר משבת: לצורך. אוכל נפש כגון שחיטה: מוגמר. בשמים על האש לגמר את הכלים ואת הבגדים: עליך אמר קרא לכל נפש דבר השוה לכל נפש. מותר ובעילה שוה לכל אבל מוגמר אינו אלא למפונקים: ומי איכא הוראה לאיסור. ומי קרי איסור הוראה משום דכל אדם רשאי להחמיר והאוסר אין זה סמיכת דברים שאפי' מן הספק שאין ההלכה ברורה לו הוא בא ואוסר אבל המתיר סומך על שמועתו או על סברת חכמתו והיא הוראה: הורוה ב"ה. משנה היא במסכת נזיר בהילני המלכה שיצא בנה למלחמה ונדרה שבע שנים בנזיר ז) בחוצה לארץ ועלתה לארץ הורוה ב"ה שתהא נזירה עוד ז' שנים אחרות: חוט השדרה שנפסק ברובו. טריפה: טעונה ברכה. ברכת חתנים: בועז אלמון הוה. דאמר מר אבצן זה בועז וכבר היו לו ל' בנים ושלשים בנות בבבא בתרא (דף צא.): האמרת שבעה. דמדאינה טעונה דקאמר רב הונא אוקימנא דאינה טעונה שבעה מכלל דטעונה דקאמר רבי אבא שבעה:

מברכין

תוספות

גבי בעילה אינו לן למשרי אע"ג דליכא לערא כיון דלא הוי פסיק רישיה לענין פתח כיון דאפשר להוציא דם בלא עשיית פתח כדמוכח לעיל (דף ה:) ומשני הכא פקיד ולא עקיר דקסבר דם חבורי מיחבר והוא הדין דהוי מצי לשנויי דלפתח הוא צריך אלא לפי מאי דקים ליה דלדם הוא צריך משני ליה ותימה דהא שמואל במלאכה שאינה צריכה לגופה סבר לה כר' יהודה כדאמרי' בפ' ח) הנחנקין (ד' פה. ושם) ובפ' כל התדיר (זבחים ד' צא.) ועוד דמדבר שאין מתכוין דשרי ר"ש ה"ל לאקשויי ולא ממלאכה שאינה צריכה לגופה כיון דרוב בקיאין ולא הוי פסיק רישיה: **מתוך** שהותרה לצורך. פירוש לצורך אוכל נפש הותרה נמי שלא לצורך אוכל נפש ובלבד שיהא לצורך הנאת היום או לצורך קיום מצוה ביו"ט כההיא דהוצאת קטן למולו וספר תורה לקרות בו ולולב לצאת בו (ביצה דף יב.) אבל שלא לצורך היום כלל לא כמו הוצאת אבנים דמיחייב והאופה מיו"ט לחול לרב חסדא דאמר לוקה (שם דף כא.) משום דלית ליה הואיל ושחיטת עולת נדבה דשרי לב"ה (שם דף כ:) היינו משום שלא יהא שלחנך מלא ושלחן רבך חסר ומוצא חמץ בתוך ביתו דאמרינן בפ"ק דפסחים (דף ו. ושם) דכופה עליו כלי ולא שרינן לשורפו משום מתוך היינו משום דאסור לשורפו מדרבנן משום מוקצה דאסור לטלטלו אבל אין לומר דאיירי כשביטלו דמכל מקום מדרבנן מצוה לשורפו והוי לצורך היום דבמצוה דרבנן נמי שרינן היכא דאיכא למימר מתוך והא דפליגי ב"ש וב"ה (ביצה דף יב:) במבשל גיד הנשה ביו"ט ואכלו דלב"ש דלית להו מתוך לוקה ולב"ה דאית להו מתוך אינו לוקה צריך לומר אע"ג דלא חשיב אוכל נפש משום איסור דרכיב עליה מכל מקום לצורך היום הוא כיון דאכיל ליה ונראה לר"י דהוצאת תינוק לטייל הוי לצורך היום ומיהו הוצאה לצורך נכרי נראה דאסור ומה שנהגו עתה להוציא לצורך נכרי היה נראה לרשב"א משום דרשות הרבים דידן לא הוי אלא כרמלית דאין רחבין ט"ז אמה וגבי יו"ט לא גזור רבנן כי היכי דלא תקון רבנן עירובי חצירות ביו"ט כדמשמע בריש פרק שני דביצה (דף טז:) דאמר יו"ט שחל להיות ערב שבת כו' רבי אומר מערבין עירובי חצירות אבל לא עירובי תחומין לפי שאתה אוסרו בדבר האסור לו ואי אתה אוסרו בדבר המותר לו אלמא לא תקון עירובי חצירות ביו"ט והוא הדין דלא גזרו בכרמלית והא דקיימא לן בפרק אמרו לו (כריתות דף יד. ושם) ובפרק קמא דביצה (דף יב. ושם) דיש עירוב והוצאה ליו"ט נראה דאיירי בעירובי תחומין ושוב חזר בו דמחצר שאינה מעורבת אין ללמוד ממנה לכרמלית דחמיר טפי כמו שפירשתי במסכת שבת (דף קל.) ועוד נראה דהא דקיימא לן דיש עירוב והוצאה ליו"ט בעירובי חצירות מיירי מדבעי למימר בפרק אמרו לו (כריתות דף יד. ושם) דאין עירוב והוצאה ליוה"כ מדתנן התם אם היתה שבת והוציאו בפיו חייב וכן בביצה (דף יב. ושם) בעי למידק דאין עירוב והוצאה ליו"ט מדשרו בית הלל להוציא קטן ולולב והיינו עירובי חצרות דהשתא מוכח לה שפיר מדשרו הוצאה דלא גזרו רבנן אעירובי חצירות אלא משום הוצאה אבל עירובי תחומין אין ענינה להוצאה והא דקאמר ואי אתה אוסרו בדבר המותר לו היינו משום דמותר להוציא לצורך: **אלא** מעתה יהא מותר לעשות מוגמר ביו"ט. ואם תאמר לדידיה נמי תקשי וכי לא סבר דאמרינן מתוך הא טעמא דב"ה הכי הוא ויש לומר שהיה סובר דטעמא דבית הלל משום דאין עירוב והוצאה כדקא ס"ד מעיקרא בביצה אע"ג דהתם פריך עלה דלמא לרב פפי לא שמיע לה ועוי"ל שהיה סובר הותרה שלא לצורך ובלבד שיהא דבר הרגיל ולהכי פריך דזה אינו רגיל טפי ממוגמר: **אמר** ליה אנא דבר הצריך לכל נפש קאמינא וצבי צריך לכל נפש. וכן ביצה וקשה לר"י דאמר בסוף פ"ב דביצה (דף כב.) מהו לכבות הנר מפני דבר אחר ומסיק דאסור הא הכא שרי משום דצריך לכל נפש וי"ל דהכא דוקא בבעילה ראשונה דמצוה היא דהוי לצורך מצות היום אבל שאר בעילות אין כל כך לצורך היום ועי"ל דכיבוי הנר מפני דבר אחר הוי כמו מכשירין דאפילו באוכל נפש אסור וכן מוכח התם דפריך עלה מהא דתניא דמכבין את הבקעת כדי שלא יתעשן הבית ומשני ההיא רבי יהודה היא דשרי מכשירי אוכל נפש כי קאמינא לרבנן: **והלכתא** מותר לבעול בתחלה בשבת. ולא חיישינן שמא ישחוט בן עוף והאמר סמכינן למיעבד סעודה בשבת:

במקהלות

מסורת הש"ס

א) [עי' תוס' לקמן ו: ד"ה אין], ב) [עירובין סה: וש"נ], ג) [פסחים ה: ביצה יב:], ד) נזיר יט:, ה) חולין מה:, ו) [לעיל ה.], ז) ומנתה בח"ל ועלתה לארץ כצ"ל. רש"ל, ח) [צ"ל בפ' כירה שבת מג.].

ליקוטי רש"י

פטור. ומותר דאין כאן תיקון ורבנן נמי לא גזור בה שבות משום צערא [שבת קז.]. מלאכה שאינה צריכה לגופה היא שהפתח היא המלאכה וזה אין צריך [לו] להיות כאן פתח מעכשיו [שם:]. מוגמר. לבונה ע"ג גחלים [ביצה כב:]. דמתוך שהותרה וכו'. הותרו נמי שלא לצורך מן התורה [שם יב:]. דבר השוה לכל נפש. וזה אינו אלא למפונקים או למי שריחו רע. צבי צריך לכל נפש הוא. דאוכל נפש הוא וראוי אף לעניים אלא שאינו מצוי להם [שם כב:]. הורה רבי. שבא מעשה לידו והורה להחמיר ולא סמך על דבריו [חולין מה:].

עין משפט נר מצוה

כו א מיי' פ"י מהל' אישות הל' ט סמג עשין מח טוש"ע אה"ע סי' סו סעי' ב:

כז ב מיי' פ"ב מהל' מזירות הל' כא:

כח ג מיי' פ"ט מהל' שחיטה הל' א סמג עשין סג טוש"ע יו"ד סי' לב סעי' א:

כט ד מיי' פ"ל מהל' שבת הל' יד סמג לאוין סה ועשין מח טוש"ע אה"ע סימן סג סעיף א וטוש"ע א"ח סי' רפ סעי' ב:

ל ה מיי' פ"ב מהל' ברכות הל' ט ומיי' פ"י מהל' אישות הל' ה סמג עשין מח טוש"ע אה"ע סי' סא סעי' ד:

לא ו ז מיי' פ"ב מהלכות ברכות הל' ט סמג שם טוש"ע שם סעי' ו:

לב ח מיי' פ"י מהלכ' אישות הל' י"ב סמג שם טוש"ע שם סי' סא סעי' ב [ועי' מ"מ]:

לג ט מיי' פ"ב מהל' ברכות ה"ט סמג שם טוש"ע שם סעי' ו:

תורה אור השלם

א) וּבַיּוֹם הָרִאשׁוֹן מִקְרָא קֹדֶשׁ וּבַיּוֹם הַשְּׁבִיעִי מִקְרָא קֹדֶשׁ יִהְיֶה לָכֶם כָּל מְלָאכָה לֹא יֵעָשֶׂה בָהֶם אַךְ אֲשֶׁר יֵאָכֵל לְכָל נֶפֶשׁ הוּא לְבַדּוֹ יֵעָשֶׂה לָכֶם: [שמות יב, טז]

ב) וַיִּקַּח עֲשָׂרָה אֲנָשִׁים מִזִּקְנֵי הָעִיר וַיֹּאמֶר שְׁבוּ פֹה וַיֵּשֵׁבוּ: [רות ד, ב]

תוספות רי"ד

א"ל והא לא כתיבא כתובה ואסרו חכמים לשהות אדם את אשתו שעה אחת בלא כתובה א"ל אתפסוה מטלטלי שיעור כתובתה. פי' שיהיה משכון בידה עד שיכתבו לה שטר כתובתה: **א"ר חלבו א"ר אדא בר זבדא אמר רב** א' בתולה וא' אלמנה טעונה ברכה [כל] שבעה. פי' טעונה ברכות כל ז' ימים ולקמן מוקי לה בדאיכא פנים חדשות: **ומי אמר רב הכי** והא"ר הונא אלמנה אינה טעונה ברכה כל ז' אלא יום א'. ל"ק כאן בבחור שנשא אלמנה כאן באלמון שנשא אלמנה. **מיתיבי** מברכים לבתולה ז' ולאלמנה יום א' מאי לאו לאלמנה שנשאת לבחור. לא לאלמון. אבל לבחור מאי ז'. א"ה ליתני מברכין לבתולה ז' ולאלמנה שנשאת לבחור ז' ולאלמנה שנשאת לאלמון יום א'. מילתא פסיקא קתני ליכא בתולה דבצירא מז' פי' ואפילו נשאת לאלמון. וליכא אלמנה דבצירא מיום א': **אלא** הא דתניא שקדו חכמים על תקנת בנות ישראל שיהא שמח עמה ג' ימים במאי אי בבחור הא אמרת ז' אם באלמון הא אמרת יום א'. איבעית אימא בבחור ז' לברכה וג' לשמחה איבע"א באלמון יום א' לברכה וג' לשמחה:

Rav Pappa responds:

אָמַר לֵיהּ – **He said to [Rav Pappi]:** עֲלֵיךְ אָמַר קְרָא – **Regarding you,** i.e. regarding your question, **the verse states:**[7] "אַךְ אֲשֶׁר יֵאָכֵל לְכָל־נֶפֶשׁ" – ***only that which is eaten by any person,*** *that alone may be performed for you,* דָּבָר הַשָּׁוֶה לְכָל נֶפֶשׁ – teaching that only **something that is common to all people** is permitted on Yom Tov.[8]

The Gemara questions this:

אָמַר לֵיהּ רַב אַחָא בְּרֵיהּ דְּרָבָא לְרַב אַשִׁי – **Rav Acha the son of Rava said to Rav Ashi:** אֶלָּא מֵעַתָּה – **But now,** if that is true, נִזְדַּמֵּן לוֹ צְבִי בְּיוֹם טוֹב – then what if **a deer became available to him on Yom Tov;** הוֹאִיל וְאֵינוֹ שָׁוֶה לְכָל נֶפֶשׁ – **since it is not common to all people** to eat venison, which is expensive and eaten only by rich people, הָכִי נַמִי דְּאָסוּר לְמִשְׁחֲטֵיהּ – **is it indeed forbidden to slaughter it?**

Rav Ashi replies:

אָמַר לֵיהּ – **He said to him:** אֲנָא דָּבָר הַצּוֹרֵךְ לְכָל נֶפֶשׁ קָאָמִינָא – **I say** that the requirement is that it be **needed by all people,** even if it not common to all people; צְבִי צָרִיךְ לְכָל נֶפֶשׁ הוּא – and **deer is needed by all people.**[9]

The Gemara presents yet another ruling concerning cohabitation with a virgin:

אָמַר רַבִּי יַעֲקֹב בַּר אִידִי – **R' Yaakov bar Idi said:** הוֹרָה רַבִּי יוֹחָנָן בְּצַיְדָּן – **R' Yochanan ruled in Sidon:** אָסוּר לִבְעוֹל בְּתְחִלָּה בְּשַׁבָּת – **It is prohibited to cohabit** with a virgin **for the first time on the Sabbath.**

The Gemara objects to the language of this decision:

וּמִי אִיכָּא הוֹרָאָה לְאִיסּוּר – **But is** the term **"ruling"** ever used **for a prohibition?**[10]

The Gemara rejects the objection by pointing to several instances where the term "ruling" is, in fact, used in reference to stringent decisions:

אִין – **Yes,** it is. וְהָתְנַן – **For we learned in a Mishnah:**[11] הוֹרוּהָ בֵּית הִלֵּל שֶׁתְּהֵא נְזִירָה עוֹד שֶׁבַע שָׁנִים אֲחֵרוֹת – BEIS HILLEL RULED FOR HER THAT SHE MUST BE A *NEZIRAH* FOR ANOTHER SEVEN YEARS.[12] Here we see the term "ruled" being used in connection with a stringent decision. וְאִי נַמִי כִּי הָא דְּתַנְיָא – **Alternatively, like that which we learned in a Baraisa:** חוּט הַשִּׁדְרָה שֶׁנִּפְסַק בְּרוּבּוֹ – An animal whose SPINAL CORD IS SPLIT IN ITS GREATER PART is a *treifah;* דִּבְרֵי רַבִּי – these are THE WORDS OF REBBI.[13] רַבִּי יַעֲקֹב אוֹמֵר – R' YAAKOV SAYS: אֲפִילּוּ נִיקַּב – EVEN if the cord is merely PIERCED the animal is a *treifah.* הוֹרָה רַבִּי כְּרַבִּי יַעֲקֹב – And REBBI himself RULED stringently IN ACCORDANCE WITH the view of R' YAAKOV. Here too, we find the term "ruled" in connection with a stringent decision.

The Gemara comments on this last Baraisa:

אָמַר רַב הוּנָא – **Rav Huna said:** אֵין הֲלָכָה כְּרַבִּי יַעֲקֹב – **The law is not in accordance with R' Yaakov;** rather, the animal is not *treifah* unless the cord is actually split in its greater part.

The Gemara cites a different version of R' Yochanan's ruling:

רַב נַחְמָן בַּר יִצְחָק מַתְנֵי הָכִי – **Rav Nachman bar Yitzchak taught it like this:** אָמַר רַבִּי אַבָּהוּ – **R' Abahu said:** שָׁאַל רַבִּי יִשְׁמָעֵאל בֶּן יַעֲקֹב דְּמִן צוֹר אֶת רַבִּי יוֹחָנָן בְּצַיְדָּן – **R' Yishmael ben Yaakov from Tyre asked R' Yochanan in Sidon,** וַאֲנָא שָׁמְעִי – **and I overheard it:** מַהוּ לִבְעוֹל בְּתְחִלָּה בְּשַׁבָּת – **What is** the law regarding **cohabiting** with a virgin **for the first time on the Sabbath?** וְאָמַר לֵיהּ אָסוּר – **And he answered him: It is forbidden.**

Having cited these various rulings the Gemara concludes with the definitive halachah:

וְהִלְכְתָא – **And the law is** מוּתָּר לִבְעוֹל בְּתְחִלָּה בְּשַׁבָּת – **that it is permitted to cohabit** with a virgin **for the first time on the Sabbath.**[14]

The Gemara turns to the topic of the blessings recited at a wedding:[15]

אָמַר רַבִּי חֶלְבּוֹ אָמַר רַב הוּנָא אָמַר רַב אַבָּא בַּר זַבְדָּא אָמַר רַב – **R' Chelbo said in the name of Rav Huna who said in the name of**

NOTES

[R' Pappi seems to be questioning the principle of *since . . .;* but this seems puzzling, inasmuch as the Mishnah in *Beitzah* (12a), cited in the previous note, explicitly espouses this principle. See *Tosafos* and other Rishonim for discussion of this issue.]

7. *Exodus* 12:16.

8. The principle that one may perform a *melachah* on Yom Tov for a food-related purpose, along with its expansion by way of the principle of *since . . .,* allow one to perform a food-related *melachah* (such as wounding, cooking or kindling) only for such purposes as are common to the generality of people, such as cohabitation. Burning incense to perfume one's clothing and utensils, however, is something that is done only by especially fastidious people and, therefore, is forbidden (*Rashi; Shitah Mekubetzes* ד״ה א״ל אנא, first explanation; cf. ibid., second explanation; see also *Meleches Yom Tov* §105 ff.).

9. That is, the criterion for applying the permit to perform food-related *melachos* on Yom Tov is that the *melachah* be done for some purpose that anyone could enjoy. Venison may be expensive, but if it were made available to him the average person could eat and enjoy it. Incense, on the other hand, is not appreciated except by very fastidious people (*Rashba*).

10. The term "ruled" does not seem to the Gemara appropriate for a stringent decision, since, even in the absence of any definitive decision, one might be stringent simply out of doubt. A lenient decision, however, requires a definite conclusion, based either on logic or tradition, and therefore is more appropriately called a "ruling" (*Rashi*).

The Gemara therefore wonders if R' Yaakov bar Idi might be mistaken in his quote of R' Yochanan; perhaps R' Yochanan actually "ruled" leniently on this issue (*Shitah Mekubetzes* ד״ה ומי איכא).

11. *Nazir* 19b.

12. This refers to an incident recorded in the Mishnah there, in which Queen Helena's son went off to war and she declared: "If my son returns safely from the war I shall be a *nezirah* for seven years." Her son returned from the war, and she undertook a term of *nezirus* of seven years, during which time she happened to be outside the Land of Israel. At the end of that time she went to the Land of Israel, where Beis Hillel ruled that she must undertake another seven-year term of *nezirus* (*Rashi*).

[A *nazir* is forbidden, among other things, to contract *tumah* from a corpse. Now, by Rabbinic decree, all the world outside of the Land of Israel is deemed *tamei* with corpse *tumah,* and, therefore, Beis Hillel penalized a *nazir* who observed his term in such a state of *tumah* by requiring him to repeat his entire term of *nezirus* in the Land of Israel (see *Tosafos* and *Rosh* to *Nazir* ibid.).]

13. [A *tereifah* is an animal that has one of a well-defined set of physical defects that will cause it to die (see *Rambam, Hil. Shechitah* ch. 5). Among the defects which render an animal *tereifah,* the Mishnah in *Chullin* (42a) reckons an animal with a split spinal cord. Rebbi rules that, in order to render the animal *tereifah,* the cord must be split in its majority. (See *Chullin* 45b for a more precise definition of what constitutes such a split.)]

14. [Regarding whether this ruling is based, as Rav maintained, on the assumption that the bleeding that results is destructive in nature (see above, 6a), or, as Rabbah maintained, on the assumption that the bleeding is unintentional and not inevitable (since most people are knowledgeable about penetrating at an angle; see above, 6b); and regarding the ramifications this has in considering whether this permit can be applied nowadays, when we can no longer say with certainty that most people are knowledgeable about this maneuver, see *Shitah Mekubetzes* to 5b ד״ה וכתבו תלמידי ה״ר יונה ז״ל; *Hagahos Asheri* and *Pnei Yehoshua* here; *Derishah, Yoreh Deah* §63.

15. The Gemara below (7b-8a) records the text of blessings that must be recited at the *kiddushin* and *nisuin* (or, *chuppah*) ceremonies. There are six blessings that are recited under the *chuppah* and the Gemara refers to these as *Bircas Chasanim,* literally: the Blessing of the Grooms. They are recited over a cup of wine (see *Maseches Soferim* 19:10 and *Even*

פטור התם פקיד ועקיר הכא פקיד ולא עקיר רבי אמי שרא למיבעל בתחלה בשבת אמרי ליה רבנן והא לא כתיבא כתובתה אמר להו (א) [א]אתפסוה מטלטלין רב זביד שרא למיבעל בתחלה בשבת איכא דאמרי רב זביד גופיה בעל בתחלה בשבת רב יהודה שרא למיבעל בתחלה ביו"ט אמר רב פפי משמיה דרבא לא תימא ביו"ט דשרי הא בשבת אסור דהוא הדין דאפילו בשבת נמי שרי (ב) ומעשה שהיה כך היה רב פפא משמיה דרבא אמר ביו"ט שרי בשבת אסור א"ל רב פפי לרב פפא מאי דעתיך מתוך שהותרה חבורה לצורך הותרה נמי שלא לצורך אלא מעתה מותר לעשות מוגמר ביו"ט (ג) דמתוך שהותרה הבערה לצורך הותרה נמי שלא לצורך אמר ליה עליך אמר קרא א) אך אשר יאכל לכל נפש דבר השוה לכל נפש אמר ליה רב אחא בריה דרבא לרב אשי אלא מעתה נזדמן לו צבי ביו"ט הואיל ואינו שוה לכל נפש ה"נ דאסור למשחטיה אמר ליה אנא דבר הצורך לכל נפש קאמינא צבי צריך לכל נפש הוא אמר רבי יעקב בר אידי הורה רבי יוחנן בצידן אסור לבעול בתחלה בשבת ומי איכא הוראה לאיסור אין והתנן (ד) הורוה בית הלל [ב]שתהא נזירה עוד שבע שנים אחרות ואי נמי כי הא דתניא (ה) [ג]חוט השדרה שנפסק ברובו דברי רבי ר' יעקב אומר אפי' ניקב הורה רבי כר' יעקב אמר רב הונא אין הלכה כר' יעקב רב נחמן בר יצחק מתני הכי אמר ר' אבהו שאל ר' ישמעאל בן יעקב דמן צור את רבי יוחנן בצידן ואנא שמעי מהו לבעול בתחלה בשבת ואמר ליה אסור והלכתא [ד]מותר לבעול בתחלה בשבת: אמר רבי חלבו אמר רב הונא א"ר אבא בר זבדא אמר רב אחת בתולה ואחת אלמנה טעונה ברכה ומי אמר רב הונא הכי והאמר רב הונא אלמנה אינה טעונה ברכה לא קשיא כאן בבחור שנשא אלמנה כאן באלמון שנשא אלמנה ואלמון שנשא אלמנה לא והאמר רב נחמן אמר לי הונא בר נתן תנא מנין [ה]לברכת חתנים בעשרה שנאמר ב) ויקח עשרה אנשים מזקני העיר ויאמר שבו פה וישבו ובועז אלמון שנשא אלמנה הוה מאי אינה טעונה ברכה דאמר רב הונא אינה טעונה ברכה כל ז' [ו]אבל יום אחד טעונה ברכה אלא הא דתניא (ו) שקדו חכמים על תקנת בנות ישראל שיהא שמח עמה ג' ימים במאי אי בבחור האמרת שבעה אי באלמון האמרת יום אחד איבעית אימא [ז]באלמון יום אחד לברכה [ח]ושלשה לשמחה ואיבעית אימא [ט]בבחור שבעה לברכה ושלשה לשמחה

מיתיבי

פטור. וקיימא לן פטור ומותר לכתחלה ביציאות שבת (דף ג.) קשיא למאן דאסר דהאי נמי להוציא דם הוא: התם. גבי ליחה: פקיד. כנוס ביחד: ועקיר. כולו מן הבשר ועומד לצאת: הכא. דם בתולים: פקיד הוא ולא עקיר. לגמרי אלא נבלע קצת בכתלים אע"פ שאינו מחובר כשאר דם האברים אלא כנוס מיהו דומה למחובר הוא שאינו מוכן לצאת כליחה: אתפסוה מטלטלי. תנו לה מטלטלין תחת ידה במשכון לשיעבוד כתובתה עד שיכתבו שטר כתובתה בשעבוד קרקעות: מאי דעתיך. למישרי יו"ט יותר מבשבת: לצורך. אוכל נפש כגון שחיטה: מוגמר. בשמים על האש לגמר את הכלים ואת הבגדים: עליך אמר קרא לכל נפש דבר השוה לכל נפש. מותר ובעילה שוה לכל אבל מוגמר אינו אלא למפונקים: ומי איכא הוראה לאיסור. ומי קרי איסור הוראה משום דכל אדם רשאי להחמיר והאוסר אין זה סמיכת דברים שאפי' מן הספק שאין ההלכה ברורה לו הוא בא ואוסר אבל המתיר סומך על שמועתו או על סברת חכמתו והיא הוראה: הורוה ב"ה. משנה היא במסכת נזיר בהילני המלכה שיצא בנה למלחמה ונדרה שבע שנים בנזיר (ז) בחולה לארץ ועלתה לארץ הורוה ב"ה שתהא נזירה עוד ז' שנים אחרות: חוט השדרה שנפסק ברובו. טריפה: טעונה ברכה. ברכת חתנים: בועז אלמון הוה. דאמר מר אבצן זה בועז וכבר היו לו ל' בנים ושלשים בנות בבבא בתרא (דף צא.): האמרת שבעה. דמדאינה טעונה דקאמר רב הונא אוקימנא דאינה טעונה שבעה מכלל דטעונה דקאמר רבי אבא שבעה:

מברכין

גבי בעילה אית לן למשרי אע"ג דליכא צערא כיון דלא הוי פסיק רישיה לענין פתח כיון דאפשר להוצאת דם בלא עשיית פתח כדמוכח לעיל (דף ה:) ומשני הכא פקיד ולא עקיר דקסבר דם חבורי מיחבר והוא הדין דהוי מצי לשנויי דלפתח הוא צריך אלא לפי מאי דקים ליה דלדם הוא צריך משני ליה ותימה דהא שמואל במלאכה שאינה צריכה לגופה סבר לה כר' יהודה כדאמרי' בפ' (ח) הנחנקין (ד' פה. ושם) ובפ' כל התדיר (זבחים ד' צא.) ועוד דמדבר שאין מתכוין דשרי ר"ש ה"ל לאקשויי ולא ממלאכה שאינה צריכה לגופה כיון דרוב בקיאין ולא הוי פסיק רישיה: **מתוך** שהותרה לצורך. פירוש לצורך אוכל נפש הותרה נמי שלא לצורך אוכל נפש ובלבד שיהא צורך הנאת היום או צורך קיום מצוה ביו"ט כההיא דהוצאת קטן למולו וספר תורה לקרות בו ולולב לצאת בו (ביצה דף יב.) אבל שלא לצורך היום כלל לא כמו הוצאת אבנים דמיחייב והאופה מיו"ט לחול לרב חסדא דאמר לוקה (שם דף כא.) משום דלית ליה הואיל ושחיטת עולת נדבה דשרי לב"ה (שם דף כ:) היינו משום שלא יהא שלחנך מלא ושלחן רבך חסר ומוצא חמץ בתוך ביתו דאמרינן בפ"ק דפסחים (דף ו. ושם) דכופה עליו כלי ולא שרינן לשורפו משום מתוך היינו משום דלאסור לשורפו מדרבנן משום מוקצה דאסור לטלטלו אבל אין לומר דאיירי כשביטלו דמכל מקום מדרבנן מצוה לשורפו והוי צורך היום דבמצוה דרבנן נמי שרינן היכא דאיכא למימר מתוך והא דפליגי ב"ש וב"ה (ביצה דף יב:) במבשל גיד הנשה ביו"ט ואכלו דלב"ש דלית להו מתוך לוקה ולב"ה דאית להו מתוך אינו לוקה צריך לומר אע"ג דלא חשיב אוכל נפש משום איסור דרביע עליה מכל מקום צורך היום הוא כיון דאכיל ליה ונראה לר"י דהוצאת תינוק לטייל הוי צורך היום ומיהו הוצאה לצורך נכרי נראה לאסור ומה שנהגו עתה להוציא לצורך נכרי היה נראה לרשב"א משום דרשות הרבים דידן לא הוי אלא כרמלית דאין רחבין ט"ז אמה וגבי יו"ט לא גזור רבנן כי היכי דלא תקון רבנן עירובי חצירות ביו"ט כדמשמע בריש פרק שני דביצה (דף טז:) דאמר יו"ט שחל להיות ערב שבת כו' רבי אומר מערבין עירובי חצירות אבל לא עירובי תחומין לפי שאתה אוסרו בדבר האסור לו ואי אתה אוסרו בדבר המותר לו אלמא לא תקון עירובי חצירות ביו"ט והוא הדין דלא גזרו בכרמלית והא דקיימא לן בפרק אמרו לו (כריתות דף יד. ושם) ובפרק קמא דביצה (דף יב. ושם) דיש עירוב והוצאה ליו"ט נראה דאיירי בעירובי תחומין ושוב חזר בו דמחצר שאינה מעורבת אין ללמוד ממנה לכרמלית דחמיר טפי כמו שפירשתי במסכת שבת (דף קח.) ועוד נראה דהא דקיימא לן דיש עירוב והוצאה ליו"ט בעירובי חצירות איירי מדבעי למימר בפרק אמרו לו (כריתות דף יד. ושם) דאין עירוב והוצאה ליוה"כ מדתנן התם אם היתה שבת והוציאו בפיו חייב וכן בביצה (דף יב. ושם) בעי למידק דאין עירוב והוצאה ליו"ט מדשרו בית הלל להוציא קטן ולולב והיינו עירובי חצרות דהשתא מוכח לה שפיר מדשרו הוצאה דלא גזרו רבנן אעירובי חצירות אלא משום הוצאה אבל עירובי תחומין אין ענינה להוצאה והא דקאמר ואי אתה אוסרו בדבר המותר לו היינו משום דמותר להוציא לצורך: **אלא** מעתה יהא מותר לעשות מוגמר ביו"ט. ואם תאמר לדידיה נמי תקשי וכי לא סבר דאמרינן מתוך הא טעמא דב"ה הכי הוא ויש לומר שהיה סובר דטעמא דבית הלל משום דאין עירוב והוצאה כדקא ס"ד מעיקרא בביצה אע"ג דהתם פריך עלה דלמא לרב פפי לא שמיע לה ועוי"ל שהיה סובר הותרה שלא לצורך ובלבד שיהא דבר הרגיל ולהכי פריך דזה אינו רגיל טפי ממוגמר: **אמר** ליה אנא דבר הצריך לכל נפש קאמינא וצבי צריך לכל נפש. וכן ביאה וקשה לר"י דאמר בסוף פ"ב דביצה (דף כב.) מהו לכבות הנר מפני דבר אחר ומסיק לאסור הא הכא שרי משום דצריך לכל נפש וי"ל דהכא דוקא בבעילה ראשונה דמצוה היא דהוי צורך מצות היום אבל שאר בעילות אין כל כך צורך היום ועי"ל דכיבוי הנר מפני דבר אחר הוי כמו מכשירין דאפילו באוכל נפש אסור וכן מוכח התם דפריך עלה מהא דתניא דמכבין את הבקעת כדי שלא יתעשן הבית ומשני ההיא רבי יהודה היא דשרי מכשירי אוכל נפש כי קאמינא לרבנן: **והלכתא** מותר לבעול בתחלה בשבת. ולא חיישינן שמא ישחוט בן עוף והא סמכינן למיעבד סעודה בשבת:

במקהלות

עין משפט נר מצוה

כו א מיי' פ"י מהל' אישות הל' ט סמג עשין מח טוש"ע אה"ע סי' סו סעי' ג:

כז ב מיי' פ"ב מהל' נזירות הל' כא:

כח ג מיי' פ"י מהל' שחיטה הל' ח סמג עשין סג טוש"ע יו"ד סי' לג סעי' א:

כט ד מיי' פ"י מהל' שבת הל' יז סמג לאוין סה ועשין מח טוש"ע אה"ע סימן סג סעיף א וטוש"ע א"ח סי' רפ סעי' ב:

ל ה מיי' פ"ב מהל' ברכות הל' ט ומיי' פ"י מהל' אישות הל' ה סמג עשין מח טוש"ע אה"ע סי' סב סעי' ד:

לא ו ז מיי' פ"ב מהלכות ברכות הל' ט סמג שם טוש"ע שם סעי' ז:

לב ח מיי' פ"י מהל' אישות הל' י"ב סמג שם טוש"ע שם סי' סד סעי' ב [ועי' מ"מ]:

לג ט מיי' פ"ב מהל' ברכות ה"ט סמג שם טוש"ע שם סעי' ו:

תורה אור השלם

א) וּבַיּוֹם הָרִאשׁוֹן מִקְרָא קֹדֶשׁ וּבַיּוֹם הַשְּׁבִיעִי מִקְרָא קֹדֶשׁ יִהְיֶה לָכֶם כָּל מְלָאכָה לֹא יֵעָשֶׂה בָהֶם אַךְ אֲשֶׁר יֵאָכֵל לְכָל נֶפֶשׁ הוּא לְבַדּוֹ יֵעָשֶׂה לָכֶם: [שמות יב, טז]

ב) וַיִּקַּח עֲשָׂרָה אֲנָשִׁים מִזִּקְנֵי הָעִיר וַיֹּאמֶר שְׁבוּ פֹה וַיֵּשֵׁבוּ: [רות ד, ב]

תוספות רי"ד

א"ל והא לא כתיבא כתובה ואסרו חכמים לשהות אדם את אשתו שעה אחת בלא כתובה א"ל אתפסוה מטלטלי שיעור כתובתה. פי' שיהיה משכון בידה עד שיכתבו לה שטר כתובתה: א"ר חלבו א"ר אדא בר זבדא אמר רב א' בתולה וא' אלמנה טעונה ברכה [כל] שבעה. פי' טעונה ברכות כל ז' ימים ולקמן מוקי לה בדאיכא פנים חדשות: ומי אמר רב הכי והא"ר הונא אלמנה אינה טעונה ברכה כל ז' אלא יום א'. ל"ק כאן בבחור שנשא אלמנה כאן באלמון שנשא אלמנה. מיתיבי מברכין לבתולה ז' ולאלמנה יום א' מאי לאו לאלמנה שנשאת לבחור. לא לאלמון. אבל לבחור מאי ז'. א"ה ליתני מברכין לבתולה ז' ולאלמנה שנשאת לבחור ז' ולאלמנה שנשאת לאלמון יום א'. מילתא פסיקא קתני ליכא בתולה דבצירא מז' ואפילו נשאת לאלמון. וליכא אלמנה דבצירא מיום א': אלא הא דתניא שקדו חכמים על תקנת בנות ישראל שיהא שמח עמה ג' ימים במאי אי בבחור הא אמרת ז' אם באלמון הא אמרת יום א'. איבעית אימא בבחור ז' לברכה וג' לשמחה איבע"א באלמון יום א' לברכה וג' לשמחה:

מסורת הש"ס

א) [עי' תוס' לקמן ט: ד"ה אין], ב) [עירובין סה: וש"נ], ג) [פסחים ה: ביצה יב.], ד) נזיר יט:, ה) חולין מה:, ו) [לעיל ה.], ז) ומנחה בחו"ל ועלתה לארץ כצ"ל. רש"ל, ח) [נ"ל בפ' כירה שבת מב.].

ליקוטי רש"י

פטור. ומותר דאין כאן תיקון ורבנן נמי לא גזור בה שבות משום צערא [שבת קז.]. מלאכה שאינה צריכה לגופה היא שמספקת היא המלאכה וזה אין צריך [לו] להיות כאן פתח [מעכשיו] [שם]. מוגמר. לבונה ע"ג גחלים [ביצה כב.]. דמתוך שהותרה וכו'. הותרו נמי שלא לצורך [שם יב.]. דבר השוה לכל נפש. חה אינו אלא למפונקים או למי שריחו רע. צבי צריך לכל נפש הוא. דאוכל נפש הוא ולאו אף לעניים אלא שאינו מצוי להם [שם כב.]. הורה רבי. שבא מעשה לידו והורה להחמיר ולא סמך על דבריו [חולין מה:].

פָּטוּר – **HE IS EXEMPT.**[1] – ? –

The Gemara answers:

הָתָם פָּקִיד וַעֲקִיר – **There,** in the case of the boil, **[the fluid] is collected** in the boil **and** is completely **detached** from the surrounding flesh. הָכָא פָּקִיד וְלָא עֲקִיר – Whereas **here,** in the case of hymenal blood, the blood **is collected but not detached;**[2] rather, it is somewhat absorbed in the vaginal walls and its release constitutes an act of wounding on the Sabbath.

The Gemara cites the first of several rulings regarding this issue:

רַבִּי אַמִּי שָׁרָא לְמִיבְעַל בִּתְחִלָּה בְּשַׁבָּת – **R' Ami permitted** a certain groom **to cohabit** with his virgin bride **for the first time on the Sabbath.**

אָמְרֵי לֵיהּ רַבָּנָן – **The Rabbis said to him:** וְהָא לֹא כְּתִיבָא כְּתוּבָּתָהּ – **But her *kesubah* was not** yet **written!**[3] – ? –

R' Ami replies:

אָמַר לְהוּ – **He said to them:** אַתְפְּסוּהָ מִטַּלְטְלִין – **Give her movable property** to secure the *kesubah* obligation.[4]

Another ruling on this issue:

רַב זְבִיד שָׁרָא לְמִיבְעַל בִּתְחִלָּה בְּשַׁבָּת – **Rav Zevid permitted cohabitation** with a virgin **for the first time on the Sabbath.** אִיכָּא דְּאָמְרֵי – And **some say** רַב זְבִיד גּוּפֵיהּ בָּעַל בִּתְחִלָּה בְּשַׁבָּת – that **Rav Zevid himself cohabited** with his virgin bride **for the first time on the Sabbath.**

Another ruling:

רַב יְהוּדָה שָׁרָא לְמִיבְעַל בִּתְחִלָּה בְּיוֹם טוֹב – **Rav Yehudah permitted** a groom **to cohabit** with his virgin bride **for the first time on Yom Tov.**

The Gemara cites a disagreement regarding how to interpret this ruling:

אָמַר רַב פַּפִּי מִשְּׁמֵיהּ דְּרָבָא – **Rav Pappi said in the name of Rava:** לֹא תֵּימָא בְּיוֹם טוֹב דִּשְׁרֵי – **Do not say that it is permitted,** according to Rav Yehudah, **on Yom Tov** only, הָא בְּשַׁבָּת אָסוּר – **but on the Sabbath it is forbidden.** דְּהוּא הַדִּין דַּאֲפִילּוּ בְּשַׁבָּת נַמִּי שָׁרֵי – **Rather, it is likewise permitted on the Sabbath.** וּמַעֲשֶׂה שֶׁהָיָה כָּךְ הָיָה – It was just that **the incident that occurred happened that way,** i.e. on Yom Tov.

Rav Pappa disagrees:

רַב פָּפָּא מִשְּׁמֵיהּ דְּרָבָא אָמַר – **Rav Pappa said in the name of Rava:** בְּיוֹם טוֹב שָׁרֵי – **It is permitted** only **on Yom Tov;** בְּשַׁבָּת אָסוּר – but **on the Sabbath it is forbidden.**

To which Rav Pappi objects:

אָמַר לֵיהּ רַב פַּפִּי לְרַב פָּפָּא – **Rav Pappi said to Rav Pappa:** מַאי דַּעְתֵּיךְ – **What is your reasoning** for distinguishing, in this regard, between the Sabbath and Yom Tov? מִתּוֹךְ שֶׁהוּתְּרָה חַבּוּרָה לְצוֹרֶךְ – Presumably, it is because you say: **Since wounding is permitted** on Yom Tov **for a** food-related **purpose,** הוּתְּרָה נַמִּי שֶׁלֹּא לְצוֹרֶךְ – **it is also permitted without a** [food-related] **purpose.**[5]

אֶלָּא מֵעַתָּה מוּתָּר לַעֲשׂוֹת מוּגְמָר בְּיוֹם טוֹב – **But now,** if that is so, **it should be permitted to make incense** burn **on Yom Tov** in order to perfume one's utensils and clothes. דְּמִתּוֹךְ שֶׁהוּתְּרָה הַבְעָרָה לְצוֹרֶךְ – **For since kindling is permitted** on Yom Tov **for a** food-related **purpose,** i.e. for cooking, הוּתְּרָה נַמִּי שֶׁלֹּא לְצוֹרֶךְ – **it is also permitted without a** [food-related] **purpose!**[6] – ? –

NOTES

1. [Since his purpose in lancing the boil is not to make an opening. Furthermore, not only is he exempt;] it is actually permitted to do so (*Rashi,* from *Shabbos* 3a).

[As for why it should not be forbidden on the grounds that the formation of the opening is an inevitable consequence of his actions, see *Tosafos* et al. here and above, 6a ד״ה האי מסוכרייתא.]

R' Ami assumes that those who forbid cohabitation with a virgin on the Sabbath do so because of the bleeding involved – which is considered an act of wounding on the Sabbath – and not because of the passageway that results. (R' Ami, apparently, assumes that the creation of a passageway is unintentional and therefore permitted, either because – following R' Shimon – unintentional acts are generally permitted on the Sabbath, or because – R' Ami assumes – something that is done to the human body can be considered an act of *building* only when it is deliberate; see *Ramban; Rashba; Shitah Mekubetzes* 6b ד״ה והקשו התוספות.) Furthermore, R' Ami assumes, the hymenal blood is physiologically analogous to the fluid in a boil, since both are a collection of fluid that is released when an egress is provided. Hence, asks R' Ami, since the Mishnah permits lancing a boil on the Sabbath (even with deliberate intent to release the fluid inside), it should likewise be permitted to cohabit with a virgin on the Sabbath (see *Ramban, Rashba, Ritva;* cf. *Tosafos*).

2. That is, the hymenal blood is not altogether detached from the vaginal walls; it is somewhat connected to them and its release, therefore, is similar to an act of wounding on the Sabbath (*Rashi*).

[Regarding whether the release of hymenal blood is considered an act of wounding – according to this view – on a Biblical level, or only Rabbinically, see *Ramban; Rashba; Chidushei Chasam Sofer.*]

3. [The *kesubah* is the document in which are recorded the legal commitments of a husband to his wife upon their marriage, the foremost feature of which is the payment awarded her in the event of their divorce or his death.] If the woman does not have a *kesubah,* the couple is not permitted to live together (see below, 57a). Thus, if the *kesubah* is not written at the time they cohabit for the first time, it will be considered an illicit act.

[Apparently, in Talmudic times the *kesubah* was sometimes written after the wedding, as was the case in this episode. See, however, *Ran* fol. 1a ד״ה או שפירסה נדה.]

4. The obligations which the Rabbis instituted should be written into the *kesubah* exist even in the absence of a written *kesubah;* indeed, there were, in Talmudic times, localities where the practice was to forgo a written *kesubah* document altogether (see below, 16b and 89a). Nonetheless, in those places where the practice was to have a written *kesubah,* the husband was not allowed to live with his wife without one, since she would not feel secure of her ability to collect the *kesubah* payment without it. R' Ami stated that for this purpose, in lieu of a written *kesubah,* it is sufficient to give her some items of value to hold as security against the *kesubah* obligation, until a written *kesubah* can be drawn up (see *Ritva*).

[This was done only as a stopgap measure, since the security of a written *kesubah* is greater than that of mortgaged movables, since a written *kesubah* secures a lien on the husband's real property (i.e. his land), which can be collected even if the husband subsequently sells the land to others, whereas the movables that the woman holds may become lost or lose their value (see *Rashi;* see also *Hagahos Asheri;* Gemara and *Tosafos* below, 56b ד״ה אין עושין; *Shulchan Aruch, Even HaEzer* 66:2 with commentaries).]

[Many Rishonim raise the question of how it was permissible to take possession of this movable property on the Sabbath, in view of the law that it is forbidden to transfer property on the Sabbath. See *Ramban* et al.]

5. [In general, the thirty-nine *melachos, labors,* that are prohibited on the Sabbath, are prohibited on Yom Tov, as well. However, in regard to Yom Tov, the Torah gives a dispensation to perform *melachos* that are needed for the preparation of food for human consumption. This is derived from the verse (*Exodus* 12:16): כָּל־מְלָאכָה לֹא־יֵעָשֶׂה בָהֶם אַךְ אֲשֶׁר יֵאָכֵל לְכָל־נֶפֶשׁ הוּא לְבַדּוֹ יֵעָשֶׂה לָכֶם, *No labor may be performed on them* [i.e. the first day and last days of Passover], *only that which is eaten by any person, that alone may be performed for you.* (See our Introduction to Tractate *Beitzah* regarding the limitations of this rule.)

The Mishnah in *Beitzah* (12a) advances a principle that greatly expands this dispensation. That is: מִתּוֹךְ שֶׁהוּתְּרָה לְצוֹרֶךְ הוּתְּרָה נַמִּי שֶׁלֹּא לְצוֹרֶךְ, *since [the melachah] was permitted for a* [food-related] *purpose, it was also permitted without a* [food-related] *purpose;* i.e. any *melachah* that is permitted in order to prepare food (for example: kindling, cooking, etc.) is likewise permitted for other, nonfood-related purposes.]

Thus, in our case, since it is permitted to wound an animal when slaughtering it for food, it is permitted to create a wound for the purpose of consummating a marriage, as well (*Rashi*).

6. Yet, the Mishnah in *Beitzah* (22b) teaches that it is forbidden to burn incense on Yom Tov in order to perfume one's clothes or utensils.

Rabbah replies:
אָמַר לֵיהּ – **He said to [Abaye]:** לֹא כְּהַלָּלוּ בַּבְלִיִּים – The Baraisa does **not** refer to people **like these Babylonians,** שֶׁאֵין בְּקִיאִין בְּהַטָּיָה – **who are not knowledgeable about** penetrating **at an angle.** אֶלָּא יֵשׁ בְּקִיאִין בְּהַטָּיָה – **Rather, there are those who are knowledgeable about** the possibility of penetrating **at an angle** in such a way that the Sabbath is not violated,[20] and the Baraisa speaks of such people; for in their case there is, indeed, no certainty that they will cause bleeding and, consequently, R' Shimon allows them to cohabit with a virgin on the Sabbath, provided they have no intent to cause bleeding.[21]

The Gemara objects to Rabbah's solution:
אִם כֵּן – **If** it is **so** that they know how to avoid rupturing the hymen, טוֹרֵד לָמָּה – **why the preoccupation** that exempts a groom from reciting the *Shema?*[22]

The Gemara answers:
לְשֶׁאֵינוֹ בָּקִי – Indeed, the exemption from *Shema* is reserved **for one who is not knowledgeable** about this maneuver.

The Gemara continues to question Rabbah's approach:
יֹאמְרוּ בָּקִי מוּתָּר – **Should they** then **say that one who is knowledgeable** about this **is permitted** to cohabit with a virgin on the Sabbath[23] שֶׁאֵינוֹ בָּקִי אָסוּר – while **one who is not knowledgeable is prohibited?**[24]

The Gemara answers:
רוֹב בְּקִיאִין הֵן – **Most people are knowledgeable** about this.[25]

The Gemara questions the idea that there is a maneuver which allows the groom to cohabit with his bride without causing her to bleed:
אָמַר לֵיהּ רָבָא בַּר רַב חָנָן לְאַבַּיֵי – **Rava bar Rav Chanan said to Abaye:** אֶלָּא מֵעַתָּה – **But then,** שׁוֹשְׁבִינִין לָמָּה – **why** have **attendants,**[26] מַפָּה לָמָּה – and **why** have **a** clean **sheet** to preserve the evidence of the bride's virginity? After all, if the groom wishes to falsely accuse his bride he can simply cohabit with her at an angle, thus avoiding any bleeding! – ? –

Abaye responds:
אָמַר לֵיהּ – **He said to him:** הָתָם שֶׁמָּא יִרְאֶה וִיאַבֵּד – **There** we are concerned that **perhaps he will see blood and destroy it.**[27]

The Gemara continues to challenge Shmuel's view that cohabitation with a virgin is prohibited on the Sabbath:
מָתִיב רַבִּי אַמִּי – **R' Ami challenged from a Mishnah:**[28] הַמֵּפִיס מוּרְסָא בְּשַׁבָּת – Regarding ONE WHO LANCES A BOIL, אִם לַעֲשׂוֹת לָהּ פֶּה – IF his intent is TO MAKE AN OPENING FOR IT,[29] חַיָּיב – HE IS LIABLE;[30] וְאִם לְהוֹצִיא מִמֶּנָּה לֵיחָה – but IF his intent is TO REMOVE the FLUID FROM IT,[31]

NOTES

20. I.e. they penetrate the vagina at an angle in such a way that [the hymen is not ruptured] and no bleeding occurs (*Rashi*); likewise, a passageway is not created (see *Rashba*). See also below, 10a note 23).

21. [Our interpretation of Rabbah's reply, and of the ensuing discussion follows *Rashi,* as understood by *Rashba* and *Ritva*; for a different understanding of *Rashi,* see *Shitah Mekubetzes* ד״ה וכן כתב הריטב״א; for other approaches see *Tosafos, Ramban* et al.; see also *Teshuvos Sho'eil U'Meishiv,* II:61 ד״ה והנה לכאורה; *Rashi* to *Zevachim* 91b ד״ה הא ר״ש.]

22. As explained earlier (see note 7), the issue that preoccupies the groom, thus exempting him from reciting the *Shema,* is whether he will be able to rupture the hymen and complete the marital act successfully. But if he knows of a maneuver that will allow him to cohabit without having to rupture the hymen at all, then why should he be preoccupied? (see *Rashi*; *Rashba*).

23. Since it is not inevitable that he will cause a wound (*Rashi*).

24. The Baraisa does not seem to make any such distinction; rather, it states categorically that it is permitted to cohabit with a virgin on the Sabbath! (see *Rashba*).

25. Therefore, the Baraisa states simply that a groom may cohabit with a virgin on the Sabbath, since we are entitled to assume that any given groom belongs to the majority of people who are knowledgable enough that they will not inevitably cause bleeding. In fact, however, a groom who lacks this knowledge would not enjoy this permit (*Rashi,* as understood by *Rashba* and *Ritva*).

From the preceding discussion it emerges that a groom who is not knowledgeable about this maneuver may not cohabit with a virgin on the Sabbath, since he will inevitably cause bleeding. It also emerges that a groom who has this knowledge is not exempt from reciting the *Shema.* The following difficulty, however, now arises: Earlier the Gemara cited a Mishnah which stated that a groom is exempt from reciting *Shema* for four nights, including Friday night. Now, of what sort of groom does this Mishnah speak? If he is knowledgeable about this maneuver then why should he be exempt from reciting *Shema?* On the other hand, if he is not, then why is he exempt from reciting the *Shema* on Friday night, since without this knowledge he cannot cohabit with his virgin bride on the Sabbath? Because of this and other difficulties, many Rishonim reject *Rashi's* explanation of our Gemara in favor of other approaches.

As for *Rashi, Rashba* suggests on his behalf that Rabbah (whose approach the Gemara is now discussing) follows the view of Abaye earlier in the Gemara, according to whom a groom is exempt on Friday night even if he is forbidden to cohabit, because he is preoccupied with his past failure to complete the marital act. Hence, the Mishnah is, indeed, referring to a groom who is not knowledgeable about this maneuver and who may not, therefore, cohabit with his bride on Friday night. He is exempt from *Shema* because he is preoccupied with his failure to cohabit on the previous nights. [As for Rava, who rejects Abaye's approach, he will maintain that even a groom who is not knowledgeable – and who will inevitably cause bleeding – may cohabit with a virgin on the Sabbath, because he considers the bleeding to be destructive in nature and, hence, permitted (see above, note 18).]

26. In Talmudic times, the bride and groom would be accompanied by attendants who would prepare the bridal bed and would prevent duplicity on the part of either the bride or the groom; that is, they would insure that the bride would not set the bed with sheets that were prestained with blood, and they would insure that the groom would not destroy any evidence of bleeding after cohabitation in order to falsely accuse his wife of not being a virgin (see *Rashi* here and below, 12a).

27. If he cohabits at an angle then her hymen will still be intact, which will give the lie to any false accusation he might level against her. Thus, the only way he can contrive an effective false accusation is to actually rupture the hymen and then destroy the evidence, and it is this that the clean sheet and the attendants are supposed to prevent (*Rashi*; see, however, *Tosafos* who object that, according to this explanation, the crux of this answer – that cohabitation at an angle will leave the hymen intact and give the lie to his accusation – is not mentioned in the Gemara; see there for another explanation of this exchange).

28. *Eduyos* 2:5.

29. I.e. he wants to "improve" the boil by making a hole that will remain [at least] until tomorrow (*Rashi*), and will serve to allow any fluid that collects to escape and to allow air in so as to promote healing (*Tosafos*).

30. Making a useful hole falls under the category of בּוֹנֶה, *building,* which is one of the thirty-nine categories of activity that are forbidden on the Sabbath. That something done to the human body can be labeled an act of "building" is evident from *Genesis* (2:22), where God is said to have "built" one of Adam's sides into a woman (*Rashi*; see also *Rashi* to *Shabbos* 107a).

31. His intent is only to remove the fluid that is currently inside the boil. Were the hole to close immediately afterwards it would not concern him (*Rashi* to *Shabbos* ibid.).

מאי לאו דאי לא בעל מצי בעיל אפילו בשבת אמר רבא לא לבר משבת אמר ליה אביי והא עד מוצאי שבת ארבעה לילות קתני אלא אמר רבא כשבעל אי כשבעל מאי קמ"ל קמ"ל דשרי למיבעל בשבת כדשמואל דאמר שמואל א) פירצה דחוקה מותר ליכנס בה בשבת ואע"פ שמשיר צרורות מתיב רב יוסף ג) א חתן פטור מקרית שמע לילה הראשון עד מוצאי שבת אם לא עשה מעשה מאי לאו דטריד דבעי למיבעל אמר ליה אביי לא דטריד דלא בעיל אמר ליה רבא ומשום טירדא פטור אלא מעתה טבעה ספינתו בים הכי נמי דפטור וכי תימא ה"נ והאמר רבי אבא בר זבדא אמר רב ג) אבל חייב בכל המצות האמורות בתורה חוץ מן ב התפילין שנא' בהן א) פאר אלא אמר רבא תנאי היא דתניא חדא אם לא עשה מעשה בראשון פטור אף בשני בשני פטור אף בשלישי ותניא אידך ראשון ושני פטור שלישי חייב ואביי התם נמי בטירדא פליגי והני תנאי כי הני תנאי דתניא הכונס את הבתולה לא יבעול בתחלה בשבת וחכמים מתירין ד) מאן חכמים אמר רבה רבי שמעון היא ה) דאמר דבר שאין מתכוין מותר אמר ליה אביי והא מודה ר' שמעון בפסיק רישיה ולא ימות אמר ליה לא כהללו בבליים שאין בקיאין בהטייה אלא יש בקיאין בהטייה א"כ טורד למה לשאינו בקי יאמרו בקי מותר שאינו בקי אסור רוב בקיאין הן אמר ליה רבא בר רב חנן לאביי אלא מעתה שושבינין למה מפה למה א"ל התם שמא יראה ויאבד מתיב רבי אמי ו) ג המפים מורסא בשבת אם לעשות לה פה חייב ואם להוציא ממנה ליחה פטור

מאי לאו. הנך ארבעה לילות עד מוצאי שבת דקתני להכי תני להו דאי לא בעל בעילה גמורה מצי למיבעל וכל דם שהוא מוציא תמיד ז) בהערותיו הוו דם בתולים ושמעינן מינה נמי דמותר לבעול בתחלה בשבת: והא ארבעה לילות עד מוצאי שבת קתני. ולא משכחת ליה לבר משבת דהא ברביעי נוסת ויש כאן לילי חמישי וששי ושבת ומוצאי שבת: אי כשבעל. ולא אתא לאורויי לן אלא היתר דם בתולים האי דנקט עד מוצאי שבת מאי קמ"ל ליתני נותנין לה ארבעה לילות על כרחך משום בעילת שבת נקט לה: שמשיר צרורות. והאי נמי דלמא מחבל פורתא ומספיקא לא אסרינן ליה: מאי לאו. האי דפטר ליה מק"ש בלילי שבת משום דטריד במצוה דבעי למיבעל והעוסק במצוה פטור מן המצוה: דטריד דלא בעל. מלטער שלא בעל: משום דטריד פטור. בתמיה ומשום לער פטור מאחר שאינו מחשב לעסוק במצוה: שנאמר בהן פאר. פארך חבוש עליך (יחזקאל כד) ואבל מעולל בעפר קרנו וראשו ואין זה פאר לתפילין: ח) [אלא אמר רבא. ודאי לא מלית לתרולי הא דחתן פטור מק"ש משום דלא מלי בעיל דא"כ לא הוה פטור דהא לא טריד בדבר מלוה: תנאי היא. בעילת מבורה בשבת ומאן דאסר לבעול בשבת כתנאי אמרה לשמעתיה דאיכא תנא אחרינא דאסר למיבעל דתנא חדא כו']: פטור. מקרית שמע: שלישי חייב. דשבת הוא ואסור לבעול: ואביי. אמר לך הנך תנאי נמי בטירדא פליגי והאי דפטר ליה מק"ש לאו משום דשרי למיבעל אלא קסבר המצטער לער של מלוה פטור מקריאת שמע ולא דמי לאבל דטריד טירדא דרשות שאין לערו מלוה אע"פ שאבילותו מלוה ומאן דמחייב סבר טירדא לא פטר ט) [ורבא אמר דמותר לבעול פליגי והני תנאי כהני תנאי]: בהטייה. שמטין לצדדין ואין מוציאים דם: אם כן. דבקיאים: טורד למה. מהו טרדו להפטר מק"ש: בקי מותר. לבעול בשבת דלא פסיק רישיה ולא ימות הוא: רוב בקיאין הן. הילכך סתמא לאו פסיק רישיה ולא ימות הוא: שושבינין למה. מאחר שיש בקיאין לבעול בלא דם הא דתניא לקמן (דף יב.) היו מעמידין להן שני שושבינין אחד לו ואחד לה כדי למשמש את החתן ואת הכלה כלומר לבקר אחריהם שלא ינהגו בה רמאות בטענת בתולים ואי בקיאין בהטייה מה שושבינין מועילין: מפה למה. לברר את הבתולים. וליטעמיך ל"ג אלא ה"ג שושבינין למה מפה למה: אמר ליה שמא יראה ויאבד. שמא לא יטה ויוליא דם ויאבדנו ויאמר לא מלאתי דם דאילו בהטייה אם בא לטעון תאמר לו עדיין בתולה אני: המפים מורסא. הפותח פה נפח שקורין קלו"ג: אם לעשות לה פה. שמתכוין ליפותה ולהיות לה פתח זה ליום מחר: חייב. שהוא מתקן פתח וחייב משום בונה ° דאשכחן בנין בבעלי חיים דכתיב ויבן את הצלע (בראשית ב):

פטור

מאי קמ"ל. במאי דנקט עד מוצאי שבת לענין רלופים ליכא למימר כדפרישית: מאי לאו דטריד דבעי למיבעל. הכא ליכא לשנויי לבר משבת כדלעיל דא"כ אינו פטור עד מוצאי שבת וקא משמע ליה לתנא טועה דפטר ליה עד מוצאי שבת אבל לעיל אפילו כי אמרינן לבר משבת ולא מצי למיבעל בשבת מכל מקום דוקא נקט עד מוצאי שבת משום דעד למוצאי שבת מולין דם בתולים היכא דעבר ובעל: והא אמר ר' אבא אבל חייב בכל המצות כו'. ואביי סבר דטירדא דליכא מלוה כלל מחייב אבל טירדא דלא מצי בעיל חשיב טירדא דמלוה כיון שטרוד במה שאינו יכול לעשות מלוה: חוץ מן התפילין שנאמר בהן פאר. ואמרינן בפרק בתרא דמועד קטן (דף טו.) מדלאמר ליה רחמנא ליחזקאל פארך חבוש עליך מכלל דלעלמא אסור ובקונטרס פי' שנאמר בהן פאר ואבל מעולל בעפר קרנו וראשו היינו ליתן טעם דלא ילפינן שאר מלות מתפילין וא"ת ומאי שנא לגבי תפילין אמרינן דדוקא ליחזקאל נאמר ולא לשאר אבלים וגבי תלמוד תורה ילפינן שאר אבלים מיחזקאל דאמרינן (שם) אבל אסור בתלמוד תורה מדאמר ליה רחמנא ליחזקאל האנק דום ויש לומר דלאסור גמרינן מדאסר רחמנא ליחזקאל לכ"ע נמי אסור אבל להתיר לא גמרינן דליה לחודיה למשרי אתא: והני תנאי כי הני תנאי. אע"ג דפליגי תנאי בהדיא בהכי מכל מקום דחיק אביי לעיל דחשיב טירדא דמלוה הא דלא מלי בעיל דניחא ליה לאוקמי מתני' כשמואל דלאסר לבעול ומוקי נמי פלוגתא דברייתא אי חשיב טירדא הא דלא מצי בעיל כדי לאוקמי כשמואל כל מה שיכול: לא כהללו בבליים שאין בקיאין בהטייה. פירוש אינו פסיק רישיה דכל העולם אינן כמו בבליים אלא בקיאין הן הילכך שרי להו למיבעל ובלבד שלא יתכונו לבעול בעילה גמורה ופריך אם כן טורד למה פירוש בשבת אמאי פטר ליה לעיל מק"ש כיון דבקיאין הן בשלמא בחול איכא טירדא לפי שמתכוין לבעול בעילה גמורה ואף לבקיאין יש טירדא לבעול בעילה גמורה כדאמר בפרק שני דברכות (דף טז. ושם) דר"ג היה פטור ומחמיר על עצמו אע"ג דבקי היה שלא היה בבלי אבל בשבת שאינו מתכוין לבעול בעילה גמורה טורד למה ומשני לשאינו בקי פי' לפי שאינו בקי בשעת ק"ש דאפי' הבקיאין בשעת מעשה קודם מעשה יראים שלא יהיו בקיאין הילכך טרודים כולם: רוב בקיאין הן. וכל חד וחד מספקינן ליה ברוב וכולם מותרים משמע הכא דרובן בקיאין בהטייה וא"ת דאמרינן בפ"ב דחגיגה (דף יד: ושם) בתולה שעיברה מהו לכהונה כגון שבדקוה על פי חבית ולא היה ריחה נודף מי חיישינן לדשמואל דאמר יכולני לבעול כמה בעילות בלא דם או דלמא באמבטי עיברה ומסיק דשמואל לא שכיח ובפרק בתרא דנדה (דף סד: ושם) נמי קאמר שאני שמואל דרב גובריה הוא והא אמרינן הכא דרוב בקיאין הן וי"ל דשמואל היה יכול לבעול בעילה גמורה שאשה מתעברת בו בלא דם אבל בהטייה אין אשה מתעברת ולהכי בההיא דחגיגה ליכא למיחש בהטייה אלא לדשמואל: אלא מעתה שושבינין למה מפה למה. פי' בקונטרס כיון שהן בקיאין לבעול בלא דם שמא יטה והיא לא תסיק אדעתה שהטה ומשני דשושבינין ומפה הם שאם לא יטה ויבעול בעילה גמורה ויאבד המפה ואם יטה ויאמר שלא מצא לה בתולים יכולה לומר עדיין בתולה אני וקשה לר"י דאינו מתרץ ממה שהקשה לו דהוי ליה לשנויי דמסקא אדעתה לומר עדיין בתולה אני ועיקר התירוץ חסר מן הספר ונראה לר"י כפירוש ר"ת דדוקא משבת קא פריך דמפה ושושבינין למה דלריך לבעול בהטייה דמעשה בכל יום שעושין שושבינין אפילו בשבת ומשני שמא יארע שלא יטה ויבעול בעילה גמורה ויאבד דם בתולים והויא דומיא דטורד למה דפריך נמי משבת: אם לעשות לה פה חייב. דפתח זה עשוי להכניס ולהוציא אויר ולהוציא ליחה: ואם להוציא ממנה ליחה פטור. בפרק שמונה שרצים (שבת דף קז: ושם) מוקמינן לה כרבי שמעון וסלקא דעתיה דרבי אמי דמותיב דדם מיפקד פקיד ולדם הוא לריך ולא לפתח ואפ"ה אסר שמואל כרבי שמעון דהוי מלאכה שאינה לריכה לגופה ולהכי פריך ממפים מורסא דכי היכי דלהוציא ממנה ליחה פטור וקיימא לן דפטור ומותר כיון דאינו לריך לפתח אף על גב דשאר מלאכה שאינה לריכה לגופה פטור אבל אסור במורסא שרי משום לער הכא נמי משום מלוה הוי לן למשרי ועוד אפילו שרינן משום לערא טפי ממשום מלוה כדפירש ר"ת לעיל פריך שפיר דהכא ודאי דהוי פסיק רישיה לענין פתח אי לאו משום לערא היה אסור אבל

גבי

עין משפט נר מצוה

כג א מיי' פ"ד מהל' ק"ש הל' א סמג עשין יח טוש"ע א"ח סי' ע סעי' ג:

כד ב מיי' פ"ד מהל' תפלין הל' יג ופ"ד מהל' אבילות הל' ט סמג עשין דרבנן ב טוש"ע א"ח סימן לח סעי' ה וטוש"ע יו"ד סי' שפח סעי' א:

כה ג מיי' פ"י מהל' שבת הל' יח סמג לאוין סה טוש"ע או"ח סי' שכח סעי' כח:

לעזי רש"י

קלו"ג. פירוש מורסא, נפח, ב"עה (מוסף הערוך ערך מורסא):

ליקוטי רש"י

חתן פטור מקרית שמע. דלא מיחייב להסיר דעתו ממחשבת מלוה ראשונה בשביל זו הבאה עליו אלא יעסוק בראשונה ויתן לבו להיות בקי בדבר. דטריד דבעי למיבעל. לבו טרוד במחשבת בעילה [סוכה כה.]. אבל חייב בכל המצות וכו' חוץ מן התפילין וכו'. אף על פי שטרוד בצערו חייב בכל המצות חוץ מן התפילין שנאמר בהם פאר ליחזקאל פארך חבוש עליך וגו' וכיון דבעו פאר ואבל מתגולל בלכלוך בעפר אין זה פאר [ברכות יא.]. ואבל לאו בר פאר הוא וכשמתפאר מראה בעצמו שאינו אבל [סוכה שם]. מאן חכמים. כלומר מאן נינהו ומאי טעמייהו [גיטין כב.]. המפים. מבקע. מורסא. קיטור"א. אם לעשות לה פה. בתוספתא תני הכי כגון לקולפה ולעשות לה פה כדרך שרופאים של עכשיו עושין דמתקן לה פתח. חייב. משום בונה פתח או משום מתקן כלי מה לי לתקן מכה מה לי לתקן כלי. ואם להוציא ממנה ליחה. של עכשיו ואינו חושש אם תחזור ותסתום כיד [שבת קז.].

מסורת הש"ס

א) נדה סד:, ב) ברכות טז., ג) סוכה כה. ברכות יא. טו: מו"ק טו. ע"ש [שמחות פ"ו], ד) [עירובין פג. וש"נ], ה) [לעיל ה: וש"נ], ו) שבת קז. ושם: עדיות פרק ב משנה ה, ז) נ"ל בהערלותיו. יעב"ץ, ח) נ"י כ"י, ט) נ"י כ"י.

גליון הש"ס

רש"י ד"ה חייב וכו' דאשכחן בנין בבע"ח. שבת לה ע"א:

תורה אור השלם

א) הֵאָנֵק דֹּם מֵתִים אֵבֶל לֹא תַעֲשֶׂה פְּאֵרְךָ חֲבוֹשׁ עָלֶיךָ וּנְעָלֶיךָ תָּשִׂים בְּרַגְלֶיךָ וְלֹא תַעְטֶה עַל שָׂפָם וְלֶחֶם אֲנָשִׁים לֹא תֹאכֵל: [יחזקאל כד, יז]

אָמַר לֵיהּ רָבָא – **Rava said to [Abaye]:** וּמִשּׁוּם טִירְדָּא פָּטוּר – **And** merely **because of** his **preoccupation** with some other matter **he is exempt** from reciting the *Shema?* אֶלָּא מֵעַתָּה – **But now,** if this were so, טָבְעָה סְפִינָתוֹ בַּיָּם – then what of **someone whose ship sank at sea;** הָכִי נַמִּי דְּפָטוּר – **is he also exempt** from reciting the *Shema,* since he is preoccupied with his misfortune?[11] וְכִי תֵּימָא הָכִי נַמִּי – **And if you** will **say** that **this is** indeed **so,** וְהָאָמַר רַבִּי אַבָּא בַּר זַבְדָּא אָמַר רַב – **why,** we see otherwise from that which **R' Abba bar Zavda said in the name of Rav:** אָבֵל חַיָּיב בְּכָל הַמִּצְוֹת הָאֲמוּרוֹת בַּתּוֹרָה – **A mourner is obligated in all the commandments stated in the Torah,** חוּץ מִן הַתְּפִילִּין – **except for** the mitzvah of **tefillin,** שֶׁנֶּאֱמַר בָּהֶן ,,פְּאֵר״ – **since the word "glory" is stated in reference to them.**[12] We see that although a mourner is certainly preoccupied with his sorrow, he is nevertheless obligated in all mitzvos, including the recitation of *Shema!* Evidently, mere preoccupation does not exempt one from recitation of the *Shema,* unless it is preparatory to the performance of some mitzvah. Consequently, the Mishnah, which exempts a groom who has not yet cohabited from reciting the *Shema* on Friday night, must maintain that he is allowed to cohabit that night, so that his preoccupation is with a mitzvah that he is about to perform; it therefore continues to pose a challenge to Shmuel! – ? –

Rava therefore offers a different defense of this view:

אֶלָּא אָמַר רָבָא – **Rather, Rava said:** תַּנָּאֵי הִיא – **It is,** in fact, a matter of **dispute among the Tannaim** whether or not one may cohabit with a virgin on the Sabbath.[13] דְּתָנָא חֲדָא – **For one Baraisa taught:** אִם לֹא עָשָׂה מַעֲשֶׂה בָּרִאשׁוֹן – IF HE DID NOT yet PERFORM THE ACT of cohabitation ON THE FIRST night [Wednesday night], פָּטוּר אַף בַּשֵּׁנִי – HE IS EXEMPT from reciting the *Shema* ON THE SECOND night [Thursday night] AS WELL. בַּשֵּׁנִי – Likewise, IF HE DID NOT yet PERFORM THE ACT of cohabitation ON THE SECOND night, פָּטוּר אַף בַּשְּׁלִישִׁי – HE IS EXEMPT from *Shema* ON THE THIRD night [Friday night]. וְתַנְיָא אִידָךְ – **But it was taught in another Baraisa:** רִאשׁוֹן וְשֵׁנִי פָּטוּר – HE IS EXEMPT from reciting the *Shema* on THE FIRST AND SECOND NIGHT, שְׁלִישִׁי חַיָּיב – but on THE THIRD NIGHT [Friday night] HE IS OBLIGATED to recite it.[14]

Abaye explains the dispute between the Baraisos diferently:[15] וְאַבַּיֵי – **But Abaye** would say to you: הָתָם נַמִּי בְּטִירְדָּא פְּלִיגֵי – **There, too, [the Baraisos] disagree about** whether his **preoccupation** with his failure to complete the act on the previous nights exempts him from reciting the *Shema.*[16]

Rava, however, as we have seen, maintains that the point of issue between the Baraisos is whether or not one may cohabit with a virgin on the Sabbath. The Gemara notes:

וְהָנֵי תַּנָּאֵי כִּי הָנֵי תַּנָּאֵי – **And** the opinions of **these Tannaim accord with** the opinions of **these** other **Tannaim;** דְּתַנְיָא – **for it was taught in a Baraisa:** הַכּוֹנֵס אֶת הַבְּתוּלָה – ONE WHO MARRIES A VIRGIN לֹא יִבְעוֹל בַּתְּחִלָּה בְּשַׁבָּת – MAY NOT COHABIT with her FOR THE FIRST TIME ON THE SABBATH. וַחֲכָמִים מַתִּירִין – BUT THE SAGES ALLOW it.[17]

The Gemara explains the basis of this dispute:

מַאן חֲכָמִים – **Who are the Sages** who allow it? אָמַר רַבָּה – **Rabbah said:** רַבִּי שִׁמְעוֹן הִיא – **It is R' Shimon,** דְּאָמַר דָּבָר שֶׁאֵין מִתְכַּוֵּין מוּתָּר – **who said that an unintended act is permitted.**[18]

Abaye objects:

אָמַר לֵיהּ אַבַּיֵי – **Abaye said to [Rabbah]:** וְהָא מוֹדֶה רַבִּי שִׁמְעוֹן בִּפְסִיק רֵישֵׁיהּ וְלֹא יָמוּת – **But R' Shimon concedes** that one is liable **in the case of an inevitable consequence.**[19] And here it is inevitable that the cohabitation will cause bleeding! – ? –

NOTES

11. Rava understands Abaye's view to be that a groom's exemption is based not upon his imminent performance of a mitzvah, but simply upon the fact that his thoughts are preoccupied. Accordingly, he asks, even someone consumed with worry about a matter that is completely unrelated to mitzvah observance, such as someone suffering a financial reversal, should be exempt from the *Shema,* since he too is unable to concentrate upon its recitation (see *Rashi* to *Succah* 25a ד״ה משום טירדא כו׳)! [As for how Abaye would respond to this challenge, see below, note 16.]

12. *Ezekiel* 24:17. Tefillin are referred to in Scripture as "glory," and it is not fitting for items so described to be affixed to the head of a mourner, which is, so to speak, soiled with the dust of mourning (*Rashi*; see *Tosafos* and *Ritva*; cf. *Rashi* to *Succah* 25b).

13. [Thus, although Shmuel's view is, indeed, contradicted by the Mishnah in *Berachos,* it finds support in the view of another Tanna who takes issue with that Mishnah.]

14. The second Baraisa, then, forbids cohabitation with a virgin on the Sabbath [hence, he must recite the *Shema* on Friday night, since he is not engaged in the performance of a mitzvah] (*Rashi*).

15. As we saw earlier, according to Abaye the Mishnah in *Berachos* – which exempts a groom on Friday night – is not inconsistent with Shmuel's view that intercourse with a virgin is forbidden on the Sabbath; likewise, he interprets the two Baraisos as being consistent with Shmuel's view, as well (see *Tosafos*).

16. That is, both Baraisos maintain, like Shmuel, that one may not cohabit with a virgin on the Sabbath. The second Baraisa, which requires the groom to recite the *Shema* on Friday night, maintains that since he is not engaged in performing a mitzvah he is not exempt; the first Baraisa maintains that since he is preoccupied with his inabililty to perform the mitzvah on the previous nights he is exempt.

As for Rava's contention that mere preoccupation – when it is not preparatory to the performance of a mitzvah – is not sufficient to exempt one from *Shema,* as evidenced by the fact that a mourner is not so exempt, Abaye would respond by distinguishing between the two cases, as follows: A groom's preoccupation on Friday night, although it is not preparatory to a mitzvah, is at least related to the performance of a mitzvah, [since it is his failure to perform the mitzvah on the previous nights that preoccupies him. In contrast,] a mourner's sorrowful and preoccupied state of mind is completely unrelated to any mitzvah observance (*Rashi,* as understood by *Shitah Mekubetzes* ד״ה והא).

[Although the observance of the laws of mourning (such as the observance of *shivah* and *sheloshim*) is certainly a mitzvah, it has no bearing on the mourner's sorrowful state of mind; for the laws of mourning are not intended for him to give vent to his grief but, rather, for him to pay respect to the deceased (see *Rashi* to *Succah* 25a; see also *Igros Moshe, Orach Chaim* I:37; see also *Rambam, Hil. Avel* 13:12, who sees in these observances a spur to repentance). Hence, the mourner's grief cannot be considered mitzvah related and it does not exempt him from reciting the *Shema*; rather, he must master his emotions and concentrate on its recital.]

17. In this Baraisa it is made explicit that the issue of cohabitation with a virgin on the Sabbath is actually the basis of a Tannaic dispute. This lends strong support to the approach of Rava, who interpreted the dispute between the two previous Baraisos as likewise revolving around this issue. Accordingly, Rishonim wonder why Abaye saw fit to take issue with Rava. See *Tosafos* et al.

18. [And since his primary intent is for his own pleasure it is permitted, even though he also causes bleeding and the opening of a passageway.]

Actually, as we saw on the previous *amud,* Rav allows cohabitation with a virgin on the Sabbath, even though he follows the view of R' Yehudah, who forbids unintended acts; he considers the bleeding and the opening of a passageway that result from the cohabitation as destructive in nature, so that no actual Sabbath violation takes place at all, intentional or otherwise. Clearly, then, Rav would not need to identify the Sages in this Baraisa with R' Shimon. Rabbah, however, considers that a constructive Sabbath violation does result from the cohabitation (either bleeding, or the creation of a passageway, or both); he therefore assumes that the Sages allow it only because these results are unintentional, and he thus identifies these Sages with R' Shimon, who allows unintentional acts (see *Ritva*).

19. See above, 6a note 6.

מאי לאו דאי לא בעל מצי בעיל אפילו בשבת אמר רבא לא לבר משבת אמר ליה אביי והא עד מוצאי שבת ארבעה לילות קתני אלא אמר רבא כשבעל אי כשבעל מאי קמ"ל קמ"ל דשרי למיבעל בשבת כדשמואל דאמר שמואל א) פירצה דחוקה מותר ליכנס בה בשבת ואע"פ שמשיר צרורות מתיב רב יוסף ג) א חתן פטור מקריאת שמע בלילה הראשון עד מוצאי שבת אם לא עשה מעשה מאי לאו דטריד דבעי למיבעל אמר ליה אביי לא דטריד דלא בעיל אמר ליה רבא ומשום טירדא פטור אלא מעתה טבעה ספינתו בים הכי נמי דפטור וכי תימא ה"נ והאמר רבי אבא בר זבדא אמר רב ג) אבל חייב בכל המצות האמורות בתורה חוץ מן ב התפילין שנא' בהן א) פאר אלא אמר רבא תנאי היא דתניא חדא אם לא עשה מעשה בראשון פטור אף בשני בשני פטור אף בשלישי ותניא אידך ראשון ושני פטור שלישי חייב ואביי התם נמי בטירדא פליגי והני תנאי כי הני תנאי דתניא הכונס את הבתולה לא יבעול בתחלה בשבת וחכמים מתירין ד) מאן חכמים אמר רבה רבי שמעון היא ה) דאמר דבר שאין מתכוין מותר אמר ליה אביי והא מודה ר' שמעון בפסיק רישיה ולא ימות אמר ליה לא כהללו בבליים שאין בקיאין בהטייה אלא יש בקיאין בהטייה א"כ טורד למה לשאינו בקי יאמרו בקי מותר שאינו בקי אסור רוב בקיאין הן אמר ליה רבא בר רב חנן לאביי אלא מעתה שושבינין למה מפה למה א"ל התם שמא יראה ויאבד מתיב רבי אמי ו) ג המפיס מורסא בשבת אם לעשות לה פה חייב ואם להוציא ממנה ליחה פטור

מאי לאו. הנך ארבעה לילות עד מוצאי שבת דקתני להכי תני להו דאי לא בעל בעילה גמורה מצי למיבעל וכל דם שהוא מוציא תמיד ז) בהערותיו הוו דם בתולים ושמעינן מינה נמי דמותר לבעול בתחלה בשבת: והא ארבעה לילות עד מוצאי שבת קתני. ולא משכחת ליה לבר משבת דהא ברביעי נישאת ויש כאן לילי חמישי וששי ושבת ומוצאי שבת: אי כשבעל. ולא אתא לאורויי לן אלא היתר דם בתולים האי דנקט עד מוצאי שבת מאי קמ"ל ליתני נותנין לה ארבעה לילות על כרחך משום בעילת שבת נקט לה: שמשיר צרורות. והאי נמי דלמא מחבל פורתא ומספיקא לא אסרינן ליה: מאי לאו. האי דפטר ליה מק"ש בלילי שבת משום דטריד במצוה דבעי למיבעל והעוסק במצוה פטור מן המצוה: דטריד דלא בעל. מצטער שלא בעל: משום דטריד פטור. בתמיה ומשום צער פטור מאחר שאינו מחשב לעסוק במצוה: שנאמר בהן פאר. פארך חבוש עליך (יחזקאל כד) ואבל מעולל בעפר קרנו וראשו ואין זה פאר לתפילין: ח) [אלא אמר רבא. ודאי לא מצית לתרוצי הא דחתן פטור מק"ש משום דלא מצי בעיל דא"כ לא הוה פטור דהא לא טריד בדבר מצוה: תנאי היא. בעילת חבורה בשבת ומאן דאסר לבעול בשבת כתנאי אמרה לשמעתיה דאיכא תנא אחרינא דאסר למיבעל דתנא חדא כו']: פטור. מקרית שמע: שלישי חייב. דשבת הוא ואסור לבעול: ואביי. אמר לך הנך תנאי נמי בטירדא פליגי והאי דפטר ליה מק"ש לאו משום דשרי למיבעל אלא קסבר המצטער צער של מצוה פטור מקריאת שמע ולא דמי לאבל דטריד טירדא דרשות שאין צערו מצוה אע"פ שאבילותו מצוה ומאן דמחייב סבר טירדא לא פטר ט) [ורבא אמר דבמותר לבעול פליגי והני תנאי כהני תנאי]: בהטייה. שמטין לצדדין ואין מוציאים דם: אם כן. דבקיאים: טורד למה. מהו טרדו להפטר מק"ש: בקי מותר. לבעול בשבת דלא פסיק רישיה ולא ימות הוא: רוב בקיאין הן. הילכך סתמא לאו פסיק רישיה ולא ימות הוא: שושבינין למה. מאחר שיש בקיאין לבעול בלא דם הא דתניא לקמן (דף יב.) היו מעמידין להן שני שושבינין אחד לו ואחד לה כדי למשמש את החתן ואת הכלה כלומר לבקר אחריהם שלא ינהגו בה רמאות בטענת בתולים ואי בקיאין בהטייה מה שושבינין מועילין: מפה למה. לברר את הבתולים. וליטעמיך ל"ג אלא ה"ג שושבינין למה מפה למה: אמר ליה שמא יראה ויאבד. שמא לא יטה ויוציא דם ויאבדנו ויאמר לא מצאתי דם דאילו בהטייה אם בא לטעון תאמר לו עדיין בתולה אני: המפיס מורסא. הפותח פה נפח שקורין קלו"ג: אם לעשות לה פה. שמתכוין ליפותה ולהיות לה פתח זה ליום מחר: חייב. שהוא מתקן פתח וחייב משום בונה ° דאשכחן בנין בבעלי חיים דכתיב ויבן את הצלע (בראשית ב):

פטור

מאי קמ"ל. במאי דנקט עד מוצאי שבת דלענין רצופים ליכא למימר כדפרישית: מאי לאו דטריד דבעי למיבעל. הכא ליכא לשנויי לבר משבת כדלעיל דא"כ אינו פטור עד מוצאי שבת וקא משוית ליה לתנא טועה דפטר ליה עד מוצאי שבת אבל לעיל אפילו כי אמרינן לבר משבת ולא מצי למיבעל בשבת מכל מקום דוקא נקט עד מוצאי שבת משום דעד למוצאי שבת תולין בדם בתולים היכא דעבר ובעל: והא אמר ר' אבא אבל חייב בכל המצות כו'. ואביי סבר דטירדא דליכא מצוה כלל מחייב אבל טירדא דלא מצי בעיל חשיב טירדא דמצוה כיון שטרוד במה שאינו יכול לעשות מצוה:

חוץ מן התפילין שנאמר בהן פאר. ואמרינן בפרק בתרא דמועד קטן (דף טו.) מדאמר ליה רחמנא ליחזקאל פארך חבוש עליך מכלל דלעלמא אסור ובקונטרס דפי' שנאמר בהן פאר ואבל מעולל בעפר קרנו ולאו היינו טעמא דלא נילף שאר מצות מתפילין וא"ת ומאי שנא גבי תפילין אמרינן דדוקא ליחזקאל נאמר ולא לשאר אבלים וגבי תלמוד תורה ילפינן שאר אבלים מיחזקאל דאמרינן (שם) אבל אסור בתלמוד תורה מדאמר ליה רחמנא ליחזקאל האנק דום וי"ל דלאסור גמרינן דמדאסר רחמנא ליחזקאל לכ"ע נמי אסור אבל להתיר לא גמרינן דליה לחודיה למשרי אתא: והני תנאי כי הני תנאי. אע"ג דפליגי תנאי בהדיא בהכי מכל מקום דחיק אביי לעיל לאשוויי טירדא דמצוה הא דלא מצי בעיל דניחא ליה לאוקמי מתני' כשמואל דאסר לבעול ומוקי נמי פלוגתא דברייתא אי חשיב טירדא הא דלא מצי בעיל כדי לאוקמי כשמואל כל מה שיכול: לא כהללו בבליים שאין בקיאין בהטייה. פירוש אינו פסיק רישיה דכל העולם אינן כמו בבליים אלא בקיאין הן הילכך שרי להו למיבעל ובלבד שלא יתכוונו לבעול בעילה גמורה ופריך אם כן טורד למה פירוש בשבת אמאי פטור ליה לעיל מק"ש כיון דבקיאין הן בשלמא בחול איכא טירדא לפי שמתכוין לבעול בעילה גמורה ואף לבקיאין יש טירדא לבעול בעילה גמורה כדאמר בפרק שני דברכות (דף טז. ושם) דר"ג היה פטור ומחמיר על עצמו אע"ג דבקי היה שלא היה בבלי אבל בשבת שאינו מתכוין לבעול בעילה גמורה טורד למה ומשני לשאינו בקי לפי שאינו בקי בשעת ק"ש דאפי' הבקיאין בשעת מעשה קודם מעשה יראים שלא יהיו בקיאין הילכך טרודים כולם: רוב בקיאין הן. וכל חד וחד מספקינן ליה ברוב וכולם מותרים משמע הכא דרובן בקיאין בהטייה וא"ת דאמרינן בפ"ב דחגיגה (דף יד: ושם) בתולה שעיברה מהו לכהונה כגון שבדקוה על פי חבית ולא היה ריחה נודף מי חיישינן לדשמואל דאמר יכולני לבעול כמה בעילות בלא דם או דלמא באמבטי עיברה ומסיק דשמואל לא שכיח ובפרק בתרא דנדה (דף סד: ושם) נמי קאמר שאני שמואל דרב גובריה הוא והא אמרינן הכא דרוב בקיאין הן וי"ל דשמואל היה יכול לבעול בעילה גמורה שאשה מתעברת בו בלא דם אבל בהטייה אין אשה מתעברת ולהכי בההיא דחגיגה ליכא למיחש בהטייה אלא לדשמואל: אלא מעתה שושבינין למה מפה למה. פי' בקונטרס כיון שהן בקיאין לבעול בלא דם שמא יטה והיא לא תסיק אדעתה שהטה ומשני לשושבינין ומפה הם שאם לא יטה ויבעול בעילה גמורה ויאבד המפה ואם יטה ויאמר שלא מצא לה בתולים יכולה לומר עדיין בתולה אני וקשה לר"י דאינו מתרץ ממה שהקשה לו דהוי ליה לשנויי דמסקא אדעתה לומר עדיין בתולה אני ועיקר התירוץ חסר מן הספר ונראה לר"י כפירוש ר"ת דדוקא משבת קא פריך דמפה ושושבינין למה דצריך לבעול בהטייה למעשה בכל יום שעושין שושבינין אפילו בשבת ומשני שמא יארע שלא יטה ויבעול בעילה גמורה ויאבד דם בתולים והויא דומיא דטורד למה דפריך נמי משבת: אם לעשות לה פה חייב. דפתח זה עשויה להכנים ולהוציא להכניס אויר ולהוציא ליחה: ואם להוציא ממנה ליחה פטור. בפרק שמונה שרצים (שבת דף קז: ושם) מוקמינן לה כרבי שמעון וסלקא דעתיה דרבי אמי דמותיב דדם מיפקד פקיד ולדם הוא צריך ולא לפתח ואפ"ה אסר שמואל כרבי שמעון דהוי מלאכה שאינה צריכה לגופה ולהכי פריך ממפיס מורסא דכי היכי דלהוציא ממנה ליחה פטור וקיימא לן דפטור ומותר כיון דאינו צריך לפתח אף על גב דשאר מלאכה שאינה צריכה לגופה פטור אבל אסור במורסא שרי משום צער הכא נמי משום מצוה הוי לן למשרי ועוד אפילו שרינן משום צערא טפי ממשום מצוה כדפירש ר"ת לעיל פריך שפיר דהכא ודאי דהוי פסיק רישיה לענין פתח אי לאו משום צערא היה אסור אבל

גבי

עין משפט נר מצוה

כג א מיי' פ"ד מהל' ק"ש הל' א סמג עשין יח טוש"ע א"ח סי' ע סעי' ג:
כד ב מיי' פ"ד מהל' תפילין הל' יג ופ"ד מהל' אבילות הל' ט סמג עשין דרבנן ב טוש"ע א"ח סימן לח סעי' ה וטוש"ע יו"ד סי' שפח סעי' א:
כה ג מיי' פ"י מהל' שבת הל' יז סמג לאוין סה טוש"ע א"ח סי' שכח סעי' כח:

לעזי רש"י

קלו"ג. פירוש מורסא, נפח, בושה (מוסף הערוך ערך מורסא):

ליקוטי רש"י

חתן פטור מקריאת שמע. דלא מחשיב להסיר דעתו ממחשבת מצוה דבעילה שבשבילו זו הבאה עליו אלא יעסק בה ויתן לבו להיות נקי בדבר. דטריד דבעי למיבעל. שכן טורד במחשבת בעילה [סוכה כה.]. אבל חייב בכל המצות וכו' חוץ מן התפילין וכו'. אף על פי שטרוד בצער חייב בכל המצות חוץ מן התפילין שנאמר בהם פאר ליחזקאל פארך חבוש עליך וגו' וכיון דכתיב ביה לאבל מתגולל בעפר אין זה פאר [ברכות יא.]. ואבל לאו כדבר הוא ובמתעסק מלאכה בעצמו שאינו אבל [סוכה שם]. מאן חכמים. כלומר מאן ניהו מאן עמהיו [גיטין כ:]. המפיס. מנקע. מורסא. קיטור"א. אם לעשות לה פה. בתוספתא תני הרי אם לנקותה ולעשות לה פה כדרך שהרופאים עושין דמתקן לה פתח. חייב. משום בונה פתח או משום מתקן כלי מה לי לתקן כבה מה לי לתקן כלי. ואם להוציא ממנה ליחה. של עכשיו ואינו חושש אם תחזור ותסתום מיד [שבת קז.].

מסורת הש"ס

א) נדה סד:, ג) ברכות טז., ג) סוכה כה. ברכות יא. טז: מו"ק טו. ע"ש [שמחות פ"ו], ד) [עירובין פג. וש"נ], ה) [לעיל ה: וש"נ], ו) שבת קז. ושם. עדיות פרק ב משנה ה, ז) נ"ל בהערלותיו. יעב"ץ, ח) נ"י כ"י, ט) נ"י כ"י.

גליון הש"ס

רש"י ד"ה חייב וכו' דאשכחן בנין בבע"ח. שבת לה ע"א:

תורה אור השלם

א) הֵאָנֵק דֹּם מֵתִים אֵבֶל לֹא תַעֲשֶׂה פְּאֵרְךָ חֲבוֹשׁ עָלֶיךָ וּנְעָלֶיךָ תָּשִׂים בְּרַגְלֶיךָ וְלֹא תַעְטֶה עַל שָׂפָם וְלֶחֶם אֲנָשִׁים לֹא תֹאכֵל: [יחזקאל כד, יז]

Rav Chisda explains how this Mishnah poses a challenge to Shmuel's view that cohabitation with a virgin is forbidden on the Sabbath:

מַאי לָאו – **Is [the Mishnah] not** implying דְּאִי לֹא בָּעַל – **that if he did not** yet successfully **cohabit** with her, מָצֵי בָּעִיל אֲפִילּוּ בְּשַׁבָּת – **he may cohabit** with her **even on the Sabbath?**[1]

Rava offers an answer:

אָמַר רָבָא – **Rava said:** לֹא לְבַר מִשַּׁבָּת – **No!** It means only that he may cohabit with her on nights **other than the Sabbath.**[2]

Abaye objects to this answer:

אָמַר לֵיהּ אַבָּיֵי – **Abaye said [to Rava]:** וְהָא עַד מוֹצָאֵי שַׁבָּת אַרְבָּעָה לֵילוֹת קָתָנֵי – **But the Mishnah states:** We give her UNTIL SATURDAY NIGHT, for a total of FOUR NIGHTS. The language of the Mishnah implies that he may cohabit with her on all four nights, including Friday night! – ? –

Rava concedes the point, and offers a different answer:

אֶלָּא אָמַר רָבָא – **Rather, Rava said:** כְּשֶׁבָּעַל – The Mishnah, in fact, refers to a case **where he had** full **intercourse** on the first night; consequently, he is permitted to cohabit on Friday night, since the hymen was already fully ruptured.[3]

The Gemara raises an objection:

אִי כְּשֶׁבָּעַל – **If he already had** full **intercourse** with her prior to the Sabbath מַאי קָא מַשְׁמַע לַן – then of **what** novel point is **[the Mishnah] informing us** by emphasizing that the four nights continue "until Saturday night"?[4]

The Gemara answers:

קָא מַשְׁמַע לַן דְּשָׁרֵי לְמִיבְעַל בְּשַׁבָּת – **It is informing us that** – once the hymen is fully ruptured – **it is permitted to cohabit on the Sabbath,** even though further bleeding may result, כִּדְשְׁמוּאֵל – **as Shmuel said.** דְּאָמַר שְׁמוּאֵל – **For Shmuel said:** פִּירְצָה דְּחוּקָה מוּתָּר לִיכָּנֵס בָּהּ בְּשַׁבָּת – **It is permitted to enter a tight breach on the Sabbath** וְאַף עַל פִּי שֶׁמַּשִּׁיר צְרוֹרוֹת – **even though it dislodges pebbles.**[5]

The Gemara continues to challenge Shmuel's view that it is forbidden to cohabit with a virgin on the Sabbath:

מֵתִיב רַב יוֹסֵף – **Rav Yosef challenged it** from the following Mishnah:[6] חָתָן פָּטוּר מִקְּרִיַּת שְׁמַע לַיְלָה הָרִאשׁוֹן עַד מוֹצָאֵי שַׁבָּת – A GROOM who marries a virgin IS EXEMPT FROM THE *SHEMA* RECITAL from THE FIRST NIGHT of his marriage UNTIL SATURDAY NIGHT אִם לֹא עָשָׂה מַעֲשֶׂה – IF HE DID NOT yet PERFORM THE ACT of cohabitation.[7] מַאי לָאו דִּטְרִיד דְּבָעֵי לְמִיבְעַל – The Mishnah implies that this exemption applies even on Friday night; but **is it** [the exemption] **not** based on the fact **that he is preoccupied because he wishes to cohabit** with her and is not sure if he will be successful in rupturing the hymen and completing the act? If so, this proves that one may cohabit with a virgin on the Sabbath! – ? –

The Gemara answers:

אָמַר לֵיהּ אַבָּיֵי – **Abaye said to him:** לֹא דִּטְרִיד דְּלֹא בָּעִיל – **No!** In fact, the groom may not cohabit; as for his exemption from reciting *Shema,* it is because **he is preoccupied** with the thought **that he has not** yet **cohabited;** that is, he is preoccupied with his failure to have completed the act on the previous nights![8]

Abaye's answer indicates that the groom's preoccupation exempts him even when it is not preparatory to performing a mitzvah.[9] Which leads to the following question:[10]

NOTES

1. Rav Chisda assumes that once full penetration is achieved, and the hymen ruptured completely, there can no longer be any basis on which to attribute bleeding during subsequent episodes of cohabitation to hymenal bleeding. Consequently, when the Mishnah states that we give her four nights following her wedding, during which we attribute any bleeding that follows cohabitation to hymenal bleeding, it must be speaking of a case in which the hymen was never fully ruptured during the first three nights; that is, of a case in which the husband did not, on the first three nights, achieve full penetration. Yet the Mishnah apparently allows cohabitation to take place on each of these four nights, even though one of these nights is Friday night, and even though – inasmuch as the hymen was never fully ruptured – hymenal bleeding will most likely occur. This would seem to prove that it is permitted to cause hymenal bleeding on the Sabbath (*Shitah Mekubetzes,* explaining *Rashi*; *Rashba*; cf. *Tosafos*).

2. That is, he may cohabit with her – and attribute any consequent bleeding to hymenal bleeding – until the last of four nights has passed, i.e. until Saturday night; he may not, however, do so on Friday night (*Ritva*).

3. Rava takes issue with Rav Chisda's basic assumption and posits that even if the groom achieved full penetration on the first night, rupturing the hymen completely, he may still continue to attribute any bleeding that follows cohabitation on the subsequent three nights to further bleeding of the hymen. It is of such a case that the Mishnah speaks (see *Rashba*; *Shitah Mekubetzes*).

4. If the Mishnah means only to teach us that the hymen may continue to bleed for four nights after it is ruptured, why does it have to emphasize that these four nights conclude on Saturday night? Obviously, the Mishnah wishes to allude to the fact that these four nights include Friday night, thereby informing us that he may even cohabit with her on the Sabbath. But if, as Rava maintains, the hymen was already fully ruptured before the Sabbath, what is the novelty in this? (*Rashi*).

5. Shmuel is saying, allegorically, that even after full penetration and rupturing of the hymen it is possible that subsequent acts of cohabitation will cause further hymenal bleeding [indeed, it is for this reasoning that for the first four nights any bleeding that occurs is not ascribed to menstruation] but we do not allow this [unlikely] possibility to bar him from having intercourse on the Sabbath. [It is this novelty that the Mishnah conveys by emphasizing that the four nights of hymenal bleeding include Friday night] (*Rashi*).

6. *Berachos* 16a.

7. That is, a groom is exempt from reciting the *Shema* until the fourth night after his wedding (regarding whether he is exempt on the fourth night itself, see *Shitah Mekubetzes* ד״ה מאי לאו), or until he cohabits with his bride – whichever comes first – because his thoughts are preoccupied with the mitzvah of procreation in which he is about to engage (see *Rambam, Commentary* to *Berachos* 2:5). This exemption is based on the principle: הָעוֹסֵק בְּמִצְוָה פָּטוּר מִן הַמִּצְוָה, *one who is occupied with one mitzvah is exempt from [performing] a [second] mitzvah* (see *Berachos* 11a for the Biblical source for this principle).

The exemption, however, applies only to someone who marries a virgin (see *Berachos* 16a), since the exemption is based on the groom's preoccupation and concern with his ability to rupture the hymen and complete the marital act successfully, without injury to himself (see *Rashi* ד״ה טורד למה; *Rashba* ד״ה ה״ג; *Shitah Mekubetzes* ד״ה ובשיטה ישנה and ד״ה וכן כתב הריטב״א; *Rashi* to *Berachos* 11a ד״ה ובלכתך בדרך and to *Succah* 25a ד״ה ובלכתך and ד״ה חתן טריד; see also *Rabbeinu Yonah* and *Meiri* to 16a; cf. *Rambam, Krias Shema* 4:1; see also *Rav* and *Tos. Yom Tov* to *Berachos* 2:5).

Once four nights have passed he is no longer exempt, even if he has not yet cohabited with her, since we assume that he has already become accustomed to his situation (*Radvaz,* cited by *Shitah Mekubetzes*; cf. *Rashba*; see also *Rambam, Hil. Krias Shema* 4:1).

[According to *Machzor Vitri* (§466) the exemption applies only to recital of *Shema* before going to sleep; a groom is, however, obligated to recite the *Shema* of the morning and evening services. Most authorities, however, assume that the exemption applies at least to the *Shema* that is recited with the evening service; regarding whether it extends also to the morning *Shema,* see *Rambam,* ibid. with *Kesef Mishneh*; *Beis Yosef, Orach Chaim* §70. Regarding whether the exemption extends to other mitzvos besides the recitation of *Shema,* see *Succah* 25b-26a with *Rashi, Baal HaMaor and Milchamos*; *Rambam* ibid. with *Kesef Mishneh* and *Kiryas Melech* ibid., Kafich ed. Regarding the disuse into which this exemption has fallen in present times see *Orach Chaim* 70:3.]

8. See *Rashi*; *Shitah Mekubetzes* ד״ה והא; cf. *Tosafos.*

9. [Since on Friday night the groom will not cohabit, and yet he is exempt merely because of his preoccupation with his failure to do so on the previous evenings.]

10. See ibid. ד״ה אלא.

מאי לאו דאי לא בעל מצי בעיל אפילו בשבת אמר רבא לא לבר משבת אמר ליה אביי והא עד מוצאי שבת ארבעה לילות קתני אלא אמר רבא כשבעל אי כשבעל מאי קמ"ל קמ"ל דשרי למיבעל בשבת כדשמואל דאמר שמואל [א] פירצה דחוקה מותר ליכנס בה בשבת ואע"פ שמשיר צרורות מתיב רב יוסף [ב] א חתן פטור מקרית שמע לילה הראשון עד מוצאי שבת אם לא עשה מעשה מאי לאו דטריד דבעי למיבעל אמר ליה אביי לא דטריד דלא בעיל אמר ליה רבא ומשום טירדא פטור אלא מעתה טבעה ספינתו בים הכי נמי דפטור וכי תימא ה"נ והאמר רבי אבא בר זבדא אמר רב [ג] אבל חייב בכל המצות האמורות בתורה חוץ מן ב התפילין שנא' בהן א) פאר אלא אמר רבא תנאי היא דתנא חדא אם לא עשה מעשה בראשון פטור אף בשני בשני פטור אף בשלישי ותניא אידך ראשון ושני פטור שלישי חייב ואביי התם נמי בטירדא פליגי והני תנאי כי הני תנאי דתניא הכונס את הבתולה לא יבעול בתחלה בשבת וחכמים מתירין [ד] מאן חכמים אמר רבה רבי שמעון היא [ה] דאמר דבר שאין מתכוין מותר אמר ליה אביי והא מודה ר' שמעון בפסיק רישיה ולא ימות אמר ליה לא כהללו בבליים שאין בקיאין בהטייה אלא יש בקיאין בהטייה א"כ טורד למה לשאינו בקי יאמרו בקי מותר שאינו בקי אסור רוב בקיאין הן אמר ליה רבא בר רב חנן לאביי אלא מעתה שושבינין למה מפה למה א"ל התם שמא יראה ויאבד מתיב רבי אמי [ו] ג המפים מורסא בשבת אם לעשות לה פה חייב ואם להוציא ממנה ליחה פטור

מאי לאו. הנך ארבעה לילות עד מוצאי שבת דקתני להכי תני להו דאי לא בעל בעילה גמורה מצי למיבעל וכל דם שהוא מוצא תמיד [ז] בהערותיו הוו דם בתולים ושמעינן מינה נמי דמותר לבעול בתחלה בשבת: והא ארבעה לילות עד מוצאי שבת קתני. ולא משכחת ליה לבר משבת דהא ברביעי נכנסת ויש כאן לילי חמישי וששי ושבת ומוצאי שבת: אי כשבעל. ולא אתא לאורויי לן אלא היתר דם בתולים האי דנקט עד מוצאי שבת מאי קמ"ל ליתני נותנין לה ארבעה לילות על כרחך משום בעילת שבת נקט לה: שמשיר צרורות. והאי נמי דלמא מחבל פורתא ומספיקא לא אסרינן ליה: מאי לאו. האי דפטר ליה מק"ש בלילי שבת משום דטריד במצוה דבעי למיבעל והעוסק במצוה פטור מן המצוה: דטריד דלא בעיל. מלטער שלא בעל: משום דטריד פטור. בתמיה ומשום לער פטור מאחר שאינו מחשב לעסוק במצוה: שנאמר בהן פאר. פארך חבוש עליך (יחזקאל כד) ואבל מעולל בעפר קרנו וראשו ואין זה פאר לתפילין: [ח] [אלא אמר רבא. ודאי לא מיית לתרוצי הא דחתן פטור מק"ש משום דלא מצי בעיל דא"כ לא הוה פטור דהא לא טריד בדבר מצוה: תנאי היא. בעילת תחלה בשבת ומאן דאסר לבעול בשבת כתנאי אמרה למתניתיה דאיכא תנא אחרינא דאסר למיבעל דתנא חדא כו']: פטור. מקרית שמע: שלישי חייב. דשבת הוא ואסור לבעול: ואביי. אמר לך הנך תנאי נמי בטירדא פליגי והאי דפטר ליה מק"ש לאו משום דשרי למיבעל אלא קסבר המצטער לער של מצוה פטור מקריאת שמע ולא דמי לאבל דטריד טירדא דרשות שאין לערו מצוה אע"פ שאבילותו מצוה ומאן דמחייב סבר טירדא לא פטר [ט] [ורבנא אמר דבמותר לבעול פליגי והני תנאי כהני תנאי]: בהטייה. שמטין לצדדין ואין מוציאים דם: אם כן. דבקיאים: טורד למה. מהו טרדו להפטר מק"ש: בקי מותר. לבעול בשבת דלא פסיק רישיה ולא ימות הוא: רוב בקיאין הן. הילכך סתמא לאו פסיק רישיה ולא ימות הוא: שושבינין למה. מאחר שיש בקיאין לבעול בלא דם הא דתניא לקמן (דף יב.) היו מעמידין להן שני שושבינין אחד לו ואחד לה כדי למשמש את החתן ואת הכלה כלומר לבקר אחריהם שלא יהגו בה רמאות בטענת בתולים ואי בקיאין בהטייה מה שושבינין מועילין: מפה למה. לבדר את הבתולים. וליטעמיך ל"ג אלא ה"ג שושבינין למה מפה למה: אמר ליה שמא יראה ויאבד. שמא לא יטה ויוליא דם ויאבדנו ויאמר לא מצאתי דם דאולי בהטייה אם לא לטעון תאמר לו עדיין בתולה אני: המפים מורסא. הפותח פה נפח שקורין קלו"ג: אם לעשות לה פה. שמתכוין ליפותה ולהיות לה פתח זה ליום מחר: חייב. שהוא מתקן פתח וחייב משום בונה [ש] דאשכחן בנין בבעלי חיים דכתיב ויבן את הצלע (בראשית ב):

מאי קמ"ל. במאי דנקט עד מוצאי שבת דלענין רצופים ליכא למימר כדפרישית: מאי לאו דטריד דבעי למיבעל. הכא ליכא לשנויי לבר משבת כדלעיל דא"כ אינו פטור עד מוצאי שבת וקא משמע ליה לתנא טובא דפטר ליה עד מוצאי שבת אבל לעיל אפילו כי אמרינן לבר משבת ולא מצי למיבעל בשבת מכל מקום דוקא נקט עד מוצאי שבת משום דעד למוצאי שבת תולין דדם בתולים היכא דעבר ובעל: והא אמר ר' אבא אבל חייב בכל המצות כו'. ואביי סבר דטירדא דליכא מצוה כלל מחייב אבל טירדא דלא מצי בעיל חשיב טירדא דמצוה כיון שטרוד במה שאינו יכול לעשות מצוה: חוץ מן התפילין שנאמר בהן פאר. ואמרינן בפרק בתרא דמועד קטן (דף טו.) מדאמר ליה רחמנא ליחזקאל פארך חבוש עליך מכלל דלעלמא אסור ובקונטרס פי' שנאמר בהן פאר ואבל מעולל בעפר קרנו וראשו היינו ליתן טעם דלא נילף שאר מצות מתפילין וא"ת ומאי שנא לגבי תפילין אמרינן דדוקא ליחזקאל נאמר ולא לשאר אבלים וגבי תלמוד תורה ילפינן שאר אבלים מיחזקאל דאמרינן (שם) אבל אסור בתלמוד תורה מדאמר ליה רחמנא ליחזקאל האנק דום וי"ל דלא לומר דלאסור גמרינן דמדאסר רחמנא ליחזקאל לכ"ע נמי אסור אבל להתיר לא גמרינן דליה לחודיה למשרי אתא: והני תנאי כי הני תנאי. אע"ג דפליגי תנאי בהדיא בהכי מכל מקום דחיק אביי לעיל לחשיב טירדא דמצוה הא דלא מצי בעיל דניחא ליה לאוקמי מתני' כשמואל דאסר לבעול ומוקי נמי פלוגתא דברייתא אי חשיב טירדא הא דלא מצי בעיל כדי לאוקמי כשמואל כל מה שיכול: לא כהללו בבליים שאין בקיאין בהטייה. פירוש אינו פסיק רישיה דכל העולם אין כמו בבליים אלא בקיאין הן הילכך שרי להו למיבעל ובלבד שלא יתכוונו לבעול בעילה גמורה ופריך אם כן טורד למה פירוש בשבת דאמאי פטור ליה לעיל מק"ש כיון דבקיאין הן בשלמא בחול איכא טירדא לפי שמתכוין לבעול בעילה גמורה ואף לבקיאין יש טירדא לבעול בעילה גמורה כדאמר בפרק שני דברכות (דף טז. ושם) דר"ג היה פטור ומחמיר על עצמו אע"ג דבקי היה שלא היה בבלי אבל בשבת שאינו מתכוין לבעול בעילה גמורה טורד למה ומשני לשאינו בקי פי' שאינו בקי בשעת ק"ש דאפי' הבקיאין בשעת מעשה קודם מעשה יראים שלא יהיו בקיאין הילכך טרודים כולם: רוב בקיאין הן. וכל חד וחד מספקינן ליה ברוב וכולם מותרים משמע הכא דרובן בקיאין בהטייה וא"ת דאמרינן בפ"ב דחגיגה (דף יד: ושם) בתולה שעיברה מהו לכהונה כגון שבדקוה על פי חבית ולא היה ריחה נודף מי חיישינן לדשמואל דאמר יכולני לבעול כמה בעילות בלא דם או דלמא דשמואל לא שכיח ומסיק דשמואל לא שכיח ובפרק בתרא דנדה (דף סד: ושם) נמי קאמר שאני שמואל דרב גובריה הוא והא אמרינן הכא דרוב בקיאין הן וי"ל דשמואל היה יכול לבעול בעילה גמורה ששה מתעברת בו בלא דם אבל בהטייה אין אשה מתעברת ולהכי בהטייה לחגיגה ליכא למיחש בהטייה אלא לדשמואל: אלא מעתה שושבינין למה מפה למה. פי' בקונטרס כיון שהן בקיאין לבעול בלא דם שמא יטה והיא לא תפסיק לדעתה שהטה ומשני דשושבינין ומפה הם שאם לא יטה ויבעול בעילה גמורה ויאבד המפה ואם יטה ויאמר שלא מצא לה בתולים יכולה לומר עדיין בתולה אני וקשה לר"י דאינו מתרץ מה שהקשה לו דהוי ליה לשנויי דמסקא לדעתה לומר עדיין בתולה אני ועיקר התירוץ חסר מן הספר ונראה לר"י כפירוש ר"ת דלדוקא קא פריך משבת מפה ושושבינין למה לצריך לבעול בהטייה דמעשה בכל יום שעושין שושבינין אפילו בשבת ומשני שמא יראה שלא יטה ויבעול בעילה גמורה ויאבד דם בתולים והוא דומיא דטורד למה דפריך נמי משבת: אם לעשות לה פה חייב. דפתח זה עשוי להכניס ולהוציא להכניס אויר ולהוציא ליחה: ואם להוציא ממנה ליחה פטור. בפרק שמונה שרצים (שבת דף קז: ושם) מוקמינן לה כרבי שמעון וסלקא דעתיה דרבי אמי דמותיב דדם מיפקד פקיד ולדם הוא דצריך ולא לפתח ואפ"ה אסר שמואל כרבי שמעון דהוי מלאכה שאינה צריכה לגופה ולהכי פריך ממפים מורסא דכי היכי דלהוציא ממנה ליחה פטור ומותר כיון דאינו צריך לפתח אף על גב דעשה מלאכה שאינה צריכה לגופה פטור אבל אסור הכא נמי גבי מורסא שרי משום צער אבל הכא לא הוה משום צער ועוד אפילו שרינן משום צערא טפי ממשום מצוה כדפירש ר"ת לעיל פריך שפיר דהכא ודאי דהוי פסיק רישיה לענין פתח אי לאו משום צערא היה אסור אבל

גבי

עין משפט נר מצוה

כג א מיי' פ"ד מהל' ק"ש הל' א סמג עשין יח טוש"ע א"ח סי' ע סעי' ג:

כד ב מיי' פ"ד מהל' תפילין הל' יג ופ"ד מהל' אבילות הל' ט סמג עשין דרבנן ב טוש"ע א"ח סימן לח סעי' ה וטוש"ע יו"ד סי' שפח סעי' א:

כה ג מיי' פ"י מהל' שבת הל' יח סמג לאוין סה טוש"ע או"ח סי' שכח סעי' מח:

לעזי רש"י

קלו"ג. פירוש מורסא, נפח, בועה (מוסף הערוך ערך מורסא):

ליקוטי רש"י

חתן פטור מקרית שמע. דלא מיחייב להסיר דעתו מכחשבת מלוה ראשונה בשביל זו הבאה עליו שלא יבעול בראשונה ויתן לבו להיות בקי בדבר. דטריד דבעי למיבעל. לבו טרוד במחשבת בעילה [סוכה כה.]. אבל חייב בכל המצות וכו' חוץ מן התפילין וכו'. אף על פי שטרוד בלערו חייב בכל המלות חוץ מן התפילין שנאמר בהם פאר ליחזקאל פארך חבוש עליך וגו' וכיון דבכו פאר ואבל מתגולל בלערו בעפר אין זה פאר [ברכות יא.]. ואבל לאו בר פאר הוא וכשמתפאר מראה בעצמו שאינו אבל [סוכה שם]. מאן חכמים. כלומר מאן ניהו ומאי טעמייהו [גיטין כב.]. המפים. מבקע. מורסא. קויטר"א אם לעשות לה פה. בתוספתא תני הכי אם לקולפה ולעשות לה פה כדרך שרופאים של עכשיו עושין דמתקן לה פתח. חייב. משום בונה פתח או משום מתקן כלי מה לי לפקן מכה מה לי לתקן כלי ואם להוציא ממנה ליחה. של עכשיו ואינו חושש אם תחזור ותסתום מיד [שבת קז.].

מסורת הש"ס

א) נדה סד:, ב) ברכות טז., ג) סוכה כה. ברכות יא. טז: מו"ק טו. ע"ש [שמחות פ"ו], ד) [עירובין פג. וש"נ], ה) [לעיל ה: וש"נ], ו) שבת קז. ושם: עדיות פרק ב משנה ה, ז) נ"ל בהערותיו. יעב"ך, ח) כ"י כ"י, ט) כ"י כ"י.

גליון הש"ס

רש"י ד"ה חייב וכו' דאשכחן בנין בבע"ח. שבת לה ע"א:

תורה אור השלם

א) הֵאָנֵק דֹּם מֵתִים אֵבֶל לֹא תַעֲשֶׂה פְּאֵרְךָ חֲבוֹשׁ עָלֶיךָ וּנְעָלֶיךָ תָּשִׂים בְּרַגְלֶיךָ וְלֹא תַעְטֶה עַל שָׂפָם וְלֶחֶם אֲנָשִׁים לֹא תֹאכֵל: [יחזקאל כד, יז]

או הלכה כר"ש א) (איתמר) בבי רב אמרי רב שרי ושמואל אסר בנהרדעא אמרי רב אסר ושמואל שרי אמר רב נחמן בר יצחק וסימניך אלו מקילין לעצמן ואלו מקילין לעצמן ורב שרי ב) והאמר רב שימי בר חזקיה משמיה דרב *האי מסוכריא דנזייתא אסור להדוקה ביומא טבא בההוא אפילו ר"ש מודה דאביי ורבא דאמרי תרוייהו מודה ר"ש ג) בפסיק רישיה ולא ימות והא אמר רב חייא בר אשי אמר רב הלכה כרבי יהודה ורב חנן בר אמי אמר שמואל הלכה כרבי שמעון ורב חייא בר אבין מתני לה בלא גברי רב אמר הלכה כר' יהודה ושמואל אמר הלכה כרבי שמעון לעולם רב כרבי יהודה סבירא ליה להך לישנא דאמר דם מיפקד פקיד מקלקל הוא אצל הפתח ולהך לישנא דאמר דם חבורי מיחבר מקלקל בחבורה הוא מתיב רב חסדא ד) תינוקת שלא הגיע זמנה לראות ונשאת ב"ש אומרים נותנין לה ארבעה לילות וב"ה אומרים ב עד שתחיה המכה הגיע זמנה לראות ונשאת בש"א נותנין לה לילה הראשון ובית הלל אומרים עד מוצאי שבת ג ארבעה לילות מאי

רש"י

או הלכה כר"ש. דמקלקל בחבורה חייב כיון דמימלי לומר הלכה כר' יהודה בדבר שאין מתכוין לאסור: **בנהרדעא.** מקומו של שמואל: **וסימניך.** שלא תטעה להחליף שמעתתא דבי רב לנהרדעא ודנהרדעא לדבי רב: **אלו מקילין לעצמן.** דבי רב שצריכים לעשות כדברי רבן אומרים שרבן התיר והנהרדעא העושים כשמואל רבן אומרים שמואל התיר: **ורב שרי.** בתמיה אלמא דבר שאין מתכוין מותר סבירא ליה: **מסוכריא דנזייתא.** סתימת נקב גיגית שמוציאין השכר לדרך הנקב וסותמין אותו בבלאי בגדים: **אסור להדוקה.** משום סחיטה: **מודה ר"ש כו'.** אבל כאן יש שבקיאים בסטייה כדלקמן: **הלכה כרבי יהודה.** דאין מתכוין: **בלא גברי.** בלא אמוראי אליבא דרב ואליבא דשמואל אלא רב ושמואל גופייהו: **להך לישנא דאמרת דם מיפקד פקיד.** והאיסור משום פתח הוא: **מקלקל הוא אצל הפתח.** ומקלקל מודה רבי יהודה: **מקלקל בחבורה הוא.** ורב סבר לה כרבי יהודה אף במקלקל בחבורה לקולא דקא פטר בה רבי יהודה: **שלא הגיע זמנה לראות.** במסכת נדה אמר אימתי הגיע זמנה לראות משיגיעו ימי הנעורים: **נותנין לה ארבעה לילות.** שכל דמים שתראה בהן מחמת תשמיש מחזיקין להו בדם בתולים: **עד שתחיה המכה.** כל זמן שאינה משמשת בלא דם לא חיתה המכה: **הגיע זמנה לראות.** ולא ראתה: **לילה הראשון.** אפילו לבעילות הרבה:

מאי

תוספות

במקלקל משום דטעם שניהם דפטורין בשאר מלאכות שבת הוי משום דבעינן מלאכת מחשבת אבל שאינו מתכוין כלל למלאכה לא משום דבעינן מלאכת מחשבת מיפטר דהא בשאר מקומות נמי מיפטר אין מתכוין כגון גבי כלאים דמוכרי כסות מוכרין כדרכן ובלבד שלא יתכוין כו' (כלאים פ"ט מ"ה) ותנן נמי נזיר חופף ומפספס כו' (נזיר דף מב.) הילכך בחבורה נמי שרי:

האי מסוכרייתא דנזייתא אסור להדוקה כו'. פירש בקונטרס וכן ר"ח ובערוך ו) בלא לישנא וכן בכלר תנאים ואמוראים דאסור משום סחיטה וקשה לר"ת דהא סחיטה משום ליבון ולא שייכא בשאר משקים דלכל דבר המלכלך את בולעו כגון יין ושכר ושמן לא שייך ליבון בסחיטתו אלא דוקא במים וראיה לדבר מדלא גזרינן בהו שמא יסחוט כמו גבי מים כדאמרינן בהלו קשרים (שבת דף קיג:) היה מהלך בשבת ופגע באמת המים כו' היכי ליעביד ליגחות במיא אתי לידי סחיטה ותניא נמי בפרק חבית (שם דף קמז:) ומסתפג באלונטית ולא יביאה בידו ומפרש בגמ' דאתי לידי סחיטה ובפ"ב דביצה (דף יח. ושם) אומר דלכ"ע אין מטבילין את הכלים ומפרש בגמרא גזירה משום סחיטה ואילו בפרק תולין (שבת דף קלט:) תנן מסננין את היין בסודרין אלמא לגבי יין לא גזרינן משום סחיטה וברים המביא (ביצה דף ל.) נמי קאמר ליפרוס סודרא עליה ולא קאמר אתי לידי סחיטה והיינו משום דלא שייך ליבון אלא גבי מים והא דאמרינן בפרק מפנין (שבת דף קכח:) אם היתה צריכה שמן חבירתה מביאה לה בשערה ופריך והא אתי לידי סחיטה ומשני אין סחיטה בשער משמע דשייך סחיטה בשמן וכן בפ' נוטל (שם דף קמג.) ספוג אם יש לו בית אחיזה מקנחין בו ואם לאו אין מקנחין בו משום דאתי לידי סחיטת שמן הנבלע בו ההיא סחיטה אור"ת דהויא משום מפרק ואסורה כמו סחיטת זיתים וענבים והכא אומר ר"ת דליכא למימר דאסור משום מפרק כיון שהנסחט הולך לאיבוד ז) אע"ג דהוי פסיק רישיה וכן פירש בערוך דכל פסיק רישיה דלא ניחא ליה שרי ועיקר ראייתו מפרק כל התדיר (זבחים דף לא: ושם) אליבא דר"ש מזלפין יין על גבי האישים אע"ג דפסיק רישיה הוא דודאי מכבה הוא כיון דלא ניחא ליה בהאי כיבוי שרי ועוד מייתי ראיה מלולב הגזול (סוכה דף לג: ושם) דקאמר ר"א בר"ש ממעטים ענבים בי"ט פי' ענבי הדס ופריך והא מתקן מנא ומוקים לה במתכוון לאכילה סבר לה כאבוה ופריך והא מודה ר"ש בפסיק רישיה כו' ומשני לא צריכא דאית ליה הושענא אחריתי אלמא כיון דלא ניחא ליה ולא חייש בהאי תיקון שרי אע"ג דפסיק רישיה הוא ונראה לר"י דלא קשה מידי דאיכא למימר דאסור לסחוט בשאר משקה משום ליבון כמו במים ומ"מ לא חיישינן בהו שמא יסחוט כיון שהטעם והריח נשארים בבגדים ומעט היה נהנה בסחיטתו ומצינן למימר נמי דאסור משום מפרק ואף ע"ג דהוי פסיק רישיה דלא ניחא ליה אסור לכתחילה לר"ש כמו במלאכה שאינה צריכה לגופה וראיות הערוך אינן ראיות דההיא דמתיר ר"ש לזלף יין על גבי האישים איכא למימר דמצוה שאני וכן ההיא דאית ליה הושענא אחריתי איכא למימר דשרי משום מצוה א"נ הכי פי' והא פסיק רישיה הוא דאית ליה הושענא אחריתי והואיל וכן שרי לר"ש דשמא לא יצטרך לה ונמצא שלא תיקן כלי והלכך לאו פסיק רישיה הוא אבל לר"י אסור דשמא יצטרך לה ואגלאי מילתא דכלי עבד ועל פי' הערוך קשה דתנן בפרק שמונה שרצים (שבת דף קז.) המפיס מורסא בשבת אם לעשות לה פה חייב ואם להוציא ממנה ליחה פטור ודוקא משום צערא פטור ומותר אבל אי לאו משום צערא היה אסור אע"ג דלא ניחא ליה בפה כלל דאי ניחא ליה מן הפה כי לא מתכוין נמי חייב וכן מחט של יד ליטול בה את הקוץ דשרי משום צערא אבל אי לאו הכי אסור אע"ג דלא ניחא ליה כלל אבל קצת קשה אי פסיק רישיה דלא ניחא ליה אסור אמאי קאמר רב בפרק חבית (שם קמה.) כבשים שסחטן לגופן פטור ומותר הואיל וא"צ למים היוצאין והשתא אע"ג דא"צ היה להיות אסור ואור"י דמצינן למימר דדוקא כבשים שרי דהוי הנסחט מהם כמו אוכלא דאיפרת ואין שם משקה עליו כדאמרינן דאפי' למימיהם פטור אבל אסור ועוד י"ל דכל דבר שאדם עושה במזיד לא שייך למימר שמא יסחוט דסברא הוא כיון דלדעת כן הוא עושה ולהכי גבי מסננין את היין לא חיישינן שמא יסחוט ואתיא שפיר האי דנדה מערמת וטובלת בבגדיה (ביצה דף יח.) וכן בפ"ח דיומא (דף עז:) ההולך להקביל פני רבו עובר עד צוארו במים ולא גזרינן שמא יסחוט לפי שלדעת כן הוא עושה ח) ועוד איכא למימר התם דמצוה שאני ובערוך פירש לשון אחר מסוכרייא דנזייתא סתימת גיגית של שכר אסור להדוקה דשמא תבטל הסתימה אצל הגיגית ויעשה כלי בשבת ואין נראה לר"י דהיכי דמי דאם בדעתו לבטל שם בשעת הנחה מאי פסיק רישיה שייך כאן מיד הוא עושה כלי דמתכוין לעשותו ואם אין בדעתו לבטלה שם א"כ לא הוי פסיק רישיה שיעשנה כלי וי"ל בדוחק שהוא מתכוין לבטלה ואינו מתכוין לעשות כלי ושייך ביה פסיק רישיה הואיל ואינו מתכוין לגמרי לעשות כלי ט): **לעולם** רב כר"י ס"ל כו'. לשמואל נמי איכא לשנויי לעולם כר"ש ס"ל להך לישנא דאמר דם מיפקד פקיד לפתח הוא צריך ולהך לישנא דאמר חבורי מחבר לדם הוא צריך: ט) **מאי** לאו דאי לא בעיל מצי בעיל. דלמאי נקט עד מוצאי שבת אי לאו דאתא לאשמועינן דמצי בעיל בשבת אע"ג דמשיר בתולים דליכא למימר דנקט עד מוצ"ש לאשמועי' דבעינן רצופין דהא לא בעינן שיהו רצופין כדתניא בפרק בתרא דנדה (דף סד: ושם) מעשה ונתן לה ד' לילות מתוך י"ב חדש והכי פי' נותנין לה ד' לילות עד מוצ"ש שיבעול בכל לילה וישיר מקצת בתולים עד מוצ"ש ואשמועינן דשרי להשיר בתולים בשבת ומשני לא לבר משבת ומוצאי שבת נקט לאשמועינן דבעינן רצופים והוה מצי למיפרך מברייתא דפרק בתרא דנדה דמוכח דאפי' מפוזרין אלא דפריך ליה מגופה דברייתא והא עד מוצאי שבת ארבעה לילות קתני וא"ת מעיקרא דמשני לבר משבת מה עלה בדעתו והא קתני בהדיא ד' לילות וי"ל דהוה ס"ד דהכי פירושו נותנין לה עד מוצאי שבת לבר משבת שהן בין הכל ד' לילות ואיהו פריך דמשמע דבעיל ד' לילות ומשני כשבעל וקמ"ל כמו שמפרש בתר הכי אע"ג דהוי פירצה דחוקה דהא אי חזיא תלינן בדם בתולין אפ"ה שרי:

מאי

עין משפט נר מצוה

כא א טוש"ע א"ח סימן שכ סעיף יח:

כב ב ג מיי' פ"ה מהל' איסורי ביאה הל' יח יט סמג לאוין קיא (טוש"ע אה"ע סימן סג סעיף א וטוש"ע י"ד סימן קצג סעיף א):

תוספות רי"ד

האי מסוכרייתא דנזייתא אסור להדוקה ביומא טבא ואפילו ר"ש מודה בהא דאביי ורבא דאמרי תרוייהו מודה ר"ש בפסיק רישי' ולא ימות. פי' המורה סתימת נקב גיגית שמוציאים ממנו השכר וסותמים אותו בבלאי בגדים אסור להדוקה משום סחיטה. ואינו נראה כלל שמה שמשימים בנקב שמוציא ממנו מים או יין בלאי בגדים אין בו משום סחיטה שאינו מוכנין לא ללבנם ולא לקבל ממנו משקה ולאיבוד אזיל א"כ אמאי ליתסר. ור' נתן בעל הערוך פי' משום ר"ח ז"ל מטלית שמשימים על הגיגית לסתום פי' (ומפרקת) [ומהדקה] המטלית שם וזהו פתרון יפה. דודאי באותו המטלית קפיד אם תשרה. א) ומה שסוחט ממנו אסור משום מלבן שדומה לסוחט בגדים שרויים. וזה שאנו משימין בברזא של חביות מתיר ר' נתן בפירוש מפני שהולך לאיבוד:

חשק שלמה על תוס' רי"ד

א) עי' בערוך ערך סבר ה' דפירש שם דלאסור משום סחיטה דניחא ליה שיזוב היין בתוך הכד ע"ש ומשמע דלאסור משום מפרק וצ"ע.

מסורת הש"ס

א) פ"א ל"ג, ב) שבת קיא. בכורות כה. [ע"ש], ג) שבת עה. קג. קיא: קז. קכ: קלג. קמג. בכורות כה. סוכה לג: [ביצה לו.], ד) נדה יא: סד:, ה) [ערך סבר], ו) [לע"ג דמלאכה שא"ל לגופה אסור לר"ש היכא דלא ניחא ליה כלל שרי טפי כ"ה הנוסחא בתשובת רא"מ סי' לד], ז) רש"ל גורס ומיהו, ח) [ועי' תוס' שבת מא: ד"ה מיחם], ט) שייך לע"ב.

ליקוטי רש"י

האי מסוכריא. בגד כורכין בברזא חבית של חרס מפני שאין הנקב שוה [שבת קיא.]. ברזא של חבית שכורכין סביבותיה נעורת [של פשתן] ומטלניות כדי [שיסתום פי] הנקב יפה [בכורות כה.]. **אסור להדוקה.** בנקב משום סחיטה ואף על גב דלא קא מכוין לסחוט אלמא לא ס"ל כר"ש בדבר שאין מתכוין [שבת שם]. בתוך החבית בכח משום סחיטה ואע"ג דאינו מתכוין לשום סחיטה אסור אפי' לר"ש דאמר במסכת שבת (דף מא:) דבר שאין מתכוין מותר [בכורות שם]. **מודה ר"ש בפסיק רישיה ולא ימות.** באומר אחתוך ראש בהמה זו בשבת ואיני רוצה שתמות דכיון דאי אפשר שלא תמות כמתכוין חשיב ליה וכי אמרינן דבר שאין מתכוין מותר כגון היכא דאפשר ליה בלא איסור כגון גורר אדם מטה כסא וספסל ובלבד שלא יתכוין לעשות חריץ ואף על גב דליכא למיחש דלמא עביד חריץ כיון דלא מתכוין להכי ואפשר לגרירה בלא חריץ כי עביד נמי חריץ דהוי מלאכה גמורה לא מיחייב אבל היכא דודאי עביד מודי [סוכה לג:]. וכיון דמהדק לה לא אפשר לה בלא סחיטה. **הלכה כרבי יהודה.** אלמא ס"ל לרב דבר שאין מתכוין אסור. **בלא גברי.** בלא רב חייא ורב חנן [בכורות שם]. **תינוקת וכו' נותנין לה ארבעה לילות.** לשמש ואפי' רואה אמרינן דם בתולים הוא [נדה סד:]. **המכה.** מכת בעילה דכל זמן שהמכה רואה דם מחמת תשמיש דם בתולים הוא [שם יא:]. **הגיע זמנה לראות.** ולא ראתה. **עד מוצאי שבת.** והיא ניסת ברביעי [שם סד:].

The Gemara proceeds to cite various Mishnahs that seem to contradict Shmuel's view that cohabiting with a virgin is forbidden on the Sabbath:[12]

מְתִיב רַב חִסְדָּא – **Rav Chisda challenged** this **from the** following **Mishnah:**[13] תִּינוֹקֶת שֶׁלֹּא הִגִּיעַ זְמַנָּהּ לִרְאוֹת וְנִשֵּׂאת – Concerning A YOUNG GIRL WHOSE TIME TO DISCHARGE blood HAS NOT ARRIVED[14] AND WHO MARRIED: בֵּית שַׁמַּאי אוֹמְרִים – BEIS SHAMMAI SAY: נוֹתְנִין לָהּ אַרְבָּעָה לֵילוֹת – WE GIVE HER FOUR NIGHTS of marital relations during which we deem her discharges *tahor.* וּבֵית הִלֵּל אוֹמְרִים – BUT BEIS HILLEL SAY: עַד שֶׁתִּחְיֶה הַמַּכָּה – We give her UNTIL THE WOUND HEALS.[15] הִגִּיעַ זְמַנָּהּ לִרְאוֹת וְנִשֵּׂאת – If HER TIME TO DISCHARGE blood HAS ARRIVED[16] AND SHE MARRIED, בֵּית שַׁמַּאי אוֹמְרִים – BEIS SHAMMAI SAY: נוֹתְנִין לָהּ לַיְלָה הָרִאשׁוֹן – WE GIVE HER THE FIRST NIGHT.[17] וּבֵית הִלֵּל אוֹמְרִים – BUT BEIS HILLEL SAY: עַד מוֹצָאֵי שַׁבָּת אַרְבָּעָה לֵילוֹת – We give her UNTIL SATURDAY NIGHT, for a total of FOUR NIGHTS.[18]

NOTES

cohabitation with a virgin on the Sabbath, even though he follows R' Shimon in allowing unintentional acts – either he maintains that the groom's primary intention is to create a passageway, or that his primary intention is to draw blood and that this blood is the result of a wound (*Tosafos* et al.).

12. As we have seen, the view that cohabitation with a virgin is forbidden on the Sabbath was championed by Shmuel, according to the version preserved in the academy of Rav, and by Rav, according to the version preserved in Nehardea. The objections that follow in the Gemara, however, are directed specifically at Shmuel. For Rav, who – in Nehardea's version – forbade such cohabitation, did so because he follows R' Yehudah's view that unintentional acts are forbidden; hence, he can simply ascribe any Mishnahs that seem to allow such cohabitation to R' Shimon, who allows unintentional acts. But when Shmuel – in the academy of Rav's version – forbade such cohabitation he did so even according to R' Shimon (whose view he follows) who allows unintentional acts. Hence, he has no such answer available (*Ritva*).

13. *Niddah* 64b.

When a virgin marries, it is to be expected that the rupturing of her hymen will cause her to bleed. (This blood is, of course, not menstrual blood, and it does not render her *tamei.*) Moreover, as it may take some time for the hymen to be completely effaced and for the wound to heal, it is quite possible that the newly wed virgin will continue to bleed for some time. Balancing the likelihood of such bleeding against the likelihood of her actually menstruating, the Rabbis detailed how long we continue to attribute the newly wed virgin's bleeding to hymenal blood – depending on her age and past history of discharge (factors that obviously affect the likelihood of her experiencing menstruation). As stated in the Mishnah there, the Rabbis divided newly wed virgins into three groups: A girl who has not reached the age of menstruation; a girl who has reached the age of menstruation but has never yet menstruated; and a girl who has menstruated in the past. Our Gemara cites that part of the Mishnah which deals with the first of these two groups.

14. [I.e. she has not reached the age of menstruation;] the Gemara in *Niddah* [5a] defines this age as the age when she becomes a *naarah* (*Rashi*). [A *naarah* is a girl between the ages of 12 and 12½ who has sprouted at least two pubic hairs.]

15. Since the young girl's time for menstruating has not arrived, we attribute her discharges to hymenal bleeding indefinitely; as long as she continues to bleed on account of cohabitation [that is, she sees blood after every cohabitation] it is presumable that the wound from the ruptured hymen has not healed and her discharges are *tahor* (*Rashi;* see *Rama, Yoreh Deah* 187:13 with *Shach* §37).

16. [I.e. she has reached the age of menstruation,] but has not yet experienced her period (*Rashi*).

17. Even if, during that night, he cohabits with her several times (*Rashi*).

18. [The Mishnah assumes that the marriage took place on Wednesday, in accordance with the rule of our Mishnah; hence, the fourth night after her wedding is Saturday night.]

או הלכה כר"ש ה) (איתמר) בבי רב אמרי רב שרי ושמואל אסר בנהרדעא אמרי רב אסר ושמואל שרי אמר רב נחמן בר יצחק וסימניך אלו מקילין לעצמן ואלו מקילין לעצמן ורב שרי ג) והאמר רב שימי בר חזקיה משמיה דרב א האי מסוכריא דנזייתא אסור להדוקה ביומא טבא בההוא אפילו ר"ש מודה דאביי ורבא דאמרי תרוייהו מודה ר"ש ג) בפסיק רישיה ולא ימות והא אמר רב חייא בר אשי אמר רב הלכה כרבי יהודה ורב חנן בר אמי אמר שמואל הלכה כרבי שמעון ורב חייא בר אבין מתני לה בלא גברי רב אמר הלכה כר' יהודה ושמואל אמר הלכה כרבי שמעון לעולם רב כרבי יהודה סבירא ליה להך לישנא דאמר דם מיפקד פקיד מקלקל הוא אצל הפתח להך לישנא דאמר דם חבורי מיחבר מקלקל בחבורה הוא מתיב רב חסדא ד) תינוקת שלא הגיע זמנה לראות ונשאת ב"ש אומרים נותנין לה ארבעה לילות וב"ה אומרים ב עד שתחיה המכה הגיע זמנה לראות ונשאת בש"א נותנין לה לילה הראשון ובית הלל אומרים עד מוצאי שבת ג ארבעה לילות מאי

רש"י

או הלכה כר"ש. דמקלקל בחבורה חייב כיון דתימלי לומר הלכה כר' יהודה בדבר שאין מתכוון דאסור: בנהרדעא. מקומו של שמואל: וסימניך. שלא תטעה להחליף שמעתתא דבי רב לנהרדעא ודנהרדעא לדבי רב: אלו מקילין לעצמן. דבי רב שצריכים לעשות כדברי רבן אומרים שרבן התיר ונהרדעא העושים כשמואל רבן אומרים שמואל התיר: ורב שרי. בתמיה אלמא דבר שאין מתכוון מותר סבירא ליה: מסוכריא דנזייתא. סתימת נקב גיגית שמוציאין השכר דרך הנקב וסותמין אותו בבלאי בגדים: אסור להדוקה. משום סחיטה: מודה ר"ש כו'. אבל כאן יש שבקיאים בהטייה כדלקמן: הלכה כרבי יהודה. באין מתכוון: בלא גברי. בלא אמוראי אליבא דרב ואליבא דשמואל אלא רב ושמואל גופייהו: להך לישנא דאמרת דם מיפקד פקיד. והאיסור משום פתח הוא: מקלקל הוא אצל הפתח. ובמקלקל מודה רבי יהודה: מקלקל בחבורה הוא. ורב סבר לה כרבי יהודה אף במקלקל בחבורה לקולא דקא פטר בה רבי יהודה: שלא הגיע זמנה לראות. במסכת נדה אמר אימתי הגיע זמנה לראות משיגיעו ימי הנעורים: נותנין לה ארבעה לילות. שכל דמים שתראה בהן מחמת תשמיש מחזקינן להו בדם בתולים: עד שתחיה המכה. כל זמן שאינה משמשת בלא דם לא חיתה המכה: הגיע זמנה לראות. ולא ראתה: לילה הראשון. אפילו לבעילות הרבה:

תוספות

או הלכה כר"ש. במקלקל משום דטעם שניהם דפטורין בשאר מלאכות שבת הוי משום דבעינן מלאכת מחשבת אבל שאינו מתכוון כלל למלאכה לא משום דבעינן מלאכת מחשבת מיפטר דהא בשאר מקומות נמי מיפטר אין מתכוון כגון גבי כלאים דמוכרי כסות מוכרין כדרכן ובלבד שלא יתכוין כו' (כלאים פ"ט מ"ה) ותנן נמי נזיר חופף ומפספס כו' (נזיר דף מב.) הילכך בחבורה נמי שרי:

האי מסוכרייתא דנזייתא אסור להדוקה כו'. פירש בקונטרס וכן ר"ח ובערוך ה) בחד לישנא וכן בסדר תנאים ואמוראים דאסור משום סחיטה וקשה לר"ת דהא סחיטה משום ליבון ולא שייכא בשאר משקים דכל דבר המלכלך את בולעו כגון יין ושכר ושמן לא שייך ליבון בסחיטתו אלא דוקא במים וראיה לדבר מדלא גזרינן בהו שמא יסחוט כמו גבי מים כדאמרינן באלו קשרים (שבת דף קיג:) היה מהלך בשבת ופגע באמת המים כו' היכי ליעביד לינחות במיא אתי לידי סחיטה ותניא נמי בפרק חבית (שם דף קמו: ושם) ומסתפג באלונטית ולא יביאה בידו ומפרש בגמ' דאתי לידי סחיטה ובפ"ב דביצה (דף יח. ושם) אומר דלכ"ע אין מטבילין את הכלים ומפרש בגמרא גזירה משום סחיטה ואילו בפרק תולין (שבת דף קלט:) תנן מסננין את היין בסודרין אלמא לגבי יין לא גזרינן משום סחיטה ובריש המביא (ביצה דף ל.) נמי קאמר ליפרוס סודרא עליה ולא קאמר אתי לידי סחיטה והיינו משום דלא שייך ליבון אלא גבי מים והא דאמרינן בפרק מפנין (שבת דף קכח:) אם היתה צריכה שמן חבירתה מביאה לה בשערה ופריך והא אתי לידי סחיטה ומשני אין סחיטה בשער משמע דשייך סחיטה בשמן וכן בפ' נוטל (שם דף קמג.) ספוג אם יש לו בית אחיזה מקנחין בו ואם לאו אין מקנחין בו משום דאתי לידי סחיטת שמן הנבלע בו ההיא סחיטה אור"ת דהויא משום מפרק ואסורה כמו סחיטת זיתים וענבים והכא אומר ר"ת דליכא למימר דאסור משום מפרק כיון שהנסחט הולך לאיבוד ו) אע"ג דהוי פסיק רישיה וכן פירש בערוך דכל פסיק רישיה דלא ניחא ליה שרי ועיקר ראייתו מפרק כל התדיר (זבחים דף צא: ושם) אליבא דר"ש מזלפין יין על גבי האישים אע"ג דפסיק רישיה הוא דודאי מכבה הוא כיון דלא ניחא ליה בהאי כיבוי שרי ועוד מייתי ראיה מלולב הגזול (סוכה דף לג: ושם) דקאמר ר"א בר"ש ממעטים ענבים בי"ט פי' ענבי הדס ופריך והא מתקן מנא ומוקים לה במתכוון לאכילה סבר לה כאבוה ופריך והא מודה ר"ש בפסיק רישיה כו' ומשני לא צריכה דאית ליה הושענא אחריתי אלמא כיון דלא ניחא ליה ולא חייש בהאי תיקון שרי אע"ג דפסיק רישיה הוא ונראה לר"י דלא קשה מידי דאיכא למימר דאסור לסחוט בשאר משקה משום ליבון כמו במים ומ"מ לא חיישינן בהו שמא יסחוט כיון שהטנופת והבריח בבגדים ומעט הוא אין נהנה בסחיטתו ומצינן למימר נמי דאסור משום מפרק ואף ע"ג דהוי פסיק רישיה דלא ניחא ליה אסור כדמפרש לר"ש כמו במלאכה שאינה צריכה לגופה ורבינו ראיות הערוך אין נראה דהתם לר"ש לזלף יין על גבי האישים איכא למימר דמצוה שאני וכן ההיא דאית ליה הושענא אחריתי איכא למימר דשרי משום מצוה א"נ הכי פי' והא פסיק רישיה הוא דאית ליה הושענא אחריתי והואיל וכן שרי לר"ש דשמא לא יצטרך לה ונמצא שלא תיקן כלי והלכך לאו פסיק רישיה הוא אבל לר"י אסור דשמא יצטרך לה ואגלאי מילתא דכלי עבד ועל פי' הערוך קשה דתנן בפרק שמונה שרצים (שבת דף קז.) המפיס מורסא בשבת אם לעשות לה פה חייב ואם להוציא ממנה ליחה פטור ודוקא משום צערא פטור ומותר אבל אי לאו משום צערא היה אסור אע"ג דלא ניחא ליה בפה כלל דאי ניחא ליה מן הפה כי לא מתכוון נמי חייב וכן מחט של יד ליטול בה את הקוץ דשרי משום צערא אבל אי לאו הכי אסור אע"ג דלא ניחא ליה כלל אבל קצת קשה אי פסיק רישיה דלא ניחא ליה אסור אמאי קאמר רב בפרק חבית (שם קמה.) כבשים שסחטן לגופן פטור ומותר הואיל ול"ל למים היוצאין והשתא אע"ג דלא"ל היה להיות אסור ואור"י דמצינן למימר דדוקא כבשים שרי דהוי הנסחט מהם כמו אוכלא דאיפרת ואין שם משקה עליו כדאמרינן דאפי' למימיהם פטור אבל אסור ועוד י"ל דכל דבר שאדם עושה במזיד לא שייך למימר שמא יסחוט דסברא הוא כיון דלדעת כן הוא עושה ולהכי גבי מסננין את היין לא חיישינן שמא יסחוט ואתיא שפיר האי דנדה מערמת וטובלת בבגדיה (ביצה דף יח.) וכן בפ"ח דיומא (דף עז:) ההולך להקביל פני רבו עובר עד צוארו במים ולא גזרינן שמא יסחוט לפי שלדעת כן הוא עושה ועוד איכא למימר התם דמצוה שאני ובערוך פירש לשון אחר מסוכרייתא דנזייתא סתימת גיגית של שכר אסור להדוקה דשמא תבטל הסתימה אצל הגיגית ויעשה כלי בשבת ואין נראה לר"י דהיכי דמי דאם בדעתו לבטל שם בשעת הנחה מאי פסיק רישיה שייך כאן מיד הוא עושה כלי דמתכוון לעשותו ואם אין בדעתו לבטלה שם א"כ לא הוי פסיק רישיה שיעשנה כלי וי"ל דבדוחק שהוא מתכוון לבטלה ואינו מתכוון לעשות כלי ושייך ביה פסיק רישיה הואיל ואינו מתכוון לגמרי לעשות כלי: ט) **לעולם** רב כר"י ס"ל כו'. לשמואל נמי איכא לשנויי לעולם כר"ש ס"ל ולהך לישנא דאמר דם מיפקד פקיד לפתח הוא צריך ולהך לישנא דאמר חבורי מחבר לדם הוא צריך: **מאי** לאו דאי לא בעיל לא מצי בעיל. דלמאי נקט עד מוצאי שבת אי לאו דאתא לאשמועינן דמצי בעיל בשבת אע"ג דמשיר בתולים ליכא למימר דנקט עד מוצ"ש לאשמועי' דבעינן רצופין דהא לא בעינן שיהו רצופין כדמוכח בפרק בתרא דנדה (דף סד: ושם) מעשה ונתן לה ד' לילות מתוך י"ב חדש והכי פי' נותנין לה ד' לילות עד מוצ"ש שיבעול בכל לילה וישיר מקצת בתולים עד מוצ"ש ואשמועינן דשרי להשיר בתולים בשבת ומשני לא לבר משבת ומוצאי שבת נקט לאשמועינן דבעינן רצופים והוה מצי למיפרך מברייתא דפרק בתרא דנדה דמוכח דלאפי' מפחרין אלא דפריך ליה מגופה דברייתא והא עד מוצאי שבת ארבעה לילות קתני וא"ת מעיקרא למשני לבר משבת מה עלה בדעתו והא קתני בהדיא ד' לילות וי"ל דהוה ס"ד דהכי פירושו נותנין לה עד מוצאי שבת לבר משבת שהן בין הכל ד' לילות ואיהו פריך דמשמע דבעיל ד' לילות ומשני כשבעל וקמ"ל כמו שמפרש בתר הכי אע"ג דהוי פירצה דחוקה דהא אי חזיא תלינן בדם בתולין אפ"ה שרי:

מאי

מסורת הש"ס

א) ס"ל א', ג"ב, ב) שבת קיא. בכורות כה. ג) שבת קג. קיא: קיז. קכ: קלג. קמג. בכורות כה. סוכה לג: [ביצה לו.], ד) נדה יא: סד:, ה) [ערך סכר], ו) [לא"ג למלאכה שא"ל לגופה אסור לר"ש היכא דלא ניחא ליה כלל שרי טפי כ"ה תוספות בתשובות רא"ם סי' לד], ז) רש"ל גורס ומיהו, ח) [ועי' תוס' שבת מא: ד"ה מיחם], ט) שייך לע"ב.

ליקוטי רש"י

האי מסוכריא. בגד כורכין בברזא חבית של חרס מפני שאין הנקב שוה [שבת קיא.]. ברזא של חבית שכורכין סביבותיה נעורת [של פשתן] ומטלניות כדי [שיסתום פיו הנקב יפה] [בכורות כה.]. אסור להדוקה. בנקב משום סחיטה ואף על גב דלא קא מכוין לסחוט אלמא לא ס"ל כר"ש בדבר שאין מתכוון [שבת שם]. בתוך החבית בכח משום סחיטה ואע"ג דאינו מתכוון לשום סחיטה אסור אפי' לר"ש דאמר במסכת שבת (דף מא:) דבר שאין מתכוון מותר [בכורות שם]. מודה ר"ש בפסיק רישיה ולא ימות. כלומר אחתוך ראש בהמה זו בשבת ואיני רוצה שתמות דכיון דלא אפשר שלא תמות כמתכוון חשיב ליה וכי מר אמרינן דבר שאין מתכוון מותר היכא דאפשר כגון גורר אדם מטה כסא וספסל ובלבד שלא יתכוין לעשות חריץ והיכא דאי אפשר לאיתחם דלאו מחשב עבר ... הלכה כרבי יהודה. אלמא ס"ל דבר שאין מתכוון אסור. בלא גברי. בלא רב חייא ורב חנן [בכורות שם]. תינוקת וכו' נותנין לה ארבעה לילות. לשמש ואפי' רואה אמרינן דם בתולים הוא [נדה סד:]. המכה. מכת בעילה דכל זמן שתהא רואה דם מחמת תשמיש דם בתולים הוא [שם יא:]. הגיע זמנה לראות. ולא ראתה. עד מוצאי שבת. והיא נשאת ברביעי [שם סד:].

עין משפט נר מצוה

כא א טוש"ע א"ח סימן שכ סעיף יח:

כב ב ג מיי' פי"א מהל' איסורי ביאה הל' יח יט סמג לאוין קיא טוש"ע אה"ע סימן סג סעיף א וטוש"ע י"ד סימן קצג סעיף א:

תוספות רי"ד

האי מסוכרייתא דנזייתא אסור להדוקה ביומא טבא ואפילו ר"ש מודה בהא דאביי ורבא דאמרי תרווייהו מודה ר"ש בפסיק רישיה ולא ימות. פי' המורה סתימת נקב גיגית שמוציאים ממנו השכר וסותמים אותו בבלאי בגדים אסור להדוקה משום סחיטה. ואינו נראה כלל שהרי שמשימים בנקב שמוציא ממנו מים או יין בלאי בגדים אין בו משום סחיטה שאינו מוכנין לא ללבנם ולא לקבל ממנו משקה ולאיבוד אזיל א"כ אמאי ליתסר. ור' נתן בעל הערוך פי' משום ר"ח ז"ל מטלית שמשימים על הגיגית לסתום פי' (ומפרקת) [ומהדקה] המטלית שם וזהו פתרון יפה. דודאי באותו המטלית קפיד אם תשרה. א) ומה שסוחט ממנו אסור משום מלבן שדומה לסוחט בגדים שרויים. וזה שאנו משימין בברזא של חביות מתיר ר' נתן בפירוש מפני שהולך לאיבוד:

חשק שלמה על תוס' רי"ד

א) עי' בערוך ערך סכר ה' דפירש שם דאסור משום סחיטה דניחא ליה שיחזור היין בתוך הכד ע"ש ומשמע דאסור משום מפרק וצ"ע.

או הֲלָכָה כְּרַבִּי שִׁמְעוֹן – or is the law in accordance with R' Shimon who holds one liable for making a wound destructively, in which case it is forbidden?[1]

The Gemara resolves the question:

בְּבֵי רַב אָמְרֵי (איתמר) – In the academy of Rav they said: **רַב שָׁרֵי וּשְׁמוּאֵל אָסַר – Rav permits** it **while Shmuel prohibits** it. **בִּנְהַרְדְּעָא אָמְרֵי – In Nehardea,** where Shmuel lived,[2] **they said: רַב אָסַר וּשְׁמוּאֵל שָׁרֵי – Rav prohibits** it **while Shmuel permits** it.

The Gemara comments on this dispute:

אָמַר רַב נַחְמָן בַּר יִצְחָק – Rav Nachman bar Yitzchak said: וְסִימָנָיךְ – And your mnemonic to remember which of these two versions was said by whom is: **אֵלּוּ מְקִילִין לְעַצְמָן וְאֵלּוּ מְקִילִין לְעַצְמָן – These are lenient for themselves and these are lenient for themselves.**[3]

The Gemara assumes that Rav permitted it because he maintains that the husband is not intent on causing a wound or creating an opening — but, rather, on his own pleasure — and Rav follows the view of R' Shimon, who permits unintentional acts.[4] Which leads to the following question:

וְרַב שָׁרֵי – But did Rav actually **permit** it? **וְהָאָמַר רַב שִׁימִי בַּר חִזְקִיָּה מִשְּׁמֵיהּ דְּרַב – But Rav Shimi bar Chizkiyah said in the name of Rav: הַאי מְסוֹכְרַיָּא דְּנַזְוְיָתָא –** Regarding **this beer-barrel stopper,**[5] **אָסוּר לְהַדּוֹקָהּ בְּיוֹמָא טָבָא – one is forbidden to push it** into place **on Yom Tov.**[6] Now in this case the perpetrator certainly does not intend to squeeze out beer from the cloth; nonetheless, Rav prohibits it. Apparently, Rav follows the view of R' Yehudah, who prohibits unintentional acts! — ? —

The Gemara answers:

בְּהַהוּא אֲפִילּוּ רַבִּי שִׁמְעוֹן מוֹדֶה – In fact, Rav follows the view of R' Shimon, who permits unintentional acts. But **in that** case of a beer-barrel stopper **even R' Shimon concedes** that it is forbidden. **דְּאַבַּיֵי וְרָבָא דְּאָמְרֵי תַּרְוַיְיהוּ – For Abaye and Rava have both said: מוֹדֶה רַבִּי שִׁמְעוֹן בִּפְסִיק רֵישֵׁיהּ וְלֹא יָמוּת – R' Shimon agrees** that one is liable **in** the case of **an inevitable consequence.**[6]

The Gemara, however, now cites incontestable evidence that Rav does not follow the view of R' Shimon:

וְהָא אָמַר רַב חִיָּיא בַּר אַשִׁי אָמַר רַב – But Rav Chiya bar Ashi said in the name of Rav that **הֲלָכָה כְּרַבִּי יְהוּדָה – the law follows R' Yehudah,** who prohibits an unintentional act. **וְרַב חָנָן בַּר אַמִּי אָמַר שְׁמוּאֵל – And Rav Chanan bar Ami said in the name of Shmuel** that **הֲלָכָה כְּרַבִּי שִׁמְעוֹן – the law follows R' Shimon,** who permits such an act. **וְרַב חִיָּיא בַּר אָבִין מַתְנֵי לָהּ בְּלָא גַּבְרֵי – And Rav Chiya bar Avin taught it** [the above dispute between Rav and Shmuel] **without** reference to other **personages,**[8] as follows: **רַב אָמַר הֲלָכָה כְּרַבִּי יְהוּדָה – Rav says** that **the law follows R' Yehudah, וּשְׁמוּאֵל אָמַר הֲלָכָה כְּרַבִּי שִׁמְעוֹן – and Shmuel says** that **the law follows R' Shimon.** Here it is made explicit that Rav does not follow R' Shimon regarding an unintentional act. How, then, can we explain Rav's permitting cohabitation with a virgin on the Sabbath?[9]

The Gemara answers:

לְעוֹלָם רַב כְּרַבִּי יְהוּדָה סְבִירָא לֵיהּ – Actually, Rav holds in accordance with R' Yehudah, who forbids unintentional acts. Nevertheless he permitted cohabiting with a virgin on the Sabbath, for one of the following reasons: **לְהַךְ לִישָּׁנָא דְּאָמַר דָּם מִיפְקָד פְּקִיד – According to that version** of our original inquiry **which said that the blood is stored** in her body, and is not considered the result of a wound, so that the only possible prohibition would be creating an opening, **מְקַלְקֵל הוּא אֵצֶל הַפֶּתַח** — we can say that Rav permitted it because he maintains that **he is acting destructively concerning the opening.**[10] **לְהַךְ לִישָּׁנָא דְּאָמַר דָּם חִבּוּרֵי מִיחַבַּר – And according to that version** of our original inquiry **which said the blood is** the result of **a wound,** so that there is also the making of a wound to be considered, **מְקַלְקֵל בְּחַבּוּרָה הוּא –** we can say, in addition, that Rav permitted it because he maintains that **he is acting destructively concerning the wound.**[11]

NOTES

1. [Actually R' Shimon himself would permit cohabiting with a virgin on the Sabbath since — the Gemara presently assumes — his primary intent is for his own pleasure and the wounding is, consequently, an unintentional act; R' Shimon, as we know, permits unintentional acts. The Gemara means only that] if we combine R' Yehudah's view that unintentional acts are forbidden with R' Shimon's view that one is liable for making a wound destructively then it follows that it is forbidden to cohabit with a virgin on the Sabbath [even assuming that his primary intent is for his own pleasure and that the wound is destructive in nature] (*Rashi*).

2. *Rashi;* see *Shabbos* 116b and *Gittin* 81a.

3. In Rav's academy, where his view was authoritative, they preserved the version in which Rav was more lenient; in Nehardea, where Shmuel flourished, his students preserved the version in which Shmuel was more lenient (*Rashi*).

[This is, of course, merely a mnemonic device; it is hardly the reason for the difference between these two versions.]

4. *Rashi; Ritva.*

5. That is, a rag that is used to plug the opening of a container in which beer is being brewed (*Rashi;* see *Maharshal;* cf. *Rashi* to *Shabbos* 111a; see also *Rashi* to *Moed Katan* 12b ד״ה לנזוי).

6. [And certainly not on the Sabbath.] This is forbidden because through pressing the cloth stopper one will squeeze out beer that it had absorbed (*Rashi*).

Rashi could mean that squeezing out the beer is a *toladah* of מְלַבֵּן, *cleaning,* since the passage of the beer through the cloth cleans it out somewhat. Alternatively, *Rashi* means that this is a *toladah* of דָּשׁ, *threshing,* for the removal of beer from within the cloth resembles the removal of grain kernels from within their husks (see *Tosafos, Ramban* et al.).

7. [Literally: its head is cut off and it should not die?] Although R' Shimon holds that one is not liable at all for a *melachah* performed unintentionally while engaged in a permitted activity, he concedes that there is liability when the forbidden labor is an inevitable consequence of the permitted action. Hence, if someone cuts off the head of a living creature on the Sabbath, he has violated the prohibition against taking a life on the Sabbath — even if he declares that he did not intend for the creature to die. Since its death is inevitable, he is considered to have willfully taken the creature's life, and he has transgressed even according to R' Shimon (*Rashi* to *Succah* 33b; *Rambam, Hil. Shabbos* 1:6). Here too, when one inserts the cloth into place, it is *inevitable* that some beer will emerge from it. (In contrast, the bleeding that results from cohabitation with a virgin is not an inevitable consequence; see above, 5b note 17.) Since even R' Shimon would agree that this is forbidden, there is no contradiction between Rav's ruling here and R' Shimon's position.

8. I.e. he attributed each statement directly to either Rav or Shmuel.

9. The question is directed at the version of Rav's view that was preserved in his academy, according to which it was Rav who permitted cohabitation with a virgin on the Sabbath. Note that according to this version the view of Shmuel is likewise problematic, since — in this version — Shmuel forbade cohabitation with a virgin on the Sabbath, even though, it now emerges, Shmuel rules with R' Shimon that unintentional acts are permitted. As for why the Gemara did ask this explicitly, see *Shitah Mekubetzes* ד״ה ה״ג ff.

According to the version preserved in Nehardea, however, there is no difficulty at all, since in that version Rav forbade cohabitation with a virgin on the Sabbath and Shmuel permitted it, which dovetails exactly with their respective positions in regard to unintentional acts.

10. See above, 5b note 16.

11. And Rav follows the view of R' Yehudah who held that one is not liable for causing a wound destructively (see above, 5b note 18).

As for Shmuel — who (in the version of the academy of Rav) forbids

accordance with R' Yehudah, who holds that an unintentional act is prohibited, and it is therefore forbidden,[21] **אוֹ הֲלָכָה כְּרַבִּי שִׁמְעוֹן – or is the law in accordance with R' Shimon,** who holds that an unintentional act is permitted? **וְאִם תִּימְצֵי לוֹמַר הֲלָכָה כְּרַבִּי יְהוּדָה – And if you conclude and say that the law is in accordance with R' Yehudah,** we can still inquire: **מְקַלְקֵל בְּחַבּוּרָה – Is he acting destructively in** making **the wound,**[22] and it is therefore permitted,[23] **אוֹ מְתַקֵּן בְּחַבּוּרָה הוּא – or is he acting constructively in** making **the wound,**[24] and it is therefore forbidden? **וְאִם תִּימְצֵי לוֹמַר מְקַלְקֵל בְּחַבּוּרָה הוּא – And,** furthermore, **if you conclude and say that he is acting destructively in** making **the wound, בִּמְקַלְקֵל הֲלָכָה כְּרַבִּי יְהוּדָה – is the law in accordance with R' Yehudah regarding one who acts destructively** in making a wound,[25]

NOTES

21. Assuming that we characterize this bleeding as constructive (*Rashi;* see below).

22. [Since he destroys the commodity of her virginity.]

23. See note 18.

24. [Since he thereby establishes her virginity.]

25. [R' Yehudah and R' Shimon disagree elsewhere (*Shabbos* 106a) regarding the liability of someone who acts destructively in causing a wound. R' Shimon maintains that although, in general, one is liable on the Sabbath only for constructive acts, causing a wound is an exception to this rule. Since making a wound, by definition, involves the loss of blood, and is therefore inherently destructive, and yet the Torah forbade it, we conclude that the Torah made an exception for this *melachah* and rendered one liable even for it even though it is done destructively. R' Yehudah disagrees; in his view causing a wound is no different than any other *melachah,* and one is liable for it only if it is done in a way that serves some constructive purpose (see *Rashi* to *Shabbos* 106a ד״ה מתני׳ ר׳ יהודה; cf. *Tosafos* and *Ramban* ad loc.).

Applying this dispute to the case at hand, if we assume R' Yehudah's view that one is not liable for making a wound destructively, and if we also assume – as the Gemara now does – that the wound involved in rupturing the hymen is destructive, it would be permitted to cause this wound on the Sabbath. [Even though R' Yehudah concedes that it is Rabbinically forbidden to make a wound (or to perform any other *melachah*) destructively, in the present case the combined factors of the wound being unintentional – since the Gemara now assumes that his primary intent is for his own pleasure – and destructive combine to permit it, as explained earlier (see note 18).]

יניח אצבעו באזניו והיינו דאמר ר' אלעזר מפני מה אצבעותיו של אדם דומות ליתידות מאי טעמא אילימא משום דמחלקן כל חדא וחדא למילתיה עבידא דאמר מר [א] זו זרת זו קמיצה זו אמה זו אצבע זה גודל אלא מה טעם משופות כיתידות שאם ישמע אדם דבר שאינו הגון יניח אצבעותיו באזניו תנא דבי רבי ישמעאל מפני מה אוזן כולה קשה והאליה רכה שאם ישמע אדם דבר שאינו הגון יכוף אליה לתוכה ת"ר [ב] אל ישמיע אדם לאזניו דברים בטלים מפני שהן נכוות תחלה לאיברים איבעיא להו מהו לבעול בתחלה בשבת דם מיפקד פקיד או חבורי מיחבר ואם תימצי לומר דם מיפקד פקיד לדם הוא צריך ושרי או דלמא לפתח הוא צריך ואסיר ואם תימצי לומר לדם הוא צריך ופתח ממילא קאתי הלכה כר"ש [ג] דאמר דבר שאין מתכוין מותר * או הלכה כרבי יהודה דאמר דבר שאין מתכוין אסור ואם תימצי לומר הלכה כר' יהודה מקלקל הוא אצל הפתח או מתקן הוא אצל הפתח איכא דאמרי ואם תימצי לומר דם חבורי מיחבר לדם הוא צריך ואסור או דלמא להנאת עצמו הוא צריך ושרי ואם תימצי לומר להנאת עצמו הוא צריך ודם ממילא קאתי הלכה כרבי יהודה או הלכה כר"ש ואם תימצי לומר הלכה כר' יהודה מקלקל בחבורה או מתקן בחבורה הוא ואם תימצי לומר מקלקל בחבורה הוא במקלקל הלכה כרבי יהודה או

רש"י

יניח אצבעו. שהיא שפויה כיתד: מ"ט. כלומר במאי דומות ליתידות: אי נימא דמחלקן. שמחולקות זו מזו ואינן מחוברות יחד: חדא חדא למילתיה. קושיא היא כל אחת יש בה צורך ואף בגורלי גבוה: זו זרת. מן הקטנה מודדין זרת של חושן: זו קמיצה. מאצבע שאצל הקטנה מתחילין לקמוץ קומץ חופה שלש אצבעות על פס ידו הקמיצה והאמה והאצבע וקומץ: זו אמה. מהגדולה מודדין אמת בנין ואמת כלים: זו אצבע. למתן דמים של חטאת דכתיב ביה באצבעו (ויקרא ד): זה גודל. לבהן יד דאהרן (שם ח) ודמצורע (שם יד): משופות. אגוישיד"ש בלעז: אליה. בשר שבסוף האוזן: נכוית תחילה לאברים. רכות ודקות ליכוות מכולם והכי נמי אמרינן במסכת ע"ז (דף לח.) האי עובד כוכבים דחריך רישא שרי למיכל אפילו מריש אודניה ולא"ם שממהר ליבשל: מהו לבעול בתחלה. לא שמיע להו הך מתניתא דלעיל[ז] א"נ שמיע להו ומיבעיא להו הלכה או אין הלכה: מיפקד פקיד. כמו פקדון כנוס ועומד ואינו נבלע בדופני הרחם להיות יוצאתו על ידי חבורה אלא שהפתח נעול בפניו ופותחין לו ויוצא: או חבורי מיחבר. דם בתולים היוצא על ידי חבורה הוא בא שהדופן מתפרק מחבורו: אם תימצי לומר מיפקד פקיד. ואין בו משום חבורה כוונת המוציאו למאי לדם הוא צריך ומתכוין להוציאו: ושרי. דהא מיפקד פקיד: או דלמא לפתח מתכוין. והרי הוא כבנין ואסור: ואם תימצי לומר לדם הוא מתכוין. ולא לפתח ומיהו על כרחך פיתחא ממילא הוי: הלכה כרבי יהודה. בדבר שאין מתכוין ואסור: או כר"ש. ומותר וא"ת פסיק רישיה ולא ימות הוא הא פרכינן לה לקמן ומשנינן יש שבקיאין בהטיה ואין דם יוצא ואף אין פתח נפתח הלכך לאו פסיק רישיה ולא ימות הוא: ואת"ל הלכה כרבי יהודה. אכתי איכא למיבעי דקיימא לן (שבת ד' קו.) כי אמר רבי יהודה במתקן אבל במקלקל אינה מלאכה ויש לשאול על פתח זה אם תקון הוא אצלה או קלקול הוא אצלה שהבתולה חשובה מן הבעולה: ואת"ל מקלקל הוא ל"ג דאי מקלקל לדברי הכל מותר שאין לך מקלקל חייב אלא חובל ומבעיר אליבא דרבי שמעון והכא לאו חובל הוא דהא בא"ל דם מיפקד פקיד בעי לה ואזיל: ודם ממילא קא הוי. הוא אינו מתכוין להוציאו אבל הוא יוצא ונמצאת חבורה נעשית שלא בכוונה: הלכה כרבי יהודה. בדבר שאינו מתכוין ושמא מתקן הוא ואסור: או הלכה כר"ש. דדבר שאין מתכוין מותר: ואם תימצי לומר הלכה כרבי יהודה. קלקול הוא ומותר או תקון הוא ואסור ואפי' אם קלקול הוא יש למצוא צד איסור אם בדבר שאין מתכוין סבירא לן כרבי יהודה ובמקלקל בחבורה סבירא לן כר"ש דמחייב דאמרינן כל המקלקלין פטורין חוץ מחובל ומבעיר ואוקימנא כר"ש בפרק האורג (שבת קו.): הלכה כרבי יהודה במקלקל. ומותר דכי אמר רבי יהודה דבר שאין מתכוין אסור במתקן אבל במקלקל לא אמר:

או

תוספות

זה גודל. פי' בקונטרס לענין בהן יד דמצורע ואין נראה דאם כן הוה ליה למימר זה בהן ועוד דאפילו לא מחלק מאי משוי על בהן שהוא קצר מכולם ונראה דלענין קמיצה קאמר כדתנן (מנחות דף יא.) מוחק בגודל מלמעלה אבל בידו אחרת לא יוכל לעשות דבעינן עבודה בימין:

מהו לבעול בתחלה בשבת. אף על גב דתקנו שתהא בתולה נשאת ברביעי מכל מקום אם אירע לו שלא בעל בליל חמישי לא חייבוהו חכמים להמתין עד יום חמישי אחר או עד יום ב' להכי בעי אם מותר לבעול בשבת אם לאו אע"ג דתניא לעיל ומפרישין חתן מן הכלה לילי שבת תחלה מפני שהוא עושה חבורה ותניא נמי באידך ברייתא בין כך ובין כך לא יבעול לא בערב שבת ולא כו' פי' בקונטרס דלא הוה ידע לה א"נ ידע לה ובעי היכי הלכתא דאיכא למימר דפליגי בה ר' יהודה ור"ש ומיהו על כרחך נראה דלא ידע הברייתא דחיישינן שמא ישחוט בן עוף דאי הוה ידע לה מאי קמיבעיא ליה הא בהא לא פליגי ר' יהודה ור"ש והא דלא פשיט מינה לבסוף משום דמשכח תנאי דפליגי עלה:

דם מיפקד פקיד או חבורי מיחבר. טעמא דחבורה לא כפרש"י דפירש בפרק שמונה שרצים (שבת קז.) דחייב משום צובע גבי ח' שרצים דתנא התם נצרר הדם אע"פ שלא יצא וקשה לר"י דבאלו טריפות (חולין מו:) בשמעתא דריאה תניא ושאר שקצים ורמשים עד שיצא מהם דם והשתא התם מאי צובע איכא הא לית להו עור וה"נ מאי צביעה איכא בהך חבורה וכן גבי חבורה דמילה לא שייך צביעה ועוד דעל כרחך לשמואל איכא טעמא אחרינא דבפרק כלל גדול (שבת עה. ושם) קאמר דשוחט לא מחייב משום צובע אלא משום נטילת נשמה אלמא טעמא דחבורה הוי משום נטילת נשמה כדקאמר שמואל התם ורב דאמר התם משום צובע אף משום צובע קאמר ונטילת נשמה אין לפרש דטעמא משום הכחשה שמחלישו ונוטל קצת נשמתו דהכא אין צריך לחלישות האשה ומיהו איסורא דקאמר הכא איכא למימר דהויא דרבנן אבל גבי מילה משמע דאיכא איסורא דאורייתא בהוצאת דם דאמרינן בפרק ר' אליעזר (שם קלג:) האי אומנא דלא מייץ סכנתא הוא ומעברינן ליה פשיטא מדקא מחללין שבת עליה מהו דתימא דם מיפקד פקיד קמ"ל דחבורי מיחבר ואי הוה משום החלשה ליכא חילול שבת דהויא מלאכה שאין צריכה לגופה דאין צורך להחליש התינוק ונראה לר"ת לפרש דהוצאת דם חשיבה נטילת נשמה כי הדם הוא הנפש וכשנוטל מקצתו נוטל מקצת נשמה וקשה לר"י דאמרי' בפרק כלל גדול (שם עה. ושם) גבי הצד חלזון והפוצעו וליחייב נמי משום נטילת נשמה ומשני מתעסק הוא אבל נטילת נשמה דכל כמה דאית ביה נשמה טפי ניחא ליה כו' ולפי זה אפילו הוא חי גמור הרי יש כאן נטילת נשמה ואומר ר"ת כי דם חלזון שצובעין בו הוא מיפקד פקיד ועל אותו אינו חייב משום נטילת נשמה ועל שאר הדם שמחובר חשיב ליה מתעסק:

לדם הוא צריך ושרי. וא"ת והא פסיק רישיה הוא לענין הפתח וי"ל שיכול להוציא הדם בלא עשיית הפתח פי' ר"ת שצריך להוציא הדם שלא יתלכלך פעם אחרת כשיבעול ולפירושו לקמן דקאמר דם חבורי מיחבר אי לדם הוא צריך ואסור אף על גב דהויא מלאכה שאינה צריכה לגופה דשריא במקום צערא גבי מורסא הכא גבי מצוה אסור ולקמן נפרש הא דפריך ממפיס מורסא לפירושו ור"י מפרש לדם הוא צריך שצריך לראות אם היא בתולה:

אם תימצי לומר הלכה כרבי יהודה מקלקל הוא אצל הפתח ושרי. פי' דרבי יהודה אית ליה דמקלקל בחבורה פטור אף על גב דפטור אבל אסור מיהו הכא מותר לכתחלה משום דאיכא תרתי מקלקל בחבורה ודבר שאינו מתכוין וקשה דבגרירה אסר ר' יהודה אע"ג דאיכא תרתי דאין מתכוין ומקלקל נמי הוי כדאמרינן בשילהי פ"ק דחגיגה (דף י.) דמוקי הך דחופר גומא ואין צריך אלא לעפרה דפטור אפי' כר' יהודה דמחייב מלאכה שאינה צריכה לגופה וטעמא דפטור משום דמקלקל הוי ובפרק י"ט (ביצה כג. ושם) אסר רבי יהודה קירוד אף על גב דאין מתכוין ומקלקל ויש לומר דהכא שרי טפי משום דאיכא נמי מצוה א"נ שלא במקום מצוה נמי היכא דאיכא תרתי שרי וגבי גרירה יש להעמיד כגון שאינו מקלקל לגמרי אלא מתקן קצת דמשוי גומות מצד אחד וגבי קירוד נמי במה שמוציא דם מיקל לבהמה קצת כמו דם הקזה [ה]:

את"ל הלכה כרבי יהודה מקלקל בחבורה הוא כו'. משמע דאי הלכה כרבי שמעון שרי אפילו הוא מתקן כיון דאין מתכוין וקשה דבשילהי פרק ספק אכל (כריתות יט: ושם) [ו] אמר לרבי שמעון הואיל ומקלקל בחבורה חייב מתעסק נמי חייב ומאי שנא דאין מתכוין פוטר רבי שמעון בחבורה טפי ממתעסק וי"ל דמתעסק שמתכוין למלאכה לא מיפטר בשבת אלא משום דאין זה מלאכת מחשבת ומשום הכי חייב לרבי שמעון מתעסק בחבורה כמו מקלקל בחבורה דמחייב רבי שמעון אע"ג דאין זה מלאכת מחשבת והכי מלין ליה במקלקל

תוספ"ת רי"ד

איבעיא ל"ו מהו לבעול בתולה בשבת. ומסיק תלמודא והלכתא מותר לבעול בתולה בשבת:

מסורת הש"ס

א) מנחות יא., ב) [מס' ד"א זוטא פ"ד], ג) ביצה כג. [שבת מא: וש"נ], ד) [דף ג:], ה) [ועי' תוס' בכורות כד: ד"ה וסיינו], ו) ליתא שם האי לישנא.

גליון הש"ס

גמ' או הלכה כר"י דאמר דשא"מ אסור. ע' פסחים כה ע"ב תד"ה לא אפשר:

לעזי רש"י

אגויישיד"ש. פירוש משופות, מחודות (רש"י ביצה דף לו ע"א ותוספות סוכה דף לו ע"ב ד"ה מקורזלות, הגהות מהרש"ל לרש"י שבת דף פא ע"א), חדות (תוספות פסחים דף מז ע"ב ד"ה אבנים), ראשן חד (רש"י שבת דף מג ע"א ד"ה מקורזלות):

ליקוטי רש"י

זו זרת. אצבע קטנה ממנה מתחיל הזרת וכ"מ למדת חשן זרת ארכה. זו קמיצה. ממנה מתחיל הקומץ מאותו אצבע שאצל הקטנה. זו אמה. ממנה מודדין כל אמות הבנין והכלים לפי שהיא ארוכה מכולן ושתי אמות היו בשושן הבירה שתי מקלות שהן אמה ובהן מודדין אמות הבנין ואותן מקלות נמדדו באותו אצבע שהוא [ארוכה]. זו אצבע. לטבל הכהן אצבעו בדם. זה גודל. לבהונות דמצורע [מנחות יא.]. הלכה כר"ש דאמר. (שבת כב. מו:) גורר אדם מטה כסא וספסל דדבר שאינו מתכוין מותר [ביצה כג.].

The Gemara explains the basis of this question:
דָּם מִיפְקַד פְּקִיד – **Is the blood** that is produced when the hymen is ruptured **stored** in her body, lacking egress, and is simply released by the rupturing of the hymen,[11] אוֹ חֲבוּרֵי מִיחַבַּר – **or is it** [the bleeding] the result of **a wound?**[12]

The Gemara elaborates on this question. The elaboration is presented in two versions, the first of which pursues what follows from assuming that the blood is simply "stored," and the second of which pursues what follows from assuming that it results from a wound.

The first version:
וְאִם תִּימְצֵי לוֹמַר דָּם מִיפְקַד פְּקִיד – **And if you conclude and say that the blood is** merely **stored** in the body, we can inquire: לְדָם הוּא צָרִיךְ וְשָׁרֵי – **Is it** primarily **the blood that he needs,**[13] **and it is** therefore, perhaps,[14] **permitted,**[15] אוֹ דִּלְמָא לְפֶתַח הוּא צָרִיךְ וַאֲסִיר – **or, perhaps, is it the opening** of a passageway in the vagina **that he needs, and it is** therefore **prohibited?**[16] וְאִם תִּימְצֵי לוֹמַר לְדָם הוּא צָרִיךְ – **And if you conclude and say that it is the blood that he needs,** וּפֶתַח מִמֵּילָא קָאָתֵי – **and the opening comes** about, so to speak, **on its own,** without his intending it, we can still inquire: הֲלָכָה כְּרַבִּי שִׁמְעוֹן דְּאָמַר דָּבָר שֶׁאֵין מִתְכַּוֵּין מוּתָּר – **Is the law in accordance with R' Shimon, who said that something that is unintended is permitted,** אוֹ הֲלָכָה כְּרַבִּי יְהוּדָה דְּאָמַר דָּבָר שֶׁאֵין מִתְכַּוֵּין אָסוּר – **or is the law in accordance with R' Yehudah, who said that something that is unintended is prohibited?**[17] וְאִם תִּימְצֵי לוֹמַר הֲלָכָה כְּרַבִּי יְהוּדָה – **And if you conclude and say that the law is in accordance with R' Yehudah,** we can yet inquire: מְקַלְקֵל הוּא אֵצֶל הַפֶּתַח – **Is he acting destructively concerning the opening** אוֹ מְתַקֵּן הוּא אֵצֶל הַפֶּתַח – **or is he acting constructively concerning the opening?**[18]

The second version:
אִיכָּא דְּאָמְרֵי – **There are those who say** it as follows: וְאִם תִּימְצֵי לוֹמַר דָּם חֲבוּרֵי מִיחַבַּר – **And if you conclude and say that the bleeding** results from **a wound,** we can then inquire: לְדָם הוּא צָרִיךְ וְאָסוּר – **Is it the blood that he needs,**[19] **and it is** therefore **forbidden,** since he is deliberately causing a wound on the Sabbath, אוֹ דִּלְמָא לַהֲנָאַת עַצְמוֹ הוּא צָרִיךְ וְשָׁרֵי – **or, perhaps, is it** only **his own pleasure that he needs** to satisfy, **and** the drawing of blood is only an unintended consequence and is, perhaps, permitted?[20] וְאִם תִּימְצֵי לוֹמַר לַהֲנָאַת עַצְמוֹ הוּא צָרִיךְ – **And if you conclude and say that he needs** only **his own pleasure,** וְדָם מִמֵּילָא קָאָתֵי – **and the blood comes,** so to speak, **on its own,** without intent, הֲלָכָה כְּרַבִּי יְהוּדָה – **is the law in**

NOTES

11. I.e. the blood is not absorbed in the body in such a way that drawing it out would be judged an act of wounding, which would be a violation of Sabbath law. Rather, it is considered to be simply "stored" [inside the body], and is released when the hymen is ruptured as if a door were opened for it (*Rashi;* see also *Shabbos* 133b with *Rashi*).

12. That is, the bleeding that accompanies cohabitation with a virgin results from a wound, for the vaginal walls tear and bleed as they are separated from each other. This would constitute an act of *wounding,* which is generally prohibited on the Sabbath (*Rashi*).

[*Rashi's* language seems to indicate that he takes the expression חֲבוּרֵי מִיחַבַּר to be derived from חַבּוּרָה, *a wound* (see *Rashi* here ד״ה או חבורי מיחבר and to *Shabbos* 133b ד״ה קמ״ל). Alternatively, it is derived from מְחוּבָּר, *connected* (see *Rashba* below, 5b ד״ה כתב רש״י). In any event, the sense is that the blood is "connected," i.e. absorbed in the vaginal walls, so that its extraction is considered an act of wounding, which is forbidden on the Sabbath (see below, 7a).]

[Wounding is forbidden on the Sabbath since it is considered a derivative (*toladah*) of the *melachah* of שׁוֹחֵט, *slaughtering* (*Rashi* to *Shabbos* 107a, first explanation; see there for another view, as well; see also *Shitah Mekubetzes* here ד״ה דם; *Pnei Yehoshua* and *Keren Orah* to *Shabbos* ibid.; for yet another view see *Rambam, Hil. Shabbos* 8:7). For the Torah says: כִּי הַדָּם הוּא הַנָּפֶשׁ, *for the blood is the life* (*Deuteronomy* 12:23); thus, the taking of blood is tantamount, in this context, to the taking of life (*Rabbeinu Tam,* cited by *Tosafos;* see also *Teshuvos Avnei Nezer, Orach Chaim* §198).]

[*Chidushei Chasam Sofer* suggests that even according to the position that the hymenal blood is the result of a wound, the rupturing of the hymen cannot be compared to the cutting of flesh. [This is apparent from the Gemara at the end of 6b, where the Gemara draws a parallel between rupturing the hymen and lancing a boil; see there.] Rather, even this view agrees that the blood is only loosely contained within the flesh. The question is how much force is needed to release it. If only a slight tear is needed, then the release of the blood is not deemed making a wound but merely opening an exit through which it may flow. If greater force is needed it is considered making a wound.]

13. I.e. is his primary purpose in this first act of cohabitation to release the blood, thus establishing his bride's virginity (see *Ri,* cited in *Tosafos; Ritva;* cf. *Rabbeinu Tam,* also cited in *Tosafos*).

14. [See *Ritva;* cf. *Rashba.*]

15. Since according to this version this is merely the release of stored blood, and is not the result of a wound (*Rashi*).

16. [The first act of cohabitation creates a passageway for future such acts. In general, the creation of a useful opening – i.e. an opening that serves as an entrance and an exit (see *Shabbos* 146a) – falls under the heading of *building,* which is forbidden on the Sabbath. Therefore, if we define his purpose as being to create this opening, then this first cohabitation is definitely forbidden on the Sabbath. If, however, his primary purpose is to release the blood, and the creation of the passageway is simply a by-product, then it may possibly be permitted; the Gemara will immediately proceed to elaborate on this last point.]

17. [Throughout the Talmud, the Tannaim R' Yehudah and R' Shimon dispute the permissibility of דָּבָר שֶׁאֵין מִתְכַּוֵּין, *something that is unintended,* that is, a permissible act that might result in an *unintended,* forbidden consequence. In the case at hand, for example, the husband's primary purpose [the Gemara now assumes] is to release the virginal blood, an act that is [according to the present line of inquiry] permitted; however, an unintended consequence of this act is the creation of a useful passageway in the vagina, which is forbidden. According to R' Yehudah, who prohibits an unintended act, this should be forbidden; whereas according to R' Shimon, who allows an unintentional act, it should be permitted.]

The Rishonim, however, raises the following difficulty: The Talmud in several places states that R' Shimon concedes that when the unintended consequence is inevitable [פְּסִיק רֵישֵׁיהּ] the act is forbidden (see below, 6a note 6). Hence in the present case even R' Shimon ought to forbid cohabitation, since an opening will inevitably be created. They answer by referring to the Gemara later [6b] which states that it is possible to cohabit with a virgin "at an angle," in such a way that no blood will be produced on that occasion; likewise, the Rishonim suggest, it is possible to cohabit with a virgin in such a way that no passageway will be created [even if blood is produced]. Thus it is not *inevitable* that he will create an opening, even if his intention is to draw blood (*Rashi,* as explained by *Shitah Mekubetzes* ד״ה ואת״ל לדם; *Tosafos; Rashba*).

18. As the Gemara states elsewhere (*Shabbos* 106a), although R' Yehudah generally holds one liable for an unintentional act, he concedes that if the unintentional act is destructive in nature he is not liable [since it is a general rule of Sabbath law that one is only liable for a *melachah* that is done constructively]. Hence, it behooves us to establish whether the opening of a passageway in the vagina should be characterized as a constructive act [since it facilitates future cohabiting], or as a destructive act, since it destroys the commodity of her virginity (see *Rashi*). Should we resolve that it is a destructive act then it would be permitted even according to R' Yehudah.

[Actually, destructive acts are permitted on the Sabbath only by Biblical law; on a Rabbinic level, they are prohibited. However, in the present case the combination of the act being both unintentional and destructive allows us to permit it outright (*Tosafos;* see there for another approach, as well; see also *Rashba; Mishneh LaMelech, Hil. Shabbos* 1:5; *Teshuvos Be'er Yitzchak, Orach Chaim* §15).]

19. [In order to establish her virginity; see above, note 13.]

20. [Assuming that unintentional acts are permitted, as R' Shimon maintains.]

יניח אצבעו באזניו והיינו דאמר ר' אלעזר מפני מה אצבעותיו של אדם דומות ליתידות מאי טעמא אילימא משום דמחלקן כל חדא וחדא למילתיה עבידא דאמר מר [א] זו זרת זו קמיצה זו אמה זו אצבע זה גודל אלא מה טעם משופות כיתידות שאם ישמע אדם דבר שאינו הגון יניח אצבעותיו באזניו תנא דבי רבי ישמעאל מפני מה אוזן כולה קשה והאליה רכה שאם ישמע אדם דבר שאינו הגון יכוף אליה לתוכה ת"ר [ב] אל ישמיע אדם לאזניו דברים בטלים מפני שהן נכוות תחלה לאיברים איבעיא להו מהו לבעול בתחלה בשבת דם מיפקד פקיד או חבורי מיחבר ואם תימצי לומר דם מיפקד פקיד לדם הוא צריך ושרי או דלמא לפתח הוא צריך ואסיר ואם תימצי לומר לדם הוא צריך ופתח ממילא קאתי הלכה כר"ש [ג] דאמר דבר שאין מתכוין מותר ° או הלכה כרבי יהודה דאמר דבר שאין מתכוין אסור ואם תימצי לומר הלכה כר' יהודה מקלקל הוא אצל הפתח או מתקן הוא אצל הפתח איכא דאמרי ואם תימצי לומר דם חבורי מיחבר לדם הוא צריך ואסור או דלמא להנאת עצמו הוא צריך ושרי ואם תימצי לומר להנאת עצמו הוא צריך ודם ממילא קאתי הלכה כרבי יהודה או הלכה כר"ש ואם תימצי לומר הלכה כר' יהודה מקלקל בחבורה או מתקן בחבורה הוא ואם תימצי לומר מקלקל בחבורה הוא במקלקל הלכה כרבי יהודה או

רש"י

יניח אצבעו. שהיא שפויה כיתד: מ"ט. כלומר במאי דומות ליתידות: אי נימא דמחלקן. שמחולקות זו מזו ואינן מחוברות יחד: חדא חדא למילתיה. קושיא היא כל אחת יש בה צורך ואף בצורכי גבוה: זו זרת. מן הקטנה מודדין זרת של חושן: זו קמיצה. מאצבע שאצל הקטנה מתחילין לקמוץ הופה שלש אצבעות על פס ידו הקמיצה והאמה והאצבע וקומץ: זו אמה. מהגדולה מודדין אמת בנין ואמת כלים: זו אצבע. למתן דמים של חטאת דכתיב ביה באצבעו (ויקרא ד): זה גודל. לבהן יד דאהרן (שם ח) ודמצורע (שם יד): משופות. אגוישיד"ש בלעז: אליה. בשר שבסוף האוזן: נכוות תחילה לאברים. רכות ודקות ליכוות מכולם והכי נמי אמרינן במסכת ע"ז (דף לח.) האי עובד כוכבים דחריך רישא שרי למיכל אפילו מריש אודניה ואע"פ שממהר ליבשל: מהו לבעול בתחלה. לא שמיע להו הך מתניתא דלעיל [ז] א"נ שמיע להו ומיבעיא להו הלכה או אין הלכה: מיפקד פקיד. כמו פקדון כנוס ועומד ואינו נבלע בדופני הרחם להיות יוצא על ידי חבורה אלא שהפתח נעול בפניו ופותחין לו ויוצא: או חבורי מיחבר. דם בתולים היוצא על ידי חבורה הוא בא שהדופן מתפרק מחבורו: אם תימצי לומר מיפקד פקיד. ואין בו משום חבורה כוונת המוציאו למאי לדם הוא צריך ומתכוין להוציאו: ושרי. דהא מיפקד פקיד: או דלמא לפתח מתכוין. והרי הוא כבנין ואסור: ואם תימצי לומר לדם הוא מתכוין. ולא לפתח ומיהו על כרחך פיתחא ממילא הוי: הלכה כרבי יהודה. בדבר שאין מתכוין ואסור: או כר"ש. ומותר וא"ת פסיק רישיה ולא ימות הוא הא פרכינן לה לקמן ומשנינן יש שבקיאין בהטיה ואין דם יוצא ואף אין פתח נפתח הלכך לאו פסיק רישיה ולא ימות הוא: ואת"ל הלכה כרבי יהודה. אכתי איכא למיבעי דקיימא לן (שבת ד' קו.) כי אמר רבי יהודה במתקן אבל במקלקל אינה מלאכה ויש לשאול על פתח זה אם תקון הוא אצלה או קלקול הוא אלא שהבתולה חשובה מן הבעולה: ואת"ל מקלקל הוא לר"ג דאי מקלקל לדברי הכל מותר שאין לך מקלקל חייב אלא חובל ומבעיר אליבא דרבי שמעון והכא לאו חובל הוא דהא באת"ל דם מיפקד פקיד בעי לה ואזיל: ודם ממילא קא הוי. הוא אינו מתכוין להוציאו אבל הוא יוצא ונמצאת חבורה נעשית שלא בכוונה: הלכה כרבי יהודה. בדבר שאינו מתכוין ושמא מתקן הוא ואסור: או הלכה כר"ש. דדבר שאין מתכוין מותר: ואם תימצי לומר הלכה כרבי יהודה. קלקול הוא ומותר או תקון הוא ואסור ואפי' אם קלקול הוא יש למצוא צד איסור אם בדבר שאין מתכוין סבירא לן כרבי יהודה ובמקלקל בחבורה סבירא לן כר"ש דמחייב דאמרינן כל המקלקלין פטורין חוץ מחובל ומבעיר ואוקימנא כר"ש בפרק האורג (שבת קו.): הלכה כרבי יהודה במקלקל. ומותר דכי אמר רבי יהודה דבר שאין מתכוין אסור במתקן אבל במקלקל לא אמר: או

תוספות

זה גודל. פי' בקונטרס לענין בהן יד דמצורע ואין נראה דאם כן הוה ליה למימר זה בהן ועוד דאפילו לא מחלק מלי משור על בהן שהוא קצר מכולם ונראה דלענין קמיצה קאמר כדתנן (מנחות דף יא.) מוחק בגודל מלמעלה אבל בידו אחרת לא יוכל לעשות דבעינן עבודה בימין:

מהו לבעול בתחלה בשבת. אף על גב דתקנו שתהא בתולה נשאת ברביעי מכל מקום אם אירע לו שלא בעל בליל חמישי לא חייבוהו חכמים להמתין עד יום חמישי אחר או עד יום ב' להכי בעי אם מותר לבעול בשבת אם לאו אע"ג דתניא לעיל ומפרישין חתן מן הכלה לילי שבת תחלה מפני שהוא עושה חבורה ותניא נמי באידך ברייתא בין כך ובין כך לא יבעול לא בערב שבת ולא כו' פי' בקונטרס דלא הוה ידע לה א"נ ידע לה ובעי היכי הלכתא דאיכא למימר דפליגי בה ר' יהודה ור"ש ומיהו על כרחך נראה דלא ידע הברייתא דחיישינן שמא ישחוט בן עוף דאי הוה ידע לה מאי קמיבעיא ליה הא בהא לא פליגי ר' יהודה ור"ש והא דלא פשיט מינה לבסוף משום דמשכח תנאי דפליגי עלה:

דם מיפקד פקיד או חבורי מיחבר. טעמא דחבורה לא כפרש"י דפירש בפרק שמונה שרצים (שבת קז.) דחייב משום צובע גבי ח' שרצים דתנא התם נצרר הדם אע"פ שלא יצא וקשה לר"י דבאלו טריפות (חולין מו:) בשמעתא דריאה תניא ושאר שקצים ורמשים עד שיצא מהם דם והשתא התם מאי צובע איכא הא לית להו עור וה"נ מאי צביעה איכא בהך חבורה וכן גבי חבורה דמילה לא שייך צביעה ועוד דעל כרחך לשמואל איכא טעמא אחרינא דבפרק כלל גדול (שבת עה. ושם) קאמר דשוחט לא מחייב משום צובע אלא משום נטילת נשמה אלמא טעמא דחבורה הוי משום נטילת נשמה כדקאמר שמואל התם ורב דאמר התם משום צובע אף משום צובע קאמר ונטילת נשמה אין לפרש דטעמא משום הכחשה שמחלישו ונוטל קצת נשמתו דהכא אין צריך לחלישות האשה ומיהו איסורא דקאמר הכא איכא למימר דהויא דרבנן אבל גבי מילה משמע דאיכא איסורא דאורייתא בהוצאת דם דאמרינן בפרק ר' אליעזר (שם קלג:) האי אומנא דלא מייץ סכנתא הוא ומעברינן ליה פשיטא מדקא מחללין שבת עליה מהו דתימא דם מיפקד פקיד קמ"ל דחבורי מיחבר ואי הוה משום החלשה ליכא חילול שבת דהויא מלאכה שאין צריכה לגופה דאין צורך להחליש התינוק ונראה לר"ת לפרש דהוצאת דם חשיבה נטילת נשמה כי הדם הוא הנפש וכשנוטל מקצתו נוטל מקצת נשמה וקשה לר"י דאמרי' בפרק כלל גדול (שם עה. ושם) גבי הצד חלזון והפוצעו וליחייב נמי משום נטילת נשמה ומשני מתעסק הוא אבל נטילת נשמה דכל כמה דאית ביה נשמה טפי ניחא ליה כו' ולפי זה אפילו הוא חי גמור הרי יש כאן נטילת נשמה ואומר ר"ת כי דם חלזון שצובעין בו הוא מיפקד פקיד ועל אותו אינו חייב משום נטילת נשמה ועל שאר הדם שמחובר חשיב ליה מתעסק:

לדם הוא צריך ושרי. וא"ת והא פסיק רישיה הוא לענין הפתח וי"ל שיכול להוציא הדם בלא עשיית הפתח פי' ר"ת שצריך להוציא הדם שלא יתלכלך פעם אחרת כשיבעול ולפירושו לקמן דקאמר דם חבורי מיחבר אי לדם הוא צריך ואסור אף על גב דהויא מלאכה שאינה צריכה לגופה דשריא במקום צערא גבי מורסא הכא גבי מצוה אסור ולקמן נפרש הא דפריך ממפיס מורסא לפירושו ור"י מפרש לדם הוא צריך שצריך לראות אם היא בתולה:

אם תימצי לומר הלכה כרבי יהודה מקלקל הוא אצל הפתח ושרי. פי' דרבי יהודה אית ליה דמקלקל בחבורה פטור אף על גב דפטור אבל אסור מיהו הכא מותר לכתחלה משום דאיכא תרתי מקלקל בחבורה ודבר שאינו מתכוין וקשה דבגרירה אסר ר' יהודה אע"ג דאיכא תרתי דאין מתכוין ומקלקל נמי הוי כדאמרינן בשילהי פ"ק דחגיגה (דף י.) דמוקי הך דחופר גומא ואין צריך אלא לעפרה דפטור אפי' כר' יהודה דמחייב מלאכה שאינה צריכה לגופה וטעמא דפטור משום דמקלקל הוי ובפרק י"ט (ביצה כג. ושם) אסר רבי יהודה קירוד אף על גב דאין מתכוין ומקלקל ויש לומר דהכא שרי טפי משום דאיכא נמי מצוה א"נ שלא במקום מצוה נמי היכא דאיכא תרתי שרי וגבי חריץ יש להעמיד כגון שאינו מקלקל לגמרי אלא מתקן קצת דמשוי גומות מלד אחד וגבי קירוד נמי במה שמוציא דם מיקל לבהמה קצת כמו דם הקזה [ה]:

את"ל הלכה כרבי יהודה מקלקל בחבורה הוא כו'. משמע דאי הלכה כרבי שמעון שרי אפילו הוא מתקן כיון דאין מתכוין וקשה דבשילהי פרק ספק אכל (כריתות יט: ושם) [ו] אמר לרבי שמעון הואיל ומקלקל בחבורה חייב מתעסק נמי חייב ומאי שנא דאין מתכוין פוטר רבי שמעון בחבורה טפי ממתעסק וי"ל דמתעסק שמתכוין למלאכה לא מיפטר בשבת אלא משום דאין זה מלאכת מחשבת ומשום הכי חייב לרבי שמעון מתעסק בחבורה כמו מקלקל בחבורה דמחייב רבי שמעון אע"ג דאין זה מלאכת מחשבת והכי תלינן ליה במקלקל

תוספות רי"ד

איבעיא להו מהו לבעול בתולה בשבת. ומסיק תלמודא דלכתחלה מותר לבעול בתולה בשבת:

מסורת הש"ס

א) מנחות יא., ב) [מס' ד"א זוטא פ"ד], ג) ביצה כג. [שבת מא: וש"נ], ד) [דף ג:], ה) [ועי' תוס' בכורות כד: ד"ה והיינו], ו) ליתא שם האי לישנא.

גליון הש"ס

גמ' או הלכה כר"י דאמר דשא"מ אסור. ע' פסחים כה ע"ב תד"ה לא אפשר:

לעזי רש"י

אגויישיד"ש. פירוש משופות, חדודות (רש"י ביצה דף לו ע"א ותוספות סוכה דף לו ע"ב ד"ה מקורזלות, הגהות מהרש"ל לרש"י שבת דף פא ע"א), חדות (תוספות פסחים דף מז ע"ב ד"ה אבנים), ראשן חד (רש"י שבת דף מג ע"א ד"ה מקורזלות):

ליקוטי רש"י

זו זרת. אצבע קטנה ממנה מתחיל הזרת וכ"מ למדת חשן זרת ארכה. זו קמיצה. ממנה מתחיל הקומץ מאותו אצבע שאצל הקטנה. זו אמה. ממנה מודדין כל אמות הבנין והכלים לפי שהיא ארוכה מכולן ושתי אמות היו בשושן הבירה שתי מקלות שהן אמה ובהן מודדין אמות הבנין ואותן מקלות נמדדו באותו אצבע שהוא [ארוכה]. זו אצבע. לטבל הכהן אצבעו בדם. זה גודל. לבהונות דמצורע [מנחות יא.]. הלכה כר"ש דאמר. (שבת כב. מו:) גורר אדם מטה כסא וספסל דדבר שאינו מתכוין מותר [ביצה כג.].

יַנִּיחַ אֶצְבָּעוֹ בְּאָזְנָיו – he should place his finger, which is tapered like a spike, **in his ears.**

The Gemara elaborates on this theme:

וְהַיְינוּ דְּאָמַר רַבִּי אֶלְעָזָר – And this is what R' Elazar said: מִפְּנֵי מָה אֶצְבְּעוֹתָיו שֶׁל אָדָם דּוֹמוֹת לִיתֵידוֹת – Why are the fingers of a person similar to spikes?

The Gemara interrupts to clarify R' Elazar's question:

מַאי טַעְמָא – In what way[1] does R' Elazar mean to equate fingers to spikes? **אִילֵימָא מִשּׁוּם דִּמְחַלְּקָן – If you say it is because they are separated** from one another like spikes, rather than being webbed together, what is R' Elazar's question? **כָּל חֲדָא וַחֲדָא לְמִילְּתֵיהּ עֲבִידָא** – Why, **each and every one** of the fingers **is used for its** own unique **purpose** – even for the needs of the Temple. **דְּאָמַר מַר – For the master said** in a Baraisa: **זוֹ זֶרֶת – THIS** smallest finger **IS** called the ***ZERES,*** and it was used to measure the breastplate worn by the Kohen Gadol;[2] **זוֹ קְמִיצָה – THIS** fourth finger **IS** called the ***KEMITZAH,*** and it was used to scoop from the *minchah* offering;[3] **זוֹ אַמָּה – THIS** middle finger **IS** called the ***AMAH,*** and from it was calculated the *amah*-measure used in building the Mishkan and its sacred vessels;[4] **זוֹ אֶצְבַּע – THIS** index finger **IS** the ***ETZBA,*** the finger used to apply sacrificial blood on the Altar;[5] **זֶה גּוּדָל** – and **THIS IS** the **THUMB,** to which sacrificial blood is applied in certain instances.[6] Obviously, then, R' Elazar could not have meant to ask why the fingers are separated!

The Gemara therefore explains R' Elazar's question as follows:

אֶלָּא מָה טַעַם מְשׁוּפּוֹת כִּיתֵידוֹת – Rather, R' Elazar meant to ask: **What is the reason [the fingers] are tapered like spikes?**

R' Elazar now answers the question:

שֶׁאִם יִשְׁמַע אָדָם דָּבָר שֶׁאֵינוֹ הָגוּן – The fingers were shaped in this manner **so that if a person will hear something that is not proper, יַנִּיחַ אֶצְבְּעוֹתָיו בְּאָזְנָיו – he will** be able to **place his fingers in his ears,** to block out the sound.

A similar thought:

תָּנָא דְּבֵי רַבִּי יִשְׁמָעֵאל – A Baraisa was taught in the academy of R' Yishmael: מִפְּנֵי מָה אוֹזֶן כּוּלָּהּ קָשָׁה וְהָאַלְיָה רַכָּה – WHY IS THE ENTIRE EAR HARD, WHILE THE LOBE of the ear **IS SOFT?**[7] **שֶׁאִם יִשְׁמַע אָדָם דָּבָר שֶׁאֵינוֹ הָגוּן – SO THAT IF A PERSON WILL HEAR SOMETHING THAT IS NOT PROPER, יָכוֹף אַלְיָה לְתוֹכָהּ – HE WILL** be able to **BEND THE LOBE INTO [THE EAR CANAL],** blocking the sound.[8]

The Gemara cites a Baraisa in conclusion:

תָּנוּ רַבָּנָן – The Rabbis taught in a Baraisa: אַל יַשְׁמִיעַ אָדָם לְאָזְנָיו דְּבָרִים בְּטֵלִים – A PERSON SHOULD NOT ALLOW HIS EARS TO HEAR IDLE TALK, מִפְּנֵי שֶׁהֵן נִכְווֹת תְּחִלָּה לְאֵיבָרִים – BECAUSE THEY (the ears) **ARE THE MOST EASILY BURNED OF THE LIMBS.**[9]

The Gemara returns to its topic of the first cohabitation with a virgin:

אִיבַּעְיָא לְהוּ – They inquired: מַהוּ לִבְעוֹל בַּתְּחִלָּה בְּשַׁבָּת – What is the law **regarding cohabiting** for the **first** time **on the Sabbath?**[10]

NOTES

1. Literally: What is the reason (see *Rashi*).

2. The Torah states that the *choshen* [breastplate] should be a *zeres* long and a *zeres* wide (see *Exodus* 28:16). This length is measured using the little finger (*Rashi*). That is, it is the distance between the thumb and little finger [the *zeres*] of a spread hand (*Aruch* ערך אצבע; cf. *Shenos Eliyahu* to *Orlah* 3:2). [This measure is equivalent to half an *amah* (see *Eruvin* 21a with *Rashi*); see note 4.]

3. [*Kemitzah* is the first of the four essential *avodos* of a *minchah's* offering.] In performing *kemitzah,* the Kohen bends the middle three fingers of his right hand over his palm to form a sort of hollow. He then digs into the flour of the *minchah* offering with the three fingers, scooping up some of the flour between his fingers and his palm (cf. *Chafetz Chaim* in *Toras HaKodashim* to *Menachos* 4a). The flour that fills this hollow is called the *kometz,* and it is eventually burned on the Altar. The scooping action is begun with the *kemitzah,* which is the finger nearest to the little finger (*Rashi*).

4. The Torah states the measurements for building the Mishkan and its vessels using the *amah* (*Rashi*).

[The *amah* is generally defined as a length equal to six *tefachim* (handbreadths) except for various measures of the Altar, where *amos* of five *tefachim* were used (see *Eruvin* 3b, *Menachos* 97a; see, however, *Rashash*). This Baraisa defines the *amah* as the distance from the tip of the middle finger to the elbow (*Rabbeinu Bachya* to *Leviticus* 8:23; *Magen Avraham, Orach Chaim* 349:2, as explained by *Shulchan Aruch HaRav* there; cf. *Pri Megadim*).] Since *Rashi* to the parallel Gemara in *Menachos* (11a) associates this *amah* with the six-*tefach amah* used for construction of the Temple, he apparently holds that the distance from the elbow to the end of the middle finger is six *tefachim.* However, many commentators hold that this actually defines the five-*tefach amah* used for the Altar. See *Shiurim shel Torah* by *R' Yisrael Yaakov Kanievsky* §6 for a lengthy discussion of this issue, including a possible alternative understanding of *Rashi.*

[It should be noted that there is also uncertainty if the half-*amah* length of the *zeres* is referring to a six-*tefach amah* or a five-*tefach amah* (see *Teshuvos HaRashba* 5:147; *Shiurim shel Torah* §5).]

5. The blood of a *chatas* offering is applied by the Kohen to the four corners of the Altar using the finger nearest the thumb (index finger). This is the אֶצְבַּע, *finger,* referred to in *Leviticus* 4:6 et al. (*Rashi*).

6. For example, Aaron the Kohen during the Inauguration service [*Leviticus* 8:23], and a *metzora* during his purification service [ibid. 14:14] (*Rashi*).

7. The upper portion of the ear is constructed with bony cartilage that makes the ear stiff and inflexible. The earlobe, on the other hand, has no cartilage, and is soft and flexible.

8. [Thus, it is clear how important it is for one to avoid hearing improper things; for God provided not one, but two sets of safeguards to prevent this from occurring.] See also *Chasam Sofer,* and *Rif* to *Ein Yaakov.*

9. [Literally: they burn first of the limbs.] Since the ears are soft and thin, they burn first. A similar idea is expressed in Tractate *Avodah Zarah* (38a) where the Gemara states that if an idolater singes the head of an animal to remove its hair, he is not deemed to have cooked any of the meat on the animal's head (which would render it impermissible), even the meat of the ears. From this Gemara, too, we see that the ears are the most easily cooked of the limbs (*Rashi*).

When one sins, he contaminates his limbs. This creates a Heavenly fire in Gehinnom that will ultimately exact retribution from the sinner. The point of the Baraisa is that when one listens to forbidden speech, his ears are the first limbs to be involved in the transgression – and they will thus be the first to be burned by the Heavenly fire (*Chafetz Chaim,* cited in *Yalkut Peirushim* to *Maseches Kesubos*). [Accordingly, the fact that the ears are *physically* the most easily burned of the limbs is mentioned by *Rashi* only to point out a parallel; viz. sins that will cause punishment to befall the ears are the most common, just as a fire that would not burn other limbs will burn the ears (ibid.; see also *Maharsha* and *Maharal* in *Chidushei Aggados*).]

[Above, the Gemara stated the importance of not listening to improper talk, which is forbidden. This Baraisa adds that one should not even listen to *idle* talk, because this can easily lead to forbidden talk (see *Maharsha;* cf. *Haflaah*).]

10. Although our Mishnah requires that a virgin be married on Wednesday – in order that the groom, should he fail to find her a virgin, be able to go to court the next morning, on Thursday – if for any reason the couple did not cohabit that night the Sages did not go so far as to require that they wait until the following Wednesday night to do so; rather, they may consummate the marriage whenever they choose. In such a case the Gemara inquires if they may even cohabit for the first time on the Sabbath (*Tosafos;* see also *Shitah Mekubetzes*).

[Although the Gemara above [3b] cited a Baraisa that explicitly prohibits cohabiting with a virgin for the first time on the Sabbath, the Amoraim who posed this question were either unaware of that Baraisa or were unsure if the halachah follows it (*Rashi, Tosafos;* cf. *Shitah Mekubetzes*).]

איבעיא להו מהו לבעול בתולה בשבת. ומסיק תלמודא והלכתא מותר לבעול בתולה בשבת:

יניח אצבעו באזניו והיינו דאמר ר' אלעזר מפני מה אצבעותיו של אדם דומות ליתידות מאי טעמא אילימא משום דמחלקן כל חדא וחדא למילתיה עבידא דאמר מר [א] זו זרת זו קמיצה זו אמה זו אצבע זה גודל אלא מה טעם משופות כיתידות שאם ישמע אדם דבר שאינו הגון יניח אצבעותיו באזניו תנא דבי רבי ישמעאל מפני מה אוזן כולה קשה והאליה רכה שאם ישמע אדם דבר שאינו הגון יכוף אליה לתוכה ת"ר [ב] אל ישמיע אדם לאזניו דברים בטלים מפני שהן נכוות תחלה לאיברים איבעיא להו מהו לבעול בתחלה בשבת דם מיפקד פקיד או חבורי מיחבר ואם תימצי לומר דם מיפקד פקיד לדם הוא צריך ושרי או דלמא לפתח הוא צריך ואסיר ואם תימצי לומר לדם הוא צריך ופתח ממילא קאתי הלכה כר"ש [ג] דאמר דבר שאין מתכוין מותר * או הלכה כרבי יהודה דאמר דבר שאין מתכוין אסור ואם תימצי לומר הלכה כר' יהודה מקלקל הוא אצל הפתח או מתקן הוא אצל הפתח איכא דאמרי ואם תימצי לומר דם חבורי מיחבר לדם הוא צריך ואסור או דלמא להנאת עצמו הוא צריך ושרי ואם תימצי לומר להנאת עצמו הוא צריך ודם ממילא קאתי הלכה כרבי יהודה או הלכה כר"ש ואם תימצי לומר הלכה כר' יהודה מקלקל בחבורה או מתקן בחבורה הוא ואם תימצי לומר מקלקל בחבורה הוא במקלקל הלכה כרבי יהודה או

רש"י

יניח אצבעו. שהיא שפויה כיתד: **מ"ש.** כלומר במאי דומות ליתידות: **אי נימא דמחלקן.** שמחולקות זו מזו ואין מחוברות יחד: **חדא חדא למילתיה.** קושיא היא כל אחת יש בה צורך ואף בצורכי גבוה: **זו זרת.** מן הקטנה מודדין זרת של חושן: **זו קמיצה.** מאצבע שאצל הקטנה מתחילין לקמוץ חופה שלש אצבעות על פס ידו הקמילה והאמה והאצבע וקומץ: **זו אמה.** מהגדולה מודדין אמת בנין ואמת כלים: **זו אצבע.** למתן דמים של חטאת דכתיב ביה באצבעו (ויקרא ד): **זה גודל.** לבהן יד דאהרן (שם ח) ודמצורע (שם יד): **משופות.** אגוישיד"ש בלעז: **אליה.** בשר שבסוף האוזן: **נכוות תחילה לאברים.** רכות ודקות ליכוות מכולם והכי נמי אמרינן במסכת ע"ז (דף לח.) האי עובד כוכבים דחריך רישא שרי למיכל אפילו מריש אודניה ואע"פ שממהר ליבשל: **מהו לבעול בתחלה.** לא שמיע להו הך מתניתא דלעיל [ז] א"נ שמיע להו ומיבעיא להו הלכה או אין הלכה: **מיפקד פקיד.** כמו פקדון כנוס ועומד ואינו נבלע בדופני הרחם להיות יוצאות על ידי חבורה אלא שהפתח נגעל בפניו ופותחין לו ויוצא: **או חבורי מיחבר.** דם בתולים היוצא על ידי חבורה הוא לא שהדופן מתפרק מחברו: **אם תימצי לומר מיפקד פקיד.** ואין בו משום חבורה כוונת המוציאו למאי לדם הוא צריך וממכוין להוציאו: **ושרי.** דהא מיפקד פקיד: **או דלמא לפתח מתכוין.** והרי הוא כבנין ואסור: **ואם תימצי לומר לדם הוא מתכוין.** ולא לפתח ומיהו על כרחך פיתחא ממילא הוי: **הלכה כרבי יהודה.** בדבר שאין מתכוין ואסור: **או כר"ש.** ומותר וא"ת פסיק רישיה ולא ימות הוא הא פרכינן לה לקמן ומשנינן יש שבקיאין בהטיה ואין דם יוצא ואף אין פתח נפתח הלכך לאו פסיק רישיה ולא ימות הוא: **ואת"ל הלכה כרבי יהודה.** אכתי איכא למיבעי דקיימא לן (שבת ד' קו.) כי אמר רבי יהודה במתקן אבל במקלקל אינה מלאכה ויש לשאול על פתח זה אם תקון הוא אצלה או קלקול הוא אצלה שהבתולה חשובה מן הבעולה: ואת"ל מקלקל הוא ל"ג דאי מקלקל לדברי הכל מותר שאין לך מקלקל חייב אלא חובל ומבעיר אליבא דרבי שמעון והכא לאו חובל הוא דהא בא"ל דם מיפקד פקיד בעי לה ואזיל: **ודם ממילא קא הוי.** הוא אינו מתכוין להוציאו אבל הוא יוצא ונמצאת חבורה נעשית שלא בכוונה: **הלכה כרבי יהודה.** בדבר שאינו מתכוין ושמא מתקן הוא ואסור: **או הלכה כר"ש.** דדבר שאין מתכוין מותר: **ואם תימצי לומר הלכה כרבי יהודה.** קלקול הוא ומותר או תקון הוא ואסור ואפי' אם קלקול הוא יש למצוא בד איסור אם בדבר שאין מתכוין סבירא לן כרבי יהודה ובמקלקל בחבורה סבירא לן כר"ש דמחייב דאמרינן כל המקלקלין פטורין חוץ מחובל ומבעיר ואוקימנא כר"ש בפרק האורג (שבת קו.): **הלכה כרבי יהודה במקלקל.** ומותר דכי אמר רבי יהודה דבר שאין מתכוין אסור במתקן אבל במקלקל לא אמר:

תוספות

זה גודל. פי' בקונטרס לבוהן יד למצורע ואין נראה דאם כן הוה ליה למימר זה בהן ועוד דאפילו לא מחלק מאי משוי על בהן שהוא קצר מכולם ונראה דלענין קמיצה קאמר כדתנן (מנחות דף יא.) מוחק בגודל מלמעלה אבל בידו אחרת לא יוכל לעשות דבעינן עבודה בימין:

מהו לבעול בתחלה בשבת. אף על גב דתקנו שתהא בתולה נשאת ברביעי מכל מקום אם אירע לו שלא בעל בליל חמישי לא חייבוהו חכמים להמתין עד יום חמישי אחר או עד יום ב' להכי בעי אם מותר לבעול בשבת אם לאו אע"ג דתניא לעיל ומפרישין חתן מן הכלה לילי שבת תחלה מפני שהוא עושה חבורה ותניא נמי באידך ברייתא בין כך ובין כך לא יבעול לא בערב שבת ולא כו' פי' בקונטרס דלא הוה ידע לה א"נ ידע לה ובעי היכי הלכתא דאיכא למימר דפליגי בה ר' יהודה ור"ש ומיהו על כרחך נראה דלא ידע הברייתא דחיישינן שמא ישחוט בן עוף דלא הוה ידע לה מאי קמיבעיא ליה הא בהא לא פליגי ר' יהודה ור"ש והא דלא פשיט מינה לבסוף משום דמסכת תנאי דפליגי עלה:

דם מיפקד פקיד או חבורי מיחבר. טעמא דחבורה לא כפרש"י דפירש בפרק שמונה שרצים (שבת קז.) דחייב משום צובע דהא גבי ח' שרצים דתנא התם נצרר הדם אע"פ שלא יצא וקשה לר"י דבאלו טריפות (חולין מו:) בשמעתא דריאה תניא ושאר שקצים ורמשים עד שיצא מהם דם והשתא התם מאי צובע איכא הא לית להו עור וה"נ מאי צביעה איכא בהך חבורה וכן גבי חבורה דמילה לא שייך צביעה ועוד דעל כרחך לשמואל איכא טעמא אחרינא דבפרק כלל גדול (שבת עה. ושם) קאמר דשוחט לא מחייב משום צובע אלא משום נטילת נשמה אלמא טעמא דחבורה הוי משום נטילת נשמה כדקאמר שמואל התם ורב דאמר התם משום צובע אף משום צובע קאמר ונטילת נשמה אין לפרש דטעמא משום הכחשה שמחלישו ונוטל קצת נשמתו דהכא אין צריך לחלישות האשה ומיהו איסורא דקאמר הכא איכא למימר דהויא דרבנן אבל גבי מילה משמע דאיכא איסורא דאורייתא בהוצאת דם דאמרינן בפרק ר' אליעזר (שם קלג:) האי אומנא דלא מייץ סכנתא הוא ומעברינן ליה פשיטא מדקא מחללין שבת עליה מהו דתימא דם מיפקד פקיד קמ"ל דחבורי מיחבר ואי הוה משום החלשה ליכא חילול שבת דהויא מלאכה שאין צריכה לגופה דאין צורך להחליש התינוק ונראה לר"ת לפרש דהוצאת דם חשיבה נטילת נשמה כי הדם הוא הנפש וכשנוטל מקצתו נוטל מקצת נשמה וקשה לר"י דאמרי' בפרק כלל גדול (שם עה. ושם) גבי הצד חלזון והפוצעו וליחייב נמי משום נטילת נשמה ומשני מתעסק הוא אצל נטילת נשמה דכל כמה דאית ביה נשמה טפי ניחא ליה כו' ולפי זה אפילו הוא חי גמור הרי יש כאן נטילת נשמה ואומר ר"ת כי דם חלזון שצובעין בו הוא מיפקד פקיד ועל אותו אינו חייב משום נטילת נשמה ועל שאר הדם שמחובר חשיב ליה מתעסק:

לדם הוא צריך ושרי. וא"ת והא פסיק רישיה הוא לענין הפתח וי"ל שיכול להוציא הדם בלא עשיית הפתח פי' ר"ת שצריך להוציא הדם שלא יתלכלך פעם אחרת כשיבעול ולפירושו לקמן דקאמר דם חבורי מיחבר אי לדם הוא צריך ואסור אף על גב דהויא מלאכה שאינה צריכה לגופה דשריא במקום צערא גבי מורסא הכא גבי מצוה אסור ולקמן נפרש הא דפריך ממפיס מורסא לפירושו ור"י מפרש לדם הוא צריך שצריך לראות אם היא בתולה:

אם תימצי לומר הלכה כרבי יהודה מקלקל הוא אצל הפתח ושרי. פי' דרבי יהודה אית ליה דמקלקל בחבורה פטור אף על גב דפטור אבל אסור מיהו הכא מותר לכתחלה משום דאיכא תרתי מקלקל בחבורה ודבר שאינו מתכוין וקשה דבגררה אסר ר' יהודה אע"ג דאיכא תרתי דאין מתכוין ומקלקל נמי הוי כדאמרינן בשילהי פ"ק דחגיגה (דף י.) דמוקי הך דחופר גומא ואין צריך אלא לעפרה דפטור אפי' כר' יהודה דמחייב מלאכה שאינה צריכה לגופה וטעמא דפטור משום דמקלקל הוי ובפרק י"ט (ביצה כג. ושם) אסר רבי יהודה קירוד אף על גב דאין מתכוין ומקלקל ויש לומר דהכא שרי טפי משום דאיכא נמי מצוה א"נ שלא במקום מצוה נמי היכא דאיכא תרתי שרי וגבי חריץ יש להעמיד כגון שאינו מקלקל לגמרי אלא מתקן קצת דמשוי גומות מלד אחד וגבי קירוד נמי במה שמוליא דם מיקל לבהמה קצת כמו דם הקזה [ה]:

את"ל הלכה כרבי יהודה מקלקל בחבורה הוא כו'. משמע דאי הלכה כרבי שמעון שרי אפילו הוא מתקן כיון דאין מתכוין וקשה דבשילהי פרק ספק אכל (כריתות יט: ושם) [ו] אמר לרבי שמעון הואיל ומקלקל בחבורה חייב מתעסק נמי חייב ומאי שנא דאין מתכוין פוטר רבי שמעון בחבורה טפי ממתעסק וי"ל דמתעסק שמתכוין למלאכה לא מיפטר בשבת אלא משום דאין זה מלאכת מחשבת ומשום הכי חייב לרבי שמעון מתעסק בחבורה כמו מקלקל בחבורה דמחייב רבי שמעון אע"ג דאין זה מלאכת מחשבת ולהכי תלינן ליה במקלקל

מסורת הש"ס

א) מנחות יא., ב) [מס' ד"א זוטא פ"ד], ג) ביצה כג. [שבת מא: וש"נ], ד) [דף ג:], ה) [ועי' תוס' בכורות כד: ד"ה והיינו], ו) ליתא שם האי לישנא.

גליון הש"ס

גמ' או הלכה כר"י דאמר דשא"מ אסור. ע' פסחים כה ע"ב תד"ה לא אפשר:

לעזי רש"י

אגויישיד"ש. פירוש משופות, חדודות (רש"י ביצה דף לו ע"א ותוספות סוכה דף לו ע"ב ד"ה מקורזלות, הגהות מהרש"ל לרש"י שבת דף פא ע"א), חדות (תוספות פסחים דף מז ע"ב ד"ה אבנים), ראשן חד (רש"י שבת דף מג ע"א ד"ה מקורזלות):

ליקוטי רש"י

זו זרת. אצבע קטנה ממנה מתחיל הזרת וכ"מ למדת חשן זרת ארכה. **זו קמיצה.** ממנה מתחיל הקומץ מאותו אצבע שאצל הקטנה. **זו אמה.** ממנה מודדין כל אמות הבנין והכלים לפי שהיא ארוכה מכולן ושתי אמות היו בשושן הבירה שתי מקלות שהן אמה ובהן מודדין אמות הבנין ואותן מקלות נמדדו באותו אצבע שהוא [ארוכה]. **זו אצבע.** לטבל הכהן אצבעו בדם. **זה גודל.** לבהונות דמצורע [מנחות יא.]. **הלכה כר"ש דאמר.** (שבת כב. מו:) גורר אדם מטה כסא וספסל דדבר שאינו מתכוין מותר [ביצה כג.].

משום חשבונות אמר ליה אביי וחשבונות של מצוה מי אסירי והא רב חסדא ורב המנונא דאמרי תרוייהו [א] חשבונות של מצוה מותר לחשבן בשבת וא"ר אלעזר [ב] פוסקין צדקה לעניים בשבת ואמר ר' יעקב אמר ר' יוחנן [ג] הולכין לבתי כנסיות ולבתי מדרשות לפקח על עסקי רבים בשבת ואמר רבי יעקב בר אידי אמר רבי יוחנן מפקחין פיקוח נפש בשבת ואמר רב שמואל בר נחמני אמר רבי יונתן הולכין לטרטייאות ולקרקייאות לפקח על עסקי רבים בשבת ותנא דבי מנשיא [ד] משדכין על התינוקת ליארס בשבת ועל התינוק ללמדו ספר וללמדו אומנות אלא אמר רבי זירא גזירה שמא ישחוט בן עוף א"ל אביי אלא מעתה יום הכפורים שחל להיות בשני בשבת ידחה גזירה שמא ישחוט בן עוף התם דלנפשיה לא טריד הכא דלאחרים טריד אי נמי התם אית ליה רווחא הכא לית ליה רווחא השתא דאתית להכי ערב שבת נמי גזירה שמא ישחוט בן עוף איבעיא להו בתולה נשאת ברביעי ונבעלת ברביעי ולא חיישינן לאיקרורי דעתא או דלמא בתולה נשאת ברביעי ונבעלת בחמישי דחיישינן לאיקרורי דעתא ת"ש דתני בר קפרא בתולה נשאת ברביעי [ה] ונבעלת בחמישי הואיל ונאמרה בו ברכה לדגים אלמנה נשאת בחמישי ונבעלת בששי הואיל ונאמרה בו ברכה לאדם טעמא משום ברכה אבל משום איקרורי דעתא לא חיישינן אי הכי אלמנה נמי תיבעל בחמישי הואיל ונאמרה בו ברכה לדגים ברכה דאדם עדיפא ליה ואי נמי משום שקדו דתניא מפני מה אמרו אלמנה נשאת בחמישי ונבעלת בששי שאם אתה אומר תיבעל בחמישי למחר משכים לאומנתו והולך לו [ו] שקדו חכמים על תקנת בנות ישראל [ז] שיהא שמח עמה שלשה ימים חמישי בשבת וערב שבת ושבת מאי איכא בין ברכה לשקדו איכא בינייהו אדם בטל אי נמי יום טוב שחל להיות בערב שבת דרש בר קפרא גדולים מעשה צדיקים יותר ממעשה שמים וארץ דאילו במעשה שמים וארץ כתיב (א) אף ידי יסדה ארץ וימיני טפחה שמים ואילו במעשה ידיהם של צדיקים כתיב (ב) מכון לשבתך פעלת ה' מקדש אדני כוננו ידיך השיב בבלי אחד ור' חייא שמו (ג) ויבשת ידיו יצרו ידו כתיב והכתיב יצרו א"ר נחמן בר יצחק יצרו אצבעותיו דכתיב (ד) כי אראה שמיך מעשה אצבעותיך ירח וכוכבים אשר כוננת מיתיבי (ה) השמים מספרים כבוד אל ומעשה ידיו מגיד הרקיע הכי קאמר מעשה ידיהם של צדיקים מי מגיד הרקיע ומאי ניהו מטר דרש בר קפרא מאי דכתיב (ו) ויתד תהיה לך על אזנך אל תקרי אזנך אלא על אוזנך שאם ישמע אדם דבר שאינו הגון

יניח

רש"י

משום חשבונות. שאם יכנוס למוצאי שבת יעשה סעודה בלילה ויחשוב בשבת מהו צריך להוציא וכתיב ודבר דבר (ישעיה נח): **מפקחים.** מוציאין לאור: **פיקוח.** פושקונברמ"ש בלעז: **טרטיאות.** פלטי מלכים ושלטונים: **ללמדו אומנות.** מצוה הוא דכתיב (קהלת ט) ראה חיים עם אשה אשר אהבת ללמוד אומנות שתחיה הימנו עם התורה ואמרינן בקידושין (דף ל:) שאביו חייב ללמדו אומנות: **שמא ישחוט בן עוף.** בשבת לצורך מוצאי שבת שיהא טרוד וישכח שהוא שבת: **שחל להיות בשני בשבת.** שצריכין להרבות בסעודה אחר השבת שהוא ערב יום כפורים: **ידחה.** לשלישי בשבת שמא ישחוט בן עוף לצורך סעודת מחר: **אית ליה רווחא.** לשחוט בלילה שהסעודה אינה עד למחר: **הכא לית ליה רווחא.** שהסעודה בלילה אחר השבת משכימה מיד: **ולא חיישינן לאיקרורי דעתא.** אם לא ימצא לה בתולים לא חיישינן שיתקרר כעסו בהאי פורתא: **ונבעלת בחמישי.** משתמש ברביעי ותיכנס ליל חמישי: **ברכה לדגים.** פרו ורבו ומלאו את המים כו' (בראשית א): **הואיל ונאמרה בו ברכה לאדם.** פרו ורבו ומלאו את הארץ (שם): **טעמא משום ברכה.** אבל מאן דלא קפיד אברכה משום איקרורי דעתא לא חיישינן משום האי פורתא: **ברכה דאדם עדיפא ליה.** ומיהו בששי לא תנשא בתולה דבזמן ארוך עד שני בשבת דאתו דייני חיישינן לאיקרורי אבל מרביעי עד חמישי לא חיישינן: **למחר משכים לאומנתו והולך.** שאין משתה אלמון באלמנה אלא יום אחד כדלקמן בפירקין (דף ז.): **חמישי בשבת.** יום חופה: **וששי בשבת.** חיבת ביאה: **אדם בטל.** למ"ד ברכה דאדם עדיפא אף זו תיבעל בששי למ"ד משום שקדו נבעלת בחמישי דהא לא ישכים לאומנתו: **גדולים מעשה צדיקים ממעשה יצירת שמים וארץ.** ומשום בר קפרא נקט לה דאיירי לעיל באגדה: **אף ידי.** חדא יד: **מקדש** מעשה ידי לדיקים הוא: **הכי קאמר.** האי ומעשה ידיו במעשה הלדיקים כתיב שקרוין מעשה שהם מעשה ידיו של הקב"ה וה"ק ומעשה ידיו דהוא מעשה הלדיקים מגיד הרקיע שהרקיע מעיד עליהם לבריות שהם לדיקים שמתפללין על הגשמים ומטר יורד: **יתד.** קביל"י בלע"ז:

תוספות

של ארבעה ארבעה טפחים שעשאן גולל לקבר המאהיל על גבי שתיהם טמא ניטלה אחת מהן המאהיל על גבי השניה טהור מפני שיש לטומאה דרך שילא מה שייך דרך שילא לפר"ת ובתוספתא דאהלות ספ"ג תניא מעשה באחד שמת בערב הפסח ולא רצו לקוברו ונכנסו הנשים וקשרו החבל בגולל משכו האנשים מבחוץ וקברוהו הנשים והלכו האנשים ועשו פסחיהן לערב משמע שלא היו יכולין הנשים לקוברו עד שמשכו האנשים מבחוץ את הגולל ואם גולל הויא מלבה למה לא קברוהו בלא מלבה עד אחר הפסח אלא ודאי הוא כסוי ארון כפירוש הקונטרס ולפי שהיה של אבן היה כבד כל כך [ג]:

שמא ישחוט בן עוף. יש גורסים בו עוף אע"ג דשבת לשון נקבה היא דכתיב (שמות לא) מחלליה מות יומת ה"נ הוי לשון זכר כל העושה בו מלאכה (שם לה) שומר שבת מחללו (ישעיה נו) ושפיר גרסינן נמי בן עוף דדרך בני אדם לשחוט הרכין והקטנים כדכתיב (ויקרא ה) שני בני יונה ובפרק קמא דקידושין (דף לו: ושם) אתיא מבן עוף מה לבן לאן שכן קבע לו כו':

אלא מעתה יום הכפורים שחל להיות בשני כו'. תימה אמאי נקט יום כפורים דלא הוי אלא לרבי יוסי הגלילי כדתנן (חולין דף פג.) בד' פרקים בשנה המוכר בהמה לחבירו צריך להודיעו אמה מכרתי לשחוט כו' וכדברי רבי יוסי הגלילי אף ערב יום הכפורים בגליל אמאי לא נקט חד מד' פרקים דהוי לכ"ע וי"ל דבערב יום הכפורים היו רגילין להרבות בעופות ובדגים כדמשמע בבראשית רבה (פי"א) גבי ההוא חייטא דזבן נונא כו' משום דהוי יום סליחה וכפרה ובהנהו ד' פרקים היו מרבים בבהמות דליכא למגזר שמא ישחוט:

אי הכי אלמנה נמי תיבעל בחמישי. פי' בשלמא אי הוה תני בברייתא דבתולה נבעלת בחמישי משום איקרורי דעתא כדקמיבעיא לן ולא משום ברכה לדגים דלא חשיבא הוי ניחא לן באלמנה דנבעלת בששי משום ברכה אבל השתא דטעמא דבתולה משום ברכה אלמנה נמי תיבעל בחמישי:

אי נמי משום שקדו. וא"ת והיכי מצי למימר משום שקדו הא בברייתא קתני בהדיא משום ברכה וי"ל דלהאי שינויא הוי פירוש הברייתא הכי אלמנה נשאת בחמישי ונבעלת בששי פי' משום שקדו כמו שמפורש בברייתא אחרת וא"ת משום ברכה דדגים היה להם להניח תקנת שקדו לא חשו לכך הואיל ובששי נמי נאמרה ברכה לאדם:

מאי איכא בין ברכה לשקדו. אע"ג דמשום ברכה לא מיקרי עבריינא מכל מקום בעי למה לי טעמא דברכה אי נמי בעי מאי איכא בין לישנא דמשני ברכה דאדם עדיפא ליה ובין לישנא דאי נמי משום שקדו ומשני דאיכא בינייהו אדם בטל אי נמי י"ט שחל להיות כו' דללישנא דטעמא דברייתא משום שקדו ולא משום ברכה הכא דליכא שקדו נבעלת אם ירצה בחמישי אבל ללישנא קמא דטעמא דברייתא משום ברכה כדמשמע פשטא דברייתא אפילו באדם בטל או בי"ט שחל להיות בערב שבת דליכא משום שקדו מכל מקום משום ברכה תבעל בששי ואפילו להאי לישנא אי לאו שתקנו משום שקדו משום ברכה לחודה לא היו קובעים יום כדפרישית לעיל גבי ותנשא באחד בשבת:

דאילו בשמים ובארץ כתיב אף ידי וגו'. דמשמע חדא אע"ג דמסיים קרא וימיני טפחה שמים ואמר בשלהי הקומץ רבה (מנחות לו: ושם) דיד היינו שמאל א"כ תרתי כתיב מ"מ בחד מעשה ליכא אלא חד אבל במעשה לדיקים בחד מעשה כמו בית המקדש כתיב תרתי ידים:

זה

מסורת הש"ס

א) שבת קנ., ב) [לעיל ב. ג. לקמן ז.], ג) [ועי' בתוס' שבת קנב: וסוכה כג. ד"ה ולא ותוס' סנהדרין מז:].

תורה אור השלם

א) אַף יָדִי יָסְדָה אֶרֶץ וִימִינִי טִפְּחָה שָׁמָיִם קֹרֵא אֲנִי אֲלֵיהֶם יַעַמְדוּ יַחְדָּו: [ישעיה מח, יג]

ב) תְּבִאֵמוֹ וְתִטָּעֵמוֹ בְּהַר נַחֲלָתְךָ מָכוֹן לְשִׁבְתְּךָ פָּעַלְתָּ יְיָ מִקְּדָשׁ אֲדֹנָי כּוֹנְנוּ יָדֶיךָ: [שמות טו, יז]

ג) אֲשֶׁר לוֹ הַיָּם וְהוּא עָשָׂהוּ וְיַבֶּשֶׁת יָדָיו יָצָרוּ: [תהלים צה, ה]

ד) כִּי אֶרְאֶה שָׁמֶיךָ מַעֲשֵׂי אֶצְבְּעֹתֶיךָ יָרֵחַ וְכוֹכָבִים אֲשֶׁר כּוֹנָנְתָּה: [תהלים ח, ד]

ה) הַשָּׁמַיִם מְסַפְּרִים כְּבוֹד אֵל וּמַעֲשֵׂה יָדָיו מַגִּיד הָרָקִיעַ: [תהלים יט, ב]

ו) וְיָתֵד תִּהְיֶה לְךָ עַל אֲזֵנֶךָ וְהָיָה בְּשִׁבְתְּךָ חוּץ וְחָפַרְתָּה בָהּ וְשַׁבְתָּ וְכִסִּיתָ אֶת צֵאָתֶךָ: [דברים כג, יד]

לעזי רש"י

פושקונברמ"ש. פירוש פיקוח, פינוי (המפולת). קביל"י:

ליקוטי רש"י

פיקוח נפש. בדבר שיש בו סכנה פקוח דיקומבימונ"ט. **לטרטייאות ולקרקייאות.** מיני פלטין הן ששם נאספו לבית הועד. **וללמדו אומנות.** דהא נמי מצוה היא דכל שאינו מלמדו אומנות מלמדו לסטות ומצוה ילפינן מקרא בקדושין בהאשה ניקנית (דף ל:) [שבת קנ.]. **מכון לשבתך.** מקדש של מטה מכוון כנגד כסא של מעלה אשר פעלת. **מקדש.** הטעם עליו זקף גדול להפרידו מתיבת השם של אחריו המקדש אשר כוננו ידיך ה'. חביב בית המקדש שהעולם נברא ביד אחת שנאמר (ישעיהו מח יג) אף ידי יסדה ארץ ומקדש בשתי ידים ואימתי יבנה בשתי ידים בזמן שה' ימלוך לעולם ועד לעתיד לבא שכל המלוכה שלו [שמות טו, יז]. **ומעשה ידיו מגיד הרקיע.** הכוכבים ואת המזלות שהם מעשה ידיו של הקב"ה אשר הם שם כמו שנאמ' (בראשית א) ויתן אותם אלהים ברקיע השמים ומשם מגידים כבודו [תהילים יט, ב]. **על אזנך.** לבד מכלי תשמישך. **אזנך.** כמו כלי זיין [דברים כג, יד].

עין משפט נר מצוה

יח א ב ג ד מיי' פכ"ד מהל' שבת הל"ה סמג לאוין סה טוש"ע או"ח סי' שו סעי' ו:

יט ה טוש"ע אה"ע סי' סד:

כ ו מיי' פ"י מהל' אישות הל' יב סמג עשין מח טוש"ע אה"ע סי' סד סעי' ג:

תוספות רי"ד

ר"ח ורב המנונא דאמרי תרוייהו חשבונות של מצוה מותר לחשבן בשבת וא"ר אלעזר פוסקין צדקה לעניים בשבת. וא"ר יעקב ב"א אר"י מפקחין פקוח נפש בשבת והולכים לב"כ ולבתי מדרשות לפקח על עסקי רבים בשבת. ותנא דבי מנשה משדכין על התינוקת לארס בשבת ועל התינוק ללמדו ספר וללמדו אומניות בשבת. וא"ר שמואל בר נחמני אר"י הולכין לטרטראות ולקרקסאות לפקח על עסקי רבים בשבת: תני בר קפרא בתולה נשאת בד' ונבעלת בה' הואיל ונאמרה בו ברכה לדגים ואלמנה נשאת בה' ונבעלת בו' הואיל ונאמרה בו ברכה לאדם ותניא מפני מה אמרו אלמנה נשאת בחמישי ונבעלת בו' שאם אתה אומר תבעל בחמישי למחר משכים הוא לאומנותו והולך. שקדו חכמים על תקנת בנות ישראל שיהא שמח עמה ג' ימים ה' בשבת ו' בשבת ושבת:

WIDOW IS MARRIED ON THURSDAY AND COHABITS ON FRIDAY? שֶׁאִם אַתָּה אוֹמֵר תִּיבָּעֵל בַּחֲמִישִׁי – BECAUSE IF YOU SAY SHE SHOULD COHABIT ON THURSDAY, לְמָחָר מַשְׁכִּים לְאוּמָּנְתּוֹ וְהוֹלֵךְ לוֹ – THE NEXT DAY [THE HUSBAND] WILL ARISE EARLY FOR HIS WORK AND GO AWAY, leaving his new bride alone.[21] שֶׁקָּדוּ חֲכָמִים עַל תַּקָּנַת בְּנוֹת יִשְׂרָאֵל – THE SAGES, however, WERE DILIGENT in promoting THE WELFARE OF JEWISH DAUGHTERS, שֶׁיְּהֵא שָׂמֵחַ עִמָּהּ שְׁלֹשָׁה יָמִים – so they legislated that the initial cohabitation should take place on Thursday night, rather than Thursday afternoon. This ensured THAT [THE GROOM] WOULD REJOICE WITH [THE BRIDE] FOR THREE DAYS: חֲמִישִׁי בְּשַׁבָּת וְעֶרֶב שַׁבָּת וְשַׁבָּת – THURSDAY, FRIDAY AND THE SABBATH.[22]

Having discovered a second reason for cohabiting with a widow on Friday, the Gemara inquires:

מַאי אִיכָּא בֵּין בְּרָכָה לְשָׁקְדוּ – What practical difference is there between the reason of the blessing and [the Sages] being diligent?

The Gemara gives two answers:

אִיכָּא בֵּינַיְיהוּ אָדָם בָּטֵל – The practical difference between them is the case of an idle man, i.e. one who does not work.[23] אִי נַמִּי יוֹם טוֹב שֶׁחָל לִהְיוֹת בְּעֶרֶב שַׁבָּת – Alternatively, a difference between them arises if they married during a week in which a Yom Tov fell on Friday.[24]

The Gemara digresses to cite another Aggadic statement of an Amora mentioned above:

דָּרַשׁ בַּר קַפָּרָא – Bar Kappara expounded: גְּדוֹלִים מַעֲשֵׂה צַדִּיקִים יוֹתֵר מִמַּעֲשֵׂה שָׁמַיִם וָאָרֶץ – The handiwork of the righteous is greater than the handiwork of God in creating the heavens and earth. דְּאִילּוּ בְּמַעֲשֵׂה שָׁמַיִם וָאָרֶץ כְּתִיב – For concerning the handiwork of the heavens and earth it is written:[25] "אַף־יָדִי יָסְדָה אֶרֶץ וִימִינִי טִפְּחָה שָׁמַיִם" – *Also, My hand has laid the foundation of the earth, and My right hand has measured out the heavens.* This verse implies that the heavens and the earth were each created using one hand. וְאִילּוּ בְּמַעֲשֵׂה יְדֵיהֶם שֶׁל צַדִּיקִים כְּתִיב – But concerning the handiwork of the righteous, it is written:[26] "מָכוֹן לְשִׁבְתְּךָ פָּעַלְתָּ ה׳ מִקְּדָשׁ אֲדֹנָי כּוֹנְנוּ יָדֶיךָ" – *The foundation of Your dwelling place that You, Hashem, have made – the Sanctuary, my Lord, that Your hands established.*[27]

The Gemara objects to this observation:

הֵשִׁיב בַּבְלִי אֶחָד וְרַבִּי חִיָּיא שְׁמוֹ – A certain Babylonian retorted, and his name was R' Chiya:[28] "וְיַבֶּשֶׁת יָדָיו יָצָרוּ" – But another verse states:[29] *And the dry land, His hands fashioned it!* We thus see that both hands are associated with creation of the earth. – ? –

The Gemara answers:

יָדוֹ כְּתִיב – The word is written without the second *yud,* so it can be interpreted "his hand," in the singular.[30]

The Gemara objects to this answer:

וְהָכְתִיב "יָצָרוּ" – But it is written: *they fashioned,* clearly indicating a plurality.[31] – ? –

The Gemara defends the answer:

אָמַר רַב נַחְמָן בַּר יִצְחָק – Rav Nachman bar Yitzchak said: יָצְרוּ אֶצְבְּעוֹתָיו – The plural verb used in the verse does not refer to two hands; rather, it means that His fingers (plural) of one hand fashioned the dry land, כְּדִכְתִיב "כִּי־אֶרְאֶה שָׁמֶיךָ מַעֲשֵׂה אֶצְבְּעֹתֶיךָ יָרֵחַ וְכוֹכָבִים אֲשֶׁר כּוֹנָנְתָּה" – as it is written:[32] *When I behold Your heavens, the work of Your fingers, the moon and the stars that You have set in place.*

The Gemara again questions the exposition of Bar Kappara:

מֵיתִיבֵי – They challenged: "הַשָּׁמַיִם מְסַפְּרִים כְּבוֹד־אֵל וּמַעֲשֵׂה יָדָיו מַגִּיד הָרָקִיעַ" – The verse states:[33] *The heavens declare the glory of God, and the firmament tells of the work of His hands.* This verse would seem to indicate that the earth is considered the work of two hands. – ? –

The Gemara answers by reinterpreting the verse:

הָכִי קָאָמַר – This is what [the verse] means: מַעֲשֵׂה יְדֵיהֶם שֶׁל צַדִּיקִים מִי מַגִּיד – Who tells of the handiwork of the righteous? הָרָקִיעַ – The firmament. וּמַאי נִיהוּ – And how is that? מָטָר – Through the rain.[34]

The Gemara cites another exposition of Bar Kappara:[35]

דָּרַשׁ בַּר קַפָּרָא – Bar Kappara expounded: מַאי דִּכְתִיב "וְיָתֵד תִּהְיֶה לְךָ עַל־אֲזֵנֶךָ" – Why is it written: *You shall have a spike in addition to your weapons (azeinecha)?*[36] אַל תִּקְרֵי "אֲזֵנֶךָ" – Do not read it *azeinecha,* meaning "your weapons," אֶלָּא עַל אוֹזְנֶךָ – but rather *oznecha,* meaning "your ears." שֶׁאִם יִשְׁמַע אָדָם דָּבָר שֶׁאֵינוֹ הָגוּן – For if a person hears something that is not proper,

NOTES

21. Since the feast mandated for the wedding of a widow takes place on the day of the wedding (see below, 7a; see also *Rashash* here), there would be no reason for the groom to stay home the day after the wedding (*Rashi*).

[Although the Gemara below (7a) states that three days of rejoicing follow the wedding of a widow, that is based on the Gemara's conclusion here (*Ritva;* see also *Rashash*).]

22. On Thursday the *chuppah* takes place, on Friday they cohabit, and on the Sabbath he stays home in any case (*Rashi*). [Although the cohabitation takes place on Thursday night, the bond of affection created by the mitzvah-cohabitation is such that he will not go away to his work on the very next morning; thus, he will stay home on Friday because of the cohabitation that took place during the previous night.]

23. According to the reason that the blessing for man is preferable to the blessing for the fish, the cohabitation should still take place on Friday. But according to the reason that the Sages were concerned for the welfare of Jewish women, they could cohabit on Thursday, since he will not go to work on Friday in any case [and they will gain the advantage of the blessing of the fish] (*Rashi*; see note 20).

24. There is thus no concern about the groom going out to work on Friday even if no cohabitation takes place on that day.

25. *Isaiah* 48:13.

26. *Exodus* 15:17.

27. Thus, Scripture refers to only one hand when describing the creation of the heavens and earth, while it states that "hands" – in the plural – established the Temple, which was built by the righteous (*Rashi*). [See *Maharsha,* who explains this; see also *Maharal* in *Chidushei Aggados*.]

Although the verse concerning Creation concludes *My right hand spread out the heavens,* we do not see *both* hands being used for any single act of creation (*Tosafos*).

28. See *Shitah Mekubetzes,* who explains why the Gemara specifies R' Chiya's nationality.

29. *Psalms* 95:5.

30. Although the word is pronounced יָדָו, *his hands,* it can also be read יָדוֹ, *his hand.* This indicates that the word is not to be expounded as a plural. [It should be noted that in our texts, the spelling of the word is indeed ידיו; see *Rashash.*]

31. The verb יָצָרוּ *(they fashioned)* is written in the plural, indicating that the subject is plural.

32. Ibid. 8:4.

33. Ibid. 19:2.

34. The handiwork of the righteous is associated with the handiwork of God. The verse thus means to state that God's handiwork – that which is produced by the righteous – is testified to by the heavens. For when the righteous pray for rain, rain descends (*Rashi*).

35. See *Chasam Sofer,* who suggests a link between the three statements of Bar Kappara cited here.

36. *Deuteronomy* 23:14. The literal meaning of the verse commands that one must carry a spike in addition to one's weapons, for the purpose of digging holes to cover bodily waste. The Gemara, though, expounds it as carrying a different meaning. See *Maharsha.*

מסורת הש"ס

א) שבת קנ., ב) [לעיל ג. ג. לקמן ז.], ג) [ועי' תוס' שבת קנב: ועוכה כב. ד"ה ולא ותוס' סנהדרין מז:].

תורה אור השלם

א) אַף יָדִי יָסְדָה אֶרֶץ וִימִינִי טִפְּחָה שָׁמָיִם קֹרֵא אֲנִי אֲלֵיהֶם יַעַמְדוּ יַחְדָּו: [ישעיה מח, יג]

ב) תְּבִאֵמוֹ וְתִטָּעֵמוֹ בְּהַר נַחֲלָתְךָ מָכוֹן לְשִׁבְתְּךָ פָּעַלְתָּ יְיָ מִקְּדָשׁ אֲדֹנָי כּוֹנְנוּ יָדֶיךָ: [שמות טו, יז]

ג) אֲשֶׁר לוֹ הַיָּם וְהוּא עָשָׂהוּ וְיַבֶּשֶׁת יָדָיו יָצָרוּ: [תהלים צה, ה]

ד) כִּי אֶרְאֶה שָׁמֶיךָ מַעֲשֵׂי אֶצְבְּעֹתֶיךָ יָרֵחַ וְכוֹכָבִים אֲשֶׁר כּוֹנָנְתָּה: [תהלים ח, ד]

ה) הַשָּׁמַיִם מְסַפְּרִים כְּבוֹד אֵל וּמַעֲשֵׂה יָדָיו מַגִּיד הָרָקִיעַ: [תהלים יט, ב]

ו) וְיָתֵד תִּהְיֶה לְךָ עַל אֲזֵנֶךָ וְהָיָה בְּשִׁבְתְּךָ חוּץ וְחָפַרְתָּה בָהּ וְשַׁבְתָּ וְכִסִּיתָ אֶת צֵאָתֶךָ: [דברים כג, יד]

לעזי רש"י

פושקונברמ"ש. פירוש פיקוח, פינוי (המפולת). קבילי"ר:

ליקוטי רש"י

פיקוח נפש. בדבר שיש בו סכנה פקוח דיקומבימינט"ש. לטרטיאות ולקרקסאות. מיני פלטין הן שאם נאספין לבית הועד. וללמדו אומנות. דהא נמי מלוה היא דכל שאינו מלמדו אומנות מלמדו לסטות ומלוה ילפינן מקרא בקדושין בהאשה ניקנית (דף ל:) [שבת קנ.]. מכון לשבתך. מקדש של מטה מכוון כנגד כסא של מעלה אשר פעלת. מקדש. הטעם עליו זקף גדול להפרידו מתיבת השם של אחריו המקדש אשר כוננו ידיך ה'. חביב בית המקדש שכשהעולם נברא ביד אחת שנאמר (ישעיהו מח יג) אף ידי יסדה ארץ ומקדש בשתי ידים ואימתי יבנה בשתי ידים בזמן שה' ימלוך לעולם ועד לעתיד לבוא שכל המלוכה שלו [שמות טו, יז]. ומעשה ידיו מגיד הרקיע. הכוכבים ואת המזלות שהם מעשה ידיו של הקב"ה אשר הם שם כמו שנאמר (בראשית א) ויתן אותם אלהים ברקיע השמים ומהם מגידים כבודו [תהלים יט, ב]. על אזנך. לבד מכלי תשמישך. אזנך. כמו כלי זיין [דברים כג, יד].

גמרא

משום חשבונות אמר ליה אביי וחשבונות של מצוה מי אסירי והא רב חסדא ורב המנונא דאמרי תרוייהו א) חשבונות של מצוה מותר לחשבן בשבת וא"ר אלעזר ב פוסקין צדקה לעניים בשבת ואמר ר' יעקב אמר ר' יוחנן ג הולכין לבתי כנסיות ולבתי מדרשות לפקח על עסקי רבים בשבת ואמר רבי יעקב בר אידי אמר רבי יוחנן מפקחין פיקוח נפש בשבת ואמר רב שמואל בר נחמני אמר רבי יונתן הולכין לטרטיאות ולקרקייאות לפקח על עסקי רבים בשבת ותנא דבי מנשיא ד משדכין על התינוקת ליארס בשבת ועל התינוק ללמדו ספר וללמדו אומנות אלא אמר רבי זירא גזירה שמא ישחוט בן עוף א"ל אביי אלא מעתה יום הכפורים שחל להיות בשני בשבת ידחה גזירה שמא ישחוט בן עוף התם דלנפשיה לא טריד הכא דלאחרים טריד אי נמי התם אית ליה רווחא הכא לית ליה רווחא השתא דאתית להכי ערב שבת נמי גזירה שמא ישחוט בן עוף איבעיא להו בתולה נשאת ברביעי ונבעלת ברביעי ולא חיישינן לאיקרורי דעתא או דלמא בתולה נשאת ברביעי ונבעלת בחמישי דחיישינן לאיקרורי דעתא ת"ש דתני בר קפרא בתולה נשאת ברביעי ה ונבעלת בחמישי הואיל ונאמרה בו ברכה לדגים אלמנה נשאת בחמישי ונבעלת בששי הואיל ונאמרה בו ברכה לאדם טעמא משום ברכה אבל משום איקרורי דעתא לא חיישינן אי הכי אלמנה נמי תיבעל בחמישי הואיל ונאמרה בו ברכה לדגים ברכה דאדם עדיפא ליה ואי נמי משום שקדו דתניא מפני מה אמרו אלמנה נשאת בחמישי ונבעלת בששי שאם אתה אומר תיבעל בחמישי למחר משכים לאומנתו והולך לו ו שקדו חכמים על תקנת בנות ישראל ז שיהא שמח עמה שלשה ימים חמישי בשבת וערב שבת ושבת מאי איכא בין ברכה לשקדו איכא בינייהו אדם בטל אי נמי יום טוב שחל להיות בערב שבת דרש בר קפרא גדולים מעשה צדיקים יותר ממעשה שמים וארץ דאילו במעשה שמים וארץ כתיב א) אף ידי יסדה ארץ וימיני טפחה שמים ואילו במעשה ידיהם של צדיקים כתיב ב) מכון לשבתך פעלת ה' מקדש אדני כוננו ידיך השיב בבלי אחד ור' חייא שמו ג) ויבשת ידיו יצרו ידו כתיב והכתיב יצרו א"ר נחמן בר יצחק יצרו אצבעותיו דכתיב ד) כי אראה שמיך מעשה אצבעותיך ירח וכוכבים אשר כוננתה מיתיבי ה) השמים מספרים כבוד אל ומעשה ידיו מגיד הרקיע הכי קאמר מעשה ידיהם של צדיקים מי מגיד הרקיע ומאי ניהו מטר דרש בר קפרא מאי דכתיב ו) ויתד תהיה לך על אזנך אל תקרי אזנך אלא על אוזנך שאם ישמע אדם דבר שאינו הגון יניח

רש"י

משום חשבונות. שאם יכנוס למוצאי שבת יעשה סעודה בלילה ויחשוב בשבת מהו צריך להוציא וכתיב ודבר דבר (ישעיה נח): מפקחים. מוציאין לאור: פיקוח. פושקונברמ"ש בלעז: טרטיאות. פלטי מלכים ושלטונים: ללמדו אומנות. מצוה הוא דכתיב (קהלת ט) ראה חיים עם אשה אשר אהבת למוד אומנות שתחיה הימנו עם התורה ואמרינן בקידושין (דף כט.) שאביו חייב ללמדו אומנות: שמא ישחוט בן עוף. בשבת לצורך מוצאי שבת שיהא טרוד וישכח שהוא שבת: שחל להיות בשני בשבת. שצריכין להרבות בסעודה אחר השבת שהוא ערב יום כפורים: ידחה. לשלישי בשבת שמא ישחוט בן עוף לצורך סעודת מחר: אית ליה רווחא. לשחוט בלילה שהסעודה אינה עד למחר: הכא לית ליה רווחא. שהסעודה בלילה אחר השבת משחשיכה מיד: ולא חיישינן לאיקרורי דעתא. אם לא ימצא לה בתולים לא חיישינן שיתקרר כעסו בהאי פורתא: ונבעלת בחמישי. משתהא ברביעי ותיכנס ליל חמישי: ברכה לדגים. פרו ורבו ומלאו את המים כו' (בראשית א): הואיל ונאמרה בו ברכה לאדם. פרו ורבו ומלאו את הארץ (שם): טעמא משום ברכה. אבל מאן דלא קפיד אברכה משום איקרורי דעתא לא חיישינן משום האי פורתא: ברכה דאדם עדיפא ליה. ומיהו בששי לא תנשא בתולה דבזמן ארוך עד שני בשבת דאתו לידי חיישינן לאיקרורי אבל מרביעי עד חמישי לא חיישינן: למחר משכים לאומנתו והולך. שאין משתה אלמון באלמנה אלא יום אחד כדלקמן בפירקין (דף ז.): חמישי בשבת. יום חופה: וששי בשבת. חיבת ביאה: אדם בטל. למ"ד ברכה דאדם עדיפא אף זו תיבעל בששי למ"ד משום שקדו נבעלת בחמישי דהא לא ישכים לאומנתו: גדולים מעשה צדיקים ממעשה יצירת שמים וארץ. ומשום בר קפרא נקט לה דאיירי לעיל באגדה: אף ידי. חדא יד: מקדש מעשה ידי צדיקים הוא: הכי קאמר. האי ומעשה ידיו במעשה הצדיקים כתיב שקרוין מעשה שלהם מעשה ידיו של הקב"ה וה"ק ומעשה ידיו דהוא מעשה הצדיקים מגיד הרקיע שהרקיע מעיד עליהם לבריות שהם צדיקים שמתפללין על הגשמים ומטר יורד: יתד. קביל"י בלע"ז:

תוספות

של ארבעה ארבעה טפחים שעשאן גולל לקבר המאהיל על גבי שתיהם טמא ניטלה אחת מהן המאהיל על גבי השניה טהור מפני שיש לטומאה דרך שילא מה שייך דרך שילא לפר"ת ובתוספתא דאהלות ספ"ג תניא מעשה באחד שמת בערב הפסח ולא רצו לקוברו ונכנסו הנשים וקשרו החבל בגולל משכו האנשים מבחוץ וקברוהו הנשים והלכו האנשים ועשו פסחיהן לערב משמע שלא היו יכולין הנשים לקוברו עד שמשכו האנשים מבחוץ את הגולל ואם גולל הויא מצבה למה לא קברוהו בלא מצבה עד אחר הפסח אלא ודאי הוא כסוי ארון כפירוש הקונטרס ולפי שהיה של אבן היה כבד כל כך ג):

שמא ישחוט בן עוף. יש גורסים בו עוף אע"ג דשבת לשון נקבה היא דכתיב (שמות לא) מחלליה מות יומת ה"נ הוי לשון זכר כל העושה בו מלאכה (שם לה) שומר שבת מחללו (ישעיה נו) ושפיר גרסינן נמי בן עוף דדרך בני אדם לשחוט הרכין והקטנים כדכתיב (ויקרא ה) שני בני יונה ובפרק קמא דקידושין (דף לו: ושם) אתיא מבן עוף מה לבן לאן שכן קבע לו כו':

אלא מעתה יום הכפורים שחל להיות בשני כו'. תימה אמאי נקט יום כפורים דלא הוי אלא לרבי יוסי הגלילי כדתנן (חולין דף פג.) בד' פרקים בשנה המוכר בהמה לחבירו צריך להודיעו אמה מכרתי לשחוט כו' וכדברי רבי יוסי הגלילי אף ערב יום הכפורים בגליל אמאי לא נקט חד מד' פרקים דהוי לכ"ע וי"ל דבערב יום הכפורים היו רגילין להרבות בעופות ובדגים כדמשמע בבראשית רבה (פי"א) גבי ההוא חייטא דזבן נונא כו' משום דהוי יום סליחה וכפרה ובהנהו ד' פרקים היו מרבים בבהמות דליכא למגזר שמא ישחוט:

אי הכי אלמנה נמי תיבעל בחמישי. פי' בשלמא אי הוה תני בברייתא דבתולה נבעלת בחמישי משום איקרורי דעתא כדקמיבעיא לן ולא משום ברכה לדגים דלא חשיבא הוי ניחא לן באלמנה דנבעלת בששי משום ברכה אבל השתא דטעמא דבתולה משום ברכה אלמנה נמי תיבעל בחמישי:

אי נמי משום שקדו. וא"ת והיכי מצי למימר משום שקדו הא בברייתא קתני בהדיא משום ברכה וי"ל דלהאי שינויא הוי פירוש הברייתא הכי אלמנה נשאת בחמישי ונבעלת בששי פי' משום שקדו כמו שמפורש בברייתא אחרת וא"ת משום ברכה דדגים היה להם להניח תקנת שקדו לא חשו לכך הואיל ובששי נמי נאמרה ברכה לאדם:

מאי איכא בין ברכה לשקדו. אע"ג דמשום ברכה לא מיקרי עברייני מכל מקום בעי למה לי טעמא דברכה אי נמי בעי מאי איכא בין לישנא דמשני ברכה דאדם עדיפא ליה ובין לישנא דאי נמי משום שקדו ומשני דאיכא בינייהו אדם בטל אי נמי י"ט שחל להיות כו' דללישנא דטעמא דברייתא משום שקדו ולא משום ברכה הכא ליכא שקדו נבעלת אם ירצה בחמישי אבל ללישנא קמא דטעמא דברייתא משום ברכה כדמשמע פשטא דברייתא אפילו באדם בטל או בי"ט שחל להיות בערב שבת ליכא משום שקדו מכל מקום משום ברכה תבעל בששי ואפילו להאי לישנא אי לאו שתקנו משום שקדו משום ברכה לחודה לא היו קובעים יום כדפרישית לעיל גבי ותנשא באחד בשבת:

דאילו בשמים ובארץ כתיב אף ידי וגו'. דמשמע חדא אע"ג דמסיים קרא וימיני טפחה שמים ואמר בשילהי הקומץ רבה (מנחות לו: ושם) דיד היינו שמאל א"כ תרתי כתיב מ"מ בחד מעשה ליכא אלא חד אבל במעשה צדיקים בחד מעשה כמו בית המקדש כתיב תרתי ידים:

זה

עין משפט נר מצוה

יח א ב ג ד מיי' פכ"ד מהל' שבת הל' ה סמג לאוין סה טוש"ע או"ח סי' שו סעי' ו:
יט ה טוש"ע אה"ע סי' סד:
כ ו מיי' פ"י מהל' אישות הל' יג סמג עשין מח טוש"ע אה"ע סי' סד סעי' ג:

תוספות רי"ד

ר"ח ורב המנונא דאמרי תרוייהו חשבונות של מצוה מותר לחשבן בשבת וא"ר אלעזר פוסקין צדקה לעניים בשבת. וא"ר יעקב ב"א אר"י מפקחין פקוח נפש בשבת והולכים לבכ"נ ולבתי מדרשות לפקח על עסקי רבים בשבת. ותנא דבי מנשה משדכין על התינוקת לארס בשבת ועל התינוק ללמדו ספר וללמדו אומניות בשבת. וא"ר שמואל בר נחמני אר"י הולכין לטרטראות ולקרקסאות לפקח על עסקי רבים בשבת: תני בר קפרא בתולה נשאת בד' ונבעלת בה' הואיל ונאמרה בו ברכה לדגים ואלמנה נשאת בה' ונבעלת בו' הואיל ונאמרה בו ברכה לאדם ותניא מפני מה אמרו אלמנה נשאת בחמישי ונבעלת בו' שאם אתה אומר תבעל בחמישי למחר משכים הוא לאומנותו והולך. שקדו חכמים על תקנות בנות ישראל שיהא שמח עמה ג' ימים ה' בשבת ו' בשבת ושבת.

to **a decree that perhaps he will** become preoccupied and **slaughter a young bird** on the Sabbath in preparation for the feast that is held on the day before Yom Kippur.[10] – ? –

The Gemara presents two answers to this challenge. The first: הָתָם דִּלְנַפְשֵׁיהּ לֹא טָרִיד – **There,** regarding Yom Kippur, **where** his preparations **are** only **for himself, he will not be preoccupied** with the preparations to the extent that he will mistakenly violate the Sabbath. הָכָא דִּלַאֲחֵרִים טָרִיד – But **here,** regarding the wedding, **where** his preparations **are for others** (the wedding guests), **he may become preoccupied** due to the many preparations necessary, and mistakenly violate the Sabbath as a result.

The second answer:

אִי נַמִּי – **Alternatively,** הָתָם אִית לֵיהּ רַוְוחָא – **there, he has sufficient time** to prepare the meal after the Sabbath, since the pre-Yom Kippur meal is not held until the next day.[11] הָכָא לֵית לֵיהּ רַוְוחָא – But **here, he does not have sufficient** time to prepare after the Sabbath, because the wedding meal is needed immediately after nightfall on Saturday night.

The Gemara concludes:

הַשְׁתָּא דְּאָתֵית לְהָכִי – **Now that you have come to this** answer, עֶרֶב שַׁבָּת נַמִּי – we can say that the reason one may not cohabit on **Friday** night is **also** גְּזֵירָה שֶׁמָּא יִשְׁחוֹט בֶּן עוֹף – because of **a decree that perhaps he will slaughter a young bird** for the wedding meal after the Sabbath begins.[12]

The Gemara seeks clarification of our Mishnah:

אִיבַּעְיָא לְהוּ – **They inquired:** בְּתוּלָה נִשֵּׂאת בִּרְבִיעִי וְנִבְעֶלֶת בִּרְבִיעִי – Does the Mishnah mean that **a virgin is married on Wednesday and she** may **cohabit** with her husband **on Wednesday,**[13] וְלֹא חָיְישִׁינָן לְאִיקְרוּרֵי דַּעְתָּא – **and we are not concerned about** his anger **cooling off** between the cohabitation on Wednesday and Thursday morning if he doubts her virginity?[14] אוֹ דִּלְמָא בְּתוּלָה נִשֵּׂאת בִּרְבִיעִי וְנִבְעֶלֶת בַּחֲמִישִׁי – **Or perhaps** the Mishnah means that **a virgin is married on Wednesday, and she** may **cohabit** with her husband only **on Wednesday night,**[15] דְּחָיְישִׁינָן לְאִיקְרוּרֵי דַּעְתָּא – **because we are concerned about** the husband's anger **cooling off** by Thursday morning if they would cohabit on Wednesday afternoon.

The Gemara resolves the question:

תָּא שְׁמַע דְּתָנֵי בַּר קַפָּרָא – **Come, learn** the answer, **for Bar Kappara taught a Baraisa** as follows: בְּתוּלָה נִשֵּׂאת בִּרְבִיעִי – A VIRGIN IS MARRIED ON WEDNESDAY וְנִבְעֶלֶת בַּחֲמִישִׁי – AND COHABITS ON WEDNESDAY NIGHT, הוֹאִיל וְנֶאֶמְרָה בּוֹ בְּרָכָה לַדָּגִים – SINCE A BLESSING TO THE FISH WAS STATED ON THAT day.[16] אַלְמָנָה נִשֵּׂאת בַּחֲמִישִׁי – A WIDOW IS MARRIED ON THURSDAY וְנִבְעֶלֶת בְּשִׁשִּׁי – AND COHABITS ON THURSDAY NIGHT הוֹאִיל וְנֶאֶמְרָה בּוֹ בְּרָכָה לָאָדָם – SINCE A BLESSING TO MAN WAS STATED ON THAT day.[17] טַעְמָא מִשּׁוּם בְּרָכָה – The Baraisa thus indicates that **the** only **reason** to cohabit on Wednesday night **is because of the blessing,** אֲבָל מִשּׁוּם אִיקְרוּרֵי דַּעְתָּא לֹא חָיְישִׁינָן – **but we are not concerned about the husband's anger cooling off** in the period from Wednesday until Thursday morning.

The Gemara questions the second half of the Baraisa:

אִי הָכִי – **If** it is **so,** that the blessing to the fish is the reason for a virgin to cohabit on Wednesday night, אַלְמָנָה נַמִּי תִּיבָּעֵל בַּחֲמִישִׁי – **a widow should also cohabit on Thursday** הוֹאִיל וְנֶאֶמְרָה בּוֹ בְּרָכָה לַדָּגִים – **since a blessing to the fish was stated on that** day.[18] – ? –

The Gemara answers:

בְּרָכָה דְּאָדָם עֲדִיפָא לֵיהּ – **The blessing for man is preferable to him.** Therefore, a widow cohabits on Thursday night.[19]

The Gemara presents a second reason why a widow cohabits on Friday rather than Thursday:

וְאִי נַמִּי מִשּׁוּם שֶׁקְּדוּ – **Alternatively, it is because [the Sages] were diligent** in promoting the welfare of Jewish women.[20] דְּתַנְיָא – **For it was taught in a Baraisa:** מִפְּנֵי מָה אָמְרוּ אַלְמָנָה נִשֵּׂאת בַּחֲמִישִׁי וְנִבְעֶלֶת בְּשִׁשִּׁי – WHY DID [THE SAGES] STATE THAT A

NOTES

moon. Thus, the court could refuse to accept the testimony of witnesses who had seen the new moon on the twenty-ninth day, and make one of the preceding months a day longer.] They would thus cause the tenth of Tishrei to fall on Tuesday (*Ritva;* see there for an alternative explanation).

10. The Gemara (*Yoma* 81b) derives that there is a mitzvah to eat on the day before Yom Kippur. Thus, if Yom Kippur falls on Monday, there is a mitzvah to eat on Sunday (*Rashi*). Accordingly, the Gemara asks why the Sages were not concerned that a person would slaughter a bird on the Sabbath to prepare for this meal.

11. *Rashi.* [*Aruch HaShulchan* (*Orach Chaim* 604:5; see also *Beur HaGra* to 604:2) infers from this Gemara that there is no mitzvah to eat on the *night* before Yom Kippur. See *Yabia Omer* (1:37) for further discussion of this issue.]

12. One who performs the initial cohabitation on Friday night will have the wedding feast on Friday afternoon; such a feast could conceivably extend into the Sabbath. And if the groom sees that he does not have sufficient food for his guests, he may forget that the Sabbath has started, and come to slaughter a bird for his guests.

[See *Pnei Yehoshua,* who discusses why the Gemara feels that it is necessary to discover another reason for the prohibition, inasmuch as a different reason (viz. that a wound will be made on Friday night) is stated explicitly in another Baraisa.]

13. That is, Wednesday during the day. [Although one is supposed to engage in marital relations only at night (see below, 65b)] relations are permitted in a darkened room even during the day (*Ramban, Rashba, Ritva*).

14. That is, if he finds that she is not a virgin on Wednesday, his anger will not cool off in the short time until Thursday morning when the courts go into session (*Rashi*).

15. Wednesday night is called the fifth day of the week, because in the Jewish calendar the night is considered the beginning of each new day (see *Rashi*). [Thus, a cohabitation performed on Wednesday night is said to have been performed on Thursday.]

16. After God created the fish on the fifth day of Creation, He said (*Genesis* 1:22): *Be fruitful and multiply, and fill the waters of the sea* (*Rashi*). This is an especially potent blessing (see *Ritva*), which is relevant to the procreation of man as well; thus, *Thursday* is, so to speak, a blessed day, auspicious for the mitzvah-cohabitation. See note 20.

17. After creating Man on the sixth day, God said (ibid. 1:28): *Be fruitful and multiply, and fill the earth* (*Rashi*).

18. If the reason that a virgin should have her first cohabitation on Thursday would be because we are concerned that the cohabitation be as close to Thursday morning (when the courts are in session) as possible, and not because of the blessing given to the fish on that day, then it would be understandable that a widow would get married on Friday (because that is the day that a blessing was given to man). But now that the Baraisa states that the reason that a virgin waits until Wednesday night is because of the blessing given to fish, the Gemara asks why a widow should not cohabit for the first time on Thursday (Wednesday night) as well (*Tosafos;* see also *Ritva*).

19. However, this is not a sufficient reason for a virgin to be married on Thursday night or Friday, because then we have to be concerned that if the husband is doubtful of her virginity his anger will cool off by the time the courts convene on Monday. But for the brief time between Wednesday and Thursday, there is no concern (*Rashi*).

20. Although the Baraisa cited by Bar Kappara seems to state that a widow cohabits on Friday because of the blessing, the real reason is because the Sages were conscientious about the welfare of Jewish women, as will be explained by another Baraisa that the Gemara proceeds to cite. Bar Kappara's Baraisa means to say that the blessing to the fish does not override the Sages' reason to have the cohabitation take place on Friday (Thursday night), because on Friday too a blessing was given – to man (*Tosafos;* see *Shitah Mekubetzes*). [See *Ritva* for why the blessing to the fish is, in fact, preferable to the blessing given to man.]

משום חשבונות אמר ליה אביי וחשבונות של מצוה מי אסירי והא רב חסדא ורב המנונא דאמרי תרוייהו [א] חשבונות של מצוה מותר לחשבן בשבת וא"ר אלעזר [ב] פוסקין צדקה לעניים בשבת ואמר ר' יעקב אמר ר' יוחנן [ג] הולכין לבתי כנסיות ולבתי מדרשות לפקח על עסקי רבים בשבת ואמר רבי יעקב בר אידי אמר רבי יוחנן מפקחין פיקוח נפש בשבת ואמר רב שמואל בר נחמני אמר רבי יונתן הולכין לטרטיאות ולקרקייאות לפקח על עסקי רבים בשבת ותנא דבי מנשיא [ד] משדכין על התינוקת ליארס בשבת ועל התינוק ללמדו ספר וללמדו אומנות אלא אמר רבי זירא גזירה שמא ישחוט בן עוף א"ל אביי אלא מעתה יום הכפורים שחל להיות בשני בשבת ידחה גזירה שמא ישחוט בן עוף התם דלנפשיה לא טריד הכא דלאחרים טריד אי נמי התם אית ליה רווחא הכא לית ליה רווחא השתא דאתית להכי ערב שבת נמי גזירה שמא ישחוט בן עוף איבעיא להו בתולה נשאת ברביעי ונבעלת ברביעי ולא חיישינן לאיקרורי דעתא או דלמא בתולה נשאת ברביעי ונבעלת בחמישי דחיישינן לאיקרורי דעתא ת"ש דתני בר קפרא בתולה נשאת ברביעי [ה] ונבעלת בחמישי הואיל ונאמרה בו ברכה לדגים אלמנה נשאת בחמישי ונבעלת בששי הואיל ונאמרה בו ברכה לאדם טעמא משום ברכה אבל משום איקרורי דעתא לא חיישינן אי הכי אלמנה נמי תיבעל בחמישי הואיל ונאמרה בו ברכה לדגים ברכה דאדם עדיפא ליה ואי נמי משום שקדו דתניא מפני מה אמרו אלמנה נשאת בחמישי ונבעלת בששי שאם אתה אומר תיבעל בחמישי למחר משכים לאומנתו והולך לו [ו] שקדו חכמים על תקנת בנות ישראל [ז] שיהא שמח עמה שלשה ימים חמישי בשבת וערב שבת ושבת מאי איכא בין ברכה לשקדו איכא בינייהו אדם בטל אי נמי יום טוב שחל להיות בערב שבת דרש בר קפרא גדולים מעשה צדיקים יותר ממעשה שמים וארץ דאילו במעשה שמים וארץ כתיב [א] אף ידי יסדה ארץ וימיני טפחה שמים ואילו במעשה ידיהם של צדיקים כתיב [ב] מכון לשבתך פעלת ה' מקדש אדני כוננו ידיך השיב בבלי אחד ור' חייא שמו [ג] וידיו יבשת יצרו ידו כתיב והכתיב יצרו א"ר נחמן בר יצחק יצרו אצבעותיו כדכתיב [ד] כי אראה שמיך מעשה אצבעותיך ירח וכוכבים אשר כוננת מיתיבי [ה] השמים מספרים כבוד אל ומעשה ידיו מגיד הרקיע הכי קאמר מעשה ידיהם של צדיקים מי מגיד הרקיע ומאי ניהו מטר דרש בר קפרא מאי דכתיב [ו] ויתד תהיה לך על אזנך אל תקרי אזנך אלא על אוזנך שאם ישמע אדם דבר שאינו הגון יניח

רש"י

משום חשבונות. שאם יכנוס למוצאי שבת יעשה סעודה בלילה ויחשוב בשבת מהו צריך להוציא וכתיב ודבר דבר (ישעיה נח): מפקחים. מוציאין לאור: פיקוח. פוסקונדרמ"ש בלעז: טרטיאות. פלטי מלכים ושלטונים: ללמדו אומנות. מלוה הוא דכתיב (קהלת ט) ראה חיים עם אשה אשר אהבת ללמוד אומנות שתחיה ימיהם עם התורה ואמרינן בקידושין (דף כט.) שאביו חייב ללמדו אומנות: שמא ישחוט בן עוף. בשבת לצורך מוצאי שבת שיהא טרוד ושכח שהוא שבת: שחל להיות בשני בשבת. שצריכין להרבות בסעודה אחר השבת שהוא ערב יום כפורים: ידחה. לשלישי בשבת שמא ישחוט בן עוף לצורך סעודת מחר: אית ליה רווחא. לשחוט בלילה שהסעודה אינה עד למחר: הכא לית ליה רווחא. שהסעודה בלילה אחר השבת משתסיכה מיד: ולא חיישינן לאיקרורי דעתא. אם לא ימצא לה בתולים לא חיישינן שיתקרר כעסו בהאי פורתא: ונבעלת בחמישי. משתמשך ברביעי ותיכנס ליל חמישי: ברכה לדגים. פרו ורבו ומלאו את המים כו' (בראשית א): הואיל ונאמרה בו ברכה לאדם. פרו ורבו ומלאו את הארץ (שם): טעמא משום ברכה. אבל מאן דלא קפיד אברכה משום איקרורי דעתא לא חיישינן משום האי פורתא: ברכה דאדם עדיפא ליה. ומיהו בששי לא תנשא בתולה דזמנא ארוך עד שני בשבת דאתו דייני חיישינן לאיקרורי אבל מרביעי עד חמישי לא חיישינן: למחר משכים לאומנתו והולך. שאין משתה אלמון באלמנה אלא יום אחד כדלקמן בפירקין (דף ז.): חמישי בשבת. יום חופה: וששי בשבת. מיגו דילה: אדם בטל. למ"ד ברכה לאדם עדיפא אף זו תיבעל בששי למ"ד משום שקדו נבעלת בחמישי דהא לא יצטרכו לאומנותו: גדולים מעשה צדיקים ממעשה יצירת שמים וארץ. ומשום בר קפרא נקט לה דאיירי לעיל באגדה: אף ידי. חדא יד: מקדש מעשה ידי לצדיקים הוא: הכי קאמר. האי ומעשה ידיו במעשה הצדיקים כתיב שקרוין מעשה שהם מעשה ידיו של הקב"ה וה"ק ומעשה ידיו דהוא מעשה הצדיקים מגיד הרקיע שהרקיע מעיד עליהם לבריות שהם צדיקים שמתפללין על הגשמים ומטר יורד: יתד. קביל"י בלע"ז:

תוספות

של ארבעה ארבעה טפחים שעשאן גולל לקבר המאהיל על גבי שתיהם טמא ניטלה אחת מהן המאהיל על גבי השניה טהור מפני שיש לטומאה דרך ניטלה מה שייך דרך שילא לפר"ת ובתוספתא דאהלות ספ"ג תניא מעשה באחד שמת בערב הפסח ולא רצו לקוברו ונכנסו הנשים וקשרו החבל בגולל משכו האנשים מבחוץ וקברוהו הנשים והלכו האנשים ועשו פסחיהן לערב משמע שלא היו יכולין הנשים לקוברו עד שמשכו האנשים מבחוץ את הגולל ואם גולל הויא מצבה למה לא קברוהו בלא מצבה עד אחר הפסח אלא ודאי הוא כסוי ארון כפירוש הקונטרס ולפי שהיה של אבן היה כבד כל כך [ג]:

שמא ישחוט בן עוף. יש גורסים בו עוף אע"ג דשבת לשון נקבה היא דכתיב (שמות לא) מחלליה מות יומת ה"ה הוי לשון זכר כל העושה בו מלאכה (שם לה) שומר שבת מחללו (ישעיה נו) ושפיר גרסינן נמי בן עוף דדרך בני אדם לשחוט הרכין והקטנים כדכתיב (ויקרא ה) שני בני יונה ובפרק קמא דקידושין (דף לו: ושם) אמיא מבן עוף מה לבן לאן שכן קבע לו כו':

אלא מעתה יום הכפורים שחל להיות בשני כו'. תימה אמאי נקט יום כפורים דלא הוי אלא לרבי יוסי הגלילי כדתנן (חולין דף פג.) בד' פרקים בשנה המוכר בהמה לחבירו צריך להודיעו אמה מכרתי לשחוט כו' וכדברי רבי יוסי הגלילי אף ערב יום הכפורים בגליל אמאי לא נקט חד מד' פרקים דהוי לכ"ע וי"ל דבערב יום הכפורים היו רגילין להרבות בעופות ובדגים כדמשמע בבראשית רבה (פי"א) גבי ההוא חייטא דזבן נונא כו' משום דהוי יום סליחה וכפרה ובהנהו ד' פרקים היו מרבים בבהמות דליכא למגזר שמא ישחוט:

אי הכי אלמנה נמי תיבעל בחמישי. פי' בשלמא אי הוה תני בברייתא דבתולה נבעלת בחמישי משום איקרורי דעתא כדקמיבעיא לן ולא משום ברכה לדגים דלא חשיבא הוי ניחא לן באלמנה דנבעלת בששי משום ברכה אבל השתא דטעמא דבתולה משום ברכה אלמנה נמי תיבעל בחמישי:

אי נמי משום שקדו. וא"ת והיכי מצי למימר משום שקדו הא בברייתא קתני בהדיא משום ברכה וי"ל דלהאי שינויא הוי פירוש הברייתא הכי אלמנה נשאת בחמישי ונבעלת בששי פי' משום שקדו כמו שמפורש בברייתא אחרת וא"ת משום ברכה דדגים היה להם להניח תקנת שקדו לא חשו לכך הואיל ובששי נמי נאמרה ברכה לאדם:

מאי איכא בין ברכה לשקדו. אע"ג דמשום ברכה לא מיקרי עברינא מכל מקום בעי למה לי טעמא דברכה אי נמי בעי מאי איכא בין לישנא דמשני ברכה דאדם עדיפא ליה ובין לישנא דאי נמי משום שקדו ומשני דאיכא בינייהו אדם בטל אי נמי י"ט שחל להיות כו' דללישנא דטעמא דברייתא משום שקדו ולא משום ברכה הכא דליכא שקדו נבעלת אם ירצה בחמישי אבל ללישנא קמא דטעמא דברייתא משום ברכה כדמשמע פשטא דברייתא אפילו באדם בטל או בי"ט שחל להיות בערב שבת דליכא משום שקדו מכל מקום משום ברכה תבעל בששי ואפילו להאי לישנא אי לאו שתקנו משום שקדו משום ברכה לחודה לא היו קובעים יום כדפרישית לעיל גבי ותנשא באחד בשבת:

דאילו בשמים ובארץ כתיב אף ידי וגו'. דמשמע חדא אע"ג דמסיים קרא וימיני טפחה שמים ואמר בשילהי הקומץ רבה (מנחות לו: ושם) דיד היינו שמאל א"כ תרתי כתיב מ"מ בחד מעשה ליכא אלא חד אבל במעשה לצדיקים בחד מעשה כמו בית המקדש כתיב תרתי ידים:

מסורת הש"ס

א) שבת קנ., ב) [לעיל ג. ג. לקמן ז.], ג) [ועי' בתוס' שבת קנב: ובסוכה כג. ד"ה ולא ותוס' סנהדרין מז:].

תורה אור השלם

א) אַף יָדִי יָסְדָה אֶרֶץ וִימִינִי טִפְּחָה שָׁמָיִם קֹרֵא אֲנִי אֲלֵיהֶם יַעַמְדוּ יַחְדָּו: [ישעיה מח, יג]

ב) תְּבִאֵמוֹ וְתִטָּעֵמוֹ בְּהַר נַחֲלָתְךָ מָכוֹן לְשִׁבְתְּךָ פָּעַלְתָּ יְיָ מִקְּדָשׁ אֲדֹנָי כּוֹנְנוּ יָדֶיךָ: [שמות טו, יז]

ג) אֲשֶׁר לוֹ הַיָּם וְהוּא עָשָׂהוּ וְיַבֶּשֶׁת יָדָיו יָצָרוּ: [תהלים צה, ה]

ד) כִּי אֶרְאֶה שָׁמֶיךָ מַעֲשֵׂי אֶצְבְּעֹתֶיךָ יָרֵחַ וְכוֹכָבִים אֲשֶׁר כּוֹנָנְתָּה: [תהלים ח, ד]

ה) הַשָּׁמַיִם מְסַפְּרִים כְּבוֹד אֵל וּמַעֲשֵׂה יָדָיו מַגִּיד הָרָקִיעַ: [תהלים יט, ב]

ו) וְיָתֵד תִּהְיֶה לְךָ עַל אֲזֵנֶךָ וְהָיָה בְּשִׁבְתְּךָ חוּץ וְחָפַרְתָּה בָהּ וְשַׁבְתָּ וְכִסִּיתָ אֶת צֵאָתֶךָ: [דברים כג, יד]

לעזי רש"י

פושקונברמ"ש. פירוש פיקוח, פינוי (המפולת). קביל"י:

ליקוטי רש"י

פיקוח נפש. בדבר שיש בו סכנה פקוח דיקומבימו"ע. לטרטייאות ולקרקייאות. מיני פלטין הן ששם נאספו לבית הועד. וללמדו אומנות. דהא נמי מלוה היא דכל שאינו מלמדו אומנות מלמדו לסטות ומלוה ילפינן מקרא בקדושין בהאשה ניקנית (דף ל:) [שבת קנ.]. מכון לשבתך. מקדש של מטה מכוון כנגד כסא של מעלה אשר פעלת. מקדש. הטעם עליו זקף גדול להפרידו מתיבת השם של אחריו המקדש אשר כוננו ידיך ה'. חביב בית המקדש שהעולם נברא ביד אחת שנאמר (ישעיהו מח יג) אף ידי יסדה ארץ ומקדש בשתי ידים ואימתי יבנה בשתי ידים בזמן שה' ימלוך לעולם ועד לעתיד לבא שכל המלוכה שלו [שמות טו, יז]. ומעשה ידיו מגיד הרקיע. הכוכבים ואת המזלות שהם מעשה ידיו של הקב"ה אשר הם שם כמו שנאמר (בראשית א) ויתן אותם אלהים ברקיע השמים והם מגידים כבודו [תהלים יט, ב]. על אזנך. לבד מכלי תשמישך. אזנך. כמו כלי זיין [דברים כג, יד].

עין משפט נר מצוה

יח א ב ג ד מיי' פכ"ד מהל' שבת הל"ה סמג לאוין סה טוש"ע או"ח סי' שו סעי' ו:

יט ה טוש"ע אה"ע סי' סד:

כ ו מיי' פ"י מהל' אישות הל' יג סמג עשין מח טוש"ע אה"ע סי' סד סעי' ג:

תוספות רי"ד

ר"ח ורב המנונא דאמרי תרוייהו חשבונות של מצוה מותר לחשבן בשבת וא"ר אלעזר פוסקין צדקה לעניים בשבת. וא"ר יעקב בר אידי א"ר מפקחין פקוח נפש בשבת והולכים לב"כ ולבתי מדרשות לפקח על עסקי רבים בשבת. ותנא דבי מנשה משדכין על התינוקת לארס בשבת ועל התינוק ללמדו ספר וללמדו אומניות בשבת. וא"ר שמואל בר נחמני א"ר הולכין לטרטראות ולקרקסאות לפקח על עסקי רבים בשבת: תני בר קפרא בתולה נשאת בד' ונבעלת בה' הואיל ונאמרה בו ברכה לדגים ואלמנה נשאת בה' ונבעלת בששי הואיל ונאמרה בו ברכה לאדם ותניא מפני מה אמרו אלמנה נשאת בחמישי ונבעלת בו' שאם אתה אומר תבעל בחמישי למחר משכים הוא לאומנותו והולך. שקדו חכמים על תקנות בנות ישראל שיהא שמח עמה ג' ימים ה' בשבת ו' בשבת ושבת:

מִשּׁוּם חֶשְׁבּוֹנוֹת – Performing the initial cohabitation on the night after the Sabbath is prohibited **because of the calculations** that will possibly be made on the Sabbath as a result.[1]

The Gemara objects, citing a series of rulings to prove that such calculations are in fact permitted:

אָמַר לֵיהּ אַבַּיֵי – **Abaye said to [R' Zeira]:** וְחֶשְׁבּוֹנוֹת שֶׁל מִצְוָה מִי אֲסִירֵי – **But are calculations** for the sake **of a mitzvah prohibited?** וְהָא רַב חִסְדָּא וְרַב הַמְנוּנָא דְּאָמְרֵי תַּרְוַיְיהוּ – **Why, Rav Chisda and Rav Hamnuna have both said:** חֶשְׁבּוֹנוֹת שֶׁל מִצְוָה מוּתָּר לְחַשְּׁבָן בְּשַׁבָּת – **It is permitted to make calculations** for the sake **of a mitzvah on the Sabbath.**[2] וְאָמַר רַבִּי אֶלְעָזָר – **And R' Elazar said:** פּוֹסְקִין צְדָקָה לַעֲנִיִּים בְּשַׁבָּת – **We may allocate charity to the poor on the Sabbath.**[3] וְאָמַר רַבִּי יַעֲקֹב אָמַר רַבִּי יוֹחָנָן – **And R' Yaakov said in the name of R' Yochanan:** הוֹלְכִין לְבָתֵּי כְנֵסִיּוֹת וּלְבָתֵּי מִדְרָשׁוֹת לְפַקֵּחַ עַל עִסְקֵי רַבִּים בְּשַׁבָּת – **We may go to synagogues and study halls to discharge matters of public** concern **on the Sabbath.**[4] וְאָמַר רַבִּי יַעֲקֹב בַּר אִידִי אָמַר רַבִּי יוֹחָנָן – **And R' Yaakov bar Idi said in the name of R' Yochanan:** מְפַקְּחִין פִּיקּוּחַ נֶפֶשׁ בְּשַׁבָּת – **We may publicize matters involving** danger **to life on the Sabbath.**[5] וְאָמַר רַב שְׁמוּאֵל בַּר נַחְמָנִי אָמַר רַבִּי יוֹנָתָן – **And R' Shmuel bar Nachmani said in the name of R' Yonasan:** הוֹלְכִין לְטַרְטִיָּאוֹת וּלְקַרְקְיָיאוֹת לְפַקֵּחַ עַל עִסְקֵי רַבִּים בְּשַׁבָּת – **We may go** even **to amphitheaters and circuses in order to discharge matters of public** concern **on the Sabbath.**[6] וְתָנָא דְּבֵי מְנַשְּׁיָא – **And a Tanna of the academy of Menashya taught:** מְשַׁדְּכִין עַל הַתִּינוֹקֶת לֵיאָרֵס בְּשַׁבָּת – **WE MAY ARRANGE A MATCH FOR A YOUNG GIRL FOR THE PURPOSE OF BETROTHAL,** even **ON THE SABBATH,** וְעַל הַתִּינוֹק לְלַמְּדוֹ סֵפֶר וּלְלַמְּדוֹ אוּמָּנוּת – **AND FOR** someone **TO TEACH A YOUNG BOY TORAH OR TO TEACH HIM A CRAFT.** There should thus be no prohibition against calculating the needs of the wedding feast on the Sabbath.[7] – ? –

The Gemara concedes the point, and presents a different reason why the initial cohabitation may not take place on Saturday night:

אֶלָּא אָמַר רַבִּי זֵירָא – **Rather, R' Zeira said:** גְּזֵירָה שֶׁמָּא יִשְׁחוֹט בֶּן עוֹף – The Sages issued **a decree** forbidding initial cohabitation on the night after the Sabbath, for fear that **perhaps he will** become preoccupied and **slaughter a young bird** on the Sabbath, in preparation for the wedding feast to be held that night.[8]

The Gemara objects:

אָמַר לֵיהּ אַבַּיֵי – **Abaye said to [R' Zeira]:** אֶלָּא מֵעַתָּה – **But now** that you are concerned that someone might become preoccupied and accidentally violate the Sabbath in order to prepare for a large meal that follows the Sabbath, יוֹם הַכִּפּוּרִים שֶׁחָל לִהְיוֹת בְּשֵׁנִי בְּשַׁבָּת יִדָּחֶה – **a Yom Kippur that falls out on Monday should be postponed** until Tuesday.[9] גְּזֵירָה שֶׁמָּא יִשְׁחוֹט בֶּן עוֹף – For allowing Yom Kippur to occur on Monday should be avoided, due

NOTES

1. If an initial cohabitation is allowed on Saturday night, it will occur that the wedding ceremony and feast will be held after the Sabbath as well (for one cannot marry on the Sabbath— see above, 3a note 29). Now, if the wedding ceremony and the feast are held on Saturday night, the groom may come to calculate during the Sabbath what he needs to spend on preparations for the feast. This is prohibited, as derived from the phrase (*Isaiah* 58:13) וְדַבֵּר דָּבָר, [*If you honor it from. . .*] *speaking words* (*Rashi*), which teaches that one's speech on the Sabbath should not be like his speech on weekdays; this includes a prohibition against speaking about business matters (*Shabbos* 113b; see *Rashi* there).

[From *Rashi* (see also *Ran*) it is clear that the Gemara is discussing a case where the wedding is also to be held on Saturday night, not just the first cohabitation (cf. *Meiri, Tosafos* below, 5b ד״ה מהו). See *Haflaah* and *Beis Aharon* for why this would be permitted, although the Mishnah taught above that a virgin must marry on Wednesday.]

2. [The Gemara in *Shabbos* (150a) derives that the prohibition against making calculations does not apply to calculations for the sake of a mitzvah, for such calculation are deemed matters of Heaven, concerning which one *may* speak on the Sabbath.] It is therefore permitted to calculate the cost of a meal for a mitzvah (e.g. a wedding meal) that will be held Saturday night or Sunday (*Meiri*). It is thus not possible to say that a person may not get married and cohabit on Saturday night because of the calculations that he might perform on the Sabbath with respect to the wedding feast.

3. One may orally divide up a charity fund, allocating specific amounts to each of its beneficiaries (see *Meiri*). One may also pledge a specific sum of one's own money to charity (see *Shulchan Aruch, Orach Chaim* 306:6 with *Rama*). [Some Rishonim, though, forbid the donation of a particular *object* to charity, because this resembles the act of consecration, which is forbidden on the Sabbath (*Meiri;* see *Ran* to *Shabbos* 150a *MHK* ed.; see also *Mishnah Berurah* ibid. §27 and §33).]

4. Even those that would not lead to mortal danger (see *Meiri;* see also *Rashash*).

5. *Tos. Rid* to *Shabbos* 150a deletes the words פִּיקּוּחַ נֶפֶשׁ, *matters involving* [danger to] *life,* because even *actions* (and not merely discussion) are permitted for the sake of protecting life. *Meiri's* text seems to have the phrase פִּיקּוּחַ רַבִּים, *matters involving the public,* instead of פִּיקּוּחַ נֶפֶשׁ. This would therefore mean that we publicize the needs of the community even when they do not involve mortal danger. However, *Tos. Rid* printed on the margin of our Gemara retains the words פִּיקּוּחַ נֶפֶשׁ.

6. One may speak to the authorities on behalf of the public if there is a matter that concerns them. Even though it is doubtful that this intervention will succeed, it is nevertheless permitted on the Sabbath (*Meiri*). [Any communal need is equivalent to a matter involving a mitzvah, and calculations concerning such matters are therefore permitted on the Sabbath (*Mishnah Berurah* 306:28).]

[It seems that although these arenas were used for purposes of public entertainment (see *Rashi* to *Avodah Zarah* 18b), they were also used for civic meetings and assemblies (see *Rashi; Shiltei HaGiborim* to *Shabbos* folio 64a §2).] See *Rashash.*

7. [There is a mitzvah to marry off one's child. Similarly,] teaching one's son a trade is a mitzvah, as the Mishnah states in *Kiddushin* 29a (see *Rashi*).

Although it is permitted to hire a tutor on the Sabbath for these purposes, one may not specify his fee (*Shulchan Aruch* ibid. 306:6; see *Beur Halachah* there ד״ה ודווקא; cf. *Shiltei HaGiborim* to *Shabbos* 150a §3).

Shitah Mekubetzes explains why the Gemara cites all six statements to prove that there would be no problem in holding the wedding meal on Saturday night — even though it could cause calculations to be performed on the Sabbath: (1) It is permitted to calculate on the Sabbath what must be spent for the meal because this is a calculation for the sake of a mitzvah. (2) It is even permitted to specify what will be served to each guest, just as it is permitted to allocate charity to each particular needy person. (3) Moreover, it is permitted to go from place to place (e.g. the meat market, the chicken market, etc.) to ensure that they will be able to supply the necessary provisions, just as one may travel to the synagogues and study halls to attend to the needs of the public. (4) It is also permitted to discuss these preparations publicly, just as we may bring to light matters of danger. (5) It is even permitted to go to gentile merchants on the Sabbath to attend to items needed for the meal, just as one may go the amphitheaters of the gentiles to take care of public needs. (6) Finally, it is permitted to do all of the above-mentioned things even for the need of an individual, just as it is permitted to arrange for someone to teach one's son a trade. See there.

8. I.e. he will be so preoccupied about the upcoming wedding that he will forget that it is the Sabbath, and violate it by slaughtering a bird for the feast (*Rashi;* cf. *Meiri;* see above, note 1).

The Gemara mentions slaughtering the bird rather than cooking it, because a bird can be slaughtered very quickly and this act is therefore subject to being performed in an instant of forgetfulness. For the same reason, the Gemara is concerned about slaughtering a bird, and not an animal, which is more difficult to slaughter (*Ritva;* see also *Tosafos* ד״ה אלא).

9. Although obviously Yom Kippur must be observed on the tenth day of Tishrei, postponement of Yom Kippur can be accomplished by manipulating the number of days in the previous months. [In Talmudic times the courts had the power to fix the length of a month at either twenty-nine or thirty days, for the new month was declared based on the court's acceptance of testimony from witnesses who had seen the new

[i.e. whether or not some unavoidable circumstance occurred], **לֹא יִבְעוֹל לֹא בְּעֶרֶב שַׁבָּת** – HE SHOULD NOT COHABIT with his virgin bride for the first time NEITHER ON THE EVE OF THE SABBATH (i.e on Friday night) **וְלֹא בְּמוֹצָאֵי שַׁבָּת** – NOR AFTER THE CONCLUSION OF THE SABBATH (on Saturday night).

The Gemara asks:

בִּשְׁלָמָא בְּעֶרֶב שַׁבָּת – **It is understandable** why he may not cohabit for the first time on **the eve of Sabbath** [i.e. Friday night], **מִשּׁוּם חַבּוּרָה** – **because** this act will create **a wound,** which is prohibited on the Sabbath.[21] **אֶלָּא בְּמוֹצָאֵי שַׁבָּת אַמַּאי לֹא** – **But why** may he **not** cohabit for the first time **after the conclusion of the Sabbath?**

The Gemara answers:

אָמַר רַבִּי זֵירָא – **R' Zeira said:**

NOTES

21. It is prohibited on the Sabbath to inflict a wound (חוֹבֵל, a *toladah* of the *av melachah* of שׁוֹחֵט, *slaughtering*). When a virgin marries, it is to be expected that cohabitation will rupture the hymen and cause her to bleed. See further below, 5b.

עין משפט
נר מצוה

יג א מיי' פי"א מהל' איסורי ביאה הל' יט סמג לאוין קיא טוש"ע יו"ד סי' קצה סעי' י:
יד ב (מיי' פ"ג מהל' אבל) סמג עשין ב טוש"ע שם סי' שפג סעי' א:
טו ג [מיי' פ"ב מהל' אבל הל' ה] טוש"ע שם סי' שעד סעי' י וסי' שפא סעי' ו:
טז ד מיי' פ"ב שם הל' ה סמג שם (טוש"ע יו"ד סי' שנד סעי' ו):
יז ה מיי' פי' מהל' אישות הל' יד טוש"ע אה"ע סי' סד סעי' ג:

גליון הש"ס

גמרא אבילותא דעלמא חמיר. ע' סוטה ו ע"א תוס' ד"ה אמר:

תוספות רי"ד

למימרא דאבילות קילא [ליה] מנדה דהא בנדה [אינה צריכה שימור אם בעל ואבילות (לא) מצרכינן שימור אע"פ שבעל. והא אר"י ב"ח א"ר פפא כל מלאכות שהאשה עושה לבעלה נדה עושה לבעלה חוץ ממזיגת הכוס והצעת המטה והרחצת פניו ידיו ורגליו ואילו גבי אבילות תניא אע"פ שאמרו אין אדם רשאי לכוף את אשתו לא להיות כוחלת ולא להיות פוקסת באמת אמ"ו מוזגת לו הכוס ומצעת לו המטה ורוחצת פני ידיו ורגליו ומסיק ר"ש מי קא מדמית אבילות דהכא לאבילות דעלמא. אבילות דעלמא חבירא ליה ולא אתי לזלזולי בה. אבל אבילות דהכא כיון דאקילו בה רבנן אתי לזלזולי בה ומאי קילותא דקתני נוהג ז' ימי המשתה ואח"כ נוהג ז' ימי אבילות: תניא כי שמת חמיו או חמותו אינו רשאי לכוף את אשתו להיות פוקסת אבל כופה מטתו ונוהג עמה אבילות ודוקא בפניה אבל שלא בפניה לא. כדא"ל רב לחייא בריה באפה נהוג אבילות שלא באפה לא תנהוג אבילות:

והצעת המטה. נראה לר"י דהצעת המטה דהכא היינו פריסת סדינין שהוא דבר של חיבה אבל הצעת כרים וכסתות שאינן דברים של חיבה שרי לנדה והביא ראיה מדתנן בפ' אע"פ (לקמן נט:) הכניסה לו ג' שפחות אינה מצעת לו המטה ואינה עושה בצמר ארבע יושבת בקתדרא ואמרינן בגמרא אע"פ שאמרו ד' יושבת בקתדרא אבל מוזגת לו כוס ומצעת לו המטה ומרחצת לו פניו ידיו ורגליו ופי' בקונטרס דהא דתנא ג' אינה מצעת לו המטה היינו הצעת כרים וכסתות דהוי דבר שיש טורח אבל מצעת לו המטה היינו פריסת סדין ולבדין דמילי דחיבה נינהו שתתכבד עליו ואין בו טורח וההיא הצעה של חיבה נראה דדוקא אסור וכן משמע דמזכירה בהדי מזיגת כוס והרחצת פניו ידיו ורגליו כי התם מיהו לספרים דל"ג במשנה אלא ואינה מצעת המטה ול"ג לו ובגמרא גרסינן לו אין ראיה משם שיהו תרי גווני הצעה דמתני' איירי בהצעת שאר מטות ובגמרא איירי בהצעת מטה לבעלה לבדו:

פוקסת. פ"ה מעברת סרק על פניה ואין נראה דאמר בפ"ב לקמן (דף ח.) לא סרק ולא פירכוס משמע דתרי מילי נינהו דפוקסת דהכא היינו פירכוס כדאמרי' בסמוך כי קתני אכיחול ואפירכוס ובשילהי המצניע (שבת צה.) קתני פוקסת ומעברת סרק על פניה ולקמן בפ"ב פ"ה פירכוס קליעת שער וקשה לר"י דבשילהי המצניע (שם צד: ושם) קתני גודלת ופוקסת אלא נראה דאמר מתיקוני נשים הוא:

ומי שאני בין אבילות דידיה לאבילות דידה. תימה דבלאו מילתא דרב יוסף הוי מצי למיפרך ברייתות אהדדי וי"ל דאי לאו הוה מילתא דרב יוסף הוה מפלגינן בין שעת חופה לשלא בשעת חופה דבשעת חופה יצרו תוקפו אע"ג דבעל אבל לרב יוסף לא מצי לפלוגי בהכי דהא בבעל חשיב ליה כאשתו ישנה דאפי' בשעת חופה אשתו ישנה עמו בנדה ובאבילות דידה ואפילו הכי באבילות דידיה קתני הוא ישן בין האנשים ולהכי פריך שפיר ולרשב"א נראה דאי לאו דרב יוסף לא הוה קשה מידי דעמו ועמה דקתני בברייתא לאו עמו במטה אלא עמה בבית אבל לרב יוסף דבאבילות דידה אשתו ישנה עמו א"כ הא דקתני נוהג עמה אבילות היינו עמה במטה דומיא דהכא באבילות דידיה הוי עמו במטה והא דמשני תני באבילות דידיה הוא ישן אינו מגיה הברייתא אלא מפרש דעמו דקתני בברייתא דהכי הוא ופריך והא עמו קתני מאי לאו עמו במטה פי' דומיא דעמה ומשני לא עמו בבית כדא"ל רב כו':

הכי קאמר וכן מי שפירסה אשתו נדה ולא בעל הוא ישן בין האנשים ואשתו ישנה בין הנשים למימרא דאבילות קילא ליה מנדה והאמר רבי יצחק בר חנינא אמר רב הונא א) [א]כל מלאכות שאשה עושה לבעלה נדה עושה לבעלה חוץ ממזיגת הכוס והצעת המטה והרחצת פניו ידיו ורגליו ואילו גבי אבילות תניא אע"פ שאמרו אין אדם רשאי לכוף את אשתו להיות כוחלת ולהיות פוקסת [ב]באמת אמרו מוזגת לו הכוס ומצעת לו המטה ומרחצת לו פניו ידיו ורגליו לא קשיא כאן באבילות דידיה כאן באבילות דידה והא אביו של חתן או אמה של כלה קתני כי קתני אשארא ומי שאני בין אבילות דידיה לאבילות דידה והתניא ב) מי שמת חמיו או חמותו [ג]אינו יכול לכוף את אשתו להיות כוחלת ולהיות פוקסת אלא כופה מטתו ונוהג עמה אבילות וכן היא שמת חמיה או חמותה אינה רשאה להיות כוחלת ולהיות פוקסת אלא כופה מטתה ונוהגת עמו אבילות תני באבילות דידיה הוא ישן בין האנשים ואשתו ישנה בין הנשים הא וכן קתני כי קתני אכיחול ואפירכוס והא עמו קתני מאי לאו עמו במטה לא עמו בבית ג) וכדאמר ליה רב לחייא בריה [ד]באפה נהוג אבילותא דלא באפה לא תנהוג אבילותא רב אשי אמר מי קמדמית אבילותא דהכא לאבילותא דעלמא ° אבילותא דעלמא חמיר ולא אתי לזלזולי ביה אבילות דהכא כיון דאקילו רבנן אתי לזלזולי ביה מאי קולא אילימא דקתני בועל בעילת מצוה ופורש התם משום דלא חל עליו אבילותא אי לרבי אליעזר ד) עד שיצא מפתח הבית אי לרבי יהושע עד שיסתם הגולל אלא דקתני נוהג שבעת ימי המשתה ואח"כ נוהג שבעת ימי אבילות אמר מר [ה]בין כך ובין כך לא יבעול לא בערב שבת ולא במוצ"ש בשלמא בערב שבת משום חבורה אלא במוצאי שבת אמאי לא אמר רבי זירא משום

ה"ק כו'. כלומר כי קאמר וכן אהוא ישן בין האנשים והיא ישנה בין הנשים קאמר ולעולם הך בשלא בעל קאי: קילא ליה. לעבור עליה מנדה דלאבילות לא מהימנת ליה ולנדה מהימנא ליה: מלאכות שהאשה עושה לבעלה. לקמן תני להו בפרק אע"פ: חוץ ממזיגת הכוס. להושיט לו: והצעת המטה והרחצת פניו כו'. שדרך קירוב וחיבה הן ובאין לידי הרגל דבר: אין אדם רשאי לכוף את אשתו. בימי אבלה כשמת אביה או אמה: פוקסת. מעברת סרק על פניה: מוזגת לו. ולא חיישינן להרגל דבר אלמא אבילות חמירא ליה: כאן באבילות דידיה. לעולם אבילות קילא ליה מנדה והכי מתניתא הכי מתרצן הא דקתני לעיל הוא ישן בין האנשים כו' באבילות דידיה והך דקתני מוזגת לו כו' באבילות דידה קאי דקתני אין אדם רשאי לכוף כו' אלמא באבילות דידה קיימינן שאינה רוצה לכחול ולפקוס והיינו טעמא דמוזגת דאם יתגבר יצרו עליו כיון דאבילות דידה הוא אינה שומעת לו: והא אביו של חתן כו'. אלמא באבילות דידיה נמי אחמיר תנא דלעיל: כי קתני. אמה של כלה אשארא אמכניסים המת לחדר אבל הוא ישן בין האנשים באבילות דמתני' קאי: ונוהגת עמו אבילות. אלמא מדלא קתני באבילות דידיה הוא ישן בין האנשים שמע מינה חמיר ליה ולא שני לן: ה"ג תני באבילות דידיה הוא ישן כו': הכי גרסינן והא עמו קתני מאי לאו עמו במטה. אלמא לאבילות דידיה נמי מהימן: לא עמו בבית. וטעמא לאו משום דמהימן נקט לה אלא לאשמועינן דאין אבילותו מוטל עליה אלא בפניו משום כבודו וכן הוא אין אבילותא מוטל עליו אלא לפניה ולכבודה: כדאמר ליה רב לחייא בריה. כשמת חמיו באפה נהוג אבילותא כו': פלוגתא דרבי אליעזר ורבי יהושע במועד קטן: גולל. זהו כסוי של ארון המת: משום

עד שיסתם הגולל. בכמה מקומות פי' רש"י דגולל הוי כיסוי ארון ודופק היינו קרשים שבצידי הארון ונקרא דופק על שם שהגולל דופק עליו וכעין זה פי' בערוך וקשה לר"ת דאמר בפרק מי שמתו (ברכות יט: ושם) מדלגין היינו על גבי ארונות ואיך היו מדלגין והלא הגולל והדופק מטמא באהל כדאמרינן בהעור והרוטב (חולין קכו: ושם) ועוד דבפרק בהמה המקשה (שם עב:) דריש על פני השדה לרבות גולל ודופק ולפ"ה הלא ארון אינו על פני השדה ואומר ה"ר דוד מנלינבורק כי לפרש"י [דריש] לרבות גולל ודופק שפירש דלא מרבינן מעל פני השדה דמטמא אלא כשפירש אבל בעוד שהוא טמון בטל אגב קרקע ולא מטמא באוהל והשתא אתי נמי שפיר ההיא דמדלגים היינו על גבי ארונות ועוד י"מ אע"ג דגולל מטמא באהל מ"מ יכולין לדלג ולטמאות עצמם בגולל דתניא במס' שמחות (פ"ד) כל טומאה שאין נזיר מגלח עליה אין כהן מוזהר עליה ואר"ת דמשובשת היא דהא רביעית דם אין נזיר מגלח עליה כדתנן בנזיר (דף נד. ושם) וכהן מוזהר עליה ועוד הקשה דתניא בעירובין (דף טו:) כל דבר שיש בו רוח חיים אין עושין ממנו לא גולל לקבר כו' ולפ"ה וכי דרך לעשות כסוי ארון מבעלי חיים ויש לומר אע"ג דאין דרך לעשות כסוי ארון מבעלי חיים מכל מקום כמה דברים אשכחן דלא שכיח ומיירי בהן הש"ס לדרוש ולקבל שכר כדאמרינן בפרק המקשה (חולין ע.) בלעתו חולדה והוציאתו והכניסתו והקיאתו ויצא מאליו מהו הדביק שני רחמים ויצא מזה לזה מהו אף על פי שלא יבא לעולם ור"ת מפרש דגולל היינו מצבה שהיא אבן גדולה ולשון גולל שייך על האבן כדכתיב וגללו את האבן (בראשית כט) ודופק הן שתי אבנים אחת לראשה ואחת לרגלה של מצבה ופעמים כשאין המצבה מזומנת מעמידין שם בהמה או דבר אחר לסימן וההיא דמדלגין לא היה שם מצבה ומחמת המת לא היו מיטמאין דרוב ארונות יש בהן פותח טפח ולא תקשה לר' יהושע מאימת חל אבילות כשאין שם מצבה די"ל דכי מהדרי אפייהו דקוברין כדאמרינן במועד קטן (דף כב.) דהנהו דלא אזלי בתר שכבא מכי מהדרי אפייהו וקשה לר"י על פירוש רבינו תם דתניא בתוספתא דאהלות בפרק ד' אמר רבי יהודה שתי אבנים גדולות של

מסורת הש"ס

א) לקמן סא., ב) מ"ק כ: שמחות פי"א, ג) ג"ז שם, ד) מ"ק כז. סנהדרין מז: [שבת קנב:].

ליקוטי רש"י

חוץ ממזיגת הכוס. כל שהוא דברים של קירוב וחיבה ומביאין לידי הרגל דבר. והצעת המטה. לפרוס סדין ולבדין דבר שאינו טורח ומשום דמילי דחיבה נינהו כדי שמתכבד עליו [לקמן סא.]. באמת אמרו. כל באמת הלכה היא ואין חולק בדבר [סוכה לח.]. הלכה היא למשה מסיני [נזיר נד:]. כוחלת. נותנת כחול בין עיניה כדי שדומות נאים [מו"ק ט:]. פוקסת. יש מרבותי אומרים מתקנת שערה במסרק או בידיה ויש שמפרשין טוחה כמין בצק על פניה וכשנוטלו מאדים הבשר [שבת צד:]. תפקום שרק על פניה טינפאנ"ל בלע"ז והוא אדום [שם סד:]. מחלקת שערה לכאן ולכאן [מו"ק שם עיי"ש]. באפה. דאיתתך כשהיא אבילה דהאי נמי כל שמתאבל עליו כגון אשתו מתאבל עמו בפניו [שם כ:]. באפה. בפניה [ב"ק נו:]. עד שיסתם הגולל. דאבילות מסיימת הגולל מיילא כדתניא באלו מגלחין. גולל. הוא הדף הנתון על הארון לכסוי ואותן שבדפנות קרי להו דופק [סנהדרין מז:]. הוא כיסוי שנותנים על ארונו [שבת קנב:].

in the case where the husband is the mourner. This would seem to indicate that there is no difference in the restrictions placed upon the couple in the two instances.[12] — ? —

The Gemara answers by emending the Baraisa:

תְּנֵי בַּאֲבֵילוּת דִידֵיהּ — **Teach in** the section of the Baraisa that refers to **his mourning** as follows: הוּא יָשֵׁן בֵּין הָאֲנָשִׁים וְאִשְׁתּוֹ יְשֵׁנָה בֵּין הַנָּשִׁים — **He sleeps among the men and his wife sleeps among the women.**

The Gemara objects:

הָא וְכֵן קָתָנֵי — **But [the Baraisa] stated:** "AND SIMILARLY, in the case of a wife whose father-in-law or mother-in-law died etc.," indicating that there is no difference whether the husband or the wife is the mourner. — ? —

The Gemara answers:

כִּי קָתָנֵי אַכִּיחוֹל וְאַפִּירְכּוּס — **When [the Baraisa] taught** this similarity between the husband and wife's states of mourning, it was referring only **to** the prohibition against the wife using **eye shadow and face powder.** But there is a distinction between the two cases as to whether the husband and wife must sleep apart.

The Gemara persists:

וְהָא עִמּוֹ קָתָנֵי — **But [the Baraisa] teaches** that when the husband's parent died, his wife observes the laws of mourning WITH HIM. מַאי לָאו עִמּוֹ בְּמִטָּה — **Does this not** imply that she can stay **with him in the** same **bed?**[13]

The Gemara answers:

לֹא עִמּוֹ בַּבַּיִת — **No!** The Baraisa means that she acts as a mourner **with him, in the house.**[14] וְכִדְאָמַר לֵיהּ רַב לְחִיָּיא בְּרֵיהּ — **And** the law that the Baraisa means to teach with this statement is **in accordance with what Rav said to Chiya his son** when Chiya's father-in-law died: בְּאַפָּהּ נְהוֹג אֲבֵילוּתָא — **In her** [i.e. your wife's] **presence, observe** the laws of **mourning;** דְּלָא בְּאַפָּהּ לָא תִנְהוֹג אֲבֵילוּתָא — but **when** you are **not in her presence, do not observe** the laws of **mourning.**[15]

The Gemara presents another solution to its original difficulty:[16]

רַב אַשִׁי אָמַר — **Rav Ashi said:** מִי קָמְדַמֵּית אֲבֵילוּתָא דְּהָכָא לַאֲבֵילוּתָא דְּעָלְמָא — **Can you compare the mourning here** concerning a just-married couple **to regular mourning?** אֲבֵילוּתָא דְּעָלְמָא חָמִיר — Actually, **regular mourning is stringent** in the eyes of people וְלָא אָתֵי לְזַלְזוּלֵי בֵּיהּ — **and they will not come to treat it lightly.**[17] אֲבֵילוּת דְּהָכָא — But concerning the **mourning here** in the case of newlyweds, כֵּיוָן דְּאַקִילוּ רַבָּנָן — **since the Rabbis ruled leniently** about it in other aspects, אָתֵי לְזַלְזוּלֵי בֵּיהּ — **[the new couple] will come to treat it lightly.**[18]

The Gemara seeks clarification of this answer:

מַאי קוּלָּא — **What is the leniency** that is found regarding the laws of mourning with respect to these newlyweds? אִילֵימָא דְּקָתָנֵי בּוֹעֵל בְּעִילַת מִצְוָה וּפוֹרֵשׁ — **If you say it is that which [the Baraisa] taught:** [THE GROOM] PERFORMS THE MITZVAH-COHABITATION [AND then SEPARATES from his bride], indicating that we allow him to cohabit, הָתָם מִשּׁוּם דְּלָא חָל עָלָיו אֲבֵילוּתָא — **there** no special leniency in the laws of mourning is involved — the reason it is permitted for him to cohabit is **because** the laws of **mourning do not** yet **take effect upon him** — אִי לְרַבִּי אֱלִיעֶזֶר עַד שֶׁיֵּצֵא מִפֶּתַח הַבַּיִת — **either according to R' Elazar until [the corpse] goes out the door of the house,** אִי לְרַבִּי יְהוֹשֻׁעַ עַד שֶׁיִּסָּתֵם הַגּוֹלֵל — **or according to R' Yehoshua** until **the top of the casket is closed** over the corpse.[19] Hence, his cohabitation before these points in time does not constitute a leniency in the laws of mourning.

The Gemara explains what the leniency is:

אֶלָּא דְּקָתָנֵי נוֹהֵג שִׁבְעַת יְמֵי הַמִּשְׁתֶּה — **Rather, it is that which [the Baraisa] taught:** [THE BRIDE AND GROOM] first OBSERVE THE SEVEN DAYS OF FEASTING וְאַחַר כָּךְ נוֹהֵג שִׁבְעַת יְמֵי אֲבֵילוּת — AND only AFTERWARDS OBSERVE SEVEN DAYS OF MOURNING.[20]

The Gemara analyzes the next section of the Baraisa that was cited above (4a):

אָמַר מַר — **The master said:** בֵּין כָּךְ וּבֵין כָּךְ — IN EITHER CASE

NOTES

12. If there was truly a distinction between the case where the husband is a mourner and the case where the wife is a mourner, as the Gemara posited above, then the Baraisa should have stated that in the case where the father-in-law or mother-in-law of the wife died, the husband and wife must sleep apart (*Rashi*).

13. That is, they may sleep together on the same overturned bed (*Rashba*). We thus see that the husband is trusted to seclude himself with his wife even when he is in mourning (*Rashi*). [This leniency applies only when the husband and wife are clothed (*Rosh*). According to *Rashba* and *Tos. HaRosh,* the phrase "with him in bed" means that her bed can be in the same room as her husband's bed. But it is prohibited for them to sleep together in the same bed even if they are clothed (see *Yoreh Deah* 383:1).]

14. The Gemara answers that the Baraisa is not discussing the husband's trustworthiness with respect to his obeying the restrictions of mourning when it states that his wife may sleep "with him." Rather, it is teaching that a wife of one who is in mourning is not subject to the restrictions of a mourner unless she is in her husband's presence, for the obligation is only out of respect for him. Similarly, when the wife is in mourning, her husband is subject to the restrictions of mourning only when he is in the presence of his wife, out of respect for her (*Rashi*).

15. The Rishonim disagree if "in her presence" means she is physically in her husband's presence, or in the same house as her husband, or if it means that she is in the same city. We are not accustomed to observe this stringency nowadays, because the assumption is that the mourner absolves his or her spouse from granting that honor (see *Ritva;* see also *Rama, Yoreh Deah* 374:6).

16. That is, the Baraisa taught above seems to state that a mourner cannot be trusted to seclude himself with his new bride (even after an initial cohabitation has been performed), even though he would be trusted with his wife who is a *niddah* in a similar situation; this implies that a person cannot be trusted to observe the laws of mourning in such a situation, while he can be trusted not to transgress the prohibition of *niddah.* The Gemara posed a seeming contradiction to this from the law that with regard to performing acts which might lead to intimacy, a mourner may perform them for her husband, while a *niddah* cannot — implying that a person is trusted with regard to the laws of mourning, while he cannot be trusted regarding the laws of *niddah.* [Above, the Gemara differentiated between the case where the husband is the mourner and the case where the wife is the mourner; the answer that the Gemara will now offer does not make this distinction.]

17. Because a person is brokenhearted when he is in mourning (*Rosh*). That is why the latter Baraisa permits a wife to mix a cup of wine for her husband, etc.

18. The earlier Baraisa therefore ruled that they must sleep separately. And since people treat mourning in this specific instance more lightly than the *niddah* prohibition, the wife must refrain from the acts that can lead to intimacy (mixing wine, making the bed, etc.) just as a *niddah* must refrain from them (*Rosh;* see *Korban Nesanel* there).

19. This moment is especially significant because from this point on, the body of the deceased will no longer be visible to his loved ones (*Yad Ramah* to *Sanhedrin* 47b).

[We have followed *Rashi* in our interpretation of the word גולל. For other interpretations, see *Tosafos.*]

20. That is (although the parent of the bride or groom has died and awaits burial), we allow the mitzvah-cohabitation to take place first, causing the couple's personal festival status to take effect, thereby allowing the mourner to postpone the restrictions of mourning that begin with the burial until after the seven days of rejoicing.

According to the conclusion of the Gemara, it makes no difference whether the bride or the groom is in mourning, and whether or not they cohabited. In all such cases, they must be separated because the mourning was treated lightly.

הכי קאמר וכן מי שפירסה אשתו נדה ולא בעל הוא ישן בין האנשים ואשתו ישנה בין הנשים למימרא דאבילות קילא ליה מנדה והאמר רבי יצחק בר חנינא אמר רב הונא [א] כל מלאכות שאשה עושה לבעלה נדה עושה לבעלה חוץ ממזיגת הכוס והצעת המטה והרחצת פניו ידיו ורגליו ואילו גבי אבילות תניא אע"פ שאמרו אין אדם רשאי לכוף את אשתו להיות כוחלת ולהיות פוקסת [ב] באמת אמרו מוזגת לו הכוס ומצעת לו המטה ומרחצת לו פניו ידיו ורגליו לא קשיא כאן באבילות דידיה כאן באבילות דידה והא אביו של חתן או אמה של כלה קתני כי קתני אשארא ומי שאני בין אבילות דידיה לאבילות דידה והתניא [ג] מי שמת חמיו או חמותו [ג] אינו יכול לכוף את אשתו להיות כוחלת ולהיות פוקסת אלא כופה מטתו ונוהג עמה אבילות וכן היא שמת חמיה או חמותה אינה רשאה להיות כוחלת ולהיות פוקסת אלא כופה מטתה ונוהגת עמו אבילות תני באבילות דידיה הוא ישן בין האנשים ואשתו ישנה בין הנשים הא וכן קתני כי קתני אכיחול ואפירכוס והא עמו קתני מאי לאו עמו במטה לא עמו בבית [ג] וכדאמר ליה רב לחייא בריה [ד] באפה נהוג אבילותא דלא באפה לא תנהוג אבילותא רב אשי אמר מי קמדמית אבילותא דהכא לאבילותא דעלמא [ה] אבילותא דעלמא חמיר ולא אתי לזלזולי ביה אבילות דהכא כיון דאקילו רבנן אתי לזלזולי ביה מאי קולא אילימא דקתני בועל בעילת מצוה ופורש התם משום דלא חל עליו אבילותא אי לרבי אליעזר [ז] עד שיצא מפתח הבית אי לרבי יהושע עד שיסתם הגולל אלא דקתני נוהג שבעת ימי המשתה ואח"כ נוהג שבעת ימי אבילות אמר מר [ה] בין כך ובין כך לא יבעול לא בערב שבת ולא במוצ"ש בשלמא בערב שבת משום חבורה אלא במוצאי שבת אמאי לא אמר רבי זירא משום

רש"י

ה"ק כו'. כלומר כי קאמר וכן להוא ישן בין האנשים והיא ישנה בין הנשים קאמר ולעולם הך בשלא בעל קאי: קילא ליה. לעבור עליה מנדה דלאבילות לא מהימנת ליה ולנדה מהימנא ליה: מלאכות שהאשה עושה לבעלה. לקמן תני להו בפרק אע"פ: חוץ ממזיגת הכוס. להושיט לו: והצעת המטה והרחצת פניו כו'. שדרך קירוב וחיבה הן ובאין לידי הרגל דבר: אין אדם רשאי לכוף את אשתו. בימי אבלה כשמת אביה או אמה: פוקסת. מעברת סרק על פניה: מוזגת לו. ולא חיישינן להרגל דבר אלמא אבילות חמירא ליה: כאן באבילות דידיה. לעולם אבילות קילא ליה מנדה והני מתניתא הכי מתרצן הא דקתני לעיל הוא ישן בין האנשים כו' באבילות דידיה והך דקתני מוזגת לו כו' באבילות דידה קאי דקתני אין אדם רשאי לכוף כו' אלמא באבילות דידה קיימינן שאינה רוצה לכחול ולפקוס והיינו טעמא דמוזגת דאם יתגבר יצרו עליו כיון דלאבילות דידה הוא אינה שומעת לו: והא אביו של חתן כו'. אלמא באבילות דידיה נמי אמר תנא דלעיל: כי קתני. אמה של כלה אשארא אמכניסים המת לחדר אבל הוא ישן בין האנשים באבילות דחתן קאי: ונוהגת עמו אבילות. אלמא מדלא קתני באבילות דידיה הוא ישן בין האנשים שמע מינה חמיר ליה ולא שני לן: ה"ג תני באבילות דידיה הוא ישן כו' הכי גרסינן והא עמו קתני מאי לאו עמו במטה. אלמא לאבילות דידיה נמי מהימן: לא עמו בבית. וטעמא לאו משום דמהימן נקט לה אלא לאשמועינן דאין אבילותו מוטל עליה אלא בפניו משום כבודו וכן הוא לא אין אבילותה מוטל עליו אלא לפניה ולכבודה: כדאמר ליה רב לחייא בריה. כשמת חמיו באפה נהוג אבילותא כו': פלוגתא דרבי אליעזר ורבי יהושע במועד קטן: גולל. זהו כסוי של ארון המת:

משום

תוספות

והצעת המטה. נראה לר"י דהצעת המטה דהכא היינו פריסת סדינין שהוא דבר של חיבה אבל הצעת כרים וכסתות שאין דברים של חיבה שרי לנדה והביא ראיה מדתנן בפ' אע"פ (לקמן נט:) הכניסה לו ג' שפחות אינה מצעת לו המטה ואינה עושה בצמר ארבע יושבת בקתדרא ואמרינן בגמרא אע"פ שאמרו ד' יושבת בקתדרא אבל מוזגת לו כוס ומצעת לו המטה ומרחצת לו פניו ידיו ורגליו ופי' בקונטרס דהא דתנא ג' אינה מצעת לו המטה היינו הצעת כרים וכסתות דהוי דבר שיש טורח אבל מצעת לו המטה היינו פריסת סדין ולבדין דמילי דחיבה נינהו שמתחבב עליו ואין בו טורח והכא הצעה של חיבה נראה דדוקא אסור וכן משמע דמזכירה בהדי מזיגת כוס והרחצת פניו ידיו ורגליו כי התם מיהו לספרים דל"ג במשנה אלא ואינה מצעת המטה ול"ג לו ובגמרא גרסינן לו אין ראיה משם שיהו תרי גווני הצעה דמתני' איירי בהצעת שאר מטות ובגמרא איירי בהצעת מטה לבעלה לבדו:

פוקסת. פ"ה מעברת סרק על פניה ואין נראה דאמר בפ"ב לקמן (דף יז.) לא סרק ולא פירכוס משמע דתרי מילי נינהו דפוקסת דהכא היינו פירכוס כדאמרי' בסמוך כי קתני אכיחול ואפירכוס ובשילהי המצניע (שבת צה.) קתני פוקסת ומעברת סרק על פניה ולקמן בפ"ב פ"ה פירכוס קליעת שער וקשה לר"י דבשילהי המצניע (שם צד: ושם) קתני גודלת ופוקסת אלא נראה דאחד מתיקוני נשים הוא:

ומי שאני בין אבילות דידיה לאבילות דידה. תימה דבלאו מילתא דרב יוסף הוי מצי למיפרך ברייתות אהדדי וי"ל דאי לאו הוה מילתא דרב יוסף הוה מפלגינן בין שעת חופה לשלא בשעת חופה דבשעת חופה יצרו תוקפו אע"ג דבעל אבל לרב יוסף לא מצי לפלוגי בהכי דהא בבעל חשיב ליה כאשתו ישנה דאפי' בשעת חופה אשתו ישנה עמו בנדה ובאבילות דידה ואפילו הכי באבילות דידיה קתני הוא ישן בין האנשים ולהכי פריך שפיר ולרשב"א נראה דאי לאו דרב יוסף לא הוה קשה מידי דעמו ועמה דקתני בברייתא לאו עמו במטה אלא עמה בבית אבל לרב יוסף דבאבילות דידה אשתו ישנה עמו א"כ הא דקתני נוהג עמה אבילות היינו עמה במטה דומיא דהכא באבילות דידיה הוי עמו במטה והא דמשני תני באבילות דידיה הוא ישן אינו מגיה הברייתא אלא מפרש דעמו דקתני בברייתא דהכי הוא ופריך והא עמו קתני מאי לאו עמו במטה פי' דומיא דעמה ומשני לא עמו בבית כדא"ל רב כו':

עד שיסתם הגולל. בכמה מקומות פי' רש"י דגולל הוי כיסוי ארון ודופק היינו קרשים שבצידי הארון ונקרא דופק על שם שהגולל דופק עליו וכעין זה פי' בערוך וקשה לר"ת דאמר בפרק מי שמתו (ברכות יט: ושם) מדלגין היינו על גבי ארונות ואיך היו מדלגין והלא הגולל והדופק מטמא באהל כדאמרינן בהעור והרוטב (חולין קכו: ושם) ועוד דבפרק בהמה המקשה (שם עב:) דריש על פני השדה לרבות גולל ודופק ולפ"ה הלא ארון אינו על פני השדה ואומר ה"ר דוד מגלינבורק כי לפרש"י [דריש] לרבות גולל ודופק שפירש דלא מרבינן מעל פני השדה דמטמא אלא כשפירש אבל בעוד שהוא טמון בטל אגב קרקע ולא מטמא באוהל והשתא אתי נמי שפיר ההיא דמדלגים היינו על גבי ארונות ועוד י"מ אע"ג דגולל מטמא באהל מ"מ יכולין לדלג ולטמאות עצמם בגולל דתניא במס' שמחות (פ"ד) כל טומאה שאין נזיר מגלח עליה אין כהן מוזהר עליה ואר"ת דמשובשת היא דהא רביעית דם אין נזיר מגלח עליה כדתנן בנזיר (דף נד. ושם) וכהן מוזהר עליה ועוד הקשה דתניא בעירובין (דף טו:) כל דבר שיש בו רוח חיים אין עושין ממנו לא גולל לקבר כו' ולפ"ה וכי דרך לעשות כסוי ארון מבעלי חיים ויש לומר אע"ג דאין דרך לעשות כסוי ארון מבעלי חיים מכל מקום כמה דברים אשכחן דלא שכיח ומיירי בהן הש"ס לדרוש ולקבל שכר כדאמרינן בפרק המקשה (חולין ע.) בלעתו חולדה והוציאתו והכניסתו והקיאתו ויצא מאליו מהו הדביק שני רחמים ויצא מזה לזה מהו אף על פי שלא יבא לעולם ור"ת מפרש דגולל היינו מצבה שהיא אבן גדולה ולשון גולל שייך על האבן כדכתיב וגללו את האבן (בראשית כט) ודופק הן שתי אבנים אחת לראשה ואחת לרגלה של מצבה ופעמים כשאין המצבה מזומנת מעמידין שם בהמה או דבר אחר לסימן וההיא דמדלגין לא היה שם מצבה ומחמת המת לא היו מיטמאין דרוב ארונות יש בהן פותח טפח ולא תקשה לר' יהושע מאימת חל אבילות כשאין שם מצבה די"ל דכי מהדרי אפייהו דקוברין כדאמרינן במועד קטן (דף כב.) דהנהו דלא אזלי בתר שכבא מכי מהדרי אפייהו וקשה לר"י על פירוש רבינו תם דתניא בתוספתא דאהלות בפרק ד' אמר רבי יהודה שתי אבנים גדולות

של

מסורת הש"ס

א) לקמן סא., ב) מ"ק כ: שמחות פי"א, ג) ג"ז שם, ד) מ"ק כ. סנהדרין מז: [שבת קנב:].

ליקוטי רש"י

חוץ ממזיגת הכוס. כל שהוא דברים של קירוב וחיבה ומביאין לידי הרגל דבר. והצעת המטה. לפרוס סדין ולבדין דבר שאינו טורח ומשום דמילי דחיבה נינהו כדי שתתחבב עליו [לקמן סא.]. באמת אמרו. כל מקום שנאמר באמת הלכה היא ואין חולק בדבר [סוכה לח.]. הלכה היא למשה מסיני [נזיר נד:]. כוחלת. נותנת כחול בין עיניה כדי שדומות נאים [מו"ק ט:]. פוקסת. יש מרבותי אומרים מתקנת שערה במסרק או בידיה ויש שמפרשין טחה כמין בצק על פניה וכשנוטלו מאדים הבשר [שבת צד:]. תפקוס סרק על פניה טינפלצ"ל בלע"ז והוא אדום [שם סד:]. מתלקת שערה לכאן ולכאן [מו"ק שם ע"ש]. באפה. לאיתתך כשהיא אבילה דהכי נמי כל שמתאבל עליו כגון אשתו מתאבל עמו בפניו [שם כ.]. באפה. בפניה [ב"ק נו:]. עד שיסתם הגולל. לאבילות מסתימת הגולל חיילא כדתניא בלא מגלחין. גולל. הוא הדף הנתון על הארון לכסוי ואותן שבדפנות קרי להו דופק [סנהדרין מז:]. הוא כיסוי שנותנים על ארונו [שבת קנב:].

עין משפט נר מצוה

יג א מיי' פי"א מהל' איסורי ביאה הל' יט סמג לאוין קיא טוש"ע יו"ד סי' קצה סעי' י:

יד ב (מיי' פ"ה מהל' אבל) סמג עשין ב טוש"ע שם סי' שפג סעי' א:

טו ג [מיי' פ"ב מהל' אבל הל' ה] טוש"ע שם סי' שעד סעי' [] וסי' שפא סעי' ו:

טז ד מיי' פ"ב שם הל' ה סמג שם (טוש"ע יו"ד סי' שעד סעי' ו):

יז ה מיי' פ"י מהל' אישות הל' ה טוש"ע אה"ע סי' סד סעי' ג:

גליון הש"ס

גמרא אבילותא דעלמא חמיר. ע' סוטה ע"א תוס' ד"ה אמר:

תוספות רי"ד

למימרא דאבילות קילא [ליה] מנדה דהא בנדה [איגד] צריכה שימור אם בעל ואבילות (לא) מצרכינן שימור אע"פ שבעל. והא אר"י ב"ח א"ר פפא כל מלאכות שהאשה עושה לבעלה נדה עושה לבעלה חוץ ממזיגת הכוס והצעת המטה והרחצת פניו ידיו ורגליו ואילו גבי אבילות תניא אע"פ שאמרו אין אדם רשאי לכוף את אשתו לא להיות כוחלת ולא להיות פוקסת באמת אמרו מוזגת לו הכוס ומצעת לו המטה ורוחצת פניו ידיו ורגליו ומסיק ר"א מי קא מדמית אבילות דהכא לאבילות דעלמא. אבילות דעלמא דמירא ליה ולא אתי לזלזולי בה. אבל אבילות דהכא כיון דאקילו בה רבנן אתי לזלזולי בה מאי קילותא דקתני נוהג ז' ימי המשתה ואח"כ נוהג ז' ימי אבילות: תניא מי שמת חמיו או חמותו אינו רשאי לכוף את אשתו להיות פוקסת אבל כופה מטתו ונוהג עמה אבילות ודוקא בפניה אבל שלא בפניה לא. כדא"ל רב לחייא בריה באפה נהוג אבילות שלא באפה לא תנהוג אבילות:

The Gemara answers:

הָכִי קָאָמַר – **This is what [the Baraisa] means:** וְכֵן מִי שֶׁפֵּירְסָה אִשְׁתּוֹ נִדָּה – **And similarly, if one's wife began to menstruate** וְלֹא בָּעַל – **and he had not** yet **cohabited** with her, הוּא יָשֵׁן בֵּין הָאֲנָשִׁים וְאִשְׁתּוֹ יְשֵׁנָה בֵּין הַנָּשִׁים – **he sleeps among the men and his wife sleeps among the women.**[1]

The Gemara asks:

לְמֵימְרָא דַּאֲבֵילוּת קִילָּא לֵיהּ מִנִּדָּה – Does this mean **to say that** a restriction pertaining to **mourning is** treated more **lightly by [a person] than** the prohibition due to **menstruation?**[2] וְהָאָמַר רַבִּי יִצְחָק בַּר חֲנִינָא אָמַר רַב הוּנָא – **But R' Yitzchak bar Chanina said in the name of Rav Huna:** כָּל מְלָאכוֹת שֶׁאִשָּׁה עוֹשָׂה לְבַעְלָהּ – **All tasks that a woman performs for her husband**[3] נִדָּה עוֹשָׂה לְבַעְלָהּ – **a *niddah* can perform for her husband,** חוּץ מִמְּזִיגַת הַכּוֹס – **except for mixing a cup** of wine to serve him, וְהַצָּעַת הַמִּטָּה – **making** his **bed,** וְהַרְחָצַת פָּנָיו יָדָיו וְרַגְלָיו – **and washing his face, hands and feet.**[4] וְאִילּוּ גַּבֵּי אֲבֵילוּת תַּנְיָא – **But regarding mourning it was taught in a Baraisa:** אַף עַל פִּי שֶׁאָמְרוּ – EVEN THOUGH [THE RABBIS] SAID: אֵין אָדָם רַשַּׁאי לָכוֹף אֶת אִשְׁתּוֹ – IT IS NOT PROPER FOR A MAN TO COMPEL HIS WIFE when she is in mourning for her mother or father לִהְיוֹת כּוֹחֶלֶת וְלִהְיוֹת פּוֹקֶסֶת – TO APPLY EYE SHADOW OR FACE POWDER,[5] בֶּאֱמֶת אָמְרוּ – IN TRUTH THEY SAID:[6] מוֹזֶגֶת לוֹ הַכּוֹס – SHE MAY MIX A CUP of wine FOR HIM, וּמַצַּעַת לוֹ הַמִּטָּה – AND MAKE THE BED FOR HIM, וּמַרְחֶצֶת לוֹ פָּנָיו יָדָיו וְרַגְלָיו – AND WASH HIS FACE, HANDS AND FEET, and we are not concerned that this will lead to cohabitation. It is thus apparent that people are more careful about the laws of mourning than the *niddah* prohibition.[7] – ? –

The Gemara answers:

לָא קַשְׁיָא – This is **not a difficulty.** Actually, everyone agrees that people treat the laws of mourning more lightly than the *niddah* prohibition. כָּאן בַּאֲבֵילוּת דִּידֵיהּ – However, **here** in the Baraisa cited above we are dealing **with his** state of **mourning;** then we have to be concerned that seclusion could lead to cohabitation even though that is not a concern regarding a *niddah.*[8] כָּאן בַּאֲבֵילוּת דִּידָהּ – But **here** in the Baraisa just cited we are dealing with **her** state of **mourning;** in that case we need not be concerned about acts of intimacy leading to cohabitation, because the wife will prevent him from cohabiting with her.[9]

The Gemara questions how the earlier Baraisa can be interpreted as referring specifically to the husband in mourning:

וְהָא אָבִיו שֶׁל חָתָן אוֹ אִמָּהּ שֶׁל כַּלָּה קָתָנֵי – **But the Baraisa taught:** "...and THE FATHER OF THE GROOM OR THE MOTHER OF THE BRIDE died." It is thus apparent that even when the woman is in mourning, the bride and groom may not be secluded, because it might lead to cohabitation. – ? –

The Gemara answers:

כִּי קָתָנֵי אַשְּׁאָרָא – **When [the Baraisa] taught** about the death of the bride's mother, it was referring **to the other** laws mentioned there.[10] But in the case where the bride is the mourner, the bride and groom may indeed be secluded together; the Baraisa's ruling that the bride and groom must sleep apart applies only when the groom is the mourner.

The Gemara questions the entire premise that the restrictions are eased when the wife is the mourner:

וּמִי שָׁאנֵי בֵּין אֲבֵילוּת דִּידֵיהּ לַאֲבֵילוּת דִּידָהּ – **But is there a difference between his** state of **mourning and her** state of **mourning?** וְהָתַנְיָא – **Why, it was taught in a Baraisa:** מִי שֶׁמֵּת חָמִיו אוֹ חֲמוֹתוֹ – ONE WHOSE FATHER-IN-LAW OR MOTHER-IN-LAW DIED אֵינוֹ יָכוֹל לָכוֹף אֶת אִשְׁתּוֹ לִהְיוֹת כּוֹחֶלֶת וְלִהְיוֹת פּוֹקֶסֶת – MAY NOT COMPEL HIS WIFE TO APPLY EYE SHADOW OR FACE POWDER. אֶלָּא כּוֹפֶה מִטָּתוֹ וְנוֹהֵג עִמָּהּ אֲבֵילוּת – RATHER, HE SHOULD OVERTURN HIS BED AND OBSERVE the laws of MOURNING WITH HER.[11] וְכֵן הִיא שֶׁמֵּת חָמִיהָ אוֹ חֲמוֹתָהּ – AND SIMILARLY, in the case of [A WIFE] WHOSE FATHER-IN-LAW OR MOTHER-IN-LAW DIED, אֵינָהּ רַשָּׁאָה לִהְיוֹת כּוֹחֶלֶת וְלִהְיוֹת פּוֹקֶסֶת – IT IS NOT PROPER FOR HER TO APPLY EYE SHADOW OR FACE POWDER. אֶלָּא כּוֹפָה מִטָּתָהּ וְנוֹהֶגֶת עִמּוֹ אֲבֵילוּת – RATHER, SHE SHOULD OVERTURN HER BED AND OBSERVE the laws of MOURNING WITH HIM. Now, the Baraisa does *not* mention any additional stringencies that apply

NOTES

1. That is, the Baraisa does not mean to teach that the laws concerning the groom or bride who is a mourner and the groom whose bride became a *niddah* are exactly the same. Rather, it is teaching that the case of a groom or bride in mourning and the case of a bride that became a *niddah* are similar in that they can both lead to the situation where the bride and groom may not be secluded with one another. However, the prohibition in the case where the wife became a *niddah* applies only when they had never cohabited (*Rashi*).

2. According to the present interpretation of the Baraisa, if the groom and bride had already cohabited, we trust the groom to be secluded with his bride when she is a *niddah,* but we do not trust him to be secluded with her if one of them is in mourning (*Rashi*).

3. The Mishnah below (59b) lists tasks that a married woman is required to perform for her husband (*Rashi*).

4. These three particular actions promote intimacy between the couple and could lead to them cohabiting in violation of the *niddah* laws (*Rashi*).

[There is actually no prohibition in a *niddah* mixing wine for her husband. Rather, she is prohibited to *serve* him the wine; the Gemara calls this "mixing the cup" (see *Rashi* ד״ה חוץ). The prohibition against a *niddah* making her husband's bed applies only in his presence, and even then only spreading the sheets is prohibited, but she may place the mattress and pillows on the bed. The prohibition of washing him includes pouring water on him even without physical contact; any type of physical contact is always prohibited between a *niddah* and her husband (see *Ritva, Tosafos*). These laws will be discussed in greater detail below, 61a.]

5. I.e. a type of dough placed on her face, which when removed gives her a [desirable] reddish complexion (*Rashi* here and *Shabbos* 94b; see *Rashi* there for an alternative explanation; cf. *Tosafos* here).

6. This expression generally introduces a statement that is universally accepted as law (see *Shabbos* 92b, *Bava Metzia* 60a, and *Rashi* to *Succah* 38a; cf. *Rashi* to *Nazir* 54b).

7. The fact that we allow the wife who is in mourning to perform these acts for her husband shows that we are not concerned that they will lead to intimacy; the Gemara now assumes that this is because people treat the laws of mourning with seriousness and would not come to transgress them.

8. The earlier Baraisa teaches that if the groom is in mourning, he should sleep with the men and the bride with the women. Since people treat the laws of mourning lightly, they may not be secluded together even after they have cohabited once; this is in contrast to *niddah* which he treats more stringently (*Rashi*).

9. The Baraisa teaching that the wife may mix her husband's wine, etc. is obviously referring to a case where the wife is in mourning, because it begins with the ruling that the husband should not compel her to use cosmetics, implying that she is in mourning. In that case she may perform the tasks mentioned above for her husband [even though a *niddah* may not] because even if these acts arouses his desire for her, she will surely not acquiesce to his desires, since she is mourning (*Rashi;* see *Rashash*). [The Gemara here assumes that the husband's desire is the more difficult to control; see below, 64b.]

10. I.e. the ruling that the corpse is removed to a room and that we proceed with the wedding, etc. (*Rashi*).

11. In Talmudic times they would overturn the mourner's bed as one of the practices of mourning (see *Moed Katan* 15a, 27a). This practice is not followed nowadays (see *Tur* and *Shulchan Aruch, Yoreh Deah* §387).

The practice of observing mourning laws when a close relative of one's spouse dies is discussed by Tannaim in Tractate *Moed Katan* (20b); see there for the reasons for this practice. See also below, notes 14 and 15.

הכי קאמר וכן מי שפירסה אשתו נדה ולא בעל הוא ישן בין האנשים ואשתו ישנה בין הנשים למימרא דאבילות קילא ליה מנדה והאמר רבי יצחק בר חנינא אמר רב הונא [א] כל מלאכות שאשה עושה לבעלה נדה עושה לבעלה חוץ ממזיגת הכוס והצעת המטה והרחצת פניו ידיו ורגליו ואילו גבי אבילות תניא אע"פ שאמרו אין אדם רשאי לכוף את אשתו להיות כוחלת ולהיות פוקסת [ב] באמת אמרו מוזגת לו הכוס ומצעת לו המטה ומרחצת לו פניו ידיו ורגליו לא קשיא כאן באבילות דידיה כאן באבילות דידה והא אביו של חתן או אמה של כלה קתני כי קתני אשארא ומי שאני בין אבילות דידיה לאבילות דידה והתניא [ג] מי שמת חמיו או חמותו [ג] אינו יכול לכוף את אשתו להיות כוחלת ולהיות פוקסת אלא כופה מטתו ונוהג עמה אבילות וכן היא שמת חמיה או חמותה אינה רשאה להיות כוחלת ולהיות פוקסת אלא כופה מטתה ונוהגת עמו אבילות תני באבילות דידיה הוא ישן בין האנשים ואשתו ישנה בין הנשים הא וכן קתני כי קתני אכיחול ואפירכום והא עמו קתני מאי לאו עמו במטה לא עמו בבית [ג] וכדאמר ליה רב לחייא בריה [ד] באפה נהוג אבילותא דלא באפה לא תנהוג אבילותא רב אשי אמר מי קמדמית אבילותא דהכא לאבילותא דעלמא [ה] אבילותא דעלמא חמיר ולא אתי לזלזולי ביה אבילות דהכא כיון דאקילו רבנן אתי לזלזולי ביה מאי קולא אילימא דקתני בועל בעילת מצוה ופורש התם משום דלא חל עליו אבילותא אי לרבי אליעזר [ד] עד שיצא מפתח הבית אי לרבי יהושע עד שיסתם הגולל אלא דקתני נוהג שבעת ימי המשתה ואח"כ נוהג שבעת ימי אבילות אמר מר [ה] בין כך ובין כך לא יבעול לא בערב שבת ולא במוצ"ש בשלמא בערב שבת משום חבורה אלא במוצאי שבת אמאי לא אמר רבי זירא משום

ה"ק כו'. כלומר כי קאמר וכן אהוא ישן בין האנשים והיא ישנה בין הנשים קאמר ולעולם הך בשלא בעל קאי: קילא ליה. לעבור עליה מנדה דאבילות לא מהימנא ליה ונדה מהימנת ליה: מלאכות שהאשה עושה לבעלה. לקמן תני להו בפרק אע"פ: חוץ ממזיגת הכוס. להושיט לו: והצעת המטה והרחצת פניו כו'. שדרך קירוב וחיבה הן ובאין לידי הרגל דבר: אין אדם רשאי לכוף את אשתו. בימי אבלה כשמת אביה או אמה: פוקסת. מעברת שרק על פניה: מוזגת לו. ולא חיישינן להרגל דבר אלמא אבילות חמירא ליה: כאן באבילות דידיה. לעולם אבילות קילא ליה מנדה והני מתניתא הכי מתרצן הא דקתני לעיל הוא ישן בין האנשים כו' באבילות דידיה והך דקתני מוזגת לו כו' באבילות דידה קאי דקתני אין אדם רשאי לכוף כו' אלמא באבילות דידה קיימינן שאינה רוצה לכחול ולפקוס והיינו טעמא דמוזגת דאם יתגבר יצרו עליו כיון דאבילות דידה הוא אינה שומעת לו: והא אביו של חתן כו'. אלמא באבילות דידיה נמי אתמר תנא דלעיל: כי קתני. אמה של כלה אשארא אמכניסים המת לחדר אבל הוא ישן בין האנשים אאבילות דחתן קאי: ונוהגת עמו אבילות. אלמא מדלא קתני באבילות דידיה הוא ישן בין האנשים שמע מינה חמיר ליה ולא שני לן: ה"ג תני באבילות דידיה הוא ישן כו': הכי גרסינן והא עמו קתני מאי לאו עמו במטה. אלמא לאבילות דידיה נמי מהימן: לא עמו בבית. וטעמא לאו משום דמהימן נקט לה אלא לאשמועינן דאין אבילותו מוטל עליה אלא בפניו משום כבודו וכן הוא אין אבילותה מוטל עליו אלא לפניה ולכבודה: כדאמר ליה רב לחייא בריה. כשמת חמיו באפה נהוג אבילותא כו': פלוגתא דרבי אליעזר ורבי יהושע במועד קטן: גולל. זהו כסוי של ארון המת:

משום

והצעת המטה. נראה לר"י דהצעת המטה דהכא היינו פריסת סדינין שהוא דבר של חיבה אבל הצעת כרים וכסתות שאינן דברים של חיבה שרי לנדה והביא ראיה מדתנן בפ' אע"פ (לקמן נט:) הכניסה לו ג' שפחות אינה מצעת לו המטה ואינה עושה בצמר ארבע יושבת בקתדרא ואמרינן בגמרא אע"פ שאמרו ד' יושבת בקתדרא אבל מוזגת לו כוס ומצעת לו המטה ומרחצת לו פניו ידיו ורגליו ופי' בקונטרס דהא דתנא ג' אינה מצעת לו המטה היינו הצעת כרים וכסתות דהוי דבר שיש טורח אבל מצעת לו המטה היינו פריסת סדין ולבדין דמילי דחיבה ניהו שמתחבב עליו ואין בו טורח והשתא הצעה של חיבה נראה דדוקא אסור וכן משמע דמזכירה בהדי מזיגת כוס והרחצת פניו ידיו ורגליו כי התם מיהו לספרים דל"ג במשנה אלא ואינה מצעת המטה ול"ג לו ובגמרא גרסינן לו אין ראיה משם שיהו תרי גווני הצעה דמתני' איירי בהצעת שאר מטות ובגמרא איירי בהצעת מטה לבעלה לבדו:

פוקסת. פ"ה מעברת שרק על פניה ואין נראה דאמר בפ"ב לקמן (דף יז.) לא שרק ולא פירכום משמע דתרי מילי ניהו דפוקסת דהכא היינו פירכום כדאמרי' בסמוך כי קתני אכיחול ואפירכום ובשילהי המצניע (שבת צה.) קתני פוקסת ומעברת שרק על פניה ולקמן בפ"ב פ"ה פירכום קליעת שער וקשה לר"י דבשילהי המצניע (שם צד: ושם) קתני גודלת ופוקסת אלא נראה דאחד מתיקוני נשים הוא:

ומי שאני בין אבילות דידיה לאבילות דידה. תימה דבלאו מילתא דרב יוסף הוי מצי למיפרך ברייתות אהדדי וי"ל דאי לאו הוה מילתא דרב יוסף הוה מפלגינן בין שעת חופה לשלא בשעת חופה דבשעת חופה יצרו תוקפו אע"ג דבעל אבל לרב יוסף לא מצי לפלוגי בהכי דהא בבעל חשיב ליה כאשתו ישנה דאפי' בשעת חופה אשתו ישנה עמו בנדה ובאבילות דידה ואפילו הכי באבילות דידיה קתני הוא ישן בין האנשים ולהכי פריך שפיר ולרשב"א נראה דאי לאו דרב יוסף לא הוה קשה מידי דעמו ועמה דקתני בברייתא לאו עמו במטה אלא עמה בבית אבל לרב יוסף דבאבילות דידה אשתו ישנה עמו א"כ הא דקתני נוהג עמה אבילות היינו עמה במטה דומיא דהכא באבילות דידיה הוי עמו במטה והא דמשני תני באבילות דידיה הוא ישן אינו מגיה הברייתא אלא מפרש דעמו דקתני בברייתא דהכי הוא ופריך והא עמו קתני מאי לאו עמו במטה פי' דומיא דעמה ומשני לא עמו בבית כדא"ל רב כו':

עד שיסתם הגולל. בכמה מקומות פי' רש"י דגולל הוי כיסוי ארון ודופק היינו קרשים שבצידי הארון ונקרא דופק על שם שהגולל דופק עליו וכעין זה פי' בערוך וקשה לר"ת דאמר בפרק מי שמתו (ברכות יט: ושם) מדלגין היינו על גבי ארונות ואיך היו מדלגין והלא הגולל והדופק מטמא באהל כדאמרינן בהעור והרוטב (חולין קכו: ושם) ועוד דבפרק בהמה המקשה (שם עב:) דריש על פני השדה לרבות גולל ודופק ולפ"ה הלא ארון אינו על פני השדה ואומר ה"ר דוד מנלינבורק כי לפרש"י [דריש] לרבות גולל ודופק שפירש דלא מרבינן מעל פני השדה דמטמא אלא כשפירש אבל בעוד שהוא טמון בטל אגב קרקע ולא מטמא באוהל והשתא אתי נמי שפיר ההיא דמדלגים היינו על גבי ארונות ועוד י"מ אע"ג דגולל מטמא באהל מ"מ יכולין לדלג ולטמאות עצמם בגולל דתניא במס' שמחות (פ"ד) כל טומאה שאין נזיר מגלח עליה אין כהן מוזהר עליה ואר"ת דמשובשת היא דהא רביעית דם אין נזיר מגלח עליה כדתנן בנזיר (דף נד. ושם) וכהן מוזהר עליה ועוד הקשה דתניא בעירובין (דף טו:) כל דבר שיש בו רוח חיים אין עושין ממנו לא גולל לקבר כו' ולפ"ה וכי דרך לעשות כסוי ארון מבעלי חיים ויש לומר אע"ג דאין דרך לעשות כסוי ארון מבעלי חיים מכל מקום כמה דברים אשכחן דלא שכיח ומיירי בהן הש"ס לדרוש ולקבל שכר כדאמרינן בפרק המקשה (חולין ע.) בלעתו חולדה והוציאתו והכניסתו והקיאתו ויצא מאליו מהו הדביק שני רחמים ויצא מזה לזה מהו אף על פי שלא יבא לעולם ור"ת מפרש דגולל היינו מצבה שהיא אבן גדולה ולשון גולל שייך על האבן כדכתיב וגללו את האבן (בראשית כט) ודופק הן שתי אבנים אחת לראשה ואחת לרגלה של מצבה ופעמים כשאין המצבה מזומנת מעמידין שם בהמה או דבר אחר לסימן וההיא דמדלגין לא היה שם מצבה ומחמת המת לא היו מיטמאין דרוב ארונות יש בהן פותח טפח ולא תקשה לר' יהושע מאימת חל אבילות כשאין שם מצבה די"ל דכי מהדרי אפייהו דקוברין כדאמרינן במועד קטן (דף כב.) דהנהו דלא אזלי בתר שכבא מכי מהדרי אפייהו וקשה לר"י על פירוש רבינו תם דתניא בתוספתא דאהלות בפרק ד' אמר רבי יהודה שתי אבנים גדולות

של

עין משפט
נר מצוה

יג א מיי' פי"א מהל' איסורי ביאה הל' יט סמג לאוין קיא טוש"ע יו"ד סי' קצה סעי' י:
יד ב (מיי' פ"ב מהל' אבל) סמג עשין ב טוש"ע שם סי' שפג סעי' א:
טו ג [מיי' פ"ב מהל' אבל הל' ה] טוש"ע שם סי' שעד סעי' ו וסי' שפא סעי' ו:
טז ד מיי' פ"ב שם הל' ה סמג שם (טוש"ע יו"ד סי' שצד סעי' ו):
יז ה מיי' פ"י מהל' אישות הל' יד טוש"ע אה"ע סי' סד סעי' ג:

גליון הש"ס

גמרא אבילותא דעלמא חמיר. ע' סוטה ז ע"א תוס' ד"ה אמר:

תוספות רי"ד

למימרא דאבילות קילא [ליה] מנדה דהא בנדה [אינה] צריכה שימור אם בעל ואבילות (לא) מצרכינן שימור אע"פ שבעל. והא אר"י ב"ח א"ר פפא כל מלאכות שהאשה עושה לבעלה נדה עושה לבעלה חוץ ממזיגת הכוס והצעת המטה והרחצת פניו ידיו ורגליו ואילו גבי אבילות תניא אע"פ שאמרו אין אדם רשאי לכוף את אשתו לא להיות כוחלת ולא להיות פוקסת באמת אמרו מוזגת לו הכוס ומצעת לו המטה ורוחצת פניו ידיו ורגליו ומסיק ר"א מי קא מדמית אבילות דהכא לאבילות דעלמא. אבילות דעלמא חמירא ליה ולא אתי לזלזולי בה. אבל אבילות דהכא כיון דאקילי בה רבנן אתי לזלזולי בה ומאי קילותא דקתני נוהג ז' ימי המשתה ואח"כ נוהג ז' ימי אבילות: תניא מי שמת חמיו או חמותו אינו רשאי לכוף את אשתו להיות פוקסת אבל כופה מטתו ונוהג עמה אבילות ודוקא בפניה אבל שלא בפניה לא. כדא"ל רב לחייא בריה באפה נהוג אבילות שלא באפה לא תנהוג אבילות:

מסורת הש"ס

א) לקמן סא., ב) מ"ק כ: שמחות פי"א, ג) ג"ז שם, ד) מ"ק כז. סנהדרין מז: [שבת קנב:].

ליקוטי רש"י

חוץ ממזיגת הכוס. כל שהוא דברים של קירוב וחיבה ומביאין לידי הרגל דבר. והצעת המטה. לפרוס סדין ולבדין דבר שאינו טורח ומשום דמילי דחיבה ניהו כדי שתתחבב עליו [לקמן סא.]. באמת אמרו. כל באמת הלכה היא ואין חולק בדבר [סוכה לח.]. הלכה היא למשה מסיני [נזיר נד:]. כוחלת. נותנת כחול בין עיניה כדי שדומות נאים [מו"ק ט:]. פוקסת. יש מרבותי אומרים מתקנת שערה במסרק או בידיה ויש שמפרשין טחה כמין בצק על פניה וכשנוטלו מאדים הבשר [שבת צד:]. תפקום שרק על פניה טיינפא"ל בלע"ז והוא אדום [שם סד:]. מחלקת שערה לכאן ולכאן [מו"ק שם עיי"ש]. באפה. דאיתתך כשהיא אבילה דהאי נמי כל שמתאבל עליו כגון אשתו מתאבל עמו בפניו [שם כ:]. באפה. בפניה [ב"ק נו:]. עד שיסתם הגולל. דאבילות מסקימת הגולל חיילא כדתניא באלו מגלחין. גולל. הוא הדף הנתון על הארון לכסוי ואותן שבדפנות קרי להו דופק [סנהדרין מז:]. הוא כיסוי שנותנים על ארונו [שבת קנב:].

ובועל בעילת מצוה ופורש ונוהג שבעת ימי המשתה ואחר כך נוהג שבעת ימי אבילות וכל אותן הימים הוא ישן בין האנשים והיא ישנה בין הנשים [א] ואין מונעין תכשיטין מן הכלה כל שלשים יום * ודוקא אביו של חתן או אמה של כלה דליכא איניש דטרח להו אבל איפכא לא אמר רפרם בר פפא אמר רב חסדא לא שנו אלא שנתן מים על גבי בשר אבל לא נתן מים על גבי בשר מזדבן אמר רבא ובכרך אע"פ שנתן מים על גבי בשר מזדבן אמר רב פפא ובכפר אע"פ שלא נתן מים על גבי בשר לא מזדבן ואלא דרב חסדא היכי משכחת לה אמר רב אשי כגון מתא מחסיא דמפקא מכרך ומפקא מכפר תניא כוותיה דרב חסדא [ב] הרי שהיה פתו אפויה וטבחו טבוח ויינו מזוג ונתן מים על גבי בשר ומת אביו של חתן או אמה של כלה מכניסין את המת לחדר ואת החתן ואת הכלה לחופה ובועל בעילת מצוה ופורש ונוהג שבעת ימי המשתה ואח"כ נוהג שבעת ימי אבילות וכל אותן הימים הוא ישן בין האנשים ואשתו ישנה בין הנשים וכן [ג] מי שפירסה אשתו נדה הוא ישן בין האנשים והיא ישנה בין הנשים [ג] ואין מונעין תכשיטין מן הכלה כל ל' יום בין כך ובין כך לא יבעול לא בערב שבת ולא במוצ"ש אמר מר הוא ישן בין האנשים והיא ישנה בין הנשים מסייע ליה לרבי יוחנן דאמר רבי יוחנן [ד] אע"פ שאמרו אין אבילות במועד אבל דברים של צינעא נוהג דרש רב יוסף בריה דרבא משמיה דרבא [ה] ל"ש אלא שלא בעל אבל בעל אשתו ישנה עמו והא הכא דבבעל עסקינן וקתני הוא ישן בין האנשים והיא ישנה בין הנשים כי קאמר [ו] אפירסה אשתו נדה הא וכן קתני הכי

רש"י

ופורש. ויקברו את המת מיד דכיון דחלה עליו חתונה הויא לגביה כרגל ולא אתיא אבילות וחיילא ונוהג שבעת ימי המשתה כו': וכל אותן הימים. של ימי המשתה ושל אבילות: הוא ישן כו'. ואין מתיחדין זה עם זה שמא יבעול ואבל אסור בתשמיש המטה כדילפינן באלו מגלחין (מו"ק דף טו:) ואף בשבעת ימי המשתה שהן כרגל נוהג הוא אבילות של דברי צינעא דהיינו איסור תשמיש כדלקמן: ואין מונעין. בשביל האבילות אין אוסרין עליה תכשיטיה שלא תתגנה על בעלה: ° כל שלשים יום. ואע"פ שהן ימי אבילות לשאר בני אדם וכל שכן משלשים ואילך: דליכא איניש דטרח. אם יפסידו מה שהכינו: שנתן מים על גבי בשר. שוב אינו ראוי למוכרו במקולין: בכרך. שכיחי אינשי טובא ויש קופלים הרבה: אלא דרב חסדא. דמפליג בין נתן ללא נתן: היכי משכחת לה. לא בכרך ולא בכפר: דמפקא מכרך ומפקא מכפר. מולאה מכלל כרך ומולאה מכלל כפר גדולה מכפר וקטנה מכרך: תניא כרב חסדא. דמוקי לה בנתן מים על גבי בשר: וכן מי שפירסה אשתו נדה. בכניסתה לחופה: הוא ישן כו'. ואין נאמנין זה עם זה: בין כך ובין כך. בין יש אונס בין אין אונס: לא יבעול. בעילה ראשונה: לא בערב שבת כו'. בליל שבת מפני שעושה חבורה: ולא במוצ"ש. לקמן מפרש: מסייע ליה. הא דקתני דאסור בתשמיש בשבעת ימי המשתה שהן לו כרגל: של צינעא. שאינו ניכר לבריות שהוא אבל בכך: לא שנו. דאין נאמנין להתייחד: אלא שלא בעל. דתקיף ליה יצריה: דבבעל עסקינן. דקתני בועל בעילת מצוה לפני קבורת המת: כי קאמר. רבא לא שנו אפירסה אשתו נדה קאמר דכיון דנדה חמורה בעל מהימן עלה דלא אתי לזלזולי באיסור כרת: הא וכן קתני. קס"ד אכולה מילתא דאבילות מדמינן ליה ובאבילות דבעל עסקינן:
ה"ק

תוספות

בועל בעילת מצוה ופורש. קודם שיקבר המת אבל לאחר שנקבר לא כדאמרינן בסמוך דברים של צינעא נוהג ודייק לה מדקתני כל אותן הימים הוא ישן בין האנשים כו' מיהו מרישא דהכא לא ה"מ למידק דדוקא כשהמת בחדר הוא דשרי בעילת מצוה דמאי לחוויי דבועל בעילת מצוה היינו אפי' לאחר שחל עליו אבילות אבל קשה לרשב"א אמאי לא דייק מדקתני ופורש מכלל דנוהג דברים של צינעא מדלא התיר אלא בעילת מצוה דוקא ואור"י דהמ"ל פורש משום דם בתולים כדאמרינן בפ' תינוקת (נדה דף סה:) אבל מהוא ישן בין האנשים דייק שפיר דהוי משום אבילות דאי משום נדות כיון דבעיל אשתו ישנה עמו כדאמר רב יוסף בסמוך ועוד דכל אותן הימים משמע דכולהו הוי חד טעמא דהיינו משום אבילות והשתא מקילינן טפי באנינות דאורייתא מבאבילות דרבנן מידי דהוה אנעילת סנדל ועטיפת הראש וכפיית המטה: בעילת מצוה. קרי לה בעילת מצוה משום דכתיב כי בועליך עושיך ואמרי' (סנהדרין דף כב:) אין אשה כורתת ברית אלא למי שעושה אותה כלי וע"י כך מידבק בה ובאין לידי פריה ורביה ולהכי קרי לה לבעילה ראשונה בעילת מצוה: אבל איפכא לא. וה"ה אם אבלים מחמת שאר קרובים תימה דאמר בפ"ג דמועד קטן (דף כג. וסס) מתה אשתו אסור לישא עד שיעברו ג' רגלים ואם אין לו בנים מותר לישא לאלתר משום פריה ורביה היינו לו בנים קטנים מותר לישא לאלתר משום פרנסתם והכא אמר אבל איפכא לא ומשמע דבאין לו בנים עסקינן מדקאמר דליכא דטרח להו משמע דבבחור איירי וי"ל דלאלתר לאו דוקא אלא כלומר מותר לאחר ז' ומיהו לבעול אסור עד לאחר ל' כדמוכח בתר הכי במעשה שמתה אשתו של יוסף הכהן ואמר לאחותה בבית הקברות לאי ופרנסי בני אחותיך ואעפ"כ לא בא עליה עד זמן מרובה מאי זמן מרובה שלשים יום מכלל דכנסה תוך ל' ותוך שבעה ודאי אסור כדמוכח הכא ומה שאמר לה בבה"ק לא היה זה כניסה אלא שידוכין בעלמא ונראה לר"י דודאי אותו שיש לו בנים קטנים מותר לישא תוך ל' כדמשמע בעובדא דיוסף הכהן אבל אותו שאין לו בנים כלל אסור לישא עד לאחר שלשים כיון שאין יכול לבעול תוך שלשים וכן משמע במס' שמחות (פ"ז) דתניא בד"א כשיש לו בנים גדולים אבל אין לו בנים או שיש לו בנים קטנים מותר לישא אחרת לאחר ל' משמע דלאסור אפי' לישא תוך שלשים ואע"ג דיש לו בנים קטנים מותר לישא תוך שלשים מ"מ נקט אחר שלשים משום אין לו בנים ור"ת ר"ל דבאין לו בנים אפי' לבעול שרי תוך שלשים אחר ז' משום פריה ורביה והיא דשמחות איירי במתייבשת כפי' ונראה דבים לו בנים קטנים שרי לישא ואפי' אם היא נמי אבילה מפני שמפרנסת בניו ואע"פ שאפשר באחרת כדמוכח בעובדא דיוסף הכהן שהיתה אבילה מאחותה ומיהו אין כל כך ראיה דשמא שאני התם לפי שהיא תרחם על בני אחותה יותר מאחרת ואע"ג דתנן בפרק החולץ (יבמות דף מא. וסס) כל הנשים יתארסו חוץ מאלמנה מפני האיבול ולא מפליג מידי משמע שאסורה אפי' למי שיש לו בנים קטנים כשהיא אבילה התם משום דבלאו הכי אסורה דצריכה להמתין ג' חדשים משום הבחנה ואור"ת דאפי' מתו אביו ואמו יכול לכנוס אחר ל' והא דאמרי' במועד קטן (דף כב:) על כל המתים נכנס לבית המשתה אחר ל' על אביו ועל אמו אחר י"ב חדשים ה"מ בשאר שמחות אבל לישא אשה שהיא מצוה יתירה מותר ואפי' יש לו בנים משום שנאמר (קהלת יא) בבקר זרע [את] זרעך ולערב אל תנח ידך והביא ראיה מדתניא סתם כל ל' יום לנישואין ולא מפליג בין אביו ואמו לשאר קרובים משמע דכולהו לאחר ל' מותר וה"ר יוסף הביא ראיה לדבריו דתנן במסכת שמחות (פ"ט) בהדיא על כל המתים אסור לילך לבית המשתה עד שישלימו ל' יום ועל אביו ועל אמו אסור כל שנים עשר חדש אא"כ היה של מצוה אלמא שרי בכל משתה של מצוה וצ"ע אי קאי נמי ארישא ושרי אפי' תוך ל' יום: כגון מתא מחסיא. תימה רב חסדא מאי דוחקיה לאוקומי בנתן מים על גבי בשר נוקמה בכפר אע"פ שלא נתן מים על גבי בשר וי"ל לומר משום דניחא ליה לרב חסדא לאוקמה ברוב עיירות שהן בינוניות וה"ק כגון מתא מחסיא ורוב עיירות ומש"ה נקט נמי בברייתא דמייתי ונתן מים על גבי בשר משום דאיירי ברוב עיירות: מסייע ליה לר' יוחנן כו'. מועד וחתן משוה אותן בכ"מ כהכיא דתניא בפ"ק דמועד קטן (דף ז: וסס) חתן שנולד בו נגע נותנין לו ז' ימי המשתה לו ולאיצטליתו ולכסותו וכן ברגל נותנין לו כל ימות הרגל: אבל דברים של צינעא נוהג. פי' חובה לעשות כן ולא רשות כדמדמיתי סייעתא מן הברייתא וא"ת רב ושמואל דאמרי בתרא בפרק בתרא דמועד קטן (דף כד.) דתשמיש המטה בשבת של ז' ימי אבילות רשות תיקשי להו ברייתא הכא ואין סברא לחלק בין מועד לשבת ומקילין בשבת טפי אלא נראה לר"י דרב ושמואל מפלגי בין חתן למועד ושבת אבל קשה דלכל אותן הימים הוא ישן בין האנשים משמע אפי' בשבת ופסקו ה"ג כר' יוחנן ופירשו אע"ג דקיימא לן כדברי המיקל באבל ה"מ בתנאי אבל באמוראי לא ואור"י דודאי נראה דהלכה כר' יוחנן מדאמר הש"ס הכא מסייע ליה לר' יוחנן:

והלעת

מסורת הש"ס

א) [יומא עח:], ד) [עי' תוס' יומא יח: ד"ה יחודי וכו' אריכות בסוגיא דהכא], ג) יומא דף עח:.

גליון הש"ס

רש"י ד"ה כל ל' יום. ע' מג"א סי' תרי"ג ס"ק י"ב:

עין משפט נר מצוה

ט א ב מיי' פי"א מהל' אבל הל' ח סמג עשין ב טוש"ע יו"ד סי' שמב וסי' שפג סעי' ב [רב אלפס כאן ובמו"ק פ"ג דף רלא.]:
י ג מיי' וסמג שם טוש"ע שם סי' שפא סעי' ו:
יא ד מיי' פי"י שם הל' ג סמג שם טוש"ע שם סי' שלט סעי' ב [עי' כ"מ]:
יב ה ו מיי' פכ"ב מהל' איסורי ביאה הל"א סמג לאוין קמ טוש"ע אה"ע סי' כב סעי' א וטוש"ע יו"ד סי' שפג סעי' ב:

תוספות רי"ד

אמר רפרם בר פפא א"ר חסדא לא שנו אלא שניתן מים ע"ג בשר אבל לא ניתן מים ע"ג בשר מיזדבן. אמר רבא ובכרך אע"פ שניתן מים על גבי בשר מיזדבן. א"ר פפא ובכפר אע"פ שלא ניתן מים ע"ג בשר לא מיזדבן. ואלא דרב חסדא היכי משכחת לה כגון מתא מחסיא דמפקא מכפר ומפקא מכרך: אמר מר הוא ישן בין האנשים וכו'. מסייע ליה לר' יוחנן דאמר ר"י אע"פ שאמרו אין אבילות במועד אבל דברים שבצנעה נוהג. פי' ז' ימי חתונות כשבעת ימי הרגל הן לו. ומפני שתשמיש המטה הוי דבר של צנעה שאין בני העולם מרגישים אסור: דרש ר"י ברי' דרבא משמיה דרבא לא שנו אלא שלא בעל שיצרו תוקפו אבל בעל אשתו ישנה עמו בבית. והא הכא בבעל עסקינן וקתני הוא ישן בין האנשים וכו'. כי קאמר ר"י אפירסה נדה. והא וכן קתני ה"ק וכן מי שפירסה אשתו נדה ולא בעל הוא ישן בין האנשים ואשתו ישנה בין הנשים פי' אבל [בעל] כל נדה דעלמא מתקיים בעלה בבית וכשמת אביו של חתן או אמה של כלה צריכי שימור:

NOT COHABIT with his virgin bride for the first time לֹא בְּעֶרֶב שַׁבָּת – NEITHER ON THE EVE OF THE SABBATH [i.e. Friday night] וְלֹא בְּמוֹצָאֵי שַׁבָּת – NOR AFTER THE CONCLUSION OF THE SABBATH (i.e. Saturday night).[21]

The Gemara elaborates on the Baraisa just cited:

אָמַר מַר – **The master said:** הוּא יָשֵׁן בֵּין הָאֲנָשִׁים וְהִיא יְשֵׁנָה בֵּין הַנָּשִׁים – HE SLEEPS AMONG THE MEN AND SHE SLEEPS AMONG THE WOMEN.

The Gemara notes:

מְסַיֵּיע לֵיהּ לְרַבִּי יוֹחָנָן – **This is a support to R' Yochanan.** דְּאָמַר רַבִּי יוֹחָנָן – **For R' Yochanan said:** אַף עַל פִּי שֶׁאָמְרוּ אֵין אֲבֵילוּת בְּמוֹעֵד – **Even though they said that there is no mourning during the festival,** אֲבָל דְּבָרִים שֶׁל צִינְעָא נוֹהֵג – **nevertheless, one must observe inconspicuous** mourning **practices.**[22]

The Gemara qualifies this ruling:

דָּרַשׁ רַב יוֹסֵף בְּרֵיהּ דְּרָבָא מִשְּׁמֵיהּ דְּרָבָא – **Rav Yosef the son of Rava expounded in the name of Rava:** לֹא שָׁנוּ אֶלָּא שֶׁלֹּא בָּעַל – **This ruling** of the Baraisa **was taught only where he** had **not** yet **cohabited** with his wife.[23] אֲבָל בָּעַל – **But if he** once **cohabited** with her, אִשְׁתּוֹ יְשֵׁנָה עִמּוֹ – then **his wife may sleep** (i.e. seclude herself) **with him.**[24]

The Gemara objects:

וְהָא הָכָא דִּבְבָעַל עָסְקִינַן – **But here** in the Baraisa **we are dealing with someone who cohabited** already [for the Baraisa directs that the groom perform the mitzvah-cohabitation before the deceased is buried], וְקָתָנֵי הוּא יָשֵׁן בֵּין הָאֲנָשִׁים וְהִיא יְשֵׁנָה בֵּין הַנָּשִׁים – **and yet [the Baraisa] teaches:** HE SLEEPS AMONG THE MEN AND SHE SLEEPS AMONG THE WOMEN! How could Rava have stated that the Baraisa's teaching applies only where he has *not* yet cohabited with his wife?

The Gemara answers:

כִּי קָאָמַר אַפֵּירְסָה אִשְׁתּוֹ נִדָּה – **When [Rava] stated** his distinction, he was referring **to** the ruling in the Baraisa concerning one **whose wife began to menstruate.**[25]

The Gemara asks:

הָא וְכֵן קָתָנֵי – **But [the Baraisa] stated:** AND SIMILARLY [in the case of a wife who began to menstruate . . .], implying that the law in that case is identical to the case where the father of the groom or the mother of the bride died.[26] – ? –

NOTES

21. He may not cohabit with her for the first time on Friday night, because this will cause her to bleed (*Rashi;* the precise nature of this prohibition is discussed at length in the Gemara below, 5b-6a). The Gemara below (4b-5a) will explain why an initial cohabitation may not be performed on Saturday night (*Rashi;* cf. *Pnei Yehoshua*).

22. I.e. although generally the laws of *aveilus* do not apply during festivals, a mourner must still observe those inconspicuous mourning practices that will not cause anyone to realize that he is in mourning [such as bathing in hot water or having marital relations] (see *Moed Katan* 24a; see also *Shulchan Aruch Yoreh Deah* 399:2 and *Orach Chaim* 548:4 with *Mishnah Berurah* §16). The Baraisa supports this ruling; for since the seven days of feasting are considered a festival for the bride and groom, and the Baraisa nevertheless states that they must sleep apart from each other, we can infer that inconspicuous mourning practices are in effect for a mourner even during a festival (*Rashi*). [See *Tosafos,* who cite sources for the law that the seven days of rejoicing are treated like a festival.]

23. In such a case, we cannot trust that he will abstain, because we are concerned that he may be seized with desire and unable to resist (*Rashi*).

24. The Gemara below will clarify which teaching of the Baraisa Rav Yosef means to qualify.

25. Since the prohibition of cohabiting with a *niddah* is stringent (in that it is subject to the punishment of *kares*), we can trust that the husband will not violate it as long as he has already cohabited with his wife once (*Rashi*). The [Rabbinic] prohibition of *aveilus,* however, is relatively lenient; thus, a mourner is prohibited to seclude himself with his wife even though they once cohabited, for his desire may prove too strong for him to control. See Gemara below (4b) for further elaboration.

26. The Gemara now assumes that the Baraisa's words ("And similarly in the case of one whose wife became a *niddah*") are teaching that the rulings concerning one whose wife is a *niddah* are exactly identical to those taught concerning the bride or groom who is a mourner. And in the case of mourning, the Baraisa states that the groom must sleep apart from his bride even though they had already cohabited [when the marriage was consummated] (*Rashi*).

מסורת הש"ס

א) [יומא עח:], ב) [עי' תוס' יומא יח: ד"ה יחודי וכו' אריכות בסוגיא דהכא], ג) יומא דף עח:.

ובועל בעילת מצוה ופורש ונוהג שבעת ימי המשתה ואחר כך נוהג שבעת ימי אבילות וכל אותן הימים הוא ישן בין האנשים והיא ישנה בין הנשים [א] ואין מונעין תכשיטין מן הכלה כל שלשים יום [א]ודוקא אביו של חתן או אמה של כלה דליכא איניש דטרח להו אבל איפכא לא אמר רפרם בר פפא אמר רב חסדא לא שנו אלא שנתן מים על גבי בשר אבל לא נתן מים על גבי בשר מזדבן אמר רבא ובכרך אע"פ שנתן מים על גבי בשר מזדבן אמר רב פפא ובכפר אע"פ שלא נתן מים על גבי בשר לא מזדבן ואלא דרב חסדא היכי משכחת לה אמר רב אשי כגון מתא מחסיא דמפקא מכרך ומפקא מכפר תניא כוותיה דרב חסדא [ב]הרי שהיה פתו אפויה וטבחו טבוח ויינו מזוג ונתן מים על גבי בשר ומת אביו של חתן או אמה של כלה מכניסין את המת לחדר ואת החתן ואת הכלה לחופה ובועל בעילת מצוה ופורש ונוהג שבעת ימי המשתה ואח"כ נוהג שבעת ימי אבילות וכל אותן הימים הוא ישן בין האנשים ואשתו ישנה בין הנשים וכן [ג]מי שפירסה אשתו נדה הוא ישן בין האנשים והיא ישנה בין הנשים [ג]ואין מונעין תכשיטין מן הכלה כל ל' יום בין כך ובין כך לא יבעול לא בערב שבת ולא במוצ"ש אמר מר הוא ישן בין האנשים והיא ישנה בין הנשים מסייע ליה לרבי יוחנן דאמר רבי יוחנן [ד]אע"פ שאמרו אין אבילות במועד אבל דברים של צינעא נוהג דרש רב יוסף בריה דרבא משמיה דרבא [ה]ל"ש אלא שלא בעל אבל בעל אשתו ישנה עמו והא הכא דבבעל עסקינן וקתני הוא ישן בין האנשים והיא ישנה בין הנשים כי קאמר [ו]אפירסה אשתו נדה הא וכן קתני הכי

רש"י

ופורש. ויקברו את המת מיד דכיון דחלה עליו אתונה הויא לגביה כרגל ולא אתיא אבילות וחיילא ונוהג שבעת ימי המשתה כו': וכל אותן הימים. של ימי המשתה ושל אבילות: הוא ישן כו'. ואין מתיחדין זה עם זה שמא יבעול ואבל אסור בתשמיש המטה כדילפינן באלו מגלחין (מו"ק דף טו:) ואף בשבעת ימי המשתה שהן כרגל נוהג הוא אבילות של דברי צינעא דהיינו איסור תשמיש כדלקמן: ואין מונעין. בשביל האבילות אין אוסרין עליה תכשיטיה שלא תתגנה על בעלה: ° כל שלשים יום. ואע"פ שהן ימי אבילות לשאר בני אדם וכל שכן משלשים ואילך: דליכא איניש דטרח. אם יפסידו מה שהכינו: שנתן מים על גבי בשר. שוב אינו ראוי למוכרו במקולין: בכרך. שכיחי אינשי טובא ויש קופלים הרבה: אלא דרב חסדא. דמפליג בין נתן ללא נתן: היכי משכחת לה. לא בכרך ולא בכפר: דמפקא מכרך ומפקא מכפר. מופלאה מכלל כרך ומופלאה מכלל כפר גדולה מכפר וקטנה מכרך: תניא כרב חסדא. דמוקי לה בנתן מים על גבי בשר: וכן מי שפירסה אשתו נדה. בכניסתה לחופה: הוא ישן כו'. ואין נאמנין זה עם זה: בין כך ובין כך. בין יש אונס בין אין אונס: לא יבעול. בעילה ראשונה: לא בערב שבת כו'. בליל שבת מפני שעושה חבורה: ולא במוצ"ש. לקמן מפרש: מסייע ליה. הא דקתני דאסור בתשמיש בשבעת ימי המשתה שהן לו כרגל: של צינעא. שאינו ניכר לבריות שהוא אבל בכך: לא שנו. דאין נאמנין להתייחד: אלא שלא בעל. דתקיף ליה יצריה: דבבעל עסקינן. דקתני בועל בעילת מצוה לפני קבורת המת: כי קאמר. רבא לא שנו אפירסה אשתו נדה קאמר דכיון דנדה חמורה בעל מהימן עלה דלא אתי לזלזולי באיסור כרת: הא וכן קתני. קס"ד אכולה מילתא דאבילות מדמינן ליה ובאבילות דבעל עסקינן: ה"ק

תוספות

בועל בעילת מצוה ופורש. קודם שיקבר המת אבל לאחר שנקבר לא כדאמרינן בסמוך דברים של צינעא נוהג ודייק לה מדקתני כל אותן הימים הוא ישן בין האנשים כו' מיהו מרישא דהכא לא ה"מ למידק דדוקא כשהמת בחדר הוא דשרי בעילת מצוה דמצי לדחויי דבועל בעילת מצוה היינו אפי' לאחר שחל עליו אבילות אבל קשה לרשב"א אמאי לא דייק מדקתני ופורש מכלל דנוהג דברים של צינעא מדלא התיר אלא בעילת מצוה דוקא ואור"י דהמ"ל פורש משום דם בתולים כדאמרינן בפ' תינוקת (נדה דף סה:) אבל מהוא ישן בין האנשים דייק שפיר דהוי משום אבילות דאי משום נדות כיון דבעיל אשתו ישנה עמו כדאמר רב יוסף בסמוך ועוד דכל אותן הימים משמע דכולהו הוי חד טעמא דהיינו משום אבילות והשתא מקילינן טפי באנינות דאורייתא מבאבילות דרבנן מידי דהוה אנעילת סנדל ועטיפת הראש וכפיית המטה: בעילת מצוה. קרי לה בעילת מצוה משום דכתיב כי בועליך עושיך ואמרי' (סנהדרין דף כב:) אין אשה כורתת ברית אלא למי שעושה אותה כלי וע"י כך מידבק בה ובאין לידי פריה ורביה ולהכי קרי לה לבעילה ראשונה בעילת מצוה: אבל איפכא לא. וה"ה אם אבלים מחמת שאר קרובים תימה דאמר בפ"ג דמועד קטן (דף כג. ושם) מתה אשתו אסור לישא עד שיעברו ג' רגלים ואם אין לו בנים מותר לישא לאלתר משום פריה ורביה הניחה לו בנים קטנים מותר לישא לאלתר משום פרנסתם והכא אמר אבל איפכא לא ומשמע דאין לו בנים עסקינן מדקאמר דליכא דטרח להו משמע דבבחור איירי וי"ל דלאלתר לאו דוקא אלא כלומר מותר לאחר ז' ומיהו לבעול אסור עד לאחר ל' כדמוכח בתר הכי במעשה שמתה אשתו של יוסף הכהן ואמר לאחותה בבית הקברות לאי ופרנסי בני אחותיך ואעפ"כ לא בא עליה עד זמן מרובה מאי זמן מרובה שלשים יום מכלל דכנסה תוך ל' ותוך שבעה ודאי אסור כדמוכח הכא ומה שאמר לה בבה"ק לא היה זה כניסה אלא שידוכין בעלמא ונראה לר"י דודאי אותו שיש לו בנים קטנים מותר לישא תוך ל' כדמשמע בעובדא דיוסף הכהן אבל אותו שאין לו בנים כלל אסור לישא עד לאחר שלשים כיון שאין יכול לבעול תוך שלשים וכן משמע במס' שמחות (פ"ז) דתניא בד"א כשיש לו בנים גדולים אבל אין לו בנים או שיש לו בנים קטנים מותר לישא אחרת לאחר ל' משמע דאסור אפי' לישא תוך שלשים ואע"ג דיש לו בנים קטנים מותר לישא תוך שלשים מ"מ נקט אחר שלשים משום אין לו בנים ור"ת ר"ל דאין לו בנים אפי' לבעול שרי תוך שלשים אחר ז' משום פריה ורביה והא דשמחות אינה מתיישבת כפי' ונראה דיש לו בנים קטנים שרי לישא ואפי' אם היא נמי אבילה מפני שמפרנסת בניו ואע"פ שאפשר באחרת כדמוכח בעובדא דיוסף הכהן שהיתה אבילה מאחותה ומיהו אין כל כך ראיה דשמא שאני התם לפי שהיא תרחם על בני אחותה יותר מאחרת ואע"ג דתנן בפרק החולץ (יבמות דף מא. ושם) כל הנשים יתארסו חוץ מאלמנה מפני האיבול ולא מפליג מידי משמע שאסורה אפי' למי שיש לו בנים קטנים כשהיא אבילה התם משום דבלאו הכי אסורה דצריכה להמתין ג' חדשים משום הבחנה ואור"ת דאפי' מתו אביו ואמו יכול לכנוס אחר ל' והא דאמרי' במועד קטן (דף כב:) על כל המתים נכנס לבית המשתה אחר ל' על אביו ועל אמו אחר י"ב חדשים ה"מ בשאר שמחות אבל לישא אשה שהיא מצוה יתירה מותר ואפי' יש לו בנים משום שנאמר (קהלת יא) בבקר זרע [את] זרעך ולערב אל תנח ידך והביא ראיה מדתניא סתם כל ל' יום לנישואין ולא מפליג בין אביו ואמו לשאר קרובים משמע דכולהו לאחר ל' מותר וה"ר יוסף הביא ראיה לדבריו דתנן במסכת שמחות (פ"ט) בהדיא על כל המתים אסור לילך לבית המשתה עד שישלימו ל' יום ועל אביו ועל אמו אסור כל שנים עשר חדש אא"כ היה של מצוה ול"ע אי קאי נמי ארישא ושרי אפי' תוך ל' יום: כגון מתא מחסיא. תימה רב חסדא מאי דוחקיה לאוקומי בנתן מים על גבי בשר נוקמה בכפר אע"פ שלא נתן מים על גבי בשר ויש לומר משום דניחא ליה לרב חסדא לאוקמה ברוב עיירות שהן בינוניות וה"ק כגון מתא מחסיא ורוב עיירות ומש"ה נקט נמי בברייתא דמייתי ונתן מים על גבי בשר משום דאיירי ברוב עיירות: מסייע ליה לר' יוחנן כו'. מועד ואתן משוה אותן בכ"מ כההיא דתניא בפ"ק דמועד קטן (דף ז: ושם) חתן שנולד בו נגע נותנין לו ז' ימי המשתה לו ולאיצטליתו ולכסותו וכן ברגל נותנין לו כל ימות הרגל: אבל דברים של צינעא נוהג. פי' חובה לעשות כן ולא רשות מדמייתי סייעתא מן הברייתא וא"ת רב ושמואל דאמרי בפרק בתרא דמועד קטן (דף כד.) דתשמיש המטה בשבת של ז' ימי אבילות רשות תיקשי להו ברייתא דהכא ואין סברא לחלק בין מועד לשבת ומקילין בשבת טפי אלא נראה לר"י דרב ושמואל מפלגי בין חתן למועד ושבת אבל קשה דכל אותן הימים הוא ישן בין האנשים משמע אפי' בשבת ופסקו ה"ג כר' יוחנן ופירשו אע"ג דקיימא לן כדברי המיקל באבל ה"מ בתנאי אבל באמוראי לא ואור"י דודאי נראה דהלכה כר' יוחנן מדאמר הש"ס הכא מסייע ליה לר' יוחנן:

והלעת

עין משפט נר מצוה

ט א ב מיי' פי"א מהל' אבל הל' ח סמג עשין ב טוש"ע יו"ד סי' שמב וסי' שפג סעי' ב [רב אלפס כאן ובמו"ק פ"ג דף רלא.]:
י ג מיי' וסמג שם טוש"ע שם סי' שפא סעי' ו:
יא ד מיי' פ"י שם הל' ג סמג שם טוש"ע שם סי' שצט סעי' ב [עי' כ"מ]:
יב ה ו מיי' פכ"ב מהל' איסורי ביאה הל"א סמג לאוין קכו טוש"ע אה"ע סי' כב סעי' א וטוש"ע יו"ד סי' שפג סעי' ב:

תוספות רי"ד

אמר רפרם בר פפא א"ר חסדא לא שנו אלא שניתן מים ע"ג בשר אבל לא ניתן מים ע"ג בשר מיזדבן. **אמר רבא** ובכרך אע"פ שניתן מים על גבי בשר מיזדבן. **א"ר פפא** ובכפר אע"פ שלא ניתן מים ע"ג בשר לא מיזדבן. ואלא דרב חסדא היכי משכחת לה כגון מתא מחסיא דמפקא מכפר ומפקא מכרך: **אמר מר** הוא ישן בין האנשים וכו'. מסייע ליה לר' יוחנן דאמר ר"י אע"פ שאמרו אין אבילות במועד אבל דברים שבצנעה נוהג. פי' ז' ימי חתונות כשבעת ימי הרגל הן לו. ומפני שתשמיש המטה הוי דבר של צנעה שאין בני העולם מרגישים אסור: **דרש ר"י ברי' דרבא משמיה דרבא** לא שנו אלא שלא בעל שיצרו תוקפו אבל בעל אשתו ישנה עמו בבית. והא הכא בבעל עסקינן וקתני הוא ישן בין האנשים וכו'. כי קאמר ר"י אפירסה נדה. והא וכן קתני ה"ק וכן מי שפירסה אשתו נדה ולא בעל הוא ישן בין האנשים ואשתו ישנה בין הנשים פי' אבל [בעל] כל נדה דעלמא מתקיים בעלה בבית וכשמת אביו של חתן או אמה של כלה צריכי שימור:

גליון הש"ס

רש"י ד"ה כל ל' יום. ע' מג"א סי' תרי"ג ס"ק י"ב:

father of the bride died], we do **not** delay the burial.[9]

The Gemara discusses what stage the wedding preparations must have already reached for the law stated by the Baraisa to apply:

אָמַר רַפְרַם בַּר פָּפָּא אָמַר רַב חִסְדָּא – Rafram bar Pappa said in the name of Rav Chisda: **לֹא שָׁנוּ אֶלָּא שֶׁנָּתַן מַיִם עַל גַּבֵּי בָּשָׂר – We were taught** that the burial is postponed **only** in an instance **where water was** already **placed on the meat** (to prepare it for cooking), since at that point the meat can longer be sold at market,[10] and it will go to waste if the wedding is postponed. **אֲבָל לֹא נָתַן מַיִם עַל גַּבֵּי בָּשָׂר – But if water had not** yet **been placed on the meat,** **מִזְדַּבַּן – it can** still **be sold,** and the wedding is therefore delayed until after the burial and mourning period.[11]

The Gemara qualifies Rav Chisda's ruling:

אָמַר רָבָא – Rava said: **וּבִכְרַךְ – In a big city,** where many people are competing to purchase any meat that is available, **אַף עַל פִּי שֶׁנָּתַן מַיִם עַל גַּבֵּי בָּשָׂר – even if water was placed on the meat,** **מִזְדַּבַּן – it can** still **be sold,** and the burial therefore cannot be delayed.[12]

The Gemara qualifies Rav Chisda's statement further:

אָמַר רַב פָּפָּא – Rav Pappa said: **וּבִכְפָר – And in a** small **village,** **אַף עַל פִּי שֶׁלֹּא נָתַן מַיִם עַל גַּבֵּי בָּשָׂר – even if water had not** yet **been put on the meat,** **לֹא מִזְדַּבַּן – it cannot be sold** so easily and the wedding should proceed as scheduled.[13]

The Gemara asks:

וְאֶלָּא דְּרַב חִסְדָּא הֵיכִי מַשְׁכַּחַת לָהּ – But now **how will you find** a case where the distinction **of Rav Chisda** (between where the water was placed on the meat and where it was not) is applicable?[14]

The Gemara answers:

אָמַר רַב אָשֵׁי – Rav Ashi said: **כְּגוֹן מָתָא מְחַסְיָא – Rav Chisda's** distinction is applicable in a place **like Masa Mechasya,** **דְּמִפְּקָא מִכְּרַךְ וּמִפְּקָא מִכְּפָר – which is excluded from** being defined as **a** big **city, but is** also **excluded from** being defined as a small **village.**[15] In such a place Rav Chisda's distinction will apply.[16]

The Gemara supports Rav Chisda's statement:

תַּנְיָא כְּוָותֵיהּ דְּרַב חִסְדָּא – A Baraisa was taught in accordance with Rav Chisda: **הֲרֵי שֶׁהָיָה פִּתּוֹ אֲפוּיָה – IF ONE'S BREAD WAS ALREADY BAKED,** **וְטִבְחוֹ טָבוּחַ – HIS [ANIMALS] SLAUGHTERED,** **וְיֵינוֹ מָזוּג – AND HIS WINE MIXED,** **וְנָתַן מַיִם עַל גַּבֵּי בָּשָׂר – AND WATER WAS PLACED ON THE MEAT,**[17] **וּמֵת אָבִיו שֶׁל חָתָן אוֹ אִמָּהּ שֶׁל כַּלָּה – AND THE FATHER OF THE GROOM OR THE MOTHER OF THE BRIDE DIED,** **מַכְנִיסִין אֶת הַמֵּת לְחֶדֶר – WE BRING THE CORPSE INTO A ROOM** **וְאֶת הֶחָתָן וְאֶת הַכַּלָּה לַחוּפָּה – AND THE GROOM AND THE BRIDE** proceed **TO THE** ***CHUPPAH.*** **וּבוֹעֵל בְּעִילַת מִצְוָה וּפוֹרֵשׁ – [THE GROOM] PERFORMS THE MITZVAH-COHABITATION AND** then **SEPARATES** from his bride. Once the marriage is consummated, the deceased is buried. **וְנוֹהֵג שִׁבְעַת יְמֵי הַמִּשְׁתֶּה – After the** burial, **[THE GROOM]** first **OBSERVES THE SEVEN DAYS OF FEASTING** with his bride, **וְאַחַר כָּךְ נוֹהֵג שִׁבְעַת יְמֵי אֲבֵילוּת – AND** only **AFTERWARD OBSERVES** the **SEVEN DAYS OF MOURNING.** **וְכָל אוֹתָן הַיָּמִים – AND** during **ALL THOSE** fourteen **DAYS** of feasting and mourning, **הוּא יָשֵׁן בֵּין הָאֲנָשִׁים – [THE GROOM] SLEEPS AMONG THE MEN** **וְאִשְׁתּוֹ יְשֵׁנָה בֵּין הַנָּשִׁים – AND HIS WIFE SLEEPS AMONG THE WOMEN.** **וְכֵן מִי שֶׁפֵּירְסָה אִשְׁתּוֹ נִדָּה – AND SIMILARLY, IF ONE'S WIFE BEGAN TO MENSTRUATE**[18] after she entered the *chuppah,* **הוּא יָשֵׁן בֵּין הָאֲנָשִׁים – HE SLEEPS AMONG THE MEN** **וְהִיא יְשֵׁנָה בֵּין הַנָּשִׁים – AND SHE SLEEPS AMONG THE WOMEN.**[19] **וְאֵין מוֹנְעִין תַּכְשִׁיטִין מִן הַכַּלָּה כָּל שְׁלֹשִׁים יוֹם – AND WE DO NOT WITHHOLD ADORNMENTS FROM THE BRIDE THE ENTIRE THIRTY DAYS.** **בֵּין כָּךְ וּבֵין כָּךְ – IN EITHER CASE** [i.e. whether or not some unavoidable circumstance occurred],[20] **לֹא יִבְעוֹל – HE SHOULD**

NOTES

9. The Gemara does not state when the wedding is held if the father of the bride or the mother of the groom [or, for that matter, any other close relative of the bride or groom] die before the wedding. According to *Tosafos,* if the groom has older children from a previous marriage he must wait until the thirty-day mourning period (*sheloshim*) has passed to marry. However, if he has not yet fulfilled the mitzvah of procreation, *Rabbeinu Tam* rules that he may marry after the seven-day period of mourning (*shivah*), and cohabit with his bride immediately. If he has already fulfilled the mitzvah of procreation but has small children that need maternal attention, he may also marry immediately after the seven days of mourning, but may not cohabit with his new bride until after *sheloshim.* Although many Rishonim dispute these laws (see *Rambam, Hil. Aveil* 6:5, *Ritva*), *Shulchan Aruch* (*Yoreh Deah* 392:1-2) sides with *Tosafos;* see the Rishonim for various details of these laws, including when one may remarry if his wife died.

[See *Rif* for a novel explanation of the Gemara's ruling in this case; see *Rosh and Ran* for a discussion of his approach.]

10. Once meat is placed in the water, it will spoil quickly and must be consumed immediately. Thus, it is difficult to find buyers who need such a large quantity of meat that will not keep.

11. [The Rabbis only allowed the burial to be delayed when postponing the wedding would cause an irretrievable loss of the wedding feast. If the meat can be sold, the funds can be used later to repurchase the feast; thus, in such a case the Rabbis did not allow the burial to be delayed.]

An apparent difficulty: The Baraisa spoke of a case where the preparations that were made included the baking of the bread, the mixing of the wine, and the slaughtering of the meat. If so, why would the fact that the meat can be sold obviate the need for postponing the wedding? The bread and the wine would still be lost! *Ritva* explains that the mixed wine [and presumably the bread as well] can always be sold, albeit at a reduced price; thus if the major loss of the meat going to waste can be averted, the wedding is not postponed. *Rashba* (to 3b), however, explains that the Baraisa is teaching that the burial is postponed if even *one* of the three components of the feast was already prepared; accordingly, Rav Chisda must be teaching here that if only the meat was prepared, the burial will not be delayed if it can be sold. See also *Bach* to *Tur Shulchan Aruch, Yoreh Deah* 342, and *Shach* to *Yoreh Deah* 342:1.

12. Since there are many people in a big city, even a large quantity of meat that cannot be kept can still be sold (see *Rashi*).

13. In a village only a limited number of customers for meat exist, and it is unlikely that a large quantity of meat can be sold, even if it will not spoil immediately.

14. It does not apply in a big city, because there it is possible to sell even meat that had water put on it, and the burial will never be postponed. And it does not apply in a small village, where it is unlikely that any meat can be sold quickly, for there the burial will always be postponed (see *Rashi*).

15. That is, it is bigger than a village, but smaller than a full-sized city (*Rashi*).

16. Actually, most towns in Talmudic times fell into this intermediate category; Masa Mechasya was only an example chosen as typical of most towns. Rav Chisda therefore interpreted the Baraisa as referring to most towns of normal size (*Tosafos*, *Ritva*).

17. This phrase, which clearly states that the Baraisa refers to a case where water was placed on the meat, is the section of the Baraisa that supports Rav Chisda's ruling. The Gemara, however, goes on to cite the entire Baraisa.

18. That is, she became a *niddah* as she entered the *chuppah* [but before any cohabitation had taken place] (*Rashi*). [See *Haflaah* here and *Rama, Yoreh Deah* 192:4 with *Taz* 192:7, who discuss *Rashi's* comment further.]

19. The husband and wife are not trusted to abstain from relations (*Rashi;* see *Shitah Mekubetzes*).

[As noted above (note 6), there is a dispute among the Rishonim about the extent of supervision needed in cases where the newlyweds are not permitted to be in seclusion together. The prevalent custom in the case of a marriage with a *niddah* is to have a young boy stay with the groom and a young girl stay with the bride (see *Rama* ibid. with commentators).]

20. *Rashi;* see, however, *Pnei Yehoshua* and *Chasam Sofer* (§562).

מסורת הש"ס

א) [יומא עח:], ב) [ע' תוס' יומא יח: ד"ה יחודי וכו' אריכות בסוגיא דהכא], ג) יומא דף עח:.

גליון הש"ס

רש"י ד"ה כל ל' יום. ע' מג"א סי' תרי"ג ס"ק י"ב:

גמרא

ובועל בעילת מצוה ופורש ונוהג שבעת ימי המשתה ואחר כך נוהג שבעת ימי אבילות וכל אותן הימים הוא ישן בין האנשים והיא ישנה בין הנשים [א] ואין מונעין תכשיטין מן הכלה כל שלשים יום [א] ודוקא אביו של חתן או אמה של כלה דליכא איניש דטרח להו אבל איפכא לא אמר רפרם בר פפא אמר רב חסדא לא שנו אלא שנתן מים על גבי בשר אבל לא נתן מים על גבי בשר מזדבן אמר רבא ובכרך אע"פ שנתן מים על גבי בשר מזדבן אמר רב פפא ובכפר אע"פ שלא נתן מים על גבי בשר לא מזדבן ואלא דרב חסדא היכי משכחת לה אמר רב אשי כגון מתא מחסיא דמפקא מכרך ומפקא מכפר תניא כוותיה דרב חסדא [ב] הרי שהיה פתו אפויה וטבחו טבוח ויינו מזוג ונתן מים על גבי בשר ומת אביו של חתן או אמה של כלה מכניסין את המת לחדר ואת החתן ואת הכלה לחופה ובועל בעילת מצוה ופורש ונוהג שבעת ימי המשתה ואח"כ נוהג שבעת ימי אבילות וכל אותן הימים הוא ישן בין האנשים ואשתו ישנה בין הנשים וכן [ג] מי שפירסה אשתו נדה הוא ישן בין האנשים והיא ישנה בין הנשים [ג] ואין מונעין תכשיטין מן הכלה כל ל' יום בין כך ובין כך לא יבעול לא בערב שבת ולא במוצ"ש אמר מר הוא ישן בין האנשים והיא ישנה בין הנשים מסייע ליה לרבי יוחנן דאמר רבי יוחנן [ד] אע"פ שאמרו אין אבילות במועד אבל דברים של צינעא נוהג דרש רב יוסף בריה דרבא משמיה דרבא [ה] ל"ש אלא שלא בעל אבל בעל אשתו ישנה עמו והא הכא דבבעל עסקינן וקתני הוא ישן בין האנשים והיא ישנה בין הנשים כי קאמר [ו] אפירסה אשתו נדה הא וכן קתני הכי

רש"י

ופורש. ויקברו את המת מיד דכיון דחלה עליו מתחלה הוא לגביה כרגל ולא אתיא אבילות ודחיא לה ונוהג שבעת ימי המשתה כו': וכל אותן הימים. של ימי המשתה ושל אבילות: הוא ישן כו'. ואין מתיחדין זה עם זה שמא יבעול ואבל אסור בתשמיש המטה כדילפינן באלו מגלחין (מו"ק דף טו:) ואף בשבעת ימי המשתה שהן כרגל נוהג הוא אבילות של דברי צינעא דהיינו איסור תשמיש כדלקמן: ואין מונעין. בשביל האבילות אין אוסרין עליה תכשיטיה שלא תתגנה על בעלה: כל שלשים יום. ואע"פ שהן ימי אבילות לשאר בני אדם וכל שכן משלשים ואילך: דליכא איניש דטרח. אם יפסידו מה שהכינו: שנתן מים על גבי בשר. שוב אינו ראוי למוכרו במקולין: בכרך. שכיחי איניש טובא ויש קופצים הרבה: אלא דרב חסדא. דמפליג בין נתן ללא נתן: היכי משכחת לה. לא בכרך ולא בכפר: דמפקא מכרך ומפקא מכפר. מוצאה מכלל כרך ומוצאה מכלל כפר גדולה מכפר וקטנה מכרך: תניא כרב חסדא. דמוקי לה בנתן מים על גבי בשר: וכן מי שפירסה אשתו נדה. בכניסתה לחופה: הוא ישן כו'. ואין נאמנין זה עם זה: בין כך ובין כך. בין יש אונס בין אין אונס: לא יבעול. בעילה ראשונה: לא בערב שבת כו'. בליל שבת מפני שעושה חבורה: ולא במוצ"ש. לקמן מפרש: מסייע ליה. הא קתני דאסור בתשמיש בשבעת ימי המשתה שהן לו כרגל: של צינעא. שאינו ניכר לבריות שהוא אבל בכך: לא שנו. דאין נאמנין להתייחד: אלא שלא בעל. דתקיף ליה יצריה: דבבעל עסקינן. דקתני בועל בעילת מצוה לפני קבורת המת: כי קאמר. רבה לא שנו אפירסה אשתו נדה קאמר דכיון דנדה חמורה בעל מהימן עלה דלא אתי לזלזולי באיסור כרת: הא וכן קתני. קס"ד אכולה מילתא דאבילות מדמינן ליה ובאבילות דבעל עסקינן: ה"ק

תוספות

בועל בעילת מצוה ופורש. קודם שיקבר המת אבל לאחר שנקבר לא כדאמרינן בסמוך דברים של צינעא נוהג ודייק לה מדקתני כל אותן הימים הוא ישן בין האנשים כו' מיהו מרישא דהכא לא ה"מ למידק דדוקא כשהמת בחדר הוא דשרי בעילת מצוה דמאי לדחויי דבועל בעילת מצוה היינו אפי' לאחר שחל עליו אבילות אבל קשה לרשב"א אמאי לא דייק מדקתני ופורש מכלל דנוהג דברים של צינעא מדלא התיר אלא בעילת מצוה דוקא ואור"י דהמ"ל פורש משום דם בתולים כדאמרינן בפ' תינוקת (נדה דף סה:) אבל מהוא ישן בין האנשים דייק שפיר דהוי משום אבילות דאי משום נדות כיון דבעל אשתו ישנה עמו כדאמר רב יוסף בסמוך ועוד דכל אותן הימים משמע דכולהו הוי חד טעמא דהיינו משום אבילות והשתא מקילין טפי בצניעות דאורייתא מבאבילות דרבנן מידי דהוה אנעילת סנדל ועטיפת הראש וכפיית המטה: **בעילת** מצוה. קרי לה בעילת מצוה משום דכתיב כי בועליך עושיך ואמרי' (סנהדרין דף כב:) אין אשה כורתת ברית אלא למי שעשאה כלי וע"י כך מידבק בה ובאין לידי פריה ורביה ולהכי קרי לה לבעילה ראשונה בעילת מצוה: **אבל** איפכא לא. וה"ה אם אבלים מחמת שאר קרובים תימה דאמר בפ"ג דמועד קטן (דף כג. וכו') מתה אשתו אסור לישא עד שיעברו ג' רגלים ואם אין לו בנים מותר לישא לאלתר משום פריה ורביה הניחה לו בנים קטנים מותר לישא לאלתר משום פרנסתם והכא אמר אבל איפכא לא ומשמע דבאין לו בנים עסקינן מדקאמר דליכא דטרח להו משמע דבבחור איירי וי"ל דלאלתר לאו דוקא אלא כלומר מותר לאחר ז' ומיהו לבעול אסור עד לאחר ל' כדמוכח בתר הכי במעשה שמתה אשתו של יוסף הכהן ואמר לאחותה בבית הקברות לאי ופרנסי בני אחותיך ואעפ"כ לא בא עליה עד זמן מרובה מאי זמן מרובה שלשים יום מכלל דכנסה תוך ל' ותוך שבעה ודאי אסור כדמוכח הכא ומה שאמר לה בבה"ק לא היה זה כניסה אלא שידוכין בעלמא ונראה לר"י דודאי אותו שיש לו בנים קטנים מותר לישא תוך ל' כדמשמע בעובדא דיוסף הכהן אבל אותו שאין לו בנים כלל אסור לישא עד לאחר שלשים כיון שאין יכול לבעול תוך שלשים וכן משמע במס' שמחות (פ"ז) דתניא בד"א כשיש לו בנים גדולים אבל אין לו בנים או שיש לו בנים קטנים מותר לישא אחרת לאחר ל' משמע דלאסור אפי' לישא תוך שלשים ואע"ג דיש לו בנים קטנים מותר לישא תוך שלשים מ"מ נקט אחר שלשים משום אין לו בנים ור"ת ר"ל דבאין לו בנים אפי' לבעול שרי תוך שלשים אחר ז' משום פריה ורביה וההיא דשמחות אינה מתיישבת כפי' ונראה דיש לו בנים קטנים שרי לישא ואפי' אם היא נמי אבילה מפני שמפרנסת בניו ואע"פ שאפשר באחרת כדמוכח בעובדא דיוסף הכהן שהיתה אבילה מאחותה ומיהו אין כל כך ראיה דשמא שאני התם לפי שהיא תרחם על בני אחותה יותר מאחרת ואע"ג דתנן בפרק החולץ (יבמות דף מא. וכו') כל הנשים יתארסו חוץ מאלמנה מפני האיבול ולא מפליג מידי משמע שאסורה אפי' למי שיש לו בנים קטנים כשהיא אבילה התם משום דבלאו הכי אסורה דצריכה להמתין ג' חדשים משום הבחנה ואור"ת דאפי' מתו אביו ואמו יכול לכנוס אחר ל' והא דאמרי' במועד קטן (דף כב:) על כל המתים נכנס לבית המשתה אחר ל' על אביו ועל אמו אחר י"ב חדשים ה"מ בשאר שמחות אבל לישא אשה שהיא מצוה יתירה מותר ואפי' יש לו בנים משום שנאמר (קהלת יא) בבקר זרע [את] זרעך ולערב אל תנח ידך והביא ראיה מדתניא סתם כל ל' יום לנישואין ולא מפליג בין אביו ואמו לשאר קרובים משמע דכולהו לאחר ל' מותר וה"ר יוסף הביא ראיה לדבריו דתנן במסכת שמחות (פ"ט) בהדיא על כל המתים אסור לילך לבית המשתה עד שישלימו ל' יום ועל אביו ועל אמו אסור כל שנים עשר חדש אא"כ היה של מצוה אלמא שרי בכל משתה של מצוה וצ"ע אי קאי נמי ארישא ושרי אפי' תוך ל' יום: **כגון** מתא מחסיא. תימה רב חסדא מאי דוחקיה לאוקומי בנתן מים על גבי בשר נוקמה בכפר אע"פ שלא נתן מים על גבי בשר ויש לומר משום דניחא ליה לרב חסדא לאוקמה ברוב עיירות שהן בינוניות וה"ק כגון מתא מחסיא ורוב עיירות ומש"ה נקט נמי בברייתא דמייתי ונתן מים על גבי בשר משום דאיירי ברוב עיירות: **מסייע** ליה לר' יוחנן כו'. מועד וחתן משוה אותן בכ"מ כההיא דתניא בפ"ק דמועד קטן (דף ז: ושם) חתן שנולד בו נגע נותנין לו ז' ימי המשתה לו ולאיצטליתו ולכסותו וכן ברגל נותנין לו כל ימות הרגל: **אבל** דברים של צינעא נוהג. פי' חובה לעשות כן ולא רשות מדמייתי סייעתא מן הברייתא וא"ת רב ושמואל דאמרי בפרק בתרא דמועד קטן (דף כד.) דתשמיש המטה בשבת של ז' ימי אבילות רשות תיקשי להו ברייתא דהכא ואין סברא לחלק בין מועד לשבת ומקילין בשבת טפי אלא נראה לר"י דרב ושמואל מפלגי בין חתן למועד ושבת אבל קשה דכל אותן הימים הוא ישן בין האנשים משמע אפי' בשבת ופסקו ה"ג כר' יוחנן ופירשו אע"ג דקיימא לן כדברי המיקל באבל ה"מ בתנאי אבל באמוראי לא ואור"י דודאי נראה דהלכה כר' יוחנן מדאמר הש"ס הכא מסייע ליה לר' יוחנן:

והלעת

עין משפט נר מצוה

ט א ב מיי' פי"א מהל' אבל הל' ח סמג עשין ב טוש"ע יו"ד סי' שמב וסי' שפג סעי' ג [רב אלפס כאן ובמו"ק פ"ג דף רלא.]:
י ג מיי' וסמג שם טוש"ע שם סי' שפא סעי' ו:
יא ד מיי' פ"י שם הל' ג סמג שם טוש"ע שם סי' שלט סעי' ג [עי' כ"מ]:
יב ה ו מיי' פכ"ב מהל' איסורי ביאה הל"א סמג לאוין קכו טוש"ע אה"ע סי' כב סעי' א וטוש"ע יו"ד סי' שפג סעי' ב:

תוספות רי"ד

אמר רפרם בר פפא א"ר חסדא לא שנו אלא שניתן מים ע"ג בשר אבל לא ניתן מים ע"ג בשר מיזדבן. **אמר רבא** ובכרך אע"פ שניתן מים על גבי בשר מיזדבן. **א"ר פפא** ובכפר אע"פ שלא ניתן מים ע"ג בשר לא מיזדבן. ואלא דרב חסדא היכי משכחת לה כגון מתא מחסיא דמפקא מכפר ומפקא מכרך: **אמר מר** הוא ישן בין האנשים וכו'. מסייע ליה לר' יוחנן דאמר ר"י אע"פ שאמרו אין אבילות במועד אבל דברים שבצנעה נוהג. פי' ז' ימי חתונות כשבעת ימי הרגל הן לו. ומפני שתשמיש המטה הוי דבר של צנעה שאין בני העולם מרגישים אסור: **דרש ר"י ברי' דרבא משמיה דרבא** לא שנו אלא שלא בעל שיצרו תוקפו אבל בעל אשתו ישנה עמו בבית. והא הכא בבעל עסקינן וקתני הוא ישן בין האנשים וכו'. כי קאמר ר"י אפירסה נדה. והא וכן קתני ה"ק וכן מי שפירסה אשתו נדה ולא בעל הוא ישן בין האנשים ואשתו ישנה בין הנשים פי' אבל [בעל] כל נדה דעלמא מתקיים בעלה בבית וכשמת אביו של חתן או אמה של כלה צריכי שימור:

וּבוֹעֵל בְּעִילַת מִצְוָה וּפוֹרֵשׁ – [THE GROOM] then **PERFORMS THE MITZVAH-COHABITATION,**[1] **AND** then **SEPARATES** from his bride.[2] Once the marriage is consummated, the deceased is buried.[3] וְנוֹהֵג שִׁבְעַת יְמֵי הַמִּשְׁתֶּה – After the burial, [THE GROOM] first **OBSERVES THE SEVEN DAYS OF FEASTING** with his bride,[4] וְאַחַר כָּךְ נוֹהֵג שִׁבְעַת יְמֵי אֲבֵילוּת – **AND** only **AFTERWARDS HE OBSERVES THE SEVEN DAYS OF MOURNING.**[5] וְכָל אוֹתָן הַיָּמִים – **AND** during **ALL THOSE** fourteen **DAYS** of feasting and mourning, הוּא יָשֵׁן בֵּין הָאֲנָשִׁים – [THE GROOM] **SLEEPS AMONG THE MEN** וְהִיא יְשֵׁנָה בֵּין הַנָּשִׁים – **AND** [THE BRIDE] **SLEEPS AMONG THE WOMEN.**[6] וְאֵין מוֹנְעִין תַּכְשִׁיטִין מִן הַכַּלָּה כָּל שְׁלֹשִׁים יוֹם – **AND WE DO NOT WITHHOLD ADORNMENTS FROM THE BRIDE THE ENTIRE THIRTY DAYS.**[7] Thus, it is to a sudden death that the earlier Baraisa refers when it teaches that in the event of "an unavoidable circumstance," the marriage can take place even on Monday, so as not to unduly delay the burial.

The Gemara elaborates on the Baraisa's permit:

וְדַוְקָא אָבִיו שֶׁל חָתָן אוֹ אִמָּהּ שֶׁל כַּלָּה – **And it is only when the father of the groom or the mother of the bride** died that the burial is delayed, דְּלֵיכָּא אִינִישׁ דְּטָרַח לְהוּ – **for there will not be anyone to bother** with preparing **for them** if the food for the wedding feast and the adornments are lost.[8] אֲבָל אִיפְּכָא לֹא – **But** in **the reverse** situation [i.e. the mother of the groom or the

NOTES

1. The first cohabitation of a man with his wife is called the mitzvah-cohabitation, because through it the wife forges the marital bond with her husband, and they are thereby enabled to fulfill the mitzvah of procreation as commanded by God (*Tosafos*).

2. The Rabbis permitted delaying the burial to allow the marriage to take place, and the cohabitation to be performed (see further below). Further cohabitation, however, is forbidden, for cohabitation is generally prohibited to an *onein* (see above, 3b note 33); furthermore, the deceased must be buried, and although the bride or groom does not enter the mourning period until the seven-day rejoicing period is complete (as the Baraisa will proceed to state – see below), cohabitation is forbidden once the burial is performed (see above, 3b note 31). Thus, the groom must separate from the bride after the initial act of cohabitation (see also *Tosafos*).

An apparent difficulty: The Sages allowed the wedding to take place before the burial so that the wedding feast would not be lost. But for what reason did they permit the mitzvah-cohabitation? *Shitah Mekubetzes* (ד״ה וכתב בעל הטורים) offers two possible explanations: (a) The permit for the bride and groom to celebrate the seven days of feasting before the seven days of mourning (see Baraisa below) hinges on the festival status that descends upon the bride and groom (see next note); and this status does not descend upon them unless the mitzvah-cohabitation is performed. (b) If it would be forbidden to perform the mitzvah-cohabitation, the *chuppah* (marriage ceremony) itself is invalid according to many opinions. [There is a practical difference between these two explanations; according to the first, the mitzvah-cohabitation must actually be performed; according to the second, it is sufficient that it *may* be performed.] According to both opinions, a second cohabitation is not permitted, for generally cohabitation is forbidden for an *onein,* as noted above.

3. The deceased can be buried immediately after the wedding and cohabitation, because after these events have occurred, the groom's (or bride's) status is like that of a person during a festival, when the laws of mourning cannot take effect. The burial therefore does not cause the laws of *aveilus* to take effect in this case, and the bride and groom can celebrate the seven days of feasting even after the burial, as the Baraisa states next (*Rashi;* see *Igros Moshe, Yoreh Deah* §226; see also note 5 below).

[*Rashi* indicates that the corpse is buried that very same day, after the wedding. Some Rishonim, though, hold that the corpse should be held until the next day, and buried then. In their view, when death and burial occur on the same day, the status of *aveilus* on that day is Biblical in nature, and such *aveilus* would take effect, deferring the festival status of the bride and groom and making it impossible to celebrate the seven days of feasting before *shivah.* Accordingly, the Sages decreed that the burial should be postponed until the following day, so the *aveilus* that is being deferred is only Rabbinic in nature. See *Rashba, Re'ah,* and *Ritva* for a discussion of this issue.]

4. When one marries a virgin, there is a mitzvah to rejoice with her for seven days (see below, 7a; *Rambam, Hil. Ishus* 10:12 and *Hil. Aveil* 1:1; *Shulchan Aruch, Even HaEzer* 64:1; see also *Rashi* to *Genesis* 29:27).

5. [The Baraisa speaks of the *groom* observing the seven days of mourning; this refers to the case where the father of the groom had died. The same law would apply to the bride in the case where the bride's mother had died.]

Although the Rabbis were lenient in this case solely for the purpose of preserving the wedding feast, they allowed the seven days of rejoicing to precede the *aveilus* as well; for once the wedding is performed, the bride and groom are viewed as celebrating a festival, and *aveilus* does not take effect (for most laws) until the festival is concluded. The seven days of rejoicing are considered part of the festival, and they are therefore celebrated before the mourning period. [The Rishonim discuss why the seven days of feasting do not serve to eliminate the *shivah* days that must be observed after they are concluded, as occurs when one loses a close relative during the last day of Yom Tov in the Diaspora, which is Rabbinic in nature; see *Rosh, Ran,* and *Ramban.*]

[It should be noted that the laws of *aveilus* that take effect following the burial of one's close relative apply for two distinct periods of time and diminish in severity. The first and stricter period is *shivah,* the initial seven-day period after the burial; the second extends from *shivah's* conclusion to the end of *sheloshim* (thirty days). For children mourning their parents there is a third mourning period, extending to the end of a full year. Now, if someone's relative died during a festival, the week of *shivah* does not begin then, but rather is postponed until after the festival. Here too, the groom (or bride) must observe the week of *shivah* after the seven days of feasting have ended.]

6. The bride and groom may not be alone together because we are concerned that he might cohabit with her, and cohabitation is prohibited for a mourner during *shivah,* as derived in *Moed Katan* (15b). And even though, as explained above, the mourning period does not take effect during the seven days of feasting, the groom (or bride) is required to observe inconspicuous mourning practices such as abstinence from marital relations even during this period, as we will learn below (*Rashi*).

[It would seem from the language of the Baraisa that the groom must stay with *two* men and the bride must also stay with *two* women. This indeed is the view of *Raavad,* cited by *Rosh.* However, other Rishonim write that it is sufficient for only one of the newlyweds to be chaperoned; and according to some opinions only one chaperone is needed (see *Shitah Mekubetzes* ד״ה הוא ישן; *Tiferes Shmuel* to *Rosh* §5; *Tur* and *Beis Yosef, Yoreh Deah* §342). There is also a dispute about how much supervision is required during the day (see there). See also below, note 19.]

7. Even though the [secondary] period of mourning under normal circumstances is thirty days (see above, note 5), a bride is not prohibited from adorning herself during the *sheloshim* period, so that she will not appear unattractive to her groom. And certainly after the *sheloshim* she may adorn herself (*Rashi*).

[From *Rashi* it appears that any *other* married woman may not adorn herself during *sheloshim;* this permit was extended only to a newlywed bride because she has not yet become fully familiar with her husband. However, this point is disputed by other Rishonim (e.g. *Rosh* and *Ran;* see also *Shulchan Aruch, Yoreh Deah* 381:6). See *Hagahos HaBach* to *Ran* for further explanation of *Rashi's* view.]

[According to *Rosh,* this section of the Baraisa does not refer to the case discussed in the Baraisa above, where the mother of the bride died before the wedding; rather, it is teaching that a new bride is never forbidden to adorn herself during the first thirty days *of her marriage,* even if she loses a close relative; this permit applies even during the *shivah* period, for the Rabbis were concerned that the newlywed bride would appear unattractive to her new husband if she were forbidden to adorn herself. Any other married woman, however, may not apply cosmetics during *shivah.*]

8. That is, if they are forced to discard the preparations made for the wedding because of a delay, there will be no one to assist the bride and groom in preparing for a new wedding (*Rashi*). [The father of the groom would customarily provide the wedding feast, and the mother of the bride would provide adornments for the bride (see *Rashi* above, 3b ד״ה אביו).]

nesday **his quartermasters arrive on Tuesday** to prepare food; thus, the wedding must be moved up to Monday.

The Gemara offers an alternative explanation of the "unavoidable circumstance" in which an individual is permitted to marry even on a Monday:[29]

וְאִיבָּעֵית אֵימָא – And if you prefer, say: מַאי מֵחֲמַת הָאוֹנֶס – What does the Baraisa mean by **"because of an unavoidable circumstance"? כִּדְתַנְיָא –** It refers to a case **such as that which is taught in a Baraisa: הֲרֵי שֶׁהָיָה פִּתּוֹ אָפוּי –** IF ONE'S BREAD WAS ALREADY BAKED, **וְטִבְחוֹ טָבוּחַ –** HIS [ANIMALS] SLAUGHTERED, **וְיֵינוֹ מָזוּג –** AND HIS WINE MIXED in preparation for the wedding feast,[30] **וּמֵת אָבִיו שֶׁל חָתָן אוֹ אִמָּהּ שֶׁל כַּלָּה –** AND THE FATHER OF THE GROOM OR THE MOTHER OF THE BRIDE DIED, we do not delay the wedding until after the burial and mourning period have elapsed.[31] Rather, the correct procedure is as follows: **מַכְנִיסִין אֶת הַמֵּת לְחֶדֶר –** WE BRING THE CORPSE INTO A ROOM[32] **וְאֶת הֶחָתָן וְאֶת הַכַּלָּה לַחוּפָּה –** AND THE GROOM AND THE BRIDE proceed TO THE *CHUPPAH*.[33]

NOTES

29. In the situation that the Gemara will now present, not allowing the wedding to take place on Monday would result in a delay in the burial of a deceased relative (see further in note 31); thus, the Sages relaxed their restriction and allowed the wedding to take place even on a Monday. See Gemara below.

30. [In Talmudic times, raw wine was extremely strong and unfit for drinking until it was mixed with water. In the Baraisa's case] water had been added to the wine in preparation for the wedding feast; once blended, the wine would quickly spoil if not consumed (*Rashi*). [Similarly, the freshly baked bread and freshly slaughtered meat would spoil if the wedding were delayed significantly.]

31. Under normal circumstances, one is not permitted to marry during the seven-day mourning period (*shivah*) that is observed upon the death of one of the seven close relatives. [In certain circumstances, the prohibition extends even beyond *shivah* – see below, 4a note 5.] In the situation described in the Baraisa, however, if the wedding were delayed until after burial and mourning, the food for the wedding feast and the [perishable] adornments used by the bride would spoil; and, because the deceased was either the father of the groom [who would customarily provide the wedding feast] or the mother of the bride [who would provide the adornments], the food and adornments would most likely not be replaced (see *Shitah Mekubetzes* to 4a ד״ה דליכא and ד״ה וז״ל הריטב״א). Therefore, in these two cases, the Rabbis were lenient and allowed postponement of the burial, so that the mourning period would not begin until after the wedding, and the feast and adornments would not be lost (*Rashi*). [See below, note 33, for further explanation.]

Although the Rabbis permitted the postponement of the burial for the reason explained above, they wished the wedding to take place as soon as possible, for the deceased could not be buried until the wedding was complete (see below, 4a), and delaying the burial is a slight to the honor of the deceased. Accordingly, the wedding would take place immediately, even if it was Monday when the death occurred. This is the meaning of the Baraisa's ruling that in the event of an unavoidable circumstance, one may marry even on a Monday (*Rashi*).

32. I.e. they would remove the deceased parent from the presence of the bride and groom, and entrust the body to the care of another for the duration of the wedding (see *Meiri,* and see *Berachos* 18a).

33. Once a deceased parent is buried, the bereaved child is an *aveil* (mourner), and the laws of mourning would preclude him (or her) from marrying, as explained above. Thus, the Rabbis decreed that the deceased should be put aside temporarily, so that the wedding can proceed (*Rashi*).

[It should be noted that although the laws of *aveilus* do not take effect until after burial (as *Rashi* states here), the laws of *aninus* (the state of a person who loses a close relative, during the period from the time of the death until the burial) *do* apply. Among the laws of *aninus* is a prohibition against cohabitation with one's spouse during this period (see *Yoreh Deah* 341:5 with commentaries; cf. *Shitah Mekubetzes* ד״ה וכתב בעל הטורים); however, in the case of the Baraisa, consummation of the marriage *is* permitted (as the Baraisa will go on to state; see below, 4a note 2). See *Ritva* here and *Tosafos* to 4a ד״ה בועל, who discuss why the Rabbis allowed the restrictions of *aninus* to be relaxed in this case, but not those of *aveilus.*]

מאי שקדו דתניא מפני מה אמרו בתולה נשאת ליום הרביעי שאם היה לו טענת בתולים היה משכים לב"ד ותנשא באחד בשבת ואם היה לו טענת בתולים היה משכים לב"ד שקדו חכמים על תקנת בנות ישראל שיהא אדם טורח בסעודה שלשה ימים אחד בשבת ושני בשבת ושלישי בשבת וברביעי כונסה ומסכנה ואילך נהגו העם לכנוס בשלישי ולא מיחו בידם חכמים ובשני לא יכנוס ואם מחמת האונס מותר ומפרישין את החתן מן הכלה לילי שבת תחלה מפני שהוא עושה חבורה מאי סכנה אילימא דאמרי בתולה הנשאת ליום הרביעי תיהרג נהגו לגמרי ניעקריה אמר רבה דאמרי בתולה הנשאת ביום הרביעי תיבעל להגמון תחלה האי סכנה אונס הוא משום דאיכא צנועות דמסרן נפשייהו לקטלא ואתיין לידי סכנה ולידרוש להו דאונס שרי איכא פרוצות ואיכא נמי כהנות וליעקרה גזירה עבידא דבטלא ותקנתא דרבנן מקמי גזירה לא עקרינן אי הכי בשלישי נמי אתי ובעיל מספיקא לא עקר נפשיה ובשני לא יכנוס ואם מחמת האונס מותר מאי אונס אילימא הא דאמרן התם קרי ליה סכנה והכא קא קרי ליה אונס ותו התם נהגו הכא מותר אמר רבא דאמרי שר צבא בא לעיר ה"ד אי דאתי וחליף ליעכב לא צריכא דאתי וקבע בג' מיהא לכנוס אספרווא דידיה בג' קאתו ואיבעית אימא מאי מחמת האונס כדתניא הרי שהיה פתו אפוי וטבחו טבוח ויינו מזוג ומת אביו של חתן או אמה של כלה מכניסין את המת לחדר ואת החתן ואת הכלה לחופה ובועל

רש"י

מאי שקדו. היכן שנינו שקדו דמקשינן לה הכא אי משום דאמר שמואל לעיל לית לן לאותביה מינה למימרא אחרינא: **ומן הסכנה ואילך.** לקמן מפרש לה: **ובשני לא יכנוס.** בשביל אותה סכנה ולאו צריך לעקור בשבילה תקנת חכמים אלא יום אחד ויהיה טורח מיהת שני ימים בצורכי סעודה: **ואם מחמת האונס.** לקמן מפרש: **תחלה.** אם ביאה ראשונה היא מפרישין אותה ממנו לילי שבת: **נהגו.** בתמיה סכנת נפשות היא ואת אמרת נהגו לכנוס ביום שלישי אבל מיעקר רביעי לגמרי לא עקרו: **ניעקריה.** ויתקנו להם ימים אחרים: **ולדרוש להו דאונס שרי.** דנבעלת באונס אינה נאסרת על בעלה דילפינן לקמן בפרק ד' (דף נא:) מוהיא לא נתפשה ולא לימסרו נפשייהו למיתה: **איכא פרוצות.** דאי מקילינן להו עבדי ברצון ונאסרות על בעליהן: **ואיכא נמי כהנות.** שנאסרות על בעליהן אף באונס ואיהו מסרן נפשייהו למיתה דאשת כהן שנאנסה אסורה לבעלה ולקמן בפרק ד' (שם) ילפינן לה: **וליעקריה.** הואיל וחזינן דאיכא סכנה: **בשלישי נמי אתי ובעיל.** כיון דידע שהתחילו לנהוג בשלישי: **מספיקא לא עקר נפשיה.** כיון דלאו קביעות גמור הוא על ידי תקנת ב"ד ספיקא היא לו אם יש נישואין היום בעיר ולא עקר נפשיה לבא בעיר: **התם נהגו.** משמע רוצים נהגו: **הכא מותר.** לא גרסינן לכתחילה והכי קא מתמה הכא מותר קתני דמשמע אם ימלך אין יחידי בבית דין ימירו לו אבל נהגו לא קתני: **שר צבא בא לעיר.** ויתטפו צורכי סעודה מאשר ימלאו: **וחליף.** לאחר רביעי: **ליעכב.** עד יום רביעי של שבת הבא: **בשלישי לכנוס.** למה נתיר לו לקדום כל כך שלא יטריח בסעודה אלא יום אחד ומיעקרא תקנתא דשקדו: **איספרווא דידיה.** חיל משרתיו המכינים לו צורכי סעודה בלשון לעז הירנ"ש: **כדתניא.** חתן שמת אביו בשני ואין יכול להמתין עד למחר שצריך להשהות את המת עד שיכנסו לחופה: **ויינו מזוג.** במים שיהא ראוי לשתיה ושוב אינו מתקיים: **אביו של חתן או אמה של כלה.** דוקא נקט אביו של חתן שהוא הטורח בצורכי סעודה ואמה של כלה היא המכינה לה תכשיטין לפיכך אם יעבור המועד שוב אין מכין להם והתירו להם להכניס את המת לחדר שלא יקברוהו דאם כן חלה אבילות על האבל בסתימת הגולל כדלקמן ושוב לא יוכל לכנוס עד שיעבור האבילות:

ופורש

תוספות

ובשני לא יכנוס. פ"ה אפילו בשעת הסכנה דאין לעקור בשבילה תקנת חכמים אלא יום אחד וקשה לר"י דאמר לקמן מאי אונס אילימא הא דאמרן התם קרי ליה כו' הוה ליה למיפרך טפי רישא לסיפא דקתני רישא ובשני לא יכנוס אפי' בשעת הסכנה ואומר ריב"א דמשום הכי לא פריך ליה משום דאיכא לפרושי ואם מחמת האונס פירוש שיש סכנה אף ביום שלישי מותר לכנוס בשני ונראה לר"י דמילתא באנפי נפשה היא ולא איירי בסכנה ובשני לא יכנוס הוא הדין בג' אלא נקט בב' משום דבעי למיתני ואם מחמת האונס מותר: **ולדרוש להו דאונס שרי.** וא"ת והא אמרינן בפ' בן סורר ומורה (סנהדרין עד. ושם) על כל עבירות יעבור ואל יהרג חוץ מעבודת כוכבים וג"ע וש"ד ותירץ ר"ת דאין חייבין מיתה על בעילת נכרי דרחמנא אפקריה לזרעיה דמילתא דכתיב (יחזקאל כג) וזרמת סוסים זרמתם ומייתי ראיה דפריך בפ' בן סורר ומורה (שם:) והא אסתר פרהסיא הואי ולא פריך והא אסתר גילוי עריות הואי משמע דמשום עריות לא הוה מיחייבא ומתוך כך התיר ר"ת לבת ישראל שהמירה ובא עליה עובד כוכבים לקיימה לאותו עובד כוכבים כשנתגייר דלא שייך למימר אחד לבעל ואחד לבועל דביאת נכרי דהויא כביאת בהמה ואין נראה לריב"ם דהא ע"י ביאת עובד כוכבים נאסרה לבעלה כדאמר הכא דאיכא פרוצות ובפ' האשה שנתארמלה (לקמן כו: ושם) גבי האשה שנתפשה בין העובדי כוכבים אמרי' דברצון אסורה לבעלה ואמר נמי במגילה (דף טו.) כאשר אבדתי אבדתי כאשר אבדתי מבית אבא אבדתי ממך אלמא לגבי בעלה לא חשיבא בעילת נכרי כביאת בהמה והוא הדין לבועל אע"ג דאין זנות לבהמה ואין ביאת בהמה פוסלת ואוסרת כדאמרי' בפ' הבא על יבמתו (יבמות נט:) ביאת נכרי הויא ביאה וכי אפקריה רחמנא לזרעיה הני מילי לענין דאין לו חייס וזרעו חשוב כזרע בהמה ויש לומר דהכי פריך ולדרוש להו דאונס שרי לפי שהאשה היא קרקע עולם ולא עבדה מעשה כדמשני בפרק בן סורר ומורה אסתר קרקע עולם היתה והא דלא פריך התם גילוי עריות הואי דפשיטא ליה דאיכא לשנויי קרקע עולם היא ואין לה למסור עצמה אבל לענין חילול השם לא היה נראה לו שיועיל טעם דקרקע עולם ומשני קרקע עולם היתה ואפילו חילול השם ליכא ובפרק מצות חליצה (שם קג. ושם) דפריך גבי יעל והא קמתהניא מעבירה ומשני טובתן של רשעים רעה היא אצל צדיקים שהטיל בה זוהמא ולא משני קרקע עולם היתה משום דהתם לא פריך אמאי לא מסרה עצמה דהא לא היה רוצה להמיתה דאדרבה היה צריך שתשמרהו אלא הכי פירושו והא מתהניא מעבירה למה משבחה הכתוב מנשים באהל תבורך ודרשינן בנזיר (דף כג: ושם) גדולה עבירה לשמה ממצוה שלא לשמה ופריך דיעל נמי הוה עבירה שלא לשמה דהא מתהניא מעבירה ומשני דלא מתהניא ועשתה עבירה לשמה כדי להציל את ישראל: **בתולה** הנשאת ברביעי תיבעל. לאו דוקא ברביעי מדפריך לקמן בשלישי נמי אתי ובעיל שאינו מתכוין אלא להנאתו אלא אגב דנקט לעיל שנשאת ברביעי תיהרג דהתם מקפידים על קביעות יום כדי להעבירם על דתם נקט ליה נמי הכא ברביעי: **ולדרוש** להו דאונס שרי. אין לפרש דפריך הכי לדרוש כו' דשוב לא יהא סכנה אלא אונס ואמאי קאמר ומסכנה ואילך דא"כ מאי משני משום פרוצות דהא אפילו לא דרשינן להו דאונס שרי לא מסרי נפשייהו דדוקא לנועות אמרינן דמסרי נפשייהו ועוד וכי משום פרוצות יניחו להרוג הנזועות אלא הכי פירושו ולדרוש להו דאונס שרי וכיון דליכא סכנה אמאי לא מיחו בידם חכמים ומשני משום פרוצות לא מיחו בידם אי נמי משום כהנות: **ותו** התם. בשלישי נהגו ואמרינן בפ' בתרא דתענית (דף כו:) מאן דאמר נהגו אורויי לא מורינן והכא בשני מותר לכתחלה ופי' הקונטרס דפירש נהגו רובא דעלמא והכא מותר יחידי ולא גרסינן לכתחלה אינו מיושב: **אי** דאתי וחליף ליעכב. פ"ה חליף לאחר ד' וליעכב עד יום ד' של שבת הבא וקשה לר"י דאם כן מאי משני לא צריכא דאתי וקבע אכתי ליעכב חדש או חדשים עד שילך על כן נראה לר"י שאם יתעכב כל יום ד' אין לו לעכב עד יום ד' אחר אלא יכנוס בג' והכי פריך אי אתי וחליף בד' גופיה ליעכב עד דחליף ומשני דאתי וקבע כל יום ד': **בשלישי** מיהא לכנוס. ולא בעי למימר דאתי שר הצבא בג' דא"כ יכנוס בד': **איספרווא** דידיה בג' אתא. אין לתמוה משום סעודה עקרינן תקנתא דרבנן ג' ימים ומשום סכנה לא עקרינן אלא יום אחד דבעילת הגמון שכיח שרגיל לבא ולבעול ואי עקרינן שני ימים אתא להשתכח אבל אונס שר צבא אינו אלא אקראי בעלמא: (לעיל) **תקנה** דרבנן מקמי גזרה לא עקרינן. כי פריך לעיל ליעקרו לא משני תקנה דרבנן מקמי גזרה כו' כדמשני הכא משום דלעיל פריך וליעקרו ויקבעו יום אחר כיון דאינו מתכוין אלא להעבירם על דת כשיקבעו יום אחר לא יחושו ולא מיעקרא תקנתא דרבנן הואיל ויהא יום אחד קבוע אבל הכא פריך וליעקרו ולא יהא שום יום קבוע שאם יקבעו יום אתי ובעיל באותו יום ולהכי משני מקמי גזרה לא עקרינן תקנה דרבנן שלא יהא שום יום קבוע: **אי** הכי בשלישי נמי אתי ובעיל. (לעיל) פי' א) אי אמרת בשלמא כדמעיקרא דאמרי בתולה שנשאת בד' תיהרג ואין מתכוונין אלא להעבירם לא יחושו אם יעשו ביום ג' אלא אי אמרת משום בעילת ההגמון כיון שמתכוין להנאתו בשלישי נמי אתי ובעיל:

בועל

תוספות רי"ד

תניא הרי שהיה פתו אפויה וטבחו טבוח ויינו מזוג ונתן מים ע"ג בשר ומת אביו של חתן או אמו של כלה מכניסין את המת לחדר ואת החתן ואת הכלה לחופה ובועל בעילת מצוה ופורש ונוהג ז' ימי משתה ואח"כ נוהג ז' ימי אבילות וכל אותן הימים הוא ישן בין האנשים והיא ישנה בין הנשים. וכן מי שפירסה אשתו נדה ואין מונעים תכשיטין מן הכלה כל ל'. **פי'** מכניסים את וכו'. שלא יקברוהו ותחול עליו האבילות בסתימות הגולל ושוב לא יוכל לכונסה עד שיעבור ז' ימי האבל. אלא כונס תחלה ואח"כ יקברו המת וכיון דחלה עליו חתונה הויא גביה כרגל שלא אתיא אבילות וחיילא עליה. **ונוהג** ז' ימי המשתה תחלה ואח"כ ז' ימי האבילות וכל אותן הימים אינו מתיחד עמה שמא יבעול. ואבל אסור בתשמיש המטה ואף בז' ימי המשתה שהן אצלו כרגל דברים של צנעה נוהג. **ואין מונעים וכו'.** ואע"פ שהיא אבילה שלא תתגנה על בעלה. ודוקא אביו של חתן הטורח בצרכי סעודה. ואמה של כלה המכינה לה לתכשיטין דליכא איניש דטרח להו. אבל איפכא לא:

מסורת הש"ס

א) [ועי' תוס' שבת קכ:].

לעזי רש"י

הירנ"ש. פירוש חיל המשרתים המכינים צורכי סעודה, מילות או גדודים הנוספים לפני שר הצבא ממקום למקום ושם מכינים לו כל צרכיו (עיין ערוך ערך אספרווא).

The Gemara answers:

אִיכָּא פְּרוּצוֹת – We are unwilling to make such an announcement because **there are brazen women** who, if we announce publicly that submitting to the governor will not cause them to become forbidden to their husbands, will cohabit with him willingly, thus committing deliberate adultery.[13] **וְאִיכָּא נַמִּי כֹּהֲנוֹת** – **Furthermore, there are the wives of Kohanim** who actually do become prohibited to their husband if they are raped,[14] and who might, therefore, resist the governor unto death. The Baraisa is therefore justified in calling this decree a "danger."

Which leads the Gemara to ask:

וְלִיעַקְרֵיהּ – **But** then marrying on Wednesday really is a mortal danger after all, and so **let us abolish it** [the institution of Wednesday marriages] altogether![15] – ? –

The Gemara answers:

גְּזֵירָה עֲבִידָא דְּבָטְלָא – **A** government **decree will eventually be revoked, וְתַקַּנְתָּא דְרַבָּנַן מִקַּמֵּי גְזֵירָה לֹא עָקְרִינַן** – **and,** therefore, **we do not abolish a Rabbinic institution in the face of a decree.**[16]

The Gemara questions its conclusion regarding the nature of this "danger":

אִי הָכִי – **If so,** that the decree was not that virgins marrying on Wednesday should be killed but, rather, that they should consort with the governor,[17] then how did it avail the people to marry on Tuesday instead? **בִּשְׁלִישִׁי נַמִּי אָתֵי וּבָעִיל** – **On Tuesday, too, he will come and have relations** with her![18]

The Gemara answers:

מִסְּפֵיקָא לֹא עָקַר נַפְשֵׁיהּ – **He will not dislodge himself** to travel to the wedding **out of doubt.**[19]

The Baraisa continued:

וּבַשֵּׁנִי לֹא יִכְנוֹס – However, even then ONE SHOULD NOT MARRY ON MONDAY,[20] **וְאִם מֵחֲמַת הָאוֹנֶס מוּתָּר** – BUT IF IT IS BECAUSE OF AN UNAVOIDABLE CIRCUMSTANCE THEN IT IS PERMITTED.

The Gemara asks:

מַאי אוֹנֶס – **What** is the **"unavoidable circumstance"** to which the Baraisa refers, which warrants moving the wedding all the way up to Monday? **אִילֵימָא הָא דַּאֲמָרַן** – **If you say** that it is **that** same "danger" **of which we** already **spoke,**[21] **הָתָם קָרֵי לֵיהּ סַכָּנָה** – why does **[the Baraisa] there** in the first case **call it a "danger," וְהָכָא קָא קָרֵי לֵיהּ אוֹנֶס** – whereas **here it calls it an "unavoidable circumstance"? וְתוּ** – **Furthermore, הָתָם נָהֲגוּ** – **there,** when it speaks of the "danger" involved in Wednesday weddings, the Baraisa says that the people **became accustomed** to marry on Tuesday, **הָכָא מוּתָּר** – whereas **here,** in the case of an "unavoidable circumstance," it says that it is **permitted** to marry on Monday, but not that this was the general custom.[22] – ? –

The Gemara answers:

אָמַר רָבָא – **Rava said: דְּאָמְרֵי שַׂר צָבָא בָּא לָעִיר** – The "unavoidable circumstance" of which the Baraisa speaks is **that they say a general is coming to town** with his army and they will despoil the feast if the wedding is held that day.[23]

The Gemara seeks further clarification:

הֵיכִי דָּמֵי – **What is the case? אִי דְּאָתֵי וְחָלִיף** – **If he is coming and leaving** soon,[24] **לִיעַכֵּב** – why not simply **delay** the wedding until next Wednesday; why should we permit the wedding to be held on Monday?[25]

The Gemara answers:

לֹא צְרִיכָא דְּאָתֵי וְקָבַע – **No,** that is not the case. Rather, **it is necessary** to move the wedding to Monday[26] in a case where **he is coming and staying** indefinitely.[27]

The Gemara asks further:

בִּשְׁלִישִׁי מֵיהָא לִכְנוֹס – **Let him** at least **marry [her] on Tuesday;** why move the wedding all the way to Monday?[28]

The Gemara answers:

אִסְפַּרְווֹא דִידֵיהּ בִּשְׁלִישִׁי קָאָתוּ – If the general is arriving on Wed-

NOTES

13. See *Rashi;* cf. *Tosafos;* see also *Shitah Mekubetzes* ד״ה ועוד הקשו.

14. The Gemara below [51b] gives the derivation for this law (*Rashi*).

15. And institute a different day in its stead (*Rashi,* as understood by *Shitah Mekubetzes* ד״ה וליעקריה כתב רש״י; cf. *Tosafos* ד״ה תקנה).

16. [Although we do countenance its being abandoned in practice until the danger passes.]

[See *Shitah Mekubetzes* (ibid.), who explains why the Gemara did not offer this reply earlier, when it posited that the decree was that any virgin who married on Wednesday was to be killed.]

17. See *Tos. HaRosh.*

18. Although, as noted earlier (note 8), the government decree was primarily antireligious in nature, and aimed specifically at Wednesday marriages, nonetheless it obviously catered to the cupidity of the governor who, we can assume, would not be denied his pleasure just because the people rescheduled their weddings for Tuesday (*Shitah Mekubetzes* ד״ה והרא״ש, explaining *Rashi;* see there for another view).

19. Since the switch to Tuesday was not an official institution [and was not universally observed], the governor would not be sure that the wedding would take place on Tuesday; he therefore will not leave his residence to come into town (*Rashi*).

20. [I.e. even if the government decreed that a virgin marrying on Wednesday must cohabit with the governor, this justified moving the wedding up one day to Tuesday, but not two days, to Monday (see above, note 4.]

21. And the Baraisa means that if the government extended the decree to Tuesday weddings then the wedding may be moved up even to Monday (see *Tosafos* ד״ה ובשני).

22. In the first case the Baraisa says that the people became accustomed to marry on Tuesday, implying this was the practice of most people; but in the second case it says only that it is permitted to marry on Monday, implying that although if an individual faced with this "unavoidable circumstance" sought permission to marry on Monday we would allow it, we would not publicize this permit to such an extent that it would become common practice (*Rashi,* as understood by *Ritva;* cf. *Tosafos*).

23. I.e. he will expropriate whatever has been prepared for the wedding meal (*Rashi*). This warrants granting a permit, on an individual basis, to move the wedding up to Monday, but – unlike the vicious government decree of which the Baraisa spoke earlier – it is not sufficiently serious a threat to publicize such a permit and make it public practice (see *Ritva*).

24. I.e. he will leave after Wednesday (*Rashi;* cf. *Tosafos*).

25. [Regarding why the Gemara did not answer that the feast was already prepared and so the wedding could not be postponed, see *Shitah Mekubetzes* ד״ה ואי בעית אימא.]

26. [The translation follows *Shitah Mekubetzes* ד״ה לא צריכא.]

27. See *Rashi;* cf. *Tosafos.*

28. [The Gemara assumes that the Baraisa speaks of a case where the general is arriving on Wednesday;] why, then, asks the Gemara, do we allow moving the wedding up two days, to Monday? Let it suffice to move it up to Tuesday, thus leaving time for at least two of the three days of preparation that the Sages – being diligent in promoting the welfare of Jewish daughters – required? (*Rashi;* cf. *Rashba;* see also *Pnei Yehoshua*).

[*Tosafos* ask why the Gemara could not answer simply that the general is, in fact, arriving on Tuesday. They offer an answer which, however, is not compatible with *Rashi's* understanding of our Gemara (see *Tos. HaRosh*). Perhaps one might suggest, according to *Rashi,* that the Gemara understands from the language of the Baraisa that both the "danger" of which it spoke earlier, and the "unavoidable circumstance" of which it speaks now, relate to Wednesday specifically, in the former case because the government decree was aimed at Wednesday weddings, and in the latter case because the general is arriving on Wednesday. The Gemara therefore seeks to understand why the Baraisa says that the former case justifies moving the wedding up by only one day, to Tuesday, while the latter case justifies moving it up by two days, to Monday.]

מאי שקדו דתניא מפני מה אמרו בתולה נשאת ליום הרביעי שאם היה לו טענת בתולים היה משכים לב"ד ותנשא באחד בשבת ואם היה לו טענת בתולים היה משכים לב"ד שקדו חכמים על תקנת בנות ישראל שיהא אדם טורח בסעודה שלשה ימים אחד בשבת ושני בשבת ושלישי בשבת וברביעי כונסה ומסכנה ואילך נהגו העם לכנוס בשלישי ולא מיחו בידם חכמים ובשני לא יכנוס ואם מחמת האונס מותר ומפרישין את החתן מן הכלה לילי שבת תחלה מפני שהוא עושה חבורה מאי סכנה אילימא דאמרי בתולה הנשאת ליום הרביעי תיהרג נהגו לגמרי ניעקריה אמר רבה דאמרי בתולה הנשאת ביום הרביעי תיבעל להגמון תחלה האי סכנה אונס הוא משום דאיכא צנועות דמסרן נפשייהו לקטלא ואתיין לידי סכנה ולידרוש להו דאונס שרי איכא פרוצות ואיכא נמי כהנות וליעקריה גזירה עבידא דבטלא ותקנתא דרבנן מקמי גזירה לא עקרינן אי הכי בשלישי נמי אתי ובעיל מספיקא לא עקר נפשיה ובשני לא יכנוס ואם מחמת האונס מותר מאי אונס אילימא הא דאמרן התם קרי ליה סכנה והכא קא קרי ליה אונס ותו התם נהגו הכא מותר אמר רבא דאמרי שר צבא בא לעיר ה"ד אי דאתי וחליף ליעכב לא צריכא דאתי וקבע בג' מיהא לכנוס אספרווא דידיה בג' קאתו ואיבעית אימא מאי מחמת האונס כדתני' הרי שהיה פתו אפוי וטבחו טבוח ויינו מזוג ומת אביו של חתן או אמה של כלה מכניסין את המת לחדר ואת החתן ואת הכלה לחופה ובועל

רש"י

מאי שקדו. היכן שנינו שקדו דמקשינן לה הכא אי משום דאמר שמואל לעיל לית לן לאותביה מינה לאמורא אחרינא: ומן הסכנה ואילך. לקמן מפרש לה: ובשני לא יכנוס. בשביל אותה סכנה ואין צריך לעקור בשבילה תקנת חכמים אלא יום אחד ויהיה טורח מיהת שני ימים בצורכי סעודה: ואם מחמת האונס. לקמן מפרש: תחלה. אם ביאה ראשונה היא מפרישין אותה ממנו לילי שבת: נהגו. בתמיה סכנת נפשות היא ואת אמרת נהגו לכנוס ביום שלישי אבל מיעקר רביעי לגמרי לא עקרו: ניעקריה. ויתקנו להם ימים אחרים: ולדרוש להו דאונס שרי. דנבעלת באונס אינה נאסרת על בעלה דילפינן לקמן בפרק ד' (דף נא:) מוהיא לא נתפשה ולא לימסרו נפשייהו למיתה: איכא פרוצות. דאי מקילינן להו עבדי ברצון ונאסרות על בעליהן: ואיכא נמי כהנות. שנאסרות על בעליהן אף באונס ואינהו מסרן נפשייהו למיתה דאשת כהן שנאנסה אסורה לבעלה ולקמן בפרק ד' (שם) ילפינן לה: וליעקריה. הואיל וזמנין דאיכא סכנה: בשלישי נמי אתי ובעיל. כיון דידע שהתחילו לנהוג בשלישי: מספיקא לא עקר נפשיה. כיון דלאו קביעות גמור הוא על ידי תקנת ב"ד ספיקא היא לו אם יש נישואין היום בעיר ולא עקר נפשיה לבא בעיר: התם נהגו. משמע רובם נהגו: הכא מותר. לא גרסינן לכתחילה והכי קא מתמה הכא מותר קתני דמשמע אם ימלך איש יחידי בבית דין יתירו לו אבל נהגו לא קתני: שר צבא בא לעיר. ויחטפו צורכי סעודה מאשר ימצאו: וחליף. לאחר רביעי: ליעכב. עד יום רביעי של שבת הבאה: בשלישי לכנוס. למה נתיר לו לקדום כל כך שלא יטריח בסעודה אלא יום אחד ומיעקרא תקנתא דשקדו: איספרווא דידיה. חיל משרתיו המכינים לו צורכי סעודה בלשון לעז הירניי"ש: כדתניא. חתן שמת אביו בשני ואין יכול להמתין עד למחר שצריך להשהות את המת עד שיכנסו לחופה: ויינו מזוג. במים שיהא ראוי לשתיה ושוב אינו מתקיים: אביו של חתן או אמה של כלה. דוקא נקט אביו של חתן שהוא הטורח בצורכי סעודה ואמה של כלה היא המכינה לה תכשיטין לפיכך אם יעבור המועד שוב אין מכין להם והתירו להם להכניס את המת לחדר שלא יקברוהו דאם כן חלה אבילות על האבל בסתימת הגולל כדלקמן ושוב לא יוכל לכנוס עד שיעבור האבילות:

ופורש

תוספות

ובשני לא יכנוס. פ"ה אפילו בשעת הסכנה דאין לעקור בשבילה תקנת חכמים אלא יום אחד וקשה לר"י דאמר לקמן מאי אונס אילימא הא דאמרן התם קרי ליה כו' הוה ליה למיפרך טפי רישא לסיפא דקתני רישא ובשני לא יכנוס אפי' בשעת הסכנה ואומר ריב"א דמשום הכי לא פריך ליה משום דאיכא לפרושי ואם מחמת האונס פירוש שיש סכנה אף ביום שלישי מותר לכנוס בשני ונראה לר"י דמילתא באנפי נפשה היא ולא איירי בסכנה ובשני לא יכנוס הוא הדין בג' אלא נקט בב' משום דבעי למיתני ואם מחמת האונס מותר: ולדרוש להו דאונס שרי. וא"ת והא אמרינן בפ' בן סורר ומורה (סנהדרין עד. ושם) על כל עבירות יעבור ואל יהרג חוץ מעבודת כוכבים וג"ע וש"ד ותירץ ר"ת דאין חייבין מיתה על בעילת מצרי דרחמנא אפקריה לזרעיה דמצרי כתיב (יחזקאל כג) וזרמת סוסים זרמתם ומייתי ראיה דפריך בפ' בן סורר ומורה (שם:) הא אסתר פרהסיא הואי ולא פריך והא אסתר גילוי עריות הויא משמע דמשום עריות לא הוה מיחייבא ומתוך כך התיר ר"ת לבת ישראל שהמירה ובא עליה עובד כוכבים לקיימה לאותו עובד כוכבים כשנתגייר דלא שייך למימר אחד לבעל ואחד לבועל בביאת מצרי דהויא כביאת בהמה ואין נראה לריב"ם דהא ע"י ביאת עובד כוכבים נאסרה לבעלה כדאמר הכא דאיכא פרוצות ובפ' האשה שנתארמלה (לקמן כו: ושם) גבי האשה שנחבשה בין העובדי כוכבים אמרי' דברצון אסורה לבעלה ואמר נמי במגילה (דף טו.) כאשר אבדתי אבדתי כאשר אבדתי מבית אבא אבדתי ממך אלמא לגבי בעלה לא חשיבא בעילת מצרי כביאת בהמה והוא הדין לבועל אע"ג דאין זנות לבהמה ואין ביאת בהמה פוסלת ואוסרת כדאמרי' בפ' הבא על יבמתו (יבמות נט:) ביאת מצרי הויא ביאה וכי אפקריה רחמנא לזרעיה הני מילי לענין דאין לו חייס חרעו חשוב כזרע בהמה ויש לומר דהכי פריך ולדרוש להו דאונס שרי לפי שהאשה היא קרקע עולם ולא עבדה מעשה כדמשני בפרק בן סורר ומורה אסתר קרקע עולם היתה והא דלא פריך התם גילוי עריות הויא דפשיטא ליה דאיכא לשנויי קרקע עולם היא ואין לה למסור עצמה אבל לענין חילול השם לא היה נראה לו שיועיל טעם דקרקע עולם ומשני קרקע עולם היתה ואפילו חילול השם ליכא ובפרק מצות חליצה (שם קג. ושם) דפריך גבי יעל והא קמתהניא מעבירה ומשני טובתן של רשעים רעה היא אצל צדיקים שהטיל בה זוהמא ולא משני קרקע עולם היתה משום דהתם לא פריך אמאי לא מסרה עצמה דהא לא היה רוצה להמיתה דאדרבה היה צריך שתשמרהו אלא הכי פירושו והא מתהניא מעבירה למה משבחה הכתוב מנשים באהל תבורך ודרשינן בנזיר (דף כג: ושם) גדולה עבירה לשמה ממצוה שלא לשמה ופריך דיעל נמי הוה עבירה שלא לשמה דהא מתהניא מעבירה ומשני דלא מתהניא ועשתה עבירה לשמה כדי להציל את ישראל: **בתולה** הנשאת ברביעי תיבעל. לאו דוקא ברביעי מדפריך לקמן בשלישי נמי אתי ובעיל שאינו מתכוין אלא להנאתו אלא אגב דנקט לעיל שנשאת ברביעי תיהרג דהתם מקפידים על קביעות יום כדי להעבירם על דתם נקט ליה נמי הכא ברביעי: **ולדרוש** להו דאונס שרי. אין לפרש דפריך הכי לדרוש כו' דשוב לא יהא סכנה אלא אונס ואמאי קאמר ומסכנה ואילך דא"כ מאי משני משום פרוצות דהא אפילו לא דרשינן להו דאונס שרי לא מסרי נפשייהו דדוקא צנועות אמרינן דמסרי נפשייהו ועוד וכי משום פרוצות יניחו להרוג הצנועות אלא הכי פירושו ולדרוש להו דאונס שרי וכיון דליכא סכנה אמאי לא מיחו בידם חכמים ומשני משום פרוצות לא מיחו בידם אי נמי משום כהנות: **ותו** התם. בשלישי נהגו ואמרינן בפ' בתרא דתענית (דף כו:) מאן דאמר נהגו אורויי לא מורינן והכא בשני מותר לכתחלה ופי' הקונטרס דפירש נהגו רובא דעלמא והכא מותר יחידי ולא גרסינן לכתחלה אינו מיושב: **אי** דאתי וחליף ליעכב. פ"ה חליף לאחר ד' וליעכב עד יום ד' של שבת הבאה וקשה לר"י דאם כן מאי משני לא צריכא דאתי וקבע אכתי ליעכב חדש או חדשים עד שילך על כן נראה לר"י שאם יתעכב כל יום ד' אין לו לעכב עד יום ד' אחר אלא יכנוס בג' והכי פריך אי אתי וחליף בד' גופיה ליעכב עד דחליף ומשני דאתי וקבע כל יום ד': **בשלישי** מיהא לכנוס. ולא בעי למימר דאתי שר הצבא בג' דא"כ יכנוס בד': **איספרווא** דידיה בג' אתא. אין לתמוה משום סעודה עקרינן תקנתא דרבנן ב' ימים ומשום סכנה לא עקרינן אלא יום אחד דבעילת הגמון שכיח שרגיל לבא ולבעול ואי עקרינן שני ימים אתא להשתכח אבל אונס שר צבא אינו אלא אקראי בעלמא: (לעיל) **תקנה** דרבנן מקמי גזרה לא עקרינן. כי פריך לעיל ליעקרוה לא משני תקנה דרבנן מקמי גזרה כו' כדמשני הכא משום דלעיל פריך וליעקרוה ויקבעו יום אחר כיון דאינו מתכוין אלא להעבירם על דת כשיקבעו יום אחר לא יחושו ולא מיעקרא תקנתא דרבנן הואיל ויהא יום אחד קבוע אבל הכא פריך וליעקרוה ולא יהא שום יום קבוע שאם יום קבוע יקבעו יום אתי ובעיל באותו יום ולהכי משני מקמי גזרה לא עקרינן תקנה דרבנן שלא יהא שום יום קבוע: (לעיל) **אי** הכי בשלישי נמי אתי ובעיל. פי' א) אי אמרת בשלמא כדמעיקרא דאמרי בתולה שנשאת בד' תיהרג ואינן מתכוונין אלא להעבירם לא יחושו אם יעשו ביום ג' אלא אי אמרת משום בעילת ההגמון כיון שמתכוין להנאתו בשלישי נמי אתי ובעיל:

בועל

תוספות רי"ד

תניא הרי שהיה פתו אפויה וטבחו טבוח ויינו מזוג ונתן מים ע"ג בשר ומת אביו של חתן או אמו של כלה מכניסין את המת לחדר ואת החתן ואת הכלה לחופה ובועל בעילת מצוה ופורש ונוהג ז' ימי משתה ואח"כ נוהג ז' ימי אבילות וכל אותן הימים הוא ישן בין האנשים והיא ישנה בין הנשים. וכן מי שפירסה אשתו נדה ואין מונעים תכשיטין מן הכלה כל ל'. פי' מכ' יום את וכו'. שלא קברוהו ותחול עליו האבילות בסתימות הגולל שוב לא יוכל לכנוס עד שיעבור ז' ימי האבל. שלא כנס תחלה ואח"כ קברו המת וכיון דחלה עליו חתונה הויא גביה כרגל שלא אתיא אבילות וחיילא עליה. ונוהג ז' ימי המשתה תחלה ואח"כ ז' ימי האבילות וכל אותן הימים אינו מתיחד עמה שמא יבעול. ואבל אסור בתשמיש המטה ואף בז' ימי המשתה שהן אצלו כרגל דברים של צנעה נוהג. ואין מונעים וכו'. ואע"פ שהיא אבילה שלא תתגנה על בעלה. ודוקא אביו של חתן הטורח בצרכי סעודה. ואמה של כלה המכינה לה לתכשיטין דליכא איניש דטרח להו. אבל איפכא לא:

א) [ועי' תוס' שבת קכ:]

לעזי רש"י

הירניי"ש. פירוש חיל המשרתים המכינים צורכי סעודה, חילות או גדודים הנוסעים לפני שר הצבא ממקום למקום ושם מכינים לו כל צרכיו (עיין ערוך ערך אספרווו):

Having questioned Rav Shmuel bar Yitzchak on the basis of the enactment of the Sages who were diligent about the welfare of Jewish daughters, the Gemara now asks:

מַאי שָׁקְדוּ – **What is** our source for saying that **[the Sages] were diligent** about the welfare of Jewish daughters?[1] דְּתַנְיָא – **For it was taught in a Baraisa:** מִפְּנֵי מָה אָמְרוּ בְּתוּלָה נִשֵּׂאת לְיוֹם הָרְבִיעִי – WHY DID THEY SAY THAT A VIRGIN SHOULD BE MARRIED ON WEDNESDAY? שֶׁאִם הָיָה לוֹ טַעֲנַת בְּתוּלִים – SO THAT IF HE HAD A CLAIM REGARDING HER VIRGINITY, הָיָה מַשְׁכִּים לְבֵית דִּין – HE WOULD GO EARLY the next morning – on Thursday – TO COURT. וְתִנָּשֵׂא בְּאֶחָד בְּשַׁבָּת – BUT, you may ask, LET HER BE MARRIED ON SUNDAY, וְאִם הָיָה לוֹ טַעֲנַת בְּתוּלִים – AND so IF HE HAD A CLAIM REGARDING HER VIRGINITY הָיָה מַשְׁכִּים לְבֵית דִּין – HE WOULD GO EARLY the next morning – on Monday – TO COURT! שָׁקְדוּ חֲכָמִים עַל תַּקָּנַת בְּנוֹת יִשְׂרָאֵל – The answer is that THE SAGES WERE DILIGENT IN PROMOTING THE WELFARE OF JEWISH DAUGHTERS, שֶׁיְּהֵא אָדָם טוֹרֵחַ בִּסְעוּדָה שְׁלֹשָׁה יָמִים – and desired THAT [THE HUSBAND] SHOULD BUSY HIMSELF WITH preparing THE wedding FEAST FOR THREE consecutive DAYS, אֶחָד בְּשַׁבָּת וְשֵׁנִי בְּשַׁבָּת וּשְׁלִישִׁי בְּשַׁבָּת – viz. SUNDAY, MONDAY, AND TUESDAY, וּבִרְבִיעִי כּוֹנְסָהּ – AND then MARRY HER ON WEDNESDAY.[2]

The Baraisa continues:

וּמִסַּכָּנָה וְאֵילָךְ – AND FROM the time of DANGER AND ONWARD, when it became dangerous to marry on Wednesday,[3] נָהֲגוּ הָעָם לִכְנוֹס בִּשְׁלִישִׁי – THE PEOPLE BECAME ACCUSTOMED TO MARRY ON TUESDAY וְלֹא מִיחוּ בְּיָדָם חֲכָמִים – AND THE SAGES DID NOT VOICE AN OBJECTION to this. וּבְשֵׁנִי לֹא יִכְנוֹס – However, even then ONE SHOULD NOT MARRY ON MONDAY.[4] וְאִם מֵחֲמַת הָאוֹנֶס מוּתָּר – BUT IF IT IS BECAUSE OF AN UNAVOIDABLE CIRCUMSTANCE[5] THEN IT IS PERMITTED to marry on Monday.

The Baraisa concludes:

וּמַפְרִישִׁין אֶת הֶחָתָן מִן הַכַּלָּה – WE SEPARATE THE GROOM FROM THE BRIDE לֵילֵי שַׁבָּת תְּחִלָּה – ON THE NIGHT OF THE SABBATH [i.e. Friday night] if this will be their FIRST act of cohabitation מִפְּנֵי שֶׁהוּא עוֹשֶׂה חַבּוּרָה – BECAUSE HE thereby MAKES A WOUND when he ruptures the hymen.[6]

The Gemara analyzes the Baraisa:

מַאי סַכָּנָה – **What** is the **danger** that caused people to abandon the Wednesday weddings? אִילֵימָא דְּאָמְרֵי בְּתוּלָה הַנִּשֵּׂאת לְיוֹם הָרְבִיעִי תֵּיהָרֵג – **If you say that [the government] said that a virgin who is married on Wednesday should be killed,** נָהֲגוּ – why is it only that **they were accustomed** to get married on Tuesday? לִגְמְרֵי נִיעַקְרֵיהּ – **We should abolish** it [the institution of Wednesday weddings] **completely.**[7] – ? –

The Gemara answers:

דְּאָמְרֵי בְּתוּלָה הַנִּשֵּׂאת בְּיוֹם הָרְבִיעִי אָמַר רַבָּה תִּיבָּעֵל לְהֶגְמוֹן תְּחִלָּה – **Rabbah said:** Rather, the decree was **that [the government] said that a virgin who is married on Wednesday should cohabit with the governor first.**[8] Since this decree did not pose a danger to life the Rabbis did not see fit to repeal one of their institutions although, as stated, they were willing to countenance its being, for the interim, abandoned in practice.

The Gemara questions the Baraisa's choice of language:[9]

הַאי סַכָּנָה – **This is a danger?** אוֹנֶס הוּא – **It is a rape,** not a danger to life! – ? –

The Gemara answers:

מִשּׁוּם דְּאִיכָּא צְנוּעוֹת – The Baraisa's term is justified **because there are modest women** דְּמָסְרָן נַפְשַׁיְיהוּ לִקְטָלָא – **who would give themselves up to death** rather than be ravished, וְאָתְיָין לִידֵי סַכָּנָה – **and** will therefore **come into** mortal **danger** by this decree.[10]

The Gemara questions this:

וְלִידְרוֹשׁ לְהוּ דְּאוֹנֶס שָׁרֵי – **But let us announce to them that** in a case of **rape** the woman **is permitted** to her husband;[11] thus, they will not resist and will not be killed. Why, then, does the Baraisa call this a situation of "danger"?[12]

NOTES

1. Although Shmuel already mentioned this enactment earlier in the Gemara [2a], that would not be sufficient grounds for the Gemara to have challenged another Amora. Such a challenge must have been based upon a Tannaic source, which the Gemara now seeks (*Rashi;* cf. *Shitah Mekubetzes*).

2. See above, 2a note 18.

3. The Gemara will soon explain what this danger was (*Rashi*).

4. The danger of marrying on Wednesday warrants displacing the wedding by one day, to Tuesday, but not by two days, to Monday, for at least if he marries on Tuesday he will have two days to prepare the wedding, whereas if he marries on Monday he will have only one day to do so (*Rashi;* cf. *Rashba* ד״ה בשלישי).

Were, however, it to become dangerous to marry on Tuesday, as well, then there would be no objection to marrying on Monday (*Shitah Mekubetzes* ד״ה ודע, explaining *Rashi;* see there for another view; cf. also *Tosafos* ד״ה איספרווא).

5. The Gemara will explain what this means (*Rashi*).

6. This will be discussed at length below, 5b.

7. The phrase "they were accustomed" indicates that the Rabbinic institution to marry on Wednesday was never repealed, although most people abandoned it in practice. But if there was a definite danger to life in marrying on Wednesday then the Rabbis ought to have themselves repealed their legislation, since it was never intended to put people in mortal danger (see *Rashi* here and below ד״ה התם נהגו; *Shitah Mekubetzes* ד״ה נהגו; cf. *Teshuvos Rivash* §373, cited by *Shitah Mekubetzes* ibid.). Therefore, rather than keeping the institution of Wednesday marriages officially in place, the Rabbis should have repealed it, and instituted that marriages take place on some other day of the week; correspondingly, they could institute that the courts, too, should convene on the day following, thus preserving the intent of the original institution of Wednesday marriages (*Rashi,* as amplified by *Chidushei Chasam Sofer*). And if the government were to realize and turn their legislation against marriages on that day, too, then the Rabbis could again move the day for weddings [and for courts convening] to yet another day (*Shitah Mekubetzes* ibid., explaining *Rashi;* see also ibid. ד״ה והרא״ש; see there for another view).

8. The decree was aimed specifically at Wednesday marriages, since its purpose was to eradicate this religious institution [of course, by its nature, such a decree involved no small measure of self-interest on the part of the governor, as well – see below, note 18] (*Shitah Mekubetzes* ד״ה דאמרינן, explaining *Rashi;* cf. *Tosafos* ד״ה בתולה; *Ramban* ד״ה ולדרוש; *Rashba* ד״ה ולדרוש).

9. [See *Ritva.*]

10. That is, there are modest women who will mistakenly imagine that their being ravished will forbid them to their husbands, and will, therefore, resist unto death, rather than succumb (see *Rashi* ד״ה ולדרוש להו; *Ritva;* see also *Shitah Mekubetzes* ד״ה ועוד הקשו).

11. The Gemara derives below (51b) that if a married woman is forced into an act of cohabitation she does not become prohibited to her husband. By making this common knowledge, we will not have to be concerned that a woman will give up her life in resisting the governor (*Rashi*).

[The following question must be addressed: The Gemara elsewhere (*Sanhedrin* 74a) states that adultery is one of the three cardinal sins (the other two being murder and idolatry) which one may not violate even on pain of death. How, then, can we discourage these women from giving up their lives in order not to have relations with the governor? To resolve this difficulty *Tosafos* distinguish between active and passive participation in the adulterous act: A man (whose role in cohabitation is, by its nature, always active) must give up his life rather than commit an adulterous act; but a woman (even a married woman) is not required to give up her life to prevent being raped (*Tosafos* ד״ה ולדרוש; see there for another answer, as well; see also *Shitah Mekubetzes*).

12. See *Re'ah,* cited in *Shitah Mekubetzes* ד״ה וז״ל הרא״ה; see also *Shitah Mekubetzes* ד״ה ועוד הקשו בתוספות; cf. *Tosafos.*

מאי שקדו דתניא מפני מה אמרו בתולה נשאת ליום הרביעי שאם היה לו טענת בתולים היה משכים לב"ד ותנשא באחד בשבת ואם היה לו טענת בתולים היה משכים לב"ד שקדו חכמים על תקנת בנות ישראל שיהא אדם טורח בסעודה שלשה ימים אחד בשבת ושני בשבת ושלישי בשבת וברביעי כונסה ומסכנה ואילך נהגו העם לכנוס בשלישי ולא מיחו בידם חכמים ובשני לא יכנוס ואם מחמת האונס מותר ומפרישין את החתן מן הכלה לילי שבת תחלה מפני שהוא עושה חבורה מאי סכנה אילימא דאמרי בתולה הנשאת ליום הרביעי תיהרג נהגו לגמרי ניעקריה אמר רבה דאמרי בתולה הנשאת ביום הרביעי תיבעל להגמון תחלה האי סכנה אונס הוא משום דאיכא צנועות דמסרן נפשייהו לקטלא ואתיין לידי סכנה ולידרוש להו דאונס שרי איכא פרוצות ואיכא נמי כהנות ולעיקריה גזירה עבידא דבטלא ותקנתא דרבנן מקמי גזירה לא עקרינן אי הכי בשלישי נמי אתי ובעיל מספיקא לא עקר נפשיה ובשני לא יכנוס ואם מחמת האונס מותר מאי אונס אילימא הא דאמרן התם קרי ליה סכנה והכא קא קרי ליה אונס ותו התם נהגו הכא מותר אמר רבא דאמרי שר צבא בא לעיר ה"ד אי דאתי וחליף ליעכב לא צריכא דאתי וקבע בג' מיהא לכנוס אספרווא דידיה בג' קאתו ואיבעית אימא מאי מחמת האונס כדתני' הרי שהיה פתו אפוי וטבחו טבוח ויינו מזוג ומת אביו של חתן או אמה של כלה מכניסין את המת לחדר ואת החתן ואת הכלה לחופה ובועל

רש"י

מאי שקדו. היכן שינו שקדו דמקשינן לה הכא אי משום דאמר שמואל לעיל לית לן לאותביה מינה לאמוראה אחרינא: ומן הסכנה ואילך. לקמן מפרש לה: ובשני לא יכנוס. בשביל אותה סכנה ואין צריך לעקור בשביל תקנת חכמים אלא יום אחד ויהיה טורח מיהת שני ימים בצורכי סעודה: ואם מחמת האונס. לקמן מפרש: תחלה. אם ביאה ראשונה היא מפרישין אותה ממנו לילי שבת: נהגו. בתמיה סכנת נפשות היא ואת אמרת נהגו לכנוס ביום שלישי אבל מיעקר רביעי לגמרי לא עקרו: ניעקריה. ויתקנו להם ימים אחרים: ולידרוש להו דאונס שרי. דנבעלת באונס אינה נאסרת על בעלה דילפינן לקמן בפרק ד' (דף נא:) מוהיא לא נתפשה ולא לימסרו נפשייהו למיתה: איכא פרוצות. דאי מקילינן להו עבדי ברצון ונאסרות על בעליהן: ואיכא נמי כהנות. שנאסרות על בעליהן אף באונס ואינהו מסרן נפשייהו למיתה דאשת כהן שנאנסה אסורה לבעלה ולקמן בפרק ד' (שם) ילפינן לה: ולעיקריה. הואיל וזמנין דליכא סכנה: בשלישי נמי אתי ובעיל. כיון דידע שהתחילו לנהוג בשלישי: מספיקא לא עקר נפשיה. כיון דלאו קביעות גמור הוא על ידי תקנת ב"ד ספיקא היא לו אם יש ישואין היום בעיר ולא עקר נפשיה לבא בעיר: התם נהגו. משמע רוצים נהגו: הכא מותר. לא גרסינן לכתחילה והכי קא מתמה הכא מותר קתני דמשמע אם ימלך איש יחידי בבית דין יתירו לו אבל נהגו לא קתני: שר צבא בא לעיר. ויתפסו צורכי סעודה מאשר ימלאו: וחליף. לאחר רביעי: ליעכב. עד יום רביעי של שבת הבא: בשלישי לכנוס. למה נתיר לו לקדום כל כך שלא יטריח בסעודה אלא יום אחד ומיעקרא תקנתא דשקדו: איספרווא דידיה. חיל משרתיו המכינים לו צורכי סעודה בלשון לעז הירני"ש: כדתניא. חתן שמת אביו בשני ואין יכול להמתין עד למחר שצריך להשהות את המת עד שיכנסו לחופה: ויינו מזוג. במים שיהא ראוי לשתיה ושוב אינו מתקיים: אביו של חתן או אמה של כלה. דוקא נקט אביו של חתן שהוא הטורח בצורכי סעודה ואמה של כלה היא המכינה לה תכשיטין לפיכך אם יעבור המועד שוב אין מכין להם והתירו להם להכניס את המת לחדר שלא יקברוהו דאם כן חלה אבילות על האבל בסתימת הגולל כדלקמן ושוב לא יוכל לכנוס עד שיעבור האבילות:

ופורש

תוספות

ובשני לא יכנוס. פ"ה אפילו בשעת הסכנה דאין לעקור בשבילה תקנת חכמים אלא יום אחד וקשה לר"י דלאמר לקמן מאי אונס אילימא הא דאמרן התם קרי ליה כו' הוה ליה למיפרך טפי רישא לסיפא דקתני רישא ובשני לא יכנוס אפי' בשעת הסכנה ואומר ריצב"א דמשום הכי לא פריך ליה משום דאיכא לפרושי ואם מחמת האונס פירוש שיש סכנה אף ביום שלישי מותר לכנוס בשני ונראה לר"י דמילתא באנפי נפשה היא ולא איירי בסכנה ובשני לא יכנוס הוא הדין בג' אלא נקט בב' משום דבעי למיתני ואם מחמת האונס מותר: **ולדרוש** להו דאונס שרי. וא"ת והא אמרינן בפ' בן סורר ומורה (סנהדרין עד. ושם) על כל עבירות יעבור ואל יהרג חוץ מעבודת כוכבים וג"ע וש"ד ותירץ ר"ת דאין חייבין מיתה על בעילת נכרי דרחמנא אפקריה לזרעיה דנכרי דכתיב (יחזקאל כג) וזרמת סוסים זרמתם ומייתי ראיה דפריך בפ' בן סורר ומורה (שם:) הא אסתר פרהסיא הואי ולא פריך והא אסתר גילוי עריות הויא משמע דמשום עריות לא הוה מיחייבא ומתוך כך התיר ר"ת לבת ישראל שהמירה ובא עליה עובד כוכבים לקיימה לאותו עובד כוכבים כשנתגייר דלא שייך למימר אחד לבעל ואחד לבועל בביאת נכרי דהויא כביאת בהמה ואין נראה לריב"ם דהא ע"י ביאת עובד כוכבים נאסרה לבעלה כדאמר הכא דאיכא פרוצות ובפ' האשה שנתארמלה (לקמן כו: ושם) גבי האשה שנחבשה בין העובדי כוכבים אמרי' דברצון אסורה לבעלה ואמר נמי במגילה (דף טו.) כאשר אבדתי אבדתי כאשר אבדתי מבית אבא אבדתי ממך אלמא לגבי בעלה לא חשיבא בעילת נכרי כביאת בהמה והוא הדין לבועל אע"ג דאין זנות לבהמה ואין ביאת בהמה פוסלת ואוסרת כדאמרי' בפ' הבא על יבמתו (יבמות נט:) ביאת נכרי הויא ביאה וכי אפקריה רחמנא לזרעיה הני מילי לענין דאין לו חייס חרעו חשוב כזרע בהמה ויש לומר דהכי פריך ולדרוש להו דאונס שרי לפי שהאשה היא קרקע עולם ולא עבדה מעשה כדמשני בפרק בן סורר ומורה אסתר קרקע עולם היתה והא דלא פריך התם גילוי עריות הויא דפשיטא ליה דאיכא לשנויי קרקע עולם היא ואין לה למסור עצמה אבל לענין חילול השם לא היה נראה לו שיועיל טעם דקרקע עולם ומשני קרקע עולם היתה ואפילו חילול השם ליכא ובפרק מצות חליצה (שם קג. ושם) דפריך גבי יעל והא קמתהניא מעבירה ומשני טובתן של רשעים רעה היא אצל צדיקים שהטיל בה זוהמא ולא משני קרקע עולם היתה משום דהתם לא פריך אמאי לא מסרה עצמה דהא לא היה רוצה להמיתה דלאדרבה היה צריך שתשמרהו אלא הכי פירושו והא מתהניא מעבירה למה משבחה הכתוב מנשים באהל תבורך ודרשינן בנזיר (דף כג: ושם) גדולה עבירה לשמה ממצוה שלא לשמה ופריך דיעל נמי הוה עבירה שלא לשמה דהא מתהניא מעבירה ומשני דלא מתהניא ועשתה עבירה לשמה כדי להציל את ישראל: **בתולה** הנשאת ברביעי תיבעל. לאו דוקא ברביעי מדפריך לקמן בשלישי נמי אתי ובעיל שאינו מתכוין אלא להנאתו אלא אגב דנקט לעיל שנשאת ברביעי תיהרג דהתם מקפידים על קביעות יום כדי להעבירם על דתם נקט ליה נמי הכא ברביעי: **ולדרוש** להו דאונס שרי. אין לפרש דפריך הכי לדרוש כו' דשוב לא יהא סכנה אלא אונס ואמאי קאמר ומסכנה ואילך דא"כ מאי משני משום פרוצות דהא אפילו לא דרשינן להו דאונס שרי לא מסרי נפשייהו דדוקא צנועות אמרינן דמסרי נפשייהו ועוד וכי משום פרוצות יניחו להרוג הצנועות אלא הכי פירושו ולדרוש להו דאונס שרי וכיון דליכא סכנה אמאי לא מיחו בידם חכמים ומשני משום פרוצות לא מיחו בידם אי נמי משום כהנות: **ותו** התם. בשלישי נהגו ואמרינן בפ' בתרא דתענית (דף כו:) מאן דאמר נהגו אורויי לא מורינן והכא בשני מותר לכתחלה ופי' הקונטרס דפירש נהגו רובא דעלמא והכא מותר יחידי ולא גרסינן לכתחלה אינו מיושב: **אי** דאתי וחליף ליעכב. פ"ה חליף לאחר ד' וליעכב עד יום ד' של שבת הבא וקשה לר"י דאם כן מאי משני לא צריכא דאתי וקבע אכתי ליעכב חדש או חדשים עד שילך על כן נראה לר"י שאם יתעכב כל יום ד' אין לו לעכב עד יום ד' אחר אלא יכנוס בג' והכי פריך אי אתי וחליף בד' גופיה ליעכב עד דחליף ומשני דאתי וקבע כל יום ד': **בשלישי** מיהא לכנוס. ולא בעי למימר דאתי שר הצבא בג' דא"כ יכנוס בד': **איספרווא** דידיה בג' אתא. אין לתמוה משום סעודה עקרינן תקנתא דרבנן ג' ימים ומשום סכנה לא עקרינן אלא יום אחד דבעילת הגמון שכיח שרגיל לבא ולבעול ואי עקרינן שני ימים אתא להשתכח אבל אונס שר צבא אינו אלא אקראי בעלמא: **תקנה** (לעיל) דרבנן מקמי גזרה לא עקרינן. כי פריך לעיל ליעקרו לא משני תקנה דרבנן מקמי גזרה כו' כדמשני הכא משום דלעיל פריך וליעקרוה ויקבעו יום אחר כיון דאינו מתכוין אלא להעבירם על דת כשיקבעו יום אחר לא יחושו ולא מיעקרא תקנתא דרבנן הואיל ויהא יום אחד קבוע אבל הכא פריך וליעקרוה ולא יהא שום יום קבוע שאם יקבעו יום אחר יבא באותו יום ולהכי משני מקמי גזרה לא עקרינן תקנה דרבנן שלא יהא שום יום קבוע: **אי** (לעיל) הכי בשלישי נמי אתי ובעיל. פי' [א] אי אמרת בשלמא כדמעיקרא דאמרי בתולה שנשאת בד' תיהרג ואין מתכוונין אלא להעבירם לא יחושו אם יעשו ביום ג' אלא אי אמרת משום בעילת ההגמון כיון שמתכוין להנאתו בשלישי נמי אתי ובעיל:

בועל

תוספות רי"ד

תניא הרי שהיה פתו אפויה וטבחו טבוח ויינו מזוג ונתן כים ע"ג בשר ומת אביו של חתן או אמו של כלה מכניסין את המת לחדר ואת החתן ואת הכלה לחופה ובועל בעילת מצוה ופורש ונוהג ד' ימי משתה ואח"כ נוהג ד' ימי אבילות וכל אותן הימים הוא ישן בין האנשים והיא ישנה בין הנשים. וכן מי שפירסה אשתו נדה ואין מונעים תכשיטין מן הכלה כל ל'. **פי'** מכניסים את וכו'. שלא יקברוהו ותחול עליו האבילות בסתימות הגולל ושוב לא יוכל לכונסה עד שיעבור ד' ימי האבל. אלא כונס תחלה ואח"כ יקברו המת וכיון דחלה עליו חתונה הויא גביה כרגל שלא אתיא אבילות וחיילא עליה. **ונוהג** ד' ימי המשתה תחלה ואח"כ ד' ימי האבילות וכל אותן הימים אינו מתיחד עמה שמא יבעול. ואבל אסור בתשמיש המטה ואף בד' ימי המשתה שהן אצלו כרגל דברים של צנעה נוהג. **ואין מונעים וכו'**. ואע"פ שהיא אבילה שלא תתגנה על בעלה. ודוקא אביו של חתן הטורח בצרכי סעודה. ואמה של כלה המכינה לה לתכשיטין דליכא איניש דטרח להו. אבל איפכא לא:

מסורת הש"ס

א) [ועי' תוס' שבת קכ:].

לעזי רש"י

הירני"ש. פירוש חייל המשרתים המכינים צורכי סעודה, חילות או גדודים הנוסעים לפני שר הצבא ממקום למקום ושם מכינים לו כל צרכיו (עיין ערוך ערך אספרווה):

זימנין דלא אניס וסברה דאניס ומיעגנא ויתבה ומשום פרוצות דאי אמרת לא ליהוי גיטא זימנין דאניס ואמרה לא אניס ואזלא ומינסבא ונמצא גט בטל ובניה ממזרים ומי איכא מידי דמדאורייתא לא להוי גט ומשום צנועות ומשום פרוצות שרינן אשת איש לעלמא אין [א]כל דמקדש אדעתא דרבנן מקדש *ואפקעינהו רבנן לקידושי מיניה אמר ליה רבינא לרב אשי תינח קדיש בכספא קדיש בביאה מאי איכא למימר שויוה רבנן לבעילתו בעילת זנות איכא דאמרי אמר רבא וכן לענין גיטין אלמא קסבר רבא יש אונס בגיטין מיתיבי הרי זה גיטיך אם לא באתי מכאן ועד שנים עשר חדש ומת בתוך שנים עשר חדש אינו גט מת הוא דאינו גט הא חלה הרי זה גט לעולם אימא לך חלה נמי אינו גט והיא גופה קמ"ל דאין גט לאחר מיתה אין גט לאחר מיתה הא תנא ליה רישא דלמא לאפוקי מדרבותינו ת"ש מעכשיו אם לא באתי מכאן ועד שנים עשר חדש ומת בתוך שנים עשר חדש הרי זה גט מאי לאו הוא הדין לחלה לא מת דוקא דלא ניחא ליה דתפול קמי יבם ת"ש מההוא דאמר להו אי לא אתינא מכאן ועד שלשים יום ליהוי גיטא אתא בסוף תלתין יומין ופסקיה מברא ואמר להו חזו דאתאי חזו דאתאי ואמר שמואל לא שמיה מתיא אונסא דשכיח שאני דכיון דאיבעי ליה לאתנויי ולא אתני איהו הוא דאפסיד אנפשיה אמר רב שמואל בר יצחק לא שנו אלא מתקנת עזרא ואילך שאין בתי דינין קבועין אלא בשני ובחמישי אבל קודם תקנת עזרא שבתי דינין קבועין בכל יום אשה נשאת בכל יום קודם תקנת עזרא מאי דהוה הוה הכי קאמר [א]אי איכא בתי דינין דקבועין האידנא כקודם תקנת עזרא אשה נשאת בכל יום הא בעינן [ג]שקדו דטריח ליה מאי

רש"י

זימנין דלא אניס. והוי גיטא: וסברה. דלמא אניס ואינו גט ותדלג להינשא: ומינסבא. וכשיבא ויאמר נאנסתי נמצא גט בטל ובניה מן האחרון ממזרים לפיכך אמרו יהא גט: דמדאורייתא לא הוי גיטא. שמצינו טענת אונס מן התורה שנאמר (דברים כב) ולנערה לא תעשה דבר: כל המקדש. כל המקדש אשה על דעת שהנהיגו חכמי ישראל בישראל הוא מקדשה שיהיו קיימין קידושין לפי דברי חכמים ויהיו בטלים לפי דברי חכמים על ידי גיטין שהכשירו חכמים: ואפקעוה רבנן לקידושין. כשיבא גט כזה אחריהם: תינח. למימר אפקעתא דקדיש בכספא דנימא גט זה עוקר הקידושין ועושה מעות מתנה מעיקרן: קדיש בביאה מאי. אפקעתא מעיקרא איכא בשלמא על ידי גט כשר אע"פ שהקידושין קיימים עד עכשיו גזירת הכתוב היא שהגט כורתו ומתיר איסורו מכאן ולהבא אבל זה שאינו גט מן התורה ואתה מכשירו מפני דעתו של זה שקידשה על דעת חכמים ושביטלו על פי חכמים צריך אתה לומר שמעיקרן לא יהו קידושין ואי קדיש בביאה ואתה עוקר קידושין למפרע מה תהא על ביאתו: שויוה רבנן לבעילתו. למפרע על ידי גט שהוא מדבריהם בעילת זנות ויש בהן כח לעשות כן שהרי הוא תלה בהן. שמעתי כל רבותי מפרשים דקדיש בכספא דקידושי דרבנן נינהו ואי אפשר לומר כן חדא דגזירה שוה היא קיחה קיחה משדה עפרון (קידושין דף ב.) וכל הלמד מגזירה שוה כמו שכתוב מפורש הוא לכל דבר ועוד אי דרבנן נינהו היאך סוקלין על ידו ומביאין חולין לעזרה על שגגתן וסוף סוף כי קא משנינן שויוה רבנן לבעילתו בעילת זנות על כרחך צריך אתה לפרש כמו שפירשתי שהקידושין נעקרין מעיקרן ולא מכאן ולהבא והמפרש לומר שויוה רבנן לכל מקדשי בביאה בעילת זנות טעות גמור הוא ובא להתיר אשת איש המתקדשת בביאה בלא גט מן הטעם הזה ולא מצינו זאת בהתלמוד: וכן לענין גיטין. אלפיכך קאי דטענינן טענת אונס בתנאי הגט להפקיעו: שבתי דינין קבועין בכל יום. כלומר שקביעות כל הימים שוה: והא בעינן שקדו. שיהא טורח בסעודה שלשה ימים: דטריח ליה. אם טרח לפני השבת ותיקן צורכי סעודה כונסה באחד בשבת או בשני בשבת: מאי

תוספות

וסברה דאניס. ומן הדין לית לן למיחש דלמא אניס הוא דרובן לא אניסי ולהכי קרי להו צנועות שמחמירים על עצמן אע"ג דמצי לאינסובי [א] וגבי פרוצות לא גרסינן וסברה דלא אניס אלא ואמרה דלא אניס פי' אפילו כשיצא הקול דלאניס אמרה דלא אניס או אפילו כשתדע היא עצמה דאניס ואחרים לא ידעו ואם תאמר מה תוך י"ב חודש נמי יהא גט מהאי טעמא דזימנין דלא מת וסברה דמת ומיעגנא ויתבה ויש לומר דמיתה קלא אית לה:

אדעתא דרבנן מקדש. לכן אומרים בשעת קידושין כדת משה וישראל:

ואפקעינהו רבנן לקידושין מינה. בריש השולח (גיטין לג.) פירשתי:

תינח דקדיש בכספא. דהפקר ב"ד היה הפקר והוו מעות מתנה וממילא יהו כל בעילותיו זנות קדיש בביאה מאי איכא למימר איך יפקיעו ביאה של קידושין ואפי' למ"ד בהאשה רבה (יבמות פט: ושם) דיש כח לחכמים לעקור דבר מן התורה היינו כגון דליכא עבירה כההיא דהאשה רבה דהדר לטיבלא אבל היכא דאיכא עבירה דמקודשת היא בביאה מאי איכא למימר ומשני שויוה רבנן בעילותיו בעילת זנות ואין כאן קידושין[ג]:

איכא דאמרי אמר רבא וכן לענין גיטין. פסק ר"ח כלישנא קמא דאין אונס בגיטין והביא ראיה מדקאמר סתמא הש"ס בריש השולח (גיטין לד. ושם) גבי ההוא דאמר אי לא נסיבנא עד תלתין יומין ליהוי גיטא כו' ואי משום אונס אין אונס בגיטין וכן נראה דאליבא דאיכא דאמרי הוו פירכי מכל הני דמייתי סייעתא ללישנא קמא ולא סמכינן אשינויי דחיקי וקשה לר"י דמסיק בפרק מי שאחזו (שם עג. ושם) דבין דאמר הרי זה גיטיך אם מתי מחולי זה בין אם אמר אם לא אעמוד מחולי זה ונפל עליו הבית או נשכו נחש או אכלו ארי דלא הוי גט אלמא דיש אונס בגיטין וליכא למימר דהתם לא מטעם דיש אונס קאמר דלא הוי גט אלא משום דבין אם מתי מחולי זה בין אם לא אעמוד משמע שימות מחמת זה החולי וכשנפל עליו הבית או נשכו נחש אינו גט דאין זה מחולי זה דהא מוכח בהדיא התם דמטעם דיש אונס הוא גבי ההוא גברא דזבין ארעא לחבריה וקביל עליה כל אונסא דאיתיליד בה כו' אמר רבא אונס דלא שכיח הוא ומייתי רבא סייעתא מהא דאכלו ארי אינו גט אלמא אונס דלא שכיח יש טענת אונס לרבא והכא קאמר רבא גופיה בלישנא קמא שהוא עיקר דאין אונס אפילו באונס דלא שכיח כדמוכח הסוגיא ואור"י דג' ענייני אונס הן דאונס דלא שכיח כלל כההיא דמי שאחזו אפי' ללישנא קמא דרבא דהכא יש אונס דלא שייך התם לתקן משום צנועות ומשום פרוצות דלעולם לא סברי צנועות דנפל עליו הבית או שהכישו נחש כיון דלא שכיח כלל ומשום פרוצות נמי ליכא למיחש כיון דלא שכיח שיעשה כן ואונס דשכיח כגון ההיא דפסקיה מברא אפילו לאיכא דאמרי אין אונס דאיבעי ליה לאתנויי אבל אונס דשכיח ולא שכיח בהא פליגי תרי לישני דרבא והלכתא כלישנא קמא דרבא כדפירשנו:

שבתי דינין קבועים בכל יום. וא"ת וכי תיקן עזרא שלא יהו בתי דינין קבועים בכל יום אלא בב' וה' בלבד ועוד קשה דאמרינן בשבת (ד' קכט: ושם) מי שיש לו זכות אבות יקיז בב' וה' וכי קודם תקנת עזרא לא היו מקיזין כל עיקר ואומר ר"ת דקודם תקנת עזרא לא היו קבועים בכל יום אלא כשהיו צריכין לשום דין היו יושבין בכל יום ויום ועזרא תיקן שיהיו קבועין בב' וה' וכל הרוצה לדון יבא וידון והיו יכולין להקיז בכל יום קודם תקנת עזרא כיון שלא היו קבועים ור"י תירץ שלא היו קבועים תחלה אלא בעיר אחת ועזרא תיקן בכל עיר ועיר בב' וה':

אשה נשאת בכל יום. קשה לרשב"א אמאי נשאת בכל יום תהא כאלמנה ותינשא בה' ותיבעל בששי לפי שנאמר בו ברכה לאדם וי"ל דמשום ברכה לא היו קובעים יום כדפרישית לעיל ובאלמנה נמי לא קבעו שתיבעל בששי משום ברכה גרידא אלא משום שקדו שיהא שמח עמה ג' ימים כדאמר לקמן (דף ה.) ובתולה דלא שייך ההוא טעמא דליכא למימר משכים לאומנתו והולך לו לפי שיש בה שבעת ימי המשתה הלכך משום ברכה גרידא לא היו קובעים יום:

אי איכא בתי דינין כו'. נראה לר"י דמכל מקום אין נשאת בששי דהא אין דינין בשבת ועתה נוהגין לישא אף בששי משום דאין ב"ד קבועין ואם יש לו טענת בתולין יכול לקבול בשבת בפני שלשה כמו בשאר ימות השבוע ועוד לפירוש הקונטרס דוקא בימיהם קבעו יום הנישואין משום שעל ידי כך יתברר הדבר ויבואו עדים מתוך שמתאספים העם לב"ד ואין שייך לומר עכשיו כך:

ובשני

מסורת הש"ס

א) יבמות ל: קי. גיטין לג. עג. בבא בתרא מח:, ב) [לעיל ב. לקמן ה.], ג) [ועי' תוס' ב"ב מח:].

גליון הש"ס

גמ' ואפקעינהו רבנן. עי' תשובת רשב"א סי' אלף קסב:

הגהות מהר"ב רנשבורג

א] תד"ה וסברה דאנים וכו' וגבי פרוצות ל"ג וכו'. עי' נדה יב ע"א תד"ה לנוע וכו':

עין משפט נר מצוה

ח א מיי' פ"י מהל' אישות הל' טו סמג עשין מח טוש"ע אה"ע סי' קד סעי' ג:

ליקוטי רש"י

אין כל דמקדש אדעתא דרבנן. תולה בדעת חכמים דהא כדת משה וישראל קאמר [יבמות צ:]. להיות קדושין תלוין כדת משה וישראל שהנהיגו חכמי ישראל והרי הם אמרו שיפקיעו כל קדושין שבישראל על ידי גט כזה הילכך פקעי שעל מנת כן קידשה [גיטין לג.]. ואפקעינהו רבנן. על ידי גט זה לקידושין מינה ושוינהו למעות דקידושין מתנה למפרע דהפקר ב"ד היה הפקר [יבמות שם]. דאע"ג דמן התורה ליהוו קידושין רבנן עקרינהו והפקירו אותן ועשו מעות מתנה ובמקום אחר מפרש דכל דמקדש אדעתא דרבנן מקדש כדת משה וישראל ורבנן אמור לא ליהוו קידושין נמצא שלא קדשה זה שהרי בדעת חכמים תלה והם אינם חפצים בקידושין הללו [רשב"ם ב"ב מח:]. תינח קדיש בכספא. איכא למימר אפקעתא דשוינהו למעות מתנה [יבמות שם]. איכא למימר דאפקעינהו לקידושין והוו מעות מתנה דהפקר ב"ד היה הפקר [שם קי.]. איכא למימר אפקעינהו לקידושין בגט דדבריהן ואמרו ליהוי מעות למפרע מתנה וממילא פקעו שהרי כשקידש ע"מ כן קידש [גיטין שם]. יכולין חכמים להפקיע הקדושין דהפקר ב"ד הפקר גבי ממון וכאילו קדשה בגזל ובחמס דמיא דלא הוו קדושין [רשב"ם שם]. קדיש בביאה. מאי הפקר ב"ד איכא למימר [יבמות קי.]. דקיימא לן בקידושין (דף ד) מכי יקח איש אשה ובעלה דאשה מתקדשת נמי בביאה מאי אפקעתא איכא למימר בהא ביאה [גיטין שם]. מאי אפקעתא איכא למימר האי ביאה מאי שויוה [יבמות צ:]. שעשה מעשה בגופה היאך יאמרו חכמים שלא תהא ביאה הרי בעל כרחנו ביאה היא [רשב"ם שם]. שויוה רבנן וכו'. כיון דבדעתא דרבנן תלה ורבנן אמור דכי יהיב לה גט כי האי תבטל ביאה דתיהוי בעילת זנות ואית דאמרי תינח קדיש בכספא דקידושי כסף דרבנן קדיש בביאה דקידושין דמדאורייתא נינהו מאי איכא למימר וטעות גדול הוא בידם דקידושי כסף דאורייתא נינהו ומג"ש דקיחה קיחה משדה עפרון גמר לה במסכת קידושין (דף ב.) וג"ש בסיני נאמרה וכל י"ג מדות ואי קידושי כסף מדרבנן מי קטלינן נפשא עלייהו דבעל ארוסה בסקילה ועוד מאי שינויא דשני שויוה רבנן כו' הא קשיא ליה היכי מצו רבנן לאפקועי מידי דאורייתא ומשני ליה שויוה רבנן הא נמי אפקעתא היא [שם צ.]. להיא ביאה למפרע ע"י גט זה בעילת זנות דאפקעו שם קידושין מינה ויש בהן כח לכך שהרי כשקידש על מנהג חוק דתם קידש כך אני מפרש בכל מקום מלבי ומרבותי קבלתי כל דמקדש אדעתא דרבנן מקדש דקידושי כסף דרבנן דלא כתיב בהדיא אלא גמרינן קיחה קיחה משדה עפרון והיינו דקפריך תינח דקדיש בכספא קדיש בביאה דכתיב בהדיא (דברים כד) כי יקח איש אשה ובעלה מאי איכא למימר היאך יכלו לעקור דבר מן התורה ומשני שויוה רבנן לבעילתו בעילת זנות של כל מקדש בביאה כדאמר התם (קידושין דף יב:) רב מנגיד אמאן דמקדש בביאה משום פריצותא ותשובות קשות יש בדבר חדא דגזירה שוה גופה תורה היא שהרי לא למדו נסקלין אלא בגזירה שוה ונותר שהוא בכרת מגזירה שוה למדנו ונערה המאורסה נהרגת בקידושי כסף ואי דרבנן מי מיקטלא ועוד דקמשני שויוה רבנן לבעילתו בעילת זנות הא דאורייתא היא וכי אמרן רב מנגיד אמאן דמקדש בביאה קידושין מיהא לא בטלי אלא הא והא דאורייתא והא דאית ברבנן כח לבטל מפני שבשעת קידושין תלה בדעתם לקדש כדת שהנהיגו חכמים בישראל [גיטין לג.]. ואית דמפרש תינח דקדיש בכספא כסף דרבנן הם אמרו והם אמרו וקידושין דדבריהן יכולין לעקור אבל קדיש בביאה דהוו קידושי דאורייתא מאי איכא למימר וטעות הוא בידם דמגזירה שוה ילפינן לקידושי כסף במסכת קדושין (דף ב.) וגם לכל דבר אתקוש הוויות להדדי ואמרינן בכריתות (דף ה.) אל תהי גזירה שוה קלה בעיניך שהרי נותר אחד מגופי תורה ולא למדה הכתוב אלא בגזירה שוה ועוד מאי האי דקמהדר ליה שויוה רבנן לבעילתו בעילת זנות הא כיון דמדאורייתא היא היאך יכולין לעשות ביאתו זנות אלא כיון דאדעתא דרבנן מקדש לא הוי קידושין דאמרי רבנן לא ליהוו קידושין ומתוך כך (נמלאת) [נעשית] מעלמה בעילת זנות [רשב"ם שם]. שקדו. עי' ליקוטי רש"י לעיל ב ע"א.

אַנַּפְשֵׁיהּ – **he has caused the loss to himself** and the *get* is valid.[24]

The Mishnah taught that virgins are married on Wednesday, in order that the husband, should he fail to find his bride a virgin, might go the next morning to court. Regarding which the Gemara comments:

אָמַר רַב שְׁמוּאֵל בַּר יִצְחָק – **Rav Shmuel bar Yitzchak stated:** לֹא שָׁנוּ אֶלָּא מִתַּקָּנַת עֶזְרָא וָאֵילָךְ – **This** ruling **was taught only from the enactment of Ezra and on,** שֶׁאֵין בָּתֵּי דִינִין קְבוּעִין אֶלָּא בְּשֵׁנִי וּבַחֲמִישִׁי – **for,** by this enactment, **the courts are convened only on Monday and Thursday.**[25] אֲבָל קוֹדֶם תַּקָּנַת עֶזְרָא – **But before the institution of Ezra,** שֶׁבָּתֵּי דִינִין קְבוּעִין בְּכָל יוֹם – **when the courts** could **convene every day,**[26] אִשָּׁה נִשֵּׂאת בְּכָל יוֹם – **a woman could get married every day,** too.

The Gemara asks:

קוֹדֶם תַּקָּנַת עֶזְרָא – What need is there to state what the law was **before the institution of Ezra?** מַאי דַּהֲוָה הֲוָה – **What was, was!** – ? –

The Gemara answers:

הָכִי קָאָמַר – **This is what [Rav Shmuel bar Yitzchak] meant:** אִי אִיכָּא בָּתֵּי דִינִין דִּקְבוּעִין הָאִידָּנָא – **If, nowadays, there are courts** in some locality **that convene** כְּקוֹדֶם תַּקָּנַת עֶזְרָא – **as they did before Ezra's enactment,**[27] אִשָּׁה נִשֵּׂאת בְּכָל יוֹם – then in that locality **a woman** (i.e. a virgin) **could be married any day** of the week.

The Gemara questions this:

הָא בְּעִינַן שָׁקְדוּ – Even if the courts do not convene on fixed days, how could a virgin be married any earlier than Wednesday; after all, **we need** to fulfill the enactment of the Sages who **"were diligent"** about the welfare of Jewish daughters and required that the husband should busy himself with preparing the wedding for at least three weekdays![28] – ? –

The Gemara answers:

דִּטְרִיחַ לֵיהּ – Rav Shmuel bar Yitzchak spoke of a case **where he** already **busied himself** with the preparations for three days before the Sabbath. In such a case, as long as the courts convene every day the marriage may take place on any weekday.[29]

NOTES

24. See ibid. note 33.

In any event the halachah follows the first version of Rava's teaching, and therefore claims of unavoidable circumstance have no force to void a conditional *get* (*Shulchan Aruch, Even HaEzer* 144:1; see there for exceptions to this rule).

25. [It was Ezra who instituted that the courts should convene every Monday and Thursday, as related in *Bava Kamma* 82a.]

26. Before Ezra's enactment the courts had no fixed day in which they convened; rather, they would convene whenever the necessity arose (*Rashi,* as explained by *Rosh; Rabbeinu Tam,* cited by *Tosafos;* cf. *Ri,* cited by *Tosafos; Ritva*).

27. I.e. without any fixed day; rather, convening as necessity demands (see previous note; *Shitah Mekubetzes* ד״ה מיהו).

28. [As we learned earlier (2a), it was for this reason that the Mishnah stated that virgins are married on Wednesday, rather than on Sunday.]

29. However, *nesuin* may not take place on Saturday, since it involves contractual obligations which make it akin to making a purchase on the Sabbath, which is forbidden (*Yerushalmi, Yoma* 1:1, cited by *Rosh; Shulchan Aruch, Even HaEzer* 64:5; regarding the prohibition to effect *kiddushin* on the Sabbath, see *Beitzah* 36b).

א) יבמות ל: קי. גיטין לג. עג. בבא בתרא מח: ב) [לעיל ב. לקמן ה.] ג) [ועי' תוס' ב"ב מח:]

גליון הש"ס

גמ' ואפקעינהו רבנן. עי' תשובת רשב"א סי' אלף קפב:

הגהות מהר"ב רנשבורג

א] תד"ה וסברה דאנים וכו' וגבי פרוצות לא"ג וכו'. ע"י נדה יב ע"א תד"ה לגוע וכו':

עין משפט נר מצוה

א א מיי' פ"י מהל' אישות הל' ט טור סמג עשין מח טוש"ע אה"ע סי' סד סעי' ג:

זימנין דלא אניס וסברה דאניס ומיעגנא ויתבה ומשום פרוצות דאי אמרת לא ליהוי גיטא זימנין דאניס ואמרה לא אניס ואזלא ומינסבא ונמצא גט בטל ובניה ממזרים ומי איכא מידי דמדאורייתא לא להוי גט ומשום צנועות ומשום פרוצות שרינן אשת איש לעלמא אין [א] כל דמקדש אדעתא דרבנן מקדש [ב] ואפקעינהו רבנן לקידושי מיניה אמר ליה רבינא לרב אשי תינח דקדיש בכספא קדיש בביאה מאי איכא למימר שויוה רבנן לבעילתו בעילת זנות איכא דאמרי אמר רבא וכן לענין גיטין אלמא קסבר רבא יש אונס בגיטין מיתיבי הרי זה גיטך אם לא באתי מכאן ועד שנים עשר חדש ומת בתוך שנים עשר חדש אינו גט מת הוא דאינו גט הא חלה הרי זה גט לעולם אימא לך חלה נמי אינו גט והיא גופה קמ"ל דאין גט לאחר מיתה הא תנא ליה רישא דלמא לאפוקי מדרבותינו ת"ש מעכשיו אם לא באתי מכאן ועד שנים עשר חדש ומת בתוך שנים עשר חדש הרי זה גט מאי לאו הוא הדין לחלה לא מת דוקא דלא ניחא ליה דתפול קמי יבם ת"ש מההוא דאמר להו אי לא אתינא מכאן ועד שלשים יום ליהוי גיטא אתא בסוף תלתין יומין ופסקיה מברא ואמר להו חזו דאתאי חזו דאתאי ואמר שמואל לא שמיה מתיא אונסא דשכיח שאני דכיון דאיבעי ליה לאתנויי ולא אתני איהו הוא דאפסיד אנפשיה אמר רב שמואל בר יצחק לא שנו אלא מתקנת עזרא ואילך שאין בתי דינין קבועין אלא בשני ובחמישי אבל קודם תקנת עזרא שבתי דינין קבועין בכל יום אשה נשאת בכל יום קודם תקנת עזרא מאי דהוה הוה הכי קאמר א אי איכא בתי דינין דקבועין האידנא כקודם תקנת עזרא אשה נשאת בכל יום הא בעינן [ג] שקדו דטריח ליה מאי

רש"י

זימנין דלא אניס. והוי גיטא: וסברה. דלמא אניס ולאו גט ותעגן ולא תנשא: ומינסבא. וכשיבא ויאמר נאנסתי נמצא גט בטל ובניה מן האחרון ממזרים לפיכך אמרו יהא גט: דמדאורייתא לא הוי גיטא. שמאינו טענת אונס מן התורה שנאמר (דברים כב) ולנערה לא תעשה דבר: כל המקדש. כל המקדש אשה על דעת שהנהיגו חכמי ישראל בישראל הוא מקדשה שיהיו קיימין קידושין לפי דברי חכמים ויהיו בטילים לפי דברי חכמים על ידי גיטין שהכשירו חכמים: ואפקעינהו רבנן לקידושין. כשיבא גט זה אחריהם: תינח. למימר אפקעתא מקדיש בכספא דנימא גט זה עוקר הקידושין ועושה מעות מתנה מעיקרן: קדיש בביאה מאי. אפקעתא מעיקרא איכא בשלמא על ידי גט כשר אע"פ שהקידושין קיימים עד עכשיו גזירת הכתוב היא שהגט כורתו ומתיר איסורו מכאן ולהבא אבל זה שאינו גט מן התורה ואתה מכשירו מפני דעתו של זה שקידשה על דעת חכמים ובטלו על פי חכמים צריך אתה לומר שמעיקרן לא יהו קידושין ואי קדיש בביאה ואתה עוקר קידושין למפרע מה תהא על ביאתו: שויוה רבנן לבעילתו. למפרע על ידי גט שהוא מדבריהם בעילת זנות ויש בהן כח לעשות כן שהרי הוא תלה בהן. שמעתי כל רבותי מפרשים דקדיש בכספא לקידושי דרבנן נינהו ואי אפשר לומר כן הלא גזירה שוה היא קיחה קיחה משדה עפרון (קידושין דף ב.) וכל הלמד מגזירה שוה כמו שכתוב מפורש הוא לכל דבר ועוד אי דרבנן נינהו היאך סוקלין על ידו ומביאין חולין לעזרה על שגגתן וסוף סוף כי קא משנינן שויוה רבנן לבעילתו בעילת זנות על כרחך צריך אתה לפרש כמו שפירשתי שהקידושין נעקרין מעיקרן ולא מכאן ולהבא והמפרש לומר שויוה רבנן לכל מקדשי בביאה בעילת זנות טעות גמור הוא וכא להתיר אשת איש המתקדשת בביאה בלא גט מן הטעם הזה ולא מצינו זאת בהתלמוד: וכן לענין גיטין. אלפיכך קאי דטענינן טענת אונס בתנאי הגט להפקיעו: שבתי דינין קבועין בכל יום. כלומר שקביעות כל הימים שוה: והא בעינן שקדו. שיהא טורח בסעודה שלשה ימים: דטריח ליה. אם טרח לפני השבת ותיקן צורכי סעודה כונסה באחד בשבת או בשני בשבת: מאי

תוספות

וסברה דאנים. ומן הדין לית לן למיחש דלמא אניס דרובן לא אניסי ולהכי קרי להו צנועות שממהרים על עצמן אע"ג דמצי לאינסובי [א] וגבי פרוצות לא גרסינן וסברה דלא אניס אלא ואמרה דלא אניס פי' אפילו כשיצא הקול דאניס אמרה דלא אניס או אפילו כשתדע היא עצמה דאניס ואחרים לא ידעו ואם תאמר מת מתוך י"ב חודש נמי יהא גט מהאי טעמא דזימנין דלא מת וסברה דמת ומיעגנא ויתבה ויש לומר דמיתה קלא אית לה:

אדעתא דרבנן מקדש. לכן אומרים בשעת קידושין כדת משה וישראל:

ואפקעינהו רבנן לקידושין מינה. בריש השולח (גיטין לג.) פירשתי:

תינח דקדיש בכספא. דהפקר ב"ד היה הפקר והוו מעות מתנה וממילא יהו כל בעילותיו זנות קדיש בביאה מאי איכא למימר איך יפקיעו ביאה של קידושין ואפי' למ"ד בהאשה רבה (יבמות פט: ושם) דיש כח לחכמים לעקור דבר מן התורה היינו כגון דליכא עבירה כההיא דהאשה רבה דהדר לטיבלא אבל היכא דאיכא עבירה דמקודשת היא בביאה מאי איכא למימר ומשני שויוה רבנן בעילותיו בעילת זנות ואין כאן קידושין ג):

איכא דאמרי אמר רבא וכן לענין גיטין. פסק ר"ח כלישנא קמא דאין אונס בגיטין והביא ראיה מדקאמר סתמא הש"ס בריש השולח (גיטין לד. ושם) גבי ההוא דאמר אי לא נסיבנא עד תלתין יומין ליהוי גיטא כו' ואי משום אונס אין אונס בגיטין וכן נראה דאליבא דאיכא דאמרי הוו פירכי מכל הני דמייתי סייעתא ללישנא קמא ולא סמכינן אשינויי דחיקי וקשה לר"י דמסיק בפרק מי שאחזו (שם עג. ושם) דבין דאמר הרי זה גיטך אם מתי מחולי זה בין אם אמר אם לא אעמוד מחולי זה ונפל עליו הבית או נשכו נחש או אכלו ארי דלא הוי גט אלמא דיש אונס בגיטין וליכא למימר דהתם לא מטעם דיש אונס קאמר דלא הוי גט אלא משום דבין אם מתי מחולי זה בין אם לא אעמוד משמע שימות מחמת זה החולי וכשנפל עליו הבית או נשכו נחש אינו גט דאין זה מחולי זה דהא מוכח בהדיא התם דמטעם דיש אונס הוא גבי ההוא גברא דזבין ארעא לחבריה וקביל עליה כל אונסא דאיתיליד בה כו' אמר רבא אונס דלא שכיח הוא ומייתי רבא סייעתא מהא דאכלו ארי אינו גט אלמא אונס דלא שכיח יש טענת אונס לרבא והכא קאמר רבא גופיה בלישנא קמא שהוא עיקר דאין אונס אפילו באונס דלא שכיח כדמוכח הסוגיא ואור"י דג' ענייני אונס הן דאונס דלא שכיח כלל כההיא דמי שאחזו אפי' ללישנא קמא דרבא דהכא יש אונס דלא שייך התם לתקן משום צנועות ומשום פרוצות דלעולם לא סברי צנועות דנפל עליו הבית או שהכישו נחש כיון דלא שכיח כלל ומשום פרוצות נמי ליכא למיחש כיון דלא שכיח שיעשה כן ואונס דשכיח כגון ההיא דפסקיה מברא אפילו לאיכא דאמרי אין אונס דאיבעי ליה לאתנויי אבל אונס דשכיח ולא שכיח בהא פליגי תרי לישני דרבא והלכתא כלישנא קמא דרבא כדפירשנו:

שבתי דינין קבועים בכל יום. וא"ת וכי תיקן עזרא שלא יהו בתי דינין קבועים בכל יום אלא בב' ובה' בלבד ועוד קשה דאמרינן בשבת (ד' קכט: ושם) מי שיש לו זכות אבות יקיז בב' ובה' וכי קודם תקנת עזרא לא היו מקיזין כל עיקר ואומר ר"ת דקודם תקנת עזרא לא היו קבועים בכל יום אלא כשהיו צריכין לשום דין היו יושבין בכל יום ויום ועזרא תיקן שיהיו קבועין בב' ובה' וכל הרוצה לדון יבא וידון והיו יכולין להקיז בכל יום קודם תקנת עזרא כיון שלא היו קבועים ור"י תירץ שלא היו קבועים תחלה אלא בעיר אחת ועזרא תיקן בכל עיר ועיר בב' ובה':

אשה נשאת בכל יום. קשה לרשב"א אמאי נשאת בכל יום תהא כאלמנה ותינשא בה' ותיבעל בששי לפי שנאמר בו ברכה לאדם וי"ל דמשום ברכה לא היו קובעים יום כדפרישית לעיל ובאלמנה נמי לא קבעו שתיבעל בששי משום ברכה גרידא אלא משום שקדו שיהא שמח עמה ג' ימים כדאמר לקמן (דף ה.) ובתולה דלא שייך ההוא טעמא דליכא למימר משכים לאומנתו והולך לו לפי שיש בה שבעת ימי המשתה הלכך משום ברכה גרידא לא היו קובעים יום:

אי איכא בתי דינין כו'. נראה לר"י דמכל מקום אין נשאת בששי דהא אין דנין בשבת ועתה נוהגין לישא אף בששי משום דאין ב"ד קבועין ואם יש לו טענת בתולין יכול לקבול בשבת בפני שלשה כמו בשאר ימות השבוע ועוד לפירוש הקונטרס דוקא בימיהם קבעו יום הנישואין משום שעל ידי כך יתברר הדבר ויבואו עדים מתוך שמתאספים העם לב"ד ואין שייך לומר עכשיו כך:

ובשני

ליקוטי רש"י

אין כל דמקדש אדעתא דרבנן. מולה בדעת חכמים דהלי כדת משה וישראל קאמר [יבמות צ:]. להיות קדושין חלין כדת משה וישראל שהנהיגו חכמי ישראל והרי הם אמרו שיפקיעו כל קדושין שישראל על ידי גט זה הילכך פקעי שעל מנת כן קידשה [גיטין לג.]. ואפקעינהו רבנן. על ידי גט זה לקדושין מינה ושויוהו דקדושין מתנה למפרע דהפקר ב"ד היה הפקר [יבמות שם]. דלאע"ג דמן התורה ליהוו קידושין רבנן עקרינהו והפקירו ממון ועשו מעות מתנה ובמקום אחר מפרש דכל דמקדש אדעתא דרבנן מקדש כדת משה וישראל ורבנן אמרו לא ליהוו קידושין נמצא דיש שלא קדשה זה שהרי בדעת חכמים תלה והם אינם מפלים בקידושין הללו [רשב"ם ב"ב מח:]. תינח קדיש בכספא. איכא למימר אפקעתא היא דשויוהו למעות מתנה [יבמות שם]. איכא למימר לאפקעינהו לקידושין והוו מעות מתנה דהפקר ב"ד היה הפקר [שם קי.]. איכא למימר אפקעינהו לקידושין בגט דדבריהן ואמרו ליהוי מעות למפרע מתנה וממילא פקעו שהרי כשקדש ע"מ כן קדיש [גיטין שם]. יכולין חכמים להפקיע קידושין דהפקר ב"ד הפקר גבי ממון ואלו קדשה בגזל ובחמס דמיה דלא הוי קדושין [רשב"ם שם]. קדיש בביאה. מאי הפקר ב"ד איכא למימר [יבמות קי.]. דקיימא לן בקידושין (דף ד) מכי יקח איש אשה ובעלה דאשה מתקדשת נמי בביאה מאי אפקעתא איכא למימר בהא ביאה [גיטין שם]. מאי אפקעתא איכא למימר האי ביאה מאי שויוה [יבמות צ:]. עשאה כגופה היאך יאמרו חכמים שלא תהא ביאה הרי בעל כרחו ביאה היא [רשב"ם שם]. שויוה רבנן וכו'. כיון דלדעתא דרבנן תלה ורבנן אמור דכי יהיב לה גט כי האי תבטל ביאה למיהוי בעילת זנות ולית דאמרי מיהו אונס קדיש בכספא דקידושי כסף דרבנן קדיש בביאה קידושין דמדאורייתא נינהו מאי איכא למימר וטעות גדול הוא בידם דקידושי כסף דאורייתא נינהו ומג"ש דקיחה קיחה משדה עפרון גמר לה במסכת קידושין (דף ב.) וג"ש בסיני נאמרה וכל י"ג מדות ואי קידושי כסף מדרבנן מי קטלינן נפשא עלייהו דבעל ארוסה בסקילה ועוד מאי שינויא דשני שויוה רבנן כו' אלא קשיא ליה היכי מצו רבנן לאפקועי מידי דאורייתא ומשני אפקעתא היא [שם צ:]. לההיא ביאה למפרע ע"י גט זה דלאפקעו שם קידושין מינה ויש בהן כח לכך שהרי כשקידש על דעת חוק דתם קידש על כל מפרש בכל מקום מלבד

ומרבותי קבלתי כל דמקדש אדעתא דרבנן מקדש דקידושי כסף דרבנן דלא כתיב בהדיא אלא גמרינן קיחה קיחה משדה עפרון והיינו דקפריך תינח דקדיש בכספא קדיש בביאה דכתיב בהדיא (דברים כד) כי יקח איש אשה ובעלה מאי איכא למימר היאך יכלו לעקור דבר מן התורה ומשני שויוה רבנן לבעילתו בעילת זנות של כל מקדש בביאה כדאמר התם (קידושין דף יב:) רב מנגיד אמאן דמקדש בביאה משום פריצותא ותשובות קשות יש גופה תורה היא שהרי לא למדו נסקלין אלא בגזירה שוה ועוד שהוא בכרת מגזירה שוה למדנו ונערה המאורסה נהרגת בקדושי כסף ואי דרבנן מי מיקטלא ועוד דקמשני שויוה רבנן לבעילתו בעילת זנות היכי הא דאורייתא היא וכי אמרן רב מנגיד אמאן דמקדש בביאה קידושין מיהא לא בטלי אלא הא והא דאורייתא והא דאית ברבנן כח לבטל מפני שבשעת קידושין תלה בדעתם לקדש כדת שהנהיגו חכמים בישראל [גיטין לג.]. ואית תינח דקדיש בכספא דקידושי כסף דרבנן הם אמרו וקידושין דדבריהן יכולין לעקור אבל קדיש בביאה דהוו קידושי דאורייתא מאי איכא למימר וטעות הוא בידם דמגזירה שוה ילפינן לקידושי כסף וגם לכל דבר אתקוש הוויות להדדי ואמרינן בכריתות (דף ה.) אל תהי גזירה שוה קלה בעיניך שהרי נותר אחד מגופי תורה ולא למדה הכתוב אלא בגזירה שוה ועוד מאי האי דקמהדר ליה שויוה רבנן לבעילתו דמדאורייתא היא היאך יכולין לעשות ביאתו זנות אלא כיון דלאדעתא דרבנן מקדש לא הוי קידושין דאמרי רבנן לא ליהוו קידושין ומתוך כך (נמצאת) [נעשית] מעצמה בעילת זנות [רשב"ם שם]. שקדו. עי' ליקוטי רש"י לעיל ב ע"ב.

Rav Ashi answers:

שַׁוְיוּהָ רַבָּנָן לִבְעִילָתוֹ בְּעִילַת זְנוּת – The Rabbis rendered his cohabitation a promiscuous cohabitation.[9]

The Gemara presents a different, and opposite, version of Rava's earlier statement:

אִיכָּא דְּאָמְרֵי – There are those who state the ruling about an unavoidable circumstance as follows: **אָמַר רָבָא – Rava said: וְכֵן לְעִנְיַן גִּיטִּין – And the same** applies **regarding *gittin;*** there, too, a claim of unavoidable circumstance is effective and voids a conditional divorce.[10]

The Gemara comments:

אַלְמָא קָסָבַר רָבָא יֵשׁ אוֹנֶס בְּגִיטִּין – Apparently Rava holds that there is force to a claim of **unavoidable circumstances with regard to** conditional ***gittin.***

The Gemara objects:[11]

מֵיתִיבֵי – They challenged this from a Mishnah:[12] **הֲרֵי זֶה גִּיטֵּיךְ** – If a man told his wife: **THIS IS YOUR *GET* אִם לֹא בָּאתִי מִכָּאן וְעַד שְׁנֵים עָשָׂר חֹדֶשׁ – IF I DO NOT RETURN WITHIN TWELVE MONTHS, וּמֵת בְּתוֹךְ שְׁנֵים עָשָׂר חֹדֶשׁ – AND HE DIED WITHIN** those **TWELVE MONTHS, אֵינוֹ גֵּט – IT IS NOT A** valid ***GET.***[13] **מֵת הוּא דְּאֵינוֹ גֵּט** – This implies that **it is** only **if he dies that it is not a** valid ***get,*** since a *get* cannot take effect after the husband's death; **הָא חָלָה הֲרֵי זֶה גֵּט – but had he** merely **become ill** and been prevented from returning on time **it is a** valid ***get,*** despite the fact that he was constrained from returning by a circumstance beyond his control.[14] – ? –

The Gemara answers:

לְעוֹלָם אֵימָא לָךְ חָלָה נַמִּי אֵינוֹ גֵּט – In fact I can still say to you that if he became ill it is also not a valid ***get.*** **וְהִיא גּוּפָהּ קָא מַשְׁמַע לָן – But** the Mishnah chose to speak of a case where the husband died – not in order to imply that the law would have been otherwise had he merely fallen ill, but, rather – because **it is informing us of this very** principle, **דְּאֵין גֵּט לְאַחַר מִיתָה – that a *get* cannot take effect after** the husband's **death.**[15]

The Gemara counters:

אֵין גֵּט לְאַחַר מִיתָה – Can the Tanna be teaching us only that **a *get* cannot take effect after** the husband's **death? הָא תָּנָא לֵיהּ רֵישָׁא – But the first part of the Mishnah** (i.e. an earlier Mishnah) already **taught that** principle![16] Clearly, then, the purpose of the latter Mishnah cannot be to reiterate a principle that we already know![17] – ? –

The Gemara answers:

דִּלְמָא לְאַפּוּקֵי מִדְּרַבּוֹתֵינוּ – Perhaps, as we said before, the latter Mishnah spoke of a case where the husband died – even though the *get* would have also been invalid had he simply fallen ill – because it wished to teach us that we may apply here the principle that a *get* cannot go into effect after the husband's death. However, the Mishnah's ultimate purpose in doing so was not to inform us of this principle itself; after all, we already know this principle from the earlier Mishnah. Rather, the Mishnah's purpose was to teach us that this principle (that the *get* cannot take effect after the husband's death) can be applied to this case, and thereby **to exclude** the view that we find elsewhere articulated by **"our Rabbis."**[18]

The Gemara attempts again to refute this version of Rava's statement:

תָּא שְׁמַע – Come, learn the end of the previously cited Mishnah:[19] **מֵעַכְשָׁיו אִם לֹא בָּאתִי מִכָּאן וְעַד שְׁנֵים עָשָׂר חֹדֶשׁ** – If a man said to his wife: This is your *get* **FROM NOW, IF I DO NOT RETURN WITHIN TWELVE MONTHS, וּמֵת בְּתוֹךְ שְׁנֵים עָשָׂר חֹדֶשׁ – AND HE DIED WITHIN** those **TWELVE MONTHS, הֲרֵי זֶה גֵּט – IT IS A** valid ***GET.***[20]

From which the Gemara infers:

מַאי לָאו הוּא הַדִּין לְחָלָה – Does this not mean that the same law would apply if **he became ill,** thus disproving Rava's thesis?[21]

The Gemara answers:

לֹא – No! מֵת דַּוְקָא – The *get* is valid **specifically** in a case where **he died, דְּלָא נִיחָא לֵיהּ דְּתִפּוֹל קַמֵּי יָבָם – for he does not wish [his wife] to fall before the *yavam.***[22]

The Gemara makes another attempt to refute Rava's thesis:

תָּא שְׁמַע – Come, learn a refutation **מֵהַהוּא דְּאָמַר לְהוּ – from the case of a certain person** who gave a *get* to his wife and **said to them: אִי לָא אָתֵינָא מִכָּאן וְעַד שְׁלֹשִׁים יוֹם – If I do not return within thirty days from now, לֶיהֱוֵי גִּיטָּא – let this be a** valid ***get.*** **אָתָא בְּסוֹף תְּלָתִין יוֹמִין – He came** back **at the end of thirty days, וּפַסְקֵיהּ מַבְרָא – but the** river **crossing stopped him. וְאָמַר לְהוּ – And he said to them** from the far side of the river: **חֲזוּ דַּאֲתַאי חֲזוּ דַּאֲתַאי – Look, I have come! Look, I have come! וְאָמַר שְׁמוּאֵל – But Shmuel said: לָא שְׁמֵיהּ מָתְיָא – It is not called an arrival** into the town, since he did not actually make it into town on time, and the *get* is valid.[23] Apparently, the fact that he was constrained from returning by circumstances beyond his control does not void the *get;* this, then, would seem to refute Rava's thesis. – ? –

The Gemara answers:

אוֹנְסָא דִּשְׁכִיחַ שָׁאנֵי – A commonly occurring constraint, such as the ferry being on the far side of the river, **is different. דְּכֵיוָן דְּאִיבָּעֵי לֵיהּ לְאַתְנוּיֵי – For since he ought to** have foreseen the possibility of the ferry being on the far side of the river when he returned **and made** some appropriate **stipulation, וְלָא אַתְנֵי – and he did not make any** such **stipulation, אִיהוּ הוּא דְּאַפְסִיד**

NOTES

9. [The Gemara retreats from its previous assumption and posits that, in fact,] the husband empowered the Rabbis to redefine the act of cohabitation that constituted the betrothal as a simple act of promiscuous copulation, without power to effect a betrothal (*Rashi*).

10. Just as Rav Yosef stated that if the husband was constrained by circumstances beyond his control from marrying his bride on time he does not become obligated to support her, so too if the condition of the *get* was fulfilled only because of circumstances beyond his control the *get* is not valid (*Rashi*). This is the exact opposite of the previous version of Rava's teaching.

11. The discussion that follows echoes that in the previous version, but on opposite lines; those sources that the Gemara cited earlier as possible sources for Rava's view are now cited as seeming refutations.

12. *Gittin* 76b.

13. See above, 2b note 12.

14. See ibid. note 13.

15. See ibid. note 14.

16. By stating (*Gittin* 72a) that if a gravely ill man gave his wife a *get* and said: "This is your *get* if I die," or "This is your *get* from this illness," or "This is your *get* after my death," the *get* is void. The Gemara quoted this Mishnah more fully in the previous version.

17. See above, 2b note 18.

18. Who disagreed with the Mishnah and, in the case where the husband gave a *get* on condition that he not return within twelve months and then died, validated the *get* and allowed the woman to marry without need of *chalitzah,* reasoning that the date of the *get* attests to its retroactive nature, as the Gemara explained in the previous version.

19. *Gittin* 76b.

20. See above, 2b notes 25-26.

21. See ibid. note 27.

22. See ibid. note 28.

23. See ibid. notes 29-32.

א) יבמות צ: קי. גיטין לג. עג. בבא בתרא מח: ב) [לעיל ב. לקמן ה.] ג) [ועי' תוס' ב"ב מח:]

עין משפט נר מצוה

ח א מיי' פ"י מהל' אישות הל' טו סמג עשין מח טוש"ע אה"ע סי' סד סעי' ג:

גליון הש"ס

גמ' ואפקעינהו רבנן. עי' תשובת רשב"א סי' אלף קסב:

הגהות מהר"ב רנשבורג

א] תד"ה וסברה דאניס וכו' וגבי פרוצות ל"ג וכו'. עי' נדה יב ע"א תד"ה נגוע וכו':

זימנין דלא אניס וסברה דאניס ומיעגנא ויתבה ומשום פרוצות דאי אמרת לא ליהוי גיטא זימנין דאניס ואמרה לא אניס ואזלא ומינסבא ונמצא גט בטל ובניה ממזרים ומי איכא מידי דמדאורייתא לא להוי גט ומשום צנועות ומשום פרוצות שרינן אשת איש לעלמא אין [א] כל דמקדש אדעתא דרבנן מקדש ° ואפקעינהו רבנן לקידושי מיניה אמר ליה רבינא לרב אשי תינח קדיש בכספא קדיש בביאה מאי איכא למימר שויוה רבנן לבעילתו בעילת זנות איכא דאמרי אמר רבא וכן לענין גיטין אלמא קסבר רבא יש אונס בגיטין מיתיבי הרי זה גיטיך אם לא באתי מכאן ועד שנים עשר חדש ומת בתוך שנים עשר חדש אינו גט מת הוא דאינו גט הא חלה הרי זה גט לעולם אימא לך חלה נמי אינו גט והיא גופה קמ"ל דאין גט לאחר מיתה אין גט לאחר מיתה הא תנא ליה רישא דלמא לאפוקי מדרבותינו ת"ש מעכשיו אם לא באתי מכאן ועד שנים עשר חדש ומת בתוך שנים עשר חדש הרי זה גט מאי לאו הוא הדין לחלה לא מת דוקא דלא ניחא ליה דתפול קמי יבם ת"ש מההוא דאמר להו אי לא אתינא מכאן ועד שלשים יום ליהוי גיטא אתא בסוף תלתין יומין ופסקיה מברא ואמר להו חזו דאתאי חזו דאתאי ואמר שמואל לא שמיה מתיא אונסא דשכיח שאני דכיון דאיבעי ליה לאתנויי ולא אתני איהו הוא דאפסיד אנפשיה אמר רב שמואל בר יצחק לא שנו אלא מתקנת עזרא ואילך שאין בתי דינין קבועין אלא בשני ובחמישי אבל קודם תקנת עזרא שבתי דינין קבועין בכל יום אשה נשאת בכל יום קודם תקנת עזרא מאי דהוה הוה הכי קאמר [ב] אי איכא בתי דינין דקבועין האידנא כקודם תקנת עזרא אשה נשאת בכל יום הא בעינן [ג] שקדו דטריח ליה מאי

רש"י

זימנין דלא אניס. והוי גיטא: **וסברה.** דלמא אניס ואינו גט ומדלג להינשא: **ומינסבא.** וכשיבא ויאמר נאנסתי נמלא גט בטל ובניה מן האחרון ממזרים לפיכך אמרו יהא גט: **דמדאורייתא לא הוי גיטא.** שמלינו טענת אונס מן התורה שנאמר (דברים כב) ולנערה לא תעשה דבר: **כל המקדש.** אשה על דעת שהנהיגו חכמי ישראל בישראל הוא מקדשה שיהיו קיימין קידושין לפי דברי חכמים ויהיו בטלים לפי דברי חכמים על ידי גיטין שהכשירו חכמים: **ואפקעוה רבנן לקידושין.** כשיבא גט כזה אחריהם: **תינח.** למימר אפקעתא דקדיש בכספא דמלא גט זה עוקר הקידושין ועושה מעות מתנה מעיקרן: **קדיש בביאה מאי.** אפקעתא מעיקרא איכא בשלמא על ידי גט כשר אע"פ שהקידושין קיימים עד עכשיו גזירת הכתוב היא שהגט כורתו ומתיר איסורו מכאן ולהבא אבל זה שאינו גט מן התורה ואתה מכשירו מפני דעתו של זה שקידשה על דעת חכמים ושביטלו על פי חכמים צריך אתה לומר שמעיקרן לא יהו קידושין ואי קדיש בביאה ואתה עוקר קידושין למפרע מה תהא על ביאתו: **שויוה רבנן לבעילתו.** למפרע על ידי גט שהוא מדבריהם בעילת זנות ויש בהן כח לעשות כן שהרי הוא תלה בהן. שמעתי כל רבותי מפרשים דקדיש בכספא דקידושי דרבנן נינהו ואי אפשר לומר כן חדא דגזירה שוה היא קיחה קיחה משדה עפרון (קידושין דף ב.) וכל הלמד מגזירה שוה כמו שכתוב מפורש הוא לכל דבר ועוד אי דרבנן נינהו היאך סוקלין על ידו ומבילין לעזרה על שגגתן וסוף סוף כי קא משנינן שויוה רבנן לבעילתו בעילת זנות על כרחך צריך אתה לפרש כמו שפירשתי שהקידושין נעקרין מעיקרן ולא מכאן ולהבא והמפרש לומר שויוה רבנן לכל מקדשי בביאה בעילת זנות טעות גמור הוא ובא להתיר אשת איש המתקדשת בביאה בלא גט מן הטעם הזה ולא מצינו זאת בהתלמוד: **וכן לענין גיטין.** אלפיכך קאי דטעינן טענת אונס בתנאי הגט להפקיעו: **שבתי דינין קבועין בכל יום.** כלומר שקביעות כל הימים שוה: **והא בעינן שקדו.** שיהא טורח בסעודה שלשה ימים: **דטריח ליה.** אם טרח לפני השבת ותיקן צורכי סעודה כונסה באחד בשבת או בשני בשבת:

תוספות

וסברה דאניס. ומן הדין לית לן למיחש דלמא אניס הוא דרבנן לא אניסי ולהכי קרי להו לנועות שמחמירים על עלמן אע"ג דמלי לאינסובי [א] וגבי פרולות לא גרסינן וסברה דלא אניס אלא ואמרה דלא אניס פי' אפילו כשיצא הקול דאניס אמרה דלא אניס או אפילו כשתדע שהיא עלמה דאניס ואחרים לא ידעו ואם תאמר מת מתוך י"ב חודש נמי יהא גט מהאי טעמא דזימנין דלא מת וסברה דמת ומיעגנא ויתבה ויש לומר דמיתה קלא אית לה: **אדעתא** דרבנן מקדש. לכן אומרים בשעת קידושין כדת משה וישראל: **ואפקעינהו** רבנן לקידושין מינה. בריש השולח (גיטין לג.) פירשתי: **תינח** דקדיש בכספא. דהפקר ב"ד היה הפקר והוו מעות מתנה וממילא יהו כל בעילותיו זנות קדיש בביאה מאי איכא למימר איך יפקיעו ביאה של קידושין ואפי' למ"ד בהאשה רבה (יבמות פט:) דיש כח לחכמים לעקור דבר מן התורה היינו כגון דליכא עבירה כההיא דהאשה רבה דהדר לטיבלא אבל היכא דאיכא עבירה דמקודשת היא בביאה מאי איכא למימר ומשני שויוה רבנן בעילותיו בעילת זנות ואין כאן קידושין: **איכא** דאמרי אמר רבא וכן לענין גיטין. פסק ר"ח כלישנא קמא דאין אונס בגיטין והביא ראיה מדקאמר סתמא הש"ס בריש השולח (גיטין לג. ושם) גבי ההוא דאמר אי לא מיגנלא עד תלתין יומין ליהוי גיטא כו' ואי משום אונס אין אונס בגיטין וכן נראה דאליבא דאיכא דאמרי הוו פירכי מכל הני דמייתי סייעתא ללישנא קמא ולא סמכינן אשינויי דחיקי וקשה לר"י דמסיק בפרק מי שאחזו (שם עג. ושם) דבין דאמר הרי זה גיטיך אם מתי מחולי זה בין אם לא אעמוד מחולי זה ונפל עליו הבית או נשכו נחש או אכלו ארי דלא הוי גט אלמא דיש אונס בגיטין וליכא למימר דהתם לא מטעם דיש אונס קאמר דלא הוי גט אלא משום דבין אם מתי מחולי זה בין אם לא אעמוד משמע שימות מחמת זה החולי וכשנפל עליו הבית או נשכו נחש אינו גט דאין זה מחולי זה דהא מוכח בהדיא התם דמטעם דיש אונס הוא גבי ההוא גברא דזבין ארעא לחבריה וקביל עליה כל אונסא דאיתיליד בה כו' אמר רבא אונס דלא שכיח הוא ומייתי רבא סייעתא מהא דאכלו ארי אינו גט אלמא אונס דלא שכיח יש טענת אונס לרבא והכא קאמר רבא גופיה בלישנא קמא שהוא עיקר דאין אונס אפילו באונס דלא שכיח כדמוכח הסוגיא ואור"י דג' ענייני אונס הן דאונס דלא שכיח כלל כההיא דמי שאחזו אפי' ללישנא קמא דרבא דהכא יש אונס דלא שייך התם לתקן משום נועות ומשום פרולות דלעולם לא סברי נועות דנפל עליו הבית או שהכישו נחש כיון דלא שכיח כלל ומשום פרולות נמי ליכא למיחש כיון דלא שכיח שיעשה כן ואונס דשכיח כגון ההיא דפסקיה מברא אפילו לאיכא דאמרי אין אונס דאיבעי ליה לאתנויי אבל אונס דשכיח ולא שכיח בהא פליגי תרי לישני דרבא והלכתא כלישנא קמא דרבא כדפירשנו: **שבתי** דינין קבועים בכל יום. וא"ת וכי תיקן עזרא שלא יהו בתי דינין קבועים בכל יום אלא בב' וה' בלבד ועוד קשה דאמרינן בשבת (ד' קכט: ושם) מי שיש לו זכות אבות יקיז בב' וה' וכי קודם תקנת עזרא לא היו מקיזין כל עיקר ואומר ר"ת דקודם תקנת עזרא לא היו קבועים בכל יום אלא כשהיו לריכין לשום דין היו יושבין בכל יום ויום ועזרא תיקן שיהיו קבועין בב' וה' וכל הרולה לדון יבא וידון והיו יכולין להקיז בכל יום קודם תקנת עזרא כיון שלא היו קבועים ור"י תירץ שלא היו קבועים תחלה אלא בעיר אחת ועזרא תיקן בכל עיר ועיר בב' וה': **אשה** נשאת בכל יום. קשה לרשב"א אמאי נשאת בכל יום תהא כאלמנה ותינשא בה' ותיבעל בששי לפי שנאמר בו ברכה לאדם וי"ל דמשום ברכה לא היו קובעים יום כדפרישית לעיל ובאלמנה נמי לא קבעו שתיבעל בששי משום ברכה גרידא אלא משום שקדו שיהא שמח עמה ג' ימים כדאמר לקמן (דף ה.) ובתולה דלא שייך ההוא טעמא דליכא למימר משכים לאומנתו והולך לו לפי שיש בה שבעת ימי המשתה הלכך משום ברכה גרידא לא היו קובעים יום: **אי** איכא בתי דינין כו'. נראה לר"י דמכל מקום אין נשאת בששי דהא אין דנין בשבת ועתה נוהגין לישא אף בששי משום דאין ב"ד קבועין ואם יש לו טענת בתולין יכול לקבול בשבת בפני שלשה כמו בשאר ימות השבוע ועוד לפירוש הקונטרס דוקא בימיהם קבעו יום הנישואין משום שעל ידי כך יתברר הדבר ויבואו עדים מתוך שמתאספים העם לב"ד ואין שייך לומר עכשיו כך:

ובשני

ומרבותי קבלתי כל דמקדש אדעתא דרבנן מקדש דקדושי כסף דרבנן דלא כתיב בהדיא אלא גמרינן קיחה קיחה משדה עפרון והיינו דקפריך תינח דקדיש בכספא קדיש בביאה דכתיב בהדיא (דברים כד) כי יקח איש אשה ובעלה מאי איכא למימר היאך יכלו לעקור דבר מן התורה ומשני שויוה רבנן לבעילתו בעילת זנות של כל מקדש בביאה כדאמר התם (קידושין דף יב:) רב מנגיד אמאן דמקדש בביאה משום פריצותא ותשובות קשות יש בדבר חדא דגזירה שוה גופה תורה היא שהרי לא למדו נסקלין אלא בגזירה שוה ונותר שהוא בכרת מגזירה שוה למדנו ונערה המאורסה נהרגת בקידושי כסף ואי דרבנן מי מיקטלא ועוד דקמשני שויוה רבנן לבעילתו בעילת זנות היכי מצו [illegible] הא דאורייתא היא וכי אמרן רב מנגיד אמאן דמקדש בביאה קידושין מיהא לא בטלי אלא הא והא דאורייתא והא דאית ברבנן כח לבטל מפני שבשעת קידושין תלה בדעתם לקדש כדת שהנהיגו חכמים בישראל [גיטין לג.] [illegible] תינח דקדיש בכספא דקידושי כסף דרבנן הם אמרו והם אמרו וקידושין דדבריהן יכולין לעקור אבל קדיש בביאה דהוו קידושי דאורייתא מאי איכא למימר וטעות הוא בידם דמגזירה שוה ילפינן לקידושי כסף [illegible] וגם לכל דבר אתקוש הוויות להדדי ואמרינן בכריתות (דף ה.) אל תהי גזירה שוה קלה בעיניך שהרי נותר אחד מגופי תורה ולא למדה הכתוב אלא בגזירה שוה ועוד מאי האי דקמהדר ליה שויוה רבנן לבעילתו [illegible] דמדאורייתא היא היאך יכולין לעשות ביאתו זנות אלא כיון דאדעתא דרבנן מקדש לא הוי קידושין דאמרי רבנן לא ליהוו קידושין ומתוך כך (נמלאת) [נעשית] מעלמה בעילת זנות [רשב"ם שם]. שקדו. עי' ליקוטי רש"י לעיל ב ע"ב.

ליקוטי רש"י

אין כל דמקדש אדעתא דרבנן. תולה בדעת חכמים דהא כדת משה וישראל קאמר [יבמות צ:]. להיות קידושין חלין כדת משה וישראל שהנהיגו חכמי ישראל והרי הם אמרו שיפקיעו כל קידושין שבישראל על ידי גט כזה הילכך פקעי שעל מנת כן קידשה [גיטין לג.]. **ואפקעינהו רבנן.** על ידי גט זה לקידושין מינה ושוינהו למעות דקידושין מתנה למפרע דהפקר ב"ד היה הפקר [יבמות שם]. דאע"ג דמן התורה ליהוו קידושין רבנן עקרינהו והפקירו אותן ועשו מעות מתנה ובמקום אחר מפרש דכל דמקדש אדעתא דרבנן מקדש כדת משה וישראל ורבנן אמור לא ליהוו קידושין נמלא שלא קדשה זה שהרי בדעת חכמים תלה והם אינם חפלים בקידושין הללו [רשב"ם ב"ב מח:]. **תינח קדיש בכספא.** איכא למימר אפקעתא דשוינהו למעות מתנה [יבמות שם]. איכא למימר דאפקעינהו לקידושין ושוו מעות מתנה דהפקר ב"ד היה הפקר [שם קי.]. איכא למימר אפקעינהו לקידושין בגט דדבריהן ואמרו ליהוי מעות למפרע מתנה וממילא פקעו שהרי כשקידש ע"מ כן קידש [גיטין שם]. יכולין חכמים להפקיע הקידושין דהפקר ב"ד הפקר גבי ממון וכאילו קדשה בגזל וכחמס דמילתא דלא הוו קדושין [רשב"ם שם]. **קדיש בביאה.** מאי [illegible]

זִימְנִין דְּלֹא אָנִיס – there are times when he would not be constrained by circumstances from returning, but, rather, willingly did not return, and the *get* is therefore valid, **וְסָבְרָה דְּאָנִיס – but she will think that he was forced** to delay and the *get* is not valid, **וּמִיעַגְנָא וְיָתְבָה – and she will sit** unmarried **as an *agunah.***[1] And, conversely, **וּמִשּׁוּם פְּרוּצוֹת – because of brazen [women], דְּאִי אָמְרַתְּ לֹא לֶיהֱוֵי גִּיטָּא – for if you say that it is not a** valid ***get,*** **זִימְנִין דְּאָנִיס – there are times when [the husband] would,** in fact, **be constrained** from returning by circumstances beyond his control, so that the *get* is not valid, **וְאָמְרָה לֹא אָנִיס – but she will say that he was not constrained,** but failed to return of his own volition, **וְאָזְלָא וּמִינַּסְבָא – and she will go and marry** another man;[2] **וְנִמְצָא גֵט בָּטֵל וּבָנֶיהָ מַמְזֵרִים – and** later, when the husband arrives and it is revealed that he was constrained from returning by circumstances beyond his control,[3] **her *get* will be discovered to be void and her children** by the new husband **to be *mamzerim.***[4] The Rabbis therefore decreed that the fact that the husband was constrained from returning should have no power to invalidate the *get;* hence, the "modest" women will have nothing to fear in remarrying and the marriage of the "brazen" women will not have any untoward consequences.

Which leads the Gemara to ask:

וּמִי אִיכָּא מִידֵי דְּמִדְּאוֹרַיְיתָא לֹא לֶהֱוֵי גֵט – But can there be such a thing that, from a Biblical standpoint, it is not a valid *get,* **וּמִשּׁוּם צְנוּעוֹת וּמִשּׁוּם פְּרוּצוֹת שָׁרֵינַן אֵשֶׁת אִישׁ לְעָלְמָא – and** yet **because of** our concern about **modest and brazen [women] we permit a married woman to the world at large,** i.e. to marry someone else?[5]

The Gemara answers:

אִין – Yes, the decree permits her to remarry, **כָּל דִּמְקַדֵּשׁ –** because **whoever betroths** a woman in Jewish marriage **אַדַּעְתָּא דְרַבָּנָן מְקַדֵּשׁ – betroths** her **subject to the will of the Rabbis, וְאַפְקְעִינְהוּ רַבָּנָן לְקִידוּשֵׁי מִינֵּיהּ – and** in this case, **the Rabbis abrogated his** original **betrothal.**[6]

The Gemara asks:

אָמַר לֵיהּ רָבִינָא לְרַב אַשִׁי – Ravina said to Rav Ashi: תִּינַח קַדֵּישׁ בְּכַסְפָּא – This explanation **is understandable if [the husband]** originally **betrothed** his wife **with money;** we can then understand how the betrothal becomes abrogated.[7] **קַדֵּישׁ בְּבִיאָה מַאי אִיכָּא לְמֵימַר – But if he betrothed her through cohabitation, what can be said** to explain how the betrothal becomes abrogated?[8]

NOTES

1. [An עֲגוּנָה, *agunah* (literally: a tied woman), is a woman who cannot remarry because she remains legally bound to her husband. This occurs when the husband is missing and it is unknown whether he is dead or alive, or when his whereabouts are known but he has abandoned his wife and she is unable to obtain a valid *get* from him.]

The pious wife will be concerned that perhaps her husband failed to return because of circumstances beyond his control, thereby voiding the *get;* she may therefore be reluctant to remarry (*Rashi*). Such apprehension goes beyond the requirements of the law; strictly speaking, once the husband fails to return on time we are entitled to assume that he did so of his own volition and the *get* is valid, and we need not concern ourselves about the relatively remote possibility that he wanted to return but was delayed by circumstances beyond his control. Nevertheless these modest women might be more stringent than the law requires (*Rashi,* as explained by *Shitah Mekubetzes* ד״ה ומלשון רש״י; *Tosafos, Rashba* et al.).

2. Actually, this "brazen woman" is doing no more than she is entitled by the letter of the law (see previous note); the Gemara refers to her as "brazen" only to distinguish her from the "modest" women of whom the Gemara spoke previously (*Rashi,* as understood by *Shitah Mekubetzes* ד״ה ומלשון רש״י; *Re'ah* cited by *Shitah Mekubetzes* ד״ה וכן כתבו הרא״ה).

Alternatively, the Gemara speaks of a woman who is actually privy to information indicating that her husband was constrained from return by circumstances beyond his control, but she suppresses this information in order to be allowed to remarry; for this reason she is termed "brazen" (*Tosafos;* see there for yet another explanation; see also *Rashba, Ritva* et al.).

3. *Rashi.*

4. [A *mamzer* is the offspring of any forbidden union that is punishable by *kares.* This includes the offspring of an adulterous association. A *mamzer* may marry only a *mamzeress* (or other *pesulei kahal,* i.e. someone who is, likewise, barred by the circumstance of their genealogy from marrying an ordinary Jew) or a convert.]

5. [What power do the Rabbis have to allow a woman to remarry on the basis of a *get* that is Biblically void? Is she not still married to the first husband by Biblical law? The Rabbis do not have the power to actively abrogate any Torah law.]

The reason the *get* is invalid, on a Biblical level, is the following: In general, the Torah does not hold a person liable for actions that he is constrained to perform against his will. This is derived from the following verse, which speaks of a betrothed maiden who was raped: *But you shall do nothing to the maiden, the maiden has committed no sin [punishable by] death* (*Deuteronomy* 22:26). Similarly, we derive from here that a *get,* even if it was drawn up and delivered with the husband's consent, is not valid if its validity came about by the husband's having been constrained to fulfill its conditions (*Rashi,* as explained by *R' Shmuel Rozovsky, Shiurei R' Shmuel* §2; cf. *Ran* to *Nedarim* 27a ד״ה קטלא שאני).

6. Whenever a man betroths a woman, he does so with the understanding that the marriage be acceptable to the Rabbis. The marriage, therefore, is maintained by the sufferance of the Rabbis, who may annul it through a *get* that they deem valid [regardless of its actual validity by Biblical law] (*Rashi*). (Regarding the mechanism by which this annulment is accomplished, see next note.) This is reflected by the standard form of the husband's betrothal declaration: "You are hereby betrothed to me . . . *in accordance with the law of Moses and Israel*" (*Rashi* to *Yevamos* 90b; *Tosafos*).

This rule is limited in scope and may not be applied except in those instances where the Gemara explicitly invokes it (*Teshuvos HaRashba* §1185; see also *Teshuvos Rivash* §339).

7. [As stated in the first Mishnah of *Kiddushin, erusin* can be effected either by giving the woman money (or some other item of value), a betrothal document, or through cohabitation for the purpose of effecting the betrothal.] Now if the husband effected *erusin* through money, then we can assume that his intent was that should the Rabbis later abrogate the marriage — which the husband has implicitly empowered them to do — then the original transfer of money, which constituted the *erusin,* should be redefined as a simple gift of money rather than as an instrument of effecting betrothal; indeed, this is the mechanism by which the marriage is annulled (*Rashi,* as explained by *Shitah Mekubetzes*).

8. Presumably the husband intended this as a marital act; how, then, can the Rabbis rescind its power to effect the marriage? (ibid.; cf. *Tosafos;* cf. also *Teshuvos Avnei Nezer, Even HaEzer* 121:30).

Now, in ordinary cases of divorce this does not present any problem. For even though the marriage was certainly in effect, the Torah decreed that a valid *get* terminates the marriage from that point forward and permits the woman to remarry. But in the case at hand the *get* itself is, by Biblical law, flawed, and its sole power derives from the husband's understanding at the time of *erusin* that the validity of his act of *erusin* is dependent upon the approval of the Rabbis, whom he empowers to redefine the act of *erusin* as a simple gift. But where the *erusin* was effected through cohabitation, the Gemara now assumes, the husband unequivocally intended it as a marital act, since he would not have wanted to engage in mere promiscuous philandering; how, then, can the marriage be annulled? (*Rashi,* as explained *Shitah Mekubetzes*).

[*Rashi* also cites another explanation of the Gemara's question, on the authority of his teachers, in which the Gemara's question is based on the assumption that betrothal by means of money is a Rabbinic institution in the first place, and can therefore be abrogated at the will of the Rabbis, whereas betrothal by means of cohabitation is a Biblical institution. *Rashi,* however, forcefully rejects this interpretation, asserting that betrothal by means of money is no less Biblically valid than any other means of betrothal; see, however, *Rambam, Hil. Ishus* 1:2 with commentaries; *Teshuvos Birkas Avraham* §44).]

months) *retroactively* from the time it was drawn up. Hence, its effective date precedes the husband's death and the *get* is valid.[22]

It was this view of "our Rabbis" that the Mishnah wished to contest, and for that reason it chose to speak of a case where the husband died, in order to indicate that, in the Mishnah's view, the effective date of such a *get* is not, as "our Rabbis" would have it, when the *get* is dated, but, rather, twelve months later, when the condition (that the husband fail to arrive) is fulfilled, by which time he is dead and we can therefore apply the principle that a *get* cannot go into effect after the husband's death.[23] Had it not wished to illustrate this principle, however, the Mishnah might, perhaps, have spoken of a case where the husband fell ill; for there too, perhaps the *get* is not valid. Thus, no proof can be brought from here for Rava's thesis that a claim of unavoidable circumstance does not invalidate a conditional *get*.

Having ruled out one possible source for Rava's thesis, the Gemara seeks another:

וְאֶלָּא מְסֵיפָא – **Rather,** it can be derived **from the end** of that Mishnah, which stated:[24] מֵעַכְשָׁיו אִם לֹא בָּאתִי מִכָּאן וְעַד שְׁנֵים עָשָׂר חֹדֶשׁ – If a man said to his wife: This is your *get* FROM NOW, IF I DO NOT RETURN WITHIN TWELVE MONTHS,[25] וּמֵת בְּתוֹךְ שְׁנֵים עָשָׂר חֹדֶשׁ – AND HE DIED WITHIN those TWELVE MONTHS, הֲרֵי זֶה גֵּט – IT IS A valid *GET*.[26]

From which the Gemara infers:

מֵת וְהוּא הַדִּין לְחָלָה – The *get* is valid if **he died and likewise if he fell ill.**[27] This, then, proves Rava's thesis.

The Gemara rejects the proof:

דִּלְמָא מֵת דַּוְקָא – **Perhaps** the *get* is valid **specifically** in a case where **he died,** דְּלָא נִיחָא לֵיהּ דְּתִפּוֹל קַמֵּי יָבָם – **for he does not wish [his wife] to fall before the** ***yavam.***[28]

The Gemara concedes the point and seeks another source for Rava's teaching:

אֶלָּא מֵהָא – **Rather,** Rava's source is **from the following:** דְּהַהוּא דְּאָמַר לְהוּ – **For a certain person once said to them:**[29] אִי לֹא אָתֵינָא מִיכָּן וְעַד תְּלָתִין יוֹמִין – **If I do not return within thirty days from now,** לֶיהֱוֵי גִּיטָּא – **let this be a** valid ***get.*** אֲתָא בְּסוֹף תְּלָתִין יוֹמִין – **He came** back **at the end of thirty days,** וּפְסַקֵיהּ מַבָּרָא – **but the** river **crossing**[30] **stopped him.**[31] אָמַר לְהוּ – **He said to them** from the far side of the river: ,,חֲזוּ דְּאָתַאי, חֲזוּ דְּאָתַאי" – **Look, I have come! Look, I have come!** אָמַר שְׁמוּאֵל – But **Shmuel said:** לָאו שְׁמֵיהּ מֵתְיָא – **It is not called an arrival** into the town, since he did not actually make it into town on time, and the *get* is valid.[32] Apparently, the fact that he was constrained from returning by circumstances beyond his control does not void the *get;* this, then, might be the source for Rava's thesis.

The Gemara rejects this source, as well:

וְדִלְמָא אוֹנְסָא דִּשְׁכִיחַ שַׁאנִי – **But perhaps a commonly occurring constraint,** such as the ferry being on the far side of the river, **is different.** דְּכֵיוָן דְּאִיבָּעֵי לֵיהּ לְאַתְנוּיֵי וְלֹא אַתְנֵי – **For since he ought to** have foreseen the possibility of the ferry being on the far side of the river when he returned **and made** some appropriate **stipulation, and he did not make any** such **stipulation,** אִיהוּ דְּאַפְסִיד אַנַּפְשֵׁיהּ – **he has caused the loss to himself** and the *get* is valid.[33]

Having failed to find an earlier source for Rava's ruling, the Gemara concludes:

אֶלָּא רָבָא סְבָרָא דְנַפְשֵׁיהּ קָאָמַר – **Rather, Rava was saying** something that he concluded by **his own reasoning,** משום צנועות ומשום פרוצות – arguing that although, in fact, by Biblical law if the husband's return is prevented by circumstances beyond his control the *get* is not valid,[34] yet by Rabbinic law it is valid **because of** our concern regarding very **modest [women] and brazen [women].** משום צנועות – That is, **because of** very **modest** (i.e. pious) **[women],** דְּאִי אָמְרַתְּ לָא לֶהֱוֵי גֵט – **for were you to say that** if the husband's return was prevented by circumstances beyond his control **it should not be a** valid ***get***

NOTES

22. [Nor, apparently, do "our Rabbis" invalidate the *get* on the grounds that the condition of the *get* was fulfilled because of an unavoidable circumstance (viz. the husband's death). Regarding why Rava did not summon this as evidence for his thesis that unavoidable circumstances do not void the validity of a conditional *get,* see *Ramban, Rashba* et al.]

23. [The Rishonim ask why the view of "our Rabbis" is not already contravened by the first Mishnah, which stated that if the husband said, "This is your *get* if I die," or some similar expression, the *get* is invalid, despite the evidence of the date that is written on it. *Ramban* suggests that perhaps even "our Rabbis" might concede that such a *get* is invalid, for the explicit declaration that it is being given "if I die" outweighs the evidence of its date and must be interpreted as meaning that the *get* will go into effect only after the husband's death. For another solution see *Tosafos.*]

24. *Gittin* 76b.

25. In this case the *get* was to take effect immediately, contingent upon the husband not returning within twelve months.

26. Because the *get* takes effect retroactively from the time of its delivery, when the husband was still alive, it is valid even though the husband died in the interim.

27. Death is certainly the most unavoidable of circumstances. Nevertheless, the Mishnah rules that the *get* is valid; certainly, then, if illness prevented him from returning the *get* would be valid (*Rashi*).

28. That is, his purpose in writing such a *get* ("if I do not return . . .") was, presumably, to prevent his wife from being subject to *yibum* in the event of his death. Obviously, then, he would not want the fact of his death to invalidate the *get,* thus defeating its entire purpose. But if he is constrained in some other way from returning, in which case he, presumably, would have rather returned and invalidated the *get,* perhaps the *get* is not valid (*Rashi;* cf. *Chidushei R' Akiva Eiger;* see also *Rashi* below, 9b ד״ה גט כריתות and *Tosafos* ad loc. ד״ה כל היוצא).

29. [Presumably, the witnesses who observed him delivering the *get* to his wife.]

30. [See *Hagahos R' Yaakov Emden* to *Sanhedrin* 109b; cf. *Yad Ramah* ad loc.]

31. The ferry was on the far side of the river, [and by the time it would cross over to ferry him across and into town the deadline would have passed].

32. Consequently, she is free to marry elsewhere and she has the status of a divorcee, who may not marry a Kohen (*Rashi;* see *Hagahos R' Elazar Moshe Horowitz*).

33. The Gemara's answer introduces a new factor: It emerges that the question of whether or not unavoidable constraint invalidates the *get* applies only where the constraint was not to be expected; but if, in the ordinary course of things, the constraint might have been expected, and yet the husband made no allowance for it, then it certainly cannot serve as a reason to invalidate the *get.*

Tosafos and many other Rishonim (see *Shitah Mekubetzes,* at length) add – on the evidence of a Gemara elsewhere (*Gittin* 73a) – that, conversely, if the circumstance that prevented the husband's return was completely unforeseeable – for example, the husband was eaten by a lion – then the *get* is certainly not valid; such an unlikely and unforeseeable event cannot possibly be considered to have been envisaged by the terms of the *get.* The debate in our Gemara concerns only such circumstances that, on the one hand, would not normally be expected, but, on the other hand, are not completely unforeseeable, either – for example, an illness.

34. [For the Scriptural source for this see below, 3a note 5.]

עין משפט
נר מצוה

ג א מיי' פ"ט מהל' גירושין הל' ח סמג עשין נ טוש"ע אה"ע סי' קמד סעי' א:
ד ב מיי' שם הל' ג (טוש"ע שם סעי' ג):
ה ג מיי' שם הל' יב סמג שם טוש"ע שם סי' קמה סעי' ח:
ו ד מיי' שם הל' יא וסמג שם טוש"ע שם סעי' ג:
ז ה מיי' שם הל' ח טוש"ע שם סעי' א:

דלא מציא אמרה ליה נסתחפה שדהו כי תיבעי לך שלא בשעת וסתה מאי כיון דלא בשעת וסתה הויא מציא אמרה ליה נסתחפה שדהו או דלמא כיון דאיכא נשי דקא משנייא וסתייהו כשעת וסתה דמי פשיט רב אחאי הגיע זמן ולא נישאו אוכלות משלו ואוכלות בתרומה לא נשאו לא קתני אלא לא נישאו היכי דמי אי דקא מעכבן אינהי אמאי אוכלות משלו ואוכלות בתרומה אלא לאו דאיתנים כי האי גוונא וקתני אוכלות משלו ואוכלות בתרומה אמר רב אשי לעולם אימא לך כל אונסא לא אכלה ודקא מעכבי אינהו ובדין הוא דאיבעי ליה למיתני לא נשאו ואיידי דתנא רישא בדידהי תנא נמי סיפא בדידהי: אמר רבא ולענין גיטין אינו כן [א] אלמא קסבר רבא אין אונס בגיטין מנא ליה לרבא הא אילימא מהא דתנן [ב] הרי זה גיטך אם לא באתי מכאן ועד שנים עשר חדש ומת בתוך שנים עשר חדש אינו גט מת הוא דאינו גט הא חלה הרי זה גט ודלמא לעולם אימא לך חלה נמי אינו גט והיא גופא קמ"ל דאין גט לאחר מיתה אין גט לאחר מיתה הא תנא ליה רישא [ג] הרי זה גיטך אם [ג] מתי הרי זה גיטך מחולי זה הרי זה גיטך לאחר מיתה לא אמר כלום דלמא לאפוקי מדרבותינו דתניא ורבותינו התירוה להנשא ואמרינן מאן רבותינו אמר רב יהודה אמר שמואל בי דינא דשרו משחא סברי לה כרבי יוסי דאמר זמנו של שטר מוכיח עליו ואלא מסיפא [ד] מעכשיו אם לא באתי מכאן ועד י"ב חדש ומת בתוך שנים עשר חדש הרי זה גט מת והוא הדין לחלה דלמא מת דוקא דלא ניחא ליה דתפול קמי יבם אלא מהא [ה] דההוא דאמר להו אי לא אתינא מיכן ועד תלתין יומין ליהוי גיטא אתא בסוף תלתין יומין [ה] ופסקיה מברא אמר להו חזו דאתאי חזו דאתאי אמר שמואל לאו שמיה מתיא ודלמא אונסא דשכיח שאני דכיון דאיבעי ליה לאתנויי ולא אתני איהו דאפסיד אנפשיה אלא רבא סברא דנפשיה קאמר משום צנועות ומשום פרוצות משום צנועות דאי אמרת לא להוי גט זימנין

מציא אמרה ליה נסתחפה שדהו. ואינו יכול לטעון דלהכי מזלה גרם דכיון דלא מיפקדא אפריה ורביה לא מיענשה כדאמרינן בהבעל על יבמתו (יבמות דף סד:) ועוד דהאשה היא שדה של הבעל ואין הבעל שדה שלה: **לפיכך** אם חלה הוא אינו מעלה לה מזונות. קשה לר"י דאמר בהחולץ (שם דף מא: ושם) עמד בדין וברח זנה משל יבם ומפרש בירושלמי ברח ה"ה חלה והכא אמרי' דחלה אין מעלה לה מזונות ואור"י דהתם חלה או ברח לאחר שעמד בדין שכבר נתחייב לה במזונות אבל הכא בחלה קודם הגעת זמן ובקונט' פי' שם דוקא ברח אבל חלה לא ואין נראה כדמשמע בירושלמי ולפירושו אין להקשות מאי קא מיבעיא לה מיבעיא אמאי לא פשיט לה מהתם דיש לומר דלרווחא נקט בחלה ומיהו טפי מיבמתו כדאמרינן ביבמות בכמה דוכתי: **פשיט** רב אחאי. לא כמו שפירש רשב"ם דהיינו רב אחאי גאון שעשה שאלתות והיה בסוף כל האמוראים ולכך משנה לשונו בכל הש"ס פרק רב אחאי פשיט רב אחאי שהרי כאן רב אשי [ו] עונה על דבריו אלא אומר רבינו תם שהוא אמורא וכל אמורא היה תופס לשונו כמו מגדף בה ר' אבהו (סנהדרין ג.) תהי בה ר' יוחנן (ב"ק קיב:) לייט עלה אביי (ברכות כט.):

לא נשאו לא קתני אלא לא נישאו. מקובלין היו כך לקרות לא נישאו ועוד דאי לא נשאו אנשים קאי ה"ל למימר נמי בלשון רבים ואוכלות משלהם: **אלא** לא נישאו. פירוש דמשמע נמי דמעכבי אינהי אבל אין לומר דמשמע דוקא דמעכבי אינהי אבל לא אינהו מדקאמר לעולם דמעכבי אינהו ואיידי דתנא רישא בדידהי כו' דמשום איידי אין לשנות טעות בסיפא: **מת** הוא דאינו גט. דאין גט לאחר מיתה הא חלה הרי זה גט דאי חלה נמי אינו גט וטעמא דהכא דאינו גט משום אונס אם כן לישמעינן חלה דהוי אונס מועט וכ"ש מת דהשתא אכתי לא אסיק אדעתיה דבמת איכא למימר ניחא ליה דלא תפול קמי יבם: **ודלמא** לעולם אימא לך חלה נמי אינו גט. ויש טענת אונס ודקאמר ליתני חלה וכ"ש מת הא דקתני מת הא קמ"ל דאין גט לאחר מיתה ואתא לאשמועינן תרוייהו דיש אונס ואין גט לאחר מיתה דאי יש אונס גרידא אתא לאשמועינן אבל יש גט לאחר מיתה הוה ליה למינקט חלה ואי אין גט לאחר מיתה גרידא הוה בעי לאשמועינן לא הוה ליה למינקט הרי זה גיטך אם לא באתי שעושה תנאי אלא הרי זה גיטך לאחר מיתה: **הרי** זה גיטך אם מתי מחולי זה לאחר מיתה. לאחר מיתה הוי טעמא דכולהו כמו אתם ולא אפוטרופסין ולא שותפין ולא אריסין ולא כל התורם את שאינו שלו (גיטין דף נב.) דכולהו הוו משום תורם את שאינו שלו וא"ת ההיא משנה גופה אמאי איצטריך הא תנן בהדיא בפ"ק דגיטין (דף יג. ושם) דאין גט לאחר מיתה דתנן האומר תנו גט זה לאשתי לא יתנו לאחר מיתה ובפרק קמא דגיטין (שם ד"ה לא) פירשנו: **דלמא** לאפוקי מדרבותינו. אבל מההיא דרישא לא שמעינן לאפוקי מדרבותינו דאיכא לאוקמה בשאין כתוב זמן בשטר והא דאמרינן (בגיטין דף פו.) שלשה גיטין פסולין וחד מינייהו שאין בו זמן הא אמרינן אם נשאת הולד כשר ומשום דאין גט לאחר מיתה קתני הכא לא אמר כלום אפילו נשאת אי נמי בשכתוב בו [ז] שבוע או שנה או חדש דאמר בפרק שני דגיטין (דף יז:) דכשר ואין זמנו מוכיח עליו אי נמי כמאומר: **דלמא** מת דוקא דלא ניחא ליה דתפול קמי יבם. וא"ת בפרק מי שאחזו (גיטין דף עג. ושם) דאמרי' אכלו ארי אין לנו פירוש אין לנו שיהא גט ואמאי לא הוי גט הא ודאי ניחא ליה דתפול קמי יבם וי"ל דבאונס לא ניחא ליה דתפול קמי יבם וגם אין סברא דלא אסיק אדעתיה שיהא גט: וסברה

פשיט רב אחאי. הך בעיא ממתניתין דקתני לא נישאו ולא קתני לא נשאו דלישתמע שהבעלים מעכבים: **אלא לא נישאו.** הן לבעלים: **ואיידי דתנא רישא בדידהי.** נותנין לבתולה שנים עשר חדש ולאלמנה שלשים יום: **ולענין גיטין אינו כן.** אלפיכך קאי דאשמעינן שעכבת האונס פוטרתו מן המזונות לענין גיטין אין טענת אונס מועלת אם נתן גט לאשתו ע"מ אם לא אבא עד זמן פלוני יהא גט [ונאנס] ולא בא הרי זה גט ואינו יכול לומר אנוס הייתי: **אלמא** קסבר **אין אונס בגטין.** אין טענת אונס בגיטין ולקמיה מפרש טעמא: **אינו גט.** ואם אין לה בנים זקוקה ליבם: **מת הוא דאינו גט.** דהא לא שויא גיטא עד י"ב חדש והוא מת בתוך הזמן ומאן קא מגרש לה מהשתא אין המתים מגרשים: **מת הוא דאינו גט.** משום דאין גט לאחר מיתה אבל משום אונס אחרינא לא מפקע גיטא אלמא אין אונס בגטין דאי סלקא דעתך חלה נמי אינו גט ניתני חלה וכל שכן מת שאין אונס גדול מזה: **היא גופא קמ"ל.** כלומר האי דתנא מת לאו לדיוקא דילה תניה למידק הא חלה הרי זה גט אלא לאשמעינן היא גופא דאין גט לאחר מיתה ואפי' בלא תנאי כגון האומר לאשתו הרי זה גיטך לאחר מותי אינו גט לפוטרה מן היבם: **זה גיטך אם מתי.** שכיב מרע שכתב גט לאשתו באחד מן הלשונות הללו זה גיטך אם מתי או זה גיטך מחולי זה משיפסוק חולי זה (מעלי) משמע והוא מת מאותו חולי לא אמר כלום שהרי משפסק אינו בחיים ואינו יכול לגרש: **דלמא.** הא דאיצטריך סיפא אם לא באתי וכו' לאפוקי מדרבותינו איצטריך דפליגי עלה ואמרי דאין גט לאחר מיתה הוא דכיון דכתוב בגט זמן כתיבתו הוא מוכיח שכך אמר לה אם לא באתי לאותו זמן יהא גט למפרע מהיום דאי לא משוה גיטא עד שנים עשר חדש למה כתב יום כתיבת הגט בתוכו לכתוב אם לא באתי לר"ח פלוני יהא גט: **התירוה לינשא.** בלא חליצה להיא דאם לא באתי: **זמנו של שטר מוכיח עליו.** לא לחנם נכתב זמנו לתוכו אם לא להודיע שמיום הכתיבה והמסירה הוא מגרשה אם לא יבא לאותו זמן הלכך אע"ג דלא כתב זה גיטך מהיום אם לא באתי כו' כמאן דכתב מהיום דמי ובבבא בתרא (דף קלו.) אמרה רבי יוסי דתנן הכותב נכסיו לבנו צריך שיכתוב מהיום ולאחר מיתה ואם לא כתב מהיום אינה מתנה רבי יוסי אומר אינו צריך: **ואלא מסיפא.** גמר רבא דאין אונס בגיטין: **הרי זה גט.** ואע"ג דאין אונס גדול ממיתה אלמא אין אונס בגיטין והוא הדין לחלה: **דלמא מת דוקא.** דכל עצמו שכתב לה גט מחמת כן כתב לה שאם ימות יהיה גט למפרע שלא תיזקק ליבם ובהאי אונסא לא ניחא ליה למיבטל גיטא אבל באונסא אחרינא דניחא ליה לבטולי גיטא ביה אימא לך יש אונס בגיטין: **ופסקיה מברא.** הנהר הפסיקו שהיתה המעבורת מלד העיר ולא יכול לעבור: **חזו דאתאי.** שבאתי: **לא שמיה מתיא.** והוי גיטא ואם רצתה תינשא לאחר וגם לכהונה נפסלת מהיום:

מסורת הש"ס

א) [גיטין ל. לד.], ב) גיטין עו: ע"ז לז., ג) גיטין עב. ב"ב קלו., ד) גיטין עו:, ה) שם לד. נדרים מ:, ו) [ועי' תוס' זבחים קב: ד"ה פרין], ז) [שבוע שנה חודש כל"ל].

ליקוטי רש"י

פשיט רב אחאי. הך בעיא ממתני' דקתני לא נישאו ולא קתני נשאו משמע שהמדמים מעכבים [רש"י משיטמ"ק]. אין אונס בגיטין. אין טענת אונס והוי גיטא [גיטין לד.]. אינו גט. דכיון דלא אמר מעכשיו משמע לאחר י"ב חדש יהא גט והרי מת בתוך הזמן ולאחר מיתה ליכא [שם עו:].

גליון הש"ס

תוס' ד"ה לא נשאו בא"ד מקובלין היו כך. וכן בנדרים דף לה ע"א ברש"י ד"ה דיקא נמי:

תוספות רי"ד

אמר רבא ולענין גיטין אינו כן. פי' לענין גיטין אין טענת אונס מועלת שאם נתן גט לאשתו שאם לא אבוא עד זמן פלוני יהא גט. ונאנס ולא בא ה"ז גט ואין יכול לומר אנוס הייתי. אלמא קסבר אין אונס בגיטין. א"ד אמר רבא וכן לענין גיטין. אלמא קסבר יש אונס בגיטין. ואע"ג דקי"ל הלכה כלישנא בתרא. הכא הלכה כלישנא קמא דהכי אמרי' בגיטין בשמעתא קמייתא דפ' השולח. הוא דא"ל אי לא נסיבנא מכאן ועד תלתין יומין להוי גיטא כי מטא יום תלתין א"ל הא טרחנא לממי נחוש לה. אי משום אונסא אין אונס לתלמודא דאין אונס בגיטין.

it is only **if he dies that it is not a** valid ***get,*** since a *get* cannot take effect after the husband's death; הָא חָלָה הֲרֵי זֶה גֵּט – **but had he** merely **become ill** and been prevented from returning on time **it is a** valid ***get.***[13]

The Gemara rejects this proof:

וְדִלְמָא לְעוֹלָם אֵימָא לָךְ חָלָה נַמִּי אֵינוֹ גֵּט – **Perhaps I can still say to you that if he became ill it is also not a** valid ***get.*** וְהִיא גּוּפָא קָא מַשְׁמַע לָן – **But** the Mishnah chose to speak of a case where the husband died – not in order to imply that the law would have been otherwise had he merely fallen ill, but, rather – because **it is informing us of this very** principle, דְּאֵין גֵּט לְאַחַר מִיתָה – **that a *get* cannot take effect after** the husband's **death.**[14]

The Gemara questions this, seeking to salvage the proof:

אֵין גֵּט לְאַחַר מִיתָה – Can the Tanna be teaching us only that **a *get* cannot take effect after** the husband's **death?** הָא תָּנָא לֵיהּ רֵישָׁא – **But the first part of the Mishnah** (i.e. an earlier Mishnah) already **taught that** principle, by stating:[15] הֲרֵי זֶה גִּיטֵּיךְ אִם מַתִּי – If a gravely ill man gives his wife a bill of divorce and tells her: THIS IS YOUR *GET* IF I DIE, הֲרֵי זֶה גִּיטֵּיךְ מֵחוֹלִי זֶה – or: THIS IS YOUR *GET* FROM THIS ILLNESS,[16] הֲרֵי זֶה גִּיטֵּיךְ לְאַחַר מִיתָה – or: THIS IS YOUR *GET* AFTER my DEATH, לֹא אָמַר כְּלוּם – HE HAS NOT SAID ANYTHING, i.e. the *get* is void, for a *get* cannot take effect after the husband's death. Clearly, then, the purpose of the latter Mishnah[17] cannot be to reiterate a principle that we already know![18]

The Gemara defends its rebuttal of the proof:

דִּלְמָא לְאַפּוּקֵי מִדְּרַבּוֹתֵינוּ – **Perhaps,** as we said before, the latter Mishnah spoke of a case where the husband died – even though the *get* would have been invalid also had he simply fallen ill – because it wished to teach us that we may apply here the principle that a *get* cannot go into effect after the husband's death. However, the Mishnah's ultimate purpose in doing so was not to inform us of this principle itself; after all, we already know this principle from the earlier Mishnah. Rather, the Mishnah's purpose was to teach us that this principle (that the *get* cannot take effect after the husband's death) can be applied to this case, and thereby **to exclude** the view that we find elsewhere articulated by **"our Rabbis."** דְּתַנְיָא – **For it was taught in a Baraisa:** וְרַבּוֹתֵינוּ הִתִּירוּהָ לְהִנָּשֵׂא – BUT OUR RABBIS PERMITTED HER TO BE MARRIED.[19]

Before explaining the reasoning behind the view of "our Rabbis," the Gemara identifies who they are:

וְאַמְרִינַן מַאן רַבּוֹתֵינוּ – **And we asked: Who are "Our Rabbis"?** אָמַר רַב יְהוּדָה אָמַר שְׁמוּאֵל – **Rav Yehudah said in the name of Shmuel:** בֵּי דִינָא דְּשָׁרוּ מִשְׁחָא – **The** members of the **court that permitted oil.**[20]

The Gemara explain the reasoning of "our Rabbis":

סְבָרֵי לָהּ כְּרַבִּי יוֹסֵי – **They held in accordance with R' Yose,** דְּאָמַר זְמַנּוֹ שֶׁל שְׁטָר מוֹכִיחַ עָלָיו – **who said that the date** that is written on a document **attests to its** retroactive nature.[21] Likewise, in the case at hand (since the date written on the *get* was, presumably, the day that it was drawn up and delivered to the wife), "our Rabbis," following the view of R' Yose, view the fact that the *get* was dated as evidence that the *get* was designed to go into effect (upon the husband's failure to arrive within twelve

NOTES

brothers (*Rashi,* as emended by *Rashash*).

[When a man dies childless, the Torah provides for one of his brothers to marry his widow. This marriage is called *yibum.* Pending this, the widow is forbidden to marry anyone else. If the brother should refuse to perform *yibum,* he must release her from her *yibum*-bond by performing the alternative rite of *chalitzah* (see *Deuteronomy* 25:5-10).]

13. The Mishnah implies that the *get* is invalidated only on account of the husband's death, on the principle that a *get* cannot go into effect after the husband's death; but had some other less drastic circumstance – such as illness – intervened to prevent his return, the divorce would be valid. For were it true that even such a circumstance as illness could invalidate the *get* then the Mishnah should have stated that fact, and left it for us to infer that certainly death – the most drastic of unavoidable circumstances – invalidates the *get.* This Mishnah thus implies that there is no force to a claim of uncontrollable circumstances with regard to a conditional *get* (*Rashi;* cf. *Ritva;* see also *Shitah Mekubetzes* ד״ה ואפשר שהתוספות).

14. The Mishnah's purpose in singling out a case where the husband died – rather than merely fell ill – was to inform us of the principle that a *get* cannot go into effect after the husband's death. [Now this principle is not necessary for the case at hand, since – at this point in the argument – we are assuming (against Rava) that a claim of unavoidable circumstance has the power to invalidate the *get;* hence, since the condition of the *get* (the husband's timely return) was brought about by an unavoidable circumstance (his death) the *get* is invalid on that account, and the principle that a *get* cannot go into effect after the husband's death need not be invoked. Rather,] the significance of this principle emerges in a case where, for example, he gave the *get* without any conditions, but stipulated that it should go into effect only after his death. Such a *get* has no validity, because of this principle that a *get* cannot go into effect after the husband's death. Hence, his widow would be subject to *yibum* (*Rashi;* see also *Tosafos;* cf. *Ramban*).

15. *Gittin* 72a.

16. I.e. after this illness passes; since, in the final event, he died before the illness was over, the implication of this stipulation is that the *get* can take effect only after his death (see *Rashi* here and to *Gittin* ibid.).

17. [Regarding someone who gave a *get* on condition that he not return within twelve months and then died.]

18. [Rather, it would seem, the purpose of the latter Mishnah in speaking of a case where the husband died – rather than fell ill – must have been to indicate that only the death of the husband invalidates the *get,* but were he prevented by illness from returning the *get* would be valid, thus proving Rava's thesis that a claim of unavoidable circumstance does not have the power to invalidate a conditional *get.*]

19. "Our Rabbis" disagreed with the Mishnah and, in the case where the husband gave a *get* on condition that he not return within twelve months and then died, they validated the *get* and allowed the woman to marry without need of *chalitzah* (*Rashi*).

20. As the Gemara recounts elsewhere (see *Avodah Zarah* 37a), R' Yehudah Nesiah and his court permitted the oil of idolaters (which had previously been forbidden by Rabbinic decree) for consumption. See also *Tosafos* to *Avodah Zarah* 36a ד״ה אשר.

21. R' Yehudah and R' Yose (cited in the Mishnah, *Bava Basra* 136a) discuss how someone can transfer property to his son yet retain rights to its produce and profits during his lifetime. An obvious method would be to have the transfer take effect after his death, but this is impossible because a person cannot transfer his property posthumously. Therefore, R' Yehudah maintains that the person must write a deed specifying that the property be transferred *from today and after my death;* this makes it clear that the property itself is transferred immediately, but the rights to its produce are retained by the father until his death. If he omitted the expression *from today,* however, the deed implies that the transfer of the property itself is to take effect posthumously, and the deed is therefore void. R' Yose disputes this, maintaining that if someone dates a deed, this clearly indicates that he wants to transfer the property from that date. The transfer is therefore valid according to R' Yose even if the man failed to include the expression *from today* in the deed; for the date takes the place of the expression *from today.*

The Gemara assumes that the above dispute pertains to our case as well. That is, R' Yose would maintain that if someone dates his *get,* he indicates that it is to take effect retroactively even if he gives it on condition of some future event (such as his failure to return within twelve months) taking place; for the date takes the place of the expression *from now* (מֵעַכְשָׁיו) [which causes the *get* to take effect retroactively when the condition is fulfilled – see Gemara below]. R' Yehudah, of course, would dispute this (*Rashi*). [See *Tosafos,* who discuss how the fact that a conditional *get* is dated can be proof that it is to take effect retroactively once the condition is fulfilled, in light of the fact that by Rabbinic decree (see *Gittin* 17b) *every get* requires a date.]

דלא מציא אמרה ליה נסתחפה שדהו כי תיבעי לך שלא בשעת וסתה מאי כיון דלא בשעת וסתה הויא מציא אמרה ליה נסתחפה שדהו או דלמא כיון דאיכא נשי דקא משנייא וסתייהו כשעת וסתה דמי פשיט רב אחאי הגיע זמן ולא נישאו אוכלות משלו ואוכלות בתרומה לא נשאו לא קתני אלא לא נישאו היכי דמי אי דקא מעכבן אינהי אמאי אוכלות משלו ואוכלות בתרומה אלא לאו דאיתנים כי האי גוונא וקתני אוכלות משלו ואוכלות בתרומה אמר רב אשי לעולם אימא לך כל אונסא לא אכלה ודקא מעכבי אינהו ובדין הוא דאיבעי ליה למיתני לא נשאו ואיידי דתנא רישא בדידהי תנא נמי סיפא בדידהי: אמר רבא ולענין גיטין אינו כן אלמא קסבר רבא אין אונס בגיטין מנא ליה לרבא הא אילימא מהא דתנן הרי זה גיטך אם לא באתי מכאן ועד שנים עשר חדש ומת בתוך שנים עשר חדש אינו גט מת הוא דאינו גט הא חלה הרי זה גט ודלמא לעולם אימא לך חלה נמי אינו גט והיא גופא קמ"ל דאין גט לאחר מיתה אין גט לאחר מיתה הא תנא ליה רישא הרי זה גיטך אם מתי הרי זה גיטך מחולי זה הרי זה גיטך לאחר מיתה לא אמר כלום דלמא לאפוקי מדרבותינו דתניא ורבותינו התירוה להנשא ואמרינן מאן רבותינו אמר רב יהודה אמר שמואל בי דינא דשרו משחא סברי לה כרבי יוסי דאמר זמנו של שטר מוכיח עליו ואלא מסיפא מעכשיו אם לא באתי מכאן ועד י"ב חדש ומת בתוך שנים עשר חדש הרי זה גט מת הוא והוא הדין לחלה דלמא מת דוקא דלא ניחא ליה דתפול קמי יבם אלא מהא דההוא דאמר להו אי לא אתינא מיכן ועד תלתין יומין ליהוי גיטא אתא בסוף תלתין יומין ופסקיה מברא אמר להו חזו דאתאי חזו דאתאי אמר שמואל לאו שמיה מתיא ודלמא אונסא דשכיח שאני דכיון דאיבעי ליה לאתנויי ולא אתני איהו דאפסיד אנפשיה אלא רבא סברא דנפשיה קאמר משום צנועות ומשום פרוצות משום צנועות דאי אמרת לא להוי גט זימנין

מציא אמרה ליה נסתחפה שדהו. ואינו יכול לטעון לאלדרכה מזלה גרם דכיון דלא מיפקדא אפריה ורביה לא מיענשא כדאמרינן בהבא על יבמתו (יבמות דף סד:) ועוד דהאשה היא שדה של הבעל ואין הבעל שדה שלה: **לפיכך** חלה הוא אינו מעלה לה מזונות. קשה לר"י דלאמר בהחולץ (שם דף מא: ושם) עמד בדין וברח זונות משל יבם ומפרש בירושלמי ברח ע"ה חלה והכא אמרי' דחלה אין מעלה לה מזונות ואור"י דהתם חלה או ברח לאחר שעמד בדין שכבר נתחייב לה במזונות אבל הכא בחלה קודם הגעת זמן ובקונטרס פי' שם דוקא ברח אבל חלה לא ואין נראה כדמשמע בירושלמי ולפירושו אין להקשות מאיכא דבעו לה מיבעיא אמאי לא פשיט לה מהתם דיש לומר דארוסתו אגידא ביה טפי מיבמתו כדאמרינן ביבמות בכמה דוכתי: **פשיט** רב אחאי. לא כמו שפירש רשב"ם דהיינו רב אחאי גאון שעשה שאלתות והיה בסוף כל האמוראים ולכך משנה לשונו בכל הש"ס פריך רב אחאי פשיט רב אחאי שהרי כאן רב אשי[ו] עונה על דבריו אלא אומר ר"ת דשמא אמורא וכל אמורא היה תופס לשונו כמו מגדף בה ר' אבהו (סנהדרין ג:) תהי בה ר' יוחנן (ב"ק קיב:) לייט עלה אביי (ברכות כט.):

לא נשאו לא קתני אלא לא נישאו. מקובלין היו כך לקרות לא נישאו ועוד דאי לא נשאו אאנשים קאי ה"ל למימר נמי בלשון רבים ואוכלות משלהם: **אלא** לא נישאו. פירוש דמשמע נמי דמעכבי אינהי אבל אין לומר דמשמע דוקא דמעכבי אינהי אבל לא אינהו מדקאמר לעולם דמעכבי אינהו ואיידי דתנא רישא בדידהי כו' דמשום איידי אין לשנות טעות בסיפא: **מת** הוא דאינו גט. דאין גט לאחר מיתה הא חלה הרי זה גט דאי חלה נמי אינו גט וטעמא דהכא דאינו גט משום אונס אם כן לישמעינן חלה דהוי אונס מועט וכ"ש מת דהשתא אכתי לא אסיק אדעתיה דבמת איכא למימר ניחא ליה דלא תפול קמי יבם: **ודלמא** לעולם אימא לך חלה נמי אינו גט. ויש טענת אונס ודקאמר ליתני חלה וכ"ש מת הא דקתני מת הא קמ"ל דאין גט לאחר מיתה ואתא לאשמועינן תרוייהו דיש אונס ואין גט לאחר מיתה דאי יש אונס גרידא אתא לאשמועינן אבל יש גט לאחר מיתה הוה ליה למינקט חלה ואי אין גט לאחר מיתה גרידא הוה בעי לאשמועינן לא הוה ליה למינקט הרי זה גיטך אם לא באתי שעושה תנאי אלא הרי זה גיטיך לאחר מיתה: **הרי** זה גיטיך אם מתי מחולי זה לאחר מיתה. לאחר מיתה הוי טעמא דכולהו כמו אתם ולא אפוטרופסין ולא שותפין ולא אריסין ולא כל התורם את שאינו שלו (גיטין דף נב.) דכולהו הוו משום תורם את שאינו שלו וא"ת ההיא משנה גופה אמאי איצטריך הא תנן בהדיא בפ"ק דגיטין (דף יג. ושם) דאין גט לאחר מיתה דתנן

פשיט רב אחאי. הך בעיא ממתניתין דקתני לא ניסאו ולא קתני לא נשאו לישמע שהבעלים מעכבים: **אלא לא נישאו**. הן לבעלים תלה העכבה בנשים: ואיידי דתנא רישא בדידהי. נותנין לבתולה שנים עשר חדש ולאלמנה שלשים יום: ולענין גיטין אינו כן. אלפיכך קאי דאשמעינן שעכבת האונס פוטרתו מן המזונות לענין גיטין אין טענת אונס מועלת אם נתן גט לאשתו ע"מ אם לא אבא עד זמן פלוני יהא גט [ונאנס] ולא בא הרי זה גט ואינו יכול לומר אנוס הייתי: אלמא קסבר אין אונס בגטין. אין טענת אונס בגיטין ולקמיה מפרש טעמא: אינו גט. ואם אין לה בנים זקוקה ליבם: מת הוא דאינו גט. דהא לא שויא גיטא עד י"ב חדש והוא מת בתוך הזמן ומאן קא מגרש לה מהשתא אין המתים מגרשים: מת הוא דאינו גט. משום דאין גט לאחר מיתה אבל משום אונס אחרינא לא מפקע גיטא אלמא אין אונס בגטין דאי סלקא דעתך חלה נמי אינו גט ניתני חלה וכל שכן מת שאין אונס גדול מזה: היא גופא קמ"ל. כלומר האי דתנא מת לאו לדיוקא דילה תניה למידק הא חלה הרי זה גט אלא לאשמעינן היא גופא דאין גט לאחר מיתה ואפי' בלא תנאי כגון האומר לאשתו הרי זה גיטיך לאחר מותי אינו גט לפוטרה מן היבם: זה גיטך אם מתי. שכיב מרע שכתב גט לאשתו באחד מן הלשונות הללו זה גיטך אם מתי או זה גיטך מחולי זה משיפסוק חולי זה (מעלי) משמע והוא מת מאותו חולי לא אמר כלום שהרי משפסק אינו בחיים ואינו יכול לגרש: דלמא. הא דאיצטריך סיפא אם לא באתי וכו' לאפוקי מדרבותינו איצטריך דפליגי עלה ואמרי דאין גט לאחר מיתה הוא דכיון דכתוב בגט זמן כתיבתו הוא מוכיח שכך אמר לה אם לא באתי לאותו זמן יהא גט למפרע מהיום דאי לא משוה גיטא עד שנים עשר חדש למה כתב יום כתיבת הגט בתוכו לכתוב אם לא באתי לר"ח פלוני יהא גט: התירוה לינשא. בלא חליצה להיא דאם לא באתי: זמנו של שטר מוכיח עליו. לא לחנם נכתב זמנו לתוכו אם לא להודיע שמיום הכתיבה והמסירה הוא מגרשה אם לא יבא לאותו זמן הלכך אע"ג דלא כתב זה גיטך מהיום אם לא באתי כו' כמאן דכתב מהיום דמי ובבבא בתרא (דף קלו.) אמרה רבי יוסי דתנן הכותב נכסיו לבנו צריך שיכתוב מהיום ולאחר מיתה ואם לא כתב מהיום אינה מתנה רבי יוסי אומר אינו צריך: ואלא מסיפא. גמר רבא דאין אונס בגיטין: הרי זה גט. ואע"ג דאין אונס גדול ממיתה אלמא אין אונס בגיטין והוא הדין לחלה: דלמא מת דוקא. דכל עצמו שכתב לה גט מחמת כן כתב לה שאם ימות יהיה גט למפרע שלא תיזקק ליבם ובהאי אונסא לא ניחא ליה למיבטל גיטא אבל באונסא אחרינא דניחא ליה לבטולי גיטא ביה אימא לך יש אונס בגיטין: ופסקיה מברא. הנהר הפסיקו שהיתה המעבורת מצד העיר ולא יכול לעבור: חזו דאתאי. שבאתי: לא שמיה מתיא. והוי גיטא ואם רצתה תינשא לאחר וגם לכהונה נפסלת מהיום: זימנין

לְעוֹלָם אֵימָא לָךְ כָּל אוֹנְסָא לֹא אָכְלָה – אָמַר רַב אַשִׁי – **Rav Ashi said:** **– Actually, I can tell you that** in the case of **any unavoidable circumstance** that delays the marriage **she does not eat** of his food. וּדְקָא מְעַכְּבֵי אִינְהוּ – **And** the Mishnah, which states that if the wedding was delayed the husband must begin supporting his bride, must therefore be referring to where **[the husbands] are** deliberately **delaying** the wedding.[5] וּבְדִין הוּא דְּאִיבָּעֵי לֵיהּ לְמִיתְנֵי לֹא נָשְׂאוּ – **And by rights [the Tanna] should have taught: "they** [the husbands] **did not marry."** וְאַיְּידֵי דְּתָנָא רֵישָׁא בִּדִידְהִי – **But since [the Tanna] taught the beginning** of the Mishnah **with respect to [the bride],**[6] תָּנָא נַמִּי סֵיפָא בִּדִידְהִי – **he taught the end** of the Mishnah **also with respect to [the bride].**[7]

In the previous discussion Rav Yosef stated that if the husband was constrained by circumstances beyond his control from marrying his bride on time he does not become obligated to support her. Regarding which, Rava makes the following observation:[8]

אָמַר רָבָא – **Rava said:** וּלְעִנְיַן גִּיטִּין אֵינוֹ כֵּן – **Regarding** ***gittin*** (bills of divorce) **this is not so.**[9]

The Gemara comments:

אַלְמָא קָסָבַר רָבָא אֵין אוֹנֶס בְּגִיטִּין – **Apparently Rava holds that there is no** force to a claim of **unavoidable circumstances with regard to** conditional ***gittin.***[10]

Which leads the Gemara to ask:

מְנָא לֵיהּ לְרָבָא הָא – **From where does Rava** know **this?** אִילֵימָא מֵהָא דִּתְנַן – **If you will say it is from that which we learned in** the following **Mishnah,** which states:[11] הֲרֵי זֶה גִּיטֵּיךְ – If a man said to his wife: THIS IS YOUR *GET* אִם לֹא בָּאתִי מִכָּאן וְעַד שְׁנֵים עָשָׂר חֹדֶשׁ – IF I DO NOT RETURN WITHIN TWELVE MONTHS, וּמֵת בְּתוֹךְ שְׁנֵים עָשָׂר חֹדֶשׁ – AND HE DIED WITHIN those TWELVE MONTHS, אֵינוֹ גֵּט – IT IS NOT A valid *GET.*[12] מֵת הוּא דְּאֵינוֹ גֵּט – This implies

דְּלָא מָצְיָא אָמְרָה לֵיהּ נִסְתַּחְפָה שָׂדְהוּ – **for she** certainly **cannot say to him: Your field became inundated.**[1] כִּי תִּיבָּעֵי לָךְ – **Rather, when should you inquire?** שֶׁלֹּא בִּשְׁעַת וִוסְתָּהּ – When she menstruated **at a time that was not her fixed period.** מַאי – **What** is the law in such a case? כֵּיוָן דְּלָא בִּשְׁעַת וִוסְתָּהּ הֲוַיָא – Do we say that **since it was not the time of her fixed period** מָצְיָא אָמְרָה לֵיהּ נִסְתַּחְפָה שָׂדְהוּ – **she can say to him that his field became inundated?** אוֹ דִּלְמָא כֵּיוָן דְּאִיכָּא נָשֵׁי דְּקָא מְשַׁנְיָיא וִוסְתַּיְיהוּ – **Or, perhaps, since there are women whose fixed periods** sometimes **change,** כִּשְׁעַת וִוסְתָּהּ דָּמֵי – **it is like** she menstruated **at the time of her fixed period.**

The Gemara seeks to resolve this issue:

פָּשִׁיט רַב אַחַאי – **Rav Achai determined** the answer by analyzing the Mishnah under discussion, which said: הִגִּיעַ זְמַן וְלֹא נִישְּׂאוּ – If THE designated TIME ARRIVED AND THEY WERE NOT MARRIED, אוֹכְלוֹת מִשֶּׁלּוֹ וְאוֹכְלוֹת בִּתְרוּמָה – THEY EAT OF HIS food, AND THEY EAT OF *TERUMAH.* לֹא נָשְׂאוּ לֹא קָתָנֵי – Now **[the Mishnah] did not say: "They** [i.e. the husbands] **did not marry . . .,"** which would imply that the delay was due to the groom; אֶלָּא לֹא נִישְּׂאוּ – **rather,** it says: THEY WERE NOT MARRIED, a formulation which includes a delay that was caused by the brides.[2] הֵיכִי דָּמֵי – **What is the case** where the brides delayed the marriage and the husbands must begin to support them? אִי דְּקָא מְעַכְּבָן אִינְהִי – **If they were** deliberately **delaying** the wedding, אַמַּאי אוֹכְלוֹת מִשֶּׁלּוֹ וְאוֹכְלוֹת בִּתְרוּמָה – **why do they eat of his food and eat of** ***terumah?***[3] אֶלָּא לָאו דְּאִיתְּנִיס כִּי הַאי גַּוְונָא – **Rather,** is the Mishnah **not** referring **to** a case **where she was constrained** from marrying **in such a manner** as in our inquiry; וְקָתָנֵי אוֹכְלוֹת מִשֶּׁלּוֹ וְאוֹכְלוֹת בִּתְרוּמָה – **and** yet **[the Mishnah] teaches:** THEY EAT OF HIS food, AND THEY EAT OF *TERUMAH?*[4]

Rav Ashi rejects this proof:

NOTES

1. The scheduled time for the wedding cannot truly be said to have arrived on a day when she was due to have her period, since this could have been foreseen; thus, the groom certainly is not obligated to support her at that point (*Shitah Mekubetzes* ד״ה והריטב״א ז״ל, explaining *Rashi;* see there for other approaches, as well).

2. [See *Tosafos* ד״ה אלא.]

Actually, the word נישאו would, in Talmudic usage, ordinarily be written without the letter י; hence, from the written (unvocalized) text of the Mishnah it could not be determined if the proper reading was נָשְׂאוּ or נִשְּׂאוּ. However, in Talmudic times the corpus of the Mishnah was committed to memory and transmitted orally; and the tradition was to read this word as נִשְּׂאוּ, rather than נָשְׂאוּ (see *Tosafos* ד״ה לא; *Rosh;* for other explanations see *Shitah Mekubetzes*).

3. [If the husband is prepared to proceed with the wedding and the wife refuses, he should not have to begin supporting her.]

4. This proves that if the wedding was delayed because the bride became ill the husband must begin supporting her (*Rashba*). [And certainly if the delay was caused by the groom taking ill he must begin supporting her.]

[The Gemara had further inquired about a case where she had an untimely onset of her period and it is possible that this case, too, is envisioned by the language of this Mishnah. However, we can only *prove* from the Mishnah that there is, at least, one case where the delay was caused by the bride and he must begin supporting her, and so we must limit ourselves to proving the one least novel such case, viz. where the bride took ill (ibid.).]

5. *Rashba; Ritva.*

6. By stating: *We give twelve months for a virgin and thirty days for a widow* (*Rashi*).

7. Note that Rav Ashi's view coincides with that of Rav Yosef on the previous *amud.*

In sum: According to Rav Yosef and Rav Ashi, the husband is not obligated to support his wife until the wedding actually takes place, unless he deliberately delayed the wedding. According to Rav Achai, if the wedding was delayed the husband must begin supporting his bride, regardless of whether the delay was caused by the husband's deliberate procrastination or by some circumstance beyond his control, such as an illness on the part of either the bride or the groom. Only if the bride deliberately delayed the wedding, or if the scheduled date of the wedding coincided with the regular onset of her period, is the husband not obligated to support her. (Rav Achai did not resolve the question of whether he must support her if she had an irregular onset of her period.)

The halachah follows the view of Rav Yosef and Rav Ashi (see *Shulchan Aruch, Even HaEzer* 56:3).

8. [See *Rashi; Ritva* to 3a ד״ה ולענין מזונות.]

9. That is, if the husband gave his wife a *get* on condition, for example, that he fail to arrive back home by a certain date, and when that date arrived he wanted to return but circumstances beyond his control prevented him from doing so, the divorce is nonetheless valid; the element of constraint cannot be used as a basis to invalidate the divorce. [Of course, the *get* had to have been originally drawn up and delivered with the husband's consent.] The Gemara will later explain the reason for this ruling (*Rashi*).

10. [It should be noted that the issue of constraint is relevant only where the husband *fulfilled* the conditions of the divorce (for example, by not returning home on time). The question then is whether or not the element of constraint undermines the fulfillment of the condition; Rava, at this point in the Gemara, maintains that it does not, while we will later encounter a view that it does. It goes without saying, however, that if the husband or wife *failed* to fulfill the condition of a *get* then the divorce is not valid, even if this failure resulted from circumstances beyond their control (*Ra'ah; Ritva;* see also *Ketzos HaChoshen* 55:1; *Kovetz Shiurim* §2,3; *Kehillos Yaakov* §1).]

11. *Gittin* 76b.

12. Since the *get* was not to go into effect until the condition (his failure to return) was fulfilled, by which time he was dead, the *get* is invalid, since it is axiomatic that a dead person cannot divorce his wife.

[Although the marriage is severed anyway by the fact of his death, the invalidity of the *get* is significant since it means that] if the husband died childless his widow would be subject to *yibum* by one of his surviving

דלא מציא אמרה ליה נתחפה שדהו כי תיבעי לך שלא בשעת וסתה מאי כיון דלא בשעת וסתה הויא מציא אמרה ליה נתחפה שדהו או דלמא כיון דאיכא נשי דקא משנייא וסתייהו כשעת וסתה דמי פשיט רב אחאי הגיע זמן ולא נישאו אוכלות משלו ואוכלות בתרומה לא נשאו לא קתני אלא לא נישאו היכי דמי אי דקא מעכבן אינהי אמאי אוכלות משלו ואוכלות בתרומה אלא לאו דאיתניס כי האי גוונא וקתני אוכלות משלו ואוכלות בתרומה אמר רב אשי לעולם אימא לך כל אונסא לא אכלה ודקא מעכבי אינהו ובדין הוא דאיבעי ליה למיתני לא נשאו ואיידי דתנא רישא בדידהו תנא נמי סיפא בדידהו: אמר רבא ולענין גיטין אינו כן אלמא קסבר רבא [א] אין אונס בגיטין מנא ליה לרבא הא אילימא מהא דתנן [ב] הרי זה גיטך אם לא באתי מכאן ועד שנים עשר חדש ומת בתוך שנים עשר חדש אינו גט מת הוא דאינו גט הא חלה הרי זה גט ודלמא לעולם אימא לך חלה נמי אינו גט והיא גופא קמ"ל דאין גט לאחר מיתה אין גט לאחר מיתה הא תנא ליה רישא [ג] הרי זה גיטך אם [ג] מתי הרי זה גיטך מחולי זה הרי זה גיטך לאחר מיתה לא אמר כלום דלמא לאפוקי מדרבותינו דתניא ורבותינו התירוה להנשא ואמרינן מאן רבותינו אמר רב יהודה אמר שמואל בי דינא דשרו משחא סברי לה כרבי יוסי דאמר זמנו של שטר מוכיח עליו ואלא מסיפא [ד] מעכשיו אם לא באתי מכאן ועד י"ב חדש ומת בתוך שנים עשר חדש הרי זה גט מת והוא הדין לחלה דלמא מת דוקא דלא ניחא ליה דתפול קמי יבם אלא מהא [ה] דההוא דאמר להו אי לא אתינא מיכן ועד תלתין יומין ליהוי גיטא אתא בסוף תלתין יומין [ו] ופסקיה מברא אמר להו חזו דאתאי חזו דאתאי אמר שמואל לאו שמיה מתיא ודלמא אונסא דשכיח שאני דכיון דאיבעי ליה לאתנויי ולא אתני איהו דאפסיד אנפשיה אלא רבא סברא דנפשיה קאמר משום צנועות ומשום פרוצות משום צנועות דאי אמרת לא להוי גט

זימנין

פשיט רב אחאי. הך בעיא ממתניתין דקתני לא נישאו ולא קתני לא נשאו לאשמע שהבעלים מעכבים: **אלא לא נישאו.** הן לבעלים תלה העכבה בנשים: **ואיידי דתנא רישא בדידהו.** נותנין לבתולה שנים עשר חדש ולאלמנה שלשים יום: **ולענין גיטין אינו כן.** אלפיך קאי דאשמעינן שעכבת האונס פוטרתו מן המזונות לענין גיטין אין טענת אונס מועלת אם נתן גט לאשתו ע"מ אם לא אבא עד זמן פלוני יהא גט [ונאנס] ולא בא הרי זה גט ואינו יכול לומר אנוס הייתי: **אלמא קסבר אין אונס בגטין.** אין טענת אונס בגיטין ולקמיה מפרש טעמא: **אינו גט.** ואם אין לה בנים זקוקה ליבם: **מת הוא דאינו גט.** דהא לא שויא גיטא עד י"ב חדש והוא מת בתוך הזמן ומאן קא מגרש לה מהשתא אין המתים מגרשים: **מת הוא דאינו גט.** משום דאין גט לאחר מיתה אבל משום אונס אחרינא לא מפקע גיטא אלמא אין אונס בגטין דאי סלקא דעתך חלה נמי אינו גט ניתני חלה וכל שכן מת שאין אונס גדול מזה: **היא גופא קמ"ל.** כלומר האי דתנא מת לאו לדיוקא דילה תניה למידק הא חלה הרי זה גט אלא לאשמעינן היא גופא דאין גט לאחר מיתה ואפי' בלא תנאי כגון האומר לאשתו הרי זה גיטך לאחר מותי אינו גט לפוטרה מן היבם: **זה גיטך אם מתי.** שכיב מרע שכתב גט לאשתו באחד מן הלשונות הללו זה גיטך אם מתי או זה גיטך מחולי זה משיפסוק חולי זה (מעלי) משמע והוא מת מאותו חולי לא אמר כלום שהרי משפסק אינו בחיים ואינו יכול לגרש: **דלמא.** הא דאיצטריך סיפא אם לא באתי וכו' לאפוקי מדרבותינו איצטריך דפליגי עלה ואמרי דאין גט לאחר מיתה הוא דכיון דכתוב בגט זמן כתיבתו הוא מוכיח שכך אמר לה אם לא באתי לאותו זמן יהא גט למפרע מהיום דאי לא משוה גיטא עד שנים עשר חדש למה כתב יום כתיבת הגט בתוכו לכתוב אם לא באתי לר"ח פלוני יהא גט: **התירוה לינשא.** בלא חליצה להיות דאם לא באתי: **זמנו של שטר מוכיח עליו.** לא לחנם נכתב זמנו לתוכו אם לא להודיע שמיום הכתיבה והמסירה הוא מגרשה אם לא יבא לאותו זמן הלכך אע"ג דלא כתב זה גיטך מהיום אם לא באתי כו' כמאן דכתב מהיום דמי ובבבא בתרא (דף קלו.) אמרה רבי יוסי דתנן הכותב נכסיו לבנו צריך שיכתוב מהיום ולאחר מיתה ואם לא כתב מהיום אינה מתנה רבי יוסי אומר אינו צריך: **ואלא מסיפא.** גמר רבא דאין אונס בגיטין: **הרי זה גט.** ואע"ג דאין אונס גדול ממיתה אלמא אין אונס בגיטין והוא הדין לחלה: **דלמא מת דוקא.** דכל עצמו שכתב לה גט מתחת כן כתב לה שאם ימות יהיה גט למפרע שלא תזקק ליבם ובהאי אונסא לא ניחא ליה למיבטל גיטא אבל באונסא אחרינא דניחא ליה לבטולי גיטא ביה אימא לך יש אונס בגיטין: **ופסקיה מברא.** הנהר הפסיקו שהיתה המעבורת מלד העיר ולא יכול לעבור: **חזו דאתאי.** שבאתי: **לא שמיה מתיא.** והוי גיטא ואם רצתה תינשא לאחר וגם לכהונה נפסלת מהיום:

זימנין

מציא אמרה ליה נתחפה שדהו. ואינו יכול לטעון דלהכי מזלה גרס דכיון דלא מיפקדא אפריה ורביה לא מיענשא כדאמרינן בהבא על יבמתו (יבמות דף סד:) ועוד דהשתא היא שדה של הבעל ואין הבעל שדה שלה: **לפיכך** חלה הוא אינו מעלה לה מזונות. קשה לר"י דאמר בהחולץ (שם דף מא: ושם) עמד בדין וברח מזונת משל יבם ומפרש בירושלמי ברח ה"ה חלה והכא אמרי' דחלה אין מעלה לה מזונות ואור"י דהתם חלה או ברח לאחר שעמד בדין שכבר נתחייב לה במזונות אבל הכא בחלה קודם הגעת זמן ובקונט' פי' שם דוקא ברח אבל חלה לא ואין נראה כדמשמע בירושלמי ולפירושו אין להקשות מאיכא דבעו לה מיבעיא אמאי לא פשיט לה מהתם דיש לומר דארוסתו אגידא ביה טפי מיבמתו כדאמרינן ביבמות בכמה דוכתי: **פשיט** רב אחאי. לא כמו שפירש רשב"ם דהיינו רב אחאי גאון שעשה שאלתות והיה בסוף כל האמוראים ולכך משנה לשונו בכל הש"ס פריך רב אחאי פשיט רב אחאי שהרי כאן רב אשי [ו] עונה על דבריו אלא אומר רבינו תם שהוא אמורא וכל אמורא היה תופס לשונו כמו מגדף בה ר' אבהו (סנהדרין ג:) תהי בה ר' יוחנן (ב"ק קיב:) לייט עלה אביי (ברכות כט.): **לא** נשאו לא קתני אלא לא נישאו. [ס] מקודלין היו כך לקרות לא נישאו ועוד דאי לא נשאו אאנשים קאי ה"ל למימר נמי בלשון רבים ואוכלות משלהם: **אלא** לא נישאו. פירוש דמשמע נמי דמעכבי אינהי אבל אין לומר דמשמע דוקא דמעכבי אינהי אבל לא אינהו מדקאמר לעולם דמעכבי אינהו ואיידי דתנא רישא בדידהי כו' דמשום איידי אין לשנות טעות בסיפא: **מת** הוא דאינו גט. דאין גט לאחר מיתה הא חלה הרי זה גט דאי חלה נמי אינו גט וטעמא דהכא דאינו גט משום אונס אם כן לישמעינן חלה דהוי אונס מועט וכ"ש מת דהשתא אכתי לא אסיק אדעתיה דמת איכא למימר ניחא ליה דלא תפול קמי יבם: **ודלמא** לעולם אימא לך חלה נמי אינו גט. ויש טענת אונס ודקאמר ליתני חלה וכ"ש מת הא דקתני מת הא קמ"ל דאין גט לאחר מיתה ואתא לאשמועינן תרוייהו דיש אונס ואין גט לאחר מיתה דאי יש אונס גרידא אתא לאשמועינן אבל יש גט לאחר מיתה הוה ליה למינקט חלה ואי אין גט לאחר מיתה גרידא הוה בעי לאשמועינן לא הוה ליה למינקט הרי זה גיטך אם לא באתי שעושה תנאי אלא הרי זה גיטך לאחר מיתה: **הרי** זה גיטך אם מתי מחולי זה לאחר מיתה. לאחר מיתה הוי טעמא דכולהו כמו אתם ולא אפוטרופסין ולא שותפין ולא אריסין ולא כל התורם את שאינו שלו (גיטין דף נב.) דכולהו הוו משום תורם את שאינו שלו וא"ת ההיא משנה גופה אמאי איצטריך הא תנן בהדיא בפ"ק דגיטין (דף יג. ושם) דאין גט לאחר מיתה דתנן האומר תנו גט זה לאשתי לא יתנו לאחר מיתה ובפרק קמא דגיטין (שם ד"ה לא) פירשנו: **דלמא** לאפוקי מדרבותינו. אבל מההיא דרישא לא שמעינן לאפוקי מדרבותינו דאיכא לאוקמה בשאין כתוב זמן בשטר והא דאמרינן (בגיטין דף פו.) שלשה גיטין פסולין וחד מינייהו שאין בו זמן הא אמרינן אם נשאת הולד כשר ומשום דאין גט לאחר מיתה קתני הכא לא אמר כלום אפילו נשאת אי נמי בשכתוב בו [ז] שבוע או שנה או חדש דאמר בפרק שני דגיטין (דף יז:) דכשר ואין זמנו מוכיח עליו אי נמי במאוחר: **דלמא** מת דוקא דלא ניחא ליה דתפול קמי יבם. וא"ת בפרק מי שאחזו (גיטין דף עג. ושם) דאמרי' אכלו ארי אין לנו פירוש אין לנו שיהא גט ואמאי לא הוי גט הא לא ניחא ליה דתפול קמי יבם וי"ל דבאונס דלא שכיח כלל לא אסיק אדעתיה שיהא גט:

וסברה

עין משפט נר מצוה

ג א מיי' פ"ט מהל' גירושין הל' ח סמג עשין נ טוש"ע אה"ע סי' קמד סעי' א:

ד ב מיי' שם הל' ג (טוש"ע שם סעי' ב:)

ה ג מיי' שם הל' יא סמג שם טוש"ע שם סי' רמה סעי' א:

ו ד מיי' שם הל' יא וסמג שם טוש"ע שם סי' קמד סעי' ג:

ז ה מיי' שם הל' ט טוש"ע שם סעי' א:

גליון הש"ס

תוס' ד"ה לא נשאו וכו' מקודלין היו כך. וכן בנדרים דף לה ע"א בר"ן ד"ה דיקא נמי:

תוספות רי"ד

אמר רבא ולענין גיטין אינו כן. פי' לענין גיטין אין טענת אונס מועלת שאם נתן גט לאשתו שאם לא אבוא עד זמן פלוני י"א גט. ונאנס ולא בא ד"ז גט ואין יכול לומר אנוס הייתי. אלמא קסבר אין אונס בגיטין. א"ד אמר רבא וכן לענין גיטין. אלמא קסבר יש אונס בגיטין. ואע"ג דקי"ל הלכה כלישנא בתרא. הכא הלכה כלישנא קמא דהכי אמרי' בגיטין בשמעתא קמייתא בפ' השולח. ההוא דא"ל אי לא נסיבנא מכאן ועד תלתין יומין להוי גיטא כי מטא יום תלתין א"ל הא טרחנא לפאי נחוש לה. אי משום אונסא אין אונס בגיטין. אלמא קסבר לה לתלמודא דאין אונס בגיטין:

מסורת הש"ס

א) [גיטין ל. לד.], ב) גיטין עו: ע"ז לז., ג) גיטין עב. ב"ב קלו., ד) גיטין עו:, ה) שם ל. לד. נדרים כז:, ו) [ועי' תוס' זבחים קב: ד"ה פריך], ז) [שבוע שנה חודש כצ"ל].

ליקוטי רש"י

פשיט רב אחאי. הך בעיא ממתני' דקתני לא נישאו ולא קתני לא נשאו משמע שהבעלים מעכבים [רש"י משיטמ"ק]. **אין אונס בגיטין.** אין טענת אונס והוי גיטא [גיטין לד.]. **אינו גט.** דכיון דלא אמר מעכשיו משמע לאחר י"ב חדש יהא גט והרי מת מתוך הזמן ולגירה ליבם [שם עו:]. [illegible]

[illegible] ... מעכשיו מהא מתנה מגופה של קרקע ופירות לאחר מיתה דאי לא בעי למיתב ליה אלא לאחר מיתה למה כתב זמן בשטר וה"נ זמנו של גט מוכיח דה"ק ליה מעכשיו יהא

[illegible] בעלמא הוא וכי לא אתא איקיים תנאה [ע"ז שם]. זמנו של שטר, שכתב בתחלתו בכך וכך בשבת אמר לנו פלוני הוו עלי עדים וקנו ממני לפלוני בני לאחר מיתתי. מוכיח עליו, שמאותו זמן התחילה המתנה דאי לא [illegible] בשטר בחנם נכתב אלא ודאי להקנות מאותו היום נכתב והכי הלכתא כרבי יוסי דאם כתב לאחר מיתה קנה אע"ג דלא כתב מהיום דהא אמר רב הלכה כר' יוסי ואע"ג דאמר בפרק המגרש (גיטין דף פה:) אתקין רב [illegible] לאפוקי מדר' יוסי דאמר זמנו של שטר מוכיח עליו הואיל ולא איתמר בהדיא התם בגיטין הדר ביה רב מהא דאמר הלכה כרבי יוסי אלא אתקין איתן לן למימר לגבי גט אשה הואיל ואין בו דבר [illegible] משום חומרא דעריות אבל גבי ממונא הלכה כר' יוסי כי י"ל כי לא אמר רב הלכה כר' יוסי אלא בשטר שיש בו קנין ורואינו בדברי הגאונים ז"ל שאמרו הכי נהיגי במתיבתא כר' יהודה אפילו בממון כתקנת רב [illegible] בידם כי הלכה כר' יהודה לא היו מניחין הלכה ומפרשין מנהג (ועוד) שלא אמרו כי הלכה אפילו בממון כתקנת רב בגיטין אלא נהגו וי"ל דכיון דחזו דסוגיא דשמעתא לקמן כר' יהודה נהגו כוותיה כן פי' רבינו [illegible] רבי יוסי גבי ממון דהא ר"נ דהלכתא כוותיה בדיני הוא דבעא מרבה בר אבוה אלמא סבירא ליה לר"נ הכי [רשב"ם ב"ב קלו.]. **מברא.** מעבר המים שלא מצא את המעבורת. **לאו שמיה מתיא.** דלא מטי עד הכא [illegible] גיטין למימר איכא א"כ יש אונס בגיטין הא אוקימנא בשמעתא קמייתא דכתובות דהאי אונסא דשכיח הוא ואיבעי ליה לאתנויי [גיטין ל.]. **דלמא אונסא דשכיח שאני.** ומעברא אונסא דמיגליא הוא דזימנין דלא [illegible] בהאי גיסא ומבעיא ליה לאפוקי אדעתיה (ודלמא אסיק אדעתיה) ואפי' הכי לא התנה משום הכי אי מיתנים בהאי זמן אמר גמר ומקני דליהוי גט אפילו עיכבו שום אונס אבל בעלמא אי איתנים פטור [נדרים כז:].

בתולה

א) א נשאת ליום הרביעי ואלמנה ליום החמישי שפעמים בשבת בתי דינין יושבין בעיירות ביום השני וביום החמישי שאם היה לו טענת בתולים היה משכים לבית דין: **גמ׳** אמר רב יוסף אמר רב יהודה אמר שמואל מפני מה אמרו בתולה נשאת ליום הרביעי לפי ששנינו ב) הגיע זמן ולא נישאו אוכלות משלו ואוכלות בתרומה יכול הגיע זמן באחד בשבת יהא מעלה לה מזונות לכך שנינו בתולה נשאת ליום הרביעי אמר רב יוסף ג) מריה דאברהם תלי תניא בדלא תניא הי תניא והי לא תניא הא תניא והא תניא אלא תלי תניא דמפרש טעמא בדתניא דלא מפרש טעמא אלא אי איתמר הכי איתמר אמר רב יהודה אמר שמואל מפני מה אמרו בתולה נשאת ליום הרביעי שאם היה לו טענת בתולים היה משכים לב"ד ותינשא באחד בשבת שאם היה לו טענת בתולים היה משכים לבית דין ד) ב שקדו חכמים על תקנת בנות ישראל שיהא טורח בסעודה שלשה ימים אחד בשבת ושני בשבת ושלישי בשבת וברביעי כונסה ועכשיו ששנינו שקדו אותה ששנינו הגיע זמן ולא נישאו אוכלות משלו ואוכלות בתרומה ג הגיע זמן באחד בשבת מתוך שאינו יכול לכנוס אינו מעלה לה מזונות לפיכך ד חלה הוא או שחלתה היא או שפירסה נדה אינו מעלה לה מזונות ואיכא דבעי לה מיבעיא חלה הוא מהו התם טעמא מאי משום דאנים והכא נמי הא אנים או דלמא התם אנים בתקנתא דתקינו ליה רבנן הכא לא ואם תמצי לומר חלה הוא מעלה לה מזונות חלתה היא מהו מצי אמר לה אנא הא קאימנא או דלמא מציא אמרה ליה נסתחפה שדהו ואם תמצי לומר אמרה ליה נסתחפה שדהו פירסה נדה מהו בשעת ווסתה לא תיבעי לך דלא

בתולה נשאת ליום הרביעי. תקנת חכמים היא שתנשא ברביעי בשבת כדמפרש טעמא: **שפעמים בשבת.** אבתולה קאי: **בשני ובחמישי.** אחת מעשר תקנות שתקן עזרא בבבא קמא בפרק מרובה (דף פב.) מפרש לכולהו ולכך תקנו שתנשא ברביעי שאם היה לו טענת בתולים ישכים לב"ד בעוד כעסו עליו ז) [ואם יש שהות בינתים יש לחוש] שמא יתפייס ותתקרר דעתו ויקיימנה ושמא היא זינתה תחתיו ונאסרה עליו כדילפינן (סוטה דף כח.) מונסתרה והיא נטמאה ומתוך שיבא לבית דין יתברר הדבר כשיצא הקול שמא יבואו עדים ובגמ׳ פריך ותינשא באחד בשבת: **גמ׳ לפי ששנינו כו׳.** לקמן מקשי עלה: **הגיע זמן ולא נישאו.** לקמן בפרק אע"פ תנן נותנין לבתולה שנים עשר חדש משתבעה הבעל והזהיר על הנישואין לפרנס עצמה בתכשיטין לפרנס קנדיר"ר בלע"ז ולאלמנה שלשים יום: **הגיע זמן.** זה ולא נישאו לחופה לקמן מפרש שעכב הבעל: **אוכלות משלו.** שהבעל חייב במזונות אשתו משהגיע זמן ב"ד כדלקמן בפרק נערה (דף נז:): **ואוכלות בתרומה.** אם כהן הוא והיא בת ישראל שהכהן מאכיל את אשתו תרומה כדיליף (לקמן דף נז:) מוכהן כי יקנה נפש: **לכך שנינו בתולה נשאת כו׳.** להודיע שתקנת חכמים מעכבתו מלכנוס ואין עכבה זו שלו: **מריה דאברהם כו׳.** תמה על דברי רבו ואמר מריה דאברהם מה זה היה לשמואל לומר כן ועוד שחלה רב יוסף ושכח תלמודו ותוהה על דברי הראשונים: **תלי תניא בדלא תניא.** תולה טעם משנה שנויה במשנה שאינה שנויה: ומקשינן לרב יוסף הי תניא והי לא תניא הא תניא והא תניא. זו שנויה וזו שנויה: **אלא תלי תניא דמפרש טעמא בדתניא דלא מפרש טעמא.** משנתינו טעמא מפורש בתוכה כדי שישכים לבית דין והגיע זמן אין שום טעם מפורש בה לומר מפני מה אם הגיע זמן באחד בשבת אינו מעלה לה מזונות: **ותינשא באחד בשבת.** כולה רב יוסף קאמר לה: **ועכשיו ששנינו שקדו.** ובשביל תקנה זו הוא מעוכב מלכנוס באחד בשבת מעתה אותה ששנינו כו׳: **לפיכך.** רב יוסף מסיים לה משמיה דנפשיה ומסבריה ואמר לפיכך הואיל ולמדנו שהמעוכב מחמת אונס אינו חייב לזונה חלה הוא כו׳: **הא קאימנא.** הנני מזומן: **נסתחפה שדהו.** לשון מטר סוחף (משלי כח) נשטפה שדך כלומר מזלך גרם כי מהיום אני מוטלת עליך לזון:

פשיט

בתולה. הא דלא קתני הבתולה כדקתני האשה נקנית היבמה נקנית (קדושין דף ב.) משום דהתם אקרא קאי כי יקח איש אשה (דברים כב) האשה הכתובה וכן היבמה אבל הכא לא קאי אקרא והא דלא תנן בפ"ק דקדושין (דף יד:) העבד עברי אף על פי דכתיב בקרא (שמות כא) כי תקנה עבד עברי משום דלא"כ ה"ל למיתני העבד העברי שאינו דבוק ואין דרך הש"ס לדבר כן ומיהו גבי איש ואשה רגילים בכל מקום לשנות בה׳ אע"ג דלא קאי אקרא כמו האשה שהלכה (יבמות דף קיד:) האשה שנתארמלה (לקמן דף טו:) האיש מדיר את בנו בנזיר (נזיר ד׳ כח:): **נשאת.** הא דלא קתני נושאין את הבתולה כמו האיש מקדש (קדושין דף מא.) לפי שעתה מקצר יותר ועוד דאי תנא הכי ה"א אפי׳ בעל כרחה כדתני (שם דף ב:) גבי הא דפריך וליתני האיש קונה ועוד דהתם אקרא קאי כי יקח איש אשה: **ליום הרביעי.** ולא בליל חמישי כדאמר בפרק בתרא דנדה (דף סה:) ו) דליכא כתובה דלא רמו בה תיגרא כ"ש אם יעשה נשואין בליל ה׳ דליכא למיחש שיטרד בנשואין וכתובה ולא יבעול: **שאם** היה לו טענת וכו׳. ואם תאמר הא תינח אשת כהן או פחותה מבת שלש דליכא אלא חד ספיקא כדאמרינן בגמרא (לקמן ט.) אבל בשאר נשים דאיכא ספק ספיקא אמאי תנשא ליום ד׳ ואומר ר"ת דלא פלוג רבנן בתקנתא ומשום אשת כהן ופחותה מג׳ תקנו בכל הנשים שינשאו ביום ד׳ ובקונטרס פי׳ שמתוך כך יתברר הדבר ויבואו עדים שזינתה ברצון וקשה לפירושו דאמרינן בגמרא (שם:) אמר אביי אף אנן נמי תנינא דהאומר פתח פתוח מצאתי נאמן לאוסרה עליו בתולה נשאת כו׳ מאי לאו דקטעין פתח פתוח והשתא היכי מייתי ראיה לפ"ה הא אע"ג דלאו נאמן מכל מקום ישכים לבית דין שמתוך כך יצא הקול ויבואו עדים ויתברר הדבר וי"ל דלא מייתי אביי ראיה לרבי אלעזר אלא שהוא בקי ומכיר אם הוא פתח פתוח דאם אינו בקי לא יצא הקול ולא יבא לידי בירור כי יאמרו שהוא טעה וסבור שמצא פתח פתוח ואינו כן ולא יחושו לדבריו ועי"ל דגם לפ"ה לא היו מתקנים שתהא נשאת ליום ד׳ משום שמא יתברר על ידי עדים אבל כיון דבאשת כהן ובפחותה מבת שלש דנאמן לאוסרה עליו תקנו שתהא נשאת ברביעי גם בשאר נשים תקנו משום שמתוך כך יצא הקול ויתברר הדבר על ידי עדים והשתא מייתי אביי שפיר ממתניתין דבאשת כהן ובפחותה מבת שלש נאמן לאוסרה עליו. ותימה דהכא משמע דמשום חששא דזנות תקנו שתהא נשאת ברביעי ובפ"ב דגטין (דף יח. ושם) איכא מ"ד דתקנו זמן בגטין משום פירי אבל משום שמא יחפה על בת אחותו לא חיישינן משום דזנות לא שכיח וי"ל דהתם קאמר זנות דאתי לידי מיתה דהיינו בהתראה ובעדים לא שכיח אי נמי הכא שלא תשב עמו באיסור כל ימיו חשו אפילו לזנות אע"ג דלא שכיח:

מפני מה אמרו בתולה נשאת ליום הרביעי לפי ששנינו כו׳. אין שואל הטעם למה נשאת ברביעי דאם כן לא הוה משני מידי אלא הכי פירושו מפני מה אמרו כלומר מאי נפקא מינה שתיקנו שנשאת ברביעי ומשני נפקא מינה לענין מזונות ותרומה ורב יוסף קא מתמה מריה דאברהם דהא נפקותא מפרשה בהדיא שאם היה לו טענת בתולים והוא מניח נפקותא זו המפורשת ותופס נפקותא אחרינא: **אלא** אי אתמר הכי אתמר א"ר יהודה אמר שמואל. ולא גרסינן רב יוסף דהא רב יוסף גופיה קאמר אלא אי איתמר: **מפני** מה אמרו כו׳. בניחותא גרסינן לה ולא בא להקשות אלא ותנשא באחד בשבת: **ותנשא** באחד בשבת. לא בעי לשנויי דנשאת ברביעי כדי שתבעל בחמישי משום ברכה שנאמרה בו לדגים כדאמרינן לקמן (דף ה.) ועוד למה לי טעם דשקדו תיפוק ליה משום ברכה ואומר ר"י דטעם דברכה אינה אלא עצה טובה ולא מקרי עבריינא אבל משום שקדו מקרי עבריינא וכן משמע לקמן דאמר טעמא משום ברכה אבל משום איקרורי דעתא לא חיישינן ומאי נפקא מינה אלא ודאי דמשום ברכה לא מקרי עבריינא:

מניח

מסורת הש"ס

א) לקמן ט:, ב) לקמן מח: נז. ע: [נדרים עג:], ג) ב"ב קלד: שבת כב. [עירובין עה:], ד) לקמן ג. ה., ה) נ"י כ"י, ו) [אין דליכא כתובה וכו׳ ליתא בנדה אך בשבת קל. ונראה כוונת התוס׳ במ"ש כדאמר בפ׳ בתרא דנדה סה: ר"ל שאמרו שם שאני כתובה דמגהי בה טפי ע׳ רש"י וערוך שם והא דכתבו דליכא כתובה הוא טעם בפ"ע].

ליקוטי רש"י

בתולה נשאת ליום הרביעי. תקנת חכמים היא שתנשא ברביעי בשבת כדמפרש טעמא בגמרא [רש"י כת"י משיטמ"ק]. **הגיע זמן.** שנים עשר חדש לבתולה משתבעה הבעל להכין עצמה לנשואין ולאלמנה שלשים יום. **ולא נישאו.** כגון שעכב החתן או אונס שלו [לקמן מח:]. **ואוכלות בתרומה.** אם כהן הוא והיא ישראלית שמשעה שקידשה אוכלת בתרומה מן התורה כדמפרש בגמרא ורבנן גזור עד השתא [לקמן נז.]. **אמר רב יוסף מריה דאברהם.** לשון תמיה הוא [שבת כב.]. רב יוסף חלה ושכח תלמודו כדאמרי׳ במסכת נדרים (דף מא.) ושמועות ששמע וכו׳ קודם חליו ועכשיו מתקשה בהן היה נותן אל לבו ותמה אם שמע כן והיה מצרן וה"ק רבש"ע אפשר ששמעתי וכו׳ שיורי גדול כזה דתלי תניא המשנה וכו׳ תולה טעמא בדבר שאינו במשנה ובברייתא וכו׳ ותולה את העיקר בטפל לו [רשב"ם ב"ב קלד:]. **שקדו.** ממהר ומנהם חברו עם לשון שקידה כמו שקד על דלתותי (משלי ח) ו"ה לשון אריכה [ירמיה א, יג]. **נסתחפה שדהו.** מזלו גרם כאדם שהמטר בא וסוחף את זרעו ועוקרו [לקמן יא:]. **נסחף,** נשטף, והפליגו גבורים כמו מטר סוחף (משלי כח) נסתחפה שדהו בלשון משנה סחפו לשון כלוי וכן הבר מטר סוחף ודונש פתר מטר סוחף כמו מעטף סוחף במערכה (ישעיה י) [שם מו, טו]. **סוחף,** שוטף, ובמשנה נסתחפה שדהו וכן נסחף אביריך (ירמיה מו) נשטפו ומעדו וכשלו [משלי כח, ג].

עין משפט נר מצוה

א א ב מיי׳ פ"י מהל׳ אישות הל׳ טו סמג עשין מח טוש"ע אה"ע סימן סד סעי׳ ג:

ב ג ד מיי׳ שם הלכה יט וסמג שם טוש"ע שם סי׳ ו סעי׳ ג:

תוספות רי"ד

בתולה נשאת ביום ד׳ ואלמנה ביום ה׳ שפעמים בשבת ב"ד יושבין בעיירות ביום ב׳ וביום ה׳ ואם היה לו טענת בתולים היה משכים לב"ד. פי׳ חכמים תקנו שתנשא הבתולה בד׳ כדי שיבעול בליל ה׳ ואם לא ימצא לה בתולים ילך בבוקר לב"ד טרם שיתקרר דעתו שיפייס עמה ויחקרו ב"ד מתי זינתה שמא תחתיו זינתה והיא אסורה לו. **שפעמים בשבת וכו׳.** פי׳ אבתולה יהיב טעמא וטעמא דאלמנה מפרש לקמן. ותקנות עזרא הוא שישבו ב"ד בעיירות בב׳ ובה׳. כדאמרינן בפ׳ מרובה מי׳ תקנות שתיקן עזרא. ואע"פ שבכל עיר ועיר היתה סנהדרין קבוע. בכל ימות השבוע היו עוסקים בתורה ובב׳ ובה׳ עוסקים בדינים. ולקמן פריך ותנשא באחד בשבת: **אמר ר"י** מפני מה אמרו בתולה נשאת בד׳ שאם היה לו טענת בתולים היה משכים לב"ד. ותנשא בא׳ בשבת ואם היה לו טענת בתולים היה משכים לב"ד שקדו חכמים על תקנות בנות ישראל שיהא טורח ג׳ ימים בסעודה א׳ בשבת שני ושלישי וברביעי כונסה. **ועכשיו ששנינו שקדו.** אותה ששנינו לקמן בפ׳ אע"פ נותנים לבתולה י"ב חודש משתבעה הבעל לפרנס א"ע. כשם שנותנים לאשה כך נותנים לאיש לפרנס א"ע ולאלמנה ל׳ יום הגיע זמן ולא נשאו אוכלות משלו. פי׳ וכגון שהבעל מעכב הגיע זמן בא׳ בשבת מתוך שאינו יכול לכנסה אינו מעלה לה מזונות לפיכך חלה הוא או שחלתה היא או שפירסה נדה אינו מעלה לה מזונות. **א"ר שמואל בר רב יצחק** ל"ש אלא מתקנות עזרא ואילך שאין ב"ד יושבין אלא בב׳ ובה׳. אבל אי איכא ב"ד קבועים בכל יום קודם תקנות עזרא אשה נשאת בכל יום והא בעינן שקדו דטריח לה. והכי אסיק רב אחא דכל אתנסא לא אכלה בין חלתה היא ובין חלה הוא. והכי הילכתא:

לעזי רש"י

קנדיר"ר. פירוש לפרנס, לספק צרכים (של בני אדם) (עיין רש"י ב"מ דף מו ע"א ד"ה ולפרנסה ורש"י גיטין דף סה ע"ב ד"ה פרנסה):

Other Amoraim are less sure of Rav Yosef's inference: וְאִיכָּא דְּבָעֵי לָהּ מִיבְּעֲיָא – **But there are those who posed this** matter **as a question,** asking: חָלָה הוּא מַהוּ – **What is [the law] if [the groom] becomes ill?** הָתָם טַעְמָא מַאי – Should we say that **there** – when the designated time arrived on Sunday – **what is the reason** that he does not have to provide support? מִשּׁוּם דַּאֲנִיס – **Because he was constrained** by a Rabbinic enactment from marrying until Wednesday, וְהָכָא נַמִּי הָא אֲנִיס – and **so too here,** where he became ill, **he is constrained** from marrying her and he should likewise not have to provide support. אוֹ דִלְמָא – **Or, perhaps** the cases are not comparable; הָתָם אֲנִיס בְּתַקַּנְתָּא דְּתַקִּינוּ לֵיהּ רַבָּנָן – **for there he was constrained by an enactment that the Rabbis instituted,** הָכָא לֹא – **whereas here,** when he is ill, this is **not** so.[22]

The Gemara continues:

וְאִם תִּמְצֵי לוֹמַר חָלָה הוּא מַעֲלֶה לָהּ מְזוֹנוֹת – **And if you conclude and say that if he became ill he does provide her with food,** חָלְתָה הִיא מַהוּ – **what is [the law] if she became ill,** rather than he? מָצֵי אָמַר לָהּ אֲנָא הָא קָאֵימְנָא – **Can he say to her: I am standing** here ready to go ahead with the wedding; I am not the cause of the delay and so I should not have to begin supporting you until the marriage can actually take place? אוֹ דִלְמָא מָצְיָא אָמְרָה לֵיהּ נִסְתַּחֲפָה שָׂדֵהוּ – **Or, perhaps, can she say to him that his field,** so to speak, **became inundated?**[23]

The Gemara continues:

וְאִם תִּמְצֵי לוֹמַר אָמְרָה לֵיהּ נִסְתַּחֲפָה שָׂדֵהוּ – **And if you conclude and say that she can say to him that his field became inundated,** פֵּירְסָה נִדָּה מַהוּ – **what is [the law] if she began to menstruate** on the day when the wedding was to take place?

The Gemara refines this last question:

בִּשְׁעַת וְסְתָּהּ – If she menstruated **at the time of her fixed period,** that is, when her period was due, לֹא תִּיבָּעֵי לָךְ – **you have no basis to inquire;**

NOTES

22. That is, where the marriage was postponed from Sunday to Wednesday because of the Rabbinic requirement that marriages take place on Wednesday, the time for the marriage cannot truly be said to have arrived until Wednesday, since that is the only day when marriages may legitimately be scheduled; therefore, the husband does not have to support her until then. But where the marriage was postponed because of the groom's illness, the scheduled time for the marriage can be said to have come and gone and, perhaps, he must begin to support his bride immediately (*Shitah Mekubetzes* ד״ה וכן מצאתי; cf. *Rashba;* see also *Chidushei R' Shmuel* §1).

23. That is, perhaps she can say to him that since the time for the marriage has arrived [and since she did not deliberately delay its taking place], he is now obligated to support her. As for any untoward circumstance (such as her illness) that prevents the marriage from taking place, it does not affect this obligation. Rather, we view it as no different than a case where someone owned a field that became flooded due to an act of God; it is just his own bad luck, and there is no one from whom he can demand redress (*Rashi,* as amplified by *Ramban* and *Rashba;* cf. *Tosafos* 2b ד״ה מציא; *Ritva*).

א) א נשאת ליום הרביעי ואלמנה ליום החמישי שפעמים בשבת בתי דינין יושבין בעיירות ביום השני וביום החמישי שאם היה לו טענת בתולים היה משכים לבית דין: גמ' אמר רב יוסף אמר רב יהודה אמר שמואל מפני מה אמרו בתולה נשאת ליום הרביעי לפי ששנינו ג) הגיע זמן ולא נישאו אוכלות משלו ואוכלות בתרומה יכול הגיע זמן באחד בשבת יהא מעלה לה מזונות לכך שנינו בתולה נשאת ליום הרביעי אמר רב יוסף ג) מריה דאברהם תלי תניא בדלא תניא הי תניא והי לא תניא הא תניא והא תניא אלא תלי תניא דמפרש טעמא בדתניא דלא מפרש טעמא אלא אי איתמר הכי איתמר אמר רב יהודה אמר שמואל מפני מה אמרו בתולה נשאת ליום הרביעי שאם היה לו טענת בתולים היה משכים לב"ד ותינשא באחד בשבת שאם היה לו טענת בתולים היה משכים לבית דין ד) ב שקדו חכמים על תקנת בנות ישראל שיהא טורח בסעודה שלשה ימים אחד בשבת ושני בשבת ושלישי בשבת וברביעי כונסה ועכשיו ששנינו שקדו אותה ששנינו הגיע זמן ולא נישאו אוכלות משלו ואוכלות בתרומה ג הגיע זמן באחד בשבת מתוך שאינו יכול לכנוס אינו מעלה לה מזונות לפיכך ד חלה הוא או שחלתה היא או שפירסה נדה אינו מעלה לה מזונות ואיכא דבעי לה מיבעיא חלה הוא מהו התם טעמא מאי משום דאנים והכא נמי הא אנים או דלמא התם אנים בתקנתא דתקינו ליה רבנן הכא לא ואם תמצי לומר חלה הוא מעלה לה מזונות חלתה היא מהו מצי אמר לה אנא הא קאימנא או דלמא מציא אמרה ליה נסתחפה שדהו ואם תמצי לומר אמרה ליה נסתחפה שדהו פירסה נדה מהו בשעת ווסתה לא תיבעי לך דלא

בתולה נשאת ליום הרביעי. תקנת חכמים היא שתנשא ברביעי בשבת כדמפרש טעמא: שפעמים בשבת. אבתולה קאי: בשני ובחמישי. אחת מעשר תקנות שתקן עזרא כבבא קמא בפרק מרובה (דף פב.) מפרש לכולהו ולכך תקנו שתנשא ברביעי שאם היה לו טוענת בתולים ישכים לב"ד בעוד כעסו עליו [ה] [ואם יש שהות בינתים יש לחוש] שמא יתפייס ותתקרר דעתו ויקיימנה ושמא היא זינתה תחתיו ונאסרה עליו כדילפינן (סוטה דף כח.) מונסתרה והיא נטמאה ומתוך שיבא לבית דין יתברר הדבר כשיצא הקול שמא יבואו עדים ובגמר' פריך ותינשא באחד בשבת: גמ' לפי ששנינו כו'. לקמן מקשי עלה: הגיע זמן ולא נישאו. לקמן בפרק אע"פ תנן נותנין לבתולה שנים עשר חדש משתבעה הבעל והזהיר על הנישואין לפרנס עצמה בתכשיטין לפרנס קנדיר"ר בלע"ז ולאלמנה שלשים יום: הגיע זמן. זה ולא נישאו לחופה לקמן מפרש שעכב הבעל: אוכלות משלו. שהבעל חייב במזונות אשתו מתקנת ב"ד כדלקמן בפרק נערה (דף מז:): ואוכלות בתרומה. אם כהן הוא והיא בת ישראל שהכהן מאכיל את אשתו תרומה כדיליף (לקמן דף נז:) מוכהן כי יקנה נפש: לכך שנינו בתולה נשאת כו'. להודיע שתקנת חכמים מעכבתו מלכנוס ואין עכבה זו שלו: מריה דאברהם כו'. תמה על דברי רבו ואמר מריה דאברהם מה זה היה לשמואל לומר כן ועוד שחלה רב יוסף ושכח תלמודו ותוהה על דבריו הראשונים: תלי תניא בדלא תניא. תולה טעם משנה שנויה במשנה שאינה שנויה: ומקשינן לרב יוסף הי תניא והי לא תניא הא תניא והא תניא. זו שנויה וזו שנויה: אלא תלי תניא דמפרש טעמא בדתניא דלא מפרש טעמא. משנתינו טעמא מפורש בתוכה כדי שישכים לבית דין והגיע זמן אין שום טעם מפורש בה לומר מפני מה אם הגיע זמן באחד בשבת אינו מעלה לה מזונות: ותינשא באחד בשבת. כולה רב יוסף קאמר לה: ועכשיו ששנינו שקדו. ובשביל תקנה זו הוא מעוכב מלכנוס באחד בשבת מעתה אותה ששנינו כו': לפיכך. רב יוסף מסיים לה משמיה דנפשיה ומסבריה ואמר לפיכך הואיל ולמדנו שהמעוכב מחמת אונס אינו חייב לזונה חלה הוא כו': הא קאימנא. הנני מזומן: נסתחפה שדהו. לשון מטר סוחף (משלי כח) נשטפה שדך כלומר מזלך גרם כי מהיום אני מוטלת עליך לזון:

פשיט

בתולה. הא דלא קתני הבתולה כדתני האשה נקנית היבמה ניקנית (קידושין דף ב.) משום דהתם אקרא קאי כי יקח איש אשה (דברים כב) האשה הכתובה וכן היבמה אבל הכא לא קאי אקרא והא דלא תנן בפ"ק דקידושין (דף יד:) העבד עברי אף על פי דכתיב בקרא (שמות כא) כי תקנה עבד עברי משום דא"כ ה"ל למתני העבד העברי שאינו דבוק ואין דרך הש"ס לדבר כן ומיהו גבי איש ואשה רגילים בכל מקום לשנות בה' אע"ג דלא קאי אקרא כמו האשה שהלכה (יבמות דף קיד:) האשה שנתארמלה (לקמן דף טו:) האיש מדיר את בנו בנזיר (נזיר ד' כח:): **נשאת.** הא דלא קתני נושאין את הבתולה כמו האיש מקדש (קידושין דף מא.) לפי שעתה מקלר יותר ועוד דאי תנא הכי ה"א אפי' בעל כרחה כדמשני (שם דף ב:) גבי הא דפריך וליתני האיש קונה ועוד דהתם אקרא קאי כי יקח איש אשה: **ליום** הרביעי. ולא בליל חמישי כדאמר בפרק בתרא דנדה (דף סה:) ו) דליכא כתובה דלא רמו בה תיגרא כ"ש אם יעשה נשואין בליל ה' דאיכא למיחש שיטרד בנשואין וכתובה ולא יבעול: **שאם** היה לו טענת וכו'. ואם תאמר הא מיגו אשת כהן או פתוחה מבת שלש דליכא אלא חד ספיקא כדאמרינן בגמרא (לקמן ט.) אבל בשאר נשים דאיכא ספק ספיקא אמאי תנשא ליום ד' ואומר ר"ת דלא פלוג רבנן בתקנתא ומשום אשת כהן ופתוחה מג' תקנו בכל הנשים שינשאו ביום ד' ובקונטרס פי' שמתוך כך יתברר הדבר ויבואו עדים שזינתה ברצון וקשה לפירושו דאמרינן בגמרא (שם:) אמר אביי אף אנן נמי תנינא דהאומר פתח פתוח מצאתי נאמן לאוסרה עליו בתולה נשאת כו' מאי לאו דקטעין פתח פתוח והשתא היכי מייתי ראיה לפ"ה הא אע"ג דאינו נאמן מכל מקום ישכים לבית דין שמתוך כך יצא הקול ויבואו עדים ויתברר הדבר וי"ל דלא מייתי אביי ראיה לרבי אלעזר אלא שהוא בקי ומכיר אם הוא פתח פתוח דאם אינו בקי לא יצא הקול ולא יבא לידי בירור כי יאמרו שהוא טעה וסבור שמצא פתח פתוח ואינו כן ולא יחושו לדבריו ועי"ל דגם לפ"ה לא היו מתקנים שתהא ניסת ליום ד' משום שמא יתברר על ידי עדים אבל כיון דבאשת כהן ובפתוחה מבת שלש דנאמן לאוסרה עליו תקנו שתהא ניסת ברביעי גם בשאר נשים תקנו משום שמתוך כך יצא הקול ויתברר הדבר על ידי עדים והשתא מייתי אביי שפיר ממתניתין דבאשת כהן ובפתוחה מבת שלש נאמן לאוסרה עליו. ותימה דהכא משמע דמשום חששא דזנות תקנו שתהא ניסת ברביעי ובפ"ב דגטין (דף יח. ושם) איכא מ"ד דתקנו זמן בגטין משום פירי אבל משום שמא יחפה על בת אחותו לא חיישינן משום דזנות לא שכיח וי"ל דהתם קאמר זנות דאתי לידי מיתה דהיינו בהתראה ובעדים לא שכיח אי נמי הכא שלא תשב עמו באיסור כל ימיו חשו אפילו לזנות אע"ג דלא שכיח:

מפני מה אמרו בתולה נשאת ליום הרביעי לפי ששנינו כו'. אין שואל הטעם למה נשאת ברביעי דאם כן לא הוה משני מידי אלא הכי פירושו מפני מה אמרו כלומר מאי נפקא מינה שתיקנו שנשאת ברביעי ומשני נפקא מינה לענין מזונות ותרומה ורב יוסף קא מתמה מריה דאברהם דהא נפקותא מפרשה בהדיא שאם היה לו טענת בתולים והוא מניח נפקותא זו המפורשת ותופס נפקותא אחרינא: **אלא** אי אתמר הכי אתמר א"ר יהודה אמר שמואל. ולא גרסינן רב יוסף דהא רב יוסף גופיה קאמר אלא אי איתמר: **מפני** מה אמרו כו'. בניחותא גרסינן לה ולא בא להקשות אלא ותנשא באחד בשבת: **ותנשא** באחד בשבת. לא בעי לשנויי דנשאת ברביעי כדי שתבעל בחמישי משום ברכה שנאמרה בו לדגים כדאמרינן לקמן (דף ה.) ועוד למה לי טעם דשקדו תיפוק ליה משום ברכה ואומר ר"י דטעם דברכה אינה אלא עצה טובה ולא מקרי עבריינא אבל משום שקדו מקרי עבריינא וכן משמע לקמן דאמר טעמא משום ברכה אבל משום איקרורי דעתא לא חיישינן ומאי נפקא מינה אלא ודאי דמשום ברכה לא מקרי עבריינא:

מגיה

מסורת הש"ס

א) לקמן ט., ב) לקמן מח. מ: ע. [נדרים עג.], ג) ב"ב קלד: שבת כג. [עירובין עה:], ד) לקמן ג. ה., ה) נ"א כ"י, ו) [כן דליכא כתובה וכו' ליתא בנדה אך בשבת קל. ונראה כוונת התוס' במ"ש כדאמר בפ' בתרא דנדה סה: ר"ל שאמרו שם שאני כתובה דמגנבי בה טפי ע' רש"י וערוך שם והא דכתבו דליכא כתובה הוא טעם בפ"ע].

ליקוטי רש"י

בתולה נשאת ליום הרביעי. תקנת חכמים היא שתנשא ברביעי בשבת כדמפרש טעמא בגמרא [רש"י כת"י משיטמ"ק]. הגיע זמן. שנים עשר חדש לבתולה משתבעה הבעל להכין עצמה לנשואין ולאלמנה שלשים יום. ולא נישאו. כגון שעכב החתן או אונס שלו [לקמן נז:]. ואוכלות בתרומה. אם כהן הוא והיא ישראלית משתבעה שקידשה אוכלת בתרומה מן התורה כדמפרש בגמרא [לקמן נז.]. אמר רב יוסף מריה דאברהם. לשון תמיה הוא [שבת כב.]. רב יוסף חלה ושכח תלמודו כדאמרי' במסכת נדרים (דף מא.) ושמועות ששמע וכו' קודם חליו ועכשיו מקשה בהן היה נותן אל לבו ותמה מה שמע כן והיה מתרגם וסבר רבא ארבע אפשר שטעה וכו' שינוי גדול מה דתלי תניא המשנה וכו' תולה טעמא בדלא תניא לדבר שאינו משנה ובבריותא וכו' ותולה את העיקר בטפל לו [רשב"ם ב"ב קלד:]. שקדו. ממהר ומנסה חברו עם לשון שמירה כדי שימהר לבקר על דלתותי (משלי ח) י"ח לשון חריפה (ירמיה ה, ו). נסתחפה שדהו. מזלך גרם כאדם שמטר על שדהו את זרעו ועוקרו [לקמן יא:]. נסחף. שנפתה והפליגו בגוריך כמו מטר סוחף (משלי כח) נסתחפה שדהו בלשון שגורה ומנסם חברו לשון כלין וכן סבר מטר סוחף ודוגם פחד מטר סוחף וזהו כמו מטר סוחף כמו מעסף פחדה במעגלה (ישעיה ז) [שם מו. טון. סוחף, סוחף ובמשנה נסתחפה שדהו וכן נסחף אביריך (ירמיה מו) נשטפו ומעדו וכשלו (משלי כח, ג)].

עין משפט נר מצוה

א א ב מיי' פ"י מהל' אישות הל' טו סמג עשין מח טוש"ע אה"ע סימן סד סעי' ג:
ב ג ד מיי' שם הלכה יט וסמג שם טוש"ע שם סי' ט סעי' ג:

תוספות רי"ד

בתולה נשאת ביום ד' ואלמנה ביום ה' שפעמים בשבת ב"ד יושבין בעיירות ביום ב' וביום ה' ואם היה לו טענת בתולים היה משכים לב"ד. פי' חכמים תקנו שתנשא הבתולה בד' כדי שיבעול בליל ה' ואם לא ימצא לה בתולים ילך בבוקר לב"ד טרם שיתקרר דעתו שיפייס עמה ויחקרו ב"ד מתי זינתה שמא תחתיו זינתה והיא אסורה לו. שפעמים בשבת וכו'. פי' אבתולה יהיב טעמא וטעמא דאלמנה מפרש לקמן. ותקנות עזרא הוא שישבו ב"ד בעיירות בב' ובה'. כדאמרינן בפ' מרובה מי' תקנות שתיקן עזרא. ואע"פ שבכל עיר ועיר היתה סנהדרין קבוע. בכל ימות השבוע היו עוסקים בתורה ובב' ובה' עוסקים בדינים. ולקמן פריך ותנשא באחד בשבת: אמר ר"י מפני מה אמרו בתולה נשאת בד' שאם היה לו טענת בתולים היה משכים לב"ד. ותנשא בא' בשבת ואם היה לו טענת בתולים היה משכים לב"ד שקדו חכמים על תקנות בנות ישראל שיהא טורח ג' ימים בסעודה א' בשבת שני ושלישי וברביעי כונסה. ועכשיו ששנינו שקדו. אותה ששנינו לקמן בפ' אע"פ נותנים לבתולה י"ב חדש משתבעה הבעל לפרנס א"ע. כשם שנותנים לאשה כך נותנים לאיש לפרנס א"ע ולאלמנה ל' יום הגיע זמן ולא נשאו אוכלות משלו. פי' וכגון שהבעל מעכב הגיע זמן בא' בשבת שמתוך שאינו יכול לכנסה אינו מעלה לה מזונות לפיכך חלה הוא או שחלתה היא או שפירסה נדה אינו מעלה לה מזונות. א"ר שמואל בר רב יצחק ל"ש אלא מתקנות עזרא ואילך שאין ב"ד יושבין אלא בב' ובה'. אבל אי איכא ב"ד קבועים בכל יום כקודם תקנות עזרא אשה נשאת בכל יום והא בעינן שקדו דטרחיה לה. והכי אסיק לה אחא דכל אתנסא לא אכלה בין חלתה היא ובין חלה הוא. והכי הילכתא:

לעזי רש"י

קנדיר"ר. פירוש לפרנס, לספק לרכוש (של בני אדם) (עיין רש"י ב"מ דף מו ע"א ד"ה ולפרנסם ורש"י גיטין דף סה ע"ב ד"ה פרנסה):

Rav Yosef questions the meaning of Shmuel's statement:[12] אָמַר רַב יוֹסֵף – **Rav Yosef said:** מָרֵיהּ דְּאַבְרָהָם – **Master of Abraham!**[13] תָּלֵי תַנְיָא בְּדְלָא תַנְיָא – **He makes [a Mishnah] that was taught dependent on [a Mishnah] that was not taught! – ? –**

The Gemara at first does not understand Rav Yosef's question: הֵי תַנְיָא וְהֵי לֹא תַנְיָא – **Which [Mishnah] was taught and which was not taught?** הָא תַנְיָא וְהָא תַנְיָא – Why, both **this [Mishnah]**[14] **was taught and that [Mishnah]**[15] **was taught! – ? –**

The Gemara explains Rav Yosef's question: אֶלָּא תָּלֵי תַנְיָא דִּמְפָרֵשׁ טַעְמָא – **Rather,** the problem is that **he** [Shmuel] **made [a Mishnah] whose reason was taught** in the Mishnah itself **dependent** בְּדְתַנְיָא דְּלָא מְפָרֵשׁ טַעְמָא – **on [a Mishnah] whose reason was not taught** in the Mishnah itself![16] – ? –

Rav Yosef therefore revises his citation of Shmuel: אֶלָּא אִי אִיתְּמַר – **Rather, if** anything **was stated** by Shmuel הָכִי אִיתְּמַר – **this is how it was stated:** אָמַר רַב יְהוּדָה אָמַר שְׁמוּאֵל – **Rav Yehudah said in the name of Shmuel:** מִפְּנֵי מָה אָמְרוּ בְּתוּלָה נִשֵּׂאת לְיוֹם הָרְבִיעִי – **Why did [the Sages] say that a virgin is married on Wednesday?** שֶׁאִם הָיָה לוֹ טַעֲנַת בְּתוּלִים – **So that if he had a claim regarding her virginity,** הָיָה מַשְׁכִּים לְבֵית דִּין – **he would go early** the next morning – on Thursday – **to court,** as the Mishnah said. וְתִינָּשֵׂא בְּאֶחָד בְּשַׁבָּת – **But,** you may ask: **Let her be married on Sunday,** שֶׁאִם הָיָה לוֹ טַעֲנַת בְּתוּלִים – **so that if he had a claim regarding her virginity,** הָיָה מַשְׁכִּים לְבֵית דִּין – **he would go early** the next morning – on Monday – **to court?** שֶׁקָּדוּ חֲכָמִים עַל תַּקָּנַת בְּנוֹת יִשְׂרָאֵל – The answer is that **the Sages were diligent in promoting the welfare of Jewish daughters** שֶׁיְּהֵא טוֹרֵחַ בִּסְעוּדָה שְׁלֹשָׁה יָמִים – and desired **that [the husband] should busy himself with** preparing **the** wedding **feast**[17] **for three** consecutive **days,** אֶחָד בְּשַׁבָּת וְשֵׁנִי בְּשַׁבָּת וּשְׁלִישִׁי בְּשַׁבָּת – viz. **Sunday, Monday, and Tuesday,** וּבָרְבִיעִי כּוֹנְסָהּ – **and** then **marry her on Wednesday.**[18] וְעַכְשָׁיו שֶׁשָּׁנִינוּ שֶׁקָּדוּ – **And,** continues Shmuel,[19] **now that we have learned that [the Sages] were diligent** in promoting the welfare of Jewish daughters, and required that the wedding take place on Wednesday, אוֹתָהּ שֶׁשָּׁנִינוּ – it follows regarding **that which we learned** in a Mishnah: הִגִּיעַ זְמַן וְלֹא נִישְׂאוּ – If THE designated TIME ARRIVED AND THEY WERE NOT MARRIED, אוֹכְלוֹת מִשֶּׁלּוֹ וְאוֹכְלוֹת בִּתְרוּמָה – THEY EAT OF HIS food, AND THEY EAT OF *TERUMAH*; הִגִּיעַ זְמַן בְּאֶחָד בְּשַׁבָּת – that if **the** designated **time arrived on Sunday,** מִתּוֹךְ שֶׁאֵינוֹ יָכוֹל לִכְנוֹס – **since [the husband] is not able to marry** her on Sunday due to the Rabbinic enactment, אֵינוֹ מַעֲלֶה לָהּ מְזוֹנוֹת – **he does not have to provide her with food** until Wednesday.

It follows from Shmuel's teaching – as revised by Rav Yosef – that if the wedding is delayed, the husband must begin providing for his wife's support only if the delay was due to his own procrastination, but not if it was due to an enactment of the Sages, which is beyond the husband's control. From which Rav Yosef draws the following inference:[20] לְפִיכָךְ חָלָה הוּא אוֹ שֶׁחָלְתָה הִיא – **Therefore,** if **he became ill, or she became ill,** and so the wedding had to be postponed, אוֹ שֶׁפֵּירְסָה נִדָּה – **or** if **she began to menstruate,** אֵינוֹ מַעֲלֶה לָהּ מְזוֹנוֹת – **he does not have to provide her with food.**[21]

NOTES

– and relies upon this to explain why our Mishnah singles out Wednesday as the appropriate day for marriage. But we still have no reason why the obligation of support itself does not set in on Sunday! The Gemara will immediately address this difficulty (*Ramban*).

12. Although Rav Yosef himself was the one who originally quoted this teaching of Rav Yehudah in the name of Shmuel, he could at first make no sense of it, so he himself questioned it. Furthermore, Rav Yosef once became seriously ill and forgot much of his learning (as the Gemara recounts in *Nedarim* 41a). Upon his recovery, he recalled a version of what he had once taught, but could not understand it himself [for his weakened memory had caused him to misquote the teaching]. He therefore wondered how he could have taught this (*Rashi;* see also *Rashbam, Bava Basra* 134b ד״ה א״ר יוסף and *Shitah Mekubetzes* here).

13. This is an expostulation, like "Master of the Universe!" (*Rashbam* ibid.).

14. I.e. our Mishnah, which requires a virgin to be married on Wednesday.

15. I.e. the Mishnah below, 57a, which Shmuel cited.

16. That is, our Mishnah states explicitly the reason a virgin must be married on Wednesday – it is so that the husband will be able to go to court the next morning if necessary. [True, this does not explain why the marriage cannot take place on Sunday, but it is a sound basis for excluding all other days, and for some unknown reason the Mishnah relies upon it to exclude Sunday as well.] The other Mishnah, however, states absolutely no reason why the husband's obligation to support his wife should not begin on Sunday (if the waiting period has ended). How can a Mishnah that contains no reason at all shed light on a Mishnah that states the reason for its ruling, and be adduced to explain why a virgin cannot be married on Sunday? (*Rashi,* with elucidation of *Ramban*).

17. I.e. the food for the feasts that take place on the seven days of celebration that follow the wedding of a virgin (see *Ramban,* cited in next note).

18. Were, however, the wedding to be scheduled on Sunday, then the food that the husband prepared before the Sabbath would not last through the Sabbath [and the seven days of celebration]. Rather, the husband would have to busy himself preparing food during the week of celebration itself, rather than spending that time with his bride. Thus the welfare of Jewish daughters is promoted by having the wedding scheduled on Wednesday (*Ramban*).

Alternatively, the welfare of Jewish daughters is promoted by this enactment because, were the wedding to be scheduled on Sunday, the husband would not prepare before the Sabbath and the wedding would be a hastily prepared affair; and, as a result of having invested so little effort in the wedding, the groom might take a cavalier attitude towards his bride and falsely impugn her virginity (*Ritva*).

19. See *Rashba.*

20. See *Rashi.* [It would make no sense for Shmuel to draw an inference from his own teaching; rather, what follows is an inference that Rav Yosef drew from the teaching that he had received from Rav Yehudah in the name of Shmuel. See, however, *Chidushei R' Akiva Eiger.*]

21. Since the delay was due to circumstances beyond the husband's control he does not have to begin to pay for her support.

The Gemara would seem to imply that if the bride began to menstruate, the wedding must indeed be delayed. Indeed, this is the view of several Rishonim, including *Ri Migash* (cited by *Ramban* and *Rashba* below, 4a) and *Rambam* (*Hil. Ishus* 10:2), and follows logically from their view that *nesuin* requires that the bride and groom be confined together (יחוד), something that is forbidden while the bride is a *niddah* (see below, 4a).

Other Rishonim, however, disagree. In their view *nesuin* does not require the bride and groom to be secluded together; rather, it is sufficient for the bride to be brought into the husband's home (*Ran*), or into the symbolic enclosure of a specially decorated canopy (*Ittur, Birchas Chasanim* §2, cited by *Beis Yosef* §61). As for our Gemara, they take it to mean, not that the husband *may not* marry her while she is a *niddah,* but, rather, that it cannot be demanded of him that he do so. That is to say, should the husband wish to delay the marriage until such a time as it can be consummated, he is within his rights and he cannot be required to support her in the meantime (*Ran*). [For a more thorough summary of the various views on this issue see *Encyclopedia Talmudis* ערך חפה.]

Alternatively, *Haflaah* suggests that if the bride became a menstruant the wedding had to be postponed because were it not, the marriage would not be consummated the night of the wedding, thus defeating the purpose of scheduling the marriage on Wednesday (viz. that the husband should be able to go to court the next day should he find his wife not a virgin). The wedding therefore had to be postponed to some other Wednesday, when the marriage could be consummated. (But see *Chidushei R' Akiva Eiger.*)

בתולה

מתני׳ **בתולה** נשאת ליום הרביעי ואלמנה ליום החמישי שפעמים בשבת בתי דינין יושבין בעיירות ביום השני וביום החמישי שאם היה לו טענת בתולים היה משכים לבית דין: **גמ׳** אמר רב יוסף אמר רב יהודה אמר שמואל מפני מה אמרו בתולה נשאת ליום הרביעי לפי ששנינו הגיע זמן ולא נישאו אוכלות משלו ואוכלות בתרומה יכול הגיע זמן באחד בשבת יהא מעלה לה מזונות לכך שנינו בתולה נשאת ליום הרביעי אמר רב יוסף מריה דאברהם תלי תניא בדלא תניא הי תניא והי לא תניא הא תניא והא תניא אלא תלי תניא דמפרש טעמא בדתניא דלא מפרש טעמא אלא אי איתמר הכי איתמר אמר רב יהודה אמר שמואל מפני מה אמרו בתולה נשאת ליום הרביעי שאם היה לו טענת בתולים היה משכים לב"ד ותינשא באחד בשבת שאם היה לו טענת בתולים היה משכים לבית דין שקדו חכמים על תקנת בנות ישראל שיהא טורח בסעודה שלשה ימים אחד בשבת ושני בשבת ושלישי בשבת וברביעי כונסה ועכשיו ששנינו שקדו אותה ששנינו הגיע זמן ולא נישאו אוכלות משלו ואוכלות בתרומה הגיע זמן באחד בשבת מתוך שאינו יכול לכנוס אינו מעלה לה מזונות לפיכך חלה הוא או שחלתה היא או שפירסה נדה אינו מעלה לה מזונות ואיכא דבעי לה מיבעיא חלה הוא מהו התם טעמא מאי משום דאנים והכא נמי הא אנים או דלמא התם אנים בתקנתא דתקינו ליה רבנן הכא לא ואם תמצי לומר חלה הוא מעלה לה מזונות חלתה היא מהו מצי אמר לה אנא הא קאימנא או דלמא מציא אמרה ליה נסתחפה שדהו ואם תמצי לומר אמרה ליה נסתחפה שדהו פירסה נדה מהו בשעת ווסתה לא תיבעי לך דלא

רש"י

בתולה נשאת ליום הרביעי. תקנת חכמים היא שתנשא ברביעי בשבת כדמפרש טעמא: שפעמים בשבת. אבתולה קאי: בשני ובחמישי. אחת מעשר תקנות שתקן עזרא בבבא קמא בפרק מרובה (דף פב.) מפרש לכולהו ולכך תקנו שתנשא ברביעי שאם היה לו טענת בתולים ישכים לב"ד בעוד כעסו עליו [ה] [ואם יש שהות בינתים יש לחוש] שמא יתפייס ותתקרר דעתו ויקיימנה ושמא היא זינתה תחתיו ונאסרה עליו כדילפינן (סוטה דף כח.) מונסתרה והיא נטמאה ומתוך שילך לבית דין יתברר הדבר כשילא הקול שמא יבואו עדים ובגמ׳ פריך ותינשא באחד בשבת: **גמ׳** לפי ששנינו כו׳. לקמן מקשי עלה: הגיע זמן ולא נישאו. לקמן בפרק אע"פ תנן נותנין לבתולה שנים עשר חדש משתבעה הבעל והזהיר על הנישואין לפרנס עלמה בתכשיטין לפרנס קנדיר"ר בלע"ז ולאלמנה שלשים יום: הגיע זמן. זה ולא נישאו לחופה לקמן מפרש שעכב הבעל: אוכלות משלו. שהבעל חייב במזונות אשתו מתקנת ב"ד כדלקמן בפרק נערה (דף מו:): ואוכלות בתרומה. אם כהן הוא והיא בת ישראל שהכהן מאכיל את אשתו תרומה כדיליף (לקמן דף נז:) מוכהן כי יקנה נפש: לכך שנינו בתולה נשאת כו׳. להודיע שתקנת חכמים מעכבתו מלכנוס ואין עכבה זו שלו: מריה דאברהם כו׳. תמה על דברי רבו ואמר מריה דאברהם מה זה היה לשמואל לומר כן ועוד שחלה רב יוסף ושכח תלמודו ותוהה על דבריו הראשונים: תלי תניא בדלא תניא. תולה טעם משנה שנויה במשנה שאינה שנויה: ומקשינן לרב יוסף הי תניא והי לא תניא הא תניא והא תניא. זו שנויה וזו שנויה: אלא תלי תניא דמפרש טעמא בדתניא דלא מפרש טעמא. מסגמינו טעמא מפורש בתוכה כדי שישכים לבית דין והגיע זמן אין שום טעם מפורש בה לומר מפני מה אם הגיע זמן באחד בשבת אינו מעלה לה מזונות: ותינשא באחד בשבת. כולה רב יוסף קאמר לה: ועכשיו ששנינו שקדו. ובשביל תקנה זו הוא מעוכב מלכנוס באחד בשבת מעתה אותה ששנינו כו׳: לפיכך. רב יוסף מסיים לה משמיה דנפשיה ומסבריה ואמר לפיכך הואיל ולמדנו שהמעוכב מחמת אונס אינו חייב לזונה חלה הוא כו׳: הא קאימנא. הנני מזומן: נסתחפה שדהו. לשון מטר סוחף (משלי כח) נשטפה שדך כלומר מזלך גרם כי מהיום אני מוטלת עליך לזון: פשיט

תוספות

בתולה. הא דלא קתני הבתולה כדתני האשה נקנית היבמה ניקנית (קדושין דף ב.) משום דהתם אקרא קאי כי יקח איש אשה (דברים כב) האשה הכתובה וכן היבמה אבל הכא לא קאי אקרא והא דלא תנן בפ"ק דקידושין (דף יד:) העבד עברי אף על פי דכתיב בקרא (שמות כא) כי תקנה עבד עברי משום דא"כ ה"ל למתני העבד העברי שאינו דבוק ואין דרך הש"ס לדבר כן ומיהו גבי איש ואשה רגילים בכל מקום לשנות בה׳ אע"ג דלא קאי אקרא כמו האשה שהלכה (יבמות דף קיד:) האשה שנתארמלה (לקמן דף טו:) האיש מדיר את בנו בנזיר (נזיר ד׳ כח:): **נשאת.** הא דלא קתני נושאין את הבתולה כמו האיש מקדש (קדושין דף מא.) לפי שעתה מקלר יותר ועוד דאי תנא הכי ה"א אפי׳ בעל כרחה כדמשני (שם דף ב:) גבי הא דפריך וליתני האיש קונה ועוד דהתם אקרא קאי כי יקח איש אשה: **ליום** הרביעי. ולא בליל חמישי כדאמר בפרק בתרא דנדה (דף סה:) [י] דליכא כתובה דלא רמו בה תיגרא כ"ש אם יעשה נשואין בליל ה׳ דאיכא למיחש שיטרד בנשואין וכתובה ולא יבעול: **שאם** היה לו טענת וכו׳. ואם תאמר הא תינח אשת כהן או פחותה מבת שלש דליכא אלא חד ספיקא כדאמרינן בגמרא (לקמן ט.) אבל בשאר נשים דאיכא ספק ספיקא אמאי תנשא ליום ד׳ ואומר ר"ת דלא פלוג רבנן בתקנתא ומשום אשת כהן ופחותה מג׳ תקנו בכל הנשים שינשאו ביום ד׳ ובקונטרס פי׳ שמתוך כך יתברר הדבר ויבואו עדים שזינתה ברלון וקשה לפירושו דאמרינן בגמרא (שם:) אמר אביי אף אנן נמי תנינא דהאומר פתח פתוח מלאתי נאמן לאוסרה עליו בתולה נשאת כו׳ מאי לאו דקטעין פתח פתוח והשתא היכי מייתי ראיה לפ"ה הא אע"ג דאינו נאמן מכל מקום ישכים לבית דין שמתוך כך יצא הקול ויבואו עדים ויתברר הדבר וי"ל דלא מייתי אביי ראיה לרבי אלעזר אלא שהוא בקי ומכיר אם הוא פתח פתוח דאם אינו בקי לא יצא הקול ולא יבא לידי בירור כי יאמרו שהוא טעה וסבור שמצא פתח פתוח ואינו כן ולא יחושו לדבריו ועי"ל דגם לפ"ה לא היו מתקנים שתהא ניסת ליום ד׳ משום שמא יתברר על ידי עדים אבל כיון דבאשת כהן ובפחותה מבת שלש דנאמן לאוסרה עליו תקנו שתהא ניסת ברביעי גם בשאר נשים תקנו משום שמתוך כך יצא הקול ויתברר הדבר על ידי עדים והשתא מייתי אביי שפיר ממתניתין דבאשת כהן ובפחותה מבת שלש נאמן לאוסרה עליו. ותימה דהכא משמע דמשום חששא דזנות תקנו שתהא ניסת ברביעי ובפ"ב דגטין (דף יז. ושם) איכא מ"ד דתקנו זמן בגטין משום פירי אבל משום שמא יחפה על בת אחותו לא חיישינן משום דזנות לא שכיח וי"ל דהתם קאמר זנות דאתי לידי מיתה דהיינו בהתראה ובעדים לא שכיח אי נמי הכא שלא תשב עמו באיסור כל ימיו חשו אפילו לזנות אע"ג דלא שכיח:

מפני מה אמרו בתולה נשאת ליום הרביעי לפי ששנינו כו׳. אין שואל הטעם למה נשאת ברביעי דאם כן לא הוה משני מידי אלא הכי פירושו מפני מה אמרו כלומר מאי נפקא מינה שתיקנו שנשאת ברביעי ומשני נפקא מינה לענין מזונות ותרומה ורב יוסף קא מתמה מריה דאברהם דהא נפקותא מפרשה בהדיא שאם היה לו טענת בתולים והוא מניח נפקותא זו המפורשת ותופס נפקותא אחרינא: **אלא** אי אתמר הכי אתמר א"ר יהודה אמר שמואל. ולא גרסינן רב יוסף דהא רב יוסף גופיה קאמר אלא אי איתמר:

מפני מה אמרו כו׳. בניחותא גרסינן לה ולא בא להקשות אלא ותנשא באחד בשבת: **ותנשא** באחד בשבת. לא בעי לשנויי דנשאת ברביעי כדי שתבעל בחמישי משום ברכה שנאמרה בו לדגים כדאמרינן לקמן (דף ה.) ועוד למה לי טעם דשקדו תיפוק ליה משום ברכה ואומר ר"י דטעם דברכה אינה אלא עלה טובה ולא מקרי עבריינא אבל משום שקדו מקרי עבריינא וכן משמע לקמן דאמר טעמא משום ברכה אבל משום איקרורי דעתא לא חיישינן ומאי נפקא מינה אלא ודאי דמשום ברכה לא מקרי עבריינא:

מאיא

מסורת הש"ס

א) לקמן ט:, ב) לקמן מח: נז. ע: [נדרים עג:], ג) ב"ב קלד: שבת כב. [עירובין עה:], ד) לקמן ג. ה., ה) נ"י כ"י, ו) [הך דליכא כתובה וכו׳ ליתא בנדה אך בשבת קל. ונראה כוונת התוס׳ במ"ש כדאמר בפ׳ בתרא דנדה סה: ר"ל שאמרו שם שאני כתובה דמגהי בה טפי ע׳ רש"י וערוך שם והא דכתבו דליכא כתובה הוא טעם בפ"ע].

ליקוטי רש"י

בתולה נשאת ליום הרביעי. תקנת חכמים היא שתנשא ברביעי בשבת כדמפרש טעמא בגמרא [רש"י כת"י משיטמ"ק]. **הגיע זמן.** שנים עשר חדש לבתולה משתבעה הבעל להכין עלמה לנשואין ולאלמנה שלשים יום. **ולא נישאו.** כגון שעכב החתן או אונס שלו [לקמן מח:]. **ואוכלות בתרומה.** אם כהן הוא והיא ישראלית משעה שקידשה אוכלת בתרומה מן התורה כדמפרש בגמרא ורבנן גזור עד השתא [לקמן נז.]. **אמר רב יוסף מריה דאברהם.** לשון תמיה הוא [שבת כב.]. רב יוסף חלה ושכח תלמודו כדאמרי׳ במסכת נדרים (דף מא.) ושמועות ששמע וכו׳ קודם חליו ועכשיו מתקשה בהן היה טוען אל לבו ותמה אם שמע כן והיה מתרלן וה"ק רבש"ע אפשר ששמעתי וכו׳ שינוי גדול כזה דתלי תניא המשנה וכו׳ תולה טעמא דלא תניא בדבר שאינו במשנה ובברייתא וכו׳ ותולה את העיקר בטפל לו [רשב"ם ב"ב קלד:]. **שקדו.** שקד, ממהר ומנחס חברו עם לשון שמירה כמו לשקוד על דלתותי (משלי ח) י"ת לשון אריבה [ירמיה ה, ו]. **נסתחפה שדהו.** מזלך גרם כאדם שהמטר בא וסוחף את זריעתו ועוקרה [לקמן יא:]. נסחף, נשטפו והחליקו גבוריך כמו מטר סוחף (משלי כח) נסתחפה שדהו בלשון משנה ומנחס חברו בלשון כליון וכן חבר מטר סוחף ודונש פתר מטר סוחף כמו מטר סועף כמו מסעף פארה במערלה (ישעיה י) [שם מו, טו]. סוחף, שוטף ובמשנה נסתחפה שדהו וכן נסחף אביריך (ירמיה מו) נשטפו ומעדו וכשלו [משלי כח, ג].

עין משפט נר מצוה

א א ב מיי׳ פ"י מהל׳ אישות הל׳ טו סמג עשין מח טוש"ע אה"ע סימן סד סעי׳ ג:

ב ג ד מיי׳ שם הלכה יט וסמג שם טוש"ע שם סי׳ ע סעי׳ ג:

תוספות רי"ד

בתולה נשאת ביום ד׳ ואלמנה ביום ה׳ שפעמים בשבת ב"ד יושבין בעיירות ביום ב׳ וביום ה׳ ואם היה לו טענת בתולים היה משכים לב"ד. פי׳ חכמים תקנו שתנשא הבתולה בד׳ כדי שיבעול בליל ה׳ ואם לא ימצא לה בתולים ילך בבוקר לב"ד טרם שיתקרר דעתו שיפייס עמה ויחקרו ב"ד מתי זינתה שמא תחתיו זינתה והיא אסורה לו. **שפעמים בשבת וכו׳.** פי׳ אבתולה יהיב טעמא וטעמא דאלמנה מפרש לקמן. ותקנות עזרא הוא שישבו ב"ד בעיירות בב׳ ובה׳. כדאמרינן בפ׳ מרובה מי׳ תקנות שתיקן עזרא. ואע"פ שבכל עיר ועיר היתה סנהדרין קבוע. בכל ימות השבוע היו עוסקים בתורה ובב׳ ובה׳ עוסקים בדינים. ולקמן פריך ותנשא באחד בשבת: **אמר ר"י** מפני מה אמרו בתולה נשאת בד׳ שאם היה לו טענת בתולים היה משכים לב"ד. ותנשא בא׳ בשבת ואם היה לו טענת בתולים היה משכים לב"ד שקדו חכמים על תקנות בנות ישראל שיהא טורח ג׳ ימים בסעודה א׳ בשבת שני ושלישי וברביעי כונסה. **ועכשיו ששנינו שקדו.** אותה ששנינו לקמן בפ׳ אע"פ נותנים לבתולה י"ב חודש משתבעה הבעל לפרנס א"ע. כשם שנותנים לאשה כך נותנים לאיש לפרנס א"ע ולאלמנה ל׳ יום הגיע זמן ולא נשאו אוכלות משלו. פי׳ וכגון שהבעל מעכב הגיע זמן בא׳ בשבת מתוך שאינו יכול לכנסה אינו מעלה לה מזונות לפיכך חלה הוא או שחלתה היא או שפירסה נדה אינו מעלה לה מזונות. **א"ר שמואל בר רב יצחק** ל"ש אלא מתקנות עזרא ואילך שאין ב"ד יושבין אלא בב׳ ובה׳. אבל אי איכא ב"ד קבועים בכל יום כקודם תקנות עזרא אשה נשאת בכל יום והא בעינן שקדו דטריח לה. והכי אסיק רב אחא דכל אונסא לא אכלה בין חלתה היא ובין חלה הוא. והכי הילכתא:

לעזי רש"י

קנדיר"ר. פירוש לפרנס, לספק לרכיס (של בני אדם) (עיין רש"י ב"מ דף מו ע"א ד"ה ואפרנסס ורש"י גיטין דף סה ע"ב ד"ה פרנסה):

Chapter One

Mishnah **בְּתוּלָה נִשֵּׂאת לְיוֹם הָרְבִיעִי – A virgin is married on Wednesday,**[1] **וְאַלְמָנָה לְיוֹם הַחֲמִישִׁי – and a widow on Thursday.**

The Mishnah explains why a virgin is married on Wednesday:[2]

שֶׁפַּעֲמַיִם בְּשַׁבָּת בָּתֵּי דִינִין יוֹשְׁבִין בָּעֲיָירוֹת – For twice a week the courts are in session in the towns,[3] **בַּיּוֹם הַשֵּׁנִי וּבַיּוֹם הַחֲמִישִׁי – on** each **Monday and Thursday.** **שֶׁאִם הָיָה לוֹ טַעֲנַת בְּתוּלִים** – One therefore marries on Wednesday **so** that **if he should have a claim regarding her virginity** **הָיָה מַשְׁכִּים לְבֵית דִּין – he would go early** the next morning **to court.**[4]

Gemara The Gemara analyzes the first statement of our Mishnah:[5]

אָמַר רַב יוֹסֵף אָמַר רַב יְהוּדָה אָמַר שְׁמוּאֵל – Rav Yosef said in the name of Rav Yehudah, who said in the name of Shmuel: **מִפְּנֵי מָה אָמְרוּ בְּתוּלָה נִשֵּׂאת לְיוֹם הָרְבִיעִי – Why did they say that a virgin is married on Wednesday?**[6] **לְפִי שֶׁשָּׁנִינוּ – Because we learned** in a Mishnah:[7] **הִגִּיעַ זְמַן וְלֹא נִישְּׂאוּ** – If, *kiddushin* having already taken place, THE TIME for *nesuin* ARRIVED AND THEY [i.e. the betrothed virgin or widow] WERE NOT MARRIED by the husband,[8] **אוֹכְלוֹת מִשֶּׁלוֹ** – THEY EAT OF HIS food,[9] **וְאוֹכְלוֹת בִּתְרוּמָה** – AND THEY EAT OF *TERUMAH*.[10] **יָכוֹל הִגִּיעַ זְמַן בְּאֶחָד בְּשַׁבָּת – It could** therefore **be** thought that **if the** designated **time arrived on Sunday** **יְהֵא מַעֲלֶה לָהּ מְזוֹנוֹת – [the husband] should** be obligated to **provide her with food** immediately. **לְכָךְ שָׁנִינוּ בְּתוּלָה נִשֵּׂאת לְיוֹם הָרְבִיעִי – We therefore learned** in our Mishnah: A VIRGIN IS MARRIED ON WEDNESDAY – the husband is not obligated to provide her with food until Wednesday.[11]

NOTES

1. I.e. the Rabbis decreed that the *nisuin* of a virgin should take place on a Wednesday; the Mishnah will shortly state the reason for this (*Rashi*). *Kiddushin,* however, may take place on any day of the week. [Regarding the distinction between *kiddushin* and *nesuin* see the General Introduction to our tractate.]

2. [The Gemara below (5a) will explain why a widow is married on Thursday.]

3. This was one of the ten enactments of Ezra the Scribe (*Rashi* from *Bava Kamma* 82a).

4. That is, the Rabbis instituted that he should marry on Wednesday in order that if he discovers on his wedding night that his bride is not a virgin he will immediately go to court, before his anger has a chance to cool. (Regarding the basis for such a claim, see below, 9a.) [The Gemara will explain why they could not just as well marry on Sunday, since the courts sit in session on Monday, too.]

Although this grievance is not sufficient grounds to forbid them to continue living together (for reasons that will be explained in the next paragraph), the publicity associated with his appearance in court may help bring to light the possible existence of witnesses who might testify that she did have an adulterous affair in the interval between *kiddushin* and *nesuin* [which, in Talmudic times, were generally separated from each other by a lengthy interval] which would render her an adulterous wife [for after *kiddushin* an act of intercourse with another man is considered adulterous], who is forbidden to her husband, as the Gemara elsewhere (*Sotah* 28a) derives from Scripture (*Rashi; cf. Tosafos* et al.).

[In the absence of such witnesses, however, the mere fact that he claims that his bride is not a virgin is not itself sufficient to forbid her to him. For even if we accept his claim as true there would remain a double doubt (סְפֵק סְפֵיקָא) whether she should be considered an adulterous wife: Firstly, we may doubt that she willingly had relations with another man; perhaps she was violated. Secondly, even if she did willingly engage in such relations, perhaps she did so while she was still single, before *kiddushin* took place. Such relations would not forbid her to her present husband. Since the rule is that cases of double doubt are decided leniently, she is not forbidden unless witnesses establish that she did, in fact, willingly commit adultery (*Rashi,* as understood by *Tosafos,* based on the Gemara below, 9a; cf. *Teshuvos R' Akiva Eiger* I:110 ד״ה אאב״ה; for exceptions to this rule see the Gemara below, ibid.).]

[As we shall see later, in times – such as today – when the courts do not convene specifically on Monday and Thursday, the requirement that a virgin marry on Wednesday does not apply.]

5. Our elucidation of the opening passage in the Gemara follows the approach of *Ramban,* which is basically taken by *Rashba, Re'ah* and *Ritva* as well, and which – according to *Ramban* himself and *Shitah Mekubetzes* (ד״ה עוד כתב הריב״ש) – is consistent with *Rashi's* terse comments here. For other approaches, see *Tosafos* and *Shitah Mekubetzes* at length. See also *Teshuvos Divrei Rivos* §239.

6. I.e. for what reason did the Rabbis enact that she should be married specifically on Wednesday?

The question seems difficult to understand, since the Mishnah itself explained the reason for the enactment – viz. so that if the husband does not find her a virgin, he will go to court the next morning, on Thursday, when it convenes. However, Shmuel means to ask why the Mishnah singles out Wednesday, when the reason it gives would allow just as well for marriage on Sunday, since the courts also convene on Monday (*Ramban;* see also *Ritva*).

7. Below, 57a.

[The Mishnah deals with a case in which a man betrothed a woman (*kiddushin*), without designating a date for the wedding (*nisuin*).] From the moment the husband asks her to prepare her clothing and adornments for the wedding she is given twelve months to prepare if she is a virgin, and thirty days if she is a widow (*Rashi*).

8. As the Gemara later explains, the Mishnah speaks of a case where the husband held up the *nisuin* (*Rashi*).

9. After *nesuin* the husband is required, by Rabbinic institution, to provide his wife with food (see below, 46b-47b); in this case, where the time for *nesuin* arrived and the husband delayed going through with the wedding, his obligation to support her goes into immediate effect, even without the *nesuin* having taken place (*Rashi*). [See *Or Same'ach* (*Hil. Ishus* 10:19), who considers whether the obligation in this case is in the nature of a penalty or is simply an implementation of the ordinary obligation of a husband to support his wife.]

[Actually, there is a dispute in the Gemara below (47b) regarding whether the obligation to support one's wife is a Biblical or a Rabbinic institution. See *Chidushei R' Reuven* for a discussion of why *Rashi* here assumes the latter view.]

10. If the husband is a Kohen she may eat *terumah,* in keeping with the law that the wife of a Kohen may eat *terumah* on his account, as the Gemara elsewhere (below, 57b) derives from Scripture. [If the woman's father is a Kohen then she may eat *terumah* in any event; the case here is where the woman's father was not a Kohen, but her husband was] (*Rashi*). [Although in general the wife of a Kohen may not eat *terumah* on her husband's account until after *nisuin,* in this case since the husband has begun supporting her she may eat *terumah* immediately; see below, 57b, for the rationale behind this ruling.]

11. The Mishnah informs us that there is a Rabbinic enactment that one must marry a virgin on Wednesday and not any other day of the week (presumably, including Sunday). Thus, if the twelve-month waiting period ends on a Sunday, the postponement of the wedding until Wednesday is due to the Rabbinic enactment and not the husband's procrastination. [He does not provide her with sustenance during this delay] (*Rashi*).

Shmuel's answer does not seem to resolve at all his question of *why* the marriage does not take place on Sunday. Rather, he seems to take for granted that the husband's obligation to support his wife begins specifically on Wednesday – even if the waiting period ended on Sunday

English. The truth is, however, that *erusin* is very different from a mere "betrothal" in that during the *erusin* stage the couple is considered legally married in most respects. The wife may not be wed to anyone else; intimate relations with any other man is considered adultery and incurs the death penalty. In addition, *erusin* can be dissolved only by a *get* (document of divorce). However, during this stage of marriage, the couple is not yet permitted to engage in marital relations.[20]

The *erusin* can be legally established by any of the following methods, if it is done for the purpose of marriage: The man gives the woman either money (or any object of value, such as a ring) or a marriage document (not to be confused with the *kesubah*), or through cohabiting with her.[21] The Rabbis, however, forbade this last method.[22]

B) *Nisuin:* The second stage of marriage is called נִשׂוּאִין, *nisuin* (full marriage). This is effected by a procedure called חוּפָּה, *chuppah,* and it completes the marriage process.

There is a controversy among the early authorities regarding the meaning of *chuppah.* One opinion is that it consists of placing a veil on the bride.[23] Others maintain that *chuppah* is performed by the groom taking the bride into his domain,[24] which may be accomplished by bringing the couple under the bridal canopy.[25] According to another view, it refers to the seclusion of the groom and bride for a short time, known as *yichud.*[26] The prevalent contemporary custom is to follow all these views by performing all three forms of *chuppah.*[27]

In earlier times, the period of *erusin* lasted a long time — usually a year.[28] Following the *erusin* ceremony, the bride returned to her father's home and remained there until the *nisuin.* Later, it became customary to perform both stages of the marriage at the wedding, which is the common practice nowadays.

◈ Stages of Development

A girl passes through three stages of legal development: minority (קְטַנּוּת); *naarus* (נַעֲרוּת); and adulthood (בַּגְרוּת). Minority lasts until she reaches the age of twelve and sprouts two pubic hairs, at which point she enters the state of *naarus.* The *naarus* state lasts for up to six months, after which she achieves the final stage of adulthood, called *bagrus.* A girl in the *naarus* state is called a *naarah.* A girl in the *bagrus* state is called a *bogeress.*

A minor girl is under her father's legal control, a *naarah* is partially under his control, and a *bogeress* is completely independent (see 46b ff).

NOTES

20. See *Rambam, Hil. Ishus* 10:1.

21. Mishnah, *Kiddushin* 2a.

22. *Kiddushin* 12b.

23. *Tosafos* to *Yoma* 13b ד״ה לחדא.

24. *Ran,* quoted by *Tos. Yom Tov* to 5:3.

25. *Beur HaGra, Even HaEzer* 55:9; *Aruch HaShulchan* there §18. See also Rishonim in our tractate, 2a.

26. *Rambam* ibid.; *Even HaEzer* 55:5.

27. *Bach* to *Even HaEzer* 61; *Beis Shmuel* there §5.

28. Mishnah, 57a.

Those who maintain that the *kesubah* was ordained by the Rabbis contend that their reason for the decree was to protect the wife against capricious divorce. Knowing that he would have to pay a substantial amount upon the dissolution of his marriage, a husband would not divorce his wife too hastily.[11] [Despite the fact that Rabbeinu Gershom has since promulgated a *cherem* (ban) that forbids a man to divorce his wife without her consent, the obligation of *kesubah* is still in effect today.[12]]

Some suggest that even those who state that the *kesubah* originates from the Torah do not actually mean that literally. Rather, their intent is that the Rabbis found Scriptural support for their own enactment.[13] Others contend that although the *kesubah* itself is of Biblical origin, its amount was not prescribed by the Torah; whatever had been agreed upon by both parties was binding. Subsequently, the Rabbis mandated a set amount for the *kesubah.*[14]

The accepted view in the Gemara and the authorities[15] is that even the *kesubah* of the virgin (and certainly that of the nonvirgin) was enacted by the Rabbis.

D) Modifying the Standard *Kesubah:* If the husband wishes, he may add to the *kesubah* as large a supplementary amount as he desires,[16] and we do not say that he may not do so lest he embarrass those who cannot afford to do the same. The groom has no right, however, to decrease the statutory amount of the *kesubah,* even with the consent of his bride. Although a permissible method of doing so is suggested in the Mishnah,[17] R' Meir contends that under no circumstances can one circumvent pledging the minimum amounts prescribed for the *kesubah.* In the words of R' Meir: *If anyone undertakes to give a virgin less than two hundred or a widow less than a hundred, their intimacy is an illicit intimacy.* The halachah follows R' Meir.[18]

E) Other Items in the *Kesubah:* Besides the statutory amount of the *kesubah* and any additional amount pledged voluntarily by the groom, the bride's dowry may also be included in the husband's responsibilities under the *kesubah.* If it is, those possessions becomes known as נִכְסֵי צֹאן בַּרְזֶל, *fixed-value* (literally: *iron sheep*) *property.* The husband assumes the responsibility of remunerating the full value of these properties — as assessed at the time the *kesubah* was written — in the event of his death or their divorce. He profits from any increase in the value of these possessions, but is also liable for their damage, depreciation or loss. They are compared to iron because of their enduring ironlike value, which the wife is assured of retaining. (Since it was customary for shepherds to accept sheep in this manner — to appraise the flock and assume responsibility for it — those properties were given the appellative *iron sheep.*)

If the woman brings at the time of marriage properties that she chooses not to enter into her *kesubah,* or she inherits or gains possession of any other belongings during the marriage, they are known as נִכְסֵי מְלוֹג, *usufructuary* (literally: plucking) *property.* They are so designated because the husband enjoys their dividends but has no rights to the properties themselves, analogous to plucking the feathers of fowl or the hair of goats, which leaves the animal itself intact. He neither profits from an increase in their value, nor is he liable for any damage, depreciation or loss The property reverts to her — in whatever condition it may be — upon their divorce or his death.[19]

The text of the *kesubah* also records the husband's pledge to provide his wife with her various needs. Also included are the obligations of his estate to her and her children after his death.

⊱§ Marriage

According to Biblical law, there are two stages to marriage. The first is known as אֵרוּסִין, *erusin,* or קִדּוּשִׁין, *kiddushin,* while the second stage is called נִשּׂוּאִין, *nisuin.*

A) *Erusin* or *Kiddushin:* These terms describe both the first stage of marriage and the act that effects it. We have sometimes translated *erusin* as *betrothal* only for lack of a better equivalent in

NOTES

11. See Gemara, 11a.
[This reason accounts only for why there should be an alimony in the event of a divorce. Even in the case of the husband's death, however, the Rabbis still awarded this amount to the widow — either to strengthen their decree by applying it to all cases in which the marriage is terminated, regardless of the reason; or, in their concern for the welfare of the widow, to assure her financial security for a reasonable period of time following the demise of her husband.]

12. *Rama, Even HaEzer* 66:3.

13. *Tosafos* to *Sotah* 27a ד״ה איש איש; see *Gemara* below, 10a.

14. See *Rif* and *Ran* to the end of the tractate.

15. See Gemara, 10a, and *Rambam, Hil. Ishus* 10:7.

16. Mishnah, 54b.

17. Ibid.

18. *Rambam, Hil. Ishus* 10:9.

19. See *Rashi* to Mishnah, *Yevamos* 66a.

מסכת כתובות / Tractate Kesubos

General Introduction

Maseches Kesubos deals with the varied aspects of the relationship between a man and his wife and their mutual obligations to each other – whether at the inception of the marriage, during the marriage, or after it is terminated by divorce or the death of one of them. This tractate takes its name from the כְּתוּבָּה, *kesubah,* the marriage contract that details the various marital and financial obligations and commitments undertaken by the two parties. This introduction will discuss briefly the nature of the *kesubah,* as well as some of the other major concepts and terms that will be encountered in the course of this volume.

◆§ The *Kesubah*

A) The Definition: The term *kesubah* literally means a document, but refers primarily not so much to the document itself but rather to the obligations of the marriage agreement. In fact, in some locales, it was not customary to commit the contract to writing at all.[1] Even in places where the custom was to record the *kesubah* in writing, if the husband neglected to do so, the *kesubah* obligations were in effect nonetheless.[2]

While this marriage agreement briefly describes the husband's obligations to his wife, its foremost feature is the dower[3] awarded the wife in the event of their divorce or the husband's death. In fact, in Mishnaic terminology the word *kesubah* generally refers not to the larger agreement, but specifically to the amount of the dower stipulated in the agreement. In contemporary parlance, however, the term *kesubah* has come to denote the document containing the marriage agreement.

B) The Amount of the *Kesubah:* Not all women receive the same amount for their settlement. A woman who marries as a virgin is entitled to two hundred *zuz.*[4] The *kesubah* of a widow or divorcee, however, is only one hundred *zuz.*[5] The amount of the *kesubah* for a woman who lost her virginity through injury rather than cohabitation is disputed by Tannaim.[6]

C) The Origin of the *Kesubah:* There is a controversy at the end of the tractate as to whether the obligation of the *kesubah* is Biblical or Rabbinical in origin.[7] Those maintaining that it is Biblical derive this from the verse dealing with a seducer, which states:[8] *He shall pay silver shekels in the amount of the settlement [made] to the virgins.* "The settlement [made] to the virgins" is understood as referring to the *kesubah.*[9] Fifty silver shekels (or *"selaim,"* in Mishnaic nomenclature) equals two hundred *dinars* or *zuz.*[10]

NOTES

1. See Gemara, 16b and 89a.

2. See Mishnah, 51a.

3. Because the words *dower* and *dowry* can be used interchangeably, we will define how these terms are used in this volume. *Dower* refers to the portion of a man's property allotted to his widow or ex-wife. *Dowry* means the money, goods or estate that a woman brings to her husband at marriage.

4. See below, 10b note 19.

5. Mishnah, 10b.

6. Mishnah, 11a.

7. See Gemara, 56b and 110b. See *Tosafos* to 10a ד״ה אמר רב נחמן.

It should be noted that there had been a custom to provide a bride with a *kesubah* even before the Torah was given. Joseph wrote one for his wife (*Kallah Rabbasi,* ch. 3; *Rashi* to *Genesis* 48:9). There was also such a practice among the gentiles (see Mishnah, 90a with *Rashi; Rashi* to *Genesis* 34:12 from *Bereishis Rabbah;* cf. *Ramban* to *Exodus* 22:15; see also *Commentary of R' Samson Raphael Hirsch* to *Exodus* ad loc.).

8. *Exodus* 22:16.

9. See *Yerushalmi* 3:5.

10. [For a detailed description of the Biblical shekel and its value in contemporary currency, see Appendix I ArtScroll *Shekalim.* See also below, 10b note 19.]

[Some see an allusion to this amount from the verse cited above, reading the word כְּמֹהַר as: כַּמָּה ר, *How much? Two hundred* (*Maharam Mintz*).]

The fact that the Torah emphasizes *the settlement [made] to "the virgins"* might also be the basis of the difference between the *kesubos* of virgins and nonvirgins (see *Hagahos Yavetz* to 56b).

מסכת כתובות
TRACTATE KESUBOS

ACKNOWLEDGMENTS

We are grateful to the distinguished *roshei hayeshivah* and rabbinic leaders שליט״א in Israel and the United States whose guidance and encouragement have been indispensable to the success of this Talmud, from its inception. They are named in volume 1 of Tractate Berachos.

A huge investment of time and resources was required to make this edition of the Talmud a reality. Only through the generous support of many people is it possible not only to undertake and sustain such a huge and ambitious undertaking, but to keep the price of the volumes within reach of the average family and student. We are grateful to them all.

The Trustees and Governors of the MESORAH HERITAGE FOUNDATION saw the need to support the scholarship and production of this and other outstanding works of Torah literature. Their names are listed on an earlier page.

JAY SCHOTTENSTEIN is chairman of the Board of Governors and has enlisted many others in support of this monumental project. In addition, he and his wife JEANIE SCHOTTENSTEIN have dedicated the HEBREW ELUCIDATION OF THE SCHOTTENSTEIN EDITION OF THE TALMUD in honor of their parents.

In addition, we are grateful to:

LAURENCE A. TISCH, JAMES S. TISCH and THOMAS J. TISCH , who have been more than gracious on numerous occasions; IRVING I. STONE, whose sponsorship of the STONE EDITION OF THE CHUMASH, SAPIRSTEIN EDITION OF RASHI, and the STONE EDITION OF TANACH is bringing a new awareness of the Torah to Jews around the world;

ELLIS A. SAFDEYE, a legendary supporter of worthy causes and a warm, treasured friend; BENJAMIN C. FISHOFF, a sensitive, visionary friend, who has brought many people under the banner of this project; LOUIS GLICK, who sponsored the ArtScroll Mishnah Series with the *Yad Avraham* commentary; JOEL L. FLEISHMAN, whose sage advice and active intervention was a turning point in our work; A. JOSEPH STERN, whose warmth and concern for people and causes are justly legendary; HIRSCH WOLF, a leader in many causes and a valued ally; SHLOMO SEGEV of Bank Leumi, who has been a responsible and effective friend; JUDAH SEPTIMUS, whose acumen and resources are devoted to numerous Torah causes; NATHAN SILBERMAN, who makes his skills and judgment available in too many ways to mention; REUVEN D. DESSLER, a leader in Torah life who brings credit to his distinguished lineage; ZVI RYZMAN, a dynamic and imaginative force for Torah life and scholarship; SOLI SPIRA, who is respected on three continents for his learning and magnanimity; DAVID RUBIN, whose generosity and vision are vital forces in his community and beyond; ABRAHAM FRUCHTHANDLER, who has placed support for Torah institutions on a new plateau. We welcome HESHE SEIF, Patron of the Seif Editions of the transliterated Siddur and Machzor, to the Board of Governors and thank him for his friendship and substantial assistance.

We are grateful, as well, to many other friends who have come forward when their help was needed most: DR. YISRAEL BLUMENFRUCHT, SHIMMIE HORN, BERNARD LAX, CPA, YEHUDAH LEVI, RABBI ARTHUR SCHICK, ELLIOT TANNENBAUM, STEVEN WEISZ, MENDY YARMISH, and HOWARD ZUCKERMAN.

We conclude with gratitude to *Hashem Yisbarach* for His infinite blessings and for the privilege of being the vehicle to disseminate His word. May this work continue so that all who thirst for His word may find what they seek in the refereshing words of the Torah.

Rabbi Nosson Scherman / Rabbi Meir Zlotowitz

Elul, 5759 / August, 1999

The Safdeye Edition of Seder Nashim

This is the first tractate published in Seder Nashim since our dear friends **Mr. and Mrs. Ellis Safdeye** became the patrons of the Seder. They are as quiet and unassuming as they are generous and visionary. In the synagogue, in the community, in the business world, the Safdeyes are equally admired, respected and beloved. They exude friendship and charm, warmth and concern, kindness and sensitivity.

As exemplary as they are in their personal and communal lives, they are dynamic and dedicated as pillars of their community. Torah study, adherence to its teachings, and the reinvigoration of the Sephardic Syrian community are the cornerstones of their lives. Thanks in great measure to the devotion of **Ellis and Altoon (Tunie) Safdeye**, their community in Flatbush is fast becoming a worthy successor to its forerunner in Aleppo. It hums with Torah study and classes for young and old. The *beit midrash* of their beloved Ateret Torah is synonymous with intense study. Ellis himself is there for hours every morning before he goes to his office — and the walls of his office are an inspiring testimony to his incredible support of countless Torah causes.

Torah study, adherence to its teachings, and the reinvigoration of the Sephardic Syrian community are the cornerstones of their lives.

As one who studies the Talmud and takes enormous pride in the Torah accomplishments of his children and grandchildren, Ellis Safdeye knows that Torah is life and that it is the very soul of the Jewish people. Mrs. Safdeye opens their home to rabbis and teachers from America and Israel. She is a living embodiment of the counsel of our Sages that one's home should a be meeting place for *chachamim*.

Ellis Safdeye knows that Torah is life and that it is the very soul of the Jewish people.

We are proud that this edition of the Talmud has a central place in the affections of the Safdeye family. Thanks to their support, tens of thousands of Jews around the world are enriching their lives through Torah study. There can be no greater source of merit. May our friendship endure and thrive for many, many years of service to those whose veins course with the eternal life of Torah study.

Patrons of this Volume

This volume is dedicated by the **Fishoff Families** in honor of their father, **R' Yechiel Ben Zion** לאויט״ and in memory of their mother **Marilyn** ע״ה. Ben Fishoff is a living legend of wisdom, generosity, sensitivity, and visionary support of Torah causes. As noted in the dedication of this volume, he is an *askan* of worldwide proportions, whose statesmanlike counsel has been sought and treasured by Klal Yisrael's greatest leaders. Marilyn Fishoff ע״ה was a woman of singular grace, charm, kindness and humility. Together they set a shining example for all who knew them, especially their devoted children. The new generations of such a distinguished family is making its own mark in the burgeoning world of Torah life and thriving institutions. We are proud to be associated with them.

He is an askan of worldwide proportions, whose statesmanlike counsel has been sought and treasured by Klal Yisrael's greatest leaders.

By dedicating this volume, the Fishoff families bring Torah knowledge to countless thousands; there can be no greater source of merit.

The Schottenstein Edition of the Talmud

They never surrendered the principles of Judaism or the love of Torah that they had absorbed in Lithuania.

This pioneering elucidation of the entire Talmud was named **THE SCHOTTENSTEIN EDITION** in memory of **EPHRAIM AND ANNA SCHOTTENSTEIN** ז״ל, of Columbus, Ohio. Mr. and Mrs. Schottenstein came to the United States as children, but they never surrendered the principles of Judaism or the love of Torah that they had absorbed in their native Lithuania. Tenacious was their devotion to the Sabbath, kashruth, and halachah; their support of needy Jews in a private, sensitive manner; their generosity to Torah institutions; and their refusal to speak ill of others.

This noble and historic gesture of dedication was made by their sons and daughters-in-law **JEROME** ז״ל **AND GERALDINE SCHOTTENSTEIN** and **SAUL AND SONIA SCHOTTENSTEIN.**

Jerome left numerous memorials of accomplishment and generosity, but surely the Schottenstein Edition of the Talmud — spanning centuries — will be the most enduring.

With the untimely passing of JEROME SCHOTTENSTEIN ז״ל, it became our sad privilege to rededicate THE SCHOTTENSTEIN EDITION to his memory, in addition to that of his parents.

Jerome Schottenstein ז״ל was a dear friend and inspirational patron. He saw the world through the lens of eternity, and devoted his mind, heart and resources to the task of assuring that the Torah would never be forgotten by its people. He left numerous memorials of accomplishment and generosity, but surely the **SCHOTTENSTEIN EDITION OF THE TALMUD** — spanning centuries — will be the most enduring.

The Schottensteins are worthy heirs to the traditions and principles of Jerome and his parents. Gracious and generous, kind and caring, they have opened their hearts to countless causes and people.

The Schottensteins are worthy heirs to the traditions and principles of Jerome and his parents. Gracious and generous, kind and caring, they have opened their hearts to countless causes and people. Quietly and considerately, they elevate the dignity and self-respect of those they help; they make their beneficiaries feel like benefactors; they imbue institutions with a new sense of mission to be worthy of the trust placed in them.

THE MESORAH HERITAGE FOUNDATION is proud and grateful to be joined with the Schottenstein family as partners in this monumental endeavor.

We pray that this great undertaking will be a source of merit for the continued health and success of the entire Schottenstein family, including the children and grandchildren:

JAY and JEANIE SCHOTTENSTEIN and their children, Joseph Aaron, Jonathan Richard, and Jeffrey Adam; **ANN and ARI DESHE** and their children, Elie Michael, David Scott, Dara Lauren, and Daniel Matthew; **SUSAN and JON DIAMOND** and their children, Jillian Leigh, Joshua Louis, and Jacob Meyer; and **LORI SCHOTTENSTEIN.**

The Schottensteins will be remembered with gratitude for as long as English-speaking Jews are nourished by the eternity of the Talmud's wisdom, for, thanks to them, millions of Jews over the generations will become closer to their heritage.

A Jew can accomplish nothing more meaningful or lasting in his sojourn on earth.

We express our appreciation to the distinguished patrons
who have dedicated volumes in the

HEBREW ELUCIDATION OF THE SCHOTTENSTEIN EDITION OF THE TALMUD

Dedicated by
JAY AND JEANIE SCHOTTENSTEIN
and their children
Joseph Aaron, Jonathan Richard, and Jeffrey Adam

SEDER ZERA'IM:	**Mrs. Margot Guez and Family** **Paul Vivianne Michelle Hubert Monique Gerard Aline Yves**
BERACHOS I:	**Jay and Jeanie Schottenstein** (Columbus, Ohio)
BERACHOS II:	**Zvi and Betty Ryzman** (Los Angeles)
SHABBOS I:	**Moshe and Hessie Neiman** (New York)
ERUVIN I:	**The Schottenstein Family** (Columbus, Ohio)
ERUVIN II:	**The Schottenstein Family** (Columbus, Ohio)
PESACHIM III:	**Morris and Devora Smith** (New York)
YOMA I:	**Peretz and Frieda Friedberg** (Toronto)
YOMA II:	**Avi Klein and Family** (New York)
BEITZAH:	**Chaim and Chava Fink** (Tel Aviv)
ROSH HASHANAH:	**Avi and Meira Schnur** (Savyon)
TAANIS:	**Mendy and Itta Klein** (Cleveland)
MOED KATTAN:	**Yisroel and Shoshana Lefkowitz** (New York)
CHAGIGAH:	**Stephen and Hadassah Weisz** (New York)
YEVAMOS I:	**Reserved**
YEVAMOS II:	**Reserved**
YEVAMOS III:	**Reserved**
KESUBOS I:	**Ben Fishoff and family** (New York)
KESUBOS II:	**Jacob and Esther Gold** (New York)
KESUBOS III:	**David and Roslyn Lowy** (Forest Hills)
NEDARIM I:	**Soli and Vera Spira** (New York / Jerusalem)
NAZIR:	**Shlomo and Esther Ben Arosh** (Jerusalem)
SOTAH:	**Motty and Malka Klein** (New York)
GITTIN I:	**Mrs. Kate Tannenbaum;** **Elliot and Debra Tannenbaum; Edward and Linda Zizmor**
KIDDUSHIN I:	**Ellis A. and Altoon Safdeye** (New York)
BAVA KAMMA I:	**Lloyd and Hadassah Keilson** (New York)
BAVA KAMMA II:	**Faivel and Roiza Weinreich** (New York)
BAVA METZIA I:	**Joseph and Rachel Leah Neumann** (Monsey)
BAVA METZIA III:	**A. George and Stephanie Saks** (New York)
SANHEDRIN I:	**Martin and Rivka Rapaport** (Jerusalem)
SANHEDRIN III:	In honor of **Joseph and Anita Wolf** (Tel Aviv)
MAKKOS:	**Hirsch and Raquel Wolf** (New York)
SHEVUOS:	**Jacques and Miriam Monderer** (Antwerp)
HORAYOS-EDUYOS:	**Woli and Chaja Stern** (Sao Paulo, Brazil)
CHULLIN II:	**Avrohom David and Chaya Baila Klein** (Monsey)
BECHOROS II:	**Howard and Chaya Balter**
ARACHIN:	**Reserved**

Pillars of The Talmud

We wish to acknowledge in this volume the friendship of the following:

In honor of the 62nd wedding anniversary of

Mayor and Esther Martin

by their children and grandchildren

Robert, Barbara, Jeffrey and Jennifer Martin

In Memoriam — לזכרון עולם

Dedicated by the Talmud Associates
to those who forged eternal links

Wealcatch — חיים דוב ב״ר זאב ואסתר בת ר׳ יוסף אייזיק ע״ה
Weiss — צבי בן יואל ע״ה
Weiss — גיטל בת ישראל ע״ה
Werdiger — ר׳ שלמה אלימלך ב״ר ישראל יצחק ע״ה
Westreich — הרב יהושע בן הרב יוסף יאסקא ז״ל
Leo Werter ע״ה
Wiesner — הרב שמעיה בן הרב זאב ע״ה
Wiesner — שרה לאה בת ר׳ צבי אריה ע״ה
Zakheim-Brecher — בתיה רחל ע״ה בת ר׳ משה יוסף שיחי׳ לאוי״ט
Zalstain — שמעון בן מרדכי יוסף הלוי ע״ה
Zimmer — ר׳ אברהם יעקב בן אהרן אליעזר ע״ה
הרב אהרן ב״ר מאיר יעקב ע״ה
הרבנית פרומא בת ר׳ חיים צבי ע״ה
Zinn — צבי יהודה בן שמעון ע״ה
Zinn — דבורה בת יחיאל מרדכי ע״ה
Leslie Zukor — ר׳ יצחק חיים ב״ר יוסף ע״ה

Scherman — הילד אברהם דוב ע״ה ב״ר זאב יוסף שיחי׳
Shafran — ר׳ יהושע ב״ר אברהם ע״ה
Shayovich — משה יעקב ב״ר נחום ועטיא פייגא בת מרדכי ע״ה
Shubow — יוסף שלום בן משה ע״ה
Silberman — ר׳ צבי ב״ר זאב הלוי ע״ה
Silberman — דבורה אסתר בת ישראל ע״ה
Silbermintz — יהושע ב״ר יוסף שמריהו ע״ה
Singer — צבי בן ר׳ חיים ע״ה
Singer — הינדי בת ר׳ שלמה ע״ה
Soclof — אברהם אבא ב״ר שמריהו ע״ה
Soclof — חיה ברכה בת צבי הירש הלוי ע״ה
Smouha — הרב אליהו בן מאיר הלוי ע״ה
Steir — משה בן מיכאל ע״ה
Steinberg — יצחק גדליה בן יהודה לייב ע״ה
Steinberg — מלכה בת מאיר לוי ע״ה
Taub — אליעזר יוסף בן מענדל ע״ה
Taub — מענדל בן אליעזר יוסף חיה בת הירש ע״ה

In Memoriam — לזכרון עולם

Dedicated by the Talmud Associates
to those who forged eternal links

Abraham — שמחה בן ר׳ יהודה לייב הכהן ע״ה
דוד חי ב״ר שלום הכהן ע״ה וחנה בת ר׳ עזרא ע״ה
אהרן בן חיים זאב ע״ה גאלדע בת ר׳ דוד ע״ה
Ashkenazy — ר׳ שלמה ב״ר יצחק זצ״ל ורעיתו עלי׳ מינדעל בת ר׳ יעקב ע״ה
Sarah T. Belz — שרה בת אהרן צבי הלוי ע״ה
Berber — משה ורחל
Bernath — מנשה ב״ר שמואל שמעלקא ע״ה Meizner — מרדכי חיים ב״ר זבולן יצחק חייא ע״ה
Blitz — דוב מאיר ב״ר דוד הכהן ע״ה
Freddy Bradfield — יעקב בן צבי ע״ה
Cooperberg — שימה רייזל בת ר׳ אהרן שלמה ע״ה
Cooperberg — אברהם אשר בן ר׳ מאיר ע״ה
Cumsky — דוב בער בן אברהם יששכר ע״ה ופעשא מאטלא בת יוסף ע״ה
צבי טעביל בן ישראל ע״ה וליבע בת דוד ע״ה
Diamant — אשר ב״ר יהושע מרדכי הכהן ע״ה
Diamant — שרה בת ר׳ אריה ע״ה
Diamant — ר׳ דוב ב״ר משה ע״ה ורייזל בת ר׳ אברהם ע״ה
Diamond — דר. ר׳ יצחק ב״ר ברוך בענדיט ע״ה
Dicker — מרדכי צבי ב״ר יעקב ע״ה
Dicker — קיילא בת ר׳ משה ע״ה
Djmal — טופיק טוביה בן משה ושושנה ע״ה
Paul and Jeannette Dubin ע״ה
Mollie Dubinsky ע״ה
Abram B. Efroymson ע״ה
Sylvia Spira Efroymson ע״ה
Einhorn — משה בן ברוך ע״ה
Eshaghian — אברהם בן דוד ע״ה
Esrig — דוד בן שלמה ע״ה וחיה אייגא בת שלום ע״ה
Feder — מלכה בת ירחמיאל הכהן ע״ה
Feiden — ישראל בן אהרן ע״ה
Feinerman — אליעזר בן יוסף ע״ה ולאה בת ישראל יצחק ע״ה
יוסף בן צבי יחזקאל ע״ה ושרה בת ר׳ משה ע״ה
Freier — ישעיה צבי ב״ר חיים אלכסנדר יוסף ע״ה
Freier — שיינדל בת ר׳ משה הלוי ע״ה
Frenkel — גרשון בן יחיאל דוד ע״ה Rottenstreich — דוד בן עקיבא ע״ה
Friedman — ר׳ אהרן ב״ר יעקב מאיר ע״ה
Frishman — מרים בת ר׳ יוסף מרדכי ע״ה
Frishman — יצחק אריה ב״ר יהודה ע״ה ומרים לאה בת ר׳ יצחק ע״ה
Gold — הרב דוב ב״ר דוד מאיר ע״ה ור׳ דוד מאיר בן הרב יעקב יצחק ע״ה
Goldman — אמו, שפרה בת ר׳ קלונימוס קלמן ע״ה
Gugenheim — החבר אפרים בן רפאל ע״ה
Gugenheim — ברײנדל בת החבר נתן הכהן ע״ה

Hanz — חיים בן מרדכי הי״ד
Henzel — אברהם בן ר׳ מנחם זאב ע״ה
Katzef — פרומה באדענה בת אלחנן ע״ה
Kleinbart — משה ב״ר אריה לייב ע״ה
Kleinbart — בתיה בת ר׳ משה אברהם ע״ה
Kriegel — רויזא מינצא בת הרב ישראל יהודה ע״ה
Kulefsky — הילד יהודה לייב בן נתן נטע ע״ה
Langer — משה בן יצחק הי״ד
Landowne — שלמה בן יוסף ע״ה
Lasry — שאול ב״ר אברהם ע״ה וזהרה אסתר בת משה ע״ה
Lazar — אליעזר שאול בן זאב מאיר ע״ה
Lefkovich — ר׳ זאב וועלוול ב״ר יצחק אייזיק ע״ה
Lemberger — יצחק בן אריה ע״ה
Leibel — יחזקאל שרגא ב״ר חיים ע״ה
Leibel — רויזא בת ר׳ אברהם משה ע״ה
Levi — הרב חיים מאיר בן ר׳ מנחם ע״ה
Levi — שושנה טייבא רייזל בת ר׳ יחזקאל גרשון ע״ה
May — ר׳ יוסף בן הרב יהודה אריה ע״ה
Neuman — יצחק אייזיק ב״ר אהרן ע״ה
Paneth — אלטע חיה שרה ע״ה בת ר׳ פנחס שיחי׳ לאוי״ט
Parnes — אריה לייבש בן יוסף יצחק ועטיא בת אשר ראובן ע״ה
Parnes — הרב אברהם זאב ב״ר ישכר ע״ה
Parsons — משה זלמן בן אהרן דוב ע״ה
Perlman — ר׳ נפתלי בנימין ב״ר משה זצ״ל ורעיתו חוה בת ר׳ שאול ע״ה
Perlowitz — הרב משה ב״ר אליעזר הלל ע״ה
Pinczower — אפרים ב״ר ישראל חיים ופייגלא בת ר׳ יעקב ע״ה
Rabin — ישראל בן נחום ע״ה
Rennert — שרה בת יצחק יעקב ע״ה
Rennert — יונה מנחם בן אהרן ע״ה
Rosenberg — חיים נחמן ב״ר דוד ולאה בת יוסף ע״ה
Sam and Leah Rosenbloom ע״ה
Roth — משה ב״ר יעקב הכהן ע״ה Weisner — יצחק ב״ר זאב ע״ה
Scharf — אליהו ב״ר משה יעקב ושרה בת אלכסנדר זיסקינד ע״ה
Scherman — ר׳ אברהם דוב ב״ר שמואל נטע ע״ה
Scherman — ליבא בת ר׳ זאב וואלף ע״ה
Schnur — אברהם יצחק בן אהרן הי״ד וחנה בת חיים יעקב ע״ה
Schoenbrun — שרגא פייבל ב״ר יעקב הכהן ומאטל אסתר בת מרדכי הלוי ע״ה
Schron — אליעזר דוב בן חיים משה ע״ה
Schron — חוה בת שמעון ע״ה
Schulman — חיים חייקל בן ר׳ שמואל ע״ה
Schulman — חיה בת הרב ישראל יהודה ע״ה
Schwebel — אברהם זכריה מנחם בן יוסף ומחלה בת ישראל מרדכי ע״ה

תנצב״ה

The Talmud Associates*

A fellowship of benefactors dedicated to
the dissemination of the Talmud

❖

Dinah Rubinoff and Family
Ms. Ruth Russ
Mr. and Mrs. Alexander Scharf
Avi and Michou Schnur
Rubin and Marta Schron
Rivie and Leba Schwebel and Family
Shlomo Segev (Smouha)
Bernard and Chaya Shafran
לזכות בניהם היקרים שיחיו:
דבורה, יעקב חיים, דוד זאב, אסתר מנוחה
Joel and Malka Shafran
לזכות בניהם היקרים שיחיו:
אשר נחמן, טובה חיה, תמר פעסיל, שרה חוה
Nathan B. and Malka Silberman
The Soclof Family
Dr. Edward L. and Judith Steinberg
Max Taub
and his son Yitzchak

Jay and Sari Tepper
Walter and Adele Wasser
Melvin, Armond and Larry Waxman
William and Noémie Wealcatch
Dr. Zelig and Evelyn (Gutwein) Weinstein
Yaakov, Daniella, Aliza and Zev
Erwin and Myra Weiss
Morry and Judy Weiss
Shlomo and Esther Werdiger
Leslie M. and Shira Westreich
Willie and Blimie Wiesner
The Yad Velvel Foundation
Moshe and Venezia Zakheim
Dr. Harry and Holly Zinn
Mrs. Edith Zukor and Family

*In formation

The Talmud Associates*

A fellowship of benefactors dedicated to
the dissemination of the Talmud

❖

Dr. Mark and Dr. Barbara Bell,
Bentzion Yosef and Mordechai Yehudah

The Belz Family

Michael and Bettina Bradfield
Gabrielle and Matthew
(London)

Nachi and Zippi Brown,
Jessica, Daniella, Shachar and Mindy
In honor of their parents and grandparents

Columbus Jewish Foundation

Milton Cooper and Family

Dr. and Mrs. David Diamond

Nahum and Feige Hinde Dicker and Family

Sophia, Alberto and Rose Djmal

Dr. Richard Dubin

Kenneth and Cochava Dubin

David and Simone Eshaghian

Louis, Reuben and Larry Feder and Family

Rabbi Judah and Ruth Feinerman

In honor of
Mr. and Mrs. Yehoshua Chaim Fischman
by their children

Mayer and Ruthy Friedman
Ari, Yitzy, Suri, Dovi

Dr. Michael and Susan Friedman
לזכות בניהם, כלתם, ונכדם; בנותיהם, וחתניהם שיחי׳

Yeshaya and Perel Friedman

Julius Frishman

David and Sally Frenkel
לזכות בניהם וכלתם היקרים שיחיו:
דניאל שמואל ומאשה שושנה, אורי גבריאל, רונית פרימיט

Sander and Tracy Gerber
לזכות בניהם היקרים יעקב עקיבא ואסתר פערל שיחי׳
שיתעלו בתורה ויראת שמים

Leon and Agi Goldenberg
In honor of the marriage of their children
Mendy and Estie Blau

Robert and Rita Gluck
לרפו״ש טויבא רחל בת פריידא שתחי׳

Shari and Jay Gold and Family

Dr. Martin and Shera Goldman and Family

Esther Henzel

Hashi and Miriam Herzka

David J. and Dora Kleinbart

In honor of
Mr. and Mrs. Label Kutoff
by their children

The Landowne Family

Ezriel and Miriam Langer

Mr. and Mrs. Chaim Leibel

Yehuda and Rasie Levi

Raphael and Blimie Manela
לזכות בניהם היקרים שיחיו:
מתתיהו, ישראל, ישעיהו, חיים משה, ושמעון

Mendy and Phyllis Mendlowitz

Robby and Judy Neuman and Family
in honor of Sid and Esther Borenstein
ובניהם: שרה מאטיל, חיה ליבה, פנחס אלימלך,
יוסף דוב, לאה פרומיט, נחמה יענטא

Naftali Binyomin and Zypora Perlman and Moshe

Kenneth Ephraim and Julie Pinczower
לרפו״ש ישראל חיים בן פייגלא שיחי׳

Dr. Douglas and Vivian Rabin

Ingeborg and Ira Leon Rennert

Alan Jay and Hindy Rosenberg

Aviva and Oscar Rosenberg

Mr. and Mrs. David Rubin and Family

*In formation

Guardians of the Talmud*

A society of visionary people who recognize the primacy of the Jewish people's commitment to intellect, ethics, integrity, law, and religion — and pursue it by presenting the treasures of the eternal Talmud in the language of today . . . for the generations of tomorrow.

❦ ❦ ❦

Milton and Rita Kramer

in honor of their 50th wedding anniversary and Milton's 80th birthday (April 1999)
and in honor of their children and grandchildren

Daniel and Gina Kramer and Children **Jonathan and Marian Kramer and Children**
Ellen Kramer Blond and Children

and in everlasting memory of their beloved parents and grandparents
Hyman S. and Fannie D. Kramer ע״ה — חיים שניאור זלמן הלוי (חזק) ופייגע דינה ע״ה
Adolph H. and Sadie A. Gross ע״ה — חיים אלטער ושרה חנה ע״ה
Morris L. and Rachel E. Kramer ע״ה — משה אליעזר הלוי ורחל עלקא ע״ה
Barney and Dvorah Cohen ע״ה — דוב בער הכהן ודבורה ע״ה
Herman M. and Leah Gross ע״ה — משולם צבי ולאה ע״ה
Peisach and Hannah Neustadter ע״ה — פסח אלכסנדר וחנה ע״ה

❦ ❦ ❦

*In formation

Guardians of the Talmud*

A society of visionary people who recognize the primacy of the Jewish people's commitment to intellect, ethics, integrity, law, and religion — and pursue it by presenting the treasures of the eternal Talmud in the language of today . . . for the generations of tomorrow.

❦ ❦ ❦

David and Jean Bernstein
Matthew Bernstein
Scott and Andrea Bernstein

in memory of
Mr. and Mrs. Harry Bernstein ע״ה
Mr. and Mrs. Joseph Furman ע״ה

❦ ❦ ❦

Alan and Myrna Cohen

in honor of
their children
Alison and Matthew

❦ ❦ ❦

Stephen and Terri Geifman
Jacquelyn and Julie

in loving memory of
משה מרדכי בן יחיאל מיכאל ז״ל — Morris M. Geifman
and in honor of
Geraldine G. Geifman

❦ ❦ ❦

Avrohom Chaim and Elisa Taub
Hadassah, Yaakov Yehuda Aryeh, Shifra, Faige, and Devorah Raizel

In loving memory of his father
ר׳ יעקב ב״ר יהודה אריה ע״ה — Taub
נפ׳ ד׳ מנחם אב תשל״ט
and in memory of the Sanz-Klausenburger Rebbe זצוק״ל
מרן הרהגה״צ ר׳ יקותיאל יהודה בהרהגה״צ ר׳ צבי זצוק״ל כ״ק אדמו״ר אבדק״ק צאנז-קלויזענבורג זי״ע
נלב״ע ש״ק פ׳ חקת, ט׳ תמוז תשנ״ד

*In formation

The Written Word is Forever

PATRONS OF THE TALMUD

TEMURAH: **Dr. and Mrs. Walter Silver**
Shlomo, Chani, and Avi Cohen
Sheri, Terri, Jennifer and Michelle Kraut
Evan and Alison Silver
in memory of our parents, and great grandparents
צבי יצחק ב״ר שמואל ע״ה — Harry Silver ע״ה
שרה פיגא בת מענדל ע״ה — Sarah Silver ע״ה
אברהם משה בן הרב שלמה זאלי ע״ה — Morris Bienenfeld ע״ה
גוטקה טובה בת אברהם דוד ע״ה — Gertrude Bienenfeld ע״ה

KEREISOS: **Mouki and Charlotte Landau** (Antwerp)
in honor of their children
Natalie and Chemi Friedman **Yanky and Miriam Landau**
Steve and Nechama Landau
and in beloved memory of their parents
חיים יעקב ב״ר יהושע ז״ל — Chaim Yaakov Landau ז״ל
אסתר בת ר׳ יעקב קאפל הכהן ע״ה — Esther Landau ע״ה
בן ציון ב״ר יצחק צבי ז״ל — Benzion Gottlob ז״ל
צילה בת ר׳ שמואל יהודה לייב ע״ה — Cila Herskovic ע״ה
and in beloved memory of our partner
מורנו הרב ר׳ יוסף יצחק בן מורנו ורבנו הרה״ג ר׳ מרדכי רוטנברג זצ״ל אבדק״ק אנטווערפן

ME'ILAH, TAMID, MIDDOS, KINNIM: **Steven and Renée Adelsberg**
Sarita David Sammy Avi
in loving memory of
שמואל שמעלקא ב״ר גדליה ז״ל — Samuel Adelsberg ז״ל
and in honor of
Helen Adelsberg Weinberg שתחי׳
and
Chaim and Rose Fraiman שיחי׳

NIDDAH I: In memory of
Joseph and Eva Hurwitz ע״ה
יוסף ב״ר מרדכי הלוי וחוה פיגא ב״ר אליעזר הלוי ע״ה
and
Lorraine Hurwitz Greenblott — לאה בילא חיה בת ר׳ יוסף ע״ה
by
Marc and Rachel Hurwitz,
Elisheva Ruchama, Michal, and Nechama Leah;
Martin and Geraldine Schottenstein Hoffman,
Jay and Jeanie Schottenstein, Ann and Ari Deshe,
Susan and Jon Diamond, and Lori Schottenstein;
and Pam and Neil Lazaroff, Frank Millman, and Dawn and Avi Petel

NIDDAH II: In memory of
Jerome Schottenstein ע״ה
יעקב מאיר חיים בן אפרים אליעזר הכהן ע״ה

PATRONS OF THE TALMUD

ZEVACHIM III: **Friends of Value City Department Stores**
In memory of
יעקב מאיר חיים בן אפרים אליעזר הכהן ע״ה — Jerome Schottenstein ע״ה

MENACHOS I: **Terumah Foundation**

MENACHOS II: **Terumah Foundation**

MENACHOS III: **Terumah Foundation**

CHULLIN I: **The Kassin Family**
in memory of
הרב יעקב שאול קצין זצ״ל — Rabbi Dr. Jacob Saul Kassin זצ״ל
The late Chief Rabbi of the Syrian-Sephardic Community
and in honor of
הרב שאול יעקב קצין שליט״א — Rabbi Saul Jacob Kassin שליט״א
Chief Rabbi of the Syrian-Sephardic Community

CHULLIN II: **Marty Silverman**
in memory of
Joseph and Fannie Silverman ע״ה and Dorothy Silverman ע״ה

CHULLIN III: **Harold and Ann Platt**
in memory of their beloved parents
אליעזר ושרה פיגא ע״ה — Eliezer and Sarah Feiga (Olshak) Platkowski ע״ה of Malkinia, Poland
ברוך ולאה ע״ה — Baruch and Laura Bienstock ע״ה of Lwow, Poland
and in memory of their entire families who perished in the Holocaust

CHULLIN IV: **Terumah Foundation**

BECHOROS I: **Howard Tzvi and Chaya Friedman**
Gabrielle and Aryeh
in memory of their father and grandfather
הרב ירחמיאל ברוך בן הרה״ח ר׳ אלעזר ז״ל — Yerachmiel Friedman ז״ל

BECHOROS II: **Howard and Chaya Balter**
Perri Naftali Aryeh
in memory of his mother and their grandmother
רחל בת ר׳ חיים ע״ה, נפ׳ ז׳ שבט תשנ״ט — **Ruth Balter** ע״ה
and in honor of their parents and grandparents שיחי׳
David Balter
Noah and Shirley Schall
and in beloved memory of their grandparents and great grandparents
ר׳ שלמה ב״ר דוד זאב ז״ל אדי בת ר׳ זאב ע״ה — Balter
ר׳ חיים ב״ר לייב ז״ל פערל בת ר׳ ביניש ע״ה — Lelling
ר׳ דוב בער ב״ר אליעזר ז״ל ליבה בת ר׳ ישראל ע״ה — Zabrowsky
ר׳ נפתלי ב״ר יעקב שלמה ז״ל שרה בת ר׳ רפאל ע״ה — Schall

ARACHIN: **Chanoch and Hadassah Weisz and Family**
in memory of his father:
לעי״נ אביו ר׳ צבי ב״ר שמחה הלוי ע״ה, נפ׳ כ״ז מנחם אב תשמ״ה — Weisz
his maternal grandfather:
לעי״נ ר׳ שלמה ב״ר יצחק ע״ה, נפ׳ ה׳ סיון תש״א — Grunwald
his maternal grandmother and their children who perished in the Holocaust:
לעי״נ מרת גנדל בת ר׳ חנוך העניך ע״ה, שנהרגה עקה״ש כ״ז סיון תש״ד הי״ד — Grunwald
ולעי״נ בניהם משה ב״ר שלמה, יעקב ב״ר שלמה, יצחק ב״ר שלמה, בנימין ב״ר שלמה,
שנהרגו עקה״ש כ״ז סיון תש״ד הי״ד

and in memory of her grandparents:
לעי״נ ר׳ חייא בן חכם ר׳ רפאל ע״ה, נפ׳ כ״ד מנחם אב תשל״ה — Aryeh
וזוגתו מרת מלכה בת ר׳ אליהו ע״ה, נפ׳ י״ח טבת תשל״ד

PATRONS OF THE TALMUD

SANHEDRIN I: **Mortimer and Barbara Klaus** **Lester and Esther Klaus**
Arthur and Vivian Klaus
in memory of their beloved parents
ר׳ שמשון ב״ר יעקב ע״ה באשא בת ר׳ מרדכי נתן ע״ה
Samuel and Bessie Klaus ע״ה
and in memory of their sister
רייזל בת ר׳ שמשון ע״ה — **Rosalie Klaus Sohn**

SANHEDRIN II: Dedicated by a fellowship of people who revere the Talmud, its sanctity and wisdom, who foster its study, and who join in helping bring its treasures to future generations, the world over.

SANHEDRIN III: **Joseph and Adina Russak**
Dr. Leonard and Bobbee Feiner
Larry and Rochelle Russak
in memory of
צבי הירש ורחל רוסק ע״ה — Mr. and Mrs. Harry Russak ע״ה
אליעזר ובריינדל דייטש ע״ה — Mr. and Mrs. Eliezer Deutsch ע״ה
יעקב ורבקה לאה פיינר ע״ה — Mr. and Mrs. Jacob Feiner ע״ה

MAKKOS: **Mr. and Mrs. Marcos Katz**
in honor of הרב אפרים לייבוש בן הרב מרדכי דוד הכהן כ״ץ שליט״א
Rabbi Ephraim Leibush Katz שליט״א

SHEVUOS: Dedicated by
Michael and Danielle Gross
(London)

AVODAH ZARAH I: **The Kuhl Family**
in memory of
יחיאל ב״ר יצחק אייזיק ע״ה — Dr. Julius Kuhl ע״ה
פרומט בת ר׳ שמואל הלוי ע״ה — Mrs. Yvonne Kuhl ע״ה
שמואל ב״ר יחיאל ע״ה — Sydney Kuhl ע״ה

AVODAH ZARAH II: In memory of
Jerome Schottenstein ע״ה
יעקב מאיר חיים בן אפרים אליעזר הכהן ע״ה

HORAYOS-EDUYOS: **Woli and Chaja Stern** (Sao Paulo, Brazil)
in memory of his parents
ר׳ צבי בן ר׳ חיים הלוי ומרת מרים ז״ל – Stern
מרת דאכא בת ר׳ פרץ ומרת ברכה ע״ה — Tager
and in memory of her parents
ר׳ דוד אריה בן ר׳ יעקב ומרת שיינדל ז״ל – Brenner
מרת איטלה בת ר׳ חיים ומרת מדל ע״ה — Stern
and in memory of their mechutanim
ר׳ ישראל מרדכי ב״ר צבי יוסף סג״ל ז״ל – Landau
ר׳ יששכר טוביה ב״ר יוסף ז״ל — Weitman
ר׳ שמואל עקיבא ב״ר שלמה צבי ז״ל — Kierszenbaum
and in honor of their children
Jacques and Ariane Stern Jaime and Ariela Landau Michäel and Annete Kierszenbaum

ZEVACHIM I: **Mr. and Mrs. Samson Bitensky**

ZEVACHIM II: **Victor Posner**

PATRONS OF THE TALMUD

BAVA KAMMA III: **Dedicated to Klal Yisrael,**
and particularly to the Six Million.

הקב״ה שוכן בתוך בני ישראל והוא חד עם כנסת ישראל

"The Holy One Blessed is He dwells among the children of Israel;
He and the congregation of Israel are one."

— *Tzidkas Hatzaddik* 179

BAVA METZIA I: **Mrs. Milton Schulman Drs. Robert and Susan Schulman**
Howard and Tzila Schulman Fred and Cindy Schulman
and Families

in memory of

מיכאל בן צבי הירש ע״ה — Milton Schulman ע״ה

BAVA METZIA II: **Donald E. and Eydie R. Garlikov, and Jennifer**

in memory of beloved son and brother

צבי שלמה בן דן ע״ה — Kenneth Scott Garlikov ע״ה

and in memory of parents and grandparents

עזריאל וועלוויל ב״ר אנשיל ע״ה טשארנא בת ר׳ אריה לייב ע״ה

Irve W. and Cecelia (Kiki) Garlikov ע״ה

and in honor of parents and grandparents, brother and uncle

מרדכי ואסתר פריידל ריטטער — Marcus and Elfrieda Ritter

נפתלי חיים ריטטער — Dr. Nathaniel Ritter

BAVA METZIA III: **The David H. Gluck Foundation**

in memory of

The Gluck Family

זאב בן דוד צבי ע״ה ואסתר בת אשר זעליג ע״ה — Zev and Esther Gluck ע״ה

ליבא, אשר זעליג, דוד צבי, שמואל, מנשה, יחזקאל שרגא ע״ה —

Lee, George, David H., Samuel C., Emanuel M., Henry ע״ה, and

יעקב יצחק בן זאב ע״ה ומיימי בת זאב ע״ה — Dr. Jack I. and Mrs. Mae Saks ע״ה

and in memory of

זאב בן חיים דוד וחיה ביילע בת יצחק יעקב ע״ה — Wolf and Chaye Beilah Saks ע״ה

יחיאל בן משה ע״ה — Elie Neustadter ע״ה

BAVA BASRA I: In memory of

מנחם מענדל בן אלימלך יהושע העשל ע״ה

חיה בת יהושע הכהן ע״ה

BAVA BASRA II: **Paul and Beth Guez and Family**

in memory of

Felix (Mazal) Guez ע״ה

BAVA BASRA III: **Irving and Frances Schottenstein**

in honor of their beloved parents

מאיר בן יהושע הכהן ע״ה ליבא בת הרב יצחק משה ע״ה — Meyer and Libbie Schottenstein

טוביה ע״ה ויבדל״ח שיינדל תחי׳ — Tobias ע״ה and Jennie Polster תחי׳

Melvin ע״ה and Lenore תחי׳ Schottenstein

in honor of their beloved parents

אברהם יוסף בן יהושע הכהן ע״ה ויבדל״ח בליה זילפה בת יצחק תחי׳

Abe J. ע״ה and Bessie (Stone) תחי׳ Schottenstein

יצחק ע״ה ויבדל״ח שרה תחי׳ — Isadore J. ע״ה and Sophie תחי׳ Green

PATRONS OF THE TALMUD

SOTAH: **Motty and Malka Klein**

In honor of their parents שיחי׳
Yidel and Suri Klein לאוי״ט
Suri Gross לאוי״ט

In memory of her father
ר׳ אשר אנשיל ב״ר משה יוסף ז״ל — Anchel Gross

And in memory of their grandparents who perished על קידוש השם in the Holocaust
ר׳ דוד ב״ר יעקב הלוי ע״ה ופערל בת ר׳ צבי ע״ה הי״ד — Klein
ר׳ מרדכי ב״ר דוד הלוי ע״ה ולאה בת ר׳ יעקב הלוי ע״ה הי״ד — Klein
ר׳ משה יוסף ב״ר בנימין צבי ע״ה ומלכה בת ר׳ יחיאל מיכל ע״ה הי״ד — Gross
ר׳ חיים אליהו ב״ר מרדכי ע״ה ויוטא בת ר׳ שלמה אליעזר ע״ה הי״ד — Gartenberg

GITTIN I: **Mrs. Kate Tannenbaum**
Elliot and Debra Tannenbaum   Edward and Linda Zizmor
and Families

commemorating the first *yahrzeit* of beloved husband, father and grandfather
ר׳ נפתלי ב״ר יהודה אריה ע״ה — Fred Tannenbaum ע״ה
נפטר ח׳ ניסן תשנ״ב

GITTIN II: **Richard and Bonnie Golding**

in honor of   Julian and Frances Golding   Lawrence Cohen and Helen Lee Cohen
and in memory of   Vivian Cohen ע״ה

Irving and Ethel Tromberg   Clarence and Jean Permut

in memory of
Benjamin and Sara Tromberg ע״ה   Harry and Lena Brown ע״ה
Molly and Julius Permut ע״ה   Lizzie and Meyer Moscovitz ע״ה

KIDDUSHIN I: **Ellis A. and Altoon Safdeye**

in memory of their beloved parents
המנוח יהודה אצלאן ומרת צלחה ויקטוריא ע״ה — Aslan and Victoria Safdeye ע״ה
המנוח יהודה ומרת מרגלית ע״ה — Judah and Margie Sultan ע״ה
and in memory of his brother יוסף ע״ה — Joseph Safdeye ע״ה

KIDDUSHIN II: **Mr. and Mrs. Ben Heller**

in memory of his father
יואל נתן ב״ר חיים הלוי ע״ה — Joseph Heller ע״ה
and in honor of his mother
צפורה שתחי׳ לאוי״ט בת ר׳ בנימין ע״ה — Fanya Gottesfeld-Heller שתחי׳

BAVA KAMMA I: **Yitzchok and Shoshana Ganger**
and Children

in memory of
ר׳ יצחק ישעיהו ב״ר שלמה זלמן ע״ה–רויזא גיטל בת ר׳ משה ע״ה — Ganger
מיכאל ב״ר אברהם מרדכי ע״ה–מרים יוכבד בת ר׳ בנימין ע״ה — Ferber
ר׳ משה דוד ב״ר יצחק זעליג מקוצק ע״ה–פיגא בת ר׳ אברהם מרדכי ע״ה — Morgenstern
ר׳ מתתיהו ב״ר שמואל דוב ע״ה–אסתר מלכה בת ר׳ אריה ליב ע״ה — Newman

BAVA KAMMA II: **William and Esther Bein, and**
Joseph Hillel, Abraham Chaim Zev, and Bella Leah

In memory of parents and grandparents
מנחם מענדל ב״ר שמואל יצחק הכהן ע״ה — Edward (Mendus) Bein ע״ה
לאה בת חיים זאב הכהן ע״ה — Ilus Hartstein Bein ע״ה
מרדכי בן יוסף ע״ה — Mordochej Szer ע״ה
בילה בת אברהם ע״ה — Baila Silber Szer ע״ה
שמואל יצחק הכהן ושרה ביין ע״ה — חיים זאב הכהן ושרה הרטשטיין ע״ה
יוסף ויענטה שער ע״ה — אברהם ואסתר זילבר ע״ה

PATRONS OF THE TALMUD

KESUBOS I: **The Fishoff Families**
in memory of their beloved mother
מינדל בת ר׳ ישראל ע״ה – Mrs. Marilyn Fishoff ע״ה
נפ׳ כד תשרי תשמ״ט
and in memory of their dear grandparents
ר׳ דוב ב״ר מנחם אשר ע״ה   מרת מירל בת ר׳ מנחם מענדל ע״ה – Fishoff
ר׳ ישראל ב״ר אברהם ע״ה   מרת חיה זיסא בת ר׳ שרגא פייוועל ע״ה – Neider

KESUBOS II **Arthur A. and Carla Rand**
in memory of their parents
ר׳ ישראל ב״ר צבי Rand ומרת ליבא מלכה ב״ר יהודה Marcus ע״ה
ר׳ שלמה ב״ר מרדכי יהודה Ratzersdorfer ומרת חוה ב״ר חיים Finkelstein ע״ה
and in honor of their children
ר׳ אריה יהושע ב״ר אליהו דוב ומרת ליבא מלכה שיחי׳ – Lydia and Lyonel S. Zuckier
ר׳ יואל אשר ב״ר חיים שלמה ומרת גנענדל חנה שיחי׳ – Gigi and Joel A. Baum
ר׳ ישראל יהודה ומרת צפורה געלא ב״ר יצחק חיים שיחי׳ – Jay J. and Cyndi Finkel-Rand
and grandchildren
דניאל יעקב, נפתלי צבי, חוה, בנימין, צפורה מרים, רחל, בתשבע Baum שיחי׳
שלמה יצחק, שירה חיה, צבי, שפרה לאה Zuckier שיחי׳
אליהו אריה לייב, יעקב שלמה, צבי, חסיה ליבא, מתתיהו דוד Rand שיחי׳

KESUBOS III **ישימך אלהים כשרה רבקה רחל ולאה**
May God make you like Sarah, Rebecca, Rachel and Leah

NEDARIM I: **Mrs. Goldy Golombeck**
Hyman P. and Elaine Golombeck   **Blanche B. Lerer**
Moishe Zvi and Sara Leifer   **Avrohom Chaim and Renee Fruchthandler**
In memory of
ר׳ משה יוסף ב״ר חיים פנחס ע״ה – Morris J. Golombeck ע״ה
and by Moishe Zvi and Sara Leifer in memory of
הרב ברוך יוסף ב״ר משה צבי ע״ה – האשה הצנועה מרים יוטא בת ר׳ לוי יצחק ע״ה
Mr. and Mrs. Baruch Leifer ע״ה

NEDARIM II: **The Warren Rothstein Family**
In honor of
Howard and Beatrice Rothstein
and in memory of
David and Esther Rothstein ע״ה   Max and Gussie Gottlieb ע״ה

NAZIR I: **Albert and Gail Nassi**
Garrett A. Nassi
Jessica Lea Nassi
in memory of
Samuel Nassi ע״ה
Albert and Leona Nassi ע״ה
Benjamin and Adell Eisenberg ע״ה
Arthur and Sarah Dector ע״ה

Daniel and Susan Kane
Jessica, Adam and Stacey
in memory of
Abraham and Rose Kanofsky ע״ה
Benjamin and Sophie Gornstein ע״ה
Elie and Irma Darsa ע״ה
Mack and Naomi Mann ע״ה

NAZIR II: **Alan and Myrna Cohen,**   **Alison and Matthew**
in memory of
Harry and Kate Cohen ע״ה   Harry and Pauline Katkin ע״ה

PATRONS OF THE TALMUD

BEITZAH: **Paul and Suzanne Peyser Irwin and Bea Peyser**
in memory of
פריידע רייזעל בת יהושע ע״ה דוד בן פינחס ע״ה — David and Rose Peyser ע״ה

ROSH HASHANAH: **Steve and Genie Savitsky David and Roslyn Savitsky**
In memory of
יואל בן אברהם ע״ה — Jerry J. Savitsky ע״ה
ישראל בן מנחם מאנעס ע״ה — Irving Tennenbaum ע״ה
שמואל בן יצחק ע״ה — George Hillelsohn ע״ה
רחל בת דוד הלוי ע״ה — Ruth Hillelsohn ע״ה
אהרן בן יהודה אריה ע״ה — Aaron Seif ע״ה

TAANIS: **David and Jean Bernstein, and Scott**
Matthew Bernstein
Albert and Gail Nassi, Jessica and Garrett
in memory of
Mr. and Mrs. Harry Bernstein ע״ה Mr. and Mrs. Joseph Furman ע״ה
Mr. Samuel Nassi ע״ה

MEGILLAH: Special Commemorative Edition published in conjunction
with the *Sh'loshim* of the patron of this edition of the Talmud
Jerome Schottenstein ע״ה
יעקב מאיר חיים בן אפרים אליעזר הכהן ע״ה

MOED KATAN: **Solomon T. and Leah Scharf**
and their children
David and Tzipi Diamond Alexander and Naomi Scharf
Joseph Scharf Dovid and Chani Scharf
לזכרון עולם
ר׳ אליהו בן משה יעקב ע״ה — R' Eliyahu Scharf ע״ה
שרה בת אלכסנדר זיסקינד ע״ה — Sara Scharf ע״ה
ר׳ יוסף בן צבי הירש ע״ה — R' Joseph Felder ע״ה

CHAGIGAH: **The Alvin E. Schottenstein Family**
In memory of
חיים אברהם יונה בן אפרים אליעזר הכהן ע״ה — Alvin E. Schottenstein ע״ה
יצחק אייזיק בן עקיבא הכהן ע״ה — Irving Altman ע״ה

YEVAMOS I: **Phillip and Ruth Wojdyslawski and Family**
In memory of his beloved parents
Abraham Michel and Ora Wojdyslawski ע״ה
ר׳ אברהם מיכאל ב״ר פינחס ע״ה
אורה בת ר׳ צבי הירש ע״ה

YEVAMOS II: **Phillip and Ruth Wojdyslawski and Family**
In memory of her beloved mother
Chaya (Cytryn) Valt ע״ה
חיה צירל בת ר׳ שלמה זלמן ע״ה

YEVAMOS III: **Phillip and Ruth Wojdyslawski and Family**
In honor of
Benjamin C. Fishoff לאוי״ט
To the public he is a leader with vision and dedication.
To us he has always been a role model, a father,
and a constant inspiration.

PATRONS OF THE TALMUD

PESACHIM III: **Lorraine and Mordy Sohn** **Ann and Pinky Sohn**
in memory of
ר׳ צבי ב״ר אלעזר ע״ה — Dr. Harry Sohn ע״ה
מרת הענדיל דבורה ב״ר אברהם שלמה ע״ה — Dora F. Sohn ע״ה
ר׳ יחזקאל ב״ר אליקים חנוך הלוי ע״ה — Harold Levine ע״ה
רייזל ב״ר שמשון ע״ה — Rosalie Sohn ע״ה

SHEKALIM: **Reserved**

YOMA I: **A. Joseph and Rochelle Stern**
Moshe Dov, Zev, Shani, Esty, and Shaye
in honor of their parents and grandparents
Eli and Frieda Stern שיחיו
Frida Weiss שתחי׳
and in memory of
ר׳ ישעי׳ בן ר׳ ישראל שמואל ווייס ז״ל

YOMA II: **A. Leibish and Edith Elbogen**
and Family
לזכר נשמות
מוה״ר אהרן בן מוה״ר יעקב קאפל עלבוגן ז״ל
וזו׳ אלטע חנה חיה מלכה בת מוה״ר חיים יצחק מאיר ע״ה
אחותי פערל עם בעלה ושבע בנים ובנות
ושלשה אחי: חיים יצחק מאיר, משה יוסף, יעקב קאפל הי״ד
בני אהרן עלבוגן שנהרגו עקד״ה
מוה״ר נתן פייטל בן מוה״ר אברהם וואלד ז״ל
וזו׳ ברכה בת מוה״ר דוד יהודה הי״ד שנאספה עקד״ה באוישוויץ

SUCCAH I: **Howard and Roslyn Zuckerman** **Steven and Shellie Zuckerman**
Leo and Rochelle Goldberg
in memory of their parents
ר׳ פסח יהודה ב״ר יצחק אייזיק ע״ה וחוה בת ר׳ יהודה לייב ע״ה — Philip and Evelyn Zuckerman ע״ה

in honor of their children
Yisroel and Shoshana Pesi Zuckerman שיחי׳
Pesach Yehudah and Asher Anshel שיחי׳
Michael (Ezra) and Lauren Zuckerman שיחי׳
Adrianne & Shawn Meller, Elliot, & Joshua Goldberg שיחי׳

in honor of their children
Glenn and Heidi, Brett, Ross and Todd שיחי׳
and
in honor of their parents
Marilyn and Aaron Feinerman שיחי׳

in memory of
ר׳ ישראל צבי ב״ר ברוך ע״ה ושיינדל בת ר׳ ישראל ע״ה — Israel and Shaindel Ray ע״ה
and in memory of Mrs. Rose Ray (Glass) ע״ה

Arthur and Randi Luxenberg
in honor of his grandfather Jesse Aronson שיחי׳
their parents Irwin and Joan Luxenberg שיחי׳ Bernard and Evelyn Beeber שיחי׳
their children Elizabeth Jewel and Jacqueline Paige שיחי׳
in memory of his grandparents
ר׳ אברהם בן אהרן מרדכי ע״ה ורחל בת משה ע״ה — Abraham and Rose Luxenberg ע״ה
and in memory of שרה צירל בת ר׳ יעקב ע״ה — Celia Aronson ע״ה

SUCCAH II: **Thomas and Lea Schottenstein** **William and Amy Schottenstein**
in memory of
אריה ליב בן אפרים אליעזר הכהן ע״ה — Leon Schottenstein ע״ה
מאיר אבנר בן דוד הלוי ע״ה — Meir Avner Levy ע״ה
and in honor of
Mrs. Jean S. Schottenstein שתחי׳ Bertram and Corinne Natelson שיחי׳
Mrs. Flory Levy שתחי׳

PATRONS OF THE TALMUD

SHABBOS II: [continued]

Rabbi Eliyahu and Yehudit Fishman
Rivka and Zvi Silberstein and Leah **Akiva Yitzchak Fishman**
Rabbi Yechiel Meir and Chagit Fishman **Rabbi Yosef and Aliza Fishman**
Talia Chanah, Ariel Yishai and Daniel
In loving memory of
ר׳ יוסף ב״ר טוביה ע״ה רודע רבקה בת ר׳ הירש מאיר ע״ה — Yosef and Rude Rivka Fishman ע״ה
and their children Yechiel Meir, Leah and Chanah הי״ד who perished in the Holocaust

SHABBOS III:

Stanley and Ellen Wasserman
and their children
Alan and Stacy Wasserman **Mark and Anne Wasserman**
Neil and Yael Wasserman **Stuart and Rivka Berger**
and families
In loving memory of
יוסף בן דוב בער ע״ה בילא בת יעקב ע״ה — Joseph and Bess Wasserman ע״ה, and
שמריהו בן משה ע״ה רבקה בת הרב יוסף הכהן ע״ה — Sascha and Regina (Czaczkes) Charles ע״ה

SHABBOS IV:

לעילוי נשמות
הורינו היקרים **ר׳ לוי ב״ר יהודה הלוי ע״ה וצירל בת ר׳ מרדכי ע״ה לוינגר**
זקנינו היקרים **ר׳ יהודה ב״ר אליעזר צבי הלוי ע״ה וטלצא בת פרומט ע״ה לוינגר**
ר׳ מרדכי ב״ר שמואל ע״ה ומלכה בת ר׳ נתן ע״ה אדלר
אחינו **שמואל הלוי ע״ה יהודה הלוי ע״ה יהונתן הלוי הי״ד**
אחותנו **לאה בת ר׳ לוי סג״ל ע״ה ובעלה ר׳ טוביה ע״ה**
גיסינו **ר׳ מיכאל ב״ר ברוך שמואל ע״ה שוויצר ר׳ שמואל ב״ר יעקב ע״ה מיכל**
ולעילוי נשמות דודינו ודודותינו ויוצאי חלוציהם שנפטרו ושנהרגו על קידוש השם הי״ד
Dedicated by **Louis and Morris Lowinger**
Teri Schweitzer **Kato Michel** **Margit Baldinger** **Eva Lowinger**

ERUVIN: [two volumes]

Jerome and Geraldine Schottenstein **Saul and Sonia Schottenstein**
Jay and Jeanie Schottenstein **Ann and Ari Deshe**
Susan and Jon Diamond **Lori Schottenstein**
in memory of
אפרים אליעזר בן יהושע הכהן ע״ה — Ephraim Schottenstein ע״ה
חנה בת צבי הירש ע״ה — Anna Schottenstein ע״ה

PESACHIM I:

Vera and Soli Spira
and Family
in memory of
ברוך בן חיים ע״ה — Baruch Spira ע״ה
בילה בת נתן שלום ע״ה — Bella Spira ע״ה
שמואל בן אברהם ע״ה — Shmuel Lebovits ע״ה
and their respective families הי״ד
who perished in the Holocaust
and in honor of
שפרה בת משה — Caroline Lebovits תחי׳

PESACHIM II:

Vera and Soli Spira
and Family
in memory of an uncle who was like a father
and a cousin who was like a brother
ישראל בן נתן שלום ע״ה — Israel Stern ע״ה
נתן שלום בן ישראל ע״ה — Noussi Stern ע״ה

PATRONS OF THE TALMUD

With generosity, vision, and devotion to the perpetuation of Torah study,
the following patrons have dedicated individual volumes of the Talmud

Reference/ Introduction: **George and Vita Kolber**
In loving memory of
Joseph and Frieda Hirschfeld **ע״ה**

BERACHOS I: In memory of
Jerome Schottenstein ע״ה
יעקב מאיר חיים בן אפרים אליעזר הכהן ע״ה

BERACHOS II: **Zvi and Betty Ryzman**
in honor of their children שיחיו
Mickey and Shelly Fenig
Elie Avi Rafi
and granddaughter Aliza

Malcolm and Joy Lyons
in honour of their parents שיחיו
Leo and Eve Lyons
Cecil and Mona Jacobs

SHABBOS I: **Nachshon and Bruria Minucha [Nuchi] Draiman and Family**
in memory of
הר״ר יהודה ליב מנדלקורן זצ״ל בן הר״ר צבי הי״ו
Rabbi Yehuda Leib Mandelcorn זצ״ל — נפטר כ׳ תמוז, תשנ״ג

SHABBOS II: **David and Bonnie Anfang** **Chaim and Ruthie Anfang**
Rachel, Julie and Elliot **Ariella Hope** **Michael Brett**
In loving memory of
ר׳ אריה ליב ב״ר דוד אביגדור ע״ה — Leib Anfang ע״ה
בשה לאה בת ר׳ אלימלך דוב ע״ה — Barbara Anfang ע״ה

Mimi and Steven Rosenbaum **Joseph and Sharon Prawer** **Alan and Louisa Prawer**
Stacey and Danny **Dena, Dovid, Alana, Naomi**
In loving memory of
ר׳ פנחס ב״ר יוסף ברוך הלוי ע״ה גילה בת אשר יונה ע״ה — Pinkus and Genia Prawer ע״ה, and
שרה בת שמעון ליב ע״ה — Sarah Cukierman ע״ה

A Hebrew edition of the Talmud Bavli is now in progress.
The Hebrew edition is dedicated by

Jay and Jeanie Schottenstein

and their children

Joseph Aaron, Jonathan Richard, and Jeffrey Adam

— in honor of their cherished loved ones who have left indelible marks on their own lives and the lives of countless others, as models of inspiration, generosity, integrity, and devotion to the noblest causes in Jewish life:
his parents **JEROME ז״ל AND GERALDINE SCHOTTENSTEIN**,
her parents **LEONARD AND HEDDY RABE**
and **SAUL AND SONIA SCHOTTENSTEIN**

❧ ❧ ❧

JAY AND JEANIE SCHOTTENSTEIN
have a perspective that transcends time and community.
Through their dedication of these editions of the Talmud, they spread Torah study around the globe and across generations.
Multitudes yet unborn will be indebted to them for their vision and generosity.

PATRONS OF THE SEDARIM

THE DAVIDOWITZ FAMILY
RENOV STAHLER ROSENWALD PERLYSKY EDITION OF SEDER NEZIKIN

is lovingly dedicated to

Rozi and Morty Davis-Davidowitz

builders of this dynasty

by their children and grandchildren

Esti and Ushi Stahler

Jamie, Danny, Duvi, Lisi, Avi, Eli, Malka and Loni

Ruki and Kal Renov

Tova, Tani, Eli, Ari, Yoni, Yael, Emi and Benji

Rivki and Lindsay Rosenwald

Doni, Joshy, Demi and Davey

Laya and Dov Perlysky

Ayala Malka, Tova Batsheva, Naftali Yonatan and Atara Yael

and is lovingly dedicated to the memory of our grandparents

Emily and Nathan Selengut ע"ה

נפתלי ב"ר יעקב ע"ה ומלכה בת ר' אלתר חיים ע"ה

THE SCHWARTZ EDITION OF SEDER KODASHIM

is lovingly dedicated by

Avrohom Yeshaya and Sally Schwartz

and their children

Ari, Moshe, Dani, and Dovi

in memory of their beloved father and grandfather

ר' יצחק ב"ר אשר ז"ל — Isaac Jarnicki ז"ל

נפ' יג' תמוז תשנ"ז

and in honor of יבלח"ט our parents and grandparents

Rabbi and Mrs. Gedalia Dov Schwartz שליט"א

Mrs. Rebecca Jarnicki שתחי'　**Mrs. Pearl Septytor שתחי'**

and in memory of our grandparents

Rabbi Eliezer and Pesha Chaya Poupko ז"ל　**Abraham Schwartz ז"ל**

Betzalel Hersh and Hendel Berliner ז"ל　**Asher and Gittel Jarnicki ז"ל**

THE WINKLER EDITION OF SEDER TOHOROS

is lovingly dedicated by

Marvin and Sherri Winkler

Jason, Eric, Sam, Nicole

in honor of their parents

Michel and Irene Winkler

in memory of their grandparents who perished in the Holocaust הי"ד

Moshe and Leah Jacobowitz ע"ה　**Joseph and Shaindel Winkler ע"ה**

and in memory of their aunt

Tera Hirsch ע"ה

PATRONS OF THE SEDARIM

Recognizing the need for the holy legacy of the Talmud
to be available to its heirs in their own language,
these generous and visionary patrons have each dedicated
one of the six Sedarim/Orders of the Talmud.

THE FORMAN EDITION OF SEDER ZERAIM

is lovingly dedicated by

Mr. and Mrs. Sam Forman, Brett and Wendy

in memory of their beloved parents and grandparents

Mr. and Mrs. George Forman ע״ה **Dr. and Mrs. Morey Chapman ע״ה**

THE HORN EDITION OF SEDER MOED

is lovingly dedicated to the memory of

ר׳ משה מניס ב״ר יעקב יצחק ע״ה — Moishe Horn ע״ה

נפטר ב׳ מנחם אב תשנ״ד

by his wife **Malkie**

his parents **Jacob ע״ה and Genia Horn שתחי׳**

and her children

Shimmie and Alissa **Devorah and Dov Elias** **Shandi and Sruli Glaser**

Ari Shana Michal Moishe Ariella

THE ELLIS A. SAFDEYE EDITION OF SEDER NASHIM

is reverently dedicated to the memory of

המנוח יהודה אצלאן ומרת צלחה ויקטוריא ע״ה

Aslan and Victoria Safdeye ע״ה

and

המנוח יהודה ומרת מרגלית ע״ה

Judah and Margie Sultan ע״ה

by their children

Ellis A. and Altoon Safdeye

and grandchildren

Alan Judah and Rachel Safdeye **Joseph and Rochelle Safdeye**
Ezra and Victoria Esses **Michael and Bobbi Safdeye**

is reverently dedicated to the memory of
the patron of this Talmud
and of countless other noble causes in Jewish life

יעקב מאיר חיים בן אפרים אליעזר הכהן ע״ה

נפטר ה׳ אדר ב׳ תשנ״ב

Jerome Schottenstein ע״ה

and to the memory of his parents

אפרים אליעזר בן יהושע הכהן ע״ה — **חנה בת צבי הירש ע״ה**

נפטר ב׳ אייר תשט״ז — נפטרה ט״ו מנחם אב תשט״ו

Ephraim and Anna Schottenstein ע״ה

by

Geraldine Schottenstein

Saul and Sonia Schottenstein

and

Jay and Jeanie Schottenstein

and their children
Joseph Aaron, Jonathan Richard, Jeffrey Adam

Ann and Ari Deshe

and their children
Elie Michael, David Scott, Dara Lauren, Daniel Matthew

Susan and Jon Diamond

and their children
Jillian Leigh, Joshua Louis, Jacob Meyer

and

Lori Schottenstein

This volume is dedicated in honor of our dear father

R' Yechiel Ben Zion Fishoff לאוי״ט

He is a living legend of wisdom, kindness, and dedication to Torah and Chassidus. His chessed is selfless; his unsolicited, unheralded generosity helps countless individuals and institutions. An *askan* of worldwide proportions, his statesmanlike counsel has been sought and treasured by Klal Yisrael's greatest leaders. The blessing of the אמרי אמת זצוק״ל has guided him from his youth and the Admorim of Gur continued to inspire his enormous achievements for Klal Yisrael and Reb Yisrael. But no less than his service to the community and its great and famous people, is his devotion and guidance to his children and grandchildren.

❦ ❦ ❦

We pay tribute to the memory of our beloved mother

Marilyn Fishoff ע״ה

מינדל בת ר׳ ישראל וחוה זיסע למשפחת ניידער ע״ה

נפטרה כ״ד תשרי, אסרו חג סוכות תשמ״ט

A scion of the Nieder-Doppelt families of respected Rizhiner chassidim, she embodied the legacy of her ancestors — the virtues of grace, warmth and sensitivity, of greeting everyone with a beautiful smile and a kind word. She was loved and admired by everyone who knew her. Our mother's dedication to her husband and children was legendary. She radiated an aristocratic charm, tempered with humility. May her legacy live on in the generations of her grandchildren, who were her life and her hope for the future.

❦ ❦ ❦

We pay tribute to the memory of
the *kedoshim* of our family, our grandparents and their children:

הרה״ח מוה״ר דוב בעריש בן מנחם אשר פישאהף ז״ל הי״ד
וזו׳ מירל בת מנחם מענדל למשפחת אורבך ע״ה הי״ד
ובניהם אהרון אשר ויעקב יצחק
ובנותיהם רבקה, בריינדל, ורחל ע״ה הי״ד
כולם נהרגו על קדוש השם ונקבע היאהרצייט כ״ה אדר ב׳

ר׳ דוב ז״ל was a great-grandson of the אגודת אזוב, who was the father of the אבני נזר. In his own right, he was one of the great chassidim of the אמרי אמת and an inspirational figure. She was the quintessential Jewish wife and mother, loyal to her Maker and devoted to her family and people.

We never knew our grandparents, but their memory remains a beacon and a vivid example of the eternal Jew. From their seeds our parents grew, and their heritage lights our way.

It is surely *Hashgachah Peratis* that the Daf Yomi study of this volume begins on the day of their *yahrzeit*. May it be a merit for their holy souls.

Meryl Gross, Regina and Yisroel Yitzchok Weinstock,
Judy and Dov Fishoff, Barbara and Naftali Gold,
Miriam and Avi Fishoff

We gratefully acknowledge the outstanding
Torah scholars who contributed to this volume:

Rabbi Yisroel Simcha Schorr, Rabbi Chaim Malinowitz
Rabbi Mordechai Marcus and **Rabbi Ephraim Zuravin**
who reviewed and commented on the manuscript,
Rabbis Hillel Danziger, Yosef Davis, Eliezer Herzka, Nesanel Kasnett,
Henoch Moshe Levin, Zev Meisels, Moshe Rosenblum,
Eli Shulman, Feivel Wahl, Yosaif Asher Weiss,
Eliyahu Cohen and **Avrohom Shereshevsky**
who edited, contributed and assisted in the production of this volume.
Rabbi Yehezkel Danziger, Editorial Director

We are also grateful to our proofreaders: Mrs. Judi Dick, Mrs. Mindy Stern, and Mrs. Faigie Weinbaum,
our typesetters: Mr. Yaakov Hersh Horowitz, Mr. Shaya Sonnenschein,
Miss Rivkie Bruck, Miss Chumie Zaidman, Mrs. Estie Dicker, Mrs. Esther Feierstein

FIRST EDITION
First Impression . . . August 1999

Published and Distributed by
MESORAH PUBLICATIONS, Ltd.
4401 Second Avenue
Brooklyn, New York 11232

Distributed in Europe by
J. LEHMANN HEBREW BOOKSELLERS
20 Cambridge Terrace
Gateshead, Tyne and Wear
England NE8 1RP

Distributed in Israel by
SIFRIATI / A. GITLER—BOOKS
10 Hashomer Street
Bnei Brak 51361

Distributed in Australia & New Zealand by
GOLDS BOOK & GIFT CO.
36 William Street
Balaclava 3183, Vic., Australia

Distributed in South Africa by
KOLLEL BOOKSHOP
Shop 8A Norwood Hypermarket
Norwood 2196, Johannesburg, South Africa

THE ARTSCROLL SERIES® / SCHOTTENSTEIN EDITION
TALMUD BAVLI / TRACTATE KESUBOS VOL. I

ISBN: 1-57819-007-X

Typography by CompuScribe at ArtScroll Studios, Ltd.
Custom bound by **Sefercraft, Inc.,** Brooklyn, N.Y.

The Schottenstein Edition

THE GEMARA: THE CLASSIC VILNA EDITION, WITH AN ANNOTATED, INTERPRETIVE ELUCIDATION, AS AN AID TO TALMUD STUDY

Published by

Mesorah Publications, ltd

THE ELLIS A. SAFDEYE EDITION OF SEDER NASHIM

מסכת כתובות

TRACTATE KESUBOS

VOLUME I

Elucidated by

Rabbi Abba Zvi Naiman (chapters 1-2)

Rabbi Mendy Wachsman (chapter 3)

under the General Editorship of

Rabbi Yisroel Simcha Schorr

and Rabbi Chaim Malinowitz

in collaboration with a team of Torah Scholars

R' Hersh Goldwurm זצ"ל

General Editor

תש"נ-תשנ"ג / 1990-1993

A PROJECT OF THE

Mesorah Heritage Foundation

THE SCHOTTENSTEIN EDITION

תלמוד בבלי

TALMUD BAVLI

The ArtScroll Series®

THE ELLIS A. SAFDEYE EDITION OF SEDER NASHIM

מסכת כתובות

TRACTATE KESUBOS

TALMUD BAVLI
תלמוד בבלי